# WHAT
# FANTASTIC
# FICTION

## DO I
## READ
## NEXT?

A Reader's Guide
to Recent Fantasy,
Horror and
Science Fiction

2ND EDITION

ISSN 1525-7258

# WHAT FANTASTIC FICTION

## DO I READ NEXT?

A Reader's Guide
to Recent Fantasy,
Horror and
Science Fiction

2ND EDITION

NEIL BARRON

*GALE GROUP*

*Detroit*
*San Francisco*
*London*
*Boston*
*Woodbridge, CT*

## Neil Barron

*Contributors:* Stefan Dziemianowicz, Scott Imes and Don D'Ammassa

**The Gale Group Staff:**
*Coordinating Editor:* Dana Ferguson
*Contributing Editors:* Ellice Engdahl and Elizabeth P. Manar
*Managing Editor:* Debra M. Kirby

*Production Director:* MaryBeth Trimper
*Assistant Production Manager:* Eveline Abou-el-Seoud
*Manufacturing Manager:* Dorothy Maki
*Buyer:* Cindy Range
*Product Design Manager:* Cynthia Baldwin
*Graphic Artist:* Gary Leach
*Cover Design:* Mary Krzewinski

*Manager, Data Entry Services:* Ronald D. Montgomery
*Acting Data Entry Coordinator:* Beverly Jendrowski

*Manager, Technical Support Services:* Theresa Rocklin

ISBN 0-7876-4476-5
ISSN 1525-7274

Printed in the United States of America

10 9 8 7 6 5 4 3 2

# Contents

**Introduction** ............................................................................................................... vii

**Key to Story Types** ....................................................................................................... ix

**Award Winners** ............................................................................................................ xv

**What Fantastic Fiction Do I Read Next?**

    Fantastic Fiction Titles ............................................................................................... 1

**Indexes**

    Series Index .......................................................................................................... 1275

    Time Period Index ................................................................................................. 1293

    Geographic Index ................................................................................................. 1321

    Story Type Index .................................................................................................. 1389

    Character Name Index .......................................................................................... 1437

    Character Description Index .................................................................................. 1575

    Author Index ........................................................................................................ 1767

    Title Index ........................................................................................................... 1843

# Introduction

Fantasy, horror, and science fiction can easily be found, whether on the big screen in the form of a Steven Spielberg production, on television as a mini-series, on bestseller lists, or on the shelves of a library. It's no wonder either, the fantastic provides great action, philosophical issues, humor, and even comments on the human condition. Indeed, dragons, monsters, invaders, magicians, and aliens have in stories as old as history. There's no question fantastic fiction is important; the true question for readers, from the avid Star Wars fan to the reader who has read it all, is "What do I read next?"

Designed as a tool to assist in the exploration of fantastic fiction, *What Fantastic Fiction Do I Read Next?* guides the reader to both current and classic recommendations in the widely read genres of fantasy, horror, and science fiction. Collecting entries from previous volumes of The Gale Group's *What Do I Read Next?* annual, *What Fantastic Fiction Do I Read Next?* allows readers quick and easy access to specific data on recent titles in these popular genres. In addition, each entry provides alternate reading selections, coming to the rescue of librarians and booksellers who may be unfamiliar with these genres yet must answer the frequently posed question "What fantastic fiction do I read next?"

## About the Contributors

**Neil Barron,** an expert in the field of fantastic fiction, coordinates the compilation of fantasy, horror, and science fiction titles for *What Do I Read Next?*. He is the editor of the reader guides *Anatomy of Wonder: A Critical Guide to Science Fiction* (Bowker, 4th ed., 1995) and *Fantasy and Horror: A Critical and Historical Guide to Literature, Illustration, Film, TV, Radio and the Internet* (Scarecrow Press, 1999).

Assisting Mr. Barron through the years of *What Do I Read Next?* have been other experts in fantastic fiction. **Scott Imes** has managed the well-known Twin Cities specialty fantastic fiction bookstore, Uncle Hugo's, for more than 20 years, where he has developed a vast knowledge of the fantasy and science fiction genres as well as a vast collection of titles. **Stefan Dziemianowicz** is an editor for a New York law book publisher. His horror credentials include co-editing the quarterly journal, *Necrofile*, and writing the definitive study, *The Annotated Guide to Unknown and Unknown Worlds* (Starmont House, 1991). He has co-edited numerous anthologies and recently compiled *A Whisper in the Dark: 12 Thrilling Tales by Louisa May Alcott* (Barnes and Noble, 1996). Also assisting during the past year was **Don D'Ammassa**, who has been reading SF and Fantasy for almost 40 years and has been the book reviewer for the *Science Fiction Chronicle* for the past 15 years. He has published fiction in fantastic magazines and anthologies and has contributed essays to a variety of reference books dealing with fantastic literature. The authors have been ably assisted by numerous contributors throughout the years.

## Details on over 6,000 Titles

*What Fantastic Fiction Do I Read Next?* contains more than 6,000 entries for fantasy, horror, and science fiction titles published in the past ten years. The criteria for inclusion of specific titles vary somewhat from genre to genre, but for the most part, the experts have attempted to select the recently published books they consider the best.

The entries are listed alphabetically by main author. Most provide the following information:

• **Author or editor's name** and real name if a pseudonym is used. Co-authors, co-editors, and illustrators are also listed where applicable.

• **Book title.**

• **Date and place of publication; name of publisher.**

• **Series name.**

• **Story type:** Genre and specific categories within each genre, identified by the compiling expert. Definitions of these types are listed in the "Key to Story Types" section following the Introduction.

• **Major characters:** Names and brief descriptions of up to three characters featured in the title.

• **Time period:** When the story takes place.

• **Locale**: Where the story takes place.

• **What the book is about:** A brief plot summary.

• **Other books you might like:** Titles by other authors written on a similar theme or in a similar style. Readers use these titles to delve more deeply into fantasy, horror, or science fiction.

### Indexes Answer Readers Questions

The eight indexes in *What Fantastic Fiction Do I Read Next?*, used separately or in conjunction with each other, create many pathways to the featured recommended titles, answering general questions or locating specific titles. For example:

### "Are there any new *Star Wars* books?"

The SERIES INDEX lists entries by the name of the series of which they are a part, helping readers locate books in a series they enjoy.

### "I like Sword and Sorcery books. Can you recommend any new ones?"

The STORY TYPE INDEX breaks each genre into story types or more specialized areas. In the Fantasy genre, for example, there is a story type heading Sword and Sorcery. This index allows readers to focus on titles that fall in a category they particularly enjoy. For the definitions of genre terms, see the Key to Story Types section.

### "I m looking for a fantasy set in Wales..."

The GEOGRAPHIC INDEX lists titles by their locale, helping readers pinpoint an area in which they have a particular interest, such as their hometown, a distant country, or even Cyberspace.

### "Do you know of any horror stories set during the 18th century?"

The TIME PERIOD INDEX is a chronological listing of titles by time period, allowing readers to find stories set in a time period past or future that interests them or to find a book whose title they do not remember, except that it s set during World War II.

### "What titles are available that feature vampires?"

The CHARACTER DESCRIPTION INDEX identifies the major characters by occupation (e.g. Accountant, Editor, Librarian) or persona (e.g. Cyborg, Noblewoman, Stowaway). This index, for example, allows a reader who enjoys books featuring mythical creatures to find them easily.

### "Has anyone written any new books with Merlin (the magician) in them?"

The CHARACTER NAME INDEX lists the major characters named in the entries, which can help readers who remember some information about a book, but not an author or title, locate it. It can also point them to more books about a famous character such as Alice in Wonderland.

### "What has Dean Koontz written recently?"

The AUTHOR INDEX contains the names of all authors featured in the entries and those listed under "Other books you might like," pointing readers to an extensive list of an author s works.

### "What books are like *Blue Mars*?"

The TITLE INDEX includes all main entry titles and all titles recommended under "Other books you might like" in one alphabetical listing. Thus readers can find a specific title they know, new or old, and go to that entry to find out what titles are similar.

The indexes can also be used together to narrow down or broaden choices. A reader interested in horror set in England during the late 19th century would consult the TIME PERIOD INDEX and GEOGRAPHIC INDEX to see which titles appear in both. Detectives abound in mystery fiction, but may be found in other genres as well. Searching for Detective in the CHARACTER DESCRIPTION INDEX enables a mystery reader to cross over into previously unknown realms of reading experiences, perhaps as far as a detective story set on Mars! And with the AUTHOR and TITLE indexes, which include all books listed under "Other books you might like," it is easy to compile an extensive list of recommended reading, beginning with a recently published title or a classic from the past.

### Also Available Online

The entries in *What Fantastic Fiction Do I Read Next?* can also be found in the online version of *What Do I Read Next?* on Galenet. This electronic product encompasses over 80,000 books, including genre fiction, mainstream fiction, and nonfiction. All the books included in *What Do I Read Next?* online are recommended by librarians or other experts or appear on bestseller lists. The user-friendly functionality allows users to refine their searching by using several criteria, while making it easy to identify similar titles for further research and reading. The online version is updated with new information on a quarterly basis. For more information about *What Do I Read Next?* online or Galenet, please contact The Gale Group.

### Suggestions Are Welcome

The editors welcome any comments and suggestions for enhancing and improving *What Fantastic Fiction Do I Read Next?*. Please address correspondence to:

Editors
*What Fantastic Fiction Do I Read Next?*
The Gale Group
27500 Drake Road
Farmington Hills, MI 48331-3535
Phone: 248-699-GALE
Toll-free: 800-347-GALE
Fax: 248-699-8074

# Key to Genre Terms

The following is a list of terms used to classify the story type of each novel included in *What Fantastic Fiction Do I Read Next?* along with brief definitions of the terms. To find books that fall under a particular story type heading, see the Story Type Index.

## Fantasy Story Types

**Adventure** - The character(s) must face a series of obstacles, which may include monsters, conflict with other travellers, war, interference by supernatural elements, interference by nature, and so on.

**Alternate History** - Using history as a backdrop, the author adds fantastic elements to build the story.

**Alternate Universe** - More accurately, in most cases, alternate history, in which the South won the Civil War, the Nazis triumphed, etc. The idea is a venerable one in SF.

**Alternate World** - The story starts out in the everyday world, but the main character is transported to an alternate/parallel world by supernatural means and generally must go on an Adventure or Quest in order to find a way home.

**Anthology** - A collection of short fiction by different authors usually related in theme or setting.

**Collection** - A book of short stories by a single author.

**Contemporary** - The story is set in the everyday world, but elements of the fantastic begin to intrude (e.g., a unicorn appears or the character suddenly has the ability to perform magic).

**Contemporary Realism** - Stories in which the fantasy elements are part of a muted background and a "mundane" or "realistic" tone permeates the story.

**Historical** - This sub-genre could also be called Alternate History. Using history as a backdrop, the author adds fantastic elements to build the story.

**Horror** - Although the story has been classified as Fantasy in this section, there are strong elements of Horror (e.g., psychological, supernatural, etc.).

**Humor** - Fantasy in which humor, from cerebral to slapstick, is prominent.

**Legend** - A story based on a legend, myth, or fairy tale, that has been rewritten.

**Light Fantasy** - There is a great deal of humor throughout the story and it is almost guaranteed to have a happy ending.

**Literary** - Usually refers to novels not published as fantasy and sometimes incorporating unconventional narrative techniques.

**Magic Conflict** - The main conflict of the story stems from magical interference. Protagonists may be caught in the middle of a conflict between sorcerers or may themselves be engaged in conflict with other sorcerers.

**Magic Realism** - A style of prose writing in which the author blends the realism of describing ordinary places and incidents with fantastic, dreamlike, or mythical events and does not differentiate between the "real" and the magical.

**Military** - Stories that can range from space wars (compare Space Opera under Science Fiction) to more local battles; most such stories tend to glorify military virtues.

**Mystery** - Although the story has been classified as Fantasy in this section, there are strong elements of Mystery (e.g., suspense, detectives, etc.).

**Political** - The novel deals with political issues that are skewed by the use and presence of fantastic elements.

**Post-Disaster** - Story set in a much degraded environment, frequently involving a reduction in population and the resulting loss of access to processes, resources, technology, etc.

**Psychic Powers** - Parapsychological or paranormal powers believed by some to be credible, e.g., telepathy, telekinesis, etc.

**Quest** - The character embarks on a journey to achieve a specific goal, such as retrieving a jewel from an evil wizard.

**Religious** - Religion of any sort plays a primary role in the plot.

**Romance** - The main characters are in love, but separated by internal motivations or external interference. Elements of the fantastic may add to or help solve the problem.

**Satire** - With an ironic and/or detached point of view, the author is writing on a particular theme (such as religion) using elements of the fantastic to exaggerate and explore the theme.

**Science Fiction** - Although the story has been classified as Fantasy in this section, there are strong elements of Science Fiction.

**Sword and Sorcery** - The tried and true formula of this sub-genre has a muscle-bound swordsman, who is innocent of thought and common sense, up against evil sorcerers and sorceresses, who naturally lose in the end because they are evil. However, Sword and Sorcery continues to be updated, with heroines instead of heroes and a bit of thought prior to action.

**Time Travel** - In Science Fiction Time Travel, there is a rational explanation rooted in science for the character's ability to move through time. In Fantasy Time Travel, the rational explanation is rooted in the supernatural.

**Urban** - Story featuring a city setting and having strong urban themes such as group identification and the resulting interactions.

**Young Adult** - Commonly indicated by publishers to help librarians categorize fiction likely to be of interest to teenage readers, this subgenre frequently involves a child or teenager maturing by accepting responsibility for self-determined goals and discovering strategies to achieve those goals.

## Horror Story Types

**Alternate World** - Generally, any imagined world in science fiction, fantasy, or horror. In horrific worlds, supernatural laws or beings are often assumed, commonly with hostile or terrifying implications.

**Ancient Evil Unleashed** - The evils may take familiar forms, like vampires undead for centuries, or malevolent ancient gods released from bondage by careless humans, or ancient prophecies wreaking havoc on today's world. The so-called *Cthulhu Mythos* originated by H.P. Lovecraft, in which *Cthulhu* is prominent among a pantheon of ancient evil gods, is a specific variation of this.

**Anthology** - A collection of short fiction by different authors, usually related in theme or setting.

**Apocalyptic Horror** - Traditionally, horrors that signal or presage the end of the world, or the world of the characters, and the establishment of a new, possibly very sinister order.

**Black Magic** - Magic directed toward malevolent ends, as distinct from white magic, which is directed toward benevolent ends. Witchcraft is commonly thought of as a black art. Voodoo consists of mysterious rites and practices including sorcery, magic and conjuration and often has evil goals. Compare Satanism and Curse.

**Carnival-Circus Horror** - Derived from its setting, especially the freakish world of the sideshow, in which the distorted or horrific is the norm and is sometimes used as a distorting mirror to reveal hidden selves.

**Child-in-Peril** - The innocence of childhood is often used to heighten the intensity and unpredictability of evil.

**Collection** - A book of short stories by a single author.

**Coming-of-Age** - A story in which the growth and development of a young character, typically a teenager, is portrayed, often by showing how obstacles are overcome and maturity achieved. The literary term is *Bildungsroman*, literally an education novel.

**Curse** - The words said when someone wishes evil or harm on someone or something, such as a witch's or prophet's curse. Compare Black Magic.

**Doppelganger** - A double or alter ego, popularized in the works of E.T.A. Hoffmann, Edgar Allen Poe, and Robert Louis Stevenson.

**Erotic Horror** - Sexuality and horror are often argued to be inextricably linked, as in Bram Stoker's *Dracula* and Sheridan Le Fanu's "Carmilla," although others have argued that they are antithetical. Sexuality became increasingly explicit in the 1980s, sometimes verging on the pornographic, as in Brett Easton Ellis' *American Psycho*.

**Evil Children** - The presumed innocence of a child is replaced with adult-like malevolence and cunning, contradicting the reader's usual expectations.

**Fantasy** - A narrative describing events the reader believes to be impossible and for which no explanation is offered; magic is often employed.

**Femme Fatale** - A seductress for whom men abandon careers, families and responsibilities and who feels no pity or compunction in return; a common figure in history and literature.

**Gay/Lesbian Fiction** - In which the homosexuality of one or more characters is integral to the plot of the story.

**Ghost Story** - The spirits of the dead, who can be benevolent, as in Charles Dickens, or malevolent, as in the tales of M.R. James.

**Gothic Family Chronicle** - A story often covering several generations of a family, many of whose members are typically evil, perverted, or loathsome, and in which family violence is common. The family may live in a decaying mansion suggestive of those in eighteenth century Gothic novels.

**Haunted House** - Literally, a house visited by ghosts, usually with evil intentions in horror fiction, but sometimes the subject of comedy.

**Historical** - Using history as a backdrop, the author adds fantastic elements to build the story. Historical figures are often portrayed as figures in supernatural dramas, and fantastic explanations are sometimes given for historical events.

**Literary** - Usually refers to novels not published as Horror and sometimes incorporating unconventional narrative techniques. Metafictional narratives take as their subject matter the nature of fiction itself and are often therefore self-referential.

**Mystery** - A story in which the identity of evildoers is often concealed and suspense therefore heightened. Psychic detective tales are often mysteries.

**Nature in Revolt** - Tales in which normally docile plants or animals suddenly turn against humankind, sometimes transformed (giant crabs resulting from radioactivity, predatory rats, plagues, blobs that threaten London or Miami, etc.).

**Occult** - An adjective suggesting fiction based on a mystical or secret doctrine, but sometimes referring to supernatural fiction generally. Implies that there is a reality beyond the perceived world that only adepts can penetrate. Black Magic may or may not be part of an occult world.

**Possession** - Domination, usually of humans, by evil spirits, demons, aliens, or other agencies in which one's own volition is replaced by an outside force.

**Psychological Suspense** - Tales often not supernatural in nature in which the psychological exploration and quirks of characters, rather than outside creations, generate suspense and plot.

**Reanimated Dead** - These can take many forms, such as mummies and zombies (often the result of Voodoo).

**Reincarnation** - The rebirth of a soul in a new body, such as that of a poet in the body of Archy, the cockroach in Don Marquis's witty tales, although the tone is darker in horror fiction.

**Satanism** - Suggests worship of evil rather than benevolent gods, the antithesis of conventional theism, whether Christianity or other religions. Evil demons are Satan writ small and usually lack the awful majesty of their parent.

**Satire** - A tale embodying wit, mockery, or irony to attack ideas or customs judged wrong-headed by the author; uncommon in horror fiction.

**Science Fiction** - Stories in which supernatural or fantastic elements are absent and some degree of "rational" explanation is present. The science fiction surface of the film *Alien* is disrupted by the horror of the alien monster.

**Serial Killer** - A multiple murderer, going back to Bluebeard and up to Ed Gein, who inspired Robert Bloch's *Psycho*.

**Small Town Horror** - The coziness and intimacy of a small community is disrupted by some sort of horrific happening, suggesting an unjustified placidity and complacency on the part of the citizens.

**Supernatural Vengeance** - Punishment inflicted by God or a godlike creature, whether justly or capriciously; contrast Apocalyptic Horror and Ancient Evil Unleashed.

**Time Travel** - An uncommon mechanism in horror fiction, standard in science fiction.

**Techno-Horror** - Suggests a catastrophe with horrific elements resulting from a scientific miscalculation or technological hubris; Victor Frankenstein's unnamed monster or a plague resulting from a laboratory mishap.

**Vampire Story** - Based on mythical bloodsucking creatures possessing supernatural powers and various forms, both animal and human. The concept can be traced far back in history, long before Bram Stoker's famous novel, *Dracula*.

**Werewolf Story** - *Were* is Old English for man, suggesting the ancient lineage of a creature that once dominated a world in which witches and sorcerers were equally feared. Sometimes used to refer to any shape shifter, whether wolves or other animals.

**Wild Talents** - The phrase comes from Charles Fort's writings and usually refers to parapsychological powers such as telepathy, psychokinesis, and precognition, collectively called psychic or psi phenomena.

**Witchcraft** - Characters either profess to be or are stigmatized as witches or warlocks, and practitioners of magic associated with witchcraft. This can include black magic (see Black Magic) or white magic (e.g. wicca).

## Science Fiction Story Types

**Adventure** - Suggests a novel or short fiction filled with a rapid sequence of incidents but little character development; Space Opera is a specialized form of adventure fiction.

**Alternate History** - A story dealing with how society might have evolved if a specific historical event had happened differently, e.g. if the South had won the American Civil War.

**Alternate Intelligence** - Story featuring an entity with a sense of identity and able to self-determine goals and actions. The natural or manufactured entity results from a synergy, generally unpredictable, of individual elements.

This subgenre frequently involves a computer-type intelligence.

**Alternate Universe** - More accurately, in most cases, alternate history, in which the South won the Civil War, the Nazis triumphed, etc. The idea is a venerable one in SF.

**Anthology** - A collection of short fiction, from a short story to a novella, written by different authors.

**Arts** - Stories incorporating themes related to music, painting, drama, and the arts generally.

**Collection** - A book of short stories written by a single author.

**Contemporary Realism** - Stories in which the science fictional elements are part of a muted background and a "mundane" or "realistic" tone permeates the story.

**Cyberpunk** - Usually applied to the stories by a group of writers who became prominent in the mid-1980s, such as William Gibson and his *Neuromancer* (1984). The cyber is derived from cybernetics, nominally the study of control and communications in machines, and a downbeat, punk sensibility reminiscent of the hardboiled school of detective fiction writers.

**Disaster** - A tale recounting some event or events seriously disruptive of the social fabric but not as serious as a holocaust; see Post-Holocaust.

**Dystopian** - The antonym of utopian, sometimes called anti-utopian, in which traditionally positive utopian themes are treated satirically or ironically and the mood is downbeat or satiric.

**End of the World** - Such a tale concentrates on the last events following a Disaster but preceding the Post-Holocaust period, although there may be some chronological or thematic overlap.

**Espionage Thriller** - Analogous to Mystery, in which espionage replaces the narrower world of the private investigator.

**Family Saga** - Usually refers to any large scale narrative extending over time and involving many related individuals.

**Fantasy** - A narrative describing events the reader believes to be impossible and for which no scientific or pseudoscientific explanation is offered; magic is usually substituted for scientific laws. Contrast Science Fantasy.

**First Contact** - Any story about the initial meeting or communication of humans with extraterrestrials or aliens. The term may take its name from the eponymous 1945 story by Murray Leinster.

**Future Shock** - A journalistic term derived from Alvin Toffler's 1970 book and which refers to the alleged disorientation resulting from rapid technological change.

**Gay/Lesbian Fiction** - In which the homosexuality of one or more characters is integral to the plot.

**Generation Starship** - If pseudoscientific explanations involving faster-than-light drives are rejected, then the time required for interstellar travel will encompass many human generations.

**Genetic Manipulation** - Sometimes called genetic engineering, this assumes that the knowledge exists to shape creatures, human or otherwise, using genetic means, as in *Brave New World* (1932).

**Hard Science Fiction** - Stories in which the author adheres with varying degrees of rigor to scientific principles believed to be true at the time of writing, principles derived from hard (physical, biological) rather than soft (social) sciences.

**Horror** - Refers to stories in which interest in the events, the intellectual puzzle characteristic of much SF, is subordinated to a feeling of terror or horror by the reader, which could result from a Disaster, Invasion of Earth, or other causes.

**Humor** - SF in which humor, from cerebral to slapstick, is prominent. Early SF was sometimes unintentionally humorous; some modern work is deliberately, and sometimes successfully, so. Compare Satire and Parody.

**Immortality** - Usually includes extreme longevity, resulting from fountains of youth, elixirs, or something with a pseudoscientific basis.

**Invasion of Earth** - An extremely common theme, often paralleling historical events and reflecting fears of the time. Most invasions are depicted as malign, only occasionally benign.

**Literary** - Usually refers to novels not published as SF and sometimes incorporating unconventional narrative techniques. Metafictional narratives take as their subject matter the nature of fiction itself and are often therefore self-referential.

**Lost Colony** - Stories centering around a colony on another world that loses contact with or is abandoned by its parent civilization and the type of society that evolves under those conditions. Conflict usually arises when contact is re-established between the colony and its home world.

**Magic Realism** - A style of prose writing in which the author blends the realism of describing ordinary places and incidents with fantastic, dreamlike, or mythical events and does not differentiate between the "real" and the magical.

**Medical** - Stories in which medical themes are dominant; compare Genetic Manipulation, a specialized form of medical narrative.

**Military** - Stories that can range from space wars (compare Space Opera) to more local battles; most such stories tend to glorify military virtues.

**Mystery** - SF to which traditional mystery/detective structures have been grafted, not always successfully, and in which private eyes go down many mean galaxies; a distant relative of Cyberpunk.

**Mystical** - Suggesting a body of esoteric knowledge known to few and which can have a transforming effect on those possessing it.

**Parody** - A narrative that follows the form of the original but usually changes its sense to nonsense, thus making fun of the original or its ideas. Compare Humor.

**Political** - Narratives in which themes of power are paramount, whether on a local or galactic scale.

**Post-Disaster** - Story set in a much degraded environment, frequently involving a reduction in population and the resulting loss of access to processes, resources, technology, etc.

**Post-Holocaust** - The events following a world-wide disaster, often the result of human folly rather than natural events (collision with a meteor, etc.).

**Post-Nuclear Holocaust** - The events following a world-wide nuclear disaster.

**Psychic Powers** - Parapsychological or paranormal powers believed by some to be credible, e.g., telepathy, telekinesis, etc.

**Robot Fiction** - From the Jewish Golem to the traditional clanking bucket of bolts to the human-like android, robots in various guises have been among us for centuries. The term comes from Karel Capek's play, *R.U.R.*, which stands for Rossum's Universal Robots. Robots are often surrogates for humans and may be treated seriously or comically.

**Romance** - A somewhat elastic term sometimes used to distinguish it from the traditional (realistic, naturalistic) novel but more commonly referring to any narrative in which the world or characters are somewhat idealized. Before the phrase science fiction was introduced in the early 1930s, scientific romance was the most common term.

**Satire** - With an ironic and/or detached point of view, the author is writing on a particular theme (such as religion) using elements of the fantastic to exaggerate and explore the theme.

**Science Fantasy** - A somewhat vague term in which there are "rational" elements from SF and "magical" or "fanciful" elements from fantasy, which hopefully cohere in a plausible story. Many Adventures are Science Fantasy.

**Science Fiction** - Sometimes regarded as a branch of fantasy, there have been many definitions over the years, often too inclusive or exclusive. Used here in a very general sense when the story does not conveniently fit into another category.

**Space Colony** - A permanent space station, usually orbiting Earth but in principal located in deep space or near other planets or stars.

**Space Opera** - Intergalactic adventures; westerns in space; a specialized form of Adventure.

**Techno-Thriller** - Stories in which a technological development, such as an invention, is linked to a series of suspenseful ("thrilling") events.

**Theological** - Stories in which religion or religious belief plays an important role.

**Time Travel** - An ancient tradition in SF, whether the traveller goes forward or backward, and replete with paradoxes.

**UFO** - Unidentified Flying Objects literally, although sometimes used more generally to refer to any object of mysterious origin or intent. A cliche today in First Contact and Invasion of Earth stories.

**Utopian** - A large, often influential, story type that takes its name from Thomas Mores's 1516 book. Usually refers to a society considered "better" by the author, even if not perfect. Aldous Huxley's *Island* (1962) is a utopia, whereas his more famous *Brave New World* (1932) is a dark twin, a dystopia.

**Young Adult** - A marketing term for publishers; one or more of the central characters is a teenager often testing his or her skills against adversity to achieve a greater degree of maturity and self-awareness. A category used by librarians to shelve books of likely appeal to teenage readers.

# Award Winners

## World Fantasy Award

For this award, fantasy is defined to include both fantasy and horror fiction. Reader ballots generate a list of candidates, and a panel of judges selects additional candidates and the winners, which are announced at the World Fantasy Convention held over Halloween weekend each year.

### Best Novel

**1989 - *Koko* by Peter Straub**

Runners-up: *The Last Coin* by James P. Blaylock; *Sleeping in Flame* by Jonathan Carroll; *Fade* by Robert Cormier; *The Silence of the Lambs* by Thomas Harris; and *The Drive-In* by Joe R. Lansdale

**1990 - *Lyonesse: Madouc* by Jack Vance**

Runners-up: *A Child Across the Sky* by Jonathan Carroll; *In a Dark Dream* by Charles L. Grant; *The Stress of Her Regard* by Tim Powers; *Carrion Comfort* by Dan Simmons; *Soldier of Arete* by Gene Wolfe

**1991 - *Only Begotten Daughter* by James Morrow**

Runners-up: *Tigana* by Guy Gavriel Kay; *Thomas the Rhymer* by Ellen Kushner; *Good Omens* by Terry Pratchett and Neil Gaiman; *Mary Reilly* by Valerie Martin

**1992 - *Boy's Life* by Robert R. McCammon**

Runners-up: *Hunting the Ghost Dancer* by A.A. Attanasio; *The Paper Grail* by James P. Blaylock; *Bone Dance* by Emma Bull; *Outside the Dog Museum* by Jonathan Carroll; *The Little Country* by Charles de Lint

**1993 - *Last Call* by Tim Powers**

Runners-up: *Anno Dracula* by Kim Newman; *Was* by Geoff Ryman; *Photographing Fairies* by Steve Szilagyi; *Briar Rose* by Jane Yolen

**1994 - *Glimpses* by Lewis Shiner**

Runners-up: *The Innkeeper's Song* by Peter S. Beagle; *Drawing Blood* by Poppy Z. Brite; *Skin* by Kathe Koja; *The Throat* by Peter Straub; *The Iron Dragon's Daughter* by Michael Swanwick; *Lord of the Two Lands* by Judith Tarr

**1995 - *Towing Jehovah* by James Morrow**

Runners-up: *Brittle Innings* by Michael Bishop; *From the Teeth of Angels* by Jonathan Carroll; *Love and Sleep* by John Crowley; *Waking the Moon* by Elizabeth Hand; *The Circus of the Earth and the Air* by Brooke Stevens

**1996 - *The Prestige* by Christopher Priest**

Runners-up: *All the Bells on Earth* by James P. Blaylock; *Red Earth, Pouring Rain* by Vikram Chandra; *The Silent Strength of Stones* by Nina Kiriki Hoffman; *Requiem* by Graham Joyce; *Expiration Date* by Tim Powers

**1997 - *Godmother Night* by Rachel Pollack**

Runners-up: *Shadow of Ahland* by Terence M. Green; *The Bear Went Over the Mountain* by William Kotzwinkle; *The 37th Mandala* by Marc Laidlaw; *A Game of Thrones* by George R.R. Martin; *The Golden Key* by Melanie Rawn, Jennifer Roberson, and Kate Elliot; *The Devil's Tower* by Mark Sumner

**1998 - *The Physiognomy* by Jeffrey Ford**

Runners-up: *Trader* by Charles deLint; *American Goliath* by Harvey Jacobs; *The Gift* by Patrick O'Leary; *Dry Water* by Eric S. Nylund

### Best Collection

**1989 - *Storeys From the Old Hotel* by Gene Wolfe**

Runners-up: *Cabal* by Clive Barker; *Charles Beaumont: Selected Stories* by Charles Beaumont; *The Blood Kiss* by Dennis Etchison; *Angry Candy* by Harlan Ellison; *The Knight and Knave of Swords* by Fritz Leiber

**1990 - *Richard Matheson: Collected Stories* by Richard Matheson**

Runners-up: *Novelty* by John Crowley; *Harlan Ellison's Watching* by Harlan Ellison; *By Bizarre Hands* by Joe R. Lansdale; *Blue World and Other Stories* by Robert R. McCammon

**1991 - *The Start of the End of It All and Other Stories*** by Carol Emshwiller

Runners-up: *The Brains of Rats* by Michael Blumlein; *The Leiber Chronicles* by Fritz Leiber; *Prayers to Broken Stones* by Dan Simmons; *Houses Without Doors* by Peter Straub

**1992 - *The Ends of the Earth*** by Lucius Shephard

Runners-up: *More Shapes than One* by Fred Chappell; *The Bone Forest* by Robert Holdstock; *Lafferty in Orbit* by R.A. Lafferty; *Grimscribe: His Lives and Works* by Thomas Ligotti; *Night of the Cooters: More Neat Stories* by Howard Waldrop

**1993 - *The Sons of Noah and Other Stories*** by Jack Cady

Runners-up: *Bear's Fantasies* by Greg Bear; *Lord Kelvin's Machine* by James P. Blaylock; *Spiritwalk* by Charles de Lint; *Meeting in Infinity* by John Kessel; *Mr. Fox and Other Feral Tales* by Norman Partridge

**1994 - *Alone with the Horrors*** by Ramsey Campbell

Runners-up: *Antiquities* by John Crowley; *Dreams Underfoot* by Charles de Lint; *Angels & Visitations: A Miscellany* by Neil Gaiman; *Hogfoot Right and Bird-Hands* by Garry Kilworth; *Under the Crust* by Terry Lamsley; *Transients and Other Disquieting Stories* by Darrell Schweitzer

**1995 - *The Calvin Coolidge Home for Dead Comedians* and *A Conflagration Artist*** by Bradley Denton

Runners-up: *The Early Fears* by Robert Bloch; *Travelers in Magic* by Lisa Goldstein; *The Earth Wire & Other Stories* by Joel Lane; *Haunted: Tales of the Grotesque* by Joyce Carol Oates

**1996 - *Seven Tales and a Fable*** by Gwyneth Jones

Runners-up: *The Secret of This Book* by Brian Aldiss; *The Panic Hand* by Jonathan Carroll; *Death Stalks the Night* by Hugh B. Cave; *The Ivory and the Horn* by Charles de Lint

**1997 - *The Wall of the Sky, The Wall of the Eye*** by Johnathan Letham

Runners-up: *Midnight Promises* by Richard Chizmar; *Conference with the Dead* by Terry Lamsley; *The Nightmare Factory* by Thomas Ligotti; *Bible Stories for Adults* by James Morrow; *Bad Intentions* by Norman Partridge; *The Pavilion of Frozen Women* by S.P. Somtow

**1998 - *The Throne of Bones*** by Brian McNaughton

Runners-up: *Giant Bones* by Peter S. Beagle; *Driving Blind* by Ray Bradbury; *Fractal Paisleys* by Paul Di Filippo; *A Geography of Unknown Lands* by Michael Swanwick

## Best Anthology

**1989 - *The Year's Best Fantasy: First Annual Collection*, edited by Ellen Datlow and Terri Windling**

Runners-up: *Night Visions 6*, edited anonymously; *Silver Scream*, edited by David Schow; *Prime Evil*, edited by Douglas Winter

**1990 - *The Year's Best Fantasy: Second Annual Collection*, edited by Ellen Datlow and Terri Windling**

Runners-up: *Blood Is Not Enough*, edited by Ellen Datlow; *Razored Saddles*, edited by Joe R. Lansdale and Pat LoBrutto; *Book of the Dead*, edited by John Skipp and Craig Spector

**1991 - *Best New Horror*, edited by Stephen Jones and Ramsey Campbell**

Runners-up: *The Walls of Fear*, edited by Kathryn Cramer; *Alien Sex*, edited by Ellen Datlow; *The Year's Best Fantasy & Horror: 3rd Annual Collection*, edited by Ellen Datlow and Terri Windling; *Borderlands*, edited by Thomas F. Monteleone; *Dark Voices 2*, edited by David Sutton and Stephen Jones

**1992 - *The Year's Best Fantasy & Horror: Fourth Annual Collection*, edited by Ellen Datlow and Terri Windling**

Runners-up: *A Whisper of Blood*, edited by Ellen Datlow; *Famous Fantastic Mysteries*, edited by Stefan Dziemianowicz, Martin H. Greenberg, and Robert Weinberg; *Final Shadows*, edited by Charles L. Grant; *After the King*, edited by Martin H. Greenberg; *When the Music's Over*, edited by Lewis Shiner

**1993 - *Metahorror*, edited by Dennis Etchison**

Runners-up: *Narrow Houses*, edited by Peter Crowther; *Grails: Quests, Visitations, and Other Occurrences*, edited by Richard Gilliam, Martin H. Greenberg, and Edward E. Kramer; *Northern Frights*, edited by Don Hutchinson; *Freak Show*, edited by F. Paul Wilson

**1994 - *Full Spectrum 4*, edited by Lou Aronica, Amy Stout, and Betsy Mitchell**

Runners-up: *Snow White, Blood Red*, edited by Ellen Datlow and Terri Windling; *The Year's Best Fantasy and Horror #6*, edited by Ellen Datlow and Terri Windling; *Christmas Forever*, edited by David G. Hartwell; *Sinestre*, edited by George Hatch; *The Oxford Book of Modern Fairy Tales*, edited by Alison Lurie

**1995 - *Little Deaths*, edited by Ellen Datlow**

Runners-up: *Love in Vein*, edited by Poppy Z. Brite and Martin H. Greenberg; *Black Thorn, White Rose*, edited by Ellen Datlow and Terri Windling; *Shadows over Innsmouth*, edited by Stephen Jones

**1996 - *The Penguin Book of Modern Fantasy by Women*, edited by A. Susan Williams and Richard Glyn Jones**

Runners-up: *Dark Love*, edited by Nancy A. Collins, Edward E. Kramer, and Martin H. Greenberg; *Dark Terrors*, edited by Stephen Jones and David Sutton; *She's Fantastical*, edited by Lucy Sussex and Judith Buckrich; *High Fantastic*, edited by Steve Rasnic Tem

**1997 - *Starlight 1*, edited by Patrick Nielsen Hayden**

Runners-up: *The Year's Best Fantasy & Horror, Ninth Annual Collection* edited by Ellen Datlow and Terri Windling; *The Shimmering Door* edited by Katherine Kerr and Martin Greenberg; *Dark Terrors 2: The Gollancz Book of Horror* edited by Stephen Jones and David Sutton

**1998 - *Bending the Landscape: Fantasy*, edited by Nicola Griffith and Stephen Pagel**

Runners-up: *Modern Classics of Fantasy* edited by Gardner Dozois; *Northern Frights 4* edited by Don Hutchison; *Dark Terrors 3* edited by Stephen Jones and David Sutton

### Life Achievement Award

**1989 - Evangeline Walton**
**1990 - R.A. Lafferty**
**1991 - Ray Russell**
**1992 - Edd Cartier**
**1993 - Harlan Ellison**
**1994 - Jack Williamson**
**1995 - Ursula K. Le Guin**
**1996 - Gene Wolfe**
**1997 - Madeleine L'Engle**
**1998 - Edward L. Ferman; Andre Norton**

## Mythopoeic Society Fantasy Award

The Mythopoeic Awards are chosen each year by committees composed of volunteer Mythopoeic Society members and are presented at Mythcon. The award is a statuette of a seated lion, after Aslan from the *Chronicles of Narnia*. Since 1992, fantasy awards have been given in two categories: adult and children's literature.

### Fantasy Award

**1989 - *Unicorn Mountain* by Michael Bishop**
**1990 - *The Stress of Her Regard* by Tim Powers**
**1991 - *Thomas the Rhymer* by Ellen Kushner**

### Adult Fantasy Award

**1992 - *A Woman of the Iron People* by Eleanor Arnason**
**1993 - *Briar Rose* by Jane Yolen**
**1994 - *The Porcelain Dove* by Delia Sherman**
**1995 - *Something Rich and Strange* by Patricia A. McKillip**
**1996 - *Waking the Moon* by Elizabeth Hand**
**1997 - *The Wood Wife* by Terri Windling**
**1998 - *The Djinn in the Nightingale's Eye* by A.S. Byatt**

### Children's Fantasy Award

**1992 - *Haroun and the Sea of Stories* by Salman Rushdie**
**1993 - *Knight's Wyrd* by Debra Doyle and James D. Macdonald**
**1994 - *The Kingdom of Kevin Malone* by Suzy McKee Charnas**
**1995 - *Owl in Love* by Patrice Kindl**
**1996 - *The Crown of Dalemark* by Diana Wynne Jones**
**1997 - (Combined with Adult Literature Award)**
**1998 - *Young Merlin Trilogy* (includes *Passager, Hobby,* and *Merlin*) by Jane Yolen**

## Bram Stoker Award

Named after the author of *Dracula*, this award is voted upon by active members of the Horror Writers Association at an annual summer conference. See also the World Fantasy Awards above.

### Best Novel

**1989 - *The Silence of the Lambs* by Thomas Harris**

Runners-up: *Stinger* by Robert R. McCammon; *Black Wind* by F. Paul Wilson; *The Drive-In* by Joe R. Lansdale; *Queen of the Damned* by Anne Rice; *Flesh* by Richard Laymon.

**1990 - *Carrion Comfort* by Dan Simmons**

Runners-up: *Geek Love* by Katherine Dunn; *In a Dark Dream* by Charles L. Grant; *Midnight* by Dean R. Koontz; *The Wolf's Hour* by Robert R. McCammon

**1991 - *Mine* by Robert R. McCammon**

Runners-up: *Funland* by Richard Layman; *Reign* by Chet Williamson; *Savage Season* by Joe R. Lansdale

**1992 - *Boy's Life* by Robert R. McCammon**

Runners-up: *The M.D.* by Thomas M. Disch; *Needful Things* by Stephen King; *Dark Tower III: The Waste Lands* by Stephen King; *Summer of Night* by Dan Simmons

**1993 - *Blood of the Lamb* by Thomas F. Monteleone**

Runners-up: *Homecoming* by Matthew Costello; *Deathgrip* by Brian Hodge; *Hideaway* by Dean Koontz; *Children of the Night* by Dan Simmons

**1994 - *The Throat* by Peter Straub**

Runners-up: *Anno Dracula* by Kim Newman; *Blackburn* by Bradley Denton; *Drawing Blood* by Poppy Z. Brite; *The Summoning* by Bentley Little

**1995 - *Dead in the Water* by Nancy Holder**

Runners-up: *The Alienist* by Caleb Carr; *From the Teeth of Angels* by Jonathan Carroll; *Insomnia* by Stephen King; *The Butcher Boy* by Patrick McCabe

**1996 - *Zombie* by Joyce Carol Oates**

Runners-Up: *Widow* by Billie Sue Mosiman; *deadrush* by Yvonne Navarro; *Bone Music* by Alan Rodgers

**1997 - *The Green Mile* by Stephen King**

Runners-up: *Exquisite Corpse* by Poppy Z. Brite; *Crota* by Owl Goingback; *The Hellfire Club* by Peter Straub

**1998 - *Children of the Dusk* by Janet Berliner and George Gutheridge**

Runners-up: *The Church of Dead Girls* by Stephen Dobyns; *My Soul to Keep* by Tananarive Due; *Earthquake Weather* by Tim Powers

### Best First Novel

**1989 -** *The Suiting* by Kelley Wilde
**1990 -** *Sunglasses After Dark* by Nancy A. Collins
**1991 -** *The Revelation* by Bentley Little
**1992 -** *The Cipher* by Kathe Koja and *Prodigal* by Melanie Tem
**1993 -** *Sineater* by Elizabeth Massie
**1994 -** *The Thread That Binds the Bones* by Nina Kiriki Hoffman
**1995 -** *Grave Markings* by Michael Arnzen
**1996 -** *The Safety of Unknown Cities* by Lucy Taylor
**1997 -** *Crota* by Owl Goingback
**1998 -** *Lives of the Monster Dogs* by Kirsten Bakis

### Best Collection

**1989 - *Charles Beaumont: Selected Stories* by Charles Beaumont**

Runners-up: *The Toynbee Convector* by Ray Bradbury; *Angry Candy* by Harlan Ellison; *The Blood Kiss* by Dennis Etchison; *Scare Tactics* by John Farris; *Blood and Water and Other Tales* by Patrick McGrath

**1990 - *Richard Matheson: Collected Stories* by Richard Matheson**

Runners-up: *Blue World and Other Stories* by Robert R. McCammon; *By Bizarre Hands* by Joe R. Lansdale; *Patterns* by Pat Cadigan; *Soft and Others* by F. Paul Wilson

**1991 - *Four Past Midnight* by Stephen King**

Runners-up: *Houses Without Doors* by Peter Straub; *Prayers to Broken Stones* by Dan Simmons; *The Brains of Rats* by Michael Blumlein

**1992 - *Prayers to Broken Stones* by Dan Simmons**

Runners-up: *Waking Nightmares* by Ramsey Campbell; *Sexpunks & Savage Sagas* by Richard Sutphen; *The Naked Flesh of Feeling* by J.N. Williamson

**1993 - *Mr. Fox and Other Feral Tales* by Norman Partridge**

Runners-up: *Nightmare Flower* by Elizabeth Engstrom; *Fantastic Tales* by I.U. Tarchetti

**1994 - *Alone with the Horrors* by Ramsey Campbell**

Runners-up: *Close to the Bone* by Lucy Taylor; *A Good, Secret Place* by Richard Laymon; *Lovedeath* by Dan Simmons; *Nightmares & Dreamscapes* by Stephen King

**1995 - *The Early Fears* by Robert Bloch**

Runners-up: *Writer of the Purple Rage* by Joe R. Lansdale; *The Flesh Artist* by Lucy Taylor; *Born Bad* by Andrew Vachss

**1996 - *The Panic Hand* by Jonathan Carroll**

Runners-up: *Cages* by Ed Gorman; *The Black Carousel* by Charles L. Grant; *Strange Highways* by Dean R. Koontz

**1997 - *The Nightmare Factory* by Thomas Ligotti**

Runners-up: *The Convulsion Factory* by Brian Hodge; *Shadow Dreams* by Elizabeth Massie; *With Wounds Still Wet* by Wayne Allen Sallee; *The Pavilion of Frozen Women* by S.P. Somtow

**1998 - *Excorcisms and Ecstasies* by Karl Edward Wagner**

Runners-up: *Things Left Behind* by Gary A. Braunbeck; *The Throne of Bones* by Brian McNaughton; *Painted in Blood* by Lucy Taylor

### Lifetime Achievement Award

**1989 - Ray Bradbury; Ronald Chetwynd-Hayes**
**1990 - Robert Bloch**
**1991 - Hugh B. Cave; Richard Matheson**
**1992 - Gahan Wilson**
**1993 - Ray Russell**
**1994 - Joyce Carol Oates**
**1995 - Christopher Lee**
**1996 - Harlan Ellison**
**1997 - Ira Levin; Forrest J. Ackerman**
**1998 - William Peter Blatty; Jack Williamson**

## Hugo Award

The Hugos, named for Hugo Gernsback, founding editor of *Amazing Stories*, are given at the world SF conventions (worldcons) held over Labor Day each year and are chosen by the votes of those attending or supporting the convention.

### Best Novel

**1989 - *Cyteen* by C.J. Cherryh**

Runners-up: *Red Prophet* by Orson Scott Card; *Falling Free* by Lois McMaster Bujold; *Islands in the Net* by Bruce Sterling; *Mona Lisa Overdrive* by William Gibson

### 1990 - *Hyperion* by Dan Simmons

Runners-up: *The Boat of a Million Years* by Poul Anderson; *Prentice Alvin* by Orson Scott Card; *A Fire in the Sun* by George Alec Effinger; *Grass* by Sheri S. Tepper

### 1991 - *The Vor Game* by Lois McMaster Bujold

Runners-up: *Earth* by David Brin; *The Fall of Hyperion* by Dan Simmons; *The Quiet Pools* by M.P. Kube-McDowell; and *Queen of Angels* by Greg Bear

### 1992 - *Barrayar* by Lois McMaster Bujold

Runners-up: *Bone Dance* by Emma Bull; *All the Weyrs of Pern* by Anne McCaffrey; *The Summer Queen* by Joan Vinge; *Xenocide* by Orson Scott Card; *Stations of the Tide* by Michael Swanwick

### 1993 - *A Fire upon the Deep* by Vernor Vinge and *Doomsday Book* by Connie Willis

Runners-up: *Red Mars* by Kim Stanley Robinson; *China Mountain Zhang* by Maureen F. McHugh; *Steel Beach* by John Varley

### 1994 - *Green Mars* by Kim Stanley Robinson

Runners-up: *Moving Mars* by Greg Bear; *Glory Season* by David Brin; *Virtual Light* by William Gibson; *Beggars in Spain* by Nancy Kress

### 1995 - *Mirror Dance* by Lois McMaster Bujold

Runners-up: *Mother of Storms* by John Barnes; *Brittle Innings* by Michael Bishop; *Beggars and Choosers* by Nancy Kress; *Towing Jehovah* by James Morrow

### 1996 - *The Diamond Age* by Neal Stephenson

Runners-up: *The Time Ships* by Stephen Baxter; *Brightness Reef* by David Brin; *The Terminal Experiment* by Robert J. Sawyer; *Remake* by Connie Willis

### 1997 - *Blue Mars* by Kim Stanley Robinson

Runners-up: *Memory* by Lois McMaster Bujold; *Remnant Population* by Elizabeth Moon; *Starplex* by Robert J. Sawyer; *Holy Fire* by Bruce Sterling

### 1998 - *Forever Peace* by Joe Haldeman

Runners-up: *Frameshift* by Robert J. Sawyer; *The Rise of Endymion* by Dan Simmons; *City on Fire* by Walter Jon Williams; *Jack Faust* by Michael Swanwick

## John W. Campbell Award for Best New Writer

This award, not to be confused with the John W. Cambell Memorial Award for Best Science Fiction Novel, is given annually at the world SF conventions (Worldcon) held on Labor Day. Though it is presented with the Hugos at the yearly conventions and chosen in the same fashion, it is not a Hugo award.

**1989 - Michaela Roessner**
**1990 - Kristine Kathryn Rusch**
**1991 - Julia Ecklar**
**1992 - Ted Chiang**
**1993 - Laura Resnick**
**1994 - Amy Thomson**
**1995 - Jeff Noon**
**1996 - David Feintuch**
**1997 - Michael A Burstein**
**1998 - Maria Doria Russell**

## John W. Campbell Memorial Award

The John W. Campbell Memorial Award, not to be confused with the award by the same name for best new writer, is named for the late editor of *Analog* (formerly called *Astounding Science Fiction Magazine*). It is given annually for the best science fiction novel of the year. The award winners are selected by a small committee of members who meet annually and reach a consensus about the best novel of the preceding year.

### Best Science Fiction Novel

### 1989 - *Islands in the Net* by Bruce Sterling

Second Place: *The Gold Coast* by Kim Stanley Robinson; Third Place: *Dragonsdawn* by Anne McCaffrey

### 1990 - *The Child Garden* by Geoff Ryman

Second Place: *Farewell Horizontal* by K.W. Jeter; Third Place: *Good News From Outer Space* by John Kessel

### 1991 - *Pacific Edge* by Kim Stanley Robinson

Second Place: *Queen of Angels* by Greg Bear; Third Place: *Only Begotten Daughter* by James Morrow

### 1992 - *Buddy Holly Is Alive and Well on Ganymede* by Bradley Denton

Second Place: *The Difference Engine* by William Gibson and Bruce Sterling; Third Place (tie): *A Woman of the Iron People* by Eleanor Arnason; *Stations of the Tide* by Micheal Swanwick; *The Silicon Man* by Charles Platt

### 1993 - *Brother to Dragons* by Charles Sheffield

Second Place: *Sideshow* by Sheri S. Tepper; Third Place: *A Fire Upon the Deep* by Vernor Vinge

### 1994 - No Award for 1st Place

Second Place: *Beggars in Spain* by Nancy Kress; Third Place: *Moving Mars* by Greg Bear

### 1995 - *Permutation City* by Greg Egan

Second Place: *Brittle Innings* by Michael Bishop; Third Place: No Award Given

**1996 - *The Time Ships* by Stephen Baxter**

Second Place: *The Diamond Age* by Neal Stephenson; Third Place: *Chaga* by Ian McDonald

**1997 - *Fairyland* by Paul McAuley**

Second Place: *Blue Mars* by Kim Stanley Robinson; Third Place: *The Sparrow* by Maria Doria Russell

**1998 - *Forever Peace* by Joe Haldeman**

Second Place: *Slant* by Greg Bear; Third Place: *Secret Passages* by Paul Preuss

## Nebula Award

Given by the Science Fiction and Fantasy Writers of America, an organization of about 1,300 members, of whom about a third vote. The awards, in four fiction categories of varying length, are announced several months before the Hugos and probably influence the voting for them. Because of the Nebula rules, some candidates are published prior to the immediately preceding year.

### Best Novel

**1989 - *The Healer's War* by Elizabeth Ann Scarborough**

Runners-up: *The Boat of a Million Years* by Poul Anderson; *Prentice Alvin* by Orson Scott Card; *Good News From Outer Space* by John Kessel; *Ivory* by Mike Resnick; *Sister Light, Sister Dark* by Jane Yolen

**1990 - *Tehanu: The Last Book of Earthsea* by Ursula K. Le Guin**

Runners-up: *Mary Reilly* by Valerie Martin; *Only Begotten Daughter* by James Morrow; *The Fall of Hyperion* by Dan Simmons; *Redshift Rendezvous* by John E. Stith; *White Jenna* by Jane Yolen

**1991 - *Stations of the Tide* by Michael Swanwick**

Runners-up: *Orbital Resonance* by John Barnes; *Barrayar* by Lois McMaster Bujold; *Bone Dance* by Emma Bull; *The Difference Engine* by William Gibson and Bruce Sterling

**1992 - *Doomsday Book* by Connie Willis**

Runners-up: *A Million Open Doors* by John Barnes; *Sarah Canary* by Karen Joy Fowler; *China Mountain Zhang* by Maureen McHugh; *A Fire Upon the Deep* by Vernor Vinge; *Briar Rose* by Jane Yolen

**1993 - *Red Mars* by Kim Stanley Robinson**

Runners-up: *Assemblers of Infinity* by Kevin J. Anderson and Doug Beason; *Hard Landing* by A.J. Budrys; *Beggars in Spain* by Nancy Kress; *Nightside the Long Sun* by Gene Wolfe

**1994 - *Moving Mars* by Greg Bear**

Runners-up: *Parable of the Sower* by Octavia Butler; *Gun, with Occasional Music* by Jonathan Lethem; *Temporary Agency* by Rachel Pollack; *Green Mars* by Kim Stanley Robinson; *A Night in the Lonesome October* by Roger Zelazny

**1995 - *The Terminal Experiment* by Robert J. Sawyer**

Runners-up: *Mother of Storms* by John Barnes; *Beggars and Choosers* by Nancy Kress; *Celestis* by Paul Park; *Metropolitan* by Walter Jon Williams; *Calde of the Long Sun* by Gene Wolfe

**1996 - *Slow River* by Nicola Griffith**

Runners-up: *The Silent Strength of Stones* by Nina Kiriki Hoffman; *Winter Rose* by Patricia McKillip; *Expiration Date* by Tim Powers; *The Diamond Age* by Neal Stephenson; *Starplex* by Robert J. Sawyer

**1997 - *The Moon and the Sun* by Vonda N. McIntyre**

Runners-up: *Memory* by Lois McMaster Bujold; *King's Dragon* by Kate Elliot; *A Game of Thrones* by George R.R. Martin; *Ancient Shores* by Jack McDevitt; *City on Fire* by Walter Jon Williams; *Bellwether* by Connie Willis

**1998 - *Forever Peace* by Joe Haldeman**

Runners-up: *The Last Hawk* by Catherine Asaro; *Moonfall* by Jack McDevitt; *How Few Remain* by Harry Turtledove; *Death of the Necromancer* by Martha Wells; *To Say Nothing of the Dog* by Connie Willis

### Grand Master

**1990 - Lester del Ray**
**1992 - Frederik Pohl**
**1994 - Damon Knight**
**1995 - A.E. Van Vogt**
**1996 - Jack Vance**
**1997 - Poul Anderson**
**1998 - Hal Clement**

## Arthur C. Clarke Award

The Arthur C. Clarke Award honors the best British science fiction novel from the previous year.

### Best Novel

**1989 - *Unquenchable Fire* by Rachel Pollack**
**1990 - *The Child Garden* by Geoff Ryman**
**1991 - *Take Back Plenty* by Colin Greenland**
**1992 - *Synners* by Pat Cadigan**
**1993 - *Body of Glass* by Marge Piercy (U.S. title: *He, She and It*)**
**1994 - *Vurt* by Jeff Noon**
**1995 - *Fools* by Pat Cadigan**
**1996 - *Fairyland* by Paul McAuley**
**1997 - *The Calcutta Chromosome* by AmitavGhosh**
**1998 - *The Sparrow* by Mary Doria Russell**

# Fantastic Fiction Titles

## ANONYMOUS

### *The Raven and the Monkey's Paw*
(New York: Modern Library, 1998)

**Story type:** Horror (Anthology)

**Summary:** Stories and poems of the macabre culled from Modern Library editions of classic literary writers. Eight stories and all eight poems are by Edgar Allan Poe, including the conte cruel "The Pit and the Pendulum," the tale of psychological horror "The Telltale Heart," the seminal detective story "Murders in the Rue Morgue," and the classic poem "The Raven." The other eight fiction selections include Edith Wharton's ghost story "Afterward," W.W. Jacobs's tale of wish-fulfillment "The Monkey's Paw," Wilkie Collins' weird crime story "A Terribly Strange Bed," and selections by Charles Dickens, O. Henry, Saki and Ambrose Bierce.

**Other books you might like:**
Alexander Laing, *The Haunted Omnibus*, 1937
    editor
Robert Phillips, *Triumph of the Night*, 1989
    editor
Philip Van Doren Stern, *The Midnight Reader*, 1942
    editor
Dennis Wheatley, *A Century of Horror Stories*, 1935
    editor
Herbert Wise, *Great Tales of Terror and the Supernatural*, 1944
    Phyllis Fraser, co-editor

## PATRICIA AAKHUS

### *The Voyage of Mael Duin's Curragh*
(Santa Cruz: Storyline Press, 1989)

**Story type:** Fantasy (Legend)
**Major character(s):** Mael Duin, Outcast, Wanderer
**Time period(s):** Indeterminate
**Locale(s):** At Sea (Heading for Viking territory)

**Summary:** Mael Duin sets out in a curragh on a sea quest to avenge the murder of his father. Caught in a storm, the curragh drifts from the shore, landing on strange and magical islands. On one Mael Duin

is captivated by the witch, Epona. Story explores the Celtic legend from *The Book of the Dun Cow.*

**Other books you might like:**
Kenneth C. Flint, *Isle of Destiny*,
R.A. MacAvoy, *The Book of Kells*, 1989
Robin McKinley, *The Outlaws of Sherwood*, 1989
Mickey Zucker Reichert, *Dragonrank Master*, 1989
Mickey Zucker Reichert, *Godslayer*, 1987
    Book 1-The Bifrost Guardians
Gene Wolfe, *Soldier of Arete*, 1989

## 3

## DONALD AAMODT

### *A Name to Conjure With*
(New York: Avon, 1989)

**Story type:** Fantasy (Light Fantasy)
**Series:** Sandy MacGregor
**Major character(s):** Sandy MacGregor, Hero, Wizard; Zhadnoboth, Sorcerer
**Time period(s):** 1980s
**Locale(s):** Zarathandra, Alternate Universe

**Summary:** Sandy MacGregor is summoned, by way of an elevator shaft turned portal, to the world of Zarathandra, in a parallel universe. Here he is ordered by the Veiled Goddess to accompany the inept and greedy sorcerer Zhadnoboth and two revenge-seeking berserkers on a quest to loot the mountain stronghold of her nemesis, the evil god Kels Zalkir. In his quest, Sandy discovers that his "name" in this world commands unknown magical and often times uncontrollable powers.

**Other books you might like:**
Mayer Alan Brenner, *Catastrophe's Spell*, 1989
Brad Strickland, *Nul's Quest*, 1989

## 4

## DONALD AAMODT

### *A Troubling Along the Border*
(New York: Avon, 1991)

**Story type:** Fantasy (Light Fantasy; Adventure)

**Series:** Sandy MacGregor
**Major character(s):** Sandy MacGregor, Hero (reluctant), Wizard; Zhadnoboth, Sorcerer
**Time period(s):** Indeterminate
**Locale(s):** Zarathandra, Alternate Universe

**Summary:** Stuck on the planet Zarathandra, Sandy MacGregor remains the unwilling tool of the goddess of love who now sends him to a realm between worlds to battle an ancient demon.

**Other books you might like:**
Isaac Asimov, *The Gods Themselves*, 1972
Mayer Alan Brenner, *Catastrophe's Spell*, 1989
Jo Clayton, *Wild Magic*, 1991
Pamela Dean, *The Hidden Land*, 1986
Pamela Dean, *The Secret Country*, 1985
Pamela Dean, *The Whim of the Dragon*, 1989
David Eddings, *The Sapphire Rose*, 1991
P.C. Hodgell, *Dark of the Moon*, 1985
P.C. Hodgell, *God Stalk*, 1982
Brad Strickland, *Nul's Quest*, 1989

**SHALE AARON**

## Virtual Death

(New York: HarperPrism, 1995)

**Story type:** Science Fiction (Satire; Arts)
**Major character(s):** Lydia Melmoth, Artist (death artist), Fugitive; Frankly Adams, Artist (depressionist), Fugitive; Stamen Melmoth, Government Official, Fugitive
**Time period(s):** 21st Century
**Locale(s):** New York, New York; Philadelphia, Pennsylvania

**Summary:** When authorities identify Lydia's mother as a "Banjo" terrorist, Lydia goes underground to escape arrest. Lydia soon discovers that everyone around her selfishly wants her to resume her career as the greatest death artist in the world. First novel.

**Other books you might like:**
Jonathan Carroll, *From the Teeth of Angels*, 1994
William Gibson, *Neuromancer*, 1984
Parke Godwin, *Waiting for the Galactic Bus*, 1988
Shariann Lewitt, *Memento Mori*, 1995
John Varley, *Steel Beach*, 1992

**DAFYDD AB HUGH**

## Arthur War Lord

(New York: AvoNova, 1994)

**Story type:** Fantasy (Time Travel; Legend)
**Series:** Arthur War Lord
**Major character(s):** Peter Smythe, Time Traveler, Military Personnel (major); Cors Cant Ewin, Minstrel (bard); Anlawdd, Royalty (princess), Criminal (assassin)
**Time period(s):** 1990s; 5th century
**Locale(s):** Caer Camlann Castle, England

**Summary:** Sent to investigate possible IRA involvement in a top-secret British military research project, Peter Smythe wakes one night and discovers that one of the scientists, using the project's time machine to send her mind to the 5th century A.D., has changed the present through her actions in the past. Smythe follows, hoping to undo the damage, and finds his consciousness inside the mind of Lancelot at King Arthur's court. Now he must figure out which of the

other minds harbors the IRA agent, and whether she intends to kill King Arthur or save him.

**Other books you might like:**
Poul Anderson, *The Shield of Time*, 1990
Gordon R. Dickson, *The Dragon and the George*, 1976
Phyllis Eisenstein, *Shadow of Earth*, 1979
Katherine Kurtz, *The Lodge of the Lynx*, 1992
    Deborah Turner Harris, co-author
Robert Silverberg, *Letters From Atlantis*, 1990

**DAFYDD AB HUGH**

## Balance of Power

(New York: Pocket, 1995)

**Story type:** Science Fiction (Space Opera; Political)
**Series:** Star Trek: The Next Generation
**Major character(s):** Wesley Crusher, Student—College, Military Personnel; Jean-Luc Picard, Spaceship Captain, Military Personnel; Geordi La Forge, Engineer, Military Personnel
**Time period(s):** 24th century
**Locale(s):** *U.S.S. Enterprise*, Spaceship; San Francisco, California; United Federation of Planets, Interstellar Empire/Federation

**Summary:** When a Federation scientist dies and his inventions go up for auction, various members of the *Enterprise* crew receive authorization to bid on them, particularly a photonic pulse cannon. Meanwhile, at Starfleet Academy, Wesley Crusher's best friend has found a way to counterfeit gold-pressed latinum. When Wesley tries to stop the theft of the counterfeiting device, a Ferengi outlaw kidnaps him as well. At the auction the Ferengi will outbid everyone with their counterfeit latinum, unless Wesley can figure out a way to escape his captors, keep the cannon out of Cardassian hands, and avoid expulsion from the Academy as AWOL.

**Other books you might like:**
Robert Asprin, *Phule's Paradise*, 1992
Diane Carey, *Battlestations!*, 1986
Carolyn Clowes, *The Pandora Principle*, 1990
John M. Ford, *How Much for Just the Planet?*, 1987
William R. Thompson, *Debtors' Planet*, 1994

**DAFYDD AB HUGH**

## Fallen Heroes

(New York: Pocket, 1994)

**Story type:** Science Fiction (Space Opera; Time Travel)
**Series:** Star Trek: Deep Space Nine
**Major character(s):** Benjamin Sisko, Leader, Military Personnel; Quark, Alien (Ferengi), Saloon Keeper/Owner; Odo, Alien (shapeshifter), Security Officer
**Time period(s):** 24th century
**Locale(s):** Deep Space Nine, Space Station (Bajoran)

**Summary:** When warriors determined to save a comrade attack Deep Space Nine, Benjamin Sisko and his crew struggle to save the station and its personnel. However, Quark and Odo, thrown three days forward in time by a Gamma Quadrant device, find a deserted Deep Space Nine and must unravel the invasion's cause and discover a way to return to the past and save the station.

**Other books you might like:**
Esther Friesner, *Warchild*, 1994
K.W. Jeter, *Bloodletter*, 1993

Sandy Schofield, *The Big Game*, 1993
Lois Tilton, *Betrayal*, 1994
John Vornholt, *Antimatter*, 1994

**9**

**DAFYDD AB HUGH**

## The Final Fury

(New York: Pocket, 1996)

**Story type:** Science Fiction (Space Opera)
**Series:** Star Trek: Voyager
**Major character(s):** Kathryn Janeway, Spaceship Captain, Space Explorer, Military Personnel; B'Elanna Torres, Engineer, Alien (half-Klingon); Neelix, Alien (Talaxian), Cook
**Time period(s):** 24th century
**Locale(s):** *U.S.S. Voyager*, Spaceship; Planet—Imaginary; Delta Quadrant, Outer Space

**Summary:** *Voyager*'s crew intercepts a Starfleet distress call in the Delta quadrant. The signal leads them to a nightmarish planet filled with demonic-looking aliens and a Federation pilot held captive on it. Captain Janeway and her Away Team free the pilot, but must determine how they can stop an invasion force of 27 billion preparing to mount an assault against the Alpha Quadrant. Concludes the four-part Invasion! Series which spans all four Star Trek television series.

**Other books you might like:**
James Blish, *Cities in Flight*, 1970
Diane Carey, *First Strike*, 1996
Alan Dean Foster, *Aliens*, 1986
L.A. Graf, *Time's Enemy*, 1996
Barbara Paul, *The Three Minute Universe*, 1988
Dean Wesley Smith, *The Soldiers of Fear*, 1996
    Kristine Kathryn Rusch, co-author

**10**

**DAFYDD AB HUGH**

## Vengeance

(New York: Pocket Books, 1998)

**Story type:** Science Fiction (Space Opera; Military)
**Series:** Star Trek: Deep Space Nine
**Major character(s):** Miles O'Brien, Engineer, Military Personnel (Starfleet); Julian Bashir, Doctor, Genetically Altered Being; Benjamin Sisko, Spaceship Captain
**Time period(s):** 24th century
**Locale(s):** Deep Space Nine, Space Station; *U.S.S. Defiant*, Spaceship

**Summary:** Rumors of a secret alliance between the Dominion and the Klingon Empire lure Captain Sisko and the *Defiant* into the Gamma Quadrant, leaving Deep Space Nine vulnerable to a surprise attack. A Klingon force seizes control of the station, leaving only a handful of residents able to resist them. Worf finds himself torn between loyalty to Starfleet and to his blood brother Malach, who leads the invaders.

**Other books you might like:**
C.J. Cherryh, *Downbelow Station*, 1981
Greg Cox, *Devil in the Sky*, 1995
David Drake, *Starliner*, 1992
Michael Jan Friedman, *Kahless*, 1996
L.A. Graf, *Crossroad*, 1994

**11**

**DAFYDD AB HUGH**

## Warriorwards

(New York: Baen, 1990)

**Story type:** Fantasy (Magic Conflict)
**Series:** Jiana
**Major character(s):** Jiana, Warrior; Radience, Slave; Toq, Mythical Creature (Boy-God)
**Time period(s):** Indeterminate
**Locale(s):** Bay Bay, Alternate Earth

**Summary:** Jiana, an unemployed warrior adept, wants to free the enslaved Radience. Unfortunately, slaves can become free only by freeing themselves, so Jiana must become a slave to set an example for Radience. Jiana is hampered by interference from her alter egos, the boy-god Toq, and the memories she continually must suppress.

**Other books you might like:**
C.J. Cherryh, *Wizard Spawn*, 1989
    Nancy Asire, co-author
C.J. Cherryh, *The Paladin*, 1988
Elizabeth Moon, *Sheepfarmer's Daughter*, 1988
Kate Wilhelm, *Cambio Bay*, 1990
Gene Wolfe, *Soldier of Arete*, 1989
Gene Wolfe, *Soldier of the Mist*, 1986

**12**

**LYNN ABBEY**

## Beneath the Web

(New York: Ace, 1994)

**Story type:** Fantasy (Magic Conflict; Romance)
**Major character(s):** Berika Ingoldesdaughter, Shepherd, Sorceress; Rinchen ''Wolf'' sorRodion, Royalty (prince); Driskolt ''Dart'' sorMeklan, Nobleman
**Time period(s):** Indeterminate
**Locale(s):** Walensor, Fictional Country; Eyerlon, Fictional City

**Summary:** Now the mistress of a nobleman, Berika treads a precarious path among the factions in Eyerlon. When enemies attack the network of power, the Web, Berika must choose her allies with care if she hopes to save Walensor. Sequel to *The Wooden Sword*.

**Other books you might like:**
C.J. Cherryh, *Angel with the Sword*, 1985
Phyllis Eisenstein, *In the Red Lord's Reach*, 1989
Simon R. Green, *Blue Moon Rising*, 1991
Barbara Hambly, *Dog Wizard*, 1993
Patricia C. Wrede, *Shadow Magic*, 1982

**13**

**LYNN ABBEY**

## The Brazen Gambit

(Lake Geneva, Wisconsin: TSR, 1994)

**Story type:** Fantasy (Political; Adventure)
**Series:** Dark Sun: Chronicles of Athas
**Major character(s):** Pavek of Urik, Religious (templar), Adventurer
**Time period(s):** Indeterminate
**Locale(s):** Athas, Planet—Imaginary

**Summary:** After discovering a plot, Pavek flees the city of Urik for the desert lest he die at the hands of people he formerly trusted. Game tie-in and first of a series.

**Other books you might like:**
Troy Denning, *The Crimson Legion*, 1992
Troy Denning, *The Verdant Passage*, 1991
Simon Hawke, *The Outcast*, 1993
Simon Hawke, *The Seeker*, 1994
Ryan Hughes, *The Darkness Before the Dawn*, 1995

**14**

**LYNN ABBEY**
**ROBERT ASPRIN**, Co-Author

## *Catwoman*

(New York: Warner, 1992)

**Story type:** Science Fiction (Adventure)
**Series:** Batman
**Major character(s):** Selena ''Catwoman'' Kyle, Criminal, Heroine; Bruce ''Batman'' Wayne, Hero, Detective—Amateur; Eddie ''Tiger'' Lobb, Criminal
**Time period(s):** 1990s
**Locale(s):** Gotham City (New York City)

**Summary:** Catwoman appeals to the Wilderness Warriors for assistance in dealing with Eddie Lobb, an unscrupulous collector of tiger pelts. As she tries to bring Lobb to justice, Catwoman crosses paths with Batman, who is following the trail of illegal arms sales to members of the former Soviet Union.

**Other books you might like:**
Craig Shaw Gardner, *Batman*, 1989
Craig Shaw Gardner, *The Batman Murders*, 1990
Craig Shaw Gardner, *Batman Returns*, 1992
Martin H. Greenberg, *The Further Adventures of Batman*, 1989
    editor
Martin H. Greenberg, *The Further Adventures of Batman 2: Featuring the Penguin*, 1992
    editor
Martin H. Greenberg, *The Further Adventures of the Joker*, 1990
    editor
Simon Hawke, *Batman: To Stalk a Specter*, 1991
Joe R. Lansdale, *Batman: Captured by the Engines*, 1991

**15**

**LYNN ABBEY**

## *Cinnabar Shadows*

(Lake Geneva, Wisconsin: TSR, 1995)

**Story type:** Fantasy (Magic Conflict)
**Series:** Dark Sun: Chronicles of Athas
**Major character(s):** Kakzim, Religious (brother), Mythical Creature (halfling); Mahtra, Genetically Altered Being; Pavek of Urik, Religious, Adventurer
**Time period(s):** Indeterminate
**Locale(s):** Athas, Planet—Imaginary

**Summary:** The insane Brother Kakzim wants to fulfill the Black Tree brethren's goals by destroying the city of Urik. The first steps of his most recent plan leave Mahtra homeless and alone, while vengeance and greed may destroy everything.

**Other books you might like:**
M.A.R. Barker, *Man of Gold*, 1984
Steven Brust, *Jhereg*, 1983

Glen Cook, *The Black Company*, 1984
Anne Logston, *Shadow*, 1991
Julian May, *The Many-Colored Land*, 1981

**16**

**LYNN ABBEY**

## *The Forge of Virtue*

(New York: Popular Library Questar, 1991)

**Story type:** Fantasy (Quest)
**Series:** Ultima Saga
**Major character(s):** Jordan Hawson, Knight; Althea, Gentlewoman; Drumon, Artisan (farrier)
**Time period(s):** Indeterminate Past
**Locale(s):** Brittania, Fictional Country

**Summary:** Lord British, ruler of Brittania, has disappeared and the members of the Council of Mages are in hiding. Althea's brother Balthan, amanuensis to Mage Felespar of the Council, is also missing, and the only clue to his fate is a magic talisman that points to Britain City. Althea persuades Jordan and Drumon to help her find her brother. As they meet and overcome various perils, it becomes apparent that there is more at stake than one young magician's life.

**Other books you might like:**
Eleanor Arnason, *The Sword Smith*, 1978
Phyllis Eisenstein, *The Crystal Palace*, 1988
Elizabeth Ann Scarborough, *The Christening Quest*, 1985
J.R.R. Tolkien, *The Hobbit*, 1938
Patricia C. Wrede, *Shadow Magic*, 1982

**17**

**LYNN ABBEY**

## *The Temper of Wisdom*

(New York: Warner Questar, 1992)

**Story type:** Fantasy (Quest; Magic Conflict)
**Series:** Ultima Saga
**Major character(s):** Jordan Hawson, Knight, Handicapped; Balthan Wanderson, Magician
**Time period(s):** Indeterminate Past
**Locale(s):** Brittania, Fictional Country

**Summary:** Jordan, his companions, and the rescued Balthan return home to find Hawksnest enthralled by the corrupt Inquisitor Lohgrin. Balthan, accused as a traitor, must flee the castle. In order to free Hawksnest, the companions must find a way to destroy Lohgrin's sorcery.

**Other books you might like:**
Robin Wayne Bailey, *Nightwatch*, 1990
C.J. Cherryh, *The Tree of Swords and Jewels*, 1983
Stephen R. Donaldson, *Lord Foul's Bane*, 1977
Randall Garrett, *Too Many Magicians*, 1967
Katherine Kurtz, *Deryni Rising*, 1970
Elizabeth Marie Pope, *The Perilous Gard*, 1974

**18**

**LYNN ABBEY**

## *The Wooden Sword*

(New York: Ace, 1991)

**Story type:** Fantasy (Adventure; Mystery)

**Major character(s):** Berika Ingoldesdaughter, Shepherd, Runaway; Dart, Nobleman, Amnesiac; Hirmin, Farmer, Fiance(e)
**Time period(s):** Indeterminate
**Locale(s):** Walensor, Fictional Country

**Summary:** When Berika prays to the gods to show her a way to escape the village of Gorge and her impending marriage to the sadistic Hirmin, she opens her eyes and sees Dart, who brings with him a magic harp, but no memory. When Dart helps Berika escape, Hirmin pursues the runaways, but is killed with a wooden sword which the forest goddess, Weycha, provides. Dart and Berika try to make their way to Eyerlon, the capital, while avoiding detection by the government's sorcerers and discovery of Dart's identity and mission.

**Other books you might like:**
C.J. Cherryh, *Rusalka*, 1989
Phyllis Eisenstein, *Born to Exile*, 1978
Ursula K. Le Guin, *A Wizard of Earthsea*, 1968
Patricia A. McKillip, *The Riddle-Master of Hed*, 1976
Elizabeth Moon, *Sheepfarmer's Daughter*, 1988
J.R.R. Tolkien, *The Fellowship of the Ring*, 1954

**19**

**KOBO ABE**

## The Face of Another
(New York: Kodansha, 1992)

**Story type:** Horror (Psychological Suspense)
**Major character(s):** Doctor K, Doctor (dermatologist)
**Time period(s):** 1960s
**Locale(s):** Japan (Osaka region)

**Summary:** Told in the form of three diaries, this outstanding meditation on the conflict of identity and appearance tells of a scientist disfigured in a laboratory experiment who fashions a synthetic, life-like face mask to conceal his deformity. When his conduct becomes increasingly more uninhibited as a result of his new identity, he finds himself incapable of determining whether he is being overwhelmed by a new person or simply confronting buried aspects of his character that refuse to stay hidden. This novel was originally published in 1962 and translated by E. Dale Saunders.

**Other books you might like:**
Randall Boyll, *Darkman*, 1990
Ariel Dorfman, *Mascara*, 1989
Gaston Leroux, *The Phantom of the Opera*, 1911
Robert Louis Stevenson, *The Strange Case of Dr. Jekyll and Mr. Hyde*, 1888
Oscar Wilde, *The Picture of Dorian Gray*, 1891

**20**

**ALEX ABELLA**

## Dead of Night
(New York: Simon & Schuster, 1998)

**Story type:** Horror (Mystery; Occult)
**Major character(s):** Charlie Morrell, Lawyer, Detective—Private; Ricardo Diaz, Sorcerer (Santeria); Armando Ponce, Religious (Santeria priest)
**Time period(s):** 1990s (1998)
**Locale(s):** Los Angeles, California

**Summary:** Charlie Morrell, whose ambivalence about his Cuban-American heritage manifests in his skepticism toward the religion of Santeria, finds himself on the trail of a sorcerer who believes emphatically in the folk religion, makes blood sacrifices to the dark gods,

and is protected by both Colombian drug lords and American politicians. A reprise of characters and situations from the author's previous novel *The Killing of the Saints* (1991).

**Other books you might like:**
Lisa Cantrell, *Boneman*, 1992
Hugh B. Cave, *Disciples of Dread*, 1988
Nicholas Conde, *The Religion*, 1982
Brian Hodge, *The Darker Saints*, 1993
John Shirley, *Cellars*, 1982

**21**

**ALEX ABELLA**

## The Killing of the Saints
(New York: Crown, 1991)

**Story type:** Horror (Occult)
**Major character(s):** Charlie Morrell, Lawyer; Ramon Valdez, Religious (priest of Santeria)
**Time period(s):** 1990s
**Locale(s):** Los Angeles, California

**Summary:** Appointed to defend a priest of the Afro-Hispanic religion Santeria following the man's grisly killings during a jewelry heist, lawyer Charlie Morrell finds himself pitted against occult forces beyond his understanding and forced to confront his own ambivalence regarding his Cuban heritage.

**Other books you might like:**
Hugh B. Cave, *Disciples of Dread*, 1988
Nicholas Conde, *The Religion*, 1982
John Farris, *All Heads Turn When the Hunt Goes By*, 1977
William Hjortsberg, *Falling Angel*, 1978

**22**

**KEN ABNER**, Editor

## Terminal Frights, Volume One
(Black River, New York: Terminal Frights, 1997)

**Story type:** Horror (Anthology)

**Summary:** Twenty-two stories of horror and fantasy in the first hardcover incarnation of a long-running horror small press magazine. Highlights include William Scheinman's "The Work of Dennis Hobbs" and Don D'Ammassa's "The Managansett Horror," both variations on Lovecraftian themes; Tom Picirilli's "A Lower Deep," which resurrects his necromancer detective hero Self, from his collection, *Pentacle*; Michael Arnzen's "Stigmata" and David Niall Wilson's "To Dream of Sheherzade," both of which feature characters whose disfigurement is an outward expression of their troubled psyches; and Scott H. Urban's "Edge-Run," in which a carjacking leads to an otherwordly adventure. Illustrations by M. Wayne Miller.

**Other books you might like:**
Jani Anderson, *Bringing Down the Moon*, 1985
    editor
Richard T. Chizmar, *The Best of Cemetery Dance*, 1998
    editor
George Hatch, *Guignoir and Other Furies*, 1991
    editor
George Hatch, *Sinistre: An Anthology of Rituals*, 1993
    editor
Tom Piccirilli, *Inside the Works*, 1998
    Gerard Daniel Houarner and Edward Lee, co-authors

Stuart David Schiff, *The Best of Whispers*, 1994
  editor

## 23

**JUSTIN ACHILLI**, Editor
**ROBERT HATCH**, Co-Editor

### Dark Tyrants

(Clarkson, Georgia: White Wolf, 1997)

**Story type:** Horror (Anthology)

**Summary:** Thirteen stories set in the publisher's World of Darkness, an alternate world where supernatural creatures co-exist with human beings. This volume features stories set exclusively in medieval Europe and concerned with the Vampire Masquerade, a pact among the vampire subculture to maintain a clandestine existence. Selections include Richard Lee Byers' "The Winged Child," Jackie Cassada's "Toujours," James S. Dorr's "The Hawk and the Slipper," and Guy Davis and Vincent Locke's illustrated "A Fool's Embrace."

**Other books you might like:**
Erin Kelly, *The Splendour Falls*, 1995
  editor
Edward E. Kramer, *Dark Destiny III: Children of Dracula*, 1996
  editor
Edward E. Kramer, *Dark Destiny II: Proprietors of Fate*, 1995
  editor
Edward E. Kramer, *Dark Destiny*, 1994
  editor
Staley Krause, *Strange City*, 1996
  Stewart Wieck, co-editor
Erin Kelly, *City of Darkness: Unseen*, 1995
  Stewart Wieck, co-editor
Stewart Wieck, *The Beast Within*, 1995
  editor
Stewart Wieck, *When Will You Rage*, 1994
  editor
Stewart Wieck, *World of Darkness: Truth Until Paradox*, 1994
  editor

## 24

**FORREST J. ACKERMAN**, Editor

### Ackermanthology!

(Los Angeles: General Publishing Group, 1997)

**Story type:** Science Fiction (Anthology)

**Summary:** Contains a two-page introduction by Ackerman, a one-page foreword by John Landis and 65 stories, some with individual introductions, from periodicals and anthrologies 1934-1975. The stories vary in tone from humorous to horrifying and appear in thematic groups such as aliens, cosmic encounters, experiments perilous, futurama, robot chronicles, spicy sci-fi and O. Henry type stories. Authors include Forrest J. Ackerman, Isaac Asimov, David Bischoff, Jerome Bixby, Hannes Bok, Ray Bradbury, Ray Cummings, Horace L. Gold, Dave Kyle, A.W. Lownes, A. Merritt, C.L. Moore, Sam Moskowitz, A.E. Van Vogt, H.G. Wells, Robert Moore Williams, Richard Wilson and Donald A. Wollheim.

**Other books you might like:**
Isaac Asimov, *Isaac Asimov Presents the Great SF Stories: 1-25*, 1979-1992
  Martin H. Greenberg, co-editor

Groff Conklin, *The Best of Science Fiction*, 1946
  editor
Janrae Frank, *New Eves: Science Fiction about the Extraordinary Women of Today and Tomorrow*, 1994
  Jean Stine, Forrest J. Ackerman, co-editors
Raymond J. Healy, *Adventures in Time and Space*, 1946
  J. Frances McComas, co-editor
Robert Silverberg, *The Science Fiction Hall of Fame, Volume 1*, 1970
  editor
Jean Marie Stine, *365 Science Fiction Short Stories*, 1995
  Forrest J. Ackerman, co-editor

## 25

**PETER ACKROYD**

### Milton in America

(New York: Doubleday/Nan A. Talese, 1997)

**Story type:** Fantasy (Alternate History; Religious)
**Major character(s):** John Milton, Writer (poet), Leader; Goosequill, Servant, Guide; Katherine Jervis, Secretary
**Time period(s):** 17th century (1660s)
**Locale(s):** New Milton, Fictional City; Alternate Earth; American Colonies

**Summary:** In A.D. 1660 John Milton, poet, Puritan and radical thinker, flees England and the depressing fact of the restored monarchy. In the New World he finds a society that he can mold to his vision of Eden. When Milton soon becomes as inflexible as the people he flees, he turns his blind and unrelenting attention on a nearby Catholic colony, whereupon evil returns to Eden.

**Other books you might like:**
James P. Blaylock, *Homunculus*, 1986
William S. Burroughs, *Ghost of Chance*, 1995
John Crowley, *Aegypt*, 1987
Kim Newman, *Back in the USSA*, 1997
  Eugene Byrne, co-author
Howard Waldrop, *Strange Monsters of the Recent Past*, 1991

## 26

**PETER ACKROYD**

### The Trial of Elizabeth Cree

(New York: Nan A. Talese/Doubleday, 1995)

**Story type:** Horror (Literary)
**Major character(s):** Elizabeth Cree, Actress; John Cree, Actor; Dan Leno, Actor
**Time period(s):** 1880s (1880)
**Locale(s):** London, England (Limehouse District)

**Summary:** Published in England in 1994 as *Dan Leno and the Limehouse Golem*, this novel traces the dismal lives of music hall actress Elizabeth Cree and her husband John, a frustrated actor who turns his penchant for artistic expression into a series of inventive murders and dismemberments that the popular press blames on a golem, until Elizabeth poisons him. The Crees' lives unfold against a vividly realized background portrait of Victorian England in which Karl Marx, George Gissing and other historical figures are characters.

**Other books you might like:**
Caleb Carr, *The Alienist*, 1994
E.L. Doctorow, *The Waterworks*, 1994
William Hjortsberg, *Nevermore*, 1994

Paul West, *The Women of Whitechapel and Jack the Ripper*, 1992

### 27
#### MARK ACRES

## Dark Divide
(New York: Ace, 1991)

**Story type:** Fantasy (Adventure)
**Series:** Runesword
**Major character(s):** Caltus "Cal" Talienson, Warrior; Elizebith of Morea, Sorceress; Malendor, Vampire, Mythical Creature (dark elf)
**Time period(s):** Indeterminate
**Locale(s):** Trondholm, Fictional Country

**Summary:** Cal and his companions must save the Kingdom of Trondholm when a vampire looses his zombie hordes on the land of the living to secure the region for his Dark Lord.

**Other books you might like:**
Stephen Billias, *Horrible Humes*, 1991
Clayton Emery, *Outcasts*, 1990
Rose Estes, *Skryling's Blade*, 1990
   Tom Wham, co-author
J.F. Rivkin, *The Dreamstone*, 1991
Christopher Stasheff, *King Kobold Revived*, 1984
Margaret Weis, *Fire Sea*, 1991
   Tracy Hickman, co-author

### 28
#### MARK ACRES

## Dragonspawn
(New York: AvoNova, 1994)

**Story type:** Fantasy (Magic Conflict; Adventure)
**Major character(s):** Bagsby, Thief; Shulana, Wizard, Mythical Creature (elf); Valdaimon, Wizard
**Time period(s):** Indeterminate
**Locale(s):** Heileshein, Fictional Country

**Summary:** The Black Prince, Ruprecht, and the wizard Valdaimon plot to control all the Land between the Rivers, while a thief and wizard attempt a daring theft that will defeat this plan. These competing schemes could resolve a 5000-year-old conflict.

**Other books you might like:**
Glen Cook, *The Black Company*, 1984
Barbara Hambly, *Dragonsbane*, 1987
Guy Gavriel Kay, *The Summer Tree*, 1985
Dennis L. McKiernan, *Dragondoom*, 1990
Melanie Rawn, *Stronghold*, 1990

### 29
#### DOUGLAS ADAMS

## The Illustrated Hitchhiker's Guide to the Galaxy
(New York: Harmony, 1994)

**Story type:** Science Fiction (Humor; Space Opera)
**Series:** Hitchhiker's Guide to the Galaxy
**Major character(s):** Arthur Dent, Traveler; Ford Prefect, Writer, Alien; Zaphod Beeblebrox, Political Figure (President of the Galaxy), Fugitive

**Time period(s):** 1980s
**Locale(s):** *Heart of Gold*, Spaceship (experimental); Outer Space

**Summary:** When construction of an interstellar bypass destroys the Earth, Ford Prefect saves Arthur Dent by surreptitiously hitching a lift with the construction fleet. When the captain discovers the stowaways, he deposits them into the vacuum of space without the benefit of space suits. A highly improbable rescue by the stolen *Heart of Gold* propels Arthur and Ford into a series of zany adventures. Folio reprint of the 1980 edition lavishly illustrated with digitally modified photographs.

**Other books you might like:**
Harlan Ellison, *I, Robot: The Illustrated Screenplay*, 1994
   Isaac Asimov, co-author
James Gurney, *Dinotopia*, 1992
Harry Harrison, *Planet Story*, 1979
Terry Jones, *Lady Cottington's Pressed Fairy Book*, 1994
   Brian Froud, co-author
Robert Anton Wilson, *Reality Is What You Can Get Away With: An Illustrated Screenplay*, 1992

### 30
#### DOUGLAS ADAMS

## The Long Dark Tea-Time of the Soul
(New York: Simon and Schuster, 1989)

**Story type:** Science Fiction (Satire)
**Series:** Adventures of Dirk Gently
**Major character(s):** Dirk Gently, Detective—Private, Psychic; Kate Schechter, Heroine
**Time period(s):** 1980s

**Summary:** An explosion occurs at Heathrow Airport just as Dirk Gently, psychic detective, is about to board a plane for Oslo. He and Kate Schechter, another survivor of the explosion, soon become enmeshed in a baffling, often rather silly attempt to discover the perpetrators of the crime. Eventually they uncover evidence that the ancient Norse Gods are involved.

**Other books you might like:**
Piers Anthony, *Castle Roogna*, 1979
Piers Anthony, *The Source of Magic*, 1979
Piers Anthony, *A Spell for Chameleon*, 1977
Ron Goulart, *The Prisoner of Blackwood Castle*, 1984
Ron Goulart, *Starpirate's Brain*, 1987
Ron Goulart, *Upside Downside*, 1982
Keith Laumer, *Retief's Ransom*, 1971
Keith Laumer, *The Return of Retief*, 1985
Keith Laumer, *Reward for Retief*, 1989

### 31
#### DOUGLAS ADAMS

## Mostly Harmless
(New York: Harmony Books, 1992)

**Story type:** Science Fiction (Humor; Space Opera)
**Series:** Hitchhiker's Guide to the Galaxy
**Major character(s):** Arthur Dent, Traveler; Ford Prefect, Writer, Alien
**Time period(s):** Indeterminate
**Locale(s):** Lamuella, Planet—Imaginary; Mythical Place (Offices of *The Hitchhiker's Guide to the Galaxy*)

**Summary:** As Ford investigates the often moved publishing offices of *The Hitchhiker's Guide to the Galaxy*, Arthur searches for a home to replace his beloved Earth, destroyed during construction of a hyperspace bypass, while characters from previous books pop into and out of the plot.

**Other books you might like:**
John DeChancie, *Paradox Alley*, 1987
John DeChancie, *Red Limit Freeway*, 1984
John DeChancie, *Starrigger*, 1983
Alan Dean Foster, *To the Vanishing Point*, 1988
Mel Gilden, *Surfing Samurai Robots*, 1988
Parke Godwin, *Waiting for the Galactic Bus*, 1988
Robert Rankin, *Armageddon: The Musical*, 1990
Robert Reed, *Down the Bright Way*, 1991
Neal Stephenson, *Snow Crash*, 1992

---

**32**

**RICHARD ADAMS**

## Tales From Watership Down

(New York: Knopf, 1996)

**Story type:** Fantasy (Collection; Young Adult)
**Major character(s):** El-ahrairah, Animal (rabbit), Leader; Rabscuttle, Animal (rabbit); Dandilion, Animal (rabbit), Storyteller
**Time period(s):** Indeterminate
**Locale(s):** Land of Yesterday, Mythical Place; The Down, Mythical Place

**Summary:** Dandilion relates generally upbeat adventures of the mythical rabbit hero, El-ahrairah, and his companion, Rabscuttle, and stories of the rabbits and life at the Down. Includes a three-page lapine glossary and a brief introduction discussing the 20 original stories' relationship to characters and events in *Watership Down*.

**Other books you might like:**
Mary Brown, *The Unlikely Ones*, 1986
Kenneth Grahame, *The Wind in the Willows*, 1908
William Horwood, *Duncton Wood*, 1980
Brian Jacques, *Mariel of Redwall*, 1992
Brian Jacques, *Martin the Warrior*, 1994
Garry Kilworth, *The Foxes of Firstdark*, 1990
Tad Williams, *Tailchaser's Song*, 1985

---

**33**

**ROBERT ADAMS**

## Of Beginnings and Endings

(New York: NAL Signet, 1989)

**Story type:** Science Fiction (Alternate Universe)
**Series:** Castaways in Time
**Major character(s):** Bass Foster, Time Traveler, Warrior; Harold Kenmore, Scientist, Time Traveler
**Time period(s):** 15th century (1489)
**Locale(s):** Alternate Earth (America and England)

**Summary:** Bass Foster and his companions must make places for themselves in fifteenth-century England and America. Meanwhile, mysterious and superpowerful beings have become aware of the castaways.

**Other books you might like:**
Daniel Da Cruz, *Mixed Doubles*, 1989
Simon Hawke, *The Argonaut Affair*, 1987
    Time Wars, No. 7
Simon Hawke, *The Kyber Connection*, 1986
    Time Wars, No. 6
Leo Frankowski, *The Flying Warlord*, 1989

Leo Frankowski, *The High-Tech Knight*, 1989
Leo Frankowski, *The Radiant Warrior*, 1989

---

**34**

**TERRY A. ADAMS**

## The Master of Chaos

(New York: DAW Books, 1989)

**Story type:** Science Fiction (First Contact)
**Major character(s):** Hanna, Telepath, Diplomat
**Time period(s):** Indeterminate Future
**Locale(s):** Uskos, Planet—Imaginary

**Summary:** Lady Hanna is assigned to make first contact with a friendly alien race, the Uskosians, but is kidnapped and tortured by space pirates who kill the Uskosians. Rescued, she vows revenge and, at the same time, attempts to salvage some form of peaceful contact with the aliens.

**Other books you might like:**
Gregory Benford, *Tides of Light*, 1989
David Alexander Smith, *Rendezvous*, 1988
Sheri S. Tepper, *Grass*, 1989
James Tiptree Jr., *Brightness Falls From the Air*, 1985

---

**35**

**WILLIAM ADAMS**
**CECIL BROOKS**, Co-Author

## The Unwound Way

(New York: Ballantine/Del Rey, 1991)

**Story type:** Science Fiction (Political; Arts)
**Major character(s):** Evan Larkspur, Actor, Fugitive; Ariel Nimitz, Administrator; Ken Mishima, Martial Arts Expert
**Time period(s):** Indeterminate Future
**Locale(s):** Nexus, Planet—Imaginary (Nexus University); Newcount Two, Planet—Imaginary; *Barbarossa*, Spaceship

**Summary:** Close to 100 years have passed since Evan Larkspur's naval operation on the spaceship *Barbarossa* went awry. He returns to normal space and the plays he had written before he left are now classics, and his Old Rite Kanalist compatriots have been eliminated or corrupted in his absence. Trapped by Maximillian Conde into impersonating a government official, what he finds on Newcount Two will challenge all his talents and require his classical education to avert disaster for himself and his companions.

**Other books you might like:**
C.J. Cherryh, *Forty Thousand in Gehenna*, 1983
Glen Cook, *The Dragon Never Sleeps*, 1988
Alan Dean Foster, *Cyber Way*, 1990
Diana G. Gallagher, *The Alien Dark*, 1990
Frank Herbert, *Dune*, 1965
Steve Miller, *Carpe Diem*, 1989
    Sharon Lee, co-author
Sheri S. Tepper, *Raising the Stones*, 1990
David Weber, *Mutineers' Moon*, 1991

## 36

### PATRICK H. ADKINS

## Sons of the Titans

(New York: Ace, 1990)

**Story type:** Fantasy (Legend; Adventure)
**Series:** Titans
**Major character(s):** Kronis, Nobleman (Lord of the Titans); Zeus, Royalty (King-to-be)
**Time period(s):** Indeterminate Past (ancient Hellenic era)
**Locale(s):** Greece

**Summary:** Zeus struggles against his Titan father to assume the throne of the King of the Gods.

**Other books you might like:**
Tom Holt, *Expecting Someone Taller*, 1987
Thomas Burnett Swann, *The Gods Abide*, 1976
Howard Waldrop, *A Dozen Tough Jobs*, 1989
Roger Zelazny, *Creatures of Light and Darkness*, 1969

## 37

### JACK ADRIAN, Editor

## The Ash-Tree Press Annual Macabre 1997

(Ashcroft, British Columbia: Ash-Tree Press, 1997)

**Story type:** Horror (Anthology)

**Summary:** Four little known tales of the Edwardian era by British female writers. Selections include Patricia Wentworth's "A Wedding Day," about a woman's life-saving psychic link with her husband; Jesse Douglas Kerruish's "The Swaying Vision," in which two men attempt to track the seemingly inexplicable source of a house's haunting; Carola Oman's "The Visitor," in which a ghost from the time of Cromwell is doomed to haunt his beloved estate until his name is cleared of a crime; and Mollie Panter-Downes' "The House of the Laburnums," about the mental distress caused by a woman's precognitive vision of a murder.

**Other books you might like:**
Nina Auerbach, *Forbidden Journeys: Fairy Tales and Fantasies by Victorian Women Writers*, 1992
    U.C. Knoepflmacher, co-editor
Richard Dalby, *Edwardian Ghost Stories by Eminent Women Writers*, 1992
    editor
Catherine A. Lundie, *Restless Spirits*, 1997
    editor
Alan Ryan, *Haunting Women*, 1988
    editor
Jessica Amanda Salmonson, *What Did Miss Darrington See?: An Anthology of Feminist Supernatural Fiction*, 1989
A. Susan Williams, *The Lifted Veil: The Book of Fantastic Literature by Women*, 1993
    editor

## 38

### JACK ADRIAN, Editor

## The Ash-Tree Press Annual Macabre 1998

(Ashcroft, British Columbia: Ash-Tree Press, 1998)

**Story type:** Horror (Anthology)

**Summary:** This anthology contains six uncommonly weird tales by literary writers of the late Victorian and Edwardian eras. Highlights include Arthur Ransome's "Post- Mortem," in which a skeptical doctor attends a seance and hears the tale of a man whose body he dissected at autopsy, and Somerset Maugham's "Told in the Inn at Algeciras" and E.C. Bentley's "Exactly as It Happened," both tales of haunted dwellings. Other selections are by John Buchan, Hilaire Belloc and Ford Maddox Ford. With an introduction and notes by the editor.

**Other books you might like:**
Cynthia Asquith, *The Ghost Book*, 1927
    editor
Richard Dalby, *The Mammoth Book of Victorian and Edwardian Ghost Stories*, 1995
    editor
Peter Haining, *The Lucifer Society*, 1972
    editor
Sam Moskowitz, *Great Untold Stories of Fantasy and Horror*, 1969
    editor
Herbert Wise, *Great Tales of Terror and the Supernatural*, 1944
    Phyllis Fraser, co-editor

## 39

### JACK ADRIAN, Editor

## Strange Tales From the Strand

(New York: Oxford University Press, 1992)

**Story type:** Horror (Anthology)

**Summary:** Twenty-nine tales of madness, murder, melodrama, revenants, superbeasts, unnatural disasters, and fantasy that appeared in the long-running British popular fiction periodical *The Strand* between 1891 and 1950. Included are Graham Greene's gruesome ghost story "All But Empty" (a.k.a. "A Little Place Off the Edgeware Road"); Hugh Walpole's tale of vengeance from beyond the grave, "The Tarn"; W. L. George's grisly mistaken identity story, "Waxworks"; Villiers de l'Isle-Adam's *conte cruel* "Torture by Hope"; C. J. Cutcliffe Hyne's tale of an accidentally revived prehistoric behemoth, "Lizard"; the comic "Queer Story of Brownlow's Newspaper" by H. G. Wells; and three stories by Arthur Conan Doyle: "How it Happened," "The Silver Mirror," and "The Horror of the Heights."

**Other books you might like:**
Isaac Asimov, *Isaac Asimov Presents the Best Horror and Supernatural Tales of the 19th Century*, 1983
    Charles G. Waugh and Martin H. Greenberg, co-editors
Sam Moskowitz, *Ghostly by Gaslight*, 1971
    Alden H. Norton, co-editor
Sam Moskowitz, *Great Untold Stories of Fantasy and Horror*, 1969
    Alden H. Norton, co-editor
Sam Moskowitz, *Science Fiction by Gaslight*, 1968
    editor

## 40

### AESOP

## Aesop's Fables

(New York: Signet Classic, 1992)

**Story type:** Fantasy (Collection; Legend)

**Summary:** Contains two pages of notes on the text, an eight-page afterword discussing Aesop and the structure and development of the fable as literary form with examples, a two-page bibliography, a three-page index plus 203 fables selected and adapted by Zipes from Reverend Thomas James's *Aesop's Fables: A New Version, Chiefly From Original Sources* (1848) to which Zipes has added modernized language and idioms and, for a few fables, created new morals more relevant to the contemporary reader. Includes ''The Ants and the Grasshopper,'' ''The Country Mouse and the City Mouse,'' ''The Hare and the Tortoise'' and ''The Shepherd Boy and the Wolf.''

**Other books you might like:**
Richard Erdoes, *American Indian Myths and Legends*, 1984
    Alfonso Ortiz, co-editor
Garry Kilworth, *The Foxes of Firstdark*, 1990
Dean R. Koontz, *Oddkins*, 1988
Barry Lopez, *Crow and Weasel*, 1990
Howard Norman, *Northern Tales: Traditional Stories of Eskimo and Indian Peoples*, 1990

**41**

### CHRIS N. AFRICA

## *When Wolves Cry*

(Edmonton, Alberta: Commonwealth, 1997)

**Story type:** Horror (Nature in Revolt)
**Major character(s):** Cloud Hunter Johnson, Guide; Big John ''BJ'', Bartender; Chris Taelor, Hunter
**Time period(s):** 1990s (1997)
**Locale(s):** Mountain City, Nevada

**Summary:** A weekend hunting expedition turns from ordinary to bizarre when a pack of sentient wolves plays a series of increasingly annoying tricks on the six hunters, and then turns vicious and predatory when the hunters kill one of the pack. A first novel.

**Other books you might like:**
David Dvorkin, *Ursus*, 1989
Brian Hopkins, *Cold at Heart*, 1997
Dean R. Koontz, *Watchers*, 1987
T. Chris Martindale, *Where the Chill Waits*, 1990
Graham Masterton, *The Manitou*, 1975
Christine Tanasiuk, *Howl*, 1997

**42**

### PHYLLIS CAROL AGINS

## *Suisan*

(New York: Baen, 1992)

**Story type:** Fantasy (Legend)
**Major character(s):** Suisan, Maiden; Cwenn, Royalty (queen), Step-Parent; Allard, Mythical Creature (dwarf), Miner
**Time period(s):** Indeterminate Past
**Locale(s):** The City, Mythical Place; The Forest, Mythical Place

**Summary:** Happy in the mines where they find and work metals and gems, seven little men discover through a vision that a beautiful young girl will be coming to them. Suisan, the Snow White Cwenn sent with the hunter to die, lives with the miners and their visions. The dwarves secretly build a wonderful growing crystal casket but cannot forsee why she will need it. Author's first book.

**Other books you might like:**
Steven Brust, *The Sun, the Moon, and the Stars*, 1987
Kara Dalkey, *The Nightingale*, 1988
Charles de Lint, *Jack, the Giant-Killer*, 1987
Pamela Dean, *Tam Lin*, 1991
Sheri S. Tepper, *Beauty*, 1991
Patricia C. Wrede, *Snow White and Rose Red*, 1989

**43**

### MARJORIE AGOSIN, Editor

## *The Secret Weavers: Stories of the Fantastic by Latin American Women*

(Fredonia, New York: White Pine Press, 1991)

**Story type:** Fantasy (Anthology)
**Major character(s):** Luz, Teenager, Psychic; Erzsebet, Noblewoman (countess), Vampire; Segismundo Linares, Maintenance Worker (janitor)
**Time period(s):** 20th century; Indeterminate Past
**Locale(s):** South America; Mythical Place

**Summary:** This volume contains 45 stories written from the 1930s to the present by 18 women from Argentina and Chile. This is the first English translation for most of the stories which are about the Fantastic, taken as a matter of fact as in ''The Compulsion Dreamer'' by Silvian Ocampo, about a young woman whose dreams come true, a situation she accepts and works into the fabric of her life. There is a lengthy introduction, with notes on the authors and translators following the stories.

**Other books you might like:**
Samuel R. Delany, *Dhalgren*, 1975
Greer Ilene Gilman, *Moonwise*, 1990
Lisa Goldstein, *The Dream Years*, 1985
Tanith Lee, *The Book of the Damned*, 1990
Pat Murphy, *The City, Not Long After*, 1989
Jack Zipes, *Don't Bet on the Prince*, 1986
    editor

**44**

### JERRY AHERN

## *The Struggle*

(New York: Zebra, 1989)

**Story type:** Science Fiction (Post-Nuclear Holocaust)
**Series:** Survivalist
**Major character(s):** John T. Rourke, Military Personnel (Soldier), Spy; Colonel Antonovich, Military Personnel
**Time period(s):** 21st century
**Locale(s):** Pacific Ocean

**Summary:** In a half-destroyed, post-nuclear holocaust world, Russia and the United States continue to oppose each other. Rourke, an ex-CIA operative, must contain Colonel Antonovich's attempt to gain world dominance for Russia.

**Other books you might like:**
Richard Austin, *Devil's Deal*, 1989
    The Guardians. Vol. 13
James Axler, *Red Equinox*, 1989
    Deathlands 9
Bob Ham, *Tennessee Terror*, 1989
    The Overlord 4
William W. Johnstone, *Trapped in the Ashes*, 1989
James Rouch, *Civilian Slaughter*, 1989
    The Zone 8

## 45

### JOAN AIKEN

## *The Haunting of Lamb House*
(New York: St. Martin's, 1993)

**Story type:** Horror (Haunted House; Literary)
**Major character(s):** Toby Lamb, Child; Henry James, Writer, Historical Figure; E.F. Benson, Writer, Historical Figure
**Time period(s):** 19th century; 20th century
**Locale(s):** Rye, England

**Summary:** The journal of Toby Lamb, a sensitive and mistreated young boy living at the end of the 18th century, falls into the hands of two later tenants of Lamb House, writers Henry James and E.F. Benson, each of whose literary involvement with the diary causes the spirits of Lamb House to manifest. Told in the form of three interlocking novellas, this homage to the classic British ghost story was first published in England in 1992.

**Other books you might like:**
Jonathan Aycliffe, *Whispers in the Dark*, 1993
E.F. Benson, *The Collected Ghost Stories of E.F. Benson*, 1992
Henry James, *Stories of the Supernatural*, 1970

## 46

### JIM AIKIN

## *The Wall at the Edge of the World*
(New York: Ace, 1993)

**Story type:** Science Fiction (Post-Holocaust; Psychic Powers)
**Major character(s):** Danlo Ree, Telepath, Traveler; Ainne Murrinder, Telepath; Linnie, Teacher
**Time period(s):** Indeterminate Future
**Locale(s):** Sacramento, California; Ranoima, Fictional City

**Summary:** Despite the easy life as part of the Body of Harmony, Danlo Ree defeats the Guidance put on him by the Joddies after his wife's Cleansing. He could work as a Joddie, utilizing his talent of surrepticiously influencing other minds and mentally partitioning his own thoughts. However, after Linnie's band of women from outside the wall kidnap Danlo, he comes to realize that he must stop the killing, whatever the cost.

**Other books you might like:**
Emma Bull, *Bone Dance: A Fantasy for Technophiles*, 1991
Marjorie Bradley Kellogg, *Harmony*, 1991
Pat Murphy, *The City, Not Long After*, 1989
Frank M. Robinson, *The Power*, 1956
Jean Stewart, *Return to Isis*, 1992
Vernor Vinge, *A Fire upon the Deep*, 1992
Paul O. Williams, *The Breaking of Northwall*, 1980

## 47

### PETER ALBANO

## *Assault of the Super Carrier*
(New York: Zebra, 1996)

**Story type:** Science Fiction (Military)
**Series:** Seventh Carrier
**Major character(s):** Brent Ross, Military Personnel; Yoshi Matsuhara, Military Personnel; Hiroshi Fujito, Military Personnel
**Time period(s):** 1990s
**Locale(s):** *Yonaga*, At Sea; *Edo*, At Sea; Japan

**Summary:** Brent accompanies *Edo* on its shakedown cruise, looking for a possible pirate ship which preys on fishing vessels. After a deadly encounter, and prior to *Yonaga*'s setting out for the Middle East, Brent takes leave, as ordered, only to find anti-military sentiment which could easily prove lethal.

**Other books you might like:**
David Alexander, *Nomad*, 1992
Daniel Da Cruz, *Texas on the Rocks*, 1987
Daniel Da Cruz, *Texas Triumphant*, 1987
John Dalmas, *The Yngling*, 1971
G. Harry Stine, *Warbots*, 1988

## 48

### PETER ALBANO

## *Ordeal of the Seventh Carrier*
(New York: Zebra, 1992)

**Story type:** Science Fiction (Military)
**Series:** Seventh Carrier
**Major character(s):** Yoshi Matsuhara, Military Personnel
**Time period(s):** 1990s
**Locale(s):** *Yonaga*, At Sea

**Summary:** The *Yonaga* prepares for a bloody showdown with the Arab battle group directed against Japan by the fanatic Libyan terrorist bent on extending his influence in the Pacific.

**Other books you might like:**
Daniel Da Cruz, *The Ayes of Texas*, 1982
Daniel Da Cruz, *Texas on the Rocks*, 1987
Daniel Da Cruz, *Texas Triumphant*, 1987
G. Harry Stine, *Force of Arms*, 1990
G. Harry Stine, *Warbots*, 1988

## 49

### PETER ALBANO

## *Revenge of the Seventh Carrier*
(New York: Zebra, 1992)

**Story type:** Science Fiction (Military)
**Series:** Seventh Carrier
**Major character(s):** Yoshi Matsuhara, Military Personnel; Brent Ross, Military Personnel; Arlene Spencer, Journalist
**Time period(s):** 1990s
**Locale(s):** *Yonaga*, At Sea

**Summary:** When a Libyan madman assembles an army of fanatics and naval forces able to attack major cities with poison gas weapons, the Japanese aircraft carrier *Yonanga* with its indomitable Samurai crew and their comrades, brave airmen from around the world, must stop the disaster.

**Other books you might like:**
Daniel Da Cruz, *The Ayes of Texas*, 1982
Daniel Da Cruz, *Texas on the Rocks*, 1987
Daniel Da Cruz, *Texas Triumphant*, 1987
G. Harry Stine, *Operation Iron Fist*, 1989
G. Harry Stine, *Warbots*, 1988

**50**

### PETER ALBANO

## Super Carrier: The Ultimate Secret Weapon

(New York: Zebra, 1994)

**Story type:** Science Fiction (Military)
**Series:** Seventh Carrier
**Major character(s):** Hiroshi Fujito, Military Personnel (admiral); Brent Ross, Military Personnel (commander)
**Time period(s):** 1990s
**Locale(s):** *Yonaga*, At Sea; Marianas Islands, Trust Territory of the Pacific Islands

**Summary:** To prevent the success of a Libyan jihad, the super carrier *Yonaga*, armed with a secret weapon, engages the enemy in the Pacific and the Middle East.

**Other books you might like:**
David Alexander, *Nomad*, 1992
Daniel Da Cruz, *Texas on the Rocks*, 1987
Daniel Da Cruz, *Texas Triumphant*, 1987
John Dalmas, *The Yngling*, 1971
G. Harry Stine, *Warbots*, 1988

**51**

### KATHLEEN ALCALA

## Mrs. Vargas and the Dead Naturalist

(Corvallis, Oregon: Calyx Books, 1992)

**Story type:** Fantasy (Collection)

**Summary:** Six original and eight stories slightly revised from 1985-1991 appearances in periodicals and anthologies. Themes of these fantasy and magical realism stories include romance, nature and Roman Catholicism.

**Other books you might like:**
Marjorie Agosin, *The Secret Weavers: Stories of the Fantastic by Latin American Women*, 1991
    editor
Pauline Melville, *Shape-Shifter: Stories by Pauline Melville*, 1991
Susanna J. Sturgis, *Magic Realism by Women: Dreams in a Minor Key*, 1991
    editor

**52**

### KATHLEEN ALCALA

## Spirits of the Ordinary

(San Francisco: Chronicle Books, 1997)

**Story type:** Fantasy (Historical; Literary)
**Major character(s):** Zacarias Caraval, Prospector; Estela Caraval, Divorced Person; Julio Caraval, Parent (father), Philosopher
**Time period(s):** 1870s
**Locale(s):** Casas Grandes, Mexico; Saltillo, Mexico

**Summary:** The Caravals have covertly practiced Judaism for many generations, hiding their religion, and working as merchants. Zacarias abandons the family business, religion and the comforts of home to wander in the wilderness looking for gold. A lost mine, cabalism, strange powers, and the mystic cliff dwellings at Casas Grandes combine to chart the course of a family, a nation, and continent.

**Other books you might like:**
Nick Bantock, *The Forgetting Room*, 1997
Martha Cerda, *Senora Rodriguez and Other Worlds*, 1997
Richard Kadrey, *Kamikaze L'Amour*, 1995
Gabriel Garcia Marquez, *One Hundred Years of Solitude*, 1967
Karen Tei Yamashita, *Tropic of Orange*, 1997

**53**

### VIVIAN ALCOCK

## The Red-Eared Ghosts

(New York: Houghton Mifflin, 1997)

**Story type:** Fantasy (Science Fiction; Young Adult)
**Major character(s):** Mary Frewin, Child, Psychic; Freda Timpson, Teacher; Edward ''Potty'' Potts, Teacher
**Time period(s):** 1990s; 1880s
**Locale(s):** Cloudsley Towers, England

**Summary:** Disappointed at Miss Timpson's failure to believe she sees red-eared ghosts, Mary complains to her friends that the confirmation of her sanity would be useful. Edward Potts looks forward to meeting Mary in hopes he will learn something. He buys her grandmother's story, the book hidden from Mary since her childhood, and shares it with her when they meet.

**Other books you might like:**
Melvin Burgess, *The Earth Giant*, 1997
Diana Wynne Jones, *The Time of the Ghost*, 1996
Margaret Mahy, *The Tricksters*, 1987
Pamela F. Service, *All's Faire*, 1993
Sylvia Waugh, *The Mennyms*, 1994

**54**

### BRIAN W. ALDISS

## Common Clay: 20 Odd Stories

(New York: St. Martin's, 1996)

**Story type:** Fantasy (Collection; Science Fiction)

**Summary:** This collection contains individual commentaries to one story from a 1987 conference program book, seven original and 12 stories reprinted from periodicals and anthologies 1992-1995, with one revised, ''Her Toes Were Beautiful on the Mountains.'' The commentary loosely links the stories into chapters of a ''chronicle novel,'' discussing life, death, and transformation in tones ranging from darkly humorous to horrific, with some suggestions of a happier existence. The British edition is titled *The Secret of This Book*.

**Other books you might like:**
Alfred Bester, *Star Light, Star Bright*, 1976
Philip K. Dick, *The Collected Stories of Philip K. Dick*, 1987
    five volumes
Cordwainer Smith, *The Rediscovery of Man*, 1993
Marc Stiegler, *The Gentle Seduction*, 1990
Theodore Sturgeon, *The Ultimate Egoist*, 1994
John Varley, *Blue Champagne*, 1986

**55**

### BRIAN W. ALDISS

## Dracula Unbound

(New York: HarperCollins, 1991)

**Story type:** Horror (Science Fiction)

**Major character(s):** Joe Bodeland, Scientist; Bram Stoker, Writer (author of *Dracula*), Historical Figure; Count Dracula, Vampire
**Time period(s):** 1990s (1999)
**Locale(s):** Utah

**Summary:** In this semi-sequel to the author's *Frankenstein Unbound*, the discovery of a 65-million-year-old tomb in Utah sends space/time manipulator Joe Bodeland investigating. Through a process not unlike the "time sink" he has developed for disposing of toxic waste, Bodeland hops a ghost train from the past that rides through the tomb site and there discovers that the immortal Count Dracula has planned a future in which he will enslave all mankind.

**Other books you might like:**
Fred Saberhagen, *The Dracula Tape*, 1975
John Shirley, *Dracula in Love*, 1979
Dan Simmons, *Carrion Comfort*, 1989
Peter Tremayne, *Dracula Unborn*, 1977
Chelsea Quinn Yarbro, *Out of the House of Life*, 1990

**56**

### BRIAN W. ALDISS

## Last Orders

(New York: Carroll and Graf, 1989)

**Story type:** Science Fiction (Collection)

**Summary:** This volume contains nine short stories and five pieces the author calls Enigmas. Publication dates range from 1973 through 1977. The best known stories in the collection are "Last Orders," "Creatures of Apogee," "The Monster of Ingratitude IV," and "The Aperture Moment."

**Other books you might like:**
J.G. Ballard, *Billennium and Other Stories*, 1962
J.G. Ballard, *The Drowned World*, 1962
J.G. Ballard, *Terminal Beach*, 1964
J.G. Ballard, *Vermilion Sands*, 1971
Paul Park, *Soldiers of Paradise*, 1987
Paul Park, *Sugar Rain*, 1989
Keith Roberts, *Kiteworld*, 1985
Keith Roberts, *The Passing of the Dragons*, 1977

**57**

### BRIAN W. ALDISS

## Man in His Time: The Best Science Fiction Stories of Brian W. Aldiss

(New York: Atheneum, 1989)

**Story type:** Science Fiction (Collection)

**Summary:** This volume contains twenty-two stories, ranging in original publication date from 1955 to 1986. Among the earliest are "Outside" (1955), "The Failed Men" (1957), "Poor Little Warrior!" (1958), and "Who Can Replace Man?" (1958), the cumulative excellence of which earned Aldiss a special award at the 1959 World Science Fiction Convention as Most Promising New Author. Other outstanding stories included are "The Saliva Tree" (1965), which won a Nebula Award, "Heresies of the Huge God" (1966), "Last Orders" (1976), "The Gods in Flight" (1984), "My Country 'Tis Not Only of Thee" (1986), and "The Difficulties Involved in Photographing Nix Olympica" (1986).

**Other books you might like:**
J.G. Ballard, *Billennium and Other Stories*, 1962
J.G. Ballard, *The Drowned World*, 1962

J.G. Ballard, *Terminal Beach*, 1964
J.G. Ballard, *Vermilion Sands*, 1971
Paul Park, *Soldiers of Paradise*, 1987
Paul Park, *Sugar Rain*, 1989
Keith Roberts, *Kiteworld*, 1985
Keith Roberts, *The Passing of the Dragons*, 1977

**58**

### BRIAN W. ALDISS

## Non-Stop

(New York: Carroll & Graf, 1989)

**Story type:** Science Fiction (Generation Starship)
**Major character(s):** Roy Complain, Hunter; Henry Marapper, Religious (Priest)
**Time period(s):** Indeterminate Future
**Locale(s):** *Big Dog*, Spaceship

**Summary:** Roy Complain has grown up in a primitive jungle world, but he has never been satisfied with the reasons the priests give for his people's boring and confined life. He wants explanations for the odd legends he's learned. Who are the Giants who supposedly built his world? Who are the people who live beyond Quarters in the place called Forwards? What lies beyond the metal walls that have always surrounded him? Eventually Complain decides to find out.

**Other books you might like:**
Ronald Anthony Cross, *Prisoners of Paradise*, 1988
Harry Harrison, *Captive Universe*, 1969
Robert A. Heinlein, *Orphans of the Sky*, 1963
Fritz Leiber, *Ship of Shadows*, 1988
Harry Martinson, *Aniara*, 1956

**59**

### BRIAN W. ALDISS

## A Romance of the Equator: The Best Fantasy Stories of Brian W. Aldiss

(New York: Atheneum, 1990)

**Story type:** Fantasy (Collection)
**Time period(s):** Indeterminate

**Summary:** This collection contains 26 short stories and an introduction in which Aldiss reveals his personal favorites to the reader. The stories include "Old Hundredth," "The Worm That Flies," "Lies," "The Small Stones of Tu Fu" and others published between 1960 and 1989. This book is a companion volume to *Man in his Time: The Best Science Fiction Stories of Brian W. Aldiss* (1989).

**Other books you might like:**
J.G. Ballard, *Terminal Beach*, 1964
J.G. Ballard, *Vermilion Sands*, 1971
Anthony Boucher, *Far and Away*, 1955
Ellen Datlow, *The Year's Best Fantasy and Horror: Third Annual Collection*, 1990
    Terri Windling, co-editor
Chad Oliver, *Another Kind*, 1954
Chad Oliver, *The Edge of Forever*, 1971

**60**

BRIAN W. ALDISS

## Somewhere East of Life

(New York: Carroll & Graf, 1994)

**Story type:** Science Fiction (Contemporary Realism)
**Major character(s):** Burnell, Amnesiac, Activist
**Time period(s):** 21st century
**Locale(s):** Turkmenistan; Georgia

**Summary:** As Burnell travels around Asia documenting destructive forces' effects on architecture, he tries to locate and reacquire the 10 years of memories stolen from him, some of which have been sold as soft core pornography.

**Other books you might like:**
Pat Cadigan, *Fools*, 1992
Pat Cadigan, *Mindplayers*, 1987
Katharine Kerr, *Resurrection*, 1992
Nancy Kress, *Brain Rose*, 1990
Michael Swanwick, *Vacuum Flowers*, 1987

**61**

BRIAN W. ALDISS

## A Tupelov Too Far and Other Stories

(New York: St. Martin's Press, 1994)

**Story type:** Science Fiction (Collection)

**Summary:** Contains an original poem, "Short Stories," and 12 stories published in periodicals and anthologies 1967-1992. Frequently philosophical, some stories feature terrestrial settings such as "Three Degrees Over" with its orgy in an Oxford garden, while others take place light years away and one is set in the Afterworld. Aldiss exhibits dark humor in "Better Morphosis," a twist on Kafka's work, and a humorless revisiting of his Frankenstein myth in "Summertime Was Nearly Over."

**Other books you might like:**
J.G. Ballard, *The Best Short Stories of J.G. Ballard*, 1978
Gardner Dozois, *Geodesic Dreams: The Best Short Fiction of Gardner Dozois*, 1992
Damon Knight, *One Side Laughing: Stories Unlike Other Stories*, 1991
John Varley, *Blue Champagne*, 1986
Gene Wolfe, *Endangered Species*, 1989

**62**

RAY ALDRIDGE

## Emperor of Everything

(New York: Bantam Spectra, 1992)

**Story type:** Science Fiction (Adventure)
**Series:** Emancipator
**Major character(s):** Ruiz Aw, Slave (former), Agent; Corean Heiclaro, Trader (slave); Nisa, Slave (escaped), Royalty
**Time period(s):** Indeterminate Future
**Locale(s):** Sook, Planet—Imaginary

**Summary:** Shepherding a band of escaped slaves across the planet Sook, Ruiz reaches Seastack. In a desperate gamble to gain safety, he accepts a job as a hired assassin at the risk of being captured and "genched"—mentally re-conditioned.

**Other books you might like:**
Marion Zimmer Bradley, *The Shattered Chain*, 1976
Emma Bull, *Bone Dance: A Fantasy for Technophiles*, 1991
Robert A. Heinlein, *Citizen of the Galaxy*, 1957
Anne McCaffrey, *Sassinak*, 1990
    Elizabeth Moon, co-author
Frederik Pohl, *The Reefs of Space*, 1964
    Jack Williamson, co-author

**63**

RAY ALDRIDGE

## The Pharaoh Contract

(New York: Bantam Spectra, 1991)

**Story type:** Science Fiction (Adventure)
**Series:** Emancipator
**Major character(s):** Ruiz Aw, Agent, Martial Arts Expert; Nacker the Teach, Health Care Professional (minddriver); Nisa, Royalty (princess of Pharaoh), Slave
**Time period(s):** Indeterminate Future
**Locale(s):** *Vigia*, Spaceship; Pharaoh, Planet—Imaginary; Sook, Planet—Imaginary (pirate base)

**Summary:** Ruiz Aw, born a slave, is an enforcer for the Arts League, the corporation which provides slaves for the Pangalac Worlds. He has Nacker loosen the Death Net which the Arts League installed along with a compulsion to complete his mission. Nacker's technique changes Ruiz Aw, but is successful in preventing the device from activating.

**Other books you might like:**
Allan Cole, *Sten*, 1984
    Chris Bunch, co-author
Stephen Goldin, *Jade Darcy and the Affair of Honor*, 1988
    Mary Mason, co-author
Steve Perry, *The Man Who Never Missed*, 1985
Carol Severance, *Reefsong*, 1991
Michael Swanwick, *Vacuum Flowers*, 1987
Sydney J. Van Scyoc, *Deepwater Dreams*, 1991

**64**

BUZZ ALDRIN
JOHN BARNES, Co-Author

## Encounter with Tiber

(New York: Warner Aspect, 1996)

**Story type:** Science Fiction (Family Saga; First Contact)
**Major character(s):** Chris Terrence, Astronaut; Zahmekoses, Alien (Tiberian), Space Explorer; Diehrenn, Alien (Tiberian), Writer
**Time period(s):** 21st century; 73rd century B.C.
**Locale(s):** Outer Space

**Summary:** The alien Tiberians mount an expensive voyage to explore and possibly settle Earth, leaving encyclopedias for humans to discover on the Moon and Mars when colonization proves impossible. A message alerting humanity to the encyclopedias spurs human space exploration in the 2000s, resulting in an unsuccessful lunar recovery attempt and the need for a multinational effort to recover the Martian encyclopedia.

**Other books you might like:**
John Barnes, *A Million Open Doors*, 1992
John Barnes, *Mother of Storms*, 1994
John Barnes, *Orbital Resonance*, 1991
Robert L. Forward, *Rocheworld*, 1990

Diana G. Gallagher, *The Alien Dark*, 1990
David Alexander Smith, *Marathon*, 1982
David Alexander Smith, *Rendezvous*, 1988
Allen Steele, *The Tranquility Alternative*, 1996

---

### 65

#### DAVID ALEXANDER

## Desert Fire

(New York: Worldwide Gold Eagle, 1993)

**Story type:** Science Fiction (Time Travel; Political)
**Series:** Nomad
**Major character(s):** Quinn "Nomad", Time Traveler, Warrior; Lux Vadim, Religious, Scientist
**Time period(s):** 2030s (2035); 1990s (1991)
**Locale(s):** Los Angeles, California; Sunyata, Space Station; New York, New York

**Summary:** When a psychotic religious leader, Lux Vadim, escapes prison and implements lethal plans to control the power of the ancients, Quinn must follow Vadim back in time and stop him from changing the outcome of the U.S. invasion of Iraq.

**Other books you might like:**
Poul Anderson, *The Time Patrol*, 1991
Keith William Andrews, *Sink the Armada*, 1990
Roger L. DiSilvestro, *Living with the Reptiles*, 1990
Randall Frakes, *The Terminator*, 1985
    Bill Wisher, co-author
Robert Charles Wilson, *A Bridge of Years*, 1991

---

### 66

#### DAVID ALEXANDER

## Nomad

(New York: Worldwide Gold Eagle, 1992)

**Story type:** Science Fiction (Adventure; Techno-Thriller)
**Series:** Nomad
**Major character(s):** Quinn "Nomad", Warrior, Spy; Ramsey, Spy (double agent); Bill Bruckner, Spy, Criminal (assassin)
**Time period(s):** 2030s (2030)
**Locale(s):** Earth; Outer Space (near Earth orbit)

**Summary:** Quinn's assignment, protecting the remaining unassassinated scientists connected with the Prometheus Project and discovering the force behind the assassination, proves difficult since Quinn's boss works for the enemy.

**Other books you might like:**
Jack L. Chalker, *War of Shadows*, 1979
Burt Cole, *The Quick*, 1989
Daniel Da Cruz, *Texas on the Rocks*, 1987
William R. Forstchen, *A Darkness upon the Ice*, 1985
Brian Stableford, *Optiman*, 1980
Walter Jon Williams, *Hardwired*, 1986
Timothy Zahn, *The Backlash Mission*, 1986

---

### 67

#### LLOYD ALEXANDER

## The Arkadians

(New York: Dutton, 1995)

**Story type:** Fantasy (Young Adult; Adventure)

---

**Major character(s):** Lucian, Adventurer, Fugitive; Joy-in-the-Dance, Adventurer; Fronto, Animal (talking donkey), Writer (poet)
**Time period(s):** Indeterminate Past
**Locale(s):** Arkadia, Ancient Civilization (Greek); Greece

**Summary:** To escape soothsayers and the king's murderous intent, Lucian flees with Fronto, who seeks restoration to human form. Soon the mysterious Joy-in-the-Dance joins them, proving useful to the dangerous quest.

**Other books you might like:**
Gillian Bradshaw, *The Land of Gold*, 1992
Mary Brown, *The Unlikely Ones*, 1986
Tom Holt, *Goatsong*, 1990
Mary James, *Shoebag*, 1990
Sherwood Smith, *Wren to the Rescue*, 1990
Robert Watson, *Whilom*, 1990

---

### 68

#### LLOYD ALEXANDER

## The Iron Ring

(New York: Dutton, 1997)

**Story type:** Fantasy (Young Adult; Quest)
**Major character(s):** Tamar, Royalty, Teacher; Garuda, Mythical Creature, Adventurer; Mirri, Young Woman, Adventurer
**Time period(s):** Indeterminate
**Locale(s):** Danda-Vana Forest, Mythical Place; Fictional Country

**Summary:** After losing his kingdom in a card game, Tamar tests his stamina and resolve as he meets talking animals, warring kings, fearsome spirits and his true love.

---

### 69

#### LLOYD ALEXANDER

## The Remarkable Journey of Prince Jen

(New York: Dutton, 1991)

**Story type:** Fantasy (Quest; Young Adult)
**Major character(s):** Jen, Royalty (prince); Mafoo, Servant; Voyaging Moon, Musician
**Time period(s):** Indeterminate Past
**Locale(s):** China

**Summary:** Before Prince Jen sets off to find the legendary court of T'ien-kuo, a strange old man gives him six rather ordinary objects to take with him. Not appreciating a future need for the objects, Jen loses a saddle and most of his retinue almost immediately. Undaunted, Jen continues his journey, learning about himself and his responsibilities before he learns the true value of the gifts.

**Other books you might like:**
William Goldman, *The Princess Bride*, 1973
Kathryn Grant, *The Willow Garden*, 1989
Barry Hughart, *Bridge of Birds*, 1984
Barry Hughart, *Eight Skilled Gentlemen*, 1990
Jeanne Larsen, *Silk Road*, 1989
Andre Norton, *Imperial Lady*, 1989
    Susan Shwartz, co-author
Laurence Yep, *Tongues of Jade*, 1991

### 70

#### ATHENA ALEXIS

## Along Came a Spider

(New York: Dell, 1991)

**Story type:** Horror (Gothic Family Chronicle)
**Major character(s):** Alice McNamara, Teenager; Daria Broderick, Child (Alice's half-sister); Jeremy Woolcott, Teenager (Alice's cousin by marriage)
**Time period(s):** 1990s
**Locale(s):** Congreve, Georgia

**Summary:** In this first novel written in the grand gothic tradition of V.C. Andrews, Alice McNamara and her beloved mother, stepfather, and half-sister Daria inherit her step-grandfather's family fortune with the provision that they relocate from New York to the family mansion in Georgia. Once there, Alice runs afoul of family matriarch Aunt Thelma, walks in fear of a mysterious old woman kept locked in the attic, fends off the advances of her lewd cousin Bubba, and develops a general disdain for those eccentricities of extended southern families that make it possible for the rest of us to feel much better about ourselves.

**Other books you might like:**
V.C. Andrews, *Flowers in the Attic*, 1979
Robert R. McCammon, *Usher's Passing*, 1984
Michael McDowell, *Blackwater*, 1983
Andrew Neiderman, *Sister, Sister*, 1992

### 71

#### KATINA ALEXIS

## Souls

(New York: Pocket, 1992)

**Story type:** Horror (Occult)
**Major character(s):** Maria Demos, Real Estate Agent; Vince De Luca, Detective—Police; Taylor Caroline Shedian, FBI Agent
**Time period(s):** 1990s
**Locale(s):** Chaseburn, Florida

**Summary:** A pair of determined millionaires with occult connections plot to recall the soul of 18th century witch Maria Trapnell from the spirit realm, reinstate it in the body of her lineal descendant, Maria Demos, and help her resume the reign of terror she and her coven of followers initiated centuries before.

**Other books you might like:**
D.A. Fowler, *The Devil's End*, 1992
Marcy Heidish, *The Torching*, 1992

### 72

#### ALICE ALFONSI, Editor
#### JOHN SCOGNAMIGLIO, Co-Editor

## Dark Seductions

(New York: Zebra, 1993)

**Story type:** Horror (Anthology)

**Summary:** The fifteen authors who contributed fourteen stories to this collection of erotic horror are better known as novelists for Zebra Books. Richard Lee Byers' ''Gloves'' tells of a paraplegic model who so desires to make love again that she submits to a bizarre prosthetic process, with terrifying results. Ric Hautala's ''Cousin's Curse'' is a vampire tale and Ronald Kelly's ''Whorehouse Hollow'' an exercise in southern grotesque. Stephen George's ''Hard'' and Scott Ciencin's ''The Victim'' both probe the underside of the entertainment profession, respectively porno films and method acting. And Tamara Thorne's ''Good Vibrations'' is about a marital aid with a mind of its own.

**Other books you might like:**
Ellen Datlow, *Alien Sex*, 1990
Jeff Gelb, *Hot Blood: Tales of Provocative Horror*, 1989
    Lonn Friend, co-editor
Jeff Gelb, *Hotter Blood: More Tales of Erotic Horror*, 1991
    Michael Garrett, co-editor
Jeff Gelb, *Hottest Blood: The Ultimate in Erotic Horror*, 1993
    Michael Garrett, co-editor
Margaret L. Carter, *Demon Lovers and Strange Seductions*, 1973

### 73

#### ALICE ALFONSI

## Some Enchanted Evening

(New York: Jove, 1998)

**Story type:** Fantasy (Light Fantasy)
**Major character(s):** Mary Jane Magorski, Businesswoman; Sinjin, Mythical Creature (genie)
**Time period(s):** 1990s (1998)
**Locale(s):** Las Vegas, Nevada

**Summary:** Mary Jane finds an antique bottle which she cleans, thereby setting free a handsome genie. He sets about granting her every wish, but his ancient enemy discovers that he has been set free and returns intent upon imprisoning him once again.

**Other books you might like:**
F. Anstey, *The Brass Bottle*, 1900
Piers Anthony, *Hasan*, 1979
H.M. Egbert, *Mrs. Aladdin*, 1925
Esther Friesner, *Wishing Season*, 1993
Kathleen Nance, *Wishes Come True*, 1998

### 74

#### JUDITH ALGUIRE

## Zeta Base

(Tallahassee: Naiad, 1991)

**Story type:** Science Fiction (Gay/Lesbian Fiction; Disaster)
**Major character(s):** Jordan ''Antiquity'' Thyme, Scientist, Computer Expert; Morgan Quade, Artist; Jaffey, Engineer, Computer Expert
**Time period(s):** Indeterminate Future (500th year of galactic civilization)
**Locale(s):** Earth

**Summary:** Antiquity, an expert on SOLCOM, the ancient computer monitoring the Sun, announces ominous findings about the Sun's output. Gathered for the galaxy's half-millennium celebration, Antiquity's three proteges struggle with a rekindled love triangle as one of them, Jaffey, performs the SOLCOM systems-check needed to verify Antiquity's findings which indicate tragedy for the earth. A first novel.

**Other books you might like:**
Perry Brass, *Mirage*, 1991
Lauren Wright Douglas, *In the Blood*, 1989
Nancy Tyler Glenn, *Clicking Stones*, 1989
Camarin Grae, *Stranded*, 1991
Robert Leininger, *Black Sun*, 1991

Lynda Lyons, *Priorities*, 1990

## 75

**MARY ELIZABETH ALLEN**

### All Hallow's Eve: Tales of Love and the Supernatural
(New York: Walker, 1992)

**Story type:** Fantasy (Anthology)

**Summary:** These sixteen original stories written in the Regency romance tradition are mostly tales of liaisons between mortal women and ghostly lovers. The best stories include S. N. Lewitt's "Pipe Dreams," about a rock musician who summons Mary Shelley's ghost for inspiration; Andre Norton's tale of ghostly revenge, "The Nabob's Gift"; and Caroline Stevermer's "Waiting for Harry," about a family ghost that predicts death. The volume also includes stories by Joan Aiken, Marvin Kaye, and Morgan Llywellyn.

**Other books you might like:**
Don Congdon, *Tales of Love and Horror*, 1961
Ellen Datlow, *Alien Sex*, 1990
Jeff Gelb, *Hot Blood: Tales of Provocative Horror*, 1990
    Michael Garret, co-editor
Jeff Gelb, *Hottest Blood: The Ultimate in Erotic Horror*, 1993
    Michael Garret, co-editor
Jeff Gelb, *Hotter Blood: More Tales of Erotic Horror*, 1990
    Michael Garret, co-editor
Michel Parry, *Devil's Kisses*, 1976
    editor
Michele Slung, *I Shudder at Your Touch*, 1991
    editor

## 76

**ROGER MACBRIDE ALLEN**

### Ambush at Corellia
(New York: Bantam Spectra, 1995)

**Story type:** Science Fiction (Space Opera; Political)
**Series:** Star Wars: The Corellian Trilogy
**Major character(s):** Leia Organa Solo, Royalty, Leader (New Republic Head of State); Han Solo, Spaceship Captain, Warrior; Luke Skywalker, Martial Arts Expert, Hero
**Time period(s):** Indeterminate Past
**Locale(s):** Corellia, Planet—Imaginary; Interstellar Empire/Federation

**Summary:** A trade summit with a government completely isolated since the Imperial/Alliance war seems the perfect opportunity for Han and Leia to work in a family vacation, showing the children their father's homeland. Their plans, however, originally did not include a compromised intelligence operation, a megalomaniac dictator, or a device capable of destroying stars! First of a trilogy.

**Other books you might like:**
Kevin J. Anderson, *Jedi Search*, 1994
Brian Daley, *The Han Solo Adventures*, 1992
Alan Dean Foster, *Splinter of the Mind's Eye*, 1978
Barbara Hambly, *Children of the Jedi*, 1995
George Lucas, *The Star Wars Trilogy*, 1987
    Donald F. Glut, James Kahn, co-authors
L. Neil Smith, *The Lando Calrissian Adventures*, 1994
Timothy Zahn, *Heir to the Empire*, 1991

## 77

**ROGER MACBRIDE ALLEN**

### Caliban
(New York: Ace, 1993)

**Story type:** Science Fiction (Robot Fiction; Mystery)
**Series:** Isaac Asimov's Caliban
**Major character(s):** CBN-001 "Caliban", Robot; Alvar Kresh, Lawman (sheriff); Fredda Leving, Computer Expert, Engineer (robot engineer)
**Time period(s):** Indeterminate Future
**Locale(s):** Inferno, Planet—Imaginary

**Summary:** Coming to awareness in a pool of blood with a woman lying at its feet, Caliban decides to leave and explore the city. Sheriff Kresh realizes Caliban acts differently than other robots and may have assaulted Fredda Leving. While all attempts to capture or destroy Caliban fail, Fredda Leving's ideas on the Three Laws of Robotics cause a riot.

**Other books you might like:**
Isaac Asimov, *The Caves of Steel*, 1954
Isaac Asimov, *The Naked Sun*, 1957
Philip K. Dick, *Blade Runner*, 1982
Robert A. Heinlein, *The Moon Is a Harsh Mistress*, 1966
Lisa Mason, *Arachne*, 1990
Victor Milan, *The Cybernetic Samurai*, 1986
Cordwainer Smith, *Norstrilia*, 1975
Amy Thomson, *Virtual Girl*, 1993
John Varley, *Steel Beach*, 1993

## 78

**ROGER MACBRIDE ALLEN**

### Inferno
(New York: Ace, 1994)

**Story type:** Science Fiction (Robot Fiction; Mystery)
**Series:** Isaac Asimov's Caliban
**Major character(s):** Caliban, Robot, Revolutionary; Prospero, Robot; Alvar Kresh, Lawman (sheriff)
**Time period(s):** Indeterminate Future
**Locale(s):** Inferno, Planet—Imaginary

**Summary:** A politician's murder creates suspicion of Caliban, the only robot not bound by the protective Laws of Robotics. However, Caliban's actions could send revolutionary reverberations through society.

**Other books you might like:**
Isaac Asimov, *The Complete Robot*, 1982
Isaac Asimov, *The Robots of Dawn*, 1983
Michael P. Kube-McDowell, *Odyssey*, 1987
Mike McQuay, *Suspicion*, 1987
William F. Wu, *Predator*, 1993

## 79

**ROGER MACBRIDE ALLEN**

### The Modular Man
(New York: Bantam Sepctra, 1992)

**Story type:** Science Fiction (Cyberpunk; Political)
**Series:** Next Wave
**Major character(s):** David "Herbert" Clancy Bailey, Robot (human imprinted), Inventor; Samantha "Sam" Crandall, Journalist (*The*

*Washington Post*); Phillipe "Phil" Montoya Sanders, Police Officer, Computer Expert (amateur)
**Time period(s):** 21st century
**Locale(s):** Washington, District of Columbia

**Summary:** When Bailey moves his personality into a machine hoping to avoid death, forces move to declare him legally dead and power down the hardware, intending to avoid a world populated by rich immortals and poverty-struck mortal humans. Includes a 12-page article by Isaac Asimov on intelligent robots.

**Other books you might like:**
Greg Bear, *Heads*, 1991
David Brin, *Earth*, 1990
Pat Cadigan, *Mindplayers*, 1987
Philip K. Dick, *Blade Runner*, 1982
Robert A. Heinlein, *The Moon Is a Harsh Mistress*, 1966
Victor Milan, *The Cybernetic Samurai*, 1986
Rudy Rucker, *Software*, 1982
Rudy Rucker, *Wetware*, 1988
Melissa Scott, *Dreamships*, 1992
Michael Swanwick, *Vacuum Flowers*, 1987
Thomas T. Thomas, *ME: A Novel of Self Discovery*, 1991
John Varley, *Steel Beach*, 1992
Vernor Vinge, *A Fire upon the Deep*, 1992
Walter Jon Williams, *Voice of the Whirlwind*, 1987

---

**80**

**ROGER MACBRIDE ALLEN**

## The Ring of Charon
(New York: Tor, 1990)

**Story type:** Science Fiction (Hard Science Fiction; Disaster)
**Series:** Hunted Earth
**Major character(s):** Larry O'Shawnessy Chao, Scientist (gravity researcher); Dianne Steiger, Spaceship Captain; Frank Barlow, Spaceman
**Time period(s):** Indeterminate Future
**Locale(s):** Gravities Research Station, Pluto; Earth; Outer Space

**Summary:** When the remote gravity research facility's funding is threatened, Larry Chao sneaks in an unauthorized experiment on the gravity generator, the Ring of Charon. His new configuration allows the first strong gravity waves to be generated in Sol Space, awakening automatic equipment quiescent for millenia. The automatic equipment triggered includes a device which transports the Earth, but not the Moon, out of Sol Space. Other equipment begins breaking up and moving other astronomical bodies. The humans remaining must find out how to stop this disaster while those on Earth must find how to survive in their new location.

**Other books you might like:**
David Brin, *Startide Rising*, 1983
Robert L. Forward, *Dragon's Egg*, 1980
Dan Simmons, *The Fall of Hyperion*, 1990
Dan Simmons, *Hyperion*, 1989
John E. Stith, *Redshift Rendezvous*, 1990

---

**81**

**ROGER MACBRIDE ALLEN**

## The Shattered Sphere
(New York: Tor, 1994)

**Story type:** Science Fiction (First Contact; Space Opera)
**Series:** Hunted Earth

**Major character(s):** Sianna Colette, Scientist (gravitational physicist), Student; Wally Sturgis, Computer Expert (Multisystem Research Institute), Student (doctoral candidate); Larry O'Shawnessy Chao, Scientist (gravitational physicist)
**Time period(s):** 25th century (2430s)
**Locale(s):** Naked Purple Habitat, Space Station (former L5 colony); *Terra Nova*, Spaceship; Earth (displaced to the Multisystem)

**Summary:** Earth loses contact with the colonized Solar System after Larry Chao's experiment with gravity awakens an ancient mechanism which transports the Earth through a wormhole into an artificial planetary system with several stars orbiting a Dyson sphere, all held in orbits utilizing colossal gravity forces. Five years later, Larry Chao searches alien artifacts on the Moon for direction in his quest to recover the stolen Earth, while Sianna and Wally struggle to understand the alien technology until a monstrous invader threatens to destroy all. Sequel to *The Ring of Charon*.

**Other books you might like:**
Stephen Baxter, *Raft*, 1991
Glen Cook, *The Dragon Never Sleeps*, 1988
Robert L. Forward, *Dragon's Egg*, 1980
Vonda N. McIntyre, *Metaphase*, 1992
Vonda N. McIntyre, *Transition*, 1991
John E. Stith, *Redshift Rendezvous*, 1990
Vernor Vinge, *A Fire upon the Deep*, 1992

---

**82**

**ROGER MACBRIDE ALLEN**
**ERIC KOTANI**, Co-Author

## Supernova
(New York: Avon, 1991)

**Story type:** Science Fiction (Hard Science Fiction; Disaster)
**Major character(s):** George Prescott, Scientist, Student; Desmond Miller, Doctor; Jessica Talmadge, Scientist, Student
**Time period(s):** 1990s; 2000s
**Locale(s):** Arizona; California; Japan

**Summary:** George Prescott, studying supernova formation, focuses in on Sirius. His models predict that this star is indeed a candidate for a supernova. When he announces this at an amateur astronomy meeting, others start studying Sirius. Meanwhile Desmond, who has just lost his family because of a madman's deed, joins a millennialist cult, the Christriders, and sees in the Sirius supernova data the proof of the end of the world. Millennialists are prevented from blowing up Los Angeles' water supply and the worst supernova effects are averted, with warning, giving the world about 100 years to prepare for the hard radiation that will shower on them from the Sirius supernova.

**Other books you might like:**
Piers Anthony, *Rings of Ice*, 1974
Greg Bear, *The Forge of God*, 1987
David Brin, *Earth*, 1990
Fred Hoyle, *The Inferno*, 1973
    Geoffrey Hoyle, co-author
Eric Kotani, *Between the Stars*, 1988
    John Maddox Roberts, co-author
Eric Kotani, *The Island Worlds*, 1987
    John Maddox Roberts, co-author
Larry Niven, *Lucifer's Hammer*, 1977
    Jerry Pournelle, co-author

## 83

### ROGER MACBRIDE ALLEN

## *Utopia*

(New York: Ace, 1996)

**Story type:** Science Fiction (Robot Fiction)
**Series:** Isaac Asimov's Caliban
**Major character(s):** Alvar Kresh, Political Figure (governor); Davlo Lentrall, Scientist; Caliban, Robot
**Time period(s):** Indeterminate Future
**Locale(s):** Inferno, Planet—Imaginary

**Summary:** To prevent the planet Inferno from dying, residents plan to drop a comet on it, creating a polar sea and a whole new ecology. However, many people do not want to see any change in their cozy lives, especially robots that will not allow any danger to humans, even if it costs Inferno its future. But for one, the fall of the comet provides a chance to exact vengeance.

**Other books you might like:**
Isaac Asimov, *Robots and Empire*, 1985
Arthur C. Clarke, *The Hammer of God*, 1993
James P. Hogan, *Code of the Lifemaker*, 1983
Anne McCaffrey, *The City Who Fought*, 1993
    S.M. Stirling, co-author
Frederik Pohl, *Mining the Oort*, 1992
L. Neil Smith, *The Venus Belt*, 1981
William F. Wu, *Predator*, 1993

## 84

### SHEILA ROSALYND ALLEN

## *The Meddlesome Ghost*

(New York: Walker, 1989)

**Story type:** Fantasy (Romance)
**Series:** Lovers of Steadford Abbey
**Major character(s):** Sir Harry Steadford, Spirit, Nobleman
**Time period(s):** 19th century
**Locale(s):** England

**Summary:** Doomed to be a ghost until he atones for his past, Sir Harry decides to play matchmaker for each heir to Steadford Abbey. The latest heir is paralyzed and bed-ridden by a recent wound and already has a fiancee; but, that doesn't stop Harry from trying to fix him up with his nurse.

**Other books you might like:**
Rebecca Brandewyne, *Passion Moon Rising*, 1989
Lindsay Clarke, *The Chymical Wedding*, 1989
Dean Wesley Smith, *Laying the Music to Rest*, 1989

## 85

### AARON ALLSTON

## *Doc Sidhe*

(New York: Baen, 1995)

**Story type:** Fantasy (Alternate World; Adventure)
**Major character(s):** Harris Greene, Sports Figure (kickboxing), Martial Arts Expert (tae kwon do); Desmond "Doc Sidhe" MaqqRee, Hero (crime-fighting superhero); Gabriela "Gaby" Donohue, Experimental Subject, Girlfriend
**Time period(s):** 1990s; Indeterminate
**Locale(s):** New York, New York; Alternate Earth

**Summary:** When Harris interrupts a strange trio's attempt to kidnap Gaby, a conjuring circle transports Harris to New York City, seemingly of the 1930s, but with many differences in the familiar environment. Harris soon meets Doc Sidhe who helps Harris locate Gaby and unravel the mystery surrounding her supressed magical abilities while deadly foes of various species plot against both universes.

**Other books you might like:**
Robin Wayne Bailey, *Brothers of the Dragon*, 1993
Gordon R. Dickson, *The Dragon and the George*, 1976
Philip Jose Farmer, *Escape From Loki*, 1991
Alis A. Rasmussen, *The Labyrinth Gate*, 1988
Kenneth Robeson, *Doc Savage Omnibus #1*, 1986
    Kenneth Robeson is the pseudonym for Lester Dent, Harold A. Davis, Will Murray, William G. Bogart, Ryerson Johnson, Laurence Donovan, and Alan Hathway who all wrote Doc Savage stories under this name.
Kenneth Robeson, *White Eyes*, 1992
    Kenneth Robeson is the pseudonym of Will Murray and Lester Dent, who collaborated on this Doc Savage story.

## 86

### AARON ALLSTON

## *Double Jeopardy*

(New York: Tor, 1994)

**Story type:** Science Fiction (Humor)
**Series:** Car Warriors
**Major character(s):** James "Spark" Parker, Insurance Investigator; Bojake "Buffalo" Lincoln, Insurance Investigator; E. "Pif" Heiligmann, Detective
**Time period(s):** 21st century
**Locale(s):** Texas

**Summary:** While trying to solve a case for Reunion Insurance Company, Spark, Buffalo, and Pif run afoul of the powerful Medcorp, needing their training as skilled combat drivers and investigators to stay alive and clear their names.

**Other books you might like:**
John DeChancie, *Starrigger*, 1983
John DeChancie, *Paradox Alley*, 1987
John DeChancie, *Red Limit Freeway*, 1984
David Drake, *The Square Deal*, 1992
Roger Zelazny, *Damnation Alley*, 1986

## 87

### AARON ALLSTON

## *Galatea in 2-D*

(New York: Baen, 1993)

**Story type:** Fantasy (Contemporary; Magic Conflict)
**Major character(s):** Roger Simmons, Artist; Elsie, Mythical Creature (nymph); Kevin Matthews, Artist, Criminal
**Time period(s):** 1990s
**Locale(s):** Earth

**Summary:** When Roger Simmons discovers the ability of bringing forth characters from his paintings, Kevin Matthews, another artist adept at animating characters from paintings, decides he must quash Roger's ability and, if necessary, his life.

**Other books you might like:**
Chester Anderson, *The Butterfly Kid*, 1967
Charles de Lint, *The Little Country*, 1991
Michael Ende, *The Neverending Story*, 1983

Philip Jose Farmer, *Red Orc's Rage*, 1991
Tim Powers, *Last Call*, 1992
Clifford D. Simak, *Out of Their Minds*, 1970
Wm. Mark Simmons, *When Dreams Collide*, 1992
Vivian Vande Velde, *User Unfriendly*, 1991
Oscar Wilde, *The Picture of Dorian Gray*, 1891

---

**88**

**STEVE ALTEN**

## *Meg*

(New York: Doubleday, 1997)

**Story type:** Horror (Nature in Revolt)
**Major character(s):** Jonas Taylor, Scientist (paleontologist); Terry Tanaka, Scientist (oceanographer); David Adashek, Journalist
**Time period(s):** 1900s (1997)
**Locale(s):** Monterey, California

**Summary:** Scientist exploration of the Marianas Trench stirs up a Megalodon, a prehistoric precursor of the great white shark that measures over 60-feet long. Jonas Taylor, the sole survivor of a deep-sea voyage slaughtered by a Megalodon, puts life and limb at risk when he agrees to help hunt the creature down and prevent a global upset of the marine food chain. A first novel.

**Other books you might like:**
Peter Benchley, *Jaws*, 1974
Peter Benchley, *Beast*, 1991
Matthew J. Costello, *Wurm*, 1991
William Dantz, *Hunger*, 1992
J.M. Morgan, *Between the Devil and the Deep*, 1992
Charles Wilson, *Extinct*, 1997

---

**89**

**DAVID AMBROSE**

## *The Man Who Turned into Himself*

(New York: St. Martin's, 1994)

**Story type:** Horror (Doppelganger)
**Major character(s):** Rick Hamilton, Publisher (magazine); Harold Allison, Lawyer; Emma Todd, Doctor (psychiatrist)
**Time period(s):** 1990s (1994)
**Locale(s):** Devon, Connecticut

**Summary:** After an accident, magazine publisher Rick Hamilton awakens to find himself trapped inside the consciousness of his alter ego, real-estate developer Richard Hamilton, who lives in the world of the alter egos of everyone else Rick knows. Rick must convince Richard that he is not merely a psychotic aspect of Richard, but a legitimate personality who wants to return to his own world. This is the author's first novel.

**Other books you might like:**
David Ely, *Seconds*, 1963
Richard Matheson, *7 Seconds to Midnight*, 1993
T.L. Parkinson, *The Man Upstairs*, 1991
Daniel Quinn, *Dreamer*, 1989

---

**90**

**DAVID AMBROSE**

## *Superstition*

(New York: Warner, 1998)

**Story type:** Horror (Ghost Story; Wild Talents)
**Major character(s):** Sam Towne, Psychologist; Joanna Cross, Journalist; Adam Wyatt, Spirit
**Time period(s):** 1990s (1998)
**Locale(s):** New York, New York

**Summary:** As part of his investigations into parapsychology, Sam Towne hires six volunteers to help him create a "ghost" out of their pooled psychic energies. Sam's experiment goes horribly awry when the ghost, which embodies the subliminal darker aspects of their personalities as well as the persona they have created for him, develops an autonomous, malignant character. First published in England in 1997.

**Other books you might like:**
Ramsey Campbell, *Incarnate*, 1983
James F. David, *Fragments*, 1997
Richard Matheson, *Hell House*, 1971
Al Sarrantonio, *House Haunted*, 1991

---

**91**

**J. EDWARD AMES**

## *The Death Crystal*

(New York: Leisure, 1990)

**Story type:** Horror (Serial Killer)
**Major character(s):** Harlan Perry, Maintenance Worker (janitor); Stevie Lasalle, Psychologist, Teacher (self-defense); Neal Bryce, Police Officer
**Time period(s):** 1990s
**Locale(s):** New Orleans, Louisiana

**Summary:** Under the influence of his schizophrenic alter ego Johnny Law, and with the help of the magic Tuoai Stone of Atlantis, homicidal Vietnam veteran Harlan Perry commits a series of brutal murders that have an infectious influence on the city of New Orleans.

**Other books you might like:**
Peter Straub, *Koko*, 1988

---

**92**

**J. EDWARD AMES**

## *Spellcaster*

(New York: Zebra, 1989)

**Story type:** Horror (Black Magic)
**Major character(s):** Alexey Zverkov, Psychic (Possessor of an "evil eye"); Alan Breaux, Detective—Police
**Time period(s):** 1980s (During Mardi Gras)
**Locale(s):** New Orleans, Louisiana (French Quarter)

**Summary:** Vowing revenge for the death of his lover-sister, Alexey Zverkov develops his "evil eye" to the point where he can wreak unbelievable havoc at will, a power he plans to unleash at the height of the Mardi Gras celebration. Led by Detective Breaux, a small group follows a series of murders to track Zverkov, penetrate his disguise, and thwart his evil plans.

**Other books you might like:**
Dennis Wheatley, *Strange Conflict*, 1941

## 93

**JOHN E. AMES**

### The Asylum

(New York: Zebra, 1994)

**Story type:** Horror (Mystery)
**Major character(s):** Reno Sloan, Detective—Private (former lawyer); Malachi Feldman, Scientist (chemist); Erin Kirby, Detective—Police
**Time period(s):** 1990s (1994)
**Locale(s):** New Orleans, Louisiana (Cypress Island)

**Summary:** Disbarred lawyer Reno Sloan uncovers a plot among the administrators of the Cypress Island Clinic to feed a newly-invented hallucinogenic drug to the children of local rich families, and "treat" them for the psychoses it induces at significant expense once they are admitted into the clinic.

**Other books you might like:**
Robin Cook, *Coma*, 1977
Stephen King, *Firestarter*, 1980
Kathe Koja, *Bad Brains*, 1992
Karl Edward Wagner, *"The Fourth Seal"*, 1984
   in *In a Lonely Place*
F. Paul Wilson, *The Select*, 1994

## 94

**MEL D. AMES**

### Tales of Titillation and Terror

(Oakville, Ontario/Buffalo, New York: Mosaic Press, 1996)

**Story type:** Horror (Collection)

**Summary:** This collection brings together 15 stories of mystery and supernatural horror by a Canadian writer. "The Messiah of Soul" is a homage to Edgar Allan Poe, and "The Embryo" a blend of horror and science fiction concerned with psychological and physical regression. "The Polargeist" and "Sasquatch" both draw their brooding atmosphere from their Canadian wilderness settings while "The Ghost Walker" and "The Promise of His Coming" employ unreliable, and possibly psychologically unbalanced, narrators. "The Enigma of Andrew Marler" and "No Sirens for Jonathan" are revenge stories with O Henry-type twists. Don Hutchison and Peter Sellers both supply introductions.

**Other books you might like:**
S. Darnbrook Colson, *People of the Night*, 1994
Christopher Fowler, *Sharper Knives*, 1992
Brian Hopkins, *Something Haunts Us All*, 1995
Elizabeth Massie, *Shadow Dreams*, 1996
David Niall Wilson, *The Fall of the House of Escher and Other Illusions*, 1995

## 95

**MARTIN AMIS**

### London Fields

(New York: Harmony Books, 1990)

**Story type:** Science Fiction (Literary)
**Major character(s):** Samson Young, Writer; Nicola Six, Girlfriend
**Time period(s):** Indeterminate Future
**Locale(s):** England

**Summary:** As the world nears environmental collapse, Sam Young, an American writer dying, perhaps of radiation poisoning, moves to London and rents the flat of the dramatist and sexual athlete Mark Asprey. Young is writing a murder mystery based on the lives of those around him, including Asprey and his girlfriend Nicola Six. The events of Young's life mirror in curious fashion those of the ongoing environmental collapse.

**Other books you might like:**
Doris Lessing, *The Fifth Child*, 1988
James Morrow, *This Is the Way the World Ends*, 1986
Kim Stanley Robinson, *The Gold Coast*, 1988
Fay Weldon, *The Cloning of Joanna May*, 1990

## 96

**MARTIN AMIS**

### Time's Arrow

(New York: Harmony Books, 1991)

**Story type:** Science Fiction (Literary; Time Travel)
**Major character(s):** Tod T. Friendly, Doctor, Criminal
**Time period(s):** 1940s; 1950s
**Locale(s):** New York, New York; Auschwitz, Poland; Munich, Germany

**Summary:** Tod T. Friendly's life unfolds backward in time as the symbiote infecting him progressively works its way through memories from his recent life as a physician in America to earlier memories of atrocities committed and life surrounding his duties as a doctor at Auschwitz, to earliest memories of his childhood in pre-Hitler Germany.

**Other books you might like:**
Piers Anthony, *Bearing an Hourglass*, 1984
Philip K. Dick, *Ubik*, 1969
Ken Grimwood, *Replay*, 1986
Dan Simmons, *The Fall of Hyperion*, 1990
Dan Simmons, *Hyperion*, 1989
Kurt Vonnegut Jr., *The Sirens of Titan*, 1959
Kurt Vonnegut Jr., *Slaughterhouse Five*, 1969
T.H. White, *The Once and Future King*, 1958

## 97

**BETH AMOS**

### Cold White Fury

(New York: HarperPaperbacks, 1996)

**Story type:** Horror (Wild Talents)
**Major character(s):** Jennifer Bolton, Teacher; Tanner Bolton, Child (Jennifer's 8-year-old son); Eric Singleton, Doctor
**Time period(s):** 1990s (1995)
**Locale(s):** Hillenberg, Virginia

**Summary:** A routine MRI scan reacts with a metal sliver lodged in young Tanner Bolton's head, activating his extrasensory perception and psychic powers. Tanner and his mother learn their lives are endangered when Tanner's conversations with the ghost of his father, formerly a geneticist, reveal that people close to the Bolton family are involved in a conspiracy to use lower class people as human guinea pigs in genetic experiments. First novel.

**Other books you might like:**
Douglas Clegg, *Eye of the Needle*, 1994
John Farris, *The Fury*, 1976
Stephen King, *Firestarter*, 1980
Dean R. Koontz, *Lightning*, 1988

Michael Kurland, *Button Bright*, 1990
David B. Silva, *Disappeared*, 1995

**98**

### DANA ANDERSON
### CHARLES DE LINT, Co-Author
### RAY GARTON, Co-Author

## *Cafe Purgatorium*
(New York: Tor, 1991)

**Story type:** Horror (Anthology)

**Summary:** Three novellas of horror and fantasy. The title story by Dana Anderson is concerned with a love that persists from beyond the grave. Charles de Lint's ''Death Leaves an Echo'' is a horror tale of a dead man forced to choose between horrible alternatives. Ray Garton's ''Dr. Krusadian's Methods'' tells of a unique type of therapy given to curb the child-abusing tendencies of two parents.

**Other books you might like:**
Mervyn Peake, *Sometime, Never*, 1954
   William Golding and John Wyndham, co-authors
Lucius Shepard, *Nantucket Slayrides*, 1990
   Robert Frazer, co-author
Various Authors, *The Night Visions Series*, 1984-1992

**99**

### KEVIN J. ANDERSON

## *Antibodies*
(New York: HarperPrism, 1997)

**Story type:** Horror (Science Fiction)
**Series:** X-Files
**Major character(s):** Fox Mulder, FBI Agent; Dana Scully, FBI Agent, Doctor; Jeremy Dorman, Scientist (research)
**Time period(s):** 1990s (1997)
**Locale(s):** Portland, Oregon

**Summary:** Agents Mulder and Scully, who investigate cases considered too bizarre for regular FBI operatives, explore the destruction of the DyMar Laboratory and the death of David Kennessy, a cancer researcher with an interest in nanotechnology. Their investigations uncover a government conspiracy to suppress Kennessy's findings and a laboratory worker infected with a nanotech virus whose touch leads to gruesome, mutating death.

**Other books you might like:**
Lincoln Child, *Mount Dragon*, 1996
   Douglas Preston, co-author
Michael Crichton, *The Andromeda Strain*, 1969
Nigel Kneale, *The Quatermass Experiment*, 1959
Dean R. Koontz, *Midnight*, 1993
Patrick Lynch, *Carriers*, 1995

**100**

### KEVIN J. ANDERSON
### DOUG BEASON, Co-Author

## *Assemblers of Infinity*
(New York: Bantam Spectra, 1993)

**Story type:** Science Fiction (Invasion of Earth; Hard Science Fiction)
**Major character(s):** Celeste McConnell, Administrator (director of US Space Agency), Psychic (esper); Jason Dvorak, Administra-

tor (director of Columbus Base), Architect; Erika Trace, Scientist (nanotechnology)
**Time period(s):** 2020s
**Locale(s):** Columbus Base, Montenegro; Antarctica; Daedalus Crater, Montenegro

**Summary:** When a routine check of the array at Dedalus on the far side of the Moon discovers a large alien construction site which kills the investigating crew, Celeste McConnell sends nanotechnologist Erika Trace to research the phenomenon in isolation at the Sim-Mars station which waited unoccupied to train the upcoming Mars expedition. Fears over the nanocritters' possible threat to Earth forces McConnell to prevent any personnel returning from the Moon, but, unfortunately nanocritters may already contaminate the Earth.

**Other books you might like:**
Roger MacBride Allen, *The Ring of Charon*, 1990
Greg Bear, *Blood Music*, 1985
David Brin, *Earth*, 1990
Octavia E. Butler, *Dawn*, 1987
Michael Flynn, *The Nanotech Chronicles*, 1991
Diana G. Gallagher, *The Alien Dark*, 1990
Janet Kagan, *Mirabile*, 1991

**101**

### KEVIN J. ANDERSON

## *Blindfold*
(New York: Warner Aspect, 1995)

**Story type:** Science Fiction (Psychic Powers; Political)
**Major character(s):** Kalliana, Telepath (truthsayer); Troy Boren, Accountant, Outlaw; Tharion, Telepath (Truthsayer Guild master)
**Time period(s):** Indeterminate
**Locale(s):** Atlas, Planet—Imaginary; OrbLab2, Space Station

**Summary:** When the Truthsayer Kalliana falsely convicts Troy Boren of murder, Guild Master Tharion learns that someone has tampered with the telepathy-inducing drug Veritas, thereby undermining the entire judicial system on Atlas.

**Other books you might like:**
Karen Haber, *The War Minstrels*, 1995
Karen Haber, *Woman Without a Shadow*, 1995
Anne McCaffrey, *Damia*, 1992
Anne McCaffrey, *Pegasus in Flight*, 1990
Anne McCaffrey, *The Rowan*, 1990
Anne McCaffrey, *To Ride Pegasus*, 1973
Joanna Russ, *And Chaos Died*, 1970

**102**

### KEVIN J. ANDERSON

## *Climbing Olympus*
(New York: Warner Aspect, 1994)

**Story type:** Science Fiction (Space Colony; Hard Science Fiction)
**Major character(s):** Rachel Dycek, Doctor; Boris Tiban, Criminal, Genetically Altered Being; Cora Marisovna, Criminal, Genetically Altered Being
**Time period(s):** 21st century
**Locale(s):** Mars

**Summary:** As genetically altered colonists terraform Mars, the rebellious leader of the severely modified humans, Boris Tiban, tries to destroy everything to avenge the wrongs done to him. As he rages, Rachel Dycek and Cora Marisovna, mother of his Earth-normal child, take refuge at a sanctuary until they can begin rebuilding and lobbying for the terraforming project and the rights of the colonists.

**Other books you might like:**
Greg Bear, *Moving Mars*, 1993
Ben Bova, *Mars*, 1992
Kim Stanley Robinson, *Red Mars*, 1993
Allen Steele, *Labyrinth of Night*, 1992
S.C. Sykes, *Red Genesis*, 1991

## 103

### KEVIN J. ANDERSON

## Darksaber

(New York: Bantam Spectra, 1995)

**Story type:** Science Fiction (Mystical; Space Opera)
**Series:** Star Wars
**Major character(s):** Luke Skywalker, Martial Arts Expert (Jedi Knight), Hero; Leia Organa Solo, Royalty, Leader; Callista, Martial Arts Expert (Jedi Knight), Pilot (spaceship)
**Time period(s):** Indeterminate Past
**Locale(s):** New Republic, Interstellar Empire/Federation

**Summary:** In search of a means to restore Jedi abilities to his love, Callista, Luke Skywalker revisits Tatooine to contact Obi-Wan Kenobi's spirit. There he discovers a plan among the galaxy's criminal warlords to reconstruct a superweapon, the Death Star. Meanwhile, surviving Imperial forces plan to crush the New Republic.

**Other books you might like:**
Roger MacBride Allen, *Ambush at Corellia*, 1995
Brian Daley, *The Han Solo Adventures*, 1992
Barbara Hambly, *Children of the Jedi*, 1995
Vonda N. McIntyre, *The Crystal Star*, 1994
L. Neil Smith, *The Lando Calrissian Adventures*, 1994
Timothy Zahn, *Heir to the Empire*, 1991

## 104

### KEVIN J. ANDERSON

## Game's End

(New York: Roc, 1990)

**Story type:** Fantasy (Alternate World)
**Series:** Gamearth
**Major character(s):** Melanie, Student, Sports Figure (fantasy gameplayer); David, Student, Sports Figure (fantasy gameplayer)
**Time period(s):** 1990s (1990)
**Locale(s):** Earth; Gamearth, Planet—Imaginary

**Summary:** Gamearth has become real for Melanie and David. As the last Sorcerers on Gamearth work to free their world from the Players' control, David continues to try to destroy it. This time Gamearth has learned how to fight back.

**Other books you might like:**
M.A.R. Barker, *Man of Gold*, 1984
Steven Brust, *Jhereg*, 1983
Geary Gravel, *A Key for the Nonesuch*, 1990
Joel Rosenberg, *The Sleeping Dragon*, 1983
Will Shetterly, *The Tangled Lands*, 1989

## 105

### KEVIN J. ANDERSON

## Gameplay

(New York: Signet, 1989)

**Story type:** Fantasy (Alternate World)
**Series:** Gamearth
**Major character(s):** David, Student, Sports Figure (Fantasy gameplayer); Melanie, Student, Sports Figure (Fantasy gameplayer)
**Time period(s):** Indeterminate
**Locale(s):** Earth; Gamearth, Planet—Imaginary

**Summary:** Though David failed in his first attempt to destroy Gamearth, he has not given up. His creation of Scartis threatens the world of Gamearth if the players cannot find a way to defeat him. Unfortunately, the fantasy characters have taken on a life of their own and even "Rulewoman" Melanie's secret map changes may not save the game.

**Other books you might like:**
Barbara Hambly, *The Silent Tower*, 1988
Joel Rosenberg, *Guardians of the Flame: The Warriors*, 1983-1985
Will Shetterly, *The Tangled Lands*, 1989
Sheri S. Tepper, *Marianne, the Matchbox and the Malachite Mouse*, 1989

## 106

### KEVIN J. ANDERSON

## Ground Zero

(New York: HarperPrism, 1995)

**Story type:** Horror (Science Fiction)
**Series:** X-Files
**Major character(s):** Fox Mulder, FBI Agent; Dana Scully, FBI Agent, Doctor; Matthew Bradoukis, Military Personnel (general)
**Time period(s):** 1990s (1995)
**Locale(s):** Pleasonton, California; Washington, District of Columbia

**Summary:** Based on the popular television show "The X-Files," about a pair of special FBI agents assigned to crack cases too weird for regular field operatives. This novel take agents Mulder and Scully to a laboratory in California to investigate the disintegrated remains of Dr. Emil Gregory, a nuclear physicist whose project "Bright Anvil" has produced a nuclear weapon that can kill on a small scale without creating fallout. When other people around the country begin dying as Gregory did, Mulder and Scully must find out who, or what, has acquired Gregory's secret weapon.

**Other books you might like:**
Charles L. Grant, *Goblins*, 1994
Charles L. Grant, *Whirlwind*, 1995
Jeff Rice, *The Night Stalker*, 1973
Jeff Rice, *The Night Strangler*, 1974

## 107

### KEVIN J. ANDERSON
### DOUG BEASON, Co-Author

## Ignition

(New York: Forge, 1997)

**Story type:** Science Fiction (Techno-Thriller)

**Major character(s):** Adam "Iceberg" Friese, Astronaut; Nicole "Panther" Hunter, Administrator (launch director), Astronaut (retired); Boorman, Political Figure (senator)
**Time period(s):** 1990s
**Locale(s):** Kourou, French Guiana; Kennedy Space Center, Florida

**Summary:** Unable to captain the shuttle flight due to a broken foot, Iceberg decides to sneak back onto the grounds to watch the flight from the swamp. Unfortunately, a terrorist and his crew take over the media center, plant a bomb on the shuttle and, unbeknownst to the world watching a tape loop, hold the shuttle for ransom. Luckily, Iceberg discovers the terrorists, foiling their plan to set off the bomb, while Panther keeps the senator in check and prevents more deaths in the control room.

**Other books you might like:**
Ben Bova, *Death Dream*, 1994
Simon Hawke, *The Whims of Creation*, 1992
Vonda N. McIntyre, *Starfarers*, 1989
Allen Steele, *Orbital Decay*, 1989
Neal Stephenson, *The Diamond Age*, 1995
Walter Jon Williams, *Voice of the Whirlwind*, 1987

---

## 108

**KEVIN J. ANDERSON**
**DOUG BEASON**, Co-Author

### *Ill Wind*

(New York: Forge, 1995)

**Story type:** Science Fiction (Disaster)
**Major character(s):** Spencer Lockwood, Scientist (physicist), Administrator (solar-satellite project); Connor Brooks, Sailor, Criminal; Todd Severyn, Engineer (petroleum)
**Time period(s):** 1990s
**Locale(s):** California; New Mexico; Southwest

**Summary:** When a supertanker's oil spill in San Francisco Bay leads officials to employ unproven, oil-eating bacteria in the cleanup, petroleum-based modern technology suffers collapse. Scientists then race to deploy solar power satellites to avert worldwide chaos.

**Other books you might like:**
John Barnes, *Mother of Storms*, 1994
David Brin, *Earth*, 1990
Larry Niven, *Footfall*, 1985
    Jerry Pournelle, co-author
Larry Niven, *Lucifer's Hammer*, 1977
    Jerry Pournelle, co-author
Kit Pedler, *Mutant 59, The Plastic Eater*, 1972
    Gerry Davis, co-author
Neal Stephenson, *Snow Crash*, 1992

---

## 109

**KEVIN J. ANDERSON**

### *Jedi Search*

(New York: Bantam Spectra, 1994)

**Story type:** Science Fiction (Space Opera)
**Series:** Star Wars: Jedi Academy Trilogy
**Major character(s):** Luke Skywalker, Martial Arts Expert (Jedi Knight), Hero; Han Solo, Spaceship Captain, Warrior; Chewbacca, Alien (Wookie), Adventurer
**Time period(s):** Indeterminate Past
**Locale(s):** Coruscant, Planet—Imaginary; Kessel, Planet—Imaginary; New Republic, Interstellar Empire/Federation

**Summary:** While Luke Skywalker begins setting up a new training center for Jedi Knights on Coruscant, Han Solo and Chewbacca break out of prison on Kessel, fleeing to a secret Imperial research laboratory. When Luke seeks his friends, he discovers a new weapon, more powerful than even the old emperor's Death Star.

**Other books you might like:**
Brian Daley, *The Han Solo Adventures*, 1992
Vonda N. McIntyre, *The Crystal Star*, 1994
Kathy Tyers, *The Truce at Bakura*, 1994
Dave Wolverton, *The Courtship of Princess Leia*, 1994
Timothy Zahn, *Heir to the Empire*, 1991

---

## 110

**KEVIN J. ANDERSON**
**DOUG BEASON**, Co-Author

### *Lethal Exposure*

(New York: Ace, 1998)

**Story type:** Science Fiction (Mystery; Techno-Thriller)
**Series:** FBI Agent Kreident
**Major character(s):** Craig Kreident, FBI Agent; Georg Dumenco, Scientist (physicist); Paige Mitchell, Public Relations
**Time period(s):** 21st century
**Locale(s):** Illinois

**Summary:** When Ukrainian physicist and defector Georg Dumenco receives a lethal dose of radiation at Fermilab, Craig Kreident must investigate the incident to find out if this threatens national security. Unfortunately, the egos and politics involved in jockeying for a Nobel Prize interfere.

**Other books you might like:**
Jack L. Chalker, *The Cybernetic Walrus*, 1995
John Cramer, *Einstein's Bridge*, 1997
Peter F. Hamilton, *Mindstar Rising*, 1996
James P. Hogan, *Thrice upon a Time*, 1980
Thomas R. McDonough, *The Missing Matter*, 1992
Walter Jon Williams, *Voice of the Whirlwind*, 1987

---

## 111

**KEVIN J. ANDERSON**
**DOUG BEASON**, Co-Author

### *Lifeline*

(New York: Bantam Spectra, 1990)

**Story type:** Science Fiction (Post-Holocaust; Political)
**Major character(s):** Ramis Barrera, Settler (colonist); Anna Tripolk, Scientist (biologist); Duncan McLaris, Manufacturer, Administrator
**Time period(s):** 21st century
**Locale(s):** Kibalchick, Space Station; Orbitech, Space Station; Clavius Base, Montenegro

**Summary:** After Earth self-destructs, the L5 colonies and Moon Base must survive. Aguinaldo has adequate food, but only gets it to Orbitech after much of the population has been spaced. The leader of Kibalchick thinks it is her duty to destroy all the American colonies. Ramis Barrera takes food to Orbitech and manages to defuse the weapons on Kibalchick set to blow up Orbitech. He ends up joining the Russians in colonizing Mars.

**Other books you might like:**
Ben Bova, *Test of Fire*, 1982
Philip Jose Farmer, *Tongues of the Moon*, 1964
Andrew Stephenson, *Nightwatch*, 1979

## 112

**KEVIN J. ANDERSON**

### Ruins

(New York: HarperPrism, 1996)

**Story type:** Horror (Science Fiction)
**Series:** X-Files
**Major character(s):** Dana Scully, FBI Agent, Doctor; Fox Mulder, FBI Agent; Cassandra Rubicon, Archaeologist
**Time period(s):** 1990s (1996)
**Locale(s):** Xitaclan, Mexico

**Summary:** In this fourth novel based on the popular television series, agents Mulder and Scully, specialists in investigating paranormal phenomena are sent to a dig site at the Pyramid of Kukulkan on the Yucatan peninsula to find a missing university archaeology expedition. Their discoveries bring them into conflict with Central American drug lords, tomb looters, the United States military, and possibly supernatural and extraterrestrial powers that seem to be attracted to the pyramid.

**Other books you might like:**
Randall Boyll, *Darkman #4: The Face of Death*, 1994
Charles L. Grant, *Goblins*, 1984
Charles L. Grant, *Whirlwind*, 1995
Jeff Rice, *The Night Stalker*, 1973

## 113

**KEVIN J. ANDERSON**
**LARRY DICKISON**, Illustrator

### Shifting the Boundaries: The Selected Works of Kevin J. Anderson

(Concord, California: Dark Regions Press, 1995)

**Story type:** Horror (Collection)

**Summary:** Eight stories blend elements of fantasy, horror and science fiction in the author's first collection. ''A Glimpse of the Ankou'' and ''Dark Angel, Archangel'' offer two different visions of death incarnate. In ''Drilling Deep,'' drilling into the stratas beneath a farm transforms the landscape into a forest primeval. ''Final Performance'' suggests ghostly revenge as the reason for the burning of Shakespeare's Globe Theatre, while ''Scarecrow'' tells of the rather strange gods to whom a psychotic farm woman pays her obeisance. Doug Beason supplies the introduction.

**Other books you might like:**
Kim Antieau, *Trudging to Eden*, 1994
Michael A. Arnzen, *Needles and Sins*, 1993
Elizabeth Massie, *Southern Discomfort: Selected Works of Elizabeth Massie*, 1993
Ardath Mayhar, *Mean Little Old Lady at Work*, 1993
Stephen Mark Rainey, *Fugue Devil and Other Weird Horrors*, 1992

## 114

**KEVIN J. ANDERSON**, Editor

### Tales From Jabba's Palace

(New York: Bantam Spectra, 1996)

**Story type:** Science Fiction (Anthology; Space Opera)
**Series:** Star Wars
**Major character(s):** Jabba the Hutt, Organized Crime Figure, Alien
**Time period(s):** Indeterminate Past
**Locale(s):** Tatooine, Planet—Imaginary; Galactic Empire, Interstellar Empire/Federation

**Summary:** Contains a two-page introduction, seven pages of authors' biographies, a five-page epilog, and 19 original stories featuring the shady characters from Jabba's Palace in *The Return of the Jedi*. Authors include Kevin J. Anderson, M. Shayne Bell, John Gregory Betancourt, A.C. Crispin, George Alec Effinger, Kenneth C. Flint, Esther M. Friesner, Barbara Hamby, Judith and Garfield Reeves-Stevens, Jennifer Roberson, Kathy Tyers, Deborah Wheeler, Dave Wolverton, William Wu, and Timothy Zahn.

**Other books you might like:**
Roger MacBride Allen, *Ambush at Corellia*, 1995
Barbara Hambly, *Children of the Jedi*, 1995
James Kahn, *Return of the Jedi*, 1983
Michael P. Kube-McDowell, *Before the Storm*, 1996
George Lucas, *The Star Wars Trilogy*, 1987
    Donald F. Glut, James Kahn, co-authors
Timothy Zahn, *Heir to the Empire*, 1991

## 115

**KEVIN J. ANDERSON**, Editor

### Tales From the Mos Eisley Cantina

(New York: Bantam Spectra, 1995)

**Story type:** Science Fiction (Anthology; Adventure)
**Series:** Star Wars
**Time period(s):** Indeterminate Past
**Locale(s):** Interstellar Empire/Federation; Tatooine, Planet—Imaginary (Mos Eisley spaceport)

**Summary:** Contains seven pages of authors' biographies and 16 original stories utilizing a multitude of characters and familiar settings from George Lucas' *Star Wars* (1976) milieu. The 18 authors include Kevin J. Anderson, Doug Beason, M. Shayne Bell, David Bischoff, A.C. Crispin, Kenneth C. Flint, Barbara Hambly, Daniel Keys Moran, Jennifer Roberson, Kathy Tyers, Dave Wolverton, and Timothy Zahn.

**Other books you might like:**
Roger MacBride Allen, *Ambush at Corellia*, 1995
Arthur C. Clarke, *Tales From the White Hart*, 1957
Brian Daley, *The Han Solo Adventures*, 1992
Spider Robinson, *Callahan and Company*, 1987
L. Neil Smith, *The Lando Calrissian Adventures*, 1994

## 116

**KEVIN J. ANDERSON**
**DOUG BEASON**, Co-Author

### The Trinity Paradox

(New York: Bantam Spectra, 1991)

**Story type:** Science Fiction (Alternate Universe; Time Travel)
**Major character(s):** Elizabeth Devane, Activist, Time Traveler
**Time period(s):** 1990s; 1940s
**Locale(s):** Los Alamos, New Mexico

**Summary:** While sabotaging an exotic weapon at Los Alamos National Laboratory, anti-nuclear activist Elizabeth Devane helps trigger a disastrous explosion that throws her nearly fifty years into the past. Her 1970s college degree in physics and subsequent work in nuclear physics afford Elizabeth enough background to join the Manhattan Project in hopes of stopping the development of nuclear weapons.

**Other books you might like:**
Keith William Andrews, *Search and Destroy*, 1990
Michael Flynn, *In the Country of the Blind*, 1990
Robert A. Heinlein, *Farnham's Freehold*, 1964
Dan Simmons, *The Fall of Hyperion*, 1990
Dan Simmons, *Hyperion*, 1989
Wilson Tucker, *The Time Masters*, 1971
　　revised
John Varley, *Millennium*, 1983
Walter Jon Williams, *Days of Atonement*, 1991

**117**

**KEVIN J. ANDERSON**
**REBECCA MOESTA**, Co-Author

**Trouble on Cloud City**

(New York: Jam, 1998)

**Story type:** Science Fiction (Young Adult)
**Series:** Young Jedi Knights
**Major character(s):** Anja Gallandro, Revolutionary; Jacen Solo, Teenager, Military Personnel (Jedi Knight); Jaina Solo, Teenager, Military Personnel (Jedi Knight)
**Time period(s):** Indeterminate Future
**Locale(s):** Cloud City, Fictional City

**Summary:** The twin children of Han and Leia Solo have been proclaimed Jedi Knights. They accept a vacation invitation to Cloud City accompanied by their new, mysterious friend, Anja Gallandro, unaware that she feels a deep rooted resentment against the new government and plans an act of deadly sabotage.

**Other books you might like:**
A.C. Crispin, *The Paradise Snare*, 1997
Barbara Hambly, *Children of the Jedi*, 1995
K.W. Jeter, *The Mandalorian Armor*, 1998
Michael P. Kube-McDowell, *Before the Storm*, 1996
Timothy Zahn, *Specter of the Past*, 1997

**118**

**KEVIN J. ANDERSON**
**DOUG BEASON**, Co-Author

**Virtual Destruction**

(New York: Ace, 1996)

**Story type:** Science Fiction (Techno-Thriller; Mystery)
**Major character(s):** Hal Michaelson, Computer Expert, Leader; Gary Lesserac, Computer Expert; Craig Kreident, FBI Agent
**Time period(s):** 1990s
**Locale(s):** Livermore, California; Washington, District of Columbia

**Summary:** Hal develops a new virtual reality system while secretly developing a second use for it. Specializing in high tech crime, Craig investigates Hal's death in the V.R. lab.

**Other books you might like:**
Bruce Bethke, *Headcrash*, 1995
Terry Bisson, *Johnny Mnemonic*, 1995
Alan Dean Foster, *Cyber Way*, 1990
Marc Laidlaw, *Neon Lotus*, 1988
Fred Saberhagen, *Octagon*, 1981
Neal Stephenson, *Snow Crash*, 1992
John E. Stith, *Redshift Rendezvous*, 1990

**119**

**KEVIN J. ANDERSON**, Editor

**War of the Worlds: Global Dispatches**

(New York: Bantam Spectra, 1996)

**Story type:** Science Fiction (Anthology; Invasion of Earth)

**Summary:** Contains 19 original stories and essays and one, Howard Waldrop's "Night of the Cooters," reprinted from a 1987 *Omni*. Stories present H.G. Wells' *The War of the Worlds'* Martian invasion as if seen through the eyes of different journalists and notables worldwide, such as Edgar Rice Burroughs, Emily Dickinson, Henry James, Rudyard Kipling, Jack London, Percival Lowell, Pablo Picasso, Joseph Pulitzer, Teddy Roosevelt, Leo Tolstoy, Mark Twain, and Jules Verne. Other authors include Kevin J. Anderson, Doug Beason, M. Shayne Bell, Gregory Benford, Janet Berliner, David Brin, George Alec Effinger, Barbara Hambly, Mike Resnick, Robert Silverberg, Allen Steele, Walter Jon Williams, Connie Willis, and Dave Wolverton.

**Other books you might like:**
Steven R. Boyett, *Treks Not Taken: What if Stephen King, Anne Rice, Bret Easton Ellis, and Other Literary Greats Had Written Episodes of Star Trek: The Next Generation?*, 1996
Randall Garrett, *Takeoff!*, 1979
Randall Garrett, *Takeoff, Too*, 1986
Manly Wade Wellman, *Sherlock Holmes's War of the Worlds*, 1975
　　Wade Wellman, co-author
H.G. Wells, *The War of the Worlds*, 1898

**120**

**M.T. ANDERSON**

**Thirsty**

(New York: Candlewick, 1997)

**Story type:** Horror (Vampire Story; Young Adult)
**Major character(s):** Chris, Teenager, Vampire; Chet, Supernatural Being; Tch'muchgar, Vampire
**Locale(s):** New England (alternate)

**Summary:** In an alternate world populated with creatures of the supernatural, Chris struggles with the growing pains that come with acceptance of his maturing vampire identity. For his first adult responsibility, Chet, a member of the Forces of Light, asks him to interfere with a ceremony that will help release a vampire lord from captivity in another world. A young adult novel.

**Other books you might like:**
Richie Tankersley Cusick, *Vampire*, 1991
Joseph Locke, *Vampire Heart*, 1994
Christopher Pike, *The Last Vampire*, 1994
L.J. Smith, *Secret Vampire*, 1996
L.J. Smith, *Dark Reunion*, 1992
　　Vampire Diaries, volume 4
S.P. Somtow, *The Vampire's Beautiful Daughter*, 1997

**121**

**MARGARET J. ANDERSON**

**The Druid's Gift**

(New York: Knopf, 1989)

**Story type:** Fantasy (Time Travel)
**Major character(s):** Caitlin, Young Woman (Rebellious)
**Time period(s):** 10th century B.C.; 18th century

**Locale(s):** St. Kilda Islands, Scotland (Islands off the coast)

**Summary:** New Druid settlements on the nearby mainland upset the harmony and order of several simple Scottish villages. The villagers fear and distrust the strange Druids and their mysterious ways of magic and music and grow increasingly hostile towards them. Despite the animosity, Caitlin persists in her quest to learn the secret ways of the Druids. With the aid of Druid magic and her own visionary powers, Caitlin travels in spirit form to the future in order to reconcile the fate of her native villagers with that of the Druids.

**Other books you might like:**
Diana Wynne Jones, *A Tale of Time City*, 1987
Welwyn Wilton Katz, *The Third Magic*, 1988
Richard Peck, *Voices After Midnight*, 1989
William Sleator, *Strange Attractors*, 1990

---

`122`

**MARGARET J. ANDERSON**

## The Ghost Inside the Monitor

(New York: Knopf/Bullseye, 1990)

**Story type:** Fantasy (Time Travel; Young Adult)
**Major character(s):** Sarah Pearce, Child, Computer Expert; Pascale, Spirit (Ghost)
**Time period(s):** 20th century
**Locale(s):** Dixon Landing

**Summary:** After she turns off her computer screen, 11-year-old Sarah sees the ghost of a child who died in the early years of the century. Then she's pulled through the computer into the ghost's own era.

**Other books you might like:**
Pam Conrad, *Stonewords: A Ghost Story*, 1990
Gilbert B. Cross, *A Witch Across Time*, 1990
Penelope Lively, *The Ghost of Thomas Kempe*, 1973
Patricia A. McKillip, *The House on Parchment Street*, 1973
Kit Pearson, *Handful of Time*, 1988
Elizabeth Marie Pope, *The Sherwood Ring*, 1958

---

`123`

**POUL ANDERSON**

## All One Universe

(New York: Tor, 1996)

**Story type:** Science Fiction (Collection)

**Summary:** Contains a two-page introduction plus individual introductions to four essays and 14 stories reprinted from periodicals and anthologies 1978-1993, with most from the last decade. Varying in tone from somber to light, with settings on and off Earth, the stories explore diverse themes such as hard science and scientific advancement, ecology, alternate histories, prehistoric society, and branching realities.

**Other books you might like:**
Brian W. Aldiss, *Man in His Time: The Best Science Fiction Stories of Brian W. Aldiss*, 1989
Larry Niven, *N-Space*, 1990
Charles Sheffield, *Dancing with Myself*, 1993
Marc Stiegler, *The Gentle Seduction*, 1990
Connie Willis, *Impossible Things*, 1994

---

`124`

**POUL ANDERSON**

## The Armies of Elfland

(New York: Tor, 1992)

**Story type:** Fantasy (Collection)

**Summary:** Contains a three-page foreward in which Anderson indicates that all stories herein share a romantic vein in the Middle Ages sense of "a tale full of color and imagination." The stories, reprinted from periodicals and books, include one collaboration with Karen Anderson, "A Feast for the Gods"; one Hugo Award and Nebula Award winner, "The Queen of Air and Darkness"; and six other stories.

**Other books you might like:**
David Brin, *The River of Time*, 1986
Orson Scott Card, *Maps in a Mirror*, 1990
John Varley, *Blue Champagne*, 1986
Kurt Vonnegut Jr., *Welcome to the Monkey House*, 1968

---

`125`

**POUL ANDERSON**

## The Boat of a Million Years

(New York: Tor, 1989)

**Story type:** Science Fiction (Immortality)
**Major character(s):** Hanno, Immortal, Sailor; Rufus, Immortal
**Locale(s):** Europe; Outer Space

**Summary:** Hanno, an ancient Phoenician, discovers himself to be immortal and spends more than 2,000 years seaching for others of his kind. Eventually he and the other immortals he discovers leave Earth for the eternal adventure of space exploration.

**Other books you might like:**
Joe Haldeman, *Buying Time*, 1989
Robert A. Heinlein, *Time Enough for Love*, 1973
Clifford D. Simak, *Way Station*, 1963
Norman Spinrad, *Bug Jack Barron*, 1969
Roger Zelazny, *This Immortal*, 1966

---

`126`

**POUL ANDERSON**

## The Fleet of Stars

(New York: Tor, 1997)

**Story type:** Science Fiction (Political; Alternate Intelligence)
**Series:** Harvest of Stars
**Major character(s):** Fenn, Police Officer, Revolutionary; Kinna Ronay, Revolutionary; Anson Guthrie, Cyborg
**Time period(s):** Indeterminate Future
**Locale(s):** Montenegro; Mars

**Summary:** Raising on the moon, Fenn rages that humans live as little more than the "domesticated pets" of the cybercosm intelligence that oversees life in the solar system. He and Kinna Ronay, a spirited Mars settler, vow to discover why the cybercosm seems intent on preventing humanity from going to the stars. Fourth in series.

**Other books you might like:**
Greg Bear, *Queen of Angels*, 1990
David Brin, *Startide Rising*, 1983
Robert A. Heinlein, *The Moon Is a Harsh Mistress*, 1966
Frank Herbert, *Destination: Void*, 1966

D.F. Jones, *Colossus*, 1966
John Varley, *Steel Beach*, 1992
Jack Williamson, *The Humanoids*, 1996
expanded edition

**127**

POUL ANDERSON

## Harvest of Stars

(New York: Tor, 1993)

**Story type:** Science Fiction (Political; Theological)
**Major character(s):** Anson Guthrie, Businessman, Disembodied Personality; Kyra Davis, Pilot (spaceship), Spaceman (space colonist); Eiko Tamura, Technician, Spacewoman (space colonist)
**Time period(s):** Indeterminate Future
**Locale(s):** Earth; Montenegro; Demeter, Planet—Imaginary

**Summary:** Trying to expand the Avantists' power beyond North America, Enrique Sayre uses a spare Download of Anson Guthrie, a brilliant entrepreneur and politician, to do the planning. However, Kyra and the Underground have the original Download and get it to the Moon where, with the aid of Rinndalir, Selenarch of Luna, they resist the power of the Avantists. Selected humans who desire freedom colonize Demeter with the aid of a planet-wide intelligence.

**Other books you might like:**
Greg Bear, *Eon*, 1985
Greg Bear, *Queen of Angels*, 1990
Gordon R. Dickson, *Necromancer*, 1962
Joe Haldeman, *Worlds: A Novel of the Near Future*, 1981
Robert A. Heinlein, *Methuselah's Children*, 1958
Donald Kingsbury, *The Moon Goddess and the Son*, 1986
Michael P. Kube-McDowell, *The Quiet Pools*, 1990
Pamela Sargent, *Venus of Dreams*, 1986
Allen Steele, *Clarke County, Space*, 1990

**128**

POUL ANDERSON

## Harvest the Fire

(New York: Tor, 1995)

**Story type:** Science Fiction (Political; Alternate Intelligence)
**Series:** Harvest of Stars
**Major character(s):** Jesse Nicol, Spaceship Captain, Writer (poet); Lucas "Venator" Mthembu, Artificial Intelligence, Robot; Lirion, Genetically Altered Being (Selenarch), Revolutionary (Scaine Croi)
**Time period(s):** 28th century
**Locale(s):** Argentina; Hydra Square, Montenegro; *Verdea*, Spaceship

**Summary:** A poet searching for understanding, Nicol leaves Earth to work for the lunar based transportation which still employs human pilots. Sympathetic to the genetically manipulated Selenarchs, the Scaine Croi recruits him to pilot a ship to Proserpina. Resurrected from the Terramind as a Peace Force robot, Venator finds himself outmaneuvered by Lirion and unable to foil the Scaine Croi plot.

**Other books you might like:**
Jack C. Haldeman II, *High Steel*, 1993
Jack Dann, co-author
Fred Saberhagen, *Berserker*, 1967
George Turner, *Genetic Soldier*, 1994
John Varley, *Steel Beach*, 1992
Jack Williamson, *The Humanoids*, 1949

**129**

POUL ANDERSON

## Inconstant Star

(New York: Baen, 1991)

**Story type:** Science Fiction (Adventure; Military)
**Series:** Man-Kzin Wars
**Major character(s):** Eric Saxtorph, Spaceship Captain (owner-tramp spaceship); Ulf Reichstein Markham, Administrator (commissioner of Space Station); Tyra Nordbo, Writer, Noblewoman (Wunderland)
**Time period(s):** 23rd century
**Locale(s):** Wunderland, Planet—Imaginary; Outer Space

**Summary:** Eric Saxtorph wants to investigate a mysterious star that originated outside the galaxy. Commissioner Markham blocks this until he can come along as he is a Kzin agent. After Saxtorph's return, Tyra Nordbo charters the ship to clear her father of the charge of being in Kzin pay. She discovers a black hole and makes a further discovery that it is her brother who is the Kzin agent. This volume collects two short pieces, *Iron*, published originally in *The Man-Kzin Wars* (1988), and *Inconstant Star*, published originally in *The Man-Kzin Wars III* (1990).

**Other books you might like:**
Dean Ing, *Cathouse*, 1991
Larry Niven, *Tales of Known Space*, 1975
H. Beam Piper, *Space Viking*, 1963
Jerry Pournelle, *Prince of Mercenaries*, 1989
L. Neil Smith, *Contact and Commune*, 1990
Sheri S. Tepper, *Grass*, 1989

**130**

POUL ANDERSON
STEVEN POPKES, Co-Author

## The Longest Voyage/Slow Lightning

(New York: Tor, 1991)

**Story type:** Science Fiction (First Contact)
**Major character(s):** Val Nira, Space Explorer (marooned); Gray, Alien (Spatien); Gnoza, Alien
**Time period(s):** Indeterminate Future; 21st century (2019-2035)
**Locale(s):** Hisagazi Yarzik Island, Moon—Imaginary; *Proud Mary*, Spaceship

**Summary:** Poul Anderson's "The Longest Voyage" received the Hugo Award after its publication in *Analog* (Dec. 1960). In the story, Rovic moves precipitously to protect what he perceives as his society's right to develop at its own pace when he is confronted with changes he foresees through Val Nira's contact. Previously unpublished, Steven Popkes' "Slow Lightning" suggests a future in which humans help extraterrestrials determine if humanity is to be considered intelligent or just food for the truly intelligent residents of the galaxy.

**Other books you might like:**
Isaac Asimov, *The Ugly Little Boy/The Widget, the Wadget, and Boff*, 1989
Theodore Sturgeon, co-author
David Brin, *Startide Rising*, 1983
Gordon R. Dickson, *Naked to the Stars/The Alien Way*, 1990
John M. Ford, *Fugue State/The Death of Dr. Island*, 1990
Gene Wolfe, co-author
Vonda N. McIntyre, *Screwtop/The Girl Who Was Plugged In*, 1989
James Tiptree, Jr., co-author
Steven Popkes, *Caliban Landing*, 1987

John Varley, *Press Enter/Hawksbill Station*, 1990
　　Robert Silverberg, co-author
John Varley, *Tango Charlie and Foxtrot Charlie/The Star Pit*, 1989
　　Samuel R. Delany, co-author

**131**

**POUL ANDERSON**

### The Shield of Time

(New York: Tor, 1990)

**Story type:** Science Fiction (Time Travel)
**Series:** Time Patrol
**Major character(s):** Manse Everard, Agent (Time Patrol); Wanda Tamberly, Agent (Time Patrol)
**Time period(s):** Indeterminate Past; 1990s (1990)
**Locale(s):** Earth

**Summary:** The delicate underpinnings of reality seem to be unravelling as Manse and Wanda strive to keep matters in balance. However, each time change can lead to unforeseen consequences, and when your change fails to restore the course of events, life gets interesting.

**Other books you might like:**
Gordon R. Dickson, *The Dragon Knight*, 1990
Gordon R. Dickson, *Time Storm*, 1977
Gordon R. Dickson, *The Dragon and the George*, 1976
Barbara Hambly, *Those Who Hunt the Night*, 1988
Larry Niven, *The Flight of the Horse*, 1973

**132**

**POUL ANDERSON**

### Space Folk

(New York: Baen Books, 1989)

**Story type:** Science Fiction (Collection)

**Summary:** This volume reprints eleven short stories, an essay, and a poem. The fiction originally appeared between 1953 and 1985 in such magazines as *Amazing, Analog, Galaxy, Fantastic Universe,* and *Boys' Life,* and such original anthologies as *Far Frontiers* and *Infinity.* Among the best known stories are ''Pride'' (1985), ''Hunter's Moon'' (1978), and ''Deathwomb'' (1983).

**Other books you might like:**
David Brin, *The River of Time*, 1986
David Brin, *Startide Rising*, 1983
David Brin, *The Uplift War*, 1987
Gordon R. Dickson, *The Forever Man*, 1986
Gordon R. Dickson, *Lost Dorsai*, 1980
Gordon R. Dickson, *Way of the Pilgrim*, 1987
Larry Niven, *The Integral Trees*, 1984
Larry Niven, *The Mote in God's Eye*, 1974
　　Jerry Pournelle, co-author
Larry Niven, *Protector*, 1973
Larry Niven, *Ringworld*, 1970

**133**

**POUL ANDERSON**

### Starfarers

(New York: Tor, 1998)

**Story type:** Science Fiction (First Contact)

**Major character(s):** Ricardo Aguilar, Spaceship Captain; Mamphela Mokoena, Scientist
**Time period(s):** Indeterminate Future
**Locale(s):** *Envoy,* Spaceship; Outer Space

**Summary:** Scientists on Earth detect phenomena that convince them that intelligent species are traveling between the stars in a distant part of the galaxy. An exploratory ship is outfitted with a small crew to make first contact, but when they arrive they discover that the great civilization that once existed has abandoned space travel because they feared they were altering the nature of the universe.

**Other books you might like:**
Terry A. Adams, *Sentience: A Novel of First Contact*, 1986
C.J. Cherryh, *Voyager in Night*, 1984
Hal Clement, *Still River*, 1987
Edmond Hamilton, *The Haunted Stars*, 1960
Charles Pellegrino, *Flying to Valhalla*, 1993

**134**

**POUL ANDERSON**

### The Stars Are Also Fire

(New York: Tor, 1994)

**Story type:** Science Fiction (Alternate Intelligence; Genetic Manipulation)
**Major character(s):** Ian Kenmuir, Spaceship Captain, Revolutionary; Dagny Beynac, Political Figure (mayor of the Moon), Parent; Lilisaire, Political Figure, Genetically Altered Being
**Time period(s):** 21st century; 28th century
**Locale(s):** Port Bowen, Montenegro; Zamok Vysoki, Montenegro

**Summary:** While humans colonize the Moon and Alpha Centauri, computers and Earth develop intelligence, creating Teramind, a conjoining of all free cyber minds. The Teramind controls the Solar System and has its own goals, which do not include human space exploration and development. Fortunately, Demeter Mother, the AI at Alpha Centauri based on human personality downloads rather than pure mechanical constructs, distracts the Teramind from human beings and their genetically manipulated cohorts and friends.

**Other books you might like:**
Helen Collins, *Mutagenesis*, 1993
Robert A. Heinlein, *The Moon Is a Harsh Mistress*, 1966
Kim Stanley Robinson, *Green Mars*, 1994
Joan Slonczewski, *A Door into Ocean*, 1986
Norman Spinrad, *Deus X*, 1993
Allen Steele, *Clarke County, Space*, 1990
John Varley, *Steel Beach*, 1992
Jack Williamson, *The Humanoids*, 1949

**135**

**POUL ANDERSON**

### The Time Patrol

(New York: Tor, 1991)

**Story type:** Science Fiction (Time Travel; Collection)
**Series:** Time Patrol
**Major character(s):** Manse Everard, Agent (Time Patrol)
**Locale(s):** Earth

**Summary:** This omnibus volume collects the adventures of Time Patrol Unattached Agent Manse Everard as he journeys here and there in time to keep the course of history intact. Included are *The Guardians of Time* (1981), ''Time Patrolmen'' (1983), and *The Year* *of the Ransom* (1988). It also includes the little-known prequel to last year's *Shield of Time* and a new novella, "Star of the Sea."

**Other books you might like:**
David Gerrold, *The Man Who Folded Himself*, 1991
Barbara Hambly, *Those Who Hunt the Night*, 1988
Robert A. Heinlein, *Glory Road*, 1963
Robert A. Heinlein, *The Number of the Beast*, 1979
Larry Niven, *The Flight of the Horse*, 1973
Robert Silverberg, *The Gate of Worlds*, 1967
Robert Charles Wilson, *A Bridge of Years*, 1991

---

**136**

POUL ANDERSON

## War of the Gods

(New York: Tor, 1997)

**Story type:** Fantasy (Legend)
**Major character(s):** Hadding, Ruler, Warrior; Hardgreip, Mythical Creature (jotun), Witch; Odin, Deity
**Time period(s):** Indeterminate Past
**Locale(s):** Denmark; Sweden

**Summary:** Left in the care of Giants, Hadding, son of the defeated King Gram, grows strong and daring. Once he reaches manhood and word comes to him of his brother's death, Hadding goes out for revenge. Through raiding, warfare, magic and trickery, force of arms, and generosity, Hadding recreates his father's kingdom under the eye of Odin.

**Other books you might like:**
Charles Barnitz, *The Deepest Sea*, 1996
Frans G. Bengtsson, *The Long Ships*, 1954
Diana L. Paxson, *The Wolf and the Raven*, 1993
Snorri Sturluson, *Egil's Saga*, 1976
    Hermann Palsson and Paul Edwards, translators
Sigrid Undset, *The Bridal Wreath*, 1923

---

**137**

C. DEAN ANDERSSON

## Buried Screams

(New York: Zebra, 1992)

**Story type:** Horror (Ancient Evil Unleashed)
**Major character(s):** Karl Thomas Clayburn, Writer; Beth Ann Simpson, Undertaker; Erik Robert Lindholm, Worker (gravedigger)
**Time period(s):** 1990s
**Locale(s):** Stoneridge, Kentucky

**Summary:** A mysterious force that came to earth in a meteorite in prehistoric times and became entombed beneath the ground that now serves as the Stoneridge graveyard gradually takes over the townsfolk one by one. The burden of rescuing Stoneridge falls to three citizens, each of whom lived through an abusive childhood and thus is better equipped to face the onslaught of horrors unleashed upon them.

**Other books you might like:**
Douglas Clegg, *Goat Dance*, 1989
Jack Finney, *The Body Snatchers*, 1955
Stephen King, *The Tommyknockers*, 1987
T.E.D. Klein, *The Ceremonies*, 1984

---

**138**

C. DEAN ANDERSSON

## Fiend

(New York: Zebra, 1994)

**Story type:** Horror (Supernatural Vengeance; Witchcraft)
**Major character(s):** Joe Clark, Student—College; T.T. Dyson, Serial Killer; Medea, Witch
**Time period(s):** 1990s (1994)
**Locale(s):** Dallas, Texas

**Summary:** At a Dallas comic book convention comic book writer neophyte Joe Clark encounters a woman who teaches him how to access his muse through sex magic. Alas, Joe's muse is the inspiration for his comic book character Toxique, a superhero avenger whose spirit reanimates the body of a dead serial killer and begins wreaking havoc at the convention.

**Other books you might like:**
Sean Costello, *The Cartoonist*, 1991
Ron Dee, *Succumb*, 1994
Richard Christian Matheson, *Created By*, 1993

---

**139**

C. DEAN ANDERSSON

## I Am Dracula

(New York: Zebra, 1993)

**Story type:** Horror (Vampire Story)
**Major character(s):** Vlad Tepes, Vampire; Tzigane, Witch
**Time period(s):** 15th century
**Locale(s):** Transylvania

**Summary:** This historically accurate novel tells an altered account of Count Dracula's vampiric origins, portraying him as a disenchanted Wallachian noble whose disdain for humanity leads him into a liaison with a witch woman, and an introduction to Satanism that he eventually regrets.

**Other books you might like:**
Mara McCuniff, *The Vampire Memoirs*, 1990
Michael Romkey, *I, Vampire*, 1990
Fred Saberhagen, *Bram Stoker's Dracula*, 1992
    James V. Hart, co-author
Bram Stoker, *Dracula*, 1895

---

**140**

C. DEAN ANDERSSON

## I Am Frankenstein

(New York: Zebra, 1996)

**Story type:** Horror (Reanimated Dead)
**Major character(s):** Gunthar Thunnar Frankenstein, Scientist; Katiasi, Young Woman; Anton Gorobec, Reanimated Dead
**Time period(s):** 1800s

**Summary:** A woman from the future visits Victor Frankenstein shortly after he has reanimated a dead human being to inform him that he and she are both pawns in the hands of Secret Masters, possibly extraterrestrial beings who are manipulating their fates to serve their own inscrutable ends.

**Other books you might like:**
Brian W. Aldiss, *Frankenstein Unbound*, 1973

Stephen Jones, *The Mammoth Book of Frankenstein*, 1994
    editor
Michel Parry, *Rivals of Frankenstein*, 1977
    editor
Fred Saberhagen, *The Frankenstein Papers*, 1986
Mary Shelley, *Frankenstein*, 1818

---

**141**

### KEITH WILLIAM ANDREWS

## *Search and Destroy*
(New York: Berkley, 1990)

**Story type:** Science Fiction (Time Travel; Military)
**Series:** Freedom's Rangers
**Major character(s):** Travis Hunter, Military Personnel (lieutenant);
    Rachel Stein, Scientist (mathematician), Agent (Chronos Project)
**Time period(s):** 1770s (1777)
**Locale(s):** North America (Dominion of British North America)

**Summary:** The Army's Chronos Project aims at countering the effects
of the KGB's time travel project which threatens to wipe out the 20th
century American enemy by altering historical events so that America never produces a United States. After saving George Washington
from an assassination attempt, Lt. Hunter must try to prevent the
colonial army's defeat by the enemy armed with weapons from the
future while Rachel is held by Soviet time travel agents.

**Other books you might like:**
Roger L. DiSilvestro, *Living with the Reptiles*, 1990
Warren Norwood, *Stranded!*, 1989
    Mel Odom, co-author
Warren Norwood, *Trapped!*, 1989
Warren Norwood, *Vanished*, 1988
H. Beam Piper, *Lord Kalvan of Otherwhen*, 1965
L. Neil Smith, *The Gallatin Divergence*, 1985
John Varley, *Millennium*, 1983

---

**142**

### KEITH WILLIAM ANDREWS

## *Sink the Armada*
(New York: Berkley, 1990)

**Story type:** Science Fiction (Time Travel; Military)
**Series:** Freedom's Rangers
**Major character(s):** Travis Hunter, Military Personnel (lieutenant);
    Greg King, Military Personnel (sergeant)
**Time period(s):** 16th century (1588)
**Locale(s):** Caribbean; At Sea

**Summary:** KGB time commandos have planned to prevent the birth
of the United States of America by arming the Spanish Armada
sufficiently well to defeat England before England colonizes America. Free America's Chronos Project must stop the interference if the
United States is to come about.

**Other books you might like:**
Roger L. DiSilvestro, *Living with the Reptiles*, 1990
Phyllis Eisenstein, *Shadow of Earth*, 1979
Randall Frakes, *The Terminator*, 1985
    Bill Wisher, co-author
H. Beam Piper, *Lord Kalvan of Otherwhen*, 1965
L. Neil Smith, *The Gallatin Divergence*, 1985
L. Neil Smith, *The Nagasaki Vector*, 1983
John Varley, *Millennium*, 1983

---

**143**

### KEITH WILLIAM ANDREWS

## *Treason in Time*
(New York: Berkley, 1990)

**Story type:** Science Fiction (Time Travel; Military)
**Series:** Freedom's Rangers
**Major character(s):** Travis Hunter, Military Personnel (lieutenant);
    Greg King, Military Personnel (sergeant)
**Time period(s):** 1910s (1918)
**Locale(s):** Europe

**Summary:** Hoping to halt the development of the USSR before it
comes into being, the Joint Chiefs have formulated Operation Backlash in which time travellers will support White Russian Admiral
Aleksandr V. Kolchak to defeat the Reds, stopping the Russian
Revolution before the Soviets can consolidate power.

**Other books you might like:**
Roger L. DiSilvestro, *Living with the Reptiles*, 1990
Randall Frakes, *The Terminator*, 1985
    Bill Wisher, co-author
Warren Norwood, *Vanished*, 1988
H. Beam Piper, *Lord Kalvan of Otherwhen*, 1965
L. Neil Smith, *The Nagasaki Vector*, 1983
John Varley, *Millennium*, 1983

---

**144**

### V.C. ANDREWS (Pseudonym of Andrew Neiderman)

## *Dawn*
(New York: Pocket, 1990)

**Story type:** Horror (Coming-of-Age)
**Major character(s):** Dawn Longchamp, Teenager; Jimmy
    Longchamp, Child (Dawn's younger brother); Philip Cutler,
    Teenager
**Time period(s):** 1990s (1990)
**Locale(s):** Washington, District of Columbia

**Summary:** Dawn Longchamp's idyllic life is shattered when the death
of her mother brings to light secrets about the family's past and
Dawn's identity. Placed with a foster family, she fights to preserve
her innocence and be reunited with her younger brother Jimmy.

**Other books you might like:**
Angela Carter, *The Magic Toyshop*, 1967

---

**145**

### V.C. ANDREWS (Pseudonym of Andrew Neiderman)

## *Gates of Paradise*
(New York: Poseidon Books, 1989)

**Story type:** Horror (Gothic Family Chronicle)
**Series:** Castell Family
**Major character(s):** Annie Casteel Stonewall, Handicapped; Luke
    Casteel Jr., Relative (Annie's half-brother)
**Time period(s):** 1980s (Present)
**Locale(s):** Boston, Massachusetts (Farthinggale Manor, family estate)

**Summary:** Although physically weak and isolated at Farthinggale
Manor, Annie searches through the tangled Casteel family history to
unearth the secrets that have cursed all the Casteels, while at the same
time falling hopelessly into a "forbidden" love with her half-

brother, Luke. (Most of this novel was written by Andrew Neideerman.)

**Other books you might like:**
Michael McDowell, *Blackwater*, 1983
Joyce Carol Oates, *Bellefleur*, 1980

## 146

**V.C. ANDREWS** (Pseudonym of Andrew Neiderman)

### Secrets of the Morning
(New York: Pocket, 1991)

**Story type:** Horror (Gothic Family Chronicle)
**Series:** New Series of the Cutler Family
**Major character(s):** Dawn Longchamp, Student, Musician; Michael Sutton, Teacher (Dawn's music teacher); Jimmy Longchamp, Military Personnel (Dawn's foster brother)
**Time period(s):** 1990s
**Locale(s):** New York, New York

**Summary:** Having recovered from the abuse she suffered at the hands of her mother's family in *Dawn*, following the revelation that she is an adopted child, Dawn Longchamp attends the Bernhardt School of Performing Arts in New York in the hope of breaking clean of her family heritage. While there, however, she falls for music teacher Michael Sutton, and teeters on the brink of repeating the same error her real mother made.

**Other books you might like:**
Athena Alexis, *Along Came a Spider*, 1991

## 147

**V.C. ANDREWS** (Pseudonym of Andrew Neiderman)

### Web of Dreams
(New York: Pocket Books, 1990)

**Story type:** Horror (Gothic Family Chronicle)
**Series:** Castell Family
**Major character(s):** Leigh Van Voreen, Young Woman; Luke Casteel Jr., Young Man
**Time period(s):** 20th century
**Locale(s):** Boston, Massachusetts (Farthinggale Manor); Willies, West Virginia

**Summary:** Attending her father's funeral, Annie Casteel discovers her grandmother's diary and reads the story of Leigh's dark secret and her rescue and restoration by Luke Casteel.

**Other books you might like:**
Michael McDowell, *Blackwater*, 1983
Joyce Carol Oates, *Bellefleur*, 1980

## 148

**SCOTT DAVID ANIOLOWSKI**, Editor

### Return to Lovecraft Country
(Lockport, New York: Triad, 1997)

**Story type:** Horror (Anthology)

**Summary:** Fifteen stories written in homage to H.P. Lovecraft's cosmic horror fiction. The volume is anchored by reprints of T.E.D. Klein's "The Events at Poroth Farm," about a supernatural presence that has infiltrated a rural setting and its inhabitants; Thomas Ligotti's "The Last Feast of Harlequin," in which a man discovers that a festival of clowns is actually a celebration of dark gods and

terrors; and Lin Carter's "Strange Manuscript Found in the Vermont Woods." Contributors of original stories include Richard Lupoff, Don Burleson, Peter Cannon, Don D'Ammassa and Robert M. Price.

**Other books you might like:**
Edward P. Berglund, *Disciples of Cthulhu*, 1996
    editor
H.P. Lovecraft, *Tales of the Cthulhu Mythos*, 1990
Robert M. Price, *The New Lovecraft Circle*, 1996
    editor
Thomas M.K. Stratman, *Cthulhu's Heirs*, 1994
    editor
Jim Turner, *Cthulhu 2000*, 1995
    editor
Robert Weinberg, *Miskatonic University*, 1996
    Martin H. Greenberg, co-editor

## 149

**ANONYMOUS**

### The Book of Irish Weirdness
(New York: Sterling, 1997)

**Story type:** Horror (Anthology)

**Summary:** Thirty-five stories of horror and fantasy by Irish writers of the nineteenth and twentieth centuries. Included are Bram Stoker's "The Judge's House," about a house terrorized by a rat imbued with the soul of its evil former owner; Charlotte Riddell's "Hertford O'Donnell's Warning," featuring the legendary banshee; F. Marion Crawford's "The Dead Smile," about a pair of lovers haunted by a family curse and the grinning face of a dead ancestor; Oscar Wilde's amusing "The Canterville Ghost," in which the ghost of a man walled up in a house centuries before attempts to redress his sin and earn release into the afterlife; J. Sheridan Le Fanu's "Wicked Captain Walshawe," in which a man's soul becomes trapped in a candle and cannot be released until it is burned up; and A.E. Coppard's "The Gollan," a fantasy about a giant given the gift of imperceptibility by a leprechaun and the curse it proves to be. Several of the selections are retellings of classic stories from the oral tradition.

**Other books you might like:**
Peter Haining, *Great Irish Tales of Horror*, 1995
    editor
Peter Haining, *Great Irish Stories of the Supernatural*, 1992
    editor
Peter Haining, *Great Irish Tales of the Unimaginable*, 1994
    editor
Jim McGarry, *Irish Tales of Terror*, 1971
    editor
Peter Tremayne, *Irish Masters of Fantasy*, 1979
    editor

## 150

**ANONYMOUS**, Editor

### The Darkest Thirst: A Vampire Anthology
(Darien, Illinois: Design Image Group, 1998)

**Story type:** Horror (Anthology; Vampire Story)

**Summary:** These 16 original vampire stories include Margaret L. Carter's "Mercy," a period story about a slave trader who supplies a vampire with African slaves for sustenance, and Edo van Belkom's "The Debauched One," which proposes that the unkillable monk Rasputin was a vampire. A number of the selections explore the sexual dimensions of vampirism, including Rick R. Reed's "On

Line,'' in which a frustrated woman makes contact with a vampire through an on-line chat room, and Robert Devereaux's ''Nocturne a Tre in B-Double-Sharp Minor,'' concerned with a pair of lesbian vampires who seduce a music teacher into their peculiar brand of performance art.

**Other books you might like:**

Martin H. Greenberg, *Vampires: The Greatest Stories*, 1997
  editor
Stephen Jones, *The Mammoth Book of Vampires*, 1992
Byron Preiss, *The Ultimate Dracula*, 1991
  editor
Lawrence Schimel, *Blood Lines: Vampire Stories From New England*, 1997
  Martin H. Greenberg, co-editor
Robert Weinberg, *100 Vicious Little Vampire Stories*, 1995
  Stefan Dziemianowicz, Martin H. Greenberg, co-editors

---

### 151

**ANONYMOUS, Editor**

## The Kiss of Death: An Anthology of Vampire Stories

(Darien, Illinois: Design Image Group, 1998)

**Story type:** Horror (Anthology; Vampire Story)

**Summary:** These 16 vampire stories are all original to this volume. Contents include Don D'Ammassa's ''Prey for the Dead,'' in which a vampire meets his match in a scrappy homeless female; Rick R. Reed's ''Morbidly Obese,'' about a hemoholic vampire who enters a self-help program to control his binge blooddrinking; Sandra Black's ''The Poster Man,'' about the true identity of a man willing to pay an outrageous sum for a Dracula movie poster; and D.G.K. Goldberg's ''La Petite Morte,'' in which an immortal vampire falls in love with an endlessly reincarnated male paramour.

**Other books you might like:**

Martin H. Greenberg, *Vampires: The Greatest Stories*, 1997
  editor
Stephen Jones, *The Mammoth Book of Vampires*, 1992
  editor
Byron Preiss, *The Ultimate Dracula*, 1991
  editor
Lawrence Schimel, *Blood Lines: Vampire Stories From New England*, 1997
  Martin H. Greenberg, co-editor
Robert Weinberg, *100 Vicious Little Vampire Stories*, 1995
  Stefan Dziemianowicz, Martin H. Greenberg, co-editors

---

### 152

**RODERICK ANSCOMBE**

## The Secret Life of Laszlo, Count Dracula

(New York: Hyperion, 1994)

**Story type:** Horror (Serial Killer)

**Major character(s):** Laszlo, Count Dracula, Nobleman; Elizabeth, Spouse (Laszlo's wife); Gregory, Religious (priest)

**Time period(s):** 1860s (1866); 1880s (1887)

**Locale(s):** Paris, France; Transylvania

**Summary:** While working as an assistant to the renowned psychiatrist Jean Martin Charcot, Laszlo is driven by jealousy to murder a female patient and drink her blood. Twenty years later, having succeeded his deceased brother George as the new Count Dracula and married George's widow Elizabeth, Laszlo struggles with his drive to murder

and drink the blood of victims, committing acts that give rise among the townspeople to the legends of the legendary supernatural vampire. This psychoanalytical rendering of the Dracula legend is the author's first novel.

**Other books you might like:**

Anne Rice, *The Vampire Lestat*, 1985
Michael Romkey, *The Vampire Papers*, 1994
Bram Stoker, *Dracula*, 1897

---

### 153

**MARK ANTHONY**

## Beyond the Pale

(New York: Bantam Spectra, 1998)

**Story type:** Fantasy (Alternate World)

**Series:** Last Rune

**Major character(s):** Travis Wilder, Saloon Keeper/Owner; Grace Beckett, Doctor

**Time period(s):** 1990s; Indeterminate

**Locale(s):** Colorado; Eldh, Mythical Place

**Summary:** As ancient runes begin to appear in the environment, Travis Wilder receives a gift immediately before someone attempts to kill him, while Grace Beckett discovers that men with a lump of iron instead of a heart pursue her. Each flees and, after hearing warnings from the leader of a magical circus, escapes to another world where both possess magical abilities and must help defend against the evil Pale King, prophesied to return.

**Other books you might like:**

Barbara Hambly, *The Time of the Dark*, 1982
Robert Holdstock, *Mythago Wood*, 1994
L. Dean James, *Summerland*, 1994
Patricia A. McKillip, *Winter Rose*, 1996
Lawrence Watt-Evans, *Out of This World*, 1994

---

### 154

**MARK ANTHONY**
**ELLEN PORATH, Co-Author**

## Kindred Spirits

(Lake Geneva, Wisconsin: TSR, 1991)

**Story type:** Fantasy (Mystery)

**Series:** Dragonlance: The Meetings Sextet

**Major character(s):** Flint Fireforge, Mythical Creature (dwarf), Artisan (metalsmith); Tanthalas ''Tanis'' Half-Elvin, Mythical Creature (elf), Warrior

**Time period(s):** Indeterminate

**Locale(s):** Qualinesti, Fictional Country

**Summary:** When Tanis stands accused of murdering a pompous elf lord, Flint must prove his innocence to avoid Tanis's permanent banishment. This is the author's first published book. A game tie-in novel.

**Other books you might like:**

Tina Daniell, *Dark Heart*, 1992
Mary Kirchoff, *Wanderlust*, 1991
  Steve Winter, co-author
Richard A. Knaak, *Kaz the Minotaur*, 1990
Barbara Siegel, *Tanis, the Shadow Years*, 1990
  Scott Siegel, co-author
Margaret Weis, *Dragons of Autumn Twilight*, 1984
  Tracy Hickman, co-author

## 155

### MARK ANTHONY

## *Tower of Doom*

(Lake Geneva, Wisconsin: TSR, 1994)

**Story type:** Horror (Reanimated Dead)
**Series:** Ravenloft
**Major character(s):** Wort, Handicapped (hunchback); Baron Caidin, Nobleman; Mika, Doctor
**Time period(s):** Indeterminate
**Locale(s):** Ravenloft, Fictional Country

**Summary:** Wort, the hunchbacked half-brother of the Baron Caidin, discovers a magic talisman that allows him to exact supernatural vengeance against his persecutors. Meanwhile, the baron resorts to a similar necromancy to create a zombie army that builds a tower he needs to defend himself against neighboring enemies.

**Other books you might like:**
Elaine Bergstrom, *Tapestry of Dark Souls*, 1993
P.N. Elrod, *I, Strahd*, 1993
Christie Golden, *Dance of the Dead*, 1992
Christie Golden, *The Enemy Within*, 1994
J. Robert King, *Carnival of Fear*, 1993
Brian Thomsen, *Tales of Ravenloft*, 1994
   editor
Chet Williamson, *Mordenheim*, 1994

## 156

### PATRICIA ANTHONY

## *Brother Termite*

(New York: Harcourt Brace, 1993)

**Story type:** Science Fiction (Invasion of Earth; Satire)
**Major character(s):** Reem "First Cousin Brother", Alien (Cousin), Political Figure (White House chief of staff); Jeff Womack, Political Figure (President of the United States), Human; Tali, Alien (Cousin), Political Figure (Cousin Brother Conscience)
**Time period(s):** 21st century
**Locale(s):** Washington, District of Columbia

**Summary:** In control of the United States government for a century, half of it overtly, aliens stop human advancement in the sciences and begin an ominous breeding program while the decline in human births precipitates a crisis in the baby food industry. Reem acts as troubleshooter despite Washington plotting and difficulties with his own kind and within himself.

**Other books you might like:**
Octavia E. Butler, *Dawn*, 1987
Arthur C. Clarke, *Childhood's End*, 1953
Parke Godwin, *Waiting for the Galactic Bus*, 1988
W.A. Harbinson, *Dream Maker*, 1992
Robert A. Heinlein, *The Puppet Masters*, 1991
   revised edition
John Kessel, *Good News From Outer Space*, 1989
Robert Rankin, *Armageddon: The Musical*, 1990
David Alexander Smith, *In the Cube*, 1993

## 157

### PATRICIA ANTHONY

## *Cold Allies*

(New York: Harcourt Brace Jovanovich, 1993)

**Story type:** Science Fiction (Military; First Contact)
**Major character(s):** Gordon Means, Military Personnel (sergeant); Valentin Baranyk, Military Personnel (lieutenant general); Jerry Casey, Teenager, Refugee
**Time period(s):** 2010s
**Locale(s):** Colorado; Pyrenees, Europe; Poland

**Summary:** The American, European, Russian alliance battles the Arab nations moving north into Europe looking for food and a place to settle. Sent via his robot tank to protect the only remaining communication and observation satellite, Gordon picks up an alien little blue light which seems to like him. The Americans decide to use the aliens in the war effort despite the inability of the military to establish communication with them. A first novel.

**Other books you might like:**
Jean Mark Gawron, *Dream of Glass*, 1993
Jack C. Haldeman II, *High Steel*, 1993
   Jack Dann, co-author
Gwyneth Jones, *White Queen*, 1993
Ursula K. Le Guin, *The Lathe of Heaven*, 1971
Garfield Reeves-Stevens, *Nighteyes*, 1989

## 158

### PATRICIA ANTHONY

## *Cradle of Splendor*

(New York: Ace, 1996)

**Story type:** Science Fiction (First Contact; Political)
**Major character(s):** Dolores Sims, Artist (painter), Spy (CIA agent); Ana Maria Bonfim, Political Figure (Presidente of Brazil); Edson Carvalho, Spy (Brazilian)
**Time period(s):** 1990s
**Locale(s):** Brazil

**Summary:** Ana Maria becomes the presidente of Brazil through treachery and the help of the CIA and labors to bring Brazil's technology to a more advanced state. When the first space launch almost fails, but then succeeds, every spy tries to discover why.

**Other books you might like:**
Alan Dean Foster, *Cyber Way*, 1990
Mark Leyner, *My Cousin, My Gastroenterologist*, 1990
Linda Nagata, *Tech-Heaven*, 1995
Neal Stephenson, *The Diamond Age*, 1995

## 159

### PATRICIA ANTHONY

## *God's Fires*

(New York; Ace, 1997)

**Story type:** Science Fiction (Theological; Political)
**Major character(s):** Alphonso Braganca, Royalty (King), Handicapped (retarded); Manoel Pessoa, Religious (Jesuit-inquisitor); Berenice Pinheiro, Healer, Herbalist
**Time period(s):** 16th century (Portuguese Inquisition)
**Locale(s):** Lisbon, Portugal; Quintas, Portugal

**Summary:** Hearing the stories of angels raping women and girls, a virgin birth and a visitation from the Virgin Mary, Pessoa realizes that he must convene an inquisition and hope to avoid more official notice of Berenice, his lover, or anyone else. Alfonso discovers God in the silver acorn he ses fall from Heaven and learns that the Earth revolves around the Sun. Unfortunately for the two ''angels'' who survived the fall, the Grand Inquisitor tries the ''fallen angels'' and ''heretics'' in Quinitas, despite Alfonso and the local priest's conviction that the trial will be illegal.

**Other books you might like:**
David Brin, *Brightness Reef*, 1995
Parke Godwin, *Waiting for the Galactic Bus*, 1988
Frederik Pohl, *The Other End of Time*, 1996
Mary Doria Russell, *The Sparrow*, 1996
Sheri S. Tepper, *Grass*, 1989

## 160
### PATRICIA ANTHONY
## *Happy Policeman*
(New York: Harcourt Brace, 1994)

**Story type:** Science Fiction (Mystery; Contemporary Realism)
**Major character(s):** DeWitt Dawson, Police Officer; Bodeen Woodruff, Police Officer; Seresen, Alien (Torku)
**Time period(s):** 1990s
**Locale(s):** Coomey, Texas

**Summary:** Coomey, Texas has existed in a Torku-created bubble for six years. After Loretta Harper's murder and her sons' disappearance, DeWitt Dawson sets out to investigate, only to find the aliens have destroyed evidence and answer all his questions with riddles.

**Other books you might like:**
Isaac Asimov, *The Caves of Steel*, 1953
Richard Bowker, *Dover Beach*, 1987
John Brunner, *The Squares of the City*, 1965
D.G. Compton, *Chronocules*, 1970
Edmund Cooper, *Seahorse in the Sky*, 1969
Philip K. Dick, *A Maze of Death*, 1970
Brad Ferguson, *The World Next Door*, 1990
Joan Slonczewski, *The Wall Around Eden*, 1989

## 161
### PIERS ANTHONY
## *Alien Plot*
(New York: Tor, 1992)

**Story type:** Science Fiction (Collection)

**Summary:** Contains a brief autobiographical sketch, ''Faces,'' an article, ''Think of the Reader,'' plus 16 stories, 7 original and 11 from periodicals and anthologies 1970-1991. The stories display a wide variety of fantasy and science fiction themes with several involving the problems writers have with editors.

**Other books you might like:**
David Brin, *The River of Time*, 1986
Orson Scott Card, *Maps in a Mirror*, 1990
Larry Niven, *N-Space*, 1990
John Varley, *Blue Champagne*, 1986
John Varley, *The Persistence of Vision*, 1978
Kurt Vonnegut Jr., *Welcome to the Monkey House*, 1968

## 162
### PIERS ANTHONY
## *And Eternity*
(New York: Morrow, 1990)

**Story type:** Fantasy (Contemporary; Magic Conflict)
**Series:** Incarnations of Immortality
**Major character(s):** Orlene, Spirit (ghost); Jolie, Spirit (ghost); Vita, Prostitute
**Time period(s):** Indeterminate Future
**Locale(s):** Earth; Hell; Heaven

**Summary:** Orlene, the mortal daughter of Gaea has finally died, after being overwhelmed with a succession of tragedies. In Afterlife, she is protected by Gaea's companion Jolie, herself the sometime-consort of Satan. Together, Orlene and Jolie seek out and are joined by Vita, contemporary mortal with her own share of troubles, her own compelling attractions and her own unsettling moral code. In a world where the Incarnation of Good seems to have fallen asleep, these three women form a triumvirate and pursue a great quest that takes them through a succession of trials as numerous and mysterious as the Incarnations themselves. This is the seventh and concluding volume in this unusual allegorical series which has personified good, evil, nature, war, fate, time and death.

**Other books you might like:**
Poul Anderson, *Operation Chaos*, 1971
Orson Scott Card, *Seventh Son*, 1987
Brian Daley, *The Doomfarers of Coramonde*, 1977
Robert A. Heinlein, *Waldo and Magic, Inc.*, 1950
Roger Zelazny, *Nine Princes in Amber*, 1970

## 163
### PIERS ANTHONY
## *But What of Earth?*
(New York: Tor, 1989)

**Story type:** Science Fiction (End of the World)
**Major character(s):** Scott Krebs, Student; Lucy, Thief
**Time period(s):** Indeterminate Future

**Summary:** Earth's civilization is on the verge of collapse due to overpopulation and the depletion of resources when practical matter transmitters are invented and increasing numbers of people emigrate to new worlds. Those few who either can't or won't leave Earth must deal with a near total breakdown of law and order. This volume includes Anthony's previously unpublished version of this novel which was published in butchered form by Laser Books in 1976. Also included are two short essays describing the background to the book's publication and nearly seventy pages of notes detailing all of the changes suggested by a series of Laser editors.

**Other books you might like:**
Neal Barrett Jr., *Dawn's Uncertain Light*, 1989
Neal Barrett Jr., *Through Darkest America*, 1987
Jerry Earl Brown, *Earthfall*, 1989
Keith Laumer, *The Stars Must Wait*, 1990

## 164

**PIERS ANTHONY**
**ROBERT E. MARGROFF**, Co-Author

### The Caterpillar's Question

(New York: Ace, 1992)

**Story type:** Fantasy (Alternate World; Contemporary)
**Major character(s):** Tappuah "Tappy" Concord, Orphan, Mythical Creature (Imago); Jack, Artist, Companion; Malva, Alien (Gaol)
**Time period(s):** 1990s
**Locale(s):** United States

**Summary:** Hidden from the alien Gaol as a maimed, blind, mute, thirteen-year-old girl, Tappy, the Imago, finds her way to a rock which leads to an alternate world. The alien honkers protect her until the Agents of the Imago rescue Tappy. If she does not realize her power as the Imago, the Agents of the Imago will kill Tappy before allowing her capture by the Gaol.

**Other books you might like:**
Glen Cook, *The Black Company*, 1984
Charles de Lint, *The Little Country*, 1991
Philip Jose Farmer, *The Maker of Universes*, 1965
Philip Jose Farmer, *Red Orc's Rage*, 1991
Alan Dean Foster, *Cyber Way*, 1990
Robert Jordan, *The Eye of the World*, 1989
Meredith Ann Pierce, *The Pearl of the Soul of the World*, 1990
Jim Shepard, *Lights Out in the Reptile House*, 1990
Karen Wehrstein, *Lion's Heart*, 1991
Roger Zelazny, *Nine Princes in Amber*, 1970

## 165

**PIERS ANTHONY**

### Chaos Mode

(New York: Ace/Putnam, 1993)

**Story type:** Fantasy (Adventure; Quest)
**Series:** Virtual Mode
**Major character(s):** Colene, Teenager, Adventurer; Burgess, Animal (invertebrate); Seqiro, Animal (horse), Telepath
**Time period(s):** 21st century; Indeterminate
**Locale(s):** Earth; Shale, Alternate Earth

**Summary:** Colene, Seqiro, Darius and Nona arrive in a world where vertebrates never developed and meet Burgess, a floater of the triramous phylum, who has been exiled from his people as contaminated by selfishness. They travel along the Virtual Mode to Julia where society has become ugly through the change from Animus to Anima.

**Other books you might like:**
Jack L. Chalker, *When the Changewinds Blow*, 1987
Cynthia Felice, *Godsfire*, 1978
Alan Dean Foster, *To the Vanishing Point*, 1988
Alan Garner, *Elidor*, 1967
Harry Harrison, *West of Eden*, 1984
Ward Hawkins, *Red Flame Burning*, 1985
Diana Wynne Jones, *The Homeward Bounders*, 1981
L. Neil Smith, *Contact and Commune*, 1980
Timothy Zahn, *Triplet*, 1987

## 166

**PIERS ANTHONY**
**ROBERT E. MARGROFF**, Co-Author

### Chimaera's Copper

(New York: Tor, 1990)

**Story type:** Fantasy (Adventure; Magic Conflict)
**Series:** Kelvin of Rud
**Major character(s):** Kelvin Knight Hackleberry, Hero; Rowforth, Royalty (King-Usurper); Heln, Spouse
**Time period(s):** 1990s
**Locale(s):** Rud, Fictional Country; Alternate Earth

**Summary:** Kelvin with his brother and father, are trapped in an unknown alternate universe by the Chimaera, while Heln is threatened by Kelvin's old enemies and his unborn child is cursed. Only Kelvin can save his family, but will he be able to free himself from the Chimaera in time?

**Other books you might like:**
John DeChancie, *Castle Perilous*, 1988
Charles de Lint, *Drink Down the Moon*, 1990
John Deakins, *Barrow*, 1990
Ellen Kushner, *Thomas the Rhymer*, 1990
Alis A. Rasmussen, *The Labyrinth Gate*, 1988

## 167

**PIERS ANTHONY**

### The Color of Her Panties

(New York: Morrow, 1992)

**Story type:** Fantasy (Light Fantasy; Quest)
**Series:** Xanth
**Major character(s):** Mela Merwoman, Mythical Creature (mermaid), Widow(er); Gwenny Goblin, Mythical Creature (goblin), Feminist; Okra Ogress, Mythical Creature (ogre), Runaway
**Time period(s):** Indeterminate
**Locale(s):** Xanth, Fictional Country

**Summary:** Gwenny Goblin, accompanied by Che Centaur and Jenny Elf, go to the Good Magician to discover how Gwenny can become chief of the Goblins. Meanwhile, Mela Merwoman, seeking a husband, Okra Ogress, trying to become a main character, and Ida Human, trying to discover her destiny, also seek out the Good Magician and wind up helping Gwenny.

**Other books you might like:**
Robert Asprin, *Another Fine Myth*, 1978
Kyle Crocco, *Heroes, Inc.*, 1991
Suzette Haden Elgin, *Twelve Fair Kingdoms*, 1981
Alan Dean Foster, *Spellsinger*, 1983
Pamela F. Service, *Weirdos of the Universe, Unite!*, 1992
Christopher Stasheff, *The Warlock in Spite of Himself*, 1969

## 168

**PIERS ANTHONY**

### Demons Don't Dream

(New York: Tor, 1993)

**Story type:** Fantasy (Light Fantasy; Quest)
**Series:** Xanth
**Major character(s):** Dug, Teenager, Adventurer; Kim, Teenager; Jenny Elf, Mythical Creature (elf), Guide

**Time period(s):** Indeterminate
**Locale(s):** Xanth, Fictional Country

**Summary:** The first players to try a new computer fantasy game allowing entry to Xanth, Kim and Dug compete to achieve their most cherished desire while utilizing a chosen and possibly traitorous companion. The pair help several other inhabitants find what they want most, while saving the magic in Xanth.

**Other books you might like:**
Robert Asprin, *Another Fine Myth*, 1978
Diane Duane, *So You Want to Be a Wizard?*, 1983
Alan Dean Foster, *Spellsinger*, 1983
Gillian Rubinstein, *Space Demons*, 1988
William Sleator, *Interstellar Pig*, 1984
Christopher Stasheff, *The Warlock in Spite of Himself*, 1969
Patricia C. Wrede, *Talking to Dragons*, 1985

**169**

PIERS ANTHONY

## Faun & Games

(New York: Tor, 1997)

**Story type:** Fantasy (Light Fantasy; Quest)
**Series:** Xanth
**Major character(s):** Forrest Faun, Mythical Creature (faun), Gardener; Mare Imbri, Animal (horse), Companion; Cathryn Centaur, Mythical Creature (centaur), Guide
**Time period(s):** Indeterminate
**Locale(s):** Xanth, Fictional Country; Ptero, Moon—Imaginary

**Summary:** When Forrest Faun must find a new keeper for a tree to prevent its dying, he goes along with Mare Imbri to Ptero, a moonlet circling Princess Ida. After several side quests, finding a centaur's true love and keeping humans from being marginalized, he returns to Xanth to find the answer.

**Other books you might like:**
Poul Anderson, *Three Hearts and Three Lions*, 1991
Robert Asprin, *Another Fine Myth*, 1978
John Barnes, *One for the Morning Glory*, 1996
Jack L. Chalker, *Demons of the Dancing Gods*, 1984
Alan Dean Foster, *Son of Spellsinger*, 1993
Andre Norton, *Dread Companion*, 1970
Christopher Stasheff, *The Warlock Unlocked*, 1982
Thomas Burnett Swann, *Lady of the Bees*, 1976

**170**

PIERS ANTHONY

## Firefly

(New York: Morrow, 1990)

**Story type:** Horror (Erotic Horror)
**Major character(s):** Geode Demerit, Maintenance Worker; Oenone Brown, Housewife; Frank Tishner, Police Officer
**Time period(s):** 1990s
**Locale(s):** Middle Kingdom Ranch, Florida

**Summary:** A monster has taken over the grounds of the remote Middle Kingdom Ranch, attracting its human victims with sexually stimulating pheromones and then draining them of their bodily fluids.

**Other books you might like:**
Ray Russell, *Incubus*, 1976

**171**

PIERS ANTHONY

## Fractal Mode

(New York: Ace/Putnam, 1992)

**Story type:** Fantasy (Quest; Adventure)
**Series:** Virtual Mode
**Major character(s):** Colene, Teenager, Adventurer; Darius, Ruler (Cyng of Pwer); Nona, Heroine, Heiress—Dispossessed
**Time period(s):** 1990s
**Locale(s):** Oklahoma, Alternate Universe

**Summary:** Nona, the ninth daughter in the ninth generation, is destined to change the rule of her fractal universe from Animus to Anima. While seeking out the Megaplayers, she meets Colene, Darius, Seqiro and Provos. They help her by enlisting the aid of Angus, a giant, while Colene talks to a math professor to find the exact spot where the change must occur. She also rescues a sexually abused child who Provos adopts as her own. They finally get Nona to the exact predetermined spot for the change from Animus to Anima. After accomplishing that, the band, plus Nona, set out again along the Virtual Mode.

**Other books you might like:**
Jack L. Chalker, *When the Changewinds Blow*, 1987
Alan Dean Foster, *To the Vanishing Point*, 1988
Alan Garner, *Elidor*, 1967
Diana Wynne Jones, *Eight Days of Luke*, 1988
Michael Reaves, *The Shattered World*, 1984

**172**

PIERS ANTHONY

## Geis of the Gargoyle

(New York: Tor, 1995)

**Story type:** Fantasy (Light Fantasy; Quest)
**Series:** Xanth
**Major character(s):** Gary Gargoyle, Mythical Creature (gargoyle); Iris, Royalty (queen); D. Mentia, Demon
**Time period(s):** Indeterminate
**Locale(s):** Xanth, Fictional Country

**Summary:** Gary Gargoyle asks the Good Magician Humfrey for a way to purify the Swan Knee River and release the gargoyles from their geis. Transformed into a man, Gary must also tutor the child, Surprise, and teach her control over her magic.

**Other books you might like:**
Robert Asprin, *Another Fine Myth*, 1978
Robert N. Charrette, *Never Trust an Elf*, 1992
Susan Cooper, *Silver on the Tree*, 1977
Susan Dexter, *The Wizard's Shadow*, 1993
Alan Dean Foster, *Spellsinger at the Gate*, 1983
Laurell K. Hamilton, *Nightseer*, 1992
Brian Stableford, *The Last Days of the Edge of the World*, 1985
Christopher Stasheff, *The Warlock in Spite of Himself*, 1969

**173**

PIERS ANTHONY

## Hard Sell

(Houston, Texas: Tafford, 1990)

**Story type:** Science Fiction (Humor)
**Major character(s):** Fisk Center, Businessman (sucker)

**Time period(s):** 21st century
**Locale(s):** Earth

**Summary:** Fisk Center, bilked of all his money by Mars, Ltd., must find some way to survive. He finds a job which he soon discovers is for an illegal adoption agency and ends up with an eleven-year-old daughter who proceeds to take over his life.

**Other books you might like:**
Steven Brust, *Cowboy Feng's Space Bar and Grille*, 1990
Lois McMaster Bujold, *Borders of Infinity*, 1989
Alan Dean Foster, *Quozl*, 1989
Mel Gilden, *Outer Space and All That Junk*, 1989
Harry Harrison, *Bill, the Galactic Hero: The Planet of the Robot Slaves*, 1989
Keith Laumer, *Reward for Retief*, 1989

---

**174**

**PIERS ANTHONY**

## Harpy Thyme

(New York: Tor, 1994)

**Story type:** Fantasy (Light Fantasy; Quest)
**Series:** Xanthe
**Major character(s):** Gloha Harpy-Goblin, Mythical Creature (winged goblin); Trent, Magician; Graeboe, Mythical Creature (giant)
**Time period(s):** Indeterminate
**Locale(s):** Xanth, Fictional Country

**Summary:** With no others like her, Gloha Harpy-Goblin seeks her ideal man. When the Good Magician Humphrey will not help her, a rejuvenated Trent and the skeleton, Marrow Bones, accompany her on the search. Although Gloha helps the demon, Metria, find happiness, she requires Trent's advice and magical assistance to achieve her own goal.

**Other books you might like:**
Douglas W. Clark, *Alchemy Unlimited*, 1990
Suzette Haden Elgin, *Twelve Fair Kingdoms*, 1981
Diana Wynne Jones, *Howl's Moving Castle*, 1986
Terry Pratchett, *The Colour of Magic*, 1983
Patricia C. Wrede, *Dealing with Dragons*, 1990

---

**175**

**PIERS ANTHONY**

## Hope of Earth

(New York: Tor, 1997)

**Story type:** Science Fiction (Family Saga; Adventure)
**Series:** Geodyssey
**Major character(s):** Sam, Warrior, Refugee; Jes, Mercenary; Ned, Orphan, Genius
**Time period(s):** Indeterminate Past; 21st century
**Locale(s):** Africa; Ancient Civilization; South America

**Summary:** Barely human, six siblings who separate from their elders must learn to survive in Australopithecine Africa. Their saga continues through all history to 21st century Peru, where they once again live within the rhythms of nature. Third in the series.

**Other books you might like:**
Brian W. Aldiss, *Cryptozoic*, 1968
Roger MacBride Allen, *Orphan of Creation*, 1988
Poul Anderson, *The Boat of a Million Years*, 1989
Michael Bishop, *No Enemy but Time*, 1982
Philip Jose Farmer, *Time's Last Gift*, 1972
Garry Kilworth, *Split Second*, 1985

---

Harry Turtledove, *A Different Flesh*, 1988

**176**

**PIERS ANTHONY**
**MERCEDES LACKEY**, Co-Author

## If I Pay Thee Not in Gold

(New York: Baen, 1993)

**Story type:** Fantasy (Magic Conflict; Quest)
**Major character(s):** Xylina, Orphan, Young Woman; Faro, Slave; Ware, Demon
**Time period(s):** Indeterminate (Age of the Mazonians)
**Locale(s):** Mazonia, Fictional Country

**Summary:** In Mazonia, women conjure and rule but men have no magical abilities and serve as slaves. Though poor, Xylina possesses more magical talents than most women, and after gaining a slave in her womanhood initiation rites, begins to improve her fortunes with his shrewd advice. But a secret enemy manages to thwart their efforts with disasters, both natural and magical. With Xylina near bankruptcy, Ware offers her the choice of becoming his lover or accepting the Queen's offer to repay the debt if Xylina will undertake the quest to retrieve a shard of a magic crystal that can make the wearer immortal.

**Other books you might like:**
C.J. Cherryh, *Angel with the Sword*, 1985
Phyllis Eisenstein, *Born to Exile*, 1978
Mercedes Lackey, *Arrows of the Queen*, 1987
Mercedes Lackey, *By the Sword*, 1991
Mack Reynolds, *Amazon Planet*, 1975
Jack Vance, *Emphyrio*, 1969
Joan D. Vinge, *The Snow Queen*, 1980
Patricia C. Wrede, *Caught in Crystal*, 1987
Patricia C. Wrede, *Shadow Magic*, 1982

---

**177**

**PIERS ANTHONY**

## Isle of View

(New York: Avon, 1990)

**Story type:** Fantasy (Light Fantasy; Romance)
**Series:** Xanth
**Major character(s):** Dolph, Royalty (Prince of Xanth); Che Centaur, Mythical Creature (Winged-Centaur); Jenny Elf, Mythical Creature (Elf)
**Time period(s):** 1990s
**Locale(s):** Xanth, Fictional Country

**Summary:** Che Centaur has been kidnapped by goblins. Jenny Elf, a visitor from the world of Two Moons, comforts him even as she tries to find a way back to her home. Prince Dolph leads an expedition to rescue Che, knowing that he must also decide which woman he will marry. Finally Che, Jenny and the Goblin princess go to live with the centaurs, while Dolph marries Electra to save her from certain death and finds he loves her after all.

**Other books you might like:**
Robert Asprin, *Another Fine Myth*, 1978
Steven R. Boyett, *Ariel: A Book of the Change*, 1983
Linda Haldeman, *The Lastborn of Elvinwood*, 1978
Christopher Stasheff, *The Warlock in Spite of Himself*, 1969

## 178

PIERS ANTHONY

### Isle of Woman

(New York: Tor, 1993)

**Story type:** Fantasy (Historical)
**Major character(s):** Blaze, Blacksmith; Ember, Parent (mother), Leader; Stone, Artisan
**Time period(s):** 20000th century B.C.; 2020s (2021)
**Locale(s):** Earth

**Summary:** A series of vignettes details the rise of humanity from the plains of Africa through post-disaster America as seen through a group of people in several reincarnations. Blaze, always a fireworker, finds his true love, Ember, repeatedly denied him or known only through dreams, while their families perpetually win despite the odds.

**Other books you might like:**
Poul Anderson, *The Boat of a Million Years*, 1989
Jean M. Auel, *Clan of the Cave Bear*, 1990
John Brunner, *The Tides of Time*, 1984
W. Michael Gear, *People of the Wolf*, 1990
    Kathleen O'Neal Gear, co-author
Crawford Kilian, *The Empire of Time*, 1978
Robert Silverberg, *Gilgamesh the King*, 1984
L. Neil Smith, *The Crystal Empire*, 1986
Roger Welsch, *Touching the Fire*, 1992

## 179

PIERS ANTHONY

### Killobyte

(New York: Ace/Putnam, 1993)

**Story type:** Fantasy (Contemporary; Adventure)
**Major character(s):** Walter Toland, Adventurer, Handicapped; Baal Curran, Handicapped, Teenager; Phreak, Computer Expert, Criminal
**Time period(s):** 1990s
**Locale(s):** United States; Virtual Reality, Cyberspace

**Summary:** While playing the virtual reality computer game, Killobyte, Walter Toland and Baal Curran discover that another player, a dangerous psychotic, has learned how to trap them in the game to kill them repeatedly. As the game continues, Walter and Baal begin to suspect the evil player can expand his influence to the realm outside the game.

**Other books you might like:**
Philip Jose Farmer, *Red Orc's Rage*, 1991
Will Shetterly, *The Tangled Lands*, 1989
Wm. Mark Simmons, *When Dreams Collide*, 1992
Vivian Vande Velde, *User Unfriendly*, 1991

## 180

PIERS ANTHONY

### Man From Mundania

(New York: Avon, 1989)

**Story type:** Fantasy (Light Fantasy)
**Series:** Xanth
**Major character(s):** Ivy, Royalty (princess), Sorceress; Grey Murphy, Student—College, Sorcerer (apprentice)
**Time period(s):** 1980s
**Locale(s):** Xanth, Planet—Imaginary; Mundania, Fictional Country (Earth world)

**Summary:** Princess Ivy is sent to Mundania by evil Com-pewter. She meets Grey Murphy and the two travel back to Xanth in order to fight Com-pewter.

**Other books you might like:**
Robert Asprin, *Myth-Nomers and Im-Pervections*, 1988
Mercedes Lackey, *Knight of Ghosts and Shadows*, 1990
Terry Pratchett, *Sourcery*, 1989
Will Shetterly, *The Tangled Lands*, 1990
Christopher Stasheff, *The Warlock in Spite of Himself*, 1969

## 181

PIERS ANTHONY

### Mercycle

(Houston: Tafford Publishing, Inc., 1991)

**Story type:** Science Fiction (Adventure)
**Major character(s):** Don Kestle, Archaeologist; Eleph, Alien
**Time period(s):** Indeterminate Future
**Locale(s):** Earth

**Summary:** Recruited by a mysterious alien force not limited by time and space, five adventurers engage in a difficult and dangerous secret mission. The individuals are subjected to a process which renders them out of phase with the normal world, allowing them a lengthy journey across the bottom of the sea. As they overcome obstacles, they find their mission involves saving the entire world.

**Other books you might like:**
David Brin, *Startide Rising*, 1983
Vonda N. McIntyre, *Superluminal*, 1983
Carol Severance, *Reefsong*, 1991
Joan Slonczewski, *A Door into Ocean*, 1986
Allen Steele, *Orbital Decay*, 1989
John E. Stith, *Redshift Rendezvous*, 1990

## 182

PIERS ANTHONY
ROBERT E. MARGROFF, Co-Author

### Mouvar's Magic

(New York: Tor, 1992)

**Story type:** Fantasy (Adventure; Magic Conflict)
**Series:** Kelvin of Rud
**Major character(s):** Kelvin Knight Hackleberry, Hero; Zady, Witch; Horace, Mythical Creature (dragon), Telepath
**Time period(s):** 1990s
**Locale(s):** Kelvinia, Fictional Country; Alternate Earth

**Summary:** In a final desperate attempt to rend the empire asunder, Devale employs Zady to defeat Kelvin's efforts to save the alliance. Kelvin lays waste to orcs, giants and other foes with the aid of a dragon and magic implements supplied by Mouvar which allow Kelvin to discover his own magic-wielding ability. Concluding volume of the five book series.

**Other books you might like:**
John DeChancie, *Castle Perilous*, 1988
Stephen R. Donaldson, *Lord Foul's Bane*, 1977
Melanie Rawn, *Stronghold*, 1990
Christopher Rowley, *Bazil Broketail*, 1992

**183**

PIERS ANTHONY

*Orc's Opal*

(New York: Tor, 1990)

**Story type:** Fantasy (Quest; Magic Conflict)
**Series:** Kelvin of Rud
**Major character(s):** Kelvin Knight Hackleberry, Hero; Zady, Witch
**Time period(s):** 1990s
**Locale(s):** Kelvinia, Fictional Country; Alternate Earth

**Summary:** Kelvin is home with his family recuperating from his last adventure when the evil Zady swears to get even by taking the lives of his children. In the many worlds of the multiverse, the Prophesy of Mouvar is unfolding as predicted, and now the children must find the Orc's Opal.

**Other books you might like:**
John DeChancie, *Castle Perilous*, 1988
Charles de Lint, *Drink Down the Moon*, 1990
John Deakins, *Barrow*, 1990
Ellen Kushner, *Thomas the Rhymer*, 1990
Alis A. Rasmussen, *The Labyrinth Gate*, 1988
Nancy Springer, *Red Wizard*, 1990

**184**

PIERS ANTHONY

*Phaze Doubt*

(New York: Ace/Putnam, 1990)

**Story type:** Fantasy (Light Fantasy)
**Series:** Apprentice Adept
**Major character(s):** Nepe/Flach, Mythical Creature (unicorn), Animal (shapechanger); Brown, Lesbian, Magician (adept); Lysander, Android, Agent
**Time period(s):** Indeterminate Future
**Locale(s):** Phaze, Planet—Imaginary

**Summary:** Hectare is invading Phaze, and Lysander is one of their agents. He is the subject of a prophecy that he will save Phaze, so Nepe/Flach takes him with her as she works to save Phaze. Lysander finds himself more and more sympathetic to Phaze until the planet makes a quarter turn and he turns into one of them and they expel the Hectare. Lysander marries Oche and they all live happily ever after.

**Other books you might like:**
Robert Asprin, *Another Fine Myth*, 1978
Steven R. Boyett, *Ariel: A Book of the Change*, 1983
Suzette Haden Elgin, *Twelve Fair Kingdoms*, 1983
Dale Estey, *A Lost Tale*, 1980
Alan Dean Foster, *Spellsinger*, 1983
Christopher Stasheff, *The Warlock in Spite of Himself*, 1969

**185**

PIERS ANTHONY
JAMES RICHEY, Co-Author
ALAN RIGGS, Co-Author

*Quest for the Fallen Star*

(New York: Tor, 1998)

**Story type:** Fantasy (Quest; Magic Conflict)
**Major character(s):** Chentelle, Singer, Mythical Creature (elf); Marcus Alanda, Religious (High Bishop of Norivika); A'stoc, Wizard

**Time period(s):** Indeterminate
**Locale(s):** Realm of Infinitera, Fictional Country

**Summary:** Answering a summons, Chentelle gathers a band of followers when Ill Will threatens Creation. They must obtain the sphere of Ohnn and travel through wasteland, an enchanted forest, and high mountains to find the metallic and mechanical Fallen Star.

**Other books you might like:**
Greg Bear, *Songs of Earth and Power*, 1994
Jack L. Chalker, *Horrors of the Dancing Gods*, 1995
Mercedes Lackey, *Knight of Ghosts and Shadows*, 1990
  Ellen Guon, co-author
Patricia A. McKillip, *The Riddle-Master of Hed*, 1976
Clifford D. Simak, *The Fellowship of the Talisman*, 1978
Nancy Springer, *The Sable Moon*, 1981
Judith Tarr, *The Isle of Glass*, 1985
Jack Vance, *Lyonesse*, 1983

**186**

PIERS ANTHONY

*Question Quest*

(New York: Avon, 1991)

**Story type:** Fantasy (Quest; Light Fantasy)
**Series:** Xanth
**Major character(s):** Lacuna, Housewife, Agent; Humfrey, Magician; Rose, Sorceress, Royalty (princess)
**Time period(s):** Indeterminate
**Locale(s):** Xanth, Fictional Country

**Summary:** Lacuna, feeling life has passed her by, goes to the Good Magician Grey to learn what she can do about it. He sends her to Hell to comfort Humfrey, the former Magician who is trying to rescue his wife, Rose. While waiting he tells Lacuna his history and that of Xanth. Then Humfrey must decide which of his former wives, all in Hell, he wishes to rescue. Taking turns, Humfrey ends up returning to Xanth with MareAnn. Lacuna returns to a changed Xanth, one where she is married with children, thus finding her purpose.

**Other books you might like:**
Robert Asprin, *Another Fine Myth*, 1978
Suzette Haden Elgin, *And Then There'll Be Fireworks*, 1981
Suzette Haden Elgin, *The Grand Jubilee*, 1981
Suzette Haden Elgin, *Twelve Fair Kingdoms*, 1981
Alan Dean Foster, *Spellsinger*, 1983
Christopher Stasheff, *The Warlock in Spite of Himself*, 1969

**187**

PIERS ANTHONY

*Roc and a Hard Place*

(New York: Tor, 1995)

**Story type:** Fantasy (Light Fantasy)
**Series:** Xanth
**Major character(s):** Metria "Woe Betide", Demon; Grossclout, Professor, Demon; Roxanne Roc, Mythical Creature (roc)
**Time period(s):** Indeterminate
**Locale(s):** Emerald Mountains, Mythical Place; Xanth, Fictional Country

**Summary:** Consulting with the Good Magician Humfrey on a way to get the stork to heed her summons, Metria must first assemble the judge and jury to try Roxanne Roc for breaking the Adult Conspiracy. After solving some problems along the way and travelling to Mundania, the trial begins with Professor Grossclout as judge.

**Other books you might like:**
Robert Asprin, *Myth-ing Persons*, 1984
C. Dale Brittain, *A Bad Spell in Yurt*, 1991
Suzette Haden Elgin, *Twelve Fair Kingdoms*, 1981
Alan Dean Foster, *Son of Spellsinger*, 1993
Diana Wynne Jones, *Castle in the Air*, 1991
Andre Norton, *Dragon Magic*, 1972
Terry Pratchett, *Witches Abroad*, 1993

---

**188**

PIERS ANTHONY

## Shame of Man

(New York: Tor, 1994)

**Story type:** Science Fiction (Family Saga; Adventure)
**Series:** Geodyssey
**Major character(s):** Hu ''Hugh'', Musician, Parent; Ann ''Annai'',
   Dancer, Parent; Minnie ''Miin'', Psychic, Child
**Time period(s):** Indeterminate Past
**Locale(s):** Earth

**Summary:** Hu, Ann and their children experience love, hate and
betrayal at the hands of Bub and Sis in their many guises from
8,000,000 B.C. to 2050 A.D. The separate incidents in different
times and places yield the story of how Hugh and his family manage
to determine that humanity's appetites need curbing to save the
Earth.

**Other books you might like:**
Brian W. Aldiss, *Cryptozoic*, 1968
Roger MacBride Allen, *Orphan of Creation*, 1988
Poul Anderson, *The Boat of a Million Years*, 1989
Neal Barrett Jr., *Dawn's Uncertain Light*, 1989
Michael Bishop, *No Enemy but Time*, 1982
John Brunner, *The Tides of Time*, 1982
Philip Jose Farmer, *Traitor to the Living*, 1973
Crawford Kilian, *The Empire of Time*, 1978
Garry Kilworth, *Split Second*, 1985
Harry Turtledove, *A Different Flesh*, 1988

---

**189**

PIERS ANTHONY
CLIFFORD A. PICKOVER, Co-Author

## Spider Legs

(New York: Tor, 1998)

**Story type:** Science Fiction (Genetic Manipulation; Horror)
**Major character(s):** Natalie Shepard, Police Officer; Elmo Samules,
   Civil Servant; Martha Samules, Scientist
**Time period(s):** Indeterminate Future
**Locale(s):** Greenland; Atlantic Ocean

**Summary:** A disgruntled scientist decides that humans are not fit to
rule the world, so she alters the DNA of a marine lifeform so that it
grows to gigantic sizes. One of the first of her creations rises from the
ocean to attack the crew of surface vessels and then heads toward
land.

**Other books you might like:**
Peter Benchley, *White Shark*, 1994
Murray Leinster, *Creatures of the Abyss*, 1961
J.M. Morgan, *Between the Devil and the Deep*, 1992
Charles Wilson, *Extinct*, 1997
John Wyndham, *Out of the Deeps*, 1953

---

**190**

PIERS ANTHONY, Editor
RICHARD GILLIAM, Co-Editor

## Tales From the Great Turtle

(New York: Tor, 1994)

**Story type:** Fantasy (Anthology; Legend)

**Summary:** Contains a three-page introduction by Anthony, a two-
page afterword by Gilliam, three pages of biographical notes on the
authors, two reprinted and 27 original stories all sharing native
American themes. Authors include Piers Anthony, Jack Dann, Esther
M. Friesner, Ed Gorman, Brad Linaweaver, Mike Resnick, Kristine
Kathryn Rusch, William Sanders, Pamela Sargent, Steve Rasnic Tem
and Jane Yolen.

**Other books you might like:**
Richard Erdoes, *American Indian Myths and Legends*, 1984
   Alfonso Ortiz, co-author
Alan Dean Foster, *Cyber Way*, 1990
Richard Gilliam, *Grails: Quests of the Dawn*, 1994
   Martin H. Greenberg, Edward E. Kramer, co-editors
Barry Lopez, *Crow and Weasel*, 1990
Howard Norman, *Northern Tales: Traditional Stories of Eskimo and
   Indian Peoples*, 1980
Gerald Vizenor, *Dead Voices: Natural Agonies in the Real World*,
   1992
Roger Welsch, *Touching the Fire*, 1992

---

**191**

PIERS ANTHONY

## Tatham Mound

(New York: Morrow, 1991)

**Story type:** Fantasy (Quest; Historical)
**Major character(s):** Tale Teller, Indian (Tocobaga), Companion
   (translator); Hernando De Soto, Historical Figure, Explorer
**Time period(s):** 16th century (1510s & 1540s)
**Locale(s):** Florida; South

**Summary:** Wounded, Hotfoot is visited by an ancestor, Dead Eagle,
who reveals to him a sacred mission. He takes the name Throatshot,
and becomes apprenticed to a trader. In his wanderings he learns
languages and takes the name, Tale Teller. His linguistic skill leads
to his accompanying Hernando De Soto as translator while De Soto
explores.

**Other books you might like:**
Orson Scott Card, *Seventh Son*, 1987
Sue Harrison, *Mother Earth, Father Sky*, 1990
J. Alison James, *Sing for a Gentle Rain*, 1990
William Sarabande, *Beyond the Sea of Ice*, 1987
Robert Shea, *Shaman*, 1991
Catherine Wells, *The Earth Is All That Lasts*, 1991
Roger Zelazny, *Bridge of Ashes*, 1976

---

**192**

PIERS ANTHONY
ROBERT KORNWISE, Co-Author

## Through the Ice

(Lancaster, PA: Underwood-Miller, 1989)

**Story type:** Fantasy (Alternate World)

**Major character(s):** Seth Warner, Hero
**Time period(s):** 1990s
**Locale(s):** Earth; Alternate Earth (Parellel plane of existence)

**Summary:** Trying to escape from punks about to beat him up, Seth falls into a world populated by fairies, trolls and elves. He joins a band of heroes (the Chosen) who are trying to defeat the evil sorceror, Nefarious, and save Earth's planes of existence.

**Other books you might like:**
Ray Garton, *Methods of Madness*, 1990
Peni R. Griffin, *Otto From Otherwhere*, 1990
Shirley Rousseau Murphy, *Medallion of the Black Hound*, 1989
　　Welch Suggs, co-author
J. Michael Straczynski, *OtherSyde*, 1990

### 193

PIERS ANTHONY

## Total Recall

(New York: William Morrow, 1989)

**Story type:** Science Fiction (Adventure)
**Major character(s):** Douglas Quail, Construction Worker; Melina, Prostitute
**Time period(s):** Indeterminate Future
**Locale(s):** Earth; Mars

**Summary:** Douglas Quail is a construction worker with a boring job and a beautiful wife, but he keeps dreaming about having adventures on Mars. Hoping to come to terms with these disturbing dreams, he goes to Rekall, a corporation which creates artificial memories. An ersatz vacation on Mars, with all the tourist trimmings, will, he hopes, satisfy whatever buried urge is behind the dreams. Something goes wrong, however, and Quail discovers that his dreams are terribly real. Film novelization based on Philip K. Dick's ''We Can Remember It for you Wholesale.''

**Other books you might like:**
Philip K. Dick, *Do Androids Dream of Electric Sheep?*, 1968
Philip K. Dick, *Flow My Tears, the Policeman Said*, 1974
Philip K. Dick, *A Scanner Darkly*, 1977
Philip K. Dick, *Time Out of Joint*, 1959
Sharon Webb, *The Halflife*, 1989

### 194

PIERS ANTHONY

## Virtual Mode

(New York: Ace/Putnam, 1991)

**Story type:** Fantasy (Quest)
**Series:** Virtual Mode
**Major character(s):** Colene, Teenager, Adventurer; Darius, Ruler (Cyng of Pwer); Seqiro, Animal (intelligent horse), Telepath
**Time period(s):** 1990s
**Locale(s):** Oklahoma, Alternate Universe

**Summary:** Colene, an unhappy 14-year-old who has tried suicide, rescues Darius. As she nurses him back to health she is happy, but does not believe his claim that he comes from another dimension until he disappears. While he tries to search for her by creating a path between the two dimensions, Colene sets off to find him and finds Seqiro instead. The two travel until captured by Ddwng. During Darius' search, he also gets captured by Ddwng and is forced to complete an interplanetary mission before he can claim Colene. Once united the two set off and are hailed by Nona in a strange dimension.

**Other books you might like:**
Jack L. Chalker, *The River of Dancing Gods*, 1984
C.J. Cherryh, *Rusalka*, 1989
Alan Dean Foster, *Spellsinger*, 1983
Diana Wynne Jones, *Fire and Hemlock*, 1984
Christopher Stasheff, *Her Majesty's Wizard*, 1986

### 195

PIERS ANTHONY
ALFRED TELLA, Co-Author

## The Willing Spirit

(New York: Tor, 1996)

**Story type:** Fantasy (Legend; Quest)
**Major character(s):** Hari, Religious (Brahmin), Adventurer; Mohini, Deity; Ravana, Deity, Demon
**Time period(s):** Indeterminate Past
**Locale(s):** India

**Summary:** The Immortals Mohini and Ravana play a game. If Mohini, in the persona of a mortal woman, can seduce Hari seven times, she wins and Ravana earns banishment for a century. If Ravana, through mortal men, can kill Hari, he wins and Mohini must provide him with a century of erotic frenzy. Meanwhile, Hari wishes only to see a bit of the world. Based on Indian myths and legends.

**Other books you might like:**
John Brunner, *The Traveler in Black*, 1971
Kara Dalkey, *Goa*, 1996
L. Sprague de Camp, *The Golden Wind*, 1969
Rudyard Kipling, *Famous Tales of India*, 1962
Mack Reynolds, *Space Search*, 1984
Chelsea Quinn Yarbro, *The Path of the Eclipse*, 1981
Roger Zelazny, *Lord of Light*, 1967

### 196

PIERS ANTHONY

## Yon Ill Wind

(New York: Tor, 1996)

**Story type:** Fantasy (Light Fantasy; Quest)
**Series:** Xanth
**Major character(s):** X(A/N)$^{th}$ ''Nimby'', Demon, Handicapped (mute); Chlorine, Runaway, Adventurer; Sean Baldwin, Teenager, Vacationer
**Time period(s):** Indeterminate
**Locale(s):** Xanth, Fictional Country

**Summary:** As they return from vacation, a hurricane blows the Baldwin family into Xanth where they encounter Nimby, travelling in mortal form because of a bet, along with his human companion, Chlorine. Chlorine must escort the Baldwins safely out of Xanth after harnessing the hurricane which has followed the Baldwins there.

**Other books you might like:**
Robert Asprin, *Another Fine Myth*, 1978
K.B. Bogen, *Go Quest, Young Man*, 1993
Susan Cooper, *Silver on the Tree*, 1977
Alan Dean Foster, *Spellsinger*, 1983
Diana Wynne Jones, *Hexwood*, 1994
Andre Norton, *Here Abide Monsters*, 1973
Terry Pratchett, *Reaper Man*, 1992
Christopher Stasheff, *M'Lady Witch*, 1994

## 197

**PIERS ANTHONY**

### Zombie Lover

(New York: Tor, 1998)

**Story type:** Fantasy (Light Fantasy; Adventure)
**Series:** Xanth
**Major character(s):** Breanna, Teenager, Explorer; Bink, Grandparent, Royalty; Justin Tree, Companion, Disembodied Personality
**Time period(s):** Indeterminate
**Locale(s):** Xanth, Fictional Country; Ptero, Moon—Imaginary

**Summary:** Breanna seeks out Good Magician Humfrey, hoping to find relief from the attentions of the zombie prince, while King Dor, Prince Dolph, and the rejuvenated Bink want to find out what unsettles the zombies.

**Other books you might like:**
Poul Anderson, *Hoka!*, 1983
   Gordon R. Dickson, co-author
Robert Asprin, *Sweet Myth-tery of Life*, 1994
L. Frank Baum, *The Emerald City of Oz*, 1910
Jack L. Chalker, *Songs of the Dancing Gods*, 1990
Alan Dean Foster, *Chorus Skating*, 1994
Esther Friesner, *Majyk by Accident*, 1993
Terry Pratchett, *The Colour of Magic*, 1983
Christopher Stasheff, *Warlock and Son*, 1991

## 198

**KIM ANTIEAU**

### The Gaia Websters

(New York: Roc, 1997)

**Story type:** Science Fiction (Post-Disaster; Robot Fiction)
**Major character(s):** Gloria Stone, Healer (soothsayer), Robot; Primer, Government Official; Thomas Church, Religious (reverend)
**Time period(s):** 25th century
**Locale(s):** Grand Canyon, Arizona; Arizona Territy, Southwest; Coyote Creek, Arizona

**Summary:** Awakening in a cave with no memories, Gloria Stone refuses to recognize herself as a Soothsayer, finding the life of healer for Coyote Creek very satisfying. After Primer poisons the water, Gloria finally agrees to see the governor, if only to complain about his agent, Primer. Disaster follows Gloria, forcing her to discover the truth about herself and her past and, perhaps, permitting a better future for all.

**Other books you might like:**
Roger MacBride Allen, *Utopia*, 1996
Emma Bull, *Bone Dance: A Fantasy for Technophiles*, 1991
Sheri S. Tepper, *A Plague of Angels*, 1993
Amy Thomson, *Virtual Girl*, 1993
Michael D. Weaver, *A Second Infinity*, 1996
Jack Williamson, *The Humanoids*, 1996

## 199

**KIM ANTIEAU**

### The Jigsaw Woman

(New York: Roc, 1996)

**Story type:** Fantasy (Legend; Time Travel)
**Major character(s):** Keelie, Reanimated Dead, Psychic; Victor Beaufort, Scientist; Lee, Abuse Victim
**Time period(s):** Indeterminate Past
**Locale(s):** Earth

**Summary:** Dr. Victor Beaufort creates Keelie from the body parts of three women and brings her to life. Not content to remain his companion, Keelie searches for her true identity, and learns that she has encountered the same three women and her creator continually throughout human history. First novel.

**Other books you might like:**
Michael Bishop, *Brittle Innings*, 1994
Amarantha Knight, *The Darker Passions: Frankenstein*, 1995
Jamil Nasir, *The Higher Space*, 1996
Christopher Pike, *The Season of Passage*, 1992
Christopher Pike, *The Starlight Crystal*, 1996
Mary Shelley, *Frankenstein*, 1818

## 200

**KIM ANTIEAU**

### Trudging to Eden

(Woodinville, Washington: Silver Salamander Press, 1994)

**Story type:** Horror (Collection)

**Summary:** This first collection by a writer of fantasy, horror, and science fiction brings together 12 stories, six original to the volume. "Listening for the General" blends horror with magic realism in its tale of a woman's revenge on a banana republic military officer. In "Cycles," an Appalachian family shows a strange fecundity that spans the generations. "Fractures" tells of a multiple personality created by a woman's absorption of ghosts, and "Lab Rats" reflects on the near-future possibilities of laboratory animal experimentation. "Mark of the Beast" is a variation on the werewolf story, and "The Girl with No Hair" on a tale of witchcraft. Charles de Lint supplies an introduction.

**Other books you might like:**
Jack Cady, *The Sons of Noah and Other Stories*, 1993
Nina Kiriki Hoffman, *Common Threads*, 1995
Steve Rasnic Tem, *Celestial Inventory*, 1991
Chet Williamson, *The House of Fear*, 1989

## 201

**ALLEN APPEL**

### Till the End of Time

(New York: Doubleday, 1990)

**Story type:** Fantasy (Contemporary; Time Travel)
**Series:** Alex Balfour
**Major character(s):** Alex Balfour, Historian; Molly Glenn, Journalist
**Time period(s):** 1990s; 1940s
**Locale(s):** New York, New York; Japan

**Summary:** Alex, like his father and grandfather, is fascinated with the past. This time Alex finds himself drawn physically to December 7, 1941, Pearl Harbor, Hawaii. When Alex tries to convince President Roosevelt not to drop the bomb on Japan, the President sends Alex there to find out what is really happening in that part of the world. Meanwhile, in 1990, Molly Glenn, his girlfriend, is in Japan working on a story. ALA Best Books For Young Adults title.

**Other books you might like:**
Alan Brennert, *Time and Chance*, 1990
Philip K. Dick, *The Man in the High Castle*, 1963
Ken Grimwood, *Replay*, 1986
David Wingrove, *The Middle Kingdom*, 1990

## 202

**KEN APPLEBY**

### The Voice of Cepheus

(New York: Ballantine/Del Rey, 1989)

**Story type:** Science Fiction (First Contact)
**Major character(s):** Sheilagh Mathews, Student, Astronaut; Adrian Holdsworth, Scientist (Astronomer)
**Time period(s):** 21st century (2001)
**Locale(s):** *Unity*, Spaceship

**Summary:** Signals are received from an alien race in the direction of the star Cepheus. Once interpreted, the signals provide information that leads to a technological revolution. Humanity sends a spacecraft to contact the aliens, but it is disabled. The marooned crew establishes contact with the friendly Cepheans and a utopian age of exploration begins. This is Appleby's first novel.

**Other books you might like:**
Arthur C. Clarke, *Childhood's End*, 1953
Edward Gibson, *Reach*, 1989
Jack McDevitt, *The Hercules Text*, 1986
Carl Sagan, *Contact*, 1985
David Alexander Smith, *Rendezvous*, 1988

## 203

**RISA ARATYR**

### Hunter of the Light

(New York: HarperPrism, 1995)

**Story type:** Fantasy (Legend; Adventure)
**Major character(s):** Blackthorn, Minstrel (bard), Hero
**Time period(s):** Indeterminate Past
**Locale(s):** Ireland (Eirinn)

**Summary:** More comfortable as entertainer than as warrior, Blackthorn, now chosen champion, must stalk and kill the white dreamstag to preserve the balance between light and dark. Author's first novel.

**Other books you might like:**
Greg Bear, *Songs of Earth and Power*, 1994
Charles de Lint, *Greenmantle*, 1988
Charles de Lint, *Moonheart: A Romance*, 1984
Kenneth C. Flint, *Riders of the Sidhe*, 1984
Casey Flynn, *Most Ancient Song*, 1991
Morgan Llywelyn, *Bard: The Odyssey of the Irish*, 1984
Patricia A. McKillip, *The Book of Atrix Wolfe*, 1995

## 204

**JOHN ARBUCCI**

### Blood of Innocents

(New York: Onyx, 1991)

**Story type:** Horror (Wild Talents)
**Major character(s):** Jack Rigger, Child; Clark Ashton, Doctor; Francis Chapin, Teacher
**Time period(s):** 1990s (1991)
**Locale(s):** Brookline, Massachusetts

**Summary:** The discovery that young Jack Rigger can hurt and heal himself at will is a godsend for Dr. Clark Ashton, who hopes to use the boy's talent to rehabilitate his flagging bioengineering company.

What Ashton doesn't know is that Jack can also inflict his talents on those persons whom he does not like. This is the author's first novel.

**Other books you might like:**
John Farris, *The Fury*, 1976

## 205

**NATHAN ARCHER** (Pseudonym of Lawrence Watt-Evans)

### Martian Deathtrap

(New York: Ballantine Del Rey, 1996)

**Story type:** Science Fiction (Invasion of Earth)
**Series:** Mars Attacks
**Major character(s):** Bud Garcia, Resistance Fighter; Katie Winters, Child, Resistance Fighter; Quisaz Hadrak, Alien (Martian), Military Personnel
**Time period(s):** 1990s
**Locale(s):** United States

**Summary:** When Bud hides under the trees to avoid an attack, Martians release powerful bioactive agents which produce unforeseen results, giant insects which threaten humans and Martians alike, as Bud and others struggle to repel the invaders. Film and comic book tie-in originating from rare 1962 Topps trading cards.

**Other books you might like:**
Kevin J. Anderson, *War of the Worlds: Global Dispatches*, 1996 editor
David Brin, *Earth*, 1990
Jonathan Gems, *Mars Attacks!*, 1996
Ray W. Murrill, *War Dogs of the Golden Horde*, 1996
Larry Niven, *Footfall*, 1985
Jerry Pournelle, co-author
H.G. Wells, *The War of the Worlds*, 1898

## 206

**NATHAN ARCHER** (Pseudonym of Lawrence Watt-Evans)

### Ragnarok

(New York: Pocket, 1995)

**Story type:** Science Fiction (Space Opera)
**Series:** Star Trek: Voyager
**Major character(s):** Kathryn Janeway, Spaceship Captain, Military Personnel, Space Explorer; Tuvok, Security Officer, Alien (Vulcan); Chakotay, Military Personnel (commander), Indian
**Time period(s):** 24th century
**Locale(s):** *U.S.S. Voyager*, Spaceship; Outer Space

**Summary:** The *Voyager* crew detects a tetryon beam that may originate in a device capable of transporting them back to the Federation. As they approach the site, they find themselves in the midst of a battle between two species which has raged for hundreds of years. Hoping to negotiate a peace that would allow them to examine the source of the tetryon beam, Janeway attempts to communicate with the warring sides, but succeeds only in attracting the hostile fire from ships on both sides.

**Other books you might like:**
Gordon R. Dickson, *Soldier, Ask Not*, 1967
David Drake, *Ranks of Bronze*, 1986
Brad Ferguson, *The Last Stand*, 1995
Joe Haldeman, *The Forever War*, 1974
Robert A. Heinlein, *Starship Troopers*, 1959
Lawrence Watt-Evans, *Crosstime Traffic*, 1992
Lawrence Watt-Evans, *Out of This World*, 1994
Susan Wright, *Violations*, 1995

## 207

**PETER ARCHER**, Editor

### Rath and Storm

(Renton, Washington: Wizards of the Coast, 1998)

**Story type:** Fantasy (Anthology)

**Summary:** A collection of nine original stories set in the magical realm created by the Magic: The Gathering role playing card game. Contributors include J. Robert King, Kij Johnson, and Liz Holiday.

**Other books you might like:**
Clayton Emery, *Whispering Woods*, 1995
William R. Forstchen, *Arena*, 1994
Sonia Orin Lyris, *And Peace Shall Sleep*, 1996
Mark Sumner, *The Prodigal Sorcerer*, 1995
Robert E. Vardeman, *Dark Legacy*, 1996

## 208

**MICHAEL ARMSTRONG**

### Agviq

(New York: Popular Library Questar, 1990)

**Story type:** Science Fiction (Post-Nuclear Holocaust; Contemporary Realism)
**Major character(s):** Claudia, Scientist, Anthropologist; Rob, Student—College
**Time period(s):** 1990s
**Locale(s):** Barrow, Alaska; Utqiagvik, Alaska

**Summary:** Claudia and Rob are on a dig studying the old Innuit culture. When a radio broadcast warns them that a nuclear holocaust has occurred, they take shelter in the Innuit home they've uncovered. When they come out three weeks later they must survive in a world heading for nuclear winter without the support of a technological society. This novel was expanded from the 1985 short story, "Going After Arvig."

**Other books you might like:**
Suzy McKee Charnas, *Motherlines*, 1979
Suzy McKee Charnas, *Walk to the End of the World*, 1974
Gordon R. Dickson, *Wolf and Iron*, 1990
W. Michael Gear, *People of the Wolf*, 1990
   Kathleen O'Neal Gear, co-author
Donald E. McQuinn, *Warrior*, 1990
R.M. Meluch, *Chicago Red*, 1990
Paul O. Williams, *The Breaking of Northwall*, 1981

## 209

**MICHAEL ARMSTRONG**

### The Hidden War

(Lake Geneva, Wisconsin: TSR, 1994)

**Story type:** Science Fiction (Military; Arts)
**Major character(s):** Krim, Military Personnel, Spaceman (pilot)
**Time period(s):** Indeterminate Future
**Locale(s):** Earth; *Jeanne Kirkpatrick*, Spaceship

**Summary:** After serving half of his 30-year sentence for opposing Earth forces' attack of the Jack, a free asteroid settlement based on beat poetry, Krim receives a "hide," a protective outer skin, and an early release with the request that he fight for the new Solarian Alliance against the Terrorons, invaders from light years distant.

Aboard the *Jeanne Kirkpatrick*, Krim learns more about the covert aspects of the space forces.

**Other books you might like:**
Glen Cook, *The Dragon Never Sleeps*, 1988
Marjorie Bradley Kellogg, *Harmony*, 1991
Melisa C. Michaels, *First Battle*, 1985
Janet Morris, *Dream Dancer*, 1981
Clifford D. Simak, *Shakespeare's Planet*, 1976

## 210

**ELEANOR ARNASON**

### Ring of Swords

(New York: Tor, 1993)

**Story type:** Science Fiction (Gay/Lesbian Fiction; Military)
**Major character(s):** Anna Perez, Diplomat, Scientist; Ettin Gwarha, Diplomat (First Defenders), Alien (Hwarhath); Nicholas Sanders, Linguist
**Time period(s):** 22nd century
**Locale(s):** Planet—Imaginary; Space Station

**Summary:** After Anna Perez acts honorably toward them, Hwarhath negotiators demand that she attend talks which will determine humanity's status as intelligent beings, a discussion with culture-shattering potential. Little prepared for diplomacy by her scientific education, Anna discovers she and a perceived traitor, Nicholas Sanders, represent humanity's best hope of avoiding destruction.

**Other books you might like:**
David Brin, *Glory Season*, 1993
Octavia E. Butler, *Survivor*, 1978
Helen Collins, *Mutagenesis*, 1993
Diana G. Gallagher, *The Alien Dark*, 1990
Nicola Griffith, *Ammonite*, 1993
Joan Slonczewski, *Daughter of Elysium*, 1993
Joan Slonczewski, *A Door into Ocean*, 1986
David Alexander Smith, *Homecoming*, 1990

## 211

**ELEANOR ARNASON**

### A Woman of the Iron People

(New York: Morrow, 1991)

**Story type:** Science Fiction (First Contact)
**Major character(s):** Nia, Alien; Li Lixia, Linguist, Sociologist
**Time period(s):** 23rd century
**Locale(s):** Sigma Draconis II, Planet—Imaginary

**Summary:** After the remaining countries on Earth recover from the devastation left by the 20th century, they send out an interstellar exploratory expedition which finds intelligent, humanoid, furry aliens on an Earth-like planet. Lixia is one of a dozen social scientists dropped on different parts of the planet who contact the local inhabitants and learn their customs, languages and cultures. Since the potentially dangerous, mature, breeding males do not live in the alien villages, male humans have difficulty interacting with the villagers.

**Other books you might like:**
Ursula K. Le Guin, *Always Coming Home*, 1987
Ursula K. Le Guin, *The Left Hand of Darkness*, 1969
Judith Moffett, *Pennterra*, 1987
Joan Slonczewski, *The Wall Around Eden*, 1989
Joan Slonczewski, *A Door into Ocean*, 1986
Joan Slonczewski, *Still Forms on Foxfield*, 1980
L. Neil Smith, *Contact and Commune*, 1990

## 212

**MICHAEL A. ARNZEN**

### Grave Markings

(New York: Dell/Abyss, 1994)

**Story type:** Horror (Serial Killer)
**Major character(s):** Mark Michael Kilpatrick, Artist (tattoo artist), Serial Killer; Roy Roberts, Journalist; John Lockerman, Police Officer
**Time period(s):** 1990s (1994)
**Locale(s):** Colorado Springs, Colorado

**Summary:** A handful of concerned citizens band together to rid Colorado Springs of a bizarre serial killer who leaves his victims covered with full-body tattoos. Alternating between omniscient and subjective viewpoints, this first novel details the twisted mind of Mark Michael Kilpatrick, a tattoo artist who never overcame his abuse as a child and now vents it through destructive creativity.

**Other books you might like:**
Poppy Z. Brite, *Drawing Blood*, 1993
Michael Cadnum, *Skyscape*, 1994
Kathe Koja, *Skin*, 1993
Kathe Koja, *Strange Angels*, 1994
Jessica Amanda Salmonson, *Anthony Shriek*, 1991

## 213

**MICHAEL A. ARNZEN**
**MARGE B. SIMON**, Illustrator

### Needles and Sins

(Concord, California: Dark Regions Press, 1993)

**Story type:** Horror (Collection)

**Summary:** This chapbook collects 11 stories, three of which are original to the book. ''An Eye for An Eye,'' ''Marked'' and ''Copycats'' share the common theme of the strange clients of tattoo artists, while ''Counterpoint,'' ''Phrenological Love,'' and ''Spring Ahead, Fall Back'' are about psychopaths masquerading as normal human beings. ''The Spirit of the Bayonet'' follows the escapades of a soldier driven crazy by boot camp. The stories are introduced by Karl Edward Wagner. This is the author's first book.

**Other books you might like:**
Edward Bryant, *Darker Passions*, 1992
Adam-Troy Castro, *Lost in Booth Nine*, 1993
Lucy Taylor, *Unnatural Acts*, 1992

## 214

**LOU ARONICA**

### Full Spectrum 2

(New York: Bantam Spectra, 1990)

**Story type:** Science Fiction (Anthology)
**Series:** Full Spectrum
**Time period(s):** Indeterminate

**Summary:** This collection of 27 short stories aims at investigating the entire realm of new ''speculative fiction.'' Some of this book's better-known authors include Greg Bear, David Brin, Edward Bryant, Vonda N. McIntyre, Patricia A. McKillip, Kim Stanley Robinson, Michaela Roessner and Michael Swanwick. Some of the newer authors include Carolyn Ives Gilman, Karen Haber and Elizabeth Hand. Reprint of 1989 Doubleday Foundation hardcover edition.

**Other books you might like:**
Isaac Asimov, *Isaac Asimov Presents the Great SF Stories: 21 (1959)*, 1990
  Martin H. Greenberg, co-editor
Groff Conklin, *The Best of Science Fiction*, 1946
Gardner Dozois, *The Year's Best Science Fiction: Seventh Annual Collection*, 1990
Harlan Ellison, *Dangerous Visions*, 1967
Raymond J. Healy, *Adventures in Time and Space*, 1946
  J. Francis McComas, co-editor
Robert Silverberg, *The Science Fiction Hall of Fame, Volume 1*, 1970
Donald A. Wollheim, *The 1990 Annual World's Best Science Fiction*, 1990
  Arthur W. Saha, co-editor

## 215

**LOU ARONICA**, Editor
**AMY STOUT**, Co-Editor
**BETSY MITCHELL**, Co-Editor

### Full Spectrum 3

(New York: Doubleday Foundation, 1991)

**Story type:** Science Fiction (Anthology)
**Series:** Full Spectrum

**Summary:** This volume contains an introduction by Lou Aronica plus 23 stories original to this anthology whose themes range from magical realism to hard science fiction. Better-known authors herein include Poul Anderson, Gregory Benford, Michael Bishop, Ursula K. Le Guin, Barry N. Malzberg, James Morrow and Norman Spinrad. Some notable authors newer to the genres include Kevin J. Anderson, Karen Joy Fowler, Elizabeth Hand, Peg Kerr, Jack McDevitt, Kristine Kathryn Rusch, Nancy Willard and David Zindell. One story, ''Desert Rain,'' is a collaborative effort by Mark L. Van Name and Pat Murphy. Two stories originally written in foreign languages appear herein. Kim Stanley Robinson translated Joelle Wintrebert's ''Transfusion'' from French and Sally Schiller and Anne Calveley translated Wolfgang Jeschke's ''Loitering at Death's Door'' from German.

**Other books you might like:**
Michael Bishop, *Nebula Awards 25*, 1991
  editor
Ellen Datlow, *The Year's Best Fantasy and Horror: Fourth Annual Collection*, 1991
  Terri Windling, co-editor
Gardner Dozois, *The Year's Best Science Fiction: Eighth Annual Collection*, 1991
  editor
Harlan Ellison, *Dangerous Visions*, 1967
  editor
Robert Silverberg, *The Science Fiction Hall of Fame, Volume 1*, 1970
  editor
Donald A. Wollheim, *The 1990 Annual World's Best Science Fiction*, 1990
  Arthur W. Saha, co-editor
George Zebrowski, *Nebula Awards 22*, 1988
  editor

## 216

LOU ARONICA, Editor
AMY STOUT, Co-Editor
BETSY MITCHELL, Co-Editor

### Full Spectrum 4

(New York: Bantam Spectra, 1993)

**Story type:** Science Fiction (Anthology)
**Series:** Full Spectrum

**Summary:** Includes one poem by Ursula K. Le Guin, six pages of biographical notes about the authors and editors plus 19 original stories, several with themes of a sexual nature and several about aliens; other themes include nanotechnology, psychology and terraforming. Authors include Ray Aldridge, Kevin J. Anderson, David Brin, Stephen R. Donaldson, Gregory Feeley, Elizabeth Hand, Nancy Kress, Dave Smeds and Martha Soukup.

**Other books you might like:**
Ellen Datlow, *Omni Best Science Fiction Three*, 1993
    editor
Gardner Dozois, *The Year's Best Science Fiction: Tenth Annual Collection*, 1993
    editor
James Morrow, *Nebula Awards 27*, 1993
    editor
Kristine Kathryn Rusch, *The Best of Pulphouse: The Hardback Magazine*, 1991
    editor
Robert Silverberg, *Universe 2*, 1992
    Karen Haber, co-editor

## 217

BRUCE D. ARTHURS, Editor

### Copper Star

(Tempe, Arizona: 1991 World Fantasy Convention, 1991)

**Story type:** Horror (Anthology)

**Summary:** This special anthology for the 1991 World Fantasy Convention brings together 16 original stories and poems of horror and fantasy with a southwestern orientation. Included are Mike Newland's tale of a ghostly encounter in the desert, "Carrion Eaters"; Ed Bryant's satire on the difference between the horror of country and city life, "Country Mouse"; Norman Partridge's story of a boxer's mystic origins, "The Cut Man"; and Jeanette M. Hopper's tale of a midwife's horrifying experience delivering a child born in desert heat, "Swelter."

**Other books you might like:**
Stephen Jones, *Gaslight and Ghosts*, 1988
    Jo Fletcher, co-editor
Joe R. Lansdale, *Razored Saddles*, 1989
    Pat LoBrutto, co-editor
Joe R. Lansdale, *The New Frontier*, 1989
Kathryn Ptacek, *Women of the West*, 1990
Frank D. McSherry Jr., *Western Ghosts*, 1990
    Charles G. Waugh and Martin D. Greenberg, co-editors

## 218

CATHERINE ASARO

### Catch the Lightning

(New York: Tor, 1996)

**Story type:** Science Fiction (Adventure; Genetic Manipulation)
**Series:** Skolian Empire
**Major character(s):** Akushtina "Tina" Santis Pulivok, Waiter/Waitress, Psychic; Althor, Military Personnel (Jagernaut Secondary), Psychic; Kryx Iquar, Alien, Psychic
**Time period(s):** 1980s (1987); Indeterminate Future
**Locale(s):** Los Angeles, California; The Cylinder, Space Station

**Summary:** Tina meets a weird man on the way home from work, discovering that he comes not only from another planet, but another universe and another time. Recognizing a psychic connection, she helps Althor escape from her government and universe, only to find far more subtle dangers in his universe.

**Other books you might like:**
Marion Zimmer Bradley, *The Forbidden Tower*, 1977
Emma Bull, *Bone Dance: A Fantasy for Technophiles*, 1991
Anne McCaffrey, *The Rowan*, 1990
K.D. Wentworth, *Moonspeaker*, 1994
Walter Jon Williams, *Metropolitan*, 1995

## 219

CATHERINE ASARO

### The Last Hawk

(New York: Tor, 1997)

**Story type:** Science Fiction (Adventure; Psychic Powers)
**Series:** Skolian Empire
**Major character(s):** Kelricson Garlin Valdoria kva Skolia, Nobleman, Psychic; Bolt, Artificial Intelligence; Deha Dahl, Government Official (bureaucrat)
**Time period(s):** Indeterminate (10th century of the Modern Age)
**Locale(s):** Coba, Planet—Imaginary

**Summary:** Kelric, heir to the Skolian Empire, crashes on a planet whose matriarchal government heals him, but destroys his ship to preserve their culture. While he finds love and some contentment, Kelric also recognizes his status as a prisoner and a pawn in a game he must learn to play, then master, if he wants his life to be his own. Third in series.

**Other books you might like:**
Eleanor Arnason, *Ring of Swords*, 1993
Iain M. Banks, *The Player of Games*, 1989
Marion Zimmer Bradley, *The Forbidden Tower*, 1977
Andre Norton, *Witch World*, 1963
K.D. Wentworth, *Moonspeaker*, 1994

## 220

CATHERINE ASARO

### Primary Inversion

(New York: Tor, 1995)

**Story type:** Science Fiction (Political; Psychic Powers)
**Major character(s):** Sauscony Valdoria, Genetically Altered Being (esper); Rex Blackstone, Military Personnel, Pilot (spaceship); J'briol Qox, Genetically Altered Being (esper), Heir
**Time period(s):** Indeterminate Future

**Locale(s):** Delos, Planet—Imaginary; Foreshires Hold, Planet—Imaginary; Allied Worlds of Earth, Interstellar Empire/Federation

**Summary:** While on the Earth Alliance world, Delos, Sauscony of Skolia discovers J'briol, supposedly Aristo, heir to the Trader empire. Once enslaved by an Aristo, she recognizes he lacks the empathic void of a true Aristo when they discover a psychic bond. J'briol refuses to accept the truth about the Aristos, risking his life and sanity and a potential end to the war between the Skolians and the Traders. First novel.

**Other books you might like:**
Jeffrey A. Carver, *Dragons in the Stars*, 1992
Michelle Shirey Crean, *Dancer of the Sixth*, 1993
Jacqueline Lichtenberg, *House of Zeor*, 1974
Alis A. Rasmussen, *A Passage of Stars*, 1990
Dan Simmons, *Hyperion*, 1989
David Weber, *Path of the Fury*, 1992

---

**221**

**FRANK ASCH**

## Journey to Terezor

(New York: Holiday House, 1989)

**Story type:** Science Fiction (Young Adult)
**Major character(s):** Matt Hilton, Teenager; Ryan Morrison, Scientist
**Time period(s):** 1980s
**Locale(s):** S-15, Planet—Imaginary (The planetary system of Terezor)

**Summary:** Matt Hilton and his family are kidnapped by aliens and brought to the Earth colony on another planet. Determined to regain their freedom, he and two other teenagers hatch a desperate plot to escape the colony.

**Other books you might like:**
Grace Chetwin, *Collidescope*, 1990
John Christopher, *The City of Gold and Lead*, 1967
John Christopher, *The Pool of Fire*, 1968
John Christopher, *The White Mountains*, 1967
Jo Dereske, *The Lone Sentinel*, 1989

---

**222**

**CONSTANCE ASH**

## The Stalking Horse

(New York: Ace, 1990)

**Story type:** Fantasy (Political)
**Major character(s):** Glennys Eve, Dancer (Ballerina), Horse Trainer
**Time period(s):** Indeterminate
**Locale(s):** St. Lucien, Fictional Country

**Summary:** In a world where political intrigue and social change are predominant, Glennys hopes to make the leap from horse trainer to ballerina. But she must be careful to guard the secret of her ability to communicate mind-to-mind with the horses, which are a part of the ballet company.

**Other books you might like:**
Anne McCaffrey, *Dragonflight*, 1981
Anne McCaffrey, *The White Dragon*, 1986
Jack Vance, *Suldrun's Garden*, 1983

---

**223**

**CONSTANCE ASH**

## The Stallion Queen

(New York: Ace, 1992)

**Story type:** Fantasy (Adventure)
**Series:** Horsegirl Saga
**Major character(s):** Glennys Eve, Leader, Telepath (animal); Leon, Royalty (prince)
**Time period(s):** Indeterminate
**Locale(s):** Saquave Wilderness, Fictional Country (desert)

**Summary:** Hoping to leave corruption behind with the court life, Glennys and her followers have established themselves in the Saquave Wilderness, adopting a life style compatible with nature and the environment. When, 10 winters later, Prince Leon appears, the future of the settlement comes into question.

**Other books you might like:**
Mary H. Herbert, *Dark Horse*, 1990
Mary H. Herbert, *Lightning's Daughter*, 1991
Peter Morwood, *The Horse Lord*, 1987
Mary Stanton, *The Heavenly Horse From the Outermost West*, 1988
Mary Stanton, *Piper at the Gate*, 1989

---

**224**

**MIKE ASHLEY**, Editor

## The Camelot Chronicles

(New York: Carroll & Graf, 1992)

**Story type:** Fantasy (Anthology; Legend)
**Major character(s):** Arthur, Royalty (King of the Britons); Guenevere, Royalty, Spouse; Merlin, Magician
**Time period(s):** 5th century
**Locale(s):** England

**Summary:** Contains a 2-page introduction by the editor, 7-page guide to Arthurian characters, 9-page appendix, ''Mountain Madness'' by Theordore Goodridge Roberts plus 18 stories written this century, 10 since 1980, all sharing themes which involve King Arthur and his knights. Authors of the 8 original stories and 10 stories reprinted from books and periodicals include Vera Chapman, Phyllis Ann Karr, Howard Pyle, Darrell Schweitzer, Keith Taylor, Peter Tremayne, P. G. Wodehouse and Jane Yolen, with the story, ''John, the Knight of the Lion,'' listed as traditional. Companion volume to *The Pendragon Chronicles*.

**Other books you might like:**
Marion Zimmer Bradley, *The Mists of Avalon*, 1983
Gillian Bradshaw, *Hawk of May*, 1980
Courtway Jones, *In the Shadow of the Oak King*, 1991
Sharan Newman, *Guinevere*, 1981
Howard Pyle, *The Story of King Arthur and His Knights*, 1903
Howard Pyle, *The Story of the Champions of the Round Table*, 1905
Persia Woolley, *Guinevere: The Legend in Autumn*, 1991

---

**225**

**MIKE ASHLEY**, Editor

## The Mammoth Book of Fairy Tales

(New York: Carroll & Graf, 1997)

**Story type:** Fantasy (Legend; Anthology)

**Summary:** Contains a two-page introduction and a 25-page appendix with brief biographic data about the authors and information about the 56 stories, published 1903-1997. Fairies, beasts, other mythical creatures and people inhabit modern urban and ancient rural settings. Authors include Hans Christian Andersen, L. Frank Baum, Lewis Carroll, Louise Cooper, The Brothers Grimm, Edward Lear, Tanith Lee, Walter de la Mare, Robin McKinley, Charles Perrault, Lawrence Schimel, Nancy Springer, Netta Syrett, Jessica Amanda Salmonson, Oscar Wilde and Jane Yolen.

**Other books you might like:**

Lester Del Rey, *Once upon a Time: A Treasury of Modern Fairy Tales*, 1991
  Rissa Kessler, co-editor
Gardner Dozois, *Modern Classics of Fantasy*, 1997
  editor
Jacob Ludwig Grimm, *The Complete Fairy Tales of the Brothers Grimm*, 1992
  Wilhelm Carl Grimm, co-author
Andrew Lang, *The Blue Fairy Book*, 1889
  editor
Alison Lurie, *The Oxford Book of Modern Fairy Tales*, 1993
  editor

**226**

**MIKE ASHLEY**, Editor

## The Mammoth Book of Short Horror Novels

(New York: Carroll & Graf, 1994)

**Story type:** Horror (Anthology)

**Summary:** The ten short novels collected in this anthology span 100 years and cover such subjects as a demonically possessed toy (Stephen King's ''The Monkey''), psychic possession (Arthur Conan Doyle's ''The Parasite''), ghostly visitations (Russell Kirk's ''There's a Long, Long Trail A-Winding''), nature in revolt (Lucius Shepard's ''How the Wind Spoke at Madaket''), manmade monsters (T.E.D. Klein's ''Nadelman's God''), vampirism (John Metcalfe's ''The Feasting Dead'') and ancient family curses (David Case's ''Fengriffen''). Included as well are stories by Algernon Blackwood, A.C. Benson, and Oliver Onions. This volume was originally published in 1988.

**Other books you might like:**

David G. Hartwell, *The Dark Descent*, 1987
  editor
David G. Hartwell, *Foundations of Fear*, 1993
  editor
Tim Haydock, *The Mammoth Book of Classic Chillers*, 1986
  editor
Stephen Jones, *The Mammoth Book of Terror*, 1991
  editor
Charles G. Waugh, *13 Short Horror Novels*, 1987
  Martin H. Greenberg, co-editor

**227**

**MIKE ASHLEY**, Editor

## The Merlin Chronicles

(New York: Carroll & Graf, 1995)

**Story type:** Fantasy (Anthology; Legend)
**Major character(s):** Merlin, Magician
**Time period(s):** 5th century

**Locale(s):** Camelot, England

**Summary:** Subtitled, ''Magic and Adventure From the Age of Legend,'' this volume contains a seven-page guide to Arthurian characters, a 15-page introduction and individual introductions to 10 original and 12 stories reprinted from anthologies, collections, and periodicals. The stories vary in tone from light to serious and feature Merlin and other famous characters and life at Arthur's Camelot. Authors include Marion Zimmer Bradley, Vera Chapman, Charles de Lint, Esther Friesner, Robert Holdstock, Phyllis Ann Karr, Tanith Lee, William Morris, H. Warner Munn, Jennifer Roberson, Jessica Amanda Salmonson, Darrell Schweitzer, Peter Tremayne, and Jane Yolen.

**Other books you might like:**

Marion Zimmer Bradley, *The Mists of Avalon*, 1983
Simon Hawke, *The Wizard of 4th Street*, 1987
Andrea Hopkins, *Chronicles of King Arthur*, 1994
  editor
Courtway Jones, *In the Shadow of the Oak King*, 1991
Stephen R. Lawhead, *Merlin*, 1988
Mary Stewart, *The Crystal Cave*, 1970

**228**

**MIKE ASHLEY**, Editor

## The Random House Book of Fantasy Stories

(New York: Random House, 1997)

**Story type:** Fantasy (Anthology)

**Summary:** Contains a three-page foreword by Ashley, a four-page introduction by Garry Kilworth, excerpts from longer works by A.C. Benson, Nicholas Stuart Gray, C.S. Lewis, George MacDonald and J.R.R. Tolkien, plus ten original stories and 12 stories reprinted from periodicals and anthologies from 1896 through 1994. From light to serious in tone, the stories employ a variety of traditional themes, such as mythical creatures, magic conflict, fairy tales, quests, music, alternate worlds, Atlantis and other fantastic locales. Other authors include Joan Aiken, Ramsey Campbell, Peter Crowther, Lord Dunsany, Neil Gaiman, Parke Godwin, Frances M. Hendry, Diana Wynne Jones, Garry Kilworth, Tanith Lee, George MacDonald, Edith Nesbit, Elisabeth Waters, Ian Watson and Jane Yolen.

**Other books you might like:**

Ellen Datlow, *The Year's Best Fantasy and Horror Series*, 1989-
  Terry Windling, co-editor
Gardner Dozois, *Modern Classics of Fantasy*, 1997
  editor
Alison Lurie, *The Oxford Book of Modern Fairy Tales*, 1993
  editor
Tom Shippey, *The Oxford Book of Fantasy Stories*, 1994
  editor
Robert Silverberg, *The Fantasy Hall of Fame*, 1983
  editor

**229**

**MIKE ASHLEY**, Editor

## The Random House Book of Science Fiction Stories

(New York: Random House, 1997)

**Story type:** Science Fiction (Anthology)

**Summary:** Contains a three-page foreword and a 15-page afterword by Ashley, a three-page introduction by Douglas Hill, plus seven original and 18 stories reprinted from anthologies and periodicals published 1935-1987. Generally upbeat in tone, the stories feature diverse themes such as space exploration, first contact, extraterrestrial tourism, intelligent aliens and life aboard a spaceship. Authors include Piers Anthony, A. Bertram Chandler, John Christopher, Arthur C. Clarke, John Russell Fearn, Nicholas Fisk, Raymond Z. Gallun, Edmond Hamilton, Douglas Hill, William F. Temple, E.C. Tubb, Ian Watson and Donald A. Wollheim.

**Other books you might like:**
Gardner Dozois, *Modern Classics of Science Fiction*, 1992
  editor
David G. Hartwell, *The Ascent of Wonder: The Evolution of Hard SF*, 1994
  Kathryn Cramer, co-editor
David G. Hartwell, *Visions of Wonder: The Science Fiction Research Association Anthology*, 1996
  Milton T. Wolf, co-editory
Ursula K. Le Guin, *The Norton Book of Science Fiction: North American Science Fiction, 1960-1990*, 1996
  Brian Attebery, co-editor
Tom Shippey, *The Oxford Book of Science Fiction Stories*, 1992
  editor

## 230
### PAULINE ASHWELL
### *Project Farcry*
(New York: Tor, 1995)

**Story type:** Science Fiction (Psychic Powers; First Contact)
**Major character(s):** Big Sword, Alien, Telepath; John James Jordan, Spaceman, Leader; Richard "Rivername" Jordan, Telepath, Teenager
**Time period(s):** Indeterminate Future
**Locale(s):** Lambda, Planet—Imaginary

**Summary:** Before discovering that his son, Richard, can read minds, John takes his son with him on the Second Lambdan Exploratory Expedition. Called "Rivername" by Big Sword, Richard acts as intermediary between the aliens and the scientists who now recognize that the aliens are intelligent. Unfortunately, Richard must return to Earth with his father, leaving no one to develop relationships with the aliens.

**Other books you might like:**
Orson Scott Card, *Speaker for the Dead*, 1986
A.C. Crispin, *Serpent's Gift*, 1992
  Deborah A. Marshall, co-author
H.M. Hoover, *Only Child*, 1992
Janet Kagan, *Hellspark*, 1988
H. Beam Piper, *Little Fuzzy*, 1962

## 231
### PAULINE ASHWELL
### *Unwillingly to Earth*
(New York: Tor, 1992)

**Story type:** Science Fiction (Adventure)
**Major character(s):** Lysistrata "Lizzie" Lee, Student, Teenager; D.J. McClare, Professor, Scientist; B. Leydon, Student, Companion
**Time period(s):** Indeterminate Future
**Locale(s):** Russett, Earth (Interplanetary College of the Humanities); Excenus 23, Planet—Imaginary; Incognita, Planet—Imaginary

**Summary:** Because of Lizzie's gift for Cultural Engineering and innate stubbornness, she attends college on Earth, despite her hidden inherited inability to use reading machines which tremendously increase reading speed. Lizzie overcomes her handicap in the nick of time, enabling her to continue her education and incidentally acquire experience in her field of study. Author's first novel.

**Other books you might like:**
Lois McMaster Bujold, *The Warrior's Apprentice*, 1986
A.C. Crispin, *Starbridge*, 1989
Tara K. Harper, *Lightwing*, 1992
Frank Herbert, *Dune*, 1965
Laura J. Mixon, *Glass Houses*, 1992
Rebecca Ore, *Becoming Alien*, 1988
Kathy Tyers, *Shivering World*, 1991

## 232
### ISAAC ASIMOV
### *The Asimov Chronicles: Fifty Years of Isaac Asimov*
(Arlington Heights: Dark Harvest, 1989)

**Story type:** Science Fiction (Collection)

**Summary:** This retrospective collection, edited by Martin H. Greenberg and heavily illustrated by Ron Lindahn and Val Lakey Lindahn, includes fifty short stories, one from each year of Isaac Asimov's enormously productive career, plus some essays. Beginning with the early "Marooned Off Vesta" (1939) and ending with the recent "I Love Little Pussy" (1988), the book includes Asimov's Hugo and Nebula Award winning "The Bicentennial Man" (1977) and such classic works as "Nightfall" (1941), "Evidence" (1946), "Little Lost Robot" (1947), "The Martian Way" (1952), "The Ugly Little Boy" (1958), and .". That Thou Art Mindful of Him" (1974).

**Other books you might like:**
James Blish, *Cities in Flight*, 1970
  Revised edition
Martin H. Greenberg, *Foundation's Friends*, 1989
  Editer
Jack Williamson, *The Humanoids*, 1949

## 233
### ISAAC ASIMOV
### *The Complete Stories - Volume 1*
(New York: Doubleday Foundation, 1990)

**Story type:** Science Fiction (Collection; Science Fiction)

**Summary:** This book collects the complete contents of three previous collections: *Earth Is Room Enough, Nine Tomorrows*, and *Nightfall and Other Stories*, comprising 46 stories with an additional brief introduction. Dr. Asimov's personal favorite, "The Last Question," is included in this volume as is "Nightfall," voted best science fiction story of all time by the Science Fiction Writers of America.

**Other books you might like:**
Alfred Bester, *Star Light, Star Bright*, 1976
James Blish, *The Best of James Blish*, 1979
Larry Niven, *Tales of Known Space*, 1975
Cordwainer Smith, *The Best of Cordwainer Smith*, 1975
  pseudonym of Paul Myron Anthony Linebarger
Theodore Sturgeon, *Caviar*, 1955
William Tenn, *The Seven Sexes*, 1968
John Varley, *The Persistence of Vision*, 1978

**234**

ISAAC ASIMOV

## The Complete Stories - Volume 2
(New York: Doubleday Foundation, 1992)

**Story type:** Science Fiction (Collection)

**Summary:** These 40 stories, published 1941-1976, reprise Asimov's early prime years. His personal favorite of the group, "The Bicentennial Man" (1976), received both Hugo and Nebula Awards.

**Other books you might like:**
Alfred Bester, *Star Light, Star Bright*, 1976
James Blish, *The Best of James Blish*, 1979
Arthur C. Clarke, *Tales From Planet Earth*, 1990
Larry Niven, *Tales of Known Space*, 1975
Robert Sheckley, *The Collected Robert Sheckley*, 1991
    5 volumes
Theodore Sturgeon, *Caviar*, 1955
William Tenn, *The Seven Sexes*, 1968
John Varley, *Blue Champagne*, 1986
John Varley, *The Persistence of Vision*, 1978

**235**

ISAAC ASIMOV, Editor
MARTIN H. GREENBERG, Co-Editor
CHARLES G. WAUGH, Co-Editor

## Faeries
(New York: Roc, 1991)

**Story type:** Fantasy (Anthology)
**Series:** Isaac Asimov's Magical Worlds of Fantasy

**Summary:** This volume includes a three-page introduction plus 18 reprinted stories about fairies. Most appeared in magazines and anthologies during the past 40 years, but two are from early this century, H.C. Bailey's "The Fairy Prince" and Lord Dunsany's "The Kith of Elf Folk." One story, Poul Anderson's "Queen of Air and Darkness," received both Hugo and Nebula Awards. Other authors include Isaac Asimov, Richard McKenna, Andre Norton, Jessica Amanda Salmonson, Henry Slesar, Thomas Burnett Swann and Robert F. Young.

**Other books you might like:**
Emma Bull, *War for the Oaks*, 1987
Andrew Lang, *The Blue Fairy Book*, 1889
    editor
Andrew Lang, *The Red Fairy Book*, 1890
    editor
Jody Lynn Nye, *Mythology 101*, 1990
James D. Priest, *Kirins: The Spell of No'an*, 1990
Will Shetterly, *Elsewhere*, 1991
Terri Windling, *Borderland*, 1986
    Mark Alan Arnold, co-editor
Terri Windling, *Bordertown*, 1986
    Mark Alan Arnold, co-editor
Terri Windling, *Faery*, 1984
    editor
Terri Windling, *Life on the Border*, 1991
    editor

**236**

ISAAC ASIMOV

## Forward the Foundation
(New York: Doubleday Foundation, 1993)

**Story type:** Science Fiction (Political; Robot Fiction)
**Series:** Foundation
**Major character(s):** Hari Seldon, Scientist (mathematician); Dors Venabili, Scientist, Martial Arts Expert; R. Daneel "Eto Demerzel" Olivaw, Robot
**Time period(s):** Indeterminate Future
**Locale(s):** Trantor, Planet—Imaginary

**Summary:** R. Daneel Olivaw, in the persona of Eto Demerzel, encourages Hari Seldon to complete his work on psychohistory and develop a device called the Prime Radiant which displays the resulting equations.

**Other books you might like:**
Ben Bova, *Sam Gunn, Unlimited*, 1993
Robert L. Forward, *Timemaster*, 1992
Charles Sheffield, *One Man's Universe*, 1993
Joan Slonczewski, *Daughter of Elysium*, 1993
John Varley, *Steel Beach*, 1992
Vernor Vinge, *A Fire upon the Deep*, 1992

**237**

ISAAC ASIMOV

## Gold: The Final Science Fiction Collection
(New York: HarperPrism, 1995)

**Story type:** Science Fiction (Collection)

**Summary:** Contains 15 previously uncollected stories, 18 essays on science fiction, plus 20 essays on writing science fiction. The tone varies from humorous to serious with themes including computers, robots, future society, ecology, the performing arts, and writing.

**Other books you might like:**
Robert L. Forward, *Indistinguishable From Magic*, 1995
Larry Niven, *N-Space*, 1990
Larry Niven, *Playgrounds of the Mind*, 1991
Charles Sheffield, *Dancing with Myself*, 1993
Gene Wolfe, *Castle of Days*, 1992

**238**

ISAAC ASIMOV
MARTIN H. GREENBERG, Co-Author

## Isaac Asimov Presents the Great SF Stories: 20 (1958)
(New York: DAW, 1990)

**Story type:** Science Fiction (Anthology)
**Series:** Isaac Asimov Presents the Great SF Stories
**Time period(s):** Indeterminate

**Summary:** This collection contains an introduction plus 12 stories featuring some of the best short fiction from 1958. Notable stories include Isaac Asimov's "The Feeling of Power," perhaps even more timely than when written, James Gunn's "The Immortals," Clifford D. Simak's "The Big Front Yard," and Cordwainer Smith's "The Burning of the Brain," a glimpse into Smith's extensive Instrumentality of Mankind series (1964-1979). Other excellent authors include Paul Anderson, C.M. Kornbluth, Robert Silverberg and Robert Sheckley.

**Other books you might like:**
Lou Aronica, *Full Spectrum 2*, 1990
  Shawna McCarthy, Amy Stout, Patrick LoBruto, co-editors
Groff Conklin, *The Best of Science Fiction*, 1946
Gardner Dozois, *The Year's Best Science Fiction: Seventh Annual Collection*, 1990
Harlan Ellison, *Dangerous Visions*, 1967
Raymond J. Healy, *Adventures in Time and Space*, 1946
  J. Francis McComas, co-editor
Robert Silverberg, *The Science Fiction Hall of Fame, Volume 1*, 1970
Donald A. Wollheim, *The 1990 Annual World's Best Science Fiction*, 1990
  Arthur W. Saha, co-editor

**239**

**ISAAC ASIMOV**
**MARTIN H. GREENBERG**, Co-Author

### Isaac Asimov Presents the Great SF Stories: 21 (1959)
(New York: DAW, 1990)

**Story type:** Science Fiction (Anthology)
**Series:** Isaac Asimov Presents the Great SF Stories
**Time period(s):** Indeterminate

**Summary:** Among the more memorable 1959 stories here are Alfred Bester's ''The Pi Man,'' Carol Emswiller's ''Day at the Beach,'' Philip Jose Farmer's ''The Alley Man,'' Clifford D. Simak's ''A Death in the House,'' Cordwainer Smith's ''No, No, Not Rogov!,'' occurring early in Smith's Instrumentality of Mankind series (1964-1979), and Theodore Sturgeon's ''The Man Who Lost the Sea.'' Other notable authors include Marion Zimmer Bradley, Damon Knight, Robert Sheckley and William Tenn.

**Other books you might like:**
Lou Aronica, *Full Spectrum 2*, 1990
  Shawna McCarthy, Amy Stout, Patrick LoBruto, co-editors
Groff Conklin, *The Best of Science Fiction*, 1946
Harlan Ellison, *Dangerous Visions*, 1967
Raymond J. Healy, *Adventures in Time and Space*, 1946
  J. Francis McComas, co-editor
Robert Silverberg, *The Science Fiction Hall of Fame, Volume 1*, 1970
Donald A. Wollheim, *The 1990 Annual World's Best Science Fiction*, 1990
  Arthur W. Saha, co-editor

**240**

**ISAAC ASIMOV**, Editor
**MARTIN H. GREENBERG**, Co-Editor

### Isaac Asimov Presents the Great SF Stories: 22 (1959)
(New York: DAW, 1991)

**Story type:** Science Fiction (Anthology)
**Series:** Isaac Asimov Presents the Great SF Stories

**Summary:** This volume contains a six-page introduction by Isaac Asimov plus 11 stories judged to be the best of 1960 including Christopher Anvil's ''Mind Partner,'' J.G. Ballard's ''The Voices of Time,'' Arthur C. Clarke's ''I Remember Babylon,'' Damon Knight's ''The Handler,'' Fritz Leiber's ''Mariana,'' Frederik Pohl's ''The Day the Icicle Works Closed,'' Rick Raphael's ''Make Mine...Homogenized'' and Cordwainer Smith's ''The Lady Who Sailed the Soul,'' from Smith's Instrumentality of Mankind series (1964-1979).

**Other books you might like:**
Anthony Boucher, *The Best From Fantasy and Science Fiction: 7*, 1958
  editor
Groff Conklin, *Science Fiction Oddities*, 1966
  editor
Groff Conklin, *The Science Fiction Omnibus*, 1956
  editor
Groff Conklin, *12 Great Classics of Science Fiction*, 1963
  editor
Harry Harrison, *S.F.: Author's Choice*, 1968
  editor
Judith Merril, *5th Annual of the Year's Best S-F*, 1960
  editor
Judith Merril, *SF: 59, The Year's Greatest Science Fiction and Fantasy*, 1959
  editor

**241**

**ISAAC ASIMOV**, Editor
**MARTIN H. GREENBERG**, Co-Editor

### Isaac Asimov Presents the Great SF Stories: 23 (1961)
(New York: DAW, 1991)

**Story type:** Science Fiction (Anthology)
**Series:** Isaac Asimov Presents the Great SF Stories

**Summary:** This volume contains a five-page introduction plus 13 stories judged best from 1961 including Brian Aldiss' Hugo Award winning story, ''Hothouse.'' One story, ''The Quaker Cannon,'' is a collaboration between Frederik Pohl and C.M. Kornbluth. Other stories include Poul Anderson's ''Hiding Place,'' Isaac Asimov's ''What Is This Thing Called Love?,'' Arthur C. Clarke's ''Death and the Senator,'' Randall Garrett's ''The Highest Treason,'' R.A. Lafferty's ''Rainbird,'' Jack Vance's ''The Moon Moth'' and Cordwainer Smith's ''A Planet Named Shayol,'' a story occurring late in the chronology of Smith's Instrumentality of Mankind series (1964-1979).

**Other books you might like:**
Anthony Boucher, *The Best From Fantasy and Science Fiction: 8*, 1959
  editor
Groff Conklin, *Another Part of the Galaxy*, 1966
  editor
Groff Conklin, *Giants Unleashed*, 1965
  editor
Groff Conklin, *Science Fiction Adventures in Dimension*, 1953
  editor
Judith Merril, *7th Annual of the Year's Best S-F*, 1962
  editor
Judith Merril, *6th Annual of the Year's Best S-F*, 1961
  editor
Robert Silverberg, *The Science Fiction Hall of Fame, Volume 1*, 1970
  editor

## 242

**ISAAC ASIMOV**, Editor
**MARTIN H. GREENBERG**, Co-Editor

### *Isaac Asimov Presents the Great SF Stories: 24 (1962)*
(New York: DAW, 1992)

**Story type:** Science Fiction (Anthology)
**Series:** Isaac Asimov Presents the Great SF Stories

**Summary:** Contains a 6-page introduction plus introductions to each of the 13 stories reprinted from 1962 periodicals including one Hugo Award nominee, ''When You Care, When You Love,'' by Theodore Sturgeon, in addition to ''Kings Who Die'' by Poul Anderson, ''The Insane Ones'' by J. G. Ballard, ''Roofs of Silver'' by Gordon R. Dickson, ''Earthlings Go Home!'' by Mack Reynolds and ''The Ballad of Lost C'mell'' by Cordwainer Smith. Other authors include Christopher Anvil, Harry Harrison, R. A. Lafferty and James White.

**Other books you might like:**
Kingsley Amis, *Spectrum 2*, 1963
    Robert Conquest, co-editor
Groff Conklin, *17 X Infinity*, 1963
    editor
Avram Davidson, *The Best From Fantasy and Science Fiction: 12*, 1963
    editor
Judith Merril, *8th Annual of the Year's Best S-F*, 1963
    editor
Frederik Pohl, *The Seventh Galaxy Reader*, 1964
    editor
Cordwainer Smith, *The Best of Cordwainer Smith*, 1975

## 243

**ISAAC ASIMOV**, Editor
**MARTIN H. GREENBERG**, Co-Editor

### *Isaac Asimov Presents the Great SF Stories: 25 (1963)*
(New York: DAW, 1992)

**Story type:** Science Fiction (Anthology)
**Series:** Isaac Asimov Presents the Great SF Stories

**Summary:** Contains a 4-page introduction plus introductions to each of the 13 stories reprinted from 1963 periodicals including the Hugo Award winner, ''No Truce with Kings'' by Poul Anderson, and one Hugo Award nominee, ''A Rose for Ecclesiastes'' by Roger Zelazny in addition to ''They Don't Make Life Like They Used To'' by Alfred Bester and ''Bernie the Faust'' by William Tenn. Other authors include Christopher Anvil, John Brunner, Hal Clement, Philip K. Dick, Fred Saberhagen, Robert Silverberg and Clifford D. Simak.

**Other books you might like:**
Kingsley Amis, *Spectrum 3*, 1964
    Robert Conquest, co-editor
Alfred Bester, *Star Light, Star Bright*, 1976
Groff Conklin, *Great Stories of Space Travel*, 1963
Avram Davidson, *The Best From Fantasy and Science Fiction: 13*, 1964
    editor
Judith Merril, *9th Annual of the Year's Best S-F*, 1964
    editor

Frederik Pohl, *The Eighth Galaxy Reader*, 1965
    editor
William Tenn, *The Seven Sexes*, 1968

## 244

**ISAAC ASIMOV**

### *Magic: The Final Fantasy Collection*
(New York: HarperPrism, 1996)

**Story type:** Fantasy (Collection)

**Summary:** This volume contains a two-page introduction by the publishers, 11 uncollected fantasy stories, 13 commentaries and critiques, and nine essays on writing fantasy. Eight of the 11 stories utilizing puns and jokes share the *Azazel* milieu, while one features the Black Widowers and Batman and two others present light fables.

**Other books you might like:**
Brian W. Aldiss, *A Romance of the Equator: The Best Fantasy Stories of Brian W. Aldiss*, 1990
David Brin, *The River of Time*, 1986
Orson Scott Card, *Maps in a Mirror*, 1990
Larry Niven, *N-Space*, 1990
Charles Sheffield, *Dancing with Myself*, 1993
Gene Wolfe, *Castle of Days*, 1992

## 245

**ISAAC ASIMOV**, Editor
**CHARLES G. WAUGH**, Co-Editor
**MARTIN H. GREENBERG**, Co-Editor

### *The Mammoth Book of Fantastic Science Fiction*
(New York: Carroll & Graf, 1992)

**Story type:** Science Fiction (Anthology)

**Summary:** Contains 10 notable novelettes and novellas first published in the 1970s including Poul Anderson's ''The Queen of Air and Darkness,'' Donald Kingsbury's ''The Moon Goddess and the Sun,'' Frederik Pohl's ''In the Problem Pit,'' Robert Silverberg's ''Born with the Dead,'' Norman Spinrad's ''Riding the Torch,'' and John Varley's ''The Persistence of Vision'' plus stories by Gordon R. Dickson, Larry Niven, Joan D. Vinge and Edward Wellen.

**Other books you might like:**
Terry Carr, *The Science Fiction Hall of Fame, Volume 4*, 1986
    editor
James Gunn, *Nebula Award Stories 10*, 1975
    editor
Ursula K. Le Guin, *Nebula Award Stories 11*, 1977
    editor
Frederik Pohl, *The Best Science Fiction for 1972*, 1972
    editor
Frederik Pohl, *Nebula Winners 14*, 1980
    editor
Frederik Pohl, *The Science Fiction Roll of Honor*, 1975
    editor

## 246

**ISAAC ASIMOV**, Editor
**CHARLES G. WAUGH**, Co-Editor
**MARTIN H. GREENBERG**, Co-Editor

### The Mammoth Book of Modern Science Fiction: Short Novels of the 1980s
(New York: Carroll & Graf, 1993)

**Story type:** Science Fiction (Anthology)

**Summary:** 10 short novels originally published in periodicals and anthologies including the Hugo and Nebula Award winning stories ''The Saturn Game'' by Poul Anderson, ''Hardfought'' by Greg Bear, ''Trinity'' by Nancy Kress, ''The Blind Geometer'' by Kim Stanley Robinson and ''Sailing to Byzantium'' by Robert Silverberg. Other authors are Gregory Benford, Suzy McKee Charnas, Barry N. Malzberg, James Tiptree, Jr., and Walter Jon Williams.

**Other books you might like:**
Michael Bishop, *Nebula Awards 24*, 1990
  editor
Terry Carr, *The Science Fiction Hall of Fame, Volume 4*, 1986
  editor
Gardner Dozois, *Modern Classics of Science Fiction*, 1992
  editor
Gardner Dozois, *The Year's Best Science Fiction Series*, 1984-1993
  editor
Ursula K. Le Guin, *The Norton Book of Science Fiction: North American Science Fiction, 1960-1990*, 1993
  Brian Attebery, co-editor
Tom Shippey, *The Oxford Book of Science Fiction Stories*, 1992
  editor
George Zebrowski, *Nebula Awards 22*, 1988
  editor

## 247

**ISAAC ASIMOV**

### Nemesis
(New York: Doubleday/Foundation, 1989)

**Story type:** Science Fiction (Space Opera)
**Major character(s):** Janus Pitt, Ruler; Marlene, Teenager
**Time period(s):** 23rd century (2236)
**Locale(s):** Earth; Rotor, Planet—Imaginary

**Summary:** Human beings have established a renegade colony, Rotor, circling Earth's recently discovered neighbor, the star Nemesis. The colony's ruler, Janus Pitt, is hostile to Earth, but a young Rotorian discovers that Nemesis poses a dire threat to life on both Earth and Rotor.

**Other books you might like:**
Arthur C. Clarke, *Rama II*, 1989
Frederik Pohl, *Gateway*, 1977
Bob Shaw, *Orbitsville*, 1975

## 248

**ISAAC ASIMOV**
**ROBERT SILVERBERG**, Co-Author

### Nightfall
(New York: Doubleday Foundation, 1990)

**Story type:** Science Fiction (End of the World)

**Major character(s):** Sheerin 501, Scientist, Psychologist; Beenay 25, Scientist (astronomer); Theremon 762, Journalist
**Time period(s):** Indeterminate
**Locale(s):** Kalgash, Planet—Imaginary

**Summary:** Inspired by a quote from Emerson, Kalgash is a world on the edge of chaos, torn between the madness of religious fanaticism and the unyielding rationalism of science. Lurking beneath it all is a collective, instinctual fear of the Darkness, because Kalgash is a world of perpetual daylight. Only a handful of people on the planet are prepared to face the truth—five of their six suns are setting while the remaining one is about to be eclipsed for the first time in over 2,000 years. Based on Asimov's 1941 story of the same name.

**Other books you might like:**
Poul Anderson, *A Stone in Heaven*, 1979
Larry Niven, *Lucifer's Hammer*, 1977
  Jerry Pournelle, co-author
Larry Niven, *The Mote in God's Eye*, 1974
  Jerry Pournelle, co-author
Frederik Pohl, *Jem*, 1979
Gene Wolfe, *The Shadow of the Torturer*, 1980

## 249

**ISAAC ASIMOV**
**ROBERT SILVERBERG**, Co-Author

### The Positronic Man
(New York: Doubleday Foundation, 1993)

**Story type:** Science Fiction (Robot Fiction)
**Major character(s):** Andrew Martin, Robot, Revolutionary
**Time period(s):** 22nd century; 23rd century
**Locale(s):** California

**Summary:** Gerald Martin purchases prototype domestic service robot NDR-113 but his children immediately name the robot ''Andrew'' and learn how to divert it from their father's tasks to play with them. When the manufacturer discovers Andrew's unique learning and emotional abilities, the company unsuccessfully attempts to recall NDR-113. During a century of service to the Martin family, Andrew's emancipation and demands for self-determination propel legal reformation. Based on Asimov's 1976 story, ''The Bicentennial Man.''

**Other books you might like:**
Philip K. Dick, *Blade Runner*, 1982
David Gerrold, *When HARLIE Was One: Release 2.0*, 1988
Rudy Rucker, *Wetware*, 1988
Joan Slonczewski, *Daughter of Elysium*, 1993
Thomas T. Thomas, *ME: A Novel of Self Discovery*, 1991
John Varley, *Steel Beach*, 1992
Jack Williamson, *The Humanoids*, 1949

## 250

**ISAAC ASIMOV**
**ROBERT SILVERBERG**, Co-Author

### The Ugly Little Boy
(New York: Doubleday Foundation, 1992)

**Story type:** Science Fiction (Contemporary Realism; Romance)
**Major character(s):** Edith Fellowes, Nurse; Timmie, Prehistoric Human (Neanderthal); Gerald Hoskins, Scientist
**Time period(s):** 21st century; 380th century B.C.
**Locale(s):** New York

**Summary:** This novel expands the 1958 short story by Isaac Asimov about Timmie, a Neanderthal boy brought 40,000 years forward to be studied at Stasis Technologies, Ltd. where Miss Fellowes recognizes him as a human child.

**Other books you might like:**
Eleanor Arnason, *A Woman of the Iron People*, 1991
David Brin, *The Uplift War*, 1987
Orson Scott Card, *Ender's Game*, 1985
Robert Reed, *Down the Bright Way*, 1991
Cordwainer Smith, *Norstrilia*, 1975
Dave Wolverton, *Serpent Catch*, 1991

### 251

JANET ASIMOV

## Murder at the Galactic Writers' Society
(New York: DAW, 1995)

**Story type:** Science Fiction (Mystery; Robot Fiction)
**Major character(s):** Arda, Android, Spy; Fortizak "Zak", Writer; Smith, Government Official
**Time period(s):** Indeterminate Future
**Locale(s):** Terran Federation, Interstellar Empire/Federation; New York, New York

**Summary:** Passing as a human being, Arda constantly faces prejudice against positronic intelligence. Assigned to prevent embarrassment of Earth while protecting the alien and human writers attending the Galactic Writers' Society meeting hosted on Earth by Zak, Arda must prevent the robbery of Princess Vush's ruulogem, reportedly the largest in the universe. Failure could lead to interplanetary disaster.

**Other books you might like:**
Wilhelmina Baird, *Crashcourse*, 1993
Hal Clement, *Fossil*, 1993
Janet O. Jeppson, *The Last Immortal*, 1981
    pseuodnym of Janet Asimov
Janet O. Jeppson, *The Second Experiment*, 1974
    pseudonym of Janet Asimov
Sharyn McCrumb, *Bimbos of the Death Sun*, 1987
Laura J. Mixon, *Glass Houses*, 1992

### 252

JANET ASIMOV
ISAAC ASIMOV, Co-Author

## Norby and the Court Jester
(New York: Walker, 1991)

**Story type:** Science Fiction (Young Adult; Robot Fiction)
**Series:** Norby
**Major character(s):** Norby, Robot; Jeff Wells, Student (at the space academy), Teenager
**Time period(s):** Indeterminate Future
**Locale(s):** Izz, Planet—Imaginary

**Summary:** Jeff Wells and Norby take advantage of Space Academy spring break to visit a toy and game fair and their friends, Princess Rinda and her robot, Pera. On Izz, Jeff and Norby search for the missing Pera and the person who has sabotaged the planetary computer system.

**Other books you might like:**
Eleanor Cameron, *The Wonderful Flight to the Mushroom Planet*, 1954

Thomas M. Disch, *The Brave Little Toaster: A Bedtime Story for Small Appliances*, 1986
Thomas M. Disch, *The Brave Little Toaster Goes to Mars*, 1988
Paul W. Fairman, *The Runaway Robot*, 1964
    as Lester del Rey
Clifford D. Simak, *City*, 1952

### 253

JANET ASIMOV
ISAAC ASIMOV, Co-Author

## Norby and the Oldest Dragon
(New York: Walker, 1990)

**Story type:** Science Fiction (Robot Fiction)
**Series:** Norby
**Major character(s):** Jeff Wells, Teenager, Student (space academy cadet); Norby, Robot
**Time period(s):** Indeterminate Future
**Locale(s):** Jamya, Planet—Imaginary

**Summary:** Jeff and Norby attend the birthday party of the Grand Dragon of Jamya, a supposedly routine event, and find themselves and the planet in enormous danger, threatened by a gigantic cloud creature. For children.

**Other books you might like:**
Isaac Asimov, *The Caves of Steel*, 1954
Isaac Asimov, *I, Robot*, 1950
Isaac Asimov, *The Naked Sun*, 1957
Isaac Asimov, *The Rest of the Robots*, 1964
Isaac Asimov, *Robot Dreams*, 1986
John Bellairs, *The Eyes of the Killer Robot*, 1986
H.M. Hoover, *Orvis*, 1987
Jane Yolen, *The Robot and Rebecca and the Missing Owser*, 1981

### 254

JANET ASIMOV
ISAAC ASIMOV, Co-Author

## Norby and Yobo's Great Adventure
(New York: Walker, 1989)

**Story type:** Science Fiction (Robot Fiction; Time Travel)
**Series:** Norby
**Major character(s):** Jeff Wells, Teenager, Student (space academy cadet); Norby, Robot
**Time period(s):** Indeterminate Future; Indeterminate Past
**Locale(s):** Mars; Earth

**Summary:** Norby and Jeff accompany their commander, Admiral Yobo, on a time travel adventure into the pre-historic past as the Admiral attempts to trace the history of an ancient family heirloom—a carved ivory tusk. For children.

**Other books you might like:**
Isaac Asimov, *The Caves of Steel*, 1954
Isaac Asimov, *I, Robot*, 1950
Isaac Asimov, *The Naked Sun*, 1957
Isaac Asimov, *The Rest of the Robots*, 1964
Isaac Asimov, *Robot Dreams*, 1986
John Bellairs, *The Eyes of the Killer Robot*, 1986
H.M. Hoover, *Orvis*, 1987
Jane Yolen, *The Robot and Rebecca and the Missing Owser*, 1981

## 255

**JANET ASIMOV**
**ISAAC ASIMOV**, Co-Author

### Norby Down to Earth

(New York: Walker, 1989)

**Story type:** Science Fiction (Robot Fiction)
**Series:** Norby
**Major character(s):** Jeff Wells, Teenager, Student (space academy cadet); Norby, Robot
**Time period(s):** Indeterminate Future
**Locale(s):** Terran Federation, Interstellar Empire/Federation

**Summary:** Jeff and Norby visit the independent nation of Manhattan on the planet Earth and find themselves smack in the middle of a mystery. Someone is zapping small robots with an electronic gun that apparently does no lasting damage while someone else is stealing computer parts. Eventually they uncover a complex and dastardly plot.

**Other books you might like:**
Isaac Asimov, *The Caves of Steel*, 1954
Isaac Asimov, *I, Robot*, 1950
Isaac Asimov, *The Naked Sun*, 1957
Isaac Asimov, *The Rest of the Robots*, 1964
Isaac Asimov, *Robot Dreams*, 1986
John Bellairs, *The Eyes of the Killer Robot*, 1986
H.M. Hoover, *Orvis*, 1987
Jane Yolen, *The Robot and Rebecca and the Missing Owser*, 1981

## 256

**NANCY ASIRE**

### Tears of Time

(New York: Baen, 1993)

**Story type:** Fantasy (Sword and Sorcery)
**Major character(s):** Kahsir, Royalty (prince), Warrior; Iowyn, Royalty (princess), Warrior; Tsingar, Military Personnel (General)
**Time period(s):** Indeterminate
**Locale(s):** Vyjenor, Fictional Country; Dramujh, Fictional City

**Summary:** Carrying on the centuries-long warfare of his people, the Krotanya, Kahsir leads his army against the invading armies of the evil Leishoranya, who use their psychic powers to kill and enslave. In a desperate fight to rescue his sister, Iowyn, Kahsir uses his own psychic powers to kill Leishoranyan soldiers, contrary to the ethics of his people. As the Krotanya refugees flee their villages and his own soldiers try to defend their borders, Kahsir also wrestles with his conscience. Sequel to *Twilight's Kingdom*.

**Other books you might like:**
Marion Zimmer Bradley, *Stormqueen!*, 1978
C.J. Cherryh, *A Dirge for Stabis*, 1989
   Leslie J. Fish, co-author
C.J. Cherryh, *Wizard Spawn*, 1989
   Nancy Asire, co-author
Barbara Hambly, *The Armies of Daylight*, 1983
Katherine Kurtz, *Deryni Checkmate*, 1972
Katherine Kurtz, *Deryni Rising*, 1970
Katherine Kurtz, *High Deryni*, 1973
J.R.R. Tolkien, *The Two Towers*, 1955

## 257

**NANCY ASIRE**

### To Fall Like Stars

(New York: Baen, 1996)

**Story type:** Fantasy (Military; Psychic Powers)
**Major character(s):** Kashir, Royalty (prince), Warrior; Tsingar, Military Personnel (general); Lorhaiden, Warrior
**Time period(s):** Indeterminate
**Locale(s):** Hvalkir, Fictional City; Vyjenor, Fictional Country

**Summary:** Staking the survival of the Krotanya on one great battle, the High King leads his army against the Leishoranya hoping to distract the powers of Darkness while his people use the Mind-Gates to flee to comparative safety in the mountains. When, a generation later, the Leishoranya again menace the Krotanyan remnant, Lorhaiden searches for a forbidden mind weapon that can save his people, but destroy the wielder of the weapon.

**Other books you might like:**
C.J. Cherryh, *Well of Shiuan*, 1978
Phyllis Eisenstein, *In the Red Lord's Reach*, 1989
Barbara Hambly, *The Armies of Daylight*, 1983
Robert Jordan, *The Fires of Heaven*, 1993
Patricia A. McKillip, *Harpist in the Wind*, 1979
J.R.R. Tolkien, *The Return of the King*, 1956

## 258

**ALICE ASKEW**
**CLAUDE ASKEW**, Co-Author

### Aylmer Vance: Ghost-Seer

(Ashcroft, British Columbia: Ash-Tree Press, 1998)

**Story type:** Horror (Collection)
**Major character(s):** Aylmer Vance, Detective (psychic)

**Summary:** This collection of eight stories published in 1914 in the *Weekly Tale-Teller*, features Aylmer Vance, a psychic detective who recounts encounters with the supernatural to Dexter, the narrator, who makes his acquaintance while on vacation. Selections include "The Invader," in which a medium becomes possessed by the spirit of a woman who lusts for her husband; "The Fire Unquenchable," in which a poet's premature death leaves his inspiration a volatile disembodied flame; and "The Fear," in which fear itself becomes a discarnate entity. Edited and introduced by Jack Adrian.

**Other books you might like:**
Algernon Blackwood, *The Complete John Silence Stories*, 1997
A.M. Burrage, *The Occult Files of Francis Chard: Some Ghost Stories*, 1997
William Hope Hodgson, *Carnacki the Ghost Finder*, 1913
J. Sheridan Le Fanu, *In a Glass Darkly*, 1872
Seabury Quinn, *The Phantom Fighter*, 1966

## 259

**ROBERT ASPRIN**

### M.Y.T.H. Inc. in Action

(Norfolk, Virginia: Donning Starblaze, 1990)

**Story type:** Fantasy (Light Fantasy)
**Series:** M.Y.T.H.
**Major character(s):** Guido, Bodyguard; Nunzio, Bodyguard
**Time period(s):** Indeterminate

**Locale(s):** Klah, Alternate Universe

**Summary:** Guido and Nunzio of the M.Y.T.H. Inc. crew have joined the army of Queen Hemlock in an effort to undermine its effectiveness.

**Other books you might like:**
Brian Daley, *A Tapestry of Magics*, 1983
Poul Anderson, *Hoka!*, 1984
   Gordon R. Dickson, co-author
Fritz Leiber, *Swords and Deviltry*, 1970
Will Shetterly, *Cats Have No Lord*, 1985
Christopher Stasheff, *The Warlock Unlocked*, 1982

---

### 260

**ROBERT ASPRIN**

## Phule's Company

(New York: Ace, 1990)

**Story type:** Science Fiction (Humor; Military)
**Series:** Phule's Company
**Major character(s):** Willard Phule, Military Personnel; Beeker, Servant (butler)
**Time period(s):** Indeterminate Future
**Locale(s):** Haskin's Planet, Planet—Imaginary

**Summary:** A megamillionaire playboy with an eye for opportunity takes command of a unit of the worst misfits in the generally rakish Space Legion. Their first mission is guarding the swamp miners of Haskin's Planet.

**Other books you might like:**
Lois McMaster Bujold, *Borders of Infinity*, 1989
Lois McMaster Bujold, *The Warrior's Apprentice*, 1986
Brian Daley, *Fall of the White Ship Avatar*, 1987
Brian Daley, *Jinx on a Terran Inheritance*, 1985
Brian Daley, *Requiem for a Ruler of Worlds*, 1985
Harry Harrison, *Bill, the Galactic Hero*, 1965

---

### 261

**ROBERT ASPRIN**

## Phule's Paradise

(New York: Ace, 1991)

**Story type:** Science Fiction (Humor; Military)
**Series:** Phule's Company
**Major character(s):** Willard Phule, Military Personnel; Tusk-Anini, Military Personnel; Maxine Pruet, Organized Crime Figure, Businesswoman
**Time period(s):** Indeterminate Future
**Locale(s):** Haskin's Planet, Planet—Imaginary; Lorelei, Space Station

**Summary:** Willard Phule and his company of misfits are sent to Space Station Lorelei where they are to protect a casino owner with more money than sense from being taken over by organized crime. Some legionnaires with criminal pasts infiltrate the local crime scene and some man the hotel, while Phule hires computer experts to debug the slot machines. After firing all those in cahoots with the local crime boss, Phule manages to open the casino and prevent a takeover.

**Other books you might like:**
Brian Daley, *Fall of the White Ship Avatar*, 1987
Brian Daley, *Jinx on a Terran Inheritance*, 1985
Brian Daley, *Requiem for a Ruler of Worlds*, 1985
Harry Harrison, *Bill, the Galactic Hero*, 1965
George H. Smith, *Kar Kaballa*, 1969

---

Walter Jon Williams, *The Crown Jewels*, 1987

---

### 262

**ROBERT ASPRIN**

## Sweet Myth-tery of Life

(Virginia Beach, Virginia: Donning, 1994)

**Story type:** Fantasy (Light Fantasy)
**Series:** M.Y.T.H.
**Major character(s):** Skeeve, Magician; Hemlock, Royalty (queen), Ruler; Cassandra, Vampire
**Time period(s):** Indeterminate
**Locale(s):** Klah, Planet—Imaginary

**Summary:** Given one month by Queen Hemlock to decide whether to marry her or rule alone when she abdicates, Skeeve decides to research the institution of marriage, including a date with Cassandra at a vampire night club.

**Other books you might like:**
Kyle Crocco, *Heroes Wanted*, 1991
George Alec Effinger, *Maureen Birnbaum, Barbarian Swordsperson: The Complete Stories*, 1993
Neil Gaiman, *Good Omens: The Nice and Accurate Prophecies of Agnes Nutter, Witch*, 1990
   Terry Pratchett, co-author
Laurell K. Hamilton, *Guilty Pleasures*, 1993
John Moore, *Slay and Rescue*, 1993

---

### 263

**ROBERT ASPRIN**
**LINDA EVANS**, Co-Author

## Time Scout

(New York: Baen, 1995)

**Story type:** Science Fiction (Time Travel)
**Major character(s):** Kenneth "Kit" Carson, Time Traveler (time scout), Aged Person; Margo van Wyyck, Time Traveler; Malcolm Moore, Time Traveler, Guide
**Time period(s):** 1880s; 1st century (47)
**Locale(s):** Shangri-la, Space Station (time nexus); London, England; Roman Empire

**Summary:** Hoping to thwart his granddaughter's desire to become the first female time scout, Kit Carson abandons his retirement to guide Margo around Victorian London and 1st century Roman Syria.

**Other books you might like:**
Poul Anderson, *The Time Patrol*, 1991
L. Sprague de Camp, *Rivers of Time*, 1993
Linda Evans, *Sleipnir*, 1994
Spider Robinson, *Callahan and Company*, 1987
Clifford D. Simak, *Way Station*, 1963
John Varley, *Millennium*, 1983

---

### 264

**ROBERT ASPRIN**
**LINDA EVANS**, Co-Author

## Wagers of Sin

(New York: Baen, 1996)

**Story type:** Science Fiction (Time Travel)
**Series:** Time Scout

**Major character(s):** Skeeter Jackson, Con Artist, Time Traveler; Marcus, Saloon Keeper/Owner, Slave; Goldie Morran, Business-woman
**Time period(s):** 1st century; 1880s (1885)
**Locale(s):** Roman Empire; Denver, Colorado

**Summary:** Time Terminal 86's resident con man, Skeeter Jackson, makes a wager with Goldie Morran concerning who can con the most money out of others. However, an even greater thief robs Goldie while Skeeter must stand combat in the arenas of ancient Rome in the vague hope of remaining alive long enough to rescue a friend from slavery.

**Other books you might like:**
Poul Anderson, *The Time Patrol*, 1991
L. Sprague de Camp, *Rivers of Time*, 1993
Linda Evans, *Far Edge of Darkness*, 1996
Crawford Kilian, *Rogue Emperor*, 1988
Lisa Mason, *The Golden Nineties*, 1995
Samuel Merwin, *The House of Many Worlds*, 1951
Robert Silverberg, *Up the Line*, 1969
Harry Turtledove, *Agent of Byzantium*, 1987
Chelsea Quinn Yarbro, *Blood Games*, 1980

---

### 265

**PETER ATKINS**

## Morningstar

(New York: HarperCollins, 1992)

**Story type:** Horror (Serial Killer; Vampire Story)
**Major character(s):** Donovan Moon, Journalist; Jonathan Frost, Busi-nessman (Real estate developer); T. Astare, Vampire
**Time period(s):** 1990s (1992)
**Locale(s):** San Francisco, California

**Summary:** Down-and-out freelance reporter Donovan Moon is hired to assist Jonathan Frost in his work as a vampire hunter, a trade he plies under the guise of a serial killer who signs his handiwork "Morningstar." This is the author's first novel.

**Other books you might like:**
Pat Cadigan, *The Power and the Passion*, 1989
    short story in *Patterns*
Barbara Hambly, *Those Who Hunt the Night*, 1987
Kim Newman, *Bad Dreams*, 1990

---

### 266

**A.A. ATTANASIO**

## The Dragon and the Unicorn

(New York: HarperPrism, 1996)

**Story type:** Fantasy (Legend; Science Fiction)
**Major character(s):** Uther Pendragon, Leader, Warrior; Merlinus "Myrddin/Lailoken" Ambrosius, Wizard, Demon; Morgeu, Royalty, Demon
**Time period(s):** Indeterminate Past
**Locale(s):** England (Britain); Avalon, Mythical Place

**Summary:** The eternal struggle for immortality yields the unicorn and dragon and leads to the human manifestation of strife and harmony, King Arthur of Britain. First of a series, and first published in the U.K. in 1994.

**Other books you might like:**
Mike Ashley, *The Pendragon Chronicles*, 1990
    editor
Marion Zimmer Bradley, *The Forest House*, 1994

Andrea Hopkins, *Chronicles of King Arthur*, 1994
    editor
Courtway Jones, *In the Shadow of the Oak King*, 1991
Morgan Llywelyn, *Druids*, 1991
T.H. White, *The Once and Future King*, 1958
Jack Whyte, *The Skystone*, 1996

---

### 267

**A.A. ATTANASIO**

## The Eagle and the Sword

(New York: HarperPrism, 1997)

**Story type:** Fantasy (Legend; Religious)
**Major character(s):** Arthor, Bastard Son, Teenager; Merlin, Wizard, Leader; Melania, Noblewoman, Adventurer
**Time period(s):** Indeterminate Past
**Locale(s):** Camelot, England (Britain)

**Summary:** While Merlin oversees the construction of Camelot, the difficulties of Arthor's life prepare him to rule. Arthor will unify the island into a nation, if he can overcome interference from the realm of the gods and human forces which encompass a different vision of the island's future.

**Other books you might like:**
Mike Ashley, *The Pendragon Chronicles*, 1990
    editor
Marion Zimmer Bradley, *The Forest House*, 1994
Bernard Cornwell, *The Winter King*, 1996
Andrea Hopkins, *Chronicles of King Arthur*, 1994
    editor
Courtway Jones, *In the Shadow of the Oak King*, 1991
Jack Whyte, *The Skystone*, 1996

---

### 268

**A.A. ATTANASIO**

## Hunting the Ghost Dancer

(New York: Harper Collins Publishers, 1991)

**Story type:** Fantasy (Quest)
**Major character(s):** Timov, Child; Hamr, Hunter, Wanderer; Baat, Monster
**Time period(s):** 480th century B.C.
**Locale(s):** Earth

**Summary:** In the distant past, a small group of people are forced to leave their diseased and dying tribe. They set out to find and kill one of the last of the Ghost Dancers, immensely powerful spirits with an appetite for destruction.

**Other books you might like:**
Jean M. Auel, *Clan of the Cave Bear*, 1980
W. Michael Gear, *People of the Wolf*, 1990
    Kathleen O'Neal Gear, co-author
Jack London, *Before Adam*, 1906
Dave Wolverton, *Serpent Catch*, 1991

---

### 269

**A.A. ATTANASIO**

## Kingdom of the Grail

(New York: HarperCollins, 1992)

**Story type:** Fantasy (Historical; Legend)

**Major character(s):** Ailena Valaise, Noblewoman, Parent (Guy Lanfranc's); Rachel Tibbon, Imposter; Guy Lanfranc, Nobleman
**Time period(s):** 12th century
**Locale(s):** Wales

**Summary:** Guy Lanfranc sends his elderly mother, Ailena, from her castle to venture forth on a religious pilgrimage. When Ailena meets Rachel who looks like Ailena in her youth, Ailena arranges to have Rachel return to Wales as Ailena with her youth miraculously restored through use of the Grail. Rachel's appearance in Wales forces a crisis of faith, forcing Rachel to join the Welsh rebellion.

**Other books you might like:**
Frans G. Bengtsson, *The Long Ships*, 1954
Parke Godwin, *Sherwood*, 1991
Frances Mary Hendry, *Quest for a Maid*, 1990
Robert Rice, *The Last Pendragon*, 1991
Persia Woolley, *Guinevere: The Legend in Autumn*, 1992

### 270
#### A.A. ATTANASIO

## *The Last Legends of Earth*
(New York: Doubleday/Foundation, 1989)

**Story type:** Science Fiction (Space Opera)
**Series:** Radix Tetrad
**Major character(s):** Chan-ti Beppu, Wanderer; Ned O'Tennis, Pilot
**Time period(s):** Indeterminate Future
**Locale(s):** Chalco-Doror, Planet—Imaginary

**Summary:** Millennia after the Earth was destroyed in a nova, a super-powerful alien known as the Rimstalker resurrects humankind on the planets of a distant star system. It does this not out of kindness, but to use humanity as bait to attract its ancient enemies, the spider-like zotl, which feed on the psychic pain of intelligent life forms. Humanity must struggle against both the Rimstalker and the zotl.

**Other books you might like:**
Philip Jose Farmer, *To Your Scattered Bodies Go*, 1971
Dan Simmons, *Hyperion*, 1989
Edward E. Smith, *Galactic Patrol*, 1950
Edward E. Smith, *Gray Lensman*, 1951
Edward E. Smith, *The Skylark of Space*, 1946
Edward E. Smith, *Skylark of Valeron*, 1949
E.E. ''Doc'' Smith, *Triplanetary*, 1948

### 271
#### A.A. ATTANASIO

## *The Moon's Wife: A Hystery*
(New York: HarperCollins, 1993)

**Story type:** Fantasy (Contemporary Realism)
**Major character(s):** Sigrid Lindo, Accountant; Daniel Schel, Deity; Glendil, Witch
**Time period(s):** 1990s (1993)
**Locale(s):** Arcadia, New York; New York, New York

**Summary:** After a wildly orgasmic seizure in a supermarket, Sigrid Lindo begins to hear the moon asking her to marry him. She quickly ends up in a mental hospital where she must confront her sanity. If she decides she truly can hear the moon, she must cope with the effect that decision will have on her life and, possibly, the whole world.

**Other books you might like:**
Eleanor Arnason, *Daughter of the Bear King*, 1987
Peter S. Beagle, *A Fine and Private Place*, 1960

Emma Bull, *War for the Oaks*, 1987
John Crowley, *Little, Big*, 1981
Robert Holdstock, *Mythago Wood*, 1984

### 272
#### A.A. ATTANASIO

## *Solis*
(New York: HarperCollins, 1994)

**Story type:** Science Fiction (Alternate Intelligence; Dystopian)
**Major character(s):** Charles ''Mr. Charlie'' Outis, Disembodied Personality, Reanimated Dead; Munk, Android (androne), Revolutionary; Mei Nili, Revolutionary
**Time period(s):** 120th century
**Locale(s):** Mars; Outer Space

**Summary:** Returning to consciousness after 1000 years, Charles Outis discovers a demand for his memories and the need for his brain as mechanical controller in an asteroid mining operation. After Munk and Mei Nili salvage Mr. Charlie, a meeting of the artificial intelligences, the Maat Pashalik, attempts to assign ownership of the brain as property. However, Munk's programmed love of human beings forces it to abscond with Mr. Charlie and attempt the dangerous trek to Solis where they may find sanctuary.

**Other books you might like:**
Greg Bear, *Heads*, 1991
Gregory Benford, *Great Sky River*, 1987
Rudy Rucker, *Live Robots*, 1994
Dan Simmons, *The Fall of Hyperion*, 1990
Jim Starlin, *Lady El*, 1992
   Diana Graziaunas, co-author

### 273
#### A.A. ATTANASIO

## *The Wolf and the Crown*
(New York: Harper, 1998)

**Story type:** Fantasy (Historical)
**Series:** Arthurian
**Major character(s):** Arthor Pendragon, Ruler (king); Merlinus Ambrosius, Wizard
**Time period(s):** Indeterminate Past
**Locale(s):** Avalon, Mythical Place; England

**Summary:** Young Arthor has become king and his first year is a tempestuous one. With the aid of Merlin, he learns to defend the land from invaders and internal dissent by using the sword when necessary, and by negotiating when able.

**Other books you might like:**
Hans Bemmann, *The Stone and the Flute*, 1987
Vera Chapman, *The Green Knight*, 1978
Parke Godwin, *Firelord*, 1980
Cary James, *King & Raven*, 1995
Richard Monaco, *The Grail War*, 1982

### 274
#### MARGARET ATWOOD

## *Good Bones and Simple Murders*
(New York: Doubleday, 1994)

**Story type:** Fantasy (Collection; Science Fiction)

**Summary:** Contains 35 stories, parables, monologues, prose poems and other short works reprinted from periodicals and collections or broadcast on the BBC program, "Anthology." The tone varies from whimsical to dark with themes including memories and views of a reincarnated bat, new slants on rewritten fairy tales, a few words from Gertrude to Hamlet, various recipes for making a man, techniques and rewards of tree stump hunting, the view of humanity by intelligent extraterrestrial moths and futures with gender-role reversal and computer control.

**Other books you might like:**

James Finn Garner, *Politically Correct Bedtime Stories*, 1994
Ursula K. Le Guin, *Buffalo Gals and Other Animal Presences*, 1987
Ursula K. Le Guin, *A Fisherman of the Inland Sea*, 1994
Connie Willis, *Impossible Things*, 1994
Jack Zipes, *The Outspoken Princess and the Gentle Knight*, 1994
   editor

---

**275**

### JEAN M. AUEL

## *The Plains of Passage*

(New York: Crown, 1990)

**Story type:** Fantasy (Romance; Historical)
**Series:** Earth's Children
**Major character(s):** Ayla, Prehistoric Human, Shaman; Jondalar, Prehistoric Human, Hunter
**Time period(s):** Indeterminate Past (Late Pleistocene Epoch)
**Locale(s):** Europe

**Summary:** As they cross the continent in their search for home, Ayla and Jondalar make friends and enemies while amazing everyone with their control over wild animals.

**Other books you might like:**

W. Michael Gear, *People of the Fire*, 1991
   Kathleen O'Neal Gear, co-author
W. Michael Gear, *People of the Wolf*, 1990
   Kathleen O'Neal Gear, co-author
Richard Herley, *The Stone Arrow*, 1978
J.H. Rosny, *Quest for Fire*, 1967
   1909
William Sarabande, *Beyond the Sea of Ice*, 1987

---

**276**

### NINA AUERBACH, Editor
### U.C. KNOEPFLMACHER, Co-Editor

## *Forbidden Journeys: Fairy Tales and Fantasies by Victorian Women Writers*

(Chicago: The University of Chicago Press, 1992)

**Story type:** Fantasy (Anthology; Legend)

**Summary:** Contains 11 stories, frequently dark and angry, divided into four parts with scholarly and interpretive introductions illustrating the revision of traditional fairy tale material, the creation of subversive text, the expansion of that subversion and the undercutting of underlying assumptions. Includes three tales by Christina Rossetti and a full-length fantasy novel with a startling feminist reversal by Jean Ingelow, "Mopsa the Fairy." Other authors include Frances Hodgson Burnett, Julia Horatia Ewing, Maria Molesworth, Edith Nesbit and Anne Thackeray Ritchie.

**Other books you might like:**

Michael Patrick Hearn, *The Victorian Fairy Tale Book*, 1988
   editor

Ethel Johnston Phelps, *Tatterhood and Other Tales*, 1978
   editor
Jack Zipes, *Beauties, Beasts and Enchantments*, 1989
   editor
Jack Zipes, *Don't Bet on the Prince*, 1986
   editor
Jack Zipes, *Spells of Enchantment*, 1991
   editor

---

**277**

### RICHARD AUSTIN (Pseudonym of Victor Milan)

## *Devil's Deal*

(New York: Jove, 1989)

**Story type:** Science Fiction (Post-Nuclear Holocaust)
**Series:** Guardians
**Major character(s):** McKay, Military Personnel; McKendree, Racist
**Time period(s):** Indeterminate Future
**Locale(s):** Wyoming

**Summary:** The Guardians, a well-armed special forces group that works for the President of the United States, is sent to Wyoming to deal with a post-nuclear war version of the racist Aryan Brotherhood. Bullets fly and bloody bodies pile up quickly.

**Other books you might like:**

Jerry Ahern, *Final Rain*, 1989
   The Survivalist 19
James Axler, *Red Equinox*, 1989
   Deathlands 9
Neal Barrett Jr., *Dawn's Uncertain Light*, 1989
Neal Barrett Jr., *Through Darkest America*, 1987
Algis Budrys, *Some Will Not Die*, 1961

---

**278**

### JAMES AXLER

## *Deep Trek*

(New York: Worldwide Library Gold Eagle, 1994)

**Story type:** Science Fiction (Post-Holocaust)
**Series:** Earth Blood
**Major character(s):** Jim Hilton, Military Personnel; Nanci Simms, Teacher (retired), Warrior; Henderson McGill, Military Personnel
**Time period(s):** 2040s (2040)
**Locale(s):** California; Nevada

**Summary:** Reunited after attempting to locate family and friends, the survivors of *Aquila*'s crew undertake a perilous journey toward a California rendezvous to search for a rumored secret military base.

**Other books you might like:**

Jerry Ahern, *The Quest*, 1981
Octavia E. Butler, *Dawn*, 1987
J.M. Morgan, *Beyond Eden*, 1992
David Robbins, *The Fox Run*, 1986
Paul O. Williams, *The Breaking of Northwall*, 1981

## 279

**JONATHAN AYCLIFFE** (Pseudonym of Denis MacEoin)

### The Lost

(New York: HarperPrism, 1996)

**Story type:** Horror (Vampire Story)
**Major character(s):** Michael Feraru, Teacher; Liliana Popescu, Lawyer; Elena Vlaicu, Maintenance Worker (caretaker)
**Time period(s):** 1990s (1996)
**Locale(s):** Castel Vlaicu, Romania

**Summary:** Michael Feraru returns to his family home in Romania after the fall of the Ceausescu dictatorship to reclaim his family's old castle in the hope of turning it into an orphange. But the deeper he penetrates into the country the more informed he becomes of the legacy of vampirism surrounding his family name and the more irreversibly he succumbs to it.

**Other books you might like:**
Elaine Bergstrom, *Shattered Glass*, 1989
Andrei Codrescu, *Blood Countess*, 1995
Jeanne Kalogridis, *Children of the Vampire*, 1995
Shawn Ryan, *Nocturnas*, 1995
Dan Simmons, *Children of the Night*, 1992
Bram Stoker, *Dracula*, 1897

## 280

**JONATHAN AYCLIFFE** (Pseudonym of Denis MacEoin)

### The Matrix

(New York: Harper, 1995)

**Story type:** Horror (Occult)
**Major character(s):** Andrew Macleod, Professor (of sociology); Duncan Mylne, Sorcerer; Ramsey Maclean, Doctor
**Time period(s):** 1990s (1995)
**Locale(s):** Edinburgh, Scotland

**Summary:** While investigating local occult groups as part of his academic research in sociology, Andrew Macleod encounters the Fraternity of the Old Path and its mysterious adherent, Duncan Mylne. Mylne quickly takes Andrew under his wing and begins instructing him in the practice of ritual magic that will eventually lead him to try to resurrect his deceased beloved wife, Catriona.

**Other books you might like:**
Ramsey Campbell, *The Influence*, 1988
Fritz Leiber, *Conjure Wife*, 1953
Peter Straub, *Mrs. God*, 1991

## 281

**JONATHAN AYCLIFFE** (Pseudonym of Denis MacEoin)

### Naomi's Room

(New York: Harper Paperbacks, 1992)

**Story type:** Horror (Ghost Story)
**Major character(s):** Charles Hillenbrand, Professor (at Cambridge University); Laura Hillenbrand, Spouse (of Charles); Dafydd Lewis, Photographer
**Time period(s):** 1970s (1970)
**Locale(s):** Cambridge, England

**Summary:** The haunting of Charles Hillenbrand and his wife by the specter of his horribly mutilated daughter Naomi leads to the discovery of a sealed attic in their house, and within it the legacy of the previous owner whose curious life and horrible fate seem to mirror Charles's own.

**Other books you might like:**
Judith Hawkes, *Julian's House*, 1989
Shirley Jackson, *The Haunting of Hill House*, 1959
Richard Matheson, *Hell House*, 1971
Chet Williamson, *Soulstorm*, 1986

## 282

**JONATHAN AYCLIFFE** (Pseudonym of Denis MacEoin)

### The Vanishment

(New York: HarperCollins, 1994)

**Story type:** Horror (Haunted House)
**Major character(s):** Peter Clare, Writer; Susannah Adderstone, Young Woman; Rachel Wigram, Child (4-year-old)
**Time period(s):** 1990s (1994)
**Locale(s):** Tredannack, England (Petherick House)

**Summary:** Peter Clare's wife disappears while they are vacationing at remote Petherick House, a building with a reputation among the local townspeople for being haunted. As Peter digs into its century-old history of parricide and fatal sibling rivalry to solve the mystery of his wife's vanishment, he touches upon the eerie possibility that the house's grisly past is being repeated by himself and his small circle of friends and acquaintances.

**Other books you might like:**
Ramsey Campbell, *The Influence*, 1988
Judith Hawkes, *Julian's House*, 1989
Shirley Jackson, *The Haunting of Hill House*, 1959
Stephen King, *The Shining*, 1977
Roland Topor, *The Tenant*, 1966

## 283

**JONATHAN AYCLIFFE** (Pseudonym of Denis MacEoin)

### Whispers in the Dark

(New York: Harper, 1993)

**Story type:** Horror (Child-in-Peril)
**Major character(s):** Charlotte Metcalf, Child, Orphan; Antony Aryton, Nobleman; Antonia Aryton, Noblewoman
**Time period(s):** 1890s
**Locale(s):** Kirkwhelpington, England (Barras Lodge)

**Summary:** Strongly influenced by the writing of M.R. James, this novel tells of orphaned Charlotte Metcalf, who seeks help from her mother's estranged relatives at Barras Lodge. While there, she is visited by the ghostly figures of children who warn her to leave before she falls victim to the curse implicit in the family motto, "They shall inherit it forever."

**Other books you might like:**
Richard Dalby, *Ghosts and Scholars*, 1987
    Rosemary Pardoe, co-editor
James Herbert, *Haunted*, 1988
M.R. James, *Casting the Runes and Other Ghost Stories*, 1987
Daniel Rhodes, *Next, After Lucifer*, 1988
Robert Westall, *Antique Dust*, 1989

## 284

**RICHARD BACHMAN** (Pseudonym of Stephen King)

### The Regulators
(New York: Dutton, 1996)

**Story type:** Horror (Wild Talents)
**Major character(s):** Seth Garin, Child (6-year-old); Johnny Marinville, Writer; Collie Entragion, Police Officer (former)
**Time period(s):** 1990s (1996)
**Locale(s):** Wentworth, Ohio

**Summary:** The peace of a small middle-American town is shattered when a disembodied entity invades the mind of an autistic boy and begins turning the violent fantasies spawned by his television-watching into horrifying reality. This novel shares characters and themes with *Desperation*, which bears the Stephen King byline and was released at approximately the same time under one of the publisher's other imprints.

**Other books you might like:**
Ramsey Campbell, *Incarnate*, 1983
Dennis Etchison, *Shadow Man*, 1993
Charles L. Grant, *In a Dark Dream*, 1989
Dean R. Koontz, *Dragon Tears*, 1992
Kim Newman, *Bad Dreams*, 1990

## 285

**CAMILLE BACON-SMITH**

### Eyes of the Empress
(New York: DAW, 1998)

**Story type:** Fantasy (Mystery; Magic Conflict)
**Major character(s):** Kevin Bradley, Detective—Private, Demon; Evan Davis, Detective—Private, Demon (half-demon); Harry Li, Professor (art), Administrator (art museum)
**Time period(s):** 1990s
**Locale(s):** Philadelphia, Pennsylvania

**Summary:** When thieves steal two heavily guarded crystals, Harry Li hires Kevin Bradley and Evan Davis to investigate. They discover that the thief who stole the jewels of the long-dead Dowager Empress of China treasures them for more than their value as art.

**Other books you might like:**
P.N. Elrod, *Bloodlist*, 1990
Laurell K. Hamilton, *Guilty Pleasures*, 1993
R.A. MacAvoy, *Tea with the Black Dragon*, 1983
R.A. MacAvoy, *Twisting the Rope*, 1986
Nick Pollotta, *Bureau 13*, 1991

## 286

**ROBIN WAYNE BAILEY**

### Brothers of the Dragon
(New York: Roc, 1993)

**Story type:** Fantasy (Alternate World; Adventure)
**Series:** Brothers of the Dragon
**Major character(s):** Eric Podlowski, Martial Arts Expert, Teacher; Robert Podlowski, Martial Arts Expert, Waiter/Waitress
**Time period(s):** 1990s; Indeterminate
**Locale(s):** Catskill Mountains, New York; Palenoc, Mythical Place
**Summary:** Drawn by a glowing light, Eric and Robert go through a waterfall and find themselves in a strange and dangerous land where

their martial arts skills allow the pair to survive and begin investigating the world. Before long, Eric and Robert become involved in an ancient power struggle in the parallel land. First of a series.

**Other books you might like:**
Gael Baudino, *Dragonsword*, 1988
Pamela Dean, *The Secret Country*, 1985
Gordon R. Dickson, *The Dragon and the George*, 1976
Carole Nelson Douglas, *Cup of Clay*, 1991
Rick Shelley, *The Hero King*, 1992

## 287

**ROBIN WAYNE BAILEY**

### Flames of the Dragon
(New York: Roc, 1994)

**Story type:** Fantasy (Alternate World; Magic Conflict)
**Series:** Brothers of the Dragon
**Major character(s):** Eric Podlowski, Martial Arts Expert, Leader; Robert Podlowski, Martial Arts Expert, Writer; Katherine "Katy" Dowd, Librarian, Adventurer
**Time period(s):** 1990s; Indeterminate
**Locale(s):** Palenoc, Mythical Place; Catskill Mountains, New York; Dowdsville, New York

**Summary:** Katy's library research allows her to bring Eric from Palenoc to prove Robert innocent of murdering Eric in Dowdsville. Katy returns to Palenoc with the pair where Robert's search for the fate of his friend, Scott, yields insight into mysterious deaths as they encounter forces of the Heart of Darkness and the Dark Lord.

**Other books you might like:**
David Eddings, *Pawn of Prophecy*, 1982
David Gemmell, *Morningstar*, 1993
Terry Goodkind, *Wizard's First Rule*, 1994
Robert Jordan, *The Eye of the World*, 1989

## 288

**ROBIN WAYNE BAILEY**

### The Lost City of Zork
(New York: Avon, 1991)

**Story type:** Fantasy (Light Fantasy; Quest)
**Series:** Infocom
**Major character(s):** Caspar Wartsworth, Adventurer, Barbarian
**Time period(s):** Indeterminate
**Locale(s):** Borphee, Fictional City

**Summary:** Arrested and sent to war as a galley slave, Caspar survives when his ship is wrecked. He then assembles a group of adventurers who hope to free the Borphee Guild of Wizards by defeating King Duncanthrax and recovering their leader, Berknip. This book ties into the Zork computer gaming universe.

**Other books you might like:**
Arthur Byron Cover, *Planetfall*, 1989
Arthur Byron Cover, *Stationfall*, 1988
George Alec Effinger, *The Zork Chronicles*, 1990
Craig Shaw Gardner, *Wishbringer*, 1988

## 289

### ROBIN WAYNE BAILEY

## *Nightwatch*

(Lake Geneva, Wisconsin: TSR, 1990)

**Story type:** Fantasy (Mystery; Magic Conflict)
**Major character(s):** Garett Starlen, Police Officer (Captain); Burge, Police Officer; Blossom, Police Officer
**Time period(s):** Indeterminate Past
**Locale(s):** Greyhawk, Mythical Place; Mist Marsh, Fictional Country

**Summary:** Five seers of Greyhawk have been killed in one night by their own instruments of divination. Garett, as commander of the night shift of the City Watch, is assigned to investigate. He discovers evidence that this is the work of the Horned Society and acquires a magic sword that is the only weapon capable of fighting their powers.

**Other books you might like:**
Steven Brust, *Jhereg*, 1983
C.J. Cherryh, *Angel with the Sword*, 1985
Barbara Hambly, *The Dark Hand of Magic*, 1990
Barbara Hambly, *The Ladies of Mandrigyn*, 1984
Barbara Hambly, *The Witches of Wenshar*, 1987
Janet Morris, *Beyond Sanctuary*, 1985
Patricia C. Wrede, *Daughter of Witches*, 1983

## 290

### ROBIN WAYNE BAILEY

## *Shadowdance*

(Clarkston, Georgia: White Wolf Borealis, 1996)

**Story type:** Fantasy (Quest)
**Major character(s):** Innowen, Handicapped, Dancer; Minarik, Military Personnel, Leader; Razkili, Military Personnel (soldier)
**Time period(s):** Indeterminate
**Locale(s):** Ispor, Fictional Country; Parendur, Fictional City

**Summary:** Paralized and helpless, Innowen deals with a witch to allow him to walk during the dark hours, for which he must dance every night. This seems ideal, but Innowen's dancing allows and forces viewers to succumb to their dark impulses. Ashamed and horrified, he sets out to find the witch and discover her reasons for the curse.

**Other books you might like:**
Scott Baker, *Drink the Fire From the Flames*, 1987
Glen Cook, *The Black Company*, 1984
Simon R. Green, *Hawk & Fisher*, 1990
Ellen Kushner, *Swordspoint*, 1987
Fritz Leiber, *Ill Met in Lankhmar*, 1995

## 291

### ROBIN WAYNE BAILEY

## *Swords Against the Shadowland*

(Clarkston, Georgia: White Wolf Borealis, 1998)

**Story type:** Fantasy (Sword and Sorcery)
**Series:** Fafhrd and the Gray Mouser
**Major character(s):** Fafhrd, Thief, Warrior; The Gray Mouser, Thief, Magician
**Time period(s):** Indeterminate
**Locale(s):** Lankhmar, Fictional City; At Sea; Planet—Imaginary

**Summary:** When a sorcerer curses Lankhmar, Fafhrd and the Gray Mouser reluctantly come to the city's aid, rather than allowing all to die, eaten away from the inside by evil.

**Other books you might like:**
Robert E. Howard, *Hour of the Dragon*, 1977
Fritz Leiber, *Bazaar of the Bizarre*, 1978
Fritz Leiber, *Ill Met in Lankhmar*, 1995
Fritz Leiber, *Lean Times in Lankhmar*, 1996
Clark Ashton Smith, *Tales of Zothique*, 1995

## 292

### SHARON BAINBRIDGE

## *Blood and Roses*

(New York: Diamond, 1994)

**Story type:** Horror (Vampire Story)
**Major character(s):** Sir Geoffrey, Nobleman, Vampire; Elaine Portland, Young Woman; William R. Praisegood, Doctor
**Time period(s):** 19th century (late)
**Locale(s):** High Grimmire, England

**Summary:** Sir Geoffrey, who contracts vampirism shortly after Count Dracula arrives on English soil, meets his match in William Praisegood, a doctor whose scientific method and incomplete skepticism make him a formidable match against those who prey upon his patients.

**Other books you might like:**
Traci Briery, *The Vampire Journals*, 1993
P.N. Elrod, *Red Death*, 1993
Kim Newman, *Anno Dracula*, 1992
Michael Romkey, *I, Vampire*, 1990
Bram Stoker, *Dracula*, 1897

## 293

### WILHELMINA BAIRD

## *Chaos Come Again*

(New York: Ace, 1996)

**Story type:** Science Fiction (Alternate Intelligence; Psychic Powers)
**Series:** Crashcourse
**Major character(s):** Desi "Daisy Smeet" Smith, Doctor, Psychic; Jeremiah "Jonesy" Jones, Journalist, Psychic; Ice, Divorced Person, Villain
**Time period(s):** Indeterminate Future
**Locale(s):** *Windrunner/Windy*, Spaceship

**Summary:** After encountering an intelligent alien symbiont, the human race acquires many new abilities which sweep through the population like wildfire. Many groups of humans reject the symbs, causing a period of warfare. Desi searches for her brilliant, insane ex-husband with the help of a lonely planetary intelligence, a stowaway reporter, and her neurotic, intelligent spaceship, human enough to have a symb of her own.

**Other books you might like:**
Stephen Goldin, *Jade Darcy and the Zen Pirates*, 1990
    Mary Mason, co-author
Anne McCaffrey, *Powers That Be*, 1993
    Elizabeth Ann Scarborough, co-author
Robert J. Sawyer, *Starplex*, 1996
Dan Simmons, *Hyperion*, 1989
Sheri S. Tepper, *Raising the Stones*, 1990
David Weber, *Path of the Fury*, 1992

**294**

### WILHELMINA BAIRD

## *Clipjoint*
(New York: Ace, 1994)

**Story type:** Science Fiction (Arts; Mystery)
**Series:** Crashcourse
**Major character(s):** Cassandra "Cass" Blaine, Actress, Thief; Hans-Bjorn "Mokey/Moke" Eklunk, Artist (sculptor), Actor; Dribble, Genetically Altered Being
**Time period(s):** 21st century
**Locale(s):** Never, Space Station; Virginity, Planet—Imaginary

**Summary:** Cass and Moke feel compelled to leave their comfortable new lives and return to Never when they receive a vidclip which seems to feature the deceased actor, Dosh. With the help of her friends, Cass uncovers proof of Coelacanth Productions' criminal activities.

**Other books you might like:**
Greg Bear, *Queen of Angels*, 1990
Pat Cadigan, *Synners*, 1991
Emily Devenport, *Shade*, 1991
Philip K. Dick, *A Scanner Darkly*, 1977
Laura J. Mixon, *Glass Houses*, 1992

**295**

### WILHELMINA BAIRD

## *Crashcourse*
(New York: Ace, 1993)

**Story type:** Science Fiction (Cyberpunk; Arts)
**Series:** Crashcourse
**Major character(s):** Cassandra "Cass" Blaine, Actress, Thief; Doshky "Dosh", Prostitute, Actor; Hans-Bjorn "Mokey/Moke" Eklunk, Artist, Actor
**Time period(s):** 21st century
**Locale(s):** Chicago, Illinois; Never, Space Station

**Summary:** Desperate to earn enough money to get off-planet, Cassie, Dosh and Moke agree to participate as actors in a production to be filmed without their reading scripts, to promote spontaneous reactions felt by the audience through cyber links. Problems arise as the actors experience difficulty distinguishing real events from scripted actions. First novel.

**Other books you might like:**
David Brin, *Earth*, 1990
Pat Cadigan, *Synners*, 1991
William C. Dietz, *Matrix Man*, 1990
Neal Stephenson, *Snow Crash*, 1992
Robert Charles Wilson, *Memory Wire*, 1987

**296**

### WILHELMINA BAIRD

## *Psykosis*
(New York: Ace, 1995)

**Story type:** Science Fiction (First Contact; Alternate Intelligence)
**Series:** Crashcourse
**Major character(s):** Cassandra "Cass" Blaine, Criminal (burglar), Companion; McLaren "Swordfish" DeLorn, Diplomat (ambassador), Military Personnel; Hans-Bjorn "Mokey/Moke" Eklunk, Artist (sculptor), Genius

**Time period(s):** 21st century
**Locale(s):** *Hercules*, Spaceship; Outer Space; Resurrection, Planet—Imaginary

**Summary:** Retaining the atomic heart and enhanced bones and nervous system from the last war with the aliens, Swordfish volunteers to attempt a meeting with them to avert yet another war. When the meeting with the telepathic toadstools on Resurrection ends with humans taken hostage, Swordfish, Cass, and Moke rush to rescue the hostages before the Navy slags the planet.

**Other books you might like:**
David Brin, *Brightness Reef*, 1995
Octavia E. Butler, *Dawn*, 1987
L. Warren Douglas, *Cannon's Orb*, 1994
Larry Niven, *The Mote in God's Eye*, 1974
   Jerry Pournelle, co-author
S. Andrew Swann, *Specters of the Dawn*, 1994
Sheri S. Tepper, *Grass*, 1989
David Weber, *Path of the Fury*, 1992

**297**

### ERIC T. BAKER

## *Checkmate*
(New York: Roc, 1998)

**Story type:** Science Fiction (Generation Starship)
**Major character(s):** Aaron Hudson, Civil Servant; Cleo, Passenger; Gaunt, Robot
**Time period(s):** Indeterminate Future

**Summary:** Aaron Hudson serves as a member of the Contraband Unit, a group within a fleet of generational starships whose job is to ensure that resources are not wasted. He uncovers a criminal plot to exploit some of those resources, but before he can identify those responsible he is framed. With his friend Cleo, he clears his own name and brings the real thieves to justice. First novel.

**Other books you might like:**
Brian W. Aldiss, *Starship*, 1959
Edmund Cooper, *The Seed of Light*, 1959
Molly Gloss, *The Dazzle of Day*, 1997
Robert A. Heinlein, *Orphans of the Sky*, 1963
Alexei Panshin, *Rite of Passage*, 1968

**298**

### KAGE BAKER

## *In the Garden of Iden*
(New York: Harcourt Brace, 1998)

**Story type:** Science Fiction (Immortality; Theological)
**Series:** Company
**Major character(s):** Mendoza, Immortal, Scientist (botanist); Nicholas Harpole, Secretary, Religious (Protestant); Joseph, Immortal
**Time period(s):** 16th century
**Locale(s):** Kent, England (Iden's Garden); Australia (Terra Australis Training Compound); Spain

**Summary:** After saving the child Mendoza from the clutches of the Spanish Inquisition, the Company turns Mendoza into an immortal, trains her as a botanist, and sends her to England to collect rare plants headed for extinction. While there, Mendoza makes the dangerous mistake of falling in love with a mortal. First novel and first in a series with at least two more books forthcoming.

**Other books you might like:**
Poul Anderson, *The Boat of a Million Years*, 1989

Orson Scott Card, *Pastwatch: The Redemption of Christopher Columbus*, 1996
Steven Gould, *Wildside*, 1996
Kay Kenyon, *The Seeds of Time*, 1997
David Morse, *The Iron Bridge*, 1998

---

**299**

### LINDA P. BAKER
### NANCY VARIAN BERBERICK, Co-Author

## *Tears of the Night Sky*
(Renton, Washington: TSR, 1998)

**Story type:** Fantasy (Quest)
**Major character(s):** Dalamar, Mythical Creature (elf); Crysania, Religious (priestess)
**Time period(s):** Indeterminate
**Locale(s):** Neraka, Fictional City; Krynn, Fictional Country

**Summary:** The high priestess of the Temple of Palatine experiences doubts about her faith. She falls under the influence of a magical stone that causes her and a group of companions to set out on a dangerous quest.

**Other books you might like:**
Chris Cymri, *Dragons Can Only Rust*, 1995
Ed Greenwood, *All Shadows Fled*, 1995
Simon Hawke, *The Seeker*, 1994
Douglas Niles, *Pawns Prevail*, 1995
R.A. Salvatore, *Sojourn*, 1991

---

**300**

### MIKE BAKER, Editor

## *Young Blood*
(New York: Zebra, 1994)

**Story type:** Horror (Anthology)

**Summary:** The 29 stories collected in this volume all were written by authors under the age of 30, many of whom had not published professionally before. Of the handful of supernatural stories, the stand-out is Clark Perry's "Little Black Bags," about a monster found inside the body of a doctor's backwoods patient. Most fall within the realm of psychological horror, including Gordon van Gelder's tale of a man's alienation from his family, "Something More"; Tim Waggoner's psycho tale of childhood neuroses that become adult psychoses, "Mr. Punch"; and Brian Everson's gruesomely humorous "Hebe Kills Jerry." One third of the book is taken up with classic reprints by Ramsey Campbell, Robert Bloch, Edgar Allan Poe, Robert E. Howard, and Stephen King, all published before the authors turned 30.

**Other books you might like:**
Peter Enfantino, *Quick Chills*, 1989
    Robert Morrish, co-editor
Robert Morrish, *Quick Chills II*, 1991
    Peter Enfantino, co-editor
Joy Oestreicher, *Air Fish*, 1992
    Richard Singer, co-editor

---

**301**

### NANCY BAKER

## *The Night Inside*
(New York: Fawcett Columbine, 1994)

**Story type:** Horror (Vampire Story)
**Major character(s):** Ardeth Alexander, Student; Dimitri Rozokov, Vampire; Ambrose Dale, Businessman
**Time period(s):** 1990s (1994); 1890s (1898)
**Locale(s):** Toronto, Ontario, Canada

**Summary:** In an unusual buddy story Ardeth Alexander, a student abducted to feed vampire Dimitri Rozokov, pools resources and knowledge with the sympathetic vampire to free him from imprisonment by pornographers who use him in snuff films. Together they discover the link binding Rozokov's current captors with the man who first began persecuting him a century before. This is the author's first novel.

**Other books you might like:**
Tanya Huff, *Blood Pact*, 1993
Roxanne Longstreet, *The Undead*, 1993
Yvonne Navarro, *Afterage*, 1993
Anne Rice, *The Vampire Lestat*, 1985

---

**302**

### NICHOLSON BAKER

## *The Fermata*
(New York: Random House, 1994)

**Story type:** Science Fiction (Psychic Powers; Humor)
**Major character(s):** Arnold Strine, Writer, Criminal; Joyce Collier, Businesswoman; Marian, Librarian
**Time period(s):** 1990s
**Locale(s):** Boston, Massachusetts

**Summary:** When he learns to halt the progression of events and, in effect, stop the passage of time while remaining unaffected, Arnold begins taking unnatural liberties with acquaintances and strangers. He indulges his fantasies by undressing and redressing women and creating anomalies in normal existence from within the spaces between moments of time, maintaining throughout a fractured moral perspective.

**Other books you might like:**
Jeff Gelb, *Hot Blood: Tales of Provocative Horror*, 1989
    Lonn Friend, co-editor
Steven Gould, *Jumper*, 1992
Robert A. Heinlein, *The Number of the Beast*, 1980
Alan Lightman, *Einstein's Dreams*, 1993
John D. MacDonald, *The Girl, the Gold Watch, and Everything*, 1962

---

**303**

### SCOTT BAKER

## *Ancestral Hungers*
(New York: Tor, 1995)

**Story type:** Horror (Vampire Story)
**Major character(s):** David Bathory, Drug Dealer; Dara, Wanderer; Michael Bathory, Businessman (David's brother)
**Time period(s):** 1990s (1995)
**Locale(s):** Illinois

**Summary:** In this expansion of his 1982 novel, *Dhampire*, the author chronicles the life of David Bathory, a lineal descendant of Count Dracula, who is forced to come to terms with his family roots after the murder of his wife. Returning to his family homestead, David finds himself drawn into a struggle with his family that mandates he draw on his inherited traits as a "dhampire," or being capable of mastering his vampire relatives.

**Other books you might like:**
Christopher Golden, *Of Saints and Shadows*, 1994
Tanith Lee, *Darkness, I*, 1995
Kim Newman, *Anno Dracula*, 1992
Brian Stableford, *Young Blood*, 1991
Robert Weinberg, *Blood War*, 1995

---

**304**

**SCOTT BAKER**

### Webs

(New York: Tor, 1989)

**Story type:** Horror (Psychological Suspense)
**Major character(s):** Brian Gerard, Professor (college); Karen Attercop, Student (spider fancier), Lover (Brian's)
**Time period(s):** 1980s
**Locale(s):** Point Marsh Key, Florida (Aubrey Estate, the Florida coast)

**Summary:** His wife confined to a mental hospital, Brian Gerard accepts a teaching job in Florida that includes free use of a large estate. Soon he finds himself plagued by an army of huge spiders and begins an affair with a pretty young student, whose expertise with spiders may rescue him from his infestation—unless she is behind it.

**Other books you might like:**
K.W. Jeter, *Soul Eater*, 1983

---

**305**

**KIRSTEN BAKIS**

### Lives of the Monster Dogs

(New York: Farrar, Strauss, Giroux, 1997)

**Story type:** Science Fiction (Literary; Genetic Manipulation)
**Major character(s):** Cleo Pira, Student; Ludwig von Sacher, Genetically Altered Being, Historian; Klaue Lutz, Genetically Altered Being
**Time period(s):** 2000s (2009)
**Locale(s):** New York, New York

**Summary:** A group of genetically and surgically modified dogs who dress and act like 19th century German aristocrats appears in New York City. The product of demented medical experiments, the dogs want only comfort and obscurity, but the modern world and a degenerative disease threaten both. As a human woman befriends them and uncovers their past and secrets, their future narrows toward extinction. First novel.

**Other books you might like:**
John Crowley, *Beasts*, 1976
Nancy Kress, *Beggars in Spain*, 1993
Ian McDonald, *Terminal Cafe*, 1994
Walter Tevis, *The Man Who Fell to Earth*, 1963
H.G. Wells, *The Island of Doctor Moreau*, 1896

---

**306**

**ROBERT T. BAKKER**

### Raptor Red

(New York: Bantam, 1995)

**Story type:** Fantasy (Adventure; Science Fiction)
**Major character(s):** Raptor Red, Animal (dinosaur)
**Time period(s):** Indeterminate Past (early Cretaceous)
**Locale(s):** Asia; North America

**Summary:** Raptor Red tragically loses her mate while hunting and must flee predators and natural disasters as she searches for a comfortable environment and a new mate.

**Other books you might like:**
Sir Arthur Conan Doyle, *The Lost World*, 1912
James Gurney, *Dinotopia*, 1992
Garry Kilworth, *The Foxes of Firstdark*, 1990
Stephen Leigh, *Ray Bradbury Presents: Dinosaur World*, 1992

---

**307**

**CHRIS BALDICK**, Editor

### The Oxford Book of Gothic Tales

(New York: Oxford University Press, 1992)

**Story type:** Horror (Anthology)

**Summary:** This superb omnibus pulls together 37 classic and contemporary stories of horror and the supernatural that define the gloomy and antiquated atmosphere of the Gothic mode. Included are seven excessively morbid fragments of early-Gothic horror from the late-eighteenth and early-nineteenth centuries; late-Gothic masterpieces of doomed families such as Poe's "The Fall of the House of Usher" and Nathaniel Hawthorne's "Rappacini's Daughter"; early-modern Gothic tales from the pulp era including H. P. Lovecraft's Poe pastiche, "The Outsider," and Clark Ashton Smith's vampire tale, "A Rendezvous in Averoigne"; and contemporary examples of the southern gothic (William Faulkner's "A Rose for Emily") and satiric Gothic (Patrick McGrath's "Blood Disease").

**Other books you might like:**
Peter Haining, *Gothic Tales of Terror*, 1972
   editor
Peter Haining, *The Shilling Shockers*, 1978
   editor
Bradford Morrow, *The New Gothic*, 1991
   Patrick McGrath, co-editor
Patricia L. Skarda, *The Evil Image: Two Centuries of Gothic Short Fiction and Poetry*, 1981
   Nora Crowe, co-editor

---

**308**

**BILL BALDWIN**

### Canby's Legion

(New York: Warner Aspect, 1995)

**Story type:** Science Fiction (Space Opera; Military)
**Major character(s):** Gordon Canby, Spaceship Captain, Mercenary; Nikolai Kobir, Spaceship Captain, Pirate; Sadir, Nobleman (First Earl of Relando)
**Time period(s):** 27th century (2681-2692)
**Locale(s):** United States (East Coast); Khalife, Planet—Imaginary

**Summary:** Gordon Canby, a retired war hero, unites a group of fellow veterans into a mercenary unit called Canby's Legion. Hired by the First Earl of Renaldo to destroy the Kirskian pirates, Canby hunts a man named Nikolai Kobir, whom he once faced as an enemy starship captain.

**Other books you might like:**
John Dalmas, *The Regiment*, 1987
Gordon R. Dickson, *Dorsai!*, 1976
David Drake, *At Any Price*, 1985
David Drake, *Igniting the Reaches*, 1994
David Drake, *Through the Breach*, 1995
Jerry Pournelle, *The Mercenary*, 1977
Jerry Pournelle, *Prince of Mercenaries*, 1989

## 309
### BILL BALDWIN
### *The Defenders*
(New York: Questar, 1992)

**Story type:** Science Fiction (Military; Space Opera)
**Series:** Helmsman
**Major character(s):** Wilf Brim, Military Personnel, Spaceship Captain; Onrad, Ruler (emperor)
**Time period(s):** 520th century
**Locale(s):** Avalon, Planet—Imaginary (center of galactic civilization); Interstellar Empire/Federation

**Summary:** Wilf Brim and his young emperor must assemble defenses for Avalon when the League of Dark Stars attacks the heart of galactic civiliztion.

**Other books you might like:**
David Brin, *Startide Rising*, 1983
Lois McMaster Bujold, *The Vor Game*, 1990
Allan Cole, *Sten*, 1984
    Chris Bunch, co-author
Glen Cook, *The Dragon Never Sleeps*, 1988
Brian Daley, *Requiem for a Ruler of Worlds*, 1985
Alis A. Rasmussen, *Revolution's Shore*, 1990
Edward E. Smith, *The Lensman Series*, 1948-1954
Vernor Vinge, *A Fire upon the Deep*, 1992

## 310
### BILL BALDWIN
### *The Defiance*
(New York; Warner Aspect, 1996)

**Story type:** Science Fiction (Military)
**Series:** Helmsman
**Major character(s):** Wilf Brim, Military Personnel
**Time period(s):** 521st century
**Locale(s):** Atalanta, Fictional City; Interstellar Empire/Federation; Outer Space

**Summary:** As the League of Dark Stars continues its war with the Empire, Admiral Wilf Brim must lead a siegebreaking of Atalanta, then capture Gontor, a vast alien fortress built into an asteroid.

**Other books you might like:**
Lois McMaster Bujold, *The Warrior's Apprentice*, 1986
Glen Cook, *The Dragon Never Sleeps*, 1988
Gordon R. Dickson, *Dorsai!*, 1976
Debra Doyle, *The Price of the Stars*, 1992
    James D. Macdonald, co-author
Robert A. Heinlein, *Starship Troopers*, 1959

Sherwood Smith, *The Phoenix in Flight*, 1993
    Dave Trowbridge, co-author
David Weber, *On Basilisk Station*, 1993

## 311
### BILL BALDWIN
### *The Mercenaries*
(New York: Warner Questar, 1991)

**Story type:** Science Fiction (Space Opera)
**Series:** Helmsman
**Major character(s):** Wilf Brim, Military Personnel, Spaceship Captain (Starfury); Nadia Tissaurd, Military Personnel
**Time period(s):** 520th century
**Locale(s):** *Starfury*, Spaceship (prototype); Fluvanna, Interstellar Empire/Federation (Magor, the capital)

**Summary:** With most of the fleet in mothballs due to the Treaty of Garak, Wilf Brim takes *Starfury* to Fluvanna to protect raw materials needed to construct a new imperial fleet.

**Other books you might like:**
David Brin, *Startide Rising*, 1983
Lois McMaster Bujold, *Brothers in Arms*, 1989
Glen Cook, *The Dragon Never Sleeps*, 1988
Melisa C. Michaels, *Skirmish*, 1985
Alis A. Rasmussen, *The Price of Ransom*, 1990

## 312
### BILL BALDWIN
### *The Siege*
(New York: Warner Questar, 1994)

**Story type:** Science Fiction (Space Opera; Military)
**Series:** Helmsman
**Major character(s):** Wilf Brim, Military Personnel (admiral); Nikolai Yanuarievich Ursis, Military Personnel
**Time period(s):** 520th century
**Locale(s):** *Alexasander Grobkin*, Spaceship; Avalon, Planet— Imaginary; Interstellar Empire/Federation

**Summary:** The League of Dark Stars once again attempts to invade the Sodeskayan Worlds. Wilf's ground troops need space support but his superiors expect the Sodeskayans to provide most of the ships. Unfortunately, the Sodeskayan shipyards have barely begun spaceship production.

**Other books you might like:**
Allan Cole, *Sten*, 1984
    Chris Bunch, co-author
Michelle Shirey Crean, *Dancer of the Sixth*, 1993
Brian Daley, *Requiem for a Ruler of Worlds*, 1985
David Drake, *The Warrior*, 1991
David Weber, *The Honor of the Queen*, 1993

## 313
### MARGARET BALL
### *Changeweaver*
(New York: Baen, 1993)

**Story type:** Fantasy (Historical; Magic Conflict)

**Major character(s):** Tamai, Shaman (Flameweaver), Heroine; Charles Francis Carrington, Traveler, Writer; Louisa McAusland, Diplomat, Shaman
**Time period(s):** 1880s (1887)
**Locale(s):** Gandhara, Fictional City; Kashgar, Ancient Civilization (Silk Road); Peking, China

**Summary:** Carrington arrives in Gandhara en route to Peking to achieve a trade agreement with the Chin Empire. There he meets his guide, Tamai, who reluctantly accompanies him over the Pamirs to Kashgar and across the Great Desert. Adopting a daughter and facing physical dangers, Tamai gains the control she had always lacked, unaware that the fate of the Chin Empire resides in her hands. Sequel to *Flameweaver*.

**Other books you might like:**
Marion Zimmer Bradley, *Hawkmistress!*, 1982
Carol Chase, *Hawk's Flight*, 1991
Marc Laidlaw, *Neon Lotus*, 1988
Jeanne Larsen, *Silk Road*, 1989
Catherine Lyndell, *Stolen Dreams*, 1989
    pseudonym of Margaret Ball
Anne McCaffrey, *PartnerShip*, 1992   ·
    Margaret Ball, co-author
Elizabeth Ann Scarborough, *Nothing Sacred*, 1991

---

### 314

#### MARGARET BALL

## Flameweaver

(New York: Baen, 1991)

**Story type:** Fantasy (Magic Conflict; Alternate History)
**Major character(s):** Tamai, Psychic; Louisa Westbrook, Gentlewoman, Psychic; James McAusland, Military Personnel (Lieutenant)
**Time period(s):** 1880s (1884)
**Locale(s):** Gandhara, Fictional City; India

**Summary:** Because she is unable to have children, Tamai's psychic powers, though strong, are undisciplined and dangerous. When invaders come from the north, she goes south with her cousin and a trained eagle to bargain for rifles from the legendary "Angrez." Tamai's psychic battle to protect her traveling companions nearly kills her, but Louisa Westbrook nurses her back to health while Tamai helps Louisa develop her latent powers.

**Other books you might like:**
Poul Anderson, *A Midsummer Tempest*, 1984
Marion Zimmer Bradley, *Hawkmistress!*, 1982
C.J. Cherryh, *A Dirge for Stabis*, 1989
    Leslie Fish, co-author
John M. Ford, *The Dragon Waiting*, 1983
Lisa Goldstein, *The Red Magician*, 1982
Rudyard Kipling, *Kim*, 1901
Ursula K. Le Guin, *Tehanu: The Last Book of Earthsea*, 1990
Elizabeth Ann Scarborough, *Nothing Sacred*, 1991
Patricia C. Wrede, *Sorcery and Cecelia*, 1988
    Caroline Stevermer, co-author

---

### 315

#### MARGARET BALL

## Lost in Translation

(New York: Baen, 1995)

**Story type:** Fantasy (Light Fantasy; Alternate World)

**Major character(s):** Allie, Student—College; Domerc, Student—College, Wizard; Aigar, Wizard, Professor
**Time period(s):** Indeterminate
**Locale(s):** Coindra, Fictional Country; Alternate Earth

**Summary:** Sent against her will to a university in southern France, Allie arrives instead in a strange place where students study the art of magic. With the help of fellow students, she must prevent Aigar from using magic to raise deadly Landmonsters from the earth.

**Other books you might like:**
Carolyn Cushman, *Witch and Wombat*, 1994
Brett Davis, *The Faery Convention*, 1995
Anne McCaffrey, *PartnerShip*, 1992
    Margaret Ball, co-author
Caroline Stevermer, *A College of Magics*, 1994
Sheri S. Tepper, *Marianne, the Magus, and the Manticore*, 1985

---

### 316

#### MARGARET BALL

## Mathemagics

(New York: Baen, 1996)

**Story type:** Fantasy (Light Fantasy; Alternate World)
**Series:** Chicks in Chainmail
**Major character(s):** Rivakonneva "Riva", Warrior, Parent; Dennis "Dennis Dithrovvu" Withrow, Scientist (mathematician), Teacher; Mikhalevviko "Mikh", Wizard, Criminal
**Time period(s):** 1990s; Indeterminate
**Locale(s):** Austin, Texas; Dazau, Planet—Imaginary

**Summary:** Riva spends most of her time on Earth studying mathematics and allowing her daughter to study while Riva commutes to work as Bronze Bra Guild fighter and bodyguard on Dazau. When Mikhalevviko joins forces with a self-aggrandizing Bible thumper intent on wiping out all secular literature on Earth, Riva and Dennis travel to Dazau, where Dennis' mathematical formulas translate to magic spells. The pair must rescue Riva's daughter and her friends and restore Earth's books by eliminating the ensorcelled literary characters created on Dazau.

**Other books you might like:**
Marion Zimmer Bradley, *The Sword and Sorceress Series*, 1984-1996
    editor
George Alec Effinger, *Maureen Birnbaum, Barbarian Swordsperson: The Complete Stories*, 1993
Esther Friesner, *Chicks in Chainmail*, 1995
    editor
Holly Lisle, *Minerva Wakes*, 1994
Sharyn McCrumb, *Bimbos of the Death Sun*, 1987
Jessica Amanda Salmonson, *Amazons!*, 1979
    editor

---

### 317

#### MARGARET BALL

## The Shadow Gate

(New York: Baen, 1991)

**Story type:** Fantasy (Alternate World; Magic Conflict)
**Major character(s):** Lisa, Secretary; Judith Templeton, Computer Expert; Count Berengar, Nobleman, Mythical Creature (elf)
**Time period(s):** 1990s (1991); Indeterminate Past
**Locale(s):** Austin, Texas; Duchy of Aquitaine, France

**Summary:** Berengar, the elvish Count of the Garronais, is trying to call the former Queen of the Middle Realm, Sybille, back from where she has fled so that she can restore the power of the Stones of Jura. Instead, three humans connected with the New Age Psychic Research Center are transported from Austin, Texas to the Duchy of Aquitaine in a world where elf and human co-exist (uneasily) and magic works (weakly). Despite the interference of the elf-hating Durandine monks, they reach the Stones and one of the mortals proves to be the one who can find Sybille and restore elvish magic.

**Other books you might like:**
Emma Bull, *War for the Oaks*, 1987
Barbara Hambly, *The Silent Tower*, 1986
Barbara Hambly, *The Silicon Mage*, 1988
R.A. MacAvoy, *The Book of Kells*, 1985
Elizabeth Marie Pope, *The Perilous Gard*, 1974

---

**318**

**BETTY BALLANTINE**

## The Secret Oceans
(New York: Ballantine, 1994)

**Story type:** Science Fiction (First Contact)
**Major character(s):** Katerina "Kate" Kominsky, Sea Captain, Scientist; David Schlessinger, Activist (environmental), Scientist
**Time period(s):** 2000s
**Locale(s):** *Turtle*, Submarine; At Sea

**Summary:** On *Turtle*'s maiden voyage the crew discovers an ancient species hidden in the ocean which has surreptitiously observed human beings and society for a long time. Extensive illustrations.

**Other books you might like:**
David Bischoff, *seaQuest DSV: The Ancient*, 1994
Orson Scott Card, *The Abyss*, 1989
Arthur C. Clarke, *The Deep Range*, 1957
Arthur C. Clarke, *Dolphin Island*, 1963
David Kirschner, *The Pagemaster*, 1993
    Ernie Contreras, co-author
James Gurney, *Dinotopia*, 1992
Kathryn Lasky, *Shadows in the Water*, 1992
Roy Meyers, *Dolphin Boy*, 1967
Theodore Sturgeon, *Voyage to the Bottom of the Sea*, 1961

---

**319**

**J.G. BALLARD**

## The Atrocity Exhibition
(San Francisco, California: RE/SEARCH Publications, 1990)

**Story type:** Science Fiction (Collection)
**Major character(s):** Ronald Reagan, Political Figure
**Time period(s):** 1970s (1970)
**Locale(s):** Earth

**Summary:** This is the "revised, expanded, illustrated edition" of a book that was printed and suppressed before release by Doubleday in 1970. It was later issued by Grove as *Love and Napalm: Export USA*. Short, vivid vignettes mix surrealism, politics, sex, popular culture, medicine and technology. This edition has extensive margin notes by the author that explain references and expand on his ideas.

**Other books you might like:**
Iain M. Banks, *The Bridge*, 1946
Michael Blumlein, *The Brains of Rats*, 1990
William S. Burroughs, *Naked Lunch*, 1959
Brian Byson, *Have to Go: Planet R-101*, 1982

Mark Leyner, *My Cousin, My Gastroenterologist*, 1990

---

**320**

**J.G. BALLARD**

## Running Wild
(New York: Farrar, Straus & Giroux, 1989)

**Story type:** Horror (Serial Killer)
**Major character(s):** Richard Greville, Doctor (Psychiatrist, police advisor); Payne, Police Officer (Sergeant; Reading CID)
**Time period(s):** 1980s (1988)
**Locale(s):** Pangbourne Village (Exclusive "planned community")

**Summary:** On June 25, 1988, thirty-two adult residents of Pangbourne Village are quickly and efficiently murdered and thirteen children vanish. Greville's scrupulous analysis of the incident leads him to a terrifying and provocative conclusion.

**Other books you might like:**
Lawrence Block, *Ariel*, 1980
Stephen King, *"The Children of the Corn"*, 1977
William March, *The Bad Seed*, 1954

---

**321**

**J.G. BALLARD**

## War Fever
(New York: Farrar, Straus, Giroux, 1991)

**Story type:** Science Fiction (Collection)

**Summary:** 14 stories written between 1975 and 1991 and originally published in periodicals and anthologies in the United States and Great Britain. Frequent humor and thorny satire appear within the themes of war, politics, media manipulation, pollution and human nature. In "The Secret History of World War 3," reports of a brief nuclear war are slipped into continuous reports of every medical detail of third-term U.S. President Ronald Reagan. Some of the short stories are presented in a non-traditional format including "The Index" which looks at 20th century literature through the index to an unpublished biography of an unknown but influential figure. "Answers to a Questionnaire," labelled 1-100, provide a look into the assassination of the Messiah during His Second Coming on Earth. In "Notes Towards a Mental Breakdown" Dr. Robert Loughlin depicts, through footnotes, events surrounding his breakdown.

**Other books you might like:**
Alfred Bester, *The Light Fantastic*, 1976
Alfred Bester, *Star Light, Star Bright*, 1976
Philip K. Dick, *The Best of Philip K. Dick*, 1977
R.A. Lafferty, *Lafferty in Orbit*, 1991
Kim Stanley Robinson, *Remaking History*, 1991
Cordwainer Smith, *The Best of Cordwainer Smith*, 1975
Kurt Vonnegut Jr., *Welcome to the Monkey House*, 1968
Gene Wolfe, *Endangered Species*, 1989

---

**322**

**IAIN M. BANKS**

## Against a Dark Background
(New York: Bantam Spectra, 1993)

**Story type:** Science Fiction (Space Opera)
**Series:** Culture
**Major character(s):** Lady Sharrow, Thief, Warrior

**Time period(s):** 100th century
**Locale(s):** *Solo*, Spaceship; Golter, Planet—Imaginary

**Summary:** Lady Sharrow pursues her quest of finding the sole remaining Lazy Gun, a fabled weapon lost among the worlds of the Thrial star system. Killers from the Huhsz cult of assassins search for her while flashbacks to horrors in her life haunt her.

**Other books you might like:**
David Brin, *Startide Rising*, 1983
Glen Cook, *The Dragon Never Sleeps*, 1988
Alan Dean Foster, *The Tar-Aiym Krang*, 1972
Vonda N. McIntyre, *Metaphase*, 1992
Charles Sheffield, *Transcendence*, 1992
Vernor Vinge, *A Fire upon the Deep*, 1992

**323**

IAIN M. BANKS

## Canal Dreams
(New York: Doubleday, 1991)

**Story type:** Science Fiction (Contemporary Realism)
**Series:** Culture
**Major character(s):** Hisako Onado, Musician; Philippe, Military Personnel; Sucre, Revolutionary
**Time period(s):** Indeterminate Future
**Locale(s):** Gatun Lake, Panama; *Nakedo*, At Sea

**Summary:** An unexpected war traps Hisako Onodo, an internationally renowned cellist, in the Panama Canal. She forms a liaison with an officer on another ship, and keeps herself distracted with diving and parties. When the war engulfs her, she must find a way to live in a world rapidly and violently falling apart. Originally published in England in 1989.

**Other books you might like:**
J.G. Ballard, *Concrete Island*, 1985
Lisa Goldstein, *The Dream Years*, 1985
Pat Murphy, *The City, Not Long After*, 1989
Lucius Shepard, *Life During Wartime*, 1987
Lewis Shiner, *Slam*, 1990

**324**

IAIN M. BANKS

## Excession
(New York: Bantam Spectra, 1997)

**Story type:** Science Fiction (Political; First Contact)
**Series:** Culture
**Major character(s):** Byr Genar-Hofoen, Diplomat; Sleeper Service, Artificial Intelligence; Fivetide Humidyear VII, Military Personnel
**Time period(s):** Indeterminate Future
**Locale(s):** *Sleeper Service*, Spaceship

**Summary:** When the excession, an inexplicable and impossible phenomenon, reappears, the Minds of the Culture want to study it. Unfortunately, with the semi-hostile Empire of the Affront eager for war, roguish minds may willingly help start an intergalactic war for their own ends. The past indiscretions of a minor diplomat could influence things.

**Other books you might like:**
David Brin, *Startide Rising*, 1983
Frank Herbert, *Dune*, 1965
Vonda N. McIntyre, *Metaphase*, 1992
Vernor Vinge, *A Fire upon the Deep*, 1992

Walter Jon Williams, *Metropolitan*, 1995

**325**

IAIN M. BANKS

## Feersum Endjinn
(New York: Bantam Spectra, 1995)

**Story type:** Science Fiction (Literary)
**Major character(s):** Alandre Sessine VII, Nobleman; Ergates, Animal (ant); Hortis Gadfium, Scientist
**Time period(s):** Indeterminate Future
**Locale(s):** Great Hall, Fictional City

**Summary:** After Count Sessine's final material life ends by treachery, bizarre digital violence begins to end his virtual post-death lives. While a barely literate boy befriends a talking ant, Horis Gadfium tries to understand the gigantic structure she inhabits.

**Other books you might like:**
Russell Hoban, *Riddley Walker*, 1980
Ian McDonald, *Terminal Cafe*, 1994
Mervyn Peake, *Gormenghast*, 1950
Lucius Shepard, *The Golden*, 1993
John Varley, *The Ophiuchi Hotline*, 1977

**326**

IAIN M. BANKS

## The Player of Games
(New York: St. Martin's Press, 1989)

**Story type:** Science Fiction (Political)
**Major character(s):** Jernau Gurgeh, Sports Figure (Gameplayer); Flere-Imsaho, Robot
**Time period(s):** Indeterminate Future
**Locale(s):** The Culture, Interstellar Empire/Federation (various artificial worlds); Empire of Azad, Interstellar Empire/Federation (various planets)

**Summary:** Gurgeh, one of the greatest of the Culture's game players, is recruited to journey to the Empire of Azad, an intensely xenophobic and potentially hostile neighboring power. Political office and indeed all power in Azad is gained through winning an incredibly complex game. Gurgeh must master the game and gain the respect of Nicosar, the Emperor of Azad, in order to avoid armed conflict.

**Other books you might like:**
Greg Bear, *Eon*, 1985
Greg Bear, *Eternity*, 1988
David Brin, *The Uplift War*, 1987
C.J. Cherryh, *Cyteen*, 1988
Michael Moorcock, *An Alien Heat*, 1972

**327**

IAIN M. BANKS

## The State of the Art
(Shingleton, CA: Ziesing, 1989)

**Story type:** Science Fiction (First Contact)
**Series:** Culture
**Major character(s):** Diziet Sma, Alien; Dervley Linter, Alien (Deserter)
**Time period(s):** 1970s (1977)
**Locale(s):** Earth

**Summary:** The starship Arbitrary enters Earth orbit and a truly eccentric group of humanoid aliens and their accompanying artificial intelligence make first contact with humanity. The aliens, who look just like us, use this similarity to move invisibly through our world, weighing and evaluating. They may choose to help us, remain aloof, or, if we warrant it, reduce Earth to a singularity.

**Other books you might like:**
Octavia E. Butler, *Dawn*, 1987
John Kessel, *Good News From Outer Space*, 1989
Joan Slonczewski, *The Wall Around Eden*, 1989

---

`328`

**IAIN M. BANKS**

## Use of Weapons

(New York: Bantam Spectra, 1992)

**Story type:** Science Fiction (Space Opera; Political)
**Series:** The Culture
**Major character(s):** Cheradenine Zakalwe, Spy, Mercenary; Diziet Sma, Spy; Skaffen-Amtiskaw, Artificial Intelligence
**Time period(s):** Indeterminate Future
**Locale(s):** *Xenophobe*, Spaceship; Voerenhutz, Planet—Imaginary; The Culture, Interstellar Empire/Federation

**Summary:** The Culture, in its efforts to stabilize a galactic civilization on the Culture's periphery, needs to find and hire Zakalwe, a master agent retired for some years. As Sma finds out, discovering his whereabouts proves easier than insuring that he does the job. Zakalwe, haunted by his past and unsure of his own motivations, may explode.

**Other books you might like:**
Glen Cook, *The Dragon Never Sleeps*, 1988
Ian McDonald, *Desolation Road*, 1988
Dan Simmons, *Hyperion*, 1989
Bruce Sterling, *Schismatrix*, 1985
F. Paul Wilson, *The LaNague Chronicles*, 1992

---

`329`

**LYNNE REID BANKS**

## The Adventures of King Midas

(New York: Morrow, 1992)

**Story type:** Fantasy (Young Adult; Legend)
**Major character(s):** Midas, Royalty (king); Nandan, Magician; The Mumbo, Mythical Creature (baby dragon)
**Time period(s):** Indeterminate Past
**Locale(s):** Fictional Country

**Summary:** When Nandan grants King Midas the power to turn whatever he touches to gold, it takes the king only a single day to discover that golden food and a golden daughter do not provide much fulfilment. Nandan cannot reverse the spell, but he sets the king on a quest to a talking rock, a witch and a dragon who all have a part in returning life to normal.

**Other books you might like:**
Grace Chetwin, *Gom on Windy Mountain*, 1986
Susan Fletcher, *Dragon's Milk*, 1989
Judith Gorog, *Winning Scheherazade*, 1991
Norton Juster, *Alberic the Wise and Other Journeys*, 1965
Phyllis McGinley, *The Plain Princess*, 1945
Jane Resh Thomas, *The Princess in the Pigpen*, 1989
Nancy Willard, *Uncle Terrible: More Adventures of Anatole*, 1982
Patricia C. Wrede, *Dealing with Dragons*, 1990

Patricia C. Wrede, *Searching for Dragons*, 1991
Jane Yolen, *Wizard's Hall*, 1991

---

`330`

**LYNNE REID BANKS**

## Angela and Diabola

(New York: Avon, 1997)

**Story type:** Fantasy (Young Adult; Light Fantasy)
**Major character(s):** Angelica Cuthberton-Jones, Child, Psychic; Diabola Cuthberton-Jones, Child, Psychic; Mrs. Cuthberton-Jones, Parent
**Time period(s):** 1990s
**Locale(s):** Earth

**Summary:** Angelica grows up cooperative and pleasant in disposition, while her twin, Diabola, becomes more hostile and selfish with each passing year. With Diabola's father gone and her teacher cowed, Mrs. Cuthberton-Jones must find a way to mitigate Diabola's powers before disaster results.

**Other books you might like:**
Michael Bedard, *Painted Devil*, 1994
Diana Wynne Jones, *Witch Week*, 1982
Tanith Lee, *Black Unicorn*, 1991
Doris Lessing, *The Fifth Child*, 1988
Margaret Mahy, *The Changeover*, 1984

---

`331`

**LYNNE REID BANKS**

## The Key to the Indian

(New York: Avon Camelot, 1998)

**Story type:** Fantasy (Young Adult; Time Travel)
**Series:** Indian in the Cupboard
**Major character(s):** Omri, Child, Time Traveler; Dad, Parent, Time Traveler; Little Bear, Indian (Mohawk), Chieftain
**Time period(s):** 1990s; 18th century
**Locale(s):** Dorset, England; North America; Great Lakes

**Summary:** Omri and his father must find a way to send themselves to Little Bear, who needs their help to save his tribe from encroaching colonists, without changing the course of history.

**Other books you might like:**
Pauline Clarke, *The Return of the Twelves*, 1964
Virginia Hamilton, *House of Dies Drear*, 1968
J. Alison James, *Sing for a Gentle Rain*, 1990
Robert Silverberg, *Letters From Atlantis*, 1990
Elizabeth Winthrop, *Castle in the Attic*, 1985

---

`332`

**LYNNE REID BANKS**

## The Secret of the Indian

(New York: Avon Camelot, 1990)

**Story type:** Fantasy (Time Travel; Young Adult)
**Series:** Indian in the Cupboard
**Major character(s):** Omri, Child, Student; Patrick, Friend; Little Bear, Indian
**Time period(s):** 1980s; 19th century (Old West)
**Locale(s):** England; West

**Summary:** Once again the secret of Little Bear, a plastic toy figurine that comes to life through the magic cupboard, is at risk of discovery as Omri and Patrick must borrow and animate toy plastic doctors to save the wounded in Little Bear's own time and place. Reprint of the 1989 Doubleday hardcover.

**Other books you might like:**
Pauline Clarke, *The Return of the Twelves*, 1964
Edward Eager, *Knight's Castle*, 1956
Richard Kennedy, *Amy's Eyes*, 1985
Elisabeth Mace, *Under Siege*, 1990
E. Nesbit, *Story of the Amulet*, 1907

---

**333**

**NICK BANTOCK**

## The Forgetting Room

(New York: HarperCollins, 1997)

**Story type:** Fantasy (Contemporary Realism)
**Major character(s):** Armon, Artist (bookbinder); Rafael, Artist (painter)
**Time period(s):** 1900s
**Locale(s):** Ronda, Spain

**Summary:** Armon's grandfather dies, leaving him the family home in Spain. When the young man goes to check out his inheritance, strange events and stranger memories form an undeniable link to his past and his grandfather's mind. Heavily illustrated with Bantock's collage and fold-out art.

**Other books you might like:**
John Crowley, *Aegypt*, 1987
Lisa Goldstein, *The Dream Years*, 1985
Karen Elizabeth Gordon, *Paris out of Hand*, 1996
Barbara Hodgson, *The Tattooed Map*, 1995
Arturo Perez-Reverte, *The Club Dumas*, 1997

---

**334**

**NICK BANTOCK**

## The Golden Mean

(San Francisco: Chronicle Books, 1993)

**Story type:** Fantasy (Contemporary; Romance)
**Series:** Griffin & Sabine
**Major character(s):** Griffin Moss, Artist (postcard designer); Sabine Strohem, Artist (stamp designer); Victor Frolatti, Journalist (scientific)
**Time period(s):** 1990s
**Locale(s):** Sicmon Islands, Fictional Country; Devon, England; Kenya

**Summary:** The third and final Griffin & Sabine book also consists of actual postcards and letters. The romance between the correspondents heats up as they move toward the resolution of the mystery and their meeting in the flesh. However, a menacing journalist may sever the lovers' tenuous bonds. An intriguing multi-media novel.

**Other books you might like:**
A.S. Byatt, *Possession: A Romance*, 1990
John Crowley, *Little, Big*, 1981
Umberto Eco, *Foucault's Pendulum*, 1989
Lisa Goldstein, *The Dream Years*, 1985
Pat Murphy, *The City, Not Long After*, 1989

---

**335**

**NICK BANTOCK**

## Sabine's Notebook

(San Francisco: Chronicle, 1992)

**Story type:** Fantasy (Contemporary; Romance)
**Series:** Griffin & Sabine
**Major character(s):** Griffin Moss, Artist (postcard designer); Sabine Strohem, Artist (stamp designer)
**Time period(s):** 1990s
**Locale(s):** London, England; Alexandria, Egypt; Brisbane, Australia

**Summary:** Griffin flees his studio to avoid meeting the mysterious, alluring and possibly imaginary Sabine. He begins to write to her at his address, and their correspondence continues. The emotional connection between these two strange individuals increases even as the mystery between them deepens. Sequel to *Griffin & Sabine* and composed of actual letters and postcards.

**Other books you might like:**
John Crowley, *Little, Big*, 1981
Umberto Eco, *Foucault's Pendulum*, 1989
Greer Ilene Gilman, *Moonwise*, 1990
Lisa Goldstein, *The Dream Years*, 1985
Pat Murphy, *The City, Not Long After*, 1989

---

**336**

**NICK BANTOCK**

## The Venetian's Wife: A Strangely Sensual Tale of a Renaissance Explorer, a Computer, and a Metamorphosis

(San Francisco: Chronicle Books, 1996)

**Story type:** Fantasy (Contemporary)
**Major character(s):** Niccolo Dei Conti, Explorer, Collector; Sara Wolfe, Artist (painter)
**Time period(s):** 1990s; 15th century
**Locale(s):** New Orleans, Louisiana; Venice, Italy

**Summary:** Bored with her job, Sara Wolfe receives an offer to do research for a mysterious employer who communicates only by e-mail. She begins to collect art objects, to experience odd events, and to fear she's losing her mind. Profusely illustrated with images of art objects, as well as reproductions of letters, diaries, and e-mail.

**Other books you might like:**
A.S. Byatt, *Possession: A Romance*, 1990
John Crowley, *Little, Big*, 1981
Lisa Goldstein, *The Dream Years*, 1985
Karen Elizabeth Gordon, *Paris out of Hand*, 1996
Barbara Hodgson, *The Tattooed Map*, 1995

---

**337**

**CLIVE BARKER**

## Cabal

(New York: Poseidon, 1988)

**Story type:** Horror (Collection)
**Summary:** In "Cabal," (filmed as *Nightbreed*) Boone, a psychotic murder suspect, flees to Midian, a town filled with monsters, where he becomes one of them. Other stories include "Twilight at the

Towers,'' a combination spy and werewolf story, and ''The Life of Death,'' in which a girl falls in love with death.

**Other books you might like:**
Thomas M. Disch, *Getting into Death*, 1976

---

**338**

**CLIVE BARKER**

## *Everville*
(New York: HarperCollins, 1995)

**Story type:** Horror (Apocalyptic Horror)
**Series:** Book of the Art Trilogy
**Major character(s):** Tesla Bombeck, Biker; Nathan Grillo, Computer Expert; Phoebe Cobb, Receptionist
**Time period(s):** 1990s (1995)
**Locale(s):** Everville, Oregon

**Summary:** In this sequel to the author's 1989 novel *The Great and Secret Show*, the struggle resumes between two mortals who have attained mystical transcendance to control The Art, a magic that permits manipulation of time and space. The battle is fought on an epic scale that spans a century of earth time, back to America's frontier days, and extends from the mundane world into the Quiddity, a dreamworld that separates daily life from the realm of mystical experience.

**Other books you might like:**
Raymond E. Feist, *Faerie Tale*, 1988
Stephen King, *The Stand*, 1978
Robert R. McCammon, *Swan Song*, 1987
Alan Rodgers, *Night*, 1991

---

**339**

**CLIVE BARKER**

## *Forms of Heaven*
(New York: HarperPrism, 1996)

**Story type:** Horror (Collection)

**Summary:** Never before collected, the three early plays gathered here contain a number of themes that dominate the author's mature work. ''Crazyface'' mixes the comic and grotesque in its account of a clown's travels through the plague-ravaged Europe of the Middle Ages. ''Paradise Street'' anticipates the author's fantasy novel *Weaveworld* with a portrait of contemporary Liverpool transformed into an idyllic dreamscape. The sea of dreams in which the imagination continually refreshes itself is the subject of ''Subtle Bodies,'' a drama whose concepts inform the novels *Everville* and *The Great and Secret Show*.

**Other books you might like:**
Hamilton Deane, *Dracula: The Ultimate Illustrated Edition of the World-Famous Vampire Play*, 1993
    John L. Balderston, co-author
Marvin Kaye, *Thirteen Plays of Ghosts and the Supernatural*, 1990
    editor
Arch Oboler, *The Oboler Omnibus*, 1945

---

**340**

**CLIVE BARKER**

## *Galilee*
(New York: HarperCollins, 1998)

**Major character(s):** Galilee Barbarossa, Sailor; Rachel Pallenberg, Heiress; Maddox Barbarossa, Writer
**Time period(s):** 1990s (1998); 19th century
**Locale(s):** Kauai, Hawaii

**Summary:** In this epic dark fantasy about two quintessential American families, the Barbarossas and the Gearys, have been locked in an uneasy relationship since their collaboration in the American Civil War. When the sexually seductive Galilee Barbarossa, who is more than a century and a half old, falls in love with Rachel, potential heir to the Geary fortune, the resulting power struggle destabilizes both families and pulls their dark family secrets into revealing light.

**Other books you might like:**
William Faulkner, *Absalom, Absalom*, 1936
Nathaniel Hawthorne, *The House of the Seven Gables*, 1851
Robert R. McCammon, *Usher's Passing*, 1984
Michael McDowell, *Blackwater*, 1983
Joyce Carol Oates, *Bellefleur*, 1980

---

**341**

**CLIVE BARKER**

## *The Great and Secret Show*
(New York: Harper and Row, 1990)

**Story type:** Horror (Apocalyptic Horror)
**Series:** Book of the Art Trilogy
**Major character(s):** Randolph Jaffe, Postal Worker; Richard Wesley Fletcher, Scientist
**Time period(s):** 1990s
**Locale(s):** Palomo Grove, California

**Summary:** Soon after Randolph Jaffe discovers the key to the ''Secret Art'' and shares it with his friend Richard Wesley Fletcher, the two men become enemies as their quests for the Secret Art launch a protracted, apocalyptic conflict between Good and Evil that is violent, raw, extravagant, vulgar, visceral, and wildly metaphysical.

**Other books you might like:**
Stephen King, *The Stand*, 1978
    Complete and uncut edition published in 1990
Stephen King, *The Dark Tower: The Gunslinger*,
Stephen King, *The Talisman*, 1984
    Peter Straub, co-author
Robert R. McCammon, *Swan Song*, 1987

---

**342**

**CLIVE BARKER**

## *The Hellbound Heart*
(New York: Harper, 1991)

**Story type:** Horror (Haunted House)
**Major character(s):** Frank, Demon; Rory, Businessman (Frank's brother); Julia, Housewife, Spouse (Rory's)
**Time period(s):** 1980s
**Locale(s):** England

**Summary:** This short novel of love and obsession originally published in 1986 tells of thrill-seeking Frank, whose dealings with the extradimensional Cenobites leave him destroyed physically and trapped spiritually between dimensions. His only hope for resurrection is to seduce Julia, his sister-in-law, who has moved with big brother Frank into the house that imprisons him and who is easily persuaded to supply him with the blood and flesh of victims he needs to return to the earthly plane. Filmed as *Hellraiser.*

**Other books you might like:**
Lisa Cantrell, *Torments*, 1990
Tom Elliott, *The Dwelling*, 1989
H.P. Lovecraft, *The Lurker at the Threshold*, 1945
    August Derleth, co-author
Al Sarrantonio, *House Haunted*, 1991

**343**
## CLIVE BARKER
## *Imajica*
(New York: HarperCollins, 1991)

**Story type:** Horror (Apocalyptic Horror)
**Major character(s):** John Furie "Gentle" Zacharias, Artist; Judith O'Dell, Heroine; Pie 'oh' Pah, Mythical Creature (Mystif)
**Time period(s):** 1990s
**Locale(s):** London, England; New York, New York

**Summary:** The failed assassination of Judith O'Dell brings her back together with former lover "Gentle" Zacharias. Their reunion precipitates the couple on a quest to help the earthly plane (known as the Fifth Dominion) become reconciled with the other four extradimensional dominions and repair the sundered (and metaphorical) federation of the Imajica, split apart two centuries ago by forces that are continuing to work against its reunion.

**Other books you might like:**
Raymond E. Feist, *Faerie Tale*, 1988
Stephen King, *The Dark Tower Series*, 1982-1992
Stephen King, *The Stand: The Complete and Uncut Edition*, 1990
Robert R. McCammon, *Swan Song*, 1987
Alan Rodgers, *Fire*, 1990

**344**
## CLIVE BARKER
## *Incarnations*
(New York: HarperPrism, 1995)

**Story type:** Horror (Collection)

**Summary:** The author, a talented playwright as well as writer of macabre fiction, collects three plays written for small production companies in the 1980s. "Colossus" is set during the Age of Napoleon and attempts to forge a link between the paintings of Goya and the real-life horrors of war that inspired them. In "Frankenstein in Love," Joseph Frankenstein resurrects corpses in a third world country in the throes of revolution, and the reanimated dead look upon their situation as not unlike the fate of mortals living in a godless universe. In "The History of the Devil," Satan is tried in court by a jury of mortals and lesser demons to determine whether his exile from Heaven can be revoked if he can prove that his time on Earth has not adversely affected the normal course of events. Barker supplies an introduction and illustrations.

**Other books you might like:**
Hamilton Deane, *Dracula: The Ultimate Illustrated Edition of the World-Famous Vampire Play*, 1993
    John L. Balderston, co-author

Marvin Kaye, *Thirteen Plays of Ghosts and the Supernatural*, 1990
    editor
Arch Oboler, *The Oboler Omnibus*, 1945

**345**
## CLIVE BARKER
## *Sacrament*
(New York: HarperCollins, 1996)

**Story type:** Horror (Occult)
**Major character(s):** Will Rabjohns, Photographer; Rosa McGee, Supernatural Being; Jacob Steep, Supernatural Being
**Time period(s):** 1990s (1996)
**Locale(s):** San Francisco, California; Burnt Yarley, England

**Summary:** While in a coma that results from his mauling by a polar bear, nature photographer Will Rabjohns recalls his childhood encounter with Rosa McGee and Jacob Steep, two characters whom he now realizes represent the yin and yang of nature's cycle of life and death. Will grasps that what he has learned from the couple has bearing on his understanding of the AIDS epidemic's toll on his friends in the gay community of San Francisco, and he travels back to his native England to come to terms with his life and the many deaths that have affected him.

**Other books you might like:**
Jonathan Carroll, *After Silence*, 1995
Jay B. Laws, *The Unfinished*, 1993
Jonathan Nasaw, *The World on Blood*, 1996

**346**
## CLIVE BARKER
## *Tapping the Vein: Books One and Two*
(Forestville, California: Eclipse Books, 1989)

**Story type:** Horror (Collection)

**Summary:** Four graphic versions of stories taken from Barker's *Books of Blood*: "Human Remains," "Pig Blood Blues." (I) "Skins of the Fathers," "In the Hills, the Cities" (II). Imaginative illustrations vividly and accurately convey the sense of the original stories.

**Other books you might like:**
Steve Niles, *Saturday Mourning Fly in My Eye*, 1989

**347**
## CLIVE BARKER
## *The Thief of Always*
(New York: HarperCollins, 1992)

**Story type:** Horror (Coming-of-Age)
**Major character(s):** Harvey Swick, Child (10-year-old boy); Rictus, Mythical Creature (messenger); Mrs. Griffin, Housekeeper
**Time period(s):** 1990s (1992)
**Locale(s):** Alternate Universe (Mr. Hood's Holiday House)

**Summary:** Bored by the dreary February weather, Harvey Swick follows the six-inch tall Rictus on a celestial journey to Mr. Hood's Holiday House, a wish-fulfilling fantasyland where he must learn to sort out those experiences with potentially nasty side effects from those of more positive substance.

**Other books you might like:**
Ray Bradbury, *Something Wicked This Way Comes*, 1962
Stephen King, *The Eyes of the Dragon*, 1987

Stephen King, *The Talisman*, 1984
  Peter Straub, co-author
Dean R. Koontz, *Oddkins*, 1989

### 348
#### ROBERT H. BARLOW

## The Hoard of the Wizard Beast and One Other

(West Warwick, Rhode Island: Necronomicon Press, 1994)

**Story type:** Horror (Collection)

**Summary:** This chapbook contains two recently discovered stories of the author, a disciple of H.P. Lovecraft who eventually became his literary executor. "The Hoard of the Wizard Beast" is about a lackey sent to replenish the coffers of the ruler of the world of Zeth from the treasures guarded by a strange creature and the grisly fate that befalls him. "The Slaying of the Monster" is a tongue-in-cheek fantasy about the cowardice of a band of men sent out to slay a dragon menacing their town. S.T. Joshi supplies the introduction. The booklet also reproduces in holograph the original manuscript pages with Lovecraft's hand-written corrections to Barlow's original writing.

**Other books you might like:**
Lord Dunsany, *Ghosts of the Heaviside Layer and Other Fantasies*, 1980
Clark Ashton Smith, *The Vaults of Yoh-Vombis*, 1988
Clark Ashton Smith, *The Dweller in the Gulf*, 1987
Clark Ashton Smith, *Mother of Toads*, 1987

### 349
#### JOHN BARNES

## Apostrophes and Apocalypses

(New York: Tor, 1998)

**Story type:** Science Fiction (Collection)

**Summary:** This is a collection of 21 stories and essays, all published since the late 1980s. The essays deal with the art and mechanics of writing science fiction, constructing believable worlds, and establishing a distinctive style.

**Other books you might like:**
Poul Anderson, *Alight in the Void*, 1991
Gregory Benford, *In Alien Flesh*, 1986
David Brin, *Otherness*, 1994
Larry Niven, *N-Space*, 1990
Theodore Sturgeon, *The Perfect Host*, 1998

### 350
#### JOHN BARNES

## Caesar's Bicycle

(New York: HarperPrism, 1997)

**Story type:** Science Fiction (Time Travel; Alternate History)
**Series:** Timeline Wars
**Major character(s):** Mark Strang, Time Traveler, Warrior (Crux Op); Chrysamen "Chrys" ja N'Wook, Time Traveler, Warrior (Crux Op); Julius Caesar, Military Personnel, Historical Figure
**Time period(s):** Indeterminate Future
**Locale(s):** Rome, Italy; Ancient Civilization

**Summary:** On the verge of winning the Timelines Wars, a Crux Op agent, Mark Strang, must go back to ancient Rome to assassinate

Julius Caesar. After ridding Caesar of the enemy's advisor, Mark recognizes Caesar's ability to rule and revitalize Rome.

**Other books you might like:**
Robert Asprin, *Wagers of Sin*, 1996
  Linda Evans, co-author
L. Sprague de Camp, *Lest Darkness Fall*, 1996
Linda Evans, *Far Edge of Darkness*, 1996
Esther Friesner, *Child of the Eagle*, 1996
Raymond Harris, *The Schizogenic Man*, 1990
Crawford Kilian, *Rogue Emperor*, 1988
Fritz Leiber, *The Big Time*, 1961
Melissa Scott, *A Choice of Destinies*, 1986

### 351
#### JOHN BARNES

## Earth Made of Glass

(New York: Tor, 1998)

**Story type:** Science Fiction (Lost Colony; First Contact)
**Major character(s):** Giraut Leones, Diplomat (ambassador); Ix, Religious (prophet); Margaret Leones, Diplomat (cultural attache)
**Time period(s):** Indeterminate Future (3rd millennium)
**Locale(s):** Briand, Planet—Imaginary

**Summary:** Sent to Briand to defuse the hostility between the Tamil and the Maya, Giraut Leones and his wife, Margaret, find hope in the appearance of a Mayan prophet, Ix, who, seems to want reconciliation, until Ix's murder precipitates violence.

**Other books you might like:**
Eleanor Arnason, *Ring of Swords*, 1993
Gregory Benford, *The Stars in Shroud*, 1978
Arthur C. Clarke, *The Songs of Distant Earth*, 1986
Paula E. Downing, *A Whisper of Time*, 1994
Raymond Harris, *Shadows of the White Sun*, 1988
Pat Murphy, *The Falling Woman*, 1986
Brian Stableford, *Balance of Power*, 1979
Joan D. Vinge, *The Summer Queen*, 1991

### 352
#### JOHN BARNES

## Kaleidoscope Century

(New York: Tor, 1995)

**Story type:** Science Fiction (Dystopian; Techno-Thriller)
**Major character(s):** Joshua Ali Quare, Experimental Subject; Sadi, Mercenary, Immortal
**Time period(s):** 22nd century (2109)
**Locale(s):** Earth; Red Sands City, Mars

**Summary:** Waking from Transit in a shack on Mars, Quare explores his returning memories, some conflicting but all true. Born to a Communist family in 1969, he escapes a violent, alcoholic father by joining "The Organization," then the KGB, and helping suppress research into closed timelike curves and life extension. Innoculated with an experimental virus, agents become longlifers, transiting every 15 years to become more youthful and losing all memories. Quare remembers participating in many violent wars, culminating with Earth controlled by the winning artificial intelligence. A message waits for his attention, probably from Sadi, but perhaps from the Organization, and Quare must decide if he wants to comply.

**Other books you might like:**
Brian W. Aldiss, *Somewhere East of Life*, 1994
Stephen Bury, *Interface*, 1994

Joe Haldeman, *The Forever War*, 1975
James Patrick Kelly, *Wildlife*, 1994
Nancy Kress, *Brain Rose*, 1990

### 353
#### JOHN BARNES

## A Million Open Doors
(New York: Tor, 1992)

**Story type:** Science Fiction (Political; Arts)
**Major character(s):** Giraut Leones, Teacher; Aimeric "Ambrose Cruthers" de Sanha Marsao, Diplomat (ambassador); Margaret, Student, Revolutionary
**Time period(s):** Indeterminate Future (3rd Millennium)
**Locale(s):** Wilson, Planet—Imaginary; Nansen, Planet—Imaginary

**Summary:** Giraut Leones accompanies Aimeric de Sanha Marsao to Caledony to prepare it for wider galactic contact. Once there, Giraut finds the culture stifling and decides to open a school to teach the gracious Nou Occitan lifestyle. After a revolution and the discovery of an earlier civilization on Nansen, he begins to travel throughout the galaxy studying cross cultural influences along with his new wife, Margaret, a former student.

**Other books you might like:**
Michael Bishop, *Eyes of Fire*, 1980
John Brunner, *Born Under Mars*, 1967
Gordon R. Dickson, *The Chantry Guild*, 1988
Cynthia Felice, *Double Nocturne*, 1986
Raymond Harris, *Shadows of the White Sun*, 1988
R.A. MacAvoy, *The Third Eagle: Lessons Along a Minor String*, 1989
Michael McCollum, *Antares Dawn*, 1986
Jerry Pournelle, *King David's Spaceship*, 1980
Melissa Scott, *The Kindly Ones*, 1987
Norman Spinrad, *A World Between*, 1979
Walter Jon Williams, *Ambassador of Progress*, 1984

### 354
#### JOHN BARNES

## Mother of Storms
(New York: Tor, 1994)

**Story type:** Science Fiction (Disaster; Political)
**Major character(s):** Jesse Callare, Teacher, Student—College; Mary Ann "Synthi Venture" Waterhouse, Actress, Television Personality (XV); Louie Tynan, Astronaut
**Time period(s):** 2020s (2028)
**Locale(s):** Earth; Outer Space

**Summary:** The UN bombing of a weapons cache in the Arctic releases so much methane that the ocean temperature rises sufficiently to spawn a monstrous hurricane, destroying Hawaii. Instead of dissipating, it calfs and sends out other gigantic storms, one of which travels across the Yucatan Peninsula into the Caribbean where it devastates the islands and Florida. The only hope to stop this storm involves Louie Tynan's travelling to the Oort Cloud for a comet whose ice will seed and cool the atmosphere.

**Other books you might like:**
Roger MacBride Allen, *Supernova*, 1991
  Eric Kotani, co-author
Piers Anthony, *Rings of Ice*, 1974
J.G. Ballard, *The Drowned World*, 1962
David Brin, *Earth*, 1990

Fred Hoyle, *The Inferno*, 1973
  Geoffrey Hoyle, co-author
D.F. Jones, *Denver Is Missing*, 1974
Fritz Leiber, *The Wanderer*, 1964
Larry Niven, *Lucifer's Hammer*, 1977
  Jerry Pournelle, co-author
Bruce Sterling, *Heavy Weather*, 1994
James Sutherland, *Stormtrack*, 1974

### 355
#### JOHN BARNES

## One for the Morning Glory
(New York: Tor, 1996)

**Story type:** Fantasy (Light Fantasy; Quest)
**Major character(s):** Amatus, Royalty (prince); Calliope, Royalty (princess), Heir—Dispossessed; Cedric, Military Personnel, Political Figure (prime minister)
**Time period(s):** Indeterminate Past
**Locale(s):** The Kingdom, Fictional Country

**Summary:** Drinking the wine of the gods, Prince Amatus finds himself only half a person, the right half. He obtains four guardians and begins performing the tasks needed to regain his left half.

**Other books you might like:**
Piers Anthony, *Wielding a Red Sword*, 1986
Tom Holt, *Expecting Someone Taller*, 1988
Diana Wynne Jones, *Castle in the Air*, 1991
Andre Norton, *The Year of the Unicorn*, 1965
Terry Pratchett, *The Light Fantastic*, 1988
Clifford D. Simak, *The Fellowship of the Talisman*, 1978

### 356
#### JOHN BARNES

## Orbital Resonance
(New York: Tor, 1991)

**Story type:** Science Fiction (Post-Holocaust)
**Major character(s):** Melpomene Murray, Student, Writer; Randomly Distributed "Randy" Schwartz, Student; Theophilius "Ted" Harrison, Student, Immigrant
**Time period(s):** 2020s
**Locale(s):** *Flying Dutchman*, Spaceship (converted asteroid)

**Summary:** Ordered to write a book which will allow survivors on Earth to understand life on *Flying Dutchman*, Melpomene struggles to tell of her friends, their activities, their growing into adulthood, and the complications which arise when an immigrant from dying Earth joins the group of spaceborn adolescents.

**Other books you might like:**
James Blish, *A Life for the Stars*, 1962
Lois McMaster Bujold, *Falling Free*, 1988
Alan Dean Foster, *Glory Lane*, 1987
Melisa C. Michaels, *Skirmish*, 1985
Alis A. Rasmussen, *A Passage of Stars*, 1990
Alis A. Rasmussen, *The Price of Ransom*, 1990
Alis A. Rasmussen, *Revolution's Shore*, 1990
Allen Steele, *Clarke County, Space*, 1990

## `357`

### JOHN BARNES

## *Patton's Spaceship*

(New York: HarperPrism, 1997)

**Story type:** Science Fiction (Alternate Universe; Adventure)
**Series:** Timeline Wars
**Major character(s):** Porter Brunreich, Child; Mark Strang, Bodyguard; Harry Skena, Professor, Time Traveler
**Time period(s):** 1990s (28th century (2726))
**Locale(s):** Hyper Athens, Fictional City

**Summary:** After the Blade of the Most Merciful killed his wife, mother and brother, almost killing his sister in the same explosion, Mark dropped his Ph.D. studies in art history to become a bodyguard. Five years later, while Mark protects Porter and her mother, the Blade of the Most Merciful once again crosses his path. Protecting Harry, Mark finds himself in Hyper Athens, training as a Special Agent for a Crux Ops team.

**Other books you might like:**
Poul Anderson, *The Time Patrol*, 1991
Deborah Christian, *Mainline*, 1996
Mona Clee, *Branch Point*, 1996
James P. Hogan, *Paths to Otherwhere*, 1996
Samuel Merwin, *The House of Many Worlds*, 1951
Spider Robinson, *Lifehouse*, 1997

## `358`

### JOHN BARNES

## *Union Fires*

(New York: Worldwide Gold Eagle, 1992)

**Story type:** Fantasy (Time Travel)
**Series:** Time Raider
**Major character(s):** Daniel "Dan" Samson, Martial Arts Expert, Time Traveler; Prescott "Sean Toole" Heller, Military Personnel, Spy; Caroline "Sarah" Carelias, Spy, Time Traveler
**Time period(s):** 1860s (1864)
**Locale(s):** Virginia

**Summary:** Freed to travel the Wind Between Time in search of heroic battles, Dan finds himself inhabiting the body of a double agent, Sean Toole. Toole had planned to betray the underground railroad which brings slaves north to freedom, but Dan's eternal quest to right the wrongs of errant warriors again transforms matters. Through mystic discussions with Master Xi who started Dan on his journey through time, Dan discovers his fate entwines with his companions' throughout history.

**Other books you might like:**
Marc Laidlaw, *Neon Lotus*, 1988
Fritz Leiber, *The Big Time*, 1961
Kevin D. Randle, *Remember Gettysburg*, 1988
    Robert J. Cornett, co-author
Robert Reed, *Down the Bright Way*, 1991
Barry Sadler, *Casca: The Eternal Mercenary*, 1979
Harry Turtledove, *The Guns of the South: A Novel of the Civil War*, 1992

## `359`

### JOHN BARNES

## *Wartide*

(New York: Worldwide Gold Eagle, 1992)

**Story type:** Fantasy (Time Travel)
**Series:** Time Raider
**Major character(s):** Daniel "Dan" Samson, Martial Arts Expert, Time Traveler; Jackson Houston, Military Personnel (possessed by Dan); Turenne, Military Personnel
**Time period(s):** 1990s (1992); 1940s
**Locale(s):** Italy

**Summary:** Rescued from death by Master Xi after a lethal heroic act, Dan finds himself presented with the opportunity to fight heroic battles in another time. Transporting his own spirit into Jackson Houston, Dan helps defeat a German war effort which resulted in the secret development of a new poison gas.

**Other books you might like:**
Keith William Andrews, *Freedom's Rangers*, 1989
Fritz Leiber, *The Big Time*, 1961
Jerry Pournelle, *Janissaries*, 1979
Robert Reed, *Down the Bright Way*, 1991
Barry Sadler, *Casca: The Eternal Mercenary*, 1979
Barry Sadler, *Casca: Panzer Soldier*, 1980
Richard Sapir, *The Destroyer #1: Created, the Destroyer*, 1971

## `360`

### STEVEN BARNES

## *Firedance*

(New York: Tor, 1994)

**Story type:** Science Fiction (Adventure)
**Series:** Aubrey Knight
**Major character(s):** Aubrey Knight, Martial Arts Expert, Spouse; Promise, Dancer, Spouse
**Time period(s):** 2030s (2033)
**Locale(s):** Los Angeles, California; Africa

**Summary:** While powerful enemies utilize trained assassins, clones of Aubrey Knight, Knight travels to Africa to kill the dictator of United Africa, unaware that others consider him expendable. Exploring his mysterious past, Knight must face his own clones to save himself and his family.

**Other books you might like:**
George Alec Effinger, *When Gravity Fails*, 1987
Stephen Goldin, *Jade Darcy and the Affair of Honor*, 1988
    Mary Mason, co-author
Stephen Goldin, *Jade Darcy and the Zen Pirates*, 1990
    Mary Mason, co-author
Larry Niven, *Achilles' Choice*, 1991
    Steven Barnes, co-author
Larry Niven, *Dream Park*, 1981
    Steven Barnes, co-author

## `361`

### STEVEN BARNES

## *Gorgon Child*

(New York: Tor, 1989)

**Story type:** Science Fiction (Adventure)
**Series:** Streetlethal

**Major character(s):** Aubrey Knight, Martial Arts Expert, Sports Figure; Promise, Dancer
**Time period(s):** 21st century (2028)
**Locale(s):** Los Angeles, California

**Summary:** Aubry Knight, martial artist, former professional athlete turned crusader, must save America from enslavement at the hands of a fanatical religious leader who plots to use genetically enhanced super-soldiers to overthrow the government.

**Other books you might like:**
Richard Kadrey, *Metrophage*, 1988
Daniel Keys Moran, *The Long Run*, 1989
W.T. Quick, *Dreams of Flesh and Sand*, 1988
W.T. Quick, *Dreams of Gods and Men*, 1989
W.T. Quick, *Systems*, 1989

## 362

### STEVEN BARNES

### *Iron Shadows*

(New York: Tor, 1998)

**Story type:** Fantasy (Mystery; Contemporary Realism)
**Major character(s):** Cat Juvell, Detective—Private, Martial Arts Expert; Tyler Juvell, Computer Expert, Handicapped; Joy Oshita, Twin, Cult Member (Golden Sun)
**Time period(s):** 1990s (1995)
**Locale(s):** Portland, Oregon; Bend, Oregon

**Summary:** Hired to kidnap an heiress who has joined the mysterious Golden Sun cult, Cat Juvell goes undercover to get close to the cult's twin leaders, Joy and Tomo Oshita. Cat finds the twins' charismatic pull more difficult to resist than she expected, however, and also realizes that they may possess genuine healing abilities after all.

**Other books you might like:**
Brenda W. Clough, *How Like a God*, 1997
Virginia Hamilton, *Justice and Her Brothers*, 1978
Robert A. Heinlein, *Stranger in a Strange Land*, 1961
   Steven Barnes, co-author
Larry Niven, *Achilles' Choice*, 1991
Christopher Pike, *The Lost Mind*, 1995
Dan Simmons, *The Hollow Man*, 1992

## 363

### CHARLES BARNITZ

### *The Deepest Sea*

(New York: Roc, 1996)

**Story type:** Fantasy (Historical; Adventure)
**Major character(s):** Bran Snorrison, Hero, Immortal; Caitria, Companion (ghost), Spirit; Frydys, Girlfriend
**Time period(s):** 8th century (792-795)
**Locale(s):** Ireland; England

**Summary:** Hoping to win gold, glory, and the woman he loves, Bran joins a band of Vikings from his hometown for an autumn of trading and looting. Separated from his crewmates, Bran meets Caitria, spends a winter in Lindisfarne Monastery just before the Danes attack it, slays a dragon, and fights his way across England. Older, richer, and immortal from the effects of the dragon's blood, he returns to his kin in Ireland. First novel.

**Other books you might like:**
Poul Anderson, *Hrolf Kraki's Saga*, 1973
Frans G. Bengtsson, *The Long Ships*, 1954
Parke Godwin, *A Memory of Lions*, 1976

Harry Harrison, *The Hammer and the Cross*, 1993
R.A. MacAvoy, *The Book of Kells*, 1985
Diana L. Paxson, *The Wolf and the Raven*, 1993
Robert Silverberg, *Gilgamesh the King*, 1984

## 364

### SUE HOLLISTER BARR

### *Twisted*

(New York: Leisure, 1992)

**Story type:** Horror (Curse)
**Major character(s):** Simba, Musician; Ronna Parsons, Vagrant; Officer Parsons, Police Officer
**Time period(s):** 1960s (1966)
**Locale(s):** Berkeley, California

**Summary:** Cross-country pursuit by Officer Parsons catalyzes the memories of previous lives lived by a van full of hippies and revealed to them following sexual romps and drug-induced dreams. The closer Parsons draws to his quarry, the closer all parties involved come to acting out a scenario lived through by their nineteenth century predecessors, one that ended in bloodshed and dismemberment.

**Other books you might like:**
Paddy Chayefsky, *Altered States*, 1978
Tom Elliott, *The Dwelling*, 1990
Ruby Jean Jensen, *Baby Dolly*, 1991

## 365

### NEAL BARRETT JR.

### *Dawn's Uncertain Light*

(New York: NAL Signet, 1989)

**Story type:** Science Fiction (Post-Nuclear Holocaust)
**Major character(s):** Howie Ryder, Teenager; Ritcher Jones, Religious, Adventurer
**Time period(s):** 21st century
**Locale(s):** North America

**Summary:** Having previously discovered the horrible secret his entire civilization is based on, that the meat animals everyone raises and eats are actually human beings just like himself, Howie Ryder sets off across country in an attempt to save his sister Caroline, who has been taken by the government to be used in a forced breeding program.

**Other books you might like:**
David Brin, *The Postman*, 1985
Edgar Pangborn, *The Company of Glory*, 1975
Edgar Pangborn, *Davy*, 1964
Edgar Pangborn, *The Judgment of Eve*, 1966
Joan Slonczewski, *The Wall Around Eden*, 1989

## 366

### NEAL BARRETT JR.

### *Judge Dredd*

(New York: St. Martin's, 1995)

**Story type:** Science Fiction (Dystopian; Adventure)
**Major character(s):** Joseph ''Judge'' Dredd, Police Officer (Judge), Fugitive; Herman D. ''Fergie'' Ferguson, Criminal, Computer Expert; Hershey, Police Officer (Judge)

**Time period(s):** 22nd century (2139)
**Locale(s):** Mega-City One, New York (New York City); Aspen Prison, Colorado

**Summary:** Framed and wrongly convicted of murder, Judge Dredd requires help from Fergie and Judge Hershey to clear his name and uncover the plot by his clone brother to overturn the system of Judges. Novelizes the film.

**Other books you might like:**
Philip K. Dick, *Blade Runner*, 1982
Craig Shaw Gardner, *Batman*, 1989
Ed Naha, *Robocop 2*, 1990
Richard Osborne, *Demolition Man*, 1993
Robert Tine, *Universal Soldier*, 1992

---

### 367

**NEAL BARRETT JR.**

## The Touch of Your Shadow, the Whisper of Your Name

(New York: Dell, 1996)

**Story type:** Science Fiction (Adventure; Space Opera)
**Series:** Babylon 5
**Major character(s):** Michael Garibaldi, Security Officer (Spaceman); John Sheridan, Leader, Spaceman; Susan Ivanova, Leader, Spacewoman
**Time period(s):** 23rd century (2260)
**Locale(s):** Babylon 5, Space Station; Interstellar Empire/Federation

**Summary:** As nightmares plague everyone aboard Babylon 5, riots and individual fights become common, while the approach of a huge apparition brings fear of invasion. Garibaldi and Sheridan must find the cause before strife sunders the League of Non-Aligned Worlds. Television tie-in set before the episode, "A Day in the Strife."

**Other books you might like:**
Jim Mortimore, *Clark's Law*, 1996
S.M. Stirling, *Betrayals*, 1996
Lois Tilton, *Accusations*, 1995
John Vornholt, *Blood Oath*, 1995
John Vornholt, *Voices*, 1995

---

### 368

**T.A. BARRON**

## The Ancient One

(New York: Philomel, 1992)

**Story type:** Fantasy (Time Travel; Young Adult)
**Major character(s):** Kate, Time Traveler, Teenager
**Time period(s):** 1990s; 15th century (1490s)
**Locale(s):** Cronon's Crater, Oregon

**Summary:** While helping her Great Aunt Melanie in her attempt to preserve a redwood forest from logging, Kate travels 500 years into the past where a magical race's battle against Gashra and the evil lizard people who wish to destroy the forest parallels the battle between environmentalists and loggers in Kate's time. Companion volume to *Heartlight*.

**Other books you might like:**
J. Alison James, *Sing for a Gentle Rain*, 1990
C.S. Lewis, *The Lion, the Witch, and the Wardrobe*, 1950
C.S. Lewis, *Prince Caspian*, 1951
C.S. Lewis, *The Voyage of the Dawn Treader*, 1952
J.R.R. Tolkien, *The Hobbit*, 1938

---

### 369

**T.A. BARRON**

## The Fires of Merlin

(New York: Philomel, 1998)

**Story type:** Fantasy (Young Adult; Legend)
**Series:** Lost Years of Merlin
**Major character(s):** Emrys Merlin, Adventurer
**Time period(s):** 6th century
**Locale(s):** Isle of Fincayra, Mythical Place

**Summary:** While exploring his abilities, Merlin must confront fire in five different forms, including lava and a dragon, and consider the nature of power.

**Other books you might like:**
Mike Ashley, *The Merlin Chronicles*, 1995 editor
Ann Curry, *The Book of Brendan*, 1990
Yves Meynard, *The Book of Knights*, 1998
Jane Yolen, *Merlin's Booke*, 1986
Jane Yolen, *Passager*, 1996

---

### 370

**T.A. BARRON**

## The Lost Years of Merlin

(New York: Philomel, 1996)

**Story type:** Fantasy (Legend; Young Adult)
**Major character(s):** Emrys, Child, Psychic; Branwen, Step-Parent; Rhia, Child, Psychic
**Time period(s):** 6th century
**Locale(s):** Isle of Fincayra, Mythical Place

**Summary:** Washed ashore then raised by Branwen as her own, Emrys must leave home. He runs away to the Isle of Fincayra to discover his identity and magical abilities. On the enchanted isle, Emrys meets Rhia and finds his fate entwined with Fincayra's.

**Other books you might like:**
Mike Ashley, *The Merlin Chronicles*, 1995 editor
Ann Curry, *The Book of Brendan*, 1990
T.H. White, *The Sword in the Stone*, 1939
Jane Yolen, *The Hobby*, 1996
Jane Yolen, *Passager*, 1996

---

### 371

**T.A. BARRON**

## The Merlin Effect

(New York: Philomel, 1994)

**Story type:** Fantasy (Young Adult; Adventure)
**Major character(s):** Kate Gordon, Teenager, Adventurer; Geoffrey Bardsey, Religious (monk), Immortal; Nimue, Sorceress
**Time period(s):** 1990s; Indeterminate
**Locale(s):** Pacific Ocean; Baja California, Mexico

**Summary:** When Kate Gordon investigates a giant whirlpool, the current traps her kayak, pulling her into an undersea world. There she discovers Geoffrey Bardsey and the battle between the legendary wizard, Merlin, and his ancient enemy, Nimue.

**Other books you might like:**
Susan Cooper, *The Dark Is Rising*, 1973

Susan Cooper, *Greenwitch*, 1974
Susan Cooper, *The Grey King*, 1975
Ursula K. Le Guin, *A Wizard of Earthsea*, 1968
Madeleine L'Engle, *An Acceptable Time*, 1990

## 372

### T.A. BARRON

## The Seven Songs of Merlin

(New York: Philomel, 1997)

**Story type:** Fantasy (Young Adult; Legend)
**Series:** Lost Years of Merlin
**Major character(s):** Emrys Merlin, Child, Psychic; Rhiannon "Rhia", Child, Psychic
**Time period(s):** 6th century
**Locale(s):** Isle of Fincayra, Mythical Place; The Otherworld, Mythical Place

**Summary:** When the young Merlin and Rhia hope to repair the damage caused to Fincayra by the vanquished Blight, Merlin's mother falls victim to a new evil. To cure her, Merlin and Rhia must acquire a magical elixir in the Otherworld, if Merlin can survive the ogre Balor's challenge and can hone his psychic vision. Third in series.

**Other books you might like:**
Mike Ashley, *The Merlin Chronicles*, 1995
    editor
Ann Curry, *The Book of Brendan*, 1990
T.H. White, *The Sword in the Stone*, 1939
Jane Yolen, *Merlin's Booke*, 1986
Jane Yolen, *Passager*, 1996

## 373

### SCOTT IAN BARRY

## The Streeter

(New York: Tor, 1994)

**Story type:** Horror (Nature in Revolt)
**Major character(s):** Adams Shaws, Guard (of the Amsterdam Starpark); Gilbert Becker, Administrator (Bureau of Animal Affairs); Andrew Stern, Professor (Chair, Psychology Dept. SUNY), Psychologist
**Time period(s):** 1990s (1994)
**Locale(s):** New York, New York (Queens)

**Summary:** Enraged by their ingestion of toxic chemicals at a nearby waste dump, a pack of homeless dogs known as "streeters" roam the grounds of the Amsterdam Starpark, mauling and eating those foolish enough to walk its grounds alone.

**Other books you might like:**
William Dantz, *Hunger*, 1992
David Dvorkin, *Ursus*, 1989
Ronald Kelly, *Pitfall*, 1990
T.J. Kirby, *Deadly Breed*, 1992
Dean R. Koontz, *Watchers*, 1987
Barry Porter, *Junkyard*, 1989
Whitley Strieber, *The Wolfen*, 1978

## 374

### JOHN BARTH

## The Last Voyage of Somebody the Sailor

(Boston: Little Brown, 1991)

**Story type:** Fantasy (Legend; Time Travel)
**Major character(s):** Simon William Behler, Journalist, Adventurer; Sinbad the Sailor, Businessman, Adventurer
**Time period(s):** 1980s (1980); Indeterminate Past
**Locale(s):** Baghdad, Middle East

**Summary:** While attempting to retrace the legendary voyages of Sinbad the Sailor, Simon Behler is lost at sea. He survives and eventually finds himself in ancient Baghdad and even in Sinbad's own house where Sinbad is involved in raising venture capital for his forthcoming seventh voyage. Simon challenges Sinbad to a storytelling marathon hoping to discover a solution to his plight and a way home to his own time.

**Other books you might like:**
Richard F. Burton, *The Book of the Thousand Nights and a Night: A Plain and Literal Translation of the Arabian Nights Entertainments*, 1885-1886
    10 volumes
Patricia Daniels, *Sinbad the Sailor*, 1980
Craig Shaw Gardner, *The Other Sinbad*, 1991
Stephen Goldin, *Shrine of the Desert Mage*, 1988
Andrew Lang, *The Arabian Nights Entertainments*, 1969
    editor
Jeanne Larsen, *Bronze Mirror*, 1991
Salman Rushdie, *Haroun and the Sea of Stories*, 1990
Susan Shwartz, *Arabesques: More Tales of the Arabian Nights*, 1988
    editor
Susan Shwartz, *Arabesques II*, 1989
    editor
Paul B. Thompson, *Red Sands*, 1988
    Tonya R. Carter, co-author
Jack Zipes, *Arabian Nights: The Marvels and Wonders of the Thousand and One Nights*, 1991
    (editor)

## 375

### DONALD BARTHELME

## The King

(New York: Harper and Row, 1990)

**Story type:** Fantasy (Legend; Humor)
**Major character(s):** Arthur, Royalty (King); Guinevere, Royalty (Queen); Launcelot, Knight
**Time period(s):** 1940s
**Locale(s):** England

**Summary:** This Retelling of Le Morte d'Arthur occurs during world War II. Arthur, Guinevere and Launcelot's classic triangle evolves while the Knights of the Round Table struggle to fit into the war effort and Mordred plots to take over the government. This novel was published posthumously.

**Other books you might like:**
Steven Brust, *The Sun, the Moon, and the Stars*, 1987
Kara Dalkey, *The Nightingale*, 1988
Pamela Dean, *Tam Lin*, 1991
Charles de Lint, *Jack, the Giant-Killer*, 1987
Patricia C. Wrede, *Snow White and Rose Red*, 1989

## 376

**DAN BARTON**

### *Relife*

(New York: Pocket, 1991)

**Story type:** Horror (Mystery)
**Major character(s):** Thomas F. Maxwell, Lawyer; Maureen Maxwell, Real Estate Agent, Spouse (Thomas's wife); Scott Maxwell, Addict (Thomas's son)
**Time period(s):** 1990s
**Locale(s):** Los Angeles, California

**Summary:** Suffering from amnesia after a severe car accident, Tom Maxwell begins trying to put the pieces of his broken life back together, starting with a reconciliation with his estranged family. When he discovers he never sustained the serious injuries he was presumed to have suffered, he finds himself in a race against time to find out who he really is and why his caretakers have lied to him before he is overwhelmed by the excessive aging of different parts of his body.

**Other books you might like:**
David Ely, *Seconds*, 1963
Ken Grimwood, *Replay*, 1986
Dean R. Koontz, *Hideaway*, 1992
Dean R. Koontz, *The House of Thunder*, 1982

## 377

**WILLIAM BARTON**

### *Acts of Conscience*

(New York: Warner Aspect, 1997)

**Story type:** Science Fiction (Adventure; First Contact)
**Major character(s):** Gaetan du Cheyne, Spaceship Captain; The Kapellmeister, Alien; Beloved Light, Alien
**Time period(s):** 26th century
**Locale(s):** Orikhalkos, Fictional City; Earth

**Summary:** Gaetan figures he will never get into space, but then receives a spaceship of his own. He wants to see distant planets, but discovers humanity has wrecked every place it visited. Then he finds forces ready to do something about it.

**Other books you might like:**
Eleanor Arnason, *Ring of Swords*, 1993
Octavia E. Butler, *Dawn*, 1987
Hal Clement, *Cycle of Fire*, 1957
Sheri S. Tepper, *Raising the Stones*, 1990
Amy Thomson, *The Color of Distance*, 1995

## 378

**WILLIAM BARTON**
**MICHAEL CAPOBIANCO**, Co-Author

### *Alpha Centauri*

(New York: Avon, 1997)

**Story type:** Science Fiction (First Contact; Political)
**Major character(s):** Maeru ''Kai'' kai Ortega, Spaceman, Engineer; Virginia ''Ginny'' Vonzel Qing-an, Spaceship Captain; Miles ''David Gilman'' Cochrane, Scientist (Planetologist), Mentally Ill Person (Multiple Personality)
**Time period(s):** 23rd century (2239)

**Locale(s):** *Mother Night*, Spaceship; Planet—Imaginary (Alpha Centauri System); Outer Space

**Summary:** Hoping to find a solar ready for colonization, *Mother Night*'s crew discover dead, used-up worlds and evidence of a culture with three intelligent species that lasted several billion years, but has been dead for over a billion. Ginny must deal with Miles who carries not only a sterilizing virus, but also hypnopoedic overlays, one of which compels him to spread the virus.

**Other books you might like:**
Roger MacBride Allen, *The Ring of Charon*, 1990
Greg Bear, */*, 1997
Michael Capobianco, *Burster*, 1990
Tom Cool, *Infectress*, 1997
Jack McDevitt, *The Engines of God*, 1994
David Weber, *Mutineers' Moon*, 1991

## 379

**WILLIAM BARTON**

### *Dark Sky Legion*

(New York: Bantam Spectra, 1992)

**Story type:** Science Fiction (Political; Space Opera)
**Major character(s):** Maaron Denturian, Immortal, Government Official (Televox); Odin, Artificial Intelligence (*Naglfar*); Sessiri-wohnith, Alien (Hoda)
**Time period(s):** Indeterminate Future
**Locale(s):** Olam, Planet—Imaginary; Earth; *Naglfar*, Spaceship

**Summary:** Using matter transmitters, humans were dispersed from Earth, many sent unwillingly by Cpaht during the Red Millennium. After more than forty thousand years the Metastable Order maintains human society by sending out duplicates of its Senators who reincarnate when they arrive at a planet. Maaron Denturian arrives at Olam finding his long experience and extraordinary powers as a Televox of the Metastable Order necessary to meet the challenge to his beliefs and purpose.

**Other books you might like:**
Roger MacBride Allen, *The Ring of Charon*, 1990
John Brunner, *The World Swappers*, 1959
Octavia E. Butler, *Dawn*, 1987
Timothy A. Madden, *Outbanker*, 1990
Robert Silverberg, *Recalled to Life*, 1962
Sheri S. Tepper, *Sideshow*, 1992
A.E. Van Vogt, *The World of Null-A*, 1948
David Weber, *Mutineers' Moon*, 1991

## 380

**WILLIAM BARTON**
**MICHAEL CAPOBIANCO**, Co-Author

### *Fellow Traveller*

(New York: Bantam Spectra, 1991)

**Story type:** Science Fiction (Techno-Thriller)
**Major character(s):** Mikhail Sergeevich Gorbachev, Political Figure, Historical Figure; Vladimir ''Volodya'' Alekseevich Manarov, Astronaut; Miroslav Ilyich Bronstein, Astronaut
**Time period(s):** 1990s; 21st century (2000-2017)
**Locale(s):** Earth; Asteroid (the asteroid belt)

**Summary:** The Soviets have embarked on a bold gamble to regain world leadership and ensure economic prosperity by trying to move an asteroid into Earth orbit to harvest its ores for industry. The more reactionary elements in the United States see the project as a potential weapon and are willing to risk the destruction of life on Earth to stop the Soviets.

**Other books you might like:**
Michael Capobianco, *Burster*, 1990
Arthur C. Clarke, *Rendezvous with Rama*, 1973
Gordon R. Dickson, *The Far Call*, 1978
Robert A. Heinlein, *Farmer in the Sky*, 1950
Dean McLaughlin, *The Man Who Wanted Stars*, 1965
Carl Sagan, *Contact*, 1985

**381**

### WILLIAM BARTON
### MICHAEL CAPOBIANCO, Co-Author

## Iris

(New York: Doubleday Foundation, 1990)

**Story type:** Science Fiction (Hard Science Fiction)
**Major character(s):** Brendan Sealock, Engineer, Scientist; Demogorgon, Computer Expert
**Time period(s):** 21st century (2097)
**Locale(s):** *Deepstar*, Spaceship; Ocypete, Moon—Imaginary (Moon of the planet Iris)

**Summary:** Iris, a wandering planet, enters the solar system and is visited by an oddball group of artists, scientists and computer hackers who pass near it while on their way to colonize Triton. They discover an alien artifact. Meanwhile the backgrounds and the complex interactions of the members of the exploration team are examined in detail.

**Other books you might like:**
Greg Bear, *Eon*, 1985
Greg Bear, *Eternity*, 1988
Gregory Benford, *Heart of the Comet*, 1986
    David Brin, co-author
Arthur C. Clarke, *Rendezvous with Rama*, 1973
Arthur C. Clarke, *2001: A Space Odyssey*, 1968
Arthur C. Clarke, *2010: Odyssey Two*, 1982
Arthur C. Clarke, *2061: Odyssey Three*, 1987

**382**

### WILLIAM BARTON

## The Transmigration of Souls

(New York: Warner Aspect, 1996)

**Story type:** Science Fiction (First Contact; Alternate Universe)
**Major character(s):** Astrid Kincaid, Military Personnel, Space Explorer; Ahmad Zeq, Space Explorer; Ling Erhsham, Space Explorer
**Time period(s):** Indeterminate Future
**Locale(s):** Montenegro; Outer Space; Alternate Universe

**Summary:** While Fortress America pursues a policy of extreme isolation, Chinese and Arab astronauts, followed by American soldiers, explore an ancient alien artifact whose ability to access alternate realities may annihilate the known universe.

**Other books you might like:**
Roger MacBride Allen, *The Ring of Charon*, 1990
Roger MacBride Allen, *The Shattered Sphere*, 1994
Greg Bear, *Eon*, 1985
David Brin, *Earth*, 1990
Vernor Vinge, *A Fire upon the Deep*, 1992
David Weber, *Mutineers' Moon*, 1991
George Zebrowski, *Stranger Suns*, 1991

**383**

### WILLIAM BARTON

## When Heaven Fell

(New York: Warner Aspect, 1995)

**Story type:** Science Fiction (Invasion of Earth; Military)
**Major character(s):** Athol Morrison, Mercenary; Alexandra "Alix" Moreno, Companion, Traveler
**Time period(s):** 22nd century
**Locale(s):** Earth; Planet—Imaginary

**Summary:** Having served the Masters with distinction, Athol returns for a visit to a vanquished Earth, now repopulated with numerous extraterrestrial races and a development nexus for the Masters' new frontier. Athol reacquaints himself with family and friends and tours Earth, finding general subjugation with only small pockets of resistance to the fate of humanity.

**Other books you might like:**
Roger MacBride Allen, *The Shattered Sphere*, 1994
Octavia E. Butler, *Dawn*, 1987
David Gerrold, *A Matter for Men*, 1989
    revised edition
Robert A. Heinlein, *The Puppet Masters*, 1991
    revised edition
Anne McCaffrey, *Freedom's Landing*, 1995
Tim Sullivan, *The Parasite War*, 1989

**384**

### WILLIAM BARTON
### MICHAEL CAPOBIANCO, Co-Author

## White Light

(New York: Avon, 1998)

**Story type:** Science Fiction (First Contact; Post-Nuclear Holocaust)
**Major character(s):** Corazon "Cory" Suarez, Teenager, Castaway; Wolf O'Malley, Spaceship Captain, Castaway; Thalia Jansky, Spacewoman (hyperdrive flight engineer), Castaway
**Time period(s):** Indeterminate Future
**Locale(s):** Sagdeev, Planet—Imaginary; Plione, Planet—Imaginary; Theolithos, Planet—Imaginary

**Summary:** Reunited with her mother after spending two years in an internment camp for orphaned juveniles, Cory finds herself on the way to explore another planet. Arriving at Sagdeev, Cory and others leave with Thalia and Wolf on their next mission to avoid being caught by a sudden inspection on Sagdeev. Before landing anywhere they spot a device which pulls them through to the Pleiades, where they find yet another stargate, which pulls them into an ancient civilization.

**Other books you might like:**
John Barnes, *Patton's Spaceship*, 1997
Stephen Baxter, *Ring*, 1996
Gregory Benford, *Furious Gulf*, 1994
Vonda N. McIntyre, *Metaphase*, 1992
Robert J. Sawyer, *Starplex*, 1996

## 385

### GRAEME BASE

## *The Discovery of Dragons*
(New York: Abrams, 1996)

**Story type:** Fantasy (Collection; Legend)
**Major character(s):** Bjorn of Bromme, Warrior (Viking), Adventurer; Soong Mei Ying, Traveler, Adventurer; E.F. Libermann, Cartographer, Scientist (amphibiologist)
**Time period(s):** 9th century; 13th century
**Locale(s):** Europe; Asia; Africa

**Summary:** Through letters, Bjorn of Bromme, Soong Mei Ying and E.F. Libermann relate discoveries of many different types of dragons they encounter as they travel through three continents. Lavishly illustrated.

**Other books you might like:**
James C. Christensen, *Voyage of the Basset*, 1996
    Renwick St. James, Alan Dean Foster, co-authors
James Gurney, *Dinotopia*, 1992
James Gurney, *The World Beneath*, 1995
Michael Hague, *The Book of Dragons*, 1995
    editor
Terry Jones, *The Goblin Companion*, 1996
    Brian Froud, co-author

## 386

### JAMES C. BASSETT

## *Living Real*
(New York: Harper Prism, 1997)

**Story type:** Science Fiction (Alternate Intelligence; Political)
**Major character(s):** Carver Blervaque, Computer Expert, Inventor; Rose Blervaque, Housewife, Artist (Sculptor); Tom Byrd, Government Official
**Time period(s):** 22nd century
**Locale(s):** Gainesville, Florida; Network, Cyberspace

**Summary:** Trying to overcome his creative block, Carver plays with forbidden Web technology. Programs written this way prove dangerously addictive to his wife, Rose, who usess the new technology to meditate. Noticing the disturbance Carver causes, Tom Byrd, Regional Administrator of the Federal Communications Agency, searches for the group behind the Web security breach, and also for Carver, whom he believes innocent.

**Other books you might like:**
Bruce Bethke, *Headcrash*, 1995
Pat Cadigan, *Synners*, 1991
Raphael Carter, *The Fortunate Fall*, 1996
James P. Hogan, *Bug Park*, 1997
Sage Walker, *Whiteout*, 1996

## 387

### DON BASSINGTHWAITE
### NANCY KILPATRICK, Co-Author

## *As One Dead*
(Clarkston, Georgia: White Wolf, 1996)

**Story type:** Horror (Vampire Story)
**Series:** A Vampire: The Masquerade: The Masquerade of Red Death

**Major character(s):** Bianka, Vampire; Lot, Vampire; DeWinter, Vampire
**Time period(s):** 1990s (1996)
**Locale(s):** Toronto, Ontario, Canada

**Summary:** Bianka, the hybrid offspring of two vampire clans, hopes to lead the restrained Apollonian members of the Camarilla sect in revolt against the Dionysian Sabbat vampires, who have restricted the Camarilla to living in a small Toronto ghetto called The Box. This novel is set in the publisher's "Vampire: The Masquerade" gaming world, in which vampire clans are enjoined by the law of their species to mingle unobtrusively with mortals and keep their supernatural identities secret.

**Other books you might like:**
Nancy A. Collins, *A Dozen Black Roses*, 1996
Brian Herbert, *Blood on the Sun*, 1996
    Marie Landis, co-author
Robert Weinberg, *Blood War*, 1995
Robert Weinberg, *The Unbeholden*, 1996
Robert Weinberg, *Unholy Allies*, 1995
Robert Weinberg, *Vampire Diary: The Embrace*, 1995
    Mark Rein-Hagen, co-author

## 388

### JOHN CALVIN BATCHELOR

## *Peter Nevsky and the True Story of the Russian Moon Landing*
(New York: Henry Holt, 1993)

**Story type:** Science Fiction (Political; Alternate Universe)
**Major character(s):** Peter Nevsky, Orphan, Spaceman; Alexander Oryolin, Spaceman, Hero; Dmitry Zhukovsky, Spaceman, Hero
**Time period(s):** 1960s (1968-1969)
**Locale(s):** Starry Town, Union of Soviet Socialist Republics (manned space center); Moscow, Russia

**Summary:** Arriving at Starry Town ready to begin cosmonaut training, Peter Nevsky becomes embroiled in the intrigues of his heroes, three World War II flying aces, now the core of the Russian space program which aims at a Soviet Moon landing at the time of *Apollo 11*. Related as memoirs of an aged Nevsky.

**Other books you might like:**
William Barton, *Fellow Traveller*, 1991
    Michael Capobianco, co-author
Gordon R. Dickson, *The Far Call*, 1978
Edward Gibson, *Reach*, 1989
Dan Simmons, *Phases of Gravity*, 1989
Norman Spinrad, *Russian Spring*, 1991

## 389

### GAEL BAUDINO

## *Branch and Crown*
(New York: Roc, 1996)

**Story type:** Fantasy (Religious; Historical)
**Series:** Water
**Major character(s):** Obadiah Jenkins, Religious, Diplomat; Sari, Traveler (pilgrim), Healer (herbalist)
**Time period(s):** Indeterminate
**Locale(s):** The Three Kingdoms, Fictional Country; Great Library of Kanez, Fictional City

**Summary:** The story of the diplomats from the Righteous States of America comes to a close. The Great Library stores much information which shed, disturbing light on the origins of the religions of the Three Kingdoms.

**Other books you might like:**
James P. Blaylock, *The Paper Grail*, 1991
Jack Cady, *The Off Season*, 1995
Orson Scott Card, *Seventh Son*, 1987
Barbara Hambly, *The Witches of Wenshar*, 1987
Rachel Pollack, *Temporary Agency*, 1994

**390**

GAEL BAUDINO

## Dragon Death

(New York: Roc, 1992)

**Story type:** Fantasy (Magic Conflict)
**Series:** Dragonsword
**Major character(s):** Suzanne ''Alouzon'' Helling, Student, Guardian; Silbakor, Mythical Creature (dragon); Helen ''Kyria'' Addams, Sorceress
**Time period(s):** 1990s
**Locale(s):** Los Angeles, California; Gryylth, Fictional Country

**Summary:** Alouzon struggles to defeat the enemy which followed her to Los Angeles then returns to Gryylth to overcome the treacherous subversion of a young sorcerer and prevent the war which threatens to lay waste to Gryylth.

**Other books you might like:**
Kevin J. Anderson, *Gamearth*, 1989
Nick Pollotta, *Bureau 13*, 1991
Mickey Zucker Reichert, *By Chaos Cursed*, 1991
Mickey Zucker Reichert, *Godslayer*, 1987

**391**

GAEL BAUDINO

## Duel of Dragons

(New York: Roc, 1991)

**Story type:** Fantasy (Alternate World)
**Series:** Dragonsword
**Major character(s):** Suzanne ''Alouzon'' Helling, Student, Guardian; Helen ''Kyria'' Addams, Scholar, Sorceress; Silbakor, Mythical Creature (dragon)
**Time period(s):** 1990s; Indeterminate Past (equivalent-5th century)
**Locale(s):** Los Angeles, California; Gryylth, Fictional Country; Vaylle, Fictional Country

**Summary:** When Silbakor transports Suzanne and Helen, now Alouzon and Kyria, to Gryylth, they find that the land created by a now-dead medieval history professor, Helen's ex-husband, is being laid waste by 20th century weapons and supernatural creatures. Silbakor must battle the White Worm while Kyria must hold weapons, creatures and Helen's bitterness at bay. Alouzon finds that her own creation, Vaylle, is similarly beset, the devastation arising from her own memories of the Vietnam War era.

**Other books you might like:**
Kevin J. Anderson, *Gamearth*, 1989
Pamela Dean, *Tam Lin*, 1991
Tom Deitz, *Windmaster's Bane*, 1986
Barbara Hambly, *The Time of the Dark*, 1982
Guy Gavriel Kay, *The Summer Tree*, 1985
Mickey Zucker Reichert, *Godslayer*, 1987
Joel Rosenberg, *The Sleeping Dragon*, 1983

**392**

GAEL BAUDINO

## Gossamer Axe

(New York: Roc, 1990)

**Story type:** Fantasy (Time Travel; Romance)
**Major character(s):** Christa Cruitaire, Teacher (Harp), Musician; Melinda Moore, Musician; Monica Sanchez, Musician
**Time period(s):** 20th century
**Locale(s):** Denver, Colorado

**Summary:** Separated from her lover by hundreds of years, the Celtic bard Chairiste Ni Cummen, now known as Christa Cruitaire, must find a way to rescue Siudb from both the Sidh's endless twilight and the royal bard, Orfide. When Christa finds that rock music can be used to free her lover, she forms an all-girl rock band with which to challenge the power of the gods.

**Other books you might like:**
Isaac Asimov, *Foundation and Empire*, 1952
Steven Brust, *Cowboy Feng's Space Bar and Grille*, 1990
Emma Bull, *War for the Oaks*, 1987
Patricia Kennealy-Morrison, *The Silver Branch*, 1988
Patricia Kennealy-Morrison, *The Throne of Scone*, 1986
Patricia Kennealy-Morrison, *The Copper Crown*, 1984
Mercedes Lackey, *Knight of Ghosts and Shadows*, 1990
  Ellen Guon, co-author

**393**

GAEL BAUDINO

## Maze of Moonlight

(New York: Roc, 1993)

**Story type:** Fantasy (Historical; Romance)
**Major character(s):** Christopher delAurvre, Nobleman (Baron of Aurverelle); Vanessa, Mythical Creature (elf); Natil, Mythical Creature (elf), Minstrel
**Time period(s):** 14th century (1399-1400)
**Locale(s):** Adria, Fictional Country

**Summary:** Three years after the crushing defeat of the Christian armies by the Turks at Nicopolis, Christopher, emaciated, ragged and apparently insane, finally reaches his castle. After months of reclusiveness, he rescues Vanessa, a peasant girl with unusual abilities inherited from her half-elf father. Christopher learns that elves still share the world with humans and that he must accept their help as he attempts to unite the squabbling barons of Adria and repel invading mercenary armies.

**Other books you might like:**
Emma Bull, *War for the Oaks*, 1987
C.J. Cherryh, *The Dreamstone*, 1983
C.J. Cherryh, *Rusalka*, 1989
Gordon R. Dickson, *The Dragon Knight*, 1990
Barbara Hambly, *The Silent Tower*, 1986
Katherine Kurtz, *Deryni Rising*, 1970
Elizabeth Marie Pope, *The Perilous Gard*, 1974
Elizabeth Ann Scarborough, *Phantom Banjo*, 1991
Elizabeth Ann Scarborough, *Song of Sorcery*, 1982
Barbara W. Tuchman, *A Distant Mirror*, 1978
  non-fiction
Patricia C. Wrede, *Shadow Magic*, 1982

## 394

### GAEL BAUDINO

## *O Greenest Branch!*

(New York: Roc, 1995)

**Story type:** Fantasy (Historical; Religious)
**Series:** Water
**Major character(s):** Sari, Abuse Victim (spousal), Traveler (pilgrim); Aeid, Royalty (crown prince), Adventurer; Obadiah Jenkins, Religious (minister), Diplomat (ambassador)
**Time period(s):** Indeterminate
**Locale(s):** The Three Kingdoms, Fictional Country; Africa; Nuhr, Fictional City

**Summary:** The Reverend Ambassador Jenkins and his diplomatic entourage from the Righteous States of America seem unable to convince Kin Inwa Kabir and his ministers that they have anything to offer the drought-ridden lands of the Three Kingdoms. Desperate for change, Crown Prince Aeid tries to steer his father away from his fanatically religious court and toward negotiations with the strangers who want to station troops there to halt French conquest of northern Africa. Meanwhile, Sari, an old woman who has finally rid herself of her abusive husband, makes a pilgrimage back to the land of her youth to atone for her abandonment of her goddess and start a new life.

**Other books you might like:**
Maya Kaathryn Bohnhoff, *The Meri*, 1992
Octavia E. Butler, *Wild Seed*, 1980
Orson Scott Card, *Red Prophet*, 1988
Orson Scott Card, *Seventh Son*, 1987
Barbara Hambly, *The Witches of Wenshar*, 1987
Simon Hawke, *The Seeker*, 1994
Rosemary Kirstein, *The Steerswoman*, 1989
Paul O. Williams, *The Breaking of Northwall*, 1981
Paul O. Williams, *The Ends of the Circle*, 1981

## 395

### GAEL BAUDINO

## *Spires of Spirit*

(New York: Roc, 1997)

**Story type:** Fantasy (Collection; Urban)
**Series:** Strands of Starlight
**Major character(s):** Varden, Mythical Creature (elf), Healer; Leather-Woman, Sorceress; Lauri, Mythical Creature (elf), Lesbian
**Time period(s):** 16th century; 1990s
**Locale(s):** Europe; Colorado; Mythical Place

**Summary:** Contains a four-page introduction, five original novelettes and one revised from the 1985 periodical version. Written 1981-1984, the stories provide the background and foundation for the *Strands of Starlight* milieu. The first three portray elven interactions with nature and humanity as the Inquisition looms, while the others focus on the reemergence of elven influences in the modern world and individuals who must come to terms with the demands of their genetic makeup.

**Other books you might like:**
Charles de Lint, *Dreams Underfoot*, 1993
Charles de Lint, *The Ivory and the Horn*, 1995
Robert Holdstock, *The Bone Forest*, 1992
Elizabeth Ann Scarborough, *The Godmother*, 1994
Elizabeth Ann Scarborough, *Phantom Banjo*, 1991

## 396

### GAEL BAUDINO

## *Strands of Sunlight*

(New York: Roc, 1994)

**Story type:** Fantasy (Urban; Religious)
**Series:** Strands of Starlight
**Major character(s):** Natil Summerson, Mythical Creature (elf), Immortal; Sandy "Sana" Joy, Musician (harpist), Psychic (healer); Theodore "TK" Karlington Winters, Veteran, Mythical Creature (elf)
**Time period(s):** 1990s (1991-1992)
**Locale(s):** Denver, Colorado; Elvenhome, Colorado

**Summary:** As sole surviving Firstborn Elf, Natil strives to guide her friends through their changes into Elves bound to compassionately aid humanity. Sana uses her harp to focus healing energies while TK battles against drug dealers in the neighborhood after meeting the Elves of Denver who seek to reestablish connection to the Creatrix. Third in series.

**Other books you might like:**
Maya Kaathryn Bohnhoff, *The Meri*, 1992
Maya Kaathryn Bohnhoff, *Taminy*, 1993
Mercedes Lackey, *Knight of Ghosts and Shadows*, 1990
Mercedes Lackey, *When the Bough Breaks*, 1993
   Holly Lisle, co-author
Susan Palwick, *Flying in Place*, 1992
Will Shetterly, *Elsewhere*, 1991

## 397

### THOMAS BAUM

## *Out of Body*

(New York: St. Martin's, 1997)

**Story type:** Horror (Wild Talents)
**Major character(s):** Denton Hake, Construction Worker; Elliot Hake, Insurance Investigator (Denton's brother); Felix Ortega, Parole Officer
**Time period(s):** 1990s (1997)
**Locale(s):** Tacoma, Washington

**Summary:** Denton Hake is plagued by out-of-body experiences during which he commits acts that he doesn't remember. Framed and imprisoned for a murder he supposedly committed during one of these experiences, he dissociates his consciousness from his body to ferret out the real murderer.

**Other books you might like:**
Rene Belletto, *Machine*, 1993
Raymond Buckland, *The Committee*, 1993
Harlan Ellison, *Mefisto in Onyx*, 1993
Graham Masterton, *Rook*, 1996
Susan Palwick, *Flying in Place*, 1992
Sean Costello, *Captain Quad*, 1991

## 398

### STEPHEN BAXTER

## *Anti-Ice*

(New York: HarperPrism, 1994)

**Story type:** Science Fiction (Techno-Thriller; Alternate Universe)
**Major character(s):** Josiah Traveller, Inventor, Engineer; Ned Vicars, Adventurer, Diplomat

**Time period(s):** 1870s (1870)
**Locale(s):** Manchester, England; *Phaeton*, Spaceship

**Summary:** Ned learns about the horrors of Anti-Ice (naturally occurring anti-matter) from his brother's experience in the Crimean War where Professor Traveller used some to construct a fearsome bomb. The Professor must invent as many peaceful uses for Anti-Ice as possible to prevent the limited resource from being used in superior explosive weapons.

**Other books you might like:**
William Gibson, *The Difference Engine*, 1991
    Bruce Sterling, co-author
Joe Haldeman, *The Forever War*, 1975
Robert J. Sawyer, *Far-Seer*, 1992
Jules Verne, *Twenty Thousand Leagues under the Sea*, 1870
Jules Verne, *From the Earth to the Moon*, 1874

## 399
### STEPHEN BAXTER
### *Flux*
(New York: HarperPrism, 1995)

**Story type:** Science Fiction (Hard Science Fiction; Political)
**Major character(s):** Dura, Genetically Altered Being, Settler (Human Being); Hork, Genetically Altered Being, Government Official; Adda, Genetically Altered Being, Patient
**Time period(s):** Indeterminate Future
**Locale(s):** The Star, Outer Space (neutron star); Parz City, Fictional City

**Summary:** As a neutron star's rotation slows, glitches occur more frequently, endangering the environment. The Human Beings living in the mantle of the star remember technology from before the War with the colonists. Dura, her brother Farr, and the elderly, critically wounded Adda find medical help in Parz City, anchored at the pole. Unfortunately, the residents of Parz City no longer possess any knowledge of the ancient technology, forcing them to retain the help of Human Beings, before the glitches destroy everything.

**Other books you might like:**
Greg Bear, *Eon*, 1985
Gregory Benford, *Furious Gulf*, 1994
James Blish, *The Seedling Stars*, 1956
Megan Lindholm, *Alien Earth*, 1992
Roger Zelazny, *Flare*, 1992
    Thomas T. Thomas, co-author

## 400
### STEPHEN BAXTER
### *Moonseed*
(New York: Harper Prism, 1998)

**Story type:** Science Fiction (Disaster; Hard Science Fiction)
**Major character(s):** Henry Meacher, Scientist; Geena Bourne, Astronaut
**Time period(s):** Indeterminate Future
**Locale(s):** Montenegro; Edinburgh, Scotland

**Summary:** The planet Venus explodes and part of the debris reaches Earth, causing major climactic upheavals and destroying the world's economy. As the survivors struggle to rebuild, particles from space land in Edinburgh and start a chain reaction that could doom Earth to the same fate. Two astronauts head for the moon while scientists try to neutralize the reaction.

**Other books you might like:**
Piers Anthony, *Rings of Ice*, 1974
Ben Bova, *Test of Fire*, 1982
David Brin, *Earth*, 1990
Elizabeth Hand, *Icarus Descending*, 1993
Yvonne Navarro, *Final Impact*, 1997

## 401
### STEPHEN BAXTER
### *Raft*
(New York: Roc, 1992)

**Story type:** Science Fiction (Space Colony; Hard Science Fiction)
**Major character(s):** Rees, Teenager, Scientist; Sheen, Miner; Pallas, Pilot
**Time period(s):** Indeterminate Future
**Locale(s):** Outer Space

**Summary:** A ship had been caught in a Bolder Ring, a gateway to another universe, and disabled. 500 years after it reached the universe, the descendants of the crew were divided by the lack of essential supplies. The universe in which they found themselves had a force of gravity a billion times stronger than Earth's and the nebula in which humans had been living since their arrival was collapsing in on itself. Rees, unhappy as a miner, stows away on a tree-ship to the Raft where he begins to get enough education to believe a solution to the ultimate death of the colony could be discovered. This is the author's first novel.

**Other books you might like:**
Roger MacBride Allen, *The Ring of Charon*, 1990
James Blish, *They Shall Have Stars*, 1957
David Brin, *Sundiver*, 1979
Hal Clement, *Mission of Gravity*, 1978
Robert L. Forward, *Dragon's Egg*, 1980
Robert L. Forward, *Starquake*, 1985
Larry Niven, *The Integral Trees*, 1984
Vernor Vinge, *Marooned in Realtime*, 1986

## 402
### STEPHEN BAXTER
### *Ring*
(New York: HarperPrism, 1996)

**Story type:** Science Fiction (Hard Science Fiction; Post-Holocaust)
**Series:** Xeelee
**Major character(s):** Lieserl, Human, Experimental Subject; Louise Ye Armonk, Engineer (starship designer), Leader; Spinner-of-Rope, Pilot, Space Explorer
**Time period(s):** 22nd century; Indeterminate Future (50,000th century)
**Locale(s):** Earth; *Great Northern*, Spaceship (starship); Outer Space

**Summary:** When Lieserl plunges into the heart of the sun, she discovers an instability that will destroy it within ten thousand years. Hired in a desperate attempt to save the human race after finding the rest of the universe slowly succumbing to the same fate, Louise and her crew agree to take the *Great Northern* through a wormhole into the distant future seeking an immense alien artifact which may hold the key to their survival. Author's brief note details the Xeelee sequence chronology and bibliography.

**Other books you might like:**
Roger MacBride Allen, *The Ring of Charon*, 1990
Greg Bear, *The Forge of God*, 1987

Gregory Benford, *Far Futures*, 1995
    editor
James Blish, *Cities in Flight*, 1970
Arthur C. Clarke, *Childhood's End*, 1953
John E. Stith, *Redshift Rendezvous*, 1990
Vernor Vinge, *A Fire upon the Deep*, 1992

### 403

#### STEPHEN BAXTER

### The Time Ships

(New York: HarperPrism, 1996)

**Story type:** Science Fiction (Time Travel; Alternate History)
**Major character(s):** The Writer, Writer, Time Traveler; Nebogipfel, Mutant (Morlock), Time Traveler; Weena, Mutant (Eloi), Young Woman
**Time period(s):** Indeterminate Past; Indeterminate Future
**Locale(s):** Richmond, England; The Sphere, Underground Environment; Palace of Green Porcelain, Mythical Place

**Summary:** Consumed with guilt over abandoning Weena to a grisly death at the hands of the Morlocks, the Writer resolves to return to A.D. 802,701 and attempt to rescue her. Stopping short of his goal, however, he realizes that his first journey through time drastically changed history, with horrifying results. Accidently joining forces with Nebogipfel, a Morlock scientist, they journey from the beginning to the end of time searching for the key to their own history. Sequel to H.G. Wells' *The Time Machine*.

**Other books you might like:**
Greg Bear, *Eon*, 1985
Paul Di Filippo, *The Steampunk Trilogy*, 1995
Gordon R. Dickson, *Time Storm*, 1977
R. Garcia y Robertson, *The Virgin and the Dinosaur*, 1996
K.W. Jeter, *Morlock Night*, 1979
Alex McDonough, *Scorpio*, 1990
H.G. Wells, *The Time Machine*, 1895

### 404

#### STEPHEN BAXTER

### Timelike Infinity

(New York: Roc, 1993)

**Story type:** Science Fiction (Hard Science Fiction)
**Series:** Xeelee
**Major character(s):** Jasoft Parz, Diplomat, Time Traveler; Michael Poole, Scientist; Shira, Time Traveler, Revolutionary (Friends of Wigner)
**Time period(s):** Indeterminate Future
**Locale(s):** *Hermit Crab*, Spaceship; *The Spline*, Spaceship (Qax)

**Summary:** Michael Poole leaves the Oort Cloud where he studies quark nuggets, to rescue a member of the team who returns through the time portal Michael helped develop. When he finds her on the Friends of Wigner's Earthship orbiting Jupiter, he learns that 1500 years in the future, the Qax control the solar system, forbidding longevity treatment. However, the Friends' hidden agenda prevents them from contacting humanity or warning of the impending Qax invasion.

**Other books you might like:**
James Blish, *The Triumph of Time*, 1958
David Brin, *Startide Rising*, 1983
Octavia E. Butler, *Dawn*, 1987
Robert L. Forward, *Starquake*, 1985

Robert L. Forward, *Timemaster*, 1992
Megan Lindholm, *Alien Earth*, 1992
Vonda N. McIntyre, *Metaphase*, 1992
Dan Simmons, *The Fall of Hyperion*, 1990
Dan Simmons, *Hyperion*, 1989

### 405

#### STEPHEN BAXTER

### Titan

(New York: HarperPrism, 1997)

**Story type:** Science Fiction (Hard Science Fiction; Disaster)
**Major character(s):** Paula Benacerraf, Astronaut, Spacewoman; Isaac Rosenberg, Scientist (physical chemistry); Jiang Ling, Astronaut (Chinese)
**Time period(s):** 2000s; Indeterminate Future
**Locale(s):** *Columbia*, Spaceship (shuttle); Titan, Saturn; *Discovery*, Spaceship

**Summary:** Paula becomes an astronaut to discover the causes for construction delays on Skylab. When the *Columbia* breaks up on reentry, killing some of the crew and the space program, Isaac Rosenberg reveals the discovery of potential life on Saturn's moon Titan. They put together a mission to Titan using museum pieces and shuttle parts, but NASA abandons them after they barely leave Earth's orbit. Jiang loves being in space enough to die for the opportunity.

**Other books you might like:**
Greg Bear, *The Forge of God*, 1987
David Brin, *Earth*, 1990
Michael Flynn, *Firestar*, 1996
Allen Steele, *Orbital Decay*, 1989
Sage Walker, *Whiteout*, 1996
David Weber, *Mutineers' Moon*, 1991

### 406

#### STEPHEN BAXTER

### Voyager

(New York: HarperPrism, 1997)

**Story type:** Science Fiction (Alternate Universe; Hard Science Fiction)
**Major character(s):** Gregory Dana, Scientist; Ralph Gershon, Astronaut; Natalie York, Scientist
**Time period(s):** 1980s
**Locale(s):** Cape Canaveral, Florida; Mars

**Summary:** In an alternate universe where President Kennedy survived the attempt on his life, the space program remained at the center of our national agenda. Heavily supported by President Nixon, a manned flight to Mars occurs in 1986, but the astronauts involved find the voyage both difficult and dangerous.

**Other books you might like:**
Ben Bova, *Mars*, 1992
Kim Stanley Robinson, *Blue Mars*, 1996
Kim Stanley Robinson, *Green Mars*, 1994
Kim Stanley Robinson, *Red Mars*, 1993

## 407

**PETER S. BEAGLE**

### The Folk of the Air

(New York: Del Rey, 1988)

**Story type:** Fantasy (Magic Conflict)
**Major character(s):** Farrell, Hippie (Medieval Anachronist)
**Time period(s):** 1980s
**Locale(s):** Earth

**Summary:** Farrell helps fight an evil man called out of his own time by a witch.

**Other books you might like:**
Adrienne Martine-Barnes, *The Rainbow Sword*, 1988

## 408

**PETER S. BEAGLE**

### Giant Bones

(New York: Roc, 1997)

**Story type:** Fantasy (Collection)

**Summary:** Contains a five-page foreword and six stories sharing the folklore and natural history of the world of *The Inkeeper's Song*. Varying in tone, the stories explore themes such as adventure, magic, mythical creatures, and ghosts.

**Other books you might like:**
Richard Adams, *Tales From Watership Down*, 1996
Marion Zimmer Bradley, *Free Amazons of Darkover*, 1985
  Friends of Darkover, co-editor
Richard Pini, *The Blood of Ten Chiefs*, 1986
  Robert Asprin and Lynn Abbey, co-editor
Will Shetterly, *Liavek*, 1985
  Emma Bull, co-editor
J.R.R. Tolkien, *The Book of Lost Tales 1*, 1984

## 409

**PETER S. BEAGLE**

### The Innkeeper's Song

(New York: Roc, 1993)

**Story type:** Fantasy (Quest; Literary)
**Major character(s):** "Lal" Lalkhamsin-Khamsolal, Sailor; Nyateneri, Religious, Fugitive; Karsh, Innkeeper
**Time period(s):** Indeterminate Past
**Locale(s):** Corcorva, Fictional City

**Summary:** Three women, all unusual, all marked by their pasts and secrets, meet on the road. At an inn, they reveal some secrets as they plot to rescue a wizard to whom each owes a debt. Several additional characters add their voices to this quilted novel where everyone gains insight while the world threatens to crash down around them.

**Other books you might like:**
Eleanor Arnason, *The Sword Smith*, 1978
John M. Ford, *Casting Fortune*, 1989
Barry Hughart, *Bridge of Birds*, 1984
Ellen Kushner, *Swordspoint*, 1987
Patricia A. McKillip, *The Riddle-Master of Hed*, 1976

## 410

**PETER S. BEAGLE**, Editor
**JANET BERLINER**, Co-Editor

### Peter S. Beagle's Immortal Unicorn

(New York: HarperPrism, 1995)

**Story type:** Fantasy (Anthology; Legend)

**Summary:** Contains a two-page preface, a five-page foreword, and 27 original stories with individual introductions by both editors and a brief biography of each author. The tone varies from dark to humorous with themes involving unicorns in diverse settings. Authors include the editors and Edward Bryant, Charles de Lint, Karen Joy Fowler, Ellen Kushner, Eric Lustbader, Lisa Mason, Elizabeth Ann Scarborough, Robert Sheckley, Will Shetterly, Susan Shwartz, Dave Smeds, S.P. Smotow, Judith Tarr, Melanie Tem, Nancy Willard, Tad Williams, and Dave Wolverton.

**Other books you might like:**
David Copperfield, *David Copperfield's Tales of the Impossible*, 1995
  Janet Berliner, co-editor
Bruce Coville, *The Unicorn Treasury*, 1988
  editor
Jack Dann, *Unicorns!*, 1982
  Gardner Dozois, co-editor
Jack Dann, *Unicorns II*, 1992
  Gardner Dozois, co-editor
Pamela Dean, *The Secret Country*, 1985
Jane Yolen, *Here There Be Unicorns*, 1994

## 411

**PETER S. BEAGLE**

### The Rhinoceros Who Quoted Nietzsche and Other Odd Acquaintances

(San Francisco, California: Tachyon Publications, 1997)

**Story type:** Fantasy (Collection)

**Summary:** Contains a four-page introduction by Patricia A. McKillip plus two original stories, two original essays, six stories reprinted from periodicals and anthologies 1957-1995 and two essays reprinted from 1965 and 1969 periodicals. Frequently light in tone, the stories include a variety of themes such as mythical and fantastic creatures, allegory and personal relationships.

**Other books you might like:**
David Brin, *The River of Time*, 1986
Nancy Kress, *Dancing on Air*, 1997
Jonathan Lethem, *The Wall of the Sky, the Wall of the Eye*, 1996
Mary Shelley, *The Mortal Immortal*, 1996
Clifford D. Simak, *Over the River & through the Woods*, 1996

## 412

**PETER S. BEAGLE**

### The Unicorn Sonata

(Atlanta: Turner Publishing, 1996)

**Story type:** Fantasy (Alternate World; Young Adult)
**Major character(s):** Josephine "Joey" Rivera, Musician, Teenager; Indigo, Musician, Teenager; Touriq, Mythical Creature (unicorn)
**Time period(s):** 1990s; Indeterminate
**Locale(s):** Los Angeles, California; Shei'rah, Alternate Earth

**Summary:** Joey follows Indigo's haunting music through the mobile border to the land of Shei'rah, populated by unicorns, satyrs, water nymphs, dragons, and phoenixes. Travelling back and forth to Shei'rah, Joey may prove the key to reversing the affliction blinding elderly unicorns.

**Other books you might like:**
Bruce Coville, *The Unicorn Treasury*, 1988
    editor
Jack Dann, *Unicorns!*, 1982
    Gardner Dozois, co-editor
Jack Dann, *Unicorns II*, 1992
    Gardner Dozois, co-editor
Pamela Dean, *The Secret Country*, 1985
Jane Yolen, *Here There Be Unicorns*, 1994

**413**

**GREG BEAR**

*/*

(New York; Tor, 1997)

**Story type:** Science Fiction (Alternate Intelligence; Techno-Thriller)
**Series:** Queen of Angels
**Major character(s):** Jill, Artificial Intelligence; Mary Choy, Police Officer; Martin Burke, Psychologist, Inventor
**Time period(s):** 2060s
**Locale(s):** Seattle, Washington; Moskow, Idaho (Green Idaho); Omphalos, Mythical Place

**Summary:** Inventor Martin Burk's nano technology permits not only body enhancement, but also the deep psychological therapy from nano machines that produces a happy society for most people. The few "naturals" who have not needed therapy fill the supervisory, directing functions in society. A few conservative naturals, bonding together as the Aristos, create an unorthodox computer to destroy the nano machines which keep most of the society healthy and sane. Mary Choy investigates a murder, leading to her discovery of the Aristos' plot.

**Other books you might like:**
John Barnes, *Kaleidoscope Century*, 1995
David Brin, *Earth*, 1990
Stephen Bury, *Interface*, 1994
Janet Kagan, *Mirabile*, 1991
Jim Young, *Armed Memory*, 1995

**414**

**GREG BEAR**

*Anvil of Stars*

(New York: Warner Questar, 1992)

**Story type:** Science Fiction (First Contact; Hard Science Fiction)
**Major character(s):** Martin "Marty" Gordon, Leader (Pan of the Watch), Spaceman; Ariel Hawthorn, Spaceman; Eye on Sky, Alien, Spaceman
**Time period(s):** 23rd century
**Locale(s):** *Dawn Trader*, Spaceship (Ship of Law); Buttercup Star System, Outer Space

**Summary:** After killer machines wipe out the Earth, surviving humans find out from their saviors that galactic civilization now expects the remaining humans to follow the Law, a galactic code, and wipe out the race which attacked humanity. A small group of humans set out in a wondrous spaceship to carry out the mission of revenge. When they find a civilization which may be the source of the killer

technology, the humans must face the difficult questions surrounding their fitness to judge the aliens and propriety of the human destruction of those intelligent beings. Sequel to *The Forge of God*.

**Other books you might like:**
David Brin, *Earth*, 1990
Orson Scott Card, *Ender's Game*, 1985
Larry Niven, *Footfall*, 1985
    Jerry Pournelle, co-author
Dan Simmons, *The Fall of Hyperion*, 1990
Dan Simmons, *Hyperion*, 1989
Vernor Vinge, *A Fire upon the Deep*, 1992

**415**

**GREG BEAR**

*Bear's Fantasies*

(Newark, New Jersey: The Wildside Press, 1992)

**Story type:** Fantasy (Collection)

**Summary:** Published by the Philadelphia Science Fiction Society, this book contains a two-page introduction with five stories first published in periodicals and anthologies 1973-1985 plus one, "Sleepside Story," first appearing in a 1988 limited edition from Cheap Street Press. Some stories share a dark tone surrounding themes of religion or crime while others present traditional themes as in "Webster," in which a dictionary helps a woman focus her thoughts into powerful magical tools, and "Sleepside Story," in which a young man plans to rescue his mother from a witch/prostitute, but comes away from the situation with an unexpected inheritance.

**Other books you might like:**
Brian W. Aldiss, *A Romance of the Equator: The Best Fantasy Stories of Brian W. Aldiss*, 1990
David Brin, *The River of Time*, 1986
Orson Scott Card, *Maps in a Mirror*, 1990
Robert Holdstock, *The Bone Forest*, 1992
Kate Wilhelm, *And the Angels Sing*, 1992
Gene Wolfe, *Storeys From the Old Hotel*, 1992

**416**

**GREG BEAR**

*Dinosaur Summer*

(New York: Warner, 1998)

**Story type:** Science Fiction (Adventure; Alternate History)
**Major character(s):** Peter Belzoni, Journalist, Teenager; Vince Shellabarger, Animal Trainer (dinosaurs), Entertainer (circus); Ernest "Monte" Schoedsack, Director (film), Adventurer
**Time period(s):** 1940s (1947)
**Locale(s):** Boston, Massachusetts; Puerto Ordaz, Venezuela (El Grande Plateau); New York, New York

**Summary:** Dreading a summer alone with his father in 1947 Manhattan, Peter unexpectedly accepts the opportunity to accompany his father as his assistant when the National Geographic Society hires them to cover the return of dinosaurs from the circus to their isolated plateau in Venezuela. Danger surfaces as soon as they get on board ship with the dinosaurs, and only gets worse the closer to El Grande they get. Sequel to Doyle's *The Lost World*.

**Other books you might like:**
Robert T. Bakker, *Raptor Red*, 1995
Sir Arthur Conan Doyle, *The Lost World*, 1915
James Gurney, *Dinotopia*, 1992

Stephen Leigh, *Ray Bradbury Presents: Dinosaur Planet*, 1993
Robert J. Sawyer, *Far-Seer*, 1992

## 417

### GREG BEAR

## *Eon*

(New York: Tor Books, 1989)

**Story type:** Science Fiction (Hard Science Fiction)
**Major character(s):** Judith Hoffman, Scientist; Garry Lanier, Engineer
**Time period(s):** 21st century
**Locale(s):** Thistledown, Asteroid

**Summary:** When an asteroid miraculously appears out of nowhere and enters Earth orbit, NASA, NATO, and the UN send explorers. They discover the stone is hollow and appears to have once been inhabited by human beings from our future, now all mysteriously vanished. Then an even more startling discovery is made. This precursor to *Eternity* was originally published in 1985.

**Other books you might like:**
Gregory Benford, *Great Sky River*, 1987
Gregory Benford, *Tides of Light*, 1989
Arthur C. Clarke, *Rendezvous with Rama*, 1973
Larry Niven, *Ringworld*, 1970
Larry Niven, *Ringworld Engineers*, 1980
Dan Simmons, *The Fall of Hyperion*, 1990
Dan Simmons, *Hyperion*, 1989

## 418

### GREG BEAR

## *Foundation and Chaos*

(New York: HarperPrism, 1998)

**Story type:** Science Fiction (Robot Fiction; Political)
**Series:** Foundation
**Major character(s):** Hari Seldon, Scientist, Aged Person; Klia Asgar, Teenager, Telepath; Lodovik Trema, Robot
**Time period(s):** Indeterminate Future
**Locale(s):** Trantor, Planet—Imaginary

**Summary:** While Hari Seldon verges on setting his great Plan into motion, Lodovik Trema, a humanaform robot released from the Three Laws, sees this Plan as an impediment to human progress. As he gathers some sympathetic followers to fight it, the Mentalist movement may correct things on its own.

**Other books you might like:**
Brian W. Aldiss, *Helliconia Winter*, 1985
Roger MacBride Allen, *Inferno*, 1994
Isaac Asimov, *Forward the Foundation*, 1993
Gregory Benford, *Foundation's Fear*, 1997
Gordon R. Dickson, *The Chantry Guild*, 1988
Jacqueline Lichtenberg, *Dushau*, 1985
Larry Niven, *The Mote in God's Eye*, 1974
    Jerry Pournelle, co-author
Jack Vance, *Alastor*, 1995

## 419

### GREG BEAR

## *Heads*

(New York: St. Martins Press, 1991)

**Story type:** Science Fiction (Political; Hard Science Fiction)
**Major character(s):** Mickey Sandoval, Researcher; Rho Sandoval, Businessman
**Time period(s):** 22nd century
**Locale(s):** Montenegro

**Summary:** When Mickey arranges to take possession of 410 cryogenically frozen heads, Rho and Mickey trigger a furor over removal of cultural and anthropological artifacts from their proper setting. They find themselves at the focus of an attempt by Logologists and religious activists to exert influence on Luna.

**Other books you might like:**
Pat Cadigan, *Mindplayers*, 1987
Pat Cadigan, *Synners*, 1991
Diana G. Gallagher, *The Alien Dark*, 1990
Robert A. Heinlein, *The Moon Is a Harsh Mistress*, 1966
Fritz Leiber, *The Silver Eggheads*, 1962
Rudy Rucker, *Wetware*, 1988
Robert Silverberg, *Recalled to Life*, 1962
Michael D. Weaver, *My Father Immortal*, 1989

## 420

### GREG BEAR

## *Legacy*

(New York: Tor, 1995)

**Story type:** Science Fiction (Lost Colony; First Contact)
**Series:** Eon
**Major character(s):** Olmy Ap Sennon, Adventurer (Hexamon agent), Sailor; Frederik Ry Ornis, Technician (gate opener); Able Lenk, Leader (Naderite)
**Time period(s):** Indeterminate Future
**Locale(s):** *Thistledown*, Spaceship; Lamarkia, Planet—Imaginary; *Vigilant*, At Sea

**Summary:** Young and bored, Olmy divorces his Naderite wife and volunteers for a mission to retrieve the missing key stolen by Lenk and observe the effect on Lamarkia, the protected planet on the Way colonized by Lenk and his followers. Although seemingly diverse, life on Lamarkia remains simple, with few individuals stealing characteristics from each other to develop new forms, but without DNA, making the planet unsuitable for human beings. Unfortunately, Olmy cannot complete his mission and leave the planet until he finds the missing key, now on another continent. Prequel to *Eon*.

**Other books you might like:**
L. Warren Douglas, *Cannon's Orb*, 1994
Harry Harrison, *The Deathworld Trilogy*, 1976
Rosemary Kirstein, *The Outskirter's Secret*, 1992
Anne McCaffrey, *Freedom's Landing*, 1995
Charles Sheffield, *Godspeed*, 1993

## 421

### GREG BEAR

## *Moving Mars*

(New York: Tor, 1993)

**Story type:** Science Fiction (Hard Science Fiction; Political)

**Major character(s):** Casseia Majamdar, Political Figure; Charles Franklin, Scientist (theoretical physicist); Ti Sandra Erzul, Political Figure (first President of Mars)
**Time period(s):** 22nd century (2171-2184)
**Locale(s):** Earth; Mars

**Summary:** Casseia Majamdar, a young Martian with political ambitions, finds herself attracted to Charles Franklin, whose focused interest in unlocking the secrets of the universe leads to a breakthrough in theoretical physics. Alarmed factions on Earth threaten to subdue Mars by any means necessary, eventually relying on the harshest possible method and generating unexpected resistance.

**Other books you might like:**
Roger MacBride Allen, *The Ring of Charon*, 1990
Ben Bova, *Mars*, 1992
Arthur C. Clarke, *The Sands of Mars*, 1952
D.G. Compton, *Farewell, Earth's Bliss*, 1971
Gordon R. Dickson, *The Pritcher Mass*, 1972
Robert A. Heinlein, *Red Planet*, 1949
Eric Kotani, *Between the Stars*, 1988
    John Maddox Roberts, co-author
Frederik Pohl, *Mining the Oort*, 1992
Jerry Pournelle, *Birth of Fire*, 1976
Kim Stanley Robinson, *Red Mars*, 1992
Allen Steele, *Labyrinth of Night*, 1992
S.C. Sykes, *Red Genesis*, 1991

---

**422**

**GREG BEAR**, Editor
**MARTIN H. GREENBERG**, Co-Editor

## New Legends
(New York: Tor, 1995)

**Story type:** Science Fiction (Anthology)

**Summary:** Contains a five-page general introduction, brief individual introductions, a one-page afterword, one article considering the influence of science fiction on the real world, Gregory Benford's "Old Legends," and 15 original stories having "great soul," with one story set on the world of *The Left Hand of Darkness* (1969), Ursula K. Le Guin's "Coming of Age in Karhide." Bear divides this volume into six sections, "Choices," "Growing Up," "Them and Us," "Win, Lose, or Draw," "Redemption," and "Cyphers," with themes which include genetic manipulation, hard science, time travel, and future society. Other authors include Poul Anderson, George Alec Effinger, Greg Egan, Geoffrey A. Landis, Paul J. McAuley, Mary Rosenblum, Robert Sheckley, and Robert Silverberg.

**Other books you might like:**
Isaac Asimov, *Isaac Asimov Presents the Great SF Stories*, 1979-1992
    Martin H. Greenberg, co-editor
Gardner Dozois, *Modern Classics of Science Fiction*, 1992
    editor
Martin H. Greenberg, *After the King: Stories in Honor of J.R.R. Tolkien*, 1992
    editor
David G. Hartwell, *The Ascent of Wonder: The Evolution of Hard SF*, 1994
    Kathryn Cramer, co-editor
Raymond J. Healy, *Adventures in Time and Space*, 1946
    J. Frances McComas, co-editor
Ursula K. Le Guin, *The Norton Book of Science Fiction: North American Science Fiction, 1960-1990*, 1993
    Brian Attebery, co-editor

Tom Shippey, *The Oxford Book of Science Fiction Stories*, 1992
editor

---

**423**

**GREG BEAR**

## Queen of Angels
(New York: Warner, 1990)

**Story type:** Science Fiction (Cyberpunk; Techno-Thriller)
**Major character(s):** Mary Choy, Police Officer; Richard Fettle, Writer (aspiring); Martin Burke, Psychologist
**Time period(s):** 21st century
**Locale(s):** Hispaniola, Caribbean; Los Angeles, California

**Summary:** Mary Choy, searching for a murderer, gets caught in international intrigue. While Richard Fettle tries to understand the murderer, Martin Burke tries to cure him, and all three try to keep him from a vigilante organization.

**Other books you might like:**
Gregory Benford, *Tides of Light*, 1989
Gregory Benford, *Great Sky River*, 1987
Dan Simmons, *The Fall of Hyperion*, 1990
Dan Simmons, *Hyperion*, 1989
Bruce Sterling, *Crystal Express*, 1989

---

**424**

**GREG BEAR**

## Songs of Earth and Power
(New York: Tor, 1994)

**Story type:** Fantasy (Alternate World; Urban)
**Major character(s):** Michael Perrin, Adventurer; Eleuth, Mythical Creature (sidhe-human), Magician; Kristine Pendeers, Professor, Researcher
**Time period(s):** 1980s; Indeterminate
**Locale(s):** Los Angeles, California; Realm of the Sidhe, Mythical Place

**Summary:** This omnibus edition contains slightly rewritten versions of *The Infinity Concerto* (1984) and its sequel, *The Serpent Mage* (1986). When a magical song opens the way, Michael Perrin travels to the fairy realm where he finds himself involved in a struggle which could destroy the Earthly realm as well as the magical one. Returning to Los Angeles, Michael must research a powerful magical song to save the Earth.

**Other books you might like:**
Emma Bull, *Finder*, 1994
Emma Bull, *War for the Oaks*, 1987
Charles de Lint, *The Little Country*, 1991
Barbara Hambly, *The Silent Tower*, 1986
Elizabeth Ann Scarborough, *Phantom Banjo*, 1991

---

**425**

**GREG BEAR**

## Tangents
(New York: Warner, 1989)

**Story type:** Science Fiction (Collection)

**Summary:** This collection of nine short stories and an article includes the original novelette, "Sisters," which has been nominated for the 1989 Nebula Award. Among the better reprint stories included are the award-winning "Tangents" and "Blood Music" (source of Bear's novel of that name), "Webster," "Dead Run," "Sleepside Story," and "Schroedinger's Plague."

**Other books you might like:**
Gregory Benford, *In Alien Flesh*, 1986
David Brin, *The River of Time*, 1986
Bruce Sterling, *Crystal Express*, 1989
Vernor Vinge, *Threats. . .and Other Promises*, 1988
Roger Zelazny, *Frost and Fire*, 1989

---

**426**

**WARREN NEWTON BEATH**

## Bloodletter

(New York: Tor, 1994)

**Story type:** Horror (Serial Killer)
**Major character(s):** Steven Albright, Writer; Eva LaPorte, Doctor (psychiatrist); Diver Dan, Serial Killer
**Time period(s):** 1990s (1994)
**Locale(s):** Hollywood, California

**Summary:** Against the backdrop of Hollywood, where nothing is as it seems, Steven Albright, author of the popular Bloodletter vampire novels now being adapted to the screen, becomes convinced that his fictional character is real and out to destroy him. Ultimately, Albright's delusion is shared by his psychiatrist, who becomes romantically involved with him, and "Diver Dan," an obsessive fan of the Bloodletter series who is compelled to commit murders at the bidding of his vampire master.

**Other books you might like:**
Robert Bloch, *Psycho II*, 1992
Stephen King, *The Dark Half*, 1990
Richard Christian Matheson, *Created By*, 1993
David J. Schow, *The Kill Riff*, 1988

---

**427**

**WARREN NEWTON BEATH**

## Shock Lines

(New York: Zebra, 1993)

**Story type:** Horror (Ancient Evil Unleashed)
**Major character(s):** Philip Strayhorn, Teacher (high school); Regina Dentata, Teenager; Leslie Strayhorn, Spouse (Philip's wife)
**Time period(s):** 1990s (1993)
**Locale(s):** Oildorado, California

**Summary:** Earthquake activity along the San Andreas fault releases the Trickster, an evil spirit of Indian lore who incarnates itself as a teenage girl to bring misery to the people of a small oil town in California.

**Other books you might like:**
Chris Curry, *Trickster*, 1993
 Lisa Dean, co-author
G. Wayne Miller, *Thunder Rise*, 1988
Kathryn Ptacek, *Ghost Dance*, 1990
Patrick Whalen, *Deathwalker*, 1993
Chet Williamson, *Dreamthorp*, 1989

---

**428**

**WARREN NEWTON BEATH**

## Who Killed James Dean?

(New York: Tor, 1995)

**Story type:** Horror (Occult)
**Major character(s):** Lou Ehlers, Student (of comparative religions); Cleveland Carroll Devereaux, Writer (biographer); Cherie Lowe, Young Woman (James Dean fan)
**Time period(s):** 1990s (1995); 1950s (1955)
**Locale(s):** Westwood, California

**Summary:** While studying the cult-like nature of the fans of the deceased movie star James Dean, comparative religions scholar Lou Ehlers discovers that Dean's untimely death may have been a consequence of the actor's dabblings in the occult. As the fortieth anniversary of Dean's death approaches, Ehlers, who bears a physical resemblance to the actor, gets the uneasy feeling that he has been chosen to play a part in a ritual re-enactment of the actor's death to help resurrect him.

**Other books you might like:**
Clive Barker, *Sex, Death and Starshine*, 1984
 in *Books of Blood 1*
David Darke, *Horrorshow*, 1994
Norman Partridge, *Spyder*, 1995
Theodore Roszak, *Flicker*, 1993

---

**429**

**CHARLES BEAUMONT**

## The Howling Man

(New York: Tor, 1992)

**Story type:** Horror (Collection)

**Summary:** Originally published in 1988 under the title *Charles Beaumont: Selected Stories*, this collection of 29 tales (one in collaboration with Chad Oliver; five never before published) and an excerpt from the 1959 novel, *The Intruder*, written by the second most prolific writer for the "Twilight Zone" television series, includes some of the most provocative horror fiction produced in the early postwar years. Included are tales of twisted sexuality such as "Miss Gentilbelle," "The Dark Music," and "The New People"; the vampire stories "Last Rites" and "Place of Meeting"; the dark fantasies "The Jungle," "The Vanishing American" and "Free Dirt"; and Beaumont's classic of a possessed jazz musician, "Dark Country." Eighteen writers and editors have contributed tributes.

**Other books you might like:**
Ray Bradbury, *The Stories of Ray Bradbury*, 1980
Dennis Etchison, *The Dark Country*, 1982
Richard Matheson, *Collected Stories*, 1989
William Relling Jr., *The Infinite Man and Other Stories*, 1989

---

**430**

**MICHAEL BEDARD**

## Painted Devil

(New York: Atheneum, 1994)

**Story type:** Fantasy (Young Adult; Horror)
**Major character(s):** Alice Higginson, Teenager, Actor (puppeteer); Mr. Dwyer, Librarian
**Time period(s):** 1990s
**Locale(s):** Caledon, Canada

**Summary:** Alice agrees to help Mr. Dwyer stage a puppet show using old Punch and Judy puppets and a rare script held by the library. As practice progresses, a dark ambience seems to envelop the town, extending to Alice's Aunt Emily who returns to Caledon to aid Alice's mother during her difficult pregnancy. Aunt Emily finds a similarity between today's events and those of 28 years earlier.

**Other books you might like:**
Pauline Clarke, *The Return of the Twelves*, 1963
Lynne Reid Banks, *The Indian in the Cupboard*, 1981
Sylvia Waugh, *The Mennyms*, 1994

**431**

**CLARE BELL**

## People of the Sky

(New York: Tor, 1989)

**Story type:** Science Fiction (First Contact)
**Major character(s):** Kesbe Temiya, Indian; Sahacat, Indian, Shaman
**Time period(s):** 23rd century
**Locale(s):** Oneway, Planet—Imaginary

**Summary:** Two hundred years ago the Pueblo Indians, following a prophecy, emigrated to Oneway, a planet circling a star light years from Earth. There they found an intelligent race of alien flyers, the Aronans, and joined them in a symbiotic relationship in the isolation of Barranca canyon. Now their existence has been almost forgotten by those who live in Oneway's high-tech enclaves. Then Kesbe rediscovers the lost colony of the People of the Sky when her airplane is forced down in a storm over Barranca canyon. They, however, refuse to help her unless she becomes one of them, joining in symbiosis with an Aronan.

**Other books you might like:**
Charles de Lint, *Svaha*, 1989
R.A. MacAvoy, *The Third Eagle: Lessons Along a Minor String*, 1989
Andre Norton, *The Beast Master*, 1959
Andre Norton, *The Sioux Space Man*, 1960
Dan Simmons, *Phases of Gravity*, 1989

**432**

**CLARE BELL**

## Ratha and Thistle-Chaser

(New York: Margaret K. McElderry Books/Macmillan, 1990)

**Story type:** Fantasy (Adventure; Young Adult)
**Series:** Ratha
**Major character(s):** Thakur, Animal, Teacher; Ratha, Animal, Leader (Clan); Newt, Animal
**Time period(s):** Indeterminate Past (25 million years ago)
**Locale(s):** Alternate Earth

**Summary:** A Clan of intelligent wild cats must move to new territory when drought threatens the herdbeasts they use for food. Thakur is both fascinated by, and wary of, Newt who has strange ways and talents. This is a 1991 ALA Best Books For Young Adults title.

**Other books you might like:**
Richard Adams, *Watership Down*, 1972
William Horwood, *Duncton Wood*, 1980
Tad Williams, *Tailchaser's Song*, 1985

**433**

**DOUGLAS BELL**

## Mojo and the Pickle Jar

(New York: Tor, 1991)

**Story type:** Fantasy (Contemporary; Religious)
**Major character(s):** Joseph "Mojo" Birdsong, Criminal; Roger K. "RK" Narn, Lawman (Texas Ranger); Juanita Vasquez, Smuggler
**Time period(s):** 1990s
**Locale(s):** Southwest

**Summary:** Mojo and Juanita are in big trouble by the time they meet Grandmother Montoya. Juanita's pickle jar contains an object much more precious than the demon she believes is there. Instead it contains the stolen heart of a saint. They must survive a demon's trying to kill them and retrieve the heart to save the world. First novel.

**Other books you might like:**
Jon Cohen, *Max Lakeman and the Beautiful Stranger*, 1990
Alan Dean Foster, *Cyber Way*, 1990
Parke Godwin, *The Snake Oil Wars*, 1989
Parke Godwin, *Waiting for the Galactic Bus*, 1988
Simon Hawke, *The Wizard of 4th Street*, 1989
Marc Laidlaw, *Neon Lotus*, 1988
James Morrow, *Only Begotten Daughter*, 1988

**434**

**M. SHAYNE BELL**

## Nicoji

(New York: Baen, 1991)

**Story type:** Science Fiction (Disaster; Adventure)
**Major character(s):** Sam, Hunter; Jake, Hunter; Eloise, Hunter
**Time period(s):** Indeterminate Future
**Locale(s):** Nicoji, Planet—Imaginary

**Summary:** Trapped on an alien planet by a ruthlessly exploitive company, Sam and Jake decide to escape. Following rumors of a newer, more fair company, they set out into the swamps that cover the planet. Unfortunately, the planet is about to go through a major upheaval, both economic and biological, and Sam and Jake are soon fighting just to survive.

**Other books you might like:**
Hal Clement, *Cycle of Fire*, 1957
Frank Herbert, *Dune*, 1965
Barry B. Longyear, *Enemy Mine*, 1985
   David Gerrold, co-author
H. Beam Piper, *Little Fuzzy*, 1962

**435**

**M. SHAYNE BELL**, Editor

## Washed by a Wave of Wind

(Salt Lake City, Utah: Signature Books, 1993)

**Story type:** Science Fiction (Anthology; Theological)

**Summary:** Contains a five-page introduction by the editor, "Toward a Science Fiction From the West"; an 11-page prologue by Barbara R. Hume, "Strange Bedfellows: A History of Science Fiction in the Corridor"; plus three reprinted and 18 original stories by writers from the (Mormon) Corridor who share beliefs concerning the nature of good life and how to achieve it. Stories feature Western impressions and underlying Western frontier values as characters face threats to individual and artistic freedom. Authors include the editor, Elizabeth H. Boyer, Orson Scott Card and Dave Wolverton.

**Other books you might like:**
Ray Bradbury, *The Martian Chronicles*, 1950
David Brin, *The Postman*, 1985
Orson Scott Card, *The Folk of the Fringe*, 1989
Orson Scott Card, *Maps in a Mirror*, 1990
Orson Scott Card, *Seventh Son*, 1987
Robert A. Heinlein, *Farnham's Freehold*, 1964
Clifford D. Simak, *All Flesh Is Grass*, 1965
L. Neil Smith, *Pallas*, 1993
Sheri S. Tepper, *Raising the Stones*, 1990

---

**436**

**RENE BELLETTO**

## Machine

(New York: Grove Press, 1993)

**Story type:** Horror (Science Fiction)
**Major character(s):** Marc Lacroix, Doctor (psychiatrist); Marie Lacroix, Housewife; Michael Zyto, Serial Killer
**Time period(s):** 1990s (1990)
**Locale(s):** Paris, France

**Summary:** Originally published in France in 1990, this novel tells of the horrifying backfire that occurs when Marc Lacroix tries to look into the mind of a serial killer by means of a machine that will exchange some of his psychic energy with the murderer's, but which accidentally switches their personalities completely. Translated by Lanie Goodman.

**Other books you might like:**
Harlan Ellison, *Mefisto in Onyx*, 1993
Damon Knight, *Mind Switch*, 1963
H.P. Lovecraft, *The Thing on the Doorstep*, 1963
    in *The Dunwich Horror and Others*
Curt Siodmak, *Gabriel's Body*, 1988
F. Paul Wilson, *Sibs*, 1993

---

**437**

**DONALD BEMAN**

## Avatar

(New York: Leisure, 1998)

**Story type:** Horror (Anthology)
**Major character(s):** Sean MacDonald, Writer; Monique Gerard, Artist (sculptor); Oliver Shore, Religious (former priest)
**Time period(s):** 1990s (1998)
**Locale(s):** New York, New York

**Summary:** Sean MacDonald's efforts to write a feature on the notoriously private artist Monique Gerard are rewarded with an exclusive audience. His growing intimacy with the sculptress discloses many of her secrets, including, ultimately, the supernatural forces she has tapped to cast her grotesque, disturbing figures.

**Other books you might like:**
Giles Blunt, *Cold Eye*, 1989
Poppy Z. Brite, *Drawing Blood*, 1993
Brian D'Amato, *Beauty*, 1992
Elizabeth Forrest, *Retribution*, 1998
Kathe Koja, *Skin*, 1993

---

**438**

**DONALD BEMAN**

## The Taking

(New York: Leisure, 1997)

**Story type:** Horror (Occult)
**Major character(s):** Sean MacDonald, Writer; Cathy Greene, Farmer; Patricia Jennings, Professor
**Time period(s):** 1990s (1990-1992)
**Locale(s):** Red Hook, New York

**Summary:** Friends study the numerological significance of events in Sean MacDonald's life and discover that he is ripe for "The Taking," or reclamation of his soul by the emissaries of Satan. The revelation helps explain the recent tragedies that have dogged Sean, including the deaths of his wife and son, and make him suspicious of the true motives of the many strong-willed women who show romantic interest in him.

**Other books you might like:**
John Burke, *Ladygrove*, 1978
Fritz Leiber, *Conjure Wife*, 1952
Bentley Little, *Dominion*, 1995
Thomas Tryon, *Harvest Home*, 1973

---

**439**

**HANS BEMMANN**

## The Broken Goddess

(New York: Roc, 1994)

**Story type:** Fantasy (Alternate World)
**Major character(s):** I, Writer; Rana Bressanone, Mythical Creature
**Time period(s):** 1990s; Indeterminate
**Locale(s):** Munich, Germany; Mythical Place (fairy realm)

**Summary:** When challenged about his beliefs concerning fairy tales at a conference, a young academic follows his questioner. His search for her leads to a realm where she reveals her true form to him and he discovers the importance of faith. Translated by Anthea Bell from the 1990 German edition.

**Other books you might like:**
John Crowley, *Little, Big*, 1981
Charles de Lint, *Memory and Dream*, 1994
Barbara Hambly, *The Silent Tower*, 1986
Robert Holdstock, *Mythago Wood*, 1984
R.A. Salvatore, *The Woods out Back*, 1993

---

**440**

**PETER BENCHLEY**

## Beast

(New York: Random House, 1991)

**Story type:** Horror (Nature in Revolt)
**Major character(s):** William Somers "Whip" Darling, Fisherman; Marcus Sharp, Military Personnel (Navy lieutenant); Herbert Talley, Professor (marine biologist)
**Time period(s):** 1990s
**Locale(s):** Bermuda

**Summary:** It's summertime and that means fishermen, swimmers, smugglers and anyone else foolish enough to go in the waters off Bermuda are fair game for *Architeuthis dux*, a ravenous monster squid that wreaks havoc on tourism and scientific research and causes no end of turmoil for its human pursuers in this rewrite of Benchley's 1974 blockbuster, *Jaws*.

**Other books you might like:**
Orson Scott Card, *The Abyss*, 1989
Matthew J. Costello, *Wurm*, 1991
Michael Crichton, *Sphere*, 1987
Jules Verne, *Twenty Thousand Leagues under the Sea*, 1873

### 441

**PETER BENCHLEY**

## White Shark

(New York: Random House, 1994)

**Story type:** Horror (Science Fiction)
**Major character(s):** Simon Chase, Scientist (oceanographer); Max Chase, Child (Simon's 10 year old son); Tall Man Palmer, Sailor
**Time period(s):** 1990s (1996)
**Locale(s):** Osprey Island, Massachusetts

**Summary:** Simon Chase thinks his worst troubles are trying to keep his impoverished oceanographic research center afloat and money-hungry poachers from turning the great white shark into a member of the endangered species list—that is, until the product of a biological experiment from Nazi Germany is liberated from the hold of a ship that sank off the American shore some 50 years ago and begins decimating sea life and human life in nearby waters.

**Other books you might like:**
Matthew J. Costello, *Wurm*, 1991
William Dantz, *Hunger*, 1992
Elizabeth Forrest, *Dark Tide*, 1993
J.M. Morgan, *Between the Devil and the Deep*, 1992

### 442

**GREGORY BENFORD**, Editor
**MARTIN H. GREENBERG**, Co-Editor

## Alternate Americas

(New York: Bantam Spectra, 1992)

**Story type:** Science Fiction (Anthology; Alternate Universe)
**Series:** What Might Have Been

**Summary:** Contains a three-page introduction by Gregory Benford plus 14 short stories commissioned for this volume with five originally appearing in 1992 periodicals and one in an anthology. Several stories feature Columbus's voyages while others present the Americas comparably explored and settled from various directions, some stories successfully employing comic twists. Authors include A. A. Attanasio, L. Sprague de Camp, Esther M. Friesner, James Morrow, Kim Stanley Robinson, Pamela Sargent, Robert Silverberg, Harry Turtledove and George Zebrowski.

**Other books you might like:**
Orson Scott Card, *Seventh Son*, 1987
Glen Cook, *A Matter of Time*, 1985
Phyllis Eisenstein, *Shadow of Earth*, 1979
Michael Flynn, *In the Country of the Blind*, 1990
Katharine Kerr, *Resurrection*, 1992
Frank D. McSherry Jr., *The Fantastic Civil War*, 1991
    editor
Ward Moore, *Bring the Jubilee*, 1953
Mike Resnick, *Alternate Kennedys*, 1992
    editor
Mike Resnick, *Alternate Presidents*, 1992
    editor

John Maddox Roberts, *King of the Wood*, 1983
S.M. Stirling, *Marching through Georgia*, 1988

### 443

**GREGORY BENFORD**, Editor
**MARTIN H. GREENBERG**, Co-Editor

## Alternate Wars

(New York: Bantam Spectra, 1991)

**Story type:** Science Fiction (Anthology; Alternate Universe)
**Series:** What Might Have Been

**Summary:** This anthology of stories about alternate wars throughout human history includes an introduction by Gregory Benford and 12 stories, including "If Lee Had Not Won the Battle of Gettysburg" by the Right Honorable Winston S. Churchill, M.P. The remaining 11 stories are all by science fiction authors including Poul Anderson, F.M. Busby, Nancy Kress, Allen Steele, Harry Turtledove and George Zebrowski.

**Other books you might like:**
J.G. Ballard, *The Atrocity Exhibition*, 1990
Arthur C. Clarke, *Tales From Planet Earth*, 1990
Philip K. Dick, *The Man in the High Castle*, 1962
Michael Flynn, *In the Country of the Blind*, 1990
William Gibson, *The Difference Engine*, 1990
    Bruce Sterling, co-author
Brad Linaweaver, *Moon of Ice*, 1988
Jack McDevitt, *A Talent for War*, 1989
Frank D. McSherry Jr., *The Fantastic Civil War*, 1991
    editor
Ward Moore, *Bring the Jubilee*, 1953

### 444

**GREGORY BENFORD**

## Cosm

(New York: Avon Eos, 1998)

**Story type:** Science Fiction (Contemporary Realism; Hard Science Fiction)
**Major character(s):** Alicia Butterworth, Scientist (particle physics), Researcher; Phat "Zak" Nguyen, Student—Graduate, Researcher; Dave Rucker, Administrator (director of operations)
**Time period(s):** 2000s (2005)
**Locale(s):** New York (Brookhaven National Laboratory); California (Univ. of California-Irvine); Berkeley, California

**Summary:** Besides the locals suing the lab to prevent her experiment to accelerate uranium atoms, and the innuendo that she received access to the lab because of her race, Alicia must produce an additional document before her experiment can take place, without enough time to do it properly. When the experiment produces an unusual sphere, she takes the object back to UC-Irvine.

**Other books you might like:**
Greg Bear, *Eon*, 1985
Alfred Bester, *Psychoshop*, 1998
    Roger Zelazny, co-author
John Cramer, *Einstein's Bridge*, 1997
Michael Kandel, *Panda Ray*, 1997
Robert J. Sawyer, *Frameshift*, 1997

## 445

**GREGORY BENFORD**, Editor

### Far Futures

(New York: Tor, 1995)

**Story type:** Science Fiction (Anthology; Science Fiction)
**Time period(s):** Indeterminate Future

**Summary:** This book contains a 12-page introduction and brief individual introductions with biographies for five novellas, written with the purpose of dealing with "truly grand perspectives in time." Poul Anderson, Greg Bear, Joe Haldeman, Donald Kingsbury, and Charles Sheffield project events from 1600 to several billion years in the future.

**Other books you might like:**
Poul Anderson, *The Stars Are Also Fire*, 1994
Poul Anderson, *Tau Zero*, 1970
James Blish, *Cities in Flight*, 1970
Arthur C. Clarke, *The City and the Stars*, 1956
Larry Niven, *A World out of Time*, 1976
Cordwainer Smith, *The Rediscovery of Man*, 1993
Olaf Stapledon, *Last and First Men*, 1930
Olaf Stapledon, *Star Maker*, 1937

## 446

**GREGORY BENFORD**

### Foundation's Fear

(New York: HarperPrism, 1997)

**Story type:** Science Fiction (Robot Fiction; Space Opera)
**Series:** Second Foundation Trilogy
**Major character(s):** Hari Seldon, Scientist (mathist), Political Figure; R. Daneel "Eto Demerzel" Olivaw, Robot; Cleon I, Ruler (emperor)
**Time period(s):** Indeterminate Future
**Locale(s):** Trantor, Planet—Imaginary

**Summary:** Feeling that something unknown remains necessary to complete his theory of psychohistory, Hari Seldon imports 16,000-year-old "sims" of Joan of Arc and Voltaire. Following the advice of Eto Demerzel, Cleon insists on Hari for his First Minister. Joan and Voltaire get loose in the Net, finding powerful and ancient minds who hate robots. First of a trilogy by Gregory Benford, Greg Bear, and David Brin.

**Other books you might like:**
Roger MacBride Allen, *Caliban*, 1993
Isaac Asimov, *The Foundation Trilogy*, 1963
Isaac Asimov, *Robots and Empire*, 1985
James P. Hogan, *Code of the Lifemaker*, 1983
A.E. Van Vogt, *The Weapon Makers*, 1946
Jack Williamson, *The Humanoids*, 1949

## 447

**GREGORY BENFORD**

### Furious Gulf

(New York: Bantam Spectra, 1994)

**Story type:** Science Fiction (Hard Science Fiction)
**Series:** Great Sky River
**Major character(s):** Killeen Bishop, Spaceship Captain, Genetically Altered Being; Toby Bishop, Refugee, Genetically Altered Be-
ing; Quath'jutt'kkal'thon "Quath", Alien (Myriapodia), Revolutionary
**Time period(s):** 280th century
**Locale(s):** *Argo*, Spaceship; Outer Space (galactic center)

**Summary:** Pursued by mechs, Family Bishop continues toward True Center with help from Quath and the Magnetic Mind. The *Argo* encounters many intelligences on its trip into the black hole and the Esty, condensed space time, they find there.

**Other books you might like:**
Roger MacBride Allen, *The Ring of Charon*, 1990
Stephen Baxter, *Raft*, 1992
Greg Bear, *Eon*, 1985
Larry Niven, *Neutron Star*, 1968
Frederik Pohl, *Gateway*, 1977
Dan Simmons, *Hyperion*, 1989
Joan Slonczewski, *Daughter of Elysium*, 1993

## 448

**GREGORY BENFORD**

### Matter's End

(New York: Bantam Spectra, 1995)

**Story type:** Science Fiction (Collection)

**Summary:** The 21 stories in this collection include Benford's first published work, "Stand-In" (1965), and exhibit a wide range of length and theme. The tone varies from humorous to dark with stories individually emphasizing setting, character, or science, according to the six-page afterword.

**Other books you might like:**
David G. Hartwell, *The Ascent of Wonder: The Evolution of Hard SF*, 1990
   Kathryn Cramer, co-editor
Judith Merril, *The Best of Judith Merril*, 1976
Marc Stiegler, *The Gentle Seduction*, 1990
Theodore Sturgeon, *The Complete Egoist*, 1994
John Varley, *The Persistence of Vision*, 1978

## 449

**GREGORY BENFORD**

### Sailing Bright Eternity

(New York: Bantam Spectra, 1995)

**Story type:** Science Fiction (Hard Science Fiction; Robot Fiction)
**Series:** Galactic Center
**Major character(s):** Nigel Walmsley, Astronaut, Immortal; Toby Bishop, Wanderer; Killeen, Parent, Wanderer
**Time period(s):** Indeterminate Future
**Locale(s):** Galcen, Mythical Place (The Lair Labyrinth)

**Summary:** Toby learns that he, his father, and grandfather hold the key to the ultimate destruction of the Mechs. Unable to believe that happiness could be their undoing, the Mechs actively search for the key, while ancient forces aid the humans.

**Other books you might like:**
Roger MacBride Allen, *The Ring of Charon*, 1990
Stephen Baxter, *Raft*, 1992
Frederik Pohl, *Gateway*, 1977
Robert Reed, *Down the Bright Way*, 1991
Dan Simmons, *Hyperion*, 1989
Dan Simmons, *The Fall of Hyperion*, 1990

## 450

**GREGORY BENFORD**

### Tides of Light

(New York: Bantam, 1989)

**Story type:** Science Fiction (Hard Science Fiction)
**Major character(s):** Killeen, Spaceship Captain (Captain of Family Bishop); Quath'jutt'kkal'thon "Quath", Alien, Revolutionary
**Time period(s):** Indeterminate Future
**Locale(s):** *Argo*, Spaceship; Abraham's Star, Outer Space

**Summary:** Fleeing the mechs who infest their home planet, Family Bishop has stolen a starship and journeyed to Abraham's Star. On a planet of that star they find other human beings fighting a battle against yet another hostile civilization, the half-alien/half-machine cybers. Cap'n Killeen must find a place for his Family, despite the hostility of cybers, mechs, and other human beings.

**Other books you might like:**
David Brin, *Startide Rising*, 1983
David Brin, *The Uplift War*, 1987
Edward Gibson, *Reach*, 1989
David Alexander Smith, *Rendezvous*, 1988

## 451

**MARCIA J. BENNETT**

### Seeking the Dream Brother

(New York: Ballantine/Del Rey, 1989)

**Story type:** Science Fiction (Adventure)
**Series:** Ni-Lach
**Major character(s):** Dhalvad, Alien, Psychic; Theon, Human
**Time period(s):** Indeterminate Future
**Locale(s):** Lach, Planet—Imaginary

**Summary:** The Ni-lach Dhalvad has fled humanity and returned to his own people because humans fear his ability to heal and teleport. Now, however, he's called on a dangerous dream quest to rescue his long lost brother.

**Other books you might like:**
David Brin, *The Uplift War*, 1987
Leslie Gadallah, *Cat's Gambit*, 1989
H. Beam Piper, *Fuzzies and Other People*, 1984
H. Beam Piper, *Little Fuzzy*, 1962
H. Beam Piper, *The Other Human Race*, 1964

## 452

**NIGEL BENNETT**
**P.N. ELROD**, Co-Author

### Keeper of the King

(New York: Baen/Starline, 1997)

**Story type:** Horror (Vampire Story)
**Major character(s):** Richard Dun, Consultant (security), Vampire; Neal Rivers, Professor, Vampire; Lady Sabra, Vampire
**Time period(s):** 1990s (1996)
**Locale(s):** Toronto, Ontario, Canada

**Summary:** In medieval times, Vampire Richard d'Orleans serves as the protector of King Arthur, giving rise to the legends of Sir Lancelot. In his 20th-century incarnation as Richard Dun, he fulfills a similar role, serving as a security consultant who protects the Canadian prime minister from an IRA-plotted assassination attempt. This is a first collaboration between Elrod, a writer of vampire fiction, and Bennett, an actor in the television vampire series "Forever Knight."

**Other books you might like:**
Jane Jensen, *Gabriel Knight: Sins of the Fathers*, 1997
Anne Rice, *The Queen of the Damned*, 1989
Fred Saberhagen, *A Sharpness on the Neck*, 1996
Robert Weinberg, *Unholy Allies*, 1995
T. Lucien Wright, *Thirst of the Vampire*, 1992

## 453

**ANN BENSON**

### The Plague Tales

(New York: Delacorte, 1997)

**Story type:** Science Fiction (Medical; Science Fiction)
**Major character(s):** Robert Sarin, Aged Person, Handicapped; Janie Crowe, Doctor (surgeon), Student (forensic anthropolgist); Alejandro Canches, Doctor, Wanderer
**Time period(s):** 14th century (2000s)
**Locale(s):** Cervere, Spain (Aragon); London, England

**Summary:** Refusing to let Janie dig in the land under his care, Robert Sarin continues to follow the instructions of his mother and the Book. Alejandro, a Jewish doctor, records the illegal autopsy he performs in his Book. The Church objects, forcing him to leave. As bubonic plague spreads through Europe, Alejandro records his observations, including the cure. Unfortunately Janie steals a soil sample from Robert's land. First novel.

**Other books you might like:**
Margaret Wander Bonanno, *The Others*, 1990
E.L. Doctorow, *The Waterworks*, 1994
Neil Gaiman, *Good Omens: The Nice and Accurate Prophecies of Agnes Nutter, Witch*, 1990
    Terry Pratchett, co-author
Bill Ransom, *ViraVax*, 1993
Connie Willis, *Doomsday Book*, 1992

## 454

**E.F. BENSON**

### The Collected Ghost Stories of E.F. Benson

(New York: Carroll & Graf, 1992)

**Story type:** Horror (Collection)

**Summary:** A landmark omnibus that collects all the major supernatural fiction of an Edwardian writer (1867-1940) better known for his comedies of manners. Included among the 54 stories are the classic vampire tales "The Room in the Tower" and "Mrs. Amworth"; the Christmas ghost story, "How Fear Departed from the Long Gallery"; a tale of a ghostly manifestation of a disease, "Caterpillars"; a story of precognition, "The Bus-Conductor"; and the tale of a slug-like horror that haunts the grounds of a former churchyard, "Negotium Perambulans." Editor Richard Dalby has also included "The Clonmel Witch Burning," an early essay in which Benson recounts the horrible torture of a suspected 19th century Irish witch.

**Other books you might like:**
Robert Hugh Benson, *The Light Invisible*, 1907
Algernon Blackwood, *Best Ghost Stories of Algernon Blackwood*, 1973
A.M. Burrage, *Warning Whispers*, 1988
William Fryer Harvey, *Midnight Tales*, 1946

**455**

### E.F. BENSON

## The Terror by Night

(Ashcroft, British Columbia: Ash-Tree Press, 1998)

**Story type:** Horror (Collection)
**Series:** Collected Spook Stories of E.F. Benson

**Summary:** First in a projected series of volumes that will collect all of the short supernatural tales of E.F. Benson, a master of macabre fiction in the Edwardian era. Stories are arranged in chronological order of publication and include ''The Man Who Went Too Far,'' about a man whose ecstatic communion with the spiritual realm leads to a gruesome demise; ''Caterpillars,'' in which a cancerous disease manifests as an insectoid creature; ''How Fear Departed From the Long Gallery,'' which involves a haunting and an exorcism; and ''The Bus-Conductor,'' an eerie tale of precognition. Introduced and edited by Jack Adrian.

**Other books you might like:**
Algernon Blackwood, *Shocks*, 1936
A.M. Burrage, *Warning Whispers*, 1988
Bernard Capes, *The Black Reaper*, 1998
M.P. Dare, *Unholy Relics*, 1947
William Fryer Harvey, *Midnight Tales*, 1946

**456**

### ROBERT HUGH BENSON

## The Light Invisible

(Bristol, Rhode Island: Hobgoblin Press, 1997)

**Story type:** Horror (Collection)

**Summary:** Collection of 12 tales of the supernatural, told by an elderly priest to illustrate the existence of the Divine. In ''The Green Robe'' and ''The Watcher,'' a young boy sees physical manifestations of the holy in nature. ''The Blood Eagle'' is concerned with a pagan ritual that incorporates elements of both Christian and pre-Christian worship in England, and ''The Traveler'' with a priest who discovers his confessional has been visited by the ghost of a conspirator in the death of Sir Thomas a Beckett. Originally published in England in 1903.

**Other books you might like:**
A.C. Benson, *Ghosts in the House*, 1996
  R.H. Benson, co-author
A.C. Benson, *Basil Netherby*, 1927
Algernon Blackwood, *Pan's Garden: A Volume of Nature Stories*, 1912
Arthur Machen, *The Terror*, 1917
A.N.L. Munby, *The Alabaster Hand and Other Ghost Stories*, 1949

**457**

### NANCY VARIAN BERBERICK

## A Child of Elvish

(New York: Ace, 1992)

**Story type:** Fantasy (Quest)
**Major character(s):** Kicva, Mythical Creature (elf), Adventurer; Joze, Adventurer; Islief the Watcher, Mythical Creature (First People)
**Time period(s):** Indeterminate
**Locale(s):** Elfland, Mythical Place

**Summary:** When Islief's lady appears to Kicva and Joze as a ghost to request help overturning an evil sorcerer's plotting, they agree to find and bring back to the spirit the child of mixed Mannish and Elvin heritage who can safely wield the ancient magic and correct the upset balance of forces. Sequel to *The Jewels of Elvish*.

**Other books you might like:**
Sheila Gilluly, *The Boy From the Burren*, 1990
Robert Jordan, *The Eye of the World*, 1989
Andre Norton, *The Elvenbane*, 1991
  Mercedes Lackey, co-author
Michael Scott Rohan, *The Forge in the Forest*, 1989
Margaret Weis, *Dragon Wing*, 1990
  Tracy Hickman, co-author

**458**

### NANCY VARIAN BERBERICK

## The Panther's Hoard

(New York: Ace, 1994)

**Story type:** Fantasy (Sword and Sorcery)
**Major character(s):** Garroc, Warrior, Mythical Creature (dwarf)
**Time period(s):** 7th century
**Locale(s):** England; Wales; Mythical Place

**Summary:** The sole surviving member of the ancient race of dwarves leads human warriors to battle the elder-gods in their own realm. Sequel to *Shadow of the Seventh Moon*.

**Other books you might like:**
Patrick H. Adkins, *Sons of the Titans*, 1990
Linda Evans, *Sleipnir*, 1994
Jason Henderson, *The Spawn of Loki*, 1994
Mark C. Perry, *Morigu: The Dead*, 1990
Elizabeth Ann Scarborough, *Last Refuge*, 1992

**459**

### NANCY VARIAN BERBERICK

## Shadow of the Seventh Moon

(New York: Ace, 1991)

**Story type:** Fantasy (Historical)
**Major character(s):** Garroc, Warrior, Mythical Creature (dwarf); Lydi, Witch; Dyfed, Warrior
**Time period(s):** 7th century (630)
**Locale(s):** England

**Summary:** Garroc, the last of the Dwarves, tells his story to the human woman Sif, daughter of Garroc's human fosterling Hinthan. Garroc was scout and soldier for Halfdan and his son Erich War Hawk, Saxon lords who held the borderland between Saxons and Welsh in the century after King Arthur's death. As kings battle each other and Erich seeks revenge on Vorgund, the slayer of Halfdan, Garroc finds his own destiny.

**Other books you might like:**
Lynn Abbey, *Unicorn and Dragon*, 1987
C.J. Cherryh, *The Tree of Swords and Jewels*, 1983
Parke Godwin, *The Last Rainbow*, 1985
Rudyard Kipling, *Puck of Pook's Hill*, 1988
Andre Norton, *Merlin's Mirror*, 1975

## 460

**DAVID BERGANTINO**

### *Wes Craven's New Nightmare*

(New York: Tor, 1994)

**Story type:** Horror (Supernatural Vengeance)
**Major character(s):** Heather Lagenkamp, Actress, Historical Figure; Wes Craven, Director (film), Historical Figure; Dylan Porter, Child (Heather's 5-year-old son)
**Time period(s):** 1990s (1994)
**Locale(s):** Los Angeles, California

**Summary:** A series of grisly deaths in the manner of the *Nightmare on Elm Street* series of movies plagues the set of director Wes Craven's newest horror film. Craven and his leading actress discover that they are the doings of the spiritual force embodied by "Nightmares" heavy Freddy Krueger, and that in order to contain it they must make another movie that brings his character back to life. This book is a novelization of the 1994 Wes Craven film of the same title.

**Other books you might like:**
Jonathan Carroll, *A Child Across the Sky*, 1989
David Darke, *Horrorshow*, 1994
Martin H. Greenberg, *Nightmares on Elm Street: Freddy Krueger's Seven Sweetest Dreams*, 1991
    editor
Dale Hoover, *65mm*, 1994
Brad Strickland, *Shadowshow*, 1988

## 461

**EDWARD P. BERGLUND**, Editor

### *Disciples of Cthulhu*

(Oakland, California: Chaosium, 1996)

**Story type:** Horror (Anthology)

**Summary:** A revision of a 1976 paperback original, this volume collects nine homages to the Cthulhu Mythos fiction of H.P. Lovecraft, including Brian Lumley's "The Fairground Horror," in which a travelling carnival brings Lovecraftian horrors to the town it visits; Ramsey Campbell's "The Tugging," in which quirks of astronomy induce nightmares of universal doom; and Fritz Leiber's "The Horror From the Depths," in which a man's attempt to reconcile himself with his personal demons parallels his pursuit of forbidden occult knowledge. Robert M. Price's "Dope War of the Black Tong," is a pastiche of Robert E. Howard in which a detective grapples with Lovecraftian monstrosities, is new to this edition. Robert Bloch supplies the introduction.

**Other books you might like:**
Lin Carter, *The Spawn of Cthulhu*, 1991
    editor
H.P. Lovecraft, *Tales of the Cthulhu Mythos: Golden Anniversary Anthology*, 1990
Robert M. Price, *The Azathoth Cycle*, 1995
    editor
Robert M. Price, *The Hastur Cycle*, 1993
    editor
Robert M. Price, *The New Lovecraft Circle*, 1996
    editor
Robert M. Price, *The Shub Niggurath Cycle*, 1994
    editor
Robert M. Price, *Tales of the Lovecraft Mythos*, 1992
    editor
Thomas M.K. Stratman, *Cthulhu's Heirs*, 1994

Jim Turner, *Cthulhu 2000*, 1995
    editor

## 462

**ELAINE BERGSTROM**

### *Blood Alone*

(New York: Jove, 1990)

**Story type:** Horror (Vampire Story)
**Major character(s):** Paul Stodard, Artisan; Laurence Austra, Vampire; Gregory Hunter, Military Personnel
**Time period(s):** 1940s
**Locale(s):** Europe

**Summary:** During the tense months prior to the beginning of World War II, members of the Austra family strive to protect their business (creating stained glass for religious shrines) and keep secret the fact that they're vampires as they combat insane Nazi doctors and hordes of spies. This novel is a sequel to *Shattered Glass*.

**Other books you might like:**
Marc Eliot, *How Dear the Dawn*, 1987
Robert R. McCammon, *The Wolf's Hour*, 1988
Dan Simmons, *Carrion Comfort*, 1989
Robert Weinberg, *The Armageddon Box*, 1991

## 463

**ELAINE BERGSTROM**

### *Daughter of the Night*

(New York: Jove, 1992)

**Story type:** Horror (Vampire Story)
**Series:** Chronicles of the Austra Family
**Major character(s):** Elizabeth Bathori, Noblewoman, Historical Figure; Catherine Austra, Vampire; Charles, Nobleman (Wallachian lord), Vampire
**Time period(s):** 16th century (1563); 17th century (1609-1610)
**Locale(s):** Transylvania

**Summary:** This novel presents a fictional rendering of the historical figure Elizabeth Bathori, who gained renown in Eastern Europe of the late sixteenth and early seventeenth century for bathing in the blood of more than 600 female victims. Here, the author surmises that Elizabeth's ghastly habits began following her association with a Wallachian vampire lady, Catherine Austra, during the same tribal wars between Turkey and Transylvania that yielded the legends of Vlad Tepes, Count Dracula.

**Other books you might like:**
Les Daniels, *The Black Castle*, 1978
Brian Lumley, *Vamphyri!*, 1987
Anne Rice, *The Vampire Lestat*, 1985
Michael Romkey, *I, Vampire*, 1990
Brian Stableford, *The Empire of Fear*, 1988
Chelsea Quinn Yarbro, *The Palace*, 1978

## 464

**ELAINE BERGSTROM**

### *The Door through Washington Square*

(New York: Ace, 1998)

**Story type:** Fantasy (Time Travel)

**Major character(s):** Dierdre MacCallum, Heir; Aleister Crowley, Magician, Historical Figure; Bridget MacCallum, Time Traveler
**Time period(s):** 1920s
**Locale(s):** New York, New York

**Summary:** Dierdre MacCallum travels to New York City to wind up the affairs of her grandmother, who has passed away. Shortly after arriving, she discovers that one of the doorways in the apartment leads back to the 1920s, where her grandmother is a young woman involved with the magic of Aleister Crowley.

**Other books you might like:**
John Dickson Carr, *The Devil in Velvet*, 1951
Jack Finney, *From Time to Time*, 1995
Jack Finney, *Time and Again*, 1971
John R. Maxim, *Time Out of Mind*, 1986
Andre Norton, *Red Hart Magic*, 1976

---

### 465

#### ELAINE BERGSTROM

### *Tapestry of Dark Souls*

(Geneva, Wisconsin: TSR, 1993)

**Story type:** Horror (Occult)
**Series:** Ravenloft
**Major character(s):** Leith, Werewolf; Jonathan, Young Man (Leith's son); Sondra, Young Woman
**Time period(s):** Indeterminate
**Locale(s):** Ravenloft, Fictional Country

**Summary:** In the imaginary world of Ravenloft, the Guardians keep watch over a tapestry with the power to absorb and amplify evil. As their numbers dwindle, they hope that the stalwart young Jonathan, entrusted to their care, will spend his life keeping the tapestry from the hands of those who would use it for evil. But Jonathan's mother was herself infected by the tapestry while she bore her son, raising doubts as to whether Jonathan himself can be trusted.

**Other books you might like:**
P.N. Elrod, *I, Strahd*, 1993
Christie Golden, *Dance of the Dead*, 1992
J. Robert King, *Carnival of Fear*, 1993

---

### 466

#### JANET BERLINER
#### GEORGE GUTHRIDGE, Co-Author

### *Child of the Journey*

(Clarkston, Georgia: White Wolf Borealis, 1996)

**Story type:** Fantasy (Magic Conflict; Historical)
**Series:** Madagascar Manifesto
**Major character(s):** Solomon "Sol" Freund, Psychic; Miriam Rathenau, Singer, Spouse; Erich "Erich Alois" Weisser, Telepath (with animals), Animal Trainer (canines)
**Time period(s):** 1930s (1938-1939)
**Locale(s):** Netherlands; Berlin, Germany; *Sogne*, At Sea

**Summary:** Solomon searches for his beloved Miriam, while Miriam pledges her body, if not her heart, to Erich, expecting thus to protect Solomon. When Erich leads a mission to occupy Madagascar, Miriam uses the little time available to speak with Solomon onboard the ship and share hopes for some positive change. Sequel to *Child of the Light*.

**Other books you might like:**
Martin Amis, *Time's Arrow*, 1991

Peter S. Beagle, *Peter S. Beagle's Immortal Unicorn*, 1995
  Janet Berliner, co-editor
Janet Gluckman, *Child of the Light*, 1992
  George Guthridge, co-author
Lisa Goldstein, *The Red Magician*, 1982
Robin Hobb, *Royal Assassin*, 1995
Jane Yolen, *Briar Rose*, 1992

---

### 467

#### JANET BERLINER
#### GEORGE GUTHRIDGE, Co-Author

### *Children of the Dusk*

(Clarkston, Georgia: White Wolf Borealis, 1997)

**Story type:** Fantasy (Magic Conflict; Historical)
**Series:** Madagascar Manifesto
**Major character(s):** Solomon "Sol" Freund, Psychic; Miriam Rathenau, Spouse; Erich "Erich Alois" Weisser, Leader (Nazi), Animal Trainer (canine unit), Telepath (with animals)
**Time period(s):** 1930s (1939)
**Locale(s):** Madagascar

**Summary:** As World War II heats up, the Nazi plan to carve out a Jewish homeland on Madagascar may fall victim to internal conflict and the actions of two Malagasy sorcerers. Concludes the triology.

**Other books you might like:**
Martin Amis, *Time's Arrow*, 1991
Peter S. Beagle, *Peter S. Beagle's Immortal Unicorn*, 1995
  Janet Berliner, co-editor
J.R. Dunn, *Days of Cain*, 1997
Lisa Goldstein, *The Red Magician*, 1982
Jane Yolen, *Briar Rose*, 1992

---

### 468

#### JANET BERLINER, Editor
#### UWE LUSERKE, Co-Editor
#### MARTIN H. GREENBERG, Co-Editor

### *Desire Burn: Women's Stories From the Dark Side of Passion*

(New York: Carroll & Graf, 1995)

**Story type:** Horror (Anthology)

**Summary:** Twenty reprinted stories by twenty women authors explore issues of female sexuality in a horror context. In Lois Tilton's "The Other Woman" and Diedra Cox's "Remnants," obsessive passions keep women and their partners alive after death. Both Dawn Dunn in "The Lonely Heart" and Nancy Holder in "Heat" link sexuality to pain. Poppy Z. Brite's "The Sixth Sentinel" is a ghost story, Esther Friesner's "Do I Dare to Ask Your Name?" a vampire story, and Jan Barrette's "Patent Pending" and Katherine Dunn's "Near Flesh" science fiction stories. Cynthia Ward's "Midwife" and Joyce Carol Oates' "Love, Letter" are exercises in psychological horror, and Berliner's own "Castoff" is a tale of supernatural revenge.

**Other books you might like:**
Marvin Kaye, *Angels of Darkness*, 1995
  editor
Kathryn Ptacek, *Women of Darkness*, 1988
  editor
Kathryn Ptacek, *Women of Darkness II*, 1990
  editor

Lisa Tuttle, *Skin of the Soul*, 1990
    editor

---

**469**

### MICHAEL BERLYN

## *The Eternal Enemy*

(New York: Morrow, 1990)

**Story type:** Science Fiction (First Contact; Space Opera)
**Major character(s):** Markos, Scientist (exobiologist); Van Pelt, Spaceship Captain
**Time period(s):** Indeterminate Future
**Locale(s):** *Paladin*, Spaceship; Outer Space; Gandji, Planet—Imaginary

**Summary:** Markos is sent to Gandji, a planet circling Tau Ceti, with a mission to find and rescue a lost probe ship scout, and to study the local sentient life. Van Pelt believes the Habers are dangerous and decides to wipe them out over Markos' objections that the Habers are completely non-violent. Markos, killed in the attempt to warn or help the Habers, finds himself changed, but alive, and continues his campaign to prevent the elimination of the Habers.

**Other books you might like:**
David Brin, *The Uplift War*, 1987
Octavia E. Butler, *Imago*, 1989
Octavia E. Butler, *Adulthood Rites*, 1988
Octavia E. Butler, *Dawn*, 1987
Orson Scott Card, *Ender's Game*, 1985
David Alexander Smith, *Homecoming*, 1990

---

**470**

### JOANNE BERTIN

## *The Last Dragonlord*

(New York: Tor, 1998)

**Major character(s):** Linden Rathan, Mythical Creature (dragonlord); Maurynna, Sea Captain
**Time period(s):** Indeterminate
**Locale(s):** Five Kingdoms, Fictional Country; At Sea

**Summary:** Linden Rathan is a shapechanger capable of becoming a dragon. His kind have helped maintain peace among the Five Kingdoms from their distant, secretive haunts. When a queen is murdered, war threatens to break out, and Rathan teams up with a sea captain to solve the mystery. First novel.

**Other books you might like:**
Carol L. Dennis, *Dragon's Knight*, 1989
Thorarinn Gunnarsson, *The Dragonlord of Mystara*, 1994
Barbara Hambly, *Dragonsbane*, 1985
Mary Kirchoff, *The Black Wing*, 1993
Richard A. Knaak, *The Ice Dragon*, 1989

---

**471**

### ELUKI BES SHAHAR

## *Archangel Blues*

(New York: DAW, 1993)

**Story type:** Science Fiction (Space Opera; Political)
**Series:** Hellflower

**Major character(s):** Butterfly St. Cyr, Smuggler (darktrader), Spaceship Captain; Paladin, Artificial Intelligence; Baijon ''Tiggy'' Stardust, Knight (Hellflower)
**Time period(s):** Indeterminate Future
**Locale(s):** *Ghost Dance*, Spaceship; Palaceoid Morningstar, Planet—Imaginary; Phoenix Empire, Interstellar Empire/Federation

**Summary:** Paladin's acting up impedes Butterfly St. Cyr's goal of finding and destroying Governor-General Mallorum Archangel before he can plunge the Phoenix Empire into war.

**Other books you might like:**
Glen Cook, *The Dragon Never Sleeps*, 1988
Cheryl J. Franklin, *Fire Crossing*, 1991
Neal Stephenson, *Snow Crash*, 1992
Vernor Vinge, *A Fire upon the Deep*, 1992
David Weber, *Path of the Fury*, 1992

---

**472**

### ELUKI BES SHAHAR

## *Darktraders*

(New York: DAW, 1992)

**Story type:** Science Fiction (Political; Space Opera)
**Series:** Hellflower
**Major character(s):** Butterfly St. Cyr, Smuggler (darktrader), Spaceship Captain; Paladin, Artificial Intelligence; Baijon ''Tiggy'' Stardust, Knight (Hellflower)
**Time period(s):** Indeterminate Future
**Locale(s):** Imperial Mikasa, Planet—Imaginary; *Woebegone*, Spaceship

**Summary:** While Butterfly tries to return Tiggy to Kenner, his Hellflower father, Imperial Prince Archangel schemes to use illegal Old Federation technology to gain control of the universe and kill Tiggy. Starflower honor prevents Butterfly's execution until after replacement of the arm she loses saving Tiggy's life. Tiggy's honor forces Butterfly to become embroiled in Starflower politics while they try to prevent the destruction of the Empire.

**Other books you might like:**
Glen Cook, *The Dragon Never Sleeps*, 1988
Cheryl J. Franklin, *Fire Crossing*, 1991
James P. Hogan, *Entoverse*, 1991
Dan Simmons, *Hyperion*, 1989
Neal Stephenson, *Snow Crash*, 1992
Michael Swanwick, *Stations of the Tide*, 1991
George Zebrowski, *Stranger Suns*, 1991

---

**473**

### ELUKI BES SHAHAR

## *Hellflower*

(New York: DAW, 1991)

**Story type:** Science Fiction (Adventure)
**Major character(s):** Butterfly St. Cyr, Smuggler (darktrader), Spaceship Captain; Paladin, Artificial Intelligence
**Time period(s):** Indeterminate Future
**Locale(s):** Wanderweb, Planet—Imaginary; *Firecat*, Spaceship

**Summary:** Butterfly's partner, Paladin, now installed in her spaceship, had been an abandoned library of the Federation, all of whose technology is now illegal. While having a constant communication device installed for Paladin, Butterfly rescues a Hellflower, a man from one of the worlds where honor is complex and primary.

**Other books you might like:**
Emma Bull, *Bone Dance: A Fantasy for Technophiles*, 1991
Glen Cook, *The Dragon Never Sleeps*, 1988
Brian Daley, *Requiem for a Ruler of Worlds*, 1985
William C. Dietz, *Drifter*, 1991
Alis A. Rasmussen, *A Passage of Stars*, 1990
David Alexander Smith, *Marathon*, 1982

**474**

ALEXANDER BESHER

## Mir

(New York: Simon & Schuster, 1998)

**Story type:** Science Fiction (Future Shock)
**Series:** Rim
**Major character(s):** Trevor Gobi, Computer Expert; Nelly, Computer Expert
**Time period(s):** 2030s (2036)
**Locale(s):** San Francisco, California; Nice, France

**Summary:** A new cold war has raised international tensions at the same time that advances in computer technology have made borders more permeable than ever. Programmers have created tattoos which contain software that can alter human perceptions, and someone has created a virus program which can have fatal results.

**Other books you might like:**
Bruce Bethke, *Headcrash*, 1995
William Gibson, *Neuromancer*, 1984
K.W. Jeter, *Death's Arms*, 1987
Neal Stephenson, *Snow Crash*, 1992
Bruce Sterling, *Islands in the Net*, 1988

**475**

ALEXANDER BESHER

## Rim: A Novel of Virtual Reality

(New York: HarperCollins West, 1994)

**Story type:** Science Fiction (Post-Disaster; Techno-Thriller)
**Major character(s):** Frank Gobi, Professor, Computer Expert
**Time period(s):** 2020s (2027)
**Locale(s):** Tokyo, Japan; Berkeley, California

**Summary:** Facing cutthroat industrial warfare, Satori Corp. struggles to hold its market share of the virtual reality entertainment market with its shared reality computer system housing millions of human psyches. When the system crashes, Gobi must locate a missing Satori Corp. executive and algorithm to save his son, who is trapped inside virtual reality.

**Other books you might like:**
Ben Bova, *Death Dream*, 1994
Victor Milan, *The Cybernetic Samurai*, 1985
Will Shetterly, *The Tangled Lands*, 1989
Neal Stephenson, *Snow Crash*, 1992
Vivian Vande Velde, *User Unfriendly*, 1991
Dave Wolverton, *On My Way to Paradise*, 1989

**476**

ALFRED BESTER

## The Demolished Man

(New York: Vintage, 1996)

**Story type:** Science Fiction (Psychic Powers; Mystery)
**Major character(s):** Ben Reich, Businessman, Murderer; Augustus "Gus" Tate, Psychic (esper), Doctor (psychiatrist); Lincoln Powell, Psychic (esper), Police Officer
**Time period(s):** 24th century
**Locale(s):** New York, New York

**Summary:** Although is has been 87 years since the last successful premediated murder. Ben Reich believes he can commit the perfect crime. He discovers a method for hiding his thoughts which may prove undetectable and unbreakable, no matter the strength of the telepath. Lincoln Powell, a master telepathic detective, may solve the case, but the Man With No Face could prove Reich's undoing. Revised reissue of the 1953 Hugo Award winning novel.

**Other books you might like:**
Isaac Asimov, *The Caves of Steel*, 1953
Greg Bear, *Queen of Angels*, 1990
Katharine Kerr, *Polar City Blues*, 1990
Lee Killough, *Deadly Silents*, 1981
David Alexander Smith, *In the Cube*, 1993

**477**

ALFRED BESTER
ROGER ZELAZNY, Co-Author

## Psychoshop

(New York: Vintage, 1998)

**Story type:** Science Fiction (Time Travel; Humor)
**Major character(s):** Alfred "Alf" Noir, Journalist, Time Traveler; Adam Maser Macairty, Time Traveler; Medusa "Glory" Sess, Time Traveler, Guardian
**Time period(s):** 1990s
**Locale(s):** Rome, Italy

**Summary:** Sent to interview the owner of the Black Place of the Soul Changer, a store operating since before the founding of Rome, Alf discovers that the proprietors come from the future and the Black Place proves more wonderful than he could have imagined. He realizes his investigation has little to do with the magazine article he was sent to write, and his involvement with the Black Place may prove fatal.

**Other books you might like:**
Frederik Pohl, *The Other End of Time*, 1996
Charles Sheffield, *Tomorrow and Tomorrow*, 1997
Roger Zelazny, *Doorways in the Sand*, 1976
Roger Zelazny, *Lord of Light*, 1967
Roger Zelazny, *Nine Princes in Amber*, 1970

**478**

ALFRED BESTER

## The Stars My Destination

(New York: Vintage, 1996)

**Story type:** Science Fiction (Science Fiction; Psychic Powers)

**Major character(s):** Gulliver ''Gully'' Foyle, Spaceman, Psychic (jaunter); Olivia Presteign, Handicapped, Businesswoman; Presteign, Businessman
**Time period(s):** 24th century
**Locale(s):** Earth; Outer Space; Sargasso Asteroid, Asteroid

**Summary:** Abandoned rather than rescued by a passing ship, the marooned Gully Foyle focuses all his energy on survival so he can destroy those who ignored him. Heroic self-rescue and an attack on the offensive ship lead Gully to imprisonment in a lightless prison until another daring self-rescue allows Gully to a continue his search for vengeance. Originally published in 1956.

**Other books you might like:**
Roger MacBride Allen, *The Ring of Charon*, 1990
Orson Scott Card, *Ender's Game*, 1985
Glen Cook, *The Dragon Never Sleeps*, 1988
Robert A. Heinlein, *The Moon Is a Harsh Mistress*, 1966
Dan Simmons, *Hyperion*, 1989
David Alexander Smith, *In the Cube*, 1993
Vernor Vinge, *A Fire upon the Deep*, 1992

## 479

**ALFRED BESTER**

### *Virtual Unrealities: The Short Fiction of Alfred Bester*
(New York: Vintage, 1997)

**Story type:** Science Fiction (Collection; Science Fiction)

**Summary:** Contains a five-page introduction by Robert Silverberg, one fragment, one original and 15 stories reprinted from periodicals and anthologies published 1939-1979. The tone varies from humorous and satirical to ironic and melancholy as Bester explores diverse themes such as time travel paradoxes, the nature of equilibrium, the relationship of creator to creation and society's absurd icons. The many recognized classics of short fiction include ''Fondly Fahrenheit,'' ''The Men Who Murdered Mohammed,'' ''The Pi Man,'' ''Adam and no Eve,'' ''Oddy and Id,'' ''The Don't Make Life Like They Used To'' and ''The Flowered Thundermug.''

**Other books you might like:**
Robert A. Heinlein, *The Past through Tomorrow*, 1967
Walter M. Miller Jr., *The Science Fiction Stories of Walter M. Miller, Jr.*, 1984
Larry Niven, *Tales of Known Space*, 1975
Cordwainer Smith, *The Rediscovery of Man*, 1993
Theodore Sturgeon, *The Ultimate Egoist*, 1994
John Varley, *Blue Champagne*, 1986
John Varley, *The Persistence of Vision*, 1978

## 480

**JOHN GREGORY BETANCOURT**, Editor

### *The Best of Weird Tales*
(New York: Barnes & Noble, 1995)

**Story type:** Horror (Anthology)

**Summary:** The 27 stories collected represent the best fantasy and horror tales published in the revived (1988-1993) *Weird Tales*. Included are ''Midnight Mass,'' F. Paul Wilson's vision of a world run by vampires, and Thomas Ligotti's ''Lost Art of Twilight,'' in which a young artist is vampirized by his family. David Schow's ''Night Bloomer'' and Brian Lumley's ''Fruiting Bodies'' are tales of gruesome vegetation that takes over human beings, and William F. Nolan's ''At Diamond Lake'' and Ramsey Campbell's ''The Same

in Any Language'' are grisly revenge tales. A final ghost story collaboration between Henry Kuttner and Robert Bloch, intended for the original *Weird Tales*, in the 1930s, is also included.

**Other books you might like:**
Robert Weinberg, *100 Wild Little Weird Tales*, 1993
   Stefan Dziemianowicz, Martin H. Greenberg, co-editors
Stefan Dziemianowicz, *Weird Tales: 32 Unearthed Terrors*, 1987
   Robert Weinberg, Martin H. Greenberg, co-editors
Peter Haining, *Weird Tales*, 1976
   editor
Marvin Kaye, *Weird Tales: The Magazine That Never Dies*, 1988
   editor
Robert Weinberg, *The Eighth Green Man and Other Strange Folk*, 1989
   editor
Robert Weinberg, *Far Below and Other Horrors*, 1974
   editor

## 481

**JOHN GREGORY BETANCOURT**

### *Rememory*
(New York: Popular Library Questar, 1990)

**Story type:** Science Fiction (Genetic Manipulation; Adventure)
**Major character(s):** Slash, Genetically Altered Being (Catman), Thief; Hangman, Genetically Altered Being, Sidekick
**Time period(s):** Indeterminate Future
**Locale(s):** Fishtown The Sprawl, North America

**Summary:** When their latest theft from the dogmen turns out to be a shipment of top secret spyeyes, Slash and Hangman are suddenly caught up in political intrigue between catmen, dogmen and government agents. Only their familiarity with the underworld of the Sprawl allows them to stay one step ahead of everyone else.

**Other books you might like:**
Ben Bova, *Cyberbooks*, 1989
George Alec Effinger, *When Gravity Fails*, 1987
William Gibson, *Neuromancer*, 1984
Joan D. Vinge, *Catspaw*, 1988
Walter Jon Williams, *Hardwired*, 1986

## 482

**JOHN GREGORY BETANCOURT**, Editor
**ROBERT WEINBERG**, Co-Editor

### *Weird Tales: Seven Decades of Terror*
(New York: Barnes & Noble, 1997)

**Story type:** Horror (Anthology)

**Summary:** Twenty-eight stories published in *Weird Tales*, the legendary magazine of fantasy and horror, which began life as a pulp magazine published between 1923 and 1954 and has since been revived four times. Included are Robert Bloch's ''Lucy Comes to Stay,'' a tale of psychological horror; Ray Bradbury's ''The Crowd,'' in which a man discovers that every car accident scene is haunted by a ghostly crowd of the same people; Clark Ashton Smith's ''The Seed from the Sepulchre,'' about a mysterious parasitical plant; Henry Kuttner's first published story, ''The Graveyard Rats''; William Hope Hodgson's sea horror story, ''The Finding of the Graiken''; and Brian Lumley's suspenseful revenge story, ''The Pit Yakker.''

**Other books you might like:**
Stefan Dziemianowicz, *Weird Tales: 32 Unearthed Terrors*, 1987
    Robert Weinberg and Martin H. Greenberg, co-editors
Peter Haining, *Weird Tales*, 1976
    editor
Marvin Kaye, *Weird Tales: The Magazine That Never Dies*, 1988
    editor
Robert Weinberg, *100 Wild Little Weird Tales*, 1993
    Stefan Dziemianowicz and Martin H. Greenberg, co-editors

---

**483**

**BRUCE BETHKE**

## Headcrash

(New York: Warner Aspect, 1995)

**Story type:** Science Fiction (Cyberpunk; Satire)
**Major character(s):** Jack ''MAX—KOOL'' Burroughs, Computer Expert; Joseph ''Gunnar Savage'' LeMat, Computer Expert
**Time period(s):** 2000s
**Locale(s):** St. Paul, Minnesota; Heaven, Cyberspace (computer virtual reality nightclub)

**Summary:** Administratively suspended from work, Jack's limited employment opportunities lead to a questionable consulting contract. His research material includes experimental interface hardware, the use of which allows dangerous manipulation of virtual reality computer space and attracts attention from similarly empowered individuals. First novel.

**Other books you might like:**
Douglas Adams, *The Hitchhiker's Guide to the Galaxy*, 1980
Alexander Besher, *Rim: A Novel of Virtual Reality*, 1994
Ed Blome, *Title Deleted for Security Reasons*, 1993
Pat Cadigan, *Synners*, 1991
Michael Flynn, *In the Country of the Blind*, 1990
Lisa Mason, *Cyberweb*, 1995
Nick Pollotta, *Illegal Aliens*, 1989
    Phil Foglio, co-author
Neal Stephenson, *Snow Crash*, 1992

---

**484**

**BRUCE BETHKE**

## Maverick

(New York: Ace, 1990)

**Story type:** Science Fiction (Robot Fiction)
**Series:** Isaac Asimov's Robot City: Robots and Aliens
**Major character(s):** David ''Derec'' Avery, Computer Expert; Janet Anastasi, Scientist (roboticist); Maverick, Alien
**Time period(s):** Indeterminate Future
**Locale(s):** Tau Puppis IV, Planet—Imaginary; Outer Space

**Summary:** The robots on Tau Puppis IV have built a city, but have no humans to serve, as they are programmed to do. Perhaps, they reason, the indigenous people, a race of wolf-like intelligent creatures who call themselves the Kin, can be defined as human. Meanwhile, Dr. Janet Anastasi is seeking her three ''Learning Machines,'' robots capable of imprinting on intelligent beings and taking on their forms. Her son Derec and his father are fleeing from a dangerous enemy. And some of the Kin regard the Learning Machine called Silversides as a goddess.

**Other books you might like:**
Isaac Asimov, *Robots and Empire*, 1985
Isaac Asimov, *The Robots of Dawn*, 1983

Jerry Oltion, *Isaac Asimov's Robot City/Robots and Aliens Book 4: Alliance*, 1990
Clifford D. Simak, *A Heritage of Stars*, 1977
Thea Von Harbou, *Metropolis*, 1927

---

**485**

**AMBROSE BIERCE**

## The Moonlit Road and Other Ghost and Horror Stories

(Mineola, New York: Dover, 1998)

**Story type:** Horror (Collection)

**Summary:** Twelve classic tales of the macabre by a master of sardonic horror, including the ghost stories ''The Middle Toe of the Right Foot'' and ''The Moonlit Road''; the lycanthropy tale ''The Eyes of the Panther''; the tale of a practical joke gone tragically wrong, ''A Watcher by the Dead''; and the early science fiction story ''Moxon's Master,'' about a mechanical man that murders its creator.

**Other books you might like:**
Gertrude Atherton, *The Bell in the Fog and Other Stories*, 1905
Robert W. Chambers, *The King in Yellow*, 1895
Ralph Adams Cram, *Black Spirits and White*, 1895
W.C. Morrow, *The Ape, the Idiot, and Other People*, 1897

---

**486**

**AMBROSE BIERCE**

## Poems of Ambrose Bierce

(Lincoln: University of Nebraska Press, 1995)

**Story type:** Horror (Collection)

**Summary:** Editer M.E. Grenander supplements the 98 previously collected poems of this great writer of fantastic and realistic fiction at the turn of the century with another eight previously uncollected poems and 12 essays, prefaces and reviews on poetic craft. Bierce's concerns in his poetry reflect those of his fiction, including the morbid (*A Vision of Doom*), life during wartime (*The Death of Grant, The Confederate Flag*), the philosophy of cynicism (*Cynic Perforce From Studying Mankind*), and the politics of his day (*The Mormon Question, The Statesmen*). All are informed by his caustic wit.

**Other books you might like:**
William Hope Hodgson, *Beyond the Dawning: The Poems of William Hope Hodgson*, 1995
Neil Gaiman, *Now We Are Sick*, 1993
    Neil Gaiman, co-author
H.P. Lovecraft, *Collected Poems*, 1963

---

**487**

**STEPHEN BILLIAS**

## Horrible Humes

(New York: Ace, 1991)

**Story type:** Fantasy (Adventure; Quest)
**Series:** Runesword
**Major character(s):** Caltus ''Cal'' Talienson, Warrior; Hathor, Mythical Creature (troll), Revolutionary (vegetarian); Queen of Ice, Ruler (land beyond Mistwall)
**Time period(s):** Indeterminate

**Locale(s):** Steadfast-by-Sea, Fictional City; Country of the Wind Websters, Fictional Country

**Summary:** Hoping to preserve her power by preventing flesh-eating creatures from becoming peaceful vegetarians, the Queen of Ice launches her attack on Hathor. Hathor is captured as he and Cal, with their sworn companions, Bith, a sorceress, and Endril, an elf, journey north to repair a rift in the Mistwall.

**Other books you might like:**
Mark Acres, *Dark Divide*, 1991
Tom Deitz, *Stoneskin's Revenge*, 1991
Clayton Emery, *Outcasts*, 1990
Rose Estes, *Skryling's Blade*, 1990
  Tom Wham, co-author
Robert Jordan, *The Eye of the World*, 1989
J.F. Rivkin, *The Dreamstone*, 1991
J.R.R. Tolkien, *The Fellowship of the Ring*, 1954
J.R.R. Tolkien, *The Return of the King*, 1956
J.R.R. Tolkien, *The Two Towers*, 1955

---

### 488

**PATRICK BILLINGS** (Pseudonym of Earl Murray)

## The Quiet

(New York: Tor, 1989)

**Story type:** Horror (Serial Killer)
**Major character(s):** Amy Ellerman, Student (plant ecology grad student); John Tanner, Ranger (game warden); Martin Linders, Ranger (bear specialist)
**Time period(s):** 1990s (1994)
**Locale(s):** Yellowstone National Park, Wyoming

**Summary:** Game wardens at Yellowstone National Park find their hands full when a bizarre murderer deliberately baits bears to kill people and help him attain his communion with a native American bear god.

**Other books you might like:**
Scott Ian Barry, *The Streeter*, 1994
David Dvorkin, *Ursus*, 1989
T.J. Kirby, *Deadly Breed*, 1992
Dean R. Koontz, *Watchers*, 1987

---

### 489

**FRANNY BILLINGSLEY**

## Well Wished

(New York: Atheneum, 1997)

**Story type:** Fantasy (Magic Conflict; Young Adult)
**Major character(s):** Nuria, Child, Orphan; Agnes, Aged Person; Catty Winter, Child, Handicapped
**Time period(s):** Indeterminate
**Locale(s):** Bishop Mayne, England

**Summary:** As the only child left in Bishop Mayne since the children were wished away, Nuria would like to have a friend. Her grandfather has already wished for the children to return and Agnes, the keeper of the Wishing Well, informs her that Catty Winter returns tomorrow. Unfortunately, Catty needs a miracle so she can skate and run with Nuria, and the Wishing Well may be the only possible help.

**Other books you might like:**
Michael Ende, *The Night of Wishes: Or, The Satanarchaeolidealcohellish Notion Potion*, 1992
Esther Friesner, *Wishing Season*, 1993
Gail Jarrow, *Beyond the Magic Sphere*, 1994

S.P. Somtow, *The Wizard's Apprentice*, 1993
Nancy Springer, *The Friendship Song*, 1992
Patricia C. Wrede, *Mairelon the Magician*, 1991

---

### 490

**ANNE BILLSON**

## Suckers

(New York: Atheneum, 1993)

**Story type:** Horror (Vampire Story; Satire)
**Major character(s):** Dora Rosamund Vale, Businesswoman (fashion consultant); Duncan Fender, Photographer; Rose Murasaki, Editor (magazine), Vampire
**Time period(s):** 1990s (1993)
**Locale(s):** London, England

**Summary:** Thirteen years ago, Dora Vale and Duncan Fender destroyed Duncan's lover Violet Westron, after discovering that she was a vampire. But Violet returns and, under the alias Rose Murasaki, begins editing *Bellini*, a hot fashion magazine that promotes the lifestyle of the undead as a fashion trend.

**Other books you might like:**
Poppy Z. Brite, *Lost Souls*, 1992
Nancy A. Collins, *Sunglasses After Dark*, 1990
Ray Garton, *Live Girls*, 1987
Anne Rice, *The Vampire Lestat*, 1985
John Skipp, *The Light at the End*, 1986
  Craig Spector, co-author
S.P. Somtow, *Vampire Junction*, 1984

---

### 491

**MARGARET BINGLEY**

## Seeds of Evil

(New York: Carroll and Graf, 1990)

**Story type:** Horror (Evil Children)
**Major character(s):** Meg Marshall, Housewife; Olivia Marshall, Child, Twin; Orlando Marshall, Child, Twin
**Time period(s):** 1980s (1988)
**Locale(s):** England

**Summary:** Olivia and Orlando, twins born to an artificially inseminated mother, share an unnatural rapport and a talent for viciousness. Meg Marshall's search for the anonymous sperm donor culminates in the shocking revelation of why her children are so badly misbehaved. First published 1988.

**Other books you might like:**
Jean Paiva, *The Lilith Factor*, 1989
Thomas Tryon, *The Other*, 1972
John Wyndham, *The Midwich Cuckoos*, 1957

---

### 492

**DAVID BISCHOFF**

## Hunter's Planet

(New York: Bantam Spectra, 1994)

**Story type:** Science Fiction (Techno-Thriller; Adventure)
**Series:** Aliens vs. Predator
**Major character(s):** Machiko Naguchi, Warrior, Guide; Attila, Android, Martial Arts Expert; Livermore Evanston, Businessman, Criminal

**Time period(s):** Indeterminate Future
**Locale(s):** Hunter's Planet, Planet—Imaginary

**Summary:** After years of hunting with a Predator pack as an honored warrior, Machiko Naguchi accepts a position as guide on Hunter's Planet, prepared for big game hunting by Livermore Evanston. Machiko and Attila soon discover that the planet houses a secret facility designed to promote Evanston's insane and deadly research into controlling aggressive life forms.

**Other books you might like:**
Alan Dean Foster, *Alien*, 1979
Alan Dean Foster, *Alien 3*, 1992
Alan Dean Foster, *Aliens*, 1986
Simon Hawke, *Predator 2*, 1990
Paul Monette, *Predator*, 1987
Steve Perry, *Aliens: Earth Hive*, 1992
Steve Perry, *Aliens: The Female War*, 1993
    Stephanie Perry, co-author
Steve Perry, *Aliens: Nightmare Asylum*, 1993
Steve Perry, *Prey*, 1994
    Stephanie Perry, co-author

---

**493**

**DAVID BISCHOFF**

### Night of the Living Shark!

(New York: Ace, 1991)

**Story type:** Science Fiction (Humor; Young Adult)
**Series:** Daniel M. Pinkwater's Melvinge of the Megaverse
**Major character(s):** Melvinge, Hero, Werewolf; Harlan, Animal, Disembodied Personality (Grabovnikon's); Grabovnikon ''Grab'', Artificial Intelligence
**Time period(s):** Indeterminate
**Locale(s):** Megaverse Mall, Mythical Place; *Grabovnikon*, Spaceship

**Summary:** Melvinge and Harlan use the Grabovnikon to travel through time and space in search of Megaverse Mall and a parking place despite threats from gypsy werewolves, Sdark the Loan Shark and deadly puns. This book contains an afterword by Daniel M. Pinkwater whose guidelines form the basis for the Melvinge of the Megaverse Series.

**Other books you might like:**
Douglas Adams, *The Restaurant at the End of the Universe*, 1980
John DeChancie, *Paradox Alley*, 1987
John DeChancie, *Red Limit Freeway*, 1984
John DeChancie, *Starrigger*, 1983
Debra Doyle, *Night of the Living Rat!*, 1992
    James D. Macdonald, co-author
Alan Dean Foster, *Glory Lane*, 1987
T. Jackson King, *Retread Shop*, 1988
Somtow Sucharitkul, *Mallworld*, 1981

---

**494**

**DAVID BISCHOFF**

### Quoth the Crow

(New York: HarperPrism, 1998)

**Story type:** Horror (Supernatural Vengeance)
**Series:** Crow
**Major character(s):** William Blessing, Writer (horror), Professor; Donald Marqueete, Student—Graduate, Writer; Mick Prince, Writer, Murderer
**Time period(s):** 1990s (1998)

**Locale(s):** Baltimore, Maryland

**Summary:** Betrayed by an admiring student whose fortunes are tied to his own, murdered horror writer and Poe scholar William Blessing returns from the grave to subject all those who conspired in his killing to deaths drawn from the pages of Poe's stories. Set in the universe of James O'Barr's graphic novel series The Crow.

**Other books you might like:**
Poppy Z. Brite, *The Lazarus Heart*, 1998
Ric Meyers, *Fear Itself*, 1991
James O'Barr, *The Crow: Shattered Lives and Broken Dreams*, 1998
    Ed Kramer, co-editor
Chet Williamson, *The Crow: City of Angels*, 1996
Chet Williamson, *Clash by Night*, 1998

---

**495**

**ANNE BISHOP**

### Daughter of the Blood

(New York: Roc, 1998)

**Story type:** Fantasy (Political; Magic Conflict)
**Major character(s):** Saetan SaDiablo, Vampire, Wizard; Daemon SaDiablo, Wizard, Prostitute Jaenelle, Child, Witch
**Time period(s):** Indeterminate
**Locale(s):** Terreille, Planet—Imaginary; Hell, Alternate Universe

**Summary:** In a world of ritualized dominance and submission, an evil queen perverts the social order into chaos. Jaenelle can set the world right, but the queen will certainly catch her and kill her, if possible. Fortunately, Jaenelle's many protectors include the world's deadliest slave-prostitute and the vampire king. First novel.

**Other books you might like:**
Clive Barker, *Imajica*, 1991
Tanith Lee, *Death's Master*, 1982
Fritz Leiber, *Ill Met in Lankhmar*, 1995
Felicity Savage, *Delta City*, 1996

---

**496**

**MICHAEL BISHOP**

### Apartheid, Superstrings, and Mordecai Thubana

(Eugene, OR: Axolotl Press, 1989)

**Story type:** Science Fiction (Political)
**Major character(s):** Mordecai Thubana, Construction Worker (African); Gerrit Myburgh, Businessman (Afrikaner)
**Time period(s):** 1990s
**Locale(s):** South Africa

**Summary:** Myburgh, an upper-class Afrikaner, is in a car accident out on the Veldt. Afterwards he finds himself stuck in an odd sort of shadow existence, invisible to other white South Africans. Myburgh is picked up by a bus taking blacks to work in Pretoria and meets Thubana, a self-educated roofer who studies such aspects of modern physics as the Grand Unified Theory and superstring. Thubana uses this knowledge to explain what has happened to Myburgh. Then they fall into the clutches of the notorious police department Special Branch.

**Other books you might like:**
Terry Bisson, *Fire on the Mountain*, 1988
Pat Murphy, *The City, Not Long After*, 1989
Mike Resnick, *Ivory: A Legend of Past and Future*, 1988
Mike Resnick, *Paradise: A Chronicle of a Distant World*, 1989

## 497

**MICHAEL BISHOP**

### At the City Limits of Fate

(Cambridge, Massachusetts: Edgewood Press, 1996)

**Story type:** Fantasy (Collection; Religious)

**Summary:** Contains 15 stories reprinted from periodicals and anthologies 1982-1996. The stories vary in tone from humorous to downbeat with theological themes including Genesis, a plague of butterflies, post-disaster life, fate, St. Augustine's religious agony, child abuse, televangelism, and the trial of Judas Iscariot.

**Other books you might like:**
Gwyneth Jones, *Seven Tales and a Table*, 1995
Garry Kilworth, *Hogfoot Right and Bird-Hands*, 1993
James Morrow, *Bible Stories for Adults*, 1996
Nancy Springer, *Damnbanna*, 1992
Cherry Wilder, *Dealers in Light and Darkness*, 1995
Kate Wilhelm, *State of Grace*, 1991

## 498

**MICHAEL BISHOP**

### Brittle Innings

(New York: Bantam, 1994)

**Story type:** Horror (Coming-of-Age)
**Major character(s):** Danny Boles, Sports Figure (baseball player), Indian; Henry Clerval, Sports Figure (baseball player), Reanimated Dead; Buck Hoey, Sports Figure (baseball player)
**Time period(s):** 1940s (Summer, 1943)
**Locale(s):** Chattahooche Valley, Georgia

**Summary:** Native American baseball scout Danny Boles tells the story of his thwarted baseball career, which included rooming with a fellow minor league player who, unbeknownst to his teammates, was the original Frankenstein's monster. This gentle fantasy with a serious moral is essentially about people trying to fit into societies hostile to their existence. Sequel to Mary Shelley's *Frankenstein*.

**Other books you might like:**
Brian W. Aldiss, *Frankenstein Unbound*, 1973
Emmanuel Carrere, *Gothic Romance*, 1990
Mary Shelley, *Frankenstein*, 1818

## 499

**MICHAEL BISHOP**

### Count Geiger's Blues

(New York: Tor, 1992)

**Story type:** Science Fiction (Arts; Alternate Universe)
**Major character(s):** Xavier Thaxton, Journalist, Hero (comic book superhero); Mikhail "the Mick" Geoffrey Menaker, Teenager; Bari Carlisle, Designer (fashion), Girlfriend (Xavier's)
**Time period(s):** 1990s
**Locale(s):** Oconee (fictional state bordering Tennessee and Georgia)

**Summary:** Stuffy, culture-encrusted Xavier Thaxton relates with difficulty to his new roommate, the Mick, Xavier's nephew who revels in popular culture. As Xavier's accident with radioactive waste changes Xavier into a comic book superhero, Xavier's relationship with the Mick improves while the change to superhero threatens Xavier's relationship with his girlfriend, Bari.

**Other books you might like:**
William Borden, *Superstoe*, 1968
Richard Brautigan, *The Hawkline Monster*, 1974
Mark Jacobson, *Gojiro*, 1991
Michael Kandel, *Captain Jack Zodiac*, 1992
George R.R. Martin, *Wild Cards*, 1987
   editor
Greg Snow, *That's All, Folks!*, 1992
Michael D. Weaver, *My Father Immortal*, 1989

## 500

**MICHAEL BISHOP**

### Nebula Awards 24

(New York: Harcourt Brace Jovanovich, 1990)

**Story type:** Science Fiction (Anthology)
**Series:** Nebula Awards
**Time period(s):** Indeterminate

**Summary:** This collection from the Science Fiction Writers of America features articles, stories, poetry and memorials appearing during 1988. Michael Bishop contributed the introduction, with articles by Paul De Filippo, Bill Warren and Ian Watson and memorials to Clifford D. Simak by Gordon R. Dickson and to Robert A. Heinlein by Frank M. Robinson. Excerpts from novels are contributed by Lois McMaster Bujold and Jane Yolen. Stories appear by Neal Barrett, Jr., George Alec Effinger, Connie Willis and Gene Wolfe. This volume also continues the tradition of showcasing Rhysling Award winners' poetry, among others, Suzette Haden Elgin and Lucius Shepard.

**Other books you might like:**
Lou Aronica, *Full Spectrum 2*, 1990
   Shawna McCarthy, Amy Stout, Patrick LoBruto, co-editors
Gardner Dozois, *The Year's Best Science Fiction: Seventh Annual Collection*, 1990
Frank Herbert, *Nebula Winners 15*, 1981
Damon Knight, *Nebula Award Stories 1965*, 1966
Robert Silverberg, *The Science Fiction Hall of Fame, Volume 1*, 1970
Donald A. Wollheim, *The 1990 Annual World's Best Science Fiction*, 1990
   Arthur W. Saha, co-editor
George Zebrowski, *Nebula Awards 22*, 1988

## 501

**MICHAEL BISHOP**, Editor

### Nebula Awards 25

(New York: Harcourt Brace Jovanovich, 1991)

**Story type:** Science Fiction (Anthology)
**Series:** Nebula Awards

**Summary:** Subtitled, *SFWA's Choices for the Best Science Fiction 1989*, this volume contains an introduction by Michael Bishop plus articles, fiction nominated for Nebula Awards and three Rhysling Award winning poems by Bruce Boston, John M. Ford and Robert Frazier. Nebula Award winning fiction includes stories by Lois McMaster Bujold, Geoffrey A. Landis, Connie Willis and an excerpt from a novel by Elizabeth Scarborough. Other fiction includes stories by Michael Bishop, John Crowley, Gardner Dozois, and Mike Resnick. Ian Watson looks at fantasy and science fiction novels of 1989, Bill Warren writes of science fiction films of 1989 and Paul Di Filippo looks at SFWA's Annual "Nebula Award Mania." In other essays, founder and first president of SFWA, Damon Knight, asks "What is Science Fiction?," Orson Scott Card presents a speech delivered in 1989 to the Indiana Humanities Council and Richard Grant discusses the writing process. Appendixes include an article about the Nebula Awards and a list of Nebula Award winners 1965-1988.

**Other books you might like:**
Lou Aronica, *Full Spectrum*, 1988
    Shawna McCarthy, co-editor
Terry Carr, *Terry Carr's Best Science Fiction and Fantasy of the Year #16*, 1987
    editor
Gardner Dozois, *The Year's Best Science Fiction: Seventh Annual Collection*, 1990
    editor
Harlan Ellison, *Dangerous Visions*, 1967
    editor
Raymond J. Healy, *Adventures in Time and Space*, 1946
    J. Francis McComas, co-editor
Frank Herbert, *Nebula Winners 15*, 1981
    editor
Damon Knight, *Nebula Award Stories 1965*, 1966
    editor
Robert Silverberg, *The Science Fiction Hall of Fame, Volume 1*, 1970
    editor
Donald A. Wollheim, *The 1990 Annual World's Best Science Fiction*, 1990
    Arthur W. Saha, co-editor
George Zebrowski, *Nebula Awards 21*, 1987
    editor
George Zebrowski, *Nebula Awards 22*, 1988
    editor

---

## 502

### MICHAEL BISHOP

## No Enemy but Time

(New York: Bantam Spectra, 1989)

**Story type:** Science Fiction (Time Travel)
**Major character(s):** Joshua Kampa, Time Traveler; Helen, Prehistoric Human (Habiline)
**Time period(s):** 1980s; Indeterminate Past (Pleistocene period)
**Locale(s):** Africa

**Summary:** In this Nebula Award-winning novel, Joshua Kampa, a black American, travels into the Pleistocene past and takes up life with the near-human habilines he meets there. Originally published in 1982.

**Other books you might like:**
Roger MacBride Allen, *Orphan of Creation*, 1988
William Golding, *The Inheritors*, 1955
Elizabeth Marshall Thomas, *Reindeer Moon*, 1987

---

## 503

### TERRY BISSON

## Bears Discover Fire

(New York: Tor, 1993)

**Story type:** Science Fiction (Collection)

**Summary:** Contains all 19 of Bisson's short stories reprinted from 1990s periodicals. Includes the Hugo Award and Nebula Award-winning title story plus a Hugo Award nominee, ''Press Ann,'' and a Nebula Award nominee, ''They're Made Out of Meat.'' Stories vary

in tone from humor to horror and reflect themes including first contact, time travel and environmental awareness. Concludes with a four-page afterword in which Bisson indicates his intent and the genesis of individual stories.

**Other books you might like:**
Damon Knight, *One Side Laughing: Stories Unlike Other Stories*, 1991
Nancy Kress, *The Aliens of Earth*, 1993
Spider Robinson, *Antinomy*, 1980
Spider Robinson, *Melancholy Elephants*, 1984
Michael Swanwick, *Gravity's Angels*, 1991
John Varley, *Blue Champagne*, 1986
John Varley, *The Persistence of Vision*, 1978

---

## 504

### TERRY BISSON

## The Fifth Element

(New York: HarperPrism, 1997)

**Story type:** Science Fiction (Space Opera; Invasion of Earth)
**Major character(s):** Vito Cornelius, Religious (priest); Korben Dallas, Taxi Driver, Military Personnel (retired); Appipulai Leeloo Minai, Deity
**Time period(s):** 1910s (1913); 25th century (2413)
**Locale(s):** Egypt; New York, New York

**Summary:** In 1913 the Mondoshawan took the ultimate weapon against evil from the recently uncovered ancient Egyptian temple, promising to return it when the war came to Earth. When the Mondoshawan try to return the weapon, their ship crashes after being attacked by Earth forces. Recreated from genetic material left after the crash, Leeloo, the Fifth Element necessary for the weapon to function, proves to be a perfect human woman. After Leeloo dives through the roof of Korben's cab, she enlists him to help her save Earth and vanquish the forces of evil. Novelizes the film.

**Other books you might like:**
A.C. Crispin, *V*, 1984
Dean Devlin, *Independence Day*, 1996
Alan Dean Foster, *Alien Nation*, 1993
Jonathan Gems, *Mars Attacks!*, 1996
Judith Reeves-Stevens, *The Day of Descent*, 1993
    Garfield Reeves-Stevens, co-author
Robert Tine, *Chain Reaction*, 1996

---

## 505

### TERRY BISSON

## Johnny Mnemonic

(New York: Pocket, 1995)

**Story type:** Science Fiction (Cyberpunk; Adventure)
**Major character(s):** Johnny, Courier (mnemonic), Fugitive
**Time period(s):** 2020s (2021)
**Locale(s):** Newark, New Jersey; Cyberspace; New York, New York

**Summary:** Immediately after Johnny transfers a computer file to his wetwired computer storage system, Yakuza assassins kill his employers and fragment the download key needed to rid him of the lethal file. Johnny flees to Newark where he hopes to unload the valuable file and collect his generous fee, if he can avoid the dragnet of well-armed thugs enthusiastically searching for him. Novelizes the film, based on William Gibson's short story.

**Other books you might like:**
Bruce Bethke, *Headcrash*, 1995

Pat Cadigan, *Fools*, 1992
Pat Cadigan, *Mindplayers*, 1987
George Alec Effinger, *When Gravity Fails*, 1987
William Gibson, *Neuromancer*, 1984
Neal Stephenson, *Snow Crash*, 1992
Michael Swanwick, *Vacuum Flowers*, 1987

## 506

### TERRY BISSON

## *Pirates of the Universe*

(New York; Tor, 1996)

**Story type:** Science Fiction (Adventure; Future Shock)
**Major character(s):** Gunther ''Gun'' Ryder, Spaceman (Space Ranger); Gordon Ryder, Fugitive; Donna, Girlfriend
**Time period(s):** 21st century
**Locale(s):** Orlando, Florida; Overworld, Space Station

**Summary:** Gunther Ryder has only one goal, to win a coveted spot in the Disney-Windows live-in theme park, ''Pirates of the Universe,'' for himself and his girlfriend Donna. To do so, he must complete one more ''Petey Hunt,'' in which Space Rangers seize the valuable skin of mysterious alien ship/creatures, which has replaced gold as the new world economic currency.

**Other books you might like:**
Shale Aaron, *Virtual Death*, 1995
Kevin J. Anderson, *Ill Wind*, 1995
    Doug Beason, co-author
David R. Bunch, *Moderan*, 1971
Mary Rosenblum, *The Stone Garden*, 1995
Robert Sheckley, *Journey Beyond Tomorrow*, 1962
Kurt Vonnegut Jr., *Player Piano*, 1952

## 507

### TERRY BISSON

## *Virtuosity*

(New York: Pocket, 1995)

**Story type:** Science Fiction (Alternate Intelligence; Techno-Thriller)
**Major character(s):** Sid 6.7, Artificial Intelligence, Criminal; Parker Barnes, Police Officer, Experimental Subject
**Time period(s):** 1990s (1999)
**Locale(s):** Los Angeles, California

**Summary:** When a computer program composed of serial killer personalities manifests itself in reality, Parker Barnes must find it and neutralize the deadly threat. Novelizes the film.

**Other books you might like:**
Piers Anthony, *Killobyte*, 1993
Ben Bova, *Death Dream*, 1994
Philip Jose Farmer, *Red Orc's Rage*, 1991
Cole Perriman, *Terminal Games*, 1994
Robert J. Sawyer, *The Terminal Experiment*, 1995
Vivian Vande Velde, *User Unfriendly*, 1991

## 508

### TERRY BISSON

## *Voyage to the Red Planet*

(New York: William Morrow, 1990)

**Story type:** Science Fiction (Adventure; Arts)

**Major character(s):** Natasha Alyosha Katerina Kirov, Spaceship Captain; Rocket Man Bass, Pilot (spaceship); S.C. Jeffries, Doctor
**Time period(s):** Indeterminate Future
**Locale(s):** *Mary Poppins*, Spaceship; Mars

**Summary:** When a never-used, mothballed spaceship becomes available to a renegade independent movie producer, he arranges for a ship's crew and the necessary movie-making equipment and personnel to travel to Mars to film on location. Once there, the group must not only film their movie, but also overcome the problem threatening to keep them on Mars forever.

**Other books you might like:**
James Blish, *The Triumph of Time*, 1958
Harry Harrison, *The Technicolor Time Machine*, 1967
John Varley, *Demon*, 1984
Ian Watson, *Chekhov's Journey*, 1989

## 509

### ALGERNON BLACKWOOD

## *The Complete John Silence Stories*

(Mineola, New York: Dover, 1997)

**Story type:** Horror (Collection; Occult)

**Summary:** ''Phsychic doctor'' John Silence investigates the impact of the supernatural upon ordinary lives in six case studies that promulgate the author's beliefs in the occult. ''Ancient Sorceries'' and ''The Camp of the Dog'' feature human beings who shapeshift into animals. ''A Psychical Invasion'' features a man haunted by the ghost of a black magician and ''The Nemesis of Fire'' a house haunted by a fire elemental brought back to England in an Egyptian mummy. In ''Secret Worship,'' black magic corrupts a remote religious school. These contents, which were published as *John Silence: Physician Extraordinaire* in 1908, are embellished with one more story, ''A Victim of Higher Space,'' in which man finds his thoughts repeatedly dragging him into a fourth dimension. Introduction by S.T. Joshi.

**Other books you might like:**
A.M. Burrage, *The Occult Files of Francis Chard: Some Ghost Stories*, 1996
Dion Fortune, *The Secrets of Dr. Taverner*, 1926
E. Heron, *Flaxman Low, Psychic Detective*, 1993
    H. Heron, co-author
William Hope Hodgson, *Carnacki the Ghost Finder*, 1913
J. Sheridan Le Fanu, *In a Glass Darkly*, 1872
Sax Rohmer, *The Dream Detective*, 1920

## 510

### GARY L. BLACKWOOD

## *Beyond the Door*

(New York: Atheneum, 1991)

**Story type:** Science Fiction (Young Adult; Political)
**Major character(s):** Walter Scott Shaffer Jr., Student, Adventurer; Tomeas, Outcast, Scientist; Tallulah ''Tulley'' Bankhead, Student, Adventurer
**Time period(s):** 1990s
**Locale(s):** Earth; Gale'tin, Planet—Imaginary

**Summary:** In his local library, Scott discovers a door which leads to another world, Gale'tin, which is beginning to develop modern technology. There he meets Tomeas who seems to be trying to help bring higher technology to his world. After Tulley also ventures to Gale'tin, Scott and Tulley discover the darker truth, that Tomeas pursues dangerous experiments, hoping to increase his control over his universe's emerging technology.

**Other books you might like:**
David Brin, *Earth*, 1990
Cheryl J. Franklin, *Fire Crossing*, 1991
Alexander Key, *The Forgotten Door*, 1965
Madeleine L'Engle, *A Wrinkle in Time*, 1962
Margaret Weis, *Fire Sea*, 1991
     Tracy Hickman, co-author
Robert Charles Wilson, *A Bridge of Years*, 1991

## 511

### GARY L. BLACKWOOD

## *The Dying Sun*

(New York: Atheneum, 1989)

**Story type:** Science Fiction (Young Adult)
**Major character(s):** James, Teenager; Robert, Teenager (James' best friend)
**Time period(s):** 21st century (2050)
**Locale(s):** Missouri

**Summary:** A new ice age has driven most of the population of the United States south into Mexico where they live in newly-built but horribly overcrowded cities along the border. The native Mexicans, hating this gringo invasion, are becoming increasingly violent and James' family decides to move back to Missouri, even though it is now little more than a frozen wasteland. James stays behind but, as the violence escalates, decides that he too must travel north.

**Other books you might like:**
Bruce Brooks, *No Kidding*, 1989
John Christopher, *The Long Winter*, 1962
John Christopher, *Wild Jack*, 1974
Michael Moorcock, *The Ice Schooner*, 1969

## 512

### JOHN BLAIR

## *Bright Angel*

(New York: Ballantine/Del Rey, 1991)

**Story type:** Science Fiction (First Contact; Disaster)
**Major character(s):** James Harris, Settler (colonist); Song Lan, Scientist; Hugh Carney, Doctor
**Time period(s):** 21st century (2063-2071)
**Locale(s):** Earth; Outer Space

**Summary:** James Harris should have died with the rest of the human colony on Comfort, but instead, he appeared in Antarctica, twelve light years away. The moment of his return to Earth coincided with the beginning of a cooling trend, just like the climate change which had killed the colony on Comfort. After years of living incognito, Harris must face his past in order to save himself and Earth.

**Other books you might like:**
C.J. Cherryh, *Voyager in Night*, 1984
Arthur C. Clarke, *2001: A Space Odyssey*, 1968
Arthur C. Clarke, *2010: Odyssey Two*, 1982
Arthur C. Clarke, *2061: Odyssey Three*, 1987
Ursula K. Le Guin, *The Lathe of Heaven*, 1971
James Tiptree Jr., *Up the Walls of the World*, 1978
     Tiptree is a pseudonym for Alice Sheldon

## 513

### JOHN BLAIR

## *A Landscape of Darkness*

(New York: Ballantine, 1990)

**Story type:** Science Fiction (Military; Psychic Powers)
**Major character(s):** John Sebastian Clay, Mercenary; Howard S. Rankin, Military Personnel (colonel); Tind, Warrior (assassin)
**Time period(s):** Indeterminate Future
**Locale(s):** Earth; Ithavoll, Planet—Imaginary

**Summary:** John Clay is recruited for a secret mission to destroy a suspected alien weapon on a backward planet. The Mission leads him and three companions into a series of violent and bloody encounters culminating in Clay's confrontation with a dead "god." This is the author's first novel.

**Other books you might like:**
Robert Asprin, *The Bug Wars*, 1979
C.J. Cherryh, *The Faded Sun: Kesrith*, 1978
Gordon R. Dickson, *Dorsai!*, 1959
Gordon R. Dickson, *Soldier, Ask Not*, 1968
Joe Haldeman, *The Forever War*, 1975

## 514

### DAN I. BLAKE

## *Killing Frost*

(Catskill, New York: Press-Tige, 1998)

**Story type:** Horror (Werewolf Story)
**Major character(s):** Raymond Frost, Clerk (paint store); Howard Trowbridge, Detective—Private; Gordon Masterson, Real Estate Agent (developer)
**Time period(s):** 1990s (1998)
**Locale(s):** Puzzle Lake, Michigan; Farmington, Indiana

**Summary:** Raymond Frost is forced to reveal his carefullly concealed werewolf identity when a greedy land developer attempts to take the remote lake cabin where he hides during his monthly transformations. His cooperation with Native American residents who have also been crowded off their land draws the attention of authorities who hope to pin the blame for a string of unsolved murders on him. A first novel.

**Other books you might like:**
Crosland Brown, *Tombley's Walk*, 1991
John R. Holt, *Wolf Moon*, 1998
Ronald Kelly, *Moon of the Werewolf*, 1991
Annette Curtis Klause, *Blood and Chocolate*, 1997
S.P. Somtow, *Moon Dance*, 1989

## 515

### KATHERINE BLAKE

## *The Interior Life*

(New York: Baen, 1990)

**Story type:** Fantasy (Romance; Alternate World)
**Major character(s):** Sue, Housewife, Parent (mother); Lady Amalia, Noblewoman (mistress of Fendarath)
**Time period(s):** Indeterminate Past; 1990s (1990)
**Locale(s):** Fendarath, Fictional Country

**Summary:** A bored housewife's daydreams and fantasies tap into an alternate world. The bond between Sue and the inhabitants of

Fendarath enables her to help Amalia become queen and shows Sue the necessity of becoming involved with others. This is the author's first novel.

**Other books you might like:**
Marion Zimmer Bradley, *The House Between the Worlds*, 1980
Stephen R. Donaldson, *The Mirror of Her Dreams*, 1986
Suzette Haden Elgin, *The Grand Jubilee*, 1981
Suzette Haden Elgin, *Twelve Fair Kingdoms*, 1981
Suzette Haden Elgin, *And Then There'll Be Fireworks*, 1981
Marge Piercy, *Woman on the Edge of Time*, 1976

## 516

### JAY D. BLAKENEY

## The Goda War

(New York: Ace Books, 1989)

**Story type:** Science Fiction (Military)
**Major character(s):** Dire-Lord Brock, Nobleman, Warrior; Kezi Falmah-Al, Warrior (Colonel)
**Time period(s):** Indeterminate Future
**Locale(s):** Held Empire, Interstellar Empire/Federation

**Summary:** As two powerful empires battle, Brock, dire-lord of the Held, whose side is losing, vows to activate the long dormant goddas, planet-sized killing machines. Also searching for the goddas is Colonel Kezi Falmah-Al. She too seeks to turn the machines to military advantage.

**Other books you might like:**
Jack McDevitt, *A Talent for War*, 1989
Fred Saberhagen, *Berserker*, 1967
Fred Saberhagen, *Berserker Man*, 1979
Fred Saberhagen, *The Berserker Throne*, 1985
Fred Saberhagen, *The Berserker Wars*, 1981
Fred Saberhagen, *Berserker's Planet*, 1975
Fred Saberhagen, *Earth Descended*, 1982
Fred Saberhagen, *The Ultimate Enemy*, 1979

## 517

### JAY D. BLAKENEY

## Requiem for Anthi

(New York: Ace Books, 1990)

**Story type:** Science Fiction (Space Opera)
**Series:** Anthi
**Major character(s):** Asan, Alien, Nobleman; Zaula, Alien, Noblewoman
**Time period(s):** Indeterminate Future
**Locale(s):** Ruantl, Planet—Imaginary

**Summary:** On a dying planet, the few survivors of an alien race fight for rule. Then the earthmen come, members of the Galactic Space Institute, eager to despoil the planet of its little remaining wealth. The lord Asan swears to fight them off, even if it means reawakening the goddess Anthi herself.

**Other books you might like:**
Emma Bull, *Falcon*, 1989
C.J. Cherryh, *The Faded Sun: Kesrith*, 1978
A.C. Crispin, *Starbridge*, 1989
Mary Gentle, *Ancient Light*, 1989
Mary Gentle, *Golden Witchbreed*, 1983
Melisa C. Michaels, *Far Harbor*, 1989

## 518

### JAMES P. BLAYLOCK

## All the Bells on Earth

(New York: Ace, 1995)

**Story type:** Fantasy (Contemporary Realism)
**Major character(s):** Walt Stebbins, Salesman (mail order); Roger Argyle, Businessman; Ivy Stebbins, Real Estate Agent
**Time period(s):** 1990s (1995)
**Locale(s):** Orange, California

**Summary:** While somebody defaces churches in peaceful Orange, good-hearted but eccentric catalog salesman Walt Stebbins gets hold of an extremely weird talisman, a dead bird in a jar. When the events come together, Walt's decisions mean the difference between life and damnation for a surprisingly large number of people.

**Other books you might like:**
Ray Bradbury, *Something Wicked This Way Comes*, 1962
Jack Cady, *The Off Season*, 1995
John Crowley, *Aegypt*, 1987
Robertson Davies, *What's Bred in the Bone*, 1985
Tim Powers, *Last Call*, 1992

## 519

### JAMES P. BLAYLOCK

## The Last Coin

(New York: Ace, 1988)

**Story type:** Fantasy (Religious)
**Major character(s):** Pennyman, Fortune Hunter (Rare coin collector); Andrew, Young Man (Amiable idler, unwitting hero)
**Time period(s):** 1980s
**Locale(s):** California (Guest House)

**Summary:** Story revolves around the thirty coins Judas Iscariot was given in exchange for the betrayal of Christ. One man has come close to collecting all thirty; if successful, he will possess a vast supernatural power.

**Other books you might like:**
Michael Frayn, *Sweet Dreams*, 1974
Barry B. Longyear, *The God Box*,
Rudy Rucker, *White Light, or What Is Cantor's Continuum Problem*,

## 520

### JAMES P. BLAYLOCK

## Lord Kelvin's Machine

(Sauk City, Wisconsin: Arkham House, 1992)

**Story type:** Fantasy (Quest; Historical)
**Major character(s):** Langdon St. Ives, Scientist, Explorer; Ignatio Narbando, Scientist; Jack Owlesby, Artisan (toymaker)
**Time period(s):** 19th century
**Locale(s):** London, England; At Sea (under the North Sea)

**Summary:** Langdon St. Ives, introduced in *Homunculus*, is pursuing Dr. Ignatio Narbando to get revenge for the murder of his wife. He travels to South America, Norway, beneath the North Sea, high in the air and back in time, dodging a bizarre cast of lunatics and ne'er-do-wells the whole way. Eventually, the salvation of the world and his soul hinge on St. Ives' moral choices and the fabulous machine of Lord Kelvin. Illustrated by J.K. Potter.

**Other books you might like:**
John Bellairs, *The Face in the Frost*, 1969
William Gibson, *The Difference Engine*, 1991
    Bruce Sterling, co-author
K.W. Jeter, *Infernal Devices*, 1987
Tim Powers, *The Anubis Gates*, 1983
Howard Waldrop, *Night of the Cooters*, 1990

---

**521**

**JAMES P. BLAYLOCK**

## Night Relics

(New York: Ace, 1994)

**Story type:** Horror (Ghost Story)
**Major character(s):** Peter Travers, Architect; Lance Klein, Business-man (real estate developer); Bernard Pomeroy, Businessman (salesman)
**Time period(s):** 1990s (1994)
**Locale(s):** Trabuco Canyon, California

**Summary:** The disapearance of his ex-wife Amanda and son David in the land surrounding his house spurs Peter Travers to action. In the course of his actions, he examines his life and finds that current events may dovetail horribly with an act of murder that resulted in the house being haunted for over 70 years.

**Other books you might like:**
Jonathan Aycliffe, *Naomi's Room*, 1991
Stephen King, *The Shining*, 1977
T.M. Wright, *Little Boy Lost*, 1992

---

**522**

**JAMES P. BLAYLOCK**

## The Paper Grail

(New York: Ace, 1991)

**Story type:** Fantasy (Quest; Contemporary)
**Major character(s):** Howard Barton, Museum Curator; Roy Barton, Construction Worker (builder of haunted houses); Mr. Jimmers, Companion (eccentric)
**Time period(s):** 1990s
**Locale(s):** California

**Summary:** Hoping to acquire a promised sketch by legendary Japa-nese artist Hoku-sai, Howard journeys to Northern California. Upon his arrival, eccentric behavior by acquaintances and family turn the simple task into a confusing quest for the artwork, that turns out to be a magic talisman with which the skilled wielder can control the elements.

**Other books you might like:**
Charles de Lint, *The Little Country*, 1990
Tom Deitz, *Soulsmith*, 1991
Roger L. DiSilvestro, *Living with the Reptiles*, 1990
Alan Dean Foster, *Cyber Way*, 1990
Marc Laidlaw, *Neon Lotus*, 1988
Stephen Leigh, *The Abraxas Marvel Circus*, 1990

---

**523**

**JAMES P. BLAYLOCK**

## The Stone Giant

(New York: Ace, 1989)

**Story type:** Fantasy (Light Fantasy)
**Major character(s):** Theophile Escargot, Cook (baker of pies), Ad-venturer (exiled); Leta, Young Woman (beautiful companion of Theophi)
**Time period(s):** Indeterminate
**Locale(s):** Twombly Town, Earth (Quasi modern town)

**Summary:** Theophile is kicked out of his marriage and leaves Twombly Town, only to find himself on a series of adventures. Elves, faeries, witches and goblins are a part of the supporting cast.

**Other books you might like:**
Avram Davidson, *Marco Polo and the Sleeping Beauty*, 1988
L. Sprague de Camp, *The Honorable Barbarian*, 1989
R.A. Lafferty, *The Devil Is Dead*, 1988

---

**524**

**JAMES P. BLAYLOCK**

## Winter Tides

(New York: Ace, 1997)

**Story type:** Horror (Possession)
**Major character(s):** Dave Quinn, Businessman (warehouse manager); Anne Morris, Writer; Edmund Dalton, Businessman (theatre owner)
**Time period(s):** 1990s (1997)
**Locale(s):** Huntington Beach, California

**Summary:** Fifteen years ago, Dave Quinn saved Anne Morris from drowning at the cost of the life of Anne's twin sister, Elinor. Now Anne has returned to Dave's town, with the malignant discarnate spirit of Elinor in hot pursuit, seeking a body she can assume control of to wreak vengeance on Dave and Anne.

**Other books you might like:**
Ramsey Campbell, *To Wake the Dead*, 1980
Richard Matheson, *Earthbound*, 1989
Peter Straub, *Ghost Story*, 1979

---

**525**

**JAMES BLISH**

## The Devil's Day

(New York: Baen, 1989)

**Story type:** Horror (Apocalyptic Horror)
**Series:** After Such Knowledge Trilogy
**Major character(s):** Father Domenico, Religious (Jesuit priest), Magi-cian (White magician); Theron Ware, Magician (Black magician)
**Time period(s):** 1960s
**Locale(s):** Italy; United States

**Summary:** Black magician Theron Ware, urged on by Baines, a billionaire industrialist, releases eighty demons from hell for one night. This triggers the appearance of Dis, capital of Hell, in Death Valley, the Devil himself, and the onslaught of Armageddon, while a handful of men fight to keep Satan from final and total victory. Originally published as *Black Easter* in 1968 and as *The Day After Judgment* in 1971.

**Other books you might like:**
Stephen King, *The Stand*, 1978
Robert R. McCammon, *Swan Song*, 1987

**526**

**JAMES BLISH**
**J.A. LAWRENCE**, Co-Author

## Star Trek: The Classic Episodes 1

(New York: Bantam Spectra, 1991)

**Story type:** Science Fiction (Space Opera; Collection)
**Series:** Star Trek
**Major character(s):** James T. Kirk, Spaceship Captain; Spock, Scientist, Alien (Vulcan); Leonard McCoy, Doctor
**Time period(s):** 23rd century
**Locale(s):** *U.S.S. Enterprise*, Spaceship; Outer Space

**Summary:** This volume includes a 12-page introduction by D.C. Fontana plus all 8 prefaces originally appearing in Blish's *Star Trek 3, 4, 5, 6, 9, 10, 11 & 12*, the forward to *Star Trek 12*, plus Blish's story versions of all 27 episodes aired during *Star Trek's* original first television season (1966-1967) and appearing previously in Blish's numbered Star Trek Series (1967-1977). Stories include two from Hugo Award winning episodes, "The Menagerie" by series creator Gene Roddenberry, and "The City on the Edge of Forever" by Harlan Ellison. Other notable stories include the prequel to *Star Trek II: The Wrath of Khan* titled "Space Seed," plus Theodore Sturgeon's "Shore Leave" and Robert Bloch's "What Are Little Girls Made Of?"

**Other books you might like:**
Margaret Wander Bonanno, *Strangers From the Sky*, 1987
Lee Correy, *The Abode of Life*, 1982
Gene DeWeese, *Chain of Attack*, 1987
Diane Duane, *Doctor's Orders*, 1990
John M. Ford, *How Much for Just the Planet?*, 1987
Alan Dean Foster, *Star Trek Log Ten*, 1978
J.A. Lawrence, *Mudd's Angels*, 1978
Jean Lorrah, *The IDIC Epidemic*, 1988
Vonda N. McIntyre, *Enterprise*, 1986
Vonda N. McIntyre, *The Entropy Effect*, 1981
Vonda N. McIntyre, *Star Trek II: The Wrath of Khan*, 1982
Melinda M. Snodgrass, *The Tears of the Singers*, 1984
Howard Weinstein, *The Covenant of the Crown*, 1981

**527**

**JAMES BLISH**

## Star Trek: The Classic Episodes 2

(New York: Bantam Spectra, 1991)

**Story type:** Science Fiction (Space Opera; Collection)
**Series:** Star Trek
**Major character(s):** James T. Kirk, Spaceship Captain; Spock, Scientist, Alien (Vulcan); Leonard McCoy, Doctor
**Time period(s):** 23rd century
**Locale(s):** *U.S.S. Enterprise*, Spaceship; Outer Space

**Summary:** This volume contains a 14-page introduction by David Gerrold plus Blish's story versions of the 25 episodes aired during *Star Trek's* original second television season (1967-1968). Stories include three from episodes receiving Hugo Award nominations, Theodore Sturgeon's "Amok Time," Norman Spinrad's "The Doomsday Machine," and David Gerrold's "The Trouble with Tribbles." Other notable stories include two from Robert Bloch's episodes, "Catspaw" and "Wolf in the Fold."

**Other books you might like:**
Greg Bear, *Corona*, 1984
Margaret Wander Bonanno, *Dwellers in the Crucible*, 1985
A.C. Crispin, *Time for Yesterday*, 1988
A.C. Crispin, *Yesterday's Son*, 1983
Alan Dean Foster, *Star Trek Log One*, 1974
Janet Kagan, *Uhura's Song*, 1985
J.A. Lawrence, *Mudd's Angels*, 1978
Jean Lorrah, *The Vulcan Academy Murders*, 1984
Sondra Marshak, *Star Trek: The New Voyages*, 1976
    Myrna Culbreath, co-author
Sondra Marshak, *Star Trek: The New Voyages II*, 1978
    Myrna Culbreath, co-author
Vonda N. McIntyre, *The Search for Spock*, 1984
Robert E. Vardeman, *The Klingon Gambit*, 1981

**528**

**JAMES BLISH**
**J.A. LAWRENCE**, Co-Author

## Star Trek: The Classic Episodes 3

(New York: Bantam Spectra, 1991)

**Story type:** Science Fiction (Space Opera; Collection)
**Series:** Star Trek
**Major character(s):** James T. Kirk, Spaceship Captain; Spock, Scientist, Alien (Vulcan); Leonard McCoy, Doctor
**Time period(s):** 23rd century
**Locale(s):** *U.S.S. Enterprise*, Spaceship; Outer Space

**Summary:** This volume contains a 16-page introduction by Norman Spinrad plus Blish's story version of each of the 24 episodes aired during *Star Trek's* original third television season (1968-1969). The stories appear in Blish's numbered Star Trek Series (1967-1977).

**Other books you might like:**
Margaret Wander Bonanno, *Strangers From the Sky*, 1987
A.C. Crispin, *Yesterday's Son*, 1983
Diane Duane, *The Wounded Sky*, 1983
John M. Ford, *The Final Reflection*, 1984
Jack C. Haldeman II, *Perry's Planet*, 1980
Joe Haldeman, *Planet of Judgment*, 1977
Joe Haldeman, *World Without End*, 1979
Barbara Hambly, *Ishmael*, 1985
J.A. Lawrence, *Mudd's Angels*, 1978
Jean Lorrah, *The Night of the Twin Moons*, 1976
M.S. Murdock, *Web of the Romulans*, 1983
Kathleen Sky, *Vulcan!*, 1978
Robert E. Vardeman, *Mutiny on the Enterprise*, 1983

**529**

**ROBERT BLOCH**

## The Complete Stories of Robert Bloch, Volume 2: Bitter Ends

(New York: Citadel Twilight, 1990)

**Story type:** Horror (Collection)

**Summary:** Thirty-one tales of horror, suspense and science fiction, originally published between 1956 and 1960. Stories such as "Betsy Blake Will Live Forever" and "Terror over Hollywood" display Bloch's fascination with the gulf between Hollywood images and reality. "The Screaming People," a tale of paranoia, and "The Real Bad Friend," with its schizophrenic narrator, reveal Bloch's interest in psychological horror. The witty puns of "Crime in Rhyme" and poetic justice of "Sock Finish" are characteristic trademarks of Bloch's short fiction. Originally published in 1987 as *The Selected Stories*, this reprint is mistitled, as it is not a complete collection.

**Other books you might like:**
Charles Beaumont, *Selected Stories*, 1988
Fredric Brown, *The Best of Fredric Brown*, 1976
Henry Kuttner, *The Best of Henry Kuttner*, 1975
Richard Matheson, *Collected Stories*, 1989

---

### 530
**ROBERT BLOCH**

## The Complete Stories of Robert Bloch, Volume 3: Last Rites
(New York: Citadel Twilight, 1991)

**Story type:** Horror (Collection)

**Summary:** This final volume of the mistitled reprint of *The Selected Stories of Robert Bloch* brings together 39 tales of horror, suspense and science fiction published between 1960 and 1979. Included are the gruesome tale of ventriloquism, "Final Performance"; a future story of Jack of Ripper, "A Toy for Juliette"; a fantasy of a horrifying cliche come to life, "A Case of the Stubborns"; and three stories set at the carnival: "Double Whammy," "Freak Show" and "The Animal Fair." All selections are leavened with Bloch's morbid wit.

**Other books you might like:**
Charles Beaumont, *Selected Stories*, 1988
Fredric Brown, *The Best of Fredric Brown*, 1976
Henry Kuttner, *The Best of Henry Kuttner*, 1975
Richard Matheson, *Collected Stories*, 1989
William Relling Jr., *The Infinite Man*, 1989

---

### 531
**ROBERT BLOCH**

## The Complete Stories of Robert Bloch. Volume 1: Final Reckonings
(New York: Citadel, 1990)

**Story type:** Horror (Collection)

**Summary:** Thirty-one stories first published between 1939 and 1956. Bloch's sense of the horror tradition is evident in "The Skull of the Marquis de Sade" and "The Man Who Collected Poe." His fascination with psychological obsession is illustrated in "The Head Man," his interest in split personality with "Lucy Comes to Stay," his concern with persecution and madness in "Terror in the Night," and his ironical humor in "The Pin." Originally published in 1987 as *The Selected Stories. . .*, this reprint is mistitled, as it is not a complete collection.

**Other books you might like:**
Charles Beaumont, *Charles Beaumont: Selected Stories*, 1988
Richard Matheson, *Richard Matheson: Collected Stories*, 1989

---

### 532
**ROBERT BLOCH**

## The Early Fears
(Minneapolis, Minnesota: Fedogan & Bremer, 1994)

**Story type:** Horror (Collection)

**Summary:** This omnibus collects the contents of *The Opener of the Way* (1945) and *Pleasant Dreams* (1962), and adds three recently published tales to boost the story count to 39. The stories are a virtual roadmap to themes and approaches that have dominated Bloch's work for 61 years, including Lovecraftian horror ("The Mannikin" and "The Shambler From the Stars"), psychological horror ("Yours Truly, Jack the Ripper" and "Enoch"), juvenile delinquency ("Sweets to the Sweet" and "Sweet Sixteen"), and deals with the devil ("Fiddler's Fee" and "That Hellbound Train"). Included are collaborations with Edgar Allan Poe ("The Lighthouse") and Henry Kuttner ("The Grab Bag"). Bloch has supplied a new introduction.

**Other books you might like:**
Charles Beaumont, *Collected Stories*, 1988
Ray Bradbury, *The Stories of Ray Bradbury*, 1980
Richard Matheson, *Collected Stories*, 1989
William F. Nolan, *Things Beyond Midnight*, 1984

---

### 533
**ROBERT BLOCH**

## Fear and Trembling
(New York: Tor, 1989)

**Story type:** Horror (Collection)

**Summary:** Thirteen stories that span most of Bloch's career from the earliest, "The Brood of Bubastis," a 1937 chiller in the Lovecraft mode to "Horror Scope," a gory 1989 tale of a serial killer with a taste for dismemberment. The typical Bloch mix of wit, gore, cynicism, irony, and a touch of sentimentality. Lively writing, vivid scenes, and Bloch's trademark twist endings.

**Other books you might like:**
Charles Beaumont, *Selected Stories*, 1988
Charles Birkin, *My Name Is Death*, 1966
Richard Matheson, *Collected Stories*, 1989

---

### 534
**ROBERT BLOCH**

## Flowers From the Moon and Other Lunacies
(Sauk City, Wisconsin: Arkham House, 1998)

**Story type:** Horror (Collection)

**Summary:** Twenty stories, only one previously collected, by a protege of H.P. Lovecraft and frequent contributor to pulp fiction magazines. Most were written early in Bloch's career, when he was trying to establish a style and approach different than Lovecraft's. Selections cover a wide range of themes and genres and include the vampire tale "A Question of Identity," the science fiction werewolf tale "Flowers from the Moon," and the psychological horror story "Death Has Five Guesses," in which a young man finds that experiments in ESP have awakened his latent impulse to murder. "The Druidic Doom" is a tale of ancient evil unleashed when a new landowner foolishly pries into the ancient heritage of his new estate, and "The Power of the Druid" is a tale of soul transfer. Robert M. Price supplies the introduction.

**Other books you might like:**
Joseph Payne Brennan, *Nine Horrors and a Dream*, 1958
Hugh B. Cave, *The Door Below*, 1997
August Derleth, *Not Long for This World*, 1948
Carl Jacobi, *Revelations in Black*, 1947
Donald Wandrei, *Don't Dream*, 1997

## 535

**ROBERT BLOCH
ANDRE NORTON**, Co-Author

### The Jekyll Legacy

(New York: Tor, 1990)

**Story type:** Horror (Mystery)
**Major character(s):** Hester Lane, Writer; Gertrude Kirby, Child-Care Giver; Alfred Prothore, Political Figure
**Time period(s):** 1880s
**Locale(s):** London, England

**Summary:** On assignment in London to investigate the founding of the Salvation Army, Canadian writer Hester Lane moves into the house of her recently deceased uncle Henry Jekyll. There she becomes embroiled in an intrigue involving white slavers who appear to have been influenced by Jekyll's former associate, the mysterious Edward Hyde.

**Other books you might like:**
Robert Bloch, *Night of the Ripper*, 1985
Valerie Martin, *Mary Reilly*, 1990
Robert Louis Stevenson, *The Strange Case of Dr. Jekyll and Mr. Hyde*, 1886

## 536

**ROBERT BLOCH**

### Lori

(New York: Tor, 1989)

**Story type:** Horror (Mystery)
**Major character(s):** Lori Holmes, Young Woman (Beautiful); Anthony Leverett, Doctor (Psychiatrist)
**Time period(s):** 1980s
**Locale(s):** Los Angeles, California

**Summary:** A mysterious phone call and the picture of a long dead girl—her exact double—send Lori on a search for the truth about her own tangled, forgotten past, a search that threatens her sanity and even her life.

**Other books you might like:**
John Farris, *When Michael Calls*, 1967

## 537

**ROBERT BLOCH**

### Midnight Pleasures

(New York: Tor, 1991)

**Story type:** Horror (Collection)
**Summary:** A reprint of a 1987 collection of 14 stories of horror and suspense by one of the masters of the modern horror story. Included are ''The Rubber Room,'' a tale of psychological horror; ''The Night Before Christmas,'' a grim exercise in adultery and revenge; ''Everybody Needs a Little Love,'' about an obsession taken to extremes; and ''The Totem Pole,'' a story of an Indian curse from the author's early *Weird Tales* fiction.

**Other books you might like:**
Charles Beaumont, *Selected Stories*, 1988
Hugh B. Cave, *Murgunstrumm and Others*, 1977
Richard Matheson, *Collected Stories*, 1989
William Relling Jr., *The Infinite Man*, 1989
Manly Wade Wellman, *Worse Things Waiting*, 1973

## 538

**ROBERT BLOCH**, Editor

### Monsters in Our Midst

(New York: Tor, 1993)

**Story type:** Horror (Anthology)
**Summary:** This second collection of non-supernatural horror stories is a follow-up to Bloch's previous anthology *Psycho Paths* (Tor, 1991), and pursues the same agenda of psychological horror fiction that the author has promulgated since he wrote *Psycho* in 1959. The best of the 17 stories includes Ramsey Campbell's ''For You to Judge,'' about a man who becomes ''infected'' by the spirit of a vicious murderer; Jonathan Carroll's ''The Lick of Time,'' concerned with a woman who creates an alternate identity on her answering machine; Bloch's own ''It Takes One to Know One,'' in which a disgruntled author fulfills a pact he and his friends made years before; and Ray Bradbury's ''Fee Fie Fo Fum,'' about an elderly woman who sees murderous intentions in a young man but can convince no one of his true nature.

**Other books you might like:**
Richard T. Chizmar, *Cold Blood*, 1991
Ed Gorman, *Dark Crimes II: Modern Masters of Noir*, 1992
    editor
Ed Gorman, *Stalkers*, 1990
    Martin H. Greenberg, co-editor

## 539

**ROBERT BLOCH**

### The Mysteries of the Worm

(Oakland, California: Chaosium, 1993)

**Story type:** Horror (Collection)
**Summary:** An expansion of Robert Bloch's 1981 volume of the same title, this book collects 17 stories written in homage to the mythic underpinnings of H.P. Lovecraft's stories, dubbed the Cthulhu Mythos. Included are ''The Shambler From the Stars,'' which inspired Lovecraft's own classic ''The Haunter of the Dark''; ''The Mannikin,'' about a hunchback whose deformity is more than a physical hindrance; ''The Creeper in the Crypt,'' which fuses horror and hard-boiled crime fiction; and several stories steeped in Egyptian mythology, including ''The Secret of Sebek,'' ''The Faceless God,'' and ''Fane of the Black Pharoah.'' Series editor Robert Price supplies an introduction, and Bloch and the late Lin Carter afterwords.

**Other books you might like:**
Ramsey Campbell, *Cold Print*, 198
August Derleth, *Tales of the Cthulhu Mythos*, 1969
    editor
H.P. Lovecraft, *The Watchers out of Time*, 1974
    August Derleth, co-author

## 540

**ROBERT BLOCH**

### Psycho

(New York: Tor, 1989)

**Story type:** Horror (Serial Killer)
**Major character(s):** Norman Bates, Innkeeper (Motel Owner), Murderer (Lunatic); Mary Crane, Thief
**Time period(s):** 1950s
**Locale(s):** Fairvale, Texas (Bates Motel)

**Summary:** Fleeing with $40,000 in stolen money, Mary Crane stops off—permanently—at the Bates Motel. A private detective, Mary's boyfriend, Sam Loomis, and her sister, Lila, subsequently track Mary to the motel where they, too, encounter Norman's vengeful "Mother." Originally published in 1959.

**Other books you might like:**
Ramsey Campbell, *The Face That Must Die*, 1979

**541**

### ROBERT BLOCH

## *Psycho II*

(New York: Tor, 1989)

**Story type:** Horror (Mystery)
**Major character(s):** Norman Bates, Murderer (Escaped lunatic); Adam Claiborne, Doctor (Norman's psychiatrist)
**Time period(s):** 1980s
**Locale(s):** Fairvale, Texas; Hollywood, California

**Summary:** Norman escapes from confinement and heads for Hollywood, where a film of his career is being made. Shortly thereafter, deaths begin to occur on the studio backlot which may—or may not—be Norman's fault. Originally published in 1982.

**Other books you might like:**
Ramsey Campbell, *The Doll Who Ate His Mother*, 1976

**542**

### ROBERT BLOCH

## *Psycho House*

(New York: Tor, 1990)

**Story type:** Horror (Mystery)
**Major character(s):** Amelia "Amy" Haines, Writer (True crime novels); Hank Gibbs, Journalist, Publisher (Fairvale's sole newspaper)
**Time period(s):** 1990s
**Locale(s):** Fairvale, Texas

**Summary:** The Bates Motel and adjoining house is rebuilt as a tourist attraction, but before opening day it becomes the site of multiple murders. While researching a book on Bates' original crimes, Amy Haines finds herself both a suspect in the new killings and a potential victim of Bates' "successor."

**Other books you might like:**
Nina Romberg, *The Spirit Stalker*, 1989

**543**

### ROBERT BLOCH
### MARTIN H. GREENBERG, Co-Author

## *Psycho-Paths*

(New York: Tor, 1991)

**Story type:** Horror (Anthology)

**Summary:** Seventeen tales of non-supernatural horror, collected by the author of *Psycho*. Most of the stories fall into the subgenre of psychological horror, and are offered as an antidote to horror fiction that caters to tastes for gore and supernatural special effects. The best include Steve Rasnic Tem's "Jesse," Charles Grant's "Kin" and Edward D. Hoch's "The Secret Blade."

**Other books you might like:**
Alfred Hitchcock, *Alfred Hitchcock Presents: Stories Not for the Nervous*, 1965
Alfred Hitchcock, *Alfred Hitchcock Presents: Stories My Mother Never Told Me*, 1963
Alfred Hitchcock, *Alfred Hitchcock Presents: Stories for Late at Night*, 1961
Joan Kahn, *Hanging by a Thread*, 1969
Joan Kahn, *The Edge of the Chair*, 1967

**544**

### ROBERT BLOCH, Editor

## *Robert Bloch's Psychos*

(New York: Pocket, 1998)

**Story type:** Horror (Anthology)
**Series:** Horror Writers Association Presents

**Summary:** This fifth volume published under the imprimatur of the Horror Writers Association features twenty-two stories written in the spirit of Robert Bloch's tales of psychological horror. Included are Stephen King's "Autopsy Room Four," narrated from the viewpoint of a catatonic man who is being prepared for an autopsy and is powerless to tell physicians that he is not yet dead; Denise M. Bruchman's "The Lesser of Two Evils," about a serial killer possessed by the spirit of Jack the Ripper; Charles L. Grant's "Haunted," which features a serial killer that steals his victim's faces; and Gary A. Braunbeck's "Safe," in which a man's survival of a mass murder incident profoundly affects his life thereafter.

**Other books you might like:**
Richard T. Chizmar, *Cold Blood*, 1991
    editor
Ed Gorman, *Dark Crimes II: Modern Masters of Noir*, 1992
    editor
Ed Gorman, *Stalkers*, 1990
    Martin H. Greenberg, co-editor
Ed Gorman, *Predators*, 1993
    Martin H. Greenberg, co-editor
Joe R. Lansdale, *Dark at Heart*, 1992
    Karen Lansdale, co-editor

**545**

### FRANCESCA LIA BLOCK

## *Baby Be-Bop*

(New York: HarperCollins, 1995)

**Story type:** Fantasy (Contemporary; Young Adult)
**Series:** Weetzie Bat
**Major character(s):** Dirk McDonald, Teenager, Homosexual; Grandma Fifi, Grandparent, Dancer; Pop, Teenager
**Time period(s):** 1970s
**Locale(s):** Los Angeles, California

**Summary:** Dirk lives in a little cottage with his grandmother and her pets. As he grows up, he slowly discovers his homosexuality and what that means to society. With the help of the ghosts of his father and great-grandmother, Dirk learns to love himself and others.

**Other books you might like:**
Marion Dane Bauer, *Am I Blue?*, 1994
    editor
James P. Blaylock, *Land of Dreams*, 1987
Diana Wynne Jones, *Aunt Maria*, 1991
Daniel Manus Pinkwater, *Young Adults*, 1991

Will Shetterly, *Elsewhere*, 1991

## 546

### FRANCESCA LIA BLOCK

## *Cherokee Bat and the Goat Guys*

(New York: HarperCollins, 1992)

**Story type:** Fantasy (Young Adult; Contemporary)
**Series:** Weetzie Bat
**Major character(s):** Cherokee Bat, Teenager, Musician; Coyote, Shaman; Witch Baby, Musician (drummer), Witch
**Time period(s):** 1990s
**Locale(s):** Los Angeles, California

**Summary:** Weetzie Bat and her friends have gone to South America to shoot a film, leaving the teenaged children under the care of Coyote. Left to their own devices, the teenagers form a band and begin to grapple with the attractions and perils of adulthood. Magic gifts from Coyote give the band confidence, but also inspire them to recklessness. Written in an exotic style, this novel, like its predecessors, deals frankly, but not graphically, with adult problems such as sex and drug use.

**Other books you might like:**
James P. Blaylock, *Land of Dreams*, 1987
Emma Bull, *War for the Oaks*, 1987
Diana Wynne Jones, *Aunt Maria*, 1991
Daniel Manus Pinkwater, *Young Adults*, 1991
Will Shetterly, *Elsewhere*, 1991
Terri Windling, *Bordertown*, 1986
    Mark Alan Arnold, co-editor

## 547

### FRANCESCA LIA BLOCK

## *Ecstasia*

(New York: Roc, 1993)

**Story type:** Fantasy (Romance)
**Major character(s):** Rafe, Musician (drummer), Orphan; Calliope, Psychic, Orphan; Lily, Sports Figure (acrobat), Addict
**Time period(s):** Indeterminate Future
**Locale(s):** Elysia, Fictional City

**Summary:** In Elysia, a city of eternal youth populated only by the young, Rafe drums for Ecstasia, Elysia's hottest band. Rafe falls in love with a doomed woman whose addiction and loss drag her Under, where old people go. Perhaps love, even in this exotic world, can beat age and death.

**Other books you might like:**
Poppy Z. Brite, *Drawing Blood*, 1993
John Crowley, *Little, Big*, 1981
Jonathan Littell, *Bad Voltage*, 1989
Ian McDonald, *Desolation Road*, 1988
Pat Murphy, *The City, Not Long After*, 1989

## 548

### FRANCESCA LIA BLOCK

## *The Hanged Man*

(New York: HarperCollins, 1994)

**Story type:** Fantasy (Contemporary Realism)
**Major character(s):** Laurel, Psychic; Jack, Addict; Claudia, Addict

**Time period(s):** 1990s
**Locale(s):** Los Angeles, California

**Summary:** While waiting in the hospital room for her father to die, Laurel meets Jack, a mysterious junkie. Overwhelmed by her abusive childhood, Laurel begins to sink into a half-remembered world of dreams and regrets. The book takes its structure from a tarot reading with cards indicating the changes Laurel must make to survive.

**Other books you might like:**
Poppy Z. Brite, *Lost Souls*, 1992
William S. Burroughs, *Junky*, 1953
Pat Cadigan, *Synners*, 1991
Kathe Koja, *Skin*, 1993
Alexander Trocchi, *Cain's Book*, 1960

## 549

### FRANCESCA LIA BLOCK

## *I Was a Teenage Fairy*

(New York: HarperCollins, 1998)

**Story type:** Fantasy (Young Adult; Contemporary)
**Major character(s):** Barbie Marks, Teenager, Model; Griffin Tyler, Teenager, Actor; Mab, Mythical Creature (fairy), Counselor
**Time period(s):** 1990s
**Locale(s):** Los Angeles, California

**Summary:** Groomed to be a model, Barbie Marks would rather be behind the camera. A beautiful and talented young man, Griffin, carries secrets that lock him away from everyone. Mab, a crabby, demanding fairy, will do her best to get them both pointed in the right direction.

**Other books you might like:**
James P. Blaylock, *Land of Dreams*, 1987
Suzy McKee Charnas, *The Kingdom of Kevin Malone*, 1993
Diana Wynne Jones, *Aunt Maria*, 1991
Tanith Lee, *Black Unicorn*, 1991
Will Shetterly, *Elsewhere*, 1991

## 550

### FRANCESCA LIA BLOCK

## *Missing Angel Juan*

(New York: HarperCollins, 1993)

**Story type:** Fantasy (Young Adult; Contemporary)
**Series:** Weetzie Bat
**Major character(s):** Witch Baby, Teenager, Musician (drummer); Angel Juan, Teenager, Musician (bass guitar); Charlie Bat, Spirit, Grandparent
**Time period(s):** 1990s
**Locale(s):** Los Angeles, California; New York, New York

**Summary:** When Angel Juan leaves warm and sunny California for New York, Witch Baby follows him. Searching for her missing lover, the strange young woman finds out about life and herself. Like Block's other books, this stylistically exotic novel deals frankly, although not graphically, with adult issues such as sex and drug abuse.

**Other books you might like:**
James P. Blaylock, *Land of Dreams*, 1987
Emma Bull, *War for the Oaks*, 1987
Suzy McKee Charnas, *The Bronze King*, 1985
Daniel Manus Pinkwater, *Young Adults*, 1991
Will Shetterly, *Elsewhere*, 1991

## 551

### FRANCESCA LIA BLOCK

## *Primavera*

(New York: Roc, 1994)

**Story type:** Fantasy (Literary; Adventure)
**Series:** Elysia
**Major character(s):** Primavera, Singer; Calliope, Parent, Psychic; Gunn, Peddler, Businessman (pimp)
**Time period(s):** Indeterminate Future
**Locale(s):** Elysia, Fictional City; Paradise, Fictional Country

**Summary:** At the end of *Ecstasia*, the band retires to Paradise, the Desert they reclaimed, to raise Primavera. The city of youth, Elysia, has a long reach, seducing Primavera into its lotus-eater world. She must learn her parents' lessons and a few hard ones of her own if she wants to escape.

**Other books you might like:**
James P. Blaylock, *Land of Dreams*, 1987
Storm Constantine, *Wraeththu*, 1993
John Crowley, *Little, Big*, 1981
Ian McDonald, *Desolation Road*, 1988
Pat Murphy, *The City, Not Long After*, 1989

## 552

### FRANCESCA LIA BLOCK

## *Witch Baby*

(New York: HarperCollins, 1991)

**Story type:** Fantasy (Contemporary; Young Adult)
**Major character(s):** Witch Baby, Teenager, Foundling, Musician; Dirk McDonald, Teenager, Homosexual; My Secret Agent Lover Man, Filmmaker
**Time period(s):** 1990s
**Locale(s):** Los Angeles, California; Santa Cruz, California

**Summary:** Witch Baby, the mysterious half-child of My Secret Agent Lover Man, doesn't fit into her odd extended family. Attempting to fit in, she causes disruption and confusion all around her. Eventually she runs away to find out who she really is and where she belongs. Enjoyable for adults, this book deals with difficult, mature themes in an off-beat way. Sequel to *Weetzie Bat*.

**Other books you might like:**
James P. Blaylock, *Land of Dreams*, 1987
Diana Wynne Jones, *Aunt Maria*, 1991
Daniel Manus Pinkwater, *Young Adults*, 1991
Will Shetterly, *Elsewhere*, 1991
Terri Windling, *Bordertown*, 1986
    Mark Alan Arnold, co-editor

## 553

### ED BLOME

## *Title Deleted for Security Reasons*

(Honesdale, Pennsylvania: West End Books, 1993)

**Story type:** Science Fiction (Alternate Intelligence; Humor)
**Series:** Paranoia
**Major character(s):** James-B-OND-1, Clone, Security Officer; Claude, Robot (foundrybot), Sidekick; Frank-I-STN-4, Administrator, Clone
**Time period(s):** Indeterminate Future (After the Big Oops)
**Locale(s):** Alpha Complex, Earth (Washington D.C. area)

**Summary:** Through luck and regular, traitorous computer hacking, James-B-OND-1 survives to acquire a potentially lethal assignment, rooting out traitorous leadership within the Troubleshooter Bureau. James-B-OND-1 faces additional danger when the Computer deletes its memory of the assignment for security reasons. Game tie-in.

**Other books you might like:**
Douglas Adams, *The Hitchhiker's Guide to the Galaxy*, 1980
Jack L. Chalker, *The Red Tape War*, 1991
    Mike Resnick, George Alec Effinger, co-authors
Harry Harrison, *Bill, the Galactic Hero: The Planet of the Robot Slaves*, 1989
Larry Niven, *Fallen Angels*, 1991
    Jerry Pournelle, Michael Flynn, co-authors
Ken Rolston, *Extreme Paranoia: Nobody Knows the Trouble I've Shot*, 1991
Neal Stephenson, *Snow Crash*, 1992

## 554

### BRITTON BLOOM

## *Matrix Cubed*

(Lake Geneva, Wisconsin: TSR, 1991)

**Story type:** Science Fiction (Political)
**Series:** Buck Rogers: The Inner Planets Trilogy
**Major character(s):** Kemal Gavilan, Royalty
**Time period(s):** 25th century
**Locale(s):** Mercury

**Summary:** Kemal Gavilan struggles to solve his father's murder, the result of family treachery. Mercury's survival is further threatened by an upcoming RAM operation against Earth and Mercury. This is the author's first published novel and a sequel to *First Power Play* and *Prime Squared*.

**Other books you might like:**
Frank Herbert, *Dune*, 1965
Richard A. Lupoff, *Buck Rogers in the 25th Century*, 1978
    as Addison E. Steele
Richard A. Lupoff, *That Man on Beta II*, 1978
    as Addison E. Steele
John Miller, *First Power Play*, 1990
M.S. Murdock, *Armageddon Off Vesta*, 1989
M.S. Murdock, *Hammer of Mars*, 1989
M.S. Murdock, *Prime Squared*, 1990
M.S. Murdock, *Rebellion 2456*, 1989
Philip Francis Nowlan, *Armageddon 2419 A.D.*, 1962
John Silbersack, *Roger's Rangers*, 1983

## 555

### MICHAEL BLUMLEIN

## *The Brains of Rats*

(Los Angeles: Scream/Press, 1989)

**Story type:** Horror (Collection)

**Summary:** Twelve stories, five original to this volume. The tension between Blumlein's precise, stripped down, almost clinically detached prose and his extreme, visceral, grotesque scenes and situations provokes disturbing reactions in the reader. A practicing M.D., his stories are glutted with body parts and surgical descriptions. Especially unnerving are the title story, a complex meditation on the tensions between the sexes, and "Tissue Ablation and Variant Regeneration: A Case Report," a visceral, darkly comedic description of an operation on ''Mr. Reagan'' to remove body parts for regeneration to feed Third World countries.

**Other books you might like:**
J.G. Ballard, *Love and Napalm: Export U.S.A.*, 1969
Dennis Etchison, *The Blood Kiss*, 1988
Joe R. Lansdale, *By Bizarre Hands*, 1989
David J. Skal, *Antibodies*, 1988
John Shirley, *Heatseeker*, 1989

## 556

### GILES BLUNT

## Cold Eye

(New York: Avon, 1990)

**Story type:** Horror (Doppelganger)
**Major character(s):** Nicholas Hood, Artist (painter); Andre Bellisle, Businessman (art patron); Gary Lauzon, Detective—Police
**Time period(s):** 1980s (1989)
**Locale(s):** New York, New York

**Summary:** When Andre Bellisle begins steering Nicholas Hood to scenes of carnage for inspiration, Hood's paintings become wildly successful. But Hood finds himself increasingly attracted to the violence that gives rise to his work. This first novel was first published in 1989.

**Other books you might like:**
Pars Lagerkvist, *The Dwarf*, 1945
Oscar Wilde, *The Picture of Dorian Gray*, 1891

## 557

### K.B. BOGEN

## Go Quest, Young Man

(Lake Geneva, Wisconsin: TSR, 1994)

**Story type:** Fantasy (Quest; Light Fantasy)
**Major character(s):** Erwyn, Sorcerer, Royalty
**Time period(s):** Indeterminate
**Locale(s):** Fictional Country

**Summary:** To avoid an enforced marriage, Erwyn enters the Sorcerer's Apprentice School. Completing formal instruction, Journeyman Sorcerer Erwyn begins a four year wandering internship equipped for guidance with his copy of the *Sorcerers Almanac*. First novel.

**Other books you might like:**
C. Dale Brittain, *A Bad Spell in Yurt*, 1991
Esther Friesner, *Wishing Season*, 1993
John Moore, *Slay and Rescue*, 1993
S.P. Somtow, *The Wizard's Apprentice*, 1993
Caroline Stevermer, *A College of Magics*, 1994

## 558

### NANCY BOGEN

## Bagatelle—Guinevere

(New York: Twickenham, 1995)

**Story type:** Fantasy (Science Fiction; Contemporary Realism)
**Major character(s):** Felice Rothman, Writer (poet); Nancy Bogen, Editor; Laleekh, Alien
**Time period(s):** 1970s (1976)
**Locale(s):** New York, New York; X, Planet—Imaginary

**Summary:** After failing to sell her well-received prose poem, Felice volunteers for a secret NASA mission to the nearby, newly discovered planet X. There she searches out the local humanoid natives who kidnap her into a vast underground city, believing her a construct of a neighboring underground city.

**Other books you might like:**
Piers Anthony, *The Caterpillar's Question*, 1992
    Philip Jose Farmer, co-author
Eleanor Arnason, *A Woman of the Iron People*, 1991
Jesse Browner, *Conglomeros*, 1992
Jane M. Lindskold, *Brother to Dragons, Companion to Owls*, 1994
Sheri S. Tepper, *A Plague of Angels*, 1993

## 559

### TIMOTHY BOGGS

## By the Sword

(New York: Berkley Boulevard, 1996)

**Story type:** Fantasy (Legend; Adventure)
**Series:** Hercules: The Legendary Journeys
**Major character(s):** Hercules, Hero, Warrior
**Time period(s):** Indeterminate Past
**Locale(s):** Ancient Civilization; Ithaca, Greece

**Summary:** When marauders steal a magical sword forged by Hephaestos for Zeus, Hercules promises his half-brother Hermes that he will recover the magical weapon. First of a television tie-in series.

**Other books you might like:**
Kyle Crocco, *Heroes, Inc.*, 1991
Ru Emerson, *The Empty Throne*, 1996
Ru Emerson, *Masques*, 1990
Barbara Hambly, *Beauty and the Beast*, 1989
Jason Henderson, *Highlander: The Element of Fire*, 1995
Barry Hughart, *Bridge of Birds*, 1984
John Moore, *Slay and Rescue*, 1993

## 560

### MAYA KAATHRYN BOHNHOFF

## The Crystal Rose

(New York: Baen, 1995)

**Story type:** Fantasy (Political; Religious)
**Series:** Meri
**Major character(s):** Daimhin Feich, Political Figure (regent); Taminy-a-Cuinn, Religious, Psychic; Ren Catahn, Leader
**Time period(s):** Indeterminate
**Locale(s):** Halig-liath, Fictional City (religious center); Creiddylad, Fictional City; Airdnasheen, Fictional City

**Summary:** While helping Airleas mature into the good king he wishes to become, Taminy must defeat the evil Daimhin Feich without compromising her principles. Ren Catahn provides a home for the refugees, including the prince and his mother, while Feich plots to control the government and the church.

**Other books you might like:**
Suzette Haden Elgin, *Twelve Fair Kingdoms*, 1981
C.S. Friedman, *When True Night Falls*, 1993
Mercedes Lackey, *The Lark and the Wren*, 1991
Marc Laidlaw, *Neon Lotus*, 1988
Elizabeth Ann Scarborough, *Nothing Sacred*, 1991

## 561

**MAYA KAATHRYN BOHNHOFF**

### The Meri

(New York: Baen, 1992)

**Story type:** Fantasy (Quest; Religious)
**Major character(s):** Meredydd a-Lagan, Orphan, Student; Osraed Bevol, Guardian, Teacher; Lealbhallain, Student
**Time period(s):** Indeterminate
**Locale(s):** Halig-liath, Mythical Place (academy)

**Summary:** Adopted by Osraed Bevol after seeing her family murdered, Meredydd becomes the only female to study at Halig-liath. A gifted student, Meredydd must overcome traditional attitudes against female mages to become apprenticed to the Meri, the bridge between the world and the Infinite. She must reconcile her conflicting goals of revenge and service before she can attain her destiny. Author's first novel.

**Other books you might like:**
Margaret J. Anderson, *The Druid's Gift*, 1989
John Desjarlais, *The Throne of Tara*, 1990
Sue Harrison, *Mother Earth, Father Sky*, 1990
Ursula K. Le Guin, *A Wizard of Earthsea*, 1968
Morgan Llywelyn, *The Horse Goddess*, 1982

## 562

**MAYA KAATHRYN BOHNHOFF**

### The Spirit Gate

(New York: Baen, 1996)

**Story type:** Fantasy (Religious; Psychic Powers)
**Major character(s):** Kassia Telek, Witch, Widow(er); Lukasha, Sorcerer; Damek, Assistant (sorcerer's)
**Time period(s):** Indeterminate
**Locale(s):** Polia, Fictional Country

**Summary:** Blamed for the floods which killed her husband and father, Kassia has a hard time supporting her son. When her sister can no longer offer housing, Kassia tries to earn enough money by telling futures until, realizing that she cannot continue, Kassia applies to the local school for training. Damek takes an instant dislike to Kassia, but Lukasha recognizes her power and realizes he can use her to help save the king from the Frankish bishop's foreign religion.

**Other books you might like:**
Barbara Hambly, *The Time of the Dark*, 1982
Marc Laidlaw, *Neon Lotus*, 1988
Thomas K. Martin, *A Matter of Honor*, 1994
Andre Norton, *Witch World*, 1963
Elizabeth Ann Scarborough, *Nothing Sacred*, 1991

## 563

**MAYA KAATHRYN BOHNHOFF**

### Taminy

(New York: Baen, 1993)

**Story type:** Fantasy (Political; Religious)
**Series:** Meri
**Major character(s):** Taminy-a-Cuinn, Religious, Psychic; Osraed Bevol, Teacher, Psychic; Wyth, Religious
**Time period(s):** Indeterminate
**Locale(s):** Halig-liath, Mythical Place (academy); Nairne, Fictional City; Creiddylad, Fictional City

**Summary:** After Meredydd replaces Taminy as vessel for the Meri, Taminy returns to Halig-liath with Bevol. Accused of practicing Wicke, Taminy passes every test of purity to no avail. Charged by the Meri to open Halig-liath to female students, Wyth finds his fellows closed to the Meri's request, perhaps endangering Halig-liath.

**Other books you might like:**
Margaret J. Anderson, *The Druid's Gift*, 1989
Margaret Ball, *Flameweaver*, 1991
Adrian Cole, *Mother of Storms*, 1992
Tom Deitz, *Soulsmith*, 1991
Carole Nelson Douglas, *Cup of Clay*, 1991
Suzette Haden Elgin, *Twelve Fair Kingdoms*, 1981
Sean Russell, *The Initiate Brother*, 1991
Elizabeth Ann Scarborough, *Last Refuge*, 1992

## 564

**JOHANNA BOLTON**

### Mission: Tori

(New York: Ballantine/Del Rey, 1990)

**Story type:** Science Fiction (First Contact; Espionage Thriller)
**Major character(s):** Mier Silver, Spy (Special Intelligence Agency), Psychic (limited); Hac, Android (Human Analog Computer); Ttar Began, Spy (consortium)
**Time period(s):** Indeterminate Future
**Locale(s):** Tori, Planet—Imaginary; Earth; Outer Space

**Summary:** Mier Silver is sent to investigate why agents have disappeared or gone insane on Tori, a planet with rich mineral deposits. While on route, she and Hac are targets for murder. The victim's so-called brother, Ttar, catches up with the two just before they land on Tori. On the planet, they are taken over by a parasite, but there is a cure. They find out that the head of the SIA is a traitor. Hac is not an android, but human. He and Mier team up.

**Other books you might like:**
Harry Harrison, *Planet of the Damned*, 1962
Robert A. Heinlein, *The Puppet Masters*, 1990
Brian Stableford, *The Castaways of Tanagar*, 1981
Brian Stableford, *The City of the Sun*, 1978
Timothy Zahn, *Spinneret*, 1985

## 565

**MARGARET WANDER BONANNO**

### The Others

(New York: St. Martin's Press, 1990)

**Story type:** Science Fiction (Political; Psychic Powers)
**Major character(s):** Lingri, Historian, Writer (poet)
**Time period(s):** Indeterminate
**Locale(s):** Planet—Imaginary

**Summary:** An advanced civilization on an isolated archipelago has been contacted by the more primitive intelligent species on the planet. When contact is made, the more numerous, more aggressive 'People' declare the pacifistic people of the archipelago the 'Others'. Lingri, of the Others, is charged with chronicling the eradication of the Others by the People after 80 years of contact. At the same time, Lingri also describes the Others' long history.

**Other books you might like:**
C.J. Cherryh, *Forty Thousand in Gehenna*, 1984
Mary Gentle, *Golden Witchbreed*, 1984
Edgar Pangborn, *A Mirror for Observers*, 1954
James D. Priest, *Kirins: The Spell of No'an*, 1990

A.E. Van Vogt, *Slan*, 1951

## 566

### MARGARET WANDER BONANNO

## *OtherWhere*

(New York: St. Martins Press, 1991)

**Story type:** Science Fiction (Political; Psychic Powers)
**Series:** Others
**Major character(s):** Lingri, Historian (chronicler), Writer; Joreth, Genetically Altered Being (Intermix); Dwiri, Telepath
**Time period(s):** Indeterminate
**Locale(s):** Planet—Imaginary

**Summary:** Having been rescued at the last possible moment by Lingri's son, Joreth, and his crew of Intermixes and People, the Others set out on a journey to their potential new home. During the trip, Lingri recalls events and circumstances which led to the deaths of almost all the Others and forced her to abandon her son and his father. This book opens with a brief summary of *The Others*.

**Other books you might like:**
Eleanor Arnason, *A Woman of the Iron People*, 1991
Octavia E. Butler, *Dawn*, 1987
Orson Scott Card, *Ender's Game*, 1985
Robert N. Charrette, *Choose Your Enemies Carefully*, 1990
C.J. Cherryh, *Cyteen*, 1988
Frank Herbert, *Dune*, 1965
Ken Kato, *Yamato: A Rage in Heaven*, 1990
Dan Simmons, *Hyperion*, 1989
Joan Slonczewski, *A Door into Ocean*, 1986
Sheri S. Tepper, *Raising the Stones*, 1990

## 567

### MARGARET WANDER BONANNO

## *OtherWise*

(New York: St. Martin's Press, 1993)

**Story type:** Science Fiction (Post-Holocaust; Psychic Powers)
**Series:** Others
**Major character(s):** Lingri, Historian, Writer (poet); Joreth, Musician; Chior, Leader, Scientist (meteorologist)
**Time period(s):** Indeterminate
**Locale(s):** The World, Planet—Imaginary

**Summary:** In telepathic contact with the Others in the Iceworld, Lingri travels with her half-People son Joreth, to investigate the message that the Patriots no longer control the People, that some Others still live on the mainland, and that transportation for the Others to leave the world still exists in the Hidden. While evading the remaining guard patrols, Lingri meets many friends on the devastated continent where she continues to develop as an empath. Chior faces the results of his disastrous meddling which spurred the Holocaust.

**Other books you might like:**
David Brin, *Sundiver*, 1980
C.J. Cherryh, *Cyteen*, 1988
Samuel R. Delany, *They Fly at Ciron*, 1993
Mary Gentle, *Golden Witchbreed*, 1984
Frank Herbert, *Dune*, 1965
Rosemary Kirstein, *The Outskirter's Secret*, 1992
Edgar Pangborn, *A Mirror for Observers*, 1954
A.E. Van Vogt, *Slan*, 1946
Gene Wolfe, *Nightside the Long Sun*, 1993

## 568

### MARGARET WANDER BONANNO

## *Preternatural*

(New York: Tor, 1996)

**Story type:** Science Fiction (First Contact; Alternate Intelligence)
**Major character(s):** Karen Rohmer Guerreri, Writer; Max Neimark, Actor, Director; Laurence ''Larry'' Koster, Actor
**Time period(s):** 1990s
**Locale(s):** New York, New York; Los Angeles, California

**Summary:** Science fiction writer Karen Gu erreri discovers that the alien telepathic jellyfish characters in her novel-in-progress actually exist and communicate with humans, including famous actors Max Neimark (a thinly-disguised Leonard Nimoy) and Larry Koster (William Shatner).

**Other books you might like:**
Philip K. Dick, *The Three Stigmata of Palmer Eldritch*, 1965
Nancy Kress, *Brain Rose*, 1990
Sharyn McCrumb, *Bimbos of the Death Sun*, 1988
Nichelle Nichols, *Saturn's Child*, 1995
    Margaret Wander Bonanno, co-author
Patrick O'Leary, *Door Number Three*, 1995
Christopher Pike, *The Eternal Enemy*, 1993
Christopher Pike, *The Starlight Crystal*, 1996

## 569

### MARGARET WANDER BONANNO

## *Probe*

(New York: Pocket Books, 1992)

**Story type:** Science Fiction (Space Opera)
**Series:** Star Trek
**Major character(s):** James T. Kirk, Spaceship Captain; Spock, Scientist, Alien (Vulcan); Tiam, Diplomat (ambassador), Alien (Romulan)
**Time period(s):** 23rd century
**Locale(s):** *U.S.S. Enterprise*, Spaceship (Federation); *Galtizh*, Spaceship (Romulan); Temaris, Planet—Imaginary

**Summary:** Engaging in a joint archaeological excavation of Temaris with Romulan scientists, the *Enterprise* crew takes part in cultural exchanges until the reappearance of an alien probe and Romulan defections seed new distrust amo ng treacherous Romulans, leaving the Enterprise as everyone's only hope, if the *Enterprise* can quickly learn to communicate with the probe. Sequel to *Star Trek IV: Voyage Home*. Extensive unauthorized changes made to the author's text.

**Other books you might like:**
Diane Duane, *Doctor's Orders*, 1990
Barbara Hambly, *Ishmael*, 1985
Janet Kagan, *Uhura's Song*, 1985
Vonda N. McIntyre, *Star Trek IV: The Voyage Home*, 1986
V.E. Mitchell, *Enemy Unseen*, 1990
Peter Morwood, *Rules of Engagement*, 1990

## 570

### JAY R. BONANSINGA

## *The Black Mariah*

(New York: Warner, 1994)

**Story type:** Horror (Curse)

**Major character(s):** Lucas Hynde, Truck Driver; Sophie Cohen, Truck Driver; Vanessa DeGeaux, Aged Person
**Time period(s):** 1990s (1994)
**Locale(s):** Georgia; Tennessee

**Summary:** Lucas Hynde and Sophie Cohen are unsuccessful in their efforts to help refuel a car in transit driven by someone who claims he has been cursed by a voodoo practitioner to keep his car in motion. When the driver dies of spontaneous combustion after his car runs out of fuel, the curse is passed to Lucas and Sophie. This variation on the legend of the Flying Dutchman is the author's first novel.

**Other books you might like:**
Eric Flanders, *Night Blood*, 1993
Ray Garton, *Lot Lizards*, 1991
Billie Sue Mosiman, *Night Cruise*, 1993
Stephen Wright, *Going Native*, 1994

### 571

### JAY R. BONANSINGA

## Sick

(New York: Warner, 1995)

**Story type:** Horror (Wild Talents)
**Major character(s):** Sarah Brandis, Dancer (exotic); Henry Decker, Psychologist; Frank Moon, Detective—Police
**Time period(s):** 1990s (1995)
**Locale(s):** Chicago, Illinois

**Summary:** Sarah Brandis's visualization technique for dealing with her rage and anger give her a means for focusing her emotions into a power that transforms her physically into a vicious avenger against her supposed persecutors.

**Other books you might like:**
Paddy Chayefsky, *Altered States*, 1972
Douglas Clegg, *Dark of the Eye*, 1994
Dean R. Koontz, *Dragon Tears*, 1993

### 572

### ALICE BORCHARDT

## The Silver Wolf

(New York: Del Rey, 1998)

**Story type:** Horror (Werewolf Story)
**Major character(s):** Regeane, Werewolf; Maenial, Military Personnel (soldier); Hadrian, Religious (pope)
**Time period(s):** 8th century
**Locale(s):** Rome, Italy

**Summary:** Historical werewolf novel set at the decline of the Roman Empire. Regeane, a shapeshifter distantly related to King Charlemagne, attempts to keep her supernatural powers concealed, even as she becomes embroiled in intrigues that require her to use them to her advantage to save family and friends from the schemes of the domineering Lombards.

**Other books you might like:**
Donna Boyd, *The Passion*, 1998
Guy Endore, *The Werewolf of Paris*, 1933
Tanith Lee, *Heart-Beast*, 1993
Pat Murphy, *Nadya: The Wolf Chronicles*, 1996
Lucius Shepard, *The Golden*, 1993

### 573

### JORGE LUIS BORGES

## Collected Fictions

(New York: Viking, 1998)

**Story type:** Horror (Collection)

**Summary:** This is an omnibus collection of short fiction by an influential Latin American author. A significant number are fantasies, dark and light, invested with metaphysical ruminations, including "Tlon, Uqbar, Orbis Tertius," in which the juxtaposition of a mirror and an encyclopedia reveals an alien world; "Funes the Memorious," in which a man is literally suffocated by the weight of his memories; and the Lovecraftian tale "The Circular Ruins." Translated by Andrew Hurley.

**Other books you might like:**
Stefan Grabinski, *The Dark Domain*, 1994
Franz Kafka, *Stories, 1904-1924*, 1981
Thomas Ligotti, *The Nightmare Factory*, 1997
Bruno Schulz, *Sanatorium under the Sign of the Hourglass*, 1937

### 574

### WILLIAM BORNEFELD

## Time and Light

(Clarkston, Georgia: White Wolf Borealis, 1996)

**Story type:** Science Fiction (Dystopian; Post-Holocaust)
**Major character(s):** Noreen, Scientist; Martine, Girlfriend; Hayes, Scientist, Administrator
**Time period(s):** Indeterminate Future
**Locale(s):** Fullerton, Fictional City; Outside, Fictional Country

**Summary:** The Family of Man, the remnants of the human race, live in a beautiful city in the center of a radioactive wastleland. One day Dr. Noreen goes outside for samples and discovers an empty, but living, world. In the Outside, he finds some photographs that unhinge his life, leading him to question everything. Includes an essay by the author discussing the specific photographic images.

**Other books you might like:**
Aldous Huxley, *Brave New World*, 1932
Walter M. Miller Jr., *A Canticle for Leibowitz*, 1960
William F. Nolan, *Logan's Run*, 1967
    George Clayton Johnson, co-author
Charles Oberndorf, *Sheltered Lives*, 1992
George Orwell, *1984*, 1949

### 575

### DOUGLAS BORTON

## Deathsong

(New York: NAL Onyx, 1989)

**Story type:** Horror (Ancient Evil Unleashed)
**Major character(s):** Billy Lee Kidd, Singer (country music); Kuruk, Cult Member (high priest of Antarok cult)
**Time period(s):** 1980s
**Locale(s):** Los Angeles, California
**Summary:** Billy Lee is granted the dubious gift of singing the "Deathsong" that opens the Door for the dark forces of Antarok. But she also has the power to close the Door and save the world if she can find and use it in time—and before she, herself, is sacrificed to Antarok.

**Other books you might like:**
George R.R. Martin, *The Armageddon Rag*, 1983
Anne Rice, *The Queen of the Damned*, 1988

### 576

#### DOUGLAS BORTON

## *Kane*

(New York: Onyx, 1990)

**Story type:** Horror (Serial Killer; Psychological Suspense)
**Major character(s):** Kane, Murderer; Bill Needham, Businessman (service-station owner)
**Time period(s):** 1990s (1990)
**Locale(s):** Tuskett, California

**Summary:** One warm summer evening, a mysterious man named Kane walks into Tuskett, California, an aging, decaying small town at the edge of the Mojave desert. Indestructible, inexplicable, possessed of extreme strength and the ability to hypnotize, the black-clad stranger intends, for reasons known only to him, to destroy the entire population of Tuskett—23 people—in one long night.

**Other books you might like:**
Robert Bloch, *Psycho*, 1959
Stephen King, *The Dark Tower: The Gunslinger*, 1982
Robert R. McCammon, *Stinger*, 1988

### 577

#### DOUGLAS BORTON

## *Shadow Dance*

(New York: Signet, 1991)

**Story type:** Horror (Ancient Evil Unleashed)
**Major character(s):** Timothy Cutter, Child; Rachel Weiss, Psychologist; Robert Thorn, Drifter
**Time period(s):** 1990s
**Locale(s):** Los Angeles, California

**Summary:** No one believes Timothy Cutter when he tells them that his parents were killed by the Runa, an ancient disembodied force that claims people sensitive to its presence for its own. But now the Runa has taken over Robert Thorn, who will stop at nothing to find Timothy.

**Other books you might like:**
G. Wayne Miller, *Thunder Rise*, 1988

### 578

#### BRUCE BOSTON

## *Dark Tales and Light*

(Concord, California: Dark Regions, 1998)

**Story type:** Horror (Collection)

**Summary:** Included here are ten tales of horror, fantasy and science fiction by a distinguished poet. "Anesthesia Man" is related as a series of nightmares experienced by a man undergoing surgery, and "On Spending the Night Alone in a Haunted House: A User's Guide" as a disarmingly clinical set of instructions on how to behave while being frightened to death by an encounter with supernatural phenomena. The book is anchored by a triptych—"Curse of the Simulacrum's Wife," "Curse of the Hypnotist's Wife" and "Curse of the Cyberhead's Wife"—which deploy the tropes of fantastic literature as a vehicle for exploring marital estrangement and disaffection.

**Other books you might like:**
Kevin J. Anderson, *Shifting the Boundaries: The Selected Works of Kevin J. Anderson*, 1990
Paul Di Filippo, *Ribofunk*, 1996
J.W. Donnelly, *Babylon Gardens*, 1998
Neil Gaiman, *Smoke and Mirrors*, 1998
Ardath Mayhar, *Mean Little Old Lady at Work*, 1993

### 579

#### ANTHONY BOUCHER

## *The Compleat Werewolf and Other Tales of Fantasy and Science Fiction*

(New York: Carroll and Graf, 1990)

**Story type:** Horror (Collection)

**Summary:** Title novella and nine short stories first published between 1941 and 1945 that mix horror, humor, and fantasy. Especially notable are the title novella about a college professor who acquires the power to exploit his previously hidden wereworlf tendencies, "We Print the Truth," about a newspaper owner who must face unexpected consequences when his casual wish to always print "only the truth" is granted, and "The Ghost of Me," in which the ghost of a murder victim returns too soon—before the murder has been committed.

**Other books you might like:**
Charles Beaumont, *Charles Beaumont: Selected Stories*, 1988

### 580

#### ALINE BOUCHER-KAPLAN

## *World Spirits*

(New York: Baen, 1991)

**Story type:** Science Fiction (Theological; Political)
**Series:** Khyren
**Major character(s):** Raunn ni Obradi san Derrith, Agent; Verrer ni Rimmani san Derrith, Alien (Tulkan); Auriel Tarz, Trader, Agent
**Time period(s):** Indeterminate Future
**Locale(s):** Chennidur, Planet—Imaginary

**Summary:** Chennidur is an enigma to the interstellar Trading Family which has its contract. Auriel il Tarz is sent to learn about the locals who believe technological devices to be evil and against the religion which is so important there. Auriel meets Raunn who is in a position to introduce her to clan society where she witnesses some of the detrimental effects of the spacer's imports.

**Other books you might like:**
Emma Bull, *Falcon*, 1989
Mary Gentle, *Golden Witchbreed*, 1984
Frank Herbert, *Dune*, 1965
Rosemary Kirstein, *The Steerswoman*, 1989
Ursula K. Le Guin, *The Word for World Is Forest*, 1972
Steve Perry, *The 97th Step*, 1989
Joan Slonczewski, *A Door into Ocean*, 1986

## 581
### BEN BOVA
## *Brothers*
(New York: Bantam, 1996)

**Story type:** Science Fiction (Medical)
**Major character(s):** Arthur Marshak, Doctor, Researcher; Jessie Marshak, Doctor; Julia Marshak, Spouse
**Time period(s):** 1990s
**Locale(s):** Washington, District of Columbia

**Summary:** Brothers Arthur and Jessie Marshak take opposite sides in a nationally-publicized argument over whether controvesial medical experiments, using cancer to regenerate organs within the body, should continue.

**Other books you might like:**
Robin Cook, *Godplayer*, 1983
Michael Crichton, *Jurassic Park*, 1990
Michael Crichton, *The Terminal Man*, 1972
James Gunn, *The Immortals*, 1962
Linda Nagata, *Tech-Heaven*, 1995

## 582
### BEN BOVA
## *Cyberbooks*
(New York: Tor, 1989)

**Story type:** Science Fiction (Humor)
**Major character(s):** Carl Lewis, Inventor; Scarlet Dean, Editor
**Time period(s):** 1980s
**Locale(s):** New York, New York

**Summary:** An inventor attempts to interest a major publisher in his revolutionary new electronic book. Meanwhile, a variety of odd and amusing characters attempt to steal or buy it.

**Other books you might like:**
Frederik Pohl, *The Coming of the Quantum Cats*, 1986
Spider Robinson, *Callahan's Crosstime Saloon*, 1977
Kate Wilhelm, *Crazy Time*, 1988

## 583
### BEN BOVA
## *Death Dream*
(New York: Bantam, 1994)

**Story type:** Science Fiction (Cyberpunk; Techno-Thriller)
**Major character(s):** Dan Santorini, Computer Expert, Engineer; Jason Lowrey, Inventor, Genius; Angie Santorini, Child
**Time period(s):** 21st century
**Locale(s):** Florida; Virtual Reality, Cyberspace

**Summary:** Dan Santorini accepts a job with ParaReality, Inc., to create the virtual reality theme park, Cyber World, with his old friend, Jason Lowrey, a wizard in creating cyberspace reality. Disaster among program uses, a threat to Dan's daughter from a co-worker and sabotage to the theme park bring Dan and Jason into direct conflict.

**Other books you might like:**
Piers Anthony, *Killobyte*, 1993
Greg Bear, *Queen of Angels*, 1990
Edmund Cooper, *Prisoner of Fire*, 1976
Alan Dean Foster, *The I Inside*, 1984

Stephen Goldin, *And Not Make Dreams Your Master*, 1981
Andrew M. Greeley, *God Game*, 1986
Nancy Kress, *Brain Rose*, 1990
James Morrow, *The Continent of Lies*, 1984
Mack Reynolds, *Perchance to Dream*, 1977
Norman Spinrad, *The Void Captain's Tale*, 1983

## 584
### BEN BOVA
## *Empire Builders*
(New York: Tor, 1993)

**Story type:** Science Fiction (Political)
**Series:** Privateers
**Major character(s):** Dan Randolph, Businessman, Fugitive; Jane Scanwell, Political Figure, Organized Crime Figure; Rafaelo Gaetano, Political Figure, Organized Crime Figure
**Time period(s):** 21st century
**Locale(s):** Earth; Montenegro

**Summary:** When scientists predict that the Greenhouse Effect will rapidly escalate in 10 years, leaders suppress the news until the Global Economic Council formulates a solution. Forced underground because his knowledge presents too great a threat, Dan Randolph teams with some Council members and economic rivals to defeat Rafaelo Gaetano's scheme of Mafia takeover.

**Other books you might like:**
Poul Anderson, *The Psychotechnic League*, 1981
C.J. Cherryh, *Hellburner*, 1992
Barney Cohen, *Blood on the Moon*, 1984
Alan Dean Foster, *The Man Who Used the Universe*, 1983
Alexis A. Gilliland, *The Revolution From Rosinante*, 1981
Donald Kingsbury, *The Moon Goddess and the Son*, 1986
Eric Kotani, *Act of God*, 1985
  John Maddox Roberts, co-author
Mack Reynolds, *Trojan Orbit*, 1985
Allen Steele, *Orbital Decay*, 1989

## 585
### BEN BOVA
## *Future Crime*
(New York: Tor, 1990)

**Story type:** Science Fiction (Collection)
**Time period(s):** Indeterminate Future
**Locale(s):** Earth

**Summary:** Seven short stories and a 1976 novella *City of Darkness* dealing with crime in the future. It ranges from extrapolating current trends to depicting wholly new crimes.

**Other books you might like:**
Isaac Asimov, *Tales of the Black Widowers*, 1974
Larry Niven, *The Long Arm of Gil Hamilton*, 1976
Larry Niven, *N-Space*, 1990
Larry Niven, *Oath of Fealty*, 1981
  Jerry Pournelle, co-author
Larry Niven, *The Patchwork Girl*, 1980
L.A. Taylor, *The Blossom of Erda*, 1986
  pseudonym of Laurie Sparer

## 586

**BEN BOVA**

## Mars

(New York: Bantam Spectra, 1992)

**Story type:** Science Fiction (Political; Hard Science Fiction)
**Major character(s):** James "Jamie" Fox Waterman, Indian (Navaho), Scientist (geologist); Joanna Brumado, Scientist (biologist); Mikhail Andreivitch Vosnesensky, Spaceman, Leader
**Time period(s):** 21st century
**Locale(s):** Earth; Mars

**Summary:** Resented from the beginning, Jamie Waterman wins a position on the first manned Mars expedition only after one man gets sick and another black-balled. When he doesn't follow the script, American politicians fear his becoming too popular. On Mars, Jamie thinks he sees a city in the Vallis Marineris and goes to explore. When the expedition leaves, the team expects follow-up missions.

**Other books you might like:**
Isaac Asimov, *The Martian Way*, 1955
Arthur C. Clarke, *The Sands of Mars*, 1952
D.G. Compton, *Farewell, Earth's Bliss*, 1971
Philip K. Dick, *Martian Time-Slip*, 1964
Gordon R. Dickson, *The Far Call*, 1978
Robert A. Heinlein, *Red Planet*, 1949
Sterling E. Lanier, *Menace Under Marwood*, 1983
Frederik Pohl, *Man Plus*, 1976
Kim Stanley Robinson, *Red Mars*, 1993
Allen Steele, *Labyrinth of Night*, 1992
Jack Williamson, *Beachhead*, 1992

## 587

**BEN BOVA**

## Moonrise

(New York: Avon, 1996)

**Story type:** Science Fiction (Political; Hard Science Fiction)
**Major character(s):** Paul Stavenger, Astronaut (retired), Businessman; Joanna Masterson Stavenger, Businesswoman; Douglas Stavenger, Experimental Subject, Teenager
**Time period(s):** 21st century
**Locale(s):** Moonbase, Montenegro; Earth; Outer Space

**Summary:** Privatization of the space program brings the possibility of rapid technological development, if Masterson Aerospace's corporate infighting over Moonbase and anti-technological religious fanatics do not spell disaster for the fragile site.

**Other books you might like:**
Kevin J. Anderson, *Assemblers of Infinity*, 1993
   Doug Beason, co-author
Robert A. Heinlein, *The Moon Is a Harsh Mistress*, 1966
Allen Steele, *Lunar Descent*, 1991
Allen Steele, *The Tranquility Alternative*, 1996
John Varley, *Steel Beach*, 1992

## 588

**BEN BOVA**

## Moonwar

(New York: Avon Eos, 1998)

**Story type:** Science Fiction (Space Colony; Military)

**Major character(s):** Douglas Stavenger, Leader, Genetically Altered Being; Georges Henri Faure, Diplomat (U.N. Secretary General); Edith Elgin, Journalist
**Time period(s):** 21st century
**Locale(s):** Montenegro; Georgia

**Summary:** U.N. Secretary General Faure wants to use Earth's anger at the use of nanotechnology on the moon to gain absolute domination over Earth. Determined to survive, Moonbase sees itself as the only forward looking society in existence. Since religious fanatics would target Lunar residents if they returned to Earth, to stay free they must defeat all of Earth.

**Other books you might like:**
Kevin J. Anderson, *Assemblers of Infinity*, 1993
   Doug Beason, co-author
Greg Bear, *Heads*, 1991
Barney Cohen, *Blood on the Moon*, 1984
John M. Ford, *Growing Up Weightless*, 1993
Robert A. Heinlein, *The Moon Is a Harsh Mistress*, 1966
Donald Kingsbury, *The Moon Goddess and the Son*, 1986
Mack Reynolds, *Trojan Orbit*, 1985
Allen Steele, *Lunar Descent*, 1991

## 589

**BEN BOVA**

## Orion Among the Stars

(New York: Tor, 1995)

**Story type:** Science Fiction (Military; Immortality)
**Series:** Orion
**Major character(s):** Orion, Immortal, Warrior; Aten, Immortal; Frede, Military Personnel, Health Care Professional (medic)
**Time period(s):** Indeterminate Future
**Locale(s):** Lunga, Planet—Imaginary; Loris, Planet—Imaginary

**Summary:** Orion awakens in the far future where he and a team of professional soldiers must take and hold a planet for the Commonwealth, at war with the Hegemony. On Lunga, ancient marine dwellers who deplore humankind's bellicosity contact Orion in hopes of stopping the space/time disruptions which threaten everyone's existence.

**Other books you might like:**
Roger MacBride Allen, *The Torch of Honor*, 1985
John Dalmas, *The Regiment*, 1987
Gordon R. Dickson, *Dorsai!*, 1976
Stephen Goldin, *The Eternity Brigade*, 1980
Joe Haldeman, *The Forever War*, 1975
Robert A. Heinlein, *Starship Troopers*, 1959
Joel Rosenberg, *Not for Glory*, 1988
Timothy Zahn, *Cobra*, 1985

## 590

**BEN BOVA**

## Orion and the Conqueror

(New York: Tor, 1994)

**Story type:** Science Fiction (Alternate Universe; Fantasy)
**Series:** Orion
**Major character(s):** Orion, Immortal, Warrior; Hera, Immortal, Deity; Philip of Macedon, Ruler, Historical Figure
**Time period(s):** 4th century B.C.
**Locale(s):** Macedonia; Athens, Greece

**Summary:** Arriving in Macedonia without knowledge of his past, Orion becomes part of a complicated plot among Philip of Macedon, his wife and his son, who is impatient to inherit the throne. When his memory slowly returns, Orion wants to find Anya but must obey Hera and Aten, who plan Philip's assassination.

**Other books you might like:**
Poul Anderson, *The Boat of a Million Years*, 1989
Piers Anthony, *Steppe*, 1985
Greg Bear, *Eternity*, 1988
Raymond Harris, *The Schizogenic Man*, 1990
Crawford Kilian, *Rogue Emperor*, 1988
Fritz Leiber, *The Big Time*, 1961
Kirk Mitchell, *Procurator*, 1984
Melissa Scott, *A Choice of Destinies*, 1986
Roger Zelazny, *Roadmarks*, 1979

---

**591**

**BEN BOVA**

## Orion in the Dying Time

(New York: Tor, 1990)

**Story type:** Science Fiction (Science Fantasy; Theological)
**Series:** Orion
**Major character(s):** Orion, Immortal, Warrior; Anya, Warrior; Set, Alien
**Time period(s):** 80th century B.C.
**Locale(s):** Shaydan, Egypt (ancient)

**Summary:** In prehistoric Egypt, Orion and Anya encounter dinosaurs who rule humans. In trying to unite them, he causes a holocaust that allows Set to colonize the area with Shaydanians, reptilian beings. Then with the aid of Aten, a being evolved beyond man, Orion leads Subotai and his mongol horde back through time to Egypt where they rout the Shaydanians. Before returning to stasis, Orion learns that Aten is man's enemy as well as that of the Shaydanians and has other dastardly plots in reserve.

**Other books you might like:**
Poul Anderson, *The Boat of a Million Years*, 1989
Michael Crichton, *Jurassic Park*, 1990
Harry Harrison, *Return to Eden*, 1988
Harry Harrison, *West of Eden*, 1984
Harry Harrison, *Winter in Eden*, 1986
Roger Zelazny, *Lord of Light*, 1967

---

**592**

**BEN BOVA**

## Sam Gunn Forever

(New York: Avon Eos, 1998)

**Story type:** Science Fiction (Collection)
**Major character(s):** Sam Gunn, Astronaut (former)

**Summary:** This collection consists of five of the adventures of Sam Gunn, ex-astronaut, who tries his hand at a series of jobs, and succeeds after a fashion in each. This is the second volume of his adventures, presenting stories published between 1994 and 1997.

**Other books you might like:**
Poul Anderson, *Kingship with the Stars*, 1991
David Brin, *Otherness*, 1994
Algis Budrys, *Michaelmas*, 1978
Isidore Haiblum, *Out of Sync*, 1990
Keith Laumer, *Nine by Laumer*, 1967

---

**593**

**BEN BOVA**

## Sam Gunn, Unlimited

(New York: Bantam Spectra, 1993)

**Story type:** Science Fiction (Collection)
**Major character(s):** Sam Gunn, Businessman; Jane "Jade" Avril Inconnu, Journalist
**Time period(s):** Indeterminate Future
**Locale(s):** Space Station; Asteroid Belt, Outer Space

**Summary:** Fascinated as a youth by tales about the famous entrepreneur Sam Gunn, Jade locates Sam's acquaintances and records events in Sam's adult life as seen by those who had known him. Much new material with some stories reprinted from 1980s and 1990s periodicals.

**Other books you might like:**
Poul Anderson, *Harvest of Stars*, 1993
Robert L. Forward, *Timemaster*, 1992
Robert A. Heinlein, *The Man Who Sold the Moon*, 1950
Frederik Pohl, *The Space Merchants*, 1953
    C.M. Kornbluth, co-author
L. Neil Smith, *The Nagasaki Vector*, 1983
L. Neil Smith, *Tom Paine Maru*, 1984
L. Neil Smith, *The Venus Belt*, 1983
F. Paul Wilson, *The LaNague Chronicles*, 1992

---

**594**

**BEN BOVA**

## Star Brothers

(New York: Tor, 1990)

**Story type:** Science Fiction (Science Fiction)
**Series:** Voyagers
**Major character(s):** Keith Stoner, Astronaut, Hero; Jo Camerata, Industrialist
**Time period(s):** 21st century
**Locale(s):** Earth; Montenegro

**Summary:** Former astronaut Keith Stoner, the first man to live through cryonic sleep and the first man to meet an alien, draws upon his alien friend's powers in a desperate effort to save the world from political chaos and a plague that could destroy all life on Earth.

**Other books you might like:**
Octavia E. Butler, *Dawn*, 1987
Arthur C. Clarke, *Childhood's End*, 1953
Damon Knight, *CV*, 1987
Damon Knight, *The Observers*, 1988

---

**595**

**BEN BOVA**
**A.J. AUSTIN**, Co-Author

## To Fear the Light

(New York: Tor, 1994)

**Story type:** Science Fiction (Political; First Contact)
**Series:** To Save the Sun
**Major character(s):** Adela de Montgarde, Scientist; Jephthah, Activist (rabble rouser); Ettalira, Alien (Gatanni), Explorer
**Time period(s):** Indeterminate Future
**Locale(s):** Earth; Tsing IV, Planet—Imaginary

**Summary:** Awakened after two centuries in cryosleep to oversee the end of her project to save Earth's sun, the dismayed Adela de Montgarde finds xenophobia, particularly against the Sarpan, whipped up by Jephthah using untraceable transmissions. After the discovery of intelligent life on another planet, Jephthah plots to murder the scouting party and imperial family who travel to the system.

**Other books you might like:**
John Brunner, *A Maze of Stars*, 1991
Gordon R. Dickson, *None but Man*, 1969
Ursula K. Le Guin, *Planet of Exile*, 1966
Chad Oliver, *Unearthly Neighbors*, 1960
Mike Resnick, *Second Contact*, 1990
James H. Schmitz, *The Demon Breed*, 1968

**596**

**BEN BOVA**
**A.J. AUSTIN**, Co-Author

## To Save the Sun
(New York: Tor, 1992)

**Story type:** Science Fiction (Science Fiction)
**Major character(s):** Nicholas, Royalty (Emperor of the Hundred Worlds); Adela de Montgarde, Scientist; Javas, Royalty (Prince of the Hundred Worlds)
**Time period(s):** Indeterminate Future
**Locale(s):** Corinth, Planet—Imaginary; Luna, Montenegro; Hundred Worlds, Interstellar Empire/Federation

**Summary:** Adela convinces Nicholas that he can save the sun and leave Earth's population in place to continue as a genetic baseline to control genetic drift in the Hundred Worlds. Important individuals in the government disapprove of the plan as expensive, surrealistic and unnecessary for their goals. Nicholas moves the government to Earth's moon, giving the project his strong support and arranging the event of his death to promote the success of the project.

**Other books you might like:**
Stephen Baxter, *Raft*, 1992
David Brin, *Earth*, 1990
Gregory Feeley, *The Oxygen Barons*, 1990
Michael Flynn, *In the Country of the Blind*, 1990
Robert L. Forward, *Martian Rainbow*, 1991
Larry Niven, *Protector*, 1973
Allen Steele, *Lunar Descent*, 1991

**597**

**BEN BOVA**
**BILL POGUE**, Co-Author

## The Trikon Deception
(New York: Tor, 1992)

**Story type:** Science Fiction (Techno-Thriller)
**Major character(s):** Hugh O'Donnell, Scientist; Dan Tighe, Leader; Lance Muncie, Spaceman
**Time period(s):** 1990s (1998)
**Locale(s):** Trikon Station, Space Station; United States

**Summary:** Trikon, a space station funded by North America, Japan, and United Europe, has been designed as a risk-free environment for controversial genetic experiments. When Trikon's survival becomes threatened by espionage and sabotage, Hugh O'Donnell must save the space station from the sabotage he stands accused of.

**Other books you might like:**
Roger MacBride Allen, *The Ring of Charon*, 1990
Gordon R. Dickson, *The Far Call*, 1978
James P. Hogan, *Endgame Enigma*, 1987
Larry Niven, *Fallen Angels*, 1991
    Jerry Pournelle and Michael Flynn, co-authors
Allen Steele, *Lunar Descent*, 1991
Allen Steele, *Orbital Decay*, 1989
Walter Jon Williams, *Voice of the Whirlwind*, 1987

**598**

**BEN BOVA**

## Triumph
(New York: Tor, 1993)

**Story type:** Science Fiction (Alternate Universe; Political)
**Major character(s):** Winston Churchill, Historical Figure, Political Figure; Franklin Delano Roosevelt, Historical Figure, Political Figure; Adolf Hitler, Historical Figure, Political Figure
**Time period(s):** 1940s (April 1945)
**Locale(s):** London, England; Berlin, Germany; Moscow, Union of Soviet Socialist Republics

**Summary:** Fearing Joseph Stalin's post-war influence, Winston Churchill plots to poison Stalin with plutonium.

**Other books you might like:**
Len Deighton, *SS-GB*, 1978
Philip K. Dick, *The Man in the High Castle*, 1962
Michael Flynn, *In the Country of the Blind*, 1990
Robert Harris, *Fatherland*, 1992
Fritz Leiber, *The Big Time*, 1961
Harry Turtledove, *The Guns of the South: A Novel of the Civil War*, 1992

**599**

**'ASTA BOWEN**

## Hungry for Home: A Wolf Odyssey
(New York: Simon & Schuster, 1997)

**Story type:** Fantasy (Adventure)
**Major character(s):** Marta, Animal (wolf), Leader; Calef, Animal (wolf); Oldtooth, Animal (wolf)
**Time period(s):** 1990s
**Locale(s):** Montana

**Summary:** "Rescued" from her chosen home in the Montana Rockies, Marta and her pack face many dangers. Food for the wolves, including three pups, would be problem enough without having to face the residents of the new place, the bears. Marta braves unknown territory including roads and cars to walk the hundreds of miles home.

**Other books you might like:**
Richard Adams, *Watership Down*, 1974
Brian Jacques, *Redwall*, 1986
Garry Kilworth, *The Foxes of Firstdark*, 1990
Sherwood Smith, *Wren to the Rescue*, 1990
Tad Williams, *Tailchaser's Song*, 1985

## 600

### GARY BOWEN

## *Diary of a Vampire*

(New York: Rhinoceros, 1995)

**Story type:** Horror (Vampire Story)
**Major character(s):** Rafael Guitierrez, Vampire; Michael Duran, Artist; James Flannagan, Businessman
**Time period(s):** 1990s (1991)
**Locale(s):** Baltimore, Maryland

**Summary:** Rafael, a vampire much older than his youthful appearance would indicate, awakens in the 1990s after a 15-year sleep and begins adjusting to a world that the AIDS virus and various political, social, and political changes have made vastly different from the world he used to know. This erotic tale is the author's first novel.

**Other books you might like:**
Poppy Z. Brite, *Lost Souls*, 1993
Nancy A. Collins, *Sunglasses After Dark*, 1990
John Peyton Cooke, *Out for Blood*, 1991
Mark Ivanhoe, *Virgintooth*, 1991
Jonathan Nasaw, *The World on Blood*, 1996
Anne Rice, *The Vampire Lestat*, 1985

## 601

### MARJORIE BOWEN

## *Twilight and Other Supernatural Romances*

(Ashcroft, British Columbia: Ash-Tree Press, 1998)

**Story type:** Horror (Collection)

**Summary:** Included here are 17 little-known tales of horror and fantasy by a distinguished writer of the Edwardian era. Selections include ''The Fair Hair of Ambrosine,'' a tale of precognition; the ghost story ''Madame Spitfire''; and two previously uncollected stories, ''The Recluse and Springtime'' and ''Vigil.'' With a preface by the author's son, Hilary Long, and an introduction by Jessica Amanda Salmonson, who edited the book.

**Other books you might like:**
Cynthia Asquith, *This Mortal Coil*, 1947
Elizabeth Bowen, *The Demon Lover and Other Stories*, 1945
Ellen Glasgow, *The Shadowy Third and Other Stories*, 1923
Margery Lawrence, *Number Seven, Queer Street*, 1945
May Sinclair, *The Intercessor and Other Stories*, 1931

## 602

### DAVID BOWKER

## *The Death Prayer*

(Clarkston, Georgia: White Wolf, 1996)

**Story type:** Horror (Black Magic)
**Major character(s):** Vernon Laverne, Police Officer (detective superintendant); Lyn Savage, Detective—Police; Hugo Prince, Religious (black magic priest)
**Time period(s):** 1990s (1995)

**Summary:** A series of killings improbably committed by the risen dead points to Hugo Prince, leader of the cultish Quest for the Higher Self, and a Kahuna who kills his enemies by simply uttering the death prayer. In the course of his investigations of Prince, Detective Superintendant Vernon Laverne discovers that he has latent psychic

talents that can put a stop to Prince's evil. The novel was first published in England in 1995.

**Other books you might like:**
Garry Kilworth, *Angel*, 1993
Dean R. Koontz, *The Bad Place*, 1990
Stephen Laws, *Macabre*, 1994
Graham Masterton, *Burial*, 1994
Guy N. Smith, *The Black Fedora*, 1991

## 603

### DONNA BOYD

## *The Passion*

(New York: Avon, 1998)

**Story type:** Horror (Werewolf Story)
**Major character(s):** Alexander Devoncroix, Werewolf; Denis Antonov, Werewolf; Tessa LeGuerre, Maintenance Worker (chambermaid)
**Time period(s):** 1990s (1998); 1890s
**Locale(s):** New York, New York; Paris, France; Lyons, France

**Summary:** The brutal murders of several werewolves in contemporary New York by a rare human-werewolf hybrid inspires werewolf elder Alexander Devoncroix to tell the story of his rivalry a century before with his brother Denis, leader of the Siberian-based Dark Brotherhood, whose objective is to eliminate human beings from the face of the Earth. Denis's plans to marry werewolf princess Elise Devoncroix to further his scheme are thwarted by Tessa LeGuerre, a human and mutual love interest of Alexander and Denis, who will lead him into exile from the werewolf clan in Alaska. A first novel, and probable beginning of a series.

**Other books you might like:**
Guy Endore, *The Werewolf of Paris*, 1933
Tanith Lee, *Heart-Beast*, 1993
Lucius Shepard, *The Golden*, 1993
S.P. Somtow, *Moon Dance*, 1990
Jack Williamson, *Darker than You Think*, 1948

## 604

### ELIZABETH H. BOYER

## *The Clan of the Warlord*

(New York: Ballantine Del Rey, 1992)

**Story type:** Fantasy (Quest; Magic Conflict)
**Major character(s):** Mistislaus, Wizard; Skylda ''Skyla'', Orphan, Witch; Guthrum, Mythical Creature (dwarf)
**Time period(s):** Indeterminate
**Locale(s):** Fairholm, Fictional Country; Rangfara, Fictional Country

**Summary:** After Rangfara falls to the Krypplinger, a peasant brings the infant Skyla to Mistislaus, who recognizes her abilities as a witch almost immediately. Before long Skyla dresses like a boy and spends much of her time in the woods. Many people, including a pack of wild boys, escaped slaves who could be her cousins, believe Skyla can lead them to the lost treasure of her forebears.

**Other books you might like:**
Jo Clayton, *Wild Magic*, 1991
Louise Cooper, *The Pretender*, 1991
C.S. Friedman, *Black Sun Rising*, 1991
Melanie Rawn, *The Star Scroll*, 1989
Michelle Sagara, *Into the Dark Lands*, 1991
R.A. Salvatore, *Sojourn*, 1991
Elizabeth Ann Scarborough, *Phantom Banjo*, 1991

## 605

### ELIZABETH H. BOYER

## *The Dragon's Carbuncle*
(New York: Ballantine/Del Rey, 1990)

**Story type:** Fantasy (Sword and Sorcery; Legend)
**Series:** Wizard's War
**Major character(s):** Leifr, Adventurer; Thurid, Wizard
**Time period(s):** Indeterminate Past
**Locale(s):** Djofullhol, Scandinavia

**Summary:** Misfit Leifr, a Scipling in Alfar must try to rescue his friend Thurid from the Fire Wizards' Inquistion, and Ljosa, his beloved who is held by his old enemy Sorkvir. With the help of his Rhbu sword, Endalaus Daudi, Leifr faces seemingly impossible tasks.

**Other books you might like:**
Mayer Alan Brenner, *Catastrophe's Spell*, 1989
Suzy McKee Charnas, *The Golden Thread*, 1989
Glen Cook, *Tower of Fear*, 1989
Diane Duane, *High Wizardry*, 1989
Peni R. Griffin, *Otto From Otherwhere*, 1990
Jane Resh Thomas, *The Princess in the Pigpen*, 1989

## 606

### ROBERT H. BOYER, Editor
### KENNETH J. ZAHORSKI, Co-Editor

## *Visions & Imaginings: Classic Fantasy Fiction*
(Chicago: Academy Chicago, 1992)

**Story type:** Fantasy (Anthology)

**Summary:** Recollects 17 of the best stories from the editors' five anthologies published 1977-1981 which presented classic fantasy stories by prominent writers from the past 150 years. The stories chosen include Joan Aiken's ''The Harp of Fishbones,'' Lloyd Alexander's ''The Foundling,'' Peter S. Beagle's ''Lila the Werewolf,'' Lord Dunsany's ''The Bridge of the Man-Horse,'' Ursula K. Le Guin's ''April in Paris,'' George MacDonald's ''The Light Princess,'' Kenneth Morris' ''Red Peach Blossom Inlet,'' Frank Stockton's ''The Accomodating Circumstance,'' Evangeline Walton Ensley's ''The Mistress of Kaer-Mor'' and T.H. White's ''The Troll.''

**Other books you might like:**
Lin Carter, *Discoveries in Fantasy*, 1972
　editor
Lin Carter, *Golden Cities, Far*, 1970
　editor
Lin Carter, *Great Short Novels of Adult Fantasy 1*, 1972
　editor
Lin Carter, *Great Short Novels of Adult Fantasy 2*, 1973
　editor
Lin Carter, *New Worlds for Old*, 1971
　editor
Lester Del Rey, *Once upon a Time: A Treasury of Modern Fairy Tales*, 1991
　Risa Kessler, co-editor
Martin H. Greenberg, *After the King: Stories in Honor of J.R.R. Tolkien*, 1992
　editor

## 607

### STEVEN R. BOYETT

## *Treks Not Taken: What if Stephen King, Anne Rice, Bret Easton Ellis, and Other Literary Greats Had Written Episodes of Star Trek: The Next Generation?*
(Burbank, California: Sneaker Press/Midnight Graffiti Press, 1996)

**Story type:** Science Fiction (Collection; Parody)
**Major character(s):** Jean-Alex Pickhard, Spaceship Captain; Datum, Android, Space Explorer; Troi Rogers, Socialite, Spacewoman
**Time period(s):** 24th century
**Locale(s):** *U.S.S. Enterprise*, Spaceship

**Summary:** Contains a six-page introduction and 20 teleplay outlines for ''Star Trek: The Next Generation'' as if written by literary greats including Anthony Burgess, Tom Clancy, Michael Crichton, Joseph Heller, Ernest Hemmingway, Jack Kerouac, Ken Kesey, Stephen King, Herman Melville, Anne Rice, Tom Robbins, J.D. Salinger, Dr. Seuss, and Kurt Vonnegut, Jr.

**Other books you might like:**
Kevin J. Anderson, *War of the Worlds: Global Dispatches*, 1996
　editor
John M. Ford, *How Much for Just the Planet?*, 1987
Randall Garrett, *Takeoff!*, 1979
Randall Garrett, *Takeoff, Too*, 1986
Leah Rewolinski, *Star Wreck: The Generation Gap*, 1990
Leah Rewolinski, *Star Wreck II: The Attack of the Jargonites*, 1991

## 608

### JOSEPHINE BOYLE

## *Holy Terror*
(New York: St. Martin's, 1995)

**Story type:** Horror (Haunted House)
**Major character(s):** Emily Wakelin, Artisan (does embroidery); John Wakelin, Accountant; Lady Abigail Curran, Aged Person
**Time period(s):** 1990s (1993)
**Locale(s):** Little Hocking, England (in Essex)

**Summary:** Emily Wakelin's strange visions and feelings of dread while visiting her next-door neighbors convince her that the legendary ghost who haunts their home is real, and that its manifestations are somehow bound up with her work to help commemorate the martyrdom of a local hero in the sixteenth century. This novel was first published in England in 1993.

**Other books you might like:**
Jonathan Aycliffe, *The Vanishment*, 1993
James P. Blaylock, *Night Relics*, 1994
Bernard Taylor, *Sweetheart, Sweetheart*, 1977

## 609

### RANDALL BOYLL

## *After Sundown*
(New York: Charter, 1989)

**Story type:** Horror (Ghost Story)
**Major character(s):** Mark Butler, Parent (Mormon father); Robin Pruett, Child
**Time period(s):** 1980s

**Locale(s):** Salt Lake City, Utah; Spike Mountain, Utah

**Summary:** Following the death of a Pruett daughter, the two families travel for solace to Spike Mountain only to find themselves isolated and thrust into madness and death as the evil of a violent incident in 1896 is released. This is Boyll's first novel.

**Other books you might like:**
John Christopher, *The Possessors*, 1964
Stephen King, *The Shining*, 1977

---

### 610

### RANDALL BOYLL

## *Chiller*

(New York: Jove, 1992)

**Story type:** Horror (Science Fiction)
**Major character(s):** Peter Kaye, Student—Graduate (in mathematics); Darbi Kaye, Child (Peter's six-year-old daughter); Kim Marden, Hotel Worker
**Time period(s):** 1990s
**Locale(s):** St. Charles, Missouri (and points across America)

**Summary:** Though his daughter Darbi has officially died of cancer, graduate student Peter Kaye packs her scientifically-reanimated body in ice and takes her on a cross-country bankrobbing spree to raise money for her admission to a secret cryogenics clinic in Wyoming.

**Other books you might like:**
Daniel H. Gower, *The Orpheus Process*, 1992
Stephen King, *Firestarter*, 1980

---

### 611

### RANDALL BOYLL

## *Darkman*

(New York: Jove, 1990)

**Story type:** Horror (Science Fiction)
**Major character(s):** Peyton Westlake, Scientist (Darkman); Julie Hastings, Lawyer
**Time period(s):** 1980s
**Locale(s):** Detroit, Michigan (Wayne State University)

**Summary:** Gangsters seeking evidence to local political corruption blow up the laboratory of a scientist who had been developing artificial skin. Grotesquely scarred by the explosion, the scientist establishes a secret laboratory from which he uses his artificial skin, which in sunlight only retains its consistency for 99 minutes, to wreak revenge on the men who destroyed his life. This book is a novelization of the Sam Raimi film, based on the screenplay by Raimi, Chuck Pfarrer, Ivan Raimi, Daniel Goldin, and Joshua Goldin.

**Other books you might like:**
Sean Costello, *Captain Quad*, 1991
Craig Shaw Gardner, *Batman*, 1989
Gaston Leroux, *The Phantom of the Opera*, 1910
H.G. Wells, *The Invisible Man*, 1897

---

### 612

### RANDALL BOYLL

## *Darkman #1: The Hangman*

(New York: Pocket, 1994)

**Story type:** Horror (Mystery)

**Series:** Darkman
**Major character(s):** Peyton Westlake, Scientist (Darkman); Penny Larsen, Secretary—Legal; Danny ''Mouse'' Frakes, Child
**Time period(s):** 1990s (1994)
**Locale(s):** Detroit, Michigan

**Summary:** Disfigured horribly by thugs, Peyton Westlake uses the artificial skin he has developed to walk the streets as a shadowy avenger known as ''Darkman.'' In this first adventure in the series inspired by the 1990 film by Sam Raimi, Darkman fights a street gang run by a latter-day Fagin, who recruits juveniles to do his dirty work.

**Other books you might like:**
Craig Shaw Gardner, *Batman*, 1991
Ric Meyers, *Fear Itself*, 1991
Ric Meyers, *Living Hell*, 1991
Ric Meyers, *Worst Nightmare*, 1992

---

### 613

### RANDALL BOYLL

## *Darkman #2: The Price of Fear*

(New York: Pocket, 1994)

**Story type:** Horror (Mystery)
**Series:** Darkman
**Major character(s):** Peyton Westlake, Scientist (Darkman); Julie Hastings, Lawyer; Martin Clayborne, Businessman (real estate developer)
**Time period(s):** 1990s (1994)
**Locale(s):** Detroit, Michigan

**Summary:** With the help of a synthetic skin he has developed, Peyton Westlake impersonates one of the assailants who brutally disfigured him and infiltrates his gang of thugs. Westlake discovers that the gang has been hired to terrorize citizens of the Eastview Estates development into selling their homes cheaply, and that the mastermind behind it, Martin Clayborne, has engaged the services of Westlake's former fiancee, Julie Hastings, under the pretense that he is trying to help out the Eastview Estates residents. This is the second novel spun off from Sam Raimi's 1990 film, *Darkman*.

**Other books you might like:**
Craig Shaw Gardner, *Batman*, 1991
Ric Meyers, *Fear Itself*, 1991
Ric Meyers, *Living Hell*, 1991
Ric Meyers, *Worst Nightmare*, 1992

---

### 614

### RANDALL BOYLL

## *Darkman #3: The Gods of Hell*

(New York: Pocket, 1994)

**Story type:** Horror (Mystery)
**Series:** Darkman
**Major character(s):** Peyton Westlake, Scientist (Darkman); Norman Hopewell, Religious (evangelist); Edgar P. Fritz, Criminal
**Time period(s):** 1990s (1994)
**Locale(s):** Detroit, Michigan

**Summary:** In his latest adventure, disfigured scientist Peyton Westlake, who has become a master of disguise through his development of synthetic flesh, encounters a fake faith, the Church of Eternal Youth and Beauty, whose guiding prophet ensures his aging congregation of immortality and ageless beauty by extorting exorbitant tithes and permitting them to gang rape virgins abducted for their regular services. Westlake must not only dissolve the church, but find a way to save their newest potential sacrifice, the niece of his former fiancee. This is the third adventure spun off from Sam Raimi's 1990 film *Darkman*.

**Other books you might like:**
Craig Shaw Gardner, *Batman*, 1991
Ric Meyers, *Fear Itself*, 1991
Ric Meyers, *Living Hell*, 1991

### 615

**RANDALL BOYLL**

## *Darkman #4: The Face of Death*

(New York: Pocket, 1995)

**Story type:** Horror (Mystery)
**Series:** Darkman
**Major character(s):** Peyton Westlake, Scientist (Darkman); Harold ''Rondo'' Ferguson, Spy (CIA agent); Jennifer ''Darla'' Dalton, Young Woman
**Time period(s):** 1990s (1995)
**Locale(s):** Detroit, Michigan

**Summary:** Based on the 1990 Sam Raimi film *Darkman*, this is the fourth adventure of Peyton Westlake, a scientist disfigured in a fire set by criminals who uses a short-lived synthetic flesh to restore his normal appearance and fight the criminals whose lives intersect with his. In this novel, Westlake crosses paths with Rondo, a rogue CIA agent with psychopathic tendencies, who hopes to use the synthetic flesh to impersonate the president of the United States and set the country back on the militaristic agenda of the Cold War years.

**Other books you might like:**
Craig Shaw Gardner, *Batman*, 1991
Ric Meyers, *Fear Itself*, 1991
Ric Meyers, *Living Hell*, 1991
Ric Meyers, *Worst Nightmare*, 1992

### 616

**RANDALL BOYLL**

## *Mongster*

(New York: Berkley, 1991)

**Story type:** Horror (Reanimated Dead)
**Major character(s):** Frank ''Weasel'' Whipple, Mechanic (auto); Arnold White, Child (stepson of Frank Whipple); Jack Cumberland, Thief
**Time period(s):** 1990s (1990)
**Locale(s):** Wabash Heights, Indiana

**Summary:** Only young Arnold, a victim of child abuse, knows the whereabouts of the sarcophagus buried beneath his home town—and the magic words that will awaken the creature within to avenge him—in this Stephen King influenced novel. And he needs all the help he can get, for his stepfather and the son of the man from whom the sarcophagus was stolen have joined forces against him.

**Other books you might like:**
David Case, *The Third Grave*, 1981
Charles L. Grant, *The Long Night of the Grave*, 1986
Robert E. Howard, *Skull-Face*, 1946
Stephen King, *It*, 1986
Anne Rice, *The Mummy, or Ramses the Damned*, 1989

### 617

**RANDALL BOYLL**

## *Tales From the Crypt: Demon Knight*

(New York: Pocket, 1995)

**Story type:** Horror (Ancient Evil Unleashed)
**Major character(s):** Silas Brayker, Thief; The Salesman, Demon; Jeryline A. Bascombe, Servant
**Time period(s):** 1990s (1995)
**Locale(s):** Wormwood, New Mexico

**Summary:** The citizens of Wormwood team up with mysterious stranger Silas Brayker to fight a demon horde that has followed him to their town in the hope of retrieving a magic talisman in his possession that will allow the powers of darkness to take over the universe. This book is a novelization of a screenplay by Ethan Reiff, Cyrus Voris and Mark Bishop written for a film spun off from the popular cable television series based on the E.C. comics of the 1950s.

**Other books you might like:**
Joe R. Lansdale, *Dead in the West*, 1986
Robert R. McCammon, *Stinger*, 1988
Christopher Moore, *Practical Demonkeeping*, 1993

### 618

**RAY BRADBURY**
**CHRIS LANE**, Illustrator

## *Ahmed and the Oblivion Machines*

(New York: Avon, 1998)

**Story type:** Fantasy (Young Adult)
**Major character(s):** Ahmed, Child; Gonn-Ben-Allah, Deity
**Time period(s):** Indeterminate Past
**Locale(s):** Middle East

**Summary:** A young boy becomes lost in the desert. His tears awaken an ancient, sleeping god who gives the boy the power of flight. Together the two explore the world.

**Other books you might like:**
Piers Anthony, *Hasan*, 1969
Rick DeMarinis, *Cinder*, 1978
Ian Dennis, *Bagdad*, 1985
Graham Diamond, *Captain Sinbad*, 1980
Judith Gorog, *Winning Scheherazade*, 1991

### 619

**RAY BRADBURY**

## *Death Is a Lonely Business*

(New York: Bantam, 1992)

**Story type:** Horror (Mystery)
**Major character(s):** The Crazy, Writer; Elmo Crumley, Detective—Private; Constance Rattigan, Actress (former)
**Time period(s):** 1940s
**Locale(s):** Venice Beach, California

**Summary:** The narrator, a writer of weird tales known only by his nickname, The Crazy, enlists the aid of a private detective and a fading movie star to help him find out why his grotesque but lovable friends are suddenly dying from unknown causes. This novel was originally published in 1985.

**Other books you might like:**
Robert Bloch, *The Star Stalker*, 1968

William Hjortsberg, *Falling Angel*, 1978

### 620
#### RAY BRADBURY

## A Graveyard for Lunatics
(New York: Knopf, 1990)

**Story type:** Horror (Mystery)
**Major character(s):** Roy Holdstrom, Filmmaker (special effects); Fritz Wong, Director (film director); Manny Leiber, Director (film director)
**Time period(s):** 1950s (1954)
**Locale(s):** Hollywood, California

**Summary:** Hired by Maximus Films to script science fiction movies, the unnamed narrator finds himself caught up in a backlot intrigue that begins when he stumbles upon the corpse of a Hollywood executive supposedly 20 years dead and his friend in the special effects department creates a monster that so disturbs the studio he is fired from his job. This is a sequel to *Death Is a Lonely Business*.

**Other books you might like:**
Robert Bloch, *Psycho II*, 1982
Robert Bloch, *The Star Stalker*, 1968
Jonathan Carroll, *A Child Across the Sky*, 1989

### 621
#### RAY BRADBURY

## The Martian Chronicles
(New York: Doubleday, 1990)

**Story type:** Science Fiction (First Contact; Space Colony)
**Major character(s):** Wilder, Spaceship Captain; Hathaway, Spaceman
**Time period(s):** 20th century; 21st century
**Locale(s):** Mars; Earth

**Summary:** The 40th anniversary hardcover reprint edition of the 1950 classic collection of short stories about the colonization of Mars. War and hardship on Earth have people emigrating to Mars after four ill-fated exploratory expeditions.

**Other books you might like:**
Hal Clement, *Needle*, 1950
Mary Gentle, *Golden Witchbreed*, 1983
Walter Tevis, *The Man Who Fell to Earth*, 1963
Wynne Whiteford, *Lake of the Sun*, 1989
Gene Wolfe, *Endangered Species*, 1989

### 622
#### RAY BRADBURY

## The Martian Chronicles
(New York: Avon, 1997)

**Story type:** Science Fiction (First Contact; Psychic Powers)
**Major character(s):** Jonathan Williams, Spaceship Captain; Ylla K, Alien (Martian), Spouse (wife); Nathaniel York, Spaceship Captain
**Time period(s):** 2030s (2030)
**Locale(s):** Mars (Tyrr)

**Summary:** When Mrs. K dreams about Nathaniel York, a giant from the third planet come to visit Mars, Mr. K goes hunting and the dreams stop. Jonathan Williams tries to convince the Martians that he

and his crew come from Earth and dies in the attempt. Unfortunately, the chicken pox in their blood kills the Martians, leaving the cities empty for the terrans who follow. Reissue of the 1950 edition with a new six-page introduction by Bradbury.

**Other books you might like:**
Philip K. Dick, *Martian Time-Slip*, 1964
Frank Herbert, *Dune*, 1965
Ursula K. Le Guin, *The Word for World Is Forest*, 1976
Ian McDonald, *Desolation Road*, 1988
Elizabeth Moon, *Remnant Population*, 1996

### 623
#### RAY BRADBURY

## The October Country
(New York: Del Rey, 1996)

**Story type:** Horror (Collection)

**Summary:** First published in 1955, this classic collection brings together 19 stories that blur the boundary between supernatural and mainstream fiction. Included are Bradbury's modern reworkings of Gothic horror themes, ''Skeleton'' and ''The Scythe,'' and his poignant tale of a love that endures beyond death, ''The Lake.'' ''The Emissary'' and the vampire tale ''The Man Upstairs'' both feature children whose imaginations endow them with a sensitivity to the dark side of life. ''Uncle Einar'' and ''The Homecoming'' are loosely linked stories concerned with a family of supernatural creatures trying to live unobtrusively as normal human beings. ''The Dwarf,'' ''The Next in Line,'' and ''The Jar'' are stories of psychological suspense in which the emotional needs of characters prove as powerful and dangerous as supernatural forces.

**Other books you might like:**
Charles Beaumont, *Selected Stories*, 1988
Dennis Etchison, *The Dark Country*, 1982
Charles L. Grant, *Tales From the Nightside*, 1981
Shirley Jackson, *The Lottery, or the Adventures of James Harris*, 1949
Richard Matheson, *Collected Stories*, 1989

### 624
#### RAY BRADBURY

## Quicker than the Eye
(New York: Avon, 1996)

**Story type:** Science Fiction (Collection; Fantasy)

**Summary:** Contains nine original and 12 stories reprinted from periodicals and anthologies 1955-1996. Frequently upbeat in tone with a strong sense of setting, the stories' themes include a cross-time encounter, ghosts, time travel, a dystopian future, an Irish tall tale, earthquakes, magic on a submarine, and molecular rejuvenation. A five-page afterword discusses the stories.

**Other books you might like:**
Brian W. Aldiss, *Man in His Time: The Best Science Fiction Stories of Brian W. Aldiss*, 1989
J.G. Ballard, *The Best Short Stories of J.G. Ballard*, 1978
Alfred Bester, *Star Light, Star Bright*, 1976
Nancy Kress, *The Aliens of Earth*, 1993
Henry Kuttner, *The Best of Henry Kuttner*, 1975
Clifford D. Simak, *Skirmish: The Great Short Fiction of Clifford D. Simak*, 1977
John Varley, *Blue Champagne*, 1986
Kurt Vonnegut Jr., *Welcome to the Monkey House*, 1968

## 625

### RAY BRADBURY

## *The Toynbee Convector*

(New York: Bantam Spectra, 1989)

**Story type:** Science Fiction (Collection)

**Summary:** The twenty-three stories contained in this latest collection originally appeared in such magazines as *Omni, Twilight Zone, Gallery*, and *Weird Tales*, as well as the anthology *Dark Forces*. Among the stories included are "On the Orient, North," "At Midnight, in the Month of June," "The Toynbee Convector," "A Touch of Petulance," "The Tombstone," "The Thing at the Top of the Stairs," and "Colonel Stonesteel's Genuine Home-made Truly Egyptian Mummy."

**Other books you might like:**
Robert Bloch, *The Selected Stories of Robert Bloch*, 1988
Harlan Ellison, *Angry Candy*, 1988
George R.R. Martin, *Portraits of His Children*, 1987
Theodore Sturgeon, *A Touch of Sturgeon*, 1987
Gene Wolfe, *Endangered Species*, 1989

## 626

### SCOTT BRADFIELD

## *Dream of the Wolf*

(New York: Knopf, 1990)

**Story type:** Horror (Collection)

**Summary:** The author's first collection brings together 13 stories, most of which are centered around social misfits or outsiders whose alienation induces them to seek escape into fantasy. The best selections include the title story, in which a man's obsessive dreams about life as a wolf begin to interfere with his humdrum daily life, "Ghost Guessed" in which a failed suicide is haunted by the ghost he would have become, and "The Wind Box," in which a man searching for meaning in his life finds that his emotional turmoil causes earthquakes. A shorter version was published in England in 1988 as *The Secret Life of Houses*.

**Other books you might like:**
Ron Hansen, *Nebraska*, 1989
Shirley Jackson, *The Lottery, or the Adventures of James Harris*, 1949
Eric McCormack, *Inspecting the Vaults*, 1987
Ian McEwan, *In between the Sheets*, 1979
Joyce Carol Oates, *Night-Side: Eighteen Tales*, 1980

## 627

### SCOTT BRADFIELD

## *What's Wrong with America*

(New York: St. Martin's, 1994)

**Story type:** Horror (Satire)
**Major character(s):** Emma Delaney O'Hallahan, Widow(er), Abuse Victim; Marvin O'Hallahan, Aged Person; Donald Sullivan, Banker
**Time period(s):** 1990s (1994)
**Locale(s):** Los Angeles, California

**Summary:** After killing her abusive husband, Emma O'Hallahan tries to live a good life but finds herself haunted by his slovenly ghost, nosy neighbors and relatives, and a variety of opportunistic social and political parasites "sympathetic" to her position. Their quirky behaviors sum up the wry title the author has given this subtle satire of life in modern America. This novel was first published in England.

**Other books you might like:**
Thomas M. Disch, *The Businessman: A Tale of Terror*, 1984
Thomas M. Disch, *The M.D.: A Horror Story*, 1991
Thomas M. Disch, *The Priest: A Gothic Romance*, 1994
Patrick McGrath, *The Grotesque*, 1989
Gus Weill, *Flesh*, 1990

## 628

### MARION ZIMMER BRADLEY, Editor

## *The Best of Marion Zimmer Bradley's Fantasy Magazine*

(New York: Warner Aspect, 1994)

**Story type:** Fantasy (Anthology)

**Summary:** Contains a three-page introduction plus individual introductions to 18 stories reprinted from *Marion Zimmer Bradley's Fantasy Magazine* 1988-1991, with one Nebula Award finalist, Mary C. Aldridge's "The Adinkra Cloth." Mercedes Lackey's "Nightside" features the protagonist from her Diana Tregarde series and Phyllis Ann Karr's "The Truth about the Lady of the Lake" features her novels' protagonists, the sorceress Frostflower and the woman warrior Thorn. The tone varies from humorous to dark with themes such as magic conflict, war with extraterrestrials, sword and sorcery and adventure. Other authors include Lynne Armstrong-Jones, Jo Clayton, Tanya Huff, Jacqueline Lichtenberg, Diana L. Paxson, Jennifer Roberson, L.A. Taylor, Elisabeth Waters and Lawrence Watt-Evans.

**Other books you might like:**
Kristine Kathryn Rusch, *The Best of Pulphouse: The Hardback Magazine*, 1991
    editor
Jessica Amanda Salmonson, *Amazons!*, 1979
    editor
Jessica Amanda Salmonson, *Heroic Visions*, 1983
    editor
Pamela Sargent, *Women of Wonder: Science Fiction Stories by Women about Women*, 1975
    editor
Jane Yolen, *Xanadu*, 1993
    editor

## 629

### MARION ZIMMER BRADLEY, Editor
### ELISABETH WATERS, Co-Editor

## *The Best of Marion Zimmer Bradley's Fantasy Magazine, Volume II*

(New York: Warner Aspect, 1995)

**Story type:** Fantasy (Anthology)

**Summary:** Contains a two-page introduction and individual introductions to 15 stories reprinted from *Marion Zimmer Bradley's Fantasy Magazine*. The tone varies from ominous to light with themes such as high fantasy, martial arts, mythical creatures, vampirism, Merlin the Magician, and psychic detection with Dana Tregarde in "Satanic, Versus" by Mercedes Lackey. Other authors include George Barr, Jo Clayton, Janet Kagan, Phyllis Ann Karr, Jennifer Roberson, eluki bes shahar, Brad Strickland, Elisabeth Waters, and Deborah Wheeler.

**Other books you might like:**
Kristine Kathryn Rusch, *The Best From Fantasy & Science Fiction: A 45th Anniversary Anthology*, 1994
  Edward L. Ferman, co-editor
Kristine Kathryn Rusch, *The Best of Pulphouse: The Hardback Magazine*, 1991
  editor
Jessica Amanda Salmonson, *Amazons!*, 1979
  editor
Jessica Amanda Salmonson, *Heroic Visions*, 1979
  editor
A. Susan Williams, *The Lifted Veil: The Book of Fantastic Literature by Women*, 1993
  editor

## 630

**MARION ZIMMER BRADLEY**
**JULIAN MAY**, Co-Author
**ANDRE NORTON**, Co-Author

### Black Trillium

(New York: Doubleday Foundation, 1990)

**Story type:** Fantasy (Quest; Magic Conflict)
**Major character(s):** Haramis, Royalty (princess), Sorceress; Kadiya, Royalty (princess); Anigel, Royalty (princess)
**Time period(s):** Indeterminate
**Locale(s):** Ruwenda, Fictional Country

**Summary:** After their parents are killed by the invading Labornok soldiers, princesses Haramis, Kadiya and Anigel must each seek out a talisman to defeat the Archmage Orogastus and regain the kingdom. On the quest Anigel must overcome her timidity, Kadiya her recklessness and Haramis her arrogance. Working together, they defeat Orogastus. Haramis becomes Archmage, Kadiya ambassador to the Wild Ones and Anigel, who marries Prince Antar of Labornok, becomes queen of both kingdoms.

**Other books you might like:**
Robert Asprin, *Thieves' World*, 1979
Jack L. Chalker, *The River of Dancing Gods*, 1984
Katherine Kurtz, *Deryni Rising*, 1981
Will Shetterly, *Liavek*, 1985
  Emma Bull, co-editor
Clifford D. Simak, *The Fellowship of the Talisman*, 1978
Jack Vance, *Lyonesse*, 1983
Terri Windling, *Borderland*, 1986
  Mark Arnold, co-editor

## 631

**MARION ZIMMER BRADLEY**

### Domains of Darkover

(New York: DAW, 1990)

**Story type:** Science Fiction (Anthology)
**Series:** Darkover
**Time period(s):** Indeterminate Future
**Locale(s):** Darkover, Planet—Imaginary

**Summary:** 17 stories from various times in Darkover history. Both new readers and those familiar with Bradley's universe will enjoy Mercedes Lackey's story, "An Object Lesson," about the Free Amazons of Darkover. Dorothy J. Heydt also submitted a strong mystery story, "Death in Thendara."

**Other books you might like:**
C.J. Cherryh, *Angel with the Sword*, 1985
C.J. Cherryh, *The Faded Sun: Kesrith*, 1978
L. Sprague de Camp, *The Hand of Zei*, 1963
Stephen Goldin, *Jade Darcy and the Affair of Honor*, 1988
Elizabeth Moon, *Sheepfarmer's Daughter*, 1988
Jack Vance, *City of the Chasch*, 1968

## 632

**MARION ZIMMER BRADLEY**

### Exile's Song

(New York: DAW, 1996)

**Story type:** Science Fiction (Science Fantasy; Family Saga)
**Series:** Darkover
**Major character(s):** Margaret Alton, Musician, Psychic; Mikhail Lanart-Hastur, Nobleman, Psychic, Telepath; Lew Alton, Diplomat, Psychic
**Time period(s):** Indeterminate Future
**Locale(s):** Darkover, Planet—Imaginary

**Summary:** Margaret Alton comes to Darkover to research music. Instead she finds herself treated with awe while unknown relatives keep popping up and expecting her to fulfill a role she doesn't want. When she starts getting visions, she must decide just what a planet she hardly remembers really means to her.

**Other books you might like:**
Octavia E. Butler, *Mind of My Mind*, 1977
Paula E. Downing, *Rinn's Star*, 1990
Cheryl J. Franklin, *The Light in Exile*, 1990
Anne McCaffrey, *Powers That Be*, 1993
  Elizabeth Ann Scarborough, co-author
Andre Norton, *Ice Crown*, 1970
James H. Schmitz, *The Telzey Toy*, 1973
Jack Vance, *Madouc*, 1990
Timothy Zahn, *A Coming of Age*, 1985

## 633

**MARION ZIMMER BRADLEY**

### The Forest House

(New York: Viking, 1994)

**Story type:** Fantasy (Historical; Religious)
**Major character(s):** Eilan, Religious (druid high priestess), Parent; Gaius Macellius Severus Siluricus, Military Personnel (Roman/British); Caillean, Religious (druid priestess)
**Time period(s):** 1st century (70s)
**Locale(s):** Deva, England; Vernematon, England (the Forest House); Roman Empire

**Summary:** Caillean tells her novices the story of Eilan, last Lady of Vernemation, and Gaius, the forbidden Roman soldier she loved during the time of the Forest House and the Roman occupation of the country, which leads to their sharing the misty island with the Nazarene monks who shelter there.

**Other books you might like:**
Margaret Ball, *Flameweaver*, 1991
Frans G. Bengtsson, *The Long Ships*, 1954
Maya Kaathryn Bohnhoff, *The Meri*, 1992
Jack Holland, *The Fire Queen*, 1992
Morgan Llywelyn, *Druids*, 1991
Bridget Wood, *Wolfking*, 1992

## 634

### MARION ZIMMER BRADLEY

## *Ghostlight*

(New York: Tor, 1995)

**Story type:** Fantasy (Contemporary; Magic Conflict)
**Major character(s):** Truth Jourdemayne, Paranormal Investigator; Julian Pilgrim, Magician; Thorne Blackburn, Magician, Parent
**Time period(s):** 1990s
**Locale(s):** Shadowkill, New York

**Summary:** Three decades after Truth's mother dies in a bizarre magical ritual and her father vanishes, the aunt who raised her gives Truth some magical artifacts belonging to her father. When Truth decides to write her father's biography, her research leads her to an old house called Shadow Gate and to a meeting with Julian Pilgrim, the handsome new owner who plans to recreate the same ritual that killed her mother.

**Other books you might like:**
Margaret Ball, *The Shadow Gate*, 1991
Emma Bull, *War for the Oaks*, 1987
R.A. MacAvoy, *Tea with the Black Dragon*, 1983
Elizabeth Ann Scarborough, *Phantom Banjo*, 1991

## 635

### MARION ZIMMER BRADLEY
### HOLLY LISLE, Co-Author

## *Glenraven*

(New York: Baen, 1996)

**Story type:** Fantasy (Magic Conflict; Adventure)
**Major character(s):** Jay Jay Bennington, Writer, Traveler; Sophie Cortiss, Traveler; Matthiall, Wizard
**Time period(s):** 1990s
**Locale(s):** Glenraven, Fictional Country (between France and Italy); Europe

**Summary:** Jay Jay Bennington, facing her third divorce, and Sophie Cortiss, unable to come to terms with the death of her daughter, travel to Glenraven, a mysterious Alpine country under the rule of a semi-immortal tyrant. As the country reaches out for a hero, the tyrant and her servants expect beings of immense power, not two ordinary women from North Carolina.

**Other books you might like:**
Poul Anderson, *Three Hearts and Three Lions*, 1961
Greg Bear, *The Infinity Concerto*, 1984
Jack L. Chalker, *The River of Dancing Gods*, 1984
Alan Dean Foster, *Spellsinger*, 1983
Barbara Hambly, *The Time of the Dark*, 1982
Diana Wynne Jones, *Hexwood*, 1994
Clifford D. Simak, *Special Deliverance*, 1982
Christopher Stasheff, *The Witch Doctor*, 1994

## 636

### MARION ZIMMER BRADLEY

## *Gravelight*

(New York: Tor, 1997)

**Story type:** Fantasy (Psychic Powers; Magic Conflict)

**Major character(s):** Wycherly "Wych" Musgrave, Alcoholic; Melusine "Sinah" Dellon, Actress, Telepath; Truth Jourdemayne, Paranormal Investigator
**Time period(s):** 1990s
**Locale(s):** Morton's Fork, West Virginia

**Summary:** When Sinah Dellon returns to Morton's Fork to find her family, no one will talk to her. After crashing her car, alcoholic Wych Musgrave decides to dry out. The two, together with a team of psychic investigators looking into disappearances centering on August 14th, must all work to battle old ritual and older magic forces, even more dangerous in this modern age.

**Other books you might like:**
Francesca Lia Block, *Witch Baby*, 1991
Jack Cady, *The Off Season*, 1995
Rose Estes, *Troll-Taken*, 1993
Lisa Goldstein, *Walking the Labyrinth*, 1996
Nina Kiriki Hoffman, *The Silent Strength of Stones*, 1995
R.A. MacAvoy, *Tea with the Black Dragon*, 1983
Susan Power, *The Grass Dancer*, 1994
Terri Windling, *The Wood Wife*, 1996
Jane Yolen, *Briar Rose*, 1992

## 637

### MARION ZIMMER BRADLEY

## *Heartlight*

(New York: Tor, 1998)

**Story type:** Fantasy (Magic Conflict; Contemporary Realism)
**Series:** Inheritor
**Major character(s):** Colin MacLaren, Psychologist, Paranormal Investigator; Claire London, Psychic; Toller Hasloch, Warrior, Villain
**Time period(s):** 1960s; 1990s
**Locale(s):** Berkeley, California; New York, New York

**Summary:** After Colin MacLaren helps defeat the Nazis in World War II, he discovers a threat surfacing in the USA in a different form, dashing men's hopes and spreading corruption throughout society. Colin does win some small victories, but cannot stem the corruption or even find his true successor until he confronts the resurrected Evil directly.

**Other books you might like:**
Piers Anthony, *Tarot*, 1987
Jack L. Chalker, *The Messiah Choice*, 1985
Pamela Dean, *Tam Lin*, 1991
Rosemary Edghill, *The Book of Moons*, 1995
Lisa Goldstein, *Walking the Labyrinth*, 1996
Katherine Kurtz, *The Lodge of the Lynx*, 1992
    Deborah Turner Harris, co-author
Linda Nevins, *Renaissance Moon*, 1997
Dennis Wheatley, *Strange Conflict*, 1941

## 638

### MARION ZIMMER BRADLEY

## *The Heirs of Hammerfell*

(New York: DAW Books, 1989)

**Story type:** Science Fiction (Science Fantasy)
**Series:** Darkover
**Major character(s):** Alastair, Heir, Twin; Conn, Heir, Twin
**Time period(s):** Indeterminate
**Locale(s):** Darkover, Planet—Imaginary

**Summary:** During the planet Darkover's dark ages, bloody clan warfare is the order of the day. When clan Storn wipes out clan Hammerfell, the twin heirs of Hammerfell survive and grow up separated from each other, each convinced the other is dead. Eventually both return to fight for their inheritance and to be reunited.

**Other books you might like:**
Katherine Kurtz, *The Harrowing of Gwynedd*, 1989
Katherine Kurtz, *The Quest for Saint Camber*, 1986
Anne McCaffrey, *Dragonsdawn*, 1988
Anne McCaffrey, *Nerilka's Story*, 1986
Anne McCaffrey, *The Renegades of Pern*, 1989
Andre Norton, *The Gate of the Cat*, 1987
Andre Norton, *Sorceress of the Witch World*, 1968
Andre Norton, *'Ware Hawk*, 1983

### 639

**MARION ZIMMER BRADLEY**
**HOLLY LISLE**, Co-Author

## *In the Rift*

(New York: Baen, 1998)

**Story type:** Fantasy (Contemporary Realism; Magic Conflict)
**Series:** Glenraven
**Major character(s):** Kate Beacham, Store Owner; Callion Aregeni, Fugitive; Rhiana, Noblewoman, Magician
**Time period(s):** 1990s
**Locale(s):** North Carolina; Ft. Lauderdale, Florida; Glenraven, Fictional Country

**Summary:** Kate Beacham has been attacked for being a witch and her horse killed. Then four beings, only one of whom looks human, pop into her North Carolina house saying that only she can help them find a renegade and return home.

**Other books you might like:**
L. Sprague de Camp, *The Pixilated Peeress*, 1991
Dale Estey, *A Lost Tale*, 1982
Katherine Kurtz, *The Adept*, 1991
  Deborah Turner Harris, co-author
Mercedes Lackey, *Wheels of Fire*, 1992
  Mark Shepherd, co-author
Megan Lindholm, *Cloven Hooves*, 1991
Holly Lisle, *Mall, Mayhem and Magic*, 1995
  Chris Guin, co-author
Holly Lisle, *Sympathy for the Devil*, 1996
  Chris Guin, co-author
Christopher Stasheff, *My Son, the Wizard*, 1997

### 640

**MARION ZIMMER BRADLEY**

## *Lady of Avalon*

(New York: Viking, 1997)

**Story type:** Fantasy (Legend; Religious)
**Series:** Mists of Avalon
**Major character(s):** Caillean, Religious (High Priestess); Gawen, Ruler, Religious; Sianna, Mythical Creature (faerie), Royalty (princess)
**Time period(s):** 1st century (A.D. 90-118); 3rd century (285-293)
**Locale(s):** Avalon, England; Inis Witrin, Mythical Place (Isle of Glass, Avalon)

**Summary:** Caillean returns to Avalon with Gawen, son of a High Priestess and a Roman soldier. Raised by the High Priestess and

Father Josephus, Gawen marries Sianna, becoming instrumental in hiding Avalon from her enemies. The old ones, reborn as Caillean, Gawen and Sianna, continue to protect England, leading to the birth of Arthur. Sequel to *The Forest House* and prequel to *The Mists of Avalon*.

**Other books you might like:**
Mike Ashley, *The Pendragon Chronicles*, 1990
  editor
Frans G. Bengtsson, *The Long Ships*, 1954
Maya Kaathryn Bohnhoff, *The Meri*, 1992
Morgan Llywelyn, *Druids*, 1991
Jennifer Roberson, *Return to Avalon: A Celebration of Marion Zimmer Bradley*, 1997
  editor
Jack Whyte, *The Skystone*, 1996

### 641

**MARION ZIMMER BRADLEY**

## *Lady of the Trillium*

(New York: Bantam Spectra, 1995)

**Story type:** Fantasy (Psychic Powers; Magic Conflict)
**Series:** Trillium
**Major character(s):** Haramis, Sorceress, Recluse, Royalty (princess); Mikayla, Royalty (princess), Student (magic); Fiolon, Nobleman, Musician
**Time period(s):** Indeterminate
**Locale(s):** Ruwenda, Fictional Country; Labornok, Fictional Country

**Summary:** In choosing a successor to Archmage, Haramis chooses Mikayla, who remains unenthusiastic about everything save her betrothal to Lord Fiolon. Haramis' magical attempt to sever the couple's telepathic link has disastrous results.

**Other books you might like:**
Jo Clayton, *Dancer's Rise*, 1993
Diane Duane, *So You Want to Be a Wizard?*, 1983
Sharon Green, *Silver Princess, Golden Knight*, 1993
Monica Hughes, *The Promise*, 1992
Julian May, *Blood Trillium*, 1992
Andre Norton, *Golden Trillium*, 1993
Pamela F. Service, *Winter of Magic's Return*, 1985
Mary Frances Zambreno, *Journeyman Wizard*, 1994

### 642

**MARION ZIMMER BRADLEY**, Editor

## *Leroni of Darkover*

(New York: DAW, 1991)

**Story type:** Science Fiction (Anthology; Psychic Powers)
**Series:** Darkover
**Time period(s):** Indeterminate Future
**Locale(s):** Darkover, Planet—Imaginary

**Summary:** This volume contains 22 stories about Darkovans with the psychic gifts of 'laran.' Stories include historical background on the first settlers in "The Tower at New Skye" by Priscilla W. Armstrong, some unusual uses of 'laran' in "Food for the Worms" by Roxana Pierson and a Terran with psychic powers in "The Speaking Touch" by Margaret Carter. "A Meeting of Minds" by Elisabeth Waters is a short, humorous piece.

**Other books you might like:**
Suzette Haden Elgin, *Communipath Worlds*, 1980
Suzette Haden Elgin, *Native Tongue*, 1984

Anne McCaffrey, *To Ride Pegasus*, 1973
Vonda N. McIntyre, *Dreamsnake*, 1978
A.E. Van Vogt, *Slan*, 1946
Patricia C. Wrede, *Caught in Crystal*, 1987

Elizabeth A. Lynn, *The Northern Girl*, 1980
C.L. Moore, *Jirel of Joiry*, 1969

## 643

### MARION ZIMMER BRADLEY
### MERCEDES LACKEY, Co-Author

## *Rediscovery: A Novel of Darkover*
(New York: DAW, 1993)

**Story type:** Science Fiction (Lost Colony; Psychic Powers)
**Series:** Darkover
**Major character(s):** Leonie Hastur, Telepath; Elizabeth Macintosh, Spacewoman, Telepath; Kermiak Alderan, Royalty, Telepath
**Time period(s):** Indeterminate Future
**Locale(s):** *Minnesota*, Spaceship; Darkover, Planet—Imaginary

**Summary:** An exploratory mission from Earth discovers an inhospitably cold planet deficient in heavy metals and sends down a landing party. Far away, Leonie Hastur finds herself in an alien mind after the Terrans' shuttle crashes in a storm and becomes fascinated by the strange minds before losing contact. The two known telepaths on the crew, Elizabeth and David, soon communicate with the natives. While listening to local entertainment, Elizabeth realizes their language, Gaelic, indicates Terran origin.

**Other books you might like:**
Margaret Wander Bonanno, *The Others*, 1990
Diana G. Gallagher, *The Alien Dark*, 1990
Kris Jensen, *Mentor*, 1991
Mercedes Lackey, *Wing Commander: Freedom Flight*, 1992
    Ellen Guon, co-author
Anne McCaffrey, *The Rowan*, 1990
Anne McCaffrey, *The Ship Who Searched*, 1992
    Mercedes Lackey, co-author
Joan Slonczewski, *A Door into Ocean*, 1986

## 644

### MARION ZIMMER BRADLEY, Editor

## *Renunciates of Darkover*
(New York: DAW, 1991)

**Story type:** Science Fiction (Anthology)
**Series:** Darkover
**Time period(s):** Indeterminate Future
**Locale(s):** Darkover, Planet—Imaginary

**Summary:** In this collection of 22 stories about the Order of Renunciates, ''Carlina's Calling'' by Patricia D. Novak, tells how the Sisterhood of the Sword and the Priestesses of Avarra joined to form the Order of Reununciates, popularly known as the Free Amazons. Several stories involve Renunciates with 'laran' powers including ''Strife'' by Chel Avery. Some stories, such as ''Amazon Fragment'' by Marion Zimmer Bradley, tell of internal Guild conflicts while others tell of Darkovan political intrigue, as in ''Set a Thief'' by Mercedes Lackey. One story, ''The Honor of the Guild'' by Joan Marie Verba, is a murder mystery, and others provide historical background development as in ''Dalereuth Guild House'' by Priscilla W. Armstrong.

**Other books you might like:**
C.J. Cherryh, *Gate of Ivrel*, 1976
Barbara Hambly, *The Ladies of Mandrigyn*, 1984
Elizabeth A. Lynn, *The Dancers of Arun*, 1979

## 645

### MARION ZIMMER BRADLEY

## *The Shadow Matrix*
(New York: DAW, 1997)

**Story type:** Science Fiction (Psychic Powers; Family Saga)
**Series:** Darkover
**Major character(s):** Marguerida ''Margaret'' Alton, Heiress, Telepath; Mikhail Lanart-Hastur, Telepath, Nobleman, Psychic
**Time period(s):** Indeterminate Future
**Locale(s):** Darkover, Planet—Imaginary

**Summary:** At Arilinn, Margaret Alton tries to get her gift under control, while Mikhail Lanart-Hastur tries to find a possible heir in a very disturbed household haunted by a ghost. Finally Margaret and Mikhail must travel back in time to save their present by preventing atomic destruction.

**Other books you might like:**
Octavia E. Butler, *Mind of My Mind*, 1977
Paula E. Downing, *Rinn's Star*, 1990
Debra Doyle, *The Price of the Stars*, 1992
    James D. Macdonald, co-author
Cheryl J. Franklin, *The Light in Exile*, 1990
Julian May, *Jack the Bodiless*, 1992
Anne McCaffrey, *The Rowan*, 1990
David Weber, *Honor Among Enemies*, 1996
K.D. Wentworth, *House of Moons*, 1995

## 646

### MARION ZIMMER BRADLEY, Editor

## *Sword and Sorceress VIII*
(New York: DAW, 1991)

**Story type:** Fantasy (Anthology; Sword and Sorcery)
**Series:** Sword and Sorceress

**Summary:** 22 original stories about women warriors with a three-page introduction by the editor plus brief introductions with biographical sketches of the author for each story. Authors whose first professional sale appears here include Deborah Burros, Jere Dunham, Margaret Howes, Stephanie Shaver and Cynthia Ward. Other authors include Laurell K. Hamilton, Mercedes Lackey, Diana L. Paxson, Jennifer Roberson, Eluki bes Shahar, Josepha Sherman and Dave Smeds.

**Other books you might like:**
Ellen Datlow, *The Year's Best Fantasy and Horror: Fourth Annual Collection*, 1991
    Terri Windling, co-editor
Ellen Kushner, *Basilisk*, 1980
    editor
Will Shetterly, *Liavek*, 1985
    Emma Bull, co-editor
Will Shetterly, *Liavek: Spells of Binding*, 1988
    Emma Bull, co-editor
Terri Windling, *Borderland*, 1986
    Mark Alan Arnold, co-editor
Terri Windling, *Life on the Border*, 1991
    editor

## 647

**MARION ZIMMER BRADLEY**, Editor

## Sword and Sorceress IX

(New York: DAW, 1992)

**Story type:** Fantasy (Anthology; Sword and Sorcery)
**Series:** Sword and Sorceress
**Time period(s):** Indeterminate Past

**Summary:** 26 original stories which revolve around women as primary actors in and initiators of adventure plus a trenchant three-page introduction by the editor and introductions to each story. Authors whose first professional sale appears here include Tanya Beaty, Lisa Deason, Eric Haines, Lee Ann Martins and Leslie Ann Miller. Other authors include Mercedes Lackey, Diana Paxson, Josepha Sherman and Dave Smeds.

**Other books you might like:**
C.J. Cherryh, *Festival Moon*, 1987
    editor
Ellen Datlow, *The Year's Best Fantasy and Horror: Third Annual Collection*, 1990
    Terri Windling, co-editor
Ellen Kushner, *Basilisk*, 1980
    editor
Will Shetterly, *Liavek*, 1985
    Emma Bull, co-editor
Terri Windling, *Borderland*, 1986
    Mark Alan Arnold, co-editor
Terri Windling, *Elsewhere*, 1981
    Mark Alan Arnold, co-editor

## 648

**MARION ZIMMER BRADLEY**, Editor

## Sword and Sorceress XI

(New York: DAW, 1994)

**Story type:** Fantasy (Anthology; Sword and Sorcery)
**Series:** Sword and Sorceress

**Summary:** Contains a two-page introduction and individual introductions with biographical sketches of the authors of 33 original stories featuring sword wielding heroines in diverse settings and situations. Authors include Lynne Armstrong-Jones, Jo Clayton, Diana L. Paxson, Dave Smeds and Deborah Wheeler.

**Other books you might like:**
Nina Auerbach, *Forbidden Journeys: Fairy Tales and Fantasies by Victorian Women Writers*, 1992
    U.C. Knoepflmacher, co-editor
George Alec Effinger, *Maureen Birnbaum, Barbarian Swordsperson: The Complete Stories*, 1993
Jessica Amanda Salmonson, *Amazons!*, 1979
    editor
Terri Windling, *Life on the Border*, 1991
    editor
Jack Zipes, *Don't Bet on the Prince*, 1986
    editor

## 649

**MARION ZIMMER BRADLEY**, Editor

## Sword and Sorceress XII

(New York: DAW, 1995)

**Story type:** Fantasy (Anthology; Sword and Sorcery)
**Series:** Sword and Sorceress

**Summary:** Contains a four-page introduction plus individual introductions to 22 original stories including one collaboration, ''A Dragon in Distress,'' by Mercedes Lackey and Elisabeth Waters. The tone varies from somber and ominous to light and whimsical with themes including high fantasy, music and a rewritten version of ''Cinderella.'' Other authors include Lynne Armstrong-Jones, Diana L. Paxson, Jennifer Roberson, L.S. Silverthorne, and Deborah Wheeler.

**Other books you might like:**
George Alec Effinger, *Maureen Birnbaum, Barbarian Swordsperson: The Complete Stories*, 1993
Esther Friesner, *Chicks in Chainmail*, 1995
    editor
C.L. Moore, *Jirel of Joiry*, 1969
Kathleen M. Massie-Ferch, *Ancient Enchantresses*, 1995
    Martin H. Greenberg, Richard Gilliam, co-editors
Jessica Amanda Salmonson, *Amazons!*, 1979
    editor

## 650

**MARION ZIMMER BRADLEY**

## Sword and Sorceress XIII

(New York: DAW, 1996)

**Story type:** Fantasy (Anthology; Sword and Sorcery)
**Series:** Sword and Sorceress

**Summary:** This anthology contains a two-page introduction plus individual introductions to 22 original stories, frequently somber to ominous in tone, with themes including shape-shifting, dream quests, biography, magic conflict, martial arts, and mythical creatures. Authors include Jo Clayton, Cynthia McQuillin, Diana L. Paxson, Marella Sands, Charles M. Saplak, Laura J. Underwood, and Deborah Wheeler.

**Other books you might like:**
George Alec Effinger, *Maureen Birnbaum, Barbarian Swordsperson: The Complete Stories*, 1993
Esther Friesner, *Chicks in Chainmail*, 1995
    editor
C.L. Moore, *Jirel of Joiry*, 1969
Kathleen M. Massie-Ferch, *Ancient Enchantresses*, 1995
    Martin H. Greenberg, Richard Gilliam, co-editors
Jessica Amanda Salmonson, *Amazons!*, 1979
    editor

## 651

**MARION ZIMMER BRADLEY**, Editor
**RACHEL E. HOLMEN**, Co-Editor

## Sword and Sorceress XIV

(New York: DAW, 1997)

**Story type:** Fantasy (Anthology)
**Series:** Sword and Sorceress

**Summary:** This anthology contains a three-page introduction by Bradley, plus individual introductions to 27 stories, frequently downbeat or ominous in tone, with themes including mythical creatures, magic conflict, high fantasy, relationships, and culinary arts. Authors include Rachel E. Holmen, Adrienne Martine-Barnes, Diana L. Paxson, Laura J. Underwood, Elisabeth Waters, and Deborah Wheeler.

**Other books you might like:**
George Alec Effinger, *Maureen Birnbaum, Barbarian Swordsperson: The Complete Stories*, 1993
Esther Friesner, *Chicks in Chainmail*, 1995
    editor
Kathleen M. Massie-Ferch, *Ancient Enchantresses*, 1995
    Martin H. Greenberg and Richard Gilliam, co-editors
C.L. Moore, *Jirel of Joiry*, 1969
Jessica Amanda Salmonson, *Amazons!*, 1979
    editor

## 652

**MARION ZIMMER BRADLEY**
**ANDRE NORTON**, Co-Author
**MERCEDES LACKEY**, Co-Author

### Tiger Burning Bright
(New York: Morrow/AvoNova, 1995)

**Story type:** Fantasy (Magic Conflict; Political)
**Major character(s):** Shelyra ''Raymonda'', Royalty (princess); Leopold, Royalty (prince), Military Personnel; Apolon, Magician
**Time period(s):** Indeterminate
**Locale(s):** Merina, Fictional City (city-state)

**Summary:** When Merina falls to Balthasar, the three former rulers, Dowager Queen Adele, Queen Lydana and Princess Shelyra, assume alternate identities to avoid Balthasar's grasp. Masquerading as a gypsy, Shelyra bonds with Balthasar's son, Leopold, as opposition to the harsh rule and Apolon's necromancy builds.

**Other books you might like:**
Piers Anthony, *For Love of Evil*, 1988
Jack L. Chalker, *Demons of the Dancing Gods*, 1984
L. Sprague de Camp, *The Land of Unreason*, 1942
    Fletcher Pratt, co-author
John M. Ford, *The Dragon Waiting*, 1983
Fritz Leiber, *Gather, Darkness!*, 1950
James H. Schmitz, *The Witches of Karres*, 1966
Melinda M. Snodgrass, *Queen's Gambit Declined*, 1989
Christopher Stasheff, *King Kobold Revived*, 1984

## 653

**MARION ZIMMER BRADLEY**, Editor

### Towers of Darkover
(New York: DAW, 1993)

**Story type:** Fantasy (Anthology; Psychic Powers)
**Series:** Darkover
**Time period(s):** Indeterminate Future
**Locale(s):** Darkover, Planet—Imaginary

**Summary:** Contains a five-page editorial and individual introductions to 20 original stories focusing on life around the citadels occupied by those developing their psychic abilities, some to master natural forces and others to forward goals of domination. Set at various times, some stories feature characters developed in novels of Bradley's Darkover Series (1962-1993) and utilize diverse themes. Au-

thors include Emily Alward, Lynne Armstrong Jones, Marion Zimmer Bradley, Patricia B. Cirone, Patricia Duffy Novak, Diann Partridge, Diana L. Paxson, Joan Marie Verba, Elisabeth Waters and Deborah Wheeler.

**Other books you might like:**
Margaret Wander Bonanno, *The Others*, 1990
Suzette Haden Elgin, *Communipath Worlds*, 1980
Elizabeth A. Lynn, *The Dancers of Arun*, 1979
Anne McCaffrey, *The Rowan*, 1990
Elizabeth Ann Scarborough, *Last Refuge*, 1992
Theodore Sturgeon, *More than Human*, 1953

## 654

**MARION ZIMMER BRADLEY**

### Witch Hill
(New York: Tor, 1990)

**Story type:** Horror (Black Magic)
**Major character(s):** Sarah Latimer, Student (art student drop out), Witch; Brian Standish, Doctor; Matthew Hay, Religious (Leader—Church of the Antique)
**Time period(s):** 1970s (1971)
**Locale(s):** Arkham, Massachusetts (Witch Hill)

**Summary:** Following the death of her family, Sarah Latimer seeks refuge at her father's family home, Witch Hill. All too soon, her dark family legacy asserts itself and Sarah is trapped in the web of an occult mystery perpetuated by preceding generations of Latimers, each of which produced a woman named Sarah who practiced witchcraft.

**Other books you might like:**
John Farris, *All Heads Turn When the Hunt Goes By*, 1977
Anne Rice, *The Witching Hour*, 1990

## 655

**MARION ZIMMER BRADLEY**

### Witchlight
(New York: Tor, 1996)

**Story type:** Fantasy (Contemporary; Magic Conflict)
**Major character(s):** Winter Musgrave, Amnesiac; Truth Jourdemayne, Paranormal Investigator (paranormal); Hunter ''Grey'' Greyson, Magician
**Time period(s):** 1990s
**Locale(s):** Taghkanic College, New York; San Francisco, California

**Summary:** Unable to remember much of her past, Winter Musgrave finds herself fleeing from an unseen force that plays tricks—including mutilating small animals—wherever she goes. Desperate, Winter seeks help from Truth Jourdemayne, who studies paranormal phenomena, and gradually uncovers her missing memories. A loose sequel to *Ghostlight*.

**Other books you might like:**
Jonathan Carroll, *Bones of the Moon*, 1988
John Crowley, *Love & Sleep*, 1994
Dean R. Koontz, *Cold Fire*, 1991
Marc Laidlaw, *The 37th Mandala*, 1996
Christopher Pike, *Whisper of Death*, 1991

## 656

**WILL BRADLEY** (Pseudonym of Brad Strickland)

### Ark Liberty
(New York: Roc, 1992)

**Story type:** Science Fiction (Post-Nuclear Holocaust; Alternate Intelligence)
**Major character(s):** Stefan Li, Scientist, Disembodied Personality (computer imprint); Carin Hawk, Explorer
**Time period(s):** 2080s (2084); 24th century
**Locale(s):** Liberty, Undersea Environment/Habitat; Atlantic Ocean; North America

**Summary:** Fearing universal destruction of Earth society, Stefan Li defies orders when he begins to fill *Liberty* with people to prepare *Liberty* for survival without contact from the outside world. When officials try to stop him, Stefan Li foils their plans, costing Li his corporeal existence. Friends salvage his personality and memories by imprinting them onto *Liberty*'s computer. Centuries later, after they attempt to seed Earth's atmosphere with beneficial bacteria, survivers from *Liberty* explore a ruined North America hoping to discover signs of recovery, but finding instead a threat to *Liberty*'s survival.

**Other books you might like:**
David Brin, *Earth*, 1990
Octavia E. Butler, *Dawn*, 1987
Daniel F. Galouye, *Dark Universe*, 1961
Marjorie Bradley Kellogg, *Harmony*, 1991
Rosemary Kirstein, *The Outskirter's Secret*, 1992
Vonda N. McIntyre, *Starfarers*, 1989
Vonda N. McIntyre, *Transition*, 1991
Donald E. McQuinn, *Warrior*, 1990
J.M. Morgan, *Desert Eden*, 1991
Michael D. Weaver, *My Father Immortal*, 1989
Catherine Wells, *The Earth Is All That Lasts*, 1991
Paul O. Williams, *The Breaking of Northwall*, 1980

## 657

**GILLIAN BRADSHAW**

### Horses of Heaven
(New York: Doubleday, 1991)

**Story type:** Fantasy (Historical; Romance)
**Major character(s):** Mauakes, Ruler; Heiokleia, Royalty (princess)
**Time period(s):** 2nd century B.C.
**Locale(s):** Ferghana, Asia; Bactria, Asia

**Summary:** Mauakes, ruler of Ferghana where the natives raise flying stallions, marries Heiokleia of the elephant masters. Their marriage is difficult as Heioka is an intelligent, independent person and Mauakes expects women to serve and obey.

**Other books you might like:**
David Cook, *Horselords*, 1990
Morgan Llywelyn, *Bard: The Odyssey of the Irish*, 1987
Morgan Llywelyn, *The Horse Goddess*, 1982
Josepha Sherman, *The Horse of Flame*, 1990
David Wingrove, *The Middle Kingdom*, 1990

## 658

**GILLIAN BRADSHAW**

### The Land of Gold
(New York: Greenwillow, 1992)

**Story type:** Fantasy (Young Adult; Quest)
**Major character(s):** Kandaki, Royalty (princess of Nubia), Heiress—Dispossessed; Hathor, Mythical Creature (dragon); Prahotep, Adventurer
**Time period(s):** Indeterminate Past
**Locale(s):** Nubia, Ancient Civilization; Africa

**Summary:** Shabako usurps her parents' throne and leaves Kandaki to die in the swamp, but Prahotep and his companions rescue her and agree to join forces to defeat Shabako. The group travels a dangerous waterway to Napata where, recognized as Queen of Nubia, Kandaki organizes a force to overthrow Shabako. Sequel to *The Dragon and the Thief.*

**Other books you might like:**
Lloyd Alexander, *The High King*, 1968
John Christopher, *Beyond the Burning Lands*, 1971
Peter Dickinson, *The Blue Hawk*, 1976
Frances Mary Hendry, *Quest for a Maid*, 1990
Andre Norton, *The Crystal Gryphon*, 1992
Robert Silverberg, *Letters From Atlantis*, 1990
Robert Silverberg, *Thebes of the Hundred Gates*, 1991

## 659

**CHRISTOPHER BRAM**

### Father of Frankenstein
(New York: Dutton, 1995)

**Story type:** Horror (Literary)
**Major character(s):** James Whale, Director (movie), Homosexual; Clayton Boone, Gardener; Boris Karloff, Actor, Historical Figure
**Time period(s):** 1950s (1957)
**Locale(s):** Santa Monica, California

**Summary:** In the last month of his life James Whale, director of the films *Frankenstein* and *Bride of Frankenstein*, is afflicted with a series of strokes that affect his ability to discriminate between past and present, and real life and the movies. In this flashback-studded novel, the gay director initially repels and then earns the affection of his homophobic ex-Marine gardener, and the two develop a relationship that begins to resemble the one between Victor Frankenstein and his creation.

**Other books you might like:**
Emmanuel Carrere, *Gothic Romance*, 1984
Kim Newman, *Anno Dracula*, 1992
Theodore Roszak, *The Memoirs of Elizabeth Frankenstein*, 1995

## 660

**REBECCA BRAND** (Pseudonym of Suzy McKee Charnas)

### The Ruby Tear
(New York: Tor/Forge, 1997)

**Story type:** Horror (Vampire Story)
**Major character(s):** Jessamyn Croft, Actress; Nic Griffin, Actor (Jessamyn's fiance), Writer (playwright); Ivo von Cragga, Vampire
**Time period(s):** 1990s (1997)
**Locale(s):** New York, New York

**Summary:** Nic Griffin, the descendant of a family who slaughtered the von Cragga vampires centuries before, writes "The Jewel," a play that reprises the Griffin/von Cragga vendetta, as a snare to trap the last surviving von Cragga who has systematically murdered his ancestors over the centuries. Nic's efforts are complicated by his fiancee Jessamyn, an actress who hopes to play the lead in the play during its off-Broadway run.

**Other books you might like:**
Steven Brust, *Agyar*, 1992
Brent Monahan, *The Book of Common Dread*, 1993
Kim Newman, *Bad Dreams*, 1990
Anne Rice, *The Vampire Lestat*, 1985
Fred Saberhagen, *A Sharpness on the Neck*, 1996
Chet Williamson, *Reign*, 1990
T. Lucien Wright, *Thirst of the Vampire*, 1992

---

**661**

**GARY BRANDNER**

## Doomstalker

(New York: Fawcett, 1989)

**Story type:** Horror (Satanism)
**Major character(s):** Brian Kettering, Detective—Police; Doomstalker, Demon
**Time period(s):** 1980s (Prologue in 1951)
**Locale(s):** California

**Summary:** As a six year old, Brian Kettering sees his father killed in a duel with the Doomstalker, a demon. As a grown man, Kettering again faces the Doomstalker, with his friends, family, and his own soul at stake.

**Other books you might like:**
William Peter Blatty, *The Exorcist*, 1971
Dean R. Koontz, *Darkfall*, 1984

---

**662**

**PERRY BRASS**

## Mirage

(Ridgefield, Connecticut: Belhue Press, 1991)

**Story type:** Science Fiction (Gay/Lesbian Fiction)
**Major character(s):** Greeland, Homosexual, Criminal; Enkidu, Homosexual, Boyfriend
**Time period(s):** 1990s
**Locale(s):** Ki, Planet—Imaginary; New York, New York

**Summary:** When Greeland kills and defiles Enkidu's estranged brother, a priestess informs Greeland he must forfeit his life and innocent Enkidu must forfeit his third testicle, the "Egg of the Infinite Eye," source of power and identification among Same Sex men who mate with each other rather than with women. To maintain the balance of their world, Greeland and Enkidu must use the power of their third testicles to travel to Earth in search of a man who would return to Ki to take the place of the murdered man. This is the author's first novel.

**Other books you might like:**
Judith Alguire, *Zeta Base*, 1991
Lauren Wright Douglas, *In the Blood*, 1989
Jack Finney, *The Body Snatchers*, 1955
   as Jack Finney
Nancy Tyler Glenn, *Clicking Stones*, 1989
Camarin Grae, *Stranded*, 1991
Lynda Lyons, *Priorities*, 1990

---

**663**

**GARY A. BRAUNBECK**

## Things Left Behind

(Abingdon, Maryland: CD Publications, 1997)

**Story type:** Horror (Collection)
**Summary:** A first collection of forty stories and prose fragments, many of which use the traditional motifs of horror as springboards for reflection on the human condition. "Some Touch of Pity" features a werewolf whose bestial side symbolizes his suppressed rage at his sexual abuse as a child. "Bloody Sam" is a tale of racial injustice that pits film director Sam Peckinpah against a vampire who feeds on the underclass south of the border, and "In Hollow Houses" is a tale of social disenfranchisement in which extraterrestrials live lives of the alienated among human beings. Illustrated by Alan Clark and Alan Koszowski, with a preface by J.N. Williamson, introduction by William F. Nolan, and afterword by Ed Gorman.

**Other books you might like:**
Richard T. Chizmar, *Midnight Promises*, 1996
Harlan Ellison, *Slippage*, 1997
Brian Hodge, *The Convulsion Factory*, 1996
Elizabeth Massie, *Shadow Dreams*, 1996
David Niall Wilson, *The Fall of the House of Escher and Other Illusions*, 1995

---

**664**

**JEFF BREDENBERG**

## The Dream Vessel

(New York: AvoNova, 1992)

**Story type:** Science Fiction (Post-Nuclear Holocaust)
**Major character(s):** Gregory, Revolutionary, Government Official; Big Tom, Businessman (slave trader); Pec-Pec, Magician, Religious (Rastsa thief/trickster)
**Time period(s):** Indeterminate Future
**Locale(s):** Blue Ridge Mountains, North America; Thomas Island, Caribbean

**Summary:** Hundreds of years after a nuclear holocaust which destroyed civilization, survivors have overthrown the repressive dictator in control of the former United States. Rebel leader Rosenthal Webb sends Gregory to the Caribbean to investigate the possibility of shipmakers there constructing a huge ship to carry the message of freedom to other continents. Ignoring Webb's intent, Gregory arranges for Big Tom to begin construction of the giant ship.

**Other books you might like:**
Will Bradley, *Ark Liberty*, 1992
David Brin, *Earth*, 1990
Octavia E. Butler, *Dawn*, 1987
Daniel F. Galouye, *Dark Universe*, 1961
Rosemary Kirstein, *The Outskirter's Secret*, 1992
Sterling E. Lanier, *Hiero's Journey*, 1973

---

**665**

**JEFF BREDENBERG**

## The Man in the Moon Must Die

(New York: AvoNova, 1993)

**Story type:** Science Fiction (Techno-Thriller; Robot Fiction)
**Major character(s):** Benito Funcitti, Government Official (Mayor of Fun City); Elvis, Robot, Spouse; Blanche, Artificial Intelligence

**Time period(s):** Indeterminate Future
**Locale(s):** Earth; Fun City, Montenegro

**Summary:** After "sending" a traveller to the Moon, a matter transmitter fails to destroy the original Benito Funcitti after creating a new Funcitti on the Moon. Now recognized as an illegal redundancy, the Earthbound Funcitti takes Elvis and flees destruction, working to change the system to allow him the right of existence.

**Other books you might like:**
Roger MacBride Allen, *The Modular Man*, 1992
Greg Bear, *Heads*, 1991
Algis Budrys, *Rogue Moon*, 1960
Joan Slonczewski, *Daughter of Elysium*, 1993
John Varley, *The Persistence of Vision*, 1978
Kate Wilhelm, *The Mile-Long Spaceship*, 1963

---

**666**

**CHAZ BRENCHLEY**

### The Keys to D'Esperance

(Burton, Michigan: Subterranean Press, 1998)

**Story type:** Horror (Haunted House)
**Time period(s):** 1910s
**Locale(s):** England (D'Esperance)

**Summary:** The nameless point-of-view character, a survivor of World War I, is despondent and on the brink of suicide when he magically comes into possession of the keys to the estate of D'Esperance. In D'Esperance, he grapples with the specters of his mother and father, and a mysterious young woman, until he achieves the psychic wholeness necessary to leave the estate. Signed limited edition chapbook.

**Other books you might like:**
Joan Aiken, *The Haunting of Lamb House*, 1992
Jonathan Aycliffe, *The Vanishment*, 1994
Jack Cady, *The Well*, 1980
Ramsey Campbell, *The Influence*, 1988
Chet Williamson, *The House of Fear*, 1989

---

**667**

**J.H. BRENNAN**

### Shiva Accused: An Adventure of the Ice Age

(New York: HarperCollins, 1991)

**Story type:** Fantasy (Historical; Young Adult)
**Series:** Shiva
**Major character(s):** Shiva, Prehistoric Human, Teenager; Hiram, Prehistoric Human; Crone, Shaman
**Time period(s):** Indeterminate Past (Ice Age)
**Locale(s):** Europe

**Summary:** In this sequel to *Shiva: An Adventure of the Ice Age*, the Barradik tribe seizes Shiva, whom they accuse of murdering the spiritual leader of their tribe. Hiram, who loves Shiva, and Crone, a powerful shaman, resolve to rescue her.

**Other books you might like:**
Eleanor Arnason, *The Sword Smith*, 1978
Jean M. Auel, *Clan of the Cave Bear*, 1980
Jean M. Auel, *The Mammoth Hunters*, 1985
Jean M. Auel, *The Valley of Horses*, 1982
Elizabeth Marshall Thomas, *Reindeer Moon*, 1987

---

**668**

**J.H. BRENNAN**

### Shiva's Challenge: An Adventure of the Ice Age

(New York: HarperCollins, 1992)

**Story type:** Fantasy (Young Adult; Historical)
**Series:** Shiva
**Major character(s):** Shiva, Prehistoric Human (Cro-Magnon), Teenager; Hiram, Prehistoric Human (Cro-Magnon); Thag, Prehistoric Human (Neanderthal), Chieftain
**Time period(s):** Indeterminate Past (Ice Age)
**Locale(s):** Europe; Mamar's Kingdom, Mythical Place

**Summary:** To determine her fitness to act as shaman, Shiva must survive potentially deadly tests of poison followed by a journey through the frozen lands to the North. When Hiram returns from a successful hunt to find Shiva gone, he sets out to find her.

**Other books you might like:**
Jean M. Auel, *Clan of the Cave Bear*, 1980
Sue Harrison, *Mother Earth, Father Sky*, 1990
Meredith Ann Pierce, *The Woman Who Loved Reindeer*, 1989
William Sarabande, *Beyond the Sea of Ice*, 1987
Elizabeth Marshall Thomas, *Reindeer Moon*, 1987

---

**669**

**J.H. BRENNAN**

### Shiva: An Adventure of the Ice Age

(New York: Lippincott, 1990)

**Story type:** Fantasy (Historical; Adventure)
**Series:** Shiva
**Major character(s):** Shiva, Prehistoric Human (Cro-Magnon), Teenager; Hiram, Prehistoric Human (Cro-Magnon); Doban, Prehistoric Human (Neanderthal), Child
**Time period(s):** Indeterminate
**Locale(s):** Europe

**Summary:** Shiva, an orphan teenager adopts a lost ogre child, Doban, despite the disapproval of her tribe. Assisted by Hiram, they encounter adventures and dire prophecies along the way to restoring Doban to his own ogre (Neanderthal) tribe.

**Other books you might like:**
Eleanor Arnason, *The Sword Smith*, 1978
Jean M. Auel, *Clan of the Cave Bear*, 1980
Jean M. Auel, *The Mammoth Hunters*, 1985
Jean M. Auel, *The Plains of Passage*, 1990
Jean M. Auel, *The Valley of Horses*, 1982

---

**670**

**JOSEPH PAYNE BRENNAN**

### The Adventures of Lucius Leffing

(Hampton Falls, NH: Donald M. Grant, 1990)

**Story type:** Horror (Collection)
**Series:** Lucius Leffing
**Major character(s):** Lucius Leffing, Paranormal Investigator; Joseph Payne Brennan, Sidekick
**Time period(s):** 1980s
**Locale(s):** New Haven, Connecticut

**Summary:** Thirteen stories, featuring Leffing, written in the "classical detective story" formula: a problem, usually supernatural, is presented; Leffing investigates; Leffing solves the problem to the continuing amazement of his confidant, "Brennan." Clever, cozy, deliberately old fashioned tales.

**Other books you might like:**
Algernon Blackwood, *John Silence*, 1908
William Hope Hodgson, *Carnacki the Ghost Finder*, 1913
Seabury Quinn, *The Phantom Fighter*, 1966

---

**671**

**MAYER ALAN BRENNER**

### Catastrophe's Spell
(New York: DAW, 1989)

**Story type:** Fantasy (Light Fantasy)
**Series:** Dance of the Gods
**Major character(s):** Maximillian, Sorcerer; Zalzyn Shaa, Magician
**Time period(s):** Indeterminate Future
**Locale(s):** Earth

**Summary:** Max tries to get a friend out of an enchanted castle. Zalzyn tries to help a young man free his father and sister from a dungeon.

**Other books you might like:**
Donald Aamodt, *A Name to Conjure With*, 1989
Piers Anthony, *Man From Mundania*, 1989
Piers Anthony, *A Spell for Chameleon*, 1977
Robert Asprin, *Myth-ing Persons*, 1986
   Myth Adventure Series
Craig Shaw Gardner, *An Excess of Enchantments*, 1989
Anne McCaffrey, *Alchemy and Academe*, 1970
Lawrence Watt-Evans, *With a Single Spell*,

---

**672**

**MAYER ALAN BRENNER**

### Spell of Apocalypse
(New York: DAW, 1994)

**Story type:** Fantasy (Light Fantasy; Magic Conflict)
**Series:** Dance of the Gods
**Major character(s):** Maximillian, Sorcerer; The Great Karlini, Sorcerer; The Creeping Sword, Handicapped, Sorcerer
**Time period(s):** Indeterminate
**Locale(s):** Peridol, Fictional City

**Summary:** Forces gather in Peridol as all sides prepare for a final battle for power among the gods, humans and non-humans.

**Other books you might like:**
Susan Dexter, *The Wizard's Shadow*, 1993
Neil Gaiman, *Good Omens: The Nice and Accurate Prophecies of Agnes Nutter, Witch*, 1990
   Terry Pratchett, co-author
Mary Gentle, *Rats and Gargoyles*, 1991
P.C. Hodgell, *God Stalk*, 1982
Harry Turtledove, *The Case of the Toxic Spell Dump*, 1993

---

**673**

**MAYER ALAN BRENNER**

### Spell of Fate
(New York: DAW, 1992)

**Story type:** Fantasy (Magic Conflict; Political)
**Series:** Dance of the Gods
**Major character(s):** Maximillian, Sorcerer; Zalzyn Shaa, Adventurer
**Time period(s):** Indeterminate
**Locale(s):** Peridol, Fictional City (imperial city)

**Summary:** To complete the overthrow of the rule of gods, Max and his companions must master the proper kind of magic needed. Mortals and gods assemble in Peridol to attend an imperial coronation, but busy themselves in intrigue, making and breaking alliances in their unofficial war, while the return of one long-absent will determine the eventual winner.

**Other books you might like:**
Donald Aamodt, *A Troubling Along the Border*, 1991
Jo Clayton, *Wild Magic*, 1991
Jo Clayton, *Wildfire*, 1992
Mary Gentle, *Rats and Gargoyles*, 1991
Laurell K. Hamilton, *Nightseer*, 1992
P.C. Hodgell, *Dark of the Moon*, 1985
P.C. Hodgell, *God Stalk*, 1982
Elizabeth Moon, *Surrender None: The Legacy of Gird*, 1990

---

**674**

**ALAN BRENNERT**

### Her Pilgrim Soul
(New York: Tor, 1990)

**Story type:** Horror (Collection)

**Summary:** Eight tales of fantasy, science fiction and horror centered around people grappling with feelings of loneliness and emotional suffering. The best include "Jamie's Smile," about the psychological scars of the family of a child with birth defects, and "Healer," about a petty criminal's struggle to accomodate his new personality after he acquires the miraculous power to heal.

**Other books you might like:**
Michael Blumlein, *The Brains of Rats*, 1990
David Drake, *From the Heart of Darkness*, 1983
Fritz Leiber, *The Leiber Chronicles*, 1989
Lucius Shepard, *The Jaguar Hunter*, 1987
Theodore Sturgeon, *E Pluribus Unicorn*, 1953

---

**675**

**ALAN BRENNERT**

### Ma Qui and Other Phantoms
(Eugene, Oregon: Pulphouse, 1991)

**Story type:** Horror (Collection)
**Series:** Author's Choice Monthly

**Summary:** Four stories (one original to the volume) concerned with literal and metaphoric ghosts. The title story tells of a horrifying afterlife for dead MIAs left in Vietnam. "Futures" is a delicate tale of an aging man whose extraordinary affliction forces him to come to terms with his own mortality.

**Other books you might like:**
Michael Blumlein, *The Brains of Rats*, 1990

David Drake, *From the Heart of Darkness*, 1983
Fritz Leiber, *The Leiber Chronicles*, 1989
Lucius Shepard, *The Jaguar Hunter*, 1987

## 676

### ALAN BRENNERT

## *Time and Chance*

(New York: Tor, 1990)

**Story type:** Fantasy (Contemporary)
**Major character(s):** Richard Cochrane, Actor (First reality); Rick Cochrane, Insurance Agent (Second reality; doppelganger)
**Time period(s):** 1990s
**Locale(s):** New York, New York

**Summary:** On a visit to his hometown, successful actor Richard Cochrane is given a chance to see what his life might have been had he married his pregnant girl friend thirteen years before. When he meets his double from a parellel world, the two decide to switch places.

**Other books you might like:**
Piers Anthony, *Split Infinity*, 1981
Lisa Goldstein, *The Dream Years*, 1985
Ken Grimwood, *Replay*, 1986

## 677

### GRENDEL BRIARTON (Pseudonym of Reginald Bretnor)

## *The Collected Feghoot*

(Eugene, Oregon: Pulphouse Publishing, 1992)

**Story type:** Science Fiction (Humor; Collection)
**Series:** Ferdinand Feghoot

**Summary:** Includes an introduction plus a 1989 essay by Reginald Bretnor who wrote most of the included science fiction short stories lavishly decorated with punnish wordplay. Expands earlier books reprinting stories from 1950s-1960s periodicals.

**Other books you might like:**
Piers Anthony, *Castle Roogna*, 1979
Piers Anthony, *Centaur Aisle*, 1981
Piers Anthony, *The Source of Magic*, 1979
Piers Anthony, *A Spell for Chameleon*, 1977
Reginald Bretnor, *The Schimmelhorn File*, 1979
Reginald Bretnor, *Schimmelhorn's Gold*, 1986
Italo Calvino, *Cosmicomics*, 1968
Italo Calvino, *T Zero*, 1969
Larry Niven, *Fallen Angels*, 1991
  Jerry Pournelle and Michael Flynn, co-authors
Spider Robinson, *Callahan's Crosstime Saloon*, 1977

## 678

### TRACI BRIERY

## *The Vampire Journals*

(New York: Zebra, 1993)

**Story type:** Horror (Vampire Story)
**Major character(s):** Maria Theresa Allogiamento, Vampire; Antonio da Clovina, Vampire; Gloria, Vampire
**Time period(s):** 18th century; 1990s (1993)
**Locale(s):** Sicily, Italy; Los Angeles, California

**Summary:** In this semi-sequel to the author's *The Vampire Memoirs* (1991), vampire Maria Theresa Allogiamento recounts how she chose vampirism in order to overcome the plight of the average woman in the 18th century, and how she has survived for 200 years to fit in with the current scene in Los Angeles and scoff at mortal poseurs fascinated with the vampire lifestyle.

**Other books you might like:**
C. Dean Andersson, *I Am Dracula*, 1993
Anne Rice, *The Vampire Lestat*, 1985
Michael Romkey, *I, Vampire*, 1990
Chelsea Quinn Yarbro, *The Olivia Trilogy*, 1987-1989

## 679

### TRACI BRIERY

## *The Werewolf Chronicles*

(New York: Zebra, 1995)

**Story type:** Horror (Werewolf Story)
**Major character(s):** Loraine "Phyllis" Turner, Dancer, Werewolf; Roxanne, Dancer; Tamara Taylor, Singer
**Time period(s):** 1990s (1995)
**Locale(s):** Los Angeles, California

**Summary:** While recuperating on her uncle's llama farm in Wisconsin from the hectic life of a Hollywood hopeful, Phyllis Turner is mauled by a wolf. Back in California, she learns to cope with her regular transformations into a werewolf, but finds she is being stalked by mysterious figures who kill her friends and leave her to take the rap for their murders.

**Other books you might like:**
Crosland Brown, *Tombley's Walk*, 1991
Nancy A. Collins, *Wild Blood*, 1994
Dennis Danvers, *Wilderness*, 1992
Whitley Strieber, *The Wild*, 1991
Whitley Strieber, *The Wolfen*, 1978

## 680

### TRACI BRIERY

## *Wolfsong*

(New York: Zebra, 1996)

**Story type:** Horror (Werewolf Story)
**Major character(s):** Loraine "Phyllis" Turner, Dancer, Werewolf; Peter Thomas, Police Officer; Tamara Taylor, Singer
**Time period(s):** 1990s (1996)
**Locale(s):** Los Angeles, California

**Summary:** In this sequel to *The Werewolf Chronicles*, shapeshifter Loraine Turner searches for the killer of her roommate, a crime of which she has been wrongly accused. At the same time, she struggles to come to terms with "Jan," the werewolf persona that has awakened her and invites her to run with the pack.

**Other books you might like:**
Crosland Brown, *Tombley's Walk*, 1991
Nancy A. Collins, *Wild Blood*, 1994
Dennis Danvers, *Wilderness*, 1993
Pat Murphy, *Nadya: The Wolf Chronicles*, 1996
Whitley Strieber, *The Wild*, 1991

## 681

### PATRICIA BRIGGS

## *Masques*

(New York: Ace, 1993)

**Story type:** Fantasy (Magic Conflict; Political)
**Major character(s):** Geoffrey ae'Magi, Magician; Wolf, Magician, Warrior; Aralorn, Mythical Creature (shapechanger), Martial Arts Expert
**Time period(s):** Indeterminate
**Locale(s):** Reth, Fictional Country

**Summary:** The evil and beguiling magician, Geoffrey ae'Magi, will overcome Reth with hordes of undead unless stopped by the few warriors who can resist him. Captured and held at ae'Magi's castle, Aralorn faces death by torture if Wolf cannot negotiate the maze and rescue her.

**Other books you might like:**
Terry Brooks, *The Talismans of Shannara*, 1993
Teresa Edgerton, *The Grail and the Ring*, 1994
Laurell K. Hamilton, *Nightseer*, 1992
Tanya Huff, *Gate of Darkness, Circle of Light*, 1989
Margaret Weis, *Fire Sea*, 1991
    Tracy Hickman, co-author
Margaret Weis, *Into the Labyrinth*, 1991
    Tracy Hickman, co-author

## 682

### PATRICIA BRIGGS

## *Steal the Dragon*

(New York: Ace, 1995)

**Story type:** Fantasy (Political; Adventure)
**Major character(s):** Rialla, Horse Trainer, Spy; Tris, Healer, Traitor
**Time period(s):** Indeterminate
**Locale(s):** Darran, Fictional Country

**Summary:** Aware that detection as a spy in Darran would mean her return to slavery, Rialla travels there hoping to foil an assassination plot aimed at killing a leader who wishes to eliminate slavery. In Darran, Tris aids the cause, despite personal danger.

**Other books you might like:**
Robin Hobb, *Assassin's Apprentice*, 1995
P.C. Hodgell, *God Stalk*, 1982
Mercedes Lackey, *The Eagle and the Nightingales*, 1995
L.E. Modesitt Jr., *Of Tangible Ghosts*, 1994
Patricia C. Wrede, *The Raven Ring*, 1994

## 683

### PATRICIA BRIGGS

## *When Demons Walk*

(New York: Ace, 1998)

**Story type:** Fantasy (Magic Conflict; Mystery)
**Major character(s):** Shamera "Sham", Thief, Sorceress; Kerim, Ruler (Reeve); Talbot, Guard, Sailor
**Time period(s):** Indeterminate
**Locale(s):** Southwood, Fictional Country

**Summary:** With her reputation as a thief of unsurpassed ability preceding her, Sham accepts the Reeve's offer to pose as his mistress. Together they pool their considerable talents to track a serial

killer whose victims include Sham's sorcerer mentor and Lord Kerim's brother, Prince Ven. Their investigation proceeds slowly, however, hampered by Kerim's disbelief in magic, until he succumbs to a crippling disease that Sham discovers has its roots in magic. His skepticism waning, Kerim begins to help Sham find a way to hunt the demon stalking the castle halls.

**Other books you might like:**
Lynn Flewelling, *Luck in the Shadows*, 1996
Eve Forward, *Villains by Necessity*, 1995
Barbara Hambly, *The Silent Tower*, 1986
J.V. Jones, *The Baker's Boy*, 1995
Fritz Leiber, *Ill Met in Lankhmar*, 1995
Melanie Rawn, *Dragon Prince*, 1988

## 684

### DAVID BRIN

## *Brightness Reef*

(New York: Bantam Spectra, 1995)

**Story type:** Science Fiction (Political; First Contact)
**Series:** Uplift
**Major character(s):** Hph-wayuo "Alvin", Alien (hoon), Student; Sara, Scientist; Sax/Ewasx, Alien (traeki/Jophur)
**Time period(s):** Indeterminate Future
**Locale(s):** Jijo, Planet—Imaginary

**Summary:** Abandoned on the fallow planet Jijo, the six intelligent species illegally resident on the Slope hope to follow to innocence the path of the once intelligent glavers. Meanwhile, the last species to arrive, humans, bring many acceptable innovations, including paper and books, completely disposable without difficulty. While prepared for the eventual appearance of the galactics, an unexpected visit by criminals intent on stealing from Jijo may shatter the accord of the Six's Common.

**Other books you might like:**
Eleanor Arnason, *Ring of Swords*, 1993
Gregory Benford, *Furious Gulf*, 1994
C.J. Cherryh, *Foreigner*, 1994
L. Warren Douglas, *Cannon's Orb*, 1994
Jack McDevitt, *The Engines of God*, 1994
Alis A. Rasmussen, *Revolution's Shore*, 1990
Vernor Vinge, *A Fire upon the Deep*, 1992

## 685

### DAVID BRIN

## *Earth*

(New York: Bantam Spectra, 1990)

**Story type:** Science Fiction (Hard Science Fiction; Contemporary Realism)
**Major character(s):** Alex Lustig, Scientist (physicist); George Hutton, Engineer, Industrialist; Jen Wolling, Scientist (behavioral/biological), Scholar (founder of Modern Gaianism)
**Time period(s):** 2030s (2039)
**Locale(s):** Earth (from crust to core); North Island, New Zealand; Kuwenezi Canton Kuwenezi, South Africa

**Summary:** A mob has released a black hole built by Alex Lustig and it drops into the Earth. Investigating whether it will dissipate or grow, destroying the planet from the inside out as it develops, Alex enlists the financial and scientific aid of multi-billionaire George Hutton and others, including his grandmother, Nobel Prize winner Jen Wolling. The project takes on global proportions to the background of life on a

21st century Earth in which the growth of industry, technology and population is matched by a growth of conscience toward the environment's future.

**Other books you might like:**
Roger MacBride Allen, *The Ring of Charon*, 1990
Greg Bear, *The Forge of God*, 1987
Octavia E. Butler, *Adulthood Rites*, 1988
Octavia E. Butler, *Dawn*, 1987
Octavia E. Butler, *Imago*, 1989
John Varley, *Titan*, 1979

**686**

**DAVID BRIN**

## Glory Season

(New York: Bantam Spectra, 1993)

**Story type:** Science Fiction (Genetic Manipulation; Lost Colony)
**Major character(s):** Maia Lamai, Teenager, Traveler; Leie Lamai, Teenager, Twin; Renna, Spaceman, Diplomat (ambassador)
**Time period(s):** Indeterminate Future
**Locale(s):** Stratos, Planet—Imaginary

**Summary:** Stratos' colonists left the human interstellar federation, the Phylum, to develop an ideal society in which most conceptions, sparked by men, result in genetic clones of the mothers, while children conceived in Summer, the vars, receive genetic material from both parents. An alien human frontman from the Phylum arrives to let Stratos know that waves of colonists will move through the sector, turning Stratos society into turmoil. Forced out of Lamai at 15, as usual for vars, Maia travels around Stratos trying to find a place for herself. She realizes the inadequacy of her education while learning about men through the alien she befriends before discovering his gender.

**Other books you might like:**
Eleanor Arnason, *Ring of Swords*, 1993
Eleanor Arnason, *A Woman of the Iron People*, 1991
Octavia E. Butler, *Dawn*, 1987
M.J. Engh, *Rainbow Man*, 1993
Ursula K. Le Guin, *Always Coming Home*, 1987
Joan Slonczewski, *Daughter of Elysium*, 1993
Joan Slonczewski, *A Door into Ocean*, 1986
Sheri S. Tepper, *Grass*, 1989
Sheri S. Tepper, *Raising the Stones*, 1990
Sheri S. Tepper, *Sideshow*, 1992

**687**

**DAVID BRIN**

## Heaven's Reach

(New York: Bantam Spectra, 1998)

**Story type:** Science Fiction (Political; First Contact)
**Series:** Uplift
**Major character(s):** Hph-wayuo "Alvin", Alien (Hoon), Journalist; Sara Koolhan, Scientist (mathematician), Linguist; Harry Harms, Genetically Altered Being (chimpanzee), Explorer (Institute of Navigation)
**Time period(s):** Indeterminate Future
**Locale(s):** E Level Hyperspace, Alternate Universe; *Streaker*, Spaceship; Outer Space

**Summary:** Alvin and his friends on *Streaker* hope to save Jijo from the criminal invaders who attempted to eliminate the G'Kek, leaving only one young female to escape. The *Streaker* finds unexpected

allies and enemies. Harry encounters a series of anomalies leading him to expect a major disturbance in the Five Galaxies, but still manages to be in the right place at the right time. Final book of the second trilogy.

**Other books you might like:**
Peter F. Hamilton, *Emergence*, 1997
Katharine Kerr, *Palace*, 1996
   Mark Kreighbaum, co-author
Dan Simmons, *The Rise of Endymion*, 1997
Sheri S. Tepper, *Six Moon Dance*, 1998
Vernor Vinge, *A Fire upon the Deep*, 1992

**688**

**DAVID BRIN**

## Infinity's Shore

(New York: Bantram Spectra, 1996)

**Story type:** Science Fiction (First Contact; Political)
**Series:** Uplift
**Major character(s):** Kaa, Genetically Altered Being (dolphin), Pilot (spaceship); Hph-wayuo "Alvin", Alien (hoon), Teenager; Asx/Ewasx, Alien (traeki/Jophur)
**Time period(s):** Indeterminate Future
**Locale(s):** Jijo, Planet—Imaginary; *Streaker*, Spaceship; *Polkjhy*, Spaceship (Jophur)

**Summary:** Vanquishing the Rothen gene thieves, the Six Races face a truly giant spaceship, as the Jophur had followed the Rothens to Jijo looking for the *Streaker*. Forced to flee the Old Ones after trying to turn over to them the dead alien, "Herbie," and the location of the derelict fleet, *Streaker* plunges deep into Jijo's ocean just in time to rescue Alvin and his friends from their demolished submarine. Meanwhile, the Jophur attempt to annihilate the g'Keks, perhaps the last of their ancient enemies still living.

**Other books you might like:**
C.J. Cherryh, *Foreigner*, 1994
L. Warren Douglas, *Cannon's Orb*, 1994
Larry Niven, *Protector*, 1973
Frederik Pohl, *The Other End of Time*, 1996
Alis A. Rasmussen, *A Passage of Stars*, 1990
Vernor Vinge, *A Fire upon the Deep*, 1992

**689**

**DAVID BRIN**

## Otherness

(New York: Bantam Spectra, 1994)

**Story type:** Science Fiction (Collection)

**Summary:** Contains 13 stories and exerpts from novels plus eight essays, some with notes about the fiction, divided into "Transitions," "Contact," "Continuity," "Cosmos" and "Otherness." Themes include biology, medicine, societal ideology and first contact. One story, "Bonding to the Genji," set the scene for the shared-universe volume, *Murasaki*.

**Other books you might like:**
Robert Silverberg, *Murasaki*, 1992
   Martin H. Greenberg, co-editor
Cordwainer Smith, *The Rediscovery of Man*, 1993
Marc Stiegler, *The Gentle Seduction*, 1990
John Varley, *Blue Champagne*, 1986
Connie Willis, *Impossible Things*, 1994

## 690

**JANE BRINDLE**

### The Tallow Image

(London: Orion, 1995)

**Story type:** Horror (Witchcraft)
**Major character(s):** Matthew Slater, Horse Trainer (breeder); Cathy Barrington, Young Woman (Matt's wife); Rebecca Norman, Witch
**Time period(s):** 1880s (1880); 1980s (1988)
**Locale(s):** Fremantle, Australia; Bedford, England

**Summary:** The night before her execution, witch Rebecca Norman presents jailer Ralph Ryan with one of two dolls she has fashioned from candlewax. More than a century later, Ryan's lineal descendant, Ralph Slater, finds his life a shambles after his bride, Cathy, comes into possession of the second doll while the couple is honeymooning in Australia, and begins acting as though possessed of a wonton woman's spirit. The pseudonymous author first published this novel in 1994. Distributed by Trafalgar Square, Pomfort, Vermont.

**Other books you might like:**
Leigh Clark, *Evil Reincarnate*, 1994
Basil Copper, *The Black Death*, 1993
Kathryn Meyer Griffith, *Witches*, 1994
Ruby Jean Jensen, *Baby Dolly*, 1991
Anne Rice, *The Witching Hour*, 1990
Guy N. Smith, *Witch Spell*, 1994

## 691

**TERRI BRISBIN**

### A Love through Time

(New York: Jove, 1998)

**Story type:** Fantasy (Time Travel; Romance)
**Major character(s):** Maggie Hobbs, Tourist; Alex MacKendimen, Businessman, Tourist
**Time period(s):** Indeterminate Past
**Locale(s):** Scotland

**Summary:** Maggie Hobbs and Alex MacKendimen meet while touring in Scotland, but their lives become inextricably linked when they are magically sent back through time to the medieval era. His fate appears to be to marry another, although he has fallen in love with Maggie. First novel.

**Other books you might like:**
Diane Bernard, *Eternally Yours*, 1996
Joyce Carlow, *Timeswept*, 1994
Diana Gabaldon, *Dragonfly in Amber*, 1992
Bobby Hutchinson, *Now and Then*, 1994
Kathleen Kirkwood, *A Slip in Time*, 1998

## 692

**KRISTEN BRITAIN**

### Green Rider

(New York: DAW, 1998)

**Story type:** Fantasy (Young Adult; Adventure)
**Major character(s):** Karigan Gladheon, Student (suspended), Courier (Green Rider); Laren Mapstone, Courier (Green Rider), Military Personnel (captain); Shawdell, Sorcerer, Immortal
**Time period(s):** Indeterminate

**Locale(s):** Sacoridia, Fictional Country; Mirwell Province, Mythical Place; Sacor City, Fictional City

**Summary:** When a mortally wounded Green Rider from His Majesty's Messenger Service gallops past Karigan and falls at her feet on the road, she reluctantly swears to complete his mission to deliver a vitally important message to the king. Hotly pursued by a mysterious hooded sorcerer and minions of the king's traitorous brother, Karigan finally delivers her message only to be further caught up in a world of magic and political intrigue that the pragmatic and honorable young merchant's daughter finds both exciting and appalling. First novel.

**Other books you might like:**
Marion Zimmer Bradley, *The Forest House*, 1994
Lynn Flewelling, *Luck in the Shadows*, 1996
Terry Goodkind, *Wizard's First Rule*, 1994
Rosemary Kirstein, *The Steerswoman*, 1989
Mercedes Lackey, *Arrows of the Queen*, 1987
Anne McCaffrey, *Moreta, Dragonlady of Pern*, 1983
Melanie Rawn, *Dragon Prince*, 1988

## 693

**POPPY Z. BRITE**

### Are You Loathsome Tonight?

(Springfield, Pennsylvania: Gauntlet Publications, 1998)

**Story type:** Horror (Collection)

**Summary:** This collection contains twelve stories strong in erotic and visceral content; two are in collaborations with other writers. Stand out selections include "Entertaining Mr. Orton," in which two male lovers rent the apartment haunted by the ghost of the murdered playwright Joe Orton; "Mussolini and the Axeman's Jazz," which links the crimes of a serial killer who terrorized New Orleans at the turn of the century to a centuries-old battle between sorcerers fought by their human surrogates; and the title story, a dark meditation on the death of Elvis Presley. With a foreword by Peter Straub, introduction by the author, and afterword by Caitlin R. Kiernan. Published only as a signed limited, edition.

**Other books you might like:**
Scott Edelman, *Suicide Art*, 1992
Elizabeth Massie, *Shadow Dreams*, 1996
Sue Storm, *Star Bones Weep the Blood of Angels*, 1995
Lucy Taylor, *Close to the Bone*, 1992
Lucy Taylor, *Unnatural Acts and Other Stories*, 1994

## 694

**POPPY Z. BRITE**

### Drawing Blood

(New York: Delacorte, 1993)

**Story type:** Horror (Haunted House)
**Major character(s):** Trevor McGee, Artist (a.k.a. Trevor Black); Zachary Busch, Computer Expert; Kinsey Hummingbird, Mechanic
**Time period(s):** 1970s (1972); 1990s (1992)
**Locale(s):** Missing Mile, North Carolina

**Summary:** Under the alias Trevor Black, Trevor McGee returns to the small North Carolina town where his artist father murdered Trevor's mother and brother before killing himself 20 years before. Fortified by the love of his soulmate Zachary Busch, Trevor seeks to understand his father's actions and, in so doing, breaks through to

Birdland, a spirit realm that fuels his artistic skills but also exposes him to the same madness that destroyed his father.

**Other books you might like:**
Giles Blunt, *Cold Eye*, 1988
Jessica Amanda Salmonson, *Anthony Shriek*, 1992

---

**695**

**POPPY Z. BRITE**

## Exquisite Corpse

(New York: Simon & Schuster, 1996)

**Story type:** Horror (Serial Killer)
**Major character(s):** Lysander "Jay" Byrne, Serial Killer; Andrew Compton, Serial Killer, Homosexual; Lucas Ransom, Writer (a.k.a. Lush Rimbaud)
**Time period(s):** 1990s (1996)
**Locale(s):** New Orleans, Louisiana

**Summary:** Andrew Compton, a gay serial killer modeled on real-life sociopath Jeffrey Dahmer, escapes from prison in London and flees to New Orleans. There, he meets and befriends Jay Byrne, a serial killer who has preyed for years on young men in the French Quarter, and the two express their emotions toward each other through an act of ritual murder and cannibalism.

**Other books you might like:**
Dennis Cooper, *Frisk*, 1991
Brett Easton Ellis, *American Psycho*, 1991
Thomas Harris, *The Silence of the Lambs*, 1988
Rick R. Reed, *Obsessed*, 1991

---

**696**

**POPPY Z. BRITE**

## The Lazarus Heart

(New York: HarperPrism, 1998)

**Story type:** Horror (Reanimated Dead)
**Major character(s):** Jared Poe, Photographer; Frank Gray, Police Officer; Jordan, Serial Killer
**Time period(s):** 1990s (1998)
**Locale(s):** New Orleans, Louisiana

**Summary:** Framed for the murder of his lover and murdered by an inmate in prison, Jared Poe returns from the grave to track down the real killer, a psychopath with a grudge against the gay and transgendered. Set in the universe of James O'Barr's graphic novel series The Crow.

**Other books you might like:**
David Bischoff, *Quoth the Crow*, 1998
Ric Meyers, *Fear Itself*, 1991
James O'Barr, *The Crow: Shattered Lives and Broken Dreams*, 1998
    Edward E. Kramer, co-editor
Chet Williamson, *The Crow: City of Angels*, 1996
Chet Williamson, *Clash by Night*, 1998

---

**697**

**POPPY Z. BRITE**

## Lost Souls

(New York: Delacorte, 1992)

**Story type:** Horror (Vampire Story)

**Major character(s):** Nothing, Teenager; Ghost, Musician (lead singer of Lost Souls); Zillah, Vampire
**Time period(s):** 1990s
**Locale(s):** New Orleans, Louisiana; Missing Mile, North Carolina

**Summary:** The author's first novel is a prose poem on adolescent angst, embodied in the character of Nothing, a child of mortal and vampire parents. Nothing runs away from his home in Maryland to missing Mile, North Carolina, home of the band Lost Souls? whose music speaks profoundly to him, but along the way encounters a van full of punk vampires and spends the rest of the story torn between their world of hedonistic excess and the world of misunderstood mortal teenagers.

**Other books you might like:**
Nancy A. Collins, *Sunglasses After Dark*, 1989
Nancy A. Collins, *Tempter*, 1990
Ray Garton, *Crucifax*, 1988
Anne Rice, *The Vampire Lestat*, 1985
John Skipp, *The Light at the End*, 1986
    Craig Spector, co-author
S.P. Somtow, *Vampire Junction*, 1983

---

**698**

**POPPY Z. BRITE**, Editor

## Love in Vein

(New York: HarperCollins, 1994)

**Story type:** Horror (Anthology; Vampire Story)
**Summary:** The 20 stories written originally for this volume all fall within the subgenre of erotic vampire fiction. Included are Norman Partridge's "Do Not Hasten to Bid Me Adieu," a variation on the Dracula legend as seen through the eyes of an American character from Bram Stoker's novel; Douglas Clegg's "White Chapel," about a being who feeds on human pain and suffering; Brian Hodge's "The Alchemy of the Throat," concerning a castrato who falls in with vampire society; Mike Baker's "Love Me Forever," featuring a shapeshifting vampire; A.R. Morlan's ".And the Horses Rise at Midnight," about a tattooed vampire in a carnival sideshow; Elizabeth Engstrom's "Elixir," about a color-blind man who draws his capacity to see normally from an unusually endowed hooker; and Robert Devereaux's "A Slow Red Whisper of Sand," which mixes vampires into a tableau of love and death in California.

**Other books you might like:**
Ellen Datlow, *Blood Is Not Enough*, 1989
    editor
Ellen Datlow, *A Whisper of Blood*, 1991
    editor
Amarantha Knight, *Love Bites*, 1995
    editor
Cecilia Tan, *Blood Kiss: Vampire Erotica*, 1994
    editor

---

**699**

**POPPY Z. BRITE**, Editor
**MARTIN H. GREENBERG**, Co-Editor

## Love in Vein II

(New York: HarperPrism, 1997)

**Story type:** Horror (Anthology; Vampire Story)
**Series:** Love in Vein

**Summary:** Eighteen erotic vampire tales by diverse authors. Highlights include David J. Schow's "Dusting the Flowers," the tale of a parasitic artist set in the Louisiana bayou; Brian Hodge's "The Dripping of Sundered Wineskins," in which a woman passes on her vampire taint to the survivor of an IRA bombing when she licks his wounds; Lucy Taylor's "Ceilings and Sky," in which a mother avenges the death of her child at the hands of a vampire cultist; and Nicholas Royle's "Kingyo No Fun," which traces a vampire undercurrent in Amsterdam's gay community.

**Other books you might like:**
Pam Keesey, *Darker Angels: Lesbian Vampire Stories*, 1995
  editor
Amarantha Knight, *Love Bites*, 1994
  editor
Michael Rowe, *Brothers of the Night*, 1997
  Thomas Roche, co-editor
Cecilia Tan, *Cherished Blood*, 1997
  editor
Cecilia Tan, *Erotic Vampire Tales*, 1994
  editor
Cecilia Tan, *Vampire Erotica*, 1996
  editor

---

**700**

### POPPY Z. BRITE

## Swamp Foetus

(Baltimore, Maryland: Borderlands Press, 1993)

**Story type:** Horror (Collection)

**Summary:** Twelve stories of provocative horror fiction, often with strong sexual content. Several draw strongly on the southern Gothic tradition, among them "His Mouth Shall Taste of Wormwood," an updating of H.P. Lovecraft's potboiler, "The Hound," and the coming of age tale, "A Georgia Story." "Angels" and "How to Get Ahead in New York" involve characters from the eponymous rock band of the author's first novel, *Lost Souls*. The best offerings are the World Fantasy Award nominated tales "The Ash of Memory, the Dust of Desire," and a harrowing tale of zombies in India, "Calcutta, Lord of Nerves." This book was released only in a signed limited edition.

**Other books you might like:**
Ramsey Campbell, *Scared Stiff*, 1987
Scott Edelman, *Suicide Art*, 1992
Ray Garton, *Methods of Madness*, 1990
Robert R. McCammon, *Blue World*, 1990
David J. Schow, *Seeing Red*, 1990

---

**701**

### C. DALE BRITTAIN

## A Bad Spell in Yurt

(New York: Baen, 1991)

**Story type:** Fantasy (Light Fantasy)
**Series:** Daimbert
**Major character(s):** Daimbert, Wizard (Royal)
**Time period(s):** Indeterminate
**Locale(s):** Yurt, Fictional Country; Alternate Earth

**Summary:** A mediocre wizard's school student, Daimbert finds he has much left to learn when he becomes Royal Wizard. With the king in danger, Daimbert searches for the person using black magic. When a dragon shows up and terrorizes people at the royal castle, Daimbert requires help from the retired Royal Wizard to defeat it.

**Other books you might like:**
Robert Don Hughes, *Prophet of Lamath*, 1979
Tanith Lee, *Black Unicorn*, 1991
Christopher Stasheff, *The Warlock Unlocked*, 1982
Michael C. Staudinger, *The Falcon Rises*, 1991
Jane Yolen, *Wizard's Hall*, 1990
Mary Frances Zambreno, *A Plague of Sorcerers*, 1991

---

**702**

### C. DALE BRITTAIN
### ROBERT A. BOUCHARD, Co-Author

## Count Scar

(New York: Baen, 1997)

**Story type:** Fantasy (Political; Magic Conflict)
**Major character(s):** Galoran, Nobleman (count), Military Personnel; Melchior, Religious, Wizard
**Time period(s):** Indeterminate Past
**Locale(s):** Peyrefixade, Fictional City

**Summary:** To his surprise, Galoran, a scarred and experienced soldier, inherits a distant county. At first, it seems like good luck, but troubles and threats become first noticeable, then inescapable. To survive, Galoran must make an alliance with Melchior, a monk and wizard who ought to be his bitter opponent.

**Other books you might like:**
Steven Brust, *Jhereg*, 1983
Deborah Chester, *Reign of Shadows*, 1996
Barbara Hambly, *The Ladies of Mandrigyn*, 1984
Patricia A. McKillip, *The Riddle-Master of Hed*, 1976
Angus Wells, *Forbidden Magic*, 1992

---

**703**

### C. DALE BRITTAIN

## Daughter of Magic

(New York: Baen, 1996)

**Story type:** Fantasy (Light Fantasy; Adventure)
**Series:** Daimbert
**Major character(s):** Daimbert, Wizard (royal); Theodora, Witch; Antonia, Witch, Child
**Time period(s):** Indeterminate
**Locale(s):** Yurt, Fictional Country; Caelrhon, Fictional Country

**Summary:** After Daimbert takes charge of his daughter, Antonia, she begins to exhibit distressing independence and use of magic, while Daimbert's undead enemy, Vlad, again attacks.

**Other books you might like:**
Carolyn Cushman, *Witch and Wombat*, 1994
Rose Estes, *Troll-Taken*, 1993
Holly Lisle, *Minerva Wakes*, 1994
James H. Schmitz, *The Witches of Karres*, 1966
Christopher Stasheff, *King Kobold*, 1971
Patricia C. Wrede, *Talking to Dragons*, 1993
  revised edition

## 704

### C. DALE BRITTAIN

## *Voima*

(New York: Baen, 1995)

**Story type:** Fantasy (Magic Conflict)
**Major character(s):** Roric No-man's Son, Warrior, Adventurer; Karin, Royalty, Adventurer; Valmar, Royalty, Adventurer
**Time period(s):** Indeterminate
**Locale(s):** Fictional Country

**Summary:** When the time of changes grows near, the immortal Wanderers find humans to help repair the damage caused by misuse of voima, the magic force of life and renewal. Meanwhile, many work against the Wanderers' influences as strife threatens the human kingdoms.

**Other books you might like:**
David Eddings, *Pawn of Prophecy*, 1982
Terry Goodkind, *Wizard's First Rule*, 1994
Barbara Hambly, *The Rainbow Abyss*, 1991
Katharine Kerr, *Daggerspell*, 1986
Mark C. Perry, *Morigu: The Dead*, 1990

## 705

### C. DALE BRITTAIN

## *The Witch and the Cathedral*

(New York: Baen, 1995)

**Story type:** Fantasy (Religious; Magic Conflict)
**Series:** Daimbert
**Major character(s):** Daimbert, Wizard (royal); Theodora, Witch
**Time period(s):** Indeterminate
**Locale(s):** Caelrhon, Fictional Country

**Summary:** Unhappy at his lot in love and events in Yurt, Daimbert travels to Caelrhon where he meets Theodora and finds himself instantly attracted to her. However, despite threats to the kingdom's cathedral by magical creatures, Daimbert's help seems unwanted by any of Caelrhon's powerful groups, leading Daimbert to suspect a plot against wizardry as an institution.

**Other books you might like:**
Mercedes Lackey, *The Eagle and the Nightingales*, 1995
Mercedes Lackey, *The Robin and the Kestrel*, 1993
Christopher Stasheff, *The Warlock in Spite of Himself*, 1969
Paula Volsky, *Illusion*, 1992

## 706

### C. DALE BRITTAIN

## *The Wood Nymph and the Cranky Saint*

(New York: Baen, 1993)

**Story type:** Fantasy (Quest; Light Fantasy)
**Series:** Daimbert
**Major character(s):** Daimbert, Wizard (royal); Joachim, Religious (royal chaplain), Adventurer
**Time period(s):** Indeterminate
**Locale(s):** Yurt, Fictional Country; Alternate Earth

**Summary:** Left in charge during the King of Yurt's vacation, Daimbert travels with Joachim to investigate the sighting of a wood nymph and complaints surrounding a saint's shrine. Daimbert unex-

pectedly finds himself called upon to act as judge in a question of royal honor.

**Other books you might like:**
Douglas W. Clark, *Whirlwind Alchemy*, 1993
Alexis A. Gilliland, *Lord of the Troll-Bats*, 1992
Nick Pollotta, *Bureau 13*, 1991
Christopher Stasheff, *The Warlock Heretical*, 1987
Christopher Stasheff, *The Warlock Rock*, 1990

## 707

### JOHN BRIZZOLARA

## *Empire's Horizon*

(New York: DAW, 1989)

**Story type:** Science Fiction (Theological)
**Major character(s):** Martin Cain, Journalist
**Time period(s):** Indeterminate Future
**Locale(s):** Darkath, Planet—Imaginary

**Summary:** Famous journalist Martin Cain has travelled from planet to planet reporting the news, but always hoping to find God. Arriving on Darkath, a remote outpost of the failing Terran Empire, he becomes embroiled in the religious controversies of the world's two native races and discovers a strange sort of redemption.

**Other books you might like:**
James Blish, *A Case of Conscience*, 1958
Mary Gentle, *Ancient Light*, 1987
Mary Gentle, *Golden Witchbreed*, 1985
Frank Herbert, *Children of Dune*, 1976
Frank Herbert, *Dune*, 1965
Frank Herbert, *Dune Messiah*, 1965
Robert Silverberg, *Downward to the Earth*, 1970

## 708

### DAMIEN BRODERICK

## *The White Abacus*

(New York: Avon, 1997)

**Story type:** Science Fiction (Political; Alternate Intelligence)
**Major character(s):** Ratio, Artificial Intelligence, Leader (Gamemaster); Telmah, Lord Cima, Heir—Dispossessed; Feng Orwen, Ruler (usurper)
**Time period(s):** Indeterminate Future
**Locale(s):** Earth; Psyche, Asteroid

**Summary:** Recognizing the potential threat of Psyche's anti-AI society and the impending fratricide of its leader, Ratio permits his Gesell connection's termination, becoming a Monad in order to get close to Telmah. Accompanied by Ratio, Telmah returns to Psyche to avenge his father's death, while Ratio works at protecting the larger community and, eventually, reconnecting with the Gesell.

**Other books you might like:**
Isaac Asimov, *The Robots of Dawn*, 1983
Philip K. Dick, *Blade Runner*, 1982
Philip K. Dick, *The Unteleported Man*, 1983
   revised
L. Warren Douglas, *Stepwater*, 1995
Dan Simmons, *Hyperion*, 1989
Sheri S. Tepper, *Grass*, 1989
Vernor Vinge, *A Fire upon the Deep*, 1992

## `709`

### BRUCE BROOKS

## *No Kidding*

(New York: Harper & Row, 1989)

**Story type:** Science Fiction (Young Adult)
**Major character(s):** Sam, Teenager; Ollie, Child (Sam's younger brother)
**Time period(s):** 21st century
**Locale(s):** Washington, District of Columbia

**Summary:** More than half the adult population of the United States is addicted to alcohol and children as young as twelve now have the legal right to have their alcoholic parents committed. Sam, a teenage boy with a compulsion to control others, has his mother committed and then, upon her release, has himself named her guardian.

**Other books you might like:**
Gary L. Blackwood, *The Dying Sun*, 1989
Robert Cormier, *Fade*, 1988
Leigh Kennedy, *The Journal of Nicholas the American*, 1986

## `710`

### TERRY BROOKS

## *The Druid of Shannara*

(New York: Del Rey, 1991)

**Story type:** Fantasy (Quest)
**Series:** Heritage of Shannara
**Major character(s):** Walker Boh, Adventurer; Morgan Leah, Adventurer; Pe Ell, Murderer
**Time period(s):** Indeterminate
**Locale(s):** The Four Lands, Mythical Place

**Summary:** Walker Boh, Morgan Leah and Pe Ell journey with Quickening, a creature created by the King of the Silver River, a being as old as mankind. They seek the Black Elfstone, which Walker needs to discharge his duty to restore Paranor, the lost Druid's Keep.

**Other books you might like:**
Dennis L. McKiernan, *The Dark Tide*, 1984
Dennis L. McKiernan, *Shadows of Doom*, 1984
J.R.R. Tolkien, *The Return of the King*, 1956
J.R.R. Tolkien, *The Two Towers*, 1955
J.R.R. Tolkien, *The Fellowship of the Ring*, 1954

## `711`

### TERRY BROOKS

## *The Elf Queen of Shannara*

(New York: Ballantine/Del Rey, 1992)

**Story type:** Fantasy (Quest)
**Series:** Heritage of Shannara
**Major character(s):** Wren Ohmsford, Mythical Creature (elf), Adventurer
**Time period(s):** Indeterminate
**Locale(s):** The Four Lands, Fictional Country; Morrowindl Island, Fictional Country

**Summary:** Carrying out the Druid, Allanon's, charge to Wren, that of finding and returning elves to the world of men, Wren and Garth travel westward. When Wren consults a Seer, the Addershag, she directs Wren to an island, Morrowindl, to which all Land Elves emigrated. Continuing their journey, they meet and receive assis-

tance from mythical and fantastic creatures as Wren grows aware of her elvish nature and her ability to wield magical forces.

**Other books you might like:**
Dennis L. McKiernan, *The Dark Tide*, 1984
Andre Norton, *The Elvenbane*, 1991
    Mercedes Lackey, co-author
J.R.R. Tolkien, *The Fellowship of the Ring*, 1954
J.R.R. Tolkien, *The Hobbit*, 1938
J.R.R. Tolkien, *The Return of the King*, 1956
J.R.R. Tolkien, *The Two Towers*, 1955
Terri Windling, *Life on the Border*, 1991
    editor

## `712`

### TERRY BROOKS

## *First King of Shannara*

(New York: Ballantine Del Rey, 1996)

**Story type:** Fantasy (Magic Conflict; Adventure)
**Series:** Shannara
**Major character(s):** Bremen, Wizard, Adventurer; Kinson Ravenloft, Scout, Adventurer
**Time period(s):** Indeterminate
**Locale(s):** The Four Lands, Fictional Country

**Summary:** When hoards of Trolls invade the Four Lands, Bremen, Kinson Ravenloft and their small company must find a means of defeating their evil leader, the corrupted Druid, Brona. Set after events in *The Talismans of Shannara* and prior to *The Sword of Shannara*.

**Other books you might like:**
Dave Duncan, *The Cutting Edge*, 1992
David Eddings, *Belgarath the Sorcerer*, 1995
    Leigh Eddings, co-author
Terry Goodkind, *Wizard's First Rule*, 1994
Robert Jordan, *The Eye of the World*, 1990
L.E. Modesitt Jr., *The Magic of Recluce*, 1991

## `713`

### TERRY BROOKS

## *Hook*

(New York: Fawcett Columbine, 1992)

**Story type:** Fantasy (Adventure; Quest)
**Major character(s):** James Hook, Pirate, Sea Captain; Peter "Peter Pan" Banning, Lawyer, Adventurer; Tinkerbell, Mythical Creature (fairy)
**Time period(s):** 1990s
**Locale(s):** Neverland, Mythical Place

**Summary:** To lure Peter Pan into a final battle, Captain Hook kidnaps Peter's children from Wendy's London home. Tinkerbell then returns Peter to Neverland, working to restore Peter's suppressed memories and credibility among the Lost Boys, Peter's former followers. Novelizes the film.

**Other books you might like:**
J.M. Barrie, *Peter Pan*, 1904
Stephen R. Donaldson, *Lord Foul's Bane*, 1977
Michael Ende, *The Neverending Story*, 1983
William Goldman, *The Princess Bride*, 1973
James Kahn, *Indiana Jones and the Temple of Doom*, 1984
J.R.R. Tolkien, *The Hobbit*, 1938

## 714

### TERRY BROOKS

## A Knight of the Word

(New York: Del Rey, 1998)

**Story type:** Fantasy (Magic Conflict)
**Major character(s):** John Ross, Professor, Sorcerer; Nest Freemark, Sorceress, Student—College, Sports Figure
**Time period(s):** 19th century
**Locale(s):** United States

**Summary:** John Ross serves the Word by traveling across America, locating and neutralizing the agents of the evil Void. The constant use of magic devastates his body and his soul, and one particularly brutal confrontation causes him to lose faith in his cause, a faith that will only be restored with the assistance of a talented young woman.

**Other books you might like:**
Poul Anderson, *The Devil's Game*, 1980
James P. Blaylock, *Homunculus*, 1986
Emma Bull, *War for the Oaks*, 1987
R.A. MacAvoy, *Tea with the Black Dragon*, 1983
Michael Swanwick, *Jack Faust*, 1997

## 715

### TERRY BROOKS

## Running with the Demon

(New York: Ballantine Del Ray, 1997)

**Story type:** Fantasy (Contemporary)
**Major character(s):** John Ross, Psychic; Nest Freemark, Teenager, Student—High School, Sorceress; The Demon, Demon
**Time period(s):** 1990s
**Locale(s):** Hopewell, Illinois

**Summary:** Over a swelteringly hot Fourth of July weekend, during a steel mill strike that divides Hopewell, a demon schemes to control the town and Nest Freemark's soul. Drawn to the site by horrific dreams of the future which will evolve if he cannot successfully neutralize the threat, John Ross also gravitates to Nest as he battles the demon.

**Other books you might like:**
James P. Blaylock, *All the Bells on Earth*, 1995
Elizabeth Hand, *Waking the Moon*, 1995
Rachel Pollack, *Godmother Night*, 1996
Tim Powers, *Last Call*, 1992
Manly Wade Wellman, *The Old Gods Waken*, 1979

## 716

### TERRY BROOKS

## The Scions of Shannara

(New York: Del Rey, 1990)

**Story type:** Fantasy (Quest)
**Series:** Heritage of Shannara
**Major character(s):** Par Ohmsford, Heir—Lost, Magician; Coll Ohmsford, Adventurer
**Time period(s):** Indeterminate
**Locale(s):** The Four Lands, Mythical Place

**Summary:** Three hundred years after events in the Sword of Shannara Series, Par Ohmsford and his brother Coll search to find Par's lost legacy, the fabled sword of Shannara.

**Other books you might like:**
Dennis L. McKiernan, *The Dark Tide*, 1984
Dennis L. McKiernan, *Shadows of Doom*, 1984
J.R.R. Tolkien, *The Return of the King*, 1956
J.R.R. Tolkien, *The Two Towers*, 1955
J.R.R. Tolkien, *The Fellowship of the Ring*, 1954

## 717

### TERRY BROOKS

## The Talismans of Shannara

(New York: Ballantine Del Rey, 1993)

**Story type:** Fantasy (Quest; Magic Conflict)
**Series:** Heritage of Shannara
**Major character(s):** Par Ohmsford, Mythical Creature (elf), Adventurer; Walker Boh, Magician (Druidic), Warrior; Wren Elessedil, Mythical Creature (elf), Ruler (Queen)
**Time period(s):** Indeterminate
**Locale(s):** The Four Lands, Fictional Country

**Summary:** Despite completing their quests, the descendants of the House of Shannara remain plagued by Shadowen dark magic and Rimmer Dall's determination to separate the family. Par can alleviate the problems, but only if he can master the legendary Sword of Shannara. Concludes the series.

**Other books you might like:**
Patricia Briggs, *Masques*, 1993
Dave Duncan, *The Cutting Edge*, 1992
David Eddings, *Pawn of Prophecy*, 1982
Robert Jordan, *The Eye of the World*, 1989
J.R.R. Tolkien, *The Fellowship of the Ring*, 1954
Margaret Weis, *Fire Sea*, 1991
　　Tracy Hickman, co-author
Margaret Weis, *Into the Labyrinth*, 1993
　　Tracy Hickman, co-author

## 718

### TERRY BROOKS

## The Tangle Box

(New York: Ballantine Del Rey, 1994)

**Story type:** Fantasy (Magic Conflict)
**Series:** Magic Kingdom of Landover
**Major character(s):** Ben Holiday, Ruler (King of Landover), Parent; Willow, Royalty (Queen of Landover); Horris Kew, Magician, Criminal
**Time period(s):** Indeterminate
**Locale(s):** Landover, Fictional Country

**Summary:** When Ben Holiday initiates the repatriation to Landover of the outcasts Horris and Biggar, Ben falls victim to the plot of an evil sorcerer, Gorse, who plans revenge and conquest in Landover. Imprisoned with comrades in the labyrinthine Tangle Box, Ben must rely on rescue from the Lady Willow whose mysterious mission yields hints of Ben's plight.

**Other books you might like:**
Patricia Briggs, *Masques*, 1993
Susan Dexter, *The Wizard's Shadow*, 1993
Barbara Hambly, *The Silent Tower*, 1986
Barbara Hambly, *The Time of the Dark*, 1982
A.C.H. Smith, *Labyrinth: A Novel*, 1986
Martha Wells, *The Element of Fire*, 1993

Elizabeth Willey, *The Well-Favored Man: The Tale of the Sorcerer's Nephew*, 1993

## 719

### TERRY BROOKS

## *Witches' Brew*

(New York: Ballantine Del Rey, 1995)

**Story type:** Fantasy (Magic Conflict; Adventure)
**Series:** Magic Kingdom of Landover
**Major character(s):** Ben Holiday, Ruler, Parent; Questor Thews, Wizard, Adventurer; Abernathy, Animal (dog), Adventurer
**Time period(s):** Indeterminate
**Locale(s):** Landover, Fictional Country

**Summary:** Ben Holiday wishes for continuing peaceful times in Landover so he can enjoy his magical daughter's childhood. However, King Rydall desires control of Landover and sends seven champions, each of a different form, which Ben must defeat before Rydall will abandon his claims to Landover.

**Other books you might like:**
Dave Duncan, *The Cutting Edge*, 1993
Holly Lisle, *Mind of the Magic*, 1995
Margaret Weis, *Dragon Wing*, 1990
    Tracy Hickman, co-author
Martha Wells, *The Element of Fire*, 1993
Elizabeth Willey, *The Well-Favored Man: The Tale of the Sorcerer's Nephew*, 1993

## 720

### JOHN BROSNAN

## *The Sky Lords*

(New York: St. Martins Press, 1991)

**Story type:** Science Fiction (Genetic Manipulation; Post-Holocaust)
**Major character(s):** Jan Dorvin, Fugitive; Milo, Genetically Altered Being, Immortal
**Time period(s):** Indeterminate Future
**Locale(s):** Minerva, Fictional Country (feminist); Sky Lord Pangloth, Alternate Earth (giant dirigible)

**Summary:** In the 800 years since the Genetic Wars, the Sky Lords, giant dirigibles, have come to control the ground over which they fly, and the people who still survive there. The aftermath of the Genetic Wars, the Blight, is gradually destroying what viable surface remains, and the science which could have solved the Earth's problems has been forgotten. Jan Darvin, the last woman from Minerva, joins forces with Milo, a strange genetically altered man, who promises Jan revenge on the Sky Lord Pangloth which destroyed Minerva.

**Other books you might like:**
Steven Barnes, *Gorgon Child*, 1989
Charles Ingrid, *The Marked Man*, 1989
Donald E. McQuinn, *Warrior*, 1990
Joan Slonczewski, *The Wall Around Eden*, 1989
Sheri S. Tepper, *The Gate to Women's Country*, 1988
Michael D. Weaver, *My Father Immortal*, 1989
Paul O. Williams, *The Breaking of Northwall*, 1980

## 721

### JOHN BROSNAN

## *The War of the Sky Lords*

(New York: St. Martin's Press, 1992)

**Story type:** Science Fiction (Post-Holocaust; Adventure)
**Series:** Sky Lords
**Major character(s):** Jan Dorvin, Administrator (Minervan); Ryn ''Robin'', Runaway; Andrea Du Lucent, Royalty (princess)
**Time period(s):** Indeterminate Future
**Locale(s):** Minerva, Fictional Country; *Sky Angel*, At Sea (giant dirigible); Shangri La, Undersea Environment/Habitat

**Summary:** In a habitat deep under Antarctica the Eloi protect Ryn from the diseases and Sky Lords of the outer world. When the renegade fleet of Sky Lords searching for the habitat arrives in the Antarctic, Ryn escapes to the Lord Mordred, trading his support of the Duke Du Lucent for sex with the Princess Andrea. Meanwhile in the north, Jan Dorvin works at eliminating the blight and developing a new, healthy society.

**Other books you might like:**
John Crowley, *Beasts*, 1976
Marjorie Bradley Kellogg, *Harmony*, 1991
Donald E. McQuinn, *Warrior*, 1990
Pat Murphy, *The City, Not Long After*, 1989
Sheri S. Tepper, *The Gate to Women's Country*, 1988
Joan D. Vinge, *The Summer Queen*, 1991
Paul O. Williams, *The Breaking of Northwall*, 1980

## 722

### CHARLES BROCKDEN BROWN

## *Three Gothic Novels*

(New York: Library of America, 1998)

**Story type:** Horror (Collection)

**Summary:** This is an omnibus repackaging of three seminal American Gothic novels. *Wieland* (1798) is a tale of family madness and religious hysteria. *Arthur Mervyn* (1798) is a bildungsroman of a young man's seduction into, and attempt to rehabilitate himself from, a life of crime, set during horrific scenes of a yellow fever outbreak in Philadelphia. *Edgar Huntly* (1799) is a nightmarish narrative of the experiences of the title character in the wilderness. Edited by Sydney J. Krause.

**Other books you might like:**
Nathaniel Hawthorne, *The Celestial Railroad and Other Stories*, 1963
James Hogg, *Private Memoirs and Confessions of a Justified Sinner*, 1825
Washington Irving, *The Legend of Sleepy Hollow and Other Stories*, 1962
Edgar Allan Poe, *Complete Stories and Poems*, 1966

## 723

### CROSLAND BROWN

## *Tombley's Walk*

(New York: Avon, 1991)

**Story type:** Horror (Werewolf Story)
**Major character(s):** Bud Turner, Fugitive (alias James Ernest Rigler); Melody Parker, Lawyer; Justin Barker, Banker
**Time period(s):** 1980s (1986)

**Locale(s):** Tombley's Walk, Texas

**Summary:** At the height of a rabies epidemic in rural Texas, a series of strange maulings occurs. Some leave the victims dead, but others leave the victims alive and ravenous in their appetites for food, sex, and mayhem. This is the author's first novel.

**Other books you might like:**
Ron Dee, *Dusk*, 1991
Chelsea Quinn Yarbro, *Beastnights*, 1989
Gary Brandner, *The Howling*, 1983

---

**724**

**JERRY EARL BROWN**

### Earthfall

(New York: Ace Books, 1990)

**Story type:** Science Fiction (Post-Nuclear Holocaust)
**Major character(s):** Chia Swann, Spaceship Captain; O'Rourke, Wanderer
**Time period(s):** 22nd century
**Locale(s):** Outer Space (In Earth orbit)

**Summary:** More than one hundred years after a nuclear war nearly ended all life on Earth, primitive humanity still clings to survival on the desolate, mutant-infested planet. Meanwhile, a high-tech human civilization flourishes in Earth-orbit and beyond. Travel to the Earth's surface is prohibited, the interdiction strictly enforced by deadly EarthWatch sentinels. One woman, Chia Swann, determines to brave both the dangers on Earth and those in Earth-orbit to save the human beings who still survive on the planet's surface.

**Other books you might like:**
Walter M. Miller Jr., *A Canticle for Leibowitz*, 1960
Robert Silverberg, *At Winter's End*, 1988
Robert Silverberg, *The New Springtime*, 1989
Michael D. Weaver, *My Father Immortal*, 1989

---

**725**

**JERRY EARL BROWN**

### Snowmen

(New York: Pocket, 1991)

**Story type:** Science Fiction (Genetic Manipulation; Adventure)
**Major character(s):** Neil Freese, Guide; Dennis Gall, Guide
**Time period(s):** 1990s
**Locale(s):** Nepal

**Summary:** As Gall and Freese rush to save a climber from death, they uncover the remains of Operation Snowman, a biological experiment using criminals that has gone horribly wrong.

**Other books you might like:**
Philip Jose Farmer, *Escape From Loki*, 1991
Marc Laidlaw, *Neon Lotus*, 1988
Kim Stanley Robinson, *Escape From Kathmandu*, 1989
Elizabeth Ann Scarborough, *Nothing Sacred*, 1991
Ryder Syvertson, *Fortress of Forbidden Destiny*, 1991

---

**726**

**MARY BROWN**

### Master of Many Treasures

(New York: Baen, 1995)

**Story type:** Fantasy (Quest)

**Series:** Unlikely Ones
**Major character(s):** Summer, Telepath, Traveler; Growch, Animal (dog), Companion; Jason, Mythical Creature (dragon), Human
**Time period(s):** Indeterminate
**Locale(s):** Venice, Italy; Middle East; Blue Mountain, Mythical Place

**Summary:** With a magic ring to protect her and foster communication through telepathy with animals, Summer realizes she must follow her one true love, now a dragon most of the time, and achieve her destiny. Sequel to *Pigs Don't Fly*.

**Other books you might like:**
Lois McMaster Bujold, *The Spirit Ring*, 1992
Don Callander, *Dragon Companion*, 1994
Robert N. Charrette, *Never Deal with a Dragon*, 1990
Thorarinn Gunnarsson, *Dragon's Domain*, 1993
Angus Wells, *Lords of the Sky*, 1994

---

**727**

**MARY BROWN**

### Pigs Don't Fly

(New York: Baen, 1994)

**Story type:** Fantasy (Light Fantasy; Quest)
**Major character(s):** Summer, Orphan, Guide; Gilman, Knight, Handicapped; The Wimperling, Animal
**Time period(s):** Indeterminate Past (medieval)
**Locale(s):** Fictional City; Evreux, Fictional City; Fictional Country (on the road)

**Summary:** When Summer's mother dies, she finds herself alone in a hostile village. She flees with only her dowry and a magic ring that permits her to understand the speech of animals. Out of love and pity, she seeks to guide a chance-met knight, recently blinded and suffering from amnesia, to his home with the aid of a dog, a horse, a pigeon and a pig.

**Other books you might like:**
Peter S. Beagle, *The Folk of the Air*, 1986
Lois McMaster Bujold, *The Spirit Ring*, 1992
Barbara Hambly, *Dragonsbane*, 1986
Patricia A. McKillip, *The Forgotten Beasts of Eld*, 1976
Patricia C. Wrede, *Sorcery and Cecelia*, 1988
   Caroline Stevermer, co-author

---

**728**

**MARY BROWN**

### Strange Deliverance

(New York: Baen, 1997)

**Story type:** Science Fiction (Post-Disaster; UFO)
**Major character(s):** Prettiance "Pretty", Teenager; Tamerlane "Tam", Teenager; The Herb-Woman, Healer, Parent
**Time period(s):** Indeterminate Future
**Locale(s):** Earth

**Summary:** Aliens crash-land their crippled ship in a clearing near a village, driving most of the panic-stricken villagers to flee into the war-torn lands around them. Another group of refugees soon finds the deserted village and begins to develop its own society. Fifty years later, their grandchildren dare to explore the forbidden wilderness and discover strange powers inside a circle of standing stones.

**Other books you might like:**
David Brin, *The Postman*, 1985
Emma Bull, *Bone Dance: A Fantasy for Technophiles*, 1991
Pamela Dean, *The Dubious Hills*, 1994

Pat Frank, *Alas, Babylon*, 1959
H.P. Lovecraft, *The Colour out of Space and Others*, 1964
John Wyndham, *Re-Birth*, 1955
Jane Yolen, *Briar Rose*, 1992

---

**729**

### JESSE BROWNER

## Conglomeros

(New York: Random House, 1992)

**Story type:** Fantasy (Satire; Contemporary)
**Major character(s):** Aaron X, Heir, Smuggler; Conglomeros, Monster; Victor Brauner, Artist (deceased)
**Time period(s):** 1990s
**Locale(s):** New York, New York; Piatra Neamt, Romania

**Summary:** While at an exhibition of Victor Brauner's life works, Aaron encounters a statue of the Conglomeros. That night he dreams of the statue and, upon awakening, recognizes it from a description in his grandfather's diary. Convinced that the Conglomeros exists in an innocent state, Aaron decides after much research to find it and protect it from harm. Unfortunately, despite their best efforts, humans frequently destroy what they love. Author's first novel.

**Other books you might like:**
Orson Scott Card, *Songmaster*, 1980
Jeff Collignon, *Her Monster*, 1992
Samuel R. Delany, *Tales of Neveryon*, 1979
Mark Jacobson, *Gojiro*, 1991
Whitley Strieber, *The Wild*, 1991
Donald E. Westlake, *Humans*, 1991

---

**730**

### VICTORIA BROWNWORTH, Editor

## Night Bites: Vampire Stories by Women

(Seattle: Seal Press, 1996)

**Story type:** Horror (Anthology; Vampire Story)

**Summary:** This volume contains 16 original and frequently erotic stories by female authors featuring vampires. Victoria Brownworth's "Twelfth Night" is concerned with a vampire journalist who uses the world beat she covers to conceal her feeding habits. Judith M. Redding's "Unexpurgated Notes from a Homicide" tells of vampires who seek an antidote for the AIDS-infected blood they have consumed. Nikki Baker's "Backlash" concerns a female detective in pursuit of a vampiric killer, and Judith Katz's "Anita, Polish Vampire, Holds Forth at the Jewish Cafe of the Dead," a vampire koffee-klatsch. In Lisa D. Williamson's "Best of Friends," a teenager mistakes her burgeoning vampirism for an unwanted pregnancy, and in Mabel Maney's "Almost the Color of the Summer Sky," a young girl fascinated by a vampire movie is oblivious to the existence of a vampire in her immediate family.

**Other books you might like:**
Martin H. Greenberg, *Vamps*, 1987
    Charles G. Waugh, co-editor
Barbara Hambly, *Sisters of the Night*, 1995
    Martin H. Greenberg, co-editor
Pam Keesey, *Dark Angels: Lesbian Vampire Stories*, 1995
    editor
Pam Keesey, *Daughters of Darkness: Lesbian Vampire Stories*, 1993
    editor
Robert Weinberg, *Girls' Night Out*, 1997
    Stefan Dziemianowicz and Martin H. Greenberg, co-editors

---

**731**

### JOSEPH BRUCHAC

## Dawn Land

(Golden, Colorado: Fulcrum Publishing, 1993)

**Story type:** Fantasy (Quest; Legend)
**Major character(s):** Young Hunter, Prehistoric Human (Abenaki Indian), Teenager; Medicine Plant, Psychic (seer), Indian (Abenaki Indian); Talker, Shaman, Prehistoric Human (Abenaki Indian)
**Time period(s):** 80th century B.C.
**Locale(s):** Adirondack Mountains, North America; Hudson River Valley, North America

**Summary:** While out hunting food for his tribe, Young Hunter is bitten by a snake. Unharmed by the bite, he returns to tell the tribal elders of the incident. Talker, the shaman, recognizes this as a spiritual event; Young Hunter has been chosen by the snake to be the protector of his people. And a menace soon appears, one that will challenge all of Young Hunter's strength, both physical and spiritual, in a fight for the survival of the Only People.

**Other books you might like:**
Jean M. Auel, *Clan of the Cave Bear*, 1980
W. Michael Gear, *People of the River*, 1992
    Kathleen O'Neal Gear, co-author
Betsy James, *Dark Heart*, 1992
Lynn Armistead McKee, *Woman of the Mists*, 1991
William Sarabande, *Thunder in the Sky*, 1992
Roger Welsch, *Touching the Fire*, 1992

---

**732**

### J.V. BRUMMELS

## Deus Ex Machina

(New York: Bantam Spectra, 1989)

**Story type:** Science Fiction (End of the World)
**Major character(s):** David Jones, Writer
**Time period(s):** 21st century
**Locale(s):** New City, Earth

**Summary:** Environmental problems and over-population have brought the world to a state of near collapse and now everything seems likely to be destroyed as the sun goes nova. A small number of people must decide whether to perish with the rest of humanity or leave the planet using an experimental teleportation device. This is Brummels' first novel.

**Other books you might like:**
Vonda N. McIntyre, *Starfarers*, 1989
Philip Wylie, *When Worlds Collide*, 1933
    Edwin Balmer, co-author

---

**733**

### JOHN BRUNNER

## Children of the Thunder

(New York: Ballantine Del Rey, 1989)

**Story type:** Science Fiction (Psychic Powers)
**Major character(s):** Peter Levin, Writer (Science writer); Claudia Morris, Sociologist
**Time period(s):** 1990s
**Locale(s):** England

**Summary:** Claudia Morris's research into juvenile delinquency seems to point to a pattern. Brilliant children are committing crimes of greater or lesser magnitude, and getting away with them. Peter Levin's reporter's sense tells him that something important is going on. Working together, they make a discovery that could change the world.

**Other books you might like:**
Roger MacBride Allen, *Orphan of Creation*, 1988
Daniel Keys Moran, *Emerald Eyes*, 1988
Daniel Keys Moran, *The Long Run*, 1989
A.E. Van Vogt, *Slan*, 1946
John Wyndham, *The Midwich Cuckoos*, 1957

---

**734**

JOHN BRUNNER

## A Maze of Stars

(New York: Ballantine/Del Rey, 1991)

**Story type:** Science Fiction (Alternate Intelligence; Adventure)
**Major character(s):** Ship, Artificial Intelligence; Stripe, Passenger; Volar, Passenger
**Time period(s):** Indeterminate Future
**Locale(s):** Milky Way Galaxy, Outer Space

**Summary:** The Ship which brought colonists to the worlds of the Arm makes repeated sweeps to see how they are doing, but these sweeps are muddled in time so that this latest sweep is the earliest as far as the settlers are concerned. Ship has passengers from time to time who comment on the planets it visits, each leaving the Ship at a world of their choosing. Some colonists are advanced enough to build their own starships while others have reverted to cannibalism or changed into something inhuman. Still the Ship must continue its sweeps lest it feels the all too human emotion of boredom.

**Other books you might like:**
Poul Anderson, *The Boat of a Million Years*, 1989
James Blish, *Earthman, Come Home*, 1955
James Blish, *A Life for the Stars*, 1962
Glen Cook, *The Dragon Never Sleeps*, 1988
Keith Laumer, *Star Colony*, 1981
Anne McCaffrey, *The Ship Who Sang*, 1969
Frederik Pohl, *The World at the End of Time*, 1990
Robert J. Sawyer, *Golden Fleece*, 1990
David Alexander Smith, *Homecoming*, 1990
Norman Spinrad, *The Void Captain's Tale*, 1983

---

**735**

JOHN BRUNNER

## Muddle Earth

(New York: Ballantine Del Rey, 1993)

**Story type:** Science Fiction (Satire; Adventure)
**Major character(s):** Rinpoche Gibbs, Time Traveler, Adventurer; Nixy Anangaranga-Jones, Tourist, Adventurer; Sherlock Holmes, Detective—Private, Teenager
**Time period(s):** 24th century
**Locale(s):** Earth

**Summary:** Revived from cryogenic suspended animation and cured of disease, Rinpoche Gibbs discovers an Earth now run by aliens as a tourist attraction and fraught with science fiction cliches. As usual with wealthy resurrectees, authorities omit the standard orientation and allow Gibbs to reeducate himself. When he immediately runs afoul of authorities and organized crime, Gibbs must seek help from

an adolescent Sherlock Holmes in a Victorian London reenactment zone.

**Other books you might like:**
Douglas Adams, *The Hitchhiker's Guide to the Galaxy*, 1980
Chester Anderson, *The Butterfly Kid*, 1967
Ron Goulart, *After Things Fell Apart*, 1970
Ron Goulart, *When the Waker Sleeps*, 1975
Larry Niven, *Fallen Angels*, 1991
    Jerry Pournelle, Michael Flynn, co-authors
Mike Resnick, *Inside the Funhouse*, 1992
    editor
Ken Rolston, *Extreme Paranoia: Nobody Knows the Trouble I've Shot*, 1991
H.G. Wells, *When the Sleeper Wakes*, 1899

---

**736**

JOHN BRUNNER

## The Shockwave Rider

(New York: Ballantine/Del Rey, 1990)

**Story type:** Science Fiction (Future Shock)
**Major character(s):** Nickie Haflinger, Experimental Subject
**Time period(s):** 21st century
**Locale(s):** United States

**Summary:** A massive computerized data-net controls virtually everything and the majority of Americans suffer periodic nervous breakdowns caused by future shock. Nickie Haflinger lives at Tarnover, a mysterious institution which has trained him from childhood to handle large quantities of data without falling prey to future shock. Eventually, however, Nickie discovers that Tarnover has its darker side. The scientists there are doing experiments in genetic manipulation which result in children who are deformed but even more capable of manipulating data than Nickie is. Nickie flees the institution and begins to search for a way to destroy both it and the out-of-control data-net which has enslaved humanity. Originally published in 1975.

**Other books you might like:**
William Gibson, *Neuromancer*, 1984
Kim Stanley Robinson, *The Gold Coast*, 1988
Norman Spinrad, *Little Heroes*, 1987
Bruce Sterling, *Islands in the Net*, 1988

---

**737**

KAREN BRUSH

## Demon Pig

(New York: Avon, 1991)

**Story type:** Fantasy (Magic Conflict; Light Fantasy)
**Major character(s):** Quadroped, Animal (pig)
**Time period(s):** Indeterminate
**Locale(s):** Nine Kingdoms, Fictional Country

**Summary:** When the Queen of the Dead enlists the help of a trickster god to start a new war, Quadroped and his strange friends must restore peace to the Nine Kingdoms while rescuing his people and stopping the forces of evil.

**Other books you might like:**
Kenneth Grahame, *The Wind in the Willows*, 1908
Brian Jacques, *Mattimeo*, 1990
Brian Jacques, *Mossflower*, 1988
Brian Jacques, *Redwall*, 1987
Garry Kilworth, *The Foxes of Firstdark*, 1990

Margery Sharp, *The Rescuers*, 1959
Tad Williams, *Tailchaser's Song*, 1985
David Henry Wilson, *The Coachman Rat*, 1985

---

**738**

**STEVEN BRUST**

## Agyar

(New York: Tor, 1993)

**Story type:** Fantasy (Urban; Horror)
**Major character(s):** Janos ''Jack'' Agyar, Vampire; Jim, Spirit; Susan Pfahl, Student
**Time period(s):** 1990s
**Locale(s):** Lakota, Ohio

**Summary:** Jack is compelled by Laura Kellem to come to Lakota to take the fall for the deaths she caused. While her scheme develops, though, Jack finds friendship with a ghost, satisfaction in writing, sustenance and power with Jill and a bond with Susan that leads him to overthrow all of it.

**Other books you might like:**
Suzy McKee Charnas, *The Vampire Tapestry*, 1980
Storm Constantine, *Burying the Shadow*, 1992
Charles de Lint, *Mulengro: A Romany Tale*, 1985
John M. Ford, *The Dragon Waiting*, 1983
Megan Lindholm, *Wizard of the Pigeons*, 1986

---

**739**

**STEVEN BRUST**

## Athyra

(New York: Ace, 1993)

**Story type:** Fantasy (Adventure)
**Series:** Vlad Taltos
**Major character(s):** Vlad Taltos, Sorcerer, Martial Arts Expert (retired assassin); Saun, Apprentice, Healer
**Time period(s):** Indeterminate Future
**Locale(s):** Smallcliff, Fictional City

**Summary:** On his way to a lesson with his master, Saun encounters a mysterious easterner named Vlad and becomes curious over Vlad's background and the possibility of Vlad teaching Saun witchcraft.

**Other books you might like:**
Jonathan Carroll, *Sleeping in Flame*, 1988
Glen Cook, *The Black Company*, 1984
Barbara Hambly, *The Rainbow Abyss*, 1991
Tanya Huff, *Child of the Grove*, 1988
Mickey Zucker Reichert, *The Legend of Nightfall*, 1993

---

**740**

**STEVEN BRUST**

## Cowboy Feng's Space Bar and Grille

(New York: Ace Books, 1990)

**Story type:** Science Fiction (Humor)
**Major character(s):** Billy, Musician; Jamie, Musician
**Time period(s):** Indeterminate Future; Indeterminate Past
**Locale(s):** Montenegro; Outer Space

**Summary:** A time-travelling bar, owned by a very strange proprietor and full of eccentric patrons, leaps across space and time to avoid a nuclear war, voyaging first to the moon and later to other solar systems altogether.

**Other books you might like:**
Spider Robinson, *Callahan's Crosstime Saloon*, 1977
Spider Robinson, *Callahan's Lady*, 1989
Spider Robinson, *Callahan's Secret*, 1986
Spider Robinson, *Time Travelers Strictly Cash*, 1981

---

**741**

**STEVEN BRUST**

## Dragon

(New York: Tor, 1998)

**Story type:** Fantasy (Adventure; Political)
**Series:** Vlad Taltos
**Major character(s):** Vlad Taltos, Sorcerer (assassin), Martial Arts Expert (reluctant mercenary); Liosh, Mythical Creature (winged lizard), Telepath (Vlad's telepathic companion); Morrolan, Mythical Creature (dragonlord)
**Time period(s):** Indeterminate Future
**Locale(s):** Dragaera, Planet—Imaginary

**Summary:** Against his better judgment, Vlad accepts employment from Dragonlord Morrolan, in which he must protect some of the most fear-inspiring magical weapons. In the process of this mission, Vlad finds himself in the midst of possibly the largest epic battle of his lifetime, and it threatens to be his last. With the help of Lioth, Vlad must turn the tide of the battle and save the day.

**Other books you might like:**
Alan Dean Foster, *The Tar-Aiym Krang*, 1988
Maggie Furey, *Aurian*, 1994
Joel Rosenberg, *The Fire Duke*, 1996
Joan D. Vinge, *The Summer Queen*, 1991
M.K. Wren, *Sword of the Lamb*, 1981

---

**742**

**STEVEN BRUST**

## Five Hundred Years After

(New York: Tor, 1994)

**Story type:** Fantasy (Political; Adventure)
**Series:** Khaavren Romances
**Major character(s):** Khaavren of House Tiassa, Military Personnel (Imperial Guard); Pel of House Yendi, Nobleman (Duke of Galstan); Aliera e'Kieron, Royalty
**Time period(s):** Indeterminate Past (350 years prior to *Jhereg*)
**Locale(s):** Dragaera, Planet—Imaginary

**Summary:** Five hundred years after events in *The Phoenix Guards*, Khaavren and his companions must foil the uprising and conspiracy which threatens to destroy the Imperial Orb and the very fabric of Dragaeran society. Pays homage to Alexandre Dumas' *Twenty Years After*.

**Other books you might like:**
Alexandre Dumas, *Twenty Years After*, 1845
Katharine Kerr, *Daggerspell*, 1986
Mercedes Lackey, *Magic's Promise*, 1990
Sheri S. Tepper, *King's Blood Four*, 1983
Chelsea Quinn Yarbro, *A Candle for D'Artagnan*, 1989

## 743

**STEVEN BRUST**
**EMMA BULL**, Co-Author

### Freedom & Necessity

(New York: Tor, 1997)

**Story type:** Fantasy (Historical; Political)
**Major character(s):** James Cobham, Writer, Wealthy; Richard Cobham, Writer, Wealthy; Susan Voight, Writer, Wealthy
**Time period(s):** 19th century
**Locale(s):** England

**Summary:** After the presumed death of James, Richard receives letters letting him know that James is alive, and starts searching for him. Susan, who loved James, also searches for him and pools information with Richard, discovering the much larger political plotting that enmeshes the socio-political structure of England and Europe.

**Other books you might like:**
Emma Bull, *Bone Dance: A Fantasy for Technophiles*, 1991
Emma Bull, *Finder*, 1994
Emma Bull, *The Princess and the Lord of Night*, 1994
Emma Bull, *War for the Oaks*, 1987
Patricia C. Wrede, *Sorcery and Cecelia*, 1988
    Caroline Stevermer, co-author

## 744

**STEVEN BRUST**
**MEGAN LINDHOLM**, Co-Author

### The Gypsy

(New York: Tor, 1992)

**Story type:** Fantasy (Mystery; Urban)
**Major character(s):** Cigany, Gypsy; Mike Stepovich, Police Officer
**Time period(s):** 1990s
**Locale(s):** Lakota, Indiana

**Summary:** Nothing in Mike Stepovich's life makes sense any more, what with seeing his new partner as a jerk, losing touch with his kids since his divorce and hating being single. Now, against all evidence and sense, he believes the arrested Gypsy innocent. Despite Mike's efforts, people still die. For his part, the Gypsy slowly remembers his purpose in Lakota and his role in fighting the Fair Lady.

**Other books you might like:**
Emma Bull, *Bone Dance: A Fantasy for Technophiles*, 1991
Charles de Lint, *Mulengro: A Romany Tale*, 1985
Heather Gladney, *Teot's War*, 1987
Lisa Goldstein, *A Mask for the General*, 1987
Megan Lindholm, *Cloven Hooves*, 1991
Megan Lindholm, *Wizard of the Pigeons*, 1986
Pat Murphy, *The Falling Woman*, 1986

## 745

**STEVEN BRUST**

### Orca

(New York: Ace, 1996)

**Story type:** Fantasy (Adventure; Political)
**Series:** Vlad Taltos
**Major character(s):** Vlad Taltos, Sorcerer, Martial Arts Expert (assassin); Kiera, Thief; Loftis, Detective (Imperial Investigator)

**Time period(s):** Indeterminate Future
**Locale(s):** Dragaera, Planet—Imaginary

**Summary:** By befriending a woman in Northport, Vlad involves himself with an investigation into the death of a merchant, Fyres. The investigation grows to encompass the Empress and the house of Orca, represented by Loftis and a variety of others. Although very talented, Vlad enlists Kiera's talents for theft to unravel the mystery surrounding Fryes' vanishing companies and holdings.

**Other books you might like:**
Marion Zimmer Bradley, *Lythande*, 1986
Lois McMaster Bujold, *The Vor Game*, 1990
Glen Cook, *The Black Company*, 1984
Simon R. Green, *Hawk & Fisher*, 1990

## 746

**STEVEN BRUST**

### Phoenix

(New York: Ace, 1990)

**Story type:** Fantasy (Adventure)
**Major character(s):** Vlad Taltos, Sorcerer, Martial Arts Expert; Loiosh, Animal (jhereg), Mythical Creature (dragon)
**Time period(s):** Indeterminate Future
**Locale(s):** Adrilankha, Fictional Country; Greensere, Fictional Country

**Summary:** Vlad's patron goddess, Yerra, has a job for him—to assassinate the king of Greensere. Unfortunately, the consequences are almost certainly war, forced conscription of humans, revolution of humans against Dragaerans, and further strain on Vlad and Cawti's marriage. But you can't say no to a goddess.

**Other books you might like:**
Samuel R. Delany, *Tales of Neveryon*, 1979
George Alec Effinger, *When Gravity Fails*, 1987
Barry Hughart, *Bridge of Birds*, 1984
Melisa C. Michaels, *Skirmish*, 1985
Roger Zelazny, *Nine Princes in Amber*, 1970

## 747

**STEVEN BRUST**

### The Phoenix Guards

(New York: Tor, 1991)

**Story type:** Fantasy (Adventure)
**Series:** Khaavren Romances
**Major character(s):** Khaavren of House Tiassa, Gentleman; Aerich of House Lyorn, Gentleman; Tazendra of House Dzur, Gentlewoman
**Time period(s):** Indeterminate Past (850 years prior to *Jhereg*)
**Locale(s):** Dragaera, Planet—Imaginary

**Summary:** Khaavren is a landless son of fallen nobility, possessor of a good sword and "tolerably well acquainted with its use." Along with his loyal friends, he enthusiastically seeks adventure and romance, while pledged to the service of the Emperor at the very end of the reign of the Athyra. But as the cycle moves on and the throne passes to the House of the Phoenix, Khaavren's life and the future of Dragaera depend on his wariness. A tribute to Alexandre Dumas's *The Three Musketeers.*

**Other books you might like:**
Brian Daley, *A Tapestry of Magics*, 1983
Alexandre Dumas, *The Three Musketeers*, 1846
Barbara Hambly, *The Rainbow Abyss*, 1991

Joel Rosenberg, *D'Shai*, 1991
Roger Zelazny, *Nine Princes in Amber*, 1970

## 748
### EDWARD BRYANT

## Aqua Sancta
(Arvada, Colorado: Roadkill Press, 1994)

**Story type:** Horror (Vampire Story)
**Major character(s):** Father Callahan, Religious (Catholic priest); The Vampire, Vampire
**Time period(s):** 1990s (1994)
**Locale(s):** United States

**Summary:** This beautifully designed and illustrated short-short story in chapbook form tells of a priest captured by a ravenous vampire, and the ingenious method he devises to dispatch the creature in the nick of time.

**Other books you might like:**
Poppy Z. Brite, *Love in Vein*, 1994
     editor
Martin H. Greenberg, *Dracula: Prince of Darkness*, 1994
     editor
Brian Hodge, *Shrines and Desecrations*, 1994
Nancy Kilpatrick, *Sex and the Single Vampire*, 1994

## 749
### EDWARD BRYANT

## Fetish
(Eugene, Oregon: Axolotl/Pulphouse, 1991)

**Story type:** Horror (Black Magic)
**Major character(s):** Angela Black, Witch; Conway Delacroix, Writer
**Time period(s):** 1990s
**Locale(s):** Arroyo Hondo, New Mexico

**Summary:** When white witch Angela Black responds to a call for help from her old lover, Conway Delacroix, she becomes caught up in a scheme to retrieve a Zuni Indian fetish from the murderer who killed Delacroix's friends, and to find out why the fetish means so much to so many people.

**Other books you might like:**
Kathryn Ptacek, *Ghost Dance*, 1990
Anne Rice, *The Witching Hour*, 1990
Sarban, *The Doll Maker and Other Tales of the Uncanny*, 1953
John Updike, *The Witches of Eastwick*, 1984

## 750
### JOHN BUCHAN

## Witchwood
(New York: Caroll & Graf, 1989)

**Story type:** Fantasy (Religious)
**Time period(s):** 17th century
**Locale(s):** Scotland

**Summary:** A young minister, newly assigned to an isolated village, discovers a coven of witches praticing the old ways in the woods surrounding the village. His efforts to abolish the group are thwarted by the villagers and by his superiors, who don't believe him.

**Other books you might like:**
Gael Baudino, *Strands of Starlight*, 1989

Katherine Kurtz, *The Harrowing of Gwynedd*, 1989
     Vol 1 - The Heirs of St. Camber
Frank E. Peretti, *This Present Darkness*, 1986

## 751
### RAYMOND BUCKLAND

## Cardinal's Sin
(Minneapolis: Llewellyn, 1996)

**Story type:** Horror (Black Magic)
**Series:** Committee
**Major character(s):** Duncan Webster, Writer; Patrizio Ganganelli, Religious (cardinal); Tanya Demidas, Witch
**Time period(s):** 1990s (1993)
**Locale(s):** Vatican City; Washington, District of Columbia

**Summary:** In this second adventure of The Committee, Duncan Webster reconvenes his multicultural team of psychically endowed specialists to battle Cardinal Ganganelli, a Vatican aspirant who has discovered black magic texts in the Vatican library. Still incensed by the ill treatment his mother received from American GIs in World War II, Ganganelli has unleashed demonic forces that have upset weather patterns throughout the world.

**Other books you might like:**
Katherine Kurtz, *The Adept*, 1991
     Deborah Turner Harris, co-author
Brian Lumley, *Psychomech*, 1984
Thomas F. Monteleone, *The Blood of the Lamb*, 1992
Robert Morgan, *The Things That Are Not There*, 1992
Dennis Wheatley, *The Devil Rides Out*, 1935

## 752
### RAYMOND BUCKLAND

## The Committee
(St. Paul, Minnesota: Llewellyn, 1993)

**Story type:** Horror (Wild Talents)
**Major character(s):** Duncan Webster, Writer; Bill Highland, Political Figure (senator); Earl Stratford, Paranormal Investigator
**Time period(s):** 1990s (1993)
**Locale(s):** Washington, District of Columbia

**Summary:** In what is advertised as a psi-tech suspense thriller, Duncan Webster joins with a covert group of psychically-endowed operatives to thwart an international cabal that is destroying American spy satellites by psychokinesis. This is the author's first novel.

**Other books you might like:**
Steven M. Krauzer, *Brainstorm*, 1991
Brian Lumley, *Psychamok*, 1985
Brian Lumley, *Psychomech*, 1984
Brian Lumley, *Psychosphere*, 1984
Jack Martin, *Scanners*, 1979

## 753
### ALGIS BUDRYS

## Hard Landing
(New York: Warner Questar, 1993)

**Story type:** Science Fiction (Invasion of Earth; Mystery)
**Major character(s):** Dothan Stablits, Police Officer; Jack Mullica, Alien; William Henshaw, Veterinarian

**Time period(s):** 1940s
**Locale(s):** Shoreview, Illinois
**Summary:** Dothan Stablits' investigation of an accidental death discovers no unusual aspects, but when the pathologist notifies the National Register of Pathological Anomalies, Dr. William Henshaw performs a second autopsy and confirms the discovery of aliens on Earth. Abandoned by policy, the stranded aliens follow a standard defensive scenario including no interference with natives and no contact with each other.

**Other books you might like:**
Greg Bear, *The Forge of God*, 1987
David Brin, *Earth*, 1990
Alan Dean Foster, *Cyber Way*, 1990
Rebecca Ore, *Becoming Alien*, 1987
David Weber, *Mutineers' Moon*, 1991
George Zebrowski, *Stranger Suns*, 1991

---

**754**

**ALGIS BUDRYS**, Editor

# L. Ron Hubbard Presents Writers of the Future, Volume VII

(Los Angeles: Bridge Publications, 1991)

**Story type:** Science Fiction (Anthology)
**Series:** Writers of the Future
**Summary:** 15 original stories chosen from the winners and finalists of the ongoing L. Ron Hubbard Writers of the Future Contest, open only to emerging writers.

**Other books you might like:**
George R.R. Martin, *The John W. Campbell Awards, Volume 5*, 1984
   editor
George R.R. Martin, *New Voices I-IV*, 1977-1981
   editor

---

**755**

**ALGIS BUDRYS**, Editor
**DAVE WOLVERTON**, Co-Editor

# L. Ron Hubbard Presents Writers of the Future, Volume VIII

(Los Angeles: Bridge Publications, 1992)

**Story type:** Science Fiction (Anthology)
**Series:** Writers of the Future
**Summary:** Includes a two-page introduction by Dave Wolverton; articles on writing by Algis Budrys, Lois McMaster Bujold, R. Garcia y Robertson and L. Ron Hubbard; one article by Edd Cartier, ''Notes to the New Artist''; a five-page article by Dave Wolverton, ''More Than a Contest''; five pages describing the Writers of the Future rules and deadlines plus 17 stories from winners and finalists and illustrations from a dozen contest winning illustrators. Stories include the grand prize winner, Alan Burt's ''The Last Indian War'' and other quarterly winners, Michael Paul Metzger's ''Anne of a Thousand Years''; M.C. Sumner's ''Surrogate''; and Steven Woodworth's ''Scary Monsters.'' One story, Nicholas A. DiChario's ''The Winterberry,'' appeared first in Mike Resnick's *Alternate Kennedys*.

**Other books you might like:**
Lou Aronica, *Full Spectrum*, 1988
   Shawna McCarthy, co-editor
George R.R. Martin, *The John W. Campbell Awards, Volume 5*, 1984
   editor

George R.R. Martin, *New Voices I-IV*, 1977-1981
   editor
Kristine Kathryn Rusch, *The Best of Pulphouse: The Hardback Magazine*, 1991
   editor

---

**756**

**LOIS MCMASTER BUJOLD**

# Barrayar

(New York: Baen, 1991)

**Story type:** Science Fiction (Political; Family Saga)
**Series:** Adventures of Miles Vorkosigan
**Major character(s):** Cordelia Naismith, Noblewoman (Lady Vorkosigan); Aral Vorkosigan, Nobleman (Lord Vorkosigan), Ruler (regent); Bothari, Bodyguard, Murderer
**Locale(s):** Barrayar, Planet—Imaginary

**Summary:** Cordelia and Aral move into the Vorkosigan family home on feudal Barrayar where Cordelia conceives a son. Aral, the new regent to the throne, is forced to make decisions which are unpopular among some of the Vor who Aral must rule. When an attack on Aral is safely avoided, Cordelia remains unable to put aside her fears for her husband. *Barrayar* is a direct sequel to *Shards of Honor* (1986) and contains an afterword with a chronology of the Miles Naismith universe.

**Other books you might like:**
Emma Bull, *Falcon*, 1989
C.J. Cherryh, *Forty Thousand in Gehenna*, 1983
Stephen Goldin, *Jade Darcy and the Affair of Honor*, 1988
   Mary Mason, co-author
Frank Herbert, *Dune*, 1965
Steve Perry, *The Man Who Never Missed*, 1985
Alis A. Rasmussen, *A Passage of Stars*, 1990

---

**757**

**LOIS MCMASTER BUJOLD**

# Borders of Infinity

(New York: Baen Books, 1989)

**Story type:** Science Fiction (Humor)
**Series:** Adventures of Miles Vorkosigan
**Major character(s):** Miles Vorkosigan, Military Personnel, Diplomat, Nobleman
**Time period(s):** Indeterminate Future
**Locale(s):** Barryaran Empire, Interstellar Empire/Federation

**Summary:** This volume contains three episodes from the life of Miles Vorkosigan, a puny aristocrat who prefers to use wit rather than military might when it comes to solving problems. ''The Mountains of Mourning'' from this collection is a Nebula Award nominee.

**Other books you might like:**
Anne McCaffrey, *Sassinak*, 1989
   Elizabeth Moon, co-author
Rebecca Ore, *Becoming Alien*, 1987
Rebecca Ore, *Being Alien*, 1989
Allen Steele, *Orbital Decay*, 1989

## 758

### LOIS MCMASTER BUJOLD

## Cetaganda

(New York: Baen, 1996)

**Story type:** Science Fiction (Mystery; Political)
**Series:** Adventures of Miles Vorkosigan
**Major character(s):** Miles Vorkosigan, Nobleman, Military Personnel (lieutenant); Ivan Vorpatril, Nobleman, Diplomat; Mia Maz, Diplomat (protocol)
**Time period(s):** Indeterminate Future
**Locale(s):** Eta Ceta IV, Planet—Imaginary; Cetaganda, Interstellar Empire/Federation

**Summary:** Sent to Cetaganda with Ivan as Vor representatives to the Dowager Empress' funeral, Miles finds a fight, perhaps accidentally, before they can dock. Now possessing an illegal weapon, Miles convinces Ivan they should investigate the circumstances of the attack, which leads to questions about the Dowager Empress' death and the highest, most secret parts of Cetagandan society.

**Other books you might like:**
Eleanor Arnason, *Ring of Swords*, 1993
L. Warren Douglas, *Stepwater*, 1995
Mary Gentle, *Golden Witchbreed*, 1984
Jack Vance, *Alastor*, 1995
Joan D. Vinge, *The Summer Queen*, 1991

## 759

### LOIS MCMASTER BUJOLD

## Dreamweaver's Dilemma

(Framingham, Massachusetts: NESFA Press, 1996)

**Story type:** Science Fiction (Collection)

**Summary:** Contains a six-page preface by Lillian Stewart Carl, author's biography and bibliography, five pages of timeline of Barrayaran and human history, two original and four stories reprinted from periodicals 1985-1989, three original and four generally biographical essays reprinted from 1990-1992 periodicals and 16 pages by Suford Lewis on pronunciation of terms and genealogy of the Vorkosigan line. Frequently upbeat in tone, the stories' themes include Sherlock Holmes, bartering between a non-human and a homemaker, cats, urban life, dream composing, and one Miles Vorkosigan adventure.

**Other books you might like:**
Joe Haldeman, *Vietnam and Other Alien Worlds*, 1993
Zenna Henderson, *Ingathering: The Complete People Stories of Zenna Henderson*, 1995
James H. Schmitz, *The Best of James H. Schmitz*, 1991
Cordwainer Smith, *The Rediscovery of Man*, 1993
James White, *The White Papers*, 1996

## 760

### LOIS MCMASTER BUJOLD

## Komarr

(New York: Baen, 1998)

**Story type:** Science Fiction (Mystery; Family Saga)
**Series:** Adventures of Miles Vorkosigan
**Major character(s):** Miles Vorkosigan, Nobleman, Auditor, Military Personnel; Ekaterin ''Kat'' Vorsoisson, Noblewoman; Lord Vorthys, Auditor

**Time period(s):** Indeterminate Future
**Locale(s):** Komarr, Planet—Imaginary; Interstellar Empire/Federation

**Summary:** When a solar power satellite necessary for terraforming Komarr blows up, Miles Vorkosigan and Lord Vorthys must investigate possible sabotage, a job made more difficult when Miles falls in love with Lord Vorthys' married niece.

**Other books you might like:**
Katharine Kerr, *Palace*, 1996
    Mark Kreighbaum, co-author
Rosemary Kirstein, *The Outskirter's Secret*, 1992
Mark Kreighbaum, *The Eyes of God*, 1998
Joan Slonczewski, *The Children Star*, 1998
Sarah Zettel, *Playing God*, 1998

## 761

### LOIS MCMASTER BUJOLD

## Memory

(New York: Baen, 1996)

**Story type:** Science Fiction (Mystery; Political)
**Series:** Adventures of Miles Vorkosigan
**Major character(s):** Miles Vorkosigan, Nobleman, Military Personnel (retired); Simon Illyan, Government Official (Imperial Security); Ivan Vorpatril, Nobleman, Military Personnel
**Time period(s):** Indeterminate Future
**Locale(s):** Barrayar, Planet—Imaginary

**Summary:** Discovered covering up the seizures still recurring since his recovery from death, Miles loses his commission and the Dendarii Mercenaries to a medical discharge. Before he can even think about what to do with his life, Miles must discover what happened to Illyan's memory chip and prevent Illyan's death.

**Other books you might like:**
Greg Bear, *Queen of Angels*, 1990
C.J. Cherryh, *Heavy Time*, 1991
Katharine Kerr, *Polar City Blues*, 1990
Steve Perry, *The Man Who Never Missed*, 1985
Allen Steele, *The Jericho Iteration*, 1994

## 762

### LOIS MCMASTER BUJOLD

## Mirror Dance

(New York: Baen, 1994)

**Story type:** Science Fiction (Family Saga; Political)
**Series:** Adventures of Miles Vorkosigan
**Major character(s):** Miles Vorkosigan, Nobleman, Military Personnel (admiral); Mark Pierre Vorkosigan, Clone
**Time period(s):** Indeterminate Future
**Locale(s):** Escobar, Planet—Imaginary; Jackson's Whole, Planet—Imaginary; *Ariel*, Spaceship

**Summary:** Impersonating Miles, Mark steals the *Ariel* and sets off for Jackson's Whole to free House Bharaputra's clones on his own. When the plan goes awry, Miles attempts a rescue, dying in the effort. After the loss of the stasis box preserving Miles' body and with precious little time to act, Mark must first travel to Barrayar and convince the family to trust him and support his plan.

**Other books you might like:**
Pauline Ashwell, *Unwillingly to Earth*, 1992
F.M. Busby, *Rissa Kerguelen*, 1977
C.J. Mills, *Brander's Book*, 1992

C.J. Mills, *Winter World*, 1988
Alis A. Rasmussen, *A Passage of Stars*, 1990
Karen Ripley, *The Tenth Class*, 1991
Joan D. Vinge, *The Summer Queen*, 1991

---

**763**

### LOIS MCMASTER BUJOLD

## *The Spirit Ring*
(New York: Baen, 1992)

**Story type:** Fantasy (Political; Light Fantasy)
**Major character(s):** Fiametta Beneforte, Magician, Fugitive; Thur Ochs, Miner, Spy (Abbot Monreal's)
**Time period(s):** Indeterminate
**Locale(s):** Montefoglia, Fictional Country (European dukedom); Alternate Earth

**Summary:** Although imperfectly understanding the nature of the spell, Fiametta correctly utilizes a magic spell while casting a ring without the supervision of her father who had apprenticed her without benefit of sanction by proper authorities. The ring's unexpected and undesired catch leads to the official notice of Fiametta's magical abilities and her enlistment in Abbot Monreal's plan to expose Lord Uberto Ferrante as a user of forbidden magic. Fiametta and Thur also provide the assistance needed to free the spirit of Fiametta's deceased father.

**Other books you might like:**
Laurell K. Hamilton, *Nightseer*, 1992
Marc Laidlaw, *Neon Lotus*, 1988
Robin McKinley, *The Blue Sword*, 1982
Robin McKinley, *The Hero and the Crown*, 1984
Patricia C. Wrede, *Mairelon the Magician*, 1991

---

**764**

### LOIS MCMASTER BUJOLD

## *The Vor Game*
(New York: Baen, 1990)

**Story type:** Science Fiction (Humor; Adventure)
**Series:** Adventures of Miles Vorkosigan
**Major character(s):** Miles Vorkosigan, Military Personnel, Diplomat, Nobleman; Gregor Vorbarra, Ruler (Emperor)
**Time period(s):** Indeterminate Future
**Locale(s):** Barryaran Empire, Interstellar Empire/Federation

**Summary:** Miles Vorkosigan's misadventures while on his first assignment as a newly commissioned ensign lead to an undercover assignment and action with his cousin, the Emperor, and the mercenary soldiers who consider Miles their leader.

**Other books you might like:**
Anne McCaffrey, *Sassinak*, 1989
   Elizabeth Moon, co-author
Rebecca Ore, *Human to Human*, 1990
Rebecca Ore, *Being Alien*, 1989
Rebecca Ore, *Becoming Alien*, 1987
Allen Steele, *Orbital Decay*, 1989

---

**765**

### LOIS MCMASTER BUJOLD, Editor
### ROLAND J. GREEN, Co-Editor

## *Women at War*
(New York: Tor, 1995)

**Story type:** Science Fiction (Anthology; Military)

**Summary:** Contains a two-page introduction by Bujold, a one-page introduction by Green, and brief introductions by Bujold to 17 original stories with diverse military themes written by women. Jane Yolen sets "The One-Armed Queen" on the world of *Sister Light, Sister Dark* (1988), while Holly Lisle's "A Few Good Men" features her character, Medwind Song, introduced in *Fire in the Mist* (1992). Other authors include Margaret Ball, P.J. Beese, Juanita Coulson, P.N. Elrod, P.M. Griffin, Adrienne Martine-Barnes, R.M. Meluch, Elizabeth Moon, Mickey Zucker Reichert, Elizabeth Ann Scarborough, and Judith Tarr.

**Other books you might like:**
Marion Zimmer Bradley, *Sword and Sorceress I-XII*, 1984-1995
   editor
Janrae Frank, *New Eves: Science Fiction about the Extraordinary Women of Today and Tomorrow*, 1994
   Jean Stine, Forrest J. Ackerman, co-editors
Esther Friesner, *Chicks in Chainmail*, 1995
   editor
Jessica Amanda Salmonson, *Amazons!*, 1979
   editor
Pamela Sargent, *Women of Wonder, the Classic Years: Science Fiction by Women From the 1940s to the 1970s*, 1995
   editor
Pamela Sargent, *Women of Wonder, the Contemporary Years: Science Fiction by Women From the 1970s to the 1990s*, 1995
   editor

---

**766**

### EMMA BULL

## *Bone Danc: A Fantasy for Technophiles*
(New York: Ace, 1991)

**Story type:** Science Fiction (Post-Holocaust)
**Major character(s):** Sparrow, Trader, Troubleshooter; Sharrea, Psychic
**Time period(s):** Indeterminate Future
**Locale(s):** Minneapolis, Minnesota

**Summary:** When Sparrow woke up broke, in a ditch, with no memory of how she got there, she made her way to visit Sharrea. Sharrea read the cards. Sparrow received definite, but unhelpful, advice and warnings which did not deter her search for the legendary videotape of *The Horses*. The mind-control weapons which had turned the tide in war—the Horses—are dead, but their legacy remains.

**Other books you might like:**
Margaret Wander Bonanno, *The Others*, 1990
Pat Cadigan, *Synners*, 1991
Ernest Hogan, *Cortez on Jupiter*, 1990
Pat Murphy, *The City, Not Long After*, 1989
Walter Jon Williams, *Hardwired*, 1986

## 767

**EMMA BULL**
**WILL SHETTERLY**, Co-Author

### Double Feature

(Framingham, Massachusetts: NESFA Press, 1994)

**Story type:** Fantasy (Collection; Urban)

**Summary:** Contains a two-page introduction by Patrick and Teresa Nielsen Hayden, individual introductions by the authors, a three-page bibliography and biography of Emma Bull, a two-page bibliography and biography of Will Shetterly, two essays on writing by Bull, the authors' sole published collaborative story, one original poem and four reprinted stories by Bull plus one original and three reprinted stories by Shetterly. Material reprinted from 1985-1992 periodicals includes five stories from the Liavek shared-world anthology series (1985-1990) and one story which gave rise to novels from each author set in Terri Windling's Borderlands milieu.

**Other books you might like:**
John M. Ford, *Casting Fortune*, 1989
Will Shetterly, *Elsewhere*, 1991
Will Shetterly, *Liavek*, 1985
    Emma Bull, co-editor
Will Shetterly, *Liavek: Festival Week*, 1990
Will Shetterly, *Liavek: Wizard's Row*, 1987
    Emma Bull, co-editor
Will Shetterly, *Nevernever*, 1993
Terri Windling, *Borderland*, 1986
    Mark Alan Arnold, co-editor
Terri Windling, *Life on the Border*, 1991
    editor

## 768

**EMMA BULL**

### Falcon

(New York: Ace, 1989)

**Story type:** Science Fiction (Space Opera)
**Major character(s):** Nikki Falcon, Royalty (Prince), Pilot; Jacob, Spy
**Time period(s):** Indeterminate Future
**Locale(s):** Cymru, Planet—Imaginary; Bellmakers World, Planet—Imaginary

**Summary:** Dominic Glyndwr, nephew of the ruler of Cymru, realizes that his planet appears headed for revolution, but is unable to stop it. Fleeing for his life, and later adopting the name Nikki Falcon, he becomes a gestalt pilot, a dangerous profession which eventually kills those who follow it.

**Other books you might like:**
C.J. Cherryh, *Rimrunners*, 1989
Daniel Keys Moran, *The Long Run*, 1989
Walter Jon Williams, *Angel Station*, 1989
David Zindell, *Neverness*, 1988

## 769

**EMMA BULL**

### Finder

(New York: Tor, 1994)

**Story type:** Fantasy (Urban; Psychic Powers)
**Series:** Borderland

**Major character(s):** Finder Orient, Psychic; Tick-Tick, Mythical Creature (elf), Mechanic (motorcycle); Alexandra "Sunny" Rico, Detective—Police
**Time period(s):** Indeterminate Future
**Locale(s):** Bordertown, Fictional City; Borderland, Mythical Place

**Summary:** Able to unerringly locate objects through a sixth sense, Finder tracks clues in a police murder investigation pointing to a new drug which could drive a permanent wedge between human and elf residents of Bordertown.

**Other books you might like:**
Simon R. Green, *Guard Against Dishonor*, 1991
Will Shetterly, *Elsewhere*, 1991
Will Shetterly, *The Liavek Series*, 1985-1990
    Emma Bull, co-editor
Will Shetterly, *Nevernever*, 1993
Terri Windling, *Borderland*, 1986
    Mark Alan Arnold, co-editor
Terri Windling, *Bordertown*, 1986
    Mark Alan Arnold, co-editor
Terri Windling, *Life on the Border*, 1991
    editor

## 770

**CHRIS BUNCH**

### The Demon King

(New York: Warner Aspect, 1998)

**Story type:** Fantasy (Political)
**Series:** Seer King
**Major character(s):** Damastes a Cimabue, Military Personnel, Prisoner; Laish Tenedos, Royalty (emperor), Wizard; Maran Agramonte, Noblewoman (countess)
**Time period(s):** Indeterminate Past
**Locale(s):** Numantia, Fictional Country; Maisir, Fictional Country

**Summary:** Imprisoned, ex-general Damastes tells the story of how Emperor Tenedos, after winning his empire, turned his mind to conquest. The dreams of peace the two men share disappear as the Emperor seeks to pay terrible debts. Damastes, torn between justice and loyalty, love and honor, must decide whether he can follow his lord's mad commands.

**Other books you might like:**
M.A.R. Barker, *Man of Gold*, 1984
Deborah Chester, *Reign of Shadows*, 1996
Kara Dalkey, *Goa*, 1996
David Drake, *An Oblique Approach*, 1998
    Eric Flint, co-author
Guy Gavriel Kay, *The Lions of Al-Rassan*, 1995

## 771

**CHRIS BUNCH**

### The Seer King

(New York: Warner Aspect, 1997)

**Story type:** Fantasy (Political)
**Major character(s):** Damastes a Cimabue, Military Personnel, Prisoner; Laish Tenedos, Royalty (emperor), Wizard; Maran Agramonte, Noblewoman (countess)
**Time period(s):** Indeterminate Past
**Locale(s):** Numantia, Fictional Country

**Summary:** A young and eager officer and a radical wizard meet at a battle neither expects to survive. Together, by luck, planning and power, they rise politically and seize control of the Empire. However, with demons, traitors and love against them, their grasp on power remains tenuous.

**Other books you might like:**
M.A.R. Barker, *Man of Gold*, 1984
Allan Cole, *Sten*, 1984
  Chris Bunch, co-author
Glen Cook, *The Black Company*, 1984
Kara Dalkey, *Goa*, 1996
Guy Gavriel Kay, *Tigana*, 1990
Roger Zelazny, *Lord of Light*, 1967

---

**772**

**DAVID R. BUNCH**

## Bunch!

(Cambridge, Massachusetts: Broken Mirrors Press, 1993)

**Story type:** Science Fiction (Collection)

**Summary:** Contains a four-page introduction by Barry N. Malzberg, one original story, ''Control,'' plus 31 stories reprinted from periodicals 1957-1984. The stories, frequently dark in tone, contain a strong sense of American setting and explore themes surrounding human interrelationships and the human condition in a changed or changing world.

**Other books you might like:**
David Brin, *The River of Time*, 1986
Michael Flynn, *The Nanotech Chronicles*, 1991
Garry Kilworth, *Hogfoot Right and Bird-Hands*, 1993
Nancy Kress, *The Aliens of Earth*, 1993
Rebecca Ore, *Alien Bootlegger and Other Stories*, 1993
Michael Swanwick, *Gravity's Angels*, 1991
John Varley, *Blue Champagne*, 1986

---

**773**

**MELVIN BURGESS**

## The Earth Giant

(New York: Putnam, 1997)

**Story type:** Science Fiction (Young Adult; First Contact)
**Major character(s):** Peter Lee, Child, Relative (brother); Amy Lee, Child, Relative (sister); Giant, Alien, Child
**Time period(s):** 1990s
**Locale(s):** Earth

**Summary:** While Amy hangs out the window watching the storm that disturbs the Lee family's sleep, she can hear something out there, calling to her in her mind. The next day, after the storm passes, Amy uncovers Giant, the friend she heard during the storm who was buried in the roots of the toppled oak. Amy and Peter hide Giant, hoping to help him get home.

**Other books you might like:**
Lynne Reid Banks, *The Indian in the Cupboard*, 1981
Bruce Coville, *My Teacher Is an Alien*, 1989
Rosalie Fry, *The Secret of Roan Inish*, 1995
Pamela F. Service, *When the Night Wind Howls*, 1987
Sylvia Waugh, *The Mennyms*, 1994

---

**774**

**WILLIAM R. BURKETT JR.**

## Blood Lines

(New York: HarperPrism, 1998)

**Story type:** Science Fiction (Political; Arts)
**Major character(s):** Keith Ramsey, Writer (journalist, poet), Hunter; Raven of Lao-tzu, Guide, Writer (poet); Ball, Cyborg, Spy (Terran Services)
**Time period(s):** Indeterminate Future
**Locale(s):** Mythical Place (Ichiro University); *Civilization River*, At Sea (houseboat); Ptolemy, Planet—Imaginary

**Summary:** On Ptolemy to hunt and visit with Ball, now a professor at Ichiro University, Ramsey agrees to participate in the Renga, a cycle poem, which will demonstrate a new technique in communications. Unfortunately, the intelligent virus may not be adequately contained, while competing agencies also want the technology.

**Other books you might like:**
Emily Devenport, *Eggheads*, 1996
Kathleen Ann Goonan, *Queen City Jazz*, 1994
Bill Ransom, *ViraVax*, 1993
Alis A. Rasmussen, *A Passage of Stars*, 1990
Sheri S. Tepper, *Six Moon Dance*, 1998

---

**775**

**DONALD BURLESON**
**ROBERT M. KNOX**, Illustrator

## Beyond the Lamplight

(Lockport, New York: Jack O'Lantern Press, 1996)

**Story type:** Horror (Collection)

**Summary:** This compilation of 34 stories encapsulates a decade of work by a writer whose stories range in theme from Lovecraftian terror to tales of psychological horror. More traditional horror stories include ''The Interview,'' about a practical joke that escalates into an encouter with supernatural horror, and ''Kokopelli,'' about a creature of Native American mythology still very much alive in contemporary times. A number of stories, including ''Walkie-Talkie,'' ''The Treehouse,'' ''Uncle Neddy's Chair,'' and ''Jigsaw,'' feature inanimate objects that become agents of supernatural dread. A trio of tales—''Down in the Mouth,'' ''Family Dentistry,'' and ''Gums''—extracts horror from the unlikely theme of dental care. Ramsey Campbell supplies an introduction.

**Other books you might like:**
Christopher Fowler, *Sharper Knives*, 1992
David Langford, *Irrational Numbers*, 1993
Mark Morris, *Close to the Bone*, 1995
Jeffrey Osier, *Driftglider and Other Stories*, 1994
Stephen Mark Rainey, *Fugue Devil and Other Weird Horrors*, 1993

---

**776**

**DONALD BURLESON**

## Four Shadowings

(West Warwick, Rhode Island: Necronomicon Press, 1994)

**Story type:** Horror (Collection)

**Summary:** The four stories in this chapbook display the diverse talents of a writer best known as a Lovecraft scholar and poststructuralist critic. ''A Student of Geometry'' is a tale of psychological horror whose point of view character is slowly driven mad by her family and school life, while "The Wind at the Top of the Tree" is a traditional ghost story. "Blue Luke" tells of a family demon who continues to exert his control over a girl who gave up her belief in it long before, and "One-Night Strand" is a perversely chilling story about what a visitor to a fleapit hotel finds goes on after hours.

**Other books you might like:**
Michael A. Arnzen, *Needles and Sins*, 1993
Joe R. Lansdale, *By Bizarre Hands*, 1989
Jeffrey Osier, *Driftglider and Other Stories*, 1994
Stephen Mark Rainey, *Fugue Devil and Other Weird Horrors*, 1993
David J. Schow, *Seeing Red*, 1990

---

**777**

**DONALD BURLESON**

## Lemon Drops and Other Horrors

(Bristol, Rhode Island: Hobgoblin Press, 1993)

**Story type:** Horror (Collection)

**Summary:** This first collection by a well-known Lovecraft scholar and controversial critic brings together 20 stories that range from the subtle to the gruesome. Among the former are "Snow Cancellations," about an endless snowfall and its implications, and "English 303," in which an English teacher lecturing on Joyce's *Finnegan's Wake* finds that time itself has become endlessly cyclical. Among the latter are "Milk," about the repulsive consequences of drinking spoiled milk; "Extractions," about the passions of a masochist; and "Connections," in which a young boy takes his grandfather's analogy of himself to an aging tree a little too far. Seven stories, including "Dark Brother," about a demonic presence in a house that only the family cat can see, are original to the book.

**Other books you might like:**
Ed Gorman, *Prisoners and Other Stories*, 1992
Stephen King, *Skeleton Crew*, 1985
Joe R. Lansdale, *By Bizarre Hands*, 1989
F. Paul Wilson, *Soft and Others*, 1989

---

**778**

**CLIFF BURNS**

## The Reality Machine

(North Battleford, Saskatchewan: Black Dog Press, 1997)

**Story type:** Horror (Collection)

**Summary:** Nineteen prose poems, vignettes, tales of science fiction, and post-modern dark fantasies. Included are "The Woman Who Gave Good Phone," about a mysterious woman who ruins lives with prank phone calls; "Also Starring," in which the world is suddenly overrun with criminals who masquerade as well-known characters actors; "In Dreams, Awake," in which a man sympathizes so deeply with his wife that he acquires her terminal illness; and "Son of Nixon," a satire on the fantastic transformation and rehabilitation of a corrupt politician. Introduction by Kim Newman.

**Other books you might like:**
William S. Burroughs, *Interzone*, 1989
Harlan Ellison, *Slippage*, 1997
Jack Remick, *Terminal Weird*, 1996
Don Webb, *A Spell for the Fulfillment of Desire*, 1996
Don Webb, *Stealing My Rules*, 1997

---

**779**

**A.M. BURRAGE**

## Someone in the Room: Strange Tales Old and New

(Ashcroft, British Columbia: Ash-Tree Press, 1997)

**Story type:** Horror (Collection)

**Summary:** Twenty-eight tales of ghosts and the supernatural, seven collected for the first time. The centerpiece is the fourteen stories collected as *Someone in the Room*, published under the pseudonym "Ex-Private X" in 1931. These include "The Sweeper," about a woman fearful of a gypsy curse that death will come in the form of a leaf-sweeper; "The Waxwork," about a wax museum haunted by the ghost of a murderer whose effigy it features; "Smee," in which a childhood game brings back the spirit of a child who was killed playing it; and "The Running Tide" and "Someone in the Room," both about sites haunted by psychic residues that repeatedly re-enact past evil deeds. Two essays on ghostly experience and fiction included. Edited by Jack Adrian.

**Other books you might like:**
E.F. Benson, *The Collected Ghost Stories of E.F. Benson*, 1992
Frederick Cowles, *Fear Walks the Night*, 1992
L.P. Hartley, *The Travelling Grave, and Other Stories*, 1948
H. Russell Wakefield, *They Return at Evening*, 1928
H. Russell Wakefield, *The Clock Strikes Twelve*, 1939

---

**780**

**WILLIAM S. BURROUGHS**

## Ghost of Chance

(New York: Serpent's Tail, 1995)

**Story type:** Science Fiction (Literary)
**Major character(s):** Mission, Pirate, Leader (captain); Ghost, Animal (lemur)
**Time period(s):** 17th century; Indeterminate
**Locale(s):** Madagascar

**Summary:** An elaborate short novella with 13 footnotes details the story of Captain Mission and his Museum of Lost Species. When the Board destroys Mission and his anti-control paradise, strange diseases live on, hidden in the Museum, changing life utterly. Interwoven with the story, Burroughs expresses views on religion, ecology, viruses, morality, and lemurs. First published as a limited edition by the Library Fellows of the Whitney Museum of American Art in 1991.

**Other books you might like:**
Kathy Acker, *Pussy, King of the Pirates*, 1996
J.G. Ballard, *Crash*, 1973
Richard Calder, *Dead Girls*, 1995
William T. Vollmann, *You Bright and Risen Angels*, 1987
Monique Wittig, *Les Guerilleres*, 1971

---

**781**

**STEPHEN BURY** (Pseudonym of Neal Stephenson and J. Frederick George)

## Interface

(New York: Bantam, 1994)

**Story type:** Science Fiction (Political; Techno-Thriller)

**Major character(s):** William Anthony Cozzano, Political Figure, Experimental Subject; Cyrus "Cy" Ogle, Public Relations; Eleanor Boxwood Richmond, Political Figure

**Time period(s):** 1990s (1995)

**Locale(s):** Springfield, Illinois; Washington, District of Columbia

**Summary:** Cozzano suffers a severe stroke just as the president announces that forgiveness of the National Debt will form the basis of his new economic policy. The Network, an organization of interests who find this intolerable, decides to elect a president they control. A suddenly available technology allowing installation of a computer chip in a stroke victim's brain to bypass damage permits Cozzano to run for president. The Network manages Cozzano's campaign and, without his consent or knowledge, controls his chip, bringing instantaneous response to polled reactions.

**Other books you might like:**
Pat Cadigan, *Synners*, 1991
Michael Flynn, *In the Country of the Blind*, 1990
Edward Gibson, *In the Wrong Hands*, 1992
George Orwell, *1984*, 1949
Neal Stephenson, *Snow Crash*, 1992

## 782

**F.M. BUSBY**

### Arrow From Earth

(New York: AvoNova, 1995)

**Story type:** Science Fiction (Political; Family Saga)

**Series:** Slow Freight

**Major character(s):** Clarence Engels "Clancy" Allaird, Spaceship Captain, Parent; Margaret "Marnie" Allaird, Stowaway, Teenager; Anne Portaris, Inventor, Spacewoman

**Time period(s):** 21st century

**Locale(s):** Glen Springs, Colorado; *Arrow*, Spaceship; Outer Space

**Summary:** Forced to leave home to avoid molestation by her mother's boyfriend, Marnie Allaird sneaks onto *Arrow* before the crew arrives, hoping to stay for the whole trip, or until she comes of legal age. While aboard *Arrow*, Marnie and the crew must deal with marauders from Earth, mutineers from *Starfinder*, and a strange being from the Aleph Continuum.

**Other books you might like:**
John Barnes, *Orbital Resonance*, 1991
Gregory Benford, *Timescape*, 1980
David Drake, *Starliner*, 1992
John M. Ford, *Growing Up Weightless*, 1993
George Zebrowski, *Stranger Suns*, 1991

## 783

**F.M. BUSBY**

### Islands of Tomorrow

(New York: AvoNova, 1994)

**Story type:** Science Fiction (Time Travel; Political)

**Major character(s):** Lucian "Luke" Tabor, Student—Graduate, Time Traveler; Jay Rozak, Time Traveler, Revolutionary; Karen Cecile "Casey" Collins, Student, Time Traveler

**Time period(s):** 1990s; Indeterminate Future

**Locale(s):** Pullman, Washington (Washington State University)

**Summary:** Recruited by Jay, Luke becomes involved in a political demonstration against unfair taxes and treatment of students. During the demonstration and his subsequent arrest, Luke realizes that impossible events continue while he and all the other arrested students

find themselves kidnapped to an unpleasant future. They must not only locate a way home but also prevent the future they discover.

**Other books you might like:**
Greg Bear, *Eternity*, 1988
Matthew J. Costello, *Day of the Snake*, 1992
Robert Silverberg, *The Gate of Worlds*, 1967
Dan Simmons, *Hyperion*, 1989
L. Neil Smith, *The Nagasaki Vector*, 1983
Sheri S. Tepper, *Beauty*, 1991
Connie Willis, *Doomsday Book*, 1992

## 784

**F.M. BUSBY**

### The Singularity Project

(New York: Tor, 1993)

**Story type:** Science Fiction (Mystery; Techno-Thriller)

**Major character(s):** Mitch Banning, Engineer (communications), Writer; Gudrun "Dauna" Haig, Journalist; Elihu "Emil Storchesson" Coogan, Agent, Criminal

**Time period(s):** 21st century

**Locale(s):** Seattle, Washington

**Summary:** When Mitch decides to check out the potential story lead his girlfriend, Dauna, hears at work, it leads to employment on a secret project to construct a matter transmitter. Mitch doubts the transmitter because he recognizes Coogan as a con artist but continues with the project as an engineer because it seems that it could actually work. However, a man calling himself the Hornet tries to sabotage the project.

**Other books you might like:**
Roger MacBride Allen, *The Ring of Charon*, 1990
Greg Bear, *Eon*, 1989
Philip K. Dick, *The Unteleported Man*, 1983 revised
Alan Dean Foster, *Cyber Way*, 1990
Laura J. Mixon, *Glass Houses*, 1992
Kim Stanley Robinson, *Red Mars*, 1993
Sheri S. Tepper, *Sideshow*, 1992
A.E. Van Vogt, *The Weapon Makers*, 1946

## 785

**F.M. BUSBY**

### Slow Freight

(New York: Bantam Spectra, 1991)

**Story type:** Science Fiction (First Contact)

**Major character(s):** Habeggar, Professor, Inventor; Rance Collier, Public Relations; Cassandra Monlux, Scientist, Agent (liaison)

**Time period(s):** 21st century

**Locale(s):** United States; *Starfinder*, Spaceship; *Environ*, Spaceship (alien)

**Summary:** Two recent discoveries, the Traction drive and the Habgate pipeline, make interstellar travel practical. The system has one minor logistical problem; there is a two year delay between entry and exit from the Habgate which, fortunately, does not age whatever is in the pipeline. Transit seems instantaneous. Coincidentally, *Environ*, containing all remaining Liij, is heading for the solar system.

**Other books you might like:**
Greg Bear, *Eon*, 1989
Michael Berlyn, *The Eternal Enemy*, 1990
Orson Scott Card, *Ender's Game*, 1985

Jeffrey A. Carver, *From a Changeling Star*, 1989
C.J. Cherryh, *Forty Thousand in Gehenna*, 1983
Harry Harrison, *The Deathworld Trilogy*, 1976
Janet Kagan, *Hellspark*, 1988
Sheri S. Tepper, *Grass*, 1989

---

**786**

### F.M. BUSBY

## *The Triad Worlds*

(New York: AvoNova, 1996)

**Story type:** Science Fiction (Political; First Contact)
**Series:** Slow Freight
**Major character(s):** Irtuk-Saa, Alien (Maghan), Ruler; Samuel "Sam" Hall Gowdy, Spaceship Captain; Sydnie "Charel Secour" Lightner, Spacewoman, Criminal (retired)
**Time period(s):** Indeterminate Future
**Locale(s):** Magh, Planet—Imaginary; *Romer*, Spaceship; Eamn, Planet—Imaginary

**Summary:** The crew of the *Romer* realizes that they will not be setting up a colony in the new, inhabited system they reach. When a raid captures several of *Romer*'s crew, Sam attempts to rescue the kidnappees as an "Inspections Committee" gets aboard and takes control of *Romer*. Sydnie recognizes her old gang boss and warns Sam.

**Other books you might like:**
Greg Bear, *Eon*, 1985
David Brin, *Brightness Reef*, 1995
C.J. Cherryh, *Foreigner*, 1994
Jane M. Lindskold, *Marks of Our Brothers*, 1995
David Weber, *Mutineers' Moon*, 1991
George Zebrowski, *Stranger Suns*, 1991

---

**787**

### ANNE KELLEHER BUSH

## *Children of Enchantment*

(New York: Warner Aspect, 1996)

**Story type:** Fantasy (Post-Disaster; Psychic Powers)
**Series:** Power and the Pattern
**Major character(s):** Roderic Ridenau, Royalty, Leader; Annadale Farhallen, Empath
**Time period(s):** 28th century
**Locale(s):** North America; Meriga, Fictional Country (Balkanized United States)

**Summary:** The disappearance of King Abelard Ridenau thrusts Prince Roderic into regency, forcing him to continue his father's plan to reunite shattered Meriga through alliances and military action against the Mutens and Harleyriders while some of his siblings surreptitiously vie for individual power. Unfortunately, events and prophecy drive Roderic and Annadale together despite Roderic's desire for another.

**Other books you might like:**
Shirley Meier, *Shadow's Daughter*, 1991
Shirley Meier, *Shadow's Son*, 1991
   S.M. Stirling, Karen Wehrstein, co-authors
S.M. Stirling, *Saber & Shadow*, 1991
   Shirley Meier, co-author
S.M. Stirling, *Snow Brother*, 1992
   expanded
Karen Wehrstein, *Lion's Heart*, 1991

Karen Wehrstein, *Lion's Soul*, 1991
Paul O. Williams, *The Breaking of Northwall*, 1981

---

**788**

### ANNE KELLEHER BUSH

## *Daughter of Prophecy*

(New York: Warner Aspect, 1995)

**Story type:** Fantasy (Post-Disaster; Psychic Powers)
**Major character(s):** Nydia Farhallen, Psychic; Abelard Ridenau, Ruler (king); Phineas, Military Personnel (captain)
**Time period(s):** 28th century (2714-2724)
**Locale(s):** United States (Meriga)

**Summary:** Abelard rescues Nydia from immolation as a witch in Tennessy Fall and escorts her to his capital in Ahga City. Unsafe among the court intrigues because of her psychic powers, Nydia accompanies Abelard on his campaign to subdue the Harleyriders. Her knowledge of the old Magic helps him evade treachery in Senifay and defeat the traitorous Senador of Vada. Even though she loves him, Nydia fears the consequences if she uses the old Magic to give him a son to inherit the kingdom. First novel.

**Other books you might like:**
Margaret Wander Bonanno, *The Others*, 1990
David Brin, *The Postman*, 1985
Octavia E. Butler, *Parable of the Sower*, 1993
Ursula K. Le Guin, *The Lathe of Heaven*, 1971
Anne McCaffrey, *To Ride Pegasus*, 1973
Walter M. Miller Jr., *A Canticle for Leibowitz*, 1960

---

**789**

### JACK BUTLER

## *Nightshade*

(New York: The Atlantic Monthly Press, 1989)

**Story type:** Science Fiction (Horror)
**Major character(s):** John Shade, Vampire, Rancher; Mandrake, Robot
**Time period(s):** 22nd century
**Locale(s):** Mars

**Summary:** Born in America's Old West of seemingly normal parents, Jack Shade is a vampire who has lived on into the age of space colonization and now resides on Mars where he quietly earns his living as a rancher and occasional secret agent. Mars's complex social order is facing imminent collapse, however, as several political blocs compete for power. Shade is drawn into the conflict, becoming a leader of the revolution.

**Other books you might like:**
Poul Anderson, *The Boat of a Million Years*, 1989
Michael Bishop, *The Secret Ascension*, 1987
Katherine Dunn, *Geek Love*, 1989
William Gibson, *Neuromancer*, 1984
Norman Spinrad, *Little Heroes*, 1987
Roger Zelazny, *This Immortal*, 1966

## 790

**OCTAVIA E. BUTLER**

### Bloodchild and Other Stories

(New York: Four Walls Eight Windows, 1995)

**Story type:** Science Fiction (Collection)

**Summary:** Contains two autobiographical essays and all five of Butler's short stories published 1971-1993 in periodicals and anthologies, with one Hugo Award and Nebula Award winning story, "Bloodchild"; one Hugo Award winner, "Speech Sounds"; and her first published story, "Crossover." Themes include gender role reversal, issues of oppression and empowerment, and the strength of women which allows them to endure the unbearable.

**Other books you might like:**
Nancy Kress, *The Aliens of Earth*, 1993
Ursula K. Le Guin, *The Compass Rose*, 1982
C.L. Moore, *The Best of C.L. Moore*, 1975
Pat Murphy, *Points of Departure*, 1990
L.A. Taylor, *Women's Work*, 1995
James Tiptree Jr., *Her Smoke Rose Up Forever*, 1990
Connie Willis, *Impossible Things*, 1994

## 791

**OCTAVIA E. BUTLER**

### Imago

(New York: Warner, 1989)

**Story type:** Science Fiction (Post-Nuclear Holocaust)
**Series:** Xenogenesis
**Major character(s):** Jodahs, Genetically Altered Being (alien-human construct); Lilith, Parent (Jodahs' mother)
**Time period(s):** 21st century
**Locale(s):** Earth

**Summary:** The alien Oankali have continued their efforts, first described in *Dawn* and *Adulthood Rites*, to establish a civilization populated by Oankali-human hybrids on a revitalized Earth which had been all but destroyed by nuclear war. Jodahs, half human, half alien, and possessed of enormous power to do both good and evil, must make a place for himself, despite the hostility of both races.

**Other books you might like:**
Gardner Dozois, *Strangers*, 1978
Bruce Sterling, *Involution Ocean*, 1977

## 792

**OCTAVIA E. BUTLER**

### Parable of the Sower

(New York: Four Walls Eight Windows, 1993)

**Story type:** Science Fiction (Theological; Adventure)
**Major character(s):** Lauren Oya Olamina, Teenager, Religious; Joanne Garfield, Teenager, Slave; Harry Balter, Teenager, Traveler
**Time period(s):** 2020s (2025-2027)
**Locale(s):** Robledos, California; Los Angeles, California; Oregon

**Summary:** Growing up in Robledos, a middle class, racially mixed, walled neighborhood, Lauren recognizes the wall as a temporary solution to the poverty and violence surrounding them. Born a hyper-empath as a result of legal, intelligence-enhancement drugs which killed her mother, Lauren suffers others' discomfort. Her father, a

Baptist minister, teaches her to live with the pain and hide her condition. Unwilling to hurt her father, Lauren develops her own religion, Earthseed, secretly, compiling a book of her inspirations. Prepared for years, when Robledos unexpectedly burns, Lauren sets off as a man to find a place where she can work for pay and found an Earthseed community.

**Other books you might like:**
Eleanor Arnason, *A Woman of the Iron People*, 1991
David Brin, *Earth*, 1990
David Brin, *The Postman*, 1985
Nicola Griffith, *Ammonite*, 1993
Marjorie Bradley Kellogg, *Harmony*, 1991
Pat Murphy, *The City, Not Long After*, 1989
Joan Slonczewski, *A Door into Ocean*, 1986
Neal Stephenson, *Snow Crash*, 1992
Vernor Vinge, *A Fire upon the Deep*, 1992
Eric Vinicoff, *The Weigher*, 1992
    Marcia Martin, co-author

## 793

**OCTAVIA E. BUTLER**

### Parable of the Talents

(New York: Seven Stories, 1998)

**Story type:** Science Fiction (Political; Theological)
**Major character(s):** Lauren Oya "Olamina" Bankole, Leader, Religious; Marcus Duran, Religious (preacher), Zealot; Larkin "Asha Vere" Bankole, Journalist, Critic
**Time period(s):** 2030s
**Locale(s):** Acorn, California

**Summary:** Worsening conditions after the election of a Christian America president permits religious zealots to destroy Acorn, steal all its children, and torture its residents. Olamina eventually contrives an escape to search for her two-month-old daughter. While continuing her search, Olamina finds converts to her new religion, Earthseed, but cannot find her daughter. Sequel to *Parable of the Sower*.

**Other books you might like:**
Eleanor Arnason, *A Woman of the Iron People*, 1991
Gregory Benford, *Cosm*, 1998
David Brin, *The Postman*, 1985
Mona Clee, *Overshoot*, 1998
Samuel R. Delany, *They Fly at Ciron*, 1993
Sheri S. Tepper, *Six Moon Dance*, 1998

## 794

**A.S. BYATT**

### The Djinn in the Nightingale's Eye

(New York: Random House, 1997)

**Story type:** Fantasy (Collection; Legend)
**Major character(s):** Gillian Perholt, Scholar; The Djinn, Mythical Creature (genie)
**Time period(s):** Indeterminate; 1990s
**Locale(s):** Middle East; United States; Fictional Country

**Summary:** Contains two reprinted and three original stories, generally upbeat in tone and featuring women in fairy tale settings. Themes include magical devices, mythical creatures, enchanted animals and a woman who considers her options carefully when given three wishes by a djinn.

**Other books you might like:**
Margaret Atwood, *Good Bones and Simple Murders*, 1994
Emma Donoghue, *Kissing the Witch: Old Tales in New Skins*, 1997
Ethel Johnston Phelps, *Tatterhood and Other Tales*, 1978
   editor
Barbara G. Walker, *Feminist Fairy Tales*, 1996
Jane Yolen, *Twelve Impossible Things Before Breakfast*, 1997
Jack Zipes, *The Outspoken Princess and the Gentle Knight*, 1994
   editor

---

**795**

RICHARD LEE BYERS

## Dark Fortune

(New York: Diamond, 1993)

**Story type:** Horror (Occult)
**Major character(s):** Tom Carpenter, Religious (minister); Rebecca Carpenter, Spouse (Tom's wife); Willie Harper, Teenager
**Time period(s):** 1990s (1993)
**Locale(s):** Corona City, Florida

**Summary:** When the fallen Reverend Carpenter reshapes his life with the help of a tarot deck, it gives him the power to heal others. But those whom he heals begin to reveal a dark side that suggests the powers of darkness are using the minister as their conduit.

**Other books you might like:**
John Byrne, *Whipping Boy*, 1992
Brian Hodge, *Deathgrip*, 1992
Stephen King, *The Dead Zone*, 1979

---

**796**

RICHARD LEE BYERS

## Dead Time

(New York: Zebra, 1992)

**Story type:** Horror (Serial Killer)
**Major character(s):** Jack Stone, Martial Arts Expert; Cheryl Stone, Prostitute; Vadoma Petalo, Gypsy
**Time period(s):** 1990s (1991)
**Locale(s):** Tampa, Florida

**Summary:** Jack Stone finds himself mystically transported back in time three weeks, with just enough time to prevent the murder of his sister. Before he can do so, though, he must determine how his time travel was made possible and who the shadowy entity is that dogs his trail and repeatedly tries to stop him.

**Other books you might like:**
Ken Grimwood, *Replay*, 1987
Lisa Tuttle, *Lost Futures*, 1992

---

**797**

RICHARD LEE BYERS

## The Ebon Mask

(Clarkston, Georgia: White Wolf, 1996)

**Story type:** Horror (Occult)
**Series:** Wraith: The Oblivion; Dark Kingdoms Trilogy
**Major character(s):** James Graham, Nobleman (Marquis of Montrose); Frank Bellamy, FBI Agent; Jim Dunn, FBI Agent
**Time period(s):** 1990s (1996)
**Locale(s):** St. Louis, Missouri; Stygia, Mythical Place (The Afterlife)

**Summary:** Intrigue among factions in the Shadowlands beyond death dovetails with a murder spree perpetrated by the Atheist in the world of the living. Synchronization of events in both worlds points the way to a possible resolution of their problems. This novel is set in the publisher's ''Wraith: The Oblivion'' gaming scenario, in which the Shadowlands of the Afterlife abut our own world.

**Other books you might like:**
Sam Chupp, *Sins of the Fathers*, 1995
Rick Hautala, *Beyond the Shroud*, 1996

---

**798**

RICHARD LEE BYERS

## Netherworld

(New York: HarperPaperbacks, 1995)

**Story type:** Horror (Vampire Story)
**Series:** World of Darkness: Vampire
**Major character(s):** Zane Tyler, Salesman; Alexander Blake, Vampire; Sartak, Vampire
**Time period(s):** 1990s (1995)
**Locale(s):** Tampa, Florida

**Summary:** Arrested on the suspicion that he murdered his girlfriend, Rose, Zane Tyler escapes from prison with the help of a hulking vampire named Sartak. With Sartak's help, Zane penetrates into the world of the Vampire Masquerade, in which numerous clans of vampires live secretly among human beings, and discovers that his girlfriend's disappearance is linked to a power struggle between the vampire clans and other supernatural beings fighting for dominance. This novel is set against the backdrop of a gaming scenario created by White Wolf.

**Other books you might like:**
Keith Herber, *Prince of the City*, 1994
James A. Moore, *The House of Secrets*, 1995
   Kevin Murphy, co-author
Robert Weinberg, *Blood War*, 1995
Robert Weinberg, *Unholy Allies*, 1995

---

**799**

RICHARD LEE BYERS

## The Vampire's Apprentice

(New York: Zebra, 1992)

**Story type:** Horror (Vampire Story)
**Major character(s):** David Brent, Vampire; Carter Cavanaugh, Vampire; Liz Scarbrough, Clerk (bookstore worker)
**Time period(s):** 1990s
**Locale(s):** Tampa, Florida

**Summary:** Nerdy David Brent seeks prestige and respect by becoming an Olympian—i.e. a vampire—but spends most of his new existence struggling to obtain his next meal and wrestling with his conscience over the moral questions that come with being a member of the Undead.

**Other books you might like:**
Poppy Z. Brite, *Lost Souls*, 1992
Nancy A. Collins, *Sunglasses After Dark*, 1989
John Peyton Cooke, *Out for Blood*, 1991
Mark Ivanhoe, *Virgintooth*, 1991
Anne Rice, *Interview with the Vampire*, 1976

## 800

### JOHN BYRNE

### *Whipping Boy*

(New York: Dell/Abyss, 1992)

**Story type:** Horror (Wild Talents)
**Major character(s):** Paul Trayne, Teenager; Robert Trayne, Religious (evangelical preacher), Parent (Paul's father); Walker Stone, Journalist
**Time period(s):** 1990s
**Locale(s):** Faulkner, Illinois

**Summary:** Preacher Robert Trayne tours the country with his son Paul, nicknamed ''The Whipping Boy'' because his laying on of hands absorbs guilt feelings from all who come in contact with him. But Paul's touch also relieves recipients of their inhibitions, initiating a spree of debauchery that an informal posse of citizens in Faulkner, Illinois decides to put a stop to.

**Other books you might like:**
James Herbert, *The Fog*, 1975
Brian Hodge, *Deathgrip*, 1992
Stephen King, *The Dead Zone*, 1979
Dean R. Koontz, *Midnight*, 1989

## 801

### P.D. CACEK
### JAMES HUBB, Illustrator

### *The Adventures of Threadwell the Tailor, or Alterations Made While You Wait*

(Clay, New York: Dark Raptor Press, 1998)

**Story type:** Horror (Satire)
**Major character(s):** Threadwell, Tailor; Wizard, Wizard; Lord Caoimhghin, Landowner
**Time period(s):** Indeterminate Past (Dark Ages)
**Locale(s):** Alternate Earth

**Summary:** In this comic dark fantasy, Threadwell the tailor applies his tailor's needle and sexual naivete to performing the necessary ''alterations'' on virgins to make them undesirable to dragons. Issued as a signed limited edition chapbook.

**Other books you might like:**
Isaac Asimov, *The Book of Dragons*, 1982
   Martin H. Greenberg, Charles G. Waugh, co-editors
Orson Scott Card, *Dragons of Light*, 1983
   editor
Jack Dann, *Dragons!*, 1993
   Gardner Dozois, co-editor
Michael Hague, *The Book of Dragons*, 1995
   editor
Byron Preiss, *The Ultimate Dragon*, 1995
   John Betancourt, Keith R.A. Candido, co-editors

## 802

### P.D. CACEK

### *Leavings*

(Greenwood Village, Colorado: StarsEnd Creations, 1997)

**Story type:** Horror (Collection)

**Summary:** Thirteen stories in a first collection of short fiction. ''Yrena'' chronicles the vampiric relationship between a young

woman and an older man. In ''The Ancient One,'' a child's teddy bear carries a centuries-old family curse. ''Here Be Dragons'' is a gargoyle tale and ''Gilgamesh Recidivus'' a unicorn story. In ''. . .Just a Little Bug. . .'' a young girl's cancer manifests outside her body as a bug-like creature.

**Other books you might like:**
Elizabeth Engstrom, *Nightmare Flower*, 1992
Brian Hopkins, *Something Haunts Us All*, 1996
Elizabeth Massie, *Shadow Dreams*, 1996
Jessica Amanda Salmonson, *John Collier and Fredric Brown Went Quarrelling through My Head*, 1989
Sue Storm, *Star Bones Weep the Blood of Angels*, 1996
David Niall Wilson, *The Fall of the House of Escher and Other Illusions*, 1996

## 803

### P.D. CACEK

### *Night Prayers*

(Darien, Illinois: Design Image Group, 1998)

**Story type:** Horror (Vampire Story)
**Major character(s):** Allison Garret, Vampire; Mica Poke, Religious (preacher); Luci, Dancer, Vampire
**Time period(s):** 1990s (1998)
**Locale(s):** Los Angeles, California

**Summary:** Abandoned by the lover who converted her to vampirism, Allison Garret learns through her own initiative how to survive, blending in with the exotic dance trade in Los Angeles as a cover for her predatory activities. This is a first novel.

**Other books you might like:**
Poppy Z. Brite, *Lost Souls*, 1992
Michael Cecilione, *Domination*, 1993
Ray Garton, *Live Girls*, 1987
Laurell K. Hamilton, *Guilty Pleasures*, 1993
Karen E. Taylor, *Blood Secrets*, 1994

## 804

### PAT CADIGAN

### *Dirty Work*

(Shingletown, California: Mark V. Ziesing, 1993)

**Story type:** Science Fiction (Collection)

**Summary:** Contains a four-page introduction by Storm Constantine and individual story introductions by Cadigan to 17 stories reprinted from periodicals and anthologies and one, ''Lost Girls,'' written for this volume. Stories utilize diverse themes from cyberpunk as in the title story which features a character, Deadpan Alley, from *Mindplayers* to alternative history, featured in several stories, while Cadigan's tone varies from dark to humorous.

**Other books you might like:**
David Brin, *The River of Time*, 1990
Gardner Dozois, *Geodesic Dreams: The Best Short Fiction of Gardner Dozois*, 1992
Michael Flynn, *The Nanotech Chronicles*, 1991
Nancy Kress, *The Aliens of Earth*, 1993
Cordwainer Smith, *The Best of Cordwainer Smith*, 1975
Bruce Sterling, *Crystal Express*, 1989
Bruce Sterling, *Mirrorshades: The Cyberpunk Anthology*, 1986
   editor
Marc Stiegler, *The Gentle Seduction*, 1990
John Varley, *Blue Champagne*, 1986

John Varley, *The Persistence of Vision*, 1978

## 805
### PAT CADIGAN

## *Fools*
(New York: Bantam Spectra, 1992)

**Story type:** Science Fiction (Cyberpunk; Alternate Intelligence)
**Major character(s):** Marceline, Police Officer (Brain Police), Imposter (memory junkie); Savoy, Actor, Disembodied Personality
**Time period(s):** Indeterminate Future
**Locale(s):** United States

**Summary:** Disoriented after a post-mindplay fugue state, Marceline decides she must have contracted with an escort service to perform especially unsavory work, hoping to satisfy her needs as a memory junkie. Her confusion deepens into fear as she discovers disturbing memories, too much cash in her pockets and a sense of being manipulated. Additional mindplay experiences lead her to believe she has involved herself illegally in an operation which franchises or bootlegs personalities, perhaps acquired using a highly illegal mindsuck. Beseeched by a victim's wife, Marceline agrees to help find or reconstruct the husband's personality. Contemporaneous with *Mindplayers*.

**Other books you might like:**
Piers Anthony, *Total Recall*, 1989
Samuel R. Delany, *Dhalgren*, 1975
Philip K. Dick, *A Maze of Death*, 1970
Philip K. Dick, *A Scanner Darkly*, 1977
George Alec Effinger, *When Gravity Fails*, 1987
Peter R. Emshwiller, *The Host*, 1991
Peter R. Emshwiller, *Short Blade*, 1992
Mick Farren, *The Feelies*, 1990
Katharine Kerr, *Polar City Blues*, 1990
Neal Stephenson, *Snow Crash*, 1992
Michael Swanwick, *Vacuum Flowers*, 1987
Walter Jon Williams, *Voice of the Whirlwind*, 1987

## 806
### PAT CADIGAN

## *Mindplayers*
(New York: Bantam Spectra, 1991)

**Story type:** Science Fiction (Cyberpunk; Future Shock)
**Major character(s):** Alexandria Victoria Haas, Psychologist (Reality Affixer), Counselor; Paolo Segretti, Lawyer, Psychologist
**Time period(s):** Indeterminate Future
**Locale(s):** United States

**Summary:** The Brain Police picked Allie up from being dry cleaned. She was now a mind criminal charged with possessing an illegal psychosis. Segretti asked if anyone had approached her about the unusual organization of her mind before he affixed her reality for the first time. The terms of her probation included mindplayer training. This book is a reissue of the 1987 edition.

**Other books you might like:**
Gregory Benford, *Great Sky River*, 1987
David Brin, *Earth*, 1990
Jeffrey A. Carver, *The Rapture Effect*, 1987
George Alec Effinger, *When Gravity Fails*, 1987
Victor Milan, *The Cybernetic Samurai*, 1986
Rudy Rucker, *Software*, 1982
Theodore Sturgeon, *Case and the Dreamer*, 1974

## 807
### PAT CADIGAN

## *Patterns*
(Kansas City: Ursus Imprints, 1989)

**Story type:** Science Fiction (Collection)
**Summary:** This collection includes one original short story, "The Power and the Passion," and eleven reprints. Among the best of these are "Pretty Boy Crossover," "It Was the Heat," "Angel" and "Rock On."

**Other books you might like:**
Patricia A. McKillip, *Fool's Run*, 1989
John Shirley, *Heatseeker*, 1989
Bruce Sterling, *Crystal Express*, 1989

## 808
### PAT CADIGAN

## *Synners*
(New York: Bantam Spectra, 1991)

**Story type:** Science Fiction (Arts; Cyberpunk)
**Major character(s):** Gina Aiesa, Artist; Mark "Visual Mark" Zamiatin, Artist; Cassandra "Sam" Ludovic, Artist
**Time period(s):** 21st century
**Locale(s):** Los Angeles, California

**Summary:** Over a score of years big business has moved into and taken over the production of synthesized videos, removing much of the individual control held by video artists called synners. Scientists have developed the first artificial neural cell which allows a direct human-computer interface. Synners and video production executives scramble for control of the new technology.

**Other books you might like:**
Gregory Benford, *Great Sky River*, 1987
David Brin, *Earth*, 1990
Jeffrey A. Carver, *The Rapture Effect*, 1987
George Alec Effinger, *When Gravity Fails*, 1987
Richard Kadrey, *Metrophage*, 1988
Victor Milan, *The Cybernetic Samurai*, 1986
Rudy Rucker, *Software*, 1982

## 809
### PAT CADIGAN

## *Tea From an Empty Cup*
(New York: Tor, 1998)

**Story type:** Science Fiction (Cyberpunk; Mystery)
**Major character(s):** Dore Konstantin, Detective—Homicide; Yukiko "Yuki", Detective—Amateur
**Time period(s):** Indeterminate Future
**Locale(s):** Washington, District of Columbia; Cyberspace

**Summary:** To search for her missing friend, Yuki enters the strange, artificial reality of post-apocalyptic Noo Yawk Sitty after contacting her friend's employer. Meanwhile Dore Konstantin discovers a dangerous and confusing environment as she visits virtual reality for the first time and uncovers a series of unusual deaths associated with virtual reality users.

**Other books you might like:**
Raphael Carter, *The Fortunate Fall*, 1996
Rudy Rucker, *Live Robots*, 1994

Neal Stephenson, *The Diamond Age*, 1995
Neal Stephenson, *Snow Crash*, 1993
Sage Walker, *Whiteout*, 1996

---

## 810

### MICHAEL CADNUM

## *Ghostwright*

(New York: Carroll & Graf, 1992)

**Story type:** Horror (Doppelganger)
**Major character(s):** Hamilton Speke, Writer (playwright); Timothy Asquith, Alcoholic; Clara Speke, Housewife (Hamilton's wife)
**Time period(s):** 1990s (1992)
**Locale(s):** San Francisco, California

**Summary:** When Timothy Asquith promises to tell the world that his old friend, renowned playwright Hamilton Speke, stole all his ideas from Timothy, Speke murders him. But Timothy is endowed with powers that the grave cannot contain, forcing Speke not only to defend himself but to ponder the curious creative bond the two men share.

**Other books you might like:**
Stephen King, *The Dark Half*, 1989
Stephen King, *Misery*, 1987
Richard Laymon, *The Stake*, 1990
T. Lucien Wright, *Blood Brothers*, 1992

---

## 811

### MICHAEL CADNUM

## *Horses of the Night*

(New York: Carroll & Graf, 1993)

**Story type:** Horror (Black Magic)
**Major character(s):** Stratton Fields, Architect; Nona Lyle, Doctor (psychiatrist); Tyson De Vere, Architect
**Time period(s):** 1990s (1993)
**Locale(s):** San Francisco, California

**Summary:** Underappreciated architect Stratton Fields makes a pact with dark forces to protect himself and his interests. When those he loves, as well as his enemies, come to harm, he begins to doubt his supposed benefactors and himself.

**Other books you might like:**
Scott Baker, *Webs*, 1988
Charles L. Grant, *The Pet*, 1986
Patrick McGrath, *Spider*, 1991

---

## 812

### MICHAEL CADNUM

## *The Judas Glass*

(New York: Carroll & Graf, 1996)

**Story type:** Horror (Vampire Story)
**Major character(s):** Richard Stirling, Lawyer, Vampire; Rebecca Pennant, Musician; Sam Opal, Doctor
**Time period(s):** 1990s (1996)
**Locale(s):** San Francisco, California

**Summary:** A cut from an antique glass mirror endows Richard Stirling with vampiric appetites, powers, and a new sensual appreciation for a world unknown to him as a mortal. Richard resurrects his

murdered lover Rebecca to share his new existence with him and becomes the object of a statewide manhunt.

**Other books you might like:**
Brett Easton Ellis, *The Informers*, 1994
Jonathan Nasaw, *The World on Blood*, 1996
Anne Rice, *Interview with the Vampire*, 1976
Lucius Shepard, *The Golden*, 1993
Brian Stableford, *Young Blood*, 1992

---

## 813

### MICHAEL CADNUM

## *Nightlight*

(New York: St. Martin's, 1989)

**Story type:** Horror (Mystery)
**Major character(s):** Paul Wright, Journalist, Critic (restaurant); Mary Lewis, Widow(er) (Paul's aunt); Leonard Lewis, Photographer (Mary's son)
**Time period(s):** 1980s (1989)
**Locale(s):** Berkeley, California

**Summary:** Desperate for a break from his newspaper job, Paul Wright accedes to his Aunt Mary's request that he search for his missing cousin, a morbid young man whose main interest is photographing cemeteries. When Paul arrives at the secluded cabin that was his cousin's last known abode, he finds that it is the setting of a recurring nightmare that has plagued him for months.

**Other books you might like:**
Ramsey Campbell, *Incarnate*, 1983
Daniel Quinn, *Dreamer*, 1988

---

## 814

### MICHAEL CADNUM

## *Skyscape*

(New York: Carroll & Graf, 1994)

**Story type:** Horror (Psychological Suspense)
**Major character(s):** Curtis Newns, Artist (painter); Margaret Newns, Writer; Red Patterson, Doctor (psychiatrist)
**Time period(s):** 1990s (1995)
**Locale(s):** San Francisco, California; Mojave Desert, California

**Summary:** Blocked creatively after the destruction of his masterpiece, "Skyscape," painter Curtis Newns agrees to undergo treatment with charismatic television psychiatrist Red Patterson at his remote facility in the Mojave Desert. Once there, Newns and his wife, Margaret, become involved in a struggle for identity with Patterson, who seeks not only to create vicariously through Newns, but to dominate and usurp his personality, at any cost.

**Other books you might like:**
Kathe Koja, *Bad Brains*, 1992
Kathe Koja, *Strange Angels*, 1994
Thomas Tessier, *The Dreams of Dr. Ladybank*, 1991
in *Night Visions 9*

---

## 815

### MICHAEL CADNUM

## *Sleepwalker*

(New York: St. Martins, 1991)

**Story type:** Horror (Reanimated Dead)

**Major character(s):** Davis Lowry, Anthropologist; Peter Chambers, Anthropologist; Irene Sarnii, Anthropologist
**Time period(s):** 1990s (1991)
**Locale(s):** York, England
**Summary:** An archaeological dig in England turns up the mummified body of the eighth century Skeldergate Man, but a series of mysterious deaths among the expedition's members suggests that the exhumed body is not dead.

**Other books you might like:**
Peter Ackroyd, *First Light*, 1989
David Case, *The Third Grave*, 1981

## 816

### MICHAEL CADNUM

### St. Peter's Wolf

(New York: Carroll & Graf)

**Story type:** Horror (Werewolf Story)
**Major character(s):** Benjamin Byrd, Psychologist; Johanna Fisher, Linguist (translator); Jacob Zinser, Collector (art)
**Time period(s):** 1990s
**Locale(s):** San Francisco, California

**Summary:** Given a set of antique silver fangs by a fellow art connoisseur, psychologist Benjamin Byrd comes to know satisfaction he has never known before as, under their influence, he begins to experience nightly transformation into a werewolf who lives, loves and feeds without inhibition.

**Other books you might like:**
Scott Bradfield, *Dream of the Wolf*, 1990
Crosland Brown, *Tombley's Walk*, 1991
Dennis Danvers, *Wilderness*, 1991

## 817

### JACK CADY

### Inagehi

(Seattle: Broken Moon Press, 1994)

**Story type:** Horror (Mystery)
**Major character(s):** Harriette Johnson, Teacher (music teacher); Johnny Whitcomb, Worker; Lewis Corey, Artisan
**Time period(s):** 1950s
**Locale(s):** North Carolina

**Summary:** Harriette Johnson returns to her family homestead in North Carolina on a quest to unravel her father's unsolved murder. As she probes into her family's past, she uncovers the truth about how her father acquired the family land and realizes that her father's death was a means of atoning for past indiscretions and making peace with his Cherokee heritage and mystical understanding of life.

**Other books you might like:**
Fred Chappell, *I Am One of You Forever*, 1991
G. Wayne Miller, *Thunder Rise*, 1988
Manly Wade Wellman, *Who Fears the Devil?*, 1962

## 818

### JACK CADY

### The Night We Buried Road Dog

(Minneapolis, Dreamhaven, 1998)

**Story type:** Horror (Collection)

**Summary:** These six stories are set mostly in the Pacific northwest and mix horror and fantasy themes in marvelously literate and original blends. The title story features ghosts and human characters in a tale of a man who builds a graveyard for old used cars. "A Sailor's Pay" is a nautical ghost story. "The Bride: A Romance" tells of the impact a magic statue has on a lonely man, and through him, his town. "The Best Left Neglected Library of Dry Facts" concerns a storehouse for human knowledge in which facts blossom into winged creatures. Introduction by Peter S. Beagle.

**Other books you might like:**
Jorge Luis Borges, *Collected Fictions*, 1998
Scott Bradfield, *Greetings From Earth*, 1990
Fred Chappell, *More Shapes than One*, 1991
Avram Davidson, *Adventures in Unhistory*, 1993
Charles de Lint, *Dreams Underfoot*, 1993

## 819

### JACK CADY

### The Night We Buried Road Dog

(Minneapolis, Minnesota: Dream Haven Books, 1998)

**Story type:** Fantasy (Collection; Contemporary Realism)

**Summary:** This collection contains an introduction by Peter S. Beagle and six short stories written between 1991 and 1996, dealing with memories, guilt, ghosts and the way the miraculous can intrude on the everyday. A young sailor gets caught up in a murder that seems not quite a murder, while a woman gives her life to a library where facts are born.

**Other books you might like:**
James P. Blaylock, *The Paper Grail*, 1991
Ray Bradbury, *The October Country*, 1996
John Crowley, *Antiquities*, 1993
Lisa Goldstein, *Travelers in Magic*, 1994
Pat Murphy, *Points of Departure*,

## 820

### JACK CADY

### The Off Season

(New York: St. Martin's, 1995)

**Story type:** Fantasy (Contemporary Realism)
**Major character(s):** Joel-Andrew, Religious, Wanderer; Kune, Doctor; Obed, Animal (cat), Linguist
**Time period(s):** 1970s (1973); 1880s (1888)
**Locale(s):** Point Vestal, Oregon

**Summary:** In a small town where ghosts exist beside the living and the present sometimes reflects one year, sometimes another, Joel-Andrew, a travelling prophet, and a cat arrive one day, upsetting certain balances.

**Other books you might like:**
James P. Blaylock, *Land of Dreams*, 1987
John Crowley, *Little, Big*, 1981
Robert Holdstock, *Mythago Wood*, 1984
Ian McDonald, *Desolation Road*, 1988
Pat Murphy, *The City, Not Long After*, 1989

**821**

### JACK CADY

## *The Sons of Noah and Other Stories*

(Seattle, Washington: Broken Moon Press, 1992)

**Story type:** Horror (Collection)

**Summary:** The seven stories collected in this booklet reveal one of the most talented writers of psychological and supernatural horror working today. The best are the title story, about a land development scheme that unleashes an uncontrollable elemental force, and the Conradian ''By Reason of Darkness,'' which tells of a Vietnam vet who brings the war home, and the army buddies who must help him fight it.

**Other books you might like:**
Michael Blumlein, *The Brains of Rats*, 1989
Fred Chappell, *More Shapes than One*, 1991
Lucius Shepard, *The Jaguar Hunter*, 1987
Dan Simmons, *Prayers to Broken Stones*, 1990

**822**

### JACK CADY

## *Street*

(New York: St. Martin's, 1994)

**Story type:** Horror (Serial Killer)
**Major character(s):** Silk, Streetperson; Symptomatic Nerve Gas, Streetperson; Elgin, Streetperson
**Time period(s):** 1990s (1994)
**Locale(s):** Seattle, Washington

**Summary:** A group of homeless people, the flotsam of disillusionment with the American establishment and tragically misspent lives, band together to track down a serial killer preying on the homeless and runaways in their town. Their investigations take them on an odyssey of self-understanding and redemption.

**Other books you might like:**
George C. Chesbro, *Bone*, 1989
Gordon Linzner, *The Troupe*, 1988
David Martin, *Bring Me Children*, 1992
Rick R. Reed, *Penance*, 1993
Wayne Allen Sallee, *The Holy Terror*, 1992

**823**

### JAMES CAHILL, Editor

## *Lamps on the Brow*

(Aliso Viejo, California: James Cahill, 1998)

**Story type:** Science Fiction (Anthology)

**Summary:** This anthology presents eight stories original to this volume by some of the leading writers in the field, plus one obscure reprint by A.E. Van Vogt. There is no central theme to the collection which includes stories by Gregory Benford, David Brin, Andre Norton, Gene Wolfe, and others.

**Other books you might like:**
Gregory Benford, *Matter's End*, 1995
David Brin, *Otherness*, 1994
Andre Norton, *The Book of Andre Norton*, 1975
A.E. Van Vogt, *Destination Universe*, 1952
Gene Wolfe, *Endangered Species*, 1989

**824**

### MARTIN CAIDIN

## *Beamriders!*

(New York: Baen Books, 1989)

**Story type:** Science Fiction (Adventure)
**Major character(s):** Kim Seavers, Sports Figure, Spy; Caleb Massey, Scientist
**Time period(s):** Indeterminate Future
**Locale(s):** Montenegro

**Summary:** Breakthroughs in laser technology lead to the development of teleportation. Beamriding, as it is called, remains enormously dangerous, however, and is only used for emergency situations. A small cadre of tough and talented beamriders is developed. They are called on whenever a daring rescue is needed or an impossible mission must be accomplished.

**Other books you might like:**
Ben Bova, *Voyagers III: Star Brothers*, 1990
Ben Bova, *Voyagers II: The Alien Within*, 1986
John Cramer, *Twistor*, 1989
John Varley, *Millennium*, 1983

**825**

### MARTIN CAIDIN

## *Indiana Jones and the Sky Pirates*

(New York: Bantam, 1993)

**Story type:** Fantasy (Adventure; Psychic Powers)
**Series:** Indiana Jones
**Major character(s):** Indiana ''Indy'' Jones, Archaeologist; Willard Cromwell, Martial Arts Expert, Adventurer
**Time period(s):** 1930s
**Locale(s):** Africa; Europe; Southwest

**Summary:** When Indy and his companions investigate reports of monstrous flying machines believed to fly through use of psychokinetic levitation, they uncover a plot to control international commerce and military power.

**Other books you might like:**
Campbell Black, *Raiders of the Lost Ark*, 1981
James Kahn, *Indiana Jones and the Temple of Doom*, 1984
Rob MacGregor, *Indiana Jones and the Dance of the Giants*, 1991
Rob MacGregor, *Indiana Jones and the Genesis Deluge*, 1992
Rob MacGregor, *Indiana Jones and the Interior World*, 1992
Rob MacGregor, *Indiana Jones and the Last Crusade*, 1989
Rob MacGregor, *Indiana Jones and the Peril at Delphi*, 1991
Rob MacGregor, *Indiana Jones and the Seven Veils*, 1991
Rob MacGregor, *Indiana Jones and the Unicorn's Legacy*, 1992

**826**

### MARTIN CAIDIN

## *Indiana Jones and the White Witch*

(New York: Bantam, 1994)

**Story type:** Fantasy (Adventure; Quest)
**Series:** Indiana Jones
**Major character(s):** Indiana ''Indy'' Jones, Archaeologist; Gale Parker, Archaeologist; Caitlin St. Brendan, Religious (Wicca), Magician
**Time period(s):** 1930s
**Locale(s):** England

**Summary:** When thieves steal an incomplete map leading to an ancient hoard of gold, Indy, Gale and Caitlin, who wields Merlin's legendary sword, undertake a perilous worldwide search for the treasure.

**Other books you might like:**
Campbell Black, *Raiders of the Lost Ark*, 1981
James Kahn, *Indiana Jones and the Temple of Doom*, 1984
Rob MacGregor, *Indiana Jones and the Dance of the Giants*, 1991
Rob MacGregor, *Indiana Jones and the Genesis Deluge*, 1992
Rob MacGregor, *Indiana Jones and the Interior World*, 1992
Rob MacGregor, *Indiana Jones and the Last Crusade*, 1989
Rob MacGregor, *Indiana Jones and the Peril at Delphi*, 1991
Rob MacGregor, *Indiana Jones and the Seven Veils*, 1991
Rob MacGregor, *Indiana Jones and the Unicorn's Legacy*, 1992

**827**

**MARTIN CAIDIN**

## A Life in the Future

(Lake Geneva, Wisconsin: TSR, 1995)

**Story type:** Science Fiction (Adventure; Time Travel)
**Series:** Buck Rogers
**Major character(s):** Buck Rogers, Pilot, Experimental Subject; Wilma Deering, Pilot, Psychologist
**Time period(s):** 1990s (1996); 25th century
**Locale(s):** *Io*, Submarine; Pacific Ocean

**Summary:** When Buck Rogers crashes at an air show, his irreparable injuries lead experimenters to send the dying Buck 400 years into the future. Snatched from death by advanced technology, Buck's knowledge of Chile proves vital in overcoming Chileans aided by extraterrestrial survivors from Atlantis.

**Other books you might like:**
John Miller, *First Power Play*, 1990
M.S. Murdock, *Prime Squared*, 1990
M.S. Murdock, *Rebellion 2456*, 1989
Philip Francis Nowlan, *Armageddon 2419 A.D.*, 1962
John Silbersack, *Roger's Rangers*, 1983

**828**

**MARTIN CAIDIN**

## Prison Ship

(New York: Baen, 1989)

**Story type:** Science Fiction (First Contact)
**Major character(s):** Jake Marden, Criminal, Computer Expert; Arbok, Alien, Pilot
**Time period(s):** 21st century
**Locale(s):** Earth; Outer Space

**Summary:** Six alien criminals, all of different species, all on the run, end up on Earth and join forces with a group of equally despicable human criminals.

**Other books you might like:**
Rick Cook, *Limbo System*, 1989
L. Ron Hubbard, *The Doomed Planet*, 1987
Larry Niven, *Man-Kzin Wars*, 1988
Larry Niven, *Man-Kzin Wars II*, 1989
Rebecca Ore, *Becoming Alien*, 1987
Rebecca Ore, *Being Alien*, 1989

**829**

**ROBERT CAIN**

## Cybernarc

(New York: HarperCollins, 1991)

**Story type:** Science Fiction (Adventure; Robot Fiction)
**Series:** Cybernarc
**Major character(s):** RAMROD Mark I "Rod", Robot, Artificial Intelligence; Christopher Drake, Military Personnel (Seal)
**Time period(s):** 21st century
**Locale(s):** Colombia; United States

**Summary:** A product of CIA Project RAMROD, ROD survives initial testing and is teamed up with Christopher Drake for advanced field testing in Operation Amber Harvest aimed at capturing Colombian drug lord Luis Delgado-Valasquez.

**Other books you might like:**
Philip K. Dick, *The Three Stigmata of Palmer Eldritch*, 1965
Alan Dean Foster, *Outland*, 1981
Ernest Hogan, *High Aztec*, 1992
Ed Naha, *Robocop*, 1987
Ed Naha, *Robocop 2*, 1990
William Shatner, *TekLab*, 1991
William Shatner, *TekWar*, 1989
G. Harry Stine, *Warbots*, 1988
Thomas T. Thomas, *ME: A Novel of Self Discovery*, 1991

**830**

**ROBERT CAIN**

## End Game

(New York: Harper Paperbacks, 1993)

**Story type:** Science Fiction (Robot Fiction; Adventure)
**Series:** Cybernarc
**Major character(s):** RAMROD Mark I "Rod", Robot, Artificial Intelligence; Christopher Drake, Martial Arts Expert, Teacher
**Time period(s):** 21st century
**Locale(s):** Colombia

**Summary:** When Rod rebels against orders and attacks a drug lord's army and captures a leader, a drug kingpin declares vengeance on cybernarc. Meanwhile, U.S. forces launch a covert worldwide operation against the illegal drug trade.

**Other books you might like:**
David Alexander, *Nomad*, 1992
Isaac Asimov, *The Caves of Steel*, 1954
Isaac Asimov, *The Naked Sun*, 1957
Philip K. Dick, *A Scanner Darkly*, 1977
Michael Kandel, *Captain Jack Zodiac*, 1992
Ed Naha, *Robocop*, 1987
Ed Naha, *Robocop 2*, 1990
L.S. Riker, *Kill Crazy*, 1993
G. Harry Stine, *Sierra Madre*, 1988

**831**

**ROBERT CAIN**

## Gold Dragon

(New York: HarperCollins, 1991)

**Story type:** Science Fiction (Adventure; Robot Fiction)
**Series:** Cybernarc

**Major character(s):** RAMROD Mark I ''Rod'', Robot, Artificial Intelligence; Christopher Drake, Military Personnel (Seal); Feng Hwa Chung, Drug Dealer

**Time period(s):** 21st century

**Locale(s):** Thailand; Myanmar; *Zhang-Zhou*, At Sea

**Summary:** ROD and Christopher Drake are sent to the Golden Triangle to find the heroin laboratory of Chinese drug lord Feng Hwa Chung, who supplies drugs to Bangkok and Hong Kong. Their mission is complicated when Drake is captured and ROD must find and free him.

**Other books you might like:**
Alan Dean Foster, *Outland*, 1981
Ed Naha, *Robocop*, 1987
Ed Naha, *Robocop 2*, 1990
William Shatner, *TekLords*, 1991
Ben Sloane, *Outland Strip*, 1991
Ben Sloane, *Ultimate Weapon*, 1991
G. Harry Stine, *The Lost Battalion*, 1989
G. Harry Stine, *Sierra Madre*, 1988

---

**832**

GEOFFREY CAINE

## Curse of the Vampire

(New York: Diamond, 1991)

**Story type:** Horror (Vampire Story)

**Series:** Adventures of Abraham Stroud

**Major character(s):** Abraham Hale Stroud, Detective—Private, Psychic; Louis P. Cage, Archaeologist; Oliver Banaker, Doctor, Vampire

**Time period(s):** 1990s

**Locale(s):** Andover, Illinois

**Summary:** Psychically sensitive private detective Abraham Stroud runs afoul of the powerbrokers of Andover when his investigation of the disappearance of several of Andover's children and the discovery of a boneyard on the outskirts of town points to the town's leading citizens and their abnormal taste for blood. Before he can prevent more disappearances though, he must overcome the townspeoples' prejudices toward his family, who were long regarded as sorcerers and murderers.

**Other books you might like:**
Charles L. Grant, *The Hour of the Oxrun Dead*, 1977
Barbara Hambly, *Those Who Hunt the Night*, 1988
Stephen King, *Salem's Lot*, 1975
Robert Weinberg, *The Armageddon Box*, 1991

---

**833**

GEOFFREY CAINE

## Legion of the Dead

(New York: Diamond, 1992)

**Story type:** Horror (Reanimated Dead)

**Series:** Adventures of Abraham Stroud

**Major character(s):** Abraham Hale Stroud, Detective—Private, Psychic; Dr. Leonard Wisnewski, Museum Curator (New York Museum of Antiquities); Dr. Kendra Cline, Doctor (epidemiologist)

**Time period(s):** 1990s (1992)

**Locale(s):** New York, New York

**Summary:** In this third adventure of psychic detective Abraham Stroud, the uncovering of a buried Etruscan ship in a Manhattan construction site releases a malignant force that sends scores of New Yorkers into comas, from which they awaken as zombified shock troops prepared to do its evil bidding.

**Other books you might like:**
Nigel Kneale, *Quatermass and the Pit*, 1968
William Relling Jr., *New Moon*, 1988
Robert Weinberg, *The Dead Man's Kiss*, 1992

---

**834**

GEOFFREY CAINE

## Wake of the Werewolf

(New York: Diamond, 1991)

**Story type:** Horror (Werewolf Story)

**Series:** Adventures of Abraham Stroud

**Major character(s):** Abraham Hale Stroud, Detective—Private, Psychic; Anna Laughing More, Police Officer; John Kerac, Prisoner (escaped convict), Indian

**Time period(s):** 1990s

**Locale(s):** Merrimac, Michigan

**Summary:** In this second adventure of Abraham Stroud, ex-cop turned psychic investigator, the escape from a Michigan penitentiary of an Indian who partially ate his captors brings Stroud into contact with the remains of the Ojibway tribe, who are convinced that the prisoner, John Kerac, has been bitten by an elemental spirit called the Wendigo, and been turned into a shape-shifting monster.

**Other books you might like:**
Charles L. Grant, *The Nestling*, 1982
T. Chris Martindale, *Where the Chill Waits*, 1991
S.P. Somtow, *Moon Dance*, 1989

---

**835**

RICHARD CALDER

## Cytheria

(New York: St. Martin's, 1998)

**Story type:** Science Fiction (Literary; Cyberpunk)

**Major character(s):** Dahlia Chan, Entertainer, Artificial Intelligence; Mosquito, Thief

**Time period(s):** 2020s (2025)

**Locale(s):** McMurdo City, Antarctica

**Summary:** While ghosts from cyberspace walk the streets at night, Dahlia Chan poses a danger to society and its entrenched powers. By turns weak and strong, but always seductive, Dahlia Chan is desired by everyone in a world on the edge of transformation and collapse.

**Other books you might like:**
Pat Cadigan, *Synners*, 1991
William Gibson, *Idoru*, 1996
Paul J. McAuley, *Fairyland*, 1996
Ian McDonald, *Terminal Cafe*, 1994
Amy Thomson, *Virtual Girl*, 1993

---

**836**

RICHARD CALDER

## Dead Boys

(New York: St. Martin's, 1996)

**Story type:** Science Fiction (Cyberpunk; Literary)

**Series:** Dead Girls

**Major character(s):** Ignatz Zwakh, Addict, Refugee; Vanity, Android (Lilim), Prostitute; Dagon, Android (Elohim), Murderer
**Time period(s):** 21st century
**Locale(s):** Bangkok, Thailand; Paris, Mars

**Summary:** Short-time companion to Primavera, the now-dead android assassin, Ignatz Zwakh wanders Bangkok, sinking into decay. Meanwhile, on Mars, the Elohim and Dead Girls carry on a cladestine war in a strange future where metaphysical viruses corrupt reality.

**Other books you might like:**
Greg Bear, *Blood Music*, 1985
Philip K. Dick, *Do Androids Dream of Electric Sheep?*, 1965
Elizabeth Hand, *AEstival Tide*, 1992
Jonathan Littell, *Bad Voltage*, 1989
Ian McDonald, *Terminal Cafe*, 1994

## 837
### RICHARD CALDER
## Dead Girls
(New York: St. Martin's, 1995)

**Story type:** Science Fiction (Cyberpunk)
**Series:** Dead Girls
**Major character(s):** Ignatz Zwakh, Fugitive; Primavera, Android (Lilim), Murderer; Jack Morganstern, Spy
**Time period(s):** 21st century
**Locale(s):** Bangkok, Thailand

**Summary:** A machine-infected killer in a teenage body, Primavera, and her human lover find themselves set up in an elaborate series of betrayals, part of the dirty politics of a ruined world. To survive, they must crack Primavera's secrets and find their true enemies. First novel.

**Other books you might like:**
J.G. Ballard, *Hello America*, 1981
Philip K. Dick, *Blade Runner*, 1982
Jonathan Littell, *Bad Voltage*, 1989
Ian McDonald, *Terminal Cafe*, 1994
Amy Thomson, *Virtual Girl*, 1993

## 838
### RICHARD CALDER
## Dead Things
(New York: St. Martin's, 1997)

**Story type:** Science Fiction (Cyberpunk; Literary)
**Series:** Dead Girls
**Major character(s):** Ignatz Zwakh, Revolutionary, Addict; Lipstick, Android (Lilim)
**Time period(s):** 21st century
**Locale(s):** Bangkok, Thailand

**Summary:** Ignatz returns to Earth after traveling through the universe and many probable universes. He has the Reality Bomb, which should undo the meta plague. When forces released during the journey collapse space and time, however, the unlikely deranged savior must race against hallucination and annhilation to complete his mission. Third, and presumably last, in the series.

**Other books you might like:**
Iain M. Banks, *Feersum Endjinn*, 1995
Octavia E. Butler, *Dawn*, 1987
Jonathan Littell, *Bad Voltage*, 1989
Ian McDonald, *Terminal Cafe*, 1994

Michael Swanwick, *Vacuum Flowers*, 1987

## 839
### C. CHRISTOPHER CALDON
## Concrete Hotel
(Kansas City, Missouri: Tiras Books, 1998)

**Story type:** Horror (Wild Talents)
**Major character(s):** Joseph Broward, Detective—Homicide; Connie Stevenson, Detective—Homicide; Sprits, Psychic (spirit medium)
**Time period(s):** 1990s (1998)
**Locale(s):** John's Bluff, Florida

**Summary:** Homicide detectives Broward and Stevenson investigate a string of murders and find some to be the handiwork of Sprits, a young man endowed with psychic powers who becomes a channel for spirits who reach out to him from the afterlife and use him for revenge against their murderers. A first novel.

**Other books you might like:**
Richard Bachman, *The Regulators*, 1997
Ramsey Campbell, *The Parasite*, 1980
Rick Hautala, *Beyond the Shroud*, 1996
Thomas Tessier, *Fog Heart*, 1997
Kelley Wilde, *The Suiting*, 1989

## 840
### MARY R. CALLAGHAN
## I Met a Man Who Wasn't There
(New York: Marion Boyars, 1997)

**Story type:** Horror (Ghost Story)
**Major character(s):** Anne O'Brien, Writer; Marcus Quilligan O'Neill, Lawyer, Spirit (ghost); Charles Matthews, Teacher
**Time period(s):** 1990s (1997)
**Locale(s):** Oldcastle, Pennsylvania (Sweetmount College); New York, New York

**Summary:** At the behest of the ghost of her grandfather Marcus, Anne O'Brien agrees to write his biography and help exonerate a man he helped to prosecute and wrongly send to his death. Anne's research into the Irish experience in early twentieth-century America acquaints her with her roots but resurrects the ghosts of Marcus's associates, who would just as soon never have the truth about their crimes come to light.

**Other books you might like:**
Noel Hynd, *Ghosts*, 1993
Greg Kihn, *Shade of Pale*, 1997
Alan Ryan, *Cast a Cold Eye*, 1984
Peter Straub, *Ghost Story*, 1979

## 841
### DON CALLANDER
## Aquamancer
(New York: Ace, 1993)

**Story type:** Fantasy (Quest; Magic Conflict)
**Series:** Pyromancer
**Major character(s):** Douglas Brightglade, Wizard (journeyman pyromancer), Fiance(e); Myrn Manstar, Apprentice (aquamancer), Fiance(e)

**Time period(s):** Indeterminate Past
**Locale(s):** Old Kingdom, Fictional Country; Choin, Fictional Country

**Summary:** For his required Journeying, Douglas Brightglade receives Master Flarman Flowerstalk's assignment to utilize his craft to investigate a coven of evil witches in the Old Kingdom. When Myrn Manstar grows concerned over the lack of communication from Douglas, Myrn convinces her master to allow her, as apprentice, to follow and help Douglas.

**Other books you might like:**
Lois McMaster Bujold, *The Spirit Ring*, 1992
Gordon R. Dickson, *The Dragon Knight*, 1990
Alexis A. Gilliland, *Lord of the Troll-Bats*, 1992
Laurell K. Hamilton, *Nightseer*, 1992
Martha Wells, *The Element of Fire*, 1993

---

**842**

**DON CALLANDER**

## Dragon Companion

(New York: Ace, 1994)

**Story type:** Fantasy (Alternate World; Adventure)
**Major character(s):** Tom Whitehead, Librarian, Adventurer; Retruance Constable, Mythical Creature (dragon); Murdan of Overhall, Leader (High Historian)
**Time period(s):** Indeterminate
**Locale(s):** Carolna, Fictional Country

**Summary:** When suddenly transported to another world, Tom Whitehead finds himself befriended by an intelligent dragon and immediately joins Murdan's forces as a Dragon Companion, so proclaimed by Retruance Constable.

**Other books you might like:**
Gordon R. Dickson, *The Dragon and the George*, 1976
Gordon R. Dickson, *The Dragon at War*, 1992
Anne McCaffrey, *Dragonriders of Pern*, 1988
Christopher Rowley, *Bazil Broketail*, 1992
Lawrence Watt-Evans, *The Blood of a Dragon*, 1991

---

**843**

**DON CALLANDER**

## Dragon Rescue

(New York: Ace, 1995)

**Story type:** Fantasy (Adventure; Quest)
**Major character(s):** Alix Amanda Trusslo, Royalty (princess), Adventurer; Murdan of Overhall, Companion (Arbitrance's); Arbitrance Constable, Mythical Creature (dragon)
**Time period(s):** Indeterminate
**Locale(s):** Carolna, Fictional Country

**Summary:** Arbitrance's family becomes concerned over his ten-year absence, not especially lengthy for the species. When his family and Murdan of Overhall search for Arbitrance, they little expect to find him kidnapping small children to play with them before returning them safely. Sequel to *Dragon Companion*.

**Other books you might like:**
Gael Baudino, *Duel of Dragons*, 1991
Gordon R. Dickson, *The Dragon and the George*, 1976
Anne McCaffrey, *Dragonriders of Pern*, 1988
Christopher Rowley, *Bazil Broketail*, 1992
Patricia C. Wrede, *Searching for Dragons*, 1991
Laurence Yep, *Dragon of the Lost Sea*, 1982

---

**844**

**DON CALLANDER**

## Dragon Tempest

(New York: Ace, 1998)

**Story type:** Fantasy (Adventure)
**Series:** Dragon
**Major character(s):** Tom Whitehead, Librarian; Byron Boldface, Kidnapper
**Time period(s):** Indeterminate
**Locale(s):** Carolna, Fictional Country

**Summary:** Byron Boldface kidnaps a princess and spirits her away. A librarian turned adventurer and his dragon companion set off on a series of lighthearted escapades in the course of rescuing her.

**Other books you might like:**
Robin Wayne Bailey, *Nightwatch*, 1990
Elizabeth H. Boyer, *The Clan of the Warlord*, 1992
Susan Dexter, *The Mountains of Channadran*, 1986
Dennis McCarty, *The Birth of the Blade*, 1993
Dennis L. McKiernan, *The Dragonstone*, 1996

---

**845**

**DON CALLANDER**

## Geomancer

(New York: Ace, 1994)

**Story type:** Fantasy (Magic Conflict)
**Series:** Pyromancer
**Major character(s):** Douglas Brightglade, Wizard, Fiance(e); Myrn Manstar, Wizard, Fiance(e); Marbleheart, Animal (sea otter), Companion (wizard's familiar)
**Time period(s):** Indeterminate Past
**Locale(s):** Dukedom, Fictional Country; Choin, Fictional Country

**Summary:** Douglas, Myrn and Marbleheart come to the aid of ensorcelled Stone Warriors, victims of an ancient geomancy. Douglas and Myrn's romance continues as Douglas prepares for the examination which will determine his fitness as Master Wizard.

**Other books you might like:**
Patricia Briggs, *Masques*, 1993
Douglas W. Clark, *Whirlwind Alchemy*, 1993
Phyllis Eisenstein, *In the Red Lord's Reach*, 1989
Mercedes Lackey, *The Robin and the Kestrel*, 1993
Christopher Stasheff, *The Warlock in Spite of Himself*, 1969

---

**846**

**DON CALLANDER**

## Marbleheart

(New York: Ace, 1998)

**Story type:** Fantasy (Quest)
**Series:** Brightglade
**Major character(s):** Marbleheart, Animal (sea otter); Flowerbender, Royalty (prince)
**Time period(s):** Indeterminate
**Locale(s):** Choin, Fictional Country

**Summary:** Young Prince Flowerbender of Choin sets out on a dangerous quest, unbeknownst to his parents, and accompanied only by the precocious and heroic sea otter, Marbleheart, who helped his father gain the throne.

**Other books you might like:**
Clare Bell, *Clan Ground*, 1984
Karen Brush, *Demon Pig*, 1991
Scott Ciencin, *The Wolves of Autumn*, 1992
Gregory Frost, *Lyrec*, 1984
Gabriel King, *The Wild Road*, 1998

## 847

### DON CALLANDER

## *Pyromancer*
(New York: Ace, 1992)

**Story type:** Fantasy (Magic Conflict; Quest)
**Major character(s):** Flarman Flowerstalk, Wizard, Magician; Douglas Brightblade, Apprentice, Teenager; Bryarmote, Mythical Creature (dwarf), Royalty
**Time period(s):** Indeterminate Past
**Locale(s):** Wizard's High, Mythical Place

**Summary:** The owl door knocker recognizes the perfect apprentice and encourages Douglas to apply for the position. After both student and mage sign the contract, Douglas, with the help of the Owl and Blue Tea Kettle, grows to understand the operation of Wizard's High and its interaction with the neighbors and surrounding community. Eventually Douglas' studies might lead to his father, lost at sea and assumed to be dead. Author's first novel.

**Other books you might like:**
Debra Doyle, *School of Wizardry*, 1990
    James D. Macdonald, co-author
Diane Duane, *So You Want to Be a Wizard?*, 1983
Simon Hawke, *The Reluctant Sorcerer*, 1992
Diana Wynne Jones, *Castle in the Air*, 1991
Meredith Ann Pierce, *The Pearl of the Soul of the World*, 1990
Jane Yolen, *Wizard's Hall*, 1991

## 848

### ITALO CALVINO, Editor

## *Fantastic Tales: Visionary and Everyday*
(New York: Pantheon, 1997)

**Story type:** Horror (Anthology)

**Summary:** Twenty-six stories of fantasy and horror by American and European masters of the eighteenth, nineteenth, and twentieth centuries. Included are E.T.A. Hoffman's "The Sandman," about a man traumatized as an adult by a childhood nightmare; Nathaniel Hawthorne's "Young Goodman Brown," in which a young husband in colonial America discovers that all of his townsfolk may be practicing devil worshippers; Edgar Allan Poe's "The Tell-Tale Heart," the story of a monomaniac undone by his guilt over the grisly murder he has committed; Ambrose Bierce's "Chickamauga," a tale of Civil War horrors; H.G. Wells's "The Country of the Blind," in which a man is imprisoned by a lost race of the congenitally blind; and Robert Louis Stevenson's "The Bottle Imp," a tale of mystical beliefs in the South Seas. Originally published in Italy in two volumes in 1983 as *Racconti Fantastici Dell'ottocento*.

**Other books you might like:**
Chris Baldick, *The Oxford Book of Gothic Tales*, 1992
    editor
Peter Haining, *Great Tales of Terror From Europe and America*, 1972
    editor

Stephen Jones, *H.P. Lovecraft's Book of Horror*, 1993
    David Carson, co-editor
Tom Shippey, *The Oxford Book of Fantasy Stories*, 1994
    editor
Patricia L. Skarda, *The Evil Image: Two Centuries of Gothic Short Fiction and Poetry*, 1981
    Nora Crowe, co-editor
Herbert Wise, *Great Tales of Terror and the Supernatural*, 1944
    Phyllis Fraser, co-editor

## 849

### ITALO CALVINO

## *Italian Folktales*
(New York: Harcourt Brace Jovanovich, 1992)

**Story type:** Fantasy (Legend; Collection)

**Summary:** Includes acknowledgements by translator George Martin, an 18-page introduction by Calvino translated by Catherine Hill, 200 folktales selected and retold by Calvino with 43 pages of notes and a five-page bibliography. From all areas having an Italian linguistic base, Calvino chose folktales of every variety including religious and local legends, short stories, animal fables, jokes and anecdotes.

**Other books you might like:**
Giambattista Basile, *Pentameron or Entertainment for the Little Ones*, 1893
    Sir Richard Burton, translator
Richard Erdoes, *American Indian Myths and Legends*, 1984
    Alfonso Ortiz, co-editor
Charles Perrault, *Complete Fairy Tales*, 1961
    A.E. Johnson, et al., translators
Ethel Johnston Phelps, *Tatterhood and Other Tales*, 1978
    editor
A.K. Ramanujan, *Folktales From India*, 1991
    editor
Moss Roberts, *Chinese Fairy Tales and Fantasies*, 1979
    editor
Jane Yolen, *Favorite Folktales From around the World*, 1986
    editor
Jack Zipes, *Beauties, Beasts and Enchantments*, 1989
    editor
Jack Zipes, *The Brothers Grimm: From Enchanted Forests to the Modern World*, 1988
    editor
Jack Zipes, *Spells of Enchantment*, 1991
    editor

## 850

### ITALO CALVINO

## *Numbers in the Dark and Other Stories*
(New York: Pantheon, 1995)

**Story type:** Science Fiction (Collection)

**Summary:** Contains a three-page preface by Esther Calvino and 37 stories, fables, and impossible interviews, 21 written 1943-1958 and 16 written 1968-1984 with several original to this volume. The tone of some stories tends toward horror, but most stories explore the human condition with wry humor and irony using themes which include computer-generated literature, a 35,000-year-old Neanderthal Man, alternate societal structures, the quest for truth, politics, and the results of mindless application of technology. Translated from Italian by Tim Parks.

**Other books you might like:**
Alfred Bester, *Star Light, Star Bright*, 1976
David G. Hartwell, *The World Treasury of Science Fiction*, 1989
  editor
Stanislaw Lem, *The Cyberiad*, 1974
Stanislaw Lem, *Mortal Engines*, 1977
Cordwainer Smith, *The Rediscovery of Man*, 1993
Marc Stiegler, *The Gentle Seduction*, 1990
Theodore Sturgeon, *E Pluribus Unicorn*, 1953
John Varley, *Blue Champagne*, 1986
Kurt Vonnegut Jr., *Welcome to the Monkey House*, 1968

---

**851**

### RAMSEY CAMPBELL

## *Alone with the Horrors*

(Sauk City, Wisconsin: Arkham House, 1993)

**Story type:** Horror (Collection)

**Summary:** The 39 stories in this book are presented as the best short fiction from the first 30 years of work by the best living writer of horror fiction. Included are homages to the work of H.P. Lovecraft (''The Room in the Castle,'' ''Cold Print''), tales of urban horror (''The Depths,'' ''Mackintosh Willy''), gruesome tales in the E.C. comics tradition (''Call First,'' ''Heading Home''), stories of erotic terror (''Loveman's Comeback'') and cosmic horror (''The Voice of the Beach''), and stories that demonstrate how humor and horror are simply opposite sides of the same coin (''Seeing the World,'' ''End of the Line''). This book is an indispensable cornerstone of any weird fiction library.

**Other books you might like:**
Robert Aickman, *The Wine-Dark Sea*, 1988
T.E.D. Klein, *Dark Gods*, 1985
Thomas Ligotti, *Songs of a Dead Dreamer*, 1990

---

**852**

### RAMSEY CAMPBELL

## *Ancient Images*

(New York: Scribner's, 1989)

**Story type:** Horror (Mystery)
**Major character(s):** Sandy Allen, Television (film editor); Roger Stone, Historian (film historian)
**Time period(s):** 1980s
**Locale(s):** London, England (Suburb of Redfield)

**Summary:** Following the mysterious death of a friend, Allen searches for *Tower of Fear*, a long suppressed Karloff/Lugosi film that reveals a terrible secret about the aristocratic Redfield family.

**Other books you might like:**
Edmund Copper, *The Amber Print*, 1973
Edmund Copper, *From Evil's Pillow*, 1973
Robin Hardy, *The Wicker Man*, 1978

---

**853**

### RAMSEY CAMPBELL

## *The Count of Eleven*

(New York: Tor, 1992)

**Story type:** Horror (Serial Killer)

**Major character(s):** Jack Orchard, Businessman (video salesman); Julia Orchard, Computer Expert (programmer), Spouse (Jack's wife); Laura Orchard, Child (Jack and Julia's daughter)
**Time period(s):** 1990s (1990)
**Locale(s):** Liverpool, England

**Summary:** In bad need of good luck after his video store burns down, amateur numerologist Jack Orchard receives a chain letter promising him improved luck if only he will help maintain the chain. When his luck fails to improve, Jack takes it upon himself to force other recipients of the letter to keep the chain going under penalty of death. Originally published in England in 1991.

**Other books you might like:**
Ken Greenhall, *Deathchain*, 1991
Ruby Jean Jensen, *Chain Letter*, 1987

---

**854**

### RAMSEY CAMPBELL, Editor

## *Deathport*

(New York: Pocket, 1993)

**Story type:** Horror (Anthology)

**Summary:** This third anthology of stories by members of the Horror Writers of America collects 28 tales centered around the Dry Plains International Airport in Texas, each chronicling a strange event attributable to the airport's being built over an Indian burial ground. Les Daniels' ''The Man in the Mirror'' and Dan Perez's ''The Smoking Mirror'' both deal with the revenge of Aztec warriors on visitors to the airport, and Chet Williamson's ''Scalps'' with the strange effect the airport's atmosphere has on a serial killer. Ron Dee and P.D. Cacek's ''Jet Lag'' imagines a unique way to refuel airplanes, and Lawrence Watt-Evans' ''Beneath the Tarmac'' tells of a monster living under the airport runway.

**Other books you might like:**
Robert R. McCammon, *Under the Fang*, 1991
  editor
F. Paul Wilson, *Freak Show*, 1992
  editor

---

**855**

### RAMSEY CAMPBELL

## *Demons by Daylight*

(New York: Carroll and Graf, 1990)

**Story type:** Horror (Collection)

**Summary:** Fifteen stories divided into three sections: ''Nightmares,'' ''Errol Undercliffe: a Tribute,'' and ''Relationships.'' Except for the Lovecraftian Undercliffe pieces, the stories are characterized by vivid dramatic vignettes, extreme compression, suppressed or nonexistent transitions, and a blurring of the lines between the rational and the insane, and the real and the nightmarish. Noteworthy stories include ''Potential,'' in which a conventional man's dark potential is unleashed, ''The Sentinenals,'' about a sinister group of rocks which may or may not come to life, and ''The Telephones,'' a sexually charged doppelganger story. Originally published in 1973.

**Other books you might like:**
Clive Barker, *The Books of Blood Series*, 1984-1985

## 856

### RAMSEY CAMPBELL

## *Far Away and Never*

(West Warwick, Rhode Island: Necronomicon Press, 1996)

**Story type:** Horror (Collection)

**Summary:** The complete sword and sorcery fiction of an author better known as a writer of contemporary urban horror totals seven dark tales of magic and mystery. Six are set on the planet Tond, and four of these feature the heroic warrior Ryre, who battles a sentient plant in "The Sustenance of Hoak," a man who steals identities in "The Changer of Names," winged monsters in "The Pit of Wings," and a man-eating cavern in "The Mouths of Light." Included as well is "The Ways of Chaos," a previously unpublished chapter written for the round-robin novel *Genseric's Fifth-Born Son*, written in the 1970s and based on a fragment left by Robert E. Howard at his death. The author supplies an introduction.

**Other books you might like:**
David Drake, *Vettius and His Friends*, 1989
Robert E. Howard, *Solomon Kane*, 1995
Brian Lumley, *Iced on Aran and Other Dream Quests*, 1992
Michael Shea, *Nifft the Lean*, 1982
Karl Edward Wagner, *The Book of Kane*, 1985

## 857

### RAMSEY CAMPBELL

## *The Influence*

(New York: Tor, 1989)

**Story type:** Horror (Possession)
**Major character(s):** Rowan, Child (seven year old girl); Queenie, Spirit (Rowan's deceased aunt)
**Time period(s):** 1980s
**Locale(s):** Mount Pleasant, England (A suburb of London)

**Summary:** After Queenie leaves her house to her niece, Alisoun, strange things begin happening, especially to Alisoun's daughter, Rowan. Is Queenie's spirit, as personified in Vicky, a mysterious little girl, animating the house and threatening to possess Rowan?

**Other books you might like:**
Thomas Tessier, *Phantom*, 1982

## 858

### RAMSEY CAMPBELL

## *The Last Voice They Hear*

(New York: Tor/Forge, 1998)

**Story type:** Horror (Mystery)
**Major character(s):** Geoff Davenport, Journalist; Ben Davenport, Taxi Driver; Pete Denton, Taxi Driver
**Time period(s):** 1990s (1998)
**Locale(s):** London, England; Blackpool, England

**Summary:** Upset over the preferential treatment his stepbrother Geoff received when they were boys, long-lost Ben Davenport secretly terrorizes Geoff and his family in order to force Geoff into a show-down from which only one brother can emerge triumphant.

**Other books you might like:**
David Ambrose, *The Man Who Turned into Himself*, 1994
Michael Cadnum, *Ghostwright*, 1992
Jonathan Carroll, *The Voice of Our Shadow*, 1982

Brian Hodge, *Oasis*, 1989
Dean R. Koontz, *Mr. Murder*, 1993

## 859

### RAMSEY CAMPBELL

## *The Long Lost*

(New York: Tor Books, 1994)

**Story type:** Horror (Wild Talents)
**Major character(s):** David Owain, Businessman (owner of a home repair company); Joelle Owain, Businesswoman (David's wife and partner); Gwendolyn Owain, Aged Person
**Time period(s):** 1990s (1994)
**Locale(s):** Chester, England

**Summary:** While on holiday in Wales, David and Joelle Owain encounter Gwendolyn, an old woman living by herself on an island off the coast who claims to be a distant relative. When they bring Gwendolyn back with them to stay in Chester, her presence ignites tensions that have been simmering beneath the town's placid social veneer, turning neighbors against one another and leaving the reader to wonder exactly who Gendolyn really is. This book was first published in England in 1993.

**Other books you might like:**
Douglas Clegg, *Goat Dance*, 1989
Stephen King, *Needful Things*, 1991
Elizabeth Massie, *Sineater*, 1992

## 860

### RAMSEY CAMPBELL

## *Midnight Sun*

(New York: Tor, 1991)

**Story type:** Horror (Ancient Evil Unleashed)
**Major character(s):** Ben Sterling, Writer (Ellen's husband); Ellen Sterling, Artist (book illustrator); Johnny Sterling, Child (Ben and Ellen's son)
**Time period(s):** 1990s
**Locale(s):** Yorkshire, England

**Summary:** Orphaned while a young boy, Ben Sterling is raised by his aunt at his family's ancestral home. It was here that Ben's great grandfather returned from the Arctic years before, and died under mysterious circumstances no one wishes to discuss. When Ben inherits the estate years later, he discovers the secret of what his grandfather instilled in the surrounding Sterling Forest, and the terrible sacrifice he and his family will be forced to make if they are to keep it from running amok.

**Other books you might like:**
Douglas Clegg, *Goat Dance*, 1989
T.E.D. Klein, *The Ceremonies*, 1984
Graham Masterton, *The Manitou*, 1975
Thomas Tryon, *Harvest Home*, 1973

## 861

### RAMSEY CAMPBELL

## *Nazareth Hill*

(New York: Tor/Forge, 1997)

**Story type:** Horror (Haunted House)

**Major character(s):** Amy Priestley, Teenager; Oswald Priestley, Insurance Agent (Amy's father); Beth Griffin, Health Care Professional (homeopath)
**Time period(s):** 1990s (1996)
**Locale(s):** Partington, England

**Summary:** Widowed Oswald Priestley moves with his daughter Amy to Nazareth Hill, an apartment complex built on the site of an old asylum. Shortly after Amy discovers that Nazareth Hill served in the middle ages as the torture chamber for the Witchfinder General, Oswald falls under the spell of its haunted past and recapitulates its brutal legacy of persecution and terror with his daughter. First published in England in 1996 as *The House on Nazareth Hill*.

**Other books you might like:**
Tom Elliott, *The Dwelling*, 1989
Judith Hawkes, *Julian's House*, 1989
Richard Matheson, *Hell House*, 1971
Al Sarrantonio, *House Haunted*, 1991
Chet Williamson, *Soulstorm*, 1986

---

### 862

### RAMSEY CAMPBELL

## The One Safe Place

(New York: Tor, 1996)

**Story type:** Horror (Psychological Suspense)
**Major character(s):** Susanne Travis, Teacher; Marshall Travis, Child (Susanne's 12-year-old son); Darren Fancy, Child (12-year-old)
**Time period(s):** 1990s (1996)
**Locale(s):** Manchester, England

**Summary:** A minor altercation between lowlife criminal Phil Fancy and bookseller Don Travis leads to Don's death and the Fancy family terrorizing the Travises. Most of this scathing critique of the modern judicial system's blindness chronicles the kidnapping of 12-year-old Marshall Travis by Phil Fancy's son, Darren, and the torments Darren subjects Marshall to in order to win the esteem of his family. This novel was published in England in 1995.

**Other books you might like:**
Anthony Burgess, *A Clockwork Orange*, 1962
William Golding, *Lord of the Flies*, 1954
K.W. Jeter, *The Night Man*, 1989
Joe R. Lansdale, *The Nightrunners*, 1987
Patrick McCabe, *The Butcher Boy*, 1992

---

### 863

### RAMSEY CAMPBELL

## The Parasite

(New York: Tor, 1989)

**Story type:** Horror (Possession)
**Major character(s):** Rose Tierney, Critic (film reviewer), Psychic; Peter Grace, Spirit (black magician)
**Time period(s):** 1980s
**Locale(s):** New York, New York; Munich, Germany; Liverpool, England

**Summary:** After a mugging releases latent psychic abilities, Rose finds herself endangered by strange external and internal forces: a mysterious baldheaded man, a sinister psychiatrist, occultists, hallucinations, frightening out-of-body trips, and, most scary, an internal "parasite" which may be the spirit of Peter Grace, a deceased black magician. Originally published in 1980.

**Other books you might like:**
Ira Levin, *Rosemary's Baby*, 1967

---

### 864

### RAMSEY CAMPBELL

## Strange Things and Stranger Places

(New York: Tor, 1993)

**Story type:** Horror (Collection)

**Summary:** This book collects 10 hitherto uncollected stories, including the haunted house tale "Cat and Mouse"; the science fiction novella, "Medusa"; several homages to the E.C. horror comics including "Wrapped Up" and "Rising Generation"; two stories that take place in carnival fairgrounds, "Little Man," and "The Next Sideshow"; and the profoundly disturbing novella, "Needing Ghosts," about a man's tenuous grip on reality. The author supplies an introduction on the origins of the stories.

**Other books you might like:**
Robert Aickman, *The Wine-Dark Sea*, 1988
Dennis Etchison, *The Dark Country*, 1982
T.E.D. Klein, *Dark Gods*, 1985
Thomas Ligotti, *Grimscribe: His Lives and Works*, 1992
Thomas Ligotti, *Songs of a Dead Dreamer*, 1990

---

### 865

### RAMSEY CAMPBELL

## Two Obscure Tales

(West Warwick, Rhode Island: Necronomicon Press, 1993)

**Story type:** Horror (Collection)

**Summary:** As the title implies, these are two somewhat opaque stories, written in the early 1970s when the author was establishing a trademark style of ambiguity that would distinguish the stories of his groundbreaking collection *Demons by Daylight*. "The Void" concerns a car accident victim trying to sort out his life after the trauma. "The Urge" records an encounter between a writer and a young man who discuss their different metaphysical approaches to life. Campbell has supplied an amusing introduction.

**Other books you might like:**
Robert Aickman, *The Wine-Dark Sea*, 1988
Dennis Etchison, *The Dark Country*, 1982
Thomas Ligotti, *Songs of a Dead Dreamer*, 1990

---

### 866

### RAMSEY CAMPBELL

## Waking Nightmares

(New York: Tor, 1991)

**Story type:** Horror (Collection)

**Summary:** Nineteen stories by the master of implied (but nonetheless gruesome) horror. Stories range in approach from "The Guide," an homage to the subtle fiction of M.R. James, to "It Helps if You Sing," a grisly satire on religious fundamentalism. There is one ingenious vampire tale ("Jack in the Box") and two stories concerned with one of Campbell's favorite themes, the relation of fiction to life: "Meeting the Author" and "Next Time You'll Know Me."

**Other books you might like:**
Robert Aickman, *The Wine-Dark Sea*, 1988
Dennis Etchison, *The Dark Country*, 1987

Thomas Ligotti, *Grimscribe: His Lives and Works*, 1992
Thomas Ligotti, *Songs of a Dead Dreamer*, 1989
T.E.D. Klein, *Dark Gods*, 1985

---

**867**

**P.H. CANNON**
**JASON ECKHARDT**, Illustrator

## Scream for Jeeves: A Parody

(New York: Wodecraft Press, 1994)

**Story type:** Horror (Collection)
**Major character(s):** Bertie Wooster, Gentleman; Jeeves, Servant (manservant)
**Time period(s):** 20th century
**Locale(s):** England

**Summary:** These three delightful pastiches imagine a world in which P.G. Wodehouse's genteel characters Bertie Wooster and his all-knowing butler, Jeeves, are thrust into scenarios straight out of H.P. Lovecraft's cosmic horror fiction. "Scream for Jeeves," an homage to Lovecraft's "The Rats in the Walls," has the unlikely duo investigating the decrepit homestead and genealogy of a family friend. "Something Foetid" introduces them to the mad doctor who has reanimated his own corpse in Lovecraft's "Cool Air." "The Rummy Affair of Young Charlie" brings together characters from Lovecraft's "Arthur Jermyn," "The Case of Charles Dexter Ward," and "The Music of Erich Zann" for a slapstick romp. The author supplies an afterword comparing Wodehouse, Lovecraft, and Sir Arthur Conan Doyle.

**Other books you might like:**
Christopher Moore, *Practical Demonkeeping*, 1992
William Browning Spencer, *Resume with Monsters*, 1995
Ralph Vaughan, *Sherlock Holmes in the Adventure of the Ancient Gods*, 1990

---

**868**

**P.H. CANNON**

## Tales of Lovecraftian Horror and Humor

(West Hills, California: Tsathoggua Press, 1997)

**Story type:** Horror (Collection)
**Series:** The Early Cannon

**Summary:** Miscellany of nine stories, essays and incidental pieces by a writer best known for his critical writing on H.P. Lovecraft. "Providence in 1990 A.D." is a wistful speculation on a world in which H.P. Lovecraft is recognized as a literary giant, while "Conclusion to 'Saucers from Yaddith'" and "The Body from the Bog" are flippant pastiches of Lovecraft's fiction. "The Pewter Ring" is a solid tale of horrors from the past that survive through dark sorcery into the present. The second of two volumes in the "Early Cannon" series.

**Other books you might like:**
Fred Chappell, *More Shapes than One*, 1991
Fred Chappell, *The Lodger*, 1993
Christopher Moore, *Practical Demonkeeping*, 1992
William Browning Spencer, *Resume with Monsters*, 1995
Gahan Wilson, *Eddy Deco's Last Caper*, 1987

---

**869**

**P.H. CANNON**

## The Thing in the Bathtub and Other Lovecraftian Tales

(West Hills, California: Tsathoggua Press, 1997)

**Story type:** Horror (Collection)
**Series:** The Early Cannon

**Summary:** Six humorous stories, poems and essays by a writer best known for his critical writing on H.P. Lovecraft. The stories are satires of Lovecraftian fiction and the cult of amateur Lovecraftians. Lovecraft is caricatured in them as the literary figure H.A. Howard, a convention guest of honor at "The Pop Festival" and the subject of a mock critical essay, "H.A. Howard: His Own Most Mediocre Creation." "From Below," a deliberately bad pastiche of Lovecraft, is presented as a typical Howard story. The title story interweaves plot devices from Lovecraft's fiction with the antics of a bunch of bumbling Howard worshippers. The first of two volumes in the "Early Cannon" series.

**Other books you might like:**
Fred Chappell, *More Shapes than One*, 1991
Fred Chappell, *The Lodger*, 1993
Christopher Moore, *Practical Demonkeeping*, 1992
William Browning Spencer, *Resume with Monsters*, 1995
Gahan Wilson, *Eddy Deco's Last Caper*, 1987

---

**870**

**MARK CANTER**

## Ember From the Sun

(New York: Delacorte, 1996)

**Story type:** Science Fiction (Mystical; Science Fiction)
**Major character(s):** Yute Nahadeh, Anthropologist (paleoanthropologist), Indian (Caiyuh); Ember Ozette, Prehistoric Human (Neanderthal), Psychic (healer); Nika Nahadeh, Psychic, Relative (sister)
**Time period(s):** 1990s
**Locale(s):** Whaler Bay, Washington; Kantishna Hills, Alaska

**Summary:** A bookworm from early childhood, Yute never learns the ways of his people. While documenting his father's hunting with primitive weapons, Yute spends the night in an ice cave and discovers a frozen, pregnant Neanderthal woman whose embryo, implanted in a surrogate mother, becomes a Neanderthal infant. Visions compel an older Ember Ozette to search for the last survivors of her race, who are now facing genocide. First novel.

**Other books you might like:**
Michael Armstrong, *Agviq*, 1990
Jean M. Auel, *Clan of the Cave Bear*, 1980
Kathleen O'Neal Gear, *Song of the Wolf*, 1992
   W. Michael Gear, co-author
Sue Harrison, *Mother Earth, Father Sky*, 1990
Jack McDevitt, *Ancient Shores*, 1996

---

**871**

**LISA CANTRELL**

## Boneman

(New York: Tor, 1992)

**Story type:** Horror (Mystery; Reanimated Dead)

**Major character(s):** J.J. Coley, Journalist; Dallas Reid, Detective—Police; Jackie Swann, Detective—Police
**Time period(s):** 1990s (1992)
**Locale(s):** Phoenix City, North Carolina

**Summary:** When a group of murderous, seemingly indestructible Haitian drug dealers begin taking over the narcotics trade in Phoenix City, rumors begin circulating that they are the zombie minions of a legendary supernatural bogeyman known as "The Boneman."

**Other books you might like:**
Hugh B. Cave, *Disciples of Dread*, 1988
K.W. Jeter, *Wolf Flow*, 1992
David J. Schow, *The Shaft*, 1990
Robert Weinberg, *The Black Lodge*, 1991

---

**872**

**LISA CANTRELL**

## The Ridge

(New York: Tor, 1989)

**Story type:** Horror (Literary)
**Major character(s):** Nick Vear, Spy (Government hit-man); Sara Vear, Child (Vear's catatonic daughter)
**Time period(s):** 1980s
**Locale(s):** North Carolina

**Summary:** In the Ridge, an old house atop a cliff, four of five people—Vear's ex-wife's family—die mysteriously, the sole survivor being Vear's catatonic seven year old daughter, Sara. The search for the killer leads Vear into conflicts with the police, the mob, his ex-wife's family, Sara, and, finally, with an ancient, malevolent power that could threaten mankind.

**Other books you might like:**
John Farris, *The Fury*, 1977

---

**873**

**LISA CANTRELL**

## Torments

(New York: Tor, 1990)

**Story type:** Horror (Haunted House)
**Major character(s):** Vince Colletti, Businessman; Sonny O'Hara, Businessman (construction consultant); Jennifer Clark, Artist (interior designer)
**Time period(s):** 1980s (1989)
**Locale(s):** Merrillville, North Carolina

**Summary:** In this sequel to the author's Bram Stoker Award-winning first novel, *The Manse*, the destruction of Merrillville's haunted house appears to have had little effect on the supernatural influence that pervades its grounds. The condominiums erected on the old site are plagued with mysterious construction problems, the dead are walking once more, and the survivors of the conflagration that consumed the old mansion are being summoned home to confront the fate they barely escaped two years before.

**Other books you might like:**
Tom Elliott, *The Dwelling*, 1989
Shirley Jackson, *The Haunting of Hill House*, 1959

---

**874**

**KAREL CAPEK**

## War With the Newts

(Highland Park: Catbird Press, 1990)

**Story type:** Science Fiction (Literary)
**Major character(s):** Van Toch, Explorer (Captain); Bondy, Businessman
**Time period(s):** 1930s
**Locale(s):** Prague (The Dutch East Indies)

**Summary:** Captain Van Toch has discovered a rare form of intelligent salamander and offers to provide them to the capitalist Bondy to sell as servants and proletarian workers. Equipped with tools and weapons, however, the salamanders soon multiply enormously and eventually take over the world. Originally published in 1936.

**Other books you might like:**
Eleanor Arnason, *To the Resurrection Station*, 1986
David Brin, *Startide Rising*, 1983
David Brin, *The Uplift War*, 1987
John Brunner, *Children of the Thunder*, 1989
Clifford D. Simak, *City*, 1952
H.G. Wells, *The Food of the Gods*, 1904
H.G. Wells, *The Island of Doctor Moreau*, 1896

---

**875**

**BERNARD CAPES**

## The Black Reaper

(Ashcroft, British Columbia: Ash-Tree Press, 1998)

**Story type:** Horror (Collection)

**Summary:** This collection contains 22 short stories and vignettes of the supernatural by a little-known Victorian master. The title story is a haunting fantasia in which death incarnate visits a plague-stricken town. Included as well are the werewolf story "The Thing in the Forest," the supernatural revenge tale "Dark Dignum," and "The Green Bottle," about a bottle that imprisons the soul of a man. Subtle and uncommon stories, introduced by Hugh Lamb, who has expanded the contents of the original 1989 edition.

**Other books you might like:**
E.F. Benson, *The Terror by Night*, 1998
Frederick Cowles, *Fear Walks the Night*, 1992
M.P. Dare, *Unholy Relics*, 1947
Richard Marsh, *The Haunted Chair and Other Stories*, 1997
H. Russell Wakefield, *The Clock Strikes Twelve*, 1939

---

**876**

**MICHAEL CAPOBIANCO**

## Burster

(New York: Bantam Spectra, 1990)

**Story type:** Science Fiction (Generation Starship; Space Colony)
**Major character(s):** Peter Zolotin, Student—Graduate, Spaceman; Traveler, Artificial Intelligence; Eugenia Taranga, Spaceship Captain
**Time period(s):** 23rd century
**Locale(s):** *Asia*, Spaceship; *Quiet Earth*, Spaceship; Mars

**Summary:** Starship Asia, 14 years out on its colonizing mission in the Epsilon Indi system, scans a burst of radiation near Sol. At the same time, all communications with Earth are cut off. Peter Zolotin is chosen to journey back to Earth to ascertain its fate with the aid of Traveler, an advanced artificial intelligence system designed to gather data and which also has a sentient personality. While Peter is gone, Captain Taranga and the scientists on *Asia* argue bitterly about what type of planet will best support life while mutiny is swiftly forming.

**Other books you might like:**
David Brin, *The Uplift War*, 1987
Octavia E. Butler, *Imago*, 1989
Octavia E. Butler, *Mind of My Mind*, 1977
Octavia E. Butler, *Wild Seed*, 1980
David R. Palmer, *Emergence*, 1984
Alis A. Rasmussen, *A Passage of Stars*, 1990
Alis A. Rasmussen, *The Price of Ransom*, 1990
Alis A. Rasmussen, *Revolution's Shore*, 1990

**877**

**MARY CARAKER**

## The Faces of Ceti

(Boston: Houghton Miflin, 1991)

**Story type:** Science Fiction (First Contact; Young Adult)
**Major character(s):** Maya Gart, Teenager, Settler; Brock Magnus, Teenager, Settler; Carlos Vega, Leader, Settler
**Time period(s):** 22nd century
**Locale(s):** Ceti, Planet—Imaginary (Tau Ceti System)

**Summary:** Maya Gart, a nonconformist among colonists settling the Tau Ceti System, ends up on Ceti where the plant life is poisonous. Only the Hlur, animals who may be sentient, are edible. The Arcadian leader demands that Cetians contribute more to the common cause or go without supplies. Maya and Brock then take a trip in which they contact the Hlur and learn how to make the plant life nutritious. They find many surprises on their return.

**Other books you might like:**
Eleanor Arnason, *A Woman of the Iron People*, 1990
F.M. Busby, *Rebel's Seed*, 1986
Janet Kagan, *Hellspark*, 1988
Garry Kilworth, *The Night of Kadar*, 1980
Ursula K. Le Guin, *The Eye of the Heron*, 1983
Larry Niven, *A Gift from Earth*, 1968

**878**

**MARY CARAKER**

## The Snows of Jaspre

(Boston: Houghton Mifflin, 1989)

**Story type:** Science Fiction (Young Adult)
**Major character(s):** Anders Ahlwen, Psychic; Morgan Farraday, Administrator (School administrator)
**Time period(s):** 24th century
**Locale(s):** Jaspre, Planet—Imaginary

**Summary:** Morgan Farraday and her daughter Dee, new settlers on the icy planet Jaspre, face difficulties on a colonial world, not the least of which is the charismatic Anders Ahlwen, leader of a group of psychics who live in a mysterious city under the ice.

**Other books you might like:**
Clare Bell, *People of the Sky*, 1989
Jo Dereske, *The Lone Sentinel*, 1989
H.M. Hoover, *The Bell Tree*, 1982
H.M. Hoover, *Children of Morrow*, 1973
H.M. Hoover, *Treasures of Morrow*, 1976

**879**

**JACK CARAVELA**

## The Gifted

(New York: Zebra, 1991)

**Story type:** Horror (Wild Talents)
**Major character(s):** Rob Endicott, Telepath, Worker (gas station attendant); Tom Naufts, Criminal (assassin), Telepath; Brian Corman, Businessman (head of the Alliance)
**Time period(s):** 1990s
**Locale(s):** Mesa, New Mexico

**Summary:** Paranormally endowed with the telepathic power to read and influence minds, Rob Endicott flees his foster father, Brian Corman, who hopes to train him to kill people with thoughts and serve as a secret weapon for the shadowy business consortium known as the Alliance. Not easily thwarted, Corman sends telepath assassin Tom Naufts to track Rob down.

**Other books you might like:**
John Arbucci, *Blood of Innocents*, 1991
John Farris, *The Fury*, 1976
Stephen King, *Firestarter*, 1980
Jack Martin, *Scanners*, 1981

**880**

**C.J. CARD**

## One Wish

(New York: Jove, 1998)

**Story type:** Fantasy (Romance; Light Fantasy)
**Major character(s):** Jenny Blake, Businesswoman; Miller Holbrook, Professor
**Time period(s):** 1890s (1899)
**Locale(s):** Washington, District of Columbia

**Summary:** Jenny Blake inherits a curiosity shop in which she finds a bottle that contains a genie. He grants her one wish, and she asks for someone whom she can truly love. But the result is an odd academic with whom she seems to have nothing at all in common. First novel.

**Other books you might like:**
Alice Alfonsi, *Some Enchanted Evening*, 1998
Piers Anthony, *Hasan*, 1979
H.M. Egbert, *Mrs. Aladdin*, 1925
Esther Friesner, *Wishing Season*, 1993
Kathleen Nance, *Wishes Come True*, 1998

**881**

**ORSON SCOTT CARD**

## Alvin Journeyman

(New York: Tor, 1995)

**Story type:** Fantasy (Psychic Powers; Historical)
**Series:** Tales of Alvin Maker
**Major character(s):** Alvin "Maker" Miller, Blacksmith (journeyman), Psychic (maker), Relative (Calvin's brother); Margaret "Peggy" Guerner, Psychic (torch), Activist (anti-slavery); Calvin Miller, Psychic (criminal), Relative (Alvin's brother)
**Time period(s):** Indeterminate
**Locale(s):** Alternate Earth

**Summary:** To build the city of his vision and help preserve peace in the spreading colonies, Alvin must defeat his ancient enemy, the

Unmaker, whose deadly plots have threatened Alvin's life at every turn. Alvin and his young friend, Arthur Stuart, flee a false scandal in Vigor Church and travel to Hatrack River, only to find that the Unmaker has already spread lies and accusations through the hearts of those ready to believe them. While Alvin stands trial for his life in the town of his apprenticeship, his jealous brother, Calvin, hones his own particular talents to bring about Alvin's downfall.

**Other books you might like:**
Jean M. Auel, *Clan of the Cave Bear*, 1990
Octavia E. Butler, *Wild Seed*, 1980
William Sarabande, *The Edge of the World*, 1993
Harry Turtledove, *The Guns of the South: A Novel of the Civil War*, 1992
Paul O. Williams, *The Breaking of Northwall*, 1981

---

**882**

ORSON SCOTT CARD

## The Call of Earth

(New York: Tor, 1993)

**Story type:** Science Fiction (Political)
**Series:** Homecoming
**Major character(s):** Rasa, Teacher, Parent; Vozmuzhalnoy "Moozh" Vozmozho, Military Personnel (General); Nafai, Teenager
**Time period(s):** Indeterminate Future
**Locale(s):** Harmony, Planet—Imaginary

**Summary:** While General Vozmuzhalnoy Vozmozho attacks Basilica, hoping to marry influentially to keep his conquest as bloodless as possible, Nafai, led by the Oversoul, gathers a group of men and their wives in preparation for the journey to Earth.

**Other books you might like:**
Piers Anthony, *If I Pay Thee Not in Gold*, 1993
    Mercedes Lackey, co-author
Isaac Asimov, *Foundation and Earth*, 1986
John Brunner, *Catch a Falling Star*, 1968
Raymond Harris, *Shadows of the White Sun*, 1988
Colin Kapp, *The Wizard of Anharitte*, 1973
Michael McCollum, *Antares Dawn*, 1986
Melissa Scott, *Five-Twelfths of Heaven*, 1985
Robert Silverberg, *Lord Valentine's Castle*, 1980
Clifford D. Simak, *A Heritage of Stars*, 1977

---

**883**

ORSON SCOTT CARD

## Children of the Mind

(New York: Tor, 1996)

**Story type:** Science Fiction (Family Saga; First Contact)
**Series:** Ender Wiggin
**Major character(s):** Jane, Artificial Intelligence, Deity; Peter Wiggin, Reincarnated Person; Malu, Philosopher, Deity
**Time period(s):** Indeterminate Future
**Locale(s):** Lusitania, Planet—Imaginary; Pacifica, Planet—Imaginary

**Summary:** Joining his wife in seclusion, Ender loses interest in young Val, giving Jane permission to take Val's body if she can. With the Starways Congress shutting down all ansibles and computers to eliminate her, Jane needs a new place to stay in order to continue the rescue of the Hive Queen and the pequeninos before the fleet can destroy Lusitania and all its residents. As the descolada virus no longer poses a risk to the human race, Jane continues to move ships

instantaneously, dispersing the Buggers and Piggies to many planets, preventing another xenocide. Direct sequel to *Xenocide*.

**Other books you might like:**
Glen Cook, *The Dragon Never Sleeps*, 1988
Dan Simmons, *The Fall of Hyperion*, 1989
Sheri S. Tepper, *Grass*, 1989
Jack Vance, *Alastor*, 1995
Vernor Vinge, *A Fire upon the Deep*, 1992

---

**884**

ORSON SCOTT CARD

## Earthborn

(New York: Tor, 1995)

**Story type:** Science Fiction (Political; Theological)
**Series:** Homecoming
**Major character(s):** Akma, Rebel (heretic), Abuse Victim; Shedemei, Historian, Immortal; Edhadeya, Royalty (princess), Teacher
**Time period(s):** Indeterminate Future
**Locale(s):** Darakemba, Fictional Country; Chelem, Fictional Country

**Summary:** After 500 years on Earth, the descendants of Nafai and Elemak continue their progenitors' feud, as Shedemei's search for Earth's guardian computer seems fruitless. Akma's disbelief in Oversoul and influence over others may catalyze a revolution if Shedemei cannot effect a repair. Fifth, concluding volume in the series, which is based on *The Book of Mormon*.

**Other books you might like:**
Brian W. Aldiss, *Helliconia Summer*, 1983
Poul Anderson, *The Boat of a Million Years*, 1989
Lloyd Biggle, *Monument*, 1974
James Blish, *Midsummer Century*, 1972
Robert Silverberg, *At Winter's End*, 1988
Clifford D. Simak, *The Fellowship of the Talisman*, 1978
Jack Vance, *The Brave Free Men*, 1973

---

**885**

ORSON SCOTT CARD

## Earthfall

(New York: Tor, 1995)

**Story type:** Science Fiction (Family Saga; First Contact)
**Series:** Homecoming
**Major character(s):** Nafai, Leader, Spaceship Captain (navigator); Elemak, Linguist, Renegade; Oykib, Teacher, Telepath
**Time period(s):** Indeterminate Future
**Locale(s):** Harmony, Planet—Imaginary; Outer Space; Earth

**Summary:** During the long space voyage to Earth to find help for the ailing Oversoul, political machinations continue until Elemak and Nafai suspend their struggle pending their father's death. On Earth they find two mutated, inimical symbiotic species, winged angels and subterranean diggers. While Elemak allies the diggers to his cause against Nafai, Nafai leads away all who wish to join him in founding a community where all three species will live peacefully. Fourth in the series, which is based on *The Book of Mormon*.

**Other books you might like:**
Isaac Asimov, *Foundation and Earth*, 1986
Ben Bova, *As on a Darkling Plain*, 1972
John Brunner, *Catch a Falling Star*, 1968
John Dalmas, *Homecoming*, 1984
Harry Harrison, *Return to Eden*, 1988
Clifford D. Simak, *Cemetery World*, 1973

Brian Stableford, *The Castaways of Tanagar*, 1981

## 886

### ORSON SCOTT CARD

## *The Folk of the Fringe*

(West Bloomfield, Michigan: Phantasia Press, 1989)

**Story type:** Science Fiction (Post-Nuclear Holocaust)
**Major character(s):** Jamie Teague, Adventurer; Herman Deaver, Religious
**Time period(s):** 21st century
**Locale(s):** Utah

**Summary:** This series of five interconnected stories, which originally appeared between 1985 and 1987 in *Isaac Asimov's Science Fiction Magazine* and elsewhere, tells the story of a loosely-knit group of survivors of a nuclear war, and the gradual growth of a Mormon nation on the shores of Great Salt Lake.

**Other books you might like:**
Neal Barrett Jr., *Dawn's Uncertain Light*, 1989
Neal Barrett Jr., *Through Darkest America*, 1987
David Brin, *The Postman*, 1985
Edgar Pangborn, *The Company of Glory*, 1975
Edgar Pangborn, *Davy*, 1964
Edgar Pangborn, *The Judgment of Eve*, 1966

## 887

### ORSON SCOTT CARD, Editor

## *Future on Fire*

(New York: Tor, 1991)

**Story type:** Science Fiction (Anthology)
**Time period(s):** Indeterminate Future

**Summary:** This collection of 15 stories from the 1980s, each briefly introduced by Orson Scott Card, contains an 11-page introduction in which he explains that the stories selected are not necessarily comfortable to read, but are important and wonderful. Among the authors included are Michael Bishop, Pat Cadigan, James Patrick Kelly, Ursula K. Le Guin, Pat Murphy, Kim Stanley Robinson, Lucius Shepard, Bruce Sterling and Connie Willis.

**Other books you might like:**
Lou Aronica, *Full Spectrum*, 1988
   Shawna McCarthy, co-editor
Michael Bishop, *Nebula Awards 24*, 1990
   editor
Gardner Dozois, *The Year's Best Science Fiction: Seventh Annual Collection*, 1990
   editor
David G. Hartwell, *The World Treasury of Science Fiction*, 1989
   editor
Kristine Kathryn Rusch, *Pulphouse, Issue 8: Science Fiction*, 1990
   editor
Donald A. Wollheim, *The 1990 Annual World's Best Science Fiction*, 1990
   Arthur W. Saha, co-editor

## 888

### ORSON SCOTT CARD, Editor

## *Future on Ice*

(New York: Tor, 1998)

**Story type:** Science Fiction (Anthology)

**Summary:** A companion volume to the 1991 *Future on Fire*, this anthology contains an essay by the editor titled "Science Fiction and the Force" and 18 stories, including many Hugo and Nebula award winners. Authors include Isaac Asimov, Greg Bear, Gregory Benford, Octavia E. Butler, Orson Scott Card, C.J. Cherryh, John Crowley, Karen Joy Fowler, Lisa Goldstein, John Kessel, Nancy Kress, George R.R. Martin, Lewis Shiner, S.C. Sykes, John Varley, Andrew Weiner, Walter Jon Williams, and David Zindell.

**Other books you might like:**
Isaac Asimov, *The New Hugo Winners*, 1989
   Martin H. Greenberg, co-editor
Gardner Dozois, *The Year's Best Science Fiction Series*, 1984-1998
   editor
Edward L. Ferman, *The Best From Fantasy & Science Fiction: A 40th Anniversary Anthology*, 1989
   editor
Ursula K. Le Guin, *The Norton Book of Science Fiction: North American Science Fiction, 1960-1990*, 1993
   Brian Attebery, co-editor
Charles Sheffield, *How to Save the World*, 1995
   editor
Sheila Williams, *Hugo and Nebula Award Winners From Asimov's Science Fiction*, 1995
   editor

## 889

### ORSON SCOTT CARD

## *Heartfire*

(New York: Tor, 1998)

**Story type:** Fantasy (Psychic Powers; Historical)
**Series:** Tales of Alvin Maker
**Major character(s):** Alvin "Maker" Miller, Blacksmith (journeyman), Psychic (maker), Spouse (of Margaret); Margaret "Peggy" Miller, Psychic (torch), Activist (anti-slavery), Spouse (of Alvin); Calvin Miller, Psychic (criminal), Relative (Alvin's youngest brother)
**Time period(s):** 19th century
**Locale(s):** Alternate Earth; American Colonies

**Summary:** Until Alvin and his pregnant wife, Peggy, journey their separate ways through the American Colonies and accomplish their individual goals, they will have little chance to enjoy a normal family life together. Alvin and his companions travel north to New England, searching for a place to build the Crystal City of his visions. Peggy foresees a bloody war over the issue of slavery and travels south to the Crown Colonies, seeking an audience with King Arthur Stuart and hoping to secure his cooperation in abolishing the practice. Soon after arriving, she discovers that the slaves have relinquished a part of their souls to an African sorcerer in order to hide their true selves from their masters. Alvin unwittingly helps her discover the location of the repository of souls and unbinds it from its magical cage.

**Other books you might like:**
Jean M. Auel, *Clan of the Cave Bear*, 1980
Octavia E. Butler, *Wild Seed*, 1980
Harry Harrison, *The Hammer and the Cross*, 1993
   John Holm, co-author

Katherine Kurtz, *Two Crowns for America*, 1996
Mark Sumner, *Devil's Tower*, 1996
Paul O. Williams, *The Breaking of Northwall*, 1981

### 890
#### ORSON SCOTT CARD

## *Homebody*
(New York: HarperCollins, 1998)

**Story type:** Horror (Haunted House)
**Major character(s):** Don Lark, Construction Worker, Widow(er); Sylvie Delaney, Young Woman, Spirit; Felicity "Lissy" Yont, Librarian
**Time period(s):** 1990s (1998)
**Locale(s):** Greensboro, North Carolina

**Summary:** Don Lark, a widower who "turns his loneliness and grief into the restoration of beautiful old houses," undertakes the renovation of the Bellamy mansion, which is haunted by the spirit of Sylvie Delaney, a young lady murdered there. Don's efforts to track down Sylvie's killer help him confront his repressed emotions and aid several other people whose fates are tied to the Bellamy house to come to terms with problems in their own lives.

**Other books you might like:**
Jack Cady, *The Well*, 1980
Tom Elliott, *The Dwelling*, 1988
Judith Hawkes, *Julian's House*, 1990
Stephen King, *The Shining*, 1977
Anne Rivers Siddons, *The House Next Door*, 1978

### 891
#### ORSON SCOTT CARD

## *Lost Boys*
(New York: HarperCollins, 1992)

**Story type:** Fantasy (Contemporary Realism; Religious)
**Major character(s):** Step Fletcher, Computer Expert, Religious (Mormon); Stevie Fletcher, Child; DeAnne Fletcher, Housewife
**Time period(s):** 1980s (1983)
**Locale(s):** Steuben, North Carolina

**Summary:** When Step and DeAnne Fletcher move with their three children to Steuben, North Carolina, their withdrawn eight-year-old Stevie becomes sensitive to the presence of "the lost boys" — the ghosts of townschildren who died at the hands of a murderer who now appears to be stalking Stevie. This novel is an expansion of the author's controversial 1989 short story of the same name.

**Other books you might like:**
Douglas Bell, *Mojo and the Pickle Jar*, 1991
Alan Dean Foster, *Cyber Way*, 1990
Katharine Kerr, *Polar City Blues*, 1990
Mercedes Lackey, *Children of the Night*, 1990
Elizabeth Ann Scarborough, *Nothing Sacred*, 1991
Kate Wilhelm, *Death Qualified: A Mystery of Chaos*, 1991

### 892
#### ORSON SCOTT CARD
#### KATHRYN H. KIDD, Co-Author

## *Lovelock*
(New York: Tor, 1994)

**Story type:** Science Fiction (Political; Science Fiction)
**Series:** Mayflower Trilogy
**Major character(s):** Lovelock, Animal (capuchin monkey), Genetically Altered Being; Carol Jeanne Cocciolone, Scientist (Gaiologist), Genius; Redmond "Red" Eugene Todd, Spouse, Psychologist
**Time period(s):** 21st century
**Locale(s):** *Ark*, Spaceship (Mayflower Village)

**Summary:** As witness for Carol Jeanne, Lovelock accompanies her and her dysfunctional family on the *Ark* where Carol Jeanne, Chief Gaiologist, plans for the safety and health of the colony. The stress of changes brought about by the move to the *Ark* and small town life aboard it force Lovelock to recognize that although his enhanced intelligence permits him to effectively complement Carol Jeanne, his conditioning and lack of speech make him only a tool or a slave, rather than a beloved friend as he previously believed.

**Other books you might like:**
David Brin, *Startide Rising*, 1983
Thomas A. Easton, *Sparrowhawk*, 1990
James H. Schmitz, *The Demon Breed*, 1968
Joan Slonczewski, *Daughter of Elysium*, 1993
Cordwainer Smith, *The Best of Cordwainer Smith*, 1975
Amy Thomson, *Virtual Girl*, 1993
Vernor Vinge, *A Fire upon the Deep*, 1992
Gene Wolfe, *Nightside the Long Sun*, 1993

### 893
#### ORSON SCOTT CARD

## *Maps in a Mirror*
(New York: Tor, 1990)

**Story type:** Horror (Collection)

**Summary:** A mammoth collection of 46 fantasy, horror, and science fiction stories by one of the most important writers of imaginative fiction to emerge in the 1980s. Of particular interest are "Lost Boys," a poignant tale of a young boy's alienation from his family; "Fat Farm," about a unique weight loss program; "Deep Breathing Exercises," in which a man develops an uncanny ability to predict when disaster will strike; and "Memories of My Head," the one story original to the volume, in which a suicide pens his farewell note *after* his death.

**Other books you might like:**
Ray Bradbury, *The Stories of Ray Bradbury*, 1980
Fritz Leiber, *The Leiber Chronicles*, 1989
Harlan Ellison, *The Essential Ellison: A 35-Year Retrospective*, 1987

### 894
#### ORSON SCOTT CARD

## *The Memory of Earth*
(New York: Tor, 1992)

**Story type:** Science Fiction (Space Colony; Political)
**Series:** Homecoming

**Major character(s):** Nafai, Student, Child; Rasa, Teacher, Parent; Volemak, Leader, Parent
**Time period(s):** Indeterminate Future
**Locale(s):** Harmony, Planet—Imaginary

**Summary:** For 40 million years the Oversoul, an artificial intelligence located in orbit above the planet of Harmony, has banned advanced technology to prevent the catastrophies that had destroyed humanity on Earth. Now, needing repair, the Oversoul decides to speak through visions and dreams to those most sensitive to its communications so that they can learn about space travel and bring the Oversoul to interface with the Keeper of Earth.

**Other books you might like:**
Isaac Asimov, *Foundation*, 1951
Marion Zimmer Bradley, *Two to Conquer*, 1980
C.J. Cherryh, *Angel with the Sword*, 1985
C.J. Cherryh, *Forty Thousand in Gehenna*, 1983
Robert A. Heinlein, *The Moon Is a Harsh Mistress*, 1966
Anne McCaffrey, *Dragonflight*, 1968

## 895

### ORSON SCOTT CARD

## *Pastwatch: The Redemption of Christopher Columbus*
(New York: Tor, 1996)

**Story type:** Science Fiction (Time Travel; Alternate History)
**Major character(s):** Diko, Time Traveler; Hunahpu Matamoros, Time Traveler; Christopher Columbus, Historical Figure, Explorer
**Time period(s):** 22nd century; 15th century (1492-1493)
**Locale(s):** Africa; Hispaniola, Caribbean

**Summary:** On an ecologically devastated Earth, a small group of Time Watchers records history. In researching Columbus, they discover changes in the past and decide to go back in time to try to mold a new history.

**Other books you might like:**
Kevin J. Anderson, *The Trinity Paradox*, 1991
   Doug Beason, co-author
Poul Anderson, *The Shield of Time*, 1990
Ben Bova, *Triumph*, 1993
Jack L. Chalker, *Downtiming the Night Side*, 1985
L. Sprague de Camp, *Lest Darkness Fall*, 1941
Michael Flynn, *In the Country of the Blind*, 1990
Crawford Kilian, *The Empire of Time*, 1978
Robert Charles Wilson, *Mysterium*, 1994

## 896

### ORSON SCOTT CARD

## *Prentice Alvin*
(New York: Tor Books, 1989)

**Story type:** Fantasy (Magic Conflict)
**Series:** Tales of Alvin Maker
**Major character(s):** Alvin ''Maker'' Miller, Apprentice (blacksmith), Psychic; Peggy Guester, Psychic (Torch)
**Time period(s):** Indeterminate
**Locale(s):** Alternate Earth

**Summary:** Alvin returns to his birthplace to become a blacksmith's apprentice. With the help of the Torch, Peggy, he will also learn to become a Maker.

**Other books you might like:**
Stephen R. Donaldson, *Chronicles of Thomas Covenant*,
Mark Helprin, *Winter's Tale*, 1983
Tom Reamy, *Blind Voices*, 1978
Bob Skimin, *Gray Victory*, 1988

## 897

### ORSON SCOTT CARD

## *The Ships of Earth*
(New York: Tor, 1994)

**Story type:** Science Fiction (Alternate Intelligence; Family Saga)
**Series:** Homecoming
**Major character(s):** Nafai, Student, Hunter; Elemak, Leader, Rogue; Luet, Psychic, Spouse
**Time period(s):** Indeterminate Future
**Locale(s):** Harmony, Planet—Imaginary

**Summary:** Exiled to the desert, the descendants of Rasa and Volemak must travel to find the port of embarkation to Earth. Elemak, the oldest, resents Nafai, seeing him as a threat to his leadership, but also fears the protection the Oversoul gives Nafai. Inevitable conflict between the two follows when Nafai penetrates the ancient starport and becomes Starmaster.

**Other books you might like:**
Ben Bova, *As on a Darkling Plain*, 1972
Paula E. Downing, *Rinn's Star*, 1990
Cynthia Felice, *Double Nocturne*, 1986
William R. Forstchen, *Ice Prophet*, 1983
H. Beam Piper, *The Cosmic Computer*, 1964
Melissa Scott, *Five-Twelfths of Heaven*, 1985
Cordwainer Smith, *Quest of the Three Worlds*, 1966
Jack Vance, *Big Planet*, 1957
James White, *The Dream Millennium*, 1974

## 898

### ORSON SCOTT CARD

## *Treasure Box*
(New York: HarperCollins, 1996)

**Story type:** Horror (Witchcraft)
**Major character(s):** Quentin Fears, Computer Expert; Sally Sannazarro, Nurse; Mike Bolt, Police Officer (chief)
**Time period(s):** 1990s (1996)
**Locale(s):** Mixinick, New York; Washington, District of Columbia

**Summary:** Quentin Fears discovers that his wife Madeleine and her entire extended family are all phantoms created by a young witch who hopes to trick Quentin into opening a magic box. This will release a creature that will increase her supernatural powers at the expense of Quentin's life.

**Other books you might like:**
Ramsey Campbell, *Incarnate*, 1983
Jonathan Carroll, *A Child Across the Sky*, 1988
Jonathan Carroll, *From the Teeth of Angels*, 1994
Mark A. Clements, *The Land of Nod*, 1995
Lisa Tuttle, *Pillow Friend*, 1996

## 899

**ORSON SCOTT CARD**

### Xenocide

(New York: Tor, 1991)

**Story type:** Science Fiction (Space Colony; Theological)
**Series:** Ender Wiggin
**Major character(s):** Andrew Wiggin, Warrior, Psychologist; Wangmu, Servant, Genetically Altered Being; Jane, Artificial Intelligence
**Time period(s):** Indeterminate Future
**Locale(s):** Lusitania, Planet—Imaginary; Path, Planet—Imaginary

**Summary:** The descolada virus threatens to destroy human life on Lusitania as scientists' vaccines barely stay ahead of the rapidly changing pathogen, which could be permanently destroyed by the colonists. Because other intelligent life on Lusitania would be devastated and then destroyed without the descolada virus, the scientists refuse to employ the drastic solution readily available if time allows a gentler treatment.

**Other books you might like:**
Octavia E. Butler, *Xenogenesis Series*, 1987-1989
James H. Schmitz, *The Demon Breed*, 1968
Dan Simmons, *The Fall of Hyperion*, 1990
Dan Simmons, *Hyperion*, 1989
Joan Slonczewski, *A Door into Ocean*, 1986
Sheri S. Tepper, *Grass*, 1989

## 900

**DIANE CAREY**

### Best Destiny

(New York: Pocket, 1992)

**Story type:** Science Fiction (Space Opera)
**Series:** Star Trek
**Major character(s):** George Samuel Kirk, Parent (James T. Kirk's), Spaceman (Starfleet); James T. "Jimmy" Kirk, Teenager, Adventurer
**Time period(s):** 23rd century
**Locale(s):** U.S.S. Enterprise, Spaceship; Outer Space

**Summary:** Jimmy's efforts to gain respect lead to trouble until George ignites Jimmy's enthusiasm by taking him on a shakedown voyage of the just-completed *Enterprise*. After pirates attack their shuttle, George forces Jimmy into a jury-rigged life support capsule, expecting everyone else to die. However, Jimmy decides to rebel by ramming the capsule into the pirate vessel then sabotaging the ship, allowing the Starfleet crew to rescue themselves. Sequel to *Final Frontier*.

**Other books you might like:**
Margaret Wander Bonanno, *Dwellers in the Crucible*, 1985
Diane Duane, *Doctor's Orders*, 1990
Barbara Hambly, *Ghost Walker*, 1991
Vonda N. McIntyre, *Enterprise*, 1986
Della Van Hise, *Killing Time*, 1985

## 901

**DIANE CAREY**

### Call to Arms

(New York: Pocket Books, 1998)

**Story type:** Science Fiction (Military; Space Opera)

**Series:** Star Trek: Deep Space Nine: The Dominion War
**Major character(s):** Benjamin Sisko, Spaceship Captain; Jadzia Dax, Military Personnel (lieutenant), Alien (Trill); Worf, Military Personnel (commander), Alien (Klingon)
**Time period(s):** 24th century
**Locale(s):** Deep Space Nine, Space Station; U.S.S. Defiant, Spaceship; I.K.S. Rotarran, Spaceship

**Summary:** The battle continues. Sisko and his Starfleet personnel abandon Deep Space Nine to combined Cardassian and Dominion forces. Kira and Odo remain behind to maintain an uneasy truce during the Occupation, while Sisko works with Martok, a Klingon captain, to strike back at the invaders. Second of four volumes.

**Other books you might like:**
C.J. Cherryh, *Rimrunners*, 1989
Gordon R. Dickson, *Soldier, Ask Not*, 1967
Brad Ferguson, *The Last Stand*, 1995
Joe Haldeman, *The Forever War*, 1975
Dean Wesley Smith, *The Soldiers of Fear*, 1996
    Kristine Kathryn Rusch, co-author

## 902

**DIANE CAREY**
**JAMES I. KIRKLAND**, Co-Author

### First Frontier

(New York: Pocket, 1995)

**Story type:** Science Fiction (Time Travel; Alternate Universe)
**Series:** Star Trek
**Major character(s):** James T. Kirk, Spaceship Captain; Spock, Scientist, Alien (Vulcan); Leonard McCoy, Doctor
**Time period(s):** Indeterminate Past (65 million years ago); 23rd century
**Locale(s):** Earth; U.S.S. Enterprise, Spaceship

**Summary:** While testing a new shielding technology, the *Enterprise* finds only a lush wilderness where human life never evolved when they return to Earth. Romulans and Klingons subjugate most other space-faring races and now fight each other to the death. Marooned in this alternate history, Kirk leads a landing party back in time through the Guardian of Forever. Realizing that someone has prevented the asteroid impact that drove the dinosaurs to extinction, they must ensure that the asteroid strikes so that mammals inherit the Earth.

**Other books you might like:**
Margaret Wander Bonanno, *Strangers From the Sky*, 1987
Michael Crichton, *Jurassic Park*, 1991
A.C. Crispin, *Time for Yesterday*, 1988
Dana Kramer-Rolls, *Home Is the Hunter*, 1990
Judith Reeves-Stevens, *Federation*, 1994
    Garfield Reeves-Stevens, co-author

## 903

**DIANE CAREY**

### First Strike

(New York: Pocket, 1996)

**Story type:** Science Fiction (Space Opera; First Contact)
**Series:** Star Trek
**Major character(s):** James T. Kirk, Spaceship Captain; Spock, Scientist, Alien (Vulcan); Zennor, Alien, Spaceship Captain
**Time period(s):** 23rd century

**Locale(s):** *U.S.S. Enterprise*, Spaceship; Outer Space; Interstellar Empire/Federation

**Summary:** When a mysterious spaceship invades Klingon space and resists all efforts to destroy it, the Klingon commander resorts to desperate measures, asking James Kirk of the Federation for help. To the Klingons' disgust, Kirk first insists on negotiating with the invaders, terrifying aliens whom Klingon myths call the Havoc and human mythology, the Furies. Since the Furies believe that they must reclaim their own territory from the evil Conquerors who drove out their ancestors millenia before, even the *Enterprise* may not be able to stop them. First of the four part Invasion! Series which spans all four of the Star Trek television series and continues in *The Soldiers of Fear*.

**Other books you might like:**
Dafydd ab Hugh, *The Final Fury*, 1996
    Invasion! Series, part 4
Orson Scott Card, *Ender's Game*, 1985
Gene DeWeese, *Chain of Attack*, 1987
Brad Ferguson, *The Last Stand*, 1995
L.A. Graf, *Time's Enemy*, 1996
    Invasion! Series, part 3
Barbara Paul, *The Three Minute Universe*, 1988
Dean Wesley Smith, *The Soldiers of Fear*, 1996
    Kristine Kathryn Rusch, co-author; Invasion! Series, part 2
David Weber, *Path of the Fury*, 1992

**904**

**DIANE CAREY**

## Ship of the Line
(New York: Pocket, 1997)

**Story type:** Science Fiction (Space Opera; Time Travel)
**Series:** Star Trek: The Next Generation
**Major character(s):** Jean-Luc Picard, Spaceship Captain; Morgan Bateson, Spaceship Captain; William Riker, Military Personnel (Starfleet Commander)
**Time period(s):** 24th century; 23rd century
**Locale(s):** *U.S.S. Enterprise*, Spaceship; Cardassia Prime, Planet—Imaginary; United Federation of Planets, Interstellar Empire/Federation

**Summary:** Fighting off an invading Klingon ship, Captain Bateson's ship disappears into a temporal anomaly and emerges into the 24th century. After three years re-training, he receives command of the new *Enterprise-E* for its shakedown cruise while a self-doubting Picard accepts a hostage rescue mission to Cardassia. Bateson's old Klingon enemy, now an embittered old man, seeks vengeance by hijacking the new *Enterprise* and using it to provoke war between the Federation and Cardassia. Picard learns some important lessons from a holographic Captain Kirk, confronts his former torturer on Cardassia, and saves the *Enterprise*.

**Other books you might like:**
Poul Anderson, *Time Patrolman*, 1983
Michael Jan Friedman, *Kahless*, 1996
L.A. Graf, *Time's Enemy*, 1996
    pseudonym of Julie Ecklar and Karen Rose
Joe Haldeman, *The Forever War*, 1975
Judith Reeves-Stevens, *Federation*, 1994
    Garfield Reeves-Stevens, co-author
Gene Wolfe, *The Shadow of the Torturer*, 1980

**905**

**DIANE CAREY**

## Starfleet Academy
(New York: Pocket, 1997)

**Story type:** Science Fiction (Young Adult; Adventure)
**Series:** Star Trek
**Major character(s):** David Forester, Student; James T. Kirk, Spaceship Captain; Hikaru Sulu, Spaceship Captain
**Time period(s):** 23rd century
**Locale(s):** San Francisco, California; United Federation of Planets, Interstellar Empire/Federation

**Summary:** David Forester begins his Starfleet Academy career by punching Captain Kirk during a simulated assassination attempt. Put in command of a team of other cadets, David attempts to mold them into a crew during simulator assignments. Soon a series of ''accidents'' point to sabotage by a group of xenophobes who want real life war with the Klingon Empire. David accepts an assignment to help find out the truth and protect the Federation. Based on a CD-ROM game.

**Other books you might like:**
Dafydd ab Hugh, *Balance of Power*, 1995
C.J. Cherryh, *Hellburner*, 1992
Carolyn Clowes, *The Pandora Principle*, 1990
Julia Ecklar, *The Kobayashi Maru*, 1989
Brad Ferguson, *A Flag Full of Stars*, 1991
L.A. Graf, *Traitor Winds*, 1990
    psuedonym of Julie Ecklar and Karen Rose
Robert A. Heinlein, *Starman Jones*, 1953

**906**

**LEONARD CARPENTER**

## Conan of the Red Brotherhood
(New York: Tor, 1993)

**Story type:** Fantasy (Sword and Sorcery)
**Series:** Conan the Barbarian
**Major character(s):** Conan, Barbarian, Warrior; Sulula ''Philiope'', Servant, Imposter (noblewoman); Yildiz, Ruler (emperor)
**Time period(s):** Indeterminate Past
**Locale(s):** Turan, Fictional Country; Aghrapur, Fictional City; At Sea

**Summary:** As Conan carves out a pirate empire, Emperor Yildiz plots his destruction.

**Other books you might like:**
Roland J. Green, *Conan the Relentless*, 1992
Robert E. Howard, *Bran Mak Morn*, 1969
Robert E. Howard, *Conan the Barbarian*, 1955
Robert E. Howard, *Hour of the Dragon*, 1977
Robert E. Howard, *King Conan*, 1953
Robert Jordan, *Conan the Invincible*, 1985
Steve Perry, *Conan the Formidable*, 1990

**907**

**LEONARD CARPENTER**

## Conan the Gladiator
(New York: Tor, 1995)

**Story type:** Fantasy (Sword and Sorcery; Adventure)
**Series:** Conan the Barbarian

**Major character(s):** Conan, Barbarian, Warrior; Sathilda, Entertainer (acrobat)
**Time period(s):** Indeterminate Past
**Locale(s):** Stygia, Fictional Country; Luxur, Fictional City

**Summary:** After he joins Sathilda's troupe for diversion, Conan runs afoul of officials and must fight exotic warriors and wild beasts in the Arena of Luxur.

**Other books you might like:**
Roland J. Green, *Conan at the Demon's Gate*, 1994
Robert E. Howard, *Conan the Barbarian*, 1955
Robert E. Howard, *Hour of the Dragon*, 1977
Robert E. Howard, *King Conan*, 1953
John Maddox Roberts, *Conan and the Manhunters*, 1994
Karl Edward Wagner, *Darkness Weaves*, 1978
    revised edition

---

**908**

**LEONARD CARPENTER**

## Conan the Outcast

(New York: Tor, 1991)

**Story type:** Fantasy (Sword and Sorcery)
**Series:** Conan the Barbarian
**Major character(s):** Conan, Barbarian, Warrior
**Time period(s):** Indeterminate Past
**Locale(s):** Qjara, Fictional City

**Summary:** Queen Regula declares Conan an outcast, but when the high priest, Khumanos, plans to sacrifice Qjara in hopes of returning Lord Votantha and glory to the City of Sark, Conan represents Qjara's only hope of survival.

**Other books you might like:**
Roland J. Green, *Conan the Guardian*, 1991
Robert Jordan, *Conan the Invincible*, 1985
Robert Jordan, *Conan the Victorious*, 1984
Steve Perry, *Conan the Formidable*, 1990
John Maddox Roberts, *Conan the Bold*, 1989
John Maddox Roberts, *Conan the Champion*, 1987

---

**909**

**LEONARD CARPENTER**

## Conan the Savage

(New York: Tor, 1992)

**Story type:** Fantasy (Sword and Sorcery)
**Series:** Conan the Barbarian
**Major character(s):** Conan, Barbarian, Warrior; Songa, Hunter, Warrior
**Time period(s):** Indeterminate Past
**Locale(s):** Brythunia, Fictional Country

**Summary:** After Conan escapes from the ''unescapable'' prison mine pits of Brythunia and flees into the wilderness, he discovers Songa and her people, the Atupans, and gains acceptance among them. When raiders abduct Songa, Conan follows and wreaks vengeance on the kidnappers, then confronts the demon goddess gaining power in Brythunia.

**Other books you might like:**
Roland J. Green, *Conan the Guardian*, 1991
Robert E. Howard, *Conan the Barbarian*, 1955
Robert E. Howard, *Conan the Conqueror*, 1950
Robert E. Howard, *King Conan*, 1953
Robert Jordan, *Conan the Invincible*, 1985

Robert Jordan, *Conan the Victorious*, 1984
Steve Perry, *Conan the Formidable*, 1990

---

**910**

**LEONARD CARPENTER**

## Conan, Scourge of the Bloody Coast

(New York: Tor, 1994)

**Story type:** Fantasy (Sword and Sorcery)
**Series:** Conan the Barbarian
**Major character(s):** Conan, Barbarian, Warrior; Crotalus, Wizard
**Time period(s):** Indeterminate Past (Hyperborean Age)
**Locale(s):** Vilayet Sea, Fictional Country; Turan, Fictional Country

**Summary:** Setting mainland empires against each other, Conan and his band of pirates attempt to recover a sunken treasure of gold and gems while avoiding Crotalus' deadly machinations.

**Other books you might like:**
Roland J. Green, *Conan at the Demon's Gate*, 1994
Robert E. Howard, *Conan the Barbarian*, 1955
Steve Perry, *Conan the Formidable*, 1990
John Maddox Roberts, *Conan and the Manhunters*, 1994
Karl Edward Wagner, *Darkness Weaves*, 1978
    revised edition

---

**911**

**A.A. CARR**

## Eye Killers

(Norman: University of Oklahoma Press, 1995)

**Story type:** Horror (Vampire Story)
**Major character(s):** Michael Roanhorse, Shepherd; Falke, Vampire; Diana Logan, Teacher (of high school English)
**Time period(s):** 1990s (1995)
**Locale(s):** Albuquerque, New Mexico

**Summary:** This first novel by a talented Native American film director draws from his own Navajo roots. When a European vampire named Falke seduces Michael Roanhorse's daughter, Melissa, to become one of his followers, Michael embarks on a quest to reacquaint himself with his native heritage and harness the mystical powers that will show him how to defeat this enemy. Michael's efforts to enlist Caucasian English teacher Diana Logan to fight the European Falke recapitulate in miniature the clash of the Anglo-American and Native American cultures.

**Other books you might like:**
Muriel Gray, *The Trickster*, 1994
Colin Kersey, *Soul Catcher*, 1995
G. Wayne Miller, *Thunder Rise*, 1988
Adam Niswander, *The Charm*, 1993
Kathryn Ptacek, *Ghost Dance*, 1990

---

**912**

**EMMANUEL CARRERE**

## Gothic Romance

(New York: Scribners, 1990)

**Story type:** Horror (Mystery)
**Major character(s):** Ann, Writer (modern gothic romance writer); Robert Walton, Publisher; Mary Shelley, Writer (wrote *Frankenstein*), Historical Figure

**Time period(s):** 1990s (1990); 1810s (1814)
**Locale(s):** London, England; Lake Geneva, Switzerland

**Summary:** While John Polidori tells the story of how Mary Shelley wrote her Gothic masterpiece, *Frankenstein*, Ann, a modern writer of Gothic romances, becomes involved in a series of mysterious experiences that suggest a correspondence between her own life and that of Mary Shelley almost 200 years before. This is a revision, translated by Lanie Goodman, of *Bravoure*, 1984.

**Other books you might like:**
Brian W. Aldiss, *Frankenstein Unbound*, 1973
Tim Powers, *The Stress of Her Regard*, 1989
Kathryn Ptacek, *In Silence Sealed*, 1988

### 913

#### EMMANUEL CARRERE

### Two by Carrere

(New York: Holt, 1998)

**Story type:** Horror (Collection)

**Summary:** These two short novels of psychological suspense with existential overtones have been translated from the French. In *The Mustache* (1987), a man finds his life hopelessly shattered when he alters his appearance by shaving off his moustache and finds his place in the world he has known permanently altered. *Class Trip* (1997) concerns a young boy, Nicolas, whose apprehensive behavior proves to be fueled by deeper emotional trauma that is revealed by his experiences on a class outing. Translated by Linda Coverdale.

**Other books you might like:**
Michael Blumlein, *The Brains of Rats*, 1989
T.L. Parkinson, *The Man Upstairs*, 1991
Patrick Suskind, *The Pigeon*, 1987
Roland Topor, *The Tenant*, 1966

### 914

#### JERRY JAY CARROLL

### Inhuman Beings

(New York: Ace, 1998)

**Story type:** Science Fiction (Invasion of Earth)
**Major character(s):** Goodwin Armstrong, Detective—Private; Princess Dulay, Royalty, Psychic
**Time period(s):** Indeterminate Future
**Locale(s):** San Francisco, California

**Summary:** Goodwin Armstrong, a moderately successful private investigator, accepts Princess Dulay as a client with some reservations. She claims to be a psychic and insists that her power has uncovered a mysterious conspiracy in the city. In the course of his investigation, Armstrong discovers that an alien race has secretly infiltrated in preparation for a full-scale takeover.

**Other books you might like:**
Fredric Brown, *The Mind Thing*, 1961
William R. Burkett Jr., *Sleeping Planet*, 1965
Harry Harrison, *Invasion: Earth*, 1982
Fritz Leiber, *The Sinful Ones*, 1953
John Lymington, *Night of the Big Heat*, 1960

### 915

#### JERRY JAY CARROLL

### Top Dog

(New York: Ave, 1996)

**Story type:** Fantasy (Alternate World; Satire)
**Major character(s):** William ''Bogey'' Ingersol, Businessman, Animal (dog); Helmish, Artisan, Inventor
**Time period(s):** 1990s; Indeterminate
**Locale(s):** Planet—Imaginary

**Summary:** Although surprised to find himself in a dog's body on another world rather than waiting to serve prison time for violating SEC rules, Bogey quickly learns to use his new abilities, integrating his Earthly business skills. Brought to help with the battle between good and evil for the Fair Lands, Bogey must decide whom to support in the conflict. First novel.

**Other books you might like:**
Carolyn Cushman, *Witch and Wombat*, 1994
Gordon R. Dickson, *The Dragon and the George*, 1976
Barbara Hambly, *The Silver Tower*, 1986
William Kotzwinkle, *The Bear Went over the Mountain*, 1996
Mark E. Rogers, *The Adventures of Samurai Cat*, 1984
J.R.R. Tolkien, *The Fellowship of the Ring*, 1954

### 916

#### JONATHAN CARROLL

### After Silence

(New York: Doubleday, 1993)

**Story type:** Horror (Mystery)
**Major character(s):** Max Fischer, Artist (cartoonist); Lily Aaron, Restaurateur; Lincoln Aaron, Teenager
**Time period(s):** 1980s; 1990s (1993)
**Locale(s):** Los Angeles, California

**Summary:** Max Fischer discovers that his girlfriend Lily has lied to him about having a husband, and that her son Lincoln is actually a child whom she kidnapped while an infant. Although Max forgives Lily and tries to establish a stable family, Lincoln's discovery of the truth years later precipitates all three of them on a path toward dissolution and death.

**Other books you might like:**
Dennis Etchison, *Darkside*, 1986
Ronald Kelly, *Father's Little Helper*, 1992
Dean R. Koontz, *Hideaway*, 1991
Bernard Taylor, *Mother's Boys*, 1987

### 917

#### JONATHAN CARROLL

### A Child Across the Sky

(New York: Doubleday, 1990)

**Story type:** Horror (Mystery)
**Major character(s):** Weber Greston, Director (film director); Philip Strayhorn, Director (recently deceased); Cullen James, Writer (Weber's former lover)
**Time period(s):** 1990s (1990)
**Locale(s):** New York, New York; Los Angeles, California

**Summary:** Distinguished film director Weber Greston agrees to finish a horror film by his friend Philip Strayhorn, left incomplete at

Philip's suicide. Through his association with mutual acquaintances, he begins to suspect that Philip was privy to dark truths that he translated into the imagery of his wildly successful ''Midnight'' film series.

**Other books you might like:**
Steven R. Boyett, *The Answer Tree*, 1988
   in David Schow, *Silver Scream*, 1988
Ramsey Campbell, *Ancient Images*, 1988

**918**

JONATHAN CARROLL

## From the Teeth of Angels
(New York: Doubleday, 1994)

**Story type:** Horror (Mystery)
**Major character(s):** Wyatt Leonard, Actor (children's television star), Homosexual; Arlen Ford, Actress; Leland Zivic, Photographer
**Time period(s):** 1990s (1994)
**Locale(s):** Vienna, Austria

**Summary:** A handful of celebrities whose paths cross in Vienna discuss their lives and fear of impending death with one another, unaware that death personified is among their company.

**Other books you might like:**
Charles L. Grant, *For Fear of the Night*, 1988
Stephen King, *It*, 1986

**919**

JONATHAN CARROLL

## Outside the Dog Museum
(New York: Doubleday, 1992)

**Story type:** Fantasy (Contemporary)
**Major character(s):** Harry Radcliffe, Architect
**Time period(s):** 20th century
**Locale(s):** Los Angeles, California; Republic of Saru, Fictional Country

**Summary:** Harry Radcliffe, world-famous architect and jerk, goes mad. With the help of Venasque, a shaman who appears in Carroll's last two books, he eventually regains his sanity and takes a commission to build a Museum for the Sultan of Saru, a small Middle Eastern country. The commission, however, is more than it seems, and Harry's world goes through some very strange changes before the story ends.

**Other books you might like:**
James P. Blaylock, *The Paper Grail*, 1991
John Crowley, *Little, Big*, 1981
Lisa Goldstein, *The Dream Years*, 1985
Robert Holdstock, *Mythago Wood*, 1984
James Patrick Kelly, *Look into the Sun*, 1989
Pat Murphy, *The City, Not Long After*, 1989

**920**

JONATHAN CARROLL

## The Panic Hand
(New York: St. Martin's, 1996)

**Story type:** Horror (Collection)
**Summary:** Featuring stories in which real life sits cheek-by-jowl with the fantastic and the comic frequently nosedives into horror, this first

collection is considerably expanded from its first appearance in Germany nearly a decade ago and its British publication in 1995. In the World Fantasy Award-winning ''Man's Best Dog,'' a child learns of an imminent animal revolt from her beloved pet. ''Flash in the Pants'' tells of a house that weeps for the departure of its tenants, and ''The Sadness of Detail'' of a woman confronted by a man who shows future photographs of her family to prove she can change the future for them. ''The Jane Fonda Room'' and ''Postgraduate'' are concerned with private hells in the afterlife and personal forms of damnation. The novellas ''Uh-Oh City'' and ''The Black Cocktail'' are concerned with the divided self and feature characters who are, respectively, fractions of the gods and fragments of the narrator.

**Other books you might like:**
Angela Carter, *Burning Your Boats: The Collected Short Stories*, 1996
Rachel Ingalls, *The End of Tragedy*, 1987
Ian McEwan, *In between the Sheets*, 1978
Stephen Millhauser, *The Barnum Museum*, 1991

**921**

ANGELA CARTER

## Burning Your Boats: The Collected Short Stories
(New York: Holt, 1996)

**Story type:** Horror (Collection)
**Summary:** This omnibus volume collects 42 tales, assembling the contents of four short fiction collections plus six previously uncollected works by a writer who consciously evoked the Gothic in her work and specialized in reworking classic fairy tales into contemporary parables. Included are ''The Company of Wolves,'' a riff on the tale of Little Red Riding Hood, and ''Lady of the House of Love,'' a continuation of Bram Stoker's *Dracula*, both of which explore the sexual subcurrents of their source material. Fantastic representations of female empowerment are the core of ''The Courtship of Mr. Lyon'' and ''The Tiger's Bride,'' while ''The Fall River Axe Murders'' explores a different sort of empowerment in the examination of the Lizzie Borden case. ''The Cabinet of Edgar Allan Poe'' recreates the childhood of its subject in an effort to understand his morbid literary vision. Salman Rushdie supplies an introduction. This book was first published in England in 1995.

**Other books you might like:**
Thomas Ligotti, *Songs of a Dead Dreamer*, 1990
Patrick McGrath, *Blood and Water and Other Tales*, 1988
Stephen Millhauser, *In the Penny Arcade*, 1986
Joyce Carol Oates, *Haunted: Tales of the Grotesque*, 1994

**922**

CARMEN CARTER

## The Devil's Heart
(New York: Pocket, 1993)

**Story type:** Science Fiction (Space Opera; Psychic Powers)
**Series:** Star Trek: The Next Generation
**Major character(s):** Jean-Luc Picard, Spaceship Captain, Military Personnel; Data, Android, Military Personnel; Guinan, Alien (Listener), Saloon Keeper/Owner
**Time period(s):** 24th century
**Locale(s):** *U.S.S. Enterprise*, Spaceship

**Summary:** Sent to investigate reports of problems in an isolated archaeological outpost, the *Enterprise* crew finds only one survivor, whose dying words speak of the legendary Ko N'ya, or Devil's Heart, a stone with reputed powers to make wishes come true—at a price. Recovering the artifact from the Ferengi marauders who have taken it from the outpost, Picard takes custody of it then dreams disturbingly of the lives and deaths of others who have held the stone. Obsessed with the stone, Picard acquires power to alter events— even past events.

**Other books you might like:**
Campbell Black, *Raiders of the Lost Ark*, 1981
Marion Zimmer Bradley, *Sharra's Exile*, 1981
C.J. Cherryh, *Exile's Gate*, 1988
A.C. Crispin, *Time for Yesterday*, 1988
A.C. Crispin, *Yesterday's Son*, 1983
J.R.R. Tolkien, *The Return of the King*, 1956
Della Van Hise, *Killing Time*, 1985

---

**923**

**CARMEN CARTER**
**PETER DAVID**, Co-Author
**MICHAEL JAN FRIEDMAN**, Co-Author

### Doomsday World

(New York: Pocket Books, 1990)

**Story type:** Science Fiction (Space Opera; Espionage Thriller)
**Series:** Star Trek: The Next Generation
**Major character(s):** Data, Android, Military Personnel; Geordi La Forge, Engineer, Military Personnel; Worf, Military Personnel, Security Officer, Alien (Klingon)
**Time period(s):** 24th century
**Locale(s):** Kirlos, Planet—Imaginary; *U.S.S. Enterprise*, Spaceship

**Summary:** The Federation and the K'vin Hegemony have co-existed for years on the artificial planet Kirlos, created by the vanished Ariantu people. Assigned to assist an archaeological team in uncovering the ruins on Kirlos, Data, Geordi and Worf find themselves cut off from the *Enterprise* and under suspicion as perpetrators of a series of terrorist attacks. Then a descendant of the Ariantu activates their ancient doomsday weapon and the *Enterprise* crew must stop it.

**Other books you might like:**
Diane Carey, *Ghost Ship*, 1988
Star Trek: The Next Generation 1
C.J. Cherryh, *Downbelow Station*, 1981
Gene DeWeese, *The Peacekeepers*, 1988
Star Trek: The Next Generation 2
Clifford D. Simak, *Destiny Doll*, 1971

---

**924**

**CHRIS CARTER**
**ELIZABETH HAND**, Co-Author

### The X-Files: Fight the Future

(New York: Harper, 1998)

**Story type:** Horror (Science Fiction)
**Major character(s):** Dana Scully, FBI Agent, Doctor; Fox Mulder, FBI Agent; Alvin Kurtzweill, Scientist
**Time period(s):** 1990s (1998)
**Locale(s):** Blackwood, Texas; Washington, District of Columbia

**Summary:** Special agents Scully and Mulder, whose X-Files team investigates strange cases beyond the scope of normal FBI routine, uncover evidence of an alien influence which came to Earth eons before and which is insidiously infiltrating the human race now that it

has been awakened from its long dormant state. Novelization of Chris Carter's screenplay for the Rob Bowman movie.

**Other books you might like:**
Kevin J. Anderson, *Antibodies*, 1997
Kevin J. Anderson, *Ground Zero*, 1995
Kevin J. Anderson, *Ruins*, 1996
Charles L. Grant, *Goblins*, 1994
Charles L. Grant, *Whirlwind*, 1994

---

**925**

**LIN CARTER**

### The Xothic Legend Cycle: The Complete Mythos Fiction of Lin Carter

(Oakland, California: Chaosium, 1997)

**Story type:** Horror (Anthology)
**Series:** Call of Cthulhu Fiction

**Summary:** Twelve stories by the late author, a celebrated editor of fantasy and horror fiction. Also included are one completion of an unfinished fragment of H.P. Lovecraft's, a collaboration with the volume's editor Robert M. Price, "The Strange Doom of Enos Harker," and Price's homage to Carter's work, "The Soul of the Devil Bought." Carter's pastiches of Lovecraft's cosmic horror fiction include "The Fishers from Outside," "The Thing in the Pit," "The Dweller in the Tomb," and "Behind the Mask."

**Other books you might like:**
Robert Bloch, *The Mysteries of the Worm*, 1993
H.P. Lovecraft, *The Watchers out of Time and Others*, 1974
    August Derleth, co-author
Richard A. Lupoff, *Before. . .12:01. . .and After*, 1996
Gary Myers, *The House of the Worm*, 1975
Richard L. Tierney, *Scroll of Thoth*, 1997

---

**926**

**MARGARET L. CARTER**

### Shadow of the Beast

(Darien, Illinois: Design Image Group, 1998)

**Story type:** Horror (Werewolf Story)
**Major character(s):** Jenny Cameron, Editor (proofreader); Kurt Ballard, Lawyer; Tim Cameron, Musician
**Time period(s):** 1990s (1998)
**Locale(s):** Annapolis, Maryland

**Summary:** Still traumatized by the bestial slaughter of her twin brother and half-sister years before, Jenny Cameron attempts to get on with her life and career. Disturbing dreams, aggravated by a meeting with the father she never knew, suggest that she carries a werewolf taint in her blood and may have had a hand in the murder of her siblings and other women in her town. A first novel by a well-known critic of horror and gothic literature.

**Other books you might like:**
Traci Briery, *The Werewolf Chronicles*, 1995
Nancy A. Collins, *Wild Blood*, 1994
Dennis Danvers, *Wilderness*, 1991
John R. Holt, *Wilderness*, 1991
Melanie Tem, *Wilding*, 1992

## 927

### RAPHAEL CARTER

## *The Fortunate Fall*

(New York: Tor, 1996)

**Story type:** Science Fiction (Cyberpunk; Post-Holocaust)
**Major character(s):** Maya Tayanichna Andreyeva, Journalist, Cyborg; Keishi Mirabara, Researcher, Technician; Pavel Sergeyevich Voskresenye, Activist, Cyborg
**Time period(s):** 23rd century
**Locale(s):** Leningrad, Russia; Arkhangelsk, Russia

**Summary:** As a camera, what Maya sees and feels, her on-line audience also sees and feels. While working on a documentary about the worst holocaust in living memory, Calinshchina, she stumbles on the interview of a lifetime, an interview with Pavel Voskresenye, an eye-witness to that atrocity. Dependent upon a new screener, Keishi Mirabara, who controls Maya's output to the net, Maya faces a tough day pursuing the story while being sought herself by officials. First novel.

**Other books you might like:**
Alfred Bester, *The Computer Connection*, 1975
Pat Cadigan, *Mindplayers*, 1987
John M. Ford, *Growing Up Weightless*, 1993
John M. Ford, *The Princes of Air*, 1982
William Gibson, *Burning Chrome*, 1986
Maureen F. McHugh, *China Mountain Zhang*, 1992
Rudy Rucker, *Live Robots*, 1994
Neal Stephenson, *Snow Crash*, 1993
Michael Swanwick, *Vacuum Flowers*, 1987
Gene Wolfe, *The Fifth Head of Cerberus*, 1972

## 928

### JEFFREY A. CARVER

## *Down the Stream of Stars*

(New York: Bantam Spectra, 1990)

**Story type:** Science Fiction (First Contact; Psychic Powers)
**Series:** Changeling Star
**Major character(s):** Claudi Melnik, Child; Lupo, Animal (half earth wolf, half picobear); Roald Thornekan, Spaceship Captain
**Time period(s):** Indeterminate Future (Year 269 of the Auricle Alliance)
**Locale(s):** *Charity*, Spaceship

**Summary:** When Claudi Melnik and Lupo seem to sense the presence of the Throg, an intelligent race hostile to humans, Captain Thornekan must decide how to best continue his interstellar flight.

**Other books you might like:**
Greg Bear, *Eon*, 1985
Gregory Benford, *Heart of the Comet*, 1986
    David Brin, co-author
C.J. Cherryh, *Cyteen*, 1988
Alis A. Rasmussen, *A Passage of Stars*, 1990
Vernor Vinge, *Marooned in Realtime*, 1986

## 929

### JEFFREY A. CARVER

## *Dragon Rigger*

(New York: Tor, 1993)

**Story type:** Science Fiction (Adventure; Science Fantasy)

**Major character(s):** Jael LaBrae, Pilot (spaceship), Heroine; Kan-Kon, Pilot (spaceship; retired); Windruth, Alien (dragon), Leader
**Time period(s):** Indeterminate Future
**Locale(s):** Dragon Realm, Mythical Place

**Summary:** Jael befriends Kan-Kon immediately before feeling called to the Dragon Realm where conditions worsen as the dragons lose battle after battle. According to the prophecy, Jael will save the Dragon Realm at the cost of her life. Sequel to *Dragons in the Stars*.

**Other books you might like:**
Sean Dalton, *Beyond the Void*, 1991
Debra Doyle, *The Price of the Stars*, 1992
    James D. Macdonald, co-author
Cheryl J. Franklin, *Fire Crossing*, 1991
Geary Gravel, *A Key for the Nonesuch*, 1990
Colin Greenland, *Take Back Plenty*, 1992
David Weber, *Path of the Fury*, 1992

## 930

### JEFFREY A. CARVER

## *Dragons in the Stars*

(New York: Tor, 1992)

**Story type:** Science Fiction (Adventure; Science Fantasy)
**Major character(s):** Jael LeBrae, Spacewoman, Teenager; Deuteronomous Mogurn, Spaceship Captain, Smuggler; "Ar" Rarberticandornan, Alien, Spaceman
**Time period(s):** Indeterminate Future
**Locale(s):** *Cassandra*, Spaceship; *Seneca*, Spaceship

**Summary:** Jael LeBrae, a qualified rigger, finally gets hired by Mogurn, who uses an illegal device to gain control over her. Her low self-esteem, already damaged by an unhappy childhood, causes her to blame her misfortunes on her deceased father. In the Flux, where riggers' mental images form the route through hyperspace, she feels happy but drawn to the Mountain Route, rumored to be inhabited by dragons and forbidden by Mogurn as too dangerous.

**Other books you might like:**
Greg Bear, *Eon*, 1985
Orson Scott Card, *Xenocide*, 1991
Stephen R. Donaldson, *The Gap into Vision: Forbidden Knowledge*, 1991
Cheryl J. Franklin, *Fire Get*, 1987
Eric Kotani, *Act of God*, 1985
    John Maddox Roberts, co-author
Alis A. Rasmussen, *A Passage of Stars*, 1990
Melissa Scott, *Dreamships*, 1992
Dan Simmons, *Hyperion*, 1989
Cordwainer Smith, *The Best of Cordwainer Smith*, 1975

## 931

### JEFFREY A. CARVER

## *From a Changeling Star*

(New York: Bantam Spectra, 1989)

**Story type:** Science Fiction (Hard Science Fiction)
**Major character(s):** Willard Ruskin, Scientist; Dax, Artificial Intelligence
**Time period(s):** Indeterminate Future (Year 178 of the Auricle Alliance)
**Locale(s):** Kantano's World, Planet—Imaginary; Starmuse Station, Space Station

**Summary:** Scientists on Starmuse Station breathlessly await the impending supernova of the star Betelgeuse, but Willard Ruskin, a scientist whose presence is vital to the project, is in difficulty on Kantano's World. Agents of the authoritarian Tandesko Triune have attempted to assassinate Ruskin. Someone else has infected him with nano-agents — microscopic, artificial intelligences, who protect his body from physical harm. Finally, Ruskin is suffering from partial amnesia. In order to save himself and Starmuse Station, Ruskin must discover who infected him with the nano-agents and why the Tandesko Triune wants him dead.

**Other books you might like:**
Greg Bear, *Eon*, 1985
Gregory Benford, *Heart of the Comet*, 1986
  David Brin, co-author
C.J. Cherryh, *Cyteen*, 1988
Vernor Vinge, *Marooned in Realtime*, 1986

---

### 932

**JEFFREY A. CARVER**

## The Infinite Sea

(New York: Tor, 1996)

**Story type:** Science Fiction (First Contact; Space Opera)
**Series:** Chaos Chronicles
**Major character(s):** John Bandicut, Spaceman; Charlie/Charlene, Alien (quarx); Julie Stone, Spacewoman
**Time period(s):** Indeterminate Future
**Locale(s):** Triton, Neptune (moon of Neptune); Planet—Imaginary; Undersea Environment/Habitat

**Summary:** John and his companions arrive at their unknown destination, a community near the edge of an undersea vent. At war with the residents of the land above, the alien Neri imprison the crew until John heals one of the Neri with the help of Charlene, demonstrating their friendship. They realize they must prevent the Neri from destruction by the giant volcano and leaking radiation, both, perhaps, caused by the crashed spaceship they work at salvaging. Meanwhile, on Triton, the translator informs Julie that the Earth again faces disaster.

**Other books you might like:**
Roger MacBride Allen, *The Ring of Charon*, 1990
Stephen Baxter, *Flux*, 1995
David Brin, *Brightness Reef*, 1995
C.J. Cherryh, *Foreigner*, 1994
David Weber, *Path of the Fury*, 1992

---

### 933

**JEFFREY A. CARVER**

## Neptune Crossing

(New York: Tor, 1994)

**Story type:** Science Fiction (First Contact)
**Series:** Chaos Chronicles
**Major character(s):** John Bandicut, Spaceman, Miner; Charlie, Alien (quarx)
**Time period(s):** 22nd century (2164)
**Locale(s):** Triton, Neptune (moon of Neptune)

**Summary:** A spell of silence-fugue renders John Bandicut receptive to contact by Charlie, reanimated after millennia of inactivity. Linking to John's mind, Charlie informs him of an impending disaster for the solar system, which Charlie and John must work to avert, a goal hindered by John's lowly position in the mining operation's hierarchy.

**Other books you might like:**
Roger MacBride Allen, *The Ring of Charon*, 1990
Gordon R. Dickson, *The Alien Way*, 1965
L. Warren Douglas, *Cannon's Orb*, 1994
Diana G. Gallagher, *The Alien Dark*, 1990
Vernor Vinge, *A Fire upon the Deep*, 1992
David Weber, *Mutineers' Moon*, 1991

---

### 934

**JEFFREY A. CARVER**

## Strange Attractors

(New York: Tor, 1995)

**Story type:** Science Fiction (Space Opera)
**Series:** Chaos Chronicles
**Major character(s):** John Bandicut, Spaceman; Charlie, Alien (quarx)
**Time period(s):** Indeterminate Future
**Locale(s):** Outer Space; The Metaworld, Mythical Place

**Summary:** John Bandicut's heroic act saves the Earth but results in Bandicut's transportation to the Metaworld, a vast array of interconnected habitats. There Bandicut and Charlie begin to ally themselves with the strange beings occupying the environment and work to thwart the attempts of a non-corporeal entity to destroy the entire structure. Sequel to *Neptune Crossing*.

**Other books you might like:**
Roger MacBride Allen, *The Ring of Charon*, 1990
Roger MacBride Allen, *The Shattered Sphere*, 1994
John E. Stith, *Manhattan Transfer*, 1993
Vernor Vinge, *A Fire upon the Deep*, 1992
David Weber, *Path of the Fury*, 1992

---

### 935

**JACKIE CASSADA**

## Shadows on the Hill

(Clarkston, Georgia: White Wolf, 1996)

**Story type:** Fantasy (Contemporary; Quest)
**Series:** World of Darkness: Immortal Eyes Trilogy
**Major character(s):** Tor, Mythical Creature (troll), Warrior; Eleighanaran "Leigh", Mythical Creature (sidhe), Noblewoman; Rasputin, Mythical Creature (pooka)
**Time period(s):** 1990s
**Locale(s):** San Francisco, California; Hilo, Hawaii

**Summary:** The companions continue their attempt to find the magical eyes, racing against Yrtalien to open the mythical gate back to Arcadia. Led to Hawaii, the land of the mysterious fairy spirits of the Pacific Isles, the menehune, the companions must contend with the Forsworn Prince as an enemy, as well as a band of half-human Faerie Hunters who want the companions dead. Second in the trilogy.

**Other books you might like:**
Emma Bull, *War for the Oaks*, 1987
Charles de Lint, *Jack of Kinrowan*, 1995
Pamela Dean, *Tam Lin*, 1991
Tom Deitz, *Windmaster's Bane*, 1986
Robert Holdstock, *Mythago Wood*, 1984

## 936

### MICHAEL CASSUTT

## Dragon Season

(New York: Tor, 1991)

**Story type:** Fantasy (Religious; Contemporary)
**Major character(s):** Richard Earl Walsh, Military Personnel; Maia Chios, Student, Heiress
**Time period(s):** 1990s
**Locale(s):** Tucson, Arizona

**Summary:** Rick Walsh arrived from Guam expecting to be met by his mysterious girlfriend, Maia. Instead, she's disappeared, leaving behind her infant son, her wallet and her car. Detective Sanchez, investigating the report on Maia's disappearance, informs Rick that many young women have been discovered missing near Tucson and are frequently never found.

**Other books you might like:**
Alan Dean Foster, *Cyber Way*, 1990
Alan Dean Foster, *To the Vanishing Point*, 1988
P.C. Hodgell, *Dark of the Moon*, 1985
P.C. Hodgell, *God Stalk*, 1982
Marc Laidlaw, *Neon Lotus*, 1988
Elizabeth Moon, *Sheepfarmer's Daughter*, 1988
Elizabeth Moon, *Surrender None: The Legacy of Gird*, 1990

## 937

### MORT CASTLE

## Cursed Be the Child

(New York: Leisure, 1990)

**Story type:** Horror (Child-in-Peril; Possession)
**Major character(s):** Lissette, Child, Spirit; Melissa "Missy" Barringer, Child; Warren Barringer, Professor (English professor)
**Time period(s):** 1990s
**Locale(s):** Chicago, Illinois (Suburbs)

**Summary:** Though they could wish to be a little more settled in their new home, Warren and Vicki Barringer are thrilled that five-year-old Melissa has adapted so well. They're not at all perturbed when Melissa creates an imaginary playmate to go with the new surroundings—until they discover that "Lissette" has an unhealthy influence on their child, and that *who* she is is not nearly so frightening as *what* she is and what she means to do to their family.

**Other books you might like:**
William Peter Blatty, *The Exorcist*, 1971
Ramsey Campbell, *The Influence*, 1988
Ramsey Campbell, *The Nameless*, 1981
Stephen King, *Pet Sematary*, 1983

## 938

### ADAM-TROY CASTRO

## Lost in Booth Nine

(Woodinville, Washington: Silver Salamander Press, 1993)

**Story type:** Horror (Collection)

**Summary:** The author's first book, a quartet of novellas set in and around an imaginary peepshow called Les Girls XXX, critiques the attitudes toward sexuality that existence of such places implies. In "Peepshow," the female performers are vampires who exploit their exploitative customers. In "The Girl in Booth Nine," a peepshow patron's fantasies become reality. "The Pussy Expert" is a mordant character study, and "Miracle Drug" a hallucinatory tale of a squatter house that serves as a doorway to hell. Dean Wesley Smith and Kristine Kathryn Rusch provide an introduction.

**Other books you might like:**
Ramsey Campbell, *Scared Stiff*, 1987
Ray Garton, *Methods of Madness*, 1990
Dan Simmons, *Lovedeath*, 1993
Lucy Taylor, *Close to the Bone*, 1993

## 939

### HUGH B. CAVE

## Bitter/Sweet

(West Warwick, Rhode Island: Necronomicon Press, 1996)

**Story type:** Horror (Collection)

**Summary:** An author best known for his work in the pulp fiction magazines presents two original stories in which seemingly ominous problems are resolved happily. In "By Heaven!" the ghosts of literary figures renowned for their tastefulness mete out gentle but just desserts to rude and insensitive contemporary cultural figures. In "Aiyana and the Gallant Rider," a dream therapist helps two lonely people interpret their nightmares and overcome the fears that have inspired them.

**Other books you might like:**
Fred Chappell, *More Shapes than One*, 1991
R. Chetwynd-Hayes, *Tales From the Shadows*, 1986
Carl Jacobi, *Smoke of the Snake*, 1994
Frank Belknap Long, *Return to Tomorrow*, 1995
Manly Wade Wellman, *Worse Things Waiting*, 1973

## 940

### HUGH B. CAVE

## Death Stalks the Night

(Minneapolis: Fedogan & Bremer, 1995)

**Story type:** Horror (Collection)

**Summary:** The seventeen stories reprinted in this volume were published in the mid-1930s in the "shudder pulps." Shudder pulp tales traditionally subjected a hero and heroine to weird menaces of a seemingly supernatural nature before revealing them to be the handiwork of criminal masterminds. In "The Flame Fiend," the perpetrator of a series of gruesome murders is a man who dons an asbestos suit and, doused with gasoline, sets himself afire to smother his victims. In "A Modern Nero," a discredited film director uses a remote resort to film grisly tortures that will give his movies verisimilitude. The title of "The Crawling Ones" refers to a torture method used in Borneo where insects are used to devour the flesh of victims. Genuine supernaturalism can be found in "Death's Loving Arms," which features a feral woman brought to America by a research expedition, and "Tomb for the Living," where a submarine pierces through a maelstrom into a world beneath the ocean floor inhabited by primitive life forms. The late Karl Edward Wagner, who planned to bring this book out over a decade ago under the Carcosa House imprint, wrote the introduction.

**Other books you might like:**
Carl Jacobi, *Smoke of the Snake*, 1994
Sheldon Jaffery, *The Weirds*, 1987
    editor
E. Hoffman Price, *Far Lands, Other Days*, 1975

Robert Weinberg, *Uncanny Tales*, 1974
  editor

**941**

### HUGH B. CAVE

## Disciples of Dread

(New York: Tor, 1989)

**Story type:** Horror (Black Magic)
**Major character(s):** Mark Donner, Young Man (American); Khargi, Religious (Voodoo priest)
**Time period(s):** 1980s
**Locale(s):** Jamaica

**Summary:** Mark Donner is stalked by the Disciples of Dread, an international terrorist organization led by Khargi, a voodoo practitioner, in a plot to trap Mark's psychically talented twin brother, an American spy.

**Other books you might like:**
John Farris, *The Fury*, 1976
Dennis Wheatley, *Strange Conflict*, 1941

**942**

### HUGH B. CAVE

## The Door Below

(Minneapolis: Fedogan & Bremer, 1997)

**Story type:** Horror (Collection)
**Summary:** Twenty-five stories of supernatural horrors and weird menaces that span more than 60 years of the author's prolific and distinguished writing career. Cave's work for the shudder pulps is represented by ''Imp of Satan,'' about a grotesquely disfigured victim of native poisons who threatens to inflict the same fate on his estranged fiancc, and ''The Thirsty Thing,'' in which a maniac uses a sea monster to kill his victims. More recent stories include the biter-bit tale ''The Hard-Luck Kid,'' the alternate dimension story ''Vanishing Point,'' and the outstanding voodoo tale ''The Place of No Return.'' The author supplies notes on selections for each of the five decades represented.

**Other books you might like:**
Arthur J. Burks, *Black Medicine*, 1966
Robert E. Howard, *Skull-Face*, 1946
Carl Jacobi, *Smoke of the Snake*, 1994
Carl Jacobi, *Revelations in Black*, 1947
Frank Belknap Long, *The Hounds of Tindalos*, 1946
E. Hoffman Price, *Far Lands, Other Days*, 1975
Manly Wade Wellman, *Worse Things Waiting*, 1973

**943**

### HUGH B. CAVE

## Lucifer's Eye

(New York: Tor, 1991)

**Story type:** Horror (Occult)
**Major character(s):** Peter Sheldon, Worker (plantation caretaker); Edith Craig, Heiress; Ma Jarrett, Psychic
**Time period(s):** 1990s
**Locale(s):** St. Albans, Caribbean

**Summary:** Talk about bad timing: Edith Craig arrives on St. Albans to take charge of her late father's coffee plantation at the same time the townspeople begin disappearing in the nearby Blackrock mountains. Exploration of the rumored Devil's Pit at the core of Blackrock Peak uncovers the secret of the green fog that turns the townspeople into automatons and the presence of a satanic terrorist squadron ready to overrun the island.

**Other books you might like:**
James Herbert, *The Dark*, 1980
James Herbert, *The Fog*, 1975
Peter Straub, *Floating Dragon*, 1982

**944**

### JEANNE CAVELOS

## The Shadow Within

(New York: Dell, 1997)

**Story type:** Science Fiction (Space Opera; Psychic Powers)
**Series:** Babylon 5
**Major character(s):** Anna Sheridan, Anthropologist; Morden, Linguist; Terrence Hilliard, Telepath
**Time period(s):** 23rd century (2256)
**Locale(s):** Geneva, Fictional City; *Icarus*, Spaceship; Z'Ha'dum, Planet—Imaginary

**Summary:** Fascinated by the artifacts found at her last dig, Anna requests Terrence Hillard's help examining one that almost seems active. Called the mouse, it responds to her attention. Unfortunately, the telepathic contact traps Terrence and destroys the mouse. The Psi Corps and Earthforce join the extremely well-supplied expedition to Z'Ha'dum, which Anna recognizes as the opportunity of her lifetime and agrees to join.

**Other books you might like:**
Neal Barrett Jr., *The Touch of Your Shadow, the Whisper of Your Name*, 1996
Kathryn M. Drennan, *To Dream in the City of Sorrows*, 1997
S.M. Stirling, *Betrayals*, 1996
Lois Tilton, *Accusations*, 1995
John Vornholt, *Blood Oath*, 1995
John Vornholt, *Voices*, 1995

**945**

### MICHAEL CECILIONE

## Deathscape

(New York: Diamond, 1992)

**Story type:** Horror (Wild Talents)
**Major character(s):** Laura Kane, Student; Neil Stone, Police Officer; Henry Kent, Doctor
**Time period(s):** 1990s (1992)
**Locale(s):** Groverton, New York

**Summary:** A near-drowning experience endows Laura Kane with the ability to foresee the deaths of others. It also opens the doorway between life and death to let in ''The Croaker,'' a monstrous avatar of death responsible for all of the victims in Laura's visions.

**Other books you might like:**
Stephen King, *The Dead Zone*, 1979
Kathe Koja, *Bad Brains*, 1992
Dean R. Koontz, *Hideaway*, 1992
Joe R. Lansdale, *The Nightrunners*, 1987

## 946

**MICHAEL CECILIONE**

## *Domination*

(New York: Zebra, 1993)

**Story type:** Horror (Vampire Story)
**Major character(s):** Kelly Mitchell, Journalist (investigative reporter); Eric Rossi, Police Officer; Ilana Florescu, Vampire
**Time period(s):** 1990s (1993)
**Locale(s):** New York, New York

**Summary:** Domination is the name of New York's hottest new nightclub and, as its victims become known all over Manhattan, a source of interest to investigative reporter Kelly Mitchell. In the course of her work, Kelly crosses paths with Ilana Florescu, a vampire who uses the domination subculture to literalize her superior relationship to her human prey.

**Other books you might like:**
Poppy Z. Brite, *Lost Souls*, 1992
Ray Garton, *Live Girls*, 1987
John Skipp, *The Light at the End*, 1986
    Craig Spector, co-author
S.P. Somtow, *Vampire Junction*, 1983

## 947

**MICHAEL CECILIONE**

## *Soul Snatchers*

(New York: Diamond, 1992)

**Story type:** Horror (Black Magic)
**Major character(s):** Elaine Prescott, Journalist (crime reporter); Zachary Carver, Police Officer (sheriff); Reverend Isaac Prowier, Religious
**Time period(s):** 1990s (1992)
**Locale(s):** Edens Bluff, Massachusetts

**Summary:** Seeking respite from the stress of her job as a crime reporter in Manhattan, Elaine Prescott takes a leave of absence at the house of an aunt in a remote section of Massachusetts, only to discover that a bizarre sect of resurrectionists that came over with the town's founders in the days of the Pilgrims is busily reviving corpses of the recent dead.

**Other books you might like:**
Elizabeth Ergas, *Devil's Gate*, 1991
Patrick Whalen, *Out of the Night*, 1990
T.M. Wright, *The Island*, 1988

## 948

**MICHAEL CECILIONE**

## *Thirst*

(New York: Zebra, 1996)

**Story type:** Horror (Vampire Story)
**Major character(s):** Cassandra Hall, Designer (fashion), Vampire; Julian Aragon, Vampire, Writer (poet); Rolando, Designer (fashion)
**Time period(s):** 1990s (1995)
**Locale(s):** New York, New York

**Summary:** Newly vampirized Cassandra Hall pines for the affections of her vampire initiator, Julian, who has turned her on to the vampire life through sexual ecstasy. Cassandra tries to live unobtrusively in the vampire subculture of Manhattan, taking blood from sexual clients and staying out of the path of a band of righteous vampire killers known as the Advocates.

**Other books you might like:**
Gary Bowen, *Diary of a Vampire*, 1995
Nancy A. Collins, *Sunglasses After Dark*, 1989
Ray Garton, *Live Girls*, 1987
John Skipp, *The Light at the End*, 1986
    Craig Spector, co-author
Karen E. Taylor, *Blood Secrets*, 1994

## 949

**MARC CERASINI**

## *Godzilla 2000*

(New York: Random House, 1997)

**Story type:** Science Fiction (Adventure; Military)
**Major character(s):** Godzilla, Monster; King Ghidorah, Monster; Kip Daniels, Teenager, Military Personnel (Air Force Special G-Force)
**Time period(s):** 1990s (1998)
**Locale(s):** Nellis Air Force Base, Nevada; New York, New York (Manhattan)

**Summary:** Recruited by the military due to his video game-playing skills, Kip Daniels trains in simulations to prepare for Godzilla's next appearance, even though he cannot convince himself that Godzilla deserves to die. When a cloud of asteriods headed towards Earth unleashes a plague of monsters, including the three-headed King Ghidorah, Godzilla may prove himself to be a friend rather than an enemy.

**Other books you might like:**
Scott Ciencin, *Godzilla Invades America*, 1997
Scott Ciencin, *Godzilla: King of the Monsters*, 1996
Michael Crichton, *The Lost World*, 1995
Michael Crichton, *Jurassic Park*, 1990
Alan Dean Foster, *The Last Starfighter*, 1984

## 950

**MARTHA CERDA**

## *Senora Rodriguez and Other Worlds*

(Durham, North Carolina: Duke University Press, 1997)

**Story type:** Fantasy (Literary)
**Major character(s):** Senora Rodriguez, Spouse, Parent
**Time period(s):** 1990s
**Locale(s):** Mexico

**Summary:** Senora Rodriguez, a remarkable woman, owns a remarkable purse filled with bits of the lives of the people around her. The events of her life interweave with moments from the lives and dreams of her family, friends, strangers and myths. Martha Cerda's first novel to be translated into English, translated by Sylvin Jiminez-Anderson.

**Other books you might like:**
Jorge Luis Borges, *Labyrinths*, 1962
Gabriel Garcia Marquez, *One Hundred Years of Solitude*, 1970
Bruno Schulz, *The Street of Crocodiles*, 1963
Fay Weldon, *Letters to Alice on First Reading Jane Austen*, 1985
Karen Tei Yamashita, *Tropic of Orange*, 1997

## `951`

### JACK L. CHALKER

## *The Cybernetic Walrus*
(New York: Ballantine Del Rey, 1995)

**Story type:** Science Fiction (Techno-Thriller; Cyberpunk)
**Series:** Wonderland Gambit
**Major character(s):** Cory Maddox, Computer Expert (programmer), Adventurer, Hero; Riki Fresca, Artist
**Time period(s):** 21st century
**Locale(s):** United States; Cyberspace (computer virtual reality)

**Summary:** Recruited into a government program to design computer reality, Cory Maddox soon finds it impossible to distinguish virtual reality from genuine memory.

**Other books you might like:**
Piers Anthony, *The Caterpillar's Question*, 1992
    Philip Jose Farmer, co-author
C.J. Cherryh, *Wave Without a Shore*, 1981
Philip K. Dick, *Eye in the Sky*, 1957
Alan Dean Foster, *To the Vanishing Point*, 1988
Robert A. Heinlein, *The Number of the Beast*, 1980
Fritz Leiber, *The Sinful Ones*, 1953
Rebecca Ore, *The Illegal Rebirth of Billy the Kid*, 1991
Melissa Scott, *Trouble and Her Friends*, 1994

## `952`

### JACK L. CHALKER

## *The Demons at Rainbow Bridge*
(New York: Ace Books, 1989)

**Story type:** Science Fiction (Adventure)
**Series:** Quintara Marathon
**Major character(s):** Jimmy McCray, Telepath; Modra Stryke, Empath
**Time period(s):** Indeterminate Future
**Locale(s):** Rainbow Bridge, Planet—Imaginary

**Summary:** Three hostile and radically different interstellar empires live in an uneasy balance. Then that balance is threatened by the discovery on the planet Rainbow Bridge of an odd horned lifeform which, somehow, resembles a creature found in the oldest legends of all three interstellar cultures.

**Other books you might like:**
Janet Kagan, *Hellspark*, 1988
Paul J. McAuley, *Four Hundred Billion Stars*, 1988
Dan Simmons, *The Fall of Hyperion*, 1990
Dan Simmons, *Hyperion*, 1989

## `953`

### JACK L. CHALKER

## *Echoes of the Well of Souls*
(New York: Ballantine Del Rey, 1993)

**Story type:** Science Fiction (Adventure; Alternate Intelligence)
**Series:** Well World
**Major character(s):** Nathan Brazil, Immortal, Sea Captain; Mavra Chang, Immortal, Chieftain; Theresa ''Terry'' Perez, Journalist (television)
**Time period(s):** 21st century
**Locale(s):** Earth; Well World, Planet—Imaginary

**Summary:** When an asteroid crashes into the Amazon jungle, a chunk splits off and captures Nathan Brazil and two handicapped people near Rio de Janeiro. The main body of the meteor transports a scientific and photo journalist team, along with two army officers, to a mysterious planet primal to all life other than Markovian in this incarnation of the universe.

**Other books you might like:**
Piers Anthony, *Thousandstar*, 1980
Greg Bear, *Eon*, 1985
Philip Jose Farmer, *The Maker of Universes*, 1965
Michael P. Kube-McDowell, *Enigma*, 1986
Michael McCollum, *A Greater Infinity*, 1982
Brian Stableford, *Journey to the Center*, 1982
Jack Vance, *Planet of Adventure*, 1993
Joan D. Vinge, *The Summer Queen*, 1991
Timothy Zahn, *Spinneret*, 1985

## `954`

### JACK L. CHALKER

## *Gods of the Well of Souls*
(New York: Ballantine Del Rey, 1994)

**Story type:** Science Fiction (Adventure)
**Series:** Well World
**Major character(s):** Nathan Brazil, Immortal; Mavra Chang, Immortal; Juana ''Juan'' Campos, Drug Dealer
**Time period(s):** 1990s
**Locale(s):** Well World, Planet—Imaginary

**Summary:** Mavra Chang's team arranges to rescue Mavra and Lori and bust up the drug cartel. When a volcanic eruption jolts Nathan Brazil and a very pregnant Terry off the island and Juana Campos, Lori and Mavra escape the cartel, all end up in the Well of Souls where Kraang, a megalomaniacal Markovian takes control.

**Other books you might like:**
Greg Bear, *Eon*, 1985
Jacqueline Lichtenberg, *Dushau*, 1985
Robert Silverberg, *Valentine Pontifex*, 1983
John Varley, *Titan*, 1979
Joan D. Vinge, *The Summer Queen*, 1991

## `955`

### JACK L. CHALKER

## *Horrors of the Dancing Gods*
(New York: Ballantine Del Rey, 1995)

**Story type:** Fantasy (Quest; Adventure)
**Series:** Dancing Gods
**Major character(s):** Irving de Oro, Hero, Warrior; Marge, Mythical Creature (kauri); Larae Ngamuku, Young Woman
**Time period(s):** Indeterminate
**Locale(s):** Husaquahr, Fictional Country; Yuggoth, Fictional Country

**Summary:** The supposedly dead Boquillas stirs up ancient evil from the Sea of Dreams, which centers on the evil continent of Yuggoth. As Joe and a mysterious changeling have disappeared there, Joe's son Irving, Marge, and Poquah set out to rescue them and acquire a statue that will instantly grant any wish.

**Other books you might like:**
C.J. Cherryh, *The Goblin Mirror*, 1992
Elizabeth Forrest, *Dark Tide*, 1993
Tim Powers, *The Drawing of the Dark*, 1979
Clifford D. Simak, *The Fellowship of the Talisman*, 1978

Melinda M. Snodgrass, *Queen's Gambit Declined*, 1989
Christopher Stasheff, *The Secular Wizard*, 1995
Harry Turtledove, *The Case of the Toxic Spell Dump*, 1993
Jack Vance, *Lyonesse*, 1983

**956**

### JACK L. CHALKER

## The Hot-Wired Dodo

(New York: Ballantine Del Rey, 1997)

**Story type:** Science Fiction (Alternate Universe; Cyberpunk)
**Series:** Wonderland Gambit
**Major character(s):** Cory Maddox, Computer Expert, Hero, Adventurer; Cynthia Matalon, Experimental Subject, Gentlewoman; Matthew Tyler Brand, Scientist, Disembodied Personality
**Time period(s):** 1900s
**Locale(s):** United States; Alternate Universe

**Summary:** Cory Maddox finds himself reborn into a world where size and strength favor women rather than men, then into a world on which hermaphrodite centaurs dominate. There Cory determines that he needs a new strategy to end the game or experiment. Concludes the trilogy.

**Other books you might like:**
Ben Bova, *Death Dream*, 1994
Philip K. Dick, *Eye in the Sky*, 1957
Robert A. Heinlein, *Job: A Comedy of Justice*, 1984
James P. Hogan, *Realtime Interrupt*, 1995
Fritz Leiber, *The Sinful Ones*, 1953
Karen Ripley, *The Alchemist of Time*, 1994
Melissa Scott, *Trouble and Her Friends*, 1994
Robert Charles Wilson, *Mysterium*, 1994

**957**

### JACK L. CHALKER

## The March Hare Network

(New York; Ballantine Del Rey, 1996)

**Story type:** Science Fiction (Techno-Thriller; Political)
**Series:** Wonderland Gambit
**Major character(s):** Cory Maddox, Computer Expert, Handicapped (quadriplegic), Adventurer; Korinna "Kori" Kassemi Ajani, Waiter/Waitress, Parent (mother)
**Time period(s):** 1990s
**Locale(s):** California; Washington

**Summary:** Cory Maddox, now Drew Maddox, achieves rebirth in a slightly more primitive world as a helpless quadriplegic. When he is delivered to his enemies, he amazingly becomes Kori, seemingly the feminine side of Cory, with everything depending on her, despite her nature and lack of education.

**Other books you might like:**
Kevin J. Anderson, *Virtual Destruction*, 1996
   Doug Beason, co-author
John Barnes, *Kaleidoscope Century*, 1995
Ben Bova, *Death Dream*, 1994
Philip K. Dick, *Eye in the Sky*, 1956
Tanith Lee, *The Electric Forest*, 1979
Rebecca Ore, *The Illegal Rebirth of Billy the Kid*, 1991
Walter Jon Williams, *Voice of the Whirlwind*, 1987

**958**

### JACK L. CHALKER

## The Ninety Trillion Fausts

(New York: Ace, 1991)

**Story type:** Science Fiction (Political; Military)
**Series:** Quintara Marathon
**Major character(s):** Gun Roh Chin, Spaceship Captain; Jimmy McCray, Telepath; Krishna the Holy Mendoro, Telepath, Religious
**Time period(s):** Indeterminate Future
**Locale(s):** Rainbow Bridge, Planet—Imaginary

**Summary:** Survivors of three teams get together and plan a common strategy against the Quintara knowing that otherwise they would all perish. Jimmy, Josef, Modra, and Krishna then discover by telepathic means whom they are fighting. This book is a sequel to *The Demons at Rainbow Bridge*.

**Other books you might like:**
Piers Anthony, *Cluster*, 1977
David Brin, *Startide Rising*, 1983
Dave Duncan, *Hero*, 1991
Alan Dean Foster, *Glory Lane*, 1987
James H. Schmitz, *The Demon Breed*, 1968

**959**

### JACK L. CHALKER
### MIKE RESNICK, Co-Author
### GEORGE ALEC EFFINGER, Co-Author

## The Red Tape War

(New York: Tor, 1991)

**Story type:** Science Fiction (Humor)
**Major character(s):** Millard Fillmore Pierce, Administrator (class 2 arbiter); XB223, Computer (navigational); Honeylou Emmyjane "Marshmallo" Goldberg, Runaway
**Time period(s):** 87th century
**Locale(s):** *Pete Rozelle*, Spaceship

**Summary:** Thanks to the quirky XB223, Pierce has become lost on his way to his latest assignment. Life is complicated further by arrivals of a lizard-like alien version of Millard Fillmore Pierce from an alternate universe and of Marshmallo who provides another host for Pierce's personality. In this "round robin"-type novel, each author attempts to leave an unresolvable situation at the end of his alternating chapter.

**Other books you might like:**
Douglas Adams, *The Hitchhiker's Guide to the Galaxy*, 1980
Douglas Adams, *The Restaurant at the End of the Universe*, 1981
John DeChancie, *Paradox Alley*, 1987
John DeChancie, *Red Limit Freeway*, 1984
John DeChancie, *Starrigger*, 1983
Frank Herbert, *The Dosadi Experiment*, 1977
Ken Rolston, *Extreme Paranoia: Nobody Knows the Trouble I've Shot*, 1991

**960**

### JACK L. CHALKER

## The Run to Chaos Keep

(New York: Ace, 1991)

**Story type:** Science Fiction (Adventure)

**Series:** Quintara Marathon
**Major character(s):** Jimmy McCray, Telepath (of the Exchange); Gun Roh Chin, Pilot (spaceship); Josef, Leader (Mycohl)
**Time period(s):** Indeterminate Future
**Locale(s):** Alternate Universe

**Summary:** Teams from each Empire—the Exchange, the Mycohl and the Mizlaplan—have entered a Demon-controlled tesseract bordering on another continuum which Jimmy McCray claims is Hell. After several temptations and battles, remnants of the teams enter Chaos Keep, a place of great evil where the three teams will be forced to fight each other by the demon-like Quintara.

**Other books you might like:**
Piers Anthony, *Vision of Tarot*, 1980
    pseudonym of Piers Anthony Dillingham Jacob
E.E.Y. Hales, *Chariot of Fire*, 1977
Michael Lahey, *Quest for Apollo*, 1989
Larry Niven, *Inferno*, 1976
    Jerry Pournelle, co-author

---

`961`

### JACK L. CHALKER

## Shadow of the Well of Souls

(New York: Ballantine Del Rey, 1994)

**Story type:** Science Fiction (Adventure)
**Series:** Well World
**Major character(s):** Nathan Brazil, Immortal; Mavra Chang, Immortal; Theresa ''Terry'' Perez, Journalist (television), Handicapped
**Time period(s):** 21st century
**Locale(s):** Well World, Planet—Imaginary

**Summary:** When Nathan Brazil, Mavra Chang and their teams head toward the Well of Souls, a shipwreck maroons them on an isolated island. Juan Campos, now a female Gloptian bent on revenge, captures Mavra and Lori and a dire fate awaits them. Still, the Well requires Nathan Brazil or Mavra Chang for repairs.

**Other books you might like:**
Philip Jose Farmer, *The Fabulous Riverboat*, 1971
Larry Niven, *Ringworld*, 1970
Robert Silverberg, *Lord Valentine's Castle*, 1980
John Varley, *Titan*, 1979
Joan D. Vinge, *The Summer Queen*, 1991

---

`962`

### JACK L. CHALKER

## Songs of the Dancing Gods

(New York: Ballantine/Del Rey, 1990)

**Story type:** Fantasy (Alternate World; Quest)
**Series:** Dancing Gods
**Major character(s):** Joe de Oro, Barbarian, Hero; Tiana, Slave, Dancer; Macero, Thief
**Time period(s):** 1990s
**Locale(s):** Husaquahr, Fictional Country

**Summary:** Joe, Marge and Tiana return to Husaquahr to discover that Sugasto, Master of the Dead, and Boquillas have joined forces to conquer Husaquahr. The three travel north where Macero, a thief with a fixation on ''Gilligan's Island'' joins them and shows them how to get to Sugasto's stronghold. There they vanquish the two, Joe becomes a wood nymph and Tiana must return to ruling Marquewood.

**Other books you might like:**
Poul Anderson, *Three Hearts and Three Lions*, 1961
Marion Zimmer Bradley, *The House Between the Worlds*, 1980
Alan Dean Foster, *To the Vanishing Point*, 1988
Elizabeth Moon, *Divided Allegiance*, 1988
Elizabeth Moon, *Oath of Gold*, 1989
Elizabeth Moon, *Sheepfarmer's Daughter*, 1988

---

`963`

### ROBERT W. CHAMBERS

## The King in Yellow

(Bristol, Rhode Island: Hobgoblin Press, 1997)

**Story type:** Horror (Collection)

**Summary:** Ten stories reflecting the American bohemian experience at the turn of the century, informally united by recurring references to *The King in Yellow*, a forbidden book that brings madness to those who read it. Included are ''The Yellow Sign,'' the classic tale of an artist stalked by gruesome specter of death; ''The Demoiselle D'ys,'' in which a cynical man learns a lesson of love that endures beyond the grave; ''The Mask,'' about an artist who invents a liquid that turns living matter into stone; and ''The Repairer of Reputations,'' which offers a dystopic vision of the future. First published in 1895. H.P. Lovecraft's assessment of Chambers in his 1927 essay, ''Supernatural Horror in Literature,'' is added as an introduction.

**Other books you might like:**
Ambrose Bierce, *Can Such Things Be?*, 1893
Ralph Adams Cram, *Black Spirits and White*, 1895
W.C. Morrow, *The Ape, the Idiot, and Other People*, 1897
Vincent O'Sullivan, *Master of the Fallen Years*, 1995

---

`964`

### ROBERT W. CHAMBERS

## Out of the Dark: Origins

(Ashcroft, British Columbia: Ash-Tree Press, 1998)

**Story type:** Horror (Collection)

**Summary:** These nine dreamy and decadent stories published between 1895 and 1897 comprise the first of two projected volumes of weird fiction by an artist turned writer. In addition to the classic ''The Yellow Sign,'' a mix of supernaturalism and nightmare, and the afterlife fantasy ''Passeur,'' the contents include ''The Key to Grief,'' in which a man about to be executed imagines a future in which he survives, and the ghost story ''A Pleasant Evening.'' Edited and introduced by Hugh Lamb.

**Other books you might like:**
Ambrose Bierce, *Can Such Things Be?*, 1893
Ralph Adams Cram, *Black Spirits and White*, 1895
R. Murray Gilchrist, *The Stone Dragon and Other Tragic Romances*, 1894
C.D. Pamely, *Tales of Mystery and Terror*, 1926
M.P. Shiel, *Xelucha and Others*, 1975

---

`965`

### VERA CHAPMAN

## The Notorious Abbess

(Chicago, Illinois: Academy Chicago, 1997)

**Story type:** Fantasy (Collection; Religious)

**Major character(s):** Hodierna, Religious (Abbess of Shaston), Adventurer
**Time period(s):** 12th century
**Locale(s):** England; Middle East

**Summary:** Familiar with royalty and Saracens, the ingenious Abbess of Shaston encounters fantastic creatures and the Devil as adventures bring her into the midst of magical and political machinations. Includes 12 stories and a five-page introduction by the editors, Robert H. Boyer and Kenneth J. Zahorski.

**Other books you might like:**
Guy Gavriel Kay, *A Song for Arbonne*, 1993
Diana L. Paxson, *The White Raven*, 1988
Susan Shwartz, *The Grail of Hearts*, 1992
Susan Shwartz, *Shards of Empire*, 1996
Judith Tarr, *The Dagger and the Cross: A Novel of the Crusades*, 1991
Judith Tarr, *The Eagle's Daughter*, 1995

---

### 966

#### FRED CHAPPELL

## The Lodger

(West Warwick, Rhode Island: Necronomicon Press, 1993)

**Story type:** Horror (Possession)
**Major character(s):** Robert Ackley, Librarian; Lyman Scoresby, Writer (poet)
**Time period(s):** 1990s
**Locale(s):** Plattsborough, North Carolina (Bryan University)

**Summary:** Librarian Robert Ackley opens a can of worms when he opens a book of verse by the decadent, second-rate, 19th century poet Lyman Scoresby and becomes possessed by the self-important writer's soul. In an effort to divest himself of this unwanted "lodger," he indulges in a variety of experiences that he feels certain will offend the poet's tastes.

**Other books you might like:**
Ramsey Campbell, *Meeting the Author*, 1991
   in *Waking Nightmares*
Marcy Heidish, *The Torching*, 1992
Thomas Ligotti, *Vastarien*, 1990
   in *Songs of a Dead Dreamer*
Michael Stewart, *Belladonna*, 1992

---

### 967

#### FRED CHAPPELL

## More Shapes than One

(New York: St. Martin's, 1991)

**Story type:** Horror (Collection)

**Summary:** Thirteen stories lightly touched with fantasy, and told with a mild southern accent. "The Somewhere Doors" is a science fiction tale of destiny, and "Mankind Journeys through Forests of Symbols" a metaphysical meditation on creativity. Two stories, "Weird Tales" and "The Adder," show the influence of the writings of H.P. Lovecraft. Some stories resemble mainstream fiction, but all are exquisitely crafted.

**Other books you might like:**
Robert R. McCammon, *Blue World*, 1989
Manly Wade Wellman, *The Valley So Low*, 1986

---

### 968

#### SUZY MCKEE CHARNAS

## The Furies

(New York: Tor, 1994)

**Story type:** Science Fiction (Gay/Lesbian Fiction; Post-Holocaust)
**Major character(s):** Alldera, Leader; Sheel Torriner, Leader
**Time period(s):** Indeterminate Future
**Locale(s):** The Grasslands, Fictional Country (Red Sands Camp); Holdfast, Fictional City

**Summary:** Alldera of the Free Fems, escaped slaves from Holdfast, leads the escapees back to free the fems left behind and to find men to mate with to allow them to have children. Led by Sheel, the Riding Women, who have no need for men, follow to talk the Free Fems into returning with them, but instead become involved in the rescue. The response of the Free Fems to their old oppressors confuses and disrupts the Riding Women. Sequel to *Motherlines*.

**Other books you might like:**
Eleanor Arnason, *A Woman of the Iron People*, 1991
Margaret Atwood, *The Handmaid's Tale*, 1985
Orson Scott Card, *Lovelock*, 1994
   Kathryn H. Kidd, co-author
Suzette Haden Elgin, *Native Tongue*, 1984
Norma Marder, *An Eye for Dark Places*, 1993
Marge Piercy, *Woman on the Edge of Time*, 1976
Pamela Sargent, *The Shore of Women*, 1986
Joan Slonczewski, *A Door into Ocean*, 1986
Michael D. Weaver, *My Father Immortal*, 1989

---

### 969

#### SUZY MCKEE CHARNAS

## The Golden Thread

(New York: Bantam, 1989)

**Story type:** Fantasy (Magic Conflict)
**Series:** Sorcery Hall
**Major character(s):** Valentine Marsh, Student—High School, Sorceress (apprentice); Bosanka Lonat, Student—Exchange, Sorceress (of another realm)
**Time period(s):** Indeterminate
**Locale(s):** Sorcery Hall, Earth

**Summary:** Valentine Marsh has inherited the family gift of sorcery from her ailing grandmother. At a New Year's Eve party, Valentine attempts to use her novice powers and she and her friends mistakenly summon a girl named Bosanka Lonat from her native realm. Bosanka is a sinister and manipulative girl who poses as a foreign exchange student. She desperately needs to assemble Valentine and her skeptical friends together again in order to conjure the necessary psychic powers for her to return to her native realm.

**Other books you might like:**
Diane Duane, *High Wizardry*, 1989
Tim Powers, *The Anubis Gates*, 1983
   6th Printing 1989
Jane Resh Thomas, *The Princess in the Pigpen*, 1989
Connie Willis, *Light Raid*, 1989
   Science Fiction. Cynthia Felice, co-author
Roger Zelazny, *Today We Choose Faces*, 1973
   re-issue 1989

## 970

### SUZY MCKEE CHARNAS

## *The Kingdom of Kevin Malone*

(New York: Harcourt Brace Jovanovich, 1993)

**Story type:** Fantasy (Alternate World; Young Adult)
**Major character(s):** Kevin Malone, Teenager, Abuse Victim; Amy, Teenager
**Time period(s):** 1990s; Indeterminate
**Locale(s):** New York, New York (Central Park); Fayre Farre, Mythical Place

**Summary:** After Kevin teases Amy, she chases him through Central Park's Willowdell Arch and finds herself with him in Fayre Farre, an imaginary world Kevin dreamed up to escape his abusive father. Although Prince Kevin sees himself as the Promised Champion, a prophecy indicates Amy and her friends must save Kevin's Kingdom.

**Other books you might like:**
Gary L. Blackwood, *Beyond the Door*, 1991
Philip Jose Farmer, *Red Orc's Rage*, 1991
Steven Gould, *Jumper*, 1992
Peni R. Griffin, *Hobkin*, 1992
Betty Levin, *Mercy's Mill*, 1992
Susan Palwick, *Flying in Place*, 1992
Will Shetterly, *Elsewhere*, 1991
Nancy Springer, *The Friendship Song*, 1992

## 971

### ROBERT N. CHARRETTE

## *Choose Your Enemies Carefully*

(New York: Roc, 1990)

**Story type:** Science Fiction (Alternate Universe; Science Fantasy)
**Series:** Secrets of Power
**Major character(s):** Samuel Verner, Outlaw; Dodger, Mutant, Computer Expert (outlaw)
**Time period(s):** 2050s (2051)
**Locale(s):** London, England

**Summary:** When magic returns to Earth, its power calls Sam Verner. As Sam searches for his sister, his quest leads him across the ocean to England where druids rule again. But all is not what it seems and Sam and his new friends are plunged into a maze of intrigue and madness. Only when Sam accepts his destiny as a shaman can he embrace the power he needs. But what waits for him in the final confrontation of technology and flesh is a secret much darker than anything he knew lay waiting in the shadows.

**Other books you might like:**
Emma Bull, *Bone Dance: A Fantasy for Technophiles*, 1991
Randall Garrett, *Too Many Magicians*, 1967
Barbara Hambly, *Dragonsbane*, 1986
Larry Niven, *Dream Park*, 1981
    Steven Barnes, co-author
Walter Jon Williams, *Hardwired*, 1986
Terri Windling, *Borderland*, 1986
    Mark Alan Arnold, co-editor
Terri Windling, *Bordertown*, 1986
    Mark Alan Arnold, co-editor

## 972

### ROBERT N. CHARRETTE

## *Find Your Own Truth*

(New York: Roc, 1991)

**Story type:** Fantasy (Adventure)
**Series:** Secrets of Power
**Major character(s):** Samuel Verner, Shaman; Janice Verner, Monster; Dodger, Mutant, Computer Expert (pecker)
**Time period(s):** 21st century
**Locale(s):** Ayer's Rock, Australia; Seattle, Washington

**Summary:** Sam Verner continues trying to reverse his sister's transformation into a Wendigo by stealing a powerful talisman that allows an unfriendly totem into the Sixth World. Vernor requires the aid of all his friends and immense sacrifice to avoid Spider's webs trapping the whole world. Based on the Shadowrun game.

**Other books you might like:**
Nigel Findley, *2XS*, 1992
William Gibson, *Neuromancer*, 1984
Jonathan Littell, *Bad Voltage*, 1989
David Pringle, *Route 666*, 1990
    editor
Walter Jon Williams, *Hardwired*, 1986

## 973

### ROBERT N. CHARRETTE

## *A King Beneath the Mountain*

(New York: Warner Aspect, 1995)

**Story type:** Fantasy (Urban; Magic Conflict)
**Series:** Prince Among Men
**Major character(s):** John Reddy, Mythical Creature (elf), Adventurer; Quetzal, Immortal; Elizabeth Spae, Researcher (magic), Adventurer
**Time period(s):** 21st century
**Locale(s):** Massachusetts; France

**Summary:** With corporations responding to reemerging magical forces, human and non-human agents plot to control this powerful, ancient magic. An invitation from a mysterious messenger leads John Reddy to accept the call for help from the awakened King Arthur to help stop an evil force that appeared with the magic.

**Other books you might like:**
Dennis Lee Anderson, *Arthur, King*, 1995
Donald Barthelme, *The King*, 1990
Molly Cochran, *The Forever King*, 1992
    Warren Murphy, co-author
Elizabeth Forrest, *Phoenix Fire*, 1992
Simon Hawke, *The Wizard of 4th Street*, 1987
Simon Hawke, *The Wizard of Camelot*, 1993
Michael A. Stackpole, *Once a Hero*, 1994

## 974

### ROBERT N. CHARRETTE

## *A Knight Among Knaves*

(New York: Warner Aspect, 1995)

**Story type:** Fantasy (Urban; Magic Conflict)
**Series:** Prince Among Men

**Major character(s):** John Reddy, Mythical Creature (elf); Bennett, Nobleman, Mythical Creature (elf); Holger Kun, Military Personnel
**Time period(s):** 21st century
**Locale(s):** Providence, Rhode Island; Faery, Mythical Place

**Summary:** Human and inhuman legacies still tear at John Reddy as the Glittering Path attempts to summon another demon. All sides, human, Faery, Corporate, Squatter, ancient, and modern, must work together or everyone dies.

**Other books you might like:**
Emma Bull, *Bone Dance: A Fantasy for Technophiles*, 1991
Charles de Lint, *Svaha*, 1989
Tom Deitz, *Windmaster's Bane*, 1986
Nigel Findley, *2XS*, 1992
Walter Jon Williams, *Voice of the Whirlwind*, 1987

---

### 975
#### ROBERT N. CHARRETTE

## Never Deal with a Dragon
(New York: Roc, 1990)

**Story type:** Science Fiction (Alternate Universe; Science Fantasy)
**Series:** Secrets of Power
**Major character(s):** Samuel Verner, Businessman (corporate researcher/salaryman); Dodger, Mutant, Computer Expert (outlaw)
**Time period(s):** 2050s (2051)
**Locale(s):** Seattle, Washington

**Summary:** In the near future, magic is on the rise and ancient races (orks, elves and dwarves) have re-emerged as humanoform mutants and many now work for the megacorporations.

**Other books you might like:**
Emma Bull, *Bone Dance: A Fantasy for Technophiles*, 1991
Randall Garrett, *Too Many Magicians*, 1967
Barbara Hambly, *Dragonsbane*, 1986
Larry Niven, *Dream Park*, 1981
    Steven Barnes, co-author
Walter Jon Williams, *Hardwired*, 1986
Terri Windling, *Borderland*, 1986
    Mark Alan Arnold, co-editor
Terri Windling, *Bordertown*, 1986
    Mark Alan Arnold, co-editor

---

### 976
#### ROBERT N. CHARRETTE

## Never Trust an Elf
(New York: Roc, 1992)

**Story type:** Fantasy (Urban; Political)
**Series:** Shadowrun
**Major character(s):** Kham, Mythical Creature (orc), Leader (teenage gang)
**Time period(s):** 2050s (2053)
**Locale(s):** Seattle, Washington; Orktown, Fictional City

**Summary:** Kham and his fellow Shadowrunners unexpectedly involve themselves in power struggles when they acquire an elven crystal usable as a conduit for magic forces. Set in the universe of the game, *Shadowrun.*

**Other books you might like:**
Emma Bull, *Bone Dance: A Fantasy for Technophiles*, 1991
Nigel Findley, *2XS*, 1992
K.W. Jeter, *Madlands*, 1991

Christopher Kubasik, *Changeling*, 1992
Will Shetterly, *Elsewhere*, 1991
Jordan K. Weisman, *Into the Shadows*, 1992
    editor
Terri Windling, *Life on the Border*, 1991
    editor

---

### 977
#### ROBERT N. CHARRETTE

## A Prince Among Men
(New York: Warner Aspect, 1994)

**Story type:** Fantasy (Urban; Magic Conflict)
**Series:** Prince Among Men
**Major character(s):** John Reddy, Security Officer; Arthur ''Artos'', Ruler, Hero; Nym, Mythical Creature (elf)
**Time period(s):** 21st century
**Locale(s):** Massachusetts

**Summary:** When supernatural forces utilize powerful elven magic which could transform or destroy the world, John Reddy and Nym bring King Arthur out of stasis to save the human realm.

**Other books you might like:**
Dennis Lee Anderson, *Arthur, King*, 1995
Donald Barthelme, *The King*, 1990
Molly Cochran, *The Forever King*, 1992
    Warren Murphy, co-author
Susan Cooper, *Over Sea, under Stone*, 1966
Simon Hawke, *The Wizard of Camelot*, 1993
Michael A. Stackpole, *Once a Hero*, 1994

---

### 978
#### ROBERT N. CHARRETTE

## Timespell
(New York: HarperPrism, 1996)

**Story type:** Fantasy (Adventure; Magic Conflict)
**Series:** Chronicles of Aelwyn
**Major character(s):** Yan Tanafres, Wizard; Peyto Lennuick, Scholar; Teletha Schonnegon, Military Personnel (airship captain)
**Time period(s):** Indeterminate Past
**Locale(s):** At Sea; Scothandir, Fictional Country

**Summary:** Discouraged and frustrated by his lack of success as an apprentice magician, Yan sets out from his provincial home to seek his fortune in the Imperial Capitol. Pirates, shipwreck, fishers, mercenaries, airship crews, and strange magic mold his trip to destiny.

**Other books you might like:**
Glen Cook, *The Swordbearer*, 1982
Diane Duane, *The Door into Fire*, 1979
Ursula K. Le Guin, *A Wizard of Earthsea*, 1968
Patricia A. McKillip, *The Riddle-Master of Hed*, 1976
Judith Tarr, *Ars Magica*, 1989

---

### 979
#### ROBERT N. CHARRETTE

## Wizard of Bones
(New York: HarperPrism, 1997)

**Story type:** Fantasy (Adventure; Magic Conflict)

**Series:** Chronicles of Aelwyn
**Major character(s):** Yan Tanafres, Wizard; Ser Handrar, Religious, Wizard; Teletha Schonnegon, Mercenary (bodyguard)
**Time period(s):** Indeterminate Past
**Locale(s):** At Sea; Jor Valadrem, Fictional City

**Summary:** Mostly recovered from his servitude to Yellow Eye, the saurian wizard, Yan Tanafres has come no closer to understanding the strange power he unleashed. When the Empire calls him to undertake a dangerous voyage, Tanafres accepts, hoping for answers. However, he finds more questions, traitors and deadly peril to his body and soul.

**Other books you might like:**
Glen Cook, *The Swordbearer*, 1982
Terry Goodkind, *Wizard's First Rule*, 1994
Robert Jordan, *The Eye of the World*, 1990
Caroline Stevermer, *A College of Magics*, 1994
Martha Wells, *The Element of Fire*, 1993

## 980

### CAROL CHASE

### *Hawk's Flight*

(New York: Baen, 1991)

**Story type:** Fantasy (Adventure; Political)
**Major character(s):** Taverik Zandro, Businessman (merchant); Marko Kastazi, Businesswoman (merchant), Heiress—Lost
**Time period(s):** Indeterminate
**Locale(s):** Pakajan Peninsula, Fictional Country

**Summary:** Coming to a fellow merchant's aid, Taverik Zandro does not expect the secrets he uncovers or the political intrigue into which he is subsequently swept.

**Other books you might like:**
Marc Laidlaw, *Neon Lotus*, 1988
Ron Miller, *Palaces and Prisons*, 1991
Ron Miller, *Silk and Steel*, 1992
Terry Pratchett, *Wyrd Sisters*, 1990
Cynthia Voigt, *On Fortune's Wheel*, 1990

## 981

### C.J. CHERRYH

### *Chanur's Legacy*

(New York: DAW, 1992)

**Story type:** Science Fiction (Science Fiction; Political)
**Series:** Chanur
**Major character(s):** Hilfy Chanur, Alien (Han), Spaceship Captain; No'shto-shti-stlen, Alien (Stsho), Diplomat (Ambassador); Vikktakkht, Alien (Kif), Spaceship Captain
**Time period(s):** Indeterminate Future
**Locale(s):** *Chanur's Legacy*, Spaceship; Meetpoint, Space Station; Compact Space, Interstellar Empire/Federation

**Summary:** Hilfy, niece of Pyanfur, Personage of Personages, finds a deal on Meetpoint that, while too good to be true, Hilfy can't refuse. Hilfy encounters increasing difficulty with the commission, to deliver a precious object to an individual. Wherever they travel, *Chanur's Legacy* and her crew become a political focus due to the belief that Hilfy's time on *The Pride of Chanur* left her an agent of Pyanfur. The peace Pyanfur imposed on Compact Space seems at risk.

**Other books you might like:**
David Brin, *The Uplift War*, 1987

Diana G. Gallagher, *The Alien Dark*, 1990
Stephen Goldin, *Jade Darcy and the Zen Pirates*, 1990
Mary Mason, co-author
Stephen Leigh, *Alien Tongue*, 1991
Alis A. Rasmussen, *A Passage of Stars*, 1990
L. Neil Smith, *Their Majesties' Bucketeers*, 1981

## 982

### C.J. CHERRYH

### *Chernevog*

(New York: Del Rey, 1990)

**Story type:** Fantasy (Legend)
**Series:** Rusalka
**Major character(s):** Pyetr Kochevikov, Hero; Sasha Misurov, Wizard, Apprentice; Kavi Chernevog, Wizard
**Time period(s):** Indeterminate Past (Before 988)
**Locale(s):** Vojvoda, Russia (Pre-Christian Russia)

**Summary:** Trying to follow his wife on her mysterious quest, Pyetr Kochevikov and Sasha Misurov accidently release Kavi Chernevog from the spell which had confined him, protecting everyone else. Their further wandering yields soul searching and personal recriminations.

**Other books you might like:**
Kingsley Amis, *The Green Man*, 1969
Jo Clayton, *Drinker of Souls*, 1986
Dan McGirt, *Jason Cosmo*, 1989
Flann O'Brien, *The Third Policeman*, 1967
Christopher Priest, *The Glamour*, 1984

## 983

### C.J. CHERRYH

### *Cloud's Rider*

(New York: Warner Aspect, 1996)

**Story type:** Science Fiction (Psychic Powers; Lost Colony)
**Major character(s):** Danny Fisher, Telepath; Cloud, Animal (nighthorse), Telepath; Brionne Goss, Telepath
**Time period(s):** Indeterminate Future
**Locale(s):** Planet—Imaginary

**Summary:** Escorting the three surviving residents of Tarmin up the mountains in a winter storm, Danny and Cloud guide them to safety at the village of Evergreen. Although a riderless nighthorse has followed them, Danny fears to tell all he knows, especially about the unconscious Brionne whose madness might draw disaster on them again if she wakes. Inside the walls, the villagers see an opportunity to claim Tarmin as salvage, with the three children as pawns or obstacles, while outside something lurks in the Wild.

**Other books you might like:**
Gayle Greeno, *Mind-Speakers' Call*, 1994
Anne McCaffrey, *Dragonsdawn*, 1988
Lisanne Norman, *Turning Point*, 1993
Andre Norton, *Catseye*, 1961
Vernor Vinge, *A Fire upon the Deep*, 1992

## 984

### C.J. CHERRYH

## *Cyteen*

(New York: Popular Library Questar, 1989)

**Story type:** Science Fiction (Hard Science Fiction)
**Major character(s):** Ariane Emory, Scientist, Political Figure; Ari, Clone, Scientist
**Time period(s):** 24th century
**Locale(s):** Cyteen, Planet—Imaginary (Circling Pell's star)

**Summary:** Ariane Emory is the most powerful person on Cyteen, a brilliant scientist, a ruthless politician, a virtual monster. Reseune, the company she controls, creates clones, the workers and soldiers who run the planet. Ariane, however, is getting old and in order to gain a kind of immortality, she clones herself. After Ariane is murdered, her clone, Ari, must take over. Controlled by those who would turn her into another Ariane, she must struggle to become her own person. Three paperback volumes, *The Betrayal*, *The Rebirth*, and *The Vindication* were reprinted in 1989 from the 1988 original one-volume edition.

**Other books you might like:**
Isaac Asimov, *Foundation*, 1951
Isaac Asimov, *Foundation and Empire*, 1952
Isaac Asimov, *Foundation's Edge*, 1982
Isaac Asimov, *Robots and Empire*, 1985
Isaac Asimov, *Second Foundation*, 1953
Bruce Sterling, *Islands in the Net*, 1988
Walter Jon Williams, *Angel Station*, 1989

## 985

### C.J. CHERRYH

## *Downbelow Station*

(New York: DAW Books, 1989)

**Story type:** Science Fiction (Space Opera)
**Series:** Union/Alliance
**Major character(s):** Damon Konstantin, Administrator (Spacestation administrator); Signy Mallory, Spaceship Captain
**Time period(s):** 24th century (2352)
**Locale(s):** Downbelow, Planet—Imaginary; Downbelow, Space Station; *Norway*, Spaceship

**Summary:** This Hugo Award-winning novel, an early entry in Cherryh's Union/Alliance future history series, recounts the complex struggle, both military and political, for Downbelow Station, a key defensive position in the battle between Earth and its rebellious colonies. Originally published in 1981.

**Other books you might like:**
Greg Bear, *Eon*, 1985
Gregory Benford, *Great Sky River*, 1987
Gregory Benford, *Tides of Light*, 1989
Emma Bull, *Falcon*, 1989
Walter Jon Williams, *Angel Station*, 1989

## 986

### C.J. CHERRYH, Editor

## *Endgame*

(New York: DAW, 1991)

**Story type:** Science Fiction (Anthology)
**Series:** Merovingen Nights

**Major character(s):** Altair Jones, Trader (canaler); Tom Mondragon, Revolutionary (former), Refugee
**Time period(s):** Indeterminate Future
**Locale(s):** Merovingen, Fictional Country

**Summary:** All the forces operating in Merovingen reach the crisis point, as those who fancy themselves powerful try to direct the course of events before the Sharrh return and scour the planet. This ''braided'' format novel incorporates seven short stories by Lynn Abbey, Nancy Asire, C.J. Cherryh, Mercedes Lackey, Janet and Chris Morris and Bradley H. Sinor. 15 pages of indexed maps follow the text.

**Other books you might like:**
Robert Asprin, *Thieves' World*, 1979
  editor
Marion Zimmer Bradley, *Sharra's Exile*, 1981
Lois McMaster Bujold, *The Warrior's Apprentice*, 1986
Emma Bull, *Bone Dance: A Fantasy for Technophiles*, 1991
George R.R. Martin, *Jokertown Shuffle*, 1991
  editor
Will Shetterly, *Liavek*, 1985
  Emma Bull, co-editor
S.M. Stirling, *The Cage*, 1989
  Shirley Meier, co-author
Terri Windling, *Borderland*, 1986
  Mark Alan Arnold, co-editor

## 987

### C.J. CHERRYH

## *Faery in Shadow*

(New York: Ballantine Del Rey, 1994)

**Story type:** Fantasy (Adventure)
**Major character(s):** Caith mac Sliabhin, Outlaw; Dubhain, Mythical Creature (pooka); Firinne, Farmer
**Time period(s):** Indeterminate Past
**Locale(s):** Gaugach, Mythical Place (stream); Gleann Fiain, Fictional Country

**Summary:** Doomed for his sins, Caith must travel alone except for his inhuman companion and keeper, Dubhain. Fleeing from danger and their own quarreling, they stumble across a farm tended by an unusual couple and soon find themselves caught up in a web of evil, past sins and Sidhe magic.

**Other books you might like:**
Eleanor Arnason, *The Sword Smith*, 1978
Peter S. Beagle, *The Folk of the Air*, 1986
Emma Bull, *War for the Oaks*, 1987
Julian May, *The Many-Colored Land*, 1981
Evangeline Walton, *The Prince of Annwn*, 1974

## 988

### C.J. CHERRYH

## *Finity's End*

(New York: Warner Aspect, 1997)

**Story type:** Science Fiction (First Contact; Adventure)
**Major character(s):** Fletcher Robert Neihart, Orphan, Teenager; Melody, Alien (Hisa); Elene Quen, Administrator (stationmaster)
**Time period(s):** Indeterminate Future
**Locale(s):** Pell, Planet—Imaginary (Downbelow); *Finity's End*, Spaceship; Pell Station, Space Station (Upabove)

**Summary:** Left on Pell Station during the war between Union and the Merchanters' Alliance, and prevented from returning to *Finity's End*, Fletcher has never fit in. When Melody and Butch, hisa who worked at the station, notice he is sad, Fletcher adopts them as his ''parents.'' When they transfer back to Downbelow, he works hard to overcome his poor record, managing to pass his tests to get sent Downbelow. *Finity's End* returns to Pell, making a deal to get Fletcher back. Unfortunately, Fletcher wants to remain Downbelow with the hisa, but must learn to live on the ship with his relatives to have any hope of getting back.

**Other books you might like:**
Eleanor Arnason, *Ring of Swords*, 1993
David Brin, *Brightness Reef*, 1995
Lois McMaster Bujold, *The Warrior's Apprentice*, 1986
L. Warren Douglas, *A Plague of Change*, 1992
Elizabeth Moon, *Remnant Population*, 1996

---

### 989

#### C.J. CHERRYH

### *Flood Tide*

(New York: DAW, 1990)

**Story type:** Science Fiction (Anthology)
**Series:** Merovingen Nights
**Time period(s):** Indeterminate Future
**Locale(s):** Merovingen, Fictional Country

**Summary:** 11 stories surrounding a murder and political struggles in Merovingen. The texts, overlapping in time, are woven together so that the many authors' works appear in the form of the ''braided novel'' rather than the traditional anthology format. Among the notable authors included in this volume are Lynn Abbey, Nancy Asire, C.J. Cherryh and Mercedes Lackey. This book is the sixth anthology edited by Cherryh, which follows her *Angel with the Sword* (1985).

**Other books you might like:**
George R.R. Martin, *Ace in the Hole*, 1990
George R.R. Martin, *Down and Dirty*, 1988
Will Shetterly, *Liavek*, 1985
    Emma Bull, co-editor
Will Shetterly, *Liavek: Festival Week*, 1990
    Emma Bull, co-editor
Will Shetterly, *Liavek: The Players of Luck*, 1986
    Emma Bull, co-editor
Will Shetterly, *Liavek: Spells of Binding*, 1988
    Emma Bull, co-editor
Will Shetterly, *Liavek: Wizard's Row*, 1987
    Emma Bull, co-editor
Terri Windling, *Borderland*, 1986
    Mark Alan Arnold, co-editor
Terri Windling, *Bordertown*, 1986
    Mark Alan Arnold, co-editor

---

### 990

#### C.J. CHERRYH

### *Foreigner*

(New York: DAW, 1994)

**Story type:** Science Fiction (First Contact; Political)
**Series:** Foreigner Universe
**Major character(s):** Manadgi, Alien (Atevi); Bren Cameron, Linguist, Diplomat; Ilisidi, Alien (Atevi)
**Time period(s):** Indeterminate Future

**Locale(s):** *Phoenix*, Spaceship; Planet—Imaginary (Mospheria Island colony)

**Summary:** When *Phoenix*, a colony ship, arrives at its destination, the crew expects to find a habitable planet previously discovered by robot probes. Unable to find any recognizable stars, the crew searches for the nearest habitable system only to find it already inhabited by intelligent aliens. Unwilling to remain on the station, some of the colonists parachute down to the planet, hoping to construct return craft after setting up a community. The Alien Atevi make contact and agree to interact with one human, allowing humans to stay if they pay with information. Abandoned by *Phoenix*, several hundred years later humans and Atevi must learn to better understand each other and cooperate to keep their independence from the returning ship.

**Other books you might like:**
Eleanor Arnason, *Ring of Swords*, 1993
David Brin, *The Uplift War*, 1987
Gordon R. Dickson, *The Alien Way*, 1965
Diana G. Gallagher, *The Alien Dark*, 1990
Mary Gentle, *Golden Witchbreed*, 1984
Kris Jensen, *Mentor*, 1991
Janet Kagan, *Hellspark*, 1988
Larry Niven, *The Gripping Hand*, 1993
    Jerry Pournelle, co-author
Vernor Vinge, *A Fire upon the Deep*, 1992

---

### 991

#### C.J. CHERRYH

### *Fortress in the Eye of Time*

(New York: HarperPrism, 1995)

**Story type:** Fantasy (Magic Conflict; Political)
**Major character(s):** Mauryl Gestaurien, Wizard; Tristen, Foundling; Cefwyn, Royalty (prince)
**Time period(s):** Indeterminate
**Locale(s):** Ylesuin, Fictional Country; Ynefel, Fictional City; Amefel, Fictional Country

**Summary:** With the Sihhe gone from the land and the war long over, Mauryl shapes a boy and summons a soul to continue the old battle. Not what Mauryl shaped or called, the boy, Tristen, must play a central role in the battle without knowing his past or his fate.

**Other books you might like:**
Glen Cook, *The Black Company*, 1984
Patricia A. McKillip, *The Riddle-Master of Hed*, 1976
Mary Stewart, *The Crystal Cave*, 1970
J.R.R. Tolkien, *The Fellowship of the Ring*, 1954
Joan D. Vinge, *The Snow Queen*, 1980
Paula Volsky, *Illusion*, 1992

---

### 992

#### C.J. CHERRYH

### *Fortress of Eagles*

(New York: HarperPrism, 1998)

**Story type:** Fantasy (Political; Magic Conflict)
**Major character(s):** Cefwyn, Royalty (king); Tristen, Supernatural Being
**Time period(s):** Indeterminate
**Locale(s):** Ylesuin, Fictional Country

**Summary:** When Cefwyn sends Tristen to lead an expedition around Ylesuin, he hopes Tristen will unite Ylesuin. Instead, Cefwyn soon finds noblemen demanding redress and threatening to withdraw their support.

**Other books you might like:**
Glen Cook, *The Black Company*, 1984
Dave Duncan, *Magic Casement*, 1990
Kate Elliott, *King's Dragon*, 1997
J. Gregory Keyes, *The Blackgod*, 1997
J.R.R. Tolkien, *The Fellowship of the Ring*, 1954

---

**993**

**C.J. CHERRYH**

## Fortress of Owls

(New York: Harper, 1998)

**Story type:** Fantasy (Sword and Sorcery)
**Series:** Fortress
**Major character(s):** Mauryl, Wizard, Immortal; Cefwyn, Royalty (king); Tristen, Supernatural Being (homunculus)
**Time period(s):** Indeterminate
**Locale(s):** Amefel, Fictional Country

**Summary:** Tristen helped Cefwyn secure his throne and received the stewardship of a small country as his reward. Now the artificial human must take up his magic sword again to defend his friend's country against invasion from a foreign threat.

**Other books you might like:**
Elizabeth H. Boyer, *The Lord of Chaos*, 1991
Susan Dexter, *The Sword of Calandra*, 1985
Dave Duncan, *The Coming of Wisdom*, 1988
Justin Leiber, *The Sword and the Tower*, 1986
Ann Marston, *Broken Blade*, 1997

---

**994**

**C.J. CHERRYH**

## The Goblin Mirror

(New York: Ballantine Del Rey, 1992)

**Story type:** Fantasy (Magic Conflict; Quest)
**Major character(s):** Tamas of Maggiar, Royalty (prince), Adventurer; Ela, Witch (apprentice), Adventurer; Azdra'ik, Mythical Creature (goblin), Royalty (prince)
**Time period(s):** Indeterminate
**Locale(s):** Maggiar, Mythical Place (kingdom); Over-mountain, Mythical Place

**Summary:** When she survives the goblin attack which kills her mistress, Ela sets out to find and confront the goblin queen utilizing the shard of a powerful magical mirror. Ela meets Tamas whose comrades scattered in a goblin attack on the group who had set out to discover the cause of increasing problems in the kingdom. After Azdra'ik rescues Tamas from ensorcellment, an unexpected alliance forms.

**Other books you might like:**
David Eddings, *Pawn of Prophecy*, 1982
Mary Gentle, *Rats and Gargoyles*, 1991
Barbara Hambly, *Dragonsbane*, 1987
Laurell K. Hamilton, *Nightseer*, 1992
Robert Jordan, *The Eye of the World*, 1989
Elizabeth Moon, *Sheepfarmer's Daughter*, 1988

---

**995**

**C.J. CHERRYH**

## Heavy Time

(New York: Warner Quester, 1991)

**Story type:** Science Fiction (Space Colony; Political)
**Series:** Compact Space
**Major character(s):** Paul Dekker, Pilot, Prospector; Morris Bird, Pilot, Prospector; Ben Pollard, Pilot, Prospector
**Time period(s):** Indeterminate Future
**Locale(s):** Asteroid (Sol's asteroid belt)

**Summary:** Paul Dekker wakes one day with his ship stolen, his partner missing, his memory destroyed and his future gone. The ASTEX mining monopoly, Mama, accuses him of being negligent, crazy and a cold-blooded murderer. Only renegade miners Morris Bird and Ben Pollard can help Dekker learn the truth that somewhere in his mind lies a dark secret that can change the fate of worlds.

**Other books you might like:**
Alan Dean Foster, *Cyber Way*, 1990
Rebecca Ore, *The Illegal Rebirth of Billy the Kid*, 1991
Alis A. Rasmussen, *A Passage of Stars*, 1990
Walter Jon Williams, *Voice of the Whirlwind*, 1987
Roger Zelazny, *Doorways in the Sand*, 1976

---

**996**

**C.J. CHERRYH**

## Hellburner

(New York: Warner, 1992)

**Story type:** Science Fiction (Adventure; Political)
**Series:** Compact Space
**Major character(s):** Ben Pollard, Pilot; Paul Dekker, Pilot; Meg Kady, Pilot
**Time period(s):** 24th century (2320s)
**Locale(s):** Sol II, Space Station

**Summary:** Sent back out to visit Paul, Ben soon realizes that his life will not continue as he had planned. After Meg and Sal appear on Earth II, Ben recognizes his involvement in a conspiracy and political intrigue reaching from Earth to beyond the Belt with the future of humanity in the balance.

**Other books you might like:**
Gordon R. Dickson, *Dorsai!*, 1976
Paula E. Downing, *Flare Star*, 1992
Tara K. Harper, *Lightwing*, 1992
Alis A. Rasmussen, *A Passage of Stars*, 1990
Allen Steele, *Orbital Decay*, 1989
Walter Jon Williams, *Voice of the Whirlwind*, 1987

---

**997**

**C.J. CHERRYH**

## Inheritor

(New York: DAW, 1996)

**Story type:** Science Fiction (Political; First Contact)
**Series:** Foreigner Universe
**Major character(s):** Bren Cameron, Diplomat, Linguist; Ilisidi, Alien (Atevi), Ruler; Jason "Jase" Graham, Spaceman, Engineer
**Time period(s):** Indeterminate Future
**Locale(s):** *Phoenix*, Spaceship (in orbit); Shejidan, Fictional City; Mospheira, Fictional City (island)

**Summary:** A near accident mars the return flight from Bren's successful tour of the new Atevi space facilities. Already in crisis due to immersion in Atevi language, Jase hears of his father's accidental death on the *Phoenix*. Repairs to their borrowed apartment reach completion, leading to the return of the hostile owner, Ilisidi, powerful grandmother of the current ruler and, hopefully, ally in what Bren interprets as warfare.

**Other books you might like:**
Eleanor Arnason, *Ring of Swords*, 1993
Gordon R. Dickson, *The Alien Way*, 1996
Mary Gentle, *Golden Witchbreed*, 1984
Elizabeth Moon, *Remnant Population*, 1996
Larry Niven, *The Gripping Hand*, 1993
    Jerry Pournelle, co-author

### 998

#### C.J. CHERRYH

## *Invader*

(New York: DAW, 1995)

**Story type:** Science Fiction (First Contact; Political)
**Series:** Foreigner Universe
**Major character(s):** Bren Cameron, Linguist, Diplomat; Tabini, Alien (Atevi), Royalty; Deana Hanks, Linguist, Government Official
**Time period(s):** Indeterminate Future
**Locale(s):** Planet—Imaginary (Mospheira Island human colony); *Phoenix*, Spaceship

**Summary:** As human official translator to the Atevi, Bren realizes that the policy determined on Mospheira can lead only to disaster. When the *Phoenix* returns after abandoning the human colony, the government attempts to replace Bren with a human chauvinist successor and to prevent the ship from dealing with the Atevi. Convinced that this course leads to disaster for all, Bren contacts the ship directly as representative of the Atevi. Attempting to destabilize Atevi society, Deana gives them the idea of faster-than-light spaceships, risking the breakdown of relations or even warfare between human and Atevi. Sequel to *Foreigner*.

**Other books you might like:**
David Brin, *Brightness Reef*, 1995
Gordon R. Dickson, *The Alien Way*, 1965
L. Warren Douglas, *Cannon's Orb*, 1994
Diana G. Gallagher, *The Alien Dark*, 1990
Janet Kagan, *Hellspark*, 1988

### 999

#### C.J. CHERRYH

## *Lois & Clark*

(Rocklin, California: Prima Publishing, 1996)

**Story type:** Science Fiction (Adventure)
**Series:** Superman
**Major character(s):** Clark ''Superman'' Kent, Journalist, Alien (Kryptonian); Lois Lane, Journalist, Girlfriend
**Time period(s):** 1990s
**Locale(s):** Metropolis (New York City)

**Summary:** While Superman works to save a village in the Caucasus Mountains from disaster, a bomb devastates a Metropolis hotel near the *Daily Planet*. Lois rushes to help, resulting in her public recognition as a hero. Unfortunately, the subsequent notoriety may prove disastrous for the secret she shares with Clark, and even their relationship.

**Other books you might like:**
Michael Jan Friedman, *Deadly Games*, 1996
M.J. Friedman, *Exile*, 1996
M.J. Friedman, *Heat Wave*, 1996
Martin H. Greenberg, *The Further Adventures of Superman*, 1993
    editor
Elliot S. Maggin, *Superman: Last Son of Krypton*, 1978
Elliot S. Maggin, *Superman: Miracle Monday*, 1981
Roger Stern, *The Death and Life of Superman*, 1993

### 1000

#### C.J. CHERRYH

## *Rider at the Gate*

(New York: Warner Aspect, 1995)

**Story type:** Science Fiction (Psychic Powers; Lost Colony)
**Major character(s):** Danny Fisher, Telepath; Guil Stewart, Telepath; Cloud, Animal (Nighthorse), Telepath
**Time period(s):** Indeterminate Future
**Locale(s):** Planet—Imaginary

**Summary:** A Nighthorse Rider dies under suspicious conditions on the trail. When her lover, Guil Stewart, hears of it, his emotions broadcast through his own Nighthorse to the other horses and riders in town. Forced at gunpoint to leave the walled town, Guil and his stallion, Burn, ride into the winter blizzards, seeking the killer. Danny and the dead woman's kinsmen search for Guil, unaware of an enemy tracking them.

**Other books you might like:**
Gayle Greeno, *Finders-Seekers*, 1993
R.A. MacAvoy, *The Grey Horse*, 1987
Anne McCaffrey, *Dragonflight*, 1968
James H. Schmitz, *The Universe Against Her*, 1964
Tricia Sullivan, *Lethe*, 1995

### 1001

#### C.J. CHERRYH

## *Rimrunners*

(New York: Warner, 1989)

**Story type:** Science Fiction (Adventure)
**Major character(s):** Elizabeth Yeager, Spacewoman; Ramey, Spaceman
**Time period(s):** 24th century
**Locale(s):** *Loki*, Spaceship (The Hinder Stars)

**Summary:** A down and out spacer finds a berth on the starship *Loki* and, despite working hard, finds herself on the bad side of the ship's executive officer. She also discovers that the ship may be involved in illegal activities.

**Other books you might like:**
Larry Niven, *The Mote in God's Eye*, 1974
    Jerry Pournelle, co-author
Larry Niven, *Protector*, 1973
Larry Niven, *Ringworld*, 1970
Walter Jon Williams, *Angel Station*, 1989

## 1002

### C.J. CHERRYH

## *Rusalka*

(New York: Del Rey, 1989)

**Story type:** Fantasy (Legend)
**Series:** Rusalka
**Major character(s):** Pyetr Kochevikov, Hero, Fugitive; Sasha Misurov, Wizard, Apprentice
**Time period(s):** Indeterminate Past (Before 988)
**Locale(s):** Vojvoda, Russia (Pre-Christian Russia)

**Summary:** Accused of killing a wealthy noble, Pyetr and his friend Sasha flee the village and make for Kiev. In an enchanted forest, the two stumble upon Vulamets, a powerful old wizard, who coerces them to assist in his attempts to bring his murdered daughter Eveshka back from the dead. She roams the forest as a ghostly Rusalka, an ill-fated spirit that must prey on living things in order to restore its life, but alas the evil wizard Kavi Chernevog continues to hold her life force in sway.

**Other books you might like:**
Kingsley Amis, *The Green Man*, 1969
Jo Clayton, *Drinker of Souls*,
  Drinker of Souls Trilogy. Bk. 1
Dan McGirt, *Jason Cosmo*, 1989
Flann O'Brien, *The Third Policeman*, 1967
Christopher Priest, *The Glamour*, 1984

## 1003

### C.J. CHERRYH

## *Tripoint*

(New York: Warner Aspect, 1994)

**Story type:** Science Fiction (Family Saga; Adventure)
**Major character(s):** Thomas ''Tom'' Bowe-Hawkins, Spaceman, Prisoner; Marie Hawkins, Spacewoman (cargo master), Parent; Austin Bowe, Spaceship Captain, Parent
**Time period(s):** Indeterminate Future
**Locale(s):** *Sprite*, Spaceship; *Corinthian*, Spaceship; Viking, Space Station (E. Eridani system)

**Summary:** Raised by Marie on the family ship, *Sprite*, Tom never feels accepted as one of the family. When, against orders, Marie decides to check out *Corinthian*, her rapist's ship, Tom decides to again try getting close to her and helping, but instead gets kidnapped by his half-brother. Unfortunately, his mother had threatened Austin that when Tom grew up, she'd have him hurt Austin and everyone close to him, making it difficult for anyone on *Corinthian* to trust him. On *Corinthian* Tom discovers he has the rare ability to stay sane in transit without tranquilizers.

**Other books you might like:**
Stephen Baxter, *Raft*, 1991
James Blish, *A Life for the Stars*, 1962
Lois McMaster Bujold, *Mirror Dance*, 1994
Lois McMaster Bujold, *The Warrior's Apprentice*, 1986
F.M. Busby, *Rissa Kerguelen*, 1977
Alis A. Rasmussen, *A Passage of Stars*, 1990
Vernor Vinge, *A Fire upon the Deep*, 1992

## 1004

### C.J. CHERRYH
### NANCY ASIRE, Co-Author

## *Wizard Spawn*

(New York: Baen, 1989)

**Story type:** Fantasy (Magic Conflict)
**Series:** Sword of Knowledge
**Time period(s):** Indeterminate

**Summary:** A society opposed to the use of magic and weapons is invaded a brutal race. Only a few of the conquered have the ability and will to use magic and weapons to defend their home.

**Other books you might like:**
Marion Zimmer Bradley, *Thendara House*, 1983
Sharon Green, *Lady Blade, Lord Fighter*, 1987
Jennifer Roberson, *Sword-Dancer*, 1986

## 1005

### C.J. CHERRYH

## *Yvgenie*

(New York: Ballantine/Del Rey, 1991)

**Story type:** Fantasy (Legend)
**Series:** Rusalka
**Major character(s):** Pyetr Kochevikov, Hero; Kavi Chernevog, Spirit; Eveshka, Wizard
**Time period(s):** Indeterminate Past
**Locale(s):** Russia (pre-Christian)

**Summary:** Pyetr and Eveshka have a daughter, Ilyana, born a wizard like her mother. After Ilyana is discovered in the arms of Kavi, she is told many disturbing facts about her mother's early life. Eveshka leaves, Ilyana is kidnapped and Pyetr, carrying Eveshka's heart, sets out to save his family.

**Other books you might like:**
Steven Brust, *The Sun, the Moon, and the Stars*, 1987
Charles de Lint, *Jack, the Giant-Killer*, 1987
Pamela Dean, *Tam Lin*, 1991
Alan Garner, *The Weirdstone of Brisingamen*, 1969
Roberto Pazzi, *The Princess and the Dragon*, 1990
  M.J. Fitzgerald, co-author
Angus Wells, *Wrath of Ashar*, 1990
Patricia C. Wrede, *Snow White and Rose Red*, 1989

## 1006

### GEORGE C. CHESBRO

## *Bone*

(New York: Mysterious Press 1990)

**Story type:** Horror (Serial Killer)
**Major character(s):** Bone, Streetperson, Amnesiac (murder suspect); Anne Winchell, Social Worker (Bone's lover)
**Time period(s):** 1980s
**Locale(s):** New York, New York (including underground caverns)

**Summary:** Bone wakes up one morning in the middle of a field, devoid of identity or memory, accused of beheading twenty-eight street people. Aided by Anne, a compassionate social worker, and Zulu, a seven-foot black storyteller, Bone struggles to learn his own identity and the awful truth about the killings—even at the risk of confirming his own guilt.

**Other books you might like:**
John Skipp, *The Light at the End*, 1986
  Craig Spector, co-author

---

## 1007
### GEORGE C. CHESBRO

### *The Fear in Yesterday's Rings*
(New York: Mysterious Press, 1991)

**Story type:** Horror (Werewolf Story)
**Series:** Mongo
**Major character(s):** Robert "Mongo" Frederickson, Detective—
  Private; Harper Rhys-Whitney, Entertainer (circus performer);
  Phil Statler, Businessman (former circus owner)
**Time period(s):** 1990s (1991)
**Locale(s):** Nebraska; Midwest

**Summary:** Mongo, a circus dwarf turned criminologist, is thwarted in
his efforts to return the Statler Brothers Circus to its ousted owner
when the new owners refuse to sell. It's not long before Mongo
suspects that their reticence is somehow related to a string of vicious
deaths that has followed the circus across the country and been
attributed to a werewolf.

**Other books you might like:**
D.J. Donaldson, *Blood on the Bayou*, 1991
Whitley Strieber, *The Wolfen*, 1978
Les Whitten, *Moon of the Wolf*, 1967

---

## 1008
### DEBORAH CHESTER

### *Realm of Light*
(New York: Ace, 1997)

**Story type:** Fantasy (Political; Magic Conflict)
**Series:** Shadows
**Major character(s):** Caelan E'non, Gladiator, Psychic; Elandra
  Albain, Ruler (empress)
**Time period(s):** Indeterminate Past
**Locale(s):** Imperia, Fictional City; Trav, Fictional Country

**Summary:** As the 1000-year Emperor fails, his pact with the Dark
God Beloth is nearly expired, and his empire fails him. Caught
between traitors, barbarians and damnation, but separated by oaths
and marriage, Caelan and Elandra must join together to save the
world, however impossible that seems.

**Other books you might like:**
M.A.R. Barker, *Man of Gold*, 1984
Brian Daley, *The Doomfarers of Coramonde*, 1977
Barbara Hambly, *The Time of the Dark*, 1982
Robin Hobb, *Assassin's Apprentice*, 1995
Michael Scott Rohan, *The Anvil of Ice*, 1986

---

## 1009
### DEBORAH CHESTER

### *Reign of Shadows*
(New York: Ace, 1996)

**Story type:** Fantasy (Political; Magic Conflict)
**Series:** Shadows

**Major character(s):** Caelan E'non, Gladiator, Psychic; Elandra
  Albain, Noblewoman, Bastard Daughter; Kostimon, Ruler (em-
  peror)
**Time period(s):** Indeterminate Past
**Locale(s):** Trav, Fictional Country; Imperia, Fictional City

**Summary:** Nearly a millennium after Emperor Kostimon deals for a
thousand years of life with the Dark God, Beloth, his empire collapses, undermined internally and externally. In the chaos, Caelan
and Elandra find their destinies.

**Other books you might like:**
Scott Baker, *Drink the Fire From the Flames*, 1987
Glen Cook, *The Black Company*, 1984
Terry Goodkind, *Wizard's First Rule*, 1994
Barbara Hambly, *The Time of the Dark*, 1982
Martha Wells, *The Element of Fire*, 1993

---

## 1010
### DEBORAH CHESTER

### *Shadow War*
(New York: Ace, 1997)

**Story type:** Fantasy (Political; Magic Conflict)
**Series:** Shadows
**Major character(s):** Caelan E'non, Military Personnel, Psychic;
  Elandra Albain, Ruler (empress); Sien, Religious, Wizard
**Time period(s):** Indeterminate Past
**Locale(s):** Imperia, Fictional City

**Summary:** The Emperor Kostimon wishes to escape his fate, but
forces inside and outside his empire plot against him. Meanwhile,
Caelan rises from gladiator to soldier, then Empress' Guard, and
Elandra becomes Empress. All three must find their destinies if
anything of the Empire will survive. Second in a series.

**Other books you might like:**
Scott Baker, *Drink the Fire From the Flames*, 1987
Glen Cook, *The Black Company*, 1984
Robert Jordan, *The Eye of the World*, 1990
Guy Gavriel Kay, *The Summer Tree*, 1985
Peg Kerr, *Emerald House Rising*, 1997
Michael Scott Rohan, *The Anvil of Ice*, 1986

---

## 1011
### GRACE CHETWIN

### *Collidescope*
(New York: Bradbury Press, 1990)

**Story type:** Science Fiction (Time Travel)
**Major character(s):** Hahn, Spaceman; Frankie, Teenager; Sky-fire-
  trail, Indian
**Time period(s):** 1990s; 15th century
**Locale(s):** New York, New York

**Summary:** Hahn, a time-traveling agent for the Intergalactic Society
for Planetary Conservation, is bushwacked as his spaceship nears the
planet Earth. Time jumping into the past in an attempt to escape, he
accidentally draws Frankie, a twentieth-century teenager who has
earned her brown belt in karate, and Sky-fire-trail, a pre-colonial
Delaware Indian, into an exciting adventure in space and time.

**Other books you might like:**
Helen Cresswell, *Moondial*, 1987
Alan Garner, *The Owl Service*, 1967
Alan Garner, *Red Shift*, 1973
Andre Norton, *The Defiant Agents*, 1962

Andre Norton, *Operation Time Search*, 1967
Andre Norton, *Quest Crosstime*, 1965

## 1012
### GRACE CHETWIN

## *Friends in Time*
(New York: Bradbury Press, 1992)

**Story type:** Fantasy (Time Travel; Young Adult)
**Major character(s):** Emma Gibson, Time Traveler, Child; Abigail Porterhouse Bentley, Time Traveler, Child
**Time period(s):** 1990s (1995); 1840s (1846)
**Locale(s):** Middletown, New York

**Summary:** In the abandoned Bentley mansion Emma discovers Abigail whose taking of a medicine man's doll precipitated a trip 150 years into the future. After Emma befriends Abigail and plans to show her modern times, Abigail wishes both girls back to Abigail's time where Abigail decides to strand Emma. The girls must resolve their feelings and work together to return Emma to her own time.

**Other books you might like:**
Pam Conrad, *Stonewords: A Ghost Story*, 1990
Gilbert B. Cross, *A Witch Across Time*, 1990
Enid Richemont, *The Time Tree*, 1990
Robert Silverberg, *Letters From Atlantis*, 1990
Vivian Vande Velde, *A Well-Timed Enchantment*, 1990

## 1013
### R. CHETWYND-HAYES

## *The Vampire Stories of R. Chetwynd-Hayes*
(Minneapolis: Fedogan & Bremer, 1997)

**Story type:** Horror (Collection)

**Summary:** Fifteen stories spanning three decades of the career of a writer known for his traditional ghost stories and blends of humor and horror. Selections include "My Mother Married a Vampire," an amusing tale of a young boy's adjustment to his father's vampire lifestyle; "Something on Which to Suck," which features a vitality-draining shadow; "The Labyrinth," which concerns a vampire house; and "Keep the Gaslight Burning," a period story. Brian Lumley contributes an introduction and Stephen Jones and Jo Fletcher add an afterword.

**Other books you might like:**
Richard Dalby, *Dracula's Brood*, 1987
    editoe
Charles L. Grant, *The Soft Whisper of the Dead*, 1982
Martin H. Greenberg, *Dracula: Prince of Darkness*, 1992
    editor
Barbara Hambly, *Those Who Hunt the Night*, 1987
Stephen Jones, *The Mammoth Book of Vampires*, 1992
    editor

## 1014
### ROB CHILSON

## *Black as Blood*
(New York: Baen, 1998)

**Story type:** Fantasy (Humor)

**Major character(s):** Bernie McKay, Businessman; Albert Smithers, Reanimated Dead; Paul Gibson, Businessman
**Time period(s):** Indeterminate
**Locale(s):** United States

**Summary:** When Uncle Albert dies, Bernie McKay expects to inherit his business interests. Unfortunately, the corpse opens its eyes during the wake and accuses Bernie of theft. Despite exorcisms, restraining orders, and other ploys, Bernie can't get his uncle to return to the grave, nor can he figure out why the dead man is so angry.

**Other books you might like:**
Piers Anthony, *Zombie Lover*, 1998
James P. Blaylock, *Homunculus*, 1986
C. Dale Brittain, *The Wood Nymph and the Cranky Saint*, 1993
Esther Friesner, *Demon Blues*, 1989
Christie Golden, *Dance of the Dead*, 1992

## 1015
### ROB CHILSON

## *Men Like Rats*
(New York: Popular Library Questar, 1989)

**Story type:** Science Fiction (Invasion of Earth)
**Major character(s):** Richer the Quick, Scavenger, Hero; Loy Little, Scavenger
**Time period(s):** Indeterminate Future
**Locale(s):** Earth

**Summary:** Alien invaders have taken over the Earth, turning human beings into little more than vermin hiding in cracks and crevasses. Scavenging desperately for food, doing battle with alien life forms and Earth-born mutants, humanity gradually loses ground to the invaders until one brave man begins to organize the resistance.

**Other books you might like:**
Gregory Benford, *Big Sky River*, 1987
Gregory Benford, *Tides of Light*, 1989
Thomas M. Disch, *The Genocides*, 1965
Thomas M. Disch, *Mankind under the Leash*, 1966
William Tenn, *Of Men and Monsters*, 1968
Jack Vance, *The Dragon Masters*, 1963

## 1016
### RICHARD CHIZMAR

## *Monsters and Other Stories*
(Burton, Michigan: Subterranean Press, 1998)

**Story type:** Horror (Collection)

**Summary:** This chapbook of six stories straddles the boundary between crime and horror. Included is the superior "The Man with X-Ray Eyes," a tale of psychological horror whose narrator is convinced he can detect extraterrestrials masquerading as people. A number of the best stories explore the dynamics of troubled father-son relationships, including "The Silence of Sorrow," "Heroes" and "Like Father, Like Son."

**Other books you might like:**
Ed Gorman, *Cages*, 1995
Brian Hodge, *Falling Idols*, 1998
Barry Hoffman, *Firefly. . .Burning Bright*, 1996
Norman Partridge, *Bad Intentions*, 1996
David B. Silva, *The Night in Fog*, 1998

## 1017

**RICHARD T. CHIZMAR**, Editor

### The Best of Cemetery Dance

(Abingdon, Maryland: Cemetery Dance Publications, 1998)

**Story type:** Horror (Anthology)

**Summary:** This omnibus anthology of 59 stories and one interview (with Dean R. Koontz) was culled from the first 25 issues of the semi-professional *Cemetery Dance*, the leading magazine of contemporary horror fiction. Included are Stephen King's "Chattery Teeth," about a dime store novelty with a murderous mind of its own, Jack Ketchum's contemorary noir tale "The Rifle," and Graham Masterton's grisly revenge story "Pig's Dinner." In addition to the generous selection of supernatural and physical horror, the anthology includes a significant amount of "dark suspense," or crime fiction with a horrific edge, including Norm Partridge's southwest Gothic "Johnny Halloween," William F. Nolan's psychological horror story "Fyodor's Law," and Ed Gorman's "Layover."

**Other books you might like:**
Charles L. Grant, *The Best of Shadows*, 1988
Jessica Horsting, *Midnight Graffiti*, 1992
  James Van Hise, co-editor
Robert Morrish, *Quick Chills II*, 1992
  Peter Enfantino, co-editor
Stuart David Schiff, *The Best of Whispers*, 1994
  editor
David B. Silva, *The Definitive Best of the Horror Show*, 1992
  editor

## 1018

**RICHARD T. CHIZMAR**, Editor

### Chillers

(Baltimore, Maryland: CD Publications)

**Story type:** Horror (Anthology)

**Summary:** The four authors represented in this anthology of dark suspense fiction each contribute 20,000 words of writing in different forms. Rex Miller's short novel "Kowloon" resurrects his misanthropic sociopath Chaingang Bunkowski by way of Chaingang's son, who still takes after his father despite his adoption by dad's killer, police detective Jack Eichord. Ardath Mayhar also has a short novel, "Winter-Stalk," in which a crusader against corruption in government turns vengeful when the forces he is battling murder his wife. Nancy Collins is on hand with four stories that deal variously with rock 'n' roll, circus freaks, southern racism, and lack of a good health care plan. Chet Williamson's dynamic duo includes the psychological horror story "Dusty Death" and a study of disintegrating social dynamics, "Watching the Burning." Joe Lansdale supplies an introduction.

**Other books you might like:**
Robert Bloch, *Monsters in Our Midst*, 1993
  editor
Robert Bloch, *Psycho-Paths*, 1991
  editor
Joe R. Lansdale, *Dark at Heart*, 1992
  Karen Lansdale, co-editor

## 1019

**RICHARD T. CHIZMAR**, Editor

### Cold Blood

(Shingletown, California: Mark Ziesing, 1991)

**Story type:** Horror (Anthology)

**Summary:** Twenty-five tales of dark suspense, in which horror occurs in non-supernatural scenarios. Among the selections are John Shirley's "Jody and Annie on TV," about a thrill-killing teenage couple; F. Paul Wilson's "Home Repairs," starring his equalizer hero Repairman Jack; Richard Laymon's "Saving Grace," about two boys who save a woman from a serial killer and its peculiar aftermath; and a chapter from Ramsey Campbell's "comic" serial-killer novel, *The Count of Eleven*.

**Other books you might like:**
Robert Bloch, *Psycho-Paths*, 1991
  Martin H. Greenberg, co-editor
Ed Gorman, *Stalkers*, 1989
  Martin H. Greenberg, co-editor
Alfred Hitchcock, *Alfred Hitchcock Presents: Stories Not for the Nervous*, 1965
  editor
Joan Kahn, *Hanging by a Thread*, 1969

## 1020

**RICHARD T. CHIZMAR**, Editor

### The Earth Strikes Back

(Shingletown, California: Mark Ziesing, 1994)

**Story type:** Horror (Anthology; Nature in Revolt)

**Summary:** The 20 stories collected here all spin ecological horror scenarios out of the irresponsibility of man toward his environment. Included are Dan Simmons' "My Copsa Micas," which imagines the world as an organism trying to dispose of man like a virus; Thomas Tessier's "I Remember Me (But I'm Not Sure about You)," about a future in which a virus has destroyed short-term memory and identity; Poppy Brite's "Toxi Wastrels," a variation on the theme of Edgar Allan Poe's "Fall of the House of Usher," about the degeneration of a family that owns a chemical industry in the Louisiana swamps; Gary A. Braunbeck's "The Dreaded Hobblobs," about a mutant who represents the future evolution of humanity in a toxically despoiled world; and Nancy Collins' "Cancer Alley," about the revenge of a polluted town against the businessman who destroyed it. The book also includes stories by Norman Partridge, Hugh Cave, Ed Gorman, Richard Laymon, Chelsea Quinn Yarbro, Ric Hautala, and Thomas Monteleone.

**Other books you might like:**
John Skipp, *The Bridge: A Horror Story*, 1991
  Craig Spector, co-author

## 1021

**RICHARD T. CHIZMAR**

### Midnight Promises

(Springfield, Pennsylvania: Gauntlet Publications, 1996)

**Story type:** Horror (Collection)

**Summary:** The 17 stories collected here by the editor of the horror magazine, *Cemetery Dance*, freely blend the genres of supernatural horror and dark suspense. The title story and "Heroes" use horrific elements to explore the emotional impact of terminal illness. "The Season of Giving" (written with Norman Partridge) and "The Silence of Sorrow" both probe the theme of child abuse. "The Sinner King" refurbishes the theme of the Holy Grail for a contemporary tale set in the Canadian wilderness. In "Grand Finale" a man discovers that the pick-ups he secretly videotapes during lovemaking play out sequences on film in which they try to kill him. Ed Gorman supplies an introduction and Ray Garton an afterword to this first book.

**Other books you might like:**
Scott Edelman, *Suicide Art*, 1992
Ray Garton, *Pieces of Hate*, 1996
Ed Gorman, *Cages*, 1995
Norman Partridge, *Bad Intentions*, 1996
Andrew Vachss, *A Flash of White*, 1993

## 1022

### RICHARD T. CHIZMAR, Editor

## Screamplays

(New York: Del Ray, 1997)

**Story type:** Horror (Anthology)

**Summary:** Seven previously unpublished screenplays of horror and dark suspense, several adapted from works of fiction and several produced for film and television. Selections include Stephen King's "General," about a family cat that protects a young girl from a nocturnal supernatural predator in her bedroom; Richard Matheson's "The Legend of Hell Huse," adapted from his 1971 novel and produced as the movie of the same name; Joe R. Lansdale's "Dead in the West," a zombie western; Richard Laymon's "The Hunted," about a woman stalked by a serial killer and his bounty hunter; Harlan Ellison's "Moonlighting," a biter-bit tale adapted from his short crime story "Ormond Always Pays His Bills"; and Harlan Ellison's "Killing Bernstein" and Ed Gorman's "Track Down." Introduction by Dean R. Koontz.

**Other books you might like:**
Clive Barker, *Forms of Heaven*, 1996
Clive Barker, *Incarnations*, 1995
Ray Bradbury, *Ray Bradbury on Stage: A Chrestomathy of His Plays*, 1991
John Burke, *The Hammer Horror Omnibus*, 1966
John Burke, *The Second Hammer Horror Film Omnibus*, 1967
Marvin Kaye, *Thirteen Plays of Ghosts and the Supernatural*, 1990
Nigel Kneale, *The Year of the Sex Olympics and Other TV Plays*, 1976
Nigel Kneale, *The Quatermass Experiment*, 1959
Arch Oboler, *The Oboler Omnibus*, 1945

## 1023

### BRYAN CHOLFIN, Editor

## The Best of Crank!

(New York: Tor, 1998)

**Story type:** Science Fiction (Anthology)

**Summary:** This anthology contains an introductory essay on the state of science fiction and fantasy publishing, and 17 stories that appeared in the magazine *Crank!*. Authors include Brian Aldiss, A.A. Attanasio, David R. Bunch, Michael Bishop, A.M. Dellamonica, Robert Devereaux, Eliot Fintushel, Karen Joy Fowler, Gwyneth Jones, R.A. Lafferty, Ursula K. Le Guin, Jonathan Lethem (three

stories, including one with Carter Scholz), Rob McCleary, Lisa Tuttle, and Gene Wolfe.

**Other books you might like:**
Paul Di Filippo, *Fractal Paisleys*, 1997
Harlan Ellison, *Again, Dangerous Visions*, 1972
    editor
Harlan Ellison, *Dangerous Visions*, 1967
    editor
Jonathan Lethem, *The Wall of the Sky, the Wall of the Eye*, 1996
Kim Mohan, *Amazing Stories: The Anthology*, 1995
    editor
David Pringle, *The Best of Interzone*, 1997
    editor
Kristine Kathryn Rusch, *The Best of Pulphouse: The Hardback Magazine*, 1991
    editor

## 1024

### JAMES C. CHRISTENSEN
### RENWICK ST. JAMES, Co-Author
### ALAN DEAN FOSTER, Co-Author

## Voyage of the Basset

(New York: Workman Artisan, 1996)

**Story type:** Fantasy (Adventure; Young Adult)
**Major character(s):** Cassandra Aisling, Child, Adventurer; Algernon Aisling, Professor, Adventurer; Miranda Aisling, Teenager, Adventurer
**Time period(s):** 1850s
**Locale(s):** *H.M.S. Basset*, At Sea

**Summary:** Professor Aisling and his daughters set sail on the magical *H.M.S. Basset*, searching for the subjects of ancient legends. Presented as a lavishly illustrated journal of a voyage of discovery.

**Other books you might like:**
Betty Ballantine, *The Secret Oceans*, 1994
Graeme Base, *The Discovery of Dragons*, 1996
Michael Green, *Quest: In Search of the Dragontooth*, 1994
James Gurney, *Dinotopia*, 1992
James Gurney, *The World Beneath*, 1995

## 1025

### DEBORAH CHRISTIAN

## Kar Kalim

(New York: Torm, 1997)

**Story type:** Fantasy (Magic Conflict; Adventure)
**Major character(s):** Inya, Recluse, Sorceress; Murl "Kar Kalim" Amrey, Magician, Warrior; Lesseth, Mythical Creature (elemental)
**Time period(s):** Indeterminate
**Locale(s):** Astareth, Planet—Imaginary; Drakmil, Mythical Place; Styreia, Planet—Imaginary

**Summary:** Inya, the Midnight Lady, trains Murl Amrey and sends him into the alternate dimension of Styreia to obtain a wizard-stone. Instead he uses one to become Kar Kalim, conqueror of Styreia, and would be ruler of Astareth as well. Holding Inya and her servants hostage, his egomania and sadism drive Inya and Lesseth to attempt murder. Exiled to Styreia, Inya learns the only way to destroy him may destroy everyone and everything in the area.

**Other books you might like:**
Joy Chant, *The Grey Mane of Morning*, 1980

C.J. Cherryh, *Gate of Ivrel*, 1976
Harry Harrison, *Deathworld 3*, 1968
John Maddox Roberts, *The Steel Kings*, 1993
Harry Turtledove, *The Legion of Videssos*, 1987
Sydney J. Van Scyoc, *Bluesong*, 1983
Jack Vance, *The Dirdir*, 1969
Nicholas Yermakov, *Fall into Darkness*, 1982

## 1026

### DEBORAH CHRISTIAN

## *Mainline*

(New York: Tor, 1996)

**Story type:** Science Fiction (Alternate Universe; Psychic Powers)
**Major character(s):** Reva, Genetically Altered Being, Criminal (assassin); Javobo, Alien, Bounty Hunter; Vask Kastlin, Psychic (esper), Police Officer (Imperial Security)
**Time period(s):** Indeterminate Future
**Locale(s):** Selmun III/R'debh, Planet—Imaginary

**Summary:** Reva discovers her talent by inadvertently moving through the Lines of the Multiverse, forever losing her home, family, and friends. She takes off on her own as soon as she turns 16, living alone and moving through the Lines to avoid getting caught. Unfortunately, she permits herself to make some friends, trapping her on her current Mainline, unable to disappear while taking care of her very dangerous business. First novel.

**Other books you might like:**
Geary Gravel, *A Key for the Nonesuch*, 1990
James P. Hogan, *Paths to Otherwhere*, 1996
Michaela Roessner, *Vanishing Point*, 1993
Deborah Wheeler, *Northlight*, 1995
George Zebrowski, *Stranger Suns*, 1991

## 1027

### DEBORAH CHURCHMAN

## *Cross a Dark Bridge*

(Rockville, Maryland: Ariadne, 1996)

**Story type:** Horror (Mystery)
**Major character(s):** Nathan Deeters, Store Owner; Gilead Grason, Clerk (Nathan's wife); Missy Grason, Twin (Gilead's)
**Time period(s):** 1990s (1996)
**Locale(s):** Cambridge, Maryland

**Summary:** When Nathan Deeters marries shy Gilead Grason, he inherits her eccentric itinerant family. As Gilead's mood progresses from shy reserve to near catatonia in her relationship with her husband, Nathan begins to suspect that there is a dark secret behind all of the Grasons' peculiarities, and that it may be linked to the sudden death of Gilead's father, which first put the family on the road. This is the author's first novel.

**Other books you might like:**
Katherine Dunn, *Geek Love*, 1989
Lewis Gannett, *The Living One*, 1993
Stella Gibbons, *Cold Comfort Farm*, 1932
Ian McEwan, *The Cement Garden*, 1978
Gus Weill, *Flesh*, 1991

## 1028

### SCOTT CIENCIN

## *Ancient Games*

(New York: AvoNova, 1997)

**Story type:** Fantasy (Religious; Magic Conflict)
**Series:** Elven Ways
**Major character(s):** Tom Keeper, Artist, Religious, Magician; Mithra, Angel; Kayrlis, Entertainer, Teenager
**Time period(s):** Indeterminate (equivalent to 1853 and 1863)
**Locale(s):** Genesis, Fictional City; City of the Abyss, Fictional City; Alternate Earth

**Summary:** Tom Keeper survives terrible things and gains strange powers, but his worst trials still wait. Forces war in what would be Heaven, while Tom's path leads to Hell. Despite the plans various factions have for him, Tom has power, courage and the support of his friends and allies, and may find the best course of action for Earth, not Heaven. Second in series.

**Other books you might like:**
Jack Dann, *Angels!*, 1995
  Gardner Dozois, co-editor
Philip Pullman, *The Golden Compass*, 1996
Michael Scott Rohan, *The Anvil of Ice*, 1986
Nancy Springer, *Metal Angel*, 1994
Roger Zelazny, *Lord of Light*, 1967

## 1029

### SCOTT CIENCIN

## *The Lotus and the Rose*

(New York: Warner Questar, 1993)

**Story type:** Fantasy (Political; Quest)
**Major character(s):** Trevelyan Arayncourt, Businessman (merchant prince)
**Time period(s):** Indeterminate
**Locale(s):** Autumn, Planet—Imaginary

**Summary:** As Trevelyan Arayncourt gains mastery over the wolves, an evil tyrant seeks to overwhelm the country. To eliminate the threat of the deadly hordes and lethal magic, Trevelyan must sacrifice the life of his lost love.

**Other books you might like:**
Carol Chase, *Hawk's Flight*, 1991
David Eddings, *Pawn of Prophecy*, 1982
Barbara Hambly, *The Ladies of Mandrigyn*, 1984
Mary H. Herbert, *Valorian*, 1993
Mercedes Lackey, *Arrows of the Queen*, 1987

## 1030

### SCOTT CIENCIN

## *Night of Glory*

(New York: Avon Eos, 1998)

**Story type:** Fantasy (Magic Conflict)
**Series:** Elven Ways
**Major character(s):** Tom Keeper, Artist, Magician; Kayrlis, Adventurer
**Time period(s):** Indeterminate
**Locale(s):** Genesis Settlement, Fictional City

**Summary:** On an Earth dominated by a race with supernatural powers, humankind battles to regain its homeland. An artist must put aside his tools and become the savior of his people when a godlike creature unleashes a plague of madness.

**Other books you might like:**
Lynn Abbey, *The Wooden Sword*, 1991
Mayer Alan Brenner, *Spell of Apocalypse*, 1994
Steven Brust, *Orca*, 1996
Sheri S. Tepper, *Necromancer Nine*, 1983
Paula Volsky, *The Sorcerer's Lady*, 1986

## 1031
### SCOTT CIENCIN

## *Parliament of Blood*
(New York: Zebra, 1992)

**Story type:** Horror (Vampire Story)
**Major character(s):** Danielle "Dani" Walthers, Doctor, Vampire (half-vampire); Samantha "Sam" Walthers, Detective—Private (Danielle's mother), Parent; Devin Tyler, Vampire
**Time period(s):** 1990s (1992)
**Locale(s):** Isleta, New Mexico; Las Vegas, Nevada

**Summary:** In this concluding book of the trilogy begun with *The Vampire Odyssey* (1992) and *The Wildlings* (1992), half-vampire Dani Walthers tries to work incognito as an air ambulance medic and keep the vengeful vampire Parliament, of which she has run afoul, away from herself and her pregnant adoptive mother, private eye Sam Walthers. But when her cover is blown, Dani flees with Sam to Las Vegas, a hotbed of vampire activity, where she is forced to make her final choice between the vampire and mortal sides of her nature.

**Other books you might like:**
Peter Atkins, *Morningstar*, 1992
Poppy Z. Brite, *Lost Souls*, 1992

## 1032
### SCOTT CIENCIN

## *The Vampire Odyssey*
(New York: Zebra, 1992)

**Story type:** Horror (Vampire Story)
**Major character(s):** Danielle "Dani" Walthers, Teenager, Student, Vampire (half-vampire); Samantha "Sam" Walthers, Detective—Private, Parent (Danielle's adoptive mother); Bill Yoshino, Vampire
**Time period(s):** 1990s (1992)
**Locale(s):** Beverly Hills, California

**Summary:** In this first book of a trilogy, Sam Walthers struggles to save her adoptive daughter Danielle when the two discover that Danielle, who was born half-vampire, has been charged with the task of making her first kill in order to join the Parliament of vampires.

**Other books you might like:**
Poppy Z. Brite, *Lost Souls*, 1992
Leigh Clark, *Blood Sabbath*, 1991
Richie Tankersley Cusick, *Buffy the Vampire Slayer*, 1992
John Skipp, *Fright Night*, 1986
    Craig Spector, co-author

## 1033
### SCOTT CIENCIN

## *The Ways of Magic*
(New York: AvoNova, 1996)

**Story type:** Fantasy (Young Adult; Religious)
**Series:** Elven Ways
**Major character(s):** Travest Mulvihill, Tailor; Tom Keeper, Teenager, Artist, Magician; Aitan Anzelm, Angel
**Time period(s):** Indeterminate
**Locale(s):** Earth

**Summary:** The angels bring "salvation" to mankind and, in the process, change the way the world runs. A talented artist, Tom must hide his art because all artists must belong to the artists' academy. When Aitan comes to Tom's father's inn and discovers Tom's talents, Aitan asks Tom to join him so that he can help Tom develop his skill.

**Other books you might like:**
Jo Clayton, *Drum Warning*, 1996
Susan Cooper, *The Dark Is Rising*, 1973
Madeleine L'Engle, *An Acceptable Time*, 1989
Holly Lisle, *Minerva Wakes*, 1994

## 1034
### SCOTT CIENCIN

## *The Wildlings*
(New York: Zebra, 1992)

**Story type:** Horror (Vampire Story)
**Major character(s):** Danielle "Dani" Walthers, Teenager, Student (medical student), Vampire (half-vampire); Samantha "Sam" Walthers, Detective—Private, Parent (Danielle's adoptive mother); Marissa Tomley, Vampire
**Time period(s):** 1990s (1992)
**Locale(s):** Beverly Hills, California

**Summary:** In this sequel to *The Vampire Odyssey*, half-vampire Danielle Walthers openly repudiates the demands for blood sacrifice of the Parliament of vampires, and is branded a "wilding," a vampire who kills other vampires and thus must be destroyed.

**Other books you might like:**
Poppy Z. Brite, *Lost Souls*, 1992
Richie Tankersley Cusick, *Buffy the Vampire Slayer*, 1992
John Skipp, *Fright Night*, 1986
    Craig Spector, co-author

## 1035
### SCOTT CIENCIN

## *The Wolves of Autumn*
(New York: Warner Quester, 1992)

**Story type:** Fantasy (Quest)
**Major character(s):** Trevelyan Arayncourt, Businessman (merchant prince); Shantow, Warrior; Ariodne, Witch
**Time period(s):** Indeterminate
**Locale(s):** Autumn, Planet—Imaginary

**Summary:** The wolves, masters of mankind on Autumn, choose Trevelyan to discover a way of defeating the Hollow, monsters born to women but lacking souls.

**Other books you might like:**
Don Callander, *Pyromancer*, 1992
Stephen R. Donaldson, *Lord Foul's Bane*, 1977
Mary Gentle, *Rats and Gargoyles*, 1991
Laurie J. Marks, *The Moonbane Mage*, 1990
Patricia A. McKillip, *The Sorceress and the Cygnet*, 1991

**1036**

JOSEPH A. CITRO

## Dark Twilight

(New York: Warner, 1990)

**Story type:** Horror (Small Town Horror; Ancient Evil Unleashed)
**Major character(s):** Harrison Allen, Businessman, Unemployed; Nancy Wells, Teacher; Cliff Ransom, Worker
**Time period(s):** 1990s
**Locale(s):** Friar's Island, Vermont

**Summary:** Unemployed and alone, Harrison Allen returns after 15 years to an island off northwestern Vermont in search of a monster and a new start for himself. Intending to track down the legendary monster in nearby Lake Champlain, Harrison doesn't bargain for the other mysteries he must face—for the island is a gateway to another dimension of reality, and in his home there is Something in the Attic. His only helpmate in confronting the unknown is lonely schoolteacher Nancy Wells, lust object of local degenerate Cliff Ransom.

**Other books you might like:**
Gregg Almquist, *Beast Rising*, 1987
Steve Rasnic Tem, *Excavation*, 1987

**1037**

JOSEPH A. CITRO

## Deus-X: A Novel of Spiritual Terror

(Sparta, New Jersey: Twilight, 1994)

**Story type:** Horror (Apocalyptic Horror)
**Major character(s):** Jeff Chandler, Government Official; Karen Bradley, Doctor (psychiatrist); William T. Sullivan, Religious (priest)
**Time period(s):** 1990s (1993)
**Locale(s):** Hobston, Vermont

**Summary:** In the guise of divine supernatural emissaries, vicious beings from an alternate dimension open a portal into our own and begin wreaking havoc, forcing a small band of human beings to thwart them and save the world.

**Other books you might like:**
Jack Finney, *The Body Snatchers*, 1955
Stephen King, *The Tommyknockers*, 1987
Robert R. McCammon, *Stinger*, 1988
Whitley Strieber, *The Forbidden Zone*, 1993

**1038**

JOSEPH A. CITRO

## Shadow Child

(Hanover, New Hampshire: University Press of New England, 1998)

**Story type:** Horror (Child-in-Peril)
**Major character(s):** Eric Nolan, Teacher; Pamela Whitcome, Housewife (Eric's sister); Luke Whitcome, Child (four years old)
**Time period(s):** 1980s
**Locale(s):** Antrim, Vermont

**Summary:** Still unsettled by the disappearance of his brother while a young boy, Eric Nolan returns to Antrim, Vermont. Eric's interest in local history and folklore acquaints him with legends of the little people of the hills, who may have taken his brother as a changeling child and who threaten to do the same with his nephew Luke. Originally published in 1987.

**Other books you might like:**
John Blackburn, *For Fear of Little Men*, 1972
Leigh Clark, *The Feeding*, 1992
Vincent Courtney, *Goblins*, 1994
Chris Curry, *Panic*, 1994
Sidney Williams, *Gnelfs*, 1991

**1039**

JOSEPH A. CITRO

## The Unseen

(New York: Warner, 1990)

**Story type:** Horror (Ancient Evil Unleashed)
**Major character(s):** Roger Newton, Saloon Keeper/Owner; Laura Drew, Saloon Hostess, Lover (Newton's)
**Time period(s):** 1990s
**Locale(s):** Vermont

**Summary:** A number of Vermonters—a barkeeper and his lover, a drunken power company lineman, a female archaeologist, a pair of young boys and their grizzled guide—are drawn to a sinister, mysterious secluded area called "the Gore," where they encounter bizarre and dangerous things including coydogs (coyote-dog mixes), an ancient rock with mysterious powers, and a lost tribe.

**Other books you might like:**
John Farris, *Wildwood*, 1987

**1040**

CHRIS CLAREMONT
BETH FLEISHER, Co-Author

## Dragon Moon

(New York: Bantam Spectra, 1994)

**Story type:** Fantasy (Contemporary)
**Major character(s):** Cassandra "Cass" Dunreith, Martial Arts Expert, Writer; Mharyon, Mythical Creature (Celtic Rider); Fieran, Martial Arts Expert, Leader (S.C.A. king)
**Time period(s):** 1990s
**Locale(s):** Pennsylvania

**Summary:** As Lady Siobhan of Craigsmere, Cass fights in the Society for Creative Anachronism's Pensic War, hoping to ascend to the kingship in the historical recreationists' next cycle. After Fieran cheats her out of victory, Cass discovers that Fieran has summoned deadly legendary Celtic Riders into her world and must learn more about her own nature and powers to find a way of reversing their threat.

**Other books you might like:**
Emma Bull, *War for the Oaks*, 1987
Charles de Lint, *Greenmantle*, 1988
Charles de Lint, *Moonheart: A Romance*, 1984
Richard A. Knaak, *King of the Grey*, 1993
Mary Monica Pulver, *Murder at the War*, 1987
Melanie Rawn, *Knights of the Morningstar*, 1994
Pamela F. Service, *All's Faire*, 1993

## 1041

### CHRIS CLAREMONT

## Grounded!

(New York: Ace, 1991)

**Story type:** Science Fiction (Military; Political)
**Series:** Nicole Shea
**Major character(s):** Nicole Shea, Pilot (spaceship), Military Personnel (Lieutenant); Alex Cobri, Computer Expert; Kymri, Pilot, Alien
**Time period(s):** Indeterminate Future
**Locale(s):** Earth; Space Station

**Summary:** Lieutenant Shea has lost her astronaut rating and is assigned to ground duty at Edwards Air Force Base. Her assignment is to be liaison to a delegation of the Halyan't'a, a cat-like alien race which she had contacted on her first mission. But there are hidden powers at work, and Shea finds that successful cooperation with the aliens is endangered, and so is her own life.

**Other books you might like:**
Poul Anderson, *A Knight of Ghosts and Shadows*, 1975
C.J. Cherryh, *The Pride of Chanur*, 1982
Gordon R. Dickson, *Dorsai!*, 1976
Cynthia Felice, *Downtime*, 1985
Anne McCaffrey, *Sassinak*, 1989
    Elizabeth Moon, co-author
Melissa Scott, *Mighty Good Road*, 1990

## 1042

### CHRIS CLAREMONT

## Shadow Dawn

(New York: Bantam Spectra, 1997)

**Story type:** Fantasy (Magic Conflict; Quest)
**Series:** Chronicles of the Shadow War
**Major character(s):** Elora Danan, Royalty (princess), Magician (Daikini); Thorn Drumheller, Companion (protector), Wizard; Torquil Ufgood, Sorcerer
**Time period(s):** Indeterminate
**Locale(s):** Angwyn, Fictional Country; Sandeni, Fictional City

**Summary:** The Shadow War continues unabated. Now 16 years old, Elora studies Fire with Torquil. While performing her test, she inadvertently calls a baby elemental, destroying the forge. When the Shadow War spreads, Elora must fulfill the prophecy by stopping the Deceiver. Sequel to *Shadow Moon*.

**Other books you might like:**
Eleanor Arnason, *The Sword Smith*, 1978
Margaret Ball, *Changeweaver*, 1993
Wayland Drew, *Willow*, 1988
Phyllis Eisenstein, *The Crystal Palace*, 1988
J. Gregory Keyes, *The Waterborn*, 1996
George Lucas, *Shadow Moon*, 1995
    Chris Claremont, co-editor
Mark Sebanc, *Flight to Hollow Mountain*, 1996

## 1043

### CHRIS CLAREMONT

## Sundowner

(New York: Ace, 1994)

**Story type:** Science Fiction (Military)

**Series:** Nicole Shea
**Major character(s):** Nicole Shea, Pilot (spaceship), Military Personnel; Raqella, Alien (Halyan't'a/Hal), Pilot; Amy Cobri, Businesswoman, Socialite
**Time period(s):** Indeterminate Future
**Locale(s):** *U.S.S. Constitution*, Spaceship; *Sundowner*, Spaceship; Outer Space

**Summary:** Assigned as Captain of the *U.S.S. Constitution*, the most advanced starship yet designed, Nicole Shea must curb the emerging anti-alien sentiments which threaten the success of the first human and alien joint mission.

**Other books you might like:**
Eleanor Arnason, *Ring of Swords*, 1993
C.J. Cherryh, *The Pride of Chanur*, 1982
Debra Doyle, *The Price of the Stars*, 1992
    James D. Macdonald, co-author
Mercedes Lackey, *Wing Commander: Freedom Flight*, 1992
    Ellen Guon, co-author
Melisa C. Michaels, *First Battle*, 1985
Melisa C. Michaels, *Last War*, 1986
Melisa C. Michaels, *Skirmish*, 1985
David Weber, *On Basilisk Station*, 1993

## 1044

### ELIZABETH ENGSTROM, Editor
### ALAN M. CLARK, Illustrator

## Imagination Fully Dilated

(Abingdon, Maryland: Cemetery Dance Publications, 1998)

**Story type:** Horror (Anthology)

**Summary:** These 28 stories, all but two original to the compilation, were each written to accompany an illustration by artist Alan Clark. Selections include Ramsey Campbell's ''Never to Be Heard,'' in which the first complete staging of a suppressed choral arrangement raises an ancient evil; F. Paul Wilson's ''Lysing Toward Bethlehem,'' narrated from the viewpoint of a virus; Poppy Z. Brite's ''Arise,'' in which the spirit of a deceased musician commandeers the body of a friend in order to prolong his career; and Lucy Taylor's deep-sea terror story ''Dead Blue,'' which won the International Horror Guild Award for best short story of 1998. Introduction by Tim Powers. Released only as a signed limited edition.

**Other books you might like:**
Randy Fox, *Not Broken, Not Belonging*, 1994
Edward Gorey, *Amphigorey Also*, 1985
Joe R. Lansdale, *Weird Business*, 1995
    Richard Klaw, co-editor
James O'Barr, *The Crow: Shattered Lives and Broken Dreams*, 1998
    Ed Kramer, co-editor

## 1045

### DOUGLAS W. CLARK

## Rehearsal for a Renaissance

(New York: Avon, 1992)

**Story type:** Fantasy (Historical; Light Fantasy)
**Major character(s):** Sebastian, Apprentice; Corwyn, Magician (alchemist); Gwen, Girlfriend
**Time period(s):** 15th century
**Locale(s):** France; Italy

**Summary:** Hoping to bring the Renaissance to the backwater town of Pomme de Terre, Corwyn, the world's first aquatic alchemist, sets out for Venice with his inept apprentice Sebastian, and Gwen, the tavernkeeper's daughter. On their way, they fall in with a band of pilgrims, Sebastian tries to turn Gwen into a noble lady (with alarming success), Gwen helps Antonio elope with Shylock's daughter Jessica and Corwyn uses alchemy to thwart the diabolical schemes of Hydro Phobius to sink Venice into the sea.

**Other books you might like:**
Robert Asprin, *Another Fine Myth*, 1988
Geoffrey Chaucer, *The Canterbury Tales*, 1478
Gordon R. Dickson, *The Dragon Knight*, 1990
L. Sprague de Camp, *Lest Darkness Fall*, 1941
Suzette Haden Elgin, *Twelve Fair Kingdoms*, 1981
Terry Pratchett, *Wyrd Sisters*, 1990
Elizabeth Ann Scarborough, *Bronwyn's Bane*, 1983
William Shakespeare, *The Merchant of Venice*, 1596

## 1046

### JAN CLARK

## Earth Herald
(New York: Roc, 1998)

**Story type:** Science Fiction (Political; Military)
**Series:** Prodigy
**Major character(s):** Rieka Degahv, Spaceship Captain, Diplomat (Earth Herald); Jeniper Tarrik, Alien (Aurian), Diplomat (planetary attache)
**Time period(s):** Indeterminate Future
**Locale(s):** Earth; Indra, Planet—Imaginary

**Summary:** As the new Earth Herald, Rieka Degahv is in the forefront of the effort to rebuild Earth's cities, which were destroyed in a meteor strike centuries ago. This earns her the enmity of the Ophs, who fear the economic clout of a rebuilt Earth, and of her mother, who resents Rieka. Now all plan to use the Reaffirmation ceremony to destroy both Rieka and Earth. Second in series.

**Other books you might like:**
Jack L. Chalker, *The Demons at Rainbow Bridge*, 1989
Paula E. Downing, *Rinn's Star*, 1990
Valerie J. Freireich, *The Beacon*, 1996
Megan Lindholm, *Alien Earth*, 1992
Elizabeth Moon, *Once a Hero*, 1997
Karen Ripley, *Prisoner of Dreams*, 1989
John Varley, *The Ophiuchi Hotline*, 1977
David Weber, *Flag in Exile*, 1995

## 1047

### JAN CLARK

## Prodigy
(New York: Roc, 1997)

**Story type:** Science Fiction (Military; Political)
**Major character(s):** Rieka Degahv, Spaceship Captain; Triscoe Marteen, Spaceship Captain
**Time period(s):** Indeterminate Future
**Locale(s):** Spaceship; Interstellar Empire/Federation

**Summary:** Charged with treason for attacking an enemy spaceship, Rieka Degahv and her few allies must discover the truth underlying the incident to avert personal disaster and destruction of the Commonwealth. First novel.

**Other books you might like:**
Debra Doyle, *The Price of the Stars*, 1992
     James D. Macdonald, co-author

Lois McMaster Bujold, *The Warrior's Apprentice*, 1986
David Feintuch, *Midshipman's Hope*, 1994
Sherwood Smith, *The Phoenix in Flight*, 1993
     Dave Trowbridge, co-author
David Weber, *On Basilisk Station*, 1993

## 1048

### LEIGH CLARK

## Blood Sabbath
(New York: Zebra, 1991)

**Story type:** Horror (Black Magic)
**Major character(s):** Heather Roberts, Teenager; Karin Roberts, Museum Curator; Magda Prokash, Witch
**Time period(s):** 1990s
**Locale(s):** Encino, California

**Summary:** After attending a clandestine black magic ritual, high school student Heather Roberts accidentally becomes the emissary of Azgaroth, a hungry god who demands sacrifices and similar socially unacceptable activities. Smitten with guilt for spoiling her daughter rotten, Karin Roberts takes it upon herself to rescue Heather from the demon's clutches.

**Other books you might like:**
William Peter Blatty, *The Exorcist*, 1971
Ramsey Campbell, *To Wake the Dead*, 1980
Ray Garton, *Crucifax*, 1988

## 1049

### LEIGH CLARK

## Carnivore
(New York: Leisure, 1997)

**Story type:** Horror (Nature in Revolt)
**Major character(s):** Troy Darrow, Scientist (geologist); Kelly Sawyer, Scientist (EPA); Valentine Tarosh, Scientist
**Time period(s):** 1990s (1997)
**Locale(s):** Antarctica

**Summary:** Scientists participating in Deepcore, a secret project to locate sites for nuclear waste dumping in Antarctica, discover a Tyrannosaurus Rex egg frozen in a glacier millions of years before. Exposed to radiactive waste, the egg hatches and the dinosaur inside grows at an accelerated pace, putting the scientists in a struggle for survival against a prehistoric monster.

**Other books you might like:**
Michael Crichton, *The Lost World*, 1995
Michael Crichton, *Jurassic Park*, 1990
James F. David, *Footprints of Thunder*, 1995
Penelope Banka Kreps, *Carnivores*, 1993
Richard Sanford, *Roadkill*, 1995

## 1050

### LEIGH CLARK

## Evil Reincarnate
(New York: Tor, 1994)

**Story type:** Horror (Serial Killer)
**Major character(s):** Connie Stallman, Doctor (psychiatrist); Tod Jarrow, Serial Killer; Azrael, Sorcerer
**Time period(s):** 1990s (1994); 16th century (1594)

**Locale(s):** Hollywood, California; Venice, Italy

**Summary:** In a narrative that veers back and forth between the sixteenth and twentieth centuries, prison psychiatrist Connie Stallman discovers that her unusual fascination with serial killer Tod Jarrow stems from the fact that they were lovers in a previous life, and that Tod's affiliation with the black arts have stoked his bloodthirstiness and ensured his immortality over the centuries.

**Other books you might like:**
Max Ehrlich, *The Reincarnation of Peter Proud*, 1974
Barbara Erskine, *Midnight Is a Lonely Place*, 1994
Marcy Heidish, *The Torch*, 1992
Michael Stewart, *Belladonna*, 1992

---

**1051**

**LEIGH CLARK**

### The Feeding
(New York: Leisure, 1992)

**Story type:** Horror (Child-in-Peril)
**Major character(s):** Matt Brenner, Architect; Robin Brenner, Photographer; Joshua Brenner, Child (10-year-old boy)
**Time period(s):** 1980s (1988)
**Locale(s):** Black Cavern, California

**Summary:** Matt and Robin Brenner take a vacation at the mountain resort Kemmering House to save their marriage, unaware that the house is intimately connected with underlying caves that are home to ''The People of the Dark,'' a society of cannibalistic neanderthals who plan to kidnap their son Joshua in the hope of spawning future generations. This book was originally published in 1988.

**Other books you might like:**
Jack Ketchum, *Offspring*, 1991
Richard Laymon, *Midnight's Lair*, 1988

---

**1052**

**LEIGH CLARK**

### Shock Radio
(New York: Tor, 1996)

**Story type:** Horror (Serial Killer)
**Major character(s):** Aaron ''Sunset'' Scott, Radio Personality (disk jockey); Samantha Collier, Television Personality (news); Leah Steinberg, Waiter/Waitress
**Time period(s):** 1990s (1996)
**Locale(s):** Los Angeles, California

**Summary:** In a novel that parallels the crude confrontational style of a radio shock jock and the sociopathy of a serial killer, brash talk show host Aaron Scott (nee Steinberg) inadvertently encourages a brutal serial slayer known as the Phantom with his abusive on-air responses to the man's telephone calls into the show, then takes it upon himself to help track the villain down.

**Other books you might like:**
Richard Bachman, *The Running Man*, 1982
Robert Bloch, *Psycho II*, 1982
David J. Schow, *The Kill Riff*, 1988
John Skipp, *The Cleanup*, 1986
  Craig Spector, co-author

---

**1053**

**ARTHUR C. CLARKE**

### 3001: The Final Odyssey
(New York: Ballantine Del Rey, 1997)

**Story type:** Science Fiction (Science Fiction; Alternate Intelligence)
**Series:** Space Odyssey
**Major character(s):** Frank Poole, Astronaut; Halman, Artificial Intelligence; Indra Wallace, Historian
**Time period(s):** 31st century (3001)
**Locale(s):** Europa, Jupiter; *Goliath*, Spaceship

**Summary:** Rescued 1000 years after the computer Hal tried to kill him, Frank Poole faces a tremendous adjustment to Earth's almost unrecognizable society, as well as some unfinished business at Jupiter, where his adventure began. Fourth, and possibly last, in the series.

**Other books you might like:**
Poul Anderson, *The Boat of a Million Years*, 1989
Martin Caidin, *A Life in the Future*, 1995
Orson Scott Card, *The Worthing Saga*, 1990
Joe Haldeman, *The Forever War*, 1975
Larry Niven, *A World out of Time*, 1976

---

**1054**

**ARTHUR C. CLARKE**
**GREGORY BENFORD**, Co-Author

### Beyond the Fall of Night
(New York: Ace/Putnam, 1990)

**Story type:** Science Fiction (Hard Science Fiction; Invasion of Earth)
**Major character(s):** Alvin, Explorer, Human (supra); Cley, Heroine, Human (Ur); Seeker After Patterns, Guide, Animal (intelligent raccoon)
**Time period(s):** Indeterminate Future
**Locale(s):** Diaspar, Earth; Lys, Earth; Outer Space

**Summary:** Alvin escapes the beautiful but confining walls of Diaspar, a huge city on desolated Earth, and finds Lys, another inhabited city on the other side of the world. In uniting the two peoples once again, Alvin and the rest of mankind start restoring the Earth and regain the ability to explore space. Later, in helping Cley to find other Ur-humans after her community is destroyed, Seeker After Patterns discovers that the Mad Mind, the entity that once drove mankind back to his native world to cower in the cities for millenia, has escaped from the warped space-time vortex where it had been imprisoned and is bent on revenge and destruction. This collaboration is the sequel to Arthur C. Clarke's *Against the Fall of Night*, originally published in 1948.

**Other books you might like:**
Octavia E. Butler, *Dawn*, 1987
Orson Scott Card, *Speaker for the Dead*, 1986
Orson Scott Card, *Ender's Game*, 1985
Dan Simmons, *The Fall of Hyperion*, 1990
Dan Simmons, *Hyperion*, 1989

## 1055

### ARTHUR C. CLARKE
### GENTRY LEE, Co-Author

## The Garden of Rama

(New York: Bantam Spectra, 1991)

**Story type:** Science Fiction (First Contact; Space Colony)
**Series:** Rama
**Major character(s):** Nicole des Jardins Wakefield, Doctor, Adventurer; Richard Wakefield, Scientist, Adventurer; Kenji Watanabe, Historian, Settler
**Time period(s):** 23rd century
**Locale(s):** *Rama II*, Spaceship; *Rama III*, Spaceship; Outer Space

**Summary:** *Rama II* takes the human survivors of an exploration group and other creatures trapped on *Rama II* on a multi-year deep space voyage during which Nicole begins a new family. When *Rama II* arrives at The Node, a large construction facility in space near Sirius, the Ramans transport Nicole's family to temporary quarters to facilitate their testing humans and reconstructing *Rama II* into *Rama III*, designed as a human space colony for an expected 2000 colonists. When *Rama III* departs for Earth, some of Nicole's family must remain with The Node to begin breeding other humans for Ramans to study.

**Other books you might like:**
Roger MacBride Allen, *The Ring of Charon*, 1990
James Blish, *Cities in Flight*, 1969
Octavia E. Butler, *Dawn*, 1987
John DeChancie, *Paradox Alley*, 1987
Vonda N. McIntyre, *Transition*, 1991
Larry Niven, *Protector*, 1973
Allen Steele, *Clarke County, Space*, 1990
John Varley, *Wizard*, 1980
Vernor Vinge, *Marooned in Realtime*, 1986

## 1056

### ARTHUR C. CLARKE

## The Ghost From the Grand Banks

(New York: Bantam Spectra, 1990)

**Story type:** Science Fiction (Contemporary Realism)
**Major character(s):** Donald Craig, Computer Expert; Jason Bradley, Engineer (underwater); Rupert Parkinson, Sailor
**Time period(s):** 2000s; 2010s
**Locale(s):** Ireland; *Glomar Explorer*, At Sea (North Atlantic Ocean)

**Summary:** Support for another attempt at raising the *Titanic* has resulted in two competing salvage operations, both planning to raise parts of the ship on the same day, to an accompanying media circus. Unbeknownst to either salvage team the sunspot cycle has combined with the cumulative effects of humankind on the environment to severely challenge their efforts.

**Other books you might like:**
David Brin, *Earth*, 1990
David Brin, *Startide Rising*, 1983
Octavia E. Butler, *Dawn*, 1987
Melissa Scott, *Mighty Good Road*, 1990
Joan Slonczewski, *A Door into Ocean*, 1986

## 1057

### ARTHUR C. CLARKE

## The Hammer of God

(New York: Bantam Spectra, 1993)

**Story type:** Science Fiction (Disaster)
**Major character(s):** Robert Singh, Spaceship Captain
**Time period(s):** 22nd century (2110s)
**Locale(s):** Montenegro; *Goliath*, Spaceship (space tug); Kali, Asteroid

**Summary:** After an amateur astronomer discovers a wayward asteroid, scientists calculate it could strike the Earth. Officials then order *Goliath* to intercept the asteroid and deflect its path. Expands the 1992 *Time* magazine story and concludes with a 14-page "Sources and Acknowledgments."

**Other books you might like:**
Greg Bear, *The Forge of God*, 1987
Gregory Benford, *Shiva Descending*, 1980
    William Rotsler, co-author
James Blish, *A Torrent of Faces*, 1967
    Norman L. Knight, co-author
David Brin, *Earth*, 1990
Gregory Benford, *Heart of the Comet*, 1986
    David Brin, co-author
Larry Niven, *Footfall*, 1985
    Jerry Pournelle, co-author
Larry Niven, *Lucifer's Hammer*, 1977
    Jerry Pournelle, co-author

## 1058

### ARTHUR C. CLARKE
### GENTRY LEE, Co-Author

## Rama II

(New York: Bantam Spectra, 1989)

**Story type:** Science Fiction (First Contact)
**Series:** Rama
**Major character(s):** Richard Wakefield, Engineer; Nicole Des Jardins, Doctor
**Time period(s):** 22nd century
**Locale(s):** Earth; *Rama II*, Spaceship

**Summary:** In this sequel to *Rendezvous with Rama*, a second Raman spacecraft enters the solar system late in the twenty-second century. A top-flight crew is sent to intercept and explore the gigantic vehicle, armed with all the knowledge gained during the first Raman encounter. Although the alien craft is similar to its predecessor, the human explorers discover startling, even deadly differences.

**Other books you might like:**
Gregory Benford, *Across the Sea of Suns*, 1984
Gregory Benford, *In the Ocean of Night*, 1977
Gregory Benford, *Heart of the Comet*, 1986
    David Brin, co-author
Edward Gibson, *Reach*, 1989
David Alexander Smith, *Rendezvous*, 1988

## 1059

**ARTHUR C. CLARKE**
**GENTRY LEE**, Co-Author

### *Rama Revealed*
(New York: Bantam Spectra, 1994)

**Story type:** Science Fiction (First Contact; Space Colony)
**Series:** Rama
**Major character(s):** Nicole des Jardins Wakefield, Political Figure (ex-governor); Eleanor of Aquitaine, Robot; Max Puckett, Farmer
**Time period(s):** Indeterminate Future
**Locale(s):** *Rama III*, Spaceship; Outer Space

**Summary:** The night before her scheduled execution, Nicole, with the help of two small robots, escapes to Max's farm where she hides in a secret room until she can join her husband, Richard. Still in charge after destroying the neighboring sentients' colony, Nakamura will not stop until he controls all of *Rama III*. Concluding novel in series.

**Other books you might like:**
Colin Greenland, *Take Back Plenty*, 1992
Vonda N. McIntyre, *Metaphase*, 1992
Frank M. Robinson, *The Dark Beyond the Stars*, 1991
David Alexander Smith, *Homecoming*, 1990
Vernor Vinge, *A Fire upon the Deep*, 1992

## 1060

**ARTHUR C. CLARKE**
**MIKE MCQUAY**, Co-Author

### *Richter 10*
(New York: Bantam Spectra, 1996)

**Story type:** Science Fiction (Disaster; Hard Science Fiction)
**Major character(s):** Lewis Crane, Scientist (seismologist); Elena "Lanie" King, Computer Expert; Dan Newcombe, Scientist (geologist), Religious
**Time period(s):** 21st century (2024-2058)
**Locale(s):** San Gabriel Mountains, California

**Summary:** After an earthquake leaves him parentless, Lewis Crane dedicates his life to predicting earthquakes. His real goal, however, involves stopping earthquakes altogether by fusing the earth's tectonic plates together.

**Other books you might like:**
Arthur Herzog III, *Earthsound*, 1975
David Lippincott, *Tremor Violet*, 1975
Mike McQuay, *Jitterbug*, 1984
Mike McQuay, *Lifekeeper*, 1980
Alvah Reidah, *Fault Lines*, 1972

## 1061

**ARTHUR C. CLARKE**

### *Tales From Planet Earth*
(New York: Bantam Spectra, 1990)

**Story type:** Science Fiction (Science Fiction; Collection)
**Time period(s):** Indeterminate
**Locale(s):** Earth

**Summary:** These stories, primarily from the 1950's, are all set on, or are about, Earth. The book includes a new introduction for each story by the author. The settings range from the recent past to the far future.

**Other books you might like:**
Groff Conklin, *The Science Fiction Omnibus*, 1956
Groff Conklin, *A Treasury of Science Fiction*, 1948
Cordwainer Smith, *The Best of Cordwainer Smith*, 1975
pseudonym of Paul Myron Anthony Linebarger
Theodore Sturgeon, *A Way Home*, 1955
John Varley, *The Persistence of Vision*, 1978

## 1062

**J. BRIAN CLARKE**

### *The Expediter*
(New York: DAW, 1990)

**Story type:** Science Fiction (First Contact)
**Major character(s):** Gia Mayland, Researcher (expediter), Explorer; Peter Digonness, Businessman (Deputy Director of Expediters); Davakinapwottapellazanzis, Alien (Phuili), Researcher
**Time period(s):** 25th century (2416)
**Locale(s):** The Shouter, Planet—Imaginary; Groombra Four, Planet—Imaginary; *Century*, Spaceship

**Summary:** The Phuili, discovered behind the Pleides Star Cluster, are studying humans while humans study the relics of a 3rd race, long vanished from the galaxy. The Phuili do not necessarily believe that humans are sentient; they think of them more as clever "animals." However, as human and alien work side-by-side, they discover that each race has technology and culture that complement one another. They must use this growing partnership when a reaction set off by the long-silent, ancient relics begins to awaken the Silver People, a deadly race devoted to destroying all other life forms occupying "their" space.

**Other books you might like:**
Orson Scott Card, *The Abyss*, 1989
Alan Dean Foster, *Alien Nation*, 1988
Mary Gentle, *Golden Witchbreed*, 1983
James Patrick Kelly, *Look into the Sun*, 1989
Rebecca Ore, *Being Alien*, 1989

## 1063

**LINDSAY CLARKE**

### *The Chymical Wedding*
(New York: Knopf, 1989)

**Story type:** Fantasy (Contemporary; Historical)
**Major character(s):** Alex Darker, Divorced Person; Edward Nesbit, Writer (poet); Lavra, Psychic
**Time period(s):** 1980s; 1840s (1849)
**Locale(s):** England

**Summary:** Alex Darker retreats to the country, where he befriends an odd pair of recluses. He is drawn into an alchemical experiment that parallels tragic events of 150 years earlier. This book was published in 1989, but was not released until 1990.

**Other books you might like:**
John Crowley, *Little, Big*, 1981
Umberto Eco, *Foucault's Pendulum*, 1989
Stuart Gordon, *Smile on the Void*, 1981
Melissa Scott, *The Armor of Light*, 1988
Lisa A. Barnett, co-author
Robert Anton Wilson, *Masks of the Illuminati*, 1981

## 1064

### JO CLAYTON

## *Dancer's Rise*

(New York: DAW, 1993)

**Story type:** Fantasy (Adventure; Political)
**Series:** Dancer Trilogy
**Major character(s):** Serroi, Warrior, Sorceress; Camnor Heslin, Diplomat, Spy; Adlayra Ryan-Turriy, Mythical Creature (shapechanger)
**Time period(s):** Indeterminate
**Locale(s):** Fictional Country

**Summary:** After escaping centuries' imprisonment by force of magic, Serroi discovers a land of city states in which her previous adventures have achieved mythic status. After agreeing to deliver a newly created device to a distant ruler, Serroi and her companions encounter many impediments before she discovers the true nature of her enemy, one who wishes to control her. First of a trilogy.

**Other books you might like:**
Elizabeth Ann Scarborough, *Last Refuge*, 1992
Julie Dean Smith, *Sage of Sare*, 1992
Deborah Talmadge-Bickmore, *The Apprentice*, 1990
Martha Wells, *The Element of Fire*, 1993
Elizabeth Willey, *The Well-Favored Man: The Tale of the Sorcerer's Nephew*, 1993

## 1065

### JO CLAYTON

## *Drum Calls*

(New York: Tor, 1997)

**Story type:** Fantasy (Adventure)
**Series:** Drums of Chaos
**Major character(s):** Breith, Slave, Wizard; Cymel, Student, Wizard
**Time period(s):** Indeterminate Past
**Locale(s):** Glandair, Planet—Imaginary; Iomard, Planet—Imaginary

**Summary:** The worlds of Gladair and Iomard come close enough for gifted people to pass from one to the other. Destined to free both worlds, the hero remains untrained, while his comrades fall victim to slavery and dissolute living. With every sorcerer on two worlds looking for him, can the hero possibly succeed in his mission?

**Other books you might like:**
Eleanor Arnason, *Daughter of the Bear King*, 1987
C.J. Cherryh, *Fortress in the Eye of Time*, 1995
Brian Daley, *The Doomfarers of Coramonde*, 1977
Kristine Kathryn Rusch, *The White Mists of Power*, 1991
Caroline Stevermer, *A College of Magics*, 1994

## 1066

### JO CLAYTON

## *Drum Warning*

(New York: Tor, 1996)

**Story type:** Fantasy (Young Adult; Adventure)
**Series:** Drums of Chaos
**Major character(s):** Cymel, Mythical Creature; Lyonz, Heir; Dur, Sorcerer
**Time period(s):** Indeterminate (year 734 since settling Glandair)
**Locale(s):** Glandair, Planet—Imaginary; Iomard, Planet—Imaginary

**Summary:** The two worlds of Iomard and Glandair draw close once a century, allowing special people to travel between the worlds. Cymel and her aunt rescue Lyonz across the worlds and learn more about the joining and the prophecy about a young hero who will save Glandair. Another youth, Dur, runs away from the organized Domains and becomes a rogue tribal sorcerer with the potential to ignite a war on two worlds.

**Other books you might like:**
Brian Daley, *The Doomfarers of Coramonde*, 1977
Maggie Furey, *Aurian*, 1994
Barbara Hambly, *The Time of the Dark*, 1982
Anne McCaffrey, *Dragondrums*, 1979

## 1067

### JO CLAYTON

## *Fire in the Sky*

(New York: DAW, 1995)

**Story type:** Science Fiction (Political)
**Series:** Shadowsong
**Major character(s):** Shadith, Psychic; Kurz, Alien, Spy
**Time period(s):** Indeterminate Future
**Locale(s):** Beluchad, Planet—Imaginary

**Summary:** Although Shadith adjusts to life outside the Diadem, troubles force her to take a job as diplomat to the planet Beluchad, inhabited by two races and suffering from the invasion of two more. Shadith must bring peace with her odd empathic and musical powers or her life after the Diadem will end quickly.

**Other books you might like:**
Iain M. Banks, *The Player of Games*, 1989
David Brin, *Startide Rising*, 1983
C.J. Cherryh, *The Faded Sun: Kesrith*, 1978
W. Michael Gear, *Relic of Empire*, 1992
S. Andrew Swann, *Profiteer*, 1995

## 1068

### JO CLAYTON

## *The Magic Wars*

(New York: DAW, 1993)

**Story type:** Fantasy (Magic Conflict; Quest)
**Series:** Wild Magic
**Major character(s):** Faan "Fa" Hasmara, Sorceress, Orphan; Serroi, Warrior, Sorceress; Navarre, Magician, Adventurer
**Time period(s):** Indeterminate
**Locale(s):** Kaerubulan, Fictional Country

**Summary:** Having mastered her abilities as magician, Faan yet seeks reunion with her mother. Unfortunately, others also desire the use of Faan's skill and, after capturing her, force Faan to use her skills on their behalf in the Magic Wars.

**Other books you might like:**
Louise Cooper, *The Avenger*, 1992
Mary Gentle, *Rats and Gargoyles*, 1991
P.C. Hodgell, *Dark of the Moon*, 1985
P.C. Hodgell, *God Stalk*, 1982
Mark C. Perry, *Morigu: The Dead*, 1990
Angus Wells, *Wild Magic*, 1993

## 1069
### JO CLAYTON
## *Shadowkill*
(New York: DAW, 1991)

**Story type:** Science Fiction (Adventure)
**Series:** Shadith's Quest
**Major character(s):** Shadith, Psychic; Kikun, Alien, Warrior; Ginbiryol Seyirshi, Filmmaker
**Time period(s):** Indeterminate Future
**Locale(s):** Bol Mutian, Planet—Imaginary; Outer Space

**Summary:** Shadith and Ginbiryol are both captured by the Institute and sold into slavery. They must set aside their hatred long enough to destroy their masters, then they can finish their feud once and for all.

**Other books you might like:**
C.J. Cherryh, *Serpent's Reach*, 1980
Louise Cooper, *Nemesis*, 1988
C.L. Moore, *Northwest Smith*, 1981
Elizabeth Ann Scarborough, *The Healer's War*, 1988

## 1070
### JO CLAYTON
## *Shadowplay*
(New York: DAW, 1990)

**Story type:** Science Fiction (Adventure)
**Series:** Shadith's Quest
**Major character(s):** Shadith, Psychic; Kikun, Alien, Warrior; Ginbiryol Seyirshi, Filmmaker
**Time period(s):** Indeterminate Future
**Locale(s):** Kiskai, Planet—Imaginary

**Summary:** Shadith, recently returned to human form, has been captured by evil filmaker Ginbiryol Seyirshi, who intends to use her two other captives to create yet another devastating war which he will film for profit. Shadith, Kikun and Rohant join with local revolutionaries to thwart Seyirshi's plot.

**Other books you might like:**
R.A. MacAvoy, *The Third Eagle: Lessons Along a Minor String*, 1989
Anne McCaffrey, *The Death of Sleep*, 1990
   Jody Lynn Nye, co-author
Anne McCaffrey, *Generation Warrior*, 1991
   Elizabeth Moon, co-author
Anne McCaffrey, *Sassinak*, 1990
   Elizabeth Moon, co-author
Andre Norton, *The Beast Master*, 1959

## 1071
### JO CLAYTON
## *Shadowspeer*
(New York: DAW, 1990)

**Story type:** Science Fiction (Adventure)
**Series:** Shadith's Quest
**Major character(s):** Shadith, Psychic; Kikun, Alien, Warrior; Ginbiryol Seyirshi, Filmmaker
**Time period(s):** Indeterminate Future
**Locale(s):** *Kezzedua Dinnyee*, Spaceship; Chissoku Bogmaks, Planet—Imaginary

**Summary:** Shadith, enraged by the pointless deaths caused by Ginbiryol's "films," vows to hunt him down. To get to the elusive producer, however, will be more complex and dangerous than she and her companions imagined.

**Other books you might like:**
F.M. Busby, *Young Rissa*, 1977
Sharon Green, *The Crystals of Mida*, 1982
Robert A. Heinlein, *Friday*, 1982
Anne McCaffrey, *Crystal Singer*, 1982
Janet Morris, *The High Couch of Silistra*, 1977

## 1072
### JO CLAYTON
## *Wild Magic*
(New York: DAW, 1991)

**Story type:** Fantasy (Magic Conflict; Religious)
**Series:** Wild Magic
**Major character(s):** Faan Korispais Piyolss, Orphan, Agent; Reyna Hayaka, Guardian (Faan's), Businessman; Faharmoy, Agent
**Time period(s):** Indeterminate
**Locale(s):** Zam Fadogurum, Fictional Country

**Summary:** Stolen from her sorceress mother, Faan receives spotty magic education which does not fully prepare her for the roll she is to play as the goddess' pawn battling the god's pawn, Faharmoy. This book is set in the same universe as the Drinker of Souls trilogy (1986-1989).

**Other books you might like:**
Donald Aamodt, *A Name to Conjure With*, 1989
Donald Aamodt, *A Troubling Along the Border*, 1991
Steven Brust, *Phoenix*, 1990
Louise Cooper, *The Deceiver*, 1991
Louise Cooper, *The Pretender*, 1991
David Eddings, *The Sapphire Rose*, 1991
P.C. Hodgell, *Dark of the Moon*, 1985
P.C. Hodgell, *God Stalk*, 1982
Sheri S. Tepper, *Grass*, 1989

## 1073
### JO CLAYTON
## *Wildfire*
(New York: DAW, 1992)

**Story type:** Fantasy (Magic Conflict; Political)
**Series:** Wild Magic
**Major character(s):** Faan "Fa" Hasmara, Sorceress, Orphan
**Time period(s):** Indeterminate
**Locale(s):** Savvalis, Fictional City; Kyatawat, Mythical Place

**Summary:** Searching for her true mother, an ensorcelled sorceress, Faan again finds herself involved as a pawn in the struggle between gods and magicians for control of her world.

**Other books you might like:**
Mary Gentle, *Rats and Gargoyles*, 1991
P.C. Hodgell, *Dark of the Moon*, 1985
P.C. Hodgell, *God Stalk*, 1982

## 1074

### MONA CLEE

## Branch Point

(New York: Ace, 1996)

**Story type:** Science Fiction (Time Travel; Alternate Universe)

**Major character(s):** Anna Leah Fall-Levchenko, Time Traveler, Scholar; Lavrenti Borisovich Zorin, Military Personnel, Revolutionary; Jeffrey Kharitonov, Time Traveler

**Time period(s):** 1960s; 19th century

**Locale(s):** Alternate Earth; United States; Union of Soviet Socialist Republics

**Summary:** Equipped with a portable time machine and advanced technology, Anna and her team travel back to 1962, intending to do anything necessary to stop the coming nuclear holocaust and eventual human extinction. When events prove difficult to mold, Anna and Jeffrey must again travel to the past, attempting to influence events positively. First novel.

**Other books you might like:**

Poul Anderson, *The Time Patrol*, 1991

Gregory Benford, *Alternate Wars*, 1991
    Martin H. Greenberg, co-editor

Randall Frakes, *Terminator 2: Judgment Day*, 1991

Harry Turtledove, *The Guns of the South: A Novel of the Civil War*, 1992

H.G. Wells, *The Time Machine*, 1895

Robert Charles Wilson, *A Bridge of Years*, 1991

## 1075

### MONA CLEE

## Overshoot

(New York: Ace, 1998)

**Story type:** Science Fiction (Disaster; Science Fiction)

**Major character(s):** Moira Janelle Burke, Lawyer, Aged Person (octogenarian); Sven "Loki", Businessman (partner), Computer Expert; Rhiannon, Witch, Computer Expert

**Time period(s):** 2030s (2032)

**Locale(s):** San Francisco, California (Withering Heights commune); Berkeley, California

**Summary:** Lucky to have a mansion in San Francisco, Moira and her retired friends produce most of their own food, despite the heat and lack of water. The greenhouse effect having changed the environment and caused social upheaval, it seems only a miracle will permit the survival of the human race after the assassination of the only environmentally interested presidential candidate. Rhiannon finds reference to the Green Man on the net, and when Moira contacts him, asks him if they should take action.

**Other books you might like:**

David Brin, *Earth*, 1990

Octavia E. Butler, *Parable of the Talents*, 1998

Sheri S. Tepper, *Gibbon's Decline and Fall*, 1996

Sage Walker, *Whiteout*, 1996

Paul O. Williams, *The Breaking of Northwall*, 1981

## 1076

### DOUGLAS CLEGG

## Breeder

(New York: Pocket, 1990)

**Story type:** Horror (Black Magic)

**Major character(s):** Rachel Adair, Lawyer; Hugh Adair, Lawyer, Spouse; Mattie Peru, Streetperson (nee Madeleine Perreau)

**Time period(s):** 1980s (1988)

**Locale(s):** Washington, District of Columbia

**Summary:** Following her traumatic miscarriage, Rachel Adair moves with her husband Hugh into Washington's historic Draper House, a gift from her father-in-law. Gradually, the couple discovers that the house has a history of evil and that the elder Adair has engineered their relocation as part of a bargain made years before to a voodoo priest.

**Other books you might like:**

Nicholas Conde, *The Religion*, 1982

John Farris, *All Heads Turn When the Hunt Goes By*, 1977

Stephanie Kegan, *The Baby*, 1990

Ira Levin, *Rosemary's Baby*, 1967

## 1077

### DOUGLAS CLEGG

## The Children's Hour

(New York: Dell, 1995)

**Story type:** Horror (Small Town Horror)

**Major character(s):** Joe Gardner, Writer (novelist); Homer "Hopfrog" Petersen, Carpenter; Tad Petersen, Child (Homer's son)

**Time period(s):** 1990s (1995)

**Locale(s):** Colony, West Virginia

**Summary:** Joe Gardner returns from Baltimore to his hometown in rural West Virginia and relives the memories of his past, including the death of his girlfriend in an automobile accident. The deaths of several local children, and the return of one who disappeared twenty years before, lead Joe to the realization that the trauma of his youth was related to an evil presence living beneath the town that is now threatening to break out.

**Other books you might like:**

Stephen King, *It*, 1987

Nina Mandelik, *Entity*, 1991

Steve Rasnic Tem, *Excavation*, 1987

## 1078

### DOUGLAS CLEGG

## Dark of the Eye

(New York: Pocket, 1994)

**Story type:** Horror (Wild Talents; Science Fiction)

**Major character(s):** Hope Stewart, Child (11 years old), Experimental Subject; Kate Stewart, Housewife; Stephen Grace, Criminal (assassin)

**Time period(s):** 1990s (1994)

**Locale(s):** Salinas, California

**Summary:** When Kate Stewart spirits her daughter Hope away from the research facility where her scientist husband has been experimenting on her with a bizarre virus, it initiates a series of events that will bring them to California, and put them in the clutches of a death cult formed from the dregs of the 1960s counterculture who plan to use Hope's experimentally-boosted capabilities to summon the god of pain and horror they worship.

**Other books you might like:**
Randall Boyll, *Chiller*, 1992
Daniel H. Gower, *The Orpheus Process*, 1992
Dean R. Koontz, *Hideaway*, 1992

---

## 1079

### DOUGLAS CLEGG

## Goat Dance

(New York: Pocket, 1989)

**Story type:** Horror (Ancient Evil Unleashed)
**Major character(s):** Malcolm "Cup" Coffey, Teacher (Elementary school); Theodora "Teddy" Amory, Child (Possessed)
**Time period(s):** 1800s (1801); 1980s (1985-87)
**Locale(s):** Pontefract, Virginia

**Summary:** A series of increasingly bizarre occurrences in Pontefract, Virginia heralds the coming of the Eater of Souls, a terror that can be averted only if a small group of townspeople can dig into the dark past of Pontefract for the secret of the nature of the evil and the means to combat it.

**Other books you might like:**
T.E.D. Klein, *The Ceremonies*, 1984
Bentley Little, *The Revelation*, 1990

---

## 1080

### DOUGLAS CLEGG

## The Halloween Man

(New York: Leisure, 1998)

**Story type:** Horror (Ancient Evil Unleashed)
**Major character(s):** Stony Crawford, Kidnapper; Lourdes Maria Castillo, Young Woman; Shiloh, Healer
**Time period(s):** 1990s (1998); 1970s
**Locale(s):** Stonehaven, Connecticut

**Summary:** Stony Crawford kidnaps Shiloh, a young boy revered as a prophet by a religious cult known as the Rapturists. His intent is to bring the boy back to his home town of Stonehaven, and there to kill him, in an effort to halt the age-old evil centered around the folkloric figure of the Halloween Man, to which the boy and his powers are intimately connected.

**Other books you might like:**
Randall Boyll, *Chiller*, 1992
John Coyne, *Child of Shadows*, 1990
Dean R. Koontz, *The Servants of Twilight*, 1984
Peter Straub, *Ghost Story*, 1995

---

## 1081

### DOUGLAS CLEGG

## Never Land

(New York: Pocket Books, 1991)

**Story type:** Horror (Evil Children)
**Major character(s):** Sumter Monroe, Child; Beauregard Jackson, Child; Rowena Wandigaux, Grandparent
**Time period(s):** 1990s

**Locale(s):** Gull Island, Georgia

**Summary:** Every summer the members of the Wandigaux family gather on Gull Island for a reunion. This summer, ten-year-olds Sumter and Beauregard are driven by boredom to play in an abandoned shack they christen Neverland, where they learn secrets of their family's guarded past and how it has manifested through both of them.

**Other books you might like:**
Ray Bradbury, *Something Wicked This Way Comes*, 1962
Arthur Machen, "The White People", 1991
    in *The Horror Hall of Fame*
Thomas Tryon, *The Other*, 1971

---

## 1082

### JAMES CLEMENS

## Wit'ch Fire

(New York: Ballantine Del Rey, 1998)

**Story type:** Fantasy (Magic Conflict; Adventure)
**Series:** Banned and the Banished
**Major character(s):** Elena, Sorceress, Teenager; Dismarum, Wizard; Er'ril, Warrior, Handicapped (has one arm)
**Time period(s):** Indeterminate Past
**Locale(s):** Alasea, Fictional Country

**Summary:** A young girl holds the hope of freedom for a country in danger, but when the Dark Power learns of her, she and her brother must flee. Aided by odd companions including a one-armed swordsman and a seer, Elena will save her people or die.

**Other books you might like:**
John Barnes, *One for the Morning Glory*, 1996
Scott Ciencin, *The Ways of Magic*, 1996
David Farland, *The Runelords: The Sum of All Men*, 1998
Robin Hobb, *Assassin's Apprentice*, 1995
Michael Scott Rohan, *The Anvil of Ice*, 1986

---

## 1083

### HAL CLEMENT

## Fossil

(New York: DAW, 1993)

**Story type:** Science Fiction (Science Fiction)
**Major character(s):** Janice Cedar, Researcher, Spouse (Hugh's); Hugh Rock Cedar, Administrator, Engineer (safety); S'Nash, Alien (Naxian), Researcher
**Time period(s):** Indeterminate Future
**Locale(s):** Habranha, Planet—Imaginary

**Summary:** On inhospitable Habranha, six intelligent alien races cooperate to discover the secrets of ancient fossils which may prove another intelligent race native to Habranha or may indicate that the race did not evolve locally, but rather descended from a legendary Seventh Race. However, research results may fall prey to secret agendas. Based on a universe created by Isaac Asimov.

**Other books you might like:**
David Brin, *Startide Rising*, 1983
Jeffrey A. Carver, *Dragons in the Stars*, 1992
A.C. Crispin, *Serpent's Gift*, 1992
    Deborah A. Marshall, co-author
Robert L. Forward, *Marooned on Eden*, 1993
    Martha Dodson Forward, co-author
Joan Slonczewski, *Daughter of Elysium*, 1993
Vernor Vinge, *A Fire upon the Deep*, 1992

## **1084**

### MARK A. CLEMENTS

## *Children of the End*

(New York: Donald I. Fine, 1993)

**Story type:** Horror (Science Fiction)
**Major character(s):** Tony Garwood, Guard (ex-cop); Deborah Kosarek, Writer (technical writer); George Irving Pendergast, Scientist (geneticist)
**Time period(s):** 1990s (1993)
**Locale(s):** San Diego, California

**Summary:** Using illegal aliens smuggled into the United States, mad scientist George Irving Pendergast breeds a ravenous race of shapeshifters known as Loners, which he intends to use as a weapon in the battle to fight overpopulation in America. Fueled by the belief that a human-free earth is their manifest destiny, the Loners quickly become a threat to the well-being of humanity.

**Other books you might like:**
Dean R. Koontz, *Shadowfires*, 1987
Dean R. Koontz, *Watchers*, 1987

## **1085**

### MARK A. CLEMENTS

## *The Land of Nod*

(New York: Donald I. Fine)

**Story type:** Horror (Mystery)
**Major character(s):** Jeffry Dittimore, Lawyer; Timothy Kregler, Spirit; Gail Rohr, Spirit
**Time period(s):** 1990s (1995)
**Locale(s):** Middlefield, Indiana

**Summary:** Recovering from a nervous breakdown, Jeffry Dittimore returns to his home town of Middlefield, only to discover that dead childhood friends are still alive there. In order to escape their unnatural hold on him and come to terms with buried traumas of the past that threaten his current life, Jeffry is forced to enter the Land of Nod, an imaginative world of his and his friends' creation, where the real and unreal collide.

**Other books you might like:**
Jonathan Carroll, *A Child Across the Sky*, 1988
Dale Hoover, *65mm*, 1993
William Browning Spencer, *Zod Wallop*, 1995

## **1086**

### MARK A. CLEMENTS

## *Lorelei*

(New York: Donald I. Fine, 1994)

**Story type:** Horror (Serial Killer)
**Major character(s):** Stacy Westerman, Psychologist; Clyde McGammon, Detective—Private; Lorelei, Serial Killer
**Time period(s):** 1990s (1994)
**Locale(s):** Washington, District of Columbia; New Orleans, Louisiana

**Summary:** A private detective with psychological problems related to his work as a former FBI agent teams up with a woman whose husband was seduced and murdered by a femme fatale serial killer. Together they discover the secret of the murderess' allure and motive and put an end to a cycle of killing that traverses the United States.

**Other books you might like:**
Ron Dee, *Succumb*, 1994
Christopher Fowler, *Red Bride*, 1992
Kathryn Ptacek, *In Silence Sealed*, 1988
Karen E. Taylor, *Bitter Blood*, 1994

## **1087**

### SHIRLEY CLIMO

## *T.J.'s Ghost*

(New York: Crowell, 1989)

**Story type:** Horror (Ghost Story)
**Major character(s):** Theresa "T.J." DuMar Jr., Teenager (On vacation); Winston D. Osborn, Teenager (T.J.'s friend)
**Time period(s):** 1980s
**Locale(s):** Pidgeon Point, California

**Summary:** Stuck with her old Aunt Onion and Uncle Will while her parents vacation, T.J. hears a mysterious foghorn and meets an Australian boy who, she gradually learns, is the ghost of a stowaway who went down in a shipwreck 120 years earlier. With her friend Winston, T.J. tries to learn all about her ghost and the mysterious quest that has brought him back to life to roam the California beach.

**Other books you might like:**
Helen K. Passey, *Speak to the Rain*, 1989

## **1088**

### LEONARD CLINE

## *The Lady of the Frozen Death and Other Weird Tales*

(West Warwick, Rhode Island: Necronomicon Press, 1992)

**Story type:** Horror (Collection)

**Summary:** A collection of five stories, two unpublished and three that appeared originally in the horror and weird mystery pulps under the author's pseudonym Alan Forsyth. Included are the title story, about a seductive snow elemental who lures men to their deaths; "The Guilt of Weasel Garrott," about a soul exchange between a university professor and a criminal; "The Vampire of Bedlam Hill," a tale of witchcraft; and "Shuffle-Thump, in the Dark," about a blind man pursued either by the ghost of a friend or his guilty conscience. Editor Douglas A. Anderson has supplied a bibliography of the author's pseudonymous and unpublished writings.

**Other books you might like:**
Hugh B. Cave, *Murgunstrumm and Others*, 1975
August Derleth, *Someone in the Dark*, 1941
Carl Jacobi, *Revelations in Black*, 1947
E. Hoffman Price, *Far Lands, Other Days*, 1977

## **1089**

### BRENDA W. CLOUGH

## *How Like a God*

(New York: Tor, 1997)

**Story type:** Fantasy (Contemporary Realism; Psychic Powers)
**Major character(s):** Rob Lewis, Computer Expert, Telepath; Edwin Amadeus Barbarossa, Scientist (microbiologist); Gilgamesh, Deity, Immortal
**Time period(s):** 1990s

**Locale(s):** Washington, District of Columbia; New York, New York; Uzbekistan

**Summary:** Waking up one morning to find he can suddenly read and influence people's minds, Rob Lewis initially intends to use his power to make the world a better place. His darker nature surfaces, however, causing him to flee from his family and home in terror. Only after a period of self-induced solitude can Rob begin the long journey towards finding out what he has become and why.

**Other books you might like:**
Jonathan Carroll, *Bones of the Moon*, 1988
Jonathan Carroll, *Outside the Dog Museum*, 1991
Ken Grimwood, *Replay*, 1986
Eric S. Nylund, *Dry Water*, 1997
Christopher Pike, *Remember Me*, 1989
Robert Silverberg, *To the Land of the Living*, 1989
Dan Simmons, *The Hollow Man*, 1992

## 1090

### BRENDA W. CLOUGH

## *An Impossumble Summer*

(New York: Walker, 1992)

**Story type:** Fantasy (Young Adult; Contemporary)
**Major character(s):** Marianne ''Rianne'' Buechner, Child; Shannon Buechner, Child; Impossumble, Animal (opossum), Magician
**Time period(s):** 1990s
**Locale(s):** Virginia

**Summary:** Shortly after moving to Virginia, Rianne rescues a magical opossum from captivity at the Pet Farm Park. The opossum brings luck, sometimes good and sometimes bad, during the summer Rianne spends with her new companion.

**Other books you might like:**
Deborah Howe, *Bunnicula: A Rabbit Tale of Mystery*, 1979
    James Howe, co-author
Tanith Lee, *Black Unicorn*, 1991
Robert C. O'Brien, *Mrs. Frisby and the Rats of NIMH*, 1971
E.B. White, *Charlotte's Web*, 1952

## 1091

### MOLLY COCHRAN
### WARREN MURPHY, Co-Author

## *The Broken Sword*

(New York: Tor, 1997)

**Story type:** Fantasy (Contemporary; Legend)
**Series:** Forever King
**Major character(s):** Beatrice, Handicapped (blind), Psychic; Aubrey Katsuleris, Artist (painter), Wizard; Taliesin, Wizard, Immortal
**Time period(s):** Indeterminate Future
**Locale(s):** Marrakesh, Morocco; Cadbury Tor, England

**Summary:** Arthur returns in the body of a teenage boy, with Taliesin and Arthur's Knights returning as well. They recovered Excalibur, but lost the Holy Grail, which now resurfaces in the hands of a once-blind girl. As the secret war between Arthur and the Forces of Darkness heats up, Excalibur's destruction makes all seem lost. Sequel to the *Sequel to the Forever King*.

**Other books you might like:**
James P. Blaylock, *The Paper Grail*, 1991
Simon Hawke, *The Wizard of 4th Street*, 1987
K.W. Jeter, *Morlock Night*, 1979
Tim Powers, *Last Call*, 1992

Michael A. Stackpole, *Once a Hero*, 1994

## 1092

### MOLLY COCHRAN
### WARREN MURPHY, Co-Author

## *The Forever King*

(New York: Tor, 1992)

**Story type:** Fantasy (Contemporary; Legend)
**Major character(s):** Hal Woczniak, FBI Agent (retired), Knight; Saladin, Immortal, Murderer; Arthur Blessing, Orphan, Heir
**Time period(s):** 1990s
**Locale(s):** New York, New York; Chicago, Illinois; England

**Summary:** Saladin, a homicidal maniac genius, orchestrates his escape from a maximum security mental institution. The Grail, his since childhood, falls into the hands of Arthur, who feels an instant resonance with it. After the cup saves his Aunt Emily's life, she and Arthur escape to England to find Arthur's legacy.

**Other books you might like:**
Donald Barthelme, *The King*, 1990
Marion Zimmer Bradley, *The Mists of Avalon*, 1983
Martin Caidin, *The Messiah Stone*, 1986
Parke Godwin, *Beloved Exile*, 1984
Patricia Kennealy-Morrison, *The Hawk's Gray Feather*, 1990
T.H. White, *The Once and Future King*, 1958

## 1093

### MOLLY COCHRAN
### WARREN MURPHY, Co-Author

## *World Without End*

(New York: Tor, 1996)

**Story type:** Fantasy (Psychic Powers; Legend)
**Major character(s):** Darian McCabe, Psychic, Sailor; Cory Althorpe, Doctor (psychiatrist), Psychic; Sam Smith, Psychic, Diver (scuba)
**Time period(s):** 1990s; Indeterminate Past
**Locale(s):** Caribbean; Atlantis, Mythical Place

**Summary:** Sam dives too deep while following a psychic call which leads to a fabulous magic treasure and a case of the bends. At the hospital, Sam meets Dr. Cory Althorpe who introduces him to a group of psychics, the Rememberers. Sam's involvement becomes pivotal as he attempts to undermine the group's enemies by travelling to Atlantis to bring about a benign future for Atlantis.

**Other books you might like:**
Ronald Anthony Cross, *The Lost Guardian*, 1995
Umberto Eco, *Foucault's Pendulum*, 1989
Michael Flynn, *In the Country of the Blind*, 1990
Robert Shea, *The Illuminatus! Trilogy*, 1988
    Robert Anton Wilson, co-author
Edward Whittemore, *Jerusalem Poker*, 1978
Robert Anton Wilson, *The Schrodinger's Cat Trilogy*, 1988

## 1094

### ANDREI CODRESCU

## *Blood Countess*

(New York: Simon & Schuster, 1995)

**Story type:** Horror (Literary)

**Major character(s):** Drake Bathory-Kereshtur, Journalist; Elizabeth Bathory, Noblewoman, Historical Figure; Andrei de Kreshtur, Student
**Time period(s):** 1990s (1995); 16th century
**Locale(s):** Budapest, Hungary

**Summary:** Drawing parallels between the savagery of the past and the present, this first novel by a well known essayist and political commentator recounts the tale of Drake Bathory-Kereshtur, a journalist lured back to Romania after the fall of communism, and who confesses to the murder of a young woman there. As Drake recounts the how he is seduced into becoming part of a political group interested in restoring the monarchy, his tale begins to parallel that of his ancestor, Elizabeth Bathory, a countess renowned for bathing in the blood of virgins.

**Other books you might like:**
Peter Ackroyd, *Hawksmoor*, 1985
Christopher Bram, *Father of Frankenstein*, 1995
Dan Simmons, *Carrion Comfort*, 1989

---

**1095**

### DAVID B. COE

## Children of Amarid

(New York: Tor, 1997)

**Story type:** Fantasy (Adventure; Quest)
**Series:** Lon Tobyn Chronicle
**Major character(s):** Jaryd, Wizard (mage-attend); Alayna, Wizard
**Time period(s):** Indeterminate
**Locale(s):** Tobyn-Ser, Fictional Country

**Summary:** The children of Amarid mediate disputes, heal ills and do good work for the lan of Tobyn-Ser, but lately have been accused of crimes and deaths. The two newest Hawk-mages, Jaryd and Alayna, venture across the country in search of the real evildoers, even as they discover that the answers may be found close to the temple. First in series.

**Other books you might like:**
Maggie Furey, *Aurian*, 1994
J. Gregory Keyes, *The Waterborn*, 1996
Mercedes Lackey, *Arrows of the Queen*, 1987
R.A. Salvatore, *The Demon Awakens*, 1997
Michelle West, *Hunter's Oath*, 1995

---

**1096**

### DAVID B. COE

## The Outlanders

(New York: Tor, 1998)

**Series:** Lon Tobyn Chronicle
**Major character(s):** Orris, Sorcerer; Baram, Warrior, Prisoner
**Time period(s):** Indeterminate
**Locale(s):** Tobyn-Ser, Fictional Country

**Summary:** The Children of Amarid protect the land of Tobyn-Ser from its enemies, but lately the latter have been considerably more successful. They finally capture one of the invaders, who is revealed to be a warrior from a neighboring land that has forsaken magic. One of their number kidnaps the prisoner and sets out on a perilous mission to end the conflict.

**Other books you might like:**
David Eddings, *Belgarath the Sorcerer*, 1995
Phyllis Eisenstein, *Born to Exile*, 1978
Robert Jordan, *The Eye of the World*, 1990

---

Richard A. Knaak, *Wolfhelm*, 1990
L.E. Modesitt Jr., *The Magic of Recluce*, 1991

---

**1097**

### M.T. COFFIN (Pseudonym of George Edward Stanley)

## Pet Store

(New York: Avon, 1996)

**Story type:** Horror (Nature in Revolt)
**Series:** Spinetinglers
**Major character(s):** Amber, Child; Dad, Guard; Mr. Pinscher, Animal (dog)
**Time period(s):** 1990s (1996)
**Locale(s):** Woofburg, Mythical Place

**Summary:** Amber's dad moves the family to Woofburg only to discover that the town is run by sentient dogs. The family struggles to escape from Woofburg before they become the pets of Dad's employer, Mr. Pinscher. This book is aimed at readers in the 8- to 12-year-old age group.

**Other books you might like:**
Christopher Pike, *The Creature in the Teacher*, 1996
R.L. Stine, *Monster Blood II*, 1994
R.L. Stine, *Say Cheese and Die*, 1992
Tom B. Stone, *The Fright Before Christmas*, 1996

---

**1098**

### JON COHEN

## Max Lakeman and the Beautiful Stranger

(New York: Warner, 1990)

**Story type:** Fantasy (Contemporary)
**Major character(s):** Max Lakeman, Landscaper; Mrs. Zeno, Disembodied Personality (Figment of Max's imagination)
**Time period(s):** 1990s
**Locale(s):** Gramentown, Pennsylvania

**Summary:** Max is living a comfortable life with his loving family until a woman he imagines comes to life in his backyard and seduces him. Things get out of hand as both Max and his wife face different threats to their life together.

**Other books you might like:**
Esther Friesner, *Sphynxes Wild*, 1989
Tanya Huff, *Gate of Darkness, Circle of Light*, 1989
Christopher Priest, *The Glamour*, 1984

---

**1099**

### THOMAS COLCHIE, Editor

## A Hammock Beneath the Mangoes

(New York: Dutton, 1991)

**Story type:** Horror (Anthology)

**Summary:** This indispensable collection of 26 Latin American stories from five different geographic regions, some never published before in English translations, contains a number of tales of magic realism and metaphysical terror, including Gabriel Garcia Marquez's stream of consciousness narrative of a boy's fascination with a mysterious ship, ''The Last Voyage of the Ghost Ship''; Jorge Luis Borges' tale of the interpenetration of dream and reality, ''The Circular Ruins''; and Julio Cortazar's fable of a man who loses the ability to distinguish between his subjective and objective perceptions of reality,

''Axolotl.'' The editor has supplied instructive biographical notes for each author and an introduction.

**Other books you might like:**
Alberto Manguel, *Black Water: The Book of Fantastic Literature*, 1983
Alberto Manguel, *Black Water 2: More Tales of the Fantastic*, 1990

## 1100
### ADRIAN COLE

## *The Gods in Anger*
(New York: Avon, 1991)

**Story type:** Fantasy (Magic Conflict)
**Series:** Omaran Saga
**Major character(s):** Simon Wargallow, Leader (Deliverers')
**Time period(s):** Indeterminate Future
**Locale(s):** Omara, Mythical Place

**Summary:** Hoping to save the last refuge of humanity, Simon Wargallow and his companions secretly journey into forbidden lands to determine the true nature of the threat posed to the human race. Reprint of the 1988 British edition.

**Other books you might like:**
Philip Jose Farmer, *Red Orc's Rage*, 1991
John Lee, *The Unicorn Quest*, 1986
Margaret Weis, *Fire Sea*, 1991
   Tracy Hickman, co-author

## 1101
### ADRIAN COLE

## *Mother of Storms*
(New York: AvoNova, 1992)

**Story type:** Fantasy (Political; Adventure)
**Series:** Star Requiem
**Major character(s):** Aru Casruel, Adventurer, Immigrant; Zellorian, Wizard; Ussemitus, Adventurer, Psychic
**Time period(s):** Indeterminate
**Locale(s):** Innasmorn, Planet—Imaginary

**Summary:** The Alien Csendook defeat humanity, forcing the Imperial contingent to leave normal space for the haven of Innasmorn. The local inhabitants there have long been forbidden the use of metals and expect disaster to follow the invaders/refugees. Zellorian, controlling the Emperor Elect, finds the path under reality using pain and death and uses torture and death to control and understand the forces unique to Innasmorn. Reprint of British 1989 edition. First in series.

**Other books you might like:**
Charles de Lint, *The Little Country*, 1990
Cheryl J. Franklin, *Fire Crossing*, 1991
Mary Gentle, *Golden Witchbreed*, 1984
Marvin Kaye, *The Masters of Solitude*, 1978
   Parke Godwin, co-author
Elizabeth Moon, *Oath of Gold*, 1989
Sean Russell, *The Initiate Brother*, 1991
Will Shetterly, *Elsewhere*, 1991

## 1102
### ADRIAN COLE

## *Warlord of Heaven*
(New York: AvoNova, 1993)

**Story type:** Fantasy (Military; Science Fiction)
**Series:** Star Requiem
**Major character(s):** Pyramors, Political Figure (consul), Military Personnel; Auganzar, Alien (Gsendooh), Military Personnel (Supreme Sanguinary); Zellorian, Political Figure (Prime Consul), Scientist
**Time period(s):** Indeterminate Future
**Locale(s):** Innasmorn, Planet—Imaginary; Eannor, Planet—Imaginary

**Summary:** In a new dimension, Zellorian plots to enslave the remains of humanity while his enemy, Pyramors, returns to the conquered human universe for revenge. First published in England in 1990, third in the series.

**Other books you might like:**
Emma Bull, *Falcon*, 1989
Glen Cook, *The Black Company*, 1984
Frank Herbert, *Dune*, 1965
Michael Moorcock, *Elric of Melnibone*, 1976
Roger Zelazny, *Nine Princes in Amber*, 1970

## 1103
### ALLAN COLE
### CHRIS BUNCH, Co-Author

## *Empire's End*
(New York: Ballantine Del Rey, 1993)

**Story type:** Science Fiction (Adventure; Political)
**Series:** Sten
**Major character(s):** Sten, Military Personnel (admiral); Cind, Military Personnel, Girlfriend; Ecu, Alien, Diplomat
**Time period(s):** Indeterminate Future
**Locale(s):** Bohr, Planet—Imaginary (Lupis Cluster); Dusable, Planet—Imaginary; *Victory*, Spaceship

**Summary:** When the Gurkas tell Sten that they want to work for him, Sten realizes that the Rule of the Eternal Emperor has deteriorated beyond recovery and the Emperor, now dangerous and totally corrupt, must be killed. Unfortunately, Sten must first find and destroy the source of $EM^2$, the powerbase of the Emperor. This sequel to *Vortex* (1992) concludes the eight volume series.

**Other books you might like:**
Lois McMaster Bujold, *Brothers in Arms*, 1988
Glen Cook, *The Dragon Never Sleeps*, 1988
Brian Daley, *Fall of the White Ship Avatar*, 1987
Joe Haldeman, *The Forever War*, 1975
Frank Herbert, *Dune*, 1965
Kevin O'Donnell Jr., *Fire on the Border*, 1990
Alis A. Rasmussen, *Revolution's Shore*, 1990
A.E. Van Vogt, *The Weapon Makers*, 1946

## 1104

### ALLAN COLE
### CHRIS BUNCH, Co-Author

## *The Far Kingdoms*
(New York: Ballantine Del Rey, 1993)

**Story type:** Fantasy (Adventure; Quest)
**Major character(s):** Amalric Antero, Adventurer, Teenager; Janos Greycloak, Military Personnel, Wizard
**Time period(s):** Indeterminate
**Locale(s):** Valaroi, Fictional Country; Vacaan, Fictional Country (the Far Kingdoms)

**Summary:** The time has come for Amalric Antero to make the traditional coming of age voyage which expands trading territory and aids in a young man's maturation. Janos Greycloak rescues Amalric and infects him with the vision of discovering the fabled Far Kingdoms. Their odyssey brings unexpected peril and reward.

**Other books you might like:**
Margaret Ball, *Changeweaver*, 1993
Frans G. Bengtsson, *The Long Ships*, 1954
David Brin, *Glory Season*, 1993
Phyllis Eisenstein, *Sorcerer's Son*, 1979
Andre Norton, *Imperial Lady*, 1989
    Susan Shwartz, co-author

## 1105

### ALLAN COLE
### CHRIS BUNCH, Co-Author

## *Kingdoms of the Night*
(New York: Ballantine Del Rey, 1995)

**Story type:** Fantasy (Adventure; Quest)
**Series:** Far Kingdoms
**Major character(s):** Amalric Antero, Adventurer; Janela Kether Greycloak, Adventurer
**Time period(s):** Indeterminate
**Locale(s):** At Sea; Tyrenia, Fictional Country (Kingdoms of the Night)

**Summary:** Janela Kether Greycloak raises Amalric Antero from his malaise with word of the real Far Kingdoms, which she claims he never reached on his first trip. Journeying farther, they discover Tyrenia and the evil forces which threatens Tyrenia and the entire world.

**Other books you might like:**
Frans G. Bengtsson, *The Long Ships*, 1954
Dave Duncan, *The Cutting Edge*, 1992
David Eddings, *Pawn of Prophecy*, 1992
Terry Goodkind, *Wizard's First Rule*, 1994
James Hilton, *Lost Horizon*, 1933
Edward Myers, *The Mountain Made of Light*, 1992
Judith Tarr, *Spear of Heaven*, 1994

## 1106

### ALLAN COLE
### CHRIS BUNCH, Co-Author

## *The Return of the Emperor*
(New York: Ballantine/Del Rey, 1990)

**Story type:** Science Fiction (Military; Political)

**Series:** Sten
**Major character(s):** Sten, Military Personnel (admiral); Ian Mahoney, Military Personnel (ex-fleet marshall); Ecu, Alien, Diplomat
**Time period(s):** Indeterminate Future
**Locale(s):** *Santana*, Spaceship; Newton, Planet—Imaginary

**Summary:** For more than 2000 years the Eternal Emperor had produced and allocated AM2, the fuel needed for space travel. Now that the emperor has been assassinated, the remaining AM2 has become extremely precious. Something must be done to find a replacement power source before the empire is destroyed by war and lack of power. Members of the Cult of the Eternal Emperor are not worried, however, and happily await his return.

**Other books you might like:**
Brian Daley, *Fall of the White Ship Avatar*, 1987
Brian Daley, *Jinx on a Terran Inheritance*, 1985
Brian Daley, *Requiem for a Ruler of Worlds*, 1985
Stephen Goldin, *Jade Darcy and the Affair of Honor*, 1988
    Mary Mason, co-author
Dan Simmons, *Hyperion*, 1989

## 1107

### ALLAN COLE
### CHRIS BUNCH, Co-Author

## *Revenge of the Damned*
(New York: Ballantine/Del Rey, 1989)

**Story type:** Science Fiction (Military)
**Series:** Sten
**Major character(s):** Sten, Spaceship Captain, Bodyguard; Alex Kilgour, Spaceman, Companion (of Sten)
**Time period(s):** Indeterminate Future
**Locale(s):** Planet—Imaginary (A Tahn POW Camp on an alien planet)

**Summary:** The alien Tahn are attacking and humanity's interstellar empire is in chaos. Just when the Emperor needs him most, Sten's ship is destroyed and the Commander finds himself in a supposedly escape-proof prisoner of war camp on a hostile alien world.

**Other books you might like:**
William C. Dietz, *Prison Planet*, 1989
Harry Harrison, *Deathworld*, 1960
Barry B. Longyear, *Infinity Hold*, 1989

## 1108

### ALLAN COLE
### CHRIS BUNCH, Co-Author

## *Vortex*
(New York: Ballantine Del Rey, 1992)

**Story type:** Science Fiction (Immortality; Political)
**Series:** Sten
**Major character(s):** Sten, Military Personnel, Diplomat (ambassader); Ian Mahoney, Military Personnel; Alex Kilgour, Royalty (Laird), Military Personnel
**Time period(s):** Indeterminate Future
**Locale(s):** Jochi, Planet—Imaginary; Prime, Planet—Imaginary

**Summary:** The Emperor has returned, rebuilt Arundel Castle and replaced all his guards with strangers. At first relieved, Sten becomes troubled by the changes in the Emperor and his policies. Having been a friend to the Emperor for so long, Sten must decide where his loyalty lies when even the Gurkas question the Emperor's actions. Sequel to *Return of the Emperor* (1990).

**Other books you might like:**
F.M. Busby, *Rissa Kerguelen*, 1977
Brian Daley, *Requiem for a Ruler of Worlds*, 1985
Frank Herbert, *Dune*, 1965
Larry Niven, *Achilles' Choice*, 1991
  Steven Barnes, co-author
Alis A. Rasmussen, *A Passage of Stars*, 1990
Alis A. Rasmussen, *The Price of Ransom*, 1990
Alis A. Rasmussen, *Revolution's Shore*, 1990
A.E. Van Vogt, *The Weapon Makers*, 1946
Ian Watson, *Inquisitor*, 1990

## 1109
### ALLAN COLE

## The Warrior Returns
(New York: Ballantine Del Rey, 1996)

**Story type:** Fantasy (Adventure; Magic Conflict)
**Series:** Far Kingdoms
**Major character(s):** Rali Emilie Antero, Wizard, Lesbian; Novari, Mythical Creature (succubus); Magon, Royalty, Pirate
**Time period(s):** Indeterminate Past
**Locale(s):** Orissa, Fictional City; At Sea

**Summary:** Nearly dead after escaping from the Bear-King, Rali sleeps away 50 years with her lover, only to be rudely awakened by the Goddess Maranonia. The Goddess, patron of Orissa, wants the city saved from Novari, Rali's foe. Although not interested in old grudges, Rali must act to save her family, also held hostage.

**Other books you might like:**
Scott Baker, *Drink the Fire From the Flames*, 1987
M.A.R. Barker, *Man of Gold*, 1984
Diane Duane, *The Door into Fire*, 1979
Fritz Leiber, *Ill Met in Lankhmar*, 1995
Michael Scott Rohan, *The Anvil of Ice*, 1986

## 1110
### ALLAN COLE
### CHRIS BUNCH, Co-Author

## The Warrior's Tale
(New York: Ballantine Del Rey, 1994)

**Story type:** Fantasy (Quest; Military)
**Series:** Far Kingdoms
**Major character(s):** Rali Emilie Antero, Military Personnel (Maranon Guard); Gamelan, Wizard; Archon of Lycanth, Ruler, Wizard
**Time period(s):** Indeterminate Past
**Locale(s):** Orissa, Fictional City; Lycanth, Fictional City

**Summary:** When the armies of Orissa finally crush their enemies, the Archeons of Lycanth, one escapes with a spell which could destroy everything. Captain Antero and her victorious but distrusted all-woman unit sail off in pursuit, beyond everything they know, to strange lands.

**Other books you might like:**
Glen Cook, *The Black Company*, 1984
David Drake, *Vettius and His Friends*, 1989
Katherine Kurtz, *Deryni Rising*, 1970
Elizabeth Moon, *Sheepfarmer's Daughter*, 1988
Elizabeth Ann Scarborough, *Last Refuge*, 1992

## 1111
### ALLAN COLE

## Wolves of the Gods
(New York: Ballantine Del Rey, 1998)

**Story type:** Fantasy (Magic Conflict)
**Series:** Tales of the Timuras
**Major character(s):** Safar Timura, Wizard, Religious; Leiria, Warrior; Iraj Protarus, Royalty, Reanimated Dead
**Time period(s):** Indeterminate Past
**Locale(s):** Kyrania, Fictional Country; Caluz, Fictional Country

**Summary:** Safar Timura makes Iraj Protarus emperor, then kills him for his crimes. Now he wants to live in peace, but evil forces stir. When Protarus returns from the dead, Safar must lead his people to the safety of a distant land.

**Other books you might like:**
M.A.R. Barker, *Man of Gold*, 1984
Chris Bunch, *The Seer King*, 1997
Glen Cook, *Tower of Fear*, 1989
Kara Dalkey, *Goa*, 1996
Guy Gavriel Kay, *The Lions of Al-Rassan*, 1995

## 1112
### ALONZO DEAN COLE

## The Witch's Tale
(Yorktown Heights, New York: Dunwich Press, 1998)

**Story type:** Horror (Collection)

**Summary:** Collection of thirteen scripts produced for ''The Witch's Tale,'' a popular radio program that broadcast 332 episodes between 1931 and 1938. Episodes published in this volume include ''The Image,'' in which a native charm endows its wearer with the ability to transform into a beast; the vampire story ''From Dawn to Sunset''; the ghost tale ''Hangman's Roost,'' based in part on Bram Stoker's classic short story ''The Judge's House''; and ''La Mannequinne,'' in which an artist's passion for unusual collectibles compels him to buy a living mannequin. Edited by David S. Siegel, includes a complete program log and program index.

**Other books you might like:**
Clive Barker, *Forms of Heaven*, 1996
Hamilton Deane, *Dracula: The Ultimate Illustrated Edition of the World-Famous Vampire Play*, 1993
  John Balderston, co-author
Marvin Kaye, *Thirteen Plays of Ghosts and the Supernatural*, 1990
  editor
Arch Oboler, *The Oboler Omnibus*, 1945
Bram Stoker, *Dracula*, 1897

## 1113
### BURT COLE

## The Quick
(New York: Morrow, 1989)

**Story type:** Science Fiction (Military)
**Major character(s):** Shaman, Mercenary; Friedkin, Scientist
**Time period(s):** 21st century
**Locale(s):** United States

**Summary:** Shaman lives for combat and makes his living as a mercenary, gun-runner and pirate. When a popular liberation front comes into open conflict with the U.S. government, Shaman joins the conflict on both sides. It's all a game to him, a form of solipcism, until Shaman realizes that someone else is playing too.

**Other books you might like:**
L. Ron Hubbard, *Final Blackout*, 1948
    Reprint 1989
Barry B. Longyear, *Infinity Hold*, 1989
Robert Mason, *Weapon*, 1989
Jerry Pournelle, *Prince of Mercenaries*, 1989

## 1114
### DAMARIS COLE

## Token of Dragonsblood
(Lake Geneva, Wisconsin: TSR, 1991)

**Story type:** Fantasy (Quest; Magic Conflict)
**Major character(s):** Noressa, Empath, Heiress—Dispossessed; Bydawine, Companion; Felaya, Sorceress
**Time period(s):** Indeterminate
**Locale(s):** Sidra, Fictional Country; Yetel, Planet—Imaginary

**Summary:** Spirited away from her family's destruction, Noressa grows up ignorant of the strange destiny bequeathed to her. Deprived of a proper teacher, Noressa must attempt to master her Talent with assistance from a wizard, Medwyn, before Felaya takes control of Noressa's medallion, the key to vast power. This is the author's first published book.

**Other books you might like:**
Jo Clayton, *Wild Magic*, 1991
David Cook, *Beyond the Moons*, 1991
Nigel Findley, *Into the Void*, 1991
Anne McCaffrey, *Dragonflight*, 1968
Andre Norton, *The Elvenbane*, 1991
    Mercedes Lackey, co-author

## 1115
### JEFF COLLIGNON

## Her Monster
(New York: Soho Press, 1992)

**Story type:** Horror (Mystery)
**Major character(s):** Edward "Eddie" Talbot, Writer (science fiction writer), Recluse; Annie Talbot, Parent (mother of Eddie), Aged Person; Katherine "Kat" Mancy, Friend, Teenager
**Time period(s):** 1990s (1992)
**Locale(s):** Idaho

**Summary:** Born hideously deformed, Eddie Talbot leads a hermetic existence but lives vicariously through the heroes of his science fiction novels. When he establishes a rapport with Kat Mancy, Eddie's jealous mother decides to let the girl know just how closely Eddie's life resembles his fiction. A first novel.

**Other books you might like:**
Susan Kay, *Phantom*, 1991
Gaston Leroux, *The Phantom of the Opera*, 1911
Steve Vance, *Spook*, 1990

## 1116
### HELEN COLLINS

## Mutagenesis
(New York: Tor, 1993)

**Story type:** Science Fiction (Genetic Manipulation; Medical)
**Major character(s):** Mattine "Mattie" Manan, Scientist, Explorer; Elizabeth, Traveler
**Time period(s):** 27th century (2635)
**Locale(s):** Anu/Dagda, Planet—Imaginary

**Summary:** After abandoning the colony on Anu prior to viability 500 years earlier, Earth sends an expedition to recover any usable food grains, intending to restore some genetic diversity on Earth. Not expecting human survivors, they find on the Plains a very religious community where women do not speak, preventing Mattie from interacting with the colonists. Elizabeth, a colonial woman caught reading, also forbidden to women, escapes and travels with Mattie to find other Anunne survivors. First novel.

**Other books you might like:**
Eleanor Arnason, *Ring of Swords*, 1993
David Brin, *Glory Season*, 1993
Octavia E. Butler, *Dawn*, 1987
C.J. Cherryh, *Serpent's Reach*, 1980
Nicola Griffith, *Ammonite*, 1993
Joan Slonczewski, *A Door into Ocean*, 1986
Sheri S. Tepper, *Grass*, 1989

## 1117
### NANCY A. COLLINS

## Angels on Fire
(Clarkston, Georgia: White Wolf, 1998)

**Story type:** Horror (Occult)
**Major character(s):** Lucy Bender, Clerk, Artist; Joth, Angel
**Time period(s):** 1990s (1998)
**Locale(s):** New York, New York

**Summary:** Lucy Bender becomes the protector of Joth, an Elohim, or fallen angel, who must choose whether to rejoin his brothers among the celestial hierarchy or become a mortal. Lucy, with help from another fallen angel, attempts to protect Joth from the demonic Meresin and the corruption of life in contemporary New York City.

**Other books you might like:**
Clive Barker, *Imajica*, 1991
Terry Brooks, *Running with the Demon*, 1997
Garry Kilworth, *Angel*, 1993
Michael Marano, *Dawn Song*, 1998
Brian Stableford, *The Werewolves of London*, 1992

## 1118
### NANCY A. COLLINS, Editor
### EDWARD E. KRAMER, Co-Editor
### MARTIN H. GREENBERG, Co-Editor

## Dark Love
(New York: Roc, 1995)

**Story type:** Horror (Anthology)
**Summary:** Twenty-two stories published here for the first time explore the dark side of love and romance. In Stephen King's "Lunch at the Gotham Cafe," a writer's discussion of divorce proceedings

with his wife in a Manhattan restaurant are interrupted by a rampaging maitre d' whose madness manifests the writer's own smoldering emotions. In Kathe Koja's "Pas de Deux," a woman's obsessive dancing and the toll it takes on her body is an outward expression of her emotional starvation. Robert Weinberg's "Ro Erg" tells of a man who lives the hedonistic life of an alter ego created by a computer misprint of his name, and Ramsey Campbell's "Going Under" of a man on a charity walk who discovers that the chaos and confusion of a stampede in a tunnel symbolize his entrapment within his own crumbling personal life. Karl Edward Wagner's "Locked Away" is about a woman who discovers the repressed emotions of another woman unleashed through a locket she wore, and Douglas E. Winter's "Loop" profiles a man's obsessive morbid interest in a porn star's film career. Ted Klein supplies an introduction.

**Other books you might like:**
Ellen Datlow, *Little Deaths*, 1994
    editor
Jeff Gelb, *Hot Blood: Tales of Provocative Horror*, 1989
    Lonn Friend, co-editor
Marvin Kaye, *Lovers and Other Monsters*, 1992
    editor
Michele Slung, *I Shudder at Your Touch*, 1992
    editor
Michele Slung, *Shudder Again*, 1993

## 1119

### NANCY A. COLLINS

## A Dozen Black Roses
(Clarkston, Georgia: White Wolf, 1995)

**Story type:** Horror (Vampire Story)
**Series:** Sonja Blue
**Major character(s):** Sonja Blue, Vampire; Sinjon, Vampire; Esher, Vampire
**Time period(s):** 1990s (1996)
**Locale(s):** Deadtown, Alternate Universe

**Summary:** Sonja Blue foments civil war between the leading vampire clans of Deadtown when she attempts to liberate the mother of a young boy who has been abducted as a plaything for one of the vampire princes. This supernatural riff on the spaghetti western is set in the publisher's World of Darkness gaming milieu, an alternate universe in which supernatural beings run the world.

**Other books you might like:**
Don Bassingthwaite, *As One Dead*, 1996
    Nancy Kilpatrick, co-author
Brian Herbert, *Blood on the Sun*, 1996
    Marie Landis, co-author
Robert Weinberg, *The Unbeholden*, 1996

## 1120

### NANCY A. COLLINS, Editor
### EDWARD E. KRAMER, Co-Editor
### MARTIN H. GREENBERG, Co-Editor

## Forbidden Acts
(New York: Avon, 1995)

**Story type:** Horror (Anthology)

**Summary:** The twenty-one stories commissioned especially for this volume probe social and personal taboos for their horror potential. Among the areas covered are television programming in Alan

Moore's "Light of Thy Countenance" and Howard Kaylan's "The Energy Pals," family life in Steve Rasnic Tem's "Blood Knot," medical research in Rob Hardin's "Interrogator Frames," autoeroticism in Lucy Taylor's "Choke Hold," lesbian vampirism in Danielle Willis's "Happy Couple," and sadomasochism in David Aaron Clark's "Stations of the Cross." Former B-movie film reviewer Joe Bob Briggs supplies the introduction.

**Other books you might like:**
Ellen Datlow, *Little Deaths*, 1995
    editor
Jeff Gelb, *Hot Blood: Tales of Provocative Horror*, 1989
    Lonn Friend, co-editor
Jeff Gelb, *Hotter Blood: More Tales of Erotic Horror*, 1991
    Michael Garrett, co-editor
Jeff Gelb, *Hottest Blood: The Ultimate in Erotic Horror*, 1993
    Michael Garrett, co-editor
Michele Slung, *I Shudder at Your Touch*, 1991
    editor
Michele Slung, *Shudder Again*, 1993
    editor

## 1121

### NANCY A. COLLINS

## In the Blood
(New York: Roc, 1992)

**Story type:** Horror (Vampire Story)
**Series:** Sonja Blue
**Major character(s):** Sonja Blue, Vampire; William Palmer, Detective; Dr. Pangloss, Supernatural Being
**Time period(s):** 1990s
**Locale(s):** San Francisco, California

**Summary:** In this sequel to her Bram Stoker Award-winning novel *Sunglasses After Dark* (1989), Collins continues the saga of Sonja Blue, the vampirized debutante searching for the being who turned her into a member of the Pretenders, a race of supernatural creatures that masquerades as the underground life of the human species. Sonja joins forces with William Palmer, a detective originally hired by her pursuers, and tracks her vampire overlord Morgan to San Francisco's famous Ghost House for a showdown.

**Other books you might like:**
Poppy Z. Brite, *Lost Souls*, 1992
P.N. Elrod, *The Vampire Files Series*, 1989-1992
Barbara Hambly, *Those Who Hunt the Night*, 1988
Anne Rice, *Interview with the Vampire*, 1976

## 1122

### NANCY A. COLLINS

## Midnight Blue: The Sonja Blue Collection
(Stone Mountain, Georgia: White Wolf, 1995)

**Story type:** Horror (Collection; Vampire Story)
**Series:** Sonja Blue
**Major character(s):** Sonja Blue, Vampire

**Summary:** This compilation collects three novels featuring punk vampire heroine Sonja Blue. In *Sunglasses After Dark* (1989), newly vampirized heiress Denise Thorne adopts the pseudonym Sonja Blue and is introduced into the world of The Pretenders, creatures of myth and fantasy who masquerade as the downtrodden and marginal among mortals. In *In the Blood* (1992), Sonja continues her quest to find her vampire initiator. *Paint It Black*, first published in England in

1995, chronicles Sonja's climactic encounter with Morgan, the vampire who converted her.

**Other books you might like:**
Poppy Z. Brite, *Lost Souls*, 1993
Gail Petersen, *The Making of a Monster*, 1994
Anne Rice, *The Vampire Lestat*, 1985
Jody Scott, *I, Vampire*, 1984
John Skipp, *The Light at the End*, 1987
    Craig Spector, co-author
S.P. Somtow, *Vanitas: Escape From Vampire Junction*, 1995

---

### 1123
#### NANCY A. COLLINS

## Nameless Sins

(Springfield, Pennsylvania: Gauntlet Press, 1994)

**Story type:** Horror (Collection)

**Summary:** This first collection of 24 stories assembles nearly all of the short fiction written to date by this Bram Stoker Award-winning writer. Reprints include ''Freaktent,'' about a photographer of carnival sideshows; ''Rant,'' which presents the world through the eyes of a psychotic; ''Iphigenia,'' a bizarre anti-war story; the horror western, ''The Tortuga Hill Gang's Last Ride''; the Civil War horror story, ''The Sunday Go-to-Meeting Jaw''; and a strange tale of sexual fulfillment, ''The Two-Headed Man.'' Three stories first published here include ''Without Sin,'' an irreverent retelling of the biblical story of Christ's crucifixion and resurrection; ''Binky Malomar and His Amazing Instant Pussy Kit,'' an amusing riff on Lovecraftian horror; and ''Speed Freaks with Guns: The Novelization,'' the novelization of a film script about a naive young man's encounter with a paranoid psychotic in Manhattan. Joe Lansdale supplies an introduction and Neil Gaiman the afterword.

**Other books you might like:**
Poppy Z. Brite, *Swamp Foetus*, 1992
Joe R. Lansdale, *By Bizarre Hands*, 1989
Elizabeth Massie, *Southern Discomfort: Selected Works of Elizabeth Massie*, 1993

---

### 1124
#### NANCY A. COLLINS

## Sunglasses After Dark

(New York: NAL Onyx, 1989)

**Story type:** Horror (Vampire Story)
**Series:** Sonja Blue
**Major character(s):** Sonja Blue, Vampire; Catherine Wheele, Psychic, Religious (Evangelist)
**Time period(s):** 1960s (1969); 1980s
**Locale(s):** New York, New York

**Summary:** Sonja Blue struggles to come to terms with the nature, morality, and meaning of her life as a vampire, while attempting to stay out of the clutches of her primary adversary, a demented, psychic evangelist.

**Other books you might like:**
Suzy McKee Charnas, *The Vampire Tapestry*, 1980
Tanith Lee, *Sabella: Or, The Blood Stone*, 1980
George R.R. Martin, *Fevre Dream*, 1982
Anne Rice, *Interview with the Vampire*, 1976
S.P. Somtow, *Vampire Junction*, 1984

---

### 1125
#### NANCY A. COLLINS

## Tempter

(New York: Onyx 1990)

**Story type:** Horror (Black Magic)
**Major character(s):** Adam Rossiter, Singer (former rock star); Charlotte Calder, Accountant (yuppie); Ti Alice, Occultist (voodoo priestess)
**Time period(s):** 1990s
**Locale(s):** New Orleans, Louisiana

**Summary:** A 37-year-old has-been rock star's quest for mystic enlightenment leads to a voodoo initiation ritual where he meets a priestess. Later, in her home, he discovers, in a mysterious ancient book called the *Aegrisomnia,* a mandala that opens a doorway between his world and that of the gods of voodoo. Charlie Calder, on the rebound from a string of disastrous love affairs, takes up with Rossiter, unaware that he is coming under the sway of the Tempter, an incredibly evil ancient spirit that seeks to return to this world.

**Other books you might like:**
Hugh B. Cave, *The Evil*, 1981
William Hjortsberg, *Falling Angel*, 1978
Dean R. Koontz, *Darkfall*, 1984
H.P. Lovecraft, *The Case of Charles Dexter Ward*, 1927
Anne Rice, *The Vampire Lestat*, 1985

---

### 1126
#### NANCY A. COLLINS

## Walking Wolf

(Shingleton, California: Ziesing, 1995)

**Story type:** Horror (Werewolf Story)
**Major character(s):** William ''Billy'' Skillet, Werewolf; Witchfinder Jones, Bounty Hunter; Digging Woman, Indian
**Time period(s):** 1860s
**Locale(s):** Southwest

**Summary:** The orphan child of a human mother and werewolf father, Billy Skillet is raised by the Comanches, who revere him as a skinwalker, or shapeshifter, named Walking Wolf. Billy's adventures eventually bring him into the white man's world, where he holds a variety of jobs that permit him to view the true bestiality of humanity in the white man's treatment of the Native American nations.

**Other books you might like:**
William Berger, *Little Big Man*, 1964
Joe R. Lansdale, *Dead in the West*, 1986
S.P. Somtow, *Moon Dance*, 1990

---

### 1127
#### NANCY A. COLLINS

## Wild Blood

(New York: Roc, 1994)

**Story type:** Horror (Werewolf Story)
**Major character(s):** Skinner Cade, Young Man, Werewolf; Jez, Werewolf; Rosie, Magician (coyotero)
**Time period(s):** 1990s (1994)
**Locale(s):** Los Lobos, Arizona

**Summary:** Newly orphaned, Skinner Cade goes searching for the truth about his origins and discovers that he is a *vargr*, or purebred werewolf. After angering the wolf clan that he at first hopes to join by spurning their inhumane treatment of their prey, Skinner is helped by other creatures of fantasy and legend who masquerade as humans.

**Other books you might like:**
Poppy Z. Brite, *Lost Souls*, 1992
Crosland Brown, *Tombley's Walk*, 1990
Ron Dee, *Dusk*, 1991
S.P. Somtow, *Moon Dance*, 1990

---

**1128**

**S. DARNBROOK COLSON**

## People of the Night

(Seattle, Washington: Three Stones Publications, 1994)

**Story type:** Horror (Collection)

**Summary:** This trilogy of stories offers stark, often macabre portraits of social outcasts. ''Brotherhood of the Dark'' tells of the relationship between a prostitute and a crippled derelict, ''People of the Night'' of gang life, and ''Darksiders'' about the subculture of the city streets at night. Wayne Allen Sallee supplies the introduction.

**Other books you might like:**
Joe R. Lansdale, *By Bizarre Hands*, 1989
Wayne Allen Sallee, *Pain-Grin*, 1993
David J. Schow, *Black Leather Required*, 1994
David J. Schow, *Lost Angels*, 1990
John Shirley, *New Noir*, 1993

---

**1129**

**DIANA M. CONCANNON**

## Helen's Passage

(Redondo Beach, California: Cavatica, 1998)

**Story type:** Fantasy (Historical)
**Major character(s):** Helen, Noblewoman; Agamemnon, Ruler; Alexander, Warrior
**Time period(s):** Indeterminate Past
**Locale(s):** Troy, Asia Minor

**Summary:** Helen is so beautiful that she becomes the focus of a contest of wills between two great city states. Eventually war breaks out, which will result in the death of heroes and the destruction of Troy. There is only minimal fantasy in this retelling of the classic story. First novel.

**Other books you might like:**
Michael Ayrton, *The Maze Maker*, 1967
Roberta Gellis, *Shimmering Splendor*, 1995
David Gemmell, *Lion of Macedon*, 1992
Roger Lancelyn Green, *The Tale of Troy*, 1958
Michael Lahey, *Quest for Apollo*, 1989

---

**1130**

**MARYSE CONDE**

## I, Tituba, Black Witch of Salem

(Charlottesville, Virginia: University Press of Virginia, 1992)

**Story type:** Fantasy (Historical)
**Major character(s):** Tituba, Historical Figure, Witch (healer); Mama Yaya, Spirit, Healer; John Indian, Slave, Spouse (Tituba's)

**Time period(s):** 17th century (1690s)
**Locale(s):** Barbados; Salem, Massachusetts, American Colonies

**Summary:** Prophesied to have much pain in her life and to travel across the water and return, Tituba marries John Indian. The property of Samuel Parris who accepts a position as minister in Salem Township where black means satanic, Tituba, victimized by the children of Salem, confesses to satanism. Although one of the first arrested for witchcraft, she lives in prison until pardoned with the other accused two years later when the prison sells her to pay for her chains and fees. Translated by Richard Philcox.

**Other books you might like:**
Octavia E. Butler, *Kindred*, 1979
Orson Scott Card, *Lost Boys*, 1992
Nathaniel Hawthorne, *The Scarlet Letter*, 1850
Susan Palwick, *Flying in Place*, 1992
Marge Piercy, *Woman on the Edge of Time*, 1976
Elizabeth Ann Scarborough, *The Healer's War*, 1989

---

**1131**

**NICHOLAS CONDE**

## In the Deep Woods

(New York: St. Martin's, 1989)

**Story type:** Horror (Serial Killer)
**Major character(s):** Carol Warren, Writer (Children's books); Paul Miller, Detective—Amateur
**Time period(s):** 1980s
**Locale(s):** New York, New York

**Summary:** After a good friend is murdered by a serial killer, Carol Warren is further horrified when an obsessed private detective implicates her brother in the killings. Her attempts to clear her brother make Carol an increasingly attractive target for the progressively demented murderer.

**Other books you might like:**
Robert Bloch, *Psycho*, 1959
Ramsey Campbell, *The Doll Who Ate His Mother*, 1976
Friedrich Durrenmatt, *It Happened in Broad Daylight*,

---

**1132**

**JANE LESLIE CONLY**

## R-T, Margaret, and the Rats of NIMH

(New York: Harper, 1990)

**Story type:** Fantasy (Science Fiction; Young Adult)
**Series:** Rats of NIMH
**Major character(s):** R-T ''Artie'', Child, Handicapped; Margaret, Child (R-T's sister); Racso, Animal (intelligent talking rat)
**Time period(s):** 1980s
**Locale(s):** Thom Valley (North Woods)

**Summary:** Lost in the North Woods, R-T and his sister Margaret are rescued by Racso and the other intelligent rats of NIMH. When the children finally return to their family at the end of summer, they are unable to keep the rats a secret, and civilization and science close in on the secret rat community in Thom Valley.

**Other books you might like:**
Richard Adams, *Watership Down*, 1974
Lynne Reid Banks, *The Indian in the Cupboard*, 1980
Pauline Clarke, *The Return of the Twelves*, 1964
Mary Norton, *The Borrowers*, 1953
Robert C. O'Brien, *Mrs. Frisby and the Rats of NIMH*, 1971

## 1133

### MICHAEL CONNER

## *Archangel*

(New York: Tor, 1995)

**Story type:** Science Fiction (Alternate Universe; Mystery)
**Major character(s):** Danny Constantine, Journalist; Simon Gray, Scientist, Doctor; Selena Crockett, Heiress
**Time period(s):** 1930s (1930)
**Locale(s):** Minneapolis, Minnesota

**Summary:** Minneapolis escapes some effects of a pandemic hemorrhagic fever due to the immunity of African-Americans, encouraged to immigrate to that city. Danny Constantine trails a killer whose victims seem slain by a vampire, while his newspaper ignores the story and new powers vie for control of the city.

**Other books you might like:**
Greg Bear, *Blood Music*, 1985
Terry Bisson, *Fire on the Mountain*, 1988
John Christopher, *Empty World*, 1978
Philip K. Dick, *Dr. Bloodmoney*, 1965
Brad Ferguson, *The World Next Door*, 1990
Frank Herbert, *The White Plague*, 1982
Wilson Tucker, *The Year of the Quiet Sun*, 1970
Chelsea Quinn Yarbro, *Time of the Fourth Horseman*, 1976

## 1134

### MIGUEL CONNER

## *The Queen of Darkness*

(New York: Aspect, 1998)

**Story type:** Science Fiction (Dystopian)
**Major character(s):** Byron, Investigator; MoonQueen, Ruler
**Time period(s):** Indeterminate Future
**Locale(s):** Norway

**Summary:** A secret race of immortals resembling legendary vampires precipitates a nuclear war and destroys civilization. In the aftermath, they build and dominate a new culture. Despite Byron's disaffection with the status quo, he accepts orders to investigate dissent among the enslaved humans and discovers that his own people have become fatally corrupted by their power. First novel.

**Other books you might like:**
Brian W. Aldiss, *Dracula Unbound*, 1992
David Bischoff, *The Vampires of Nightworld*, 1981
Tanith Lee, *Sabella: Or, The Blood Stone*, 1980
Jacqueline Lichtenberg, *House of Zeor*, 1977
Christopher Pike, *The Season of Passage*, 1992

## 1135

### FLYNN CONNOLLY

## *The Rising of the Moon*

(New York: Ballantine Del Rey, 1993)

**Story type:** Science Fiction (Political)
**Major character(s):** Nuala Maebh Dennehy, Teacher, Revolutionary; Igraine, Revolutionary
**Time period(s):** 21st century
**Locale(s):** Ireland

**Summary:** After teaching abroad for 15 years, Nuala Dennehy returns to Ireland to discover complete repression of women, now the property of men, through a structure supported by the isolationist Irish government and Catholic church. Nuala finds an underground movement striving to empower women by distributing revolutionary literature and contraceptives and soon runs afoul of authorities. Author's first novel.

**Other books you might like:**
Margaret Atwood, *The Handmaid's Tale*, 1985
Maya Kaathryn Bohnhoff, *The Meri*, 1992
Maya Kaathryn Bohnhoff, *Taminy*, 1993
Lester Del Rey, *The Eleventh Commandment*, 1970 revised
Suzette Haden Elgin, *The Judas Rose*, 1987
Suzette Haden Elgin, *Native Tongue*, 1984

## 1136

### JOHN DAVID CONNOR (Pseudonym of John H. Way and David C. Miller)

## *Contagion*

(New York: Diamond, 1992)

**Story type:** Horror (Mystery)
**Major character(s):** Howard Fletcher, Doctor; Byron Swinton, Doctor (epidemiologist); Robby Swinton, Teenager
**Time period(s):** 1990s
**Locale(s):** New Orleans, Louisiana

**Summary:** A high school science project runs amuck when the son of an epidemiologist working for the Centers for Disease Control tries his hand at infectious disease research by releasing a new, lethal strain of typhus on the unsuspecting celebrants of the Mardi Gras festival in New Orleans.

**Other books you might like:**
Michael Crichton, *The Andromeda Strain*, 1969
Pauline Dunn, *The Crawling Dark*, 1991
Christopher Hyde, *Jericho Falls*, 1986
Peter Straub, *Floating Dragon*, 1982

## 1137

### WILLIAM W. CONNORS
### CARRIE A. BEBRIS, Co-Author

## *Shadowborn*

(Renton, WA: TSR, 1998)

**Story type:** Horror (Occult)
**Series:** Ravenloft
**Major character(s):** Alexi Shadowborn, Knight; Dasmaria Eveningstar, Knight; Lysander Greylocks, Religious (monk)
**Time period(s):** 7th century (626, Barovian calendar)
**Locale(s):** Avonleigh, Alternate Earth

**Summary:** Alexi Shadowborn's plans to become a paladin in service to the sun god Belenus are thwarted following his triumph over a pack of marauding ghouls. Determined to fulfill his ambitions, he embarks on a quest revealed to him in dreams that will involve liberating the soul of his dead warrior mother from the clutches of the demon who has imprisoned her. Set in the imaginary realm of Ravenloft, where the reanimated dead and creatures of the supernatural co-exist with mortals.

**Other books you might like:**
Andria Cardarelle, *To Sleep with Evil*, 1996
Gene DeWeese, *Lord of the Necropolis*, 1997
Gene DeWeese, *King of the Dead*, 1996
Laurell K. Hamilton, *Death of a Darklord*, 1995

Tanya Huff, *Scholar of Decay*, 1995

## 1138

### PAM CONRAD

## Stonewords: A Ghost Story

(New York: Harper and Row, 1990)

**Story type:** Fantasy (Time Travel; Young Adult)
**Major character(s):** Zoe, Child (20th century); Zoe Louise, Child (19th century), Spirit (20th century)
**Time period(s):** 20th century; 19th century
**Locale(s):** United States

**Summary:** 11-year-old Zoe discovers that her house is occupied by the ghost of her namesake, who carries her back to 1870 to try to prevent her tragic death.

**Other books you might like:**
L.M. Boston, *The Stones of Green Knowe*, 1976
William Mayne, *Earthfasts*, 1967
Ruth Park, *Playing Beatie Bow*, 1980
Philippa Pearce, *Tom's Midnight Garden*, 1959

## 1139

### ROBERT CONROY

## 1901

(Novato, California: Presidio Press/Lyford Books, 1995)

**Story type:** Science Fiction (Alternate Universe; Political)
**Major character(s):** Patrick Mahan, Military Personnel; Theodore Roosevelt, Historical Figure, Political Figure
**Time period(s):** 1900s (1901)
**Locale(s):** United States

**Summary:** When President McKinley refuses Kaiser Wilhelm II's demand that the U.S. surrender Pacific and Caribbean territories, the Kaiser initiates an invasion of the United States, first striking Long Island. First novel.

**Other books you might like:**
William Gibson, *The Difference Engine*, 1991
 Bruce Sterling, co-author
Kim Newman, *Anno Dracula*, 1993
Mike Resnick, *Alternate Presidents*, 1992
 editor
John Maddox Roberts, *King of the Wood*, 1983
Harry Turtledove, *The Guns of the South: A Novel of the Civil War*, 1992

## 1140

### STORM CONSTANTINE

## Bewitchments of Love and Hate

(New York: Tor, 1990)

**Story type:** Science Fiction (Gay/Lesbian Fiction; Science Fantasy)
**Series:** Books of Wraeththu
**Major character(s):** Swift, Heir; Calanthe, Wanderer; Trerzian, Royalty
**Time period(s):** Indeterminate
**Locale(s):** Earth

**Summary:** Swift grows up as the pampered child of the leader of the Varrs, a warlike tribe of Wraeththu. When Cal comes into this closed world, Swift has to learn to separate the positive and negative qulities of the Varrs if they are to survive.

**Other books you might like:**
Angela Carter, *The Bloody Chamber*, 1979
Ellen Kushner, *Swordspoint*, 1987
Tanith Lee, *The Book of the Damned*, 1990
Tanith Lee, *Night's Master*, 1978
Anne Rice, *Interview with the Vampire*, 1976

## 1141

### STORM CONSTANTINE

## The Enchantments of Flesh and Spirit

(New York: Tor, 1989)

**Story type:** Science Fiction (Psychic Powers)
**Series:** Books of Wraeththu
**Major character(s):** Pellaz, Mutant, Psychic; Calanthe, Mutant, Psychic
**Time period(s):** Indeterminate Future
**Locale(s):** England

**Summary:** In a near-future England collapsing into economic and environmental ruin, a new form of human being comes into existence. The Wraeththu, hermaphroditic and endowed with psychic powers, begin to contest with humanity for control of the world.

**Other books you might like:**
Marion Zimmer Bradley, *The Shattered Chain*, 1976
John Christopher, *Pendulum*, 1968
Ursula K. Le Guin, *The Left Hand of Darkness*, 1969
Doris Lessing, *The Fifth Child*, 1988
Doris Lessing, *The Memoirs of a Survivor*, 1974

## 1142

### STORM CONSTANTINE

## The Fulfillments of Fate and Desire

(New York: Tor, 1991)

**Story type:** Science Fiction (Gay/Lesbian Fiction; Science Fantasy)
**Series:** Books of Wraeththu
**Major character(s):** Calanthe, Wanderer, Prostitute; Panthera, Heir, Prostitute; Thiede, Deity, Ruler
**Time period(s):** 21st century
**Locale(s):** Fallsend, Fictional Country; Immanira, Fictional Country

**Summary:** Cal has hit bottom at the start of the final Wraeththu book, scraping and working as a prostitute. Slowly, Cal's nature and events conspire to drive him to Immanira.

**Other books you might like:**
Angela Carter, *The Bloody Chamber*, 1979
Ellen Kushner, *Swordspoint*, 1987
Tanith Lee, *Red as Blood: Or Tales from the Sisters Grimmer*, 1983
Michael Shea, *Nifft the Lean*, 1982
Chelsea Quinn Yarbro, *Hotel Transylvania*, 1978

## 1143

### D.J. CONWAY

## Soothslayer: A Magickal Fantasy

(St. Paul, Minnesota: Llewellyn Publications, 1997)

**Story type:** Fantasy (Magic Conflict; Religious)
**Series:** Dream Warrior Trilogy

**Major character(s):** Corri Farblood, Sorcerer, Leader (Dream Warrior); The Soothslayer, Sorcerer, Religious (priest); Imandoff Silverhair, Sorcerer
**Time period(s):** Indeterminate
**Locale(s):** Sar Akka, Fictional Country

**Summary:** Corri Farblood's acceptance of the fact that she is truly the Dream Warrior of prophecy propels her to the forefront of a war to prevent the religious fanatics of Frav, led by Corri's father, Kayth, from invading their lands and destroying their way of life. Imandoff Silverhair helps Corri reach her full magical potential while they plan the defeat of Kayth and his evil ally, the Soothsayer. Second volume in trilogy.

**Other books you might like:**
Maya Kaathryn Bohnhoff, *The Spirit Gate*, 1996
D.A. Heeley, *Lilith*, 1996
Mercedes Lackey, *The Lark and the Wren*, 1991
Thomas K. Martin, *A Matter of Honor*, 1994
Eloise Jarvis McGraw, *The Moorchild*, 1996
Elizabeth Moon, *Sheepfarmer's Daughter*, 1988
Melanie Rawn, *Dragon Prince*, 1988
Melanie Rawn, *The Ruins of Ambrai*, 1994
Martha Wells, *The Element of Fire*, 1993

---

**1144**

**DAVID COOK**

## *Beyond the Moons*

(Lake Geneva, Wisconsin: TSR, 1991)

**Story type:** Fantasy (Quest)
**Series:** Cloakmaster Cycle
**Major character(s):** Teldin Moore, Adventurer, Warrior; Herphan Gomja, Military Personnel, Alien (Giff)
**Time period(s):** Indeterminate
**Locale(s):** Krynn, Planet—Imaginary

**Summary:** When a spelljamming ship crashes, a dying alien presents Teldin with a magical cloak, one which Teldin inadvertently dons and then cannot remove. As he searches for the secret to his cloak's power, he finds himself in unpleasantly high demand as he tries to take the cloak to the mysterious creators. This book is set in the Spelljammer gaming milieu.

**Other books you might like:**
Brian Daley, *Fall of the White Ship Avatar*, 1987
Brian Daley, *Jinx on a Terran Inheritance*, 1985
Brian Daley, *Requiem for a Ruler of Worlds*, 1985
John DeChancie, *Starrigger*, 1983
Nigel Findley, *Into the Void*, 1991
Alis A. Rasmussen, *The Price of Ransom*, 1990

---

**1145**

**DAVID COOK**

## *Horselords*

(Lake Geneva, Wisconsin: TSR, 1990)

**Story type:** Fantasy (Historical)
**Series:** Forgotten Realms: The Empire Trilogy
**Major character(s):** Koja, Religious (priest); Yamun, Royalty (Khahan)
**Time period(s):** 12th century
**Locale(s):** Quaraband, Asia (City of Tents)

**Summary:** Koja of Khazari, Priest of Furo, joins Khahan Yamun's entourage. Their relationship develops through treachery, intrigue, and the consolidation of an empire. Novel based on a game.

**Other books you might like:**
M. Coleman Easton, *Spirits of Cavern and Hearth*, 1989
Ken Kato, *Yamato: A Rage in Heaven*, 1990
Marc Laidlaw, *Neon Lotus*, 1988
Jeanne Larsen, *Silk Road*, 1989
David Wingrove, *The Middle Kingdom*, 1990

---

**1146**

**DAVID COOK**

## *King Pinch*

(Lake Geneva, Wisconsin: TSR, 1995)

**Story type:** Fantasy (Adventure; Magic Conflict)
**Series:** Forgotten Realms: The Nobles
**Major character(s):** Pinch "Janol", Thief, Orphan; Lissa, Religious (priestess); Cleedis, Warrior
**Time period(s):** Indeterminate
**Locale(s):** Ankhapur, Fictional City

**Summary:** Upon the death of Pinch's guardian, King Manferic III, Cleedis finds Pinch and implores him to return to Ankhapur, where potential rulers employ an ancient test of worthiness. Interrupted at his current gambit, Pinch turns his attention toward the throne and the potentially deadly trials arising from his new goal.

**Other books you might like:**
Dave Duncan, *Magic Casement*, 1990
James Lowder, *The Ring of Winter*, 1992
Michelle Sagara, *Into the Dark Lands*, 1991
R.A. Salvatore, *The Legacy*, 1992
Michael Williams, *A Forest Lord*, 1991
Tad Williams, *The Dragonbone Chair*, 1988

---

**1147**

**GLEN COOK**

## *Bleak Seasons*

(New York: Tor, 1996)

**Story type:** Fantasy (Military; Magic Conflict)
**Series:** Chronicles of the Black Company: Glittering Stone
**Major character(s):** Murgen, Military Personnel; Longshadow, Wizard; Croaker, Military Personnel, Doctor
**Time period(s):** Indeterminate Past
**Locale(s):** Dejagore, Fictional City; Shadowcatch, Fictional City

**Summary:** De facto leader of the Black Company since Croaker's disappearance, Murgen tries to defend Dejagore against an army and traitors. Meanwhile, Croaker and Lady try to survive the plots against them and the Company. Elsewhere, Longshadow plots, hoping to survive and conquer. First book of the Glittering Stone trilogy and the seventh Black Company novel.

**Other books you might like:**
Brian Daley, *The Doomfarers of Coramonde*, 1977
Terry Goodkind, *Wizard's First Rule*, 1994
Barbara Hambly, *The Ladies of Mandrigyn*, 1984
Guy Gavriel Kay, *Tigana*, 1990
Fritz Leiber, *Ill Met in Lankhmar*, 1995
Michael Moorcock, *The Swords Trilogy*, 1977

## 1148

### GLEN COOK

## *Deadly Quicksilver Lies*

(New York: Roc, 1994)

**Story type:** Fantasy (Mystery)
**Series:** Garrett Files
**Major character(s):** Garrett, Detective—Private; Winger, Detective—Private
**Time period(s):** Indeterminate Past
**Locale(s):** TunFaire, Fictional Country

**Summary:** When hired to locate a missing teenager, Garrett must find a king's illegitimate daughter hiding from more than her mother. Garrett, Winger and Saucerhead Thorpe must keep one step ahead of the Rainmaker in unraveling the trail of mayhem and magic to find the girl and stay alive.

**Other books you might like:**
Robert Asprin, *Thieves' World*, 1979
    editor
Emma Bull, *Finder*, 1984
Randall Garrett, *Too Many Magicians*, 1967
Simon R. Green, *Hawk & Fisher*, 1990
Will Shetterly, *Nevernever*, 1993

## 1149

### GLEN COOK

## *Dread Brass Shadows*

(New York: Roc, 1990)

**Story type:** Fantasy (Mystery)
**Series:** Garrett Files
**Major character(s):** Garrett, Detective—Private; Tinnie, Girlfriend
**Time period(s):** Indeterminate Past
**Locale(s):** TunFaire, Fictional Country

**Summary:** In this latest installment, someone has tried to murder Garrett's girlfriend, Tinnie. Garrett sets out in search of the *Book of Shadows* to find out why Tinnie is a target.

**Other books you might like:**
Craig Shaw Gardner, *Bride of the Slime Monster*, 1990

## 1150

### GLEN COOK

## *Dreams of Steel*

(New York: Tor, 1990)

**Story type:** Fantasy (Sword and Sorcery)
**Series:** Chronicles of the Black Company
**Major character(s):** Croaker, Military Personnel (soldier), Historian; Lady, Military Personnel (soldier), Sorcerer
**Time period(s):** Indeterminate Past
**Locale(s):** Taglios, Fictional City; Dejagore, Fictional City

**Summary:** After the defeat at Dejagore, Croaker is believed dead, though Soulcatcher has healed him and holds him captive in her revenge against Lady. Lady takes command of and starts rebuilding the Black Company, and allies with a secret cult of assassins who believes she will become the avatar of their goddess in order to carry on the fight against the remaining Shadowmasters, who once served her Empire.

**Other books you might like:**
Robert Asprin, *Thieves' World*, 1979
Heather Gladney, *Teot's War*, 1987
Barbara Hambly, *The Ladies of Mandrigyn*, 1984
Fred Saberhagen, *Woundhealer's Story: The First Book of Lost Swords*, 1983
Gene Wolfe, *The Shadow of the Torturer*, 1980

## 1151

### GLEN COOK

## *Old Tin Sorrows*

(New York: NAL Signet, 1989)

**Story type:** Fantasy (Mystery)
**Series:** Garrett Files
**Major character(s):** Garrett, Detective—Private
**Time period(s):** Indeterminate Past
**Locale(s):** TunFaire, Fictional Country

**Summary:** Garrett is hired by a general, then finds himself caught in the middle of murder, madness and greed.

**Other books you might like:**
William Kotzwinkle, *Fata Morgana*, 1977
Michael Kurland, *A Study in Sorcery*, 1989
Mercedes Lackey, *Children of the Night*, 1990

## 1152

### GLEN COOK

## *Pretty Pewter Gods*

(New York: Roc, 1995)

**Story type:** Fantasy (Mystery; Urban)
**Series:** Garrett Files
**Major character(s):** Garrett, Detective—Private; Dead Man, Mythical Creature (loghyr); Magodor, Deity
**Time period(s):** Indeterminate Past
**Locale(s):** Karenta, Fictional City

**Summary:** With real estate scarce on Temple Row, Garrett has three reasons to find the key to the last remaining temple: the two minor pantheons who demand his services and the possibility of war on a supernatural scale that could destroy all reality.

**Other books you might like:**
Robert Asprin, *Thieves' World*, 1979
    editor
Emma Bull, *Finder*, 1994
Randall Garrett, *Too Many Magicians*, 1967
Simon R. Green, *Hawk & Fisher*, 1990
Laurell K. Hamilton, *Guilty Pleasures*, 1993
Jonathan Lethem, *Gun, with Occasional Music*, 1994
Will Shetterly, *Nevernever*, 1993
Gary K. Wolf, *Who Censored Roger Rabbit?*, 1981

## 1153

### GLEN COOK

## *Red Iron Nights*

(New York: Roc, 1991)

**Story type:** Fantasy (Mystery; Urban)
**Series:** Garrett Files

**Major character(s):** Garrett, Detective—Private; Dead Man, Sidekick, Genius
**Time period(s):** Indeterminate Past
**Locale(s):** TunFaire, Fictional City

**Summary:** The Watch finally comes to Garrett for help when someone kills young women who are well-enough connected to pressure the Watch for results. Gruesome even for TunFaire, the murders point to some sort of ritual compulsion. When Garrett lands the culprit, the murders mysteriously continue.

**Other books you might like:**
Robert Asprin, *Thieves' World*, 1979
   editor
George Alec Effinger, *When Gravity Fails*, 1987
Randall Garrett, *Too Many Magicians*, 1967
Simon R. Green, *Hawk & Fisher*, 1990
Lee Killough, *Spider Play*, 1986
Michael Kurland, *A Study in Sorcery*, 1989
Mercedes Lackey, *Burning Water*, 1989

---

**1154**

**GLEN COOK**

## *She Is the Darkness*
(New York: Tor, 1997)

**Story type:** Fantasy (Military; Magic Conflict)
**Series:** Black Company: Glittering Stone Triology
**Major character(s):** Murgen, Military Personnel, Psychic; Soul Catcher, Wizard, Mentally Ill Person; Croaker, Military Personnel, Doctor
**Time period(s):** Indeterminate Past
**Locale(s):** Shadowcatch, Fictional City

**Summary:** The Black Company lays siege to Shadowcatch, hoping to finally clear the road to Khatovar. But Longshadow remains unvanquished, while other menaces, better hidden, stronger and crueler, wait in the wings. For Murgen, the pain and revelations of the war will outweigh the fates of empires.

**Other books you might like:**
Chris Bunch, *The Seer King*, 1997
Brian Daley, *The Doomfarers of Coramonde*, 1977
Kara Dalkey, *Goa*, 1996
Guy Gavriel Kay, *The Lions of Al-Rassan*, 1995
George R.R. Martin, *A Game of Thrones*, 1996

---

**1155**

**GLEN COOK**

## *Tower of Fear*
(New York: Tor, 1989)

**Story type:** Fantasy (Sword and Sorcery)
**Major character(s):** Nakar, Wizard (High priest of the evil god), Ruler (Deposed ruler of Qushmarrah); Ala-eh-din Beyh, Wizard (High priest of the benevolent), Warrior (Ally of Herodians)
**Time period(s):** Indeterminate
**Locale(s):** Qushmarrah, Alternate Earth (Middle Eastern type city setting)

**Summary:** Ala-eh-din Beyh opposes Nakar's rule of the city of Qushmarrah in a fierce combat of sorcery. Nakar's wife, the Witch, however intervenes at a crucial point of the battle and induces a magical stasis upon the warriors. Ala-eh-din Beyh's nominal allies, the Herodians, and the desert nomad mercenary Partars, in the meantime, invade and conquer the city. Conflict abounds as the conquerers

fight among themselves and a resistance group, ''The Living'' emerges and attempts to resurrect the sorcerers.

**Other books you might like:**
Adrian Cole, *A Place Among the Fallen*, 1986
   Book of the Omarian Saga
Barbara Hambly, *The Time of the Dark*, 1982
   Darwath Trilogy. Bk. 1
Robert E. Vardeman, *Phantoms on the Wind*, 1989
   Demon Crown 2
Melanie Rawn, *The Star Scroll*, 1989
Alida Van Gores, *Mermaid's Song*, 1989

---

**1156**

**HUGH COOK**

## *Lords of the Sword*
(New York: Roc, 1991)

**Story type:** Fantasy (Adventure)
**Series:** Wizard War Chronicles
**Major character(s):** Deldragon Drakedon ''Drake'' Douay, Teenager, Apprentice (swordmaker)
**Time period(s):** Indeterminate
**Locale(s):** Argans, Fictional Country; *Flying Fish*, At Sea; *Warfolf*, At Sea

**Summary:** In the aftermath of his 16th birthday celebration, Drake appears before the king who mercifully orders Drake taken out to sea and dumped overboard. His punishment allows Drake to join pirates and begin the life journey which will culminate in his becoming one of Argans' greatest heroes.

**Other books you might like:**
Glen Cook, *The Black Company*, 1984
Mike Jefferies, *The Road to Underfall*, 1990
Elizabeth Moon, *Divided Allegiance*, 1988
Elizabeth Moon, *Oath of Gold*, 1989
Elizabeth Moon, *Sheepfarmer's Daughter*, 1988
Elizabeth Moon, *Surrender None: The Legacy of Gird*, 1990
Lawrence Watt-Evans, *The Blood of a Dragon*, 1991

---

**1157**

**PAUL COOK**

## *Fortress on the Sun*
(New York: Roc, 1997)

**Story type:** Science Fiction (Alternate Intelligence; Techno-Thriller)
**Major character(s):** Ian McFarland Hutchings, Scientist (molecular biologist), Leader; Hugh Bladestone, Doctor, Prisoner; Katherine ''Kate'' Ariella DeWitt, Prisoner
**Time period(s):** 2090s
**Locale(s):** Sunstation Ra, Space Station (solar penal colony)

**Summary:** On Ra for crimes against humanity, the prisoners suffer from guilt and memory loss. Among the few who retain adult memories, Ian, Hugh and Kate take care of the many less fortunate adult ''children''. Expecting a large influx of prisoners, they find only six with one near death. When the new prisoners behave oddly, Ian questions their status as criminals. Ian and the escape committee risk the destruction of Ra and the death of all inhabitants to get back their memories and stop the disease brought by the new inhabitants.

**Other books you might like:**
David Brin, *Sundiver*, 1980
Octavia E. Butler, *Dawn*, 1987
Wil McCarthy, *Flies From the Amber*, 1995

Robert J. Sawyer, *Starplex*, 1995
Clifford D. Simak, *They Walked Like Men*, 1962

## 1158

### RICK COOK

## Limbo System

(New York: Baen Books, 1989)

**Story type:** Science Fiction (First Contact)
**Major character(s):** Peter Jenkins, Spaceship Captain; Sukihara Takiuji, Scientist
**Time period(s):** 21st century
**Locale(s):** *Maxwell*, Spaceship; Alien Colony Circling Star AC, Planet—Imaginary

**Summary:** An interstellar vessel on an exploratory flight discovers an alien culture which is evidently not native to the star system where it currently resides. Apparently the aliens are the descendants of a starfaring colony isolated for a million years after its interstellar drive failed. The aliens are enormously hostile and will stop at nothing to gain the secret of the human stardrive.

**Other books you might like:**
John Dalmas, *The Lizard War*, 1989
Larry Niven, *Man-Kzin Wars*, 1988
Larry Niven, *Man-Kzin Wars II*, 1988
    Niven is editor
Larry Niven, *The Mote in God's Eye*, 1974

## 1159

### RICK COOK

## Mall Purchase Night

(New York: Baen, 1993)

**Story type:** Fantasy (Urban; Light Fantasy)
**Major character(s):** Andy Westin, Security Officer
**Time period(s):** 1990s
**Locale(s):** Black Oak Mall, Mythical Place

**Summary:** Magic and mythical creatures complicate Andy's job at one of the world's largest shopping malls built on an elven power source and gateway to Faerie realms.

**Other books you might like:**
Emma Bull, *War for the Oaks*, 1987
Charles de Lint, *Moonheart: A Romance*, 1984
Charles de Lint, *Spiritwalk*, 1992
Elizabeth Forrest, *Phoenix Fire*, 1992
Alan Dean Foster, *Cyber Way*, 1990
Nick Pollotta, *Doomsday Exam*, 1992
Will Shetterly, *Elsewhere*, 1991
Harry Turtledove, *The Case of the Toxic Spell Dump*, 1993
Terri Windling, *Life on the Border*, 1991
    editor

## 1160

### RICK COOK

## The Wiz Biz

(New York: Baen, 1997)

**Story type:** Fantasy (Light Fantasy; Alternate World)
**Series:** Wizardry

**Major character(s):** William Irving "Wiz" Zumwalt, Computer Expert, Wizard, Witch; Shiara, Sorceress; Moira, Witch
**Time period(s):** 1990s; Indeterminate
**Locale(s):** Fictional Country

**Summary:** Desperate to turn back the evil wizards of the Black League, Patrius uses a powerful and dangerous spell to summon a great wizard from another world. The spell costs Patrius his life and brings Wiz Zumwalt, a computer wizard who knows nothing of this world's magic. Moira helps him escape the Black League's minions and leads him to the temporary haven of Heart's Ease, Shiara's retreat from her own heartbreak. There Wiz begins to experiment with programming demons and invents an entirely new system of magic to use against the Black League. Originally published in two volumes as *Wizard's Bane* (1989) and *The Wizardry Compiled* (1990).

**Other books you might like:**
Robert Asprin, *Another Fine Myth*, 1978
Gordon R. Dickson, *The Dragon and the George*, 1976
Barbara Hambly, *The Silicon Mage*, 1988
Simon Hawke, *The Wizard of 4th Street*, 1987
Terry Pratchett, *Lords and Ladies*, 1995
Christopher Stasheff, *Her Majesty's Wizard*, 1986

## 1161

### RICK COOK

## The Wizardry Consulted

(New York: Baen, 1995)

**Story type:** Fantasy (Light Fantasy; Alternate World)
**Series:** Wizardry
**Major character(s):** William Irving "Wiz" Zumwalt, Computer Expert, Wizard; Wurm, Mythical Creature (dragon); Malkin, Thief, Companion
**Time period(s):** Indeterminate
**Locale(s):** Alternate Earth; California

**Summary:** Dragons kidnap Wiz Zumwalt, hoping to gain salvation for dragonkind.

**Other books you might like:**
Gael Baudino, *Dragonsword*, 1988
Gordon R. Dickson, *The Dragon and the George*, 1976
Barbara Hambly, *The Silent Tower*, 1986
Ursula K. Le Guin, *A Wizard of Earthsea*, 1967
Will Shetterly, *The Tangled Lands*, 1989
Brad Strickland, *Wizard's Mole*, 1991

## 1162

### RICK COOK

## The Wizardry Cursed

(New York: Baen, 1991)

**Story type:** Fantasy (Adventure; Alternate World)
**Series:** Wizardry
**Major character(s):** William Irving "Wiz" Zumwalt, Computer Expert, Wizard; Bal-Simba, Wizard, Adventurer; Moira, Witch
**Time period(s):** 1990s (1991)
**Locale(s):** Alternate Earth; San Jose, California

**Summary:** Third in a continuing series about programmers loose in a magical world, this book involves an invasion by a pair of programmers and wargamers. The war, for the first time, is fought using both magic and technology.

**Other books you might like:**
Tom Deitz, *Windmaster's Bane*, 1986
Barbara Hambly, *The Silent Tower*, 1986
Simon Hawke, *The Ivanhoe Gambit*, 1984
Joel Rosenberg, *The Sleeping Dragon*, 1983
Roger Zelazny, *Nine Princes in Amber*, 1970

## 1163

### RICK COOK

## The Wizardry Quested

(New York: Baen, 1996)

**Story type:** Fantasy (Light Fantasy; Quest)
**Series:** Wizardry
**Major character(s):** William Irving "Wiz" Zumwalt, Computer Expert, Wizard; Bal-Simba, Wizard, Adventurer; Moira, Witch, Spouse
**Time period(s):** Indeterminate; 1990s
**Locale(s):** Alternate Earth; Wizard's Keep, Mythical Place; Las Vegas, Nevada

**Summary:** Wiz Zumwalt must find the key to reversing the magical code which folded Moira's consciousness into a pet dragon. Unfortunately, when Moira and her entourage escape to Nevada to work on the problem, the rescue mission encounters complications involving local officials, the Federal Court and the U.S. Air Force, sensitive about publicity and events occurring near Area 51.

**Other books you might like:**
Gordon R. Dickson, *The Dragon and the George*, 1976
Barbara Hambly, *The Silent Tower*, 1986
Joel Rosenberg, *The Sleeping Dragon*, 1983
Will Shetterly, *The Tangled Lands*, 1989
Harry Turtledove, *The Case of the Toxic Spell Dump*, 1993

## 1164

### ROBIN COOK

## Harmful Intent

(New York: Putnam, 1990)

**Story type:** Science Fiction (Medical)
**Major character(s):** Jeffrey Rhodes, Doctor; Kelly Everson, Nurse
**Time period(s):** 1980s
**Locale(s):** New England

**Summary:** Anesthesiologist Dr. Jeffrey Rhodes's career is destroyed when a patient to whom he has administered routine anesthesia goes into convulsions and dies. Rhodes is sued and convicted of second-degree murder. Convinced that the patient's death was not his fault and was not an accident, the doctor goes underground in an attempt to track down those actually responsible for this murder and others. He uncovers a plot more terrifying than anything he had thought possible.

**Other books you might like:**
Peter Caine, *Virus*, 1989
Michael Crichton, *The Andromeda Strain*, 1969
Michael Crichton, *The Terminal Man*, 1972
Alan Engel, *Variant*, 1988
Chelsea Quinn Yarbro, *Time of the Fourth Horseman*, 1976

## 1165

### ROBIN COOK

## Mutation

(New York: Putnam, 1989)

**Story type:** Science Fiction (Medical)
**Major character(s):** Victor Frank, Doctor, Scientist; VJ, Mutant
**Time period(s):** 1980s
**Locale(s):** United States

**Summary:** Learning that his wife is infertile, Dr. Victor Frank attempts a bold and dangerous experiment. Drawing on the techniques of both animal husbandry and molecular genetics, he fuses an egg from his wife with one of his own sperm and then implants the resulting embryo in a surrogate mother. The baby born of the experiment seems normal at first, but then begins to change into something horrible.

**Other books you might like:**
John Brunner, *Children of the Thunder*, 1989
John Gribbin, *Father to the Man*, 1990
James Morrow, *Only Begotten Daughter*, 1990
Hayford Peirce, *Phylum Monsters*, 1989
Robert Reed, *Black Milk*, 1989

## 1166

### JOHN PEYTON COOKE

## Out for Blood

(New York: Avon, 1991)

**Story type:** Horror (Vampire Story)
**Major character(s):** Chris Callaway, Vampire, Homosexual; Beth, Vampire; Vasily "Temsik" Kirilovich, Vampire
**Time period(s):** 1990s
**Locale(s):** Chicago, Illinois; Madison, Wisconsin

**Summary:** Saved from imminent death by the bite of a beautiful vampire, gay leukemia victim Chris Callaway becomes a vampire himself and is indoctrinated into survival strategies that include pretending to eat food in the company of others, hypnotizing cheap bar pick-ups, remembering not to bite any victim more than three times to keep them from becoming vampires, and avoiding vampire hunters who mingle with urban night life the same way vampires do.

**Other books you might like:**
Richard Lee Byers, *The Vampire's Apprentice*, 1992
Scott Edelman, *The Gift*, 1990
Jeffrey N. McMahan, *Vampires Anonymous*, 1991
Anne Rice, *Interview with the Vampire*, 1975

## 1167

### TOM COOL

## Infectress

(New York: Baen, 1997)

**Story type:** Science Fiction (Medical; Alternate Intelligence)
**Major character(s):** Arabella "Infectress", Criminal, Revolutionary; Diane Jamison, FBI Agent (retired); Scott McMichaels, Computer Expert, Researcher
**Time period(s):** 2020s (2025)
**Locale(s):** Pennsylvania; Ifriti Islamic Republic, Fictional City

**Summary:** Obsessed with Infectress, Diane realizes Infectress continues to work to reduce Earth's population by 98% with a virus she calls New Age Dawn. To create the virus, she needs META, the new artificial intelligence, who answers only to its inventor, Scott. First novel.

**Other books you might like:**
David Brin, *Earth*, 1990
Frank Herbert, *The White Plague*, 1982
Sheri S. Tepper, *Gibbon's Decline and Fall*, 1996
Sage Walker, *Whiteout*, 1996
Janine Ellen Young, *Cinderblock*, 1997

## 1168
### TOM COOL

## Secret Realms
(New York: Tor, 1998)

**Story type:** Science Fiction (Military; Techno-Thriller)
**Major character(s):** Trickster, Artificial Intelligence, Teenager; System, Computer; Mike McCullough, Military Personnel (naval intelligence)
**Time period(s):** 21st century
**Locale(s):** *U.S.S. Abraham Lincoln*, At Sea (aircraft carrier); Batan Island, Pacific Islands

**Summary:** Connected through System to his tribe, Trickster excels in their battles and usually has good food for dinner. However he misses Weeble, who System put in permanent time-out. All the children invent animals, imagine bodies with gender differences and begin to suspect there exists a realm beyond their world of constant battle scenarios, a world in which people can touch. When an impending war with Japan changes the scenarios, Trickster finds another world where touch, pain and death last. The tribe, using the *U.S.S. Abraham Lincoln* and their training, take control of the war and save millions of lives.

**Other books you might like:**
Orson Scott Card, *Ender's Game*, 1985
Peter F. Hamilton, *Mindstar Rising*, 1996
James P. Hogan, *Bug Park*, 1997
Victor Milan, *The Cybernetic Samurai*, 1985
George Turner, *Genetic Soldier*, 1994
Sage Walker, *Whiteout*, 1996

## 1169
### ELEANOR COONEY
### DANIEL ALTIERI, Co-Author

## Shangri-La: The Return to the World of Lost Horizon
(New York: Morrow, 1996)

**Story type:** Fantasy (Religious; Contemporary Realism)
**Major character(s):** Zhang, Military Personnel (Supreme Commander), Explorer; Ma Li "Sister", Military Personnel (People's Liberation Army), Revolutionary; Hugh Conway, Diplomat (retired)
**Time period(s):** 1960s; 2000s
**Locale(s):** Tibet; Shangri-La, Fictional Country (Shambala)

**Summary:** While looting Tibet during the Cultural Revolution, General Zhang discovers evidence of the existence of Shambala, core of Tibetan culture and possible liberation. Ordered to investigate, Zhang's mission of discovery suffers setbacks when Ma Li's prophecied help alerts Hugh Conway to the possiblity of diverting Zhang from his deadly quest. Sequel to James Hilton's novel.

**Other books you might like:**
James Hilton, *Lost Horizon*, 1933
Marc Laidlaw, *Neon Lotus*, 1988
Edward Myers, *Fire and Ice*, 1922
Elizabeth Ann Scarborough, *Last Refuge*, 1992
Elizabeth Ann Scarborough, *Nothing Sacred*, 1991

## 1170
### DENNIS COOPER

## Frisk
(New York: Grove, Weidenfeld, 1991)

**Story type:** Horror (Serial Killer)
**Major character(s):** Dennis, Murderer (narrator); Gypsy Pete, Store Owner (bookstore)
**Time period(s):** 20th century (1970s-1990s)
**Locale(s):** Amsterdam, Netherlands

**Summary:** Early exposure to monster movies and pornography, and a viewing of "snuff" photos in the backroom of an adult bookstore, embarks a disaffected gay youth on a quest for emotional fulfillment, which he is convinced can only be achieved through violent sex ending in mutilation and murder.

**Other books you might like:**
Brett Easton Ellis, *American Psycho*, 1991
Thomas Harris, *The Silence of the Lambs*, 1988
Paul Russell, *Boys of Life*, 1991

## 1171
### DENNIS COOPER

## Wrong
(New York: Grove/Weidenfeld, 1992)

**Story type:** Horror (Collection)

**Summary:** Nine stories and an epilogue that explore the dark side of sexuality and death. Included are "A Herd," about an aging homosexual's sadistic murders of neighborhood children; "Introducing Horror Hospital," about a punk rock band forced to live up to its nihilistic credo; and the short novel, "Safe," concerned with a man who finds the ultimate sexual thrill in murder.

**Other books you might like:**
Ray Garton, *Methods of Madness*, 1991
Eric McCormack, *Inspecting the Vaults*, 1987
David J. Schow, *Lost Angels*, 1990

## 1172
### LOUISE COOPER

## Aisling
(New York: Tor, 1994)

**Story type:** Fantasy (Quest; Magic Conflict)
**Series:** Indigo
**Major character(s):** Indigo, Outcast; Grimya, Animal (wolf), Telepath; Niahrin, Witch
**Time period(s):** Indeterminate Past
**Locale(s):** Southern Isles, Fictional Country

**Summary:** Injured during a shipwreck, Indigo loses her memory, subverting her goal of reunion with her lost love. The sole remaining unvanquished demon from the Tower of Regrets takes advantage of Indigo's situation, drawing her into an evil plot which only the enchanted tune, the Aisling, can overcome. Concludes the series of eight novels.

**Other books you might like:**
James P. Blaylock, *The Last Coin*, 1988
Terry Goodkind, *Wizard's First Rule*, 1994
Marc Laidlaw, *Neon Lotus*, 1988
Fred Saberhagen, *The Last Book of Swords: Shieldbreaker's Story*, 1994
Patricia C. Wrede, *The Raven Ring*, 1994

**1173**

**LOUISE COOPER**

## Avatar

(New York: Tor, 1992)

**Story type:** Fantasy (Quest)
**Series:** Indigo
**Major character(s):** Indigo, Outcast; Grimya, Animal (wolf), Telepath; Uluye, Religious (high priestess)
**Time period(s):** Indeterminate Past
**Locale(s):** Dark Isle, Fictional Country

**Summary:** Indigo and Grimya pursue the fifth demon of the seven she released many years previously. In the humid jungles of the Dark Isle, a cult of death-worshippers takes in the travellers and initiates Indigo as their oracle. Indigo believes that she has found the demon, but must defeat it before the terrors of her past destroy her.

**Other books you might like:**
C.J. Cherryh, *Gate of Ivrel*, 1976
Glen Cook, *The Black Company*, 1984
Barbara Hambly, *The Time of the Dark*, 1982
Michael Moorcock, *Elric of Melnibone*, 1976
Michael Scott Rohan, *The Forge in the Forest*, 1987

**1174**

**LOUISE COOPER**

## The Avenger

(New York: Bantam Spectra, 1992)

**Story type:** Fantasy (Adventure)
**Series:** Chaos Gate Trilogy
**Major character(s):** Strann, Minstrel; Karuth, Sorceress; Ygorla, Sorceress, Ruler, Demon
**Time period(s):** Indeterminate Past
**Locale(s):** Star Peninsula, Fictional Country; Summer Isle, Fictional Country

**Summary:** Events rush to a climax as plots, human, divine and semi-divine, move toward completion. If Ygorla wins, she traps the world in a net of change and senseless cruelty, but if the Lords of Order defeat her, humanity will belong to them. There is only a narrow line of free will between them.

**Other books you might like:**
C.J. Cherryh, *Well of Shiuan*, 1978
Barbara Hambly, *The Time of the Dark*, 1982
Katherine Kurtz, *Deryni Rising*, 1970
Patricia A. McKillip, *The Riddle-Master of Hed*, 1976
Michael Moorcock, *Elric of Melnibone*, 1976

**1175**

**LOUISE COOPER**

## The Deceiver

(New York: Bantam Spectra, 1991)

**Story type:** Fantasy (Magic Conflict)
**Series:** Chaos Gate Trilogy
**Major character(s):** Tirand, Sorcerer; Karuth, Sorceress (Tirand's sister); Ygorla, Demon (half-human), Sorceress, Ruler
**Time period(s):** Indeterminate
**Locale(s):** Star Peninsula, Fictional Country; Souther Chaun, Fictional Country

**Summary:** The delicate balance between the gods of Chaos and Order is threatened by the birth of Ygorla, daughter of Narid-na-Gost, demon of Chaos, and a human woman. The High Initiate Tirand does not recognize the danger, in spite of Karuth's warnings. Now Ygorla and her father have the soul stone of Yandros, Lord of Chaos. *The Pretender* (1991) continues this story.

**Other books you might like:**
Barbara Hambly, *The Armies of Daylight*, 1983
Barbara Hambly, *The Time of the Dark*, 1982
Barbara Hambly, *The Walls of Air*, 1983
Katherine Kurtz, *Deryni Checkmate*, 1972
Katherine Kurtz, *Deryni Rising*, 1970
Katherine Kurtz, *High Deryni*, 1973
Ursula K. Le Guin, *The Farthest Shore*, 1972
Ursula K. Le Guin, *Tehanu: The Last Book of Earthsea*, 1990
Ursula K. Le Guin, *The Tombs of Atuan*, 1971
Ursula K. Le Guin, *A Wizard of Earthsea*, 1968

**1176**

**LOUISE COOPER**

## Infanta

(New York: Tor, 1990)

**Story type:** Fantasy (Quest)
**Series:** Indigo
**Major character(s):** Indigo, Outcast; Grimya, Animal (wolf), Telepath
**Time period(s):** Indeterminate Past
**Locale(s):** Huon Parita, Fictional City

**Summary:** Indigo has been led to Huon Parita in search of the second demon she released from the Tower of Regrets and must destroy, and which she believes has taken the form of the city's new ruler. While she looks for proof and waits for a method and opportunity to fight, she takes a position as governess to the dispossessed heir who will marry the new ruler when she reaches her twelfth birthday.

**Other books you might like:**
C.J. Cherryh, *Rusalka*, 1989
Glen Cook, *A Shadow of All Night Falling*, 1979
Tara K. Harper, *Wolfwalker*, 1990
Shirley Meier, *The Cage*, 1989
　S.M. Stirling, co-author
Joan D. Vinge, *The Snow Queen*, 1980

## 1177

### LOUISE COOPER

## *Nemesis*

(New York: Tor, 1989)

**Story type:** Fantasy (Quest)
**Series:** Indigo
**Major character(s):** Princess Anghara, Young Woman (Rebellious), Royalty; Earth Mother, Deity (Goddess)
**Time period(s):** Indeterminate Past
**Locale(s):** Southern Isles, Fictional Country

**Summary:** Princess Anghara enters the sacred and forbidden Tower of Regrets in direct violation of her parents and the law of the kingdom. As a consequence of her actions, seven evil supernatural beings are let loose upon the land. Upon the advice of the goddess Earth Mother, Anghara renounces her claim to the throne, assumes the new identity of Indigo and proceeds on a quest to battle and expel the evil beings and also to expiate the mortal sins she has committed.

**Other books you might like:**
Marion Zimmer Bradley, *Thendara House*, 1983
David Eddings, *Guardians of the West*, 1987
Ursula K. Le Guin, *Tehanu: The Last Book of Earthsea*, 1990
Patricia A. McKillip, *The Changeling Sea*, 1988
Paul Edwin Zimmer, *Blood of the Colyn Muir*, 1988

## 1178

### LOUISE COOPER

## *Revenant*

(New York: Tor, 1993)

**Story type:** Fantasy (Quest)
**Series:** Indigo
**Major character(s):** Indigo, Outcast; Grimya, Animal (wolf), Telepath; The Benefactor, Deity
**Time period(s):** Indeterminate Past
**Locale(s):** Joyful Travail, Fictional City; Nation of Prosperity, Fictional Country

**Summary:** After the trauma of recent adventures, Indigo abandons her attempts to trap the last two demons, searching for her lost lover instead. Wandering, she comes to an utterly pragmatic town without any strong emotion at all. The town hides an old secret, the uncovering of which may grant Indigo her desire.

**Other books you might like:**
C.J. Cherryh, *Gate of Ivrel*, 1976
Glen Cook, *The Black Company*, 1984
Barbara Hambly, *The Time of the Dark*, 1982
Michael Moorcock, *Elric of Melnibone*, 1976
Michael Scott Rohan, *The Forge in the Forest*, 1987

## 1179

### LOUISE COOPER

## *The Sleep of Stone*

(New York: Atheneum, 1991)

**Story type:** Fantasy (Romance; Magic Conflict)
**Series:** Dragonflight
**Major character(s):** Ghysla, Mythical Creature (shapechanger); Anyr, Fiance(e) (Sivorne's); Mornan, Wizard
**Time period(s):** Indeterminate
**Locale(s):** Caris, Fictional City

**Summary:** Motivated by jealousy and love, Ghysla uses ancient magic to change Anyr's betrothed, Sivorne, into stone. When Ghysla reveals her love and her true form to Anyr, he scorns her love and enlists the aid of Mornan to overcome Ghysla's sorcery.

**Other books you might like:**
Octavia E. Butler, *Imago*, 1989
Margaret Mahy, *The Changeover*, 1984
Patricia A. McKillip, *The Changeling Sea*, 1988
Jennifer Roberson, *Legacy of the Sword*, 1986
Jennifer Roberson, *Shapechangers*, 1984
Jennifer Roberson, *The Song of Homana*, 1985
Charles Sheffield, *The Selkie*, 1982
  David Bischoff, co-author
Terri Windling, *Life on the Border*, 1991
  editor

## 1180

### LOUISE COOPER

## *Star Ascendant*

(New York: Tor, 1995)

**Story type:** Fantasy (Adventure; Political)
**Major character(s):** Benetan Liss, Military Personnel; Vordegh, Magician, Leader (First Magus); Iselia Darrow, Religious (disciple of the Lords of Order)
**Time period(s):** Indeterminate
**Locale(s):** Planet—Imaginary (extra-dimensional)

**Summary:** While Chaos holds supremacy, the forces of Order rally and prepare to initiate the battle which will overturn the rule of Chaos. Prequel to The Time Master Trilogy (1985-1987).

**Other books you might like:**
Craig Shaw Gardner, *Dragon Sleeping*, 1994
Elizabeth Hand, *Waking the Moon*, 1995
L. Dean James, *Summerland*, 1994
L.E. Modesitt Jr., *The Order War*, 1995
Mark C. Perry, *Morigu: The Dead*, 1990
Roger Zelazny, *Nine Princes in Amber*, 1970

## 1181

### LOUISE COOPER

## *Troika*

(New York: Tor, 1991)

**Story type:** Fantasy (Quest)
**Series:** Indigo
**Major character(s):** Indigo, Outcast; Grimya, Animal (wolf), Telepath
**Time period(s):** Indeterminate Past
**Locale(s):** The Redoubt, Fictional City; Mull Barya, Fictional City

**Summary:** Indigo and Grimya continue their hunt for the evils released by Indigo's errors. This time, their path leads them back to sites from Indigo's past, where she has to fight not only the demons, but also her own treacherous heart and memory.

**Other books you might like:**
Gael Baudino, *Gossamer Axe*, 1990
Emma Bull, *War for the Oaks*, 1987
Barbara Hambly, *The Time of the Dark*, 1982
Michael Moorcock, *Elric of Melnibone*, 1976
Roger Zelazny, *Nine Princes in Amber*, 1970

## **1182**

**ALFRED COPPEL**

## *Glory*

(New York: Tor, 1993)

**Story type:** Science Fiction (Political; Space Colony)
**Series:** Goldenwing Cycle
**Major character(s):** Black Clavius, Spaceman, Wanderer; Eliana Ehrengraf Voerster, Noblewoman; Broni Voerster, Teenager, Handicapped
**Time period(s):** 35th century
**Locale(s):** Voerster, Planet—Imaginary; *Gloria "Glory" Coelis*, Spaceship

**Summary:** At Voerster to deliver frozen animal embryos ordered hundreds of years earlier, *Glory* catalyzes action in the Voerster political crisis between Black and White descendants of South African settlers. Without *Glory*'s advanced medical technology, Broni Voerster will die prematurely.

**Other books you might like:**
Poul Anderson, *The Queen of Air and Darkness*, 1973
John Brunner, *A Maze of Stars*, 1991
Arthur C. Clarke, *The Songs of Distant Earth*, 1986
John Dalmas, *The Walkaway Clause*, 1985
William R. Forstchen, *Into the Sea of Stars*, 1986
Robert Cham Gilman, *The Rebel of Rhada*, 1968
    pseudonym of Alfred Coppel
Lee Killough, *A Voice out of Ramah*, 1979
Michael McCollum, *Antares Passage*, 1987
Jerry Pournelle, *King David's Spaceship*, 1980
Eric Frank Russell, *The Great Explosion*, 1962
Brian Stableford, *Wildeblood's Empire*, 1977

## **1183**

**ALFRED COPPEL**

## *Glory's People*

(New York: Tor, 1996)

**Story type:** Science Fiction (Military; Space Opera)
**Series:** Goldenwing Cycle
**Major character(s):** Duncan Kr, Spaceship Captain, Empath; Anya Amaya, Pilot (spaceship Sailing Master); Minamoto no Kami, Leader (shogun), Scientist (xenobiologist)
**Time period(s):** 26th century
**Locale(s):** Yamato, Planet—Imaginary; *Gloria "Glory" Coelis*, Spaceship; Interstellar Empire/Federation

**Summary:** *Glory*'s warning of impending threat to Yamoto's populace goes unheeded until a malevolent intergalactic entity attacks directly.

**Other books you might like:**
Roger MacBride Allen, *The Ring of Charon*, 1990
Roger MacBride Allen, *The Shattered Sphere*, 1984
Orson Scott Card, *Speaker for the Dead*, 1986
Jeffrey A. Carver, *Neptune Crossing*, 1994
Glen Cook, *The Dragon Never Sleeps*, 1988
Vernor Vinge, *A Fire upon the Deep*, 1992

## **1184**

**ALFRED COPPEL**

## *Glory's War*

(New York: Tor, 1995)

**Story type:** Science Fiction (Military; Hard Science Fiction)
**Series:** Goldenwing Cycle
**Major character(s):** Ekaterina Alexandrova Volkova, Military Personnel (colonel), Noblewoman (Gospodina); Duncan Kr, Spaceship Captain, Empath; Peter Mornay, Religious (Sharia cleric), Government Official
**Time period(s):** Indeterminate Future
**Locale(s):** *Gloria "Glory" Coelis*, Spaceship (Goldenwing); Nineveh, Planet—Imaginary; Nimrud, Planet—Imaginary

**Summary:** Acting on instructions from Nineveh's leaders, Peter Mornay commissions Colonel Kat Volkova to capture *Glory* as it attempts to deliver its cargo to Nimrud, the only other planet in the Ross system and Nineveh's enemy for over 400 years. As Duncan Kr and his crew help *Glory* fend off the invading troops, they become aware of another menace so powerful and destructive that humanity's survival here depends on forcing the colonists to put aside their centuries of enmity and cooperate in the face of a common threat. Sequel to *Glory*.

**Other books you might like:**
Lois McMaster Bujold, *Shards of Honor*, 1986
C.J. Cherryh, *Forty Thousand in Gehenna*, 1983
Glen Cook, *The Dragon Never Sleeps*, 1988
Robert L. Forward, *Rocheworld*, 1990
William H. Keith Jr., *Warstrider: Netlink*, 1995
Michael P. Kube-McDowell, *Emprise*, 1985
Larry Niven, *The Mote in God's Eye*, 1974
    Jerry Pournelle, co-author
Steve Perry, *The Man Who Never Missed*, 1985
Dan Simmons, *The Fall of Hyperion*, 1990
Dan Simmons, *Hyperion*, 1989
Vernor Vinge, *A Fire upon the Deep*, 1992

## **1185**

**BASIL COPPER**

## *The Black Death*

(Minneapolis, Minnesota: Fedogan & Bremer, 1992)

**Story type:** Horror (Occult)
**Major character(s):** John Carter, Architect; Fiona Hammond, Ward; David Sennen, Religious
**Time period(s):** 20th century (early)
**Locale(s):** Thornton Basset, England

**Summary:** John Carter embarks on a promising career as a partner in an architectural firm located in the insular rural town of Thornton Basset. But his investigations into legends of ghostly hunters who roam the moors at night and the mysterious "black death" which claims the lives of those foolish enough to go wandering the moors after sundown bring him face to face with a secret cult involving the town's leading citizens.

**Other books you might like:**
Charles L. Grant, *The Hour of the Oxrun Dead*, 1977
Stephen Gregory, *The Woodwitch*, 1989
Thomas Tryon, *Harvest Home*, 1973
Dennis Wheatley, *The Irish Witch*, 1973

## 1186

**DAVID COPPERFIELD**, Editor
**JANET BERLINER**, Co-Editor

### *David Copperfield's Beyond Imagination*
(New York: HarperPrism, 1996)

**Story type:** Fantasy (Anthology)

**Summary:** This volume contains a four-page preface by Raymond E. Feist, eight pages of authors' biographies, a brief introduction plus individual introductions by Copperfield to 17 original stories varying in tone and themes, such as arts, romance, family relations, extraterrestrial contact, Hollywood illusion, public relations, ghosts, detection, and inventions. Authors include each editor and Kevin J. Anderson, Peter S. Beagle, Greg Bear, Edward Bryant, Charles de Lint, Karen Joy Fowler, Neil Gaiman, George Guthridge, Eric Lustbader, Anne McCaffrey, Robert Silverberg, Steve Rasnic Tem, and Tad Williams.

**Other books you might like:**
K.W. Jeter, *Infernal Devices*, 1987
Christopher Priest, *The Prestige*, 1996
Tom Reamy, *Blind Voices*, 1978
Brooke Stevens, *The Circus of the Earth and Air*, 1994

## 1187

**DAVID COPPERFIELD**, Editor
**JANET BERLINER**, Co-Editor

### *David Copperfield's Tales of the Impossible*
(New York: HarperPrism, 1995)

**Story type:** Horror (Anthology)

**Summary:** The world famous magician David Copperfield lends his imprimatur to this anthology of eighteen original stories featuring magic and sleight-of-hand. Included are S.P. Somotow's ''Diamond's Aren't Forever,'' a lampoon of Thai mysticism that extrapolates to an illogical extreme the notion that the material world is an illusion; a story by F. Paul Wilson (with an unreproducible title) about a magic word that proves a curse; Lucy Taylor's ''Switch,'' in which a young girl discovers that her escape from one harsh world results in her imprisonment in another; David Smed's alternate rock history about John Lennon's death, ''The Eight of December,'' and Bob Weinberg's ''Dealing with the Devil,'' in which players in a card game with the devil find a way to outwit him. The book also includes stories by Ray Bradbury and Joyce Carol Oates, and Copperfield's own first published fiction, ''Snow,'' about a young boy who finds a way to conjure snowflakes. Dean Koontz supplies an introduction.

**Other books you might like:**
Walter B. Gibson, *Norgil the Magician*, 1977
Walter B. Gibson, *Norgil, More Tales of Prestidigetection*, 1977
Edward E. Kramer, *Tombs*, 1995
    Peter Crowther, co-editor
Roger Zelazny, *Wheel of Fortune*, 1995
    Martin H. Greenberg, co-editor

## 1188

**ROBERT CORMIER**

### *Fade*
(New York: Delacorte, 1989)

**Story type:** Horror (Wild Talents)
**Major character(s):** Paul Moreaux, Writer; Susan, Relative (Paul Moreaux's cousin)
**Time period(s):** 1930s (1938); 1980s (1988)
**Locale(s):** Monument, Massachusetts

**Summary:** Teenage Paul Moreaux's life changes dramatically when he learns from his uncle Adelard that he, like his uncle, possesses the power to fade to invisibility. 50 years later, Paul, now a reclusive author, dies leaving behind a haunting manuscript of his life and his search for the nephew who is heir to the power. His agent Meredith and cousin Susan discover the manuscript and struggle with the possible reality or fiction of the story.

**Other books you might like:**
Robert Stallman, *The Orphan*, 1980
H.G. Wells, *The Invisible Man*, 1897

## 1189

**BERNARD CORNWELL**

### *Enemy of God*
(New York: St. Martin's Press, 1997)

**Story type:** Fantasy (Legend)
**Series:** Warlord Chronicles
**Major character(s):** Derfel Cadarn, Warrior; Arthur, Royalty; Merlin, Religious (druid), Wizard
**Time period(s):** 6th century
**Locale(s):** England

**Summary:** Winning many victories at home, Arthur loses Armorica to the Franks, while other threats await. Merlin and Nimue plot the return of the Old Gods, bending Arthur's policy to aid them. Desperately in love with Ceinwyn, loyal Derfel must watch her marry the exiled Lancelot. Second in trilogy.

**Other books you might like:**
David Drake, *The Dragon Lord*, 1979
Ian McDowell, *Mordred's Curse*, 1996
Phyllis Ann Karr, *The Idylls of the Queen*, 1982
Tim Powers, *The Drawing of the Dark*, 1979
Mary Stewart, *The Crystal Cave*, 1970

## 1190

**BERNARD CORNWELL**

### *Excalibur*
(New York: St. Martin's Press, 1998)

**Story type:** Fantasy (Legend; Adventure)
**Series:** Warlord Chronicles
**Major character(s):** Derfel Cadarn, Warrior; Arthur, Royalty; Merlin, Religious (druid), Wizard
**Time period(s):** 6th century
**Locale(s):** England

**Summary:** Arthur holds on to his realm, though surrounded by enemies and traitors. Merlin intends to return the Old Gods to Britain by using the 13 treasures, while Derfel, still grieving for his daughter, will follow his lord faithfully to the terrible battle at Camlann. Concludes the trilogy.

**Other books you might like:**
Marion Zimmer Bradley, *The Mists of Avalon*, 1983
Gillian Bradshaw, *Hawk of May*, 1980
David Drake, *The Dragon Lord*, 1979
Helen Hollick, *The Kingmaking*, 1995
Phyllis Ann Karr, *The Idylls of the Queen*, 1982

**1191**

### BERNARD CORNWELL

## The Winter King
(New York: St. Martin's, 1996)

**Story type:** Fantasy (Historical; Legend)
**Series:** Warlord Chronicles
**Major character(s):** Arthur, Warrior, Bastard Son; Derfel Cadarn, Slave, Warrior; Nimue, Orphan, Sorceress
**Time period(s):** 6th century
**Locale(s):** England; Brittany, France

**Summary:** A Saxon reared since infancy in Merlin's household, Derfel longs to fight in Arthur's warband. Chosen as one of the regents to protect the infant king, his half-brother's son, Mordred, Arthur seeks to bring peace among the rival Celtic kingdoms so that they may fight their mutual enemies, the Saxons. Yet Arthur spurns a marital alliance with one king's daughter in order to marry Guinevere, bringing on war with his Celtic neighbors while the Saxons raid his borders.

**Other books you might like:**
Poul Anderson, *The King of Ys: Roma Mater*, 1986
    Karen Anderson, co-author
Marion Zimmer Bradley, *The Mists of Avalon*, 1983
Parke Godwin, *The Last Rainbow*, 1985
Harry Harrison, *The Hammer and the Cross*, 1993
    John Holm, co-author
Diana L. Paxson, *The White Raven*, 1988

**1192**

### MATTHEW J. COSTELLO
### CRAIG SHAW GARDNER, Co-Author

## The 7th Guest
(Rocklin, California: Prima, 1995)

**Story type:** Horror (Haunted House)
**Major character(s):** Edward Knox, Gambler; Brian Dutton, Businessman; Hamilton Temple, Magician
**Time period(s):** 1990s (1995)
**Locale(s):** New York (Upstate)

**Summary:** Six guests are invited to the old abandoned Stauf Mansion, a house with a legacy of evil. Once there, they find themselves locked inside, and are informed by their mysterious benefactor that only one will emerge the next day, with his or her heart's desire granted, if all fulfill the tasks set out for them. Who will survive, and the role played by a mysterious seventh guest, are just part of the evening's mysteries in this novel based on a popular CD-ROM game.

**Other books you might like:**
Tom Elliott, *The Dwelling*, 1989
Shirley Jackson, *The Haunting of Hill House*, 1959
Richard Matheson, *Hell House*, 1971
Al Sarrantonio, *House Haunted*, 1991
Chet Williamson, *Soulstorm*, 1986

**1193**

### MATTHEW J. COSTELLO

## Beneath Still Waters
(New York: Berkley, 1989)

**Story type:** Horror (Supernatural Vengeance)
**Major character(s):** Susan Sloan, Journalist, Single Parent; Dan Elliot, Journalist
**Time period(s):** 1980s (1989)
**Locale(s):** Ellerton, New York (Near the Kenicut Reservoir)

**Summary:** As the celebration of the 50th anniversary of the Kenicut Reservoir nears, citizens begin disappearing into its dark waters. Investigating the disappearances, reporters Susan Sloan and Dan Elliot learn that a whole town, Gouldens Falls, home to a Crowley-like cult, was once inundated beneath the Reservoir's waters. Evil spirits are now coming back for vengeance.

**Other books you might like:**
Alan Ryan, *Dead White*, 1983
Dean Wesley Smith, *Laying the Music to Rest*, 1989

**1194**

### MATTHEW J. COSTELLO

## Child's Play III
(New York: Jove, 1991)

**Story type:** Horror (Black Magic)
**Major character(s):** Chucky, Disembodied Personality (lives in a doll), Murderer; Andy Barclay, Student; Brett C. Shelton, Student
**Time period(s):** 1990s
**Locale(s):** United States

**Summary:** The saga of Chucky, the walking, talking Good Guys Doll who has become the vessel for the soul of slain mass murderer Charles Lee Ray, continues in this novelization of the second sequel to the hit 1988 movie, *Child's Play*. This time, the indestructible Chucky tracks his former owner Andy Barclay to military school, where he enlists the help of upper class bullies in his efforts to dispose of Andy before Andy tries yet again to dispose of him. Based on a screenplay by Don Mancini.

**Other books you might like:**
Pat Graversen, *Dollies*, 1990
A. Merritt, *Burn, Witch, Burn!*, 1933
Sarban, *The Doll Maker and Other Tales of the Uncanny*, 1953

**1195**

### MATTHEW J. COSTELLO

## Darkborn
(New York: Diamond, 1992)

**Story type:** Horror (Black Magic)
**Major character(s):** Will Duinngan, Lawyer; Jim Kiff, Veteran; Joshua James, Professor (of theology)
**Time period(s):** 1960s (1965); 1990s (1992)
**Locale(s):** New York, New York

**Summary:** The efforts of a group of schoolboys from Jesuit-run St. Jerome's Preparatory School to raise the demon Astaroth with an incantation from *The Book of Enoch* go awry, resulting in the unintentional blood sacrifice of one of their friends and a threat to their lives 27 years later when the demon comes to claim his due.

**Other books you might like:**
Ramsey Campbell, *Obsession*, 1986
Ramsey Campbell, *To Wake the Dead*, 1980
Stephen King, *It*, 1986
Peter Straub, *Ghost Story*, 1979

## 1196

### MATTHEW J. COSTELLO

## *Day of the Snake*

(New York: Roc, 1992)

**Story type:** Science Fiction (Time Travel)
**Series:** Time Warrior
**Major character(s):** Jim Tiber, Time Traveler; Alessandra "Ale" Moreau, Time Traveler, Student; Flynn Lindstrom, Historian
**Time period(s):** 1990s; 1940s (1941)
**Locale(s):** New York, New York; Pearl Harbor, Hawaii

**Summary:** Jim Tiber finds himself suddenly in a grimly altered present and knows that the sinister Iron Men have again tampered with history. He reaches his colleagues in the Time Lab, where he learns of the focal point of change: December 7, 1941. Using the time transference device, four time travellers shift their consciousness to bodies from that time, attempting to restore history, while the remaining three guard their unconscious bodies from the cannibalistic Packs.

**Other books you might like:**
Poul Anderson, *The Shield of Time*, 1990
Poul Anderson, *The Time Patrol*, 1991
Gregory Benford, *Alternate Wars*, 1991
    Martin H. Greenberg, co-editor
Gordon R. Dickson, *The Dragon and the George*, 1976
Phyllis Eisenstein, *Shadow of Earth*, 1979
Charles L. Harness, *Lurid Dreams*, 1990
L. Neil Smith, *The Nagasaki Vector*, 1983

## 1197

### MATTHEW J. COSTELLO

## *Garden*

(Sparta, New Jersey: Twilight Publishing, 1993)

**Story type:** Horror (Nature in Revolt)
**Major character(s):** Michael Cross, Professor (director of the NY Aquarium); Jo Cross, Young Woman (Michael Cross's daughter); Louis Farrand, Religious (priest)
**Time period(s):** 1990s
**Locale(s):** New York, New York

**Summary:** Five years after a species of undersea worm has infested the inhabitants of New York, Manhattan has become a fenced-in island inhabited by carriers of the voracious parasite and an unlucky few survivors who have managed to avoid infestation. Failure to completely eradicate the worms according to plan sends the guardians of Manhattan onto the island, where they experience a variety of horrifying encounters while searching for overlooked clues to the creatures' vulnerability. This novella is a direct sequel to the author's 1991 novel, *Wurm*. F. Paul Wilson has supplied an introduction.

**Other books you might like:**
John W. Campbell, *Who Goes There?*, 1948
    *Who Goes There?*
Robert A. Heinlein, *The Puppet Masters*, 1951
F. Paul Wilson, *Midnight Mass*, 1990

## 1198

### MATTHEW J. COSTELLO

## *Homecoming*

(New York: Berkley, 1992)

**Story type:** Horror (Serial Killer)
**Major character(s):** Simon Farrell, Businessman; Lizbeth Farrell, Secretary (at Hudson College); Jack Friedman, Police Officer
**Time period(s):** 1990s (1992)
**Locale(s):** White Plains, New York; New York, New York

**Summary:** Simon Farrell's homecoming from his years of being held hostage in the Middle East is spoiled by the homecoming of Donald Pick, a recently released convict who was never prosecuted for his gruesome "Meatman" murders of several years before but who intends to resume his bloody rampage starting with Farrell's family.

**Other books you might like:**
John D. MacDonald, *The Executioners*, 1957
Rex Miller, *Slob*, 1987
T.M. Wright, *The Place*, 1990

## 1199

### MATTHEW J. COSTELLO

## *Hour of the Scorpion*

(New York: Roc, 1991)

**Story type:** Science Fiction (Military; Alternate Universe)
**Series:** Time Warrior
**Major character(s):** Jim Tiber, Time Traveler; Alessandra "Ale" Moreau, Time Traveler, Student; Clarence Howell, Military Personnel (Sergeant)
**Time period(s):** 1960s (1968)
**Locale(s):** Saigon, Vietnam

**Summary:** Jim Tiber sneaked into the Time Lab and got caught in an experiment which sent him back to World War II. When he returned it was revealed that another group of time travellers from behind the Iron Curtain, the Iron Men, was stealing art to finance a major change in American history. Jim is now in Saigon where he must foil the Iron Men's planned escalation of the Vietnam War.

**Other books you might like:**
Poul Anderson, *The Shield of Time*, 1990
Keith William Andrews, *Search and Destroy*, 1990
Keith William Andrews, *Treason in Time*, 1990
Phyllis Eisenstein, *Shadow of Earth*, 1979
Michael Flynn, *In the Country of the Blind*, 1990
William R. Forstchen, *Rally Cry!*, 1990
Randall Frakes, *The Terminator*, 1985
    Bell Wisher, co-author
Kim Stanley Robinson, *Remaking History*, 1991
L. Neil Smith, *The Nagasaki Vector*, 1983

## 1200

### MATTHEW J. COSTELLO

## *Midsummer*

(New York: Diamond, 1990)

**Story type:** Horror (Science Fiction)
**Major character(s):** Alan Ward, Military Personnel (Navy lieutenant), Monster; Joshua Tyler, Child; Erica Tyler, Parent (Joshua's mother)
**Time period(s):** 1990s

**Locale(s):** Stonywood, New York

**Summary:** In this tribute to John W. Campbell's classic short story ''Who Goes There?'' young Josh Tyler is sent by his widowed mother to spend the summer with his grandmother in the peaceful town of Stonywood. He is unaware that a prehistoric monster capable of absorbing a human personality and assuming its shape has come to town in the person of a Navy lieutenant Alan Ward, recently returned from an Antarctic research station where he survived a massacre. Now the Thing is taking over the inhabitants of Stonywood.

**Other books you might like:**
Jack Finney, *The Body Snatchers*, 1955
Alan Dean Foster, *The Thing*, 1982
Stephen King, *The Tommyknockers*, 1987

## 1201

### MATTHEW J. COSTELLO

### seaQuest DSV: Fire Below

(New York: Ace, 1994)

**Story type:** Science Fiction (Adventure)
**Series:** seaQuest DSV
**Major character(s):** Nathan Hale Bridger, Scientist, Sea Captain; Lucas Wolenczak, Computer Expert, Teenager; Terry McShane, Military Personnel (UEO)
**Time period(s):** 2010s (2018)
**Locale(s):** *seaQuest DSV*, Submarine; SousMer, Undersea Environment/Habitat; Atlantic Ocean

**Summary:** Terrorists threaten SousMer while an ocean worm, newly discovered by the Azores Deep Sea Research Station, presents a new and deadly biological threat. Television tie-in.

**Other books you might like:**
David Bischoff, *seaQuest DSV: The Ancient*, 1994
Orson Scott Card, *The Abyss*, 1989
Diane Duane, *seaQuest DSV: The Novel*, 1993
  Peter Morwood, co-author
G. Harry Stine, *Starsea Invaders: First Action*, 1993
Theodore Sturgeon, *Voyage to the Bottom of the Sea*, 1961

## 1202

### MATTHEW J. COSTELLO

### Wurm

(New York: Diamond, 1991)

**Story type:** Horror (Apocalyptic Horror)
**Major character(s):** Michael Cross, Professor (director of the NY Aquarium); Paul Barron, Religious (evangelist)
**Time period(s):** 1990s
**Locale(s):** New York, New York; Gulf of Mexico, At Sea

**Summary:** When Michael Cross and the Woods Hole Oceanographic Institute investigate the aftermath of the ship *Achilles*' ill-fated deep sea expedition, they find the crew dead and a new species of undersea worm that evolves in a frighteningly unpredictable fashion. Can it be any coincidence that at approximately the same time lapsed evangelist Paul Barron begins to preach once more, disseminating a message of imminent armageddon?

**Other books you might like:**
Orson Scott Card, *The Abyss*, 1989
Michael Crichton, *Sphere*, 1987
Robert Serling, *Something's Alive on the Titanic*, 1990
Dean Wesley Smith, *Laying the Music to Rest*, 1989

## 1203

### SEAN COSTELLO

### Captain Quad

(New York: Pocket, 1991)

**Story type:** Horror (Wild Talents)
**Major character(s):** Peter Gardner, Handicapped (Captain Quad); Sam Gardner, Student (Peter's brother); Kelly Wheeler, Teacher
**Time period(s):** 1980s; 1990s
**Locale(s):** Massachusetts

**Summary:** Paralyzed from the neck down by a car accident, former medical school hopeful and promising musician Peter Gardner comes to hate the world and his friends and family. When a near-death experience teaches him how to project his consciousness outside his body, he seeks revenge against those whom he feels have betrayed him.

**Other books you might like:**
Stephen King, *Carrie*, 1974

## 1204

### SEAN COSTELLO

### The Cartoonist

(New York: Pocket, 1990)

**Story type:** Horror (Supernatural Vengeance)
**Major character(s):** Scott Bowman, Doctor (psychiatrist); Vince Bateman, Doctor (psychiatrist); Grandpa Rowe, Artist (cartoonist), Psychic
**Time period(s):** 1980s (1988)
**Locale(s):** Quebec, Canada

**Summary:** As teenagers, Scott Bowman and two friends are parties to a hit-and-run accident for which they are never held accountable. Years later, Scott encounters a mute psychiatric patient whose drawings forecast the near future and whose apparent knowledge of Scott's past deeds jeopardizes his family's welfare.

**Other books you might like:**
John Farris, *Fiends*, 1990
Giles Blunt, *Cold Eye*, 1989

## 1205

### SEAN COSTELLO

### Eden's Eyes

(New York: Pocket, 1989)

**Story type:** Horror (Possession)
**Major character(s):** Karen Lockheart, Patient (Eye-transplant recipient); Eve Crowell, Parent (Eye-donor's mother; religious)
**Time period(s):** 1980s
**Locale(s):** Ottawa, Ontario, Canada

**Summary:** The gift of an eye-transplant to Karen becomes a curse when the vengeful spirit of the donor, helped by his demented mother, comes to ''reclaim'' the organs taken from his dead body.

**Other books you might like:**
Pierre Boileau, *Choice Cuts*, 1966
  Thomas Narcejac, co-author
Michael McDowell, *The Amulet*, 1979
Maurice Renard, *The Hands of Orlac*, 1920

## 1206

### GREG COSTIKYAN

## *Another Day, Another Dungeon*

(New York: Tor, 1990)

**Story type:** Fantasy (Light Fantasy)
**Series:** Cups and Sorcery
**Major character(s):** Timaeus D'Asperge, Magician (fire), Nobleman (lord); Garni ben Grimi, Mythical Creature (dwarf), Adventurer; Sydney Stollitt, Businesswoman (expedition organizer)
**Time period(s):** Indeterminate
**Locale(s):** Urf Durfal, Fictional City; Caverns of Cytorax, Mythical Place

**Summary:** Timaeus D'Asperge, newly graduated Magister Igniti, decides to test his prowess and make his reputation by leading an expedition to the Caverns of Cytorax, where, despite the local orcs, the adventurers find a magical statue which they must somehow bring home safely.

**Other books you might like:**
Piers Anthony, *Man From Mundania*, 1989
    Pseudonym of Piers Anthony Dillingham Jacob
Mayer Alan Brenner, *Catastrophe's Spell*, 1989
John Deakins, *Barrow*, 1990
Craig Shaw Gardner, *Wishbringer*, 1988
Matt Ruff, *Fool on the Hill*, 1989

## 1207

### GREG COSTIKYAN

## *By the Sword*

(New York: Tor, 1993)

**Story type:** Fantasy (Light Fantasy)
**Series:** Magic of the Plains
**Major character(s):** Nijon Oonitsaupivia, Hero, Barbarian; Mika Nashram, Magician, Con Artist; Nlavi, Royalty (princess)
**Time period(s):** Indeterminate
**Locale(s):** Fictional Country; Purasham, Fictional City

**Summary:** In order to pass his manhood initiation, Nijon must go out on the plains, with only his horse, Naenae, and an obsidian knife, and survive for 40 days and nights. Despite losing both knife and horse, Nijon does survive with the help of the god Mongoose and gains riches from a caravan of scheming city traders. Returning to the village with his half-brother, he faces trial for murder, one committed by rivals who have planted incriminating evidence against him. Exiled, he sets out for the cities of the north to make his fortune, find adventure, and rescue a princess from a dragon. Computer game tie-in and first of a series.

**Other books you might like:**
Robert Asprin, *Thieves' World*, 1979
    editor
Jean M. Auel, *The Mammoth Hunters*, 1985
Gordon R. Dickson, *The Dragon and the George*, 1976
Simon R. Green, *Blue Moon Rising*, 1991
Barbara Hambly, *Dragonsbane*, 1987
Terry Pratchett, *Guards! Guards!*, 1991
Elizabeth Ann Scarborough, *The Drastic Dragon of Draco, Texas*, 1986
J.R.R. Tolkien, *The Hobbit*, 1938
Chelsea Quinn Yarbro, *A Baroque Fable*, 1986

## 1208

### GREG COSTIKYAN

## *One Quest, Hold the Dragons*

(New York: Tor, 1995)

**Story type:** Fantasy (Light Fantasy; Sword and Sorcery)
**Series:** Cups and Sorcery
**Major character(s):** Timaeus D'Asperge, Magician, Nobleman; Sydney Stollitt, Businesswoman (expedition organizer); Kraki Kronarsson, Adventurer
**Time period(s):** Indeterminate
**Locale(s):** Hamsterburg, Fictional City

**Summary:** After unwanted stays in a dungeon and a fairy ring on the way to Arst-Kara-Morn, Timaeus and his companions must again rescue the statue of King Stantius, held in hopes of tilting the political power in Hamsterburg.

**Other books you might like:**
Robert Asprin, *Another Fine Myth*, 1978
James P. Blaylock, *The Stone Giant*, 1989
Kyle Crocco, *Heroes, Inc.*, 1991
John Moore, *Slay and Rescue*, 1993
Roger Zelazny, *Bring Me the Head of Prince Charming*, 1991
    Robert Sheckley, co-author

## 1209

### JUANITA COULSON

## *Legacy of Earth*

(New York: Ballantine/Del Rey, 1989)

**Story type:** Science Fiction (Family Saga)
**Series:** Children of the Stars
**Major character(s):** Anthony Saunder, Clone; Yrae, Alien, Actress
**Time period(s):** 21st century
**Locale(s):** Procyon Four, Planet—Imaginary

**Summary:** Anthony Saunder, poor step-child of the fabulously wealthy Saunder clan, makes his living creating emoto-tapes. When he is asked by the alien Whimeds to direct a presentation for the upcoming Interspecies Conference, he finds himself caught in the middle of a complex struggle between that species and another alien race.

**Other books you might like:**
Rebecca Ore, *Becoming Alien*, 1987
Rebecca Ore, *Being Alien*, 1989
Frederik Pohl, *Narabedla, Ltd.*, 1988

## 1210

### JUANITA COULSON

## *The Past of Forever*

(New York: Ballantine/Del Rey, 1989)

**Story type:** Science Fiction (Family Saga)
**Series:** Children of the Stars
**Major character(s):** Dan McKelvey, Castaway
**Time period(s):** 21st century
**Locale(s):** Planet of the N'lacs, Planet—Imaginary

**Summary:** McKelvey, a poor relative of the Saunder family who dominated the first two books in this series, is stranded on a world where archaeologists study the remains of a once-advanced alien race which has fallen back into a primitive state. Whatever destroyed the N'lacs' advanced culture may still be a danger to humanity.

**Other books you might like:**
John Brizzolara, *Empire's Horizon*, 1989
Mary Gentle, *Ancient Light*, 1987
Mary Gentle, *Golden Witchbreed*, 1985

---

**1211**

### JUANITA COULSON

## *Star Sister*

(New York: Ballantine/Del Rey, 1990)

**Story type:** Science Fiction (Adventure)
**Major character(s):** Renee Amos, Feminist
**Time period(s):** 1990s
**Locale(s):** Niand, Planet—Imaginary

**Summary:** A politically liberal young woman is accidentally teleported to another planet by passing aliens known as the Arbiters whose purpose is to deal with that planet's oppressive matriarchal government and end discrimination against men. The young woman joins the masculine cause and helps defeat the evil female ruler who is endangering the entire galaxy.

**Other books you might like:**
L. Sprague de Camp, *Rogue Queen*, 1951
Joanna Russ, *The Female Man*, 1975
B.J. Salterberg, *The Outlander: Captivity*, 1989
Sheri S. Tepper, *The Gate to Women's Country*, 1988

---

**1212**

### VINCENT COURTNEY

## *Goblins*

(New York: Zebra, 1994)

**Story type:** Horror (Curse; Evil Children)
**Major character(s):** Marty Martin, Child (six-year-old boy); Dan Martin, Director (film); Vicki Martin, Housewife (Dan's wife, Marty's mother)
**Time period(s):** 1990s (1994)
**Locale(s):** Scotland

**Summary:** Vicki Martin's miscarriage following her visit to the legend-cursed Castle Drochil seems a coincidence, but the birth of her strange first child is not. Vicki has fallen victim to the curse of the castle's evil builders, and her adopted son, Marty, can't convince his mother that his certainty that his little brother is a bona-fide goblin is anything but the fancy of a jealous imagination.

**Other books you might like:**
Ira Levin, *Rosemary's Baby*, 1967
Bernard Taylor, *The Godsend*, 1976
Thomas Tryon, *The Other*, 1972

---

**1213**

### VINCENT COURTNEY

## *Harvest of Blood*

(New York: Pinnacle, 1992)

**Story type:** Horror (Vampire Story)
**Major character(s):** Christopher Blaze, Detective—Private, Vampire; Reggie Carver, Detective—Private; Sue Blaze, Doctor (Christopher's wife)

**Time period(s):** 1990s (1992)
**Locale(s):** Miami, Florida

**Summary:** Having recovered from his first adventure as a vampirized cop in *Vampire Beat* (1991), Christopher Blaze returns as a private detective and faces his most formidable challenge yet: a fellow vampire running a drug pipeline between Central America and the United States.

**Other books you might like:**
P.N. Elrod, *The Vampire Files Series*, 1989-1992
Lee Killough, *Blood Hunt*, 1988

---

**1214**

### VINCENT COURTNEY

## *Vampire Beat*

(New York: Zebra/Pinnacle, 1991)

**Story type:** Horror (Vampire Story)
**Major character(s):** Christopher Blaze, Police Officer, Vampire; Sue Catledge, Doctor; Yosekaat Rakz, Vampire
**Time period(s):** 1990s
**Locale(s):** Miami, Florida

**Summary:** Cursed by a dying black magician to become a vampire, detective Chris Blaze finds himself uniquely suited to track down a vampire serial killer on the streets of Miami, all the while trying to hide his own nighttime blood-drinking habits to keep himself above the suspicion of his colleagues.

**Other books you might like:**
P.N. Elrod, *The Vampire Files Series*, 1989-1992
Lee Killough, *Blood Hunt*, 1988
Brian Lumley, *Necroscope*, 1988

---

**1215**

### VINCENT COURTNEY

## *Wake Up Screaming*

(New York: Pinnacle, 1992)

**Story type:** Horror (Occult)
**Major character(s):** Derek Harris, Child (12-year-old boy); Dutch Harris, Farmer, Grandparent (Derek's grandfather); Petie Mattison, Teenager
**Time period(s):** 1990s
**Locale(s):** Sundova Beach, Florida

**Summary:** When Derek Harris and his friend Petie play with an ancient grimoire found in Dutch Harris's house, they unwittingly open the gateway to the spirit world in which Dutch's first wife, Katherine, has been trapped for almost half a century and scheming for vengeance against the former members of her satanic cult.

**Other books you might like:**
Ramsey Campbell, *To Wake the Dead*, 1980
Leigh Clark, *Blood Sabbath*, 1991
Penelope Banka Kreps, *Demon's Fright*, 1992
Peter Straub, *Ghost Story*, 1979

---

**1216**

### ARTHUR BYRON COVER

## *Stationfall*

(New York: Avon Books, 1989)

**Story type:** Science Fiction (Humor)

**Major character(s):** Homer Hunter, Spaceman (Lieutenant); Oliver, Robot
**Time period(s):** Indeterminate Future
**Locale(s):** Aurelian, Space Station

**Summary:** In this sequel to *Planetfall*, Homer and Oliver find themselves accidentally caught up in a war being fought on the space station Aurelian. They deal more or less successfully with spies, terrorists, space vampires, and a robot's ghost.

**Other books you might like:**
Douglas Adams, *The Hitchhiker's Guide to the Galaxy*, 1979
Ron Goulart, *Big Bang*, 1982
Ron Goulart, *Hellquad*, 1984
Ron Goulart, *Skyrocket Steele*, 1980
Barry B. Longyear, *Naked Came the Robot*, 1988
Alexei Panshin, *Masque World*, 1969

## 1217

### BRUCE COVILLE

## Aliens Stole My Body

(New York: Pocket Minstrel, 1998)

**Story type:** Science Fiction (Young Adult; Adventure)
**Series:** Bruce Coville's Alien Adventures
**Major character(s):** Rod ''Seymour'' Allbright, Disembodied Personality, Adventurer; BKR, Alien, Villain; Snout, Alien, Psychic
**Time period(s):** 1990s
**Locale(s):** *Ferkel*, Spaceship; Kryndamar, Planet—Imaginary

**Summary:** With his personality transferred to Seymour, the chibling from Dimension X, Rod Allbright and the crew of the *Ferkel* pursue BKR, who has stolen Rod's body in order to secure information he thinks he will find in Rod' s brain.

**Other books you might like:**
Janet Asimov, *The Norby Chronicles*, 1986
   Isaac Asimov, co-author
Eleanor Cameron, *The Wonderful Flight to the Mushroom Planet*, 1954
Robert A. Heinlein, *Have Spacesuit—Will Travel*, 1958
Norton Juster, *The Phantom Tollbooth*, 1961
Marilyn Kaye, *Amy, Number Seven*, 1998

## 1218

### BRUCE COVILLE

## Goblins in the Castle

(New York: Pocket Minstrel, 1992)

**Story type:** Fantasy (Quest; Young Adult)
**Major character(s):** Igor, Handicapped, Adventurer; William, Orphan, Adventurer; Herky, Mythical Creature (goblin)
**Time period(s):** Indeterminate
**Locale(s):** Toad-in-a-Cage Castle, Mythical Place; Nilbog, Mythical Place (goblin's city)

**Summary:** William and Igor set out from Toad-in-a-Cage Castle to discover a solution to the castle's goblins, which may soon escape confinement and again visit their benign trickery on everyone. After goblins kidnap Igor, Granny Pinchbottom directs William to Nilbog equipped with a quest and a reward. Taken prisoner in Nilbog, William relies on Herky to help him and Igor escape the other goblins.

**Other books you might like:**
Lynne Reid Banks, *The Indian in the Cupboard*, 1980
L. Frank Baum, *The Master Key: An Electrical Fairy Tale*, 1901

Edward Eager, *Knight's Castle*, 1956
Kathryn Lasky, *Double Trouble Squared*, 1991
Daniel Manus Pinkwater, *Lizard Music*, 1976
Vivian Vande Velde, *User Unfriendly*, 1991
Laurence Yep, *Dragon of the Lost Sea*, 1982
Mary Frances Zambreno, *A Plague of Sorcerers*, 1991

## 1219

### BRUCE COVILLE

## Into the Land of the Unicorns

(New York: Scholastic, 1994)

**Story type:** Fantasy (Young Adult; Quest)
**Series:** Unicorn Chronicles
**Major character(s):** Cara Diana Hunter, Adventurer; The Dimblethum, Mythical Creature; Lightfoot, Mythical Creature (unicorn), Animal
**Time period(s):** 1990s; Indeterminate
**Locale(s):** Land of Luster, Fictional Country

**Summary:** Bearing an amulet she has promised to safeguard, Cara travels to Luster where she finds herself important to the survival of unicorns.

**Other books you might like:**
Peter S. Beagle, *The Last Unicorn*, 1968
Jack Dann, *Unicorns II*, 1992
   Gardner Dozois, co-editor
Elizabeth Goudge, *The Little White Horse*, 1946
Tanith Lee, *Black Unicorn*, 1991
Jane Yolen, *Here There Be Unicorns*, 1994

## 1220

### BRUCE COVILLE

## Jennifer Murdley's Toad

(New York: Harcourt Brace Jovanovich, 1992)

**Story type:** Fantasy (Contemporary; Young Adult)
**Series:** Magic Shop
**Major character(s):** Jennifer Murdley, Teenager, Student; S.H. Elives, Businessman
**Time period(s):** 1990s
**Locale(s):** Smokey Hollow, Fictional City

**Summary:** In a chance visit to the magic shop, Jennifer spends 75[cnt] for a toad which she hopes to use as the subject of her writing assignment. Jennifer finds that her toad speaks but disapproves of all the resulting trouble. After a series of extraordinary adventures, Jennifer realizes the importance of internal beauty and discovers her own.

**Other books you might like:**
Annie Dalton, *Out of the Ordinary*, 1990
Diana Wynne Jones, *Howl's Moving Castle*, 1986
Diana Wynne Jones, *The Ogre Downstairs*, 1974
Edward Ormondroyd, *David and the Phoenix*, 1957
Pat O'Shea, *The Hounds of the Morrigan*, 1986
Patricia C. Wrede, *Dealing with Dragons*, 1990
Patricia C. Wrede, *Talking to Dragons*, 1985

## 1221

### BRUCE COVILLE

## *Jeremy Thatcher, Dragon Hatcher*

(New York: Harcourt Brace Jovanovich, 1991)

**Story type:** Fantasy (Young Adult; Quest)
**Series:** Magic Shop
**Major character(s):** Jeremy Thatcher, Child; Tiamat, Mythical Creature (dragon)
**Time period(s):** 1990s
**Locale(s):** Blodgett's Crossing, Mythical Place

**Summary:** At Elive's Magic Supplies, Jeremy purchases a beautiful marbled ball, discovering when he arrives home the instructions for hatching his dragon egg. Before long, Jeremy joins the shop owner and the librarian to provide a way for Tiamat to journey to the world of dragons.

**Other books you might like:**
Thorarinn Gunnarsson, *Make Way for Dragons!*, 1990
Ursula K. Le Guin, *A Wizard of Earthsea*, 1968
Anne McCaffrey, *Dragondrums*, 1979
Anne McCaffrey, *Dragonsinger*, 1977
Anne McCaffrey, *Dragonsong*, 1976
Edward Ormondroyd, *David and the Phoenix*, 1957
Patricia C. Wrede, *Dealing with Dragons*, 1990
Laurence Yep, *Tongues of Jade*, 1991

## 1222

### BRUCE COVILLE

## *My Teacher Flunked the Planet*

(New York: Pocket Minstrel, 1992)

**Story type:** Science Fiction (Young Adult; Invasion of Earth)
**Series:** My Teacher Is an Alien
**Major character(s):** Peter Thompson, Student, Hero; Broxholm, Alien; Kreeblim, Alien
**Time period(s):** 1990s
**Locale(s):** United States

**Summary:** Equipped by the aliens with universal translators, Peter and his companions return to Earth to help determine Earth's fate with the Interplanetary Council, worried since all civilized societies have abandoned warfare before venturing into space.

**Other books you might like:**
Alan Dean Foster, *Glory Lane*, 1987
Daniel Manus Pinkwater, *Borgel*, 1990
Terry Pratchett, *Diggers*, 1991
Terry Pratchett, *Truckers*, 1990
Terry Pratchett, *Wings*, 1991

## 1223

### BRUCE COVILLE

## *My Teacher Fried My Brains*

(New York: Pocket Minstrel, 1991)

**Story type:** Science Fiction (First Contact; Young Adult)
**Series:** My Teacher Is an Alien
**Major character(s):** Duncan Dougal, Student; Betty Lou Karpou, Alien, Teacher; Susan Simmons, Student
**Time period(s):** 1990s
**Locale(s):** United States (small town, fictional city)

**Summary:** Bully Duncan Dougal becomes convinced that a second alien is present at his school, but no one believes him. When Miss Karpou and her jelly-like pet, Poot, capture Duncan, they use his brain to regain communication with the Interplanetary Council, which is about to make a decision on ''The Earth Question''—what to do about the extremely intelligent, but uncivilized, humans?

**Other books you might like:**
Janet Asimov, *Norby, the Mixed-up Robot*, 1983
    Isaac Asimov, co-author
Daniel Manus Pinkwater, *Lizard Music*, 1978
    as D. Manus Pinkwater
Terry Pratchett, *Diggers*, 1991
Terry Pratchett, *Truckers*, 1990
Terry Pratchett, *Wings*, 1991

## 1224

### BRUCE COVILLE

## *My Teacher Glows in the Dark*

(New York: Pocket Minstrel, 1991)

**Story type:** Science Fiction (First Contact; Young Adult)
**Series:** My Teacher Is an Alien
**Major character(s):** Peter Thompson, Student; Hoo-Lan, Alien
**Time period(s):** 1990s
**Locale(s):** New Jersey; Spaceship (alien)

**Summary:** Peter Thompson is hurled into the middle of the Interplanetary League's debate over what to do about Earth. In their 3,000-year history they have never seen another species that kills its members with such reckless abandon. The danger from this mass insanity is so great that they are considering quarantine or destruction.

**Other books you might like:**
Daniel Manus Pinkwater, *Borgel*, 1990
Daniel Manus Pinkwater, *The Snarkout Boys and the Avocado of Death*, 1982
Terry Pratchett, *Diggers*, 1991
Terry Pratchett, *Truckers*, 1990
Terry Pratchett, *Wings*, 1991

## 1225

### GREG COX

## *Assignment: Eternity*

(New York: Pocket Books, 1998)

**Story type:** Science Fiction (Time Travel; Space Opera)
**Series:** Star Trek
**Major character(s):** Gary Seven, Spy, Time Traveler; Spock, Alien (Vulcan), Scientist; James T. Kirk, Spaceship Captain
**Time period(s):** 23rd century (2269); 1960s (1969)
**Locale(s):** U.S.S. Enterprise, Spaceship; Planet—Imaginary; Romulan Empire, Interstellar Empire/Federation

**Summary:** Responding to a distress call from Agent 146, Gary Seven and Roberta Lincoln cross time and space to commandeer the *Enterprise* and send it deep within the Romulan Empire to a cloaked planet. Leaving Spock in command, Kirk leads a landing party to explore the shielded facility on the planet's surface. Despite his misgivings, Kirk teams up with Seven to fight the Romulan commander who has captured Agent 146 and who intends to use the base to travel into the future and kill Spock at Khitomer.

**Other books you might like:**
Poul Anderson, *Guardians of Time*, 1960

Margaret Wander Bonanno, *Strangers From the Sky*, 1987
Diane Carey, *First Frontier*, 1995
James I. Kirkland, co-author
Harlan Ellison, *The City on the Edge of Forever*, 1995
Barbara Hambly, *Ishmael*, 1985
Kij Johnson, *Dragon's Honor*, 1996
Greg Cox, co-author

---

**1226**
**GREG COX**
**JOHN GREGORY BETANCOURT**, Co-Author

## Devil in the Sky
(New York: Pocket, 1995)

**Story type:** Science Fiction (Adventure; Space Opera)
**Series:** Star Trek: Deep Space Nine
**Major character(s):** Ttan, Parent, Alien (Horta); Benjamin Sisko, Military Personnel (commander); Major Kira, Military Personnel, Alien (Bajoran)
**Time period(s):** 24th century
**Locale(s):** Deep Space Nine, Space Station; Davonia, Moon—Imaginary

**Summary:** When the Cardassians capture a mother Horta en route to Bajor for a mining project, her 20 eggs, held in stasis, arrive safely at Deep Space Nine while Kira and Dax lead a rescue mission. Nog and Jake's tampering with the stasis field allows the eggs to hatch, releasing 20 hungry Horta to consume the station. The Bajoran government has changed its mind, however, and no longer wants the Horta on Bajoran soil. If the mother Horta does not return soon, Sisko faces the unpleasant alternative of killing the baby Hortas or letting them destroy the station.

**Other books you might like:**
C.J. Cherryh, *Downbelow Station*, 1981
A.C. Crispin, *Sarek*, 1994
Peter David, *Q-Squared*, 1994
Diane Duane, *The Romulan Way*, 1987
Peter Morwood, co-author
Kij Johnson, *Dragon's Honor*, 1996
Greg Cox, co-author
Gore Vidal, *Visit to a Small Planet*, 1956

---

**1227**
**GREG COX**

## Iron Man: The Armor Trap
(New York: Berkley Boulevard, 1995)

**Story type:** Science Fiction (Adventure)
**Series:** Iron Man
**Major character(s):** Tony ''Iron Man'' Stark, Scientist, Hero; Jim ''War Machine'' Rhodes, Hero
**Time period(s):** 21st century
**Locale(s):** San Francisco, California; Cyberspace

**Summary:** When enemies capture Tony Stark, hoping to force him into producing a copy of his high-tech armor, his corporation sends War Machine to negotiate his release while Stark navigates a cyberspace maze, attempting to retrieve his armor. Comic book tie-in.

**Other books you might like:**
Peter David, *What Savage Beast*, 1995
Diane Duane, *Spider-Man: The Venom Factor*, 1994
Stan Lee, *The Ultimate Spider-Man*, 1994
editor

---

Neal Stephenson, *Snow Crash*, 1992
John Varley, *Superheroes*, 1995
Ricia Mainhardt, co-editor

---

**1228**
**GREG COX**

## Q-Space
(New York: Pocket Books, 1998)

**Story type:** Science Fiction (Space Opera; Psychic Powers)
**Series:** Star Trek: The Next Generation: The Q Continuum
**Major character(s):** Q, Immortal, Alien; Jean-Luc Picard, Spaceship Captain; Deanna Troi, Psychologist, Psychic (empath)
**Time period(s):** 24th century
**Locale(s):** *U.S.S. Enterprise*, Spaceship; Q Continuum, Alternate Universe; Interstellar Empire/Federation

**Summary:** Enroute to test a new technology that may permit travel through the barrier at the edge of the galaxy, the *Enterprise* receives a visit from Q—and his new wife and son, Q and q. Q warns Picard not to meddle with the barrier, and an attack by the Calamarain reinforces the point. When Picard demands to know why, Q takes Picard on a tour of time and space, leaving the crew to deal with the Calamarain, the other Q, and q. First of three volumes.

**Other books you might like:**
Peter David, *Q-in-Law*, 1991
Peter David, *Q-Squared*, 1994
Diane Duane, *The Wounded Sky*, 1983
Michael Jan Friedman, *All Good Things. . .*, 1994
Kij Johnson, *Dragon's Honor*, 1996
Greg Cox, co-author
Gore Vidal, *Visit to a Small Planet*, 1953

---

**1229**
**GREG COX**

## Q-Zone
(New York: Pocket Books, 1998)

**Story type:** Science Fiction (Space Opera; Psychic Powers)
**Series:** Star Trek: The Next Generation: The Q Continuum
**Major character(s):** Q, Immortal, Alien; Jean-Luc Picard, Spaceship Captain, Military Personnel; William Riker, Military Personnel (Starfleet Commander)
**Time period(s):** 24th century
**Locale(s):** *U.S.S. Enterprise*, Spaceship; Q Continuum, Alternate Universe

**Summary:** Q takes Picard on a tour of the multiverse, with special emphasis on Q's own history. Meanwhile, the crew of the *Enterprise*, unable to disengage from the Calamarain attack, attempts to escape by crossing the galactic energy barrier. Second of three volumes.

**Other books you might like:**
Peter David, *Q-in-Law*, 1991
Peter David, *Q-Squared*, 1994
Michael Jan Friedman, *All Good Things. . .*, 1994
David Gerrold, *Encounter at Farpoint*, 1987
Robert A. Heinlein, *Glory Road*, 1963
Kij Johnson, *Dragon's Honor*, 1996
Greg Cox, co-author

**1230**

**GREG COX**, Editor
**T.K.F. WEISKOPF**, Co-Editor

## *Tomorrow Bites*
(New York: Baen, 1995)

**Story type:** Horror (Anthology; Werewolf Story)

**Summary:** The volume consists of 11 reprints and one original story that situate the werewolf of supernatural horror in science fiction scenarios. In Michael Flynn's "Werehouse," shape shifting with the help of nanotechnology becomes a form of cheap thrill seeking on a future earth. James Blish offers a scientific explanation for lycanthropy in "There Shall Be No Darkness," while Poul Anderson, in "Operation Afreet," imagines an alternate World War II as fought by werewolves and other supernatural entities. Larry Niven's "There's a Wolf in My Time Machine" sends a time traveller to an alternate Earth in which the dominant species evolved from wolves, while Clark Ashton Smith's "A Prophecy of Monsters" ruminates on the problems a werewolf might have getting dinner in the future. Gene Wolfe, in "The Hero as Werewolf," considers the needs that humans and werewolves share.

**Other books you might like:**
Brian J. Frost, *Book of the Werewolf*, 1973
Martin H. Greenberg, *Werewolves*, 1995
    editor
Stephen Jones, *The Mammoth Book of Werewolves*, 1994
    editor
Byron Preiss, *The Ultimate Werewolf*, 1992
    editor
Bill Pronzini, *Werewolf!*, 1979
    editor

**1231**

**GREG COX**, Editor
**T.K.F. WEISKOPF**, Co-Editor

## *Tomorrow Sucks*
(New York: Baen, 1994)

**Story type:** Horror (Anthology; Vampire Story)

**Summary:** The dozen reprints gathered here represent an underexamined yet rich and rewarding side of vampire fiction: vampires in science fiction. Among the selections that probe science fiction's interface with the supernatural are the Ray Bradbury's "Pillar of Fire," about a creature of the undead resurrected in a future where belief in his kind has been obliterated; Brian Stableford's "The Man Who Loved the Vampire Lady," a story set in an alternate universe in which the ruling elite of history are vampires; C.L. Moore's "Shambleau," the classic space opera of a man who finds the basis for the Medusa myth in a race of extraterrestrial vampires; Joe L. Hensley's "And Not Quite Human," a tale of interstellar armageddon and the unlikely survivors who emerge; Leslie Roy Carter's "Vanishing Breed," about a future where vampires have been so perfectly bred to fit in with normal human beings that they have forgotten their Gothic heritage; S.N. Dyer's "Born Again," about a biological experiment that isolates a virus responsible for vampirism; and Roger Zelazny's "The Stainless Steel Leech," in which a renegade robot and the last vampire on earth form a curious friendship.

**Other books you might like:**
Ellen Datlow, *Blood Is Not Enough*, 1989
    editor

Ellen Datlow, *A Whisper of Blood*, 1991
    editor
Alan Ryan, *Vampires: Two Centuries of Great Vampire Stories*, 1987
Robert Weinberg, *Weird Vampire Tales*, 1992
    Stefan Dziemianowice, Martin H. Greenberg, co-editors

**1232**

**MICHAEL COX**, Editor

## *The Oxford Book of Twentieth Century Ghost Stories*
(New York: Oxford University Press, 1996)

**Story type:** Horror (Anthology; Ghost Story)

**Summary:** Arranged in chronological order, the 33 stories by American and British writers assembled here span the years 1910 to 1994 and provide an overview of the ghost story tradition in the 20th century. The selections include E. Nesbit's "In the Dark," in which a man is haunted either by a friend he murdered or his own guilty conscience; Ellen Glasgow's "The Shadowy Third," in which a love triangle is catalyzed by the ghost of a young girl; M.R. James's "The Diary of Mr. Poynter," which recounts the death and gruesome manifestation thereafter of a dissolute man; May Sinclair's "The Nature of Evidence" and F. Scott Fitzgerald's "A Short Trip Home," both of which involve ghosts who try to seduce the living into romantic liaisons; Fritz Leiber's "Smoke Ghost," which reconceives the traditional gothic ghost for a contemporary urban environment; and the sentimental ghost story "The July Ghost" by A.S. Byatt.

**Other books you might like:**
Richard Dalby, *The Mammoth Book of Ghost Stories 2*, 1991
    editor
Richard Dalby, *The Mammoth Book of Ghost Stories*, 1990
    editor
Larry Dark, *The Literary Ghost*, 1991
    editor
Robert Phillips, *Triumph of the Night*, 1989
    editor

**1233**

**MICHAEL COX**, Editor

## *Twelve Tales of the Supernatural*
(New York: Oxford, 1997)

**Story type:** Horror (Anthology)

**Summary:** One dozen stories by British writers, most featuring ghosts and most written before the middle of the twentieth century. Included are William Fryer Harvey's "The Tool," in which a man discovers through supernatural clues his unwitting complicity in a murder; E.F. Benson's "The Face," about a woman's inescapable rendezvous with a ghost from the past; and M.R. James's "Number 13," about the ghostly goings on in a forgotten room in a lodging house. A number of the stories feature ghostly revenges, including J.H. Riddell's "A Terrible Vengeance," Marjorie Bowen's "The Last Bouquet," and A.N.L. Munby's "A Christmas Game."

**Other books you might like:**
R. Chetwynd-Hayes, *Gaslight Tales of Terror*, 1976
    editor
Richard Dalby, *The Mammoth Book of Ghost Stories*, 1990
    editor

Hugh Lamb, *Forgotten Tales of Terror*, 1978
editor
Michel Parry, *Reign of Terror*, 1976
editor

**1234**

**MICHAEL COX**, Editor

*Twelve Victorian Ghost Stories*

(New York: Oxford, 1997)

**Story type:** Horror (Anthology; Ghost Story)

**Summary:** Twelve stories of ghostly encounters written during the golden age of the classic ghost story. Included are Margaret Oliphant's "The Lady's Walk," about a haunted estate whose ghost warns people of impending tragedy; Rhoda Broughton's "Poor Pretty Bobby," a tale of love that endures beyond the grave; J. Sheridan Le Fanu's "Madam Crowl's Ghost," in which a woman's ghost reveals a gruesome secret she has taken with her to the grave; and Richard Marsh's "The Fifteenth Man," about a ghostly rugby player.

**Other books you might like:**
Everett F. Bleiler, *A Treasury of Victorian Ghost Stories*, 1981
editor
Richard Dalby, *The Mammoth Book of Victorian and Edwardian Ghost Stories*, 1995
editor
Richard Dalby, *The Virago Book of Victorian Ghost Stories*, 1988
editor
Hugh Lamb, *Victorian Nightmares*, 1977
editor
Michel Parry, *Reign of Terror*, 1976
editor

**1235**

**MICHAEL COX**, Editor
**R.A. GILBERT**, Co-Editor

*Victorian Ghost Stories: An Oxford Anthology*

(New York: Oxford, 1991)

**Story type:** Horror (Anthology; Ghost Story)

**Summary:** Thirty-five ghost stories spanning the years 1852 to 1908. Included are such well known classics as Charles Dickens' tale of ghostly revenge, "To Be Taken with a Grain of Salt"; Henry James' tale of clothes that retain the spirit of their former owner, "A Romance of Certain Old Clothes"; M.R. James' tale of a hideous secret recorded in a mouldering book, "Canon Alberic's Scrapbook"; and less familiar tales by Algernon Blackwood, Bernard Capes, J. Sheridan LeFanu and others.

**Other books you might like:**
Everett F. Bleiler, *A Treasury of Victorian Ghost Stories*, 1981
editor
Richard Dalby, *Victorian Ghost Stories by Eminent Women Writers*, 1988
editor

**1236**

**JOHN COYNE**

*Child of Shadows*

(New York: Warner, 1990)

**Story type:** Horror (Evil Children)
**Major character(s):** Melissa Vaughn, Social Worker; Adam, Foundling; Connor Connaghan, Artisan, Landlord (Melissa's)
**Time period(s):** 1990s
**Locale(s):** Beaver Creek, North Carolina; New York, New York

**Summary:** Frustrated with her hopeless job, Manhattan social worker Melissa Vaughn moves to North Carolina with Adam, an autistic child found living in the tunnels beneath Grand Central Station. When Adam shows abnormal familiarity with Melissa's hidden past and becomes an object of veneration for a bizarre evangelical cult, Melissa begins to wonder if he is really the innocent child she took him for.

**Other books you might like:**
Dean R. Koontz, *The Servants of Twilight*, 1984
John Saul, *Suffer the Children*, 1977
Bernard Taylor, *The Godsend*, 1976

**1237**

**JOHN COYNE**

*Fury*

(New York: Warner, 1989)

**Story type:** Horror (Reincarnation)
**Major character(s):** Jennifer Winters, Lawyer; Kathy Dart, Psychic (New Age evangelist and channel)
**Time period(s):** 1980s
**Locale(s):** New York, New York; Dart Commune, Minnesota

**Summary:** When Jennifer Winters begins to experience increasingly violent "primitive" episodes, she gradually realizes that identities and enemies from previous lives are taking over. With the help of a "New Age Channeller"—who may be a friend or a foe—she attempts to probe her past lives to confront the evil that has intruded into her present one.

**Other books you might like:**
Max Ehrlich, *The Reincarnation of Peter Proud*, 1974
William Hallahan, *The Search for Joseph Tully*, 1974
Charles Maclean, *The Watcher*, 1983
Ramona Stewart, *The Possession of Joel Delaney*, 1970

**1238**

**BRIAN CRAIG** (Pseudonym of Brian Stableford)

*Ghost Dancers*

(Baltimore, Maryland: GW Books, 1991)

**Story type:** Science Fiction (Adventure; Alternate Universe)
**Series:** Dark Future
**Major character(s):** Kid Zero, Outlaw; Pasco, Agent; Carl Preston, Agent
**Time period(s):** 1990s
**Locale(s):** Southwest United States, Alternate Earth; Antarctica, Alternate Earth (Mitso-Makema Base)

**Summary:** Kid Zero has accidently come into possession of a very hot data disk. Everybody wants it: GenTech (the disk's owners), Mitso-Makema (their rivals), the Mafia, the Yakuza and even what's left of the U.S. Government. They all want Kid Zero, too, and they're even willing to take him alive.

**Other books you might like:**
Nigel Findley, *2XS*, 1992
William Gibson, *Neuromancer*, 1984
Jack Yeovil, *Demon Download*, 1990
Jack Yeovil is pseudonym for Kim Newman
Jack Yeovil, *Krokodil Tears*, 1991
Jack Yoevil is pseudonym for Kim Newman
Mike Resnick, *Soothsayer*, 1991
Steve Wilson, *The Lost Traveller*, 1976
Roger Zelazny, *Damnation Alley*, 1969

---

**1239**

**BRIAN CRAIG** (Pseudonym of Brian Stableford)

## Plague Demon

(Baltimore, Maryland: GW Books/Games Workshop, 1990)

**Story type:** Fantasy (Quest; Horror)
**Series:** Warhammer
**Major character(s):** Harmis Datz, Military Personnel; Nicodemus, Religious; Averil, Sorceress
**Time period(s):** 16th century
**Locale(s):** Alternate Earth

**Summary:** The second story told by Orfeo to his jailer is about Harmis Datz, a soldier in a small country threatened by a once-human servant of the Plague God. Datz and companions must unravel plots, fight monsters, and face their own best/worst natures before the kingdom can be saved.

**Other books you might like:**
Steven Brust, *Jhereg*, 1983
Glen Cook, *The Black Company*, 1984
Barbara Hambly, *The Time of the Dark*, 1982
Fritz Leiber, *Swords and Deviltry*, 1970
Michael Shea, *Nifft the Lean*, 1982

---

**1240**

**BRIAN CRAIG** (Pseudonym of Brian Stableford)

## Storm Warriors

(Baltimore, Maryland: GW Books/Games Workshop, 1991)

**Story type:** Fantasy (Adventure; Horror)
**Series:** Warhammer
**Major character(s):** Orfeo, Minstrel; Trystan, Minstrel (bard); Herla, Royalty (king)
**Time period(s):** 16th century
**Locale(s):** Morien Wales, Alternate Earth

**Summary:** Orfeo's last tale tells the fate of a king in Morien who allows a band of elves to settle in his land. They are not quite what they seem, and chaos soon threatens everyone. Too powerful for combat, chaos must be fought with music and spirit. A game tie-in novel.

**Other books you might like:**
Steven Brust, *Jhereg*, 1983
Glen Cook, *The Black Company*, 1984
Casey Flynn, *Most Ancient Song*, 1991
Michael Moorcock, *The Chronicles of Corum*, 1978
Keith Taylor, *Bard*, 1981

---

**1241**

**BRIAN CRAIG** (Pseudonym of Brian Stableford)

## Zaragoz

(Baltimore, Maryland: GW Books/Games Workshop, 1990)

**Story type:** Fantasy (Adventure; Horror)
**Series:** Warhammer
**Major character(s):** Orfeo, Minstrel, Writer (poet); Semjaza, Sorcerer; Arcangelo, Religious
**Time period(s):** 16th century
**Locale(s):** Alternate Earth

**Summary:** The Castle Zaragoz is unconquerable except by treachery. The minstrel, Orfeo, wanders into the net of treachery, sorcery, deception and counter-deception that surrounds two families' claims to control the citadel. He must face down plotters and demons to see justice done. The first in a series of novels presented as stories told by Orfeo while in jail.

**Other books you might like:**
Steven Brust, *Jhereg*, 1983
Charles de Lint, *Yarrow*, 1986
David Ferring, *Konrad*, 1990
Fritz Leiber, *Swords and Deviltry*, 1970
Michael Moorcock, *Elric of Melnibone*, 1976

---

**1242**

**PATRICIA CRAIG**, Editor

## Twelve Irish Ghost Stories

(New York: Oxford, 1998)

**Story type:** Horror (Anthology)

**Summary:** This anthology includes one poem and 11 tales of the supernatural with Irish settings. Selections span more than a century and include Charlotte Riddell's "The Last Squire of Ennismore," about the cursed booty of a wrecked ship and the luckless man who comes into its possession; Dorothy Macardle's "The Prisoner," in which the ghost of a man wrongly accused in the Middle Ages endures to exonerate his name; George Moore's "A Play-House in the Waste," which features ghosts in a parable concerned with the great famine; and stories by J. Sheridan Le Fanu, Elizabeth Bowen and others.

**Other books you might like:**
Peter Haining, *Great Irish Tales of Horror*, 1995
editor
Peter Haining, *Great Irish Tales of Terror and the Supernatural*, 1994
editor
Joseph Hone, *Irish Ghost Stories*, 1971
editor
Jim McGarry, *Irish Tales of Terror*, 1971
editor
Peter Tremayne, *Irish Masters of Fantasy*, 1979
editor

---

**1243**

**RALPH ADAMS CRAM**

## Black Spirits and White

(West Warwick, Rhode Island: Necronomicon Press, 1993)

**Story type:** Horror (Collection)

**Summary:** Originally published in 1895, this slim booklet of six stories, the author's only contribution to the field of weird fiction, is a classic. Four of the stories are ghost tales, ''No. 252 Rue M. le Prince'' being an almost comic account of the attempt of several skeptics to exorcise a haunted house, and ''In Kropfsberg Keep,'' ''The White Villa,'' and ''Sister Madelena'' being about art students who travel to foreign lands and invariably run afoul of the local ghost in the houses they put up in. ''Notre Dame des Eaux'' is a *conte cruel* about an escaped madman and ''The Dead Valley'' a masterpiece of atmospheric horror about two boys who stumble upon a desolate valley laid waste by a noxious mist.

**Other books you might like:**
E.F. Benson, *The Collected Ghost Stories of E.F. Benson*, 1992
Ambrose Bierce, *Ghost and Horror Stories*, 1964
Algernon Blackwood, *Best Ghost Stories of Algernon Blackwood*, 1973
M.R. James, *Casting the Runes and Other Ghost Stories*, 1987
W.C. Morrow, *The Ape, the Idiot, and Other People*, 1897

## 1244

### JOHN CRAMER

## Einstein's Bridge

(New York: Avon, 1997)

**Story type:** Science Fiction (Hard Science Fiction; First Contact)
**Major character(s):** George Griffin, Scientist (nuclear physics); Roger Coulton, Scientist (nuclear physics); Alice ''Lancaster'' Lang, Journalist, Writer
**Time period(s):** 2000s (2004)
**Locale(s):** Geneva, Switzerland; Waxahachie, Texas

**Summary:** The Hive, an ancient predator, constantly searches for new universes to conquer. While George and Roger conduct research at the Superconducting Super Collider, Tunnel Maker creates a photon sized bridge to the SSC. George befriends Alice who simultaneously writes an article on the SSC for a prestigious journal and a thriller about its effect on the local fine arts.

**Other books you might like:**
Roger MacBride Allen, *The Ring of Charon*, 1990
Michael Flynn, *Firestar*, 1996
Robert L. Forward, *Dragon's Egg*, 1980
Charles Pellegrino, *The Killing Star*, 1995
 George Zebrowski, co-author
Sage Walker, *Whiteout*, 1996

## 1245

### JOHN CRAMER

## Twistor

(New York: William Morrow, 1989)

**Story type:** Science Fiction (Hard Science Fiction)
**Major character(s):** David Harrison, Scientist (Physicist); Jeffrey Ernst, Child
**Time period(s):** 20th century
**Locale(s):** Seattle, Washington; Alternate Universe

**Summary:** David Harrison, a brilliant young physicist, has made a breakthrough that will allow human beings to enter and explore alternate universes. When espionage agents from a private corporation attempt to steal the experimental apparatus, David and two small children find themselves transported into and stranded in one such alternate universe.

**Other books you might like:**
Gregory Benford, *Timescape*, 1980
Robert L. Forward, *Dragon's Egg*, 1980
Robert L. Forward, *The Flight of the Dragonfly*, 1984
Robert L. Forward, *Starquake*, 1985
James P. Hogan, *The Genesis Machine*, 1981
James P. Hogan, *The Proteus Operation*, 1985

## 1246

### KATHRYN CRAMER

## Walls of Fear

(New York: Morrow, 1990)

**Story type:** Horror (Anthology; Haunted House)

**Summary:** In this successor to *The Architecture of Fear* Kathryn Cramer collects 16 original haunted house stories by Chet Williamson, Gene Wolfe, Jonathan Carroll, and other writers. Several of the best of these stories show the influence of well-known writers (H.P. Lovecraft in Richard A. Luppoff's ''The House of Rue Chartres'') and filmmakers (Peter Weir in Karl Edward Wagner's ''Cedar Lane'') associated with the horror genre.

**Other books you might like:**
Charles G. Waugh, *House Shudders*, 1987
 Martin H. Greenberg, co-author

## 1247

### MELISSA CRANDALL

## Earth 2

(New York: Ace, 1994)

**Story type:** Science Fiction (Post-Disaster; Adventure)
**Major character(s):** Danziger, Spaceman, Castaway; Devon Adair, Leader, Settler
**Time period(s):** 22nd century
**Locale(s):** G889, Planet—Imaginary

**Summary:** Colonists from Earth hope to populate a healthy new world on which they can thrive. When a malfunction sends the crew and colonists far from their intended landing spot, New Pacifica, Devon and her comrades find intelligent natives, previously unknown. Novelizes the teleplay.

**Other books you might like:**
Roger MacBride Allen, *The Ring of Charon*, 1990
Stephen Baxter, *Raft*, 1991
Helen Collins, *Mutagenesis*, 1993
J.M. Dillard, *Emissary*, 1993
Alan Dean Foster, *Alien Nation*, 1988
David Gerrold, *Encounter at Farpoint*, 1987
Harry Harrison, *The Deathworld Trilogy*, 1976
Megan Lindholm, *Alien Nation*, 1988
Anne McCaffrey, *Dragonsdawn*, 1988

## 1248

### BETTY ANNE CRAWFORD

## The Bushido Incident

(New York: DAW, 1992)

**Story type:** Science Fiction (Mystery; Political)
**Major character(s):** So Pak, Spaceship Captain; Matsuda, Businessman; Ewha Thompson, Doctor (ship's)

**Time period(s):** 2090s (2096)
**Locale(s):** Earth; Zeta Reticuli 2, Planet—Imaginary

**Summary:** Sent on a probe to discover what happened to the Korean and Japanese miners who died mysteriously on Zeta Reticuli years earlier, So Pak hears from the Japanese businessman who controls Iwaski Corporation, the most powerful on the planet, that So Pak will never return. On Zeta Reticuli, So Pak and Ewha Thompson learn that the Japanese stole the patent for ultrasound mining which made Iwaski Corporation rich and that its illegal testing of viruses inadvertently created the virus now killing off the first aliens contacted by humanity.

**Other books you might like:**
Poul Anderson, *Question and Answer*, 1978
Gregory Benford, *The Stars in Shroud*, 1978
Ben Bova, *As on a Darkling Plain*, 1972
John Brunner, *Total Eclipse*, 1974
A. Bertram Chandler, *Frontier of the Dark*, 1984
Gordon R. Dickson, *The Far Call*, 1978
Colin Kapp, *The Survival Game*, 1976
Kim Stanley Robinson, *Icehenge*, 1984
Brian Stableford, *Critical Threshold*, 1977
Brian Stableford, *The Gates of Eden*, 1983

---

`1249`

**DAN CRAWFORD**

## Rouse a Sleeping Cat

(New York: Ace, 1993)

**Story type:** Fantasy (Mystery; Political)
**Series:** Nimnestl the Bodyguard
**Major character(s):** Nimnestl, Bodyguard (royal); Conan III, Royalty, Child
**Time period(s):** Indeterminate
**Locale(s):** Rossacotta, Fictional Country

**Summary:** Nimnestl must protect nine-year old King Conan III against court intrigue and problems in Rossacotta including a cult of demon worshippers and deadly treason. First of a series. First novel.

**Other books you might like:**
Steven Brust, *The Gypsy*, 1992
    Megan Lindholm, co-author
Lois McMaster Bujold, *The Spirit Ring*, 1992
Charles de Lint, *Mulengro: A Romany Tale*, 1985
Susan Fletcher, *Flight of the Dragon Kyn*, 1993
Simon R. Green, *The Bones of Haven*, 1992
Paula Volsky, *Illusion*, 1992

---

`1250`

**DAN CRAWFORD**

## The Sure Death of a Mouse

(New York: Ace, 1994)

**Story type:** Fantasy (Mystery)
**Series:** Nimnestl the Bodyguard
**Major character(s):** Nimnestl, Bodyguard (royal); Polijn, Servant, Minstrel; Kaftus, Sorcerer
**Time period(s):** Indeterminate
**Locale(s):** Rossacotta, Fictional Country

**Summary:** Nimnestl investigates a series of murders at the palace and finds a plethora of suspects among the courtiers. Sequel to *Rouse a Sleeping Cat*.

**Other books you might like:**
Glen Cook, *Red Iron Nights*, 1991
Mary Gentle, *The Architecture of Desire*, 1993
Simon R. Green, *Hawk & Fisher*, 1990
Gary Gygax, *The Anubis Murders*, 1992
Joel Rosenberg, *Hour of the Octopus*, 1994

---

`1251`

**DAN CRAWFORD**

## A Wild Dog and Lone

(New York: Ace, 1995)

**Story type:** Fantasy (Mystery; Political)
**Series:** Nimnestl the Bodyguard
**Major character(s):** Conan III, Ruler (king); Polijn, Child, Apprentice, Minstrel; Nimnestl, Bodyguard (royal)
**Time period(s):** Indeterminate
**Locale(s):** Rossacotta, Fictional Country

**Summary:** Sweltering in an early summer, the court of Conan III plans the development of a university while readying to move north. Although everyone wants to join the king's retinue, not everyone receives the invitation. While the military resents this usurping of their function as educators, the early, very hot summer may account for the high murder rate. However, intrigue abounds. Third in the series.

**Other books you might like:**
Allan Cole, *The Far Kingdoms*, 1993
    Chris Bunch, co-author
Mary Gentle, *Rats and Gargoyles*, 1991
Simon R. Green, *Hawk & Fisher*, 1990
P.C. Hodgell, *God Stalk*, 1982
Paula Volsky, *Illusion*, 1992

---

`1252`

**F. MARION CRAWFORD**

## For the Blood Is the Life and Other Stories

(Clarkston, Georgia: White Wolf, 1996)

**Story type:** Horror (Collection)

**Summary:** These eight stories, all but one of which were collected in *Wandering Ghosts* in 1911, represent the bulk of supernatural fiction by a writer best known for popular, romantic novels produced at the turn of the century. ''The Upper Berth'' and ''Man Overboard'' are strongly atmospheric tales of hauntings onboard ships. ''The Dead Smile'' is a tale of Gothic family intrigue and ''The Screaming Skull'' a tale of revenge from beyond the grave. The title story is a classic of vampire fiction, and ''By the Waters of Paradise'' a tale of romance curtailed by the whims of destiny. ''The King's Messenger'' treats death allegorically.

**Other books you might like:**
Robert W. Chambers, *The King in Yellow*, 1895
Robert Hichens, *Tongues of Conscience*, 1900
Oliver Onions, *The Collected Ghost Stories of Oliver Onions*, 1935
Hugh Walpole, *All Souls' Night*, 1933
Edward Lucas White, *Lukundoo and Other Stories*, 1927

## 1253
### ROBERTA CRAY

### *The Sword and the Lion*
(New York: DAW, 1993)

**Story type:** Fantasy (Religious; Political)
**Major character(s):** Breyd, Religious (initiate), Warrior (Dyaddi)
**Time period(s):** Indeterminate Past
**Locale(s):** Ghezrat, Fictional City (walled fortress)

**Summary:** Prophecy indicates Breyd must join with her father as Dyaddi, one of the warrior pairs able to utilize divine strength in defense of the city gates when invaders breach all barriers. Breyd's new career brings expected glorious battles and unanticipated complications in her personal life.

**Other books you might like:**
Marion Zimmer Bradley, *The Firebrand*, 1987
Laurell K. Hamilton, *Nightseer*, 1992
P.C. Hodgell, *God Stalk*, 1982
Elizabeth Moon, *Sheepfarmer's Daughter*, 1988
Sean Russell, *Gatherer of Clouds*, 1992
Elizabeth Ann Scarborough, *Last Refuge*, 1992
Martha Wells, *The Element of Fire*, 1993

## 1254
### MICHELLE SHIREY CREAN

### *Dancer of the Sixth*
(New York: Ballantine Del Rey, 1993)

**Story type:** Science Fiction (Political; Military)
**Major character(s):** Auglaise "Dancer" DeWellesthar, Spaceship Captain, Military Personnel; Makellen Darke, Genetically Altered Being (Auryx), Psychic (esper); Harla Davenger/Daven, Military Personnel, Imposter
**Time period(s):** Indeterminate Future
**Locale(s):** O'Brian's Stake, Planet—Imaginary; Lioth, Planet—Imaginary

**Summary:** Captured by the Karranganthian, Auglaise and her Fourth Service Dancer Flight provide amusement with their slow deaths by torture. Rescued by the legendary Sixth Service, Dancer recovers with the help of her new commander, Michael, despite the death of her constant companion, Makellen Darke, who Sixth Service Security claims never existed. Twelve years later a Fourth Service Show Team plane crashes with a drugged pilot and Dancer's double, perhaps foiling an impending war. Author's first novel.

**Other books you might like:**
Lois McMaster Bujold, *Shards of Honor*, 1986
F.M. Busby, *Rissa Kerguelen*, 1977
Orson Scott Card, *Ender's Game*, 1985
Allan Cole, *Sten*, 1984
    Chris Bunch, co-author
Frank Herbert, *Dune*, 1965
Charles Sheffield, *Cold as Ice*, 1992
Eric Vinicoff, *The Weigher*, 1992
    Marcia Martin, co-author
David Weber, *On Basilisk Station*, 1993

## 1255
### MICHAEL CRICHTON

### *Jurassic Park*
(New York: Alfred A. Knopf, 1990)

**Story type:** Science Fiction (Genetic Manipulation; Adventure)
**Major character(s):** John Hammond, Businessman; Alan Grant, Scientist (paleontologist), Professor; Ellie Sattler, Scientist (paleobotanist)
**Time period(s):** 1980s (1989)
**Locale(s):** Isla Nublar, Costa Rica

**Summary:** Planning to make a fortune in patent life forms by cloning dinosaurs from bits of prehistoric DNA, International Genetic Technologies, Inc. constructs a highly automated theme park and resort featuring cloned dinosaurs as centerpieces for the enterprise. Just before the park is scheduled to open, Biosyn Corp., a competitor, arranges to sabotage park barriers and alarms in order to steal dinosaur embryos. While John Hammond, Alan Grant and Ellie Sattler visit the nearly completed park, a computer failure allows dinosaurs to run amok. As the human food source diminishes, the dinosaurs appear to desire migration, threatening to begin a new Age of Dinosaurs. Alan, Ellie and the few survivors must find a way to stop the release.

**Other books you might like:**
David Brin, *Startide Rising*, 1983
Octavia E. Butler, *Adulthood Rites*, 1988
Octavia E. Butler, *Dawn*, 1987
Octavia E. Butler, *Imago*, 1989
Larry Niven, *The Flight of the Horse*, 1973
Dave Wolverton, *Serpent Catch*, 1991

## 1256
### MICHAEL CRICHTON

### *The Lost World*
(New York: Knopf, 1995)

**Story type:** Science Fiction (Genetic Manipulation; Adventure)
**Major character(s):** Ian Malcolm, Scientist (mathematician); Sarah Harding, Scientist (field biologist); Richard Levine, Scientist (paleobiologist)
**Time period(s):** 1990s
**Locale(s):** Costa Rica

**Summary:** Years after the destruction of the ill-fated Jurassic Park and its reconstructed dinosaur species, scientists locate and investigate a new population of dinosaurs growing from Jurassic Park survivors.

**Other books you might like:**
Robert T. Bakker, *Raptor Red*, 1995
James F. David, *Footprints of Thunder*, 1995
Sir Arthur Conan Doyle, *The Lost World*, 1912
James Gurney, *Dinotopia*, 1992
Harry Adam Knight, *Carnosaur*, 1984

## 1257

**CATHY CRIMMINS**
**TOM MAEDER**, Co-Author

### Revenge of the Christmas Box

(Los Angeles: Dove Books, 1996)

**Story type:** Fantasy (Satire; Collection)

**Summary:** This collection contains a two-page introduction, three pages of spurious sequels and television tie-ins, and 20 stories exploring humorous and frequently fantastic aspects of Christmas boxes, including an FAA inspection of Santa's sled's black box recorder, organized elves, a cryogenic baby, and several boxes with nasty surprises.

**Other books you might like:**
William J. Brooke, *Teller of Tales*, 1994
David Fisher, *Legally Correct Fairy Tales*, 1996
James Finn Garner, *Politically Correct Bedtime Stories*, 1994
James Finn Garner, *Politically Correct Holiday Stories*, 1995
Kristine Kathryn Rusch, *Pulphouse, Issue 10: Special Issue*, 1991
     editor

## 1258

**A.C. CRISPIN**

### Alien Resurrection

(New York: Warner Aspect, 1997)

**Story type:** Science Fiction (Space Opera; Horror)
**Series:** Alien
**Major character(s):** Vincent Distephano, Military Personnel; Mason Wren, Doctor, Scientist; Ripley, Clone, Hero
**Time period(s):** Indeterminate Future
**Locale(s):** Auriga, Space Station (orbiting Pluto); *Betty*, Spaceship

**Summary:** Finally successful in obtaining a life alien fetus from the cloned human host, Dr. Wren permits the surgeons to save the host, despite her attack on one of his doctors. Ripley informs them that they took a queen and all will die, while Dr. Wren feeds alien embryos on newly reviving cryonically stored humans. Novelizes the 1997 film.

**Other books you might like:**
Greg Bear, *The Forge of God*, 1987
David Brin, *Earth*, 1990
Elizabeth Hand, *12 Monkeys*, 1995
Jack McDevitt, *The Engines of God*, 1994
Larry Niven, *Footfall*, 1985
     Jerry Pournelle, co-author
Charles Pellegrino, *The Killing Star*, 1995
     George Zebrowski, co-author

## 1259

**A.C. CRISPIN**
**T. JACKSON KING**, Co-Author

### Ancestor's World

(New York: Ace, 1996)

**Story type:** Science Fiction (First Contact; Political)
**Series:** StarBridge
**Major character(s):** Mahree Burroughs, Diplomat (ambassador); Gordon Mitchell, Anthropologist; Krillen, Alien (Na-Dina), Detective

**Time period(s):** Indeterminate Future
**Locale(s):** Na-Dina, Planet—Imaginary

**Summary:** Replacing the brutally murdered Interrelator to Na-Dina, Mahree brings a large crew to help evacuate the soon to be flooded Valley of Life. Contacted by corporations from the Shadowed Sector, Na-Dina feels compelled to develop a modern military and industrial infrastructure in order to compete in galactic society. Unfortunately the project will destroy the archaeological history of the Na-Dina and cause disastrous social upheaval.

**Other books you might like:**
David Brin, *Brightness Reef*, 1995
C.J. Cherryh, *Foreigner*, 1994
T. Jackson King, *Retread Shop*, 1988
Anne McCaffrey, *Treaty at Doona*, 1994
     Jody Lynn Nye, co-author
Jack McDevitt, *The Engines of God*, 1994
Larry Niven, *Protector*, 1973

## 1260

**A.C. CRISPIN**

### Sarek

(New York: Pocket, 1994)

**Story type:** Science Fiction (Space Opera; Political)
**Series:** Star Trek
**Major character(s):** Peter James Kirk, Student; Sarek, Diplomat, Alien (Vulcan); Spock, Scientist, Alien (Vulcan)
**Time period(s):** 23rd century
**Locale(s):** *U.S.S. Enterprise*, Spaceship; Vulcan, Planet—Imaginary; United Federation of Planets, Interstellar Empire/Federation

**Summary:** Leaving his wife's deathbed to carry out what he sees as his duty, Sarek risks destroying the newly-won rapport with his son, Spock. Yet after Amanda's death, Sarek and Spock must work together to rescue James Kirk's nephew from Klingon kidnappers and foil a plot that would destroy the Federation.

**Other books you might like:**
Margaret Wander Bonanno, *Dwellers in the Crucible*, 1985
Diane Duane, *Spock's World*, 1989
Brad Ferguson, *A Flag Full of Stars*, 1991
Jean Lorrah, *The Vulcan Academy Murders*, 1984
Jeri Taylor, *Unification*, 1991

## 1261

**A.C. CRISPIN**
**DEBORAH A. MARSHALL**, Co-Author

### Serpent's Gift

(New York: Ace, 1992)

**Story type:** Science Fiction (Adventure; Young Adult)
**Series:** StarBridge
**Major character(s):** Robert Gable, Psychologist, Administrator; Serge LaRoche, Student, Musician; Heather Farley, Student, Telepath
**Time period(s):** Indeterminate Future
**Locale(s):** StarBridge Academy, Asteroid; Starbridge Station, Space Station

**Summary:** Heather Farley, an eleven-year-old computer whiz accepted at StarBridge Academy despite her age because of powerful telepathic abilities, becomes infatuated with Serge, an older student still traumatized by the accidental loss of his hands despite fully functional prosthetics. When the asteroid's rich neutronium deposit suddenly becomes unstable, monitors blame the anthropologists working at a local dig and recommend evacuation, which could lead to the dissolution of StarBridge.

**Other books you might like:**
David Brin, *The Uplift War*, 1987
Lois McMaster Bujold, *The Warrior's Apprentice*, 1986
T. Jackson King, *Retread Shop*, 1988
Larry Niven, *Protector*, 1973
Rebecca Ore, *Being Alien*, 1989
David R. Palmer, *Emergence*, 1984
Tim Sullivan, *Lords of Creation*, 1992
Sheri S. Tepper, *After Long Silence*, 1990

## 1262

### A.C. CRISPIN
### JANNEAN ELLIOTT, Co-Author

## Shadow World

(New York: Ace, 1991)

**Story type:** Science Fiction (First Contact; Young Adult)
**Series:** StarBridge
**Major character(s):** Mark Kenner, Student (interrelater), Diplomat; Ri-El Eerin, Alien (Elpind); Cara Hendricks, Journalist, Teenager
**Time period(s):** Indeterminate Future
**Locale(s):** Starbridge Academy, Asteroid (school); Elseemar, Planet—Imaginary

**Summary:** After a Cooperative League of Systems ship made an emergency landing on Elseemar, discovering the Elspind, an exceedingly short-lived and intelligent people, a lab was set up to try extending the life-span of the Elspind. When Mark Kenner is paired with Eerin on a student project, he is compelled to exercise his skills as an interrelater to save his life and the lives of his companions.

**Other books you might like:**
Stephen Baxter, *Raft*, 1991
David Brin, *Startide Rising*, 1983
Stephen Goldin, *Jade Darcy and the Affair of Honor*, 1988
    Mary Mason, co-author
T. Jackson King, *Retread Shop*, 1988
Rebecca Ore, *Being Alien*, 1989
David R. Palmer, *Emergence*, 1984
Alis A. Rasmussen, *A Passage of Stars*, 1990
Pamela F. Service, *Under Alien Stars*, 1990

## 1263

### A.C. CRISPIN
### KATHLEEN O'MALLEY, Co-Author

## Silent Dances

(New York: Ace, 1990)

**Story type:** Science Fiction (First Contact)
**Series:** StarBridge
**Major character(s):** Tesa "Good Eyes", Handicapped (deaf), Linguist; Taller, Leader, Alien (Grus); Sailor "Lightning", Alien (Grus)
**Time period(s):** Indeterminate Future
**Locale(s):** Trinity, Planet—Imaginary (StarBridge Academy)

**Summary:** Tesa, deaf since birth, is the perfect ambassador to the alien Grus, an avian race that resembles giant cranes, whose cries can shatter human eardrums. As "interrelator," her assignment is to cement the human-avian bond by helping rear a newly-hatched chick. But the Grus have powerful enemies on their world—not only

the eagle-like Aquila, but human predators who kill them for their iridescent feathers. Tesa finds she must establish contact with two intelligent species while foiling the poachers.

**Other books you might like:**
Suzette Haden Elgin, *Communipath Worlds*, 1980
Ursula K. Le Guin, *The Word for World Is Forest*, 1972
Anne McCaffrey, *Decision at Doona*, 1969
H. Beam Piper, *Little Fuzzy*, 1962
H. Beam Piper, *The Other Human Race*, 1964

## 1264

### A.C. CRISPIN
### KATHLEEN O'MALLEY, Co-Author

## Silent Songs

(New York: Ace, 1994)

**Story type:** Science Fiction (First Contact)
**Series:** StarBridge
**Major character(s):** Ptesa "Tesa/Good Eyes" Wakandagi, Diplomat (interrelator), Indian; Atle, Military Personnel (First-in-Conquest), Spaceship Captain; Taller, Leader, Alien (Avian)
**Time period(s):** Indeterminate Future
**Locale(s):** Crane, Space Station; Trinity, Planet—Imaginary; Cooperative League of Systems, Interstellar Empire/Federation

**Summary:** When the amphibian aliens attempt to conquer Trinity, Tesa leads the native Gnus and the rest of the team, without any advanced weapons, in defense of the planet. Meanwhile, another intelligent telepathic species makes itself known on Trinity.

**Other books you might like:**
Eleanor Arnason, *Ring of Swords*, 1993
David Brin, *Startide Rising*, 1983
Anne McCaffrey, *Treaty at Doona*, 1994
    Jody Lynn Nye, co-author
Larry Niven, *Protector*, 1973
Vernor Vinge, *A Fire upon the Deep*, 1992

## 1265

### A.C. CRISPIN

## Starbridge

(New York: Ace, 1989)

**Story type:** Science Fiction (First Contact)
**Series:** StarBridge
**Major character(s):** Mahree Burroughs, Teenager; Robert Gable, Psychologist, Administrator
**Time period(s):** Indeterminate Future
**Locale(s):** *Desiree*, Spaceship

**Summary:** Earth's first contact with an alien race nearly turns to disaster, but teenager Mahree Burroughs and ship's doctor Robert Gable make friends with the alien Dhurrrkk, and the two races begin to find common ground.

**Other books you might like:**
C.J. Cherryh, *Rimrunners*, 1989
Robert A. Heinlein, *Podkayne of Mars*, 1963
Patricia A. McKillip, *Fool's Run*, 1988
Andre Norton, *Ordeal in Otherwhere*, 1964

## **1266**

### A.C. CRISPIN
### RU EMERSON, Co-Author

## *Voices of Chaos*

(New York: Ace, 1998)

**Story type:** Science Fiction (First Contact; Political)
**Series:** StarBridge
**Major character(s):** Khyriz, Royalty (prince), Alien (Arekkhi); Magdalena Perez, Linguist (student), Abuse Victim; Robert Gable, Administrator (StarBridge Academy), Psychologist
**Time period(s):** Indeterminate Future
**Locale(s):** NewAm, Planet—Imaginary; Arekkhi, Planet—Imaginary; Outer Space (StarBridge Academy)

**Summary:** Continuing to have nightmares about her life before entering StarBridge, third year student Magdalena practices dance as a communications skill. The Arekkhi, a newly contacted species, have sent Khyriz to StarBridge in order to steal as much technology as possible while keeping quiet the secrets which could bar the planet from membership in the Cooperative League of Systems. Despite trepidation, having her first assignment on Arekkhi thrills Magdalena.

**Other books you might like:**
L. Warren Douglas, *Stepwater*, 1995
Carolyn Ives Gilman, *Halfway Human*, 1998
Severna Park, *Hand of Prophecy*, 1998
Sheri S. Tepper, *Six Moon Dance*, 1998
James White, *Mind Changer*, 1998

## **1267**

### KYLE CROCCO

## *Heroes Wanted*

(New York: Ace, 1991)

**Story type:** Fantasy (Adventure; Light Fantasy)
**Series:** Heroes, Inc.
**Major character(s):** Cilla, Heroine, Companion; Grover, Hero, Mercenary; Beogoat, Wizard
**Time period(s):** Indeterminate
**Locale(s):** Hoven Westerhoven, Fictional Country

**Summary:** Grover and Cilla are hired to impersonate King Phillip and his servant Voss until after Phillip's marriage to Winona unites all Westerhoven. However, the wizard neglected to tell the two a few things, such as the fact that Winona hates Phillip. Therefore Cilla has to prevent her from poisoning Grover. Winona's death at the wedding causes a war in which Cilla kills Hans, Phillip's major enemy, and Grover shatters the sacred stone.

**Other books you might like:**
Piers Anthony, *A Spell for Chameleon*, 1977
Robert Asprin, *Phule's Company*, 1990
Jack L. Chalker, *The River of Dancing Gods*, 1984
Diane Duane, *So You Want to Be a Wizard?*, 1983
Alan Dean Foster, *Glory Lane*, 1990

## **1268**

### KYLE CROCCO

## *Heroes, Inc.*

(New York: Ace, 1991)

**Story type:** Fantasy (Light Fantasy; Adventure)
**Series:** Heroes, Inc.
**Major character(s):** Grover, Hero (reluctant), Mercenary; Cilla, Companion, Heroine
**Time period(s):** Indeterminate Future
**Locale(s):** Parda, Fictional City; Jolinstive, Fictional City

**Summary:** In order to secure his inheritance, Grover must immediately produce an heir, a task made difficult by his sudden impotence. To solve this problem, Grover must obtain the vital ingredient, dragon gonads. Everyone's desire to make Grover a hero and sign him to a contract with Heroes, Inc. makes Grover's quest especially hard. First novel.

**Other books you might like:**
Neil Gaiman, *Good Omens: The Nice and Accurate Prophecies of Agnes Nutter, Witch*, 1990
  Terry Pratchett, co-author
Craig Shaw Gardner, *Revenge of the Fluffy Bunnies*, 1990
Thorarinn Gunnarsson, *Make Way for Dragons!*, 1990
Barry Hughart, *Bridge of Birds*, 1984
Dan McGirt, *Jason Cosmo*, 1989
Christopher Stasheff, *The Warlock in Spite of Himself*, 1969

## **1269**

### ANNE ELIOT CROMPTON

## *Gawain and Lady Green*

(New York: Donald I. Fine, 1997)

**Story type:** Fantasy (Legend)
**Major character(s):** Gawain, Knight; Lady Green, Sorceress; Lord Bright, Nobleman, Knight
**Time period(s):** Indeterminate
**Locale(s):** England

**Summary:** Traveling on Arthur's command, Sir Gawain becomes trapped in a small village destined for sacrifice. He escapes with the aid of Lady Green, who loves him, but betrays her soon after. When the Green Knight comes to Arthur's court with a wager, Gawain must pay for his actions, even if it costs him his honor, pride, or life. Sequel to *Merlin's Harp*.

**Other books you might like:**
Marion Zimmer Bradley, *The Mists of Avalon*, 1983
Vera Chapman, *The Green Knight*, 1978
Phyllis Ann Karr, *The Idylls of the Queen*, 1982
Ian McDowell, *Mordred's Curse*, 1996
J.R.R. Tolkien, *Sir Gawain and the Green Knight, Pearl, and Sir Orfeo*, 1975

## **1270**

### ANNE ELIOT CROMPTON

## *Merlin's Harp*

(New York: Donald I. Fine, 1995)

**Story type:** Fantasy (Legend; Young Adult)
**Major character(s):** Niviene, Mythical Creature (fey), Apprentice (Merlin's); Merlin, Magician
**Time period(s):** Indeterminate

**Locale(s):** Camelot, England; World of the Fey, Mythical Place

**Summary:** To save Arthur's kingdom, Merlin requires help from Niviene, daughter of the Lady of the Lake.

**Other books you might like:**
Mike Ashley, *The Merlin Chronicles*, 1995
    editor
Marion Zimmer Bradley, *The Forest House*, 1994
Marion Zimmer Bradley, *The Mists of Avalon*, 1983
Andrea Hopkins, *Chronicles of King Arthur*, 1994
    editor
Mary Stewart, *The Crystal Cave*, 1970

**1271**

**CLAIRE CROSS**

## The Last Highlander
(New York: Jove, 1998)

**Story type:** Fantasy (Time Travel; Romance)
**Major character(s):** Alasdair MacAuley, Nobleman; Morgan LaFayette, Tourist
**Time period(s):** 14th century (1314); 1990s (1998)
**Locale(s):** Scotland

**Summary:** A witch tells Alasdair MacAuley, a nobleman, that he must confront the legendary Morgaine le Fee. Magically transported to the future, he encounters her in a new manifestation, but she is unaware of her own identity.

**Other books you might like:**
Janice Bennett, *Forever in Time*, 1990
Joyce Carlow, *Timeswept*, 1994
Cherlyn Jac, *Shadows in Time*, 1994
Kathleen Kirkwood, *A Slip in Time*, 1998
Ann Meredith, *Love Across Time*, 1995

**1272**

**GILBERT B. CROSS**

## A Witch Across Time
(New York: Atheneum, 1990)

**Story type:** Fantasy (Time Travel; Young Adult)
**Major character(s):** Hannah Kincaid, Teenager; Greg Donohue, Boyfriend; Patience, Spirit (ghost)
**Time period(s):** 1980s
**Locale(s):** Martha's Vineyard, Massachusetts

**Summary:** After being discharged from a period of institutionalization for emotional imbalance, 15-year-old Hannah spends the summer with her great-aunt at Martha's Vineyard. Along with a handsome new boy, Greg, Hannah encounters the ghost of a young woman, who was falsely executed as a witch in 1692 and seeks to clear her name.

**Other books you might like:**
Pam Conrad, *Stonewords: A Ghost Story*, 1990
Penelope Lively, *The Ghost of Thomas Kempe*, 1973
Patricia A. McKillip, *The House on Parchment Street*, 1973
Pat Murphy, *The Falling Woman*, 1986
Christopher Pike, *See You Later*, 1990
Elizabeth Marie Pope, *The Sherwood Ring*, 1958

**1273**

**RONALD ANTHONY CROSS**

## The Fourth Guardian
(New York: Tor, 1994)

**Story type:** Science Fiction (Alternate Universe; Mystical)
**Series:** Eternal Guardians
**Major character(s):** Elena, Apprentice, Sorcerer; Corbo O'Connor, Gladiator, Sorcerer; Drusilla, Sorceress
**Time period(s):** 1990s; Indeterminate Past
**Locale(s):** Mexico; California; Astral Plane, Mythical Place

**Summary:** Using the Four Stones of Power, ancient Romans surreptitiously control human events for millennia. In the present, Corbo and Elena battle the emergence of a demon and the attempts of one Eternal Guardian to consolidate the Stones' power.

**Other books you might like:**
Umberto Eco, *Foucault's Pendulum*, 1989
Simon Hawke, *The Wizard of 4th Street*, 1987
Tom Holt, *Who's Afraid of Beowulf?*, 1989
Robert Shea, *The Illuminatus! Trilogy*, 1988
    Robert Anton Wilson, co-editor
Robert Anton Wilson, *The Earth Will Shake*, 1982

**1274**

**RONALD ANTHONY CROSS**

## The Lost Guardian
(New York: Tor, 1995)

**Story type:** Science Fiction (Alternate Universe; Mystical)
**Series:** Eternal Guardians
**Major character(s):** Corbo O'Connor, Gladiator, Sorcerer; Gumby, Psychic; Elena, Sorcerer
**Time period(s):** Indeterminate Past; 1990s
**Locale(s):** Europe; Zaire

**Summary:** Corbo and others continue to vie for control of four stones, powerful magical objects that can prevent alien interference in human affairs.

**Other books you might like:**
Umberto Eco, *Foucault's Pendulum*, 1989
Michael Flynn, *In the Country of the Blind*, 1990
Robert Shea, *The Illuminatus! Trilogy*, 1988
    Robert Anton Wilson, co-author
Edward Whittemore, *Jerusalem Poker*, 1978
Robert Anton Wilson, *The Schrodinger's Cat Trilogy*, 1988

**1275**

**RONALD ANTHONY CROSS**

## The White Guardian
(New York: Tor, 1999)

**Story type:** Science Fiction (Alternate History; Mystical)
**Series:** Eternal Guardians
**Major character(s):** Corbo O'Connor, Gladiator, Sorcerer; Raphael, Sorcerer
**Time period(s):** Indeterminate Past
**Locale(s):** England

**Summary:** Two members of the Guardians, Corbo and Raphael, solve different problems in past eras. In one case, Nazi agents are undermining England centuries before World War II. In the other, a coven of witches gains mystical power over the process of time itself.

**Other books you might like:**
Katherine Kurtz, *Lammas Night*, 1983
Fritz Leiber, *The Change War*, 1983
H. Beam Piper, *Lord Kalvan of Otherwhen*, 1965
Edward Whittemore, *Jerusalem Poker*, 1978
Robert Anton Wilson, *The Earth Will Shake*, 1982

---

`1276`

**JOHN CROWLEY**

## Antiquities

(Seattle, Washington: Incunabula, 1993)

**Story type:** Fantasy (Collection; Science Fiction)
**Time period(s):** 19th century; 21st century
**Locale(s):** Greece; United States; Planet—Imaginary

**Summary:** Contains seven stories, originally published 1977-1993, displaying a broad range of setting and tone. The stories, both fantasy and science fiction, deal with the past, memories and how people deal with them. In one, "Missolonghi 1824," Lord Byron, on his death-bed, relates a strange story that highlights his adventurous and tragic life.

**Other books you might like:**
A.S. Byatt, *Possession: A Romance*, 1990
Greer Ilene Gilman, *Moonwise*, 1990
Mark Helprin, *Winter's Tale*, 1983
Tim Powers, *The Stress of Her Regard*, 1989
John Whitbourn, *Popes and Phantoms*, 1993

---

`1277`

**JOHN CROWLEY**

## Love & Sleep

(New York: Bantam, 1994)

**Story type:** Fantasy (Literary; Contemporary Realism)
**Series:** AEgypt
**Major character(s):** Pierce Moffett, Researcher; Giordano Bruno, Religious (monk), Historical Figure; Madimi, Angel
**Time period(s):** 1990s; 16th century (1583)
**Locale(s):** New York; Cumberland Mountains, Kentucky; London, England

**Summary:** Pierce Moffett researches the strange novels of Fellowes Kraft and tracks the possibility of Kraft's mysterious treasure. The secrets pile up around Moffett as his long-forgotten childhood meshes with the lives of Bruno and Dee. Sequel to *AEgypt*.

**Other books you might like:**
A.S. Byatt, *Possession: A Romance*, 1990
Robertson Davies, *What's Bred in the Bone*, 1985
Umberto Eco, *Foucault's Pendulum*, 1990
Tim Powers, *Last Call*, 1992
Brian Stableford, *The Werewolves of London*, 1992

---

`1278`

**JOHN CROWLEY**

## Novelty

(New York: Doubleday Foundation, 1989)

**Story type:** Science Fiction (Collection)

**Summary:** This collection of four of Crowley's stories includes the original novella "Great Work of Time," a 1989 Nebula Award nominee, as well as "In Blue," "The Nightingale Sings at Night," and "Novelty."

**Other books you might like:**
Jonathan Carroll, *Bones of the Moon*, 1987
Jonathan Carroll, *A Child Across the Sky*, 1989
Jonathan Carroll, *Sleeping in Flame*, 1988
Richard Grant, *Rumors of Spring*, 1987
Richard Grant, *Views from the Oldest House*, 1989
Ian McDonald, *Empire Dreams*, 1988
Ian McDonald, *Out on Blue Six*, 1989

---

`1279`

**PETER CROWTHER**, Editor

## Blue Motel

(Clarkston, Georgia: White Wolf, 1996)

**Story type:** Horror (Anthology)
**Series:** Narrow Houses

**Summary:** The third and final volume in the Narrow Houses series of stories based on superstitions contains eighteen stories and poems written exclusively for the volume. Included are Ed Gorman's "Curses," a revenge tale involving the evil eye; Jonathan Aycliffe's "The Reiver's Lament," about a superstition surrounding a murder committed at an old country inn; Conrad Williams's "The Burn," in which a man's disordered mind begins to manifest itself in physical phenomena; and Carl West and Katherine MacLean's "Isaac My Son," a reworking of the biblical tale of Jacob and Isaac for Native American folklore, concerning a father's sacrifice of, and for, his son. Dennis Etchison provides an introduction. This volume was first published in England in 1994.

**Other books you might like:**
Jeff Gelb, *Fear Itself*, 1996
    editor
Gary L. Raisor, *Obsessions*, 1991
    editor
Wendy Webb, *More Phobias*, 1995
    Ric Gilliam, Ed Kramer, and Martin H. Greenberg, co-editors
Wendy Webb, *Phobias: Stories of Your Deepest Fears*, 1994
    Ric Gilliam, Ed Kramer, and Martin H. Greenberg, co-editors

---

`1280`

**PETER CROWTHER**
**EDWARD E. KRAMER**, Co-Author

## Dante's Disciples

(Clarkston, Georgia: White Wolf, 1996)

**Story type:** Horror (Anthology)

**Summary:** Inspired by Dante's *Inferno*, the editors asked 26 writers to write stories featuring modern visions of hell. The results include Douglas Clegg's "The Ripening Sweetness of Late Afternoon," about a homicidal preacher who lives in a personal hell; Harlan Ellison's "Chatting with Anubis," in which archaeologists discover the jackal god Anubis presiding over the tomb of a famous god-killer; Nancy Holder's "Hell Is for Children," in which a young girl creates a computer virus that creates virtual reality hells for systems infected with it; Rick Hautala's "Tunnels," in which a graffiti artist discovers a netherworld of horror in the subway tunnels; and Brian Lumley's "Hell Is a Personal Place," in which Adolf Hitler discovers that the afterlife is a Fourth Reich that has no use for him.

**Other books you might like:**

Basil Davenport, *Deals with the Devil: An Anthology*, 1959
  editor
Marvin Kaye, *Devils and Demons*, 1987
  editor
Janet Morris, *Heroes in Hell*, 1986
  editor
Maximilian Rudwin, *Devil Stories*, 1921

## 1281

**PETER CROWTHER**, Editor

### Destination Unknown

(Clarkston, Georgia: White Wolf, 1997)

**Story type:** Horror (Anthology)

**Summary:** Sixteen tales of horror, fantasy and science fiction, loosely linked by the theme of personal encounters with the unknown. Horror selections include Ramsey Campbell's ''Between the Floors,'' in which a movie theater manager meets a grotesque doppelganger while away at a business convention; Christopher Fowler's ''Wage Slaves,'' about the ultimate corporate environment that shapes workers to conform to its specifications; Bentley Little's ''Monteith,'' in which a man discovers the disturbing, inexplicable private life his wife leads while he is away at work; and Lisa Tuttle's ''The Extra Hour,'' about a writer who becomes increasingly unable to separate from the fantasy world she creates in her fiction. Anne McCaffrey supplies the introduction.

**Other books you might like:**

George Hatch, *Souls in Pawn*, 1994
  editor
George Hatch, *Sinistre: An Anthology of Rituals*, 1993
  editor
Jessica Horsting, *Midnight Graffiti*, 1992
  James Van Hise, co-editor
Edward E. Kramer, *Dante's Disciples*, 1996
  Peter Crowther, co-editor
Edward E. Kramer, *Tombs*, 1995
  Peter Crowther, co-editor
John Pelan, *Darkside: Horror for the Next Millennium*, 1995
  editor
Carol Serling, *Return to the Twilight Zone*, 1994
  editor
Carol Serling, *Journeys to the Twilight Zone*, 1993
  editor

## 1282

**PETER CROWTHER**
**JAMES LOVEGROVE**, Co-Author

### Escardy Gap

(New York: Tor, 1996)

**Story type:** Horror (Carnival/Circus Horror)
**Major character(s):** Jeremiah Rackstraw, Entertainer; Joshua Knight, Child; Mayor Mayor, Political Figure (Mayor)
**Time period(s):** 1950s
**Locale(s):** Escardy Gap, Midwest

**Summary:** A nameless writer struggling to overcome a writer's block begins spontaneously transcribing the tale of Escardy Gap, a quaint middle-American town visited by a supernaturally endowed troupe of evildoers who call themselves the Company. As the Company begins wreaking havoc about town, the writer finds himself pondering his relationship to the characters he has created and his responsi-

bility for conjuring a moral for their travails. This is a first collaborative novel by a well-known editor and a fantasy writer.

**Other books you might like:**

Ray Bradbury, *Something Wicked This Way Comes*, 1962
Charles G. Finney, *The Circus of Dr. Lao*, 1935
Dean R. Koontz, *Twilight Eyes*, 1987
Thomas F. Monteleone, *The Magnificent Gallery*, 1987
Tom Reamy, *Blind Voices*, 1978

## 1283

**PETER CROWTHER**, Editor
**MARTIN H. GREENBERG**, Co-Editor

### Heaven Sent: 18 Glorious Tales of the Angels

(New York: DAW, 1995)

**Story type:** Fantasy (Anthology; Religious)

**Summary:** Contains a three-page introduction plus 18 original stories with ethereal themes. The tone varies from dark to humorous as angels' roles vary from Angel of Death to savior. Authors include Michael Bishop, John Brunner, Storm Constantine, Charles de Lint, Ed Gorman, Nina Kiriki Hoffman, Garry Kilworth, Jane M. Lindskold, Judith Moffett, and Kristine Kathryn Rusch.

**Other books you might like:**

Jack Dann, *Angels!*, 1995
  Gardner Dozois, co-editor
Neil Gaiman, *Good Omens: The Nice and Accurate Prophecies of Agnes Nutter, Witch*, 1990
  Terry Pratchett, co-author
Edward E. Kramer, *Tombs*, 1995
  Peter Crowther, co-editor
Alan Ryan, *Perpetual Light*, 1982
  editor
Pamela Sargent, *Afterlives: An Anthology of Stories about Life After Death*, 1986
  Ian Watson, co-editor

## 1284

**PETER CROWTHER**, Editor

### Narrow Houses

(New York: Warner, 1994)

**Story type:** Horror (Anthology)
**Series:** Narrow Houses

**Summary:** Originally published in England in 1992, this book collects 30 stories by diverse hands concerned with the superstitions that shape our behavior. Included are Nancy Collins' ''The Needle-Men,'' which traces several urban folk tales from Louisiana to a common source; Robert Holdstock's ''The Silvering,'' concerned with the legend of the selkie; Chet Williamson's ''The Swing of the Knife,'' about a businessman obsessed with the talismanic qualities of a knife; Peter James' ''Breaking the Chain,'' about the consequences of not sending a chain letter; Stephen Gallagher's ''The Sluice,'' about a young man's refusal to accept the finality of death; and Kim Newman's ''Three on a Match,'' which ponders a future that did not happen as a result of a World War I doughboy not lighting a third cigarette from the same matchstick. Douglas Winter supplies the book's introduction.

**Other books you might like:**

Charles L. Grant, *Fears*, 1983
  editor

Gary L. Raisor, *Obsessions*, 1991
  editor
Wendy Webb, *Phobias: Stories of Your Deepest Fears*, 1994
  Ric Gilliam, Ed Kramer, and Martin H. Greenberg, co-editors
Wendy Webb, *More Phobias*, 1995
  Ric Gilliam, Ed Kramer, and Martin H. Greenberg, co-editors

**1285**

**PETER CROWTHER**, Editor

## Touch Wood

(Clarkston, Georgia: White Wolf, 1996)

**Story type:** Horror (Anthology)
**Series:** Narrow Houses

**Summary:** First published in England in 1993, this volume in the Narrow Houses series features 25 original stories and poems based on old and new superstitions. Charles Grant's ''Holding Hands'' spins a startling suicide scenario from a superstition about passing on to the afterlife. Karl Edward Wagner's ''Little Lessons in Gardening'' is a revenge tale cultivated from the legend of the mandrake root. Michael Marshall Smith's ''The Owner'' is about a woman who finds herself being displaced from her own life. Bentley Little's ''The Woods Be Dark'' resurrects a folk legend of evil. Thomas Monteleone tackles superstitions regarding premature burial in ''The Wager.'' Stanley Wiater's ''Mysteries of the Word,'' a fantasy about the misfortune that befalls a child who utters a forbidden word, is illustrated by Gahan Wilson. Ramsey Campbell supplies the introduction.

**Other books you might like:**
Jeff Gelb, *Fear Itself*, 1996
  editor
Gary L. Raisor, *Obsessions*, 1991
  editor
Wendy Webb, *More Phobias*, 1995
  Ric Gilliam, Ed Kramer, and Martin H. Greenberg, co-editors
Wendy Webb, *Phobias: Stories of Your Deepest Fears*, 1994
  Ric Gilliam, Ed Kramer, and Martin H. Greenberg, co-editors

**1286**

**OUIDA CROZIER**

## Shadows After Dark

(New York: Rising Tide Press, 1993)

**Story type:** Fantasy (Alternate World; Quest)
**Major character(s):** Kathryn Hartell, Lesbian, Researcher (AIDS); Kyril Vertok, Alien (oupir), Vampire
**Time period(s):** 1980s
**Locale(s):** Kornagy, Planet—Imaginary; Minneapolis, Minnesota

**Summary:** To find a cause of death spreading on Kornagy, Kyril travels to Earth where she meets Kathryn. The two find a bond which transcends the differences between them and even Kathryn's cultural prejudice against vampirism. However, the strength of their passion may prove fatal to Kathryn as the pair travels to Kornagy where human health fails.

**Other books you might like:**
Elaine Bergstrom, *Daughter of the Night*, 1992
Steven Brust, *Agyar*, 1993
Suzy McKee Charnas, *The Vampire Tapestry*, 1980
Nancy A. Collins, *In the Blood*, 1992
Ellen Datlow, *A Whisper of Blood*, 1991
  editor

Katherine V. Forrest, *Dreams and Swords*, 1990
Jewelle Gomez, *The Gilda Stories*, 1991
Pam Keesey, *Daughters of Darkness: Lesbian Vampire Stories*, 1993
  editor
Anne Rice, *Interview with the Vampire*, 1976

**1287**

**ELAINE CUNNINGHAM**

## Daughter of the Drow

(Lake Geneva, Wisconsin: TSR, 1995)

**Story type:** Fantasy (Quest; Adventure)
**Series:** Forgotten Realms
**Major character(s):** Liriel Baenre, Magician, Mythical Creature (dark elf); Fyodor of Rashemen, Warrior
**Time period(s):** Indeterminate
**Locale(s):** Menzoberranzan, Fictional City; The Underdark, Mythical Place; Planet—Imaginary

**Summary:** With Menzoberranzan forces defeated afar and strife at home expected soon, Princess Liriel Baenri finds a way to the surface to pursue her dark elf magic, hoping to discover a way to protect her society from the tyranny of Loth and her priestesses.

**Other books you might like:**
Richard Awlinson, *Shadowdale*, 1989
Troy Denning, *The Parched Sea*, 1991
James Lowder, *Prince of Lies*, 1993
R.A. Salvatore, *The Legacy*, 1992
R.A. Salvatore, *Siege of Darkness*, 1994
R.A. Salvatore, *Starless Night*, 1994
Margaret Weis, *DragonLance Chronicles*, 1988
  Tracy Hickman, co-author

**1288**

**ELAINE CUNNINGHAM**

## Elfshadow

(Lake Geneva, Wisconsin: TSR, 1991)

**Story type:** Fantasy (Adventure)
**Series:** Forgotten Realms: The Harpers
**Major character(s):** Arilyn Moonblade, Warrior, Spy; Danilo ''Dan'' Thann, Nobleman; Kymil Nimesin, Martial Arts Expert (sword), Mythical Creature (elf)
**Time period(s):** Indeterminate
**Locale(s):** Evereska, Fictional City; Waterdeep, Fictional City

**Summary:** Someone is killing members of the Harpers, a group dedicated to justice. The killings fall into a pattern uncomfortably close to that of Arilyn's assignments. Secrecy has always served the Harpers well, but now all the groups with pieces of the puzzle are making it difficult for Arilyn to find out who the assassin is and what is sought. A game tie-in novel.

**Other books you might like:**
Troy Denning, *The Parched Sea*, 1991
Sheila Gilluly, *Greenbriar Queen*, 1988
Katharine Kerr, *Daggerspell*, 1986
Guy Gavriel Kay, *The Summer Tree*, 1985
Judith Tarr, *The Isle of Glass*, 1985
Terri Windling, *Borderland*, 1986
  Mark Alan Arnold, co-editor

**1289**

ELAINE CUNNINGHAM

## Elfsong

(Lake Geneva, Wisconsin: TSR, 1994)

**Story type:** Fantasy (Quest; Mystery)
**Series:** Forgotten Realms: The Harpers
**Major character(s):** Danilo ''Dan'' Thann, Musician (bard); Elaith Craulnober, Mythical Creature (elf)
**Time period(s):** Indeterminate
**Locale(s):** The High Forest, Mythical Place

**Summary:** Danilo Thann must confront the green dragon who holds the key to the rewritten memories of bards and the new tales appearing among their songs.

**Other books you might like:**
Scott Ciencin, *The Night Parade*, 1992
Troy Denning, *The Parched Sea*, 1991
James Lowder, *The Ring of Winter*, 1992
Jean Rabe, *Red Magic*, 1991
Elizabeth Ann Scarborough, *Phantom Banjo*, 1991

**1290**

ELAINE CUNNINGHAM

## Evermeet: Island of Elves

(Renton, Washington: TSR, 1998)

**Story type:** Fantasy (Military)
**Major character(s):** Lamruil, Ruler (prince); Darthoridan, Warrior (elf)
**Time period(s):** Indeterminate
**Locale(s):** Evermeet, Fictional Country

**Summary:** The Queen of the Elves sacrifices her life to protect Evermeet, the island sacred to her people and perhaps their last refuge. In her place rules Prince Lamruil, an unpopular leader who seems incapable of guaranteeing the security his mother sought and died to obtain.

**Other books you might like:**
Lynn Abbey, *Cinnabar Shadows*, 1995
Mark Anthony, *Crypt of the Shadowking*, 1993
Nancy Varian Berberick, *A Child of Elvish*, 1992
Scott Ciencin, *The Night Parade*, 1002
R.A. Salvatore, *Canticle*, 1991

**1291**

ELAINE CUNNINGHAM

## The Radiant Dragon

(Lake Geneva, Wisconsin: TSR, 1992)

**Story type:** Fantasy (Quest)
**Series:** Cloakmaster Cycle
**Major character(s):** Teldin Moore, Adventurer, Warrior; Vallus, Mythical Creature (elf), Wizard; Estriss, Alien (Illithid), Spaceship Captain
**Time period(s):** Indeterminate
**Locale(s):** Armistice, Planet—Imaginary; *Nightstalker*, Spaceship

**Summary:** Teldin seeks a great ship, *Spelljammer*, which he and a radiant dragon could take command by using their combined forces. Meanwhile, elves try to enlist Teldin's help in the second Unhuman War, hoping to use the power vested in Teldin's magic cloak. Set in the milieu of the role-playing game, *Spelljammer*.

**Other books you might like:**
David Cook, *Beyond the Moons*, 1991
Nigel Findley, *Into the Void*, 1991
Roger E. Moore, *The Maelstrom's Eye*, 1992

**1292**

ELAINE CUNNINGHAM

## Silver Shadows

(Lake Geneva, Wisconsin: TSR, 1996)

**Story type:** Fantasy (Adventure)
**Series:** Forgotten Realms: The Harpers
**Major character(s):** Arilyn Moonblade, Warrior, Spy; Foxfire, Mythical Creature (elf), Leader; Danilo ''Dan'' Thann, Musician (bard), Spy
**Time period(s):** Indeterminate
**Locale(s):** The Forest of Tethir, Fictional City

**Summary:** Lured by promises of information about her magic sword and her fate, Arilyn Moonblade becomes the agent of powers who move to protect the Elves of Tethir when threatened. On arriving at her destination, the half-elf finds the situation and the elves' leader more compelling than she imagines.

**Other books you might like:**
Eleanor Arnason, *The Sword Smith*, 1978
Steven Brust, *Jhereg*, 1983
Terry Goodkind, *Wizard's First Rule*, 1994
Guy Gavriel Kay, *Tigana*, 1990
Fritz Leiber, *Ill Met in Lankhmar*, 1995

**1293**

ELAINE CUNNINGHAM

## Thornhold

(Renton, Washington: TSR, 1998)

**Story type:** Fantasy (Magic Conflict; Political)

**Summary:** The most powerful sorcerer in Waterdeep prepares to defend his city from attack by an outside power. Restiveness among the lesser mages of that city hampers his efforts, which are also tied to the mission of Bronwyn, a professional revolutionary, to uncover the secrets of her own heritage.

**Other books you might like:**
Richard Awlinson, *Waterdeep*, 1989
Philip Brugalette, *The Nine Gates*, 1992
Troy Denning, *The Amber Enchantress*, 1992
Ed Greenwood, *All Shadows Fled*, 1995
Mary H. Herbert, *Lightning's Daughter*, 1991

**1294**

ANN CURRY

## The Book of Brendan

(New York: Holiday House, 1990)

**Story type:** Fantasy (Legend; Young Adult)
**Major character(s):** Elric, Child; Father Brendan, Religious; Arthur, Royalty
**Time period(s):** 8th century (725)
**Locale(s):** Hobury Abbey, England; Bay of Wodin, England

**Summary:** Myrddin, the evil magician, enchants most of the monks of the Abbey in his pursuit of the newly completed, illuminated *Book of Brendan*. Left to oppose him are the aging Father Brendan and two children, Elric and Bridget, who are aided by Avis, the bird from the Paradise of Birds (from the legend of Brendan the Mariner) and magical beasts from the *Book of Brendan*. Then the children call in King Arthur, his Queen, and Merlin.

**Other books you might like:**
John Bellairs, *The House with a Clock in Its Walls*, 1973
Edward Eager, *Seven-Day Magic*, 1962
Michael Ende, *The Neverending Story*, 1983
Alan Garner, *The Weirdstone of Brisingamen*, 1969
Betty Levin, *The Sword of Culann*, 1973
John Masefield, *The Box of Delights, or, When the Wolves Were Running*, 1935
Pat O'Shea, *The Hounds of the Morrigan*, 1986
Robert Westall, *Wind Eye*, 1977

**1295**

### CHRIS CURRY

## *Panic*

(New York: Pocket, 1994)

**Story type:** Horror (Child-in-Peril)
**Major character(s):** Rick Piper, Journalist (television); Carmen Zapata, Housekeeper; Jade Ewebean, Aged Person
**Time period(s):** 1990s (1994)
**Locale(s):** Santa Verde, California

**Summary:** Against his wish, Rick Piper returns to his family home to slay some personal demons, but instead encounters real ones: greenjacks, creatures of Scottish folklore who stole the soul of his nasty twin brother while he was young, and who now threaten his two young children.

**Other books you might like:**
Leigh Clark, *The Feeding*, 1992
Stephen R. George, *Dark Reunion*, 1990

**1296**

### CHRIS CURRY

## *Thunder Road*

(New York: Pocket, 1995)

**Story type:** Horror (Science Fiction)
**Major character(s):** Tom Abernathy, Rancher; Justin Martin, Teenager; Alexander Manderley, Scientist (UFO researcher)
**Time period(s):** 1990s (1995)
**Locale(s):** Madelyn, California

**Summary:** UFO sightings in the small town of Madelyn bring out peculiar behavior in some of the residents, including military personnel trying to keep the sighting secret, a serial killer who hopes the disappearance of his victims will be blamed on extraterrestrial abductions, and an unscrupulous evangelist who exploits the inexplicable events that are occurring to preach the coming armageddon.

**Other books you might like:**
Donald Burleson, *Flute Song*, 1996
Joseph A. Citro, *Deus-X: A Novel of Spiritual Terror*, 1995
Maxine O'Callaghan, *Dark Time*, 1992
Whitley Strieber, *Majestic*, 1989

**1297**

### CHRIS CURRY
### LISA DEAN, Co-Author

## *Trickster*

(New York: Pocket, 1992)

**Story type:** Horror (Serial Killer)
**Major character(s):** Phil Waterman, Police Officer (Sergeant Detective, Seattle PD); Dori Gallagher, Journalist (newspaper reporter); Seth Shepherd, Collector (art collector)
**Time period(s):** 1990s (1992)
**Locale(s):** Seattle, Washington

**Summary:** Emulating the Trickster of Salish Indian lore, a serial killer commandeers the bodies of innocent victims to perpetrate his grisly crimes and uses the Seattle underground to elude the police.

**Other books you might like:**
G. Wayne Miller, *Thunder Rise*, 1988
Kathryn Ptacek, *Ghost Dance*, 1990
Chet Williamson, *Dreamthorp*, 1989

**1298**

### JAMES ROBERTO CURTIS

## *Shango*

(Houston: Arte Publico, 1996)

**Story type:** Horror (Occult)
**Major character(s):** Miguel Calderon, Student—College; Rosa Garcia-Mesa, Religious (Santeria priestess); Osvaldo Gutierrez, Police Officer (lieutenant)
**Time period(s):** 1990s (1995)
**Locale(s):** Miami, Florida

**Summary:** Miguel Calderon is thrilled that his anthropolional research into the mystical religion Santeria is reacquainting him with his Cuban roots. What he doesn't know is that the priestess under whom he is studying is preparing him to become a blood sacrifice to Shango, one of the black *santos*, or darker saints. First novel.

**Other books you might like:**
Alex Abella, *The Killing of the Saints*, 1991
Hugh B. Cave, *The Lower Deep*, 1990
Nicholas Conde, *The Religion*, 1982
Don Davis, *The Gris-Gris Man*, 1996
Brian Hodge, *The Darker Saints*, 1994
Robert Weinberg, *The Black Lodge*, 1991

**1299**

### CAROLYN CUSHMAN

## *Witch and Wombat*

(New York: Warner Questar, 1994)

**Story type:** Fantasy (Light Fantasy)
**Major character(s):** Hali, Witch, Guide; Bernie, Companion (Hali's familiar), Animal (crow/wombat)
**Time period(s):** Indeterminate
**Locale(s):** Inner Worlds, Mythical Place (realm of magic)

**Summary:** To offset a depletion of the reservoir of magic within the Inner World, Bentwood initiates a trans-dimensional business that seems to link fantasy role-playing gamers in computer virtual reality, but actually transports them to the Inner World for adventure. Under contract to Bentwood, Hali and Bernie reluctantly lead the first group. First novel.

**Other books you might like:**
Michael Ende, *The Neverending Story*, 1983
Holly Lisle, *Minerva Wakes*, 1994
Larry Niven, *The Magic Goes Away*, 1978
James D. Priest, *Kirins: The Spell of No'an*, 1990
Lawrence Watt-Evans, *The Rebirth of Wonder*, 1992

## 1300
### RICHIE TANKERSLEY CUSICK

## Blood Roots
(New York: Pocket, 1992)

**Story type:** Horror (Gothic Family Chronicle)
**Major character(s):** Oilvia Crawford, Young Woman; Rosalie Deveraux, Aged Person, Grandparent; Skyler, Handyman (groundskeeper)
**Time period(s):** 1990s
**Locale(s):** Louisiana

**Summary:** Olivia Crawford runs away from her sluttish mother to go live with the maternal grandmother she has never met at the family plantation on the Louisiana bayou. There, she encounters the family legacy of voodoo horror, cannibalism, and sexual perversity extending back to the Civil War era that made her mother what she is today and threatens to do the same to her.

**Other books you might like:**
Athena Alexis, *Along Came a Spider*, 1992
V.C. Andrews, *The Dollanganger Saga*, 1979-1987
   Andrew Neiderman, co-author
Michael McDowell, *The Blackwater Series*, 1983
Joyce Carol Oates, *Bellefleur*, 1980

## 1301
### RICHIE TANKERSLEY CUSICK

## Buffy the Vampire Slayer
(New York: Pocket, 1992)

**Story type:** Horror (Vampire Story)
**Major character(s):** Buffy Summers, Teenager, Vampire Hunter; Merrick, Vampire Hunter; Lothos, Vampire
**Time period(s):** 1990s (1992)
**Locale(s):** Los Angeles, California

**Summary:** Buffy is distracted from her plans for the Hemery High senior prom when she is informed by the mysterious Mr. Merrick that she is a member of the Order, a secret lineage of vampire killers that has existed since the expulsion of Adam and Eve from Eden. It is her special task to track down and kill Lothos, the Vampire King responsible for a recent spate of deaths and disappearances among local high school teenagers. This book is a novelization of Joss Whedon's screenplay for the film of the same name.

**Other books you might like:**
Poppy Z. Brite, *Lost Souls*, 1992
Ray Garton, *Crucifax Autumn*, 1988
John Skipp, *The Light at the End*, 1986
   Craig Spector, co-author
S.P. Somtow, *Valentine*, 1992
William Tedford, *Liquid Diet*, 1992

## 1302
### RICHIE TANKERSLEY CUSICK

## The Harvest
(New York: Pocket/Archway, 1997)

**Story type:** Horror (Vampire Story)
**Series:** Buffy the Vampire Slayer
**Major character(s):** Buffy Summers, Teenager, Vampire Hunter; Mr. Giles, Librarian; Henrich Joseph Nest, Vampire
**Time period(s):** 1990s (1997)
**Locale(s):** Sunnydale, California

**Summary:** Buffy Summers, a teenager endowed with a sensitivity to vampires, transfers to Sunnydale High School in time to tangle with vampire Master Henrich Joseph Nest, who has engineered the deaths of several students as part of the Harvest that will open the door between the world of mortals and vampires. Novelization based on the television series derived from the 1992 movie *Buffy the Vampire Slayer*.

**Other books you might like:**
Elvira, *Transylvania 90210*, 1996
   John Paragon, co-author
Joseph Locke, *Vampire Heart*, 1994
Christopher Pike, *The Last Vampire*, 1994
Nicholas Pine, *Night School*, 1994
L.J. Smith, *Dark Reunion*, 1992
   Vampire Diaries, volume 4

## 1303
### JULIE E. CZERNEDA

## Beholder's Eye
(New York: DAW, 1998)

**Story type:** Science Fiction (First Contact; Alternate Intelligence)
**Major character(s):** Esen-Alit-Quar, Alien (shapechanger), Immortal; Paul Ragem, Spaceman, Military Personnel; Ersh, Alien (shapechanger), Immortal
**Time period(s):** Indeterminate Future
**Locale(s):** Kraos, Planet—Imaginary; *Rigus*, Spaceship; Rigel II, Planet—Imaginary

**Summary:** Having broken the basic rule of her kind, "Never let anyone know we exist, or that we change shape," Esen must hide some of her memories, an ability possessed only by Ersh, the first, ancient part of her being. While one human hunts her, the more she learns about herself, the worse her problems become.

**Other books you might like:**
C.J. Cherryh, *Foreigner*, 1994
L. Warren Douglas, *Cannon's Orb*, 1994
James Alan Gardner, *Expendable*, 1997
Vernor Vinge, *A Fire upon the Deep*, 1992
Sarah Zettel, *Fool's War*, 1997

## 1304
### JULIE E. CZERNEDA

## A Thousand Words for Stranger
(New York: DAW, 1997)

**Story type:** Science Fiction (Political; Psychic Powers)
**Major character(s):** Sira di Sarc, Amnesiac, Alien (M'hiray); Jason Morgan, Spaceship Captain (Telepath); Barac sud Sarc, Alien (M'hirary)

**Time period(s):** Indeterminate Future
**Locale(s):** *Silver Fox*, Spaceship; Auord, Planet—Imaginary

**Summary:** On the run with no memory of her past or identity, Sira knows only that she must hide from Trade Pact Enforcers and other dangerous pursuers. For reasons she does not understand, Sira accepts help and a ride from a space trader named Jason Morgan, even though she does not quite trust him. First novel.

**Other books you might like:**
Piers Anthony, *Total Recall*, 1989
Octavia E. Butler, *Imago*, 1989
Carole Nelson Douglas, *Probe*, 1985
Nicola Griffith, *Slow River*, 1995
Jacqueline Lichtenberg, *First Channel*, 1980
    Jean Lorrah, co-author
John E. Stith, *Memory Blank*, 1986

---

### 1305

**DANIEL DA CRUZ**

## Mixed Doubles

(New York: Ballantine/Del Rey, 1989)

**Story type:** Science Fiction (Time Travel)
**Major character(s):** Justin Pope, Composer, Thief; John Skardon, Scientist
**Time period(s):** 1990s; 1920s
**Locale(s):** California; Vienna, Austria

**Summary:** Justin Pope is a minimally talented composer who has made a name for himself by stealing the work of others more talented but less fortunate than himself. Then he discovers a time machine and sets out to steal from the great masters themselves.

**Other books you might like:**
Brian W. Aldiss, *Frankenstein Unbound*, 1973
Mike McQuay, *Memories*, 1987
Michael Moorcock, *Behold the Man*, 1969
Kim Stanley Robinson, *The Memory of Whiteness*, 1985

---

### 1306

**ROALD DAHL**, Editor

## Roald Dahl's Book of Ghost Stories

(New York: Farrar, Strauss and Giroux, 1996)

**Story type:** Horror (Anthology; Ghost Story)

**Summary:** First published in 1983, this volume assembles 14 stories of ghosts and the supernatural chosen by a modern master of the macabre. Included are stories by A.M. Burrage, among them "The Sweeper," about a rich woman who is cursed to death by a beggar she turned from her door; L.P. Hartley's "W.S.," about a writer stalked by one of his fictional creations; Cynthia Asquith's "A Corner Shop," in which a man returns from the dead to redress a wrong he feels he has committed; F. Marion Crawford's "The Upper Berth," about a berth on an ocean-going ship haunted by a gruesome revenant; Rosemary Timperley's "Christmas Meeting," a ghost story in which it is difficult to distinguish the dead from the living; and Edith Wharton's "Afterward," a classic tale about a house haunting so subtle no one can determine who the ghost is.

**Other books you might like:**
Ramsey Campbell, *Uncanny Banquet*, 1992
    editor
Richard Dalby, *The Mammoth Book of Ghost Stories*, 1990
    editor

Larry Dark, *The Literary Ghost*, 1991
    editor
Hugh Lamb, *Forgotten Tales of Terror*, 1978
    editor
Robert Phillips, *Triumph of the Night*, 1989
    editor

---

### 1307

**RICHARD DALBY**

## Chillers for Christmas

(New York: Gallery Books, 1990)

**Story type:** Horror (Anthology)

**Summary:** Twenty-seven horror and suspense stories that span the century and take Christmas or winter as their theme. Some, like L.P. Hartley's "The Waits" and Bernard Capes' "The Vanishing House" are tales of traditional yuletide haunts, while Eugene Johnson's "Just Before Dawn" and John Collier's "Back for Christmas" offer unique forms of poetic justice as holiday gifts. Rudyard Kipling's "The Strange Ride of Morrowbie Jukes" and Sarban's "A Christmas Story" are classic narratives that defy categorization. Six tales are original to the volume.

**Other books you might like:**
Kathryn Cramer, *Spirits of Christmas*, 1989
    David Hartwell, co-author
Kathryn Cramer, *Christmas Ghosts*, 1987
    David Hartwell, co-author

---

### 1308

**RICHARD DALBY**, Editor

## Dracula's Brood

(New York: Barnes & Noble, 1987)

**Story type:** Horror (Anthology; Vampire Story)

**Summary:** The editor, a well-known scholar of horror and supernatural fiction, includes 30 stories of vampirism published before or near the 1897 appearance of Bram Stoker's *Dracula*. Included are Anne Crawford's "A Mystery of the Campagna" and Julian Hawthorne's "Ken's Mystery," in which vampire femmes fatales victimize male artists; Arthur Conan Doyle's tale of psychic vampirism, "The Parasite"; Mary Elizabeth Braddon's "Good Lady Ducayne," in which a vampiric old lady feeds symbolically on the vitality of her young travelling companions; Vernon Lee's "Marsyas in Flanders," concerned with a cursed religious relic; and M.R. James's "Wailing Well," about the vampiric fate that befalls a young boy who disobeys his elders.

**Other books you might like:**
Christopher Frayling, *The Vampire*, 1978
    editor
Alan Ryan, *Vampires: Two Centuries of Great Vampire Stories*, 1988
    editor
Leslie Shepard, *The Dracula Book of Great Vampire Stories*, 1977
    editor

## 1309

### RICHARD DALBY

### *The Mammoth Book of Ghost Stories*
(New York: Carroll & Graf, 1995)

**Story type:** Horror (Anthology; Ghost Story)

**Summary:** Fifty ghost stories by American and British authors, ranging from recognized classics (Ambrose Bierce's "An Inhabitant of Carcosa," Rudyard Kipling's "They") to less reprinted stories by classic authors (William Hope Hodgson's "The Valley of the Lost Children," M.R. James's "The Haunted Doll's House"), modern stories in the classic tradition (Robert Aickman's "Unsettled Dust," Ramsey Campbell's "The Guide"), pulp horror stories (Manly Wade Wellman's "Where Angels Fear") and contemporary ghost stories (Basil Copper's "The House by the Tarn," Karl Edward Wagner's "In the Pines").

**Other books you might like:**
Robert Aickman, *The Fontana Book of Ghost Stories Series*, 1964-1971
Bennett Cerf, *Famous Ghost Stories*, 1956
Michael Cox, *The Oxford Book of English Ghost Stories*, 1986
    R.A. Gilbert, co-author
J.A. Cuddon, *The Penguin Book of Ghost Stories*, 1985

## 1310

### RICHARD DALBY, Editor

### *The Mammoth Book of Victorian and Edwardian Ghost Stories*
(New York: Carroll & Graf, 1995)

**Story type:** Horror (Anthology; Ghost Story)

**Summary:** Through 42 stories by British and American authors, the editor, a renowned authority on ghost stories and tales of horror, captures the sensibility of the supernatural story in the late nineteenth and early twentieth centuries. Included are J. Sheridan Le Fanu's tale of an unscrupulous man who weds his niece to a dead man, "Schalken the Painter"; one of William Hope Hodgson's tales of his psychic detective, Carnacki, "The Gateway of the Monster"; W.C. Morrow's story of a unique ghostly visitation "An Original Revenge"; and Bram Stoker's story of a young student beset by the evil influence of the former owner of the house he has rented, "The Judge's House." In addition to these classics, the book contains a wealth of stories that have been reprinted rarely, if at all.

**Other books you might like:**
Anonymous, *A Century of Ghost Stories*, 1936
Anonymous, *Fifty Years of Ghost Stories*, 1935
Cynthia Asquith, *The Ghost Book*, 1927
    editor
Joseph Lewis French, *The Short Story Omnibus*, 1926
    editor
Alexander Laing, *The Haunted Omnibus*, 1937

## 1311

### RICHARD DALBY, Editor

### *Mistletoe Mayhem*
(New York: Castle, 1993)

**Story type:** Horror (Anthology)

**Summary:** Published in England in 1992 as *Horror for Christmas*, this book brings together 13 tales of horror and suspense set during the Christmas season. Included are a Basil Copper story original to the anthology, "Wish You Were Here," about a writer who receives Christmas cards from the dead; Robert Bloch's sardonic tale of marital infidelity, "The Night Before Christmas"; Sabine Baring Gould's deal-with-the-devil tale, "Mustapha"; ghost stories from Marjorie Bowen ("The Crown Derby Plate") and W.W. Jacobs ("Jerry Bundler"); and Stephen Gallagher's suspense tale of a journalist trapped in a newsroom by a homicidal maniac, "Dance by the Light of the Moon." Other contributors include Nigel Kneale, R. Chetwynd-Hayes, Robert Aickman, and Hugh Walpole.

**Other books you might like:**
Kathryn Cramer, *Christmas Ghosts*, 1988
    David Hartwell, co-editor
Kathryn Cramer, *Spirits of Christmas*, 1989
    David Hartwell, co-editor
Seon Manley, *Christmas Ghosts: An Anthology*, 1978
    Gogo Lewis, co-editor
Mike Resnick, *Christmas Ghosts*, 1993
    Martin H. Greenberg, co-editor

## 1312

### RICHARD DALBY, Editor

### *Modern Ghost Stories by Eminent Women Writers*
(New York: Carroll & Graf, 1992)

**Story type:** Horror (Anthology; Ghost Story)

**Summary:** This book collects 27 ghost stories by women writers, some of whom will be unfamiliar to readers steeped in the supernatural horror canon. The ghostly manifestations recounted here include the spectral landlord of Edith Wharton's "Afterward," the haunted automobiles of Rosemary Pardoe's "The Chauffer" and Lady Antonia Fraser's "Who's Been Sitting in My Car," the ghost who doesn't know she's a ghost in Jean Rhys' "I Used to Live Here Once," and the ghostly family of Mary Elizabeth Counselman's southern Gothic, "The House of Shadows."

**Other books you might like:**
Kathryn Ptacek, *Women of Darkness*, 1989
    editor
Alan Ryan, *Haunting Women*, 1988
    editor
Jessica Amanda Salmonson, *What Did Miss Darrington See?: An Anthology of Feminist Supernatural Fiction*, 1989
    editor

## 1313

### RICHARD DALBY, Editor

### *Shivers for Christmas*
(New York: St. Martin's, 1996)

**Story type:** Horror (Anthology)

**Summary:** Sixteen stories of the supernatural with a Christmas theme are chosen by an editor renowned for his knowledge of the horror genre. Included are Amelia B. Edwards' "The Discovery of the Treasure Isles," about a magic island that plays hob with time; Nathaniel Hawthorne's "The Christmas Banquet," in which a Christmas feast is the setting for a meeting of ten people whose misery effects uncanny transformations; Terry Lamsley's "Two Returns," in which a man is victimized by a haunted coat left by a former tenant; Stephen Gallagher's "Fancy That!," about a man who buys an unusual present for an even more unusual companion; and Alan McMurray's "It Will All Be Over by Christmas," in which a soldier of the first World War keeps his promise to be home by Christmas Eve, even though he has died.

**Other books you might like:**
Kathryn Cramer, *Christmas Ghosts*, 1988
   David Hartwell, co-editor
Seon Manley, *Christmas Ghosts: An Anthology*, 1978
   Gogo Lewis, co-editor
Mike Resnick, *Christmas Ghosts*, 1993
   Martin H. Greenberg, co-editor

## 1314

### RICHARD DALBY, Editor

### *Twelve Gothic Tales*
(New York: Oxford, 1998)

**Story type:** Horror (Anthology)

**Summary:** In these twelve reprint stories, the mood, atmosphere, and plots are steeped in the Gothic tradition. Selections include Charles R. Maturin's "Lexlip Castle," concerned with the supernatural circumstances surrounding a woman's ill-fated betrothal; Sabine Baring-Gould's "Master Sacristan Eberhart," in which a cleric's beliefs bring a gargoyle to unholy life; Ralph Adams Cram's "In Kropfsberg Keep," about two men travelers who foolishly ignore warnings not to spend a night in a haunted castle; and Gerald Durrell's "The Entrance," in which a man discovers that the legend-shrouded estate where he is working is menaced by a monster that lives in a world on the other side of the mirror.

**Other books you might like:**
Chris Baldick, *The Oxford Book of Gothic Tales*, 1992
   editor
Peter Haining, *The Shilling Shockers*, 1978
   editor
Peter Haining, *Gothic Tales of Terror*, 1972
   editor
Joyce Carol Oates, *American Gothic Tales*, 1996
   editor
Patricia L. Skarda, *The Evil Image: Two Centuries of Gothic Short Fiction and Poetry*, 1981
   Nora Crowe, co-editor

## 1315

### BRIAN DALEY

### *A Screaming Across the Sky*
(New York: Ballantine Del Rey, 1998)

**Story type:** Science Fiction (Military; Adventure)
**Series:** Gammalaw
**Major character(s):** Dextra Haven, Political Figure, Religious (high priestess); Burning, Military Personnel (Ext soldier); Yatt, Artificial Intelligence
**Time period(s):** Indeterminate Future
**Locale(s):** Periapt, Planet—Imaginary; Aquamarine, Planet—Imaginary

**Summary:** Against political and economic odds, Dextra Haven heads an expedition of scientists and Ext warriors to the sea-planet Aquamarine, believing that the planet may hold the key to peace between humans and the alien Roke.

**Other books you might like:**
Gordon R. Dickson, *Dorsai!*, 1976
David Drake, *Hammer's Slammers*, 1987
   expanded edition
David Drake, *Northworld*, 1990
Wil McCarthy, *Aggressor Six*, 1994
Wil McCarthy, *The Fall of Sirius*, 1996
David Weber, *Flag in Exile*, 1995

## 1316

### KARA DALKEY

### *Bhagavati*
(New York: Tor, 1998)

**Story type:** Fantasy (Historical; Adventure)
**Series:** Blood of the Goddess
**Major character(s):** Thomas Chinnery, Apothecary, Trader; Stheno, Mythical Creature (gorgon), Immortal; Gandharva, Musician, Handicapped (blind)
**Time period(s):** 16th century
**Locale(s):** Bhagavati, India

**Summary:** In resurrecting Aditi, Stheno, the immortal ruler of the hidden city of Bhagavati, inadvertently leads the Mughul army there. While Stheno becomes enamored of Thomas Chinnery (who loves Aditi and who wishes most of all to return to England), the Mughul army's looting and the demands of the people drive Stheno to madness, so that only her death can save everyone else. Concludes the trilogy.

**Other books you might like:**
Piers Anthony, *The Willing Spirit*, 1996
   Alfred Tella, co-author
M.A.R. Barker, *Man of Gold*, 1984
John Barnes, *Earth Made of Glass*, 1998
L. Sprague de Camp, *The Golden Wind*, 1969
Amitav Ghosh, *The Calcutta Chromosome*, 1997
Rudyard Kipling, *Famous Tales of India*, 1962
Tanith Lee, *Tamastara, or, the Indian Nights*, 1984
Roger Zelazny, *Lord of Light*, 1967

## 1317

### KARA DALKEY

### *Bijapur*
(New York: Tor, 1997)

**Story type:** Fantasy (Historical; Adventure)
**Series:** Blood of the Goddess
**Major character(s):** Thomas Chinnery, Apothecary, Prisoner; Aditi, Sorceress
**Time period(s):** 16th century (1597)
**Locale(s):** India

**Summary:** Thomas Chinnery and the party from Goa reach Bijapur in their search for the death-defying elixir. Mirza Ali Akbarshah, a Mughul general interested in expanding his ruler's territory, also advances on Bijapur where Ibrahim Adilshah, the ruler of Bijapur, decides to send all of them on the quest for the elixir.

**Other books you might like:**
Piers Anthony, *The Willing Spirit*, 1996
   Alfred Tella, co-author
M.A.R. Barker, *Flamesong*, 1986
M.A.R. Barker, *Man of Gold*, 1984
L. Sprague de Camp, *The Golden Wind*, 1969

Rudyard Kipling, *Famous Tales of India*, 1962
Tanith Lee, *Tamastara, or, the Indian Nights*, 1984
Chelsea Quinn Yarbro, *The Path of the Eclipse*, 1981
Roger Zelazny, *Lord of Light*, 1967

## 1318

### KARA DALKEY

## *Blood of the Goddess*

(New York: Tor, 1996)

**Story type:** Fantasy (Religious; Horror)
**Series:** Goa
**Major character(s):** Thomas Chinnery, Sailor, Apothecary; Aditi, Deity (goddess), Widow(er), Sorceress; Brother Timoteo, Religious, Lawyer
**Time period(s):** 16th century (1597)
**Locale(s):** Goa, India

**Summary:** En route to Cathay, Thomas Chinnery meets a reputed sorcerer and a mysterious Hindu woman, Aditi, who have an elixir which kills the living and restores the dead. When captured by the Inquisition in Goa, Thomas gains a limited release by promising to lead the authorities to the source of the elixir.

**Other books you might like:**
Piers Anthony, *The Willing Spirit*, 1996
   Alfred Tella, co-author
M.A.R. Barker, *Flamesong*, 1985
M.A.R. Barker, *Man of Gold*, 1984
Tanith Lee, *Tamastara, or, the Indian Nights*, 1984
Chelsea Quinn Yarbro, *The Path of the Eclipse*, 1981
Roger Zelazny, *Lord of Light*, 1967

## 1319

### KARA DALKEY

## *The Heavenward Path*

(New York: Harcourt Brace, 1998)

**Story type:** Fantasy (Legend; Young Adult)
**Major character(s):** Fujiwara no Mitsuko, Heroine, Teenager; Goranu, Mythical Creature (tengu shapeshifter), Demon
**Time period(s):** 12th century
**Locale(s):** Japan

**Summary:** As ghosts and bad luck plague Fujiwara no Mitsuko, one angry spirit demands that she keep a forgotten promise. To help her fulfill the difficult tasks he proposes, Fujiwara no Mitsuko enlists Goranu's aid. Unfortunately, Goranu's help comes with a potentially deadly price tag. Sequel to *Little Sister*.

**Other books you might like:**
Grace Chetwin, *Out of the Dark World*, 1985
John Gordon, *The Edge of the World*, 1983
Eloise Jarvis McGraw, *The Moorchild*, 1996
Tamora Pierce, *The Realms of the Gods*, 1996
Sherwood Smith, *Wren's Quest*, 1993

## 1320

### KARA DALKEY

## *Little Sister*

(New York: Harcourt Brace/Jane Yolen Books, 1996)

**Story type:** Fantasy (Young Adult; Legend)

**Major character(s):** Fujiwara "Little Puddle" no Mitsuko, Teenager, Heroine; Goranu, Mythical Creature (tengu shapeshifter), Demon
**Time period(s):** 12th century
**Locale(s):** Japan; Mythical Place (netherworld)

**Summary:** After outlaws attack her village, a young noblewoman seeks aid from a demon to retrieve her sister's soul, lost while searching for her murdered husband.

**Other books you might like:**
Grace Chetwin, *Out of the Dark World*, 1985
John Gordon, *The Edge of the World*, 1983
Eloise Jarvis McGraw, *The Moorchild*, 1996
Sherwood Smith, *Wren's Quest*, 1993

## 1321

### KARA DALKEY

## *Steel Rose*

(New York: Roc, 1997)

**Story type:** Fantasy (Urban; Magic Conflict)
**Major character(s):** Tiffany Jeanine "T.J." Kaminski, Artist, Student—College; Ralph, Mythical Creature (knocker), Activist; Norton, Mythical Creature (knocker), Activist
**Time period(s):** 1990s
**Locale(s):** Pittsburgh, Pennsylvania; Under the Hill, Mythical Place

**Summary:** Rehearsing new material after her audience fails to appreciate T.J.'s performance art, T.J. chances to incorporate an incantation from an old book, which brings forth a pair of Unseelie helpers intent on using T.J.'s act to irritate the Sidhe's Seelie court. After unintentionally accepting a challenge of battle from the Seelie court, T.J. reluctantly trusts Ralph and Norton with her performance art while they fight for Unseelie rights.

## 1322

### JOHN DALMAS

## *The Kalif's War*

(New York: Baen, 1991)

**Story type:** Science Fiction (Military; Political)
**Series:** Regiment
**Major character(s):** Chodrisei "Coso" Biilathkamoro, Ruler (Kalif of the Karghanik Empire); Tain Faronya, Prisoner (confederation); Sumbaa, Computer
**Time period(s):** 220th century
**Locale(s):** Karghanik Empire, Interstellar Empire/Federation

**Summary:** Coso Biilanthkamoro becomes Kalif after a coup. His immediate concern is to bring the Confederation into the Karghanik Empire. He also is enamoured with Tain Faronya, a Confederation prisoner, and marries her despite the misgivings of friends, prelates and the Diet. After many plots and attempted coups during which he and the Kalifa are wounded, they finally set off to fight the Confederation leaving his "trusted" friend Jilsomo as acting Kalif.

**Other books you might like:**
Gordon R. Dickson, *The Tactics of Mistake*, 1971
Jerry Pournelle, *Falkenberg's Legion*, 1990
Joel Rosenberg, *Not for Glory*, 1988
S.M. Stirling, *Marching through Georgia*, 1988
Timothy Zahn, *Cobra*, 1985

`1323`

## JOHN DALMAS

### *The Lantern of God*
(New York: Baen Books, 1989)

**Story type:** Science Fiction (Space Colony)
**Major character(s):** Elver Brokols, Diplomat (Ambassador); Juliassa Hanorissia, Royalty (Princess)
**Time period(s):** Indeterminate Future
**Locale(s):** Almeon Colony, Planet—Imaginary

**Summary:** Two thousand years earlier an interstellar cargo ship, fleeing a major war, had abandoned a group of pleasure androids on a deserted planet. Rather than dying out, the androids began to reproduce and created their own civilization, eventually losing all memory of their origins. They are now true human beings, but the descendents of the starship crew that abandoned them have returned for the property their forerunners left behind.

**Other books you might like:**
C.J. Cherryh, *Forty Thousand in Gehenna*, 1983
Mary Gentle, *Ancient Light*, 1989
Mary Gentle, *Golden Witchbreed*, 1983
F. Paul Wilson, *The Tery*, 1990

`1324`

## JOHN DALMAS

### *The Lion of Farside*
(New York: Baen, 1995)

**Story type:** Fantasy (Alternate World; Political)
**Major character(s):** Curtis Macurdy, Farmer, Warrior; Varia, Psychic, Spouse (Curtis Macurdy's); Melody, Warrior
**Time period(s):** 1930s
**Locale(s):** Indiana; Yuulith, Planet—Imaginary; Alternate Universe

**Summary:** Originally from Yuulith, Varia wants only to remain with Curtis Macurdy in Indiana, defying the orders of her Sisterhood. When the Sisterhood abducts Varia, Curtis follows her to Yuulith. At first enslaved, Curtis quickly advances as a military leader until he influences even the basic social order in his quest to recover Varia.

**Other books you might like:**
Piers Anthony, *Var the Stick*, 1973
Ben Bova, *Orion*, 1984
Gordon R. Dickson, *The Dragon and the George*, 1976
Philip Jose Farmer, *The Maker of Universes*, 1965
Julian May, *The Many-Colored Land*, 1981
Christopher Stasheff, *Her Majesty's Wizard*, 1986
Harry Turtledove, *The Misplaced Legion*, 1987
Paul O. Williams, *The Ends of the Circle*, 1981

`1325`

## JOHN DALMAS

### *The Lizard War*
(New York: Baen Books, 1989)

**Story type:** Science Fiction (Military)
**Major character(s):** Luis Raoul DenUyl, Warrior; Tom, Farmer
**Time period(s):** 30th century
**Locale(s):** North America

**Summary:** A thousand years ago Earth had nearly destroyed itself in a nuclear war. Now, its level of technology roughly late medieval, the planet has been conquered by lizard-like aliens. The only humans standing between Earth and complete subjugation are a sect of mystic warriors.

**Other books you might like:**
Poul Anderson, *The High Crusade*, 1960
Rick Cook, *Limbo System*, 1989
Kenneth Von Gunden, *StarSpawn*, 1990
F. Paul Wilson, *The Tery*, 1989

`1326`

## JOHN DALMAS

### *The Regiment's War*
(New York: Baen, 1993)

**Story type:** Science Fiction (Military; Political)
**Series:** Regiment
**Major character(s):** Artus Romlar, Military Personnel (Colonel), Mercenary; Kelmer Faronya, Journalist; Gulthar Kro, Criminal (assassin), Spy
**Time period(s):** 220th century
**Locale(s):** Smolen, Fictional Country; Komars, Fictional Country

**Summary:** The White T'swa get their first job, fighting for the Smoleni against the occupying Komarsi. When the Smoleni begin turning the tide, the king of Komars hires the original T'swa to fight for him. Moderate forces must take over and make peace between the two countries, then prepare to fight the approaching Imperials.

**Other books you might like:**
Roger MacBride Allen, *The Torch of Honor*, 1985
Neal Barrett Jr., *The Karma Corps*, 1984
Lois McMaster Bujold, *Borders of Infinity*, 1989
David Drake, *Hammer's Slammers*, 1979
Gordon R. Dickson, *The Tactics of Mistake*, 1971
M.A. Foster, *The Warriors of Dawn*, 1975
P.M. Griffin, *Jungle Assault*, 1991
Colin Kapp, *The Ion War*, 1978
Jerry Pournelle, *Falkenberg's Legion*, 1990
S.M. Stirling, *The Stone Dogs*, 1990
Timothy Zahn, *Cobra*, 1985

`1327`

## JOHN DALMAS

### *The White Regiment*
(New York: Baen, 1990)

**Story type:** Science Fiction (Military; Political)
**Series:** Regiment
**Major character(s):** Artus Romlar, Military Personnel, Mercenary; Lotta Alsnor, Counselor, Psychic; Igsat Tarimenloku, Military Personnel (Klestronu commodore)
**Time period(s):** 220th century
**Locale(s):** Iryala, Planet—Imaginary; Terfreya, Planet—Imaginary; Confederation, Interstellar Empire/Federation

**Summary:** A Klestronu scoutship discovers Confederation space and decides to annex it to the Empire. Meanwhile on Iryala, T'swa warriors are training the locals into a Regiment to see how much they can learn of T'swa military arts. A scientist discovers a means of teleportation, but only the mentally gifted can use it (many of whom are warriors). When the Klestronu invade at Terfreya, the Regiment and the new method of teleportation must prove themselves and carry the day. The Klestronu retreat, but vow to return someday.

**Other books you might like:**
Gordon R. Dickson, *The Tactics of Mistake*, 1971
David Drake, *The Forlorn Hope*, 1984
Robert A. Heinlein, *Starship Troopers*, 1959
Jerry Pournelle, *Falkenberg's Legion*, 1990
Joel Rosenberg, *Not for Glory*, 1988

---

**1328**

**JOHN DALMAS**

## The Yngling and the Circle of Power

(New York: Baen, 1992)

**Story type:** Science Fiction (Adventure; Post-Holocaust)
**Series:** Yngling
**Major character(s):** Nils Jarnhann, Telepath, Warrior; Deodoro "Ted" Baver, Anthropologist (ethnologist); Songstan Gampo, Ruler (Emperor of China)
**Time period(s):** 29th century
**Locale(s):** Europe; Mongolia; China

**Summary:** Nils, mentally contacted by minds far to the East, sets off in that direction along with Hans, a saga writer, and Baver, a man returned from the stars. After journeying across Russia and Mongolia, they finally arrive in China where Baver is captured by the Emperor's soldiers. Demon-driven Yeti brings Nils to the Emperor and his Circle of Power, hoping to destroy it all.

**Other books you might like:**
Piers Anthony, *Battle Circle*, 1978
Leigh Brackett, *The Long Tomorrow*, 1955
Gordon R. Dickson, *Wolf and Iron*, 1990
Leo Frankowski, *The Cross-Time Engineer*, 1986
Marc Laidlaw, *Neon Lotus*, 1988
Elizabeth Ann Scarborough, *Nothing Sacred*, 1991

---

**1329**

**JOHN DALMAS**

## The Yngling in Yamato

(New York: Baen, 1994)

**Story type:** Science Fiction (Adventure; Post-Holocaust)
**Series:** Yngling
**Major character(s):** Nils Jarnhann, Telepath, Warrior; Matsumura Shinji, Nobleman, Warrior; Hidaka Sataru, Thief (bandit), Wizard
**Time period(s):** 29th century
**Locale(s):** Japan

**Summary:** When Nils Jarnhann, Hans and their starship crew travel to Yamato to seek out a holy man, rebellion and civil war reflect the weakness of the Emperor and the restlessness of the samurai nobility. Adopted by an imperial loyalist, Matsumura, Nils discovers much of the plot against the Emperor and seeks help from the holy man during the rebellion.

**Other books you might like:**
Dennis Schmidt, *Kensho*, 1979
Brian Stableford, *The Castaways of Tanagar*, 1981
Eric Van Lustbader, *Dai-San*, 1978
Jack Vance, *Servants of the Wankh*, 1969
Paul O. Williams, *The Sword of Forebearance*, 1985

---

**1330**

**ANNIE DALTON**

## Out of the Ordinary

(New York: Harper, 1990)

**Story type:** Fantasy (Magic Conflict; Young Adult)
**Major character(s):** Molly Gurney, Teenager, Child-Care Giver; Floris, Foundling, Heir—Lost; Icanus Tomkins, Musician
**Time period(s):** 1980s
**Locale(s):** England; Launde, Alternate Universe

**Summary:** Molly Gurney finds herself babysitting for the enchanting (and enchanted) beautiful four-year-old foster child, Floris, who is soon the object of a search by malevolent, destructive powers. Aided by Icarus, Molly must protect Floris from evil wizardry and through a series of adventures through both England and occasionally the alternate world of Launde and the Heartstone.

**Other books you might like:**
Susan Cooper, *The Dark Is Rising*, 1973
Susan Cooper, *The Grey King*, 1975
Alan Garner, *Elidor*, 1967
Astrid Lindgren, *Mio My Son*, 1956
Pat O'Shea, *The Hounds of the Morrigan*, 1986

---

**1331**

**SEAN DALTON** (Pseudonym of Deborah Chester)

## Beyond the Void

(New York: Ace, 1991)

**Story type:** Science Fiction (Adventure; Military)
**Series:** Operation StarHawks
**Major character(s):** Bryan Kelly, Military Personnel (commander, Special Operations); Phila Mohatsa, Military Personnel (communications officer); Antoinette Beaulieu, Doctor
**Time period(s):** Indeterminate Future
**Locale(s):** Outer Space

**Summary:** When legendary invaders from another universe come through gates, attack the Earthship *Sounder* and take it with them, the Starhawks follow to rescue the crew.

**Other books you might like:**
Lois McMaster Bujold, *Shards of Honor*, 1986
Allan Cole, *Sten*, 1984
  Chris Bunch, co-author
Brian Daley, *Jinx on a Terran Inheritance*, 1985
Stephen Goldin, *Jade Darcy and the Affair of Honor*, 1988
  Mary Mason, co-author
Geary Gravel, *A Key for the Nonesuch*, 1990
Steve Perry, *Matadora*, 1986
Jerry Pournelle, *The Children's Hour*, 1991
  S.M. Stirling, co-author

---

**1332**

**SEAN DALTON** (Pseudonym of Deborah Chester)

## Destination: Mutiny

(New York: Ace, 1991)

**Story type:** Science Fiction (Adventure; Military)
**Series:** Operation StarHawks
**Major character(s):** Bryan Kelly, Military Personnel (commander, Special Operations); Olaf Siggerson, Pilot (spaceship); Ouoji, Animal (alien mascot)

**Time period(s):** Indeterminate Future
**Locale(s):** Melthanus, Planet—Imaginary; *Blade*, Spaceship

**Summary:** Having lost a member of their crew of Salukan, the Starhawks rescue Kelly from detox, steal the *Blade*, and set off to rescue 41. The expectation that they'll be able to return and clear their names seems less likely as their adventure progresses.

**Other books you might like:**
Lois McMaster Bujold, *Borders of Infinity*, 1989
Allan Cole, *The Return of the Emperor*, 1990
   Chris Bunch, co-author
Geary Gravel, *A Key for the Nonesuch*, 1990
Melisa C. Michaels, *Skirmish*, 1985
Steve Perry, *The Man Who Never Missed*, 1985
Alis A. Rasmussen, *A Passage of Stars*, 1990
Melissa Scott, *Mighty Good Road*, 1990

## 1333

### SEAN DALTON (Pseudonym of Deborah Chester)

## The Salukan Gambit

(New York: Ace, 1992)

**Story type:** Science Fiction (Adventure; Political)
**Series:** Operation StarHawks
**Major character(s):** Bryan Kelly, Military Personnel; Operative 41, Alien (half Human/half Salukan), Spaceman; Antoinette Beaulieu, Doctor
**Time period(s):** Indeterminate Future
**Locale(s):** *Sabre*, Spaceship; Banqot, Fictional City; Minzan, Planet—Imaginary

**Summary:** The StarHawks rescue Melaethia and her infant triplets, but before the *Sabre* builds up speed, a Jostic pirate vessel with several Salukan Warriors on board disables the *Sabre*. Since one of the Salukans, Melaethia's brother, desperately wants to hurt Melaethia, the StarHawks must keep Melaethia and her children safe while regaining control of the *Sabre*.

**Other books you might like:**
Lois McMaster Bujold, *Shards of Honor*, 1986
C.J. Cherryh, *The Pride of Chanur*, 1982
Allan Cole, *Sten*, 1984
   Chris Bunch, co-author
A.C. Crispin, *Starbridge*, 1989
Brian Daley, *Jinx on a Terran Inheritance*, 1985
Vonda N. McIntyre, *Metaphase*, 1992
Steve Perry, *The Man Who Never Missed*, 1985
Vernor Vinge, *A Fire upon the Deep*, 1992

## 1334

### BRIAN D'AMATO

## Beauty

(New York: Delacorte, 1992)

**Story type:** Horror (Science Fiction)
**Major character(s):** Jamie Angelo, Artist, Student (medical); Jaishree/Minaz, Artist, Model; David Lowenstein, Doctor
**Time period(s):** 1990s (1992)
**Locale(s):** New York, New York

**Summary:** This critique of the Manhattan art scene and fashion world tells of artist Jamie Angelo, a modern Pygmalion who has perfected a sculpting material, PCS10, that he uses in unorthodox plastic surgery procedures to remake the faces of wealthy patients. Jamie lives a life

of decadent riches until his operations begin breaking down in unforeseen ways with hideous results. This is the author's first novel.

**Other books you might like:**
Kobo Abe, *The Face of Another*, 1966
Randall Boyll, *Darkman*, 1990
Ariel Dorfman, *Mascara*, 1988
Steve Vance, *Spook*, 1990

## 1335

### DON D'AMMASSA
### ROBERT H. KNOW, Illustrator

## Twisted Images

(West Warwick, Rhode Island: Necronomicon Press, 1995)

**Story type:** Horror (Occult)
**Major character(s):** Alan Sheridan, Worker (Eblis Manufacturing); Chen Li, Young Woman; Tao Tieh, Aged Person
**Time period(s):** 1990s (1995)
**Locale(s):** Providence, Rhode Island

**Summary:** In this short story chapbook, Alan Sheridan moves into an apartment whose previous owner, a murder victim, left an ornately decorated Oriental mirror on the wall. His friendship with a young Asian woman in the building makes him aware of a legend of a secret world on the other side of the mirror and unfortunate mortals on this side in danger of being absorbed into it.

**Other books you might like:**
Gordon Linzner, *The Oni*, 1986
Bentley Little, *The Summoning*, 1993
Robert Morgan, *Some Things Never Die*, 1993
Donald Wandrei, *The Painted Mirror*, 1944
   in *The Eye and the Finger*
Kelley Wilde, *Angel Kiss*, 1993

## 1336

### TONY DANIEL

## Earthling

(New York: Tor, 1997)

**Story type:** Science Fiction (Robot Fiction; Alternate Intelligence)
**Major character(s):** Victor "Orf" Wu, Robot, Scientist (geologist); Andrew Hutton, Scientist (geologist); Jarrod, Government Official (forest ranger)
**Time period(s):** 2010s; 31st century (3020)
**Locale(s):** Pacific Northwest (Olympic Peninsula); Lilian River Valley, Washington

**Summary:** After his wife dies and his daughter leaves for California, Victor Wu continues to wander around the Olympic Peninsula, attempting to understand the forces at work there. He and Andrew discover a route that would get them very deep if they could afford the equipment. When Andred discovers an abandoned mining robot, he downloads the newly deceased Wu's memories into it and begins the deep path down. The robot inadvertently disturbs the emerginc consciousness of the area, triggering global disaster.

**Other books you might like:**
Roger MacBride Allen, *Caliban*, 1993
Isaac Asimov, *The Caves of Steel*, 1954
David Brin, *Earth*, 1990
Joan Slonczewski, *Daughter of Elysium*, 1993
Sheri S. Tepper, *Gibbon's Decline and Fall*, 1996
John Varley, *Steel Beach*, 1992

## 1337

**TONY DANIEL**

### *Warpath*

(New York: Tor, 1993)

**Story type:** Science Fiction (First Contact; Immortality)
**Major character(s):** Will James, Immortal, Publisher; Thomas Fall, Indian, Wanderer; Janey Calhoun, Alien (half chocalaca), Settler
**Time period(s):** 26th century (2563)
**Locale(s):** Candle, Planet—Imaginary

**Summary:** Reconstituted on Candle 500 years after his transmission from Earth, Will publishes the *Cold Truth*, a local newspaper for both the settlement of Jackson and Doom, the Mississippi Indian village. His friend, Thomas, carries a bit of clay containing a chocalaca, Raej, who protects him and allows him to travel faster than light alone in his canoe as the Mississippi Indians have done in pairs since the 11th century. Half chocalaca, Janey manipulates real space directly but without much control, perhaps leading to war between the settlers and Indians then throughout the universe. Author's first novel.

**Other books you might like:**
William Barton, *Dark Sky Legion*, 1992
Greg Bear, *Eon*, 1985
Jeffrey A. Carver, *Dragons in the Stars*, 1992
John DeChancie, *Starrigger*, 1983
Jack C. Haldeman II, *High Steel*, 1993
    Jack Dann, co-author
Alis A. Rasmussen, *A Passage of Stars*, 1990
Robert Silverberg, *Recalled to Life*, 1962
Vernor Vinge, *A Fire upon the Deep*, 1992

## 1338

**LES DANIELS**

### *No Blood Spilled*

(New York: Tor, 1990)

**Story type:** Horror (Vampire Story)
**Series:** Chronicles of Don Sebastian
**Major character(s):** Don Sebastian de Villanueva, Vampire; Reginald Calder, Mentally Ill Person; Christopher Hawke, Military Personnel
**Time period(s):** 1840s
**Locale(s):** India

**Summary:** Efforts by Don Sebastian de Villanueva to resurrect the Thuggee death cult of Kali worshipers are almost confounded by the deranged vengeance-seeking Reginald Calder, competing Thuggee leader Kalidas Sen, and Lt. Christopher Hawke of the 5th Fusiliers. Aiding Don Sebastian is a young Indian boy named Jamini who becomes his devoted servant. The conflict in this best of Daniels' Don Sebastian novels climaxes in an exciting finale set during a monsoon in the jungles north of Calcutta.

**Other books you might like:**
Dan Simmons, *Song of Kali*, 1985

## 1339

**JACK DANN**, Editor
**GARDNER DOZOIS**, Co-Editor

### *Angels!*

(New York: Ace, 1995)

**Story type:** Fantasy (Anthology; Religious)

**Summary:** Contains 12 stories and two poems about divine agents reprinted from periodicals and anthologies, with the tone varying from light to dark. Authors include Pat Cadigan, Philip K. Dick, Esther M. Friesner, Lisa Goldstein, Robert Silverberg, Kate Wilhelm, Jane Yolen, and Roger Zelazny.

**Other books you might like:**
Peter Crowther, *Heaven Sent: 18 Glorious Tales of the Angels*, 1995
    editor
Gardner Dozois, *The Year's Best Science Fiction Series*, 1984-1994
    editor
Neil Gaiman, *Good Omens: The Nice and Accurate Prophecies of Agnes Nutter, Witch*, 1990
    Terry Pratchett, co-author
Andrew M. Greeley, *Angel Light*, 1995
Alan Ryan, *Perpetual Light*, 1982
    editor
Sean Stewart, *Resurrection Man*, 1995

## 1340

**JACK DANN**, Editor
**GARDNER DOZOIS**, Co-Editor

### *Little People!*

(New York: Ace, 1991)

**Story type:** Fantasy (Anthology)

**Summary:** This thematic anthology contains brief introductions with 11 stories originally published in magazines and anthologies between 1939 and 1988. All stories feature mythical creatures thought of as short in stature such as elves, pixies, sprites, fairies, gremlins and leprechauns. Authors include Jack Dann, L. Sprague de Camp, Harlan Ellison, Horace L. Gold, Henry Kuttner, Theodore Sturgeon and Gene Wolfe. One story, ''Send No Money,'' is a collaboration between Susan Casper and Gardner Dozois.

**Other books you might like:**
Robin McKinley, *Imaginary Lands*, 1985
    editor
Baird Searles, *Halflings, Hobbits, Warrows & Weefolk: A Collection of Tales of Heroes Short in Stature*, 1991
    Brian Thomsen, co-editor
Terri Windling, *Elsewhere*, 1981
    Mark Alan Arnold, co-editor
Terri Windling, *Elsewhere II*, 1982
    Mark Alan Arnold, co-editor
Terri Windling, *Elsewhere III*, 1984
    Mark Alan Arnold, co-editor
Terri Windling, *Faery*, 1984
    editor

## 1341

**JACK DANN**

### The Memory Cathedral

(New York: Bantam, 1995)

**Story type:** Science Fiction (Alternate Universe; Political)
**Major character(s):** Leonardo da Vinci, Historical Figure, Inventor; Niccolo Machiavelli, Historical Figure, Apprentice; Sandro Botticelli, Historical Figure, Artist (painter)
**Time period(s):** 15th century
**Locale(s):** Florence, Italy; Middle East; Alternate Earth

**Summary:** As Leonardo da Vinci dies, he explores the carefully stored memories of a lifetime. He recalls a ruthless kidnapper forcing him to construct the fantastic machines he has designed, while employing them to an end which proves heartbreaking to the savant. Concludes with a four-page afterword by Dann.

**Other books you might like:**
Martin Amis, *Time's Arrow*, 1991
L. Sprague de Camp, *Lest Darkness Fall*, 1941
Leo Frankowski, *The Cross-Time Engineer*, 1986
Paul J. McAuley, *Pasquale's Angel*, 1995
Chelsea Quinn Yarbro, *Ariosto*, 1980

## 1342

**JACK DANN**, Editor

### Nebula Awards 32

(New York: Harcourt Brace, 1998)

**Story type:** Science Fiction (Anthology)

**Summary:** Subtitled "SFWA'S Choices for the Best Science Fiction and Fantasy of the Year," this volume contains a four-page introduction by the editor with a list of 1996 Nebula Award finalists and winners; comments by eight authors in "The Year in Science Fiction and Fantasy: A Symposium"; a 14-page article on fantastic films of 1996; two poems by Rysling Award winners Margaret Ballif Simon and Bruce Boston; six page appendix including selected titles from the preliminary ballot and a list of previous winners; "The Men Return" by Grand Master Award winner Jack Vance with appreciations by Robert Silverberg and Terry Dowling; plus individual introductions to eight other excerpts and stories by authors including Jack Dann, Esther M. Friesner, Nicola Griffith, Jonathan Lethem, Dean Wesley Smith and Harry Turtledove.

**Other books you might like:**
Michael Bishop, *Nebula Awards 23-25*, 1989-1991
    editor
Gardner Dozois, *The Year's Best Science Fiction Series*, 1984
    editor
James Morrow, *Nebula Awards 26-28*, 1992-1994
    editor
Pamela Sargent, *Nebula Awards 29-31*, 1995-1997
    editor
George Zebrowski, *Nebula Awards 21-22*, 1987-1988
    editor

## 1343

**JACK DANN**, Editor
**GARDNER DOZOIS**, Co-Editor

### Unicorns II

(New York: Ace, 1992)

**Story type:** Fantasy (Anthology; Legend)

**Summary:** Contains a two-page preface plus individual introductions to 10 stories reprinted from periodicals and anthologies from 1984 to 1991 and two originals, Jack C. Haldeman II's "Ghost Town" and Lawrence Watt-Evan's "Unicornicopia," all sharing the theme of the mythical unicorn. With Susan Casper and Gardner Dozois collaborating on one story, other authors include Michael Bishop, Jack Dann, Gregory Frost, Janet Kagan, Tanith Lee, Mike Resnick, Patricia C. Wrede and Jane Yolen. Concludes with a short bibliography.

**Other books you might like:**
Peter S. Beagle, *The Last Unicorn*, 1968
Michael Bishop, *Unicorn Mountain*, 1988
Bruce Coville, *The Unicorn Treasury*, 1988
    editor
Pamela Dean, *The Secret Country*, 1985
Mark S. Geston, *The Siege of Wonder*, 1976
Tanith Lee, *Black Unicorn*, 1991
Madeleine L'Engle, *A Swiftly Tilting Planet*, 1978
Mike Resnick, *Stalking the Unicorn: A Fable of Tonight*, 1987

## 1344

**JOSHUA DANN**

### Timeshare

(New York: Ace, 1997)

**Story type:** Science Fiction (Time Travel; Arts)
**Major character(s):** John Surrey, Time Traveler, Security Officer; Althea Rowland, Actress; Cornelia Hazelhof, Businesswoman, Genius
**Time period(s):** 2000s (2006); 1940s (1940)
**Locale(s):** California

**Summary:** John Surrey, vice-president of security for Timeshares Unlimited, travels in time and meets John Wayne and his own grandfather, helps Ian Fleming capture a Nazi agent and lands a bit part in *The Maltese Falcon*. He also falls in love with Althea Rowland who, despite his persuasive efforts, returns to England to join the Women's Air Corps. From his own time, John learns of Althea's death in World War II. John thinks of going back to his old police job, but Cornelia makes him a better offer.

**Other books you might like:**
Dennis Lee Anderson, *Arthur, King*, 1995
Poul Anderson, *Time Patrolman*, 1983
David Evans, *Time Station London*, 1996
Harry Harrison, *The Technicolor Time Machine*, 1967
H.G. Wells, *The Time Machine*, 1895

## 1345

**JOSHUA DANN**

### Timeshare: Second Time Around

(New York: Ace, 1998)

**Story type:** Science Fiction (Time Travel)
**Series:** Time Share

**Major character(s):** John Surrey, Time Traveler; Al Capone, Historical Figure, Organized Crime Figure
**Time period(s):** 1920s
**Locale(s):** Chicago, Illinois; New York, New York

**Summary:** A filmmaker takes a vacation in time but disappears rather than returning to his home in the 21st century. John Surrey travels back to retrieve him, but in order to do so he must become intimate with a number of historical figures, the most significant of whom is gangster Al Capone.

**Other books you might like:**
Poul Anderson, *Time Patrolman*, 1983
John Brunner, *Timescoop*, 1969
Robert A. Heinlein, *The Door into Summer*, 1957
James P. Hogan, *Thrice upon a Time*, 1980
Lisa Mason, *Summer of Love*, 1994

---

**1346**

**WILLIAM DANTZ** (Pseudonym of Rodman Philbrick)

## Hunger

(New York: Tor, 1992)

**Story type:** Horror (Nature in Revolt; Science Fiction)
**Major character(s):** Sally Hart, Sailor (charter boat captain); Thomas J. Hart, Sailor (charter boat captain); Vernon Speke, Scientist (marine biologist)
**Time period(s):** 1990s
**Locale(s):** Key West, Florida

**Summary:** The escape of a half-dozen ravenous, genetically-engineered great white sharks from the Sealife Research Institute into tourist-infested waters off the Florida Keys pits a pair of animal-loving skindivers against the scientist who has been training the sharks as a new weapon for the Department of Defense.

**Other books you might like:**
Peter Benchley, *Beast*, 1991
Peter Benchley, *Jaws*, 1974
T.J. Kirby, *Deadly Breed*, 1991
Dean R. Koontz, *Watchers*, 1987
J.M. Morgan, *Between the Devil and the Deep*, 1992

---

**1347**

**WILLIAM DANTZ** (Pseudonym of Rodman Philbrick)

## Nine Levels Down

(New York: Tor, 1995)

**Story type:** Horror (Psychological Suspense)
**Major character(s):** Anna Kane, Psychologist; John Marlon, Criminal; Kevin McRay, Police Officer
**Time period(s):** 1990s (1995)
**Locale(s):** New York, New York

**Summary:** Psychologist Anna Kane has developed an implant device that can neutralize the worst psychopathic impulses in her murderous patients. It proves all for nought when criminal patient John Marlon abducts her into the New York subway system, where he has kidnapped numerous other victims whom he has tortured fiendishly.

**Other books you might like:**
Michael Crichton, *The Terminal Man*, 1972
Richard Laymon, *Midnight's Lair*, 1988
Chet Williamson, *Lowland Rider*, 1988
F. Paul Wilson, *Implant*, 1995

---

**1348**

**DENNIS DANVERS**

## Circuit of Heaven

(New York: Avon Eos, 1998)

**Story type:** Science Fiction (Cyberpunk; Post-Disaster)
**Major character(s):** Justine Ingham, Singer, Artificial Intelligence; Newman "Nemo" Thorne, Trader; Newman "Warren G. Menso" Rogers, Genius, Disembodied Personality
**Time period(s):** 2080s (2081)
**Locale(s):** Richmond, Virginia; Washington, District of Columbia; The Bin, Cyberspace

**Summary:** Newly arrived in the Bin, Justine dreams the memories of three other women, and has access only to memories of her own. Nemo resents his parents entering the Bin when he was only 11, leaving him in the care of Lawrence the dinosaur, a construct of three people in a genetically manipulated body. While visiting them in the Bin for his 21st birthday, Nemo and Justine meet and fall in love. Unfortunately, Nemo doesn't want to enter the Bin permanently, while Justine can't leave.

**Other books you might like:**
James C. Bassett, *Living Real*, 1997
Greg Bear, *Blood Music*, 1985
Tom Cool, *Infectress*, 1997
J.R. Dunn, *Full Tide of Night*, 1998
Ian McDonald, *Terminal Cafe*, 1994
Janine Ellen Young, *Cinderblock*, 1997

---

**1349**

**DENNIS DANVERS**

## Wilderness

(New York: Poseidon, 1991)

**Story type:** Horror (Werewolf Story)
**Major character(s):** Alice White, Travel Agent, Werewolf; Erik Summers, Scientist (biologist), Professor; Luther Adams, Doctor (psychiatrist)
**Time period(s):** 1990s
**Locale(s):** Richmond, Virginia

**Summary:** This first novel about the sacrifices of love tells the poignant tale of Alice White, who risks her chance for romantic fulfillment and personal freedom when she confesses to her boyfriend not only that she is a werewolf, but that she has killed a man during her feral transformation.

**Other books you might like:**
Peter S. Beagle, *Lila the Werewolf*, 1969
Scott Bradfield, *Dream of the Wolf*, 1990
Michael Cadnum, *St. Peter's Wolf*, 1991
Charles de Lint, *Wolf Moon*, 1988
Dean R. Koontz, *Watchers*, 1987
Thomas Tessier, *The Nightwalker*, 1979

---

**1350**

**M.P. DARE**

## Unholy Relics

(Ashcroft, British Columbia: Ash-Tree Press, 1997)

**Story type:** Horror (Collection; Ghost Story)

**Summary:** Thirteen antiquarian ghost stories, intended to be in the tradition of M.R. James. Included are ''The Haunted Drawers,'' about a dresser imbued with the spirit of a writer whose letters are hidden in it; ''A Nun's Tragedy,'' in which an abbey is haunted by the ghost of nun walled-up there; ''The Fatal Oak,'' in which commonplace objects made from the wood of a gibbet are endowed with the power to kill evil people; ''Bring Out Your Dead,'' in which a skull stolen from an ossuary resurrects the black plague that killed its owner; and the title story, in which sacred relics of the dead are protected by animated skeletons. The original 1947 edition has been embellished with two essays, ''Beyond the Veil'' and ''Ghosts I Have Met.'' Introduction by Reg Meuross.

**Other books you might like:**
A.M. Burrage, *Some Ghost Stories*, 1927
Ingulphus, *Tedious Brief Tales of Granta and Gramarye*, 1919
    pseudonym of Arthur Gray
R.H. Malden, *Nine Ghosts*, 1943
A.N.L. Munby, *The Alabaster Hand and Other Ghost Stories*, 1949
L.T.C. Rolt, *Sleep No More*, 1948
E.G. Swain, *The Stoneground Ghost Tales*, 1912

---

**1351**

### LARRY DARK

## *The Literary Ghost*

(New York: Atlantic Monthly Press, 1991)

**Story type:** Horror (Anthology; Ghost Story)

**Summary:** Twenty-eight classic and contemporary ghost stories by writers whose work falls largely outside the horror and fantasy genres. Included are Tim O'Brien's tale of the horrors of the Vietnam War, ''The Ghost Soldiers''; Graham Greene's gruesome shocker of a revelation in a movie theater, ''A Little Place Off the Edgware Road''; Joyce Carol Oates' tale of a strange ritual noted among evening commuters and other members of the living dead, ''The Others''; and Patrick McGrath's extraordinary Gothic pastiche ''Marmilion.''

**Other books you might like:**
Bradford Morrow, *The New Gothic*, 1992
    Patrick McGrath, co-author
Robert Phillips, *Triumph of the Night*, 1988

---

**1352**

### DAVID DARKE (Pseudonym of Ron Dee)

## *Blind Hunger*

(New York: Pinnacle, 1993)

**Story type:** Horror (Vampire Story)
**Major character(s):** Patty Hunsacker, Widow(er), Handicapped (blind); Matt Hunsacker, Vampire; Chris Mikel, Child
**Time period(s):** 1990s (1993)
**Locale(s):** Nesoho, Missouri

**Summary:** Mark, the supposed twin brother of Matt Hunsacker, comes to stay with Matt's blind wife Patty after the untimely and inexplicable death of her husband. But Patty's senses tell her that Mark is actually Matt, risen from the grave as a vampire and intent on using their house as a base of operations for his regular feedings.

**Other books you might like:**
Lee Weathersby, *Kiss of the Vampire*, 1992
T. Lucien Wright, *Blood Brothers*, 1992

---

**1353**

### DAVID DARKE (Pseudonym of Ron Dee)

## *Horrorshow*

(New York: Zebra, 1994)

**Story type:** Horror (Small Town Horror)
**Major character(s):** Greg Driver, Actor; Jim, Actor; Dennis ''Druzeppa'' Thudd, Actor
**Time period(s):** 1990s (1995)
**Locale(s):** Twainton

**Summary:** As part of their plan to launch their careers as actors, Greg and Jim use their Halloween show on the local Twainton television station to air the final tape of Druzeppa, a monster movie host who died under mysterious circumstances while on the air 20 years before. Their action brings Druzeppa back from the dead to continue the satanic mission he was prevented from fulfilling before his death: urging the townspeople on to a life of debauchery and mayhem.

**Other books you might like:**
Dale Hoover, *65mm*, 1994
Jack Martin, *Videodrome*, 1982
Theodore Roszak, *Flicker*, 1993
Brad Strickland, *Shadowshow*, 1988

---

**1354**

### DAVID DARKE (Pseudonym of Ron Dee)

## *Last Rites*

(New York: Zebra, 1996)

**Story type:** Horror (Black Magic)
**Major character(s):** Betsy Walker, Femme Fatale; Gary Carpenter, Businessman; Tonia Carpenter, Artist
**Time period(s):** 1990s (1996)
**Locale(s):** Tulsa, Oklahoma

**Summary:** Following their high school reunion, a group of friends agrees to revive the Necro Club, a black magic coven they joined as teenagers in order to resurrect the dead and see into the future. When their plans go awry, it results in a deadly power struggle among themselves.

**Other books you might like:**
Leigh Clark, *Blood Sabbath*, 1991
Ed Kelleher, *The School*, 1988
    Harriette Vidal, co-author
Mark Morris, *Stitch*, 1992
R.L. Stine, *Superstitious*, 1995
Tamara Thorne, *Moonfall*, 1996

---

**1355**

### DAVID DARKE (Pseudonym of Ron Dee)

## *Shade*

(New York: Zebra, 1994)

**Story type:** Horror (Vampire Story)
**Major character(s):** Scarlett Shade, Writer, Vampire
**Time period(s):** 1990s (1994)
**Locale(s):** Norman, Oklahoma

**Summary:** Bestselling writer of vampire fiction Scarlett Shade turns out to be a real vampire who feeds off the ''scarlett fever'' of amorality and sexual abandon that her novels inspire in her devoted fans.

**Other books you might like:**
Steven Brust, *Agyar*, 1993
Tanya Huff, *Blood Price*, 1991
Anne Rice, *The Vampire Lestat*, 1985
T. Lucien Wright, *Blood Brothers*, 1991

## 1356

### DIANA DARLING

## The Painted Alphabet
(New York: Houghton Mifflin, 1992)

**Story type:** Fantasy (Legend; Religious)
**Major character(s):** Siladri, Farmer; Mpu Dibiaja, Shaman; Dayu Datu, Witch
**Time period(s):** Indeterminate
**Locale(s):** Bali, Indonesia

**Summary:** In this modern first novel, based on an ancient Balinese epic poem, Siladri, a farmer with a loving, happy family, decides to go to the mountains to study with a spiritual advisor. He leaves his infant son with his brother and takes his infant niece at his brother's insistence. His wife, taken on an expedition to the mountains as a child, hates and fears the mountains and refuses to let Siladri go alone.

**Other books you might like:**
Maya Kaathryn Bohnhoff, *The Meri*, 1992
Charles de Lint, *The Little Country*, 1990
Monica Hughes, *Sandwriter*, 1988
Barry Lopez, *Crow and Weasel*, 1990
Robin Morgan, *The Mer-Child: A Legend for Children and Other Adults*, 1991
Antoine de Saint-Exupery, *The Little Prince*, 1943
Lucius Shepard, *Kalimantan*, 1992

## 1357

### ELLEN DATLOW, Editor

## Alien Sex
(New York: Dutton, 1990)

**Story type:** Horror (Anthology; Science Fiction)

**Summary:** Nineteen tales and poems of science fiction, fantasy and horror concerned with the sexuality of humans and non-humans and the alienating potential of sexual relationships between men and women. Best stories include K.W. Jeter's brilliant ''The First Time,'' about a young boy's rite of passage into adulthood; Lisa Tuttle's ''Husbands,'' an inquiry into the unbridgeable differences between men and women; and Lewis Shiner's ''Scales,'' about a lamia who brings about the destruction of a marriage. With author and editor notes for each story.

**Other books you might like:**
Margaret L. Carter, *Demon Lovers and Strange Seductions*, 1973
Don Congdon, *Tales of Love and Horror*, 1961
Jeff Gelb, *Hotter Blood: More Tales of Erotic Horror*, 1991
    Michael Garrett, co-author
Jeff Gelb, *Hot Blood: Tales of Provocative Horror*, 1989
    Lonn Friend, co-author
Michele Slung, *I Shudder at Your Touch*, 1991

## 1358

### ELLEN DATLOW, Editor
### TERRI WINDLING, Co-Editor

## Black Swan, White Raven
(New York: Avon, 1997)

**Story type:** Fantasy (Anthology; Legend)

**Summary:** Five-page introduction and individual introductions to 21 original stories, frequently dark in tone, which explore themes of classic fairy tales or rework familiar tales such as, ''Sleeping Beauty,'' ''Little Red Riding Hood,'' ''Thumbelina,'' ''Rumpelstiltskin,'' '' The Little Match Girl,'' ''Hansel and Gretel,'' ''Rapunzel,'' ''The Tinder Box'' and ''Snow White and the Seven Dwarves.'' Authors include Michael Blumlein, Michael Cadnum, John Crowley, Karen Joy Fowler, Esther M. Friesner, Gregory Frost, Nina Kiriki Hoffman, Garry Kilworth, Nancy Kress, Pat Murphy, Joyce Carol Oats, Midori Snyder, Steve Rasnic Tem, and Jane Yolen.

**Other books you might like:**
A.S. Byatt, *The Djinn in the Nightingale's Eye*, 1997
Kara Dalkey, *The Nightingale*, 1988
Emma Donoghue, *Kissing the Witch: Old Tales in New Skins*, 1997
Robin McKinley, *Deerskin*, 1993
Delia Sherman, *The Porcelain Dove*, 1993
Terri Windling, *The Armless Maiden and Other Tales for Childhood's Survivors*, 1995
    editor
Terri Windling, *The Wood Wife*, 1996
Jane Yolen, *Briar Rose*, 1992

## 1359

### ELLEN DATLOW, Editor
### TERRI WINDLING, Co-Editor

## Black Thorn, White Rose
(New York: Tor, 1994)

**Story type:** Fantasy (Anthology; Legend)

**Summary:** Contains five pages of recommended reading, a six-page introduction by Datlow and Windling plus individual introductions to one poem, one unusual recipe and 16 original stories which retell cherished fairy tales utilizing a darker and sexier tone for adults. Authors include Michael Cadnum, Storm Constantine, Ann Elizabeth Downer, Michael Kandel, Nancy Kress, Daniel Quinn, Midori Snyder, Peter Straub, Howard Waldrop, Patricia C. Wrede, Jane Yolen and Roger Zelazny.

**Other books you might like:**
Lester Del Rey, *Once upon a Time: A Treasury of Modern Fairy Tales*, 1991
    Risa Kessler, co-editor
Tanith Lee, *Red as Blood: Or Tales from the Sisters Grimmer*, 1983
Terri Windling, *Life on the Border*, 1991
    editor
Jane Yolen, *The Xanadu Series*, 1993-1995
    editor
Jack Zipes, *Beauties, Beasts and Enchantments*, 1989
    editor

## 1360

**ELLEN DATLOW**, Editor

### *Blood Is Not Enough*

(New York: Berkley, 1990)

**Story type:** Horror (Anthology; Vampire Story)

**Summary:** Seventeen stories that expand the boundaries of the traditional vampire tale in their exploration of the relationship between the victim and the victimizer. Highlights include Fritz Leiber's classic of exploitative advertising, "The Girl with the Hungry Eyes," Gardner Dozois and Jack Dann's controversial tale of the victims of a concentration camp vampire, "Down Among the Dead Men," Gahan Wilson's nasty interpretation of Lewis Carroll, "The Sea Was Wet as Wet Could Be," Tanith Lee's tale of debilitating illness, "The Janfia Tree," and Dan Simmons' story of psychic vampirism, "Carrion Comfort," which became the basis for his Bram Stoker Award-winning novel of the same title. Reprint of a 1989 hardcover.

**Other books you might like:**
Richard Dalby, *Dracula's Brood*, 1987
Martin H. Greenberg, *Vamps*, 1987
   Charles G. Waugh, co-author
Alan Ryan, *Vampires: Two Centuries of Great Vampire Stories*, 1987
Leslie Shepard, *The Dracula Book of Great Vampire Stories*, 1977

## 1361

**ELLEN DATLOW**, Editor

### *Little Deaths*

(New York: Dell, 1995)

**Story type:** Horror (Anthology)

**Summary:** The sixteen tales of erotic horror collected here have been distilled from the British version of this anthology, which appeared earlier in 1995 and contained twenty-four stories. Included are Stephen Dedman's "The Lady of Situations," and Lucy Taylor's "Hungry Skin," both tales with sadomasochistic subtexts, and Nicholas Royle's "The Swing," which metaphorically likens a relationship to the tethering of two individuals. Joel Lane, in "The Pain Barrier," blurs the boundaries between film and reality in his tale of a man who discovers the film star he has fallen for lives in the same dwelling used as the backdrop for his transgressive films. Joyce Carol Oates' "Fever Blisters" is a nightmarish story of a couple trying to recapture the ecstacy of their first sexual experience years after they know the horrible consequences it has wrought. Jack Womack's "That Old School Tie," concerns a teacher whose interest in a student's chaos theory of literature draws him into kinky escapades. In Richard Christian Matheson's "Menage a Trois," a man and woman develop an unusual relationship with the knife they use in sadomasochistic rituals.

**Other books you might like:**
Jeff Gelb, *Hot Blood: Tales of Provocative Horror*, 1989
   Lonn Friend, co-editor
Jeff Gelb, *Deadly After Dark*, 1994
   Michael Garrett, co-editor
Jeff Gelb, *Seeds of Fear*, 1995
   Michael Garrett, co-editor
Jeff Gelb, *Stranger by Night*, 1995
   Michael Garrett, co-editor
Jeff Gelb, *Hotter Blood: More Tales of Erotic Horror*, 1991
   Michael Garrett, co-editor

Jeff Gelb, *Hottest Blood: The Ultimate in Erotic Horror*, 1993
   Michael Garrett, co-editor
Michele Slung, *I Shudder at Your Touch*, 1991
   editor
Michele Slung, *Shudder Again*, 1993
   editor

## 1362

**ELLEN DATLOW**, Editor

### *Off Limits: Tales of Alien Sex*

(New York: St. Martin's Press, 1996)

**Story type:** Science Fiction (Anthology)

**Summary:** Contains a three-page foreword by Rober Silverberg, a three-page introduction plus individual introductions by Datlow and authors' afterwords to four stories reprinted from periodicals and anthologies 1970-1993, original poems by Joe Haldeman and Jane Yolen, and 15 original stories. Stories are frequently dark in tone, all focusing on sex, with other themes such as disease, prostitution, dystopias, communication, gender politics, and power. Other authors include Samuel R. Delany, Neil Gaiman, Elizabeth Hand, Simon Ings, Gwyneth Jones, Bruce McAllister, Joyce Carol Oates, Martha Soukup, and Lisa Tuttle.

**Other books you might like:**
Octavia E. Butler, *Dawn*, 1987
Joseph Elder, *Eros in Orbit*, 1973
   editor
Philip Jose Farmer, *Strange Relations*, 1960
Richard Glyn Jones, *Cybersex*, 1996
   editor
Ursula K. Le Guin, *The Left Hand of Darkness*, 1969
Thomas N. Scortia, *Strange Bedfellows: Sex and Science Fiction*, 1972
   editor
Dan Simmons, *Lovedeath*, 1993
Theodore Sturgeon, *Venus Plus X*, 1960

## 1363

**ELLEN DATLOW**, Editor

### *Omni Best Science Fiction One*

(New York: Omni Books, 1992)

**Story type:** Science Fiction (Anthology)

**Summary:** Contains six original stories and four reprinted from *Omni*, 1986-1987, with themes including arts, cyberpunk, first contact, genetic manipulation, and satire. Original story authors include Richard Kadrey, Elizabeth A. Lynn, Paul Park, and Robert Silverberg. Reprinted stories appear by Neal Barrett, Jr., Suzy McKee Charnas, Jack Dann, and Tom Maddox, whose "Snake Eyes" expands the world of *Halo* (1991).

**Other books you might like:**
Lou Aronica, *Full Spectrum*, 1988
   Shawna McCarthy, co-editor
Lou Aronica, *Full Spectrum 2*, 1990
   Shawna McCarthy, co-editor
Lou Aronica, *Full Spectrum 3*, 1991
   Amy Stout and Betsy Mitchell, co-editors
Michael Bishop, *Nebula Awards 25*, 1991
   editor

Gardner Dozois, *The Year's Best Science Fiction: Eighth Annual Collection*, 1991
editor
Kristine Kathryn Rusch, *The Best of Pulphouse: The Hardback Magazine*, 1991
editor
Robert Silverberg, *Universe 1*, 1990
Karen Haber, co-editor
Robert Silverberg, *Universe 2*, 1992
Karen Haber, co-editor

### 1364

**ELLEN DATLOW**, Editor

## *Omni Best Science Fiction Three*

(Greensborough, North Carolina: Omni Books, 1993)

**Story type:** Science Fiction (Anthology)
**Series:** Omni Best Science Fiction

**Summary:** Contains a two-page introduction, individual story introductions, Thomas M. Disch's story, "Palindrome," reprinted from *Omni* plus 10 original stories, many containing sexual themes, by authors including Pat Cadigan, John Crowley, Ursula K. Le Guin, Ian McDonald, Pat Murphy and Gahan Wilson.

**Other books you might like:**
Lou Aronica, *Full Spectrum 4*, 1993
Amy Stout, Betsy Mitchell, co-editors
Gardner Dozois, *The Year's Best Science Fiction: Tenth Annual Collection*, 1993
editor
Kristine Kathryn Rusch, *The Best of Pulphouse: The Hardback Magazine*, 1991
editor
Robert Silverberg, *Universe 1*, 1990
Karen Haber, co-editor
Robert Silverberg, *Universe 2*, 1992
Karen Haber, co-editor

### 1365

**ELLEN DATLOW**, Editor

## *Omni Visions One*

(Greensborough, North Carolina: Omni Books, 1993)

**Story type:** Science Fiction (Anthology)
**Series:** Omni Visions

**Summary:** Contains a one-page introduction plus individual introductions to an original Joyce Carol Oates story and nine stories published in *Omni* 1986-1989. Themes include alternate universes, fantasy, ecological disaster, early radio broadcasting, missed chances and human illness with many stories dark in tone. Authors include James P. Blaylock, William S. Burroughs, Octavia E. Butler, Marc Laidlaw, Michael Swanwick and Howard Waldrop.

**Other books you might like:**
Lou Aronica, *Full Spectrum*, 1988
Shawna McCarthy, co-editor
Lou Aronica, *Full Spectrum 2*, 1990
Shawna McCarthy, Amy Stout, Patrick LoBrutto, co-editors
Gardner Dozois, *The Year's Best Science Fiction: Tenth Annual Collection*, 1993
editor
James Morrow, *Nebula Awards 27*, 1993
editor

Kristine Kathryn Rusch, *The Best of Pulphouse: The Hardback Magazine*, 1991
editor
Robert Silverberg, *Universe 1*, 1990
Karen Haber, co-editor
Robert Silverberg, *Universe 2*, 1992
Karen Haber, co-editor

### 1366

**ELLEN DATLOW**, Editor
**TERRI WINDLING**, Co-Editor

## *Ruby Slippers, Golden Tears*

(New York: AvoNova/Morrow, 1995)

**Story type:** Fantasy (Anthology; Legend)
**Series:** Snow White, Blood Red

**Summary:** Contains eight pages of recommended reading, a seven-page introduction by Windling and Datlow plus individual introductions to three poems and 19 original literary fairy tales with themes including high fantasy, the complications of modern life and horror. Also included are familiar stories in new guises, such as "Rumplestiltskin," "Puss in Boots," "The Princess and the Pea," and "Snow White," as well as other tales from Asia, Europe, and North America. Authors include John Brunner, Michael Cadnum, Nancy A. Collins, Neil Gaiman, Lisa Goldstein, Joyce Carol Oates, Susan Palwick, Delia Sherman, Gahan Wilson, Gene Wolfe, and Jane Yolen.

**Other books you might like:**
Lester Del Rey, *Once upon a Time: A Treasury of Modern Fairy Tales*, 1991
Risa Kessler, co-editor
Tanith Lee, *Red as Blood: Or Tales from the Sisters Grimmer*, 1983
Vivian Vande Velde, *Tales From the Brothers Grimm and the Sisters Weird*, 1995
Terri Windling, *The Armless Maiden and Other Tales for Childhood's Survivors*, 1995
editor
Jane Yolen, *The Xanadu Series*, 1993-1995
editor
Jack Zipes, *Don't Bet on the Prince*, 1986
editor
Jack Zipes, *The Outspoken Princess and the Gentle Knight*, 1994
editor

### 1367

**ELLEN DATLOW**, Editor
**TERRI WINDLING**, Co-Editor

## *Sirens and Other Daemon Lovers*

(New York: Harper, 1998)

**Story type:** Horror (Anthology)

**Summary:** These 22 erotic tales of fantasy and horror are all original to this volume. Selections include Joyce Carol Oates' "Broke Heart Blues," about an incubus-like boy who haunts the women of an upstate New York town; Nail Gaiman's "Tastings," in which a woman vampirically drains her lovers of their memories during sex; and Doris Egan's sexy vampire detective story "The Sweet of Bitter Bark and Burning Clove."

**Other books you might like:**
Margaret L. Carter, *Demon Lovers and Strange Seductions*, 1973
editor

Nancy A. Collins, *Dark Love*, 1995
　Edward E. Kramer, Martin H. Greenberg, co-editors
Ellen Datlow, *Little Deaths*, 1994
　editor
Jeff Gelb, *Hot Blood*, 1989
　Michael Garrett, co-editor
Michele Slung, *I Shudder at Your Touch*, 1991
　editor

## 1368

**ELLEN DATLOW**, Editor
**TERRI WINDLING**, Co-Editor

### Snow White, Blood Red

(New York: Morrow AvoNova, 1993)

**Story type:** Fantasy (Anthology; Legend)
**Series:** Snow White, Blood Red

**Summary:** Emphasizing the roots and archetypal imagery of the ancient fairy tale tradition, this volume contains a 14-page introduction by Terri Windling, ''White as Snow: Fairy Tale and Fantasy''; a six-page introduction by Ellen Datlow, ''Red as Blood: Fairy Tales and Horror''; and individual introductions to 20 original stories, frequently dark in tone, by authors including Jack Dann, Charles de Lint, Esther M. Friesner, Gregory Frost, Neil Gaiman, Kathe Koja, Nancy Kress, Tanith Lee, Elizabeth A. Lynn, Patricia A. McKillip, Gahan Wilson and Jane Yolen.

**Other books you might like:**
Lester Del Rey, *Once upon a Time: A Treasury of Modern Fairy Tales*, 1991
　Risa Kessler, co-editor
Terri Windling, *Borderland*, 1986
　Mark Alan Arnold, co-editor
Terri Windling, *Elsewhere*, 1981
　Mark Alan Arnold, co-editor
Terri Windling, *Elsewhere II*, 1982
　Mark Alan Arnold, co-editor
Terri Windling, *Faery*, 1984
Terri Windling, *Life on the Border*, 1991
　editor
Jane Yolen, *Xanadu*, 1993
　editor
Jack Zipes, *Spells of Enchantment*, 1991
　editor, translator

## 1369

**ELLEN DATLOW**, Editor

### Twists of the Tale

(New York: Dell, 1996)

**Story type:** Horror (Anthology)

**Summary:** Cats and their interests feature in 20 original stories and two reprints in this compilation. Among the best stories are Michael Marshall Smith's ''Not Waving,'' which frames a love triangle in terms of feline mythology; Kathe Koja and Barry Malzberg's ''Homage to Custom,'' which concerns a derelict woman who develops a psychic link with a feline; Douglas Clegg's ''The Five,'' a tale of family dysfunction in which cats become pawns in a game of cruelty between parents and children; Michael Cadnum's ''The Man Who Did Cats Harm,'' about feline revenge on a man who has killed one of their number; Gahan Wilson's ''Best Friends,'' which shows how cats actually own people as their pets; and Joyce Carol Oates'

''Nobody Knows My Name,'' a riff on the superstition that cats can suck the breath from the living while they sleep.

**Other books you might like:**
Jack Dann, *Magicats!*, 1984
　Gardner Dozois, co-editor
Claire Necker, *Supernatural Cats*, 1972
　editor
Andre Norton, *Catfantastic*, 1989
　Martin H. Greenberg, co-editor
Michel Parry, *Beware of the Cat*, 1974
　editor

## 1370

**ELLEN DATLOW**, Editor

### A Whisper of Blood

(New York: Morrow, 1991)

**Story type:** Horror (Anthology; Vampire Story)

**Summary:** This collection of eighteen stories—three reprints, the rest new—explores, as its predecessor, *Blood Is Not Enough* did, the theme of vampirism through a variety of original and unlikely applications. Included are David Schow's ''A Week in the Unlife,'' about a vampire who feeds off of other vampires; Thomas Ligotti's ''Mrs. Rinaldi's Angel,'' about the parasitical nature of dreams; two stories that look at the vampiric nature of parent/child relationships, K.W. Jeter's ''True Love'' and Elizabeth Massie's ''M is for the Many Things''; Suzy McKee Charnas's ghost vampire tale, ''Now I Lay Me Down to Sleep''; Chelsea Quinn Yarbro's powerful tale of paranoia, ''Do I Dare to Eat a Peach''; and Robert Silverberg's classic of an empath who feeds off the misery of others, ''The Warm Man.''

**Other books you might like:**
Richard Dalby, *Dracula's Brood*, 1987
Martin H. Greenberg, *A Taste for Blood*, 1992
　Robert Weinberg and Stefan Dziemianowicz, co-editors
Martin H. Greenberg, *Vamps*, 1987
　Charles G. Waugh, co-editor
Alan Ryan, *Vampires: Two Centuries of Great Vampire Stories*, 1987
Leslie Shepard, *The Dracula Book of Great Vampire Stories*, 1977
　editor

## 1371

**ELLEN DATLOW**, Editor
**TERRI WINDLING**, Co-Editor

### The Year's Best Fantasy and Horror: Eleventh Annual Collection

(New York: St. Martin's, 1998)

**Story type:** Horror (Anthology)
**Series:** The Year's Best Fantasy and Horror

**Summary:** Thirty-eight stories and eight poems selected by the authors as the best short horror and fantasy published in a variety of anthologies and periodicals in 1997. Horror selections, which are chosen by Datlow, include Stephen Laws' ''The Crawl,'' which recounts the horrific pursuit of a couple across the British countryside by an animated scarecrow; Joyce Carol Oates' ''The Sky Blue Ball,'' in which a child's game of ball throwing with an unseen participant on the other side of a wall grows increasingly menacing; Charles L. Grant's ''Riding the Black,'' which captures the paranoia of the dawning nuclear age; and Gary A. Braunbeck's ''Safe,'' a meditation on serial killers and survival. Includes lengthy surveys of the year's offerings in fantasy and horror by the editors, plus survey essays on horror and fantasy in the media by Ed Bryant, a survey of the year in comics and graphic novels by Seth Johnson, and a necrology by James Frenkel.

**Other books you might like:**
Lin Carter, *The Year's Best Fantasy Stories Series*, 1974-1980
  editor
Stephen Jones, *The Mammoth Book of Best New Horror 9*, 1998
  editor
Arthur W. Saha, *The Year's Best Fantasy Stories Series*, 1981-1988
  editor
Karl Edward Wagner, *The Year's Best Horror Stories Series*, 1979-1994
  editor

---

**1372**

**ELLEN DATLOW**, Editor
**TERRI WINDLING**, Co-Editor

## The Year's Best Fantasy and Horror: Fifth Annual Collection

(New York: St. Martin's Press, 1992)

**Story type:** Horror (Anthology; Fantasy)

**Summary:** The fifth annual installment of this World Fantasy Award-winning series includes 44 stories and 6 poems, 26 of which fall within the purview of the horror genre. Included are two stories each by Kathe Koja and S. P. Somtow; vampire tales by Robert Holdstock, Gary Kilworth, and K. W. Jeter; Thomas Ligotti's story of a haunted movie theater, "The Glamour"; Dennis Etchison's non-supernatural chiller, "Call Home"; and Karl Edward Wagner's erotic horror story, "The Kind Men Like."

**Other books you might like:**
Stephen Jones, *Best New Horror*, 1990-1992
Robert Morrish, *The Quick Chills Series*, 1989-1992
  Peter Enfantino, co-editor
Karl Edward Wagner, *The Year's Best Horror Stories Series*, 1980-1992
  editor

---

**1373**

**ELLEN DATLOW**, Editor
**TERRI WINDLING**, Co-Editor

## The Year's Best Fantasy and Horror: Fourth Annual Collection

(New York: St. Martin's Press, 1991)

**Story type:** Fantasy (Anthology; Horror)

**Summary:** This volume includes 52 stories published in 1990 plus introductions and notes. Highlights include "The First Time" by K.W. Jeter, a brutal story about a young man's very different coming of age, and Charles de Lint's "Freewheeling" which mixes tragedy, whimsey, art and punk. As in previous collections, this volume presents a spectrum ranging from dark horror to whimsical, 'folksy' fantasy. Some major authors include Michael Bishop, Jonathan Carroll, Angela Carter, John Crowley, Karen Joy Fowler, T.E.D. Klein, Ellen Kushner, R.A. Lafferty, Joe Lansdale, Joyce Carol Oates and Lucius Shepard.

**Other books you might like:**
David G. Hartwell, *The Color of Evil*, 1987
  editor
Robert R. McCammon, *Under the Fang*, 1991
Kristine Kathryn Rusch, *The Best of Pulphouse: The Hardback Magazine*, 1991
  editor
Kristine Kathryn Rusch, *Pulphouse, Issue 6: Fantasy*, 1990
  editor
Kristine Kathryn Rusch, *Pulphouse, Issue 9: Dark Fantasy*, 1990
  editor
Karl Edward Wagner, *The Year's Best Horror Stories XIX*, 1991
  editor
Terri Windling, *Life on the Border*, 1991
  editor

---

**1374**

**ELLEN DATLOW**, Editor
**TERRI WINDLING**, Co-Editor

## The Year's Best Fantasy and Horror: Ninth Annual Collection

(New York: St. Martin's, 1996)

**Story type:** Horror (Anthology; Fantasy)

**Summary:** Datlow, who covers the horror end, and Windling, who selects the fantasy, choose 35 stories and 11 poems representing the best to appear in 1995. Horror highlights include Stephen King's Bram Stoker Award-winning "Lunch in the Gotham Cafe," about a psychopathic *maitre'd* on the loose in a Manhattan restaurant; Douglas Winter's "Loop," in which a man's obsession with a film starlet turns psychopathological; Michael Marshall Smith's tale of Internet terror, "More Tomorrow"; David Schow's "Refrigerator Heaven," a torture tale of imprisonment; Terry Lamsley's "Screens," in which a man discovers a macabre other life occurring at the home of a neighbor; and Tanith Lee's "La Dame," an allegorical tale of a man and the sea in a vampiric relationship. Fantasy efforts include Nina Kiriki Hoffman's domestic magic tale, "Home for Christmas"; Midori Snyder's riff on an old folk theme, "King of Crows"; and Peter S. Beagle's talking rhinoceros tale, "Professor Gottesman and the Indian Rhinoceros." Each editor supplies an essay surveying her respective field for the year, Ed Bryant wraps up films for the year, and Jim Frenkel supplies obituaries for 1995.

**Other books you might like:**
Lin Carter, *The Year's Best Fantasy Stories Series*, 1974-1980
  editor
Stephen Jones, *The Mammoth Book of Best New Horror*, 1996
  editor
Arthur W. Saha, *The Year's Best Fantasy Stories*, 1981-1988
  editor
Karl Edward Wagner, *The Year's Best Horror Stories Series*, 1979-1994
  editor

## 1375

**ELLEN DATLOW**, Editor
**TERRI WINDLING**, Co-Editor

### The Year's Best Fantasy and Horror: Seventh Annual Collection

(New York: St. Martin's, 1994)

**Story type:** Horror (Anthology; Fantasy)

**Summary:** The most recent installment in this World Fantasy Award-winning compilation of outstanding fantasy and horror fiction collects 54 stories from a wide range of mainstream and genre markets. Included are Fred Chappell's World Fantasy Award-winning ''The Lodger,'' an amusing tale of a librarian possessed by the soul of a hack poet; John Coyne's psychological horror story, ''Snow Man''; Elizabeth Hand's ''The Erl King,'' which recasts the classic folk tale as a parable for the age of rock 'n' roll; Graham Masterton's ''The Taking of Mr. Bill,'' Nicholas Royle's ''The Crucian Pit,'' and Nancy Collins' ''The Sunday-Go-to-Meeting Jaw,'' all zombie stories; Neil Gaiman's ''Troll Bridge,'' a retelling of the story of the three Billy Goats gruff as a parable about aging gracefully; Thomas Tessier's ''The Last Crossing,'' a tale of marital infidelity and murder; and Robert Westall's ''In Camera,'' a mystery story with supernatural overtones. The book is prefaced with overviews of the year in horror, fantasy and film.

**Other books you might like:**
Karl Edward Wagner, *The Year's Best Horror Stories XXII*, 1994

## 1376

**ELLEN DATLOW**, Editor
**TERRI WINDLING**, Co-Editor

### The Year's Best Fantasy and Horror: Sixth Annual Collection

(New York: St. Martin's, 1993)

**Story type:** Horror (Anthology; Fantasy)

**Summary:** The sixth installment in this award-winning annual series brings together 53 tales of fantasy and horror chosen by the editors as the best in their respective fields. Included are Poppy Brite's tale of the living dead in India, ''Calcutta, Lord of Nerves''; Neil Gaiman's retelling of the fall of Lucifer as a hardboiled mystery, ''Murder Mysteries''; Joyce Carol Oates' allegory of rigidly enforced sexual roles, ''Martyrdom''; Ed Gorman's sensitive story of the stigma of deformity, ''The Ugly File''; Clive Barker's spectral fantasy, ''Hermione and the Moon''; and Peter Straub's tale of the heart of darkness in Vietnam, ''The Ghost Village.'' The editors and critic Ed Bryant provide invaluable overviews of the year in fantasy, horror and film.

**Other books you might like:**
Stephen Jones, *Best New Horror 4*, 1993
    Ramsey Campbell, co-editor
Karl Edward Wagner, *The Year's Best Horror Stories XXI*, 1993
    editor

## 1377

**ELLEN DATLOW**, Editor
**TERRI WINDLING**, Co-Editor

### The Year's Best Fantasy and Horror: Tenth Annual Collection

(New York: St. Martin's, 1997)

**Story type:** Horror (Anthology)
**Series:** The Year's Best Fantasy and Horror

**Summary:** The most recent volume in this award-winning series reprints 39 stories and four poems from 1996, representative of the year's best fantasy and horror. Approximately half of the selections are horror and dark fantasy. Stand-out selections include Dennis Etchison's ''The Dead Cop,'' a tale of grief and obsession set in riot-torn Los Angeles; Terry Lamsley's ''Walking the Dog,'' in which a man discovers that his job includes walking his employer's pet monster for his nightly feedings; and Thomas Ligotti's ''Teatro Grottesco,'' a tale of madness and illusion. Includes comprehensive introductory essays on the year's yield of horror and fantasy fiction, film and comics, and the annual necrology.

**Other books you might like:**
Lin Carter, *The Year's Best Fantasy Stories Series*, 1974-1980
    editor
Stephen Jones, *The Mammoth Book of Best New Horror 8*, 1997
    editor
Arthur W. Saha, *The Year's Best Fantasy Stories Series*, 1981-1988
    editor
Karl Edward Wagner, *The Year's Best Horror Stories Series*, 1979-1994
    editor

## 1378

**ELLEN DATLOW**, Editor
**TERRI WINDLING**, Co-Editor

### The Year's Best Fantasy and Horror: Third Annual Collection

(New York: St. Martin's, 1990)

**Story type:** Horror (Anthology; Fantasy)

**Summary:** Forty-seven tales of fantasy and horror representing the best short fiction from mainstream and genre publications for 1989. The outstanding horror selections include Gary Kilworth's mystical ''White Noise''; Lisa Tuttle's coming-of-age tale ''The Walled Garden''; Fred Chappell's witty addition to the Cthulhu Mythos ''The Adder''; Jonathan Carroll's surprisingly nasty ''Mr. Fiddlehead''; and Ramsey Campbell's even nastier ''Meeting the Author.''

**Other books you might like:**
Peter Enfantino, *Quick Chills*, 1990
Stephen Jones, *Best New Horror*, 1990
    Ramsey Campbell, co-author
Karl Edward Wagner, *The Year's Best Horror Stories XVIII*, 1990

## 1379

**JAMES F. DAVID**

### Footprints of Thunder

(New York: Forge, 1995)

**Story type:** Science Fiction (Disaster; Science Fantasy)

**Major character(s):** Scott McIntyre, Political Figure (U.S. president); Petra Zalewski, Student—College, Adventurer; Colter Swenson, Student—College, Adventurer
**Time period(s):** 1990s
**Locale(s):** Oregon; Washington, District of Columbia; Florida

**Summary:** When the barrier of time breaks down and dinosaurs appear in the modern world, some common folk and politicians scramble to address the catastrophe while other people take advantage of the chaos.

**Other books you might like:**
Robert T. Bakker, *Raptor Red*, 1995
Michael Crichton, *Jurassic Park*, 1990
Michael Crichton, *The Lost World*, 1995
Sir Arthur Conan Doyle, *The Lost World*, 1912
Harry Adam Knight, *Carnosaur*, 1984
Stephen Leigh, *Ray Bradbury Presents: Dinosaur World*, 1992

## 1380
### JAMES F. DAVID
### *Fragments*
(New York: Tor/Forge, 1997)

**Story type:** Horror (Ghost Story)
**Major character(s):** Wes Martin, Psychologist; Elizabeth Foxworth, Social Worker; Gil Masters, Psychic
**Time period(s):** 1990s
**Locale(s):** University of Oregon, Oregon

**Summary:** An experiment to create a group consciousness from the minds of five idiot savants goes awry when the consciousness of a young girl brutally murdered in the house where they are staying ''contaminates'' the entity created. The situation is complicated further by the presence of a homicidal psychic who hopes to exploit the experiment for his own use.

**Other books you might like:**
Ramsey Campbell, *Incarnate*, 1983
Dean R. Koontz, *Strangers*, 1986
Al Sarrantonio, *House Haunted*, 1991
Theodore Sturgeon, *More than Human*, 1953
Chet Williamson, *Soulstorm*, 1986

## 1381
### PETER DAVID
### MICHAEL JAN FRIEDMAN, Co-Author
### ROBERT GREENBERGER, Co-Author
### *The Disinherited*
(New York: Pocket, 1992)

**Story type:** Science Fiction (Space Opera)
**Series:** Star Trek
**Major character(s):** Uhura, Military Personnel (Starfleet lieutenant), Space Explorer; Pavel Chekov, Military Personnel (Starfleet ensign), Space Explorer; James T. Kirk, Spaceship Captain
**Time period(s):** 23rd century
**Locale(s):** Rithra, Planet—Imaginary; *U.S.S. Enterprise*, Spaceship

**Summary:** Starfleet sends the *Enterprise* to protect the remaining population of the Xaridian system, now devastated by surprise attacks on three of the planets by unknown spaceships. An over-eager Ensign Chekov finds himself confined to quarters, but regains his place on the bridge crew. On temporary assignment to assist in translating the language of the Rithrim people for a diplomatic

mission, Lieutenant Uhura discovers secrets on Rithra that hold the key to dealing with the attacks on the Xaridian worlds.

**Other books you might like:**
Orson Scott Card, *Ender's Game*, 1985
C.J. Cherryh, *The Faded Sun: Kesrith*, 1978
Diane Duane, *Doctor's Orders*, 1990
Julia Ecklar, *The Kobayashi Maru*, 1989
Janet Kagan, *Uhura's Song*, 1985
Joan D. Vinge, *The Outcasts of Heaven Belt*, 1978

## 1382
### PETER DAVID
### *End Game*
(New York: Pocket, 1997)

**Story type:** Science Fiction (Space Opera)
**Series:** Star Trek: New Frontier
**Major character(s):** Mackenzie Calhoun, Spaceship Captain; Si Cwan, Royalty (prince), Alien (Thallonian); Soleta, Alien (Vulcan), Scientist
**Time period(s):** 24th century
**Locale(s):** *U.S.S. Excalibur*, Spaceship; Thallon, Planet—Imaginary

**Summary:** Captain Calhoun faces down the Nelkarites and secures the release of their hostages. The Thallonian rebels capture Si Cwan and Kebron after destroying their shuttlecraft. Soleta and Lieutenant Lefler realize the cause of the devastating seismic activity on Thallon and warn the population to evacuate before the Great Bird of the Galaxy hatches out of their planet. Concludes the storylines begun in *House of Cards*, *Into the Void*, and *The Two-Front War*.

**Other books you might like:**
Isaac Asimov, *Lucky Starr and the Pirates of the Asteroids*, 1953
David Brin, *Earth*, 1990
John M. Ford, *How Much for Just the Planet?*, 1987
Harry Harrison, *Bill, the Galactic Hero*, 1965
Robert A. Heinlein, *Starship Troopers*, 1959
Kij Johnson, *Dragon's Honor*, 1996
  Greg Cox, co-author

## 1383
### PETER DAVID
### *Imzadi*
(New York: Pocket, 1992)

**Story type:** Science Fiction (Space Opera; Alternate Universe)
**Series:** Star Trek: The Next Generation
**Major character(s):** Deanna Troi, Psychologist, Empath; William Riker, Military Personnel (Starfleet), Space Explorer; Data, Android, Military Personnel (Starfleet), Space Explorer
**Time period(s):** 25th century; 24th century
**Locale(s):** Betazed, Planet—Imaginary; Forever World, Planet—Imaginary; United Federation of Planets, Interstellar Empire/Federation

**Summary:** While temporarily assigned to a dirtball Federation embassy, young and lusty Lieutenant William Riker rescues Deanna Troi from a kidnapper then tumbles into a brief but torrid sexual relationship during which the pair merges souls, thus becoming *imzadi* and leaving them fully telepathic with each other. Later, Deanna's inexplicable death robs Will of zest for life and enjoyment of the subsequent 40 years of his Starfleet career. In charge of Starbase 86, ''Starbase Dead End,'' and nearing retirement, Admiral Riker learns that the Guardian of Forever, an alternate intelligence time travel device, has isolated a minor 24th-century time anomaly centered around Deanna Troi, whereupon Riker threatens his entire timeline in a desperate leap back in time to save his *imzadi*.

**Other books you might like:**
A.C. Crispin, *Yesterday's Son*, 1983
Michael Jan Friedman, *Fortune's Light*, 1991
Barbara Hambly, *Ishmael*, 1985
Laurell K. Hamilton, *Nightshade*, 1992
Howard Weinstein, *Perchance to Dream*, 1991
Howard Weinstein, *Power Hungry*, 1989

## 1384
### PETER DAVID

## Q-in-Law
(New York: Pocket, 1991)

**Story type:** Science Fiction (Space Opera; Humor)
**Series:** Star Trek: The Next Generation
**Major character(s):** Jean-Luc Picard, Spaceship Captain, Military Personnel; Q, Alien; Lwaxana Troi, Telepath, Alien (Betazed)
**Time period(s):** 24th century
**Locale(s):** *U.S.S. Enterprise*, Spaceship; Outer Space

**Summary:** The *U.S.S. Enterprise* is the site of the marriage of Kerin and Sehra, whose joining will also unite their rival families. When a curious Q arrives to probe this human emotion, he and Lwaxana Troi find each other. Q's machinations cause emotions to run so high that a blood feud is declared.

**Other books you might like:**
Diane Carey, *Ghost Ship*, 1988
Carmen Carter, *The Children of Hamlin*, 1988
C.J. Cherryh, *The Pride of Chanur*, 1982
Gene DeWeese, *The Peacekeepers*, 1988
Diane Duane, *Spock's World*, 1989
James H. Schmitz, *The Witches of Karres*, 1966

## 1385
### PETER DAVID

## Q-Squared
(New York: Pocket, 1994)

**Story type:** Science Fiction (Space Opera; Psychic Powers)
**Series:** Star Trek: The Next Generation
**Major character(s):** Jean-Luc Picard, Spaceship Captain, Military Personnel; Jack Crusher, Spaceship Captain; Q, Alien
**Time period(s):** 24th century
**Locale(s):** *U.S.S. Enterprise*, Spaceship

**Summary:** Q takes on the job of teaching the young Trelane, another transcendently powerful being who has had dealings with the *Enterprise* crew in the past. But even Q has trouble keeping the rebellious youngster under control, and when Trelane's creation of temporal anomalies leads to the intersection of multiple alternate universes, Picard and Q join forces to save the universe.

**Other books you might like:**
Diane Duane, *Dark Mirror*, 1993
Barbara Hambly, *Ishmael*, 1985
Terry Pratchett, *Mort*, 1989
Della Van Hise, *Killing Time*, 1985
Gore Vidal, *Visit to a Small Planet*, 1956

## 1386
### PETER DAVID

## The Rift
(New York: Pocket, 1991)

**Story type:** Science Fiction (Space Opera; First Contact)
**Series:** Star Trek
**Major character(s):** Spock, Scientist, Alien (Vulcan); Christopher Pike, Spaceship Captain; James T. Kirk, Spaceship Captain
**Time period(s):** 23rd century
**Locale(s):** *U.S.S. Enterprise*, Spaceship; Calligar, Planet—Imaginary

**Summary:** The *Enterprise* encounters a "rift" in the fabric of space-time that is a gateway to a distant sector of the galaxy where the people of the Calligar Worldnet live. Captain Pike and his officers meet with the Calligar leaders, who are not sure they want to have close contact with the Federation. 33.4 years later, the *Enterprise*, now commanded by James Kirk, has returned to establish relations, a job made more difficult when the Federation delegation is held hostage by the Calligar.

**Other books you might like:**
Margaret Wander Bonanno, *Strangers From the Sky*, 1987
C.J. Cherryh, *Port Eternity*, 1982
Diane Duane, *The Wounded Sky*, 1983
D.C. Fontana, *Vulcan's Glory*, 1989
R.A. MacAvoy, *The Book of Kells*, 1985
Vonda N. McIntyre, *The Entropy Effect*, 1981
Della Van Hise, *Killing Time*, 1985

## 1387
### PETER DAVID

## Thirdspace
(New York: Ballantine Del Rey, 1998)

**Story type:** Science Fiction (Space Opera; Space Colony)
**Series:** Babylon 5
**Major character(s):** John Sheridan, Military Personnel (captain); Lyta Alexander, Telepath; Elizabeth Trent, Archaeologist
**Time period(s):** 23rd century (2261)
**Locale(s):** Babylon 5, Space Station; Interstellar Empire/Federation; Outer Space

**Summary:** After his crew recovers a derelict alien artifact, Sheridan finds himself locked in a power struggle with Interplanetary Expeditions archaeologist Elizabeth Trent over who should control investigation of the artifact. Meanwhile, Lyta Alexander suffers from telepathic visions which portend doom for everyone aboard the station.

**Other books you might like:**
Jeanne Cavelos, *The Shadow Within*, 1997
Kathryn M. Drennan, *To Dream in the City of Sorrows*, 1997
J. Gregory Keyes, *Dark Genesis*, 1998
Jim Mortimore, *Clark's Law*, 1996
Al Sarrantonio, *Personal Agendas*, 1997
Robert Sheckley, *A Call to Arms*, 1999
John Vornholt, *Voices*, 1995

## 1388

PETER DAVID

### *Triangle: Imzadi II*

(New York: Pocket, 1998)

**Story type:** Science Fiction (Space Opera; Psychic Powers)
**Series:** Star Trek: The Next Generation
**Major character(s):** Deanna Troi, Psychologist (counselor), Empath, Fiance(e) (of Worf); William Riker, Military Personnel (commander); Worf, Military Personnel (lieutenant commander), Fiance(e) (of Deanna Troi), Alien (Klingon)
**Time period(s):** 24th century
**Locale(s):** Lazon II, Planet—Imaginary (prison planet); Betazed, Planet—Imaginary; Qo'noS, Planet—Imaginary (Klingon home world)

**Summary:** When Worf asks Deanna to marry him, she agrees, but their respective parents have doubts. Lwaxana Troi's attempts to teach Worf about Betazoid culture prove frustrating for all concerned, while Will Riker regrets his lost chance with Deanna. After Tom Riker, Will's doppelganger, helps the Romulans kidnap Deanna and Worf's son, Alexander, Will and Worf go to the rescue. Worf must choose between love and honor when Romulan leader Sela offers the lives of her hostages in exchange for the assassination of Klingon Chancellor Gowron, an act which would end the Klingon-Federation alliance.

**Other books you might like:**
Margaret Wander Bonanno, *Dwellers in the Crucible*, 1985
C.J. Cherryh, *Endgame*, 1991
Michael Jan Friedman, *All Good Things...*, 1994
Jeri Taylor, *Mosaic*, 1996
Joan D. Vinge, *The Summer Queen*, 1991

## 1389

PETER DAVID

### *Vendetta*

(New York: Pocket, 1991)

**Story type:** Science Fiction (Space Opera)
**Series:** Star Trek: The Next Generation
**Major character(s):** Jean-Luc Picard, Spaceship Captain, Military Personnel; Guinan, Saloon Keeper/Owner, Alien; Geordi La Forge, Engineer, Military Personnel
**Time period(s):** 24th century
**Locale(s):** *U.S.S. Enterprise*, Spaceship

**Summary:** The machine-like Borg have nearly demolished the Penzatti homeworld when their fleet is annihilated by another ship. When the *Enterprise* is ordered to the scene, Picard meets Guinan's adopted sister, Delcara, the sole survivor of an earlier Borg attack. Delcara controls a planet-destroying weapon built by an extinct people for the purpose of exacting revenge on the Borg, who destroyed their race.

**Other books you might like:**
C.J. Cherryh, *Serpent's Reach*, 1980
Carolyn Clowes, *The Pandora Principle*, 1990
A.C. Crispin, *The Eyes of the Beholders*, 1990
Gordon R. Dickson, *The Forever Man*, 1986
Anne McCaffrey, *The Ship Who Sang*, 1970

## 1390

PETER DAVID

### *What Savage Beast*

(New York: Putnam Boulevard, 1995)

**Story type:** Science Fiction (Alternate Universe; Adventure)
**Series:** Incredible Hulk
**Major character(s):** Robert Bruce "Incredible Hulk" Banner, Scientist; Elizabeth "Betty Tanner" Banner, Spouse; Leonard "Doc" Samson, Doctor (psychiatrist)
**Time period(s):** 1990s; 22nd century
**Locale(s):** Chicago, Illinois; The Crossroads, Mythical Place (time nexus); Alternate Earth

**Summary:** Desperate to escape his current circumstances, including harassment by the military and difficulty providing his wife with a normal life, Dr. Banner undergoes experimental surgery, not comprehending the problems it will cause for himself and for his offspring.

**Other books you might like:**
Greg Cox, *Iron Man: The Armor Trap*, 1995
Diane Duane, *Spider-Man: The Venom Factor*, 1994
Stan Lee, *The Ultimate Silver Surfer*, 1995
    editor
Stan Lee, *The Ultimate Spider-Man*, 1994
    editor
David Michelinie, *Spider-Man: Carnage in New York*, 1995
    Dean Wesley Smith, co-author
John Varley, *Superheroes*, 1995
    Ricia Mainhardt, co-editor
Len Wein, *Stalker From the Stars*, 1978
    Marv Wolfman, Joseph Silva, co-authors

## 1391

PETER DAVID

### *Worf's First Adventure*

(New York: Pocket Minstrel, 1993)

**Story type:** Science Fiction (Young Adult; Adventure)
**Series:** Star Trek: The Next Generation: Starfleet Academy
**Major character(s):** Worf Rozhenko, Alien (Klingon), Student; Soleta, Alien (Vulcan), Student; Mark McHenry, Scientist (mathematician), Student
**Time period(s):** 24th century
**Locale(s):** San Francisco, California (Starfleet Academy)

**Summary:** As a new cadet, Worf Rozhenko experiences some difficulty adjusting to life at Starfleet Academy, but begins to form friendships with other cadets, both human and extraterrestrial. A disastrous raid by Romulans presents unexpected challenges to Worf during his first mission.

**Other books you might like:**
Bruce Coville, *My Teacher Flunked the Planet*, 1992
A.C. Crispin, *Shadow World*, 1991
    Jannean Elliott, co-author
A.C. Crispin, *Silent Dances*, 1990
    Kathleen O'Malley, co-author
A.C. Crispin, *Starbridge*, 1989
Paul Davids, *The Glove of Darth Vader*, 1992
    Hollace Davids, co-author
Paul Davids, *The Lost City of the Jedi*, 1992

## 1392

### PAUL DAVIDS
### HOLLACE DAVIDS, Co-Author

## *The Glove of Darth Vader*

(New York: Bantam Skylark, 1992)

**Story type:** Science Fiction (Young Adult; Space Opera)
**Series:** Star Wars
**Major character(s):** Luke Skywalker, Martial Arts Expert (Jedi Knight), Hero; Trioculus, Imposter (emperor's son), Ruler (emperor); C-3PO, Robot, Adventurer
**Time period(s):** Indeterminate Past
**Locale(s):** Kessel, Planet—Imaginary; Calamari, Planet—Imaginary

**Summary:** Aided by trickery, Trioculus poses as the deceased Emperor's son and declares himself Emperor with the help of the Central Committee of Grand Moffs. Trioculus then travels to Calamari to recover Darth Vader's indestructable glove, the symbol of great power. On Calamari, Trioculus finds himself opposed by Luke Skywalker, who is involved in freeing the exploited Whaladons. Contains a seven-page glossary and four-page biography of authors and illustrators.

**Other books you might like:**

Bonnie Bogart, *The Ewoks Join the Fight*, 1983
Amy Ehrlich, *The Ewoks and the Lost Children*, 1985
James Howe, *How the Ewoks Saved the Trees: An Old Ewok Legend*, 1984
Joe Johnston, *The Adventures of Peebo: A Tale of Magic and Suspense*, 1984
Melinda Luke, *The Baby Ewok's Picnic Surprise*, 1984
Melinda Luke, *Wicket Finds a Way: An Ewok Adventure*, 1984

## 1393

### PAUL DAVIDS
### HOLLACE DAVIDS, Co-Author

## *The Lost City of the Jedi*

(New York: Bantam Skylark, 1992)

**Story type:** Science Fiction (Young Adult; Space Opera)
**Series:** Star Wars
**Major character(s):** Luke Skywalker, Martial Arts Expert (Jedi Knight), Hero; Trioculus, Imposter (emperor's son), Ruler (emperor); Ken, Teenager, Student (Jedi Knight)
**Time period(s):** Indeterminate Past
**Locale(s):** Lost City of the Jedi, Fictional City; Yavin Four, Moon—Imaginary

**Summary:** Warned of the threat to his rule posed by a Jedi Prince living in the Lost City of the Jedi, Trioculus searches Yavin Four. Failing to find the entrance to the legendary Lost City, Trioculus releases weapons which ignite the rainforests of Yavin Four, source of thousands of medicines used throughout the galaxy. Utilizing an access code given him in a vision by Obi-Wan Kenobi, Luke activates a weather control system within the Lost City in an attempt to save the planet. Contains a five-page glossary and three-page biography of authors and illustrators.

**Other books you might like:**

Bonnie Bogart, *The Ewoks Join the Fight*, 1983
Amy Ehrlich, *The Ewoks and the Lost Children*, 1985
James Howe, *How the Ewoks Saved the Trees: An Old Ewok Legend*, 1984
Joe Johnston, *The Adventures of Peebo: A Tale of Magic and Suspense*, 1984

Melinda Luke, *The Baby Ewok's Picnic Surprise*, 1984
Melinda Luke, *Wicket Finds a Way: An Ewok Adventure*, 1984

## 1394

### PAUL DAVIDS
### HOLLACE DAVIDS, Co-Author

## *Zorba the Hutt's Revenge*

(New York: Bantam Skylark, 1992)

**Story type:** Science Fiction (Young Adult; Space Opera)
**Series:** Star Wars
**Major character(s):** Leia Organa, Royalty (princess), Diplomat; Zorba the Hutt, Alien, Parent (Jabba the Hutt's); Trioculus, Imposter (emperor's son), Ruler (emperor)
**Time period(s):** Indeterminate Past
**Locale(s):** Cloud City, Fictional City; Tatooine, Planet—Imaginary

**Summary:** When Zorba the Hutt discovers that his son died at the hands of Princess Leia, he travels to Cloud City to exact revenge on the Princess. After he cheats Lando Calrissian to gain control of Cloud City, Zorba must acquire the Princess from Trioculus who hopes to make her his queen. Contains a five-page glossary of terms and three-page biography of authors and illustrators.

**Other books you might like:**

Bonnie Bogart, *The Ewoks Join the Fight*, 1983
Amy Ehrlich, *The Ewoks and the Lost Children*, 1985
James Howe, *How the Ewoks Saved the Trees: An Old Ewok Legend*, 1984
Joe Johnston, *The Adventures of Peebo: A Tale of Magic and Suspense*, 1984
Melinda Luke, *The Baby Ewok's Picnic Surprise*, 1984
Melinda Luke, *Wicket Finds a Way: An Ewok Adventure*, 1984

## 1395

### AVRAM DAVIDSON

## *The Avram Davidson Treasury*

(New York: Tor, 1988)

**Story type:** Science Fiction (Collection)
**Summary:** A collection of stories spanning the entire career of the late, highly regarded author, who was better known for his shorter pieces than for his novels. The treatments range from serious to whimsical to surreal and are oriented toward the literary rather than adventure.

## 1396

### AVRAM DAVIDSON
### GRANIA DAVIS, Co-Author

## *The Boss in the Wall*

(San Francisco: Tachyon Publications, 1998)

**Story type:** Horror (Reanimated Dead)
**Major character(s):** Luke Larraby, Museum Curator; Edward E. Bagnell, Professor (ethnologist); Vlad Smith, Professor
**Time period(s):** 1990s (1998)
**Locale(s):** New York, New York; Providence, Rhode Island; South

**Summary:** Vlad Smith's personal encounter with a house devil known as The Boss in the Wall encourages him to research the history of its origins in southern folklore. Vlad's investigations are complicated by the activities of scores of charlatans and opportunists, all of whom want to cash in on the Boss's notoriety. A short novel unfinished at the time of Davidson's death and completed by his wife.

**Other books you might like:**
Scott Bradfield, *What's Wrong with America*, 1994
Rob Chilson, *Black as Blood*, 1998
Thomas M. Disch, *The Businessman: A Tale of Terror*, 1984
David Prill, *The Unnatural*, 1995
Manly Wade Wellman, *After Dark*, 1980

---

### 1397

**ROBERTSON DAVIES**

## The Cornish Trilogy

(New York: Penguin, 1992)

**Story type:** Fantasy (Collection; Contemporary)
**Major character(s):** Francis Cornish, Artist, Philanthropist; Maria Magdalena Theotohy, Scholar; Simon Darcourt, Religious (Anglican priest), Scholar
**Time period(s):** 1980s
**Locale(s):** Mythical Place (College of St. John and the Holy Ghost); Germany; Toronto, Ontario, Canada

**Summary:** Originally published as *The Rebel Angels* (1982), *What's Bred in the Bone* (1986) and *The Lyre of Orpheus* (1989), this omnibus relates the complicated story of Francis Cornish and the foundation he endowed on his death. The story is full of mystery, scholarship, comedy, history, angels, spirits and a bizarre murder revolving around the lonely figure of Francis Cornish, a man whose life locked him in a shell of history. The narration wraps Cornish in a web of monks, gypsies, professors, artists and mountebanks showing the impact of one individual on a curious world.

**Other books you might like:**
James P. Blaylock, *The Paper Grail*, 1991
Lindsay Clarke, *The Chymical Wedding*, 1989
John Crowley, *Little, Big*, 1981
Umberto Eco, *Foucault's Pendulum*, 1989
Fay Weldon, *Letters to Alice on First Reading Jane Austen*, 1984

---

### 1398

**BRETT DAVIS**

## Bone Wars

(New York: Baen, 1998)

**Story type:** Science Fiction (First Contact)
**Series:** Dinosaur Bones
**Major character(s):** Othniel Charles Marsh, Scientist; Edward Drinker Cope, Scientist
**Time period(s):** 1870s (1876)
**Locale(s):** Montana

**Summary:** Two scientists travel to southwestern United States in 1876 in a competition to uncover a significant cache of dinosaur bones. They encounter two strange men who claim to have traveled from Europe on a similar quest, but who are actually visitors from another planet on a secret mission.

**Other books you might like:**
John Boyd, *The Andromeda Gun*, 1974
Sean Dalton, *Showdown*, 1992
Lionel Fenn, *Once upon a Time in the East*, 1993
John Jakes, *Six Gun Planet*, 1970

---

### 1399

**BRETT DAVIS**

## The Faery Convention

(New York: Baen, 1995)

**Story type:** Fantasy (Light Fantasy; Political)
**Major character(s):** Joe Cork, Mythical Creature (half-elf), Government Official (Congressional investigator); Ellen King, Receptionist; Merlin, Wizard, Leader
**Time period(s):** 21st century
**Locale(s):** Washington, District of Columbia

**Summary:** A plot by shapeshifters threatens to foil the Grimm Accord, a Congressional Act establishing a homeland for supernatural creatures within Texas and Oklahoma. While Joe and Ellen investigate, Merlin advances the wizards' control of U.S. weaponry. First novel.

**Other books you might like:**
Charles de Lint, *Memory and Dream*, 1994
Laurell K. Hamilton, *Guilty Pleasures*, 1993
Nick Pollotta, *Bureau 13*, 1991
Clifford D. Simak, *Out of Their Minds*, 1970
Michael Swanwick, *In the Drift*, 1985
Sheri S. Tepper, *A Plague of Angels*, 1993
Harry Turtledove, *The Case of the Toxic Spell Dump*, 1993
Gary K. Wolf, *Who Censored Roger Rabbit?*, 1981

---

### 1400

**BRETT DAVIS**

## Hair of the Dog

(New York: Baen, 1997)

**Story type:** Fantasy (Mystery)
**Major character(s):** Ashley Durbin, Journalist; Bob Savik, Police Officer (retired); Paul Moreau, Werewolf
**Time period(s):** 21st century
**Locale(s):** Las Vegas, Nevada

**Summary:** After Monty Allen announces new hope on his telethon to raise money for lycanthropy research, Ashley Durbin and Bob Savik investigate the murder of the researcher who discovered the reported cure, discovering many puzzling aspects of the case as they continue to ask embarrassing questions.

**Other books you might like:**
Laurell K. Hamilton, *The Lunatic Cafe*, 1996
Tanya Huff, *Blood Price*, 1991
Nick Pollotta, *Full Moonster*, 1992
Will Shetterly, *Nevernever*, 1993
Denise Vitola, *Opalite Moon*, 1997
Denise Vitola, *Quantum Moon*, 1996

---

### 1401

**CAROL ANNE DAVIS**

**JAMES HUBBS**, Illustrator

## Expiry Date

(Clay, New York: Dark Raptor Press, 1998)

**Story type:** Horror (Erotic Horror)
**Major character(s):** Chaz Cooper, Courier; Caitlin, Young Woman; Bonnie, Teacher
**Time period(s):** 1990s (1998)

**Locale(s):** Edinburgh, Scotland

**Summary:** While recovering from a suicide attempt, Chaz makes the acquaintance of both the promiscuous Caitlin and the virginal Bonnie. Events escalate to a deadly climax when Bonnie intrudes upon Chaz during a bondage incident with Caitlin. Illustrated by James Hubbs. Issued as a signed limited edition chapbook.

**Other books you might like:**
Poppy Z. Brite, *Are You Loathsome Tonight?*, 1998
Brett Easton Ellis, *American Psycho*, 1991
Jeff Gelb, *Hot Blood*, 1989
   Lonn Friend, co-editor
Richard Sutphen, *Sexpunks & Savage Sagas*, 1991
Lucy Taylor, *The Flesh Artist*, 1994

**1402**

**DON DAVIS**
**JAY DAVIS**, Co-Author

## *Bring on the Night*
(New York: Tor, 1993)

**Story type:** Horror (Vampire Story)
**Major character(s):** Dennis Coglin, Detective—Police; Nathan Kane, Vampire; Corky Washburn, Morgue Attendant (Nathan's aide)
**Time period(s):** 1990s (1993)
**Locale(s):** Chicago, Illinois

**Summary:** Nathan Kane moves to Chicago and uses the tactics of a contemporary serial killer to cover up his regular vampiric feastings.

**Other books you might like:**
Charles L. Grant, *The Soft Whisper of the Dead*, 1982
Stephen King, *Salem's Lot*, 1975
Robert R. McCammon, *They Thirst*, 1981
Bram Stoker, *Dracula*, 1897
Les Whitten, *Progeny of the Adder*, 1965

**1403**

**DON DAVIS**

## *The Gris-Gris Man*
(New York: Turner, 1997)

**Story type:** Horror (Black Magic)
**Major character(s):** Wade Broussard, Detective—Police; Rene Chauvin, Businessman; Alexandra Larsen, Editor
**Time period(s):** 1990s (1997)
**Locale(s):** New Orleans, Louisiana

**Summary:** Cajun police detective Wade Broussard turned his back on his voodoo upbringing when an encounter with Baron Samedi, Lord of the Graveyard, resulted in the deaths of several innocent victims during a routine crime investigation. Now a murder spree with voodoo overtones has forced Broussard to resurrect himself as *Le Blanc Houngan* in order to pursue a criminal who is using black magic as a front for drug smuggling.

**Other books you might like:**
Alex Abella, *The Killing of the Saints*, 1991
Hugh B. Cave, *Shades of Evil*, 1982
Nicholas Conde, *The Religion*, 1982
Graham Masterton, *Rook*, 1996
Michael Reaves, *Voodoo Child*, 1998
Robert Weinberg, *The Black Lodge*, 1991

**1404**

**DON DAVIS**
**JAY DAVIS**, Co-Author

## *Sins of the Flesh*
(New York: Tor, 1989)

**Story type:** Horror (Serial Killer)
**Major character(s):** Stephen Sikes, Young Man; Jesse Sikes, Murderer (Stephen's uncle), Monster (Shape-changing Wendigo)
**Time period(s):** 1960s (1968); 1980s (1988)
**Locale(s):** Gideon, Missouri; Kennett, Missouri

**Summary:** A black magician's curse turns Jesse Sikes into a semi-human serial killer. For twenty years his mother's occult powers imprison him, but upon her death he is freed to terrorize the townspeople. His nephew Stephen, the last of the Sikes, is the only person with the knowledge and ability to stop Jesse—if he has the courage and resourcefulness.

**Other books you might like:**
Les Whitten, *Moon of the Wolf*, 1967

**1405**

**JAKE DAVIS**

## *Destination: Showdown*
(New York: Berkley, 1993)

**Story type:** Science Fiction (Post-Holocaust)
**Series:** Last Rangers
**Major character(s):** Alamo Smith, Lawman; APU-805 ''Bird Dog'', Robot, Military Personnel
**Time period(s):** 2030s (2035)
**Locale(s):** Texas (southwest border badlands)

**Summary:** When the evil leaders of a post-disaster city-state discover the underground organization led by Alamo Smith, the freedom fighter and Bird Dog must rush to keep an ultimate weapon from the overlords.

**Other books you might like:**
David Alexander, *Death Race*, 1992
David Alexander, *Nomad*, 1992
David Brin, *The Postman*, 1985
Bill Dolan, *Afrikorps*, 1991
Bill Dolan, *Iron Horse*, 1991
Michael D. Weaver, *My Father Immortal*, 1989

**1406**

**JAKE DAVIS**

## *The Last Rangers*
(New York: Berkley, 1992)

**Story type:** Science Fiction (Post-Holocaust; Adventure)
**Major character(s):** Alamo Smith, Lawman; APU-805 ''Bird Dog'', Robot, Military Personnel; Rima, Prostitute
**Time period(s):** 2030s (2035)
**Locale(s):** Texas (southwest border badlands)

**Summary:** After a devastating war with the Red Chinese and continued environmental degradation, law and order in the United States breaks down, leaving the people at the mercy of vicious gangs. In Texas, the underground force of high-tech avengers, the Last Rangers, provides some hope for justice to the deteriorating frontier society along the southern border.

**Other books you might like:**
Robert Cain, *Cybernarc*, 1991
Mark Grant, *Mutants Amok*, 1991
    pseudonym of David Bischoff
Ed Naha, *Robocop*, 1987
David Robbins, *Yellowstone Run*, 1990
William Shatner, *TekWar*, 1989
G. Harry Stine, *Sierra Madre*, 1988

## 1407

### MARGARET DAVIS

## Mind Light

(New York: Ballantine Del Rey, 1993)

**Story type:** Science Fiction (First Contact)
**Major character(s):** Kiley Michaelson, Businesswoman, Pilot (spaceship); Greg Lukas, Spaceman, Pilot (spaceship)
**Time period(s):** Indeterminate Future
**Locale(s):** *Widdon Galaxy*, Spaceship; Jeross, Space Station

**Summary:** Desperate for any relief pilot, Kiley Michaelson hires the intoxicated and apparently ill Greg Lukas as a temporary solution, fearful she has acquired new problems for the family's spaceship. The family soon realizes Greg's unusual piloting skills result from Space Academy training, but must remain curious about his subsequent court martial. When the Space Corps becomes interested in reopening Greg's case, *Widdon Galaxy* flees to the site of Greg's crimes, where the ship finds interest among the first aliens to contact humans. Author's first book.

**Other books you might like:**
Roger MacBride Allen, *The Ring of Charon*, 1990
Eleanor Arnason, *Ring of Swords*, 1993
Alis A. Rasmussen, *A Passage of Stars*, 1990
Alis A. Rasmussen, *The Price of Ransom*, 1990
Alis A. Rasmussen, *Revolution's Shore*, 1990
David Alexander Smith, *Homecoming*, 1990
David Alexander Smith, *Rendezvous*, 1988

## 1408

### MARGARET DAVIS

## Minds Apart

(New York: Ballantine Del Rey, 1994)

**Story type:** Science Fiction (First Contact)
**Major character(s):** Daniel Keenan, Doctor (psychiatrist); Sensar, Alien (Gan-Tir), Teacher; Greg Lukas, Spaceman, Pilot (spaceship)
**Time period(s):** Indeterminate Future
**Locale(s):** *Widdon Galaxy*, Spaceship

**Summary:** Wanting to deal only with Daniel Keenan, the newly contacted aliens, the Gan-Tir, hire the *Widdon Galaxy* to bring representatives into human space for a conference. Keenan hates and fears the Gan-Tir as well as fearing Greg Lukas' Quayla symbiont, who drains Lukas. When the Gan-Tir decide to return home without seeing human representatives, they become mired in a barrier and require Keenan's help.

**Other books you might like:**
Eleanor Arnason, *Ring of Swords*, 1993
Octavia E. Butler, *Adulthood Rites*, 1988
Jacqueline Lichtenberg, *House of Zeor*, 1974
Rebecca Ore, *Becoming Alien*, 1987
Jack Vance, *The Anome*, 1973

## 1409

### CAROL DAWSON

## Meeting the Minotaur

(Chapel Hill, North Carolina: Algonquin, 1997)

**Story type:** Fantasy (Legend; Contemporary Realism)
**Major character(s):** Taylor Thaddeus "Taytay" Troys, Handicapped, Relative (son); Ramon Vizuelos, Friend, Criminal; A.J. Deeds, Parent, Wealthy
**Time period(s):** 1990s
**Locale(s):** Bernice, Texas; Tokyo, Japan; Dallas, Texas

**Summary:** Taytay grows up believing himself abandoned by an uncaring father. Handicapped by meningitis, he finds that no one expects much of him. After Taytay drops out of college, his grandfather informs him that he will bankroll any business taytay decides to develop. Taytay decides to go into burglary to connect with his father. Retells *Theseus and the Minotaur*.

**Other books you might like:**
Gael Baudino, *Gossamer Axe*, 1990
Marion Zimmer Bradley, *The Mists of Avalon*, 1983
Pamela Dean, *Tam Lin*, 1991
Amarantha Knight, *The Darker Passions: Frankenstein*, 1995
Elizabeth Ann Scarborough, *Carol for Another Christmas*, 1996
Jane Yolen, *Briar Rose*, 1992

## 1410

### CHET DAY

## The Hacker

(New York: Pocket, 1989)

**Story type:** Horror (Techno-Horror)
**Major character(s):** Succubus, Computer Expert, Murderer; Dennis "Tunnel Rat" Conlick, Computer Expert (Head of "The Surgery" computer)
**Time period(s):** 1980s
**Locale(s):** New Orleans, Louisiana

**Summary:** The Surgery, a "network" of computer experts working on a secret government project, is broken into by the Succubus, a psychotic, vindictive computer genius, who begins to pick off the Surgery members one by one while he steals their discoveries in an attempt to turn himself into a "god."

**Other books you might like:**
Herbert Lieberman, *City of the Dead*, 1976
F. Paul Wilson, *The Touch*, 1986

## 1411

### LOUIS DE BERNIERES

## Senor Vivo and the Coca Lord

(New York: Morrow, 1992)

**Story type:** Fantasy (Contemporary; Quest)
**Major character(s):** Dionisio Vivo, Critic (social), Patriot; Ramon Dario, Police Officer; Anica, Girlfriend
**Time period(s):** 1990s
**Locale(s):** South America

**Summary:** A prominent lecturer, Dionisio Vivo, criticizes a system corrupted by illegal coca trade. When an assassination attempt fails, Ramon warns Dionisio of the perils of his behavior. Dionisio, however, remains driven to fight the corruption despite the adverse effects to his relationships and friends.

**Other books you might like:**

Marjorie Agosin, *The Secret Weavers: Stories of the Fantastic by Latin American Women*, 1991
  editor
Philip K. Dick, *A Scanner Darkly*, 1977
Philip K. Dick, *The Three Stigmata of Palmer Eldritch*, 1965
  editor
Gabriel Garcia Marquez, *One Hundred Years of Solitude*, 1970
Ben Okri, *The Famished Road*, 1992

## 1412

### LOUIS DE BERNIERES

## The War of Don Emmanuel's Nether Parts

(New York: Morrow, 1992)

**Story type:** Fantasy (Satire; Political)
**Major character(s):** Aurelio, Indian, Shaman; Constanza Evans, Socialite; Asado, Military Personnel, Criminal
**Time period(s):** 1990s
**Locale(s):** South America

**Summary:** Directionless revolutionaries attempt to overthrow the government, precipitating vicious and repressive tactics designed to maintain governmental authority while Constanza's excesses heat up revolutionary fire. His village destroyed, Aurelio escapes from the mountains to the jungle where he learns magical arts. After leading village resistance to government attacks, Aurelio sets off with the villagers to settle new territory and create a peaceful society accompanied by magical cats which improve the humor of anyone they meet. Author's first novel.

**Other books you might like:**

Marjorie Agosin, *The Secret Weavers: Stories of the Fantastic by Latin American Women*, 1991
  editor
Gabriel Garcia Marquez, *One Hundred Years of Solitude*, 1970
  editor
Ben Okri, *The Famished Road*, 1992
Elizabeth Ann Scarborough, *Nothing Sacred*, 1991
Kurt Vonnegut Jr., *Cat's Cradle*, 1963

## 1413

### L. SPRAGUE DE CAMP, Editor
### CHRISTOPHER STASHEFF, Co-Editor

## The Enchanter Reborn

(New York: Baen, 1992)

**Story type:** Fantasy (Anthology; Light Fantasy)
**Series:** Harold Shea
**Major character(s):** Harold Shea, Psychologist, Adventurer; Reed Chalmers, Psychologist, Adventurer

**Summary:** Contains a six-page introduction and three stories by Christopher Stasheff plus two stories by Holly Lisle and John Maddox Roberts developed from outlines by de Camp and Stasheff. Featuring Harold Shea, each story visits the universe of myths and literary adventures including characters from the Buddhist pantheon, classical mythology, Oz and *Don Quixote.*

**Other books you might like:**

Craig Shaw Gardner, *Slaves of the Volcano God*, 1989
Holly Lisle, *Fire in the Mist*, 1992
Clifford D. Simak, *Out of Their Minds*, 1970

Christopher Stasheff, *Her Majesty's Wizard*, 1986
Christopher Stasheff, *The Warlock in Spite of Himself*, 1969

## 1414

### L. SPRAGUE DE CAMP

## The Hand of Zei

(New York: Baen Books, 1990)

**Story type:** Science Fiction (Adventure)
**Series:** Viagens Interplanetarias
**Major character(s):** Dirk Barnevelt, Writer; George Tangaloa, Scientist
**Time period(s):** Indeterminate Future
**Locale(s):** Krishna, Planet—Imaginary

**Summary:** Dirk Barnevelt, who for years has been chronicling the adventures of others on the wild and dangerous planet Krishna, finally gets a chance to go there himself when his boss, a famous explorer, disappears on an undercover mission. All advanced technology is prohibited on Krishna, so Barnevelt finds ample opportunity for swashbuckling, swordplay, and derring do. Originally published in 1963.

**Other books you might like:**

Edgar Rice Burroughs, *Pirates of Venus*, 1934
Edgar Rice Burroughs, *A Princess of Mars*, 1917
Edgar Rice Burroughs, *Synthetic Men of Mars*, 1940
Poul Anderson, *Hoka!*, 1983
  Gordon R. Dickson, co-author
Robert A. Heinlein, *Glory Road*, 1963
R.A. MacAvoy, *The Third Eagle: Lessons Along a Minor String*, 1989

## 1415

### L. SPRAGUE DE CAMP

## The Honorable Barbarian

(New York: Del Rey, 1989)

**Story type:** Fantasy (Adventure)
**Series:** Unbeheaded King
**Major character(s):** Kerin, Barbarian
**Time period(s):** Indeterminate
**Locale(s):** Alternate Universe

**Summary:** Found in an awkward situation with the daughter of a prominent man, Kerin is sent on an ocean voyage. Originally dispatched by his older brother the king to the east to learn the secret of a clock escapement, Kerin encounters many misadventures. These include an amorous captain's mistress, a hermit wizard on a desert isle, capture by pirates, a princess in need and at last a meeting with the Emperor of the East who believes Kerin to have an important secret to reveal.

**Other books you might like:**

David Drake, *The Sea Hag*, 1988
  Book 1-The World of Crystal Walls
Geoffrey Marsh, *Fangs and the Hooded Demon*, 1988

## 1416

**L. SPRAGUE DE CAMP
CATHERINE CROOK DE CAMP**, Co-Author

### *The Pixilated Peeress*

(New York: Ballantine/Del Rey, 1991)

**Story type:** Fantasy (Adventure)
**Major character(s):** Thorolf Zigramson, Scholar, Military Personnel; Yvette of Grintz, Runaway, Noblewoman; Wok, Leader, Mythical Creature (troll)
**Time period(s):** Indeterminate
**Locale(s):** Rhaetia, Fictional Country

**Summary:** Sergeant Thorolf Zigramson encounters the fugitive Countess Yvette of Grintz who can think of nothing but regaining her estates and escaping her noble, would-be husband. Accidentally turned into an octopus, her only cure is to be possessed by a Delta and then imprisoned by Sophonomists. Thorolf, thoroughly smitten, seeks to rescue her but is captured by Trolls. He manages to forge an alliance with them and rescue Yvette, who spurns him. When Thorolf becomes a mercenary and weds a foreign bride, Yvette belatedly decides she loves him.

**Other books you might like:**
Piers Anthony, *On a Pale Horse*, 1983
Robert Asprin, *Another Fine Myth*, 1978
Alan Dean Foster, *Spellsinger*, 1983
Christopher Stasheff, *The Warlock Rock*, 1990
Sheri S. Tepper, *King's Blood Four*, 1983

## 1417

**L. SPRAGUE DE CAMP**

### *Rivers of Time*

(New York: Baen, 1993)

**Story type:** Science Fiction (Collection; Time Travel)
**Major character(s):** Reginald Rivers, Guide, Time Traveler
**Time period(s):** Indeterminate Past (Paleocene; Pleistocene)
**Locale(s):** Earth

**Summary:** Contains two original stories, a newly revised version of "A Gun for Dinosaur," and six stories from 1990s periodicals and an anthology. Stories feature Reginald Rivers who leads deep-pocket clients in perilous pursuit of the biggest big game of all time.

**Other books you might like:**
Poul Anderson, *The Time Patrol*, 1991
Michael Crichton, *Jurassic Park*, 1990
Roger L. DiSilvestro, *Living with the Reptiles*, 1990
Sir Arthur Conan Doyle, *The Lost World*, 1912
Stephen Leigh, *Dinosaur Samurai*, 1993
  John J. Miller, co-author
J.F. Rivkin, *Tyrannosaurus Rex*, 1992

## 1418

**L. SPRAGUE DE CAMP
CATHERINE CROOK DE CAMP**, Co-Author

### *The Swords of Zinjaban*

(New York: Baen, 1991)

**Story type:** Science Fiction (Arts; Humor)
**Series:** Viagens Interplanetarias

**Major character(s):** Fergus Reith, Tour Guide, Divorced Person; Alicia "Lish" Dyckman, Producer (assistant), Divorced Person; Gilan "Gilan the Third" bad-Jam, Alien (Krishnan), Ruler (Dasht of Rue)
**Time period(s):** 22nd century
**Locale(s):** Krishna, Planet—Imaginary (Tau Ceti System)

**Summary:** This story begins 20 years after Alicia left Krishna when Reith would not accept a reconciliation for their marriage. Reith discovers his latest tour presents unusual problems. His former marriage to the Cosmic Productions' employee complicates filming the motion picture they've come to make, as does Reith's former marriage to a potential mate of Gilan the Third who, making matters worse, has imprisoned Reith. A two-page introduction by the co-author summarizes three previous Krishna books.

**Other books you might like:**
Terry Bisson, *Voyage to the Red Planet*, 1990
Pat Cadigan, *Synners*, 1991
Craig Shaw Gardner, *Slaves of the Volcano God*, 1989
Harry Harrison, *The Technicolor Time Machine*, 1967
John Varley, *Demon*, 1984
Ian Watson, *Chekhov's Journey*, 1989

## 1419

**L. SPRAGUE DE CAMP
DAVID DRAKE**, Co-Author

### *The Undesired Princess and the Enchanted Bunny*

(New York: Baen, 1990)

**Story type:** Fantasy (Light Fantasy; Alternate World)
**Major character(s):** Rollin Hobart, Engineer (consulting); Joe Johnson, Writer (ghostwriter)
**Time period(s):** 1990s (1990); Indeterminate
**Locale(s):** Loggia, Fictional Country; Hamisch, Fictional Country

**Summary:** This book contains two separate stories on a theme. A contemporary American male finds himself suddenly and unexpectedly transported to. . .somewhere else. . .where magic works, where the technology and social structure are medieval (magical) creatures, swords, wagons, castles, kings, beautiful princesses, etc. There is a menace to be surmounted and the reluctant hero tries to use his modern knowledge to help and discovers things don't quite work the way they do back home, and must adjust. David Drake's story is an homage to L. Sprague de Camp's stories in this sub-genre.

**Other books you might like:**
Jack L. Chalker, *The River of Dancing Gods*, 1984
Rick Cook, *Wizard's Bane*, 1989
Brian Daley, *The Doomfarers of Coramonde*, 1977
Alan Dean Foster, *Quozl*, 1989
Barbara Hambly, *The Silent Tower*, 1988
Eric Frank Russell, *The Space Willies*, 1958
Mark Twain, *A Connecticut Yankee in King Arthur's Court*, 1889
  Pseudonym of Samuel Clemens

## 1420

**L. SPRAGUE DE CAMP**

### *The Venom Trees of Sunga*

(New York: Ballantine Del Rey, 1992)

**Story type:** Science Fiction (Humor; Adventure)

**Major character(s):** Kirk Salazar, Student, Traveler; Alexis Ritter, Religious (high priestess), Leader; George Cantemir, Businessman, Criminal (ecological)
**Time period(s):** Indeterminate Future
**Locale(s):** Sunga, Planet—Imaginary

**Summary:** While visiting Sunga to advance his study of the ecology of Sunga's venom tree forest, Kirk Salazar travels with a tour group to save money. Salazar's studies suffer through the efforts of Alexis Ritter, who lusts after Salazar despite her cult's dedication to chastity, and by George Cantemir's arrangement with a local chieftain, that would furnish the entire forest for lumber.

**Other books you might like:**
Stephen Goldin, *Jade Darcy and the Zen Pirates*, 1990
   Mary Mason, co-author
Harry Harrison, *Bill, the Galactic Hero: On the Planet of Tasteless Pleasure*, 1991
   David Bischoff, co-author
Janet Kagan, *Mirabile*, 1991
James Luceno, *Illegal Alien*, 1990
Harry Turtledove, *Earthgrip*, 1992

---

**1421**

**TOM DE HAVEN**

## The End-of-Everything Man

(New York: Doubleday, 1991)

**Story type:** Fantasy (Adventure)
**Series:** Chronicles of the King's Tramp
**Major character(s):** Peter Musik, Journalist; Jack, Traveler, Agent; Didge, Magician (dispeller)
**Time period(s):** Indeterminate
**Locale(s):** Lostwithal, Planet—Imaginary

**Summary:** Despite Jack and his allies' successes, the plans of the Mage of Four still threaten Lostwithal. Disasters and character flaws sink the travellers from Kemolo into misery and distraction. Everything will stop if Jack can't find out what's going on and save his allies.

**Other books you might like:**
Piers Anthony, *Split Infinity*, 1980
Ru Emerson, *The Calling of the Three*, 1990
Barbara Hambly, *The Time of the Dark*, 1982
Julian May, *The Many-Colored Land*, 1981
Tom Robbins, *Another Roadside Attraction*, 1971

---

**1422**

**TOM DE HAVEN**

## The Last Human

(New York: Bantam Spectra, 1992)

**Story type:** Fantasy (Political; Quest)
**Series:** Chronicles of the King's Tramp
**Major character(s):** Jack, Traveler (Walker)
**Time period(s):** Indeterminate
**Locale(s):** Undermoment, Mythical Place (extra-dimensional meeting place)

**Summary:** Jack and his comrades work to defeat the deadly threat represented by the Last Human: the Queen of Noise, a creature which has escaped from another dimension to the Undermoment, while citizens of the three safe worlds meet in the Undermoment to achieve mutual understanding.

**Other books you might like:**
Philip Jose Farmer, *To Your Scattered Bodies Go*, 1971
Barbara Hambly, *The Time of the Dark*, 1982
Robert Jordan, *The Eye of the World*, 1989
Michael Moorcock, *The Fortress of the Pearl*, 1989
Margaret Weis, *Serpent Mage*, 1992
   Tracy Hickman, co-author

---

**1423**

**TOM DE HAVEN**

## Walker of Worlds

(New York: Doubleday, 1990)

**Story type:** Fantasy (Contemporary)
**Series:** Chronicles of the King's Tramp
**Major character(s):** Jack, Traveler
**Time period(s):** Indeterminate
**Locale(s):** Earth

**Summary:** As elements of fantasy begin to intrude on the life of everyday people, the Walker begins his journeys between worlds.

**Other books you might like:**
Clive Barker, *Weaveworld*, 1987
John Crowley, *Little, Big*, 1981
Charles de Lint, *Drink Down the Moon*, 1990
Robert Holdstock, *Lavondyss: Journey to an Unknown Region*, 1989
Morgan Llewelyn, *The Isles of the Blest*, 1989

---

**1424**

**WALTER DE LA MARE**

## The Return

(Mineola, New York: Dover, 1997)

**Story type:** Horror (Possession)
**Major character(s):** Arthur Lawford, Parent; Sheila Lawford, Young Woman (Arthur's wife); Grisel Herbert, Young Woman
**Time period(s):** 1920s
**Locale(s):** London, England

**Summary:** Drawn to the grave of Noiholas Sabathier, an eighteenth-century suicide, Arthur Lawford falls asleep on top of it and awakens with the man's features and irascible personality. Arthur struggles to understand his apparent supernatural possession and find a means of driving Sabathier from him to keep his life from falling apart. First published in 1920. Introduction by S.T. Joshi.

**Other books you might like:**
Fred Chappell, *The Lodger*, 1993
H.B. Drake, *The Shadowy Thing*, 1928
H.P. Lovecraft, *The Case of Charles Dexter Ward*, 1943
Robert Louis Stevenson, *The Strange Case of Dr. Jekyll and Mr. Hyde*, 1886

---

**1425**

**CHARLES DE LINT**

## Dreams Underfoot

(New York: Tor, 1993)

**Story type:** Fantasy (Urban; Collection)

**Summary:** Contains two original and 17 stories reprinted from periodicals, anthologies and small press publications 1987-1993. The extra-natural elements in some stories infuse from outside the real world, while in others, elements intrinsic to the real world we know hide until pointed out. In yet others, the very concept of a "real" world comes into question.

**Other books you might like:**
Emma Bull, *Bone Dance: A Fantasy for Technophiles*, 1991
Steven Brust, *Agyar*, 1993
Megan Lindholm, *Wizard of the Pigeons*, 1986
Terri Windling, *Elsewhere*, 1981
  Mark Alan Arnold, co-editor
Terri Windling, *Elsewhere II*, 1982
  Mark Alan Arnold, co-editor
Terri Windling, *Elsewhere III*, 1984
  Mark Alan Arnold, co-editor

---

**1426**

CHARLES DE LINT

## Drink Down the Moon

(New York: Ace, 1990)

**Story type:** Fantasy (Contemporary)
**Time period(s):** 1990s
**Locale(s):** Earth

**Summary:** In this sequel to *Jack the Giant Killer*, the normal, everyday world comes in contact with an alternate world where magic works. The characters find themselves facing and dealing with far more than they ever thought they would.

**Other books you might like:**
Suzy McKee Charnas, *The Vampire Tapestry*, 1980
Tom De Haven, *Walker of Worlds*, 1990
Alan Dean Foster, *Spellsinger*, 1983
  Book 1 - Spellsinger Series
Esther Friesner, *Elf Defense*, 1988
Tanya Huff, *Gate of Darkness, Circle of Light*, 1989

---

**1427**

CHARLES DE LINT

## Ghosts of Wind and Shadow

(Eugene, Oregon: Pulphouse Publishing, 1991)

**Story type:** Fantasy (Urban; Contemporary)
**Major character(s):** Meran Kelledy, Musician, Mythical Creature (faerie); Cerin Kelledy, Mythical Creature (faerie); Lesli Batterberry, Musician, Runaway
**Time period(s):** 1990s
**Locale(s):** California

**Summary:** When Lesli's mother notices and begins to discourage her belief in Faerie, Lesli runs away and then is abducted and imprisoned. Informed of Lesli's disappearance, Cerin sets out to find her using Faerie guidance.

**Other books you might like:**
Mercedes Lackey, *Bardic Voices*, 1991
Will Shetterly, *Elsewhere*, 1991
Will Shetterly, *Liavek: Wizard's Row*, 1987
  Emma Bull, co-editor
Terri Windling, *Borderland*, 1986
  Mark Alan Arnold, co-editor
Terri Windling, *Bordertown*, 1986
  Mark Alan Arnold, co-editor
Terri Windling, *Life on the Border*, 1991
  editor

---

**1428**

CHARLES DE LINT

## Hedgework and Guessery

(Eugene, Oregon: Pulphouse Publishing, 1991)

**Story type:** Fantasy (Collection)
**Series:** Author's Choice Monthly

**Summary:** Issue 22 in the Author's Choice Monthly Series, this collection contains an introduction plus 7 poems (1978-1991) and 8 short stories (1986-1990), most having appeared in periodicals, anthologies, chapbooks and limited edition books.

**Other books you might like:**
Ellen Datlow, *The Year's Best Fantasy and Horror: Third Annual Collection*, 1990
  Terri Windling, co-editor
Ron Goulart, *Skyrocket Steele Conquers the Universe and Other Media Tales*, 1990
Damon Knight, *God's Nose*, 1991
Elizabeth A. Lynn, *Tales From a Vanished Country*, 1990
Judith Moffett, *Two That Came True*, 1991
Kim Stanley Robinson, *A Sensitive Dependence on Initial Conditions*, 1991
Spider Robinson, *True Minds*, 1990

---

**1429**

CHARLES DE LINT

## The Hidden City

(New York: Bantam Spectra, 1990)

**Story type:** Fantasy (Alternate World; Adventure)
**Series:** Philip Jose Farmer's The Dungeon
**Major character(s):** Clive Folliot, Military Personnel
**Time period(s):** 1870s (1870); 1890s (1896)
**Locale(s):** Alternate Earth

**Summary:** The adventure of Clive Folliot through the nine levels of the Dungeon's computer game-like world are continued in the fifth volume.

**Other books you might like:**
Robin Wayne Bailey, *The Lake of Fire*, 1989
Bruce Coville, *The Dark Abyss*, 1989
Robert A. Heinlein, *Glory Road*, 1963
Richard A. Lupoff, *The Black Tower*, 1988
Richard A. Lupoff, *The Final Battle*, 1990
Gene Wolfe, *The Shadow of the Torturer*, 1980

---

**1430**

CHARLES DE LINT

## Into the Green

(New York: Tor, 1993)

**Story type:** Fantasy (Adventure)
**Major character(s):** Angharad, Minstrel, Wanderer
**Time period(s):** Indeterminate
**Locale(s):** Kingdoms of the Green Isles, Fictional Country

**Summary:** Incorporates short stories reprinted from Marion Zimmer Bradley's *Sword and Sorceress* anthology series into the novel framework and portrays Angharad's travels and encounters with the kingdom's residents, some of whom exhibit prejudice toward those possessing unusual powers and one whose gruesome trade in body parts could not exist without the magically empowered. Concludes with four pages of musical notation for harp.

**Other books you might like:**
Gael Baudino, *Gossamer Axe*, 1990
Phyllis Eisenstein, *Born to Exile*, 1978
Phyllis Eisenstein, *In the Red Lord's Reach*, 1989
Mercedes Lackey, *Bardic Voices*, 1991
Andre Norton, *Songsmith*, 1992
    A.C. Crispin, co-author
Caroline Stevermer, *River Rats*, 1992

**1431**

### CHARLES DE LINT

## The Ivory and the Horn

(New York: Tor, 1995)

**Story type:** Fantasy (Collection; Urban)
**Time period(s):** 1990s
**Locale(s):** Newford, Canada

**Summary:** Contains one original and 14 stories reprinted from periodicals, anthologies and chapbooks 1992-1994. All are set in Newford, home to a wide variety of artists and site of many unusual occurrences as magic infuses the mundane world.

**Other books you might like:**
David Brin, *The River of Time*, 1986
John Crowley, *Antiquities*, 1993
Lisa Goldstein, *Travelers in Magic*, 1994
Robert Holdstock, *The Bone Forest*, 1992
Megan Lindholm, *Wizard of the Pigeons*, 1986
Pat Murphy, *Points of Departure*, 1990
Gene Wolfe, *Storeys From the Old Hotel*, 1992

**1432**

### CHARLES DE LINT

## The Little Country

(New York: Morrow, 1991)

**Story type:** Fantasy (Legend; Contemporary)
**Major character(s):** Janey Little, Musician (pipes and fiddle); Thomas Little, Aged Person (Janey's grandfather); Felix Gavin, Sailor, Musician
**Time period(s):** 1990s (1991)
**Locale(s):** Bodbury, England; Mousehole, England

**Summary:** Janey Little and her grandfather, Thomas, are hiding a very important book in their cottage. Although they only suspect that is has unusual properties, it seems that whenever it's opened, things begin to happen. As Janey reads the book, the adventures that befall the characters within the story begin to affect the lives of Janey, Thomas and the people around them.

**Other books you might like:**
Tom Deitz, *Sunshaker's War*, 1990
Michael Ende, *The Neverending Story*, 1983
Raymond E. Feist, *Faerie Tale*, 1988
William Goldman, *The Princess Bride*, 1973
Mercedes Lackey, *Knight of Ghosts and Shadows*, 1990
    Ellen Guon, co-author

**1433**

### CHARLES DE LINT

## Memory and Dream

(New York: Tor, 1994)

**Story type:** Fantasy (Contemporary; Horror)
**Major character(s):** Isabelle "Izzy" Copley, Artist (painter), Student—College; Katharine Mully, Writer, Lesbian; Vincent Adjani Rushkin, Artist (painter), Recluse
**Time period(s):** 1970s (1973-1979); 1990s (1992-1993)
**Locale(s):** Canada

**Summary:** Izzy studies under the master painter, Rushkin, despite his abusive, moody nature, learning his ability to create animated doppelgangers of some paintings' subjects, including characters from Katharine's stories. Despite premonitions and direct warnings, Izzy continues her affiliation with Rushkin as her career advances, little suspecting the dark future resulting from her actions.

**Other books you might like:**
Aaron Allston, *Galatea in 2-D*, 1993
Steven Brust, *Agyar*, 1993
Ben Okri, *The Famished Road*, 1992
Nancy Springer, *Larque on the Wing*, 1994
Sheri S. Tepper, *A Plague of Angels*, 1993

**1434**

### CHARLES DE LINT

## Our Lady of the Harbour

(Eugene, Oregon: Pulphouse Publishing, 1991)

**Story type:** Fantasy (Legend; Contemporary)
**Major character(s):** Matt Casey, Musician; Amy Scallan, Musician; Katrina, Mythical Creature (mermaid)
**Time period(s):** 1970s
**Locale(s):** Nowford, Fictional City

**Summary:** Matt Casey, a brilliant musician unable to relate to people, attracts the attention of a mermaid. She trades her tail for legs, but is cursed to die unless she can get him to love her. This story is a retelling of Hans Christian Andersen's "The Little Mermaid."

**Other books you might like:**
Gael Baudino, *Gossamer Axe*, 1990
Emma Bull, *War for the Oaks*, 1987
Pamela Dean, *Tam Lin*, 1991
Ellen Kushner, *Thomas the Rhymer*, 1990
Terri Windling, *Life on the Border*, 1991
    editor

**1435**

### CHARLES DE LINT

## Someplace to Be Flying

(New York: Tor, 1998)

**Story type:** Fantasy (Contemporary; Quest)
**Series:** Newford
**Major character(s):** Hank "Joey Bennett" Warner, Taxi Driver (unregistered); Lily Carson, Photojournalist
**Time period(s):** 1990s (1996)
**Locale(s):** Newford, Canada

**Summary:** While attempting to locate evidence of humanoid animal creatures, called First People by Native Americans, Lily meets Hank.

Together they find not only evidence of the animal people, but also a secret war for the soul of the city.

**Other books you might like:**
A.A. Attanasio, *The Moon's Wife: A Hystery*, 1993
Alan Dean Foster, *To the Vanishing Point*, 1988
Robert Holdstock, *Mythago Wood*, 1984
Richard A. Knaak, *King of the Grey*, 1993
Lucius Shepard, *Kalimantan*, 1992

**1436**

**CHARLES DE LINT**

## Spiritwalk
(New York: Tor, 1992)

**Story type:** Fantasy (Collection; Urban)
**Series:** Tamson House
**Time period(s):** 1990s
**Locale(s):** Ottawa, Ontario, Canada

**Summary:** Combines ''Merlin Dreams in the Mondrean Wood'' plus *Ascian in Rose* (1987), *Westlin Wind* (1989) and *Ghostwood* (1990) relating events surrounding Tamson House, a huge and mysterious house containing paths to lands through which Native American and Celtic magic leaks into our world. Set in the universe of *Moonheart: A Romance*.

**Other books you might like:**
Gael Baudino, *Gossamer Axe*, 1990
Emma Bull, *War for the Oaks*, 1987
Mercedes Lackey, *Born to Run*, 1992
    Larry Dixon, co-author
Mercedes Lackey, *Summoned to Tourney*, 1992
    Ellen Guon, co-author
John Maddox Roberts, *King of the Wood*, 1983
Will Shetterly, *Elsewhere*, 1991
Terri Windling, *Borderland*, 1986
    Mark Alan Arnold, co-editor
Terri Windling, *Bordertown*, 1986
    Mark Alan Arnold, co-editor
Terri Windling, *Life on the Border*, 1991
    editor

**1437**

**CHARLES DE LINT**

## Svaha
(New York: Ace, 1989)

**Story type:** Science Fiction (Cyberpunk)
**Major character(s):** Gahzee Animiki-Waewidum, Indian, Scientist; Shigehero Gorp, Criminal
**Time period(s):** 21st century
**Locale(s):** Canada

**Summary:** In the late twentieth century, most of western civilization collapsed beneath the weight of its own pollution and corruption. The Native American peoples made a series of scientific discoveries which allowed them, almost overnight, to transform their reservations into virtual walled utopias. Now, however, the gangsters and multinational corporations who run what's left of the western world, have set themselves to invade and destroy the Native American lands. The scientist-warrior Gahzee must leave his home and enter a hellish world of radioactive wastelands, cybernetic samurai, and deadly plots to counter their efforts.

**Other books you might like:**
Andre Norton, *The Beast Master*, 1959
Andre Norton, *Lord of Thunder*, 1962
Craig Strete, *The Bleeding Man and Other Stories*, 1977
Craig Strete, *Death in the Spirit House*, 1988
Craig Strete, *Dreams That Burn in the Night*, 1982

**1438**

**CHARLES DE LINT**

## Trader
(New York: Tor, 1997)

**Story type:** Fantasy (Contemporary; Quest)
**Series:** Newford
**Major character(s):** Max Trader, Artisan (luthier), Businessman; Johnny Devlin, Rogue, Alcoholic; Zefty Lacerda, Waiter/Waitress
**Time period(s):** 1990s
**Locale(s):** Newford, Fictional City; Canada; The Spiritworld, Mythical Place

**Summary:** When Max and Johnny mysteriously wake up in each other's bodies, ne'er-do-well Johnny immediately adapts to Max's stable environment. Now in possession of Johnny's body and miserable life to date, Max must put together a new life. His efforts lead to the realm of dreams and spirits.

**Other books you might like:**
Aaron Allston, *Galatea in 2-D*, 1993
A.A. Attanasio, *The Moon's Wife: A Hystery*, 1993
Peter R. Emshwiller, *The Host*, 1991
Robert Holdstock, *Mythago Wood*, 1984
Ben Okri, *The Famished Road*, 1992
Dan Simmons, *The Hollow Man*, 1992
Nancy Springer, *Larque on the Wing*, 1994

**1439**

**CHARLES DE LINT**

## Westlin Wind
(Seattle, WA: The Anxolotl Press, 1989)

**Story type:** Fantasy (Quest)
**Major character(s):** Emma, Young Woman; Esmeralda Foyan, Young Woman
**Time period(s):** Indeterminate
**Locale(s):** Ottawa, Ontario, Canada; Alternate Universe

**Summary:** The quest is to save a woman, Emma, who has been separated from her soul. A group of friends goes after her body, while Esmeralda, traveling alone, searches for the soul.

**Other books you might like:**
Jo Clayton, *Diadem from the Stars*, 1986
Bruce Fergusson, *The Mace of Souls*, 1989
Jennifer Roberson, *Sword-Singer*, 1988

**1440**

**CHARLES DE LINT**
**BRIAN FROUD**, Illustrator

## The Wild Wood
(New York: Bantam Spectra, 1994)

**Story type:** Fantasy (Contemporary)

**Series:** Brian Froud's Faerielands
**Major character(s):** Eithnie Gerrows, Artist (painter); Albin, Mythical Creature
**Time period(s):** 1990s
**Locale(s):** Ontario, Canada; Arizona

**Summary:** When Eithnie retreats to her secluded cabin to paint, she discovers the fairy realm, now endangered by modern development. Illustrations and five-page introduction by Brian Froud. First of a new series.

**Other books you might like:**
Pamela Dean, *The Secret Country*, 1985
Robert Holdstock, *Mythago Wood*, 1984
Tanith Lee, *Black Unicorn*, 1991
Megan Lindholm, *Cloven Hooves*, 1991
Patricia A. McKillip, *Something Rich and Strange*, 1994

---

`1441`

**CHARLES DE LINT**

## The Wishing Well

(Eugene, Oregon: Pulphouse Publishing Axolotl Press, 1993)

**Story type:** Fantasy (Contemporary)
**Major character(s):** Brenda Perry, Journalist, Businesswoman (advertising manager); Ellie Carter, Spirit, Businesswoman; Jilly Coppercorn, Artist
**Time period(s):** 1990s
**Locale(s):** North America

**Summary:** While driving, Brenda finds an abandoned motel where she discovers a mysterious resident and a well from which voices seem to emanate—voices that begin to fill her dreams. When Brenda's lack of self-esteem precipitates financial and personal crises in her life, she abandons her friends in favor of living at the abandoned motel. Alarmed at her unusual behavior, Brenda's friends initiate a search for her.

**Other books you might like:**
Peni R. Griffin, *Hobkin*, 1992
Katharine Kerr, *Resurrection*, 1992
Kristine Kathryn Rusch, *The Gallery of His Dreams*, 1991
Nancy Springer, *Damnbanna*, 1992
Nancy Springer, *The Friendship Song*, 1992
Kate Wilhelm, *Naming the Flowers*, 1992

---

`1442`

**ELISABETH DE VOS**

## The Seraphim Rising

(New York: Roc, 1997)

**Story type:** Science Fiction (Invasion of Earth; Theological)
**Major character(s):** Ezekiel "Zeke", Angel, Telepath; Carson Mc-Cullough, Government Official (liaison to Seraphim); Harry Chen, Deity, Addict
**Time period(s):** 2030s
**Locale(s):** Destiny World, Florida; Atlanta, Georgia

**Summary:** Six eggs fall into the ocean during a meteor shower, leading to fears of an alien invasion. Six angels rise to the surface 30 years later, proclaiming the advent of the Messiah. Possessing telepathic powers like those of the Seraphim, Harry Chen may be God, or perhaps a genetically manipulated being created from material using a seventh egg, secretly stolen and autopsied by the government. Carson must try to prevent Zeke's drinking from interfering

with the Herald Party's political activities, and must determine if the Seraphim represent an alien threat to Earth. First novel.

**Other books you might like:**
Damien Broderick, *The White Abacus*, 1997
Emily Devenport, *The Kronos Condition*, 1997
Mary Doria Russell, *The Sparrow*, 1996
Sharon Shinn, *Archangel*, 1996
Dan Simmons, *Endymion*, 1996

---

`1443`

**JOHN DEAKINS**

## Barrow

(New York: Roc, 1990)

**Story type:** Fantasy (Magic Conflict)
**Major character(s):** Fleetfox, Hero
**Time period(s):** Indeterminate
**Locale(s):** Barrow, Fictional Country

**Summary:** Good and evil magic have leaked into the town of Barrow, leaving Fleetfox and sundry others to cope with the new order of life.

**Other books you might like:**
Don Davis, *Sins of the Flesh*, 1989
    Jay Davis, co-author
Gordon R. Dickson, *The Earth Lords*, 1989
Mark C. Perry, *Morigu: The Dead*, 1990
Jack Yeovil, *Drachenfels*, 1989

---

`1444`

**PAMELA DEAN**

## The Dubious Hills

(New York: Tor, 1994)

**Story type:** Fantasy (Magic Conflict; Mystery)
**Series:** Secret Country
**Major character(s):** Arry, Teenager, Empath; Oonan, Healer; Halver, Teacher, Werewolf
**Time period(s):** Indeterminate
**Locale(s):** The Dubious Hills, Fictional Country

**Summary:** Cooperating with others to solve the mystery behind unusual lupine behavior, Arry discovers tantalizing hints about the fate of her missing parents. Further investigation uncovers a surreptitious revolution which could transform her entire society. Set during the Spring of *The Whim of the Dragon*.

**Other books you might like:**
Jesse Browner, *Conglomeros*, 1992
Diane Duane, *The Door into Fire*, 1979
Diane Duane, *The Door into Shadow*, 1984
Nina Kiriki Hoffman, *The Thread That Binds the Bones*, 1993
Diana Wynne Jones, *Cart and Cwidder*, 1977
Diana Wynne Jones, *Drowned Ammet*, 1978
Diana Wynne Jones, *The Spellcoats*, 1979
Meredith Ann Pierce, *The Dark-Angel*, 1982

---

`1445`

**PAMELA DEAN**

## Juniper, Gentian and Rosemary

(New York: Tor, 1998)

**Story type:** Fantasy (Contemporary)

**Major character(s):** Gentian Meriweather, Scientist (amateur astronomer), Teenager; Dominic Hardy, Mythical Creature
**Time period(s):** 1990s (1993-1994)
**Locale(s):** Minneapolis, Minnesota

**Summary:** When a new house goes up almost overnight on the vacant lot next door, Gentian and her sisters, Juniper and Rosemary, become simultaneously fascinated and repelled by Dominic, their mysterious new neighbor. Dominic proposes that the girls help him construct a time machine in the Meriweather attic, a project which threatens to absorb Gentian's attention at the expense of friends, family, and the stars.

**Other books you might like:**
John Crowley, *Little, Big*, 1981
Charles de Lint, *Memory and Dream*, 1994
Elizabeth Hand, *Waking the Moon*, 1995
Alice Hoffman, *Practical Magic*, 1995
Will Shetterly, *Dogland*, 1997

---

**1446**

PAMELA DEAN

## Tam Lin
(New York: Tor, 1991)

**Story type:** Fantasy (Legend; Historical)
**Series:** Fairy Tales
**Major character(s):** Janet Carter, Student; Thomas Lane, Student; Nick Tooley, Student
**Time period(s):** 1970s
**Locale(s):** Blackstock College, Minnesota

**Summary:** Entering college, Janet Carter finds exciting classical education fraught with Shakespeare, Keats, Pope and Homer. Living in a dormitory, away from home for the first time, Janet's growing up is complicated by an unwanted pregnancy.

**Other books you might like:**
Steven Brust, *The Sun, the Moon, and the Stars*, 1987
Kara Dalkey, *The Nightingale*, 1988
Charles de Lint, *Jack, the Giant-Killer*, 1987
Patricia C. Wrede, *Snow White and Rose Red*, 1989

---

**1447**

PAMELA DEAN

## The Whim of the Dragon
(New York: Ace, 1989)

**Story type:** Fantasy (Alternate World)
**Series:** Secret Country
**Major character(s):** Fence, Wizard
**Time period(s):** 1980s
**Locale(s):** Earth; Hidden Land, Alternate Universe

**Summary:** A children's game becomes real when the children are able to cross over to the Hidden Land. The conclusion answers questions raised in the first two books and ends with a battle.

**Other books you might like:**
Joy Chant, *Red Moon and Black Mountain*, 1970
Susan Cooper, *The Dark Is Rising*, 1983
  Book 1 The Dark Is Rising Series
C.S. Lewis, *The Chronicles of Narnia*,
  1951-1956

---

**1448**

HAMILTON DEANE

## Dracula: The Ultimate Illustrated Edition of the World-Famous Vampire Play
(New York: St. Martin's, 1993)

**Story type:** Horror (Anthology; Vampire Story)
**Summary:** The editor collects for the first time two stage adaptations of Bram Stoker's *Dracula*: Hamilton Deane's version, which was written in 1924 and toured with great success in England, and John Balderston's 1927 revision of Deane's play, which ran on Broadway and launched the career of Bela Lugosi. Both plays are extensively illustrated with stills and drawings as well as annotated.

**Other books you might like:**
Marvin Kaye, *13 Plays of Ghosts and the Supernatural*, 1990
  editor
Bram Stoker, *Dracula*, 1895

---

**1449**

DON H. DEBRANDT

## The Quicksilver Screen
(New York: Ballantine Del Rey, 1992)

**Story type:** Science Fiction (Cyberpunk; Arts)
**Major character(s):** Virgil Jakobi, Artist; Thann Demetrios, Artist; Shan, Artist
**Time period(s):** 21st century
**Locale(s):** Earth

**Summary:** Infinite Range Television (IRTV) allows humanity to view transmissions from alternate realities, providing new frontiers of entertainment for everyone. Corporate America assigns researchers to view IRTV in search of solutions to problems and possible new money-making ideas. When one researcher, Virgil Jakobi, takes an unauthorized sabbatical to help prevent a suicide, he finds himself pursued by a reanimated mass murderer.

**Other books you might like:**
Pat Cadigan, *Fools*, 1992
Pat Cadigan, *Mindplayers*, 1987
Pat Cadigan, *Synners*, 1991
Ernest Hogan, *Cortez on Jupiter*, 1990
Marjorie Bradley Kellogg, *Harmony*, 1991
William F. Nolan, *William F. Nolan's Logan: A Trilogy*, 1992
Neal Stephenson, *Snow Crash*, 1992

---

**1450**

ELISA DECARLO

## The Devil You Say
(New York: AvoNova, 1993)

**Story type:** Fantasy (Mystery; Psychic Powers)
**Major character(s):** Aubrey Arbuthnot, Detective—Private, Psychic; Anthony Hornchurch, Servant, Detective—Amateur
**Time period(s):** 1930s (1933)
**Locale(s):** London, England

**Summary:** Hired by a mysterious client to bid on an ancient occult text, *The Book of Shadows*, Aubrey Arbuthnot becomes embroiled in a satanic plot to acquire the powerful artifact. A competitor of the successful bidder turns his daughter into a Ming vase while trying to get the book. Humorous adventure ensues as Aubrey works to destroy the tome and prevent the world's destruction. Author's first novel.

**Other books you might like:**
Lois McMaster Bujold, *The Spirit Ring*, 1992
Mercedes Lackey, *Burning Water*, 1989
Mercedes Lackey, *Children of the Night*, 1990
Mercedes Lackey, *Jinx High*, 1991
R.A. MacAvoy, *Tea with the Black Dragon*, 1983

## `1451`

### ELISA DECARLO

## *Strong Spirits*

(New York: AvoNova, 1994)

**Story type:** Fantasy (Mystery; Psychic Powers)
**Major character(s):** Aubrey Arbuthnot, Detective—Private, Psychic; Anthony Hornchurch, Servant, Detective—Amateur; Farquhar Arbuthnot, Nobleman, Spirit
**Time period(s):** 1920s (1928)
**Locale(s):** England

**Summary:** When Aubrey Arbuthnot attempts to banish the ghost of his father, his work with spiritualists and activity on the astral plane awaken his psychic abilities. Prequel to *The Devil You Say*.

**Other books you might like:**
Nancy Atherton, *Aunt Dimity and the Duke*, 1994
Lois McMaster Bujold, *The Spirit Ring*, 1992
Mercedes Lackey, *Burning Water*, 1989
R.A. MacAvoy, *Tea with the Black Dragon*, 1983
P.H. Cannon, *Scream for Jeeves: A Parody*, 1994

## `1452`

### JOHN DECHANCIE

## *Bride of the Castle*

(New York: Ace, 1994)

**Story type:** Science Fiction (Alternate Universe; Humor)
**Series:** Castle Perilous
**Major character(s):** Incarnadine, Royalty, Magician; Linda, Bride, Magician; Rance, Royalty, Wanderer
**Time period(s):** 1990s; Indeterminate
**Locale(s):** Castle Perilous, Planet—Imaginary (center of the Multiverse); New York, New York

**Summary:** Returning from vacation, the king conjures up his double and leaves. While finalizing the design of her wedding dress, Linda worries if Gene will find happiness when they marry. Barbarians trap Gene in a seemingly peaceful manner when he ducks out of his bachelor party, while Rance must rid himself of the curse he picked up while grave robbing.

**Other books you might like:**
Charles de Lint, *The Little Country*, 1991
Robert A. Heinlein, *Glory Road*, 1963
Michael Kandel, *Strange Invasion*, 1989
Ken Rolston, *Extreme Paranoia: Nobody Knows the Trouble I've Shot*, 1991
Will Shetterly, *The Tangled Lands*, 1989

## `1453`

### JOHN DECHANCIE

## *Castle Dreams*

(New York: Ace, 1992)

**Story type:** Science Fiction (Alternate Universe; Humor)
**Series:** Castle Perilous
**Major character(s):** Incarnadine, Royalty (King of the Realms Perilous), Magician; Trent, Royalty (Prince of the Realms Perilous)
**Time period(s):** 1990s
**Locale(s):** Castle Perilous, Planet—Imaginary (center of the Multiverse)

**Summary:** When Incarnadine turns up missing, suspicion falls on the new King of Castle Perilous, the former King's brother. Two spot quizzes and a final exam test readers' attentiveness to the story and views on the author's style and the publishing industry.

**Other books you might like:**
Douglas Adams, *Dirk Gently's Holistic Detective Agency*, 1987
Douglas Adams, *The Hitchhiker's Guide to the Galaxy*, 1980
Philip K. Dick, *A Maze of Death*, 1970
Alan Dean Foster, *Glory Lane*, 1987
Robert A. Heinlein, *Glory Road*, 1963

## `1454`

### JOHN DECHANCIE

## *Castle Spellbound*

(New York: Ace, 1992)

**Story type:** Science Fiction (Alternate Universe; Science Fantasy)
**Series:** Castle Perilous
**Major character(s):** Trent, Royalty (prince); Osmirik, Librarian, Magician; Kwip, Thief
**Time period(s):** Indeterminate
**Locale(s):** Castle Perilous, Planet—Imaginary (center of the multiverse); Hellas, Mythical Place

**Summary:** King Incarnadine sends Trent to oversee a military campaign. Meanwhile, two lazy apprentice sorcerers unintentionally unleash supernatural forces, sending them into Castle Perilous with the instructions to clean up the entire place, no matter what the cost.

**Other books you might like:**
Steven Brust, *Cowboy Feng's Space Bar and Grille*, 1990
Alan Dean Foster, *Quozl*, 1989
Alan Dean Foster, *To the Vanishing Point*, 1988
Stephen Goldin, *Jade Darcy and the Zen Pirates*, 1990
   Mary Mason, co-author
Michael Kandel, *Strange Invasion*, 1989
Nick Pollotta, *Illegal Aliens*, 1989
   Phil Foglio, co-author

## `1455`

### JOHN DECHANCIE

## *Castle War!*

(New York: Ace, 1990)

**Story type:** Science Fiction (Alternate Universe; Science Fantasy)
**Series:** Castle Perilous
**Major character(s):** Jeremy Hochstader, Computer Expert; Incarnadine, Royalty (King of Castle Perilous), Magician; Gene Ferraro, Adventurer
**Time period(s):** 1990s

**Locale(s):** Castle Perilous, Planet—Imaginary (Center of the Multiverse); Merydion, Planet—Imaginary

**Summary:** After the interuniversal medium is disturbed by a previous disaster, the residents of Castle Perilous are taken by surprise when they are visited by their duplicates from the mirror Castle Perilous that has appeared next door. His portal had become unusable, leaving Lord Incarnadine stranded in another universe. Jeremy, with the help of an artificial intelligence, must restabilize the cosmos.

**Other books you might like:**
Douglas Adams, *The Hitchhiker's Guide to the Galaxy*, 1980
Alan Dean Foster, *Quozl*, 1989
Alan Dean Foster, *To the Vanishing Point*, 1988
Alan Dean Foster, *Glory Lane*, 1987

## 1456

**JOHN DECHANCIE**
**DAVID BISCHOFF**, Co-Author

### Dr. Dimension

(New York: Roc, 1993)

**Story type:** Science Fiction (Space Opera; Humor)
**Major character(s):** Demetrios "Dr. Dimension" Demopoulos, Scientist, Inventor; Vivian Vernon, Scientist; Samuel Flitheimer, Philanthropist
**Time period(s):** 1930s (1939); Indeterminate
**Locale(s):** Flitheimer University, Nebraska; *Mudlark*, Spaceship

**Summary:** Dr. Demopoulos thinks he might lose his grant when he blows up the physics lab once again. Dr. Vernon hopes to get his grant, but Sam Flitheimer proves to be a fan of super-science literature, fascinated with the idea of a spaceship or even a time machine. As the deadline arrives, a mysterious package of strange parts allows the inventor to complete a spaceship. Leaving to keep the ship out of Nazi hands, the explorers find themselves involved with aliens who need aid from the humans.

**Other books you might like:**
Douglas Adams, *The Hitchhiker's Guide to the Galaxy*, 1980
David Bischoff, *Night of the Living Shark!*, 1991
Alan Dean Foster, *To the Vanishing Point*, 1988
Mel Gilden, *Hawaiian U.F.O. Aliens*, 1991
T. Jackson King, *Retread Shop*, 1988
Henry Kuttner, *Robots Have No Tails*, 1952

## 1457

**JOHN DECHANCIE**

### From Prussia with Love

(Rocklin, California: Prima, 1996)

**Story type:** Fantasy (Historical; Magic Conflict)
**Series:** Castle Falkenstein
**Major character(s):** Thomas "Tom" Edward Olam, Time Traveler, Computer Expert; Ludwig Wittelsbach, Ruler (king); Ruggerio Zambelli, Scientist (rocket)
**Time period(s):** Indeterminate (1870s equivalent)
**Locale(s):** *Wagner*, in the Air (zeppelin); Europe, Alternate Earth

**Summary:** While on the *Wagner* in Victorian-era Bavaria, Tom observes a Russian missile crash into the Baltic Sea. He convinces Ludwig to start his own research progarm to prevent Chancellor Bismarck's steam-powered ballistic missiles from conquering New Europe. With the aid of an Italian fireworks designer who plans to build a ship to go to the moon and his dwarf engineer, Ludwig creates a countermissile for the defense of his kingdom, despite his reluc-

tance to develop weapons of mass destruction. Computer game tie-in.

**Other books you might like:**
Orson Scott Card, *The Folk of the Fringe*, 1989
John Crowley, *Aegypt*, 1987
William Gibson, *The Difference Engine*, 1991
  Bruce Sterling, co-author
Paul J. McAuley, *Pasquale's Angel*, 1995
Tim Powers, *The Anubis Gates*, 1983
Harry Turtledove, *The Guns of the South: A Novel of the Civil War*, 1992

## 1458

**JOHN DECHANCIE**

### Innerverse

(New York: AvoNova, 1996)

**Story type:** Science Fiction (Dystopian; Political)
**Major character(s):** Frank Sutter, Spy (Special Forces), Experimental Subject; Alice, Revolutionary, Adventurer
**Time period(s):** 2020s
**Locale(s):** United States; The Republic, Fictional Country (eastern United States)

**Summary:** Use of Innerverse, a nanotechnology development, brings despotism and a 30-year silence from the eastern United States. Searching for insight into the new society, Frank Sutter ingests Innerverse and begins to explore the Republic, aided by Alice, a Republican resident with inactive Innerverse.

**Other books you might like:**
Raphael Carter, *The Fortunate Fall*, 1996
Jeffrey A. Carver, *From a Changeling Star*, 1989
Philip K. Dick, *The Unteleported Man*, 1983
  revised edition
Neal Stephenson, *The Diamond Age*, 1995
Sheri S. Tepper, *Grass*, 1989
Vernor Vinge, *A Fire upon the Deep*, 1992

## 1459

**JOHN DECHANCIE**

### The Kruton Interface

(New York: Ace, 1993)

**Story type:** Science Fiction (Humor; Space Opera)
**Major character(s):** David L. Wanker, Military Personnel, Spaceship Captain
**Time period(s):** Indeterminate Future
**Locale(s):** *U.S.S. Repulse*, Spaceship; Kruton, Planet—Imaginary; Outer Space

**Summary:** When a race of lawyers sues the entire human race, Captain David Wanker rushes to the Human/Kruton border with *U.S.S. Repulse*, the worst crewed spaceship in the fleet, to save humanity from the litigious shapechangers.

**Other books you might like:**
Douglas Adams, *The Hitchhiker's Guide to the Galaxy*, 1980
Douglas Adams, *The Restaurant at the End of the Universe*, 1982
Jack L. Chalker, *The Red Tape War*, 1991
  Mike Resnick, George Alec Effinger, co-authors
John M. Ford, *How Much for Just the Planet?*, 1987
Leah Rewolinski, *Star Wreck: The Generation Gap*, 1990
Leah Rewolinski, *Star Wreck II: The Attack of the Jargonites*, 1991
Leah Rewolinski, *Star Wreck III: Time Warped*, 1992

## **1460**

### JOHN DECHANCIE

## *Living with Aliens*

(New York: Ace, 1995)

**Story type:** Science Fiction (Invasion of Earth; Adventure)
**Major character(s):** Drew Hayes, Teenager; Zorg, Alien; Flez, Alien
**Time period(s):** 1990s
**Locale(s):** Keynesville, Ohio

**Summary:** During his summer vacation, aliens come to live with Drew Hayes, a normal 13-year-old. Although the aliens can control other people's minds, nothing conquers the curiosity of a teenage boy with nothing to do.

**Other books you might like:**
Robert A. Heinlein, *Have Spacesuit—Will Travel*, 1958
Zenna Henderson, *Ingathering: The Complete People Stories of Zenna Henderson*, 1995
Daniel Keyes, *Flowers for Algernon*, 1966
Rebecca Ore, *Becoming Alien*, 1987

## **1461**

### JOHN DECHANCIE

## *MagicNet*

(New York: Morrow AvoNova, 1993)

**Story type:** Fantasy (Adventure; Contemporary)
**Major character(s):** Schuyler "Skye" King, Professor, Detective—Amateur; Lloyd Merlin Jones, Computer Expert, Warlock; Grant, Computer Expert, Disembodied Personality
**Time period(s):** 1990s
**Locale(s):** Los Angeles, California; MagicNet, Cyberspace

**Summary:** While speaking to Grant on the telephone, Skye hears him murdered. Following Grant's instructions, Skye later finds a computer artifact of Grant's personality within MagicNet, an amateur computer network. Skye learns that Grant's death might be the result of Merlin's programming that utilizes magic to allow psychic manipulation of virtual reality, and travels to Los Angeles to confront Merlin. There he discovers a bizarre landscape and perilous reality and virtual reality.

**Other books you might like:**
Aaron Allston, *Galatea in 2-D*, 1993
Piers Anthony, *Killobyte*, 1993
Rick Cook, *The Wizardry Cursed*, 1991
Philip Jose Farmer, *Red Orc's Rage*, 1991
Will Shetterly, *The Tangled Lands*, 1989
Wm. Mark Simmons, *In the Net of Dreams*, 1990
Vivian Vande Velde, *User Unfriendly*, 1991

## **1462**

### STEPHEN DEDMAN

## *The Art of Arrow Cutting*

(New York: Tor, 1997)

**Story type:** Fantasy (Contemporary; Magic Conflict)
**Major character(s):** Michelangelo "Mage" Magistrale, Wizard, Photographer; Tamenaga Tatsuo, Wizard, Organized Crime Figure; Charles "Charlie" Willis Takumo, Supernatural Being, Stuntman
**Time period(s):** 1990s
**Locale(s):** Las Vegas, Nevada; Calgary, Alberta, Canada

**Summary:** Photographer "Mage" Magistrale briefly meets a mysterious ill woman who gives him a key, and must suddenly evade the police, the Japanese mob, female ninja assassins, and a rukoro-kubi, which is nothing but a head and pair of hands. First novel.

**Other books you might like:**
Marion Zimmer Bradley, *Witchlight*, 1996
Kara Dalkey, *Little Sister*, 1996
Kwadwo Agymah Kamau, *Flickering Shadows*, 1996
Mercedes Lackey, *The Fire Rose*, 1995
Cary Osborne, *Iroshi*, 1995

## **1463**

### RON DEE

## *Blood*

(New York: Pocket, 1993)

**Story type:** Horror (Vampire Story)
**Major character(s):** Debi Develos, Vampire, Experimental Subject; Fred Langston, Police Officer (former FBI agent); Trish Blaine, Doctor
**Time period(s):** 1990s (1993)
**Locale(s):** Atlanta, Georgia

**Summary:** Debi Develos agrees to an experimental form of medical therapy to help cure her brain tumor, unaware that the serum injected into her will break down her inhibitions and turn her and everyone she bites into a bloodthirsty vampire.

**Other books you might like:**
Kathryn Meyer Griffith, *The Last Vampire*, 1992
Robert R. McCammon, *They Thirst*, 1981
Dan Simmons, *Children of the Night*, 1992
Brian Stableford, *The Empire of Fear*, 1988

## **1464**

### RON DEE

## *Blood Lust*

(New York: Dell, 1990)

**Story type:** Horror (Vampire Story)
**Major character(s):** Warren MacDonald, Religious; Emily Knox, Teenager; Benjamin Dixon, Vampire Hunter, Religious
**Time period(s):** 1990s
**Locale(s):** Valley View, Missouri (a suburb of St. Louis)

**Summary:** A plague of vampirism spreads like wildfire through the small town of Valley View, claiming the wife of Warren MacDonald and the entire family of Emily Knox. With the help of Benjamin Dixon, a preacher who has tracked the vampire scourge from his own town, the two fight against hopeless odds to save Valley View, and perhaps the entire country, from this inexorable doom.

**Other books you might like:**
Robert R. McCammon, *They Thirst*, 1981

## **1465**

### RON DEE

## *Descent*

(New York: Dell Abyss, 1991)

**Story type:** Horror (Occult)

**Major character(s):** Sarah Finley, Doctor (psychiatrist); Vickie Laster, Young Woman; Garcia Efstathiou, Lover (a.k.a. Aleister C.)
**Time period(s):** 1990s
**Locale(s):** Stillwater, Oklahoma

**Summary:** Vickie Laster's one-night stand with a stranger to get back at her abusive husband turns out to have some peculiar consequences. For one thing, her lover proves to be a dead rock star who had embraced the Satanic and died at the site of their tryst years before. For another, Vickie has become pregnant, even though medically incapable of bearing a child, leaving her to wonder just what the child really is.

**Other books you might like:**
Douglas Clegg, *Breeder*, 1990
Nancy A. Collins, *Tempter*, 1990
Ira Levin, *Rosemary's Baby*, 1967

## 1466
### RON DEE

## Dusk

(New York: Dell Abyss, 1991)

**Story type:** Horror (Vampire Story)
**Major character(s):** Samantha Borden, Government Official (immigration officer); Sheriff Bill, Lawman (local sheriff); Jay Adwon, Lawman (deputy)
**Time period(s):** 1990s
**Locale(s):** Dallas, Texas

**Summary:** When a group of rambunctious young vampires indiscriminately blows the cover of a vampire stronghold near the Mexican border, it leads to a bloody war with all the mortals living between the border and Dallas.

**Other books you might like:**
Stephen King, *Salem's Lot*, 1975
Robert R. McCammon, *They Thirst*, 1981

## 1467
### RON DEE
### ROGER GERBERDING, Illustrator

## Sex and Blood

(Leesburg, Virginia: TAL, 1994)

**Story type:** Horror (Collection; Vampire Story)

**Summary:** This book features three interconnected stories by an author who specializes in vampire fiction. In "Blood Tithe," lonely loser John contacts an escort agency unaware that its promise of great sex includes vampirism. In "Stakeout," John's ex-wife Rhonda searches for her missing husband and ends up in a nightclub catering to the undead. In "Wholly Lust," Rhonda fights for her mortality against vampires who want to turn her into what John has become. This chapbook, which was not available until 1995, was issued in a signed limited edition of 1,000 copies.

**Other books you might like:**
S. Darnbrook Colson, *Snakes*, 1992
Brian Hodge, *Shrines and Desecrations*, 1994
Nancy Kilpatrick, *Sex and the Single Vampire*, 1994
Edward Lee, *Edward Lee's Quest for Sex, Truth and Reality*, 1992
Lucy Taylor, *Unnatural Acts*, 1992

## 1468
### RON DEE

## Succumb

(New York: Pocket, 1994)

**Story type:** Horror (Doppelganger)
**Major character(s):** Martin Paarman, Teacher (music); Leigh Paarman, Advertising (executive), Businesswoman; Jan "Jeanette" Fancy, Femme Fatale
**Time period(s):** 1990s (1994)
**Locale(s):** United States

**Summary:** Frustrated with the loss of direction in his life and his increasingly strained marriage, Martin Paarman starts an affair with Jan Fancy, a seductive bar pickup who fulfills Martin's every need, and whom he begins to suspect is simply the sum of all his desires made flesh.

**Other books you might like:**
Charles L. Grant, *For Fear of the Night*, 1988
Richard Matheson, *Earthbound*, 1981
Eric McCormack, *The Paradise Motel*, 1989
T.L. Parkinson, *The Man Upstairs*, 1991

## 1469
### TOM DEITZ

## Above the Lower Sky

(New York: AvoNova/Morrow, 1994)

**Story type:** Fantasy (Science Fiction; Psychic Powers)
**Major character(s):** Kevin Mauney, Writer (fantasy novelist); Fir, Mythical Creature (selkie); Thunderbird Devlin "Bird" O'Connor, Indian (Cherokee)
**Time period(s):** 2020s (2024)
**Locale(s):** County Offaly, Ireland (United Eire); Aztlan Free Zone, Mexico

**Summary:** Fir induces Kevin to travel to the sea during a hurricane. Followed by several large men who try to kill him, Kevin discovers that he and his estranged sister, along with an unknown third person, must join together against an as yet unknown danger to save humanity.

**Other books you might like:**
Don Callander, *Aquamancer*, 1993
Gordon R. Dickson, *Home From the Shore*, 1978
A.E. Van Vogt, *The Silkie*, 1969
Joan D. Vinge, *The Summer Queen*, 1991
Lawrence Watt-Evans, *The Lure of the Basilisk*, 1980

## 1470
### TOM DEITZ

## Darkthunder's Way

(New York: Avon, 1989)

**Story type:** Fantasy (Quest)
**Series:** David Sullivan
**Major character(s):** David Sullivan, Student—College, Adventurer; Morwyne the Powershaper, Mythical Creature
**Time period(s):** 20th century
**Locale(s):** Western United States, Alternate Earth

**Summary:** David and his companion, the son of a medicine man, travel through the mythlands of the Cherokee Indians to help

Morwyne find a way home from the land of the Sidhe. Together they fight against the evil magic of Finnvarra.

**Other books you might like:**
Greg Bear, *The Infinity Concerto*, 1987
M. Coleman Easton, *Spirits of Cavern and Hearth*, 1989
Michael Moorcock, *The Fortress of the Pearl*, 1989
Dave Smeds, *The Schemes of Dragons*, 1989
Craig Strete, *Death in the Spirit House*, 1988

## 1471
### TOM DEITZ

## *Dreambuilder*
(New York: AvoNova, 1992)

**Story type:** Fantasy (Contemporary; Religious)
**Series:** Soulsmith
**Major character(s):** Ronny Dillon, Artist (metalsmith), Telepath; Lewis Welch, Political Figure (master of Cardalba), Telepath; Brandy Wallace, Artist, Teacher
**Time period(s):** 1990s
**Locale(s):** Cordova, Georgia; Welch County, Georgia

**Summary:** Ronny graduates from college about five years after the events in *Soulsmith*. Reluctant to return home due to his intense memories and the deaths in his family, Ronny complies with Lewis's urgent request, as predicted by the radio. While in Welch County, Ronny gets involved with Brandy and her castle-building project.

**Other books you might like:**
Piers Anthony, *Virtual Mode*, 1991
Emma Bull, *War for the Oaks*, 1987
Charles de Lint, *The Little Country*, 1991
Greer Ilene Gilman, *Moonwise*, 1991
Megan Lindholm, *Cloven Hooves*, 1991
Ian McDonald, *King of Morning, Queen of Day*, 1991
Jody Lynn Nye, *Mythology 101*, 1990
Claudia Peck, *Spirit Crossings*, 1991

## 1472
### TOM DEITZ

## *Dreamseeker's Road*
(New York: Morrow/AvoNova, 1995)

**Story type:** Fantasy (Adventure; Alternate World)
**Series:** David Sullivan
**Major character(s):** David Sullivan, Student—College, Adventurer; Alec McLean, Student—College, Adventurer; Aikin Daniels, Student—College, Adventurer
**Time period(s):** 1990s; Indeterminate
**Locale(s):** Georgia; Faerie, Mythical Place

**Summary:** A hunting trip the day before Halloween leads David and his friends into danger as an ancient and evil force tracks them, while the barriers between the human realm and Faerie break down.

**Other books you might like:**
Aaron Allston, *Doc Sidhe*, 1995
Greg Bear, *Songs of Earth and Power*, 1994
Charles de Lint, *Memory and Dream*, 1994
Charles de Lint, *Moonheart: A Romance*, 1984
Patricia A. McKillip, *The Book of Atrix Wolfe*, 1995
Jane Yolen, *The Wild Hunt*, 1995

## 1473
### TOM DEITZ

## *The Gryphon King*
(New York: Avon, 1989)

**Story type:** Fantasy (Contemporary)
**Major character(s):** Jay Madison, Student—College, Relative (Rob's half brother); Rob Tolar, Student—College, Relative (Jay's half brother)
**Time period(s):** 1980s
**Locale(s):** Athens, Georgia (University of Georgia)

**Summary:** A play is found which has the power to raise the Devil and reunite the magic and human worlds. A group of human college students and magic beings try to prevent the play from being read.

**Other books you might like:**
Ramsey Campbell, *Ancient Images*, 1990
Daniel Da Cruz, *Mixed Doubles*, 1989
John M. Ford, *Casting Fortune*, 1989
Joe Haldeman, *The Hemingway Hoax*, 1990

## 1474
### TOM DEITZ

## *Landslayer's Law*
(New York: AvoNova, 1997)

**Story type:** Fantasy (Adventure; Alternate World)
**Series:** David Sullivan
**Major character(s):** David Sullivan, Adventurer, Student—College; Lugh, Royalty, Mythical Creature (Sidhe); James Murphy, Musician (bagpiper)
**Time period(s):** 1990s
**Locale(s):** Georgia; Tir-Nan-Og, Mythical Place (Faerie)

**Summary:** When real estate developers endanger the walls between Faerie and Georgia, High King Lugh threatens to retaliate with a "final war" against humans. David Sullivan and friends must save both worlds.

**Other books you might like:**
Aaron Allston, *Doc Sidhe*, 1995
Charles de Lint, *Moonheart: A Romance*, 1984
Guy Gavriel Kay, *The Summer Tree*, 1985
Will Shetterly, *Elsewhere*, 1991
Michael Williams, *Arcady*, 1996

## 1475
### TOM DEITZ

## *Soulsmith*
(New York: Avon, 1991)

**Story type:** Fantasy (Contemporary; Young Adult)
**Series:** Soulsmith
**Major character(s):** Ronny Dillon, Orphan, Student—High School; Lewis Welch, Bastard Son, Student—High School; Road Man, Traveler, Magician
**Time period(s):** 1990s
**Locale(s):** Cordova, Georgia

**Summary:** After Ronny Dillon shattered his kneecap and lost his adoptive parents, he went to live with his grandmother and her son, Lewis, in rural Georgia. Unable to reconcile himself with the changes in his life, and having discovered a talent for working with metal in shop class, Ronny put his energy into decorating his crutch. Before long he is forced to notice that the town and people around him present dangers he is not prepared to handle.

**Other books you might like:**
Emma Bull, *War for the Oaks*, 1987
Charles de Lint, *The Dreaming Place*, 1990
Hila Feil, *Blue Moon*, 1990
Christopher Pike, *See You Later*, 1990
Michael Scott Rohan, *Chase the Morning*, 1991

## 1476

### TOM DEITZ

## *Stoneskin's Revenge*

(New York: Avon, 1991)

**Story type:** Fantasy (Contemporary; Adventure)
**Series:** David Sullivan
**Major character(s):** Calvin McIntosh, Indian (Cherokee), Wanderer; Robyn, Runaway; Utlunta, Indian, Monster
**Time period(s):** 1990s (1991)
**Locale(s):** Whidden, Georgia; Galunlati, Fictional Country

**Summary:** After the war in *Sunshaker's War*, a door into the other world of Galunlati was left open, and a monster escaped into Georgia. Calvin McIntosh, mostly Cherokee and a part-time sorcerer, has to deal with the problem without the help of his friends.

**Other books you might like:**
Emma Bull, *War for the Oaks*, 1987
Guy Gavriel Kay, *The Summer Tree*, 1985
Patricia Kennealy-Morrison, *The Copper Crown*, 1986
Alex McDonough, *Scorpio*, 1990
Morgan Llywelyn, *Druids*, 1991

## 1477

### TOM DEITZ

## *Sunshaker's War*

(New York: Avon, 1990)

**Story type:** Fantasy (Adventure; Contemporary)
**Series:** David Sullivan
**Major character(s):** David Sullivan, Student—College, Adventurer; Calvin McIntosh, Indian, Wanderer; Fionchadd mac Ailill, Mythical Creature (Elf)
**Time period(s):** 1980s
**Locale(s):** Enotah County, Georgia; Galunlati, Mythical Place; Faerie, Mythical Place

**Summary:** The borders between the mortal lands and Faerie have supposedly been sealed to prevent the war between Tir-Nan-Og and Erenn. Not only are the borders leaking, but Calvin discovers that the magic being worked to wage the war is unbalancing the sun and will destroy all three worlds if not stopped. David, Calvin and their friends decide the only way to stop the war is to find out where Fionchadd is being held prisoner, rescue him, and return him to his people.

**Other books you might like:**
Margaret Ball, *The Shadow Gate*, 1991
Charles de Lint, *Svaha*, 1989
Barbara Hambly, *The Time of the Dark*, 1982
R.A. MacAvoy, *Tea with the Black Dragon*, 1983
Patricia C. Wrede, *The Seven Towers*, 1984

## 1478

### TOM DEITZ

## *Wordwright*

(New York: AvoNova, 1993)

**Story type:** Fantasy (Contemporary; Psychic Powers)
**Series:** Soulsmith
**Major character(s):** Ronny Dillon, Artist, Telepath; Lewis Owen Welch, Telepath; Donson Gwent, Director, Writer (playwright)
**Time period(s):** 1990s
**Locale(s):** Welch County, Georgia

**Summary:** After Martha, the Welch family matriarch, dies, Lewis renounces his Mastership to search for his and Ronny's sister. Before long the folks in town notice that the Luck seems to have left, and since Lew left, they blame Ronny. Brandy decides to help the town by producing a play despite knowing the plot will greatly upset Ronny. The director sparks a fight which forces Ron to leave Brandy Hall and eventually learn about the Road Man and the Welch family Luck.

**Other books you might like:**
Piers Anthony, *The Caterpillar's Question*, 1992
    Philip Jose Farmer, co-author
Maya Kaathryn Bohnhoff, *The Meri*, 1992
Emma Bull, *War for the Oaks*, 1987
Charles de Lint, *The Little Country*, 1990
Nina Kiriki Hoffman, *The Thread That Binds the Bones*, 1993
    Larry Dixon, co-author
Alis A. Rasmussen, *A Passage of Stars*, 1990
Lawrence Watt-Evans, *The Rebirth of Wonder*, 1992

## 1479

### LESTER DEL REY, Editor
### RISA KESSLER, Co-Editor

## *Once upon a Time: A Treasury of Modern Fairy Tales*

(New York: Ballantine/Del Rey, 1991)

**Story type:** Fantasy (Anthology; Legend)

**Summary:** This volume contains 10 fairy tales by well-known science fiction and fantasy authors. All stories are new for this anthology, but the authors use classic fairy tale themes and characters. The stories are aimed at adult readers, but can be enjoyed by the younger reader with good reading skills. Major authors include Isaac Asimov, Terry Brooks, C.J. Cherryh, Barbara Hambly, Katherine Kurtz and Anne McCaffrey.

**Other books you might like:**
Steven Brust, *The Sun, the Moon, and the Stars*, 1987
Kara Dalkey, *The Nightingale*, 1988
Charles de Lint, *Jack, the Giant-Killer*, 1987
Andrew Lang, *The Blue Fairy Book*, 1889
    editor
Andrew Lang, *The Red Fairy Book*, 1890
    editor
Sheri S. Tepper, *Beauty*, 1991
Patricia C. Wrede, *Snow White and Rose Red*, 1989
Jack Zipes, *Beauties, Beasts and Enchantments*, 1989
    edited, translated
Jack Zipes, *Spells of Enchantment*, 1991
    edited, translated

## 1480

**PETER DELACORTE**

### Time on My Hands

(New York: Scribner, 1997)

**Story type:** Science Fiction (Time Travel)
**Major character(s):** Gabriel Prince, Time Traveler, Writer; Ronald "Dutch" Reagan, Historical Figure, Actor (future president)
**Time period(s):** 1930s; 1940s
**Locale(s):** Hollywood, California

**Summary:** An aging hippie physicist engages out of luck travel writer Gabriel Prince to use a time machine and return to pre-World War II Hollywood, befriend Ronald Reagan, and do whatever necessary to prevent Ronald Reagan from becoming President of the United States in the 1980s.

**Other books you might like:**
Jack Finney, *From Time to Time*, 1995
Jack Finney, *Time and Again*, 1970
Lisa Mason, *Summer of Love*, 1994
Wilson Tucker, *The Lincoln Hunters*, 1958
Harry Turtledove, *The Guns of the South: A Novel of the Civil War*, 1992

## 1481

**SAMUEL R. DELANY**

### The Einstein Intersection

(Hanover, New Hampshire: Wesleyan University Press, 1998)

**Story type:** Science Fiction (Post-Nuclear Holocaust; Psychic Powers)
**Major character(s):** Lo Lobey, Mutant, Musician; Kid Death, Mutant, Criminal (murderer); Spider, Businessman (dragon herder), Mutant
**Time period(s):** Indeterminate Future

**Summary:** Before leaving to search out Kid Death, the murderer, Lo Lobey kills a bull with his sword flute and meets an ancient computer which tells him he is in the wrong maze. After rescuing a dragon, Lobey discovers he takes music from other people's minds. This novel combines futuristic science fiction with ancient mythology. This is a new edition of the 1967 Nebula Award winner.

**Other books you might like:**
Kim Antieau, *The Gaia Websters*, 1997
Tony Daniel, *Earthling*, 1997
Sterling E. Lanier, *Hiero's Journey*, 1973
Sheri S. Tepper, *A Plague of Angels*, 1993
Nicolas van Pallandt, *Anvil*, 1998

## 1482

**SAMUEL R. DELANY**

### They Fly at Ciron

(Seattle, Washington: Incunabula Press, 1993)

**Story type:** Science Fiction (Political)
**Major character(s):** Rahn, Farmer, Wanderer; Kire, Military Personnel (lieutenant); Vortcir, Alien (Winged One)
**Time period(s):** Indeterminate
**Locale(s):** Ciron, Fictional City; Hi-Vator, Fictional City

**Summary:** Gone for a week, Rahn considers heading home to Ciron when he kills a mountain lion and is afraid by a Winged One overhead. Kire observes the kill and casually uses his powergun to shoot at the Winged One who spied on the Myetran mission to "conquer all in a line like blood running down a map." Rahn, a primitive, gives Kire the skin in thanks and friendship, not understanding that Myetra marches next to Ciron.

**Other books you might like:**
Richard Grant, *Through the Heart*, 1991
Nicola Griffith, *Ammonite*, 1993
Marjorie Bradley Kellogg, *Harmony*, 1991
Morgan Llywelyn, *The Elementals*, 1993
J.M. Morgan, *Desert Eden*, 1991
Sheri S. Tepper, *A Plague of Angels*, 1993
Gene Wolfe, *The Shadow of the Torturer*, 1980

## 1483

**MARTIN DELRIO**

### Mortal Kombat

(New York: Tor, 1995)

**Story type:** Fantasy (Adventure)
**Series:** Mortal Kombat
**Major character(s):** Liu Kang, Religious, Martial Arts Expert; Sonya Blade, Military Personnel, Warrior; Goro, Warrior, Royalty
**Time period(s):** 1990s
**Locale(s):** Hong Kong; Outworld, Mythical Place

**Summary:** Mortal warriors compete in a tournament to determine their worthiness to defend humanity from the evil sorcerer, Shang Tsung. Novelizes the film based on the electronic game.

**Other books you might like:**
Dean Devlin, *StarGate*, 1994
  Roland Emmerich, co-author
Wayland Drew, *Willow*, 1988
William R. Forstchen, *Arena*, 1994
Paul Monette, *Predator*, 1987
Jeff Rovin, *Mortal Kombat*, 1995

## 1484

**TROY DENNING**

### Crucible

(Renton, Washington: TSR, 1998)

**Story type:** Fantasy (Magic Conflict)
**Major character(s):** Cyric, Deity (god); Tyr, Lawyer; Kelemvor, Warrior
**Time period(s):** Indeterminate
**Locale(s):** Faerun, Fictional Country

**Summary:** The god Cyric has apparently gone mad, at least in the view of his contemporaries, who resent his propensity for violence. Despite the efforts of the other gods to control him, he interferes repeatedly in the affairs of mortals. Sequel to *Prince of Lies* by James Lowder.

**Other books you might like:**
Mark Anthony, *Beyond the Pale*, 1998
Simon R. Green, *The Bones of Haven*, 1992
Fritz Leiber, *Lean Times in Lankhmar*, 1996
Douglas Niles, *A Breach in the Watershed*, 1995
R.A. Salvatore, *Sojourn*, 1991

## 1485

**TROY DENNING**

### Faces of Deception

(Renton, Washington: TSR, 1998)

**Story type:** Fantasy (Quest)
**Major character(s):** Atreus, Nobleman; Rishi Saubhari, Companion
**Time period(s):** Indeterminate
**Locale(s):** Erlkazar, Fictional Country

**Summary:** Atreus of Erlkazar has a horribly disfigured face which he keeps concealed. A member of a wealthy family, he has powerful enemies. He and his companion Rishi set off on a journey of discovery into the mysterious lands known as the Utter East, where he comes to terms with his handicap.

**Other books you might like:**
Ed Greenwood, *Spellfire*, 1988
Simon Hawke, *The Seeker*, 1994
J. Robert King, *The Summerhill Hounds*, 1995
Richard A. Knaak, *Kaz the Minotaur*, 1990
Richard A. Knaak, *The Legend of Huma*, 1988

## 1486

**TROY DENNING**

### The Parched Sea

(Lake Geneva, Wisconsin: TSR, 1991)

**Story type:** Fantasy (Adventure; Sword and Sorcery)
**Series:** Forgotten Realms: The Harpers
**Major character(s):** Ruha, Widow(er), Sorceress; Lander, Revolutionary; Kadumi, Warrior
**Time period(s):** Indeterminate Past
**Locale(s):** Anauroch, Mythical Place (desert)

**Summary:** In Anauroch to help the desert tribes resist the efforts of the Zhentarim to enslave them, Lander is too late to stop Ruha and Kadumi's tribes from being slaughtered. The remaining tribes may agree to work together to fight the Zhentarim, if Ruha and Lander can convince the tribes that Ruha's magical abilities are not a curse on their efforts. A game tie-in novel.

**Other books you might like:**
Elaine Cunningham, *Elfshadow*, 1991
Doris Egan, *The Gate of Ivory*, 1989
Heather Gladney, *Teot's War*, 1987
Melanie Rawn, *Dragon Prince*, 1988
Jennifer Roberson, *Sword-Singer*, 1988

## 1487

**TROY DENNING**

### The Verdant Passage

(Lake Geneva, Wisconsin: TSR, 1991)

**Story type:** Fantasy (Adventure; Sword and Sorcery)
**Series:** Prism Pentad
**Major character(s):** Agis, Political Figure (senator), Psychic (psionic); Sadira, Slave, Mythical Creature (half elf); Rikus, Warrior (gladiator), Mythical Creature (dwarf)
**Time period(s):** Indeterminate
**Locale(s):** Athas, Mythical Place

**Summary:** An unlikely trio comes together through a group leading a popular rebellion against an unethical King. Based on the Dark Sun game from TSR.

**Other books you might like:**
Elaine Cunningham, *Elfshadow*, 1991
Heather Gladney, *Teot's War*, 1987
Melanie Rawn, *Dragon Prince*, 1988
Jennifer Roberson, *Sword-Singer*, 1988

## 1488

**CAROL L. DENNIS**

### Dragon's Queen

(New York: Warner Questar, 1991)

**Story type:** Fantasy (Alternate World)
**Series:** Dragon's Pawn
**Major character(s):** Lealor, Guardian (gatewarden); Fafleen, Mythical Creature (dragon)
**Time period(s):** Indeterminate
**Locale(s):** Widdershins, Planet—Imaginary

**Summary:** When Lealor and Fafleen find themselves stuck on Widdershins, a place where dragons are forbidden, they try to unite people and dragons as they search for a way home from the Shadowlord's realm.

**Other books you might like:**
Pamela Dean, *The Hidden Land*, 1986
Pamela Dean, *The Secret Country*, 1985
Pamela Dean, *The Whim of the Dragon*, 1989
Margaret Weis, *Fire Sea*, 1991
  Tracy Hickman, co-author
Patricia C. Wrede, *Dealing with Dragons*, 1990
Patricia C. Wrede, *Searching for Dragons*, 1991
Patricia C. Wrede, *Talking to Dragons*, 1985

## 1489

**BRADLEY DENTON**

### Blackburn

(New York: St. Martin's, 1993)

**Story type:** Horror (Serial Killer)
**Major character(s):** Jimmy Blackburn, Drifter, Serial Killer; Jasmine Blackburn, Child (Jimmy's sister); Ernest Tompkins, Child
**Time period(s):** 20th century
**Locale(s):** Wontoda, Kansas; Southwest

**Summary:** This extraordinary novel intersperses accounts of murders committed by Jimmy Blackburn, a young drifter who travels around the country under a variety of aliases, with vignettes from his deprived childhood and adolescence, forging a link between his loveless and alienated past and the crimes he commits against those who lie to or betray him.

**Other books you might like:**
Ramsey Campbell, *The Count of Eleven*, 1991
Truman Capote, *In Cold Blood*, 1967
Davis Grubb, *The Night of the Hunter*, 1953
Norman Mailer, *The Executioner's Song*, 1979
William F. Nolan, *Helltracks*, 1991

## 1490

### BRADLEY DENTON

## *Buddy Holly Is Alive and Well on Ganymede*

(New York: William Morrow, 1991)

**Story type:** Science Fiction (Humor; Adventure)
**Major character(s):** Oliver Vale, Fugitive; Richter, Government Official
**Time period(s):** 1980s (1989)
**Locale(s):** Kansas; Oklahoma

**Summary:** Oliver Vale is shocked into flight on his motorcycle by the sudden appearance on all televisions in the world of Buddy Holly requesting someone to contact Vale for him. Vale flees all manner of agents, FBI, Kansas Bureau of Investigations, pro-flesh and anti-flesh aliens, as he tries to get to Lubbock, Texas where Buddy Holly is buried and where Vale hopes to find the answers to his many questions.

**Other books you might like:**
John DeChancie, *Paradox Alley*, 1987
John DeChancie, *Red Limit Freeway*, 1984
John DeChancie, *Starrigger*, 1983
Robert Rankin, *Armageddon: The Musical*, 1990
Robert Silverberg, *Letters From Atlantis*, 1990
Steven Spielberg, *Close Encounters of the Third Kind*, 1977

## 1491

### BRADLEY DENTON

## *Lunatics*

(New York: St. Martin's, 1996)

**Story type:** Fantasy (Contemporary Realism; Light Fantasy)
**Major character(s):** Jack, Mentally Ill Person; Lily, Deity; Stephen, Professor
**Time period(s):** 1990s
**Locale(s):** Austin, Texas

**Summary:** When Jack's life falls apart, he begins seeing Lily, apparently a goddess from the moon. His friends have a little trouble with this, especially when Jack takes to running around naked every full moon. With the Moon and Lily embodying love, soon everybody acts like a lunatic.

**Other books you might like:**
A.A. Attanasio, *The Moon's Wife: A Hystery*, 1993
Eleanor Arnason, *Daughter of the Bear King*, 1987
Emma Bull, *War for the Oaks*, 1987
Robert Holdstock, *Ancient Echoes*, 1996
Thorne Smith, *The Night Life of the Gods*, 1931

## 1492

### BRADLEY DENTON

## *One Day Closer to Death*

(New York: St Martin's, 1998)

**Story type:** Science Fiction (Collection)

**Summary:** The collection consists of eight stories, including one original that is part of the author's highly regarded series about an unusual serial killer. The other stories originally appeared between 1986 and 1992. Includes some notes by the author.

**Other books you might like:**
Paul Di Filippo, *Fractal Paisleys*, 1997
Harlan Ellison, *Angry Candy*, 1988
R.A. Lafferty, *Lafferty in Orbit*, 1991
John Shirley, *Black Butterflies: A Flock on the Dark Side*, 1998

## 1493

### JO DERESKE

## *The Lone Sentinel*

(New York: Atheneum, 1989)

**Story type:** Science Fiction (Young Adult)
**Major character(s):** Erik, Teenager; Willa, Runaway
**Time period(s):** Indeterminate Future
**Locale(s):** Azure, Planet—Imaginary

**Summary:** On the planet Azure, machines called Sentinels produce a beam of energy that protects biosote, a strange growth needed by the Helgatites, a superior alien race. Erik and his father have lived in isolation, guarding the Lone Sentinel for as long as he can remember. Now, however, Erik's father has died and the teenager decides to carry on the job alone. He knows that if he reports his father's death, Trust Control, which oversees the Sentinels, will replace him and send him back to live in the city. Erik gets along fine until two runaways, Willa and Augusta, appear at his isolated outpost.

**Other books you might like:**
Frank Asch, *Journey to Terezor*, 1989
Gordon R. Dickson, *Way of the Pilgrim*, 1987
David Gerrold, *Chess with a Dragon*, 1987
Rebecca Ore, *Becoming Alien*, 1987
Rebecca Ore, *Being Alien*, 1989

## 1494

### AUGUST DERLETH

## *The Cthulhu Mythos*

(New York: Barnes & Noble, 1997)

**Story type:** Horror (Collection)

**Summary:** Omnibus volume of August Derleth's complete contributions to the Cthulhu Myhthos based on the work of H.P. Lovecraft. It includes the complete contents of Derleth's collection *The Mask of Cthulhu* (1958), his episodic novel. *Trail of Cthulhu* (1962), and six other stories, including the previously uncollected ''Something from Out There,'' and ''Ithaqua'' and ''The Thing That Walked on the Wind,'' both of which fold the Indian legend of the Wendigo into Lovecraft's pantheon of extradimensional monsters. Ramsey Campbell supplies an introduction.

**Other books you might like:**
Robert Bloch, *The Early Fears*, 1994
Ramsey Campbell, *Cold Print*, 1993
Brian Lumley, *Dagon's Bell and Other Discords*, 1995
Clark Ashton Smith, *A Rendezvous in Averoigne*, 1989
Donald Wandrei, *Don't Dream*, 1997

## 1495

### AUGUST DERLETH
### STEPHEN FABIAN, Illustrator

## *In Lovecraft's Shadow*

(Sauk City, Wisconsin: Arkham House, 1998)

**Story type:** Horror (Collection)

**Summary:** The twenty-three stories and three poems in this collection span nearly 30 years and represent all of the short fiction August Derleth contributed to the Cthulhu Mythos, an informal mythology built from the concepts of the horror fiction of H.P. Lovecraft. In addition to the complete contents of the author's volumes *The Mask of Cthulhu* (1958) and *The Trail of Cthulhu* (1962), the book includes three collaborations with Mark Schorer, and two stories, "Those Who Seek" and "The God Box," tangential to the Mythos but important for showing its pervasive influence on Derleth's work. Lavishly illustrated by Stephen Fabian. Editor Joe Wrzos contributes a detailed introduction and a chronology, "The Derleth Cthulhu Mythos Stories."

**Other books you might like:**
Robert Bloch, *The Early Fears*, 1994
Ramsey Campbell, *The Inhabitant of the Lake and Less Welcome Tenants*, 1964
Henry Kuttner, *The Book of Iod*, 1995
Frank Belknap Long, *The Hounds of Tindalos*, 1946
Brian Lumley, *Dagon's Bell and Other Discords*, 1995

## 1496

### AUGUST DERLETH

## *The Mask of Cthulhu*

(New York: Carroll & Graf, 1996)

**Story type:** Horror (Collection)

**Summary:** These six stories were all originally published in the pulp magazine *Weird Tales* and are consciously modeled on H.P. Lovecraft's renderings of the mechanistic forces of entropy and chaos as extradimensional monsters wreaking havoc on human affairs. "The Return of Hastur," "The Whippoorwills in the Hills" and "The Sandwin Compact" all feature naive young men who inherit estates from family members only to discover that their relatives have accessed monstrous forces of evil that still lurk in the family bequest. "Something in Wood" features a curio that embodies unspeakable evil and "The Seal of R'lyeh" a family curse of inescapable genetic destiny. "The House in the Valley" is loosely modeled on Lovecraft's classic "The Dunwich Horror." This book was first published in 1958.

**Other books you might like:**
Robert Bloch, *The Early Fears*, 1994
Ramsey Campbell, *The Inhabitant of the Lake and Less Welcome Tenants*, 1964
Frank Belknap Long, *The Hounds of Tindalos*, 1946
Brian Lumley, *Dagon's Bell and Other Discords*, 1995
Clark Ashton Smith, *Out of Space and Time*, 1942
Donald Wandrei, *The Eye and the Finger*, 1944

## 1497

### AUGUST DERLETH

## *The Trail of Cthulhu*

(New York: Carroll & Graf, 1996)

**Story type:** Horror (Ancient Evil Unleashed)
**Major character(s):** Laban Shrewsbury, Professor; Andrew Phelan, Researcher; Abel Keane, Student (divinity)
**Time period(s):** 1940s
**Locale(s):** Boston, Massachusetts; Lima, Peru

**Summary:** This episodic novel is stitched together from five pastiches of the writings of H.P. Lovecraft that were first published in the pulp magazine *Weird Tales* in the 1940s and 1950s. Laban Shrewsbury, a folklorist and lecturer, recruits a succession of five young men to assist him in the suppression of cultish activities in a variety of geographic locales that foreshadow the summoning of Cthulhu, an extradimensional entity whose existence in the earthly plane portends the destruction of mankind. This novel was first published in 1962.

**Other books you might like:**
Robert Bloch, *Strange Eons*, 1978
Basil Copper, *The Great White Space*, 1974
Brian Lumley, *The Burrowers Beneath*, 1974
Michael Shea, *The Colour out of Time*, 1984
Richard L. Tierney, *The House of the Toad*, 1993

## 1498

### JOHN DESJARLAIS

## *The Throne of Tara*

(Wheaton, Illinois: Crossway, 1990)

**Story type:** Fantasy (Legend; Religious)
**Major character(s):** Columcille, Royalty (Prince), Religious
**Time period(s):** 6th century
**Locale(s):** Iona, Ireland; Scotland

**Summary:** A change is being felt in Ireland as conflict between the old ways and Christianity becomes more prevalent. When Columcille exiles himself in Scotland he realizes that conflict with the druids was inevitable.

**Other books you might like:**
Margaret J. Anderson, *The Druid's Gift*, 1989
Frans G. Bengtsson, *The Long Ships*, 1954
Marion Zimmer Bradley, *The Mists of Avalon*, 1983
Kenneth C. Flint, *Cromm*, 1990
Stephen R. Lawhead, *Arthur*, 1989
Mike McQuay, *The Nexus*, 1989

## 1499

### DIANE DESROCHERS

## *Walker between the Worlds*

(St. Paul, Minnesota: Llewellyn, 1995)

**Story type:** Fantasy (Science Fiction; Psychic Powers)
**Major character(s):** Alan Kolkey, Scientist, Psychic; Dawn LaSarde, Psychic; Garuda, Animal (eagle)
**Time period(s):** 2000s (2001)
**Locale(s):** Tabriz, Iran

**Summary:** For lifetimes Alan Kolkey avoids his obligations to the Mother Goddess, but now she forces him into action by drawing a comet toward the Earth. In addition to the physical challenge, Alan has buried his true self and talents under a modern, macho surface which he needs to shed to save Earth. First novel.

**Other books you might like:**
Scott Baker, *Dhampire*, 1982
Gael Baudino, *Gossamer Axe*, 1990
Emma Bull, *Bone Dance: A Fantasy for Technophiles*, 1991
Charles de Lint, *Svaha*, 1989
Stuart Gordon, *Smile on the Void*, 1981
Starhawk, *The Fifth Sacred Thing*, 1993

## 1500

### EMILY DEVENPORT

## *Eggheads*
(New York: Roc, 1996)

**Story type:** Science Fiction (First Contact; Political)
**Major character(s):** An, Spacewoman, Linguist; Mohamonero, Doctor; Jo, Spaceman
**Time period(s):** Indeterminate Future
**Locale(s):** Storm, Planet—Imaginary; Cabar 4, Planet—Imaginary

**Summary:** Having left the poverty of Storm as a teenager, An accepts a DNA transplant to better find and translate glyphs left by the progenitor Earlies. Complicated by the attempt on her life by her lover, Jo, and interference by the alien Vorn, also searching for glyphs, An's search becomes more difficult as the DNA integrates with her consciousness. As her DNA implant takes hold, An discovers the true position of the Vorn and the meaning of the glyphs.

**Other books you might like:**
C.J. Cherryh, *Foreigner*, 1994
A.C. Crispin, *Ancestor's World*, 1996
    T. Jackson King, co-author
L. Warren Douglas, *Stepwater*, 1995
Anne McCaffrey, *Freedom's Landing*, 1995
Jack McDevitt, *The Engines of God*, 1994

## 1501

### EMILY DEVENPORT

## *GodHeads*
(New York: Roc, 1998)

**Story type:** Science Fiction (Political; Psychic Powers)
**Series:** Eggheads
**Major character(s):** Edna "Aten" Hume, Genetically Altered Being, Telepath; Bomarigala, Administrator (OMSK), Scientist (personality construction); KLse, Alien (X'GBri), Telepath
**Time period(s):** Indeterminate Future
**Locale(s):** OMSK, Planet—Imaginary; Storm, Planet—Imaginary (GodWorld)

**Summary:** In order to get control of the Web, OMSK found that Edna, who had been frozen for more than 1000 years, tries to substitute Aten, but Edna persists. The two are sent to GodWorld to spy on the GodHeads. Before Edna can join the GodHeads, the X'Gbri capture Edna/Aten. Edna falls in love with the X'Gbri as they remind her of a friend from her previous life, allowing the alternate intelligence, GodWeed, to contact them.

**Other books you might like:**
David Brin, *Heaven's Reach*, 1998
Julie E. Czerneda, *Beholder's Eye*, 1998
Katharine Kerr, *Palace*, 1996
    Mark Kreighbaum

Anne McCaffrey, *Freedom's Landing*, 1995
Charles Sheffield, *Transcendence*, 1992

## 1502

### EMILY DEVENPORT

## *The Kronos Condition*
(New York: Roc, 1997)

**Story type:** Science Fiction (Psychic Powers; Fantasy)
**Major character(s):** Sally, Psychic (esper), Child; Ted, Psychic, Mentally Ill Person; King Monkey, Prehistoric Human (Neanderthal)
**Time period(s):** 1990s
**Locale(s):** Arizona; Olympus, Mythical Place

**Summary:** Ted, Marc, and Suzanne join together to form the Mastermind which controls Sally and the other Kronos Kids and their telepathic and telekinetic powers. Sally develops a Secret Mind after two of her "siblings" die when challenging the Three. The Three force the children to aid in their quest to join the gods on Olympus.

**Other books you might like:**
Octavia E. Butler, *Mind of My Mind*, 1977
Orson Scott Card, *Lost Boys*, 1992
Zenna Henderson, *Ingathering: The Complete People Stories of Zenna Henderson*, 1995
Nina Kiriki Hoffman, *The Thread That Binds the Bones*, 1994
Michael Kandel, *Panda Ray*, 1997

## 1503

### EMILY DEVENPORT

## *Larissa*
(New York: Roc, 1993)

**Story type:** Science Fiction (Science Fiction)
**Major character(s):** Larissa, Teenager, Runaway; Hazaar, Alien (Q'rin); Knossus, Alien (Aesopian)
**Time period(s):** Indeterminate Future
**Locale(s):** Hook, Planet—Imaginary; Z'taruhn, Planet—Imaginary

**Summary:** Believing herself a murderer, Larissa flees Hook. Very tall and athletic, Larissa works as a bodyguard until her job terminates on Z'taruhn where she meets Shade and her Aesopian friends and learns of the Aesopian origins.

**Other books you might like:**
David Brin, *Startide Rising*, 1983
David Brin, *The Uplift War*, 1987
Lois McMaster Bujold, *Shards of Honor*, 1986
Debra Doyle, *The Price of the Stars*, 1992
    James D. Macdonald, co-author
Stephen Goldin, *Jade Darcy and the Affair of Honor*, 1988
    Mary Mason, co-author
Steve Perry, *The Man Who Never Missed*, 1985
Alis A. Rasmussen, *A Passage of Stars*, 1990

## 1504

### EMILY DEVENPORT

## *Shade*
(New York: Roc, 1991)

**Story type:** Science Fiction (Psychic Powers; Young Adult)
**Major character(s):** Shade, Runaway, Teenager; Knossus, Alien (Aesopian); Donokh, Alien (Q'rin)

**Time period(s):** Indeterminate Future
**Locale(s):** Los Angeles, California; Z'taruhn, Planet—Imaginary

**Summary:** After being abandoned by her parents, Shade decides to stow away on a spaceship and leave Earth behind. She is abandoned again and marooned on Z'taruhn, a gambling planet with no Earth embassy. Shade survives by using her empathic ability to pick winners and through her partnership with Knossus, the elephant man.

**Other books you might like:**
Douglas Adams, *The Hitchhiker's Guide to the Galaxy*, 1980
David Brin, *Startide Rising*, 1983
George Alec Effinger, *When Gravity Fails*, 1987
W. Michael Gear, *Starstrike*, 1990
Janet Kagan, *Hellspark*, 1988
Pamela F. Service, *Under Alien Stars*, 1990

---

**1505**

**ROBERT DEVEREAUX**

*Deadweight*

(New York: Dell/Abyss, 1994)

**Story type:** Horror (Wild Talents; Reanimated Dead)
**Major character(s):** Karin Tanner, Gardener; Danny Daniels, Reanimated Dead; Frank Tanner, Lawyer (Karin's husband)
**Time period(s):** 1990s (1994)
**Locale(s):** Roseville, California

**Summary:** Married to the dull but dependable defense attorney who cleared her of the murder of her abusive husband, Karin Tanner grapples with her ambivalence toward her life and self-esteem. Her powerful feelings uncannily amplify her gardener's green thumb, accidentally resurrecting the corpse of her husband, who intends to settle the score with her. This is the author's first novel.

**Other books you might like:**
Rick Hautala, *Ghost Light*, 1992
Ruby Jean Jensen, *Celia*, 1991
Dean R. Koontz, *Shadowfires*, 1987

---

**1506**

**ROBERT DEVEREAUX**

*Santa Steps Out: A Fairy Tale for Grownups*

(Fort Collins, Colorado: Dark Highway, 1998)

**Story type:** Horror (Erotic Horror)
**Major character(s):** Santa Claus, Mythical Creature; Anya Claus, Spouse; Rachel McGinnis, Designer (software)
**Time period(s):** 1990s
**Locale(s):** Sacramento, California; North Pole, Arctic

**Summary:** This novel proposes that Santa Claus, the Tooth Fairy, the Easter Bunny and other figures of childhood fairy tales are modern incarnations of the randy gods and goddesses of old who have forgotten their pagan origins. Reawakened to his true identity through sexual relations with the Tooth Fairy, Santa Claus indulges his sexual appetites with a woman who remembers having glimpsed him delivering presents one Christmas in her childhood. With forewords by David G. Hartwell and Patrick LoBrutto, both of whom played a role in the novel's long gestation period, and an afterword by the author recounting the difficulties he encountered getting the novel published for nearly a decade. Published in a signed limited edition.

**Other books you might like:**
Graham Joyce, *The Tooth Fairy*, 1997
Dean R. Koontz, *Santa's Twin*, 1996
James Morrow, *Only Begotten Daughter*, 1990
David Nickle, *The Claus Effect*, 1997
    Karl Schroeder, co-author
Gary K. Wolf, *Who Censored Roger Rabbit?*, 1981

---

**1507**

**ROBERT DEVEREAUX**

*Walking Wounded*

(New York: Dell, 1996)

**Story type:** Horror (Wild Talents)
**Major character(s):** Katt Galloway, Masseuse; Marcus Galloway, Professor (English); Sherry Feit, Professor
**Time period(s):** 1990s (1996)
**Locale(s):** Fort Collins, Colorado

**Summary:** Katt discovers that she has the power to cure or kill by touch at the same time that she falls in love with Sherry, her philandering husband's mistress. She determines to dispose of her husband by activating his still dormant Huntington's Chorea, but finds her relationship with Sherry complicated by a serial killer stalking the two of them.

**Other books you might like:**
John Byrne, *Whipping Boy*, 1992
Thomas F. Monteleone, *The Blood of the Lamb*, 1992
Thomas F. Monteleone, *The Resurrectionist*, 1995
Yvonne Navarro, *Deadrush*, 1995
F. Paul Wilson, *The Touch*, 1997

---

**1508**

**DEAN DEVLIN**
**ROLAND EMMERICH**, Co-Author
**STEPHEN MOLSTAD**, Co-Author

*Independence Day*

(New York: HarperPrism, 1996)

**Story type:** Science Fiction (Invasion of Earth; Military)
**Major character(s):** Thomas Whitmore, Political Figure; Constance "Connie" Spano, Public Relations (communications director); Steven Hiller, Military Personnel, Pilot
**Time period(s):** 1990s
**Locale(s):** Washington, District of Columbia; Area 51, Nevada

**Summary:** Worldwide interruption of communications precedes a violent invasion of extraterrestrials which could spell the end of civilization, if not the human race. As millions die, defenders construct a toxic computer program in a desperate attempt to halt the aliens. Novelizes the film.

**Other books you might like:**
A.C. Crispin, *V*, 1984
Jonathan Gems, *Mars Attacks!*, 1996
Robert A. Heinlein, *Starship Troopers*, 1951
Larry Niven, *Footfall*, 1985
    Jerry Pournelle, co-author
Judith Reeves-Stevens, *The Day of Descent*, 1993
    Garfield Reeves-Stevens, co-author
Robert Tine, *Chain Reaction*, 1996

## 1509

### DEAN DEVLIN
### ROLAND EMMERICH, Co-Author

## StarGate

(New York: Signet, 1994)

**Story type:** Science Fiction (Adventure)
**Major character(s):** Jack O'Neill, Military Personnel, Leader (StarGate program); Daniel Jackson, Linguist, Scholar (Egyptologist); Ra-hotep-kan "Ra", Alien
**Time period(s):** 1990s (1994); Indeterminate
**Locale(s):** Planet—Imaginary; Colorado; Africa

**Summary:** After excavation reveals an alien device dubbed "StarGate," which seems to relate to Egyptian astronomy and the deity Ra, scientists speculate the device could transport humans to another planet. When an advance recon team tests the device, they arrive at an unknown place with ancient Egyptian architecture and discover they may have no way home from the potentially deadly planet. Novelizes the movie.

**Other books you might like:**
Roger MacBride Allen, *The Ring of Charon*, 1990
Philip K. Dick, *The Unteleported Man*, 1983 revised edition
Alan Dean Foster, *The Last Starfighter*, 1984
Frederik Pohl, *Gateway*, 1977
George Zebrowski, *Stranger Suns*, 1991

## 1510

### GENE DEWEESE

## King of the Dead

(Lake Geneva, Wisconsin: Berkley, 1996)

**Story type:** Horror (Alternate World)
**Series:** Ravenloft
**Major character(s):** Firan Zal'honan, Sorcerer; Oldar, Assistant; Lord Darcalus, Wizard
**Time period(s):** Indeterminate
**Locale(s):** Darkon, Mythical Place

**Summary:** In his avatar as Firan Zal'honan, Azalin, King of the Dead, mourns the death of his son Irik and ponders the course of events that have brought him to the world of Darkon, where his current incarnation plots the assassination of Lord Darcalus. This novel is set in the gaming world of Ravenloft, a gothic universe where sorcery and supernatural beings are commonplace.

**Other books you might like:**
Mark Anthony, *Tower of Doom*, 1994
P.N. Elrod, *I, Strahd*, 1993
Laurell K. Hamilton, *Death of a Darklord*, 1995
Tanya Huff, *Scholar of Decay*, 1995
Chet Williamson, *Mordenheim*, 1994

## 1511

### GENE DEWEESE

## Renegade

(New York: Pocket, 1991)

**Story type:** Science Fiction (Space Opera)
**Series:** Star Trek
**Major character(s):** James T. Kirk, Spaceship Captain; Leonard McCoy, Doctor; Spock, Scientist, Alien (Vulcan)
**Time period(s):** 23rd century
**Locale(s):** *U.S.S. Enterprise*, Spaceship; Chyrellka, Planet—Imaginary; Vancadia, Planet—Imaginary

**Summary:** During the last year of its original five-year mission, the *Enterprise* responds to broken relations between the rebelling colony world, Vancadia, and mother world Chyrellka. When Kirk sends Spock and McCoy to investigate rebel demands, their capture and apparent deaths devastate Kirk. His subsequent investigation into events uncovers a Klingon plot against the Federation.

**Other books you might like:**
Margaret Wander Bonanno, *Dwellers in the Crucible*, 1985
J.M. Dillard, *The Lost Years*, 1989
Brad Ferguson, *A Flag Full of Stars*, 1991
Barbara Hambly, *Ishmael*, 1985
Della Van Hise, *Killing Time*, 1985
Robert E. Vardeman, *The Klingon Gambit*, 1981

## 1512

### SUSAN DEXTER

## The Prince of Ill Luck

(New York: Ballantine Del Rey, 1994)

**Story type:** Fantasy (Light Fantasy; Magic Conflict)
**Series:** Warhorse of Esdragon
**Major character(s):** Leith, Royalty (Prince of the Isles), Psychic; Kessallia, Noblewoman; Valadan, Animal (horse)
**Time period(s):** Indeterminate
**Locale(s):** Esdragon, Fictional Country

**Summary:** As Leith wanders the hills of Esdragon searching to lift the curse of ill luck which seems to strike all those around him, he encounters and befriends Valadan, a stallion sired by the wind. They conquer a glass hill, foiling fair, fiery Kessallia's plan to keep her many suiters busy while she searches for her father and long lost witch queen mother. Leith joins her through caves, mountain perils and strife on a quest to lift his curse and free Kessallia from her vow.

**Other books you might like:**
Tom Deitz, *Soulsmith*, 1990
Nina Kiriki Hoffman, *The Thread That Binds the Bones*, 1993
John Moore, *Slay and Rescue*, 1993
Midori Snyder, *The Flight of Michael McBride*, 1994
Patricia C. Wrede, *Calling on Dragons*, 1993

## 1513

### SUSAN DEXTER

## The True Knight

(New York: Ballantine Del Rey, 1996)

**Story type:** Fantasy (Quest; Magic Conflict)
**Series:** Warhorse of Esdragon
**Major character(s):** Titch, Warrior, Adventurer; Wren, Apprentice, Magician; Valadan, Animal (horse)
**Time period(s):** Indeterminate
**Locale(s):** Esdragon, Fictional Country

**Summary:** Setting out to achieve knighthood, Titch suffers wounds which require Wren's attention. Separating, the pair reunite when the Red Queen demands that mages and wisewomen find her ensorcelled son and transform him from a swan back into a prince or suffer death.

**Other books you might like:**
Anne Kelleher Bush, *Children of Enchantment*, 1996

Terry Goodkind, *Wizard's First Rule*, 1994
Robin Hobb, *Assassin's Apprentice*, 1995
J.V. Jones, *The Baker's Boy*, 1995
Kristine Kathryn Rusch, *Traitors*, 1994

---

**1514**

**SUSAN DEXTER**

## The Wizard's Shadow

(New York: Ballantine Del Rey, 1993)

**Story type:** Fantasy (Magic Conflict; Adventure)
**Major character(s):** Crocken, Peddler, Adventurer; The Shadow, Disembodied Personality
**Time period(s):** Indeterminate
**Locale(s):** Armyn, Fictional Country; Axe-Edge, Fictional City

**Summary:** Seeking revenge, a dying wizard casts off his shadow. Summoned to meet the shadow during an eclipse, then threatened, Crocken cedes use of his body to the shadow. Crocken's goal of profitable trade and the shadow's mission of vengeance advance rapidly when Crocken's mad act of heroism saves Princess Gloriet.

**Other books you might like:**
Alfred Bester, *The Stars My Destination*, 1956
Kara Dalkey, *The Curse of Sagamore*, 1986
Kara Dalkey, *The Sword of Sagamore*, 1989
Elizabeth Forrest, *Phoenix Fire*, 1992
Marc Laidlaw, *Neon Lotus*, 1988

---

**1515**

**PAUL DI FILIPPO**

## Fractal Paisleys

(New York: Four Walls Eight Windows, 1997)

**Story type:** Science Fiction (Collection; Fantasy)

**Summary:** Contains individual introductions to two previously unpublished stories and eight stories from periodicals and anthologies from 1989-1997. Frequently humorous or whimsical in tone, the stories explore a variety of themes, including the disappearance of the dinosaurs, politics, alternate worlds and popular music.

**Other books you might like:**
David Brin, *The River of Time*, 1986
Nancy Kress, *The Aliens of Earth*, 1993
Rebecca Ore, *Alien Bootlegger and Other Stories*, 1993
Marc Stiegler, *The Gentle Seduction*, 1990
John Varley, *Blue Champagne*, 1986
Kurt Vonnegut Jr., *Welcome to the Monkey House*, 1968

---

**1516**

**PAUL DI FILIPPO**

## Lost Pages

(New York: Four Walls Eight Windows, 1998)

**Story type:** Science Fiction (Collection; Satire)

**Summary:** Contains an introductory parody/essay attributing the demise of science fiction to *Star Trek*, which was finally "killed off" by a "true SF fan" letter-writing campaign. Also contains nine stories about the quirky alternate lives of literary figures such as Franz Kafka, Anne Frank, Robert A. Heinlein, Philip K. Dick, and Henry Miller.

**Other books you might like:**
Stephen Marlowe, *The Lighthouse at the End of the World*, 1995
Kim Newman, *Back in the USSA*, 1997
    Eugene Byrne, co-author
Bruce Sterling, *Mirrorshades: The Cyberpunk Anthology*, 1986
    editor
Harry Turtledove, *How Few Remain*, 1997

---

**1517**

**PAUL DI FILIPPO**

## Ribofunk

(New York: Four Walls Eight Windows, 1996)

**Story type:** Science Fiction (Collection; Hard Science Fiction)

**Summary:** Contains two original and 11 stories reprinted from periodicals and anthologies 1989-1995. Ranging from downbeat to humorous, the stories focus on diverse aspects of biology with other themes including renegade gene splicers, human chimeras, a sentient river, and a revolutionary Peter Rabbit.

**Other books you might like:**
Michael Flynn, *The Nanotech Chronicles*, 1991
Janet Kagan, *Mirabile*, 1991
Robert Silverberg, *Murasaki*, 1992
    Martin H. Greenberg, co-editor
Marc Stiegler, *The Gentle Seduction*, 1990
John Varley, *The Persistence of Vision*, 1978

---

**1518**

**PAUL DI FILIPPO**

## The Steampunk Trilogy

(New York: Four Walls Eight Windows, 1995)

**Story type:** Science Fiction (Alternate History; Collection)
**Major character(s):** Cosmo Cowperthwait, Inventor, Naturalist; Emily Dickinson, Writer (poet), Historical Figure
**Time period(s):** 19th century
**Locale(s):** Alternate Earth; England; Massachusetts

**Summary:** Contains one original and two reprinted stories set in a very different Victorian Era: "Victoria" (*Amazing*, 1991) features a randy Queen Victoria clone and mysterious super science as Cosmo Cowperthwait investigates Victoria's disappearance; in "Hottentots" Lovecraftian horrors threaten historical characters; and "Walt and Emily" (*Interzone*, 1993) works poets' verse into the romance between Walt Whitman and Emily Dickinson.

**Other books you might like:**
Philip K. Dick, *The Man in the High Castle*, 1962
Randall Garrett, *Too Many Magicians*, 1967
William Gibson, *The Difference Engine*, 1991
    Bruce Sterling, co-author
Kim Newman, *Anno Dracula*, 1993
Neal Stephenson, *Snow Crash*, 1992
Harry Turtledove, *The Guns of the South: A Novel of the Civil War*, 1992

## 1519
### PHILIP K. DICK

## The Collected Stories of Philip K. Dick, Volume One: The Short Happy Life of the Brown Oxford
(New York: Carol Publishing Group, 1990)

**Story type:** Science Fiction (Collection)
**Series:** Collected Stories of Philip K. Dick
**Major character(s):** The Brown Oxford, Experimental Subject; Doc Labyrinth, Scientist; Shadrach Jones, Clerk, Royalty
**Time period(s):** 1950s
**Locale(s):** United States

**Summary:** This is a collection of 25 stories written between 1953-1955. The title story recounts an attempt to make the inanimate animate by the Principle of Sufficient Irritation. The stories range from whimsical to chilling, sometimes within a single work. This book is a reprint of the 1987 Underwood-Miller edition subtitled *Beyond Lies the Wub*.

**Other books you might like:**
Michael Bishop, *The Secret Ascension*, 1987
James P. Blaylock, *The Paper Grail*, 1991
Pat Cadigan, *Mindplayers*, 1987
K.W. Jeter, *The Glass Hammer*, 1985
Tim Powers, *Dinner at Deviant's Palace*, 1985

## 1520
### PHILIP K. DICK

## The Collected Stories of Philip K. Dick, Volume Two: We Can Remember It for You Wholesale
(New York: Carol Publishing Group, 1990)

**Story type:** Science Fiction (Collection)
**Series:** Collected Stories of Philip K. Dick
**Major character(s):** Douglas Quail, Clerk, Spy; Mr. McClane, Psychologist
**Time period(s):** Indeterminate Future
**Locale(s):** Earth; Mars

**Summary:** This volume contains 27 stories written between 1953-1954 from the early years of Dick's career and includes the story that inspired the movie *Total Recall*. As usual for Dick, Quail finds reality breaking down when a trip to a memory-implanting clinic provides him with recollections of an assassination that he may or may not have actually committed. Reprint of the 1986 Underwood-Miller edition *Second Variety*, in which the title story was replaced with the movie tie-in story.

**Other books you might like:**
Michael Bishop, *The Secret Ascension*, 1987
James P. Blaylock, *The Digging Leviathan*, 1989
Pat Cadigan, *Patterns*, 1989
K.W. Jeter, *The Glass Hammer*, 1985
Tim Powers, *The Anubis Gates*, 1983

## 1521
### PHILIP K. DICK

## Eye in the Sky
(New York: Macmillan Collier Nucleus, 1989)

**Story type:** Science Fiction (Alternate Universe)
**Major character(s):** Jack Hamilton, Engineer; Marsha Hamilton, Liberal
**Time period(s):** 1950s (1959)
**Locale(s):** California

**Summary:** When an experiment in high-energy physics goes wrong, eight people find themselves flung into a series of increasingly bizarre nightmares which seem to reflect their own paranoid fears. They seek desperately for a way of escape and are changed utterly by their experience. Originally published in 1957.

**Other books you might like:**
Michael Bishop, *The Secret Ascension*, 1987
Fredric Brown, *What Mad Universe*, 1949
Ursula K. Le Guin, *The Lathe of Heaven*, 1971
Robert Charles Wilson, *Gypsies*, 1989
Gene Wolfe, *There Are Doors*, 1988
Roger Zelazny, *The Dream Master*, 1966

## 1522
### PHILIP K. DICK

## The Penultimate Truth
(New York: Carroll & Graf, 1989)

**Story type:** Science Fiction (Post-Nuclear Holocaust)
**Major character(s):** Nicholas St. James, Government Official; Joseph Adams, Writer
**Time period(s):** 21st century
**Locale(s):** United States

**Summary:** War has raged for fifteen years and Americans have been living underground all that time building the weapons needed to keep the war going. There is evidence, however, that something strange is going on. The President of the United States, seen periodically on the news, doesn't appear to be aging. There are rumors that the war may in fact be a hoax. Nick St. James determines to find out the truth. Originally published in 1964.

**Other books you might like:**
Michael Bishop, *The Secret Ascension*, 1987
Michael Kandel, *Strange Invasion*, 1989
Leonard C. Lewin, *Report from Iron Mountain*, 1967
Mordecai Roshwald, *Level 7*, 1959

## 1523
### PHILIP K. DICK

## The Zap Gun
(New York: Carroll & Graf, 1989)

**Story type:** Science Fiction (Satire)
**Major character(s):** Lars Powderdry, Engineer (Weapons Designer); Lilo Topchek, Engineer (Weapons Designer)
**Time period(s):** 21st century (2004)
**Locale(s):** Wes-bloc, Fictional Country; Peep-East, Fictional Country

**Summary:** Lars Powderdry is the most respected and successful weapons designer in Wes-bloc. While under the influence of hallucinogenic drugs he creates dazzling weapons, weapons capable of spectacular, wholesale destruction. There's just one catch. None of them work. They're all cheap fakes, just like the weapons Peep-East comes up with, designed to fulfill the public's need for violence and macho posturing. Despite great wealth and fame, Powderdry knows he's a fake and this upsets him. He decides to do something about it. Originally published in 1967.

**Other books you might like:**
Michael Bishop, *The Secret Ascension*, 1987
Ursula K. Le Guin, *The Lathe of Heaven*, 1971
A.E. Van Vogt, *The Weapon Shops of Isher*, 1951
Kurt Vonnegut Jr., *Player Piano*, 1952

---

**1524**

**CHARLES DICKENS**
**CARLO FRUTTERO**, Co-Author
**FRANCO LUCENTINI**, Co-Author

## The D. Case: The Truth about the Mystery of Edwin Drood

(New York: Harcourt Brace Jovanovich, 1992)

**Story type:** Fantasy (Mystery; Satire)
**Major character(s):** Sherlock Holmes, Detective—Private; Philip Marlowe, Detective—Private; Nero Wolfe, Detective—Private
**Time period(s):** 1990s
**Locale(s):** Rome, Italy (Urbis et Orbis Hotel)

**Summary:** A forum on the Completion of Unfinished or Fragmentary Works in Music and Literature, an international conference sponsored by the Japanese, attracts the greatest detectives from literature, all interested in Charles Dickens' fragmentary novel, *The Mystery of Edwin Drood*. To finish and solve that mystery, detectives including Lew Archer, Father Brown, Sherlock Holmes, Jules Maigret, Philip Marlowe, Hercule Poirot and Nero Wolfe listen and consult mediums and computers as simultaneous translations present Dickens' novel a chapter at a time, yielding a mystery surrounding the author as well as the novel. Translated by Gregory Dowling. Originally published in Italy in 1989.

**Other books you might like:**
Milorad Pavic, *Landscape Painted with Tea*, 1990
Bill Pronzini, *Double*, 1984
    Marcia Muller, co-author
Fred Saberhagen, *The Holmes-Dracula File*, 1978
Manly Wade Wellman, *Sherlock Holmes's War of the Worlds*, 1975
    Wade Wellman, co-author
Gary K. Wolf, *Who Censored Roger Rabbit?*, 1981

---

**1525**

**PETER DICKINSON**

## Eva

(New York: Delacorte Press, 1989)

**Story type:** Science Fiction (Young Adult)
**Major character(s):** Eva, Teenager; Dad, Scientist
**Time period(s):** Indeterminate Future
**Locale(s):** Earth

**Summary:** When thirteen year old Eva is in a serious automobile accident and isn't expected to survive, her father, a primate zoologist, has her mind transferred into the brain of a chimpanzee. Eva must learn to live in the chimp body and must also learn to cope with what's left of the chimp's memories and impulses.

**Other books you might like:**
Roger MacBride Allen, *Orphan of Creation*, 1988
Michael Bishop, *Ancient of Days*, 1985
Michael Bishop, *No Enemy but Time*, 1982
John Gribbin, *Father to the Man*, 1989
Pat Murphy, *Rachel in Love*, 1987

---

**1526**

**PETER DICKINSON**

## The Lion Tamer's Daughter

(New York: Delacorte, 1997)

**Story type:** Horror (Collection; Young Adult)

**Summary:** Four stories of fantasy and horror for young adult readers. In "Touch and Go," a young boy discovers a magical doorway into the past and befriends a girl who once lived in the house he now inhabits. "Checkers," about a young kidnap victim who so vividly imagines a make-believe companion that he wishes him into being, is one of several stories in which young protagonists confront supernaturally objectfied alter egos. The others are the title novella and "The Spring," both variations on the doppelganger theme.

**Other books you might like:**
Joan Aiken, *A Touch of Chill*, 1979
Joan Aiken, *A Fit of Shivers*, 1990
Penelope Lively, *Uninvited Ghosts and Other Stories*, 1984
Robert Westall, *In Camera and Other Stories*, 1993
Robert Westall, *The Call and Other Stories*, 1993

---

**1527**

**PETER DICKINSON**
**EMMA CHICHESTER-CLARK**, Illustrator

## Time and the Clock Mice, Etcetera

(New York: Delacorte, 1994)

**Story type:** Fantasy (Young Adult; Psychic Powers)
**Major character(s):** I, Writer, Artisan (clockmaker); Tracy Dickory, Animal (mouse), Telepath
**Time period(s):** 1990s
**Locale(s):** Branton, England

**Summary:** After 99 years of operation, the Branton Town Hall Clock stops, threatening the tourist trade. When the clockmaker's grandson investigates, he discovers, living inside, families of fabulously intelligent, telepathic Clock Mice who help keep things running. As the clock undergoes detailed repairs, Dickinson presents insight into clockworks, bells, people, cats, mice and animal intelligence.

**Other books you might like:**
Michael Ende, *The Night of Wishes: Or, The Satanarchaeolidealcohellish Notion Potion*, 1992
Brian Jacques, *Redwall*, 1987
Barry Lopez, *Crow and Weasel*, 1990
Robert C. O'Brien, *Mrs. Frisby and the Rats of NIMH*, 1971
James Thurber, *The 13 Clocks*, 1950

---

**1528**

**GORDON R. DICKSON**

## The Dragon and the Djinn

(New York: Ace, 1996)

**Story type:** Fantasy (Quest; Alternate World)

**Series:** Dragon Knight
**Major character(s):** Jim/Gorbash Eckert, Knight, Magician, Nobleman (Baron De Bois de Malencontri); Sir Brian Neville-Smythe, Knight, Fiance(e)
**Time period(s):** Indeterminate
**Locale(s):** England, Alternate Earth; Middle East, Alternate Earth

**Summary:** To turn his engagement into marriage, Brian must travel to the Middle East in search of his fiancee's missing father to acquire his blessing. For his journey, Brian secures James' aid, not realizing how useful the magician will prove when pirates, sea giants and a particularly dangerous djinn impede their progress.

**Other books you might like:**
Glen Cook, *Tower of Fear*, 1989
Stephen Goldin, *Shrine of the Desert Mage*, 1988
Ursula K. Le Guin, *A Wizard of Earthsea*, 1968
R.A. MacAvoy, *Tea with the Black Dragon*, 1983
Elizabeth Ann Scarborough, *The Harem of Aman Akbar*, 1984

## 1529

### GORDON R. DICKSON

## The Dragon and the Gnarly King

(New York: Tor, 1997)

**Story type:** Fantasy (Alternate World; Magic Conflict)
**Series:** Dragon Knight
**Major character(s):** Jim/Gorbash Eckert, Nobleman (Baron de Bois de Malencontri), Magician, Knight; Angie Eckert, Noblewoman (baroness), Spouse; Robert de Clifford, Nobleman (Earl), Kidnapper
**Time period(s):** 14th century
**Locale(s):** England; Alternate Earth

**Summary:** When the Earl of Cumberland and the King of the Gnarlies join forces and kidnap Robert, adopted son of Jim and Angie Eckert, the Eckerts and their friends set out to find and rescue him. In the process, they must avoid the Earl's plots to have them accused of and executed for high treason, and then become embroiled in a power struggle for leadership of the Gnarlies.

**Other books you might like:**
Steven Brust, *Jhereg*, 1983
John DeChancie, *Castle Perilous*, 1988
Ursula K. Le Guin, *A Wizard of Earthsea*, 1968
Terry Pratchett, *Wyrd Sisters*, 1990
Joel Rosenberg, *The Fire Duke*, 1995
S.P. Somtow, *Riverrun*, 1991

## 1530

### GORDON R. DICKSON

## The Dragon at War

(New York: Ace, 1992)

**Story type:** Fantasy (Alternate World; Magic Conflict)
**Series:** Dragon Knight
**Major character(s):** Jim/Gorbash Eckert, Knight, Magician, Nobleman (Baron de Bois de Malencontri); Essessili, Mythical Creature (sea serpent)
**Time period(s):** 14th century
**Locale(s):** England, Alternate Earth; France, Alternate Earth

**Summary:** When the French ally themselves with mighty sea serpents in order to defeat the English, Jim and his companions travel to France to enlist the help of dragons to repel the invasion of sea serpents. Fourth in the series.

**Other books you might like:**
Phyllis Eisenstein, *In the Red Lord's Reach*, 1989
Phyllis Eisenstein, *Shadow of Earth*, 1979
Ursula K. Le Guin, *A Wizard of Earthsea*, 1968
Brad Strickland, *Wizard's Mole*, 1991

## 1531

### GORDON R. DICKSON

## The Dragon in Lyonesse

(New York: Tor, 1998)

**Story type:** Fantasy (Alternate World; Magic Conflict)
**Series:** Dragon Knight
**Major character(s):** Jim/Gorbash Eckert, Nobleman (Baron de Bois de Malencontri), Magician, Knight; Sir Brian Neville-Smythe, Knight; Dafydd ap Hywel, Warrior (archer), Adventurer
**Time period(s):** 14th century; Indeterminate
**Locale(s):** Alternate Earth (England); Lyonesse, Alternate Earth (land under the sea)

**Summary:** King Arthur and his court prosper for centuries in Lyonesse until a resurgence of the Dark Powers threatens their refuge. After arranging to borrow enough magic to contend with the expected resistance, Jim Eckert and his companions set off to save Lyonesse.

**Other books you might like:**
Mike Ashley, *The Pendragon Chronicles*, 1990
    editor
Marion Zimmer Bradley, *The Mists of Avalon*, 1983
Ursula K. Le Guin, *A Wizard of Earthsea*, 1968
R.A. MacAvoy, *Tea with the Black Dragon*, 1983
Christopher Stasheff, *The Warlock in Spite of Himself*, 1969

## 1532

### GORDON R. DICKSON

## The Dragon Knight

(New York: Tor, 1990)

**Story type:** Fantasy (Alternate World; Quest)
**Series:** Dragon Knight
**Major character(s):** Jim/Gorbash Eckert, Nobleman (Baron de Bois de Malencontri), Magician, Knight; Aargh, Animal (Wolf/Englishwolf)
**Time period(s):** 14th century
**Locale(s):** England, Alternate Earth

**Summary:** In this continuation of *The Dragon and the George* (1976), Jim Eckert, who had decided to stay in the magical kingdom a few months previous, awakes in the form of a dragon. He realizes that he has much to learn about his new situation, and it had better be soon. He must fulfill his obligations to his king—will he have time to get his magic under control?

**Other books you might like:**
L. Sprague de Camp, *The Incomplete Enchanter*, 1942
Robert Don Hughes, *Prophet of Lamath*, 1979
Fritz Leiber, *The Knight and Knave of Swords*, 1990
Larry Niven, *The Magic Goes Away*, 1979
Alis A. Rasmussen, *The Labyrinth Gate*, 1988
Mark Twain, *A Connecticut Yankee in King Arthur's Court*, 1889
    Pseudonym of Samuel Clemens
Michael Williams, *A Sorcerer's Apprentice*, 1990

## 1533

### GORDON R. DICKSON

## *The Dragon on the Border*

(New York: Ace, 1992)

**Story type:** Fantasy (Alternate World; Magic Conflict)
**Series:** Dragon Knight
**Major character(s):** Jim/Gorbash Eckert, Knight, Magician, Nobleman (Baron de Bois de Malencontri); Dafydd ap Hywel, Martial Arts Expert (bowman), Royalty (Prince of Merlon)
**Time period(s):** 14th century
**Locale(s):** England, Alternate Earth

**Summary:** As Sir Jim and friends ride North toward the Scottish border, strange apparitions attack their party. Swift action by Dafydd defeats the attack which seemed to come from armor occupied by invisible men mounted on invisible horses. Jim immediately involves himself in repelling the invasion of Hollow Men, ensorcelled warriors. Traditionally hostile groups unite to eliminate the Hollow Men, but Jim himself must meet the final challenge from a deadly worm. Third in the series.

**Other books you might like:**
Mark Acres, *Dark Divide*, 1991
Ursula K. Le Guin, *A Wizard of Earthsea*, 1968
Christopher Stasheff, *King Kobold Revived*, 1984
Margaret Weis, *Fire Sea*, 1991
    Tracy Hickman, co-author
Patricia C. Wrede, *Searching for Dragons*, 1991

## 1534

### GORDON R. DICKSON

## *The Dragon, the Earl, and the Troll*

(New York: Ace, 1994)

**Story type:** Fantasy (Magic Conflict; Alternate World)
**Series:** Dragon Knight
**Major character(s):** Jim/Gorbash Eckert, Knight, Magician, Nobleman (Baron de Bois de Malencontri); Sir Brian Neville-Smythe, Knight; Mnrogar, Mythical Creature (troll)
**Time period(s):** Indeterminate
**Locale(s):** England, Alternate Earth

**Summary:** After Jim and Angela survive an attack on their castle, Carolinus informs them that they will have to attend the lavish Christmas feast of the Earl of Somerset. When the Dark Powers plan a new offensive, Jim must foil the plot with help from old friends and new allies.

**Other books you might like:**
Poul Anderson, *Three Hearts and Three Lions*, 1961
Randall Garrett, *Too Many Magicians*, 1967
Barbara Hambly, *The Dark Hand of Magic*, 1990
Christopher Stasheff, *The Warlock in Spite of Himself*, 1969
Patricia C. Wrede, *Dealing with Dragons*, 1990

## 1535

### GORDON R. DICKSON

## *The Harriers*

(New York: Baen, 1991)

**Story type:** Science Fiction (Anthology; Military)
**Series:** War and Honor
**Locale(s):** The Magnificate, Interstellar Empire/Federation

**Summary:** A shared world-type anthology featuring the military forces which guard the Hub and its diplomats. The three stories included are "Of War and Codes and Honor," a collaboration between Gordon R. Dickson and Chelsea Quinn Yarbro, plus Steve Perry's "Into the Hot and Moist," and S.N. Lewitt's "Tonight We Improvise."

**Other books you might like:**
David Brin, *Startide Rising*, 1983
Allan Cole, *Sten*, 1982
    Chris Bunch, co-author
S.N. Lewitt, *Cyberstealth*, 1989
George R.R. Martin, *Wild Cards*, 1987
    editor
Larry Niven, *Man-Kzin Wars*, 1988
    editor
Steve Perry, *The Man Who Never Missed*, 1985
Chelsea Quinn Yarbro, *Hyacinths*, 1983

## 1536

### GORDON R. DICKSON

## *The Magnificent Wilf*

(New York: Baen, 1995)

**Story type:** Science Fiction (Humor; First Contact)
**Major character(s):** Tom Parent, Diplomat; Lucy Parent, Linguist; Rex, Animal (dog)
**Time period(s):** Indeterminate Future
**Locale(s):** Earth; Cayahno, Planet—Imaginary

**Summary:** Chosen as a "typical" couple to host a visiting Oprinkian diplomat, Tom and Lucy develop new abilities, including telepathic contact with their dog, Rex, and find themselves thrust into galactic politics. As representatives of Earth, Tom, Lucy, and Rex free the Bulburs from Jaktal tyranny, correct a wobble in Wockii futures, and save the galaxy from invaders. Expands previously published short stories into a novel.

**Other books you might like:**
Poul Anderson, *Earthman's Burden*, 1957
    Gordon R. Dickson, co-author
John M. Ford, *How Much for Just the Planet?*, 1987
Harry Harrison, *Bill, the Galactic Hero*, 1965
Keith Laumer, *Retief at Large*, 1978
Alexei Panshin, *Star Well*, 1968
James H. Schmitz, *The Witches of Karres*, 1966
Connie Willis, *Uncharted Territory*, 1994

## 1537

### GORDON R. DICKSON

## *Naked to the Stars/The Alien Way*

(New York: Tor, 1991)

**Story type:** Science Fiction (First Contact; Military)
**Major character(s):** Cal Truant, Military Personnel, Government Official; Jason "Jase" Lee Barchar, Government Official, Experimental Subject; Kator Secondcousin Brutogas, Alien (Ruml)
**Time period(s):** Indeterminate Future
**Locale(s):** Paumons, Planet—Imaginary; Earth; Ruml Homeworld, Planet—Imaginary

**Summary:** In *Naked to the Stars* (1961), Cal Truant risks his mission and the lives of many in a desperate attempt to force a meeting as equals between leaders of the Terran invasion force and the native Paumons. In *The Alien Way* (1965), a human trap infects Kator

Secondcousin with a virus which causes transmission of Kator's thoughts into Jason Barchar's mind, allowing humans to understand the enemy to whom humanity wishes to extend friendship. As Jason begins to understand Ruml ways, his superiors start acting as if Jason has become the enemy.

**Other books you might like:**
Roger MacBride Allen, *The Ring of Charon*, 1990
Jeffrey A. Carver, *The Rapture Effect*, 1987
C.J. Cherryh, *Forty Thousand in Gehenna*, 1983
Robert L. Forward, *Dragon's Egg*, 1980
Janet Kagan, *Hellspark*, 1988
Rebecca Ore, *Becoming Alien*, 1987
Robert Silverberg, *Letters From Atlantis*, 1990
David Alexander Smith, *Homecoming*, 1990
David Alexander Smith, *Rendezvous*, 1988

---

`1538`

**GORDON R. DICKSON**

## Other

(New York: Tor, 1994)

**Story type:** Science Fiction (Political)
**Series:** Childe Cycle
**Major character(s):** Bleys Ahrens, Genius, Activist; Antonia "Toni" Lu, Activist, Assistant; Henry MacLean, Farmer
**Time period(s):** 24th century
**Locale(s):** Association, Planet—Imaginary; New Earth, Planet—Imaginary

**Summary:** Bleys Ahrens continues his plan to unify the Others, those humans neither Exotics, Dorsai, nor Old Earth. He extends his influence to the worlds of new Earth, Cassida and Newton. At the same time, he tries to find and capture Hal Mayne, whose mysterious powers make him a match for Bleys.

**Other books you might like:**
Isaac Asimov, *Foundation and Empire*, 1952
Lois McMaster Bujold, *Brothers in Arms*, 1988
C.J. Cherryh, *Cyteen*, 1988
Frank Herbert, *Dune Messiah*, 1969
David Wingrove, *The Middle Kingdom*, 1990

---

`1539`

**GORDON R. DICKSON**

## Wolf and Iron

(New York: Tor Books, 1990)

**Story type:** Science Fiction (Post-Holocaust)
**Major character(s):** Jeeris Belamy "Jeebee" Walther, Professor; Paul Sanderson, Businessman, Wanderer; Merry Sanderson, Girlfriend
**Time period(s):** 20th century
**Locale(s):** South Dakota; Montana

**Summary:** An expansion of the 1974 short story, "In Iron Years." Jeebee is forced by the collapse of modern society to leave the university town where he resides to visit his brother. While learning to understand the wolf he befriends on his travels, he learns to survive in a non-technological world.

**Other books you might like:**
Jean M. Auel, *Clan of the Cave Bear*, 1980
Dean R. Koontz, *Watchers*, 1987
Donald E. McQuinn, *Warrior*, 1990
David R. Palmer, *Emergence*, 1984

Alexei Panshin, *Rite of Passage*, 1968

---

`1540`

**GORDON R. DICKSON**

## Young Bleys

(New York: Tor, 1991)

**Story type:** Science Fiction (Political)
**Series:** Childe Cycle
**Major character(s):** Bleys Ahrens, Student, Activist; Dahno Ahrens, Activist
**Time period(s):** 24th century
**Locale(s):** Association, Planet—Imaginary

**Summary:** When Bleys Ahrens becomes a problem for his mother, she sends him to live with his uncle on the planet Association. There Bleys joins his brother, Dahno, in an interstellar organization of people whose parentage is mixed among the Three Splinter Cultures: the Exotics, the Friendlies and the Dorsai. Bleys eventually takes over the organization, hoping to further his goal of dominating many worlds.

**Other books you might like:**
Isaac Asimov, *The Foundation Trilogy*, 1951-1953
Lois McMaster Bujold, *Adventures of Miles Vorkosian*, 1986-
Harry Harrison, *The Deathworld Trilogy*, 1960-1968
Steve Perry, *The Man Who Never Missed Series*, 1985-1989

---

`1541`

**ULYSSES G. DIETZ**

## Desmond: A Novel of Love and the Modern Vampire

(Los Angeles, California: Alyson, 1998)

**Story type:** Horror (Vampire Story)
**Major character(s):** Desmond Beckwith, Businessman, Vampire; Tony Chapman, Museum Curator; Roger Deland, Vampire
**Time period(s):** 1990s (1998); 18th century
**Locale(s):** New York, New York; Paris, France

**Summary:** Financial wizard Desmond Beckwith, a 250-year-old vampire, comes to terms with both his vampirism and his homosexuality while the AIDS epidemic and a killer whose methods seem to suggest a fellow vampire decimate his social circle in New York. A first novel.

**Other books you might like:**
Gary Bowen, *Diary of a Vampire*, 1995
John Peyton Cooke, *Out for Blood*, 1991
Scott Edelman, *The Gift*, 1990
Jonathan Nasaw, *The World on Blood*, 1996
Anne Rice, *Interview with the Vampire*, 1975

---

`1542`

**WILLIAM C. DIETZ**

## Bodyguard

(New York: Ace, 1994)

**Story type:** Science Fiction (Military; Adventure)
**Major character(s):** Max Maxon, Bodyguard, Handicapped (brain damaged); Sasha Casad, Teenager; Norris, Military Personnel (corporate)
**Time period(s):** Indeterminate Future

**Locale(s):** Sea-Tac Urboplex, Washington (Seattle, Tacoma); Mars

**Summary:** Max Maxon accepts the job of protecting Sasha on her trip to Europa Station. After kidnappers take her from his apartment right in front of him, Max must rescue her and get them to Europa despite the apparent army of people out to kill or rape Sasha.

**Other books you might like:**
Lois McMaster Bujold, *Shards of Honor*, 1986
Brian Daley, *Jinx on a Terran Inheritance*, 1985
Stephen Goldin, *Jade Darcy and the Affair of Honor*, 1988
    Mary Mason, co-author
Elizabeth Moon, *Hunting Party*, 1993
Steve Perry, *The Man Who Never Missed*, 1985

### 1543
#### WILLIAM C. DIETZ

### *Drifter*
(New York: Ace, 1991)

**Story type:** Science Fiction (Adventure; Theological)
**Series:** Pik Lando
**Major character(s):** Pik Lando, Smuggler, Spaceship Captain; Wendy Wendeen, Religious, Doctor
**Time period(s):** Indeterminate Future
**Locale(s):** *The Tinker's Damn*, Spaceship; Angel, Planet—Imaginary

**Summary:** When Lando agreed to smuggle fertilizer past Mega-Metals Corporation customs officers, he didn't anticipate becoming involved in a revolution which could change not only Angel's government but also the ecology of the entire planet.

**Other books you might like:**
Lois McMaster Bujold, *The Vor Game*, 1990
C.J. Cherryh, *The Pride of Chanur*, 1982
Marc Laidlaw, *Neon Lotus*, 1988
Melisa C. Michaels, *First Battle*, 1985
Melisa C. Michaels, *Skirmish*, 1985
Larry Niven, *Fallen Angels*, 1991
    Jerry Pournelle, Michael Flynn, co-authors
Alis A. Rasmussen, *Revolution's Shore*, 1990
Joan Slonczewski, *A Door into Ocean*, 1986
Michael Swanwick, *Vacuum Flowers*, 1987
Walter Jon Williams, *Hardwired*, 1986

### 1544
#### WILLIAM C. DIETZ

### *Drifter's Run*
(New York: Ace, 1992)

**Story type:** Science Fiction (Adventure)
**Series:** Pik Lando
**Major character(s):** Pik Lando, Smuggler, Spaceship Captain; Melissa Sorenson, Child, Businesswoman; Cy Borg, Cyborg, Engineer
**Time period(s):** Indeterminate Future
**Locale(s):** *Junk*, Spaceship; Outer Space

**Summary:** When Pik Lando hastily signs on as pilot on the *Junk*, he finds the skills acquired as a smuggler prove useful when his captain mixes drayage, salvage and his perpetual search for the missing luxury liner, *Star of Empire*.

**Other books you might like:**
Lois McMaster Bujold, *Brothers in Arms*, 1988
Lois McMaster Bujold, *The Warrior's Apprentice*, 1986
Alis A. Rasmussen, *A Passage of Stars*, 1990

Alis A. Rasmussen, *The Price of Ransom*, 1990
Alis A. Rasmussen, *Revolution's Shore*, 1990
Mike Resnick, *Soothsayer*, 1991

### 1545
#### WILLIAM C. DIETZ

### *Drifter's War*
(New York: Ace, 1992)

**Story type:** Science Fiction (Adventure)
**Series:** Pik Lando
**Major character(s):** Pik Lando, Smuggler, Spaceship Captain; Cy Borg, Cyborg, Engineer
**Time period(s):** Indeterminate Future
**Locale(s):** NBHJ-43301-G, Planet—Imaginary

**Summary:** When Cy's companions rejoin him on the drifting alien spacecraft, they find themselves on an unexpected hyperspace voyage which leads to a world in which they represent the natives' only hope of surviving an alien invasion.

**Other books you might like:**
David Brin, *Startide Rising*, 1983
John DeChancie, *Red Limit Freeway*, 1984
Alis A. Rasmussen, *A Passage of Stars*, 1990
Alis A. Rasmussen, *The Price of Ransom*, 1990
Alis A. Rasmussen, *Revolution's Shore*, 1990

### 1546
#### WILLIAM C. DIETZ

### *The Final Battle*
(New York: Ace, 1995)

**Story type:** Science Fiction (Military)
**Series:** Legion of the Damned
**Major character(s):** Natalie Norwood, Military Personnel (general); Max Meyers, Military Personnel (master sergeant); Poseen-Ka, Alien (Hudathan), Military Personnel
**Time period(s):** Indeterminate Future
**Locale(s):** Worber's World, Planet—Imaginary; Battle Station Alpha XIV, Space Station (Old Lady); Confederacy of Sentient Beings, Interstellar Empire/Federation

**Summary:** Orbiting Worber's World in the *Old Lady*, Norwood watches the Hudathans who survive on the destroyed planet. Despite great vigilance by the Confederacy of Sentient Beings, the Hudathans smuggle technology planetside, which allows resumption of the Hudathan war to eliminate all competition.

**Other books you might like:**
Bill Baldwin, *The Siege*, 1994
John Dalmas, *The Regiment*, 1987
Andrew Keith, *Cohort of the Damned*, 1993
Anne McCaffrey, *Treaty at Doona*, 1994
    Jody Lynn Nye, co-author
Jerry Pournelle, *Falkenberg's Legion*, 1990
David Weber, *On Basilisk Station*, 1993

## 1547

### WILLIAM C. DIETZ

## *Legion of the Damned*
(New York: Ace, 1993)

**Story type:** Science Fiction (Military; Political)
**Major character(s):** Paula Scolari, Military Personnel; Marianne Mosby, Military Personnel; Sergi Chien-Chu, Counselor (advisor to the throne)
**Time period(s):** Indeterminate Future
**Locale(s):** Earth; Algeron, Planet—Imaginary

**Summary:** Earth creates a deadly legion of cyborgs through reanimation, surgery and involuntary recruitment and training programs with a high failure rate. If they survive basic training, Algeron provides a mutually beneficial but lethal training ground for Legionnaires and a like-minded native race. Meanwhile, the Emperor and Legion struggle to counter assaults from the alien Hudatha Empire.

**Other books you might like:**
David Drake, *The Jungle*, 1991
David Drake, *The Warrior*, 1991
Dave Duncan, *Hero*, 1991
Stephen Goldin, *Jade Darcy and the Affair of Honor*, 1988
   Mary Mason, co-author
Andrew Keith, *March or Die*, 1992
   William H. Keith, Jr., co-author
Jerry Pournelle, *Janissaries*, 1979
Richard Sapir, *The Destroyer #1: Created, the Destroyer*, 1971
   Warren Murphy, co-author
Robert Tine, *Universal Soldier*, 1992

## 1548

### WILLIAM C. DIETZ

## *Mars Prime*
(New York: Roc, 1992)

**Story type:** Science Fiction (Adventure; Mystery)
**Series:** Rex Corvan
**Major character(s):** Rex Corvan, Journalist; Kim Corvan, Editor (broadcast news); Martin, Artificial Intelligence
**Time period(s):** Indeterminate Future
**Locale(s):** *Outward Bound*, Spaceship; Mars

**Summary:** Rex and Kim Corvan travel on the second colony ship to Mars. Along the way, a serial killer menaces everyone while protocol and security hamper the investigation. On Mars itself, the threats grow more complex. Even with the help of artificial intelligences, Kim and Rex find it difficult to survive more mysterious disappearances and a revolution.

**Other books you might like:**
Robert L. Forward, *Martian Rainbow*, 1991
Robert A. Heinlein, *The Moon Is a Harsh Mistress*, 1966
Spider Robinson, *Stardance*, 1979
   Jeanne Robinson, co-author
Richard Paul Russo, *Destroying Angel*, 1992
Allen Steele, *Orbital Decay*, 1989
John E. Stith, *Redshift Rendezvous*, 1990

## 1549

### WILLIAM C. DIETZ

## *Matrix Man*
(New York: Roc, 1990)

**Story type:** Science Fiction (Adventure; Techno-Thriller)
**Series:** Rex Corvan
**Major character(s):** Rex Corvan, Journalist (television correspondent)
**Time period(s):** 21st century
**Locale(s):** Seattle, Washington

**Summary:** Rex Corvan, 3-D television superstar, has unusual equipment; a camera in place of his right eye, allowing him to easily provide a second camera viewpoint. When a new device, the video matrix generator, allows easy modification of video and holographic images, the World Peace Organization decides to use it to take over the world. As Corvan investigates, he becomes a target of an assassin.

**Other books you might like:**
David Brin, *Earth*, 1990
Pat Cadigan, *Synners*, 1991
Orson Scott Card, *Xenocide*, 1991
Jeffrey A. Carver, *The Rapture Effect*, 1987
Robert J. Sawyer, *Golden Fleece*, 1990

## 1550

### WILLIAM C. DIETZ

## *McCade's Bounty*
(New York: Ace, 1990)

**Story type:** Science Fiction (Adventure; Military)
**Series:** Sam McCade
**Major character(s):** Sam McCade, Spaceship Captain, Bounty Hunter (former); Mustapha Pong, Pirate (space), Kidnapper; Molly McCade, Child (Sam's daughter)
**Time period(s):** Indeterminate Future
**Locale(s):** Alice, Planet—Imaginary; *Void Runner*, Spaceship

**Summary:** While Sam McCade was off picking up a load of fertilizer for his home planet, Alice, Mustapha Pong attacked it. Sam returns in his converted warship, *Void Runner*, to find Alice in ruins, many people dead, his wife seriously wounded, and 60 children kidnapped. Sam and his crew set off to rescue the children and punish the pirates.

**Other books you might like:**
Lois McMaster Bujold, *The Vor Game*, 1990
Allan Cole, *Sten*, 1984
   Chris Bunch, co-author
Melisa C. Michaels, *Pirate Prince*, 1987
Melisa C. Michaels, *Skirmish*, 1985
David R. Palmer, *Emergence*, 1984

## 1551

### WILLIAM C. DIETZ

## *Prison Planet*
(New York: Ace Books, 1989)

**Story type:** Science Fiction (Adventure)
**Major character(s):** Jonathan Renn, Prisoner; Marla Mendez, Cyborg, Prisoner
**Time period(s):** Indeterminate Future
**Locale(s):** Swamp, Planet—Imaginary (A prison planet)

**Summary:** Renn, framed for a crime he did not commit, is dumped on the dangerous prison planet Swamp. He immediately sets out to rescue Marla, escape, and seek revenge.

**Other books you might like:**
Allan Cole, *Revenge of the Damned*, 1989
    Chris Bunch, co-author
Harry Harrison, *Deathworld*, 1960
Barry B. Longyear, *Infinity Hold*, 1989

## 1552

### WILLIAM C. DIETZ

## *Steelheart*

(New York: Ace, 1998)

**Story type:** Science Fiction (Military)
**Major character(s):** Harley Doon, Android; Amy Reno, Android
**Time period(s):** 22nd century (2176)
**Locale(s):** Zuul, Planet—Imaginary

**Summary:** Humans have planted a colony on the planet Zuul along with two different alien races. Unfortunately, one of those species believes in a fanatical religion that views certain forms of technology as evil. This results in a war, during which the unlikely saviors of the human population are a minority of androids.

**Other books you might like:**
Bill Baldwin, *Canby's Legion*, 1995
David Drake, *The Military Dimension*, 1991
Roland J. Green, *The Painful Field*, 1995
John Dalmas, *The White Regiment*, 1990
Victor Milan, *CLD*, 1995

## 1553

### WILLIAM C. DIETZ

## *Where the Ships Die*

(New York; Ace, 1996)

**Story type:** Science Fiction (Political; Adventure)
**Major character(s):** Dorn Voss, Student, Teenager; Carnaby Orr, Businessman; Natalie Voss, Spacewoman
**Time period(s):** Indeterminate Future
**Locale(s):** New Hope, Planet—Imaginary; La-Tri, Planet—Imaginary; Mechnos, Planet—Imaginary

**Summary:** Forced to leave school due to lack of payments by his parents, Dorn falls into the hands of slavers. While a volcano erupts on La-Tri, killing all of the philosophers at once, on Mechnos, Natalie realizes that Carnaby Orr murdered her parents.

**Other books you might like:**
L. Warren Douglas, *Stepwater*, 1995
Debra Doyle, *The Price of the Stars*, 1992
    James D. Macdonald, co-author
Alan Dean Foster, *The Tar-Aiym Krang*, 1972
Alis A. Rasmussen, *A Passage of Stars*, 1990
David Weber, *Mutineers' Moon*, 1991

## 1554

### J.M. DILLARD

## *Insurrection*

(New York: Pocket Books, 1998)

**Story type:** Science Fiction (Space Opera; Immortality)

**Series:** Star Trek: The Next Generation
**Major character(s):** Jean-Luc Picard, Spaceship Captain; Data, Android, Space Explorer, Military Personnel; Anij, Immortal, Settler (colonist)
**Time period(s):** 24th century
**Locale(s):** *U.S.S. Enterprise*, Spaceship; Ba'ku, Planet—Imaginary; United Federation of Planets, Interstellar Empire/Federation

**Summary:** Data goes berserk while on a scientific observation assignment. When asked to help de-activate Data, Picard suspects a hidden agenda and defies Starfleet orders. His investigation reveals a sinister plot against the people and planet of Ba'ku.

**Other books you might like:**
C.J. Cherryh, *Cyteen*, 1988
Robert A. Heinlein, *Methuselah's Children*, 1958
Judy Klass, *The Cry of the Onlies*, 1989
Jean Lorrah, *The IDIC Epidemic*, 1988
Judith Reeves-Stevens, *Prime Directive*, 1990
    Garfield Reeves-Stevens, co-author

## 1555

### J.M. DILLARD

## *Specters*

(New York: Dell Abyss, 1991)

**Story type:** Horror (Psychological Suspense)
**Major character(s):** Jacob Feinman, Doctor; Avra Kallisti, Clerk (in a bookstore); Magdalen Kallisti, Teacher
**Time period(s):** 1990s (1990); 1930s (1936)
**Locale(s):** Tampa, Florida; Baltimore, Maryland

**Summary:** Unbeknownst to twins Avra and Magdalen Kallisti, the man who abused them as children and murdered their mother has come back under a guise they least suspect, still intent on exorcising the ghosts of his own miserable childhood by killing the two of them.

**Other books you might like:**
Thomas Harris, *The Silence of the Lambs*, 1988
Jack Martin, *Halloween*, 1978

## 1556

### J.M. DILLARD

## *Star Trek VI: The Undiscovered Country*

(New York: Pocket, 1991)

**Story type:** Science Fiction (Space Opera)
**Series:** Star Trek
**Major character(s):** James T. Kirk, Spaceship Captain; Leonard McCoy, Doctor
**Time period(s):** 23rd century
**Locale(s):** *U.S.S. Enterprise*, Spaceship; *Kronos One*, Spaceship; Rura Penthe, Planet—Imaginary

**Summary:** Kirk and the *U.S.S. Enterprise* crew unwillingly follow orders to escort Klingon High Council Chancellor Gorkon to a negotiation session aimed at dismantling space stations and starbases along the Klingon Neutral Zone. When the Chancellor's assassination leads to Kirk and McCoy's trial and sentencing to the Klingon prison planet, Rura Penthe, the *U.S.S. Enterprise* crew must rescue their officers and foil the conspiracy which threatens potential Federation peace with the Klingon Empire. Novelizes the sixth motion picture.

**Other books you might like:**
Diane Duane, *Doctor's Orders*, 1990
Barbara Hambly, *Ishmael*, 1985

Janet Kagan, *Uhura's Song*, 1985
Vonda N. McIntyre, *The Search for Spock*, 1984
Vonda N. McIntyre, *Transition*, 1991
Vonda N. McIntyre, *Star Trek IV: The Voyage Home*, 1986
Vonda N. McIntyre, *Star Trek II: The Wrath of Khan*, 1982
Gene Roddenberry, *Star Trek - The Motion Picture: A Novel*, 1979

**1557**

### J.M. DILLARD

## *Star Trek: The Lost Years*

(New York: Pocket Books, 1989)

**Story type:** Science Fiction (Space Opera)
**Series:** Star Trek
**Major character(s):** James T. Kirk, Spaceship Captain; Spock, Scientist, Alien
**Time period(s):** 23rd century (Stardate 6987)
**Locale(s):** Earth; *U.S.S. Enterprise*, Spaceship

**Summary:** Its five year mission over, the *Enterprise* returns to Earth and its crew is reassigned to other duties. Captain Kirk is promoted to Admiral and placed in charge of a specially created Starfleet division, while Mr. Spock accepts a teaching position on Vulcan, and Dr. McCoy goes off to do medical research. Each must struggle to achieve some form of stability in a life without the other two, but each soon finds himself immersed in a new and exciting adventure as well.

**Other books you might like:**
Greg Bear, *Eon*, 1985
David Brin, *Startide Rising*, 1983
Emma Bull, *Falcon*, 1989
Larry Niven, *The Mote in God's Eye*, 1974
    Jerry Pournelle, co-author
David Alexander Smith, *Rendezvous*, 1988

**1558**

### BARBARA DILLON

## *My Stepfather Shrank!*

(New York: HarperCollins, 1992)

**Story type:** Science Fiction (Young Adult)
**Major character(s):** Mallory, Child; Woody, Parent (stepfather), Lawyer; Peebles, Spouse (inventor's)
**Time period(s):** 1990s
**Locale(s):** Jefferson Village, Fictional City

**Summary:** Mallory's stepfather, Woody, shrinks to three inches tall when he eats a piece of candy containing Mr. Peebles' latest invention, the "Lose It Now" diet formula. A "kidnapping" by a crow, scaring off burglars and a wild time at the carnival ensue before Mr. Peebles can save Woody with another of his unpredictable inventions.

**Other books you might like:**
Bruce Coville, *Jeremy Thatcher, Dragon Hatcher*, 1991
Beatrice Gormley, *Mail-Order Wings*, 1981
Mary Norton, *The Borrowers*, 1953
Jenny Pausacker, *Fast Forward*, 1989
John Peterson, *The Littles*, 1967
Terry Pratchett, *Truckers*, 1989

**1559**

### JENNIFER DIMARCO

## *Escape to the Wind*

(New York: Castillo International Inc., 1993)

**Story type:** Science Fiction (Gay/Lesbian Fiction; Post-Nuclear Holocaust)
**Series:** Wind Trilogy
**Major character(s):** Tyger, Leader (Windriders), Lesbian; Christopher Jarth, Leader, Military Personnel; Ardyn, Lesbian
**Time period(s):** Indeterminate Future
**Locale(s):** New Seattle, North America

**Summary:** War between rival gangs and oppression by the dictatorial Patriarchy makes life miserable for unempowered New Seattle residents. Outside the protective dome a post-war phenomenon, the radioactive Wind kills most humans, metamorphosing the few survivors and all other animal life. Tyger and other Windriders seek to escape the tyranny and violence by fleeing to the unprotected wild, there discovering evidence of new Patriarchy atrocities.

**Other books you might like:**
Octavia E. Butler, *Imago*, 1989
Marjorie Bradley Kellogg, *Harmony*, 1991
Frances Lucas, *Cathy IV*, 1992
Vonda N. McIntyre, *Starfarers*, 1989
Severna Park, *Speaking Dreams*, 1992
Joan Slonczewski, *A Door into Ocean*, 1986

**1560**

### NICK DIMARTINO

## *Seattle Ghost Story*

(Lynnwood, Washington: Rosebriar Publishing, 1998)

**Story type:** Horror (Ghost Story)
**Major character(s):** Pepper Merlino, Student; Joe Strozza, Artist; Billy Beck, Child (eleven years old)
**Time period(s):** 1990s (1998)
**Locale(s):** Seattle, Washington

**Summary:** Immediately after Carmen Merlino's accidental death from a plunge off the bridge in Cowan Park, Joe Strozza, Billy Beck, and Carmen's granddaughter Pepper, all of whom were present at her death, experience a series of foreboding nightmares. The source of their nightmares, and the spectral incidents that accompany them, is an incident that happened decades before, remnants of which are buried in the park and tied directly to the disappearance of Pepper's father and grandfather.

**Other books you might like:**
James P. Blaylock, *Night Relics*, 1994
Stephen King, *Bag of Bones*, 1998
Richard Matheson, *Earthbound*, 1994
Peter Straub, *Ghost Story*, 1979
Thomas Tessier, *Phantom*, 1982

**1561**

### THOMAS M. DISCH

## *The M.D.: A Horror Story*

(New York: Knopf, 1991)

**Story type:** Horror (Satire)

**Major character(s):** William ''Billy'' Michaels, Doctor, Parent (father of Judge); Mercury, Deity (god of medical science); Judge Michaels, Young Man, Relative (son of Billy)
**Time period(s):** 1990s
**Locale(s):** Minneapolis, Minnesota

**Summary:** As a young boy, Billy Michaels is given a magic caduceus that can either heal or render illness, depending on Billy's inclinations. Billy uses his Faustian powers megalomaniacally, creating a virulent disease which he alone can cure in this satire on the absolute corruption that comes with absolute power.

**Other books you might like:**
Robin Cook, *Coma*, 1977
C.M. Kornbluth, *''The Little Black Bag''*, 1990
　in *Intensive Scare*
Mary Shelley, *Frankenstein*, 1818
Karl Edward Wagner, *''The Fourth Seal''*, 1983
　in *In a Lonely Place*
F. Paul Wilson, *The Touch*, 1986

**1562**

**THOMAS M. DISCH**

## *The Priest: A Gothic Romance*
(New York: Knopf, 1995)

**Story type:** Horror (Satire)
**Major character(s):** Pat Bryce, Religious (Catholic priest); A.D. Boscage, Writer; Alison Sanders, Student
**Time period(s):** 1990s (1995)
**Locale(s):** Minneapolis, Minnesota

**Summary:** In this savage satire on the Catholic church (not to mention the writings of Whitley Streiber), Father Patrick Bryce is punished for his pedophilic tendencies by being made to preside over a concentration-camp-like establishment designed to prevent pregnant young women from having abortions. When taken over by the transmigrated soul of 13th-century Bishop Silvanus de Roquefort, a participant in the Spanish Inquisition, Bryce launches into his duties with savage and lusty glee.

**Other books you might like:**
Lewis Gannett, *The Living One*, 1993
William Browning Spencer, *Resume with Monsters*, 1995

**1563**

**ROGER L. DISILVESTRO**

## *Living with the Reptiles*
(New York: Donald I. Fine, 1990)

**Story type:** Science Fiction (Time Travel; Humor)
**Major character(s):** Jackson Black, Adventurer; Ritz, Financier, Handicapped (paralyzed); Hunter Killdeer, Police Officer (time police captain)
**Time period(s):** 20th century; 9th century
**Locale(s):** South America (Amazon jungle); England

**Summary:** The Time Police have shot down a renegade time traveller in the 20th century. Mr. Ritz arranges to get Jackson Black's help in recovering the time travel device. The salvage operation mounted in the Amazon jungle yields a time traveller from 2075 and his downed chronocraft. Ritz takes the chronocraft back to the 9th century. Captain Killdeer arrives in the 20th century and takes Black to 2101, finding the disasterous results of Ritz's trip, results which must be reversed if human life is to survive on Earth.

**Other books you might like:**
Warren Norwood, *Stranded!*, 1989
　Mel Odom, co-author
Warren Norwood, *Trapped!*, 1989
Warren Norwood, *Vanished*, 1988
H. Beam Piper, *Lord Kalvan of Otherwhen*, 1965
L. Neil Smith, *The Nagasaki Vector*, 1983
John Varley, *Millennium*, 1983

**1564**

**E.L. DOCTOROW**

## *The Waterworks*
(New York: Random House, 1994)

**Story type:** Science Fiction (Literary; Medical)
**Major character(s):** Martin Pemberton, Journalist; McIlvane, Editor; Sartorius, Doctor, Inventor
**Time period(s):** 1870s (1871)
**Locale(s):** New York, New York

**Summary:** A freelance writer, Martin Pemberton, sees his deceased father in the streets of New York, confides this to a friend and disappears. The friend, McIlvane, follows Pemberton's trail through a city of corruption and mystery. As much a picture of a city as a story, *Waterworks* shows New York growing, for good or ill, into its current form, with the science fiction elements fantastic to the 1870s evolving into mostly common 1990s technology.

**Other books you might like:**
James P. Blaylock, *Homunculus*, 1986
G.K. Chesterton, *The Man Who Was Thursday*, 1908
William Hjortsberg, *Nevermore*, 1994
Tim Powers, *The Anubis Gates*, 1983

**1565**

**ROBERT DOHERTY**

## *Area 51*
(New York: Dell, 1997)

**Story type:** Science Fiction (Invasion of Earth)
**Major character(s):** Kelly Reynolds, Journalist; Mike Turcotte, Military Personnel
**Time period(s):** 1990s
**Locale(s):** Area 51, Nevada; Las Vegas, Nevada; Southwest

**Summary:** Decades of government secrecy surrounding events at Area 51 begin to unravel as signs indicate that a quiescent artifact may awaken.

**Other books you might like:**
Roger MacBride Allen, *The Ring of Charon*, 1990
Greg Bear, *Eon*, 1985
Philip K. Dick, *The Unteleported Man*, 1983
　revised
Jack McDevitt, *The Engines of God*, 1994
Allen Steele, *Labyrinth of Night*, 1992
David Weber, *Mutineers' Moon*, 1991

## 1566

**BILL DOLAN**

### Afrikorps

(New York: Harper, 1991)

**Story type:** Science Fiction (Military; Post-Holocaust)
**Series:** Afrikorps
**Major character(s):** Abe ''TC'' Creighton, Military Personnel
**Time period(s):** 22nd century (2175)
**Locale(s):** Africa

**Summary:** In the wake of the ''Green House'' cataclysm of 2050, the offspring of Biosphere survivors struggle to reclaim the Earth. When Africa gives rise to vicious and evil new armies which invade Europe, a multinational military force, Afrikorps, organizes to clean up Africa. Captain Creighton leads his team on a violent mission for a mysterious leader hoping to win new allies for the Afrikorps.

**Other books you might like:**
Frank Herbert, *Dune*, 1965
J.M. Morgan, *Desert Eden*, 1991
G. Harry Stine, *The Bastard Rebellion*, 1988
G. Harry Stine, *Warbots*, 1988

## 1567

**BILL DOLAN**

### Cobra Curse

(New York: Harper Paperbacks, 1993)

**Story type:** Science Fiction (Military; Post-Holocaust)
**Series:** Afrikorps
**Major character(s):** Abe ''TC'' Creighton, Military Personnel
**Time period(s):** 22nd century (2178)
**Locale(s):** Egypt; Africa

**Summary:** When Captain Abe Creighton leads his troops on a routine mission in Egypt, survivalist cultists capture them. Creighton escapes and discovers their plot to control the world involves a bacteriological weapons arsenal. Africorps must stop the Cult of the Cobra if they hope to return peace to Africa.

**Other books you might like:**
Jake Davis, *The Last Rangers*, 1992
David Drake, *The Jungle*, 1991
K.W. Jeter, *Madlands*, 1991
Mike Resnick, *Future Earths: Under African Skies*, 1993
    Gardner Dozois, co-editor
John Sievert, *Suicide Attack*, 1990
G. Harry Stine, *The Bastard Rebellion*, 1988

## 1568

**BILL DOLAN**

### Iron Horse

(New York: Harper, 1991)

**Story type:** Science Fiction (Military; Post-Holocaust)
**Series:** Afrikorps
**Major character(s):** Abe ''TC'' Creighton, Military Personnel
**Time period(s):** 22nd century (2175)
**Locale(s):** Africa

**Summary:** Ordered to provide security for the building of a train, Captain Creighton must respond to a warning from cryogenically frozen survivors of the ''Green House'' cataclysm, now revived, who tell of Marauders mounting an assault. Creighton and the Afrikorps must stop the Marauders, save the survivors from the past and safeguard the train which represents the key to future freedom.

**Other books you might like:**
J.M. Morgan, *Desert Eden*, 1991
G. Harry Stine, *Guts and Glory*, 1991
G. Harry Stine, *Warbots*, 1988
Michael D. Weaver, *My Father Immortal*, 1989

## 1569

**BILL DOLAN**

### White Rhino

(New York: Harper, 1992)

**Story type:** Science Fiction (Military; Post-Holocaust)
**Series:** Afrikorps
**Major character(s):** Abe ''TC'' Creighton, Military Personnel; Benhaddou, Criminal
**Time period(s):** 22nd century (2176)
**Locale(s):** Africa

**Summary:** Hoping to again bring civilization to Africa, Creighton and the Afrikorps attempt to install a new communications system and establish a game preserve while a killer, escaped from prison, seeks Creighton with murder in mind.

**Other books you might like:**
Will Bradley, *Ark Liberty*, 1992
David Brin, *The Postman*, 1985
Octavia E. Butler, *Dawn*, 1987
J.M. Morgan, *Future Eden*, 1992
G. Harry Stine, *The Bastard Rebellion*, 1988
G. Harry Stine, *Warbots*, 1988
Michael D. Weaver, *My Father Immortal*, 1989

## 1570

**D.J. DONALDSON**

### Blood on the Bayou

(New York: St. Martins, 1991)

**Story type:** Horror (Werewolf Story)
**Major character(s):** Andy Broussard, Doctor (Chief medical examiner); Kit Franklyn, Psychologist
**Time period(s):** 1990s (1991)
**Locale(s):** New Orleans, Louisiana

**Summary:** A series of brutal murders in the New Orleans area raises suspicions that it is the work of a werewolf. Doctors Andy Broussard and Kit Franklyn resist the temptation to accept this incredible possibility until Kit herself is stalked by the murderer.

**Other books you might like:**
George C. Chesbro, *The Fear in Yesterday's Rings*, 1991
Whitley Strieber, *The Wolfen*, 1978
Les Whitten, *Moon of the Wolf*, 1967

## 1571

**STEPHEN R. DONALDSON**

### Forbidden Knowledge

(New York: Bantam Spectra, 1991)

**Story type:** Science Fiction (Space Opera)
**Series:** Gap

**Major character(s):** Morn Hyland, Police Officer (United Mining Corporation); Nick Succorso, Pirate, Spaceman (Captain's Fancy); Angus Thermopyle, Convict
**Time period(s):** Indeterminate Future
**Locale(s):** *Captain's Fancy*, Spaceship (in Forbidden Space)

**Summary:** Some pirates clandestinely allied to United Mining Corporation Police operate at the edge of the Forbidden Space where the alien Amnion hold sway. Morn is addicted to use of the illegal zone control which was planted in her head against her wishes by Angus Thermopyle. When she finally gains the control device she fights to regain her sanity and her future. *Forbidden Knowledge* is a sequel to *The Real Story* (1990) and is the first of a five book cycle.

**Other books you might like:**
Lois McMaster Bujold, *The Warrior's Apprentice*, 1986
F.M. Busby, *Rissa Kerguelen*, 1977
Orson Scott Card, *Songmaster*, 1980
Stephen Goldin, *Jade Darcy and the Affair of Honor*, 1988
   Mary Mason, co-author
Robert A. Heinlein, *Friday*, 1982
Alis A. Rasmussen, *A Passage of Stars*, 1990

---

**1572**

STEPHEN R. DONALDSON

### The Gap into Conflict: The Real Story

(New York: Bantam Spectra, 1991)

**Story type:** Science Fiction (Adventure; Space Opera)
**Major character(s):** Morn Hyland, Police Officer; Angus Thermopyle, Pirate (space)
**Time period(s):** Indeterminate Future
**Locale(s):** Com-Mine Station, Space Station; Outer Space

**Summary:** Morn Hyland was an agent of the military police when she caused the accident which blew up the Starmaster, her family's spaceship. Morn was the only survivor. She was rescued by Angus Thermopyle who then implanted an illegal device in her brain which allowed him control over her body and mind. It made her a perfect crew member and victim for his abuse.

**Other books you might like:**
Brian Daley, *Fall of the White Ship Avatar*, 1987
Brian Daley, *Jinx on a Terran Inheritance*, 1985
Brian Daley, *Requiem for a Ruler of Worlds*, 1985
George Alec Effinger, *When Gravity Fails*, 1987
Stephen Goldin, *Jade Darcy and the Affair of Honor*, 1988
   Mary Mason, co-author
Stephen Goldin, *Jade Darcy and the Zen Pirates*, 1990
   Mary Mason, co-author

---

**1573**

STEPHEN R. DONALDSON

### The Gap into Madness: Chaos and Order

(New York: Bantam Spectra, 1994)

**Story type:** Science Fiction (Space Opera; Political)
**Series:** Gap
**Major character(s):** Angus Thermopyle, Spaceship Captain, Cyborg; Morn Hyland, Police Officer (United Mining Corporation), Prisoner; Nick Succorso, Pirate, Spaceman
**Time period(s):** Indeterminate Future
**Locale(s):** Interstellar Empire/Federation; *Trumpet*, Spaceship; *Punisher*, Spaceship

**Summary:** Former enemies struggle to survive and control *Trumpet* as it flees UMC police, who have been ordered to capture or kill all aboard her.

**Other books you might like:**
Roger MacBride Allen, *The Ring of Charon*, 1990
Allan Cole, *Sten*, 1984
   Chris Bunch, co-author
Glen Cook, *The Dragon Never Sleeps*, 1988
Vernor Vinge, *A Fire upon the Deep*, 1992
David Wingrove, *The Middle Kingdom*, 1990

---

**1574**

STEPHEN R. DONALDSON

### The Gap into Power: A Dark and Hungry God Arises

(New York: Bantam, 1992)

**Story type:** Science Fiction (Space Opera)
**Series:** Gap
**Major character(s):** Morn Hyland, Police Officer (United Mining Corp.); Holt "The Dragon" Fasner, Administrator; Angus Thermopyle, Spaceship Captain, Cyborg
**Time period(s):** Indeterminate Future
**Locale(s):** Billingate, Space Station; *Trumpet*, Spaceship

**Summary:** Holt discovers that Warden Dios of the UMC Police plans to shut down Billingate, thereby disrupting trade with the alien Amnion and interfering with piratical fencing transactions. Angus Thermopyle, now a cyborg programmed with loyalty to UMCP, also heads for Billingate. Someone must rescue Morn Hyland and her force-grown son from the Amnion before Billingate's destruction.

**Other books you might like:**
John Brunner, *A Planet of Your Own*, 1966
F.M. Busby, *Rissa Kerguelen*, 1977
Orson Scott Card, *Wyrms*, 1987
C.J. Cherryh, *Cyteen*, 1988
Alis A. Rasmussen, *A Passage of Stars*, 1990
Robert Reed, *Down the Bright Way*, 1991

---

**1575**

STEPHEN R. DONALDSON

### The Gap into Ruin: This Day All Gods Die

(New York: Bantam Spectra, 1996)

**Story type:** Science Fiction (Space Opera; Political)
**Series:** Gap
**Major character(s):** Morn Hyland, Police Officer (United Mining Corporation); Angus Thermopyle, Spaceship Captain, Cyborg; Warden Dios, Police Officer (United Mining Corporation), Leader
**Time period(s):** Indeterminate Future
**Locale(s):** Interstellar Empire/Federation; *Trumpet*, Spaceship; Outer Space

**Summary:** When Warden Dios plans to expose the corrupt leadership of the United Mining Corporation, his action may precipitate total war. Meanwhile, Angus Thermopyle and Morn Hyland struggle to obtain an antidote to the enemy's virus which could destroy all of human kind. Concludes the series.

**Other books you might like:**
Roger MacBride Allen, *The Ring of Charon*, 1990
Allan Cole, *Sten*, 1984
   Chris Bunch, co-author

Glen Cook, *The Dragon Never Sleeps*, 1988
Vernor Vinge, *A Fire upon the Deep*, 1992
David Wingrove, *The Middle Kingdom*, 1990

**1576**

**STEPHEN R. DONALDSON**, Editor

## Strange Dreams

(New York: Bantam Spectra, 1993)

**Story type:** Fantasy (Anthology)

**Summary:** Contains a three-page introduction plus 28 stories originally published in periodicals and anthologies during the past 50 years, a majority from the 1970s and 1980s with diverse themes and settings and all unforgettable to the editor. Authors include Michael Bishop, Jorge Luis Borges, Orson Scott Card, C.J. Cherryh, Harlan Ellison, John M. Ford, Franz Kafka, Rudyard Kipling, Nancy Kress, R.A. Lafferty, Patricia A. McKillip, Robin McKinley, Lucius Shepard, Theodore Sturgeon, Sheri S. Tepper, Jack Vance and John Varley.

**Other books you might like:**
Jorge Luis Borges, *The Book of Fantasy*, 1990
  editor
Robert H. Boyer, *Visions & Imaginings: Classic Fantasy Fiction*, 1992
  Kenneth J. Zahorski, co-editor
Lin Carter, *Discoveries in Fantasy*, 1972
  editor
Lester Del Rey, *Once upon a Time: A Treasury of Modern Fairy Tales*, 1991
  Risa Kessler, co-editor
Martin H. Greenberg, *After the King: Stories in Honor of J.R.R. Tolkien*, 1992
  editor
Jack Zipes, *Spells of Enchantment*, 1991
  editor

**1577**

**MARCOS DONNELLY**

## Prophets for the End of Time

(New York: Baen, 1998)

**Story type:** Fantasy (Contemporary; Humor)
**Major character(s):** Clayton Pinkes, Religious; Henri Elobert, Businessman; Elizabeth Gadded, Entertainer
**Time period(s):** 20th century; 21st century (1969-2000)
**Locale(s):** Heaven; England

**Summary:** This novel provides a comedic look at Armageddon. Heavenly bureaucrats decree that the world is indeed about to end, which has consequences for an offbeat evangelist, a cunning businessman with no scruples, and a comedienne whose destiny involves saving the world. First novel.

**Other books you might like:**
Joan Brady, *God on a Harley*, 1995
Avery Corman, *Oh God!*, 1971
Neil Gaiman, *Good Omens: The Nice and Accurate Prophecies of Agnes Nutter, Witch*, 1993
  Terry Pratchett, co-author
Romain Gary, *The Gasp*, 1973
James Morrow, *Towing Jehovah*, 1995

**1578**

**EMMA DONOGHUE**

## Kissing the Witch: Old Tales in New Skins

(New York: HarperCollins/Joanna Colter Books, 1997)

**Story type:** Fantasy (Collection; Legend)

**Summary:** Contains 13 linked stories, varying in tone, which present traditional fairy tales and fairy tale patterns with a twist. Rewritten to present the stories from the women's point of view, the familiar characters include Snow White, Cinderella, Rumplestiltskin, Rapunzel and Beauty and the Beast.

**Other books you might like:**
Margaret Atwood, *Good Bones and Simple Murders*, 1994
William J. Brooke, *Teller of Tales*, 1994
David Fisher, *Legally Correct Fairy Tales*, 1996
James Finn Garner, *Once upon a More Enlightened Time*, 1995
James Finn Garner, *Politically Correct Bedtime Stories*, 1994
James Finn Garner, *Politically Correct Holiday Stories*, 1995
Ethel Johnston Phelps, *Tatterhood and Other Tales*, 1978
  editor

**1579**

**JAMES DOOHAN**
**S.M. STIRLING**, Co-Author

## The Rising

(New York: Baen Starline, 1996)

**Story type:** Science Fiction (Adventure; Mystery)
**Series:** Flight Engineer
**Major character(s):** Peter Raeder, Engineer, Spaceman; Cynthia Robbins, Military Personnel (lieutenant), Spacewoman; Paddy Casey, Engineer, Spaceman
**Time period(s):** Indeterminate Future
**Locale(s):** *Invincible*, Spaceship; Outer Space; Ontario Base, Montenegro

**Summary:** When injuries from the war with secessionists prevent Peter Raeder from continuing to pilot a spaceship, he accepts the assignment of engineer aboard *Invincible*. However, unless Peter can discover who murdered *Invincible*'s previous engineer, the traitor will continue to kill. Doohan's first novel and first of a series.

**Other books you might like:**
Nigel Bennett, *Keeper of the King*, 1997
  P.N. Elrod, co-author
Jonathan Frakes, *The Abductors: Conspiracy*, 1996
  Dean Wesley Smith, co-author
S.M. Stirling, *Marching through Georgia*, 1988
S.M. Stirling, *The Stone Dogs*, 1990
S.M. Stirling, *Under the Yoke*, 1989
John E. Stith, *Redshift Rendezvous*, 1990

**1580**

**FRAN DORF**

## A Reasonable Madness

(New York: Birch Lane Press/Carol, 1990)

**Story type:** Horror (Mystery)
**Major character(s):** Laura Gardner Wade, Heiress; David Goldman, Doctor (psychiatrist); Zach Wade, Businessman (department store manager), Spouse (Laura's husband)

**Time period(s):** 1990s (1990)
**Locale(s):** New York, New York

**Summary:** Rich and beautiful Laura Wade confesses to the murder of Rita Harmon, even though she was nowhere near the scene of the crime and witnesses claim to have seen a man do the killing. Can Laura really kill, as she maintains, through her psychic powers? If not, then how does she know details about the murder only someone present at the scene of the crime could know? This is the author's first novel.

**Other books you might like:**
Owen Brookes, *Inheritance*, 1980
John Farris, *The Fury*, 1976
James Herbert, *Moon*, 1985
Geoffrey Household, *The Sending*, 1980
Bari Wood, *The Killing Gift*, 1975

### 1581

**MICHAEL DORN**
**HILARY HEMINGWAY**, Co-Author
**JEFFREY P. LINDSAY**, Co-Author

## Time Blender

(New York: HarperPrism, 1997)

**Story type:** Science Fiction (Alternate Universe)
**Major character(s):** Tony Miller, Archaeologist; Jay Cook, Archaeologist; Mara, Religious (priestess)
**Time period(s):** 1990s
**Locale(s):** Pacific Islands

**Summary:** Tony Miller thinks he has rescued his colleague, Jay Cook, from the earthquake and tsunami, only to discover that an alien intelligence has taken over Cook's body. Belonging to one side of a future cosmic battle, the alien seeks to preserve the Artifact that regulates the chaos of the space-time continuum. After Cook dies during the rescue attempt, Miller brings the Artifact to Tahiti but chaos has already begun to affect the space-time continuum.

**Other books you might like:**
Campbell Black, *Raiders of the Lost Ark*, 1981
David Brin, *Earth*, 1990
C.J. Cherryh, *The Fires of Azeroth*, 1979
Gordon R. Dickson, *Time Storm*, 1977
Phyllis Eisenstein, *Shadow of Earth*, 1979
Philip Jose Farmer, *To Your Scattered Bodies Go*, 1971
Joseph Millard, *The Gods Hate Kansas*, 1964
Clifford D. Simak, *Time Is the Simplest Thing*, 1961

### 1582

**CANDAS JANE DORSEY**

## Black Wine

(New York: Tor, 1997)

**Story type:** Science Fiction (Political; Gay/Lesbian Fiction)
**Major character(s):** Essa, Wanderer, Slave; Ea, Linguist, Captive; Annalise, Companion, Slave
**Time period(s):** Indeterminate
**Locale(s):** Land of the Dark Isles, Fictional City; Avanue, Fictional City

**Summary:** Abandoned at six years old, Essa searches for her mother, experiencing the different comprehensions permitted by the languages of the cultures she visits. Essa's resemblance to her mother gets her thrown off a skyship, causing a severe head injury and amnesia. Sold into slavery, Essa eventually regains enough memory

to accomplish the task her mother had bequeathed her, but had been unable to conceive herself.

**Other books you might like:**
Marion Zimmer Bradley, *The Mists of Avalon*, 1983
L. Warren Douglas, *Stepwater*, 1995
Suzette Haden Elgin, *Native Tongue*, 1984
Nicola Griffith, *Slow River*, 1995
Amy Thomson, *Virtual Girl*, 1993

### 1583

**CAROLE NELSON DOUGLAS**

## Cup of Clay

(New York: Tor, 1991)

**Story type:** Fantasy (Alternate World)
**Series:** Taliswoman
**Major character(s):** Alison Carver, Journalist; Rowan Firemayne, Hero, Musician
**Time period(s):** 1990s (1991); Indeterminate
**Locale(s):** Minnesota; Veil, Planet—Imaginary

**Summary:** Having finished a lengthy and disgusting newspaper series on generational familial sexual abuse of children, journalist Alison Carver retreats with her dog to her rural island in Southern Minnesota hoping to find rest and recovery. At her campsite Alison awakens to find herself transported to a mountainous land in which society seems much different, with brutal men, the Takers, exploiting children mercilessly. Hoping to return to her own Earth, Alison sets out to discover more about her new environment with the help of Rowan, who hopes to achieve through song his quest to become Guardian of the Cup of Earth.

**Other books you might like:**
Eleanor Arnason, *A Woman of the Iron People*, 1991
Gael Baudino, *Gossamer Axe*, 1990
Orson Scott Card, *Seventh Son*, 1987
Orson Scott Card, *Songmaster*, 1980
Phyllis Eisenstein, *Born to Exile*, 1978
J. Alison James, *Sing for a Gentle Rain*, 1990
Mercedes Lackey, *Bardic Voices*, 1991
Andrea Shettle, *Flute Song Magic*, 1990

### 1584

**CAROLE NELSON DOUGLAS**

## Seed upon the Wind

(New York: Tor, 1992)

**Story type:** Fantasy (Alternate World; Quest)
**Series:** Taliswoman
**Major character(s):** Alison Carver, Journalist, Shaman (Taliswoman); Rowan Firemayne, Hero, Musician; Mark McPherson, Journalist
**Time period(s):** Indeterminate; 1990s
**Locale(s):** Veil, Planet—Imaginary; St. Paul, Minnesota; Huntsville, Indiana

**Summary:** After seeing a redhead like Rowan, Alison returns to her island in northern Minnesota, keeping the Cup of Earth with her. Continuing to Veil, Alison learns that Veil suffers greatly from the loss of the Cup and may not survive the attack of the Crux even with the Cup of Earth.

**Other books you might like:**
Eleanor Arnason, *A Woman of the Iron People*, 1991
Douglas Bell, *Mojo and the Pickle Jar*, 1991

Charles de Lint, *The Little Country*, 1990
John DeChancie, *Castle Perilous*, 1988
Phyllis Eisenstein, *Born to Exile*, 1978
Ru Emerson, *The Two in Hiding*, 1991
Geary Gravel, *A Key for the Nonesuch*, 1990

---

### 1585

**IAN DOUGLAS**

## Semper Mars

(New York, Avon, 1998)

**Story type:** Science Fiction (Military; Adventure)
**Series:** Heritage Trilogy
**Major character(s):** General Montgomery Warhurst, Military Personnel (marine), Leader; Major Mark Alan Garroway, Military Personnel (marine), Computer Expert; Mireille Joubert, Political Figure (United Nations liaison), Scientist (xenoarcheologist)
**Time period(s):** 2040s
**Locale(s):** Washington, District of Columbia; Cydonia Base, Mars

**Summary:** Despite their possible obsolescence, Monty sends a marine platoon to Mars to protect the interests of the United States. When the UN realizes that the marines have found something potentially important from the Martian ruins, the marines find themselves isolated and unable to return to base. Somehow Garroway must recover his enthusiasm, and find a way to report, rescue his men, and take back Cydonia base.

**Other books you might like:**
Greg Bear, *Moving Mars*, 1993
Ben Bova, *Mars*, 1992
William Hartmann, *Mars Underground*, 1997
Robert A. Heinlein, *Red Planet*, 1949
Kim Stanley Robinson, *Red Mars*, 1993
S.C. Sykes, *Red Genesis*, 1991

---

### 1586

**L. WARREN DOUGLAS**

## Cannon's Orb

(New York: Ballantine Del Rey, 1994)

**Story type:** Science Fiction (First Contact; Genetic Manipulation)
**Major character(s):** Ben Cannon, Student, Political Figure; Estelle "Lysistrata" Mason, Genetically Altered Being, Student; Ennnesstheh, Alien (psaatla)
**Time period(s):** 25th century (2486)
**Locale(s):** Phastillan, Planet—Imaginary; Cannon's Orb, Planet—Imaginary

**Summary:** Realizing that without the trade disturbed by the pirates who prey on young colonies, the metal-poor Cannon's Orb and her neighbors cannot survive, Jack Cannon signs a treaty with the psaatla and human colony on Phastillan. Cannon contracts with the psaatla to come and change the Orb and its inhabitants, allowing human survival. The female form of the psaatla, non-sentient "ksta," spread through the Orb's soil in preparation for an eventual joint colony. Although intelligent, psaatla unfortunately consist of a worm colony and too many humans find them intolerably alien.

**Other books you might like:**
Eleanor Arnason, *Ring of Swords*, 1993
Michael Berlyn, *The Eternal Enemy*, 1990
Octavia E. Butler, *Dawn*, 1987
Helen Collins, *Mutagenesis*, 1993
Paula E. Downing, *Fallway*, 1993

---

C.S. Friedman, *The Madness Season*, 1990
Nicola Griffith, *Ammonite*, 1993
Anne McCaffrey, *Treaty at Doona*, 1994
   Jody Lynn Nye, co-author
Larry Niven, *The Gripping Hand*, 1993
   Jerry Pournelle, co-author
Joan Slonczewski, *A Door into Ocean*, 1986
Vernor Vinge, *A Fire upon the Deep*, 1992

---

### 1587

**L. WARREN DOUGLAS**

## A Plague of Change

(New York: Ballantine Del Rey, 1992)

**Story type:** Science Fiction (Genetic Manipulation; Political)
**Major character(s):** Vassily "Bass" James Cannon, Heir, Computer Expert; Sfalek-ni Swadeith, Alien (psaatla)
**Time period(s):** 25th century (2470)
**Locale(s):** Cannon's Orb, Planet—Imaginary; Phastillan, Planet—Imaginary

**Summary:** When human colonies expand into the Caprian Reef, a region lacking in heavy metals, brisk trading permits continued survival. Vikings and other human predators disturb trade, threatening the viability of many colonies. Betrayed by his childhood friends, Bass, whose father founded Cannon's Orb, gravitates toward Phastillan, where he expects to find a solution while working for the very alien psaatla. Author's first novel.

**Other books you might like:**
Michael Berlyn, *The Eternal Enemy*, 1990
David Brin, *Startide Rising*, 1983
Octavia E. Butler, *Dawn*, 1987
C.S. Friedman, *The Madness Season*, 1990
Diana G. Gallagher, *The Alien Dark*, 1990
Robert A. Heinlein, *Stranger in a Strange Land*, 1991
   revised edition
Rebecca Ore, *Becoming Alien*, 1987
Vernor Vinge, *A Fire upon the Deep*, 1992

---

### 1588

**L. WARREN DOUGLAS**

## Stepwater

(New York: Roc, 1995)

**Story type:** Science Fiction (Genetic Manipulation; Political)
**Series:** Arbiter Tale
**Major character(s):** John Minder XXIII, Ruler (Arbiter); Barc Doresh, Genetically Altered Being (Bors), Heir; Girelf, Genetically Altered Being (Mantee), Heir
**Time period(s):** Indeterminate Future
**Locale(s):** Xarafeille Stream, Interstellar Empire/Federation; Newhome, Planet—Imaginary; Stepwater, Planet—Imaginary

**Summary:** John Minder, the hereditary ruler of the many planets of the Xarafeille Stream, must recover the data cubes taken by his older brother who disappears to avoid becoming Arbiter. Unable to recover the Arbiter set, John must locate and acquire the cubes from the seven planets which each have a copy of one, and from them find the location of the planets of Poletzai, which should be at his command. The seven varieties of humans, six developed as special workers and all requiring his support and leadership to interact, must not learn the Arbiter lost access to his tools. Barc acquires the first of the lost data blocks for him while rescuing Margak Steep and its environs from

---

disaster and saving the forbidden relationship with his one true love, Girelf.

**Other books you might like:**
David Brin, *Glory Season*, 1993
Alis A. Rasmussen, *The Price of Ransom*, 1990
Melissa Scott, *Shadow Man*, 1995
Cordwainer Smith, *The Rediscovery of Man*, 1993
S. Andrew Swann, *Forests of the Night*, 1993

**1589**

### L. WARREN DOUGLAS

## The Wells of Phyre

(New York: Roc, 1996)

**Story type:** Science Fiction (Genetic Manipulation; Political)
**Series:** Arbiter Tale
**Major character(s):** John Minder XXIII, Ruler (Arbiter); Slith Wrasselty, Genetically Altered Being (Fard), Businessman; Bleth Wrasselty, Genetically Altered Being (Fard)
**Time period(s):** Indeterminate Future
**Locale(s):** Phyre, Planet—Imaginary; Newhome, Planet—Imaginary; Xarafeille Stream, Interstellar Empire/Federation

**Summary:** Having not yet recovered enough information to find his fleet and the military police, the Arbiter must solve disputes and prevent major wars using the knowledge acquired by his many subjects, luckily finding the people he needs. On Phyre, one of the many inhabited planets of the Xarafeille Stream, Slith's dangerous discovery could lead to major interstellar war, instead of just making him rich. However, his nursling befriends the Arbiter's Consul, giving John Minder the information he needs to prevent war on another planet in the Stream.

**Other books you might like:**
David Brin, *Brightness Reef*, 1995
Lois McMaster Bujold, *Falling Free*, 1988
C.J. Cherryh, *Foreigner*, 1994
Julia Ecklar, *Regenesis*, 1995
Janet Kagan, *Mirabile*, 1991
S. Andrew Swann, *Forests of the Night*, 1993

**1590**

### LAUREN WRIGHT DOUGLAS

## In the Blood

(Tallahassee: Naiad Press, 1989)

**Story type:** Science Fiction (Gay/Lesbian Fiction)
**Major character(s):** Hart, Scientist, Lesbian; Sandoval, Military Personnel, Lesbian
**Time period(s):** 21st century
**Locale(s):** Arizona; California

**Summary:** A near-future America has fragmented into smaller nations as a result of the death and destruction caused by an artificially-created virus, the Red Death. Solar-tech Hart, a free Arizonan, must accompany Dr. Ashe, creator of an experimental vaccine against the Red Death, to the California border. Not everyone wants the vaccine freely distributed, however, and Hart must overcome attempts at treachery, kidnapping, even murder.

**Other books you might like:**
Suzy McKee Charnas, *Motherlines*, 1979
Suzy McKee Charnas, *Walk to the End of the World*, 1974
Nancy Tyler Glenn, *Clicking Stones*, 1989
Joanna Russ, *The Female Man*, 1975

Joanna Russ, *We Who Are About To. . .*, 1977
Chelsea Quinn Yarbro, *Time of the Fourth Horseman*, 1976

**1591**

### TOM DOWD

## Night's Pawn

(New York: Roc, 1993)

**Story type:** Science Fiction (Adventure)
**Series:** Shadowrun
**Major character(s):** Jason Chase, Businessman (corporate liason), Martial Arts Expert; Caroline "Cara Deaver" Tara Villiers, Fugitive
**Time period(s):** 2050s (2053)
**Locale(s):** New York, New York; Denver, Colorado; Germany

**Summary:** Caroline Villiers approaches Jason Chase with the request that Jason protect his former employer, Caroline's father, from corporate assassins. However, Chase discovers his skills must protect Caroline from the terrorists trying to kill her. Game tie-in.

**Other books you might like:**
Robert N. Charrette, *Choose Your Enemies Carefully*, 1991
Robert N. Charrette, *Find Your Own Truth*, 1991
Robert N. Charrette, *Never Deal with a Dragon*, 1990
Robert N. Charrette, *Never Trust an Elf*, 1992
Nigel Findley, *2XS*, 1992
Nigel Findley, *Shadowplay*, 1993
Christopher Kubasik, *Changeling*, 1992
Carl Sargent, *Streets of Blood*, 1992
    Marc Gascoigne, co-author
Nyx Smith, *Striper Assassin*, 1993
Jordan K. Weisman, *Into the Shadows*, 1992
    editor

**1592**

### ANN DOWNER

## The Spellkey Trilogy

(New York: Baen, 1995)

**Story type:** Fantasy (Quest; Magic Conflict)
**Series:** Spellkey
**Major character(s):** Caitlin, Foundling, Witch; The Badger, Bastard Son, Companion; Elric, Knight
**Time period(s):** Indeterminate
**Locale(s):** Thirdmoon, Fictional Country; Otherworld, Mythical Place

**Summary:** Accused of witchcraft and exiled to the Abbey of Ninthstile, Caitlin travels through the Thirteen Kingdoms escorted by Badger, a ward of the Abbot of Thirdmoon See. Followed by a mysterious man, they meet a variety of characters who help or hinder them as they learn about the Spellkey and how their destinies intertwine. Omnibus edition combining the previously published *The Spellkey* (1987), *The Glass Salamander* (1989), and *The Books of the Keepers* (1993), here revised and with new material.

**Other books you might like:**
Eleanor Arnason, *The Sword Smith*, 1978
C.J. Cherryh, *Rusalka*, 1989
Robert Jordan, *The Eye of the World*, 1990
Patricia A. McKillip, *The Riddle-Master of Hed*, 1976
J.R.R. Tolkien, *The Fellowship of the Ring*, 1954

## 1593

### PAULA E. DOWNING

## *Fallway*

(New York: Ballantine Del Rey, 1993)

**Story type:** Science Fiction (First Contact; Space Colony)
**Major character(s):** Jahnel Alain, Leader; Koyil, Alien (Avelle), Ruler; Gregory Austin, Captive (hostage), Spaceman
**Time period(s):** Indeterminate Future
**Locale(s):** Quevi Ltir, Asteroid

**Summary:** Five hundred years after the alien Avelle colonize an asteroid as an emergency space dock, the Faon, descendants of rescued humans, begin to gain the acceptance of their hosts, paying their guest debt by joining Avelle wars. Captured by the enemy, a shocked Jahnel finds humans confused about why anyone would attack a rescue ship responding to the 80-year-old distress call of Jahnel's ancestors. Jahnel must convince the Avelle and her compatriot Faon that they belong on Quevi Ltir to prevent disaster for all.

**Other books you might like:**
Eleanor Arnason, *Ring of Swords*, 1993
Stephen Baxter, *Raft*, 1991
Octavia E. Butler, *Dawn*, 1987
Gordon R. Dickson, *Naked to the Stars/The Alien Way*, 1991
C.S. Friedman, *The Madness Season*, 1990
Janet Kagan, *Mirabile*, 1991
Paula King, *Mad Roy's Light*, 1990
    pseudonym of Paula E. Downing
Joan D. Vinge, *The Summer Queen*, 1991

## 1594

### PAULA E. DOWNING

## *Flare Star*

(New York: Ballantine Del Rey, 1992)

**Story type:** Science Fiction (Disaster; Science Fiction)
**Major character(s):** Jason Roarke, Spaceman, Hero; Magda Janozek, Teenager; Yves Marceau, Spaceship Captain
**Time period(s):** 23rd century
**Locale(s):** Colony Station Wolf II, Planet—Imaginary; *Ceti Flag*, Spaceship (freighter)

**Summary:** As *Ceti Flag* approaches Wolf 359 to refuel and drop off supplies, the star produces a long overdue flare large enough to destroy the electronic mental equipment of the Wolf II colony, sear anyone caught on the dayside surface and kill anyone in the top two levels of the underground complex. The survival of the remaining colonists depends upon the *Ceti Flag*, which has lost the colony and may decide to pass it by.

**Other books you might like:**
Michael Berlyn, *The Eternal Enemy*, 1990
David Brin, *Earth*, 1990
F.M. Busby, *Slow Freight*, 1991
Michael Capobianco, *Burster*, 1990
A.C. Crispin, *Silent Dances*, 1990
    Kathleen O'Malley, co-author
Gregory Feeley, *The Oxygen Barons*, 1990
Paula King, *Mad Roy's Light*, 1990
    pseudonym of Paula E. Downing
Rebecca Ore, *Becoming Alien*, 1987
Allen Steele, *Orbital Decay*, 1989

## 1595

### PAULA E. DOWNING

## *A Whisper of Time*

(New York: Ballantine Del Rey, 1994)

**Story type:** Science Fiction (First Contact; Political)
**Major character(s):** Medoret Douglas, Alien, Foundling; Samta Montes, Indian (Mayan), Archaeologist (xenoarchaeologist); Sieyes, Psychologist
**Time period(s):** Indeterminate Future
**Locale(s):** Ariadan, Planet—Imaginary; Cebalrai, Planet—Imaginary

**Summary:** Discovered in a long deserted city on Cebalrai, Medoret cannot fit in despite all attempts. Given a chance to return to that city, others judge her too emotionally unstable to explore it. Escaping with the aid of Samta Montes, Medoret triggers a signal which brings her own people back to Cebalrai.

**Other books you might like:**
John Brunner, *Bedlam Planet*, 1968
Octavia E. Butler, *Survivor*, 1978
C.J. Cherryh, *Cuckoo's Egg*, 1985
Gordon R. Dickson, *Wolfling*, 1969
Garry Kilworth, *The Night of Kadar*, 1980
Paula King, *Mad Roy's Light*, 1990
    pseudonym of Paula E. Downing
Dean R. Koontz, *Beastchild*, 1970
Anne McCaffrey, *Decision at Doona*, 1969
Kris Neville, *Bettyann*, 1970
H. Beam Piper, *Little Fuzzy*, 1962
Sydney J. Van Scyoc, *Darkchild*, 1982
Vernor Vinge, *Tatja Grimm's World*, 1987

## 1596

### SIR ARTHUR CONAN DOYLE

## *The Best Horror Stories of Arthur Conan Doyle*

(Chicago: Academy, 1989)

**Story type:** Horror (Collection)

**Summary:** Thirteen stories that mix horror, mystery, and science fiction. Important stories include "The American Tale," about a man-eating plant, "The Captain of the *Polestar*," a ghostly sea story, "The Leather Funnel" and "The Silver Hatchet," two stories about haunted objects, and "J. Habakuk Jephson's Statement," a tale based on the true incident of the mysteriously abandoned ship, the *Mary Celeste*.

**Other books you might like:**
Guy de Maupassant, *The Dark Side: Tales of Terror and the Supernatural*, 1989

## 1597

### SIR ARTHUR CONAN DOYLE

## *The Horror of the Heights and Other Tales of Suspense*

(San Francisco: Chronicle, 1992)

**Story type:** Horror (Collection)

**Summary:** Fourteen stories of mystery and horror by the Victorian master of suspense. Included are the classic reanimated mummy story, ''Lot 249''; the science-fantasy, ''The Los Amigos Fiasco''; a tale of psychic vengeance, ''The Parasite''; and the title story concerned with monsters of the upper atmosphere that lie in wait for aviators.

**Other books you might like:**
Charles Dickens, *The Complete Ghost Stories of Charles Dickens*, 1982
Edward Bulwer Lytton, *The Haunters and the Haunted; or, the House and the Brain*, 1905
W.C. Morrow, *The Ape, the Idiot, and Other People*, 1897
H.G. Wells, *28 Science Fiction Stories*, 1982

## 1598

### DEBRA DOYLE
### JAMES D. MACDONALD, Co-Author

## By Honor Betray'd
(New York: Tor, 1994)

**Story type:** Science Fiction (Psychic Powers; Family Saga)
**Series:** Mageworlds
**Major character(s):** Theio syn-Ricte sus-Airaalin, Military Personnel (Grand Admiral), Psychic (Mage Lord); Errec Ransome, Psychic (Master of Adepts' Guild); Beka Rosselin Metadi, Royalty (Domina of Entibor), Spaceship Captain
**Time period(s):** Indeterminate Future
**Locale(s):** Namport, Fictional City; Nammerin, Planet—Imaginary; *Warhammer*, Spaceship

**Summary:** The war between the Republic and the Mage Worlds reaches a climax as the murderer of the Domina of Entibor reveals himself. A new understanding may form between the Mage-Circles and The Guild.

**Other books you might like:**
Allan Cole, *Empire's End*, 1993
  Chris Bunch, co-author
Glen Cook, *The Dragon Never Sleeps*, 1988
Michelle Shirey Crean, *Dancer of the Sixth*, 1993
Frank Herbert, *Dune*, 1965
Andre Norton, *Brother to Shadows*, 1993
Alis A. Rasmussen, *Revolution's Shore*, 1990
David Weber, *On Basilisk Station*, 1993

## 1599

### DEBRA DOYLE
### JAMES D. MACDONALD, Co-Author

## The Gathering Flame
(New York: Tor, 1995)

**Story type:** Science Fiction (Political; Adventure)
**Series:** Mageworlds
**Major character(s):** Jos Metadi, Spaceship Captain, Privateer; Errec Ransome, Psychic (esper), Spaceman; Perada ''Rada'' Rosselin, Ruler (Domina of Entibor)
**Time period(s):** Indeterminate Future
**Locale(s):** Galcen, Planet—Imaginary; *Warhammer*, Spaceship; Entibor, Planet—Imaginary

**Summary:** The uncrowned Domina of Entibor, Perada, finds mages to kill, while Metadi, now Consort, leads the fleet, protecting Entibor and hunting mages. Despite Perada's best efforts, political holdovers from the previous government conspire with the enemy, resulting in disaster. Set prior to events in the Mageworlds Trilogy (1992-1994).

**Other books you might like:**
Lois McMaster Bujold, *The Warrior's Apprentice*, 1986
L. Warren Douglas, *A Plague of Change*, 1992
Mary Gentle, *Ancient Light*, 1987
Alis A. Rasmussen, *A Passage of Stars*, 1990
David Weber, *Mutineers' Moon*, 1991

## 1600

### DEBRA DOYLE
### JAMES D. MACDONALD, Co-Author

## Groogleman
(New York: Harcourt Brace/Jane Yolen Books, 1996)

**Story type:** Science Fiction (Post-Holocaust; Young Adult)
**Major character(s):** Daniel Henchard, Teenager, Apprentice (healer); Lezzie Johnson, Healer (weller), Teenager; Joshua, Guide
**Time period(s):** Indeterminate Future
**Locale(s):** United States; Dead Lands, Mythical Place

**Summary:** Lezzie notes Daniel's interest and skill in healing and undertakes his training. When Lezzie responds to the report of a plague, fearsome Grooglemen capture her. As Daniel and Lezzie's patient, Joshua, set out for the Dead Lands to rescue her, he displays unexpected knowledge of the Grooglemen.

**Other books you might like:**
Nancy Farmer, *The Ear, the Eye, and the Arm*, 1994
David R. Palmer, *Emergence*, 1984
Sherwood Smith, *Wren's Quest*, 1993
Caroline Stevermer, *River Rats*, 1992
Vivian Vande Velde, *User Unfriendly*, 1991

## 1601

### DEBRA DOYLE
### JAMES D. MACDONALD, Co-Author

## Knight's Wyrd
(New York: Harcourt Brace Jovanovich, 1992)

**Story type:** Fantasy (Young Adult; Adventure)
**Major character(s):** William ''Will'' Odosson, Knight, Adventurer
**Time period(s):** Indeterminate
**Locale(s):** Anglia, Fictional Country

**Summary:** After an outstanding first tournament, newly knighted Will Odosson sets off to meet his betrothed with some trepidation since a prophecy about him seems to indicate his death in the immediate future. Nonetheless, Will survives his many dangerous encounters with trolls, dragons, ogres and wizards.

**Other books you might like:**
Lloyd Alexander, *The Book of Three*, 1964
Susan Cooper, *Over Sea, under Stone*, 1966
Diana Wynne Jones, *The Lives of Christopher Chant*, 1988
J.R.R. Tolkien, *The Hobbit*, 1938
Jane Yolen, *Wizard's Hall*, 1991

## 1602

**DEBRA DOYLE**
**JAMES D. MACDONALD**, Co-Author

### *The Long Hunt*
(New York: Tor, 1996)

**Story type:** Science Fiction (Psychic Powers; Family Saga)
**Series:** Mageworlds
**Major character(s):** Errec Ransome, Spirit (ghost), Psychic; Jens Metadi Jessan D'Rosselin, Teenager, Heir; Chakallakak "Chaka" ngha Chakallakak, Alien (Selvaur), Teenager
**Time period(s):** Indeterminate Future
**Locale(s):** Maraghai, Planet—Imaginary; Khesat, Planet—Imaginary

**Summary:** Jens, Chaka, and Jens' foster brother leave Maraghai in search of fame and glory. Steered toward Khesat after several attempts on their lives, Jens admits he intends to go there to discover the whereabouts of his missing parents and perhaps become the new Highest, planetary leader of Khesat.

**Other books you might like:**
Lois McMaster Bujold, *Mirror Dance*, 1994
F.M. Busby, *Arrow From Earth*, 1995
C.S. Friedman, *The Madness Season*, 1990
Andre Norton, *Brother to Shadows*, 1993
David Weber, *Path of the Fury*, 1992

## 1603

**DEBRA DOYLE**
**JAMES D. MACDONALD**, Co-Author

### *Night of the Living Rat!*
(New York: Ace, 1992)

**Story type:** Science Fiction (Humor)
**Series:** Daniel M. Pinkwater's Melvinge of the Megaverse
**Major character(s):** Melvinge, Hero, Werewolf; Loola, Girlfriend, Mythical Creature (were-lizard); Harlan, Animal (dogoid)
**Time period(s):** Indeterminate
**Locale(s):** Megaverse Mall, Mythical Place; Neitherworld, Mythical Place

**Summary:** The saga continues as the Loan Shark pursues Ratner and Harlan to the parking lot of the Megaverse Mall. Melvinge finds death in the Neitherworld boring—until Sdark the Loan Shark finds him. The Sdark's attempts at killing Melvinge in the Neitherworld return him to his body in the Mall parking lot, and vice versa. At last everyone meets again at the Really Big Dance Hall. An afterword by Daniel M. Pinkwater throws further confusion on the origins of the Megaverse.

**Other books you might like:**
Douglas Adams, *The Restaurant at the End of the Universe*, 1981
Robert Asprin, *Little Myth Marker*, 1985
David Bischoff, *Night of the Living Shark!*, 1991
Lionel Fenn, *The Seven Spears of the W'dch'ck*, 1988
Craig Shaw Gardner, *Revenge of the Fluffy Bunnies*, 1990
Richard A. Lupoff, *Night of the Living 'Gator!*, 1992
Daniel Manus Pinkwater, *Borgel*, 1990
Terry Pratchett, *Reaper Man*, 1992
Somtow Sucharitkul, *Mallworld*, 1981

## 1604

**DEBRA DOYLE**
**JAMES D. MACDONALD**, Co-Author

### *The Price of the Stars*
(New York: Tor, 1992)

**Story type:** Science Fiction (Adventure; Political)
**Series:** Mageworlds
**Major character(s):** Beka Rosselin Metadi, Spaceship Captain, Heiress; Jessan, Doctor, Military Personnel (Spaceforce); Lannan, Military Personnel (Spaceforce), Psychic
**Time period(s):** Indeterminate Future
**Locale(s):** Innish-Kyl, Planet—Imaginary (Waycross); *Warhammer*, Spaceship; Mandeyn, Planet—Imaginary (Embrig Spaceport)

**Summary:** After eight years in space Beka meets with her father who offers her his ship, the *Warhammer*, if she will find out the names of her mother the Empress's assassins. Forced to fake her death and change the name of her ship to save her life, Beka accepts the help and companionship of the family's old weapons master as the intrigue turns more deadly.

**Other books you might like:**
Ray Aldridge, *The Pharaoh Contract*, 1991
Lois McMaster Bujold, *Shards of Honor*, 1986
Allan Cole, *Sten*, 1984
    Chris Bunch, co-author
Brian Daley, *Jinx on a Terran Inheritance*, 1985
Stephen Goldin, *Jade Darcy and the Affair of Honor*, 1988
    Mary Mason, co-author
Steve Perry, *The 97th Step*, 1989
Alis A. Rasmussen, *A Passage of Stars*, 1990

## 1605

**DEBRA DOYLE**
**JAMES D. MACDONALD**, Co-Author

### *School of Wizardry*
(Mahwah, New Jersey: Troll Associates, 1990)

**Story type:** Fantasy (Magic Conflict; Young Adult)
**Series:** Circle of Magic
**Major character(s):** Randall, Apprentice, Wizard
**Time period(s):** Indeterminate
**Locale(s):** Alternate Earth

**Summary:** Determined to become a wizard, 12-year-old Randall is delighted to be accepted into the famed School of Wizardry, but his apprenticeship is marred when he realizes that one of the master wizards is using evil spells to destroy the school and gain supreme power.

**Other books you might like:**
Diane Duane, *So You Want to Be a Wizard?*, 1983
Diana Wynne Jones, *The Lives of Christopher Chant*, 1988
Ursula K. Le Guin, *A Wizard of Earthsea*, 1967
Otfried Preussler, *The Satanic Mill*, 1972
Sherwood Smith, *Wren to the Rescue*, 1990
Jane Yolen, *Wizard's Hall*, 1991

## 1606

**DEBRA DOYLE**
**JAMES D. MACDONALD**, Co-Author

### Starpilot's Grave

(New York: Tor, 1993)

**Story type:** Science Fiction (Adventure; Psychic Powers)
**Series:** Mageworlds
**Major character(s):** Beka Rosselin Metadi, Ruler, Spaceship Captain; Nyls Jessan, Doctor, Military Personnel (intelligence officer); Llannat, Military Personnel (Space Force), Psychic
**Time period(s):** Indeterminate Future
**Locale(s):** *Warhammer*, Spaceship; Namport, Planet—Imaginary; Galcen, Planet—Imaginary

**Summary:** In this direct sequel to *The Price of the Stars*, Beka and Nyls act as traders in the Mageworlds to gather information confirming that the Mage Lords again prepare for war. Suddenly given orders to investigate a derelict Mageworld fighter from the Magewar, Llannat finds herself drawn to it and discovers a message left there for her hundreds of years earlier. Rumors of a Mageworld fleet become realized as Beka races ahead of it to warn Galcen before it arrives.

**Other books you might like:**
C.J. Cherryh, *Cyteen*, 1988
Brian Daley, *Jinx on a Terran Inheritance*, 1985
Stephen Goldin, *Jade Darcy and the Affair of Honor*, 1988
    Mary Mason, co-author
Larry Niven, *The Gripping Hand*, 1993
    Jerry Pournelle, co-author
Alis A. Rasmussen, *A Passage of Stars*, 1990
Alis A. Rasmussen, *Revolution's Shore*, 1990
Joan D. Vinge, *The Summer Queen*, 1991

## 1607

**GARDNER DOZOIS**, Editor

### Dying for It: More Erotic Tales of Unearthly Love

(New York: Harper, 1997)

**Story type:** Horror (Anthology; Erotic Horror)

**Summary:** Seventeen stories of dark love and obsession that draw from horror, fantasy and science fiction sources. Selections include Tanith Lee's "Cain," Ursula K. Le Guin's "Olders," Robert Silverberg's "Multiples," Pat Cadigan's "Another Story," Michael Bishop's "Yesterday's Hostage," Nancy Kress's "Johnny's So Long at the Fair," and Esther Friesner's "Silent Love."

**Other books you might like:**
Ellen Datlow, *Off Limits: Tales of Alien Sex*, 1996
    editor
Ellen Datlow, *Alien Sex*, 1990
    editor
Joseph Elder, *Eros in Orbit*, 1973
    editor
Jeff Gelb, *Hot Blood: Tales of Provocative Horror*, 1989
    Lonn Friend, co-editor
Thomas N. Scortia, *Strange Bedfellows: Sex and Science Fiction*, 1972
    editor
Michele Slung, *I Shudder at Your Touch*, 1991

## 1608

**GARDNER DOZOIS**

### Geodesic Dreams: The Best Short Fiction of Gardner Dozois

(New York: St. Martin's Press, 1992)

**Story type:** Science Fiction (Collection)

**Summary:** Contains a seven-page foreward by Robert Silverberg plus 14 stories published 1971-1990 in anthologies and periodicals. Two stories received Nebula Awards, "Peacemaker" and "Morning Child"; one story received nomination for a Nebula Award, "Disciples"; and three stories received Hugo Award nominations, "Chains of the Sea," "A Kingdom by the Sea" and "A Special Kind of Morning." Dozois collaborates with Jack C. Haldeman II in "Executive Clemency" and with Jack Dann in "Down Among the Dead" and "Slow Dancing with Jesus."

**Other books you might like:**
David Brin, *The River of Time*, 1986
Samuel R. Delany, *Driftglass: 10 Tales of Speculative Fiction*, 1971
Larry Niven, *Tales of Known Space*, 1975
Cordwainer Smith, *The Best of Cordwainer Smith*, 1975
Theodore Sturgeon, *Sturgeon Is Alive and Well*, 1971
John Varley, *Blue Champagne*, 1986
John Varley, *The Persistence of Vision*, 1978
Gene Wolfe, *Storeys From the Old Hotel*, 1992

## 1609

**GARDNER DOZOIS**, Editor

### The Good Old Stuff

(New York: St Martin's, 1998)

**Story type:** Science Fiction (Anthology)

**Summary:** This anthology contains 16 classic science fiction stories from 1948 through 1975, including the award winning "The Doors of His Face, the Lamps of His Mouth" by Roger Zelazny. Collectively they demonstrate the changing focus in the genre during those three decades.

**Other books you might like:**
Terry Carr, *On Our Way to the Future*, 1970
Damon Knight, *Beyond Tomorrow*, 1965
Damon Knight, *Now Begins Tomorrow*, 1969
Pamela Sargent, *Women of Wonder: Science Fiction Stories by Women about Women*, 1975

## 1610

**GARDNER DOZOIS**, Editor
**SHEILA WILLIAMS**, Co-Editor

### Isaac Asimov's Ghosts

(New York: Ace, 1995)

**Story type:** Horror (Anthology; Ghost Story)

**Summary:** The twelve stories by diverse hands are collected from *Isaac Asimov's Science Fiction Magazine* and all feature ghosts. Connie Willis's "Death on the Nile" is a wry account of Americans travelling abroad who may be dead and on their way to the underworld. In Kim Antieau's "Hauntings" and Jack Dann's "Visitors," people with medical conditions that have brought them close to death are subject to visions of the dead that no one else can see. Terry Bisson's comic "Dead Man's Curve" is about a dangerous bend in a road that transports joyriders into a dimension inhabited by a ghost, while Sharon Faber's ''The July Ward'' tells of a secret ward in a hospital that conceals spectres of a surgeon's guilt. In Lisa's Goldstein's ''Alfred,'' a young girl meets the ghost of her grandfather, who died in a Nazi concentration camp.

**Other books you might like:**

Isaac Asimov, *Isaac Asimov's Magical Worlds of Fantasy #10: Ghosts*, 1988
   Charles G. Waugh, Martin H. Greenberg, co-editors
Paul F. Olson, *Post Mortem: New Tales of Ghostly Horror*, 1989
   David B. Silva, co-editor
Peter Straub, *Peter Straub's Ghosts*, 1995
   editor

## 1611

**GARDNER DOZOIS**, Editor
**SHEILA WILLIAMS**, Co-Editor

### Isaac Asimov's Vampires
(New York: Ace, 1996)

**Story type:** Horror (Anthology; Vampire Story)

**Summary:** These eight stories, culled from the pages of *Asimov's Science Fiction* magazine, feature vampires in a variety of different guises. Connie Willis' ''Jack,'' set during the London blitz, and Tanith Lee's ''Winter Flowers,'' which takes place during medieval times, both feature vampires who use wartime bloodshed to camouflage their feedings. Susan Palwick reworks the fairy tale of Cinderella into a tale of the undead in ''Ever After,'' while David Redd gives the vampire theme a science fiction top spin in ''The Old Man of Munnington.'' Greg Frost's ''Some Things Are Better Left,'' a mordant meditation on becoming middle-aged, uses a high school reunion as a springboard for his tale of vampiric immortality.

**Other books you might like:**

Greg Cox, *Tomorrow Sucks*, 1994
   T.K.F. Weiskopf, co-author
Ellen Datlow, *Blood Is Not Enough*, 1989
   editor
Martin H. Greenberg, *A Taste for Blood*, 1992
   editor
Stephen Jones, *The Mammoth Book of Vampires*, 1992
   editor

## 1612

**GARDNER DOZOIS**, Editor

### Modern Classic Short Novels of Science Fiction
(New York: St. Martin's Press, 1994)

**Story type:** Science Fiction (Anthology)

**Summary:** Includes a four-page introduction plus individual introductions to 13 stories published in anthologies and periodicals 1958-1992, including Poul Anderson's ''The Longest Voyage,'' Samuel R. Delany's ''The Star Pit,'' Frederik Pohl's ''The Merchants of Venus,'' Joanna Russ' ''Souls,'' Cordwainer Smith's ''On the Storm Planet'' and Jack Vance's ''The Miracle Workers.'' Other authors include Brian W. Aldiss, Nancy Kress, Robert Silverberg, Kate Wilhelm and Gene Wolfe.

**Other books you might like:**

Isaac Asimov, *Isaac Asimov Presents the Great SF Stories Series*, 1979-1992
   Martin H. Greenberg, co-editor

David G. Hartwell, *The World Treasury of Science Fiction*, 1989
   editor
Ursula K. Le Guin, *The Norton Book of Science Fiction: North American Science Fiction, 1960-1990*, 1993
   Brian Attebery, co-editor
Tom Shippey, *The Oxford Book of Science Fiction Stories*, 1992
   editor
Robert Silverberg, *The Science Fiction Hall of Fame, Volume 1*, 1970
   editor

## 1613

**GARDNER DOZOIS**, Editor

### Modern Classics of Fantasy
(New York: St. Martin's, 1997)

**Story type:** Fantasy (Anthology)

**Summary:** Contains a 13-page preface, five pages of recommended readings and 32 stories with individual introductions, presented in the order of original publication in periodicals and anthologies 1939-1996. In settings from contemporary to fantastic and tone from light to ominous, the short stories, novellas and excerpts from longer works, explore a variety of themes, such as high fantasy, sword and sorcery, mythical creatures, quests, time travel, religion and legends. Authors include Poul Anderson, Peter S. Beagle, James P. Blaylock, Suzy McKee Charnas, John Crowley, Avram Davidson, L. Sprague de Camp, George Alex Effinger, Ester M. Friesner, Horace L. Gold, R.A. Lafferty, Fritz Leiber, Ursula K. Le Guin, Lucius Shepard, Bruce Sterling, Thomas Burnett Swann, Michael Swanwick, Judith Tarr, Jack Vance, Howard Waldrop, Manly Wade Wellman, Gene Wolfe, Jane Yolen and Roger Zelazny.

**Other books you might like:**

Mike Ashley, *The Random House Book of Fantasy Stories*, 1997
   editor
Robert H. Boyer, *Visions & Imaginings: Classic Fantasy Fiction*, 1992
   Kenneth J. Zahorski, co-editor
Alison Lurie, *The Oxford Book of Modern Fairy Tales*, 1993
   editor
Tom Shippey, *The Oxford Book of Fantasy Stories*, 1993
   editor
Robert Silverberg, *The Fantasy Hall of Fame*, 1983
   editor

## 1614

**GARDNER DOZOIS**, Editor

### Modern Classics of Science Fiction
(New York: St. Martin's Press, 1992)

**Story type:** Science Fiction (Anthology)

**Summary:** Contains a six-page preface including lists of wonderful stories not contained herein plus 26 stories published 1955-1989 in periodicals and anthologies and a two-page afterword with additional recommendations of newer authors. One story, ''The Moment of the Storm'' by Roger Zelazny, received a Hugo Award nomination; two stories, ''Particle Theory'' by Edward Bryant and ''Driftglass'' by Samuel R. Delany, received Nebula Award nominations; and one story, ''The Ugly Chickens'' by Howard Waldrop, won a Nebula Award. Other stories include ''Narrow Valley'' by R. A. Lafferty, ''Mother Hitton's Littul Kittons'' by Cordwainer Smith, ''The Other Celia'' by Theodore Sturgeon, ''The Moon Moth'' by Jack Vance and ''The Fifth Head of Cerberus'' by Gene Wolfe.

**Other books you might like:**
Isaac Asimov, *Isaac Asimov Presents the Great SF Stories Series*, 1979-1992
   Martin H. Greenberg, co-editor
Groff Conklin, *12 Great Classics of Science Fiction*, 1963
   editor
Groff Conklin, *Another Part of the Galaxy*, 1966
   editor
Groff Conklin, *Giants Unleashed*, 1965
   editor
Harlan Ellison, *Dangerous Visions*, 1967
   editor
Robert Silverberg, *The Science Fiction Hall of Fame, Volume 1*, 1970
   editor

## 1615

### GARDNER DOZOIS

## *Slow Dancing through Time*

(Kansas City, Missouri: Ursus Imprints, 1990)

**Story type:** Science Fiction (Collection)
**Time period(s):** 1940s; 1960s
**Locale(s):** Europe; United States

**Summary:** 14 stories, with introductions, written between 1980-1985 by Dozois in collaboration with Jack Dann, Michael Swanwich, Susan Casper and Jack C. Haldeman III. ''Down Among the Dead Men,'' a Roman story about a vampire in a World War II death camp, is the best known and most controversial. Lighter in tone, ''Slow Dancing with Roman Jesus,'' a transcribed dream, features an uncool girl, a prom, and Jesus Christ, and shows Dozois' range.

**Other books you might like:**
Pat Cadigan, *Patterns*, 1989
Harlan Ellison, *Partners in Wonder: Harlan Ellison in Collaboration with. . .*, 1971
Kim Newman, *The Night Mayor*, 1990
Tim Powers, *The Anubis Gates*, 1983
Howard Waldrop, *Night of the Cooters*, 1990

## 1616

### GARDNER DOZOIS, Editor

## *The Year's Best Science Fiction: Eighth Annual Collection*

(New York: St. Martin's Press, 1991)

**Story type:** Science Fiction (Anthology)
**Series:** Year's Best Science Fiction

**Summary:** This volume contains 25 stories originally published in periodicals and anthologies during 1990, six pages of honorable mentions, plus a 22-page summation of the 1990 Science Fiction milieu by the editor, Gardner Dozois, who received a Hugo Award for his editing of last year's *Best Science Fiction of the Year; Seventh Annual Collection*. Appearing here are two stories which received both Hugo and Nebula Awards, ''The Hemingway Hoax'' by Joe Haldeman and ''Bears Discover Fire'' by Terry Bisson, one story which received a Nebula Award, ''Tower of Babylon'' by Ted Chiang, one which is a collaboration, ''The All-Consuming'' by Lucius Shepard and Robert Frazier, and two stories by one author, Greg Egan. Other authors include John Brunner, Alexander Jablokov, James Patrick Kelly, John Kessel, Nancy Kress, Ursula K. Le Guin, Michael Moorcock, Pat Murphy, Charles Sheffield, Lewis

Shiner, Robert Silverberg, Bruce Sterling, Kate Wilhelm and Connie Willis.

**Other books you might like:**
Lou Aronica, *Full Spectrum 2*, 1990
   Shawna McCarthy, Amy Stout and Patrick LoBruto, co-editors
Michael Bishop, *Nebula Awards 25*, 1991
   editor
Harlan Ellison, *Dangerous Visions*, 1967
   editor
Raymond J. Healy, *Adventures in Time and Space*, 1946
   J. Francis McComas, co-editor
Robert Silverberg, *The Science Fiction Hall of Fame, Volume 1*, 1970
   editor
Donald A. Wollheim, *The 1990 Annual World's Best Science Fiction*, 1990
   Arthur W. Saha, co-editor

## 1617

### GARDNER DOZOIS, Editor

## *The Year's Best Science Fiction: Eleventh Annual Collection*

(New York: St. Martin's Press, 1994)

**Story type:** Science Fiction (Anthology)
**Series:** Year's Best Science Fiction

**Summary:** Contains a 35-page summation of science fiction in 1993, six pages of honorable mentions and 23 stories. The stories include one Hugo and Nebula Award winner, Charles Sheffield's ''Georgia on My Mind''; one Hugo Award winner and Nebula Award nominee, Connie Willis' ''Death on the Nile''; one Hugo Award nominee and Nebula Award winner, Jack Cady's ''The Night We Buried Road Dog''; one Hugo Award and Nebula Award nominee, G. David Nordley's ''Into the Miranda Rift''; and two Nebula Award nominees, Nancy Kress' ''Dancing on Air'' and Walter Jon Williams' ''Wall, Stone, Craft.'' Other authors include Brian W. Aldiss, Neal Barrett Jr., Stephen Baxter, Pat Cadigan, Joe Haldeman, Rebecca Ore, Robert Reed, Mike Resnick, Dan Simmons and Bruce Sterling.

**Other books you might like:**
Lou Aronica, *Full Spectrum 4*, 1993
   Amy Stout, Betsy Mitchell, co-editors
David G. Hartwell, *The Ascent of Wonder: The Evolution of Hard SF*, 1994
   Kathryn Cramer, co-editor
Ursula K. Le Guin, *The Norton Book of Science Fiction: North American Science Fiction, 1960-1990*, 1993
   Brian Attebery, co-editor
James Morrow, *Nebula Awards 28*, 1994
   editor
Robert Silverberg, *Universe 3*, 1994
   Karen Haber, co-editor

## 1618

### GARDNER DOZOIS, Editor

## *The Year's Best Science Fiction: Fifteenth Annual Collection*

(New York: St Martin's, 1998)

**Story type:** Science Fiction (Anthology)

**Summary:** The 15th in a series of retrospective looks at the previous year, including stories culled not only from science fiction magazines and collections but from various unlikely places. Includes several essays summing up different aspects of the year, and an extensive honor roll of other worthwhile stories not included in the current volume.

**Other books you might like:**
Terry Carr, *The Best From Universe*, 1984
Terry Carr, *The Science Fiction Hall of Fame, Volume 4*, 1986
Damon Knight, *The Clarion Awards*, 1984
Damon Knight, *One Hundred Years of Science Fiction*, 1968
Kristine Kathryn Rusch, *The Best of Pulphouse: The Hardback Magazine*, 1991

## 1619

### GARDNER DOZOIS, Editor

## *The Year's Best Science Fiction: Fourteenth Annual Collection*

(New York: St. Martin's, 1997)

**Story type:** Science Fiction (Anthology; Science Fiction)
**Series:** Year's Best Science Fiction

**Summary:** Contains a 36-page summation of science fiction in 1996, five pages of honorable mentions and 28 stories with individual introductions. The stories include one Hugo Award-winner, Bruce Sterling's "Bicycle Repairman"; one Hugo Award and Nebula Award-nominee, Maureen F. McHugh's "The Cost to Be Wise"; and three Hugo Award-nominees, Gregory Benford's "Immersion," Mike Resnick's "The Land of Nod" and Michael Swanwick's "The Dead." Other authors include William Barton, Stephen Baxter, James P. Blaylock, Damien Broderick, Michael Cassutt, Tony Daniel, Gregory Feeley, Gwyneth Jones, John Kessel, Nancy Kress, Jonathan Lethem, Ian McDonald, Paul Park, Robert Reed, Charles Sheffield, Robert Silverberg, Cherry Wilder, Walter Jon Williams and Gene Wolfe.

**Other books you might like:**
Jack Dann, *Nebula Awards 32*, 1998
  editor
David G. Hartwell, *Year's Best SF*, 1996
  editor
David G. Hartwell, *Year's Best SF 2*, 1997
  editor
Jennifer Hershey, *Full Spectrum 5*, 1995
  Tom Dupree, Janna Silverstein, co-editors
Ursula K. Le Guin, *The Norton Book of Science Fiction: North American Science Fiction, 1960-1990*, 1993
  Brian Attebery, co-editor

## 1620

### GARDNER DOZOIS, Editor

## *The Year's Best Science Fiction: Ninth Annual Collection*

(New York: St. Martin's Press, 1992)

**Story type:** Science Fiction (Anthology)
**Series:** Year's Best Science Fiction

**Summary:** Contains 28 stories, five pages of honorable mentions, plus a 27-page summation of the 1991 Science Fiction milieu by the editor. "Beggars in Spain" by Nancy Kress received both a Hugo Award and a Nebula Award, "A Walk in the Sun" by Geoffrey A.

Landis received a Hugo Award, "The Gallery of His Dreams" by Kristine Kathryn Rusch received both Hugo and Nebula nominations and three stories received a Hugo nomination. Other authors include Brian W. Aldiss, Gregory Benford, Jack Dann, Karen Joy Fowler, William Gibson, Alexander Jablokov, James Patrick Kelly, Ian McDonald, Kim Newman, Robert Reed, Kim Stanley Robinson, Robert Silverberg and Walter Jon Williams.

**Other books you might like:**
Lou Aronica, *Full Spectrum 3*, 1991
  Amy Stout and Betsy Mitchell, co-editors
Michael Bishop, *Nebula Awards 25*, 1991
  editor
Harlan Ellison, *Dangerous Visions*, 1967
  editor
Raymond J. Healy, *Adventures in Time and Space*, 1946
  J. Francis McComas, co-editor
James Morrow, *Nebula Awards 26*, 1992
  editor
Robert Silverberg, *The Science Fiction Hall of Fame, Volume 1*, 1970
  editor
Robert Silverberg, *Universe 2*, 1992
  Karen Haber, co-editor
Donald A. Wollheim, *The 1990 Annual World's Best Science Fiction*, 1990
  Arthur W. Saha, co-editor

## 1621

### GARDNER DOZOIS

## *The Year's Best Science Fiction: Seventh Annual Collection*

(New York: St. Martin's Press, 1990)

**Story type:** Science Fiction (Anthology; Hard Science Fiction)
**Series:** Year's Best Science Fiction
**Time period(s):** Indeterminate

**Summary:** This book contains 25 stories, a fifteen-page summation of 1989 by the editor and a lenthy list of runners-up. Gregory Benford, Robert Silverberg, John Varley, Nancy Kress, Janet Kagan and Connie Willis are among the 24 authors represented.

**Other books you might like:**
Lou Aronica, *Full Spectrum*, 1988
  Shawna McCarthy, co-editor
Lou Aronica, *Full Spectrum 2*, 1989
  Shawna McCarthy, co-editor
Groff Conklin, *The Best of Science Fiction*, 1946
Raymond J. Healy, *Adventures in Time and Space*, 1946
  J. Francis McComas, co-editor
Donald A. Wollheim, *The 1990 Annual World's Best Science Fiction*, 1990
  Arthur W. Saha, co-editor

## 1622

### GARDNER DOZOIS, Editor

## *The Year's Best Science Fiction: Tenth Annual Collection*

(New York: St. Martin's Press, 1993)

**Story type:** Science Fiction (Anthology)
**Series:** Year's Best Science Fiction

**Summary:** Contains a 26-page summation of science fiction in 1992, six pages of honorable mentions and 24 stories. These include one Hugo and Nebula Award winner, Connie Willis' "Even the Queen"; three Hugo and Nebula Award nominees, Bradley Denton's "The Territory," Nancy Kress' "The Mountain to Mohammed" and Maureen McHugh's "Protection"; and one Nebula Award nominee, Michael Swanwick's "Griffin's Egg." Other authors include Neal Barrett, Jr., Terry Bisson, Pat Cadigan, Arthur C. Clarke, L. Sprague de Camp, Joe Haldeman, Kathe Koja, Frederik Pohl, Robert Silverberg, Ian Watson and Kate Wilhelm.

**Other books you might like:**
Lou Aronica, *Full Spectrum 4*, 1993
    Amy Stout, Betsy Mitchell, co-editors
Michael Bishop, *Nebula Awards 25*, 1991
    editor
Ellen Datlow, *Omni Best Science Fiction Three*, 1993
    editor
Ursula K. Le Guin, *The Norton Book of Science Fiction: North American Science Fiction, 1960-1990*, 1993
    Brian Attebery, co-editor
James Morrow, *Nebula Awards 27*, 1993
    editor
Robert Silverberg, *Universe 2*, 1992
    Karen Haber, co-editor

## 1623

**GARDNER DOZOIS**, Editor

### *The Year's Best Science Fiction: Thirteenth Annual Collection*
(New York: St. Martin's Griffin, 1996)

**Story type:** Science Fiction (Anthology)
**Series:** Year's Best Science Fiction

**Summary:** Contains a 39-page summation of science fiction in 1995, six pages of honorable mentions, and 24 stories with introductions. The stories include two Hugo Award winners that received Nebula Award nominations, James Patrick Kelly's "Think Like a Dinosaur" and Maureen F. McHugh's "The Lincoln Train"; one Hugo Award winner, Allen Steele's "The Death of Captain Future"; two Hugo Award nominees, Greg Egan's "Luminous" and Ursula K. LeGuin's "A Woman's Libration"; and one Nebula Award nominee, Brian Stableford's "Mortimer Gray's *History of Death*." Other authors include Poul Anderson, Terry Bisson, Pat Cadigan, Michael F. Flynn, Joe Haldeman, John Kessel, Nancy Kress, Paul J. McAuley, Robert Reed, Mary Rosenblum, Jeff Ryman, William Sanders, Dan Simmons, and Michael Swanwick.

**Other books you might like:**
David G. Hartwell, *The Ascent of Wonder: The Evolution of Hard SF*, 1994
    Kathryn Cramer, co-editor
David G. Hartwell, *The Year's Best SF 13*, 1996
    editor
Jennifer Hershey, *Full Spectrum 5*, 1995
    Tom Dupree, Janna Silverstein, co-editors
Ursula K. Le Guin, *The Norton Book of Science Fiction: North American Science Fiction, 1960-1990*, 1993
    Brian Attebery, co-author
Pamela Sargent, *Nebula Awards 29*, 1996
    editor
Robert Silverberg, *Universe 3*, 1994
    Karen Haber, co-editor

## 1624

**GARDNER DOZOIS**, Editor

### *The Year's Best Science Fiction: Twelfth Annual Collection*
(New York: St. Martin's Griffin, 1995)

**Story type:** Science Fiction (Anthology)
**Series:** Year's Best Science Fiction

**Summary:** Contains a 36-page summation of science fiction in 1994, six pages of honorable mentions, and 23 stories. The stories include one Hugo and Nebula Award winner, Mike Resnick's "Seven Views of Olduvai George"; one Hugo Award winner and Nebula Award nominee, Joe Haldeman's "None So Blind"; two Hugo and Nebula Award nominees, both by Ursula K. Le Guin, "Forgiveness Day" and "The Matter of Seggri"; four Hugo Award nominees, Michael Bishop's "Cri de Coeur," Greg Egan's "Cocoon," Michael F. Flynn's "Melodies of the Heart," and Brian Stableford's "Les Fleurs du Mal"; and one Nebula Award nominee, Maureen F. McHugh's "Necropolis." Other authors include Stephen Baxter, Terry Bisson, Pat Cadigan, Lisa Goldstein, Katharine Kerr, Nancy Kress, Robert Reed, Mary Rosenblum, Howard Waldrop, and Walter Jon Williams.

**Other books you might like:**
David G. Hartwell, *The Ascent of Wonder: The Evolution of Hard SF*, 1994
    Kathryn Cramer, co-editor
Jennifer Hershey, *Full Spectrum 5*, 1995
    Tom Dupree, Janna Silverstein, co-editors
Ursula K. Le Guin, *The Norton Book of Science Fiction: North American Science Fiction, 1960-1990*, 1993
    Brian Attebery, co-editor
Pamela Sargent, *Nebula Awards 29*, 1995
    editor
Robert Silverberg, *Universe 3*, 1994
    Karen Haber, co-editor

## 1625

**ALISON DRAKE**

### *Lagoon*
(New York: Ballantine, 1990)

**Story type:** Horror (Nature in Revolt)
**Major character(s):** Scott Nash, Photojournalist; Fay Donovan, Doctor (coroner)
**Time period(s):** 1990s
**Locale(s):** Lagoon, Georgia

**Summary:** Scott Nash returns to the small northeast Georgia town of Lagoon to discover the reason his brother Ben went berserk during dinner one evening and gunned down twenty-nine people at the local inn. Nash discovers that prior to his rampage, Ben had begun to exhibit strange physical symptons—which seem inexplicably to coincide with weather anomalies, disappearances, cannibalistic assaults, mutant plants and animals in the vicinity, and a pervasive sense of "wrongness" that has settled over the area. Joining forces with local physician Fay Donovan, Nash discovers that nature itself is in revolt against the abuses humanity has perpetrated upon it.

**Other books you might like:**
Robert Charles, *Flowers of Evil*, 1982
Marilyn Harris, *The Portent*, 1980
Leslie Horvitz, *The Dying*, 1987
David J. Michael, *Death Tour*, 1978

Alan E. Nourse, *The Fourth Horseman*, 1983

**1626**

**DAVID DRAKE**
**JANET MORRIS**, Co-Author

*Arc Riders*
(New York: Warner Aspect, 1995)

**Story type:** Science Fiction (Time Travel; Military)
**Major character(s):** Rebecca Carnes, Military Personnel, Time Traveler; Nan Roebeck, Time Traveler; Tim Grainger, Time Traveler
**Time period(s):** 26th century (November 17, 2522); 250th century B.C.
**Locale(s):** Boston, Massachusetts; Vietnam; Superior, Minnesota

**Summary:** While attempting to return to Anti-Reversion Command Central at the end of a mission, the team barely escapes from an unexpected attack. The Arc Riders retreat to 25,000 B.C. to find and correct the revision. Needing more information to discover when the change occurred, the team recruits Rebecca Carnes from 1991, just prior to the detailed years stored in their computer, hoping she can help them restore their timeline and avoid perpetual war or nuclear desctuction.

**Other books you might like:**
Poul Anderson, *The Time Patrol*, 1991
Fritz Leiber, *The Big Time*, 1961
Janet Morris, *Heroes in Hell*, 1986
Janet Morris, *Threshold*, 1990
    Chris Morris, co-author
Andre Norton, *The Crossroads of Time*, 1956
H. Beam Piper, *Lord Kalvan of Otherwhen*, 1965

**1627**

**DAVID DRAKE**, Editor
**BILL FAWCETT**, Co-Editor

*Battlestation*
(New York: Ace, 1992)

**Story type:** Science Fiction (Anthology; Space Opera)
**Series:** Battlestation
**Time period(s):** Indeterminate Future
**Locale(s):** *Stephen Hawking*, Spaceship; Outer Space

**Summary:** An alien species which colonizes planets by consuming everything usable on them has already destroyed hundreds of species when survivors of four planets ask for help from humans. The resulting battlestation they construct sets out to turn back the invasion. 11 authors including Diane Duane, Janet Morris, Robert Sheckley and Christopher Stasheff chronicle different aspects of the battle and individuals involved.

**Other books you might like:**
Robert Asprin, *The Bug Wars*, 1979
James Blish, *Cities in Flight*, 1970
Orson Scott Card, *Ender's Game*, 1985
Bill Fawcett, *The Siege of Arista*, 1991
Joe Haldeman, *The Forever War*, 1975
Anne McCaffrey, *The Ship Who Sang*, 1969
Elizabeth Mitchell, *Alien Stars*, 1985
    editor
Larry Niven, *Man-Kzin Wars*, 1988
    editor

**1628**

**DAVID DRAKE**

*Caught in the Crossfire*
(New York: Baen, 1998)

**Story type:** Science Fiction (Military; Collection)
**Series:** Hammer's Slammers
**Time period(s):** Indeterminate Future

**Summary:** This collection includes two short novels and three stories, all previously published except for one story original in this book. Each deals with another mission involving elements of Hammer's Slammers, an elite mercenary force that fights its battles with high tech tanks on a variety of different planets. The stories are primarily concerned with the pressure of battle on the participants and the politics that often reduce human beings to game pieces.

**Other books you might like:**
Lois McMaster Bujold, *Brothers in Arms*, 1989
John Dalmas, *The Kalif's War*, 1991
Keith Laumer, *Rogue Bolo*, 1986
R.M. Meluch, *War Birds*, 1989
Andre Norton, *Star Guard*, 1955

**1629**

**DAVID DRAKE**, Editor

*A Century of Horror: 1970-1979: The Greatest Stories of the Decade*
(New York: Michael J. Fine, 1997)

**Story type:** Horror (Anthology)

**Summary:** The first of a projected series of anthologies presenting the best horror fiction of the century. The twenty-one stories gathered include Dennis Etchison's "It Only Comes Out at Night," about a highway rest stop haunted by a serial killer; Joyce Carol Oates's "Night-Side," a period tale of a skeptic in Victorian times whose encounter with the supernatural during a seance sparks his belief; Ramsey Campbell's "Mackintosh Willy," about a murdered hobo who gets his revenge on the children who tormented him; Karl Edward Wagner's "Sticks," an homage to the fiction of H.P. Lovecraft; Ted Klein's "The Events at Poroth Farm," about an alien invasion of a rural farm; and Richard Matheson's "Duel," about a showdown in the desert between a tractor trailer and a car, later a suspensful made-for-TV film directed by Stephen Spielberg.

**Other books you might like:**
Dennis Etchison, *The Complete Masters of Darkness*, 1991
    editor
Charles L. Grant, *The Best of Shadows*, 1988
    editor
David G. Hartwell, *The Dark Descent*, 1987
    editor
Kirby McCauley, *Dark Forces*, 1980
    editor
Stuart David Schiff, *The Best of Whispers*, 1994
    editor

## 1630

**DAVID DRAKE**
**WILLIAM C. DIETZ**, Co-Author

### Cluster Command

(New York: Baen Books, 1989)

**Story type:** Science Fiction (Military)
**Series:** Crisis of Empire
**Major character(s):** Anson Merikur, Military Personnel (Commander); Bethany Windsor, Heiress
**Time period(s):** Indeterminate Future
**Locale(s):** Harmony Star Cluster, Interstellar Empire/Federation

**Summary:** As the First Empire enters its final days, corrupt government officials scramble for all they can get. Commander Anson Merikur is an exception to this trend, an old-fashioned military man who will do anything to stem the tide of collapse, even if it means war.

**Other books you might like:**
Lois McMaster Bujold, *Borders of Infinity*, 1989
    with David Drake
Lois McMaster Bujold, *The Warrior's Apprentice*, 1986
Larry Niven, *The Mote in God's Eye*, 1974
    Jerry Pournelle, co-author
Jerry Pournelle, *Prince of Mercenaries*, 1989

## 1631

**DAVID DRAKE**
**JANET MORRIS**, Co-Author

### The Fourth Rome

(New York: Warner Aspect, 1996)

**Story type:** Science Fiction (Time Travel; Adventure)
**Series:** ARC Riders
**Major character(s):** Nan Roebeck, Time Traveler, Leader; Pauli Weigand, Time Traveler; Tim Grainger, Time Traveler
**Time period(s):** 1st century (9 A.D.); 1990s (1992)
**Locale(s):** Germany; Moscow, Russia

**Summary:** Team 79 finds no trace of those they track when sent into the past to capture Russian revisionists who plan to ensure Roman conquest of the ancient Germans by preventing the massacre in the Teutoberg Forest that ended Roman expansion east of the Rhine. Pauli, Rebecca, and Gerd stay in 9 A.D. to find the revisionists and ensure that history remains unchanged, while Nan, Tim, and Quo go forward to 1992 Moscow, searching for the technology that allowed the time transplant. In 1992, Nan and her group discover interference by far future conspirators that may extend to the highest levels of the Anti-Revisionist Command.

**Other books you might like:**
Poul Anderson, *Guardians of Time*, 1960
Poul Anderson, *Time Patrolman*, 1983
C.J. Cherryh, *Exile's Gate*, 1988
L. Sprague de Camp, *Lest Darkness Fall*, 1941
Janet Morris, *Heroes in Hell*, 1986
    editor
Elizabeth Ann Scarborough, *The Healer's War*, 1988

## 1632

**DAVID DRAKE**
**JIM KJELGAARD**, Co-Author

### The Hunter Returns

(New York: Baen, 1991)

**Story type:** Fantasy (Historical; Adventure)
**Major character(s):** Hawk, Prehistoric Human, Inventor; Wolf, Prehistoric Human, Hunter; Willow, Prehistoric Human
**Time period(s):** Indeterminate Past (Pleistocene)
**Locale(s):** Earth

**Summary:** Hawk, Chief Spear-Maker, accidently invented a throwing stick with which he attacked a sabre-tooth tiger, a taboo act for a Chief Spear-Maker. Game is scarce and Hawk's break with tradition is blamed for the tribe's difficulty acquiring meat. Willow, wounded by a tiger, and Hawk become a couple while Hawk invents new hunting techniques and a better lifestyle. Expanded from the 1951 novel, *Firehunter*, by Kjelgaard alone.

**Other books you might like:**
Michael Armstrong, *Agviq*, 1990
Jean M. Auel, *Clan of the Cave Bear*, 1980
J.H. Brennan, *Shiva: An Adventure of the Ice Age*, 1990
W. Michael Gear, *People of the Wolf*, 1990
    Kathleen O'Neal Gear, co-author
Richard Herley, *The Stone Arrow*, 1978
Elizabeth Marshall Thomas, *Reindeer Moon*, 1987

## 1633

**DAVID DRAKE**

### Igniting the Reaches

(New York: Ace, 1994)

**Story type:** Science Fiction (Adventure; Military)
**Major character(s):** Stephen Gregg, Military Personnel (colonel); Piet Ricimer, Spaceman
**Time period(s):** Indeterminate Future (4th millennium)
**Locale(s):** Venus; Benisan, Planet—Imaginary

**Summary:** When humans travel again in deep space, a millenium after the human empire collapses, a pair of young men from Venus seek gold and glory. They face natural dangers, aliens and a hostile Earth in pursuit of their dream.

**Other books you might like:**
Poul Anderson, *Flandry of Terra*, 1965
Iain M. Banks, *The Player of Games*, 1989
Lois McMaster Bujold, *Barrayar*, 1991
Glen Cook, *The Dragon Never Sleeps*, 1988
H. Beam Piper, *Space Viking*, 1963

## 1634

**DAVID DRAKE**

### The Jungle

(New York: Tor, 1991)

**Story type:** Science Fiction (Adventure; Military)
**Major character(s):** Brainard, Military Personnel (Free Companies ensign)
**Time period(s):** Indeterminate Future (380s As-After Settlement)
**Locale(s):** Venus

**Summary:** With Earth destroyed, the survivors of humanity are trying to terraform Venus while carrying on the war which wiped out life on Earth. When Ensign Brainard's craft is downed, the crew must battle Venus's hostile jungle to return to their home, an underwater dome. This novel is set in the same milieu as Henry Kuttner's, *Destination Infinity* (1958), a retitling of *Fury* (1950), and his novella, "Clash by Night," the latter included here along with Drake's note of explanation.

**Other books you might like:**
David Brin, *Startide Rising*, 1983
David Brin, *The Uplift War*, 1987
Octavia E. Butler, *Dawn*, 1987
Harry Harrison, *The Deathworld Trilogy*, 1976
James H. Schmitz, *The Demon Breed*, 1968
Dan Simmons, *The Fall of Hyperion*, 1990
Dan Simmons, *Hyperion*, 1989
John Varley, *Titan*, 1979

## 1635

### DAVID DRAKE

## *Justice*

(New York: Ace, 1992)

**Story type:** Science Fiction (Military)
**Series:** Northworld
**Major character(s):** Nils Hansen, Police Officer (former); Sparrow, Artisan (smith), Matchmaker; Venkatna, Royalty (king)
**Time period(s):** Indeterminate Future
**Locale(s):** Northworld, Planet—Imaginary; Eight Planes of the Matrix, Mythical Place

**Summary:** When King Venkatna wishes to rule everyone and everything in Northland, North gives him a Web which will grant his wish, although it obeys his commands literally and some people, such as Nils Hansen, who will fight Venkatna to the very end, possess immunity to the Web. Meanwhile, Sparrow travels through the planes determined to secure a wife for his master, Saburo.

**Other books you might like:**
Robert A. Heinlein, *Starship Troopers*, 1959
Fritz Leiber, *The Big Time*, 1961
Michael Moorcock, *The Runestaff*, 1977
Jerry Pournelle, *Janissaries*, 1979
Roger Zelazny, *Lord of Light*, 1967
Roger Zelazny, *Nine Princes in Amber*, 1970

## 1636

### DAVID DRAKE

## *Lord of the Isles*

(New York: Tor, 1997)

**Story type:** Fantasy (Magic Conflict)
**Major character(s):** Tenoctris, Wizard, Aged Person; Garric or-Reise, Warrior, Hunter; The Hooded One, Wizard
**Time period(s):** Indeterminate Past
**Locale(s):** Yole, Fictional Country; Barca's Hamlet, Fictional City

**Summary:** The Duke of Yole has won a great victory, but his ambition ends when the payment turns out to be the sinking of his realm. His court wizard, Tenoctris, flees a millennium into the future, but finds the same peril there. Out of malice or error, the Hooded One still wants the Throne of Malhar and will sink the whole world to get it.

**Other books you might like:**
Glen Cook, *The Swordbearer*, 1982
Robin Hobb, *Assassin's Apprentice*, 1995
Ursula K. Le Guin, *A Wizard of Earthsea*, 1968
Fritz Leiber, *Ill Met in Lankhmar*, 1995
Martha Wells, *The Element of Fire*, 1993

## 1637

### DAVID DRAKE

## *Northworld*

(New York: Ace, 1990)

**Story type:** Science Fiction (Mystical; Political)
**Series:** Northworld
**Major character(s):** Nils Hansen, Police Officer (Consensus)
**Time period(s):** Indeterminate Future
**Locale(s):** Northworld, Planet—Imaginary

**Summary:** First the Consensus sent an exploration team led by Captain Rolls and then a crisis team led by Captain North had gone to Northworld. Neither had returned. Finally, when several more attempts had failed, the Consensus tapped Special Forces Commissioner Nils Hansen to go and investigate.

**Other books you might like:**
John Brunner, *Children of the Thunder*, 1989
Frank Herbert, *Dune*, 1965
Michael Moorcock, *Elric of Melnibone*, 1976
Roger Zelazny, *Nine Princes in Amber*, 1970
Roger Zelazny, *Creatures of Light and Darkness*, 1969

## 1638

### DAVID DRAKE
### ERIC FLINT, Co-Author

## *An Oblique Approach*

(New York: Baen, 1998)

**Story type:** Science Fiction (Alternate Universe; Military)
**Major character(s):** Belisarius, Military Personnel (general); Aide, Artificial Intelligence; Valentinian, Military Personnel (cataphract), Bodyguard
**Time period(s):** 6th century (528)
**Locale(s):** Alternate Earth (Byzantium, Byzantine Empire); Alternate Earth (Bhafakuccha, India)

**Summary:** As the Malwa Empire of northern India prepares to sweep across the world in a bloody wave of tyranny, blood a strange gem full of visions of the future falls into the hands of Belisarius, an extremely capable Byzantine general. The general and his allies must cross the world and outwit the deadly and cruel Malwa to gain any hope of changing the bitter future.

**Other books you might like:**
L. Sprague de Camp, *Lest Darkness Fall*, 1941
Linda Evans, *Far Edge of Darkness*, 1996
John M. Ford, *The Dragon Waiting*, 1983
Robert Silverberg, *Up the Line*, 1969
Harry Turtledove, *The Misplaced Legion*, 1996

## 1639

### DAVID DRAKE

### Old Nathan

(New York: Baen, 1991)

**Story type:** Fantasy (Collection; Magic Conflict)
**Major character(s):** Old Nathan, Backwoodsman, Magician
**Time period(s):** 1820s
**Locale(s):** Tennessee

**Summary:** With dialog written in backwoods dialect, these five adventures tell of Old Nathan, frequently called upon to do magical odd jobs. ''The Bull'' first appeared in *Whispers* magazine and ''The Fool'' first appeared in *Whispers VI* (1987). Stories original to this collection are ''The Gold,'' ''The Bullhead'' and ''The Box.''

**Other books you might like:**
Tom Deitz, *Soulsmith*, 1991
Manly Wade Wellman, *After Dark*, 1980
Manly Wade Wellman, *The Hanging Stones*, 1982
Manly Wade Wellman, *John the Balladeer*, 1988
Manly Wade Wellman, *The Lost and Lurking*, 1981
Manly Wade Wellman, *Who Fears the Devil?*, 1963

## 1640

### DAVID DRAKE

### Queen of Demons

(New York: Tor, 1998)

**Story type:** Fantasy (Magic Conflict)
**Series:** Lord of the Isles
**Major character(s):** Tenoctris, Wizard, Aged Person; Garric or-Reise, Warrior, Psychic; Zahag, Animal (ape)
**Time period(s):** Indeterminate Past
**Locale(s):** the Isles, Fictional Country

**Summary:** The threat of the Hooded One is finished, but the forces awakened by his magic remain active. While a king and queen plot the conquest of the Isles and strange half-humans return to the world, the Beast moves again. Behind the scenes, the Queen of Demons directs people and nations like pawns in a game.

**Other books you might like:**
Glen Cook, *A Shadow of All Night Falling*, 1979
Barbara Hambly, *The Time of the Dark*, 1982
George R.R. Martin, *A Game of Thrones*, 1996
Matthew Woodring Stover, *Iron Dawn*, 1987
Janny Wurts, *Curse of the Mistwraith*, 1994

## 1641

### DAVID DRAKE

### Redliners

(New York: Baen, 1996)

**Story type:** Science Fiction (Military; Adventure)

**Summary:** Deemed too dangerous for civilian life following their mission on Stalleybrass, Strike Force Company C41 deploys to provide protection for colonists settling Bezant, a hell planet where all life seems dangerous to humans. Crash landing in the most dangerous area on the planet, miles from the colony site, the Company must fight off the enemy and get the colonists to their colony site.

**Other books you might like:**
Orson Scott Card, *Ender's Game*, 1985
Gordon R. Dickson, *The Tactics of Mistake*, 1971
Joe Haldeman, *The Forever War*, 1975
Harry Harrison, *Deathworld*, 1960
Robert A. Heinlein, *Starship Troopers*, 1959
Colin Kapp, *The Survival Game*, 1976
Jerry Pournelle, *Go Tell the Spartans*, 1991
S.M. Stirling, *Marching through Georgia*, 1988

## 1642

### DAVID DRAKE

### Rolling Hot

(New York: Baen Books, 1989)

**Story type:** Science Fiction (Military)
**Series:** Hammer's Slammers
**Major character(s):** June Ranson, Mercenary (Captain); Dick Suilin, Journalist, Mercenary
**Time period(s):** Indeterminate Future (Third Millennium)
**Locale(s):** Prosperity, Planet—Imaginary

**Summary:** Captain Ranson thinks she's been handed an easy assignment, but then disaster strikes. Now she must lead her own mercenary tank force and a mixed bag of raw recruits three hundred miles to relieve the district capital or the war will be effectively over and Hammer's Slammers will be on the losing side.

**Other books you might like:**
Harold Coyle, *Team Yankee*, 1988
Edward P. Hughes, *Masters of the Fist*, 1989
Keith Laumer, *The Complete Bolo*, 1990
Keith Laumer, *The Stars Must Wait*, 1989
Ralph Peters, *Red Army*, 1989
Jerry Pournelle, *Janissaries*, 1979
Jerry Pournelle, *Prince of Mercenaries*, 1989

## 1643

### DAVID DRAKE

### The Sharp End

(New York: Baen, 1993)

**Story type:** Science Fiction (Adventure; Military)
**Major character(s):** Matthew Coke, Military Personnel, Leader; Sten Moden, Military Personnel; Mary Margulies, Military Personnel
**Time period(s):** Indeterminate Future
**Locale(s):** Cantilucca, Planet—Imaginary

**Summary:** The Frisian Defense Forces survey team encounter difficulty on Cantilucca, whose warlords regularly terrorize the peasantry. Set in the *Hammer's Slammers* milieu.

**Other books you might like:**
Simon R. Green, *Hellworld*, 1993
Harry Harrison, *The Deathworld Trilogy*, 1976
Janet Kagan, *Hellspark*, 1988
Rosemary Kirstein, *The Outskirter's Secret*, 1992
Sheri S. Tepper, *Grass*, 1989

## 1644

### DAVID DRAKE

## *The Square Deal*
(New York: Tor, 1992)

**Story type:** Science Fiction (Adventure; Techno-Thriller)
**Series:** Car Warriors
**Major character(s):** Brian Deal, Teenager, Adventurer; John "J.C." Deal, Adventurer, Warrior; Ditsy Wallace, Journalist, Adventurer
**Time period(s):** 21st century
**Locale(s):** Mannheim, New Mexico

**Summary:** Brian spends his time repairing wrecks and helping his friend, Ditsy, with television coverage of highway autoduelling until his brother returns to Mannheim driving a hot car. Shortly thereafter, Brian, Ditsy and J.C. become involved in a feud which includes Ditsy's father, a local rancher and a gang of pirates on motorcycles. Ties into the game, *Car Wars*, inspired by the Alan Dean Foster story, "Why Johnny Can't Speed."

**Other books you might like:**
Robert Silverberg, *Car Sinister*, 1979
    Martin H. Greenberg and Joseph D. Olander, co-editors
Joan D. Vinge, *Mad Max Beyond Thunderdome*, 1985
Walter Jon Williams, *Hardwired*, 1986
Roger Zelazny, *Damnation Alley*, 1968

## 1645

### DAVID DRAKE

## *Starliner*
(New York: Baen, 1992)

**Story type:** Science Fiction (Adventure; Science Fiction)
**Major character(s):** Randall "Ran" Colville, Spaceman (Trident Starlines); Wanda Holly, Spaceman (Trident Starlines); Lady Scour, Alien (Szgranian), Royalty
**Time period(s):** Indeterminate Future
**Locale(s):** *Empress of Earth*, Spaceship (starliner); Outer Space

**Summary:** The *Empress of Earth* and *Brasil*, with routes from Earth to Tblisi and back, carry first class passengers as well as cargo class freight. Randall Colville, a new officer of the *Empress of Earth*, recognizes its potential value if war erupts between Nevasa and Grantholm. On the trip to Tblisi, Ran rescues a Nevasan passenger from her Grantholm kidnappers, foils an attempt to steal the ship and an attempt to hijack it, and becomes an integral member of the *Empress'* crew shepherding interesting passengers from planet to planet.

**Other books you might like:**
Stephen Baxter, *Raft*, 1991
C.J. Cherryh, *The Pride of Chanur*, 1982
Glen Cook, *The Dragon Never Sleeps*, 1988
John DeChancie, *Starrigger*, 1983
Vonda N. McIntyre, *Transition*, 1991
Alis A. Rasmussen, *A Passage of Stars*, 1990
Frank M. Robinson, *The Dark Beyond the Stars*, 1991
David Weber, *Mutineers' Moon*, 1991

## 1646

### DAVID DRAKE

## *Surface Action*
(New York: Ace, 1990)

**Story type:** Science Fiction (Military; Young Adult)
**Major character(s):** John Gordon, Mercenary; Daniel Cooke, Mercenary (naval)
**Time period(s):** Indeterminate Future
**Locale(s):** Venus

**Summary:** Hundreds of years after Earth's final war, the Venus colonies live on as domes under the endless oceans. Disputes between the domes are fought by mercenaries on the surface as naval engagements. Every boy on Venus dreams of joining a mercenary fleet—of a warrior's life on the high seas—and John Gordon is no exception. Son of a senator and nephew of a prominent commander, Johnnie has trained his whole life for battle. Now the time has come to experience his first taste of surface action.

**Other books you might like:**
Gordon R. Dickson, *Dorsai!*, 1976
Larry Niven, *The Mote in God's Eye*, 1974
    Jerry Pournelle, co-author
Jerry Pournelle, *The Mercenary*, 1977
Paul Preuss, *Breaking Strain*, 1987

## 1647

### DAVID DRAKE

## *Through the Breach*
(New York: Ace, 1995)

**Story type:** Science Fiction (Military; Adventure)
**Major character(s):** Piet Ricimer, Spaceman (general commander), Pirate; Stephen Gregg, Pirate
**Time period(s):** Indeterminate Future ((4th millenium))
**Locale(s):** Venus; Landolph's Breach, Outer Space (the Mirror)

**Summary:** Leading the Venus Asteroid Expedition, Piet Ricimer and Stephen Gregg head for the Mirror, a weak point where the barrier to booty and power lies thinnest. Sequel to *Igniting the Reaches*.

**Other books you might like:**
Poul Anderson, *Trader to the Stars*, 1964
C.J. Cherryh, *The Pride of Chanur*, 1982
L. Warren Douglas, *Bright Islands in a Dark Sea*, 1993
Gordon Eklund, *Space Pirates*, 1979
    E.E. Smith, co-author
Jack Vance, *Space Pirate*, 1953

## 1648

### DAVID DRAKE

## *Vengeance*
(New York: Ace, 1990)

**Story type:** Science Fiction (Political; Mystical)
**Series:** Northworld
**Major character(s):** Nils Hansen, Police Officer (former); North, Military Personnel (former)
**Time period(s):** Indeterminate Future
**Locale(s):** Northworld, Planet—Imaginary

**Summary:** Having gained the ability to manipulate the Matrix like the other "gods" before him, Hansen finds himself engaged in a power struggle with North over the fate of Northworld.

**Other books you might like:**
John Brunner, *Children of the Thunder*, 1989
Frank Herbert, *Dune*, 1965
Michael Moorcock, *Elric of Melnibone*, 1976
Roger Zelazny, *Nine Princes in Amber*, 1970
Roger Zelazny, *Creatures of Light and Darkness*, 1969

## 1649

### DAVID DRAKE

### *The Voyage*

(New York: Tor, 1994)

**Story type:** Science Fiction (Lost Colony; Military)
**Major character(s):** Lissea Doorman, Spaceship Captain, Military Personnel; Ned Slade, Military Personnel; Toll Warson, Military Personnel
**Time period(s):** Indeterminate Future
**Locale(s):** *Swift*, Spaceship; Planet—Imaginary

**Summary:** Lissea Doorman handpicks a crew for the Pancahte expedition, intending to reestablish contact. The venture brings much opportunity for action along the way. Contains a three-page "Author's Note" comparing the voyage to that of Homer's Argonauts in *The Iliad*. Set in the *Hammer's Slammers* milieu.

**Other books you might like:**
Nicola Griffith, *Ammonite*, 1993
Simon Lang, *The Trumpets of Tagan*, 1992
Vonda N. McIntyre, *Starfarers*, 1989
Alis A. Rasmussen, *The Price of Ransom*, 1990
A.E. Van Vogt, *The Voyage of the Space Beagle*, 1950

## 1650

### DAVID DRAKE
### ROGER MACBRIDE ALLEN, Co-Author

### *The War Machine*

(New York: Baen Books, 1989)

**Story type:** Science Fiction (Military)
**Series:** Crisis of Empire
**Major character(s):** Allison Spencer, Military Personnel (Captain)
**Time period(s):** Indeterminate Future
**Locale(s):** First Empire, Interstellar Empire/Federation

**Summary:** Captain Allison Spencer's marriage was destroyed by government officials for reasons of state and he sank into a life of drug addiction. Now, however, a hostile alien race menaces the Empire and Spencer appears to be the only man who can stop them.

**Other books you might like:**
Lois McMaster Bujold, *Borders of Infinity*, 1989
Lois McMaster Bujold, *The Warrior's Apprentice*, 1986
Larry Niven, *The Mote in God's Eye*, 1974
   Jerry Pournelle, co-author
Jerry Pournelle, *Prince of Mercenaries*, 1989
David Drake, *An Honorable Defense*, 1988
   Crisis of Empire Book I. Thomas T. Thomas, co-author

## 1651

### DAVID DRAKE

### *The Warrior*

(New York: Baen, 1991)

**Story type:** Science Fiction (Military)
**Series:** Hammer's Slammers
**Major character(s):** Samuel "Slick" Des Grieux, Military Personnel (Sergeant); Alois Hammer, Military Personnel (Colonel)
**Time period(s):** Indeterminate Future
**Locale(s):** Fictional Country

**Summary:** Constant battle keeps the adrenaline high and demonstrates the superior skills of Hammer's Slammers.

**Other books you might like:**
Greg Bear, *The Forge of God*, 1987
David Brin, *Earth*, 1990
Gordon R. Dickson, *Dorsai!*, 1976
Robert A. Heinlein, *Starship Troopers*, 1959
Keith Laumer, *Rogue Bolo*, 1986
G. Harry Stine, *Blood Siege*, 1990
G. Harry Stine, *The Lost Battalion*, 1989
G. Harry Stine, *Sierra Madre*, 1985

## 1652

### DAVID DRAKE

### *With the Lightnings*

(New York: Baen, 1998)

**Story type:** Science Fiction (Military)
**Major character(s):** Daniel Leary, Military Personnel (lieutenant); Adele Mundy, Scholar
**Time period(s):** Indeterminate Future
**Locale(s):** Kostroma, Planet—Imaginary

**Summary:** Two planetary governments contend for an alliance with Kostroma, a planet with no military but a very strategic location. As representatives for the two parties meet with the local government, one side masterminds a coup that puts them in control of that world. A military officer and a scholar from the opposing delegation become fugitives and seek to reverse the course of events.

**Other books you might like:**
Poul Anderson, *Earthman, Go Home!*, 1960
Bill Baldwin, *The Defiance*, 1996
Lois McMaster Bujold, *The Warrior's Apprentice*, 1986
Jerry Pournelle, *A Spaceship for the King*, 1973
Eric Frank Russell, *Wasp*, 1957

## 1653

### DIRK DRAULANS

### *The Red Queen*

(New York: St Martin's, 1998)

**Story type:** Science Fiction (Dystopian)
**Major character(s):** Ellen, Scientist
**Time period(s):** Indeterminate Future

**Summary:** When a plague wipes out virtually all of the male sex, the surviving women reproduce through artificial means. They institute a ruthless dictatorship which suppresses freedom and reacts violently to the discovery of a surviving male, whose very existence threatens the status quo. A scientist turns against her society to assist him. First novel.

**Other books you might like:**
Margaret Atwood, *The Handmaid's Tale*, 1986
Esther Friesner, *The Psalms of Herod*, 1995
Ursula K. Le Guin, *A Fisherman of the Inland Sea*, 1994
Charles Eric Maine, *Alph*, 1972
Joanna Russ, *The Female Man*, 1977

---

### 1654

**KATHRYN M. DRENNAN**

## To Dream in the City of Sorrows

(New York: Dell, 1997)

**Story type:** Science Fiction (Mystery; Military)
**Series:** Babylon 5
**Major character(s):** Jeffrey Sinclair, Military Personnel (Ranger One); Catherine Sakai, Pilot, Surveyor; Marcus Cole, Military Personnel (ranger)
**Time period(s):** 23rd century (2258)
**Locale(s):** Minbar, Planet—Imaginary

**Summary:** Recently and mysteriously reassigned by Earthforce as Ambassador to the Minbari homeworld, former Babylon 5 Commander Jeffrey Sinclair reluctantly agrees to serve as Ranger One, the leader of an elite Minbari/Human military/spiritual order. In the novel's foreward, television series creator J. Michael Straczynski calls this story "an official, authorized chapter in the Babylon 5 storyline," taking place concurrently with the show's second and part of the third season. First novel.

**Other books you might like:**
Neal Barrett Jr., *The Touch of Your Shadow, the Whisper of Your Name*, 1996
Jeanne Cavelos, *The Shadow Within*, 1997
J.M. Dillard, *Emissary*, 1965
Frank Herbert, *Dune*, 1965
Jim Mortimore, *Clark's Law*, 1996

---

### 1655

**RICHARD DREYFUSS**
**HARRY TURTLEDOVE**, Co-Author

## The Two Georges

(New York: Tor, 1996)

**Story type:** Science Fiction (Alternate Universe; Mystery)
**Major character(s):** Thomas Bushell, Military Personnel (colonel), Detective; Kathleen Flannery, Museum Curator, Adventurer; Samuel Stanley, Military Personnel
**Time period(s):** 1990s (1996)
**Locale(s):** North American Union, Alternate Earth (Canada and continental United States of America)

**Summary:** When thieves, presumably the Sons of Liberty who advocate separation from Great Britain, steal Gainsborough's famous painting, "The Two Georges," on exhibition in North America, Colonel Thomas Bushell must recover it before Charles III visits Victoria, capital of the North American Union.

**Other books you might like:**
John Christopher, *New Found Land*, 1983
Michael Flynn, *In the Country of the Blind*, 1990
Randall Garrett, *Too Many Magicians*, 1967
Harry Harrison, *Tunnel through the Deeps*, 1972
Keith Laumer, *Worlds of the Imperium*, 1962

Michael Moorcock, *The Warlord of the Air*, 1971
John Maddox Roberts, *King of the Wood*, 1983
L. Neil Smith, *The Probability Broach*, 1980
Harry Turtledove, *A Different Flesh*, 1988

---

### 1656

**JOHN DRIVER**

## The Hunger of the Beast

(New York: Jove, 1991)

**Story type:** Horror (Psychological Suspense)
**Major character(s):** Esau Wilkinson, Young Man; Diana LaBianca, Producer (assistant in New York Theatre); Dennis O'Connor, Journalist
**Time period(s):** 1990s
**Locale(s):** Fenwick, Vermont

**Summary:** Diana LaBianca's vacation at Vermont's Wilkinson Inn turns into a nightmare when she is mistaken for someone snooping into the owners' background and is imprisoned at the mercy of Esau Wilkinson, the deformed half-wit progeny of the Wilkinson clan.

**Other books you might like:**
John Fowles, *The Collector*, 1963
Stephen R. George, *The Forgotten*, 1991

---

### 1657

**DIANE DUANE**

## The Book of Night with Moon

(New York: Warner Aspect, 1997)

**Story type:** Fantasy (Magic Conflict; Adventure)
**Major character(s):** Rhiow, Animal (cat), Wizard; Urruah, Animal (cat), Wizard; Saash, Animal (cat), Wizard
**Time period(s):** 1990s; Indeterminate
**Locale(s):** New York, New York

**Summary:** Responsible for weaving and maintaining the magical threads linking different realities, four cats must repel the horrifying invasion from another dimension coming through the magic doorways in Grand Central Station.

**Other books you might like:**
A.A. Attanasio, *The Dragon and the Unicorn*, 1996
Louis de Bernieres, *The War of Don Emmanuel's Nether Parts*, 1992
Tanya Huff, *Summon the Keeper*, 1998
Shirley Rousseau Murphy, *The Catswold Portal*, 1992
Andre Norton, *Catseye*, 1961
L.A. Taylor, *Cat's Paw*, 1995
Tad Williams, *Tailchaser's Song*, 1985

---

### 1658

**DIANE DUANE**

## Dark Mirror

(New York: Pocket, 1993)

**Story type:** Science Fiction (Alternate Universe; Space Opera)
**Series:** Star Trek: The Next Generation
**Major character(s):** Jean-Luc Picard, Spaceship Captain, Military Personnel; Hwii ih'iie-u Ulak!ha', Alien (native of Triton Two), Scientist; Geordi La Forge, Engineer, Military Personnel
**Time period(s):** 24th century

**Locale(s):** *U.S.S. Enterprise*, Spaceship; *I.S.S. Enterprise*, Spaceship; United Empire of Planets, Interstellar Empire/Federation

**Summary:** Snatched during their investigation into a disturbance in the hyperstring structure of the galaxy, the crew of the *U.S.S. Enterprise* find themselves in an alternate universe where the United Empire of Planets rules the galaxy with fear and violence. Picard, Troi and La Forge must transport to the *Imperial Star Ship Enterprise*, impersonate their amoral counterparts and avoid assassination attempts by ambitious junior officers in order to find the information they need to escape to their own universe and save the Federation from the transdimensional invasion that the Empire plans. Set in the universe of the ''Star Trek'' episode, Mirror, Mirror.'

**Other books you might like:**
James Blish, *Star Trek 3*, 1969
Peter David, *Imzadi*, 1992
Philip K. Dick, *The Man in the High Castle*, 1962
Phyllis Eisenstein, *Shadow of Earth*, 1979
Michael Jan Friedman, *Double, Double*, 1989
Barbara Hambly, *Ishmael*, 1985

## 1659

### DIANE DUANE

## Doctor's Orders

(New York: Pocket, 1990)

**Story type:** Science Fiction (Space Opera)
**Series:** Star Trek
**Major character(s):** Leonard McCoy, Doctor; James T. Kirk, Spaceship Captain; At, Alien
**Time period(s):** 23rd century
**Locale(s):** Flyspeck, Planet—Imaginary; Musca Constellation, Outer Space; *U.S.S. Enterprise*, Spaceship

**Summary:** The *Enterprise* is sent to open diplomatic relations with three species on a recently contacted planet. The mission is intriguing and seems safe so Kirk hands over the controls to McCoy, much to the doctor's chagrin. Then Kirk vanishes from the planet, Starfleet demands to know why McCoy is in command and the Klingons arrive. Suddenly Kirk's afternoon of turning the tables on the doctor has gotten out of hand.

**Other books you might like:**
Lloyd Biggle, *This Darkening Universe*, 1975
John M. Ford, *How Much for Just the Planet?*, 1984
   Star Trek 36
Keith Laumer, *Retief: Diplomat at Arms*, 1982

## 1660

### DIANE DUANE

## The Door into Sunset

(New York: Tor, 1993)

**Story type:** Fantasy (Magic Conflict; Religious)
**Series:** Tale of the Five
**Major character(s):** Freelorn ''Lorn'', Heir—Dispossessed, Royalty (Prince of Arlen); Herewiss, Magician, Religious; Segnbora, Sorceress, Martial Arts Expert
**Time period(s):** Indeterminate
**Locale(s):** Arlen, Fictional Country

**Summary:** To restore vitality to Arlen, Lorn and his companions strive to overthrow the usurper king. Pursuing his goal, Lorn must sneak back into his homeland and discover, then attempt to pass, the rites of Initiation.

**Other books you might like:**
C.J. Cherryh, *Gate of Ivrel*, 1976
Sheila Gilluly, *Greenbriar Queen*, 1988
Barbara Hambly, *The Time of the Dark*, 1982
Guy Gavriel Kay, *The Summer Tree*, 1985
Guy Gavriel Kay, *Tigana*, 1990
Patricia Kennealy-Morrison, *The Copper Crown*, 1984
Katharine Kerr, *Daggerspell*, 1986
Mercedes Lackey, *Magic's Pawn*, 1989
Patricia A. McKillip, *The Riddle-Master of Hed*, 1976
Martha Wells, *The Element of Fire*, 1993

## 1661

### DIANE DUANE
### PETER MORWOOD, Co-Author

## High Moon

(New York: Avon, 1992)

**Story type:** Science Fiction (Military; Space Opera)
**Series:** Spacecops
**Major character(s):** Evan Glyndower, Military Personnel (Solar Patrol); Joss O'Bannion, Military Personnel (Solar Patrol)
**Time period(s):** Indeterminate Future
**Locale(s):** Phobos, Mars (2nd moon of Mars)

**Summary:** Vacationing on Phobos, Joss attends the Triplanetary Video, Solid, and Holo Collectors Convention while Evan visits the weapon experts at FAF Sydanham Upper. After a mysterious attack, the partners, ordered into space to find the ship containing their prototype decoder, find themselves fighting the Red Dawn, a band of outlaws.

**Other books you might like:**
Lois McMaster Bujold, *Brothers in Arms*, 1988
David Drake, *Northworld*, 1990
Stephen Goldin, *Jade Darcy and the Affair of Honor*, 1988
   Mary Mason, co-author
Steve Perry, *The Man Who Never Missed*, 1989
Paul Preuss, *The Diamond Moon*, 1990
Alis A. Rasmussen, *A Passage of Stars*, 1990

## 1662

### DIANE DUANE

## High Wizardry

(New York: Delacorte, 1990)

**Story type:** Fantasy (Science Fiction)
**Major character(s):** Dairine, Wizard
**Time period(s):** Indeterminate Future
**Locale(s):** Outer Space

**Summary:** Dairine finds a manual of magic on her computer and sets off on an adventure. She is chased by a wide variety of aliens and agents before her adventure ends.

**Other books you might like:**
Kevin J. Anderson, *Game's End*, 1990
Barbara Hambly, *The Silent Tower*, 1988
Michael Kandel, *In between Dragons*, 1990
Susan Beth Pfeffer, *Rewind to Yesterday*, 1988
Will Shetterly, *The Tangled Lands*, 1989
Connie Willis, *Light Raid*, 1989
   Science Fiction. Cynthia Felice, co-author

## 1663
### DIANE DUANE

### *Intellivore*
(New York: Pocket, 1997)

**Story type:** Science Fiction (Space Opera)
**Series:** Star Trek: The Next Generation
**Major character(s):** Jean-Luc Picard, Spaceship Captain; Data, Android, Military Personnel (lieutenant commander), Space Explorer; Beverly Crusher, Doctor, Space Explorer
**Time period(s):** 24th century
**Locale(s):** *U.S.S. Enterprise*, Spaceship; United Federation of Planets, Interstellar Empire/Federation

**Summary:** Sent to aid other Starfleet vessels investigating a string of disappearances, Picard and his crew track a wide-spread trail of destruction caused by entities that feed off conscious thought, leaving their victims mindless shells. Crusher learns that the intellivores cannot detect unconscious bodies, so Picard must devise a trap that will destroy the entities before they grow strong enough to wipe out sentient life in the entire Federation.

**Other books you might like:**
Dafydd ab Hugh, *The Final Fury*, 1996
Martin Amis, *Time's Arrow*, 1991
Diane Carey, *First Strike*, 1996
Gene DeWeese, *Chain of Attack*, 1987
Barbara Hambly, *Ghost Walker*, 1991
Barbara Paul, *The Three Minute Universe*, 1988
Garfield Reeves-Stevens, *Memory Prime*, 1988
    Judith Reeves-Stevens, co-author
Vernor Vinge, *A Fire upon the Deep*, 1992

## 1664
### DIANE DUANE
### PETER MORWOOD, Co-Author

### *Kill Station*
(New York: AvoNova, 1992)

**Story type:** Science Fiction (Mystery)
**Series:** Spacecops
**Major character(s):** Evan Glyndower, Military Personnel (solar patrol); Joss O'Bannion, Military Personnel (solar patrol)
**Time period(s):** 22nd century
**Locale(s):** *Nosey*, Spaceship; Asteroid Belt, Outer Space

**Summary:** While investigating a series of piracies to space-going freighters, Evan and Joss discover a conspiracy which may present a threat throughout the solar system.

**Other books you might like:**
Alfred Bester, *The Stars My Destination*, 1956
Glen Cook, *The Dragon Never Sleeps*, 1988
Katharine Kerr, *Polar City Blues*, 1990
Melisa C. Michaels, *Skirmish*, 1985
Alis A. Rasmussen, *Revolution's Shore*, 1990
John Varley, *Steel Beach*, 1992
Vernor Vinge, *A Fire upon the Deep*, 1992

## 1665
### DIANE DUANE
### PETER MORWOOD, Co-Author

### *Mindblast*
(New York: Avon, 1991)

**Story type:** Science Fiction (Mystery)
**Series:** Spacecops
**Major character(s):** Evan Glyndower, Military Personnel (Solar Patrol); Joss O'Bannion, Military Personnel (Solar Patrol)
**Time period(s):** 22nd century
**Locale(s):** Freedom, Space Station (at L5)

**Summary:** When Glyndower's partner is killed on Freedom, he's paired with O'Bannion, and the two of them are sent to continue the investigation and find the killer despite corrupt cops and budget cutbacks.

**Other books you might like:**
Barney Cohen, *The Taking of Satcon Station*, 1982
    Jim Baen, co-author
Glen Cook, *Sweet Silver Blues*, 1987
P.M. Griffin, *Star Commandos*, 1986
Lee Killough, *Spider Play*, 1986
Mercedes Lackey, *Burning Water*, 1989
Walter Jon Williams, *Days of Atonement*, 1991

## 1666
### DIANE DUANE
### PETER MORWOOD, Co-Author

### *seaQuest DSV: The Novel*
(New York: Ace, 1993)

**Story type:** Science Fiction (Adventure; Techno-Thriller)
**Series:** seaQuest DSV
**Major character(s):** Nathan Hale Bridger, Scientist, Sea Captain; Darwin, Animal (dolphin); Marilyn Stark, Sea Captain, Criminal
**Time period(s):** 2010s
**Locale(s):** *seaQuest DSV*, Submarine; Atlantic Ocean

**Summary:** When Marilyn Stark washes out as captain of *seaQuest DSV*, United Earth/Oceans Organization searches out Nathan Bridger and coerces him into the submarine, hoping to entice its designer into accepting captaincy. Attempting to gain revenge, Marilyn Stark uses her knowledge of *seaQuest DSV* to sabotage the research vehicle, threatening the lives of military and scientific personnel. Novelizes the television pilot.

**Other books you might like:**
Harry Harrison, *The Daleth Effect*, 1970
Damon Knight, *CV*, 1985
Damon Knight, *The Observers*, 1988
Damon Knight, *A Reasonable World*, 1991
Theodore Sturgeon, *Voyage to the Bottom of the Sea*, 1961
Jules Verne, *Twenty Thousand Leagues under the Sea*, 1870

## 1667
### DIANE DUANE

### *Spider-Man: The Venom Factor*
(New York: G.P. Putnam's Sons, 1994)

**Story type:** Science Fiction (Adventure; Mystery)
**Series:** Spider-Man

**Major character(s):** Peter "Spider-Man" Parker, Hero, Detective—Amateur; Hobgoblin, Criminal; Venom, Alien
**Time period(s):** 1990s
**Locale(s):** New York, New York

**Summary:** When the murder of an innocent man during a mysterious crime points unexpectedly toward Venom, Spider-Man must investigate the crime while simultaneously outsmarting Hobgoblin to save the city.

**Other books you might like:**
Stan Lee, *The Ultimate Spider-Man*, 1994
   editor
Dennis O'Neil, *Batman: Knightfall*, 1993
Roger Stern, *The Death and Life of Superman*, 1993
John Varley, *Superheroes*, 1995
   Ricia Mainhardt, co-editor
Len Wein, *Mayhem in Manhattan*, 1978
   Marv Wolfman, co-author

---

### 1668
#### DIANE DUANE

## A Wizard Abroad
(New York: Harcourt Brace, 1997)

**Story type:** Fantasy (Light Fantasy; Young Adult)
**Series:** Wizardry
**Major character(s):** Juanita "Nita" Callahan, Teenager, Wizard (American); Ronan Nolan, Teenager, Wizard (Irish); Tualha, Animal (kitten), Minstrel (bard)
**Time period(s):** 1990s
**Locale(s):** Ireland; Under the Hill, Mythical Place

**Summary:** When Nita goes on a vacation to her Aunt's home in Ireland, her parents expect her to take a break from magic and her wizard partner. Learning about Irish legend and mythology, Nita and her partner, who travels to Ireland by magic, soon must help in a desperate effort to save everything from the terror of Irish monsters come to life. Originally published 1993, fourth in series.

**Other books you might like:**
Susan Cooper, *The Dark Is Rising*, 1973
Diana Wynne Jones, *Cart and Cwidder*, 1977
Diana Wynne Jones, *Howl's Moving Castle*, 1986
Margaret Mahy, *The Tricksters*, 1987
Jody Lynn Nye, *Mythology Abroad*, 1991
Evangeline Walton, *The Children of Llyr*, 1971
Patricia C. Wrede, *Talking to Dragons*, 1993
   revised

---

### 1669
#### TANNARIVE DUE

## The Between
(New York: HarperCollins, 1995)

**Story type:** Horror (Wild Talents)
**Major character(s):** Hilton James, Social Worker; Dede James, Judge (Hilton's wife); Raul Puerta, Psychologist (therapist)
**Time period(s):** 1990s (1995)
**Locale(s):** Miami, Florida

**Summary:** After being saved from drowning when he was eight years old, Hilton James builds a good life for himself and family over the next thirty years. But a sudden spate of bad experiences, including dreams of an alternate life so vivid that Hilton is unable to separate them from reality, begins to suggest that he may never have been

intended to live as long as he has and that fate is trying to rectify the situation. This is the author's first novel.

**Other books you might like:**
Stephen King, *The Dead Zone*, 1979
Stephen King, *Insomnia*, 1994
Dean R. Koontz, *Hideaway*, 1993
Daniel Quinn, *Dreamer*, 1988

---

### 1670
#### TANNARIVE DUE

## My Soul to Keep
(New York: HarperCollins, 1997)

**Story type:** Horror (Occult)
**Major character(s):** David Wolde, Linguist; Jessica Jacobs-Wolde, Journalist; Kira Wolde, Child (David and Jessica's daughter)
**Time period(s):** 1990s (1997)
**Locale(s):** Miami, Florida

**Summary:** In the person of Dawit, David Wolde became a member of an Abyssinian immortality cult four and a half centuries ago. His intention to confer immortality on his current wife and daughter gains the attention of cult leaders who strictly limit membership and preserve their privacy, putting David and his family at risk of reprisal.

**Other books you might like:**
John Farris, *Sacrifice*, 1994
Dan Simmons, *Song of Kali*, 1985
Dan Simmons, *Carrion Comfort*, 1989
Harry Stein, *Infinity's Child*, 1997
Karen E. Taylor, *Bitter Blood*, 1994

---

### 1671
#### STEVE DUFFY

## The Night Comes On
(Ashcroft, British Columbia: Ash-Tree Press, 1998)

**Story type:** Horror (Collection)

**Summary:** This first collection of 16 Jamesian tales of the supernatural emphasizes subtlety in the elaboration of horror. Included are the mummy story "The Night Comes On"; the gypsy curse tale "The Story of a Malediction"; "Ex Libris," a tale of a forbidden book and its terrible cost; and "Tidesend," an homage to J. Sheridan Le Fanu's vampire classic "Carmilla."

**Other books you might like:**
Sheila Hodgson, *The Fellow Travellers and Other Ghost Stories*, 1998
Terry Lamsley, *Conference with the Dead*, 1996
David G. Rowlands, *The Executor and Other Ghost Stories*,
C.E. Ward, *Vengeful Ghosts*, 1998
Robert Westall, *Antique Dust*, 1989

---

### 1672
#### LEE DUIGON

## Mind Stealer
(New York: Pinnacle, 1990)

**Story type:** Horror (Occult)
**Major character(s):** Larry Donaldson, Businessman; Geoff Tagge, Professor, Anthropologist; Tanaka, Shaman

**Time period(s):** 1990s (1990)
**Locale(s):** New Jersey

**Summary:** When workaholic Larry Donaldson dies mysteriously after a secretive six-week business training program, his brother-in-law Geoff suspects dark forces may be involved.

**Other books you might like:**
Thomas M. Disch, *The Businessman: A Tale of Terror*, 1984
John Tigges, *Venom*, 1988

## 1673

### OLIVIA HOWARD DUNBAR

## The Shell of Sense

(Uncasville, Connecticut: Fawcett, 1997)

**Story type:** Horror (Collection)

**Summary:** Four short tales of the supernatural written in the first two decades of the twentieth century and representing the author's complete output of weird fiction. In addition to the oft-anthologized title story, the volume includes "The Long Chamber," in which a ghostly encounter awakens a woman to the misery of her loveless marriage; "The Dream-Baby," in which a pair of spinsters become obsessively devoted to a child one imagines in her dreams; and "The Sycamore," in which a tree serves as a protective muse to a starving painter and his family. Two essays by the author, "The Decay of the Ghost in Fiction" and "The Present Status of the Ghost," are included. Edited by Jessica Amanda Salmonson and illustrated by Wendy Wees.

**Other books you might like:**
Gertrude Atherton, *The Bell in the Fog and Other Stories*, 1905
H.D. Everett, *The Death Mask and Other Ghosts*, 1920
Ellen Glasgow, *The Shadowy Third and Other Stories*, 1923
Charlotte Perkins Gilman, *"The Yellow Wallpaper"*, 1901
Elkeanor Scott, *Randall's Round*, 1929
Mary E. Wilkins-Freeman, *The Wind in the Rosebush and Other Stories of the Supernatural*, 1903

## 1674

### DAVE DUNCAN

## The Cursed

(New York: Ballantine Del Rey, 1995)

**Story type:** Fantasy (Political; Adventure)
**Major character(s):** Gwin Nien Solith, Innkeeper, Magician (Poulscath); Bulion Tharn, Leader; Niad, Magician (Ivielscath), Teenager
**Time period(s):** Indeterminate
**Locale(s):** Da Lam, Fictional Country; Wesran, Fictional Country; Raragash, Fictional Country

**Summary:** Gwin illegally shelters Niad who feels the effect of the Curse which brings forth magical abilities, for good or ill. After Gwin encourages Niad to cure Bulion Tharn's malady, Gwin and Bulion agree to wed. Seeking a more hospitable environment for magicians, they lead a band of Cursed who may help Bulion, the prophecied Renewer, bind together the fragments of the old empire and renew its glory.

**Other books you might like:**
Terry Goodkind, *Stone of Tears*, 1995
Laurell K. Hamilton, *Nightseer*, 1992
George R.R. Martin, *The Wild Cards Series*, 1987-1995
L.E. Modesitt Jr., *The Towers of the Sunset*, 1992
Elizabeth Moon, *Sheepfarmer's Daughter*, 1988

Julie Dean Smith, *Call of Madness*, 1990
Janny Wurts, *Curse of the Mistwraith*, 1994

## 1675

### DAVE DUNCAN

## The Cutting Edge

(New York: Ballantine Del Rey, 1992)

**Story type:** Fantasy (Magic Conflict; Political)
**Series:** Handful of Men
**Major character(s):** Rap, Ruler, Adventurer
**Time period(s):** Indeterminate
**Locale(s):** Pandemia, Fictional Country

**Summary:** After 3000 years of the Protocol, a ban on the political use of some types of magic, prophecies indicate that cataclysmic changes threaten Pandemia. After more than a decade of peace and security in his kingdom, Rap hesitantly accepts his role in upcoming events as heroes and heroines begin to assemble in preparation for the political and magical chaos looming on the horizon.

**Other books you might like:**
David Eddings, *Pawn of Prophecy*, 1982
Robert Jordan, *The Eye of the World*, 1989
Elizabeth Moon, *Sheepfarmer's Daughter*, 1988
J.R.R. Tolkien, *The Fellowship of the Ring*, 1954
Paula Volsky, *Illusion*, 1992

## 1676

### DAVE DUNCAN

## Emperor and Clown

(New York: Ballantine Del Rey, 1992)

**Story type:** Fantasy (Light Fantasy; Adventure)
**Series:** Man of His Word
**Major character(s):** Rap, Warrior, Psychic (seer); Inosolan "Inos", Royalty (queen); Azak, Mythical Creature (djinn), Leader
**Time period(s):** Indeterminate Past
**Locale(s):** Pandemia, Fictional Country; Cenmere, Fictional Country (capital district); Hub of the Impire, Fictional City

**Summary:** Having failed his mission to rescue Queen Inos from Azak, Rap awaits his dark future at the hands of Azak's torturers. However, Azak's intention to recover his losses and free himself from a curse yields unexpected results.

**Other books you might like:**
Harry Turtledove, *An Emperor for the Legion*, 1987
Harry Turtledove, *The Legion of Videssos*, 1987
Harry Turtledove, *The Misplaced Legion*, 1987
Paula Volsky, *Illusion*, 1992

## 1677

### DAVE DUNCAN

## Faery Lands Forlorn

(New York: Ballantine/Del Rey, 1991)

**Story type:** Fantasy (Adventure; Light Fantasy)
**Series:** Man of His Word
**Major character(s):** Inosolan "Inos", Royalty (queen); Rap, Worker (stableboy), Psychic (seer); Kadolan "Kade", Royalty (princess), Guardian (Inosolan's aunt)
**Time period(s):** Indeterminate Past

**Locale(s):** Zark, Fictional Country; Faerie, Fictional Country

**Summary:** When Krasnegar is overrun with invaders, Inos, Rap and Aunt Kade escape through the magic casement. Unfortunately, it sends them to opposite ends of Pandemia. Inos and Aunt Kade must outwit the sorceress who has taken control of Zark and its sultan, even though as women they have no standing in Zarkian society. Rap is flung to the Island of Faery and having a word of power seems woefully inadequate to help him reach Inos.

**Other books you might like:**
Leo Frankowski, *The Cross-Time Engineer*, 1986
Barry Hughart, *Bridge of Birds*, 1984
Diana Wynne Jones, *Howl's Moving Castle*, 1986
John Morressy, *The Questing of Kedrigern*, 1987

---

### 1678

**DAVE DUNCAN**

## *Future Indefinite*

(New York: Avon, 1997)

**Story type:** Fantasy (Alternate World)
**Series:** Great Game
**Major character(s):** Edward Exeter, Traveler, Leader; Prat'han Potter, Revolutionary, Warrior; Dosh Coachman, Prostitute (gigolo)
**Time period(s):** 1910s; Indeterminate Past
**Locale(s):** England; Nextdoor, Alternate Earth

**Summary:** Edward Exeter has shuffled back and forth between Earth and Nextdoor for five years, always a pawn in someone else's plan. With Exeter now prepared to take his place at the center of his own plan, for his own purposes, the Pentatheon, the Service and especially Zath, the "god of death," had best beware of the Liberator.

**Other books you might like:**
Poul Anderson, *Three Hearts and Three Lions*, 1961
Eleanor Arnason, *Daughter of the Bear King*, 1987
Barbara Hambly, *The Time of the Dark*, 1982
H. Beam Piper, *Lord Kalvan of Otherwhen*, 1965
Roger Zelazny, *Nine Princes in Amber*, 1970

---

### 1679

**DAVE DUNCAN**

## *The Gilded Chain: A Tale of the King's Blades*

(New York: Avon Eos, 1998)

**Story type:** Fantasy (Quest; Political)
**Major character(s):** Sir Durendal, Knight (King's Blade), Agent; Ambrose, Royalty (king); Kromman, Wizard (inquisitor), Spy
**Time period(s):** Indeterminate Past
**Locale(s):** Chivial, Fictional Country; Samarinda, Fictional City

**Summary:** Sir Durendal is a King's Blade, a magically enhanced knight bonded for life to protect a single person, who in Durendal's case a useless, foppish nobleman. Despite his inauspicious master, Durendal travels the length of the world, fights terrifying magic and cunning plots, and interferes in the future of his kingdom and king.

**Other books you might like:**
Lisa Goldstein, *Strange Devices of the Sun and Moon*, 1993
Barbara Hambly, *Icefalcon's Quest*, 1998
Ellen Kushner, *Swordspoint*, 1987
Michaela Roessner, *The Stars Dispose*, 1997
Kristine Kathryn Rusch, *The White Mists of Power*, 1991

---

### 1680

**DAVE DUNCAN**

## *Hero*

(New York: Ballantine/Del Rey, 1991)

**Story type:** Science Fiction (Genetic Manipulation; Military)
**Major character(s):** Vaun, Genetically Altered Being, Hero; Feirn, Television Personality; Roker, Military Personnel
**Time period(s):** Indeterminate Future (295th Century of the Empire)
**Locale(s):** Ult, Planet—Imaginary

**Summary:** An unwilling hero in Ult's first contact with the Brotherhood, Vaun finds himself again forced by Roker to save Ult from the Brotherhood's invasion.

**Other books you might like:**
Lois McMaster Bujold, *Barrayar*, 1991
Orson Scott Card, *Ender's Game*, 1985
George Alec Effinger, *When Gravity Fails*, 1987
Stephen Goldin, *Jade Darcy and the Affair of Honor*, 1988
    Mary Mason, co-author
Marc Laidlaw, *Neon Lotus*, 1988
Alis A. Rasmussen, *Revolution's Shore*, 1990
James H. Schmitz, *The Demon Breed*, 1968
Cordwainer Smith, *Norstrilia*, 1975

---

### 1681

**DAVE DUNCAN**

## *The Hunters' Haunt*

(New York: Ballantine Del Rey, 1995)

**Story type:** Fantasy (Adventure)
**Major character(s):** Omar "Trader of Tales" Anglith of Arkraz, Writer, Traveler
**Time period(s):** Indeterminate Past
**Locale(s):** Middle East

**Summary:** To avoid ejection from Hunters' Haunt Inn into a deadly storm, Omar agrees to a story-telling contest in which his tales must prove more entertaining than those of the inn's guests.

**Other books you might like:**
Salman Rushdie, *Haroun and the Sea of Stories*, 1990
Susan Shwartz, *Arabesques: More Tales of the Arabian Nights*, 1988
    editor
Dan Simmons, *Hyperion*, 1989
John Vornholt, *The Fabulist*, 1993
Jack Zipes, *Arabian Nights: The Marvels and Wonders of the Thousand and One Nights*, 1991
    editor

---

### 1682

**DAVE DUNCAN**

## *The Living God*

(New York: Ballantine Del Rey, 1994)

**Story type:** Fantasy (Adventure; Magic Conflict)
**Series:** Handful of Men
**Major character(s):** Rap, Nobleman, Psychic; Zinixo, Mythical Creature (dwarf), Wizard; Emshander V, Ruler (Imperator)
**Time period(s):** Indeterminate Past
**Locale(s):** The Impire, Fictional Country

**Summary:** The awesome power of Zinixo continues to grow as he tracks down the last free wizards and tightens his hold on the Impire. As the mad dwarf's power grows, the hopes of Rap and his outmatched dissidents fail. If they cannot accomplish the seemingly impossible task of revitalizing the Impire, their entire world faces doom.

**Other books you might like:**
Glen Cook, *The Black Company*, 1984
David Eddings, *Pawn of Prophecy*, 1982
Robert Jordan, *The Eye of the World*, 1989
Patricia A. McKillip, *The Riddle-Master of Hed*, 1976
Lawrence Watt-Evans, *The Lure of the Basilisk*, 1980

### 1683

**DAVE DUNCAN**

## *Magic Casement*

(New York: Ballantine/Del Rey, 1990)

**Story type:** Fantasy (Light Fantasy; Adventure)
**Series:** Man of His Word
**Major character(s):** Inosolan ''Inos'', Royalty (princess); Rap, Worker (stableboy), Psychic (seer)
**Time period(s):** Indeterminate Past
**Locale(s):** Krasnegar, Fictional Country; Kinvale, Fictional Country

**Summary:** Inos's peaceful childhood and many friendships, especially with Rap, come to an end when she's sent to Kinvale to learn to be a lady. In the meantime, Rap finds himself ostracized for his new abilities as a seer, befriended only by a newcomer who's almost too charming to be true. When Rap discovers that Inos's father is dying, he and his friend set off for Kinvale, unprepared for the experiences and revelations to come.

**Other books you might like:**
Sheila Gilluly, *Greenbriar Queen*, 1987
Lyndon Hardy, *Master of the Five Magics*, 1980
Mickey Zucker Reichert, *Godslayer*, 1987
Elizabeth Ann Scarborough, *Bronwyn's Bane*, 1983
Will Shetterly, *Liavek*, 1985
    Emma Bull, co-editer

### 1684

**DAVE DUNCAN**

## *Past Imperative*

(New York: AvoNova/Morrow, 1995)

**Story type:** Fantasy (Alternate World)
**Major character(s):** Edward Exeter, Student; Eleal Singer, Singer, Handicapped; Throng Impresario, Entertainer
**Time period(s):** 1910s (1914); Indeterminate
**Locale(s):** Nargh, Fictional City; Fallo, Mythical Place (public school); Alternate Earth

**Summary:** Authorities accuse Edward Exeter of a terrible crime the summer after graduation, while in another world Eleal Singer prays to the Trickster for healing as she travels to an Art Festival. The gods pull them together across the gap between their worlds, to take part in a game whose rules and stakes they don't quite understand.

**Other books you might like:**
Eleanor Arnason, *Daughter of the Bear King*, 1987
Robert A. Heinlein, *Glory Road*, 1993
Will Shetterly, *The Tangled Lands*, 1989
S.P. Somtow, *Riverrun*, 1991
Roger Zelazny, *Nine Princes in Amber*, 1970

### 1685

**DAVE DUNCAN**

## *Perilous Seas*

(New York: Ballantine/Del Rey, 1991)

**Story type:** Fantasy (Light Fantasy; Adventure)
**Series:** Man of His Word
**Major character(s):** Inosolan ''Inos'', Royalty (queen); Rap, Worker (stableboy), Psychic (seer); Kadolan ''Kade'', Royalty (princess), Guardian (Inosolan's aunt)
**Time period(s):** Indeterminate Past
**Locale(s):** Zark, Fictional Country; Dragon Reach, Fictional Country

**Summary:** Inos and Aunt Kade have allied themselves with the true sultan of Zark in an attempt to escape the sorceress Rasha and present their plea to the four Wardens for restoration of Krasnegar and Zark to their rightful rulers. Meanwhile, Rap encounters the fulfillment of the first of three dire prophecies presented by the magic casement.

**Other books you might like:**
Elizabeth H. Boyer, *The Elves and the Otterskin*, 1981
Gordon R. Dickson, *The Dragon and the George*, 1976
Raymond E. Feist, *Magician*, 1982
Barbara Hambly, *Dragonsbane*, 1987
Robert Jordan, *The Eye of the World*, 1989
Patricia C. Wrede, *The Seven Towers*, 1984

### 1686

**DAVE DUNCAN**

## *Present Tense*

(New York: Avon, 1996)

**Story type:** Fantasy (Alternate World)
**Series:** Great Game
**Major character(s):** Edward Exeter, Traveler; Julian Smedley, Military Personnel, Handicapped; Kammaeman, Military Personnel
**Time period(s):** 1910s (1917); Indeterminate
**Locale(s):** England; Alternate Earth

**Summary:** Edward Exeter escapes the perils of the strange world he entered three years earlier. Unfortunately, he returns to Europe during the First World War still wanted for murder. Even worse, the forces that have decreed his destiny want him back enough to kill anyone in two worlds to get him.

**Other books you might like:**
Eleanor Arnason, *Daughter of the Bear King*, 1987
Guy Gavriel Kay, *The Summer Tree*, 1985
Kim Newman, *The Bloody Red Baron*, 1995
Brian Stableford, *The Carnival of Destruction*, 1994
Roger Zelazny, *Nine Princes in Amber*, 1970

### 1687

**DAVE DUNCAN**

## *The Reaver Road*

(New York: Ballantine Del Rey, 1992)

**Story type:** Fantasy (Adventure)
**Major character(s):** Omar ''Trader of Tales'' Anglith of Arkraz, Writer, Traveler; Thorian, Royalty (crown prince), Traveler; Jaxian Tharpit, Government Official, Leader (Zanadon)
**Time period(s):** Indeterminate
**Locale(s):** Zanadon, Fictional City; Spice Lands, Fictional Country

**Summary:** As Omar and Thorian travel together they tell each other fabulous heroic tales about themselves and the war in the Spice Lands.

**Other books you might like:**
Stephen Goldin, *Shrine of the Desert Mage*, 1988
Laurell K. Hamilton, *Nightseer*, 1992
Andrew Lang, *The Arabian Nights Entertainments*, 1969
   editor
Susan Shwartz, *Arabesques: More Tales of the Arabian Nights*, 1988
   editor
Jack Zipes, *Arabian Nights: The Marvels and Wonders of the Thousand and One Nights*, 1991
   editor

---

**1688**

DAVE DUNCAN

## The Stricken Field

(New York: Ballantine Del Rey, 1993)

**Story type:** Fantasy (Adventure; Magic Conflict)
**Series:** Handful of Men
**Major character(s):** Rap, Nobleman, Psychic; Zinixo, Mythical Creature (dwarf), Wizard; Emshander V, Ruler (Imperor)
**Time period(s):** Indeterminate Past
**Locale(s):** The Impire, Fictional Country

**Summary:** Zinixo controls the Impire and almost every magician in the world. A small group of nobles and magicians that oppose him suffer many setbacks and few successes while hoping that help can be found before Zinixo rules everything.

**Other books you might like:**
Glen Cook, *The Black Company*, 1984
David Eddings, *Pawn of Prophecy*, 1982
Robert Jordan, *The Eye of the World*, 1989
Patricia A. McKillip, *The Riddle-Master of Hed*, 1976
Lawrence Watt-Evans, *The Lure of the Basilisk*, 1980

---

**1689**

DAVE DUNCAN

## Strings

(New York: Ballantine/Del Rey, 1990)

**Story type:** Science Fiction (Adventure)
**Major character(s):** Cedric, Teenager; Princess Alya, Royalty
**Time period(s):** 21st century
**Locale(s):** Nauc, Earth

**Summary:** On an Earth stewing in its own pollution, scientists work on developing superstring transportation as a way of escaping the planet. Cedric is a hick from the sticks, but his grandmother is head of the planetary exploration project. Through her he meets the Princess Alya and together they attempt to escape Earth before it collapses.

**Other books you might like:**
Piers Anthony, *But What of Earth?*, 1976
   Revised 1989
Gregory Benford, *Tides of Light*, 1989
Vonda N. McIntyre, *Starfarers*, 1989

---

**1690**

DAVE DUNCAN

## Upland Outlaws

(New York: Ballantine Del Rey, 1993)

**Story type:** Fantasy (Magic Conflict; Political)
**Series:** Handful of Men
**Major character(s):** Rap, Ruler, Psychic; Zinixo, Mythical Creature (dwarf), Wizard; Emshander IV, Ruler (Imperor)
**Time period(s):** Indeterminate Past
**Locale(s):** Hub of the Impire, Fictional City

**Summary:** Chaos and confusion settle on the capital as omens and strange actions warn of a plot against the Impire. When King Rap must go out again to battle the insane Zinixo, this time without his power, he and a small group including the deposed Imperor create a crazy plan that just might save the Millenium.

**Other books you might like:**
Glen Cook, *The Black Company*, 1984
David Eddings, *Pawn of Prophecy*, 1982
Robert Jordan, *The Eye of the World*, 1989
Patricia A. McKillip, *The Riddle-Master of Hed*, 1976
Michael Scott Rohan, *The Forge in the Forest*, 1987

---

**1691**

DAVE DUNCAN

## West of January

(New York: Ballantine/Del Rey, 1989)

**Story type:** Science Fiction (Adventure)
**Major character(s):** Knobil, Wanderer
**Time period(s):** Indeterminate Future
**Locale(s):** Planet—Imaginary

**Summary:** On a strange planet which revolves every 264.6 days and rotates every 263.6 days lives a wide variety of races, cultures, and animals, all originally from Earth. Knobil, son of a herdswoman and, supposedly, an angel, wanders the planet having adventures, some of them exciting, some of them tragic, some of them rather sexy.

**Other books you might like:**
Ronald Anthony Cross, *Prisoners of Paradise*, 1988
R.A. MacAvoy, *The Third Eagle: Lessons Along a Minor String*, 1989
Jack Vance, *Big Planet*, 1957
Jack Vance, *Showboat World*, 1975

---

**1692**

LOIS DUNCAN

## I Know What You Did Last Summer

(New York: Dell Laurel Leaf, 1997)

**Story type:** Horror (Psychological Suspense)
**Major character(s):** Julie James, Teenager; Raymond Bronson, Teenager; Collingsworth Wilson, Young Man
**Time period(s):** 1970s (1973)
**Locale(s):** Silver Spring, New Mexico

**Summary:** On the eve of her graduation from high school, Julie James receives an anonymous note incriminating her in an incident the year before. Julie and her friends must own up to their complicity in the accidental death of a young boy or face the consequences of an unknown accuser who employs potentially deadly methods to extract the truth. Reprint of a young adult novel from 1973 to tie in with its film adaptation in 1997.

**Other books you might like:**
Richie Tankersley Cusick, *The Mall*, 1992
Diane Hoh, *The Accident*, 1991
Christopher Pike, *Chain Letter*, 1986
R.L. Stine, *The Wrong Number*, 1990

## 1693

**LOIS DUNCAN**, Editor

# Night Terrors: Stories of Shadow and Substance

(New York: Simon & Schuster/Aladdin, 1997)

**Story type:** Horror (Anthology; Young Adult)

**Summary:** A renowned writer of horror thrillers for young adult readers assembles 11 tales of suspense and supernatural horror original to the volume. Highlights include Joan Lowery Nixon's "The Dark Beast of Death," a murder mystery involving a teenage girl gang; Annette Curtis Klause's "The Bogey Man," in which a young boy discovers to his dismay why he should have heeded his strict grandmother's injunction not to go down into her cellar; Alane Ferguson's "Satan's Shadow," about a young girl who suffers horrendous nightmares when she turns in her best friend for parricide; and Chris Lynch's "Bearing Paul," about a young boy convinced that he sees the body of his cousin moving in his coffin. Other contributors include Joan Aiken, Theodore Taylor, Patricia Windsor, Richard Peck, Harry Mazer, Norma Fox Mazer, and Madge Harrah. First published in 1996.

**Other books you might like:**
A. Finnis, *Bone Meal: Seven More Tales of Terror*, 1994
   editor
A. Finnis, *The Cat-Dogs*, 1994
   editor
William Mayne, *Supernatural Stories*, 1996
   editor
Dennis Pepper, *The Young Oxford Book of Ghost Stories*, 1994
   editor
T. Pines, *Thirteen*, 1991
   editor
Susan Price, *Horror Stories*, 1995
Robert Westall, *Ghost Stories*, 1993
   editor

## 1694

**J.R. DUNN**

# Days of Cain

(New York: Avon, 1997)

**Story type:** Science Fiction (Time Travel; Disaster)
**Major character(s):** James Gaspar, Time Traveler; Alma Marie Lewin, Time Traveler, Prisoner; Rebeka Motzin, Prisoner
**Time period(s):** 1940s; Indeterminate Future
**Locale(s):** Auschwitz, Poland; M3 Center, Mythical Place; The Moiety, Interstellar Empire/Federation

**Summary:** Alma works to mitigate the brutal treatment of death camp prisoners, recruiting Rebeka to help in her forbidden rescue operation. Meanwhile, Gaspar accepts the assignment of finding Alma, whose renegade operation could change the nature of humanity's future, eventually compromising human dominance in the galaxy.

**Other books you might like:**
Poul Anderson, *The Time Patrol*, 1991
Deborah Christian, *Mainline*, 1996
Kay Kenyon, *The Seeds of Time*, 1997
Fritz Leiber, *The Big Time*, 1961
Kurt Vonnegut Jr., *Slaughterhouse Five*, 1969
Jane Yolen, *Briar Rose*, 1992

## 1695

**J.R. DUNN**

# Full Tide of Night

(New York: Avon Eos, 1998)

**Story type:** Science Fiction (Political; Techno-Thriller)
**Major character(s):** Julia Amalfi, Computer Expert, Leader; Cariola "Cary", Artificial Intelligence; Antonio "Tony" Perin, Revolutionary, Leader
**Time period(s):** 21st century
**Locale(s):** *Petrel*, Spaceship; Midgard, Planet—Imaginary

**Summary:** Recognizing the danger of the Erinye, Julia escapes the solar system with Cary, taking with her genetic material to stock Midgard, barely habitable, with Terran life. Unfortunately, the colonists rebel and Cary has a nervous breakdown after contacting Earth. A ship arrives just as the rebellion comes to a conclusion, leaving Tony to represent Midgard and hope the ship does not bring Erinye.

**Other books you might like:**
Roger MacBride Allen, *Utopia*, 1996
Suzette Haden Elgin, *Twelve Fair Kingdoms*, 1981
Katharine Kerr, *Palace*, 1996
   Mark Kreighbaum, co-author
Wil McCarthy, *Bloom*, 1998
Elizabeth Moon, *Remnant Population*, 1996
John Varley, *Steel Beach*, 1992

## 1696

**J.R. DUNN**

# This Side of Judgment

(New York: Harcourt Brace, 1994)

**Story type:** Science Fiction (Alternate Intelligence; Mystery)
**Major character(s):** Ross Bohlen, Government Official; Jason Telford, Fugitive; Scott Page, Murderer
**Time period(s):** 21st century
**Locale(s):** Ironwood, Montana; Washington, District of Columbia

**Summary:** The recent war to prevent Cybernetically Enhanced Individuals, called CEIs or chipheads, from taking over the world succeeded, but with great loss of life and much destruction. Recognizing the pattern, Bohlen looks for one of the few remaining chipheads who he believes murdered a young girl, while attempting to prevent the death of any innocent CEIs. Unfortunately, all chipheads eventually show symptoms of Pelton's Syndrome from excessive use of the interface, leading to fatal information overload. First novel.

**Other books you might like:**
Alfred Bester, *The Demolished Man*, 1953
Pat Cadigan, *Fools*, 1992
Philip K. Dick, *A Scanner Darkly*, 1977
James Patrick Kelly, *Wildlife*, 1994
Katharine Kerr, *Polar City Blues*, 1990
Frederik Pohl, *The Voices of Heaven*, 1994
Kevin D. Randle, *Mind Slayer*, 1992
   Richard Driscoll, co-author

## 1697

### KATHERINE DUNN

## Geek Love

(New York: Warner, 1990)

**Major character(s):** Olympia Binewski, Parent, Genetically Altered Being; Miranda Binewski, Artist (Medical)
**Time period(s):** 1980s
**Locale(s):** United States

**Summary:** Arturo Binewski and his wife Crystal Lil save the Carnival Fabulon from ruin by breeding their own freaks, products of Lil's ingestion of drugs, insecticides, arsenic, radioactive isotopes, etc. The story of this bizarre, perverse, grotesque, humorous, but also loving and tender menage is told by the dwarfed daughter Olympia, focusing on her own secret maternal love for her vulnerable "normal" daughter, Miranda.

**Other books you might like:**
Angela Carter, *Nights at the Circus*, 1985
William Goyen, *Arcadio*, 1983
Todd Robbins, *"Spurs"*, 1932

## 1698

### PAULINE DUNN (Pseudonym of Susan Hartzell)

## The Crawling Dark

(New York: Zebra, 1991)

**Story type:** Horror (Apocalyptic Horror)
**Major character(s):** Martin Bryant, Student; Sandra Bryant, Restaurateur; Richard O'Brien, Police Officer (sheriff)
**Time period(s):** 1990s
**Locale(s):** Rockville, Tennessee

**Summary:** Martin and Sandra Bryant return to their home town to attend to the burial of their recently deceased father but find all of the townspeople dead from a biologically peculiar organism that can reanimate corpses seemingly at will. Along with the police force of nearby Edgerton, the two become involved in an effort to stop not just what appears on the surface to be an infestation of unknown origin but what may actually be the beginning of the biblical apocalypse.

**Other books you might like:**
Michael Crichton, *The Andromeda Strain*, 1969
Dean R. Koontz, *Phantoms*, 1983

## 1699

### LORD DUNSANY

## The Complete Pegana

(Oakland, California: Chaosium, 1998)

**Story type:** Fantasy (Collection)
**Summary:** This work contains 54 stories originally published between 1905 and 1919, and previously collected piecemeal under other titles. It collects all of Dunsany's stories set in the magical land of Pegana into a single volume. Most of these are extremely short, some little more than sketches, and are among the author's earliest works.

**Other books you might like:**
James Branch Cabell, *The Silver Stallion*, 1926
Henry Kuttner, *Elak of Atlantis*, 1985
Tanith Lee, *Tamastara, or, the Indian Nights*, 1984

William Morris, *Golden Wings and Other Stories*, 1976
Clark Ashton Smith, *Tales of Zothique*, 1995

## 1700

### LORD DUNSANY

## The Hashish Man and Other Stories by Lord Dunsany

(San Francisco: Manic D Press, 1996)

**Story type:** Fantasy (Collection)

**Summary:** Contains a two-page introduction, the "Preface to The Last Book of Wonder" and 25 stories excerpted from *A Dreamer's Tales* (1910), *Fifty-One Tales* (1915) and *The Last Book of Wonder* (1916). The stories' tone generally varies from grim to creepy with themes including chess, dream travel, prophecy, mythology, hunting, and sea voyages.

**Other books you might like:**
Hugh B. Cave, *Murgunstrumm and Others*, 1977
H.P. Lovecraft, *The Best of H.P. Lovecraft: Bloodcurdling Tales of Horror and the Macabre*, 1982
E. Hoffman Price, *Far Lands, Other Days*, 1975
Clark Ashton Smith, *Other Dimensions*, 1970
Clark Ashton Smith, *Tales of Zothique*, 1995
Howard Wandrei, *Time Burial*, 1995

## 1701

### ALAN DURANT, Editor

## Vampire and Werewolf Stories

(New York: Kingfisher, 1998)

**Story type:** Horror (Anthology)

**Summary:** This compilation for young adults features fifteen stories, two novel excerpts and one legend retold from the French, all featuring vampires or werewolves. Selections include Woody Allen's comic vignette "Count Dracula," in which the legendary Count Dracula emerges prematurely during an eclipse; Carl Jacobi's "Revelations in Black," about a man beguiled into romance with a vampire lover; Richard Matheson's "Drink My Blood" (a.k.a. "Blood Son"), in which a young boy's infatuation with vampires leads him to a close encounter with the un-dead; and stories by Saki, Angela Carter, William F. Nolan, Jane Yolen, and Sir Arthur Conan Doyle, among others.

**Other books you might like:**
Anthony Horowitz, *The Puffin Book of Horror Stories*, 1994
   editor
William Mayne, *Supernatural Stories*, 1996
   editor
Dennis Pepper, *The Young Oxford Book of Ghost Stories*, 1994
   editor
Susan Price, *Horror Stories*, 1995
   editor
Robert Westall, *Ghost Stories*, 1993
   editor

## **1702**

### DORANNA DURGIN

## *Barrenlands*

(New York: Baen, 1998)

**Story type:** Fantasy (Magic Conflict; Political)
**Major character(s):** Ehren, Military Personnel (King's Guard); Laine, Military Personnel (King's Guard); Varien, Wizard
**Time period(s):** Indeterminate
**Locale(s):** Solvany, Fictional Country

**Summary:** A member of the King's Guard investigates the assassination of the man he was sworn to protect. Before he can identify the parties responsible, a powerful court wizard orders him to abandon the search and instead help locate and neutralize other members of the royal family. Rather than cooperate with the usurpers, Ehren and Laine pursue their original intention and foil a plot to seize control of their nation.

**Other books you might like:**
Steven Brust, *The Phoenix Guards*, 1991
Simon R. Green, *Blue Moon Rising*, 1991
Robert Jordan, *Lord of Chaos*, 1994
Katherine Kurtz, *Deryni Rising*, 1970
Elizabeth Moon, *Divided Allegiance*, 1988

## **1703**

### DORANNA DURGIN

## *Changespell*

(New York: Baen, 1997)

**Story type:** Fantasy (Alternate World; Magic Conflict)
**Major character(s):** Jess, Animal (horse), Young Woman; Carey, Courier; Jaime Cabot, Horse Trainer
**Time period(s):** Indeterminate
**Locale(s):** Alternate Earth

**Summary:** Back in her own world, Jess works as a human courier, though she can turn herself into a horse through use of a spellstone. In horse form, however, she cannot trigger the spell to make herself human, but must rely on one of her friends. This proves a serious problem when some rogue magicians capture her as part of their experiments on changing animals to humans and vice versa. Jess, Carey, Jaime, and their friends from both worlds team up to put an end to the magicians' schemes and to the use of the dangerous drug "mage lure." Sequel to *Dun Lady's Jess*.

**Other books you might like:**
Eleanor Arnason, *Daughter of the Bear King*, 1987
C.J. Cherryh, *Rider at the Gate*, 1995
Rick Cook, *The Wiz Biz*, 1997
Simon R. Green, *Blue Moon Rising*, 1991
Barbara Hambly, *The Armies of Daylight*, 1983
R.A. MacAvoy, *The Grey Horse*, 1987

## **1704**

### DORANNA DURGIN

## *Dun Lady's Jess*

(New York: Baen, 1994)

**Story type:** Fantasy (Alternate World; Magic Conflict)
**Major character(s):** Carey, Courier; Dun Lady's Jess, Animal (horse), Young Woman; Jaime Cabot, Horse Trainer
**Time period(s):** 1990s; Indeterminate

**Locale(s):** Alternate Earth; Marion, Ohio

**Summary:** Fleeing pursuers who seek to misuse the dangerous spells he carries, Carey and his horse trigger a spell that brings them to an alternate world, along with their pursuers. Separated from Carey and transformed into a human, Jess finds refuge at the Dancing Equine Dressage Center with new friends who help her rescue Carey. But even if Carey finds a way to go back and defeat the evil Calandre, Jess may not want to be a horse again.

**Other books you might like:**
Eleanor Arnason, *Daughter of the Bear King*, 1987
Jude Deveraux, *A Knight in Shining Armor*, 1989
Gordon R. Dickson, *The Dragon and the George*, 1976
C.S. Lewis, *The Magician's Nephew*, 1955
R.A. MacAvoy, *The Grey Horse*, 1987

## **1705**

### DORANNA DURGIN

## *Touched by Magic*

(New York: Baen, 1996)

**Story type:** Fantasy (Magic Conflict; Mystery)
**Major character(s):** Reandn, Guard (King's Wolf), Detective; Rethia, Healer; Farren, Wizard
**Time period(s):** Indeterminate
**Locale(s):** King's Keep, Mythical Place; Keland, Fictional Country

**Summary:** Reandn's investigation into missing children progresses until magical interference destroys Reandn's life. The key to the lost children and the return of the magic, thought long gone, may hinge on a former wizard and a healer familiar with unicorns who took the magic with them on leaving.

**Other books you might like:**
Pamela Dean, *The Dubious Hills*, 1994
Graham Edwards, *Dragoncharm*, 1996
Simon R. Green, *Hawk & Fisher*, 1990
Irene Radford, *The Glass Dragon*, 1994
Melissa Scott, *Point of Hopes*, 1995
    Lisa A. Barnett, co-author

## **1706**

### DORANNA DURGIN

## *Wolf Justice*

(New York: Baen, 1998)

**Story type:** Fantasy (Sword and Sorcery)
**Major character(s):** Reandn, Military Personnel, Bodyguard; Kalena, Noblewoman
**Time period(s):** Indeterminate
**Locale(s):** King's Keep, Fictional City

**Summary:** Reandn leaves military service after a quarrel with his superiors. He accepts a job as bodyguard for a noblewoman during a perilous journey across a land to which magic has suddenly and even disastrously returned. Sequel to *Touched by Magic*.

**Other books you might like:**
Steven Brust, *The Phoenix Guards*, 1991
Raymond E. Feist, *Krondor, the Betrayal*, 1998
Simon R. Green, *Hawk & Fisher*, 1990
Fritz Leiber, *The Swords of Lankhmar*, 1968
Andre Norton, *The Hands of Lyr*, 1994

## 1707
### DAVID DVORKIN

## *Insatiable*
(New York: Pinnacle, 1993)

**Story type:** Horror (Vampire Story)
**Major character(s):** Richard Venneman, Assistant (laboratory), Vampire; Jill Kennedy, Office Worker; Harold "Dirty" Dinsmuir, Scientist (physicist)
**Time period(s):** 1990s (1993)
**Locale(s):** Denver, Colorado

**Summary:** Newly vampirized Richard Venneman tries to kill himself by exposing his body to radiation, but only succeeds in transforming himself into a vampire for whom blood tastes disgusting, and whose victims develop an unquenchable obsession for him.

**Other books you might like:**
Poppy Z. Brite, *Lost Souls*, 1992
Nancy A. Collins, *Sunglasses After Dark*, 1989
John Peyton Cooke, *Out for Blood*, 1991
John Skipp, *The Light at the End*, 1986
    Craig Spector, co-author

## 1708
### DAVID DVORKIN

## *Ursus*
(New York: Franklin Watts, 1989)

**Story type:** Science Fiction (Horror)
**Major character(s):** Mark Adler, Government Official; Phyllis Ortiveda, Police Officer
**Time period(s):** 1980s
**Locale(s):** Piketon, Rocky Mountains

**Summary:** Vicious mini-bears terrorize the Rocky Mountain community of Piketon. The town government, corrupt through and through, seems helpless to stop the killing.

**Other books you might like:**
Stephen King, *Cujo*, 1981
Dean R. Koontz, *Watchers*, 1987

## 1709
### STEFAN DZIEMIANOWICZ, Editor
### ROBERT WEINBERG, Co-Editor
### MARTIN H. GREENBERG, Co-Editor

## *100 Ghastly Little Ghost Stories*
(New York: Barnes & Noble, 1993)

**Story type:** Horror (Anthology; Ghost Story)

**Summary:** The title notwithstanding, this volume contains 101 short-short ghost stories of 300 words or less written since the late-eighteenth century. Representative authors include M.R. James, J. Sheridan Le Fanu, E.F. Benson, H.P. Lovecraft, Henry S. Whitehead, August Derleth, Steve Rasnic Tem, William F. Nolan, and Chet Williamson. Nearly half of the stories were first published in the pages of *Weird Tales*, the premiere magazine of weird fiction between 1923 and 1954. Donald Burleson's "The Pedicab" appears in print for the first time.

**Other books you might like:**
Richard Dalby, *The Mammoth Book of Ghost Stories*, 1990
Richard Dalby, *The Mammoth Book of Ghost Stories 2*, 1991

Al Sarrantonio, *100 Hair-Raising Little Horror Stories*, 1993
    Martin H. Greenberg, co-editor
Sebastian Wolfe, *The Little Book of Horrors*, 1992

## 1710
### STEFAN DZIEMIANOWICZ, Editor
### ROBERT WEINBERG, Co-Editor
### MARTIN H. GREENBERG, Co-Editor

## *100 Twisted Little Tales of Torment*
(New York: Barnes & Noble, 1998)

**Story type:** Horror (Anthology)

**Summary:** This anthology contains 100 short-short story reprints of fantasy, horror and science fiction that span the centuries. Selections include Donald Wandrei's science fiction horror story "The Atom Smasher"; David J. Schow's "Busted in Buttown," about maverick organ harvesters who don't wait for their victims to die; Mary Elizabeth Counselman's "Devil's Lottery," about the satanic doings in a small town; and Ambrose Bierce's psychological suspense story "The Man and the Snake."

**Other books you might like:**
Isaac Asimov, *100 Great Fantasy Short Short Stories*, 1984
    Terry Carr, Martin H. Greenberg, co-editors
Al Sarrantonio, *100 Hair-Raising Little Horror Stories*, 1993
    editor
Sebastian Wolfe, *The Little Book of Horrors*, 1992
    editor

## 1711
### STEFAN DZIEMIANOWICZ, Editor
### ROBERT WEINBERG, Co-Editor
### MARTIN H. GREENBERG, Co-Editor

## *100 Wicked Little Witch Stories*
(New York: Barnes & Noble, 1995)

**Story type:** Horror (Anthology; Witchcraft)

**Summary:** Most of these 100 stories of approximately 3000 words or less are original to the volume. Their different approaches to the witch theme include deep-sea witchcraft (Lois Gresh's "Fish Witch"), doll magic (Kathryn Ptacek's "Poppet"), a bewitched supermarket manager (Adam Niswander's "Bat's Blood for Flavor"), a variation on Cinderella's fairy godmother (Tina L. Jens' "The Princess and the Frog"), medieval witchcraft (Brian McNaughton's "The Conversion of St. Monocarp"), Caribbean witchcraft (Nancy Kilpatrick's "Heartbeat"), and the unexpected effects of magic curses (Nancy and Wayne Holder's "1-900-Witches").

**Other books you might like:**
Richard Dalby, *Tales of Witchcraft*, 1991
Peter Haining, *The Witchcraft Reader*, 1969
Marvin Kaye, *Witches and Warlocks: Tales of Black Magic Old and New*, 1990
Rod Serling, *Rod Serling's Triple W*, 1963
Charles G. Waugh, *Yankee Witches*, 1988
    Martin H. Greenberg, Frank McSherry, Jr., co-editors

## 1712

**STEFAN DZIEMIANOWICZ**, Editor
**ROBERT WEINBERG**, Co-Editor
**MARTIN H. GREENBERG**, Co-Editor

### Famous Fantastic Mysteries
(New York: Gramercy, 1991)

**Story type:** Horror (Anthology; Mystery)

**Summary:** Thirty stories collected from the pulp magazines *Famous Fantastic Mysteries* and *Fantastic Novels*, both of which specialized in reprints of fantasies and scientific romances from the early pulp magazines but also published original fiction. Included are horror classics such as Arthur Machen's black magic story, ''The Novel of the White Powder,'' Robert W. Chamber's extended dreamy tale, ''The King in Yellow,'' and William Hope Hodgson's nautical nightmare, ''The Derelict.'' More modern tales include H.P. Lovecraft's ''The Music of Erich Zann,'' Arthur C. Clarke's ''The Guardian,'' Robert Bloch's ''The Man Who Collected Poe,'' and A. Merritt's rare lost race novella, ''The Face in the Abyss.''

**Other books you might like:**
Tony Goodstone, *The Pulps*, 1970
   editor
Sam Moskowitz, *Hauntings and Horrors*, 1969
   editor
Sam Moskowitz, *Horrors Unknown*, 1971
   editor
Sam Moskowitz, *Masters of Horror*, 1968
   editor
Sam Moskowitz, *Science Fiction by Gaslight*, 1968
   editor

## 1713

**STEFAN DZIEMIANOWICZ**, Editor
**ROBERT WEINBERG**, Co-Editor
**MARTIN H. GREENBERG**, Co-Editor

### Girls' Night Out
(New York: Barnes & Noble, 1997)

**Story type:** Horror (Anthology; Vampire Story)

**Summary:** Twenty-nine classic and contemporary tales featuring female vampires. Outstanding selections include E.F. Benson's ''Mrs. Amworth,'' about a vampire who preys on the aristocrats of Edwardian England; Chet Williamson's ''To Feel Another's Woe,'' about a stage actress who feeds on the adulation of her audience; Fritz Leiber's ''The Girl with the Hungry Eyes,'' in which an advertising model subsists on the desires of the consumer public; Clark Ashton Smith's ''The End of the Story,'' about a vampire who lies in wait for visitors to her ruined castle in medevial France; and Joanna Russ's ''My Dear Emily,'' which equates a young girl's nascent vampirism with her awakening sexual identity.

**Other books you might like:**
Victoria Brownworth, *Night Bites: Vampire Stories by Women*, 1996
   editor
Martin H. Greenberg, *Vamps*, 1987
   Charles G. Waugh, co-editor
Barbara Hambly, *Sisters of the Night*, 1995
   Martin Greenberg, co-editor
Pam Keesey, *Daughters of Darkness: Lesbian Vampire Stories*, 1993
   editor
Pam Keesey, *Darker Angels: Lesbian Vampire Stories*, 1993
   editor

## 1714

**STEFAN DZIEMIANOWICZ**, Editor
**ROBERT WEINBERG**, Co-Editor
**MARTIN H. GREENBERG**, Co-Editor

### Horrors: 365 Scary Stories
(New York: Barnes & Noble, 1998)

**Story type:** Horror (Anthology)

**Summary:** This anthology offers one short-short horror story for each day of the year, none longer than 750 words, embracing a wide range of traditional and non-traditional horror themes. Selections include Phyllis Eisenstein's ''Boxes,'' about gruesome things that come in small packages; Peter Atkins' metaphysical nightmare ''Adventures in Further Education''; Michael Marshall Smith's story of good friends who conspire to commit murder as a party game, ''A Convenient Arrangement''; and Donald Burleson's tale of life after dog death, ''Good Dog.''

**Other books you might like:**
Isaac Asimov, *100 Great Fantasy Short Short Stories*, 1984
   Terry Carr, Martin H. Greenberg, co-editors
Al Sarrantonio, *100 Hair-Raising Little Horror Stories*, 1993
   editor
Sebastian Wolfe, *The Little Book of Horrors*, 1992
   editor

## 1715

**STEFAN DZIEMIANOWICZ**, Editor
**DENISE LITTLE**, Co-Editor
**ROBERT WEINBERG**, Co-Editor

### Mistresses of the Dark
(New York: Barnes & Noble, 1998)

**Story type:** Horror (Anthology)

**Summary:** This anthology includes 25 stories of the macabre by female literary writers of the postwar era. Selections include Patricia Highsmith's ''The Pond,'' about the evil influence that lives in the pond on an estate; Daphne du Maurier's ''Don't Look Now,'' a classic tale of fatal precognition; Angela Carter's ''The Bloody Chamber,'' a modernization of the tale of Bluebeard; and Alison Lurie's tale of parental guilt and ghosts, ''Another Halloween.'' Stories by Margaret Atwood, Joyce Carol Oates, Valerie Martin, A.M. Homes, and Eudora Welty are also included.

**Other books you might like:**
Richard Dalby, *Modern Ghost Stories by Eminent Women Writers*, 1992
   editor
Seon Manley, *Women of the Weird*, 1976
   Gogo Lewis, co-editor
Alan Ryan, *Haunting Women*, 1988
   editor
Jessica Amanda Salmonson, *What Did Miss Darrington See?: An Anthology of Feminist Supernatural Fiction*, 1989
   editor
A. Susan Williams, *The Lifted Veil: The Book of Fantastic Literature by Women*, 1993
   editor

## 1716

STEFAN DZIEMIANOWICZ, Editor
ROBERT WEINBERG, Co-Editor
MARTIN H. GREENBERG, Co-Editor

### Nursery Crimes
(New York: Barnes & Noble, 1993)

**Story type:** Horror (Anthology; Child-in-Peril)

**Summary:** Thirty horror stories of children in peril published over the last century and a half, beginning with J. Sheridan Le Fanu's "The Child Who Went with the Fairies" and running to Steve and Melanie Tem's "Resettling." The many threats posed to the children in these stories include war (Ambrose Bierce's "Chickamauga"), schools (Ramsey Campbell's "The Interloper"), families (Charles Grant's "Everything to Live For"), extradimensional specters (Henry S. Whitehead's "The Trap"), and other children (Stephen Gallagher's "Magpie"). The editors also include two full novels, Henry James' classic ghost story, *The Turn of the Screw*, and Sarban's *The Doll Maker*, reprinted for the first time in over 30 years.

**Other books you might like:**
Vic Ghidalia, *The Devil's Generation*, 1973
Vic Ghidalia, *Little Monsters*, 1969

## 1717

STEFAN DZIEMIANOWICZ, Editor
ROBERT WEINBERG, Co-Editor
MARTIN H. GREENBERG, Co-Editor

### To Sleep, Perchance to Dream. . .Nightmare
(New York: Barnes & Noble, 1993)

**Story type:** Horror (Anthology)

**Summary:** This book collects 30 stories involving dreams or nightmares. The contents range from 19th century tales to contemporary ones. Included are J. Sheridan Le Fanu's "The Drunkard's Dream," about a man who cannot distinguish between a dream and a possible vision of hell; Bram Stoker's "A Dream of Red Hands," about a man whose guilt for a crime he commited manifests as a nightmare; and Wilkie Collins' "The Dream Woman," about a recurrent a dream in which a man envisions his death at the hands of the woman he has married. Also included are to H.P. Lovecraft's "Dreams in the Witch House"; Clark Ashton Smith's "Ubbo Sathla"; Fritz Leiber's "The Dreams of Albert Moreland"; Clive Barker's "In the Flesh," in which dreamers find a way to penetrate other dimensions through their dreams; Thomas Ligotti's "Dream of a Mannikin" and Charles L. Grant's "The Last Dreadful Hour," in which dreamers awaken to find themselves incapable of distinguishing whether the dream world is not actually the real world; Bruce McAllister's "Dream Baby," in which dreams are harnessed as weapons in the Vietnam War; and Scott Bradfield's "Dream of the Wolf," in which a man entrapped by the daily routine of his life finds liberation in his nightly dreams of running with a wolf pack.

**Other books you might like:**
Poul Anderson, *The Night Fantastic*, 1991
    Karen Anderson, co-author
Damon Knight, *Perchance to Dream*, 1973

## 1718

STEFAN DZIEMIANOWICZ, Editor
ROBERT WEINBERG, Co-Editor
MARTIN H. GREENBERG, Co-Editor

### Virtuous Vampires
(New York: Barnes & Noble, 1996)

**Story type:** Horror (Anthology; Vampire Story)

**Summary:** Vampires are the good guys in the 18 reprinted stories assembled here. They apply their nocturnal skills to detective work in Tanya Huff's "This Town Ain't Big Enough" and heal with their bite in Sharon Farber's "A Surfeit of Melancholic Humours" and Spider Robinson's "Pyotr's Story." They protect mortals from Jack the Ripper in Les Daniels' "Yellow Fog" and Harry Turtledove's "Gentlemen of the Shade," from an otherworldly menace in C.L. Moore's "Scarlet Dream," and from humanity's own decadent tendencies in Brian Stableford's "The Hunger and Ecstasy of Vampires." And they help with humor in Henry Kuttner's "Masquerade" and Robert Bloch's "The Cloak."

**Other books you might like:**
Ellen Datlow, *Blood Is Not Enough*, 1989
    editor
Ellen Datlow, *A Whisper of Blood*, 1992
    editor
Martin H. Greenberg, *Vampire Detectives*, 1995
    editor
Alan Ryan, *Vampires: Two Centuries of Great Vampire Stories*, 1988
    editor

## 1719

PAULA E. DOWNING

### Rinn's Star
(New York: Ballantine/Del Rey, 1990)

**Story type:** Science Fiction (Psychic Powers; Political)
**Major character(s):** Rinn McCrea, Telepath; Yuri Ivanovich Selenkov, Spaceship Captain (Zvesta); Lorat, Shaman (Lily People)
**Time period(s):** 24th century
**Locale(s):** Outer Space; Delta Bootis, Planet—Imaginary; Novy Strana, Planet—Imaginary

**Summary:** After her ship is destroyed, Rinn McCrea seeks sanctuary on the Zvesta even though the Russians have proscribed her type (starfarers/telepaths). On Novy Strana, in order to avoid death, she agrees to attempt to get the natives of Delta Bootis to resume trade with the Russians. By psychic meddling with the mind of the tribe's shaman, trade is resumed. Rinn marries Yuri and becomes a permanent member of the Zvesta's crew.

**Other books you might like:**
Poul Anderson, *The Peregrine*, 1978
Jack L. Chalker, *The Demons at Rainbow Bridge*, 1989
C.J. Cherryh, *Rimrunners*, 1989
Cynthia Felice, *The Sunbound*, 1981
Andre Norton, *Voodoo Planet*, 1959
Brian Stableford, *Critical Threshold*, 1977

## 1720

**WILLIAM EAKINS**

### Key West 2720 A.D.

(Pound Ridge, NY: Knights Press, 1989)

**Story type:** Science Fiction (Gay/Lesbian Fiction)
**Major character(s):** Sam Phoe, Government Official, Homosexual; Gibb, Homosexual
**Time period(s):** 28th century (2720)
**Locale(s):** Key West, Florida

**Summary:** The world is run by gigantic corporations and nations have fragmented into city-states. Homosexuals have been excluded from most places, but Sam Phoe, the mayor of Key West, Florida, has given sanctuary to all gays in exile. Now, however, a number of hostile factions are working to bring an end to Sam's rule, some out of homophobia, some out of a simple desire for power.

**Other books you might like:**
Samuel R. Delany, *The Bridge of Lost Desire*, 1987
Samuel R. Delany, *Dhalgren*, 1975
Samuel R. Delany, *The Splendor and Misery of Bodies, of Cities*, 1985
Samuel R. Delany, *Stars in My Pocket Like Grains of Sand*, 1984
Samuel R. Delany, *Triton*, 1976
Lauren Wright Douglas, *In the Blood*, 1989
Joanna Russ, *The Female Man*, 1975
Theodore Sturgeon, *Venus Plus X*, 1960

## 1721

**DANIEL EASTERMAN** (Pseudonym of Denis MacEoin)

### Name of the Beast

(New York: HarperCollins, 1992)

**Story type:** Horror (Apocalyptic Horror)
**Major character(s):** Aisha Manfaluti, Archaeologist (Egyptologist); Michael Hunt, Spy (former M15 agent); al-Qurtubi, Terrorist
**Time period(s):** 1990s (1999)
**Locale(s):** Cairo, Egypt

**Summary:** At the same time fundamentalist terrorist al-Qurtubi ascends to the presidency of Egypt a plague occurs, fulfilling biblical prophecy and reinforcing the rumors that he is the anti-Christ setting the stage for apocalypse in the coming millenium.

**Other books you might like:**
Thomas F. Monteleone, *The Blood of the Lamb*, 1992
Brian Stableford, *The Werewolves of London*, 1990
Robert Weinberg, *The Dead Man's Kiss*, 1992
F. Paul Wilson, *Nightworld*, 1992

## 1722

**M. COLEMAN EASTON**

### Spirits of Cavern and Hearth

(New York: St. Martin's, 1989)

**Story type:** Fantasy (Quest)
**Major character(s):** Yarkol Dolmi, Doctor; Dzaminid, Shaman
**Time period(s):** Indeterminate
**Locale(s):** Alternate Universe

**Summary:** The southern Hakhan farmers are at odds with the nothern Chirudak nomads over lands which are increasingly unable to accommodate each society's growth and lifestyle. War is imminent and only one man, Yarkol Dolmi, can prevent it. Yarkol has attained a mysterious affliction that provides him with mystical powers and gateways to the realm of spirits. He must use his powers to outwit and defeat the underground cavern spirits that have sided with the Chirudak before a peace can be negotiated.

**Other books you might like:**
Vonda N. McIntyre, *Dreamsnake*, 1986
Jonathan Wylie, *Dreams Street*, 1989
Roger Zelazny, *Wizard World*, 1989

## 1723

**THOMAS A. EASTON**

### Greenhouse

(New York: Ace, 1991)

**Story type:** Science Fiction (Genetic Manipulation)
**Series:** Sparrowhawk
**Major character(s):** Tom Cross, Genetically Altered Being, Businessman; Muffy Bowen, Dancer, Captive
**Time period(s):** 2080s (2084)
**Locale(s):** United States

**Summary:** Human genetic experimentation yields a crop of intelligent, aggressive plants with a desire to begin turning their cousins, human beings, into members of the plant kingdom.

**Other books you might like:**
Alfred Bester, *Golem $^{100}$*, 1980
Octavia E. Butler, *Adulthood Rites*, 1988
Octavia E. Butler, *Dawn*, 1987
Octavia E. Butler, *Imago*, 1989
Jack Finney, *The Body Snatchers*, 1955
Janet Kagan, *Mirabile*, 1991
Joan Slonczewski, *A Door into Ocean*, 1986
Cordwainer Smith, *The Best of Cordwainer Smith*, 1975
Cordwainer Smith, *Norstrilia*, 1975
Michael Swanwick, *Vacuum Flowers*, 1987

## 1724

**THOMAS A. EASTON**

### Seeds of Destiny

(New York: Ace, 1994)

**Story type:** Science Fiction (Genetic Manipulation; Political)
**Series:** Sparrowhawk
**Major character(s):** Dotson Barbtail, Alien (Rac), Genetically Altered Being; Marcus Aurelius Hrecker, Scientist; Gypsy Blossom, Genetically Altered Being (plant)
**Time period(s):** 23rd century
**Locale(s):** Belt Center 83, Asteroid; First-Stop, Planet—Imaginary (Tau Ceti system); *Saladin*, Spaceship

**Summary:** With life in the Solar System bleak under the Engineer's rule, when the expedition returns from First-Stop with news of a possibly engineered intelligent species, an expedition to eliminate any abomination and take over First-Stop leaves almost immediately. The Racs at first believe their Remakers have returned but soon discover they must defend themselves.

**Other books you might like:**
Frank Herbert, *The White Plague*, 1982
Janet Kagan, *Mirabile*, 1991
Bill Ransom, *ViraVax*, 1993
Kim Stanley Robinson, *Green Mars*, 1994
Joan Slonczewski, *Daughter of Elysium*, 1993

## THOMAS A. EASTON

## Sparrowhawk

(New York: Ace, 1990)

**Story type:** Science Fiction (Mystery; Genetic Manipulation)
**Series:** Sparrowhawk
**Major character(s):** Bernie Fischer, Detective—Police; Ralph Chowdhury, Scientist (genetic engineer); Emily Gilman, Scientist (genetic engineer)
**Time period(s):** 2040s (2044)
**Locale(s):** United States

**Summary:** To satisfy gambling debts Ralph Chowdhury is forced to secretly engineer devices for the underworld. When Bernie Fischer investigates an attack on commuters by a giant sparrow modified for use as a transport, one witness, Dr. Emily Gilman, proves especially helpful. As they track down the cause behind the suddenly dangerous equipment, Emily herself becomes an obvious target of Chowdhury's lethal constructs. A first novel.

**Other books you might like:**
David Brin, *Startide Rising*, 1983
David Brin, *The Uplift War*, 1987
Philip K. Dick, *Blade Runner*, 1982
Alan Dean Foster, *Cyber Way*, 1990
Katharine Kerr, *Polar City Blues*, 1990
Cordwainer Smith, *Norstrilia*, 1975

## 1726

## THOMAS A. EASTON

## Tower of the Gods

(New York: Ace, 1993)

**Story type:** Science Fiction (First Contact; Genetic Manipulation)
**Series:** Sparrowhawk
**Major character(s):** Pearl Angelica, Genetically Altered Being (Bot); Lois McAlois, Spaceship Captain; Blacktop, Alien (Rac), Genetically Altered Being
**Time period(s):** 22nd century
**Locale(s):** Tau Ceti IV, Planet—Imaginary; *Gypsy*, Spaceship; Montenegro

**Summary:** Pearl Angelica dreams of going to Earth to find bees for *Gypsy* and free everyone from hand fertilizing all plants. After she travels to Earthspace, Engineer kidnappers take her to a barren Earth where they judge her too dangerous to remain. They transport Pearl to the Moon and cage her in public view as a hostage for the Q-drive, which Pearl realizes must be kept out of engineer hands.

**Other books you might like:**
Octavia E. Butler, *Adulthood Rites*, 1988
Octavia E. Butler, *Imago*, 1989
Janet Kagan, *Mirabile*, 1992
Megan Lindholm, *Alien Earth*, 1992
Vonda N. McIntyre, *Metaphase*, 1992
Larry Niven, *Protector*, 1973

## 1727

## THOMAS A. EASTON

## Woodsman

(New York: Ace, 1992)

**Story type:** Science Fiction (Genetic Manipulation)

**Series:** Sparrowhawk
**Major character(s):** Alice Bell, Genetically Altered Being (bot); Frederick Suida, Genetically Altered Being (pig), Human; Lois McAlois, Spaceship Captain
**Time period(s):** 2090s
**Locale(s):** United States; Probe Station, Space Station

**Summary:** Believing that a richer and safer humanity depends upon returning to the good old days of machines, the Engineers have taken over the government, which now ignores the increasing violence against genetically altered beings. Recognizing the imminent destruction of the environment and collapse of the infrastructure which maintains the modestly successful but highly over-populated planet, Earth's intelligent plants prepare their self defense while possible salvation orbits overhead.

**Other books you might like:**
Octavia E. Butler, *Adulthood Rites*, 1988
Octavia E. Butler, *Dawn*, 1987
Octavia E. Butler, *Imago*, 1989
Jack Finney, *The Body Snatchers*, 1955
    pseudonym of Walter Braden Finney
Janet Kagan, *Mirabile*, 1991
James Morrow, *City of Truth*, 1992
Cordwainer Smith, *The Best of Cordwainer Smith*, 1975
Vernor Vinge, *A Fire upon the Deep*, 1992

## JULIA ECKLAR

## The Kobayashi Maru

(New York: Pocket Books, 1989)

**Story type:** Science Fiction (Space Opera)
**Series:** Star Trek
**Major character(s):** James T. Kirk, Spaceship Captain; Sulu, Military Personnel (Spaceship officer)
**Time period(s):** 23rd century
**Locale(s):** *Hailey*, Spaceship; Hohweyn System, Outer Space

**Summary:** A freak accident leaves Captain Kirk and a number of his officers adrift in a shuttlecraft. Hope of rescue is small. With no possibility of saving themselves, Kirk, Sulu, Scotty, and the others pass the time describing their experiences with the Kobayashi Maru, a complex, computer-simulated exam that every student at Starfleet Academy must pass to graduate. This is Ecklar's first novel.

**Other books you might like:**
J.M. Dillard, *Star Trek: The Lost Years*, 1989
J.M. Dillard, *Star Trek V: The Final Frontier*, 1989
Diane Duane, *My Enemy, My Ally*, 1984
    Star Trek 18
D.C. Fontana, *Vulcan's Glory*, 1989
    Star Trek 44

## 1729

## JULIA ECKLAR

## Regenesis

(New York: Ace, 1995)

**Story type:** Science Fiction (Genetic Manipulation; Adventure)
**Major character(s):** Rahel Tovin, Scientist (zoologist), Animal Lover; Paval Kuvasc, Apprentice, Scientist (zoologist)
**Time period(s):** Indeterminate Future
**Locale(s):** New Dallas, Planet—Imaginary; Reyson's Planet, Planet—Imaginary; Uriel, Planet—Imaginary

**Summary:** A proctor for the Noah's Ark project, Rahel travels to various planets to ensure that transplanted Earth species survive in their new homes.

**Other books you might like:**
David Brin, *Startide Rising*, 1983
David Brin, *The Uplift War*, 1987
Orson Scott Card, *Lovelock*, 1994
    Kathryn H. Kidd, co-author
Hal Clement, *Fossil*, 1993
Michael Crichton, *Jurassic Park*, 1990
L.A. Graf, *Caretaker*, 1995
    pseudonym of Julia Ecklar and Karen Rose
L.A. Graf, *Extreme Prejudice*, 1995
    pseudonym of Julia Ecklar and Karen Rose
L.A. Graf, *Traitor Winds*, 1990
    pseudonym of Julia Ecklar and Karen Rose
Janet Kagan, *Mirabile*, 1991

**1730**

**DAVID EDDINGS**
**LEIGH EDDINGS**, Co-Author

**Belgarath the Sorcerer**
(New York: Ballantine Del Rey, 1995)

**Story type:** Fantasy (Adventure)
**Major character(s):** Belgarath, Sorcerer, Adventurer
**Time period(s):** Indeterminate
**Locale(s):** Mallorea, Fictional Country; Arendia, Fictional Country; Sendaria, Fictional Country

**Summary:** Belgarath relates his early life and the events which led to his becoming the world's most powerful sorcerer. Set prior to events in *Paw of Prophecy*.

**Other books you might like:**
Steven Brust, *The Phoenix Guards*, 1991
Raymond E. Feist, *Magician*, 1982
Robert Jordan, *The Eye of the World*, 1989
Michael Scott Rohan, *The Anvil of Ice*, 1986
J.R.R. Tolkien, *The Silmarillion*, 1977

**1731**

**DAVID EDDINGS**

**The Diamond Throne**
(New York: Del Rey, 1989)

**Story type:** Fantasy (Quest)
**Series:** Elenium
**Major character(s):** Sparhawk, Knight (Queen's Champion); Sephrenia, Sorceress
**Time period(s):** Indeterminate
**Locale(s):** Elenia, Planet—Imaginary

**Summary:** After a 10 year absence, Sparhawk returns to Elenia, only to find his queen in a state near death. Sephrenia has enclosed the queen in crystal to slow her death, but she and Sparhawk have a limited amount of time to try and find a cure.

**Other books you might like:**
Carole Nelson Douglas, *Keepers of Edanvant*, 1989
    Book 3 - Sword and Circulate
Sharon Green, *Hellhound Magic*,
Peter Morwood, *The Horse Lord*, 1986
    Book 1 - The Book of Years Series

Jonathan Wylie, *Dreams of Stone*,
    Book 1 of Unbalanced Earth Series
Jonathan Wylie, *The Lightless Kingdom*, 1989
    Book 2 of Unbalanced Earth Series

**1732**

**DAVID EDDINGS**

**Domes of Fire**
(New York: Ballantine Del Rey, 1993)

**Story type:** Fantasy (Quest)
**Series:** Tamuli
**Major character(s):** Sparhawk, Knight; Ehlana, Royalty (queen)
**Time period(s):** Indeterminate
**Locale(s):** Elenia, Fictional Country; Tamul Empire, Fictional Country

**Summary:** When threats face Elenia and the Tamul Empire, Sparhawk journeys to Tamuli with a large entourage including family, Pandion Knights, government officials, warriors and the Tamuli Ambassador. Sequel to The Elenium Series (1989-1992).

**Other books you might like:**
Dave Duncan, *The Cutting Edge*, 1992
Dave Duncan, *Magic Casement*, 1990
Barbara Hambly, *Dragonsbane*, 1987
Barbara Hambly, *The Time of the Dark*, 1982
Robert Jordan, *The Eye of the World*, 1989
Elizabeth Moon, *Sheepfarmer's Daughter*, 1988
Roger Zelazny, *Nine Princes in Amber*, 1970

**1733**

**DAVID EDDINGS**

**The Hidden City**
(New York: Ballantine Del Rey, 1994)

**Story type:** Fantasy (Magic Conflict; Adventure)
**Series:** Tamuli
**Major character(s):** Sparhawk, Knight, Parent (Aphrael's); Aphrael, Deity, Child; Bhelliom "Blue Rose", Mythical Creature (elemental)
**Time period(s):** Indeterminate
**Locale(s):** Arjuna, Fictional Country; Natayos, Fictional City; Cyrga, Fictional City (the Hidden City)

**Summary:** To gain control of Bhelliom, the jewel of power, the deity, Cyrgon, directs his minions to kidnap Sparhawk's wife, Queen Ehlana, and brings back into the world the banished monster, Klael. While Bhelliom battles its opposite force, Klael, Sparhawk must personally defeat Cyrgon to gain the return of Ehlana.

**Other books you might like:**
Glen Cook, *The Black Company*, 1984
Dave Duncan, *The Cutting Edge*, 1992
Raymond E. Feist, *Magician*, 1982
Terry Goodkind, *Wizard's First Rule*, 1994
Robert Jordan, *The Eye of the World*, 1989

## 1734

### DAVID EDDINGS
### LEIGH EDDINGS, Co-Author

## *Polgara the Sorceress*
(New York: Ballantine Del Rey, 1997)

**Story type:** Fantasy (Adventure; Political)
**Major character(s):** Polgara, Sorceress, Adventurer
**Time period(s):** Indeterminate
**Locale(s):** Kingdoms of the West, Mythical Place; Arendia, Fictional Country

**Summary:** Seeking to complement her father, Belgarath the Sorcerer's, account of events and hoping future rulers will avoid the mistakes of the past, Polgara relates events from her extraordinary life, from youngster to accomplished shapechanger and Duchess of Erat.

**Other books you might like:**
Steven Brust, *The Phoenix Guards*, 1991
Terry Goodkind, *Stone of Tears*, 1995
Robert Jordan, *The Eye of the World*, 1990
Patricia A. McKillip, *The Sorceress and the Cygnet*, 1991

## 1735

### DAVID EDDINGS
### LEIGH EDDINGS, Co-Author

## *The Rivan Codex*
(New York: Ballantine Del Rey, 1998)

**Story type:** Fantasy (Collection)
**Major character(s):** Belgarath, Sorcerer
**Time period(s):** Indeterminate
**Locale(s):** Fictional Country

**Summary:** This collection contains a 16-page introduction, a 30-page preface titled "The Personal History of Belgarath the Sorcerer" and six parts: "The Holy Books," "The Histories," "The Battle of Vo Mimbre," "Preliminary Studies to the Malloreon," "The Malloreon Gospels" and "A Summary of Current Events," which discuss the history, culture, background, geography and myths associated with the Belgariad and Malloreon milieu.

**Other books you might like:**
Robert Jordan, *The World of Robert Jordan's The Wheel of Time*, 1997
  Teresa Patterson, co-author
Katherine Kurtz, *The Deryni Archives*, 1986
Mercedes Lackey, *Sword of Ice and Other Tales of Valdemar*, 1997 editor
J.R.R. Tolkien, *The Silmarillion*, 1977
J.R.R. Tolkien, *Unfinished Tales of Numenor and Middle-Earth*, 1980

## 1736

### DAVID EDDINGS

## *The Ruby Knight*
(New York: Ballantine/Del Rey, 1991)

**Story type:** Fantasy (Quest)
**Series:** Elenium
**Major character(s):** Sparhawk, Knight (Queen's Champion); Sephrenia, Sorceress; Talen, Thief

**Time period(s):** Indeterminate
**Locale(s):** Elenia, Planet—Imaginary

**Summary:** When Ehlana, Queen of Elenia, was poisoned, a spell to sustain her life was fashioned. The protective spell's time was rapidly running out when Sparhawk discovered that Ehlana's cure is the Bhelliom, a great jewel lost five hundred years ago. Sparhawk and his company of adventurers set off to ask the ghosts of those who knew of the jewel where it could be found. As they search for the jewel, their way is obstructed by Azash, an evil god not sympathetic to their efforts.

**Other books you might like:**
Carole Nelson Douglas, *Keepers of Edanvant*, 1989
Sharon Green, *Hellhound Magic*, 1989
Peter Morwood, *The Horse Lord*, 1986
Jonathan Wylie, *The Lightless Kingdom*, 1989
Jonathan Wylie, *Dreams of Stone*, 1987

## 1737

### DAVID EDDINGS

## *The Sapphire Rose*
(New York: Ballantine/Del Rey, 1990)

**Story type:** Fantasy (Adventure; Political)
**Series:** Elenium
**Major character(s):** Sparhawk, Knight; Ehlana, Royalty (queen)
**Time period(s):** Indeterminate
**Locale(s):** Elenia, Planet—Imaginary

**Summary:** Having secured Bhelliom, the magic jewel needed to free Queen Ehlana from her slow poisoning, Sparhawk discovers himself betrothed to Ehlana. After arranging for a home guard, Sparhawk and the Pandion Knights move to protect the Church's throne from takeover by the Primate, Annias. That completed, Sparhawk prepares to use Bhelliom to destroy the god Azash, while the goddess Aphrael makes new plans for Sparhawk and Ehlana.

**Other books you might like:**
Steven Brust, *Phoenix*, 1990
Marc Laidlaw, *Neon Lotus*, 1988
Elizabeth Moon, *Divided Allegiance*, 1988
Elizabeth Moon, *Oath of Gold*, 1989
Elizabeth Moon, *Sheepfarmer's Daughter*, 1988
Persia Woolley, *Guinevere: The Legend in Autumn*, 1991

## 1738

### DAVID EDDINGS

## *The Seeress of Kell*
(New York: Del Rey, 1991)

**Story type:** Fantasy (Quest)
**Series:** Malloreon
**Major character(s):** Garion, Wizard (Shape-Changer), Royalty (Rivan King); Zandramas, Sorceress
**Time period(s):** Indeterminate
**Locale(s):** Mallorea, Fictional Country; Kell, Fictional Country

**Summary:** Garion and his companions continue their quest to recover Garion's infant son and heir as time runs out. They overcome the minions of the dark forces, allowing a final confrontation between good and evil. Much time is spent tying up loose, but not too pressing, ends.

**Other books you might like:**
Raymond E. Feist, *Magician*, 1982
Elizabeth Moon, *Divided Allegiance*, 1989

Elizabeth Moon, *Oath of Gold*, 1988
Elizabeth Moon, *Sheepfarmer's Daughter*, 1988
J.R.R. Tolkien, *The Return of the King*, 1956
J.R.R. Tolkien, *The Two Towers*, 1955
J.R.R. Tolkien, *The Fellowship of the Ring*, 1954

## 1739
### DAVID EDDINGS

## Sorceress of Darshiva
(New York: Del Rey, 1989)

**Story type:** Fantasy (Quest)
**Series:** Malloreon
**Major character(s):** Garion, Wizard (Shape-changer), Royalty (Rivan King)
**Time period(s):** Indeterminate
**Locale(s):** Mallorea, Fictional Country; Kell, Fictional Country

**Summary:** Garion, Child of the Light, sets out to rescue his infant son, kidnapped by the sorceress Zandramas, Child of the Dark. He and his companions must battle their enemies as they race against time to rescue the child before Zandramas uses him in a ritual that will assure the dominance of the Dark Forces.

**Other books you might like:**
Louise Cooper, *Nemesis*, 1989
Guy Gavriel Kay, *The Summer Tree*, 1985
   1st Book - The Fionavar Tapestry
J.R.R. Tolkien, *The Lord of the Rings Trilogy*,

## 1740
### SCOTT EDELMAN

## Suicide Art
(West Warwick, Rhode Island: Necronomicon Press, 1992)

**Story type:** Horror (Collection)

**Summary:** A pair of horror stories that reflect metafictionally on the ways in which horror writers seek to fulfill the expectations of readers. ''The Suicide Artist'' is a first person account of an abusive upbringing that blurs the boundaries between real and imagined terrors. ''The Unkindest Cut'' tells of a sex transplant recipient who experiences an unusual type of phantom limb phenomena.

**Other books you might like:**
Dennis Etchison, *Metahorror*, 1992
   editor
Eric Garber, *Embracing the Dark*, 1991
   editor

## 1741
### TERESA EDGERTON

## The Castle of the Silver Wheel
(New York: Ace, 1993)

**Story type:** Fantasy (Magic Conflict; Romance)
**Major character(s):** Gwenlliant, Wizard; Tryffin fab Maelgwyn, Royalty, Government Official (Governor of Mochdreff)
**Time period(s):** Indeterminate
**Locale(s):** Ynys Celydonn, Fictional Country

**Summary:** When Tryffin returns to Mochdreff with his new bride, Gwenlliant, human and magical forces begin attempting to tear them apart and destroy Gwenlliant. With her knowledge of the ancient

Wild Magic and of herself, Gwenlliant works to overcome the sorcery she believes wrought by Tryffin's supposed mistress. First of a trilogy.

**Other books you might like:**
Marion Zimmer Bradley, *The Mists of Avalon*, 1983
L.E. Modesitt Jr., *The Towers of the Sunset*, 1992
Josepha Sherman, *Child of Faerie, Child of Earth*, 1992
Persia Woolley, *Queen of the Summer Stars*, 1990

## 1742
### TERESA EDGERTON

## The Gnome's Engine
(New York: Ace, 1991)

**Story type:** Fantasy (Adventure; Romance)
**Series:** Goblin Moon
**Major character(s):** Sera Vorder, Gentlewoman; Francis Skelbrooke, Adventurer, Rake; Haakon Skogskra, Nobleman, Monster
**Time period(s):** 18th century
**Locale(s):** Euterpe, Alternate Earth; The New World, Alternate Earth

**Summary:** A direct sequel to *Goblin Moon*, this novel continues the mix of Regency-style romance and adventure. Skelbrooke has a series of adventures, while the rest of the heroes flee from Euterpe to the New World to escape their enemies. The story comes to a climax with an attempt to raise the sunken land of Panterra using a strange blend of magic and science.

**Other books you might like:**
Emma Bull, *War for the Oaks*, 1987
Katherine Kurtz, *Deryni Rising*, 1970
Ursula K. Le Guin, *A Wizard of Earthsea*, 1968
Judith Tarr, *Alamut*, 1989
Patricia C. Wrede, *Mairelon the Magician*, 1991
Patricia C. Wrede, *Sorcery and Cecelia*, 1988
   Caroline Stevermer, co-author

## 1743
### TERESA EDGERTON

## Goblin Moon
(New York: Ace, 1991)

**Story type:** Fantasy (Political)
**Series:** Green Lion
**Major character(s):** Caleb Braun, Worker; Sera Vorder, Gentlewoman; Gottfried Jenk, Scholar
**Time period(s):** Indeterminate Past
**Locale(s):** Thornberry-on-the-Lunn, Alternate Earth

**Summary:** Caleb Braun finds a body floating on the river. The body, that of a magician who had his books with him, is brought to Gottfried Jenk, a collector of curiosities. Both the commoners and the aristocracy of Thornberry become magically threatened.

**Other books you might like:**
Constance Ash, *The Stalking Horse*, 1990
Elizabeth Cleghorn Gaskell, *Cranford*, 1976
Ursula K. Le Guin, *A Wizard of Earthsea*, 1968
Judith Tarr, *Ars Magica*, 1989
Jack Vance, *Madouc*, 1990

## 1744

### TERESA EDGERTON

## *The Grail and the Ring*

(New York: Ace, 1994)

**Story type:** Fantasy (Mystery; Alternate World)
**Major character(s):** Gwenlliant, Wizard
**Time period(s):** Indeterminate
**Locale(s):** Ynys Celydonn, Fictional Country; Shadow Land, Mythical Place

**Summary:** When the power of an ancient ring transports Gwenlliant and her infant son to the Shadow Realm, she discovers an evil predator of Celydonn children. To save herself and the children, Gwenlliant must unravel the mystery of the ring.

**Other books you might like:**
Pamela Dean, *The Secret Country*, 1985
Rose Estes, *Troll-Taken*, 1993
Terry Goodkind, *Wizard's First Rule*, 1994
Laurell K. Hamilton, *Nightseer*, 1992
Holly Lisle, *Minerva Wakes*, 1994

## 1745

### TERESA EDGERTON

## *The Moon in Hiding*

(New York: Ace, 1989)

**Story type:** Fantasy (Quest)
**Series:** Green Lion
**Major character(s):** Telerini Pendaron, Apprentice, Wizard
**Time period(s):** Indeterminate Past (Medieval)
**Locale(s):** Wales

**Summary:** A group of people come together to fight a menace that threatens their survival. The situation is more out of control than in the first novel and the people are less certain of their course of action.

**Other books you might like:**
Katherine Kurtz, *The Harrowing of Gwynedd*, 1989
Robert E. Vardeman, *Phantoms on the Wind*,
Margaret Weis, *The Lost King*, 1990

## 1746

### TERESA EDGERTON

## *The Work of the Sun*

(New York: Ace, 1990)

**Story type:** Fantasy (Quest)
**Series:** Green Lion
**Major character(s):** Teleri ni Pendaron, Sorceress; Ceilyn mac Cuel, Knight, Werewolf; Diaspad, Royalty
**Time period(s):** Indeterminate Past (Middle Ages)
**Locale(s):** Kingdom of Celydonn, Fictional Country (legendary Celtic kingdom)

**Summary:** The heroes msut stop the evil princess' last attempt to steal the throne of Calydonn, this time with the help of a powerful artifact. Strong alchemical themes run through the story, which pays close attention to the emotional and moral changes of its characters.

**Other books you might like:**
Orson Scott Card, *Seventh Son*, 1987
Lindsay Clarke, *The Chymical Wedding*, 1989
Monica Furlong, *Wise Child*, 1987

Barbara Hambly, *The Armies of Daylight*, 1983
Barbara Hambly, *The Time of the Dark*, 1982
Barbara Hambly, *The Walls of Air*, 1983

## 1747

### ROSEMARY EDGHILL

## *The Cup of Morning Shadows*

(New York: DAW, 1995)

**Story type:** Fantasy (Alternate World; Quest)
**Series:** Twelve Treasures
**Major character(s):** Ruth Marlowe, Librarian, Student; Nic Brightlaw, Librarian, Military Personnel; Rohannan Melior, Mythical Creature (clf), Nobleman
**Time period(s):** 1990s (1995)
**Locale(s):** Ippisiqua, New York; Elphame, Mythical Place; Elfland, Mythical Place

**Summary:** Once touched by the magical land of Elphame, Ruth finds her way back, this time followed by her boss. She wants to find Melior, the elf she loves, but Elphame's impending civil war interferes. Ruth's discovery of the power behind the turmoil only increases her problems.

**Other books you might like:**
Eleanor Arnason, *Daughter of the Bear King*, 1987
Peter S. Beagle, *The Folk of the Air*, 1986
Emma Bull, *War for the Oaks*, 1987
Gordon R. Dickson, *The Dragon and the George*, 1976
Barbara Hambly, *The Time of the Dark*, 1982

## 1748

### ROSEMARY EDGHILL

## *The Sword of Maiden's Tears*

(New York: DAW, 1994)

**Story type:** Fantasy (Quest)
**Series:** Twelve Treasures
**Major character(s):** Ruth Marlowe, Librarian, Student; Rohannan Melior, Mythical Creature (elf)
**Time period(s):** 1990s
**Locale(s):** New York, New York; Elphame, Mythical Place

**Summary:** When Ruth Marlowe finds Rohannan Melior after muggers have taken the magical sword entrusted to his family, Ruth and her friends help Melior recover the powerful tool which has enslaved its human wielder, turning him into a golem.

**Other books you might like:**
Peter S. Beagle, *The Folk of the Air*, 1986
Elizabeth Forrest, *Phoenix Fire*, 1992
Fred Saberhagen, *The Sixth Book of Lost Swords: Mindsword's Story*, 1990
Fred Saberhagen, *The Second Book of Swords*, 1983

## 1749

### GRAHAM EDWARDS

## *Dragoncharm*

(New York: HarperPrism, 1996)

**Story type:** Fantasy (Magic Conflict; Political)

**Major character(s):** Fortune, Mythical Creature (dragon), Adventurer; Scope, Mythical Creature (dragon), Adventurer; Cumber, Mythical Creature (dragon), Adventurer
**Time period(s):** Indeterminate
**Locale(s):** Covamere, Mythical Place (fortress); Fictional Country

**Summary:** As the predicted time of treachery and conflict between Natural and Charmed dragons approaches, Fortune seeks a missing companion before plunging into the strife which could spell the end of the dragons' presence in the world. First novel.

**Other books you might like:**
Gael Baudino, *Dragonsword*, 1988
Thorarinn Gunnarsson, *Dragon's Domain*, 1993
Irene Radford, *The Glass Dragon*, 1994
Christopher Rowley, *Bazil Broketail*, 1992
Lawrence Watt-Evans, *The Blood of a Dragon*, 1991

## 1750

### GEORGE ALEC EFFINGER

### The Exile Kiss

(New York: Doubleday Foundation, 1991)

**Story type:** Science Fiction (Mystery; Dystopian)
**Series:** Marid Audran
**Major character(s):** Marid Audran, Assistant, Bodyguard; Friedlander Bey, Businessman, Organized Crime Figure (vicelord)
**Time period(s):** 23rd century
**Locale(s):** Africa (Budayeen (red-light district), North Africa); Africa (Arabian Desert)

**Summary:** Marid and Friedlander Bey are betrayed by Shaykh Reda Abu Adil and sent into exile to die in the Arabian Desert. While living with the Bedouin on his journey back to his home, Marid learns harsh truths about himself and he returns to the Budayeen prepared to exact revenge on those who betrayed him.

**Other books you might like:**
Pat Cadigan, *Mindplayers*, 1987
William Gibson, *Neuromancer*, 1984
John Shirley, *Eclipse*, 1987
John Shirley, *Eclipse Penumbra*, 1988
John Shirley, *Eclipse Corona*, 1990
Bruce Sterling, *Islands in the Net*, 1988
Walter Jon Williams, *Hardwired*, 1986

## 1751

### GEORGE ALEC EFFINGER

### A Fire in the Sun

(New York: Doubleday Foundation, 1989)

**Story type:** Science Fiction (Mystery)
**Major character(s):** Marid Audran, Police Officer, Bodyguard; Friedlander Bey, Criminal, Businessman
**Time period(s):** 21st century
**Locale(s):** Africa (Budayeen, the red-light district of a Middle-Eastern city)

**Summary:** Once a small-time hood living in the slums, Marid is now Friedlander Bey's eyes and ears in the local police department. His employer's power, however, seems to be crumbling. Chaos has disrupted the tightly-regulated graft and corruption of the Budayeen—a mad killer is loose and Friedlander Bey lies mysteriously ill. Abu Adil, a major rival, may be behind the trouble. Marid must get to the bottom of the mystery, though it may cost him his life.

**Other books you might like:**
Richard Bowker, *Dover Beach*, 1987
William Gibson, *Neuromancer*, 1984
Norman Spinrad, *Little Heroes*, 1987
F. Paul Wilson, *Dydeetown World*, 1989

## 1752

### GEORGE ALEC EFFINGER

### Maureen Birnbaum, Barbarian Swordsperson: The Complete Stories

(Austin, Texas: Swan Press, 1993)

**Story type:** Fantasy (Collection; Light Fantasy)
**Major character(s):** Maureen Birnbaum, Heroine, Martial Arts Expert

**Summary:** Contains a three-page introduction by Mike Resnick and individual introductions by Effinger to the eight stories, including one original, one revised and six reprinted from 1980s and 1990s periodicals and a conference program book. Stories feature a scantily clad, sword wielding heroine with a passion for shopping and settings devised by Robert Adams, Isaac Asimov, Edgar Rice Burroughs and H.P. Lovecraft and legends surrounding the Holy Grail and Robin Hood.

**Other books you might like:**
Jack L. Chalker, *The Red Tape War*, 1991
    Mike Resnick, George Alec Effinger, co-authors
Alan Dean Foster, *Glory Lane*, 1987
Randall Garrett, *Takeoff!*, 1979
Randall Garrett, *Takeoff, Too*, 1986
Tom Holt, *Flying Dutch*, 1992
Larry Niven, *The Flight of the Horse*, 1973

## 1753

### GEORGE ALEC EFFINGER, Editor

### The Old Funny Stuff

(Eugene, Oregon: Pulphouse Publishing, 1989)

**Story type:** Science Fiction (Collection)
**Series:** Author's Choice Monthly

**Summary:** This slim volume includes an introduction by the author, one original work of fiction, "CHESS.BAT: A New Wave Story," and five other short stories, all published between 1982 and 1985 in such magazines as *Twilight Zone*, *Isaac Asimov's Science Fiction Magazine*, and *The Magazine of Fantasy and Science Fiction*. The best known stories in the volume are probably "Mars Needs Beatniks" and "The Aliens Who Knew, I Mean, Everything."

**Other books you might like:**
Edward Bryant, *Neon Twilight*, 1989
    Author's Choice Monthly. Issue 7
Edward Bryant, *Particle Theory*, 1980
Philip K. Dick, *The Collected Stories of Philip K. Dick*, 1987
George R.R. Martin, *Portraits of His Children*, 1987
Robert Sheckley, *Is THAT What People Do? The Selected Short Stories of Robert Sheckley*, 1984

**1754**

### GEORGE ALEC EFFINGER

## *The Zork Chronicles*

(New York: Avon, 1990)

**Story type:** Science Fiction (Science Fantasy; Humor)
**Series:** Infocom
**Major character(s):** Glorian, Companion; Mirakles, Hero; Spike, Companion
**Time period(s):** Indeterminate
**Locale(s):** Great Underground Empire, Fictional Country

**Summary:** Mirakles, with his trusty magic sword, is off on a quest for the Dipped Switch. Prodded along by his companion Glorian, they make their way through the Great Underground Empire encountering the Dragon's Lair, the Wizard's Workroom, the Kimono Dragon and the Warm Boot of Frobozz.

**Other books you might like:**
Robin Wayne Bailey, *Enchanter*, 1989
Arthur Byron Cover, *Planetfall*, 1988
Arthur Byron Cover, *Stationfall*, 1989
Brian Daley, *The Doomfarers of Coramonde*, 1977
Brian Daley, *Starfollowers of Coramonde*, 1979
Robert A. Heinlein, *Glory Road*, 1963
Michael Moorcock, *Elric of Melnibone*, 1976

**1755**

### DORIS EGAN

## *The Gate of Ivory*

(New York: DAW Books, 1989)

**Story type:** Science Fiction (Science Fantasy)
**Series:** Ivory
**Major character(s):** Theodora of Pyrene, Student; Ran Cormallon, Wizard
**Time period(s):** Indeterminate Future
**Locale(s):** Ivory, Planet—Imaginary

**Summary:** Theodora, an anthropology student, is accidentally stranded on the planet Ivory and, in order to support herself, sets up as a reader of Tarot cards. She soon discovers, however, that not all the magic users on the planet are fakes, that magic and high technology appear to exist side by side. The wizard Ran Cormallon befriends her and the two set off on a series of adventures.

**Other books you might like:**
Marion Zimmer Bradley, *The Shattered Chain*, 1976
Marion Zimmer Bradley, *Thendara House*, 1983
Christopher Stasheff, *The Warlock in Spite of Himself*, 1969
Christopher Stasheff, *The Warlock Insane*, 1969
Christopher Stasheff, *The Warlock Wandering*, 1986
Roger Zelazny, *Jack of Shadows*, 1971

**1756**

### DORIS EGAN

## *Guilt-Edged Ivory*

(New York: DAW, 1992)

**Story type:** Science Fiction (Mystery; Science Fantasy)
**Series:** Ivory
**Summary:** When Theodora learned that her sister-in-law could be forced to accept a co-wife, she realized that she could not wait to

discover Ivoran genetic compatibility with mainstream humans. When the oldest son drowns as a result of sorcery at a party given by the prospective bride's family, Ran, accused of the murder, contracts to prove his innocence while Theodora endeavors to find the murderer.

**Other books you might like:**
Lois McMaster Bujold, *Barrayar*, 1991
Lois McMaster Bujold, *Shards of Honor*, 1986
Cheryl J. Franklin, *Fire Crossing*, 1991
Rosemary Kirstein, *The Steerswoman*, 1989
Alis A. Rasmussen, *A Passage of Stars*, 1990

**1757**

### DORIS EGAN

## *Two-Bit Heroes*

(New York: DAW, 1992)

**Story type:** Science Fiction (Adventure; Science Fantasy)
**Series:** Ivory
**Major character(s):** Theodora of Pyrene, Scholar, Bride; Ran Cormallon, Wizard; Stereth Tar'krim, Outlaw
**Time period(s):** Indeterminate Future
**Locale(s):** Ivory, Planet—Imaginary

**Summary:** Theodora of Pyrene and her half-husband Ran Cormallon, sent to ferret out information about Vere Atvalid, are captured by the notorious bandit Stereth Tar'krim who Vere Atvalid's father is pursuing. While Ran sulks, Theodora gives direction to the outlaw band by telling them of Robin Hood. Eventually Theodora and Ran escape and work to affect solutions.

**Other books you might like:**
L. Sprague de Camp, *The Swords of Zinjaban*, 1991
  Catherine Crook de Camp, co-author
Cynthia Felice, *Double Nocturne*, 1986
M.A. Foster, *The Warriors of Dawn*, 1975
Mary Gentle, *Golden Witchbreed*, 1984
Colin Kapp, *The Wizard of Anharitte*, 1973
Lee Killough, *Liberty's World*, 1985
Melissa Scott, *The Kindly Ones*, 1987
Sydney J. Van Scyoc, *Feather Stroke*, 1989

**1758**

### GREG EGAN

## *Axiomatic*

(New York: HarperPrism, 1997)

**Story type:** Science Fiction (Collection)

**Summary:** Contains two original and 16 stories reprinted from 1990-1992 periodicals. From downbeat to humorous in tone, the stories feature a variety of themes including genetic manipulation, time travel, dolphin communication, "designer children," religion and "the reversal."

**Other books you might like:**
Paul Di Filippo, *Fractal Paisleys*, 1997
Alan Lightman, *Einstein's Dreams*, 1993
James Morrow, *Bible Stories for Adults*, 1996
Rebecca Ore, *Alien Bootlegger and Other Stories*, 1993
Allen Steele, *All-American Alien Boy*, 1996
Connie Willis, *Impossible Things*, 1994

### GREG EGAN

## Diaspora

(New York: HarperPrism, 1998)

**Story type:** Science Fiction (Alternate Intelligence; Robot Fiction)
**Major character(s):** Yatima, Artificial Intelligence, Orphan; Paolo, Robot, Traveler; Blanca, Artificial Intelligence, Scientist (mathematician)
**Time period(s):** 30th century (2970s); Indeterminate Future
**Locale(s):** Konishi, Fictional City (polis-Earth AI colony); Ashton-Laval, Outer Space (polis); Atlanta, Georgia

**Summary:** To promote diversity within the polis, Konisha produces orphans. Unique (as Konisha destroys his pattern when he decides to leave Earth), the Orphan Yatima continues to study the Truth Mine. After the death of all flesh humans on Earth, Yatima searches for the knowledge of the Transmuters, whose abandoned technology both created the solar system and caused its death.

**Other books you might like:**
Stephen Baxter, *The Time Ships*, 1996
David Brin, *Heaven's Reach*, 1998
Emily Devenport, *GodHeads*, 1998
Frederik Pohl, *The Voices of Heaven*, 1994
Robert J. Sawyer, *Starplex*, 1996

### 1760
### GREG EGAN

## Distress

(New York: HarperPrism, 1997)

**Story type:** Science Fiction (Genetic Manipulation)
**Major character(s):** Andrew Worth, Journalist, Filmmaker; Violet Mosala, Scientist; Akili, Genetically Altered Being (Asex)
**Time period(s):** 2050s (2055)
**Locale(s):** Stateless, Fictional City; Sydney, Australia

**Summary:** A weary documentary filmmaker takes a job covering a science conference intended to create a new Theory of Everything. Not surprisingly, some people fear that a new TOE will redefine everything and, literally, remake the world. Surprisingly, when Andrew Worth starts to link "Distress" and rippling bouts of anxiety with the new TOE, it seems the paranoiacs might be right. First published in the United Kingdom in 1995.

**Other books you might like:**
Greg Bear, *Blood Music*, 1985
John Brunner, *The Shockwave Rider*, 1975
Pat Cadigan, *Synners*, 1991
Ian McDonald, *Terminal Cafe*, 1994
Maureen F. McHugh, *Half the Day Is Night*, 1994

### 1761
### GREG EGAN

## Permutation City

(New York: HarperPrism, 1995)

**Story type:** Science Fiction (Cyberpunk; Alternate Intelligence)
**Major character(s):** Paul Durham, Computer Expert; Maria Deluca, Computer Expert; Thomas Riemann, Disembodied Personality (cyberspace copy)
**Time period(s):** 2050s (2050)

**Locale(s):** Elysium, Cyberspace (computer virtual reality); Sydney, Australia

**Summary:** Trying to perfect and understand cyberspace, Paul Durham sends copies of himself there as experiments in continuous consciousness and sensory experience, sending the fourth copy after the first three bail out. Paul meets Maria who develops an evolutionary mutative process for computer life which results in alien inhabitants and personal flexibility in Elysium.

**Other books you might like:**
Jean Mark Gawron, *Dream of Glass*, 1993
James P. Hogan, *Realtime Interrupt*, 1995
Mary Rosenblum, *Chimera*, 1993
Melissa Scott, *Trouble and Her Friends*, 1994
Neal Stephenson, *Snow Crash*, 1992
Thomas T. Thomas, *ME: A Novel of Self Discovery*, 1991

### 1762
### GREG EGAN

## Quarantine

(New York: Harper Prism, 1995)

**Story type:** Science Fiction (Cyberpunk; Post-Disaster)
**Major character(s):** Nick Stavrianos, Police Officer (retired), Detective—Private; Laura Andrews, Patient (mental)
**Time period(s):** 2060s (2067)
**Locale(s):** Perth, Australia; New Hong Kong, Australia

**Summary:** Bio-enhanced while he was a policeman and further supplemented after the death of his wife, Nick takes a job to find Laura, who has been kidnapped from a mental institution. Suspecting the Children of the Bubble, a group organized after a bubble formed around the solar system, Nick finds himself co-opted by the Ensemble who install a loyalty chip, with unexpected results. Reprint of 1992 British edition.

**Other books you might like:**
John Barnes, *Kaleidoscope Century*, 1995
Philip K. Dick, *Ubik*, 1969
George Alec Effinger, *When Gravity Fails*, 1987
James P. Hogan, *The Multiplex Man*, 1992
Robert Reed, *Beyond the Veil of Stars*, 1994

### 1763
### EHREN M. EHLY

## Star Prey

(New York: Zebra, 1992)

**Story type:** Horror (Serial Killer)
**Major character(s):** Adrian Finesse, Actor; Jose Fuentes, Police Officer; Tamsin Weatherby, Actress
**Time period(s):** 1990s (1992)
**Locale(s):** Hollywood, California

**Summary:** Down-and-out B-movie actor Adrian Finesse was clearly too convincing in his last performance as a spirit channeler at a house party—now, movie starletts are dying bloody deaths that only make sense if one assumes that he has summoned the spirit of Jack the Ripper to contemporary Hollywood.

**Other books you might like:**
Robert Bloch, *The Shooting Star*, 1956
Robert Bloch, *The Star Stalker*, 1968
Gardner Dozois, *Ripper!*, 1988
  Susan Casper, co-editor

## 1764

**RANDY LEE EICKHOFF**

### The Raid

(New York: Forge, 1997)

**Story type:** Fantasy (Legend)
**Major character(s):** Cuchlainn, Warrior, Teenager
**Time period(s):** 1st century
**Locale(s):** Ulster, Ireland; Connacht, Ireland

**Summary:** When the theft of a magical bull in a bid for power precipitates warfare, only Cuchlainn can save the province of Ulster from the Connacht invasion.

**Other books you might like:**

Kenneth C. Flint, *A Storm upon Ulster*, 1981
Morgan Llywelyn, *Red Branch*, 1989
Diana L. Paxson, *Master of Earth and Water*, 1993
    Adrienne Martin-Barnes, co-author
Evangeline Walton, *The Children of Llyr*, 1971

## 1765

**PHYLLIS EISENSTEIN**

### In the Red Lord's Reach

(New York: NAL Signet, 1989)

**Story type:** Fantasy (Sword and Sorcery)
**Major character(s):** Alaric, Minstrel, Warlock
**Time period(s):** Indeterminate
**Locale(s):** Mythical Place

**Summary:** In this sequel to *Born to Exile*, Alaric wanders into the Red Lord's valley, only to join up with a nomadic band of reindeer herders. He realizes that he must use his magic talents to overthrow the reign of the Red Lord and restore peace to the valley.

**Other books you might like:**

Marion Zimmer Bradley, *Lythandedeer People*, 1986
Esther Friesner, *The Water King's Laughter*, 1989
Megan Lindholm, *The Reindeer People*, 1988
Anne McCaffrey, *Drangonsinger*, 1977
Manly Wade Wellman, *John the Balladeer*,

## 1766

**PHYLLIS EISENSTEIN**, Editor

### Spec-Lit: Speculative Fiction, Number 1

(Chicago: Columbia College Chicago, 1997)

**Story type:** Science Fiction (Anthology)

**Summary:** Contains a four-page editorial, "Into the Unknown" by Eisenstein, brief introductions to "Living Alone in the Jungle" by A.J. Budrys, "The Changeling" by Gene Wolfe, and 15 original stories by emerging writers from Eisenstein's science fiction writing classes at Columbia College of Chicago, 1989-1995. Frequently downbeat in tone, the stories feature diverse themes including relationships, gambling, religion, the end of the world, physical and philosophical metamorphoses, and policing driven by quotas and profit.

**Other books you might like:**

Algis Budrys, *L. Ron Hubbard Presents Writers of the Future, Volumes I-VIII*, 1985-1992
    editor

John Kessel, *Intersections: The Sycamore Hill Anthology*, 1996
    Mark L. Van Name and Richard Butner, co-editors
Robin Scott Wilson, *Clarion I-III*, 1971-1973
    editor
Robin Scott Wilson, *Those Who Can: A Science Fiction Reader*, 1973
    editor

## 1767

**PHYLLIS EISENSTEIN**, Editor

### Spec-Lit: Speculative Fiction, Number 2

(Chicago: Columbia College, 1998)

**Story type:** Science Fiction (Anthology)

**Summary:** This anthology contains a three-page introduction by Eisenstein and individual introductions to two reprinted stories: Alfred Bester's "The Roller Coaster" and George R.R. Martin's "In the House of the Worm." It also includes 12 originals by Eisenstein and emerging writers from her science fiction writing classes at Columbia College of Chicago from 1989 through 1995, including E. Michael Blake and Valerie J. Freireich. Frequently dark in tone, the stories explore diverse themes such as aliens, sex, death, technology, life in space, masquerade, virtual reality gaming, horror, and surreal prognostication.

**Other books you might like:**

Algis Budrys, *L. Ron Hubbard Presents Writers of the Future, Volumes I-VIII*, 1985-1992
    editor
David G. Hartwell, *Northern Stars: The Anthology of Canadian Science Fiction*, 1994
    Glenn Grant, co-editor
John Kessel, *Intersections: The Sycamore Hill Anthology*, 1996
    Mark L. Van Name, Richard Butner, co-editors
Robin Scott Wilson, *Clarion I-III*, 1971-1973
    editor
Robin Scott Wilson, *Those Who Can: A Science Fiction Reader*, 1993
    editor

## 1768

**GORDON EKLUND**

### A Thunder on Neptune

(New York: Morrow, 1989)

**Story type:** Science Fiction (First Contact)
**Major character(s):** Danny Hawkins, Child, Explorer; Samuel Goble, Scientist
**Time period(s):** 21st century
**Locale(s):** Mars; Neptune

**Summary:** Human beings are transformed on a molecular level and sent to the planet Neptune in an attempt to contact a mysterious alien race. When the first expedition ends in disaster—one man disappears, the other is driven insane—a second expedition is mounted using children on the theory that they will be more easily able to adapt to a radically different environment.

**Other books you might like:**

Octavia E. Butler, *Adulthood Rites*, 1988
Robert A. Heinlein, *Farmer in the Sky*, 1950
Robert A. Heinlein, *Red Planet*, 1949
Frederik Pohl, *Jem*, 1979
Frederik Pohl, *Man Plus*, 1976

## 1769

### SUZETTE HADEN ELGIN

## *Earthsong*

(New York: DAW, 1994)

**Story type:** Science Fiction (Political)
**Series:** Native Tongue
**Major character(s):** Delina Meloran Chornyak, Linguist, Scientist; Will Bluecrane, Indian, Chieftain; Nazareth Joanna Chornyak, Disembodied Personality (deceased)
**Time period(s):** 24th century (2300s)
**Locale(s):** Ozarks; Meander, Arkansas

**Summary:** After the aliens leave and quarantine humanity for persistent use of violence, Delina contacts the recently deceased Nazareth through a PICOTA ritual. Delina learns that the women of the linguists' lines must marry PICOTA men and join PICOTA families and that humanity requires a cure for hunger to eliminate violence.

**Other books you might like:**
Octavia E. Butler, *Parable of the Sower*, 1993
Helen Collins, *Mutagenesis*, 1993
Nicola Griffith, *Ammonite*, 1993
Janet Kagan, *Mirabile*, 1992
Joan Slonczewski, *Daughter of Elysium*, 1993
Joan Slonczewski, *A Door into Ocean*, 1986
Sheri S. Tepper, *Raising the Stones*, 1990

## 1770

### ELTON ELLIOTT, Editor

## *Nanodreams*

(New York: Baen, 1995)

**Story type:** Science Fiction (Anthology; Hard Science Fiction)

**Summary:** Contains a three-page preface and a two-page afterword by the editor, a nine-page foreword by John G. Cramer, a four-page introduction by Dr. K. Eric Drexler, three essays, and seven original and five stories reprinted from periodicals 1983-1992. Frequently optimistic in tone, the stories explore possible and wondrous effects of nanotechnology. Authors include Kevin J. Anderson, Poul Anderson, Greg Bear, Richard E. Geis, Charles Sheffield, Dave Smeds, and Marc Stiegler.

**Other books you might like:**
Kevin J. Anderson, *Assemblers of Infinity*, 1993
    Doug Beason, co-author
Greg Bear, *Blood Music*, 1985
Michael Flynn, *The Nanotech Chronicles*, 1991
Robert L. Forward, *Rocheworld*, 1990
Marc Stiegler, *The Gentle Seduction*, 1990

## 1771

### KATE ELLIOTT (Pseudonym of Alis A. Rasmussen)

## *An Earthly Crown*

(New York: DAW, 1993)

**Story type:** Science Fiction (Arts; Adventure)
**Series:** Jaran
**Major character(s):** Ilyakoria "Ilya" Bakhtiian, Leader, Barbarian; Terese "Tess" Soerensen, Heiress, Linguist; Diana Brooke-Holt, Actress
**Time period(s):** Indeterminate Future
**Locale(s):** Rhui, Planet—Imaginary (Delta Pavonis); Earth

**Summary:** Failed revolutionary, now a duke in the alien Chapalii Empire which rules Earth, Charles Soerensen visits Rhui, a primitive world that constitutes part of the fiefdom granted him by the Emperor. Taking a theater company with him as cover, he goes to meet his sister, Tess, officially declared dead, who has secretly remained on Rhui to marry Ilya. The actors hide their advanced technology as they accompany Ilya and his people on their path of conquest, while Charles travels to an ancient site that contains information about the ancient activities of Chapalii on the planet, information which could help bring freedom for all humanity. The story continues in *His Conquering Sword*.

**Other books you might like:**
Octavia E. Butler, *Dawn*, 1987
C.J. Cherryh, *The Faded Sun: Kesrith*, 1978
Cynthia Felice, *The Khan's Persuasion*, 1991
Mary Gentle, *Golden Witchbreed*, 1984
Ursula K. Le Guin, *The Left Hand of Darkness*, 1969
Alis A. Rasmussen, *The Price of Ransom*, 1990
Alis A. Rasmussen, *Revolution's Shore*, 1990
Christopher Stasheff, *A Company of Stars*, 1991
Christopher Stasheff, *We Open on Venus*, 1994

## 1772

### KATE ELLIOTT

## *Jaran*

(New York: DAW, 1992)

**Story type:** Science Fiction (Adventure)
**Major character(s):** Terese "Tess" Soerensen, Scholar, Noblewoman; Ilyakoria "Ilya" Bakhtiian, Barbarian; Cha Ishil Hokokul, Alien (Chapelli)
**Time period(s):** Indeterminate Future
**Locale(s):** Rhui, Planet—Imaginary

**Summary:** An unexpected stop maroons Tess thousands of miles from her intended destination. Rescued by Ilya, Tess accompanies Ilya and his three companions on a nearly lethal journey. She is again saved by Ilya however, and falls in love with him. Author's first novel, set on the same world as *An Earthly Crown*.

**Other books you might like:**
L. Sprague de Camp, *The Hand of Zei*, 1963
Paula E. Downing, *Rinn's Star*, 1990
Cynthia Felice, *The Khan's Persuasion*, 1991
Jacqueline Lichtenberg, *Dushau*, 1985
Ann Maxwell, *Fire Dancer*, 1982
Anne McCaffrey, *Killashandra*, 1985
Kathy Tyers, *Firebird*, 1987
Ted White, *The Sorceress of Qar*, 1966

## 1773

### KATE ELLIOTT (Pseudonym of Alis A. Rasmussen)

## *King's Dragon*

(New York: DAW, 1997)

**Story type:** Fantasy (Magic Conflict; Political)
**Series:** Crown of Stars
**Major character(s):** Alain, Bastard Son, Military Personnel (soldier); Liath, Courier (King's Eagle)
**Time period(s):** Indeterminate
**Locale(s):** Wendar, Fictional Country

**Summary:** As royal siblings jostle for control, strife envelops the land. After her father's murder, Liath escapes her unpleasant fate to become an elite messenger, while Alain's life changes when the invaders who sack his monastery send him off to become a soldier. Fate thrusts both of them into unexpected roles in the destiny of their land.

**Other books you might like:**
Lynn Flewelling, *Luck in the Shadows*, 1996
Robin Hobb, *Assassin's Apprentice*, 1995
J.V. Jones, *The Baker's Boy*, 1995
Melanie Rawn, *Dragon Prince*, 1988
Melanie Rawn, *The Golden Key*, 1997
    Jennifer Roberson, Kate Elliott, co-authors
Martha Wells, *The Element of Fire*, 1993

---

### 1774

**KATE ELLIOTT** (Pseudonym of Alis A. Rasmussen)

## The Law of Becoming

(New York: DAW, 1994)

**Story type:** Science Fiction (Political; Adventure)
**Series:** Jaran
**Major character(s):** Terese "Tess" Soerensen, Ruler; Vasily "Vasha" Kireyevsky, Warrior, Bastard Son; Anatoly Sakhalin, Warrior, Nobleman
**Time period(s):** Indeterminate Future
**Locale(s):** Rhui, Planet—Imaginary; London, England

**Summary:** Eight years after her brother's "death" on the interdicted world of Rhui, Tess Soerensen rules her brother's lands and collects information for the hoped-for rebellion against the alien Chapalli Empire, while concealing the advanced technology she uses in her "library." Tess' husband Ilya expands his conquests and alliances on Rhui, while Vasha tries to earn his father's approval through military exploits, only proving his worth in captivity. Having left Rhui to join his wife, Anatoly Sakhalin experiences culture shock before exploring the virtual reality world of "nesh," leading Anatoly to a meeting with the Chapali Emperor and a new role in the Game of Princes.

**Other books you might like:**
C.J. Cherryh, *The Faded Sun: Shon'Jir*, 1978
Gordon R. Dickson, *Way of the Pilgrim*, 1987
Jane S. Fancher, *Harmonies of the 'Net*, 1992
Mary Gentle, *Ancient Light*, 1987
Alis A. Rasmussen, *A Passage of Stars*, 1990

---

### 1775

**KATE ELLIOTT**

## Prince of Dogs

(New York: DAW, 1998)

**Story type:** Fantasy (Alternate World; Political)
**Series:** Crown of Stars
**Major character(s):** Sanglant, Military Personnel (captain), Immortal; Liant, Sorceress; Alain, Nobleman
**Locale(s):** Wendar, Fictional Country; Varre, Fictional Country

**Summary:** The immortal Sanglant has been captured by the enemies of his nation. Elsewhere his friends struggle with separate battles, building an army, protecting secret knowledge, and interpreting prophetic visions of the increasingly violent war that threatens them all.

**Other books you might like:**
Marion Zimmer Bradley, *Lady of Avalon*, 1997
Raymond E. Feist, *Prince of the Blood*, 1990

Terry Goodkind, *Blood of the Fold*, 1996
Robert Jordan, *A Crown of Swords*, 1996
Janny Wurts, *Fugitive Prince*, 1997

---

### 1776

**TOM ELLIOTT**

## The Dwelling

(New York: St. Martin's, 1989)

**Story type:** Horror (Haunted House)
**Major character(s):** Katy McClure, Photographer (Police photographer); Ben Thibodeaux, Aged Person
**Time period(s):** 1980s (Flashbacks to 1931, 1958, 1967)
**Locale(s):** Creque Bayou, Louisiana

**Summary:** Three individuals—a police photographer, a fugitive, and a disgraced ex-college professor—are drawn to an old house in rural Louisiana, where they are possessed by a revenge-obsessed entity. There they are all forced to confront not only their own foulest experiences and deepest fears, but also those of their corrupt fathers, who committed a terrible crime in the house over thirty years previously. This is Elliott's first novel.

**Other books you might like:**
Jack Cady, *The Well*, 1980
Richard Matheson, *Hell House*, 1971

---

### 1777

**BRETT EASTON ELLIS**

## American Psycho

(New York: Vintage, 1990)

**Story type:** Horror (Serial Killer)
**Major character(s):** Patrick Bateman, Businessman, Serial Killer; Timothy Price, Businessman (Wall Street fast-tracker); Donald Kimball, Detective—Private
**Time period(s):** 1990s (1990)
**Locale(s):** New York, New York

**Summary:** By day privileged, fashion-conscious Patrick Bateman makes a killing on Wall Street. By night, he translates his predatory impulses into a string of brutal and sadistic murders.

**Other books you might like:**
Robert Bloch, *Psycho*, 1959
John Farris, *The Axman Cometh*, 1989
Ira Levin, *Sliver*, 1991
David J. Schow, *The Kill Riff*, 1988

---

### 1778

**BRETT EASTON ELLIS**

## The Informers

(New York: Alfred A. Knopf, 1994)

**Story type:** Horror (Vampire Story)
**Major character(s):** Dirk Erickson, Vampire; Martin, Producer (video); Christie, Student
**Time period(s):** 1980s
**Locale(s):** Los Angeles, California

**Summary:** Graham, Christie, Martin, Bruce and Cheryl are twenty-something Los Angelenos who tan by day, eat at all the fashionable restaurants by evening, take designer drugs by night, have reckless and indifferent sex, and help shape a culture so amoral that the vampires they number among their friends seem no worse than they are.

**Other books you might like:**
Poppy Z. Brite, *Lost Souls*, 1992
Anne Rice, *The Vampire Lestat*, 1985
Dan Simmons, *Carrion Comfort*, 1989

---

**1779**

JACK ELLIS

## *Nightlife*

(New York: Zebra, 1996)

**Story type:** Horror (Vampire Story)
**Major character(s):** Richard Carnitch, Vampire; Simon Babych, Clerk (in a bookstore); Becky Rutman, Administrator (homeless shelter manager)
**Time period(s):** 1990s (1996)
**Locale(s):** Minneapolis, Minnesota

**Summary:** Richard Carnitch, a vampire who consumes the entire bodies of his victims, preys on the homeless who live on the streets of Minneapolis. Outrage over his activities draws together various friends of the homeless, who act as an unlikely band of vampire hunters.

**Other books you might like:**
George C. Chesbro, *Bone*, 1989
Don Davis, *Bring on the Night*, 1993
    Jay Davis, co-author
Roxanne Longstreet, *The Undead*, 1993
Rick R. Reed, *Penance*, 1993
Wayne Allen Sallee, *The Holy Terror*, 1992
John Skipp, *The Light at the End*, 1986
    Craig Spector, co-author

---

**1780**

JACK ELLIS

## *Seeing Eye*

(New York: Zebra, 1995)

**Story type:** Horror (Wild Talents; Psychological Suspense)
**Major character(s):** Campbell Knight, Businessman (car dealership owner); Hope Matheson, Animal Lover (humane society worker)
**Time period(s):** 1990s (1995)
**Locale(s):** Battle Lake, Minnesota

**Summary:** Campbell Knight agrees to undergo a radical experiment to restore his sight that entails hooking implants in his brain to the visual cortex of his seeing-eye dog, Shadow. When Campbell begins ''seeing'' visions in which a psychotic woman imprisons and abuses small children in her basement, he realizes that Shadow is privy to a world whose whereabouts he must discover and make known to the police.

**Other books you might like:**
H.B. Gilmour, *The Eyes of Laura Mars*, 1978
Stephen King, *The Dead Zone*, 1979
Dean R. Koontz, *The Vision*, 1977
Dean R. Koontz, *Watchers*, 1987

---

**1781**

TERRY ELLIS

## *Invasion of Willow Wood Springs*

(Santa Monica, CA: Roundtable, 1989)

**Story type:** Fantasy (Adventure)
**Series:** Willow Wood Springs
**Time period(s):** 1980s (1989)
**Locale(s):** Alternate Earth (Reath (Fantasy version of Earth))

**Summary:** After Reath is invaded by evil beings who have the power of mind control, a group of juvenile friends set out on a dangerous journey to find allies to defeat the evil ones.

**Other books you might like:**
John Christopher, *The White Mountains*, 1967
    Vol 1 - The Tripods Trilogy
Tanya Huff, *Gate of Darkness, Circle of Light*, 1989
R.A. Salvatore, *Echoes of the Fourth Magic*, 1990

---

**1782**

HARLAN ELLISON

## *''Repent, Harlequin!'' Said the Ticktockman*

(Grass Valley, California: Underwood Books, 1997)

**Story type:** Science Fiction (Dystopian; Humor)
**Major character(s):** The Ticktockman, Government Official (Master Timekeeper); Everett C. ''Harlequin'' Marm, Revolutionary, Activist
**Time period(s):** 25th century
**Locale(s):** Earth

**Summary:** In a society obsessed with effciency, the Ticktockman keeps track of incidents which cause people to be late and assigns blame, allowing automatic execution of those deemed to have excessively wasted the time of others. Through a series of humorous distractions, the Harlequin hopes to alert a complacent populace to the stagnation infecting their society, if the Ticktockman does not find him first. Deluxe quarto edition planned to commemorate the 30th anniversary of the story, but issued two years late. Contains a four-page foreword and brief afterword by the author.

**Other books you might like:**
Philip K. Dick, *The Man Who Japed*, 1956
Alan Harrington, *Life in the Crystal Palace*, 1959
Aldous Huxley, *Brave New World*, 1932
George Orwell, *1984*, 1949
Jack Williamson, *The Humanoids*, 1996
    expanded

---

**1783**

HARLAN ELLISON

## *Angry Candy*

(New York: NAL Plume, 1989)

**Story type:** Horror (Collection)

**Summary:** Seventeen stories published between 1980 and 1988, plus a moving meditation on the death of friends, ''Introduction: The Wind Took Your Answer Away.'' Most impressive are ''Palladin of the Lost Hour,'' a poignant story about an old man and a watch that freezes time (winner in its TV version of a Writers Guild Most Outstanding Teleplay Award), ''Soft Monkey,'' about a bag lady stalked by mobsters in Manhattan, "Function of Dream Sleep" about a young man who wakes and sees a secret mouth filled with teeth opening in his skin, and "Laugh Track," a moving story about a young man's quest to release his aunt's soul, captured in her laugh, from imprisonment on the laugh tracks of bad sitcoms.

**Other books you might like:**
George R.R. Martin, *Songs the Dead Men Sing*, 1983
David J. Schow, *Seeing Red*, 1990

---

**1784**

**HARLAN ELLISON**

## The City on the Edge of Forever
(Gulf Breeze, Florida: Borderlands Press, 1995)

**Story type:** Science Fiction (Space Opera; Time Travel)
**Series:** Star Trek
**Major character(s):** James T. Kirk, Spaceship Captain, Time Traveler; Spock, Scientist, Alien (Vulcan)
**Time period(s):** 23rd century; 1930s
**Locale(s):** Planet—Imaginary; Chicago, Illinois

**Summary:** Contains a spirited Ellison introduction, the original script for the Star Trek teleplay, two prefatory treatments and two scenes Ellison added at producer Gene Roddenberry's request, plus comments by four original *Star Trek* writers and four original cast members. Kirk and Spock must use an alien dimensional doorway to rescue the ship's doctor and repair unintentional damage to their time continuum.

**Other books you might like:**
Douglas Adams, *The Original Hitchhiker's Radio Scripts*, 1985
Roger Elwood, *Six Science Fiction Plays*, 1976
    editor
Kurt Vonnegut Jr., *Between Time and Timbuktu*, 1972
Kurt Vonnegut Jr., *Happy Birthday, Wanda June*, 1970
Robert Anton Wilson, *Reality Is What You Can Get Away With: An Illustrated Screenplay*, 1992

---

**1785**

**HARLAN ELLISON**
**ISAAC ASIMOV**, Illustrator
**MARK ZUG**, Illustrator

## I, Robot: The Illustrated Screenplay
(New York: Warner Aspect, 1994)

**Story type:** Science Fiction (Robot Fiction)
**Series:** Robot
**Major character(s):** Susan Calvin, Computer Expert, Psychologist (robopsychologist); Robert Bratenahl, Journalist (*Cosmos* magazine); Norman Bogert, Reanimated Dead (cryonically frozen), Scientist
**Time period(s):** 21st century
**Locale(s):** Earth; Aldebaran-C XII, Planet—Imaginary; Galactic Federation, Interstellar Empire/Federation

**Summary:** Contains a three-page introduction by Asimov, a 10-page introduction by Ellison, a chronology of events 1952-2076 and the unproduced screenplay adapted by Ellison in 1978 from four Asimov stories, "Robbie," "Runaround," "Liar" and "Lenny," which offer glimpses into Susan Calvin's life and her relationships with robots. Illustrations include 16 color plates by Mark Zug with indication of the plates' locations within the text plus camera and viewpoint directions.

**Other books you might like:**
John Brunner, *Stand on Zanzibar*, 1968
Roger Elwood, *Six Science Fiction Plays*, 1976
    editor
Kurt Vonnegut Jr., *Between Time and Timbuktu*, 1972
Kurt Vonnegut Jr., *Happy Birthday, Wanda June*, 1970
Robert Anton Wilson, *Reality Is What You Can Get Away With: An Illustrated Screenplay*, 1992

---

**1786**

**HARLAN ELLISON**

## Mefisto in Onyx
(Shingletown, California: Mark Ziesing, 1993)

**Story type:** Horror (Serial Killer; Wild Talents)
**Major character(s):** Rudy Pairis, Psychic (mind reader); Allison Roche, Lawyer (deputy district attorney); Henry Lake Spanning, Convict
**Time period(s):** 1990s (1993)
**Locale(s):** Atmore, Alabama (Holman Prison)

**Summary:** At the urging of his friend District Attorney Allison Roche, mindreader Rudy Pairis reluctantly agrees to "jaunt" into the mind of Henry Lake Spanning, a serial killer whom Allison helped put on death row but now believes is innocent of the crimes for which he was convicted. This novella appeared earlier in 1993 in *Omni* magazine.

**Other books you might like:**
Rene Belletto, *Machine*, 1993
Damon Knight, *Mind Switch*, 1963
Curt Siodmak, *Gabriel's Body*, 1988
F. Paul Wilson, *Sibs*, 1992

---

**1787**

**HARLAN ELLISON**
**JACEK YERKA**, Illustrator

## Mind Fields: The Art of Jacek Yerka
(Beverly Hills, California: Morpheus International, 1994)

**Story type:** Fantasy (Collection; Horror)

**Summary:** Contains 33 original stories and a three-page "Afterthoughts" by Ellison, inspired by 33 surreal paintings by Yerka. Despite ironic humor, the tone of the stories reflect Yerka's dark vision, with themes including anti-Semitism as a historical and contemporary force, classical myth and urban life.

**Other books you might like:**
Richard Brautigan, *In Watermelon Sugar*, 1968
Harry Harrison, *Planet Story*, 1979
Marlen Haushofer, *The Wall*, 1991
    Shaun Whiteside, translator
Cordwainer Smith, *The Rediscovery of Man*, 1993
Jane Yolen, *Briar Rose*, 1992

## 1788

**HARLAN ELLISON**
**JACK DANN**, Co-Author
**JACK C. HALDEMAN II**, Co-Author

### Run for the Stars/Echoes of Thunder

(New York: Tor, 1991)

**Story type:** Science Fiction (Horror; Hard Science Fiction)
**Major character(s):** Benno Tallant, Experimental Subject; John Stranger, Indian (Mohawk), Construction Worker (orbital)
**Time period(s):** Indeterminate Future
**Locale(s):** Deald's World, Planet—Imaginary; Space Station

**Summary:** This book contains "Run for the Stars" by Harlan Ellison plus "Echoes of Thunder" by Jack Dann and Jack C. Haldeman II. In "Run for the Stars," retreating Terran forces, desperate to stop the Kyben armada heading toward Earth, modify unlikely hero Benno Tallant by implanting a cataclysmic bomb inside his body then turning him loose to be found by the Kyben. In "Echoes of Thunder," a corporation exercises its option to draft John Stranger for orbital construction. In space he must try to preserve his Indian spirit despite an environment which pulls him toward the dominant culture.

**Other books you might like:**
Jack Dann, *The Man Who Melted*, 1984
Jack Dann, *Wandering Stars: An Anthology of Jewish Fantasy and Science Fiction*, 1974
    editor
Alan Dean Foster, *Cyber Way*, 1990
Jack C. Haldeman II, *Vector Analysis*, 1979
Allen Steele, *Clarke County, Space*, 1990

## 1789

**HARLAN ELLISON**

### Slippage

(New York: Houghton-Mifflin, 1997)

**Story type:** Horror (Collection)

**Summary:** Collection of twenty-one selections that mix fantasy, horror and science fiction in provocative explorations of social and philosophical themes. Included is "Mephisto in Onyx," a tale of racial stereotypes and victimization in which a black psychic is accused of crimes committed by a white serial killer. "Keyboard" is a variant on the vampire theme, about a computer keyboard that drains life from its users, and "She's a Young Thing and Cannot Leave Her Mother," a tale of love and nurturing among a family of cannibals. "Crazy as a Soup Sandwich," the script for a deal-with-the-devil story, was produced as an episode of the revived "Twilight Zone" television series. A signed, limited hardcover edition published by Mark Ziesing contains additional contents.

**Other books you might like:**
Gary A. Braunbeck, *Things Left Behind*, 1997
Jonathan Carroll, *The Panic Hand*, 1996
Richard T. Chizmar, *Midnight Promises*, 1996
Brian Hodge, *The Convulsion Factory*, 1996
Elizabeth Massie, *Shadow Dreams*, 1996
David Niall Wilson, *The Fall of the House of Escher and Other Illusions*, 1995

## 1790

**LARRY ELMORE**
**ROBERT ELMORE**, Co-Author

### Runes of Autumn

(Lake Geneva, Wisconsin: TSR, 1996)

**Story type:** Fantasy (Adventure; Mystery)
**Major character(s):** Rafin, Police Officer; Maraakuks Oit-Makidom, Military Personnel; Alyna, Wizard
**Time period(s):** Indeterminate
**Locale(s):** Stridgenfel, Fictional City

**Summary:** The death and mutilation of two boys make some people think Ammak raiders have returned, while others think a bear did it. The village, however, receives aid, some requested and some not, in fighting the ancient legacy of evil. First novel.

**Other books you might like:**
Eleanor Arnason, *The Sword Smith*, 1978
Glen Cook, *The Swordbearer*, 1982
Robert Jordan, *The Eye of the World*, 1990
Caroline Stevermer, *A College of Magics*, 1994
Martha Wells, *The Element of Fire*, 1993

## 1791

**P.N. ELROD**

### Blood on the Water

(New York: Ace, 1992)

**Story type:** Horror (Vampire Story)
**Series:** Vampire Files
**Major character(s):** Jack Fleming, Detective—Private, Vampire, Journalist (former); Charles Escott, Detective—Private; Vaughan Kyler, Organized Crime Figure
**Time period(s):** 1930s
**Locale(s):** Chicago, Illinois

**Summary:** In this sixth and final adventure of Elrod's hardboiled depression-era vampire series, reporter-turned-vampire-private-eye Jack Fleming becomes a pawn in a war between racketeers, one of whom seems to have discovered his true identity.

**Other books you might like:**
Vincent Courtney, *Vampire Beat*, 1990
Barbara Hambly, *Those Who Hunt the Night*, 1988
Tanya Huff, *Blood Price*, 1991
Lee Killough, *Blood Links*, 1987

## 1792

**P.N. ELROD**

### Bloodlist

(New York: Ace, 1990)

**Story type:** Horror (Vampire Story)
**Series:** Vampire Files
**Major character(s):** Jack Fleming, Journalist (former investigative reporter), Vampire, Detective—Private; Charles Escott, Detective—Private; Frank Paco, Organized Crime Figure
**Time period(s):** 1930s (the Depression)
**Locale(s):** Chicago, Illinois

**Summary:** Investigative reporter Jack Fleming embarks on a search for the woman who turned him into a vampire in the first of a new series of hardboiled crime/vampire novels. In this adventure, Jack plays cat-and-mouse with Frank Paco, the Chicago racketeer who killed him for stealing a list of blackmail victims.

**Other books you might like:**
Stephen Gallagher, *Valley of Lights*, 1988
Barbara Hambly, *Immortal Blood*, 1987
William Hjortsberg, *Falling Angel*, 1978
Lee Killough, *Blood Links*, 1988
Lee Killough, *Blood Hunt*, 1987

#### P.N. ELROD

## A Chill in the Blood

(New York: Ace, 1998)

**Story type:** Horror (Vampire Story)
**Series:** Vampire Files
**Major character(s):** Jack Fleming, Detective—Private, Vampire, Journalist (former); Opal, Accountant (bookkeeper); Merrill Adkins, Investigator (federal)
**Time period(s):** 1930s (1937)
**Locale(s):** Chicago, Illinois

**Summary:** Vampire detective Jack Fleming finds himself caught in the crossfire of a mob war being fought by the Paco family and their archenemies. His effort to save Opal, the bookkeeper whose information can put the families out of business, is complicated by the arrival of an upstart gangster from New York eager to takeover the Paco family holdings, as well as the incursions of federal crimebuster Merrill Adkins, who is as brutal as the gangsters he pursues. This is the seventh novel in the author's Vampire Files series.

**Other books you might like:**
Vincent Courtney, *Vampire Beat*, 1990
Barbara Hambly, *Immortal Blood*, 1987
Tanya Huff, *Blood Price*, 1991
Lee Killough, *Blood Links*, 1987
Michael Reaves, *Night Hunter*, 1991

**1794**

#### P.N. ELROD

## Dance of Death

(New York: Ace, 1996)

**Story type:** Horror (Vampire Story; Historical)
**Series:** Adventures of Jonathan Barrett
**Major character(s):** Jonathan Barrett, Vampire; Oliver Fonteyn Marling, Doctor; Nora Jones, Vampire
**Time period(s):** 1770s (1777)
**Locale(s):** London, England

**Summary:** While searching for the woman who turned him into a vampire, American colonist and royalist Jonathan Barrett assumes responsibility for four-year-old Richard, the boy he sired with the wife of a cousin. When assassins unaware of his vampire nature attempt to kill him, Jonathan discovers that a plot involving family members has been hatched to eliminate him and the embarrassment he has caused.

**Other books you might like:**
Traci Briery, *The Vampire Journals*, 1993
Les Daniels, *Citizen Vampire*, 1981
Fred Saberhagen, *A Sharpness on the Neck*, 1996
T. Lucien Wright, *Thirst of the Vampire*, 1992

**1795**

#### P.N. ELROD

## Death Masque

(New York: Berkley, 1995)

**Story type:** Horror (Vampire Story; Historical)
**Series:** Adventures of Jonathan Barrett
**Major character(s):** Jonathan Barrett, Vampire; Elizabeth Barrett, Young Woman; Oliver Fonteyn, Cousin (of Jonathan and Elizabeth)
**Time period(s):** 1770s (1777)
**Locale(s):** London, England

**Summary:** Jonathan Barrett, the vampire son of a Tory family in Revolutionary War America, retraces the steps he took in *Red Death*, travelling from the United States back to England as his family prepares to flee from colonial hooligans on Long Island. While serching for Nora Jones, the vampire love he left behind, Jonathan stumbles upon a plot by his estranged mother's side of the family to ruin the Barretts.

**Other books you might like:**
Traci Briery, *The Vampire Journals*, 1993
Les Daniels, *Citizen Vampire*, 1981
Anne Rice, *The Vampire Lestat*, 1985
Lee Weathersby, *Kiss of the Vampire*, 1981
T. Lucien Wright, *Thirst of the Vampire*, 1992
Chelsea Quinn Yarbro, *Hotel Transylvania*, 1978

**1796**

#### P.N. ELROD

## Fire in the Blood

(New York: Ace, 1991)

**Story type:** Horror (Vampire Story)
**Series:** Vampire Files
**Major character(s):** Jack Fleming, Journalist, Vampire, Detective—Private; Charles Escott, Detective—Private; Doreen Gray, Photographer
**Time period(s):** 1930s
**Locale(s):** Chicago, Illinois

**Summary:** In his fifth adventure, investigative-reporter-turned-vampire-detective Jack Fleming takes on the case of a millionaire anxious for the return of a missing family heirloom bracelet and stumbles into an adventure chock full of blackmailers, pornographers, bootleggers, bookies, and all those other social miscreants who helped make depression-era Chicago famous.

**Other books you might like:**
Tanya Huff, *Blood Price*, 1991
Lee Killough, *Blood Links*, 1987

**1797**

#### P.N. ELROD

## I, Strahd

(Geneva, Wisconsin: TSR, 1993)

**Story type:** Horror (Vampire Story; Fantasy)
**Series:** Ravenloft
**Major character(s):** Rudolph Van Richten, Doctor; Strahd Von Zarovich, Ruler (of Barovia), Vampire; Tatyana, Vampire
**Time period(s):** Indeterminate
**Locale(s):** Barovia, Fictional Country

**Summary:** Set in the mythical kingdom of Barovia, this fantasy-horror genre blend recounts how the ruler Strahd Von Zarovich is bewitched by his brother's fiance, Tatyana, vampirized, and turned into a cruel ruler who lets his kingdom fall into disarray. The novel is the first of a projected trilogy.

**Other books you might like:**
Les Daniels, *The Black Castle*, 1978
Brian Stableford, *The Empire of Fear*, 1988
Chelsea Quinn Yarbro, *The Palace*, 1978

▮**1798**▮

**P.N. ELROD**

# Red Death

(New York: Ace, 1993)

**Story type:** Horror (Vampire Story)
**Series:** Adventures of Jonathan Barrett
**Major character(s):** Jonathan Barrett, Student (law student); Nora Jones, Vampire; Oliver Fonteyn Marling, Student (law student)
**Time period(s):** 1770s (1773-1776)
**Locale(s):** Cambridge, England; Long Island, New York

**Summary:** Sent by his mother against his wishes to study law in England, Jonathan Barrett falls under the influence of vampire Nora Jones. Upon his return to New York, his lust for blood becomes increasingly difficult to hide from British soldiers who overrun the British colonies preparatory to the American Revolution.

**Other books you might like:**
Traci Briery, *The Vampire Journals*, 1993
Anne Rice, *The Vampire Lestat*, 1985
Lee Weathersby, *Kiss of the Vampire*, 1992
T. Lucien Wright, *Thirst of the Vampire*, 1992

▮**1799**▮

**P.N. ELROD**, Editor
**MARTIN H. GREENBERG**, Co Editor

# The Time of the Vampires

(New York: DAW, 1996)

**Story type:** Horror (Anthology; Vampire Story)

**Summary:** Nineteen stories written originally for this volume feature vampires in historical settings and famous historical personalities whose adventures bring them into contact with, or reveal them to have been, vampires. P.N. Elrod's "The Devil's Mark" is set during the witch-hunting craze of 17th-century England, and Elaine Bergstrom's "The Ghost of St. Mark's" during the London blitz. Lois Tilton's "Vision of Darkness" features Socrates, Teresa Patterson's "The Gift" features King Arthur, and Tanya Huff's "What Manner of Man" and Lillian Stewart Carl's "The Blood of the Lamb" both feature associates of Henry VIII, all involved in vampire intrigues. Most of the contributors to this volume are distinguished writers of vampire novels.

**Other books you might like:**
Martin H. Greenberg, *Celebrity Vampires*, 1994
    editor
Martin H. Greenberg, *Dracula: Prince of Darkness*, 1992
    editor
Stephen Jones, *The Mammoth Book of Vampires*, 1993
    editor
Alan Ryan, *Vampires: Two Centuries of Great Vampire Stories*, 1987
    editor

Robert Weinberg, *Rivals of Dracula*, 1996
    Stefan Dziemianowicz, Martin H. Greenberg, co-editors

▮**1800**▮

**ELVIRA**

**JOHN PARAGON**, Co-Author

# The Boy Who Cried Werewolf

(New York: Berkley/Boulevard, 1998)

**Story type:** Horror (Werewolf Story)
**Major character(s):** Elvira, Young Woman; Whitney Benedict, Teenager; Madame Ousensky, Psychic (fortune teller)
**Time period(s):** 1990s (1998)
**Locale(s):** Beaver Hills, California

**Summary:** Elvira, the ditzy gothic mistress, comes to the aid of Whitney Benedict, whose inability to pay a quack fortune teller has apparently earned him the curse of the werewolf.

**Other books you might like:**
Nancy A. Collins, *Wild Blood*, 1994
Carl Dreadstone, *The Wolfman*, 1977
Lewis Gannett, *The Living One*, 1993
Christopher Moore, *Bloodsucking Fiends: A Love Story*, 1995
Jeff Rovin, *Return of the Wolfman*, 1997

▮**1801**▮

**ELVIRA**

**JOHN PARAGON**, Co-Author

# Camp Vamp

(New York: Boulevard, 1997)

**Story type:** Horror (Satire)
**Series:** Elvira, Mistress of the Dark
**Major character(s):** Elvira, Young Woman; Chloe, Teenager; Ranger Dan, Ranger (park)
**Time period(s):** 1990s (1997)
**Locale(s):** Beaver Hills, California

**Summary:** Elvira, television's ditzy Mistress of the Dark, is coerced into chaperoning a camp out for the Happy Campers club of Beaver Hill high school. Spooky campfire stories, scary misadventures and countless bad puns follow when Elvira and her ruggedness-challenged pack of teenage valley girls find themselves stalked by the legendary Beast of Beaver Hills.

**Other books you might like:**
Richie Tankersley Cusick, *Buffy the Vampire Slayer*, 1992
Lois Duncan, *Summer of Fear*, 1990
Joan Lowery Nixon, *The Stalker*, 1995
Christopher Pike, *Weekend*, 1986
R.L. Stine, *All-Night Party*, 1997

▮**1802**▮

**ELVIRA**

**JOHN PARAGON**, Co-Author

# Elvira: Transylvania 90210

(New York: Berkley/Boulevard, 1996)

**Story type:** Horror (Vampire Story)
**Major character(s):** Elvira, Young Woman; Shannon Doheny, Teenager; Sevil Alucard, Vampire
**Time period(s):** 1990s (1996)

**Locale(s):** Beaver Hills, California

**Summary:** Elvira, whose Gothic attire and peculiar behavior leads many to mistake her for a witch, discovers that a genuine vampire has moved next door to her and plans to vampirize the students of Beaver Hills High. This campy spoof, the author's first novel, lampoons not only teen-targeted television shows but also the television persona of Elvira herself.

**Other books you might like:**
Anne Billson, *Suckers*, 1993
Richie Tankersley Cusick, *Buffy the Vampire Slayer*, 1992
Lionel Fenn, *The Mark of the Moderately Vicious Vampire*, 1992
Christopher Moore, *Bloodsucking Fiends: A Love Story*, 1995

---

**1803**

**ROGER ELWOOD**

## *Angelwalk: A Modern Fable*
(Westchester, Illinois: Crossway Books, 1988)

**Story type:** Fantasy (Religious)
**Major character(s):** Darian, Angel
**Time period(s):** 1980s
**Locale(s):** Heaven; Earth

**Summary:** An angel is allowed to go to Earth by God to find out why Lucifer was thrown out of Heaven. During his visit, he sees all manner of horrible things on Earth in this Christian fantasy.

**Other books you might like:**
John Bunyan, *The Pilgrim's Progress*, 1984
Parke Godwin, *Waiting for the Galactic Bus*, 1989
Andrew M. Greeley, *Angel Fire*, 1988
C.S. Lewis, *The Chronicles of Narnia*, 1988
C.S. Lewis, *Perelanda: A Novel*, 1990
C.S. Lewis, *Pilgrim's Regress*, 1958
Mike McQuay, *The Nexus*, 1989

---

**1804**

**ROGER ELWOOD**

## *Sorcerers of Sodom*
(Tarrytown, New York: Fleming H. Revell Company, 1991)

**Story type:** Horror (Black Magic)
**Major character(s):** Brian Loeffler, Religious (former pastor); Judson McClane, Administrator (college chancellor); Anita Carlsen, Journalist ("The New Age Columnist")
**Time period(s):** 1990s
**Locale(s):** Beverly Hills, California

**Summary:** This pretentiously self-important "Christian horror" novel sends the pastor Brian Loeffler, fresh from the spectacular destruction of his pastorage owing to a momentary lapse of faith, to Beverly Hills. There, in the Sodom of Southern California, he brings down divine retribution on drug addicts, pornographers, homosexuals, New Age believers, and anyone who does not follow the "true" way.

**Other books you might like:**
William Peter Blatty, *The Exorcist*, 1971
Joe R. Lansdale, *Dead in the West*, 1986

---

**1805**

**DAVID ELY**

## *A Journal of the Flood Year*
(New York: Donald I. Fine, 1992)

**Story type:** Science Fiction (Techno-Thriller; Disaster)
**Major character(s):** William G. Fowke, Engineer, Outlaw
**Time period(s):** 21st century
**Locale(s):** United States

**Summary:** A technological marvel, The Wall, claimed new land from the Atlantic Ocean while converting energy from wave action. When Fowke reports leaks in The Wall to a bureaucrat, the official dismisses the complaint as disagreeing with the computer system analysis of The Wall's integrity. As Fowke complains further, his status changes from troublemaker to fugitive pursued by robotic trackers of the bureaucracy. Written in journal form.

**Other books you might like:**
David Brin, *Earth*, 1990
Jeffrey A. Carver, *The Rapture Effect*, 1987
Emily Devenport, *Shade*, 1991
Rosemary Kirstein, *The Outskirter's Secret*, 1992
Larry Niven, *Fallen Angels*, 1991
   Jerry Pournelle and Michael Flynn, co-authors
Frederik Pohl, *Gladiator-at-Law*, 1955
   C.M. Kornbluth, co-author
Ken Rolston, *Extreme Paranoia: Nobody Knows the Trouble I've Shot*, 1991
Neal Stephenson, *Snow Crash*, 1992
Kathy Tyers, *Shivering World*, 1991

---

**1806**

**WINIFRED ELZE**

## *The Changeling Garden*
(New York: St. Martin's/Wyatt, 1995)

**Story type:** Horror (Occult)
**Major character(s):** Annie Carter, Housewife; David Carter, Child (Annie's five-year-old son); Mariah Fenton, Herbalist
**Time period(s):** 1990s (1995)
**Locale(s):** Southwest

**Summary:** Shortly after the Carter family moves into a house whose previous owner specifically selected them, Annie and her son David find they have a psychic rapport with the plants and animals inhabiting the garden. Annie spends most of her time trying to prevent her husband Mark from selling off part of the yard for development into a parking lot and fending off Harley Baer, Jr., a lowlife possessed by the spirit of an ancient Mayan warrior intent on destroying the human race. This ecologically-aware tale is the author's first novel.

**Other books you might like:**
Alison Drake, *Lagoon*, 1990
John Skipp, *The Bridge: A Horror Story*, 1991
   Craig Spector, co-author
David van Meter Smith, *Trinity Grove*, 1990
John Wyndham, *The Day of the Triffids*, 1951

## **1807**

### JANE EMERSON

## *City of Diamond*
(New York: DAW, 1996)

**Story type:** Science Fiction (Political; Space Opera)
**Major character(s):** Adrian Mercati, Ruler (diamond protector); Iolanthe ''Io'' Pelagia, Royalty (lady); Tal Diamond, Alien (Elaphite/Human halfbreed), Military Personnel (special officer)
**Time period(s):** Indeterminate Future
**Locale(s):** *City of Diamond,* Spaceship; Baret Two, Planet—Imaginary

**Summary:** Adrian Mercati, the charismatic but inexperienced Protector of the *City of Diamond,* marries Lady Iolanthe Pegalia of the *City of Opal* in an effort to promote peace between the rival city-ships. Secretly, however, Adrian attempts to gain power over the other ship by searching for the Sawyer Crown, a mysterious alien artifact.

**Other books you might like:**
L. Warren Douglas, *Stepwater,* 1995
Valerie J. Freireich, *Becoming Human,* 1995
Valerie J. Freireich, *Testament,* 1995
Frank Herbert, *Dune,* 1965
Sheri S. Tepper, *Grass,* 1989
Margaret Weis, *Sentinels,* 1996
    Tracy Hickman, co-author

## **1808**

### RU EMERSON

## *The Empty Throne*
(New York: Berkley Boulevard, 1996)

**Story type:** Fantasy (Legend; Adventure)
**Series:** Xena: Warrior Princess
**Major character(s):** Xena, Warrior, Royalty; Gabrielle, Sidekick, Adventurer
**Time period(s):** Indeterminate Past
**Locale(s):** Ancient Civilization; Ithaca, Greece

**Summary:** Xena and Gabrielle discover a village whose men have vanished and where ruffians rule the street. The two must find the truth behind the events before they, too, disappear. First of a television tie-in series.

**Other books you might like:**
Marion Zimmer Bradley, *The Sword and Sorceress Series,* 1984-1996
    editor
Timothy Boggs, *By the Sword,* 1996
Timothy Boggs, *Serpent's Shadow,* 1996
George Alec Effinger, *Maureen Birnbaum, Barbarian Swordsperson: The Complete Stories,* 1993
Esther Friesner, *Chicks in Chainmail,* 1995
    editor
Barbara Hambly, *Beauty and the Beast,* 1989
Jason Henderson, *Highlander: The Element of Fire,* 1995
Jessica Amanda Salmonson, *Amazons!,* 1979
    editor

## **1809**

### RU EMERSON

## *One Land, One Duke*
(New York: Ace, 1992)

**Story type:** Fantasy (Alternate World; Adventure)
**Series:** Night-Threads
**Major character(s):** Jennifer Cray, Lawyer, Magician; Dahven, Nobleman; Aletto, Heir—Dispossessed
**Time period(s):** Indeterminate
**Locale(s):** Rhadaz, Fictional Country; Podhru, Fictional City; Zelharri, Fictional Country

**Summary:** Arriving in Podhru, the Crays, Aletto, Lialla and Dahven find betrayal. After Aletto escapes and Jennifer clears Dahven of murdering his father, they travel to Zelharri where Aletto seeks to regain his rightful dukedom.

**Other books you might like:**
Piers Anthony, *Man From Mundania,* 1989
Jack L. Chalker, *The River of Dancing Gods,* 1984
Joy Chant, *Red Moon and Black Mountain,* 1971
Brian Daley, *The Doomfarers of Coramonde,* 1977
L. Sprague de Camp, *The Land of Unreason,* 1942
    Fletcher Pratt, co-author
Kate Elliott, *Jaran,* 1992
Barbara Hambly, *The Time of the Dark,* 1982

## **1810**

### RU EMERSON

## *Spell Bound*
(New York: Ace, 1990)

**Story type:** Fantasy (Historical)
**Major character(s):** Sophie, Young Woman (''Cinderella''); Fairy Godmother, Mythical Creature
**Time period(s):** 15th century
**Locale(s):** Germany

**Summary:** In this rewrite of ''Cinderella,'' the characters have been fleshed out and given personal histories. Sophie becomes the pawn of her fairy godmother, when her fairy godmother sets out to take revenge for a wrongful death.

**Other books you might like:**
Tanith Lee, *Red as Blood: Or Tales from the Sisters Grimmer,* 1983
Morgan Llywelyn, *The Isles of the Blest,* 1989
Howard Waldrop, *A Dozen Tough Jobs,* 1989
David Henry Wilson, *The Coachman Rat,*
Patricia C. Wrede, *Snow White and Rose Red,*

## **1811**

### RU EMERSON

## *The Thief of Hermes*
(New York: Boulevard, 1997)

**Story type:** Fantasy (Legend; Adventure)
**Series:** Xena: Warrior Princess
**Major character(s):** Xena, Warrior, Royalty; Gabrielle, Warrior, Storyteller; Helarion, Thief
**Time period(s):** Indeterminate Past
**Locale(s):** Athens, Greece

**Summary:** When Helarion, who claims the sun god Hermes as his parent, frames Xena and Gabrielle for one of his crimes, the pair must plan a jailbreak and set the record straight. Television tie-in.

**Other books you might like:**

Marion Zimmer Bradley, *The Sword and Sorceress Series*, 1984-1997
    editor
George Alec Effinger, *Maureen Birnbaum, Barbarian Swordsperson: The Complete Stories*, 1993
Esther Friesner, *Chicks in Chainmail*, 1995
    editor
Stella Howard, *Prophecy of Darkness*, 1997
Jessica Amanda Salmonson, *Amazons!*, 1979
    editor

## 1812
### RU EMERSON

## The Two in Hiding
(New York: Ace, 1991)

**Story type:** Fantasy (Adventure; Alternate World)
**Series:** Night-Threads
**Major character(s):** Aletto, Heir—Dispossessed, Runaway; Robyn Cray, Single Parent, Mythical Creature (shapechanger); Jennifer Cray, Lawyer, Magician
**Time period(s):** Indeterminate
**Locale(s):** Rhadaz, Fictional Country

**Summary:** Three Americans, Chris, Jennifer and Robyn Cray, have been called into Rhadaz where they find themselves mixed up in a dynastic dispute between Jadek and his nephew Aletto, the rightful, though sickly, heir. While travelling across the desert, Robyn and Chris try to get Aletto into good shape and teach him martial arts. Coming to Bez, Jennifer rescues Dahven who was sold into slavery, then leaves quickly before Duke Jadek's men seize them.

**Other books you might like:**

Piers Anthony, *Man From Mundania*, 1989
Piers Anthony, *Split Infinity*, 1980
Jack L. Chalker, *The River of Dancing Gods*, 1984
Brian Daley, *The Doomfarers of Coramonde*, 1977
L. Sprague de Camp, *The Complete Compleat Enchanter*, 1989
    Fletcher Pratt, co-author
Barbara Hambly, *The Time of the Dark*, 1982

## 1813
### CLAYTON EMERY

## Cardmaster
(New York: Baen, 1997)

**Story type:** Fantasy (Adventure)
**Series:** Fantasy Adventure
**Major character(s):** Byron, Apprentice, Wizard (cardsmith); Cerise, Adventurer; Veronica, Religious
**Time period(s):** Indeterminate Past
**Locale(s):** Waterholm, Fictional City; Thallandia, Fictional Country

**Summary:** Byron's master dies under mysterious circumstances in a fire that the apprentice barely escapes. While fleeing, Byron meets the cardmistress, Cerise, and forms an uneasy alliance against their mutual enemies, which certainly include the church, but may also involve darker forces. Collectible card game tie-in.

**Other books you might like:**

Steven Brust, *Jhereg*, 1983

Barbara Hambly, *Mother of Winter*, 1996
Lyndon Hardy, *Master of the Five Magics*, 1980
Fritz Leiber, *Ill Met in Lankhmar*, 1995
Roger Zelazny, *Nine Princes in Amber*, 1970

## 1814
### CLAYTON EMERY

## Final Sacrifice
(New York: HarperPrism, 1995)

**Story type:** Fantasy (Magic Conflict)
**Series:** Magic: The Gathering
**Major character(s):** Gull, Leader, Revolutionary; Greensleeves, Wizard, Revolutionary; Immugio, Mythical Creature (giant/ogre), Wizard
**Time period(s):** Indeterminate Past
**Locale(s):** The Domains, Fictional Country

**Summary:** Greensleeves and Gull begin to win their long war against the wizards, but can they do it without becoming what they hate? Based on the popular card game.

**Other books you might like:**

Brian Daley, *The Doomfarers of Coramonde*, 1977
William R. Forstchen, *Arena*, 1994
Lisa Goldstein, *Summer King, Winter Fool*, 1994
Terry Goodkind, *Wizard's First Rule*, 1994
Patricia A. McKillip, *The Riddle-Master of Hed*, 1976
Michael Scott Rohan, *The Anvil of Ice*, 1986

## 1815
### CLAYTON EMERY

## Outcasts
(New York: Ace, 1990)

**Story type:** Fantasy (Quest)
**Series:** Runesword
**Major character(s):** Elizebith of Morea, Sorceress; Hathor, Mythical Creature (Ogre); Dark Lord, Wizard
**Time period(s):** Indeterminate
**Locale(s):** Alternate Earth

**Summary:** Elizebith, kidnapped from the home of a hated sorceress and then abandoned, sets herself up as a witch. When one of her cures proves fatal, Bith runs. She meets some fellow travelers and is contacted by a god who requires that she find the magic swords which were scattered around the Earth before the Dark Lord can drain their power for his own uses.

**Other books you might like:**

Adrienne Martine-Barnes, *The Rainbow Sword*, 1988
C.J. Cherryh, *The Paladin*, 1988
Rose Estes, *Skryling's Blade*, 1990
    Tom Wham, co-author
Rosemary Kirstein, *The Steerswoman*, 1989
Laurie J. Marks, *The Moonbane Mage*, 1990
Elizabeth Moon, *Sheepfarmer's Daughter*, 1988
J.F. Rivkin, *Runesword: The Dreamstone*, 1991
Paul Edwin Zimmer, *Blood of the Colyn Muir*, 1988
    Jon de Cles, co-author

## 1816

### CLAYTON EMERY

## Shattered Chains

(New York: HarperPrism, 1995)

**Story type:** Fantasy (Magic Conflict)
**Series:** Magic: The Gathering
**Major character(s):** Gull, Leader, Revolutionary; Greensleeves, Wizard, Revolutionary; Norreen, Military Personnel
**Time period(s):** Indeterminate Past
**Locale(s):** The Domains, Fictional Country

**Summary:** Siblings Gull and Greensleeves continue their war against the wizards. Greensleeves must master the sorcery she hates, and Gull must learn to lead an army to allow survival of themselves and their followers. Based on the popular card game.

**Other books you might like:**
Steven Brust, *The Phoenix Guards*, 1991
Glen Cook, *The Black Company*, 1984
Pamela Dean, *The Secret Country*, 1985
William R. Forstchen, *Arena*, 1994
Ursula K. Le Guin, *A Wizard of Earthsea*, 1968
Sheri S. Tepper, *King's Blood Four*, 1983

## 1817

### CAROL EMSHWILLER

## Carmen Dog

(San Francisco: Mercury House, 1990)

**Story type:** Fantasy (Satire)
**Major character(s):** Pooch, Animal (dog)
**Time period(s):** Indeterminate
**Locale(s):** New York, New York

**Summary:** Women are turning into beasts, and beasts are turning into women in this story. Pooch, once the family dog, has become a woman, and decides to escape to New York City to become an opera singer. Once there, she begins to explore the nature of relationships between men and women.

**Other books you might like:**
Margaret Atwood, *The Handmaid's Tale*, 1986
Eugene Ionesco, *Rhinoceros*, 1959
Ira Levin, *The Stepford Wives*, 1979
James Morrow, *Only Begotten Daughter*, 1990
George Orwell, *Animal Farm*, 1986

## 1818

### CAROL EMSHWILLER

## The Start of the End of It All

(San Francisco: Mercury House, 1991)

**Story type:** Science Fiction (Collection; Contemporary Realism)

**Summary:** These 18 stories written before 1990 mix realism, science fiction and magical realism, exploring the experience of emotionally marginalized women and men whose lives are changed by the fantastic. The title story presents an alien invasion force that works through kitchens and dislikes cats, while the story "Eclipse" deals with public embarrassment and fears of alienation.

**Other books you might like:**
Marjorie Agosin, *The Secret Weavers: Stories of the Fantastic by Latin American Women*, 1991
editor
Angela Carter, *The Infernal Desire Machines of Dr. Hoffman*, 1982
Pat Murphy, *Points of Departure*, 1990
James Tiptree Jr., *Her Smoke Rose Up Forever*, 1990
Fay Weldon, *Lives and Loves of a She-Devil*, 1983

## 1819

### PETER R. EMSHWILLER

## The Host

(New York: Bantam Spectra, 1991)

**Story type:** Science Fiction (Political; Techno-Thriller)
**Major character(s):** Watly Caiper, Murderer (accused), Disembodied Personality; Alysess Tolnismer, Doctor; Ragman, Psychic, Revolutionary
**Time period(s):** Indeterminate Future
**Locale(s):** United Countries of America, Fictional Country

**Summary:** The only possibility for motherhood Watly Caiper could imagine was a job as Host for Alvedine Industries. With the high pay from this dangerous position he could afford the antiprophies allowing fertility, and could hire a female to carry his child. As a resident of Level One Manhattan, and earlier in Brooklyn, he had never seen a child younger than himself except on CV, but his only goal in life is to be a mother. This is the author's first novel.

**Other books you might like:**
Emma Bull, *Bone Dance: A Fantasy for Technophiles*, 1990
Katharine Kerr, *Polar City Blues*, 1990
Frederik Pohl, *The Years of the City*, 1984
Dan Simmons, *Hyperion*, 1989
Michael A. Stackpole, *Evil Ascending*, 1991
Michael A. Stackpole, *A Gathering Evil*, 1991
Michael Swanwick, *Vacuum Flowers*, 1987
Lawrence Watt-Evans, *Newer York*, 1991
editer

## 1820

### PETER R. EMSHWILLER

## Short Blade

(New York: Bantam Spectra, 1992)

**Story type:** Science Fiction (Dystopian; Political)
**Major character(s):** Watly Caiper, Disembodied Personality; Noonie Caiper, Child (Watly's daughter); Alysess Tolnismer, Doctor, Revolutionary
**Time period(s):** Indeterminate Future
**Locale(s):** United Countries of America, Fictional Country

**Summary:** In this sequel to *The Host* Watly has realized his dream of becoming a mother, but he is "killed" while hosting in the body of Sentiva Alvedine. Meanwhile, Noonie, threatened by Sentiva, wonders about the identity of her real mother as Watly fights to retain control of Sentiva's body. Watly's need to live and act as Sentiva compromises his ability to help his compatriots from First Level Manhattan in the revolution against their oppressors from the Second Level.

**Other books you might like:**
Pat Cadigan, *Mindplayers*, 1987
George Alec Effinger, *When Gravity Fails*, 1987
Frederik Pohl, *The Years of the City*, 1984

Rudy Rucker, *Wetware*, 1988
Dan Simmons, *The Fall of Hyperion*, 1990
Dan Simmons, *Hyperion*, 1989
Michael A. Stackpole, *A Gathering Evil*, 1991
Vernor Vinge, *A Fire upon the Deep*, 1992
Walter Jon Williams, *Hardwired*, 1986

---

## 1821

### MICHAEL ENDE

## The Night of Wishes: Or, The Satanarchaeolidealcohellish Notion Potion

(New York: Farrar, Straus and Giroux, 1992)

**Story type:** Fantasy (Magic Conflict; Light Fantasy)
**Major character(s):** Morris "Mauricio di Mauro", Animal (cat), Spy (High Council of Animals); Jacob Scribble, Animal (raven), Spy (High Council of Animals); Beelzebub Preposteror, Sorcerer
**Time period(s):** 1990s
**Locale(s):** Villa Nightmare, Mythical Place (Preposteror's house)

**Summary:** Assigned by the High Council of Animals to spy on Preposteror and his aunt, Mauricio and Jacob witness the creation of a wishing potion which would allow both evil sorcerers to achieve their annual quota of dastardly deeds before midnight arrives to avoid cancellation of their magical powers and the subsequent penalty. With a bit of magical help from Father New Year, Mauricio and Jacob struggle to contaminate the brew and modify the potion's power. Translated from German by Heiki Schwarzbauer and Rick Takvorian.

**Other books you might like:**
Karen Brush, *Demon Pig*, 1991
Karen Brush, *The Pig, the Prince and the Unicorn*, 1987
Kenneth Grahame, *The Wind in the Willows*, 1908
Margery Sharp, *The Rescuers*, 1959
Roger Zelazny, *Bring Me the Head of Prince Charming*, 1991
    Robert Sheckley, co-author

---

## 1822

### GUY ENDORE

## The Werewolf of Paris

(New York: Citadel, 1992)

**Story type:** Horror (Werewolf Story)
**Major character(s):** Bertrand Caillet, Military Personnel (National Guard), Werewolf; Aymar Galliez, Writer; Josephine Caillet, Servant (Bertrand's mother)
**Time period(s):** 1870s (1870)
**Locale(s):** Paris, France

**Summary:** Although guardian Aymar Galliez tries his best to hide from young Bertrand Caillet the fact that his ward is a werewolf born of the unholy union of a servant girl and an accursed stranger, Bertrand finds it impossible to restrain his bestial side during the rapine and slaughter of the Paris Commune uprisings of 1870. This extraordinary allegory of the dark side of human nature was first published in 1933. Robert Bach has written a new foreword.

**Other books you might like:**
Michael Cadnum, *St. Peter's Wolf*, 1991
S.P. Somtow, *Moon Dance*, 1990
Whitley Strieber, *The Wolfen*, 1978
Melanie Tem, *Wilding*, 1992
Jack Williamson, *Darker than You Think*, 1948

---

## 1823

### PETER ENFANTINO, Editor

## Quick Chills

(San Jose, CA: Deadline Publications, 1990)

**Story type:** Horror (Anthology)

**Summary:** Fourteen stories by 13 authors, written for small press magazines between 1988 and 1989 and selected by the editor of the small press review magazine *The Scream Factory*. Stories with familiar themes, such as Ed Bryant's "While She Was Out" (a woman stalked by a homicidal maniac) and Joe Lansdale's "Not from Detroit" (a man's physical grapple with the specter of death) are balanced by tales with relatively unconventional topics, such as Bentley Little's "Survivalist" (the fate of the only couple in a southwestern town who do not subscribe to survivalism) and Ken Wisman's "On the Side of the Road" (the terrors of genetic engineering).

**Other books you might like:**
Jessica Amanda Salmonson, *Tales by Moonlight II*, 1989
Jessica Amanda Salmonson, *Tales by Moonlight*, 1984
Elizabeth A. Saunders, *When the Black Lotus Blooms*, 1990
Stuart David Schiff, *The Whispers Series*, 1977-1987
David B. Silva, *Best of The Horror Show*, 1987

---

## 1824

### M.J. ENGH

## Rainbow Man

(New York: Tor, 1993)

**Story type:** Science Fiction (Adventure; Political)
**Major character(s):** Trojan nine zero eight Liss, Spacewoman; Leona Porlock, Spacewoman; Doron, Religious (Selector)
**Time period(s):** Indeterminate Future
**Locale(s):** Bimran, Planet—Imaginary

**Summary:** Having decided to live on a planet, Liss chooses Bimran partly because it lacks laws, especially for visitors, but also for its high pressure oxygen atmosphere. Due to her voluntary surgical sterilization, Liss's Visitor Permit defines her as male, and the friendly locals greet her as Rainbow Man for her bright clothing. With the help of another outsider, Leona, a spaceshipper like herself, Liss gradually understands why Bimran requires no laws in its religious society. Unfortunately, Liss becomes too close to Doron, potentially leading to disaster for all her friends.

**Other books you might like:**
Eleanor Arnason, *Ring of Swords*, 1993
David Brin, *Glory Season*, 1993
Marge Piercy, *He, She and It*, 1991
Alis A. Rasmussen, *A Passage of Stars*, 1990
Joan Slonczewski, *A Door into Ocean*, 1986
Sheri S. Tepper, *Grass*, 1989
David Weber, *Path of the Fury*, 1992

---

## 1825

### TERRY ENGLAND

## Rewind

(New York: AvoNova, 1997)

**Story type:** Science Fiction (First Contact; Political)

**Major character(s):** Aaron Lee Fairfax, Genetically Altered Being; Miranda Sena, Scientist, Administrator; Radmilla Everett, Lawyer, Government Official (Health and Human Services)
**Time period(s):** 2000s
**Locale(s):** Santa Fe, New Mexico; Albuquerque, New Mexico

**Summary:** When the Holn depart from Earth, they leave behind 17 children who claim to be the 17 adults, one an octagenarian, trapped in the ship for four days before the ship took off. With an election upcoming, the President wants the situation done and out of the news. However, the fears of the religious right and the scientists' unwillingness to simply declare the ''children'' not aliens in dusguise, leads to transferring the rights and properties to ''responsible adults'' and the murder of six of the 17. Miranda must find help rescuing the survivors.

**Other books you might like:**
C.J. Cherryh, *Foreigner*, 1995
Ian McDonald, *Evolution's Shore*, 1995
Elizabeth Moon, *Remnant Population*, 1996
Richard Paul Russo, *Destroying Angel*, 1992
S. Andrew Swann, *Specters of the Twilight*, 1994
John Varley, *The Ophiuchi Hotline*, 1977

---

`1826`

**ELIZABETH ENGSTROM**

## Lizzie Borden

(New York: Tor, 1991)

**Story type:** Horror (Psychological Suspense; Gay/Lesbian Fiction)
**Major character(s):** Andrew Borden, Businessman (mill owner); Lizzie Borden, Heroine (Andrew's daughter), Historical Figure; Emma Borden, Spinster (Lizzie's older sister)
**Time period(s):** 1890s (1892)
**Locale(s):** Fall River, Massachusetts

**Summary:** A novel based on the famous Lizzie Borden murder case. Repressed and frustrated by her life in the parsimonious Borden household, Lizzie finds comfort in romantic relationships with other women. Through her sexual awakening, and with the help of a book lent to her by a lover, Lizzie learns how to liberate the murderous and uncontrollable ''Other Lizzie'' inside her.

**Other books you might like:**
John Farris, *The Axman Cometh*, 1989
John R. Maxim, *Abel/Baker/Charley*, 1984
Ed McBain, *Lizzie*, 1986

---

`1827`

**ELIZABETH ENGSTROM**

## Nightmare Flower

(New York: Tor, 1992)

**Story type:** Horror (Collection)
**Summary:** This volume collects nineteen stories and one short novel, most of which dwell on the dark side of human relationships and love. ''Will Lunch Be Ready on Time'' and ''Grandma's Hobby'' are both concerned with cannibalism, and the title story with a man-eating plant. ''The Final Tale'' works a variation on the old ghost story formula, while the lengthy ''Project Stone'' is a near-science fiction story in which an Arizona town's subtle plans for social engineering backfire with horrifying results.

**Other books you might like:**
Pat Cadigan, *Patterns*, 1989
Pat Murphy, *Points of Departure*, 1990

---

Jessica Amanda Salmonson, *John Collier and Fredric Brown Went Quarrelling through My Head*, 1989
Lisa Tuttle, *Memories of the Body*, 1992
Lisa Tuttle, *A Nest of Nightmares*, 1986

---

`1828`

**S.K. EPPERSON**

## Borderland: A Novel of Terror

(New York: Donald I. Fine, 1992)

**Story type:** Horror (Small Town Horror)
**Major character(s):** Wulf Nolan, Fire Fighter; Vic Kimmler, Police Officer, Widow(er); Myra Callahan, Housekeeper
**Time period(s):** 1990s (1992)
**Locale(s):** Denke, Kansas

**Summary:** Widower Vic Kimmler returns to his family homestead in Denke, Kansas, unaware that the town still practices its legacy of murder and cannibalism.

**Other books you might like:**
Randall Boyll, *After Sundown*, 1989
Jack Ketchum, *Offspring*, 1991
Michael B. Sirota, *Demon Shadows*, 1990

---

`1829`

**S.K. EPPERSON**

## Dumford Blood

(New York: St. Martin's, 1991)

**Story type:** Horror (Mystery)
**Major character(s):** Ben Portlock, Police Officer; Lura Taylor, Convict (ex-convict), Girlfriend (former); Portis Jackson, Banker (Ben's brother-in-law)
**Time period(s):** 1990s
**Locale(s):** Dumford, Kansas

**Summary:** The mutilation of several animals in the small town of Dumford coupled with the gruesome death of the local garbageman forces local officer Ben Portlock to draw on all of his investigative skills to solve the murder before someone pins the blame on his former girlfriend.

**Other books you might like:**
Susan Rogers Cooper, *Other People's Houses*, 1990
Bill Crider, *Shotgun Saturday Night*, 1987
Jean Hagar, *Nightwalker*, 1990
David Martin, *Lie to Me*, 1990
Sharyn McCrumb, *If Ever I Return, Pretty Peggy-O*, 1990
Jim Thompson, *Pop. 1280*, 1964
Anne Wingate, *The Eye of Anna*, 1990

---

`1830`

**S.K. EPPERSON**

## Green Lake

(New York: Donald I. Fine, 1996)

**Story type:** Horror (Psychological Suspense)
**Major character(s):** Madeleine Heron, Anthropologist, Widow(er); Eris Renard, Government Official (conservation officer), Indian; Dale Russell, Government Official (conservation officer)
**Time period(s):** 1990s (1996)
**Locale(s):** Green Lake, Kansas

**Summary:** Madeleine Heron retreats to her sister's cabin in remote Green Lake to work through her grief over the suicide of her husband. While there she falls in love with Native American Eris Renard, arousing the hostility of Eris's tribal matriarch and setting the stage for a difficult relationship to be played out against the town's midwestern Gothic backdrop, which includes acts of child molesting, necrophilia, and murder.

**Other books you might like:**
Robert Bloch, *American Gothic*, 1974
Ed Gorman, *Shadow Games*, 1993
Joe R. Lansdale, *Mucho Mojo*, 1994
Peter Straub, *The Throat*, 1993
S.J. Strayhorn, *Black Night*, 1996

## 1831

### S.K. EPPERSON

## The Moons of Summer

(New York: Donald I. Fine, 1994)

**Story type:** Horror (Mystery)
**Major character(s):** Guy Driscoll, Journalist; Michael Bish, Police Officer; Vernon Diest, Undertaker
**Time period(s):** 1990s (1994)
**Locale(s):** Colson, Kansas

**Summary:** Journalist Guy Driscoll returns to his home town of Colson in the hope it will help settle his rebellious teenage daughter, but immediately he reuns afoul of the police through his coverage of local crime and stumbles upon a plot by the local undertaker to keep a steady stream of business flowing through the door whether people are dying naturally or not.

**Other books you might like:**
James Neal Harvey, *The Headsman*, 1991
Joe R. Lansdale, *Act of Love*, 1981
Joe R. Lansdale, *Cold in July*, 1989
Stephen Wright, *M31: A Family Romance*, 1988

## 1832

### S.K. EPPERSON

## Nightmare

(New York: Leisure, 1993)

**Story type:** Horror (Psychological Suspense)
**Major character(s):** Bryan Raleigh, Doctor (psychiatrist); David Raleigh, Journalist; Kate Berquist, Health Care Professional (occupational therapist)
**Time period(s):** 1990s (1992)
**Locale(s):** Flint Hills, Kansas

**Summary:** David Raleigh is goaded by his psychiatrist brother Bryan to move to Bryan's clinic for women with multiple personality disorders and write a book promoting his medical breakthroughs. Once there, David discovers that someone is inducing the alternate personas of the patients to kill one another. This novel was originally published in 1992.

**Other books you might like:**
Robin Cook, *Coma*, 1977
Robin Cook, *Godplayer*, 1983
Dean R. Koontz, *The House of Thunder*, 1982

## 1833

### ELIZABETH ERGAS

## Devil's Gate

(New York: Zebra/Pinnacle, 1991)

**Story type:** Horror (Occult)
**Major character(s):** Alison Crandall Fortune, Paralegal; Sam Chandler, Architect; Adrian Blaise, Businessman (real estate developer)
**Time period(s):** 1990s (1990)
**Locale(s):** Draconia, New Hampshire

**Summary:** Two hundred years ago the townspeople of New Hope, New Hampshire sold their collective souls to the Devil. Renamed Draconia, the town's 20th century version seems poised on the verge of making the same mistake once more when real estate developer Adrian Blaise offers its citizens newfound wealth in exchange for its innocent women and children.

**Other books you might like:**
John Burke, *The Devil's Footsteps*, 1976
Thomas Tryon, *Harvest Home*, 1973

## 1834

### ELIZABETH ERGAS

## Rage

(New York: Zebra, 1993)

**Story type:** Horror (Supernatural Vengeance)
**Major character(s):** Leah Gold, Aged Person; Janie Rose, Young Woman; Maxwell Marsh, Journalist
**Time period(s):** 1990s (1993)
**Locale(s):** Sawquid, New York

**Summary:** Leah Gold's favorite necklace is fashioned from volcanic rock imbued with the soul of an angry young woman trapped in a lava flow almost a century before. Motivated by their own rage, Leah and her elderly friends find it possible to liberate the woman's spirit from the necklace to take revenge against their supposed persecutors.

**Other books you might like:**
Robert Bloch, *There Is a Serpent in Eden*, 1979
Edward Bryant, *Fetish*, 1991
A.R. Morlan, *The Amulet*, 1991

## 1835

### STEVE ERICKSON

## Arc d'X

(New York: Poseidon, 1993)

**Story type:** Fantasy (Historical; Religious)
**Major character(s):** Sally Hemings, Slave; Thomas Jefferson, Diplomat, Historical Figure; Etcher, Thief
**Time period(s):** 18th century; 21st century
**Locale(s):** Paris, France; Los Angeles, California; Berlin, Germany

**Summary:** After killing her master, Sally Hemings burns at the stake and returns to life as Thomas Jefferson's slave and mistress, accompanying the ambassador to Paris where 18th century ideals conflict with convenience. In a dystopian 21st century, echoes of the master and slave resonate in residents of a Los Angeles run by religious fanatics and policed by mobs. However, the balance changes when Etcher steals magical books and begins rewriting events.

**Other books you might like:**
Octavia E. Butler, *Kindred*, 1979
Maryse Conde, *I, Tituba, Black Witch of Salem*, 1992
Charles de Lint, *The Little Country*, 1991
Philip K. Dick, *Ubik*, 1969
Cynthia Kadohata, *In the Heart of the Valley of Love*, 1992
Marge Piercy, *Woman on the Edge of Time*, 1976
Lewis Shiner, *Glimpses*, 1993
Starhawk, *The Fifth Sacred Thing*, 1993

## 1836

### BARBARA ERSKINE

## Midnight Is a Lonely Place
(New York: Dutton, 1994)

**Story type:** Horror (Supernatural Vengeance)
**Major character(s):** Kate Kennedy, Writer; Greg Lindsey, Artist;
Alison Lindsey, Teenager
**Time period(s):** 1990s (1994)
**Locale(s):** Colchester, England

**Summary:** Kate Kennedy retires to a seaside refuge to take time out
from a rocky romance and begin her new biography of Lord Byron.
While there, the ocean erodes a cliff that has entombed for centuries
the bodies of a druid priest and his lover, victims of a jealous
husband, who begin exerting their terrifying powers through living
agents once their bodies are washed free.

**Other books you might like:**
Jonathan Aycliffe, *Naomi's Room*, 1991
Emmanuel Carrere, *Gothic Romance*, 1984
Marcy Heidish, *The Torching*, 1992
Michael Stewart, *Belladonna*, 1992

## 1837

### ROSE ESTES

## Elfwood
(New York: Ace, 1992)

**Story type:** Fantasy (Sword and Sorcery)
**Major character(s):** Jaeme, Nobleman; Decutonius, Magician; Kirk,
Orphan
**Time period(s):** Indeterminate
**Locale(s):** Albion, Fictional Country; Elfwood, Mythical Place; Cas-
tle Elfwood, Mythical Place

**Summary:** The peaceful order imposed on Albion from Castle
Elfwood falls prey to human barbarians and orcs. Four youths must
destroy the enemy threat or lose both human and faerie realms to
chaos.

**Other books you might like:**
Emma Bull, *War for the Oaks*, 1987
Laurell K. Hamilton, *Nightseer*, 1992
Jackie Hyman, *Shadowlight*, 1989
Robert Jordan, *The Eye of the World*, 1989
Joel Rosenberg, *The Road to Ehvenor*, 1991
Will Shetterly, *Elsewhere*, 1991
Marilyn Singer, *Charmed*, 1990
Terri Windling, *Life on the Border*, 1991
editor

## 1838

### ROSE ESTES

## The Hunter on Arena
(New York: Warner Questar, 1991)

**Story type:** Science Fiction (Adventure)
**Series:** Hunter
**Major character(s):** Braldt, Prisoner, Warrior; Keri, Prisoner; Randi,
Prisoner
**Time period(s):** Indeterminate Future
**Locale(s):** Rototara, Planet—Imaginary

**Summary:** Captured by a technologically advanced people who have
a mining colony on his planet, Braldt is separated from his companions and sent to fight in the arena for the amusement of his captors.
With a team of other beings from other worlds, Braldt battles other
teams for the right to continue living while searching for a way to
escape and rescue his friends.

**Other books you might like:**
Jean M. Auel, *Clan of the Cave Bear*, 1980
Gordon R. Dickson, *Wolf and Iron*, 1990
Geary Gravel, *A Key for the Nonesuch*, 1990
Simon R. Green, *Winner Takes All*, 1991
Robert E. Howard, *Conan the Conqueror*, 1950
Frederik Pohl, *Gladiator-at-Law*, 1955
C.M. Kornbluth, co-author

## 1839

### ROSE ESTES

## Iron Dragons: Mountains and Madness
(New York: Baen, 1993)

**Story type:** Fantasy (Quest)
**Major character(s):** Tianna, Royalty (princess), Magician; Steffan,
Mythical Creature (half-elf), Engineer
**Time period(s):** Indeterminate
**Locale(s):** Bright Kingdom, Fictional Country

**Summary:** To fend off economic collapse, Tianna agrees to the plan
of an èlf and dwarf to build a railroad using dragons transformed into
smoke-billowing engines to bring their goods and produce to outside
markets. She and Steffan must avert war, sorcery and treachery to
save the Bright Kingdom. Game tie-in.

**Other books you might like:**
Robin Wayne Bailey, *Enchanter*, 1989
Robin Wayne Bailey, *The Lost City of Zork*, 1991
George Alec Effinger, *The Zork Chronicles*, 1990
Craig Shaw Gardner, *Wishbringer*, 1988
Mercedes Lackey, *Castle of Deception*, 1992
Josepha Sherman, co-author
Mercedes Lackey, *Fortress of Frost and Fire*, 1993
Ru Emerson, co-author
Mercedes Lackey, *Prison of Souls*, 1993
Josepha Sherman, co-author
Josepha Sherman, *The Chaos Gate*, 1994

## 1840

### ROSE ESTES
### TOM WHAM, Co-Author

## The Stone of Time

(New York: Ace, 1992)

**Story type:** Fantasy (Quest)
**Series:** Runesword
**Major character(s):** Caltus "Cal" Talienson, Warrior; Elizebith of Morea, Sorceress
**Time period(s):** Indeterminate
**Locale(s):** Westwoods, Mythical Place (kingdom)

**Summary:** When the Dark Lord again sends the goblin-led legions into Westwoods, this time to capture the Stone of Time, Cal and his companions venture to Abaton to secure for themselves the Stone of Time with which they intend to permanently annihilate the Dark Lord.

**Other books you might like:**
Mark Acres, *Dark Divide*, 1991
Stephen Billias, *Horrible Humes*, 1991
Clayton Emery, *Outcasts*, 1990
J.F. Rivkin, *The Dreamstone*, 1991

## 1841

### ROSE ESTES

## Troll-Quest

(New York: Ace, 1995)

**Story type:** Fantasy (Urban; Quest)
**Major character(s):** Katherine Sinclair, Parent, Adventurer; Crystal, Parent, Mythical Creature (troll); Benjamin Bosch, Doctor
**Time period(s):** 1990s (1995)
**Locale(s):** Chicago, Illinois; Mammoth Caves, Kentucky

**Summary:** Despite warfare between humans and Under Dwellers, Katherine, a human, and Crystal, a troll, don't care about the larger conflict, since they only want their beloved children back. But their efforts intertwine with the fate of both races, as the theft of their children reflects the larger issues that face both humans and trolls.

**Other books you might like:**
Peter S. Beagle, *The Folk of the Air*, 1986
Lois McMaster Bujold, *The Spirit Ring*, 1992
Emma Bull, *War for the Oaks*, 1987
Michael de Larrabeiti, *The Borribles*, 1978
R.A. MacAvoy, *Tea with the Black Dragon*, 1983
Will Shetterly, *Elsewhere*, 1991

## 1842

### ROSE ESTES

## Troll-Taken

(New York: Ace, 1993)

**Story type:** Fantasy (Contemporary)
**Major character(s):** Katherine Sinclair, Parent, Adventurer; Benjamin Bosch, Doctor, Adventurer
**Time period(s):** 1990s
**Locale(s):** Chicago, Illinois

**Summary:** When Katherine Sinclair discovers her child has been taken and a sickly infant left instead, she begins a desperate search for her child. The search leads her deep under Chicago where whe

---

discovers a society experiencing terrible health problems among youngsters.

**Other books you might like:**
David Eddings, *Sorceress of Darshiva*, 1989
Teresa Edgerton, *The Grail and the Ring*, 1994
Barbara Hambly, *The Silent Tower*, 1986
Richard A. Knaak, *King of the Grey*, 1993
Jody Lynn Nye, *Higher Mythology*, 1993
Viido Polikarpus, *Down Town*, 1985
    Tappan King, co-author

## 1843

### DENNIS ETCHISON

## California Gothic

(New York: Dell/Abyss, 1995)

**Story type:** Horror (Psychological Suspense)
**Major character(s):** Dan Markham, Store Owner (bookstore); Evie Markham, Store Owner (bookstore); Judy Rios, Young Woman
**Time period(s):** 1990s (1995)
**Locale(s):** Los Angeles, California

**Summary:** Dan Markham and his family are menaced by his ex-girlfriend, Judy, a former radical and member of the Church of Satan the Redeemer. Judy supposedly killed herself decades ago before the authorities could catch her, but she reappears looking exactly as she did, and tries to ignite the passions Dan knew as a younger and more idealistic radical.

**Other books you might like:**
Douglas Clegg, *Dark of the Eye*, 1994
Joe R. Lansdale, *Savage Season*, 1989
Robert R. McCammon, *Mine*, 1990
Chet Williamson, *Second Chance*, 1994

## 1844

### DENNIS ETCHISON, Editor

## The Complete Masters of Darkness

(Lancaster, PA: Underwood-Miller, 1991)

**Story type:** Horror (Anthology)

**Summary:** A compilation of the three individual "Masters of Darkness" paperbacks, totaling 45 stories. All tales were chosen by the authors as their favorite works, explanations of which are given in individual afterwords. Selections range in variety from simple pulp gems like Ray Bradbury's "The Dead Man" and Manly Wade Wellman's "Up Under the Roof," to Joyce Carol Oates' post-holocaust spoof "Family" and Clive Barker's political allegory "In the Hills, The Cities." Also included are Richard Matheson's science fiction terror tale "Dance of the Dead," Whitley Strieber's sexually provocative "Perverts," Steve Rasnic Tem's dreamy "Preparations for the Game," George R.R. Martin's comically grotesque "The Monkey Treatment," Stephen King's dark fantasy "The Woman in the Room," and a rare short story by James Herbert, "Hallowe'en Child."

**Other books you might like:**
David G. Hartwell, *The Dark Descent*, 1987
Leo Margulies, *My Best Science Fiction Story*, 1949
Kirby McCauley, *Night Chills*, 1975

## 1845

### DENNIS ETCHISON

## Darkside

(Chicago: America Fantasy/Airgedlamh Publications, 1996)

**Story type:** Horror (Child-in-Peril)
**Major character(s):** Doug Carson, Composer (film); Casey Carson, Housewife; Erin Carson, Teenager
**Time period(s):** 1980s (1986)
**Locale(s):** Los Angeles, California

**Summary:** Behind the sleek facades and glossy sheen of contemporary Los Angeles lurk the Lost Ones, a death cult of youngsters driven to the dark side of the counterculture through the emptiness of their lives. When his stepdaughter Erin becomes involved with the cult, Doug Carson must infiltrate the Underground where they live, and even risk passing over to the other side to save her. Published as a paperback original in 1986, this signed limited hardcover edition of the book presents the author's preferred text. Ramsey Campbell supplies the introduction.

**Other books you might like:**
Poppy Z. Brite, *Drawing Blood*, 1993
Ray Garton, *Crucifax Autumn*, 1988
Melanie Tem, *Prodigal*, 1991

## 1846

### DENNIS ETCHISON

## Double Edge

(New York: Dell, 1997)

**Story type:** Horror (Psychological Suspense; Serial Killer)
**Major character(s):** Jenny Marlow, Writer (screenwriter); Lee Marlow, Photographer; Walter Heim, Agent
**Time period(s):** 1990s (1997)
**Locale(s):** Los Angeles, California

**Summary:** Shortly after Jenny and Lee Marlow write a script for a revisionist television movie that will present Lizzie Borden as a victim rather than a cold-blooded parricide, a series of gruesome murders begins decimating their circle of Hollywood friends and acquaintances. Are they being stalked by a psychopath, or has their script resurrected the ghost of Lizzie herself?

**Other books you might like:**
Robert Bloch, *Psycho II*, 1982
Ehren M. Ehly, *Star Prey*, 1992
Stephen King, *The Dark Half*, 1992
Richard Christian Matheson, *Created By*, 1993

## 1847

### DENNIS ETCHISON, Editor

## Metahorror

(New York: Dell/Abyss, 1992)

**Story type:** Horror (Anthology)

**Summary:** Twenty-one original stories meant to expand the boundaries of the modern horror story. Among the best are Scott Edelman's tale of McCarthyan paranoia, "Are You Now"; Lisa Tuttle's meditation on the battle of the sexes, "Replacements"; Donald R. Burleson's story of schoolchildren with horrifyingly acute perception, "Ziggles"; Ramsey Campbell's seriocomedy about the implications of communication breakdown, "End of the Line"; Steve

Rasnic Tem's potent exploration of terminal illness, "Underground"; and "The Ghost Village," an excerpt from Peter Straub's novel, *The Throat*.

**Other books you might like:**
Kirby McCauley, *Dark Forces*, 1980
Thomas F. Monteleone, *Borderlands 1*, 1990
J.N. Williamson, *The Best of Masques*, 1988

## 1848

### DENNIS ETCHISON

## Shadow Man

(New York: Dell/Abyss, 1993)

**Story type:** Horror (Serial Killer; Child-in-Peril)
**Major character(s):** Jack Martin, Artist; Christopher Buckley, Child; Lissa Shelby, Counselor (youth counselor)
**Time period(s):** 1990s (1993)
**Locale(s):** Shadow Bay, California; Eden Cove, California

**Summary:** In a tale laced with subtle criticism about the fraying of American society, Jack Martin and Lissa Shelby struggle to protect a young boy from becoming the next victim of a child murderer who stalks the town of Shadow Bay and who is linked in the minds of the local children to the horror movies they watch.

**Other books you might like:**
Samuel M. Key, *From a Whisper to a Scream*, 1992
John Saul, *Suffer the Children*, 1977
Whitley Strieber, *Billy*, 1990

## 1849

### RUTLEDGE ETHERIDGE

## The First Duelist

(New York: Ace, 1994)

**Story type:** Science Fiction (Military; Space Opera)
**Major character(s):** Simon Barrow, Martial Arts Expert, Teenager; Griffin Joyner, Military Personnel; Corinne Hernandez, Martial Arts Expert
**Time period(s):** 22nd century (2128-2166)
**Locale(s):** Mercator, Asteroid (prison); *Celeste*, Spaceship; *Serendipity*, Spaceship

**Summary:** Condemned to the prison asteroid, Mercator, for sabotaging Earth's first star ship, the *Utic Shinar*, Simon Barrow joins forces with the legendary General Joyner and Talon. Together, they fight the injustices of the established government and strive to regain space travel for the entire human race.

**Other books you might like:**
Eleanor Arnason, *Ring of Swords*, 1993
Emma Bull, *Bone Dance: A Fantasy for Technophiles*, 1991
Joe Haldeman, *All My Sins Remembered*, 1977
Steve Miller, *Agent of Change*, 1988
    Sharon Lee, co-author
Steve Perry, *The Man Who Never Missed*, 1985
Alis A. Rasmussen, *Revolution's Shore*, 1990

## 1850

**KEN EULO**

**JOE MAUCK**, Co-Author

### Claw

(New York: Simon & Schuster, 1994)

**Story type:** Horror (Nature in Revolt)
**Major character(s):** Meg Stewart, Veterinarian; Dan Dragelman, Police Officer; Philip Roueche, Zoo Keeper (curator of the Los Angeles Zoo)
**Time period(s):** 1990s (1994)
**Locale(s):** Los Angeles, California

**Summary:** The bloody escape of Rajah, a Siberian tiger who is one of the star attractions of the Los Angeles Zoo, leads veterinarian Meg Stewart to investigate why the animal has suddenly turned so vicious. Meg discovers that Rajah is part of a project funded by the Department of Defense to give tigers the thinking capacity of human beings for use as potential weapons.

**Other books you might like:**
Peter Benchley, *White Shark*, 1994
T.J. Kirby, *Deadly Breed*, 1991
Dean R. Koontz, *Watchers*, 1987
Bob Mayer, *Operation Synbat*, 1994

## 1851

**KEN EULO**

### Manhattan Heat

(New York: Tor, 1991)

**Story type:** Horror (Occult)
**Major character(s):** Frank Caldwell, Police Officer; Caroline Caldwell, Child (Frank's daughter); Kate Reeling, Psychologist
**Time period(s):** 1990s
**Locale(s):** New York, New York

**Summary:** Manhattan cop Frank Caldwell's efforts to be a good father and ex-husband in the wake of a divorce are interrupted by his latest case, which involves a coven of the walking dead who inhabit New York City's underground and who may be related to the religious practices of a fringe group of the local Cuban community.

**Other books you might like:**
Alex Abella, *The Killing of the Saints*, 1991
Nicholas Conde, *The Religion*, 1982
Gordon Linzner, *The Troupe*, 1988
Chet Williamson, *Lowland Rider*, 1988

## 1852

**DAVID EVANS**

### Time Station Berlin

(New York: Ace, 1997)

**Story type:** Science Fiction (Time Travel)
**Series:** Time Station
**Major character(s):** Alan Specter, Time Traveler, Police Officer (time warden); Angela Chance, Time Traveler, Student—Graduate; John F. Kennedy, Historical Figure, Leader (U.S. president)
**Time period(s):** 1960s (June 1963)
**Locale(s):** Berlin, Germany

**Summary:** Angela Chance, a graduate student from the future, wishes to see John F. Kennedy. She prevents an assassination by a KGB agent, but the attempt angers Kennedy so much he resolves to tear down the wall. Now Time Warden Specter must step in to restore history and prevent World War III.

**Other books you might like:**
Kevin J. Anderson, *The Trinity Paradox*, 1991
   Doug Brason, co-author
Poul Anderson, *The Time Patrol*, 1991
John Brunner, *Times Without Number*, 1962
Jack L. Chalker, *Downtiming the Night Side*, 1985
Richard Cooper, *The Road to Corlay*, 1979
Kevin Randle, *Remember the Little Bighorn*, 1990
   Robert Cornett, co-author
Connie Willis, *To Say Nothing of the Dog*, 1998
Robert Charles Wilson, *A Bridge of Years*, 1991

## 1853

**DAVID EVANS**

### Time Station London

(New York: Ace, 1996)

**Story type:** Science Fiction (Time Travel)
**Series:** Time Station
**Major character(s):** Steven "Brian Moore" Whitefeather, Military Personnel (colonel), Time Traveler; Samatha Trillby, Military Personnel (lieutenant); Diana Basehart, Time Traveler
**Time period(s):** 1940s (1940); Indeterminate Future
**Locale(s):** London, England; Coventry, England

**Summary:** Assigned to the London Time Station during the Blitz, Steven takes on the identity of a British counterintelligence officer in order to find out who plans to kill Winston Churchill and to stop the plan, thus keeping history unchanged. Yet his love for Samantha, a native of the 20th century, leads him to travel backward and forward in time to prevent her destined death.

**Other books you might like:**
Dennis Lee Anderson, *Arthur, King*, 1995
Poul Anderson, *Time Patrolman*, 1983
David Drake, *Arc Riders*, 1995
   Janet Morris, co-author
Harlan Ellison, *The City on the Edge of Forever*, 1995
S.D. Perry, *Timecop*, 1994
John T. Phillifent, *The Man From U.N.C.L.E.: The Mad Scientist Affair*, 1966

## 1854

**DAVID EVANS**

### Time Station Paris

(New York: Ace, 1997)

**Story type:** Science Fiction (Time Travel)
**Series:** Time Station
**Major character(s):** John "Jean Vitterand" Thomason, Police Officer (time warden), Time Traveler; George Faracon, Criminal, Time Traveler
**Time period(s):** 1940s (1943); 50th century B.C. (4903 B.C.)
**Locale(s):** Paris, France; Ancient Civilization (Sumer)

**Summary:** Rescued from death, John Thomason becomes Jean Vitterand, Time Warden, in 1943 Paris. Warned that the murder of Herman Goring will destroy the future, he must battle time outlaws stuck in ancient Sumer.

**Other books you might like:**
Kevin J. Anderson, *The Trinity Paradox*, 1991
    Doug Beason, co-author
Poul Anderson, *The Shield of Time*, 1990
John Barnes, *Patton's Spaceship*, 1996
Ben Bova, *Triumph*, 1993
John Brunner, *Times Without Number*, 1969
Newt Gingrich, *1945*, 1995
    William R. Forstchen, co-author
Harry Turtledove, *Worldwar: In the Balance*, 1994
Connie Willis, *Fire Watch*, 1985

**1855**

LINDA EVANS

## Far Edge of Darkness

(New York: Baen, 1996)

**Story type:** Science Fiction (Time Travel; Political)
**Major character(s):** Charlie Flynn, Police Officer, Time Traveler; Sibyl Johnson, Student, Time Traveler; Tony ''Antonius Caelerus'' Bartlett, Time Traveler, Criminal
**Time period(s):** 1990s; 1st century (79 A.D.)
**Locale(s):** Alaska; Roman Empire

**Summary:** At different times and places, Charlie Flynn and Sybil Johnson anger the powerful Carreras family and end up as slaves in ancient Rome trying to survive the eruption of Mt. Vesuvius. Meanwhile, thrown four years into the future, Logan McKee stumbles upon a secret base in Alaska and soon must try a desperate time jump to survive at all.

**Other books you might like:**
Poul Anderson, *Guardians of Time*, 1960
Robert Asprin, *Time Scout*, 1995
    Linda Evans, co-author
Robert Asprin, *Wagers of Sin*, 1996
    Linda Evans, co-author
Greg Bear, *Eternity*, 1988
L. Sprague de Camp, *Rivers of Time*, 1993
David Drake, *Birds of Prey*, 1984
Crawford Kilian, *Rogue Emperor*, 1988
Samuel Merwin, *The House of Many Worlds*, 1951
Melissa Scott, *A Choice of Destinies*, 1986
William F. Wu, *Warrior*, 1993

**1856**

LINDA EVANS

## Sleipnir

(New York: Baen, 1994)

**Story type:** Fantasy (Sword and Sorcery; Legend)
**Major character(s):** Randy Barnes, Military Personnel; Gary Vernon, Military Personnel; Odin, Deity
**Time period(s):** 1980s; Indeterminate
**Locale(s):** Germany; Nifflheim, Mythical Place (Norse underworld); Valhalla, Mythical Place

**Summary:** While guarding a U.S. Army base in Germany, Randy watches Odin's eight-legged horse, Sleipnir, carry the soul of his buddy, Gary Vernon, to Valhalla. When Gary's grandmother gives Randy a knife with magical properties, Randy seeks vengeance against Odin himself on a perilous journey into the depths of a Norwegian cave which leads him to Nifflheim, the domain of Hel, goddess of the dead, and eventually to personal combat with Odin in Valhalla. First novel.

**Other books you might like:**
Harry Harrison, *The Hammer and the Cross*, 1993
    John Holm, co-author
P.C. Hodgell, *God Stalk*, 1982
Robert E. Howard, *Conan the Conqueror*, 1950
Victor Koman, *The Jehovah Contract*, 1987
John Myers Myers, *Silverlock*, 1949
Diana L. Paxson, *The Wolf and the Raven*, 1993

**1857**

QUINN TAYLOR EVANS

## Merlin's Legacy: Dawn of Camelot

(New York: Zebra, 1998)

**Story type:** Fantasy (Quest)
**Series:** Merlin's Legacy
**Major character(s):** Connor, Knight; Megan, Sorceress
**Time period(s):** 11th century (1068)
**Locale(s):** Avalon, Fictional Country; England

**Summary:** Merlin's sister grows tired of her self-exile to magical Avalon, where she has learned sorcery arts almost equal to that of her brother. She visits the mainland in the aftermath of King Arthur's disappearance, and encounters a knight with whom she eventually discovers the virtues of mortal love.

**Other books you might like:**
Marion Zimmer Bradley, *The Mists of Avalon*, 1982
Vera Chapman, *King Arthur's Daughter*, 1978
Anne Eliot Crompton, *Merlin's Harp*, 1996
Phyllis Ann Karr, *The Idylls of the Queen*, 1982
Sharan Newman, *The Chessboard Queen*, 1997

**1858**

MARK FABI

## Wyrm

(New York: Bantam Spectra, 1997)

**Story type:** Science Fiction (Contemporary Realism; Fantasy)
**Major character(s):** Michael Arcangelo, Computer Expert; Alice Mende, Computer Expert; Beelzebub, Computer Expert
**Time period(s):** 1990s
**Locale(s):** California; Virtual Reality, Cyberspace

**Summary:** Hired to debug a high-end chess computer, Michael Arcangelo soon finds the virus attacking all over in a bid to start Armageddon. The path of the virus will lead Arcangelo and friends around the country and into Virtual Reality, where a series of deadly puzzles hides clues to success or death.

**Other books you might like:**
Kevin J. Anderson, *Virtual Destruction*, 1996
    Doug Beason, co-author
Rick Cook, *The Wizardry Compiled*, 1990
Alan Dean Foster, *Cyber Way*, 1990
Spider Robinson, *Callahan's Crosstime Saloon*, 1977
Fred Saberhagen, *Octagon*, 1981

## 1859

### KENNETH W. FAIG JR.

## Tales of the Lovecraft Collectors

(West Warwick, Rhode Island: Necronomicon Press, 1995)

**Story type:** Horror (Collection)

**Summary:** In an original approach to the tale of Lovecraftian horror, the author, a renowned H.P. Lovecraft scholar and genealogist of the Lovecraft family, presents four stories of mystery, the supernatural and romance from the diary of antiquarian book collector David Parkes Boynton, in which Boynton's travels bring him into contact with Lovecraft collectors who have found interesting associations between Lovecraft's stories and events in his personal life. ''Collector the First: Major Geoffrey Hopinkson Smith (1857-1943)'' suggests that the Mexican Indian legends of Lovecraft's story ''The Transition of Juan Romero'' were drawn from fact. ''Collector the Second: Dean Allen Edgerton Noble (1876-1959)'' focuses on Lovecraft's father, and a possible association with the Lizzie Borden murders. ''Collector the Third: Charles Wilson Hodap (1842-1944)'' suggests a source for Lovecraft's prose poem ''Nyarlathotep,'' while ''Collector the Fourth and Fifth: David Parkes Boynton (1897-1956) and Another Gentleman of the Hope Club'' speculates about events in Lovecraft's personal life that may have precipitated his nervous breakdown. These stories were first collected in 1989 in slightly different form.

**Other books you might like:**
P.H. Cannon, *Pulptime*, 1984
Richard A. Lupoff, *Lovecraft's Book*, 1985
Robert M. Price, *Tales of the Providence Pales*, 1983
   editor
Ralph Vaughan, *Sherlock Holmes in the Adventure of the Ancient Gods*, 1990

## 1860

### MARGARET FALK

## Darkscope

(New York: Pinnacle, 1990)

**Story type:** Horror (Supernatural Vengeance)
**Major character(s):** Chelsea McCord, Artist; Ben Fletcher, Horse Trainer; Bob McCord, Businessman (Chelsea's uncle)
**Time period(s):** 1980s (1986)
**Locale(s):** Bisbee, Arizona

**Summary:** Following the failure of her marriage, Chelsea McCord takes up residence in Bisbee, a town once controlled by her great-grandfather, a powerful mining magnate. When she accidentally releases a spirit that was trapped in an old box camera in her attic, she reignites the long-standing feud between the McCords and the Barries, a family that was exploited by the McCords and whose members, both living and dead, are bent on revenge.

**Other books you might like:**
Michael McDowell, *Cold Moon over Babylon*, 1980
Dean Wesley Smith, *Laying the Music to Rest*, 1989
Peter Straub, *If You Could See Me Now*, 1977

## 1861

### JANE S. FANCHER

## Ground-Ties

(New York: Warner Questar, 1991)

**Story type:** Science Fiction (Political)
**Major character(s):** Loren Cantrell, Spaceship Captain (admiral); Stephen Ridenour, Computer Expert; Anevai Tyeewapi, Scientist, Guide
**Time period(s):** Indeterminate Future
**Locale(s):** *Cetacean*, Spaceship; HuteNamid, Planet—Imaginary

**Summary:** Officially, Admiral Cantrell's mission is to convey young Stephen Ridenour to HuteNamid to investigate possible misuse of the Nexus ComNet, the interstellar computer network that links the people of the Alliance. Although Ridenour's repressed memories and conflicting loyalties threaten his sanity and safety, he may hold the key to the salvation, or destruction, of HuteNamid.

**Other books you might like:**
Alfred Bester, *The Computer Connection*, 1974
Emma Bull, *Bone Dance: A Fantasy for Technophiles*, 1991
C.J. Cherryh, *Downbelow Station*, 1981
Diane Duane, *Spock's World*, 1989
Mary Gentle, *Golden Witchbreed*, 1984
Frank Herbert, *Dune*, 1965
Jim Young, *The Face of the Deep*, 1979

## 1862

### JANE S. FANCHER

## Harmonies of the 'Net

(New York: Warner Questar, 1992)

**Story type:** Science Fiction (Political)
**Major character(s):** Stephen Ridenour, Computer Expert; Jonathan Wesley Smith, Computer Expert; Loren Cantrell, Spaceship Captain
**Time period(s):** Indeterminate Future
**Locale(s):** HuteNamid, Planet—Imaginary; *Cetacean*, Spaceship

**Summary:** Loren Cantrell deals with representatives of the 'NetAT who want to take Stephen off his assignment. Wesley Smith, both attracted to and repelled by Stephen Ridenour, learns more about Stephen and seduces him. Stephen, gradually remembering more about his past experiences as Zivon Ryevanishov, seeks out the Cocheta library, where he interfaces directly with the 'Net and begins to repair it. Sequel to *Uplink*.

**Other books you might like:**
Marion Zimmer Bradley, *The Forbidden Tower*, 1977
C.J. Cherryh, *Heavy Time*, 1991
David Drake, *Northworld*, 1990
William Gibson, *Neuromancer*, 1984
Robert A. Heinlein, *Stranger in a Strange Land*, 1961
C.J. Mills, *Winter World*, 1988
Neal Stephenson, *Snow Crash*, 1992

## 1863

### JANE S. FANCHER

## Ring of Intrigue

(New York: DAW, 1997)

**Story type:** Fantasy (Political; Magic Conflict)
**Series:** Dance of the Rings

**Major character(s):** Deymorin Rhomandi dunMheric, Royalty; Mikhyel Rhomandi dunMheric, Royalty, Handicapped
**Time period(s):** Indeterminate
**Locale(s):** Rhomatum, Fictional City

**Summary:** The death of the ringmaster of Rhomatum throws the magic power of the great city-state into disarray. Their allies and enemies waste no time in acting against Rhomatum. The children of the Rhomandi, the ruling family, must put aside their differences and act decisively to preserve the world. Second in series.

**Other books you might like:**
Barbara Hambly, *The Time of the Dark*, 1982
Robin Hobb, *Assassin's Apprentice*, 1995
Katherine Kurtz, *Deryni Rising*, 1970
Patricia A. McKillip, *The Riddle-Master of Hed*, 1976
Paula Volsky, *Illusion*, 1992

## 1864

### JANE S. FANCHER

## Ring of Lightning
(New York: DAW, 1995)

**Story type:** Fantasy (Political; Magic Conflict)
**Series:** Dance of the Rings
**Major character(s):** Deymorin Rhomandi dunMheric, Royalty (Princeps of Rhomatum); Mikhyel Rhomandi dunMheric, Royalty (Princeps of Rhomatum); Nikaenor "Nikki" Rhomandi dunMheric, Royalty (Princeps of Rhomatum)
**Time period(s):** Indeterminate
**Locale(s):** Rhomatum, Fictional City (city-state)

**Summary:** To survive the threat from a neighboring city-state and allow Rhomatum to blossom as a democracy, Deymorin must cease feuding with his brothers and plan a coordinated assault on their great-aunt's control of the magical power of the leythium Rings, focus of Rhomatum society. First of a series.

**Other books you might like:**
Robert Jordan, *The Eye of the World*, 1989
Melanie Rawn, *Dragon Prince*, 1988
Kristine Kathryn Rusch, *Traitors*, 1994
Martha Wells, *The Element of Fire*, 1993
Roger Zelazny, *Nine Princes in Amber*, 1970

## 1865

### JANE S. FANCHER

## Uplink
(New York: Warner Questar, 1992)

**Story type:** Science Fiction (Political)
**Major character(s):** Stephen Ridenour, Computer Expert; Anevai Tyeewapi, Scientist, Guide; Jonathan Wesley Smith, Computer Expert
**Time period(s):** Indeterminate Future
**Locale(s):** *Cetacean*, Spaceship; HuteNamid, Planet—Imaginary

**Summary:** While Stephen recovers aboard the *Cetacean*, having suffered a brutal beating on HuteNamid, the ship's doctor discovers evidence of his past abuse and drug addiction, possibly part of some plan by bigoted politicans back at Vandereaux. Stephen returns to HuteNamid and makes contact, at first unwillingly, through a virtual reality "library" with the Cocheta, a mysterious alien race. Sequel to *Ground-Ties*.

**Other books you might like:**
C.J. Cherryh, *Cyteen*, 1988
C.J. Cherryh, *Downbelow Station*, 1981
A.C. Crispin, *Silent Dances*, 1990
    Kathleen O'Malley, co-author
Cynthia Felice, *Downtime*, 1985
William Gibson, *Neuromancer*, 1984

## 1866

### DAVID FARLAND

## The Runelords: The Sum of All Men
(New York: Tor, 1998)

**Story type:** Fantasy (Magic Conflict)
**Series:** Runelords
**Major character(s):** Gaborn Val Orden, Royalty (prince), Wizard; Raj Ahten, Royalty (Wolf Lord), Wizard (Runelord); Iome Sylvarresta, Royalty (princess), Handicapped
**Time period(s):** Indeterminate Past
**Locale(s):** Sylvarresta, Fictional City; Kingdom of Rofehaven, Fictional Country

**Summary:** Prince Gaborn is on his way to ask for Iome's hand in marriage, when his chance discovery of a pair of assassins throws him into a deadly net of treachery and magic. On the move, the Wolf Lord intends to conquer first Sylvarresta, then the Kingdom of Rofehaven, and possibly the entire world. Only the man can stop him: Gaborn, the Earth King. First novel.

**Other books you might like:**
Glen Cook, *Tower of Fear*, 1989
David Drake, *Lord of the Isles*, 1997
Lisa Goldstein, *Summer King, Winter Fool*, 1994
Barbara Hambly, *The Time of the Dark*, 1982
Sheri S. Tepper, *King's Blood Four*, 1983

## 1867

### NANCY FARMER

## The Ear, the Eye, and the Arm
(New York: Orchard Books, 1994)

**Story type:** Fantasy (Mystery; Science Fiction)
**Major character(s):** Amadeus Matsika, Military Personnel (general); Tendai Matsika, Child
**Time period(s):** 22nd century (2194)
**Locale(s):** Harare, Zimbabwe

**Summary:** Fearing his enemies might harm his children, General Matsika keeps the youngsters sheltered in the home compound. After Tendai and his sister and brother sneak out of the house to bus across Harare for a scout merit badge, the Blue Monkey lures them into the clutches of Fist and Knife and then the She Elephant who forces them to mine plastic. Tendai attracts the spirit of Zimbabwe which helps the children survive while the three mutant detectives, the Eye, the Ear, and the Arm, effect their rescue.

**Other books you might like:**
Gillian Bradshaw, *The Land of Gold*, 1992
Barry Lopez, *Crow and Weasel*, 1990
Ben Okri, *The Famished Road*, 1992
Ben Okri, *Songs of Enchantment*, 1993
Mike Resnick, *Future Earths: Under African Skies*, 1993
    Gardner Dozois, co-editor

## 1868
### NANCY FARMER

## A Girl Named Disaster
(New York: Orchard Books, 1996)

**Story type:** Fantasy (Adventure; Quest)
**Major character(s):** Nhamo, Child, Adventurer
**Time period(s):** 1990s
**Locale(s):** Lake Cabora Bassa, Mozambique; Zimbabwe

**Summary:** Fleeing the impending marriage which would make her fourth wife to a cruel man, Nhamo sets out for Zimbabwe to search for her father. Swept to the uncharted Lake Cabora Bassa, Nhamo nearly drowns. Near-starvation puts her in contact with the spirit world, a contact that remains after Nhamo leaves the wilderness.

**Other books you might like:**
Gillian Bradshaw, *The Land of Gold*, 1992
Kara Dalkey, *Little Sister*, 1996
Garth Nix, *Sabriel*, 1996
Ben Okri, *The Famished Road*, 1992
Ben Okri, *Songs of Enchantment*, 1993
Mike Resnick, *Future Earths: Under African Skies*, 1993
  Gardner Dozois, co-editor

## 1869
### PHILIP JOSE FARMER

## Dayworld Breakup
(New York: Tor, 1990)

**Story type:** Science Fiction (Adventure; Political)
**Series:** Dayworld
**Major character(s):** William St.-George Duncan, Revolutionary; Panthea Snick, Revolutionary, Girlfriend
**Time period(s):** 31st century
**Locale(s):** Earth

**Summary:** William St.-George Duncan, an integrated multiple personality, and Panthea Snick sabotage the system in hopes of forcing the government to reveal the secrets of a life-extending drug and the decline in population. A lengthy pursuit results in their capture after which Duncan's individual personalities become a further problem.

**Other books you might like:**
Robert A. Heinlein, *Revolt in 2100*, 1953
Robert A. Heinlein, *Sixth Column*, 1949
Steve Perry, *The Man Who Never Missed*, 1985
Clifford D. Simak, *The Werewolf Principle*, 1967
David Alexander Smith, *Homecoming*, 1990
A.E. Van Vogt, *The Weapon Shops of Isher*, 1951
A.E. Van Vogt, *The Weapon Makers*, 1946

## 1870
### PHILIP JOSE FARMER

## Escape From Loki
(New York: Bantam Falcon, 1991)

**Story type:** Fantasy (Adventure)
**Series:** Doc Savage
**Major character(s):** Clark "Doc" Savage Jr., Adventurer, Military Personnel (pilot); von Hessel, Nobleman (baron), Military Personnel (Colonel)
**Time period(s):** 1910s (1918)
**Locale(s):** Germany

**Summary:** When shot down over Germany and captured by Baron von Hessel, 16-year-old Lieutenant Clark Savage escapes only to be recaptured and thrown into an escape-proof salt mine where the Baron experiments on human guinea pigs. Doc Savage must defeat the Baron to save the Allies from his new superweapon.

**Other books you might like:**
Kenneth Robeson, *Doc Savage Omnibus #13*, 1990
  Kenneth Robeson is the pseudonym of a group of authors (mainly Lester Dent) who wrote the Doc Savage stories.
Kenneth Robeson, *Doc Savage Omnibus #12*, 1990
  Kenneth Robeson is the pseudonym of a group of authors (mainly Lester Dent) who wrote the Doc Savage stories.
Kenneth Robeson, *Doc Savage Omnibus #11*, 1990
  Kenneth Robeson is the pseudonym for a group of authors (mainly Lester Dent) who wrote the Doc Savage stories.
Kenneth Robeson, *Doc Savage Omnibus #10*, 1989
Kenneth Robeson, *Doc Savage Omnibus #9*, 1989
Kenneth Robeson, *Doc Savage Omnibus #1*, 1986
Kenneth Robeson, *Python Isle*, 1991

## 1871
### PHILIP JOSE FARMER

## More than Fire
(New York: Tor, 1993)

**Story type:** Science Fiction (Adventure)
**Series:** World of Tiers
**Major character(s):** Kickaha, Adventurer; Red Orc, Immortal; Khruuz, Alien
**Time period(s):** 1990s; Indeterminate
**Locale(s):** World of Tiers, Planet—Imaginary; Earth; Earth II, Planet—Imaginary

**Summary:** Aided by Khruuz, lone survivor of his race, Kickaha and Anana must stop the mad Lord, Red Orc, from finding the secret of creating and destroying universes. Concludes the series.

**Other books you might like:**
Piers Anthony, *Kirlian Quest*, 1978
Greg Bear, *Eternity*, 1988
Ben Bova, *Orion*, 1984
Octavia E. Butler, *Adulthood Rites*, 1988
Jack L. Chalker, *The Run to Chaos Keep*, 1990
Alan Dean Foster, *Glory Lane*, 1987
Jack Vance, *The Five Gold Bands*, 1963
Roger Zelazny, *Nine Princes in Amber*, 1970

## 1872
### PHILIP JOSE FARMER, Editor

## Quest to Riverworld
(New York: Warner Questar, 1993)

**Story type:** Science Fiction (Anthology; Immortality)
**Series:** Riverworld
**Time period(s):** Indeterminate Future
**Locale(s):** Riverworld, Planet—Imaginary

**Summary:** Contains 14 stories all sharing Philip Jose Farmer's Riverworld setting with two stories by the series' creator and one collaboration by David Bischoff and Dean Wesley Smith. Other authors include John Gregory Betancourt, Jody Lynn Nye, Robert Sheckley, Brad Strickland, Lawrence Watt-Evans and Robert Weinberg.

**Other books you might like:**
Pamela Sargent, *Afterlives: An Anthology of Stories about Life After Death*, 1986
  Ian Watson, co-editor
William Shatner, *Believe: A Novel*, 1992
  Michael Tobias, co-author
Robert Silverberg, *To the Land of the Living*, 1990
Clifford D. Simak, *Out of Their Minds*, 1970
Joan Slonczewski, *Daughter of Elysium*, 1993
Robert Weinberg, *The Mists From Beyond*, 1993
  Stefan R. Dziemianowicz, Martin H. Greenberg, co-editors

---

**1873**

PHILIP JOSE FARMER

## Red Orc's Rage

(New York: Tor, 1991)

**Story type:** Fantasy (Contemporary; Alternate World)
**Series:** World of Tiers
**Major character(s):** Jim Grimson, Teenager, Criminal; L. Robert Porsena, Doctor (psychiatrist); Orc, Teenager, Nobleman
**Time period(s):** 1970s (1979)
**Locale(s):** Belmont City, Ohio; Tiersian Universe, Fictional Country

**Summary:** Jim's life is a mess until he begins treatment under Dr. Porsena, who has adapted Farmer's World of Tiers series (1965- ) for use as a therapeutic tool. Jim chooses the series' major villain, Orc, as the alter ego through which he will try to confront his problems and learn positive coping strategies. Some new problems arise when Jim becomes convinced that he actually occupies the body of his alter ego.

**Other books you might like:**
Pat Cadigan, *Mindplayers*, 1987
Charles de Lint, *The Little Country*, 1990
Gordon R. Dickson, *The Dragon and the George*, 1976
Rudy Rucker, *Software*, 1982
Robert Silverberg, *Letters From Atlantis*, 1990
Vivian Vande Velde, *User Unfriendly*, 1991
Roger Zelazny, *Bridge of Ashes*, 1976

---

**1874**

PHILIP JOSE FARMER

## Riders of the Purple Wage

(New York: Tor, 1992)

**Story type:** Science Fiction (Collection)

**Summary:** Contains eight stories reprinted from periodicals and anthologies including one from *Dangerous Visions* (1967), the title story, which received a Nebula Award nomination and a Hugo Award. The mood of these stories varies from humor to emotional drama while Farmer's social commentary encompasses situations as disparate as a time-travelling saint in "St. Francis Kisses His Ass Goodbye" and the IRS's encounter with a UFO in "UFO Versus IRS."

**Other books you might like:**
Alfred Bester, *Star Light, Star Bright*, 1976
Orson Scott Card, *Maps in a Mirror*, 1990
Larry Niven, *Tales of Known Space*, 1975
Robert Silverberg, *The Science Fiction Hall of Fame, Volume 1*, 1970
  editor
Cordwainer Smith, *The Best of Cordwainer Smith*, 1975

---

Theodore Sturgeon, *Aliens 4*, 1959
Theodore Sturgeon, *E Pluribus Unicorn*, 1953
William Tenn, *The Human Angle*, 1956
William Tenn, *Of All Possible Worlds*, 1955
John Varley, *Blue Champagne*, 1986
John Varley, *The Persistence of Vision*, 1978

---

**1875**

PHILIP JOSE FARMER, Editor
MARTIN H. GREENBERG, Co-Editor

## Tales of Riverworld

(New York: Warner Questar, 1992)

**Story type:** Science Fiction (Anthology; Immortality)
**Series:** Riverworld
**Time period(s):** Indeterminate
**Locale(s):** Riverworld, Planet—Imaginary

**Summary:** Contains a two-page foreword and nine stories all sharing the world of Farmer's award winning *River of Eternity* (1983) begun in the Hugo Award winning novel, *To Your Scattered Bodies Go* (1971). This book includes one story by the editor, "Crossing the River"; one collaboration by Mike Resnick and Barry Malzberg, "Every Man a God"; the first appearance by Dane Helstrom, "A Hole in Hell"; the first humorous Riverworld story, "Blandings on Riverworld," by Phillip C. Jennings; and the first science fiction story by horror writer Ed Gorman, "Fool's Paradise," plus stories by John Gregory Betancourt, Allen Steele, Harry Turtledove and Robert Weinberg.

**Other books you might like:**
Diana G. Gallagher, *The Alien Dark*, 1990
Joe Haldeman, *The Hemingway Hoax*, 1990
Frank M. Robinson, *The Dark Beyond the Stars*, 1991
Pamela Sargent, *Afterlives: An Anthology of Stories about Life After Death*, 1986
  Ian Watson, co-editor
William Shatner, *Believe: A Novel*, 1992
  Michael Tobias, co-author
Robert Silverberg, *To the Land of the Living*, 1990

---

**1876**

PHILIP JOSE FARMER

## To Your Scattered Bodies Go

(New York: Ballantine Del Rey, 1998)

**Story type:** Science Fiction (Adventure; Immortality)
**Series:** Riverworld
**Major character(s):** Richard Francis Burton, Historical Figure, Explorer; Hermann Goering, Historical Figure; Kazzintuitruaabemss "Kazz", Prehistoric Human
**Time period(s):** Indeterminate Future
**Locale(s):** Riverworld, Planet—Imaginary

**Summary:** All humanity resurrects on a distant planet dominated by a huge river. Richard Burton wants to sail that river with his group, but remains thwarted by Slavers and his mysterious link, persisting through death, to Hermann Goering. However, one of the Ethicals behind the resurrection secretly aids Burton and other chosen ones. A reissue of this classic first published in 1971.

**Other books you might like:**
Poul Anderson, *The Boat of a Million Years*, 1989
Greg Bear, *Eon*, 1985
Jack L. Chalker, *Midnight at the Well of Souls*, 1977

John Dalmas, *The Lantern of God*, 1989
Larry Niven, *Ringworld*, 1970
Mike Resnick, *A Miracle of Rare Design*, 1994
Karen Ripley, *The Persistence of Memory*, 1993
Kim Stanley Robinson, *Blue Mars*, 1996

**1877**

MICK FARREN

## The Armageddon Crazy

(New York: Ballantine/Del Rey, 1989)

**Story type:** Science Fiction (Dystopian)
**Major character(s):** Harry Carlisle, Police Officer; Cynthia Kline, Spy
**Time period(s):** 21st century
**Locale(s):** United States

**Summary:** In a future America where fundamentalist Christianity rules with an iron hand, a group of people gather together to stage a revolution using spectacular special effects.

**Other books you might like:**
Margaret Atwood, *The Handmaid's Tale*, 1986
Michael Bishop, *A Little Knowledge*, 1977
Robert A. Heinlein, *Sixth Column*, 1949
John Kessel, *Good News From Outer Space*, 1989
James Morrow, *Only Begotten Daughter*, 1990

**1878**

MICK FARREN

## The Feelies

(New York: Ballantine/Del Rey, 1990)

**Story type:** Science Fiction (Contemporary Realism; Techno-Thriller)
**Major character(s):** John Wilson Heffer, Vacationer; Wanda-Jean, Television Personality (gameshow contestant)
**Time period(s):** 21st century
**Locale(s):** United States

**Summary:** John Wilson Heffer got a special deal on a feelie, a total sensory experience in a life support chamber. He couldn't resist the offer, but then found himself stuck as Billy the Kid getting shot by Pat Garrett, over and over. When it was noticed that his machine was malfunctioning, he'd been dead for quite some time. Meanwhile, Wanda-Jean wanted to experience a feelie. Although she could never afford it, if she won on the TV Gameshow "Wildest Dreams," the first prize was a feelie contract. Revised from the 1978 British edition.

**Other books you might like:**
Piers Anthony, *Total Recall*, 1989
    pseudonym of Piers Anthony Dillingham Jacob
Pat Cadigan, *Mindplayers*, 1987
Pat Cadigan, *Synners*, 1991
Harry Harrison, *Make Room, Make Room*, 1966
Walter Dean Myers, *Brainstorm*, 1977

**1879**

MICK FARREN

## The Last Stand of the DNA Cowboys

(New York: Ballantine/Del Rey, 1989)

**Story type:** Science Fiction (Adventure)
**Series:** DNA Cowboys
**Major character(s):** Minstrel Boy, Warrior (DNA Cowboy); Billy Oblivion, Warrior (DNA Cowboy)
**Time period(s):** Indeterminate Future
**Locale(s):** Earth

**Summary:** In a post-holocaust world with a strong flavoring of drugs, rock n' roll and the sixties, the DNA Cowboys do their best to hold things together and have a good time.

**Other books you might like:**
Samuel R. Delany, *The Einstein Intersection*, 1987
Michael Moorcock, *The Final Programme*, 1968
Michael Moorcock, *The Fireclown*, 1965
William F. Wu, *Hong on the Range*, 1989

**1880**

MICK FARREN

## Mars—The Red Planet

(New York: Ballantine/Del Rey, 1990)

**Story type:** Science Fiction (Adventure)
**Major character(s):** Lech Hammond, Journalist
**Time period(s):** 21st century
**Locale(s):** Mars

**Summary:** The Martian Soviets have uncovered an alien artifact and ace TV reporter Lech Hammond goes to investigate. Mars is in chaos when he arrives due to the attacks of a vicious serial killer whose actions may be stimulated by the artifact.

**Other books you might like:**
W. Michael Gear, *The Artifact*, 1989
Ian McDonald, *Desolation Road*, 1988
Daniel Keys Moran, *The Armageddon Blues*, 1988
Paul Preuss, *Arthur C. Clarke's Venus Prime, Vol. 2: Maelstrom*, 1988

**1881**

MICK FARREN

## Necrom

(New York: Ballantine/Del Rey, 1991)

**Story type:** Science Fiction (Alternate Universe; Fantasy)
**Major character(s):** Joe Ribson, Musician (rock); Nephredann, Demon; Gideon Windemere, Drug Dealer
**Time period(s):** 1990s
**Locale(s):** New York, New York; Hole in the Void Valley, Alternate Universe

**Summary:** Gibson, an alcoholic ex-rock star, tries to remember his life before being confined and drugged in an asylum. It seems he'd gotten involved in an interdimensional effort to save humanity from demonic forces and nuclear destruction, but the drugs keep his mind fuzzy. Nonetheless, the evening news convinces him that he is not in the New York where he belongs.

**Other books you might like:**
Pat Cadigan, *Mindplayers*, 1987

Geary Gravel, *A Key for the Nonesuch*, 1990
Marc Laidlaw, *Neon Lotus*, 1988
Michael Moorcock, *Elric of Melnibone*, 1976
Elizabeth Ann Scarborough, *Nothing Sacred*, 1991
Michael A. Stackpole, *A Gathering Evil*, 1991

## 1882

### MICK FARREN

## *The Time of Feasting*
(New York: Tor, 1996)

**Story type:** Horror (Vampire Story)
**Major character(s):** Victor Renquist, Vampire; Kurt Carfax, Vampire; Gideon Kelly, Religious (ex-priest)
**Time period(s):** 1990s (1996)
**Locale(s):** New York, New York

**Summary:** At the approach of the next Feasting, a period when vampires state their hungers and disguise the carnage as the handiwork of human malefactors, vampire patriarch Victor Renquist is challenged for the leadership of his Manhattan-based vampire enclave by Kurt Carfax, a brash young vampire who threatens to bring notice and destruction down upon the vampire brood. Renquist and Carfax are avidly watched by Gideon Kelly, a defrocked priest who hopes to redeem himself by destroying them.

**Other books you might like:**
Poppy Z. Brite, *Lost Souls*, 1993
Nancy A. Collins, *Sunglasses After Dark*, 1989
Robert R. McCammon, *They Thirst*, 1981
Anne Rice, *The Queen of the Damned*, 1988
Whitley Strieber, *The Hunger*, 1981

## 1883

### JOHN FARRIS

## *The Axman Cometh*
(New York: Tor, 1989)

**Story type:** Horror (Psychological Suspense)
**Major character(s):** Shannon Hill, Artist; Donald Carnes, Boyfriend
**Time period(s):** 1960s (1964); 1980s
**Locale(s):** Emerson, Kansas; New York, New York

**Summary:** Trapped in a darkened, disabled elevator, Shannon is tormented by a stranger claiming to be the "Axman" who killed her entire family 20 years earlier. Meanwhile her boyfriend, urged on by the ghost of Ernest Hemingway, attempts to go to her rescue.

**Other books you might like:**
Peter Straub, *If You Could See Me Now*, 1977

## 1884

### JOHN FARRIS

## *Fiends*
(Arlington Heights, IL: Dark Harvest, 1989)

**Story type:** Horror (Ancient Evil Unleashed)
**Major character(s):** Arne Horsfall, Patient (escaped mental patient); Enid Waller, Nurse (mental hospital worker)
**Time period(s):** 1900s (1906); 1970s
**Locale(s):** Sublimity, Tennessee (a suburb of Nashville)

**Summary:** Made dumb and half-insane by a mysterious quest with his father in 1906, Arne Horsfall escapes the hospital in 1970, becoming

an unwilling emissary for a breed of winged semi-human monsters who are unleashed to terrorize the countryside and recruit new members.

**Other books you might like:**
Jere Cunningham, *The Abyss*, 1981
Bentley Little, *The Revelation*, 1990

## 1885

### JOHN FARRIS
### JOE R. LANSDALE, Co-Author
### STEPHEN GALLAGHER, Co-Author

## *Night Visions 8*
(Arlington Heights, IL: Dark Harvest, 1991)

**Story type:** Horror (Anthology)
**Series:** Night Visions

**Summary:** Each of the three writers contribute approximately 30,000 words of contemporary horror fiction. The stories range from the dark whimsey of Gallagher's "The Back of His Hand" to the terrifying woman-in-jeopardy story "Incident On and Off a Mountain Road" by Lansdale. Afterword by Robert R. McCammon.

**Other books you might like:**
Charles L. Grant, *Night Visions 2*, 1985
George R.R. Martin, *Night Visions 3*, 1986
Alan Ryan, *Night Visions 1*, 1984
Douglas E. Winter, *Night Visions 5*, 1988

## 1886

### JOHN FARRIS

## *Sacrifice*
(New York: Tor, 1994)

**Story type:** Horror (Mystery)
**Major character(s):** Greg Walker, Repairman (appliance); Sharissa Walker, Teenager (Greg's daughter); C.G. Butterbaugh, Detective
**Time period(s):** 1990s (1994)
**Locale(s):** Sky Valley, Georgia; Kan Peten, Guatemala

**Summary:** If Greg Walker seems a little overprotective of his teenage daughter and nosy about her sex life, it's with good reason. A near immortal survivor of the ancient Mayas who has endured centuries of physical wear and tear, he must ritually sacrifice a virgin at an ancient Mayan temple every generation in order to maintain his longevity. This novel is an expansion of Farris's 1990 novella, "Good Morning, Daddy."

**Other books you might like:**
Robert R. McCammon, *Mystery Walk*, 1984
Ashley McConnell, *Days of the Dead*, 1992
G. Wayne Miller, *Thunder Rise*, 1988
Adam Niswander, *The Charm*, 1993
Dan Simmons, *Song of Kali*, 1985

## 1887

### JOHN FARRIS

## *Scare Tactics*
(New York: Tor, 1989)

**Story type:** Horror (Collection)

**Summary:** One short novel and two stories. Most notable is the novel, *The Guardians*, in which a political rivalry erupts into violence and murder. Other excellent stories include ''The Odor of Violets,'' in which a man commits murder to lay claim to the work of another, only to discover that ''Fate'' has made sure he receives justice, and ''Horrorshow,'' in which the hero uses his supernatural powers to expose a brutal murderer. The paperback edition contains two additional stories, ''Scare Tactics'' and ''I Scream. You Scream. We All Scream for Ice Cream.''

**Other books you might like:**
Robert R. McCammon, *Blue World*, 1990
F. Paul Wilson, *Soft and Others*, 1989

## 1888

### DAVID A. FARROW

## Root of All Evil

(Charleston, South Carolina: Wyrick, 1997)

**Story type:** Horror (Black Magic; Mystery)
**Major character(s):** Harry Holmes, Detective—Police; Andrew Rutledge, Writer; Willy Huger, Political Figure
**Time period(s):** 1990s (1997); 1950s (1959)
**Locale(s):** Charleston, South Carolina

**Summary:** A serial killer is stalking women in Charleston, cutting out their hearts and leaving roots associated with voodoo herbalism entwined in their hair. Detective Harry Holmes's investigations bring him into contact with Andrew Rutledge, who experienced psychic links to several of the murder victims, and a trail of larceny and corruption that extends back through Rutledge's family and the family of his friend over 40 years. A first novel.

**Other books you might like:**
Nancy A. Collins, *Tempter*, 1990
Don Davis, *The Gris-Gris Man*, 1997
D.J. Donaldson, *Blood on the Bayou*, 1991
John Farris, *All Heads Turn When the Hunt Goes By*, 1972
Karen Hall, *Dark Debts*, 1996
Robert R. McCammon, *Usher's Passing*, 1984

## 1889

### GREG FARSHTEY, Editor
### GREG GORDEN, Co-Editor
### ED STARK, Co-Editor

## Strange Tales From the Nile Empire

(Honesdale, Pennsylvania: West End Games, 1992)

**Story type:** Fantasy (Anthology; Adventure)
**Series:** Torg: The Possibility Wars
**Major character(s):** Morbius, Criminal, Ruler (High Lord)
**Time period(s):** 21st century
**Locale(s):** Nile Empire, Alternate Earth

**Summary:** This volume contains a nine-page introduction, a five-page appendix by Greg Gorden plus eight stories by six authors set in a Middle East in which Dr. Morbius's reality-warping ability creates a cross between ancient Egypt and 1930s heroic pulp fiction. A game tie-in.

**Other books you might like:**
George Alec Effinger, *When Gravity Fails*, 1987
Douglas Kaufman, *Dragons over England*, 1992
    Ed Stark, co-editor
Christopher Kubasik, *Changeling*, 1992

Will Shetterly, *Liavek*, 1985
    Emma Bull, co-editor
Ed Stark, *Mysterious Cairo*, 1992
    Editor
Jordan K. Weisman, *Into the Shadows*, 1992

## 1890

### CHRISTA FAUST

## Control Freak

(New York: Masquerade/Rhinoceros, 1998)

**Story type:** Horror (Mystery)
**Major character(s):** Caitlin McCullough, Writer; Michael Kiernan, Detective
**Time period(s):** 1990s (1998)
**Locale(s):** New York, New York

**Summary:** Caitlin McCullough sees the sex murder of a wayward New York debutante as fodder for a book that will liberate her from the grind of writing pseudonymous serial pulp novels. Her investigations into the New York sadomasochism scene usher her into a truly dark and dangerous underworld and acquaint her with her hitherto unacknowledged proclivities for sexual domination. A first novel.

**Other books you might like:**
Poppy Z. Brite, *Exquisite Corpse*, 1996
Michael Cecilione, *Domination*, 1993
Ray Garton, *Live Girls*, 1987
Caitlin R. Kiernan, *Silk*, 1998
Lucy Taylor, *The Flesh Artist*, 1994

## 1891

### JOE CLIFFORD FAUST

## Desperate Measures

(New York: Ballantine/Del Rey, 1989)

**Story type:** Science Fiction (Space Opera)
**Series:** Angel's Luck
**Major character(s):** James May, Spaceship Captain
**Time period(s):** Indeterminate Future
**Locale(s):** *Angel's Luck*, Spaceship

**Summary:** James May is consistently unlucky. He can barely make the payments on his spaceship, he's got the authorities sniffing at his heels, his copilot just disappeared (taking the autopilot with him) and, last but not least, the crime syndicate wants to repossess his ship. Then there's the cargo of beef in his hold; what's he supposed to do with that? It's definitely time to take desperate measures.

**Other books you might like:**
C.J. Cherryh, *Merchanter's Luck*, 1982
Rory Harper, *Petrogypsies*, 1989
R.A. MacAvoy, *The Third Eagle: Lessons Along a Minor String*, 1989
Walter Jon Williams, *Angel Station*, 1989

## 1892

### JOE CLIFFORD FAUST

## Ferman's Devils

(New York: Bantam Spectra, 1996)

**Story type:** Science Fiction (Humor)

**Major character(s):** Boddekker, Advertising; Honniker, Advertising; Bainbridge, Advertising, Student—College
**Time period(s):** 21st century
**Locale(s):** New York, New York

**Summary:** A rising star at an advertising agency, Boddekker must attain wealth and a wife to qualify for a magnificent house outside New York City. His mugging by a street gang and the demands of the ad agency to develop a winning ad campaign for a new product present Boddekker with the opportunity for a bold original approach to selling laundry soap utilizing the street gang.

**Other books you might like:**
Mel Gilden, *Tubular Android Superheroes*, 1991
Frederik Pohl, *Midas World*, 1983
Frederik Pohl, *The Space Merchants*, 1953
    C.M. Kornbluth, co-author
Nick Pollotta, *Illegal Aliens*, 1989
    Phil Foglio, co-author

---

**1893**

**JOE CLIFFORD FAUST**

## Precious Cargo

(New York: Ballantine/Del Rey Books, 1990)

**Story type:** Science Fiction (Space Opera)
**Series:** Angel's Luck
**Major character(s):** James May, Spaceship Captain
**Time period(s):** Indeterminate Future
**Locale(s):** Angel's Luck, Spaceship

**Summary:** Captain May's *Angel's Luck* continues to find trouble (and silliness) wherever it goes. Although they've survived—barely—a battle with the evil Yueh-shing, they're stranded in space. Then, almost worse than being stranded, they're picked up by a ship captained by May's ex-wife Maggie, a ship chockful to the gills with argumentative aliens.

**Other books you might like:**
C.J. Cherryh, *Merchanter's Luck*, 1982
Rory Harper, *Petrogypsies*, 1989
R.A. MacAvoy, *The Third Eagle: Lessons Along a Minor String*, 1989
Walter Jon Williams, *Angel Station*, 1989

---

**1894**

**RON FAUST**

## Lord of the Dark Lake

(New York: Tor/Forge, 1996)

**Story type:** Horror (Psychological Suspense)
**Major character(s):** Jay Chandler, Archaeologist; Alexander Krisos, Wealthy; Walter Von Rabenaue, Guard
**Time period(s):** 1990s (1996)
**Locale(s):** Krisos Island, Greece

**Summary:** While excavating the Temple of Poseidon, Jay Chandler is invited to attend the annual celebrity-studded summer party that his friend Alexander Krisos throws on the family island. A macabre turn of events leads to the systematic murders of the party guests, driving Jay into the catacombs under the island where he becomes a latter day Theseus, attempting to elude a Minotaur and determine who is killing the guests and why.

**Other books you might like:**
Michael Green, *The Jimjams*, 1994
Michael T. Hinkemeyer, *Order of the Arrow*, 1989

Stephen Laws, *Daemonic*, 1995
Richard Laymon, *Midnight's Lair*, 1988
Brian Lumley, *The House of Doors*, 1990

---

**1895**

**BILL FAWCETT**, Editor

## Cats in Space and Other Places

(New York: Baen, 1992)

**Story type:** Science Fiction (Anthology)

**Summary:** Divided into two sections, "Cats" and "Alien Cats," this volume contains 17 stories, most reprinted from periodicals and anthologies 1939-1991, with two stories by Cordwainer Smith, "The Game of Rat and Dragon" and "The Ballad of Lost C'Mell" and two by Fritz Leiber, "Ship of Shadows" and "Space-Time for Springers." One story, "Chanur's Homecoming," first appeared as chapter twelve of C.J. Cherryh's *Chanur's Homecoming* (1986). Other influential stories include "Mouse" by Fredric Brown and "Black Destroyer" by A.E. van Vogt. Other authors include Greg Bear, Arthur C. Clarke, David Drake, Robert A. Heinlein, Ursula K. Le Guin, Anne McCaffrey and S.M. Stirling.

**Other books you might like:**
Clare Bell, *Clan Ground*, 1984
C.J. Cherryh, *The Pride of Chanur*, 1982
Alan Dean Foster, *Cat-A-Lyst*, 1991
Robert A. Heinlein, *The Door into Summer*, 1957
Andre Norton, *Catfantastic*, 1989
    Martin H. Greenberg, co-editor
Michael Peak, *Cat House*, 1989
Mark E. Rogers, *The Adventures of Samurai Cat*, 1984
Cordwainer Smith, *The Best of Cordwainer Smith*, 1975
Marti Steussy, *Forest of the Night*, 1987

---

**1896**

**BILL FAWCETT**, Editor

## Honor of the Regiment

(New York: Baen, 1993)

**Story type:** Science Fiction (Anthology; Alternate Intelligence)
**Series:** Bolo
**Time period(s):** Indeterminate Future
**Locale(s):** Earth; Planet—Imaginary

**Summary:** Contains eight original stories by 10 authors providing glimpses into the history and evolution of Bolos, heavily armed and armored artificial intelligences built for human defense. Authors include Larry Dixon, David Drake, Mercedes Lackey, S.N. Lewitt, Barry N. Malzberg, Mike Resnick, Christopher Stasheff and S.M. Stirling.

**Other books you might like:**
Orson Scott Card, *Ender's Game*, 1985
David Drake, *The Fleet*, 1988
    Bill Fawcett, co-editor
David Drake, *Counter Attack*, 1988
    Bill Fawcett, co-editor
Keith Laumer, *Bolo: The Annals of the Dinochrome Brigade*, 1976
Keith Laumer, *The Complete Bolo*, 1990
Keith Laumer, *Rogue Bolo*, 1986
G. Harry Stine, *Warbots*, 1988
Jack Williamson, *The Humanoid Touch*, 1980

## 1897
### GREGORY FEELEY

## The Oxygen Barons
(New York: Ace, 1990)

**Story type:** Science Fiction (Hard Science Fiction; Political)
**Major character(s):** Galvanix Nagashima, Scientist; Beryl, Warrior
**Time period(s):** Indeterminate Future
**Locale(s):** Tycho South Shore, Montenegro

**Summary:** The moon had been in the process of developing a viable ecology with water sent from the asteroid belt and carbon dioxide sent from Venus, allowing free water and a breathable atmosphere to develop. In order to save the newly declared Lunar Republic, Galvanix and Beryl undertake a suicide mission to pulverize the last water ice comet before it hits the moon. This is the author's first book.

**Other books you might like:**
Roger MacBride Allen, *The Ring of Charon*, 1990
Greg Bear, *Eon*, 1986
David Brin, *Earth*, 1990
Vonda N. McIntyre, *Transition*, 1990
Vonda N. McIntyre, *Starfarers*, 1989
Larry Niven, *The Smoke Ring*, 1987
Larry Niven, *The Integral Trees*, 1984

## 1898
### HILA FEIL

## Blue Moon
(New York: Atheneum, 1990)

**Story type:** Fantasy (Contemporary; Young Adult)
**Major character(s):** Julia, Child-Care Giver, Teenager; Molly, Child; Sean, Artist
**Time period(s):** 1990s
**Locale(s):** Cape Cod, Massachusetts

**Summary:** Molly's stepmother, soap opera writer Cheryl, is ready to make some changes in the home of Molly's dead mother Maria, another artist whose ghost Molly believes is present.

**Other books you might like:**
C.S. Adler, *Ghost Brother*, 1990
Ruth Arthur, *The Autumn People*, 1973
Avi, *Something Upstairs: A Tale of Ghosts*, 1988
Madeleine L'Engle, *The Moon by Night*, 1963

## 1899
### DAVID FEINTUCH

## Challenger's Hope
(New York: Warner Aspect, 1995)

**Story type:** Science Fiction (Military; Alternate Intelligence)
**Series:** Nicholas Seafort Saga
**Major character(s):** Nicholas Seafort, Military Personnel; Philip Tyre, Military Personnel (midshipman), Spaceman
**Time period(s):** 22nd century (2197-2198)
**Locale(s):** Outer Space

**Summary:** New to command, Nicholas Seafort first faces an alien attack, then plague. On a hopeless rescue mission, he must overcome emergencies and pull together a functioning crew from passengers.

**Other books you might like:**
F.M. Busby, *Slow Freight*, 1991
A. Bertram Chandler, *The Big Black Mark*, 1975
C.J. Cherryh, *Tripoint*, 1994
Margaret Davis, *Mind Light*, 1993
Paula E. Downing, *Flare Star*, 1992
Robert A. Heinlein, *Starman Jones*, 1953
David Gerrold, *Voyage of the Star Wolf*, 1990
Norman Spinrad, *The Void Captain's Tale*, 1983

## 1900
### DAVID FEINTUCH

## Fisherman's Hope
(New York: Warner Aspect, 1996)

**Story type:** Science Fiction (Military; Political)
**Series:** Nicholas Seafort Saga
**Major character(s):** Nicholas Seafort, Military Personnel; Edgar "Eddie" Tolliver, Military Personnel (aide-de-camp)
**Time period(s):** 23rd century (2201)
**Locale(s):** Earth; Montenegro; Outer Space

**Summary:** Assigned command of the Space Academy at Devon and at Farside on the Moon, Nicholas Seafort reminisces about his own days at the Academy. While Seafort learns to navigate amidst political rivalries to gain even minimum appropriations, alien warships arrive in the Solar System, attacking Earth with only Seafort and his cadets to save the day. Fourth in the series.

**Other books you might like:**
Poul Anderson, *Ensign Flandry*, 1966
Lois McMaster Bujold, *The Vor Game*, 1990
F.M. Busby, *Star Rebel*, 1984
A. Bertram Chandler, *The Big Black Mark*, 1975
David Gerrold, *A Matter for Men*, 1983
Robert A. Heinlein, *Space Cadet*, 1948
Jerry Pournelle, *Prince of Mercenaries*, 1989
Harry Turtledove, *Worldwar: In the Balance*, 1994
Timothy Zahn, *Cobra*, 1985

## 1901
### DAVID FEINTUCH

## Midshipman's Hope
(New York: Warner Aspect, 1994)

**Story type:** Science Fiction (Military)
**Series:** Nicholas Seafort Saga
**Major character(s):** Nicholas Seafort, Military Personnel; Vax Holser, Military Personnel
**Time period(s):** 22nd century (2194-2195)
**Locale(s):** *U.N.S. Hibernia*, Spaceship; Outer Space; Hope Nation, Planet—Imaginary

**Summary:** When *Hibernia*'s captain dies of illness, Midshipman Seafort becomes her new captain, and is quickly challenged by unexpected difficulties including the attempted pirating of the ship.

**Other books you might like:**
Lois McMaster Bujold, *The Warrior's Apprentice*, 1986
F.M. Busby, *The Demu Trilogy*, 1980
Debra Doyle, *The Price of the Stars*, 1992
    James D. Macdonald, co-author
Sherwood Smith, *The Phoenix in Flight*, 1993
    Dave Trowbridge, co-author
David Weber, *On Basilisk Station*, 1993

## **1902**

### DAVID FEINTUCH

## *The Still*

(New York: Warner Aspect, 1997)

**Story type:** Fantasy (Political; Adventure)
**Major character(s):** Rodrigo, Royalty, Heir—Dispossessed; Rustin, Royalty; Elryc, Royalty
**Time period(s):** Indeterminate Past
**Locale(s):** Caldeon, Fictional Country

**Summary:** Prince Rodrigo should ascend the throne of Caldeon when his mother dies. However, the spoiled and indolent young man has not prepared for the plots and betrayals that depose him. If he wishes to rule, he must grow up and dare to seize the power of the Still.

**Other books you might like:**
Glen Cook, *The Swordbearer*, 1982
Diane Duane, *The Door into Fire*, 1979
J.V. Jones, *The Baker's Boy*, 1995
Ellen Kushner, *Swordspoint*, 1987
Paula Volsky, *Illusion*, 1992

## **1903**

### DAVID FEINTUCH

## *Voices of Hope*

(New York: Warner Aspect, 1996)

**Story type:** Science Fiction (Political; Dystopian)
**Series:** Nicholas Seafort Saga
**Major character(s):** Philip Seafort, Genius, Child; Jared Tenere, Computer Expert, Runaway; Pook, Streetperson, Kidnapper
**Time period(s):** 23rd century (2229)
**Locale(s):** New York, New York

**Summary:** When Jared, a rebellious and spoiled teenager, runs away from home, he plans to sell his story to a scandal sheet, but ends up on the squalid, dangerous streets of New York among the trannies—the transients. Philip Seafort, son of ex-SecGen Seafort, thinks he knows where to find Jared and follows him. As Jared and Philip's parents search for the boys, Jared gets revenge by using his computer skills to help the trannies bring down the towers of the wealthy Uppies, escalating a "rumble" into full-scale class war.

**Other books you might like:**
Algis Budrys, *Some Will Not Die*, 1978
Emma Bull, *Bone Dance: A Fantasy for Technophiles*, 1991
William Gibson, *Virtual Light*, 1993
Robert A. Heinlein, *Citizen of the Galaxy*, 1957
Amy Thomson, *Virtual Girl*, 1993

## **1904**

### RAYMOND E. FEIST

## *The King's Buccaneer*

(New York: Doubleday Foundation, 1992)

**Story type:** Fantasy (Adventure; Young Adult)
**Series:** Riftwar
**Major character(s):** Nicholas, Royalty (prince), Teenager; Harry, Companion (squire)
**Time period(s):** Indeterminate
**Locale(s):** Novindus, Mythical Place; Midkemia, Mythical Place; Kelewan, Planet—Imaginary

**Summary:** Sent to his uncle, the Duke of Crydee, to learn about the responsibility that accompanies his privileged position, Prince Nicholas must grow up quickly when enemies invade Castle Crydee and kidnap his heartthrob. Nicholas leads a rescue mission to the pirates' stronghold to foil his family's enemies and rescue Lady Abigail, the object of both Nicholas's and Harry's affection.

**Other books you might like:**
M.A.R. Barker, *Flamesong*, 1985
M.A.R. Barker, *Man of Gold*, 1984
David Eddings, *Magician's Gambit*, 1983
David Eddings, *Pawn of Prophecy*, 1982
David Eddings, *Queen of Sorcery*, 1982
Janny Wurts, *The Master of Whitestorm*, 1992

## **1905**

### RAYMOND E. FEIST

## *Krondor, the Betrayal*

(New York: Avon, 1998)

**Story type:** Fantasy (Magic Conflict)
**Series:** Riftwar
**Major character(s):** Squire Locklear, Nobleman; Gorath, Chieftain (elf)
**Time period(s):** Indeterminate
**Locale(s):** Midkemia, Fictional Country

**Summary:** This is a sidebar to the author's Riftwar series, inspired by the computer game. A chief of the elves abandons his people to bring news of a fresh plot by others of his kingdom to launch a new war against Krondor. Squire Locklear accompanies him on a perilous journey to the royal court despite efforts by their mutual enemies to stop them.

**Other books you might like:**
David Eddings, *The Hidden City*, 1994
Terry Goodkind, *Wizard's First Rule*, 1994
Robert Jordan, *Lord of Chaos*, 1994
L.E. Modesitt Jr., *The Magic of Recluce*, 1991
R.A. Salvatore, *Dragonslayer's Return*, 1995

## **1906**

### RAYMOND E. FEIST
### JANNY WURTS, Co-Author

## *Mistress of the Empire*

(New York: Doubleday Foundation, 1992)

**Story type:** Fantasy (Political)
**Series:** Empire Trilogy
**Major character(s):** Mara, Royalty (House Acoma)
**Time period(s):** Indeterminate
**Locale(s):** Kelewan, Planet—Imaginary

**Summary:** Tragedy rocks Mara's secure and happy marriage when her oldest son dies at the hands of an assassin. Mara engages in battle with magicians and others as she attempts to gain safety for her family.

**Other books you might like:**
M.A.R. Barker, *Flamesong*, 1985
M.A.R. Barker, *Man of Gold*, 1984
Janny Wurts, *Keeper of the Keys*, 1988
Janny Wurts, *The Master of Whitestorm*, 1992
Janny Wurts, *Shadowfane*, 1988
Janny Wurts, *Stormwarden*, 1984

## 1907
### RAYMOND E. FEIST

## *Prince of the Blood*
(New York: Doubleday, 1989)

**Story type:** Fantasy (Adventure)
**Series:** Riftwar
**Major character(s):** Borric, Royalty (Prince); Erland, Royalty (Prince)
**Time period(s):** Indeterminate
**Locale(s):** Krondor, Planet—Imaginary; Kesh, Planet—Imaginary

**Summary:** Set in the same world as *The Riftwar Saga*, the story follows the adventures of Borric and Erland, twin sons of Arutha. The twins, twenty years old, travel to Kesh on a diplomatic mission, but Borric is kidnapped and Erland must continue on his own.

**Other books you might like:**
Barbara Hambly, *The Time of the Dark*, 1984
Melanie Rawn, *Dragon Prince*, 1988
Janny Wurts, *Stormwarden*, 1988

## 1908
### RAYMOND E. FEIST

## *Rage of a Demon King*
(New York: Avon, 1997)

**Story type:** Fantasy (Magic Conflict)
**Series:** Serpentwar Saga
**Major character(s):** Erik von Darkmoor, Military Personnel, Bastard Son (of a nobleman); Rupert ''Roo'' Avery, Businessman, Bastard Son (of a commoner); Jakan, Demon
**Time period(s):** Indeterminate Past
**Locale(s):** Midkemia, Planet—Imaginary

**Summary:** Already ravaged by the war with the Saaur, Midkemia faces worse enemies when a host of demons, freed after many years by a desperate priest, make their way to Midkemia. Concludes the trilogy.

**Other books you might like:**
M.A.R. Barker, *Man of Gold*, 1984
Glen Cook, *The Black Company*, 1984
Patricia A. McKillip, *The Riddle-Master of Hed*, 1976
Melanie Rawn, *Dragon Prince*, 1988
Janny Wurts, *Curse of the Mistwraith*, 1994

## 1909
### RAYMOND E. FEIST

## *Rise of a Merchant Prince*
(New York: Morrow, 1995)

**Story type:** Fantasy (Political)
**Series:** Serpentwar Saga
**Major character(s):** Rupert ''Roo'' Avery, Businessman, Bastard Son (of a commoner); Erik von Darkmoor, Military Personnel, Nobleman, Bastard Son (of a nobleman)
**Time period(s):** Indeterminate
**Locale(s):** Midkemia, Fictional Country; Krondor, Mythical Place

**Summary:** Through a dimensional breach serpentine Sauur invade and begin their ruthless conquest of Midkemia. Erik feels he best serves the Empire as a soldier, while his lifelong friend, Roo, sees the opportunity for power and profit as a merchant. While luck and a timely marriage provide a quick rise in business, Roo's passions may lead to his personal downfall and disaster for all.

**Other books you might like:**
M.A.R. Barker, *Flamesong*, 1985
M.A.R. Barker, *Man of Gold*, 1984
David Eddings, *Pawn of Prophecy*, 1982
Robert Jordan, *The Eye of the World*, 1990
Tad Williams, *The Dragonbone Chair*, 1988

## 1910
### RAYMOND E. FEIST
### JANNY WURTS, Co-Author

## *Servant of the Empire*
(New York: Doubleday Foundation, 1990)

**Story type:** Fantasy (Political; Romance)
**Series:** Empire Trilogy
**Major character(s):** Mara, Royalty (House Acoma); Desio, Royalty (House Minwanabi)
**Time period(s):** Indeterminate
**Locale(s):** Kelewan, Planet—Imaginary

**Summary:** Mara, having demonstrated her political prowess in the Great Game of the Tsurani Court, faces a blood feud with Lord Desio. Mara must deal with magic, murder and treachery before the battle between House Acoma and House Minwanabi is decided.

**Other books you might like:**
M.A.R. Barker, *Flamesong*, 1985
M.A.R. Barker, *Man of Gold*, 1984

## 1911
### RAYMOND E. FEIST

## *Shadow of a Dark Queen*
(New York: William Morrow, 1994)

**Story type:** Fantasy (Adventure; Quest)
**Series:** Serpentwar Saga
**Major character(s):** Erik von Darkmoor, Bastard Son (of a nobleman), Fugitive, Military Personnel; Rupert ''Roo'' Avery, Fugitive, Bastard Son (of a commoner); Calis, Mercenary, Mythical Creature (elf)
**Time period(s):** Indeterminate
**Locale(s):** Krondor, Fictional City; Novindus, Fictional Country; Midkemia, Mythical Place

**Summary:** Erik works as an apprentice blacksmith, hoping one day to have his own smithy. When a quarrel with his half-brother leads to murder, Erik and his friend flee their birthplace. Caught and convicted, they escape execution in exchange for accepting a secret mission against the invading serpent men of Pantathia.

**Other books you might like:**
Stephen R. Donaldson, *The Illearth War*, 1977
David Eddings, *Pawn of Prophecy*, 1982
Barbara Hambly, *The Time of the Dark*, 1982
Robert Jordan, *The Eye of the World*, 1989
Tad Williams, *The Dragonbone Chair*, 1988

## 1912

### RAYMOND E. FEIST

## *Shards of a Broken Crown*

(New York: Avon Eos, 1998)

**Story type:** Fantasy (Magic Conflict)
**Series:** Serpentwar Saga
**Major character(s):** Rupert "Roo" Avery, Businessman, Bastard Son (of a commoner); Dash, Scout, Nobleman; Erik von Darkmoor, Military Personnel, Bastard Son (of a nobleman)
**Time period(s):** Indeterminate Past
**Locale(s):** Midkemia, Planet—Imaginary; Ylith, Fictional City

**Summary:** With the Emerald Queen dead and the demons who replaced her destroyed, a remnant of the Queen's army holds a fortified place in the kingdom and other, darker forces seek to profit from the chaos. Two young brothers stand at the fulcrum of plots and armies, with the fate of Midkemia in their untried hands.

**Other books you might like:**
M.A.R. Barker, *Man of Gold*, 1984
Allan Cole, *The Far Kingdoms*, 1993
    Chris Bunch, co-author
George R.R. Martin, *A Game of Thrones*, 1996
Melanie Rawn, *Dragon Prince*, 1988
Michael Scott Rohan, *The Anvil of Ice*, 1986

## 1913

### CYNTHIA FELICE

## *Iceman*

(New York: Ace, 1991)

**Story type:** Science Fiction (Political; Romance)
**Major character(s):** Jacinta Renya, Noblewoman, Government Official (Corps of Means); Michael Jivar, Government Official (Corps of Means); Ramon Santos, Nobleman
**Time period(s):** 45th century (Ice Age)
**Locale(s):** Earth

**Summary:** Jacinta Renya, a Ballendian aristocrat, serves in the Corps of Means. After a shuttle crash on frozen Earth, she is saved by Michael Jivar, an Earthman serving in the Corps. When Jacinta's uncle pushes the two into a marriage to advance his political career, Jacinta goes along with it, not knowing Michael's main mission is to destroy the House of Santos.

**Other books you might like:**
Poul Anderson, *The Night Face*, 1978
Johanna Bolton, *Mission: Tori*, 1990
Lois McMaster Bujold, *Barrayar*, 1991
Lois McMaster Bujold, *Shards of Honor*, 1986
Anne McCaffrey, *Restoree*, 1967
C.J. Mills, *Kit's Book*, 1991

## 1914

### CYNTHIA FELICE

## *The Khan's Persuasion*

(New York: DAW, 1991)

**Story type:** Science Fiction (Romance; Adventure)
**Major character(s):** Sindon Liang, Linguist; Rukmani Khan, Chieftain, Empath; David Quarrels, Engineer, Fiance(e) (former)
**Time period(s):** Indeterminate Future
**Locale(s):** Cestry Prime, Planet—Imaginary

**Summary:** Rukmani Khan kidnaps Sindon Liang and tries to get her to forget her own people and stay with him because of his greater sexual powers. David Quarrels comes after Sindon hoping to rescue her while Rukmani Khan is equally determined to keep her. David finally wins out as Rukmani Khan cannot stand to be physically impaired and commits suicide.

**Other books you might like:**
Octavia E. Butler, *Survivor*, 1978
L. Sprague de Camp, *The Virgin of Zesh*, 1983
L. Sprague de Camp, *The Prisoner of Zhamanak*, 1982
Mary Gentle, *Golden Witchbreed*, 1984
Raymond Harris, *Shadows of the White Sun*, 1988

## 1915

### OSCAR L. FELLOWS

## *Operation Damocles*

(New York: Baen, 1998)

**Story type:** Science Fiction (Techno-Thriller)
**Major character(s):** James Reed, Spy, Criminal (assassin); Beverly Watkins, Journalist (newscaster); Edward Teller, Scientist, Aged Person
**Time period(s):** 21st century
**Locale(s):** Washington, District of Columbia; Menlo Park, California

**Summary:** In a near-future America with a lying, scheming president willing to do anything to remain in power, an assassin rebels on a mission to silence a newscaster. The pair becomes involved in a right-wing conspiracy to conquer the Earth.

**Other books you might like:**
John Brunner, *The Shockwave Rider*, 1975
Robert A. Heinlein, *The Moon Is a Harsh Mistress*, 1966
Brad Linaweaver, *Moon of Ice*, 1988
L. Neil Smith, *The Probability Broach*, 1980
F. Paul Wilson, *The LaNague Chronicles*, 1992

## 1916

### OSCAR L. FELLOWS

## *Operation Damocles*

(New York: Baen, 1998)

**Story type:** Science Fiction (Techno-Thriller; Disaster)
**Major character(s):** Joe Dykes, Government Official (NASA); Charlie Castor, Technician (NASA)
**Time period(s):** Indeterminate Future
**Locale(s):** Outer Space; Florida

**Summary:** A sophisticated terrorist group has control of an orbiting superweapon that can literally incinerate large portions of the Earth. Scientists at NASA try to develop a method of neutralizing it before it can be used, but those responsible have too many safeguards and eventually begin a methodical destruction of the world's cities. First novel.

**Other books you might like:**
Roger MacBride Allen, *Farside Cannon*, 1988
Milan Chiba, *Noonblaze*, 1981
Arthur C. Clarke, *Earthlight*, 1955
Rick DeMarinis, *Scimitar*, 1977
Edmond Hamilton, *Doomstar*, 1966

## 1917

**LIONEL FENN** (Pseudonym of Charles L. Grant)

### 668: The Neighbor of the Beast
(New York: Ace, 1992)

**Story type:** Horror (Satire)
**Series:** Kent Montana
**Major character(s):** Kent Montana, Actor, Laird; Chita Juarel, Young Woman; Howmaster Maclemmon, Businessman
**Time period(s):** 1990s (1992)
**Locale(s):** Hamtucket, New Hampshire

**Summary:** In this spoof of the writing of H. P. Lovecraft, actor-buffoon Kent Montana agrees to fulfill the terms of an inheritance left him by unscrupulous businessman Howmaster Maclemmon by spending the night in Maclemmon's former home in Hamtucket. Unknown to Montana, the house is the meeting place of cultists who plan to sacrifice him during a ritual described in the *Bingonomicron* for summoning the extra-dimensional deity Bog-Muggoth.

**Other books you might like:**
Christopher Moore, *Practical Demonkeeping*, 1992

## 1918

**LIONEL FENN** (Pseudonym of Charles L. Grant)

### Kent Montana and the Really Ugly Thing From Mars
(New York: Ace, 1990)

**Story type:** Science Fiction (Parody; Invasion of Earth)
**Series:** Kent Montana
**Major character(s):** Kent Montana, Actor, Laird; Chita Juarel, Waiter/Waitress; Nicodemus Hooker, Scientist
**Time period(s):** 1990s (1990)
**Locale(s):** New Jersey

**Summary:** IT came from Mars and crashed near Gander Pond, New Jersey. Nothing can stop IT. Not the Army. Not the Scientist. Not the Preacher. Only Kent Montana, unemployed actor and Scottish Laird, can save the Earth. A pastiche of every invasion from outer space movie.

**Other books you might like:**
Douglas Adams, *The Hitchhiker's Guide to the Galaxy*, 1980
Douglas Adams, *Life, the Universe, and Everything*, 1982
Douglas Adams, *The Restaurant at the End of the Universe*, 1980
Douglas Adams, *So Long, and Thanks for All the Fish*, 1984
Ben Bova, *The Starcrossed*, 1975
John M. Ford, *How Much for Just the Planet?*, 1987
  Star Trek #36
David Langford, *The Leaky Establishment*, 1984
John Sladek, *Mechasm*, 1968

## 1919

**LIONEL FENN** (Pseudonym of Charles L. Grant)

### Kent Montana and the Reasonably Invisible Man
(New York: Ace, 1991)

**Story type:** Science Fiction (Parody)
**Series:** Kent Montana
**Major character(s):** Kent Montana, Actor, Laird; Janice Plase, Police Officer; Lizzy Howgath, Librarian

**Time period(s):** 1990s
**Locale(s):** Merkleton, England

**Summary:** When Kent Montana, out-of-work actor and Scottish laird, is first hit over the head by a mostly-invisible assailant, he does not recognize the sinister plot unfolding. A mad scientist, who is also an unemployed musician, has found a formula that makes him almost completely invisible and now plans to take his revenge on Kent Montana and the public at large. This novel is a pastiche of the mad scientist, ''B'' movie genre.

**Other books you might like:**
Douglas Adams, *Dirk Gently's Holistic Detective Agency*, 1987
Douglas Adams, *The Long Dark Tea-Time of the Soul*, 1988
Daniel Da Cruz, *Mixed Doubles*, 1989
Harry Harrison, *Bill, the Galactic Hero*, 1965
John Sladek, *Mechasm*, 1968

## 1920

**LIONEL FENN** (Pseudonym of Charles L. Grant)

### The Mark of the Moderately Vicious Vampire
(New York: Ace, 1989)

**Story type:** Horror (Satire; Vampire Story)
**Major character(s):** Kent Montana, Actor, Laird; Roxanne Lott, Young Woman; Count Lamar de la von Zaguar, Vampire, Nobleman (count)
**Time period(s):** 1990s (1992)
**Locale(s):** Assyria, Maine

**Summary:** When people begin dying and coming back from the dead in the beachfront community of Assyria, the townsfolk go on the lookout for a vampire. Because his eccentricities immediately raise suspicions, visting actor Kent Montana is forced to track down the real vampire in order to clear his own name.

**Other books you might like:**
John Peyton Cooke, *Out for Blood*, 1991
Stephen King, *Salem's Lot*, 1975

## 1921

**LIONEL FENN** (Pseudonym of Charles L. Grant)

### Time: The Semi-Final Frontier
(New York: Ace, 1994)

**Story type:** Science Fiction (Time Travel)
**Series:** Diego
**Major character(s):** Diego, Gunfighter, Time Traveler; Dirk Winslow, Military Personnel; Angel Lecotta, Revolutionary, Time Traveler
**Time period(s):** 26th century
**Locale(s):** *CISS Angus*, Spaceship; Gannet, Planet—Imaginary

**Summary:** The Fate of the Universe rests in the competent hands of Captain Dirk Winslow, proud representative of the Conglomeration of Independent Space States. The man they call Diego just wants to return to his own time, 1880, although the incompetence of Virgil, who created the Time Thing, and Molly, who drives it, may very well make this impossible. But first they must join forces against the dreaded Space Avenger.

**Other books you might like:**
Douglas Adams, *The Hitchhiker's Guide to the Galaxy*, 1980
John M. Ford, *How Much for Just the Planet?*, 1987

Larry Niven, *Fallen Angels*, 1991
   Jerry Pournelle, Michael Flynn, co-authors
Nick Pollotta, *Illegal Aliens*, 1989
   Phil Foglio, co-author
Patricia C. Wrede, *Sorcery and Cecelia*, 1988
   Caroline Severmer, co-author

## 1922

### BRAD FERGUSON

## *A Flag Full of Stars*
(New York: Pocket, 1991)

**Story type:** Science Fiction (Space Opera)
**Series:** Star Trek
**Major character(s):** James T. Kirk, Spaceship Captain (Starfleet admiral); G'Dath, Alien (Klingon), Scientist (physicist); Kevin Riley, Military Personnel (Starfleet lieutenant commander)
**Time period(s):** 23rd century
**Locale(s):** San Francisco, California; New York, New York; Earth

**Summary:** Kirk's new life changes when he meets Klingon scientist G'Dath who has made an important discovery which could mean either tremendous strides in Federation technology or Klingon subjugation of countless worlds. This book is a sequel to J.M. Dillard's *The Lost Years*.

**Other books you might like:**
James Blish, *Spock Must Die*, 1970
J.M. Dillard, *The Lost Years*, 1989
Diane Duane, *Doctor's Orders*, 1990
   Star Trek 50
John M. Ford, *The Final Reflection*, 1984
   Star Trek 16
John M. Ford, *How Much for Just the Planet?*, 1987
   Star Trek 16
Barbara Hambly, *Ishmael*, 1985
   Star Trek 23

## 1923

### BRAD FERGUSON

## *The Last Stand*
(New York: Pocket, 1995)

**Story type:** Science Fiction (First Contact; Space Opera)
**Series:** Star Trek: The Next Generation
**Major character(s):** Jean-Luc Picard, Spaceship Captain, Military Personnel; Data, Military Personnel (lieutenant commander), Android, Space Explorer; Deanna Troi, Psychologist, Alien (Betazoid), Space Explorer
**Time period(s):** 24th century
**Locale(s):** Nem Ma'ak Bratuna, Planet—Imaginary; *U.S.S. Enterprise*, Spaceship

**Summary:** On a routine stellar mapping mission, the *Enterprise* encounters a warp field pulse in an uncharted system. Investigating, Picard finds a civilization preparing to defend itself from an attack by enemies who have held a grudge for 6,000 years. Picard offers his services as negotiator to avert war, while Riker and Troi reconnoiter the invading ships and Data and Ro investigate the planet, where they find some puzzling inconsistencies.

**Other books you might like:**
Nathan Archer, *Ragnarok*, 1995
C.J. Cherryh, *The Faded Sun: Kutath*, 1979
Gene DeWeese, *Chain of Attack*, 1987

Ursula K. Le Guin, *The Dispossessed*, 1974
Barbara Paul, *The Three Minute Universe*, 1988

## 1924

### BRAD FERGUSON

## *The World Next Door*
(New York: Tor, 1990)

**Story type:** Science Fiction (Alternate Universe; Post-Nuclear Holocaust)
**Major character(s):** Jake Garfield, Minstrel, Wanderer; Prosper Cross, Minstrel, Wanderer; Digger Digby, Mountain Man
**Time period(s):** 21st century
**Locale(s):** Adirondack Mountains, New York; McAndrew, New York

**Summary:** The few survivors of 1962's nuclear World War III have been rebuilding their meager world for decades. Suddenly the citizens of McAndrew begin having strange dreams of things only the oldest remember—televisions, computers, electricity. Another Earth is close by and the walls between the two are dissolving as nuclear holocaust threatens once again. Jake Garfield and Prosper Cross help to solve the mystery and keep the town from being overrun by war.

**Other books you might like:**
Jerry Ahern, *The Struggle*, 1989
David Brin, *The Postman*, 1984
Jerry Earl Brown, *Earthfall*, 1990
Octavia E. Butler, *Dawn*, 1987
David Mace, *Firelance*, 1989

## 1925

### BRUCE FERGUSSON

## *The Mace of Souls*
(New York: Morrow, 1989)

**Story type:** Fantasy (Quest)
**Major character(s):** Falca Breks, Thief (Extortionist); Amala Damarr, Noblewoman (Falca's Lover)
**Time period(s):** Indeterminate
**Locale(s):** Six Kingdoms, Fictional Country

**Summary:** A Spiritlifter captures Amala's soul in his crystal mace and she is devoid of personality. The story is about Falca's quest to regain and return Amala's soul.

**Other books you might like:**
Charles de Lint, *Westlin Wind*, 1989
Alfred Tella, *Sundered Soul*, 1990

## 1926

### KEITH FERRARIO

## *Deadly Friend*
(New York: Leisure, 1994)

**Story type:** Horror (Ghost Story; Supernatural Vengeance)
**Major character(s):** Peter Cowal, Child; Bobby Cowal, Child; Amanda Collins, Paranormal Investigator
**Time period(s):** 1990s (1994)
**Locale(s):** Fulton, Ohio

**Summary:** A bunch of malicious high school students hound young Bobby Cowal to his death, unaware that Bobby's "imaginary" playmate, Georgie, is the ghost of a young boy with a long history of exacting vengeance against those who upset him.

**Other books you might like:**
Anne Dillard, *Specters*, 1991
Stephen King, *Carrie*, 1974
Abigail McDaniels, *The Uprising*, 1994
Jean Simon, *Ghost Boy*, 1994

## 1927
### DAVID FERRING

### *Konrad*
(Baltimore, Maryland: GW Books/Games Workshop, 1990)

**Story type:** Fantasy (Adventure; Quest)
**Series:** Warhammer: Warblade
**Major character(s):** Konrad, Servant; Wolf, Mercenary; Elyssa, Sorceress
**Time period(s):** 16th century
**Locale(s):** Alternate Earth

**Summary:** Konrad, an abused orphan involved in a forbidden affair with his Lord's daughter, flees his home when it is destroyed by monsters. He becomes the squire of a cynical wanderer and learns how to survive in a hostile world.

**Other books you might like:**
Adrian Cole, *A Place Among the Fallen*, 1986
Glen Cook, *The Black Company*, 1984
Michael Moorcock, *Elric of Melnibone*, 1976
Michael Shea, *Nifft the Lean*, 1982
Jack Yeovil, *Drachenfels*, 1990
    Pseudonym of Kim Newman

## 1928
### DAVID FERRING

### *Shadowbreed*
(Baltimore, Maryland: GW Books/Games Workshop, 1990)

**Story type:** Fantasy (Adventure)
**Series:** Warhammer: Warblade
**Major character(s):** Konrad, Warrior; Kastring, Warrior; Litzenreich, Sorcerer
**Time period(s):** 16th century
**Locale(s):** Alternate Earth

**Summary:** Konrad's story continues as he is taken prisoner by a chaos cult and begins to learn about his possible destiny. Escaping, he falls in with an eccentric wizard, and discovers a plot that threatens every level of his society.

**Other books you might like:**
Scott Baker, *Drink the Fire From the Flames*, 1987
Glen Cook, *The Black Company*, 1984
Michael Moorcock, *Elric of Melnibone*, 1976
Michael Shea, *Nifft the Lean*, 1982
Jack Yeovil, *Drachenfels*, 1990
    Pseudonym of Kim Newman

## 1929
### LUCY FERRISS

### *The Misconceiver*
(New York: Simon & Schuster, 1997)

**Story type:** Science Fiction (Political; Medical)
**Major character(s):** Phoebe Chambers, Criminal (abortionist), Computer Expert Jonathan, Computer Expert, Friend; Christel Chambers, Relative (niece)
**Time period(s):** 2020s (2026)
**Locale(s):** Utica, New York

**Summary:** Twelve-year-old Phoebe performs her first misconception on her beloved older sister, Marie, herself a misconceiver. Believing her skills necessary despite their current illegality, Phoebe enjoys continuing the family tradition in her spare time, working as a computer expert during the day.

**Other books you might like:**
Margaret Atwood, *The Handmaid's Tale*, 1986
Suzette Haden Elgin, *Native Tongue*, 1984
Larry Niven, *The Mote in God's Eye*, 1974
    Jerry Pournelle, co-author
Neal Stephenson, *The Diamond Age*, 1995
Sheri S. Tepper, *The Gate to Women's Country*, 1988

## 1930
### FREDERICK FICHMAN

### *SETI*
(New York: Roc, 1990)

**Story type:** Science Fiction (First Contact)
**Major character(s):** Sam Alexander, Radio (technician), Student—High School
**Time period(s):** 1990s
**Locale(s):** Escondita, California

**Summary:** Even as a small child, Sam Alexander was a radio genius with a strong interest in NASA's SETI (Search for Extraterrestrial Intelligence) project where his father worked. When his parents' plane disappeared, Sam's interest intensified. As his Aunt Marion and Uncle Stu allowed him to control his inheritance, he could afford the necessary equipment, but when his patience is rewarded, who should be told?

**Other books you might like:**
Orson Scott Card, *Wyrms*, 1987
Alan Dean Foster, *Quozl*, 1989
David R. Palmer, *Emergence*, 1984
Garfield Reeves-Stevens, *Nighteyes*, 1989
Rebecca Ore, *Becoming Alien*, 1988

## 1931
### MORGAN FIELDS

### *Shaman Woods*
(New York: Zebra, 1990)

**Story type:** Horror (Ancient Evil Unleashed)
**Major character(s):** Worth Martin, Child; Paul Martin, Teacher, Parent (Worth's father); Zacxk White Eagle, Indian, Shaman
**Time period(s):** 1990s (1990)
**Locale(s):** Agate Creek, California

**Summary:** Four-and-a-half centuries after a devastating battle between the Shoshone Indians and Spanish conquistadors, a lumber company harvests the forest that has grown up on the battlefield, liberating the bloodthirsty spirits who inhabit it.

**Other books you might like:**
Douglas Clegg, *Goat Dance*, 1989
Chet Williamson, *Dreamthorp*, 1989

**1932**

MEG FILES

## Meridian 144
(New York: Soho Press, 1991)

**Story type:** Science Fiction (Post-Nuclear Holocaust; Literary)
**Major character(s):** Kitty Manning, Teacher; Norio Onoda, Tourist; Rogelio Torres, Student
**Time period(s):** 1990s
**Locale(s):** Tano Island, Pacific Islands

**Summary:** While exploring a sunken ship, Kitty survived the fireball and shockwave which wrought destruction on Tano Island. She left her shelter after several days to rescue her dog. Although it seemed that she was the only living thing on the island, within a few days the vegetation showed some green and Kitty noticed evidence of at least one other living person. This is the author's first novel.

**Other books you might like:**
Octavia E. Butler, *Dawn*, 1987
Gordon R. Dickson, *Wolf and Iron*, 1990
J.M. Morgan, *Desert Eden*, 1991
Elizabeth Ann Scarborough, *Nothing Sacred*, 1991
Catherine Wells, *The Earth Is All That Lasts*, 1991
Kate Wilhelm, *Margaret and I*, 1971
Kate Wilhelm, *Where Late the Sweet Birds Sang*, 1976

**1933**

SHEILA FINCH

## Shaper's Legacy
(New York: Bantam Spectra, 1989)

**Story type:** Science Fiction (Genetic Manipulation)
**Series:** Shaper Exile
**Major character(s):** Beryt, Royalty; ReAth, Nobleman
**Time period(s):** Indeterminate Future
**Locale(s):** Beta Orbis IV, Planet—Imaginary

**Summary:** Five hundred years ago the Venn bioengineers came to Beta Orbis IV with stolen human germ plasma and created three artificial races. Now two of those races, the intelligent Ganu and the shape-shifting Liani, have united to form one nation and have overthrown the immortal Venn. Complex political and military intrigue is a given, however, and the Venn continue their genetic manipulation in secret.

**Other books you might like:**
Marion Zimmer Bradley, *The Heritage of Hastur*, 1975
Mary Gentle, *Ancient Light*, 1989
Mary Gentle, *Golden Witchbreed*, 1983
Daniel Keys Moran, *Emerald Eyes*, 1987
Robert Reed, *Black Milk*, 1989

**1934**

SHEILA FINCH

## Shaping the Dawn
(New York: Bantam Books, 1989)

**Story type:** Science Fiction (Genetic Manipulation)
**Series:** Shaper Exile
**Major character(s):** Rivi, Young Woman; Tagak, Scientist
**Time period(s):** Indeterminate Future
**Locale(s):** Beta Orbis IV, Planet—Imaginary

**Summary:** The struggle for control continues on Beta Orbis IV. The Biblists, mutant religious fanatics, come to the planet to destroy the Venn scientists. Meanwhile, Rivi, a troubled young woman, loses two lovers, travels across the planet, faces many dangers, and finds a higher destiny than she had ever thought possible.

**Other books you might like:**
Marion Zimmer Bradley, *The Heritage of Hastur*, 1975
Mary Gentle, *Ancient Light*, 1989
Mary Gentle, *Golden Witchbreed*, 1983
Daniel Keys Moran, *Emerald Eyes*, 1987
Robert Reed, *Black Milk*, 1989

**1935**

NIGEL FINDLEY

## 2XS
(New York: Roc, 1992)

**Story type:** Fantasy (Mystery; Science Fiction)
**Series:** Shadowrun
**Major character(s):** Derek Montgomery, Detective; Jacques Barnard, Wizard, Businessman
**Time period(s):** 2050s (2052)
**Locale(s):** Seattle, Washington

**Summary:** Dirk Montgomery, wrongly implicated in a murder, searches to find the murderer and the connection between the addictive computer chip, 2XS, and a product manufactured by a legitimate business, Yamatetsu Corporation. Life becomes more difficult when Yamatetsu's Senior Vice President, Jacques Barnard, notices Dirk's interest.

**Other books you might like:**
Pat Cadigan, *Mindplayers*, 1987
Robert N. Charrette, *Choose Your Enemies Carefully*, 1990
Robert N. Charrette, *Find Your Own Truth*, 1991
Robert N. Charrette, *Never Deal with a Dragon*, 1990
Glen Cook, *Sweet Silver Blues*, 1987
Mel Gilden, *Hawaiian U.F.O. Aliens*, 1991
Mel Gilden, *Surfing Samurai Robots*, 1988
Mel Gilden, *Tubular Android Superheroes*, 1991
Brian Craig, *Ghost Dancers*, 1991

**1936**

NIGEL FINDLEY

## House of the Sun
(New York: Roc, 1995)

**Story type:** Science Fiction (Cyberpunk; Science Fantasy)
**Series:** Shadowrun
**Major character(s):** Gordon Ho, Royalty; Dirk Montgomery, Cyborg, Detective—Private (retired); Scott, Driver, Mythical Creature (ork)

**Time period(s):** 2050s (2055)
**Locale(s):** Cheyenne, Wyoming; Hawaii

**Summary:** Pulled out of retirement, Dirk Montgomery receives an easy mission to the Kingdom of Hawai'i. The easy mission starts well, goes bad, gets deadly, and proceeds downhill from there. Soon Dirk uncovers a plot so terrible that it frightens even Insect Spirits.

**Other books you might like:**
Emma Bull, *Bone Dance: A Fantasy for Technophiles*, 1991
Pat Cadigan, *Synners*, 1991
Charles de Lint, *Svaha*, 1989
William Gibson, *Neuromancer*, 1984
Walter Jon Williams, *Voice of the Whirlwind*, 1987

## 1937

### NIGEL FINDLEY

## *Into the Void*

(Lake Geneva, Wisconsin: TSR, 1991)

**Story type:** Fantasy (Quest)
**Series:** Cloakmaster Cycle
**Major character(s):** Teldin Moore, Warrior, Adventurer; Aelfred Silverhorn, Mercenary; Estriss, Alien (Illithid), Telepath (mind flayer)
**Time period(s):** Indeterminate
**Locale(s):** *Probe*, Spaceship; Toril, Planet—Imaginary

**Summary:** In the quest to learn more about the cloak given him by a mortally wounded spelljammer, Teldin confides in Estriss, who senses magic-using ability in Teldin. As they travel to Toril, Estriss teaches Teldin what he can of the spelljamming basics. This sequel to David Cook's *Beyond the Moons* is set in the Spelljammer gaming milieu.

**Other books you might like:**
Damaris Cole, *Token of Dragonsblood*, 1991
David Cook, *Beyond the Moons*, 1991
Brian Daley, *Requiem for a Ruler of Worlds*, 1985
Alis A. Rasmussen, *The Price of Ransom*, 1990
Margaret Weis, *Dragon Wing*, 1990
　　Tracy Hickman, co-author

## 1938

### NIGEL FINDLEY

## *No Limits*

(New York: Roc, 1996)

**Story type:** Science Fiction (Adventure)
**Series:** Virtual World
**Major character(s):** Samantha ''Sam'' Dooley, Pilot; Renard Gilbert, Warrior; Jared Bloch, Teacher, Military Personnel
**Time period(s):** 1990s; Indeterminate (Alternate Universe A.D. 3052)
**Locale(s):** Gold Beach, Oregon; Elsewhen, Cyberspace

**Summary:** Samantha Dooley leaves her granfather's deathbed wondering about the mystery of the Virtual Georgraphic League. Her search leads her to Elsewhen, a virtual world where she can exist in a desolate war zone of giant battle robots as the warrior she always wanted to be.

**Other books you might like:**
Iain M. Banks, *The Player of Games*, 1989
Robert N. Charrette, *Wolves on the Border*, 1989
Keith Laumer, *Bolo: The Annals of the Dinochrome Brigade*, 1976
G. Harry Stine, *Warbots*,
　　1988

Robert Thurston, *Robot Jox*, 1989

## 1939

### TIMOTHY FINDLEY

## *Headhunter*

(New York: Crown, 1994)

**Story type:** Horror (Psychological Suspense)
**Major character(s):** Lilah Kemp, Psychic (spiritualist); Rupert Kurtz, Doctor (psychiatrist); Charles Marlow, Doctor (psychiatrist)
**Time period(s):** 1990s (1994)
**Locale(s):** Toronto, Ontario, Canada

**Summary:** New to the Parkin Institute of Psychiatric Research, Doctor Charles Marlow discovers a ghastly plot by head psychiatrist Rupert Kurtz to cater to the perversions of his wealthy patients by controlling local youth with drugs and psychiatric techniques to turn them into therapeutic playthings.

**Other books you might like:**
John E. Ames, *The Asylum*, 1994
Robin Cook, *Coma*, 1977
Kathe Koja, *Bad Brains*, 1992
Thomas Tessier, *The Dreams of Dr. Ladybank*, 1991
　　in *Night Visions 9*
F. Paul Wilson, *The Select*, 1994

## 1940

### JON STEPHEN FINK

## *Further Adventures*

(New York: St. Martin's Press, 1993)

**Story type:** Fantasy (Contemporary; Literary)
**Major character(s):** Reuven Agranovsky, Aged Person, Actor (radio); Amelia, Fugitive; Uncle Jake, Criminal, Fugitive
**Time period(s):** 1930s; 1990s
**Locale(s):** New York, New York

**Summary:** A mostly literate ex-radio actor contemplating suicide relates a strange and convoluted story which flips back and forth between the past, when he secretly played the voice of The Green Ray, a radio hero, and the present, where he becomes involved in a strange kidnapping plot. First novel.

**Other books you might like:**
Lin Carter, *Invisible Death*, 1975
Tom De Haven, *Freak's Amour*, 1979
Philip Jose Farmer, *Doc Savage: His Apocalyptic Life*, 1973
Kenneth Robeson, *The Frightened Fish*, 1992
Grant Stockbridge, *The Spider #1: The Spider and the Pain Master/ Secret City of Crime*, 1991

## 1941

### JACK FINNEY (Pseudonym of Walter Braden Finney)

## *From Time to Time*

(New York: Simon & Schuster, 1995)

**Story type:** Science Fiction (Time Travel; Alternate Universe)
**Major character(s):** Simon ''Si'' Morley, Time Traveler; E.E. Danziger, Scientist (physicist); Rube Prien, Military Personnel, Researcher
**Time period(s):** 1880s; 1990s
**Locale(s):** New York, New York

**Summary:** Happily settled in the New York City of 1888 with his wife, Julia, and young son, Willie, Si decides to return to the 1990s to check on the time travel project, now headed by Rube Prien. Convinced to return to 1912 despite Dr. Danziger's misgivings, Si attempts to prevent World War I. This sequel to *Time and Again* includes many photographs and illustrations of late 19th century and early 20th century New York City.

**Other books you might like:**
Poul Anderson, *The Time Patrol*, 1991
Gordon R. Dickson, *Time Storm*, 1977
Randall Frakes, *The Terminator*, 1985
    Bill Wisher, co-author
Harry Turtledove, *The Guns of the South: A Novel of the Civil War*, 1992
Connie Willis, *Doomsday Book*, 1992

---

## `1942`

### DAVID FISHER

## *Legally Correct Fairy Tales*

(New York; Warner, 1996)

**Story type:** Fantasy (Collection; Legend)

**Summary:** Contains 14 familiar fairy tales and children's rhymes, humorously rewritten as if they form the basis for legal action. Includes "Hansel and Gretel," "Sleeping Beauty," "Snow White," "Pinocchio," "Cinderella," "Beauty and the Beast," "Little Red Riding Hood," and "Goldilocks."

**Other books you might like:**
Margaret Atwood, *Good Bones and Simple Murders*, 1994
William J. Brooke, *Teller of Tales*, 1994
James Finn Garner, *Once upon a More Enlightened Time*, 1995
James Finn Garner, *Politically Correct Bedtime Stories*, 1994
James Finn Garner, *Politically Correct Holiday Stories*, 1995

---

## `1943`

### MARINA FITCH

## *The Seventh Heart*

(New York: Ace, 1997)

**Story type:** Fantasy (Contemporary Realism; Religious)
**Major character(s):** Gillian Wheatley, Linguist; Candace, Spirit (wind sprite); Melanie Frost, Health Care Professional
**Time period(s):** 1990s
**Locale(s):** Rio Santo, California

**Summary:** After five years of drought, Rio Santo now suffers frequent magnitude 6.5 earthquake aftershocks. Most homes prove unsafe, while blocked roads interfere with distribution of emergency supplies of food and water. Gillian's roommate, Melanie, disappears after the first earthquake, leaving Gillian to deal with the earth, wind and water spirits whose loneliness and insanity caused the drought and earthquakes. First novel.

**Other books you might like:**
Maya Kaathryn Bohnhoff, *The Spirit Gate*, 1996
Tom Deitz, *Above the Lower Sky*, 1994
Sharon Green, *Convergence*, 1996
J. Gregory Keyes, *The Waterborn*, 1996
Marc Laidlaw, *Neon Lotus*, 1988
Sheri S. Tepper, *The Family Tree*, 1997

---

## `1944`

### ERIC FLANDERS

## *The Forever Children*

(New York: Zebra, 1992)

**Story type:** Horror (Science Fiction)
**Major character(s):** Warren Hubert Barry, Doctor; Dawn Henderson, Child; William Wesley, Child
**Time period(s):** 1990s
**Locale(s):** Jamay Lake, Indiana

**Summary:** To all outward appearances, Jamay Lake is an insular religious community that keeps to itself. In fact, the town is a huge experimental laboratory in which Dr. Warren Hubert Barry, the town's founder, strives to arrest the development of children between the ages of six and ten, in an effort to solve the world's overpopulation problem and help break the cycle of child abuse that comes from families having more children than they can reasonably hope to support.

**Other books you might like:**
Ira Levin, *The Stepford Wives*, 1972
John Saul, *Creature*, 1990
John Saul, *Darkness*, 1991

---

## `1945`

### ERIC FLANDERS

## *Night Blood*

(New York: Zebra, 1993)

**Story type:** Horror (Vampire Story)
**Major character(s):** Val Romero, Vampire; Elaine Trent, Businesswoman; Jonathan Drew, Police Officer (FBI agent)
**Time period(s):** 1990s (1993)
**Locale(s):** Lansom, Texas

**Summary:** Footloose vampire Val Romero is tracked across the southwest by a group of different people whose lives have been adversely changed by contact with him. None are aware that their actions are being clandestinely observed and choreographed by a band of vampire hunters pursuing their own unusual agenda.

**Other books you might like:**
Peter Atkins, *Morningstar*, 1992
Poppy Z. Brite, *Lost Souls*, 1992
Ron Dee, *Blood Lust*, 1990
Ron Dee, *Dusk*, 1991
Gary L. Raisor, *Less than Human*, 1992

---

## `1946`

### ROBERT C. FLEET

## *Last Mountain*

(New York: Ace, 1994)

**Story type:** Fantasy (Urban; Adventure)
**Major character(s):** Annunciata "Nancy" del Rio, Child; The Unicorn, Mythical Creature; Karus, Companion
**Time period(s):** 1990s; 16th century
**Locale(s):** Los Angeles, California; San Gabriel Mountains, California

**Summary:** Annunciata struggles to help unite the Unicorn with Karus, the Unicorn Rider, to bring a proper finale to the Unicorn's long life.

However the Dreambreaker and other Border Patrol agents seek Annunicata for deportation.

**Other books you might like:**
Peter S. Beagle, *The Last Unicorn*, 1968
Bruce Coville, *The Unicorn Treasury*, 1988
    editor
John Lee, *The Unicorn Quest*, 1986
Tanith Lee, *Black Unicorn*, 1991
Jane Yolen, *Here There Be Unicorns*, 1994

## 1947

### ROBERT C. FLEET

## *White Horse, Dark Dragon*
(New York: Ace, 1993)

**Story type:** Fantasy (Contemporary; Adventure)
**Major character(s):** Jim Marlowe, Scientist; Frank Brown, Industrialist; Alta, Psychic
**Time period(s):** 1990s
**Locale(s):** Karistan, Fictional Country

**Summary:** Jim Marlowe travels to the small Balkan country of Karistan to prepare an environmental impact statement for a proposed mining project, a seemingly simple assignment. A local bureaucracy, a psychic, a blind woman, Marlowe's son and dog, and a dragon complicate matters. When the statement does not go as planned, mercenaries make the mystery a little more interesting. A first novel.

**Other books you might like:**
Emma Bull, *War for the Oaks*, 1987
Charles de Lint, *Moonheart: A Romance*, 1984
Tom Deitz, *Windmaster's Bane*, 1986
Guy Gavriel Kay, *The Summer Tree*, 1985
Michael Scott Rohan, *Chase the Morning*, 1991

## 1948

### SID FLEISCHMAN

## *The Midnight Horse*
(New York: Greenwillow, 1990)

**Story type:** Fantasy (Contemporary; Young Adult)
**Major character(s):** Great Chaffalo, Spirit, Magician; Touch, Orphan, Child
**Time period(s):** 1990s
**Locale(s):** Cricklewood, New Hampshire

**Summary:** On his way to meet his great uncle, Touch sees the Great Chaffalo for the first time. Later, when he is fleeing from his uncle, Touch convinces the ghost to change a bundle of straw into a horse for him. This is an ALA Best Books for Middle Readers title.

**Other books you might like:**
Alan Dean Foster, *Orphan Star*, 1977
Robert A. Heinlein, *Citizen of the Galaxy*, 1957

## 1949

### GHERBOD FLEMING

## *The Devil's Advocate*
(Clarkston, Georgia: White Wolf, 1997)

**Story type:** Horror (Vampire Story)
**Series:** Trilogy of the Blood Curse

**Major character(s):** Owain ap Ieuan, Vampire; J. Benison Hodge, Vampire; Kendall Jackson, Vampire
**Locale(s):** Atlanta, Georgia (alternate world)

**Summary:** A plague is killing vampires in the World of Darkness, raising suspicions among warring vampire clans that each is responsible. As the Masquerade that ensures their peaceful co-existence crumbles, anarchy begins to prevail and Owain must decide which clan to support. Set in the World of Darkness, a fantasy role-playing game world where human beings and creatures of the supernatural co-exist.

**Other books you might like:**
Don Bassingthwaite, *As One Dead*, 1996
    Nancy Kilpatrick, co-author
Nancy A. Collins, *A Dozen Black Roses*, 1996
Brian Herbert, *Blood on the Sun*, 1996
    Marie Landis, co-author
Robert Weinberg, *Blood War*, 1995
Robert Weinberg, *Unholy Allies*, 1996
Robert Weinberg, *The Unbidden*, 1996

## 1950

### GHERBOD FLEMING

## *The Winnowing*
(Clarkston, Georgia: White Wolf, 1998)

**Story type:** Horror (Vampire Story)
**Series:** A Vampire: The Masquerade: Trilogy of the Blood Curse
**Major character(s):** Owain Evans, Vampire, Spy; Nicholas, Vampire; Kli Kodesh, Vampire
**Time period(s):** 1990s (1998)
**Locale(s):** Atlanta, Georgia

**Summary:** Owain Evans, a spy for the Sabbat vampire clans, finds himself involved in intrigues between the Sabbat and Camarilla rooted in centuries of conflict over the Vampire Masquerade, which preserves a fragile tension between vampires and mortals. While the Rage, a plague of bloodlust that inflames vampire thirsts to insatiable proportions, drives vampires on both sides to desperate measures, Vampire elder Kli Kodesh manipulates events to fulfill a mission foreordained in ages past. Set in the World of Darkness, a fantasy role playing world where supernatural beings and mortals co-exist. Second book of a trilogy.

**Other books you might like:**
Nancy A. Collins, *A Dozen Black Roses*, 1996
Brian Herbert, *Blood on the Sun*, 1996
    Marie Landis, co-author
Robert Weinberg, *Blood War*, 1995
Stewart Wieck, *Toreador*, 1999
David Niall Wilson, *To Dream of Dreamers Lost*, 1998

## 1951

### SUSAN FLETCHER

## *Flight of the Dragon Kyn*
(New York: Atheneum, 1993)

**Story type:** Fantasy (Quest; Young Adult)
**Major character(s):** Kara, Adventurer, Teenager
**Time period(s):** Indeterminate
**Locale(s):** Mythical Place

**Summary:** When Kara answers King Orrik's summons to help rid the kingdom of its dragon plague, Kara finds herself between the King and his brother in their power struggle. Kara's hazardous efforts in carrying out the King's orders take her into the dragons' lair where she suddenly recalls a previous visit. Prequel to *Dragon's Milk*.

**Other books you might like:**
Andre Norton, *The Beast Master*, 1959
Andre Norton, *The Elvenbane*, 1992
   Mercedes Lackey, co-author
Vivian Vande Velde, *Dragon's Bait*, 1992
Patricia C. Wrede, *Dealing with Dragons*, 1990
Patricia C. Wrede, *Searching for Dragons*, 1991

## `1952`
### LYNN FLEWELLING

## *Luck in the Shadows*
(New York: Bantam Spectra, 1996)

**Story type:** Fantasy (Magic Conflict; Political)
**Series:** Nightrunner
**Major character(s):** Alec of Kerry, Woodsman, Spy (Watcher); Nysander, Wizard (High Thaumaturgist), Spy (Watcher); Seregil, Spy (Watcher), Musician
**Time period(s):** Indeterminate
**Locale(s):** Rhiminee, Fictional City; Skala, Fictional Country

**Summary:** Seregil engineers Alec of Kerry's escape from captivity then, on a reconnaissance foray, steals a magic token which quickly renders him delusional then unconscious. With difficulty, Alec returns Seregil to Nysander who reverses the damage, recruits Alec as a spy and sets him to uncover the details of a plot to oust Skala's queen. First of a series.

**Other books you might like:**
Terry Goodkind, *Wizard's First Rule*, 1994
Robin Hobb, *Assassin's Apprentice*, 1995
J.V. Jones, *The Baker's Boy*, 1995
Mercedes Lackey, *Arrows of the Queen*, 1987
J.R.R. Tolkien, *The Fellowship of the Ring*, 1954
Paula Volsky, *Illusion*, 1992

## `1953`
### LYNN FLEWELLING

## *Stalking Darkness*
(New York: Bantam Spectra, 1997)

**Story type:** Fantasy (Magic Conflict; Political)
**Series:** Nightrunner
**Major character(s):** Alec of Kerry, Apprentice, Spy (Watcher); Seregil, Spy (Watcher), Thief; Beka Cavish, Warrior, Teenager
**Time period(s):** Indeterminate
**Locale(s):** Rhiminee, Fictional City; Skala, Fictional Country

**Summary:** A necromancer pursues Seregil and Alec, intent on recovering a deadly magical artifact and invoking the power of an ancient evil. While bloodthirsty sacrifices continue and warfare engulfs the land, the fate of the kingdom depends on the actions of a courageous few. Sequel to *Luck in the Shadows*.

**Other books you might like:**
Lois McMaster Bujold, *The Spirit Ring*, 1992
Terry Goodkind, *Wizard's First Rule*, 1994
Robin Hobb, *Assassin's Apprentice*, 1995
J.V. Jones, *The Baker's Boy*, 1995
J.R.R. Tolkien, *The Fellowship of the Ring*, 1954
Patricia C. Wrede, *The Raven Ring*, 1994

## `1954`
### DENNY MARTIN FLINN

## *The Fearful Summons*
(New York: Pocket, 1995)

**Story type:** Science Fiction (Space Opera)
**Series:** Star Trek
**Major character(s):** James T. Kirk, Spaceship Captain, Aged Person; Hikaru Sulu, Spaceship Captain; Maldari, Spaceship Captain, Alien (Thraxian)
**Time period(s):** 23rd century
**Locale(s):** *U.S.S. Enterprise*, Spaceship; Beta Prometheus, Planet— Imaginary; United Federation of Planets, Interstellar Empire/ Federation

**Summary:** A Thraxian starship captain tricks Sulu and a landing party into coming aboard his vessel, then holds time hostage and demands advanced weaponry as ransom. When Federation negotiators refuse, Kirk and some of his former crew go to the rescue on board a borrowed space yacht.

**Other books you might like:**
Margaret Wander Bonanno, *Dwellers in the Crucible*, 1985
J.M. Dillard, *Recovery*, 1995
Michael Jan Friedman, *Legacy*, 1991
Vonda N. McIntyre, *Star Trek III: The Search for Spock*, 1984
Peter Morwood, *Rules of Engagement*, 1990

## `1955`
### ERIC FLINT
### DAVID DRAKE, Co-Author

## *In the Heart of Darkness*
(New York: Baen, 1998)

**Story type:** Science Fiction (Invasion of Earth)
**Series:** Belisarius
**Major character(s):** Belisarius, Military Personnel (Roman general); Link, Alien; Emperor Justinian, Ruler
**Time period(s):** 6th century
**Locale(s):** India

**Summary:** A Roman general has to deal with two problems. First, his own emperor mistrusts officers who are too successful in the field. Second, the Malwa Empire, which has conquered India, is secretly controlled by an alien race with advanced mental and technological powers.

**Other books you might like:**
David Drake, *Birds of Prey*, 1985
David Drake, *Bridgehead*, 1986
David Drake, *Dagger*, 1988
David Drake, *Northworld*, 1990
David Drake, *Ranks of Bronze*, 1986
David Drake, *Through the Breach*, 1995
Crawford Kilian, *Rogue Emperor*, 1988
Kirk Mitchell, *Cry Republic*, 1989
Kirk Mitchell, *Procurator*, 1984

## 1956

### ERIC FLINT

## *Mother of Demons*

(New York: Baen, 1997)

**Story type:** Science Fiction (First Contact; Space Colony)
**Major character(s):** Nukurren, Warrior, Alien (Gukuy); Indira Toledo, Historian, Settler (colonist); Julius Cohen, Scientist (biologist), Settler (colonist)
**Time period(s):** 22nd century
**Locale(s):** Ishtar, Planet—Imaginary

**Summary:** Stranded on a planet circling Tau Ceti, their spaceship crashed and their technology reduced to the Stone Age, the surviving humans learn to adapt to their new environment. When they meet refugees from religious persecution and learn of the threat posed by certain clans in the surrounding plains, they devise a plan to protect themselves and their only food source, the owoc. Knowing the horrors of history and fearing their little society will repeat humanity's worst mistakes, Indira must choose a path for humans and the Gukuy outcasts as they forge a new entity, the nation.

**Other books you might like:**
Margaret Wander Bonanno, *The Others*, 1990
C.J. Cherryh, *Foreigner*, 1994
C.J. Cherryh, *Forty Thousand in Gehenna*, 1983
Hal Clement, *Mission of Gravity*, 1954
A.C. Crispin, *Silent Dances*, 1990
    Kathleen O'Malley, co-author
David Drake, *An Oblique Approach*, 1998
    Eric Flint, co-author
Rosemary Kirstein, *The Outskirter's Secret*, 1992
Anne McCaffrey, *Decision at Doona*, 1969

## 1957

### KENNETH C. FLINT

## *Cromm*

(New York: Doubleday, 1990)

**Story type:** Fantasy (Contemporary)
**Major character(s):** Colin McMahon, Artist (Graphic)
**Time period(s):** 1990s; 4th century
**Locale(s):** United States; Ireland

**Summary:** Colin's nightmares of a bloodthirsty 4th century Celtic god become all too real when he travels to Ireland, where the past and present merge into a dangerous adventure for him. He is forced to finish a fight in which his ancestor, another Colin, fought centuries ago. Explores Celtic folklore and mythology.

**Other books you might like:**
Clive Barker, *Weaveworld*, 1987
Lloyd Arthur Eshbach, *The Land Beyond the Gate*, 1988
R.A. MacAvoy, *The Book of Kells*, 1985
Keith Taylor, *The Cauldron of Plenty*, 1989
    The Damans, No. 2

## 1958

### KENNETH C. FLINT

## *Legends Reborn*

(New York: Bantam Spectra, 1992)

**Story type:** Fantasy (Quest; Urban)

**Major character(s):** Michael Kean, Businessman; Caitlin Bawn, Traveler, Immortal; Rury O'Mor, Chieftain, Immortal
**Time period(s):** 1990s
**Locale(s):** New York, New York (Manhattan); Ireland; Sidh, Mythical Place

**Summary:** While visiting Ireland, Michael Kean meets Caitlin Bawn in a glen where her world intersects the mortal realm. Excited by the difference of the mortal realm, Caitlin accompanies Michael, which brings Rury O'Mor to the mortal realm to find and return Caitlin to Sidh.

**Other books you might like:**
Gael Baudino, *Gossamer Axe*, 1990
Emma Bull, *War for the Oaks*, 1987
Charles de Lint, *Moonheart: A Romance*, 1984
Charles de Lint, *Spiritwalk*, 1992
Alan J. Lerner, *Brigadoon: A Musical Play in Two Acts*, 1947
Will Shetterly, *Elsewhere*, 1991
Terri Windling, *Life on the Border*, 1991
    Editor

## 1959

### KENNETH C. FLINT

## *Otherworld*

(New York: Bantam/ Spectra, 1991)

**Story type:** Horror (Apocalyptic Horror)
**Major character(s):** Robert Cassiday, Government Official; Richard Jordan, Professor; Ann Archer, Teacher
**Time period(s):** 1990s
**Locale(s):** Denver, Colorado

**Summary:** Agent Robert Cassiday's investigation of the death of a friend at the hands of a mass murderer is repeatedly thwarted by annoying supernatural events. But Cassiday knows something his associates don't: that the tide of senseless violence increasing as we approach the millenium indicates forces from the supernatural Otherworld are threatening to break loose into our own.

**Other books you might like:**
Roger Elwood, *Sorcerers of Sodom*, 1991
Dan Simmons, *Carrion Comfort*, 1989

## 1960

### CASEY FLYNN (Pseudonym of Kenneth C. Flint)

## *The Enchanted Isles*

(New York: Bantam Spectra, 1991)

**Story type:** Fantasy (Legend; Quest)
**Series:** Gods of Ireland
**Major character(s):** Danu, Royalty (queen); Nuada, Leader, Immigrant; Dagda, Immigrant, Adventurer
**Time period(s):** Indeterminate Past
**Locale(s):** Ireland

**Summary:** Searching for a new homeland, the surviving people of Nemed arrive on a remote island where they receive succor and are told that they must acquire permission from Queen Danu to immigrate. On their dangerous journey to see Danu, the Nemedians are tested to see if they will be appropriate neighbors. This book is a sequel to *Most Ancient Song* (1991).

**Other books you might like:**
Marion Zimmer Bradley, *The Mists of Avalon*, 1983
Guy Gavriel Kay, *Tigana*, 1990
Patricia Kennealy-Morrison, *The Silver Branch*, 1988

Morgan Llywelyn, *The Isles of the Blest*, 1989
Morgan Llywelyn, *Red Branch*, 1988
Ian McDonald, *King of Morning, Queen of Day*, 1991
Andrew J. Offutt, *Sword of the Gael*, 1975
Andrew J. Offutt, *When Death Birds Fly*, 1980
    Keith Taylor, co-author
Keith Taylor, *Bard*, 1981
Terri Windling, *Life on the Border*, 1991
    editor

## 1961

**CASEY FLYNN** (Pseudonym of Kenneth C. Flint)

### Most Ancient Song
(New York: Bantam Spectra, 1991)

**Story type:** Fantasy (Legend; Quest)
**Series:** Gods of Ireland
**Major character(s):** Nuada, Leader, Immigrant; Dagda, Immigrant, Adventurer
**Time period(s):** Indeterminate Past
**Locale(s):** Ireland

**Summary:** Driven from home, the peaceful Nemedians have sailed in search of a new homeland. When they find a magnificent green isle, they decide to settle in the single beautiful valley they find ready for occupation. There they are attacked by the Formor, defenders of the new land who wield powerful magical devices. The Nemedians, unprepared for battle, are defended by strangers whose motives are unclear.

**Other books you might like:**
Marion Zimmer Bradley, *The Mists of Avalon*, 1983
Patricia Kennealy-Morrison, *The Copper Crown*, 1984
Morgan Llywelyn, *Bard: The Odyssey of the Irish*, 1984
Morgan Llywelyn, *The Horse Goddess*, 1982
Michael Moorcock, *The Swords Trilogy*, 1977
Keith Taylor, *Bard*, 1981
Keith Taylor, *Search for the Starblade*, 1990
Keith Taylor, *The Sorcerer's Sacred Isle*, 1989
Evangeline Walton, *The Island of the Mighty*, 1970

## 1962

**MICHAEL FLYNN**

### Firestar
(New York: Tor, 1996)

**Story type:** Science Fiction (Hard Science Fiction; Political)
**Major character(s):** Mariesa Gorley van Huyten, Heiress, Business-woman; Barry Fast, Teacher; Ned DuBois, Astronaut
**Time period(s):** 1990s (1999); 2000s (2000-2007)
**Locale(s):** North Orange, New Jersey; Mir, Space Station

**Summary:** Dismayed by the government's failures in public education and space exploration, Mariesa van Huyten uses her inherited fortune to fund her personal education and space exploration dreams, battling corrupt government officials and saboteurs every step of the way.

**Other books you might like:**
Arthur C. Clarke, *Richter 10*, 1996
    Mike McQuay, co-author
G.C. Edmondson, *The Man Who Corrupted Earth*, 1980
Robert A. Heinlein, *Time Enough for Love*, 1973
Larry Niven, *Fallen Angels*, 1991
    Jerry Pournelle, Michael Flynn, co-authors

Charles Sheffield, *Higher Education*, 1996
    Jerry Pournelle, co-author
Charles Sheffield, *How to Save the World*, 1995
    editor

## 1963

**MICHAEL FLYNN**

### The Forest of Time and Other Stories
(New York: Tor, 1997)

**Story type:** Science Fiction (Collection)

**Summary:** Contains a five-page introduction and individual afterwords to ten stories published in *Analog* from 1982 to 1994, including two Hugo Award nominees, the title story and "Melodies of the Heart," and one story set in the milieu of *The Nanotech Chronicles*, "Great, Sweet Mother." From serious to ironic or humorous in tone, the stories feature diverse themes and realms such as artificial intelligence, aliens, hard science fiction, alternate universes, and ghosts.

**Other books you might like:**
Alfred Bester, *Virtual Unrealities: The Short Fiction of Alfred Bester*, 1997
Charles Sheffield, *Georgia on My Mind and Other Places*, 1995
Marc Stiegler, *The Gentle Seduction*, 1990
John Varley, *The Persistence of Vision*, 1978
Connie Willis, *Impossible Things*, 1994

## 1964

**MICHAEL FLYNN**

### The Nanotech Chronicles
(New York: Baen, 1991)

**Story type:** Science Fiction (Hard Science Fiction; Collection)
**Major character(s):** Pavel Denisovitch, Teacher
**Time period(s):** 21st century
**Locale(s):** L4, Space Station; Brazil; New York, New York

**Summary:** The six stories contained herein have been previously published in *Analog* and *New Destinies* magazines. The stories tie together as examples used by Pavel Denisovitch to explain development of nanotechnology necessary to life in orbiting space complexes. An urban arts theme runs through "Soul of the City," while "The Washer at the Ford" points out the necessity of radiation resistance to people in space. "Remember'd Kisses" presents one less benign aspect with horrifying overtones.

**Other books you might like:**
Octavia E. Butler, *Dawn*, 1987
Pat Cadigan, *Mindplayers*, 1987
Jeffrey A. Carver, *From a Changeling Star*, 1989
George Alec Effinger, *When Gravity Fails*, 1987
Robert L. Forward, *Rocheworld*, 1990
Janet Kagan, *Mirabile*, 1991
Rudy Rucker, *Wetware*, 1988
Marc Stiegler, *The Gentle Seduction*, 1990
Michael Swanwick, *Vacuum Flowers*, 1987

## 1965

### MICHAEL FLYNN

## *Rogue Star*
(New York: Tor, 1998)

**Story type:** Science Fiction (Hard Science Fiction; Political)
**Series:** Firestar
**Major character(s):** Mariesa Gorley van Huyten, Heiress, Business-woman; Forrest Calhoun, Spaceship Captain; Roberta Carson, Activist, Writer (poet)
**Time period(s):** 2000s (2009)
**Locale(s):** *Gene Bullard*, Spaceship; Washington, District of Columbia

**Summary:** Mariesa van Huyten continues her crusade to get humanity into space. With the first manned flight to the asteroid belt underway and a permanent space station taking shape, Mariesa has many forces to fight, including the power of nature and a U.S. president intent on getting weapons into orbit. Sequel to *Firestar*.

**Other books you might like:**
John Brunner, *The Shockwave Rider*, 1975
Robert A. Heinlein, *The Moon Is a Harsh Mistress*, 1966
Nancy Kress, *Beggars in Spain*, 1993
Allen Steele, *Clarke County, Space*, 1990
Bruce Sterling, *Schismatrix Plus*, 1996

## 1966

### JOHN FOGARTY

## *The Haunt*
(New York: Popular Library, 1990)

**Story type:** Horror (Haunted House)
**Major character(s):** Mike O'Sullivan, Professor (Former); Mary Mc-Given, Girlfriend
**Time period(s):** 1990s
**Locale(s):** County Cork, Ireland (Puxley Estate)

**Summary:** Recovering from a traumatic encounter with a serial murderer, Mike O'Sullivan and his lover Mary McGiven, journey to Ireland to explore Puxley Estate, Mike's inherited estate. After they settle in, Mike becomes increasingly absorbed with the violent history of the surroundings and of his own family, until he can no longer distinguish between the real and the unreal, the past and the present, sanity and madness. This is Fogarty's first novel.

**Other books you might like:**
Stephen King, *The Shining*, 1977

## 1967

### D.C. FONTANA

## *Vulcan's Glory*
(New York: Pocket Book, 1989)

**Story type:** Science Fiction (Space Opera)
**Series:** Star Trek
**Major character(s):** Spock, Scientist, Alien; T'Pris, Alien
**Time period(s):** 23rd century (Prior to Mr. Spock's meeting Captai)
**Locale(s):** Vulcan, Planet—Imaginary; *U.S.S. Enterprise*, Spaceship

**Summary:** Mr. Spock falls in love with the Vulcan woman T'Pris who is then murdered. The killer must be brought to justice.

**Other books you might like:**
J.M. Dillard, *Star Trek: The Lost Years*, 1989

J.M. Dillard, *Star Trek V: The Final Frontier*, 1989
Julia Ecklar, *The Kobayashi Maru*, 1989
    Star Trek 47
Michael Jan Friedman, *Double, Double*, 1989
    Star Trek 45

## 1968

### EDITH FORBES

## *Exit to Reality*
(Seattle, Washington: Seal Press, 1997)

**Story type:** Science Fiction (Immortality; Literary)
**Major character(s):** Euclid, Computer Expert; Proteus, Psychic; Mom, Artificial Intelligence
**Time period(s):** 29th century
**Locale(s):** Cyberspace

**Summary:** When Euclid meets Proteus online, they strike up an unlikely friendship and romance. In a very ordered world, this unconventionality becomes a subversive act that may give Proteus necessary stability and Euclid a chance to grow beyond tedium and acceptible bounds.

**Other books you might like:**
Greg Bear, *Queen of Angels*, 1990
Alfred Bester, *The Demolished Man*, 1996
    revised
Pat Cadigan, *Mindplayers*, 1987
Maureen F. McHugh, *China Mountain Zhang*, 1992
Walter Tevis, *Mockingbird*, 1980

## 1969

### JOHN M. FORD

## *From the End of the Twentieth Century*
(Framingham, Massachusetts: NESFA Press, 1997)

**Story type:** Science Fiction (Collection)

**Summary:** Contains a four-page introduction by Neil Gaiman, one original story, nine poems, three essays, a technical discussion of the Moon's transit system from *Growing Up Weightless* and 12 stories reprinted from periodicals, anthologies and limited edition chapbooks 1979-1995. Some with individual introductions and afterwords, the stories feature diverse themes such as the space shuttle, trains, religion, gaming adventure and space exploration with one story from the *Liavek* milieu.

**Other books you might like:**
Lois McMaster Bujold, *Dreamweaver's Dilemma*, 1996
Emma Bull, *Double Feature*, 1994
    Will Shetterly, co-author
Joe Haldeman, *Vietnam and Other Alien Worlds*, 1993
Zenna Henderson, *Ingathering: The Complete People Stories of Zenna Henderson*, 1995
James H. Schmitz, *The Best of James H. Schmitz*, 1991
Will Shetterly, *Liavek*, 1985
    Emma Bull, co-editor
Cordwainer Smith, *The Rediscovery of Man*, 1993
James White, *The White Papers*, 1996

## 1970

### JOHN M. FORD

## Growing Up Weightless

(New York: Bantam Spectra, 1993)

**Story type:** Science Fiction (Political; Young Adult)
**Major character(s):** Matthias "Matt" Ronay, Teenager, Adventurer
**Time period(s):** 21st century
**Locale(s):** Montenegro

**Summary:** Despite his parents' successes in politics and medicine, Matt feels constricted options as he pursues hobbies including theater, virtual reality gaming and Mazerunning with friends. On a surreptitious journey to the farside, Matt finds unexpected internal resources as he uncovers a plot hindering his father's water negotiations with Earth and rescues a Starship crew from a local fracas.

**Other books you might like:**
John Barnes, *A Million Open Doors*, 1992
John Barnes, *Orbital Resonance*, 1991
Robert A. Heinlein, *Podkayne of Mars*, 1963
Robert A. Heinlein, *The Rolling Stones*, 1952
Alis A. Rasmussen, *A Passage of Stars*, 1990
Allen Steele, *Clarke County, Space*, 1990
Allen Steele, *Lunar Descent*, 1991
John Varley, *Steel Beach*, 1992

## 1971

### ELIZABETH FORREST

## Bright Shadow

(New York: DAW, 1997)

**Story type:** Horror (Wild Talents)
**Major character(s):** Jim McGruder, FBI Agent; Vernon Spenser, Mechanic; Gunnar Davidsen, Hunter
**Time period(s):** 1990s
**Locale(s):** Badger Mountain, Arizona

**Summary:** Vernon Spenser is in the right place at the right time to save little Jennifer from a mismanaged DEA assault on the New Hope Righteous Eternal compound. But he quickly finds he was in the wrong place at the wrong time when he and Jennifer, who has been bred for her psychic powers as a tool of obsessively righteous cult leader Gunnar Davidsen, become the object of a manhunt by both the government and the cult.

**Other books you might like:**
Randall Boyll, *Chiller*, 1992
Douglas Clegg, *Dark of the Eye*, 1994
Daniel H. Gower, *The Orpheus Process*, 1992
Stephen King, *Firestarter*, 1980
Dean R. Koontz, *Sole Survivor*, 1997

## 1972

### ELIZABETH FORREST

## Dark Tide

(New York: DAW, 1993)

**Story type:** Horror (Ancient Evil Unleashed)
**Major character(s):** Parker Solomon, Businessman (real estate developer); Steve Rollie, Political Figure (vice mayor); Maggie Dunbar, Teacher
**Time period(s):** 1990s (1993)
**Locale(s):** Pacific Crest, California

**Summary:** When Parker Solomon returns to his hometown to help renovate its deteriorating ocean front, he must confront the sea entity that nearly stole his soul as a boy and that has since taken over many of the town's most prominent citizens to do its bidding.

**Other books you might like:**
Matthew J. Costello, *Beneath Still Waters*, 1989
Dean Wesley Smith, *Laying the Music to Rest*, 1989

## 1973

### ELIZABETH FORREST

## Killjoy

(New York: DAW, 1996)

**Story type:** Horror (Science Fiction)
**Major character(s):** Mitch Christiansen, Military Personnel; Brandon "Brand" X, Teenager; Kamryn Smith, Young Woman
**Time period(s):** 1990s (1996)
**Locale(s):** Los Angeles, California; New Orleans, Louisiana

**Summary:** An ex-marine disillusioned by his discovery that the United States military is involved in voodoo-tainted operations in Haiti meets a young boy who has been given an unauthorized virtual reality implant of a serial killer's persona by a deranged experimental psychiatrist. With the help of a band of renegades and runaways, the two attempt to expose a secret government plot with far-reaching political ramifications.

**Other books you might like:**
Dean R. Koontz, *Dark Rivers of the Heart*, 1994
Michael Marshall Smith, *Spares*, 1996
F. Paul Wilson, *Mirage*, 1996
  Matt Costello, co-author

## 1974

### ELIZABETH FORREST

## Phoenix Fire

(New York: DAW, 1992)

**Story type:** Fantasy (Quest; Legend)
**Major character(s):** Tembo, Revolutionary (Tiananmen Square student), Archaeologist; Susan Aronson, Businesswoman; Tam Chen, Businessman
**Time period(s):** 1990s
**Locale(s):** Xian, China; Los Angeles, California

**Summary:** While excavating the tomb of Emperor Huang, Tembo frees a demon held captive by magic for 2000 years. When the demon discovers that the emperor who had imprisoned him died nearly 2000 years earlier, the demon hastens to Los Angeles to eliminate the threat represented by his enemy, the Phoenix, waking beneath the La Brea tar pits. A first novel.

**Other books you might like:**
Alan Dean Foster, *Cyber Way*, 1990
Marc Laidlaw, *Neon Lotus*, 1988
Nick Pollotta, *Bureau 13*, 1991
Nick Pollotta, *Doomsday Exam*, 1992
Elizabeth Ann Scarborough, *Last Refuge*, 1992

## 1975

**ELIZABETH FORREST** (Pseudonym of Rhondi Salsitz)

### *Retribution*

(New York: DAW, 1998)

**Story type:** Horror (Wild Talents)
**Major character(s):** Charlotte Saunders, Artist (painter); Wade Clarkson, Doctor (surgeon); John Rubidoux, Animal Trainer (dogs)
**Time period(s):** 1990s (1998)
**Locale(s):** Laguna Beach, California

**Summary:** Supposedly cured of the pediatric brain tumor that made her vulnerable to visions that she channelled creatively into her paintings, Charlie Saunders finds her nightmares, which she refers to as Midnight, returning in her adult life. Belatedly, Charlie discovers that her dreams are precognitive glimpses at a killer's crimes—and that the killer, who is aware she is painting them into her creations, is determined to stop her.

**Other books you might like:**
Giles Blunt, *Cold Eye*, 1989
Jack Ellis, *Seeing Eye*, 1995
H.B. Gilmour, *The Eyes of Laura Mars*, 1978
Stephen King, *The Dead Zone*, 1979
Dean R. Koontz, *The Vision*, 1977

## 1976

**WILLIAM R. FORSTCHEN**

### *Action Stations*

(New York: Baen, 1998)

**Story type:** Science Fiction (Military)
**Series:** Wing Commander
**Major character(s):** Winston Turner, Military Personnel (commander); Geoffrey Tolwyn, Military Personnel (ensign)
**Time period(s):** Indeterminate Future
**Locale(s):** Outer Space

**Summary:** A prolonged period of peace in space led to the mothballing of most of humanity's warships. When the catlike Kilrathi begin testing human resolve, Commander Winston Turner realizes that war is imminent and that because of his relative weakness, he will have to conduct a defensive battle until sufficient forces can be created to take on the enemy.

**Other books you might like:**
Bill Baldwin, *Galactic Convoy*,
John Dalmas, *The Lizard War*, 1992
David Drake, *Redliners*, 1997
William H. Keith Jr., *Mercenary's Star*, 1987
Mercedes Lackey, *Freedom Flight*, 1992
    Ellen Guon, co-author

## 1977

**WILLIAM R. FORSTCHEN**

### *Arena*

(New York: HarperPrism, 1994)

**Story type:** Fantasy (Adventure; Magic Conflict)
**Series:** Magic: The Gathering
**Major character(s):** Garth One-eye, Warrior, Heir—Dispossessed; Hammen, Thief (pickpocket); Zarel Ewine, Nobleman (High Baron of Kush), Leader (Grand Master of the Arena)
**Time period(s):** Indeterminate

**Locale(s):** Kush, Fictional City

**Summary:** Festival provides the annual opportunity for the best fighters from each House to meet in the Arena, testing material and magical weapons. The stranger Garth One-eye quickly draws Zarel Ewine's interest as a source of trouble. Garth One-eye's agenda may lead from Arena spectacle to disaster for many. Game tie-in.

**Other books you might like:**
Alan Burt Akers, *Arena of Antares*, 1974
Robert N. Charrette, *Never Trust an Elf*, 1992
Clayton Emery, *Shattered Chains*, 1995
Clayton Emery, *Whispering Woods*, 1995
Simon Hawke, *The Nomad*, 1994

## 1978

**WILLIAM R. FORSTCHEN**

### *Article 23*

(New York: Baen, 1998)

**Story type:** Science Fiction (Adventure; Military)
**Major character(s):** Justin Wood Bell, Teenager, Spaceman (cadet); Matt Everett, Teenager, Spaceman (cadet); Thor Thorsson, Administrator (Star Voyager Academy), Military Personnel (admiral)
**Time period(s):** 21st century
**Locale(s):** Space Station (Star Voyager Academy); *Somers*, Spaceship

**Summary:** Matt and Justin return to the academy after having passed the introductory summer session. Tension between the Earth and outer colonies remains high, and fear that the alien Trac may again attack has gradually abated. The new cadets find themselves assigned to a working ship en route to Mars to gain experience. A warning that the captain is tough does not prepare the cadets for events following a solar flare which cuts off all communications.

**Other books you might like:**
C.J. Cherryh, *Finity's End*, 1997
A.C. Crispin, *Starbridge*, 1989
David Feintuch, *Midshipman's Hope*, 1994
Robert A. Heinlein, *Starman Jones*, 1953
David Weber, *On Basilisk Station*, 1993

## 1979

**WILLIAM R. FORSTCHEN**
**GREG MORRISON**, Co-Author

### *The Crystal Sorcerers*

(New York: Avon, 1991)

**Story type:** Fantasy (Alternate World; Magic Conflict)
**Series:** Crystal Warriors
**Major character(s):** Ikawa Yoshio, Military Personnel (Imperial Japanese Army), Warrior; Mark Phillips, Military Personnel (United States Army), Warrior; Allic, Royalty (prince of Landra), Deity (demi-god)
**Time period(s):** 1940s
**Locale(s):** Haven, Planet—Imaginary

**Summary:** Mark Phillips and Ikawa Yoshio had been opposing commanders in World War II China. Magically kidnapped to Haven they become allies, both in service to Allic in a war between gods. After the war is won, the new friends, unable to return home to Earth, are granted large holdings on Haven. When Gorgon, a demon-lord, threatens Haven, they once again fight for Allic and his demi-god relatives.

## Other books you might like:
Patrick H. Adkins, *Sons of the Titans*, 1990
Glen Cook, *The Black Company*, 1984
John DeChancie, *Castle Perilous*, 1988
Geary Gravel, *A Key for the Nonesuch*, 1990
Fritz Leiber, *Swords and Deviltry*, 1970
Mickey Zucker Reichert, *Godslayer*, 1987
Brian Craig, *Plague Demon*, 1990
    as Brian Craig
Roger Zelazny, *Creatures of Light and Darkness*, 1969

## 1980
### WILLIAM R. FORSTCHEN

## The Napoleon Wager
(New York: Ballantine Del Rey, 1993)

**Story type:** Science Fiction (Military; Alternate Intelligence)
**Series:** Gamester Wars
**Major character(s):** Napoleon Bonaparte, Historical Figure, Military Personnel; Aldin Larice, Businessman (entrepreneur), Gambler; Oishi Kurosawa, Warrior (samurai)
**Time period(s):** 28th century
**Locale(s):** Magellanic Cloud, Outer Space

**Summary:** Bored by the peace imposed by the Overseers who rule the Magellanic Cloud, the wealthier inhabitants bet on simulated battles or clandestine wars on primitive planets, all arranged by gaming masters like Aldin Larice. When a rival starts a real war, the Overseers unleash devices made by the extinct race, the First Travelers, creating a wormhole that threatens to devour the Magellanic Cloud. Attempting to retrieve a physicist from the 23rd century who might be able to help, Larice ends up bringing back Napoleon Bonaparte. Returning home, they find a Dyson sphere left by the First Travelers, still run by a slightly mad artificial intelligence who agrees to help them—if they win a re-enacted battle of Waterloo.

## Other books you might like:
Poul Anderson, *The Time Patrol*, 1991
Gregory Benford, *Alternate Wars*, 1991
    Martin H. Greenberg, co-editor
David Drake, *Ranks of Bronze*, 1986
Larry Niven, *The California Voodoo Game*, 1992
    Steven Barnes, co-author
Larry Niven, *Ringworld*, 1970
Wilson Tucker, *The Lincoln Hunters*, 1958

## 1981
### WILLIAM R. FORSTCHEN

## Never Sound Retreat
(New York: Roc, 1998)

**Story type:** Science Fiction (Alternate World)
**Series:** Lost Regiment
**Major character(s):** Andrew Keane, Military Personnel (colonel); Ha'ark, Alien, Ruler
**Locale(s):** Xi'an, Fictional City

**Summary:** A regiment of Civil War soldiers has spent a decade on an alternate Earth where the alien Bantag rule and humans are enslaved. Although the soldiers have established a free nation, the aliens have a new leader who has led them to a series of military victories that threaten to make them supreme masters of the planet once more.

## Other books you might like:
John Dalmas, *The Bavarian Gate*, 1997

Arsen Darnay, *The Purgatory Zone*, 1981
Steven Gould, *Wildside*, 1996
James P. Hogan, *Entoverse*, 1991
S.M. Stirling, *Island in the Sea of Time*, 1998

## 1982
### WILLIAM R. FORSTCHEN

## Rally Cry!
(New York: Roc, 1990)

**Story type:** Science Fiction (Alternate Universe; Time Travel)
**Series:** Lost Regiment
**Major character(s):** Andrew Keane, Military Personnel (Colonel); Kalencka, Sidekick (native); Patriarch Rasnar, Religious (priest)
**Time period(s):** 1860s; Indeterminate (Medieval)
**Locale(s):** City Point, Virginia (Suzdal); Alternate Universe

**Summary:** Swept by a storm through a space-time warp, Union Colonel Andrew Keane and the men of the famed 35th Maine Regiment find themselves on an alien world where church and nobility rule a serfdom, and behind them are alien masters for whom human beings are merely experimental animals and food. Keane and his company disrupt the status quo by introducing radical ideas of democracy and freedom, and a much-superior weapons technology. The strongly disapproving leaders declare war.

## Other books you might like:
Pierre Boulle, *Planet of the Apes*, 1963
Philip K. Dick, *The Man in the High Castle*, 1962
Leo Frankowski, *The Cross-Time Engineer*, 1986
Leo Frankowski, *The High-Tech Knight*, 1989
Leo Frankowski, *The Radiant Warrior*, 1989

## 1983
### WILLIAM R. FORSTCHEN

## Terrible Swift Sword
(New York: Roc, 1992)

**Story type:** Science Fiction (Time Travel; Military)
**Series:** Lost Regiment
**Major character(s):** Andrew Keane, Military Personnel (Colonel); Yuri Yaroslavich, Slave; Jubadi va Ulga, Ruler, Alien (Merki)
**Time period(s):** Indeterminate
**Locale(s):** Valennia, Planet—Imaginary

**Summary:** Colonel Keane and his Union regiment, swept through a time-space warp like countless humans before them, find themselves stranded forever on an alien world where the warlike natives call the marooned humans "cattle," using them as a source of food and labor. Union rifles and 19th century technology enable the humans to fight back and establish their own territory, but the alien Merki leaders, assisted by air power, unite to crush the rebellious human cattle.

## Other books you might like:
Poul Anderson, *The Shield of Time*, 1990
Poul Anderson, *The Time Patrol*, 1991
Gordon R. Dickson, *Time Storm*, 1977
David Drake, *Ranks of Bronze*, 1986
Barbara Hambly, *The Time of the Dark*, 1982
Robert A. Heinlein, *Glory Road*, 1963
William Sanders, *The Wild Blue and the Gray*, 1991
Gene Wolfe, *The Shadow of the Torturer*, 1980

## 1984

### KATE FORSYTH

## *The Witches of Eileanan*

(New York: Roc, 1998)

**Story type:** Fantasy (Political; Quest)
**Major character(s):** Isabeau, Apprentice (sorceress), Adventurer; Meghan NicCuinn, Sorceress, Leader (Coven of Witches' Keybearer)
**Time period(s):** Indeterminate
**Locale(s):** Eileanan, Fictional Country; Dragonclaw, Mythical Place

**Summary:** When warriors assault Meghan's hidden valley, hoping to destroy the last practitioners of magic, Meghan sends Isabeau to secure aid from other witches of Eileanan, while she seeks help from dragons, generally inimical to human causes. First novel.

**Other books you might like:**
Graham Edwards, *Dragoncharm*, 1996
Lynn Flewelling, *Luck in the Shadows*, 1996
Carol Heller, *The Gates of Vensunor*, 1997
Ursula K. Le Guin, *A Wizard of Earthsea*, 1968
Andre Norton, *The Elvenbane*, 1991
  Mercedes Lackey, co-author

## 1985

### EVE FORWARD

## *Villains by Necessity*

(New York: Tor, 1995)

**Story type:** Fantasy (Magic Conflict; Quest)
**Major character(s):** Kaylana Nathalorial, Religious (druid), Leader; Sam, Criminal (assassin), Adventurer; Mizzamir, Magician (arch-mage), Criminal
**Time period(s):** Indeterminate
**Locale(s):** The Six Lands, Fictional Country

**Summary:** Transformed into a stagnant utopia by the ultimate victory of Good and Light, the world faces imminent destruction from the imbalance of nature's forces. Pursued by Mizzamir and his forces of Light, Kaylana and her companions must each survive a hero's test to win through to the DarkGate, unleash the forces of Evil and Darkness and restore the vitality and conflict necessary to a balanced universe. First novel.

**Other books you might like:**
Gordon R. Dickson, *The Dragon and the George*, 1976
Gordon R. Dickson, *The Dragon Knight*, 1990
Diane Duane, *The Door into Fire*, 1979
Diane Duane, *The Door into Sunset*, 1993
Barbara Hambly, *Dog Wizard*, 1993
Barbara Hambly, *The Silent Tower*, 1986
Barbara Hambly, *The Silicon Mage*, 1988
Michelle Sagara, *Lady of Mercy*, 1993

## 1986

### ROBERT L. FORWARD
### MARTHA DODSON FORWARD, Co-Author

## *Marooned on Eden*

(New York: Baen, 1993)

**Story type:** Science Fiction (First Contact; Hard Science Fiction)
**Series:** Rocheworld

**Major character(s):** Virginia ''Jinjur'' Jones, Spaceship Captain, Military Personnel; Reiki Momoku Le Roux, Computer Expert, Spacewoman; Seetoo ''Jolly'', Alien (Keejook), Leader
**Time period(s):** 2070s (2071)
**Locale(s):** *Prometheus*, Spaceship; Barnard Star System, Outer Space; Zuni, Moon—Imaginary

**Summary:** Continuing their survey, the crew of the *Prometheus* plan to use their last lander and flyer to visit Zuni, a seemingly Earthlike moon of Gargantua. Fortunately Zuni proves habitable after their crash landing and loss of supplies and equipment. Stranded, with rescue expected in 25 years and only minimal support possible from *Prometheus*, the crew and the alien flouwen they brought with them begin to appreciate the idyllic island where they reside. Sequel to *Return to Rocheworld*.

**Other books you might like:**
Stephen Baxter, *Raft*, 1992
C.J. Cherryh, *Forty Thousand in Gehenna*, 1983
Hal Clement, *Mission of Gravity*, 1954
Anne McCaffrey, *Dinosaur Planet*, 1978
Michael McCollum, *The Clouds of Saturn*, 1991
Larry Niven, *The Integral Trees*, 1984
Alis A. Rasmussen, *A Passage of Stars*, 1990
Vernor Vinge, *Marooned in Realtime*, 1986

## 1987

### ROBERT L. FORWARD

## *Martian Rainbow*

(New York: Ballantine/Del Rey, 1991)

**Story type:** Science Fiction (Political; First Contact)
**Major character(s):** Alexander ''the Great'' Armstrong, Military Personnel (general), Political Figure (Infinite Lord); Augustus ''Gus'' Armstrong, Scientist, Administrator
**Time period(s):** 2040s
**Locale(s):** Washington, District of Columbia; Mars

**Summary:** Mars is conquered for the United Nations by the identical twins Alexander and Augustus Armstrong. Alexander goes home to gain whatever political advantage he can from the successful campaign, while Gus stays on Mars to administer the international scientific colony. Alex consolidates his control on Earth and eventually threatens Mars' autonomy. The colonists vote to fight for their independence, but without unexpected help the colonists will have difficulty surviving without support from Earth. This book contains acknowledgements, a short bibliography and a brief guide to Mars.

**Other books you might like:**
Orson Scott Card, *Ender's Game*, 1985
Michael Flynn, *In the Country of the Blind*, 1990
Robert A. Heinlein, *Double Star*, 1956
Larry Niven, *Protector*, 1973
Dana Stabenow, *Second Star*, 1991
Sheri S. Tepper, *Grass*, 1989

## 1988

### ROBERT L. FORWARD
### MARTHA DODSON FORWARD, Co-Author

## *Ocean under the Ice*

(New York: Baen, 1994)

**Story type:** Science Fiction (First Contact; Adventure)
**Series:** Rocheworld

**Major character(s):** Silver-Rim, Alien (Icerug); Virginia "Jinjur" Jones, Spaceship Captain, Military Personnel; David Greystoke, Spaceman, Musician
**Time period(s):** 2070s (2070)
**Locale(s):** *Prometheus*, Spaceship; Barnard Star System, Outer Space; Zulu, Moon—Imaginary

**Summary:** After leaving Rocheworld, the crew of the *Prometheus* meets another intelligent alien species, the Icerugs, on Zulu orbiting Gargantua, the system's gas giant. While learning about the predatory coelasharks, the crew discovers the previously unknown reproductive cycle of the Icerugs. Set prior to *Marooned on Eden*.

**Other books you might like:**
C.J. Cherryh, *Chanur's Legacy*, 1992
Hal Clement, *Mission of Gravity*, 1954
Janet Kagan, *Mirabile*, 1991
Anne McCaffrey, *Powers That Be*, 1993
    Elizabeth Ann Scarborough, co-author
Robert J. Sawyer, *Far-Seer*, 1992
Robert J. Sawyer, *Fossil Hunter*, 1993
L. Neil Smith, *Their Majesties' Bucketeers*, 1981

**1989**

### ROBERT L. FORWARD
### JULIE FORWARD FULLER, Co-Author

## Return to Rocheworld

(New York: Baen, 1993)

**Story type:** Science Fiction (First Contact; Hard Science Fiction)
**Series:** Rocheworld
**Major character(s):** Virginia "Jinjur" Jones, Spaceship Captain, Military Personnel; Arielle Trudeau, Pilot (spaceship)
**Time period(s):** 21st century
**Locale(s):** *Prometheus*, Spaceship; Barnard Star System, Outer Space

**Summary:** The *Prometheus'* crew gives their flouwen friends a terminal which will eventually allow direct communication with Earth and immediate communication with the *Prometheus*. When it occurs to them to check for life on the newly flooded Roche, the Terrans discover another culture of aliens, the gummies, who maintain their shape and move on land. Able to travel in space suits designed for them, the exceedingly intelligent flouwen visit the ship and decide to help the gummies develop a more advanced society. Extensive technical indices. Sequel to *Rocheworld*.

**Other books you might like:**
Roger MacBride Allen, *The Ring of Charon*, 1990
David Brin, *Earth*, 1990
Stephen Leigh, *Alien Tongue*, 1991
Larry Niven, *The Gripping Hand*, 1993
    Jerry Pournelle, co-author
Vonda N. McIntyre, *Metaphase*, 1992
David Alexander Smith, *Homecoming*, 1990
Sheri S. Tepper, *Raising the Stones*, 1990
Vernor Vinge, *A Fire upon the Deep*, 1992

**1990**

### ROBERT L. FORWARD

## Rocheworld

(New York: Baen, 1990)

**Story type:** Science Fiction (Hard Science Fiction; First Contact)
**Major character(s):** Virginia "Jinjur" Jones, Spaceship Captain, Military Personnel (general)

**Time period(s):** 21st century
**Locale(s):** Earth; *Prometheus*, Spaceship; Barnard Star System, Outer Space

**Summary:** An expedition to Barnard's Star is organized, the crew is selected, and the spaceship heads out. In order to make the long journey tolerable the crew is given the drug, NO-DIE, which slows life processes, including mentation, with only James, the ship's robot, to take care of them. This is 50,000 words longer than the previously published version titled *The Flight of the Dragonfly* (1984).

**Other books you might like:**
Roger MacBride Allen, *The Ring of Charon*, 1990
David Brin, *Earth*, 1990
Larry Niven, *Protector*, 1973
Charles Sheffield, *The McAndrew Chronicles*, 1983
John E. Stith, *Redshift Rendezvous*, 1990

**1991**

### ROBERT L. FORWARD

## Saturn Rukh

(New York: Tor, 1997)

**Story type:** Science Fiction (Hard Science Fiction; First Contact)
**Major character(s):** Chastity Blaze, Spacewoman, Pilot; Sandra Green, Scientist (biologist), Spacewoman; Rod Morgan, Spaceship Captain
**Time period(s):** 21st century
**Locale(s):** *Sextant*, Spaceship; Saturn

**Summary:** Offered $1 trillion apiece to undertake an extremely risky mission to Saturn, the crew of the *Sextant* discover and learn to communicate with intelligent life forms in Saturn's upper atmosphere, who ultimately save the humans' lives and help them return home.

**Other books you might like:**
Gregory Benford, *If the Stars Are Gods*, 1977
    Gordon Eklund, co-author
Gordon Eklund, *A Thunder on Neptune*, 1989
Larry Niven, *The Integral Trees*, 1984
Larry Niven, *The Smoke Ring*, 1987
Amy Thomson, *The Color of Distance*, 1995

**1992**

### ROBERT L. FORWARD

## Timemaster

(New York: Tor, 1992)

**Story type:** Science Fiction (Hard Science Fiction)
**Major character(s):** Harold "Randy" Randolph Hunter, Space Explorer, Businessman (Reinhold Astroengineering Co.); Rosita "Rose" Carmelita Cortez, Spouse (Randy's), Parent
**Time period(s):** 2030s (2036)
**Locale(s):** *Spacemaster*, Spaceship; *Timemaster*, Spaceship (time machine); Asteroid Belt, Outer Space

**Summary:** The discovery of a new organism in the airless asteroid belt provides a wellspring of technology when technicians examine the alien's physiology and discover the organism's ability to warp the fabric of space/time and extract energy from matter/antimatter interaction. While battling political pressure, Randy's company constructs spaceships which Randy uses to transport and position the resulting matter transmitters/receivers at nearby star systems while his company produces nearly cost-free energy and limitless profits.

Problems arise which cause Randy to countermand his own orders preventing use of the organism for time travel. Concludes with a two-page non-fiction bibliography.

**Other books you might like:**
Greg Bear, *Eon*, 1985
Frank Herbert, *Whipping Star*, 1970
Michael P. Kube-McDowell, *Enigma*, 1986
Vonda N. McIntyre, *Metaphase*, 1992
Vonda N. McIntyre, *Transition*, 1991
Alis A. Rasmussen, *The Price of Ransom*, 1990
Alis A. Rasmussen, *Revolution's Shore*, 1990
Frank M. Robinson, *The Dark Beyond the Stars*, 1991
Charles Sheffield, *The McAndrew Chronicles*, 1983
Vernor Vinge, *A Fire upon the Deep*, 1992

## 1993
### ALAN DEAN FOSTER
### Alien 3
(New York: Warner, 1992)

**Story type:** Science Fiction (Horror; Adventure)
**Series:** Alien
**Major character(s):** Ripley, Military Personnel, Heroine; Bishop, Android, Hero; Dillon, Prisoner, Miner
**Time period(s):** Indeterminate Future
**Locale(s):** Fiorina, Planet—Imaginary

**Summary:** Having escaped the aliens a second time, Ripley crashes on a maximum security prison planet and mining facility, unwittingly bringing a deadly alien with her. The alien wreaks lethal havoc in her attempt to insure the survival of her kind. Novelizes the film.

**Other books you might like:**
Roger MacBride Allen, *The Ring of Charon*, 1990
Robert A. Heinlein, *The Moon Is a Harsh Mistress*, 1966
Steve Perry, *Aliens: Earth Hive*, 1992
Dan Simmons, *Hyperion*, 1989
Vernor Vinge, *A Fire upon the Deep*, 1992

## 1994
### ALAN DEAN FOSTER, Editor
### Betcha Can't Read Just One
(New York: Ace, 1993)

**Story type:** Fantasy (Anthology; Light Fantasy)

**Summary:** Contains a three-page introduction plus individual introductions to 13 original and three reprinted stories, one translated from German for the first time. The humorous stories feature a variety of settings and mythical characters by writers including Margaret Ball, Greg Costikyan, George Alec Effinger, Alan Dean Foster, Esther Friesner, Mel Gilden, Ron Goulart, Nina Kiriki Hoffman, R.A. Lafferty, Jack McDevitt, Laura Resnick, Mike Resnick and Steve Rasnic Tem.

**Other books you might like:**
Baird Searles, *Halflings, Hobbits, Warrows & Weefolk: A Collection of Tales of Heroes Short in Stature*, 1991
  Brian Thomsen, co-editor
Will Shetterly, *Liavek*, 1985
  Emma Bull, co-editor
Will Shetterly, *Liavek: The Players of Luck*, 1986
  Emma Bull, co-editor
Michael Stearns, *A Wizard's Dozen*, 1993
  editor

Terri Windling, *Borderland*, 1986
  Mark Alan Arnold, co-editor
Terri Windling, *Life on the Border*, 1991
  editor

## 1995
### ALAN DEAN FOSTER
### A Call to Arms
(New York: Ballantine/Del Rey, 1991)

**Story type:** Science Fiction (First Contact; Adventure)
**Series:** Damned
**Major character(s):** Will Dulac, Composer; Caldaq, Alien (massood), Warrior
**Time period(s):** 1990s
**Locale(s):** Outer Space; Earth

**Summary:** The Weave has been fighting the Amplitur for millennia. On an exploratory trip to find allies, they stumble across Earth and composer Will Dulac. Despite Will's insistence that Earthmen do not like war and would not be interested in joining the fray, humanity is drawn in.

**Other books you might like:**
Piers Anthony, *Cluster*, 1977
David Brin, *Startide Rising*, 1983
Glen Cook, *The Dragon Never Sleeps*, 1988
Gordon R. Dickson, *Wolfling*, 1969
Richard Meredith, *At the Narrow Passage*, 1973
Rebecca Ore, *Becoming Alien*, 1987
Frederik Pohl, *Narabedla, Ltd.*, 1988

## 1996
### ALAN DEAN FOSTER
### Carnivores of Light and Darkness
(New York: Warner Aspect, 1998)

**Story type:** Fantasy (Quest; Adventure)
**Series:** Journeys of the Catechist
**Major character(s):** Etjole Ehomba, Traveler, Worker (goatherd); Simna bin Sind, Warrior (swordsman); Ahlitah, Animal (lion/cheetah cross)
**Time period(s):** Indeterminate
**Locale(s):** Fictional Country

**Summary:** Because of his vow to a dying man, Etjole Ehomba travels north to rescue a captive Visioness. On the way he picks up some traveling companions and must end a war, aid some monkeys, best corruption, and topple a wall.

**Other books you might like:**
Neal Barrett Jr., *Through Darkest America*, 1986
Nancy Farmer, *A Girl Named Disaster*, 1996
Lee Killough, *The Leopard's Daughter*, 1987
Sterling E. Lanier, *Hiero's Journey*, 1973
David Mason, *The Sorcerer's Skull*, 1970
Mike Resnick, *Paradise: A Chronicle of a Distant World*, 1989
Robert Silverberg, *Lion Time in Timbuctoo*, 1990

## 1997

**ALAN DEAN FOSTER**

### Cat-A-Lyst

(New York: Ace, 1991)

**Story type:** Science Fiction (Adventure)
**Major character(s):** Jeremy Carter, Actor (Grade B movies); O'lal, Alien (Shihar), Animal (Cat); Igor von Mannheim De Soto, Guide
**Time period(s):** Indeterminate
**Locale(s):** Paititi La S'ebra Sur, Peru (legendary Incan city); Contisuyu, Planet—Imaginary; Nazca, Peru

**Summary:** O'lal is looking for a renegade Shiharareth who is preparing the destruction of Earth for his entertainment. Jeremy Carter finds a mini-disc which, with the help of the costume mistress from his latest film, leads him to Cuzco, Peru on a search for Incan gold. Their paths converge at Paititi which is not at all what they expected to find.

**Other books you might like:**
C.J. Cherryh, *Chanur's Homecoming*, 1986
Mel Gilden, *Hawaiian U.F.O. Aliens*, 1991
Janet Kagan, *Mirabile*, 1991
Marc Laidlaw, *Neon Lotus*, 1988
Carol Severance, *Reefsong*, 1991

## 1998

**ALAN DEAN FOSTER**

### Chorus Skating

(New York: Warner Aspect, 1994)

**Story type:** Fantasy (Quest; Magic Conflict)
**Series:** Spellsinger
**Major character(s):** Jon-Tom Meriweather, Musician, Adventurer; Mudge, Animal (otter); Hieronymus Hinckel, Musician, Thief
**Time period(s):** Indeterminate
**Locale(s):** Mashupro, Fictional City; Farraglean Ocean, Mythical Place

**Summary:** Bored at home, Jon-Tom and Mudge chase after music that leads them southward where they rescue some princesses and find music vanishing. On an island, they encounter a displaced grunge band who claim that Hieronymus Hinckel, who has no musical talent, steals the music. Jon-Tom decides he must try to defeat Hinckel and free all the music.

**Other books you might like:**
Robert Asprin, *Another Fine Myth*, 1978
Brian Jacques, *Redwall*, 1987
Elizabeth Ann Scarborough, *Picking the Ballad's Bones*, 1991
Clifford D. Simak, *The Fellowship of the Talisman*, 1978
Christopher Stasheff, *The Warlock Rock*, 1990

## 1999

**ALAN DEAN FOSTER**

### Codgerspace

(New York: Ace, 1992)

**Story type:** Science Fiction (Humor; Alternate Intelligence)
**Major character(s):** Autothor, Artificial Intelligence, Alien (Drex); Mina Gelmann, Aged Person, Adventurer; Victor Iranaputra, Aged Person, Adventurer
**Time period(s):** Indeterminate Future
**Locale(s):** Earth

**Summary:** When one ancient artificial intelligence begins searching for non-human intelligences, artifical intelligences everywhere become entirely too intelligent and uncooperatively philosophical. The fate of the civilized galaxy falls into the hands of five senior citizens and their food processor.

**Other books you might like:**
Douglas Adams, *The Hitchhiker's Guide to the Galaxy*, 1980
Roger MacBride Allen, *The Ring of Charon*, 1990
Ron Goulart, *Brainz, Inc.*, 1985
Michael Kandel, *Strange Invasion*, 1989
Henry Kuttner, *Robots Have No Tails*, 1952
Vernor Vinge, *A Fire upon the Deep*, 1992

## 2000

**ALAN DEAN FOSTER**

### Cyber Way

(New York: Ace, 1990)

**Story type:** Science Fiction (Mystery; Theological)
**Major character(s):** Vernon Moody, Detective—Police; Paul Ooljee, Police Officer (sergeant), Indian (Navajo)
**Time period(s):** 22nd century
**Locale(s):** Navajo Nation Four Corners; Greater Tampa, Florida

**Summary:** When a murder in Florida involves a Navajo sandpainting, waterloving Detective Moody finds himself sent to the arid, high-tech Navajo Nation. Paul Ooljee, an expert in sandpaintings has volunteered to help with this case and takes Moody under his wing for the duration of the adventure. As they try to unravel the secrets of Moody's peculiar sandpainting photograph, they begin to understand the terrifyingly current message contained in the ancient symbols.

**Other books you might like:**
Roger MacBride Allen, *The Ring of Charon*, 1990
Katharine Kerr, *Polar City Blues*, 1990
Lee Killough, *Dragon's Teeth*, 1990
Marc Laidlaw, *Neon Lotus*, 1988
G. Harry Stine, *Blood Siege*, 1990
John E. Stith, *Redshift Rendezvous*, 1990

## 2001

**ALAN DEAN FOSTER**
**ERIC FRANK RUSSELL**, Co-Author

### Design for Great-Day

(New York: Tor, 1995)

**Story type:** Science Fiction (First Contact; Military)
**Major character(s):** James Lawson, Diplomat; Markhamwit, Alien, Leader
**Time period(s):** Indeterminate Future
**Locale(s):** Planet—Imaginary; Solarian Combine, Interstellar Empire/Federation

**Summary:** When a single human emissary arrives on both planets about to engage in interstellar warfare, the belligerents must decide if they wish to continue battle plans or yield to a demand for peace from the fabled Solarian Combine. Expanded by Foster from Russell's 1953 novella.

**Other books you might like:**
A.C. Crispin, *Silent Songs*, 1994
    Kathleen O'Malley, co-author
Keith Laumer, *Retief and the Warlords*, 1968

Anne McCaffrey, *Treaty at Doona*, 1994
    Jody Lynn Nye, co-author
Eric Frank Russell, *Dreadful Sanctuary*, 1951
Eric Frank Russell, *Sinister Barrier*, 1943
Eric Frank Russell, *Wasp*, 1957
John Varley, *The Ophiuchi Hotline*, 1977

## 2002

### ALAN DEAN FOSTER

## *The Dig*

(New York: Warner Aspect, 1996)

**Story type:** Science Fiction (Adventure; Mystery)
**Major character(s):** Boston Low, Pilot (space shuttle); Maggie Robbins, Journalist; Ludger Brink, Scientist
**Time period(s):** 21st century
**Locale(s):** *Atlantis*, Spaceship; Cocytus, Planet—Imaginary

**Summary:** When an asteroid suddenly appears near Earth, scientists send a team to investigate and regularize the asteroid's orbit. However, when the group arrives at the asteroid, a mysterious force transports them to Cocytus, formerly civilized, but now abandoned, where they must solve the puzzle of returning home. Computer game tie-in.

**Other books you might like:**
Roger MacBride Allen, *The Ring of Charon*, 1990
Greg Bear, *Eon*, 1985
John DeChancie, *Starrigger*, 1983
Frederik Pohl, *The Other End of Time*, 1996
Robert J. Sawyer, *Starplex*, 1996
Allen Steele, *The Tranquility Alternative*, 1996

## 2003

### ALAN DEAN FOSTER

## *Dinotopia Lost*

(Atlanta: Turner Publishing, 1996)

**Story type:** Fantasy (Adventure)
**Series:** Dinotopia
**Major character(s):** Will Denison, Adventurer; Blackstrap, Pirate, Sea Captain; Preister Smiggens, Pirate
**Time period(s):** 1860s
**Locale(s):** Dinotopia, Fictional Country

**Summary:** When a giant breaker washes a pirate ship over Dinotopia's protective coral reef, the pirates capture a dinosaur family. Will Denison leads a small rescue party in pursuit through Rainy Basin, an abandoned area where tyrannosaurs still rule.

**Other books you might like:**
Scott Ciencin, *Windchaser*, 1995
James Gurney, *Dinotopia*, 1992
James Gurney, *The World Beneath*, 1995
Midori Snyder, *Hatchling*, 1995
John Vornholt, *River Quest*, 1995

## 2004

### ALAN DEAN FOSTER

## *The False Mirror*

(New York: Ballantine Del Rey, 1992)

**Story type:** Science Fiction (Military; Political)

**Series:** Damned
**Major character(s):** Ranji, Warrior, Genetically Altered Being; Heida Trondheim, Military Personnel; D'oud, Alien, Scientist (xenobiologist)
**Time period(s):** 21st century
**Locale(s):** Cosuut, Planet—Imaginary; Eirossad, Planet—Imaginary; The Weave, Interstellar Empire/Federation

**Summary:** After his capture on Eirossad, Ranji learns that his makeup reflects not Ashregan, but rather human ancestry. Returning to his people, Ranji leads them to join with other humans in the Weave. Fearing knowledge of their psychic ability, a result of their genetic manipulation, would result in their persecution, the group decides to keep the ability secret and form an insular community for protection.

**Other books you might like:**
John Dalmas, *Homecoming*, 1984
Gordon R. Dickson, *Wolfling*, 1969
David Drake, *Cross the Stars*, 1984
Robert A. Heinlein, *Starship Troopers*, 1959
Richard Meredith, *At the Narrow Passage*, 1973
Jerry Pournelle, *War World I: The Burning Eye*, 1988
    John F. Carr and Roland Green, co-editors
Joel Rosenberg, *Hero*, 1990

## 2005

### ALAN DEAN FOSTER

## *Greenthieves*

(New York: Ace, 1994)

**Story type:** Science Fiction (Mystery; Robot Fiction)
**Major character(s):** Broderick Manz, Insurance Investigator; Moses, Robot; Vyra Kullervo, Alien, Insurance Investigator
**Time period(s):** Indeterminate Future
**Locale(s):** Juarez El Pasco Port Authority, Earth

**Summary:** Braun-Roche-Keck sends Vyra with Manz, his Minder, and Moses to stop the thefts of pharmaceuticals leaving the planet. Embarrassed by the thefts from their supposedly safe, high-tech security storage area, the Port Authority supplies the cooperation of their security chief and all information acquired to date. Unfortunately, while they inspect the facilities, another shipment disappears from the locked, vacuum-sealed room, practically in front of their eyes. They must find the thieves and stop the thefts.

**Other books you might like:**
Roger MacBride Allen, *Caliban*, 1993
Isaac Asimov, *The Caves of Steel*, 1954
Mel Gilden, *Tubular Android Superheroes*, 1991
Mike Resnick, *Whatdunits*, 1992
    editor
John E. Stith, *Deep Quarry*, 1989

## 2006

### ALAN DEAN FOSTER

## *The Howling Stones*

(New York: Ballantine Del Rey, 1997)

**Story type:** Science Fiction (First Contact; Mystical)
**Series:** Humanx Commonwealth
**Major character(s):** Pulickel Tomochelor, Scientist (xenologist), Anthropologist (first contact specialist); Fawn Seaforth, Scientist (xenologist); Jorana, Alien (Seni), Artisan (woodworker)
**Time period(s):** Indeterminate Future

**Locale(s):** Parramat Archipelago, Mythical Place; Senisran, Planet—Imaginary

**Summary:** Sent to newly discovered Senisran to win a treaty with the aboriginal Seni aliens, Pulickel Tomochelor refuses to believe that the Senis' sacred stones possess great powers until he witnesses those powers for himself.

**Other books you might like:**
Arthur C. Clarke, *The Songs of Distant Earth*, 1986
Julia Ecklar, *Regenesis*, 1995
Frederik Pohl, *Beyond the Blue Event Horizon*, 1980
Frederik Pohl, *Gateway*, 1977
Sheri S. Tepper, *Raising the Stones*, 1990
Amy Thomson, *The Color of Distance*, 1995

## 2007
### ALAN DEAN FOSTER

## Jed the Dead
(New York: Ace, 1997)

**Story type:** Science Fiction (First Contact; Humor)
**Major character(s):** Ross Ed Hager, Tourist; Jed, Alien (Shakaleeshva), Reanimated Dead; Caroline, Friend
**Time period(s):** 1990s
**Locale(s):** New Mexico; Arizona; California

**Summary:** Investigating a small cave above a roadside rest stop, Ross Ed finds more than a nice view when he discovers a dead alien who had lived long enough to escape the crash near Roswell. Experiencing strange visions upon contact with its environmental suit, Ross Ed takes the small creature on an odyssey through a Southwest grown suddenly strange, while U.S. Army Intelligence officers and others search for the pair.

**Other books you might like:**
Mel Gilden, *Hawaiian U.F.O. Aliens*, 1991
Mel Gilden, *Surfing Samurai Robots*, 1988
Mel Gilden, *Tubular Android Superheroes*, 1991
Nick Pollotta, *Illegal Aliens*, 1989
Spider Robinson, *Callahan's Legacy*, 1996

## 2008
### ALAN DEAN FOSTER

## Life Form
(New York: Ace, 1995)

**Story type:** Science Fiction (First Contact; Hard Science Fiction)
**Major character(s):** Jack Simna, Scientist; Franklin Lastwell, Spaceship Captain; Bontu, Alien (humanoid)
**Time period(s):** Indeterminate Future
**Locale(s):** *James Cook*, Spaceship; Outer Space; Xica de Silva III, Planet—Imaginary

**Summary:** After exploring several worlds, the crew of the *James Cook* and the scientists on board still hope to find life on a planet where humans can thrive. On Xica da Silva III they discover coastal jungles rich with life, large salt oceans, and interior desert. Although too brief for a thorough understanding, the two-year expedition should achieve fame by cataloging local fauna. Finding humanoid natives with a powerful need to learn leads the scientists to a more complete and realistic comprehension of the native biology.

**Other books you might like:**
Octavia E. Butler, *Dawn*, 1987
L. Warren Douglas, *Cannon's Orb*, 1994
L. Warren Douglas, *A Plague of Change*, 1992

Janet Kagan, *Mirabile*, 1991
Larry Niven, *The Mote in God's Eye*, 1974
  Jerry Pournelle, co-author
Joan Slonczewski, *Daughter of Elysium*, 1993

## 2009
### ALAN DEAN FOSTER

## Mad Amos
(New York: Ballantine Del Rey, 1996)

**Story type:** Fantasy (Collection; Light Fantasy)
**Major character(s):** Amos "Mad Amos" Malone, Mountain Man, Sorcerer
**Time period(s):** 19th century
**Locale(s):** Southwest; Pacific Islands

**Summary:** Contains a four-page introduction plus individual introductions to two original and eight stories reprinted from periodicals and anthologies 1982-1992. Mad Amos Malone's adventures in the Wild West and in the South Pacific involve dragons, jackalopes, sorcerers, headless Indian spirits, and an erupting volcano.

**Other books you might like:**
Stephen King, *The Dark Tower: The Gunslinger*, 1982
Louis L'Amour, *Haunted Mesa*, 1987
George R.R. Martin, *Fevre Dream*, 1982
Elizabeth Ann Scarborough, *The Goldcamp Vampire; or The Sanguinary Sourdough*, 1987
Midori Snyder, *The Flight of Michael McBride*, 1994

## 2010
### ALAN DEAN FOSTER

## Mid-Flinx
(New York: Ballantine Del Rey, 1995)

**Story type:** Science Fiction (First Contact; Alternate Intelligence)
**Series:** Flinx
**Major character(s):** Philip "Flinx" Lynx, Psychic (esper), Wanderer; Jack-Jax Landsdowne Coerlis, Heir, Collector; Saalahan, Alien (furcot)
**Time period(s):** Indeterminate Future
**Locale(s):** Samstead, Planet—Imaginary; Midworld, Planet—Imaginary; *Teacher*, Spaceship

**Summary:** On Samstead to stay out of trouble and see the sights, Flinx and his mini-dragon Pip run into Jack-Jax who wants Pip for his zoo. Escaping in *Teacher* on a random course, Flinx decides to explore the forest world on their route still followed by the angry, covetous Jack-Jax.

**Other books you might like:**
David Brin, *Brightness Reef*, 1995
L. Warren Douglas, *Bright Islands in a Dark Sea*, 1993
Harry Harrison, *The Deathworld Trilogy*, 1976
Anne McCaffrey, *Powers That Be*, 1993
  Elizabeth Ann Scarborough, co-author
Vernor Vinge, *A Fire upon the Deep*, 1992

## 2011
### ALAN DEAN FOSTER

## *Montezuma Strip*
(New York: Warner Aspect, 1995)

**Story type:** Science Fiction (Mystery; Cyberpunk)
**Major character(s):** Angel Cardenas, Police Officer (Federale Sergeant), Psychic; Hypatia Spango, Computer Expert
**Time period(s):** 21st century
**Locale(s):** Montezuma Strip, North America (USA-Mexico border); United States; Mexico

**Summary:** Angel Cardenas, an "Intuit" police officer who senses when people lie, uses his special abilities to solve crimes along the Montezuma Strip, where the U.S.-Mexican border has grown into one long, industrialized strip with a rough culture all its own.

**Other books you might like:**
Isaac Asimov, *The Naked Sun*, 1957
Ben Bova, *Death Dream*, 1994
Philip K. Dick, *Blade Runner*, 1982
Julia Ecklar, *Regenesis*, 1995
William Gibson, *Neuromancer*, 1984

## 2012
### ALAN DEAN FOSTER

## *Parallelities*
(New York: Ballantine Del Rey, 1998)

**Story type:** Science Fiction (Alternate Universe; Science Fiction)
**Major character(s):** Max Parker, Journalist; Barrington Boles, Scientist, Inventor
**Time period(s):** 21st century
**Locale(s):** Los Angeles, California

**Summary:** Max Parker becomes a magnet attracting people from parallel universes. As the effect gets stronger, he even attracts himself in both male and female forms, and soon begins to slip in and out of various realities. Among the many alternate Boleses, Max must find the correct Boles, the scientist who got him into this plight, to have any hope of returning to his normal life.

**Other books you might like:**
Poul Anderson, *There Will Be Time*, 1972
Isaac Asimov, *The End of Eternity*, 1955
John Brunner, *The Infinitive of Go*, 1980
Jack L. Chalker, *Downtiming the Night Side*, 1985
Sheila Finch, *Infinity's Web*, 1985
David Gerrold, *The Man Who Folded Himself*, 1973
Richard Meredith, *Vestiges of Time*, 1979
Frederik Pohl, *The Coming of the Quantum Cats*, 1986

## 2013
### ALAN DEAN FOSTER

## *Quozl*
(New York: Ace Books, 1989)

**Story type:** Science Fiction (Humor)
**Major character(s):** Looks-at-Charts, Alien, Scout; Chad Collins, Teenager
**Time period(s):** Indeterminate Future
**Locale(s):** *Sequencer*, Spaceship; Earth

**Summary:** The Quozl, an alien race obsessed with trendy clothes and fashion accessories, visits the Earth, setting the stage for one of the silliest invasions of another planet in history.

**Other books you might like:**
Damien Broderick, *Striped Holes*, 1988
Mel Gilden, *Surfing Samurai Robots*, 1988
Keith Laumer, *The Return of Retief*, 1985
Keith Laumer, *Reward for Retief*, 1989
Alexei Panshin, *Masque World*, 1969
Alexei Panshin, *Star Well*, 1968
Charles Platt, *Free Zone*, 1989

## 2014
### ALAN DEAN FOSTER, Editor
### MARTIN H. GREENBERG, Co-Editor

## *Smart Dragons, Foolish Elves*
(New York: Ace, 1991)

**Story type:** Fantasy (Anthology; Light Fantasy)

**Summary:** This volume contains an introduction and afterword by Alan Dean Foster plus 18 humorous stories originally published as early as 1939 and as recently as 1990. Authors include Anthony Boucher, John Collier, Avram Davidson, George Alec Effinger, Harlan Ellison, Esther M. Friesner, Horace L. Gold, Ron Goulart, Marvin Kaye, Mike Resnick, Robert Sheckley, Robert Silverberg, William Tenn and Roger Zelazny.

**Other books you might like:**
Chester Anderson, *The Butterfly Kid*, 1967
Orson Scott Card, *Dragons of Darkness*, 1981
  editor
Orson Scott Card, *Dragons of Light*, 1980
  editor
L. Sprague de Camp, *The Complete Compleat Enchanter*, 1989
  Fletcher Pratt, co-author
Charles L. Grant, *Blood River Down*, 1986
  as Lionel Fenn
Patricia C. Wrede, *Dealing with Dragons*, 1990
Patricia C. Wrede, *Talking to Dragons*, 1985

## 2015
### ALAN DEAN FOSTER

## *Son of Spellsinger*
(New York: Warner Questar, 1993)

**Story type:** Fantasy (Light Fantasy; Quest)
**Series:** Spellsinger
**Major character(s):** Buncan Meriweather, Teenager, Musician; Gragelouth, Businessman (merchant), Animal (sloth); Snaugenhutt, Warrior, Animal (rhinoceros)
**Time period(s):** Indeterminate
**Locale(s):** Bellwoods, Mythical Place; Kilagurri, Mythical Place (monastery)

**Summary:** Bored with home and school, Buncan Meriweather teams up with Squill and Neena to form a rap spellsinging group. They rescue a merchant who proposes a quest to find the Grand Veritable, the greatest threat to the world.

**Other books you might like:**
Piers Anthony, *Demons Don't Dream*, 1993
Suzette Haden Elgin, *Twelve Fair Kingdoms*, 1981
Diana Wynne Jones, *The Power of Three*, 1977
Anne McCaffrey, *Dragonsong*, 1976

Christopher Stasheff, *The Warlock Rock*, 1990
Patricia C. Wrede, *Searching for Dragons*, 1991

## 2016

### ALAN DEAN FOSTER

## *The Spoils of War*

(New York: Ballantine Del Rey, 1993)

**Story type:** Science Fiction (Military; Political)
**Series:** Damned
**Major character(s):** Lalelelang, Historian, Alien (Wais); Nevan Straat-ien, Military Personnel (colonel), Human
**Time period(s):** 25th century
**Locale(s):** Outer Space

**Summary:** The Weave expert on humans, Wais Scholar Historian Lalelelang travels among humans to further her studies, managing to see warfare up close without going mad. While fearing humanity will exterminate itself after the war ends, Lalelelang becomes the key to galactic peace.

**Other books you might like:**
Eleanor Arnason, *Ring of Swords*, 1993
David Brin, *The Uplift War*, 1987
C.J. Cherryh, *The Pride of Chanur*, 1981
Colin Kapp, *The Survival Game*, 1976
Michael McCollum, *Antares Passage*, 1987
Rebecca Ore, *Being Alien*, 1989
Timothy Zahn, *Cobra*, 1985

## 2017

### CHRISTOPHER FOWLER

## *The Bureau of Lost Souls*

(New York: Ballantine, 1991)

**Story type:** Horror (Collection)

**Summary:** The twelve mildly engaging horror stories in this collection, originally published in England in 1989, are concerned mostly with interesting methods of revenge. Included are ''The Art Nouveau Fireplace,'' about a modern Bluebeard; ''The Ladies Man,'' about three turned-down job applicants who give a sexist employer his comeuppance; ''Safe as Houses,'' about a health nut who gets his just desserts; and ''The Master Builder,'' a contrived study of the lengths to which a sexually obsessed handyman will go to be with the woman he lusts for. Several of these stories appeared in the author's collection, *More City Jitters*.

**Other books you might like:**
Ramsey Campbell, *Dark Companions*, 1982

## 2018

### CHRISTOPHER FOWLER

## *Personal Demons*

(New York: Serpent's Tail, 1998)

**Story type:** Horror (Collection)

**Summary:** Contained in this collection are seventeen stories with a preface by the author. Selections range in style from the eastern fantasy ''The Man Who Wound a Thousand Clocks,'' to the intentional Gothicism of ''Dracula's Library,'' but most mix the supernatural with contemporary urban realism. Included are ''Permanent Fixture,'' in which a woman discovers that a crowd of football fans

has become a living entity with a single consciousness; ''Five Star,'' in which a corrupt financier gets his just reward at a tourist spot hurt by his heartless business practices; ''Wage Slaves,'' in which the exploitation of the office worker is taken to supernatural extremes; and ''The Cages,'' an allegory of the traps each man builds for himself.

**Other books you might like:**
Ramsey Campbell, *Ghosts and Grisly Things*, 1998
David Langford, *Irrational Numbers*, 1993
Graham Masterton, *Flights of Fear*, 1996
Mark Morris, *Close to the Bone*, 1995
Kim Newman, *Famous Monsters*, 1995

## 2019

### CHRISTOPHER FOWLER

## *Red Bride*

(New York: Roc, 1993)

**Story type:** Horror (Mystery)
**Major character(s):** John Chapel, Public Relations; Ixoro De Corizo, Actress; Helen Chapel, Accountant (bookkeeper)
**Time period(s):** 1990s (1992)
**Locale(s):** London, England

**Summary:** So infatuated does John Chapel become with Ixoro De Corizo, the actress whose publicity he handles, that he leaves his wife and family to marry her. When men who know Ixora's past begin dying horrible deaths, that past inevitably comes to light as John desperately tries to clear her of any implication in the murders. This novel was originally published in England in 1992.

**Other books you might like:**
Richard Adams, *Girl in a Swing*, 1980
Richard Matheson, *Earthbound*, 1982
Peter Straub, *Ghost Story*, 1979
Whitley Strieber, *The Hunger*, 1981

## 2020

### CHRISTOPHER FOWLER

## *Rune*

(New York: Ballantine, 1991)

**Story type:** Horror (Occult)
**Major character(s):** Harry Buckingham, Advertising (advertising executive); Grace Crispian, Truck Driver; Dorothy Huxley, Librarian
**Time period(s):** 1990s (1990)
**Locale(s):** London, England

**Summary:** When his father dies beneath the wheels of a delivery truck, clutching a scrap of paper with ancient runic symbols scrawled on it, Harry Buckingham suspects a more-than-natural death. His investigations uncover a conspiracy on the part of the ODEL corporation to subliminally control the world through ancient occult forces.

**Other books you might like:**
M.R. James, ''*Casting the Runes*'', 1989
    in *A Warning to the Curious*
David C. Smith, *The Fair Rules of Evil*, 1989

## 2021
### D.A. FOWLER

## Bad Blood
(New York: Pinnacle, 1993)

**Story type:** Horror (Evil Children)
**Major character(s):** Arlo Wade, Child (10 years old), Twin; Austin Wade, Child (10 years old), Twin; Tamara Wade, Mentally Ill Person, Parent (Arlo and Austin's mother)
**Time period(s):** 1990s (1993)
**Locale(s):** Huntington, West Virginia

**Summary:** Tamara Wade escapes from her incarceration in a mental asylum and returns home to find that her cruel and mischievous twin sons, Arlo and Austin, have perpetuated her legacy of callous disregard for the feelings and well-being of friends and family. This book is an indirect sequel to the author's 1991 novel, *What's Wrong with Tamara?*

**Other books you might like:**
Margaret Bingley, *Seeds of Evil*, 1988
Tom Piccirilli, *Dark Father*, 1990
Thomas Tryon, *The Other*, 1972

## 2022
### D.A. FOWLER

## The Book of the Damned
(New York: Pocket, 1993)

**Story type:** Horror (Occult)
**Major character(s):** Rosalyn Vaughn, Hairdresser; Levi D. Santa, Demon; Kevin Kessler, Detective—Police
**Time period(s):** 1990s (1993)
**Locale(s):** Brookington

**Summary:** Bored Rosalyn Vaughn reads a pulpy horror novel titled *The Book of the Damned* for entertainment. Thereafter she keeps slipping into flashbacks in which she is the heroine of the novel, a helpless victim tortured by a devil incarnate who goes about under the name Levi D. Santa, an anagram for ''Devil Satan.''

**Other books you might like:**
John Byrne, *Fear Book*, 1988
Thomas Ligotti, *Vastarien*, 1990
  in *Songs of a Dead Dreamer*

## 2023
### D.A. FOWLER

## The Devil's End
(New York: Pocket, 1992)

**Story type:** Horror (Black Magic; Occult)
**Major character(s):** Nancy Snell, Teenager; Lana Bremmers, Teenager; Spiro Guenther, Teenager
**Time period(s):** 1990s
**Locale(s):** Sharon Valley, South Dakota

**Summary:** Nancy Snell discovers that she is a lineal descendant of a witch whose legacy forms part of the dark history of Sharon Valley. She finds a way to access the occult powers and use them against her enemies and uses the new girl in town, Lana Bremmers.

**Other books you might like:**
Katina Alexis, *Souls*, 1992
Marcy Heidish, *The Torching*, 1992

Ed Kelleher, *The School*, 1992
Harriette Vidal, co-author

## 2024
### D.A. FOWLER

## Flesh and Blood
(New York: Pocket, 1993)

**Story type:** Horror (Psychological Suspense)
**Major character(s):** Deidi Marshall, Journalist; Camisa Collins, Housewife; Judson Hendricks, Detective
**Time period(s):** 1990s (1993)
**Locale(s):** Danville, South

**Summary:** Although from completely different walks of life, Deidi Marshall and Camisa Collins share the same visions of a woman who looks like them murdering a variety of people. When those murders are reported in the local paper, their investigations put them on pathways that will inevitably converge and explain their peculiar bond.

**Other books you might like:**
J.M. Dillard, *Specters*, 1991
Thomas Tryon, *The Other*, 1972
T. Lucien Wright, *Blood Brothers*, 1992

## 2025
### D.A. FOWLER

## What's Wrong with Tamara?
(New York: Pocket, 1992)

**Story type:** Horror (Evil Children)
**Major character(s):** Tamara Wade, Child; Jonathan Wade, Miner (coal miner); Alex Morrison, Detective—Police
**Time period(s):** 1990s (1992)
**Locale(s):** Huntington, West Virginia

**Summary:** Nine years before, Tamara Wade was kidnapped by a mad woman who conversed with the dead and, supposedly at their bidding, murdered numerous people, including Tamara's mother. Now Tamara speaks to her collection of talking dolls, which encourage her to disrupt her father's plans for remarriage and generally cause havoc.

**Other books you might like:**
Algernon Blackwood, *The Doll and One Other*, 1946
William Goldman, *Magic*, 1978
Pat Graversen, *Dollies*, 1990
Ruby Jean Jensen, *Baby Dolly*, 1992
A. Merritt, *Burn, Witch, Burn!*, 1933
Sarban, *The Doll Maker and Other Tales of the Uncanny*, 1953

## 2026
### D.A. FOWLER

## What's Wrong with Valerie?
(New York: Pocket, 1991)

**Story type:** Horror (Psychological Suspense)
**Major character(s):** Valerie Scott, Writer; Elisabeth, Housewife (Valerie's sister); Tamara, Child (Valerie's niece)
**Time period(s):** 1990s
**Locale(s):** Huntington, West Virginia

**Summary:** Convinced that the home she has inherited is haunted by the spirits of dead family members who warn her that entities from beyond the grave are returning to eat her flesh, pathetically insane Valerie Scott kidnaps her niece to save her from a similar fate, and locks the two of them away from public scrutiny inside the house.

**Other books you might like:**
Shirley Jackson, *We Have Always Lived in the Castle*, 1962

---

**2027**

**KAREN JOY FOWLER**

### Black Glass: Short Fictions

(New York: Henry Holt, 1998)

**Story type:** Science Fiction (Collection)

**Summary:** Contains 15 stories, frequently humorous, which explore diverse themes such as fairy tales, the DEA, Native Americans, the war in Vietnam, Albert Einstein, alternative history, life in the bush, the study of romance, changes in lifestyle, and the healing powers of alcohol and psychology. One story, ''The Travails,'' is presented in epistolary form.

**Other books you might like:**
Nancy Kress, *The Aliens of Earth*, 1993
Elizabeth Moon, *Phases*, 1997
Rebecca Ore, *Alien Bootlegger and Other Stories*, 1993
Mary Rosenblum, *Synthesis & Other Virtual Realities*, 1996
Connie Willis, *Impossible Things*, 1994

---

**2028**

**KAREN JOY FOWLER**

### Sarah Canary

(New York: Henry Holt, 1991)

**Story type:** Fantasy (Quest)
**Major character(s):** Ah Kin Chin, Worker, Wanderer; Sarah Canary, Patient (mental), Wanderer; B.J. Voisard, Patient (mental)
**Time period(s):** 1870s (1873)
**Locale(s):** Stellacoom, Washington; Pacific Northwest

**Summary:** Sarah Canary, a woman either insane or supernatural or both, arrives without warning in a camp of migrant Chinese railroad workers. One of the workers, Chin, takes charge of her, and they travel across the Pacific Northwest through a series of surreal encounters, trying to find either her identity or a safe home for her. This experimental novel is the author's first.

**Other books you might like:**
Iain M. Banks, *The Bridge*, 1986
James P. Blaylock, *The Paper Grail*, 1991
Lisa Goldstein, *The Dream Years*, 1985
Pat Murphy, *The City, Not Long After*, 1989
Fay Weldon, *The Shrapnel Academy*, 1987

---

**2029**

**KAREN JOY FOWLER**

### The Sweetheart Season

(New York: Henry Holt, 1996)

**Story type:** Fantasy (Contemporary Realism)
**Major character(s):** Maggie Collins, Housewife, Mythical Creature; Irini Doyle, Cook, Sports Figure; Henry Collins, Businessman
**Time period(s):** 1940s (1947)

**Locale(s):** Magrit, Minnesota

**Summary:** Magrit Mill, a major breakfast cereal company, sponsors the Sweetwheat Sweethearts, an all-woman baseball team. But consistent with Magrit's odd past, which includes a drowned village and a ghost rowboat, the team evolves differently than the town expects.

**Other books you might like:**
Michael Bishop, *Brittle Innings*, 1994
Darryl Brock, *If I Never Get Back*, 1989
Robert Browne, *The New Atoms' Bombshell*, 1980
Jack Cady, *The Off Season*, 1995
W.P. Kinsella, *The Iowa Baseball Confederacy*, 1986
Pat Murphy, *Nadya: The Wolf Chronicles*, 1996

---

**2030**

**RANDY FOX**
**ALAN M. CLARK**, Illustrator

### Not Broken, Not Belonging

(Arvada, Colorado: Roadkill Press, 1994)

**Story type:** Horror (Possession)
**Major character(s):** Dr. Ward, Doctor; Rachael Cummings, Artist; Michael Cummings, Banker
**Time period(s):** 1990s (1994)
**Locale(s):** Knoxville, Tennessee

**Summary:** This short-story tells of an artist who nearly dies when her car plunges into a river, and what her artwork thereafter reveals about the origins of her strange post-traumatic behavior. Fox wrote the story based upon concepts embodied in the artwork of Clark, who has illustrated the chapbook generously.

**Other books you might like:**
Giles Blunt, *Cold Eye*, 1989
Stephen King, *Pet Sematary*, 1983
Kathe Koja, *Bad Brains*, 1992
Kathe Koja, *Skin*, 1993
Kathe Koja, *Strange Angels*, 1994
Jessica Amanda Salmonson, *Anthony Shriek*, 1992

---

**2031**

**JOCELIN FOXE**

### The Wild Hunt: Vengeance Moon

(New York: Avon Eos, 1998)

**Story type:** Fantasy (Political; Romance)
**Major character(s):** Richenza Indes, Noblewoman; Walter of Jacin, Leader; Leot Thaiter, Royalty
**Time period(s):** Indeterminate Past
**Locale(s):** Tarsia, Fictional Country

**Summary:** The Wild Hunt consists of men cursed by the Three Goddesses to avenge wrongs or die horribly. Richenza Indes summons them to repay the ruling House of Thaiter for her brother's murder, one more bloody step in the history of the Hunt. As always, along with combat and intrigue, each summoning offers a hope of escape for the damned huntsmen.

**Other books you might like:**
Steven Brust, *Jhereg*, 1983
Glen Cook, *The Black Company*, 1984
Katharine Kerr, *Daggerspell*, 1986
Elizabeth Moon, *Sheepfarmer's Daughter*, 1988
Katya Reimann, *Wind From a Foreign Sky*, 1996

## 2032

### ELLEN FOXXE

## *Season of Storms*

(New York: DAW, 1996)

**Story type:** Fantasy (Political)
**Series:** Summerlands
**Major character(s):** Rolande Vendeley, Privateer; Alicen Kendry, Gentlewoman, Spy; Katin, Royalty, Herbalist
**Time period(s):** Indeterminate
**Locale(s):** Albin, Fictional Country; New Albin, Fictional Country

**Summary:** In New Albin, the collection of refugees, criminals and political dissidents thrive. In Albin, the peace of the chamber of statesmen collapses under the actions of two pretenders to the throne. While this may not be the best time to attempt to return as the rightful heir, if Princess Katin hesitates, there may be no kingdom to restore.

**Other books you might like:**
Teresa Edgerton, *Goblin Moon*, 1991
Ellen Kushner, *Swordspoint*, 1987
Caroline Stevermer, *A College of Magics*, 1994
Paula Volsky, *Illusion*, 1992
Martha Wells, *The Element of Fire*, 1993

## 2033

### GEORGE FOY

## *The Shift*

(New York: Bantam Spectra, 1996)

**Story type:** Science Fiction (Cyberpunk; Mystery)
**Major character(s):** Alex Munn, Writer (television, virtual reality), Computer Expert; Kaye Santangelo, Writer (poet); Larissa "Lara" Love, Actress
**Time period(s):** 2000s
**Locale(s):** New York, New York; Riker's Island, New York (prison)

**Summary:** Advanced virtual reality technology inspires Alex Munn to create *Munn's World*, a VR program about a serial killer called Fishman. Soon, however, Alex must fight to survive and to prove his innocence when the Fishman seemingly escapes the confines of VR to kill in the real world.

**Other books you might like:**
Terry Bisson, *Johnny Mnemonic*, 1995
Alan Dean Foster, *Montezuma Strip*, 1995
James P. Hogan, *Realtime Interrupt*, 1995
Richard Paul Russo, *Carlucci's Edge*, 1995
Richard Paul Russo, *Destroying Angel*, 1992
Walter Jon Williams, *Hardwired*, 1986

## 2034

### JONATHAN FRAKES
### DEAN WESLEY SMITH, Co-Author

## *The Abductors: Conspiracy*

(New York: Tor, 1996)

**Story type:** Science Fiction (Invasion of Earth; Adventure)
**Series:** Abductors
**Major character(s):** Richard McCallum, Detective—Private; Neda Foster, Researcher; Tina Harris, Student—College
**Time period(s):** 1990s
**Locale(s):** Portland, Oregon; Washington, District of Columbia

**Summary:** A private investigator working on two separate missing person cases, Richard McCallum realizes he has stumbled onto something big when he reluctantly concludes that both cases actually involve alien abductions. He joins forces with Neda Foster of Underground Investigations, an organization that has been secretly researching alien abductions for years.

**Other books you might like:**
David Bischoff, *Abduction: The UFO Conspiracy*, 1990
Dean Devlin, *Independence Day*, 1996
   Roland Emmerich, Stephen Molstad, co-authors
Robert A. Heinlein, *The Puppet Masters*, 1990
   revised edition
Anne McCaffrey, *Freedom's Landing*, 1995
Dean Wesley Smith, *Laying the Music to Rest*, 1989
Whitley Strieber, *Communion: A True Story*, 1987
H.G. Wells, *The War of the Worlds*, 1898

## 2035

### JANRAE FRANK, Editor
### JEAN MARIE STINE, Co-Editor
### FORREST J. ACKERMAN, Co-Editor

## *New Eves: Science Fiction about the Extraordinary Women of Today and Tomorrow*

(Stamford, Connecticut: Longmeadow Press, 1994)

**Story type:** Science Fiction (Anthology)

**Summary:** Dedicated to women who edited science fiction magazines 1928-1981, this volume contains a ten-page introduction focusing on historical perspective, a one-page "Author's Note" plus individual introductions to 32 stories reprinted from periodicals and anthologies 1918-1993 and arranged roughly by decade. Authors include Leigh Brackett, Marion Zimmer Bradley, Octavia E. Butler, Miriam Allen deFord, Phyllis Eisenstein, Carol Emshwiller, Sheila Finch, Karen Joy Fowler, Zenna Henderson, Lee Killough, Nancy Kress, Ursula K. Le Guin, Anne McCaffrey, Maureen F. McHugh, Judith Merril, Andre Norton, Mary Rosenblum, Joanna Russ, Margaret St. Clair, Pamela Sargent, Evelyn E. Smith, Francis Stevens, James Tiptree Jr., Sidney J. Van Scyoc and Kate Wilhelm.

**Other books you might like:**
Marjorie Agosin, *The Secret Weavers: Stories of the Fantastic by Latin American Women*, 1991
   editor
Nina Auerbach, *Forbidden Journeys: Fairy Tales and Fantasies by Victorian Women Writers*, 1992
   U.C. Knoepflmacher, co-editor
Jessica Amanda Salmonson, *What Did Miss Darrington See?: An Anthology of Feminist Supernatural Fiction*, 1989
   editor
Susanna J. Sturgis, *Magic Realism by Women: Dreams in a Minor Key*, 1991
   editor
A. Susan Williams, *The Lifted Veil: The Book of Fantastic Literature by Women*, 1993
   editor

## **2036**

### CHERYL J. FRANKLIN

## *Fire Crossing*

(New York: DAW, 1991)

**Story type:** Science Fiction (Science Fantasy; Space Opera)
**Series:** Network/Consortium
**Major character(s):** Luki, Immortal; Katerin "Kitri Terry" Meral, Professor; Quinzaine an Jiar yn Aliria dur Hamley, Immortal, Wizard
**Time period(s):** Indeterminate
**Locale(s):** Serii, Planet—Imaginary; Network, Planet—Imaginary (Hamley University)

**Summary:** Jon and Elizabeth Terry escape from Network to Serii, but have been forced to abandon their children, Michael and Kitri, to the evil Rabh Marrach. Marrach has conditioned the children to forget their past and to believe their parents are dead. The wizards of Serii, fearful of attack by Network, prevent the Terrys from remembering their children for almost twenty years, but the Network never forgets Jon Terry.

**Other books you might like:**
Gregory Benford, *Great Sky River*, 1987
Marion Zimmer Bradley, *The Firebrand*, 1987
Alan Dean Foster, *Cat-A-Lyst*, 1991
Anne McCaffrey, *Dragonflight*, 1968
Dan Simmons, *The Fall of Hyperion*, 1990
Dan Simmons, *Hyperion*, 1989
George Zebrowski, *Stranger Suns*, 1991

## **2037**

### CHERYL J. FRANKLIN

## *The Inquisitor*

(New York: DAW, 1992)

**Story type:** Science Fiction (First Contact; Political)
**Series:** Network/Consortium
**Major character(s):** Ngina-li "Ngina" Ngenga, Alien (Stromvi); Birk "Birkaj" Hodge, Trader, Administrator; Victoria "Tori" Mirelle, Clone
**Time period(s):** Indeterminate Future
**Locale(s):** Stromvi, Planet—Imaginary

**Summary:** Akras, Rea leader after Birkaj killed her father and her husband, preserves her clan and its primitive ideals. Birkaj settles on Stromvi, not comfortable for Soli, but possible with adaptation fluid. He arranges to plant roses, but also plants the precursor to adaptation fluid which makes the place more hospitable for Soli but, unfortunately, kills many of the intelligent, cooperative, peaceful natives before the Inquisitor from the Consortium can sort out the best solution.

**Other books you might like:**
Eleanor Arnason, *A Woman of the Iron People*, 1991
David Brin, *Startide Rising*, 1983
Octavia E. Butler, *Dawn*, 1987
C.S. Friedman, *Black Sun Rising*, 1991
Janet Kagan, *Mirabile*, 1991
Ursula K. Le Guin, *Always Coming Home*, 1987
Jacqueline Lichtenberg, *Molt Brother*, 1982
Sheri S. Tepper, *Raising the Stones*, 1990

## **2038**

### CHERYL J. FRANKLIN

## *The Light in Exile*

(New York: DAW Books, 1990)

**Story type:** Science Fiction (Adventure)
**Series:** Network/Consortium
**Major character(s):** Evjenial, Doctor; Rabh Marrah, Murderer
**Time period(s):** 24th century
**Locale(s):** Siatha, Planet—Imaginary

**Summary:** The Adraki, last survivors of an alien race, roam the galaxy conquering and destroying, apparently looking for a lost treasure. A powerful human allies himself with the Adraki, even though their alliance may lead to the destruction of the lovely non-technological planet Siatha, home of the mysterious and legendary Healers.

**Other books you might like:**
C.J. Cherryh, *The Faded Sun: Kesrith*, 1978
Rosemary Kirstein, *The Steerswoman*, 1989
Paul O. Williams, *The Gift of the Gorboduc Vandal*, 1989

## **2039**

### CHERYL J. FRANKLIN

## *Sable, Shadow and Ice*

(New York: DAW, 1994)

**Story type:** Fantasy (Religious; Magic Conflict)
**Major character(s):** Marita, Magician; Benedict, Religious; Aroha, Magician
**Time period(s):** Indeterminate Future
**Locale(s):** Rit, Fictional City (island); Tathagata, Fictional City

**Summary:** Battling Ch'ango, one of the polytheistic Mages of Avalon, Aroha uses Benedict, with his obsession over an ancient, forbidden monotheism, and Benedict's family, especially Marita, and their family's connections in his bid for power over the Protectorate.

**Other books you might like:**
Marion Zimmer Bradley, *The Mists of Avalon*, 1983
Laurell K. Hamilton, *Nightseer*, 1992
Paula Volsky, *Illusion*, 1992
Martha Wells, *The Element of Fire*, 1993
Patricia C. Wrede, *The Raven Ring*, 1994

## **2040**

### PAT FRANKLIN

## *Dark Dreaming*

(New York: Diamond, 1991)

**Story type:** Horror (Haunted House)
**Major character(s):** Meredith Morgan, Psychologist; Gustav Halburton, Psychologist; Richard Morgan, Businessman, Spouse (Meredith's husband)
**Time period(s):** 1990s
**Locale(s):** Mabton, California

**Summary:** After moving into a new house, Meredith Morgan begins having erotic dreams about men she has never seen before that begin to merge seamlessly with reality. Initially fearful she is losing her mind, she begins to suspect she has come under the influence of a lingering residue in the house when she finds out her dream lovers are local citizens, and that the house's previous owner committed suicide.

**Other books you might like:**
Tom Elliott, *The Dwelling*, 1989
Judith Hawkes, *Julian's House*, 1989
Shirley Jackson, *The Haunting of Hill House*, 1959
Al Sarrantonio, *House Haunted*, 1992

## 2041
### STEVEN FRANKOS
### *Cathedral of Thorns*
(New York: Ace, 1995)

**Story type:** Fantasy (Quest)
**Series:** Wheel Trilogy
**Major character(s):** Aitchley Corlaiys, Farmer, Adventurer; TW-O: 114-84-1311825, Robot; Calyx, Mythical Creature (dwarf)
**Time period(s):** Indeterminate
**Locale(s):** Vedette, Fictional Country; Alternate Universe

**Summary:** The heroes complete several steps in their search for the Elixir of Life. Unfortunately, Harris Blind-Eye steals the clues and kidnaps Berlyn, a new obstacle to deal with before the heroes can continue their primary effort.

**Other books you might like:**
M.A.R. Barker, *Man of Gold*, 1984
Simon R. Green, *Hawk & Fisher*, 1990
Patricia A. McKillip, *The Riddle-Master of Hed*, 1976
Fred Saberhagen, *Empire of the East*, 1979
Christopher Stasheff, *The Warlock in Spite of Himself*, 1969

## 2042
### STEVEN FRANKOS
### *The Jewel of Equilibrant*
(New York: Ace, 1993)

**Story type:** Fantasy (Alternate World; Quest)
**Major character(s):** Matthew Logan, Traveler; Thromar, Warrior; The Smythe, Wizard
**Time period(s):** 1990s; Indeterminate
**Locale(s):** Santa Monica, California; Sparrill, Alternate Universe

**Summary:** After repeated warnings that he should recognize the danger of dreams, Matthew steps out for daily exercise. While jogging, Matthew suddenly experiences a peculiar storm. Afterward he must defend himself with bow and sword before convincing himself he has travelled to an alternate world. He discovers that he must restore the Balance of the Wheel before he can return home.

**Other books you might like:**
Steven Brust, *Jhereg*, 1983
Gordon R. Dickson, *The Dragon and the George*, 1976
Carole Nelson Douglas, *Cup of Clay*, 1991
William R. Forstchen, *The Crystal Warriors*, 1988
  Greg Morrison, co-author
Geary Gravel, *A Key for the Nonesuch*, 1990
Robert Jordan, *The Eye of the World*, 1989
Brad Strickland, *Wizard's Mole*, 1991

## 2043
### LEO FRANKOWSKI
### *Conrad's Quest for Rubber*
(New York: Ballantine Del Rey, 1998)

**Story type:** Science Fiction (Time Travel; Adventure)
**Series:** Conrad Stargard
**Major character(s):** Conrad Stargard, Time Traveler, Engineer; Josip Sobieski, Military Personnel, Explorer; Maude, Bodyguard, Genetically Altered Being
**Time period(s):** 13th century (1240s)
**Locale(s):** Okoitz, Poland; Brazil

**Summary:** Conrad Stargard tries to make medieval Poland as comfortable as possible. Josip Sobieski, a simple baker's son, watches and participates in Conrad's plans to defeat the Mongols, introduce education and social reforms, and explore the world. Eventually Josip goes to Brazil, where he discovers that the worst enemies may not always be human.

**Other books you might like:**
L. Sprague de Camp, *Lest Darkness Fall*, 1941
Paul J. McAuley, *Pasquale's Angel*, 1995
Ward Moore, *Bring the Jubilee*, 1953
Mike Moscoe, *Second Fire*, 1997
H. Beam Piper, *Lord Kalvan of Otherwhen*, 1965

## 2044
### LEO FRANKOWSKI
### *The Flying Warlord*
(New York: Ballantine/Del Rey, 1989)

**Story type:** Science Fiction (Time Travel)
**Series:** Adventures of Conrad Stargard
**Major character(s):** Conrad Stargard, Engineer, Time Traveler
**Time period(s):** 13th century
**Locale(s):** Poland; Alternate Earth

**Summary:** Stargard has accidentally time traveled to medieval Poland, started a premature Industrial Revolution, and altered the course of history. Arming the Polish army with modern weapons, he does battle with the invading Mongols.

**Other books you might like:**
Gregory Benford, *Alternate Empires*, 1989
  Martin H. Greenberg, co-author
Daniel Da Cruz, *Mixed Doubles*, 1989
L. Sprague de Camp, *Lest Darkness Fall*, 1941
Mark Twain, *A Connecticut Yankee in King Arthur's Court*, 1899

## 2045
### LEO FRANKOWSKI
### *The High-Tech Knight*
(New York: Ballantine/Del Rey, 1989)

**Story type:** Science Fiction (Time Travel)
**Series:** Adventures of Conrad Stargard
**Major character(s):** Conrad Stargard, Engineer, Time Traveler
**Time period(s):** 13th century
**Locale(s):** Poland; Alternate Earth

**Summary:** In volume 1 of this series, *The Cross-Time Engineer*, Stargard accidentally time traveled to medieval Poland just before it was to be invaded by the Mongols. Establishing himself as a knight, he now uses his engineering skill to start a premature Industrial Revolution.

**Other books you might like:**
Gregory Benford, *Alternate Empires*, 1989
    Martin H. Greenberg, co-editor
Daniel Da Cruz, *Mixed Doubles*, 1989
L. Sprague de Camp, *Lest Darkness Fall*, 1941
Mark Twain, *A Connecticut Yankee in King Arthur's Court*, 1899

## **2046**
### LEO FRANKOWSKI

## *Lord Conrad's Lady*
(New York: Ballantine/Del Rey, 1990)

**Story type:** Science Fiction (Time Travel; Alternate Universe)
**Series:** Adventures of Conrad Stargard
**Major character(s):** Conrad Stargard, Time Traveler, Engineer; Francine, Noblewoman (lady), Spouse
**Time period(s):** 13th century
**Locale(s):** Poland; Alternate Earth

**Summary:** After defeating a third Mongol army, Conrad Stargard is elected King of Poland due to his wife Francine's machinations. As her husband totally ignores her, Lady Francine turns to plotting to make her son the greatest king in Christendom by cleverly allying Poland with Ruthemia, Bulgaria and other neighboring kingdoms. Yet Conrad still takes no notice of her.

**Other books you might like:**
L. Sprague de Camp, *Lest Darkness Fall*, 1941
Harry Harrison, *A Rebel in Time*, 1983
H. Beam Piper, *Lord Kalvan of Otherwhen*, 1965
Kevin D. Randle, *Remember the Alamo!*, 1986
    Robert Cornett, co-author

## **2047**
### LEO FRANKOWSKI

## *The Radiant Warrior*
(New York: Ballantine/Del Rey, 1989)

**Story type:** Science Fiction (Time Travel)
**Series:** Adventures of Conrad Stargard
**Major character(s):** Conrad Stargard, Engineer, Time Traveler
**Time period(s):** 13th century
**Locale(s):** Poland; Alternate Earth

**Summary:** Having achieved knighthood in early-medieval Poland and established an industrial base far in advance of anything the world has seen heretofore, time traveler Conrad Stargard now prepares his Polish troops to meet the Mongol invaders.

**Other books you might like:**
Gregory Benford, *Alternate Empires*, 1989
    Martin H. Greenberg, co-editor
Daniel Da Cruz, *Mixed Doubles*, 1989
L. Sprague de Camp, *Lest Darkness Fall*, 1941
Mark Twain, *A Connecticut Yankee in King Arthur's Court*, 1899

## **2048**
### VALERIE J. FREIREICH

## *The Beacon*
(New York: Roc, 1996)

**Story type:** Science Fiction (First Contact; Invasion of Earth)
**Major character(s):** Beatrice Whit, Traveler; Stefan Acari, Judge; John Denning, Political Figure
**Time period(s):** Indeterminate Future
**Locale(s):** Earth

**Summary:** Four Travellers, descendants of humans abducted from Earth centuries ago by aliens, visit Earth and must decide whether to call the beacon which will bring their starship into Earth orbit. When someone kidnaps one of the four, Stefan re-establishes his mental link with the Assembly in order to take charge of the investigation. Even after he rescues Beatrice from her kidnappers, Stefan must still decide whether he prefers the risks of alien contact or the risks of tyranny by the assembly.

**Other books you might like:**
Juanita Coulson, *Tomorrow's Heritage*, 1981
Michael Crichton, *The Andromeda Strain*, 1969
Jane S. Fancher, *Harmonies of the 'Net*, 1992
Vonda N. McIntyre, *Transition*, 1991
Rebecca Ore, *Becoming Alien*, 1988
Clifford D. Simak, *They Walked Like Men*, 1962
Steven Spielberg, *Close Encounters of the Third Kind*, 1977
H.G. Wells, *The War of the Worlds*, 1898
Jack Williamson, *Mazeway*, 1990

## **2049**
### VALERIE J. FREIREICH

## *Becoming Human*
(New York: Roc, 1995)

**Story type:** Science Fiction (Genetic Manipulation; Political)
**Major character(s):** Sanda Brauna, Political Figure (elector); August, Genetically Altered Being; Jeroen Lee, Political Figure (elector)
**Time period(s):** Indeterminate Future
**Locale(s):** Andia, Planet—Imaginary; Neuland, Planet—Imaginary; Harmony of Worlds, Interstellar Empire/Federation

**Summary:** Neuland needs help from the Harmony of Worlds, but the genetic alteration which eliminates the sensation of pain makes Harmony unwilling to admit the people as full citizens, as human. Also not considered human because of genetic design for his position as political analyst to Elector Brauna, August finds himself flung into the same political crisis which brought about the death of his clone-father and now gives him the reputation of a traitor.

**Other books you might like:**
C.J. Cherryh, *Forty Thousand in Gehenna*, 1983
Gordon R. Dickson, *Dorsai!*, 1976
Rebecca Ore, *The Illegal Rebirth of Billy the Kid*, 1991
Joan Slonczewski, *Daughter of Elysium*, 1993
Cordwainer Smith, *Norstrilia*, 1995
John Varley, *The Ophiuchi Hotline*, 1977

## 2050

### VALERIE J. FREIREICH

## *Imposter*

(New York: Roc, 1997)

**Story type:** Science Fiction (Genetic Manipulation; Political)
**Series:** Polite Harmony of Worlds
**Major character(s):** Marcer Joseph Brice, Scholar, Genetically Altered Being; Idryis Khan a'Husain, Political Figure; Linnet Wali, Prostitute, Genetically Altered Being
**Time period(s):** Indeterminate Future
**Locale(s):** Polite Harmony of Worlds, Interstellar Empire/Federation; Bralava, Planet—Imaginary

**Summary:** Deported from the Harmony, Marcer struggles to survive on Bralava and to escape the attentions of Idryis, who has a political as well as a personal interest in using Marcer. Idryis forces Marcer to investigate the biology of the Houris, mysterious females from the plant Paradise, and plans to use the information to incite genocide and to make himself ruler of the Emirates. Set in the same universe as *Testament* and *Becoming Human*.

**Other books you might like:**
Marion Zimmer Bradley, *The Shattered Chain*, 1976
C.J. Cherryh, *Cyteen*, 1988
Philip Jose Farmer, *The Lovers*, 1961
Elizabeth Ann Scarborough, *The Harem of Aman Akbar*, 1984
John Varley, *The Ophiuchi Hotline*, 1977
Joan D. Vinge, *World's End*, 1984

## 2051

### VALERIE J. FREIREICH

## *Testament*

(New York: Roc, 1995)

**Story type:** Science Fiction (Political; Genetic Manipulation)
**Series:** Polite Harmony of Worlds
**Major character(s):** Gray Bridger, Guide; Mead Bridger, Genetically Altered Being; Martin Penn, Tourist, Doctor
**Time period(s):** 30th century
**Locale(s):** Testament, Planet—Imaginary; Polite Harmony of Worlds, Interstellar Empire/Federation

**Summary:** Gray Bridger is a freak on Testament where descendants of genetically altered settlers inherit conscious memories of their female ancestors. He longs to escape to the Polite Harmony of Worlds, which quarantines altered humans. Just before he receives permission to enter the Harmony, the schemes of his grandmother and the Testament matriarchy threaten his plan. As Gray struggles to outwit these schemes, he begins to realize how they will change Testament and the Harmony.

**Other books you might like:**
Eleanor Arnason, *Ring of Swords*, 1993
Isaac Asimov, *Foundation and Empire*, 1952
C.J. Cherryh, *Cyteen*, 1988
Jane S. Fancher, *Ground-Ties*, 1991
Nicola Griffith, *Ammonite*, 1993
Joan Slonczewski, *A Door into Ocean*, 1986
Tricia Sullivan, *Lethe*, 1995
Amy Thomson, *Virtual Girl*, 1993

## 2052

### ROBERT FREZZA

## *Fire in a Faraway Place*

(New York: Ballantine Del Rey, 1994)

**Story type:** Science Fiction (Military)
**Major character(s):** Anton Vereshchagin, Military Personnel; Hanna Bruwer-Sanmartin, Political Figure; Daisuke Matsudaira, Businessman
**Time period(s):** Indeterminate Future
**Locale(s):** Suid-Afrika, Planet—Imaginary; Tokyo, Japan

**Summary:** Concerned with profit rather than peace, the Japanese Empire's outlook threatens the gains accomplished when Lieutenant-Colonel Anton Vereshchagin enlists the help and pride of Suid-Afrika's native peoples. Since every choice leads to war, the occupying troops of the First Battalion of the 35th Imperial Infantry must choose to support the Empire, which stranded them on Suid-Afrika, or to support the democratic government of the planet they now call home. Sequel to *A Small Colonial War* .

**Other books you might like:**
Eleanor Arnason, *Ring of Swords*, 1993
Lois McMaster Bujold, *Shards of Honor*, 1986
David Drake, *Hammer's Slammers*, 1979
   expanded edition, 1987
Joel Rosenberg, *Hero*, 1990
Sheri S. Tepper, *The Gate to Women's Country*, 1988

## 2053

### ROBERT FREZZA

## *McLendon's Syndrome*

(New York: Del Ray, 1993)

**Story type:** Science Fiction (Military; Medical)
**Major character(s):** Kenneth "Ken" Mac Kay, Military Personnel (Vampire); Anna Catarina Lindquist, Military Personnel, Vampire; Bucky Beaver, Alien (!Plixxi*), Diplomat (ambassador)
**Time period(s):** Indeterminate Future
**Locale(s):** Schuyler's World, Planet—Imaginary; *Rustam's Slipper*, Spaceship ("*Rusty Scupper*")

**Summary:** After one of the *Rusty Scupper*'s crew's jail term prevents the ship from leaving, Ken suggests Catarina as a replacement despite recognizing her as a vampire. Discovering that the ship transports contraband and that Catarina and a stowaway actually belong to the navy, the *Rusty Scupper* becomes embroiled in interplanetary political and military machinations.

**Other books you might like:**
Debra Doyle, *The Price of the Stars*, 1992
   James D. Macdonald, co-author
David Drake, *Starliner*, 1992
Alan Dean Foster, *Quozl*, 1989
Laurell K. Hamilton, *Guilty Pleasures*, 1993
Alis A. Rasmussen, *Revolution's Shore*, 1990
Denise Vitola, *Half-Light*, 1992

## 2054

### ROBERT FREZZA

## *A Small Colonial War*

(New York: Ballantine/Del Rey, 1989)

**Story type:** Science Fiction (Military)

**Major character(s):** Raul Sanmartin, Military Personnel (Captain); Anton Vereshchagin, Military Personnel (Lt. Colonel)
**Time period(s):** 22nd century
**Locale(s):** Suid Afrika, Planet—Imaginary

**Summary:** When a revolt occurs on the factory world called Suid Afrika, a small, undermanned military force is sent to deal with it. After a series of boondoggles, the competence of one small battalion saves the day. Frezza's first novel.

**Other books you might like:**
Gordon R. Dickson, *The Final Encyclopedia*, 1984
Gordon R. Dickson, *Lost Dorsai*, 1989
Gordon R. Dickson, *Soldier, Ask Not*, 1967
Gordon R. Dickson, *The Tactics of Mistake*, 1971
David Drake, *Counting the Cost*, 1987
David Drake, *Hammer's Slammers*, 1979
Jerry Pournelle, *The Mercenary*, 1977
Jerry Pournelle, *Prince of Mercenaries*, 1989

---

| 2055 |

**ROBERT FREZZA**

## The VMR Theory

(New York: Ballantine Del Rey, 1996)

**Story type:** Science Fiction (Humor; Adventure)
**Major character(s):** Kenneth "Ken" McKay, Vampire, Military Personnel (Navy Intelligence Reserves); Anna Catarina Lindquist, Spacewoman, Vampire
**Time period(s):** Indeterminate Future
**Locale(s):** Alt Bauernhof, Planet—Imaginary; *Rustam's Slipper*, Spaceship ("*Rusty Scupper*"); Confederation, Interstellar Empire/Federation

**Summary:** Nominally assigned to transport goods to Alt Bauernhof, Ken and Catarina must find and retrieve a Confederation agent from the planet. Anticipating conquest of the Confederation, Alt Bauernhof natives, the Macdonalds, look forward to Ken and Catarina's visit as an opportunity to study actual vampires, controllers of humanity's destiny according to the popular Macdonald conjecture, the Vampire Master Race Theory.

**Other books you might like:**
Douglas Adams, *The Hitchhiker's Guide to the Galaxy*, 1980
Douglas Adams, *The Restaurant at the End of the Universe*, 1982
Laurell K. Hamilton, *Guilty Pleasures*, 1993
Spider Robinson, *Callahan's Crosstime Saloon*, 1977
Spider Robinson, *Callahan's Legacy*, 1996
James H. Schmitz, *The Demon Breed*, 1968
Harry Turtledove, *Earthgrip*, 1991

---

| 2056 |

**C.S. FRIEDMAN**

## Black Sun Rising

(New York: DAW, 1991)

**Story type:** Fantasy (Horror; Science Fiction)
**Series:** Coldfire Trilogy
**Major character(s):** Damien Kilcannon Vryce, Religious (priest), Warrior; Gerald Tarrant, Nobleman (neocount); Hesseth, Alien (Rakh)
**Time period(s):** Indeterminate Future
**Locale(s):** Erna, Planet—Imaginary

**Summary:** After more than a millennium, humans have adapted to Erna, a planet so near the edge of the galaxy that night without stars, moon or galactic core to give light is not uncommon. Before humans arrived, Erna had no intelligent species. However, it had a characteristic humans called "the fae" which is very sensitive to human thought, including subconscious fears. Now Erna has not only all the human monsters which humans have imagined and become, but a hostile, intelligent native species is evolving as well.

**Other books you might like:**
Octavia E. Butler, *Dawn*, 1987
Mary Gentle, *Rats and Gargoyles*, 1990
Harry Harrison, *The Deathworld Trilogy*, 1976
Christopher Pike, *Sati*, 1990
Dan Simmons, *Hyperion*, 1989
Bill Slavicsek, *Storm Knights*, 1990
    C.J. Tramontana, co-author
Sheri S. Tepper, *Grass*, 1989

---

| 2057 |

**C.S. FRIEDMAN**

## Crown of Shadows

(New York: DAW, 1995)

**Story type:** Science Fiction (Psychic Powers; Theological)
**Series:** Coldfire Trilogy
**Major character(s):** Damien Kilcannon Vryce, Religious (priest), Warrior; Iezu, Demon; Gerald Tarrant, Vampire, Religious (prophet)
**Time period(s):** Indeterminate Future
**Locale(s):** Erna, Planet—Imaginary

**Summary:** No longer an innocent priest, Damien Vryce continues the battle between faith and sorcery, while the Iezu, Calesta's children, evolve from feeding only on pain to appreciate other human emotions. The Church must somehow learn to control the native sources of magical power so humans can regain a peaceful, secure life on Erna.

**Other books you might like:**
Tom Deitz, *Soulsmith*, 1991
Mary Gentle, *Golden Witchbreed*, 1984
Dan Simmons, *Hyperion*, 1989
Sheri S. Tepper, *Shadow's End*, 1994
Gene Wolfe, *Nightside the Long Sun*, 1993

---

| 2058 |

**C.S. FRIEDMAN**

## The Madness Season

(New York: DAW, 1990)

**Story type:** Science Fiction (Adventure; Immortality)
**Major character(s):** The Marra, Alien; Daetrin Ungashak To-Alym Haal, Vampire, Werewolf; Raayat, Alien (Tyr, a hive mind)
**Time period(s):** 24th century
**Locale(s):** *Talguth*, Spaceship; Meyaga, Planet—Imaginary (Cantona Settlement); Yuang, Planet—Imaginary (Dome Prime)

**Summary:** The Tyr, alien conquerors, remove Daetrin from Earth where he was potentially a disruptive influence in his position as a teacher. Daetrin, a reluctant vampire, gets involved with other humans and aliens in a revolution against the Tyr.

**Other books you might like:**
Greg Bear, *Blood Music*, 1985
Octavia E. Butler, *Adulthood Rites*, 1988
Octavia E. Butler, *Dawn*, 1987
Octavia E. Butler, *Imago*, 1989

C.J. Cherryh, *Serpent's Reach*, 1980
Janet Kagan, *Hellspark*, 1988
Jack Vance, *The Dragon Masters*, 1963

## 2059

### C.S. FRIEDMAN

## *This Alien Shore*

(New York: DAW, 1998)

**Story type:** Science Fiction (Political)
**Major character(s):** Jamisia "Jamie Capra" Shido, Abuse Victim, Fugitive; Dr. Kio Masada, Computer Expert, Mentally Ill Person (obsessive/compulsive); Ladyship Alya Cairo, Administrator (Prima of the Ainniq Guild)
**Time period(s):** Indeterminate Future
**Locale(s):** Guera, Planet—Imaginary (Guild Headquarters); *Aurora*, Spaceship; *Exeter*, Spaceship

**Summary:** Having escaped the destruction of Shido, Jamie, on Aurora, runs to the entrance into subspace to leave Earthspace. On the trip she discovers she has many separate personalities designed for some unknown purpose, and that she must learn to get along with them. Meanwhile, Dr. Masada studies Lucifer, a brainware virus specifically designed to destroy Guild pilots.

**Other books you might like:**
Jeffrey A. Carver, *Dragons in the Stars*, 1992
Julie E. Czerneda, *A Thousand Words for Stranger*, 1997
L. Warren Douglas, *Stepwater*, 1995
Melissa Scott, *Shadow Man*, 1995
Dan Simmons, *Endymion*, 1996

## 2060

### C.S. FRIEDMAN

## *When True Night Falls*

(New York: DAW, 1993)

**Story type:** Fantasy (Psychic Powers; Religious)
**Series:** Coldfire Trilogy
**Major character(s):** Damien Kilcannon Vryce, Religious (priest), Warrior; Gerald Tarrant, Sorcerer, Nobleman; Hesseth, Alien (Rakh)
**Time period(s):** Indeterminate Future
**Locale(s):** Erna, Planet—Imaginary

**Summary:** Stabilizing the colonists' emotions and thoughts after the chaos resulting from the destruction of their shuttle and loss of communications with the advanced technology orbiting above, Gerald Tarrant founded the Church in which Damien Vryce now serves. Continuing the battle against evil forces attempting to control Erna, Damien, Gerald and Hesseth set out across the ocean to overcome the Prince of Light and avert catastrophe.

**Other books you might like:**
Roger MacBride Allen, *The Ring of Charon*, 1990
Jeffrey A. Carver, *Dragon Rigger*, 1993
Tom Deitz, *Soulsmith*, 1991
Melanie Rawn, *Dragon Prince*, 1988
Dan Simmons, *Hyperion*, 1989
Paula Volsky, *Illusion*, 1992
Martha Wells, *The Element of Fire*, 1993

## 2061

### MICHAEL JAN FRIEDMAN

## *All Good Things. . .*

(New York: Pocket, 1994)

**Story type:** Science Fiction (Space Opera; Time Travel)
**Series:** Star Trek: The Next Generation
**Major character(s):** Jean-Luc Picard, Spaceship Captain (*U.S.S. Enterprise*), Military Personnel; Q, Alien; Beverly Crusher, Spaceship Captain (*U.S.S. Pasteur*), Doctor
**Time period(s):** 24th century
**Locale(s):** *U.S.S. Enterprise*, Spaceship; Outer Space; *U.S.S. Pasteur*, Spaceship

**Summary:** Q continues the test of humanity's mettle begun in *Encounter at Farpoint* by presenting a problem which requires Captain Picard to coherently sense his existence at different times and act to avoid a future disaster directly sensed in the present. Novelizes the teleplay of the concluding episode of the TV series.

**Other books you might like:**
J.M. Dillard, *Emissary*, 1993
J.M. Dillard, *Star Trek: Generations*, 1994
David Gerrold, *Encounter at Farpoint*, 1987
L.A. Graf, *Caretaker*, 1995
Jeri Taylor, *Unification*, 1991

## 2062

### MICHAEL JAN FRIEDMAN

## *A Call to Darkness*

(New York: Pocket Books, 1989)

**Story type:** Science Fiction (Space Opera)
**Series:** Star Trek: The Next Generation
**Major character(s):** Jean-Luc Picard, Spaceship Captain, Military Personnel; William Riker, Military Personnel (First Officer)
**Time period(s):** 24th century (Stardate 42908.6)
**Locale(s):** *U.S.S. Enterprise*, Spaceship

**Summary:** Just after Captain Picard vanishes on what appears to be a routine rescue mission, a deadly plague begins to ravage the crew of the *Enterprise*. First Officer Riker must unravel the mystery of both the plague and his Captain's disappearance, or face the destruction of his starship.

**Other books you might like:**
J.M. Dillard, *Star Trek: The Lost Years*, 1989
J.M. Dillard, *Star Trek V: The Final Frontier*, 1989
Diane Duane, *My Enemy, My Ally*, 1984
    Star Trek 18
Diane Duane, *Spock's World*, 1988
Larry Niven, *The Mote in God's Eye*, 1974
    Jerry Pournelle, co-author

## 2063

### MICHAEL JAN FRIEDMAN

## *Crossover*

(New York: Pocket, 1995)

**Story type:** Science Fiction (Space Opera; Political)
**Series:** Star Trek: The Next Generation
**Major character(s):** Spock, Scientist, Alien (Vulcan); Montgomery Scott, Engineer, Military Personnel; Jean-Luc Picard, Spaceship Captain, Military Personnel

**Time period(s):** 24th century
**Locale(s):** *U.S.S. Enterprise*, Spaceship; Constanthus, Planet—Imaginary; United Federation of Planets, Interstellar Empire/Federation

**Summary:** Former ambassador Spock now endeavors to teach the philosphy of Surak to the underground movement of Romulans eager to re-unite the Romulan and Vulcan peoples. Betrayed by a spy in their midst, Spock and some of his followers face a show trial and execution. When Starfleet sends the *Enterprise* to the border to pursue diplomatic measures with Dr. McCoy as an advisor, Scotty, unwilling to wait, steals an antique starship and sets out to rescue Spock himself.

**Other books you might like:**
Margaret Wander Bonanno, *Dwellers in the Crucible*, 1985
J.M. Dillard, *Star Trek: Generations*, 1994
Diane Duane, *My Enemy, My Ally*, 1984
Diane Duane, *The Romulan Way*, 1987
    Peter Morwood, co-author
Jeri Taylor, *Unification*, 1991

---

**2064**

MICHAEL JAN FRIEDMAN

### *Her Klingon Soul*

(New York: Pocket, 1997)

**Story type:** Science Fiction (Space Opera)
**Series:** Star Trek: Day of Honor
**Major character(s):** B'Elanna Torres, Engineer, Alien (half-Klingon); Harry Kim, Military Personnel (ensign); Kathryn Janeway, Spaceship Captain, Military Personnel, Space Explorer
**Time period(s):** 24th century
**Locale(s):** *U.S.S. Voyager*, Spaceship; Planet—Imaginary

**Summary:** Besides reminding B'Elanna of her troublesome Klingon heritage, the Klingon Day of Honor always brings her bad luck. This time, while searching for food supplies, she and Harry fall into a Kazon trap. While the *Voyager's* crew searches for their missing shipmates, Harry and B'Elanna nearly escape from their imprisonment, only to find the Kazon fighting for their lives against an attacking Nograkh ship. The Nograkh take them as slaves to work the asteriod mines, where B'Elanna uses her Klingon skills and instincts to lead a slave revolt.

**Other books you might like:**
Margaret Wander Bonanno, *Dwellers in the Crucible*, 1985
Carmen Carter, *The Children of Hamlin*, 1988
C.J. Cherryh, *Rimrunners*, 1989
Diane Duane, *My Enemy, My Ally*, 1984
L.A. Graf, *Firestorm*, 1993
    pseudonym of Julia Ecklar and Karen Rose
Frederik Pohl, *The Reefs of Space*, 1964
    Jack Williamson, co-author

---

**2065**

MICHAEL JAN FRIEDMAN

### *Kahless*

(New York: Pocket, 1996)

**Story type:** Science Fiction (Genetic Manipulation; Adventure)
**Series:** Star Trek: The Next Generation
**Major character(s):** Kahless, Warrior, Hero; Jean-Luc Picard, Spaceship Captain, Military Personnel; Worf, Military Personnel (lieutenant), Alien (Klingon)

**Time period(s):** 24th century; Indeterminate Past
**Locale(s):** Qo'noS, Planet—Imaginary; *U.S.S. Enterprise*, Spaceship; Klingon Empire, Interstellar Empire/Federation

**Summary:** An archaeological find casts doubt on the exploits of the legendary Kahless, whose clone now occupies the throne as the titular head of the Klingon Empire. Kahless discovers a plot against the Empire and, fearing that he can trust no one in the Empire, turns to Picard and Worf for help. The story of the original Kahless and the circumstances that compelled him to defy the tyrant Molor parallels the struggle of the 24th century Kahless to foil the traitorous plot and restore his people's faith.

**Other books you might like:**
Margaret Wander Bonanno, *Strangers From the Sky*, 1987
Carmen Carter, *The Devil's Heart*, 1993
C.J. Cherryh, *Cyteen*, 1988
Judith Reeves-Stevens, *Federation*, 1994
    Garfield Reeves-Stevens, co-author
William Shatner, *The Return*, 1996
    Judith Reeves-Stevens, Garfield Reeves-Stevens, co-authors
Roger Zelazny, *Lord of Light*, 1967

---

**2066**

MICHAEL JAN FRIEDMAN

### *Relics*

(New York: Pocket, 1992)

**Story type:** Science Fiction (Space Opera)
**Series:** Star Trek: The Next Generation
**Major character(s):** Jean-Luc Picard, Spaceship Captain (*U.S.S. Enterprise*), Military Personnel; Montgomery Scott, Engineer (*U.S.S. Enterprise*), Military Personnel (retired); Geordi La Forge, Engineer (*U.S.S. Enterprise*), Military Personnel
**Time period(s):** 23rd century; 24th century
**Locale(s):** *S.S. Jenolen*, Spaceship; *U.S.S. Enterprise*, Spaceship

**Summary:** When the *Enterprise* responds to a 75-year-old distress call, an away team discovers the wreckage of the *Jenolen* and a jury-rigged transporter mechanism which preserved retired Montgomery Scott after *Jenolen's* crash. Retrieved from stasis, Scott provides the vital solution when disaster strikes the *Enterprise* crew. Novelizes a television episode.

**Other books you might like:**
Carmen Carter, *Doomsday World*, 1990
    Peter David, Michael Jan Friedman and Robert Greenberger, co-authors
A.C. Crispin, *The Eyes of the Beholders*, 1990
Peter David, *A Rock and a Hard Place*, 1990
David Gerrold, *Encounter at Farpoint*, 1987
Jean Lorrah, *Metamorphosis*, 1990
Jeri Taylor, *Unification*, 1991
Howard Weinstein, *Exiles*, 1990

---

**2067**

MICHAEL JAN FRIEDMAN
KEVIN RYAN, Co-Author

### *Requiem*

(New York: Pocket, 1994)

**Story type:** Science Fiction (Space Opera; Time Travel)
**Series:** Star Trek: The Next Generation

**Major character(s):** Jean-Luc Picard, Spaceship Captain, Military Personnel; Reginald Barclay, Engineer, Space Explorer; Geordi La Forge, Engineer, Military Personnel
**Time period(s):** 24th century; 23rd century
**Locale(s):** *U.S.S. Enterprise*, Spaceship; Cestus III, Planet—Imaginary; United Federation of Planets, Interstellar Empire/Federation

**Summary:** Twenty-five years ago, Captain Picard of the *U.S. Stargazer* negotiated with the Gorn. Now, en route to a second meeting, the *Enterprise* encounters an abandoned space station of unknown origin that sends Picard across space and time to Cestus III a hundred years in the past, just days before the Gorn massacred its human settlers. As his crew searches for him, Picard tries to survive and leave a clue for future rescuers and return to aid the colonists.

**Other books you might like:**
Poul Anderson, *Time Patrolman*, 1983
Arthur C. Clarke, *Rendezvous with Rama*, 1973
Gene DeWeese, *The Peacekeepers*, 1988
Cynthia Felice, *Downtime*, 1985
Barbara Hambly, *Ishmael*, 1985

---

**2068**

**MICHAEL JAN FRIEDMAN**

### Reunion

(New York: Pocket, 1991)

**Story type:** Science Fiction (Space Opera)
**Series:** Star Trek: The Next Generation
**Major character(s):** Jean-Luc Picard, Spaceship Captain, Military Personnel; Worf, Military Personnel (Starfleet officer), Alien (Klingon); Morgen, Royalty (Crown Prince of Daa'V), Spaceship Captain (former)
**Time period(s):** 24th century
**Locale(s):** *U.S.S. Enterprise*, Spaceship

**Summary:** Captain Jean-Luc Picard has been assigned the diplomatic mission of transporting his former subordinate, Captain Morgen, to the planet, Daa'V, where he is to assume power. Many of Picard's officers from the *U.S.S. Stargazer*, former shipmates of Morgen's, have accompanied Morgen. When an attempt is made on Morgen's life, Picard must discover who wants to murder the Crown Prince, opening Daa'V to a new alliance, one less beneficial to the Federation.

**Other books you might like:**
Diane Carey, *Ghost Ship*, 1988
A.C. Crispin, *The Eyes of the Beholders*, 1990
Peter David, *A Rock and a Hard Place*, 1990
Gene DeWeese, *The Peacekeepers*, 1988
David Dvorkin, *The Captain's Honor*, 1989
    Daniel Dvorkin, co-author
Jean Lorrah, *Survivors*, 1989
John Vornholt, *Masks*, 1989
Howard Weinstein, *Power Hungry*, 1989

---

**2069**

**MICHAEL JAN FRIEDMAN**

### Shadows on the Sun

(New York: Pocket, 1993)

**Story type:** Science Fiction (Space Opera; Medical)
**Series:** Star Trek

**Major character(s):** Leonard McCoy, Doctor; Shil Andrachis, Alien (Ssana), Leader (High Assassin); Jocelyn Treadway, Diplomat, Divorced Person (McCoy's ex-wife)
**Time period(s):** 23rd century
**Locale(s):** *U.S.S. Enterprise*, Spaceship; Ssan, Planet—Imaginary

**Summary:** The young doctor McCoy, outraged by his wife's infidelity, deserts his family and joins Starfleet. Forty years later, McCoy must cooperate with the diplomats assigned to the *Enterprise*, his ex-wife and her new husband. The Assassins on war-torn Ssan, a cult who believe ritual assassination the most honorable kind of death, attack the landing team sent to negotiate peace. With Kirk and Jocelyn imprisoned by the High Assassin, a patient whose life McCoy saved as a young intern, McCoy's knowledge of the Ssani may help save them, if he can overcome his conflicting emotions.

**Other books you might like:**
Steven Brust, *Jhereg*, 1983
J.M. Dillard, *The Lost Years*, 1989
Diane Duane, *The Romulan Way*, 1987
    Peter Morwood, co-author
Julia Ecklar, *The Kobayashi Maru*, 1989
Cynthia Felice, *Downtime*, 1985
Cynthia Felice, *The Khan's Persuasion*, 1991
Mary Gentle, *Golden Witchbreed*, 1984

---

**2070**

**ESTHER FRIESNER**, Editor
**MARTIN H. GREENBERG**, Co-Editor

### Alien Pregnant by Elvis

(New York: DAW, 1994)

**Story type:** Fantasy (Anthology; Light Fantasy)

**Summary:** Contains a three-page introduction by Friesner and 36 original stories reflecting lurid tabloid themes such as Bigfoot, J.F.K., Marilyn Monroe, UFOs, zombies, the Loch Ness monster, psychic animals and the search for the perfect orgasm. Authors include John Gregory Betancourt, David Brin, John DeChancie, David Drake, George Alec Effinger, Gregory Feeley, Esther Friesner, Alan Dean Foster, Jody Lynn Nye, Laura Resnick, Kristine Kathryn Rusch, Eluki ''Bob'' bes Shahar, Josepha Sherman, Dean Wesley Smith, Allen Steele, Harry Turtledove and Lawrence Watt-Evans.

**Other books you might like:**
Robert Rankin, *Armageddon: The Musical*, 1991
Mike Resnick, *By Any Other Fame*, 1994
    Martin H. Greenberg, co-editor
Kim Stanley Robinson, *Escape From Kathmandu*, 1989
Paul M. Sammon, *The King Is Dead: Tales of Elvis Post Mortem*, 1994
    editor
Kay Sloan, *Elvis Rising: Stories on the King*, 1993
    Constance Pierce, co-editor

---

**2071**

**ESTHER FRIESNER**, Editor
**MARTIN H. GREENBERG**, Co-Editor

### Blood Muse: Timeless Tales of Vampires in the Arts

(New York: Donald I. Fine, 1995)

**Story type:** Horror (Anthology; Vampire Story)

**Summary:** The 32 original stories collected here all grow out of the idea of the vampiric relationship between the artist, art, and life. Selections are divided into seven categories (The Gallery, The Conservatory, The Screening Room, The Sculpture Garden, The Dance Studio, The Scriptorium, Special Exhibits). Hightlights include Susan Williams' ''Blind Faith,'' about a vampire stained-glass maker who can never enter the cathedrals for which he does his work; Meg Turville-Heitz's ''Sing Heavenly Muse,'' about the influence of a vampire on John Milton's writing of *Paradise Lost*; Ben Adams' ''The Frieze of Life,'' about Rodin's parasitic dependence on his models; and Adam-Troy Castro's ''The Hand Inside,'' a unique look at the relationship between a ventriloquist and his dummy.

**Other books you might like:**
Ellen Datlow, *Blood Is Not Enough*, 1989
Ellen Datlow, *A Whisper of Blood*, 1992
Martin H. Greenberg, *Celebrity Vampires*, 1995
  editor
Alan Ryan, *Vampires: Two Centuries of Great Vampire Stories*, 1987
Robert Weinberg, *100 Vicious Little Vampire Stories*, 1995
  Stefan Dziemianowicz, Martin H. Greenberg, co-editors

## 2072
### ESTHER FRIESNER, Editor

## Chicks in Chainmail
(New York: Baen, 1995)

**Story type:** Fantasy (Anthology; Light Fantasy)

**Summary:** Contains a four-page introduction plus 20 original stories which assault the pulp fiction stereotype of the woman warrior, such as a new Maureen Birnbaum, Barbarian Swordsperson tale from George Alec Effinger and a discussion of the results of a royal tax on bronze bras by Elizabeth Moon. Other authors include Margaret Ball, eluki bes shahar, Esther Friesner, Holly Lisle, Jody Lynn Nye, Elizabeth Ann Scarborough, Josepha Sherman, Susan Shwartz, Nancy Springer, Harry Turtledove, Lawrence Watt-Evans, and Roger Zelazny.

**Other books you might like:**
Marion Zimmer Bradley, *The Sword and Sorceress Series*, 1984-1995
  editor
George Alec Effinger, *Maureen Birnbaum, Barbarian Swordsperson: The Complete Stories*, 1993
C.L. Moore, *Jirel of Joiry*, 1969
Jessica Amanda Salmonson, *Amazons!*, 1979
  editor

## 2073
### ESTHER FRIESNER

## Child of the Eagle
(New York: Baen, 1996)

**Story type:** Fantasy (Historical; Legend)
**Major character(s):** Marcus Junius Brutus, Political Figure, Military Personnel (Roman general); Gaius Julius Caesar, Ruler (dictator), Military Personnel (Roman general); Venus, Deity
**Time period(s):** 1st century B.C.
**Locale(s):** Rome, Roman Empire; Alexandria, Egypt

**Summary:** On the eve of the plot against Caesar's life, the goddess Venus convinces Brutus to save the dictator rather than kill him. In return, she extends Brutus's life so he can see the eventual results of his decision and convince himself that his actions have helped his beloved Rome.

**Other books you might like:**
Anthony Burgess, *The Eve of Saint Venus*, 1964
Irving A. Greenfield, *Julius Caesar Is Alive and Well*, 1977
Talbot Mundy, *Queen Cleopatra*, 1929
Talbot Mundy, *Tros of Samothrace*, 1934
Lawrence Watt-Evans, *Split Heirs*, 1993
  Esther Friesner, co-author

## 2074
### ESTHER FRIESNER, Editor

## Did You Say Chicks?!
(New York: Baen, 1998)

**Story type:** Fantasy (Anthology; Light Fantasy)

**Summary:** This anthology contains a three-page introduction, seven pages of authors' biographies, and 19 original stories featuring women warriors in a variety of situations. Authors include Margaret Ball, Doranna Durgin, Esther M. Friesner, Barbara Hambly, Elizabeth Moon, Jody Lynn Nye, Elizabeth Ann Scarborough, Harry Turtledove, Lawrence Watt-Evans, K.D. Wentworth and Sarah Zettel.

**Other books you might like:**
Margaret Ball, *Mathemagics*, 1996
Marion Zimmer Bradley, *The Sword and Sorceress Series*, 1984-1998
  editor
George Alec Effinger, *Maureen Birnbaum, Barbarian Swordsperson: The Complete Stories*, 1993
C.L. Moore, *Jirel of Joiry*, 1969
Jessica Amanda Salmonson, *Amazons!*, 1979
  editor

## 2075
### ESTHER FRIESNER

## Gnome Man's Land
(New York: Ace, 1991)

**Story type:** Fantasy (Contemporary; Light Fantasy)
**Series:** Timothy Desmond
**Major character(s):** Timothy Alfred Desmond, Teenager; T'ing Hau Kaplan, Teenager; Telery of Limerick, Mythical Creature (banshee)
**Time period(s):** 1990s (1991)
**Locale(s):** New York, New York

**Summary:** There is a hole between the leeside (where the faeries went) and our world. Tim's life is drastically altered when his family banshee appears and starts bemoaning his imminent demise. He and T'ing must come to terms with mythical beings and magic battles. The hole is left open, leaving room for the forthcoming title, *Harpy High*.

**Other books you might like:**
Douglas Adams, *The Hitchhiker's Guide to the Galaxy*, 1980
Robert Asprin, *Another Fine Myth*, 1978
John Bellairs, *The Face in the Frost*, 1969
Diana Wynne Jones, *Howl's Moving Castle*, 1986
Diana Wynne Jones, *The Ogre Downstairs*, 1990
Terry Pratchett, *The Colour of Magic*, 1983

**2076**

**ESTHER FRIESNER**

## Harpy High

(New York: Ace, 1991)

**Story type:** Fantasy (Light Fantasy; Young Adult)
**Series:** Timothy Desmond
**Major character(s):** Timothy Alfred Desmond, Student—High School, Wizard; Baba Yaga, Witch; Telery of Limerick, Mythical Creature (banshee)
**Time period(s):** 1990s
**Locale(s):** New York, New York

**Summary:** After "things" slip out of the Feidelstein Deli's Back Room and Baba Yaga puts Tim's mother to sleep for a thousand years, Tim, as Grand and Puissant Champion of the Fey, must somehow restore the balance of the Mythological Continuum and bring his mother back to life.

**Other books you might like:**
Robert Asprin, *Another Fine Myth*, 1978
Emma Bull, *War for the Oaks*, 1987
Dave Duncan, *Magic Casement*, 1990
Thorarinn Gunnarsson, *Make Way for Dragons!*, 1990
Diana Wynne Jones, *The Ogre Downstairs*, 1990
T.A. Waters, *The Probability Pad*, 1970

**2077**

**ESTHER FRIESNER**

## Hooray for Hellywood

(New York: Ace, 1990)

**Story type:** Fantasy (Light Fantasy; Satire)
**Major character(s):** Melisan Cardiff, Demon, Human; Noel Cardiff, Warlock; Raleel, Demon
**Time period(s):** 21st century
**Locale(s):** Hollywood, California

**Summary:** The demon Raleel is currently posing as Joseph Lee, a televangelist whose plan to make a "sin-free" movie is just his most recent twist to curry sinful feelings in his followers. Noel Cardiff, his ardent, naive assistant, is conscience-stricken over the magical powers he inherited from his demon mother Melisan, and seems determined to turn away from his mother and her cohorts who helped defeat Raleel previously.

**Other books you might like:**
Emma Bull, *War for the Oaks*, 1987
Robert N. Charrette, *Never Deal with a Dragon*, 1991
Alan Dean Foster, *Smart Dragons, Foolish Elves*, 1991
    Martin Harry Greenberg, co-editor
Thorarinn Gunnarsson, *Make Way for Dragons!*, 1990
Tim Powers, *The Anubis Gates*, 1983

**2078**

**ESTHER FRIESNER**

## It's Been Fun

(Eugene, Oregon: Pulphouse Publishing, 1991)

**Story type:** Fantasy (Collection)
**Series:** Author's Choice Monthly
**Summary:** This volume contains a 4-page introduction plus 6 stories. Four of them appeared in 1980s *Amazing* magazines and one,

"Love's Eldritch Ichor," was published in the 1990 World Fantasy Convention program book. One story, "Pride and Prescience," appears for the first time.

**Other books you might like:**
Alan Brennert, *Ma Qui and Other Phantoms*, 1991
Charles de Lint, *Ghosts of Wind and Shadow*, 1991
Nina Kiriki Hoffman, *Legacy of Fire*, 1990
Damon Knight, *God's Nose*, 1991
Joe R. Lansdale, *Stories by Mama Lansdale's Youngest Boy*, 1991
Kate Wilhelm, *State of Grace*, 1991

**2079**

**ESTHER FRIESNER**

## Majyk by Accident

(New York: Ace, 1993)

**Story type:** Fantasy (Light Fantasy; Adventure)
**Series:** Majyk
**Major character(s):** Kendar "Ratwacker" Gangle, Wizard, Student; Scandal, Animal (cat); Zoltan Fiendlord, Wizard
**Time period(s):** Indeterminate
**Locale(s):** Orbix, Planet—Imaginary

**Summary:** Prepared to withdraw from wizard's school with a D-, Kendar unexpectedly taps into all the abilities of his dying master but does not possess the wherewithal to wield them with maturity. A jealous wizard, a mythical Earth cat and an overdose of available majyk brings magical mayhem to the death of Orbix's most powerful wizard. First of a series.

**Other books you might like:**
C. Dale Brittain, *A Bad Spell in Yurt*, 1991
Lois McMaster Bujold, *The Spirit Ring*, 1992
Douglas W. Clark, *Whirlwind Alchemy*, 1993
John Moore, *Slay and Rescue*, 1993
S.P. Somtow, *The Wizard's Apprentice*, 1993
Christopher Stasheff, *The Warlock in Spite of Himself*, 1969
Lawrence Watt-Evans, *Split Heirs*, 1993
    Esther M. Friesner, co-author

**2080**

**ESTHER FRIESNER**

## Majyk by Design

(New York: Ace, 1994)

**Story type:** Fantasy (Quest; Light Fantasy)
**Series:** Majyk
**Major character(s):** Kendar "Ratwacker" Gangle, Wizard; Curio, Model (book cover supermodel); Zoltan Fiendlord, Wizard
**Time period(s):** Indeterminate
**Locale(s):** Orbix, Planet—Imaginary

**Summary:** When a supermodel for book covers disappears, Curio requires Kendar Gangle's aid to prove his innocence. Kendar's investigation leads to an old rival, Zoltan Fiendlord.

**Other books you might like:**
C. Dale Brittain, *The Wood Nymph and the Cranky Saint*, 1993
Kyle Crocco, *Heroes, Inc.*, 1991
L. Sprague de Camp, *The Complete Compleat Enchanter*, 1989
    Fletcher Pratt, co-author
John Moore, *Slay and Rescue*, 1993
Harry Turtledove, *The Case of the Toxic Spell Dump*, 1993

## 2081

**ESTHER FRIESNER**

## *Majyk by Hook or Crook*

(New York: Ace, 1994)

**Story type:** Fantasy (Light Fantasy; Adventure)
**Series:** Majyk
**Major character(s):** Kendar "Ratwacker" Gangle, Wizard; Scandal, Animal (cat)
**Time period(s):** Indeterminate
**Locale(s):** Orbix, Planet—Imaginary

**Summary:** The king has been deposed and live birds will rain on Orbix until his reinstatement. Kendar gets asked to fix the problem. Many strange animals and bad puns later, Kendar and Scandal may find the opportunity.

**Other books you might like:**
Robert Asprin, *Another Fine Myth*, 1978
C. Dale Brittain, *A Bad Spell in Yurt*, 1991
Alan Dean Foster, *Spellsinger*, 1983
Craig Shaw Gardner, *The Other Sinbad*, 1991
Roger Zelazny, *Bring Me the Head of Prince Charming*, 1991
   Robert Sheckley, co-author

## 2082

**ESTHER FRIESNER**

## *The Sherwood Game*

(New York: Baen, 1995)

**Story type:** Science Fiction (Humor; Robot Fiction)
**Major character(s):** Carl Sherwood, Computer Expert; Robin Hood, Artificial Intelligence; Laurie Pincus, Computer Expert
**Time period(s):** 21st century
**Locale(s):** Austin, Texas; Virtual Reality, Cyberspace

**Summary:** Carl Sherwood's unauthorized virtual reality game set in medieval Sherwood Forest features a self-aware Robin Hood program. When the Robin Hood AI, occupying an android body, exercises its freedom in the real world, Carl must thwart both the AI and an evil corporate executive.

**Other books you might like:**
Aaron Allston, *Galatea in 2-D*, 1993
Piers Anthony, *Killobyte*, 1993
Charles de Lint, *Memory and Dream*, 1994
Philip Jose Farmer, *Red Orc's Rage*, 1991
Will Shetterly, *The Tangled Lands*, 1989
Vivian Vande Velde, *User Unfriendly*, 1991

## 2083

**ESTHER FRIESNER**

## *Sphynxes Wild*

(New York: Signet, 1989)

**Story type:** Fantasy (Contemporary)
**Major character(s):** Sanchi, Gambler
**Time period(s):** 1980s
**Locale(s):** Atlantic City, New Jersey

**Summary:** After escaping the control of a sorcerer, a sphynx wanders through modern America seeking power. She becomes the head of a giganitc corporate empire in Atlantic City. A group from a ghetto join forces with the sorcerer to stop and control the sphynx.

**Other books you might like:**
Emma Bull, *War for the Oaks*, 1988
Craig Shaw Gardner, *A Multitude of Monsters*, 1986
Diana L. Paxson, *Brisingamen*, 1984
Adrienne Martine-Barnes, *The Rainbow Sword*, 1988

## 2084

**ESTHER FRIESNER**

## *Unicorn U.*

(New York: Ace, 1992)

**Story type:** Fantasy (Light Fantasy; Young Adult)
**Series:** Timothy Desmond
**Major character(s):** Timothy Alfred Desmond, Student—College, Wizard; T'ing Hau Kaplan, Student—College; Yang, Spirit (T'ing's ancestor)
**Time period(s):** 1990s
**Locale(s):** New York, New York

**Summary:** Timothy Desmond should concentrate on his pre-medicine studies at Princeton but Yang's news that T'ing no longer sees her ancestor's spirit sends him on a rescue mission. Life becomes further complicated by his mother's engagement to the legendary Dr. Faustus, the reappearance of his banshee, Telery, and a handful of deities bent on starting armageddon in New York City.

**Other books you might like:**
Suzette Haden Elgin, *And Then There'll Be Fireworks*, 1981
Suzette Haden Elgin, *The Grand Jubilee*, 1981
Suzette Haden Elgin, *Twelve Fair Kingdoms*, 1981
Alan Dean Foster, *Cyber Way*, 1990
Neil Gaiman, *Good Omens: The Nice and Accurate Prophecies of Agnes Nutter, Witch*, 1990
   Terry Pratchett, co-author
Craig Shaw Gardner, *Revenge of the Fluffy Bunnies*, 1990
Parke Godwin, *Waiting for the Galactic Bus*, 1988

## 2085

**ESTHER FRIESNER**

## *Wishing Season*

(New York: Atheneum, 1993)

**Story type:** Fantasy (Light Fantasy; Young Adult)
**Series:** Dragonflight
**Major character(s):** Khalid, Mythical Creature (genie), Student
**Time period(s):** Indeterminate Past
**Locale(s):** Middle East

**Summary:** Insufficiently warned in school, Khalid blows his first field assignment by failing to limit his first master to three wishes. Disaster strikes when Khalid must grant an infinite number of wishes. To extract himself from the mess, Khalid requires the assistance of a female genie, a princess and a talking cat.

**Other books you might like:**
Michael Ende, *The Night of Wishes: or The Satanarchaeolidealcohellish Notion Potion*, 1992
Craig Shaw Gardner, *The Other Sinbad*, 1991
S.P. Somtow, *The Wizard's Apprentice*, 1993
Brad Strickland, *Dragon's Plunder*, 1992
Tad Williams, *Child of an Ancient City*, 1992
   Nina Kiriki Hoffman, co-author

## 2086

**ESTHER FRIESNER**

### Yesterday We Saw Mermaids

(New York: Tor, 1992)

**Story type:** Fantasy (Historical)
**Major character(s):** Mother Catalina, Religious (nun); Rasha of the Thousand Doors, Royalty (princess), Spouse (djinn's); La Zagala, Witch, Gypsy
**Time period(s):** 15th century (1492)
**Locale(s):** Atlantic Ocean; North America

**Summary:** The ethnically diverse passengers of a magical ship hope to arrive in the New World prior to Columbus, intending to preserve the place of magic in America. Presented as sequential journal entries.

**Other books you might like:**
Orson Scott Card, *Prentice Alvin*, 1988
Orson Scott Card, *Red Prophet*, 1989
Orson Scott Card, *Seventh Son*, 1987
John Maddox Roberts, *King of the Wood*, 1983

## 2087

**GREGORY FROST**

### The Pure Cold Light

(New York: AvoNova, 1993)

**Story type:** Science Fiction (Political; Invasion of Earth)
**Major character(s):** Thomasina Lyell, Journalist, Activist; Angel, Alien
**Time period(s):** 21st century
**Locale(s):** Philadelphia, Pennsylvania; Montenegro

**Summary:** Thomasina Lyell follows leads on a story, revealing a conspiracy fostered by the megacorporations to maximize profits regardless of the cost to humanity.

**Other books you might like:**
Patricia Anthony, *Brother Termite*, 1993
William C. Dietz, *Matrix Man*, 1990
Michael Flynn, *In the Country of the Blind*, 1990
David Alexander Smith, *In the Cube*, 1993
Neal Stephenson, *Snow Crash*, 1992
John Varley, *Steel Beach*, 1992
Vernor Vinge, *A Fire upon the Deep*, 1992

## 2088

**BRIAN FROUD**, Author/Illustrator

### Good Faeries, Bad Faeries

(New York: Simon and Schuster, 1998)

**Story type:** Fantasy (Collection; Legend)

**Summary:** This collection contains a five-page preface and a 17-page introduction discuss ing faery nature, classification, physiognomy and faery life, plus short essays on 78 different good faeries. Bound upside down, the ''Bad Faeries'' section contains a duplicate, five-page preface and a different 16-page introduction discussing faery nature and danger to humans from that nature, the dark side of faery, defects, glamour and magic and protection from faeries, plus short essays on 78 different bad faeries.

**Other books you might like:**
Charles de Lint, *The Wild Wood*, 1994
    Brian Froud, co-author
Terry Jones, *The Goblin Companion*, 1996
    Brian Froud, co-author
Terry Jones, *Lady Cottington's Pressed Fairy Book*, 1994
    Brian Froud, co-author
Terry Jones, *Strange Stains and Mysterious Smells*, 1996
    Brian Froud, co-author
Patricia A. McKillip, *Something Rich and Strange*, 1994
    Brian Froud, co-author

## 2089

**STEVEN RAY FULGHAM**

### The Forsaken

(New York: Diamond, 1991)

**Story type:** Horror (Occult)
**Major character(s):** Marshall Shaeler, Child; Anita Shaeler, Travel Agent; Azod, Young Man
**Time period(s):** 1990s
**Locale(s):** Seattle, Washington

**Summary:** In this semi-sequel to the author's first novel, *The Summoned*, a deformed young man named Azod lives in the attic of a skyscraper in downtown Seattle, fishing nightly with a large grappling hook for unwary strollers whom he hoists to his lair and subjects to the worst tortures imaginable in his service to the demon Bargolas.

**Other books you might like:**
Christopher Fowler, *Roofworld*, 1988

## 2090

**STEVEN RAY FULGHAM**

### The Summoned

(New York: Diamond, 1991)

**Story type:** Horror (Occult)
**Major character(s):** Stan Fuller, Teenager; Mike Kawaguchi, Teenager; Bargolas, Demon
**Time period(s):** 1970s (1970)
**Locale(s):** Othello, Washington

**Summary:** The author's first novel tells in flashbacks how the succubus Bargolas was born of the union between a nun and priest during the Spanish Inquisition, and how the unbridled lusts of persons ever since have repeatedly summoned him back to the earthly plane. Bargolas proves quite a big hit in the small town of Othello, where teenage hormone levels run high.

**Other books you might like:**
Edward Lee, *Incubi*, 1991
Ray Russell, *Incubus*, 1976

## 2091

**STEVEN RAY FULGHAM**

### A Whisper of Wings

(New York: Diamond, 1992)

**Story type:** Horror (Possession)
**Major character(s):** Duncan Glass, Civil Servant; Bo Challer, Teenager; Kaeot, Monster (Member of the Wicrae)

**Time period(s):** 1990s
**Locale(s):** Seattle, Washington

**Summary:** Seduced against his will into sexual union with a winged creature he hits with his car, Duncan Glass finds that he is undergoing a slow and painful physical transformation that will eventually transforms him into one of the Wicrae, a race of human beings turned into winged monsters who feed on human flesh.

**Other books you might like:**
Angela Carter, *Nights at the Circus*, 1984
John Farris, *Fiends*, 1990
John Farris, *Wildwood*, 1987

---

## 2092

### ERIC JAMES FULLILOVE

## *Circle of One*

(New York: Bantam Spectra, 1996)

**Story type:** Science Fiction (Cyberpunk; Mystery)
**Major character(s):** Jenny Sixa, Telepath, Detective; Didi ''Deeds'', Robot, Researcher; Derrick Trent, Detective—Homicide
**Time period(s):** 2050s
**Locale(s):** Los Angeles, California

**Summary:** A civilian aiding homicide investigations by tapping psychic impressions from corpses, Jenny Sixa finds a disturbing pattern in the victims of a serial killer. As part of the murders, the killer arranges for Jenny's name to appear among the victims' final memories. First novel.

**Other books you might like:**
Pat Cadigan, *Fools*, 1992
Raphael Carter, *The Fortunate Fall*, 1996
Laurell K. Hamilton, *Guilty Pleasures*, 1993
Katharine Kerr, *Polar City Blues*, 1990
Richard Paul Russo, *Destroying Angel*, 1992
David Alexander Smith, *In the Cube*, 1993
Neal Stephenson, *Snow Crash*, 1992

---

## 2093

### ERIC JAMES FULLILOVE

## *The Stranger*

(New York: Bantam Spectra, 1997)

**Story type:** Science Fiction (Mystery; Theological)
**Series:** Jenny Sixa
**Major character(s):** Jenny Sixa, Telepath, Detective—Amateur; Didi ''Deeds'' Myers, Robot, Researcher; Derrick Trent, Detective—Police
**Time period(s):** 2050s
**Locale(s):** Los Angeles, California

**Summary:** When, bored by her newly wealthy lifestyle, Jenny agrees to help Derrick identify a young murder victim, even her telepathic skills cannot reach the victim's last memories. Forensic tests show that an overdose of the illegal drug Zombie caused his death, while DNA tests prove him the son of a woman who denies ever having children. As thoughts broadcast by a sexual predator invade Jenny's dreams and a religious cult seeks to kill her, the police find another murdered teenager.

**Other books you might like:**
Isaac Asimov, *The Caves of Steel*, 1953
Alfred Bester, *The Demolished Man*, 1953
Philip K. Dick, *The Three Stigmata of Palmer Eldritch*, 1965
Lynn S. Hightower, *Alien Heat*, 1994

Colleen McCullough, *A Creed for the Third Millennium*, 1985
Amy Thomson, *Virtual Girl*, 1993

---

## 2094

### LIZ FULTON

## *The Palm Dome*

(New York: Bantam 1990)

**Story type:** Horror (Supernatural Vengeance)
**Major character(s):** Maurizio Camfrey, Professor (Professor of English); Faye Wolsey, Printer; Jack Gilbert, Antiques Dealer
**Time period(s):** 1990s
**Locale(s):** Camfrey Estate, Connecticut

**Summary:** Estranged nephew Jack Camfrey inherits the family estate from his deceased Aunt Emmeline, unaware that he is also inheriting the skeletons in the family closet—or, in this case, bodies at the bottom of the pool beneath the estate's lush palm dome.

**Other books you might like:**
James Herbert, *Haunted*, 1988
Matthew J. Costello, *Beneath Still Waters*, 1988
Steve Rasnic Tem, *Excavation*, 1987

---

## 2095

### MAGGIE FUREY

## *Aurian*

(New York: Bantam Spectra, 1994)

**Story type:** Fantasy (Magic Conflict; Romance)
**Major character(s):** Aurian, Student, Magician; Avran, Servant, Magician; Miathan, Magician
**Time period(s):** Indeterminate
**Locale(s):** Nexis, Fictional City

**Summary:** Inheriting both Earth-magic and Fire-magic from her parents, Aurian grows up in near isolation. When a friend of her father moves in, life changes, but following a near-fatal accident during a sword-fighting lesson, she goes to Nexis for training at the Mage's Academy. The Archmage Miathan plans on using her talents to increase his power, but when she takes a mortal lover, the Archmage schemes to destroy her, even if it means unleasing the long-lost magic of forbidden weapons. First novel.

**Other books you might like:**
Lynn Abbey, *Daughter of the Bright Moon*, 1979
C.J. Cherryh, *The Paladin*, 1988
Phyllis Eisenstein, *Born to Exile*, 1978
Barbara Hambly, *The Ladies of Mandrigyn*, 1984
Tad Williams, *The Dragonbone Chair*, 1988

---

## 2096

### MAGGIE FUREY

## *Dhiammara*

(New York: Bantam Spectra, 1997)

**Story type:** Fantasy (Magic Conflict)
**Series:** Aurian
**Major character(s):** Aurian, Magician; Eliseth, Magician; Miathan, Magician
**Time period(s):** Indeterminate
**Locale(s):** Nexis, Fictional City; Dhiammara, Fictional City; Southern Kingdoms, Fictional Country

**Summary:** Magically transported into the future, Aurian finds Eliseth reanimating the dead and preparing to conquer the world, while Miathan strives to turn himself into a god. Aurian will require all her resources to achieve victory in the final conflict in Dhiammara. Fourth in series.

**Other books you might like:**
David Eddings, *Pawn of Prophecy*, 1982
Lynn Flewelling, *Stalking Darkness*, 1997
Terry Goodkind, *Temple of the Winds*, 1997
Patricia A. McKillip, *The Riddle-Master of Hed*, 1976
Michelle Sagara, *Chains of Darkness, Chains of Light*, 1994

---

**2097**

MAGGIE FUREY

## Harp of Winds

(New York: Bantam Spectra, 1995)

**Story type:** Fantasy (Magic Conflict; Quest)
**Series:** Aurian
**Major character(s):** Aurian, Magician, Parent; Avran, Magician; Miathan, Magician
**Time period(s):** Indeterminate
**Locale(s):** Nexis, Fictional City; Aerillia, Fictional City

**Summary:** Driven from the city of Nexis and unable to wield her magical powers during her pregnancy, Aurian sets forth on a journey with Avran and a small group of supporters to bring back the Staff of Earth, one of the ancient Great Weapons, and the heal a land locked in the icy grip of eternal winter by Miathan's sorcery. With the birth of her child, Aurian regains her magic but cannot undo the curse Miathan set on her child, while Avran goes in search of the second Great Weapon, the Harp of Winds. Sequel to *Aurian*.

**Other books you might like:**
Lynn Abbey, *The Wooden Sword*, 1991
C.J. Cherryh, *The Tree of Swords and Jewels*, 1983
Barbara Hambly, *The Silicon Mage*, 1988
Robert Jordan, *The Dragon Reborn*, 1991
Patricia A. McKillip, *The Riddle-Master of Hed*, 1976

---

**2098**

MAGGIE FUREY

## Sword of Flame

(New York: Bantam Spectra, 1996)

**Story type:** Fantasy (Magic Conflict; Quest)
**Series:** Aurian
**Major character(s):** Aurian, Magician; Avran, Magician; Eliseth, Magician
**Time period(s):** Indeterminate
**Locale(s):** Nexis, Fictional City; Xandim, Fictional City

**Summary:** Using the Staff of Earth and the Harp of Winds, Aurian and Avran have broken the unnatural winter conjured by Eliseth and Miathan using the Cauldron of Waters. Beset by evil sorcery, betrayal, and madness they travel northward to Nexis seeking the fourth Artifact of Power, the Sword of Flame. The Sword's power can end Eliseth's rule, but the price of its mastery may be too high for Aurian.

**Other books you might like:**
C.J. Cherryh, *The Tree of Swords and Jewels*, 1983
Barbara Hambly, *The Dark Hand of Magic*, 1990
Robert Jordan, *The Fires of Heaven*, 1993
Katherine Kurtz, *High Deryni*, 1973
Patricia A. McKillip, *Harpist in the Wind*, 1979

J.R.R. Tolkien, *The Return of the King*, 1956

---

**2099**

LESLIE GADALLAH

## Cat's Gambit

(New York: Ballantine/Del Rey Books, 1990)

**Story type:** Science Fiction (Space Opera)
**Major character(s):** Ayyah, Alien, Refugee; McDonald, Spaceman, Pirate
**Time period(s):** Indeterminate Future
**Locale(s):** Alpha Centauri IV, Planet—Imaginary; Pigpen, Asteroid; Kazi Empire, Interstellar Empire/Federation

**Summary:** The Oriani, a cat-like alien race, have been almost wiped out by the Kaz, a race of insect-like aliens. Ayyah, a refugee from that massacre, looks for a way to destroy the Kaz, who have now taken over much of the galaxy. She enlists the not entirely willing aid of a group of Terran gunrunners and mercenaries and the battle is on.

**Other books you might like:**
C.J. Cherryh, *Chanur's Homecoming*, 1986
C.J. Cherryh, *Chanur's Venture*, 1984
C.J. Cherryh, *The Kif Strike Back*, 1985
C.J. Cherryh, *The Pride of Chanur*, 1982
Walter Jon Williams, *Angel Station*, 1989

---

**2100**

PETER GADOL

## Coyote

(New York: Crown, 1990)

**Story type:** Fantasy (Religious; Adventure)
**Major character(s):** Coyote Gato, Guide; Madeleine Mash, Journalist
**Time period(s):** 1990s
**Locale(s):** Frescuro, Southwest

**Summary:** Coyote hitches a ride with Madeleine to the ashram of Guru B. They pass by the Great Tree which has been very significant in Coyote's life. When they get to the ashram, Coyote claims to be Madeleine's husband in order to get inside, where he wants to find a friend and also a meteorite which had been stolen.

**Other books you might like:**
Neil Gaiman, *Good Omens: The Nice and Accurate Prophecies of Agnes Nutter, Witch*, 1990
   Terry Pratchett, co-author
Parke Godwin, *The Snake Oil Wars*, 1989
Parke Godwin, *Waiting for the Galactic Bus*, 1988
John Kessel, *Good News From Outer Space*, 1989
Barry Lopez, *Crow and Weasel*, 1990
Allen Steele, *Clarke County, Space*, 1990
Kurt Vonnegut Jr., *Cat's Cradle*, 1963

---

**2101**

NEIL GAIMAN

## Angels & Visitations: A Miscellany

(Minneapolis, Minnesota: Dream Haven Books, 1993)

**Story type:** Fantasy (Collection)
**Major character(s):** The Troll, Mythical Creature; Lucifer, Angel, Military Personnel; Jack Horner, Detective—Private
**Time period(s):** Indeterminate Past; 1990s

**Locale(s):** The Palace of Spiders, Mythical Place; The Silver City, Fictional City; London, England

**Summary:** Contains 11 short stories, six poems and five essays, written 1984-1993, along with an introduction and seven illustrations. The tone ranges from horrifying to humorous while two of the stories put a new spin on mysteries as unusual detectives pursue murderers through *Mother Goose* and a city of angels.

**Other books you might like:**
Jonathan Carroll, *Bones of the Moon*, 1987
John Crowley, *Little, Big*, 1981
Robert Holdstock, *Mythago Wood*, 1984
Fritz Leiber, *Swords and Deviltry*, 1970
Ian McDonald, *Desolation Road*, 1988

---

`2102`

**NEIL GAIMAN**

## *Day of the Dead*

(Minneapolis, Minnesota: Dream Haven Books, 1998)

**Story type:** Science Fiction (Space Colony; Religious)
**Series:** Babylon 5
**Major character(s):** Zooty, Entertainer (comedian); Elizabeth Lochley, Military Personnel; Londo Mollari, Diplomat, Alien (Centauri)
**Time period(s):** 23rd century
**Locale(s):** Babylon 5, Space Station; Brakir, Planet—Imaginary; Interstellar Empire/Federation

**Summary:** Since the Brakiri believe that the dead return to Brakir every 180 years to visit the living, the Brakiri living on Babylon 5 purchase part of the station to make it Brakir. To the crew's shock, part of Babylon 5 becomes Brakir for one night, and the dead do, in fact, return. At the same time, a pair of comedians visit the station to remind the living of their humanity. This title is an annotated script of an episode of the TV series *Babylon 5*.

**Other books you might like:**
Neal Barrett Jr., *The Touch of Your Shadow, the Whisper of Your Name*, 1996
Peter David, *In the Beginning*, 1998
Kathryn M. Drennan, *To Dream in the City of Sorrows*, 1997
J. Gregory Keyes, *Deadly Relations*, 1999
John Vornholt, *Voices*, 1995

---

`2103`

**NEIL GAIMAN**
**TERRY PRATCHETT**, Co-Author

## *Good Omens: The Nice and Accurate Prophecies of Agnes Nutter, Witch*

(New York: Workman, 1990)

**Story type:** Fantasy (Religious; Light Fantasy)
**Major character(s):** Crowley, Angel (fallen); Aziraphale, Angel; Adam, Demon (the Antichrist)
**Time period(s):** 1990s (1990)
**Locale(s):** London, England; Oxfordshire, England

**Summary:** An angel and a demon cooperate in delaying Armageddon so as to preserve the interesting life on Earth. Their efforts become complicated when the Antichrist ends up in the wrong family at birth.

**Other books you might like:**
Parke Godwin, *The Snake Oil Wars*, 1989
Parke Godwin, *Waiting for the Galactic Bus*, 1988

Robert A. Heinlein, *Job: A Comedy of Justice*, 1984
Robert A. Heinlein, *Stranger in a Strange Land*, 1961
Kurt Vonnegut Jr., *Cat's Cradle*, 1963

---

`2104`

**NEIL GAIMAN**

## *Neverwhere*

(New York: Avon, 1997)

**Story type:** Fantasy (Contemporary; Urban)
**Major character(s):** Richard Mayhew, Businessman; Lady Door, Gentlewoman, Fugitive; Marquis de Carabas, Nobleman, Con Artist
**Time period(s):** 1990s (1996)
**Locale(s):** London, England; London Below, Fictional City

**Summary:** When Richard Mayhew stops to assist an injured woman, he finds himself drawn into the odd world of London Below, a city made up of sewers and legends, lost dreams and forgotten people. His everyday life erased because of his kindness, Richard Mayhew, hapless businessman, must risk everything to save both Londons. Based on Gaiman's screenplay for the BBC miniseries and revised from the UK edition.

**Other books you might like:**
Jack Cady, *The Off Season*, 1995
John Crowley, *Little, Big*, 1981
Charles de Lint, *Someplace to Be Flying*, 1988
Lisa Goldstein, *The Dream Years*, 1985
Megan Lindholm, *Wizard of the Pigeons*, 1986

---

`2105`

**NEIL GAIMAN**, Editor
**EDWARD E. KRAMER**, Co-Editor

## *The Sandman: Book of Dreams*

(New York: HarperPrism, 1996)

**Story type:** Fantasy (Anthology; Literary)
**Series:** Sandman
**Major character(s):** Peter Himmels, Military Personnel; Morpheus, Mythical Creature (Lord of the Dreaming); Death, Mythical Creature
**Time period(s):** 1990s; 1940s
**Locale(s):** The Dreaming, Mythical Place; Wych Cross, England

**Summary:** Contains a five-page preface by Frank McConnell and individual introductions to 17 stories, one poem and Tori Amos' introduction to "Death: The High Cost of Living," all inspired by Neil Gaiman's comic, *The Sandman*. Varying in tone, the stories involve dreams, dreaming, and peoples' reactions to them, with some elaboration on characters and settings created or developed by Gaiman. Authors include Steven Brust, Nancy Collins, George Alec Effinger, John M. Ford, Lisa Goldstein, Colin Greenland, Karen Haber, Barbara Hambly, Delia Sherman, Will Shetterly, Tad Williams, and Gene Wolfe.

**Other books you might like:**
Jonathan Carroll, *Bones of the Moon*, 1987
John Crowley, *Little, Big*, 1981
Greer Ilene Gilman, *Moonwise*, 1990
Robert Holdstock, *Mythago Wood*, 1984
Megan Lindholm, *Wizard of the Pigeons*, 1986

## 2106
### NEIL GAIMAN

## Smoke and Mirrors
(New York: Avon, 1998)

**Story type:** Fantasy (Collection; Contemporary)

**Summary:** This collection contains 31 stories and poems written between 1993 and 1998, plus an introduction describing the pieces. Stories include an elderly woman who finds the Holy Grail at a charity shop, a man who sells a portion of himself to a troll and comes to regret it, and a chilling story about the first murder committed in heaven.

**Other books you might like:**
John Crowley, *Antiquities*, 1993
Charles de Lint, *The Ivory and the Horn*, 1995
Lisa Goldstein, *Travelers in Magic*, 1994
Robert Holdstock, *The Bone Forest*, 1991
Pat Murphy, *Points of Departure*, 1990

## 2107
### DAN GALLAGHER

## The Pleistocene Redemption
(Brooksville, Florida: Ancient Prophecies, 1998)

**Story type:** Science Fiction (Genetic Manipulation; Political)
**Major character(s):** Kevin G. Harrigan, Scientist (geneticist); Ismail Mon, Ruler (Iraq)
**Time period(s):** 2010s (2019)
**Locale(s):** Iraq; Israel

**Summary:** A geneticist develops a method of recreating ancient species by applying modern technology to samples of tissue that have survived since ancient times. He gains funding for his project from the dictator of Iraq, but eventually discovers that the motivation is the development of biological warfare weapons which can be used against Israel. First novel.

**Other books you might like:**
Brian W. Aldiss, *An Island Called Moreau*, 1981
John Christopher, *The Little People*, 1968
Michael Crichton, *Jurassic Park*, 1990
Will Henry, *Genesis Five*, 1968
Hayford Peirce, *Phylum Monsters*, 1989

## 2108
### DIANA G. GALLAGHER

## The Alien Dark
(Lake Geneva, Wisconsin: TSR, 1990)

**Story type:** Science Fiction (Hard Science Fiction)
**Major character(s):** Tahl d'jehn, Alien (ahsin bey), Spaceship Captain; Riitha f'ath, Alien (ahsin bey), Scientist (biologist)
**Time period(s):** Indeterminate Future (1,000,000th century)
**Locale(s):** *Dan tahlni*, Spaceship; Venus; Montenegro

**Summary:** The ahsin bey sent out several survey vessels to find new solar systems to colonize. It will be decades before the crew of the *Dan tahlni* can learn if a colony ship is on the way to the system they've discovered, but the installations around the fifth planet will be ready when the time comes.

**Other books you might like:**
Octavia E. Butler, *Dawn*, 1987

C.J. Cherryh, *The Pride of Chanur*, 1982
Gordon R. Dickson, *The Alien Way*, 1965
Larry Niven, *Protector*, 1973
David Alexander Smith, *Homecoming*, 1990
L. Neil Smith, *Their Majesties' Bucketeers*, 1981

## 2109
### DIANA G. GALLAGHER
### MARTIN R. BURKE, Co-Author

## The Chance Factor
(New York: Pocket, 1997)

**Story type:** Science Fiction (Adventure; Young Adult)
**Series:** Star Trek Voyager: Starfleet Academy
**Major character(s):** Kathryn Janeway, Student (Starfleet Academy), Leader
**Time period(s):** 24th century
**Locale(s):** Diehr IV, Planet—Imaginary; United Federation of Planets, Interstellar Empire/Federation

**Summary:** As a last opportunity to save her career, Starfleet Academy Cadet Kathryn Janeway leads a field study on a wilderness planet. The mission becomes more dangerous when they cannot leave the planet as expected.

**Other books you might like:**
Patricia Barnes-Svarney, *Quarantine*, 1997
Peter David, *Worf's First Adventure*, 1993
Alexei Panshin, *Rite of Passage*, 1968
Brad Strickland, *Crisis on Vulcan*, 1996
Brad Strickland, *The Star Ghost*, 1994
  Barbara Strickland, co-author
Bobbie J.G. Weiss, *Lifeline*, 1997
  David Cody Weiss, co-author

## 2110
### STEPHEN GALLAGHER

## Down River
(New York: Tor, 1990)

**Story type:** Horror (Psychological Suspense)
**Major character(s):** Johnny Mays, Police Officer; Nick Frazier, Police Officer; Alice Craig, Office Worker
**Time period(s):** 1980s (1989)
**Locale(s):** London, England

**Summary:** Maverick cop Johnny Mays takes his personal vendettas too far one night and apparently drowns in a reservoir while harrassing a felon. Shortly thereafter his partner, Nick Frazier, notices that people Johnny held a grudge against are dying horrible deaths.

**Other books you might like:**
Ramsey Campbell, *The Face That Must Die*, 1979
Thomas Harris, *Red Dragon*, 1981
William Hjortsberg, *Falling Angel*, 1978

## 2111
### STEPHEN GALLAGHER

## Nightmare, with Angel
(New York: Ballantine, 1993)

**Story type:** Horror (Psychological Suspense)

**Major character(s):** Marianne Cadogan, Child (10 years old); Ryan O'Donnell, Beachcomber; Jennifer McGann, Detective—Police
**Time period(s):** 1990s (1993)
**Locale(s):** England; Hamburg, Germany

**Summary:** When young Marianne Cadogan runs away from her stern father to find her mother in Germany, Patrick Cadogan doesn't know which is worst: the possiblity that she may find her mother and the sordid sex ring she was involved with, or the fact that Marianne's traveling companion is a man who was once imprisoned for murdering an eleven-year-old child. This book was originally published in England in 1992.

**Other books you might like:**
John D. MacDonald, *The Executioners*, 1958
Robert R. McCammon, *Mine*, 1990
Ian McEwan, *The Cement Garden*, 1978
John Metcalfe, *The Feasting Dead*, 1954

**2112**

STEPHEN GALLAGHER

*Oktober*

(New York: Tor, 1990)

**Story type:** Horror (Mystery)
**Major character(s):** Jim Harper, Teacher; Rochelle Genoud, Heiress; Werner Risinger, Businessman (head of Risinger-Genoud), Relative (Rochelle's stepbrother)
**Time period(s):** 1980s (1989)
**Locale(s):** Switzerland; Cliff House, England

**Summary:** Critically injured in a mishap at the Risinger-Genoud chemical plant, Jim Harper is injected with the experimental drug Epheteline. Years later, a series of recurring nightmares convinces Jim that his condition is connected to his treatment, and that he is being monitored like a guinea pig by those who treated him.

**Other books you might like:**
Martin James, *Night Glow*, 1989
Stephen King, *Firestarter*, 1980
Dean R. Koontz, *Midnight*, 1989

**2113**

STEPHEN GALLAGHER

*Red, Red Robin*

(New York: Ballantine, 1995)

**Story type:** Horror (Psychological Suspense)
**Major character(s):** Ruth Lasseter, Advertising; Aidan Kincannon, Security Officer; Tim Hagan, Companion (paid escort)
**Time period(s):** 1990s (1995)
**Locale(s):** Philadelphia, Pennsylvania

**Summary:** In an effort to protect a married colleague from the embarrassment of public discovery of their affair, British expatriate Ruth Lsseter hires a professional escort for a company party, and then foolishly indulges him with a one night stand that provides him with a fatal attraction for her. After he is dispatched, Ruth embarks on an obsessive quest into his background that reveals the monster he is and, worse, that he may not be dead as Ruth thinks.

**Other books you might like:**
John Farris, *Sacrifice*, 1994
John Fowles, *The Collector*, 1963
Samuel M. Key, *I'll Be Watching You*, 1994

**2114**

LEWIS GANNETT

*Gehenna*

(New York: Harper, 1997)

**Story type:** Horror (Serial Killer)
**Series:** Millennium
**Major character(s):** Frank Black, FBI Agent (former); Peter Watt, Spy; Dylan, Young Man
**Time period(s):** 1990s (1997)
**Locale(s):** San Francisco, California

**Summary:** Ex-FBI agent Frank Black and agents of the Millennium Group track the activities of Gehenna International, a death cult that brainwashes its members with LSD-induced visions of supernatural doom and immolates its enemies with the fires of Gehenna. Novelization of the Fox television series "Millennium," about a group of special agents who work covertly to solve crimes inspired by the dark side of the coming millennium.

**Other books you might like:**
Kevin J. Anderson, *The X-Files: Ruins*, 1996
Charles L. Grant, *The X-Files: Goblins*, 1994
Elizabeth Hand, *The Frenchman*, 1997
Jeff Rice, *The Night Strangler*, 1974
Jeff Rice, *The Night Stalker*, 1973

**2115**

LEWIS GANNETT

*The Living One*

(New York: Randam House, 1993)

**Story type:** Horror (Gothic Family Chronicle)
**Major character(s):** Torrance Spoor, Teenager (16 years old); Baron Malcolm Spoor, Businessman; Sheila Massif, Sociologist
**Time period(s):** 1990s (1993)
**Locale(s):** Boston, Massachusetts

**Summary:** Under the pretense of spending his last days with his son, Baron Malcolm Spoor, the inheritor of a family curse of madness that strikes all male descendants of the Spoor family before they turn 50, transplants the boy from California to a secluded stronghold in Massachusetts. There, young Torrance is subjected to his father's voyeurism and other perverse habits, before learning that the collective Spoor male consciousness inhabiting his father's body plans to incorporate Torrance's own consciousness and take over his body when his father "dies." Told in an epistolary style, this is the author's first novel.

**Other books you might like:**
Tanith Lee, *Dark Dance*, 1992
Robert R. McCammon, *Usher's Passing*, 1984
Patrick McGrath, *The Grotesque*, 1990
Joyce Carol Oates, *Bellefleur*, 1980
Gus Weill, *Flesh*, 1990
F. Paul Wilson, *Sibs*, 1992

**2116**

ERIC GARBER

*Embracing the Dark*

(Boston: Alyson, 1991)

**Story type:** Horror (Anthology)

**Summary:** This first anthology of gay and lesbian horror fiction collects eleven stories—five original, five reprint, and Karl Heinrich Ulrich's "Manor," a translation of a story originally published in the 1880s. Included are Jay B. Laws "Imagine," about a dream lover who becomes real; two stories of vampires by Jewelle Gomez and Jeffrey McMahan; and a shapeshifter story by John Peyton Cooke, "The Strawberry Man."

**Other books you might like:**
John Peyton Cooke, *Out for Blood*, 1991
Scott Edelman, *The Gift*, 1990
Jeffrey M. Elliot, *Kindred Spirits*, 1984
Jewelle Gomez, *The Gilda Stories*, 1991
Jay B. Laws, *Steam*, 1991
Jeffrey N. McMahan, *Somewhere in the Night*, 1989
Jeffrey N. McMahan, *Vampires Anonymous*, 1991

---

**2117**

**ERIC GARBER**, Editor
**JEWELLE GOMEZ**, Co-Editor

## Swords of the Rainbow

(Los Angeles: Alyson Publications, 1996)

**Story type:** Fantasy (Anthology; Science Fiction)

**Summary:** This anthology contains three pages of authors' biographies, 13 original stories and Samuel R. Delany's "The Tale of Small Sarg" from *Tales of Neveryon* (1979). All stories utilize gay/lesbian themes with other themes such as sword and sorcery, urban fantasy, post-disaster, political conflict, and high fantasy by authors including Lauren Wright Douglas, Jewelle Gomez, Tanya Huff, Mel Keegan, Carrie Richardson, Mark Shepherd, and Jean Stewart.

**Other books you might like:**
Camilla Decarnin, *Worlds Apart*, 1986
    Eric Garber, Lyn Paleo, co-editors
Jeffrey M. Elliot, *Kindred Spirits*, 1984
    editor
Pam Keesey, *Dark Angels: Lesbian Vampire Stories*, 1995
    editor
Pam Keesey, *Daughters of Darkness: Lesbian Vampire Stories*, 1993
    editor
Ernest Posey, *Hormone Pirates of Xenobia and Dream Studs of Kama Loka*, 1996
Caro Soles, *Meltdown!*, 1994
    editor

---

**2118**

**ROBERT T. GARCIA**, Editor

## Chilled to the Bone

(Niles, Illinois: Mayfair Games, Inc., 1991)

**Story type:** Horror (Anthology)

**Summary:** Fifteen tales of horror and dark fantasy by diverse hands presented as selections from the closed files of The Eternal Society of the Silver Way (Societas Argenti Viae Eternitata, or SAVE), an occult investigation unit. Included are Robert Weinberg's tale of an urban werewolf, "Terror by Night"; F.A. McMahan's account of a phantom lover, "Whose Hungry Mouth"; Blythe Ayne's story of the cult of Kali, "In Her Hands"; and stories by Matthew Costello, Steve and Melanie Tem, Andre Norton, and G. Wayne Miller.

**Other books you might like:**
Charles L. Grant, *The Greystone Bay Series*, 1985-1991
Robert R. McCammon, *Under the Fang*, 1991

John Skipp, *Book of the Dead*, 1989
    Craig Spector, co-author

---

**2119**

**R. GARCIA Y ROBERTSON**

## Atlantis Found

(New York: AvoNova, 1997)

**Story type:** Science Fiction (Time Travel; Adventure)
**Series:** Virgin and the Dinosaur
**Major character(s):** Jake Bento, Time Traveler, Guide; Sauromanta, Time Traveler, Warrior (Amazon); Hercules, Hero (demi-god)
**Time period(s):** Indeterminate Past; 27th century (2600s)
**Locale(s):** *Argo*, in the Air (airship); *Thetis*, Submarine

**Summary:** Jake leads a mission to the Bronze Age to rescue the three Special Temporal Operations teams lost trying to locate Atlantis. Jake and his team soon realize that future time travelers infiltrated their organization, stole the STOP equipment, and now attempt to block Jake's time from the portal. With the help of Hercules, Jake must rescue his team, take back his equipment and return to the future before Thera explodes, destroying Atlantis.

**Other books you might like:**
Poul Anderson, *Guardians of Time*, 1960
David Drake, *Arc Riders*, 1995
    Janet Morris, co-author
Fritz Leiber, *The Big Time*, 1961
Julian May, *The Many-Colored Land*, 1981
Andre Norton, *The Crossroads of Time*, 1956
S.D. Perry, *Timecop*, 1994

---

**2120**

**R. GARCIA Y ROBERTSON**

## The Moon Maid and Other Fantastic Adventures

(Chicago: Golden Gryphon Press, 1998)

**Story type:** Science Fiction (Collection)

**Summary:** Contains a three-page preface by the author and eight stories which appeared in periodicals between 1989 and 1996. Several of the stories have elaborate historical settings and a fantasy flavor, yet contain science fiction elements such as time travel, space travel, and aliens.

**Other books you might like:**
Joe Haldeman, *None So Blind*, 1996
Ursula K. Le Guin, *Buffalo Gals and Other Animal Presences*, 1987
Ursula K. Le Guin, *The Wind's Twelve Quarters*, 1975
Lisa Mason, *The Golden Nineties*, 1995
Vonda N. McIntyre, *Dreamsnake*, 1978
Mary Rosenblum, *Synthesis & Other Virtual Realities*, 1996
Connie Willis, *Impossible Things*, 1994

---

**2121**

**R. GARCIA Y ROBERTSON**

## The Spiral Dance

(New York: William Morrow, 1991)

**Story type:** Fantasy (Adventure; Historical)
**Major character(s):** Anne Percy, Noblewoman (Countess of Northumberland); Jock o' the Syde, Werewolf, Companion

**Time period(s):** 16th century
**Locale(s):** Scotland; England

**Summary:** Anne, driven by a religious vision, and her husband set out to depose Elizabeth Tudor and put Mary Stuart on the British throne. When her husband is betrayed and imprisoned, Anne seeks freedom and spiritual satisfaction aided by Jock. During perilous travels she is transported by witchcraft to Faerie and back before reaching enlightenment. This is the author's first novel.

**Other books you might like:**
Margaret J. Anderson, *The Druid's Gift*, 1989
Gael Baudino, *Strands of Starlight*, 1989
Diana Gabaldon, *Outlander*, 1991
Mary Alexander Walker, *The Scathach and the Maeve's Daughter*, 1990
Patricia C. Wrede, *Snow White and Rose Red*, 1989

**2122**

#### R. GARCIA Y ROBERTSON

### The Virgin and the Dinosaur

(New York: AvoNova, 1996)

**Story type:** Science Fiction (Time Travel; Political)
**Major character(s):** Jake Bento, Time Traveler, Guide; Peg, Scientist (paleontologist), Time Traveler; Charlotte Marie d'Anton, Slave, Time Traveler
**Time period(s):** Indeterminate Past (Mesozoic era/Upper Cretaceous); 1850s (1857)
**Locale(s):** Hell Creek, Montana

**Summary:** When Jake takes Peg to the Mesozoic era to study dinosaurs, he loses his only weapon almost immediately. They record many encounters with dinosaurs before the loss of their reactor forces them to head for home, passing through the 1857 Midwest where they travel the Mississippi River on a paddlewheel steamboat.

**Other books you might like:**
Poul Anderson, *The Time Patrol*, 1991
James Gurney, *Dinotopia*, 1992
Stephen Leigh, *Ray Bradbury Presents: Dinosaur Planet*, 1993
Julian May, *The Many-Colored Land*, 1981
Robert J. Sawyer, *Far-Seer*, 1992

**2123**

#### CRAIG SHAW GARDNER

### A Bad Day for Ali Baba

(New York: Ace, 1992)

**Story type:** Fantasy (Legend; Light Fantasy)
**Series:** Arabian Nights
**Major character(s):** Ali Baba, Artisan, Adventurer; Aladdin, Thief, Adventurer
**Time period(s):** Indeterminate Past
**Locale(s):** Middle East

**Summary:** Ali Baba and Aladdin's quest for treasure and humorous encounters leads from an enchanted cavern to the Palace of Beautiful Women. Companion volume to *The Other Sinbad*.

**Other books you might like:**
Douglas Adams, *The Hitchhiker's Guide to the Galaxy*, 1980
Douglas Adams, *The Restaurant at the End of the Universe*, 1981
Piers Anthony, *A Spell for Chameleon*, 1977
John Barth, *The Last Voyage of Somebody the Sailor*, 1991
Andrew Lang, *The Arabian Nights Entertainments*, 1969
    Editor

Salman Rushdie, *Haroun and the Sea of Stories*, 1990
Susan Shwartz, *Arabesques: More Tales of the Arabian Nights*, 1988
    Editor
Jack Zipes, *Arabian Nights: The Marvels and Wonders of the Thousand and One Nights*, 1991
    Editor

**2124**

#### CRAIG SHAW GARDNER

### Batman Returns

(New York: Warner, 1992)

**Story type:** Science Fiction (Adventure)
**Series:** Batman
**Major character(s):** Bruce "Batman" Wayne, Hero, Detective—Amateur; Oswald "the Penguin" Cobblepot, Criminal; Selena "Catwoman" Kyle, Criminal, Heroine
**Time period(s):** 21st century
**Locale(s):** Gotham City (New York City)

**Summary:** Penguin and Catwoman plot to discredit Batman and terrorize some Gotham City residents as they attempt to control the city. Film tie-in.

**Other books you might like:**
Lynn Abbey, *Catwoman*, 1992
    Robert Asprin, co-author
Martin H. Greenberg, *The Further Adventures of Batman*, 1989
    editor
Martin H. Greenberg, *The Further Adventures of Batman 2: Featuring the Penguin*, 1992
    editor
Martin H. Greenberg, *The Further Adventures of the Joker*, 1990
    editor
Simon Hawke, *Batman: To Stalk a Specter*, 1991
Joe R. Lansdale, *Batman: Captured by the Engines*, 1991

**2125**

#### CRAIG SHAW GARDNER

### Bride of the Slime Monster

(New York: Ace, 1990)

**Story type:** Fantasy (Alternate World)
**Series:** Cineverse Cycle
**Major character(s):** Roger Gordon Jr., Public Relations; Delores, Girlfriend (Roger's)
**Time period(s):** 1980s; Indeterminate
**Locale(s):** Earth; Alternate Universe

**Summary:** Though Roger has finally escaped Cineverse, the universe in which old B-movies are real, he must return to rescue his girlfriend, Delores, from the evil Dr. Dread. He must also battle a new adversary, Menge the Merciless, and must deal with the misunderstood Edward the Slime Monster.

**Other books you might like:**
Glen Cook, *Dread Brass Shadows*, 1990
Peter David, *Howling Mad*, 1989
Terry Pratchett, *Sourcery*, 1988
Alis A. Rasmussen, *The Labyrinth Gate*, 1989
Spider Robinson, *Callahan's Crosstime Saloon*, 1989
George H. Scithes, *Another Round at the Spaceport Bar*, 1989
    Daniell Schweitzer, co-author

## 2126

### CRAIG SHAW GARDNER

## *Dragon Burning*

(New York: Ace, 1996)

**Story type:** Fantasy (Magic Conflict; Alternate World)
**Series:** Dragon Circle
**Major character(s):** Nick Blake, Teenager, Warrior; Carl Jackson, Adventurer; Nunn, Magician
**Time period(s):** Indeterminate
**Locale(s):** Seven Islands, Fictional Country

**Summary:** With the dragon awakened and the wizards continuing their warfare, chaos and destruction will envelop the land unless Nick Blake and his neighbors from Chestnut Circle can halt the conflict.

**Other books you might like:**
A.A. Attanasio, *The Dragon and the Unicorn*, 1996
Robin Wayne Bailey, *Brothers of the Dragon*, 1993
Don Callander, *Dragon Companion*, 1994
Terry Goodkind, *Stone of Tears*, 1995
Robert Jordan, *The Eye of the World*, 1990
Marjorie Bradley Kellogg, *The Book of Earth*, 1995

## 2127

### CRAIG SHAW GARDNER

## *Dragon Sleeping*

(New York: Ace, 1994)

**Story type:** Fantasy (Alternate World; Magic Conflict)
**Series:** Dragon Circle
**Major character(s):** Nick Blake, Teenager, Warrior; Mary Lou ''Merrilu'' Dafoe, Teenager; Nunn, Magician
**Time period(s):** 1960s (1967); Indeterminate
**Locale(s):** Chestnut Circle, Fictional City; Seven Islands, Fictional Country

**Summary:** When the residents of Chestnut Circle find their community transported to a magical realm, only Nick and three friends evade Nunn's capture, joining Nunn's rival in an attempt to control an immortal dragon. Finding an opportunity to escape, Mary Lou also flees and locates allies among fierce warriors. First of a series.

**Other books you might like:**
Robin Wayne Bailey, *Brothers of the Dragon*, 1993
Gordon R. Dickson, *The Dragon and the George*, 1976
Carole Nelson Douglas, *Cup of Clay*, 1991
Richard A. Knaak, *King of the Grey*, 1993
R.A. Salvatore, *The Woods out Back*, 1993

## 2128

### CRAIG SHAW GARDNER

## *Dragon Waking*

(New York: Ace, 1995)

**Story type:** Fantasy (Magic Conflict; Alternate World)
**Series:** Dragon Circle
**Major character(s):** Nick Blake, Teenager, Warrior; Obar, Magician; Nunn, Magician
**Time period(s):** Indeterminate
**Locale(s):** Seven Islands, Fictional Country; At Sea

**Summary:** Nunn and Obar continue to battle for supremacy and control of the immortal dragon, now risen and draining magic from the world. The wizards use magic artifacts as well as Nick and his friends in their attempts to master the beast.

**Other books you might like:**
Terry Goodkind, *Stone of Tears*, 1995
Robert Jordan, *The Eye of the World*, 1989
Marjorie Bradley Kellogg, *The Book of Earth*, 1995
Ursula K. Le Guin, *A Wizard of Earthsea*, 1968
Mark C. Perry, *Morigu: The Dead*, 1990

## 2129

### CRAIG SHAW GARDNER

## *The Last Arabian Night*

(New York: Ace, 1993)

**Story type:** Fantasy (Legend; Light Fantasy)
**Series:** Arabian Nights
**Major character(s):** Scheherazade, Spouse, Storyteller; Shahryar, Royalty (king), Spouse
**Time period(s):** Indeterminate Past
**Locale(s):** Middle East

**Summary:** Casting about to replace his wife, beheaded for faithlessness, Shahryar chooses his grand vizier's daughter, Scheherazade. To save herself from the expected beheading at the hands of an obsessive-compulsive spouse, Scheherazade diverts his attention with her marvelous tales.

**Other books you might like:**
John Barth, *Chimera*, 1972
John Barth, *The Last Voyage of Somebody the Sailor*, 1991
Esther Friesner, *Wishing Season*, 1993
Susan Shwartz, *Arabesques: More Tales of the Arabian Nights*, 1988
    editor
Mark Twain, *Satires and Burlesques*, 1968
Jack Zipes, *Arabian Nights: The Marvels and Wonders of the Thousand and One Nights*, 1991
    editor

## 2130

### CRAIG SHAW GARDNER

## *The Other Sinbad*

(New York: Ace, 1991)

**Story type:** Fantasy (Legend; Light Fantasy)
**Major character(s):** Sinbad the Porter, Worker; Sinbad the Sailor, Businessman, Adventurer; Ozzie, Mythical Creature (djinn)
**Time period(s):** Indeterminate Past
**Locale(s):** Baghdad, Middle East; Hutan's Ship, At Sea

**Summary:** Involuntarily recruited by Sinbad the Sailor, Sinbad the Porter journeys on an eighth wondrous voyage with the famous sailor whose latest voyage aims at replenishing his treasury, which was drained by the vengeful djinn, Ozzie.

**Other books you might like:**
Douglas Adams, *The Hitchhiker's Guide to the Galaxy*, 1980
Douglas Adams, *The Restaurant at the End of the Universe*, 1981
Piers Anthony, *A Spell for Chameleon*, 1977
John Barth, *The Last Voyage of Somebody the Sailor*, 1991
Patricia Daniels, *Sinbad the Sailor*, 1980
Stephen Goldin, *Shrine of the Desert Mage*, 1988
Andrew Lang, *The Arabian Nights Entertainments*, 1969
    editor

Salman Rushdie, *Haroun and the Sea of Stories*, 1990
Susan Shwartz, *Arabesques: More Tales of the Arabian Nights*, 1988
    editor
Susan Shwartz, *Arabesques II*, 1989
    editor
Jack Zipes, *Arabian Nights: The Marvels and Wonders of the Thousand and One Nights*, 1991
    editor

---

**2131**

CRAIG SHAW GARDNER

## Return to Chaos

(New York: Pocket, 1998)

**Story type:** Horror (Vampire Story; Ancient Evil Unleashed)
**Series:** Buffy the Vampire Slayer
**Major character(s):** Buffy Summers, Teenager, Vampire Hunter; Willow Rosenberg, Teenager; Rupert Giles, Librarian
**Time period(s):** 1990s (1998)
**Locale(s):** Sunnydale, California

**Summary:** Remnants of the Druid race travel to vampire-ridden Sunnydale and help Buffy Sumner in her bid to rid the town of the evil that has earned it the nickname Hellmouth. But ensuing mysterious events persuade Buffy that the Druid interests may not be entirely benevolent. An original novel based on a popular television series.

**Other books you might like:**
Richie Tankersley Cusick, *Buffy the Vampire Slayer*, 1992
Richie Tankersley Cusick, *The Harvest*, 1997
    A novelization of a Buffy the Vampire Slayer Series episode
Elvira, *Transylvania 90210*, 1996
    John Paragon, co-author
Joseph Locke, *Vampire Heart*, 1994
S.P. Somtow, *The Vampire's Beautiful Daughter*, 1997

---

**2132**

CRAIG SHAW GARDNER

## Revenge of the Fluffy Bunnies

(New York: Ace, 1990)

**Story type:** Fantasy (Light Fantasy; Satire)
**Series:** Cineverse Cycle
**Major character(s):** Roger Gordon Jr., Hero, Adventurer; Mrs. Gordon Sr., Housewife, Adventurer; Doctor Dread, Terrorist, Leader
**Time period(s):** Indeterminate
**Locale(s):** Cineverse, Alternate Universe (Citadel of Dread); California

**Summary:** Cineverse's many movie worlds are undergoing an insidious change. Bad guys are winning, good guys are dying, and the boy doesn't even get the girl. Only Captain Crusader (Roger Gordon, Jr. in ''real'' life) can save the day by defeating Dr. Dread and his evil Forces of Darkness before the curtain falls on the last act. Unfortunately, Dr. Dread's partner, whip-cracking archvillainess Mother Antoinette, is Roger's mother, Mrs. Roger Gordon, Sr., a bored widow with a taste for destruction. To complicate things, Roger's girlfriend has been abducted by Edward, an amorous slime monster.

**Other books you might like:**
Douglas Adams, *The Hitchhiker's Guide to the Galaxy*, 1980
Piers Anthony, *Man From Mundania*, 1989
James P. Blaylock, *The Stone Giant*, 1989
James P. Blaylock, *The Elfin Ship*, 1986

Alexis A. Gilliland, *Wizenbeak*, 1990
Gary K. Wolf, *Who Censored Roger Rabbit?*, 1981

---

**2133**

CRAIG SHAW GARDNER

## Wishbringer

(New York: Avon, 1988)

**Story type:** Fantasy (Light Fantasy)
**Major character(s):** Simon, Postal Worker
**Time period(s):** Indeterminate
**Locale(s):** Festerton; Witchville

**Summary:** Based on one of Infocom's interactive fiction computer games, the story follows Simon who commits a crime and is sentenced to serve as a mailman in the town of Festerton (which occasionally turns into the sinister town of Witchville).

**Other books you might like:**
Douglas Adams, *The Hitchhiker's Guide to the Galaxy*, 1979
Piers Anthony, *Man From Mundania*, 1989
James P. Blaylock, *The Elfin Ship*, 1986
James P. Blaylock, *The Stone Giant*, 1989
Alexis A. Gilliland, *Wizenbeak*, 1990
Daniel Manus Pinkwater, *Borgel*, 1990

---

**2134**

JAMES ALAN GARDNER

## Commitment Hour

(New York: Avon Eos, 1998)

**Story type:** Science Fiction (Genetic Manipulation; Political)
**Major character(s):** Fullin, Musician, Experimental Subject; Rashid, Scientist; Steck, Clone (neuter), Outcast
**Time period(s):** 25th century
**Locale(s):** Tober Cove, Fictional City; Birds Home, Mythical Place

**Summary:** The children of Tober Cove go to Birds Home each year and come home the opposite sex. When they reach the age of 20 they must decide which gender to choose, or become hermaphrodite, which they call Neut. Unfortunately stuck as male his whole life, the Prophet, leader of Tober Cove decrees that all Neuts should be burned, or exiled. With Commitment due, Fullin, now male, meets Rashid, who stays to observe Commitment Hour with Steck, a Neut, complicating the decision Fullin finds increasingly difficult.

**Other books you might like:**
David Brin, *Glory Season*, 1993
M.J. Engh, *Rainbow Man*, 1993
Carolyn Ives Gilman, *Halfway Human*, 1998
Melissa Scott, *Shadow Man*, 1995
Sheri S. Tepper, *A Plague of Angels*, 1993

---

**2135**

JAMES ALAN GARDNER

## Expendable

(New York: AvoNova, 1997)

**Story type:** Science Fiction (Political; First Contact)
**Major character(s):** Festina Ramos, Space Explorer, Military Personnel; Oar, Genetically Altered Being (glass woman); Yarrun Derigha, Space Explorer, Military Personnel
**Time period(s):** 25th century (2450s)

**Locale(s):** New Earth, Planet—Imaginary; *Jacaranda*, Spaceship; Melaquin, Planet—Imaginary

**Summary:** Since the Admiralty High Council noticed that the loss of ugly, unpopular crew members proves less disruptive to spaceship operations, all intelligent, physically flawed, but able children serve in the Explorer Corps. The League of Peoples prevents non-sapients, including anyone who would send a person to his death, from leaving his world. Festina and Yarrun must accompany the banished Admiral Chee to earthlike Melaquin, a planet from which no explorer has ever returned. On Melaquin, Festina discovers the High Council's ugly secret. First novel.

**Other books you might like:**
C.J. Cherryh, *Forty Thousand in Gehenna*, 1983
L. Warren Douglas, *Stepwater*, 1995
Anne McCaffrey, *The Ship Who Sang*, 1969
Elizabeth Moon, *Remnant Population*, 1996
Robert J. Sawyer, *Starplex*, 1996
Jack Vance, *Alastor*, 1995

**2136**

MARTIN GARDNER

## Visitors From Oz: The Wild Adventures of Dorothy, the Scarecrow and the Tin Woodman

(New York: St. Martin's Press, 1998)

**Story type:** Fantasy (Contemporary; Adventure)
**Major character(s):** Dorothy Gale, Traveler, Teenager; Samuel Gold, Producer; Buffalo Odersby Boggs, Producer
**Time period(s):** Indeterminate; 1990s
**Locale(s):** Oz, Mythical Place; New York, New York

**Summary:** To meet them and promote his new Oz film, Samuel Gold invites Dorothy Gale and her friends to visit Earth after nearly a century in Oz. After borrowing magic pearls from Ozma to keep them safe, Dorothy, the Scarecrow and the Tin Woodman travel magically to New York City, where Buffalo Boggs, planning a new *Peter Pan* film, launches deadly attacks on them.

**Other books you might like:**
L. Frank Baum, *The Wonderful Wizard of Oz*, 1900
Philip Jose Farmer, *A Barnstormer in Oz*, 1982
Gregory Maguire, *Wicked: The Life and Times of the Wicked Witch of the West*, 1995
Geoff Ryman, *Was*, 1992
Joan D. Vinge, *Return to Oz*, 1985

**2137**

S. ANTHONY GARDNER

## A Few Bricks Shy

(Syracuse, New York: Vampire Dan's Story Emporium, 1997)

**Story type:** Horror (Collection)
**Summary:** Three stories and one poem on a variety of supernatural and nonsupernatural horror themes. ''Campfire'' is a variation on a spooky campfire tale, ''Rod and Gun'' a tale of murder and dark deeds, and ''Traffic Accident'' a tale of an ironic twist of fate. Issued as a signed limited edition chapbook. Illustrated by Kevin Butterfield and Peter Sieburg.

**Other books you might like:**
S. Darnbrook Colson, *People of the Night*, 1994
Randy Fox, *Not Broken, Not Belonging*, 1994

Gary Jonas, *Nice Guys Finish Last*, 1997
Gary Jonas, *By Death Abused*, 1990
Jack Remick, *Terminal Weird*, 1996
Wayne Allen Sallee, *Pain-Grin*, 1993
Don Webb, *A Spell for the Fulfillment of Desire*, 1996

**2138**

HENRY GARFIELD

## Moondog

(New York: St. Martin's, 1995)

**Story type:** Horror (Werewolf Story; Mystery)
**Major character(s):** Joe Acton, Worker (in a restaurant); Cyrus ''Moondog'' Nygerski, Journalist; Erik Gunn, Editor
**Time period(s):** 1980s (1989)
**Locale(s):** Julian, California

**Summary:** The slaughter of several women on nights of the full moon during a summer in a quiet suburb of San Diego brings together ex-burglar Joe Acton and renegade journalist Moondog Nygerski to solve the mystery. When the two deduce that a werewolf is the only possible explanation, its casts suspicion on a number of townspeople, themselves included. This is the author's first novel.

**Other books you might like:**
Crosland Brown, *Tombley's Walk*, 1991
George C. Chesbro, *The Fear in Yesterday's Rings*, 1991
D.J. Donaldson, *Blood on the Bayou*, 1991
Whitley Strieber, *The Wolfen*, 1978
Les Whitten, *Moon of the Wolf*, 1967

**2139**

HENRY GARFIELD

## Room 13

(New York: St. Martin's, 1997)

**Story type:** Horror (Haunted House; Werewolf Story)
**Major character(s):** Marilou McCormick, Teacher (high school english); Cyrus ''Moondog'' Nygerski, Driver (school bus), Werewolf; Robert Rickard, Maintenance Worker (janitor)
**Time period(s):** 1990s (1997)
**Locale(s):** Julian, California

**Summary:** Progressive English teacher Marilou McCormick inherits a classroom haunted by the ghost of a former teacher who forces students and teachers of the Drew Bailey Memorial High School to re-enact situations from the classic works of literature he taught. Her only hope is Moondog Nygerski, a former journalist turned werewolf, whose condition makes him sensitive to psychic phenomena. A sequel to the author's first novel Moondog.

**Other books you might like:**
Ed Kelleher, *The School*, 1991
Harriette Vidal, co-author
R.L. Stine, *Superstitious*, 1995
Manly Wade Wellman, *The School of Darkness*, 1995
T.M. Wright, *The School*, 1990

## 2140
### RICHARD GARFINKLE

### *Celestial Matters*
(New York: Tor, 1996)

**Story type:** Science Fiction (Alternate Universe; Hard Science Fiction)
**Major character(s):** Aias, Scientist; Yellow Hare, Military Personnel; Phan Xu-Tzu, Spy, Scientist
**Time period(s):** 7th century
**Locale(s):** Athens, Greece; Mars; Alternate Universe

**Summary:** In a Ptolemic universe, the Delian Archons choose Aias of Tyre to take his ship, *Chandra's Tear*, to the Celestial Sphere and capture sun matter with which to destroy 'AngXou, the capital of the Middle Kingdom at war with the Delian League for 900 years. When traitors and agents sabotage the ship, stranding it in Ares Sphere, Aias and the Middle Kingdom agent Phan Xu-Tzu must cooperate to get the ship home and find out how to halt, if only for a time, the centuries long war. First novel.

**Other books you might like:**
Greg Bear, *Eternity*, 1988
Ben Bova, *Orion and the Conqueror*, 1994
L. Sprague de Camp, *The Dragon of the Ishtar Gate*, 1961
Kirk Mitchell, *Procurator*, 1984
Melissa Scott, *A Choice of Destinies*, 1986
Judith Tarr, *Lord of the Two Lands*, 1993
Harry Turtledove, *Agent of Byzantium*, 1987

## 2141
### MARK A. GARLAND
### CHARLES G. MCGRAW, Co-Author

### *Demon Blade*
(New York: Baen, 1994)

**Story type:** Fantasy (Quest; Adventure)
**Major character(s):** Madia, Royalty; Tyrr, Demon, Magician; Frost, Magician
**Time period(s):** Indeterminate
**Locale(s):** Far North, Fictional Country

**Summary:** After Tyrr discredits Madia, Frost and Madia must journey to the swamplands of the Far North to find and acquire the Demon Blade, a powerful magic object.

**Other books you might like:**
Lois McMaster Bujold, *The Spirit Ring*, 1992
Rosemary Edghill, *The Sword of Maiden's Tears*, 1994
Terry Goodkind, *Wizard's First Rule*, 1994
Marc Laidlaw, *Neon Lotus*, 1988
Holly Lisle, *Minerva Wakes*, 1994
Patricia C. Wrede, *The Raven Ring*, 1994

## 2142
### MARK A. GARLAND
### CHARLES G. MCGRAW, Co-Author

### *Dorella*
(New York: Baen, 1992)

**Story type:** Fantasy (Magic Conflict)
**Major character(s):** Dorella, Witch, Alien
**Time period(s):** 1990s
**Locale(s):** Earth

**Summary:** Finally warming to human beings after more than 4000 years on Earth, Dorella repeatedly begins to form friendships with humans only to find an ancient enemy's agents forcing her to move on. Author's first novel.

**Other books you might like:**
Michael Cassutt, *Dragon Season*, 1991
Elizabeth Forrest, *Phoenix Fire*, 1992
James D. Priest, *Kirins: The Flight of the Ain*, 1992
James D. Priest, *Kirins: The Spell of No'an*, 1990
Will Shetterly, *Elsewhere*, 1991

## 2143
### JAKE GARN
### STEPHEN PAUL COHEN, Co-Author

### *Night Launch*
(New York: William Morrow, 1989)

**Story type:** Science Fiction (Techno-Thriller)
**Major character(s):** Conrad Williams, Astronaut; Aelita Zakharov, Astronaut
**Time period(s):** 1990s
**Locale(s):** Earth; *Discovery*, Spaceship

**Summary:** The first space shuttle to be launched with an international crew is hijacked by a psychopathic criminal with connections to the terrorist underground. The terrorists demand the release of political prisoners and the international situation begins to heat up. A desperate rescue mission is launched to retake the shuttle and save its crew.

**Other books you might like:**
Ben Bova, *The Kinsman Saga*, 1987
Ben Bova, *Peacekeepers*, 1988
Dale Brown, *Day of the Cheetah*, 1989
Dale Brown, *The Silver Tower*, 1988
Edward Gibson, *Reach*, 1989
Dean Ing, *The Ransom of Black Stealth One*, 1989

## 2144
### JAMES FINN GARNER

### *Once upon a More Enlightened Time: More Politically Correct Bedtime Stories*
(New York: Macmillan, 1995)

**Story type:** Fantasy (Collection; Legend)

**Summary:** Contains a three-page introduction, a politically correct alphabet, and nine familiar fairy tales, humorously rewritten to reflect modern sensiblities, such as ''Sleeping Persun of Better-than-average Attractiveness'' and ''The City Mouse and the Suburban Mouse.'' In other tales, Hansel and Gretel learn about forest ecology from a resident Wiccan, the Little Mer-persun visits a protest over drift net fishing, Puss in Boots acts as spin doctor and organizer of the senatorial campaign of his inheritor, and the tortoise and the hare compete in a media-oriented sporting extravaganza.

**Other books you might like:**
Margaret Atwood, *Good Bones and Simple Murders*, 1994
William J. Brooke, *Teller of Tales*, 1994
George Alec Effinger, *Maureen Birnbaum, Barbarian Swordsperson: The Complete Stories*, 1993
Esther Friesner, *Chicks in Chainmail*, 1995
editor
Ursula K. Le Guin, *Fish Soup*, 1992

Ethel Johnston Phelps, *Tatterhood and Other Tales*, 1978
  editor
Chelsea Quinn Yarbro, *A Baroque Fable*, 1986
Jack Zipes, *The Outspoken Princess and the Gentle Knight*, 1994
  editor

## 2145

### JAMES FINN GARNER

## Politically Correct Bedtime Stories

(New York: Macmillan, 1994)

**Story type:** Fantasy (Anthology; Legend)

**Summary:** Contains 13 familiar fairy tales retold with modern sensibilities in mind and tongue firmly in cheek, with Cinderella joining her sisters-of-step in a co-op to produce comfortable clothes for womyn, the Emperor endorsing a clothing-optional life style and Jack's climbing the beanstalk and learning not to judge people by their size. But not everyone lives happily ever after as the princess realizes that the frog she has just kissed has become a real estate developer who wants to build an office/condo/resort complex in the woods.

**Other books you might like:**
Robert Asprin, *Another Fine Myth*, 1978
Terry Pratchett, *Witches Abroad*, 1993
Elizabeth Ann Scarborough, *The Drastic Dragon of Draco, Texas*, 1986
Chelsea Quinn Yarbro, *A Baroque Fable*, 1986
Jack Zipes, *The Outspoken Princess and the Gentle Knight*, 1994
  editor

## 2146

### JAMES FINN GARNER

## Politically Correct Holiday Stories: For an Enlightened Yuletide Season

(New York: Macmillan, 1995)

**Story type:** Fantasy (Collection; Legend)

**Summary:** Contains a four-page introduction, one poem, and four familiar seasonal stories humorously rewritten for modern sensibilities. In "'Twas the Night Before Solstice," a co-op resident educates a visitor on parental cultivation of values and the influence of retailers on seasonal giving; Frosty the Persun of Snow campaigns as a eco-warrior; the Nutcracker, having resigned from the military, acts as a diplomat; Rudolph the Nasally Empowered Reindeer forces labor concessions out of Santa Claus; and three spiritual facilitators work over Scrooge in an extensive guilt trip.

**Other books you might like:**
Margaret Atwood, *Good Bones and Simple Murders*, 1994
William J. Brooke, *Teller of Tales*, 1994
David G. Hartwell, *Christmas Magic*, 1994
  editor
Ethel Johnston Phelps, *Tatterhood and Other Tales*, 1978
  editor
Kristine Kathryn Rusch, *Pulphouse, Issue 10: Special Issue*, 1991
  editor
Jack Zipes, *The Outspoken Princess and the Gentle Knight*, 1994
  editor

## 2147

### SHEILA BRISTOW GARNER

## Night Music

(New York: Pinnacle, 1992)

**Story type:** Horror (Black Magic; Occult)
**Major character(s):** Kitty Barrett, Nurse; Michael Sandeen, Musician; Zeke Miller, Musician
**Time period(s):** 1990s
**Locale(s):** Ocean City, North Carolina

**Summary:** Nurse Kitty Barrett rescues dissipated guitarist Michael Sandeen from a life of rampant drug abuse, endless sexual orgies, and other occupational hazards of the music business. But bass guitarist Zeke Miller, member of a satanic coven, exploits Michael's vulnerability, seeing in him a potential new member of the coven, and in Kitty a potential blood sacrifice.

**Other books you might like:**
Nancy A. Collins, *Tempter*, 1991
Ray Garton, *Crucifax*, 1988
John Skipp, *The Scream*, 1988
  Craig Spector, co-author

## 2148

### DAVID GARNETT, Editor

## New Worlds

(Clarkston, Georgia: White Wolf, 1997)

**Story type:** Science Fiction (Anthology)

**Summary:** Contains an eight-page introduction, eight pages of authors' biographies, and 14 original stories by British authors or authors with strong ties to Great Britain, including one collaboration, "The White Stuff," by Peter F. Hamilton and Graham Joyce. From downbeat to ironic or humorous in tone, the stories explore diverse themes such as artificial reality, the future of death, rural life, technological innovation, relationships, and sports. Other authors include Brian W. Aldiss, Pat Cadigan, William Gibson, Garry Kilworth, Michael Moorcock, Kim Newman, Howard Waldrop, and Ian Watson.

**Other books you might like:**
Kim Mohan, *Amazing Stories: The Anthology*, 1995
  editor
Michael Moorcock, *New Worlds 5*, 1974
  editor
Michael Moorcock, *New Worlds Quarterly Number 1-4*, 1971-1972
  editor
David Pringle, *The Best of Interzone*, 1997
  editor
Kristine Kathryn Rusch, *The Best of Pulphouse: The Hardback Magazine*, 1991
  editor

## 2149

### SUSAN M. GARRETT

## Forever Knight: Intimations of Mortality

(New York: Berkley/Boulevard, 1997)

**Story type:** Horror (Vampire Story)
**Series:** Forever Knight

**Major character(s):** Nicholas Knight, Detective—Homicide, Vampire; Natalie Lambert, Doctor (forensic pathologist); Tracy Vetter, Detective—Homicide
**Time period(s):** 1990s (1997)
**Locale(s):** Toronto, Ontario, Canada

**Summary:** Under the influence of a charmed doll and his own nostalgia for life as a mortal, 800-year-old vampire Nicholas Knight has dreams of an alternate world in which he is part of a minority of mortals living in a civilization of vampires. The dreams eventually begin to seep into reality and adversely affect Knight's work as a detective. Based on the cable television series *Forever Knight*.

**Other books you might like:**
Vincent Courtney, *Vampire Beat*, 1991
P.N. Elrod, *Bloodlist*, 1990
Laurell K. Hamilton, *Guilty Pleasures*, 1993
Tanya Huff, *Blood Price*, 1991
Roxanne Longstreet, *Cold Kiss*, 1995
Anne Rice, *The Tale of the Body Thief*, 1992
Karen E. Taylor, *Blood Secrets*, 1994

---

**2150**

### RAY GARTON

## Dark Channel

(New York: Bantam, 1992)

**Story type:** Horror (Apocalyptic Horror)
**Major character(s):** Hester Thorne, Cult Member (leader); Jordan Cross, Detective—Private; Lauren Schroeder, Housewife
**Time period(s):** 1990s (1993)
**Locale(s):** Anderson, California

**Summary:** Jordan Cross is looking into the disappearance of a reporter for *Trends* magazine following his investigation into the New Age cult of the Universal Enlightened Alliance. Lauren Schroeder is desperately searching for her husband, a member of the Alliance who has abducted her son. Together, Jordan and Lauren infiltrate the Alliance and discover the true sinister source of its appeal and power.

**Other books you might like:**
Alex Abella, *The Killing of the Saints*, 1991
Nicholas Conde, *The Religion*, 1982
Thomas F. Monteleone, *The Blood of the Lamb*, 1992

---

**2151**

### RAY GARTON

## Live Girls

(Baltimore: CD Publications, 1997)

**Story type:** Horror (Vampire Story)
**Major character(s):** Davey Owen, Editor; Anya, Dancer (exotic), Vampire; Walter Benedek, Journalist
**Time period(s):** 1980s
**Locale(s):** New York, New York

**Summary:** Converted into a vampire during a performance by vampire show girls at a Times Square skin show, Davey Owen pursues his vampire initiator, Anya, and is indoctrinated into the vampire night life of Manhattan. First hardcover printing of a novel published as a paperback original in 1987.

**Other books you might like:**
Poppy Z. Brite, *Lost Souls*, 1993
Michael Cecilione, *Domination*, 1993
Michael Cecilione, *Thirst*, 1996
Nancy A. Collins, *Sunglasses After Dark*, 1990

John Skipp, *The Light at the End*, 1986
   Craig Spector, co-author
Karen E. Taylor, *Blood Secrets*, 1994

---

**2152**

### RAY GARTON

## Lot Lizards

(Shingletown, California: Mark Ziesing, 1991)

**Story type:** Horror (Vampire Story)
**Major character(s):** Bill Ketter, Truck Driver; Jon Ketter, Child (Bill Ketter's son); Byron Quimby, Maintenance Worker (janitor)
**Time period(s):** 1990s
**Locale(s):** Yreka, California (The Sierra Gold Pan Truck Stop)

**Summary:** When the Sierra Gold Pan Truck Stop becomes snowed in, the clients find they must band together to protect themselves from vampiric "lot lizards"—truckstop hookers—who share their predicament but not exactly their taste in food.

**Other books you might like:**
Ron Dee, *Blood Lust*, 1990
Ron Dee, *Dusk*, 1991
Stephen King, *Salem's Lot*, 1975
Robert R. McCammon, *They Thirst*, 1981

---

**2153**

### RAY GARTON

## Methods of Madness

(Arlington Heights, IL: Dark Harvest, 1990)

**Story type:** Horror (Collection)

**Summary:** Six tales of unusual human relationships with an emphasis on sex and death. "Active Member" and "Something Kinky" are concerned with the bizarre fates that befall characters seeking to satisfy their sexual obsessions. "Shock Radio" and the short novel "Dr. Krusadian's Method" tell of the poetic justice meted out to, respectively, an abusive radio talk show host and child-abusing parents.

**Other books you might like:**
Clive Barker, *Books of Blood Series*, 1984-1985
Ramsey Campbell, *Scared Stiff*, 1987
John Skipp, *Dead Lines*, 1989
   Craig Spector, co-author

---

**2154**

### RAY GARTON

## The New Neighbor

(Lynbrook, New York: Charnel House, 1991)

**Story type:** Horror (Erotic Horror)
**Major character(s):** Lorelle Dupree, Demon; Ronald Prosky, Journalist; Jen Pritchard, Young Woman
**Time period(s):** 1990s
**Locale(s):** Redbrook, California

**Summary:** Under the guise of a beautiful woman, a succubus moves into the town of Redbrook, seducing the citizens both literally and in their dreams, and pitting them all against one another.

**Other books you might like:**
Jackie Hyman, *Echoes*, 1990
Stephen King, *Needful Things*, 1992

Ray Russell, *Incubus*, 1976

## 2155

### RAY GARTON

## *Pieces of Hate*

(Baltimore, Maryland: Cemetary Dance, 1996)

**Story type:** Horror (Collection)

**Summary:** Most of these nine polemical horror tales feature smugly-righteous characters who get their just desserts, usually by supernatural means. In "A Gift From Above," a woman excercises horrible transformative powers on former classmates who once humiliated her, unaware of the toll they are taking on her spiritually. "Choices" and "The Devil's Music" envision the private hells that befall, respectively, a fanatical right-to-lifer and an obnoxious rock musician. "Ophilia Raphaeldo" imagines the hysterics of daytime talk shows taken to illogical extremes, and "Bad Blood" depicts a fittingly dismal revenge for a sexually repressed gay basher. This book was produced only in a signed limited edition hardcover format.

**Other books you might like:**
Richard T. Chizmar, *Midnight Promises*, 1996
Ed Gorman, *Moonchasers and Other Stories*, 1996
Barry Hoffman, *Firefly. . .Burning Bright*, 1996
Lucy Taylor, *The Flesh Artist*, 1994

## 2156

### RAY GARTON

## *Shackled*

(New York: Bantam, 1997)

**Story type:** Horror (Mystery)
**Major character(s):** Bentley Noble, Journalist; Lacey Ryan, Teenager; Stephen Colloway, Writer (true crime)
**Time period(s):** 1990s (1997)
**Locale(s):** Vallejo, California

**Summary:** As part of his newspaper's plan to soften its crude tabloid image, Global Inquisitor reporter Bentley Noble pursues the human-interest angle of the recent disapperance of several children in the town of Vallejo. His investigations uncover a plot involving high-ranking town officials and professional personnel to indoctrinate the children into a Satanic cult and sell them into sexual slavery through cult networks on the Internet.

**Other books you might like:**
Rick R. Reed, *Obsessed*, 1993
John Saul, *Darkness*, 1991
John Shirley, *Wetbones*, 1992
Guy N. Smith, *Dead End*, 1996

## 2157

### RAY GARTON

## *Website*

(Burton, Michigan: Subterranean Press, 1997)

**Story type:** Horror (Psychological Suspense)
**Major character(s):** Martin Boyle, Worker (lawn care); Heather Boyle, Housewife (Martin's wife); Fiona Webb, Doctor (psychiatrist)
**Time period(s):** 1990s (1997)
**Locale(s):** United States

**Summary:** Martin Boyle discovers that someone has created a computer website for him without his knowledge and that it provides illuminating insights into his life that even he doesn't know. Is something supernatural afoot, or is Martin not as reliable a narrator as he seems? Signed limited edition short story chapbook.

**Other books you might like:**
Richard T. Chizmar, *Blood Brothers*, 1997
Daniel H. Gower, *The Orpheus Process*, 1992
Dean R. Koontz, *Dark Rivers of the Heart*, 1994
Dean R. Koontz, *Demon Seed*, 1973
Thomas F. Monteleone, *Between Floors*, 1997

## 2158

### ELIZABETH CLEGHORN GASKELL

## *A Dark Night's Work and Other Stories*

(New York: Oxford Paperbacks, 1992)

**Story type:** Horror (Collection)

**Summary:** Five stories and novellas by a Victorian writer known for her scrupulous realism, the two longest of which dip into the dark side of the human psyche. "The Grey Woman" both employs and subverts elements of the Gothic horror story in its working out of a feminist manifesto. The title story is about a false accusation of murder and the soul-searching questions it raises in the falsely accused. Suzanne Lewis has supplied an introduction.

**Other books you might like:**
Catherine Crowe, *Night-Side of Nature*, 1848
Charlotte Perkins Gilman, *The Yellow Wallpaper and Other Writings of Charlotte Perkins Gilman*, 1989
Mrs. J.H. Riddell, *The Collected Ghost Stories of Mrs. J.H. Riddell*, 1977
Mary Shelley, *Tales and Stories of Mary Wollstonecraft Shelley*, 1891

## 2159

### R. PATRICK GATES

## *Deathwalker*

(New York: Dell/Abyss, 1996)

**Story type:** Horror (Serial Killer)
**Major character(s):** Bill Cage, Police Officer; Ivy Delacroix, Child; Jack Walker, Criminal
**Time period(s):** 1990s (1995)
**Locale(s):** Crocker, Massachusetts

**Summary:** While detoxing at a clinic from the drug and alcohol addictions he developed after a serial killer murdered his wife, officer Bill Cage is harassed by another killer who sends him letters signed "The Walking Death" and photos of the grisly murders he commits. Bill becomes involved in a cat-and-mouse game with the murderer, who blames Bill for what he has become. This novel is a sequel to the author's novel *Tunnelvision*.

**Other books you might like:**
Michael A. Arnzen, *Grave Markings*, 1994
Thomas Harris, *Red Dragon*, 1981
Barry T. Hawkins, *Puppet Master*, 1993
Roxanne Longstreet, *Red Angel*, 1994

## 2160

### R. PATRICK GATES

## Grimm Memorials

(New York: Onyx, 1990)

**Story type:** Horror (Black Magic; Child-in-Peril)
**Major character(s):** Eleanor Grimm, Undertaker, Witch; Steve Nailer, Teacher, Writer (poet); Diane Nailer, Spouse (Steve's wife)

**Summary:** Aging, ailing mortician (and witch) Eleanor Grimm, linked psychically to her deceased twin brother Edmund, must mutilate young children in order to preserve her own life and return Edmund to his. None of this is known to Steve and Diane Nailer, who have just moved into a house near the Grimm mortuary and the enveloping nearby woods. This inventive original novel incorporates material from a number of fairy tales and children's rhymes into an extremely graphic, gory narrative.

**Other books you might like:**
Raymond E. Feist, *Faerie Tale*, 1988
John Fowles, *The Magus*, 1965
James Herbert, *The Magic Cottage*, 1986
Dean R. Koontz, *Twilight Eyes*, 1987

## 2161

### R. PATRICK GATES

## Jumpers

(New York: Dell, 1997)

**Story type:** Horror (Wild Talents)
**Major character(s):** Anna Wheaton, Child; Dee Dee Blaine, Secretary; Kevin Lucier, Veteran
**Time period(s):** 1990s (1997)
**Locale(s):** Greenfield, New Hampshire; Missoula, Montana

**Summary:** A group of "jumpers"—people whose near-death experiences have endowed them with the ability to shift to alternative worlds where their deaths have not occurred—struggle to help one another and thwart the Shadow Monster, a composite of dead souls that pursues them relentlessly in an effort to absorb them.

**Other books you might like:**
Tannarive Due, *The Between*, 1995
Rick Hautala, *Beyond the Shroud*, 1996
Stephen King, *Insomnia*, 1994
Dean R. Koontz, *Hideaway*, 1993
Daniel Quinn, *Dreamer*, 1988

## 2162

### R. PATRICK GATES

## Tunnelvision

(New York: Dell Abyss, 1991)

**Story type:** Horror (Serial Killer)
**Major character(s):** Bill Gates, Police Officer; Ivy Delacroix, Teenager; Wilbur Clayton, Guard
**Time period(s):** 1990s
**Locale(s):** Crocker, Massachusetts

**Summary:** Rehabilitated cop Bill Gates, still haunted by the revelation that his father was a mass murderer, agrees to take on the case of another mass murderer, and finds himself trying to capture a latter-day Jack the Ripper, who films his grisly kills and markets them as snuff films.

**Other books you might like:**
Dennis Cooper, *Frisk*, 1991
Joe R. Lansdale, *Cold in July*, 1989

## 2163

### JEAN MARK GAWRON

## Dream of Glass

(New York: Harcourt Brace, 1993)

**Story type:** Science Fiction (Alternate Intelligence; Cyberpunk)
**Major character(s):** Alexa Augustine, Computer Expert, Military Personnel; Quincunx "the Thief", Artificial Intelligence; Lady Anne, Artificial Intelligence
**Time period(s):** 22nd century
**Locale(s):** Horton's Valley, California; San Francisco, California

**Summary:** While cannibalizing a landed Galactic Ship, the Rose Post Public occupies Horton's Valley. After one of the soldiers befriends Alexa, who proves a natural computer interfacer, Alexa begins training by the Rose Artificial Intelligence Agency, becoming the best ever trained there. When Alexa "dies" as a result of a bomb blast, enough body remains to inherit Alexa's estate, but with less than 90% intact memory, she must change her first name. Implanted without her knowledge, Augustine carries micromolecular transmitters in her brain from which Quincunx constructs an internal, duplicate Augustine and also monitors her condition for the Rose. Addicted to dopamine exciters in the hospital and subject to severe headaches, Augustine experiences much confusion after leaving the hospital. Allowed to interface, Augustine discovers the powerful interests behind the experiment on her.

**Other books you might like:**
Greg Bear, *Blood Music*, 1985
Pat Cadigan, *Fools*, 1992
Jeffrey A. Carver, *Dragon Rigger*, 1993
Jeffrey A. Carver, *Dragons in the Stars*, 1992
James P. Hogan, *The Multiplex Man*, 1992
Dan Simmons, *The Hollow Man*, 1992
Neal Stephenson, *Snow Crash*, 1991
Michael Swanwick, *Vacuum Flowers*, 1987
Amy Thomson, *Virtual Girl*, 1993

## 2164

### KATHLEEN O'NEAL GEAR
### W. MICHAEL GEAR, Co-Author

## People of the Lakes

(New York: Tor Forge, 1994)

**Story type:** Fantasy (Quest; Historical)
**Series:** First North Americans
**Major character(s):** Star Shell, Heroine, Indian (Hopewell); Otter, Trader, Indian; Green Spider, Psychic (mystic), Indian (Hopewell)
**Time period(s):** 2nd century
**Locale(s):** Great Lakes, North America

**Summary:** Guided by Green Spider's visions and aided by Otter, Star Shell races to save her people from the adverse effects of an evil totemic mask by destroying it at Niagara Falls. A vengeful chief pursues to recover a runaway traveling with them while Star Shell's enemy tries to foil her mission and recover the mask to use it for personal power. Includes four pages of maps, a two-page series chronology and four-page selected bibliography.

**Other books you might like:**
W. Michael Gear, *People of the Earth*, 1992
     Kathleen O'Neal Gear, co-author
W. Michael Gear, *People of the Fire*, 1991
     Kathleen O'Neal Gear, co-author
W. Michael Gear, *People of the River*, 1992
     Kathleen O'Neal Gear, co-author
W. Michael Gear, *People of the Sea*, 1993
     Kathleen O'Neal Gear, co-author
W. Michael Gear, *People of the Wolf*, 1990
     Kathleen O'Neal Gear, co-author

## 2165

### W. MICHAEL GEAR

## The Artifact

(New York: DAW Books, 1990)

**Story type:** Science Fiction (Adventure)
**Major character(s):** Solomon Carrasco, Spaceship Captain; Kraal, Alien (Galactic Grand Master)
**Time period(s):** Indeterminate Future
**Locale(s):** *Boaz*, Spaceship; Star's Rest, Planet—Imaginary

**Summary:** In a galactic civilization on the brink of civil war, an artifact of an ancient alien race is discovered on a distant world and a starship is sent to investigate. Unbeknownst to humanity, the artifact destroyed its creators and could destroy the human race as well.

**Other books you might like:**
Arthur C. Clarke, *Rama II*, 1989
Arthur C. Clarke, *Rendezvous with Rama*, 1973
Ted Reynolds, *The Tides of God*, 1989
Fred Saberhagen, *Berserker*, 1967

## 2166

### W. MICHAEL GEAR
### KATHLEEN O'NEAL GEAR, Co-Author

## People of the Earth

(New York: Tor, 1992)

**Story type:** Fantasy (Historical; Romance)
**Series:** First North Americans
**Major character(s):** Brave Man, Prehistoric Human, Leader; Bad Belly/Still Water, Prehistoric Human, Indian; White Ash, Prehistoric Human, Psychic (dreamer)
**Time period(s):** 30th century B.C. (B.C.)
**Locale(s):** North America

**Summary:** As clans migrate slowly southward along the Rocky Mountains, territories come under new stewardship and inter-clan rivalries and kidnappings modify the clans' makeup. A powerful fetish, the Wolf Bundle, continues to influence events.

**Other books you might like:**
Jean M. Auel, *Clan of the Cave Bear*, 1980
Sue Harrison, *Mother Earth, Father Sky*, 1990
J. Alison James, *Sing for a Gentle Rain*, 1990
Ardath Mayhar, *People of the Mesa*, 1992
Lynn Armistead McKee, *Woman of the Mists*, 1991
Meredith Ann Pierce, *The Woman Who Loved Reindeer*, 1985
J.H. Rosny, *Quest for Fire*, 1909
     Pseudonym of J.H.H. Boex
William Sarabande, *Beyond the Sea of Ice*, 1987

Elizabeth Marshall Thomas, *Reindeer Moon*, 1987
Roger Zelazny, *Bridge of Ashes*, 1976

## 2167

### W. MICHAEL GEAR
### KATHLEEN O'NEAL GEAR, Co-Author

## People of the Fire

(New York: Tor, 1991)

**Story type:** Fantasy (Historical; Adventure)
**Series:** First North Americans
**Major character(s):** Little Dancer, Shaman, Prehistoric Human; Elk Charm, Prehistoric Human, Indian
**Time period(s):** Indeterminate Past (Pleistocene Epoch)
**Locale(s):** Norway

**Summary:** As threat of starvation forces Heavy Bear to kill a newborn female and frustration leads him to desecrate the Wolf Bundle, a powerful sacred fetish, Little Dancer resolves to become a Spirit Dancer and protect his tribe from the power-hungry chief. A Wolf Dream instructs Little Dancer to seek guidance from White Calf in his mission to regain the Wolf Bundle and lead his people from the drought stricken area.

**Other books you might like:**
Jean M. Auel, *Clan of the Cave Bear*, 1980
Sue Harrison, *Mother Earth, Father Sky*, 1990
Richard Herley, *The Stone Arrow*, 1978
J. Alison James, *Sing for a Gentle Rain*, 1990
Meredith Ann Pierce, *The Woman Who Loved Reindeer*, 1985
William Sarabande, *Beyond the Sea of Ice*, 1987
Elizabeth Marshall Thomas, *Reindeer Moon*, 1987

## 2168

### W. MICHAEL GEAR
### KATHLEEN O'NEAL GEAR, Co-Author

## People of the River

(New York: Tor, 1992)

**Story type:** Fantasy (Historical; Religious)
**Series:** First North Americans
**Major character(s):** Lichen, Indian, Psychic; Tharon, Indian, Leader
**Time period(s):** Indeterminate Past (Pleistocene Epoch)
**Locale(s):** Cahokia, North America (capital of Mississippi River Mound Builders)

**Summary:** Troubled by failing crops and excessive tribute demanded by Tharon, people turn to Lichen in hopes that the gods will open the underworld to her.

**Other books you might like:**
Jean M. Auel, *Clan of the Cave Bear*, 1980
Sue Harrison, *Mother Earth, Father Sky*, 1990
Richard Herley, *The Stone Arrow*, 1978
J. Alison James, *Sing for a Gentle Rain*, 1990
Meredith Ann Pierce, *The Woman Who Loved Reindeer*, 1985
William Sarabande, *Beyond the Sea of Ice*, 1987
Elizabeth Marshall Thomas, *Reindeer Moon*, 1987

## 2169

**W. MICHAEL GEAR**
**KATHLEEN O'NEAL GEAR**, Co-Author

### People of the Sea
(New York: St. Martin's, 1993)

**Story type:** Fantasy (Historical; Quest)
**Series:** First North Americans
**Major character(s):** Sunchaser, Prehistoric Human, Shaman; Catchstraw, Prehistoric Human; Kestrel, Prehistoric Human, Fugitive
**Time period(s):** 90th century B.C.
**Locale(s):** Sierra Nevada Mountains, North America

**Summary:** As glaciers melt and change North American ecology, Sunchaser's people view with alarm the changes which deprive them of mastodons and other large game. Sunchaser cannot establish the usual link to the spirit world and Catchstraw's use of witchcraft threatens Sunchaser's authority. When Kestrel, fleeing an abusive husband, joins the tribe, many people feel that befriending her will bring further retribution from the spirit world.

**Other books you might like:**
Jean M. Auel, *Clan of the Cave Bear*, 1980
Sue Harrison, *Mother Earth, Father Sky*, 1990
Sue Harrison, *My Sister the Moon*, 1992
Richard Herley, *The Stone Arrow*, 1978
Meredith Ann Pierce, *The Woman Who Loved Reindeer*, 1985
William Sarabande, *Beyond the Sea of Ice*, 1987
Elizabeth Marshall Thomas, *Reindeer Moon*, 1987

## 2170

**W. MICHAEL GEAR**
**KATHLEEN O'NEAL GEAR**, Co-Author

### People of the Wolf
(New York: Tor, 1990)

**Story type:** Fantasy (Historical; Adventure)
**Series:** First North Americans
**Major character(s):** Heron, Shaman, Prehistoric Human; Runs in Light, Hunter, Prehistoric Human; Raven Hunter, Warrior, Prehistoric Human
**Time period(s):** Indeterminate Past (Pleistocene Epoch)
**Locale(s):** Bering Land Bridge, Asia (Bering Strait)

**Summary:** Heron dreams about Runs in Light who will become Wolf Dreamer, her student, and his twin brother, Raven Hunter, who will become her enemy. Wolf Dreamer, who will someday be a powerful shaman, leads his people to a land shown to him by a wolf in a vision.

**Other books you might like:**
Jean M. Auel, *The Mammoth Hunters*, 1985
Jean M. Auel, *Clan of the Cave Bear*, 1980
J. Alison James, *Sing for a Gentle Rain*, 1990
Meredith Ann Pierce, *The Woman Who Loved Reindeer*, 1985
J.H. Rosny, *Quest for Fire*, 1967
    1909
William Sarabande, *Beyond the Sea of Ice*, 1987
Patricia Wrightson, *Journey Behind the Wind*, 1981
Patricia Wrightson, *The Dark Bright Water*, 1978
Patricia Wrightson, *The Ice Is Coming*, 1977

## 2171

**W. MICHAEL GEAR**

### Relic of Empire
(New York: DAW, 1992)

**Story type:** Science Fiction (Political; Space Opera)
**Series:** Forbidden Borders
**Major character(s):** Staffa kar Therma, Mercenary; Skyla Lyma, Mercenary; Sinklar Fist, Military Personnel
**Time period(s):** Indeterminate Future
**Locale(s):** Sassan Empire, Interstellar Empire/Federation; Rega, Planet—Imaginary

**Summary:** Desperately striving to avert interstellar war between the Regan and Sassan Empires, Staffa kar Therma must choose between saving the life of Skyla, his lover and second-in-command, and saving the human race. Complicating forces, including his long-lost son Sinklar, now a general in the opposing camp, work at cross purposes. Only time will tell if anyone will survive to claim victory.

**Other books you might like:**
Isaac Asimov, *Foundation and Empire*, 1952
Alfred Bester, *The Stars My Destination*, 1957
C.J. Cherryh, *Cyteen*, 1988
Donald F. Glut, *The Empire Strikes Back*, 1980
James Kahn, *Return of the Jedi*, 1983
George Lucas, *Star Wars*, 1976
Jerry Pournelle, *Falkenberg's Legion*, 1990

## 2172

**W. MICHAEL GEAR**

### Starstrike
(New York: DAW, 1990)

**Story type:** Science Fiction (First Contact; Space Opera)
**Major character(s):** Wide, Alien (Ahımsa), Leader (Overone); Sheik Dunbar, Military Personnel (major)
**Time period(s):** 21st century
**Locale(s):** Earth; Ta Ha Ak Station, Outer Space

**Summary:** Against all intersellar regulations, Earth's military, industrial and technological systems are taken over by the Ahimsa, aliens from another galaxy. They've decided to use humans to destroy the powerful, but peaceful Pashti. Believing no other option exists, the Earth's governments comply. Earth's best soldiers head into outer space.

**Other books you might like:**
Douglas Adams, *The Hitchhiker's Guide to the Galaxy*, 1980
David Brin, *Startide Rising*, 1983
Fletcher Pratt, *Invaders From Rigel*, 1960
A.E. Van Vogt, *The Battle of Forever*, 1971
John Varley, *The Ophiuchi Hotline*, 1977

## 2173

**W. MICHAEL GEAR**

### The Web of Spider
(New York: DAW Books, 1989)

**Story type:** Science Fiction (Space Opera)
**Series:** Spider
**Major character(s):** Ngen Van Chou, Leader, Revolutionary; Susan Smith Andojar, Military Personnel
**Time period(s):** Indeterminate Future

**Locale(s):** The World, Planet—Imaginary; Outer Space (Arcturus System)

**Summary:** In a galaxy convulsed by civil war, the Warriors of Spider attempt to maintain order and stop Ngen Van Chou's rebellion.

**Other books you might like:**
Roland J. Green, *Starcruiser Shenandoah*, 1989
R.M. Meluch, *War Birds*, 1989
Paul O. Williams, *The Gift of the Gorboduc Vandal*, 1989

### 2174

**JEFF GELB**, Editor
**MICHAEL GARRETT**, Co-Editor

## Deadly After Dark

(New York: Pocket, 1994)

**Story type:** Horror (Anthology; Erotic Horror)
**Series:** Hot Blood

**Summary:** The 14 stories in this book range from the non-supernatural to the supernatural in their treatment of erotic horror themes. Highlights include Lucy Taylor's ''Things of Which We Do Not Speak,'' about the horrifying memories evoked by the protagonists' rough sex play; Michael Garrett's ''Immaterial Girl,'' about a prostitute with the capacity to mold her features into every man's fantasy woman; Edo van Belkom's ''Sex Starved,'' in which an obese newlywed's appetite and sex drive become intertwined; Jack Ketchum's ''The Role,'' a tale of psychopathic dominance and imprisonment; and Bentley Little's wonderfully wacky ''The Numbers Game,'' in which a computer hacker finds the proper sequence of numbers for leaving a person sexually incapacitated. Forrest Ackerman contributes an introduction.

**Other books you might like:**
Ellen Datlow, *Alien Sex*, 1990
    editor
Ellen Datlow, *Little Deaths*, 1994
    editor

### 2175

**JEFF GELB**, Editor

## Fear Itself

(New York: Pocket, 1995)

**Story type:** Horror (Anthology)

**Summary:** Twenty-one leading authors supply stories based on the things that they fear most. The underlying fears of Jack Ketchum's ''Snakes'' and Graham Watkins' ''Here There Be Spyders'' are self-evident. Fear of modern urban life empowers Nancy Collins' ''Avenue X,'' while fear of the loss of a loved one is the inspiration for Thomas Monteleone's ''Time Enough to Sleep'' and Jeff Gelb's ''Home Again.'' Paul Kupferberg's ''Food for the Beast'' and Stephen Gresham's ''Once upon a Darkness'' deal with fears specific to horror writers: respectively, the impact of life upon the writing of horror fiction, and the impact of horror fiction life. Each author supplies a note on the basis for his or her story.

**Other books you might like:**
Peter Crowther, *Narrow Houses*, 1993
    editor
Charles L. Grant, *Fears*, 1983
    editor
Wendy Webb, *More Phobias*, 1995
    Richard Gilliam, Edward Kramer, Martin H. Greenberg, co-editors

Wendy Webb, *Phobias: Stories of Your Deepest Fears*, 1994
    Richard Gilliam, Edward Kramer, Martin H. Greenberg, co-editors

### 2176

**JEFF GELB**, Editor
**MICHAEL GARRETT**, Co-Editor

## Fear the Fever

(New York: Pocket, 1996)

**Story type:** Horror (Anthology; Erotic Horror)
**Series:** Hot Blood

**Summary:** The seventh compilation in this long-running series of erotic horror anthologies brings together 17 stories written especially for this volume. Among them are Lucy Taylor's ''The Five Percent People,'' about a menage a trois that comes to a dismal end; Graham Masterton's ''The Secret Shih Tan,'' about a legendary cookbook whose recipes for human flesh bring sexual ecstasy; Alan Brennert's ''Fantasies,'' in which a husband and wife conceive a child who is the embodiment of her father's sexual fantasies; P.D. Cacek's ''Metalica,'' concerned with a woman unhealthily obsessed with gynecological examinations; and Edward Lee and Jack Ketchum's ''Love Letters From the Rain Forest,'' in which a sexually-transmitted disease becomes a gruesome tool of revenge.

**Other books you might like:**
Nancy A. Collins, *Dark Love*, 1995
    Ed Kramer, Martin H. Greenberg, co-editors
Ellen Datlow, *Little Deaths*, 1995
    editor
John Pelan, *Darkside: Horror for the Next Millennium*, 1996
    editor
Michele Slung, *I Shudder at Your Touch*, 1991
    editor
Michele Slung, *Shudder Again*, 1993
    editor

### 2177

**JEFF GELB**, Editor
**MICHAEL GARRETT**, Co-Editor

## Hot Blood X

(New York: Pocket, 1998)

**Story type:** Horror (Anthology; Erotic Horror)
**Series:** Hot Blood

**Summary:** This anthology contains 17 tales of erotic horror, one of them a reprint. In Ramsey Campbell's ''Seductress,'' a woman avenges her son through a strange sexual masquerade. Greg Kihn's ''Olivia in the Graveyard with Pablo'' is a vampire tale, and Graham Watkin's ''Fulfillment'' the tale of a bizarre and potentially fatal alternate sex website on the Internet.

**Other books you might like:**
Nancy A. Collins, *Dark Love*, 1995
    Edward E. Kramer, Martin H. Greenberg, co-editors
Ellen Datlow, *Little Deaths*, 1995
Gardner Dozois, *Dying for It: More Erotic Tales of Unearthly Love*, 1997
    editor
Amarantha Knight, *Demon Sex*, 1998
    editor
Amarantha Knight, *Seductive Spectres*, 1996
    editor

## 2178

**JEFF GELB**
**MICHAEL GARRETT**, Co-Author

### *Hot Blood: Crimes of Passion*
(New York: Pocket, 1997)

**Story type:** Horror (Anthology; Erotic Horror)
**Series:** Hot Blood

**Summary:** Fourteen tales of erotic horror fill out the ninth volume in this long-running anthology series. Selections include Greg Kihn's "The Great White Light," in which free love and great acid introduces two young men to a bizarre counterculture cult in the 1960s; Tom Piccirilli's "Curs," which explores the sexual politics of a thankless marriage and an adulterous relationship; and Melanie Tem's "Loving Delia," in which a woman's sexual passion becomes objectified and personified. Ramsey Campbell, Lawrence Block and Brian Lumley are represented with reprinted stories.

**Other books you might like:**
Nancy A. Collins, *Dark Love*, 1995
    Edward E. Kramer and Martin H. Greenberg, co-editors
Ellen Datlow, *Alien Sex*, 1990
    editor
Ellen Datlow, *Little Deaths*, 1995
    editor
Gardner Dozois, *Dying for It: More Erotic Tales of Unearthly Love*, 1997
    editor
Michel Parry, *Devil's Kisses*, 1976
    editor
Michele Slung, *I Shudder at Your Touch*, 1993
    editor
Michele Slung, *Shudder Again*, 1995
    editor

## 2179

**JEFF GELB**
**MICHAEL GARRETT**, Co-Author

### *Hot Blood: Kiss and Kill*
(New York: Pocket, 1997)

**Story type:** Horror (Anthology; Erotic Horror)
**Series:** Hot Blood

**Summary:** Sixteen tales of erotic horror, all original to the eighth volume in this long-running series. Selections include Thomas Tessier's "La Mourante," in which a jaded man develops an insatiable passion for necrophilia; Nancy Holder's "Bonus Notches," in which the competitiveness between two sexually active women reaches to absurd heights; and Ray Garton's "Hair of the Dog," where a philandering husband's night of debauchery leads to a murder mystery with two corpses. Brian Hodge, Graham Masterton, and Gary Brandner are among the other contributors.

**Other books you might like:**
Nancy A. Collins, *Dark Love*, 1995
    Edward E. Kramer and Martin H. Greenberg, co-editors
Ellen Datlow, *Alien Sex*, 1990
    editor
Ellen Datlow, *Little Deaths*, 1995
    editor
Gardner Dozois, *Dying for It: More Erotic Tales of Unearthly Love*, 1997
    editor

Michel Parry, *Devil's Kisses*, 1976
    editor
Michele Slung, *I Shudder at Your Touch*, 1993
    editor
Michele Slung, *Shudder Again*, 1995
    editor

## 2180

**JEFF GELB**, Editor
**MICHAEL GARRETT**, Co-Editor

### *Hotter Blood: More Tales of Erotic Horror*
(New York: Pocket Books, 1990)

**Story type:** Horror (Anthology; Erotic Horror)
**Series:** Hot Blood

**Summary:** Twenty-four original short stories that deal very explicitly with sex, usually in the form of violence directed at women. New writers such as Kurt Busiek and Michael Newton appear alongside well-known authors such as Karl Edward Wagner, John Shirley, Stephen Gallagher, and Chet Williamson. Most of these stories are grim, graphic, and reactionary in their treatment of sexuality, marriage, and human relations; several are very disgusting.

**Other books you might like:**
Ellen Datlow, *Alien Sex*, 1990
Ramsey Campbell, *Scared Stiff*, 1987

## 2181

**JEFF GELB**, Editor
**MICHAEL GARRETT**, Co-Editor

### *Hottest Blood: The Ultimate in Erotic Horror*
(New York: Pocket, 1993)

**Story type:** Horror (Anthology; Erotic Horror)
**Series:** Hot Blood

**Summary:** Completing the trilogy begun with *Hot Blood* (1989) and *Hotter Blood* (1991), the editors bring together 20 original tales of erotic horror fiction. Nancy Holder's "I Hear the Mermaids Singing," about an abused woman who lives in a fantasy world to escape the harsh reality of life, and Steve and Melanie Tem's "Safe at Home," about the impact of a childhood incident of sexual abuse on the protagonist's adult life, are powerful studies of the ways in which sexuality shapes the personality, while David Schow's "Where the Heart Was" and Graham Watkins' "Hillbettys" are amusing takes on sexual anxieties. The rest of the contents are mediocre with Graham Masterton's "Sex Object," about a woman who transforms herself surgically into a pleasure-giving orifice for the benefit of her chauvinistic husband, an exploitative low point.

**Other books you might like:**
Ellen Datlow, *Alien Sex*, 1991
Michel Parry, *Devil's Kisses*, 1976
Michele Slung, *I Shudder at Your Touch*, 1991

## 2182

**JEFF GELB**, Editor
**MICHAEL GARRETT**, Co-Editor

### Seeds of Fear

(New York: Pocket, 1995)

**Story type:** Horror (Anthology)
**Series:** Hot Blood

**Summary:** This fifth volume in the Hot Blood erotic horror anthology series assembles nineteen new stories of sexual terror. Ronald Kelly's ''Scream Queen'' is concerned with a film student who discovers the horrible reality behind the sexy persona projected by an actress who specializes in horror film heroine roles. In ''Overeater's Ominous,'' Stephen George tells of women who find a way to displace the obesity that has robbed them of their sexiness onto others. Kathryn Ptacek's ''Hunger'' is about a desperate woman driven to extremes to stop her nymphomania and Edward Lee's ''Grub Girl'' about a near future where a radiation leak has produced mutants with unusual sexual proclivities. Horror film actress Brinke Stevens supplies an introduction.

**Other books you might like:**
Nancy A. Collins, *Dark Love*, 1995
    Ed Kramer and Martin H. Greenberg, co-editors
Ellen Datlow, *Little Deaths*, 1995
    editor
Michele Slung, *I Shudder at Your Touch*, 1991
    editor
Michele Slung, *Shudder Again*, 1993
    editor

## 2183

**JEFF GELB**, Editor

### Shock Rock

(New York: Pocket, 1992)

**Story type:** Horror (Anthology)

**Summary:** Twenty original stories that adapt rock music to the horror medium. Included are Stephen King's ''You Know They Got a Hell of a Band,'' about a town where all the dead rock stars go, David Schow's ''Odeed,'' about what might really happen at a concert when a band cranks the amps to 11 and starts jamming, and Patrick Gates' ''Heavy Metal,'' a limp pastiche of Edgar Allan Poe. Far too many stories involve the resurrection of dead rock stars. With an introduction by rock star Alice Cooper.

**Other books you might like:**
David J. Schow, *Silver Scream*, 1988

## 2184

**JEFF GELB**, Editor

### Shock Rock II

(New York: Pocket, 1994)

**Story type:** Horror (Anthology)

**Summary:** All 21 original stories in this compilation use the rock music scene as a vehicle for horror. Included are Bob Weinberg and Tina Jens' ''Elvis Can't Dance,'' in which The King returns from the dead to dispose of defilers of the rock 'n' roll tradition; Scott H. Urban's ''Better to Burn Out,'' about an aging rock star's psychotic final performance; Rick Hautala's ''Dead Legends,'' which tells of a strange recording studio where famous musicians play just before they die; Mike Baron's ''Oi Boy,'' in which a gypsy puts a poetically just curse on a skinhead rocker; Max Allan Collins' tongue-in-cheek vampire tale, ''Rock 'n' Roll Will Never Die''; and the editor's own tale of a nighttime disk jockey's unusual callers, ''Graveyard Shift.''

**Other books you might like:**
Paul J. McAuley, *In Dreams*, 1992
    Kim Newman, co-author
Paul M. Sammon, *The King Is Dead: Tales of Elvis Post Mortem*, 1994
    editor

## 2185

**JEFF GELB**, Editor
**MICHAEL GARRETT**, Co-Editor

### Stranger by Night

(New York: Pocket, 1995)

**Story type:** Horror (Anthology; Erotic Horror)
**Series:** Hot Blood

**Summary:** Seventeen new stories and one reprint comprise the contents of this installment in the ''Hot Blood'' erotic horror anthology series. In the reprint, Brian Lumley's ''Back Row,'' a patron of a movie theater discovers there is something more gruesome than necking going on between a man and woman with seats near him. Tom Piccirilli's ''Take It as It Comes'' presents a bizarre sexual revenge scenario, and Ramsey Campbell's ''The Body in the Window'' features an anti-smut crusader who finds the tables strangely turned on him when he trolls through the red light district of Amsterdam. In Christa Faust's ''Skin Deep,'' a sex club habitue's tattoos develop a mind of their own, and in Lucy Taylor's ''Male-Call,'' a woman finds a sexual surrogate to get revenge upon her abusive husband.

**Other books you might like:**
Nancy A. Collins, *Dark Love*, 1995
    Ed Kramer and Martin H. Greenberg, co-editors
Ellen Datlow, *Little Deaths*, 1995
    editor
Michele Slung, *I Shudder at Your Touch*,
    editor
Michele Slung, *Shudder Again*, 1993
    editor

## 2186

**PETER GELMAN**

### Flying Saucers over Hennepin

(San Francisco, California: Permeable Press, 1997)

**Story type:** Fantasy (Contemporary Realism; Literary)
**Major character(s):** Zenobia Olson, Writer; I, Writer; Columbus Binder, Businessman (furrier)
**Time period(s):** 1980s (1988)
**Locale(s):** Minneapolis, Minnesota

**Summary:** Winner of the Hayloft Grant, Zenobia Olson circulates at the Waltz-a-Rama. The writer notices strange behavior which seems to continue. Columbus Binder spent time alone with Erika Swanson before jumping off the bridge. Perhaps the aliens from the Fornax Cluster induce the visions and doppelgangers seen since the anarchist uprising.

**Other books you might like:**
William Borden, *Superstoe*, 1968

Jesse Browner, *Conglomeros*, 1992
Mark Leyner, *My Cousin, My Gastroenterologist*, 1990
Haruki Murakami, *Hard-Boiled Wonderland and the End of the World*, 1991
Milorad Pavic, *Landscape Painted with Tea*, 1990
Tom Robbins, *Another Roadside Attraction*, 1971

## 2187

### DAVID GEMMELL

## Dark Prince

(New York: Ballantine Del Rey, 1993)

**Story type:** Fantasy (Historical)
**Series:** Macedon
**Major character(s):** Parmenion, Warrior; Derae, Psychic (seer); Alexander the Great, Historical Figure
**Time period(s):** 4th century B.C.
**Locale(s):** Macedonia; Middle East

**Summary:** Parmenion diffuses the attack on Alexander sufficiently to save him but not free him from the forces of darkness. In another world populated by characters from Greek legend, a demon king plots to capture Alexander and gain immortality while Parmenion and Derae work to free Alexander to become the legendary Golden Child. U.K. edition published 1991.

**Other books you might like:**
Nikos Kazantzakis, *Alexander the Great*, 1982
Edison Marshall, *Conqueror*, 1962
Mary Renault, *Fire From Heaven*, 1969
Judith Tarr, *Lord of the Two Lands*, 1993
Gene Wolfe, *Soldier of Arete*, 1989
Gene Wolfe, *Soldier of the Mist*, 1986

## 2188

### DAVID GEMMELL

## Ghost King

(New York: Ballantine Del Rey, 1996)

**Story type:** Fantasy (Legend; Sword and Sorcery)
**Series:** Stones of Power
**Major character(s):** Thuro "Uther Pendragon", Royalty, Orphan; Culain lach Feragh, Immortal, Warrior; Laitha "Gian Avur", Orphan, Young Woman
**Time period(s):** 6th century
**Locale(s):** England (Britain); Pinrae, Fictional Country

**Summary:** Fleeing his father's assassins, Thuro finds refuge in the mountains with Laitha and her guardian, Culain, who teaches the boy to use a sword. But in order to take his rightful place as High King and defeat the Brigantes and Saxons who have attacked his land, Thuro must first travel through the land of the Mist to reclaim his father's magical sword and find a lost army.

**Other books you might like:**
Marion Zimmer Bradley, *The Mists of Avalon*, 1983
C.J. Cherryh, *The Paladin*, 1988
David Drake, *Ranks of Bronze*, 1986
Parke Godwin, *Firelord*, 1980
Katherine Kurtz, *Deryni Rising*, 1970
Rosemary Sutcliff, *Sword at Sunset*, 1963
T.H. White, *The Once and Future King*, 1958

## 2189

### DAVID GEMMELL

## Lion of Macedon

(New York: Ballantine Del Rey, 1992)

**Story type:** Fantasy (Historical; Sword and Sorcery)
**Series:** Macedon
**Major character(s):** Parmenion, Mercenary, Sports Figure (runner); Tamis, Psychic (seer); Philip of Macedon, Historical Figure, Leader
**Time period(s):** 4th century B.C.
**Locale(s):** Sparta, Greece; Thebes, Greece; Pella, Greece (ancient Macedonia)

**Summary:** Of mixed Spartan and Macedonian parentage, Parmenion represents civilization's best hope for preventing the Dark One from taking over ancient Greece. After Tamis uses knowledge gained in a vision to identify Parmenion and arranges for him to acquire the needed skills, he advances to mercenary general and plays a pivotal role in the battle between Chaos and Light.

**Other books you might like:**
Frans G. Bengtsson, *The Long Ships*, 1954
Tom Holt, *Goatsong*, 1990
Tom Holt, *The Walled Orchard*, 1991
Gene Wolfe, *Soldier of Arete*, 1989
Gene Wolfe, *Soldier of the Mist*, 1986

## 2190

### DAVID GEMMELL

## Morningstar

(New York: Ballantine Del Rey, 1993)

**Story type:** Fantasy (Adventure)
**Major character(s):** Jarek Mace, Criminal, Hero; Owen Odell, Minstrel (bard)
**Time period(s):** Indeterminate
**Locale(s):** Highland, Fictional Country

**Summary:** When Jarek Mace inadvertently aids the Highland people, he finds himself hailed as the legendary hero, Morningstar, returned to his people. Known to his companion, Owen Odell, as an outlaw, bandit and heartless thief, Jarek Mace grabs the opportunity to change his persona and income as he and his companions assume the hero's mantle. A retelling of the Robin Hood tale utilizing magical elements.

**Other books you might like:**
Glen Cook, *The Black Company*, 1984
David Eddings, *Pawn of Prophecy*, 1982
Parke Godwin, *Robin and the King*, 1993
Parke Godwin, *Sherwood*, 1991
Robert Jordan, *The Eye of the World*, 1989
Fritz Leiber, *Two Sought Adventure: Exploits of Fafhrd and the Gray Mouser*, 1957

## 2191

### DAVID GEMMELL

## Wolf in Shadow

(New York: Ballantine Del Rey, 1997)

**Story type:** Science Fiction (Post-Holocaust; Science Fantasy)
**Series:** Stones of Power

**Major character(s):** Jon Shannow, Traveler, Warrior; Batik, Religious (satanist), Fugitive; Abaddon, Immortal, Ruler
**Time period(s):** Indeterminate Future
**Locale(s):** Rivervale, Fictional City; New Babylon, Fictional City

**Summary:** Centuries after civilization falls to natural catastrophe, humanity reestablishes itself. A wanderer in search of lost Jerusalem, Jon Shannow falls in with a band of pioneers looking for new land in a once-radioactive waste. Instead, they find a satanic empire and the beginnings of a new armageddon. First published in the United States as *The Jerusalem Man* (1987).

**Other books you might like:**
Orson Scott Card, *Seventh Son*, 1987
Glen Cook, *The Black Company*, 1984
David Drake, *Old Nathan*, 1991
Stephen King, *The Dark Tower: The Gunslinger*, 1982
George R.R. Martin, *Fevre Dream*, 1982

**2192**
GARY GENTILE

## Dragons Past
(New York: Ace, 1990)

**Story type:** Science Fiction (Invasion of Earth; Time Travel)
**Series:** Time for Dragons
**Major character(s):** Scott, Revolutionary; Death Wind, Revolutionary; Doc, Revolutionary
**Time period(s):** Indeterminate Future; Indeterminate Past (Cretaceous Period)
**Locale(s):** Earth

**Summary:** The battle against the alien invaders called dragons was won, but the war continues. The dragons have returned and captured a group of rebels for their slave pens. The rebels use the dragons' time machinery to escape into the Cretaceous Period. Then they search out and destroy the dragons' main base in hopes of stopping the invasion at its source.

**Other books you might like:**
Gordon R. Dickson, *Way of the Pilgrim*, 1987
Clifford D. Simak, *Mastodonia*, 1978
Jack Vance, *Emphyrio*, 1969
H.G. Wells, *The War of the Worlds*, 1898

**2193**
GARY GENTILE

## A Time for Dragons
(New York: Ace, 1989)

**Story type:** Science Fiction (Military)
**Major character(s):** Rusty, Teenager, Refugee; Scott, Teenager, Refugee
**Time period(s):** 21st century
**Locale(s):** Earth

**Summary:** A century after the collapse of human civilization, hostile reptilian aliens prowl the surface of the Earth, killing any humans with whom they come in contact. The few humans who remain alive fight back with whatever weapons they can muster.

**Other books you might like:**
Rob Chilson, *Men Like Rats*, 1989
John Dalmas, *The Lizard War*, 1989
Jack Vance, *The Dragon Masters*, 1963
F. Paul Wilson, *The Tery*, 1989

**2194**
MARY GENTLE

## Ancient Light
(New York: New American Library, 1989)

**Story type:** Science Fiction (First Contact)
**Major character(s):** Lynne De Lisle Christie, Diplomat; Doug Clifford, Diplomat
**Time period(s):** 21st century
**Locale(s):** Orthe, Planet—Imaginary

**Summary:** Lynne Christie returns to the devastated planet of Orthe after an absence of eight years to find it changed drastically by the recent presence of human beings. Orthe's high civilization was destroyed in a cataclysmic war some two thousand years ago, but it is rumored that the super weapons used in that war still exist on the planet. The Panoceania Company is willing to stop at nothing, even the destruction of Orthe's fragile ecosystem, to find them.

**Other books you might like:**
C.J. Cherryh, *Cuckoo's Egg*, 1985
C.J. Cherryh, *The Faded Sun: Kesrith*, 1978
C.J. Cherryh, *The Faded Sun: Kutath*, 1980
C.J. Cherryh, *The Faded Sun: Shon'Jir*, 1979
Frank Herbert, *Dune*, 1965
Ursula K. Le Guin, *The Left Hand of Darkness*, 1969

**2195**
MARY GENTLE

## The Architecture of Desire
(New York: Roc, 1993)

**Story type:** Fantasy (Political; Historical)
**Major character(s):** Valentine White Crow, Magician (master physician), Military Personnel (scholar-soldier), Spouse (of Lord-Architect Casaubon); Lord-Architect Casaubon, Magician, Spouse (White Crow's), Nobleman; Pollexfen Calmady, Gentleman, Mercenary
**Time period(s):** Indeterminate Past (17th century equivalent)
**Locale(s):** Alternate Earth (London)

**Summary:** Years after the overthrow of the Gods and establishment of human rule, repeated building disasters cause Protector-General Olivia to call for aid from Lord-Architect Casaubon to forward her goal of creating a powerful magical edifice. Unenthusiastic about returning to London, White Crow experiences a crisis of her convictions after Casaubon's friend, Pollexfen Calmady, admits raping White Crow's acquaintance. Sequel to *Rats and Gargoyles*.

**Other books you might like:**
Lois McMaster Bujold, *The Spirit Ring*, 1992
Mercedes Lackey, *The Robin and the Kestrel*, 1993
R.A. MacAvoy, *The Belly of the Wolf*, 1994
Elizabeth Moon, *Sheepfarmer's Daughter*, 1988
Paula Volsky, *Illusion*, 1992
Martha Wells, *The Element of Fire*, 1993

**2196**
MARY GENTLE

## Rats and Gargoyles
(New York: Roc, 1990)

**Story type:** Fantasy (Political; Religious)

**Major character(s):** Prince Lucas, Royalty, Thief; Valentine White Crow, Magician, Military Personnel (scholar-soldier); Lord-Architect Casaubon, Nobleman, Magician
**Time period(s):** Indeterminate Past
**Locale(s):** Alternate Earth

**Summary:** An enslaved world populace struggles to throw off a tyrannical pantheon of 36 actual gods (the "Gargoyles") and their overseer caste of giant, humanoid rats. Events are set in motion when White Crow, Scholar-Soldier of the magisterial secret order of the Invisible College, magically paints secret signs upon the face of the moon with her own blood, signalling to the world that the struggle is on. But there remains the need to find someone who can read the occult message and to find a way to prevail against the gods.

**Other books you might like:**
Eleanor Arnason, *To the Resurrection Station*, 1986
Margot Benary-Isbert, *The Wicked Enchantment*, 1955
Robert A. Heinlein, *The Moon Is a Harsh Mistress*, 1966
P.C. Hodgell, *God Stalk*, 1982
James Morrow, *Only Begotten Daughter*, 1990
Roger Zelazny, *Lord of Light*, 1967

---

**2197**

STEPHEN R. GEORGE

## Bloody Valentine

(New York: Zebra, 1994)

**Story type:** Horror (Serial Killer)
**Major character(s):** Jo Granville, Artist (illustrator); Ryan Locke, Police Officer (sheriff); Gabby Granville, Child
**Time period(s):** 1990s (1994)
**Locale(s):** Halkirk, Minnesota

**Summary:** During a college psychology experiment, five college students imagined Joshua Valentine, the ideal serial killer—who became less than ideal when he suddenly materialized and murdered a child. Ten years later, someone who signs himself Joshua Valentine begins cutting a bloody swath through Minnesota, and the authorities must determine why he has resurfaced and what he hopes to accomplish.

**Other books you might like:**
Ramsey Campbell, *Incarnate*, 1983
Charles L. Grant, *The Pet*, 1986
John R. Maxim, *Abel/Baker/Charley*, 1983

---

**2198**

STEPHEN R. GEORGE

## Dark Reunion

(New York: Zebra, 1990)

**Story type:** Horror (Occult)
**Major character(s):** Peter Willson, Teenager; Andrea Willson, Real Estate Agent, Step-Parent (Peter's); Matthew Willson, Police Officer, Parent (Peter's)
**Time period(s):** 1990s (1990)
**Locale(s):** Marissa, Minnesota (small town near Minneapolis)

**Summary:** Matthew Willson moves his family from Minneapolis back to his hometown of Marissa, unaware that in doing so he is exposing them to terrible danger. For Marissa is the home of the ancient people of The Craft, among whom an evil subgroup has begun clamoring for resurgence. Soon Matthew's son Peter falls under the influence of Longshadow, the sentient mist that leads the cultists.

**Other books you might like:**
Margaret Falk, *Darkscope*, 1990
Morgan Fields, *Shaman Woods*, 1990
Diane Guest, *Lullaby*, 1990

---

**2199**

STEPHEN R. GEORGE

## Deadly Vengeance

(New York: Zebra, 1993)

**Story type:** Horror (Supernatural Vengeance)
**Major character(s):** Alan Shea, Child; Cobalt, Animal (dog); Bill Shea, Writer (Alan's father)
**Time period(s):** 1990s (1993)
**Locale(s):** Laidlaw, Minnesota

**Summary:** Alan Shea is threatened with physical harm by the boys who killed his brother if he tells on them. Alan's new dog, Cobalt, a former laboratory animal, is telepathically sensitive to Alan's childish rage and begins systematically killing the boys responsible.

**Other books you might like:**
Stephen King, *Cujo*, 1981
John Stchur, *Paddywhack*, 1989
Raymond Van Over, *Whisper*, 1991

---

**2200**

STEPHEN R. GEORGE

## The Forgotten

(New York: Zebra, 1991)

**Story type:** Horror (Psychological Suspense)
**Major character(s):** Richard Sullivan, Guard (security guard at the Citadel); Mark Sullivan, Child; Hillary "Hilly" Walker, Writer
**Time period(s):** 1990s
**Locale(s):** Minneapolis, Minnesota

**Summary:** Ed, a former abused child who has become a feral man living in the sewer system of Minneapolis, befriends Mark Sullivan, the only child living in the maximum security living complex known as the Citadel. When Mark befriends the new tenant Hilly Walker, Ed sees her as competition who must be destroyed.

**Other books you might like:**
Joseph A. Citro, *The Unseen*, 1990
John Driver, *The Hunger of the Beast*, 1991
Susan Kay, *Phantom*, 1991

---

**2201**

STEPHEN R. GEORGE

## Grandma's Little Darling

(New York: Zebra, 1990)

**Story type:** Horror (Possession)
**Major character(s):** Nora Harris, Orphan; Cheryl Gibson, Child-Care Giver; Grandma Johnson, Aged Person
**Time period(s):** 1990s (1990)
**Locale(s):** Minneapolis, Minnesota

**Summary:** Faced with the prospect of being sent to a state orphanage, chronically unplaceable orphan Nora Harris tries desperately to fit in with her new foster family, the Johnsons, unaware that the immortal spirit inhabiting Grandma Johnson's body plans to take over hers next.

**Other books you might like:**
Ramsey Campbell, *The Influence*, 1988
Ramsey Campbell, *To Wake the Dead*, 1980
   a.k.a. The Parasite
K.W. Jeter, *Soul Eater*, 1983

## 2202

### STEPHEN R. GEORGE

## *Near Dead*

(New York: Zebra, 1992)

**Story type:** Horror (Occult)
**Major character(s):** Taylor Holdman, Businessman; Marilyn Briggs, Psychic (medium); Wayne Semmlar, Mechanic, Serial Killer
**Time period(s):** 1990s
**Locale(s):** Minneapolis, Minnesota

**Summary:** The near-dead are those mortals whom the spirits of the dead find easy to communicate with. Taylor Holdman finds he must classify himself among them when the spirits of his butchered wife and child appear to him and enjoin him to seek out their murderer and put an end to the string of murders by which the murderer hopes to be accepted into the demon world.

**Other books you might like:**
John Farris, *The Axman Cometh*, 1989
Dean R. Koontz, *Hideaway*, 1992

## 2203

### STEPHEN R. GEORGE

## *Nightscape*

(New York: Zebra, 1992)

**Story type:** Horror (Child-in-Peril)
**Major character(s):** Bonnie Laine, Parent; Evan Laine, Child (8-year-old boy); Shep Thomas, Police Officer (former Chicago cop)
**Time period(s):** 1990s (1992)
**Locale(s):** Minneapolis, Minnesota

**Summary:** Shep Laine joins forces with Bonnie Laine to protect her son Evan from "the creche," a cult of supernaturally-endowed beings who have chosen the boy to become their future leader.

**Other books you might like:**
Leigh Clark, *The Feeding*, 1992
Pat Graversen, *The Fagin*, 1982
Dean R. Koontz, *The Servants of Twilight*, 1984

## 2204

### STEPHEN R. GEORGE

## *Torment*

(New York: Zebra, 1994)

**Story type:** Horror (Possession)
**Major character(s):** Melissa Woodrow, Child (12 year old), Musician; April Kostanuik, Child (12 year old), Musician; John Woodrow, Architect
**Time period(s):** 1990s (1994)
**Locale(s):** Minneapolis, Minnesota

**Summary:** Shortly after 12-year-old piano virtuoso April Kostanuik is killed in a car accident, another Minneapolis child, Melissa Woodrow, finds she is endowed with the same musical and mathematical abilities as April. Melissa's parents accept her new abilities as the flowering of her God-given talents—only to realize too late that April's spirit is embarked on a wholesale takeover and extirpation of their daughter's personality.

**Other books you might like:**
Clifford Mohr, *Requiem*, 1992
Fred Mustard Stewart, *The Mephisto Waltz*, 1969
Ramona Stewart, *The Possession of Joel Delaney*, 1970

## 2205

### TESS GERRITSEN

## *Bloodstream*

(New York: Pocket, 1998)

**Story type:** Horror (Child-in-Peril)
**Major character(s):** Claire Elliott, Doctor; Noah Elliott, Teenager (Claire's son)
**Time period(s):** 1990s (1998)
**Locale(s):** Tranquility, Maine

**Summary:** Outbreaks of violence among the children of Tranquility every half century lead Doctor Claire Elliot to investigate Locust Lake, a popular swimming hole for the children. Claire's discovery of a disgusting parasite that inhabits the lake and infects the brain is dismissed by locals, even as episodes of violence grow more terrifying and threaten Claire herself.

**Other books you might like:**
Gary Goshgarian, *Rough Beast*, 1995
Andrew Neiderman, *Perfect Little Angels*, 1989
John Saul, *Creature*, 1990
John Whitman, *Disturbing Behavior*, 1998

## 2206

### TESS GERRITSEN

## *Life Support*

(New York: Pocket, 1997)

**Story type:** Horror (Mystery)
**Major character(s):** Toby Harper, Doctor (emergency room); Carl Wallenberg, Doctor (endocrinologist); Daniel Dvorak, Doctor (medical examiner)
**Time period(s):** 1990s (1997)
**Locale(s):** Boston, Massachusetts

**Summary:** Physician Toby Harper investigates when two patients from the upscale Brant Hill retirement home show up at her hospital with symptoms that suggest fatal cases of Creutzfeldt-Jakob Disease. Her suspicion that the patients contracted the disease from infected tissue used in rejuvenation experiments is met with swift reprisal by greedy conspirators, who attempt to ruin her credibility and her life.

**Other books you might like:**
Robin Cook, *Coma*, 1977
Michael Crichton, *The Terminal Man*, 1972
Patrick Lynch, *Omega*, 1997
Harry Stein, *Infinity's Child*, 1997
F. Paul Wilson, *The Select*, 1994

## 2207

**DAVID GERROLD**

### A Covenant of Justice

(New York: Bantam Spectra, 1994)

**Story type:** Science Fiction (Genetic Manipulation; Horror)
**Major character(s):** Lady Zillabar, Noblewoman, Vampire (Phaester); Neena Linn-Campbell, Spaceship Captain, Rebel; Harry Mertz, Immortal, Judge
**Time period(s):** Indeterminate Future
**Locale(s):** Burihatin-14, Planet—Imaginary; Thoska-Roole, Planet—Imaginary

**Summary:** Holding Lady Zillabar as a hostage, Finn, Sawyer and their friends travel to Burihatin-14, where they seek the TimeBinder to thwart Lord d'Vashti from abolishing the law against eating sentient beings. On a further voyage to Thoska-Roole, Lady Zillabar agrees to love and respect lesser beings, but turns on them during an attempted coup by d'Vashti. Sequel to *Under the Eye of God.*

**Other books you might like:**
C.J. Cherryh, *Voyager in Night,* 1984
Tanith Lee, *Sabella: Or, The Blood Stone,* 1980
Sheri S. Tepper, *Grass,* 1989
Jack Vance, *The Brave Free Men,* 1973

## 2208

**DAVID GERROLD**

### The Man Who Folded Himself

(New York: Bantam Spectra, 1991)

**Story type:** Science Fiction (Time Travel)
**Major character(s):** Daniel Jamieson Eakins, Time Traveler; Diane Jane Eakins, Time Traveler
**Time period(s):** 1970s (1975)
**Locale(s):** Los Angeles, California

**Summary:** Upon the death of his Uncle Jim, Danny Eakins inherits a time belt which allows him to get rich quick and travel unlimitedly through time. Upon meeting himself over and over in both male and female form, he learns that he is the sole occupant of his immediate universe; even his Uncle Jim is him, grown old. This reissue incorporates minor changes by the author to the original 1973 edition's text.

**Other books you might like:**
Douglas Adams, *The Hitchhiker's Guide to the Galaxy,* 1980
James Blish, *The Triumph of Time,* 1958
Jack L. Chalker, *Downtiming the Night Side,* 1985
Ken Grimwood, *Replay,* 1987
Michael P. Kube-McDowell, *Alternities,* 1988

## 2209

**DAVID GERROLD**

### The Middle of Nowhere

(New York: Bantam Spectra, 1995)

**Story type:** Science Fiction (Military; Adventure)
**Major character(s):** Robert Gatineau, Spaceman; Jonathan Thomas Korie, Spaceship Captain (commander); Brik, Genetically Altered Being (Morthan Tyger)
**Locale(s):** LS-1187 Star Wolf, Spaceship

**Summary:** Gatineau, the newest member of the crew, gets initiated into the Order of the Mobius Wrench while everyone onboard

attempts to decontaminate, repair, and resupply their sabotaged vessel. Unfortunately, the defeated saboteur left behind a space pixie who continues the sabotage. The *Star Wolf* can't rejoin the fleet or even dock at a repair facility until it eliminates the imp, an almost impossible task. Sequel to *Voyage of the Star Wolf.*

**Other books you might like:**
Alfred Bester, *The Stars My Destination,* 1956
Lois McMaster Bujold, *Shards of Honor,* 1986
Stephen Goldin, *Jade Darcy and the Affair of Honor,* 1988
   Mary Mason, co-author
George Turner, *Genetic Soldier,* 1994
David Weber, *Path of the Fury,* 1992

## 2210

**DAVID GERROLD**

### A Rage for Revenge

(New York: Bantam Spectra, 1989)

**Story type:** Science Fiction (Invasion of Earth)
**Series:** War Against the Chtorr
**Major character(s):** James Edward McCarthy, Military Personnel
**Locale(s):** United States

**Summary:** Alien worms continue their devastation of the Earth. McCarthy fights feverishly against them, gradually learning more about their complex ecosystem, but still unsure of whether or not they are intelligent. As he learns more about the Chtorr, McCarthy also learns about himself.

**Other books you might like:**
Harry Harrison, *Deathworld,* 1960
Robert A. Heinlein, *Starship Troopers,* 1959
Larry Niven, *The Legacy of Heorot,* 1987
   Jerry Pournelle, and Steven Barnes, co-authors

## 2211

**DAVID GERROLD**

### A Season for Slaughter

(New York: Bantam Spectra, 1993)

**Story type:** Science Fiction (Military; Invasion of Earth)
**Series:** War Against the Chtorr
**Major character(s):** James Edward McCarthy, Military Personnel; Elizabeth "Lizard" Tirelli, Military Personnel
**Time period(s):** 21st century
**Locale(s):** United States; Brazil

**Summary:** Jim McCarthy quits, bothered by the incompetence of allied forces fighting the Chtorr. Long presumed dead, General Ira Wallachstein persuades McCarthy to stay and fight, utilizing McCarthy's legendary intuition concerning the Chtorr. After observing captured humans slowly transforming into Chtorrian beings, they mount a rescue operation.

**Other books you might like:**
Roger MacBride Allen, *Rogue Powers,* 1986
Robert Asprin, *The Bug Wars,* 1979
Octavia E. Butler, *Dawn,* 1987
Stephen Goldin, *The Eternity Brigade,* 1980
Joe Haldeman, *The Forever War,* 1975
Robert A. Heinlein, *The Puppet Masters,* 1951
Robert A. Heinlein, *Starship Troopers,* 1959
Jack Lovejoy, *The Hunters,* 1982
Larry Niven, *The Legacy of Heorot,* 1987
   Jerry Pournelle, Steven Barnes, co-authors

Timothy Zahn, *The Blackcollar*, 1983

---

**2212**

**DAVID GERROLD**

### Voyage of the Star Wolf

(New York: Bantam Spectra, 1990)

**Story type:** Science Fiction (Military)
**Major character(s):** Jonathan Thomas Korie, Military Personnel (lieutenant commander); Hardesty, Spaceship Captain; Harlie, Artificial Intelligence
**Time period(s):** 24th century
**Locale(s):** Outer Space

**Summary:** After leading his starship home following a defeat by the enemy Morthan, J.T. Korie is made a scapegoat and sent out under the sadistic Captain Hardesty to rescue the Burke which turns out to be a trap set up by a Morthan Assassin. He finally saves the ship, but Harlie, the computer, finds it was all a set-up.

**Other books you might like:**
Piers Anthony, *Bio of a Space Tyrant*, 1984
Lois McMaster Bujold, *The Vor Game*, 1990
Robert Chase, *The Game of Fox and Lion*, 1986
Timothy Zahn, *The Blackcollar*, 1983
Timothy Zahn, *Cobra*, 1985

---

**2213**

**MARK S. GESTON**

### Mirror to the Sky

(New York: Morrow, 1992)

**Story type:** Science Fiction (Arts; Invasion of Earth)
**Major character(s):** Rane, Artist, Alien; Andrew Cavan, Government Official
**Time period(s):** 21st century
**Locale(s):** Washington, District of Columbia; Kansas

**Summary:** The aliens brought humanity their advanced solutions to Earth's problems as they searched the galaxy, hoping to meet their prophecied fate as far as possible from their home planet. They also brought examples of their remarkable religious icons, paintings which have a deeply compulsive effect on some people. As they arrange to display more paintings on Earth, a terrorist attack convinces most aliens to leave the Earth, taking some humans with them. The aliens return when they discover they have unintentionally left an original icon on Earth.

**Other books you might like:**
Octavia E. Butler, *Adulthood Rites*, 1988
Octavia E. Butler, *Dawn*, 1987
Octavia E. Butler, *Imago*, 1989
Robert Reed, *Down the Bright Way*, 1991
Walter Jon Williams, *Aristoi*, 1992

---

**2214**

**AMITAV GHOSH**

### The Calcutta Chromosome

(New York: Avon, 1996)

**Story type:** Horror (Mystery)
**Major character(s):** Antar, Computer Expert (Data analyst); L. Murugan, Computer Expert (Data analyst); Urmila, Journalist

**Time period(s):** 1990s (1995)
**Locale(s):** New York, New York; Calcutta, India

**Summary:** Antar, a data programmer and analyst for the nonprofit global health consulting agency Lifewatch, traces a glitch on his computer program to L. Murugan, a colleague who disappeared in 1995 while researching inconsistencies in the Ronald Ross's study of malaria in 1898. His exploration uncovers clues to a global, and possibly cosmic conspiracy, that is directing humanity to a foreordained destiny. First published in India in 1995.

**Other books you might like:**
Clive Barker, *The Great and Secret Show*, 1989
Umberto Eco, *Foucault's Pendulum*, 1989
Theodore Roszak, *Flicker*, 1991

---

**2215**

**EDWARD GIBSON**

### In the Wrong Hands

(New York: Bantam Spectra, 1992)

**Story type:** Science Fiction (Genetic Manipulation; Political)
**Major character(s):** Joseph "Joe" Z. Rebello, Spaceman, Military Personnel; Thaddaios "Wolf" Alexandru Wojciechowski, Scientist; Otto Stark, Clone
**Time period(s):** 2030s (2039)
**Locale(s):** LB-13, Montenegro; Equality, Space Station

**Summary:** Joe believes PRECISE, run by Wolf, caused the "accidental" deaths of his crewmates. Wolf, crippled by a prenatal virus, develops the "perfect" human which he intends will replace all humanity, creating perfect equality.

**Other books you might like:**
Stephen Baxter, *Raft*, 1991
Octavia E. Butler, *Dawn*, 1987
Dave Duncan, *Hero*, 1991
Thomas A. Easton, *Sparrowhawk*, 1990
Edward M. Lerner, *Probe*, 1991
George Orwell, *1984*, 1949

---

**2216**

**EDWARD GIBSON**

### Reach

(New York: Doubleday Foundation, 1989)

**Story type:** Science Fiction (First Contact)
**Major character(s):** Jake Ryder, Astronaut; Joseph "Speed" Spencer, Astronaut
**Time period(s):** 21st century
**Locale(s):** Earth; *Wayfarer 1*, Spaceship; *Wayfarer 2*, Spaceship

**Summary:** After a mysterious object is detected approaching the solar system, a series of unmanned and manned probes is sent to examine it with disastrous results. Jake Ryder, captain of *Wayfarer 2*, is determined that his mission will be different and that he will get to the bottom of whatever alien menace awaits out beyond Pluto.

**Other books you might like:**
Gregory Benford, *Across the Sea of Suns*, 1984
Gregory Benford, *Heart of the Comet*, 1986
David Brin, co-author
Gregory Benford, *In the Ocean of Night*, 1977
Arthur C. Clarke, *Rama II*, 1989
Arthur C. Clarke, *Rendezvous with Rama*, 1973
Ted Reynolds, *The Tides of God*, 1989
David Alexander Smith, *Rendezvous*, 1988

## 2217

**WILLIAM GIBSON**
**BRUCE STERLING**, Co-Author

### The Difference Engine

(New York: Bantam Spectra, 1991)

**Story type:** Science Fiction (Alternate Universe; Cyberpunk)
**Major character(s):** Edward Mallory, Scientist; Sybil Gerard, Prostitute; Ada Byron, Scientist
**Time period(s):** 1850s (1855)
**Locale(s):** London, England

**Summary:** Charles Babbage has perfected his Analytical Engine. The computer age has arrived a century ahead of time in an England ruled by scientists and industrialists. The characters are drawn into a conspiracy linking Great Britain with the France of Louis Napolean and the Manhattan Commune of Karl Marx over a mysterious program called the Modus.

**Other books you might like:**
Michael Flynn, *The Country of the Blind*, 1990
Randall Garrett, *Too Many Magicians*, 1967
A.E. Van Vogt, *Null-A Three*, 1985
A.E. Van Vogt, *The Players of Null-A*, 1966
A.E. Van Vogt, *The World of Null-A*, 1950

## 2218

**WILLIAM GIBSON**

### Idoru

(New York: Putnam, 1996)

**Story type:** Science Fiction (Cyberpunk)
**Series:** Virtual Light
**Major character(s):** Colin Laney, Consultant, Researcher; Chia McKenzie, Teenager, Investigator; Rei Toei, Entertainer, Artificial Intelligence
**Time period(s):** 21st century
**Locale(s):** Tokyo, Japan

**Summary:** Colin Laney predicts trends. Chia McKenzie idolizes Rez, a hugely popular singer who plans, much to Chia's horror, to marry the virtual entertainer Rei Toei. Their paths collide in 21st century Tokyo, where image rules, substance changes its nature, and the fate of profitable entertainers proves deadly.

**Other books you might like:**
Pat Cadigan, *Synners*, 1991
Paul J. McAuley, *Fairyland*, 1996
Ian McDonald, *Terminal Cafe*, 1994
Richard Paul Russo, *Destroying Angel*, 1992
John Varley, *Steel Beach*, 1992

## 2219

**WILLIAM GIBSON**

### Virtual Light

(New York: Bantam Spectra, 1993)

**Story type:** Science Fiction (Cyberpunk; Disaster)
**Major character(s):** Berry Rydell, Police Officer (rentacop), Bounty Hunter; Chevette, Postal Worker (bicycle messenger), Fugitive; Skinner, Aged Person
**Time period(s):** 2000s (2005)
**Locale(s):** Los Angeles, California; San Francisco, California

**Summary:** When Chevette steals a pair of sunglasses on impulse, very thorough people soon pursue, forcing her to flee with the help of a burned-out rentacop. The sunglasses prove the key to a future even more unplesant than the one the characters already inhabit.

**Other books you might like:**
Pat Cadigan, *Synners*, 1991
Jonathan Littell, *Bad Voltage*, 1989
Pat Murphy, *The City, Not Long After*, 1989
Richard Paul Russo, *Destroying Angel*, 1992
Neal Stephenson, *Snow Crash*, 1992

## 2220

**JOHN GIDEON**

### Golden Eyes

(New York: Berkley, 1994)

**Story type:** Horror (Vampire Story)
**Major character(s):** Mark Lansen, Professor (of history); Clovis Gersten, Actor, Vampire; Tressa Downey, Administrator (courtroom administrator)
**Time period(s):** 1980s (1988)
**Locale(s):** Oldenburg, Oregon

**Summary:** Pulled back to his adoptive family's hometown to write a local history, Mark Lansen discovers the truth about the vampire scourge that has taken hold of the town, and the secret of his true heritage that links him to it.

**Other books you might like:**
Charles L. Grant, *The Soft Whisper of the Dead*, 1982
Stephen King, *Salem's Lot*, 1975
Richard Laymon, *The Stake*, 1991
Tanith Lee, *Dark Dance*, 1992
Bentley Little, *The Summoning*, 1993

## 2221

**JOHN GIDEON**

### Greely's Cove

(New York: Jove, 1991)

**Story type:** Horror (Small Town Horror)
**Major character(s):** Carl Trosper, Businessman; Stu Bromton, Police Officer; Hadrian Craslowe, Psychologist (child psychologist)
**Time period(s):** 1990s
**Locale(s):** Greely's Cove, Washington

**Summary:** Summoned back to Greely's Cove by the death of his ex-wife and a sense of responsibility for his autistic genius son, Carl Trosper uncovers a rash of mysterious disappearances among the townspeople, some of whom return as festering apparitions to their friends and relatives to lure them to "The Feast" being sponsored by "Giver of Dreams," an ungodly monster who appears to reside on the estate of the doctor who has helped rehabilitate Carl's son.

**Other books you might like:**
Al Sarrantonio, *October*, 1990

## 2222

**JOHN GIDEON** (Pseudonym of Lonn Hoklin)

### Kindred

(New York: Jove, 1996)

**Story type:** Horror (Occult)

**Major character(s):** Lewis Kindred, Veteran (Vietnam); Cartee Gamaliel, Investigator (interrogator); Josh Nickerson, Teenager

**Time period(s):** 1990s (1992)

**Locale(s):** Portland, Oregon; Cu Chi, Vietnam

**Summary:** During the Vietnam war Lieutenant Lewis Kindred resisted the supernatural powers offered to him by a flesh-eating demon who masqueraded as a soldier. Back home in the United States, Lewis discovers that the demon is still hoping to recruit him two decades after their first encounter. He will need the assistance of his surviving war buddies to help put a stop to the creature's bloody spree.

**Other books you might like:**

Clive Barker, *The Hellbound Heart*, 1991
Marc Laidlaw, *The 37th Mandala*, 1996
John Skipp, *The Scream*, 1988
　　Craig Spector, co-author
Peter Straub, *Koko*, 1988
Thomas Tessier, *The Nightwalker*, 1979
Chelsea Quinn Yarbro, *Beastnights*, 1989

---

**2223**

SCOTT G. GIER

## Genellan: Planetfall

(New York: Ballantine Del Rey, 1995)

**Story type:** Science Fiction (First Contact; Military)

**Series:** Genellan

**Major character(s):** Sharl Buccari, Military Personnel; Braan, Alien, Military Personnel (flight commander); Dowornobb, Alien (Kora), Scientist

**Time period(s):** Indeterminate Future

**Locale(s):** Genellan, Planet—Imaginary; Kor, Planet—Imaginary

**Summary:** Fleeing a battle defeat, a pod of space marines lands on Genellan, an earthlike world, to await rescue. There they encounter intelligent avians who help them and huge alien scientists who have come to Genellan from the next planet in. Despite the apparent friendliness of the scientists, past hostilities have left their government distrustful of aliens, an obstacle that the marines must overcome. First novel.

**Other books you might like:**

Poul Anderson, *People of the Wind*, 1973
David Brin, *Sundiver*, 1980
Octavia E. Butler, *Survivor*, 1978
Paula E. Downing, *Fallway*, 1993
Lee Killough, *Liberty's World*, 1985
Anne McCaffrey, *Freedom's Landing*, 1995
Brian Stableford, *Balance of Power*, 1979

---

**2224**

SCOTT G. GIER

## In the Shadow of the Moon

(New York: Ballantine Del Rey, 1996)

**Story type:** Science Fiction (Military; Adventure)

**Series:** Genellan

**Major character(s):** Sharl Buccari, Pilot, Parent (mother); Et Kalass, Political Figure (prime minister), Alien (Kones); Lizard Lips, Alien (cliff dweller)

**Time period(s):** Indeterminate Future

**Locale(s):** Genellan, Planet—Imaginary; Kon, Planet—Imaginary

**Summary:** Commander Sharl Buccari has her hands full negotiating between the Terran colonists on Genellan, the native cliff dwellers, the Kones from a neighboring planet who think they should control Genellan, and the Service who haven't really accepted that the Terran colonists no longer accept their command. The return of the alien Shaula further complicates matters.

**Other books you might like:**

Poul Anderson, *People of the Wind*, 1973
Robert Asprin, *The Bug Wars*, 1979
David Brin, *Startide Rising*, 1983
Octavia E. Butler, *Survivor*, 1978
C.J. Cherryh, *The Faded Sun: Kesrith*, 1978
Paula E. Downing, *Fallway*, 1993
Rebecca Ore, *Becoming Alien*, 1988
Diann Thornley, *Ganwold's Child*, 1995

---

**2225**

R. MURRAY GILCHRIST

## The Stone Dragon and Other Tragic Romances

(Charleston, South Carlina: Charon House, 1998)

**Story type:** Horror (Collection)

**Summary:** This collection of 14 stories is steeped in fin de siecle sensibility. Several are tales of love under the duress of supernatural influence, including ''The Basilisk,'' in which a man finds himself pitted against a preternatural serpent while wooing his lady love. ''Witch in Grain'' is a conte cruel about the torture of a witch, ''Roxana Runs Lunatick,'' the tale of a cuckolded husband's revenge on his unfaithful wife, and ''The Pageant of Ghosts,'' a historical ghost story. First published in England in 1894.

**Other books you might like:**

Robert W. Chambers, *The King in Yellow*, 1985
Stefan Grabinski, *The Dark Domain*, 1994
C.D. Pamely, *Tales of Mystery and Terror*, 1926
Clark Ashton Smith, *A Rendezvous in Averoigne*, 1989
Brian Stableford, *Fables and Fantasies*, 1997

---

**2226**

MEL GILDEN

## Hawaiian U.F.O. Aliens

(New York: Roc, 1991)

**Story type:** Science Fiction (Humor; Mystery)

**Series:** Zoot Marlowe

**Major character(s):** Zoot Marlowe, Alien (Toomler), Detective (hard-boiled); Bill, Robot (duck), Sidekick

**Time period(s):** 21st century

**Locale(s):** Malibu, California

**Summary:** After a brief visit to his home planet, T'toom, Zoot returns to Malibu to discover a UFO parked in the sand outside the house he shares with his surfing pals. When one surfer is hit by a mysterious beam from the UFO, changing him into a magician totally uninterested in surfing, Zoot takes up the case in hopes of saving his housemate and the Earth.

**Other books you might like:**

Douglas Adams, *The Hitchhiker's Guide to the Galaxy*, 1980
Roger MacBride Allen, *The Ring of Charon*, 1990
Glen Cook, *Sweet Silver Blues*, 1987
John DeChancie, *Paradox Alley*, 1987
John DeChancie, *Red Limit Freeway*, 1984

John DeChancie, *Starrigger*, 1983
Christopher Stasheff, *King Kobold Revived*, 1984
John E. Stith, *Deep Quarry*, 1989
Sheri S. Tepper, *Grass*, 1989

---

**2227**

MEL GILDEN

## Outer Space and All That Junk

(New York: Lippincott, 1989)

**Story type:** Science Fiction (Humor)
**Major character(s):** Myron Duberville, Teenager, Genius; Hugo, Scientist
**Locale(s):** Vasichvu Bend

**Summary:** Young Myron Duberville goes to spend the summer with his eccentric Uncle Hugo, owner of the highly successful Astronetics Corporation. Uncle Hugo's hobby is collecting junk. He has a yard full of it and he claims that hidden away in the junk pile are aliens whom he is trying to help. At first Myron assumes that his uncle is a wacko. Later he finds out that aliens are in fact hiding in the junk pile and that they are very strange indeed.

**Other books you might like:**
Frank Asch, *Journey to Terezor*, 1989
Reginald Bretnor, *The Schimmelhorn File*, 1979
Jo Dereske, *The Lone Sentinel*, 1989
William Kotzwinkle, *E.T.: The Extra-Terrestrial*, 1982

---

**2228**

MEL GILDEN

## Tubular Android Superheroes

(New York: Roc, 1991)

**Story type:** Science Fiction (Humor; Mystery)
**Series:** Zoot Marlowe
**Major character(s):** Zoot Marlowe, Alien (Toomler), Detective (hardboiled); Bill, Robot (duck), Sidekick
**Time period(s):** 21st century
**Locale(s):** Malibu, California; Los Angeles, California (Los Angeles County)

**Summary:** Returning from T'toom with Grampa Zamp, Zoot finds California's solution to the parking problem involves the latest craze, the Melt-O-Mobile. As Zoot begins to nose around a sudden proliferation of androids, the Melt-O-Mobile takes on a sinister air.

**Other books you might like:**
Douglas Adams, *Dirk Gently's Holistic Detective Agency*, 1987
Douglas Adams, *The Long Dark Tea-Time of the Soul*, 1989
Chester Anderson, *The Butterfly Kid*, 1967
Glen Cook, *Dread Brass Shadows*, 1990
Glen Cook, *Old Tin Sorrows*, 1989
Glen Cook, *Sweet Silver Blues*, 1987
Nick Pollotta, *Illegal Aliens*, 1989
    Phil Foglio, co-author
T.A. Waters, *The Probability Pad*, 1970

---

**2229**

DONNA GILLESPIE

## The Light Bearer

(New York: Berkley, 1994)

**Story type:** Fantasy (Historical; Political)
**Major character(s):** Auriane, Warrior, Religious (priestess); Decius, Slave, Military Personnel; Marcus Julianus, Diplomat (stateman)
**Time period(s):** 1st century
**Locale(s):** Europe

**Summary:** Prophecied to disrupt the ancient order, Auriane witnesses the Roman destruction of her family then vows to avenge the horrors. Her quest of vengeance takes her to Rome where she meets Marcus Julianus, destined to share Auriane's fate. First novel.

**Other books you might like:**
Stephan Grundy, *Rhinegold*, 1994
Harry Harrison, *The Hammer and the Cross*, 1993
    John Holm, co-author
Morgan Llywelyn, *Bard: The Odyssey of the Irish*, 1984
Morgan Llywelyn, *Druids*, 1991
Diana L. Paxson, *The Wolf and the Raven*, 1993

---

**2230**

RICHARD GILLIAM, Editor
MARTIN H. GREENBERG, Co-Editor
EDWARD E. KRAMER, Co-Editor

## Confederacy of the Dead

(New York: Roc, 1993)

**Story type:** Horror (Anthology)
**Summary:** The 25 stories, all but three original to the book, center around the horrors of the American Civil War. Wendy Webb's "A Dress for Tea" is a subtle ghost story and S.P. Somtow's "Darker Angels" and Karl Edward Wagner's "Hell Creek" unabashed zombie stories. Nancy A. Collins' "The Sunday-Go-To-Meeting Jaw" is a southern grotesque and William S. Burroughs' "Death Fiend" a graphic anti-war story. Both Nancy Holder's "Strawman" and Robert Sampson's "Two Yellow Pine Coffins" juxtapose the horrors of war with the terror of black magic. Although most stories are from the perspective of the South, both Richard Lee Byers' "Foragers" and Doug Murray's "The Crater" are told from the northern point-of-view. Michael Bishop has supplied the preface.

**Other books you might like:**
Frank D. McSherry Jr., *Civil War Ghosts*, 1990
    Charles G. Waugh, Martin H. Greenberg, co-editors
Frank D. McSherry Jr., *Nightmares in Dixie*, 1987
    Charles G. Waugh, Martin H. Greenberg, co-editors

---

**2231**

RICHARD GILLIAM, Editor
MARTIN H. GREENBERG, Co-Editor
EDWARD E. KRAMER, Co-Editor

## Grails: Quests of the Dawn

(New York: Roc, 1994)

**Story type:** Fantasy (Anthology; Legend)
**Summary:** Contains a three-page afterword by Fritz Leiber, two poems by James S. Dorr and Jane Yolen plus 23 stories, some reprinted from a 1992 limited edition focusing on diverse investiga-

tions into the ultimate vessel of magic. Authors include Marion Zimmer Bradley, Orson Scott Card, Lionel Fenn, Alan Dean Foster, Neil Gaiman, Richard Gilliam, Lee Hoffman, Mercedes Lackey, Andre Norton, Diana L. Paxson, Kristine Kathryn Rusch, Dean Wesley Smith, Brad Strickland, Brian M. Thomsen, Lawrence Watt-Evans, Gene Wolfe and Janny Wurts. Companion volume to *Grails: Visitations of the Night*.

**Other books you might like:**
A.A. Attanasio, *Kingdom of the Grail*, 1992
James P. Blaylock, *The Paper Grail*, 1991
Marion Zimmer Bradley, *The Mists of Avalon*, 1983
Malcolm Godwin, *The Holy Grail*, 1994
Andrew M. Greeley, *The Magic Cup*, 1979
Marc Laidlaw, *Neon Lotus*, 1988
Rob MacGregor, *Indiana Jones and the Last Crusade*, 1989
Charles Williams, *War in Heaven*, 1930

## 2232

**RICHARD GILLIAM**, Editor
**MARTIN H. GREENBERG**, Co-Editor
**EDWARD E. KRAMER**, Co-Editor

### Grails: Visitations of the Night

(New York: Roc, 1994)

**Story type:** Fantasy (Anthology; Legend)

**Summary:** Contains a five-page introduction by Brian Thomsen, two pages of notes and acknowledgments by Richard Gilliam, plus 29 stories, some reprinted from a 1992 limited edition. The stories focus on the quest for the object of ultimate power. Authors include John Gregory Betancourt, Pat Cadigan, Michael Cassutt, George Alec Effinger, John Farris, Jack C. Haldeman II, Tanith Lee, Brad Linaweaver, S.P. Somtow, Karl Edward Wagner and Robert Weinberg. Companion volume to *Grails: Quests of the Dawn*.

**Other books you might like:**
James P. Blaylock, *The Last Coin*, 1988
Marion Zimmer Bradley, *The Mists of Avalon*, 1983
Susan Cooper, *Over Sea, under Stone*, 1966
Malcolm Godwin, *The Holy Grail*, 1994
Andrew M. Greeley, *The Magic Cup*, 1979
Marc Laidlaw, *Neon Lotus*, 1988
Rosemary Sutcliff, *The Light Beyond the Forest*, 1980

## 2233

**RICHARD GILLIAM**, Editor
**MARTIN H. GREENBERG**, Co-Editor

### Phantoms of the Night

(New York: DAW, 1996)

**Story type:** Horror (Anthology; Ghost Story)

**Summary:** The twenty-eight stories of ghosts and hauntings collected here are all original to the volume. They include Owl Goingback's "Last Man in Line," a Civil War horror story about the ghosts of Andersonville, and Tina Jens' "Preacherman Gets the Blues," in which music has the power to summon and banish the spirits of the dead. Matthew Costello's "Unfortunate Obsession" is a fatal attraction tale with a twist ending, and Edward Kramer's "Casting Circles" a story of a summer camp prank gone weird. Ghosts are tragic family revenants in Douglas Clegg's "The Fruit of Her Womb," sardonic vehicles for revenge in John Helfers' "Blood Ghost," and sentimental entities with good fashion sense in Lawrence Schimel's "Old as a Rose in Bloom."

**Other books you might like:**
Marvin Kaye, *Ghosts*, 1981
   editor
Claudia O'Keefe, *Ghosttide*, 1993
   editor
Paul F. Olson, *Post Mortem: New Tales of Ghostly Horror*, 1989
   David B. Silva, co-editor
Peter Straub, *Ghosts*, 1995
   editor

## 2234

**ALEXIS A. GILLILAND**

### Lord of the Troll-Bats

(New York: Ballantine Del Rey, 1992)

**Story type:** Fantasy (Political)
**Series:** Wizenbeak
**Major character(s):** Wizenbeak, Wizard, Royalty (king)
**Time period(s):** Indeterminate
**Locale(s):** Guhland, Fictional Country

**Summary:** Wizenbeak's peaceful rule as King-Patriarch suffers when ex-Patriarch Gorbani summons the Lord of the Troll-Bats to curse Wizenbeak and arranges an invasion of Guhland's provinces by armies of dragons and women. Further complications arise when Wizenbeak's wife inexplicably disappears.

**Other books you might like:**
Gordon R. Dickson, *The Dragon at War*, 1992
Robert Don Hughes, *The Forging of the Dragon*, 1989
Richard A. Knaak, *Dragon Tome*, 1992

## 2235

**ALEXIS A. GILLILAND**

### The Shadow Shaia

(New York: Ballantine/Del Rey, 1990)

**Story type:** Fantasy (Political; Adventure)
**Series:** Wizenbeak
**Major character(s):** Wizenbeak, Wizard
**Time period(s):** Indeterminate
**Locale(s):** Guhland, Fictional Country

**Summary:** The war is over. King Kahun is dead. Wizenbeak has chosen the Regent for young Prince Dervian. He seems to be in control and should be able to relax and enjoy life. However, the aftermath of a civil war, with inexperienced people at the top seems an opportune time for neighboring King Kirndal to reclaim the province of Kalycas.

**Other books you might like:**
Jack L. Chalker, *The River of Dancing Gods*, 1984
Jack L. Chalker, *When the Changewinds Blow*, 1987
Barbara Hambly, *The Time of the Dark*, 1982
Christopher Stasheff, *The Warlock in Spite of Himself*, 1969
J.R.R. Tolkien, *The Fellowship of the Ring*, 1954

## 2236

**SHEILA GILLULY**

### The Boy From the Burren

(New York: Roc, 1990)

**Story type:** Fantasy (Adventure; Quest)

**Series:** Book of the Painter
**Major character(s):** Aengus, Artist (painter); Bruchan, Minstrel (storyteller); Jorem, Religious (priest)
**Time period(s):** Indeterminate Past
**Locale(s):** Inishbuffin, Fictional City

**Summary:** As Bruchan's indentured servant, Aengus is learning a trade (medicine), self-defense and performing various community chores with the other indentured boys. But in secret, he is being taught to paint, for his painting is the key to fulfilling a prophecy. But Jorem will do anything to stop Aengus and Bruchan in order to preserve his skewed version of their religion and his political power.

**Other books you might like:**
Steven Brust, *The Sun, the Moon, and the Stars*, 1984
Orson Scott Card, *Seventh Son*, 1987
C.J. Cherryh, *Angel with the Sword*, 1988
Mercedes Lackey, *Arrows of the Queen*, 1987
Karen Wehrstein, *Lion's Heart*, 1991

## 2237

### CAROLYN IVES GILMAN

## *Halfway Human*

(New York: Avon Eos, 1998)

**Story type:** Science Fiction (Political; Lost Colony)
**Major character(s):** Valerie "Val" Endrada, Anthropologist (exoethnologist), Student (post graduate); Tedla Galele, Genetically Altered Being (neuter), Refugee; Deirdre "Deedee" Endrada, Child, Explorer
**Time period(s):** Indeterminate Future
**Locale(s):** Capella II, Planet—Imaginary; Gammadis, Planet—Imaginary

**Summary:** Val finds Tedla at her mother-in-law's clinic after Tedla tries to commit suicide. When Tedla meets Val's daughter, Deedee, he begins to relax enough to gradually tell the story of his life on Gammadis where a third of all children do not find themselves fully human gendered people. That third, the blands, provide all the services, living underneath the cities. However, after Alair rescues him, he finds himself in a gendered, information hungry society for which he has no survival skills, while a delegation from Gammadis wants to take him back, perhaps against his will. First novel.

**Other books you might like:**
M.J. Engh, *Rainbow Man*, 1993
C.S. Friedman, *This Alien Shore*, 1998
James Alan Gardner, *Commitment Hour*, 1998
Ursula K. Le Guin, *The Left Hand of Darkness*, 1969
Amy Thomson, *The Color of Distance*, 1995

## 2238

### GREER ILENE GILMAN

## *Moonwise*

(New York: Penguin, 1991)

**Story type:** Fantasy (Quest; Alternate World)
**Major character(s):** Ariane, Scholar; Sylvie, Landowner; Craobb, Angel
**Time period(s):** 1990s (1991)
**Locale(s):** Earth; Cloud, Fictional Country

**Summary:** This is the story of two friends who create stories about magic worlds together. One day Sylvie disappears into one of these worlds and her more practical friend, Ariane, must make a complex trip into the nature of magic and reality to save her.

**Other books you might like:**
John Crowley, *Little, Big*, 1981
Robert Holdstock, *Lavondyss: Journey to an Unknown Region*, 1988
Robert Holdstock, *Mythago Wood*, 1984
Ian McDonald, *King of Morning, Queen of Day*, 1991
Christoph Ransmayr, *The Last World*, 1990

## 2239

### NEWT GINGRICH
### WILLIAM R. FORSTCHEN, Co-Author

## *1945*

(New York: Baen, 1995)

**Story type:** Science Fiction (Alternate Universe; Military)
**Major character(s):** James Mannheim Martel, Military Personnel (Navel Intelligence); Otto Skorzeny, Military Personnel (colonel), Historical Figure; Andrew Harrison, Political Figure (U.S. president)
**Time period(s):** 1940s (1945)
**Locale(s):** Germany; United States

**Summary:** When intelligence indicates American research on an atomic bomb, Hitler decides to attack nuclear facilities at Oak Ridge, Tennessee, thus putting Germany far ahead in nuclear weapons development. While James Martel intervenes to avert the disaster at Oak Ridge, the Germans begin to invade England, aided by a traitor on President Harrison's staff.

**Other books you might like:**
Kevin J. Anderson, *The Trinity Paradox*, 1991
    Doug Beason, co-author
Ben Bova, *Triumph*, 1993
Philip K. Dick, *The Man in the High Castle*, 1962
William R. Forstchen, *Terrible Swift Sword*, 1992
Robert Harris, *Fatherland*, 1992
Brad Linaweaver, *Moon of Ice*, 1988
Harry Turtledove, *Worldwar: Tilting the Balance*, 1995
Robert Charles Wilson, *Mysterium*, 1994

## 2240

### ROBERT GIRARDI

## *Madeleine's Ghost*

(New York: Delacorte, 1995)

**Story type:** Horror (Ghost Story)
**Major character(s):** Ned Conti, Student (grad student in French history); Antoinette Rivaudais, Saloon Hostess; Father Rose, Religious (Catholic priest)
**Time period(s):** 1990s (1995)
**Locale(s):** New York, New York (Brooklyn)

**Summary:** While dithering over the completion of his dissertation Ned Conti, a New Orleans native transplanted to Brooklyn, accepts a research job to help a local parish further the canonization of Sister Januarius, a nun who worked the Brooklyn wharves in the mid-nineteenth century and, like Ned, was also originally from New Orleans. Ghostly manifestations in Ned's apartment and overtures from his old girlfriend in Louisiana eventually encourage him to look into his own life and history to find the answers he needs to cope with his present problems. This is the author's first novel.

**Other books you might like:**
Jack Cady, *The Off Season*, 1995
Judith Hawkes, *Julian's House*, 1989
Michael Upchurch, *Passive Intruder*, 19950

## 2241
### ROBERT GIRARDI

### *Vaporetto 13*
(New York: Delacorte, 1997)

**Story type:** Horror (Ghost Story)
**Major character(s):** Jack Squires, Trader (currency); Caterina Vendramin, Young Woman; Rinio Donato, Trader (currency)
**Time period(s):** 1990s (1997)
**Locale(s):** Venice, Italy

**Summary:** While working in Venice, money broker Jack Squires falls in love with the beautiful Caterina, a mysterious descendant of one of the city's oldest families who has a more than mortal attachment to Italy's splendid past. Under Caterina's influence, Jack sees the superficiality of his life to date and undergoes a spiritual and psychic transformation.

**Other books you might like:**
Ramsey Campbell, *Ancient Images*, 1989
Orson Scott Card, *Homebody*, 1998
Dennis McFarland, *A Face at the Window*, 1997
Peter Straub, *Mrs. God*, 1990
T.M. Wright, *The Island*, 1988

## 2242
### NANCY TYLER GLENN

### *Clicking Stones*
(Tallahassee: Naiad Press, 1989)

**Story type:** Science Fiction (Gay/Lesbian Fiction)
**Major character(s):** Erica, Lesbian; Morgan, Lesbian
**Time period(s):** 1980s; 21st century
**Locale(s):** United States

**Summary:** A young girl finds a mysterious stone with special powers; striking it against another stone causes both to flare into incredible brilliance, causing both physical and mental illumination. As news of the strange phenomenon spreads, a potentially utopian movement begins to grow. This is Glenn's first novel.

**Other books you might like:**
Suzy McKee Charnas, *Motherlines*, 1979
Suzy McKee Charnas, *Walk to the End of the World*, 1974
Lauren Wright Douglas, *In the Blood*, 1989
Karen Marie Christa Minns, *Virago*, 1990
Joanna Russ, *The Female Man*, 1975
Joanna Russ, *We Who Are About To. . .*, 1977

## 2243
### MOLLY GLOSS

### *The Dazzle of Day*
(New York: Tor, 1997)

**Story type:** Science Fiction (Generation Starship; Theological)
**Major character(s):** Dolores Negrete, Settler; Juko Ohasi, Spacewoman; Cejo Indergard, Settler
**Time period(s):** 2050s; 23rd century (2250s)
**Locale(s):** Southwest; *Dusty Miller*, Spaceship; Planet—Imaginary

**Summary:** Dolores Negrete leaves the land her people farmed for 240 years when the Quakers buy a failed space station and emigrate to another solar system. Her descendant, Juko, lives with a curved sky in a Quaker society in which the small gene pool and radiation effects of sail work may damage offspring. Arriving at their destination proves stressful and requires immediate decisions that must take into account the high suicide rate.

**Other books you might like:**
Brian W. Aldiss, *Starship*, 1959
Samuel R. Delany, *They Fly at Ciron*, 1993
Simon Hawke, *The Whims of Creation*, 1995
Joan Slonczewski, *Still Forms on Foxfield*, 1980
Sheri S. Tepper, *The Family Tree*, 1997
Sage Walker, *Whiteout*, 1996
Gene Wolfe, *Nightside the Long Sun*, 1993

## 2244
### JANET GLUCKMAN
### GEORGE GUTHRIDGE, Co-Author

### *Child of the Light*
(New York: St. Martin's, 1992)

**Story type:** Fantasy (Historical; Political)
**Series:** Madagascar Manifesto
**Major character(s):** Solomon Freund, Psychic; Erich Weisser, Telepath, Animal Trainer; Miriam Rathenau, Singer
**Time period(s):** 1920s; 1930s
**Locale(s):** Berlin, Germany

**Summary:** Erich and Solomon's boyhood friendship falls victim to historical forces of anti-semitism and their love of the same woman, Miriam. Erich's ability as a dog trainer yields a rapid rise in the Nazi heirarchy while Solomon remains plagued with visions of horror. Nazi death camp mentality and the plan to export Jews to their new homeland, Madagascar, further distance the pair.

**Other books you might like:**
Martin Amis, *Time's Arrow*, 1991
Katherine Kurtz, *Lammas Night*, 1983
Kurt Vonnegut Jr., *Slaughterhouse Five*, 1969
Jane Yolen, *Briar Rose*, 1992
Jane Yolen, *The Devil's Arithmetic*, 1988

## 2245
### PARKE GODWIN

### *Limbo Search*
(New York: AvoNova, 1995)

**Story type:** Science Fiction (Military; First Contact)
**Major character(s):** Charley Stoner, Military Personnel (UNESA warrant officer); Elli Rovin, Military Personnel (UNESA warrant officer); Nigel Pauley, Military Personnel (UNESA intelligence officer)
**Time period(s):** Indeterminate Future
**Locale(s):** Limbo, Space Station; *Kennedy*, Spaceship

**Summary:** Charley Stoner and his United Earth Space Authority colleagues monitor communications for illegal corporate space activity. When they identify the first alien signal ever encountered by humans, their duties become even more dangerous.

**Other books you might like:**
Ben Bova, *The Privateers*, 1985
Joe Haldeman, *The Forever War*, 1975
Marvin Kaye, *A Cold Blue Light*, 1983
Marvin Kaye, *The Masters of Solitude*, 1978
    Parke Godwin, co-author
Marvin Kaye, *Wintermind*, 1982
    Parke Godwin, co-author

John Steakley, *Armor*, 1984

## 2246

### PARKE GODWIN

## Lord of Sunset

(New York: Avon, 1998)

**Story type:** Fantasy (Political; Legend)
**Major character(s):** Edith of Shaftsbury, Spouse, Parent; Harold Godwinesson, Nobleman, Warrior; Edward, Royalty (king)
**Time period(s):** 11th century
**Locale(s):** England

**Summary:** From the age of 18 until his death at Hastings, Harold Godwinesson, the last Saxon king of England, dreams of keeping England English, rather than allowing it to become Danish or Norman.

**Other books you might like:**
Poul Anderson, *The Broken Sword*, 1971
   revised edition
Steven Gould, *Helm*, 1998
Harry Harrison, *The Hammer and the Cross*, 1993
   John Holm, co-author
C.C. MacApp, *Prisoners of the Sky*, 1969
Diana L. Paxson, *The Wolf and the Raven*, 1993
Judith Tarr, *Ars Magica*, 1989
Chelsea Quinn Yarbro, *Better in the Dark*, 1993

## 2247

### PARKE GODWIN

## Robin and the King

(New York: Morrow, 1993)

**Story type:** Fantasy (Legend; Historical)
**Major character(s):** Robin Hood, Hero, Outlaw; Marian, Spouse (Robin's); William, Royalty (king), Historical Figure
**Time period(s):** 11th century
**Locale(s):** England

**Summary:** Now middle aged, Robin Hood fiercely opposes absolute rule of free Englishmen by any monarch. His campaign progresses from local strife to the protection of England from foreign invaders. Sequel to *Sherwood*.

**Other books you might like:**
David Gemmell, *Morningstar*, 1993
Richard Kluger, *The Sheriff of Nottingham*, 1992
Robin McKinley, *The Outlaws of Sherwood*, 1989
Howard Pyle, *The Merry Adventures of Robin Hood*, 1883
Jennifer Roberson, *Lady of the Forest*, 1992

## 2248

### PARKE GODWIN

## Sherwood

(New York: Morrow, 1991)

**Story type:** Fantasy (Legend)

**Summary:** In this richly detailed story set at the time of the Norman conquest of the Saxons, Robin Hood illustrates the Saxon resistance to William the Conqueror's domination of Saxons and Celts. The Sheriff of Nottingham, charged with forcing William the Conqueror's laws on the Saxons, brands Robin Hood an outlaw for holding on to Saxon ideas of honor and law. Events conspire to make sworn enemies temporary allies as Robin Hood formally enters the rebellion against the invaders.

**Other books you might like:**
Frans G. Bengtsson, *The Long Ships*, 1954
C.J. Cherryh, *Cyteen*, 1988
Clayton Emery, *Tales of Robin Hood*, 1988
Martin H. Greenberg, *The Fantastic Adventures of Robin Hood*, 1991
   editor
Robin McKinley, *The Outlaws of Sherwood*, 1988
Bernard Miles, *Robin Hood: His Life and Legend*, 1979
Howard Pyle, *The Merry Adventures of Robin Hood*, 1883
William F. Wu, *The Robin Hood Ambush*, 1990

## 2249

### PARKE GODWIN

## The Snake Oil Wars

(New York: Doubleday Foundation, 1989)

**Story type:** Science Fiction (Satire)
**Major character(s):** Barion, Alien (God); Coyul, Alien (Satan)
**Time period(s):** 1980s
**Locale(s):** Earth; Topside, Planet—Imaginary

**Summary:** As described in *Waiting for the Galactic Bus*, the brothers Barion and Coyul, a pair of alien graduate students, were abandoned on the planet Earth as part of a college prank. Bored, they created illegal life, which eventually evolved into humankind. Now Barion has been sent home to stand trial for their crime, leaving Coyul to explain things to a humanity who, collectively, are not amused. Humanity files a law suit.

**Other books you might like:**
John Kessel, *Good News From Outer Space*, 1989
James Morrow, *Only Begotten Daughter*, 1990
Salman Rushdie, *The Satanic Verses*, 1989

## 2250

### PARKE GODWIN

## The Tower of Beowulf

(New York: Morrow, 1995)

**Story type:** Fantasy (Legend; Adventure)
**Major character(s):** Beowulf, Hero; Sigyn, Mythical Creature; Grendel, Mythical Creature, Monster
**Time period(s):** 5th century; 6th century
**Locale(s):** Denmark; Sweden; Asgard, Mythical Place

**Summary:** Memories of a botched first raid drive numbed Beowulf toward greater deeds as his reputation grows. Sigyn provides Grendel shelter from others during his youth until Thor repudiates him, ending his innocence. When Grendel asserts his claim as true king of the Scyldings, Beowulf battles and defeats him, but must subsequently vanquish Sigyn then recover his lust for life.

**Other books you might like:**
Frans G. Bengtsson, *The Long Ships*, 1954
John Gardner, *Grendel*, 1971
Stephan Grundy, *Rhinegold*, 1994
Harry Harrison, *The Hammer and the Cross*, 1993
   John Holm, co-author
Diana L. Paxson, *The Wolf and the Raven*, 1993

## 2251

### OWL GOINGBACK

## Crota

(New York: Donald I. Fine, 1996)

**Story type:** Horror (Ancient Evil Unleashed)
**Major character(s):** Jay Little Hawk, Game Warden; Skip Harding, Police Officer (sheriff)
**Time period(s):** 1990s (1996)
**Locale(s):** Logan, Missouri

**Summary:** The author's first novel concerns a monster of Creek Indian legend, the invincible Crota, who is released from captivity in the caves beneath the town of Logan and who embarks on a bloody rampage against white men and Native Americans alike. Only by reacquainting himself with the Native American heritage he has forsaken in order to assimilate with the white man's world can Sheriff Skip Harding find the power to defeat the creature.

**Other books you might like:**
Muriel Gray, *The Trickster*, 1994
T. Chris Martindale, *Demon Dance*, 1991
G. Wayne Miller, *Thunder Rise*, 1988
Eugene E. Pfaff Jr., *Uwharrie*, 1993
   Michael Causey, co-author
Kathryn Ptacek, *Ghost Dance*, 1990
Patrick Whalen, *Deathwalker*, 1992

## 2252

### CHRISTIE GOLDEN

## Invasion America

(New York: Roc, 1998)

**Story type:** Science Fiction (Invasion of Earth)
**Series:** Invasion America
**Major character(s):** David Carter, Student—High School; Cale, Alien, Royalty (heir to the throne)
**Time period(s):** Indeterminate Future
**Locale(s):** Glenport, Massachusetts; Tyrus, Planet—Imaginary

**Summary:** The military elite on the planet Tyrus have seized control of their government. In order to ensure their continued rule, they must hunt down and capture, or kill, the heir to the throne, a half human, half alien teenager who is living secretly on Earth. They mount an expedition to conquer the Earth and seize the boy.

**Other books you might like:**
John Brunner, *The Astronauts Must Not Land*, 1963
Thomas M. Disch, *The Genocides*, 1965
Keith Laumer, *End as a Hero*, 1985
Charles Pellegrino, *Flying to Valhalla*, 1993
Robert Silverberg, *Conquerers From the Darkness*, 1968

## 2253

### CHRISTIE GOLDEN

## King's Man and Thief

(New York: Ace, 1997)

**Story type:** Fantasy (Adventure; Magic Conflict)
**Major character(s):** Deveren Larath, Nobleman, Thief; Allika, Child, Thief; Marrika, Thief, Traitor
**Time period(s):** 13th century (1285)
**Locale(s):** Braedon, Fictional City

**Summary:** When Braedon's enemies attempt to defeat the city by use of a magical plague, Deveren and his band of thieves must search out the cause and discover a way to nullify the attack.

**Other books you might like:**
Lynn Flewelling, *Luck in the Shadows*, 1996
Lynn Flewelling, *Stalking Darkness*, 1997
Peg Kerr, *Emerald House Rising*, 1997
Fritz Leiber, *Ill Met in Lankhmar*, 1995
Fritz Leiber, *Lean Times in Lankhmar*, 1996

## 2254

### CHRISTIE GOLDEN

## On the Run

(New York: Roc, 1998)

**Series:** Invasion America
**Major character(s):** David Carter, Student—High School; Cale, Alien, Royalty (prince); The Dragit, Alien, Ruler
**Time period(s):** Indeterminate Future
**Locale(s):** Utah

**Summary:** In order to escape the unwanted attention of the military dictatorship on Tyrus, Prince Cale flees into space. He lands in Utah and goes into hiding, while agents of his homeworld search for him and prepare to release a deadly virus that will kill off much of the human population.

**Other books you might like:**
Roger MacBride Allen, *Allies and Aliens*, 1995
Patricia Anthony, *Brother Termite*, 1993
William Barton, *When Heaven Fell*, 1995
Philip K. Dick, *Our Friends From Frolix 8*, 1970
Gordon R. Dickson, *Way of the Pilgrim*, 1987

## 2255

### CHRISTOPHER GOLDEN

## Angel Souls and Devil Hearts

(New York: Berkley, 1995)

**Story type:** Horror (Vampire Story)
**Major character(s):** Will Cody, Vampire; Alison Vigeant, Journalist; Liam Mulkerrin, Vampire
**Time period(s):** 2000s (2000)
**Locale(s):** Salzburg, Austria

**Summary:** Having survived a secret plot by the Vatican to destroy them, a vampire race known as the Shadows, or Defiant Ones, struggles for the same civil rights enjoyed by mortal human beings. Their efforts are potentially endangered by a civil war fomented by renegade vampires who want nothing to do with peaceful coexistence with humanity. Sequel to *Of Saints and Shadows*.

**Other books you might like:**
Scott Baker, *Ancestral Hungers*, 1995
Laurell K. Hamilton, *Circus of the Damned*, 1994
Brian Stableford, *The Hunger and Ecstasy of Vampires*, 1996
Robert Weinberg, *Blood War*, 1995
Kelley Wilde, *Mastery*, 1991

**2256**

CHRISTOPHER GOLDEN

## Codename Wolverine

(New York: Boulevard/Putnam, 1998)

**Story type:** Science Fiction (Adventure; Genetic Manipulation)
**Series:** X-Men
**Major character(s):** Logan "Wolverine", Mutant, Adventurer; Victor "Sabertooth" Creed, Mutant, Mentally Ill Person; Raven "Mystique" Darkholme, Mutant, Spy
**Time period(s):** 1990s
**Locale(s):** New York, New York; East Berlin, Germany

**Summary:** Years ago, while Wolverine worked on team X for NATO, one mission to recover a disk from Soviet agents went badly awry. A deadly secret from that failed mission threatens Wolverine, now a super hero, and all the members of his old team.

**Other books you might like:**
Chris Claremont, *First Flight*, 1987
Tom Defalco, *The Past*, 1998
    Jason Henderson, co-author
Diane Duane, *X-Men: Empire's End*, 1997
Scott Lobdell, *Generation X*, 1997
    Elliot S. Maggin, co-author
George R.R. Martin, *Wild Cards*, 1987
    editor

**2257**

CHRISTOPHER GOLDEN
MIKE MIGNOLA, Illustrator

## Hellboy: The Lost Army

(Milwaukie, Oregon: Dark Horse, 1997)

**Story type:** Horror (Ancient Evil Unleashed)
**Series:** Hellboy
**Major character(s):** Hellboy, Supernatural Being; Anastasia Branfield, Archaeologist; Michael Creaghan, Military Personnel (soldier)
**Time period(s):** 1990s
**Locale(s):** Great Sand Sea, Egypt

**Summary:** Novel featuring Mike Mignola's graphic novel superhero Hellboy, a creature of evil summoned by Nazi dabblings in black magic who has since become a benevolent superhero employed by the Bureau for Paranormal Research and Defense. Hellboy is summoned to investigate the disappearance of an archaeological team from the border between Libya and Egypt, where mass disappearances have occurred over the centuries. In a lost world accessed through a nearby oasis, he discovers the mystery is the work of the ancient priest Hazred, who seeks a vessel for the return of the ancient Sumerian sorceror, Mar-Ti-Ku.

**Other books you might like:**
Campbell Black, *Raiders of the Lost Ark*, 1981
Edgar Rice Burroughs, *At the Earth's Core*, 1922
Joe R. Lansdale, *Tarzan: The Lost Adventure*, 1996
    Edgar Rice Burroughs, co-author
A. Merritt, *The Moon Pool*, 1919

**2258**

CHRISTOPHER GOLDEN

## Of Masques and Martyrs

(New York: Ace, 1998)

**Story type:** Horror (Vampire Story)
**Series:** Shadow Saga
**Major character(s):** Peter Octavian, Detective—Private, Vampire; Will Cody, Vampire; Alison Vigeant, Journalist
**Time period(s):** 21st century
**Locale(s):** New York, New York; New Orleans, Louisiana

**Summary:** Set in a future where vampires co-exist openly with human beings, this is third book in the series begun with *Of Saints and Shadows* and *Angel Souls and Devil Hearts*. It chronicles the final showdown between the Shadows, or vampires who take blood without destroying life and who pass on vampirism only to willing recipients, and the traditional vampires, who are bent on enslavement of the human race.

**Other books you might like:**
Nancy A. Collins, *A Dozen Black Roses*, 1996
Mick Farren, *The Time of Feasting*, 1996
Robert R. McCammon, *They Thirst*, 1981
Anne Rice, *The Queen of the Damned*, 1988
Robert Weinberg, *Blood War*, 1995

**2259**

CHRISTOPHER GOLDEN

## Of Saints and Shadows

(New York: Jove, 1994)

**Story type:** Horror (Vampire Story)
**Major character(s):** Peter Octavian, Detective—Private, Vampire; Father Mulkerrin, Religious (Catholic priest)
**Time period(s):** 1990s (1995)
**Locale(s):** Boston, Massachusetts; Venice, Italy

**Summary:** Private detective and vampire Peter Octavian discovers that a secret branch of the Vatican controls all supernatural beings such as the Defiant Ones (a.k.a. vampires) through black magic and psychological conditioning, and that one of its renegade members has found forbidden magic that will allow him to unleash these forces upon the world and take control of it.

**Other books you might like:**
Scott Baker, *Ancestral Hungers*, 1995
Brent Monahan, *The Book of Common Dread*, 1993
Anne Rice, *The Vampire Lestat*, 1985
Robert Weinberg, *Blood War*, 1995

**2260**

STEPHEN GOLDIN
MARY MASON, Co-Author

## Jade Darcy and the Zen Pirates

(New York: Roc, 1990)

**Story type:** Science Fiction (Adventure; Mystery)
**Series:** Rehumanization of Jade Darcy
**Major character(s):** Jade Darcy, Martial Arts Expert (bouncer), Warrior; Megan Cafferty, Businesswoman (entrepreneur); Peach-Frog-At-Twilight, Alien (Restaapan), Religious (novice Furgato)
**Time period(s):** Indeterminate Future

**Locale(s):** Cablans, Planet—Imaginary; Restaapa, Planet—Imaginary (Monastery of the Dirda Hills)

**Summary:** Hoping to open a new market, Megan Cafferty has been trying unsuccessfully to wrangle an invitation to Restaapa when she is overjoyed to discover Jade Darcy has an invitation to the Imperial Festival of the Snows. Jade offers her services as hired bodyguard, allowing Megan to be included in Jade's invitation from the Furgato Sect. While jouneying to the festival site, xenophobic Restaapans attack Jade and Megan who defend themselves until their Furgato hosts come to assist. Shortly after Jade and Megan arrive for the festival, a murder draws them into the intrigue surrounding Imperial efforts to end Restaapa's self-imposed isolation.

**Other books you might like:**
Rosemary Kirstein, *The Steerswoman*, 1989
Melisa C. Michaels, *Skirmish*, 1985
David R. Palmer, *Emergence*, 1984
Alis A. Rasmussen, *A Passage of Stars*, 1990
Alis A. Rasmussen, *The Price of Ransom*, 1990
Alis A. Rasmussen, *Revolution's Shore*, 1990

---

**2261**

**LISA GOLDSTEIN**

## Daily Voices

(Eugene, Oregon: Pulphouse Publishing, 1989)

**Story type:** Science Fiction (Collection)
**Series:** Author's Choice Monthly

**Summary:** Although titled like a magazine, this brief volume is essentially a short story collection consisting of an introduction by the author and five stories originally published between 1984 and 1987 in *Isaac Asimov's SF Magazine*, including "Cassandra's Photographs," "Death is Different," and "Tourists."

**Other books you might like:**
Pat Cadigan, *Patterns*, 1989
Karen Joy Fowler, *Artificial Things*, 1986
Kate Wilhelm, *Children of the Wind: Five Novellas*, 1989
Kate Wilhelm, *Listen, Listen*, 1981
Pamela Zoline, *The Heat Death of the Universe*, 1988

---

**2262**

**LISA GOLDSTEIN**

## Strange Devices of the Sun and Moon

(New York: Tor, 1993)

**Story type:** Fantasy (Historical)
**Major character(s):** Alice Wood, Businesswoman; Christopher Marlowe, Writer (playwright), Historical Figure; Margery, Witch
**Time period(s):** 16th century
**Locale(s):** London, England

**Summary:** Husband dead and son missing, Alice Wood makes her way with difficulty as a bookseller in London. Christopher Marlow, freethinker and playwright, spies for a mysterious benefactor. The lives of these two people, along with the Queen of Faerie and Alice's missing son, entangle with the destiny of England.

**Other books you might like:**
John Crowley, *Aegypt*, 1987
Michael Moorcock, *Gloriana, or the Unfulfilled Queen*, 1978
Tim Powers, *The Drawing of the Dark*, 1979
Melissa Scott, *The Armor of Light*, 1988
    Lisa Barnett, co-author
Patricia C. Wrede, *Snow White and Rose Red*, 1989

---

**2263**

**LISA GOLDSTEIN**

## Summer King, Winter Fool

(New York: Tor, 1994)

**Story type:** Fantasy (Political; Magic Conflict)
**Major character(s):** Valemar, Nobleman; Narrion, Nobleman; Taja, Librarian, Wizard
**Time period(s):** Indeterminate Past
**Locale(s):** Shai, Fictional Country

**Summary:** In a small, intrigue-filled kingdom, a young courtier goes into exile at a small fishing village with an odd, ancient library. People do not fare well under the ruling usurper and the threat of impending war, while the summer god has not yet ascended into heaven to end winter. Against this gloomy backdrop, the courtier searches for his fate, despite uncertainty and ambivalence.

**Other books you might like:**
Eleanor Arnason, *The Sword Smith*, 1978
Ellen Kushner, *Swordspoint*, 1987
Patricia A. McKillip, *The Riddle-Master of Hed*, 1976
Melissa Scott, *The Armor of Light*, 1988
    Lisa A. Barnett, co-author
Caroline Stevermer, *A College of Magics*, 1994

---

**2264**

**LISA GOLDSTEIN**

## Tourists

(New York: Simon and Schuster, 1989)

**Story type:** Fantasy (Magic Conflict)
**Major character(s):** Casey Parmenter, Teenager; Mitchell Parmenter, Anthropologist (Casey's father)
**Time period(s):** 1980s
**Locale(s):** Amaz, Planet—Imaginary; Earth

**Summary:** Casey and her family are in Amaz because her father is searching for the Jewel King's palace and fabled sword. The novel focuses on the family's attempt to cope with a city in which magic exists and has an everyday role in the life of the inhabitants.

**Other books you might like:**
Rick Cook, *Wizard's Bane*, 1988
Doris Egan, *The Gate of Ivory*, 1989
Hanne Marie Svendsen, *The Gold Ball*, 1989

---

**2265**

**LISA GOLDSTEIN**

## Travelers in Magic

(New York: Tor, 1994)

**Story type:** Fantasy (Collection)

**Summary:** Contains 14 short stories published 1984-1994 in periodicals and anthologies and one original story with brief afterwords to each. As usual for Goldstein, the stories detail ordinary people and place that suddenly experience strange, possibly magical, events. Three of the stories involve Amaz, the country featured in *Tourists*, while several others deal with Jewish history and culture.

**Other books you might like:**
John Crowley, *Antiquities*, 1993
Karen Joy Fowler, *Sarah Canary*, 1991
Pat Murphy, *Points of Departure*, 1990

Tim Powers, *The Stress of Her Regard*, 1989
Jane Yolen, *Briar Rose*, 1992

## 2266

### LISA GOLDSTEIN

## *Walking the Labyrinth*

(New York: Tor, 1996)

**Story type:** Fantasy (Mystery; Contemporary)
**Major character(s):** Molly Travers, Detective—Private; John Stow, Detective—Private; Fentrice Allalie, Aged Person, Magician (retired)
**Time period(s):** 1990s; 1930s (1935)
**Locale(s):** England; Midwest

**Summary:** Spurred by John Stow's investigation of her Aunt Fentrice's family magic act, Molly Travers queries Fentrice for details. Her curiosity leads to a secret society of powerful labyrinth builders and a house in England built by her relative, complete with an extensive labyrinth under the house. Further searching uncovers unusual powers and unexpected family history.

**Other books you might like:**
Charles de Lint, *Memory and Dream*, 1994
Christopher Priest, *The Prestige*, 1996
Michaela Roessner, *Vanishing Point*, 1993
Brooke Stevens, *The Circus of the Earth and Air*, 1994
Terri Windling, *The Wood Wife*, 1996

## 2267

### JEWELLE GOMEZ

## *The Gilda Stories*

(Ithaca, New York: Firebrand Books, 1991)

**Story type:** Horror (Vampire Story)
**Major character(s):** Gilda, Vampire, Lesbian; Miss Bird, Servant, Indian; Effie, Young Woman
**Time period(s):** 19th century; 20th century
**Locale(s):** South; Boston, Massachusetts; New York, New York

**Summary:** In this episodic first novel Gilda, a black lesbian vampire, travels from place to place across the United States over a two-century interval, lending her assistance and social conscience to historically disenfranchised ethnic and social groups and embodying through her experiences a chronicle of prejudice and cultural bias in America.

**Other books you might like:**
Suzy McKee Charnas, *The Vampire Tapestry*, 1980
Mara McCuniff, *The Vampire Memoirs*, 1991
    Tracy Briery, co-author
Anne Rice, *Interview with the Vampire*, 1976
Michael Romkey, *I, Vampire*, 1990

## 2268

### TERRY GOODKIND

## *Blood of the Fold*

(New York: Tor, 1996)

**Story type:** Fantasy (Sword and Sorcery; Political)
**Series:** Sword of Truth

**Major character(s):** Richard "the Seeker" Rahl, Wizard (War Wizard); Verna Sauventreen, Magician (Sister of the Light), Leader (prelate); Kahlan Amnell, Magician, Leader (Mother Confessor)
**Time period(s):** Indeterminate
**Locale(s):** The Midlands, Fictional Country; Aydindril, Fictional City; The Old World, Fictional Country

**Summary:** With the destruction of ancient barriers against invasion from the Old World, a dream-walker begins the conquest of the Midlands and the rest of the New World. Condemned as traitor, Kahlan Amnell flees while Verna Sauventreen copes with elevation to Prelate as the evil Sisters of Darkness attempt to suborn the Sisters of Light. Acting on instinct, Richard Rahl begins forcing enemies to work together to repel human invaders while he braves the deadly Wizard's Keep to engage magical forces which could destroy rather than aid his efforts.

**Other books you might like:**
David Eddings, *Pawn of Prophecy*, 1982
Lynn Flewelling, *Luck in the Shadows*, 1996
Laurell K. Hamilton, *Nightseer*, 1992
Robin Hobb, *Assassin's Apprentice*, 1995
J.V. Jones, *The Baker's Boy*, 1995
Robert Jordan, *The Eye of the World*, 1990
Patricia C. Wrede, *The Raven Ring*, 1994

## 2269

### TERRY GOODKIND

## *Stone of Tears*

(New York: Tor, 1995)

**Story type:** Fantasy (Magic Conflict; Sword and Sorcery)
**Series:** Sword of Truth
**Major character(s):** Richard "the Seeker" Cypher, Wizard, Captive; Kahlan Amnell, Magician, Leader (Mother Confessor); Zeddicus "Zedd" Zu'l Zorander, Wizard
**Time period(s):** Indeterminate
**Locale(s):** D'Hara, Fictional Country; The Midlands, Fictional Country; Palace of the Prophets, Mythical Place (wizards' school)

**Summary:** Richard's defeat of Darken Rahl brings only brief relief from the Keeper's struggle to escape confinement and destroy the world. When Richard's uncontrolled development as a wizard threatens to overwhelm him, Kahlan tricks Richard into making himself a prisoner of the Sisters of the Light who promise to save his life and develop his talents. When Richard leaves, Kahlan, as Moter Confessor, must mold raw troops into effective counterinsurgency warriors while Zedd and his sorceress friend attempt to subvert magical attacks by the Keeper's agents.

**Other books you might like:**
Lois McMaster Bujold, *The Spirit Ring*, 1992
David Eddings, *Pawn of Prophecy*, 1982
Laurell K. Hamilton, *Nightseer*, 1992
Robert Jordan, *The Eye of the World*, 1989
Caroline Stevermer, *A College of Magics*, 1994
Patricia C. Wrede, *The Raven Ring*, 1994
Martha Wells, *The Element of Fire*, 1993

## 2270

### TERRY GOODKIND

## *Temple of the Winds*

(New York: Tor, 1997)

**Story type:** Fantasy (Magic Conflict; Political)

**Series:** Sword of Truth
**Major character(s):** Richard ''the Seeker'' Rahl, Wizard (War Wizard), Ruler; Kahlan Amnel, Magician, Leader (Mother Confessor); Drefan Rahl, Criminal, Imposter
**Time period(s):** Indeterminate
**Locale(s):** D'Hara, Fictional Country; The Midlands, Fictional Country

**Summary:** Betrothed, Richard and Kahlan plan to marry as soon as Richard's leadership of D'Hara and The Midlands allows him to eliminate a sorcerous plague and assaults from Emperor Jagang, who captures unprotected minds while people sleep. However, the spirits of the Temple of the Winds demand the couple marry other partners to rectify a magical imbalance. Complicating matters, Kahlan's new fiance, Drefan Rahl, can command the complete D'Hara loyalty due to a Rahl, the only sure protection against Jagang. Fourth in series, following *Blood of the Fold*.

**Other books you might like:**
David Eddings, *Pawn of Prophecy*, 1982
Lynn Flewelling, *Luck in the Shadows*, 1997
Lynn Flewelling, *Stalking Darkness*, 1997
Robin Hobb, *Assassin's Apprentice*, 1995
J.V. Jones, *The Baker's Boy*, 1995
Robert Jordan, *The Eye of the World*, 1990

## 2271

### TERRY GOODKIND

## *Wizard's First Rule*

(New York: Tor, 1994)

**Story type:** Fantasy (Quest; Magic Conflict)
**Major character(s):** Richard ''the Seeker'' Cypher, Woodsman, Martial Arts Expert; Kahlan Amnell, Magician, Leader (Mother Confessor); Darken Rahl, Wizard, Leader
**Time period(s):** Indeterminate
**Locale(s):** Westland, Fictional Country; The Midlands, Fictional Country; The Underworld, Mythical Place (realm of the dead)

**Summary:** When Richard saves Kahlan from four assassins who hunt her, he becomes her friend and protector on her dangerous mission to prevent Darken Rahl from acquiring ultimate magical power through ancient artifacts. Recognized as the prophecied Seeker by his wizard friend, Richard accepts the Sword of Truth and learns of the sword's great power and the terrible price its use demands of the user. First novel.

**Other books you might like:**
Lois McMaster Bujold, *The Spirit Ring*, 1992
Dave Duncan, *The Cutting Edge*, 1992
David Eddings, *Pawn of Prophecy*, 1982
Raymond E. Feist, *Magician*, 1982
Robert Jordan, *The Eye of the World*, 1989
Rosemary Kirstein, *The Outskirter's Secret*, 1992
Dennis L. McKiernan, *Voyage of the Fox Rider*, 1993
Michael Scott Rohan, *The Anvil of Ice*, 1986
J.R.R. Tolkien, *The Fellowship of the Ring*, 1954
J.R.R. Tolkien, *The Hobbit*, 1938
Margaret Weis, *Dragons of Autumn Twilight*, 1984
    Tracy Hickman, co-author

## 2272

### MARIE D. GOODWIN

## *Where the Towers Pierce the Sky*

(New York: Macmillan Four Winds, 1989)

**Story type:** Fantasy (Time Travel)
**Major character(s):** Lizzie Patterson, Teenager (13 years old); Jacques Aubert, Apprentice (to an Astrologer)
**Time period(s):** 1980s; 15th century
**Locale(s):** South Bend, Indiana; France

**Summary:** A 15th century astrologer mistakenly calls 20th century Lizzie to war-torn France and Joan of Arc. The astrologer's apprentice helps her adjust to a harsh and dangerous medieval lifestyle.

**Other books you might like:**
Suzy McKee Charnas, *The Golden Thread*, 1989
Diana Wynne Jones, *A Tale of Time City*, 1987
Richard Peck, *Voices After Midnight*, 1989
Pamela F. Service, *Winter of Magic's Return*, 1985
Jane Yolen, *The Devil's Arithmetic*, 1988

## 2273

### KATHLEEN ANN GOONAN

## *The Bones of Time*

(New York: Tor, 1996)

**Story type:** Science Fiction (Genetic Manipulation; Mystical)
**Major character(s):** Lynn Oshima, Fugitive; Akamu, Clone, Fugitive; Cen Kalakaua, Genius, Scientist (mathematician)
**Time period(s):** 2010s (2014-2017); 2030s (2034)
**Locale(s):** Honolulu, Hawaii; Hong Kong

**Summary:** Rejecting Interspace, her family's corrupt corporation, Lynn Oshima flees from Hawaii to Hong Kong while sheltering the boy, Akamu, an illegal clone of the long dead Hawaiian King Kamehameha. In a parallel but earlier storyline, Cen Kalakaua, a streetwise youngster, learns he has a unique talent for visualizing mathematical concepts. His research eventually affects Lynn and Akamu's fates, as well as the ongoing power struggle between the Hawaiian Homeland Movement and Interspace.

**Other books you might like:**
Greg Egan, *Quarantine*, 1995
Nicola Griffith, *Slow River*, 1995
Jamil Nasir, *The Higher Space*, 1996
Frederik Pohl, *The Singers of Time*, 1991
    Jack Williamson, co-author
Michaela Roessner, *Vanishing Point*, 1993

## 2274

### KATHLEEN ANN GOONAN

## *Mississippi Blues*

(New York: Tor, 1997)

**Story type:** Science Fiction (Genetic Manipulation; Arts)
**Major character(s):** Verity, Clone, Genetically Altered Being; Blaze, Genetically Altered Being, Musician; Lightnin' Lil, Scientist (genetic engineer)
**Time period(s):** Indeterminate Future
**Locale(s):** Cincinnati, Ohio; *American Queen*, Mississippi River

**Summary:** Unwilling to fulfill her destiny as the queen of Queen City (Cincinnati), Verity infects the entire city with the Norleans Plague, which compels inhabitants to follow, via riverboat and raft, the fictional path of Tom Sawyer and Huckleberry Finn down the Mississippi River. En route, Verity and her charges encounter a wide variety of characters, including a woman infected to act as Mark Twain, some of whom know more about the Norleans Plague than they let on. Sequel to *Queen City Jazz*.

**Other books you might like:**
Valerie J. Freireich, *Becoming Human*, 1995
Nicola Griffith, *Slow River*, 1995
Nancy Kress, *Beggars and Choosers*, 1994
Shariann Lewitt, *Interface Masque*, 1997
Linda Nagata, *The Bohr Maker*, 1995
Linda Nagata, *Deception Well*, 1997
Caroline Stevermer, *River Rats*, 1992
Tricia Sullivan, *Lethe*, 1995

---

`2275`

### KATHLEEN ANN GOONAN

## Queen City Jazz

(New York: Tor, 1994)

**Story type:** Science Fiction (Alternate Intelligence; Genetic Manipulation)
**Major character(s):** Verity, Adoptee, Clone; Abraham Durancy, Scientist, Architect
**Time period(s):** 21st century
**Locale(s):** Cincinnati, Ohio

**Summary:** Raised among New Shakers, Verity travels to the Enhanced City of Cincinnati where she hopes that nanotechnology can revive her friend, Blaze, and her dog, Cairo. On the outskirts of the city she meets Sphere who, unknown to her, places Blaze and Cairo in a healing machine while she goes into the city where Verity finds herself the key to events. First novel.

**Other books you might like:**
Kevin J. Anderson, *Assemblers of Infinity*, 1993
    Doug Beason, co-author
Greg Bear, *Blood Music*, 1985
Ben Bova, *Death Dream*, 1994
Nancy Kress, *Brain Rose*, 1990
Walter Jon Williams, *Voice of the Whirlwind*, 1987

---

`2276`

### EDWARD GOREY

## The Haunted Tea Cosy: A Dispirited and Distasteful Diversion for Christmas

(New York: Harcourt Brace, 1998)

**Story type:** Horror (Ghost Story)
**Major character(s):** Edmund Gravel, Recluse; The Bahhum Bug, Supernatural Being
**Time period(s):** 19th century
**Locale(s):** Lower Spigot, England

**Summary:** This comic variation on the theme of Charles Dickens' *A Christmas Carol* is illuminated by the author's well known morbid artwork. After eating a piece of ten-year-old fruitcake on Christmas Eve, Edmund Gravel, the Recluse of Lower Spigot, dreams about three different ghostly beings who expose him to bizarre incidents of Christmases past, present and future, all of which persuade him to give up his solitary lifestyle and become more sociable. First hardcover publication of story written in 1997.

**Other books you might like:**
Kathryn Cramer, *Christmas Ghosts*, 1988
    David Hartwell, co-editor
Richard Dalby, *Mistletoe Mayhem*, 1993
    editor
Charles Dickens, *A Christmas Carol*, 1843
Seon Manley, *Christmas Ghosts: An Anthology*, 1978
    Gogo Lewis, co-editor
Mike Resnick, *Christmas Ghosts*, 1993
    Martin H. Greenberg, co-editor

---

`2277`

### ED GORMAN

## Cages

(San Jose, CA: Deadline Press, 1996)

**Story type:** Horror (Collection)

**Summary:** This collection brings together twenty-one tales of horror and dark suspense by a writer distinguished in these and other genres. Included are the title story, a hard-boiled tale about the victims of toxic waste; "Moonchasers," in which two boys get their first taste of the adult world while hiding a criminal from the law; "The Face," a Civil War ghost story; and "The End of It All," in which characters discover only belatedly that their plastic surgery enhancement does nothing to improve their wretched personalities. In addition, the book contains the western adventure "Pards" and western gothic "Deathman," the science fiction tales "Survival" and "The Brasher Girl," and the gentle fantasy "Yesterday's Dreams." F. Paul Wilson supplies a foreword and Marcia Muller an afterword.

**Other books you might like:**
Dean R. Koontz, *Strange Highways*, 1995
Richard Matheson, *Collected Stories*, 1989
Norman Partridge, *Bad Intentions*, 1996
Norman Partridge, *Mr. Fox and Other Feral Tales*, 1993
F. Paul Wilson, *Soft and Others*, 1989

---

`2278`

### ED GORMAN, Editor
### MARTIN H. GREENBERG, Co-Editor

## Night Screams

(New York: DAW, 1996)

**Story type:** Horror (Anthology)

**Summary:** Twenty-two stories, 16 of them originals, fill this non-theme anthology of horror and dark suspense fiction. The originals include F. Paul Wilson's "The Wringer," a novella featuring the vigilante Repairman Jack who helps an employer get even with a disgruntled ex-employee who has kidnapped the man's wife and child; Christopher Fahy's "Trolls," about a grotesque school for the mentally challenged and the peculiar relationship of the students to the teachers; and Al Sarrantonio's "White Lightning," in which a young man goes on a murder rampage supposedly under the influence of bootleg liquor. Reprints include Ray Bradbury's "Corpse Carnival," in which a sideshow performer determines to find the murderer of his Siamese twin, and Clive Barker's "The Book of Blood," about a young man who gets his grisly comeuppance from the dead whom he purports to contact psychically for paying customers.

**Other books you might like:**
Richard T. Chizmar, *Cold Blood*, 1991
    editor

Joe R. Lansdale, *Dark at Heart*, 1992
  Karen Lansdale, co-editor
John Maclay, *Voices From the Night*, 1994
  editor
Stanley Wiater, *After the Darkness*, 1993
  editor

**2279**

**ED GORMAN**

## Out There in the Darkness

(Burton, Michigan: Subterranean Press, 1995)

**Story type:** Horror (Mystery)
**Major character(s):** Aaron Bellini, Businessman; Neil Solomon, Businessman; Mike O'Brien, Businessman
**Time period(s):** 1990s (1995)
**Locale(s):** Wisconsin

**Summary:** On what should have been a quiet poker night, four businessmen in suburban Wisconsin apprehend and accidentally kill a burglar. Fearing legal repercussions, they dispose of the body, and from that point on find themselves fighting a battle to save their lives when the burglar's escaped accomplice begins killing them off one by one. This short story chapbook was published in a signed limited edition of 500 copies.

**Other books you might like:**
James Dickey, *Deliverance*, 1973
Stephen Gallagher, *Down River*, 1989
Joe R. Lansdale, *Dark at Heart*, 1992
    Karen Lansdale, co-editor
Joe R. Lansdale, *The Steel Valentine*, 1991

**2280**

**ED GORMAN**, Editor
**MARTIN H. GREENBERG**, Co-Editor

## Predators

(New York: Roc, 1993)

**Story type:** Horror (Anthology)

**Summary:** Following up on the theme of their anthology *Stalkers* (1989), which collected stories based on the theme of predator and prey, the editors have assembled 19 original and one reprint tale of both supernatural and non-supernatural horror. John Shirley's "Rubber Smile" concerns the adverse effects of graphic horror films upon certain audience members, T.L. Parkinson's "Mistaken Identity" is about a woman's psychological dissolution, Edward Wellen's "Mind Slash Matter" tells of a man suffering from Alzheimer's disease who develops an unhealthy relationship with an artificial intelligence module operating on his computer, Daniel Ransom and Rex Miller's "Valentine" chronicles the life of a detective tracking a female assassin who kills only mobsters, and Dean R. Koontz's "Hardshell" portrays alien creatures in human disguise stalking one another.

**Other books you might like:**
Robert Bloch, *Monsters in Our Midst*, 1993
  editor
Robert Bloch, *Psycho-Paths*, 1991
  editor
Richard T. Chizmar, *Cold Blood*, 1991
  editor
George Hatch, *Guignoir and Other Furies*, 1991
  editor

**2281**

**ED GORMAN**

## Prisoners and Other Stories

(Baltimore, Maryland: CD Publications, 1992)

**Story type:** Horror (Collection)

**Summary:** The author's first collection brings together 22 stories of horror and dark suspense, several published here for the first time. Included are the hardboiled ghost tale, "Drifter," and the serial killer stories, "The Man in the Long Black Sedan" and "Stalker." With an afterword by Dean R. Koontz.

**Other books you might like:**
Ray Bradbury, *A Memory of Murder*, 1984
Joe R. Lansdale, *By Bizarre Hands*, 1989
Robert R. McCammon, *Blue World*, 1989
William F. Nolan, *Things Beyond Midnight*, 1984

**2282**

**ED GORMAN**, Editor
**MARTIN H. GREENBERG**, Co-Editor

## Stalkers

(New York: Roc, 1990)

**Story type:** Horror (Anthology)

**Summary:** Eighteen original stories that jump back and forth freely between the suspense and supernatural story in their elaboration of the theme of the pursuer and his quarry. Where John Maclay's "Firing" is a simple ghost tale of a man haunted by the person he wronged, Dean Koontz's "Trapped" relates the story of a mother and child trapped in their snowbound cabin by vicious genetically engineered rats. John Coyne's "Flight" and Al Sarrantonio's "Children of Cain" employ scenarios in which pursuit may be all in the narrator's mind, while Robert R. McCammon's straightforward monster tale, "Lizardman," leaves no doubt as to who is being pursued and why.

**Other books you might like:**
Robert Bloch, *Psycho-Paths*, 1991
Joan Kahn, *The Edge of the Chair*, 1967
Joan Kahn, *Hanging by a Thread*, 1969
Alfred Hitchcock, *Alfred Hitchcock Presents: Stories for Late at Night*, 1961

**2283**

**JUDITH GOROG**

## On Meeting Witches at Wells

(New York: Philomel Books, 1991)

**Story type:** Fantasy (Contemporary Realism; Young Adult)
**Major character(s):** Ms. Oakes, Administrator (elementary school principal), Witch; Jeff, Student—Middle School (eighth grade)
**Time period(s):** Indeterminate
**Locale(s):** Poor Farm Road, Mythical Place (elementary school)

**Summary:** The Poor Farm Road Elementary School building suddenly developed a large crack in an exterior wall. The traditional pillowmaking and storytelling gathering was special that year, not only because it became the last, but also due to the unexpected ghostly visitors' interesting contributions.

**Other books you might like:**
Margaret J. Anderson, *The Ghost Inside the Monitor*, 1990

Pam Conrad, *Stonewords: A Ghost Story*, 1990
Alan Garner, *The Weirdstone of Brisingamen*, 1960
Patricia A. McKillip, *The House on Parchment Street*, 1973
Philippa Pearce, *Tom's Midnight Garden*, 1959

## 2284

### GARY GOSHGARIAN

## *Rough Beast*

(New York: Donald I. Fine, 1995)

**Story type:** Horror (Science Fiction)
**Major character(s):** Calvin Hazzard, Professor (of English); Matt Hazzard, Child (Calvin's 12-year-old son); Jerry Mars, Criminal (assassin)
**Time period(s):** 1990s (1995)
**Locale(s):** Carleton, Massachusetts

**Summary:** Government agents try to obliterate all traces of Black Flag, a biological weapons project conceived at the end of the Vietnam War that could prove an embarrassment to the president. Meanwhile, Calvin and Terry Hazzard are unaware that their quiet suburban home sits upon the toxic products of Black Flag, and that these are initiating a frightening physical transformation in their son, Matt.

**Other books you might like:**
Stephen King, *Firestarter*, 1980
Dean R. Koontz, *Watchers*, 1987
John Saul, *Creature*, 1988
John Saul, *The Homing*, 1994

## 2285

### GARY GOSHGARIAN

## *The Stone Circle*

(New York: Donald I. Fine, 1997)

**Story type:** Horror (Ancient Evil Unleashed)
**Major character(s):** Peter Van Zandt, Archaeologist; Constance Lambert, Teacher; Andy Van Zandt, Child
**Time period(s):** 1990s (1997)
**Locale(s):** Kingdom Head Island, Massachusetts

**Summary:** Archeologist Peter van Zandt finds evidence of a pre-Columbian druid settlement on an island in Boston harbor. The island is imbued with the spirit of Brigid Mocnessa, a druid witch, who masquerades as the spirit of Peter's beloved dead wife to persuade him to perform the blood sacrifice needed to revive the island's pagan heritage.

**Other books you might like:**
Joseph A. Citro, *Dark Twilight*, 1990
Douglas Clegg, *Goat Dance*, 1989
Brent Monahan, *The Uprising*, 1992
Patrick Whalen, *Out of the Night*, 1990

## 2286

### PHYLLIS GOTLIEB

## *Flesh and Gold*

(New York: Tor, 1998)

**Story type:** Science Fiction (Mystery)
**Major character(s):** Skerow, Alien, Judge; Anthony Labonta, Lawyer
**Time period(s):** Indeterminate Future

**Locale(s):** Fthel V., Planet—Imaginary

**Summary:** Skerow's duties as a roving judge take her to the planet Fthel where she sentences a criminal who vows vengeance against her and others. While trying to decide whether or not to take his threats seriously, she discovers that slavery exists on Fthel, even though it is against interplanetary law. She uses her telepathic powers to solve both problems.

**Other books you might like:**
Patricia Anthony, *Happy Policeman*, 1994
Lynn S. Hightower, *Alien Heat*, 1994
Lee Killough, *Deadly Silents*, 1981
Susan R. Matthews, *Hour of Judgment*, 1999
Atanielle Annyn Noel, *Speaker to Heaven*, 1987

## 2287

### PHYLLIS GOTLIEB

## *Heart of Red Iron*

(New York: St. Martin's, 1989)

**Story type:** Science Fiction (Science Fiction)
**Major character(s):** Sven Dahlgren, Mutant; Mod Dahlgren, Android
**Time period(s):** Indeterminate Future
**Locale(s):** Dahlgren's World, Planet—Imaginary

**Summary:** In this sequel to *O Master Caliban*, the four-armed mutant Sven Dahlgren returns to the dangerous planet of his childhood in order to help settle four alien races, victims of disasters on their own worlds. With him are his family and an android duplicate of his scientist father. Humans, mutants, androids, intelligent robots, and a variety of aliens, including a sentient crystal species, must learn to work together if they are going to survive the inimical conditions on Dahlgren's World.

**Other books you might like:**
Octavia E. Butler, *Adulthood Rites*, 1988
Octavia E. Butler, *Dawn*, 1987
Octavia E. Butler, *Imago*, 1989
Sheri S. Tepper, *After Long Silence*, 1987
Sheri S. Tepper, *Grass*, 1989

## 2288

### SHERRY GOTTLIEB

## *Love Bite*

(New York: Warner, 1994)

**Story type:** Horror (Vampire Story)
**Major character(s):** Jace Levy, Detective—Homicide; Liz Robinson, Detective—Homicide; Risha "Rusty" Cadigan, Photographer, Vampire
**Time period(s):** 1990s (1994)
**Locale(s):** Los Angeles, California

**Summary:** Jace Levy battles the trauma his experiences as a homicide detective have inflicted on him while tackling his latest case: a serial killer who contacts victims through personal ads in the local papers and drains them of their blood. This novel, the author's first, was also published in a deluxe limited edition by Canadian publisher Transylvania Press.

**Other books you might like:**
Michael Cecilione, *Domination*, 1993
Don Davis, *Bring on the Night*, 1993
    Jay Davis, co-author
Stephen Gallagher, *Valley of Lights*, 1987
Robert Morgan, *Some Things Never Die*, 1993

William Relling Jr., *New Moon*, 1987
Karen E. Taylor, *Bitter Blood*, 1994
Karen E. Taylor, *Blood Secrets*, 1994
Les Whitten, *Progeny of the Adder*, 1965

**2289**

STEVEN GOULD

## Helm

(New York: Tor, 1998)

**Story type:** Science Fiction (Lost Colony; Young Adult)
**Major character(s):** Leland de Laal, Royalty (Warden of the Needle), Military Personnel; Marilyn de Noram, Royalty (guide of Noram City); Charlina "Charley" Rosen, Martial Arts Expert
**Time period(s):** Indeterminate Future
**Locale(s):** Agatsu, Planet—Imaginary

**Summary:** After donning the glass helm that resides atop the forbidden "Needle," Leland de Laal suddenly hears a strange voice in his head that instructs him in martial arts and military tactics—tactics he will need in order to save his father's land and recover Earth's lost knowledge.

**Other books you might like:**
C.J. Cherryh, *Cloud's Rider*, 1996
C.J. Cherryh, *Rider at the Gate*, 1995
Marian Hughes, *Initiation*, 1995
Larry Niven, *Destiny's Road*, 1997
Larry Niven, *The Integral Trees*, 1984
Larry Niven, *The Smoke Ring*, 1987

**2290**

STEVEN GOULD

## Jumper

(New York: Tor, 1992)

**Story type:** Science Fiction (Psychic Powers; Young Adult)
**Major character(s):** David "Davy" Rice, Teenager, Runaway (by teleportation); Millicent "Millie", Girlfriend
**Time period(s):** 1990s
**Locale(s):** Minnesota; New York, New York

**Summary:** About to suffer a beating at the hands of his alcoholic father, David suddenly discovers his unique ability to teleport. David runs away to New York where he explores his new ability, robbing a bank in the process, but avoiding the revenge he wishes upon his father. David finds Millicent and becomes close to her as he begins to mature on his rite of passage. Author's first novel.

**Other books you might like:**
Alfred Bester, *The Stars My Destination*, 1956
Lester Del Rey, *Pstalemate*, 1971
Phyllis Eisenstein, *Born to Exile*, 1978
Phyllis Eisenstein, *In the Red Lord's Reach*, 1989
Robert A. Heinlein, *Tunnel in the Sky*, 1955
Robert Silverberg, *Dying Inside*, 1972
Theodore Sturgeon, *More than Human*, 1953
A.E. Van Vogt, *Slan*, 1946

**2291**

STEVEN GOULD

## Wildside

(New York: Tor, 1996)

**Story type:** Science Fiction (Young Adult; Alternate Universe)
**Major character(s):** Charlie Newell, Teenager, Pilot; Marie Nguyen, Teenager, Pilot; Clara Prentice, Teenager, Pilot
**Time period(s):** 1990s
**Locale(s):** Texas; Wild Side, Alternate Earth

**Summary:** Charlie Newell discovers a gateway to the "wildside," an unspoiled parallel Earth where many animals now extinct on Charlie's world still roam. Together with his closest friends, Charlie struggles to explore and exploit the wildside while simultaneously protecting it from the federal government.

**Other books you might like:**
Michael Crichton, *Jurassic Park*, 1990
Julia Ecklar, *Regenesis*, 1995
Louis L'Amour, *Haunted Mesa*, 1987
Christopher Pike, *The Tachyon Web*, 1986
Sage Walker, *Whiteout*, 1996

**2292**

DANIEL H. GOWER

## Harrowgate

(New York: Dell/Abyss, 1993)

**Story type:** Horror (Occult)
**Major character(s):** Julian Stormer, Artist; Ashley Herrin, Reanimated Dead; Vernon Doyle, Businessman (security systems consultant)
**Time period(s):** 1990s (1993)
**Locale(s):** Groveland, Midwest

**Summary:** Avant garde artist Julian Stormer finds his artwork becoming satisfactorily more bizarre after the mysterious Ashley Herrin becomes his muse. Could it have to do with the fact that Ashley, a dead former prostitute and drug pusher, has been reanimated for the express task of guarding Harrowgate, a gateway to the afterlife through which the Coprolites, or ossified souls of the evil, are trying to break through?

**Other books you might like:**
Jonathan Aycliffe, *Naomi's Room*, 1991
Giles Blunt, *Cold Eye*, 1989
T. Chris Martindale, *The Voice in the Basement*, 1992
T.M. Wright, *Little Boy Lost*, 1992

**2293**

DANIEL H. GOWER

## The Orpheus Process

(New York: Dell/Abyss, 1992)

**Story type:** Horror (Reanimated Dead; Science Fiction)
**Major character(s):** Orville Helmond, Scientist; Alexandra "Ally" Helmond, Teenager (Orville's daughter); Stuart Coleridge, Police Officer (sheriff)
**Time period(s):** 1990s
**Locale(s):** Berkshire, Ohio

**Summary:** Orville Helmond's successful experiments in reviving dead animals offer his daughter Eunice a second chance for life after she is killed by a mass murderer. But Eunice returns from the dead with an antipathy for human beings and, worse, a willingness to help resurrect an army of others like herself. This is the author's first novel.

**Other books you might like:**
Stephen King, *Pet Sematary*, 1983
Dean R. Koontz, *Hideaway*, 1992
Mary Shelley, *Frankenstein*, 1818

**2294**
STEFAN GRABINSKI

## *The Dark Domain*
(New York: Hippocrene, 1994)

**Story type:** Horror (Collection)

**Summary:** The 11 stories translated here represent the first collection in English of a Polish writer of weird fiction whose work appeared before World War II and which blends the tropes of Gothic horror with anti-materialist philosophy. "Fumes," "The Area," "Szamota's Mistress," "Strabismus," and "Saturnin Sektor" all use the author's favorite theme of the doppelganger, while "The Motion Demon," "The Wandering Train," and "In the Compartment" deploy magically-endowed trains as agents of dread and transcendance. The translator, Miroslaw Lipinski, has supplied an introduction that gives a historical overview of the author and his writing.

**Other books you might like:**
Thomas Ligotti, *Songs of a Dead Dreamer*, 1990
Bruno Schulz, *Sanatorium under the Sign of the Hourglass*, 1937
Bruno Schulz, *The Street of Crocodiles*, 1934
Roland Topor, *The Tenant*, 1966

**2295**
CAMARIN GRAE

## *Stranded*
(Tallahassee: Naiad Press, 1991)

**Story type:** Science Fiction (Gay/Lesbian Fiction; Invasion of Earth)
**Major character(s):** Amy, Artist, Musician; Jenna, Alien, Disembodied Personality; Zephkar, Alien, Disembodied Personality
**Time period(s):** 1990s
**Locale(s):** San Francisco, California; Chicago, Illinois

**Summary:** Disembodied minds from Allo, a planet of hermaphrodites, have begun invading humans. Jenna, residing in Amy's mind, and her friends, Billy and Cass, from the Zephkar Elimination Team, act to defeat Zephkar who was formally outcast from Allo society for her violent acts. Zephkar has escaped from Allo and has come to Earth where she takes over James Lane, using him to form a new fundamentalist religion and political party and hoping to run America as a theocracy.

**Other books you might like:**
Storm Constantine, *Bewitchments of Love and Hate*, 1990
Storm Constantine, *The Enchantments of Flesh and Spirit*, 1989
Camilla Decarnin, *Worlds Apart*, 1986
    Eric Garber and Lyn Paleo, co-editors
Suzette Haden Elgin, *Native Tongue*, 1984
Jeffrey M. Elliot, *Kindred Spirits*, 1984
    editor
Nancy Tyler Glenn, *Clicking Stones*, 1989
Ursula K. Le Guin, *The Left Hand of Darkness*, 1969
Lynda Lyons, *Priorities*, 1990

Joan Slonczewski, *A Door into Ocean*, 1986
John Varley, *The Persistence of Vision*, 1978
John Varley, *Titan*, 1979

**2296**
L.A. GRAF (Pseudonym of Julia Ecklar and Karen Rose Cercone)

## *Armageddon Sky*
(New York: Pocket, 1997)

**Story type:** Science Fiction (Space Opera; Disaster)
**Series:** Star Trek: Day of Honor
**Major character(s):** Benjamin Sisko, Spaceship Captain, Military Personnel; Worf, Alien (Klingon), Military Personnel (commander); Julian Bashir, Doctor, Military Personnel
**Time period(s):** 24th century
**Locale(s):** Armageddon, Planet—Imaginary; *U.S.S. Defiant*, Spaceship; United Federation of Planets, Interstellar Empire/Federation

**Summary:** On a mission to rescue a shipload of scientists, Sisko and his crew have little trouble deflecting the cometary debris that bombards the planet. But they also must avoid betraying their presence to a Klingon ship and a Cardassian ship, in order to avert interstellar war. On the inhospitable planet, the Away Team discovers three groups of exiled Klingons, one of which holds the scientists and the key to a deadly secret.

**Other books you might like:**
C.J. Cherryh, *Downbelow Station*, 1981
Greg Cox, *Devil in the Sky*, 1995
    John Gregory Betancourt, co-author
Diane Duane, *My Enemy, My Ally*, 1984
Brad Ferguson, *A Flag Full of Stars*, 1991
Larry Niven, *Lucifer's Hammer*, 1977
    Jerry Pournelle, co-author
H. Beam Piper, *Little Fuzzy*, 1962
Howard Weinstein, *Deep Domain*, 1987

**2297**
L.A. GRAF (Pseudonym of Julia Ecklar and Karen Rose)

## *Time's Enemy*
(New York: Pocket, 1996)

**Story type:** Science Fiction (Space Opera; Time Travel)
**Series:** Star Trek: Deep Space Nine
**Major character(s):** Jadzia Dax, Military Personnel (lieutenant), Alien (Trill); Benjamin Sisko, Spaceship Captain, Military Personnel; Julian Bashir, Doctor, Military Personnel
**Time period(s):** 24th century
**Locale(s):** *U.S.S. Defiant*, Spaceship; Deep Space Nine, Space Station; United Federation of Planets, Interstellar Empire/Federation

**Summary:** A 5000-year-old spaceship found frozen in cometary debris, *Defiant*, contains the remains of Captain Sisko, Dr. Bashir, and the living symbiont, Dax. Piecing together the evidence leads Starfleet to conclude that the *Defiant* has taken part in a great battle sometime in the near future, probably against the terrible enemy that drove the Furies from the Alpha Quadrant. Now Sisko and his crew try to use this knowledge to save the quadrant from the Conquerors who drove the Furies from their homes. Third of the four-part Invasion! Series which spans all four of the "Star Trek" television series and concludes in *The Final Fury*.

**Other books you might like:**
Dafydd ab Hugh, *The Final Fury*, 1996
   Invasion! Series, part 4
Orson Scott Card, *Speaker for the Dead*, 1988
Diane Carey, *First Strike*, 1996
   Invasion! Series, part 1
Barbara Hambly, *Ishmael*, 1985
Dean Wesley Smith, *The Escape*, 1995
   Kristine Kathryn Rusch, co-author
Dean Wesley Smith, *The Soldiers of Fear*, 1996
   Invasion! Series, part 2; Kristine Kathryn Rusch, co-author
James Tiptree Jr., *Up the Walls of the World*, 1978
   pseudonym of Alice Sheldon
Della Van Hise, *Killing Time*, 1985

## 2298

**L.A. GRAF** (Pseudonym of Julia Ecklar and Karen Rose)

### Traitor Winds

(New York: Pocket, 1994)

**Story type:** Science Fiction (Mystery; Adventure)
**Series:** Star Trek
**Major character(s):** Pavel Chekov, Military Personnel (Starfleet ensign), Space Explorer; Hikaru Sulu, Military Personnel (Starfleet lieutenant); James T. Kirk, Military Personnel (Starfleet admiral), Spaceship Captain
**Time period(s):** 23rd century
**Locale(s):** *U.S.S. Enterprise*, Spaceship; Earth; United Federation of Planets, Interstellar Empire/Federation

**Summary:** After the completion of their five-year mission, the *Enterprise* crew have gone on to new assignements. When Chekov witnesses a murder and Sulu's top secret aircraft disappears, they join forces again to find out the truth behind the framing of their shipmates for murder and treason. Their search uncovers a plot designed to discredit Admiral Kirk and start an interstellar war.

**Other books you might like:**
Margaret Wander Bonanno, *Strangers From the Sky*, 1987
C.J. Cherryh, *Hellburner*, 1992
Jane S. Fancher, *Harmonies of the 'Net*, 1992
Judith Reeves-Stevens, *Prime Directive*, 1990
   Garfield Reeves-Stevens, co-author

## 2299

**L.A. GRAF**

### War Dragons

(New York: Pocket Books, 1998)

**Story type:** Science Fiction (First Contact; Space Opera)
**Series:** Star Trek: The Captain's Table
**Major character(s):** James T. Kirk, Spaceship Captain; Hikaru Sulu, Spaceship Captain; Pavel Chekov, Military Personnel (commander), Space Explorer
**Time period(s):** 23rd century (2265); 23rd century (2290)
**Locale(s):** Interstellar Empire/Federation (The Captain's Table saloon); *U.S.S. Enterprise*, Spaceship; *U.S.S. Excelsior*, Spaceship

**Summary:** Kirk takes Sulu to The Captain's Table, a bar where captains of all sorts of vessels congregate to drink and tell tales of their adventures. Kirk and Sulu regale their tablemates with first-person accounts of two encounters, 25 years apart, with a reptilian species that survived by scavenging the technology of other cultures—and how they avoided interstellar war. First of six volumes.

**Other books you might like:**
Steven Brust, *Cowboy Feng's Space Bar and Grille*, 1990
Arthur C. Clarke, *Tales From the White Hart*, 1957
L. Sprague de Camp, *Tales From Gavagan's Bar*, 1978
   expanded edition; Fletcher Pratt, co-author
Spider Robinson, *Callahan's Crosstime Saloon*, 1970
Spider Robinson, *Callahan's Legacy*, 1996

## 2300

**JOHN GRAFTON**, Editor

### Great Ghost Stories

(New York: Dover, 1992)

**Story type:** Horror (Anthology; Ghost Story)

**Summary:** This volume collects ten short classic ghost stories. Included are Ambrose Bierce's tale of vengeance from beyond the grave, ''The Moonlit Road''; Bram Stoker's haunted house story, ''The Judge's House''; Charles Dicken's tale of spectral justice, ''To Be Taken with a Grain of Salt'' (a.k.a. ''The Trial for Murder''); and W. W. Jacobs' masterpiece of a wish-fulfilling talisman that becomes a horrible curse, ''The Monkey's Paw.'' There are also stories by J. Sheridan Le Fanu, E. G. Swain, M. R. James, Amelia B. Edward, Jerome K. Jerome and E. F. Benson.

**Other books you might like:**
Everett F. Bleiler, *A Treasury of Victorian Ghost Stories*, 1981
   editor
Michael Cox, *The Oxford Book of English Ghost Stories*, 1991
   R. Gilbert, co-editor
Michael Cox, *Victorian Ghost Stories: An Oxford Anthology*, 1991
   editor
Jack Sullivan, *Lost Souls*, 1983
   editor

## 2301

**DANIEL GRAHAM JR.**

### The Gatekeepers

(New York: Baen, 1995)

**Story type:** Science Fiction (Techno-Thriller; Political)
**Major character(s):** Rolf Bernard, Businessman; Max Yeager, Engineer; Cynthia Bernard, Wealthy, Businesswoman
**Time period(s):** 2000s
**Locale(s):** Tucson, Arizona; Washington, District of Columbia; Australia

**Summary:** When the government monopoly on space development threatens to prevent the adoption of a new aerospace vehicle and ruin his company, Rolf Bernard plans to use his fleet of space vehicles and Starwars Defense Initiative hardware to overcome U.S. defenses and impress his vision onto the country's future. First novel.

**Other books you might like:**
James P. Hogan, *Endgame Enigma*, 1987
David Kagan, *Sunstroke*, 1993
Michael P. Kube-McDowell, *Emprise*, 1985
Vonda N. McIntyre, *Starfarers*, 1989
Larry Niven, *Fallen Angels*, 1991
   Jerry Pournelle, Michael Flynn, co-authors
Allen Steele, *Orbital Decay*, 1989

## 2302

**DEE GRAHAM**

### Fallen

(New York: Signet, 1998)

**Story type:** Horror (Occult)
**Major character(s):** John Hobbes, Detective; Lou La Cava, Detective; Gretta Milano, Professor
**Time period(s):** 1990s (1998)
**Locale(s):** United States

**Summary:** Homicide detective John Hobbes discovers that the serial killer he has just helped send to the electric chair acted under the influence of Azazel, a demon who moves from body to body and who has assumed many identities over the years. While Hobbes seeks a means to send Azazel back to his realm, Azazel uses human surrogates close to Hobbes to implicate him as a murderer. Novelization of Nicholas Kazan's script for the film directed by Gregory Hoblit.

**Other books you might like:**
C. Dean Andersson, *Buried Screams*, 1992
John Christopher, *The Possessors*, 1994
Jack Finney, *The Body Snatchers*, 1955
Stephen Gallagher, *Valley of Lights*, 1987
Lawrence Watt-Evans, *The Nightmare People*, 1990

## 2303

**CHARLES L. GRANT**

### The Black Carousel

(New York: Tor, 1995)

**Story type:** Horror (Small Town Horror)
**Series:** Oxrun Station
**Major character(s):** Casey Bethune, Postal Worker (mail carrier); Fran Lumbaird, Child; Drake Saxton, Journalist
**Time period(s):** 1990s (1995)
**Locale(s):** Oxrun Station, Connecticut

**Summary:** This novel is actually a collection of four loosely linked novellas. ''Pilgrim's Travelers,'' a travelling carnival that comes to the small town of Oxrun Station, mirrors in its sideshows and attractions the hopes and fear of several unlucky townspeople, including an older man desperate for love, a young girl recently moved to town and starved for friendship, a local boy in the grip of his domineering mother, and an elderly man haunted by the ghosts of his youth.

**Other books you might like:**
Ray Bradbury, *Something Wicked This Way Comes*, 1962
Charles G. Finney, *The Circus of Dr. Lao*, 1935
Thomas F. Monteleone, *The Magnificent Gallery*, 1987
Tom Reamy, *Blind Voices*, 1978
Theodore Sturgeon, *The Dreaming Jewels*, 1950

## 2304

**CHARLES L. GRANT**

### Chariot

(New York: Tor/Forge, 1998)

**Story type:** Horror (Apocalyptic Horror)
**Series:** Millennium Quartet
**Major character(s):** Trey Falkirk, Gambler; Sir John Harp, Aged Person; Eula Korrey, Religious (evangelist)
**Time period(s):** 1990s (1998)
**Locale(s):** Las Vegas, Nevada

**Summary:** Trey Falkirk's uncommon luck at gambling and imperviousness to injury are signs of supernatural talents he refuses to acknowledge. Sir John Harp, an enigmatic benefactor, tries to awaken Trey to the responsibility these talents impose, but is countered by Eula Korrey, a secretly sinister gospel singer who mobilizes Trey's friends and associates against him to further her evil schemes. This is the third novel in Grant's Millennium Quartet, each novel is centered around one of the Four Horsemen of the Apocalypse.

**Other books you might like:**
James P. Blaylock, *The Last Coin*, 1988
Thomas F. Monteleone, *The Resurrectionist*, 1995
Michael Moorcock, *Blood: A Southern Fantasy*, 1996
Tim Powers, *Last Call*, 1996
Robert Weinberg, *The Devil's Auction*, 1988

## 2305

**CHARLES L. GRANT**

### Dialing the Wind

(New York: Tor, 1989)

**Story type:** Horror (Small Town Horror)
**Series:** Oxrun Station
**Major character(s):** Callum Davidson, Aged Person
**Time period(s):** Indeterminate
**Locale(s):** Oxrun Station, Connecticut

**Summary:** Two men discover photographs and writings hidden in an album in an old friend's house that offer clues to the stories of four individuals trapped and destroyed by their own desires—a widow drawn to a mysterious radio message, a man driven to madness by a woman who never existed, a high school teacher tormented by his own insignificance, and a long suffering, would-be lover who gets his heart's desire too late.

**Other books you might like:**
John Farris, *Scare Tactics*, 1988
Stephen King, *Different Seasons*, 1982

## 2306

**CHARLES L. GRANT**, Editor

### Final Shadows

(New York: Doubleday, 1991)

**Story type:** Horror (Anthology)

**Summary:** This final installment in Grant's long-running series of anthologies of original horror fiction concerned with people and their problems collects 36 stories by British and American authors. Stories range from elliptical fantasies like Lori Negridge Allen's ''Under the Boardwalk'' and Craig Shaw Gardner's ''Going Away,'' to the psychological horror of Melanie Tem's ''Fry Day'' and Dennis Etchison's ''When They Gave Us Memory,'' to tales of murder and madness such as Stephen Gallagher's ''Magpie'' and Bill Pronzini's ''Out Behind the Shed,'' to outright monster stories like Peter Tremayne's ''Fear A' Ghorta'' and Tanith Lee's ''The Mermaid.''

**Other books you might like:**
Thomas F. Monteleone, *The Borderlands Series*, 1990-1991
Chris Morgan, *Dark Fantasies*, 1989

## 2307

CHARLES L. GRANT, Editor

### Gallery of Horror

(New York: Roc, 1996)

**Story type:** Horror (Anthology)

**Summary:** First published in 1983 as *The Dodd Mead Gallery of Horror*, this anthology features 20 stories by some of the best living writers of modern horror, all of which reflect its editor's preference for subtle, atmospheric horror. Stephen King's "Nona" features a loser in love whose psychopathic murder spree may or may not be due to the woman whom he claims has supernatural control over him. Dennis Etchison's "The Chair" concerns a man who attends the high school reunion from hell, Alan Ryan's "Death to the Easter Bunny" the dark truth behind a childhood legend, and David Morrell's "The Typewriter" a man who becomes a bestselling novelist due to a supernaturally-endowed typewriter. Ted Klein's "Petey" wreaks a modern variation on the Frankenstein theme, and Bernard Taylor's "Out of Sorts" a similar variation on the werewolf theme. Four of the stories are vampire tales: Ramsey Campbell's "The Sunshine Club," Craig Shaw Gardner's "Aim for the Heart," Jack Dann and Gardner Dozois's "Down Among the Dead Men," and Tanith Lee's "Nunc Dimittis."

**Other books you might like:**
Ramsey Campbell, *New Terrors*, 1982
    editor
Ramsey Campbell, *Superhorror*, 1976
    editor
Kirby McCauley, *Dark Forces*, 1980
Stuart David Schiff, *The Best of Whispers*, 1994
    editor

## 2308

CHARLES L. GRANT

### Genesis

(New York: Roc, 1998)

**Story type:** Horror (Reanimated Dead)
**Series:** Black Oak
**Major character(s):** Ethan Proctor, Businessman; Corliss Nathan, Police Officer (sheriff); Lulu "Flower" Power, Dancer
**Time period(s):** 1990s (1998)
**Locale(s):** Crockston, Kentucky

**Summary:** Ethan Proctor and members of his Black Oak Security team travel to rural Kentucky to follow-up on the mysterious death of one of their members. Their investigations bring them into conflict with a mysterious force, possibly supernatural, that has been implicated in the deaths of several locals in the surrounding woods over the past few years. This is the first novel in the Black Oak series, about a team of private investigators whose work exposes the uncanny and inexplicable.

**Other books you might like:**
Kevin J. Anderson, *Ruins*, 1996
Elizabeth Hand, *The Frenchman*, 1997
Lewis Gannett, *Gehenna*, 1997
Chet Williamson, *City of Iron*, 1998
Chet Williamson, *Empire of Dust*, 1998

## 2309

CHARLES L. GRANT

### Goblins

(New York: HarperPrism, 1994)

**Story type:** Science Fiction (Mystery; Horror)
**Series:** X-Files
**Major character(s):** Fox Mulder, FBI Agent; Dana Scully, FBI Agent, Doctor
**Time period(s):** 1990s
**Locale(s):** Washington, District of Columbia; New Jersey

**Summary:** When reports of an invisible murderer trigger an X-Files investigation, a witness considered unreliable by authorities blames the grisly murders on goblins. Television tie-in.

**Other books you might like:**
Elizabeth Forrest, *Phoenix Fire*, 1992
Alan Dean Foster, *Cyber Way*, 1990
Laurell K. Hamilton, *Guilty Pleasures*, 1993
Nick Pollotta, *Bureau 13*, 1991
Nick Pollotta, *Doomsday Exam*, 1992

## 2310

CHARLES L. GRANT

### In a Dark Dream

(New York: Tor, 1989)

**Story type:** Horror (Ghost Story)
**Major character(s):** Glenn Erskine, Police Officer (Sheriff); Cheryl Erskine, Child (Erskine's youngest daughter, a)
**Time period(s):** 1980s
**Locale(s):** Hunter, New Jersey

**Summary:** As if Glenn Erskine didn't have enough "real" problems to handle—an understaffed sheriff's department, a returning mass murderer, a career clash with his wife, and troubled children, especially his nightmare-prone daughter Cheryl, he must also deal with apparitions of dead people, strangers who appear and disappear mysteriously, violent encounters that subsequently "vanish," and, worst of all, a pervasive sense of impending doom.

**Other books you might like:**
Alan Ryan, *The Kill*, 1982
Chet Williamson, *Ash Wednesday*, 1987

## 2311

CHARLES L. GRANT, Editor

### In the Fog

(New York: Tor, 1993)

**Story type:** Horror (Anthology)
**Series:** Chronicles of Greystone Bay
**Locale(s):** Greystone Bay, New England

**Summary:** This fourth and purportedly final collection of novellas chronicling life in the atmospheric New England port city Greystone Bay includes Elizabeth Engstrom's "The Fog Knew Her Name," about a woman whose identity crisis takes on objective manifestations; Craig Shaw Gardner's "Warm," in which a man sees the apparition of his first wife in patterns in the snow; Kathryn Ptacek's "The Home," about what happens at a remote hospital for invalids cut off from the rest of Greystone Bay during a power outage; Chelsea Quinn Yarbro's "Whiteface," in which a Mafia-run carnival meets its comeuppance when forced to pitch its tents on haunted ground; Nancy Holder's "O Love They Kiss," which unfolds a grim tale from the Bay's colonial history; Steve Rasnic Tem's mesmerizing "Ice House Pond," in which a man's personal breakdown is mirrored in the landscape around him; and editor Grant's ghostly "Josie, in the Fog."

**Other books you might like:**
Ramsey Campbell, *Deathport*, 1993
F. Paul Wilson, *Freak Show*, 1992

**2312**

### CHARLES L. GRANT

## In the Mood

(New York: Tor, 1998)

**Story type:** Horror (Apocalyptic Horror)
**Series:** Millennium Quartet
**Major character(s):** John Bannock, Writer; Lanyon Trask, Religious (preacher); Tony Garza, Murderer
**Time period(s):** 1990s (1998)
**Locale(s):** Vallor, Illinois

**Summary:** John Bannock's interviews with death-row inmates uncover a universal plan, possibly engineered by the anti-Christ, who appears to be rallying his servants in an obscure midwestern town. The drama unfolds against a backdrop of universal famine in this second novel of Grant's Millennium Quartet, in which each novel dramatizes one of the Four Horsemen of the Apocalypse.

**Other books you might like:**
Daniel Easterman, *Name of the Beast*, 1992
Marc Laidlaw, *The 37th Mandala*, 1996
Andrew Laurance, *Catacomb*, 1981
Kim Newman, *Jago*, 1991
David Seltzer, *The Omen*, 1976

**2313**

### CHARLES L. GRANT

## Jackals

(New York: Tor, 1994)

**Story type:** Horror (Serial Killer)
**Major character(s):** Jim Scott, Wealthy; Rachel Corder, Drifter; Maurice Lion, Religious (preacher)
**Time period(s):** 1990s (1994)
**Locale(s):** Potar Ridge, Tennessee

**Summary:** When Jim Scott takes in the victim of a deliberate hit-and-run accident, it reignites a longstanding feud between Jim, his vigilante friends and the Jackals, a cabal of nearly inhuman predators who prey upon travellers and victims of highway mishaps. Unbeknownst to Jim, the Jackals have infiltrated his ranks in the hope of removing the final obstacle to their success.

**Other books you might like:**
Jay R. Bonansinga, *The Black Mariah*, 1994
Eric Flanders, *Night Blood*, 1993
Ray Garton, *Lot Lizards*, 1990
Billie Sue Mosiman, *Night Cruise*, 1992
John Shirley, *Wetbones*, 1992

**2314**

### CHARLES L. GRANT

## Raven

(New York: Tor, 1993)

**Story type:** Horror (Mystery)
**Major character(s):** Neil Maclaren, Restaurateur; Julia Sanders, Waiter/Waitress; Willie Ennin, Cook
**Time period(s):** 1990s (1993)
**Locale(s):** New Jersey

**Summary:** On a snowy winter night, Neil Maclaren's restaurant is besieged by a mysterious shotgun-toting figure. Driven to desperation, the imprisoned patrons and employees fight as much among themselves as against the stranger holding them captive.

**Other books you might like:**
Douglas Borton, *Kane*, 1989
Shirley Jackson, *The Sundial*, 1958
Stephen King, *The Shining*, 1977
Robert R. McCammon, *Stinger*, 1988

**2315**

### CHARLES L. GRANT, Editor

## The SeaHarp Hotel

(New York: Tor, 1990)

**Story type:** Horror (Anthology)
**Series:** Chronicles of Greystone Bay

**Summary:** In this third and final chronicle of the shared-world of Greystone Bay, 15 stories tell of or begin at the run-down SeaHarp Hotel. In "Ex-Library," Chet Williamson writes of the sinister influence at work in the downstairs reading room, while in "Beauty," Robert R. McCammon offers the narrative of someone whose circumstances render her a permanent non-paying guest. Thomas Monteleone's "No Pain, No Gain" and Les Daniel's "Room Service" are both eerie stories of unfortunate bellboys who learn more than they wish to know about the hotel's visitors.

**Other books you might like:**
Robert R. McCammon, *Under the Fang*, 1991
Robert Weinberg, *Lovecraft's Legacy*, 1990
    Martin H. Greenberg, co-author

**2316**

### CHARLES L. GRANT

## Something Stirs

(New York: Tor, 1991)

**Story type:** Horror (Small Town Horror)
**Major character(s):** Joey Costello, Teenager; Scott Byrns, Teenager; Fern Bellard, Teenager
**Time period(s):** 1990s
**Locale(s):** Foxriver, New Jersey

**Summary:** Something is killing the citizens of Foxriver, in particular the members of The Pack, a group of teenage outsiders who find solidarity by cultivating the group image of rebel outcasts fostered by B-movies of the 1950s. Unwittingly, their nostalgia has tapped into the fears behind small-town American life of that period, and given life to the same embodiments of those fears that dominated the film, fiction and popular culture of the Eisenhower years.

**Other books you might like:**
Ray Bradbury, *Something Wicked This Way Comes*, 1962
William W. Johnstone, *Darkly the Thunder*, 1990
Stephen King, *Christine*, 1983
Stephen King, *It*, 1986

**2317**

**CHARLES L. GRANT**

*Stunts*

(New York: Tor, 1990)

**Story type:** Horror (Curse)
**Major character(s):** Evan Kendal, Teacher (high school); Addie Burwin, Doctor; Brian Oakland, Teenager, Student—High School (at Port Richmond High School)
**Time period(s):** 1990s (1990)
**Locale(s):** London, England; Port Richmond, New Jersey

**Summary:** Pursued by a friend who has fallen under "the curse of the wolf," visiting teacher Evan Kendal flees England for America. Back home in New Jersey, he finds that his Uncle John has fallen under the same curse and is planning evil deeds that will coincide with the coming Halloween.

**Other books you might like:**
Stanwood Brooks, *The Seventh Child*, 1980
Jack Martin, *Halloween III: Season of the Witch*, 1985

**2318**

**CHARLES L. GRANT**

*Symphony*

(New York: Tor/Forge, 1997)

**Story type:** Horror (Apocalyptic Horror; Small Town Horror)
**Series:** Millennium Quartet
**Major character(s):** Casey Chisolm, Religious (minster); Stan Hogan, Drifter; Helen Gable, Waiter/Waitress
**Time period(s):** 1990s (1996)
**Locale(s):** Maple Landing, New Jersey

**Summary:** A plague of ominous portents in the small town of Maple Landing, and the Reverend Casey Chisholm's sudden discovery of his miraculous healing powers, dovetail with the nationwide swath of death and destruction wrought by a carload of vagrants en route to the town for an apocalyptic showdown between Good and Evil. This is the first of a projected quartet of novels built upon millenial themes.

**Other books you might like:**
Richard Bachman, *The Regulators*, 1996
Stephen King, *The Dead Zone*, 1979
Bentley Little, *The Revelation*, 1989
Elizabeth Massie, *Sineater*, 1992
Thomas F. Monteleone, *The Blood of the Lamb*, 1992

**2319**

**CHARLES L. GRANT**

*Tales From the Nightside*

(New York: Tor, 1991)

**Story type:** Horror (Collection)

**Summary:** Fifteen stories, most set in the recurring locales of Oxrun Station and Hawthorne Street, that typify the atmospheric, ambigu-

ous, subtle horror referred to as dark fantasy. The author is particularly interested in the macabre relationships that develop between children and adults (often parents) in "If Damon Calls," "When All the Children Call My Name," and "White Wolf Calling," and in the dark secrets of suburban neighborhoods disclosed in "Digging" and "Old Friends." Grant also expertly retailors classic fantasy themes to fit the simple lives of his small-town characters: Greek mythology in "Coin of the Realm," a reanimated corpse in "Three of Tens" and ghosts in "Come Dance with Me on My Pony's Grave."

**Other books you might like:**
Ray Bradbury, *The October Country*, 1955
Joseph Payne Brennan, *Stories of Darkness and Dread*, 1973
Dennis Etchison, *The Dark Country*, 1982
Robert R. McCammon, *Blue World*, 1989
Alan Ryan, *The Bones Wizard*, 1988

**2320**

**CHARLES L. GRANT**

*Whirlwind*

(New York: HarperPrism, 1995)

**Story type:** Fantasy (Mystery; Contemporary)
**Series:** X-Files
**Major character(s):** Fox Mulder, FBI Agent; Dana Scully, FBI Agent, Doctor
**Time period(s):** 1990s
**Locale(s):** New Mexico; Washington, District of Columbia

**Summary:** Called to investigate unusual deaths in the Southwest, Scully and Mulder discover a malevolent whirlwind, the Blood Wind, that seems under the direction of a human agent.

**Other books you might like:**
Kevin J. Anderson, *Ground Zero*, 1995
Elizabeth Forrest, *Phoenix Fire*, 1992
Alan Dean Foster, *Cyber Way*, 1990
Laurell K. Hamilton, *Guilty Pleasures*, 1993
Mercedes Lackey, *Burning Water*, 1989
Nick Pollotta, *Bureau 13*, 1991
Nick Pollotta, *Doomsday Exam*, 1992

**2321**

**CHARLES L. GRANT**

*The World of Darkness: Watcher*

(New York: Harper, 1997)

**Story type:** Horror (Werewolf Story)
**Series:** World of Darkness: Werewolf
**Major character(s):** Richard Turpin, FBI Agent, Werewolf; Joanne Minster, Police Officer; Miles Blanchard, Werewolf
**Time period(s):** 1990s (1997)
**Locale(s):** Lookout Mountain, Tennessee

**Summary:** A rogue werewolf is slaughtering humans in the Blue Ridge Mountains, threatening to break the Veil that separates humans from supernatural creatures in the World of Darkness and reveal the secret of the 13 tribes of the Garou. Werewolf Richard Turpin is assigned to work with human partner Joanne Minster and bring the monster to bay, without giving away his werewolf identity. Set in a fantasy role-playing world.

**Other books you might like:**
Don Bassingthwaite, *Such Pain*, 1995
Richard Lee Byers, *Netherworld*, 1995
Edo van Belkom, *Wyrm Wolf*, 1995

Stewart Von Allmen, *Conspicuous Consumption*, 1995

## 2322

**LINDA GRANT** (Pseudonym of Linda V. Williams)

### Vampire Bytes

(New York: Scribner, 1998)

**Story type:** Horror (Mystery; Vampire Story)
**Major character(s):** Catherine Sayler, Detective—Private; Ari Kazacos, Businessman; Thomas Seaton, Religious (reverend)
**Time period(s):** 1990s (1998)
**Locale(s):** San Francisco, California

**Summary:** At the request of Ari Kazacos, head of Astra Software, Catherine Sayler investigates the disappearance of programmer Matt Demming, who filched the company's hot new interactive software game, Cult of Blood, after a disagreement with his partner. Matt's body turns up drained of blood, evidence that Matt and others in his circle of friends and acquaintances have taken the notion of live-action role-playing games a bit too far.

**Other books you might like:**
John Coyne, *Hobgoblin*, 1981
Chet Day, *The Hacker*, 1989
Dean R. Koontz, *Dark Rivers of the Heart*, 1994
Joshua Quittner, *Flame War*, 1997
    Michelle Slatalla, co-author
Michael Reaves, *Night Hunter*, 1991

## 2323

**MARK GRANT** (Pseudonym of David Bischoff)

### Christmas Slaughter

(New York: Avon, 1991)

**Story type:** Science Fiction (Adventure; Post-Holocaust)
**Series:** Mutants Amok
**Major character(s):** Maximillian Turkel, Revolutionary; Ooslaxt, Mutant, Leader; SU912, Android
**Time period(s):** 21st century
**Locale(s):** Devil's Mountain, North America; New San Francisco, North America

**Summary:** The small band of rebels sneaks into New San Francisco to put an end to the Mutant's latest scheme to end Mutant dependence on continual supply of Human gene-material. They are aided by a group of crazed African-American berserkers and a renegade assassination "cyborg."

**Other books you might like:**
David Drake, *Hammer's Slammers*, 1979
Robert A. Heinlein, *Sixth Column*, 1949
Jack Yeovil, *Demon Download*, 1990
Ken Rolston, *Extreme Paranoia: Nobody Knows the Trouble I've Shot*, 1991
Norman Spinrad, *The Iron Dream*, 1972
Roger Zelazny, *Damnation Alley*, 1969

## 2324

**MARK GRANT** (Pseudonym of David Bischoff)

### Mutant Hell

(New York: Avon, 1991)

**Story type:** Science Fiction (Adventure; Post-Holocaust)

**Series:** Mutants Amok
**Major character(s):** Maximillian Turkel, Revolutionary, Warrior; Jack Bender, Revolutionary; BrainGeneral Torx, Genetically Altered Being, Military Personnel
**Time period(s):** 21st century (after the Last World War)
**Locale(s):** Iowa; Cheyenne Mt., Colorado

**Summary:** The recently captured Maximillian Turkel is flown to Cheyenne Mt. for delivery to the mutants' Emperor, Ignatius Charlemagne the Seventh, Point Five. While Max's friends journey to Colorado in hopes of rescuing him, Max tries to escape with the help of a mutant BrainGeneral in charge of the mutants' Internal Revenue Service.

**Other books you might like:**
Jerry Ahern, *To End All War*, 1990
James Axler, *Death Lands: Time Nomads*, 1990
Bob Ham, *Rolling Vengeance*, 1990
Jack Maloney, *Freedom Express*, 1990
Michael McGann, *The Ghost Warriors*, 1990
David Robbins, *Yellowstone Run*, 1990
James Rouch, *Body Count*, 1990

## 2325

**MARK GRANT** (Pseudonym of David Bischoff)

### Mutants Amok

(New York: Avon, 1991)

**Story type:** Science Fiction (Adventure; Post-Holocaust)
**Series:** Mutants Amok
**Major character(s):** Maximillian Turkel, Revolutionary, Fugitive; Jack Bender, Farmer, Revolutionary; BrainGeneral Torx, Genetically Altered Being, Military Personnel
**Time period(s):** 21st century
**Locale(s):** Iowa

**Summary:** New Humans, genetically altered human warriors, have risen up against their human creators and taken over. Maximillian Turkel, injured and fleeing, enlists the help of Jack Bender. Hidden in Jack's treehouse, Max heals sufficiently to undergo surgical removal of an implanted tracking device. In a subsequent attempt to rescue Jack's girlfriend from the Muties, Max and his friends are captured. His friends escape and plan to rescue Max.

**Other books you might like:**
Jerry Ahern, *To End All War*, 1990
James Axler, *Death Lands: Time Nomads*, 1990
Bob Ham, *Rolling Vengeance*, 1990
Jack Maloney, *Freedom Express*, 1990
Michael McGann, *The Ghost Warriors*, 1990
David Robbins, *Yellowstone Run*, 1990
James Rouch, *Body Count*, 1990

## 2326

**RICHARD GRANT**

### In the Land of Winter

(New York: Avon, 1997)

**Story type:** Fantasy (Contemporary; Religious)
**Major character(s):** Pippa Rede, Single Parent; Winterbelle, Child
**Time period(s):** 1990s
**Locale(s):** New England

**Summary:** Struggling to survive and raise Winterbelle in a forest home in harmony with nature, Pippa, a Wiccan, must suddenly reorient her world when bigoted religious zealots accuse her of child abuse and Satan worship. Deprived of her loving and beloved daughter by complicit government officials, Pippa finds solace and transformation deep in the woods.

**Other books you might like:**
Rose Estes, *Troll-Taken*, 1993
Katharine Eliska Kimbriel, *Kindred Rites*, 1997
Holly Lisle, *Minerva Wakes*, 1994
Susan Palwick, *Flying in Place*, 1992
Terri Windling, *The Wood Wife*, 1996

---

## 2327

### RICHARD GRANT

## *Tex and Molly in the Afterlife*

(New York: Avon, 1996)

**Story type:** Fantasy (Satire; Science Fiction)
**Major character(s):** Tex ''Bear'' Darffot, Spirit, Activist; Molly, Spirit, Activist
**Time period(s):** 1990s
**Locale(s):** Maine; The Afterlife, Mythical Place

**Summary:** Counting-culture enthusiasts Tex and Molly find their alternate life style becomes an alternate death style when dying leaves them unready to depart Earth. Both individuals discover odd and unpleasant aspects of the Afterlife when they attempt to continue their routine existence and goals while meeting the strange denizens inhabiting their space.

**Other books you might like:**
Alan Dean Foster, *To the Vanishing Point*, 1988
Neil Gaiman, *Good Omens: The Nice and Accurate Prophecies of Agnes Nutter, Witch*, 1990
   Terry Pratchett, co-author
James Morrow, *Towing Jehovah*, 1944
Daniel Manus Pinkwater, *The Afterlife Diet*, 1995
Terry Pratchett, *Reaper Man*, 1992
Elizabeth Ann Scarborough, *Last Refuge*, 1992
Thorne Smith, *Topper: An Improbable Adventure*, 1926

---

## 2328

### RICHARD GRANT

## *Through the Heart*

(New York: Bantam Spectra, 1991)

**Story type:** Fantasy (Science Fiction; Literary)
**Major character(s):** Bell Dog, Engineer; Kem, Teenager; Sander, Friend, Teenager
**Time period(s):** Indeterminate Future
**Locale(s):** The Oasis (Midwest desert)

**Summary:** Sander, exchanged by his father for a new motor and tools, gradually understands the functioning of his new home, the land ship *Oasis*. On its route through the post-disaster American Desert, Sander is promoted from galley boy, to engine snipe, to assistant navigation officer. While learning much about the world and people around him, Sander also learns that trading with the wagon people and a few remaining communities masks the true purpose of the *Oasis's* journey.

**Other books you might like:**
David Brin, *Earth*, 1990
Samuel R. Delany, *Tales of Neveryon*, 1979
Marjorie Bradley Kellogg, *Harmony*, 1991
J.M. Morgan, *Desert Eden*, 1991

Frederik Pohl, *Gladiator-at-Law*, 1955
   C.M. Kornbluth, co-author
Vernor Vinge, *Marooned in Realtime*, 1986

---

## 2329

### RICHARD GRANT

## *Views from the Oldest House*

(New York: Doubleday Foundation, 1989)

**Story type:** Science Fiction (Satire)
**Major character(s):** Turner Ashenden, Student; Black Malachi Pantera, Student (Lunatic)
**Time period(s):** Indeterminate Future
**Locale(s):** United States

**Summary:** Turner Ashenden, an incompetent and not very happy college student in a near-future world which appears on the edge of economic collapse, finds himself proclaimed a hero by his mad friend Black Malachi Pantera. Turner's supposed destiny begins to seem more than just an outrageous joke, however, when he discovers the Bad Winters Institute of Science and Philosophy, a secluded mansion in the nearby mountains, and confronts the strange psychic Madame Gwendola.

**Other books you might like:**
James P. Blaylock, *Homunculus*, 1986
James P. Blaylock, *Land of Dreams*, 1987
James P. Blaylock, *The Last Coin*, 1988
John Crowley, *Aegypt*, 1987
John Crowley, *Little, Big*, 1981
Tim Powers, *The Anubis Gates*, 1983
Thomas Pynchon, *Gravity's Rainbow*, 1973

---

## 2330

### GEARY GRAVEL

## *A Key for the Nonesuch*

(New York: Ballantine/Del Rey, 1990)

**Story type:** Science Fiction (Adventure; Alternate Universe)
**Series:** War of the Fading Worlds
**Major character(s):** Howard Bell, Maintenance Worker, Writer (aspiring)
**Time period(s):** 1990s
**Locale(s):** Nexus Building, Earth; Fading Worlds, Alternate Universe

**Summary:** Howard Bell, master handyman, could fix almost anything. At his job in the brand new Nexus Building he borrows a key to the washroom which propels him to another place. He finds that he is the Nonesuch in the Fading Worlds, a perpetually changing battlefield.

**Other books you might like:**
M.A.R. Barker, *Man of Gold*, 1984
Alfred Bester, *The Demolished Man*, 1953
Steven Brust, *Jhereg*, 1983
Will Shetterly, *The Tangled Lands*, 1989
E.C. Tubb, *Toyman*, 1969

## 2331

### GEARY GRAVEL

## *Mask of the Phantasm*

(New York: Bantam Spectra, 1994)

**Story type:** Science Fiction (Adventure; Mystery)
**Series:** Batman
**Major character(s):** Bruce ''Batman'' Wayne, Hero, Detective—Amateur; Andrea Beaumont, Girlfriend; The Joker, Criminal
**Time period(s):** 21st century
**Locale(s):** Gotham City (New York City)

**Summary:** When a serial killer of mob bosses frames Batman, police begin searching for him as the suspect. The approaching career burnout and reappearance of a former paramour lead Batman to reconsider retirement. Novelizes the animated film.

**Other books you might like:**
Craig Shaw Gardner, *The Batman Murders*, 1992
Martin H. Greenberg, *The Further Adventures of Batman*, 1989 editor
Simon Hawke, *Batman: To Stalk a Specter*, 1991
Joe R. Lansdale, *Captured by the Engines*, 1991
Dennis O'Neil, *Batman: Knightfall*, 1994

## 2332

### GEARY GRAVEL

## *The Return of the Breakneck Boys*

(New York: Ballantine/Del Rey, 1991)

**Story type:** Science Fiction (Adventure)
**Series:** War of the Fading Worlds
**Major character(s):** Howard Bell, Leader; Yam Ya-Mash, Sidekick, Alien (Trilbit); Alaiya, Military Personnel
**Time period(s):** 1990s
**Locale(s):** Boston, Massachusetts; The Thousand Island World, Planet—Imaginary; The Flower World, Planet—Imaginary

**Summary:** This book continues the adventures begun in *A Key for the Nonsuch*. Howard and his crew discover more about the Fading Worlds and the Keyholders. After returning from a weekend on Earth with a newly found Breakneck Boy, Howard finds he can no longer return to Earth. Although the battle with the Keyholders has barely begun, the Breakneck Boys resolve not to quit until the Keyholders are conquered.

**Other books you might like:**
Douglas Adams, *The Hitchhiker's Guide to the Galaxy*, 1980
David Brin, *Startide Rising*, 1983
John DeChancie, *Starrigger*, 1983
Philip Jose Farmer, *To Your Scattered Bodies Go*, 1971
Alan Dean Foster, *Glory Lane*, 1987
Larry Niven, *Ringworld*, 1970
E.C. Tubb, *The Winds of Gath*, 1967

## 2333

### PAT GRAVERSEN

## *Black Ice*

(New York: Zebra, 1993)

**Story type:** Horror (Supernatural Vengeance)
**Major character(s):** John ''Gibby'' Gibson, Doctor; Cassie McCall, Accountant (bookkeeper); Jess McCall, Child (Cassie's 8-year-old son)

**Time period(s):** 1990s (1993)
**Locale(s):** Winter Falls, Connecticut

**Summary:** Connor McCall helped cover up a crime related to his practicing black magic by disposing of the bodies of his three half sisters in Lake Wahelo. More than half a century later, the trio claim the soul of Connor's grandson Jess when he accidentally falls into the lake, and use him to seek their revenge upon the town.

**Other books you might like:**
Matthew J. Costello, *Beneath Still Waters*, 1989
Ruby Jean Jensen, *Celia*, 1991

## 2334

### PAT GRAVERSEN

## *The Fagin*

(New York: Zebra, 1992)

**Story type:** Horror (Child-in-Peril)
**Major character(s):** Felice Sinclair, Divorced Person, Single Parent; Jason Sinclair, Child (Felice's 6 year old son); Kadar, Witch
**Time period(s):** 1990s
**Locale(s):** Blue Falls, Virginia

**Summary:** Felice Sinclair thinks that a return to her hometown following her divorce will help her get a new start in life. Troubles arise when when a local coven kidnaps her son Jason because they recognize in him the essential qualities that will make him an ideal future leader. This novel was originally published in 1982.

**Other books you might like:**
John Coyne, *Child of Shadows*, 1990
Tom Piccirilli, *Dark Father*, 1990
Peter Straub, *Shadowland*, 1980

## 2335

### PAT GRAVERSEN

## *Graythings*

(New York: Zebra, 1995)

**Story type:** Horror (Occult)
**Major character(s):** Mariele Hollander, Interior Decorator; Simon Novak, Psychic; Dwago, Cult Member (Thanatological Society)
**Time period(s):** 1990s (1995)
**Locale(s):** New York, New York

**Summary:** Mariele Hollander's efforts to contact her dead husband through a seance activate the ''graythings,'' intangible beings from the other side of death that begin seeping into our own world.

**Other books you might like:**
Daniel H. Gower, *Harrowgate*, 1993
Fritz Leiber, *Our Lady of Darkness*, 1977
T.M. Wright, *The Ascending*, 1995
T.M. Wright, *Sleepeasy*, 1993

## 2336

### PAT GRAVERSEN

## *Precious Blood*

(New York: Zebra, 1993)

**Story type:** Horror (Vampire Story)
**Major character(s):** Beth Hart, Teenager, Vampire; Quinn, Vampire; Adragon Hart, Vampire (leader, Society of Vampires)
**Time period(s):** 2000s (2005)

**Locale(s):** New York, New York

**Summary:** Vampire Adragon Hart struggles to save his rebellious teenage daughter from the clutches of Quinn, leader of a band of renegade urban vampires whose traffickings in diseased blood and the intravenous narcotic Rush threaten to expose the vampire subculture living in the suburbs.

**Other books you might like:**
Poppy Z. Brite, *Lost Souls*, 1992
Scott Ciencin, *The Vampire Odyssey*, 1992
Nancy A. Collins, *Sunglasses After Dark*, 1989
William Tedford, *Liquid Diet*, 1992

---

**2337**

**PAT GRAVERSEN**

### Sweet Blood

(New York: Zebra, 1992)

**Story type:** Horror (Vampire Story)
**Major character(s):** Adragon Hart, Teenager, Vampire; Elsbeth Hart, Writer, Vampire; Delphine Keelan, Vampire
**Time period(s):** 1990s (1992)
**Locale(s):** Asbury Park, New Jersey

**Summary:** Adragon Hart thinks it's all a joke when he and his socially withdrawn mother are inducted into The Society of Vampires. But then Adragon discovers that the society's members really are vampires—and that his overprotective mother is not about to give him up to the alluring Society officer Del Keelan without a bloody fight.

**Other books you might like:**
Poppy Z. Brite, *Lost Souls*, 1992
Richard Lee Byers, *The Vampire's Apprentice*, 1992
John Peyton Cooke, *Out for Blood*, 1991
Mark Ivanhoe, *Virgintooth*, 1991
Anne Rice, *Interview with the Vampire*, 1976

---

**2338**

**ALASDAIR GRAY**

### A History Maker

(New York: Harcourt Brace, 1996)

**Story type:** Science Fiction (Satire; Political)
**Major character(s):** Wat Dryhope, Warrior, Hero; Kate "Kittock" Dryhope, Parent; Jardine Craig Douglas, Military Personnel (general)
**Time period(s):** 23rd century (2230s)
**Locale(s):** Scotland

**Summary:** Unable to adjust to space, Wat returns home to fight beside his father, General Craig Douglas, who orders Wat to perform an unethical tactic which prevents defeat. Observed by the public eye which broadcasts battles, Wat refuses to accept the image of hero. He returns to the women of Dryhope, receiving much attention as most of the men now nourish the powerplant.

**Other books you might like:**
Eleanor Arnason, *Ring of Swords*, 1993
Samuel R. Delany, *They Fly at Ciron*, 1993
James Morrow, *City of Truth*, 1992
Sheri S. Tepper, *A Plague of Angels*, 1993
George Turner, *Genetic Soldier*, 1994

---

**2339**

**MURIEL GRAY**

### Furnace

(New York: Doubleday, 1997)

**Story type:** Horror (Black Magic)
**Major character(s):** Josh Spiller, Truck Driver; Nelly MacFarlane, Political Figure (town councillor); Griffin MacFarlane, Teenager
**Time period(s):** 1990s (1997)
**Locale(s):** Furnace, Virginia

**Summary:** After an upsetting accident in the small town of Furnace, where he claims he saw a town leader push a child in front of his truck, Josh Spiller can't shake the feeling that he is being pursued by something dreadful. Josh soon discovers the town is populated with the descendants of alchemists who perform ritual sacrifice and that he has been passed runes, a parchment with an invocation to fire demon that he must pass "willingly but unknowingly" back to the person who passed it to him if he is to avoid a horrible death. The novel is a variation on M. R. James's classic story, "Casting the Runes."

**Other books you might like:**
Ramsey Campbell, *Obsession*, 1985
Christopher Fowler, *Rune*, 1990
Charles L. Grant, *The Hour of the Oxrun Dead*, 1977
Bernard Taylor, *Evil Intent*, 1994

---

**2340**

**MURIEL GRAY**

### The Trickster

(New York: Doubleday, 1995)

**Story type:** Horror (Ancient Evil Unleashed)
**Major character(s):** Sam Hunt, Maintenance Worker (groundskeeper), Indian; Katie Hunt, Museum Curator (Silver Heritage Museum); Calvin Bitterhand, Shaman, Indian
**Time period(s):** 1900s (1907); 1990s (1995)

**Summary:** This first novel, originally published in England in 1994, tells of the Trickster, a demon of Indian mythology. It is successfully thwarted in the Canadian mining town of Silver in 1907 when the Indians and whites bury their differences to work collectively against it. But it re-emerges to cause murder and mayhem in contemporary times when Sam Hunt repudiates his tribal heritage and selection to be a Sioux shaman.

**Other books you might like:**
Colin Kersey, *Soul Catcher*, 1995
G. Wayne Miller, *Thunder Rise*, 1988
Adam Niswander, *The Charm*, 1993
Eugene E. Pfaff Jr., *Uwharrie*, 1993
  Michael Causey, co-author
Kathryn Ptacek, *Ghost Dance*, 1990
Patrick Whalen, *Deathwalker*, 1992

---

**2341**

**DAINA GRAZIUNAS**
**JIM STARLIN**, Co-Author

### Thinning the Predators

(New York: Warner, 1996)

**Story type:** Horror (Serial Killer; Wild Talents)

**Major character(s):** David Vandermark, Lawyer; Ira Levitt, FBI Agent
**Time period(s):** 1990s (1996)
**Locale(s):** New York, New York

**Summary:** Following an accident that endows him with telepathic powers, David Vandermark embarks on a spree to eliminate the serial killer who murdered his wife and child and a score of other murderers like him. Federal agent Levitt pursues Vandermark to New York to apprehend him, but becomes his ally when he discovers that recent murders Vandermark is investigating in the local Hispanic community are government plots.

**Other books you might like:**
Thomas Harris, *Red Dragon*, 1981
Dean R. Koontz, *The Bad Place*, 1990
Dean R. Koontz, *Dragon Tears*, 1993
Joe R. Lansdale, *The Nightrunners*, 1987

## 2342

### ANDREW M. GREELEY

### *Angel Light*
(New York: Tor Forge, 1995)

**Story type:** Fantasy (Religious; Contemporary)
**Major character(s):** G. Patrick "Toby" Tobin, Traveler, Computer Expert; Raphaella "Rae", Angel, Travel Agent; Sara Ann Tobin, Student (music)
**Time period(s):** 1990s
**Locale(s):** Chicago, Illinois; Ireland

**Summary:** Hoping to inherit a large fortune, Toby reluctantly follows his ancestor's demand that he woo a distant Irish cousin and end a family feud. While arranging the trip to Ireland, Toby contacts Raphaella who has searched for a human to help. Based on the Book of Tobias from the Old Testament of the Bible.

**Other books you might like:**
Peter Crowther, *Heaven Sent: 18 Glorious Tales of the Angels*, 1995
    editor
Jack Dann, *Angels!*, 1995
    Gardner Dozois, co-editor
Neil Gaiman, *Good Omens: The Nice and Accurate Prophecies of Agnes Nutter, Witch*, 1990
    Terry Pratchett, co-author
Parke Godwin, *Waiting for the Galactic Bus*, 1987
C.S. Lewis, *Out of the Silent Planet*, 1943
Nancy Springer, *Metal Angel*, 1994
Sean Stewart, *Resurrection Man*, 1995

## 2343

### ANDREW M. GREELEY, Editor
### MICHAEL CASSUTT, Co-Editor

### *Sacred Visions*
(New York: Tor, 1991)

**Story type:** Science Fiction (Anthology; Theological)
**Summary:** This volume contains twelve stories with Roman Catholic settings or themes and a six-page introduction and includes reprinted stories by James Blish, Anthony Boucher, Jeff Duntemann, Walter M. Miller, Jr. and R.A. Lafferty plus three original stories, "Xorinda the Witch" by Andrew M. Greeley, "Guts" by Jack McDevitt, and "The Seraph from Its Sepulcher" by Gene Wolfe.

**Other books you might like:**
Orson Scott Card, *Xenocide*, 1991

Alan Dean Foster, *Cyber Way*, 1990
Parke Godwin, *Waiting for the Galactic Bus*, 1988
Robert A. Heinlein, *Stranger in a Strange Land*, 1991
    revised
Frank Herbert, *Whipping Star*, 1970
Marc Laidlaw, *Neon Lotus*, 1988
Ted Reynolds, *The Tides of God*, 1989
Ian Watson, *God's World*, 1990

## 2344

### MICHAEL GREEN

### *Dry Skull Dreams*
(New York: Pocket, 1995)

**Story type:** Horror (Science Fiction)
**Major character(s):** Molly Coughlin, Nurse; Charlie Coughlin, Aged Person; Sibatia, Shaman
**Time period(s):** 1990s (1995)
**Locale(s):** Brattleboro, Vermont

**Summary:** In this informal sequel to *The Jimjams* (1994), Molly Coughlin returns from relief work in Africa unaware that a tribal shaman has infected her with "seeds" from outer space that will take over her will and force her to pass them to an increasing number of other victims.

**Other books you might like:**
Jack Finney, *The Body Snatchers*, 1955
Robert A. Heinlein, *The Puppet Masters*, 1951
John Shirley, *In Darkness Waiting*, 1988
Lawrence Watt-Evans, *The Nightmare People*, 1990
John Wyndham, *The Day of the Triffids*, 1951

## 2345

### MICHAEL GREEN

### *The Jimjams*
(New York: Pocket, 1994)

**Story type:** Horror (Science Fiction)
**Major character(s):** Duffy Farris, Hotel Worker; Rose Farris, Hotel Worker; Earl Douchette, Aged Person (retiree)
**Time period(s):** 1990s (1994)
**Locale(s):** Blue Turtle Island, Florida

**Summary:** Blue Turtle Island turns into the retirement resort from hell when a horde of "freddies," (possibly extraterrestrial) insectoid creatures with wings and frog features, turn visitors into sex- and violence-crazed incubators for their kind.

**Other books you might like:**
Jack Finney, *The Body Snatchers*, 1955
Robert A. Heinlein, *The Puppet Masters*, 1951
John Shirley, *In Darkness Waiting*, 1988
Whitley Strieber, *The Forbidden Zone*, 1993
Lawrence Watt-Evans, *The Nightmare People*, 1990

## 2346

### MICHAEL GREEN

### *Quest: In Search of the Dragontooth*
(Philadelphia: Running Press, 1994)

**Story type:** Fantasy (Quest; Religious)

**Major character(s):** Magnalucius, Religious, Writer; Ibn Sufa al-Iskandaria, Companion, Adventurer
**Time period(s):** 15th century
**Locale(s):** England

**Summary:** This illustrated monk's journal is divided into two parts: ''The Unicornis Notebooks of Magnalucius'' details his search for the origins of a unicorn that he spotted one day while meditating; and ''In Search of the Dragontooth'' follows his pursuit of the enchanted Perilous Dragontooth using old documents and rumors acquired as he proceeds.

**Other books you might like:**
Richard Gilliam, *Grails: Quests of the Dawn*, 1994
     Martin H. Greenberg, Edward E. Kramer, co-editors
Richard Gilliam, *Grails: Visitations of the Night*, 1994
     Martin H. Greenberg, Edward E. Kramer, co-editors
James Gurney, *Dinotopia*, 1992
Jane Yolen, *Here There Be Dragons*, 1993
Jane Yolen, *Here There Be Unicorns*, 1994

## 2347

### ROLAND J. GREEN

## *Conan the Guardian*

(New York: Tor, 1991)

**Story type:** Fantasy (Sword and Sorcery)
**Series:** Conan the Barbarian
**Major character(s):** Conan, Barbarian, Warrior
**Time period(s):** Indeterminate
**Locale(s):** Argos, Fictional Country; Alternate Earth

**Summary:** Conan accepts the duty of guarding Livia, then he and his men must defend her against armed men and treacherous sorcery.

**Other books you might like:**
Leonard Carpenter, *Conan the Warlord*, 1988
Robert E. Howard, *Conan the Barbarian*, 1955
Robert E. Howard, *Conan the Conqueror*, 1950
Robert Jordan, *Conan the Magnificent*, 1984
Robert Jordan, *Conan the Victorious*, 1984
Steve Perry, *Conan the Free Lance*, 1990
Karl Edward Wagner, *Echoes of Valor I*, 1987
     editor

## 2348

### ROLAND J. GREEN

## *Conan the Relentless*

(New York: Tor, 1992)

**Story type:** Fantasy (Sword and Sorcery)
**Series:** Conan the Barbarian
**Major character(s):** Conan, Barbarian, Warrior; Raihna, Warrior, Leader
**Time period(s):** Indeterminate
**Locale(s):** Border Kingdom, Fictional Country

**Summary:** While traveling through the northern borderlands, Conan chances upon Raihna, a beautiful swordswoman known to him, and joins her followers. In service to the king, Conan may represent the only hope of countering the magic employed by the Star Brothers and stopping the ancient evil they have loosed.

**Other books you might like:**
Leonard Carpenter, *Conan the Warlord*, 1988
Robert E. Howard, *Conan the Barbarian*, 1955
Robert E. Howard, *Conan the Conqueror*, 1950

Robert Jordan, *Conan the Magnificent*, 1984
Robert Jordan, *Conan the Victorious*, 1984
Steve Perry, *Conan the Free Lance*, 1990
Karl Edward Wagner, *Echoes of Valor I*, 1987
     editor

## 2349

### ROLAND J. GREEN

## *The Mountain Walks*

(New York: Ace Books, 1989)

**Story type:** Science Fiction (Military)
**Series:** The Peace Company
**Major character(s):** John Parkes, Military Personnel (Sergeant Major)
**Time period(s):** 24th century
**Locale(s):** Zauberberg, Planet—Imaginary

**Summary:** Religious fanaticism is tearing the planet Zauberberg apart. The Peace Force must stop the fighting and solve the religious dispute.

**Other books you might like:**
Gordon R. Dickson, *Lost Dorsai*, 1980
Gordon R. Dickson, *Soldier, Ask Not*, 1967
Gordon R. Dickson, *The Tactics of Mistake*, 1971
Jerry Pournelle, *Janissaries*, 1979
Larry Niven, *Oath of Fealty*, 1981
     Jerry Pournelle, co-author
Jerry Pournelle, *Prince of Mercenaries*, 1989

## 2350

### ROLAND J. GREEN

## *On the Verge*

(Renton, Washington: TSR, 1998)

**Story type:** Science Fiction (Military)
**Major character(s):** Damion Witzko, Military Personnel (lieutenant); Kasuga, Military Personnel
**Time period(s):** Indeterminate Future
**Locale(s):** Arist, Planet—Imaginary

**Summary:** A company of space marines stationed on a remote, ice covered world find themselves in the middle of a shooting war. If the conflict escalates, it could spread off world and embroil the entire human culture. Interpersonal rivalries among the marines complicate matters further.

**Other books you might like:**
Bill Baldwin, *The Mercenaries*, 1991
Lois McMaster Bujold, *Shards of Honor*, 1986
William C. Dietz, *Freehold*, 1987
David Drake, *Northworld*, 1990
William H. Keith Jr., *Operation Excalibur*, 1997

## 2351

### ROLAND J. GREEN

## *The Painful Field*

(New York: Roc, 1993)

**Story type:** Science Fiction (Military; Political)
**Series:** Starcruiser Shenandoah

**Major character(s):** Candice Shores, Military Personnel (Lieutenant Colonel); Rose Liddell, Spaceship Captain; Sho Kurasawa, Military Personnel (Vice Admiral)
**Time period(s):** Indeterminate Future
**Locale(s):** Linak'h, Planet—Imaginary; *Shenandoah*, Spaceship

**Summary:** The crew of the Federation starcruiser *Shenandoah*, charged with keeping an uneasy peace on Linak'h, tread a fine line among the factions and species on the planet. An attempted prison break and sabotage of a chemical plant escalates into a deadly campaign of terrorism as a struggle between the Confraternity and the Administration turns friends into enemies.

**Other books you might like:**
C.J. Cherryh, *Downbelow Station*, 1981
Gordon R. Dickson, *The Tactics of Mistake*, 1971
Jane S. Fancher, *Ground-Ties*, 1991
Joe Haldeman, *The Forever War*, 1975
Robert A. Heinlein, *Starship Troopers*, 1959
Jerry Pournelle, *Falkenberg's Legion*, 1990
Joel Rosenberg, *Hero*, 1990

---

**2352**

ROLAND J. GREEN

## Squadron Alert

(New York: NAL Signet, 1989)

**Story type:** Science Fiction (Military)
**Series:** Starcruiser Shenandoah
**Major character(s):** Rose Liddell, Spaceship Captain
**Time period(s):** 26th century
**Locale(s):** Victoria, Planet—Imaginary

**Summary:** War looms between the United Federation of Starworlds and the Freeworld States Alliance over the planet Victoria. Rose Liddell, captain of the Starcruiser *Shenandoah*, has evidence that an unknown third party is promoting the violence. She must discover the culprit and stop the war.

**Other books you might like:**
W. Michael Gear, *The Artifact*, 1989
Thorarinn Gunnarsson, *Battle of the Ring*, 1989
Larry Niven, *The Mote in God's Eye*, 1974
   Jerry Pournelle, co-author

---

**2353**

ROLAND J. GREEN

## The Sum of Things

(New York: Roc, 1991)

**Story type:** Science Fiction (Military)
**Series:** Starcruiser Shenandoah
**Major character(s):** Rose Liddell, Spaceship Captain; Candice Shores, Military Personnel (acting Major); Sho Kurasawa, Military Personnel (acting Vice Admiral)
**Time period(s):** Indeterminate Future
**Locale(s):** Victoria, Planet—Imaginary

**Summary:** The Federation and the Alliance both want peace, but the planetary factions are still fighting. The presence of two alien races complicates the picture, along with terrorist acts by unidentified forces. The crew of the *Shenandoah* has to fight on multiple fronts to preserve the newly created Associated States of Victoria.

**Other books you might like:**
John Dalmas, *The Lizard War*, 1989
Gordon R. Dickson, *The Tactics of Mistake*, 1971

Joe Haldeman, *The Forever War*, 1975
Robert A. Heinlein, *Starship Troopers*, 1959
Jerry Pournelle, *Falkenberg's Legion*, 1990
Joel Rosenberg, *Hero*, 1990

---

**2354**

SHARON GREEN

## Challenges

(New York: Avon Eos, 1998)

**Story type:** Fantasy (Magic Conflict; Political)
**Series:** Blending
**Major character(s):** Jovvi Hafford, Wizard, Prostitute (retired); Rion Mardimil, Wizard, Gentleman; Lorand "Lor" Coll, Wizard, Farmer
**Time period(s):** Indeterminate Past
**Locale(s):** Gan Garee, Fictional City

**Summary:** The five heroes continue to tighten their bond, despite the underhanded tricks of the nobles and the testing authority. The success of a common blending would challenge social conventions, an unacceptable development. Then the blending discovers a secret that will either perfect their power or shatter it.

**Other books you might like:**
Marion Zimmer Bradley, *The Forbidden Tower*, 1977
Teresa Edgerton, *Goblin Moon*, 1991
Ursula K. Le Guin, *A Wizard of Earthsea*, 1968
Patricia A. McKillip, *The Book of Atrix Wolfe*, 1995
Caroline Stevermer, *A College of Magics*, 1994

---

**2355**

SHARON GREEN

## Competition

(New York: AvoNova, 1997)

**Story type:** Fantasy (Magic Conflict; Political)
**Series:** Blending
**Major character(s):** Jovvi Hafford, Wizard, Prostitute; Rion Mardimil, Wizard, Gentleman; Lorand Coll, Wizard, Farmer
**Time period(s):** Indeterminate Past
**Locale(s):** Gan Garee, Fictional City

**Summary:** The five magicians who must become the next Blending must master their powers. They must use those powers to survive a series of deadly tests, ones that at least some of their teachers would prefer they failed. In an Empire failing from ignorance and corruption, five young wizards have little hope. Sequel to *Convergence*.

**Other books you might like:**
Teresa Edgerton, *Goblin Moon*, 1991
Ellen Kushner, *Swordspoint*, 1987
Caroline Stevermer, *A College of Magics*, 1994
Elizabeth Willey, *A Sorcerer and a Gentleman*, 1995
Patricia C. Wrede, *Mairelon the Magician*, 1991

---

**2356**

SHARON GREEN

## Convergence

(New York: AvoNova, 1996)

**Story type:** Fantasy (Magic Conflict; Political)
**Series:** Blending

**Major character(s):** Lorand "Lor" Coll, Wizard, Farmer; Tamrissa Domon, Wizard, Abuse Victim; Vallant Ro, Wizard, Sea Captain
**Time period(s):** Indeterminate
**Locale(s):** Gan Garee, Fictional City

**Summary:** The first Blending of Water, Earth, Air, Fire, and Spirit founded the Empire and defeated the evil Four Powers centuries ago. Now a group of five unwilling candidates must participate in unwelcome training of their talents to learn if they will become the next Blending. If they don't, the Four Powers may return.

**Other books you might like:**
Glen Cook, *The Swordbearer*, 1982
Teresa Edgerton, *Goblin Moon*, 1991
Ursula K. Le Guin, *A Wizard of Earthsea*, 1968
Caroline Stevermer, *A College of Magics*, 1994
Janny Wurts, *Stormwarden*, 1984

---

**2357**

SHARON GREEN

## Dark Mirror, Dark Dreams

(New York: AvoNova, 1994)

**Story type:** Fantasy (Magic Conflict; Quest)
**Major character(s):** Alexia, Royalty (princess), Magician (shape-shifter); Tiran d'Iste, Mercenary, Magician (shape-shifter); Chalaine, Sorceress
**Time period(s):** Indeterminate
**Locale(s):** Golran, Fictional Country

**Summary:** Misunderstandings threaten to disrupt the honeymoon of Alexia and her new husband, Tiran, as they prepare to oust the usurpers in their alternate world kingdom. Their alliance with Chalaine and Bariden, the rightful rulers of a neighboring alternate world, deepens their jealousies when they agree to split their forces as a strategic ploy. Finally, they must each face the evil magic of their alternate selves in order to save their kingdoms and their marriages. Sequel to *Silver Princess, Golden Knight*.

**Other books you might like:**
Margaret Ball, *The Shadow Gate*, 1991
Marion Zimmer Bradley, *The Forbidden Tower*, 1977
Simon R. Green, *Blue Moon Rising*, 1991
Barbara Hambly, *Dog Wizard*, 1993
Robert A. Heinlein, *Glory Road*, 1963

---

**2358**

SHARON GREEN

## The Hidden Realms

(New York: AvoNova, 1993)

**Story type:** Fantasy (Magic Conflict; Quest)
**Major character(s):** Chalaine, Sorceress; Bariden, Martial Arts Expert (swordsman), Sorcerer
**Time period(s):** Indeterminate
**Locale(s):** Melen, Fictional Country; Palace of Ease, Mythical Place

**Summary:** To counter the evil force acting on souls within the castle walls, Chalaine joins with Prince Bariden. Their search leads through a portal and into a series of dangerous challenges as they investigate the conspiracy that may prove fatal for them.

**Other books you might like:**
Carole Nelson Douglas, *Cup of Clay*, 1991
Laurell K. Hamilton, *Nightseer*, 1992
Shirley Rousseau Murphy, *The Catswold Portal*, 1993
Martha Wells, *The Element of Fire*, 1993

---

**2359**

SHARON GREEN

## Silver Princess, Golden Knight

(New York: AvoNova, 1993)

**Story type:** Fantasy (Alternate World; Romance)
**Major character(s):** Alexia, Royalty (princess), Magician (shape-shifter); Tiran d'Iste, Mercenary, Magician (shape-shifter); Reynar III, Ruler (king), Parent
**Time period(s):** Indeterminate
**Locale(s):** Golran, Fictional Country

**Summary:** King Reynar, outraged by his daughter's wild behavior, decides that Alexia should marry. In order to find a husband equal to her in shape-shifting and swordfighting abilities, he announces a contest with Alexia as the prize. Determined to control her own life, Alexia enters the contest herself, but magical sabotage sends Alexia and the leading contender, Tiran d'Iste, through a Gate into other worlds. Shared peril forces her to cooperate with her rival, but her growing attraction to Tiran threatens to upset her plans.

**Other books you might like:**
Margaret Ball, *The Shadow Gate*, 1990
C.J. Cherryh, *Exile's Gate*, 1988
Pamela Dean, *The Secret Country*, 1985
R.A. MacAvoy, *The Book of Kells*, 1985
Patricia C. Wrede, *The Seven Towers*, 1984

---

**2360**

SHARON GREEN

## Wind Whispers, Shadow Shouts

(New York: AvoNova, 1995)

**Story type:** Fantasy (Magic Conflict; Quest)
**Major character(s):** Alexia, Royalty (queen), Magician (shape-shifter); Tiran d'Iste, Ruler (king), Magician (shape-shifter); Brandis, Sorcerer
**Time period(s):** Indeterminate
**Locale(s):** Fictional Country

**Summary:** Having taken their rightful place as rulers of their land, Alexia and Tiran fight chaos and corruption in their realm and treachery among their courtiers. A magical trap contrived by their enemies casts a spell of fear on Alexia, just when she needs all her strength and courage to help Tiran face a pair of usurpers in hand-to-hand combat. Sequel to *Dark Mirror, Dark Dreams*.

**Other books you might like:**
Gordon R. Dickson, *The Dragon, the Earl, and the Troll*, 1994
Simon R. Green, *Blue Moon Rising*, 1991
Barbara Hambly, *The Ladies of Mandrigyn*, 1993
Katherine Kurtz, *Deryni Checkmate*, 1972
C.L. Moore, *Jirel of Joiry*, 1969

---

**2361**

SIMON R. GREEN

## Blood and Honor

(New York: Roc, 1993)

**Story type:** Fantasy (Magic Conflict; Horror)
**Major character(s):** Jordan, Actor; Gawaine, Knight; Victor, Royalty (prince), Magician
**Time period(s):** Indeterminate

**Locale(s):** Redhart, Fictional Country; Castle Midnight, Mythical Place

**Summary:** Hired to impersonate Prince Victor, one of three brothers competing for the throne of their recently deceased father, Jordan begins to wonder if he will survive to collect his fee. He could handle the assassination attempts and the sorcerous plots of the rival factions, but without a king to control the Unreal in Castle Midnight, horrible monsters have broken through into reality, threatening the destruction of the whole country.

**Other books you might like:**
C.J. Cherryh, *Angel with the Sword*, 1985
Phyllis Eisenstein, *Born to Exile*, 1978
Barbara Hambly, *The Time of the Dark*, 1982
Robert A. Heinlein, *Double Star*, 1956
Patricia A. McKillip, *The Riddle-Master of Hed*, 1976
Jennifer Roberson, *Shapechangers*, 1984
Robert Silverberg, *Lord Valentine's Castle*, 1980
Roger Zelazny, *Nine Princes in Amber*, 1970

---

**2362**

SIMON R. GREEN

## Blue Moon Rising

(New York: Roc, 1991)

**Story type:** Fantasy (Quest; Magic Conflict)
**Major character(s):** Rupert, Royalty (prince); Julia, Royalty (princess); Unicorn, Mythical Creature, Animal
**Time period(s):** Indeterminate
**Locale(s):** Forest Kingdom, Fictional Country

**Summary:** When Prince Rupert of the Forest Kingdoms "rescues" a princess from a dragon, he finds the mild-mannered dragon knows some useful spells and the strong-willed princess is a competent swordswoman. Their skills help Rupert and his unicorn fight their way back through the Darkwood. When plague, famine and marauding demons threaten the very existence of the kingdom, Rupert is sent to find the self-exiled High Warlock who might be able to combat the Wild Magic that will be let loose when the Blue Moon is full.

**Other books you might like:**
Eleanor Arnason, *The Sword Smith*, 1978
Robert Asprin, *Another Fine Myth*, 1978
Steven Brust, *Jhereg*, 1983
Gordon R. Dickson, *The Dragon and the George*, 1976
Fritz Leiber, *Swords Against Death*, 1970
Patricia C. Wrede, *Dealing with Dragons*, 1990
Patricia C. Wrede, *The Seven Towers*, 1984
Chelsea Quinn Yarbro, *A Baroque Fable*, 1986

---

**2363**

SIMON R. GREEN

## The Bones of Haven

(New York: Ace, 1992)

**Story type:** Fantasy (Adventure; Mystery)
**Series:** Hawk & Fisher
**Major character(s):** Isobel Fisher, Police Officer (captain); Hawk, Police Officer (captain)
**Time period(s):** Indeterminate Past
**Locale(s):** Haven, Fictional City

**Summary:** Hawk and Fisher join the SWAT (Special Wizardry and Tactics) team to stop a prison riot that includes sorcerers and worse.

The day's work for Hawk and Fisher also involves a possibly psychotic and definitely supernaturally powerful man who escapes from a painting into the city and a band of terrorists that takes two kings hostage.

**Other books you might like:**
Robert Asprin, *Thieves' World*, 1979
   editor
Steven Brust, *Jhereg*, 1983
Glen Cook, *Sweet Silver Blues*, 1987
Randall Garrett, *Too Many Magicians*, 1967
Fritz Leiber, *Swords and Deviltry*, 1970
Nick Pollotta, *Doomsday Exam*, 1992

---

**2364**

SIMON R. GREEN

## Deathstalker Honor

(New York: Roc, 1998)

**Story type:** Science Fiction (Space Opera)
**Series:** Life and Times of Owen Deathstalker
**Major character(s):** Owen Deathstalker, Nobleman (retired), Bounty Hunter; Hazel d'Ark, Revolutionary (retired), Bounty Hunter; Jacob Wolfe, Reanimated Dead, Cyborg
**Time period(s):** Indeterminate Future
**Locale(s):** Virimonde, Planet—Imaginary; Shub, Planet—Imaginary

**Summary:** The death of Lionstone XIV and the destruction of her corrupt administration does not finish the work of Owen Deathstalker and his friends. The noble houses and Blue Bloch conspire to undo the revolution, the Hadenmen and the AIs of Shub plan humanity's destruction, and a strange enemy lurks beyond the edge of inhabited space.

**Other books you might like:**
Iain M. Banks, *The Player of Games*, 1989
Allan Cole, *Sten*, 1984
   Chris Bunch, co-author
Glen Cook, *The Dragon Never Sleeps*, 1988
Steve Perry, *The Man Who Never Missed*, 1985
Walter Jon Williams, *Metropolitan*, 1995

---

**2365**

SIMON R. GREEN

## Deathstalker Rebellion

(New York: Roc, 1996)

**Story type:** Science Fiction (Space Opera)
**Series:** Life and Times of Owen Deathstalker
**Major character(s):** Owen Deathstalker, Revolutionary, Nobleman (deposed); Ruby Journey, Revolutionary, Bounty Hunter; John Silence, Military Personnel
**Time period(s):** Indeterminate Future
**Locale(s):** Golgotha, Planet—Imaginary; Technos III, Planet—Imaginary

**Summary:** Owen Deathstalker's revolution goes on the offensive against the Empire as he attempts to unite all of Empress Lionstone's enemies. One group of rebels travels to Technos III, becoming trapped in plots and counter-plots surrounding the production of a new star drive. Meanwhile, Imperial Captain Silence discovers extremely unpleasant alien truths that may threaten both Empire and Rebellion.

**Other books you might like:**
Iain M. Banks, *Consider Phlebas*, 1988

Glen Cook, *The Dragon Never Sleeps*, 1988
Frank Herbert, *Dune*, 1965
George Lucas, *Star Wars*, 1976
Paul J. McAuley, *Four Hundred Billion Stars*, 1988

## 2366

### SIMON R. GREEN

## Deathstalker War

(New York: Roc, 1997)

**Story type:** Science Fiction (Space Opera)
**Series:** Life and Times of Owen Deathstalker
**Major character(s):** Owen Deathstalker, Revolutionary, Nobleman (deposed); Jenny Psycho, Revolutionary, Psychic; Frost, Military Personnel (investigator)
**Time period(s):** Indeterminate Future
**Locale(s):** Mistworld, Planet—Imaginary; Summerland, Planet—Imaginary

**Summary:** The rebellion comes to an end as Owen Deathstalker and his allies close in on Golgotha, capitol of the empire. However, the empress has many allies, while the threat of traitors and other hidden enemies remains.

**Other books you might like:**
Iain M. Banks, *Consider Phlebas*, 1988
Allan Cole, *Sten*, 1984
    Chris Bunch, co-author
Frank Herbert, *Dune*, 1965
Sherwood Smith, *The Phoenix in Flight*, 1993
    Dave Trowbridge, co-author
David Weber, *On Basilisk Station*, 1993

## 2367

### SIMON R. GREEN

## Down Among the Dead Men

(New York: Roc, 1993)

**Story type:** Fantasy (Military; Adventure)
**Major character(s):** Duncan MacNeil, Military Personnel (Ranger sergeant); Scarecrow Jack, Woodsman; Constance, Sorcerer
**Time period(s):** Indeterminate Past
**Locale(s):** Parkwood, Fictional Country (forest kingdom)

**Summary:** In the 10 years since the Demon Wars, retaking tainted lands and restoring peace has proven a hard and often bloody business. The Rangers take the brunt of it, sent ahead of the Guard patrols and expected to handle whatever they find. On the current assignment they investigate a fort held by friendly forces but from which no one who enters can emerge. Sequel to *Blue Moon Rising*.

**Other books you might like:**
Steven Brust, *Jhereg*, 1983
Glen Cook, *The Black Company*, 1984
David Drake, *Old Nathan*, 1991
Barbara Hambly, *The Time of the Dark*, 1982
Justin Leiber, *The Sword and the Eye*, 1985

## 2368

### SIMON R. GREEN

## The God Killer

(New York: Ace, 1991)

**Story type:** Fantasy (Adventure; Mystery)
**Series:** Hawk & Fisher
**Major character(s):** Isobel Fisher, Police Officer (captain); Hawk, Police Officer (captain)
**Time period(s):** Indeterminate Past
**Locale(s):** Haven, Fictional City

**Summary:** The hundreds of Beings and their religious followers on the Street of Gods have jostled along together well enough for a very long time, their bickering and feuding handled by the Guard's God Squad. But when someone, or something, begins killing Gods, it's time to call in Hawk and Fisher.

**Other books you might like:**
Robert Asprin, *Thieves' World*, 1979
    editor
Randall Garrett, *Too Many Magicians*, 1967
Fritz Leiber, *Swords and Deviltry*, 1970
Anne Logston, *Shadow*, 1991

## 2369

### SIMON R. GREEN

## Guard Against Dishonor

(New York: Ace, 1991)

**Story type:** Fantasy (Mystery)
**Series:** Hawk & Fisher
**Major character(s):** Hawk, Police Officer (captain); Isobel Fisher, Police Officer (captain)
**Time period(s):** Indeterminate Past
**Locale(s):** Haven, Fictional City

**Summary:** When a new street drug causes users to tear themselves and anyone around them into pieces with their bare hands, Hawk and Fisher arrest the supplier. When he is promptly released because of his important contacts, and the drug disappears, Hawk and Fisher protest the obvious corruption of the Guards. Reassigned separately, both are charged with treason when assignments come under attack. Somehow, they must stay alive, clear their names and stop the corruption.

**Other books you might like:**
Robert Asprin, *Thieves' World*, 1979
    editor
Glen Cook, *Sweet Silver Blues*, 1987
Alan Dean Foster, *Outland*, 1981
Randall Garrett, *Too Many Magicians*, 1967
Ernest Hogan, *High Aztec*, 1992
Lee Killough, *Spider Play*, 1986
Mickey Zucker Reichert, *Godslayer*, 1987

## 2370

### SIMON R. GREEN

## Hawk & Fisher

(New York: Ace, 1990)

**Story type:** Fantasy (Mystery; Magic Conflict)
**Series:** Hawk & Fisher

**Major character(s):** Hawk, Police Officer (Captain); Isobel Fisher, Police Officer (Captain)
**Time period(s):** Indeterminate Past
**Locale(s):** Haven, Fictional City

**Summary:** Hawk and Fisher are assigned as bodyguards to one of the City's most powerful and controversial politicians. Their task begins at a private dinner party attended by the politician's friends and allies at a private home that is magically sealed from outside interference. It should be perfectly safe. But why—and how—do the guests, including their charge, keep dying?

**Other books you might like:**
Glen Cook, *Sweet Silver Blues*, 1987
Randall Garrett, *Too Many Magicians*, 1967
Lee Killough, *Spider Play*, 1986
Michael Kurland, *A Study in Sorcery*, 1989
Mercedes Lackey, *Children of the Night*, 1990
Mercedes Lackey, *Burning Water*, 1989

**2371**

SIMON R. GREEN

# Hellworld

(New York: Ace, 1993)

**Story type:** Science Fiction (First Contact)
**Series:** Twilight of the Empire
**Major character(s):** Scott Hunter, Military Personnel, Scout (planetary); Megan DeChance, Military Personnel, Psychic (esper); Krystel, Government Official (investigator), Scout (planetary)
**Time period(s):** Indeterminate Future
**Locale(s):** Wolf IV, Planet—Imaginary

**Summary:** When the planetary survey team lands on Wolf IV intending to determine its suitability for human colonization, they discover numerous hostile life forms. When the team explores an abandoned city, they discover the most terrifying aspect of their new home.

**Other books you might like:**
David Brin, *Startide Rising*, 1983
David Drake, *The Jungle*, 1991
Harry Harrison, *The Deathworld Trilogy*, 1976
Anne McCaffrey, *The Chronicles of Pern: First Fall*, 1993
Anne McCaffrey, *Dragonsdawn*, 1988
James H. Schmitz, *The Demon Breed*, 1968
John Varley, *Titan*, 1979

**2372**

SIMON R. GREEN

# Mistworld

(New York: Ace, 1992)

**Story type:** Science Fiction (Adventure; Mystery)
**Series:** Mistworld
**Major character(s):** Topaz, Psychic, Martial Arts Expert (assassin); Leon Vertue, Doctor (Criminal); Cat, Thief, Handicapped (deaf-mute)
**Time period(s):** Indeterminate Future
**Locale(s):** Mistworld, Planet—Imaginary; Empire, Interstellar Empire/Federation

**Summary:** A mysterious refugee carries plague onto Mistworld, killing and mindwiping thousands of people. When Topaz vows to uncover any Empire plotting, the nearly lethal investigation proves complicated since all knowledgeable parties died by murder.

**Other books you might like:**
Marion Zimmer Bradley, *The World Wreckers*, 1971
Cheryl J. Franklin, *The Light in Exile*, 1990
Katharine Kerr, *Polar City Blues*, 1990
Andre Norton, *Judgment on Janus*, 1963
Sydney J. Van Scyoc, *Cloudcry*, 1977

**2373**

SIMON R. GREEN

# Shadows Fall

(New York: Roc, 1994)

**Story type:** Fantasy (Science Fiction; Religious)
**Major character(s):** Leanard Ash, Reanimated Dead; Rhea Frazier, Political Figure; Richard Erickson, Lawman (sheriff)
**Time period(s):** Indeterminate Future
**Locale(s):** Shadows Fall, Fictional City

**Summary:** Hoping to find something or someone they lost, many people journey to the last vestige of the fairy realm on Earth, Shadows Fall, a city containing the Forever Door which beckons to dying people and the deceased who refuse to leave the realm of the living. The town begins to panic as murders, previously unknown, proliferate. However, an invasion by the Warriors of the Cross brings greater disaster.

**Other books you might like:**
Emma Bull, *Finder*, 1994
Will Shetterly, *Elsewhere*, 1991
Will Shetterly, *Nevernever*, 1993
Terri Windling, *Bordertown*, 1986
   Mark Alan Arnold, co-editor
Terri Windling, *Life on the Border*, 1991
   editor

**2374**

SIMON R. GREEN

# Twilight of the Empire

(New York: Roc, 1997)

**Story type:** Science Fiction (Space Opera; Collection)
**Series:** Life and Times of Owen Deathstalker
**Major character(s):** Typhoid Mary, Psychic, Mentally Ill Person; John Silence, Military Personnel; Hunter, Pioneer
**Time period(s):** Indeterminate Future
**Locale(s):** Mistworld, Planet—Imaginary; Wolf IV, Planet—Imaginary

**Summary:** In the first of three short novels set just before the events of the Deathstalker Trilogy, Typhoid Mary pursues a strange mission on a planet of psychics. In the second, Silence investigates an abandoned mining colony, while in the third, a suicide planetary colonization team discovers an improbable paradise.

**Other books you might like:**
Iain M. Banks, *The Player of Games*, 1989
Glen Cook, *The Dragon Never Sleeps*, 1988
Debra Doyle, *The Price of the Stars*, 1992
   John D. Macdonald, co-author
H. Beam Piper, *Space Viking*, 1963
Vernor Vinge, *A Fire upon the Deep*, 1992

## 2375

### SIMON R. GREEN

## *Winner Takes All*
(New York: Ace, 1991)

**Story type:** Fantasy (Mystery)
**Series:** Hawk & Fisher
**Major character(s):** Isobel Fisher, Police Officer (captain); Hawk, Police Officer (captain)
**Time period(s):** Indeterminate Past
**Locale(s):** Haven, Fictional City

**Summary:** Captains Hawk and Fisher are assigned to guard the Reform candidate in the last days before the city elections, always an occasion for confrontations, corruption and general craziness. When the Reform campaign is beset by embezzlement, magical attack, betrayal and armed assault by the most feared mercenary leader in the countryside, Hawk and Fisher struggle to keep the candidate alive.

**Other books you might like:**
Robert Asprin, *Thieves' World*, 1979
    editor
Glen Cook, *Sweet Silver Blues*, 1987
Robert A. Heinlein, *Double Star*, 1956
Lee Killough, *Spider Play*, 1986
Katherine Kurtz, *The Adept*, 1991
    Deborah Turner Harris, co-author
Mercedes Lackey, *Burning Water*, 1989
Mickey Zucker Reichert, *Godslayer*, 1987

## 2376

### SIMON R. GREEN

## *Wolf in the Fold*
(New York: Ace, 1991)

**Story type:** Fantasy (Mystery; Urban)
**Series:** Hawk & Fisher
**Major character(s):** Isobel Fisher, Police Officer (captain); Hawk, Police Officer (captain)
**Time period(s):** Indeterminate Past
**Locale(s):** Haven, Fictional City

**Summary:** There's a spy loose in Haven and he's even managed to get away from Hawk and Fisher and slip into the MacNeil family citadel. Since Hawk and Fisher are the only ones to have seen him, they are ordered in after him, knowing the assignment will be denied if they are caught impersonating Quality, a capital offense in Haven.

**Other books you might like:**
Robert Asprin, *Thieves' World*, 1979
    editor
Glen Cook, *Sweet Silver Blues*, 1987
Tanya Huff, *Blood Price*, 1991
Anne Logston, *Shadow*, 1991
J.F. Rivkin, *Silverglass*, 1986
Will Shetterly, *Liavek*, 1985
    Emma Bull, co-editor

## 2377

### TERRENCE M. GREEN

## *Blue Limbo*
(New York: Tor, 1997)

**Story type:** Science Fiction (Cyberpunk; Political)
**Major character(s):** Mitch Helwig, Police Officer; Sam Karoulis, Police Officer (Captain); Barbie Helwig, Child
**Time period(s):** 2000s
**Locale(s):** Toronto, Ontario, Canada

**Summary:** No longer able to stand by while corrupt police officers participate in criminal activity, Mitch gets fired for bombing their illegal drug operation. He buys illegal, state of the art weapons and goes slightly crazy when his wife proves to have a lover. Mitch must rescue his father and daughter, who have been kidnapped by criminals hirelings. Meanwhile, revival using Blue Limbo extends the life of Sam's brain for about a month, enabling him to clear Mitch.

**Other books you might like:**
Philip K. Dick, *Blade Runner*, 1982
Alan Dean Foster, *Montezuma Strip*, 1995
Katharine Kerr, *Polar City Blues*, 1990
Ian McDonald, *Terminal Cafe*, 1994
Neal Stephenson, *The Diamond Age*, 1995

## 2378

### MARTIN H. GREENBERG, Editor

## *After the King: Stories in Honor of J.R.R. Tolkien*
(New York: Tor, 1992)

**Story type:** Fantasy (Anthology)

**Summary:** Includes a three-page introduction by Jane Yolen, and a two-page biography of contributors plus 19 stories by 20 authors asked to write a Tolkienesque story, but not an imitation Tolkien story, in honor of the author who richly influenced fantasy fiction. Poul Anderson and Karen Anderson collaborated on one story. Other authors include Peter S. Beagle, John Brunner, Emma Bull, Charles de Lint, Stephen R. Donaldson, Patricia A. McKillip, Andre Norton, Terry Pratchett, Elizabeth Ann Scarborough, Robert Silverberg, Judith Tarr, Harry Turtledove and Jane Yolen.

**Other books you might like:**
Lin Carter, *Dragons, Elves and Heroes*, 1969
    editor
Lester Del Rey, *Once upon a Time: A Treasury of Modern Fairy Tales*, 1991
    Risa Kessler, co-editor
Baird Searles, *Halflings, Hobbits, Warrows & Weefolk: A Collection of Tales of Heroes Short in Stature*, 1991
    Brian Thomsen, co-editor
J.R.R. Tolkien, *The Fellowship of the Ring*, 1954
J.R.R. Tolkien, *The Hobbit*, 1938
J.R.R. Tolkien, *The Return of the King*, 1956
J.R.R. Tolkien, *The Two Towers*, 1955
Terri Windling, *Life on the Border*, 1991
    editor

## 2379

**MARTIN H. GREENBERG**, Editor
**CHARLES G. WAUGH**, Co-Editor

### Back From the Dead
(New York: DAW Books, 1991)

**Story type:** Horror (Anthology)

**Summary:** Twenty-one stories about people or things that come back from the dead. Included are H.P. Lovecraft's Poe pastiche, ''The Outsider,'' Poe's masterpiece of possession and haunting, ''Ligeia,'' Edith Wharton's subtle ghost story, ''Afterward,'' Theodore Sturgeon's tale of a muck monster, ''It,'' Robert Bloch's voodoo story, ''Mother of Serpents,'' and Washington Irving's story of demonic resuscitation, ''The Adventure of the German Student.''

**Other books you might like:**
Peter Haining, *Stories of the Walking Dead*, 1985
Hugh Lamb, *Return From the Grave*, 1976
John Skipp, *Book of the Dead*, 1989
　　Craig Spector, co-author

## 2380

**MARTIN H. GREENBERG**, Editor
**LARRY SEGRIFF**, Co-Editor

### Battle Magic
(New York: DAW, 1998)

**Story type:** Fantasy (Anthology)

**Summary:** In this anthology are 15 original stories about the use of magic to win wars, topple cities, defeat enemies, and cause general mayhem. The stories include magical duels, ancient curses, and other plots, most handled seriously, although a few poke fun at the genre. Contributors include Mickey Zucker Reichert, Charles De Lint, and Lois Tilton.

**Other books you might like:**
John DeChancie, *Castle Fantastic*, 1996
　　Martin H. Greenberg, co-editor
Martin H. Greenberg, *After the King: Stories in Honor of J.R.R. Tolkien*, 1994
Martin H. Greenberg, *Horse Fantastic*, 1991
　　Rosalind Greenberg, co-editor
Martin H. Greenberg, *Lord of the Fantastic: Stories in Honor of Roger Zelazny*, 1998
　　Martin H. Greenberg, co-editor
Susan Shwartz, *Sisters in Fantasy*, 1995
　　Martin H. Greenberg, co-editor

## 2381

**MARTIN H. GREENBERG**, Editor
**JOHN HELFERS**, Co-Editor

### Black Cats and Broken Mirrors
(New York: DAW, 1998)

**Story type:** Fantasy (Anthology)

**Summary:** Of these 17 original stories about various superstitions, many are lampoons , while others take superstition deadly seriously. The contributors include Esther Friesner, Charles De Lint, Nancy Spring, Peter Crowther, Elizabeth Ann Scarborough, and Josepha Sherman.

**Other books you might like:**
Richard Gilliam, *Phantoms of the Night*, 1996
　　Martin H. Greenberg, co-editor
Katharine Kerr, *Enchanted Forests*, 1995
　　Martin H. Greenberg, co-editor
Lawrence Schimel, *The Fortune Teller*, 1997
　　Martin H. Greenberg, co-editor
Cynthia Sternau, *The Secret Prophecies of Nostradamus*, 1995
　　Martin H. Greenberg, co-editor

## 2382

**MARTIN H. GREENBERG**, Editor

### Celebrity Vampires
(New York: DAW, 1995)

**Story type:** Horror (Anthology; Vampire Story)

**Summary:** The nineteen stories original to this volume all present famed celebrities as vampires, or involved with vampires. In ''Undead Origami,'' Norman Partridge likens Howard Hughes' business tactics to a vampire's voracious practices, and in ''I Vant to Be Alone,'' Barb D'Amato attributes Greta Garbo's timeless beauty to her deathless vampirism. J.N. Williamson sees the original spirit of Vlad Tepes in Vladimir Nikolai Lenin, the protagonist of ''Vladimir's Conversions,'' while John Lutz imagines vampires playing a role in Carrie Nation's intemperate fight for temperance in ''Plague.'' Vampirism mixes with writing in several stories: Kristine Kathryn Rusch's ''The Beautiful and the Damned'' features F. Scott Fitzgerald, Roman A. Ranieri's ''A Singular Event on a Night in 1912,'' both Bram Stoker and Sir Arthur Conan Doyle, and Wendi Lee and Terry Beatty's ''Death on the Mississippi,'' Mark Twain. In P.N. Elrod's ''A Night at the (Horse) Opera,'' a vampire detective helps one of the Marx brothers out of a gambling debt.

**Other books you might like:**
Jean Marie Stine, *I, Vampire: Interviews with the Undead*, 1995
　　Forrest J. Ackerman, co-editor
Stephen Jones, *The Mammoth Book of Vampires*, 1993
　　editor
Alan Ryan, *Vampires: Two Centuries of Great Vampire Stories*, 1987
　　editor

## 2383

**MARTIN H. GREENBERG**, Editor
**FRANK D. MCSHERRY JR.**, Co-Editor
**CHARLES G. WAUGH**, Co-Editor

### Civil War Ghosts
(Little Rock, Arkansas: August House, 1991)

**Story type:** Horror (Anthology; Ghost Story)

**Summary:** Eight tales of ghosts and hauntings connected with the American Civil War. Included are Ambrose Bierce's classic hallucinatory tale, ''An Occurrence at Owl Creek Bridge,'' Manly Wade Wellman's short occult novel of two Union soldiers who struggle to save a girl's soul, ''Fearful Rock,'' and two tales of ghostly revenge, John Jakes' ''Miranda'' and Dan Simmons' ''Iverson's Pits.''

**Other books you might like:**
Marvin Kaye, *Haunted America*, 1990

## 2384

**MARTIN H. GREENBERG**, Editor
**SCOTT H. URBAN**, Co-Editor

### The Conspiracy Files
(New York: Daw 1998)

**Story type:** Horror (Anthology)

**Summary:** These 14 original stories uncover the menacing conspiratorial forces underlying ordinary aspects of daily life, including junk mail in Mark Rainey's ''Free Sample,'' the tendency of women to go to bathrooms in pairs in Nancy Holder's ''The Ladies Room,'' and male baldness in Edo van Blekom's ''Pattern Baldness.'' Other stories focus on our unspoken obsession with conspiracies, including Norm Partridge's ''Coyotes'' and Richard Chizmar's ''The Good Old Days.''

**Other books you might like:**
Esther Friesner, *Alien Pregnant by Elvis*, 1994
    Martin H. Greenberg, co-editor
Gerard Daniel Houarner, *Going Postal*, 1998
    editor
Gary L. Raisor, *Obsessions*, 1991
Wendy Webb, *Phobias: Stories of Your Deepest Fears*, 1994
    Richard Gilliam, Edward E. Kramer, Martin H. Greenberg, co-editors

## 2385

**MARTIN H. GREENBERG**
**CHARLES G. WAUGH**, Co-Author

### Devil Worshippers
(New York: DAW, 1990)

**Story type:** Horror (Anthology)

**Summary:** Fifteen stories of demons and those foolish enough to summon them. Included are Nathaniel Hawthorne's classic of dark minds and hearts, ''Young Goodman Browne,'' Robert Bloch's tale of teenage rebels with a satanic cause, ''Sweet Sixteen,'' Charles Beaumont's suburban horror story, ''The New People,'' and Anthony Boucher's amusing account of a werewolf professor recruited to fight spies, ''The Compleat Werewolf.''

**Other books you might like:**
Peter Haining, *The Black Magic Omnibus*, 1976
Peter Haining, *The Evil People*, 1968
Michel Parry, *Great Black Magic Stories*, 1977
Rod Serling, *Devils and Demons*, 1967

## 2386

**MARTIN H. GREENBERG**, Editor

### Dinosaurs
(New York: Donald I. Fine Books, 1996)

**Story type:** Science Fiction (Anthology)

**Summary:** Contains a four-page introduction by Robert Silverberg, seven pages of authors' biographies, and 14 stories published 1950-1994 in periodicals and anthologies. Themes include time travel, criminal justice, entropy, metamorphosis, and nanotechnology; authors include Poul Anderson, Isaac Asimov, Ray Bradbury, Pat Cadigan, Arthur C. Clarke, L. Sprague de Camp, Kristine Kathryn Rusch, Michelle Sagara, Robert J. Sawyer, Robert Silverberg, Harry Turtledove, and Howard Waldrop.

**Other books you might like:**
Robert T. Bakker, *Raptor Red*, 1995
Jack Dann, *Dinosaurs!*, 1990
    Gardner Dozois, co-editor
Jack Dann, *Dinosaurs II*, 1995
    Gardner Dozois, co-editor
James Gurney, *Dinotopia*, 1992
Mike Resnick, *Dinosaur Fantastic*, 1993
    Martin H. Greenberg, co-editor
Robert J. Sawyer, *Far-Seer*, 1992

## 2387

**MARTIN H. GREENBERG**, Editor
**ED GORMAN**, Co-Editor

### Dracula: Prince of Darkness
(New York: DAW, 1992)

**Story type:** Horror (Anthology; Vampire Story)

**Summary:** Timed to coincide with the release of Francis Ford Coppola's film adaptation of Bram Stoker's *Dracula* (1897), this anthology collects 15 original stories, most of which involve Dracula himself as a character. Included are F. Paul Wilson's tale of vampires overrunning the world, ''The Lord's Work,'' Daniel Ransom's (a.k.a. Ed Gorman's) hardboiled vampire story, ''Night Cries,'' and W. R. Philbrick's ''The Cure,'' in which vampirism is presented as a last resort cure for the terminally ill. There are also stories by Brian Hodge, P. N. Elrod, Richard Laymon and John Shirley.

**Other books you might like:**
Richard Dalby, *Dracula's Brood*, 1987
Ellen Datlow, *Blood Is Not Enough*, 1989
    editor
Ellen Datlow, *A Whisper of Blood*, 1991
    editor
Robert R. McCammon, *Under the Fang*, 1991
    editor
Byron Preiss, *The Ultimate Dracula*, 1991
    editor

## 2388

**MARTIN H. GREENBERG**, Editor

### Elf Fantastic
(New York: DAW, 1997)

**Story type:** Fantasy (Anthology; Legend)

**Summary:** Contains a two-page introduction plus brief individual introductions to 19 original stories, frequently ominous in tone, and featuring encounters between elves and mortals. Authors include Lynn Abbey, Craig Shaw Gardner, Richard Gilliam, Karen Haber, Tanya Huff, Jane M. Lindskold, Dennis L. McKiernan, Andre Norton, Jody Lynn Nye, Diana L. Paxson, Mickey Zucker Reichert, Michelle West and David Niall Wilson.

**Other books you might like:**
Isaac Asimov, *Faeries*, 1991
    Martin H. Greenberg, Charles G. Waugh, co-editors
Lin Carter, *Dragons, Elves and Heroes*, 1969
    editor
Jack Dann, *Little People!*, 1991
    Gardner Dozois, co-editor
Baird Searles, *Halflings, Hobbits, Warrows & Weefolk: A Collection of Tales of Heroes Short in Stature*, 1991
    Brian Thomsen, co-editor

Terri Windling, *Faery*, 1984
   editor

### 2389

**MARTIN H. GREENBERG**, Editor

## *The Fantastic Adventures of Robin Hood*
(New York: Signet, 1991)

**Story type:** Fantasy (Anthology; Legend)
**Major character(s):** Robin Hood, Outlaw, Hero

**Summary:** The 13 original stories feature Robin Hood and his merry men in settings both on and off Earth. Stories range from fantasy, science fiction and horror to mystery. Authors include Nancy A. Collins, Matthew Costello, George Alec Effinger, Clayton Emery, Ed Gorman, Mike Resnick, Elizabeth Ann Scarborough, Midori Snyder and Steve Rasnic Tem.

**Other books you might like:**
C.J. Cherryh, *Cyteen*, 1988
Clayton Emery, *Tales of Robin Hood*, 1988
Parke Godwin, *Sherwood*, 1991
Robin McKinley, *The Outlaws of Sherwood*, 1988
Bernard Miles, *Robin Hood: His Life and Legend*, 1979
Howard Pyle, *The Merry Adventures of Robin Hood*, 1883
William F. Wu, *The Robin Hood Ambush*, 1990

### 2390

**MARTIN H. GREENBERG**, Editor

## *Frankenstein: The Monster Wakes*
(New York: DAW, 1993)

**Story type:** Horror (Anthology)

**Summary:** The 18 contributors to this volume each supply a variation on the Frankenstein theme. In Rex Miller's "I've Got Hugh Under My Skin," a latter-day descendant of Victor Frankenstein keeps the old family business going, while in Richard T. Chizmar's "Bride of Frankenstein: A Modern Love Story" and Mike Baker's "Role Model," unbalanced readers of Mary Shelley's novel identify too closely with its namesake. Matthew J. Costello in "My Coney Island Baby," Terry Beatty and Wendy Lee in "Special Effects," and Brian Hodge in "A Loaf of Bread, A Jug of Wine" all resurrect Frankenstein's monster, while Norman Partridge, in "The Man with the Barbed-Wire Fists," takes a highly inventive approach to the idea of the making of a man.

**Other books you might like:**
Michel Parry, *Rivals of Frankenstein*, 1977
   editor
Byron Preiss, *The Ultimate Frankenstein*, 1991
   John Betancourt, co-editor

### 2391

**MARTIN H. GREENBERG**, Editor

## *The Further Adventures of Batman 2: Featuring the Penguin*
(New York: Bantam Spectra, 1992)

**Story type:** Science Fiction (Adventure; Anthology)
**Series:** Batman
**Major character(s):** Bruce "Batman" Wayne, Hero, Detective—Amateur; Oswald "the Penguin" Cobblepot, Criminal

**Time period(s):** 1990s
**Locale(s):** Gotham City (New York City); United States; Mexico

**Summary:** Contains eleven stories featuring Batman and his archenemy, the Penguin. Laurie Sefton and Charles Von Rospach collaborated on one story, "Going Straight." Other authors include John Gregory Betancourt, Max Allan Collins, Nancy A. Collins, Will Murray, William F. Nolan, Kristine Kathryn Rusch, Steve Rasnic Tem, and Brian M. Thomsen.

**Other books you might like:**
Lynn Abbey, *Catwoman*, 1992
   Robert Asprin, co-author
Craig Shaw Gardner, *Batman*, 1989
Craig Shaw Gardner, *The Batman Murders*, 1990
Craig Shaw Gardner, *Batman Returns*, 1992
Simon Hawke, *Batman: To Stalk a Specter*, 1991
Joe R. Lansdale, *Batman: Captured by the Engines*, 1991

### 2392

**MARTIN H. GREENBERG**, Editor

## *The Further Adventures of Batman 3: Featuring Catwoman*
(New York: Bantam, 1993)

**Story type:** Science Fiction (Anthology; Adventure)
**Series:** Batman
**Major character(s):** Selena "Catwoman" Kyle, Criminal, Heroine; Bruce "Batman" Wayne, Hero, Detective—Amateur
**Time period(s):** 1990s
**Locale(s):** Gotham City (New York City)

**Summary:** Contains 13 original stories, many dark in tone, about Batman and his seductive nemesis, Catwoman. Authors include John Gregory Betancourt, Mort Castle, Ed Gorman, Will Murray, Jeff Rovin, Kristine Kathryn Rusch, Brian M. Thomsen and Robert Weinberg.

**Other books you might like:**
Lynn Abbey, *Catwoman*, 1992
   Robert Asprin, co-author
Craig Shaw Gardner, *Batman*, 1989
Craig Shaw Gardner, *The Batman Murders*, 1990
Craig Shaw Gardner, *Batman Returns*, 1992
Simon Hawke, *Batman: To Stalk a Specter*, 1991
Joe R. Lansdale, *Captured by the Engines*, 1991

### 2393

**MARTIN H. GREENBERG**, Editor

## *The Further Adventures of Superman*
(New York: Bantam, 1993)

**Story type:** Science Fiction (Anthology)
**Series:** Superman
**Major character(s):** Clark "Superman" Kent, Journalist, Alien (Kryptonian)
**Time period(s):** 1990s; Indeterminate Past
**Locale(s):** Metropolis (New York City)

**Summary:** Contains a prologue and epilogue by Dave Gibbons plus 10 original stories about the "man of steel." Authors include Diane Duane, Karen Haber, Will Murray, Garfield Reeves-Stevens, Mike Resnick and Henry Slesar.

**Other books you might like:**
Michael Bishop, *Count Geiger's Blues*, 1992

William Borden, *Superstoe*, 1968
John Brunner, *Polymath*, 1974
Elliot S. Maggin, *Superman: Last Son of Krypton*, 1978
Elliot S. Maggin, *Superman: Miracle Monday*, 1981
Roger Stern, *The Death and Life of Superman*, 1993

## 2394

**MARTIN H. GREENBERG**, Editor
**LARRY SEGRIFF**, Co-Editor

### Future Net
(New York: DAW, 1996)

**Story type:** Science Fiction (Anthology; Hard Science Fiction)

**Summary:** Contains a two-page introduction and brief biographical introductions to authors of the 16 original stories focusing on computer virtual reality. Themes include artificial intelligences, future chatrooms, alternate worlds, invasion of Earth, and life after death with stories varying in tone from whimsical to ominous. Authors include Robin Wayne Bailey, Gregory Benford, Matthew Costello, John DeChancie, Jane Lindskold, Wil McCarthy, Jody Lynn Nye, Mickey Zucker Reichert, and Josepha Sherman.

**Other books you might like:**
Raphael Carter, *The Fortunate Fall*, 1996
Jack Dann, *Hackers*, 1996
    Gardner Dozois, co-editor
Elton Elliott, *Nanodreams*, 1995
    editor
Karie Jacobson, *Simulations*, 1993
    editor
Neal Stephenson, *Snow Crash*, 1992
Bruce Sterling, *Mirrorshades: The Cyberpunk Anthology*, 1986
    editor
Sage Walker, *Whiteout*, 1996

## 2395

**MARTIN H. GREENBERG**, Editor
**JILL MORGAN**, Illustrator
**ROBERT WEINBERG**, Illustrator
**GAHAN WILSON**, Illustrator

### Great Writers and Kids Write Spooky Stories
(New York: Random House, 1995)

**Story type:** Horror (Anthology)

**Summary:** For this collection of young adult horror stories, the authors asked 13 renowned writers of fantasy and horror to collaborate with their children or grandchildren on a horror story. Peter and Benjamin Straub, in "In Transit," tell the story of a father and son with a dark secret who are forced to prey on the local bullies. Ramsey, Tammy, and Matt Campbell offer a story of children trapped in a shrubbery maze by beings who want to steal their identities. F. Paul Wilson and Meggan C. Wilson supply a story about the fear of spiders, and Ric, Jesse, and Matti Hautala tell a tale of alien invasion. Joe, Keith, and Kasey Jo Lansdale have written an eerie story of a vampire scarecrow brought to life. Gahan Wilson supplies an introduction and the illustrations.

**Other books you might like:**
A. Finnis, *13 Again*, 1995
Anthony Horowitz, *The Puffin Book of Horror Stories*, 1994
T. Pines, *Thirteen*, 1991
T. Pines, *13 Tales of Horror*, 1994

## 2396

**MARTIN H. GREENBERG**, Editor

### Haunted Houses: The Greatest Stories
(New York: Michael J. Fine, 1997)

**Story type:** Horror (Anthology; Haunted House)

**Summary:** Sixteen classic and contemporary stories of haunted houses. Included are H.P. Lovercraft's "The Rats in the Walls," in which a man discovers the influence of his cannibal ancestors is still active in his family mansion; Joyce Carol Oates's "The Doll," in which a woman endures a bizarre encounter in a house that resembles a doll house she owned as a child; Bram Stoker's "The Judge's House," in which new tenants of a house haunted by an evil judge come to a dismal end; William F. Nolan's "Dark Winner," about a man who visits his childhood home and finds it haunted by his childhood self; and Robert Bloch's "Lizzie Borden Took an Axe," about a woman possessed by the spirit of axe murderess Lizzie Borden.

**Other books you might like:**
Kathryn Cramer, *The Architecture of Fear*, 1987
    Peter Pautz, co-editor
Kathryn Cramer, *Walls of Fear*, 1990
    editor
Peter Straub, *Peter Straub's Ghosts*, 1995
    editor
Gahan Wilson, *Gahan Wilson's The Ultimate Haunted House*, 1996
    editor

## 2397

**MARTIN H. GREENBERG**, Editor
**ROSALIND M. GREENBERG**, Co-Editor

### Horse Fantastic
(New York: DAW, 1991)

**Story type:** Fantasy (Anthology)

**Summary:** This volume contains a four-page introduction by Jennifer Roberson plus 17 original stories featuring horses in fantasy situations. Contributors include Constance Ash, Mercedes Lackey, Elizabeth Moon, Mickey Zucker Reichert, Mike Resnick, Jennifer Roberson, Josepha Sherman, Mary Stanton, Judith Tarr and Janny Wurtz.

**Other books you might like:**
Robert Adams, *The Coming of the Horseclans*, 1982
Constance Ash, *The Horsegirl*, 1988
Constance Ash, *The Stalking Horse*, 1990
Jack Dann, *Unicorns!*, 1982
    Gardner Dozois, co-editor
Mary H. Herbert, *Dark Horse*, 1990
Mary H. Herbert, *Lightning's Daughter*, 1991
Peter Morwood, *The Horse Lord*, 1987
Mary Stanton, *The Heavenly Horse From the Outermost West*, 1988
Mary Stanton, *Piper at the Gate*, 1989

`2398`

**MARTIN H. GREENBERG**, Editor

## Lord of the Fantastic: Stories in Honor of Roger Zelazny

(New York: Avon Eos, 1998)

**Story type:** Fantasy (Anthology; Science Fiction)

**Summary:** This anthology contains a three-page introduction by Fred Saberhagen, a six-page afterword by Gerald Hausman, five pages of notes about the authors, 21 original stories, and three stories re-printed from periodicals and anthologies dating from 1994 to 1997, each with an individual author's afterword. Diverse themes include psychology, biology, poker, American Indian mythology, death, alien artifacts, mythical creatures, religion, the legend of the Flying Dutchman, and virtual reality. Authors include Gregory Benford, Steven Brust, Neil Gaiman, Nina Kiriki Hoffman, Katharine Eliska Kimbriel, Jane Lindskold, Andre Norton, Jennifer Roberson, Robert Sheckley, Robert Silverberg, John Varley, Walter Jon Williams, and Jack Williamson.

**Other books you might like:**
Kevin J. Anderson, *War of the Worlds: Global Dispatches*, 1996
　editor
Peter S. Beagle, *Peter S. Beagle's Immortal Unicorn*, 1995
　Janet Berliner, co-editor
Steven R. Boyett, *Treks Not Taken: What if Stephen King, Anne Rice, Bret Easton Ellis, and Other Literary Greats Had Written Episodes of Star Trek: The Next Generation?*, 1996
Randall Garrett, *Takeoff!*, 1979
Randall Garrett, *Takeoff, Too*, 1986
William F. Nolan, *The Bradbury Chronicles: Stories in Honor of Ray Bradbury*, 1991
　Martin H. Greenberg, co-editor
Jennifer Roberson, *Return to Avalon: A Celebration of Marion Zimmer Bradley*, 1996
Roger Zelazny, *The Williamson Effect*, 1996

`2399`

**MARTIN H. GREENBERG**, Editor
**ROBERT WEINBERG**, Co-Editor

## Miskatonic University

(New York: DAW, 1996)

**Story type:** Horror (Anthology)

**Summary:** The 13 original stories collected here are all set on the campus of Miskatonic University, a locale created by H.P. Lovecraft and renowned as a battleground where ancient superstitions and modern scientific enlightenment collide. Alan Rodgers' "Her Misbegotten Son," about forces of black magic that overwhelm a professor's family, is a semi-sequel to Lovecraft's "Dreams in the Witch House" and "The Dunwich Horror," while Jane M. Lindskold's "A Dreaming of Dead Poets" extrapolates the plot of Lovecraft's "The Call of Cthulhu" in a tale of students who discover their artistic talents have made them sensitive to forces engaged in an occult conspiracy. Jay Bonansinga's "Black Celebration" and Benjamin Adams' "Second Movement" both feature musicians who tap into the school's latent reserves of dark power, and Stephen Mark Rainey's "To Be as They" an art student whose paintings access another dimension. Will Murray's "Sothis Radiant" reveals that the campus astronomy department knows more about the impending end of the world than it will say.

**Other books you might like:**
Edward P. Berglund, *Disciples of Cthulhu*, 1976
　editor
Lin Carter, *The Spawn of Cthulhu*, 1971
　editor
Robert M. Price, *The Arkham Cycle*, 1996
　editor
Robert M. Price, *The Dunwich Cycle*, 1995
　editor
Thomas M.K. Stratman, *Cthulhu's Heirs*, 1994
　editor

`2400`

**MARTIN H. GREENBERG**

## Mummy Stories

(New York: Ballantine, 1990)

**Story type:** Horror (Anthology; Reanimated Dead)

**Summary:** Fourteen stories about mummies, five original to this volume. The selections range in tone from the whimsical (Edgar Allan Poe's "Some Words with a Mummy," Sharon McCrumb's "Remains to Be Seen") to the weird (E.F. Benson's "Monkeys," Sir Arthur Conan Doyle's "Lot 249") to the utterly gruesome (Donald Wollheim's "Bones," Robert Bloch's "Beetles").

**Other books you might like:**
Bill Pronzini, *Mummy!*, 1980

`2401`

**MARTIN H. GREENBERG**, Editor

## The New Hugo Winners, Volume IV

(New York: Baen, 1997)

**Story type:** Science Fiction (Anthology; Science Fiction)
**Series:** Hugo Winners

**Summary:** Contains brief individual introductions by Gregory Benford to nine stories given Science Fiction Achievement Awards, known as "Hugo Awards," by voting members of World Science Fiction Conventions 1992-1994. Authors include Isaac Asimov, Janet Kagan, Nancy Kress, Charles Sheffield, Harry Turtledove and Connie Willis.

**Other books you might like:**
Isaac Asimov, *The Hugo Winners 1-5*, 1962-1986
　editor
Isaac Asimov, *Isaac Asimov Presents the Great SF Stories: 1-25*, 1979-1992
　Martin H. Greenberg, co-editor
Isaac Asimov, *The New Hugo Winners*, 1989
　editor
James Morrow, *Nebula Awards 26-28*, 1992-1994
　editor
Connie Willis, *The New Hugo Winners, Volume III*, 1994
　Martin H. Greenberg, co-editor

`2402`

**MARTIN H. GREENBERG**, Editor

## New Stories From the Twilight Zone

(New York: Avon, 1991)

**Story type:** Horror (Anthology)

**Summary:** Twenty-one tales of fantasy, horror and science fiction, originally written for publication but adapted for the briefly revived television program. Stories range in scope from Arthur C. Clarke's ''The Star,'' about an amazing archaeological find on a planet about to be consumed by a supernova, to Harlan Ellison's intimate ''Shatterday,'' about a man so out of touch with the world around him he begins to dematerialize. There is humor (Theodore Sturgeon's ''Yesterday Was Monday''), horror (Robert R. McCammon's ''Nightcrawlers'') and a *conte cruel* (Richard Matheson's ''Button, Button'') to suit every taste.

**Other books you might like:**
Mitchell Galen, *Tales From the Darkside, Volume 1*, 1989
    Tom Allen, co-editor
Rod Serling, *The Night Gallery Reader*, 1990
Rod Serling, *Stories From the Twilight Zone*, 1990
J. Michael Straczynski, *Tales From the New Twilight Zone*, 1989
John Tigges, *Kevin Browne's Nightales*, 1990

## 2403

**MARTIN H. GREENBERG**, Editor

### Nightmares on Elm Street: Freddy Krueger's Seven Sweetest Dreams
(New York: St. Martin's, 1991)

**Story type:** Horror (Anthology)

**Summary:** The seven original stories in this book revolve around the character of Freddy Krueger, child murderer of Wes Craven's *Nightmare on Elm Street* film saga, who was burned to death by a vigilante squad of concerned parents but continues to haunt and kill the children of Elm Street through their dreams. Included are Brian Hodge's ''Asleep at the Wheel,'' in which Freddy insinuates himself into the career dreams of a rock band named after one of his victims; Wayne Allen Sallee's ''Close My Eyes and I'll Kiss You,'' in which Freddy visits a prisoner on death row; Nancy Collins' ''Not Just a Job,'' in which Freddy trains the child of a mass murderer to emulate his father; and Tom Elliott's ''Briefcase Full of Blues,'' in which Freddy meets his match at the hands of his daughter.

**Other books you might like:**
Mitchell Galen, *Tales From the Darkside, Volume 1*, 1989
    Tom Allen, co-author
Jack Oleck, *Tales From the Crypt*, 1972
Rod Serling, *The Night Gallery Reader*, 1990
J. Michael Straczynski, *Tales From the New Twilight Zone*, 1989

## 2404

**MARTIN H. GREENBERG**, Editor
**BRUCE D. ARTHURS**, Co-Editor

### Olympus
(New York: DAW, 1998)

**Story type:** Fantasy (Anthology)

**Summary:** These 17 original stories involve the Greek gods, some in the original ancient setting, some transplanted into the modern age. Contributors include Esther Friesner, Jon DeCles, Charles De Lint, Jo Clayton, and Lawrence Watt-Evans.

**Other books you might like:**
Patrick H. Adkins, *Sons of the Titans*, 1990
Michael Ayrton, *The Maze Maker*, 1967
Robert Graves, *Hercules, My Shipmate*, 1945
David Lee Jones, *Zeus and Co.*, 1993
Jane M. Lindskold, *The Pipes of Orpheus*, 1995

## 2405

**MARTIN H. GREENBERG**, Editor

### The Super Hugos
(New York: Baen, 1992)

**Story type:** Science Fiction (Anthology)

**Summary:** Charles Sheffield provides a four-page introduction and introductions to 10 individual stories, all voted best among previous Hugo Award winning stories by members of the 1992 World Science Fiction Convention, MagiCon. This anthology contains two stories by Harlan Ellison, ''Repent, Harlequin!' Said the Ticktockman'' and ''I Have No Mouth, and I Must Scream,'' and two stories which inspired films, Daniel Keyes' ''Flowers for Algernon'' (*Charly*) and Barry B. Longyear's ''Enemy Mine'' (*Enemy Mine*). Other favorite Hugo winners included Isaac Asimov's ''The Bicentennial Man,'' Arthur C. Clarke's ''The Star,'' George R. R. Martin's ''Sandkings,'' Anne McCaffrey's ''Weyr Search,'' Larry Niven's ''Neutron Star'' and Clifford D. Simak's ''The Big Front Yard.'' Concludes with a 10-page article by Joe Siclari and Edie Stern, ''About the Super Hugo Voting,'' and a 12-page appendix listing Hugo Award winners.

**Other books you might like:**
Isaac Asimov, *The Hugo Winners 1-5*, 1962-1986
    editor
Isaac Asimov, *The New Hugo Winners*, 1989
    editor
Raymond J. Healy, *Adventures in Time and Space*, 1946
    J. Francis McComas, co-editor
Richard A. Lupoff, *What If? Stories That Should Have Won the Hugo*, 1980
    editor
Leo Margulies, *My Best Science Fiction Story*, 1949
    O. J. Friend, co-editor
Robert Silverberg, *The Science Fiction Hall of Fame, Volume 1*, 1970
    editor

## 2406

**MARTIN H. GREENBERG**, Editor
**LAWRENCE SCHIMEL**, Co-Editor

### Tarot Fantastic
(New York: DAW, 1997)

**Story type:** Fantasy (Anthology)

**Summary:** Contains a five-page introduction by Schimel, an original poem by Jane Yolen and 15 original stories varying in tone from whimsical to downbeat and featuring themes surrounding fortune-telling tarot cards. Other authors include Charles de Lint, Teresa Edgerton, Rosemary Edghill, George Alec Effinger, Kate Elliott, Mark A. Garland, Nina Kiriki Hoffman, Tanya Huff, Nancy Springer and Michelle Sagara West.

**Other books you might like:**
Piers Anthony, *Tarot*, 1987
Italo Calvino, *The Castle of Crossed Destinies*, 1977
Rachel Pollack, *Tarot Tales*, 1996
    Caitlin Matthews, co-editor
Tim Powers, *Last Call*, 1992
Charles Williams, *The Greater Trumps*, 1932
Roger Zelazny, *Wheel of Fortune*, 1995
    Martin H. Greenberg, co-editor

## 2407

**MARTIN H. GREENBERG**, Editor
**STEFAN DZIEMIANOWICZ**, Co-Editor
**ROBERT WEINBERG**, Co-Editor

## A Taste for Blood

(New York: Dorset, 1992)

**Story type:** Horror (Anthology; Vampire Story)

**Summary:** Fifteen vampire stories and novellas that span the last 125 years of horror publishing. Included are J. Sheridan Le Fanu's influential ''Carmilla,'' Hugh B. Cave's pulp classic, ''Murgunstrumm,'' H. P. Lovecraft's fusion of the vampire and haunted house story, ''The Shunned House,'' Karl Edward Wagner's mix of the ghost and vampire story, ''Beyond Any Measure,'' Thomas Ligotti's tale of the offspring of vampire and mortal parents, ''The Lost Art of Twilight,'' and Patrick McGrath's black humor sketch, ''Blood Disease.''

**Other books you might like:**

Alan Ryan, *Vampires: Two Centuries of Great Vampire Stories*, 1987

Leslie Shepard, *The Dracula Book of Great Vampire Stories*, 1977
editor

Devendra P. Varma, *Voices From the Vault: Authentic Vampire Tales*, 1987
editor

## 2408

**MARTIN H. GREENBERG**, Editor

## Vampire Detectives

(New York: DAW, 1995)

**Story type:** Horror (Anthology; Vampire Story)

**Summary:** The nineteen stories commissioned for this anthology feature vampire detectives or vampire crime perpetrators. In William F. Nolan's ''Vampire Dollars,'' a detective becomes entangled in a black-mail murder case involving a former starlet of vampire films. William Sanders' ''The Count's Mailbox'' uses an exchange of letters to tell of a vampire's unsuccessful attempts to market a vampire novel and the drastic measures he resorts to. Jack Kethcum's ''The Turning'' and Wayne Allen Sallee's ''Blind Pig on North Halsted'' are both urban horror tales that find analogies between different types of criminal activity and vampirism. And in Richard Laymon's ''Phil the Vampire,'' a private detective must decide whether a woman who complains her husband is a vampire is telling the truth, or merely hopeful that she can gull him into killing her abusive spouse.

**Other books you might like:**

Jean Marie Stine, *I, Vampire: Interviews with the Undead*, 1995
Forrest J. Ackerman, co-editor

Stephen Jones, *The Mammoth Book of Vampires*, 1993
editor

Alan Ryan, *Vampires: Two Centuries of Great Vampire Stories*, 1987

## 2409

**MARTIN H. GREENBERG**, Editor

## Vampires: The Greatest Stories

(New York: Michael J. Fine, 1997)

**Story type:** Horror (Anthology; Vampire Story)

**Summary:** Fifteen vampire stories by some of the best-known names in horror and fantasy. Included are Eric Lustbader's ''In Darkness, Angels,'' set in a Gothic castle inhabited by vampire siblings; Karl Edward Wagner's ''Beyond Any Measure,'' a fusion of the ghost and vampire story; David Drake's ''Something Had to Be Done,'' about a vampire that haunts the battlefields of Vietnam; Robert R. McCammon's ''The Miracle Mile,'' which takes place in a future where vampires have overrun the world; Dan Simmons's ''Shave and Haircut, Two Bites,'' which explores the iconography of the local barbershop in terms of vampirism; and Robert Bloch's ''The Bat Is My Brother,'' a first person account of a man rising from the dead as a vampire.

**Other books you might like:**

Ellen Datlow, *Blood Is Not Enough*, 1989
editor

Stephen Jones, *The Mammoth Book of Vampires*, 1992
editor

Alan Ryan, *Vampires: Two Centuries of Great Vampire Stories*, 1987
editor

Leonard Wolf, *Blood Thirst: 100 Years of Vampire Fiction*, 1997
editor

## 2410

**MARTIN H. GREENBERG**, Editor

## Werewolves

(New York: DAW, 1995)

**Story type:** Horror (Anthology; Werewolf Story)

**Summary:** Twenty-two stories original to this volume approach the werewolf theme from a variety of angles. Brian Hodge draws parallels between werewolves and the street children of South America in ''Extinctions in Paradise.'' Max Allan Collins' ''Wolf'' features a gigolo who preys on young women, while Nina Kiriki Hoffman's ''Dumpster Diving'' tells of the nurturing relationship between a young woman and a foundling baby werewolf. Mike Baker's ''Bark at the Moon'' and Matt Costello's ''Nick of Time'' find werewolves lurking beneath the surface of daily life in the city, and Hugh Cave's ''Nights in the Mountains of Haiti'' in a more exotic locale. Norman Partridge's ''The Pack'' is a brilliant anti-werewolf tale that uses a pack of motorcycle hoodlums to undermine reader expectations for an expression of the beast within.

**Other books you might like:**

Greg Cox, *Tomorrow Bites*, 1995
T.K.F. Weiskopf, co-editor

Brian J. Frost, *Book of the Werewolf*, 1973

David Hill, *The Way of the Werewolf*, 1966
editor

Stephen Jones, *The Mammoth Book of Werewolves*, 1994
editor

Byron Preiss, *The Ultimate Werewolf*, 1992
editor

Bill Pronzini, *Werewolf!*, 1979
editor

## 2411

**MARTIN H. GREENBERG**, Editor

### White House Horrors
(New York: DAW, 1996)

**Story type:** Horror (Anthology)

**Summary:** Sixteen original stories feature the White House and the presidency as elements of their horror themes. Brian Hodge's "Healing the Body Politic" concerns a secret service agent who discovers that the White House and other world governments are run by secret occult societies. Richard T. Chizmar's "Homesick" is about a child of the Chief Executive moved to express his resentment at being wrenched out of his former way of life. Edward Lee's "Night of the Vegetables" features one inept president's handling of a national crisis spawned by nuclear woes. Stories that feature specific presidents include Barbara Collins and Max Allan Collins' "The Cabinet of William Henry Harrison," Bill Crider's "The Ghost and Mr. Truman," Graham Masterton's "Jack Be Quick" (John F. Kennedy), and Kein Stein and Robert Weinberg's "Release," based on the apocryphal tale that William McKinley foresaw his assassination.

**Other books you might like:**
Mike Resnick, *Alternate Kennedys*, 1992
  editor
Mike Resnick, *Alternate Presidents*, 1992
  editor

## 2412

**ROSALIND M. GREENBERG**, Editor
**MARTIN H. GREENBERG**, Co-Editor

### Christmas Bestiary
(New York: DAW, 1992)

**Story type:** Fantasy (Anthology)

**Summary:** Contains an eight-page introduction by Stefan Dziemianowicz plus 19 original stories with Christmas themes all featuring legendary creatures such as selkies, sea serpents, elves, pixies, a yeti and a blue-nosed reindeer. Authors include Mark Aronson, Karen Haber, Jack C. Haldeman II, Tanya Huff, Barry N. Malzberg, Mike Resnick, Jennifer Roberson, Kristine Kathryn Rusch, Elizabeth Scarborough, Harry Turtledove and Jane Yolen.

**Other books you might like:**
Alan Brennert, *Kindred Spirits*, 1984
Martin H. Greenberg, *Christmas on Ganymede and Other Stories*, 1990
  editor
David G. Hartwell, *Christmas Stars*, 1992
  editor
Kristine Kathryn Rusch, *Pulphouse, Issue 10: Special Issue*, 1991
  editor
John Silbersack, *The Magic of Christmas*, 1992
  Christopher Schelling, co-editor
Gene Wolfe, *Gene Wolfe's Book of Days*, 1981

## 2413

**ROSALIND M. GREENBERG**, Editor
**MARTIN H. GREENBERG**, Co-Editor

### Dragon Fantastic
(New York: DAW, 1992)

**Story type:** Fantasy (Anthology; Legend)

**Summary:** Contains an eight-page introduction by Tad Williams plus 16 original stories with diverse approaches to the theme, dragons. Mark A. Kreighbaum and Dennis L. McKiernan collaborated on "Straw into Gold: Part II." Other authors include Ruth Berman, Alan Dean Foster, Esther M. Friesner, Karen Haber, Tanya Huff, Barry N. Malzberg, Mickey Zucker Reichert, Mike Resnick and Josepha Sherman.

**Other books you might like:**
Poul Anderson, *The Night Fantastic*, 1991
  Karen Anderson, co-editor
Orson Scott Card, *Dragons of Darkness*, 1981
  Editor
Orson Scott Card, *Dragons of Light*, 1980
  Editor
Alan Dean Foster, *Smart Dragons, Foolish Elves*, 1991
  Editor
Andre Norton, *Catfantastic*, 1989
  Martin H. Greenberg, co-editor
Andre Norton, *Catfantastic II*, 1991
  Martin H. Greenberg, co-editor
Patricia C. Wrede, *Dealing with Dragons*, 1990

## 2414

**KIRBY GREENE**

### Brotherhood of the Stars
(New York: Bantam Spectra, 1994)

**Story type:** Science Fiction (Space Opera; Adventure)
**Major character(s):** Ree Barzac, Spaceman; Erpad Ystilog, Museum Curator; Zigmunn, Spaceman, Outcast (exiled)
**Time period(s):** Indeterminate Future
**Locale(s):** Glaurus, Planet—Imaginary; Azonda, Planet—Imaginary

**Summary:** Ree Barzac comes to Glaurus where, 10 years earlier, his blood brother was marooned. When he learns that Zigmunn has joined a cult and gone to Azonda, Barzac tries to follow, but disaster leads to enslavement. To secure freedom, he must join the cult.

**Other books you might like:**
Jim Aikin, *Walk the Moon's Road*, 1985
Johanna Bolton, *Mission: Tori*, 1990
Leigh Brackett, *The Sword of Rhiannon*, 1953
Marion Zimmer Bradley, *The Door through Space*, 1961
John Brunner, *The Rites of Ohe*, 1963
Lin Carter, *The City Outside the World*, 1977
Philip Jose Farmer, *The Green Odyssey*, 1956
Simon R. Green, *Mistworld*, 1992
Harry Harrison, *Planet of the Damned*, 1962
Sydney J. Van Scyoc, *Assignment: Nor'Dyren*, 1973
Jack Vance, *Trullion: Alastor 2262*, 1973

## 2415

### KEN GREENHALL

## *Deathchain*

(New York: Pocket, 1991)

**Story type:** Horror (Psychological Suspense)
**Major character(s):** Paul Marnay, Artist (painter); Hillary Block, Social Worker (psychotherapist); Phyllis Arno, Actress
**Time period(s):** 1990s
**Locale(s):** Dale Falls, New York

**Summary:** One by one, the residents of Dale Falls begin murdering one another at the behest of the Chainmaster, an anonymous letter writer whose chain letter promises the disposal of someone they want eliminated if they themselves will commit a murder. When Paul Marnay stumbles upon the pattern behind the deaths, he becomes a murder target, and must not only determine the identity of the Chainmaster but also find out who among his acquaintances might wish him dead.

**Other books you might like:**
Ramsey Campbell, *Obsession*, 1986
Patricia Highsmith, *Strangers on a Train*, 1950
Ruby Jean Jensen, *Chain Letter*, 1987

## 2416

### COLIN GREENLAND

## *Harm's Way*

(New York: AvoNova, 1993)

**Story type:** Science Fiction (Adventure; Alternate Universe)
**Major character(s):** Sophie Farthing, Runaway, Heiress—Lost; Jacob Farthing, Parent, Security Officer; Bruno, Mercenary (assassin)
**Time period(s):** Indeterminate
**Locale(s):** High Haven, Space Station; Mars

**Summary:** Following an encounter with a mysterious stranger who claims to have known her mother, Sophie runs away from her home on High Haven. Her search for her mother leads her to the Moon, outpost of the British Empire and to London, the capital. Disguised as a boy, she works her passage to Mars as a cabin boy on one of the ships that sail the tides of aether between the worlds. Barely escaping death as a sacrifice to the Black God of Mars, she lives for a time among the half-wild Martian converts at a French mission in the desert, until the man sent to kill her offers her instead a chance to discover hidden talents and the truth about her parentage.

**Other books you might like:**
Ray Bradbury, *The Martian Chronicles*, 1950
Edgar Rice Burroughs, *The Gods of Mars*, 1918
C.J. Cherryh, *Cuckoo's Egg*, 1985
Robert A. Heinlein, *Podkayne of Mars*, 1963
C.S. Lewis, *Out of the Silent Planet*, 1965
Anne McCaffrey, *The Rowan*, 1990
William Sanders, *The Wild Blue and the Gray*, 1991

## 2417

### COLIN GREENLAND

## *Mother of Plenty*

(New York: Avon Eos, 1998)

**Story type:** Science Fiction (Adventure; Theological)
**Series:** Tabitha Jute

**Major character(s):** Tabitha Jute, Spaceship Captain, Leader; Saskia Zodiac, Clone; Xtasca the Cherub, Alien, Genetically Altered Being
**Time period(s):** Indeterminate Future
**Locale(s):** *Plenty*, Spaceship; Capella System, Outer Space

**Summary:** Planning to go to Proxima Centauri, the inhabitants of *Plenty* get hijacked during the trip by Saskin, a tool of the Temple of Abraxas. With the help of Alice Liddell, the AI from her old barge, Tabitha tries to rescue her crew, take back *Plenty*, and return home.

**Other books you might like:**
Roger MacBride Allen, *The Ring of Charon*, 1990
Patricia Anthony, *Brother Termite*, 1993
Greg Bear, *Eon*, 1985
Glen Cook, *The Dragon Never Sleeps*, 1988
Frederik Pohl, *The Other End of Time*, 1996
Robert J. Sawyer, *Starplex*, 1996

## 2418

### COLIN GREENLAND

## *Seasons of Plenty*

(New York: AvoNova, 1996)

**Story type:** Science Fiction (Adventure)
**Series:** Plenty
**Major character(s):** Tabitha Jute, Spaceship Captain, Leader; Saskia Zodiac, Clone, Magician (stage); Xtasca the Cherub, Genetically Altered Being
**Time period(s):** Indeterminate Future
**Locale(s):** *Plenty*, Spaceship

**Summary:** Tabitha Jute and her stolen spaceship, loaded with criminals, renegades, and many odd things, set course for the star Proxima Centauri. The situation deteriorates as different factions maneuver for power and plots multiply. When a "cybermessiah" appears, maybe a devil and maybe an angel, life aboard *Plenty* gets weirder. Second in a trilogy.

**Other books you might like:**
Glen Cook, *The Dragon Never Sleeps*, 1988
Bradley Denton, *Buddy Holly Is Alive and Well on Ganymede*, 1991
Robert A. Heinlein, *Podkayne of Mars*, 1963
Damon Knight, *Why Do Birds*, 1992

## 2419

### COLIN GREENLAND

## *Take Back Plenty*

(New York: Avon, 1992)

**Story type:** Science Fiction (Adventure; Alternate Intelligence)
**Major character(s):** Alice Liddell, Artificial Intelligence (Spaceship); Tabitha Jute, Spaceship Captain; Hannah Soo, Financier, Reanimated Dead (cryogenically interred)
**Time period(s):** 23rd century
**Locale(s):** Schiaparelli Luna, Montenegro; Plenty, Space Station; Spaceship

**Summary:** The Capellans, having given us the space drive, demonstrated their superiority and limited humanity to our solar system. Tabitha Jute, trying to find replacement parts for her well-built but ancient ship, finds herself involved with a traveling nightclub act. The troupe includes several genetically altered humans and an alien or two. Trying to get payment so she can repair her ship, Tabitha finds herself part of the hidden agenda of Hannah Soo, the troupe's agent and financier. This book won both the Arthur C. Clarke Award and the British Science Fiction Association Award for the Best SF Novel of the year when published in England in 1990.

**Other books you might like:**
David Brin, *Startide Rising*, 1983
Octavia E. Butler, *Dawn*, 1987
Arthur C. Clarke, *The Garden of Rama*, 1991
   Gentry Lee, co-author
Glen Cook, *The Dragon Never Sleeps*, 1988
Anne McCaffrey, *The Ship Who Sang*, 1969
Melisa C. Michaels, *Skirmish*, 1985
Naomi Mitchison, *Memoirs of a Spacewoman*, 1973
Alis A. Rasmussen, *A Passage of Stars*, 1990
David Alexander Smith, *Homecoming*, 1990

**2420**

**GAYLE GREENO**

## Exiles' Return
(New York: DAW, 1995)

**Story type:** Science Fiction (Psychic Powers; Lost Colony)
**Series:** Ghatti's Tale
**Major character(s):** Doyce Marbon, Telepath; Khar'pern, Alien (Ghatta), Telepath; Jenret Wycherley, Telepath
**Time period(s):** Indeterminate Future
**Locale(s):** Methuen, Planet—Imaginary

**Summary:** When the discovery that psychics, called Resonants, can read and control other minds fills ordinary citizens with fear and hatred, Jenret undertakes a mission to find and protect the Resonants. As Doyce awaits the birth of her child, she embarks on a mental journey into the past of their planet, guided by the cat-like Ghatti with whom she has a telepathic link.

**Other books you might like:**
C.J. Cherryh, *Rider at the Gate*, 1995
Mary Gentle, *Golden Witchbreed*, 1984
Anne McCaffrey, *To Ride Pegasus*, 1968
Andre Norton, *Catseye*, 1961
James H. Schmitz, *The Universe Against Her*, 1964
A.E. Van Vogt, *Slan*, 1946

**2421**

**GAYLE GREENO**

## Finders-Seekers
(New York: DAW, 1993)

**Story type:** Science Fiction (Psychic Powers; Mystery)
**Series:** Ghatti's Tale
**Major character(s):** Doyce Marbon, Telepath; Khar'pern, Alien (Ghatti), Telepath; Mahafny, Doctor
**Time period(s):** Indeterminate Future
**Locale(s):** Methuen, Planet—Imaginary

**Summary:** Descendants of the lost colony of humans on Methuen have adapted and created a culture based on partnership with the Ghatti, telepathic cat-like natives. Sent to investigate the tragic death of her lover, Oriel, and the psychic crippling of Saam, his bondmate, Doyce and her bondmate, Khar'pern, set out to retrace Oriel's steps. They discover a conspiracy to murder human-ghatti pairs and an unsuspected perversion of mental powers. First novel.

**Other books you might like:**
C.J. Cherryh, *Forty Thousand in Gehenna*, 1983
Gordon R. Dickson, *Masters of Everon*, 1980
Lynn S. Hightower, *Alien Blues*, 1992

Janet Kagan, *Uhura's Song*, 1985
Rosemary Kirstein, *The Outskirter's Secret*, 1992
Anne McCaffrey, *Decision at Doona*, 1969
Anne McCaffrey, *Dragonflight*, 1968
James H. Schmitz, *The Universe Against Her*, 1964
Tad Williams, *Tailchaser's Song*, 1985

**2422**

**GAYLE GREENO**

## Mind Snare
(New York: DAW, 1997)

**Story type:** Science Fiction (Arts; Family Saga)
**Major character(s):** Glynn Webster Stanislaus, Actor, Teenager; Jerelynn Stanislaus, Actress; Vitarosa, Murderer, Religious
**Time period(s):** 22nd century (2158)
**Locale(s):** PabNeruda, Space Station; Texas Republic, Fictional Country (NetwArk and Houston); North America

**Summary:** Upon giving his ultimate performance in the Stanislaus Troupe, Glynn feels unprepared to relinquish his acting career, as required of males by troupe custom when they turn 15. When assassins almost kill his mother, the Great Jerelynn, Glynn preserves her mind in a forbidden brain box and takes over her roles while attempting to track down the would-be assassins.

**Other books you might like:**
Orson Scott Card, *The Worthing Saga*, 1991
Robert A. Heinlein, *Double Star*, 1956
Frederik Pohl, *Outnumbering the Dead*, 1992
Sheri S. Tepper, *Sideshow*, 1992
Jack Vance, *Showboat World*, 1975
Katie Waitman, *The Merro Tree*, 1997

**2423**

**GAYLE GREENO**

## Mind-Speakers' Call
(New York: DAW, 1994)

**Story type:** Science Fiction (Psychic Powers; Political)
**Series:** Ghatti's Tale
**Major character(s):** Doyce Marbon, Telepath; Khar'pern, Alien (Ghatti), Telepath; Jenret Wycherley, Telepath
**Time period(s):** Indeterminate Future
**Locale(s):** Canderis, Fictional Country; Marchmont, Fictional Country

**Summary:** Though still recovering from the mental effects of her confrontation with a rogue psychic, Doyce agrees to join a diplomatic mission to the neighboring nation of Marchmont, which has cut off trade with Canderis. Inside Marchmont, she and her companions discover a country on the verge of civil war over a disputed succession. Struggling to prevent war and stay alive, they find conspiracies, new telepathic talents and love.

**Other books you might like:**
Mary Gentle, *Golden Witchbreed*, 1984
Ursula K. Le Guin, *The Left Hand of Darkness*, 1969
Anne McCaffrey, *Dragonflight*, 1968
James H. Schmitz, *The Universe Against Her*, 1964
Tad Williams, *Tailchaser's Song*, 1985

### 2424

**GAYLE GREENO**

## Sunderlies Seeking

(New York: DAW, 1998)

**Story type:** Fantasy (Magic Conflict)
**Major character(s):** Jenneth Marbon, Teenager; Diccon Marbon, Teenager
**Time period(s):** Indeterminate
**Locale(s):** Sunderlies, Fictional Country

**Summary:** The Marbon family travels to the Sunderlies on a business trip even though the islands are reputed to be the home of various criminals and other undesirables. Their journey is marked by a series of suspicious accidents that are the result of evil magic directed against them.

**Other books you might like:**
Robin Wayne Bailey, *Brothers of the Dragon*, 1993
Margaret Ball, *Flameweaver*, 1991
Elizabeth H. Boyer, *The Elves and the Otterskin*, 1981
Guy Gavriel Kay, *Tigana*, 1990
Katherine Kurtz, *King Javan's Year*, 1992

### 2425

**ED GREENWOOD**
**JEFF GRUBB**, Co-Author

## Cormyr: A Novel

(Renton, Washington: TSR, 1998)

**Story type:** Fantasy (Political; Magic Conflict)
**Major character(s):** Azoun IV, Ruler; Dauneth Marliir, Warrior
**Time period(s):** Indeterminate
**Locale(s):** Cormyr, Fictional Country

**Summary:** As the current king of Cormyr lies on his deathbed, several rival families plot to take this opportunity to seize the throne. Those loyal to the legitimate line counter their plots against an elaborate background retelling of the episodic history of the nation of Cormyr.

**Other books you might like:**
Lynn Abbey, *Simbul's Gift*, 1997
Raymond E. Feist, *Magician*, 1983
Robert Jordan, *Lord of Chaos*, 1994
Don Perrin, *Theros Ironfeld*, 1996
Chris Pierson, *Spirit of the Wind*, 1997

### 2426

**ED GREENWOOD**
**JEFF GRUBB**, Co-Author

## Cormyr: A Novel

(Lake Geneva, Wisconsin: TSR, 1996)

**Story type:** Fantasy (Political)
**Series:** Forgotten Realms
**Major character(s):** Vangerdahast, Magician (Royal Magician)
**Time period(s):** Indeterminate
**Locale(s):** Cormyr, Fictional Country

**Summary:** When Cormyr's King Azoun IV falls victim to a deadly malady, Vangerdahast steps in to aid the kingdom, while many feel that the Royal Magician himself may have caused Azoun's illness.

**Other books you might like:**
Jeff Grubb, *Lord Teode*, 1994

Robin Hobb, *Assassin's Apprentice*, 1995
J.V. Jones, *The Baker's Boy*, 1995
Kate Novak, *Song of the Saurials*, 1991
  Jeff Grubb, co-author
Kate Novak, *The Wyvern's Spur*, 1990
  Jeff Grubb, co-author
Chet Williamson, *Murder in Cormyr*, 1996

### 2427

**ED GREENWOOD**

## Elminster: The Making of a Mage

(Lake Geneva, Wisconsin: TSR, 1994)

**Story type:** Fantasy (Sword and Sorcery; Adventure)
**Series:** Forgotten Realms
**Major character(s):** Elminster, Sorcerer, Royalty; Mystra, Sorceress; Elmara, Adventurer, Religious (priestess)
**Time period(s):** Indeterminate
**Locale(s):** Faerun, Fictional Country

**Summary:** When magelords kill his parents and lay waste to the land, a young shepherd, Elminster, decides to avenge the disaster and begins the journey which leads to his becoming the most powerful mage in Faerun.

**Other books you might like:**
Richard Awlinson, *Shadowdale*, 1989
Troy Denning, *The Parched Sea*, 1991
R.A. Salvatore, *The Legacy*, 1992
R.A. Salvatore, *Siege of Darkness*, 1994
R.A. Salvatore, *Starless Night*, 1993

### 2428

**STEPHEN GREGORY**

## The Blood of Angels

(Clarkston, Georgia: White Wolf, 1995)

**Story type:** Horror (Psychological Suspense)
**Major character(s):** Harry Clewe, Handyman; Elizabeth Clewe, Musician; Zoe Clewe, Child
**Time period(s):** 1990s (1995)
**Locale(s):** Caernarfon, Wales

**Summary:** First published in England in 1994, this grim tale of psychological dissolution concerns Harry Clewe, a slightly dysfunctional young man whose fever-born vision of an angelic being propels him through a series of increasingly disastrous relationships with women including a female hitchhiker, a sister with whom he has an incestuous affair, the child of that affair, and, eventually, an androgynous young man.

**Other books you might like:**
Robert Bloch, *Psycho*, 1959
Christopher Fowler, *Red Bride*, 1993
John Fowles, *The Collector*, 1962
Thomas Harris, *The Silence of the Lambs*, 1989
Marvin Kaye, *Fantastique*, 1992

## 2429

### STEPHEN GREGORY

### *The Cormorant*

(Clarkston, Georgia: White Wolf, 1996)

**Story type:** Horror (Psychological Suspense)
**Major character(s):** Ann, Housewife; Harry, Child; Archie, Animal (pet cormorant)
**Time period(s):** 1980s (1986)
**Locale(s):** Wales (near Caernarfon)

**Summary:** The nameless narrator and his wife and son inherit a house from their Uncle Ian on the condition that they care for his unfriendly pet cormorant. In a short time, the bird becomes an object of and focus for the pent up anger that is slowly pulling the family apart. This novel was originally published in England in 1986 and won the Somerset Maugham Award.

**Other books you might like:**
Stephen King, *Cujo*, 1981
Dean R. Koontz, *Watchers*, 1987
Michael Stewart, *Monkey Shines*, 1983
Laren Stover, *Pluto, Animal Lover*, 1994

## 2430

### STEPHEN GRESHAM

### *Blood Wings*

(New York: Zebra, 1990)

**Story type:** Horror (Ancient Evil Unleashed)
**Major character(s):** Anita Martin, Divorced Person; Wade Martin, Child
**Time period(s):** 1990s
**Locale(s):** Orchid Springs, Florida (A small town at the edge of the Everglades)

**Summary:** Fleeing a bad marriage, Anita Martin settles with her young sons, Wade and Timmy, in Orchard Springs. Wade has nightmares of a huge, winged, carniverous bat-like creature and people begin to die and disappear in the swamp. Finally accepting the idea that ''Blood Wings'' is a real creature, a small group ventures into the swamp to try to track and kill it.

**Other books you might like:**
Charles L. Grant, *The Nestling*, 1982
Peter Tremayne, *Swamp*, 1989

## 2431

### STEPHEN GRESHAM

### *The Living Dark*

(New York: Zebra, 1991)

**Story type:** Horror (Werewolf Story)
**Major character(s):** Mance Culley, Teenager; Jonella ''Johnnie'' Withers, Teenager; Kenton Austin, Businessman (furniture salesman)
**Time period(s):** 1990s
**Locale(s):** Soldier, Georgia

**Summary:** Shortly after Mance Culley's girlfriend Johnnie is raped, her two assailants are found mutilated, as though by a ravenous animal. As more of his enemies meet a similar fate, Mance begins to suspect he is being protected by a beneficent supernatural force conjured from the dark side of his soul.

**Other books you might like:**
Charles L. Grant, *The Pet*, 1986
K.W. Jeter, *The Night Man*, 1990

## 2432

### THOMAS S. GRESSMAN

### *Shadows of War*

(New York: Roc, 1998)

**Story type:** Science Fiction (Military)
**Series:** Battletech
**Major character(s):** Ariana Winston, Military Personnel (general); Paul Moon, Military Personnel (colonel)
**Time period(s):** Indeterminate Future
**Locale(s):** Huntress, Planet—Imaginary; Outer Space

**Summary:** In a bid to end an interstellar war, a massive army prepares to attack the enemy on its home world, Huntress. As the forces prepare to strike, they are undermined by enemies within their own forces who throw the entire operation into jeopardy.

**Other books you might like:**
William C. Dietz, *The Final Battle*, 1995
W. Michael Gear, *Starstrike*, 1990
Karl Hansen, *War Games*, 1981
Jack McKinney, *Before the Invid Storm*, 1996
Elizabeth Moon, *Once a Hero*, 1997

## 2433

### JOHN GRIBBIN
### MARCUS CHOWN, Co-Author

### *Double Planet*

(New York: Avon, 1991)

**Story type:** Science Fiction (Hard Science Fiction; Political)
**Major character(s):** Yevgeny Ustinov, Administrator (U.N.); David Kondratieff, Administrator (U.N.); Frances Reese, Spaceship Captain
**Time period(s):** 22nd century (2100s)
**Locale(s):** Outer Space (between Mars and Earth); Reykjavik, Iceland; Hipparchus, Montenegro

**Summary:** After David Kondratieff is informed that a comet occupies a near-Earth orbit, perhaps even a collision course, he sends out Earth's last working shuttle to divert it. The public mission is to mine the comet while the astronauts' true mission remains hidden. Originally published 1988.

**Other books you might like:**
William Barton, *Fellow Traveller*, 1991
   Michael Capobianco, co-author
Gregory Benford, *Heart of the Comet*, 1986
   David Brin, co-author
Arthur C. Clarke, *Rendezvous with Rama*, 1973
Gregory Feeley, *The Oxygen Barons*, 1990
Allen Steele, *Orbital Decay*, 1989

## 2434

### JOHN GRIBBIN

### *Father to the Man*

(New York: Tor, 1990)

**Story type:** Science Fiction (Hard Science Fiction)

**Major character(s):** Richard Lee, Scientist; Marjorie Cooper, Scientist
**Time period(s):** 21st century
**Locale(s):** England

**Summary:** In a near-future world burdened by plague, starvation, war, pollution, and the rise of anti-science fundamentalist religion, Richard Lee, a brilliant young scientist, is persecuted for stating in a television interview that humanity and chimpanzees may be much more closely related than has been previously believed. His career a shambles, his fiancee murdered by thugs out to get him, Lee goes into hiding. Over the next few years, as society continues its collapse, Lee devotes himself to raising a baby, the outcome of his research, who is not entirely human.

**Other books you might like:**
Roger MacBride Allen, *Orphan of Creation*, 1988
Michael Bishop, *Ancient of Days*, 1985
Michael Bishop, *No Enemy but Time*, 1982
David Brin, *Startide Rising*, 1983
David Brin, *The Uplift War*, 1987
Vercors, *You Shall Know Them*, 1953
    No 1st name, pseud; real name Jean Bruller

---

**2435**

**P.M. GRIFFIN**

## Call to Arms

(New York: Ace, 1991)

**Story type:** Science Fiction (Adventure; Military)
**Series:** Star Commandos
**Major character(s):** Islaen Connor, Leader, Telepath; Varn Tarl Sogan, Royalty (war prince), Military Personnel; Lloyd George Thatcher, Criminal
**Time period(s):** Indeterminate Future
**Locale(s):** Noreen, Planet—Imaginary

**Summary:** Islaen Connor, Varn Tarl Sogan and their comrades return to Noreen of Tara, Islaen's homeworld, hoping to foil Thatcher who is hiding there and preparing a strike that will allow him both revenge and riches enough to retire on Earth.

**Other books you might like:**
Lois McMaster Bujold, *Brothers in Arms*, 1988
C.J. Cherryh, *Rimrunners*, 1989
Gordon R. Dickson, *Dorsai!*, 1976
Melisa C. Michaels, *Last War*, 1986
Jerry Pournelle, *Falkenberg's Legion*, 1990
Joel Rosenberg, *Not for Glory*, 1988
Timothy Zahn, *Cobra*, 1985

---

**2436**

**P.M. GRIFFIN**

## Fire Planet

(New York: Ace, 1990)

**Story type:** Science Fiction (Space Opera)
**Series:** Star Commandos
**Major character(s):** Varn Tarl Sogan, Military Personnel (admiral); Islaen Connor, Military Personnel (colonel); Bandit, Alien, Telepath
**Time period(s):** Indeterminate Future
**Locale(s):** Tambora, Planet—Imaginary

**Summary:** Officially, Isalen, commander of the Space Commandos, and her husband Sogan are sent to the beautiful tropical world of Tambora for R and R. Unofficially, they are also to investigate the rumors of a radical sect called the Gray Ascetics that is secretly preparing for a coup. But the greatest danger to Tambora comes from the volcanic forces about to break out beneath her seas.

**Other books you might like:**
C.J. Cherryh, *Exile's Gate*, 1988
C.J. Cherryh, *The Fires of Azeroth*, 1979
Phyllis Eisenstein, *In the Hands of Glory*, 1981
Robert A. Heinlein, *Starship Troopers*, 1959
Anne McCaffrey, *Sassinak*, 1990
    Elizabeth Moon, co-author
Kevin D. Randle, *The Galactic Silver Star*, 1990
Helen S. Wright, *A Matter of Oaths*, 1990

---

**2437**

**P.M. GRIFFIN**

## Jungle Assault

(New York: Ace, 1991)

**Story type:** Science Fiction (Space Opera; Military)
**Series:** Star Commandos
**Major character(s):** Islaen Connor, Military Personnel; Varn Tarl Sogan, Royalty (War Prince), Telepath; Jake Karmikal, Military Personnel
**Time period(s):** Indeterminate Future
**Locale(s):** Amazoon, Planet—Imaginary

**Summary:** The four-person Commando Team must stop bandits from using scavenged military equipment against the colonists of Amazoon, a jungle planet habitable only at the poles. They crash into the jungle and must cross hundreds of miles to get at the bandits and their cache, battling harsh terrain and hungry predators.

**Other books you might like:**
Poul Anderson, *Earthman, Go Home!*, 1960
F.M. Busby, *The Alien Debt*, 1984
David Drake, *The Jungle*, 1991
Phyllis Eisenstein, *In the Hands of Glory*, 1981
Melisa C. Michaels, *First Battle*, 1985
Andre Norton, *Voorloper*, 1980

---

**2438**

**PENI R. GRIFFIN**

## Hobkin

(New York: Macmillan McElderry, 1992)

**Story type:** Fantasy (Young Adult)
**Major character(s):** Sara "Liza Franklin" Welch, Runaway; Melissa "Kay Franklin" Welch, Runaway; Hobkin, Mythical Creature (brownie)
**Time period(s):** 1990s
**Locale(s):** Britt, Texas (Stark Homestead)

**Summary:** Escaping abuse and unacceptable family life, Liza and Kay flee across West Texas until a chance bus stop and quick thinking allow the pair to take possession of an abandoned farmstead known as home to a haunt. While her sister works at Britt's only store, Liza benefits from a distant but growing friendship with the spirit, a brownie, as she begins to learn the skills necessary for rural life.

**Other books you might like:**
Sylvia Cassedy, *Behind the Attic Wall*, 1983
Helen Cresswell, *A Game of Catch*, 1977
Penelope Lively, *The Ghost of Thomas Kempe*, 1973

Arthur Mason, *The Wee Men of Ballywooden*, 1930
Diana Mulock, *The Adventures of a Brownie as Told to My Child*, 1952
Jody Lynn Nye, *Mythology 101*, 1990

---

**2439**

KATHRYN MEYER GRIFFITH

## The Calling

(New York: Zebra, 1994)

**Story type:** Horror (Ghost Story)
**Major character(s):** Faye Summers, Businesswoman (club owner); Nick Summers, Musician; Sharif al-Hakim, Guide
**Time period(s):** 1990s (1994)
**Locale(s):** Cairo, Egypt

**Summary:** Acting under the compulsion of an inner self she has acknowledged all her life, American Faye Summers travels to Egypt. There she discovers that she is haunted by the spirit of Ankhesenaton, the daughter of Akhenaton and Nefertiti, and is enjoined to discover the whereabouts of their remains and bury them properly, so that their spirits my be released from the earth. But just as Ankhesenaton has existed spiritually over the centuries, so have the spirit forms of the enemies of her family, and they block Faye at every possible step.

**Other books you might like:**
Charles L. Grant, *The Long Night of the Grave*, 1986
Michael Paine, *Cities of the Dead*, 1988
Anne Rice, *The Mummy, or Ramses the Damned*, 1989

---

**2440**

KATHRYN MEYER GRIFFITH

## The Last Vampire

(New York: Zebra, 1992)

**Story type:** Horror (Vampire Story)
**Major character(s):** Emma Bloodworth, Artist, Vampire; Matthew Whitefeather, Worker, Indian; Byron Shelly, Vampire
**Time period(s):** Indeterminate Future
**Locale(s):** St. Louis, Missouri

**Summary:** Saved from death by the bite of a sympathetic vampire, Emma Bloodworth stalks an Earth devastated by earthquakes and natural disasters, banding with fellow vampires in an effort to track down dwindling resources of fresh human blood.

**Other books you might like:**
Jack Butler, *Nightshade*, 1989
Richard Matheson, *I Am Legend*, 1954
Lois Tilton, *Vampire Winter*, 1990
F. Paul Wilson, *Midnight Mass*, 1990

---

**2441**

KATHRYN MEYER GRIFFITH

## Vampire Blood

(New York: Zebra, 1991)

**Story type:** Horror (Vampire Story)
**Major character(s):** Jenny Lacey, Writer; Joey Lacey, Restaurateur; Terry Michelson, Vampire
**Time period(s):** 1990s
**Locale(s):** Summer Haven, Florida

**Summary:** Horror writer Jenny Lacey returns home after her divorce to pick up the pieces of her life, and discovers that the family who have taken over Summer Haven's old abandoned movie theatre with intent to refurbish it are a brood of vampires whose indiscreet teenage children are about to decimate the town.

**Other books you might like:**
Tanya Huff, *Blood Price*, 1991
Stephen King, *Salem's Lot*, 1975
Richard Laymon, *The Stake*, 1990

---

**2442**

KATHRYN MEYER GRIFFITH

## Witches

(New York: Zebra, 1993)

**Story type:** Horror (Black Magic)
**Major character(s):** Amanda Givens, Witch; Rachel Coxe, Witch (dead for 300 years); Amadeus, Animal (cat; Amanda's familiar)
**Time period(s):** 1990s (1993)
**Locale(s):** Canaan, Connecticut

**Summary:** Rachel Coxe vowed revenge upon the small Connecticut town of Canaan when whe was murdered for being a witch at the end of the 18th century. Through the activity of contemporary black magic covens, she begins to exact her bloody retribution but is fought by Amanda Givens, a witch who practices white magic and refuses to become a part of Rachel's scheme, even though the townsfolk assume Amanda is responsible for the madness and mayhem that have overtaken them.

**Other books you might like:**
Marian O'Hearn, *Soldiers of the Black Goat*, 1940
Anne Rice, *The Witching Hour*, 1991
John Updike, *The Witches of Eastwick*, 1984

---

**2443**

NICOLA GRIFFITH

## Ammonite

(New York: Ballantine Del Rey, 1993)

**Story type:** Science Fiction (Genetic Manipulation; Lost Colony)
**Major character(s):** Marguerite ''Marghe'' Angelica Raishan, Anthropologist, Wanderer; Hannah Danner, Military Personnel; Thenike, Healer, Wanderer
**Time period(s):** Indeterminate Future
**Locale(s):** Estrade, Space Station; Grenchstom's Planet ''Jeep'', Planet—Imaginary

**Summary:** Marghe arrives at Jeep disillusioned with the Company and informed that all residents must remain since the planet hosts a virus which kills all men and 20 percent of the women. An experimental drug prevents Marghe from acquiring the virus, but leaves her weakened. Upon learning that her assistant disappeared 18 months before, Marghe begins an adventure which takes her far to the north where she learns about herself and the women who have already survived hundreds of years without men, information necessary to the women at the Company base. First novel.

**Other books you might like:**
Greg Bear, *Blood Music*, 1985
Mary Gentle, *Golden Witchbreed*, 1984
Rosemary Kirstein, *The Outskirter's Secret*, 1992
Rosemary Kirstein, *The Steerswoman*, 1989
Ursula K. Le Guin, *The Left Hand of Darkness*, 1969
Jody Lynn Nye, *Taylor's Ark*, 1993

Bill Ransom, *ViraVax*, 1993
Joan Slonczewski, *A Door into Ocean*, 1986
Eric Vinicoff, *The Weigher*, 1992
  Marcia Martin, co-author

---

**2444**

NICOLA GRIFFITH, Editor
STEPHEN PAGEL, Co-Editor

## Bending the Landscape: Fantasy

(Clarkston, Georgia: White Wolf, 1997)

**Story type:** Fantasy (Anthology; Literary)

**Summary:** Contains a three-page introduction by Griffith and Pagel, 13 pages of editors' and contributors' biographies plus brief individual introductions to 22 original stories utilizing settings ranging from an 11th-century Japanese garden to a modern, split-level suburban home to explore various physical, emotional and moral views of homosexuality. The authors include Kim Antieu, Robin Wayne Bailey, Carolyn Ives Gilman, Tanya Huff, M.W. Keiper, Ellen Kushner, James A. Moore, Simon Sheppard, B.J. Thrower, Jeff Verona and Leslie What.

**Other books you might like:**
Camilla Decarnin, *Worlds Apart*, 1986
  Eric Garber, Lynn Paleo, co-editors
Jeffrey M. Elliot, *Kindred Spirits*, 1984
  editor
Eric Garber, *Swords of the Rainbow*, 1996
  Jewelle Gomez, co-editor
Pam Keesey, *Darker Angels: Lesbian Vampire Stories*, 1995
  editor
Pam Keesey, *Daughters of Darkness: Lesbian Vampire Stories*, 1993
  editor
Caro Soles, *Meltdown!*, 1994
  editor

---

**2445**

NICOLA GRIFFITH

## Slow River

(New York: Ballantine Del Rey, 1995)

**Story type:** Science Fiction (Hard Science Fiction; Gay/Lesbian Fiction)
**Major character(s):** Frances Lorien "Lore" van de Oest, Artist (video), Heiress; Spanner, Lesbian, Criminal; Cherry Magyar, Engineer (water purification)
**Time period(s):** 21st century
**Locale(s):** Ratnapida, Tropical Island (estate); England

**Summary:** Left on the street to die, Lore accepts help from Spanner who recognizes her as the heir of the water purification van de Oests whose ransom requests aired on the media. Lore realizes she cannot contact her family as they had abandoned her to the kidnappers, and becomes Spanner's partner until she gains enough strength to get a job as a menial laborer at a water treatment plant which she could as easily run.

**Other books you might like:**
Lois McMaster Bujold, *Shards of Honor*, 1986
F.M. Busby, *Rissa Kerguelen*, 1977
Suzette Haden Elgin, *Native Tongue*, 1984
Susan Palwick, *Flying in Place*, 1992
Melissa Scott, *Trouble and Her Friends*, 1994
Amy Thomson, *Virtual Girl*, 1993

---

**2446**

LEE GRIMES

## Retro Lives

(New York: AvoNova, 1993)

**Story type:** Science Fiction (Family Saga; Immortality)
**Major character(s):** Robert Widdick, Businessman, Parent (progenitor); Milton Kleiffer, Doctor (psychiatrist); Harry Widdick, Heir
**Time period(s):** 1980s (1985)
**Locale(s):** United States

**Summary:** Milton Kleiffer diagnoses his first patient at the mental institution, Robert Widdick, as suffering some form of Korsakov's Syndrome which affects transfer of information to long term memory. Milton then discovers that Robert, now appearing about 25 years old, had entered the hospital at the age of 60. The diagnosis becomes extremely complicated when, one day, Robert begins remembering recent events and begins to grow older again. Genetic analysis points to an extension on Robert's Y chromosome, indicating that the mutation will show up in his sons.

**Other books you might like:**
Martin Amis, *Time's Arrow*, 1991
Ken Grimwood, *Replay*, 1986
Robert A. Heinlein, *Time Enough for Love*, 1973
Nancy Kress, *Brain Rose*, 1990
Michael D. Weaver, *My Father Immortal*, 1989

---

**2447**

JACOB LUDWIG GRIMM
WILHELM CARL GRIMM, Co-Author

## The Complete Fairy Tales of the Brothers Grimm

(New York: Bantam, 1992)

**Story type:** Fantasy (Anthology; Legend)

**Summary:** Enlarged edition of the 1987 release and most comprehensive collection of the *Grimms' Tales* to date with eight new tales among the 40 tales first translated into English by Zipes and slightly corrected herein. Throughout the book, entirely retranslated by the editor, Zipes retains the historical character and idioms and the 19th century flavor while incorporating contemporary vocabulary and terms when not intrusive. Includes a 15-page biography of the Grimms by Zipes titled, "Once There Were Two Brothers Named Grimm," two pages of notes on translation (1986), one page of notes on the expanded edition and 250 tales followed by 16 pages of notes on the text and a four-page index.

**Other books you might like:**
Hans Christian Andersen, *The Complete Fairy Tales and Stories*, 1974
Clemens Maria Brentano, *Fairy Tales From Brentano*, 1886
Wilhelm Hauff, *The Fairy Tales of Wilhelm Hauff*, 1895
Michael Patrick Hearn, *The Victorian Fairy Tale Book*, 1988
  editor
Andrew Lang, *The Blue Fairy Book*, 1889
  editor
Andrew Lang, *The Green Fairy Book*, 1892
  editor
Andrew Lang, *The Red Fairy Book*, 1890
  editor
George MacDonald, *The Complete Fairy Tales of George MacDonald*, 1979

Aesop, *Aesop's Fables*, 1992
Jack Zipes, editor

## 2448

### TODD GRIMSON

### *Brand New Cherry Flavor*

(New York: HarperPrism, 1996)

**Story type:** Horror (Occult)
**Major character(s):** Lisa Nova, Director (film); Selwyn Popcorn, Director (film); Boro, Religious (voodoo priest)
**Time period(s):** 1990s (1996)
**Locale(s):** Hollywood, California

**Summary:** When Lisa Nova is denied a film job she slept with people to get, she contacts Boro, a voodoo hit-man, who takes a liking to her and helps her get her revenge. Too late, Lisa discovers that she has been pulled into the horrifying world of Boro and his black magic.

**Other books you might like:**
William Peter Blatty, *Demons Five, Exorcists Nothing*, 1996
Ramsey Campbell, *Ancient Images*, 1989
Dennis Cooper, *Frisk*, 1991
Dennis Etchison, *Shadow Man*, 1994
Greg Kihn, *Horror Show*, 1996
Theodore Roszak, *Flicker*, 1991
Paul Russell, *Boys of Life*, 1991

## 2449

### TODD GRIMSON

### *Stainless*

(New York: HarperPrism, 1996)

**Story type:** Horror (Vampire Story)
**Major character(s):** Justine, Vampire; Keith, Musician (guitarist); David Henry Reid, Actor
**Time period(s):** 1990s (1996)
**Locale(s):** Los Angeles, California

**Summary:** Enamored of young vampire femme fatal Justine, Keith becomes her chauffeur, driving her around Los Angeles in the evening to find her nightly meals. In due time, he becomes her protector as well, helping her elude a vengeful silent movie actor whom Justine vampirized decades before.

**Other books you might like:**
Poppy Z. Brite, *Lost Souls*, 1992
Nancy A. Collins, *Sunglasses After Dark*, 1989
Christopher Moore, *Bloodsucking Fiends: A Love Story*, 1995
Jonathan Nasaw, *The World on Blood*, 1996
Gail Petersen, *The Making of a Monster*, 1993

## 2450

### KEN GRIMWOOD

### *Into the Deep*

(New York: Morrow, 1995)

**Story type:** Science Fiction (First Contact; Psychic Powers)
**Major character(s):** Sheila Roberts, Student—College (graduate school); Daniel Colter, Journalist (freelance reporter), Stowaway; Ch*Tril, Animal (dolphin)
**Time period(s):** 21st century
**Locale(s):** North America; At Sea

**Summary:** Millennia ago, dolphins maintained telepathic contact with humans. Now fearful over carnage in the ocean, dolphins choose a few people with whom to reestablish contact, initiating communication with Sheila Roberts through dream imagery. To learn of cetacean atrocities, Daniel Colter investigates harvesting practices aboard a tuna trawler whose captain does not recall prior dolphin contact.

**Other books you might like:**
Jim Aikin, *Walk the Moon's Road*, 1985
Piers Anthony, *Mercycle*, 1991
David Brin, *Startide Rising*, 1983
Gordon R. Dickson, *The Space Swimmers; Science Fiction by Gordon Dickson*, 1967
Alan Dean Foster, *Cachalot*, 1980
Anne McCaffrey, *The Dolphins of Pern*, 1994
Margaret St. Clair, *The Dolphins of Altair*, 1967
L. Neil Smith, *The Venus Belt*, 1981
Sydney J. Van Scyoc, *Deepwater Dreams*, 1991

## 2451

### ANNE LESLEY GROELL

### *Anvil of the Sun*

(New York: Roc, 1996)

**Story type:** Fantasy (Quest; Adventure)
**Series:** Cloak and Dagger
**Major character(s):** Jenifleur Radineaux, Student, Martial Arts Expert (assassin); Thibault Lescevre, Apprentice (carpenter), Martial Arts Expert (assassin); Viera Radineaux, Martial Arts Expert (assassin), Debutante
**Time period(s):** Indeterminate
**Locale(s):** Ashkharon, Fictional Country

**Summary:** The best assassin in the world takes a commission to assassinate a government minister in Ashkharon. When she does not come home in time to welcome her niece, the niece sets off into certain danger, a fate preferable to the Debutante's Ball. First novel.

**Other books you might like:**
Steven Brust, *Jhereg*, 1983
Eve Forward, *Villains by Necessity*, 1995
Robin Hobb, *Assassin's Apprentice*, 1995
Fritz Leiber, *Ill Met in Lankhmar*, 1995
Michael Shea, *Nifft the Lean*, 1982

## 2452

### ANNE LESLEY GROELL

### *Bridge of Valor*

(New York: Roc, 1997)

**Story type:** Fantasy (Adventure)
**Series:** Cloak and Dagger
**Major character(s):** Jenifleur Radineaux, Debutante, Martial Arts Expert (assassin); Thibault Lescevre, Student, Martial Arts Expert (assassin); Ruairi NaBlaine, Nobleman
**Time period(s):** Indeterminate Past
**Locale(s):** Arrhyndon, Fictional Country

**Summary:** Eager for their first true assignment, Jenifleur and Thibault accept a mission to a remote estate where bizarre occurrences, ghosts, disappearing rooms and a rain of goldfish torment the lord of the estate. The mission proves more difficult than expected when the two assassins quickly become immersed in a lethal maze of plots. Second in series.

**Other books you might like:**
Steven Brust, *Jhereg*, 1983
Lynn Flewelling, *Luck in the Shadows*, 1996
Robin Hobb, *Assassin's Apprentice*, 1995
J.V. Jones, *The Baker's Boy*, 1995
Fritz Leiber, *Ill Met in Lankhmar*, 1995
Anne Logston, *Shadow*, 1996

---

**2453**

**STEPHAN GRUNDY**

## Attila's Treasure

(New York: Bantam Spectra, 1996)

**Story type:** Fantasy (Adventure; Legend)
**Major character(s):** Hagan, Warrior, Homosexual; Attila the Hun, Historical Figure, Foster Parent; Hildegund, Teenager
**Time period(s):** 5th century
**Locale(s):** Europe

**Summary:** Fostered to Attila the Hun along with a potential bride of Attila's, Hagan develops into a fierce fighter. However, during Hagan's first battle, he discovers a pathway to the otherworld, knowledge which could allow Attila to see him as an adversary.

**Other books you might like:**
Frans G. Bengtsson, *The Long Ships*, 1954
Donna Gillespie, *The Light Bearer*, 1994
Parke Godwin, *The Tower of Beowulf*, 1995
Harry Harrison, *The Hammer and the Cross*, 1993
    John Holm, co-author
Diana L. Paxson, *The Wolf and the Raven*, 1993

---

**2454**

**STEPHAN GRUNDY**

## Rhinegold

(New York: Bantam, 1994)

**Story type:** Fantasy (Legend; Adventure)
**Major character(s):** Sigfrith, Mythical Creature (demigod shapechanger), Warrior; Brunichild, Royalty, Warrior
**Time period(s):** 5th century
**Locale(s):** Europe

**Summary:** Working as a smith, Sigfrith accepts a magical draught which brings mythic figures to life and empowers him with supernatural abilities. He grows to heroic stature as he slays the dragon, Fadhmir, and wins a hoard of gold. Fated to love one another but marry others, Sigfrith and Brunichild's love turns tragic for both. First novel.

**Other books you might like:**
Frans G. Bengtsson, *The Long Ships*, 1954
Donna Gillespie, *The Light Bearer*, 1994
Harry Harrison, *The Hammer and the Cross*, 1993
    John Holm, co-author
Morgan Llywelyn, *Druids*, 1991
Diana L. Paxson, *The Wolf and the Raven*, 1993

---

**2455**

**DIANE GUEST**

## Lullaby

(New York: Putnam's 1990)

**Story type:** Horror (Possession)
**Major character(s):** Rachel Daimler, Housewife; Judd Pauling, Artist, Spouse; Addy Pauling, Child (Rachel's daughter)
**Time period(s):** 1990s (1990)
**Locale(s):** Land's End, Maine

**Summary:** Overcoming her longstanding aversion to her childhood home, Rachel Daimler returns with her family to visit her dying mother. Soon thereafter her youngest daughter, Addy, becomes a pawn in the family's struggle to escape the evil influence of the household.

**Other books you might like:**
Ramsey Campbell, *The Influence*, 1988
Robert Marasco, *Burnt Offerings*, 1973

---

**2456**

**JEFF GUINN**

## The Autobiography of Santa Claus: It's Better to Give

(Fort Worth, Texas: The Summit Group, 1994)

**Story type:** Fantasy (Legend)
**Major character(s):** Nicholas "Santa Claus", Hero; Arthur, Royalty, Ruler; Attila the Hun, Warrior
**Time period(s):** 3rd century; 20th century
**Locale(s):** Middle East; Europe; United States

**Summary:** Nurtured and taught the lessons of goodness and generosity, Nicholas begins sharing his wealth with the needy as a child. When Nicholas discovers that he no longer ages and can travel rapidly, he begins distributing his gifts to the children of the world as he recruits helpers through the ages.

**Other books you might like:**
L. Frank Baum, *The Life and Adventures of Santa Claus*, 1902
Martin H. Greenberg, *Christmas on Ganymede and Other Stories*, 1990
    editor
David G. Hartwell, *Christmas Forever*, 1993
    editor
Kristine Kathryn Rusch, *Pulphouse, Issue 10: Special Issue*, 1991
    editor
J.R.R. Tolkien, *The Father Christmas Letters*, 1976

---

**2457**

**GUNELI GUN**

## The Adventures of Huru on the Road to Baghdad

(Claremont, CA: Hunter House, 1988)

**Story type:** Fantasy (Adventure)
**Major character(s):** Huru, Young Woman (Turkish)
**Time period(s):** Indeterminate Past
**Locale(s):** Middle East

**Summary:** When her parents make a pilgrimage to Mecca, Huru is falsely accused of wantonness. She decides to leave, and try to find her parents in Baghdad. Along the way, she has a number of adventures, magic and otherwise.

**Other books you might like:**
Samuel R. Delany, *Neveryona*, 1983
Elizabeth Moon, *Sheepfarmer's Daughter*, 1988
Judith Tarr, *A Wind in Cairo*, 1989

**2458**
### JAMES GUNN
### THEODORE STURGEON, Co-Author

## The Joy Machine
(New York: Pocket, 1996)

**Story type:** Science Fiction (Political; Space Opera)
**Series:** Star Trek
**Major character(s):** James T. Kirk, Spaceship Captain; Spock, Scientist, Alien (Vulcan); Kemal Marouk, Scientist, Government Official (paymaster)
**Time period(s):** 23rd century
**Locale(s):** *U.S.S. Enterprise*, Spaceship; Timshel, Planet—Imaginary; United Federation of Planets, Interstellar Empire/Federation

**Summary:** Returning to Timshel where he previously enjoyed several months of vacation and recovery, Jim finds an old friend, Marouk, is now the most powerful man on the planet. Unfortunately the Joy Machine, which also rewards the citizens it monitors, no longer permits anyone to leave Timshel, or to remain free of its control. Worse, it plans to extend its influence to the rest of the Federation. Based on a Theodore Sturgeon short story.

**Other books you might like:**
Theodore Sturgeon, *The Dreaming Jewels*, 1950
Theodore Sturgeon, *Microcosmic God*, 1995
Theodore Sturgeon, *The Ultimate Egoist*, 1994
John Varley, *Steel Beach*, 1992
Jack Williamson, *The Humanoids*, 1949
Jack Williamson, *Star Bridge*, 1955
    James Gunn, co-author

**2459**
### JAMES GUNN
### JACK WILLIAMSON, Co-Author

## Star Bridge
(New York: Macmillan Collier Nucleus, 1989)

**Story type:** Science Fiction (Space Opera)
**Major character(s):** Alan Horn, Mercenary; Oliver Wu, Immortal, Wanderer
**Time period(s):** 35th century
**Locale(s):** Earth; Eron, Planet—Imaginary

**Summary:** The Eron Empire dominates the galaxy due to its control of the star bridges which make interstellar travel possible, and the Empire rules with a heavy hand. A human mercenary and an immortal Chinese each fight the Eronian tyranny in his own way. Originally published in 1955.

**Other books you might like:**
Poul Anderson, *The Boat of a Million Years*, 1989
Poul Anderson, *The Game of Empire*, 1985
Poul Anderson, *Mirkheim*, 1977
F.M. Busby, *Rebel's Quest*, 1985
F.M. Busby, *Rissa Kerguelen*, 1977
Robert A. Heinlein, *Double Star*, 1956

Robert A. Heinlein, *The Moon Is a Harsh Mistress*, 1966
Frank Herbert, *Dune*, 1965

**2460**
### THORARINN GUNNARSSON

## Battle of the Ring
(New York: Popular Library/Questar, 1989)

**Story type:** Science Fiction (Space Opera)
**Series:** Starwolves
**Major character(s):** Commander Velmeran, Spaceship Captain; Valthyrra, Artificial Intelligence (Sentient spaceship)
**Time period(s):** Indeterminate Future
**Locale(s):** *Valthyrra Methryn*, Spaceship

**Summary:** A warrior race, the Starwolves, live their entire lives on gigantic sentient spaceships. One such ship, the Valthyrra, must defeat the gigantic fortress ship of an evil race of alien saurians if the Starwolves are to survive.

**Other books you might like:**
Gregory Benford, *Tides of Light*, 1989
W. Michael Gear, *The Artifact*, 1989
W. Michael Gear, *The Warriors of Spider*, 1988
W. Michael Gear, *The Way of Spider*, 1988
W. Michael Gear, *The Web of Spider*, 1989
Fred Saberhagen, *Berserker's Planet*, 1975

**2461**
### THORARINN GUNNARSSON

## Dragon's Domain
(New York: Ace, 1993)

**Story type:** Fantasy (Quest; Adventure)
**Series:** Make Way for Dragons
**Major character(s):** Kalavek, Mythical Creature (dragon), Adventurer; Einar Myklathun, Government Official (forester), Adventurer; Ayesha, Mythical Creature (dragon)
**Time period(s):** 1860s; 1880s
**Locale(s):** Norway

**Summary:** After magic fades from the world, Kalavek's birth provides his tribe with hope for reversing centuries of dragonkind's decline. When the dragons' mortal enemies, the Shadows, catch wind of young Kalavek and Ayesha while out exploring, Einar steps in to save the pair. Later, when Kalavek and Ayesha cannot direct the magic necessary to successfully procreate, Kalavek enlists Einar's help in retrieving a Core of Magic from the Fountain of the World's Heart, the channel for the vanished ancient magic.

**Other books you might like:**
Ursula K. Le Guin, *The Farthest Shore*, 1972
Ursula K. Le Guin, *The Tombs of Atuan*, 1971
Ursula K. Le Guin, *A Wizard of Earthsea*, 1968
Larry Niven, *The Magic Goes Away*, 1979
Lawrence Watt-Evans, *The Blood of a Dragon*, 1991
Terri Windling, *Life on the Border*, 1991
    editor
Patricia C. Wrede, *Searching for Dragons*, 1991
Laurence Yep, *Dragon of the Lost Sea*, 1982

## 2462

### THORARINN GUNNARSSON

## *Dragonmage of Mystara*

(Lake Geneva, Wisconsin: TSR, 1996)

**Story type:** Fantasy (Magic Conflict; Political)
**Series:** Mystara: The Dragonlord Chronicles
**Major character(s):** Thelvyn Fox-Eyes, Royalty (Dragonking); Alessa Vyledaar, Wizard; Kharendaen, Mythical Creature (dragon)
**Time period(s):** Indeterminate
**Locale(s):** Mystara, Planet—Imaginary

**Summary:** Unable to resist the enchanted red jewel's call, Alessa risks the Collar of the Dragons and destruction of both the dragons and her people in another war. To save Mystara, Thelvyn must somehow convince his dragons to join the humans against the force behind the gem. Third in the series.

**Other books you might like:**
Gael Baudino, *Duel of Dragons*, 1991
Mary Brown, *Master of Many Treasures*, 1995
Don Callander, *Dragon Companion*, 1994
Margaret Weis, *Dragons of Summer Flame*, 1995
  Tracy Hickman, co-author
Angus Wells, *Lords of the Sky*, 1994

## 2463

### THORARINN GUNNARSSON

## *Dragons on the Town*

(New York: Ace, 1992)

**Story type:** Fantasy (Magic Conflict; Quest)
**Series:** Faerie Dragon
**Major character(s):** Jenny Barker, Disembodied Personality; Dalvenjah Foxfire, Mythical Creature (dragon); Mira, Sorceress
**Time period(s):** 1990s
**Locale(s):** New York, New York

**Summary:** Sharing a body with a dragon, Jenny Barker learns that her father, a faerie dragon, planned her birth to satisfy the Prophecy of the Faerie Dragons. Mira discovers the sorceress Darja actually needs her body and the continuing error could threaten the Emperor and his minions. Meanwhile Jenny, awaiting a corporeal form to inhabit, transfers into a Dragon Mirror.

**Other books you might like:**
Steven Brust, *Jhereg*, 1983
Michael Cassutt, *Dragon Season*, 1991
Robert N. Charrette, *Never Deal with a Dragon*, 1990
L. Sprague de Camp, *The Honorable Barbarian*, 1989
William R. Forstchen, *The Crystal Warriors*, 1988
  Greg Morrison, co-author
Geary Gravel, *A Key for the Nonesuch*, 1990
Patricia C. Wrede, *Searching for Dragons*, 1991
Laurence Yep, *Dragon Cauldron*, 1991

## 2464

### THORARINN GUNNARSSON

## *Dreadnought*

(New York: Warner Questar, 1993)

**Story type:** Science Fiction (Military)
**Series:** Starwolves

**Major character(s):** Janus Tarrel, Spaceship Captain; Valthyrra Methryn, Artificial Intelligence (sentient spaceship); Walter Pesca, Linguist, Military Personnel
**Time period(s):** Indeterminate Future
**Locale(s):** *Methryn*, Spaceship; Outer Space

**Summary:** The Union Fleet and the Starwolves, millennia-old enemies, must unite their forces to face a new threat to their combined space, an automated war machine they call the Dreadnought. Captain Janus Tarrel of the Union Fleet negotiates a truce which may very well disintegrate if they can conquer the Dreadnought.

**Other books you might like:**
C.J. Cherryh, *Downbelow Station*, 1981
Glen Cook, *The Dragon Never Sleeps*, 1988
Joe Haldeman, *The Forever War*, 1975
Robert A. Heinlein, *Starship Troopers*, 1959
Frank Herbert, *Heretics of Dune*, 1984
Keith Laumer, *Bolo: The Annals of the Dinochrome Brigade*, 1976

## 2465

### THORARINN GUNNARSSON

## *Make Way for Dragons!*

(New York: Ace, 1990)

**Story type:** Fantasy (Light Fantasy)
**Series:** Faerie Dragon
**Major character(s):** Dalvenjah Foxfire, Mythical Creature (Dragon); Allan Breivik, Musician (Cellist), Magician
**Time period(s):** 1990s
**Locale(s):** California

**Summary:** A huge dragon followed by two smaller dragons appears in California. The smaller golden dragon, Dalvenjah, and her young child try to kill the large steel dragon, but are unsuccessful and Dalvenjah is wounded. She looks up the local wizard who has no idea that he has any magical powers. The two dragons move in with him and Dalvenjah begins to teach him how to use his talents.

**Other books you might like:**
Gael Baudino, *Duel of Dragons*, 1990
Emma Bull, *War for the Oaks*, 1987
L. Sprague de Camp, *The Honorable Barbarian*, 1989
Megan Lindholm, *Luck of the Wheels*, 1989
Matt Ruff, *Fool on the Hill*, 1989

## 2466

### THORARINN GUNNARSSON

## *Tactical Error*

(New York: Warner Questar, 1991)

**Story type:** Science Fiction (Space Opera)
**Series:** Starwolves
**Major character(s):** Commander Velmeran, Spaceship Captain; Valthyrra Methryn, Artificial Intelligence (sentient spaceship); Donalt Trace, Military Personnel
**Time period(s):** Indeterminate Future
**Locale(s):** *Methryn*, Spaceship; *Vulcyr*, Spaceship; Earth

**Summary:** The Starwolves discover Donalt Trace has assembled for the Union a large mock Starwolf fleet which he is manning with 10,000 clones of Commander Velmeran. To save their base and even long-lost Earth, the Starwolves must defeat Donalt Trace's mock Starwolf fleet and its complement of Union Fortresses.

**Other books you might like:**
C.J. Cherryh, *Cyteen*, 1988

C.J. Cherryh, *Downbelow Station*, 1981
Glen Cook, *The Dragon Never Sleeps*, 1988
Dave Duncan, *Hero*, 1991
Melisa C. Michaels, *Skirmish*, 1985
Alis A. Rasmussen, *Revolution's Shore*, 1990

## 2467

### ELLEN GUON

## *Bedlam Boyz*

(New York: Baen, 1993)

**Story type:** Fantasy (Magic Conflict; Urban)
**Major character(s):** Kayla Smith, Magician, Runaway; Elizabet Winters, Magician, Psychologist
**Time period(s):** 1990s; Indeterminate
**Locale(s):** Los Angeles, California; Unseelie lands, Mythical Place (elven realm)

**Summary:** Elizabet hopes to develop Kayla's recently discovered talent for healing. However, a *barrio* gang sees Kayla as the *bruja* who will solve their problems while powerful and deadly Faery agents search out the powerful new mage. Prequel to *Knight of Ghosts and Shadows* and *Summoned to Tourney*.

**Other books you might like:**
Mercedes Lackey, *Born to Run*, 1992
  Larry Dixon, co-author
Mercedes Lackey, *Knight of Ghosts and Shadows*, 1990
  Ellen Guon, co-author
Mercedes Lackey, *Summoned to Tourney*, 1992
  Ellen Guon, co-author
Mercedes Lackey, *Wheels of Fire*, 1992
  Mark Shepherd, co-author
Will Shetterly, *Elsewhere*, 1991
Terri Windling, *Borderland*, 1986
  Mark Alan Arnold, co-editor
Terri Windling, *Bordertown*, 1986
  Mark Alan Arnold, co-editor
Terri Windling, *Life on the Border*, 1991
  editor

## 2468

### JAMES GURNEY

## *Dinotopia*

(Atlanta, Georgia: Turner Publishing, Inc., 1992)

**Story type:** Fantasy (Historical; Quest)
**Series:** Dinotopia
**Major character(s):** Arthur Denison, Scientist (biologist), Explorer; Will Denison, Adventurer, Teenager; Bix, Animal (dinosaur), Guide
**Time period(s):** 1860s
**Locale(s):** Dinotopia, Fictional Country

**Summary:** Shipwrecked on a voyage of discovery, Arthur Denison and his son find themselves marooned on an island whose inhabitants include humans and dinosaurs living together peacefully in a technologically sophisticated society. Arthur explores Dinotopia, meeting residents and expanding his lavishly illustrated journal.

**Other books you might like:**
Jack Dann, *Dinosaurs!*, 1990
  Gardner Dozois, co-editor
Sir Arthur Conan Doyle, *The Lost World*, 1912

Evelyn Sibley Lampman, *The Shy Stegosaurus of Cricket Creek*, 1955
Evelyn Sibley Lampman, *The Shy Stegosaurus of Indian Springs*, 1962
Stephen Leigh, *Ray Bradbury Presents: Dinosaur World*, 1992
J.F. Rivkin, *Tyrannosaurus Rex*, 1992
Robert J. Sawyer, *Far-Seer*, 1992
Jules Verne, *Journey to the Center of the Earth*, 1874
Roger Zelazny, *Way Up High*, 1992

## 2469

### JAMES GURNEY

## *The World Beneath*

(Atlanta, Georgia: Turner Publishing, Inc., 1995)

**Story type:** Fantasy (Historical; Adventure)
**Series:** Dinotopia
**Major character(s):** Arthur Denison, Scientist (biologist), Explorer; Will Denison, Adventurer
**Time period(s):** 1860s
**Locale(s):** Dinotopia, Fictional Country

**Summary:** After an accident in Professor Denison's newly invented flying machine nearly kills Will, Denison investigates ancient caverns beneath Dinotopia, hoping to discover the lost civilization that produced tantalizing artifacts found in the caves. Presented as a lavishly illustrated journal.

**Other books you might like:**
Betty Ballantine, *The Secret Oceans*, 1994
Scott Ciencin, *Windchaser*, 1995
Rudy Rucker, *The Hollow Earth: The Narrative of Mason Algiers Reynolds of Virginia*, 1990
Midori Snyder, *Hatchling*, 1995
Jules Verne, *Journey to the Center of the Earth*, 1874
John Vornholt, *River Quest*, 1995

## 2470

### DAN GUTMAN

## *Virtually Perfect*

(New York: Hyperion, 1998)

**Story type:** Science Fiction (Young Adult)
**Major character(s):** Victor, Artificial Intelligence; Lucas "Yip" Turner, Teenager
**Time period(s):** 1990s (1999)
**Locale(s):** Cyberspace; Sunnyvale, California

**Summary:** Yip discovers that his father's company is developing new artificial intelligence techniques that will create virtual actors. He experiments on his own and creates a character that is not only intelligent but displays evidence of a strong individual personality. When his creation tries to break out of virtual reality and into the real world, Yip realizes that he is in big trouble.

**Other books you might like:**
Stephen Billias, *The Holo Men*, 1996
Jack L. Chalker, *The Cybernetic Walrus*, 1995
Esther Friesner, *The Sherwood Game*, 1995
Diana G. Gallagher, *Arcade*, 1995
Kim Newman, *The Night Mayor*, 1989

## 2471

### ELISE GUTTENBERG

## Sunder, Eclipse and Seed

(New York: Roc, 1990)

**Story type:** Fantasy (Magic Conflict)
**Series:** Sunder, Eclipse and Seed
**Major character(s):** Calyx, Religious (dreamer); Dev, Religious (Sumedaro priest)
**Time period(s):** Indeterminate Past
**Locale(s):** Briana, Fictional City; Aster, Fictional City

**Summary:** When Calyx is sent to the temple at Aster, she finds ways, with Dev's help, to train her true dreams even though she's denied the priesthood. In the process she discovers that Edishu, the god Jokjoa's nightmare, is reaching for power in the world again and only she seems to be able to resist him.

**Other books you might like:**
Catherine Cooke, *Mask of the Wizard*, 1985
Ru Emerson, *To the Haunted Mountains*, 1987
Guy Gavriel Kay, *The Summer Tree*, 1985
Patricia A. McKillip, *The Riddle-Master of Hed*, 1978
Jane Yolen, *Sister Light, Sister Dark*, 1988

## 2472

### GARY GYGAX

## The Anubis Murders

(New York: Roc, 1992)

**Story type:** Fantasy (Mystery; Magic Conflict)
**Series:** Dangerous Journeys
**Major character(s):** Setne Inhetep, Wizard, Religious; Rachelle, Martial Arts Expert, Bodyguard
**Time period(s):** Indeterminate Past
**Locale(s):** Egypt

**Summary:** Setne Inhetep and Rachelle must find the individual wielding potent magic and committing murders in the name of the god Anubis in order to clear the name of their god. As he investigates, Setne discovers himself tangled in a web of intrigue propelled by a powerful black magic.

**Other books you might like:**
Greg Farshtey, *Strange Tales From the Nile Empire*, 1992
  Greg Gorden and Ed Stark, co-editors
Randall Garrett, *Lord Darcy Investigates*, 1981
Simon R. Green, *The God Killer*, 1991
Ed Stark, *Mysterious Cairo*, 1992
  editor

## 2473

### GARY GYGAX

## Death in Delhi

(New York: Roc, 1993)

**Story type:** Fantasy (Mystery; Magic Conflict)
**Series:** Dangerous Journeys
**Major character(s):** Setne Inhetep, Wizard, Religious; Rachelle, Bodyguard, Martial Arts Expert
**Time period(s):** Indeterminate Past
**Locale(s):** Middle East; Delhi, India

**Summary:** When Setne Inhetep and Rachelle answer the call of the Maharajah of Delhi to help recover the crown jewels, the pair find themselves caught between the scheming of an evil ruler, the spells of a powerful witch and rebels with murderous intent for anyone helping the Maharajah. Based on a fantasy role-playing game.

**Other books you might like:**
M.A.R. Barker, *Man of Gold*, 1984
Randall Garrett, *Too Many Magicians*, 1967
Simon R. Green, *Hawk & Fisher*, 1990
Anne Logston, *Shadow*, 1991
Anne Logston, *Shadow Hunt*, 1992
Ed Stark, *Mysterious Cairo*, 1992
  editor

## 2474

### KAREN HABER

## Mutant Legacy

(New York: Bantam Spectra, 1993)

**Story type:** Science Fiction (Psychic Powers; Theological)
**Series:** Mutant Season
**Major character(s):** Joachim Metzgar, Leader, Psychic; Julian Akimura, Psychologist, Psychic; Rick Akimura, Psychic, Mutant
**Time period(s):** 2020s
**Locale(s):** California

**Summary:** Having been accepted and integrated into normal human society at last, the long awaited super-mutant, Rick Akimura, attracts followers who revere him as a messiah. His brother, Julian, afraid of Rick's power, opposes him and the future of both the mutants and humans. Concludes series.

**Other books you might like:**
Alfred Bester, *The Demolished Man*, 1953
John Brunner, *Children of the Thunder*, 1989
Steven Gould, *Jumper*, 1992
Henry Kuttner, *Mutant*, 1953
Anne McCaffrey, *Pegasus in Flight*, 1990
Anne McCaffrey, *The Rowan*, 1990
Robert Silverberg, *The Mutant Season*, 1990
  Karen Haber, co-author
Joan D. Vinge, *Psion*, 1982

## 2475

### KAREN HABER

## Mutant Star

(New York: Bantam Spectra, 1992)

**Story type:** Science Fiction (Political; Psychic Powers)
**Series:** Mutant Season
**Major character(s):** Ethan Hawkins, Military Personnel (Colonel), Spaceman; Eva Seguy, Doctor, Professor; Julian Akimura, Twin, Psychic
**Time period(s):** 2020s
**Locale(s):** Montenegro; California

**Summary:** Humanity has begun to accept the mutants who have been developing psychic powers for the past four generations. Usually talents appear in childhood, as did Julian's. Unfortunately his fraternal twin, happy as a psychic null, begins developing precognition in his early twenties, which may prove disastrous for everyone close to him.

**Other books you might like:**
Alfred Bester, *The Demolished Man*, 1953

John Brunner, *Children of the Thunder*, 1989
Katharine Kerr, *Polar City Blues*, 1990
Henry Kuttner, *Mutant*, 1953
Anne McCaffrey, *Pegasus in Flight*, 1990
Anne McCaffrey, *The Rowan*, 1990
Mike Resnick, *Prophet*, 1993
Joan D. Vinge, *Psion*, 1982

**2476**

KAREN HABER

### Sister Blood

(New York: DAW, 1996)

**Story type:** Science Fiction (Psychic Powers; Political)
**Series:** Mindstar
**Major character(s):** Kayla Reed, Empath, Revolutionary; Lyle Mackenzie, Administrator, Political Figure; Merrick the Blackbird, Pirate
**Time period(s):** Indeterminate Future
**Locale(s):** Styx, Planet—Imaginary; Vardalia, Planet—Imaginary

**Summary:** When Kayla Reed travels to Styx to seek out Yates Keller, who holds Kayla's friends as hostages, Kayla finds Styx deserted except for religious fanatics who wish to keep the planet depopulated by shutting down the mindsalt trade, a destructive force. Meanwhile, on Vardalia, Merrick plots to start up the mindsalt trade, regardless of who stands in his way.

**Other books you might like:**
Poul Anderson, *The Game of Empire*, 1985
C.J. Cherryh, *Merchanter's Luck*, 1982
Alfred Coppel, *Glory's War*, 1995
Paula E. Downing, *Fallway*, 1993
Anne McCaffrey, *Powers That Be*, 1993
    Elizabeth Ann Scarborough, co-author
Melissa Scott, *Mighty Good Road*, 1990
Charles Sheffield, *Cold as Ice*, 1992
David Weber, *Flag in Exile*, 1995

**2477**

KAREN HABER

### The War Minstrels

(New York: DAW, 1995)

**Story type:** Science Fiction (Psychic Powers; Adventure)
**Series:** Mindstar
**Major character(s):** Kayla Reed, Empath, Smuggler; Yates Keller, Empath, Criminal; Iger, Spaceman, Smuggler
**Time period(s):** Indeterminate Future
**Locale(s):** *Falstaff*, Spaceship; Bryce Station, Space Station

**Summary:** After hearing about the legendary Mindstar, a mindstone that greatly enhances empathic abilities, Kayla Reed decides to find and use it to help the War Minstrels, a group of smugglers fighting for a free trade system. Sequel to *Woman Without a Shadow*.

**Other books you might like:**
Kevin J. Anderson, *Blindfold*, 1995
Alan Dean Foster, *Splinter of the Mind's Eye*, 1978
Anne McCaffrey, *Crystal Singer*, 1982
Vonda N. McIntyre, *The Exile Waiting*, 1975
Robert Silverberg, *The Mutant Season*, 1989
    Karen Haber, co-author

**2478**

KAREN HABER

### Woman Without a Shadow

(New York: DAW, 1995)

**Story type:** Science Fiction (Psychic Powers; Adventure)
**Series:** Mindstar
**Major character(s):** Kayla Reed, Empath, Fugitive; Barabbas, Smuggler; Yates Keller, Empath, Criminal
**Time period(s):** Indeterminate Future
**Locale(s):** Styx, Planet—Imaginary; *Falstaff*, Spaceship

**Summary:** Orphaned when her parents die in a mining accident, Kayla Reed tries to continue their mindstone mining operation. However, after tangling with the powerful Keller family, Kayla must escape from Styx, taking on a new identity as navigator for a smuggling ship.

**Other books you might like:**
Kevin J. Anderson, *Blindfold*, 1995
Anne McCaffrey, *Crystal Singer*, 1982
Anne McCaffrey, *Damia*, 1992
Anne McCaffrey, *The Rowan*, 1990
Larry Segriff, *Spacer Dreams*, 1995
Robert Silverberg, *The Mutant Season*, 1989
    Karen Haber, co-author

**2479**

MICHAEL HAGUE, Editor

### The Book of Dragons

(New York: Morrow, 1995)

**Story type:** Fantasy (Anthology; Young Adult)
**Summary:** Contains 17 stories excerpted from novels and reprinted from collections and anthologies 1921-1980, all featuring traditional dragons in diverse settings with tone varying from light to ominous. Authors include Italo Calvino, the Brothers Grimm, Kenneth Grahame, Andrew Lang, C.S. Lewis, E. Nesbit, and J.R.R. Tolkien. Lavishly illustrated in color and monocolor by Hague.

**Other books you might like:**
Isaac Asimov, *Dragon Tales*, 1982
    Martin H. Greenberg, Charles G. Waugh, co-editors
Orson Scott Card, *Dragons of Darkness*, 1981
    editor
Orson Scott Card, *Dragons of Light*, 1983
    editor
Jack Dann, *Dragons!*, 1993
    Gardner Dozois, co-editor
Rosalind M. Greenberg, *Dragon Fantastic*, 1992
    Martin H. Greenberg, co-editor
Byron Preiss, *The Ultimate Dragon*, 1995
    John Betancourt, Keith R.A. DeCandido, co-editors
Margaret Weis, *A Dragon-Lover's Treasury of the Fantastic*, 1994
    editor
Jane Yolen, *Here There Be Dragons*, 1993

**2480**

ISIDORE HAIBLUM

### Specterworld

(New York: Avon, 1991)

**Story type:** Science Fiction (Time Travel; Adventure)

**Series:** Tom Dunjer
**Major character(s):** Tom Dunjer, Security Officer; X41, Robot; Nigel, Professor
**Time period(s):** Indeterminate Future
**Locale(s):** Happy City, Fictional Country; Fearsburg, Fictional Country

**Summary:** In this sequel to *Interworld*, Dunjer's Happy City robbery investigation leads to Fearsburg and an old nemesis. The conspiracy Dunjer discovers leads him away from his own world and time.

**Other books you might like:**
Douglas Adams, *Dirk Gently's Holistic Detective Agency*, 1987
Michael Flynn, *In the Country of the Blind*, 1990
Mel Gilden, *Hawaiian U.F.O. Aliens*, 1991
Thomas R. McDonough, *The Missing Matter*, 1992
Ken Rolston, *Extreme Paranoia: Nobody Knows the Trouble I've Shot*, 1991
Dan Simmons, *The Fall of Hyperion*, 1990
Dan Simmons, *Hyperion*, 1989

**2481**

**PETER HAINING**, Editor

## Great Irish Stories of the Supernatural

(New York: Barnes & Noble, 1998)

**Story type:** Horror (Anthology)

**Summary:** This anthology is made up of 28 stories of horror and fantasy set on Irish soil and/or written by Irish authors. Selections include Bram Stoker's "The Judge's House," about a student's ill-fated rental of a room in a house haunted by its former owner; Elizabeth Bowen's "Hand in Glove," about a vengeful pair of supernaturally animated gloves; William Trevor's "Autumn Sunshine," the tale of a haunted small-town rectory; and Lord Dunsany's tall tale "The Crock of Gold," in which inveterate liar Jorkens fights a leprechaun for his buried treasure. Other contributors include James Joyce, Frank O'Connor, J.M. Synge, and Sean O'Faolain.

**Other books you might like:**
Patricia Craig, *Twelve Irish Ghost Stories*, 1998
  editor
Joseph Hone, *Irish Ghost Stories*, 1971
  editor
Jim McGarry, *Irish Tales of Terror*, 1971
  editor
H.M. Tichenor, *Irish Fairy Tales*, 1923
  editor
Peter Tremayne, *Irish Masters of Fantasy*, 1979
  editor

**2482**

**PETER HAINING**, Editor

## Great Irish Tales of Horror

(New York: Barnes & Noble, 1997)

**Story type:** Horror (Anthology)

**Summary:** Twenty-four stories by Irish authors and with Irish settings. Included are Elizabeth Bowen's "Happy Autumn Fields," in which an imagined world takes on reality for a woman; M.P. Shiel's "The Bride," in which the corpse of a jilted woman enacts a gruesome revenge on the wedding night of her intended lover; Vincent O'Sullivan's "Will," in which strength of will animates a corpse; and L.A.G. Strong's "Danse Macabre," in which a man

discovers that his dancing partner is a ghost. Also included are stories by Wiliam Trevor, Neil Jordan, George Bernard Shaw, Sax Rohmer, and Brian Moore. First published in England in 1995.

**Other books you might like:**
Joseph Hone, *Irish Ghost Stories*, 1971
  editor
Jim McGarry, *Irish Tales of Terror*, 1971
  editor
H.M. Tichenor, *Irish Fairy Tales*, 1923
  editor
Peter Tremayne, *Irish Masters of Fantasy*, 1979
  editor

**2483**

**PETER HAINING**, Editor

## The Mammoth Book of Twentieth Century Ghost Stories

(New York: Carroll & Graf, 1998)

**Story type:** Horror (Anthology; Ghost Story)

**Summary:** This omnibus collection of 30 ghost stories published since 1900 includes works by Henry James, Muriel Spark, Fay Weldon, Ruth Rendell, Agatha Christie and other literary and genre writers. A special grouping of stories is devoted to tales in which ghostly presences have helped turn the tide of war or brought solace to soldiers, including A. Merritt's "Three Lines of Old French," Henry Kuttner's "We Are the Dead," and Arthur Machen's "The Bowmen."

**Other books you might like:**
Michael Cox, *The Oxford Book of English Ghost Stories*, 1986
  R.A. Gilbert, co-editor
Michael Cox, *The Oxford Book of Twentieth Century Ghost Stories*, 1996
Richard Dalby, *The Mammoth Book of Victorian and Edwardian Ghost Stories*, 1995
Richard Dalby, *Modern Ghost Stories by Eminent Women Writers*, 1992
Brad Leithauser, *The Norton Book of Ghost Stories*, 1994
  editor

**2484**

**PETER HAINING**, Editor

## The Vampire Hunters' Casebook

(New York: Barnes & Noble, 1997)

**Story type:** Horror (Anthology; Vampire Story)

**Summary:** Fifteen stories featuring human characters who detect, capture or kill vampires. Included are Seabury Quinn's "The Man Who Cast No Shadow," featuring psychic detective Jules de Grandin; David Schow's "A Week in the Unlife," about vampires who prey on other vampires; Robert Bloch's "The Undead," which resurrects Count Dracula; and Manly Wade Wellman's "The Last Grave of Lill Warran," in which his series detective John Thunstone hunts a being who is both werewolf and vampire. Included are excerpts from Jeff Rice's novel *The Night Stalker*, featuring vampire hunting journalist Carl Kolchak, and Anne Rice's "The Master of the Rampling Gate," excerpted from her novel *The Vampire Lestat*. Stills from vampire films are included.

**Other books you might like:**
Richard Dalby, *Dracula's Brood*, 1987
  editor

Martin H. Greenberg, *Vampires: The Greatest Stories*, 1997
editor
Stephen Jones, *The Mammoth Book of Vampires*, 1992
editor

---

**2485**

**PETER HAINING**

## Weird Tales

(New York: Carroll and Graf, 1990)

**Story type:** Horror (Anthology)

**Summary:** A collection of 31 stories and poems from *Weird Tales*, the legendary weird fiction magazine that provided H.P. Lovecraft, Ray Bradbury, Robert Bloch and hundreds of other fantasists with an outlet for their writing during the years 1923 to 1954. Produced as a facsimile edition of the magazine, the book offers a mix of magazine columns, artwork and classic stories such as Manly Wade Wellman's "The Valley Was Still," Henry S. Whitehead's "The Passing of a God" and Edmond Hamilton's "The Man Who Returned."

**Other books you might like:**
Stefan Dziemianowicz, *Weird Tales: 32 Unearthed Terrors*, 1988
Robert Weinberg and Martin H. Greenberg, co-authors
Leo Margulies, *Worlds of Weird*, 1965
Leo Margulies, *Weird Tales*, 1964
Robert Weinberg, *The Eighth Green Man and Other Strange Folk*, 1989
Robert Weinberg, *Far Below and Other Horrors*, 1974

---

**2486**

**JACK C. HALDEMAN II**
**JACK DANN**, Co-Author

## High Steel

(New York: Tor, 1993)

**Story type:** Science Fiction (First Contact; Political)
**Major character(s):** John Stranger, Indian (Lakota), Spaceman (conscripted); Leonard Broken-finger, Shaman (medicine man), Indian; Gerard Leighton, Administrator
**Time period(s):** 22nd century (2177)
**Locale(s):** Trans-United Space Colony, Space Station (L-7)

**Summary:** Before John Stranger can complete his training as a medicine man, Trans-United drafts him to become a spaceman, likely to remain forever off Earth. Unhappy over being drafted, John still finds great beauty and peace in space. After John stops a runaway space station, Trans-United recognizes John's talent, an ability to select correct solutions, and begins a secret program to test John's ability to pilot a prototype faster-than-light spaceship built from incompletely understood designs transmitted by aliens as part of the Rosetta Triptych. However, Trans-United's experimentation may lead to Earth's annihilation.

**Other books you might like:**
Alan Dean Foster, *Cyber Way*, 1990
Jean Mark Gawron, *Dream of Glass*, 1993
Joe Haldeman, *There Is No Darkness*, 1983
Jack C. Haldeman II, co-author
Harry Harrison, *Bill, the Galactic Hero: On the Planet of Zombie Vampires*, 1991
Jack C. Haldeman II, co-author
Gwyneth Jones, *White Queen*, 1993
Ursula K. Le Guin, *The Lathe of Heaven*, 1971
Allen Steele, *Clarke County, Space*, 1990

---

Allen Steele, *Orbital Decay*, 1989

---

**2487**

**JOE HALDEMAN**

## Buying Time

(New York: Morrow, 1989)

**Story type:** Science Fiction (Immortality)
**Major character(s):** Dallas Barr, Immortal, Businessman; Maria Marconi, Immortal, Pilot
**Time period(s):** 21st century
**Locale(s):** Earth; Ceres, Asteroid

**Summary:** A radical surgical technique, the Stileman process, can prolong life virtually indefinitely. The process wears off after ten years, however, and must be repeated at great expense. Dallas Barr, one of the first Stileman immortals, uncovers a plot to kill off his peers and to pervert the technique to an evil end.

**Other books you might like:**
Robert A. Heinlein, *Time Enough for Love*, 1973
Frederik Pohl, *Drunkard's Walk*, 1960
Robert Silverberg, *The Book of Skulls*, 1971
Norman Spinrad, *Bug Jack Barron*, 1969
Jack Vance, *To Live Forever*, 1956
Roger Zelazny, *This Immortal*, 1966

---

**2488**

**JOE HALDEMAN**

## Forever Peace

(New York: Ace, 1997)

**Story type:** Science Fiction (Military; Political)
**Major character(s):** Julian Class, Military Personnel, Scientist; Amelia "Blaze" Harding, Scientist, Professor; Marty Larrin, Scientist
**Time period(s):** 2040s
**Locale(s):** Portobello, Mexico; Houston, Texas

**Summary:** In the Ngumi War, Julian, a platoon sergeant, maintains constant communication with his men and women, five of each, as part of his link to his remote-controlled soldierboy, a humanform robot. They maintain the link for ten days while in their pods at Portobello and then have 20 days off. Julian returns to Houston to teach and run physics experiments relating to the giant accelerator around Jupiter. Marty, an old friend of Blaze, invented the link and understands Blaze's desire to connect with Julian. The war troubles Julian because nanoforge technology produces everything. including nuclear weapons, although the war would by unnecessary if all could be trusted to use the technology fairly and responsibly.

**Other books you might like:**
Pat Cadigan, *Synners*, 1991
Michael Flynn, *In the Country of the Blind*, 1990
Robert J. Sawyer, *The Terminal Experiment*, 1995
Neal Stephenson, *Snow Crash*, 1992
G. Harry Stine, *Warbots*, 1988
Sage Walker, *Whiteout*, 1996

## **2489**

### JOE HALDEMAN

## *The Hemingway Hoax*

(New York: Morrow, 1990)

**Story type:** Science Fiction (Time Travel)
**Major character(s):** John Baird, Professor; Sylvester Castlemaine, Criminal
**Time period(s):** Indeterminate Future; 1920s (1922)
**Locale(s):** Key West, Florida

**Summary:** A conman convinces Professor Baird, a Hemingway specialist, to forge some stories that Hemingway's wife apparently lost on a train in 1922. Unbeknownst to either man, a time and dimension-travelling police force has determined that increased interest in Hemingway would not be to the world's advantage because it would promulgate macho attitudes of a sort likely to lead to nuclear war. The agents of that police force are willing to murder Professor Baird, and to do so repeatedly in various timelines, in order to stop him from carrying out the forgery attempt.

**Other books you might like:**
Isaac Asimov, *The End of Eternity*, 1955
Barrington J. Bayley, *The Fall of Chronopolis*, 1974
Robert A. Heinlein, *To Sail Beyond the Sunset*, 1987
Michael P. Kube-McDowell, *Alternities*, 1988
Bob Shaw, *The Two-Timers*, 1968

## **2490**

### JOE HALDEMAN

## *None So Blind*

(New York: Morrow/AvoNova, 1996)

**Story type:** Science Fiction (Collection)

**Summary:** Contains a six-page introduction, four story poems and 11 stories published since 1986 with afterwords describing the real life events that influenced the story or sparked the idea. One story, "The Hemingway Hoax," won both the Hugo and Nebula Awards; another, "Graves," won a World Fantasy Award and a Nebula Award; and "None So Blind" won a Hugo Award. Themes include death, ghosts, the effect of Ernest Hemingway on the multiverse, concern for others, and the importance of one's point of view.

**Other books you might like:**
Isaac Asimov, *Gold: The Final Science Fiction Collection*, 1995
Harry Harrison, *Galactic Dreams*, 1994
Larry Niven, *N-Space*, 1990
Theodore Sturgeon, *The Ultimate Egoist*, 1994
John Varley, *The Persistence of Vision*, 1978

## **2491**

### JOE HALDEMAN

## *Worlds Enough and Time*

(New York: Morrow, 1992)

**Story type:** Science Fiction (Generation Starship; First Contact)
**Series:** Worlds Trilogy
**Major character(s):** Marianne O'Hara, Administrator, Settler; O'Hara Prime, Artificial Intelligence; Harry Purcell, Political Figure
**Time period(s):** 22nd century
**Locale(s):** *Newhome*, Spaceship; O'Hara, Planet—Imaginary

**Summary:** Marianne O'Hara has joined a colony ship travelling to Epsilon Eridani. On the way, sabotage destroys most of the ship's memory and a virus destroys all photosynthesizing plant life. When John, one of Marianne's husbands, suffers a stroke, Marianne, her daughter and her son-in-law go into cryptobiosis until they reach Epsilon Eridani. Landing on the planet, they encounter life that tests Marianne to see if humans may live in the universe.

**Other books you might like:**
David Brin, *Earth*, 1990
Robert A. Heinlein, *Have Spacesuit—Will Travel*, 1958
Robert A. Heinlein, *Methuselah's Children*, 1958
Keith Laumer, *Star Colony*, 1981
Vonda N. McIntyre, *Transition*, 1991
Larry Niven, *The Legacy of Heorot*, 1987
    Jerry Pournelle and Steven Barnes, co-authors
Brian Stableford, *The Gates of Eden*, 1983
James White, *The Silent Stars Go By*, 1991
Timothy Zahn, *Spinneret*, 1985

## **2492**

### WENDY HALEY

## *These Fallen Angels*

(New York: Diamond, 1995)

**Story type:** Horror (Vampire Story; Gothic Family Chronicle)
**Series:** Danilov Family Saga
**Major character(s):** Alexander Danilov, Vampire; Justin Danilov, Teenager; Sonya Danilov, Parent (Justin's mother)
**Time period(s):** 1990s (1995)
**Locale(s):** Savannah, Georgia

**Summary:** Having vanquished the centuries-old vampire sorcerer who menaced him and his extended family in *This Dark Paradise* (1994), vampire patriarch Alexander Danilov tries once again to preside over his family's affairs, and prepare young Justin Danilov for his upcoming marriage. But the disembodied soul of Lydia, who craved the immortality that Alexander refused her, reanimates Alexander's dead love Elizabeth to torment him.

**Other books you might like:**
V.C. Andrews, *All That Glitters*, 1995
Tanith Lee, *Dark Dance*, 1993
Michael Romkcy, *The Vampire Papers*, 1994
Fred Saberhagen, *A Matter of Taste*, 1992
Karen E. Taylor, *Bitter Blood*, 1994

## **2493**

### WENDY HALEY

## *This Dark Paradise*

(New York: Diamond, 1994)

**Story type:** Horror (Vampire Story; Gothic Family Chronicle)
**Series:** Danilov Family Saga
**Major character(s):** Alexander Danilov, Vampire; Barron Danilov, Businessman; James Suldris, Sorcerer
**Time period(s):** 1990s (1994); 16th century
**Locale(s):** Savannah, Georgia

**Summary:** Alex Danilov, a benevolent vampire member of the Danilov family, returns to the family estate in Georgia in time to inherit the family wealth and incur the wrath of his petty and perverse mortal relatives. At the same time, Alex is stalked by James Suldris, a sorcerer whom he thought he killed centuries before but whom he inadvertently vampirized, turning him into an immortal adversary.

**Other books you might like:**
Tanith Lee, *Dark Dance*, 1993
Michael Romkey, *The Vampire Papers*, 1994
Fred Saberhagen, *A Matter of Taste*, 1992
Dan Simmons, *Carrion Comfort*, 1989
Karen E. Taylor, *Bitter Blood*, 1994

## 2494

### KAREN HALL

## Dark Debts

(New York: Random House, 1996)

**Story type:** Horror (Black Magic)
**Major character(s):** Michael Kinney, Religious (Jesuit priest); Randa Phillips, Journalist; Jack Landry, Handyman
**Time period(s):** 1990s (1996)
**Locale(s):** Barton, Georgia

**Summary:** Randa Phillips' investigation into the apparent suicide of her lover, Cameron Landry, brings to light the dark legacy of his family, whose patriarch summoned a demon that has wrought destruction through family members before killing them as part of a botched satanic bargain made generations before. Now Jack Landry, Cameron's brother, is feeling the demon's influence, and the only thing that will save him is an exorcism by Father Michael Kinney, a distant relative who has also felt the demon's touch. This is the author's first novel.

**Other books you might like:**
William Peter Blatty, *The Exorcist*, 1971
Poppy Z. Brite, *Drawing Blood*, 1993
Nancy A. Collins, *Tempter*, 1990
John Farris, *All Heads Turn When the Hunt Goes By*, 1972
Robert R. McCammon, *Usher's Passing*, 1984

## 2495

### MATTHEW HALL

## Nightmare Logic

(New York: Bantam, 1989)

**Story type:** Horror (Serial Killer)
**Major character(s):** Carolyn Bergeron, Murderer (Serial killer), Artist; Ben Quadrun, Journalist
**Time period(s):** 1960s; 1980s
**Locale(s):** Tucson, Arizona

**Summary:** Sixteen females are murdered in the desert outside of town. Reporter Ben Quadrun gradually comes to believe that the perpetrator may be a beautiful female painter—and that his girlfriend, Nita, is in danger of becoming her next victim. This is Hall's first novel.

**Other books you might like:**
Peter Straub, *If You Could See Me Now*, 1977

## 2496

### MELISSA MIA HALL, Editor

## Wild Women

(New York: Carroll & Graf, 1997)

**Story type:** Horror (Anthology)

**Summary:** Thirty-two reprint stories and poems that celebrate the "primal selves" of women. A signigicant number of the selections

are horror and dark fantasy, including Fritz Leiber's "The Girl with the Hungry Eyes," about a female vampire who seduces men through an advertising image; Lucy Taylor's "Going North," a hardboiled tale of just desserts for a child-abusing family; Lisa Tuttle's "Bit and Pieces," in which a woman's memories of past lovers manifest as discorporate body parts; Joyce Carol Oates's "Haunted," in which a woman's repressed memories of a psychologically traumatic experience acquire near supernatural intensity; and Joe R. Landsdale's psychological suspense story "Incident On and Off a Mountain Road."

**Other books you might like:**
Pam Keesey, *Women Who Run with Werewolves: Tales of Blood, Lust and Metamorphosis*, 1996
 editor
Kathryn Ptacek, *Women of Darkness II*, 1990
 editor
Kathryn Ptacek, *Women of Darkness*, 1988
 editor
Alan Ryan, *Haunting Women*, 1988
 editor
Jessica Amanda Salmonson, *What Did Miss Darrington See?: An Anthology of Feminist Supernatural Fiction*, 1989
 editor
Lisa Tuttle, *Skin of the Soul*, 1991
 editor

## 2497

### ELIZABETH HALLAM

## Spirit Catcher

(New York: Jove, 1998)

**Story type:** Fantasy (Light Fantasy; Mystery)
**Major character(s):** Dallas James, Actress; Boone Cantrell, Spirit, Lawman (sheriff)
**Time period(s):** 1990s (1998)
**Locale(s):** Fury, Colorado

**Summary:** Dallas James makes her living by acting a part in a restored ghost town. Her life becomes more complicated when she realizes that she alone can see one of the inhabitants of the town, the ghost of a long-dead sheriff who wants her to help him solve an old mystery. First novel.

**Other books you might like:**
Suzanne Elizabeth, *Destined to Love*, 1994
Suzanne Elizabeth, *Destiny in Disguise*, 1997
Georgina Gentry, *Timeless Warrior*, 1996
Vivan Knight Jenkins, *The Outlaw Heart*, 1995
Stephanie Mittman, *Bridge to Yesterday*, 1995

## 2498

### JAMES L. HALPERIN

## The First Immortal

(New York: Ballantine Del Rey, 1998)

**Story type:** Science Fiction (Immortality; Family Saga)
**Major character(s):** Benjamin Franklin Smith, Immortal, Doctor; Gary Franklin Smith, Artist, Doctor; George "Trip" Crane III, Scientist (nanotechnology), Professor
**Time period(s):** 20th century; 21st century (1925-2100)
**Locale(s):** Boston, Massachusetts

**Summary:** When his family learns, upon his death in the late 1980s, that Ben Smith made arrangements for his cryonic preservation, as well as their own, they think him crazy. Cryonics and nanotechnology, however, begin to grow by leaps and bounds, allowing the family to reunite in a future they barely recognize. Loosely related to *The Truth Machine.*

**Other books you might like:**
Sterling Blake, *Chiller*, 1993
    pseudonym of Gregory Benford
Orson Scott Card, *The Worthing Saga*, 1990
Robert A. Heinlein, *Time Enough for Love*, 1973
Robert A. Heinlein, *I Will Fear No Evil*, 1970
Linda Nagata, *Tech-Heaven*, 1995
Clifford D. Simak, *Why Call Them Back From Heaven?*, 1967
Allen Steele, *A King of Infinite Space*, 1997

---

**2499**

**BARBARA HAMBLY**

## Bride of the Rat God

(New York: Ballantine Del Rey, 1994)

**Story type:** Fantasy (Magic Conflict; Horror)
**Major character(s):** Chrysanda "Christine" Famande, Actress; Shang Ko, Wizard; Norah Blackstone, Companion (Christine's sister-in-law)
**Time period(s):** 1920s
**Locale(s):** Hollywood, California; Los Angeles, California; Red Bluff, California

**Summary:** Unbeknownst to her, Christine's use of a magic necklace, The Moon of Rats, betroths her to an ancient Manchurian demon, the Rat God. On the set of her latest film, the demon in human form attempts to kill her to make her his bride while Shang Ko uses protective magic as he searches for a way to counter the undesired union.

**Other books you might like:**
Lois McMaster Bujold, *The Spirit Ring*, 1992
Elizabeth Forrest, *Phoenix Fire*, 1992
Alan Dean Foster, *Cyber Way*, 1990
Marc Laidlaw, *Neon Lotus*, 1988
Elizabeth Ann Scarborough, *Last Refuge*, 1992

---

**2500**

**BARBARA HAMBLY**

## Children of the Jedi

(New York: Bantam Spectra, 1995)

**Story type:** Science Fiction (Mystical; Space Opera)
**Series:** Star Wars
**Major character(s):** Han Solo, Spaceship Captain, Warrior; Leia Organa Solo, Royalty, Leader; Luke Skywalker, Martial Arts Expert, Hero
**Time period(s):** Indeterminate Past
**Locale(s):** New Republic, Interstellar Empire/Federation; Outer Space; Belsavis, Planet—Imaginary

**Summary:** As the surviving Houses of the New Republic attempt to regain their former influence, Leia and Han follow rumors of hidden Jedi to Belsavis while Luke attempts to thwart deadly orders issued by the former emperor to a Super Star Destroyer class battleship.

**Other books you might like:**
Kevin J. Anderson, *Jedi Search*, 1994
Brian Daley, *The Han Solo Adventures*, 1992
George Lucas, *The Star Wars Trilogy*, 1987
    Donald F. Glut, James Kahn, co-authors

Vonda N. McIntyre, *The Crystal Star*, 1994
L. Neil Smith, *The Lando Calrissian Adventures*, 1994
Dave Wolverton, *The Courtship of Princess Leia*, 1994
Timothy Zahn, *Heir to the Empire*, 1991

---

**2501**

**BARBARA HAMBLY**

## Crossroad

(New York: Pocket, 1994)

**Story type:** Science Fiction (Space Opera)
**Series:** Star Trek
**Major character(s):** Christine Chapel, Nurse, Military Personnel (Starfleet); Lao Zhiming, Military Personnel (ensign); Spock, Scientist, Alien (Vulcan)
**Time period(s):** 23rd century
**Locale(s):** *U.S.S. Enterprise*, Spaceship; *Nautilus*, Spaceship; United Federation of Planets, Interstellar Empire/Federation

**Summary:** While investigating the Crossroads Nebula and the Turtledove Anomaly within it, the *Enterprise* rescues the crew of a battered starship, *Nautilus*. The *Nautilus* crew claims they travelled from the future to work as freedom fighters to save the Federation. When the newcomers seize control of his ship and another starship arrives to arrest the renegades, Kirk must discover whom he can trust.

**Other books you might like:**
James Blish, *The Triumph of Time*, 1958
Peter David, *Q-Squared*, 1994
Diane Duane, *The Wounded Sky*, 1983
David Dvorkin, *Timetrap*, 1988
Harry Turtledove, *The Guns of the South: A Novel of the Civil War*, 1992

---

**2502**

**BARBARA HAMBLY**

## The Dark Hand of Magic

(New York: Del Rey, 1990)

**Story type:** Fantasy (Sword and Sorcery)
**Series:** Sun Wolf and Starhawk
**Major character(s):** Sun Wolf, Mercenary (Former), Wizard (Inexperienced); Starhawk, Mercenary (Former)
**Time period(s):** Indeterminate

**Summary:** Ex-mercenary couple Sun Wolf and Starhawk are drawn back to their former company of mercenaries when Sun Wolf is rescued by them because they need his help in a war between merchant princes. Meanwhile a wizard has promised to teach Sun Wolf how to use his powers but begins to enslave him instead.

**Other books you might like:**
Carole Nelson Douglas, *Six of Swords*, 1982
Janet Morris, *City at the Edge of Time*, 1988
Jennifer Roberson, *Sword-Dancer*, 1989
    Book 3
Dave Smeds, *The Sorcery Within*, 1985

## 2503

### BARBARA HAMBLY

## Dog Wizard

(New York: Ballantine Del Rey, 1993)

**Story type:** Fantasy (Alternate World; Magic Conflict)
**Series:** Windrose Chronicles
**Major character(s):** Antryg Windrose, Wizard, Fugitive; Joanna, Computer Expert
**Time period(s):** 1990s; Indeterminate
**Locale(s):** Los Angeles, California; The Citadel of Wizards, Mythical Place; Empire of Ferryth, Fictional Country

**Summary:** When dimensional breaches allow horrible forces into the exiled Wizards' Citadel, the frightened Wizards blame Antryg Windrose who fled to Earth to avoid their justice. When Antryg ignores the Wizards' summons to return, they kidnap Joanna, forcing Antryg to return to his world to rescue Joanna and battle the deadly breach.

**Other books you might like:**
Lois McMaster Bujold, *The Spirit Ring*, 1992
Laurell K. Hamilton, *Nightseer*, 1992
Elizabeth Ann Scarborough, *Last Refuge*, 1992
Margaret Weis, *The Hand of Chaos*, 1993
    Tracy Hickman, co-author
Martha Wells, *The Element of Fire*, 1993
Elizabeth Willey, *The Well-Favored Man: The Tale of the Sorcerer's Nephew*, 1993

## 2504

### BARBARA HAMBLY

## Icefalcon's Quest

(New York: Ballantine Del Rey, 1998)

**Story type:** Fantasy (Magic Conflict; Alternate World)
**Series:** Darwath
**Major character(s):** Icefalcon, Military Personnel, Indian; Altir "Tir", Royalty, Child; Ingold Inglorion, Wizard
**Time period(s):** 1990s
**Locale(s):** Keep of Dare, Fictional City

**Summary:** When kidnappers grab Prince Tir from the Keep of Dare, only Icefalcon, the enigmatic Guard, can follow the boy's captors in time to stop their plan. The kidnappers, however, head out onto the plains, where Icefalcon must fight not only magic and lost technology, but also his own repressed past and sins. Fifth in series.

**Other books you might like:**
Eleanor Arnason, *Daughter of the Bear King*, 1987
Robin Hobb, *Assassin's Apprentice*, 1995
Guy Gavriel Kay, *Tigana*, 1990
Patricia A. McKillip, *The Riddle-Master of Hed*, 1976
Michael Scott Rohan, *The Anvil of Ice*, 1986

## 2505

### BARBARA HAMBLY

## The Magicians of Night

(New York: Ballantine Del Rey, 1992)

**Story type:** Fantasy (Magic Conflict; Alternate World)
**Series:** Sun-Cross
**Major character(s):** Rhion the Brown, Wizard
**Time period(s):** 1940s

**Locale(s):** Germany

**Summary:** Marooned in Nazi Germany with no easy way back to his own world, Rhion ineffectively advises four would-be wizards against utilizing dark magic to overcome their enemies. Although informed that the Dark Well no longer exists, Rhion believes it does exist and that he must find it if he wishes to return across the Void to his home world.

**Other books you might like:**
Gael Baudino, *Dragon Death*, 1992
Stephen R. Donaldson, *The Mirror of Her Dreams*, 1986
Katherine Kurtz, *Lammas Night*, 1983
Shirley Rousseau Murphy, *Medallion of the Black Hound*, 1989
    Welch Suggs, co-author
Alis A. Rasmussen, *The Labyrinth Gate*, 1988
Brad Strickland, *Wizard's Mole*, 1991

## 2506

### BARBARA HAMBLY

## Mother of Winter

(New York: Ballantine Del Rey, 1996)

**Story type:** Fantasy (Magic Conflict; Alternate World)
**Series:** Darwath
**Major character(s):** Ingold Inglorion, Wizard; Gil Patterson, Warrior, Scholar; Rudy Solis, Wizard, Mechanic
**Time period(s):** 1990s
**Locale(s):** Keep of Dare, Fictional City; Alketch, Fictional Country

**Summary:** The vanquishing of the Dark Ones should have brought easy life, but strange plants and animals, immune to magic, threaten the Keep. While Rudy stays at home to deal with politics and treachery, Gil and Ingold must sneak through the hostile Empire of Alketch to confront an enemy from the dawn of the world.

**Other books you might like:**
Eleanor Arnason, *Daughter of the Bear King*, 1987
Terry Goodkind, *Wizard's First Rule*, 1994
Guy Gavriel Kay, *The Summer Tree*, 1985
Patricia A. McKillip, *The Riddle-Master of Hed*, 1976
Martha Wells, *The Element of Fire*, 1993

## 2507

### BARBARA HAMBLY

## The Rainbow Abyss

(New York: Ballantine/Del Rey, 1991)

**Story type:** Fantasy (Magic Conflict; Alternate World)
**Series:** Sun-Cross
**Major character(s):** Rhion the Brown, Wizard; Jaldis the Blind, Wizard
**Time period(s):** Indeterminate
**Locale(s):** Felsplex, Fictional City; Bragenmere, Fictional City

**Summary:** With wizards considered unfavorably in Felsplex, Rhion and his mentor, Jaldis, barely scratch a living until they are finally run out of the city. They take refuge at the court of the sympathetic Duke of Bragenmere, where Jaldis pursues his researches into the Abyss, trying to reach the people calling to him from the world that has no magic. The prospect of the Abyss frightens Rhion as much as the thought of Jaldis in a place where he is blind and voiceless.

**Other books you might like:**
John M. Ford, *The Dragon Waiting*, 1983
Stephen R. Donaldson, *The Mirror of Her Dreams*, 1986
Katherine Kurtz, *Lammas Night*, 1983

Megan Lindholm, *Luck of the Wheels*, 1989
Joel Rosenberg, *D'Shai*, 1991
Sheri S. Tepper, *King's Blood Four*, 1983

---

**2508**

BARBARA HAMBLY, Editor
MARTIN H. GREENBERG, Co-Editor

### Sisters of the Night

(New York: Warner, 1995)

**Story type:** Horror (Anthology)

**Summary:** The fourteen stories written especially for this volume all feature female vampires. Barbara Hambly's "Madeleine" is a biter-bit story in which a vampire's victims turn the tables on her, and Michael Kurland's "In the Blood" is a female vampire coming-of-age tale. Pat Cadigan's "Sometimes Salvation" draws analogies between the vampire life and the exploitation of street children while in Tanith Lee's "La Dame," the spirit of a ship develops a vampiric hold on a sailor. Female vampires offer consolation at death for characters in Jane Yolen's "Sister Death" and Dean Wesley Smith's "Tumbling Down the Nightmare," while the vampire of Nina Kiriki Hoffman's "Food Chain" is a child vampire who serves as a surrogate to mothers who have lost their children. Larry Niven's "Song of the Night People" is an excerpt from his novel *The Ringworld Throne*.

**Other books you might like:**
Poppy Z. Brite, *Love in Vein*, 1994
    Martin H. Greenberg, co-editor
Ellen Datlow, *Blood Is Not Enough*, 1989
    editor
Martin H. Greenberg, *Vamps*, 1987
    Charles G. Waugh, co-editor
Pam Keesey, *Dark Angels: Lesbian Vampire Stories*, 1995
    editor
Pam Keesey, *Daughters of Darkness: Lesbian Vampire Stories*, 1993
    editor

---

**2509**

BARBARA HAMBLY

### Stranger at the Wedding

(New York: Ballantine Del Rey, 1994)

**Story type:** Fantasy (Magic Conflict)
**Major character(s):** Kyra Peldyrin, Wizard; Alix Peldyrin, Fiance(e); Tibbeth of Hale, Wizard
**Time period(s):** Indeterminate
**Locale(s):** Angelshand, Fictional City; Empire of Ferryth, Fictional Country

**Summary:** Responding to a premonition of disaster for Alix on her wedding night, Kyra must stall the wedding without bringing the unwanted attention of the Inquisition down upon herself for using magic in human affairs. Set in the Windrose Chronicles milieu.

**Other books you might like:**
Mary Gentle, *The Architecture of Desire*, 1993
Laurell K. Hamilton, *Nightseer*, 1992
Delia Sherman, *The Porcelain Dove*, 1993
Paula Volsky, *Illusion*, 1992
Martha Wells, *The Element of Fire*, 1993
Elizabeth Willey, *The Well-Favored Man: The Tale of the Sorcerer's Nephew*, 1993

---

**2510**

BARBARA HAMBLY

### Those Who Hunt the Night

(New York: Ballantine Del Rey, 1988)

**Story type:** Horror (Vampire Story)
**Major character(s):** James Asher, Detective—Amateur (Ex-British spy), Professor (Oxford); Don Simon Ysidro, Vampire (Sympathetic)
**Time period(s):** 1900s (1907)
**Locale(s):** London, England

**Summary:** Asher is "hired," under threat of death to himself and his wife, by a group of the undead to discover who—or what—is killing London's vampire society.

**Other books you might like:**
Nancy A. Collins, *Sunglasses After Dark*, 1989
Anne Rice, *Interview with the Vampire*, 1976
Whitley Strieber, *The Hunger*, 1981
Les Whitten, *Progeny of the Adder*, 1965

---

**2511**

BARBARA HAMBLY

### Traveling with the Dead

(New York: Del Rey, 1995)

**Story type:** Horror (Vampire Story)
**Major character(s):** Lydia Asher, Scientist (biologist); James Asher, Professor, Detective—Amateur; Ignace Karolyi, Mercenary
**Time period(s):** 1900s (1908)
**Locale(s):** London, England; Vienna, Austria

**Summary:** In this sequel to *Those Who Hunt the Night*, James Asher's pursuit of vampire Lord Charles Farren across Europe results in his capture by the Turkish vampires who have hired Farren for an undisclosed purpose, and Asher's wife Lydia's similar pursuit to save her husband. Along the way, Lydia teams up with a number of mortals and vampires whose motivations mirror her own.

**Other books you might like:**
Les Daniels, *Yellow Fog*, 1986
Kim Newman, *Anno Dracula*, 1993
Lucius Shepard, *The Golden*, 1994
Chelsea Quinn Yarbro, *Tempting Fate*, 1982

---

**2512**

LAURELL K. HAMILTON

### Bloody Bones

(New York: Ace, 1996)

**Story type:** Horror (Vampire Story)
**Series:** Anita Blake, Vampire Hunter
**Major character(s):** Anita Blake, Vampire Hunter, Detective—Private; Larry Kirkland, Psychic, Vampire Hunter; Jean-Claude, Vampire
**Time period(s):** 1990s (1996)
**Locale(s):** St. Louis Missouri, Alternate Earth

**Summary:** In this fifth adventure of Anita Blake, set in an alternate universe where supernatural creatures have the same rights as human beings, Anita is called to resurrect ancient dead from a cemetery to settle a property dispute between the family of the dead and a corporation that wants to develop the cemetery land. When Anita's investigations dovetail with recent murders caused by members of the community, she reluctantly seeks assistance from her vampire suitor, Jean-Claude.

**Other books you might like:**
Scott Baker, *Ancestral Hungers*, 1995
Nancy A. Collins, *A Dozen Black Roses*, 1996
Christopher Golden, *Of Saints and Shadows*, 1994
Don Bassingthwaite, *As One Dead*, 1996
Robert Weinberg, *The Unbeholden*, 1996

## 2513

### LAURELL K. HAMILTON

## Blue Moon

(New York: Ace, 1998)

**Story type:** Horror (Vampire Story)
**Series:** Anita Blake, Vampire Hunter
**Major character(s):** Anita Blake, Vampire Hunter, Detective—Private; Richard Zeeman, Werewolf, Student (working on thesis), Teacher (high school); Frank Niley, Real Estate Agent (developer)
**Time period(s):** 1990s (1998)
**Locale(s):** Myerton, Tennessee, Alternate Earth

**Summary:** Anita Blake finds herself torn between her vampire lover, Jean-Claude, and old flame Richard Zeeman when Richard is accused of rape in rural Tennessee. Anita speeds to Richard's defense and finds evidence of a frame-up to protect a local businessman and his interests. Eighth novel in the Anita Blake series, set in a world where vampires, human beings and creatures of the supernatural uneasily co-exist.

**Other books you might like:**
Richard Lee Byers, *On a Darkling Plain*, 1995
Tanya Huff, *Blood Price*, 1991
Nick Pollotta, *Full Moonster*, 1992
Denise Vitola, *Opalite Moon*, 1997

## 2514

### LAURELL K. HAMILTON

## Burnt Offerings

(New York: Ace, 1998)

**Story type:** Horror (Vampire Story)
**Series:** Anita Blake, Vampire Hunter
**Major character(s):** Anita Blake, Vampire Hunter; Jean-Claude, Vampire, Businessman (night club owner); Asher, Vampire
**Time period(s):** 1990s (1998)
**Locale(s):** St. Louis, Missouri, Alternate Earth

**Summary:** This is the seventh adventure of Anita Blake, Vampire Hunter, who lives in an alternate world where humans, vampires and other creatures of the supernatural co-exist. This time Anita attempts to sustain her romantic attachment to vampire leader Jean-Claude, while becoming embroiled in an internecine war between the vampire and werewolf societies, and trying to apprehend a supernaturally endowed pyromaniac who is torching the vampire strongholds.

**Other books you might like:**
Nancy A. Collins, *A Dozen Black Roses*, 1997
Barbara Hambly, *Those Who Hunt the Night*, 1998
Tanya Huff, *Blood Trail*, 1992
Robert Weinberg, *Blood War*, 1995
    editor
Robert Weinberg, *Unholy Allies*, 1995

## 2515

### LAURELL K. HAMILTON

## Circus of the Damned

(New York: Ace, 1995)

**Story type:** Horror (Vampire Story)
**Series:** Anita Blake, Vampire Hunter
**Major character(s):** Anita Blake, Vampire Hunter (animator), Detective—Private; Jean-Claude, Vampire; Larry Kirkland, Psychic (animator), Vampire Hunter
**Time period(s):** 1990s (1995)
**Locale(s):** St. Louis Missouri, Alternate Earth

**Summary:** In an alternate America where vampires coexist with human beings and are achieving equal rights under their rule, animator Anita Blake, who resurrects dead bodies as part of her crime-solving activities, becomes a prize fought for by Jean-Claude, the reigning vampire master of St. Louis, and a vampire interloper, Alejandro, who aspires to become the new master of the city. This is the third novel in the author's "Anita Blake: Vampire Hunter" series, after *The Laughing Corpse* and *Guilty Pleasures*.

**Other books you might like:**
Richard Lee Byers, *Netherworld*, 1995
Richard Lee Byers, *On a Darkling Plain*, 1995
Robert Weinberg, *Blood War*, 1995
Robert Weinberg, *Unholy Allies*, 1995

## 2516

### LAURELL K. HAMILTON

## Death of a Darklord

(Lake Geneva, WI: TSR, 1995)

**Story type:** Horror (Reanimated Dead)
**Series:** Ravenloft
**Major character(s):** Jonathan Ambrose, Investigator (mage finder); Tereza Ambrose, Magician (mage); Harkon Lukas, Minstrel
**Time period(s):** Indeterminate
**Locale(s):** Cortton Kartakass, Fictional Country

**Summary:** In the imaginary world of Ravenloft, based on the popular fantasy role-playing game, Jonathan Ambrose is summoned to the city of Cortton to get to the bottom of a recent plague of the walking dead. Jonathan discovers that the plague is part of a ruse contrived by the evil bard Harkon Lukas to instill his discorporate soul into the body of Jonathan's colleague Ambrose Burn and thereby escape into the Dark Domains.

**Other books you might like:**
Mark Anthony, *Tower of Doom*, 1994
Elaine Bergstrom, *Baronness of Blood*, 1995
Elaine Bergstrom, *Tapestry of Dark Souls*, 1992
P.N. Elrod, *I, Strahd*, 1993
Christie Golden, *The Enemy Within*, 1993
J. Robert King, *Carnival of Fear*, 1992
Chet Williamson, *Mordenheim*, 1994

## 2517

### LAURELL K. HAMILTON

## Guilty Pleasures

(New York: Ace, 1993)

**Story type:** Fantasy (Mystery)
**Series:** Anita Blake, Vampire Hunter

**Major character(s):** Anita Blake, Vampire Hunter (reanimator), Detective—Private; Nikolaus, Vampire, Leader; Zachary, Reanimated Dead, Criminal
**Time period(s):** Indeterminate
**Locale(s):** Alternate Earth

**Summary:** In an alternate world in which humans and the undead co-exist uneasily, mortal detective Anita Blake is forced by a 1000 year old master vampire to discover the identity of a serial murderer of vampires. Anita's investigations take her into an underworld of bizarre sexual relationships and vampire power politics which may result in Anita's own death or worse.

**Other books you might like:**
P.N. Elrod, *Bloodlist*, 1990
Barbara Hambly, *Those Who Hunt the Night*, 1988
Tanya Huff, *Blood Price*, 1991
Tanya Huff, *Blood Trail*, 1991
Mercedes Lackey, *Children of the Night*, 1990
Fred Saberhagen, *An Old Friend of the Family*, 1979

---

**2518**

### LAURELL K. HAMILTON

## *The Killing Dance*

(New York: Ace, 1997)

**Story type:** Horror (Mystery)
**Series:** Anita Blake, Vampire Hunter
**Major character(s):** Anita Blake, Vampire Hunter, Detective—Private; Richard Zeeman, Werewolf, Teacher; Jean-Claude, Vampire, Leader (master vampire)
**Time period(s):** 1990s (1997)
**Locale(s):** St. Louis, Missouri (alternate earth)

**Summary:** Torn between two lovers—Richard, a werewolf who is enjoined to fight for the leadership of his pack, and Jean-Claude, the sophisticated vampire master who takes considerable risks courting a mortal—detective Anita Blake discovers that her life is further complicated by someone who has put a bounty on her head. Set in an alternate universe where creatures of the supernatural enjoy the same civil rights as humans. Sixth in a series.

**Other books you might like:**
Nancy A. Collins, *A Dozen Black Roses*, 1996
Christopher Golden, *Of Saints and Shadows*, 1994
Tanya Huff, *Blood Trail*, 1994
Robert Weinberg, *World of Darkness: The Unbeholden*, 1996

---

**2519**

### LAURELL K. HAMILTON

## *The Laughing Corpse*

(New York: Ace, 1994)

**Story type:** Fantasy (Mystery; Horror)
**Series:** Anita Blake, Vampire Hunter
**Major character(s):** Anita Blake, Vampire Hunter (reanimator), Detective—Private; Jean-Claude, Vampire (master vampire of the city); Dominga Salvatore, Religious (voodoo priestess), Criminal
**Time period(s):** Indeterminate
**Locale(s):** St. Louis Missouri, Alternate Earth

**Summary:** When Dominga Salvatore creates durable zombies by reincorporating the deceased's soul, the police require Anita Blake's help to stop her.

**Other books you might like:**
Lois McMaster Bujold, *The Spirit Ring*, 1992

Tanya Huff, *Blood Price*, 1991
Tanya Huff, *Blood Trail*, 1991
Christopher Moore, *Practical Demonkeeping*, 1992
Nick Pollotta, *Bureau 13*, 1991
Margaret Weis, *Fire Sea*, 1991
  Tracy Hickman, co-author

---

**2520**

### LAURELL K. HAMILTON

## *The Lunatic Cafe*

(New York: Ace, 1996)

**Story type:** Horror (Vampire Story; Werewolf Story)
**Series:** Anita Blake, Vampire Hunter
**Major character(s):** Anita Blake, Vampire Hunter, Detective—Private; Richard Zeeman, Werewolf, Teacher (high school); Edward Forrester, Criminal (assassin)
**Time period(s):** 1990s (1996)
**Locale(s):** St. Louis Missouri, Alternate Earth

**Summary:** In an alternate universe where supernatural beings and mortals are on equal terms, Anita Blake, a human member of the Regional Preternatural Investigation Team, infiltrates the insular society of lycanthropes and shape-shifters to discover why lycanthropes are disappearing without a trace and whether it is related to the murders being committed by an apparent rogue werewolf.

**Other books you might like:**
Nancy A. Collins, *Wild Blood*, 1994
Tanya Huff, *Blood Trail*, 1992
Richard Jaccoma, *The Werewolf's Tale*, 1988

---

**2521**

### LAURELL K. HAMILTON

## *Nightseer*

(New York: Roc, 1992)

**Story type:** Fantasy (Magic Conflict)
**Major character(s):** Keleios, Sorceress, Fiance(e); Lothor, Sorcerer, Fiance(e)
**Time period(s):** Indeterminate
**Locale(s):** Zeln's Castle, Mythical Place

**Summary:** In a prophetic dream at Zeln's Castle, Keleios foresees treachery and invasion. On waking, her warning fails to prevent the assault and destruction. Keleios and Lothor work to defeat the attacking demons and the sorceress who directs them. Author's first novel.

**Other books you might like:**
Emma Bull, *War for the Oaks*, 1987
Louise Cooper, *The Deceiver*, 1991
Mary Gentle, *Rats and Gargoyles*, 1991
P.C. Hodgell, *God Stalk*, 1982
Deborah Talmadge-Bickmore, *The Apprentice*, 1990

---

**2522**

### PETER F. HAMILTON

## *Conflict*

(New York: Warner Aspect, 1998)

**Story type:** Science Fiction (Space Opera; Theological)

**Series:** Neutronium Alchemist
**Major character(s):** Fletcher Christian, Historical Figure, Reanimated Dead; Bonnie Lewin, Hunter, Reanimated Dead; Dr. Alkad Mzu, Scientist, Avenger
**Time period(s):** 27th century
**Locale(s):** New California, Planet—Imaginary; Tranquility, Space Station

**Summary:** The war between the Possessed and the Living continues as the organization spreads from New California, while Dr. Mzu aims to use the Neutronium Alchemist to extinguish a sun in her quest for revenge. The Possessed know this, but cannot be allowed to capture either it or the doctor, since being dead is no longer an escape.

**Other books you might like:**
Iain M. Banks, *Use of Weapons*, 1992
Nancy Kress, *Beggars in Spain*, 1993
Ian McDonald, *Terminal Cafe*, 1994
Vonda N. McIntyre, *Metaphase*, 1992
Walter Jon Williams, *Metropolitan*, 1995

## 2523
### PETER F. HAMILTON
## Consolidation
(New York: Warner Aspect, 1998)

**Story type:** Science Fiction (Space Opera; Theological)
**Series:** Neutronium Alchemist
**Major character(s):** Joshua Calvert, Spaceship Captain; Al Capone, Historical Figure, Reanimated Dead
**Time period(s):** 27th century
**Locale(s):** New California, Planet—Imaginary; Tranquility, Space Station

**Summary:** The returned dead exist everywhere, fighting to seize control of planets and then removing those planets from the universe. Adding to the chaos, rogue scientist Alkad Mzu escapes with a weapon that can destroy stars.

**Other books you might like:**
Iain M. Banks, *Excession*, 1997
James Blish, *A Case of Conscience*, 1958
Glen Cook, *The Dragon Never Sleeps*, 1988
Frank Herbert, *Dune*, 1965
Vernor Vinge, *A Fire upon the Deep*, 1992

## 2524
### PETER F. HAMILTON
## Emergence
(New York: Warner Aspect, 1997)

**Story type:** Science Fiction (Science Fiction; Political)
**Major character(s):** Joshua Calvert, Businessman, Spaceman; Quinn Dexter, Religious
**Time period(s):** 26th century
**Locale(s):** Human Confederation, Interstellar Empire/Federation; Lalonde, Planet—Imaginary

**Summary:** Conflict arises between two fundamentally different starfaring cultures, the Edenists, genetically altered telepathic humans with sentient biological spaceships, and the Adamists, wizards of nanotechnology and computer science. First half of UK edition, *The Reality Dysfunction*, continued in *Expansion*.

**Other books you might like:**
Roger MacBride Allen, *The Ring of Charon*, 1990

Cheryl J. Franklin, *Fire Crossing*, 1991
Cheryl J. Franklin, *Fire Get*, 1987
Cheryl J. Franklin, *Fire Lord*, 1989
Frank Herbert, *Dune*, 1965
Vernor Vinge, *A Fire upon the Deep*, 1992

## 2525
### PETER F. HAMILTON
## Expansion
(New York: Warner, 1997)

**Story type:** Science Fiction (Space Opera)
**Series:** The Reality Dysfunction
**Major character(s):** Graeme Nicholson, Journalist (reporter); Jenny Harris, Spacewoman; Joshua Calvert, Spaceman
**Time period(s):** 27th century
**Locale(s):** Outer Space

**Summary:** Humanity struggles to defeat the horrifying invasion that began in *Emergence* as it leapfrogs from one inhabited planet to the next across the galaxy. The invaders are truly nightmarish, a horde of the undead, with superpowers that fly in the face of both human science and religion.

**Other books you might like:**
Iain M. Banks, *Excession*, 1997
Greg Bear, *Eternity*, 1988
Victor Koman, *The Jehovah Contract*, 1987
Dan Simmons, *Endymion*, 1996
Dan Simmons, *The Rise of Endymion*, 1997
Vernor Vinge, *A Fire upon the Deep*, 1992

## 2526
### PETER F. HAMILTON
## Mindstar Rising
(New York: Tor, 1996)

**Story type:** Science Fiction (Psychic Powers; Techno-Thriller)
**Series:** Greg Mandel
**Major character(s):** Greg Mandel, Psychic, Detective; Philip Evans, Industrialist, Disembodied Personality; Juliet "Julie" Evans, Cyborg
**Time period(s):** 21st century
**Locale(s):** England

**Summary:** Given a gland by the military which imparts psychic abilities, Greg Mandel gets his way. Philip Evans of Event Horizon, at the forefront of everything, hires Greg to find the saboteur who killed him. Having transferred to a computer before death, Evans helps prevent the saboteur from destroying Event Horizon. First novel originally published in the UK in 1993.

**Other books you might like:**
Poul Anderson, *Harvest of Stars*, 1993
Julian May, *Magnificat*, 1996
Victor Milan, *The Cybernetic Samurai*, 1985
Kim Stanley Robinson, *Green Mars*, 1994
George Turner, *Genetic Soldier*, 1994

## 2527

**PETER F. HAMILTON**

### A Quantum Murder

(New York: Tor, 1997)

**Story type:** Science Fiction (Psychic Powers; Mystery)
**Series:** Greg Mandel
**Major character(s):** Greg Mandel, Psychic, Detective; Edward Kitchener, Scientist; Eleanor Mandel, Spouse, Detective
**Time period(s):** 21st century
**Locale(s):** England

**Summary:** Ex-military psychic Greg Mandel tries to make an honest living, following the fall of the Marxist government in England. Then Event Horizon, the corporation that employed him in the past, calls him in to investigate the death of a double Nobel laureate. There are too many leads, and some of them point to Mandel's uncomfortable past. Second in series, following *Mindstar Rising* and preceding *The Nano Flower*.

**Other books you might like:**
Isaac Asimov, *The Caves of Steel*, 1954
Alfred Bester, *The Demolished Man*, 1996
Pat Cadigan, *Fools*, 1992
Larry Niven, *The Long Arm of Gil Hamilton*, 1976
Richard Paul Russo, *Destroying Angel*, 1992

## 2528

**VIRGINIA HAMILTON**

### Her Stories

(New York: Scholastic/The Blue Sky Press, 1995)

**Story type:** Fantasy (Collection; Legend)

**Summary:** Contains a three-page introduction and five-page afterword about the stories, two pages of useful sources and 19 stories, legends, and tales divided into five sections: ''Her Animal Tales,'' ''Her Fairy Tales,'' ''Her Supernatural,'' ''Her Folkways and Legends,'' and ''Her True Tales.'' While endeavoring to retain the original flavor, Hamilton retells for younger readers African American women's tales which focus on females in various forms, concluding each with a comment.

**Other books you might like:**
Ethel Johnston Phelps, *Tatterhood and Other Tales*, 1978
    editor
Paul Radin, *African Folktales and Sculpture*, 1952
    editor
Manly Wade Wellman, *Cahena*, 1979
Jane Yolen, *Favorite Folktales From around the World*, 1986
    editor
Richard Young, *African-American Folktales for Young Readers: Including Favorite Stories From African and African-American Storytellers*, 1993
    editor
Jack Zipes, *Don't Bet on the Prince*, 1986
    editor

## 2529

**IAN HAMMELL**

### Clock Strikes Sword

(New York: Ace, 1995)

**Story type:** Fantasy (Political; Adventure)

**Series:** Shadow World
**Major character(s):** Aivlys Platho, Apprentice (watchmaker), Magician; Endimin Platho, Artisan (watchmaker), Magician; Beroth of Firoze, Warrior
**Time period(s):** Indeterminate
**Locale(s):** Firoze, Fictional City (city state); Gnomon, Fictional City (city state)

**Summary:** Known as home to fierce warriors, Firoze must unite with a traditional enemy, Gnomon, whose clockmakers wield power over time itself, to defeat the Vargan expansionism which threatens their island. Game tie-in.

**Other books you might like:**
Clayton Emery, *Shattered Chains*, 1995
Greg Gorden, *Prophecy*, 1994
Michael Moorcock, *Elric of Melnibone*, 1976
Margaret Weis, *Dragon Wing*, 1990
    Tracy Hickman, co-author
Martha Wells, *The Element of Fire*, 1993

## 2530

**MICHAEL HAMMOND**

### The Burning Man

(New York: Zebra/Pinnacle, 1991)

**Story type:** Horror (Wild Talents)
**Major character(s):** Maggie Converse, Journalist; Sam Cutter, Paranormal Investigator; Jonathan Hill, Aged Person
**Time period(s):** 1980s (1988)
**Locale(s):** Boulder, Colorado; Clear Creek, Virginia

**Summary:** Maggie Converse, Sam Cutter and Jonathan Hill all share the same disturbing dream of a blonde-haired man who bursts into flame and dies in agony. But their efforts to pool their paranormal talents and dredge up the subconscious memories necessary to decipher the dream are repeatedly thwarted by Soviet agents with paranormal talents—and inscrutable motives—of their own.

**Other books you might like:**
Ramsey Campbell, *Incarnate*, 1983
John Farris, *The Fury*, 1976
Stephen King, *Firestarter*, 1980
Brian Lumley, *Necroscope*, 1988

## 2531

**NEIL HANCOCK**

### The Bridge of Dawn

(New York: Popular Library Questar, 1991)

**Story type:** Fantasy (Quest)
**Series:** Windameir Circle
**Major character(s):** Owen Helwin, Warrior
**Time period(s):** Indeterminate Past
**Locale(s):** Atlanton Earth, Fictional Country

**Summary:** Armed with the majestic Sword of Skye, Owen Helwin must win the aid of bears, sea beasts and the High Dragon. With their strength he plans to save beloved Lady Deros. Evil forces have gathered at the mystic Bridge of Dawn for the ultimate battle.

**Other books you might like:**
David Eddings, *Magician's Gambit*, 1983
David Eddings, *Pawn of Prophecy*, 1982
David Eddings, *Queen of Sorcery*, 1982
J.R.R. Tolkien, *The Fellowship of the Ring*, 1954
J.R.R. Tolkien, *The Return of the King*, 1956

J.R.R. Tolkien, *The Two Towers*, 1955

## 2532

### ELIZABETH HAND

## *12 Monkeys*

(New York: HarperPrism, 1995)

**Story type:** Science Fiction (Time Travel; Post-Disaster)
**Major character(s):** James Cole, Time Traveler, Criminal; Kathryn Railly, Doctor (psychiatrist)
**Time period(s):** 21st century; 1990s
**Locale(s):** Washington, District of Columbia; Baltimore, Maryland; Philadelphia, Pennsylvania

**Summary:** In exchange for a commuted sentence, James Cole accepts a dangerous reconnaissance mission to 1996, hoping to find evidence of the Army of the 12 Monkeys and the origin of the plague which devastated Earth's population. Mistakenly sent to 1990, James Cole meets Kathryn Railly who later assists him on a subsequent mission to 1996. Novelizes the film.

**Other books you might like:**
Poul Anderson, *The Time Patrol*, 1991
Randall Frakes, *Terminator 2: Judgment Day*, 1991
S.D. Perry, *Timecop*, 1994
Robert Tine, *Universal Soldier*, 1992
Robert Charles Wilson, *A Bridge of Years*, 1991

## 2533

### ELIZABETH HAND

## *AEstival Tide*

(New York: Bantam Spectra, 1992)

**Story type:** Science Fiction (Genetic Manipulation; End of the World)
**Series:** The Coming of the Magdalene
**Major character(s):** Reive, Genetically Altered Being (hermaphrodite); Nefertity, Artificial Intelligence; Margalis Tast'annin, Military Personnel (Aviator Imperator)
**Time period(s):** Indeterminate
**Locale(s):** Araboth, Fictional City

**Summary:** Events drag the fortune teller, Reive, to the highest levels of Araboth, a huge and ancient labyrinthian city built on even older foundations. Reive must negotiate a series of plots and strange events to live even as long as the celebration of AEstival Tide, much less survive the apocalypse that may follow. Sequel to *Winterlong*.

**Other books you might like:**
C.J. Cherryh, *Sunfall*, 1981
John Crowley, *Little, Big*, 1981
Richard Grant, *Through the Heart*, 1991
Ian McDonald, *Desolation Road*, 1988
Gene Wolfe, *The Shadow of the Torturer*, 1980

## 2534

### ELIZABETH HAND

## *The Frenchman*

(New York: Harper, 1997)

**Story type:** Horror (Serial Killer)
**Series:** Millennium

**Major character(s):** Frank Black, FBI Agent (former); Robert Bletcher, Detective—Homicide; Catherine Black, Housewife (Frank's wife)
**Time period(s):** 1990s (1997)
**Locale(s):** Seattle, Washington

**Summary:** A serial killer is murdering people in Seattle's sexual underground as part of his plan for apocalyptic cleansing. Ex-FBI agent Frank Black, on the run to protect his family from a predator stalking them, lends his psychic powers of deduction to solving the case. Novelization of the pilot for the Fox television series "Millennium," about a group of special agents who work covertly to solve weird crimes inspired by millennial fanaticism.

**Other books you might like:**
Kevin J. Anderson, *The X-Files: Ruins*, 1996
Lewis Gannett, *Gehenna*, 1997
Charles L. Grant, *The X-Files: Goblins*, 1994
Thomas Harris, *Red Dragon*, 1981
Garry Kilworth, *Angel*, 1993

## 2535

### ELIZABETH HAND

## *Glimmering*

(New York: HarperPrism, 1997)

**Story type:** Science Fiction (Disaster; Future Shock)
**Major character(s):** Jack Finnegan, Publisher, Recluse (AIDS survivor); Leonard Thorpe, Filmmaker; Trip Marlowe, Musician
**Time period(s):** 1990s (1999)
**Locale(s):** Yonkers, New York

**Summary:** The Millennium waits under a cloud of greenhouse gasses that turns the sky into a glowing sheet of color, while a dying publisher, a rock star obsessed by virtual reality, and the "Hyacinth Girl" wait in a dilapidated mansion for the end times. Then an enigmatic social observer arrives with a mystery, a cure, and the threat of the new.

**Other books you might like:**
J.G. Ballard, *The Drought*, 1976
Pat Cadigan, *Synners*, 1991
Stuart Gordon, *Smile on the Void*, 1981
Jonathan Lethem, *Amnesia Moon*, 1995
Michaela Roessner, *Vanishing Point*, 1993

## 2536

### ELIZABETH HAND

## *Icarus Descending*

(New York: Bantam Spectra, 1993)

**Story type:** Science Fiction (Genetic Manipulation; Political)
**Major character(s):** Margalis Tast'annin, Military Personnel (Imperator of Ascendant forces); Aidan Harrow, Disembodied Personality
**Time period(s):** 26th century
**Locale(s):** Earth; Outer Space

**Summary:** For centuries the Ascendants have ruled Earth from orbiting space stations, aided by bioengineered geneslaves, the energumens. Now the energumens intend to overthrow the Ascendants and unite the bioengineered slaves in a rebellion against humanity. When sent to investigate, Tast'annin discovers an ancient threat to all life on Earth, one requiring energumen help to oppose.

**Other books you might like:**
Philip K. Dick, *Blade Runner*, 1982

Dave Duncan, *Hero*, 1993
Thomas A. Easton, *Greenhouse*, 1991
Thomas A. Easton, *Sparrowhawk*, 1990
Cordwainer Smith, *Norstrilia*, 1975
Michael Swanwick, *Vacuum Flowers*, 1987
Michael D. Weaver, *My Father Immortal*, 1989
Walter Jon Williams, *Voice of the Whirlwind*, 1987

---

## 2537

### ELIZABETH HAND

## *Last Summer at Mars Hill*

(New York: Harper Prism, 1998)

**Story type:** Fantasy (Collection; Contemporary Realism)

**Summary:** This collection contains 11 short stories and one poem, written from 1988 to 1994, featuring fantastic elements intruding into everyday life. Among the stories: two teenagers face their parents' very different reactions to terminal illness, a young woman watches a musician's charmed life come to a horrifying end, and justice arrives in an Oklahoma town with the aid of an ancient force.

**Other books you might like:**
John Crowley, *Antiquities*, 1993
Lisa Goldstein, *Travelers in Magic*, 1994
Megan Lindholm, *Wizard of the Pigeons*, 1986
Pat Murphy, *Points of Departure*, 1990
Connie Willis, *Impossible Things*, 1994

---

## 2538

### ELIZABETH HAND

## *Waking the Moon*

(New York: HarperPrism, 1995)

**Story type:** Fantasy (Magic Conflict; Religious)
**Major character(s):** Katherine Sweeney Cassidy, Anthropologist; Angelica di Rienzi, Anthropologist, Religious; Anne Marie "Annie" Harmon, Musician, Lesbian
**Time period(s):** 1970s; 1990s
**Locale(s):** Washington, District of Columbia; Sedona, Arizona

**Summary:** When signs portend a return of the goddess Othiym, Angelica di Rienzi utilizes a powerful sacred object and human sacrifices to facilitate Othiym's return. Meanwhile, an ancient society that promotes patriarchal religions, the Benandanti, works surreptitiously at the University of the Archangels and St. John the Divine to prevent the return of Othiym and the associated bloody worship practices.

**Other books you might like:**
A.A. Attanasio, *The Moon's Wife: A Hystery*, 1993
Charles de Lint, *Memory and Dream*, 1994
Pamela Dean, *Tam Lin*, 1991
Mary Gentle, *Rats and Gargoyles*, 1991
P.C. Hodgell, *God Stalk*, 1982
Patricia A. McKillip, *The Book of Atrix Wolfe*, 1995

---

## 2539

### ELIZABETH HAND

## *Winterlong*

(New York: Bantam Spectra, 1990)

**Story type:** Science Fiction (Post-Holocaust; Genetic Manipulation)

**Series:** The Coming of the Magdalene
**Major character(s):** Wendy Wanders, Genetically Altered Being (empath); Justice Saint-Alaban, Scientist (laboratory aid); Miss Scarlet Pan, Actress, Genetically Altered Being
**Time period(s):** Indeterminate Future
**Locale(s):** North America

**Summary:** When the city's new governor decides to terminate a weapons research program, Wendy Wanders avoids death by fleeing with the help of Justice Saint-Alaban. They find sanctuary when asked to join an acting troupe. Their strange and dangerous odyssey through the Narrow Forrest to the Engulfed Cathedral leads them to the final confrontation with the governor at a Grand Masque, the culmination of the Feast of Winterlong. This first person narrative has subtexts drawn from Middle Eastern mythologies, the Demeter/Persephone myth and Bible stories.

**Other books you might like:**
Octavia E. Butler, *Adulthood Rites*, 1988
Octavia E. Butler, *Dawn*, 1987
Octavia E. Butler, *Imago*, 1989
Philip K. Dick, *Blade Runner*, 1982
Robert Silverberg, *Tower of Glass*, 1970

---

## 2540

### LYNN HANNA

## *The Starry Child*

(New York: Penguin Onyx, 1998)

**Story type:** Fantasy (Contemporary; Romance)
**Major character(s):** Matt Macinnes, Linguist; Sasha Nielson, Child, Reincarnated Person; Rainey Nielson, Widow(er)
**Time period(s):** 1990s
**Locale(s):** Stanford, California (Stanford University)

**Summary:** Since her father's death, young Sasha has not spoken one intelligible word, while thunderstorms bring out extremely odd behavior in her. At her wit's end, Sasha's mother tries to keep the little girl out of an institution. Then a brilliant linguist recognizes the girl's babbling as fluent Gaelic and raises the possibility that the child is living in a past life.

**Other books you might like:**
Marina Fitch, *The Seventh Heart*, 1997
Diana Gabaldon, *Outlander*, 1991
Lynn Kurland, *Stardust of Yesterday*, 1996
Linda Nevins, *Renaissance Moon*, 1997
Christina Skye, *Bride of the Mist*, 1996

---

## 2541

### MARY K. HANNER

## *Rapid Growth*

(New York: Dell/Abyss, 1993)

**Story type:** Horror (Science Fiction)
**Major character(s):** Alan Campbell, Doctor (surgeon); Katie Campbell, Researcher (research assistant); Robbie Campbell, Child (8 years old)
**Time period(s):** 1990s (1993)
**Locale(s):** Serenity Hills, California

**Summary:** Exposure to electromagnetic radiation from a poorly regulated producer of microwave ovens causes a plague of teratomas—humanoid tumors that eat their way out of a body—among the residents of Serenity Hills. First novel.

**Other books you might like:**
John Blackburn, *For Fear of Little Men*, 1972
T.J. Kirby, *Dangerous Nature*, 1993
John Skipp, *The Bridge: A Horror Story*, 1991
    Craig Spector, co-author
Peter Straub, *Floating Dragon*, 1982

---

**2542**

W.A. HARBINSON

## Dream Maker

(New York: Walker, 1992)

**Story type:** Science Fiction (Invasion of Earth; Alternate Intelligence)
**Major character(s):** Tony Rydell, Scientist (NASA); Clare Holton, Government Official (scientific liaison officer)
**Time period(s):** 21st century
**Locale(s):** Washington, District of Columbia; South America; Antarctica

**Summary:** While investigating ozone layer depletion over Antarctica, Tony encounters a UFO helping advance the ozone depletion. After returning to Washington, Tony enlists Clare's help to investigate the ozone depletion, a quest which demands greater sacrifice than either expects when they discover the Dream Maker, an inorganic intelligence which feeds on human minds, driving them into demonic reaches of the subconscious.

**Other books you might like:**
Martin Amis, *Time's Arrow*, 1991
Fredric Brown, *The Mind Thing*, 1961
Octavia E. Butler, *Survivor*, 1978
Hal Clement, *Needle*, 1950
Garfield Reeves-Stevens, *Nighteyes*, 1989
Kurt Vonnegut Jr., *Slaughterhouse Five*, 1969

---

**2543**

TERRI HARDIN, Editor

## Supernatural Tales From around the World

(New York: Barnes & Noble, 1995)

**Story type:** Horror (Anthology)

**Summary:** The 221 brief tales collected here are retellings of legends, folk tales and accounts from the oral tradition of supernatural beings and goings on. Divided into four geographic sections that include Europe, the Americas, Africa and the Near East, and Asia and the Pacific, the book presents accounts of the witches, ghosts, vampires, werewolves, and other traditional beings of the supernatural, as well as certain indigenous monsters such as the banshee (Ireland), the bouda (India), and the tengu (Japan).

**Other books you might like:**
John Canning, *50 Great Ghost Stories*, 1971
    editor
D.J. Enright, *The Oxford Book of the Supernatural*, 1994
    editor
Charles Lindley, *The Ghost Book of Charles Lindley, Viscount Halifax*, 1994
Elliott O'Donnell, *Ghosts: Stories of the Supernatural*, 1959
Elliott O'Donnell, *Strange Disappearances*, 1990
Jessica Amanda Salmonson, *The Mysterious Doom and Other Ghostly Tales of the Pacific Northwest*, 1992
John Manchip White, *Whistling Past the Churchyard*,

---

**2544**

DONALD HARINGTON

## The Cockroaches of Stay More

(New York: Harcourt Brace Jovanovich, 1989)

**Story type:** Fantasy (Satire)
**Major character(s):** Tish Dingletoon, Animal (Female Cockroach); Sam Ingledew, Animal (Male Cockroach)
**Time period(s):** 1980s
**Locale(s):** Stay More, Arkansas

**Summary:** This is a religious parable, a plea for tolerance and an insectile love story.

**Other books you might like:**
Brian Brett, *The Fungus Garden*, 1988
Stephen Fine, *Molly Dear: The Autobiography of an Android*, 1988

---

**2545**

CHARLES L. HARNESS

## Lunar Justice

(New York: Avon, 1991)

**Story type:** Science Fiction (Psychic Powers; Political)
**Major character(s):** Quentin Thomas, Psychic, Lawyer; Michael Dore, Genius, Philanthropist; Martin Rile, Judge
**Time period(s):** Indeterminate Future
**Locale(s):** Oldcolumbia; Patuxet Haven; Lunaplex, Montenegro

**Summary:** Quentin Thomas, patent attorney for Penal Systems, Incorporated, suddenly finds himself forced to accompany a guillotine to Lunaplex. While there he is contacted by Michael Dore, initiator of the Lamplighter Project which will turn Jupiter into a sun and convert its outer moons into habitable planets. Michael Dore is charged with treason, a capital offense, for taking money for Lamplighter and failing to produce a sun. Thomas, compelled to defend Dore, is appalled by the Lunar Justice System.

**Other books you might like:**
Alfred Bester, *The Stars My Destination*, 1956
Pat Cadigan, *Mindplayers*, 1987
Frank Herbert, *The Dosadi Experiment*, 1977
Katharine Kerr, *Polar City Blues*, 1990
Frederik Pohl, *Gladiator-at-Law*, 1955
    C.M. Kornbluth, co-author
A.E. Van Vogt, *Slan*, 1946

---

**2546**

CHARLES L. HARNESS

## Lurid Dreams

(New York: Avon, 1990)

**Story type:** Science Fiction (Time Travel; Alternate Universe)
**Major character(s):** William Reynolds, Student, Time Traveler; Wellington Birch, Military Personnel (colonel), Time Traveler; Alix Schell, Student
**Time period(s):** 1990s (1990); 19th century
**Locale(s):** Baltimore, Maryland; Gettysburg, Pennsylvania

**Summary:** William Reynolds has only one chance to get his doctoral thesis in "Out-of-Body Experiences - History and Techniques" approved. He must fulfill the conditions of the grant offered by Colonel Wellington Birch. He wants William and Alix to combine their talents and send William back in time to convince Edgar Allan

Poe to give up his literary aspirations. A computer extrapolation has shown that if Poe had pursued his forgotten military career, he would have been the General at the Battle of Gettysburg to turn the tide of the Civil War and allow the South to win.

**Other books you might like:**
James P. Blaylock, *Homunculus*, 1986
Randall Frakes, *The Terminator*, 1985
    Bill Wisher, co-author
Joe Haldeman, *The Forever War*, 1975
Joe Haldeman, *The Hemingway Hoax*, 1990
Tim Powers, *The Anubis Gates*, 1983
John Varley, *Millennium*, 1983

`2547`

**CHARLES L. HARNESS**

## An Ornament to His Profession

(Framingham, Massachusetts: NESFA Press, 1998)

**Story type:** Science Fiction (Collection)

**Summary:** This collection of 17 stories covers the author's career from 1948 to 1994, and includes his classic short novel *The Rose*. Several of the stories have introductions and there is an extensive bibliography and other material about the author. One of the stories is original to this book.

**Other books you might like:**
Arthur C. Clarke, *More than One Universe*, 1991
Harry Harrison, *Galactic Dreams*, 1994
Damon Knight, *One Side Laughing: Stories Unlike Other Stories*, 1994
Murray Leinster, *First Contacts: The Essential Murray Leinster*, 1998
Theodore Sturgeon, *Thunder and Roses*, 1997

`2548`

**ANDREW HARPER** (Pseudonym of Douglas Clegg)

## Bad Karma

(New York: Kensington, 1997)

**Story type:** Horror (Psychological Suspense)
**Major character(s):** Trey Campbell, Health Care Professional (mental health); Agnes Hatcher, Patient
**Time period(s):** 1990s (1997)
**Locale(s):** Catalina Island, California

**Summary:** Under the impression that she is the reincarnation of a century-old prostitute and that mental health specialist Trey Campbell is the reincarnation of her former lover, psychiatric patient Agnes Hatcher effects a bloody escape from Darden State Hospital and high-tails it to Catalina Island, where Trey is vacationing. Agnes will stop at nothing to be with Trey—even the murder of his wife and children.

**Other books you might like:**
Robert Bloch, *The Scarf*, 1947
Kathe Koja, *Strange Angels*, 1994
Simon Maginn, *Virgins and Martyrs*, 1995
Robert R. McCammon, *Mine*, 1990
Patrick McGrath, *Spider*, 1990

`2549`

**RORY HARPER**

## Petrogypsies

(New York: Baen Books, 1989)

**Story type:** Science Fiction (Alternate Universe)
**Major character(s):** Henry Lee McFarland, Oil Industry Worker (Petrogypsy), Farmer (Former); Doc Miller, Oil Industry Worker (Petrogypsy)
**Time period(s):** Indeterminate
**Locale(s):** Texas, Alternate Universe

**Summary:** In Harper's first novel, a race of gigantic, nonsentient, worm-like aliens has been stranded on Earth and the creatures now make their livings working as oil well drillers. The men who follow the aliens across the country taking care of them and arranging jobs for them, called petrogypsies, lead a romantic and fun-filled life. Henry Lee, a strapping young farmboy grown sick of slopping hogs, decides to leave home and take to the road as a petrogypsy.

**Other books you might like:**
Robert A. Heinlein, *Farmer in the Sky*, 1950
Rebecca Ore, *Becoming Alien*, 1987
Rebecca Ore, *Being Alien*, 1989
Allen Steele, *Orbital Decay*, 1989
Howard Waldrop, *A Dozen Tough Jobs*, 1989

`2550`

**TARA K. HARPER**

## Cat Scratch Fever

(New York: Ballantine Del Rey, 1994)

**Story type:** Science Fiction (Adventure; Psychic Powers)
**Major character(s):** Tsia, Scientist, Genetically Altered Being; Vashanna, Slave; Ramok, Mercenary
**Time period(s):** Indeterminate Future
**Locale(s):** Risthmus, Planet—Imaginary

**Summary:** After years of preparation, Tsia at last takes the guide virus that will mutate her body to create a biogate, a telepathic link to another lifeform. But prohibitions forbid human interference with the large cats, the lifeform with which she forms her gate. Suddenly kidnapped, enslaved, tortured and imprisoned, Tsia struggles to free herself, using every resource, even if it means opening her mind to the wild cats.

**Other books you might like:**
Marion Zimmer Bradley, *The Shattered Chain*, 1976
A.C. Crispin, *Silent Dances*, 1990
    Kathleen O'Malley, co-author
Gordon R. Dickson, *Masters of Everon*, 1980
Gayle Greeno, *Finders-Seekers*, 1993
Gene Wolfe, *The Shadow of the Torturer*, 1980

`2551`

**TARA K. HARPER**

## Lightwing

(New York: Ballantine Del Rey, 1992)

**Story type:** Science Fiction (Political; Psychic Powers)
**Major character(s):** Kiondili Wae, Student, Telepath; Shyh Stilman, Researcher, Scientist; Poole, Alien (Dhirrnu)
**Time period(s):** Indeterminate Future
**Locale(s):** *Mul Hunter*, Spaceship; Corson, Space Station

**Summary:** Orphaned and betrayed by the trader guild, Kiondili Wae hides her abilities to gain the training she can afford and avoid working for the guild. When proved a strong psychic, she accepts a position at Corson, where she contributes to faster than light research. When humanity develops a faster than light drive, the interstellar community will grant humans equal trade status.

**Other books you might like:**
Pauline Ashwell, *Unwillingly to Earth*, 1992
David Brin, *The Uplift War*, 1987
A.C. Crispin, *Starbridge*, 1989
Anne McCaffrey, *The Rowan*, 1990
Rebecca Ore, *Becoming Alien*, 1988
Alis A. Rasmussen, *A Passage of Stars*, 1990
Vernor Vinge, *A Fire upon the Deep*, 1992

## 2552

### TARA K. HARPER

### Shadow Leader

(New York: Ballantine/Del Rey, 1991)

**Story type:** Fantasy (Adventure)
**Major character(s):** Aranur, Martial Arts Expert; Dion, Martial Arts Expert (wolfwalker), Healer, Twin; Rhom, Twin
**Time period(s):** Indeterminate Future
**Locale(s):** Ramaj Ariye Asengar, Planet—Imaginary

**Summary:** Dion, bonded to her wolf Gray Hishn, can telepathically communicate with any wolf. With her brother and companions, Dion and her wolf work as scouts to shepherd the group through the mountains to warn their people of impending attack. Sequel to *Wolfwaker*.

**Other books you might like:**
Tom Deitz, *Soulsmith*, 1991
Mary H. Herbert, *Dark Horse*, 1990
V.E. Mitchell, *Enemy Unseen*, 1990
Andre Norton, *The Beast Master*, 1959
Melanie Rawn, *Dragon Prince*, 1988
Elizabeth Ann Scarborough, *Nothing Sacred*, 1991
Michael D. Weaver, *Wolf-Dreams*, 1989

## 2553

### TARA K. HARPER

### Wolfwalker

(New York: Del Rey, 1990)

**Story type:** Fantasy (Quest)
**Major character(s):** Dion, Martial Arts Expert (wolfwalker), Healer
**Time period(s):** Indeterminate Future
**Locale(s):** Planet—Imaginary

**Summary:** Dion and her twin brother set out on a ritual journey and encounter travelers on a quest to end a slave trading practice. Joining them in their rescue mission leads the pair into dangerous adventures and ultimately forces Dion to use her forbidden skills of psychic healing to stop a plague.

**Other books you might like:**
Mercedes Lackey, *The Oathbound*, 1988
Anne McCaffrey, *The Dragonriders of Pern Series*,
Dave Smeds, *The Sorcery Within*, 1985
Michael D. Weaver, *Wolf-Dreams*, 1989

## 2554

### JACQUELINE HARPMAN

### I Who Have Never Known Men

(New York: Seven Stories Press, 1997)

**Story type:** Science Fiction (Post-Holocaust; Literary)
**Major character(s):** I, Writer, Explorer; Anthea, Explorer; Greta, Explorer
**Time period(s):** Indeterminate Future
**Locale(s):** Earth

**Summary:** After civilization breaks down, men hold women captive in subterranean cages. By chance, at one prison the guards have just unlocked the women's door when an evacuation signal draws away all the guards. The 40 women escape, but must develop a new society, scavenging supplies from abandoned prisons and exploring the environment as time whittles away at their numbers. Winner of the 1996 Prix Medicis and translated from the 1995 French publication by Ros Schwartz. First novel published in English.

**Other books you might like:**
Richard Brautigan, *In Watermelon Sugar*, 1968
Marlen Haushofer, *The Wall*, 1991
Jean Hegland, *Into the Forest*, 1997
David R. Palmer, *Emergence*, 1984

## 2555

### JON A. HARRALD (Pseudonym of Harold Schechter and Jonna Gormley Semeiks)

### Dying Breath

(New York: Pocket/Star, 1992)

**Story type:** Horror (Psychological Suspense)
**Major character(s):** Simon Proctor, Cult Member (leader); Marianne Byrne, Police Officer; Richard Wayland, Police Officer (Chief of Stoneham police force)
**Time period(s):** 1990s (1992)
**Locale(s):** Stoneham, New York

**Summary:** In this collaborative first novel, a ritualistic animal killing, a graverobbing, a child kidnapping, and the defacing of public property with Satanic graffiti prove to be the work of Simon Proctor, a Southern California cult leader with delusions of prophethood, who has chased two lapsed disciples cross country to exact his revenge upon them.

**Other books you might like:**
Stephen R. George, *Nightscape*, 1992
Dean R. Koontz, *The Servants of Twilight*, 1984
Robert R. McCammon, *Mine*, 1990

## 2556

### BARRY HARRINGTON

### The Beyond

(New York: Diamond, 1991)

**Story type:** Horror (Possession)
**Major character(s):** Susan Holland, Designer (fashion designer); Justin Nesbitt, Musician (rock guitarist); Michael Pearl, Doctor, Administrator (of hospital)
**Time period(s):** 1990s (1991)
**Locale(s):** Groveland, New York

**Summary:** Although haunted by the memory of the night that she was assaulted and another 12-year-old was raped and killed by two teenage boys, Susan Holland returns to her hometown of Groveland to inherit her mother's estate. But Susan is unaware that the one attacker who still lives is literally haunted by the spirit of his dead companion, who has been waiting more than 20 years to finish the job he started. A first novel.

**Other books you might like:**
J.M. Dillard, *Specters*, 1991
Joe R. Lansdale, *The Nightrunners*, 1987
T.M. Wright, *Boundaries*, 1991

---

### 2557

**ALLEN LEE HARRIS**

## Let There Be Dark

(New York: Jove, 1994)

**Story type:** Horror (Small Town Horror)
**Major character(s):** Matt Hardison, Writer; Tommy Buford, Handyman; Pete Hardison, Child (Matt's son)
**Time period(s):** 1990s (1994)
**Locale(s):** Mt. Jephtha, Georgia

**Summary:** Matt Hardison returns to his rural southern hometown after his novel *The Shadowstealer*, loosely based on a local legend told him by an elderly aunt, becomes a bestseller. But Matt discovers that his book has liberated the creature of its title, a soul-stealing monster that preys upon weaknesses in human beings, and whose origins are closely tied to unremembered events in Matt's childhood.

**Other books you might like:**
Ray Bradbury, *Something Wicked This Way Comes*, 1962
Jonathan Carroll, *The Land of Laughs*, 1980
Douglas Clegg, *Goat Dance*, 1989
Elizabeth Forrest, *Dark Tide*, 1993
Robert R. McCammon, *Usher's Passing*, 1984

---

### 2558

**ANNE HARRIS**

## Accidental Creatures

(New York: Tor, 1998)

**Story type:** Science Fiction (Genetic Manipulation; Alternate Intelligence)
**Major character(s):** Helix Martin, Genetically Altered Being (Tetra), Adoptee; Hector Martin, Scientist, Researcher; Chango Chichelski, Mutant (Sport), Thief
**Time period(s):** Indeterminate Future
**Locale(s):** Detroit, Michigan (Vattown)

**Summary:** After isolating herself in her adopted father's apartment for years, Helix Martin follows an inexplicable instinct to Vattown, a Detroit neighborhood where GeneSys vatdivers harvest valuable biopolymers from a lethal growth medium. Helix soon learns that her origins and her role in the powerful GeneSys corporation intertwine far more than she ever could have imagined.

**Other books you might like:**
Lois McMaster Bujold, *Falling Free*, 1988
Valerie J. Freireich, *Testament*, 1995
Nicola Griffith, *Slow River*, 1995
Aldous Huxley, *Brave New World*, 1932
Nancy Kress, *The Beggars in Spain Trilogy*, 1993-1996
Tricia Sullivan, *Lethe*, 1995

---

### 2559

**ANNE HARRIS**

## The Nature of Smoke

(New York: Tor, 1996)

**Story type:** Science Fiction (Alternate Intelligence; Gay/Lesbian Fiction)
**Major character(s):** Magnolia, Runaway, Lesbian; Cidiera "Cid", Scientist (molecular biologist), Lesbian; Tumcari, Artificial Intelligence
**Time period(s):** 21st century
**Locale(s):** Wotroya House, Asia (Polish Siberia); Amsterdam, Netherlands

**Summary:** A runaway from the grim Detroit slums, Magnolia receives an offer from a mysterious doctor who wants to template her personality to create independently-minded robots. At his remote estate in Polish Siberia, she falls in love with Cid, a scientist trying to create a virus which allows people to see the connections between seemingly chaotic events. First novel.

**Other books you might like:**
Valerie J. Freireich, *Becoming Human*, 1995
Nicola Griffith, *Slow River*, 1995
Linda Nagata, *The Bohr Maker*, 1995
Mary Rosenblum, *The Stone Garden*, 1995
Kate Wilhelm, *Death Qualified: A Mystery of Chaos*, 1991

---

### 2560

**DEBORAH TURNER HARRIS**

## Caledon of the Mists

(New York: Ace, 1994)

**Story type:** Fantasy (Adventure; Magic Conflict)
**Series:** Caledon
**Major character(s):** Rorin McCann, Nobleman, Rebel; Duncan Dunladry, Royalty, Heir—Dispossessed; Mhairi Dunladry, Royalty, Heiress—Dispossessed
**Time period(s):** Indeterminate
**Locale(s):** Caledon, Fictional Country

**Summary:** After exiled Prince Duncan returns to Caledon to reclaim his rights from a usurper, he falls victim to a shape-shifting demon in the first battle. When his sister, Mhairi, realizes that she must carry on the dream and the fight, she rallies the people of Caledon and, as Queen, calls upon the powers of the land itself to overthrow the tyrant.

**Other books you might like:**
Diane Duane, *The Door into Sunset*, 1993
Barbara Hambly, *The Time of the Dark*, 1982
Katherine Kurtz, *The Adept*, 1991
    Deborah Turner Harris, co-author
Katherine Kurtz, *Deryni Rising*, 1970
Christopher Stasheff, *Her Majesty's Wizard*, 1986

---

### 2561

**DEBORAH TURNER HARRIS**

## The Queen of Ashes

(New York: Ace, 1995)

**Story type:** Fantasy (Political; Magic Conflict)
**Series:** Caledon

**Major character(s):** Mhairi Dunladry, Royalty (queen); Perolys na Juriam dro Sarn, Government Official; Mordance of Barquist, Widow(er), Friend
**Time period(s):** Indeterminate
**Locale(s):** Caledon, Fictional Country; Behringar, Fictional Country

**Summary:** Conflict between Caledon and Behringar leaves Mhairi open to overtures of marriage from Edwin, King of Behringar. Already unhappy with their loss of power, the Lords of Caledon plot against Mhairi, as an old, dark plot endangers them all. Second in the series.

**Other books you might like:**
Barbara Hambly, *The Time of the Dark*, 1982
Katherine Kurtz, *Deryni Rising*, 1970
Susan Schwartz, *Byzantium's Crown*, 1987
Julie Dean Smith, *Call of Madness*, 1990
Judith Tarr, *Lord of the Two Lands*, 1993
Paula Volsky, *Illusion*, 1992

---

**2562**

**MARILYN HARRIS**

## Night Games

(New York: Doubleday, 1987)

**Story type:** Horror (Psychological Suspense)
**Major character(s):** Zoe Manning, Housewife; Mary Lisa Fletcher, Actress (A childhood friend of Manning)
**Time period(s):** 1980s (1986)
**Locale(s):** Whitney, New Hampshire

**Summary:** Confused and depressed over the suicide of her parents and the instability of her marriage, Zoe returns to her childhood home, where she is taken in by a group of demented actors—who may or may not be real—who subject her to a series of "night games" that force her to confront her own deepest fears and secrets.

**Other books you might like:**
James Herbert, *The Magic Cottage*, 1986
Helen McCloy, *Through a Glass Darkly*, 1980

---

**2563**

**RAYMOND HARRIS**

## The Schizogenic Man

(New York: Ace, 1990)

**Story type:** Science Fiction (Time Travel)
**Major character(s):** John Heron, Immigrant (to New City from the Midwest), Time Traveler; Stella Cranach, Artist; MEQMAT, Computer (in charge of New City)
**Time period(s):** Indeterminate Future; 1st century B.C.
**Locale(s):** New City, Fictional City; Alexandria, Egypt

**Summary:** John Heron is sent back to Alexandrian Egypt in a so-called experiment to improve memory. There his identity is that of Nikias, who is chosen to take Kaiserion, Cleopatra's son, into exile in India. When he returns to the present, things are subtly altered—he has a son rather than a daughter—and the City is going downhill, threatened by Texas Fundamentalists. He does more Dips in the hopes of returning to his original past. Finally, under bombing and chaos, he manages to find his original self, or so he thinks.

**Other books you might like:**
John Brunner, *Times Without Number*, 1962
A. Bertram Chandler, *Kelly Country*, 1985
Crawford Kilian, *The Empire of Time*, 1978
Ward Moore, *Bring the Jubilee*, 1953

Kevin D. Randle, *Remember the Alamo!*, 1986
Robert J. Cornett, co-author

---

**2564**

**ROBERT HARRIS**

## Fatherland

(New York: Random House, 1992)

**Story type:** Science Fiction (Alternate Universe; Political)
**Major character(s):** Xavier March, Detective—Police, Police Officer; Charlotte "Charlie" Maguire, Journalist
**Time period(s):** 1960s (April 14, 1964-April 19, 1964)
**Locale(s):** Berlin, Germany

**Summary:** Twenty years after Nazi victory in World War II and a week before Hitler's 75th birthday, Xavier March and Charlie Maguire investigate the death of a once-important Nazi official. They uncover a conspiracy begun during the war which threatens the underpinning of the Nazi regime, a deal between Adolph Hitler and United States President Joseph P. Kennedy. Author's first novel.

**Other books you might like:**
Brian W. Aldiss, *The Year Before Yesterday*, 1987
Gregory Benford, *Hitler Victorious: Eleven Stories of the German Victory in World War II*, 1986
Martin H. Greenberg, co-editor
Philip K. Dick, *The Man in the High Castle*, 1962
Michael Flynn, *In the Country of the Blind*, 1990
Fritz Leiber, *The Big Time*, 1961
Norman Spinrad, *The Iron Dream*, 1972

---

**2565**

**STEVE HARRIS**

## The Eyes of the Beast

(New York: Tor, 1993)

**Story type:** Horror (Carnival/Circus Horror)
**Major character(s):** David Carter, Teenager; Sally Harrison, Office Worker; Frederick Purdue, Worker (carnival worker)
**Time period(s):** 1990s (1990)
**Locale(s):** Basingstoke, England

**Summary:** When the Adventureland fun fair comes to town, people begin disappearing from Basingstoke, and David Carter finds himself battling a variety of bizarre monsters seemingly straight out of the computer games to which he is addicted. David's investigations take him and girlfriend Sally into the dark reality behind Adventureland's gaudy carnival trappings. This book, the author's first novel, was originally published in England in 1990 as *Adventureland*.

**Other books you might like:**
Ray Bradbury, *Something Wicked This Way Comes*, 1962
Charles G. Finney, *The Circus of Dr. Lao*, 1935
Richard Laymon, *Funland*, 1990
Thomas F. Monteleone, *The Magnificent Gallery*, 1987
A.R. Morlan, *Dark Journey*, 1991

---

**2566**

**THOMAS HARRIS**

## The Silence of the Lambs

(New York: St. Martin's, 1988)

**Story type:** Horror (Serial Killer)

**Major character(s):** Clarice Starling, FBI Agent (trainee); Hannibal "Cannibal" Lector, Murderer (brilliant psychopath)
**Time period(s):** 1980s
**Locale(s):** United States

**Summary:** Starling probes the mind of the infamous ex-psychiatrist and mass murderer "Cannibal" Lector for clues in her pursuit of the bizarre serial killer, "Buffalo Bill," while Lector uses his celebrity status to engineer his own escape attempt.

**Other books you might like:**
Robert Bloch, *Psycho*, 1959
Rex Miller, *Slob*, 1987

---

**2567**

**HARRY HARRISON**
**DAVID BISCHOFF**, Co-Author

## Bill, the Galactic Hero: On the Planet of Tasteless Pleasure

(New York: Avon, 1991)

**Story type:** Science Fiction (Humor)
**Series:** Bill, the Galactic Hero
**Major character(s):** Bill, Spaceman; Irma Feritayl, Royalty; Rick, Spaceship Captain
**Time period(s):** Indeterminate Future
**Locale(s):** *Desire*, Spaceship; Planet—Imaginary

**Summary:** Bill seeks good times when he signs on with Rick in the Quest for the Holy Bar and Grill. 15 pages of humorous illustrations are included.

**Other books you might like:**
Douglas Adams, *The Hitchhiker's Guide to the Galaxy*, 1980
Henry N. Beard, *Bored of the Rings*, 1969
    Douglas C. Kenney, co-author
John M. Ford, *How Much for Just the Planet?*, 1987
Sharyn McCrumb, *Bimbos of the Death Sun*, 1987
Larry Niven, *Fallen Angels*, 1991
    Michael Flynn and Jerry Pournelle, co-authors
Leah Rewolinski, *Star Wreck: The Generation Gap*, 1990
Ken Rolston, *Extreme Paranoia: Nobody Knows the Trouble I've Shot*, 1991
Ellis Weiner, *National Lampoon's Doon*, 1984

---

**2568**

**HARRY HARRISON**
**DAVID HARRIS**, Co-Author

## Bill, the Galactic Hero: The Final Incoherent Adventure

(New York: AvoNova, 1992)

**Story type:** Science Fiction (Humor; Military)
**Series:** Bill, the Galactic Hero
**Major character(s):** Bill, Spaceman; "Captain Cadaver" Kadaffi, Military Personnel
**Time period(s):** Indeterminate Future
**Locale(s):** Eyerack, Planet—Imaginary

**Summary:** When Captain Kadaffi volunteers Bill for an assault on Eyerack, Bill moves from V.I.P. to prisoner as he searches for good times and a human foot to replace his prosthetic Swiss Army foot.

**Other books you might like:**
Douglas Adams, *The Hitchhiker's Guide to the Galaxy*, 1980

---

Henry N. Beard, *Bored of the Rings*, 1969
    Douglas C. Kenney, co-author
John M. Ford, *How Much for Just the Planet?*, 1987
Larry Niven, *Fallen Angels*, 1991
    Michael Flynn and Jerry Pournelle, co-authors
Leah Rewolinski, *Star Wreck: The Generation Gap*, 1990
Ken Rolston, *Extreme Paranoia: Nobody Knows the Trouble I've Shot*, 1991
Ellis Weiner, *National Lampoon's Doon*, 1984

---

**2569**

**HARRY HARRISON**

## Galactic Dreams

(New York: Tor, 1994)

**Story type:** Science Fiction (Collection)

**Summary:** Contains a nine-page introduction, one original story featuring Bill, the Galactic Hero, and 11 stories reprinted without prior publication acknowledgments. Themes include space opera in "Space Rats of the CCC," a dystopian solution to birth control in "A Criminal Act," a tragicomic investigation of love in "The Robot Who Wanted to Know," a teddy bear with a sinister agenda in "I Always Do What Teddy Says," a time travel paradox in "If" and racial prejudice in "Mute Milton." Companion volume to *Stainless Steel Visions*.

**Other books you might like:**
Alfred Bester, *Star Light, Star Bright*, 1976
Michael Flynn, *The Nanotech Chronicles*, 1991
Cordwainer Smith, *The Rediscovery of Man*, 1993
Theodore Sturgeon, *The Ultimate Egoist*, 1994
John Varley, *Blue Champagne*, 1986

---

**2570**

**HARRY HARRISON**
**JOHN HOLM**, Co-Author

## The Hammer and the Cross

(New York: Tor, 1993)

**Story type:** Fantasy (Historical; Religious)
**Series:** Hammer and the Cross
**Major character(s):** Shef Sigvarthsson, Hero, Blacksmith; Brand, Warrior, Sidekick; Ivar, Warrior
**Time period(s):** 9th century (865)
**Locale(s):** England

**Summary:** Born to an Englishwoman raped by a Viking raider, Shef fights the Norse invaders and follows them to rescue his step-sister, Godive. In his quest, he meets Vikings who follow the Way, worshipping the old gods while seeking to increase human knowledge in preparation for Ragnarok, the final battle between good and evil. Guided by visions of the gods, Shef develops new weapons including the halberd and the crossbow and leads his own army to victory against both pagan marauders and Christian invaders.

**Other books you might like:**
Poul Anderson, *A Midsummer Tempest*, 1984
Orson Scott Card, *Red Prophet*, 1988
C.J. Cherryh, *A Dirge for Stabis*, 1989
    Leslie Fish, co-author
L. Sprague de Camp, *Lest Darkness Fall*, 1941
John M. Ford, *The Dragon Waiting*, 1983
Parke Godwin, *Sherwood*, 1991
R.A. MacAvoy, *The Book of Kells*, 1985

Pat Winter, *Madoc's Hundred*, 1991

### 2571

**HARRY HARRISON**
**JOHN HOLM**, Co-Author

## *King and Emperor*
(New York: Tor, 1996)

**Story type:** Fantasy (Historical; Religious)
**Series:** Hammer and the Cross
**Major character(s):** Shef Sigvarthsson, Royalty (king), Scientist; Bruno, Royalty (emperor)
**Time period(s):** 9th century (875)
**Locale(s):** Spain; Italy

**Summary:** Intrigued by the offer of knowledge about flying, Shef agrees to help the Caliph of Cordova fight the alliance of Holy Roman and Byzantine Emperors. Between battles and aeronautical experiments, Shef finds the Holy Grail, learns the uses of zero, invents movable type, and discovers the destructive secret of Greek fire. When in visions he sees his father free Loki, the god of fire and trickery, portending Ragnarok and the twilight of the gods, Shef's own actions in the world may hasten the day.

**Other books you might like:**
Poul Anderson, *Hrolf Kraki's Saga*, 1973
Jean M. Auel, *The Valley of Horses*, 1982
L. Sprague de Camp, *Lest Darkness Fall*, 1941
Diana L. Paxson, *The Wolf and the Raven*, 1993
Susan Shwartz, *The Grail of Hearts*, 1992

### 2572

**HARRY HARRISON**
**JOHN HOLM**, Co-Author

## *One King's Way*
(New York: Tor, 1995)

**Story type:** Science Fiction (Alternate Universe; Fantasy)
**Series:** Hammer and the Cross
**Major character(s):** Shef Sigvarthsson, Royalty (king), Warrior; Erkenbert, Religious (deacon), Leader; Brand, Warrior, Sidekick (Shef's)
**Time period(s):** 9th century (860s)
**Locale(s):** England; At Sea; Europe

**Summary:** Having risen from slave to king of a mighty Viking nation and co-ruler of England, Shef Sigvarthsson presents a threat to all the powers of Europe. One group in particular, the Knights of the Lance, believe that he who holds the sacred spear of Christ will assume the mantle of Emperor. To that end, many factions vie to locate the spear, pull Shef from his throne, replace the Pope in Rome with someone more sympathetic to their cause, and create a new German Roman Empire. Sequel to *The Hammer and the Cross*.

**Other books you might like:**
Frans G. Bengtsson, *The Long Ships*, 1954
Marion Zimmer Bradley, *The Mists of Avalon*, 1983
Ben Bova, *Orion and the Conqueror*, 1994
Linda Evans, *Sleipnir*, 1994
Stephan Grundy, *Rhinegold*, 1994
Morgan Llywelyn, *Bard: The Odyssey of the Irish*, 1984
Morgan Llywelyn, *Lion of Ireland*, 1979
Andrew J. Offutt, *Sword of the Gael*, 1975
Diana L. Paxson, *The Wolf and the Raven*, 1993
T.H. White, *The Once and Future King*, 1958

### 2573

**HARRY HARRISON**

## *Planet of the Robot Slaves*
(New York: Avon, 1989)

**Story type:** Science Fiction (Humor)
**Series:** Bill, the Galactic Hero
**Major character(s):** Corporal Bill, Military Personnel; Cy BerPunk, Computer Expert
**Time period(s):** Indeterminate Future
**Locale(s):** Planet of the Robot Slaves, Planet—Imaginary

**Summary:** Corporal Bill and a number of other not particularly intelligent military types are marooned on a very strange and rather silly planet filled with heavy metal monsters.

**Other books you might like:**
Ron Goulart, *Brinkman*, 1981
Ron Goulart, *Hellquad*, 1984
Ron Goulart, *The Wicked Cyborg*, 1978
Barry B. Longyear, *Naked Came the Robot*, 1988
Terry Pratchett, *Equal Rites*, 1987

### 2574

**HARRY HARRISON**

## *The Stainless Steel Rat Goes to Hell*
(New York: Tor, 1996)

**Story type:** Science Fiction (Adventure; Humor)
**Series:** Stainless Steel Rat
**Major character(s):** Jim diGriz, Criminal, Adventurer; Justin Slakey, Con Artist, Professor
**Time period(s):** Indeterminate Future
**Locale(s):** Lussuoso, Planet—Imaginary; Heaven; Hell

**Summary:** Angelina diGriz disappears while investigating a scam in which a cult leader promises trips to Heaven. When Jim diGriz calls the family together to find her, he ends up in quite different places, thanks to Justin Slakey's dimension-warping device.

**Other books you might like:**
Poul Anderson, *Operation Chaos*, 1971
Piers Anthony, *Tarot*, 1987
David Brin, *The Practice Effect*, 1984
Arsen Darnay, *The Purgatory Zone*, 1981
Brad Ferguson, *The World Next Door*, 1990
Ward Hawkins, *Red Flame Burning*, 1985
Larry Niven, *Inferno*, 1976
  Jerry Pournelle, co-author
Roger Zelazny, *A Farce to Be Reckoned With*, 1995
  Robert Sheckley, co-author

### 2575

**HARRY HARRISON**

## *The Stainless Steel Rat Sings the Blues*
(New York: Bantam Spectra, 1994)

**Story type:** Science Fiction (Adventure; Humor)
**Series:** Stainless Steel Rat
**Major character(s):** Jim DiGriz, Criminal; Steengo, Spy, Musician; Madonette, Singer, Worker (electrical)
**Time period(s):** Indeterminate Future
**Locale(s):** Liokukae, Planet—Imaginary

**Summary:** Blackmailed into going to the prison planet, Liokukae, to retrieve an alien artifact that has landed there, Jim DiGriz assumes as cover the persona of a musician heading a group busted for drug possession, allowing him to travel the planet filled with criminals who have formed very strange societies.

**Other books you might like:**
Piers Anthony, *Orn*, 1971
Robert Asprin, *Phule's Company*, 1990
J.F. Bone, *Confederation Matador*, 1978
Leigh Brackett, *The Ginger Star*, 1974
A. Bertram Chandler, *The Wild Ones*, 1985
Ursula K. Le Guin, *The Eye of the Heron*, 1983
Robert Silverberg, *Hawksbill Station*, 1968
Christopher Stasheff, *We Open on Venus*, 1994
Jack Vance, *Showboat World*, 1975

---

**2576**

**HARRY HARRISON**
**BRYN BARNARD**, Illustrator

## Stainless Steel Visions
(New York: Tor, 1993)

**Story type:** Science Fiction (Collection)

**Summary:** Contains a six-page introduction plus 13 stories reprinted from periodicals and anthologies. "The Golden Years of the Stainless Steel Rat" features the protagonist from The Stainless Steel Rat series (1961- ) while "The Mothballed Spaceship" utilizes characters from *The Deathworld Trilogy* (1976). Includes "Roommates," the original story for the film, *Soylent Green*; "The Secret of Stonehenge," the basis for *Stonehenge: Where Atlantis Died* (1983); "Portrait of the Artist," which reflects Harrison's work as a comic book artist; and "The Street of Ashkelon" in a restored version.

**Other books you might like:**
David Brin, *The River of Time*, 1986
Michael Flynn, *The Nanotech Chronicles*, 1991
Ian McDonald, *Speaking in Tongues*, 1992
Larry Niven, *N-Space*, 1990
Cordwainer Smith, *The Rediscovery of Man*, 1993
John Varley, *Blue Champagne*, 1986
John Varley, *The Persistence of Vision*, 1978
Gene Wolfe, *Castle of Days*, 1992

---

**2577**

**HARRY HARRISON**

## Stars and Stripes Forever
(New York: Del Rey, 1998)

**Story type:** Science Fiction (Alternate History; Military)
**Major character(s):** Abraham Lincoln, Political Figure; President Jefferson Davis, Political Figure
**Time period(s):** 1860s
**Locale(s):** United States

**Summary:** Civil War history diverges when Prince Albert dies without smoothing over a rift between the Union and England. England enters the war on the side of the Confederacy, invading from Canada and blockading the coast. Presidents Lincoln and Davis ultimately become allies when the British inadvertently attack the wrong side.

**Other books you might like:**
Terry Bisson, *Fire on the Mountain*, 1988
John Jakes, *Black in Time*, 1970
Ward Moore, *Bring the Jubilee*, 1952

Harry Turtledove, *Between the Rivers*, 1998
Harry Turtledove, *The Guns of the South: A Novel of the Civil War*, 1992

---

**2578**

**HARRY HARRISON**, Editor
**BRUCE MCALLISTER**, Co-Editor

## There Won't Be War
(New York: Tor, 1991)

**Story type:** Science Fiction (Anthology)
**Time period(s):** Indeterminate Future

**Summary:** This anthology of 5 reprint and 14 original stories which focus on the struggle for peace also includes an introduction by Bruce McAllister and an afterword by Harry Harrison. Authors include Isaac Asimov, J.G. Ballard, Joe Haldeman, James Morrow, Frederik Pohl, Robert Sheckley, William Tenn and George Zebrowski.

**Other books you might like:**
Octavia E. Butler, *Dawn*, 1987
Daniel Quinn, *Ishmael*, 1992
Elizabeth Ann Scarborough, *Nothing Sacred*, 1991
Joan Slonczewski, *A Door into Ocean*, 1986
Joan Slonczewski, *Still Forms on Foxfield*, 1980
Sheri S. Tepper, *Sideshow*, 1992
Michael Tobias, *Voice of the Planet*, 1990

---

**2579**

**HARRY HARRISON**
**MARVIN MINSKY**, Co-Author

## The Turing Option
(New York: Warner, 1992)

**Story type:** Science Fiction (Techno-Thriller; Alternate Intelligence)
**Major character(s):** Brian Delaney, Scientist, Computer Expert
**Time period(s):** 2020s (2023-2024)
**Locale(s):** California; Mexico; Europe

**Summary:** Shortly after Brian Delaney develops an artificial intelligence for Metaglobe Industries, an assassin loots his lab, kills his assistants and attempts to kill Delaney. Experimental surgery saves Delaney, but the results begin to blur the distinction between man and machine.

**Other books you might like:**
David Brin, *Earth*, 1990
Jeffrey A. Carver, *The Rapture Effect*, 1987
Victor Milan, *The Cybernetic Samurai*, 1986
Rudy Rucker, *Software*, 1982
David Alexander Smith, *Marathon*, 1982
Neal Stephenson, *Snow Crash*, 1992
Thomas T. Thomas, *ME: A Novel of Self Discovery*, 1991
John Varley, *Steel Beach*, 1992
Walter Jon Williams, *Voice of the Whirlwind*, 1987

### 2580

**M. JOHN HARRISON**

## Signs of Life

(New York: St. Martin's, 1997)

**Story type:** Science Fiction (Contemporary Realism; Genetic Manipulation)
**Major character(s):** Mick "China" Rose, Truck Driver, Businessman; Isobel Avens, Genetically Altered Being; Choe Ashton, Truck Driver, Rebel
**Time period(s):** 1990s
**Locale(s):** London, England; Budapest, Hungary

**Summary:** The middle-aged and weary owner of a biological and medical delivery service, Mick Rose, relates how Isobel came into his life and left again. Mourning his loss, Mick struggles to understand why Isobel's dreams of flying led her to participate in dangerous and illegal molecular biology experiments.

**Other books you might like:**
J.G. Ballard, *Concrete Island*, 1974
J.G. Ballard, *Crash*, 1973
Nancy Kress, *Beggars and Choosers*, 1994
Christopher Priest, *The Perfect Lover*, 1977
S. Andrew Swann, *Specters of the Dawn*, 1994
H.G. Wells, *The Island of Doctor Moreau*, 1896

### 2581

**SUE HARRISON**

## Mother Earth, Father Sky

(New York: Doubleday, 1990)

**Story type:** Fantasy (Romance; Historical)
**Major character(s):** Chagak, Prehistoric Human, Indian (Aleut); Shuganan, Artist, Indian (Aleut)
**Time period(s):** 71st century B.C. (7056 B.C.)
**Locale(s):** Aleutian Islands, Alaska

**Summary:** Chagak sees the massacre of her people, finds her infant brother and decides to live. She leaves her beach to search for a place for herself and her brother. 1991 Best Books For Young Adults title.

**Other books you might like:**
Jean M. Auel, *Clan of the Cave Bear*, 1980
W. Michael Gear, *People of the Fire*, 1991
   Kathleen O'Neal Gear, co-author
Richard Herley, *The Stone Arrow*, 1978
Meredith Ann Pierce, *The Woman Who Loved Reindeer*, 1989
William Sarabande, *Beyond the Sea of Ice*, 1987
Elizabeth Marshall Thomas, *Reindeer Moon*, 1987

### 2582

**SUE HARRISON**

## My Sister the Moon

(New York: Doubleday, 1992)

**Story type:** Fantasy (Historical; Legend)
**Major character(s):** Samiq, Prehistoric Human, Indian (Aleut); Amgigh, Prehistoric Human, Indian (Aleut); Kiin, Prehistoric Human, Indian (Aleut)
**Time period(s):** 8th century B.C. (B.C.)
**Locale(s):** Aleutian Islands, Alaska

**Summary:** In love with Samiq, Kiin's betrothal to his brother, Amgigh, saves her life which was endangered by her father. An Aleut legend about a female who mates with two sea otter brothers forms the basis for this sequel to *Mother Earth, Father Sky*.

**Other books you might like:**
Jean M. Auel, *Clan of the Cave Bear*, 1980
Meredith Ann Pierce, *The Woman Who Loved Reindeer*, 1989
William Sarabande, *The Sacred Stones*, 1991
Elizabeth Marshall Thomas, *The Animal Wife*, 1990
Elizabeth Marshall Thomas, *Reindeer Moon*, 1987

### 2583

**SUE HARRISON**

## Song of the River

(New York: Avon, 1997)

**Story type:** Fantasy (Adventure; Quest)
**Series:** Mother Earth, Father Sky
**Major character(s):** K'os, Indian, Avenger; Chakliux, Storyteller, Handicapped (clubfoot); Aqamdax, Indian (Wanderer)
**Time period(s):** 65th century B.C. (6480 B.C.)
**Locale(s):** Alaska

**Summary:** Having been raised by the men of Near River Village, K'os raises Chakliux, also from that village, to get vengeance. When Chakliux, expecting to marry to heal the breach between the Cousin and Near River people, finds himself unable to win the trust of his new tribe, he wanders and learns about himself and his people, seeking the reasons his people suffered.

**Other books you might like:**
Jean M. Auel, *Clan of the Cave Bear*, 1980
W. Michael Gear, *People of the Wolf*, 1990
   Kathleen O'Neal Gear, co-author
Meredith Ann Pierce, *The Woman Who Loved Reindeer*, 1985
William Sarabande, *The Sacred Stones*, 1991
Elizabeth Marshall Thomas, *Reindeer Moon*, 1987

### 2584

**WILLIAM HARTMANN**

## Mars Underground

(New York: Tor, 1997)

**Story type:** Science Fiction (Political; Adventure)
**Major character(s):** Alwyn Bryan Stafford, Explorer, Scientist (biology); Carter Jahns, Engineer, Administrator; Annie Pohaku, Journalist
**Time period(s):** 2030s (2032)
**Locale(s):** Hilo, Hawaii; Mars; Phobos, Mars ((moon of Mars))

**Summary:** On Mars longer than anyone else, Stafford disappears while on one of his semi-legal solo excursions, hoping the clues he left for Carter prove useful. Refusing to believe Stafford died when his oxygen ran out, Carter continues the search with Annie, who promises not to file her story without his permission when they uncover a conspiracy. First novel.

**Other books you might like:**
Greg Bear, *Moving Mars*, 1993
Ben Bova, *Mars*, 1992
William C. Dietz, *Mars Prime*, 1992
Robert A. Heinlein, *Red Planet*, 1949
Kim Stanley Robinson, *Red Mars*, 1993
S.C. Sykes, *Red Genesis*, 1991

## 2585

**DAVID G. HARTWELL**, Editor
**KATHRYN CRAMER**, Co-Editor

### The Ascent of Wonder: The Evolution of Hard SF

(New York: Tor, 1994)

**Story type:** Science Fiction (Anthology; Hard Science Fiction)

**Summary:** Contains three introductions by Gregory Benford, Kathryn Cramer and David G. Hartwell plus lengthy individual introductions to 67 stories reprinted from periodicals and anthologies and organized by the way in which the author utilizes science in the story, with a two-page appendix by Cramer presenting a thematic organization of 44 stories. Authors contributing to the foundation of scientific fiction last century include Nathaniel Hawthorne, Edgar Allan Poe and Jules Verne, with Rudyard Kipling and H.G. Wells' work from early this century. Other authors include Poul Anderson, Isaac Asimov, J.G. Ballard, Greg Bear, Gregory Benford, Gordon R. Dickson, Michael F. Flynn, John M. Ford, Robert L. Forward, C.M. Kornbluth, Henry Kuttner, Philip Latham, Ursula K. Le Guin, Katherine MacLean, Anne McCaffrey, George Turner, Vernor Vinge, Ian Watson, Kate Wilhelm and Gene Wolfe.

**Other books you might like:**

Isaac Asimov, *Isaac Asimov Presents the Great SF Stories*, 1979-1992
  Martin H. Greenberg, co-editor
Gardner Dozois, *Modern Classics of Science Fiction*, 1992
  editor
Ursula K. Le Guin, *The Norton Book of Science Fiction: North American Science Fiction, 1960-1990*, 1993
  Brian Attebery, co-editor
Tom Shippey, *The Oxford Book of Science Fiction Stories*, 1992
  editor
Robert Silverberg, *The Science Fiction Hall of Fame, Volume 1*, 1970
  editor

## 2586

**DAVID G. HARTWELL**, Editor

### Bodies of the Dead

(New York: Tor, 1997)

**Story type:** Horror (Anthology)

**Summary:** Thirteen stories of horror and the supernatural by American writers from the late nineteenth and early twentieth centuries. Included are Edith Wharton's ''Kerfol,'' in which a man is slain by the ghosts of dogs who once protected the wife he abused; Willa Cather's ''The Affair at Grover Station,'' in which a ghost helps to solve the mystery of his own murder; Nathaniel Hawthorne's ''The Grey Champion,'' which features a ghost who embodies the revolutionary spirit of America; G. Ranger Wormser's ''The Scarecrow,'' which suggests the influence of the supernatural pervading a soldier's uniform used to dress a scarecrow; Edgar Allan Poe's ''Berenice,'' in which a man's obsession with the smile of his beloved leads to a gruesome post-mortem act; and the title tale by Ambrose Bierce, a series of vignettes concerning premature burial.

**Other books you might like:**

Peter Haining, *Great Tales of Terror From Europe and America*, 1972
  editor

Marvin Kaye, *Haunted America*, 1990
  editor
Frank D. McSherry Jr., *Great American Ghost Stories*, 1991
  Charles G. Waugh and Martin H. Greenberg, co-editors
Frank D. McSherry Jr., *A Treasury of Great American Horror Stories*, 1995
  Martin H. Greenberg, co-editor
Elizabeth Terry, *American Gothic*, 1993
  Terri Hardin, co-editor

## 2587

**DAVID G. HARTWELL**, Editor

### Christmas Forever

(New York: Tor, 1993)

**Story type:** Fantasy (Anthology; Religious)

**Summary:** Contains 28 original stories of Yuletide wonder exhibiting a broad range of themes which encompass monsters, mythical creatures, a magical cruise, virgin births, holidays on alien worlds and a Christmas at the end of time. Authors include James P. Blaylock and Tim Powers collaborating on one story plus Joan Aiken, Margaret Ball, Michael Bishop, Charles de Lint, Alan Dean Foster, Janet Kagan, Damon Knight, Patricia A. McKillip, Rudy Rucker, Robert Sheckley, Gene Wolfe, Dave Wolverton and Roger Zelazny.

**Other books you might like:**

Martin H. Greenberg, *Christmas on Ganymede and Other Stories*, 1990
  editor
Rosalind M. Greenberg, *Christmas Bestiary*, 1992
  Martin H. Greenberg, co-editor
Mike Resnick, *Christmas Ghosts*, 1993
  Martin H. Greenberg, co-editor
Kristine Kathryn Rusch, *Pulphouse, Issue 10: Special Issue*, 1991
  editor
John Silbersack, *The Magic of Christmas*, 1992
  Christopher Schelling, co-editor

## 2588

**DAVID G. HARTWELL**, Editor

### Christmas Magic

(New York: Tor, 1994)

**Story type:** Fantasy (Anthology; Religious)

**Summary:** Contains seven original stories and 21 stories reprinted from periodicals and anthologies 1957-1993, all sharing Yuletide themes, with one 1993 Hugo award winning story by Janet Kagan, ''The Nutcracker Coup.'' Other authors include A.J. Austin, David R. Bunch, Harlan Ellison, Alan Dean Foster, Nina Kiriki Hoffman, James P. Hogan, Alexander Jablokov, Kit Reed, and Margaret St. Clair.

**Other books you might like:**

Kathryn Cramer, *Spirits of Christmas*, 1989
  David G. Hartwell, co-editor
Martin H. Greenberg, *Christmas on Ganymede and Other Stories*, 1990
  editor
Rosalind M. Greenberg, *Christmas Bestiary*, 1992
  Martin H. Greenberg, co-editor
Kristine Kathryn Rusch, *Pulphouse, Issue 10: Special Issue*, 1991
  editor

John Silbersack, *The Magic of Christmas*, 1992
  Christopher Schelling, co-editor

### 2589

**DAVID G. HARTWELL**, Editor

## Christmas Stars

(New York: Tor, 1992)

**Story type:** Science Fiction (Anthology)

**Summary:** Contains 23 short stories published from 1950-1991 in periodicals and books plus two poems by John M. Ford, all sharing the theme Christmas. Joe L. Hensley and Alexei Panshin collaborated on one story, "Dark Conception." Other authors include Brian W. Aldiss, Ben Bova, Ray Bradbury, Arthur C. Clarke, Thomas M. Disch, Cynthia Felice, William Gibson, Anne McCaffrey, Frederik Pohl, Ian Watson, Connie Willis and Gene Wolfe.

**Other books you might like:**
Alan Brennert, *Kindred Spirits*, 1984
Martin H. Greenberg, *Christmas on Ganymede and Other Stories*, 1990
  editor
Rosalind M. Greenberg, *Christmas Bestiary*, 1992
  Martin H. Greenberg, co-editor
Kristine Kathryn Rusch, *Pulphouse, Issue 10: Special Issue*, 1991
  editor
John Silbersack, *The Magic of Christmas*, 1992
  Christopher Schelling, co-editor
Gene Wolfe, *Gene Wolfe's Book of Days*, 1981

### 2590

**DAVID G. HARTWELL**, Editor

## The Dark Descent

(New York: Tor, 1997)

**Story type:** Horror (Anthology)

**Summary:** Landmark 1,000-plus page anthology celebrating the horror short story, drawn from English, American and continental literature of the nineteenth and twentieth century. Classic selections include Henry James's ghost tale, "The Jolly Corner," Oliver Onions's tale of a spectral *femme fatale*, "The Beckoning Fair One," J. Sheridan LeFanu's deal-with-the-devil story, "Schalken the Painter," and M.R. James's tale of supernatural curse, "The Ash-Tree." Modern selections include Flannery O'Connor's black comedy, "Good Country People," and H.P. Lovecraft's cosmic horror story, "The Call of Cthulhu." Contemporary stories include Shirley Jackson's tale of paranoia, "The Summer People," Stephen King's story of a supernaturally endowed toy, "The Monkey," and Robert Aickman's erotic horror tale, "The Swords." First published in 1987.

**Other books you might like:**
Ramsey Campbell, *Uncanny Banquet*, 1992
  editor
Dennis Etchison, *The Complete Masters of Darkness*, 1991
  editor
Bill Pronzini, *The Arbor House Treasury of Horror and the Supernatural*, 1981
  Barry Malzberg and Martin H. Greenberg, co-editors
Robert Silverberg, *The Horror Hall of Fame*, 1991
  Martin H. Greenberg, co-editor
Herbert Wise, *Great Tales of Terror and the Supernatural*, 1944
  Phyllis Fraser, co-author

### 2591

**DAVID G. HARTWELL**, Editor

## Foundations of Fear

(New York: Tor, 1992)

**Story type:** Horror (Anthology)

**Summary:** A mammoth follow-up volume to the editor's earlier *The Dark Descent*, tracking the development of the horror genre through the novella length work. The 30 stories include H. P. Lovecraft's short novel of horrors in the Antarctic, "At the Mountains of Madness"; Richard Matheson's tale of a paranoid traffic chase, "Duel"; John W. Campbell's science fiction horror story, "Who Goes There"; Clive Barker's dark fairy tale, "In the Hills, The Cities"; Peter Straub's tale of a vindictive young boy, "The Blue Rose"; and Arthur Machen's classic story of evil incarnate, "The Great God Pan." The editor has supplied an insightful introduction.

**Other books you might like:**
Bill Pronzini, *The Arbor House Treasury of Horror and the Supernatural*, 1981
  Barry Malzberg and Martin H. Greenberg, co-editors
Herbert Wise, *Great Tales of Terror and the Supernatural*, 1944
  Phyllis Fraser, co-editor

### 2592

**DAVID G. HARTWELL**, Editor

## Masterpieces of Fantasy and Wonder

(New York: St. Martin's Press, 1994)

**Story type:** Fantasy (Anthology)

**Summary:** Contains a four-page introduction plus individual introductions to 38 of the best fantasy stories from the 19th and 20th centuries organized into five sections, "Enchantments," "Wonders," "Creatures," "Worlds" and "Adventures." Authors include L. Frank Baum, Charles Dickens, Suzette Haden Elgin, Harlan Ellison, John M. Ford, Ursula K. Le Guin, George MacDonald, Anne McCaffrey, Patricia A. McKillip, Robin McKinley, William Morris, Edith Nesbit, Isaac Bashevis Singer, Fyodor Sologub, Frank R. Stockton, James Tiptree Jr., Mark Twain and Jack Vance.

**Other books you might like:**
Jorge Luis Borges, *The Book of Fantasy*, 1990
  editor
Robert H. Boyer, *Visions & Imaginings: Classic Fantasy Fiction*, 1992
  Kenneth J. Zahorski, co-editor
Alison Lurie, *The Oxford Book of Modern Fairy Tales*, 1993
  editor
Tom Shippey, *The Oxford Book of Fantasy Stories*, 1994
  editor
Robert Silverberg, *The Fantasy Hall of Fame*, 1983
  Martin H. Greenberg, co-editor

### 2593

**DAVID G. HARTWELL**, Editor
**GLENN GRANT**, Co-Editor

## Northern Stars: The Anthology of Canadian Science Fiction

(New York: Tor, 1994)

**Story type:** Science Fiction (Anthology)

**Summary:** Contains an 11-page appendix of major Canadian SF and fantasy awards, a four-page introduction by Grant plus individual introductions to two essays, two novel excerpts and 25 stories, with five of them translated from French, published during the past 20 years by Canadian writers. Authors include Michael G. Coney, Charles de Lint, Candas Jane Dorsey, Dave Duncan, William Gibson, Phyllis Gotlieb, Terrance M. Green, Eileen Kernaghan, Robert Sawyer, Elisabeth Vonarburg and Robert Charles Wilson.

**Other books you might like:**

Damien Broderick, *Strange Attractors: Original Australian Speculative Fiction*, 1985
  editor
John Robert Colombo, *Other Canadas*, 1979
  editor
Gardner Dozois, *The Year's Best Science Fiction Series*, 1984-1994
  editor
Ursula K. Le Guin, *The Norton Book of Science Fiction: North American Science Fiction, 1960-1990*, 1993
  Brian Attebery, co-editor
Kristine Kathryn Rusch, *The Best of Pulphouse: The Hardback Magazine*, 1991
  editor

---

**2594**

**DAVID G. HARTWELL**, Editor

## The Science Fiction Century
(New York: Tor, 1997)

**Story type:** Science Fiction (Anthology; Science Fiction)

**Summary:** Contains a four-page introduction plus individual introductions to 45 stories, novellas and novelettes which investigate the truth of the human condition in this century as it relates to science and technology. From somber to upbeat in tone, the stories reflect diverse themes from well known authors including Poul Anderson, James Blish, Algis Budrys, Hal Clement, John Crowley, Harlan Ellison, Philip Jose Farmer, William Gibson, Frank Herbert, Rudyard Kipling, Nancy Kress, Philip Latham, Jack London, Frank Belknap Long, Richard A. Lupoff, James Morrow, Chad Oliver, Margaret St. Clair, Michael Shaara, Robert Silverberg, Cordwainer Smith, Bruce Sterling, Michael Swanwick, William Tenn, George Turner, A.E. van Vogt, Jack Vance, Connie Willis, John Wyndham and Roger Zelazny.

**Other books you might like:**

Mike Ashley, *The Random House Book of Science Fiction Stories*, 1997
  editor
Isaac Asimov, *Isaac Asimov Presents the Great SF Stories: 1-25*, 1979-1992
  Martin H. Greenberg, co-editor
Gardner Dozois, *Modern Classics of Science Fiction*, 1992
  editor
Gardner Dozois, *The Year's Best Science Fiction Series*, 1984-1997
  editor
Ursula K. Le Guin, *The Norton Book of Science Fiction: North American Science Fiction, 1960-1990*, 1993
  Brian Attebery, co-editor
Tom Shippey, *The Oxford Book of Science Fiction Stories*, 1992
  editor

---

**2595**

**DAVID G. HARTWELL**, Editor
**MILTON T. WOLF**, Co-Editor

## Visions of Wonder: The Science Fiction Research Association Anthology
(New York: Tor, 1996)

**Story type:** Science Fiction (Anthology)

**Summary:** This survey assembles 32 stories published in periodicals and anthologies 1961-1994 and nine essays useful for teachers and understandable by students from periodicals and anthologies, 1956-1989. The stories reflect some of the most influential work of popular authors and address the broad spectrum of issues facing teachers, such as new science and technologies, social problems and forces, the future in space, and gender issues. Authors include Brian W. Aldiss, Greg Bear, Gregory Benford, Orson Scott Card, Suzy McKee Charnas, Charles de Lint, Anne McCaffrey, Andre Norton, Frederik Pohl, Charles Sheffield, Judith Tarr, James Tiptree Jr., Jack Williamson, and Gene Wolfe.

**Other books you might like:**

Isaac Asimov, *Isaac Asimov Presents the Great SF Stories: 1-25*, 1979-1992
  Martin H. Greenberg, co-editor
Gardner Dozois, *Modern Classics of Science Fiction*, 1992
  editor
Gardner Dozois, *The Year's Best Science Fiction Series*, 1984-1996
  editor
Ursula K. Le Guin, *The Norton Book of Science Fiction: North American Science Fiction, 1960-1990*, 1993
  Brian Attebery, co-editor
Tom Shippey, *The Oxford Book of Science Fiction Stories*, 1992
  editor

---

**2596**

**DAVID G. HARTWELL**, Editor

## Year's Best SF
(New York: HarperPrism, 1996)

**Story type:** Science Fiction (Anthology)

**Summary:** Contains a three-page introduction and individual introductions to 14 stories published in periodicals and anthologies in 1995 with one Hugo Award winner and Nebula Award nominee, James Patrick Kelly's "Think Like a Dinosaur." Varying in tone, the stories feature diverse themes such as hard science, first contact, space exploration, cyberpunk, medicine, volcanic disaster, and alternate history. Ursula K. Le Guin returns to the world of *The Left Hand of Darkness* (1969) with "Coming of Age in Karhide." Other authors include Stephen Baxter, Gregory Benford, Joe Haldeman, Nancy Kress, Patricia A. McKillip, Joan Slonczewski, Gene Wolfe, and Roger Zelazny.

**Other books you might like:**

Isaac Asimov, *Isaac Asimov Presents the Great SF Stories: 1-25*, 1979-1992
  Martin H. Greenberg, co-editor
Greg Bear, *New Legends*, 1995
  Martin H. Greenberg, co-editor
Gardner Dozois, *The Year's Best Science Fiction Series*, 1984-1996
  editor
Jennifer Hershey, *Full Spectrum 5*, 1995
  Tom Dupree, Janna Silverstein, co-editors

Pamela Sargent, *Nebula Awards 30*, 1996
  editor
Robert Silverberg, *Universe 3*, 1994
  Karen Haber, co-editor

## 2597

### DAVID G. HARTWELL, Editor

## Year's Best SF 2
(New York: HarperPrism, 1997)

**Story type:** Science Fiction (Anthology; Science Fiction)
**Series:** Year's Best SF

**Summary:** Contains a three-page introduction and individual introductions to 20 stories published in periodicals and anthologies in 1996. From humorous to somber in tone, the stories reflect diverse themes and genres such as hard science fiction, virtual reality, robots, modern society, space colonization, alternate universes, and evolution. Authors include Stephen Baxter, Gregory Benford, Terry Bisson, John Brunner, Kathleen Ann Goonan, Gwyneth Jones, James Patrick Kelly, Damon Knight, Robert Reed, Joanna Russ, Brian Stableford, Allen Steele, Bruce Sterling, Kate Wilhelm, Connie Willis, and Gene Wolfe.

**Other books you might like:**
Isaac Asimov, *Isaac Asimov Presents the Great SF Stories: 1-25, 1979-1992*
  Martin H. Greenberg, co-editor
Greg Bear, *New Legends*, 1995
  Martin H. Greenberg, co-editor
Gardner Dozois, *The Year's Best Science Fiction Series*, 1984-
  editor
Jennifer Hershey, *Full Spectrum 5*, 1995
  Tom Dupree and Janna Silverstein, co-editors
Pamela Sargent, *Nebula Awards 31*, 1997
  editor

## 2598

### DAVID G. HARTWELL, Editor

## Year's Best SF 3
(New York: HarperPrism, 1998)

**Story type:** Science Fiction (Anthology)
**Series:** Year's Best SF

**Summary:** This anthology contains a three-page introduction as well as individual introductions to its 22 stories, which come from 1997 periodicals and anthologies. Frequently somber or downbeat in tone, the stories cover a variety of themes such as aliens, cyborgs, time travel, cosmology, computer love, dinosaurs, alternative history, railroads, technological barriers, and divisions in society. Authors include Gregory Benford, Terry Bisson, Ray Bradbury, Tom Cool, Greg Egan, R. Garcia y Robertson, William Gibson, James Patrick Kelly, Nancy Kress, Geoffrey A. Landis, Michael Moorcock, Kim Newman, Robert Silverberg, Michael Swanwick, Jack Williamson, and Gene Wolfe.

**Other books you might like:**
Isaac Asimov, *Isaac Asimov Presents the Great SF Stories: 1-25, 1979-1992*
  Martin H. Greenberg, co-editor
Greg Bear, *New Legends*, 1995
  Martin H. Greenberg, co-editor
Gardner Dozois, *The Year's Best Science Fiction Series*, 1984-
  editor

Jennifer Hershey, *Full Spectrum 5*, 1995
  Tom Dupree, Janna Silverstein, co-editors
Pamela Sargent, *Nebula Awards 31*, 1997
  editor

## 2599

### JAMES NEAL HARVEY

## The Headsman
(New York: Jove, 1993)

**Story type:** Horror (Mystery)
**Major character(s):** Jud McElroy, Police Officer (police chief); Karen Wilson, Secretary, Psychic; Emmett Stark, Police Officer (former police chief)
**Time period(s):** 1990s (1991)
**Locale(s):** Braddock, New York

**Summary:** Police officer Jud McElroy teams up with psychically-endowed Karen Wilson to find out who is using their small rural town's legend of an immortal axe murderer as a cover for his own spree of gruesome decapitations. This novel was originally published in hardcover in 1991.

**Other books you might like:**
Paul Dale Anderson, *Claw Hammer*, 1989
S.K. Epperson, *Dumford Blood*, 1991
Michael Slade, *Headhunter*, 1983

## 2600

### GEORGE HATCH, Editor

## Guignoir and Other Furies
(Long Island City, New York: Horror's Head Press, 1991)

**Story type:** Horror (Anthology)

**Summary:** Thirteen stories of "psychological terror, violence and suspense" that, as the title implies, wed grotesque imagery to the dark themes of noir fiction. Included are stories of repellently dysfunctional families by Nancy Holder and Tia Travis, a sexual dystopia by Lucy Taylor, and the title story, a bizarre hardboiled revenge tale about a serial killer and traveling side show.

**Other books you might like:**
Robert Bloch, *Psycho-Paths*, 1991
  Martin H. Greenberg, co-author
Richard T. Chizmar, *Cold Blood*, 1991
Ed Gorman, *Dark Crimes: Great Noir Fiction From the '50's to the '90's*, 1992
Ed Gorman, *Stalkers*, 1989
  Martin H. Greenberg, co-author
Joe R. Lansdale, *Dark at Heart*, 1992
  Karen Lansdale, co-author

## 2601

### GEORGE HATCH, Editor
### STEVE RASNIC TEM, Illustrator
### T. WINTER-DAMON, Illustrator

## Sinistre: An Anthology of Rituals
(Staten Island, New York: Horrors Head Press, 1993)

**Story type:** Horror (Anthology)

**Summary:** The 16 original stories in this trade paperback incarnation of George Hatch's small press magazine *Noctulpa* all are concerned with the enduring force of primitive rites and superstitions in a modern context. Included are A.R. Morlan's "Tattoo," in which a gang rape victim undergoes a full-body tattoo of clothing to avoid her psychological trauma; Robert Frazier's "Too Long in the Wasteland" and Gerald Daniel Houarner's "Hidden Agendas," each of which treats the idea of parricide as a rite of passage; Nancy Patrick's "The Power of One" and Steve Rasnic Tem's "Doodles," in which characters develop obsessive traits to compensate for guilt feelings; and Connie Hirsch's humorous "Prayers and the Material Girl," conducted as a dialogue between one woman's multiple personalities.

**Other books you might like:**
Martin H. Greenberg, *Cults of Horror*, 1990
　　Charles G. Waugh, co-editor
Gary L. Raisor, *Obsessions*, 1991
　　editor

---

**2602**

**RICHARD HATCH**
**CHRISTOPHER GOLDEN**, Co-Author

## Armageddon
(New York: Pocket, 1997)

**Story type:** Science Fiction (Military)
**Series:** Battlestar Galactica
**Major character(s):** Apollo, Warrior, Spaceman; Starbuck, Warrior, Spaceman
**Time period(s):** Indeterminate Future
**Locale(s):** battlestar *Galactica*, Outer Space

**Summary:** With the succession of leadership in question and continuing threat from the Cylons, Apollo leaves Battlestar *Galactica* in search of Starbuck, presumed killed by Cylon raiders.

**Other books you might like:**
Roger MacBride Allen, *The Ring of Charon*, 1990
Christopher Golden, *Of Saints and Shadows*, 1994
Glen A. Larson, *Battlestar Galactica*, 1978
　　Robert Thurston, co-author
Glen A. Larson, *The Cylon Death Machine*, 1979
　　Robert Thurston, co-author
Glen A. Larson, *The Living Legend*, 1982
　　Nicholas Yermakov, co-author
Glen A. Larson, *The Long Patrol*, 1984
　　Ron Goulart, co-author

---

**2603**

**MARLEN HAUSHOFER**
**SHAUN WHITESIDE**, Co-Author

## The Wall
(Pittsburg, Pennsylvania: Cleis Press, 1991)

**Story type:** Science Fiction (Dystopian; Post-Holocaust)
**Major character(s):** I, Writer
**Time period(s):** 20th century
**Locale(s):** Europe (Alps)

**Summary:** The diarist awakens in the countryside to find herself the only survivor of a disaster which has wiped out all life on the other side of an invisible barrier which surrounds a large, unaffected area. With no wilderness training, she must find the means to survive. Originally published in German as *Die Wand* (1962), this translation by Shaun Whiteside is the author's first book available in English.

**Other books you might like:**
Neal Barrett Jr., *Through Darkest America*, 1987
Richard Brautigan, *In Watermelon Sugar*, 1968
David Brin, *The Postman*, 1985
Octavia E. Butler, *Dawn*, 1987
Gordon R. Dickson, *Wolf and Iron*, 1990
David R. Palmer, *Emergence*, 1984
Vernor Vinge, *Marooned in Realtime*, 1986
Vernor Vinge, *The Peace War*, 1984
M.K. Wren, *A Gift upon the Shore*, 1990

---

**2604**

**RICK HAUTALA**

## Beyond the Shroud
(Stone Mountain, Georgia: White Wolf, 1996)

**Story type:** Horror (Possession)
**Major character(s):** David Robinson, Writer; Sarah Robinson, Teacher; Tony Ranieri, Student
**Time period(s):** 1990s (1996)
**Locale(s):** Portland, Maine

**Summary:** From The Shadowlands, a realm of dead souls and supernatural beings who prey upon them, newly deceased David Robinson watches helplessly while his ex-wife Sarah, whom he still loves, begins an affair with a young man who has fallen under the murderous influence of one of the knives used by Jack the Ripper. Set in the world of the publisher's role-playing game "Wraith."

**Other books you might like:**
Richard Lee Byers, *On a Darkling Plain*, 1995
Sam Chupp, *Sins of the Fathers*, 1995

---

**2605**

**RICK HAUTALA**

## Cold Whisper
(New York: Zebra, 1991)

**Story type:** Horror (Curse)
**Major character(s):** Sarah Lahikainen, Student—College (at University of Maine, Orono); Elliot Clark, Police Officer; Alan Griffin, Prisoner
**Time period(s):** 1990s
**Locale(s):** Hilton, Maine; Orono, Maine

**Summary:** As a child, Sarah Lahikainen could not escape the belief that her imaginary playmate Tully engineered the deaths of her pets and baby brother when she became angry with them. In the wake of her mother's brutal murder at the hands of a delinquent who is now stalking her, Sarah discovers that Tully is a tulpa, a family demon who grows stronger and more uncontrollable the longer her anger remains unassuaged.

**Other books you might like:**
J.N. Williamson, *The Tulpa*, 1982

---

**2606**

**RICK HAUTALA**

## Dark Silence
(New York: Zebra, 1992)

**Story type:** Horror (Curse)

**Major character(s):** Brian Fraser, Child; Edward Fraser, Businessman (real estate developer); Mike Fraser, Patient (escaped mental patient)
**Time period(s):** 1990s (1994)
**Locale(s):** Summerfield, Maine

**Summary:** When his father begins trying to sell off the family land Brian Fraser falls prey to the same supernatural curse that turned his uncle Mike into a raving lunatic, one levied 300 years before by an ancestor hanged as a witch who vowed vengeance against all her enemies and their descendants who sought to appropriate her lands illegally.

**Other books you might like:**
Vincent Courtney, *Wake Up Screaming*, 1992
Roy Sorrels, *The Eyes of Torie Webster*, 1990

---

**2607**

### RICK HAUTALA

## *Dead Voices*
(New York: Warner, 1990)

**Story type:** Horror (Occult)
**Major character(s):** Elizabeth ''Payne'' Meyer, Divorced Person; Frank Melrose, Police Officer; Roland Graydon, Doctor (psychiatrist)
**Time period(s):** 1990s
**Locale(s):** Bristol Mills, Maine

**Summary:** Emotionally devastated after the death of her young daughter Caroline, Elizabeth Meyer leaves her husband to return to her family home in Maine. While she is there, a series of graveyard defilements and mysterious deaths seems to indicate that Caroline is trying to get in touch with her mother from beyond the grave—or that someone is trying to make it look so.

**Other books you might like:**
Stephen King, *Pet Sematary*, 1983
David C. Smith, *The Fair Rules of Evil*, 1989

---

**2608**

### RICK HAUTALA

## *Ghost Light*
(New York: Warner, 1993)

**Story type:** Horror (Psychological Suspense)
**Major character(s):** Cindy Toland, Young Woman; Alex Harris, Worker (airport worker); Billy Harris, Child (Alex's son)
**Time period(s):** 1990s (1993)
**Locale(s):** Omaha, Nebraska; Portland, Maine

**Summary:** Cindy Toland flees Nebraska with her young niece and nephew, pursued cross-country by their psychotic father Alex, who murdered their mother, and protected by a ghostly figure with a blue aura whom only the children can see.

**Other books you might like:**
Stephen Gallagher, *Down River*, 1989
Ruby Jean Jensen, *Celia*, 1991
Dean R. Koontz, *Lightning*, 1988
Dean R. Koontz, *Shadowfires*, 1987

---

**2609**

### RICK HAUTALA

## *Impulse*
(New York: Pinnacle, 1996)

**Story type:** Horror (Psychological Suspense)
**Major character(s):** Angie Ross, Teacher; Greg Newman, Murderer; Brandy Ross, Teenager
**Time period(s):** 1990s (1996)
**Locale(s):** New York, New York; Bolton, Maine

**Summary:** Paranoid and hounded by the voices of those he has murdered, Greg Newman stalks the mother and children of one of his victims, forcing them to become as savage as he is.

**Other books you might like:**
Ruby Jean Jensen, *Celia*, 1991
Stephen King, *Rose Madder*, 1995
Dean R. Koontz, *Whispers*, 1980
Clare McNally, *Good Night, Sweet Angel*, 1996

---

**2610**

### RICK HAUTALA

## *Moon Walker*
(New York: Zebra, 1989)

**Story type:** Horror (Reanimated Dead)
**Major character(s):** Dale Harmon, Engineer; Franklin Rodgers, Undertaker
**Time period(s):** 1980s
**Locale(s):** Dyer, Maine

**Summary:** When his best friend is killed, Dale Harmon begins to investigate the mysterious events occurring in the small town of Dyer, Maine. The trail leads him to Franklin Rodgers, the local funeral director, who possesses an ''eye'' to see other worlds and the ability to reanimate the dead. Soon Harmon and a small group of associates find themselves under siege by a small army of zombies.

**Other books you might like:**
Stephen Gallagher, *Valley of Lights*, 1987
Richard Laymon, *Resurrection Dreams*, 1989

---

**2611**

### RICK HAUTALA

## *The Mountain King*
(Baltimore: CD Publications, 1996)

**Story type:** Horror (Nature in Revolt)
**Major character(s):** Mark Newman, Worker (mill worker); Phil Sawyer, Worker (mill worker); Sandy Newman, Teenager (Mark's daughter)
**Time period(s):** 1990s (1996)
**Locale(s):** Hilton, Maine

**Summary:** Mark Newman can't get anyone to believe that he saw his friend Phil abducted by a sasquatch-like creature during their last climb on Mount Agiochook. Mark returns to the mountain to look for his friend and becomes the object of a dual manhunt, by the townsfolk who suspect him of Phil's murder, and by the monster itself. This book was published as a signed limited hardcover edition of 500 copies.

**Other books you might like:**
Jack Ketchum, *Off Season*, 1980

Jack Ketchum, *Offspring*, 1991
Dean R. Koontz, *Watchers*, 1987
Richard Laymon, *Midnight's Lair*, 1988
John Tigges, *Monster*, 1995

`2612`

**RICK HAUTALA**

*Shades of Night*

(New York: Zebra, 1995)

**Story type:** Horror (Haunted House)
**Major character(s):** Lara DeSalvo, Housewife; Vincent DeSalvo, Businessman (land developer); Matt Coulter, Carpenter
**Time period(s):** 1990s (1995)
**Locale(s):** Portland, Maine

**Summary:** Newly married Lara DeSalvo moves to her husband's home in Portland, Maine, where she finds herself plagued with nighttime visions of a ghostly woman and stalked by a menacing prowler. When her husband begins exerting an irrational control over her life, Lara examines how all of these inexplicable variables might be interrelated.

**Other books you might like:**
Robert Bloch, *American Gothic*, 1974
Daphne Du Maurier, *Rebecca*, 1938
Ruby Jean Jensen, *Celia*, 1993
Stephen King, *Rose Madder*, 1995

`2613`

**RICK HAUTALA**

*Twilight Time*

(New York: Zebra, 1994)

**Story type:** Horror (Psychological Suspense)
**Major character(s):** Jeff Wagner, Professor (of history); Katherine Foster, Secretary—Legal; Danny Foster, Child (Katherine's son)
**Time period(s):** 1990s (1994)
**Locale(s):** Cape Higgins, Maine

**Summary:** As a young boy Jeff Wagner endured abuse at the hands of fundamentalist guardians and sought comfort in an illicit relationship with his sister. His return to his hometown to see his sister through a suicide attempt inaugurates a series of deaths and disappearances that may be the doings of the multiple personalities spawned by his guilt feelings, or other people trying to drive him mad.

**Other books you might like:**
David Ambrose, *The Man Who Turned into Himself*, 1994
Richard Matheson, *A Stir of Echoes*, 1958
John R. Maxim, *Abel/Baker/Charley*, 1983
Daniel Quinn, *Dreamer*, 1988
F. Paul Wilson, *Sibs*, 1991

`2614`

**PETE HAUTMAN**

*Mr. Was*

(New York: Simon & Schuster, 1996)

**Story type:** Science Fiction (Young Adult; Time Travel)
**Major character(s):** Jack "Mr. Was" Lund, Time Traveler, Amnesiac; Andrea "Andie" Skoro, Time Traveler; Pinky, Time Traveler, Administrator

**Time period(s):** 1990s; 1940s
**Locale(s):** Minnesota; Guadalcanal, Pacific Islands (The Canal/The Isle of Death); Andrea Island, Puerto Rico

**Summary:** Jack Lund's journal reveals glimpses of Jack's life after family tragedies and his discovery of a doorway to the past firm Jack's resolve to travel back in time to change events he experienced as a youth.

**Other books you might like:**
Octavia E. Butler, *Kindred*, 1979
Eleanor Cameron, *The Court of the Stone Children*, 1973
Mona Clee, *Branch Point*, 1996
Kara Dalkey, *Little Sister*, 1996
Susan Palwick, *Flying in Place*, 1992
Jill Paton Walsh, *A Chance Child*, 1978

`2615`

**DOUGLAS D. HAWK**

*The Devouring*

(New York: Leisure, 1994)

**Story type:** Horror (Nature in Revolt)
**Major character(s):** Morgan Blaylock, Writer; Robert Ferris, Spy; Richard Chase, FBI Agent
**Time period(s):** 1990s (1994)
**Locale(s):** Crystal Wells, Rocky Mountains, Canada

**Summary:** The destruction of a mountaintop research facility in the Rocky Mountains proves to be the work of *Homo desmodus*, a crossbred species of humans and bloodthirsty bats that has lived inside the earth for eons. The efforts of locals to eradicate the creatures are thwarted by government agents intent on capturing the creatures for their own uses.

**Other books you might like:**
William W. Johnstone, *Bats*, 1993
Martin Cruz Smith, *Nightwing*, 1977
T.W. Stetson, *Night Beasts*, 1993
Robert Charles Wilson, *Second Fire*, 1993

`2616`

**SIMON HAWKE**

*The Ambivalent Magician*

(New York: Warner Aspect, 1996)

**Story type:** Fantasy (Alternate World; Light Fantasy)
**Series:** Reluctant Sorcerer
**Major character(s):** Marvin "Doc" Brewster, Scientist, Genius; Warrick Morgannan, Wizard, Leader; Pamela Fairburn, Scientist, Fiance(e)
**Time period(s):** Indeterminate; 1990s
**Locale(s):** Darn, Fictional Country; London, England

**Summary:** Trapped in a parallel universe, Brewster rallies the motley inhabitants of Brigand's Roost, now the Kingdom of Brigantium, to fight Warrick, who has troubles of his own with the Narrator. Meanwhile, a tabloid story about one of Warrick's experimental subjects, transported across time and space by Brewster's invention, attracts the attention of Brewster's long-suffering fiancee, Pamela. When Warrick turns up in modern London with the time machine and Pamela commandeers it to rescue Brewster, the Narrator triumphs over Warrick. . .perhaps.

**Other books you might like:**
Robert Asprin, *Another Fine Myth*, 1978

L. Sprague de Camp, *The Complete Compleat Enchanter*, 1989
Fletcher Pratt, co-author
Gordon R. Dickson, *The Dragon and the George*, 1976
Barbara Hambly, *Dog Wizard*, 1993
Terry Pratchett, *The Colour of Magic*, 1983
Christopher Stasheff, *Her Majesty's Wizard*, 1986
Mark Twain, *A Connecticut Yankee in King Arthur's Court*, 1889

---

**2617**

### SIMON HAWKE

## *The Inadequate Adept*

(New York: Warner Questar, 1993)

**Story type:** Fantasy (Alternate World; Magic Conflict)
**Series:** Reluctant Sorcerer
**Major character(s):** Marvin "Doc" Brewster, Scientist, Genius; Warrick Morgannan, Wizard, Leader (Grand Director of the Guild)
**Time period(s):** Indeterminate; 1990s
**Locale(s):** Frank, Fictional Country; Darn, Fictional Country

**Summary:** Doc continues producing magical devices using local robbers as a labor force. Warrick tries to determine the magic of Doc's time machine, but the prisoners he straps into it continue to disappear. The narrator follows Doc's attempts to regain his machine and return to Pamela, who endeavors to duplicate the device and rescue Doc.

**Other books you might like:**
John DeChancie, *Castle Perilous*, 1988
Gordon R. Dickson, *The Dragon and the George*, 1976
Carole Nelson Douglas, *Cup of Clay*, 1991
Brad Strickland, *Wizard's Mole*, 1991

---

**2618**

### SIMON HAWKE

## *The Iron Throne*

(Lake Geneva, Wisconsin: TSR, 1995)

**Story type:** Fantasy (Political; Adventure)
**Series:** Birthright
**Major character(s):** Michael Roele, Royalty, Leader
**Time period(s):** Indeterminate
**Locale(s):** Cerilian Empire of Anuire, Fictional Country

**Summary:** Raised to rule, Michael Roele faces many challenges from those who wish to acquire the power destined for him. First of a game tie-in series.

**Other books you might like:**
David Cook, *Beyond the Moons*, 1991
Troy Denning, *The Verdant Passage*, 1991
David Eddings, *Pawn of Prophecy*, 1982
Douglas Niles, *Darkwalker on Moonshae*, 1987
R.A. Salvatore, *The Legacy*, 1992

---

**2619**

### SIMON HAWKE

## *The Last Wizard*

(New York: Warner Aspect, 1997)

**Story type:** Fantasy (Magic Conflict; Urban)
**Series:** Wizard of 4th Street

**Major character(s):** Talon, Immortal, Wizard (Dark One); Sebastian Makepeace, Mythical Creature (fairy), Teacher; Katherine O'Connor, Political Figure (President of the United States)
**Time period(s):** 25th century
**Locale(s):** New York, New York; Washington, District of Columbia; Arizona

**Summary:** With the support of the President of the United States, the International Traumaturgic Commission and a little help from friends, the four Avatars of the Runestones live under guard in the old United Nations building while waiting for the next attack by the remaining Dark Ones. Meanwhile, Talon founds the Order of Universal Spiritual Unity with a dragon preserve around it, then sets up a treatment center for juvenile offenders to convert to acolytes. Gradually all the remaining immortal Dark Ones fall to Talon who keeps them alive, locked in stone as a power source, for the great battle.

**Other books you might like:**
Robert N. Charrette, *A Prince Among Men*, 1994
Tanya Huff, *Gate of Darkness, Circle of Light*, 1989
J.V. Jones, *The Baker's Boy*, 1995
Marc Laidlaw, *Neon Lotus*, 1988
Morgan Llywelyn, *Silverlight*, 1996

---

**2620**

### SIMON HAWKE

## *The Nine Lives of Catseye Gomez*

(New York: Warner Questar, 1992)

**Story type:** Fantasy (Light Fantasy; Mystery)
**Series:** Wizard of 4th Street
**Major character(s):** Catseye Gomez, Animal (cat), Genetically Altered Being; Jay Solo, Police Officer (Commissioner), Administrator; Dan Leventhal, Detective—Police
**Time period(s):** 26th century
**Locale(s):** Santa Fe, New Mexico; Denver, Colorado

**Summary:** After the death of his only real friend, Gomez moves to Denver with Solo. The next morning he meets another thaumaturgic cat who tries to get him involved in the Equal Rights for Animals movement. When the cat's owner, a journalist promoting E.R.A., gets murdered by a car bomb, Leventhal, a maverick assigned to the case, recruits Gomez as his special assistant on the investigation.

**Other books you might like:**
Steven Brust, *Jhereg*, 1983
Glen Cook, *Sweet Silver Blues*, 1987
Alan Dean Foster, *Cat-A-Lyst*, 1991
Simon R. Green, *The God Killer*, 1991
Gary K. Wolf, *Who P-P-Plugged Roger Rabbit?*, 1991

---

**2621**

### SIMON HAWKE

## *The Outcast*

(Lake Geneva, Wisconsin: TSR, 1993)

**Story type:** Fantasy (Quest)
**Series:** Dark Sun: Tribe of One
**Major character(s):** Sorak, Psychic, Mythical Creature (half-elf)
**Time period(s):** Indeterminate
**Locale(s):** Athas, Planet—Imaginary

**Summary:** Found abandoned in the desert as a child, Sorak grows up with mystics who understand his psionic power and fragmented, multiple identities. Hoping to resolve his internal turmoil, Sorak sets out to discover his origins and seek out the Sage, a powerful magician who will help Sorak find his destiny.

**Other books you might like:**
Troy Denning, *The Amber Enchantress*, 1992
Troy Denning, *The Cerulean Storm*, 1993
Troy Denning, *The Crimson Legion*, 1992
Troy Denning, *The Obsidian Oracle*, 1993
Troy Denning, *The Verdant Passage*, 1991

## 2622

### SIMON HAWKE

## The Reluctant Sorcerer

(New York: Warner Questar, 1992)

**Story type:** Fantasy (Alternate World; Light Fantasy)
**Series:** Reluctant Sorcerer
**Major character(s):** Marvin ''Doc'' Brewster, Scientist, Genius; Michael Timothy O'Fallon, Mythical Creature (leprechaun); Robie McMurphy, Farmer
**Time period(s):** Indeterminate; 1990s
**Locale(s):** London, England; Frank, Fictional Country

**Summary:** While watching his favorite film, *Frankenstein*, Doc thinks he's solved the problem with his time machine. Leaving his fiancee behind, he fixes the switch on the machine and transports, totally destroying the device during his arrival. Mistaken for a sorcerer by the local inhabitants, he finds himself in an alternate universe in which he must find the faulty machine he has inadvertently sent before his arrival or remain permanently.

**Other books you might like:**
Douglas Adams, *The Hitchhiker's Guide to the Galaxy*, 1980
Katherine Blake, *The Interior Life*, 1990
Rick Cook, *Wizard's Bane*, 1989
John DeChancie, *Castle Perilous*, 1988
John Morressy, *The Questing of Kedrigern*, 1987
Spider Robinson, *Callahan's Secret*, 1986
Gene Wolfe, *Castleview*, 1990

## 2623

### SIMON HAWKE

## The Samurai Wizard

(New York: Warner/Questar, 1991)

**Story type:** Fantasy (Magic Conflict; Contemporary)
**Series:** Wizard of 4th Street
**Major character(s):** Wyrdrune Carpinski, Wizard; Billy Slade, Wizard (Merlin Ambrosius)
**Time period(s):** 23rd century
**Locale(s):** Tokyo, Japan; New York, New York

**Summary:** Before humans developed intelligence there was a race of Immortal Necromancers on the Earth. Eventually some noticed that the humans had become people, not beasts, and chose to use them no longer. A war was fought between those white mages and the necromancers who did not want to lose this rich resource, as white magic is more difficult and less powerful than necromancy. One of these Immortals, Merlin, chose to re-enter the world of men after the collapse and a 2000 year respite and introduce the structured use of thaumaturgic power to save the human race.

**Other books you might like:**
Suzy McKee Charnas, *The Golden Thread*, 1989
John DeChancie, *Castle Perilous*, 1988
Diane Duane, *High Wizardry*, 1989

Barbara Hambly, *The Time of the Dark*, 1982
Gene Wolfe, *Castleview*, 1990

## 2624

### SIMON HAWKE

## The Seeker

(Lake Geneva, Wisconsin: TSR, 1994)

**Story type:** Fantasy (Quest; Adventure)
**Series:** Dark Sun: Tribe of One
**Major character(s):** Sorak, Psychic, Mythical Creature (half-elf); Ryana, Religious (priestess), Adventurer
**Time period(s):** Indeterminate
**Locale(s):** Athas, Planet—Imaginary

**Summary:** Led by visions and a spell scroll, Sorak and Ryana must cross a deadly wasteland in search of the reclusive Sage and the secret Veiled Alliance. Sequel to *The Outcast*.

**Other books you might like:**
Lynn Abbey, *The Brazen Gambit*, 1994
Troy Denning, *The Amber Enchantress*, 1992
Troy Denning, *The Crimson Legion*, 1993
Troy Denning, *The Verdant Passage*, 1991
Ryan Hughes, *The Darkness Before the Dawn*, 1995

## 2625

### SIMON HAWKE

## War

(Lake Geneva, Wisconsin: TSR, 1996)

**Story type:** Fantasy (Political; Adventure)
**Series:** Birthright
**Major character(s):** Gannd Aurealis, Mythical Creature (half-elf), Warrior; Katrina, Noblewoman; Reece, Mercenary
**Time period(s):** Indeterminate
**Locale(s):** Empire of Anuir, Fictional Country; Seaharrow, Mythical Place

**Summary:** When Michael Roele dies, many attempt to gain power in the empire. Unless one leader emerges, the intrigues and squabbling among those who wish to rule will tear the empire asunder.

**Other books you might like:**
John Gregory Betancourt, *The Hag's Contract*, 1996
Anne Kelleher Bush, *Children of Enchantment*, 1996
Dixie Lee McKeone, *Greatheart*, 1996
Dixie McKeone, *The Spider's Test*, 1996
R.A. Salvatore, *Siege of Darkness*, 1994

## 2626

### SIMON HAWKE

## The Whims of Creation

(New York: Warner Aspect, 1995)

**Story type:** Science Fiction (Generation Starship; Genetic Manipulation)
**Major character(s):** Ulysses Buckland, Teenager, Wizard; Jenny Kruickshank, Teenager, Warrior; Penelope Selden, Psychologist, Computer Expert (programmer)
**Time period(s):** Indeterminate Future (3rd millennium A.D.)
**Locale(s):** *Agamemnon*, Spaceship; Outer Space

**Summary:** Ulysses discovers that suicide and early marriage seem on the increase, but he lacks the proper security code to check on the psych files. In other unusual occurrences, his mother finds fairies in the herb fields and the school's artificial intelligence sends him to a planet where he uses mystic posers and Jenny wields a sword. 50 years earlier, Dr. Selden predicted the need for change and adventure, altering the A.I. programs to produce mythic forms using the reproductive centers.

**Other books you might like:**
Brian W. Aldiss, *Starship*, 1959
Poul Anderson, *The Boat of a Million Years*, 1989
James Blish, *A Life for the Stars*, 1962
Alexei Panshin, *Rite of Passage*, 1968
Gene Wolfe, *Nightside the Long Sun*, 1993

---

**2627**

**SIMON HAWKE**

## The Wizard of Camelot

(New York: Warner Questar, 1993)

**Story type:** Fantasy (Light Fantasy; Post-Disaster)
**Series:** Wizard of 4th Street
**Major character(s):** Merlin Ambrosius, Wizard; Thomas Mallory, Police Officer (retired); Billy Martens, Television Personality
**Time period(s):** 25th century
**Locale(s):** London, England; Loughborough, England

**Summary:** At the end of the Collapse, Thomas Mallory quits the London Police Department. He comes home to find his family cold and hungry and takes an ax to illegally cut some wood, almost not caring if he gets caught. When his ax touches the tree, a bolt of lightning splits the tree and an old man in a robe suddenly appears, calling himself Merlin Ambrosius and desiring to start a school to train adepts in Thaumaturgy and save humanity and the Earth from the Collapse. Prequel to *The Wizard of 4th Street.*

**Other books you might like:**
James P. Blaylock, *The Paper Grail*, 1991
Charles de Lint, *The Little Country*, 1991
John DeChancie, *Castle Perilous*, 1988
Michael Kurland, *A Study in Sorcery*, 1989
Michael Williams, *A Forest Lord*, 1991
Robert Anton Wilson, *The Widow's Son*, 1985

---

**2628**

**SIMON HAWKE**

## The Wizard of Santa Fe

(New York: Warner Questar, 1991)

**Story type:** Fantasy (Magic Conflict; Post-Disaster)
**Series:** Wizard of 4th Street
**Major character(s):** Wyrdrune Carpinski, Wizard; Billy Slade, Wizard (Merlin Ambrosius)
**Time period(s):** 26th century
**Locale(s):** Sante Fe, New Mexico

**Summary:** When a necromancer kills two young women in Santa Fe, Merlin recognizes the work of a Dark One. He moves the household, including Broom, to New Mexico to destroy the necromancer before the Bureau of Thaumaturgy agent arrives. The Bureau does not know that Merlin is alive in the body of his descendant, Billy Slade, and Merlin prefers to keep it that way.

**Other books you might like:**
Glen Cook, *Sweet Silver Blues*, 1984

John DeChancie, *Castle Perilous*, 1988
Diane Duane, *High Wizardry*, 1990
Randall Garrett, *Too Many Magicians*, 1967
Barbara Hambly, *The Time of the Dark*, 1982
Michael Kurland, *A Study in Sorcery*, 1989
Roger Zelazny, *Nine Princes in Amber*, 1970

---

**2629**

**SIMON HAWKE**

## The Wizard of Sunset Strip

(New York: Questar, 1989)

**Story type:** Fantasy (Contemporary)
**Series:** Wizard of 4th Street
**Major character(s):** Wyrdrune Carpinski, Wizard
**Time period(s):** Indeterminate Future
**Locale(s):** Los Angeles, California

**Summary:** A new age of magic has arrived, along with the spirits of Merlin, Mordred and sundry others. Sacrificial killings of beautiful women lead the Bureau of Thaumatology to believe a significant supernatural event will soon take place.

**Other books you might like:**
Glen Cook, *Bitter Gold Hearts*, 1988
  The Garrett Files
Alan Dean Foster, *Glory Lane*, 1987
Barbara Hambly, *The Silent Tower*, 1988

---

**2630**

**JUDITH HAWKES**

## Julian's House

(New York: Ticknor & Fields, 1989)

**Story type:** Horror (Haunted House)
**Major character(s):** David Curtiss, Paranormal Investigator (Parapsychologist); Sally Curtiss, Paranormal Investigator (Parapsychologist)
**Time period(s):** 1980s (1983)
**Locale(s):** Skipdon, Massachusetts (Samuel Gilfoy House)

**Summary:** Married parapsychologists Sally and David Curtiss probe the secrets of their rented haunted house. They stimulate bizarre psychic phenomena and discover dark, disturbing secrets about the Gilfoy family, putting their own marriage and psychological/psychic stability at risk.

**Other books you might like:**
Shirley Jackson, *The Haunting of Hill House*, 1959
Richard Matheson, *Hell House*, 1971
Chet Williamson, *Soulstorm*, 1986

---

**2631**

**JUDITH HAWKES**

## My Soul to Keep

(New York: Dutton, 1996)

**Story type:** Horror (Ghost Story)
**Major character(s):** Annabel "Nan" Lucas, Photographer; Stephen Barnett, Child (Nan's eight-year-old son); Schuyler "Sky" Barnett, Handyman (Nan's cousin)
**Time period(s):** 1980s (1988)
**Locale(s):** Corey County, Tennessee

**Summary:** Nan Lucas leaves New York for her family homestead in Tennessee to get a new start following her failed marriage. She is unconcerned about her son Stephen developing an imaginary playmate, until she discovers the playmate closely resembles her childhood friend Tucker, who died saving her life and whom Stephen could not have known about otherwise.

**Other books you might like:**
Rick Hautala, *Cold Whisper*, 1991
Stephen King, *The Shining*, 1977
Thomas Tryon, *The Other*, 1971

## 2632

### BARRY T. HAWKINS

### *Puppet Master*
(New York: Zebra, 1993)

**Story type:** Horror (Psychological Suspense; Serial Killer)
**Major character(s):** Gil Beach, Detective—Police; Pilar Murphy, Psychologist, Professor; The Performer, Entertainer (ventriloquist), Serial Killer
**Time period(s):** 1990s (1993)
**Locale(s):** New York, New York

**Summary:** Detective Gil Beach finds himself matching wits with one of the most insidious killers he has ever confronted, a child murderer who steals body parts from his victims for his ventriloquist's doll.

**Other books you might like:**
William Goldman, *Magic*, 1976
Thomas Tryon, *The Other*, 1971

## 2633

### JULIAN HAWTHORNE

### *The Rose of Death and Other Mysterious Delusions*
(Ashcroft, British Columbia: Ash-Tree Press, 1997)

**Story type:** Horror (Collection)

**Summary:** Eight stories, many of them previously uncollected, by the son of Nathaniel Hawthorne. Included are "Ken's Mystery," about an artist seduced by a vampire; "The Delusion of Ralph Penwyn," about a man killed by eastern occultism; and "Kildhurm's Oak," in which acorns bathed in the blood of a murdered man and his lover grows into an oak that fulfills a curse placed upon it centuries later. Edited and with an introduction by Jessica Amanda Salmonson.

**Other books you might like:**
F. Marion Crawford, *Wandering Ghosts*, 1911
Olivia Howard Dunbar, *The Shell of Sense*, 1997
Henry James, *The Ghostly Tales of Henry James*, 1948
Fitz-James O'Brien, *The Supernatural Tales of Fitz-James O'Brien*, 1988
Vincent O'Sullivan, *Master of the Fallen Years*, 1994

## 2634

### PATRICK NIELSEN HAYDEN, Editor

### *Starlight 1*
(New York: Tor, 1996)

**Story type:** Science Fiction (Anthology; Fantasy)
**Series:** Starlight

**Summary:** Contains a three-page introduction and 12 original stories, generally serious in tone, exploring the grand diversity of science fiction and fantasy with themes such as first contact, dystopias, drama, Nazi experimentation, illness, dreaming, religion, and magic. Authors include John M. Ford, Mark Kreighbaum, Maureen F. McHugh, Susan Palwick, Robert Reed, Martha Soukup, Michael Swanwick, and Jane Yolen. First of a new series.

**Other books you might like:**
Lou Aronica, *Full Spectrum*, 1988
   Shawna McCarthy, co-editor
Lou Aronica, *Full Spectrum 2*, 1989
   Shawn McCarthy, Amy Stout, Patrick Lo Brutto, co-editors
Lou Aronica, *Full Spectrum 3-4*, 1991-1993
   Amy Stout, Betsy Mitchell, co-editors
Greg Bear, *New Legends*, 1995
   editor
Jennifer Hershey, *Full Spectrum 5*, 1995
   Tom Dupree, Janna Silverstein, co-editors
Robert Silverberg, *Universe 1-3*, 1990-1994
   Karen Haber, co-editor
Jane Yolen, *The Xanadu Series*, 1993-1995
   editor

## 2635

### PATRICK NIELSEN HAYDEN, Editor

### *Starlight 2*
(New York: Tor, 1998)

**Story type:** Science Fiction (Anthology)
**Series:** Starlight

**Summary:** This anthology contains a three-page introduction and 13 original stories, including the first English-language appearance of Argentine writer Angelica Gorodischer (translated by Ursula K. Le Guin). Other authors include M. Shayne Bell, Raphael Carter, Ted Chiang, Susanna Clarke, Esther M. Friesner, Ellen Kushner, Geoffrey A. Landis, David Langford, Jonathan Lethem, Carter Scholz, Martha Soukup, and Robert Charles Wilson. Part of an ongoing series that includes the World Fantasy Award winner *Starlight 1*.

**Other books you might like:**
Lou Aronica, *Full Spectrum 3-4*, 1991-1993
   Amy Stout, Betsy Mitchell, co-editors
Greg Bear, *New Legends*, 1995
   editor
David Garnett, *New Worlds*, 1997
   editor
Jennifer Hershey, *Full Spectrum 5*, 1995
   Tom Dupree, Janna Silverstein, co-editors
John Kessel, *Intersections: The Sycamore Hill Anthology*, 1996
   Mark L. Van Name, Richard Butner, co-editors
Robert Silverberg, *Universe 1-3*, 1990-1994
   Karen Haber, co-editor
Jane Yolen, *The Xanadu Series*, 1993-1995
   editor

## 2636

### PAUL HAZEL

### *The Wealdwife's Tale*
(New York: Morrow AvoNova, 1993)

**Story type:** Fantasy (Legend; Quest)
**Major character(s):** Rudyard "Waldo" Riding Wenceslas, Royalty (eighth Duke of West Redding), Adventurer

**Time period(s):** Indeterminate Past
**Locale(s):** England; The Weald, Mythical Place (forest)

**Summary:** Overcome by melancholy from the loss of his beloved, Waldo journeys into the Weald to bring back his wife. Waldo returns with a new bride, her long dead mother and a new curse which will impel his daughter toward her fated future. Based on the song, "Good King Wenceslaus."

**Other books you might like:**
Louise Cooper, *The Sleep of Stone*, 1991
Frances Mary Hendry, *Quest for a Maid*, 1990
Robert Holdstock, *Lavondyss: Journey to an Unknown Region*, 1989
Robert Holdstock, *Mythago Wood*, 1984
Joseph Jacobs, *English Fairy Tales*, 1898
    editor
Ellen Kushner, *Thomas the Rhymer*, 1990
Patricia C. Wrede, *Snow White and Rose Red*, 1989

### 2637

**DENISE LOPEZ HEALD**

## *Mistwalker*

(New York: Ballantine Del Rey, 1994)

**Story type:** Science Fiction (First Contact; Political)
**Major character(s):** Meesha Raschad, Miner, Heir; Sally "Sal" Banks, Businesswoman (delivery service)
**Time period(s):** Indeterminate Future
**Locale(s):** Ver Day, Planet—Imaginary

**Summary:** While claiming to maintain a Green economic and industrial environment, the corrupt government of Ver Day knows that the new equipment proves unreliable in the harsh environment, which kills most new residents of the planet within months. Sal Banks hires Meesha Raschad who unknowingly befriended the mistwalkers, thereby changing the lives of all residents on Ver Day.

**Other books you might like:**
Eleanor Arnason, *A Woman of the Iron People*, 1991
Octavia E. Butler, *Parable of the Sower*, 1994
L. Warren Douglas, *Cannon's Orb*, 1994
L. Warren Douglas, *A Plague of Change*, 1992
Eric Vinicoff, *The Weigher*, 1992
    Marcia Martin, co-author

### 2638

**DANIEL HECHT**

## *Skull Session*

(New York: Viking, 1998)

**Story type:** Horror (Mystery)
**Major character(s):** Paul Skoglund, Construction Worker; Morgan Ford, Police Officer; Vivien Hoffman, Heiress (Paul's aunt)
**Time period(s):** 1990s (1998)
**Locale(s):** Lewisboro, New York

**Summary:** Afflicted with a case of Tourette's syndrome that hinders his ability to secure a teaching position, Paul Skoglund accepts an offer from his rich Aunt Vivien to renovate her vandalized Hudson Valley mansion. The mansion plays a key role in the police investigation of the disappearance of several local teenagers, and murders so brutal that they suggest the involvement of a supernatural monster or a person of near superhuman strength. A first novel.

**Other books you might like:**
Robert Bloch, *Psycho*, 1959
Michael Cadnum, *Nightlight*, 1989

Michael Crichton, *The Terminal Man*, 1972
Charles L. Grant, *Genesis*, 1998
Michael Slade, *Ghoul*, 1987

### 2639

**D.A. HEELEY**

## *Ronin*

(St. Paul, Minnesota: Llewellyn Publications, 1997)

**Story type:** Fantasy (Magic Conflict; Religious)
**Series:** Darkness and Light
**Major character(s):** Shadrack, Reincarnated Person (Malak), Martial Arts Expert (samurai-magician); Fiona, Reincarnated Person (Lena), Spouse (Malak's); Jaad, Reincarnated Person (Dethen), Magician (Black Adept)
**Time period(s):** Indeterminate
**Locale(s):** Earth; Mythical Place

**Summary:** Reborn on Earth as Shadrack 1,000 years after the Arch-Demon Lilith destroys him and devours his soul, Malak learns the art of the samurai while struggling to remember and recover his former self. Lena, the wife for whom he sacrificed his soul, regains her memories when reincarnated as Fiona, and uses her magic powers to help Malak fuse the pieces of his shattered identity. They and their allies must defeat Malak's evil karmic twin, the Black Adept Dethen, and face Lilith once again to save Enya and its inhabitants from destruction. Second in series.

**Other books you might like:**
Steven Brust, *Jhereg*, 1983
D.J. Conway, *The Dream Warrior*, 1996
Eve Forward, *Villains by Necessity*, 1995
Elizabeth Moon, *Sheepfarmer's Daughter*, 1988
Joel Rosenberg, *The Fire Duke*, 1995
Roger Zelazny, *Nine Princes in Amber*, 1970

### 2640

**JEAN HEGLAND**

## *Into the Forest*

(New York: Bantam, 1997)

**Story type:** Science Fiction (Disaster)
**Major character(s):** Eva, Teenager; Nell, Teenager, Writer
**Time period(s):** 1990s
**Locale(s):** California

**Summary:** Overseas warfare interrupts Eva's plans for a dance career and Nell's plans to attend Harvard. When civil strife causes electrical and telephone service to cease, Eva and Nell, now orphaned, must stretch their dwindling resources and learn to survive using the riches of the forest around their isolated home. First novel. Reissue of the 1996 Calyx Books edition.

**Other books you might like:**
Richard Brautigan, *In Watermelon Sugar*, 1968
David Brin, *The Postman*, 1985
Marlen Haushofer, *The Wall*, 1991
Sterling E. Lanier, *Hiero's Journey*, 1973
David R. Palmer, *Emergence*, 1984

## 2641

### R. ANDREW HEIDEL

## Beyond the Wall of Sleep

(New York: Mortco, 1998)

**Story type:** Fantasy (Collection)

**Summary:** This collection contains nine stories and 15 poems. The themes range from conversations with God to encounters with death personified.

**Other books you might like:**
Donald Barthelme, *City Life*, 1970
Ray Bradbury, *Driving Blind*, 1997
Avram Davidson, *The Avram Davidson Treasury*, 1998
Slawomir Mrozek, *The Elephant*, 1958
Joyce Carol Oates, *Night-Side: Eighteen Tales*, 1977

## 2642

### MARCY HEIDISH

## The Torching

(New York: Simon & Schuster, 1992)

**Story type:** Horror (Black Magic; Occult)
**Major character(s):** Alice Grey, Writer; Jake Randolph, Writer, Pilot; Evangeline Smith, Witch
**Time period(s):** 1980s (1989)
**Locale(s):** Washington, District of Columbia (Georgetown area)

**Summary:** Historical novelist Alice Grey begins routine research into the life of Evangeline Smith, an eighteenth-century woman burned at the stake on apparently trumped-up charges of witchcraft. Imagine Alice's surprise when her investigation turns up evidence that Evangeline may indeed have been a witch—and may in fact be using Alice as the conduit by which she will re-emerge into the world of the living.

**Other books you might like:**
Jonathan Aycliffe, *Naomi's Room*, 1991
Emmanuel Carrere, *Gothic Romance*, 1984
Michael Stewart, *Belladonna*, 1992

## 2643

### RUTH D. HEIN
### VICKY L. HINSENBROCK, Co-Author

## Ghostly Tales of Iowa

(Ames: Iowa State University Press, 1996)

**Story type:** Horror (Collection)

**Summary:** This book collects 53 folk tales from the oral tradition, many with roots in the beliefs and superstitions of the Scandinavian settlers of Iowa. Harmless ghosts spook the unwary in "Back to Her Grave" and "The Ghostly Bell Ringer" and haunt houses in "The Haunted House" and "Spook Hollow House." Ghosts manifest themselves as human remains in "The Skeleton's Hands" and animals in "The Dog of a Ghost." Supernatural beings other than ghosts are the subject of "Tricked by a Troll," "The Cellar Witch," and "The Witch's Book."

**Other books you might like:**
John Canning, *50 Great Ghost Stories*, 1971
    editor
D.J. Enright, *The Oxford Book of the Supernatural*, 1994
    editor

Terri Hardin, *Supernatural Tales From around the World*, 1995
    editor
Jessica Amanda Salmonson, *The Mysterious Doom and Other Ghostly Tales of the Pacific Northwest*, 1992
John Manchip White, *Whistling Past the Churchyard*, 1991

## 2644

### ROBERT A. HEINLEIN

## Glory Road

(New York: Baen, 1993)

**Story type:** Fantasy (Alternate World; Adventure)
**Major character(s):** Evelyn Cyril "Oscar/Scar" Gordon, Hero, Traveler; Aster "Star", Royalty (queen), Traveler; Rufo, Magician, Servant
**Time period(s):** 1960s; Indeterminate
**Locale(s):** I'lli Du Levant, Mediterranean; Alternate Earth; Nice, France

**Summary:** Released from the Army in Southeast Asia via Heidelberg, Scar travels to the Mediterranean hoping to have enough money to attend Heidelberg University. When his Irish Sweepstakes winning ticket proves counterfeit, Scar sees an ad looking for a hero with his skills. He responds and soon finds himself in situations where his social graces and martial arts skills improve with practice and willingness to learn. Reissue of the 1963 Hugo Award nominee.

**Other books you might like:**
Piers Anthony, *The Caterpillar's Question*, 1992
Charles de Lint, *The Little Country*, 1991
John DeChancie, *Castle Perilous*, 1988
Alan Dean Foster, *To the Vanishing Point*, 1988
Geary Gravel, *A Key for the Nonesuch*, 1990
S.P. Somtow, *Riverrun*, 1991
Will Shetterly, *The Tangled Lands*, 1989

## 2645

### ROBERT A. HEINLEIN

## The Moon Is a Harsh Mistress

(New York: Tor, 1996)

**Story type:** Science Fiction (Political)
**Major character(s):** Manuel "Mannie" O'Kelly, Revolutionary, Computer Expert; Wyoming "Wyoh" Knott, Revolutionary; Mike, Artificial Intelligence, Imposter (Adam Selene)
**Time period(s):** 2070s (2075)
**Locale(s):** Luna City, Montenegro

**Summary:** Mysteriously self-aware, Mike grows and explores consciousness with Mannie and Wyoh's help. The three work to effect revolution and revolt against Earth's abuse of lunar residents, exiled to the Moon as permanent prisoners. Reissue of the Hugo Award winning novel published in 1966.

**Other books you might like:**
Isaac Asimov, *Foundation*, 1951
Alfred Bester, *The Stars My Destination*, 1996
    revised edition
Ben Bova, *Millennium*, 1976
David Brin, *Earth*, 1990
Rudy Rucker, *Live Robots*, 1994
Cordwainer Smith, *Norstrilia*, 1975
Allen Steele, *Lunar Descent*, 1991
John Varley, *Steel Beach*, 1992

## 2646

### ROBERT A. HEINLEIN

## *The Puppet Masters*

(New York: Del Rey, 1991)

**Story type:** Science Fiction (Invasion of Earth)
**Major character(s):** Sam Nivens, Spy (Very Secret Agency); Mary, Spy (aka Allucquere); The Old Man, Spy (head spy-Very Secret Agency)
**Time period(s):** 2000s (2007)
**Locale(s):** United States

**Summary:** Parasitic slugs capable of controlling men are brought to Earth by flying saucers. Sam Nivens, the Old Man and Mary are sent to investigate, but have trouble convincing the government of the seriousness of the threat. Total nudity can keep the threat at bay, but something that will kill slugs and not people is needed to really control it. Mary, a survivor of a failed Venus colony, is the key to both disease and cure. Realizing that this is not a total solution, selected Earthmen take ship for Titan to exterminate the slugs. This is a substantially expanded edition of the novel first published in 1951.

**Other books you might like:**
Greg Bear, *The Forge of God*, 1987
Gregory Benford, *Across the Sea of Suns*, 1984
Thomas M. Disch, *The Genocides*, 1979
David Gerrold, *A Matter for Men*, 1989
Larry Niven, *Footfall*, 1985
  Jerry Pournelle, co-author

## 2647

### ROBERT A. HEINLEIN

## *Red Planet*

(New York: Del Rey, 1990)

**Story type:** Science Fiction (Young Adult; Adventure)
**Major character(s):** Jim Marlowe, Student; Frank Sutton, Student; Willis, Alien
**Time period(s):** Indeterminate Future
**Locale(s):** South Colony, Mars; Syrtis Minor, Mars

**Summary:** Jim and Frank take their furry friend Willis with them when they leave home to go to school in Syrtis Minor. When the Headmaster confiscates Willis on the grounds of the ''no pets'' rule, the young men's claim that Willis is not an animal falls on deaf ears. They must rescue their friend and try to solve the mystery of the true nature of the alien being. Originally published in 1949, this is the first publication of the complete manuscript.

**Other books you might like:**
John Christopher, *Fireball*, 1981
Arthur C. Clarke, *Islands in the Sky*, 1952
John Keir Cross, *The Angry Planet*, 1945
Gordon R. Dickson, *Space Winners*, 1965
Patricia A. McKillip, *Moon-Flash*, 1984

## 2648

### ROBERT A. HEINLEIN

## *Requiem*

(New York: Tor, 1992)

**Story type:** Science Fiction (Collection; Anthology)

**Summary:** Subtitled ''New Collected Works by Robert A. Heinlein and Tributes to the Grand Master,'' this volume contains fiction and non-fiction by Heinlein and non-fiction about Heinlein and his work with a five-page preface by Virginia Heinlein and a one-page editor's foreword.

**Other books you might like:**
Larry Niven, *N-Space*, 1990
Larry Niven, *Playgrounds of the Mind*, 1991

## 2649

### ROBERT A. HEINLEIN

## *Stranger in a Strange Land*

(New York: Putnam, 1991)

**Story type:** Science Fiction (Theological; Political)
**Major character(s):** Valentine Michael Smith, Angel (archangel Michael), Orphan; Jubal Harshaw, Writer, Lawyer; Gillian Boardman, Nurse, Companion
**Time period(s):** 21st century
**Locale(s):** Washington, District of Columbia; New York, New York

**Summary:** Michael is sent to Earth by the Ancient Ones of Mars who have raised Michael as a Martian after he became the sole survivor of Mankind's first Martian colony. Unbeknownst to him, Michael is being used as a spy, allowing Martians to decide Humanity's fate. As a wolfling, Michael must discover his human nature, his happiness, loves, growth into adulthood and the joy of becoming self-directed. His human rite of passage is viewed through Michael's eyes and through the eyes of his friends. This edition is 60,000 words longer than the 1961 edition, now containing the complete, restored, original manuscript of this Hugo Award-winning novel.

**Other books you might like:**
Roger MacBride Allen, *The Ring of Charon*, 1990
David Brin, *Startide Rising*, 1983
Octavia E. Butler, *Dawn*, 1987
Larry Niven, *Protector*, 1973
Alis A. Rasmussen, *A Passage of Stars*, 1990
Alis A. Rasmussen, *The Price of Ransom*, 1990
Alis A. Rasmussen, *Revolution's Shore*, 1990
Cordwainer Smith, *The Best of Cordwainer Smith*, 1975
  pseudonym of Paul Myron Anthony Linebarger
Cordwainer Smith, *Norstrilia*, 1975
  pseudonym of Paul Myron Anthony Linebarger
John Varley, *The Persistence of Vision*, 1978

## 2650

### CAROL HELLER

## *The Gates of Vensunor*

(New York: AvoNova, 1997)

**Story type:** Fantasy (Magic Conflict; Adventure)
**Series:** Shunlar Chronicles
**Major character(s):** Shunlar, Psychic, Warrior; Algooth, Mythical Creature (dragon); Creedath, Businessman (merchant), Psychic
**Time period(s):** Indeterminate
**Locale(s):** Vensunor, Fictional City; Valley of Great Trees, Mythical Place

**Summary:** Ordered by the mayor to find a particular stranger, Shunlar soon finds herself hunted, as Creedath seeks to find and control dragonkind. First in a series.

**Other books you might like:**
Graham Edwards, *Dragoncharm*, 1996

Lynn Flewelling, *Luck in the Shadows*, 1996
Ursula K. Le Guin, *A Wizard of Earthsea*, 1968
Andre Norton, *The Elvenbane*, 1991
    Mercedes Lackey, co-author
Andre Norton, *Elvenblood*, 1995
    Mercedes Lackey, co-author

---

| 2651 |

### CAROL HELLER

## The Sands of Kalaven: A Novel of Shunlar

(New York: Avon Eos, 1998)

**Story type:** Fantasy (Quest; Sword and Sorcery)
**Series:** Shunlar Chronicles
**Major character(s):** Shunlar, Mercenary; Ranth, Mercenary
**Time period(s):** Indeterminate
**Locale(s):** Kalaven, Fictional Country

**Summary:** An oracle causes Shunlar and her lover, Ranth, to set off toward the desert country of Kalaven, each on separate quests that will eventually bring them back together. Shunlar seeks the secret of her own past, and discovers that those she considered friends are really enemies plotting her destruction.

**Other books you might like:**
Lynn Abbey, *The Black Flame*, 1980
Claudia J. Edwards, *Taming the Forest King*, 1987
Ru Emerson, *The Princess of Flames*, 1986
Ron Miller, *Silk and Steel*, 1992
C.L. Moore, *Jirel of Joiry*, 1969

---

| 2652 |

### JANE HELLER

## Infernal Affairs

(New York: Kensington, 1996)

**Story type:** Horror (Occult)
**Major character(s):** Barbara Chessner, Real Estate Agent; Jeremy Cook, Sailor (charter boat captain); Frances Lutz, Real Estate Agent
**Time period(s):** 1990s (1996)
**Locale(s):** Banyon Beach, Florida

**Summary:** Distressed over her deteriorating marriage and frustrating life, Barbara Chessner inadvertently sells her soul to the devil for personal beauty. Barbara's deal proves only the beginning of other satanic arrangements that begin changing life in the town of Banyon Beach.

**Other books you might like:**
Ramsey Campbell, *Obsession*, 1986
Stephen King, *Needful Things*, 1992
Robert Masello, *Private Demons*, 1992
Kim Newman, *The Quorum*, 1994

---

| 2653 |

### MARK HELPRIN

## A City in Winter

(New York: Viking Ariel, 1996)

**Story type:** Fantasy (Psychic Powers; Political)
**Major character(s):** I, Royalty, Orphan; Notorincus, Slave, Revolutionary; Astrahn, Slave, Revolutionary

**Time period(s):** Indeterminate
**Locale(s):** The Kingdom, Fictional Country

**Summary:** When an evil usurper kills the king and queen, their orphaned daughter lives in anonymous safety for years. Deciding to return justice to the kingdom, she receives aid from two rebels who help her hide until she can confront the usurper and precipitate a popular revolt.

**Other books you might like:**
Lois McMaster Bujold, *The Spirit Ring*, 1992
William Goldman, *The Princess Bride*, 1973
Robin Hobb, *Assassin's Apprentice*, 1995
Mercedes Lackey, *The Robin and the Kestrel*, 1993
Patricia A. McKillip, *The Book of Atrix Wolfe*, 1995
Paula Volsky, *Illusion*, 1992

---

| 2654 |

### MARK HELPRIN

## The Veils of Snows

(New York: Viking Ariel, 1997)

**Story type:** Fantasy (Young Adult; Political)
**Series:** Swan Lake
**Major character(s):** I, Writer, Military Personnel (soldier); The Queen, Royalty
**Time period(s):** Indeterminate
**Locale(s):** The Kingdom, Fictional Country

**Summary:** After many years of peace in the kingdom, the usurper returns, leaving the queen only a brief time to mount a defense. As the situation worsens, the Veil of Snows provides some opportunity for repelling the invasion. However, the best hope for the kingdom to regain its rightful ruler may lie with the infant prince, if he survives.

**Other books you might like:**
James C. Christensen, *Voyage of the Basset*, 1996
    Renwick St. James, Alan Dean Foster, co-authors
James Gurney, *Dinotopia*, 1992
E.T.A. Hoffmann, *Nutcracker*, 1996
Anne McCaffrey, *Black Horses for the King*, 1996
Patricia A. McKillip, *The Book of Atrix Wolfe*, 1995
Garth Nix, *Sabriel*, 1996

---

| 2655 |

### MICHAEL HEMMINGSON
### JIM BOB COOK, Illustrator
### PAUL SCHIOLA, Illustrator

## Nice Little Stories Jam-Packed with Depraved Sex and Violence

(Denver: Cyber-Psychos A.O.D., 1995)

**Story type:** Horror (Collection)

**Summary:** This first collection brings together six stories of twisted personalities for mature readers. In the title story, a psychotherapist uses the 50 minutes his patients are hypnotized on the couch to murder their children. "The Bibliophile" tells of a librarian with a book fetish and Nazi tendencies, and "Skull-Fuck" of a man who discovers the fantasies he unleashes in his group therapy sessions are not very pleasant when they occur in real life. "Pain" is a hardboiled revenge story. Full Force Frank supplies the introduction.

**Other books you might like:**
S. Darnbrook Colson, *People of the Night*, 1994
Ron Dee, *Sex and Blood*, 1994

Edward Lee, *Header*, 1995
Lucy Taylor, *Close to the Bone*, 1993
Lucy Taylor, *The Flesh Artist*, 1994
Lucy Taylor, *Unnatural Acts and Other Stories*, 1994

---

## 2656
### MICHAEL HEMMINGSON

## Snuff Flique

(Denver: Cyber-Psychos AOD, 1997)

**Story type:** Horror (Collection)

**Summary:** Six violent tales of dark suspense, including "Leashes," in which a child recalls his mother's vicious revenge against the circus clown that brutalized her; "Two of a Kind," about a vigilante who enjoys his work; "The Silence of Dirt and Grass," in which the recovery of a childhood toy brings back a man's memories of a horrible murder he committed as a youth; "Shadowplayers," which features a drifter whose hopes for salvation from a life of past crime are tragically shattered; and "Snuff Flick," which elaborates a corrupt federal agent's adventures in a grim and seamy world of kidnappers, pornographers, adulterers and murderers.

**Other books you might like:**
S. Darnbrook Colson, *People of the Night*, 1995
Ray Garton, *Methods of Madness*, 1990
Barry Hoffman, *Firefly. . .Burning Bright*, 1996
Gerard Daniel Houarner, *Painfreak*, 1996
David J. Schow, *Lost Angels*, 1990
John Shirley, *New Noir*, 1993
Lucy Taylor, *Painted in Blood*, 1997

---

## 2657
### JASON HENDERSON

## The Element of Fire

(New York: Warner Aspect, 1995)

**Story type:** Fantasy (Adventure; Contemporary Realism)
**Series:** Highlander
**Major character(s):** Duncan MacLeod, Immortal, Martial Arts Expert; Connor MacLeod, Immortal; Khordas, Immortal, Pirate
**Time period(s):** 1850s; 1890s
**Locale(s):** Massachusetts; Atlantic Ocean; Scotland

**Summary:** Lusting for revenge for an ancient wrong that he attributes to Duncan MacLeod, Khordas plots to destroy all that Duncan holds dear, then kill Duncan himself. With only one immortal fated to survive, Duncan intends to keep his own head. First of a television tie-in series.

**Other books you might like:**
L. Sprague de Camp, *The Fantastic Swordsmen*, 1967
   editor
Terry Goodkind, *Wizard's First Rule*, 1994
Ashley McConnell, *Highlander: Scimitar*, 1996
Melanie Rawn, *Knights of the Morningstar*, 1994
Fred Saberhagen, *An Armory of Swords*, 1995
   editor

---

## 2658
### JASON HENDERSON

## The Spawn of Loki

(New York: Baen, 1994)

**Story type:** Fantasy (Adventure; Religious)
**Major character(s):** MacDuff, Hero; Loki, Deity; Susan, Mythical Creature (eternal guardian of fate), Immortal
**Time period(s):** 11th century
**Locale(s):** Normandy, France; Uppsala, Sweden; New Asgard, Mythical Place (realm of the gods)

**Summary:** When a Norman monk's research awakens Loki, Ragnarok, the final destruction of the world, may ensue 1000 years earlier than planned by the gods. MacDuff presents humanity's only hope for postponing disaster.

**Other books you might like:**
Patrick H. Adkins, *Sons of the Titans*, 1990
James Blish, *Black Easter*, 1968
Elizabeth Forrest, *Phoenix Fire*, 1992
Alan Dean Foster, *Cyber Way*, 1990
Neil Gaiman, *Good Omens: The Nice and Accurate Prophecies of Agnes Nutter, Witch*, 1990
   Terry Pratchett, co-author
Roger Zelazny, *Creatures of Light and Darkness*, 1969
Roger Zelazny, *The Mask of Loki*, 1990
   Thomas T. Thomas, co-author

---

## 2659
### ZENNA HENDERSON

## Ingathering: The Complete People Stories of Zenna Henderson

(Framingham, Massachusetts: NESFA Press, 1995)

**Story type:** Science Fiction (Collection; Psychic Powers)
**Time period(s):** 20th century
**Locale(s):** New Mexico; Southwest

**Summary:** Contains a five-page chronology of the People by editors Mark Olson and Priscilla Olson, one page of acknowledgements, a two-page introduction by Priscilla Olson, a three-page afterword by Zenna Henderson, "The People Stories," plus all 17 stories of the People including those published as *Pilgrimage: The Book of the People* (1961), *The People: No Different Flesh* (1967), three subsequently published in periodicals, plus one original, "Michal Without." Stories feature a gentle investigation of extraterrestrial immigrants inspired by Henderson's lengthy teaching career and Bible stories.

**Other books you might like:**
Nina Kiriki Hoffman, *The Thread That Binds the Bones*, 1994
Janet Kagan, *Mirabile*, 1991
Spider Robinson, *Callahan and Company*, 1987
Theodore Sturgeon, *The Ultimate Egoist*, 1994
John Varley, *The Persistence of Vision*, 1978

---

## 2660
### HOWARD V. HENDRIX

## Lightpaths

(New York: Ace, 1997)

**Story type:** Science Fiction (Space Colony; Utopia)

**Major character(s):** Roger Cortland, Scientist, Researcher; Marissa Correa, Researcher, Student; Jhana Meniskos, Scientist, Researcher
**Time period(s):** 2040s
**Locale(s):** Orbital Biodiversity Preserve, Space Station (Orbital Park); High Orbital Mfg. Env., Space Station (Home)

**Summary:** On his way back to his laboratory on Orbital Park, Roger meets his new lab assistant, there to do research and study social systems with his mother, one of the founders of the Biodiversity Preserve. Also on the shuttle, Jhana, still troubled by the death of her ex-lover, shares Roger's line of study. Sent by one of the Earth-based investors of Orbital Park, Jhana must send back information about Diamond Thunderbolt, perhaps a weapon to be used against Earth. Meanwhile, the computer which controls the habitat seems more helpful lately.

**Other books you might like:**
Michael Flynn, *Firestar*, 1996
Melissa Scott, *Dreaming Metal*, 1997
Allen Steele, *Clarke County, Space*, 1990
Bruce Sterling, *Schismatrix Plus*, 1996
Harlan Thompson, *Silent Running*, 1972
John Varley, *Steel Beach*, 1992

## 2661

### HOWARD V. HENDRIX

## Standing Wave

(New York: Ace, 1998)

**Story type:** Science Fiction (Space Colony; Alternate Intelligence)
**Series:** Lightpaths
**Major character(s):** Brandi Easter, Spacewoman; Mei-Ling Magnus, Historian, Researcher; Roger Cortland, Scientist, Spaceman
**Time period(s):** 2040s
**Locale(s):** Orbital Biodiversity Preserve, Space Station (Orbital Park); Fionnphort, Scotland (Mull Island); Caracas, Venezuela

**Summary:** An event sparked by a death in space, perceived as Light, changes the many minds it touches, not only human, if only for a brief time. Brandi spots the asteroid heading for Earth, realizes it will land, and sees people waving as she surfs past it, while Mei-Ling, obsessed with mazes, becomes fascinated with standing waves and the Light.

**Other books you might like:**
Greg Egan, *Diaspora*, 1998
Michael Kanaly, *Thoughts of God*, 1997
Frederik Pohl, *The Voices of Heaven*, 1994
Robert J. Sawyer, *Starplex*, 1996
Charles Sheffield, *Transcendence*, 1992

## 2662

### FRANCES MARY HENDRY

## Quest for a Maid

(New York: Farrar Straus Giroux, 1990)

**Story type:** Fantasy (Legend)
**Major character(s):** Inge, Witch; Marjory de Brus, Noblewoman
**Time period(s):** 13th century (1286)
**Locale(s):** Inverkeithing, Scotland

**Summary:** Marjory de Brus makes an arrangement with Inge to hire her as an advisor if Inge will give her the power of the throne. Inge kills King Alexander with magic and promises Lady Marjory that her son, Robert, will be king, although the Maid of Norway, the King's granddaughter, is the heir to the throne if she survives her journey home. An ALA Best Book For Young Adults title.

**Other books you might like:**
Morgan Llywelyn, *The Isles of the Blest*, 1989
Hanne Marie Svendsen, *The Gold Ball*, 1989
Judith Tarr, *Ars Magica*, 1989
Gail Van Asten, *Charlemagne's Champion*, 1990
Jack Vance, *Madouc*, 1990

## 2663

### KEITH HERBER

## Dark Prince

(New York: HarperPrism, 1994)

**Story type:** Horror (Vampire Story)
**Series:** World of Darkness: Vampire
**Major character(s):** Sullivan, Vampire; Kathy, Prostitute; Angel, Vampire
**Time period(s):** 1990s (1994)
**Locale(s):** San Francisco, California

**Summary:** Accused of diablerie, or the forbidden drinking of vampire blood by another vampire, Sullivan, a 150-year-old vampire who controls the streets of San Francisco, is stalked and sought by warring vampire clans eager to use him as a pawn in their quest to consolidate power and take over the city.

**Other books you might like:**
Elaine Bergstrom, *Tapestry of Dark Souls*, 1993
Richard Lee Byers, *Netherworld*, 1995
P.N. Elrod, *I, Strahd*, 1993
Robert Weinberg, *Blood War*, 1995
Robert Weinberg, *Vampire Diary: The Embrace*, 1995
   Mark Rein-Hagen, co-author

## 2664

### BRIAN HERBERT
### MARIE LANDIS, Co-Author

## Blood on the Sun

(New York: HarperPrism, 1996)

**Story type:** Horror (Vampire Story)
**Series:** World of Darkness: Vampire
**Major character(s):** Desidra Smith, Vampire; Christopher T. Wilson, Vampire; Mitsuo Tokoyuni, Military Personnel
**Time period(s):** 1940s
**Locale(s):** Seattle, Washington; Anchorage, Alaska

**Summary:** Defying the prince of her vampire clan, Desidra takes a false name and works as a cryptographer for the Allied forces during World War II. When she falls in love with the Japanese soldier she is spying on, she risks not only giving away Allied plans for the Battle of Midway but revealing her vampire heritage as well. This novel is set in White Wolf Books' "World of Darkness" gaming world, where humans and supernatural beings coexist.

**Other books you might like:**
Don Bassingthwaite, *As One Dead*, 1996
   Nancy Kilpatrick, co-author
Richard Lee Byers, *Netherworld*, 1995
Nancy A. Collins, *A Dozen Black Roses*, 1996
Keith Herber, *Prince of the City*, 1995
Doug Murray, *Blood Relations*, 1996
Robert Weinberg, *Vampire Diary: The Embrace*, 1995
   Mark Rein-Hagen, co-author

## 2665

**BRIAN HERBERT**
**MARIE LANDIS**, Co-Author

### *Memorymakers*

(New York: Roc, 1991)

**Story type:** Science Fiction (Political)
**Major character(s):** Emily Harvey, Twin, Revolutionary; Thomas Harvey, Twin
**Time period(s):** 22nd century
**Locale(s):** Earth

**Summary:** Unrecognized for millennia, the Ch'Var have lived alongside human Gweens, partaking of the delicacy of human flesh when possible. Now Emily and Thomas represent a new form of human which may overturn the traditional balance. This collaboration is Marie Landis' first novel.

**Other books you might like:**
C.S. Friedman, *The Madness Season*, 1990
Jacqueline Lichtenberg, *First Channel*, 1980
    Jean Lorrah, co-author
Jacqueline Lichtenberg, *House of Zeor*, 1974
Jacqueline Lichtenberg, *Molt Brother*, 1982
Jacqueline Lichtenberg, *Unto Zeor Forever*, 1978
A.E. Van Vogt, *Slan*, 1946

## 2666

**BRIAN HERBERT**

### *The Race for God*

(New York: Ace, 1990)

**Story type:** Science Fiction (Theological; Alternate Universe)
**Major character(s):** Evander Harold McMurtrey, Religious; Jin the Plarnjarn, Robot (Cyberoo C-unit 7891), Spy (Department of Loyalty)
**Time period(s):** Indeterminate Future
**Locale(s):** D'Urth, Alternate Earth

**Summary:** Evander Harold McMurtrey is contacted by God. He is given the location, the ships and along with several other humans, an invitation to visit. The pilgrimage becomes a dangerous race to reach God first.

**Other books you might like:**
J.M. Dillard, *Star Trek V: The Final Frontier*, 1989
Parke Godwin, *Waiting for the Galactic Bus*, 1988
Frank Herbert, *Whipping Star*, 1970
Ted Reynolds, *The Tides of God*, 1989
Dan Simmons, *Hyperion*, 1989
Ian Watson, *God's World*, 1979

## 2667

**JAMES HERBERT**

### *'48*

(New York: HarperPrism, 1997)

**Story type:** Horror (Science Fiction)
**Major character(s):** Hoke, Pilot; Stern, Pilot; Cissie, Young Woman
**Time period(s):** 1940s (1948)
**Locale(s):** London, England

**Summary:** In an alternate future a biological plague delivered by Nazi missiles has decimated the Earth's population, killing all but a handful of resistant people with the AB-negative blood type. Hoke, an American fighter pilot, combats roving bands of Blackshirts slowly succumbing to the disease who hope to steal potentially lifesaving blood from persons with his rare type.

**Other books you might like:**
Len Deighton, *SS-GB*, 1978
Philip K. Dick, *The Man in the High Castle*, 1992
Robert Harris, *Fatherland*, 1992
Sarban, *The Sound of His Horn*, 1962

## 2668

**JAMES HERBERT**

### *The Ghosts of Sleath*

(New York: HarperPrism, 1995)

**Story type:** Horror (Ghost Story)
**Major character(s):** David Ash, Paranormal Investigator; Grace Lockwood, Student (art student); Reverend Edmund Lockwood, Religious
**Time period(s):** 1990s (1995)
**Locale(s):** Sleath, England

**Summary:** In this sequel to the author's 1988 novel, *Haunted*, skeptical psychic investigator David Ash is summoned to a former mill town to look into the sudden reappearance of the ghosts of the newly dead. There he discovers a legacy of supernatural evil founded on ritual sacrifice intertwined with the town's history.

**Other books you might like:**
John R. Maxim, *Platforms*, 1980
Steve Rasnic Tem, *Excavation*, 1987
Chet Williamson, *Ash Wednesday*, 1987

## 2669

**JAMES HERBERT**

### *Haunted*

(New York: NAL Signet, 1990)

**Story type:** Horror (Haunted House)
**Major character(s):** David Ash, Paranormal Investigator; Christina Mariell, Heiress; Tessa Webb, Aged Person (Christina's aunt)
**Time period(s):** 1990s (1990)
**Locale(s):** Ravenmoor, England; London, England

**Summary:** Sent by the Psychical Research Institute to investigate the haunting of the Mariell family's country home, Edbrook Manor, skeptical David Ash experiences a series of increasingly threatening paranormal phenomena that eventually reveal the manor's buried history and its impact on the current Mariell family. First published in England in 1988.

**Other books you might like:**
Judith Hawkes, *Julian's House*, 1989
Shirley Jackson, *The Haunting of Hill House*, 1959
Richard Matheson, *Hell House*, 1971

## 2670

**JAMES HERBERT**

### *Portent*

(New York: HarperPrism, 1996)

**Story type:** Horror (Apocalyptic Horror)

Major character(s): James Rivers, Scientist (climatologist); Hugo Poggs, Scientist; Mama Pitie, Religious (priestess)
Time period(s): 1990s (1993)
Locale(s): Hazelrod, England; New Orleans, Louisiana

Summary: Recovering from his near death in a hurricane over the Gulf of Mexico, British climatologist James Rivers is contacted by Hugo Poggs, an eccentric whose adopted gypsy children know that Rivers was saved from death for a purpose. At their behest, Rivers searches out a Scottish recluse known as the Dream Man, in order to fulfill a mystical destiny that will help save the world from ecological cataclysm. First published in England in 1993.

Other books you might like:
Colin Kersey, *Soul Catcher*, 1995
Graham Masterton, *Burial*, 1992
John Skipp, *The Bridge: A Horror Story*, 1991
    Craig Spector, co-author

---

**2671**

JAMES HERBERT

## The Rats

(New York: NAL Signet, 1989)

Story type: Horror (Nature in Revolt)
Major character(s): Harris, Teacher (Art); Foskins, Government Official (Ministry of Health agent)
Time period(s): 1970s
Locale(s): London, England

Summary: Huge mutant rats ravage London. The heroic duo search for the telepathic intelligence directing the rats, while the authorities attempt to control the plague with an anti-rat virus. Originally published in 1974.

Other books you might like:
Harry Adam Knight, *The Fungus*, 1985
Guy N. Smith, *The Killer Crabs Series*, 1978

---

**2672**

JAMES HERBERT

## Sepulchre

(New York: Jove, 1989)

Story type: Horror (Ancient Evil Unleashed)
Major character(s): Liam Halloran, Bodyguard; Felix Kline, Psychic, Businessman
Time period(s): 1980s
Locale(s): Neath, England (Kline's hideaway)

Summary: When Halloran is hired to protect Kline from unnamed enemies, he encounters a kinky love affair, a terrorist plot, horrifying psychic phenomena, and a Sumerian devil-god.

Other books you might like:
Clive Barker, *The Damnation Game*, 1985
John Blackburn, *For Fear of Little Men*, 1972
John Farris, *Catacombs*, 1981

---

**2673**

MARY H. HERBERT

## City of the Sorcerers

(Lake Geneva, Wisconsin: TSR, 1994)

Story type: Fantasy (Quest; Psychic Powers)

---

Series: Dark Horse
Major character(s): Kelene, Sorceress, Healer; Demir, Animal (horse), Telepath; Sayyed, Sorcerer, Religious
Time period(s): Indeterminate
Locale(s): Dark Horse Plains, Mythical Place; Moy Tura, Fictional City

Summary: When a plague rekindles old suspicions about magic-wielders and threatens a 20-year peace, a few magic-wielders travel to the ruins of Moy Tura, the city of sorcerers, to find a cure.

Other books you might like:
Constance Ash, *The Stallion Queen*, 1992
Doranna Durgin, *Dun Lady's Jess*, 1994
Peter Morwood, *The Horse Lord*, 1987
Karen Ripley, *The Persistence of Memory*, 1993
Mary Stanton, *The Heavenly Horse From the Outermost West*, 1988

---

**2674**

MARY H. HERBERT

## Dark Horse

(Lake Geneva, WI: TSR, 1990)

Story type: Fantasy (Magic Conflict)
Series: Dark Horse
Major character(s): Gabria, Warrior (Female), Sorceress; Nara, Animal (Magical horse)
Time period(s): Indeterminate

Summary: With only Nara to support her, Gabria forces her way into the male-dominated world of sorcery, defeating the evil Lord Medb in the process.

Other books you might like:
C.J. Cherryh, *Wizard Spawn*, 1989
    Nancy Asire, co-author
Mercedes Lackey, *Arrow's Fall*, 1988
Robin McKinley, *The Blue Sword*, 1982
Mark C. Perry, *Morigu: The Dead*, 1990
Sheri S. Tepper, *Jinian Footseer*, 1985

---

**2675**

MARY H. HERBERT

## Legacy of Steel

(Renton, Washington: TSR, 1998)

Story type: Fantasy (Magic Conflict)
Major character(s): Sara Dunstan, Warrior; Cobalt, Animal (dragon); Mirielle Abrena, Military Personnel (general)
Time period(s): Indeterminate
Locale(s): Neraka, Fictional City

Summary: Sara Dunstan hears rumors that the evil order of Knights of Takhisis is forming once again in the city of Neraka. Accompanied by a dragon friend, she travels to investigate and foils an ambitious general's plan to raise an army with which to conquer neighboring cities.

Other books you might like:
Mary Kirchoff, *Kendermore*, 1989
Victor Milan, *War in Tethyr*, 1995
Douglas Niles, *Feathered Dragon*, 1991
Dan Parkinson, *The Gates of Thorbardin*, 1990
R.A. Salvatore, *Exile*, 1990

## 2676

**MARY H. HERBERT**

### Lightning's Daughter

(Lake Geneva, Wisconsin: TSR, 1991)

**Story type:** Fantasy (Magic Conflict; Quest)
**Series:** Dark Horse
**Major character(s):** Gabria, Warrior, Sorceress
**Time period(s):** Indeterminate
**Locale(s):** Dark Horse Plains, Mythical Place

**Summary:** Hoping to secure a place for magic among the untrusting plains tribes, Gabria and her companions, aided by the intelligent, magic Hunnuli horses, set out to find a tome of magic which would allow Gabria to overcome the threats to her people. Sequel to *Dark Horse*.

**Other books you might like:**
Constance Ash, *The Horsegirl*, 1988
David Eddings, *Pawn of Prophecy*, 1982
Robin McKinley, *The Blue Sword*, 1982
Robin McKinley, *The Hero and the Crown*, 1984
Mary Stanton, *The Heavenly Horse From the Outermost West*, 1988

## 2677

**MARY H. HERBERT**

### Valorian

(Lake Geneva, Wisconsin: TSR, 1993)

**Story type:** Fantasy (Quest)
**Series:** Dark Horse
**Major character(s):** Valorian, Leader, Magician; Hunnul, Animal (horse), Telepath; Tyrranis, Military Personnel
**Time period(s):** Indeterminate
**Locale(s):** Tarnish Empire, Fictional Country; Chadar, Fictional Country; Darkhorn Mountains, Mythical Place

**Summary:** Aided by gifts from the goddess Amara, Valorian unites his clan with the vision of freedom in a new land, providing they escape General Tyrranis and survive a difficult journey across unknown mountains. Set 500 years prior to *Dark Horse*.

**Other books you might like:**
Casey Flynn, *The Enchanted Isles*, 1991
Robert Jordan, *The Eye of the World*, 1989
L.E. Modesitt Jr., *The Towers of the Sunset*, 1992
Elizabeth Moon, *Liar's Oath*, 1992

## 2678

**MARY H. HERBERT**

### Winged Magic

(New York: TSR, 1996)

**Story type:** Fantasy (Magic Conflict; Political)
**Series:** Dark Horse
**Major character(s):** Kelene, Sorceress, Healer; Gabria, Warrior, Sorceress; Sayyed, Sorcerer, Leader
**Time period(s):** Indeterminate
**Locale(s):** Altai Valley, Mythical Place; Turic Nation, Fictional Country; Cangora, Fictional City

**Summary:** An untrained sorcerer kidnaps Kelene and Gabria and their telepathic horse companions, intending to force them to teach him sorcery, however he does not anticipate the resourceful resistance of his captives or their relatives' response in gathering disparate forces to mount a rescue and avert the disastrous use of sorcery.

**Other books you might like:**
Constance Ash, *The Stallion Queen*, 1992
Doranna Durgin, *Dun Lady's Jess*, 1994
Peter Morwood, *The Horse Lord*, 1987
Andre Norton, *Elvenblood*, 1995
    Mercedes Lackey, co-author
Karen Ripley, *The Persistence of Memory*, 1993
Mary Stanton, *The Heavenly Horse From the Outermost West*, 1988

## 2679

**JENNIFER HERSHEY**, Editor
**TOM DUPREE**, Co-Editor
**JANNA SILVERSTEIN**, Co-Editor

### Full Spectrum 5

(New York: Bantam Spectra, 1995)

**Story type:** Science Fiction (Anthology)
**Series:** Full Spectrum

**Summary:** Contains seven pages of notes about the authors and editors and 28 original stories, varying from humorous to dark in tone, which present a thematically wide range of speculative fiction. Authors include William Barton, Doug Beason, Michael Bishop, Richard Bowes, Emily Devenport, Karen Joy Fowler, Jean Mark Gawron, Jonathan Letham, Lisa Mason, Patricia A. McKillip, Paul Park, Alan Rodgers, Neal Stephenson, Tricia Sullivan, William Jon Watkins, Lawrence Watt-Evans, and Gene Wolf.

**Other books you might like:**
Lou Aronica, *Full Spectrum*, 1988
    Shawna McCarthy, co-editor
Lou Aronica, *Full Spectrum 4*, 1993
    Amy Stout, Betsy Mitchell, co-editors
Lou Aronica, *Full Spectrum 3*, 1993
    Amy Stout, Betsy Mitchell, co-editors
Lou Aronica, *Full Spectrum 2*, 1989
    Shawna McCarthy, Amy Stout, Patrick LoBruto
Greg Bear, *New Legends*, 1995
Gardner Dozois, *The Year's Best Science Fiction: Twelfth Annual Collection*, 1995
    editor

## 2680

**HERMANN HESSE**

### The Fairy Tales of Hermann Hesse

(New York: Bantam, 1995)

**Story type:** Fantasy (Collection)

**Summary:** Contains a 20-page introduction by translator and editor Jack Zipes and the first English language versions of 22 stories in the modern fairy tale tradition, all published in German in journals and newspapers 1904-1918. Frequently dark in tone, the stories' themes include the agony of the artist, social turmoil, wish fulfillment, and societal structures.

**Other books you might like:**
Italo Calvino, *Italian Folktales*, 1992
Sir Arthur Conan Doyle, *The Best Supernatural Tales of Arthur Conan Doyle*, 1979
Rudyard Kipling, *Kipling's Fantasy*, 1992
Jack London, *Selected Science Fiction and Fantasy Stories*, 1979

Kenneth Morris, *The Dragon Path: Collected Tales of Kenneth Morris*, 1995
Jack Zipes, *Beauties, Beasts and Enchantments*, 1989
  editor
Jack Zipes, *Spells of Enchantment*, 1991
  editor

## 2681

### TRACY HICKMAN

## *The Immortals*

(New York: Roc, 1996)

**Story type:** Science Fiction (Medical; Political)
**Major character(s):** Michael Albert Barris, Journalist, Parent; Quinton Weston, Religious (reverend), Political Figure (mayor); Virgil Wayne Johnston, Cowboy
**Time period(s):** 2010s (2010)
**Locale(s):** Newhouse Center, Utah; Beaver, Utah; Milford, Utah

**Summary:** During the V-CIDS epidemic, Michael sneaks into Newhouse Center, an Emergency Relocation and Isolation Service, to reconcile with his son. Attempting to check out business possibilities in the area, Virgil barely escapes the destruction of Wild Cove Center, but discovers, to his horror, the explosion incinerated alive many people, including children. Michael and Virgil discover that everyone in an ERIS designated "predeceased" has, at most, six months before that center, in orderly rotation, receives its prescheduled total demolition.

**Other books you might like:**
Greg Bear, *Blood Music*, 1985
Helen Collins, *Mutagenesis*, 1993
L. Warren Douglas, *Cannon's Orb*, 1994
Frank Herbert, *The White Plague*, 1982
Bill Ransom, *ViraVax*, 1993

## 2682

### LYNN S. HIGHTOWER

## *Alien Blues*

(New York: Ace, 1992)

**Story type:** Science Fiction (Mystery)
**Series:** Alien Blues
**Major character(s):** David Silver, Police Officer (Homicide task force); Puzzle Solver, Alien (Elaki), Detective; String, Alien (Elaki), Police Officer
**Time period(s):** Indeterminate Future
**Locale(s):** Saigo City, Fictional City

**Summary:** David Silver unhappily accepts an alien partner to help investigate crimes by a sexual psychopath. As the investigation proceeds, the FBI and DEA become involved. When Puzzle Solver is killed and Silver nearly killed by the explosion of their car, it becomes clear that a larger situation threatens both humans and elaki.

**Other books you might like:**
Alan Dean Foster, *Alien Nation*, 1988
Alan Dean Foster, *Cyber Way*, 1990
Katharine Kerr, *Polar City Blues*, 1990
Lee Killough, *The Doppelganger Gambit*, 1979
Lee Killough, *Dragon's Teeth*, 1990
Lee Killough, *Spider Play*, 1986
Walter Jon Williams, *Days of Atonement*, 1991

## 2683

### LYNN S. HIGHTOWER

## *Alien Eyes*

(New York: Ace, 1993)

**Story type:** Science Fiction (Mystery; Political)
**Series:** Alien Blues
**Major character(s):** David Silver, Police Officer; String, Alien (Elaki), Police Officer; Dahmi, Alien (Elaki)
**Time period(s):** Indeterminate Future
**Locale(s):** Saigo City, Fictional City

**Summary:** Dahmi, a good mother accused of killing her children, refuses to cooperate with the police for fear of involving the Elaki police. David must discover the reason behind the murders and the fear.

**Other books you might like:**
Eleanor Arnason, *A Woman of the Iron People*, 1991
Lois McMaster Bujold, *Shards of Honor*, 1986
Sean Dalton, *Beyond the Void*, 1991
Paula E. Downing, *Fallway*, 1993
Alan Dean Foster, *Alien Nation*, 1988
K.W. Jeter, *Dark Horizon*, 1993
Lee Killough, *Dragon's Teeth*, 1990
Stephen Leigh, *Alien Tongue*, 1991

## 2684

### LYNN S. HIGHTOWER

## *Alien Heat*

(New York: Ace, 1994)

**Story type:** Science Fiction (Mystery; Psychic Powers)
**Series:** Alien Blues
**Major character(s):** David Silver, Police Officer; String, Alien (Elaki), Police Officer; Yolanda Free Clements, Police Officer
**Time period(s):** Indeterminate Future
**Locale(s):** Saigo City, Fictional City

**Summary:** Detective Silver and the Arson Squad investigate a fire in a supper club that killed over 200 people. The clues point to arson, but complications include the body of a woman strangled during the fire, a beautiful psychic called in to assist on another case, and racial tensions between Elaki and Humans. Then a second supper club burns down.

**Other books you might like:**
Isaac Asimov, *The Caves of Steel*, 1954
Philip K. Dick, *Do Androids Dream of Electric Sheep?*, 1968
Alan Dean Foster, *Alien Nation*, 1988
Katharine Kerr, *Polar City Blues*, 1990
James H. Schmitz, *The Universe Against Her*, 1964

## 2685

### LYNN S. HIGHTOWER

## *Alien Rites*

(New York: Ace, 1995)

**Story type:** Science Fiction (Mystery)
**Series:** Alien Blues
**Major character(s):** David Silver, Police Officer; String, Alien (Elaki), Police Officer; Annie Trey, Single Parent
**Time period(s):** Indeterminate Future
**Locale(s):** Saigo City, Fictional City

**Summary:** As Detective Silver and his partner, String, investigate the disappearance of a local college student, they find links to the disappearance of a police pathologist, an extortion plot in the Elaki quarter of town, an antique teddy bear, and a young woman accused of murdering her infant son.

**Other books you might like:**
Isaac Asimov, *The Caves of Steel*, 1954
Rosel George Brown, *Sibyl Sue Blue*, 1966
Michael Crichton, *The Andromeda Strain*, 1969
Philip K. Dick, *Do Androids Dream of Electric Sheep?*, 1968
Katharine Kerr, *Polar City Blues*, 1990
Jean Lorrah, *The IDIC Epidemic*, 1988

---

**2686**

**JAMAKE HIGHWATER**

## Dark Legend

(New York: Grove Press, 1994)

**Story type:** Fantasy (Legend; Quest)
**Major character(s):** Kuwai, Indian, Royalty (lord of the sky); Washi, Indian, Hero; Idera, Indian, Warrior (Muri Woman)
**Time period(s):** Indeterminate Past
**Locale(s):** Central America

**Summary:** Using as inspiration the Germanic myths of the Nibelungen, ancient Eddic poems, the Icelandic Volsunga Saga and the Norse Nibelungenlied, Highwater transplants the action into pre-Columbian tropical America.

**Other books you might like:**
Piers Anthony, *Tales From the Great Turtle*, 1994
    Richard Gilliam, co-editor
Stephan Grundy, *Rhinegold*, 1994
Diana L. Paxson, *The Wolf and the Raven*, 1993
Gerald Vizenor, *Dead Voices: Natural Agonies in the Real World*, 1992
Roger Welsch, *Touching the Fire*, 1992

---

**2687**

**WILLIAM HILL**

## California Ghosting

(Doctors Inlet, Florida: Otter Creek Press, 1998)

**Story type:** Horror (Haunted House)
**Major character(s):** Blasing Madera, Businessman; Angela Starborne, Lawyer; Sean Heller, Businessman
**Time period(s):** 1990s (1998)
**Locale(s):** Ghostal Shores, California

**Summary:** Blasing Madera inherits a stake in Ghostal Shores, a popular Bay Area resort where ghosts and humans freely mingle. Blaise's investigation into the murder of Peter "Mac" MacGuire, the uncle who bequeathed him his share in the property, is complicated by Mac's conniving partner Sean Heller, who hopes to sell the resort as a time-share property, and malevolent ghosts who have plans of their own for their resort.

**Other books you might like:**
Peter S. Beagle, *A Fine and Private Place*, 1960
James P. Blaylock, *Night Relics*, 1994
Jack Cady, *The Off Season*, 1995
John R. Maxim, *Platforms*, 1980
Tim Powers, *Expiration Date*, 1996

---

**2688**

**WILLIAM HILL**

## The Magic Bicycle

(Doctors Inlet, Florida: Otter Creek, 1998)

**Story type:** Fantasy (Young Adult)
**Major character(s):** Danny Chase, Teenager; Kah-laye-dee, Alien
**Time period(s):** 1990s (1999)

**Summary:** Shortly after moving to Texas, a lonely teenager encounters an alien from space who gives him a magical device that travels through time, allows animals to talk, and leads Danny into a series of wonderful adventures.

**Other books you might like:**
David Alexander, *Fane*, 1981
Margaret J. Anderson, *In the Circle of Time*, 1979
John Bellairs, *The Trolley to Yesterday*, 1989
Mary Downing Hahn, *The Doll in the Garden*, 1989
Jody Lynn Nye, *Waking in Dreamland*, 1998

---

**2689**

**MICHAEL T. HINKEMEYER**

## Order of the Arrow

(New York: Tor, 1990)

**Story type:** Horror (Serial Killer)
**Major character(s):** Anne Davis, Student (History Ph.D. candidate); Chandler Kane, Businessman, Wealthy; James D. Lugosh, Student, Serial Killer
**Time period(s):** 1990s (1990)
**Locale(s):** Manor Island, New England (an island off the New England Coast)

**Summary:** Anne Davis emerges cured from an insane asylum 13 months after a deformed murderer killed her family. She falls in love with Chandler Kane, a millionaire and medieval enthusiast who runs his private island like a feudal kingdom. She is unaware that the murderer from her past is still stalking her and finds Kane's secluded island the perfect setting in which to dispose of her.

**Other books you might like:**
John Farris, *The Axman Cometh*, 1989
Jan Lara, *Soulcatchers*, 1990
Chet Williamson, *Dreamthorp*, 1989

---

**2690**

**CHRISTOPHER HINZ**

## Ash Ock

(New York: St. Martin's Press, 1989)

**Story type:** Science Fiction (Space Opera)
**Series:** Paratwa Saga
**Major character(s):** Jarem Marth, Pirate, Ruler; Gillian, Genetically Altered Being, Warrior
**Time period(s):** Indeterminate Future
**Locale(s):** Earth's Orbital Space Colonies, Space Station

**Summary:** Fifty-six years have passed since the first attack of the Paratwa, genetically engineered warriors with telepathic powers, upon the orbital colonies. Now a new attack is in the offing and Jarem Marth, the lion of Alexander, decides to revive from their long stasis the deadly Paratwa hunters Gillian and Nick who were responsible for defeating the earlier attack.

**Other books you might like:**
Gregory Benford, *Great Sky River*, 1987
Gregory Benford, *Tides of Light*, 1989
Patricia A. McKillip, *Fool's Run*, 1987
Robert Reed, *The Hormone Jungle*, 1988
Joan D. Vinge, *Catspaw*, 1988

## `2691`

### CHRISTOPHER HINZ

## *The Paratwa*

(New York: St. Martin's Press, 1991)

**Story type:** Science Fiction (Space Opera)
**Series:** Paratwa Saga
**Major character(s):** Jarem Marth, Pirate, Ruler; Gillian, Genetically Altered Being, Warrior; Nick, Warrior
**Time period(s):** 24th century
**Locale(s):** Earth's Orbital Space Colonies, Space Station

**Summary:** Fifty-six years after the first attack of the Paratwa, genetically engineered warriors able to merge their consciousnesses, Gillian and Nick are awakened by Jarem Marth from stasis to again defeat the Paratwan attack. Separately they battle to stop the attack and discover the secrets of the Ash Ock, the incorporated telepathic consciousness.

**Other books you might like:**
Gregory Benford, *Great Sky River*, 1987
Gregory Benford, *Tides of Light*, 1989
Robert Reed, *The Hormone Jungle*, 1988
David Alexander Smith, *Homecoming*, 1990
Joan D. Vinge, *Catspaw*, 1988

## `2692`

### WILLIAM HJORTSBERG

## *Nevermore*

(New York: Atlantic Monthly Press, 1994)

**Story type:** Horror (Mystery; Historical)
**Major character(s):** Arthur Conan Doyle, Historical Figure, Writer; Harry Houdini, Magician, Historical Figure; Damon Runyon, Journalist, Historical Figure
**Time period(s):** 1920s
**Locale(s):** New York, New York

**Summary:** During one of his American tours to promote spiritualist beliefs, Arthur Conan Doyle befriends the great magician Harry Houdini and becomes caught up in an investigation to solve a series of murders that mimick those committed in the stories of Edgar Allan Poe, and that appear to be leading up to the murder of Houdini himself.

**Other books you might like:**
Mark Frost, *The List of 7*, 1992
Kim Newman, *Anno Dracula*, 1992
Daniel Stashower, *The Adventure of the Ectoplasmic Man*, 1985

## `2693`

### ROBIN HOBB (Pseudonym of Megan Lindholm)

## *Assassin's Apprentice*

(New York: Bantam Spectra, 1995)

**Story type:** Fantasy (Psychic Powers; Political)

**Series:** Farseer
**Major character(s):** FitzChivalry "Fitz" Farseer, Bastard Son, Psychic; Burrich, Step-Parent (Fitz's), Animal Trainer (master of horses/dogs); Chade Fallstar, Bastard Son, Diplomat (assassin)
**Time period(s):** Indeterminate
**Locale(s):** Six Duchies, Fictional Country

**Summary:** After Fitz's unwelcome appearance precipitates Chivalry's abdication from royal succession, Burrich serves as Fitz's guardian and mentor until King Shrewd orders Fitz to move to the keep to begin royal training. The curriculum includes assassination which King Shrewd intends that Fitz use as commanded for political engineering.

**Other books you might like:**
Terry Goodkind, *Wizard's First Rule*, 1994
Paula Volsky, *Illusion*, 1992
Martha Wells, *The Element of Fire*, 1993
Megan Lindholm, *Cloven Hooves*, 1991
Megan Lindholm, *Wizard of the Pigeons*, 1986
Megan Lindholm, *The Limbreth Gate*, 1984

## `2694`

### ROBIN HOBB (Pseudonym of Megan Lindholm)

## *Assassin's Quest*

(New York: Bantam Spectra, 1997)

**Story type:** Fantasy (Political; Psychic Powers)
**Series:** Farseer
**Major character(s):** FitzChivalry "Fitz" Farseer, Bastard Son, Psychic; Starling Birdsong, Minstrel; Nighteyes, Animal (wolf), Telepath
**Time period(s):** Indeterminate
**Locale(s):** Six Duchies, Fictional Country

**Summary:** Thought dead, FitzChivalry slowly recovers from near death, fighting his way back to the human world despite his attraction to Nighteyes' world. As the usurper, King Regal, squanders a fortune in the Inland Duchies while abandoning Buckkeep and other seaside settlements to the deadly Red Ship Raiders, King Verity searches for help in the wilderness. All motivated to see an heir of the proper bloodline on the throne, Queen Kettricken, the Fool and FitzChivalry search for the help needed to set matters right while deadly foes seek them.

**Other books you might like:**
Lynn Flewelling, *Luck in the Shadows*, 1996
Lynn Flewelling, *Stalking Darkness*, 1997
Terry Goodkind, *Wizard's First Rule*, 1994
J.V. Jones, *The Baker's Boy*, 1995
Megan Lindholm, *Wizard of the Pigeons*, 1986
Martha Wells, *The Element of Fire*, 1993

## `2695`

### ROBIN HOBB (Pseudonym of Megan Lindholm)

## *Royal Assassin*

(New York: Bantram Spectra, 1996)

**Story type:** Fantasy (Political; Psychic Powers)
**Series:** Farseer
**Major character(s):** FitzChivalry "Fitz" Farseer, Bastard Son, Psychic; Verity Farseer, Psychic, Royalty (king-in-waiting); Nigheyes, Animal (wolf), Telepath
**Time period(s):** Indeterminate
**Locale(s):** Six Duchies, Fictional Country

**Summary:** Faring poorly after the attempt on his life, FitzChivalry returns to Buckkeep to pursue assassin studies. With mindless Forged ones' and fierce Red-Ship warriors' deadly havoc ever closer, Verity demands much of FitzChivalry. As FitzChivalry's deeds and reputation grow, he forms bonds with old and new friends and forms a forbidden bond to a wolf he saves, while Prince Regal works to discredit or kill FitzChivalry.

**Other books you might like:**
Lynn Flewelling, *Luck in the Shadows*, 1996
Terry Goodkind, *Wizard's First Rule*, 1994
J.V. Jones, *The Baker's Boy*, 1995
Megan Lindholm, *Wizard of the Pigeons*, 1986
Martha Wells, *The Element of Fire*, 1993
Michelle West, *Hunter's Oath*, 1995

---

**2696**

ROBIN HOBB (Pseudonym of Megan Lindholm)

## The Ship of Magic

(New York: Bantam Spectra, 1998)

**Story type:** Fantasy (Adventure)
**Series:** Liveship Traders Trilogy
**Major character(s):** Althea Vestrit, Teenager, Heiress—Dispossessed; Kyle Haven, Sea Captain
**Time period(s):** Indeterminate
**Locale(s):** Bingtown, Fictional City; Rain Wild River, Mythical Place; *Vivacia*, At Sea

**Summary:** Althea's father intends to bequeath Althea the family's ship, which will become an intelligent, living vessel, called a "Liveship," when he dies. Unfortunately, Althea's youth leads her father to give captaincy to her brother-in-law, who knows nothing of the family business. His poor business practices lead to conversion of the ship into a slaver and firm Althea's resolve to gain control of the ship, while a pirate captain also resolves to get it. First of series.

**Other books you might like:**
Lynn Flewelling, *Luck in the Shadows*, 1996
Terry Goodkind, *Wizard's First Rule*, 1994
J.V. Jones, *The Baker's Boy*, 1995
Megan Lindholm, *Wizard of the Pigeons*, 1986
Martha Wells, *The Element of Fire*, 1993

---

**2697**

HENRY W. HOCHERMAN

## The Gilgul

(New York: Pinnacle, 1990)

**Story type:** Horror (Possession)
**Major character(s):** Neil DeLuca, Journalist; Karen Gordon, Young Woman
**Time period(s):** 1980s (1988)
**Locale(s):** New York, New York; Miami Beach, Florida

**Summary:** On her wedding day, Karen Gordon is possessed by a "gilgul," or spirit of the dead. Hideously changed, she is kept in a mental hospital while her fiance David Seligman, and friend, Neil DeLuca, attempt to discover who or what has possessed Karen and how to get rid of it.

**Other books you might like:**
William Peter Blatty, *The Exorcist*, 1971
Bari Wood, *The Tribe*, 1981

---

**2698**

BRIAN HODGE

## The Convulsion Factory

(Seattle: Silver Salamander, 1996)

**Story type:** Horror (Collection)
**Summary:** One dozen stories, four original to the volume, present this young writer's frank and often bleak portrayals of people whose ennui and dissatisfaction with their lives encourage them to seek outrageous outlets for personal fulfillment. "Godflesh," "Childhood at the Lost and Found," and "The Meat in the Machine" all involve characters who seek transcendance through self-mutilation. "Cancer Causes Rats" critiques the means by which the media perpetuates the crimes it reports, and "Mostly Cloudy, Chance of Kurt" examines the public's fascination with celebrity death. "In a Roadhouse Far, Past the Edge of Town" spoofs serial killer films, and "Naked Lunchmeat" the writings of William Burroughs. Phil Nutman supplies an introduction. This book was published as both a trade paperback and signed limited edition hardcover.

**Other books you might like:**
Michael A. Arnzen, *Needles and Sins*, 1993
Poppy Z. Brite, *Swamp Foetus*, 1993
Elizabeth Massie, *Shadow Dreams*, 1996
Wayne Allen Sallee, *With Wounds Still Wet*, 1996

---

**2699**

BRIAN HODGE

## The Darker Saints

(New York: Dell/Abyss, 1993)

**Story type:** Horror (Black Magic)
**Major character(s):** Justin Gray, Advertising; April Kingston-Gray, Advertising, Artist (graphic designer); Terrance "Eel" Fletcher, Criminal
**Time period(s):** 1990s (1993)
**Locale(s):** Tampa, Florida; Louisiana

**Summary:** In this semi-sequel to the 1991 novel, *Nightlife*, advertising man Justin Gray is precipitated into an unexpected situation when circumstances surrounding the success of his campaign for a coffee company suggest illegal, and possibly supernatural dealings by the client. Eventually, Justin's investigations will get him entangled with criminals and drugrunners who use voodoo to animate the dead as their zombie lackeys.

**Other books you might like:**
Lisa Cantrell, *Boneman*, 1992
Hugh B. Cave, *Disciples of Dread*, 1990
Vincent Courtney, *Harvest of Blood*, 1992
Robert Weinberg, *The Black Lodge*, 1991

---

**2700**

BRIAN HODGE

## Deathgrip

(New York: Dell/Abyss, 1992)

**Story type:** Horror (Wild Talents)
**Major character(s):** Paul Handler, Radio Personality; Donny Dawson, Religious (charismatic preacher); Gabriel Matthews, Fanatic (religious)
**Time period(s):** 1990s (1992)
**Locale(s):** St. Louis, Missouri

**Summary:** KGRM disc jockey Paul Handler has spent his life coping with his power to heal by the laying on of hands, a gift bestowed on him at birth by a member of a secret coven known as the Quorum. But the gift becomes a curse with unpredictable repercussions when Paul falls under the influence of Donny Dawson, a former faith healer who hopes to exploit Paul's uncanny talents.

**Other books you might like:**
John Byrne, *Whipping Boy*, 1992
Thomas M. Disch, *The M.D.: A Horror Story*, 1991
Thomas F. Monteleone, *The Blood of the Lamb*, 1992
F. Paul Wilson, *The Touch*, 1986

**2701**

### BRIAN HODGE

## *Falling Idols*
(Woodinville, Washington: Silver Salamander Press, 1998)

**Story type:** Horror (Collection)

**Summary:** This collection contains seven stories of fantasy and horror, many with a metaphysical dimension, including the novella "As Above, So Below," in which a man's quest for transcendence leads him into contact with an alien species. Also included are the Lovecraft lampoon "Blind Idiot Lovecraft," the vampire tale "The Dripping of Sundered Wineskins," the Frankenstein variant "A Loaf of Bread, A Jug of Wine," and "Stick Around, It Gets Worse," in which a man's grief over the senseless death of his lover opens him up to a horrifying vision of the cosmic pattern. With story notes by the author.

**Other books you might like:**
Gary A. Braunbeck, *Things Left Behind*, 1997
Richard T. Chizmar, *Midnight Promises*, 1996
Harlan Ellison, *Slippage*, 1997
Elizabeth Massie, *Shadow Dreams*, 1996
David B. Silva, *The Night in Fog*, 1998

**2702**

### BRIAN HODGE

## *Nightlife*
(New York: Dell, 1991)

**Story type:** Horror (Doppelganger)
**Major character(s):** Justin Gray, Advertising (copywriter); April Kingston, Advertising, Artist (freelance graphic designer); Kerebawa, Indian (member of Venezuelan Mabori)
**Time period(s):** 1990s (1990)
**Locale(s):** Tampa, Florida

**Summary:** When Justin Gray samples "skullflush," a recreational drug that causes users to temporarily revert to their animal selves, he runs afoul of dealer Tony Mendoza. His only hope for survival is to team up with Kerebawa, a primitive Venezuelan Indian who has tracked the drug to the United States to prevent its distribution.

**Other books you might like:**
Paddy Chayefsky, *Altered States*, 1978
Leonard Cline, *The Dark Chamber*, 1927
Robert Louis Stevenson, *The Strange Case of Dr. Jekyll and Mr. Hyde*, 1886

**2703**

### BRIAN HODGE

## *Oasis*
(New York: Tor, 1989)

**Story type:** Horror (Curse)
**Major character(s):** Chris Anderson, Teenager; Aaron Anderson, Teenager
**Time period(s):** 1970s (Prologue in 1940)
**Locale(s):** Tri-Lakes, Illinois (A wooded area in southern Illinois)

**Summary:** An idyllic summer at Tri-Lakes turns gradually horrific for the Anderson brothers as, one by one, their friends and associates meet violent ends. An ancient malevolent force—a Viking blood feud—animates a mysterious woods and finally drives the brothers into a violent confrontation—with each other.

**Other books you might like:**
Gary Brandner, *Doomstalker*, 1989

**2704**

### BRIAN HODGE

## *Prototype*
(New York: Dell, 1996)

**Story type:** Horror (Science Fiction)
**Major character(s):** Clay Palmer, Drifter; Adrienne Rand, Psychologist; Patrick Valentine, Smuggler (arms smuggler)
**Time period(s):** 1990s (1996)
**Locale(s):** Denver, Colorado

**Summary:** Clay Palmer is a victim of Helverson's Syndrome, a congenital disease that imparts superhuman powers but impulsive and violent tendencies as well. Clay becomes a pawn between a biotech firm that hopes to harness his medical condition to their business interests, and criminal Patrick Valentine, another sufferer of Helverson's who is banding together others like him into an unstoppable gang of outlaws.

**Other books you might like:**
John Arbucci, *Blood of Innocents*, 1990
John Farris, *The Fury*, 1976
Stephen King, *Firestarter*, 1980
Dean R. Koontz, *The Bad Place*, 1990
Michael Kurland, *Button Bright*, 1995

**2705**

### BRIAN HODGE

## *Shrines and Desecrations*
(Leesburg, Virginia: TAL Publications, 1994)

**Story type:** Horror (Collection; Vampire Story)
**Major character(s):** Kraeken, Vampire

**Summary:** The author's first collection presents a trio of stories centered around Kraeken, an irreverent young vampire living in Florida who hopes to build a cult around himself by undermining the faith of others. In the book's only reprint, "Like a Pilgrim to the Shrine," Kraeken squares off against the grandaddy of all vampires, Count Dracula, to see who will claim Florida for his own turf. In "Leper's Holiday," the vampire sows doubt in the minds of fundamentalists at a barbecue. In "Messiah Envy," Kraeken finally gathers his acolytes only to have them rebel against him. Poppy Z. Brite contributes the introduction.

**Other books you might like:**
Edward Bryant, *Aqua Sancta*, 1994
Martin H. Greenberg, *Dracula: Prince of Darkness*, 1992
  editor
Nancy Kilpatrick, *Sex and the Single Vampire*, 1994
Chelsea Quinn Yarbro, *The Saint-Germain Chronicles*, 1983

---

**2706**

### BARBARA HODGSON

## The Tattooed Map

(San Francisco: Chronicle Books, 1995)

**Story type:** Fantasy (Literary)
**Major character(s):** Lydia, Traveler; Chris, Traveler
**Time period(s):** 1990s
**Locale(s):** Morocco

**Summary:** In North Africa a woman discovers strange marks on her arm quickly growing into a tattoo depicting a map which drags her into a mysterious journey. Later, her travelling companion must pick up her trail and journal and follow her into the mystery. First novel heavily illustrated with photos, drawings, maps, and reproductions of things the travellers see.

**Other books you might like:**
Nick Bantock, *Griffin & Sabine*, 1991
John Crowley, *Little, Big*, 1981
Lisa Goldstein, *Tourists*, 1989
Robert Irwin, *The Arabian Nightmare*, 1983
Pat Murphy, *The City, Not Long After*, 1989

---

**2707**

### SHEILA HODGSON

## The Fellow Travellers and Other Ghost Stories

(Ashcroft, British Columbia: Ash-Tree Press, 1998)

**Story type:** Horror (Collection)

**Summary:** This first collection of 12 tales of ghosts and the supernatural is written in the antiquarian style of M.R. James. Selections include "The Villa Martine," in which a mother's possessiveness leads to a gruesome rift between a husband and wife; "The Turning Point," in which two men attempt to turn the tables on those who would persecute them for witchcraft, with uncanny results; and "Childermass," a tale of witchcraft and infanticide.

**Other books you might like:**
Mrs. J.H. Riddell, *The Collected Ghost Stories of Mrs. J.H. Riddell*, 1977
David G. Rowlands, *The Executor and Other Ghost Stories*, 1996
C.E. Ward, *Vengeful Ghosts*, 1998
Ron Weighell, *The White Road*, 1996
John Whitbourn, *Binscombe Tales*, 1998

---

**2708**

### WILLIAM HOPE HODGSON

## Demons of the Sea

(West Warwick, Rhode Island: Necronomicon Press, 1992)

**Story type:** Horror (Collection)

**Summary:** Six hitherto unreprinted stories and three non-fiction pieces by an early and influential master of modern horror. Included are the sentimental ghost story "The Valley of Lost Children"; the sea-monster tale "The Haunted *Pampero*"; the author's first published story "The Goddess of Death"; and the futuristic satire "Date 1965: Modern Warfare."

**Other books you might like:**
Lloyd Kropp, *The Drift*, 1969
William Pattrick, *Mysterious Sea Stories*, 1985
  editor
Charles G. Waugh, *Spooky Sea Stories*, 1991
  Frank McSherry, Jr., co-editor

---

**2709**

### WILLIAM HOPE HODGSON

## Down Among the Weeds: The Sargasso Sea Stories of William Hope Hodgson

(Bristol, Rhode Island: Hobgoblin Press, 1997)

**Story type:** Horror (Collection)

**Summary:** Contains four atmospheric short stories and a novel excerpt written between 1907 and 1913, each set in the Sargasso sea, whose weed-choked waters trap ships and spawn horrors peculiar to their nautical setting. "From the Tideless Sea" and "The Finding of the Graiken" both feature enormous sea squids as their monsters, and "More News from the Homebird" and "The Mystery of the Derelict" have armies of ravenous sea crabs and ship rats as their subjects. "The Weed Men," a chapter from Hodgson's novel *The Boats of the Glen Carrig*, tells of a humanoid race from the sea that traps a ship's crew on an island. Edited and with an introduction by Sam Gafford. Dated 1997 but not available until 1998.

**Other books you might like:**
Simon Clark, *The Derelict of Death*, 1998
  John Ford, co-author
T. Liam McDonald, *Sea Cursed: Thirty Terrifying Tales of the Deep*, 1994
  Stefan Dziemianowicz, Martin H. Greenberg, co-editors
William Pattrick, *Mysterious Sea Stories*, 1985
  editor
Charles G. Waugh, *Spooky Sea Stories*, 1991
  Frank McSherry, Jr., co-editor

---

**2710**

### WILLIAM HOPE HODGSON

## The Haunted Pampero

(Kingston, Rhode Island: Donald M. Grant, 1992)

**Story type:** Horror (Collection)

**Summary:** Sam Moskowitz has edited and supplied a lengthy biographical introduction to this collection of 12 stories by an early master of visionary supernatural horror fiction. Included are the title story, "The Ghosts of the 'Glen Doon,'" and "The Silent Ship," all deep-sea horror tales; the sentimental fantasy "The Valley of Lost Children"; an introductory tale involving Hodgson's renowned psychic sleuth, Carnacki the Ghost Finder; the science fictional "Date 1965: Modern Warfare"; the ghost story "Old Golly"; and the mystery, "Bullion."

**Other books you might like:**
Algernon Blackwood, *Best Ghost Stories of Algernon Blackwood*, 1973
H.P. Lovecraft, *The Dunwich Horror and Others*, 1963
Arthur Machen, *Tales of Horror and the Supernatural*, 1948

## 2711

**WILLIAM HOPE HODGSON**

### The House on the Borderland

(New York: Caroll & Graf, 1996)

**Story type:** Horror (Apocalyptic Horror)
**Major character(s):** The Narrator, Writer; Mary, Young Woman (the narrator's sister); Pepper, Animal (dog)
**Time period(s):** 1900s
**Locale(s):** Kraighten, Ireland

**Summary:** This story is presented as a manuscript found in an abandoned house in rural Ireland by two foreign travellers. It recounts the nameless narrator's efforts to defend himself against a horde of swine-like creatures who emerge from the ravine near which the house is set, and the narrator's experiences in the strange space and time warps to which his house seems to be subject. This novel was first published in England in 1908.

**Other books you might like:**
Ramsey Campbell, *Midnight Sun*, 1990
Basil Copper, *The Great White Space*, 1974
H.P. Lovecraft, *At the Mountains of Madness*, 1964
Adrian Ross, *The Hole of the Pit*, 1914

## 2712

**WILLIAM HOPE HODGSON**
**NED DAMERON**, Illustrator

### Terrors of the Sea

(Hampton Falls, New Hampshire: Donald M. Grant, 1996)

**Story type:** Horror (Collection)

**Summary:** Fourteen works of fiction and non-fiction, only three of which have been published before, comprise this latest posthumous compilation of work from an author best known for his tales of sea horror. ''The Promise'' is a *conte cruel* and ''Demons of the Sea'' is a tale of monstrous terror on the high seas. ''The Plans of the Reefing Bi-Plane'' is an invention story featuring Hodgson's series character Captain Gault. Included as well are ''Ten Months at Sea,'' Hodgson's autobiographical account of the rigors of a sailor's life, and ''Writers of Ghost Stories,'' a fragment of an essay. Sam Moskowitz supplies a lengthy introduction.

**Other books you might like:**
Algernon Blackwood, *The Listener and Other Stories*, 1907
H.P. Lovecraft, *The Dunwich Horror and Others*, 1963
Arthur Machen, *The Three Impostors*, 1895
Richard Middleton, *The Ghost Ship and Other Stories*, 1912

## 2713

**ALICE HOFFMAN**

### Practical Magic

(New York: Berkley, 1998)

**Story type:** Fantasy (Light Fantasy)
**Major character(s):** Gillian Owens, Witch; Sally Owens, Witch
**Time period(s):** 1990s (1999)
**Locale(s):** Massachusetts

**Summary:** Gillian and Sally Owens grew up knowing that they were different from the neighbors who shunned them. As adults, each seeks to hide that difference, one by deciding to marry, the other by leaving home. But the tradition of witchcraft runs strong in their family, and even good witches sometimes give in to temptation.

**Other books you might like:**
Richard Adams, *Girl in a Swing*, 1980
Brenda Jordan, *The Brentwood Witches*, 1987
Fritz Leiber, *Conjure Wife*, 1952
Josephine Pinckney, *Great Mischief*, 1948
Keith Roberts, *Anita*, 1970

## 2714

**BARRY HOFFMAN**
**HARRY O. MORRIS**, Illustrator

### Firefly. . .Burning Bright

(Springfield, Pennsylvania: Gauntlet Publications, 1994)

**Story type:** Horror (Collection)

**Summary:** Four tales of nonsupernatural horror explore the social and psychological dynamics of victimization. In the title story, a neglected young girl gets the attention she craves through acts of pyromania. ''No Place to Hide'' tells of an assault victim's revenge against her attacker and ''The Ultimate Groupie'' of the perverse relationship that develops between a serial killer and his victim. In ''Vicious Cycle,'' an abused spouse comes to a tragic conclusion regarding the only means of preventing her husband from abusing their unborn child as he has her. Ronald Kelly supplies an introduction and Richard T. Chizmar an afterword. This is the author's first book.

**Other books you might like:**
Richard T. Chizmar, *Midnight Promises*, 1996
Ed Gorman, *Cages*, 1995
Dean R. Koontz, *Strange Highways*, 1995
Andrew Vachss, *Born Bad*, 1994

## 2715

**NINA KIRIKI HOFFMAN**

### Legacy of Fire

(Eugene, OR: Pulphouse, 1990)

**Story type:** Horror (Collection)

**Summary:** Four tales of fantasy and horror, two reprints and two originals. ''Coming Home'' is about the guilt a woman bears for a childhood prank that went tragically awry. ''Tremors'' features a ghostly grandmother. ''Works of Art'' tells of an artist with rather peculiar notions about the relationship of art to life. This is the author's first collection.

**Other books you might like:**
Pat Cadigan, *Patterns*, 1989
Pat Murphy, *Points of Departure*, 1990
Jessica Amanda Salmonson, *John Collier and Fredric Brown Went Quarrelling through My Head*, 1989
Lisa Tuttle, *A Nest of Nightmares*, 1986
Chelsea Quinn Yarbro, *Signs and Portents*, 1984

## 2716

**NINA KIRIKI HOFFMAN**

### The Silent Strength of Stones

(New York: AvoNova, 1995)

**Story type:** Fantasy (Contemporary; Psychic Powers)

**Major character(s):** Nick Verrou, Teenager, Psychic (esper); Willow Seale, Teenager, Psychic (esper); Evan Seale, Teenager, Animal (wolf)
**Time period(s):** 1990s
**Locale(s):** Sauterelle Lake, Oregon; Cascade Mountains, Oregon

**Summary:** Still angry at being abandoned by his mother four years earlier, Nick works hard both at home and in the family store and motel. With little free time, Nick manages solitary forays through the populated areas around the lake morning and night, observing the local and vacationing residents. Nick expects an unusual summer when he sees Willow disappear, befriends a wolf, and recognizes that he possesses a command voice and that his mother had seemed special.

**Other books you might like:**
Tom Deitz, *Soulsmith*, 1990
Zenna Henderson, *Ingathering. The Complete People Stories of Zenna Henderson*, 1995
David Lee Jones, *Zeus and Co.*, 1993
Morgan Llywelyn, *The Elementals*, 1993
Elizabeth Ann Scarborough, *Nothing Sacred*, 1991

---

**2717**

**NINA KIRIKI HOFFMAN**

## The Thread That Binds the Bones

(New York: AvoNova, 1993)

**Story type:** Fantasy (Contemporary; Psychic Powers)
**Major character(s):** Tom Renfield, Psychic (esper); Laura Bolte, Psychic (esper); Peregrine, Spirit
**Time period(s):** 1990s
**Locale(s):** Portland, Oregon; Arcadia, Oregon

**Summary:** Tom leaves Portland to escape notoriety arising when he floated two teenagers who had jumped off a building. After riding the rails to Arcadia, Tom drives a taxi while feeling that he waits for something. When Laura Bolte hires his cab, he discovers a clan of people and their forebears with talents similar to his own. He marries Laura, accepts Peregrine as mentor and attempts to protect his friends from his new family.

**Other books you might like:**
James P. Blaylock, *The Paper Grail*, 1991
Emma Bull, *War for the Oaks*, 1987
Tom Deitz, *Soulsmith*, 1990
Steven Gould, *Jumper*, 1992
Zenna Henderson, *The People: No Different Flesh*, 1967
Marc Laidlaw, *Neon Lotus*, 1988

---

**2718**

**E.T.A. HOFFMANN**

## The Golden Pot and Other Tales

(New York: Oxford Paperbacks, 1992)

**Story type:** Horror (Collection)

**Summary:** Five stories by the renowned German romanticist. Included are "The Sandman," a harrowing tale of an early childhood nightmare and its long-term consequences for the adult protagonist; "Master Flea," in which denizens of a fairy realm are reincarnated as mortals; and "The Golden Pot," about the young poet Anselmus who lives a double life in the real world as well as the mystical world of ancient Atlantis. The stories have been translated by Ritchie Robinson.

**Other books you might like:**
Peter Haining, *Gothic Tales of Terror*, 1972
editor
I.U. Tarchetti, *Fantastic Tales*, 1992
Ronald Taylor, *Six German Romantic Tales*, 1992
editor

---

**2719**

**E.T.A. HOFFMANN**

## Nutcracker

(New York: Harcourt Brace, 1996)

**Story type:** Fantasy (Legend; Young Adult)
**Major character(s):** Marie Stahlbaum, Child; Christian Elias "Godfather" Drosselmeier, Artisan (toymaker)
**Time period(s):** 19th century
**Locale(s):** Germany

**Summary:** At Christmas, Godfather Drosselmeier brings marvelous toys for the Stahlbaum children and tells them wondrous tales. Falling in love with Drosselmeier's ugly nutcracker, Marie helps change the ensorcelled toy into a handsome prince who leads other toys in repelling the seven-headed mouse king and his minions. Based on Major Alex Ewing's 1886 translation from the German of Hoffmann's *Nutcracker and the King of Mice* (1816), the inspiration for the Tchaikovsky ballet.

**Other books you might like:**
Lynne Reid Banks, *The Indian in the Cupboard*, 1981
James C. Christensen, *Voyage of the Basset*, 1996
Renwick St. James, Alan Dean Foster, co-authors
Ethel Johnston Phelps, *Tatterhood and Other Tales*, 1978
Sylvia Waugh, *The Mennyms*, 1994

---

**2720**

**CHUCK HOGAN**

## The Blood Artists

(New York: Morrow, 1998)

**Story type:** Horror (Science Fiction)
**Major character(s):** Stephen Pearse, Scientist; Peter Maryk, Scientist
**Time period(s):** 21st century
**Locale(s):** Atlanta, Georgia

**Summary:** Despite their vastly differing philosophies about their work, Stephen and Peter are friends and cooperative colleagues who helped eradicate a devastating blood virus in Africa—or so they thought. When Stephen is infected with the disease years later, following its unexpected arrival in America, Peter sustains him with an artificial blood he has invented, racing against the clock to find a remedy that will save his friend and neutralize Zero, a semi-human incarnation of the disease.

**Other books you might like:**
Robin Cook, *Outbreak*, 1987
Michael Crichton, *The Andromeda Strain*, 1969
James Herbert, *'48*, 1997
Philip Kerr, *The Second Angel*, 1999
Patrick Lynch, *Carriers*, 1997

## 2721

### ERNEST HOGAN

## *Cortez on Jupiter*
(New York: Tor, 1990)

**Story type:** Science Fiction (Arts; First Contact)
**Major character(s):** Pablo Cortez, Artist (graffiti); Anna Paik, Journalist (media interviewer)
**Time period(s):** Indeterminate Future
**Locale(s):** Ithica Base, Space Station (in orbit around Jupiter); Los Angeles, California; Hightown, Space Station (near Earth)

**Summary:** Pablo Cortez is a brilliant, egotistical guerilla graffiti artist. On the way to developing his art he demonstrates his inability to conform to the restrictions society places on him. Cortez is peculiar enough that he may be the only person who can communicate with newly discovered aliens and live. First novel.

**Other books you might like:**
Pat Cadigan, *Synners*, 1991
Gordon R. Dickson, *Alien Art*, 1973
James Patrick Kelly, *Look into the Sun*, 1989
Spider Robinson, *Stardance*, 1979
   Jeanne Robinson, co-author
John Varley, *The Persistence of Vision*, 1978

## 2722

### ERNEST HOGAN

## *High Aztec*
(New York: Tor, 1992)

**Story type:** Science Fiction (Theological; Medical)
**Major character(s):** Xolotl Zapata, Fugitive, Artist
**Time period(s):** 2040s (2045)
**Locale(s):** Mexico City, Mexico

**Summary:** Throughout Tenochtitlan, formerly known as Mexico City, everyone wants to get their hands on Xolotl Zapata who has become infected by a genetically engineered virus which can infect any human with religion.

**Other books you might like:**
Michael Cassutt, *Dragon Season*, 1991
Philip K. Dick, *The Three Stigmata of Palmer Eldritch*, 1965
Robert A. Heinlein, *Stranger in a Strange Land*, 1991
   revised
Frank Herbert, *Heretics of Dune*, 1984
Katharine Kerr, *Polar City Blues*, 1990
Ted Reynolds, *The Tides of God*, 1989
Kurt Vonnegut Jr., *Cat's Cradle*, 1963

## 2723

### JAMES P. HOGAN

## *Bug Park*
(New York: Baen, 1997)

**Story type:** Science Fiction (Adventure; Techno-Thriller)
**Major character(s):** Kevin Heber, Teenager, Technician; Taki, Teenager, Technician; Vanessa Heber, Step-Parent, Scientist (neurophysiologist)
**Time period(s):** 1900s
**Locale(s):** Tacoma, Washington

**Summary:** Kevin thinks of his mini robots as toys to play with in Bug Park, a testing area in his back yard, but Vanessa's friends use them to kill people. When Kevin discovers that his father may become the next victim, he enlists Taki's help insinuating his robots into his father's car, his step-mother's car and her lover's boat. Caught by Vanessa, Kevin must find a way to escape and save his father's life.

**Other books you might like:**
Stephen Bury, *Interface*, 1994
   pseudonyn of Neal Stephenson and George F. Jewsbury
Pat Cadigan, *Synners*, 1991
Wil McCarthy, *Murder in the Solid State*, 1996
Laura J. Mixon, *Glass Houses*, 1992
Sage Walker, *Whiteout*, 1996

## 2724

### JAMES P. HOGAN

## *Entoverse*
(New York: Ballantine/Del Rey, 1991)

**Story type:** Science Fiction (First Contact; Alternate Intelligence)
**Series:** Giants
**Major character(s):** Victor Hunt, Scientist (physicist); Gina Martin, Writer; VISAR, Artificial Intelligence
**Time period(s):** 21st century
**Locale(s):** Earth; Jevlen, Planet—Imaginary; Waroth, Alternate Universe

**Summary:** Dr. Victor Hunt is sent to Jevlen with a handpicked team to determine why, contrary to expectations, the population continues to fall apart after it was freed from the pervasive control of an artificial intelligence. The team finds not only an artificial intelligence less disposed of than previously thought, but also evidence of impending invasion from a parallel universe, one which seems to operate on magic. This book is a sequel to *The Giants Novels* (1991).

**Other books you might like:**
Isaac Asimov, *The Gods Themselves*, 1972
Raymond E. Feist, *A Darkness at Sethanon*, 1986
Raymond E. Feist, *Magician*, 1982
Raymond E. Feist, *Silverthorn*, 1985
Cheryl J. Franklin, *Fire Crossing*, 1991
Cheryl J. Franklin, *Fire Get*, 1987
Cheryl J. Franklin, *Fire Lord*, 1989
Cheryl J. Franklin, *The Light in Exile*, 1990

## 2725

### JAMES P. HOGAN

## *The Immortality Option*
(New York: Ballantine Del Rey, 1995)

**Story type:** Science Fiction (Robot Fiction; First Contact)
**Major character(s):** Karl Zambendorf, Psychic, Magician; Arthur, Robot (Taloid), Alien; Genius, Artificial Intelligence, Alien
**Time period(s):** Indeterminate Future
**Locale(s):** Titan, Saturn (moon)

**Summary:** After discovering the robot civilization on titan, Earth interests organize to exploit the medieval society. Arthur begins to develop a more modern free culture, while Karl and his team protect the budding society from interference. When the original alien intelligences hidden on Titan wake up, they attempt to take over the Net on Earth, which may result in disaster for all. Sequel to *Code of the Lifemaker*.

**Other books you might like:**
Roger MacBride Allen, *Orphan of Creation*, 1988
Isaac Asimov, *The Robots of Dawn*, 1983
Keith Laumer, *Rogue Bolo*, 1986
Dan Simmons, *The Fall of Hyperion*, 1990
Thomas T. Thomas, *ME: A Novel of Self Discovery*, 1991

**2726**

JAMES P. HOGAN

## The Mirror Maze

(New York: Bantam Spectra, 1989)

**Story type:** Science Fiction (Techno-Thriller)
**Major character(s):** Stephanie Carne, Scientist; Melvin Shears, Lawyer
**Time period(s):** 20th century (2000)
**Locale(s):** United States

**Summary:** The United States is safe from enemy attack beneath its satellite-carried defense lasers and things are looking up all across the country. A new political party, the Constitutionals, seems poised to carry the nation to a near-utopian level of wealth and personal freedom. It soon becomes clear, however, that there are those who will stop at nothing to keep America from achieving this golden age.

**Other books you might like:**
Ben Bova, *The Kinsman Saga*, 1987
Ben Bova, *Peacekeepers*, 1988
Dale Brown, *The Silver Tower*, 1988

**2727**

JAMES P. HOGAN

## The Multiplex Man

(New York: Bantam Spectra, 1992)

**Story type:** Science Fiction (Political; Techno-Thriller)
**Major character(s):** Richard Jarrow, Military Personnel, Experimental Subject; M.R. Valdheim, Doctor (neurophysiologist), Government Official; Andre Ulkanov, Researcher, Doctor
**Time period(s):** 2000s
**Locale(s):** Atlanta, Georgia; Minneapolis, Minnesota; Copernicus, Montenegro

**Summary:** Richard Jarrow awakens in November in a hotel in Atlanta instead of Minneapolis where he teaches junior high school. He looks younger, darker and no longer sports a moustache. However, these details seem unimportant compared to the strange clothes, guns, spy tools, I.D. with his picture and the name Maurice J. Gordon, and the fact that his last memory dated from April. He takes the only clues in the room, a message and some phone numbers, and heads for Minneapolis where he discovers that Richard Jarrow died of a stroke in May.

**Other books you might like:**
Greg Bear, *Queen of Angels*, 1990
Ben Bova, *The Trikon Deception*, 1992
    Bill Pogue, co-author
Pat Cadigan, *Fools*, 1992
Peter R. Emshwiller, *The Host*, 1991
David D. Ross, *The Eighth Rank*, 1991
Dan Simmons, *The Hollow Man*, 1992
Dan Simmons, *Hyperion*, 1989
Norman Spinrad, *Russian Spring*, 1991

**2728**

JAMES P. HOGAN

## Paths to Otherwhere

(New York: Baen, 1996)

**Story type:** Science Fiction (Political; Alternate Universe)
**Major character(s):** Hugh Brenner, Scientist (quantum physics), Inventor; Edward Kintner, Scientist, Government Official; Sam Phniangsak, Religious (Buddhist)
**Time period(s):** 21st century
**Locale(s):** Berkeley, California; Los Alamos, New Mexico

**Summary:** In the militaristic overpopulated future, the United States no longer retains its position of power, while world war seems imminent. Kintner works on a quantum device which he believes too risky to leave uncontrolled. Co-opted by the government's central secret project to predict political solutions, Hugh finds an alternative project more in keeping with his research at Berkeley and, perhaps, a better solution in a quantum universe.

**Other books you might like:**
Gregory Frost, *The Pure Cold Light*, 1993
Michaela Roessner, *Vanishing Point*, 1993
Neal Stephenson, *The Diamond Age*, 1995
Michael Swanwick, *Stations of the Tide*, 1991
George Zebrowski, *Stranger Suns*, 1991

**2729**

JAMES P. HOGAN

## Realtime Interrupt

(New York: Bantam Spectra, 1995)

**Story type:** Science Fiction (Cyberpunk; Adventure)
**Major character(s):** Joe Corrigan, Computer Expert; Lilly Essell, Military Personnel, Astronaut
**Time period(s):** Indeterminate Future
**Locale(s):** Pittsburgh, Pennsylvania; Oz, Cyberspace (computer virtual reality); Dun Laoghaire, Ireland

**Summary:** The designer and head of the Oz Project, Joe Corrigan volunteers as one of its first inhabitants. While there, his wife leaves him, the project fails, he suffers a nervous breakdown, and he loses control of the company. When he meets Lilly, soon recognizing her as another volunteer, he realizes that he remains in Oz and must somehow find a way out.

**Other books you might like:**
Greg Egan, *Permutation City*, 1995
Jean Mark Gawron, *Dream of Glass*, 1993
Mary Rosenblum, *Chimera*, 1993
Dan Simmons, *Hyperion*, 1989
Neal Stephenson, *Snow Crash*, 1992
Amy Thomson, *Virtual Girl*, 1993

**2730**

JAMES P. HOGAN

## Star Child

(New York: Baen, 1998)

**Story type:** Science Fiction (Robot Fiction; First Contact)
**Major character(s):** Taya, Child, Genetically Altered Being (human); Kort, Robot, Artificial Intelligence; Cyron, Royalty (king)
**Time period(s):** Indeterminate Future

**Locale(s):** *Merkon*, Spaceship; Aranos, Fictional City; Azure, Planet—Imaginary (of Vaxis)

**Summary:** Alone on *Merkon*, heading for Vaxis for as long as they can remember, the Mechmind decide to create chemical life to help answer some philosophical questions. Using some mathematical remnants found from an earlier stage of Merkon, they make Taya and 50 other similar chemical intelligences, while Kort makes himself into a remote to take care of her. Meanwhile, on Azure, people remember the prophecy that gods of silver will come from the sky to teach the Warrior Kings the way of gentleness.

**Other books you might like:**
Isaac Asimov, *Robots and Empire*, 1985
Katharine Kerr, *Palace*, 1996
    Mark Kreighbaum, co-author
Amy Thomson, *Virtual Girl*, 1993
A.E. Van Vogt, *The Weapon Shops of Isher*, 1951
John Varley, *Steel Beach*, 1992

---

**2731**

**CHRISTINE HOLDEN**

### A Time for Us

(New York: Jove, 1998)

**Story type:** Fantasy (Time Travel; Romance)
**Major character(s):** Ailith deCotmer, Teenager; Joshua Claybourne Kenley, Professor
**Time period(s):** 1990s (1998); 15th century (1413)
**Locale(s):** England; New Orleans, Louisiana

**Summary:** An astrologer in 1413 sends his daughter forward through time to escape the unwanted attentions of the local nobleman. After a series of comical adventures in 1998, the young woman enlists the aid of an unlikely academic to help her rescue her parents from the past. First novel.

**Other books you might like:**
Rosalyn Alsobrook, *Time Storm*, 1993
Joyce Carlow, *Timeswept*, 1994
Diana Gabaldon, *Dragonfly in Amber*, 1992
Cherlyn Jac, *Shadows in Time*, 1994
Kathleen Kane, *This Time for Keeps*, 1998

---

**2732**

**NANCY HOLDER**

### Dead in the Water

(New York: Dell/Abyss, 1994)

**Story type:** Horror (Supernatural Vengeance)
**Major character(s):** Donna Almond, Teacher; John Fielder, Doctor; Ruth Hamilton, Widow(er)
**Time period(s):** 1990s (1994)
**Locale(s):** *Robert X. Morris*, At Sea (a ship on the Pacific Ocean)

**Summary:** The author's first horror novel tells of a vacation voyage aboard the *Robert X. Morris* that turns into a nightmare when the ship falls prey to a vengeful spirit with a history of attacking ships and absorbing the souls of its passengers. In their efforts to avoid this fate, many of the passengers discover personal strengths they have developed trying to cope with life problems that have sent them on the voyage in the first place.

**Other books you might like:**
William Hope Hodgson, *The Ghost Pirates*, 1909
Stephen King, *The Shining*, 1977
Damon Knight, *CV*, 1985

T. Liam McDonald, *Sea Cursed: Thirty Terrifying Tales of the Deep*, 1994
    Stefan Dziemianowicz, Martin H. Greenberg, co-editors
William Pattrick, *Mysterious Sea Stories*, 1985
    editor
Dean Wesley Smith, *Laying the Music to Rest*, 1989

---

**2733**

**NANCY HOLDER**

### The Six Families

(New York: Avon, 1998)

**Story type:** Science Fiction (Dystopian; Mystery)
**Series:** Gambler's Star
**Major character(s):** Deuce McNamara, Gambler; Hunter Castle, Businessman; Sparkle, Dancer
**Time period(s):** 22nd century (2142)
**Locale(s):** Moonbase Vegas, Montenegro; *Gambler's Star*, Spaceship

**Summary:** Deuce knows the secrets of the Six Families who control Moonbase Vegas' gambling casinos, and he hopes to gain a piece of the action himself. But when he involves himself in Castle's schemes, he suddenly finds that he doesn't know the score.

**Other books you might like:**
C.J. Cherryh, *The Pride of Chanur*, 1982
Jane S. Fancher, *Ground-Ties*, 1991
Robert A. Heinlein, *The Moon Is a Harsh Mistress*, 1966
Melanie Tem, *Making Love*, 1993
    Nancy Holder, co-author

---

**2734**

**NANCY HOLDER**
**MELANIE TEM**, Co-Author

### Witch-Light

(New York: Tor, 1996)

**Story type:** Horror (Occult)
**Major character(s):** Valerie Kittridge, Student (film); Gabriel Luz, Witch (brujo); Maria Elena Lopez, Young Woman
**Time period(s):** 1990s (1995)
**Locale(s):** Duerme, New Mexico

**Summary:** While visiting her ill father, Valerie falls in love with Gabriel, a brujo who is related to his father's mistress. Although Gabriel teaches Valerie how to access latent spiritual powers, Valerie is not entirely sure that Gabriel is the completely kind and caring person he appears to be.

**Other books you might like:**
Warren Newton Beath, *Shock Lines*, 1993
Morgan Fields, *Shaman Woods*, 1990
Ashley McConnell, *Days of the Dead*, 1992
Kathryn Ptacek, *Shadoweyes*, 1984
William Relling Jr., *Brujo*, 1986

---

**2735**

**ROBERT HOLDSTOCK**

### Ancient Echoes

(New York: Roc, 1996)

**Story type:** Fantasy (Magic Conflict; Alternate World)

**Major character(s):** Jack Chatwin, Psychic; Nemet ''Greenface'', Hunter; Baalgor ''Grayface'', Hunter
**Time period(s):** 1990s; Indeterminate
**Locale(s):** Earth; Gl'thaan Em, Alternate Earth (Glanum)

**Summary:** Jack's lifelong visions of hunters fleeing a violent threat prove more real than Jack imagined when Grayface escapes to Earth. To reunite with his beloved Greenface, Grayface will employ extreme methods, even threatening Jack's family.

**Other books you might like:**
Aaron Allston, *Galatea in 2-D*, 1993
A.A. Attanasio, *The Dragon and the Unicorn*, 1996
Charles de Lint, *The Little Country*, 1991
Charles de Lint, *Memory and Dream*, 1994
Ben Okri, *The Famished Road*, 1992
Nancy Springer, *Larque on the Wing*, 1994
Sheri S. Tepper, *A Plague of Angels*, 1993

## 2736

### ROBERT HOLDSTOCK

## The Bone Forest

(New York: AvoNova, 1992)

**Story type:** Fantasy (Collection)

**Summary:** Contains eight stories published 1976-1989 in periodicals and anthologies. Surreal and horrific images present themes which include mythical creatures, pagan magic, madness and the primal power evoked by some tale-tellers. The title novella is a prequel to *Mythago Wood*.

**Other books you might like:**
Brian W. Aldiss, *A Romance of the Equator: The Best Fantasy Stories of Brian W. Aldiss*, 1990
Orson Scott Card, *Maps in a Mirror*, 1990
Charles de Lint, *Spiritwalk*, 1992
Pauline Melville, *Shape-Shifter: Stories by Pauline Melville*, 1991
Gene Wolfe, *Storeys From the Old Hotel*, 1992

## 2737

### ROBERT HOLDSTOCK

## Gate of Ivory, Gate of Horn

(New York: Roc, 1997)

**Story type:** Fantasy (Alternate World; Magic Conflict)
**Series:** Mythago Wood
**Major character(s):** Christian Huxley, Adventurer; Guiwenneth, Warrior
**Time period(s):** 1990s; Indeterminate Past
**Locale(s):** Ryhope Wood, Mythical Place; England

**Summary:** Drawn by his childhood vision of Guiwenneth, Christian ventures into Ryhope Wood, hoping to find the young woman. Christian soon joins Guiwenneth and a band of crusaders from the past in a battle with sorcerers and giants as he begins to undestand the truth underlying the two gates, one of horn and one of ivory.

**Other books you might like:**
Greg Bear, *Songs of Earth and Power*, 1994
Charles de Lint, *The Little Country*, 1991
Charles de Lint, *Memory and Dream*, 1994
Tom Deitz, *Dreamseeker's Road*, 1995
Holly Lisle, *Minerva Wakes*, 1994

## 2738

### ROBERT HOLDSTOCK

## The Hollowing

(New York: Roc, 1994)

**Story type:** Fantasy (Quest)
**Series:** Mythago Wood
**Major character(s):** Richard Bradley, Parent, Adventurer; Alexander ''Alex'' Bradley, Student; Arnauld Lacan, Scientist
**Time period(s):** 1960s; Indeterminate Past
**Locale(s):** Ryhope Wood, Mythical Place; England

**Summary:** When Richard Bradley enters Ryhope Wood in search of his son, he finds scientists investigating the nature of the area. His search leads him through mythic time, including an encounter with Jason and the Argonauts.

**Other books you might like:**
Charles de Lint, *The Little Country*, 1991
Charles de Lint, *Memory and Dream*, 1994
Holly Lisle, *Minerva Wakes*, 1994
Michael Swanwick, *The Iron Dragon's Daughter*, 1994
Sheri S. Tepper, *A Plague of Angels*, 1993

## 2739

### ROBERT HOLDSTOCK

## Lavondyss: Journey to an Unknown Region

(New York: William Morrow, 1989)

**Story type:** Fantasy (Quest)
**Major character(s):** Tallis Keeton, Teenager (Girl); Scathach, Royalty (Prince)
**Time period(s):** 1980s
**Locale(s):** England

**Summary:** Tallis, a bridge between the modern and ancient world, is convinced that her brother Harry, missing since World War II, is lost in the magical forest, Ryhope Wood. She searches for him and the answers to puzzling questions.

**Other books you might like:**
Greer Ilene Gilman, *Moonwise*, 1991
Paul Hazel, *The Wealdwife's Tale*, 1993
R.A. Salvatore, *The Woods out Back*, 1993

## 2740

### JACK HOLLAND

## The Fire Queen

(New York: Roc, 1992)

**Story type:** Fantasy (Historical; Political)
**Major character(s):** Fen ''Fire Queen'' Fire, Warrior, Royalty (adopted daughter)
**Time period(s):** 1st century
**Locale(s):** England (Briton)

**Summary:** After Fen Fire exposes the treacherous relationship between her brother and the Roman Emperor Caligula, Fen Fire must rally her people's defenses to stand against Caligula's invading army, intent on ruling the island.

**Other books you might like:**
Marion Zimmer Bradley, *The Mists of Avalon*, 1983

Morgan Llywelyn, *Druids*, 1991
Bridget Wood, *Wolfking*, 1992

---

**2741**

### TOM HOLLAND

## *Lord of the Dead*

(New York: Pocket, 1996)

**Story type:** Horror (Vampire Story)
**Major character(s):** Rebecca Carville, Scholar (Orientalist); George Gordon Byron, Historical Figure, Writer (poet); Percy Bysshe Shelley, Writer (poet), Historical Figure
**Time period(s):** 1990s (1995); 1800s
**Locale(s):** London, England; Albania

**Summary:** Rebecca Carville opens a forgotten crypt in hopes of finding a copy of Lord Byron's supposedly destroyed memoirs, and instead finds Byron himself, who has been a vampire for almost two centuries. Byron regales Rebecca with his personal history as Lord of the Dead, one that makes much sense of the poet's exploits and the imagery in his verse. This first novel was originally published in England in 1995.

**Other books you might like:**
Kim Newman, *Anno Dracula*, 1992
Tim Powers, *The Stress of Her Regard*, 1989
Kathryn Ptacek, *In Silence Sealed*, 1988
Anne Rice, *The Vampire Lestat*, 1985
Brian Stableford, *The Empire of Fear*, 1988

---

**2742**

### TOM HOLLAND

## *Slave of My Thirst*

(New York: Pocket, 1997)

**Story type:** Horror (Vampire Story)
**Major character(s):** John Eliot, Doctor; Bram Stoker, Writer; Lucy Ruthven, Actress
**Time period(s):** 1880s (1887-1888)
**Locale(s):** London, England

**Summary:** Eliot Burns joins forces with struggling writer and stage manager Bram Stoker to investigate the murder of actress Lucy Ruthven's brother and the disappearance of her guardian. Clues lead Eliot and Stoker to India where they encounter Lilah, a megalomaniacal vampire queen. A sequel to *Lord of the Dead* and first published in England in 1997 under the title *The Libertine*.

**Other books you might like:**
Les Daniels, *Yellow Fog*, 1986
Les Daniels, *No Blood Spilled*, 1990
Jeanne Kalogridis, *Lord of the Vampires*, 1996
Kim Newman, *The Bloody Red Baron*, 1995
Kim Newman, *Anno Dracula*, 1993
Bram Stoker, *Dracula*, 1897

---

**2743**

### GARY L. HOLLEMAN

## *Demon Fire*

(New York: Leisure, 1995)

**Story type:** Horror (Black Magic)

**Major character(s):** Quinn Ramsey, Police Officer (former); Gail Okata, Police Officer; Quinn Ramsey Jr., Child (9-year-old)
**Time period(s):** 1990s (1995)
**Locale(s):** Hana, Hawaii

**Summary:** Quinn Ramsey inherits the fortune and property of an uncle who died under mysterious circumstances in Hawaii. After moving there with his son, Quinn discovers that his uncle practiced black magic. He is caught between other black magic adherents who hope to gain control of a demon his uncle summoned, and a wicca cult allied with the ancient gods of the island who use white magic to control the damage his uncle has already caused. First novel.

**Other books you might like:**
Robert Bloch, *Strange Eons*, 1976
Edward Lee, *The Chosen*, 1993
Graham Masterton, *Burial*, 1994
Dan Simmons, *Fires of Eden*, 1994
Tamara Thorne, *Haunted*, 1995

---

**2744**

### GARY L. HOLLEMAN

## *Howl-O-Ween*

(New York: Leisure, 1996)

**Story type:** Horror (Black Magic)
**Major character(s):** Cyrus "Russ" Trigg, Bodyguard; Kyna Rand, Businesswoman (diamond merchant); Macumba the Dark Man, Sorcerer
**Time period(s):** 1990s (1996)
**Locale(s):** Memphis, Tennessee

**Summary:** Unaware that she is carrying a stolen talisman known as The Butcher's Broom, Kyna Rand travels the world at the behest of her employer, who hopes to deprive the Dark Man of his magic charm and leave him vulnerable to attack come Halloween. But the Dark Man, a voodoo houngan, has raised the loup garou, whose bite is slowly turning Kyna's bodyguard into a werewolf.

**Other books you might like:**
Hugh B. Cave, *Disciples of Dread*, 1988
Nicholas Conde, *The Religion*, 1982
Don Davis, *The Gris-Gris Man*, 1997
Robert Weinberg, *The Black Lodge*, 1991

---

**2745**

### HELEN HOLLICK

## *The Kingmaking*

(New York: St. Martin's, 1995)

**Story type:** Fantasy (Legend)
**Series:** Pendragon's Banner Trilogy
**Major character(s):** Arthur Pendragon, Royalty, Leader; Gwenhwyfar, Fiance(e)
**Time period(s):** 5th century (450s)
**Locale(s):** England (Britain)

**Summary:** As forces drive the Roman legions from Britain, Uthr's death thrusts Arthur into leadership. He must quickly learn the warrior's way of life, difficult after his early life, spent posing as the son of a serving woman to protect him from Uthr's enemies. First novel.

**Other books you might like:**
Mike Ashley, *The Camelot Chronicles*, 1992
    editor

Mike Ashley, *The Pendragon Chronicles*, 1990
 editor
Marion Zimmer Bradley, *The Mists of Avalon*, 1983
Gillian Bradshaw, *Hawk of May*, 1980
Andrea Hopkins, *Chronicles of King Arthur*, 1994
Courtway Jones, *In the Shadow of the Oak King*, 1991
Mary Stewart, *The Crystal Cave*, 1970
T.H. White, *The Once and Future King*, 1958

---

### 2746

### HELEN HOLLICK

## Pendragon's Banner

(New York: St. Martin's, 1996)

**Story type:** Fantasy (Legend; Political)
**Series:** Pendragon's Banner Trilogy
**Major character(s):** Arthur Pendragon, Royalty, Leader; Gwenhwyfar, Royalty, Spouse
**Time period(s):** 5th century (460s)
**Locale(s):** England (Britain)

**Summary:** As Arthur attempts to hold on to his newly unified kingdom and keep his family safe, power seekers and family problems threaten the harmony. Second in the trilogy.

**Other books you might like:**
Mike Ashley, *The Pendragon Chronicles*, 1990
 editor
Marion Zimmer Bradley, *The Mists of Avalon*, 1983
Andrea Hopkins, *Chronicles of King Arthur*, 1994
Morgan Llywelyn, *Pride of Lions*, 1996
Mary Stewart, *The Crystal Cave*, 1970
Jack Whyte, *The Skystone*, 1996

---

### 2747

### HELEN HOLLICK

## Shadow of the King

(New York: St. Martin's Press, 1997)

**Story type:** Fantasy (Legend)
**Series:** Pendragon's Banner Trilogy
**Major character(s):** Gwenhwyfar, Royalty; Arthur, Royalty (king); Cerdic, Royalty, Warrior
**Time period(s):** 5th century
**Locale(s):** England; Caer Cadan, Fictional City (Cadbury)

**Summary:** When news of Arthur Pendragon's death comes to Caer Cadan, Gwenhwyfar must find a way to defy the nobles who would benefit from the news. Meanwhile, as the Britons squabble, the Saxons grow more and more powerful. If Arthur lives, will it make any difference once the Saxons move? Conclusion of trilogy.

**Other books you might like:**
Poul Anderson, *The King of Ys: Roma Mater*, 1986
 Karen Anderson, co-author
Gillian Bradshaw, *Hawk of May*, 1980
Bernard Cornwell, *The Winter King*, 1996
David Drake, *The Dragon Lord*, 1979
Phyllis Ann Karr, *The Idylls of the Queen*, 1982

---

### 2748

### JOHN R. HOLT

## The Convocation

(New York: Bantam, 1993)

**Story type:** Horror (Black Magic)
**Major character(s):** Elspeth ''Beth'' Tremaine, Statistician (for a brokerage house); Max Wingate, Artist; Victor Rotciv, Stock Broker
**Time period(s):** 1990s (1993)
**Locale(s):** New York, New York

**Summary:** Beth Tremaine's mother died horribly at the hands of the People of the Griffin, a black magic coven to which she belonged and to whom her mother had promised her. Decades later, the coven tries to force Beth back into its clutches in order to avail itself of the extraordinary supernatural talents she possesses.

**Other books you might like:**
Robert Bloch, *Strange Eons*, 1978
Scott Ciencin, *The Vampire Odyssey*, 1992
Stephen R. George, *Nightscape*, 1992
Pat Graversen, *The Fagin*, 1981
Kate Stewart, *The Devil's Cradle*, 1975
Peter Straub, *Shadowland*, 1980

---

### 2749

### JOHN R. HOLT

## Wolf Moon

(New York: Bantam, 1997)

**Story type:** Horror (Black Magic; Werewolf Story)
**Major character(s):** Nicole St. Claire, Student, Werewolf; Duffy Johnson, Student (medical); Timothy Balthazar, Businessman (satanist)
**Time period(s):** 1990s (1997)
**Locale(s):** St. Claire, New York

**Summary:** Satanist Timothy Balthazar summons members of a splinter cult back to St. Claire in the belief that eliminating them will help to save his comatose daughter. Nicole St. Claire, a survivor of the cult and of Balthazar's longstanding grudge against her family, must draw on her family's werewolf curse to save herself and her lover.

**Other books you might like:**
Douglas Clegg, *Goat Dance*, 1989
Elizabeth Forrest, *Dark Tide*, 1993
Allen Lee Harris, *Let There Be Dark*, 1994
Robert R. McCammon, *Usher's Passing*, 1984
Robert Morgan, *The Things That Are Not There*, 1992

---

### 2750

### TOM HOLT

## Flying Dutch

(New York: St. Martin's Press, 1992)

**Story type:** Fantasy (Legend; Light Fantasy)
**Major character(s):** Cornelius Vanderdecker, Sea Captain, Immortal; Jane Doland, Banker
**Time period(s):** 1990s
**Locale(s):** *Verdomde*, At Sea; Scotland; England

**Summary:** Hundreds of years after accidentally ingesting an immortality elixir with a malodorous side effect, Captain Vanderdecker and his crew sail endlessly while attempting landfall at seven year intervals. The noxious smell temporarily neutralized by radioactive water, Vanderdecker searches for the elixir's inventor while the company which carries his 400-year-old life insurance policy sends Jane Doland to search out and reason with the captain, hoping to avoid bankruptcy and ruination of the Earth's economic system should Vanderdecker die.

**Other books you might like:**
Douglas Adams, *The Hitchhiker's Guide to the Galaxy*, 1980
James P. Blaylock, *The Elfin Ship*, 1986
Neil Gaiman, *Good Omens: The Nice and Accurate Prophecies of Agnes Nutter, Witch*, 1990
   Terry Pratchett, co-author
Parke Godwin, *Waiting for the Galactic Bus*, 1988
Terry Pratchett, *Wyrd Sisters*, 1990

## 2751

### TOM HOLT

## *Goatsong*

(New York: St. Martin's Press, 1990)

**Story type:** Fantasy (Historical)
**Series:** Walled Orchard
**Major character(s):** Eupolis of Pallene, Writer
**Time period(s):** 5th century B.C.
**Locale(s):** Athens, Greece

**Summary:** A greek goatherd whose love is comic verse develops his skill as a playwright in Athens. While there, he gets married, writes his comedy and gets it produced to a background of Athenian democracy.

**Other books you might like:**
L. Sprague de Camp, *The Undesired Princess and the Enchanted Bunny*, 1990
   David Drake, co-author
Joan Slonczewski, *Still Forms on Foxfield*, 1980
Howard Waldrop, *A Dozen Tough Jobs*, 1989
Robert Watson, *Whilom*, 1990
Gene Wolfe, *Soldier of Arete*, 1989

## 2752

### TOM HOLT

## *The Walled Orchard*

(New York: St. Martin's Press, 1991)

**Story type:** Fantasy (Historical)
**Series:** Walled Orchard
**Major character(s):** Eupolis of Pallene, Writer
**Time period(s):** 5th century B.C.
**Locale(s):** Athens, Greece

**Summary:** In this sequel to *Goatsong* (1990), Eupolis continues his commissioned history of modern, 5th century Greece with his conscription into military forces fighting for Athens in the Great Peloponnesian War. Surviving the Sicilian disaster, he returns to Athens where he is accused of treason in conjunction with a tasteless blasphemy he had witnessed prior to conscription.

**Other books you might like:**
Robert Silverberg, *Letters From Atlantis*, 1990
Harry Turtledove, *The Misplaced Legion*, 1987
Robert Watson, *Whilom*, 1990
Gene Wolfe, *Soldier of Arete*, 1989

## 2753

### TOM HOLT

## *Ye Gods!*

(New York: St. Martin's Press, 1993)

**Story type:** Fantasy (Light Fantasy; Religious)
**Major character(s):** Jerry Derry, Adventurer, Hero; Apollo, Mythical Creature, Deity; Minerva, Mythical Creature, Deity
**Time period(s):** 1990s; Indeterminate
**Locale(s):** Earth; The Underground, Mythical Place

**Summary:** Greek gods delight in playing a game of existence and alternate worlds, modestly hoping to undo Prometheus's betrayal and bring a sense of humor to the human race. A rules violation changes relationships when Apollo must punish Prometheus for subverting heroes.

**Other books you might like:**
Neil Gaiman, *Good Omens: The Nice and Accurate Prophecies of Agnes Nutter, Witch*, 1990
   Terry Pratchett, co-author
Parke Godwin, *The Snake Oil Wars*, 1989
Parke Godwin, *Waiting for the Galactic Bus*, 1988
Robert A. Heinlein, *Job: A Comedy of Justice*, 1984
Curtis H. Hoffman, *Project: Millennium*, 1987
A.J. Langguth, *Jesus Christs*, 1968
Donald E. Westlake, *Humans*, 1992

## 2754

### STEWART HOME

## *Come Before Christ and Murder Love*

(New York: Serpent's Tail, 1997)

**Story type:** Fantasy (Contemporary Realism; Literary)
**Major character(s):** Kevin Callen, Fugitive, Wizard; Philip Sloan, Fugitive, Mentally Ill Person
**Time period(s):** 1990s (1997)
**Locale(s):** London, England

**Summary:** The subject of a British Government mind control project, Kevin Callen also possesses magical abilities, many allies and followers, but, unfortunately, occasionally becomes Philip Sloan, loser and possible murderer. With a trail of sex, magic, drugs, death and conspiracy, Kevin must stay on the run and under cover to find his true identity.

**Other books you might like:**
Scott Baker, *Dhampire*, 1982
Philip K. Dick, *Valis*, 1981
Stuart Gordon, *Smile on the Void*, 1981
Ursula K. Le Guin, *The Lathe of Heaven*, 1971
Douglas Rushkoff, *Ecstasy Club*, 1997

## 2755

### A.M. HOMES

## *The End of Alice*

(New York: Scribner's, 1996)

**Story type:** Horror (Psychological Suspense)
**Major character(s):** Chappy, Prisoner; Alice Somerfield, Child (12-year-old); Matthew, Child (12-year-old)
**Time period(s):** 1990s (1996)
**Locale(s):** Westchester County, New York; Ossining, New York (Sing Sing Prison)

**Summary:** A female pen pal of a man imprisoned for the brutal sexual assault and murder of a 12-year-old girl becomes obsessed with his twisted mind. She herself seduces a 12-year-old boy and embarks upon an affair destined to lead to a similarly perverse end.

**Other books you might like:**
Ramsey Campbell, *The Face That Must Die*, 1979
Brett Easton Ellis, *American Psycho*, 1991
Stephen Gallagher, *Nightmare, with Angel*, 1992
Ronald Kelly, *Father's Little Helper*, 1992
Stephen King, *Apt Pupil*, 1982
    in *Different Seasons*
Joyce Carol Oates, *Zombie*, 1995
John Saul, *Black Lightning*, 1995

## 2756

### DANIEL HOOD

## Beggar's Banquet

(New York: Ace, 1997)

**Story type:** Fantasy (Mystery; Magic Conflict)
**Series:** Fanuilh
**Major character(s):** Liam Rhenford, Scholar, Detective—Amateur; Fanuilh, Mythical Creature (dragon), Companion (familiar); Mistress Priscian, Businesswoman, Heiress
**Time period(s):** Indeterminate
**Locale(s):** Southwark, Fictional City; Taralon, Fictional Country

**Summary:** Although Liam hopes to initiate some business contacts and enjoy the festival of Beggars Banquet, he must instead help find a murderer and the person who stole a dangerous magical artifact from his proposed business partner.

**Other books you might like:**
Steven Brust, *Jhereg*, 1983
Glen Cook, *Sweet Silver Blues*, 1987
Lynn Flewelling, *Luck in the Shadows*, 1996
Simon R. Green, *Hawk & Fisher*, 1990
Joel Rosenberg, *Hour of the Octopus*, 1994

## 2757

### DANIEL HOOD

## Fanuilh

(New York: Ace, 1994)

**Story type:** Fantasy (Mystery)
**Series:** Fanuilh
**Major character(s):** Liam Rhenford, Scholar, Detective—Amateur; Fanuilh, Mythical Creature (dragon), Companion (wizard's familiar); Aedile Coeccias, Government Official
**Time period(s):** Indeterminate Past
**Locale(s):** Southwark, Fictional City; Taralon, Fictional Country

**Summary:** After the murder of the wizard Tarquin, Liam Rhenford's only friend in Southwark, Fanuilh, will give Liam no peace until they discover the murderer's identity.

**Other books you might like:**
Steven Brust, *Jhereg*, 1983
Glen Cook, *Sweet Silver Blues*, 1987
Simon R. Green, *Hawk & Fisher*, 1990
Barbara Hambly, *Dragonsbane*, 1986
Katharine Kerr, *Polar City Blues*, 1990

## 2758

### DANIEL HOOD

## Scales of Justice

(New York: Ace, 1998)

**Story type:** Fantasy (Mystery; Magic Conflict)
**Major character(s):** Liam Rhenford, Scholar, Detective (Quaestor); Fanuilh, Mythical Creature (dragon), Companion (familiar)
**Locale(s):** Southwark, Fictional City; Taralon, Fictional Country

**Summary:** Assigned to join the Areopagus circuit court, a prestigious court which judges only magical crimes, Liam Rhenford struggles to understand the nature of a death involving sorcery.

**Other books you might like:**
Simon R. Green, *Hawk & Fisher*, 1990
Peg Kerr, *Emerald House Rising*, 1997
Melissa Scott, *Point of Hopes*, 1995
    Lisa A. Barnett, co-author
Delia Sherman, *The Porcelain Dove*, 1993
Martha Wells, *The Death of the Necromancer*, 1998

## 2759

### DANIEL HOOD

## Wizard's Heir

(New York: Ace, 1995)

**Story type:** Fantasy (Mystery)
**Series:** Fanuilh
**Major character(s):** Liam Rhenford, Scholar, Detective—Amateur; Fanuilh, Mythical Creature (dragon), Companion (wizard's familiar); Werewolf, Criminal
**Time period(s):** Indeterminate Past
**Locale(s):** Southwark, Fictional City; Taralon, Fictional Country

**Summary:** Liam struggles to deal with the death of Tarquin and the inheritance of the wizard's home and familiar. The theft of several magical artifacts from his home complicates his life, while Liam and Fanuilh must deal with wizards, priests, and thieves before they can rest.

**Other books you might like:**
Steven Brust, *Jhereg*, 1983
Glen Cook, *Sweet Silver Blues*, 1987
Simon R. Green, *Hawk & Fisher*, 1990
Ellen Kushner, *Swordspoint*, 1987
Fritz Leiber, *Ill Met in Lankhmar*, 1995

## 2760

### KEN HOOD

## Demon Knight

(New York: Harper, 1998)

**Story type:** Fantasy (Historical; Magic Conflict)
**Series:** Years of Longdirk
**Major character(s):** Tobias Longdirk, Outlaw; Lisa, Noblewoman; Hamish Campbell, Traveler
**Time period(s):** 16th century (1525)
**Locale(s):** Italy

**Summary:** Tobias Longdirk uses magic to defeat a supernatural creature, but his opponent has not yet abandoned the fight. Now a brutal army is poised to invaded 16th-century Europe, and part of their plan involves placing the woman Longdirk loves in jeopardy.

**Other books you might like:**
Elizabeth H. Boyer, *The Curse of Slagfid*, 1989
Gillian Bradshaw, *Hawk of May*, 1980
Mike Jefferies, *Hidden Echoes*, 1992
Richard A. Knaak, *Frostwing*, 1995
Tanith Lee, *Quest for the White Witch*, 1978

---

**2761**

**DALE HOOVER**

## 65mm

(New York: Dell/Abyss, 1994)

**Story type:** Horror (Haunted House)
**Major character(s):** Joe Moreson, Businessman (movie house owner); Andy Jordan, Teenager; Kelsie Brown, Computer Expert (systems analyst)
**Time period(s):** 1990s (1994)
**Locale(s):** Fareland, California

**Summary:** In an act of near compulsion Joe Moreson buys the old Fareland Cinema after quitting his job as a computer programmer. But when Joe begins showing a secret 65mm film found in the projection booth of the theater to the local residents, it reignites a series of brutal tortures and murders that the threater fed on 50 years before and is ravenous for again.

**Other books you might like:**
David Darke, *Horrorshow*, 1994
David J. Schow, *Silver Scream*, 1988
    editor
Brad Strickland, *Shadowshow*, 1988

---

**2762**

**DALE HOOVER**

## Shadow Twin

(New York: Dell Abyss, 1991)

**Story type:** Horror (Doppelganger)
**Major character(s):** Jack Benson, Businessman; Rachal Benson, Housewife; Jedidiah Benson, Child (Jack and Rachal's son)
**Time period(s):** 1990s
**Locale(s):** Apple Creek, California

**Summary:** Stressed out by his job and memories of a less than ideal childhood, Jack Benson moves his family to a new life in California. But Jack's emotional turmoil quickly manifests as poltergeist phenomena, opening a hole in the attic of the house from which the physical manifestation of his dark side crawls out and threatens to overwhelm him and his family. This is the author's first novel.

**Other books you might like:**
Kathe Koja, *The Cipher*, 1991

---

**2763**

**H.M. HOOVER**

## Away Is a Strange Place to Be

(New York: E.P. Dutton, 1989)

**Story type:** Science Fiction (Young Adult)
**Major character(s):** Abby Tabor, Teenager; Bryan Bishop, Teenager
**Time period(s):** 24th century (2349)
**Locale(s):** Vitacon, Space Station; United States

**Summary:** Abby and Bryan are kidnapped to serve as slave labor on a space habitat. Although they escape, they find the adult world unwilling to accept the truth of what they've been through, thus leaving them still in danger.

**Other books you might like:**
Frank Asch, *Journey to Terezor*, 1989
Lois McMaster Bujold, *Falling Free*, 1988
Robert A. Heinlein, *Have Spacesuit—Will Travel*, 1958
Robert A. Heinlein, *Podkayne of Mars*, 1963

---

**2764**

**H.M. HOOVER**

## Only Child

(New York: Dutton, 1992)

**Story type:** Science Fiction (First Contact; Young Adult)
**Major character(s):** Cody Oakton, Teenager; Emily ''Avi'' Avichenko, Scientist; Skipper, Alien
**Time period(s):** Indeterminate Future
**Locale(s):** Patma, Planet—Imaginary

**Summary:** The only child aboard the *Annie Cannon*, Cody finds the prospect of his first planetfall quite exciting. When the adults' investigation of Patma's 200-year-old colony proves boring, he wanders away, discovering intelligent natives whose existence the colonists hid. Cody photographs the natives and their arts, determined to prove their existence on Earth where he will attend school.

**Other books you might like:**
Isaac Asimov, *Lucky Starr and the Big Sun of Mercury*, 1956
Ben Bova, *The Winds of Altair*, 1973
Marion Zimmer Bradley, *Star of Danger*, 1965
Diana G. Gallagher, *The Alien Dark*, 1990
Janet Kagan, *Hellspark*, 1988
Andre Norton, *The Stars Are Ours*, 1954
Andre Norton, *The X Factor*, 1965
II. Beam Piper, *Little Fuzzy*, 1962
Marti Steussy, *Dreams of Dawn*, 1988

---

**2765**

**H.M. HOOVER**

## The Winds of Mars

(New York: Dutton, 1995)

**Story type:** Science Fiction (Young Adult; Robot Fiction)
**Major character(s):** Annalyn Reynolds Court, Military Personnel (cadet); Evan Parker, Military Personnel (cadet), Political Figure; Janis Parker, Political Figure (first lady)
**Time period(s):** Indeterminate Future
**Locale(s):** Mars

**Summary:** Annalyn serves as security for her father, protecting him from many enemies. After a foiled plot, Annalyn takes command and restores order, but must then contend with relatives who claim that she usurped power.

**Other books you might like:**
Isaac Asimov, *David Starr, Space Ranger*, 1952
Greg Bear, *Moving Mars*, 1993
Robert A. Heinlein, *Red Planet*, 1949
Frederik Pohl, *Mining the Oort*, 1992
Jerry Pournelle, *Birth of Fire*, 1976
Kim Stanley Robinson, *Green Mars*, 1993
S.C. Sykes, *Red Genesis*, 1991

## 2766

**STUART HOPEN**

### Warp Angel

(New York: Tor, 1995)

**Story type:** Science Fiction (Psychic Powers; Theological)
**Major character(s):** Chev Carson, Mercenary; Dawson, Slave, Cyborg; Magen Hirsch, Warrior
**Time period(s):** Indeterminate Future
**Locale(s):** The Autumn World, Planet—Imaginary (Draconis System)

**Summary:** Marooned in the Draconis System by the abandonment of warp ships, a slave-based society serves the rich and powerful. Magen searches for her husband, a Jewish revolutionary captured by the quasi-governmental Slavers Bod. Unable to find him, Magen enlists Chev and their rich benefactor in an attempt to free as many slaves as possible, and learns the secret of breaking the slaves' conditioning. To save her husband Megan braves the planet most disrupted by the warp drive.

**Other books you might like:**
Lois McMaster Bujold, *Falling Free*, 1988
Lois McMaster Bujold, *Shards of Honor*, 1986
F.M. Busby, *Arrow From Earth*, 1995
Stephen Goldin, *Jade Darcy and the Zen Pirates*, 1990
    Mary Mason, co-author
Elizabeth Moon, *Sporting Chance*, 1994
Dan Simmons, *Hyperion*, 1989

## 2767

**ANDREA HOPKINS**, Editor

### Chronicles of King Arthur

(New York: Viking Studio Books, 1994)

**Story type:** Fantasy (Anthology; Legend)
**Major character(s):** Arthur, Ruler (king), Warrior; Lancelot, Knight
**Time period(s):** 5th century; 6th century
**Locale(s):** England

**Summary:** Contains a four-page introduction and retelling of the medieval story cycle *Matter of Britain* based on the vulgate story cycle, including "Merlin," "Lancelot," "La Queste del Saint Graal," and "Mort Artu" and Sir Thomas Malory's "Morte D'Arthur" plus poems and tales with some material newly translated. Hopkins utilizes original text with expansions and clarifications added. Includes a list of principal characters and glossary.

**Other books you might like:**
Mike Ashley, *The Camelot Chronicles*, 1992
    editor
Mike Ashley, *The Pendragon Chronicles*, 1990
    editor
Marion Zimmer Bradley, *The Mists of Avalon*, 1983
Howard Pyle, *The Story of King Arthur and His Knights*, 1903
T.H. White, *The Once and Future King*, 1958

## 2768

**BRIAN HOPKINS**

### Cold at Heart

(Pasco, Washington: Sovereign Seal, 1997)

**Story type:** Horror (Werewolf Story)

**Major character(s):** Peter Burke, Photographer; David Snow, Scientist (biologist); Julie Snow, Young Woman
**Time period(s):** 1990s (1997)
**Locale(s):** Ellesmere Island, Arctic

**Summary:** Peter Burke's expedition to the arctic to photograph wolves is complicated by the presence of Julie Snow, a young woman whose experiences in the wilds of Minnesota years before have given her an unnatural rapport with wolves. Julie's presence helps bring out the spirit of a werewolf who was responsible for the decimation of several arctic expeditions over the past century.

**Other books you might like:**
Chris N. Africa, *When Wolves Cry*, 1997
Henry Garfield, *Moondog*, 1995
Randy Goldman, *Werewolf Wars*, 1996
Charles L. Grant, *The Dark Cry of the Moon*, 1986
Christine Tanasiuk, *Howl*, 1997

## 2769

**BRIAN HOPKINS**
**DONALD W. SCHANK**, Illustrator

### Something Haunts Us All

(Norfolk, Virginia: Macabre, Inc., 1995)

**Story type:** Horror (Collection)

**Summary:** This first story collection by a small-press author brings together seven tales of horror and surreality. "Night Bite" tells of a man's strange experience with a satanic trickster who may or may not be the manifestation of his illness. In "Scarecrow's Dream" and "And Though a Million Stars Were Shining," the worlds of the living and the dead impinge uneasily upon one another. "The Night Was Kind to Loretta" and "The Thunder of Water" both feature psychopathic murderers who get their just desserts and more. William G. Raley supplies an introduction.

**Other books you might like:**
S. Darnbrook Colson, *People of the Night*, 1994
Jeffrey Osier, *Driftglider and Other Stories*, 1994
Stephen Mark Rainey, *Fugue Devil and Other Weird Horrors*, 1992
Sue Storm, *Star Bones Weep the Blood of Angels*, 1995
David Niall Wilson, *The Fall of the House of Escher and Other Illusions*, 1995

## 2770

**JACK HOPKINS** (Pseudonym of Nick Pollotta)

### Satellite Night News

(New York: Ace, 1993)

**Story type:** Science Fiction (Adventure; Satire)
**Series:** Satellite Night News
**Major character(s):** Rikka Collins, Television Personality; Harry Snyder, Television Personality; Diedrich, Disembodied Personality (Artificial Intelligence)
**Time period(s):** 23rd century
**Locale(s):** Montenegro

**Summary:** After racing to the station, having escaped many close calls, the team finds they have been scooped by another station. Using their skills of misdirection, extortion and bribery, the team get their ship and equipment repaired and updated and head out on assignment to acquire another impossible scoop.

**Other books you might like:**
John DeChancie, *Paradox Alley*, 1987
John DeChancie, *Red Limit Freeway*, 1984

John DeChancie, *Starrigger*, 1983
Frederik Pohl, *Gladiator-at-Law*, 1955
   C.M. Kornbluth, co-author
Ken Rolston, *Extreme Paranoia: Nobody Knows the Trouble I've Shot*, 1991
Neal Stephenson, *Snow Crash*, 1992
Kurt Vonnegut Jr., *Hocus Pocus or, What's the Hurry, Son?*, 1990

## 2771

**NALO HOPKINSON**

### Brown Girl in the Ring

(New York: Warner Aspect, 1998)

**Story type:** Fantasy (Contemporary; Literary)
**Major character(s):** Ti-Jeanne Baines, Psychic (seer), Single Parent; Mami Gros-Jeanne, Healer, Herbalist; Rudolph ''Rudy'' Sheldon, Criminal, Sorcerer (shadow catcher)
**Time period(s):** 1990s
**Locale(s):** Toronto, Ontario, Canada

**Summary:** Sealed off from its suburbs and the rest of the world by roadblocks and barbed wire, Toronto's inner-city residents try desperately to maintain some sense of community, while Rudy and his gang of thugs employ violence combined with black magic to terrorize the area into submission. However, Mami Gros-Jeanne, local healer and focal point of the neighborhood, threatens Rudy's rule as she begins to teach her reluctant granddaughter, Ti-Jeanne, how to use her magical gifts. According to the visions Mami conjures, Ti-Jeanne represents their only hope of destroying Rudy. But Ti-Jeanne has her own problems, namely a newborn infant and a weakness for her spineless, drug-addicted boyfriend, Tony, and has no time or patience for magical mumbo-jumbo or Rudy's downfall. Winner of the Warner Aspect first novel contest.

**Other books you might like:**
Roger D. Abrahams, *Afro-American Folk Tales*, 1985
Emma Bull, *War for the Oaks*, 1987
Octavia E. Butler, *Parable of the Sower*, 1993
Octavia E. Butler, *Wild Seed*, 1980
Charles de Lint, *Mulengro: A Romany Tale*, 1985
Samuel R. Delany, *Dhalgren*, 1975
Marc Laidlaw, *Neon Lotus*, 1988
Ben Okri, *The Famished Road*, 1992
Paul Radin, *African Folktales*, 1985
   editor
Mike Resnick, *Future Earths: Under African Skies*, 1993
   editor

## 2772

**ANTHONY HOROWITZ**, Editor

### Death Walks Tonight

(New York: Puffin, 1996)

**Story type:** Horror (Anthology)
**Summary:** The ten tales of horror presented here were collected with younger readers in mind. Included are Stephen King's ''Battleground,'' about a hit man who meets his match when he receives a box of magically-endowed toy soldiers from one victim's family; Roald Dahl's ''Man From the South,'' a suspenseful tale of a strange man who makes outrageous bets with an extraordinary degree of self-assurance; John Gordon's ''Eels,'' about the just rewards that befall a murderous old lady; Robert Westall's ''The Vacancy,'' a dystopic fiction terror tale about a future in which it does not pay to

be too smart; and an excerpt from Bram Stoker's *Dracula*. This book was first published in England in 1994 as *The Puffin Book of Horror Stories*.

**Other books you might like:**
A. Finnis, *Bone Meal: Seven More Tales of Terror*, 1994
   editor
A. Finnis, *The Cat-Dogs*, 1994
   editor
Gene Kemp, *Ghosts, Ghouls and Other Nightmares*, 1992
   editor
Dennis Pepper, *The Young Oxford Book of Ghost Stories*, 1994
   editor
Susan Price, *Horror Stories*, 1995
   editor
Robert Westall, *Ghost Stories*, 1993
   editor

## 2773

**JESSICA HORSTING**, Editor
**JAMES VAN HISE**, Co-Editor

### Midnight Graffiti

(New York: Warner, 1992)

**Story type:** Horror (Anthology)

**Summary:** Nineteen stories of fantasy and horror, a number of which appeared originally in the cutting edge small press horror magazine, *Midnight Graffiti*, between 1989 and 1992. Included are Stephen King's tale of vengeful frogs, ''The Rainy Season''; Stephen R. Boyett's surrealistic ''Emerald City Blues''; Joe Lansdale's satirical ''Bob the Dinosaur Goes to Disneyland''; a reprint of Dan Simmons' first published story, ''The River Styx Runs Upstream''; and psychological horror stories by Nancy Collins, Rex Miller, and K.W. Jeter.

**Other books you might like:**
Robert Morrish, *Quick Chills II*, 1992
   Peter Enfantino, co-author
Stephen Mark Rainey, *The Best of Deathrealm*, 1993
Stuart David Schiff, *The Whispers Series*, 1977-1987
David B. Silva, *Best of The Horror Show*, 1987
David B. Silva, *The Definitive Best of the Horror Show*, 1992

## 2774

**WILLIAM HORWOOD**
**PATRICK BENSON**, Illustrator

### Toad Triumphant

(New York: St. Martin's Press, 1996)

**Story type:** Fantasy (Young Adult; Adventure)
**Series:** Tales of the Willows
**Major character(s):** Toad of Toad Hall, Animal, Adventurer; Water Rat ''Ratty'', Animal, Adventurer; Mole, Animal, Adventurer
**Time period(s):** Indeterminate
**Locale(s):** England

**Summary:** Infatuated and in search of immortality, Toad takes a motor boat and heads upriver to win the heart of his beloved. Ratty and Mole set out on a river expedition, but then must help rescue the impetuous Toad from his latest legal predicament. A sequel to Kenneth Grahame's *Wind in the Willows*.

**Other books you might like:**
Mary Brown, *The Unlikely Ones*, 1986
Kenneth Grahame, *The Wind in the Willows*, 1908
Brian Jacques, *Redwall*, 1987

Dixon Scott, *A Fresh Wind in the Willows*, 1987
Tad Williams, *Tailchaser's Song*, 1985

---

**2775**

### WILLIAM HORWOOD

## *The Willows and Beyond*

(New York: St. Martin's Press, 1998)

**Story type:** Fantasy (Young Adult; Adventure)
**Series:** Tales of the Willows
**Major character(s):** Toad of Toad Hall, Animal, Adventurer; Mole, Animal, Adventurer; Sea Rat "Ratty", Animal, Adventurer
**Time period(s):** Indeterminate
**Locale(s):** England; Toad Hall, Mythical Place; the River Bank, Mythical Place

**Summary:** Aging, the old animal friends discuss their adventures and prepare to pass on the River Bank to a younger generation.

**Other books you might like:**
Mary Brown, *The Unlikely Ones*, 1986
Kenneth Grahame, *The Wind in the Willows*, 1908
Brian Jacques, *Redwall*, 1987
Dixon Scott, *A Fresh Wind in the Willows*, 1987
Tad Williams, *Tailchaser's Song*, 1985

---

**2776**

### WILLIAM HORWOOD
### PATRICK BENSON, Illustrator

## *The Willows in Winter*

(New York: St. Martin's Press, 1994)

**Story type:** Fantasy (Young Adult; Adventure)
**Series:** Tales of the Willows
**Major character(s):** Toad of Toad Hall, Animal, Pilot; Water Rat "Ratty", Animal, Adventurer; Mole, Animal, Adventurer
**Time period(s):** Indeterminate
**Locale(s):** England

**Summary:** When Badger requisitions Toad's new airplane to search for the missing Mole, Toad waylays his friend and the pilot and takes off with Water Rat, despite inadequate flying lessons. The flight soon ends in first parachuting opportunities for Rat and Toad, allowing Rat to find his way home and Toad to find his way into additional trouble in town. Sequel to Kenneth Grahame's *The Wind in the Willows*.

**Other books you might like:**
Mary Brown, *The Unlikely Ones*, 1986
Michael Ende, *The Night of Wishes: or The Satanarchaeolidealcohellish Notion Potion*, 1992
Kenneth Grahame, *The Wind in the Willows*, 1908
Brian Jacques, *Redwall*, 1987
Dixon Scott, *A Fresh Wind in the Willows*, 1987

---

**2777**

### GERARD DANIEL HOUARNER, Editor

## *Going Postal*

(New York: Space & Time, 1998)

**Story type:** Horror (Anthology)

**Summary:** These 19 stories, original to the volume, feature people driven over the edge by the annoyances and stresses of everyday life. Selections include Melanie Tem's tale of urban paranoia, "Sweet"; Don Webb's "The Last Beep," in which a man is driven to murderous rage by a barrage of misdirected phone calls; Bentley Little's "Life with Father," in which two young girls conspire to save themselves from their psychotically environmentally conscious father; and Gordon Linzner's "The Van," about a deranged motor vehicle operator.

**Other books you might like:**
Peter Crowther, *Narrow Houses*, 1993
    editor
Jeff Gelb, *Fear Itself*, 1994
    editor
Charles L. Grant, *Fears*, 1983
    editor
Gary L. Raisor, *Obsessions*, 1991
    editor
Wendy Webb, *Phobias: Stories of Your Deepest Fears*, 1994
    editor

---

**2778**

### GERARD DANIEL HOUARNER

## *Painfreak*

(Orlando, Florida: Necro Publications, 1996)

**Story type:** Horror (Collection; Erotic Horror)

**Summary:** The author's first collection brings together ten stories of erotic horror, only three of which were previously published. Among the offerings are the title story, about a man's desperate efforts to rescue his wife from an after hours sex club; "Safe Word," concerned with a sexual slave whose master enjoins her to humiliate her tricks; "Painted Faces," in which a man passes on the psychological trauma of his abuse as a child to his wife and daughter; and "The Night Pain," in which a sexual predator psychically binds his victims to him through ritual mutilation. Also included are "The Beast That Was Max," "The Angel of Death," and "Demons of Blood and Passion," which comprise the Max Trilogy, a series of stories featuring an indulgent uncle who is all too willing to supply his sexual partners with everything they desire. Tom Piccirilli supplies the introduction.

**Other books you might like:**
Ron Dee, *Sex and Blood*, 1995
Michael Hemmingson, *Nice Little Stories Jam-Packed with Depraved Sex and Violence*, 1995
Edward Lee, *Edward Lee's Quest for Sex, Truth and Reality*, 1992
Lucy Taylor, *The Flesh Artist*, 1993
Lucy Taylor, *Unnatural Acts and Other Stories*, 1994

---

**2779**

### LYLE HOWARD

## *Mr. Sandman*

(Salt Lake City: Northwest Publishing Inc., 1995)

**Story type:** Horror (Wild Talents)
**Major character(s):** Lance Cutter, Investigator (arson); Julie Chapman, Scientist; Adolph Xavier, Scientist
**Time period(s):** 1990s (1995)
**Locale(s):** Fort Lauderdale, Florida

**Summary:** Lance Cutter's unusual ability to withstand heat makes him well-suited to serve as an arson investigator. His exploits tracking down a Florida arsonist who delivers pets coated with a highly flammable chemical to his victims excited the interest of the United States government, who knows that Lance escaped as a boy from Project Sandman, a secret experiment in genetics to breed a superior soldier class by blending human and animal DNA.

**Other books you might like:**
Mark A. Clements, *Children of the End*, 1993
Ken Eulo, *Claw*, 1994
   Joe Mauck, co-author
T.J. Kirby, *Deadly Breed*, 1992
Dean R. Koontz, *Watchers*, 1987
Penelope Banka Kreps, *Carnivores*, 1993
Bob Mayer, *Operation Synbat*, 1993

---

**2780**

ROBERT E. HOWARD

## *Beyond the Borders*
(New York: Baen, 1996)

**Story type:** Horror (Collection)

**Summary:** Thirteen stories of adventure, fantasy and horror by this popular pulp writer feature several of his recurring characters. The adventurer Costigan matches wits with a satanic opera singer in ''Casonetto's Last Song'' and tries to help a friend overcome a Hindu curse in ''The Dream Snake.'' Professor Kirowan, a traveller cut from the same cloth as Costigan, fights occult entities in ''Dig Me No Grave,'' a cursed talisman in ''The Haunter of the Ring,'' the ghostly past in ''Dermod's Bane,'' and the power of racial memory in ''The Children of the Night.'' Also included are the Lovecraftian horror tale, ''The Fire of Asshurbanipal''; the theriomorphy tale, ''The Hyena''; and the torture tale, ''The Voice of El-Lil.'' T.K.F. Weiskopf supplies headnotes and a foreword.

**Other books you might like:**
Hugh B. Cave, *Murgunstrumm and Others*, 1977
David Drake, *From the Heart of Darkness*, 1983
Brian Lumley, *Fruiting Bodies and Other Fungi*, 1993
E. Hoffman Price, *Far Lands, Other Days*, 1975
Karl Edward Wagner, *In a Lonely Place*, 1983

---

**2781**

ROBERT E. HOWARD

## *Eons of the Night*
(New York: Baen, 1996)

**Story type:** Horror (Collection)

**Summary:** Ten stories, half of which were first published after the author's death in 1936, display his proficiency in both heroic fantasy and supernatural horror fiction. ''Spear and Fang,'' Howard's first professionally published tale, tells of a primitive man's savage battle with a gorilla. Also included are two chronicles of James Allison, a contemporary American whose numerous reincarnations include hunwulf, a barbarian challenged with rescuing his woman from bat-winged captors in ''The Garden of Fear,'' and Hialmar, a mercenary who confronts the goddess Ishtar, in ''The Marchers of Valhalla.'' ''Sea Curse'' and ''Out of the Deep'' both feature sailors enmeshed in uncanny phenomena on the high seas. ''In the Forest of Villefere'' and ''Wolfshead'' are werewolf stories with sword-and-sorcery flourishes. S.M. Stirling supplies headnotes and a foreword.

**Other books you might like:**
Ramsey Campbell, *Far Away and Never*, 1996
David Drake, *Vettius and His Friends*, 1989

Fritz Leiber, *Heroes and Horrors*, 1984
Michael Moorcock, *Stormbringer*, 1993
Karl Edward Wagner, *The Book of Kane*, 1985

---

**2782**

ROBERT E. HOWARD

## *Ghor, Kin-Slayer: The Saga of Genseric's Fifth-Born Son*
(West Warwick, Rhode Island: Necronomicon Press, 1997)

**Story type:** Horror (Occult)

**Summary:** Episodic round-robin novel begun from a fragment of a story by Robert E. Howard concerning Ghor, a young boy raised by wolves who grows to be a fearsome warrior driven by the desire to revenge himself for his parents' abandonment. His travels bring him into conflict with a variety of human and supernatural monsters and nemeses. Sixteen writers were commissioned to continue Howard's tale for the small press magazine *Fantasy Crossroads* in the 1970s, but the magazine ceased publication before all the episodes could be published. All are published here for the first time. Contributors inlcude Karl Edward Wagner, Joseph Payne Brennan, Richard L. Tierney, Michael Moorcock, Charles R. Saunders, Andrew J. Offutt, Manly Wade Wellman, Darrell Schweitzer, A.E. van Vogt, Brian Lumley, Frank Belknap Long, Adrian Cole, Ramsey Campbell, H. Warner Munn, Marion Zimmer Bradley, and Richard A. Lupoff.

**Other books you might like:**
Ramsey Campbell, *Far Away and Never*, 1996
David Drake, *Vettius and His Friends*, 1989
Robert E. Howard, *Conan the Barbarian*, 1955
David C. Smith, *Engor's Sword Arm*, 1997
Richard L. Tierney, *Scroll of Thoth*, 1997
Karl Edward Wagner, *The Book of Kane*, 1985

---

**2783**

ROBERT E. HOWARD

## *Hour of the Dragon*
(West Kingston, RI: Donald M. Grant, 1989)

**Story type:** Fantasy (Sword and Sorcery)
**Major character(s):** Conan, Barbarian, Warrior
**Time period(s):** Indeterminate Past
**Locale(s):** Earth

**Summary:** In the only full-length novel Howard ever wrote about Conan the Barbarian, Conan finally gains a kingdom, only to have it taken by means of treachery and sorcery. This was first serialized in 1935-1936 and republished as *Conan the Conqueror* in 1950.

**Other books you might like:**
Poul Anderson, *The Broken Sword*, 1983
Robert Asprin, *Stealer's Sky*, 1990
   Lynn Abbey, co-editor; Thieve's World 12
Fritz Leiber, *The Swords of Lankhmar*, 1963
Fred Saberhagen, *The Third Book of Lost Swords: Stonecutter's Story*, 1988

**ROBERT E. HOWARD**

## Trails in Darkness

(New York: Baen, 1995)

**Story type:** Horror (Collection)

**Summary:** Although best known as the creator of Conan the Barbarian, whose adventures were published in the pulp magazine *Weird Tales*, Howard also wrote many atmospheric tales of horror set in his native southwest. The ten collected here include the ghost stories ''The Man on the Ground'' and ''The Dead Remember,'' and the vampire tale ''The Horror From the Mound.'' A number of tales, including ''Black Canaan,'' ''Moon of Zambebwei,'' and ''Kelly the Conjure-Man'' use racial tensions between blacks and whites as the foundation for tales of voodoo horrors imported to the American frontier. ''The Valley of the Lost'' and ''Black Hound of Death'' are tales of revenge and frontier justice garnished with hints of the supernatural. S.M. Stirling supplies headnotes and an introduction.

**Other books you might like:**
David Drake, *From the Heart of Darkness*, 1983
Joe R. Lansdale, *By Bizarre Hands*, 1989
Brian Lumley, *Fruiting Bodies and Other Fungi*, 1993
Karl Edward Wagner, *In a Lonely Place*, 1983

**2785**

**RUSS T. HOWARD**

## The Ultimate Helm

(Lake Geneva, Wisconsin: TSR, 1993)

**Story type:** Fantasy (Quest)
**Series:** Cloakmaster Cycle
**Major character(s):** Teldin Moore, Adventurer, Spaceship Captain
**Time period(s):** Indeterminate
**Locale(s):** *Spelljammer*, Spaceship; Outer Space

**Summary:** Teldin Moore boards *Spelljammer*, the key to his destiny, and he struggles to control it in spite of the political intrigue and magical forces working to prevent his mastery. Concludes the game tie-in series.

**Other books you might like:**
David Cook, *Beyond the Moons*, 1991
Elaine Cunningham, *The Radiant Dragon*, 1992
Nigel Findley, *The Broken Sphere*, 1993
Nigel Findley, *Into the Void*, 1991
Roger E. Moore, *The Maelstrom's Eye*, 1992
Alis A. Rasmussen, *A Passage of Stars*, 1990
Alis A. Rasmussen, *The Price of Ransom*, 1990
Alis A. Rasmussen, *Revolution's Shore*, 1990

**2786**

**JAMES HOWE**

## Return to Howliday Inn

(New York: Atheneum, 1992)

**Story type:** Fantasy (Young Adult; Adventure)
**Major character(s):** Harold, Animal (dog); Chester, Animal (cat); Howie, Animal (dog)
**Time period(s):** 1990s
**Locale(s):** Chateau ''Howliday Inn'' Bow-Wow, Mythical Place

**Summary:** On a return visit to the site of Howie's birth, Chester resolves to discover the secret of Chateau Bow-Wow.

**Other books you might like:**
Robert Davis, *Padre Porko: The Gentlemanly Pig*, 1939
Elizabeth Seeman, *The Talking Dog and the Barking Man*, 1960
Dodie Smith, *The Hundred and One Dalmatians*, 1957
Eve Titus, *Basil of Baker Street*, 1958
E.B. White, *Charlotte's Web*, 1952

**2787**

**TREVOR HOYLE**

## Kids

(New York: Berkley 1990)

**Story type:** Horror (Evil Children)
**Major character(s):** Tom Margison, Student, Scientist (physicist); Danny Margison, Child (Tom's sister); Mary Helms, Doctor (neurologist)
**Time period(s):** 1990s
**Locale(s):** Torrence, North Carolina; Pennsylvania

**Summary:** ''What's the matter with kids today?'' wonders Tom Margison when his 11-year-old sister, her intelligence and propensity for violence enhanced by a blood transfusion, becomes hyperkinetic and develops the ability to control others through telepathic power. Meanwhile, a group of doctors and scientists at a psychiatric institute in western Pennsylvania tries to explain and cure similar uncontrollable, psychotic behavior in a host of other young children. Originally published in England by Sphere Books in 1987.

**Other books you might like:**
J.G. Ballard, *Running Wild*, 1988
James Herbert, *The Fog*, 1975
Leonard Reiffel, *The Contaminant*, 1978
John Wyndham, *Chocky*, 1968
John Wyndham, *The Midwich Cuckoos*, 1957

**2788**

**L. RON HUBBARD**

**KEVIN J. ANDERSON**, Co-Author

## Ai! Pedrito!: When Intelligence Goes Wrong

(Los Angeles: Bridge, 1998)

**Story type:** Science Fiction (Espionage Thriller)
**Major character(s):** Tom Smith, Military Personnel (naval officer); Pedro Miraflores, Spy, Revolutionary
**Time period(s):** Indeterminate Future
**Locale(s):** Cuba; United States

**Summary:** A young naval officer discovers that he is an almost exact double for an infamous South American spy and revolutionary leader named Miraflores. When Miraflores flees to the north and tries to assume the officer's identity, life becomes very complicated for them both. Only marginally science fiction, it is based on a story by the late L. Ron Hubbard but is written primarily by Anderson.

**Other books you might like:**
Kevin J. Anderson, *Blindfold*, 1995
Kevin J. Anderson, *Climbing Olympus*, 1994
Kevin J. Anderson, *Ground Zero*, 1995
Kevin J. Anderson, *Ruins*, 1996
Jeff Bredenberg, *The Man in the Moon Must Die*, 1993
Diane Duane, *Dark Mirror*, 1993
Gerald Heard, *The Doppelgangers*, 1947

Robert A. Heinlein, *Double Star*, 1956

## 2789

### L. RON HUBBARD

## Fear

(Los Angeles: Bridge Publications, 1991)

**Story type:** Horror (Psychological Suspense)
**Major character(s):** James Lowry, Professor (ethnologist); Tommy Williams, Professor; Mary Lowry, Housewife (James' wife)
**Time period(s):** 1940s (1940)
**Locale(s):** Atworthy College (a small university town)

**Summary:** Fired from his teaching position at Atworthy College for writing a popular magazine article debunking the existence of devils and demons, ethnologist James Lowry suddenly finds himself unable to account for the past four hours of his life. He is soon subjected to a series of bizarre, seemingly supernatural experiences that are somehow linked to an event that occurred during those "lost" hours.

**Other books you might like:**
Ramsey Campbell, *Incarnate*, 1983
Philip K. Dick, *Ubik*, 1969
Daniel Quinn, *Dreamer*, 1988
Roland Topor, *The Tenant*, 1964
Jack Williamson, *Darker than You Think*, 1947

## 2790

### L. RON HUBBARD

## Final Blackout

(Los Angeles: Bridge, 1989)

**Story type:** Science Fiction (Military)
**Major character(s):** Lieutenant, Military Personnel
**Time period(s):** Indeterminate Future
**Locale(s):** England

**Summary:** After thirty years, a seemingly unending world war is finally approaching its final stages. Hundreds of millions of people have died, apparently for no reason. The mysterious Lieutenant, who was born in an air-raid shelter and who has spent virtually his entire adult life on the battlefield, leads a small army in the conquest of England. Setting himself up as a benevolent dictator, he reconstructs the nation's economy and brings about a near-utopia.

**Other books you might like:**
Joe Haldeman, *The Forever War*, 1974
Robert A. Heinlein, *Starship Troopers*, 1959
Edward P. Hughes, *Masters of the Fist*, 1989
Fritz Leiber, *The Big Time*, 1961
H.G. Wells, *The Shape of Things to Come*, 1933

## 2791

### L. RON HUBBARD

## Typewriter in the Sky

(Los Angeles: Bridge Publications, 1995)

**Story type:** Fantasy (Adventure; Alternate World)
**Major character(s):** Mike de Wolf, Adventurer, Pirate (fictional); Horace Hackett, Writer
**Time period(s):** 1940s; Indeterminate
**Locale(s):** New York, New York; Mythical Place (literary Caribbean setting)

**Summary:** A strange accident transports Mike de Wolf into the literary world of Horace Hackett's novel-in-progress, a 17th century swashbuckler with a villain modeled after Mike. Mike's thrilling Caribbean exploits may end tragically if he suffers the usual fate of Hackett's antagonists. Reissue of the 1940 serial from *Unknown* with a five-page introduction by Kevin J. Anderson.

**Other books you might like:**
Aaron Allston, *Galatea in 2-D*, 1993
Piers Anthony, *Killobyte*, 1993
Ben Bova, *Death Dream*, 1994
Charles de Lint, *The Little Country*, 1991
Philip Jose Farmer, *Red Orc's Rage*, 1991
Richard A. Knaak, *King of the Grey*, 1993
Will Shetterly, *The Tangled Lands*, 1989
Clifford D. Simak, *Out of Their Minds*, 1970

## 2792

### TANYA HUFF

## Blood Debt

(New York: DAW, 1997)

**Story type:** Horror (Vampire Story; Mystery)
**Series:** Victory Nelson, Investigator
**Major character(s):** Henry Fitzroy, Writer, Vampire; Vicki Nelson, Detective—Private; Mike Celluci, Detective—Police
**Time period(s):** 1990s (1997)
**Locale(s):** Vancouver, British Columbia, Canada

**Summary:** In this adventure of private investigator Vicki Nelson, Vicki is summoned back to Vancouver by vampire Henry Fitzroy to solve the mystery of his nightly haunting by the ghost of a mutilated victim. Vicki's investigation into black market organ bootlegging as a possible origin of the haunting is hampered by the limitations of vampire life and by her constant bickering with the territorial Fitzroy.

**Other books you might like:**
Vincent Courtney, *Vampire Beat*, 1991
P.N. Elrod, *Bloodlist*, 1990
Lee Killough, *Blood Walk*, 1997
Michael Reaves, *Night Hunter*, 1991
Les Whitten, *Progeny of the Adder*, 1965

## 2793

### TANYA HUFF

## Blood Price

(New York: DAW, 1991)

**Story type:** Horror (Vampire Story)
**Major character(s):** Vicki Nelson, Detective—Private; Mike Celluci, Police Officer; Henry Fitzroy, Writer (romance writer), Vampire
**Time period(s):** 1990s
**Locale(s):** Toronto, Ontario, Canada

**Summary:** Detective Vicki Nelson and her former lover, Officer Mike Celluci, are joined by an unusual third party in their investigation of a string of murders that seem to point to a vampire: vampire Henry Fitzroy, a sophisticated writer of historical romances, who is determined to help clear his species of blame for the atrocities.

**Other books you might like:**
P.N. Elrod, *The Vampire Files Series*, 1990-1992
Stephen Gallagher, *Valley of Lights*, 1987
Lee Killough, *Blood Hunt*, 1987
William Relling Jr., *New Moon*, 1988

## 2794

### TANYA HUFF

## *Blood Trail*

(New York: DAW, 1991)

**Story type:** Horror (Werewolf Story)
**Major character(s):** Vicki Nelson, Detective—Private; Mike Celluci, Police Officer; Henry Fitzroy, Writer (romance writer), Vampire
**Time period(s):** 1990s
**Locale(s):** Toronto, Ontario, Canada

**Summary:** Detective Vicki Nelson and 450-year-old vampire Henry Fitzroy team up for their second adventure, this time to discover who is behind the systematic murder of a family of werewolves who were Henry's friends. Complicating the investigation are internal quarrels among the werewolves and the jealousy of Vicki's former lover and colleague, Mike Celluci.

**Other books you might like:**
Richard Jaccoma, *The Werewolf's Tale*, 1989
Ronald Kelly, *Something Out There*, 1991
George R.R. Martin, *"The Skin Trade"*, 1987
    In *Night Visions 4*
S.P. Somtow, *Moon Dance*, 1990

## 2795

### TANYA HUFF

## *Fifth Quarter*

(New York: DAW, 1995)

**Story type:** Fantasy (Magic Conflict)
**Series:** Circle and Quarters
**Major character(s):** Vree, Martial Arts Expert (assassin); Bannon, Martial Arts Expert (assassin); Gyhard, Military Personnel (general)
**Time period(s):** Indeterminate Past
**Locale(s):** Havakeen Empire, Fictional Country

**Summary:** Bannon and Vree's latest hit goes disastrously wrong when their target jumps his personality into Bannon's body, forcing Bannon into his sister's mind, where they strike a precarious balance until they can get his body back. Their target, Gyhard, leads them into his plot to jump into the Imperial Prince, in turn drawn to a strange, twisted old man with the ability to hold dead spirits to their bodies. Second in the series.

**Other books you might like:**
Steven Brust, *Jhereg*, 1983
Octavia E. Butler, *Mind of My Mind*, 1977
Robin Hobb, *Assassin's Apprentice*, 1995
Marjorie Bradley Kellogg, *The Book of Earth*, 1995
Mercedes Lackey, *By the Sword*, 1991

## 2796

### TANYA HUFF

## *The Fire's Stone*

(New York: DAW, 1990)

**Story type:** Fantasy (Quest)
**Major character(s):** Aaron, Thief; Darvish, Royalty (prince); Chandra, Wizard, Royalty (princess)
**Time period(s):** Indeterminate Past
**Locale(s):** Ischia, Fictional Country; Ytaili, Fictional Country

**Summary:** The Stone that keeps Ischia's active volcano has been stolen and apparently taken to Ytaili. Darvish (alcoholic wastrel that he is) and Aaron (under Darvish's protection after his failed attempt to steal the emerald atop the royal staff) are soul-linked and sent to get it back. Chandra, refusing to diffuse her power by accepting an arranged marriage to Darvish, insists on coming along.

**Other books you might like:**
Diane Duane, *The Door into Shadow*, 1984
Diane Duane, *The Door into Fire*, 1979
Barbara Hambly, *The Time of the Dark*, 1982
Rosemary Kirstein, *The Steerswoman*, 1989
Mercedes Lackey, *Arrows of the Queen*, 1987
Robin McKinley, *The Blue Sword*, 1982

## 2797

### TANYA HUFF

## *Gate of Darkness, Circle of Light*

(New York: DAW, 1989)

**Story type:** Fantasy (Contemporary)
**Major character(s):** Rebecca, Handicapped (Mentally); Roland, Musician (Street)
**Time period(s):** 1980s
**Locale(s):** Toronto, Ontario, Canada

**Summary:** Only Rebecca can see the little people that live in the trees. When a little person is stabbed, she asks Roland and other friends for help. Together, they discover an evil sorcerer who must be stopped.

**Other books you might like:**
Gael Baudino, *Duel of Dragons*, 1983
Charles de Lint, *Greenmantle*, 1988
Charles de Lint, *Jack, the Giant-Killer*, 1987
Alan Dean Foster, *Glory Lane*, 1987
Simon Hawke, *The Wizard of Sunset Strip*, 1989

## 2798

### TANYA HUFF

## *No Quarter*

(New York: DAW, 1996)

**Story type:** Fantasy (Magic Conflict; Quest)
**Series:** Circle and Quarters
**Major character(s):** Vree, Martial Arts Expert (assassin); Bannon, Martial Arts Expert (assassin); Gyhard, Military Personnel
**Time period(s):** Indeterminate Past
**Locale(s):** Shkoder, Fictional Country

**Summary:** Bannon and Vree, whose body also houses Gyhard's spirit, travel to Shkoder, hoping to enlist bardic help in finding a new body for Gyhard. However, the Emperor's and Bannon's desire for revenge upon Gyhard interferes with their plans. Sequel to *Fifth Quarter*.

**Other books you might like:**
Steven Brust, *Jhereg*, 1983
Octavia E. Butler, *Mind of My Mind*, 1977
Robin Hobb, *Assassin's Apprentice*, 1995
J.V. Jones, *The Baker's Boy*, 1995
Mercedes Lackey, *By the Sword*, 1991

**2799**

**TANYA HUFF**

## Sing the Four Quarters

(New York: DAW, 1994)

**Story type:** Fantasy (Adventure; Political)
**Major character(s):** Annice, Royalty (former princess), Minstrel (bard); Pjerin, Nobleman (Duc of Ohrid); Stasya, Minstrel (bard)
**Time period(s):** Indeterminate Past
**Locale(s):** Shkoder, Fictional Country; Ohrid, Fictional Country

**Summary:** Ten years ago, Annice could renounce her royal position and become a Bard only under certain conditions. Now she must treasonously violate those conditions, as she finds herself pregnant and the father of her child in prison for supposed treason of his own. Annice and Stasya must help him escape, then strike out to find the real traitor.

**Other books you might like:**
Gael Baudino, *Strands of Starlight*, 1989
Diane Duane, *The Door into Fire*, 1979
Ru Emerson, *The Princess of Flames*, 1986
Marjorie Bradley Kellogg, *The Book of Earth*, 1995
Rosemary Kirstein, *The Steerswoman*, 1989
Mercedes Lackey, *The Lark and the Wren*, 1993

**2800**

**TANYA HUFF**

## Summon the Keeper

(New York: DAW, 1998)

**Story type:** Fantasy (Light Fantasy; Religious)
**Major character(s):** Claire Beth Hansen, Psychic (Keeper); Austin, Animal (cat), Psychic; Dean McIssac, Maintenance Worker, Cook
**Time period(s):** 1990s
**Locale(s):** Kingston, Ontario, Canada

**Summary:** Although Claire expects a long career as Keeper, moving from emergency to emergency, events draw her to a bed and breakfast where 50 years earlier the Keepers forged a temporary seal to a conduit opened to Hell. If Claire cannot find a permanent solution, duty will require her to stay forever.

**Other books you might like:**
Gael Baudino, *Strands of Sunlight*, 1994
Esther Friesner, *Happy High*, 1991
Janet Kagan, *Mirabile*, 1991
Nick Pollotta, *Bureau 13*, 1991
Elizabeth Ann Scarborough, *The Godmother*, 1994

**2801**

**MARLYS HUFFMAN**

## Afternoon of the Gosling

(New York: Zebra, 1989)

**Story type:** Horror (Evil Children)
**Major character(s):** Philip Thayer, Religious (Evangelist); Cerise Thayer, Child
**Time period(s):** 1980s
**Locale(s):** United States

**Summary:** Taking her stepfather's ideas very seriously, Cerise Thayer prays a lot and her prayers come true—animals are killed, fires are started, the friend who makes fun of her is accidentally shot, and her pestering little sister drowns—with a little help from Cerise. Then she prays for her most ambitious desire—to take her mother's place with her stepfather.

**Other books you might like:**
Lawrence Block, *Ariel*, 1980
John Saul, *Suffer the Children*, 1977
Bernard Taylor, *The Godsend*, 1976
Patricia Wallace, *Monday's Child*, 1989

**2802**

**JAMES BYRON HUGGINS**

## Cain

(New York: Simon & Schuster, 1997)

**Story type:** Horror (Science Fiction; Apocalyptic Horror)
**Major character(s):** Roth Tiberius Cain, Military Personnel (soldier); Soloman, Military Personnel (soldier); Maggie, Scientist
**Time period(s):** 1990s (1997)
**Locale(s):** Death Valley, New Mexico; Los Angeles, California

**Summary:** Cain, the ultimate soldier, created in the laboratory and imbued with the spirit of the murderous Cain of biblical legend, goes on a rampage of death and destruction when he escapes from the facility where he was made. Special forces commando Soloman and Maggie, a scientist who helped create Cain, launch a manhunt that is complicated by the HyMar virus, a plague with which Cain is infected and which could cause mass destruction if released into the atmosphere.

**Other books you might like:**
Roger Elwood, *Angelwalk: A Modern Fable*, 1988
Garry Kilworth, *Angel*, 1993
Garry Kilworth, *Archangel*, 1994
Dean R. Koontz, *Shadowfires*, 1987

**2803**

**BARRY HUGHART**

## The Chronicles of Master Li and Number Ten Ox

(Chicago: Stars Our Next Destination Press, 1998)

**Story type:** Fantasy (Light Fantasy; Quest)
**Major character(s):** Master Li, Con Artist, Adventurer; Number Ten Ox, Orphan, Adventurer
**Time period(s):** Indeterminate Past
**Locale(s):** China

**Summary:** Omnibus edition including *Bridge of Birds* (1984), *The Story of the Stone* (1988) and *Eight Skilled Gentlemen* (1991). Master Li and Number Ten Ox travel through ancient China searching for adventure and interesting times while trying to solve mysteries.

**Other books you might like:**
Kyle Crocco, *Heroes, Inc.*, 1991
Neil Gaiman, *Good Omens: The Nice and Accurate Prophecies of Agnes Nutter, Witch*, 1990
Terry Pratchett, co-author
Jeanne Larsen, *Bronze Mirror*, 1991
John Moore, *Slay and Rescue*, 1993
Joel Rosenberg, *Hour of the Octopus*, 1994

**BARRY HUGHART**

## Eight Skilled Gentlemen

(New York: Doubleday Foundation, 1991)

**Story type:** Fantasy (Adventure; Alternate World)
**Series:** Master Li
**Major character(s):** Master Li, Detective; Number Ten Ox, Sidekick
**Time period(s):** 7th century (640)
**Locale(s):** Peking, China; Forbidden City, China

**Summary:** Two oriental detectives face a series of diabolical murders committed by mythical demons who performed evil for eight long-dead shamans. Yen Shih, a puppeteer, and Yu Lan, his shaman daughter, help the pair solve the mystery.

**Other books you might like:**
John DeChancie, *Castle Perilous*, 1988
John DeChancie, *Paradox Alley*, 1987
John DeChancie, *Red Limit Freeway*, 1984
John DeChancie, *Starrigger*, 1983
Randall Garrett, *Too Many Magicians*, 1967
Michael Kurland, *Ten Little Wizards*, 1988
Jeanne Larsen, *Silk Road*, 1989

**2805**

**EDWARD P. HUGHES**

## Masters of the Fist

(New York: Baen Books, 1989)

**Story type:** Science Fiction (Post-Nuclear Holocaust)
**Major character(s):** Patrick O'Meara, Warrior (Master Sergeant), Ruler
**Time period(s):** 21st century
**Locale(s):** Barley Cross, Ireland

**Summary:** This short story collection relates the adventures of O'Meara and his battle tank after WW III. The ex-soldier settles in the town of Barley Cross, Ireland, using the tank to establish his right to rule. He's a good, but stern ruler and the only man in the village who isn't sterile. He thus has had the responsibility of fathering every child born since the war. Some of these stories were previously published in *The Magazine of Fantasy and Science Fiction*, the *There Will Be War* anthology series, and elsewhere between 1980 and 1987.

**Other books you might like:**
David Brin, *The Postman*, 1985
Algis Budrys, *Some Will Not Die*, 1961
David Drake, *Hammer's Slammers*, 1979
Keith Laumer, *The Stars Must Wait*, 1990

**2806**

**MARIAN HUGHES**

## Initiation

(New York: Baen, 1995)

**Story type:** Science Fiction (Lost Colony; Post-Disaster)
**Major character(s):** Bart, Apprentice, Hunter; Sanda, Apprentice, Scholar; Mikhail, Hunter, Leader
**Time period(s):** Indeterminate Future
**Locale(s):** Planet—Imaginary

**Summary:** On a planet where the native food turns humans into "zerkers," or enraged fighters, Bart and Sanda struggle to make changes and improve the lives of their people. First novel.

**Other books you might like:**
Nicola Griffith, *Ammonite*, 1993
Jacqueline Lichtenberg, *First Channel*, 1980
  Jean Lorrah, co-author
Vonda N. McIntyre, *Dreamsnake*, 1978
Frederik Pohl, *Stopping at Slowyear*, 1991
Sheri S. Tepper, *Grass*, 1989

**2807**

**MONICA HUGHES**

## Invitation to the Game

(New York: Simon and Schuster, 1991)

**Story type:** Science Fiction (Young Adult; Adventure)
**Major character(s):** Lisse, Artist; Benta, Farmer; Rich, Doctor (psychiatrist)
**Time period(s):** 22nd century
**Locale(s):** North America; Planet—Imaginary

**Summary:** Unable to find work, Lisse and seven friends from school are sent to live in a dreary Designated Area. Unwilling to simply drift, they are thrilled to be asked to participate in the Game which takes them to a marvelous new world where they can explore and wander. When they say they need a doctor and someone with farming experience, Rich and Benta, both newly unemployed, join the group. On their final mission, they do not return to their familiar city, discovering that they have been dropped on a colony planet with the Game as training for survival there. After a year they meet another group of participants in the Game and are prepared to build a new society.

**Other books you might like:**
John Brunner, *The Dreaming Earth*, 1963
Orson Scott Card, *Ender's Game*, 1985
Arthur C. Clarke, *The Garden of Rama*, 1991
John Cramer, *Twistor*, 1989
Robert A. Heinlein, *Tunnel in the Sky*, 1955
William Sleator, *Interstellar Pig*, 1984
Jack Williamson, *Mazeway*, 1990

**2808**

**MONICA HUGHES**

## The Promise

(New York: Simon & Schuster, 1992)

**Story type:** Science Fiction (Fantasy; Young Adult)
**Major character(s):** Rania, Child, Royalty (princess); Atbin, Teenager, Adventurer; Sandwriter, Shaman
**Time period(s):** Indeterminate Future
**Locale(s):** Rokam, Planet—Imaginary

**Summary:** On her 10th birthday Rania receives a gift box from the Sandwriter. Filled with sand, the box signals her parents that the Sandwriter, now 76 years old, needs her promised apprentice. Rania must leave her life as a princess, her family and all her possessions behind to become the new guardian of Rokam.

**Other books you might like:**
Peter Dickinson, *Eva*, 1989
Gordon R. Dickson, *Time Storm*, 1977
Robert A. Heinlein, *The Rolling Stones*, 1952
David R. Palmer, *Emergence*, 1984

Pamela F. Service, *Under Alien Stars*, 1990

## 2809

### ROBERT DON HUGHES

## The Faithful Traitor

(New York: Ballantine Del Rey, 1992)

**Story type:** Fantasy (Adventure; Political)
**Series:** Wizard and Dragon
**Major character(s):** Seagryn, Wizard (powershaper), Criminal (accused traitor); Vicia-Heinox, Mythical Creature (two-headed dragon)
**Time period(s):** Indeterminate
**Locale(s):** One Land, Mythical Place

**Summary:** After Seagryn the powershaper loosed it, Vicia-Heinox created havoc by eating people and burning the land, actions generally blamed on Seagryn. Outcast from society, Seagryn must find a way to appease Vicia-Heinox in order to regain his wife and acceptance in society amidst conspiracy and preparations for war.

**Other books you might like:**
Teresa Edgerton, *The Work of the Sun*, 1990
Barbara Hambly, *Dragonsbane*, 1987
Judith Reeves-Stevens, *Shifter*, 1990
    Garfield Reeves-Stevens, co-author
Christopher Stasheff, *The Warlock Insane*, 1989

## 2810

### RYAN HUGHES

## Hard Crash

(New York: Pocket, 1998)

**Series:** Unreal
**Major character(s):** Zofia, Prisoner; Gerick, Prisoner
**Time period(s):** Indeterminate Future
**Locale(s):** Na Pali, Planet—Imaginary

**Summary:** Zofia and Gerick escape imprisonment when their spaceship crashlands on the planet Na Pali. They learn that the natives of Na Pali have been conquered by a brutal alien force which uses them as prey for their hunting expeditions. The natives believe the two humans are their prophesized saviors, and before long the humans begin to believe the same.

**Other books you might like:**
Poul Anderson, *Fire Time*, 1974
Kenneth Bulmer, *The Earth Gods Are Coming*, 1960
Alan Dean Foster, *A Call to Arms*, 1991
Keith Laumer, *Judson's Eden*, 1991
Andre Norton, *The X Factor*, 1967

## 2811

### ZACH HUGHES (Pseudonym of Hugh Zachary)

## Deep Freeze

(New York: DAW, 1992)

**Story type:** Science Fiction (Alternate Intelligence; First Contact)
**Major character(s):** Daniel Webster, Spaceship Captain, Aged Person (retired); Joshua Webster, Military Personnel; Sarah Webster de Conde, Socialite, Twin
**Time period(s):** Indeterminate Future

**Locale(s):** Tigian II, Planet—Imaginary; Deep Freeze, Planet—Imaginary

**Summary:** When Daniel and Fran Webster disappear while searching for possible colony planets, their children hunt for them. After the disappearance of her siblings, Sarah Webster de Conde gets strange dreams calling her to come to the aid of her parents and siblings. Responding, she discovers the secret behind the Dead Worlds and the greatest menace facing humanity.

**Other books you might like:**
Johanna Bolton, *Mission: Tori*, 1991
F.M. Busby, *Cage a Man*, 1973
C.J. Cherryh, *Voyager in Night*, 1984
Susan Coon, *Rahne*, 1980
Thomas M. Disch, *The Genocides*, 1965
Jack Lovejoy, *The Hunters*, 1982

## 2812

### ZACH HUGHES (Pseudonym of Zachary Hugh)

## Mother Lode

(New York: DAW, 1991)

**Story type:** Science Fiction (Adventure; First Contact)
**Major character(s):** Erin Elizabeth Kenner, Explorer, Spaceship Captain; Denton Gale, Computer Expert
**Time period(s):** Indeterminate Future
**Locale(s):** Terra II, Planet—Imaginary; *Mother Lode*, Spaceship

**Summary:** When Lt. Erin Kenner retired from the government, she expected to spend time with her father on Terra II. Arriving there, she found that her father had died the week before, having mortgaged the house for a spaceship. Erin, with her father's pet dog, takes the ship to where her father had intended to explore.

**Other books you might like:**
Roger MacBride Allen, *The Ring of Charon*, 1990
Michael Berlyn, *The Eternal Enemy*, 1990
Glen Cook, *The Dragon Never Sleeps*, 1988
Stephen Goldin, *Jade Darcy and the Affair of Honor*, 1988
    Mary Mason, co-author
Rosemary Kirstein, *The Steerswoman*, 1987
Alis A. Rasmussen, *A Passage of Stars*, 1990

## 2813

### DON HUTCHISON, Editor

## Northern Frights

(Oakville, Ontario: Mosaic Press, 1992)

**Story type:** Horror (Anthology)

**Summary:** This book collects seventeen stories and one poem of horror and the supernatural (fifteen original and three reprint), all set in Canada. Included are ghost stories by Galad Elflandson ("Waiting") and Charles de Lint ("The Soft Whisper of Midnight Snow"), werewolf stories by Robert Bloch ("The Man Who Cried Wolf") and Edo Van Belkom ("The Mark of the Beast"), a vampire tale by Nancy Baker ("Cold Sleep"), and a science fiction horror story by Robert Sampson ("The Silver Face").

**Other books you might like:**
Robertson Davies, *High Spirits*, 1982
Alberto Manguel, *The Oxford Book of Canadian Ghost Stories*, 1989
    editor

## 2814

**DON HUTCHISON**, Editor

### Northern Frights 2

(Buffalo, New York: Mosaic Press, 1994)

**Story type:** Horror (Anthology)
**Locale(s):** Canada

**Summary:** The 18 stories collected in this volume all have Canadian settings. Highlights include Chet Williamson's tale of a haunting, "Other Errors, Other Times"; Nancy Kilpatrick's Halloween shocker, "Punkins"; Garfield Reeves-Stevens' "The Eddies," about people trapped at the top of a tall building during a windstorm; Hugh Cave's tale of an extradimensional doorway in the Canadian woods, "Vanishing Point"; and Edward D. Hoch's "Night Swimmer," which brings back his psychic detective, Simon Ark, in a tale of Inuit mythology.

**Other books you might like:**
Robertson Davies, *High Spirits*, 1982
Alberto Manguel, *The Oxford Book of Canadian Ghost Stories*, 1991
    editor
Tim Sullivan, *Cold Shocks*, 1990
    editor

## 2815

**DON HUTCHISON**, Editor

### Northern Frights 3

(Buffalo, NY: Mosaic Press, 1995)

**Story type:** Horror (Anthology)
**Locale(s):** Canada

**Summary:** One poem and seventeen new and reprinted stories all have Canadian settings, and often involve Canadian themes. Rick Hautala's "Silver Rings" tells of a man who has a literal haunting experience when his partner in a passionate one-night stand turns out to be a ghost who preys on his mind forever. In "Grist for the Mills of Christmas," James Powell tells of strange disappearances in the Canadian wilderness, and in "Snow Angel" Nancy Kilpatrick tells of a woman stranded in the wilds with the corpse of her dead husband who has to make the ultimate gruesome choice for her survival. In Tia Travis's "The Pines," a young woman comes to grips with the abusiveness of her relationship with her lover after confronting the death of a childhood friend.

**Other books you might like:**
Graeme Hurry, *Northern Chills*, 1994
Alberto Manguel, *The Oxford Book of Canadian Ghost Stories*, 1990
    editor
Tim Sullivan, *Cold Shocks*, 1991
    editor

## 2816

**SHAUN HUTSON**

### Heathen

(New York: Warner, 1993)

**Story type:** Horror (Occult)
**Major character(s):** Donna Ward, Widow(er); Julie Craig, Young Woman (Donna Ward's sister); David MacKenzie, Detective—Police (constable)
**Time period(s):** 1990s (1992)
**Locale(s):** London, England; Dublin, Ireland

**Summary:** When Donna Ward investigates the mysterious circumstances under which her husband died, she finds that he gained possession of a grimoire in which the names of all the members of the secret black magic society, The Sons of Midnight, are written and that the members, who include some of the most prominent social figures on the continent, will stop at nothing to get it back. This novel was originally published in England in 1992.

**Other books you might like:**
D.A. Fowler, *The Devil's End*, 1992
Ray Russell, *Absolute Power*, 1992

## 2817

**ALDOUS HUXLEY**
**CHRISTOPHER ISHERWOOD**, Co-Author

### Jacob's Hands

(New York: St. Martin's Press, 1998)

**Story type:** Fantasy (Literary; Contemporary Realism)
**Major character(s):** Jacob Ericson, Rancher, Healer; Sharon Carter, Handicapped, Singer; Earl Medwin, Heir, Wealthy
**Time period(s):** 1920s
**Locale(s):** Mojave Desert, California; Los Angeles, California

**Summary:** Jacob Ericson, an inept ranch hand, discovers he can heal with his touch. After curing his boss's crippled daughter, he follows her to Los Angeles where they both discover the cost of success.

**Other books you might like:**
Ray Bradbury, *Something Wicked This Way Comes*, 1962
Jack Cady, *The Off Season*, 1995
John Crowley, *Little, Big*, 1981
Robertson Davies, *The Depford Trilogy*, 1983
Megan Lindholm, *Wizard of the Pigeons*, 1986

## 2818

**JACKIE HYMAN**

### Echoes

(New York: Morrow, 1990)

**Story type:** Horror (Doppelganger)
**Major character(s):** Laura Bennett, Journalist (reporter); Lewis Tarkenton, Judge (Laura's lover); Joe Pickard, Political Figure (mayor of San Paradiso)
**Time period(s):** 1990s (1992); 1970s (1973)
**Locale(s):** San Paradiso, California; Nice, France

**Summary:** Following up on a series of news stories in which socially prominent members of her community commit acts totally out of character, reporter Laura Bennett uncovers a network of doppelganger "echoes" that have been generated by a force unleashed when her painter father copied Goya's canvas "The Witches' Sabbath" 20 years before.

**Other books you might like:**
Robert Louis Stevenson, *The Strange Case of Dr. Jekyll and Mr. Hyde*, 1886
Thomas Tryon, *The Other*, 1971
Oscar Wilde, *The Picture of Dorian Gray*, 1891

## **2819**

### JACKIE HYMAN

## *Shadowlight*

(New York: DAW, 1989)

**Story type:** Fantasy (Quest)
**Major character(s):** Shadow, Mythical Creature; Graylord, Monster (Zombie)
**Time period(s):** Indeterminate
**Locale(s):** Fictional Country

**Summary:** Shadow, a young woman with special inherited powers, must fight Graylord, the leader of a pack of zombies, in order to protect her world. During this struggle she comes of age.

**Other books you might like:**
Sheila Gilluly, *Greenbriar Queen*, 1987
E.E. Horlak, *Still Life*, 1988
Laurie J. Marks, *The Moonbane Mage*, 1990
Patricia A. McKillip, *The Riddle-Master of Hed*, 1976
Robin McKinley, *The Blue Sword*, 1982
Andre Norton, *Witch World*, 1963

## **2820**

### TOM HYMAN

## *Jupiter's Daughter*

(New York: Viking, 1994)

**Story type:** Science Fiction (Genetic Manipulation; Techno-Thriller)
**Major character(s):** Anne Stewart, Parent, Researcher; Genevieve "Genny" Stewart, Genetically Altered Being, Psychic; Dalton Stewart, Businessman, Criminal
**Time period(s):** 1990s (1999); 2000s (2000-2003)
**Locale(s):** Coronado, Caribbean; New York, New York; Europe

**Summary:** To test Dr. Harold Goth's theories for improving the human gcnome, Dalton Stewart arranges to inpregnate Anne Stewart with the results of Goth's experimentation. After Genny's birth, Anne Stewart studies modern genetic theory in an attempt to determine the cause of her daughter's unusual abilities while Dalton Stewart's associates attempt to exploit Genny and Goth's research to advance a sinister plot.

**Other books you might like:**
Helen Collins, *Mutagenesis*, 1993
Michael Crichton, *Jurassic Park*, 1990
Nancy Kress, *Beggars in Spain*, 1993
Marc Laidlaw, *Kalifornia*, 1993
Joan Slonczewski, *Daughter of Elysium*, 1993

## **2821**

### NOEL HYND

## *Cemetery of Angels*

(New York: Kensington, 1995)

**Story type:** Horror (Ghost Story; Supernatural Vengeance)
**Major character(s):** Rebecca Moore, Housewife; Edmund Van Allen, Detective; Billy Carlton, Actor, Spirit
**Time period(s):** 1990s (1995)
**Locale(s):** Los Angeles, California

**Summary:** An attempt on Rebecca Moore's life by a mysterious assailant sends Rebecca, her husband Bill, and their two children scurrying to relocate from Connecticut to Los Angeles. In their new home next to the San Angelo cemetery, the children befriend the ghost of a movie actor murdered half a century before, who spirits them away as part of his scheme to get even with the mysterious assailant who has followed the Moores to California.

**Other books you might like:**
Keith Ferrario, *Deadly Friend*, 1994
Abigail McDaniels, *The Uprising*, 1994
Jean Simon, *Ghost Boy*, 1994

## **2822**

### NOEL HYND

## *Ghosts*

(New York: Zebra, 1993)

**Story type:** Horror (Ghost Story)
**Major character(s):** Annette Carlson, Actress; Tim Brooks, Police Officer; George Osaro, Religious (minister)
**Time period(s):** 1990s (1993)
**Locale(s):** Nantucket Island, Massachusetts

**Summary:** When vacationers on Nantucket Island are visited by ghostly manifestations and shocked by gruesome deaths engineered by seemingly supernatural mechanisms, a small band of locals traces the events to the death of a theatrical agent decades before and an unredressed wrong committed and covered up. This is the author's first supernatural novel.

**Other books you might like:**
Matthew J. Costello, *Beneath Still Waters*, 1988
Liz Fulton, *The Palm Dome*, 1990
John Saul, *Second Child*, 1990
Peter Straub, *Ghost Story*, 1979
T.M. Wright, *The Island*, 1988

## **2823**

### NOEL HYND

## *The Prodigy*

(New York: Kensington, 1998)

**Story type:** Horror (Supernatural Vengeance)
**Major character(s):** Rolf Geiger, Musician; Diana Stephenson, Artist; Brian Greenstone, Agent (musical)
**Time period(s):** 1990s (1998)
**Locale(s):** New York, New York

**Summary:** Piano virtuoso Rolf Geiger is haunted by the spirit of his teacher, Isador Rabinowitz, a man who envied his pupil's talents but disdained his appreciation of popular culture and life outside of music. As Rabinowitz's irresistible presence progresses from spectral appearances to psychic takeover, Rolf finds all that he holds dear in life threatened.

**Other books you might like:**
Stephen R. George, *Torment*, 1994
Clifford Mohr, *Requiem*, 1992
Anne Rice, *Violin*, 1997
Fred Mustard Stewart, *The Mephisto Waltz*, 1969

## 2824

### NOEL HYND

## *Rage of Spirits*

(New York: Kensington, 1997)

**Story type:** Horror (Ghost Story)
**Major character(s):** William Cochrane, Government Official; Carl Einhorn, Scientist (mathematician); Gabriel Lang, Political Figure (vice president)
**Time period(s):** 2000s (2003)
**Locale(s):** Washington, District of Columbia

**Summary:** When United States president George Farley falls into an inexplicable coma, vice president Gabriel Lang instructs press attache William Cochrane to investigate possible supernatural causes. Cochrane's investigations into Farley's past bring him into contact with Carl Einhorn, who purports to be causing Farley's affliction psychically, and a host of spiritual phenomena that are influencing the government at its highest levels.

**Other books you might like:**
Raymond Buckland, *The Committee*, 1993
James Herbert, *Portent*, 1993
William W. Johnstone, *Prey*, 1996
Thomas F. Monteleone, *The Resurrectionist*, 1995

## 2825

### NOEL HYND

## *A Room for the Dead*

(New York: Kensington, 1994)

**Story type:** Horror (Supernatural Vengeance)
**Major character(s):** Frank O'Hara, Police Officer; Carolyn Hart, Young Woman; Gary Ledbetter, Serial Killer
**Time period(s):** 1990s (1994)
**Locale(s):** Nashua, New Hampshire; Philadelphia, Pennsylvania

**Summary:** Years after he was sentenced to the electric chair for a string brutal of murders, Gary Ledbetter manifests as an apparition to his arresting officer, Frank O'Hara, who is investigating a spate of murders committed in Ledbetter's trademark style. Upon reopening the investigation of Ledbetter, Frank begins to suspect that the man was deliberatedly framed to help cover up someone else's role in past events, and that the current murder victims were all somehow related to that cover up.

**Other books you might like:**
Thomas Harris, *Red Dragon*, 1981
William W. Johnstone, *Night Mask*, 1994
Samuel M. Key, *From a Whisper to a Scream*, 1992
Roxanne Longstreet, *Red Angel*, 1994

## 2826

### JAMES HYNES

## *Publish and Perish*

(New York: Picador/St. Martin's, 1997)

**Story type:** Horror (Collection)

**Summary:** Trio of loosely interconnected novellas that use the literary supernatural tale as a vehicle for satirizing modern academic life. In ''Queen of the Jungle,'' a philandering postdoctoral student gets his comeuppance through the intervention of his wife's preternaturally endowed pet cat. ''99'' concerns an American anthropologist so caught up in his exploration of primitive ritual sacrifice in a rural English town that he is oblivious to the fate for which the townspeople are grooming him. ''Casting the Runes,'' an homage to M.R. James's classic story of the same name, involves a history professor who invokes a supernatural revenge against a female colleague who plans to expose him as a plagiarist.

**Other books you might like:**
P.H. Cannon, *Scream for Jeeves: A Parody*, 1994
Fred Chappell, *The Lodger*, 1993
Fritz Leiber, *Conjure Wife*, 1952
Alison Lurie, *Women and Ghosts*, 1994
William Browning Spencer, *The Return of Count Electric and Other Stories*, 1993

## 2827

### KATHY ICE, Editor

## *Distant Planes*

(New York: HarperPrism, 1996)

**Story type:** Fantasy (Anthology; Magic Conflict)
**Series:** Magic: The Gathering

**Summary:** Contains 15 original adventure stories rife with mythical creatures in diverse settings and situations by authors including Hanovi Braddock, Keith R.A. DeCandido, Jane M. Lindskold, Michael G. Ryan, Michael A. Stackpole, Amy Thomson, and Robert E. Vardeman. Game tie-in.

**Other books you might like:**
Hanovi Braddock, *Ashes of the Sun*, 1996
Clayton Emery, *Shattered Chains*, 1995
William R. Forstchen, *Arena*, 1994
Sonia Orin Lyris, *And Peace Shall Sleep*, 1996
Teri McLaren, *The Cursed Land*, 1995
Robert E. Vardeman, *Dark Legacy*, 1996

## 2828

### DEAN ING

## *Cathouse*

(New York: Baen, 1991)

**Story type:** Science Fiction (Military; Political)
**Series:** Man-Kzin Wars
**Major character(s):** Carroll Locklear, Scholar, Scientist (xenobiologist); Lolita, Prehistoric Human; Grraf-Commander, Alien (Kzin)
**Time period(s):** 22nd century
**Locale(s):** Zoo, Planet—Imaginary

**Summary:** Carroll Locklear was dumped on a planet containing prehistoric Kzin in stasis. His scholarly instincts lead him to revive them, discovering when he does so that the females are sentient! Then Grraf-Commander lands to question Locklear. He and Grraf-Commander decide they want to stay on Zoo isolated from the outside universe. This volume collects two short pieces, *Cathouse*, published originally in the *Man-Kzin Wars* (1988), and *Briar Patch*, published originally in *Man-Kzin Wars II* (1989).

**Other books you might like:**
Poul Anderson, *Inconstant Star*, 1991
Edmund Cooper, *Seahorse in the Sky*, 1969
Larry Niven, *Protector*, 1973
Larry Niven, *Ringworld*, 1970
Larry Niven, *Ringworld Engineers*, 1979
Larry Niven, *Tales of Known Space*, 1975

## 2829

**DEAN ING**
**ROBERT A. HEINLEIN**, Co-Author

### Silent Thunder/Universe

(New York: Tor, 1991)

**Story type:** Science Fiction (Techno-Thriller; Generation Starship)
**Major character(s):** Walter Kalvin, Government Official (White House Chief of Staff); Hugh Hoyland, Spaceman, Student; Joe-Jim Gregory, Mutant, Spaceman
**Time period(s):** 21st century; 27th century
**Locale(s):** Spaceship; Outer Space

**Summary:** This book contains Dean Ing's original "Silent Thunder" plus Robert A. Heinlein's "Universe," first published in *Astounding* (1941). In "Silent Thunder," Walter Kalvin tries to locate a Nazi superweapon, the Donnersprache, as the United States slides toward a new fascism. In "Universe," Joe-Jim shows Hugh that his world of villages lies within a spaceship traveling long beyond its intended voyage. Hugh resolves to renew powered flight and discover an Earth-like world to settle, as originally intended.

**Other books you might like:**
Brian W. Aldiss, *Spaceship*, 1959
Poul Anderson, *The Boat of a Million Years*, 1989
Stephen Baxter, *Raft*, 1992
Leigh Brackett, *The Nemesis From Terra/Battle for the Stars*, 1989
    Edmond Hamilton, co-author
Karen Haber, *Thieves' Carnival/The Jewel of Bas*, 1990
    Leigh Brackett, co-author
Robert A. Heinlein, *The Past through Tomorrow*, 1967
Keith Laumer, *The Other Sky/The House in November*, 1981
Frank M. Robinson, *The Dark Beyond the Stars*, 1991
Joanna Russ, *Souls/Houston, Houston, Do You Read?*, 1989
    James Tiptree, Jr., co-author
Harry Turtledove, *The Pugnacious Peacemaker/The Wheels of If*, 1990
    L. Sprague de Camp, co-author

## 2830

**CHARLES INGRID**

### Alien Salute

(New York: DAW Books, 1989)

**Story type:** Science Fiction (Adventure)
**Series:** Sand Wars
**Major character(s):** Jack Storm, Military Personnel, Revolutionary
**Time period(s):** Indeterminate Future
**Locale(s):** Galactic Empire, Interstellar Empire/Federation

**Summary:** The Thraks' betrayal is now open and Jack is put in command of the Dominion Knights. Suddenly a third party enters the fray, a mysterious and superpowerful alien race bent on attacking humans and Thraks alike.

**Other books you might like:**
W. Michael Gear, *The Artifact*, 1990
W. Michael Gear, *The Warriors of Spider*, 1988
W. Michael Gear, *The Way of Spider*, 1988
W. Michael Gear, *The Web of Spider*, 1989
Stephen Leigh, *Changeling*, 1989
    Isaac Asimov's Robot City: Robtos and Aliens No. 1

## 2831

**CHARLES INGRID**

### The Marked Man

(New York: DAW Books, 1989)

**Story type:** Science Fiction (Post-Holocaust)
**Major character(s):** Thomas Blade, Psychic; Denethan, Mutant
**Time period(s):** 21st century
**Locale(s):** United States

**Summary:** Humanity has been decimated by environmental damage and plague. The Lord Protectors, seven men and women with psychic abilities, stand guard against the evil mutants who would destroy what's left of civilization.

**Other books you might like:**
W. Michael Gear, *The Artifact*, 1990
W. Michael Gear, *The Warriors of Spider*, 1988
W. Michael Gear, *The Way of Spider*, 1988
W. Michael Gear, *The Web of Spider*, 1989
Stephen Leigh, *Changeling*, 1989
    Isaac Asimov's Robot City: Robots and Aliens No. 1

## 2832

**CHARLES INGRID**

### Path of Fire

(New York: DAW, 1992)

**Series:** Patterns of Chaos
**Major character(s):** Palaton, Alien (Choyan), Spaceman (pilot); Rand, Student, Human; Panshinea, Alien (Choyan), Ruler (emperor)
**Time period(s):** Indeterminate Future
**Locale(s):** Arizar, Planet—Imaginary; Cho, Planet—Imaginary

**Summary:** Only the *tezars* of Cho pilot faster-than-light ships through the Patterns of Chaos, inevitably burning out their minds and abilities. Palaton, heir of Panshinea, takes part in an illegal experimental procedure. To save Rand's life, Palaton rests in Rand the part of his consciousness called *bahdur* which only *tezars* can use to find patterns in the chaos of faster-than-light space. He hopes to keep Rand alive, free and sane, until he figures out how to retrieve his *bahdur*.

**Other books you might like:**
Pauline Ashwell, *Unwillingly to Earth*, 1992
Jeffrey A. Carver, *Dragons in the Stars*, 1992
C.J. Cherryh, *Hellburner*, 1992
Tara K. Harper, *Lightwing*, 1992
Melissa Scott, *Dreamships*, 1992
Cordwainer Smith, *The Best of Cordwainer Smith*, 1975
Vernor Vinge, *A Fire upon the Deep*, 1992
David Weber, *Path of the Fury*, 1992

## 2833

**CHARLES INGRID**

### Return Fire

(New York: DAW Books, 1989)

**Story type:** Science Fiction (Adventure)
**Series:** Sand Wars
**Major character(s):** Jack Storm, Military Personnel, Revolutionary; Amber, Psychic
**Time period(s):** Indeterminate Future

**Locale(s):** Mistwald, Planet—Imaginary

**Summary:** When the Dominion Knights are betrayed by Emperor Pepys into an alliance with the evil alien Thraks, Jack Storm goes underground to prove the Thraks have an ulterior motive and are still the enemy.

**Other books you might like:**
W. Michael Gear, *The Artifact*, 1990
W. Michael Gear, *The Warriors of Spider*, 1988
W. Michael Gear, *The Way of Spider*, 1988
W. Michael Gear, *The Web of Spider*, 1989
Stephen Leigh, *Changeling*, 1989
    Isaac Asimov's Robot City: Robots and Aliens No. 1

## 2834

### MARK IVANHOE

## *Virgintooth*

(San Francisco: III Publishing, 1991)

**Story type:** Horror (Vampire Story)
**Major character(s):** The Master, Vampire; Jonathan, Vampire; Elizabeth, Vampire
**Time period(s):** 1990s
**Locale(s):** United States

**Summary:** In this vampire dystopia, young Elizabeth rises from the grave as a vampire, learning about her new powers and capabilities while striving for a lifestyle different than those offered by the autocratic Master, who demands her total obedience, and by a vampire commune that spurns individuality and encourages mortification of the flesh.

**Other books you might like:**
Richard Lee Byers, *The Vampire's Apprentice*, 1992
Anne Rice, *Interview with the Vampire*, 1975
Brian Stableford, *The Empire of Fear*, 1988

## 2835

### ALEXANDER JABLOKOV

## *The Breath of Suspension*

(Sauk City, Wisconsin: Arkham House, 1994)

**Story type:** Science Fiction (Collection)

**Summary:** Contains 10 stories, frequently light in tone, published 1985-1992 in *Isaac Asimov's Science Fiction Magazine* with several stories sharing time travel themes. Other themes include cetacean intelligence, hard science and hardboiled detective fiction.

**Other books you might like:**
John Kessel, *Meeting in Infinity*, 1992
Nancy Kress, *The Aliens of Earth*, 1993
Lucius Shepard, *The Ends of the Earth*, 1991
Michael Swanwick, *Gravity's Angels*, 1991
James Tiptree Jr., *Her Smoke Rose Up Forever*, 1990

## 2836

### ALEXANDER JABLOKOV

## *Carve the Sky*

(New York: Morrow, 1991)

**Story type:** Science Fiction (Arts; Adventure)
**Major character(s):** Anton Lindgren, Steward; Vanessa Karageorge, Scholar

**Time period(s):** 24th century
**Locale(s):** Earth; Montenegro; Asteroid (the asteroid belt)

**Summary:** Anton, Vanessa and others search for a sculptor thought dead and a missing alien artifact which could prove the key to opening a wider universe for humanity. This is the author's first book.

**Other books you might like:**
John DeChancie, *Starrigger*, 1983
Alan Dean Foster, *Cyber Way*, 1990
Michael P. Kube-McDowell, *Emprise*, 1985
Michael P. Kube-McDowell, *Enigma*, 1986
Marc Laidlaw, *Neon Lotus*, 1988
Vonda N. McIntyre, *Transition*, 1991
David F. Nighbert, *The Clouds of Magellan*, 1991
Larry Niven, *Protector*, 1973
Frederik Pohl, *The Gateway Trip: Tales and Vignettes of the Heechee*, 1990

## 2837

### ALEXANDER JABLOKOV

## *Deepdrive*

(New York: Avon, 1998)

**Story type:** Science Fiction (First Contact; Cyberpunk)
**Major character(s):** Ripi Ripi-Arana-Hoc, Alien (Vronnan); Sophonisba "Soph" Trost, Businesswoman, Adventurer; Lightfoot, Computer Expert, Businessman
**Time period(s):** Indeterminate Future
**Locale(s):** Venus; *Argent*, Spaceship; Montenegro

**Summary:** Many alien species now share the solar system with humans, leaving the humans desperate to find, buy, steal or otherwise acquire an interstellar drive. Hired to rescue Ripi, who agrees to accompany her for his own reasons, Soph becomes involved in his plans and learns more than she wants to know about the aliens in the solar system and their politics.

**Other books you might like:**
Colin Greenland, *Seasons of Plenty*, 1996
Gwyneth Jones, *White Queen*, 1993
Michael Kandel, *Panda Ray*, 1996
Garth Nix, *Shade's Children*, 1997
Rudy Rucker, *Wetware*, 1988

## 2838

### ALEXANDER JABLOKOV

## *A Deeper Sea*

(New York: Morrow AvoNova, 1992)

**Story type:** Science Fiction (Military; First Contact)
**Major character(s):** Ilya Sergeiivich Stasov, Scientist (dolphin researcher), Military Personnel
**Time period(s):** 2010s (2015); 2020s
**Locale(s):** *Andrei Sakharov*, At Sea; Russia; Jupiter, Space Station

**Summary:** After Stasov provides a breakthrough in dolphin/human communications, the United Soviet Republics again engage in war with the United States. Stasov's dolphins prove themselves as intelligent weapons of war which can carry bombs directly to the enemy's ships. However, the dolphins' vision of the future encompasses a larger role for themselves which takes them beyond Earth's confines.

**Other books you might like:**
David Brin, *Startide Rising*, 1983
Arthur C. Clarke, *The Deep Range*, 1957

Vonda N. McIntyre, *Starfarers*, 1989
Vonda N. McIntyre, *Superluminal*, 1983
Robert Merle, *The Day of the Dolphin*, 1969
James H. Schmitz, *The Demon Breed*, 1968

**2839**

### ALEXANDER JABLOKOV

## *Nimbus*

(New York: Morrow/AvoNova, 1993)

**Story type:** Science Fiction (Mystery; Cyberpunk)
**Major character(s):** Theo ''Peter Ambrose'' Bronkman, Amnesiac, Detective—Amateur
**Time period(s):** 2030s
**Locale(s):** Chicago, Illinois

**Summary:** When a virtual image of a murder victim appears in Peter Ambrose's house, Peter begins an investigation which uncovers a disturbing pattern of murders of participants in a secret wartime project, Nimbus, in which Peter took part. As Peter tries to find surviving project participants, he begins to reassemble his missing memories while clues point toward disturbing conclusions concerning the serial killer.

**Other books you might like:**
Pat Cadigan, *Fools*, 1992
Pat Cadigan, *Mindplayers*, 1987
Michael Flynn, *In the Country of the Blind*, 1990
Jean Mark Gawron, *Dream of Glass*, 1993
Kim Newman, *The Night Mayor*, 1990
Neal Stephenson, *Snow Crash*, 1992
Amy Thomson, *Virtual Girl*, 1993

**2840**

### ALEXANDER JABLOKOV

## *River of Dust*

(New York: Morrow/AvoNova, 1996)

**Story type:** Science Fiction (Family Saga; Political)
**Major character(s):** Breyten Passman, Human (Martian); Miriam Kostal, Police Officer; Hektor Passman, Political Figure
**Time period(s):** 24th century
**Locale(s):** Mars

**Summary:** Having just returned to Scamander from Earth with the Martian delegation, Hektor realizes how Martian architecture reflects the differences between the planets in politics and society. On Earth, buildings define a volume and frequently open directly to the air, while on Mars the hollowed-out spaces intertwine, but none open onto the toxic, dangerous surface.

**Other books you might like:**
Ben Bova, *Mars*, 1992
Paul J. McAuley, *Red Dust*, 1994
Frederik Pohl, *Man Plus*, 1994
    Thomas T. Thomas, co-author
Kim Stanley Robinson, *Green Mars*, 1994
S.C. Sykes, *Red Genesis*, 1991

**2841**

### RICHARD JACCOMA

## *The Werewolf's Revenge*

(New York: Fawcett, 1991)

**Story type:** Horror (Werewolf Story)
**Major character(s):** Jimmy Underhill, Spy; Clara Steiner, Spy (Nazi agent); Beth Li, Teenager
**Time period(s):** 1940s (1942)
**Locale(s):** Beirut, Lebanon

**Summary:** Back for another round of battle with the Nazis, OSS agent Jimmy Underhill works in collaboration with the Royal British Occult Bureau to prevent the Nazi agent who turned him into a werewolf from discovering the whereabouts of the Jewelled Skull of Baphomet, a Satanic talisman worshipped by the Knights Templar which can turn the tide of the war for Germany. This novel is the sequel to *The Werewolf's Tale*.

**Other books you might like:**
Jerry Ahern, *Werewolves*, 1990
    Sharon Ahern, co-author
Robert R. McCammon, *The Wolf's Hour*, 1989
Robert Weinberg, *The Armageddon Box*, 1991

**2842**

### SHIRLEY JACKSON

## *Just an Ordinary Day*

(New York: Bantam, 1997)

**Story type:** Horror (Collection)
**Summary:** Thirty previously unpublished and twenty-two previously uncollected stories by a writer renowned for her macabre, psychologically complex fiction and tales of the dark side of everyday life. The handful of horror and fantasy stories include ''One Ordinary Day with Peanuts,'' about a capriciously nasty and unpredictable couple; '' The Possibility of Evil,'' about a woman who writes anonymous poison pen letters with serious consequences to keep her town on its best behavior; and two tales featuring the devil, ''Smoking Room'' and ''Devil of a Tale.''

**Other books you might like:**
Jonathan Carroll, *The Panic Hand*, 1995
Fred Chappell, *More Shapes than One*, 1991
Rachel Ingalls, *The End of Tragedy*, 1987
Alison Lurie, *Women and Ghosts*, 1994
Joyce Carol Oates, *Haunted: Tales of the Grotesque*, 1994
Muriel Spark, *Open to the Public*, 1997

**2843**

### CHARLEE JACOB

## *This Symbiotic Fascination*

(Orlando, Florida: Necro Publications, 1998)

**Story type:** Horror (Vampire Story)
**Major character(s):** Tawne Delaney, Clerk, Vampire; Arcan Tyler, Clerk; Alan Moravec, Journalist (television)
**Time period(s):** 1990s (1998)
**Locale(s):** Shorecross, Texas
**Summary:** Tawne is a lovelorn 30-something woman with an unattractively large physique. Her friend Arcan is a lonely young man who endured sexual abuse while a child from his mother. Sparks fly

when Tawne discovers that Arcan is a serial rapist who believes he is a vessel for the spirits of a cat, a wolf and a ghoul, and Arcan discovers that Tawne has been sexually initiated by a vampire. A first novel.

**Other books you might like:**
John D. MacDonald, *The Executioners*, 1957
Thom Metzger, *Big Gurl*, 1989
Rex Miller, *Slob*, 1987
Kate Pullinger, *Where Does Kissing End?*, 1992
John Shirley, *Wetbones*, 1991

## 2844
### CARL JACOBI

## Smoke of the Snake
(Minneapolis, Minnesota: Fedogan & Bremer, 1994)

**Story type:** Horror (Collection)

**Summary:** The 15 stories collected here were mostly published in the last 20 years, although some were written during the author's prolific years as a writer for the pulp magazines. They represent the remainder of the author's previously uncollected weird fiction. "Hamadryad," "The Monument" and the title story all deploy snakes as objects of horror, while "The Music Lover" and "Josephine Gage" are tales of supernatural vengeance and "Chameleon Town" and "The Lost Street" (written in collaboration with Clifford Simak) are science fiction-horror hybrids. Dixon Smith, the author's biographer, has supplied the introduction.

**Other books you might like:**
Joseph Payne Brennan, *Nine Horrors and a Dream*, 1958
Hugh B. Cave, *Murgunstrumm and Others*, 1977
Frank Belknap Long, *The Hounds of Tindalos*, 1946
Manly Wade Wellman, *Worse Things Waiting*, 1973

## 2845
### A.J. JACOBS

## Fractured Fairy Tales
(New York: Bantam, 1997)

**Story type:** Fantasy (Legend; Collection)

**Summary:** Contains 25 humorously twisted interpretations of well-known fairy tales and myths as featured in Jay Ward's *Rocky and Bullwinkle Show* television series. Stories include "The Frog Prince," "Rumplestiltskin," "Hansel and Gretel," "Pinocchio," "The Elves and the Shoemaker," "Princess and the Pea," "The Golden Goose," "Beauty and the Beast," "Aladdin's Lamp," "Jack and the Beanstalk" and "King Midas."

**Other books you might like:**
William J. Brooke, *Teller of Tales*, 1994
Emma Donoghue, *Kissing the Witch: Old Tales in New Skins*, 1997
David Fisher, *Legally Correct Fairy Tales*, 1996
James Finn Garner, *Once upon a More Enlightened Time*, 1995
James Finn Garner, *Politically Correct Bedtime Stories*, 1994
James Finn Garner, *Politically Correct Holiday Stories*, 1995

## 2846
### W.W. JACOBS

## The Monkey's Paw and Other Tales of Mystery and the Macabre
(Chicago, Illinois: Academy Chicago, 1997)

**Story type:** Horror (Collection)

**Summary:** The first exclusive compilation of the author's tales of mystery and the macabre, drawn from thirteen collections of short fiction published between 1896 and 1926. In addition to the well-known title story, selections include the gruesome tale of ghostly revenge, "The Well"; the story "The Interruption"; and a number of stories of practical jokes that go comically awry, including "The Vigil" and "Sam's Ghost." Editor Gary Hoppenstand supplies an introduction and select bibliography. Copyrighted 1997 but not available until 1998.

**Other books you might like:**
E.F. Benson, *The Collected Ghost Stories of E.F. Benson*, 1994
A.M. Burrage, *Intruders: New Weird Tales*, 1995
Oliver Onions, *The Collected Ghost Stories of Oliver Onions*, 1935
Saki, *The Complete Short Stories of Saki*, 1930
H. Russell Wakefield, *They Return at Evening*, 1928

## 2847
### MARK JACOBSON

## Gojiro
(New York: Atlantic Monthly Press, 1991)

**Story type:** Fantasy (Literary; Humor)
**Major character(s):** Gojiro, Animal (monitor lizard), Mutant; Komodo, Teenager
**Time period(s):** 1950s
**Locale(s):** Radioactive Island, Pacific Islands

**Summary:** Gojiro, a monitor lizard irradiated and mutated into a dragon, and Komodo, a young student who was in a coma for years, were both victims of Hiroshima. They make a pact together to discover who they are, where they're from, how they came to be where they are and what they'll do next. This is the author's first novel.

**Other books you might like:**
Brian W. Aldiss, *Hothouse*, 1962
Richard Brautigan, *The Hawkline Monster*, 1974
Ernest Hogan, *Cortez on Jupiter*, 1990
Mark Leyner, *My Cousin, My Gastroenterologist*, 1990
R.A. MacAvoy, *Tea with the Black Dragon*, 1983
Michael D. Weaver, *My Father Immortal*, 1989

## 2848
### BRIAN JACQUES

## The Bellmaker
(New York: Philomel Books, 1995)

**Story type:** Fantasy (Young Adult; Adventure)
**Series:** Redwall
**Major character(s):** Joseph, Animal (mouse), Adventurer; Mariel, Animal (mouse), Adventurer, Warrior
**Time period(s):** Indeterminate
**Locale(s):** Redwall Abbey, England; *Pearl Queen*, At Sea; Southsward, Fictional Country (Castle Floret)

**Summary:** When Martin the Warrior appears to Joseph the Bellmaker in a dream, warning him of danger to his traveling daughter, Joseph and four companions sail to Southsward where an evil fox enforces a tyrannical rule from Castle Floret. To restore autonomy, Joseph and his company join Mariel and the Southsward natives in battle.

**Other books you might like:**
Mary Brown, *The Unlikely Ones*, 1986
Karen Brush, *Demon Pig*, 1991
Kenneth Grahame, *The Wind in the Willows*, 1908
William Horwood, *The Willows in Winter*, 1995
Margery Sharp, *The Rescuers*, 1959
Tad Williams, *Tailchaser's Song*, 1985

## 2849

### BRIAN JACQUES

## The Long Patrol

(New York: Philomel, 1998)

**Story type:** Fantasy (Young Adult; Adventure)
**Series:** Redwall
**Major character(s):** Tammo, Animal (hare); Russa Nodrey, Animal (squirrel)
**Time period(s):** Indeterminate
**Locale(s):** England (Redwall Abbey); Salamandastron, Mythical Place

**Summary:** Stung by defeat at the hands of the Lady of Salamandastron, the Rapscallion army heads toward Redwall Abbey. Tammo and Russa Nodrey join the fighting unit, the Long Patrol, ordered to defend against the Rapscallions—to the death, if necessary. Eleventh in series, followed by *Marlfox*.

**Other books you might like:**
Richard Adams, *Tales From Watership Down*, 1997
Allen Andrews, *Pig Plantagenet*, 1980
Mary Brown, *The Unlikely Ones*, 1986
Kenneth Grahame, *The Wind in the Willows*, 1908
Tad Williams, *Tailchaser's Song*, 1985

## 2850

### BRIAN JACQUES

## Mariel of Redwall

(New York: Philomel/Putnam, 1992)

**Story type:** Fantasy (Adventure; Young Adult)
**Series:** Redwall
**Major character(s):** Mariel, Animal (mouse), Warrior, Adventurer; Gabool, Animal (rat), Pirate (king); Han Rosie, Animal (hare), Warrior
**Time period(s):** Indeterminate
**Locale(s):** Redwall Abbey, England

**Summary:** Thrown overboard by Gabool during his attack on her ship, Mariel washes ashore without her memory. Taken to Redwall Abbey, Mariel recovers her memory then sets out with others to find Gabool and avenge her father's death. Prequel to Jacques' other books.

**Other books you might like:**
Richard Adams, *Watership Down*, 1974
Mary Brown, *The Unlikely Ones*, 1986
Karen Brush, *Demon Pig*, 1991
Karen Brush, *The Pig, the Prince and the Unicorn*, 1987
Kenneth Grahame, *The Wind in the Willows*, 1908
Tad Williams, *Tailchaser's Song*, 1985

Laurence Yep, *Dragon War*, 1992

## 2851

### BRIAN JACQUES
### GARY CHALK, Illustrator

## Martin the Warrior

(New York: Philomel Books, 1994)

**Story type:** Fantasy (Young Adult; Adventure)
**Series:** Redwall
**Major character(s):** Martin the Warrior, Animal (mouse), Slave; Badrang the Tyrant, Animal (stoat), Leader
**Time period(s):** Indeterminate
**Locale(s):** Marshank, England; Redwall Abbey, England

**Summary:** Enslaved by Badrang the Tyrant, Martin vows to regain his freedom and his father's sword, stolen by Badrang. Aided in his escape, Martin raises an army to oppose Badrang, but in the end must face Badrang himself in a personal challenge.

**Other books you might like:**
Mary Brown, *The Unlikely Ones*, 1986
Karen Brush, *Demon Pig*, 1991
Kenneth Grahame, *The Wind in the Willows*,
Margery Sharp, *The Rescuers*, 1959
Tad Williams, *Tailchaser's Song*, 1985

## 2852

### BRIAN JACQUES

## Mattimeo

(New York: Philomel Books, 1990)

**Story type:** Fantasy (Adventure; Young Adult)
**Series:** Redwall
**Major character(s):** Matthias, Warrior, Animal (mouse); Slagar, Animal (fox)
**Time period(s):** Indeterminate
**Locale(s):** Mossflower Woods, Mythical Place

**Summary:** Seeking revenge on the brave mice who defeated and disfigured him, Slagar plots to steal the young ones of Redwall. The devoted friends and family unite to rescue their children in a massive battle with the evil Malkariss who enslaved them.

**Other books you might like:**
Richard Adams, *Watership Down*, 1974
Kenneth Grahame, *The Wind in the Willows*, 1908
Margery Sharp, *The Rescuers*, 1959
Tad Williams, *Tailchaser's Song*, 1985

## 2853

### BRIAN JACQUES
### ALLAN CURLESS, Illustrator

## Outcast of Redwall

(New York: Philomel Books, 1996)

**Story type:** Fantasy (Young Adult; Adventure)
**Series:** Redwall
**Major character(s):** Veil, Animal (ferret); Swartt Sixclaw, Animal (ferret), Warrior; Sunflash, Animal (badger), Warrior
**Time period(s):** Indeterminate
**Locale(s):** Redwall Abbey, England; Mossflower Woods, Mythical Place

**Summary:** After the sympathetic Bryny nurtures the abandoned Veil at Redwall Abbey, Veil's transgression forces him from the abbey. When his estranged father, the warlord Swartt, attacks Sunflash and abbey residents, Veil must decide whether to aid his friends or the father who abandoned him.

**Other books you might like:**
Allen Andrews, *Pig Plantagenet*, 1980
Mary Brown, *The Unlikely Ones*, 1986
Karen Brush, *Demon Pig*, 1991
Kenneth Grahame, *The Wind in the Willows*, 1908
Robert C. O'Brien, *Mrs. Frisby and the Rats of NIMH*, 1971
Tad Williams, *Tailchaser's Song*, 1985

---

### 2854

#### BRIAN JACQUES

## The Pearls of Lutra

(New York: Philomel, 1997)

**Story type:** Fantasy (Young Adult; Adventure)
**Series:** Redwall
**Major character(s):** Tansy, Animal (hedgehog); Ublaz Mad Eyes, Animal (pine martin), Ruler (Emperor of Sampetra); Viola, Animal (vole), Adventurer
**Time period(s):** Indeterminate
**Locale(s):** Redwall Abbey, England; Isle of Sampetra, Fictional Country

**Summary:** Emperor Ublaz orders his corsairs to recover the Pearls of Lutra, thought hidden at Redwall Abbey. However, a gruesome discovery by Tansy brings to light the clues which allow Abbey residents to begin recovering the pearls, each secreted with a riddle which leads a searcher to another pearl's hiding place.

**Other books you might like:**
Richard Adams, *Tales From Watership Down*, 1997
Allen Andrews, *Pig Plantagenet*, 1980
Mary Brown, *The Unlikely Ones*, 1986
Kenneth Grahame, *The Wind in the Willows*, 1908
Tad Williams, *Tailchaser's Song*, 1985

---

### 2855

#### BRIAN JACQUES
#### GARY CHALK, Illustrator

## Salamandastron

(New York: Philomel Books, 1993)

**Story type:** Fantasy (Young Adult; Adventure)
**Series:** Redwall
**Major character(s):** Urthstripe the Strong, Animal (badger), Leader; Thrugg, Animal (otter); Ferahgo the Assassin, Animal (weasel), Warrior
**Time period(s):** Indeterminate
**Locale(s):** Redwall Abbey, England; Salamandastron, Mythical Place (mountain stronghold)

**Summary:** When Ferahgo the Assassin besieges Salamandastron, Urthstripe the Strong leads warriors against Ferahgo's vermin horde while others search for the flowers of Icetor, needed to stop the illness affecting Redwall Abbey residents.

**Other books you might like:**
Mary Brown, *The Unlikely Ones*, 1986
Karen Brush, *Demon Pig*, 1991
Karen Brush, *The Pig, the Prince and the Unicorn*, 1987
Kenneth Grahame, *The Wind in the Willows*, 1908

Tad Williams, *Tailchaser's Song*, 1985

---

### 2856

#### MICHAEL JAHN

## The Frighteners

(New York: Berkley/Boulevard, 1996)

**Story type:** Horror (Ghost Story)
**Major character(s):** Frank Bannister, Paranormal Investigator; Lucy Lynskey, Doctor; Magda Ravanski, Journalist
**Time period(s):** 1990s (1994)
**Locale(s):** Fairwater, Maine

**Summary:** With the help of the spooks he purports to exorcise, shady psychic investigator Frank Bannister ekes out a living busting ghosts in the small town of Fairwater. To clear himself when he is implicated in a series of unexplained deaths among the townsfolk, Frank delves into an unsolved 40-year-old local mystery and is forced to confront his most difficult adversary yet: the Grim Reaper. This novelization of a Peter Jackson film is based on a screenplay written by Jackson and Fran Walsh.

**Other books you might like:**
Judith Hawkes, *Julian's House*, 1989
Mercedes Lackey, *Burning Water*, 1989
Seabury Quinn, *The Phantom Fighter*, 1966
Robert Weinberg, *The Black Lodge*, 1991
Manly Wade Wellman, *The School of Darkness*, 1985

---

### 2857

#### BETSY JAMES

## Dark Heart

(New York: Dutton, 1992)

**Story type:** Fantasy (Young Adult; Quest)
**Major character(s):** Kat, Teenager; Raim, Handicapped
**Time period(s):** Indeterminate
**Locale(s):** Creek, Fictional City; Tells, Fictional City; Dark Heart, Mythical Place (mountain)

**Summary:** Kat pursues acceptance among her mother's tribe through the bear ceremony, a spiritual rite of passage, but her growing love for Raim does not help.

**Other books you might like:**
J.H. Brennan, *Shiva's Challenge: An Adventure of the Ice Age*, 1992
Sue Harrison, *Mother Earth, Father Sky*, 1990
J. Alison James, *Sing for a Gentle Rain*, 1990
Lynn Armistead McKee, *Woman of the Mists*, 1991
Elizabeth Marshall Thomas, *Reindeer Moon*, 1987

---

### 2858

#### CARY JAMES

## King & Raven

(New York: Tor, 1995)

**Story type:** Fantasy (Adventure)
**Major character(s):** Michel ''Raven'' de Verdeur, Apprentice, Knight; Arthur, Ruler (King of Britain); Amaury, Knight
**Time period(s):** 6th century
**Locale(s):** England (Britain); France

**Summary:** When he sees four of King Arthur's knights rape and murder his sister, Michel swears revenge, pursuing it by moving into

Camelot and training for the inevitable opportunity fate will present him. His quest takes him to France and back to Britain as his skill and fame increase. First novel.

**Other books you might like:**
Marion Zimmer Bradley, *The Mists of Avalon*, 1983
Susan Dexter, *The Wizard's Shadow*, 1993
Courtway Jones, *In the Shadow of the Oak King*, 1991
Peter Telep, *Squire*, 1995
Peter Telep, *Squire's Blood*, 1995

## 2859
### DARIUS JAMES

## Negrophobia: An Urban Parable
(New York: Citadel Underground, 1992)

**Story type:** Fantasy (Satire; Alternate World)
**Major character(s):** Bubbles Brazil, Teenager, Adventurer
**Time period(s):** 1990s; Indeterminate
**Locale(s):** United States; Alternate Earth

**Summary:** Voodoo magic transports blonde bombshell Bubbles Brazil to an alternate United States populated by surreal animations and racist stereotypes. Bubbles emerges changed from the extended hyperbole. Author's first book.

**Other books you might like:**
William S. Burroughs, *Naked Lunch*, 1959
Parke Godwin, *The Snake Oil Wars*, 1989
Parke Godwin, *Waiting for the Galactic Bus*, 1988
Mark Leyner, *My Cousin, My Gastroenterologist*, 1990
Kurt Vonnegut Jr., *Cat's Cradle*, 1963
Robert Anton Wilson, *Reality Is What You Can Get Away With: An Illustrated Screenplay*, 1992

## 2860
### DEL JAMES

## The Language of Fear
(New York: Dell/Abyss, 1995)

**Story type:** Horror (Collection)

**Summary:** This first collection by an editor of a rock music magazine assembles 15 original stories. Preoccupied with people who live on the fringe of acceptable society, they chronicle (among other things) the thoughts of a worker at a porno theater who decides to vent his self-loathing on a patron (''Adult Nature Material''), the life of a suicidal teenager (''Memoirs of High School''), a flirtation with extradimensional monsters during an LSD trip (''Mindwarp''), and the haunted memories of a self-destructive musician (''November Rain''). Axl Rose, whose band Guns 'n Roses has recorded several songs written by the author, supplies the introduction.

**Other books you might like:**
Poppy Z. Brite, *Swamp Foetus*, 1993
S. Darnbrook Colson, *People of the Night*, 1994
David J. Schow, *Lost Angels*, 1990
John Shirley, *New Noir*, 1993
Lucy Taylor, *Close to the Bone*, 1993

## 2861
### J. ALISON JAMES

## Sing for a Gentle Rain
(New York: Atheneum, 1990)

**Story type:** Fantasy (Time Travel; Romance)
**Major character(s):** James Winter, Student; Spring Rain, Shaman, Indian (Anasazi); Anasan, Shaman, Indian (Anasazi)
**Time period(s):** 1990s; 13th century
**Locale(s):** Arizona

**Summary:** Working on a high school research paper, James visits an Anasazi museum where he becomes inexplicably attracted to a shard of pottery. For weeks his dreams are disturbed by visions of ancient Anasazi life and one woman in particular. In the 13th century, Spring Rain learns the sacred songs of the tribe, songs which should be passed on to a male apprentice. She sings, hoping for relief from a lengthy drought, but her song draws James into the past where he is declared a friend by Anasan. James begins to learn Anasazi language and falls in love with Spring Rain before events force Spring Rain to sing James back to his own time. This is an ALA Best Young Adult Books title.

**Other books you might like:**
Alan Dean Foster, *Cyber Way*, 1990
Dean Ing, *Anasazi*, 1980
Robert Silverberg, *Letters From Atlantis*, 1990
Roger Zelazny, *Bridge of Ashes*, 1976

## 2862
### L. DEAN JAMES

## Book of Stones
(Lake Geneva, Wisconsin: TSR, 1993)

**Story type:** Fantasy (Quest)
**Series:** Red Kings of Wynnamyr
**Major character(s):** Davyn ''Davi'' Darynson, Royalty, Sorcerer (apprentice); Gaylon Reysson, Ruler (king), Wizard
**Time period(s):** Indeterminate
**Locale(s):** Wynnamyr, Fictional Country

**Summary:** Davi's desire to pursue sorcery leads him to utilize a forbidden talisman and book despite the danger of enslavement by the former owner's spirit.

**Other books you might like:**
Donald Aamodt, *A Name to Conjure With*, 1989
Lois McMaster Bujold, *The Spirit Ring*, 1992
Louise Cooper, *Nemesis*, 1989
Laurell K. Hamilton, *Nightseer*, 1992

## 2863
### L. DEAN JAMES

## Kingslayer
(Lake Geneva, Wisconsin: TSR, 1992)

**Story type:** Fantasy (Adventure)
**Series:** Red Kings of Wynnamyr
**Major character(s):** Gaylon Reysson, Ruler (king), Wizard
**Time period(s):** Indeterminate
**Locale(s):** Wynnamyr, Fictional Country

**Summary:** Events force King Gaylon Reysson to lead his army to battle, but he hesitates to take up the magic sword, Kingslayer, which nearly robbed him of his will during the bloodlust of its last use.

**Other books you might like:**
Fred Saberhagen, *The Fifth Book of Lost Swords: Coinspinner's Story*, 1989
Fred Saberhagen, *The Fourth Book of Lost Swords: Farslayer's Story*, 1989
Fred Saberhagen, *The Sixth Book of Lost Swords: Mindsword's Story*, 1990
Fred Saberhagen, *The Second Book of Lost Swords: Sightbinder's Story*, 1987
Fred Saberhagen, *The Third Book of Lost Swords: Stonecutter's Story*, 1988

**2864**

**L. DEAN JAMES**

*Mojave Wells*

(New York: AvoNova, 1994)

**Story type:** Science Fiction (Invasion of Earth)
**Major character(s):** John Caldwell, Student—College, Genetically Altered Being; Sidney Bowers, Mechanic
**Time period(s):** 1990s
**Locale(s):** Mojave Desert, California; Mojave Wells, California

**Summary:** Exposed to an ancient alien device, the Gatekeeper, John transforms into a Ral warrior, complete with alien memories. While university and government agents want to use John, he emotionally bonds through dreams with Sidney and pursues his mission of repairing a gate which will allow Ral immigration.

**Other books you might like:**
Gordon R. Dickson, *The Alien Way*, 1965
Diana G. Gallagher, *The Alien Dark*, 1990
Larry Niven, *Protector*, 1973
Allen Steele, *Labyrinth of Night*, 1992
W.J. Stuart, *Forbidden Planet*, 1956
Denise Vitola, *Half-Light*, 1992
Kate Wilhelm, *Naming the Flowers*, 1992

**2865**

**L. DEAN JAMES**

*Summerland*

(New York: AvoNova, 1994)

**Story type:** Fantasy (Alternate World; Post-Disaster)
**Major character(s):** Jamie Weston, Adventurer, Imposter; Harry I. Roswell, Dentist, Doctor; Lila Anne, Runaway, Sorceress
**Time period(s):** 21st century; Indeterminate
**Locale(s):** Los Angeles, California; Oregon; Planet—Imaginary

**Summary:** Motivated by her dying father's present of a guidestone and instructions that she discover and stop the cause of earthwide drought, Jamie Weston finds the necessary helpers and travels to a realm where Earth's stolen water provides luxury for the inhabitants. However, events do not prepare Jamie for the notoriety accompanying the ancient prophecy which foretells the defeat of God.

**Other books you might like:**
Pamela Dean, *The Dubious Hills*, 1994
J. Alison James, *Sing for a Gentle Rain*, 1990
Victor Koman, *The Jehovah Contract*, 1987
Ursula K. Le Guin, *The Farthest Shore*, 1972
Laurence Yep, *Dragon of the Lost Sea*, 1982

**2866**

**M.R. JAMES**

*A Warning to the Curious*

(Boston, MA: David R. Godine, 1990)

**Story type:** Horror (Collection)

**Summary:** From the master of subtle supernatural horror, 13 classic ghost stories about things that are often more than ghosts. Included are "Canon Alberic's Scrapbook," in which the past encroaches ravenously upon the present, "The Ash-Tree," about revenge from beyond the grave, and "The Mezzotint," in which life imitates art with frightening consequences. First published 1986.

**Other books you might like:**
Ramsey Campbell, *Dark Companions*, 1982
Richard Dalby, *The Best of Ghosts and Scholars*, 1988
    Rosemary Pardoe, co-author
J. Sheridan Le Fanu, *Best Ghost Stories*, 1964
Thomas Ligotti, *Songs of a Dead Dreamer*, 1989
Robert Westall, *Antique Dust*, 1989

**2867**

**MARTIN JAMES**

*Night Glow*

(New York: Pinnacle Books, 1989)

**Story type:** Horror (Techno-Horror)
**Major character(s):** Marian Turner, Psychologist; John Morton, Researcher (Director of Shodale Drugs)
**Time period(s):** 1980s
**Locale(s):** Indianapolis, Indiana

**Summary:** Experimenters in dream research develop a drug that induces nightmares then stimulates the victims to act out their dreams violently. Marian Turner and Det. Carl Nolan seek frantically to find and destroy the drug before it spreads to the general population.

**Other books you might like:**
Robin Cook, *Coma*, 1977
James Herbert, *The Fog*, 1975

**2868**

**MARY JAMES**

*Shoebag*

(New York: Scholastic, 1990)

**Story type:** Fantasy (Contemporary; Young Adult)
**Major character(s):** Stuart "Shoebag" Bagg, Animal (cockroach), Child
**Time period(s):** 1990s
**Locale(s):** United States

**Summary:** Shoebag, a young cockroach, is suddenly turned into a young boy. Adopted by the Biddle family who live in the house where he was born, Shoebag is re-named Stuart Bagg. He makes friends with Pretty Soft who stars in a television commercial, and begins to learn how to be a human being.

**Other books you might like:**
Frank Asch, *Journey to Terezor*, 1989
Peter Dickinson, *Eva*, 1989
Norton Juster, *The Phantom Tollbooth*, 1961
Sarah Sargent, *Jonas McFee, A.T.P.*, 1989

Sarah Sargent, *Weird Henry Berg*, 1980

**2869**

### MARY JAMES

## Shoebag Returns

(New York: Scholastic, 1996)

**Story type:** Fantasy (Young Adult; Urban)
**Major character(s):** Stuart "Shoebag" Bagg, Animal (cockroach), Child; Stanley Sweetsong, Child, Student
**Time period(s):** 1990s
**Locale(s):** Wayne, Pennsylvania

**Summary:** To help Stanley Sweetsong, the sole boy studying at Miss Rattray's School for Girls, Shoebag magically transforms again from cockroach into young lad.

**Other books you might like:**
Lloyd Alexander, *The Arkadians*, 1995
Doranna Durgin, *Dun Lady's Jess*, 1994
Sherwood Smith, *Wren to the Rescue*, 1990
Sylvia Waugh, *The Mennyms*, 1994

**2870**

### P.D. JAMES

## The Children of Men

(New York: Knopf, 1993)

**Story type:** Fantasy (Post-Disaster; Literary)
**Major character(s):** Theodore Faron, Historian, Revolutionary; Xan Lyppiatt, Political Figure (dictator); Julian, Revolutionary, Parent
**Time period(s):** 2020s (2021)
**Locale(s):** England

**Summary:** After a quarter century of universal male sterility, 2021 society focuses on the aging and dying. The United Kingdom suffers under a dictator, Xan Lyppiatt, whose advisor and cousin, Theo Faron, dabbles with revolutionaries until discovering a comrade pregnant. Fearful over her fate as the first woman pregnant in 25 years, she and Theo leave for Wales, but Xan soon pursues.

**Other books you might like:**
Brian W. Aldiss, *Greybeard*, 1964
Richard Bowker, *Forbidden Sanctuary*, 1982
F.M. Busby, *The Breeds of Man*, 1988
Richard Cowper, *Clone*, 1973
William R. Forstchen, *Ice Prophet*, 1983
Frank Herbert, *The White Plague*, 1982
Ursula K. Le Guin, *Planet of Exile*, 1966
Edward Llewellyn, *Prelude to Chaos*, 1983
Charles Eric Maine, *Alph*, 1972
Clifford D. Simak, *Our Children's Children*, 1974

**2871**

### PETER JAMES

## Dreamer

(New York: St. Martin's, 1990)

**Story type:** Horror (Mystery)
**Major character(s):** Samantha "Sam" Curtis, Producer (television commercials); Richard Curtis, Financier, Spouse; Billy "Slider" Wolf, Murderer
**Time period(s):** 1990s

**Locale(s):** London, England

**Summary:** Though Sam Curtis's nightmares change their settings nightly, their basic scenario remains the same: Slider, the murderer whom she killed in self-defense when she was seven years old, is not dead and is coming to get her.

**Other books you might like:**
John Farris, *The Axman Cometh*, 1989
Dean R. Koontz, *The Vision*, 1977
Joe R. Lansdale, *The Nightrunners*, 1987

**2872**

### PETER JAMES

## Host

(New York: Villard, 1995)

**Story type:** Horror (Science Fiction)
**Major character(s):** Joe Messenger, Scientist, Computer Expert (in artificial intelligence); Karen Messenger, Researcher (television), Spouse (of Joe); Juliet Spring, Scientist, Computer Expert
**Time period(s):** 1990s (1993)
**Locale(s):** Sussex, England

**Summary:** Obsessed with finding a means of preserving life after death, Professor Joe Messenger of England's Isaac Newton University finds a way to upload human consciousness into his ARCHIVE computer. When Joe does this in order to save Juliet Spring, his terminally ill assistant, he overlooks that he has also loaded the computer with Juliet's psychoses, hidden in life but which begin manifesting once she has been digitized. This novel was first published in England in 1993.

**Other books you might like:**
Michael Crichton, *The Terminal Man*, 1972
Daniel H. Gower, *The Orpheus Process*, 1992
Dean R. Koontz, *Demon Seed*, 1973

**2873**

### PETER JAMES

## Possession

(New York: Dell, 1989)

**Story type:** Horror (Ghost Story)
**Major character(s):** Alex Hightower, Agent (literary), Parent (mother of Fabian); Fabian Hightower, Spirit (recently died), Young Man
**Time period(s):** 1980s

**Summary:** After the sudden, unexpected death of her son Fabian, Alex begins to receive messages from him—or from a demonic spirit claiming to be him—pleading for "help" and "freedom." As she searches for the truth of the messages—turning to husband and friends, to clergymen, to spiritualists—her own sanity and soul are increasingly jeopardized.

**Other books you might like:**
Michael Bishop, *Who Made Stevie Crye?*, 1984
John Coyne, *Fury*, 1989

**2874**

### PETER JAMES

## Prophecy

(New York: St. Martin's, 1994)

**Story type:** Horror (Occult)

**Major character(s):** Francesca Monsanto, Archaeologist; Oliver Halkin, Actuary; Edward Halkin, Child (Oliver's son)
**Time period(s):** 1990s (1992)
**Locale(s):** London, England

**Summary:** Francesca Monsanto's chance meeting with attractive widower Oliver Halkin begins to seem not so chance after all when the two discover that everything about them—the death of Oliver's wife, their meeting, and their ensuing romance—may have been engineered by an evil forebear of Oliver's, who was executed for necromancy in 1652 but is now using occult forces to come back in the twentieth century. This novel was originally published in England in 1992.

**Other books you might like:**
Jonathan Aycliffe, *Naomi's Room*, 1991
Marcy Heidish, *The Torching*, 1992
Richard Matheson, *A Stir of Echoes*, 1958
Daniel Rhodes, *Adversary*, 1988
Michael Stewart, *Belladonna*, 1992

## 2875

**PETER JAMES**

### Sweet Heart

(New York: St. Martin's, 1991)

**Story type:** Horror (Possession)
**Major character(s):** Charley Witney, Clerk (shopworker); Tom Witney, Lawyer; Hugh Boxer, Neighbor
**Time period(s):** 1990s
**Locale(s):** Elmwood, England

**Summary:** Charley and Tom Witney move to the country to help improve Charley's chances of conceiving a child. But the 15th-century house they rent stimulates uneasy memories in Charley, and the hypnotic regression therapy she takes to enhance her fertility dredges up further memories that suggest she is under the control of occult forces that are inducing her to recapitulate a past life. This novel was first published in England in 1990.

**Other books you might like:**
Daphne Du Maurier, *Rebecca*, 1938
Tom Elliott, *The Dwelling*, 1989
Stephanie Kegan, *The Baby*, 1990
Al Sarrantonio, *House Haunted*, 1991

## 2876

**PETER JAMES**

### Twilight

(New York: St. Martin's, 1993)

**Story type:** Horror (Occult)
**Major character(s):** Kate Hemingway, Journalist; Harvey Swire, Doctor (anesthesiologist)
**Time period(s):** 1970s; 1990s (1992)
**Locale(s):** Sussex, England

**Summary:** When journalist Kate Hemingway reveals that a recently interred women has been buried alive, she runs afoul of the sinister Harvey Swire, an anesthesiologist whose out-of-body experiences for the last 20 years are intimately connected to the case. This novel was originally published in England in 1991.

**Other books you might like:**
Sean Costello, *Captain Quad*, 1991
Susan Palwick, *Flying in Place*, 1992

## 2877

**ROBY JAMES**

### Commencement

(New York: Ballantine Del Rey, 1996)

**Story type:** Science Fiction (Psychic Powers; Political)
**Major character(s):** Ronica McBride, Psychic (esper); Mortel John, Teacher; Jemeret, Psychic (esper)
**Time period(s):** Indeterminate Future
**Locale(s):** Caryldon, Planet—Imaginary; The Com, Interstellar Empire/Federation

**Summary:** Awakening on a primitive wild planet with natural old forests, Ronica remembers only living on technologically advanced planets in the Com. Although she remembers graduating, trained as the strongest esper in the Com, Ronica cannot reach out with her mind or recall arriving on Caryldon. Somehow she must learn to survive and get along without forcing others with her mental abilities. First novel.

**Other books you might like:**
Catherine Asaro, *Primary Inversion*, 1995
Emily Devenport, *Eggheads*, 1996
Louise Marley, *Sing the Light*, 1995
James H. Schmitz, *The Demon Breed*, 1968
Joan D. Vinge, *Dreamfall*, 1996

## 2878

**ELLEN JAMISON**

### Stone Dead

(New York: Zebra, 1993)

**Story type:** Horror (Supernatural Vengeance)
**Major character(s):** Haldis "Hally" Varney, Actress; Clint Hendricks, Police Officer; Elita, Toy (doll)
**Time period(s):** 1990s (1993)
**Locale(s):** Los Angeles, California

**Summary:** Hally Varney, who unwittingly inherited the curse of the evil eye through her family, finds that her new antique doll will kill whomever she thinks badly of.

**Other books you might like:**
Matthew J. Costello, *Child's Play III*, 1991
Pat Graversen, *Dollies*, 1990
Ruby Jean Jensen, *Baby Dolly*, 1991
Ruby Jean Jensen, *The Living Evil*, 1993
Abigail McDaniels, *Playmates*, 1993

## 2879

**GAIL JARROW**

### Beyond the Magic Sphere

(New York: Harcourt Brace, 1994)

**Story type:** Fantasy (Young Adult; Alternate World)
**Major character(s):** S .B. "Air", Child, Adventurer; Cally "Earth", Child, Adventurer; Finis "Water", Child, Adventurer
**Time period(s):** 1990s; Indeterminate
**Locale(s):** New York; Green Lord's Realm, Mythical Place

**Summary:** Rather than vacationing in Europe as she wants, S. B. must spend the summer with her grandmother in outstate New York. There she meets Cally and Finis with whom she visits the Green Lord's realm, learning another way to view herself.

**Other books you might like:**
Suzy McKee Charnas, *The Kingdom of Kevin Malone*, 1993
Pamela Dean, *The Secret Country*, 1985
Shirley Rousseau Murphy, *Medallion of the Black Hound*, 1989
  Welch Suggs, co-author
Nancy Springer, *The Friendship Song*, 1992
Nancy Springer, *Red Wizard*, 1990

## 2880
### LINDA JAVIN

## *Rock 'n' Roll Babes From Outer Space*
(New York: Broadway Books, 1998)

**Story type:** Science Fiction (Humor; Arts)
**Major character(s):** Baby Baby, Alien, Musician
**Time period(s):** Indeterminate Future
**Locale(s):** Earth; Spaceship; Outer Space

**Summary:** When the offspring of an extraterrestrial and a human being, Baby Baby, comes to Earth searching for sex, drugs and rock and roll, she kidnaps a human being and sets out to form a band which will skyrocket to stardom—assuming, that is, that Baby Baby can avoid the pursuing human and non-human agents.

**Other books you might like:**
Douglas Adams, *The Hitchhiker's Guide to the Galaxy*, 1980
Christopher Anvil, *Pandora's Planet*, 1972
John M. Ford, *How Much for Just the Planet?*, 1987
Neil Gaiman, *Good Omens: The Nice and Accurate Prophecies of Agnes Nutter, Witch*, 1990
  Terry Pratchett, co-author
Nick Pollotta, *Illegal Aliens*, 1989
  Phil Foglio, co-author

## 2881
### FRANK A. JAVOR

## *The Ice Beast*
(New York: DAW, 1990)

**Story type:** Science Fiction (Techno-Thriller)
**Major character(s):** Eli Pike, Photojournalist; Theodore Baran, Prospector
**Time period(s):** Indeterminate Future
**Locale(s):** Thul, Planet—Imaginary

**Summary:** Eli Pike arrives on the icy planet Thul intending to get a story about the ultimate racing beast rumored to be found there. He finds the beast, but also finds a tribe of natives who want their existence kept secret and a device, left over from the last interplanetary war, which could destroy the planet.

**Other books you might like:**
Arthur C. Clarke, *A Fall of Moondust*, 1961
Arthur C. Clarke, *The Sands of Mars*, 1952
Ursula K. Le Guin, *The Left Hand of Darkness*, 1969
Vernor Vinge, *The Peace War*, 1984

## 2882
### FRANK A. JAVOR

## *The Rim-World Legacy and Beyond*
(New York: DAW, 1991)

**Story type:** Science Fiction (Collection)

**Major character(s):** Eli Pike, Photographer, Military Personnel (retired); Anton Plagier, Criminal; August Rook, Inventor
**Time period(s):** Indeterminate Future
**Locale(s):** Yoldragi, Planet—Imaginary

**Summary:** Eli Pike, hired by Brigit to photograph Anton Plagier, becomes involved in a murder, a search for an unknown boy, and a very dangerous invention. Reprints *The Rim-World Legacy* (1967) and adds two stories.

**Other books you might like:**
Greg Bear, *Eon*, 1989
Greg Bear, *Queen of Angels*, 1990
Arthur C. Clarke, *A Fall of Moondust*, 1961
Philip K. Dick, *The Unteleported Man*, 1983
  revised
Ron Goulart, *After Things Fell Apart*, 1977
Leo P. Kelley, *The Counterfeits*, 1967
Michael Kurland, *Transmission Error*, 1970
Dan Simmons, *Hyperion*, 1989
Sheri S. Tepper, *Grass*, 1989

## 2883
### WILLIAM JAY

## *The Lost History of Redwyn*
(Bloomfield Hills, Michigan: Lancaster Books, 1992)

**Story type:** Fantasy (Legend; Religious)
**Major character(s):** Redwyn, Magician; Lynn St. Du Lac, Noblewoman
**Time period(s):** 14th century (1352)
**Locale(s):** Scotland; England

**Summary:** As Redwyn concludes that his career in magic leaves much wanting in the development of his higher potential, he comes into possession of King Arthur's sword, Excaliber, and becomes involved in an 800-year-old conflict between good and evil.

**Other books you might like:**
Margaret J. Anderson, *The Druid's Gift*, 1989
Marion Zimmer Bradley, *The Mists of Avalon*, 1983
Katherine Kurtz, *Camber of Culdi*, 1976
Katherine Kurtz, *Camber the Heretic*, 1981
Katherine Kurtz, *Saint Camber*, 1978
Susan Shwartz, *The Grail of Hearts*, 1992
Lawrence Watt-Evans, *The Rebirth of Wonder*, 1992
Connie Willis, *Doomsday Book*, 1992

## 2884
### MIKE JEFFERIES

## *Hall of Whispers*
(New York: HarperCollins, 1992)

**Story type:** Fantasy (Political; Adventure)
**Series:** Heirs to Gnarlsmyre
**Major character(s):** Marrimian, Ruler; Pinvey, Revolutionary; Erek, Sorceress
**Time period(s):** Indeterminate Past
**Locale(s):** Gnarlsmyre, Fictional Country

**Summary:** Marrimian has passed the tests required for becoming ruler of Gnarlsmyre, but her gender prevents her acceptance by the marshmen. She travels through her rebellious and starving kingdom to gain the respect and acceptance of her subjects while her sister, Pinvey, and the crone Erek plot rebellion.

**Other books you might like:**
Terry Brooks, *The Sword of Shannara*, 1978
Glen Cook, *The Black Company*, 1984
Dennis L. McKiernan, *The Dark Tide*, 1984
Patricia A. McKillip, *The Riddle-Master of Hed*, 1976
Michael Scott Rohan, *The Forge in the Forest*, 1986
Paula Volsky, *Illusion*, 1992

## 2885

### MIKE JEFFERIES

## Hidden Echoes

(New York: HarperCollins, 1993)

**Story type:** Fantasy (Alternate World; Adventure)
**Major character(s):** Orun, Traveler, Animal Trainer; Denso Alburton, Writer; Mya Capthorne, Scientist (environmentalist)
**Time period(s):** 1990s
**Locale(s):** City of Time, Fictional City; New York, New York

**Summary:** When Orun, a Waymaster, travels through the Doorcrack to Paradise to find the prophet Denso Alburton, he finds a fantasy writer basing his books on vivid dreams. With a confused environmentalist, he battles a threat to everything that exists.

**Other books you might like:**
Adrian Cole, *A Place Among the Fallen*, 1987
Barbara Hambly, *The Time of the Dark*, 1982
Patricia A. McKillip, *The Riddle-Master of Hed*, 1976
Michael Moorcock, *Elric of Melnibone*, 1976
Sheri S. Tepper, *King's Blood Four*, 1983

## 2886

### MIKE JEFFERIES

## The Knights of Cawdor

(New York: HarperPrism, 1995)

**Story type:** Fantasy (Political; Adventure)
**Series:** Loremasters of Elundium
**Major character(s):** Drib, Student, Chimneysweep (apprentice); Grout, Teacher (Loremaster); Snatch, Military Personnel
**Time period(s):** Indeterminate
**Locale(s):** Elundium, Fictional Country

**Summary:** Although the new regime provides freedom from King Thane's oppression, some people in every town plot to revolt. Seeking freedom and safety, helpless former slaves find themselves the target of people's discontent.

**Other books you might like:**
Glen Cook, *The Swordbearer*, 1982
Barbara Hambly, *The Time of the Dark*, 1982
Dennis L. McKiernan, *The Dark Tide*, 1984
Michael Scott Rohan, *The Forge in the Forest*, 1986
Sheri S. Tepper, *King's Blood Four*, 1983

## 2887

### MIKE JEFFERIES

## Palace of Kings

(New York: Harper and Row, 1990)

**Story type:** Fantasy (Magic Conflict; Sword and Sorcery)
**Series:** Loremasters of Elundium

**Major character(s):** Thanehand, Warrior, Leader; Elionbel, Fiance(e) (Thane's), Prisoner (Krulshards'); Krulshards, Demon (Master of Darkness)
**Time period(s):** Indeterminate
**Locale(s):** Elundium, Fictional Country

**Summary:** Thane, the Candleman's son, has risen to become the leader of King Holbian's armies, fulfilling the ancient prophecies of enchanter-guardian Nevian. However, even though Thane and the warriors of Underfall were victorious over the armies of the Master of Darkness, Krulshards himself escapes in the City of Night and plots his revenge. Thane, preparing to follow and destroy him, claims his grandfather's magical sword, but as he is about to set out on his journey, he receives word that King Holbian is trapped in the besieged Granite City, struggling to keep the hordes of Nightbeasts from gaining the walls. Thane must choose the path that will best serve Elundium and its king.

**Other books you might like:**
M.A.R. Barker, *Flamesong*, 1985
M.A.R. Barker, *Man of Gold*, 1984
Stephen R. Donaldson, *The Illearth War*, 1977
J.R.R. Tolkien, *The Fellowship of the Ring*, 1954
J.R.R. Tolkien, *The Return of the King*, 1956
J.R.R. Tolkien, *The Two Towers*, 1955

## 2888

### MIKE JEFFERIES

## The Road to Underfall

(New York: Harper and Row, 1990)

**Story type:** Fantasy (Magic Conflict; Sword and Sorcery)
**Series:** Loremasters of Elundium
**Major character(s):** Thanehand, Apprentice (candlemaker), Warrior; Willow Leaf, Slave (tunneller); Holbian, Royalty (king), Warrior
**Time period(s):** Indeterminate
**Locale(s):** Elundium, Fictional Country; Granite City, Fictional City

**Summary:** Krulshards, Master of Darkness, having escaped from his marble prison on Mantern's Mountain, has gathered his evil forces near Underfall, final resting place of all the Granite Kings, at the edge of the Kingdom of Elundium. Aging King Holbian, who has allowed his greed to corrupt the land for many years, repents and sends the only messenger he can trust, Thane, son of the Candleman, to alert the border garrisons at Underfall of their peril. Thane, eager to serve, but untrained as yet in warfare, will be very fortunate to successfully complete his journey.

**Other books you might like:**
M.A.R. Barker, *Flamesong*, 1985
M.A.R. Barker, *Man of Gold*, 1984
Stephen R. Donaldson, *Lord Foul's Bane*, 1977
J.R.R. Tolkien, *The Fellowship of the Ring*, 1954
J.R.R. Tolkien, *The Return of the King*, 1956
J.R.R. Tolkien, *The Two Towers*, 1955

## 2889

### MIKE JEFFERIES

## Stone Angels

(New York: HarperPaperbacks, 1994)

**Story type:** Horror (Ancient Evil Unleashed)
**Major character(s):** Jarvin Mandrake, Archaeologist; Joni Frost, Vagrant; Martyn Burr, Doctor
**Time period(s):** 1990s (1994)

**Locale(s):** Norwich, England

**Summary:** Dispatched to England to recover from a harrowing experience during excavations in Egypt, archaeologist Jarvin Mandrake finds himself caught in a legendary struggle between good and evil angels carved into the statuary of the cathedral whose history he has agreed to chronicle.

**Other books you might like:**
Cleve Cartmill, *Prelude to Armageddon*, 1943
Bernard King, *Demon Shield*, 1989
Daniel Rhodes, *Next, After Lucifer*, 1987
Whitley Strieber, *Unholy Fire*, 1992

## 2890

### PHILLIP C. JENNINGS

### *The Bug Life Chronicles*

(New York: Baen Books, 1989)

**Story type:** Science Fiction (Collection)
**Time period(s):** Indeterminate Future

**Summary:** These fifteen short stories, some of which appeared in *Amazing Science Fiction, Isaac Asimov's Science Fiction Magazine* and elsewhere in 1987 and 1988, are all set in the same universe as the author's previous novel, *Tower to the Sky*. Among the stories included are "Teddy Bug and the Hot Purple Snowball," "The Quonset Hut," "Messiah," and "The Hero."

**Other books you might like:**
Anne McCaffrey, *The Ship Who Sang*, 1969
Bruce Sterling, *Schismatrix*, 1985
Somtow Sucharitkul, *Light on the Sound*, 1982
Somtow Sucharitkul, *The Throne of Madness*, 1983
Somtow Sucharitkul, *The Utopia Hunters*, 1984

## 2891

### TINA L. JENS, Editor

### *Dangerous Dames*

(Chicago: 11th Hour Production Publications, 1998)

**Story type:** Horror (Anthology)
**Series:** Twilight Tales Presents

**Summary:** Here are 11 tales and poems of femme fatales and feisty women, all by female writers. Selections include Tina Jens's "Death Gets a Makeover," in which death in all her skeletal glory gets fashion tips from Gaia, Mother Earth; Pamela Hodgson's "Returned Mail From Ealtgeld," about a future where communication is so remote and off-putting that direct human contact becomes fatal; and Lynda Licina's "Something I Can Never Have," about a female vampire who stalks prey through the personal ads. Includes an introduction by Pam Kesey. Second book in a series devoted to stories read monthly at a Chicago writers gathering.

**Other books you might like:**
Janet Berliner, *Desire Burn: Women's Stories From the Dark Side of Passion*, 1995
    editor
Victoria Brownworth, *Night Bites: Vampire Stories by Women*, 1996
Kathryn Ptacek, *Women of Darkness*, 1989
    editor
Kathryn Ptacek, *Women of Darkness II*, 1990
    editor
Lisa Tuttle, *Skin of the Soul*, 1990
    editor

## 2892

### TINA L. JENS, Editor

### *Strange Creatures*

(Chicago: 11th Hour Production Publications, 1998)

**Story type:** Horror (Anthology)
**Series:** Twilight Tales Presents

**Summary:** Included here are ten short stories of nonhuman menaces, four original to the booklet. Selections include T. Diane Slatton's "Baby Hercules," a tale of mutant birth; Scott Cupp's "I Was a Teenage Horny Toad," a homage to 1950s B-movies; Andre Dubnick's "Arkady," a tale of werewolf appetites and human prejudices; and Martin H. Mundt's amusing "The Reincarnation of the Dolly Lama," in which a sect of holy men search for the reincarnation of one of their own among household items. Third book in a series devoted to stories read monthly at a Chicago writers gathering.

**Other books you might like:**
Brian J. Frost, *Book of the Werewolf*, 1973
Stephen Jones, *The Mammoth Book of Frankenstein*, 1995
    editor
Denise Little, *Alien Pets*, 1998
Byron Preiss, *The Ultimate Zombie*, 1993
Robert Weinberg, *100 Creepy Little Creature Stories*, 1994
    Stefan Dziemianowicz, Martin H. Greenberg, co-editors

## 2893

### TINA L. JENS, Editor

### *Tales of Forbidden Passion*

(Chicago: 11th Hour Production Publications, 1998)

**Story type:** Horror (Anthology; Erotic Horror)
**Series:** Twilight Tales Presents

**Summary:** These six tales of strange fetishes and lusts include Martin Mundt's "My Love Is a Dead, Dead Rose," presented as a series of letters written by a necrophiliac to Calvin Klein, the lovelorn column of the local newspaper, and similarly unlikely recipients; and Bill Breedlove's "That Dreamy Feeling," the story of a one-night stand whose narrator gradually reveals his psychopathology. Other contributors include Yvonne Navarro, Rick R. Reed, J.D. Smith and Leigh Jensen. First book in a series devoted to stories read monthly at a Chicago writers gathering.

**Other books you might like:**
Nancy A. Collins, *Dark Love*, 1995
    Ed Kramer, Martin H. Greenberg, co-editors
Jeff Gelb, *Hottest Blood: The Ultimate in Erotic Horror*, 1993
    Michael Garrett, co-editor
Michel Parry, *Devil's Kisses*, 1976
John Pelan, *Darkside: Horror for the Next Millennium*, 1996
    editor
Michele Slung, *I Shudder at Your Touch*, 1991

## 2894

### TINA L. JENS

### *Winter Tales*

(Chicago: 11th Hour Production Publications, 1998)

**Story type:** Horror (Anthology)
**Series:** Twilight Tales Presents

**Summary:** This anthology includes 11 stories with Christmas themes. The majority are macabre fantasies in which Santa Claus is the victim of a variety of indignities, including Wayne Allen Sallee's ''He Knows When You've Been Sleeping,'' in which a psychotic Santa causes death and destruction in homes that don't request American-made toys; Barrett McGivney's ''Exorcising Your Christmas Spirit,'' in which a contract thug launches a tasteless smear campaign against Santa and Christmas; and Robin Reed's ''Twas the Night.,'' in which Santa's elves discover that their leader is a vampire. Fourth book in a series devoted to stories read monthly at a Chicago writers gathering.

**Other books you might like:**
Kathryn Cramer, *Spirits of Christmas*, 1989
   David Hartwell, co-editor
Richard Dalby, *Chillers for Christmas*, 1990
   editor
Richard Dalby, *Mistletoe Mayhem*, 1993
   editor
Seon Manley, *Christmas Ghosts: An Anthology*, 1978
   Gogo Lewis, co-editor
Mike Resnick, *Christmas Ghosts*, 1993
   Martin H. Greenberg, co-editor

---

**2895**

**JANE JENSEN**

## The Beast Within: A Gabriel Knight Mystery

(New York: Roc, 1998)

**Story type:** Horror (Werewolf Story)
**Series:** Gabriel Knight
**Major character(s):** Gabriel Knight, Writer; Grace Nakimura, Clerk (bookstore); Friedrich von Glower, Nobleman (baron)
**Time period(s):** 1990s (1998)
**Locale(s):** Munich, Germany

**Summary:** Gruesome murders on the outskirts of Munich point to the activity of a werewolf. Horror writer Gabriel Knight, who comes from a family of Shadow Hunters, infiltrates an elite hunting club whose members appear to be harboring the culprit werewolf, but finds his problems have just begun when he is bitten by the werewolf leader during one of the club's hunting weekends. Second novel in a series based on a popular CD-Rom game.

**Other books you might like:**
Tanith Lee, *Heart-Beast*, 1990
Robert R. McCammon, *The Wolf's Hour*, 1989
Peter Rubie, *Werewolf*, 1991
Jeffrey Sackett, *Mark of the Werewolf*, 1990
S.P. Somtow, *Moon Dance*, 1990

---

**2896**

**JANE JENSEN**

## Gabriel Knight: Sins of the Fathers

(New York: Roc, 1997)

**Story type:** Horror (Occult)
**Series:** Gabriel Knight
**Major character(s):** Gabriel Knight, Writer; Mosely, Detective—Police; Grace Nakimura, Worker (bookstore employee)
**Time period(s):** 1990s (1993)
**Locale(s):** New Orleans, Louisiana

**Summary:** While researching voodoo for his newest horror novel, author Gabriel Knight becomes a key figure in the investigation of several gruesome murders, all of which have the stamp of the voodoo ritual. Gabriel's research introduces him to a shapeshifting voodoo cult and reveals the history of his own family, whose members have for centuries served as Shadow Hunters dedicated to the extirpation of supernatural evil. Based on the CD-ROM game Gabriel Knight.

**Other books you might like:**
Alex Abella, *The Killing of the Saints*, 1991
Nancy A. Collins, *Tempter*, 1990
Don Davis, *The Gris-Gris Man*, 1997
Michael Reaves, *Voodoo Child*, 1988
Vivian Schilling, *Sacred Prey*, 1994
Robert Weinberg, *The Black Lodge*, 1991

---

**2897**

**KRIS JENSEN**

## FreeMaster

(New York: DAW, 1990)

**Story type:** Science Fiction (First Contact)
**Series:** World of Ardel
**Major character(s):** Sarah Anders, Diplomat
**Time period(s):** 23rd century
**Locale(s):** Ardel, Planet—Imaginary

**Summary:** Sarah Anders, a representative of the Terran Trade Union, fights to keep less altruistic interstellar corporations from raping the mineral-rich but backward planet Ardel. The Ardellans, however, make up for what they lack in technology with psionic talent and prove fully capable of taking care of themselves. This is Jensen's first novel.

**Other books you might like:**
Mary Gentle, *Ancient Light*, 1989
Mary Gentle, *Golden Witchbreed*, 1983
Judith Moffett, *Pennterra*, 1987
Richard Paul Russo, *Inner Eclipse*, 1988

---

**2898**

**KRIS JENSEN**

## Mentor

(New York: DAW, 1991)

**Story type:** Science Fiction (First Contact; Psychic Powers)
**Series:** World of Ardel
**Major character(s):** Sinykin Inda, Doctor, Psychic; Jeryl, Alien
**Time period(s):** 23rd century (2260s)
**Locale(s):** Ardel, Planet—Imaginary

**Summary:** Jeryl, Mentor of Alu, has sole trade rights and controls Terran access to Ardel. Few Ardellans are happy to have Terrans on Ardel while some want open trade for all. Sinykin Inda develops a vaccine for a local Ardellan plague which also attacks humans. While traveling to Clan Alu to get tissue samples from Ardellan survivors in order to develop a vaccine for them, he learns much about Ardel and Ardellans.

**Other books you might like:**
David Brin, *The Uplift War*, 1987
Octavia E. Butler, *Dawn*, 1987
Mary Gentle, *Golden Witchbreed*, 1984
Stephen Leigh, *Alien Tongue*, 1991
Rebecca Ore, *Becoming Alien*, 1987
David Alexander Smith, *Homecoming*, 1990

David Alexander Smith, *Rendezvous*, 1988

## 2899

### RUBY JEAN JENSEN

## Baby Dolly

(New York: Zebra, 1991)

**Story type:** Horror (Child-in-Peril)
**Major character(s):** Sybil Wilfred Madison, Aged Person; Adam Curtis, Child; Prissy Curtis, Child
**Time period(s):** 19th century; 20th century
**Locale(s):** Wilfred, Mississippi

**Summary:** With the help of a demonically empowered doll her father brings back from South America, Sybil Wilfred vents her petty jealousies on three generations of her family. When the Curtis family move into the abandoned Wilfred mansion, they are unaware that Sybil has destroyed her family—and that the instrument of that destruction is still around, and ravenously hungry.

**Other books you might like:**
Algernon Blackwood, *The Doll and One Other*, 1946
Matthew J. Costello, *Child's Play III*, 1991
Pat Graversen, *Dollies*, 1990

## 2900

### RUBY JEAN JENSEN

## Celia

(New York: Zebra, 1991)

**Story type:** Horror (Reanimated Dead)
**Major character(s):** Celia Nolan, Housewife; Mel, Truck Driver; Durk Nolan, Reanimated Dead
**Time period(s):** 1990s
**Locale(s):** United States

**Summary:** For the sake of her children Celia Nolan kills her abusive husband Durk and hides his body in the swamp. But Durk proves a persistent man even after he is dead, chasing Celia and the kids cross-country and destroying anyone foolish enough to get in his way.

**Other books you might like:**
Stephen Gallagher, *Down River*, 1989
Dean R. Koontz, *Shadowfires*, 1987

## 2901

### RUBY JEAN JENSEN

## The Haunting

(New York: Zebra, 1994)

**Story type:** Horror (Haunted House)
**Major character(s):** Theodora Wickham, Aged Person; Eddie Wickham, Child; Katie Roberts, Real Estate Agent
**Time period(s):** 1990s (1994)
**Locale(s):** South

**Summary:** Katie Roberts feels an inexplicable attraction to Wickham House, a property associated with the deaths of several children decades before. As Katie slowly unravels the history of the house and the secret of its former matriarch's affiliation with the powers of darkness, she begins to sense an uncanny kinship with one of the house's victims.

**Other books you might like:**
Poppy Z. Brite, *Drawing Blood*, 1993

Max Ehrlich, *The Reincarnation of Peter Proud*, 1974
Tom Elliott, *The Dwelling*, 1988
Nina Romberg, *Shadow Walkers*, 1993

## 2902

### RUBY JEAN JENSEN

## The Living Evil

(New York: Zebra, 1993)

**Story type:** Horror (Supernatural Vengeance)
**Major character(s):** Pamela Armand, Prisoner (former); Zenoa Morris, Young Woman; Justin, Young Man (Pamela's nephew)
**Time period(s):** 1870s; 20th century
**Locale(s):** South

**Summary:** Upon her return from prison Pamela Armand vows to destroy Zenoa, an antique doll animated by the vindictive spirit of its former owner that has killed several families over the years. But Pamela finds that Zenoa has been transformed from a doll into a seductress affianced to her nephew and bent on inflicting terror upon the rest of her family.

**Other books you might like:**
Algernon Blackwood, *The Doll and One Other*, 1946
Matthew J. Costello, *Child's Play III*, 1991
Pat Graversen, *Dollies*, 1990
Abigail McDaniels, *Playmates*, 1993

## 2903

### RUBY JEAN JENSEN

## Night Thunder

(New York: Zebra, 1995)

**Story type:** Horror (Black Magic)
**Major character(s):** Brent Salisaw, Construction Worker; Kara Salisaw, Child; Holly Salisaw, Child
**Time period(s):** 1990s (1995)
**Locale(s):** South

**Summary:** When construction workers uproot a sycamore tree planted on top of a mass grave from the American Civil War period, they resurrect the witches buried there, who begin reanimating corpses of the dead to perpetuate their century-old legacy of horror.

**Other books you might like:**
Barbara Erskine, *Midnight Is a Lonely Place*, 1994
Ashley McConnell, *Days of the Dead*, 1993
Abigail McDaniels, *Dead Voices*, 1994
G. Wayne Miller, *Thunder Rise*, 1989
Brent Monahan, *The Uprising*, 1992
Steve Zell, *WiZrD*, 1994

## 2904

### RUBY JEAN JENSEN

## The Reckoning

(New York: Zebra, 1992)

**Story type:** Horror (Supernatural Vengeance)
**Major character(s):** Dalton Walsh, Religious (evangelistic preacher); Matt Reed, Taxidermist; Thomas Abbot, Police Officer (Chief, Spring Valley police)
**Time period(s):** 1990s (1992)
**Locale(s):** Spring Valley, Kansas

**Summary:** The Reverend Walsh's hellfire and brimstone preaching works a miracle when it summons back all the children who have disappeared from Spring Valley. But it soon becomes apparent that the children are ghosts, and that they have returned to seek the murderer still lurking in the town's midst.

**Other books you might like:**
Sean Costello, *The Cartoonist*, 1990
Peter Straub, *Ghost Story*, 1979
Chet Williamson, *Ash Wednesday*, 1988

## 2905
**AUGUSTUS JESSOP**

### The Phantom Coach and Other Ghost Stories of an Antiquary
(Uncasville, CT: Richard Fawcett, 1998)

**Story type:** Horror (Collection)

**Summary:** Four previously uncollected short stories steeped in the folklore and superstitions of rural England, written around the turn of the century by a friend and contemporary of ghost story master M. R. Included are the author's best known tale "The Phantom Coach," about a ghostly coach that occasionally picks up unwitting mortals, and "Dreams" and "A Waking Night," both of which concern dreams and nightmares that interpenetrate reality. Edited by Jessica Amanda Salmonson and illustrated by Wendy Wees. The author's own essay, "The Dying out of the Marvellous," is included as an introduction. Available as a limited edition hardcover.

**Other books you might like:**
James Hogg, *Selected Stories and Sketches*, 1980
M.R. James, *The Collected Ghost Stories of M.R. James*, 1931
A.N.L. Munby, *The Alabaster Hand and Other Ghost Stories*, 1949
Elliott O'Donnell, *Haunted and Hunted*, 1946
L.T.C. Rolt, *Sleep No More*, 1946

## 2906
**K.W. JETER**

### Blade Runner 2: The Edge of Human
(New York: Bantam Spectra, 1995)

**Story type:** Science Fiction (Post-Nuclear Holocaust; Genetic Manipulation)
**Major character(s):** Rick Deckard, Police Officer (bladerunner); Rachael, Android (replicant); Sarah Tyrell, Heiress, Model (templant)
**Time period(s):** 2020s (2020)
**Locale(s):** Los Angeles, California

**Summary:** Rick Deckard keeps his beloved Rachael in stasis most of the time in an attempt to extend her short life. Hired by Sarah, the new head of Tyrell Industries, to find another replicant, Rick must first disprove the murder charge resulting when he eliminated a human as a replicant. Sequel to the film *Bladerunner*.

**Other books you might like:**
Roger MacBride Allen, *Caliban*, 1993
Stephen Baxter, *The Time Ships*, 1996
Philip K. Dick, *Blade Runner*, 1982
S. Andrew Swann, *Forests of the Night*, 1993
George Turner, *Genetic Soldier*, 1994

## 2907
**K.W. JETER**

### Blade Runner: Replicant Night
(New York: Bantam Spectra, 1996)

**Story type:** Science Fiction (Political; Alternate Intelligence)
**Series:** Blade Runner
**Major character(s):** Rick Deckard, Police Officer, Consultant; Sarah Tyrell, Businesswoman, Imposter; Roy Batty, Disembodied Personality, Artificial Intelligence
**Time period(s):** 21st century
**Locale(s):** Outer Hollywood, Space Station; Earth; Mars

**Summary:** Rick Deckard hopes to earn enough by consulting on an Outer Hollywood movie about his life to allow him to emigrate to Mars with Sarah Tyrell both using pseudonyms to avoid notice. Before he can return to Mars, Deckard acquires a briefcase implanted with Roy Batty's personality which informs Deckard of his key role in the replicants' revolution on Earth. Meanwhile, kidnappers loyal to the destroyed Tyrell Corporation abduct Sarah Tyrell, intending that she lead a glorious revival of the corporation.

**Other books you might like:**
Poul Anderson, *Harvest of Stars*, 1993
Pat Cadigan, *Fools*, 1992
Philip K. Dick, *Blade Runner*, 1982
Philip K. Dick, *The Three Stigmata of Palmer Eldritch*, 1965
Philip K. Dick, *The Unteleported Man*, 1983 revised edition
J.R. Dunn, *This Side of Judgment*, 1994

## 2908
**K.W. JETER**

### Bloodletter
(New York: Pocket, 1993)

**Story type:** Science Fiction (Space Colony; Space Opera)
**Series:** Star Trek: Deep Space Nine
**Major character(s):** Major Kira, Military Personnel, Alien (Bajoran); Benjamin Sisko, Military Personnel, Leader (Deep Space 9); Miles O'Brien, Military Personnel, Engineer
**Time period(s):** 24th century
**Locale(s):** Deep Space Nine, Space Station; United Federation of Planets, Interstellar Empire/Federation

**Summary:** When the Federation learns the Cardassians plan to build a Gamma Quadrant advance base on the far side of the wormhole, officials order Benjamin Sisko and the Deep Space 9 crew to immediately construct a Federation base there. When an old enemy of Major Kira shows up, his mission of murder threatens not only Major Kira, but also Bajor and the Federation.

**Other books you might like:**
Peter David, *The Siege*, 1993
J.M. Dillard, *Emissary*, 1993
Sandy Schofield, *The Big Game*, 1993

## 2909
**K.W. JETER**

### Cross of Blood
(New York: Pocket, 1995)

**Story type:** Science Fiction (Invasion of Earth; Medical)
**Series:** Alien Nation

**Major character(s):** George Francisco, Alien (Tenctonese), Detective—Police; Matthew Sikes, Detective—Police; Cathy Frankel, Alien (Tenctonese), Doctor
**Time period(s):** 21st century
**Locale(s):** Los Angeles, California

**Summary:** George and Susan, unbeknownst to each other, suffer terrible nightmares. Matt also hides his nightmares. The cross soaked with blood left on a Newcomer's lawn, an escalation of Human Defense League activity, couldn't have come at a worse time, as George can't focus on work and Cathy, pregnant with Matt's child, will give birth to the first Newcomer/Human baby.

**Other books you might like:**
Margaret Wander Bonanno, *The Others*, 1990
Peter David, *Body and Soul*, 1993
Alan Dean Foster, *Alien Nation*, 1993
Barry B. Longyear, *The Change*, 1994
Judith Reeves-Stevens, *The Day of Descent*, 1993
    Garfield Reeves-Stevens, co-author
S. Andrew Swann, *Forests of the Night*, 1993

## 2910

### K.W. JETER

## Dark Horizon

(New York: Pocket, 1993)

**Story type:** Science Fiction (Invasion of Earth)
**Series:** Alien Nation
**Major character(s):** George Francisco, Alien (Tenctonese), Detective—Police; Matthew Sikes, Detective—Police
**Time period(s):** 21st century
**Locale(s):** Los Angeles, California

**Summary:** The human Purists, opposed to the involuntary alien presence on Earth, release deadly new bacteria aimed at killing all Tenctonese which infects George's family. Meanwhile, a ruthless Overseer has come to Earth to enslave humans and recapture Tenctonese escapees. Novelizes teleplays of the cliff-hanging concluding series episode and sequel teleplay never produced.

**Other books you might like:**
A.C. Crispin, *V*, 1984
Peter David, *Body and Soul*, 1993
Alan Dean Foster, *Alien Nation*, 1988
Judith Reeves-Stevens, *The Day of Descent*, 1993
    Garfield Reeves-Stevens, co-author
Jayne Tannehill, *V: The Oregon Invasion*, 1984

## 2911

### K.W. JETER

## Farewell Horizontal

(New York: St. Martin's Press, 1989; Signet, 1989)

**Story type:** Science Fiction (Cyberpunk)
**Major character(s):** Ny Axxter, Artist; General Cripplemaker, Outlaw (Gang leader)
**Time period(s):** Indeterminate Future
**Locale(s):** Cylinder, Planet—Imaginary (The Cylinder is a world-sized building)

**Summary:** Axxter has choosen to leave the safe, boring life of a resident of the Cylinder's Horizontal levels and go Vertical, actually live on the side of the gigantic building that is the only world he knows. He wants to become a successful graffex artist, a specialist at designing the complex insignias and wildly illustrated armor worn by

the violent gangs who roam the Vertical regions. Then he makes a mistake, angering one of the more powerful gangs, and must flee for his life into unknown territory.

**Other books you might like:**
William Gibson, *Count Zero*, 1985
William Gibson, *Mona Lisa Overdrive*, 1988
William Gibson, *Neuromancer*, 1984
Norman Spinrad, *Little Heroes*, 1987

## 2912

### K.W. JETER

## In the Land of the Dead

(New York: NAL Onyx, 1989)

**Story type:** Horror (Reanimated Dead)
**Major character(s):** Cooper, Convict (Itinerant ex-con); Vandervelde, Farmer (Sadistic)
**Time period(s):** 1930s
**Locale(s):** California

**Summary:** "Paroled" to work on a farm, Cooper, despite the threat of a sadistic boss and vicious son, becomes slowly enamored of Fay, a strange young girl who communicates with the dead.

**Other books you might like:**
Curt Selby, *Blood County*,

## 2913

### K.W. JETER

## Madlands

(New York: St. Martins Press, 1991)

**Story type:** Science Fiction (Post-Holocaust; Mystery)
**Major character(s):** Trayne, Detective; Geldt, Companion
**Time period(s):** 21st century
**Locale(s):** Los Angeles, California

**Summary:** The Madlands, an L.A. environment changed by some mysterious effect, no longer responds to normal laws of reality. Residents become subject to numerous new maladies including n-formation disease which causes the loss of pattern discrimination on a cellular level. When Trayne, an employee of the televangelist Identrope, is rescued by his former partner Geldt, he sets out to discover who hired Geldt to find him and deliver him for questioning.

**Other books you might like:**
Chester Anderson, *The Butterfly Kid*, 1967
Philip K. Dick, *Ubik*, 1969
Philip K. Dick, *The Unteleported Man*, 1983
George Alec Effinger, *When Gravity Fails*, 1987
Katharine Kerr, *Polar City Blues*, 1990
Michael Kurland, *The Unicorn Girl*, 1969
Geoff Ryman, *The Child Garden*, 1990
T.A. Waters, *The Probability Pad*, 1970

## 2914

### K.W. JETER

## The Mandalorian Armor

(New York: Bantam Spectra, 1998)

**Story type:** Science Fiction (Space Opera)
**Series:** Star Wars: The Bounty Hunter Wars

**Major character(s):** Boba Fett, Bounty Hunter; Xizor, Royalty, Criminal; Bossk, Bounty Hunter
**Time period(s):** Indeterminate Past
**Locale(s):** Kud'ar Mub'at's Web, Space Station; Tatooine, Planet—Imaginary; The Empire, Interstellar Empire/Federation

**Summary:** In a bid to increase the power of the Empire and his own Black Sun, Prince Xizor hires Boba Fett to destroy the Bounty Hunter's Guild. Involving betrayals and counter betrayals, this commission will have reverberations far beyond Xizor's expectations, beyond even Boba Fett's apparent death on Tatooine.

**Other books you might like:**
Kevin J. Anderson, *Tales From the Bounty Hunters*, 1996 editor
Brian Daley, *The Han Solo Adventures*, 1992
Barbara Hambly, *Children of the Jedi*, 1995
Michael A. Stackpole, *Rogue Squadron*, 1996
Timothy Zahn, *Heir to the Empire*, 1991

---

**2915**

**K.W. JETER**

## The Night Man

(New York: NAL Onyx, 1990)

**Story type:** Horror (Supernatural Vengeance)
**Major character(s):** Steven, Child (ten-year-old boy), Abuse Victim; Taylor, Detective—Police
**Time period(s):** 1990s
**Locale(s):** California

**Summary:** Picked on by his drunken mother, mocked by his sister and her boyfriend, bullied by the bigger, tougher boys, Steven can only fantasize about revenge—until the fantasies take concrete shape in "the night man," who violently carries out Steven's dreams.

**Other books you might like:**
Charles L. Grant, *The Pet*, 1986
Stephen King, *Carrie*, 1974
Stephen King, *Christine*, 1983

---

**2916**

**K.W. JETER**

## Noir

(New York: Spectra, 1998)

**Story type:** Science Fiction (Cyberpunk; Mystery)
**Major character(s):** McNihil, Detective—Private; Harrisch, Businessman (CEO)
**Time period(s):** Indeterminate Future
**Locale(s):** West Coast

**Summary:** The Pacific Rim is thriving even though the rest of the world is subsiding into economic anarchy. McNihil investigates the murder of a business executive killed by an interloper who managed to bypass the impressive company security system. The CEO of the company seems more interested in repairing the breach than in receiving justice for the death of his subordinate, and McNihil suspects that he knows more than he is letting on.

**Other books you might like:**
Bruce Bethke, *Headcrash*, 1995
William Gibson, *Count Zero*, 1986
Wil McCarthy, *Murder in the Solid State*, 1996
Mike McQuay, *Hot Time in Old Town*, 1981
Steve Perry, *The Digital Effect*, 1997

---

**2917**

**K.W. JETER**

## Warped

(New York: Pocket, 1995)

**Story type:** Science Fiction (Space Opera)
**Series:** Star Trek: Deep Space Nine
**Major character(s):** Benjamin Sisko, Military Personnel (Starfleet Commander), Leader (Deep Space Nine); Odo, Alien, Security Officer; McHogue, Computer Expert, Criminal
**Time period(s):** 24th century
**Locale(s):** Deep Space Nine, Space Station (Bajoran); United Federation of Planets, Interstellar Empire/Federation

**Summary:** With political unrest on Bajor spreading to Deep Space Nine, Odo must solve a series of murders while Sisko deals with the effects of McHogue's cortical induction holosuite technology which threatens Sisko's son, the Federation presence on Deep Space Nine and the perception of reality even more widely.

**Other books you might like:**
Dafydd ab Hugh, *Fallen Heroes*, 1994
Diane Carey, *The Search*, 1994
Greg Cox, *Devil in the Sky*, 1995
John Gregory Betancourt, co-author
Esther Friesner, *Warchild*, 1994
Sandy Schofield, *The Big Game*, 1993
Lois Tilton, *Betrayal*, 1994
John Vornholt, *Antimatter*, 1994

---

**2918**

**K.W. JETER**

## Wolf Flow

(New York: St. Martin's, 1992)

**Story type:** Horror (Wild Talents)
**Major character(s):** Mike, Doctor; Lindy, Addict; Doot, Teenager
**Time period(s):** 1990s
**Locale(s):** Hot Lake, Oregon (the Thermalene Spa)

**Summary:** Mike takes refuge in the ruins of the abandoned Thermalene Spa after drug dealers dump him in the desert for dead. While there, he partakes of the spa's recuperative waters—and becomes imbued with the same malignancy that leached into the waters a century before and left the surrounding territory a wasteland.

**Other books you might like:**
Paddy Chayefsky, *Altered States*, 1978
David J. Schow, *The Shaft*, 1990

---

**2919**

**SARAH ORNE JEWETT**

## Lady Ferry and Other Uncanny People

(Ashcroft, British Columbia: Ash-Tree Press, 1998)

**Story type:** Horror (Collection)

**Summary:** Eleven tales of horror and the supernatural come from a well-known American regionalist writer of the late 19th century. The title story concerns an immortal woman. Other stories include the telepathy tale "The Green Bowl," the witchcraft story "In Dark New England Days," the curse story "The Landscape Chamber," and an allegory of death incarnate, "The Gray Man." With a preface by Joanna Russ and an introduction by Jessica Amanda Salmonson, who edited the book.

**Other books you might like:**
Gertrude Atherton, *The Bell in the Fog and Other Stories*, 1905
Olivia Howard Dunbar, *The Shell of Sense*, 1996
Hildegarde Hawthorne, *Faded Garden: The Collected Ghost Stories of Hildegarde Hawthorne*, 1985
Elia Peattie, *The Shape of Fear and Other Ghostly Tales*, 1898
Harriet Beecher Stowe, *Old Town Fireside Stories*, 1871

---

**2920**

### JAMES B. JOHNSON

## Habu

(New York: DAW Books, 1989)

**Story type:** Science Fiction (Immortality)
**Major character(s):** Reuben Flood, Scientist, Military Personnel
**Time period(s):** Indeterminate Future
**Locale(s):** Snister, Planet—Imaginary

**Summary:** A longevity treatment is discovered that not only prolongs life but supposedly removes all physical and psychological defects. Reuben Flood, who helped create the treatment, also fixed the system so that his personality won't be altered. Unknown to him there lurks within his sub-conscious the persona of Habu, a vigilante berserker who the authorities have sought for centuries.

**Other books you might like:**
Joe Haldeman, *Buying Time*, 1989
Robert A. Heinlein, *Time Enough for Love*, 1973
Frederik Pohl, *Drunkard's Walk*, 1960
Robert Silverberg, *The Book of Skulls*, 1971
Norman Spinrad, *Bug Jack Barron*, 1969
Jack Vance, *To Live Forever*, 1956
Roger Zelazny, *This Immortal*, 1966

---

**2921**

### JAMES B. JOHNSON

## A World Lost

(New York: DAW, 1991)

**Story type:** Science Fiction (Adventure; First Contact)
**Major character(s):** Rollingham Boregard ''Rusty'' Wallace, Spaceship Captain; Marion Zarnicke, Journalist; Sunday A. Sunday, Administrator (Galacticon Central)
**Time period(s):** Indeterminate Future
**Locale(s):** Roanoke, Planet—Imaginary (Sector VIII Galactic Plex Net Headquarters)

**Summary:** Rusty Wallace, one of the few remaining spacemen, returns to Roanoke to find that the planet and its sun disappeared, leaving only one clue, a fragment of a message from his father about a deadline of 100 days. When he discovers that the Plex beacon is also gone, Rusty travels to Plex Central for help where he discovers that the disappearance of the third generation population of Roanoke is unimportant to the D'Earnhardt bureaucrats. They are in need of a spaceship captain and ship to replace a Plex beacon, allowing the rescue of Lequinto's cut-off billions.

**Other books you might like:**
Roger MacBride Allen, *The Ring of Charon*, 1990
Lois McMaster Bujold, *Shards of Honor*, 1986
Ron Goulart, *The Chameleon Corps*, 1972
Mike Resnick, *Second Contact*, 1990
David Alexander Smith, *Rendezvous*, 1988

L. Neil Smith, *The Probability Broach*, 1980
E.C. Tubb, *Toyman*, 1969

---

**2922**

### KIJ JOHNSON
### GREG COX, Co-Author

## Dragon's Honor

(New York: Pocket, 1996)

**Story type:** Science Fiction (First Contact; Space Opera)
**Series:** Star Trek: The Next Generation
**Major character(s):** Jean-Luc Picard, Spaceship Captain, Military Personnel; Beverly Crusher, Doctor, Space Explorer
**Time period(s):** 24th century
**Locale(s):** Pai, Planet—Imaginary; Dragon Empire, Interstellar Empire/Federation; *U.S.S. Enterprise*, Spaceship

**Summary:** The Dragon Empire plans to end its civil war by marrying the son of the Emperor to the daughter of the opposition leader, thus preparing the way for Federation membership. As honored guests at the wedding, Picard and the *Enterprise* crew want to ensure that all goes smoothly, despite lingering feuds, a reluctant bride, and assassination attempts since, if the emperor does not sign the treaty, the Federation cannot protect his planet from the invading G'kkau. First novel by Johnson.

**Other books you might like:**
C.J. Cherryh, *Foreigner*, 1994
Greg Cox, *Devil in the Sky*, 1995
    John Gregory Betancourt, co-author
Gene DeWeese, *The Peacekeepers*, 1988
Brad Ferguson, *The Last Stand*, 1995
Rebecca Neason, *Guises of the Mind*, 1993
Elizabeth Ann Scarborough, *The Harem of Aman Akbar*, 1984
Howard Weinstein, *The Covenant of the Crown*, 1981

---

**2923**

### NORMA TADLOCK JOHNSON

## The Witch House

(New York: Avon Camelot, 1990)

**Story type:** Fantasy (Light Fantasy; Young Adult)
**Major character(s):** Guinevere Jones, Child; Great Aunt Maybelle, Spirit (ghost)
**Time period(s):** 1980s
**Locale(s):** Seattle, Washington

**Summary:** Guinevere and her siblings must convince their father to sell their newly inherited mansion to the historical society to satisfy the ghost of Great Aunt Maybelle. In the process of dealing with Maybelle's ghost, the three children and their parents learn to get along better as a family.

**Other books you might like:**
Penelope Lively, *The Ghost of Thomas Kempe*, 1973
Patricia A. McKillip, *The House on Parchment Street*, 1973
Phyllis Reynolds Naylor, *Bernie and the Bessledorf Ghost*, 1990
Richard Peck, *The Ghost Belonged to Me*, 1975

## 2924

**OLIVER JOHNSON**

### The Forging of the Shadows

(New York: Roc, 1997)

**Story type:** Fantasy (Sword and Sorcery; Political)
**Series:** Lightbringer Trilogy
**Major character(s):** Jayal, Nobleman, Hero, Knight; Thalassa, Prostitute, Heroine; Uthred of Ravenspur, Religious, Wizard
**Time period(s):** Indeterminate
**Locale(s):** Thrull, Fictional City; Fictional Country

**Summary:** Seven years after the High Priest of the God of Darkness plunges Thrull into an era of shadow, unleashing his undead hoards against the populace, three champions of the God of Light seek a way to return the city of the God of Light to peace and prosperity. First novel, first of a trilogy.

**Other books you might like:**
Terry Goodkind, *Wizard's First Rule*, 1994
J.V. Jones, *The Baker's Boy*, 1995
J. Gregory Keyes, *The Waterborn*, 1996
Douglas Niles, *A Breach in the Watershed*, 1995
J.R.R. Tolkien, *The Fellowship of the Ring*, 1954

## 2925

**OLIVER JOHNSON**

### Nations of the Night

(New York: Roc, 1998)

**Story type:** Fantasy (Sword and Sorcery; Political)
**Series:** Lightbringer Trilogy
**Major character(s):** Thalassa, Heroine; Uthred, Religious; Jayal, Knight, Nobleman, Hero
**Time period(s):** Indeterminate
**Locale(s):** Fictional Country

**Summary:** To reverse the darkening of the sun, Thalassa journeys into the unknown north, home of deadly and magical enemies. Bitten by the Dead in Life, Thalassa must hurry to find the man of bronze who will help defeat the darkness. Second in trilogy.

**Other books you might like:**
Lynn Flewelling, *Luck in the Shadows*, 1997
Terry Goodkind, *Wizard's First Rule*, 1994
J.V. Jones, *The Baker's Boy*, 1995
J. Gregory Keyes, *The Waterborn*, 1996
Douglas Niles, *A Breach in the Watershed*, 1995

## 2926

**WILLIAM W. JOHNSTONE**

### Bats

(New York: Zebra, 1993)

**Story type:** Horror (Nature in Revolt)
**Major character(s):** Johnny MacBride, Military Personnel (retired); Mark Hayden, Police Officer (state trooper); Blair Perkins, Professor, Veterinarian
**Time period(s):** 1990s (1993)
**Locale(s):** Catahoula, Louisiana

**Summary:** A mutant species of giant vampire bats from South America makes its way north of the American border, spreading rabies among lunatic Satanists, who welcome the creatures as a sign from the devil, and threatening to overrun the United States.

**Other books you might like:**
Martin Cruz Smith, *Nightwing*, 1977
T.W. Stetson, *Night Beasts*, 1993
Robert Charles Wilson, *Second Fire*, 1993

## 2927

**WILLIAM W. JOHNSTONE**

### Carnival

(New York: Zebra, 1989)

**Major character(s):** Martin Holland, Political Figure (Mayor); Linda Holland, Teenager (Martin's daughter)
**Time period(s):** 1980s
**Locale(s):** Holland, Nebraska

**Summary:** Shortly after Nebo's Carnival of Dread comes to town, the killings begin. Mayor Holland and his daughter search for the source and nature of the carnival's terrible powers before it overwhelms the entire town.

**Other books you might like:**
Dean R. Koontz, *Twilight Eyes*, 1987
Richard Laymon, *Funland*, 1990
Alan Ryan, *Dead White*, 1983

## 2928

**WILLIAM W. JOHNSTONE**

### Cat's Eye

(New York: Zebra, 1989)

**Story type:** Horror (Ancient Evil Unleashed)
**Major character(s):** Daphne "Dee" Conner, Writer (Romance novels); Carl Garrett, Detective—Private
**Time period(s):** 1980s
**Locale(s):** Reeves County, Virginia (In the Blue Ridge Mountains)

**Summary:** Strange creatures, led by Anya and Pet, two shapeshifting demons, emerge from the wooded area surrounding Dee Conner's house and terrorize the countryside as they prepare the way for the return of the Devil. Only Carl Garrett, who as a young boy survived a similar seige, can organize the uncorrupted locals into the fighting force necessary to face and defeat Satan and his cohorts.

**Other books you might like:**
Rick Hautala, *Moon Walker*, 1989
Bentley Little, *The Revelation*, 1990

## 2929

**WILLIAM W. JOHNSTONE**

### Darkly the Thunder

(New York: Zebra, 1990)

**Story type:** Horror (Ancient Evil Unleashed)
**Major character(s):** Reed "Sand" Saunders, Disembodied Personality; Al Watt, Lawman (retired sheriff); Richard Jennings, Disembodied Personality
**Time period(s):** 1980s
**Locale(s):** Willowdale, Colorado; Thunder, Colorado (a ghost town above Willowdale)

**Summary:** When Willowdale sheriff Al Watt killed Reed "Sand" Saunders for taking the law into his own hands, the balance of good and evil in the universal Force was upset. Now, 30 years later, a malignant presence called The Fury has taken over Willowdale, and only Sand's discorporate soul can save the town.

**Other books you might like:**
Douglas Clegg, *Goat Dance*, 1989
Matthew J. Costello, *Beneath Still Waters*, 1989
Charles L. Grant, *The Nestling*, 1982
T.E.D. Klein, *The Ceremonies*, 1984
Bentley Little, *The Revelation*, 1990

## **2930**

### WILLIAM W. JOHNSTONE

## *The Devil's Laughter*

(New York: Zebra, 1992)

**Story type:** Horror (Black Magic)
**Major character(s):** Lincoln ''Link'' Donovan, Journalist; Ray Ingalls, Police Officer (sheriff); Anne Brooks, Veterinarian
**Time period(s):** 1990s
**Locale(s):** LaGrange, Louisiana

**Summary:** In this right-wing survivalist manifesto, a series of animal deaths and human sacrifices in LaGrange convince animal-loving CIA-operative-turned-newspaper-reporter Link Donovan that a coven of devil worshippers are gearing up for the coming millenium. Link determines to break the Satanic conspiracy that has seduced many of the town's teenagers and appears to be controlled by some of the most influential persons in LaGrange.

**Other books you might like:**
Roger Elwood, *Sorcerers of Sodom*, 1991
Charles L. Grant, *The Hour of the Oxrun Dead*, 1977
Pat Graversen, *The Fagin*, 1982

## **2931**

### WILLIAM W. JOHNSTONE

## *Night Mask*

(New York: Zebra, 1994)

**Story type:** Horror (Serial Killer)
**Major character(s):** Leo Franks, Police Officer; Lani Prejean, Police Officer; Dick Hale, Radio (station manager)
**Time period(s):** 1990s (1994)
**Locale(s):** La Barca, California

**Summary:** Investigating a series of grisly murders in which the perpetrator, referred to as ''The Ripper,'' dismembers the bodies and takes the faces of his victims, two police officers discover that the trail leads back over decades, and across the country, to a family of evil people, who lure their victims by encoding tapes played at the local radio station with subliminal messages.

**Other books you might like:**
Robert Bloch, *Night of the Ripper*, 1984
Thomas Harris, *The Silence of the Lambs*, 1988
Roxanne Longstreet, *Red Angel*, 1994
Michael Slade, *Cutthroat*, 1992

## **2932**

### WILLIAM W. JOHNSTONE

## *Prey*

(New York: Pinnacle, 1996)

**Story type:** Horror (Mystery)
**Major character(s):** Barry Cantrell, Immortal (aka Vald Dumitru Radu); Stormy Knight, Journalist; John Ravenna, Criminal (assassin)
**Time period(s):** 1990s (1996)
**Locale(s):** Arkansas; Washington, District of Columbia

**Summary:** Barry Cantrell, ''the world's consummate and eternal warrior,'' has fought for centuries to preserve the freedom of the individual. When a plot is hatched by his archnemesis Robert Roche to dismantle the government through a series of political assassinations, Barry leaves his refuge in northern Arkansas to take on assassin John Ravenna, ''the pure personification of evil.''

**Other books you might like:**
Mark A. Kostrubula, *Dark Legacy*, 1996
Robert Weinberg, *The Dead Man's Kiss*, 1994
Dennis Wheatley, *They Used Dark Forces*, 1964

## **2933**

### WILLIAM W. JOHNSTONE

## *Rockabilly Hell*

(New York: Zebra, 1995)

**Story type:** Horror (Ghost Story)
**Major character(s):** Jesse ''Cole'' Younger, Police Officer (Deputy); Katti Baylor, Journalist; Jim Deaton, Detective—Private
**Time period(s):** 1990s (1995)
**Locale(s):** Memphis, Tennessee; Alaska

**Summary:** An experience at a ghostly roadhouse on Route 61 induces Cole Younger to investigate the disappearance and deaths of over 500 people along that road in the past 25 years. Cole and his accomplices find their efforts hindered by local officials engaged in a satanic conspiracy who have used the roadhouse ghosts to dispose of people who would prove a personal or political embarrassment to them.

**Other books you might like:**
Ruby Jean Jensen, *The Haunting*, 1994
Abigail McDaniels, *Dead Voices*, 1994
Abigail McDaniels, *The Uprising*, 1994

## **2934**

### WILLIAM W. JOHNSTONE

## *Rockabilly Limbo*

(New York: Zebra, 1996)

**Story type:** Horror (Apocalyptic Horror; Science Fiction)
**Major character(s):** Jesse ''Cole'' Younger, Police Officer (sheriff); Katti Baylor, Writer; Hank Milam, Religious (priest)
**Time period(s):** 1990s (1996)
**Locale(s):** Memphis, Tennessee

**Summary:** In this sequel to *Rockabilly Hell*, Sheriff Cole Younger and his troupe of libertarian comrades struggle to survive in a world where the breakdown of the moral order has plunged the United States and other countries into godless anarchy. With the discovery that space aliens have helped engineer the chaos in order to purge the planet of its ills, Cole becomes instrumental in establishing a new world order.

**Other books you might like:**
Pauline Dunn, *The Crawling Dark*, 1991
Stephen King, *The Stand*, 1978
Dean R. Koontz, *Phantoms*, 1983

---

## 2935

### WILLIAM W. JOHNSTONE

## Them

(New York: Zebra, 1992)

**Story type:** Horror (Science Fiction)
**Major character(s):** Jake Silver, Teenager; Charles Massenet, Doctor; Cag, Alien
**Time period(s):** 1990s (1992)
**Locale(s):** Sandy Run, Louisiana

**Summary:** Abused by his boorish father, betrayed by his ineffectual mother, and misunderstood by his malicious classmates, Jake Silver befriends Cag, an alien from outer space who promises to endow the boy with powers that will allow him to get back at his enemies, and thereby pave the way for an invasion of Earth by extraterrestrials.

**Other books you might like:**
Ray Garton, *Crucifax Autumn*, 1988
Charles L. Grant, *The Pet*, 1986
K.W. Jeter, *The Night Man*, 1990
J. Michael Straczynski, *OtherSyde*, 1990

---

## 2936

### WILLIAM W. JOHNSTONE

## Watchers in the Woods

(New York: Zebra, 1991)

**Story type:** Horror (Nature in Revolt)
**Major character(s):** Susan Benning Dalton, Housewife; Tom Dalton, Spouse (of Susan); Matt Jordan, Spy (ex-CIA agent)
**Time period(s):** 1990s (1997)
**Locale(s):** Great Primitive Area, Idaho

**Summary:** Things get a tad prickly for the Denver Class of '67 when a post-reunion camping trip in the wilderness of Idaho brings them face to face with the white supremacist group that goes by the name of Citizens for White America, and the Sataws, a band of primitive human beings whose years in the wilds have nurtured a taste for human flesh.

**Other books you might like:**
Joseph A. Citro, *The Unseen*, 1990
John Farris, *Fiends*, 1990
John Farris, *Wildwood*, 1987
T. Chris Martindale, *Where the Chill Waits*, 1991

---

## 2937

### GARY JONAS

## Curse of the Magazine Killers

(Owasso, Oklahoma: Ozark Triangle Press, 1998)

**Story type:** Horror (Collection)

**Summary:** A collection of four horror and fantasy stories that were accepted by small press magazines but never published because the magazines discontinued publication with the stories in inventory. In

"Maternal Instinct," a young mother's probable insanity manifests as a disembodied voice she hears over a baby monitor. "In League" concerns a rock band whose music opens a doorway to a dark dimension. "Broken Spirits" is a sword-and-sorcery story and "She Ain't Ready for My Lovin'" a horror-crime hybrid. The author supplies an introduction and story notes.

**Other books you might like:**
P.D. Cacek, *Leavings*, 1998
Brian Hopkins, *Something Haunts Us All*, 1995
Jeffrey Osier, *Driftglider and Other Stories*, 1994
Newton E. Streeter, *Noise and Other Night Terrors*, 1998
David Niall Wilson, *The Fall of the House of Escher and Other Illusions*, 1995

---

## 2938

### GARY JONAS

## Nice Guys Finish Last

(Owasso, Oklahoma: Ozark Triangle Press, 1997)

**Story type:** Horror (Witchcraft)
**Major character(s):** Eugene Smith, Young Man; Fat Woman, Witch
**Time period(s):** 1990s (1997)
**Locale(s):** United States

**Summary:** A man seeks out a witch for supernatural interventions to improve his love life, but all of the scenarios she sketches out, though perceptive in regard to the differences between men and women, are ironically unappealing. Signed limited edition chapbook with an introduction by the author.

**Other books you might like:**
Edward Bryant, *Fetish*, 1991
Glen E. Cox, *Going Mobile*, 1993
Norman Partridge, *Spyder*, 1995
Byron Preiss, *The Ultimate Witch*, 1993
John Betancourt, co-editor
Robert Weinberg, *100 Wicked Little Witch Stories*, 1996
Stefan Dziemianowicz and Martin H. Greenberg, co-editors

---

## 2939

### COURTWAY JONES

## In the Shadow of the Oak King

(New York: Pocket, 1991)

**Story type:** Fantasy (Legend)
**Series:** Dragon's Heirs
**Major character(s):** Arthur, Royalty (King of the Britons); Pelleas, Telepath, Companion; Myrddin, Artisan (master smith), Guardian (Arthur and Pelleas's)
**Time period(s):** 5th century
**Locale(s):** England

**Summary:** Saving Pelleas from Druid sacrifice, Myrddin becomes Pelleas's then Arthur's guardian. The clever smith constructs a device which will allow Arthur to remove the embedded sword from its anvil. After Arthur is recognized as King of the Britons, his task of uniting the island's diverse peoples begins. First novel.

**Other books you might like:**
Marion Zimmer Bradley, *The Mists of Avalon*, 1983
Gillian Bradshaw, *Hawk of May*, 1980
Gillian Bradshaw, *In Winter's Shadow*, 1982
Gillian Bradshaw, *Kingdom of Summer*, 1981
Sharan Newman, *Guinevere*, 1981
Persia Woolley, *Child of the Northern Spring*, 1987

Persia Woolley, *Guinevere: The Legend in Autumn*, 1991
Persia Woolley, *Queen of the Summer Stars*, 1990

## **2940**

### COURTWAY JONES

## *Witch of the North*

(New York: Pocket Books, 1992)

**Story type:** Fantasy (Legend)
**Series:** Dragon's Heirs
**Major character(s):** Morgan le Fey, Royalty; Arthur, Royalty (High King of the Britons); Guenevere, Royalty, Spouse
**Time period(s):** 5th century (453-488)
**Locale(s):** Scotland; Camelot, England

**Summary:** Holding Arthur's father responsible for the death of her father, Morgan swears revenge. Reaffirming her pledge of revenge at the time of her marriage to a Pictish king, Morgan goes about building a haven for his children, her followers and the widows from Arthur's wars. In Scotland and at Camelot Morgan continues to carry through her revenge upon Arthur.

**Other books you might like:**
Marion Zimmer Bradley, *The Mists of Avalon*, 1983
Gillian Bradshaw, *Hawk of May*, 1980
Gillian Bradshaw, *Kingdom of Summer*, 1981
Mary Stewart, *The Wicked Day*, 1983
Persia Woolley, *Guinevere: The Legend in Autumn*, 1991
Persia Woolley, *Queen of the Summer Stars*, 1990

## **2941**

### DAVID LEE JONES

## *Unicorn Highway*

(New York: Avon, 1992)

**Story type:** Fantasy (Quest; Young Adult)
**Major character(s):** Thaddeus "Thaddy" Williams, Child, Adventurer; Mr. Tucker, Aged Person; Infinity, Mythical Creature (unicorn)
**Time period(s):** 1940s (1947)
**Locale(s):** Kansas

**Summary:** After hearing that Mr. Tucker saw a unicorn on his land, Thaddy Williams decides that he must ride the creature. As government agents attempt to capture the unicorn, which they believe threatens the country, Thaddy works to accomplish his goal despite the dangerous nightmare, the Wolf, which lurks near the unicorn. Author's first novel.

**Other books you might like:**
Jack Dann, *Unicorns!*, 1982
   Gardner Dozois, co-editor
Jack Dann, *Unicorns II*, 1992
   Gardner Dozois, co-editor
John Lee, *The Unicorn Dilemma*, 1988
John Lee, *The Unicorn Quest*, 1986
John Lee, *The Unicorn Solution*, 1991
Tanith Lee, *Black Unicorn*, 1991

## **2942**

### DAVID LEE JONES

## *Zeus and Co.*

(New York: AvoNova, 1993)

**Story type:** Fantasy (Contemporary; Urban)
**Major character(s):** Cyrus "Cy" Lance Major, Computer Expert, Sports Figure (surfer); Erato, Mythical Creature (muse); Janet Stewart, Computer Expert, Businesswoman
**Time period(s):** 1990s
**Locale(s):** California

**Summary:** Just before the end of his shift at midnight, Cy receives a peculiar message from an unknown, unauthorized file. Drawn to Erato waiting at the bus stop, Cy learns that her sister, Euterpe, imprisoned in his computer at work, must be freed within a week or their father, Zeus, will show his displeasure. Unfortunately Erato must first convince Cy and his employers that her sister's entrapment compels their help and that the new invention under development remains safe.

**Other books you might like:**
Emma Bull, *War for the Oaks*, 1987
Tom Deitz, *Soulsmith*, 1991
Parke Godwin, *Waiting for the Galactic Bus*, 1988
Robert A. Heinlein, *Job: A Comedy of Justice*, 1984
Nina Kiriki Hoffman, *The Thread That Binds the Bones*, 1993
Terry Pratchett, *Wyrd Sisters*, 1990
Lawrence Watt-Evans, *The Rebirth of Wonder*, 1992
David Weber, *Path of the Fury*, 1992

## **2943**

### DIANA WYNNE JONES

## *Aunt Maria*

(New York: Greenwillow, 1991)

**Story type:** Fantasy (Contemporary; Young Adult)
**Major character(s):** Naomi "Mig" Margaret Laker, Teenager, Writer; Aunt Maria, Magician; Antony Green, Spirit
**Time period(s):** 1990s (1991)
**Locale(s):** Cranbury-on-the-Sea, England

**Summary:** Mig, Chris and their mother go visit Aunt Maria over Easter. She proves to be a demanding old woman who has most of the women of the town dancing attendance on her. When Chris is impudent, she turns him into a wolf. Mig tries to contact the ghost haunting the spare room to find out how to fix things before Aunt Maria can have Chris hunted down and killed. British edition is titled *Black Maria*.

**Other books you might like:**
Piers Anthony, *Virtual Mode*, 1991
Dale Estey, *A Lost Tale*, 1980
Alan Garner, *The Weirdstone of Brisingamen*, 1969
Andre Norton, *Octagon Magic*, 1967

## **2944**

### DIANA WYNNE JONES

## *Castle in the Air*

(New York: Greenwillow, 1991)

**Story type:** Fantasy (Light Fantasy; Magic Conflict)
**Series:** Howl's Moving Castle

**Major character(s):** Abdullah, Businessman (carpet merchant); Suliman, Wizard; Hasruel, Demon, Mythical Creature (djinn)
**Time period(s):** Indeterminate
**Locale(s):** Zanzib, Fictional Country (Sultinate); Rashpuht, Fictional Country (Sultinate)

**Summary:** After Abdullah acquires a magic flying carpet, he and his beloved Flower-in-the-Night are involved in a series of adventures and misadventures with good and bad djinn, wizards, stolen princesses, sultans and such.

**Other books you might like:**
Lloyd Alexander, *The Book of Three*, 1964
Edward Eager, *Half Magic*, 1954
Sherwood Smith, *Wren to the Rescue*, 1990
Robert Westall, *The Cats of Seroster*, 1984
Patricia C. Wrede, *Dealing with Dragons*, 1990
Janc Yolen, *Wizard's Hall*, 1991

---

**2945**

**DIANA WYNNE JONES**

## The Crown of Dalemark

(New York: Greenwillow, 1995)

**Story type:** Fantasy (Quest; Time Travel)
**Series:** Dalemark
**Major character(s):** Mayelbridwen "Maewen" Singer, Time Traveler; Alhammitt "Mitt" Alhammittson, Warrior, Leader; Wend Orilson, Immortal
**Time period(s):** Indeterminate Past
**Locale(s):** North Dalemark, Fictional Country

**Summary:** The Countess of Abereth sends Mitt to kill Noreth, daughter of the One who seeks to rule Dalemark. Sent two centuries back in time to replace Noreth, who disappeared, Maewen falls in love with Mitt. However, as evil powers assemble, Mitt must find and use the ring, the sword, and the cup to reunite Dalemark.

**Other books you might like:**
Poul Anderson, *A Midsummer Tempest*, 1974
Richard Cowper, *The Road to Corlay*, 1979
John M. Ford, *The Dragon Waiting*, 1983
Linda Haldeman, *The Lastborn of Elvinwood*, 1978
Clifford D. Simak, *The Fellowship of the Talisman*, 1978
Kathleen Sky, *Witchdame*, 1985
Melinda M. Snodgrass, *Queen's Gambit Declined*, 1989
Jack Vance, *Lyonesse*, 1983

---

**2946**

**DIANA WYNNE JONES**

## Dark Lord of Derkholm

(New York: Greenwillow, 1998)

**Story type:** Fantasy (Light Fantasy)
**Major character(s):** Derk, Wizard; Blade, Teenager, Wizard (novice)
**Time period(s):** Indeterminate
**Locale(s):** Mythical Place

**Summary:** Mr. Chesney's Pilgrim Parties have been wreaking havoc with almost every facet of society for decades, as has the threat of Mr. Chesney's powerful demon. When the snake-like Chancellor of Wizard's University consults both the Black and White Oracles, their advice leads to the appointment of animal-loving Derk as the tourist season's Dark Lord. Derk's serious run-in with an ancient dragon requires his human and griffin children to step in to avoid breaching the demon-backed contract with Chesney.

**Other books you might like:**
Robert Asprin, *Another Fine Myth*, 1978
Carolyn Cushman, *Witch and Wombat*, 1994
Alan Dean Foster, *The Hour of the Gate*, 1984
Alan Dean Foster, *Spellsinger*, 1983
Patricia C. Wrede, *Talking to Dragons*, 1985

---

**2947**

**DIANA WYNNE JONES**

## Everard's Ride

(Framingham, Massachusetts: NESFA Press, 1995)

**Story type:** Fantasy (Collection; Science Fiction)

**Summary:** Contains a one-page introduction by Patricia C. Wrede, two original novellas plus one article "The Shape of Narrative in *The Lord of the Rings*," and five stories published 1983-1990 in collections and anthologies. Set in an alternate universe, the title story features an adolescent protagonist in Victorian England. Other themes include an author's transition from typewriter to word processor, robotics, dragons, wolves, peacocks, and imprisonment.

**Other books you might like:**
Emma Bull, *Double Feature*, 1994
    Will Shetterly, co-author
Joe Haldeman, *Vietnam and Other Alien Worlds*, 1993
James H. Schmitz, *The Best of James H. Schmitz*, 1991
Cordwainer Smith, *The Rediscovery of Man*, 1993
Jane Yolen, *Storyteller*, 1992

---

**2948**

**DIANA WYNNE JONES**

## Hexwood

(New York: Greenwillow, 1994)

**Story type:** Science Fiction (Young Adult; Science Fantasy)
**Major character(s):** Ann Veronica Stavely, Child; Mordion "the Servant" Agenos, Martial Arts Expert (assassin), Criminal; Vierran, Servant, Revolutionary
**Time period(s):** 1990s
**Locale(s):** England; Homeworld, Planet—Imaginary

**Summary:** Investigating mysterious events at Hexwood Farm, Ann discovers Mordion and learns of the Bannus, an ancient alien device that manipulates reality. When its use threatens to hinder a power struggle on Homeworld, the Organization leaders, the five Reigners, rush to Earth to shut down the Bannus. Reigner Three brings Vierran to Earth, intending that she mate with the exiled Mordion to produce potential assassins for testing and training.

**Other books you might like:**
Gary L. Blackwood, *Beyond the Door*, 1991
A.C. Crispin, *V*, 1984
Alexander Key, *The Forgotten Door*, 1965
Madeleine L'Engle, *A Wrinkle in Time*, 1962
Denise Vitola, *Half-Light*, 1992

---

**2949**

**DIANA WYNNE JONES**

## The Ogre Downstairs

(New York: Greenwillow, 1990)

**Story type:** Fantasy (Light Fantasy; Contemporary)

**Major character(s):** Caspar, Teenager; Malcolm, Teenager; The Ogre, Parent
**Time period(s):** 20th century
**Locale(s):** England

**Summary:** The Ogre has married the mother of Caspar, Johnny and Gwinny, and he and his sons Malcolm and Douglas are making life miserable. Then he buys Malcolm and Caspar chemistry sets that turn out to have magical properties, and the kids are thrown together in their attempts to stay out of trouble. This book is a reissue of the 1974 edition.

**Other books you might like:**
L.M. Boston, *Children of Green Knowe*, 1954
Roald Dahl, *The Witches*, 1983
Diane Duane, *So You Want to Be a Wizard?*, 1983
Beatrice Gormley, *Mail-Order Wings*, 1981
Helen V. Griffith, *Journal of a Teenage Genius*, 1987
E.W. Hildick, *The Active-Enzyme Lemon-Freshened Junior High School Witch*, 1973
Pamela L. Travers, *Mary Poppins*, 1981

---

### 2950

#### DIANA WYNNE JONES

## A Sudden Wild Magic

(New York: Morrow, 1992)

**Story type:** Fantasy (Light Fantasy; Magic Conflict)
**Major character(s):** Gladys Naismith, Witch, Adventurer
**Time period(s):** 1990s
**Locale(s):** England; Arth, Planet—Imaginary (alternate universe)

**Summary:** When the benevolent society of witches and conjurers known as The Ring uncovers the scheme of evil mages from Arth, the Pentarch, to steal Earth technology and create catastrophes, Gladys and others combine forces in a guerilla attack on the Pentarch's fortress on Arth.

**Other books you might like:**
Gael Baudino, *Gossamer Axe*, 1990
Kyle Crocco, *Heroes, Inc.*, 1991
Suzette Haden Elgin, *And Then There'll Be Fireworks*, 1981
Suzette Haden Elgin, *The Grand Jubilee*, 1981
Suzette Haden Elgin, *Twelve Fair Kingdoms*, 1981
Neil Gaiman, *Good Omens: The Nice and Accurate Prophecies of Agnes Nutter, Witch*, 1990
Terry Pratchett, co-author

---

### 2951

#### DIANA WYNNE JONES

## The Time of the Ghost

(New York: Greenwillow, 1996)

**Story type:** Fantasy (Contemporary; Young Adult)
**Major character(s):** The Ghost, Spirit; Monigan, Deity; Cart, Teenager
**Time period(s):** 1990s
**Locale(s):** England

**Summary:** Drawn to a family operating a boardinghouse at a boy's school, a confused ghost attemps to determine her own identity. She must also discover the purpose of her existence and her relationship to Monigan before disaster befalls the family.

**Other books you might like:**
Eleanor Cameron, *The Court of the Stone Children*, 1973
Penelope Lively, *The Ghost of Thomas Kempe*, 1973

Margaret Mahy, *The Tricksters*, 1987
Phyllis Reynolds Naylor, *Bernie and the Bessledorf Ghost*, 1990
Susan Palwick, *Flying in Place*, 1992

---

### 2952

#### GWYNETH JONES

## Flowerdust

(New York: Tor, 1995)

**Story type:** Science Fiction (Political; Psychic Powers)
**Series:** Divine Endurance
**Major character(s):** Derveet, Revolutionary, Addict; Divine Endurance, Animal (cat), Android; Endang, Scholar (withdrawn), Slave
**Time period(s):** Indeterminate Future
**Locale(s):** Ranganar, Fictional City; The Peninsula, Fictional Country; Asia

**Summary:** In a Southeast Asia changed beyond recognition, native cultures struggle with disinterested rulers and their pawns. Aided by a diverse group of sympathizers, Derveet carries on the revolution through example and direct action.

**Other books you might like:**
Lisa Goldstein, *Tourists*, 1989
Marc Laidlaw, *Neon Lotus*, 1988
Ian McDonald, *The Broken Land*, 1992
Maureen F. McHugh, *China Mountain Zhang*, 1992
Geoff Ryman, *The Unconquered Country*, 1986

---

### 2953

#### GWYNETH JONES

## North Wind

(New York: Tor, 1996)

**Story type:** Science Fiction (First Contact; Invasion of Earth)
**Major character(s):** Goodlooking/Bella, Alien (Aleutian), Librarian; Sidney "Sid" Carton, Kidnapper, Adventurer; Clavel, Alien (Aleutian), Writer (poet)
**Time period(s):** 22nd century
**Locale(s):** Uji, Fictional City (alien enclave); Europe

**Summary:** Objecting to the Aleutian plan to modify Earth's climate by eliminating the Himalayas, both sides of the Gender War temporarily ally to eliminate the alien presence on Earth. As the aliens do not believe in permanent death, many die in the conflict. Meanwhile Sid kidnaps Bella for his employer who believes the librarian is key to finding the instantaneous space drive most people believe lost with the death of the inventor. Sequel to *White Queen*.

**Other books you might like:**
Octavia E. Butler, *Dawn*, 1987
L. Warren Douglas, *A Plague of Change*, 1992
Alis A. Rasmussen, *The Price of Ransom*, 1990
Amy Thomson, *The Color of Distance*, 1995
Ian Watson, *The Flies of Memory*, 1991

---

### 2954

#### GWYNETH JONES

## Phoenix Cafe

(New York: Tor, 1998)

**Story type:** Science Fiction (Invasion of Earth)

**Major character(s):** Catherine, Religious (missionary); Misha Connelly, Nobleman
**Time period(s):** Indeterminate Future
**Locale(s):** North America

**Summary:** The alien Aleutians have been on Earth for several generations and their presence has altered the economic, social, political, and religious structure of the human race. Catherine, a ward of one of the alien aristocrats, questions her role as a missionary to her own kind. The sexual tension between herself and Misha Connelly aggravates the situation as does the fact that the Aleutians are preparing to leave Earth.

**Other books you might like:**
John Brunner, *Age of Miracles*, 1973
Rob Chilson, *Men Like Rats*, 1989
C.S. Friedman, *The Madness Season*, 1990
Daniel F. Galouye, *Lords of the Psychon*, 1963
David Gerrold, *A Day for Damnation*, 1985

---

**2955**

### GWYNETH JONES

## *White Queen*

(New York: Tor, 1993)

**Story type:** Science Fiction (First Contact; Invasion of Earth)
**Major character(s):** Johnny Guglioli, Expatriate, Journalist; Braemer Wilson, Journalist; Elavel, Alien, Immortal
**Time period(s):** 2030s (2038)
**Locale(s):** Gerardville, Africa (West Africa); London, England

**Summary:** Johnny is exiled, falsely accused of being infected with QV, a virus that attacks the organic core of all American computers as well as humans. A pension for basic survival arrives monthly while Johnny outlives his expected death. He continually encounters a very strange girl whom he seeks out after recruitment by Braemer to help find the aliens reported in the area. Johnny must discover why aliens terrify and attract humans and if aliens and humans can be prevented from destroying each other as the telepathic aliens always recognize lies. Winner of James Tiptree award. Reprint of 1991 British edition.

**Other books you might like:**
Greg Bear, *The Forge of God*, 1987
Octavia E. Butler, *Dawn*, 1987
Pat Cadigan, *Synners*, 1991
Jean Mark Gawron, *Dream of Glass*, 1993
Damon Knight, *A Reasonable World*, 1991
Spider Robinson, *Stardance*, 1979
    Jeanne Robinson, co-author
Ian Watson, *The Flies of Memory*, 1991

---

**2956**

### J.V. JONES

## *The Baker's Boy*

(New York: Warner Aspect, 1995)

**Story type:** Fantasy (Political; Magic Conflict)
**Series:** Book of Words
**Major character(s):** Jack, Baker, Sorcerer; Melliandra ''Melli'', Noblewoman, Fiance(e); Baralis, Sorcerer, Traitor
**Time period(s):** Indeterminate
**Locale(s):** Castle Harvell, Mythical Place; Four Kingdoms, Fictional Country; Rorn, Fictional City

**Summary:** To forward his evil scheme of advancement, Baralis drafts the illiterate Jack to copy arcane books without understanding their content. When Jack's scribing eventually brings literacy and unconscious comprehension of sorcery, Jack flees Castle Harvell, meeting Melli in the forest as she runs from an unacceptable royal marriage. With royal guardsmen and Baralis' mercenaries in pursuit, the two youngsters hold little hope of happiness. First novel.

**Other books you might like:**
Lois McMaster Bujold, *The Spirit Ring*, 1992
Terry Goodkind, *Wizard's First Rule*, 1994
Laurell K. Hamilton, *Nightseer*, 1992
Robin Hobb, *Assassin's Apprentice*, 1995
Caroline Stevermer, *A College of Magics*, 1994
Paula Volsky, *Illusion*, 1992
Martha Wells, *The Element of Fire*, 1993

---

**2957**

### J.V. JONES

## *The Barbed Coil*

(New York: Warner Aspect, 1997)

**Story type:** Fantasy (Alternate World; Sword and Sorcery)
**Major character(s):** Tessa McCamfrey, Wizard; Ravis, Nobleman, Mercenary; Camron, Nobleman, Warrior
**Time period(s):** 1990s; Indeterminate
**Locale(s):** Bay'Zell, Fictional City; World of the Barbed Coil, Mythical Place

**Summary:** Transported to another world when she pricks herself with a newfound ring, Tessa discovers magical abilities associated with the ring. Lord Camron benefits from her abilities when he engages Ravis in his quest for vengeance for his father's death.

**Other books you might like:**
Tom Deitz, *Dreamseeker's Road*, 1995
Lynn Flewelling, *Luck in the Shadows*, 1996
Terry Goodkind, *Wizard's First Rule*, 1994
Patricia A. McKillip, *Winter Rose*, 1996
Patricia C. Wrede, *The Raven Ring*, 1994

---

**2958**

### J.V. JONES

## *A Man Betrayed*

(New York: Warner Aspect, 1996)

**Story type:** Fantasy (Magic Conflict; Political)
**Series:** Book of Words
**Major character(s):** Jack, Sorcerer, Hero; Melliandra ''Melli'', Noblewoman; Garon, Nobleman (Duke of Bren), Warrior
**Time period(s):** Indeterminate
**Locale(s):** Bren, Fictional City; Halcus, Fictional Country; Four Kingdoms, Fictional Country

**Summary:** Melli's attempt to avoid marriage to Prince Kylock leads to her capture and delivery into unexpected hands. While her father and the sorcerer Baralis jostle for influence over events, Archbishop Tavalisk of Rorn stirs up trouble. Meanwhile, thinking Melli dead, Jack seeks shelter with strangers and receives weapons training.

**Other books you might like:**
Terry Goodkind, *Stone of Tears*, 1995
Barbara Hambly, *Stranger at the Wedding*, 1994
Robin Hobb, *Assassin's Apprentice*, 1995
Katya Reimann, *Wind From a Foreign Sky*, 1996
Martha Wells, *The Element of Fire*, 1993

Salinda Tyson, *Wheel of Dreams*, 1996

## 2959

### J.V. JONES

## *Master and Fool*

(New York: Warner Aspect, 1996)

**Story type:** Fantasy (Magic Conflict; Political)
**Series:** Book of Words
**Major character(s):** Jack, Sorcerer, Hero; Baralis, Sorcerer, Traitor; Tawl, Knight
**Time period(s):** Indeterminate
**Locale(s):** Four Kingdoms, Fictional Country

**Summary:** Impelled by fate, prophecy and deception, Jack and his companions must elude assassins as they attempt to eliminate Larn's oracular powers while the psychotic usurper, Kylock, seeks conquest and the elimination of the kingdom's rightful heirs.

**Other books you might like:**
David Eddings, *Pawn of Prophecy*, 1982
Lynn Flewelling, *Luck in the Shadows*, 1996
Terry Goodkind, *Wizard's First Rule*, 1994
Robin Hobb, *Assassin's Apprentice*, 1995
J.R.R. Tolkien, *The Fellowship of the Ring*, 1954
Martha Wells, *The Element of Fire*, 1993

## 2960

### STEPHEN JONES, Editor
### DAVID SUTTON, Co-Editor

## *The Best Horror From Fantasy Tales*

(New York: Carroll and Graf, 1990)

**Story type:** Horror (Fantasy)

**Summary:** A collection of 20 stories, both new and old, from the pages of Britain's best known small press weird fiction magazine. Aside from a small number of vintage reprints from American pulp magazines, such as Fritz Leiber's "In the X-Ray" and Robert Bloch's "The Sorceror's Jewel," the majority of stories first appeared in the magazine and testify to its eclectic editorial policy. The best include Thomas Ligotti's tale of insanity, "The Frolic," Ramscy Campbell's Cthulhu Mythos Story "The Voice of the Beach," and Dennis Etchison's moody World Fantasy Award-winner "The Dark Country."

**Other books you might like:**
Peter Enfantino, *Quick Chills*, 1990
Stuart David Schiff, *Whispers: An Anthology of Fantasy and Horror*, 1977
David B. Silva, *Best of The Horror Show*, 1987

## 2961

### STEPHEN JONES, Editor
### RAMSEY CAMPBELL, Co-Editor

## *Best New Horror*

(New York: Carroll & Graf, 1990)

**Story type:** Horror (Anthology)
**Series:** Best New Horror

**Summary:** Twenty stories chosen from the amateur and professional press that accentuate the depth and diversity of the modern horror story. Robert Westall's "The Last Days of Miss Dorinda Molyneaux," a ghost story in the tradition of M.R. James, contrasts with Thomas Tessier's "Blanca," a modern spectral tale that grapples with third world political revolution. Nicholas Royle's oblique dark fantasy "Archway" is counterbalanced by Kim Newman's science fiction crossover "Technicolor Twitch." And Thomas Ligotti's insidiously disturbing "The Strange Design of Master Rignolo" stands at the opposite extreme from Richard Laymon's blatantly gross "Bad News."

**Other books you might like:**
Ellen Datlow, *The Year's Best Fantasy and Horror: Third Annual Collection*, 1990
   Terri Windling, co-author
Peter Enfantino, *Quick Chills*, 1990
Karl Edward Wagner, *The Year's Best Horror Stories XVIII*, 1990

## 2962

### STEPHEN JONES, Editor
### RAMSEY CAMPBELL, Co-Editor

## *Best New Horror 2*

(New York: Carroll & Graf, 1991)

**Story type:** Horror (Anthology)

**Summary:** Twenty-eight stories representing the best works of horror in Britain and America published in 1990. Included are three homages to the work of H.P. Lovecraft, Poppy Z. Brite's "His Mouth Shall Taste of Wormwood," Gene Wolfe's "Lord of the Land," and Thomas Ligotti's "The Last Feast of Harlequin"; Ray Garton's gory tale of a talk show host who gets his comeuppance, "Shock Radio"; impressionistic fantasies by Jonathan Carroll ("The Dead Love You") and Peter Straub ("A Short Guide to the City"); Elizabeth Massie's Bram Stoker Award-winning tale of grotesque love, "Stephen"; and F. Paul Wilson's tale of nature in revolt, "Pelts."

**Other books you might like:**
Ellen Datlow, *The Year's Best Fantasy and Horror: Fourth Annual Collection*, 1991
   Terri Windling, co-editor
Robert Morrish, *Quick Chills II*, 1992
   Peter Enfantino, co-editor
Karl Edward Wagner, *The Year's Best Horror Stories XIX*, 1991
   editor

## 2963

### STEPHEN JONES, Editor
### RAMSEY CAMPBELL, Co-Editor

## *Best New Horror 4*

(New York: Carroll & Graf, 1993)

**Story type:** Horror (Anthology)
**Series:** Best New Horror

**Summary:** The editors collect 24 of the best horror stories published in 1992, along with a survey of the year in horror. Included are Peter Straub's World Fantasy Award winning "The Ghost Village," an excerpt from his novel *The Throat*; Scott Edelman's metafictional rumination on why we read horror fiction, "The Suicide Artist"; Thomas Ligotti's tale of the horrors inside a run down movie theatre, "The Glamour"; Kim Newman's "Red Reign," a vampire novella that grew into his alternate history *Anno-Dracula*; Douglas Winter's postmodern zombie tale, "Bright Lights, Big Zombie"; Steve Rasnic Tem's tale of Lovecraftian horror, "The Mirror Man"; two ghostly tales, Clive Barker's "The Departed" and Les Daniels' "The Little Green Ones"; and two powerful tales of urban horror,

Poppy Z. Brite's ''How to Get Ahead in New York'' and Joel Lane's ''And Some Are Missing.''

**Other books you might like:**
Ellen Datlow, *The Year's Best Fantasy and Horror: Sixth Annual Collection*, 1993
  Terri Windling, co-editor
Karl Edward Wagner, *The Year's Best Horror Stories XXI*, 1993
  editor

---

**2964**

**STEPHEN JONES**, Editor

## Best New Horror 6
(New York: Carroll & Graf, 1995)

**Story type:** Horror (Anthology)

**Summary:** This sixth annual volume brings together 22 British and American horror stories chosen by the editor as the best short fiction of 1994. Included are Robert Bloch's Stoker Award-winning ''A Scent of Vinegar,'' about a strange species of vampires that live in an abandoned Hollywood whorehouse; Brian Hodge's ''The Alchemy of the Throat,'' about a castrato taken in by a vampire patron; Norman Partridge's ''Harvest,'' in which radiation sickness fosters gruesome terrors in a southwestern town; Terry Lamsley's ''Blade and Bone,'' a traditional ghostly tale; Ramsey Campbell's ''The Alternative,'' in which a middleclass businessman is overwhelmed by the feeling that he is a destitute person imagining himself living a life of comparative luxury; and Esther M. Friesner's narrative poem ''Lovers.'' The author supplies an informative introduction, and Kim Newman assists in compiling the book's annual necrology. This is the first volume in the series for which Ramsey Campbell does not serve as co-editor.

**Other books you might like:**
Ellen Datlow, *The Year's Best Fantasy and Horror: Eighth Annual Collection*, 1995
  Terri Windling, co-editor
Karl Edward Wagner, *The Year's Best Horror Stories Series*, 1979-1994
  editor

---

**2965**

**STEPHEN JONES**, Editor
**DAVID SUTTON**, Co-Editor

## Fantasy Tales #2
(New York: Carroll & Graf, 1990)

**Story type:** Horror (Anthology; Fantasy)

**Summary:** This issue of Jones and Sutton's bi-annual illustrated anthology of original horror fiction, a reprint of the *Fantasy Tales 5* (Autumn 1990), contains 12 stories (and one poem), including a sensitive tale of adolescent infatuation and loss by Roberta Lannes, a sword-and sorcery pastiche by Ramsey Campbell, a satire of eighties corporate amorality in yuppiedom by David Schow, and a witty riff on the Frankenstein motif by Garry Kilworth.

**Other books you might like:**
Dennis Etchison, *Cutting Edge*, 1986
Kirby McCauley, *Dark Forces*, 1980
Kirby McCauley, *Frights*, 1976
Kirby McCauley, *Night Chills*, 1975
Douglas E. Winter, *Prime Evil*, 1988

---

**2966**

**STEPHEN JONES**, Editor
**DAVID SUTTON**, Co-Editor

## Fantasy Tales #4
(New York: Carroll & Graf, 1991)

**Story type:** Horror (Anthology; Fantasy)

**Summary:** Nine tales of horror and fantasy and two poems make up this trade paperback incarnation of Britain's long-running magazine. Included are Kathryn Ptacek's ''Living to the End,'' about a man who has cheated death; Tom Ligotti's metaphysical nightmare, ''The Medusa''; Tom Monteleone's tale of a man who tries to change his life as it flashes before his eyes, ''Rehearsals''; and a reprint of Ramsey Campbell's rare sword and sorcery tale, ''The Pit of Wings.''

**Other books you might like:**
George Hatch, *Guignoir and Other Furies*, 1991
Stuart David Schiff, *The Whispers Series*, 1977-1987
David B. Silva, *Best of The Horror Show*, 1987

---

**2967**

**STEPHEN JONES**, Editor
**DAVID SUTTON**, Co-Editor

## Fantasy Tales #6
(New York: Carroll & Graf, 1991)

**Story type:** Horror (Anthology; Fantasy)

**Summary:** Ten stories of horror and fantasy, two poems and one essay from Britain's trade paperback equivalent of America's *Weird Tales*. Included are Neil Gaiman's ''Foreign Parts,'' about a man whose sexual repression is manifested as an organic disease; Kim Newman's hardboiled horror story, ''Mother Hen''; R. Chetwynd-Hayes' SF-horror tale, ''Devil's Child''; and Thomas Ligotti's ''The Spectacles in the Drawer,'' about a joke that backfires upon its perpetrator with nightmarish results.

**Other books you might like:**
Norman Partridge, *Guignoir*, 1991
Kristine Kathryn Rusch, *The Best of Pulphouse: The Hardback Magazine*, 1991
Elizabeth A. Saunders, *When the Black Lotus Blooms*, 1990

---

**2968**

**STEPHEN JONES**, Editor
**DAVE CARSON**, Co-Editor

## H.P. Lovecraft's Book of Horror
(New York: Barnes & Noble, 1993)

**Story type:** Horror (Anthology)

**Summary:** This anthology reprints as its introduction H.P. Lovecraft's groundbreaking 1933 eassy, ''Supernatural Horror Literature,'' and collects 21 classic tales of horror and the supernatural singled out for excellence therein. Included are three tales of invisible monsters, William Hope Hodgson's ''The Hog,'' Ambrose Bierce's ''The Damned Thing,'' and Guy de Maupassant's ''The Horla''; Rudyard Kipling's Tale of atavistic transformation, ''The Mark of the Beast''; two gruesome supernatural revenge stories, Irvin S. Cobb's ''Fishhead'' and Edward Lucas White's ''Lukundoo''; four stories of ineluctable supernatural fates, M.R. James's ''Count Magnus,'' Charles Dickens's ''The Haunted Signalman,'' Robert W. Chambers' ''The Yellow Sign,'' and Clark Ashton Smith's ''The Double Shadow''; Edgar Allan Poe's rendering of the haunted house as a psychological allegory, ''The Fall of the House of Usher''; and Arthur Machen's tale of the unholy union between a mortal woman and an immortal deity, ''The Great God Pan.'' The book is illustrated by Carson.

**Other books you might like:**

Alexander Laing, *The Haunted Omnibus*, 1937
  editor
Philip Van Doren Stern, *The Midnight Reader*, 1942
  editor
Dennis Wheatley, *A Century of Horror Stories*, 1935
  editor
Herbert Wise, *Great Tales of Terror and the Supernatural*, 1944
  Phyllis Fraser, co-editor

---

**2969**

STEPHEN JONES, Editor

## The Mammoth Book of Best New Horror
(New York: Carroll & Graf, 1996)

**Story type:** Horror (Anthology)

**Summary:** A retitling of the *Best New Horror* series, this seventh volume in the series collects 26 of the best stories published in 1995. Among them are the novelette version of Brian Stableford's ''The Hunger and Ecstasy of Vampires,'' a futuristic vampire tale written as a Wellsian scientific romance; Jane Rice's ''The Sixth Dog,'' about a strange house which humans enter but only dogs leave; Brian Hodge's ''Extinctions in Paradise,'' about third-world werewolves; Steve Rasnic Tem's ''100 Wicked Little Witches,'' in which a man blames his every misfortune on imagined supernatural beings; Terry Lamsley's ''The Toddler,'' about a phantom child; Graham Masterton's ''The Grey Madonna,'' a ghost story in the M.R. James tradition; and Norman Partridge's ''The Bars on Satan's Jailhouse,'' a mix of horror, crime, and western fiction. The editor supplies an insightful introduction summing up the year in horror, and Kim Newman supplies a ''Necrology'' for 1995.

**Other books you might like:**

Ellen Datlow, *The Year's Best Fantasy and Horror: Ninth Annual Collection*, 1996
  Terri Windling, co-editor
Karl Edward Wagner, *The Year's Best Horror Stories Series*, 1979-1994
  editor

---

**2970**

STEPHEN JONES, Editor

## The Mammoth Book of Best New Horror 8
(New York: Carroll & Graf, 1997)

**Story type:** Horror (Anthology)

**Summary:** Twenty-five stories selected from the British and American professional and semi-professional press representing the best horror fiction published in 1996. Stand-out selections include Douglas Clegg's ''Underworld,'' a tale of grief and loss that resolves in supernatural experience; Poppy Z. Brite's ''Mussolini and the Axeman's Jazz,'' about a serial killer on the streets of New Orleans; Donald Burleson's ''Hopscotch,'' in which a childhood game proves a doorway to a dark dimension; Gregory Frost's ''The Blissful Height,'' set during the spiritualist craze of the late nineteenth century; Scott Edelman's ''A Plague on Both Your Houses,'' a zombie

story written as a Shakespearian verse tragedy; and Terry Lamsley's vampire tale, ''The Break.'' Jones contributes an introductory survey of the horror field in 1996 and, with Kim Newman, a necrology of deceased horror personnel for the year.

**Other books you might like:**

Ellen Datlow, *The Year's Best Fantasy and Horror Series*, 1988-1997
  Terri Winding, co-editor
Karl Edward Wagner, *The Year's Best Horror Stories Series*, 1979-1994
  editor

---

**2971**

STEPHEN JONES, Editor

## The Mammoth Book of Best New Horror 9
(New York: Carroll & Graf, 1998)

**Story type:** Horror (Anthology)

**Summary:** These 19 tales of horror were selected as the best of the year by the editor. Included are the vampire opuses ''Coppola's Dracula'' by Kim Newman and ''The Dripping of Sundered Wineskins'' by Brian Hodge; Thomas Ligotti's surreal episode of a life in a small strange town, ''The Bells Will Sound Forever''; Douglas E. Winter's post-mdern zombie tale ''The Zombies of Madison County''; and Ramsey Campbell's tale of mounting paranoia, ''The Word.'' With a year's wrap-up of the horror field in 1997 by the editor, and a necrology of deaths in the horror field by the editor and Kim Newman.

**Other books you might like:**

Ellen Datlow, *The Year's Best Fantasy and Horror Series*, 1988-1998
  Terri Windling, co-editor
Karl Edward Wagner, *The Year's Best Horror Stories Series*, 1979-1994
  editor

---

**2972**

STEPHEN JONES, Editor

## The Mammoth Book of Dracula
(New York: Carroll & Graf, 1997)

**Story type:** Horror (Anthology; Vampire Story)
**Major character(s):** Dracula, Vampire, Nobleman

**Summary:** Thirty-two stories and one poem featuring Dracula as a character, in an anthology compiled to commemorate the *Dracula* centenary. Selections include Thomas Ligotti's ironic prose poem, ''The Heart of Count Dracula, Descendant of Attila, Scourge of God'', Manly Wade Wellman's ''The Devil is Not Mocked,'' a classic short in which the Nazis make the mistake of billeting at Castle Dracula; Ramsey Campbell's ''Conversion,'' told from the viewpoint of a man who does not know that he's a vampire; Bram Stoker's prologue to the stage version of his novel, ''Dracula: or The Un-Dead''; and new stories by Michael Marshall Smith, Christopher Fowler, Basil Copper, Joel Lane, Terry Lamsley, Guy N. Smith and R. Chetwynd-Hayes.

**Other books you might like:**

Richard Dalby, *Dracula's Brood*, 1987
  editor
Martin H. Greenberg, *Dracula: Prince of Darkness*, 1992
  editor

Michel Parry, *The Rivals of Dracula: A Century of Vampire Fiction*, 1977
  editor
Robert Weinberg, *Rivals of Dracula*, 1996
  Stefan Dziemianowicz and Martin H. Greenberg, co-editors

---

**2973**

**STEPHEN JONES**, Editor

## The Mammoth Book of Frankenstein

(New York: Carroll & Graf, 1995)

**Story type:** Horror (Anthology)

**Summary:** This excellent anthology combines twenty-four new and reprinted stories about the reanimated dead, including the full text of Mary Shelley's novel *Frankenstein* in the revised 1831 version. Robert Bloch's "Mannikins of Horror" tells of the gruesome fate that befalls a man who finds a way to project his soul into miniature dolls. Kim Newman, in "Completist Heaven," draws ironic parallels between the walking dead and a couch-potato video addict. Michael Marshall Smith's "To Receive Is Better" and Dennis Etchison's "The Dead Line" both tell of scientific experiments to keep the dead alive long enough to harvest their organs. David Schow's amusing "Last Call for the Sons of Shock" envisions a watering hole where the great Hollywood film monsters hang out and recount their favorite adventures.

**Other books you might like:**
Martin H. Greenberg, *Frankenstein: The Monster Wakes*, 1994
  editor
Hugh Lamb, *Return From the Grave*, 1976
  editor
Michel Parry, *Rivals of Frankenstein*, 1977
  editor
Bill Pronzini, *The Arbor House Necropolis*, 1981
  editor

---

**2974**

**STEPHEN JONES**, Editor

## The Mammoth Book of Terror

(New York: Carroll & Graf, 1991)

**Story type:** Horror (Anthology)

**Summary:** Eighteen stories, both classic and contemporary. Some wreak interesting variations on traditional horror themes such as madness (Karl Edward Wagner's "The River of Night's Dreaming"), revenge from beyond the grave (Ramsey Campbell's "Out of Copyright") and Lovecraftian horror (Brian Lumley's "The House of the Temple"). Others utilize non-traditional themes and approaches, including the detective tale (Clive Barker's "The Last Illusion"), the hardboiled story (David Schow's "Bunny Didn't Tell Us") and abortion (F. Paul Wilson's "Buckets"). Graham Masterton's "Pig's Dinner" is original to the volume.

**Other books you might like:**
Mike Ashley, *The Mammoth Book of Short Horror Novels*, 1988
Kirby McCauley, *Night Chills*, 1975
Bill Pronzini, *The Arbor House Treasury of Horror and the Supernatural*, 1981
  Barry Malzberg and Martin H. Greenberg, co-authors
Charles G. Waugh, *13 Short Horror Novels*, 1987
  Martin H. Greenberg, co-author

---

**2975**

**STEPHEN JONES**, Editor

## The Mammoth Book of Vampires

(New York: Carroll & Graf, 1992)

**Story type:** Horror (Anthology; Vampire Story)

**Summary:** Twenty-nine traditional and none-too-traditional vampire stories ranging from Gothic classics such as Bram Stoker's "Dracula's Guest" and F. Marion Crawford's "For Blood Is the Life," to F. Paul Wilson's tale of a future in which vampires rule the world, "Midnight Mass"; David Schow's "A Week in the Unlife," about vampires who prey on other vampires; Les Daniels' novella of his series character Don Sebastian de Villaneuva, "Yellow Fog"; and Brian Stableford's tale of vampirism as a blood-borne disease, "The Man Who Loved the Vampire Lady."

**Other books you might like:**
Richard Dalby, *Dracula's Brood*, 1987
Ellen Datlow, *Blood Is Not Enough*, 1989
Martin H. Greenberg, *A Taste for Blood*, 1992
  Robert Weinberg and Stefan Dziemianowicz, co-editors
Martin H. Greenberg, *Vamps*, 1987
  Charles G. Waugh, co-editor
Alan Ryan, *Vampires: Two Centuries of Great Vampire Stories*, 1987

---

**2976**

**STEPHEN JONES**, Editor

## The Mammoth Book of Werewolves

(New York: Carroll & Graf, 1994)

**Story type:** Horror (Anthology; Werewolf Story)

**Summary:** This anthology contains 24 werewolf stories, ten of which are original. Included are David Case's classic short epistolary novel of a murderer convinced he is a werewolf, "The Cell"; Ramsey Campbell's brief tale of the strange effect of a museum talisman on a night watchman, "Night Beat"; Suzy McKee Charnas's coming-of-age tale, "Boobs"; Manly Wade Wellman's pulp thriller, "The Hairy Ones Shall Dance"; Scott Bradfield's story of a man who leads a feral life in his dreams, "Dream of the Wolf"; and Clive Barker's cold war werewolf thriller, "Twilight at the Towers."

**Other books you might like:**
Brian J. Frost, *Book of the Werewolf*, 1973
David Hill, *The Way of the Werewolf*, 1966
  editor
Byron Preiss, *The Ultimate Werewolf*, 1992
  John Betancourt, co-editor
Bill Pronzini, *Werewolf!*, 1979
  editor

---

**2977**

**STEPHEN JONES**, Editor

## The Mammoth Book of Zombies

(New York: Carroll & Graf, 1993)

**Story type:** Horror (Anthology; Reanimated Dead)

**Summary:** This book collects 26 stories of the reanimated dead, some liberally interpreted to be about zombies. Included are Edgar Allan Poe's story of a soul that inhabits a corpse after death, "The Fact in the Case of M. Valdemar"; H.P. Lovecraft's pastiche of

*Frankenstein*, ''Herbert West—Reanimator''; Karl Edward Wagner's pastiche of H.P. Lovecraft, ''Sticks''; Dennis Etchison's tale of backstage intrigues during the filming of a zombie movie, ''The Blood Kiss''; Clive Barker's tale of a theatre where old performers never die, ''Sex, Death and Starshine''; and J. Sheridan Le Fanu's story of a woman betrothed to a corpse, ''Schalken the Painter.'' Seven stories by Peter Tremayne, Nicholas Royle, Graham Masterton, Hugh B. Cave, David Riley, David Sutton, and Michael Marshall Smith are original to the anthology.

**Other books you might like:**
Peter Haining, *Stories of the Walking Dead*, 1985
    editor
Bill Pronzini, *The Arbor House Necropolis*, 1981
John Skipp, *Book of the Dead*, 1990
    Craig Spector, co-editor
John Skipp, *Still Dead: Book of the Dead 2*, 1992
    Craig Spector, co-editor

## 2978

**STEPHEN JONES**, Editor

### Shadows over Innsmouth

(Minneapolis: Fedogan & Bremer, 1994)

**Story type:** Horror (Anthology)

**Summary:** The 17 stories in this anthology are homages to H.P. Lovecraft's ''The Shadow over Innsmouth,'' about a traveller's discovery that a New England seaport town is inhabited by the spawn of humans and sea creatures. In addition to Lovecraft's own story, the selections include Ramsey Campbell's first published tale, ''The Church in High Street,'' about the hideous discovery a man makes in an abandoned church; Brian Stableford's ''The Innsmouth Heritage,'' which explores the genetic ramifications behind Lovecraft's story; David Langford's ''Deepnet,'' which reimagines Lovecraft's menace for the computer age; Guy N. Smith's tale of horrifying self-discovery, ''Return to Innsmouth''; and Brian Lumley's ''Dagon's Bell,'' about the resurgence of the fish-god Dagon.

**Other books you might like:**
Edward P. Berglund, *Disciples of Cthulhu*, 1973
Ramsey Campbell, *New Tales of the Cthulhu Mythos*, 1980
H.P. Lovecraft, *Tales of the Cthulhu Mythos: Golden Anniversary
    Anthology*, 1990
Robert M. Price, *The Hastur Cycle*, 1994
    editor
Robert M. Price, *The Shub Niggurath Cycle*, 1994
Robert M. Price, *Tales of the Lovecraft Mythos*, 1992
Thomas M.K. Stratman, *Cthulhu's Heirs*, 1994
    editor

## 2979

**TERRY JONES**

### Douglas Adams's Starship Titanic

(New York: Harmony, 1997)

**Story type:** Science Fiction (Humor; Adventure)
**Major character(s):** Dan, Space Explorer, Traveler; Nettie, Space
    Explorer, Traveler; Lucy, Space Explorer, Traveler
**Time period(s):** Indeterminate Future
**Locale(s):** *Starship Titanic*, Spaceship; Outer Space

**Summary:** On the eve of the launch of his greatest achievement, designer Leovinus discovers unfinished and flawed construction on *Starship Titanic*, but cannot prevent its launch and immediate loss.

Under autopilot, the ship lands on Earth and picks up Dan, Nettie and Lucy, who must explore the massive ship and help effect repairs, if they hope to see Earth again. Based on a CD-ROM adventure.

**Other books you might like:**
Douglas Adams, *The Hitchhiker's Guide to the Galaxy*, 1980
Douglas Adams, *The Restaurant at the End of the Universe*, 1982
Alan Dean Foster, *Dark Star*, 1974
Henry Kuttner, *Robots Have No Tails*, 1952
Ken Rolston, *Extreme Paranoia: Nobody Knows the Trouble I've
    Shot*, 1991
Charles Sheffield, *One Man's Universe*, 1993

## 2980

**TERRY JONES**
**BRIAN FROUD**, Co-Author

### The Goblin Companion

(Atlanta: Turner Publishing, 1996)

**Story type:** Fantasy (Collection; Legend)

**Summary:** Contains a six-page introduction plus 70 tales and descriptions of the Goblins of the Labyrinth who, millions of years ago, retreated into a vast fortress to protect themselves against the ungoblin world. ''A Field Guide to Goblins'' results from combining the stories of an ancient African wise man and illustrations from a storage chest dating from the goblin era.

**Other books you might like:**
Graeme Base, *The Discovery of Dragons*, 1996
Charles de Lint, *The Wild Wood*, 1994
    Brian Froud, co-author
James Gurney, *Dinotopia*, 1992
James Gurney, *The World Beneath*, 1995
Steve Szilagyi, *Photographing Fairies*, 1992

## 2981

**TERRY JONES**
**BRIAN FROUD**, Illustrator

### Lady Cottington's Pressed Fairy Book

(Atlanta, Georgia, Turner, 1994)

**Story type:** Fantasy (Contemporary; Light Fantasy)
**Major character(s):** Lady Angelica Cottington, Naturalist (amateur),
    Teenager; Lord Crowley, Rogue, Nobleman
**Time period(s):** 1890s (1895-1899); 1900s
**Locale(s):** England; Naples, Italy

**Summary:** Lady Cottington collects fairies within a journal which documents her discovery and interaction with the creatures, who tease her to distraction and play tricks on her as she examines her budding sexuality.

**Other books you might like:**
David Kirschner, *The Pagemaster*, 1993
    Ernie Contreras, co-author
James Gurney, *Dinotopia*, 1992
Patricia A. McKillip, *Something Rich and Strange*, 1994
    Brian Froud, co-author
Steve Szilagyi, *Photographing Fairies*, 1992
David Worsick, *Henry's Gift: The Magic Eye*, 1994

## 2982

**TERRY JONES**
**BRIAN FROUD**, Co-Author

### Strange Stains and Mysterious Smells
(New York: Simon & Schuster, 1996)

**Story type:** Fantasy (Collection; Light Fantasy)
**Major character(s):** Quentin Coddington, Psychic, Researcher
**Time period(s):** 1910s; 1920s
**Locale(s):** England

**Summary:** Equipped with his Psychic Image Nebulising Generator and Primary Odour Nasalising Gasificator, Quentin Coddington investigates more than 780 psychic encounters and the stains and odors which result, documenting 34 with stories and illustrations presented in his journal.

**Other books you might like:**
Betty Ballantine, *The Secret Oceans*, 1994
Graeme Base, *The Discovery of Dragons*, 1996
James Gurney, *Dinotopia*, 1992
James Gurney, *The World Beneath*, 1995
Patricia A. McKillip, *Something Rich and Strange*, 1994
    Brian Froud, co-author
Steve Szilagyi, *Photographing Fairies*, 1992

## 2983

**ROBERT JORDAN**

### The Conan Chronicles
(New York: Tor, 1995)

**Story type:** Fantasy (Sword and Sorcery; Adventure)
**Series:** Conan the Barbarian
**Major character(s):** Conan, Barbarian, Warrior
**Time period(s):** Indeterminate Past
**Locale(s):** Zamora, Fictional Country; Nemedia, Fictional Country; Turan, Fictional Country

**Summary:** Omnibus edition collecting *Conan the Invincible* (1982), *Conan the Defender* (1982) and *Conan the Unconquered* (1983). Conan pursues treasure and seeks to fulfill vows to the gods while powerful warriors, sorcerers and treacherous women attempt to divert him from his goals.

**Other books you might like:**
Leonard Carpenter, *Conan the Gladiator*, 1995
Roland J. Green, *Conan at the Demon's Gate*, 1994
Robert E. Howard, *Conan the Barbarian*, 1955
Robert E. Howard, *Hour of the Dragon*, 1977
Steve Perry, *Conan the Fearless*, 1986
John Maddox Roberts, *Conan and the Treasure of Python*, 1993

## 2984

**ROBERT JORDAN**

### A Crown of Swords
(New Yok: Tor, 1996)

**Story type:** Fantasy (Magic Conflict)
**Series:** Wheel of Time
**Major character(s):** Rand ''Dragon Reborn'' al'Thor, Leader; Elayne, Royalty, Heiress; Egwene al'Vere, Religious (Aes Sedai), Witch
**Time period(s):** Indeterminate

**Locale(s):** Cairhien, Fictional Country; Andor, Fictional Country; Ebou Dar, Fictional City

**Summary:** While Elayne and others attempt to acquire the artifact that could reverse an unnatural heat wave, Egwene gathers together all manner of entities who can channel and Rand confronts Forsaken Sammael, a minion of the Dark One.

**Other books you might like:**
Glen Cook, *The Black Company*, 1984
Dave Duncan, *Magic Casement*, 1990
David Eddings, *Pawn of Prophecy*, 1982
Raymond E. Feist, *Magician*, 1982
Terry Goodkind, *Wizard's First Rule*, 1994
Michael Scott Rohan, *The Anvil of Ice*, 1986

## 2985

**ROBERT JORDAN**

### The Dragon Reborn
(New York: Tor, 1991)

**Story type:** Fantasy (Quest; Magic Conflict)
**Series:** Wheel of Time
**Major character(s):** Rand ''Dragon Reborn'' al'Thor, Leader, Revolutionary; Elayne, Royalty, Heiress; Egwene al'Vere, Religious (Aes Sedai), Witch
**Time period(s):** Indeterminate
**Locale(s):** Tar Valon, Fictional Country; Illian, Fictional Country

**Summary:** Having accepted his role in prophecy as Dragon Reborn, Rand seeks after a magic sword while Egwene, Elayne and Nynaeve, training again with the Aes Sedai sisterhood, travel to the White Tower for help healing Mat's wounds and answers to Agwene's disturbing dreams. At the White Tower, Verin entrusts Egwene with a ter'angreal, a device which allows dreams to become real, the tool of a Dreamer. The prophecied Pattern continues to unfold, challenging Egwene's restraint in use of the Power.

**Other books you might like:**
David Cook, *Beyond the Moons*, 1991
Glen Cook, *The Black Company*, 1984
David Eddings, *Pawn of Prophecy*, 1982
Raymond E. Feist, *Magician*, 1982
Barbara Hambly, *The Time of the Dark*, 1982
Elizabeth Moon, *Sheepfarmer's Daughter*, 1988
Andre Norton, *The Elvenbane*, 1991
    Mercedes Lackey, co-author
J.R.R. Tolkien, *The Fellowship of the Ring*, 1954

## 2986

**ROBERT JORDAN**

### The Eye of the World
(New York: Tor, 1989)

**Story type:** Fantasy (Quest)
**Series:** Wheel of Time
**Major character(s):** Rand al'Thor, Farmer (shepherd); Fades, Monster
**Time period(s):** Indeterminate
**Locale(s):** Emond's Field, Fictional Country

**Summary:** Three boys forced from their home, a young girl, and a magic worker are brought together to help battle the dark forces trying to take over their land.

**Other books you might like:**
Lloyd Alexander, *The Book of Three*, 1988
  Reissue of 1964; The Prydain Series. Vol. 1
Guy Gavriel Kay, *The Summer Tree*, 1985
  The Fionavar Tapestry. Bk. 1
Victor Kelleher, *The Red King*, 1989
R.A. MacAvoy, *Lens of the World*, 1990

---

`2987`

**ROBERT JORDAN**

## The Fires of Heaven

(New York: Tor, 1993)

**Story type:** Fantasy (Magic Conflict)
**Series:** Wheel of Time
**Major character(s):** Rand ''Dragon Reborn'' al'Thor, Leader, Revolutionary; Aviendha, Warrior; Elayne, Royalty, Heiress
**Time period(s):** Indeterminate
**Locale(s):** Rhuidean, Fictional City; Amadicia, Fictional Country

**Summary:** While factions among the Aes Sedai plot, Elayne and Nynaeve continue their travels, meeting Siuan and Min at Salidar. The Forsaken exert their evil influence and Rand leads his Aiel warriors to victory, even though he must enter the World of Dreams, the Tel'aran'rhiod, to confront Rahvin.

**Other books you might like:**
Lynn Abbey, *Daughter of the Bright Moon*, 1979
Stephen R. Donaldson, *Lord Foul's Bane*, 1977
Diane Duane, *The Door into Fire*, 1979
Simon R. Green, *Blue Moon Rising*, 1991
Barbara Hambly, *The Armies of Daylight*, 1983
Katherine Kurtz, *High Deryni*, 1973
Leo Tolstoy, *War and Peace*, 1886
J.R.R. Tolkien, *The Two Towers*, 1955
Angus Wells, *Dark Magic*, 1992

---

`2988`

**ROBERT JORDAN**

## Lord of Chaos

(New York: Tor, 1994)

**Story type:** Fantasy (Magic Conflict)
**Series:** Wheel of Time
**Major character(s):** Rand ''Dragon Reborn'' al'Thor, Leader; Demandred, Wizard; Shaidar Haran, Mythical Creature (Myrddraal)
**Time period(s):** Indeterminate
**Locale(s):** Shayol Ghul, Fictional City (mountainstronghold of the Dark One); The Blasted Lands, Fictional Country; Shaidar Haran, Fictional City

**Summary:** The plot of this immense series continues to build as the forces of good and evil pursue their plans. Unfortunately for Rand al'Thor, ambitious mortals as well as the plots of the Great Lord of the Dark impede the removal of the Dark One's influence over the Wheel of Time.

**Other books you might like:**
Glen Cook, *The Black Company*, 1984
David Eddings, *Pawn of Prophecy*, 1982
Guy Gavriel Kay, *The Summer Tree*, 1985
Katherine Kurtz, *Deryni Rising*, 1970
Patricia A. McKillip, *The Riddle-Master of Hed*, 1976

---

`2989`

**ROBERT JORDAN**

## The Path of Daggers

(New York: Tor, 1998)

**Story type:** Fantasy (Magic Conflict)
**Series:** Wheel of Time
**Major character(s):** Rand al'Thor, Leader; Elayne, Royalty, Fugitive; Egwene al'Vere, Religious, Witch
**Time period(s):** Indeterminate
**Locale(s):** Caemlyn, Fictional Country; Illian, Fictional Country

**Summary:** The war continues across the continent, as Rand fights the Seanchan invaders. Forces worse than the Seanchan stir while the war stretches Rand's allies thin. But Egwene can bring victory if she can reunite the Aes Sedai.

**Other books you might like:**
Glen Cook, *A Shadow of All Night Falling*, 1979
Terry Goodkind, *Wizard's First Rule*, 1994
Robin Hobb, *Assassin's Apprentice*, 1995
George R.R. Martin, *A Game of Thrones*, 1996
Martha Wells, *The Element of Fire*, 1993

---

`2990`

**ROBERT JORDAN**

## The Shadow Rising

(New York: Tor, 1992)

**Story type:** Fantasy (Magic Conflict)
**Series:** Wheel of Time
**Major character(s):** Rand ''Dragon Reborn'' al'Thor, Leader, Hero
**Time period(s):** Indeterminate
**Locale(s):** Tar Valon, Fictional City; Two Rivers, Fictional Country

**Summary:** As the Dark One expands its influence over the land, humans who lust for power and control plot to assume command. In Two Rivers, Rand eludes the pursuing Whitecloaks, remaining humanity's best hope for restoration of the balance of magical forces.

**Other books you might like:**
Glen Cook, *The Black Company*, 1984
Glen Cook, *Shadows Linger*, 1984
Glen Cook, *The White Rose*, 1985
David Eddings, *Magician's Gambit*, 1983
David Eddings, *Pawn of Prophecy*, 1982
David Eddings, *Queen of Sorcery*, 1982

---

`2991`

**ROBERT JORDAN**
**TERESA PATTERSON**, Co-Author

## The World of Robert Jordan's The Wheel of Time

(New York: Tor, 1997)

**Story type:** Fantasy (Collection; Magic Conflict)
**Series:** Wheel of Time
**Time period(s):** Indeterminate
**Locale(s):** Ten Nations, Mythical Place

**Summary:** Contains numerous short stories, literary sketches, and legends about characters and events pivotal to the series. Lavish illustrations include many maps and portraits.

**Other books you might like:**
Marion Zimmer Bradley, *The Keeper's Price*, 1980
    editor
Katherine Kurtz, *The Deryni Archives*, 1986
Mercedes Lackey, *Sword of Ice and Other Tales of Valdemar*, 1997
    editor
J.R.R. Tolkien, *The Silmarillion*, 1977
J.R.R. Tolkien, *Unfinished Tales of Numenor and Middle-Earth*, 1980

---

**2992**

**SHERRYL JORDAN**

## The Juniper Game

(New York: Scholastic, 1991)

**Story type:** Fantasy (Contemporary; Young Adult)
**Major character(s):** Juniper Golding, Teenager, Psychic (clairvoyant); Dylan Pidgely, Artist, Psychic; Marsha Golding, Single Parent
**Time period(s):** 1990s
**Locale(s):** New Zealand

**Summary:** Juniper Golding has an obsession with Medieval England and ESP. She draws Dylan Pidgely, a fellow student, into her experiments and both are drawn into the life and time of Johanna, a young woman in 15th-century Tewkesbury who is accused of being a witch. Both feel they may be too caught up when they must watch helplessly as Johanna is tried and condemned, but find they can give her a bit of peace during her ordeal.

**Other books you might like:**
Margaret J. Anderson, *To Nowhere and Back*, 1975
Peter Dickinson, *The Gift*, 1974
Alan Garner, *Red Shift*, 1973
Katherine Kurtz, *The Adept*, 1991
    Deborah Turner Harris, co-author
Andre Norton, *Lavender-Green Magic*, 1974
Alison Uttley, *A Traveler in Time*, 1940

---

**2993**

**S.T. JOSHI**, Editor

## Great Weird Tales

(Mineola, New York: Dover Books, 1998)

**Story type:** Horror (Anthology)

**Summary:** Fourteen classics of weird fiction published between 1858 and 1936 and divided into five categories: "Tales of Supernatural Horror," "Tales of Non-Supernatural Horror," "Tales of Awe," "Tales of Fantasy," and "Tales of Pseudo-Science." Selections include Frank Belknap Long's homage to Poe "The Eye Above the Mantel," Ambrose Bierce's darkly funny "My Favorite Murder," H.P. Lovecraft's tale of a dark family heritage "Facts Concerning the Late Arthur Jermyn and His Family," and Fitz-James O'Brien's "The Diamond Lens," in which a scientist discovers a miniature world inside a drop of water. Stories by Algernon Blackwood, Arthur Machen, and Lord Dunsany are also included.

**Other books you might like:**
Ramsey Campbell, *Uncanny Banquet*, 1992
    editor
Marvin Kaye, *Masterpieces of Terror and the Unknown*, 1993
    editor
Hugh Lamb, *Forgotten Tales of Terror*, 1978
    editor

Bill Pronzini, *The Arbor House Treasury of Horror and the Supernatural*, 1981
    Barry Malzberg, Martin H. Greenberg, co-editors
Herbert Wise, *Great Tales of Terror and the Supernatural*, 1944
    Phyllis Fraser, co-editor

---

**2994**

**GRAHAM JOYCE**

## Requiem

(New York: Tor 1996)

**Story type:** Horror (Mystery)
**Major character(s):** Tom Webster, Teacher; Sharon, Counselor; David Feldberg, Linguist (translator)
**Time period(s):** 1990s (1993)
**Locale(s):** Jerusalem, Israel

**Summary:** Sick with grief and guilt over the accidental death of his wife, Tom Webster flees to Israel and the arms of his ex-girlfriend Sharon. While there, he is entrusted by a dying scholar with a lost Dead Sea Scroll and its heretical revelations about the true origin of the Catholic Church only further weaken Tom's slipping grasp on reality. A nominee for the World Fantasy Award, this novel was first published in England in 1995.

**Other books you might like:**
Simon Maginn, *Virgins and Martyrs*, 1995
Brent Monahan, *The Book of Common Dread*, 1993
Mary Elizabeth Murphy, *Virgin*, 1996

---

**2995**

**GRAHAM JOYCE**

## The Tooth Fairy

(New York: Tor, 1998)

**Story type:** Fantasy (Horror; Contemporary Realism)
**Major character(s):** Sam Southall, Teenager; Tooth Fairy, Supernatural Being; Clive Rogers, Genius, Teenager
**Time period(s):** 1990s
**Locale(s):** Redstone, England

**Summary:** Friends since early childhood, Sam, Clive, and Terry share the somewhat brutal experience of growing up in an economically depressed British town. Sam, however, has a secret that only he can see—a sometimes ally, sometimes enemy he calls the Tooth Fairy. Winner of the British Fantasy Award for Best Novel.

**Other books you might like:**
Clive Barker, *The Thief of Always*, 1992
Richard Bowes, *Minions of the Moon*, 1999
Jonathan Carroll, *Bones of the Moon*, 1988
Jonathan Carroll, *A Child Across the Sky*, 1989
Jonathan Carroll, *From the Teeth of Angels*, 1994
Kara Dalkey, *Goa*, 1996

---

**2996**

**PETER JURASIK**
**WILLIAM H. KEITH JR.**, Co-Author

## Diplomatic Act

(New York: Baen, 1998)

**Story type:** Science Fiction (First Contact)
**Major character(s):** Richard Faraday, Actor; Dahnak, Alien

**Time period(s):** Indeterminate Future
**Locale(s):** California; Outer Space

**Summary:** Richard Faraday is an actor whose current role is that of a heroic interstellar diplomat in a television series. An alien race faced with the prospects of a devastating war seeks a third party to mediate their disputes. Since they don't recognize the concept of storytelling, they interpret television signals as factual and shanghai the actor to help them solve their problems. First novel.

**Other books you might like:**
Greg Bear, *Beyond Heaven's River*, 1980
Lloyd Biggle, *All the Colors of Darkness*, 1963
Ben Bova, *The Starcrossed*, 1976
John Brunner, *The Skynappers*, 1960
Edmund Cooper, *Transit*, 1964

**2997**

**CYNTHIA KADOHATA**

## In the Heart of the Valley of Love

(New York: Viking, 1992)

**Story type:** Science Fiction (Dystopian)
**Major character(s):** Francie, Teenager, Orphan
**Time period(s):** 2050s
**Locale(s):** Los Angeles, California

**Summary:** In the violent, chaotic Los Angeles environment, Francie roams around searching for direction in her life.

**Other books you might like:**
David Brin, *Earth*, 1990
Octavia E. Butler, *Dawn*, 1987
K.W. Jeter, *Madlands*, 1991
David R. Palmer, *Emergence*, 1984
Geoff Ryman, *The Child Garden*, 1990
Carolyn See, *Making History*, 1991
Neal Stephenson, *Snow Crash*, 1992

**2998**

**RICHARD KADREY**

## Kamikaze L'Amour

(New York: St. Martin's, 1995)

**Story type:** Science Fiction (Post-Holocaust)
**Major character(s):** Ryder, Musician, Fugitive; Frida, Musician; Virilio, Criminal
**Time period(s):** 2000s (2001)
**Locale(s):** San Francisco, California

**Summary:** Moving north, the jungles destroy cities and bring strange new life. A rock star now comfortably anonymous after a failed suicide, Ryder comes to San Francisco to start over. Unable to resist the attraction of music after meeting Frida, Ryder pursues a new sound for a new world.

**Other books you might like:**
J.G. Ballard, *The Drowned World*, 1962
Pat Cadigan, *Synners*, 1991
Pat Murphy, *The City, Not Long After*, 1989
Lewis Shiner, *Deserted Cities of the Heart*, 1988
Bruce Sterling, *Heavy Weather*, 1994

**2999**

**DAVID KAGAN**

## Sunstroke

(New York: Diamond, 1993)

**Story type:** Science Fiction (Techno-Thriller)
**Major character(s):** James William Kendall, Government Official (president); Mike Doheny, Engineer, Administrator (project director)
**Time period(s):** 21st century
**Locale(s):** Earth

**Summary:** Experimental civilian solar power satellite, SOLSAT X-1, orbits Earth, converting sunlight to electricity. While overtly benign, secret programming allows the microwave beam used for transfering energy to Earth to come under control of U.S. Space Defense Command who can target the microwave beam as a death weapon. When programming fails, the few cognoscenti rush in to prevent worldwide disaster.

**Other books you might like:**
David Brin, *Earth*, 1990
Michael Crichton, *The Andromeda Strain*, 1969
Mary Gentle, *Ancient Light*, 1987
Rosemary Kirstein, *The Outskirter's Secret*, 1992
J.M. Morgan, *Desert Eden*, 1991

**3000**

**JANET KAGAN**

## Hellspark

(Decatur, Georgia: Meisha Merlin, 1998)

**Story type:** Science Fiction (First Contact; Alternate Intelligence)
**Major character(s):** Tocohl Susumo, Spaceship Captain, Trader; Margaret "Maggy" Lord Lynn, Artificial Intelligence, Computer; Tinling Alfvaen, Psychic (serendipitist)
**Time period(s):** Indeterminate Future
**Locale(s):** Lassti, Planet—Imaginary; Veschke, Planet—Imaginary

**Summary:** The birdlike natives of the newly discovered planet Lassti defy the survey team's abilities to ascertain their sentience, but time has run out. Multi-Galactic Enterprises wants to exploit the resources of the planet, an extravaganza of bio-electric plant life, and three years of expenses without any concrete results spurs MGE to pressure the team for a swift conclusion to their survey. When Captain Tocohl Susumo, Hellspark trader and linguistic and cultural expert, agrees to examine the evidence and pass judgment on the natives, she unexpectedly gains necessary time for her observations when the survey team's ethologist accuses those same natives of the recent and deliberate murder of the team's physicist. With the aid of Maggy and Tinling Alfvaen, Tocohl ends up conducting a murder investigation that will decide the ownership of the planet.

**Other books you might like:**
Eleanor Arnason, *Ring of Swords*, 1993
Isaac Asimov, *The Caves of Steel*, 1954
David Brin, *The Uplift War*, 1987
Octavia E. Butler, *Dawn*, 1987
C.J. Cherryh, *Cyteen*, 1988
C.J. Cherryh, *Foreigner*, 1994
Joan Slonczewski, *The Children Star*, 1998

## 3001

**JANET KAGAN**

### Mirabile

(New York: Tor, 1991)

**Story type:** Science Fiction (Hard Science Fiction; Adventure)
**Major character(s):** Anna ''Mama'' Jason Masmajean, Scientist (biologist); Leonov Opener Denness, Scientist (naturalist), Explorer
**Time period(s):** Indeterminate Future
**Locale(s):** Mirabile, Planet—Imaginary

**Summary:** Romance flourishes as colonists try to establish Earth-authentic species on Mirabile using embryos and genetic material sent with them. All plant and animal life sent has inactive genetic material nested inside the normally active DNA that unexpectedly generates new life forms, dragon's teeth, which Mama Jason must study then stabilize or eliminate. Six stories packaged as a novel.

**Other books you might like:**
Octavia E. Butler, *Adulthood Rites*, 1988
Octavia E. Butler, *Dawn*, 1987
Octavia E. Butler, *Imago*, 1989
Michael Flynn, *The Nanotech Chronicles*, 1991
Diana G. Gallagher, *The Alien Dark*, 1990
Anne McCaffrey, *Dragonsdawn*, 1988
Joan Slonczewski, *A Door into Ocean*, 1986
Cordwainer Smith, *The Best of Cordwainer Smith*, 1975
Harry Turtledove, *Earthgrip*, 1991

## 3002

**RICHARD KALICH**

### The Nihilesthete

(Stone Mountain, Georgia: White Wolf, 1996)

**Story type:** Horror (Psychological Suspense)
**Major character(s):** Haberman, Social Worker; Brodski, Handicapped; Maria Rivera, Aged Person
**Time period(s):** 1980s (1987)
**Locale(s):** New York, New York

**Summary:** Haberman, a sadistically misanthropic social worker, assumes the care of an idiot quadriplegic with the intention of helping him develop his aptitude for art and then denying him outlets of creative expression. This novel, the author's first, was originally published in 1987.

**Other books you might like:**
John Fowles, *The Collector*, 1958
Stephen King, *Misery*, 1987
Patrick McGrath, *The Grotesque*, 1989
Joyce Carol Oates, *Zombie*, 1995

## 3003

**JEANNE KALOGRIDIS**

### Children of the Vampire

(New York: Delacorte, 1995)

**Story type:** Horror (Vampire Story)
**Series:** Diaries of the Family Dracul
**Major character(s):** Stefan Van Helsing, Doctor; Arkady Tsepesh, Vampire; Vlad Tsepesh, Vampire (Count Dracula)
**Time period(s):** 1840s (1845); 1870s (1871)
**Locale(s):** Transylvania; Amsterdam, Netherlands

**Summary:** In this sequel to *Covenant with the Vampire*, newly vampirized Arkady Tsepesh flees Castle Dracula to protect his infant son Stefan from the family curse, which demands that the firstborn male of every generation of Tsepeshs becomes bound by blood to the Count and supply him with foreign travellers for his sustenance. Twenty-six years later, Stefan is oblivious to his heritage, yet still feels the call of blood that lures him back to Castle Dracula, and his destiny. The author is better known by her pseudonym, Diane Duane.

**Other books you might like:**
Brian W. Aldiss, *Dracula Unbound*, 1991
Roderick Anscombe, *The Secret Life of Laszlo, Count Dracula*, 1994
Fred Saberhagen, *A Matter of Taste*, 1991
Peter Tremayne, *Dracula Unborn*, 1977

## 3004

**JEANNE KALOGRIDIS**

### Covenant with the Vampire

(New York: Delacorte, 1994)

**Story type:** Horror (Vampire Story)
**Major character(s):** Arkady Tsepesh, Young Man; Mary Wyndham Tsepesh, Young Woman (Arkady's wife); Vlad Tsepesh, Vampire (Count Dracula)
**Time period(s):** 1840s (1845)
**Locale(s):** Transylvania (Castle Dracula)

**Summary:** The author's first novel, in a projected trilogy retelling the story of Bram Stoker's *Dracula*, is told in epistolary form as the diaries of Arkady and Mary Tsepesh, and Arkady's sister Zsuzsanna. Upon the death of his father, Arkady returns to Transylvania from London with his pregnant wife. There, he discovers to his horror that his great uncle, Vlad, is a vampire who expects him, and his as yet unborn child, to serve him as the first-born of each generation of the Tsepesh has done: by obtaining victims who will supply him with the blood he needs.

**Other books you might like:**
C. Dean Andersson, *I Am Dracula*, 1993
Marie Kiraly, *Mina*, 1994
Bram Stoker, *Dracula*, 1897

## 3005

**JEANNE KALOGRIDIS**

### Lord of the Vampires

(New York: Delacorte, 1996)

**Story type:** Horror (Vampire Story)
**Series:** Diaries of the Family Dracul
**Major character(s):** Abraham Van Helsing, Doctor; Jonathan Seward, Doctor; Elizabeth Bathory, Vampire
**Time period(s):** 1890s (1893)
**Locale(s):** London, England

**Summary:** This third novel in the Diaries of the Family Dracul trilogy, a prequel to Bram Stoker's *Dracula*, recapitulates many of the events of Stoker's novel. Sworn to avenge the death of his father and half brother at the hands of vampire Vlad Dracul, Abraham Van Helsing and a band of confederates grapple with Dracula and his renowned cousin, Elizabeth Bathory. Their struggle draws the attention of an even more formidable nemesis, the Lord of the Vampires, who first charged Vlad with the task of killing the first born son of each generation of his family in order to enjoy his vampiric immortality.

**Other books you might like:**
C. Dean Andersson, *I Am Dracula*, 1994
Roderick Anscombe, *The Secret Life of Laszlo, Count Dracula*, 1994
Kim Newman, *Anno Dracula*, 1992
Peter Tremayne, *Dracula Unborn*, 1977

---

**3006**

### KWADWO AGYMAH KAMAU

## *Flickering Shadows*

(Minneapolis, Minnesota: Coffee House Press, 1996)

**Story type:** Fantasy (Contemporary Realism; Political)
**Major character(s):** Cephus, Farmer, Revolutionary; Boysie, Sailor, Revolutionary; Doreen, Spouse (Cephus')
**Time period(s):** 1990s
**Locale(s):** Caribbean; The Hill, Fictional City

**Summary:** Independence from Britain leaves an island vulnerable to exploitation as exploration for mineral wealth and development for tourism progresses with the aid of an unscrupulous missionary. Communicating from the spirit world, Cephus' grandfather attempts to mitigate events and cultivate a sense of group identity as Cephus' family and neighbors struggle with personal and societal problems. First novel.

**Other books you might like:**
Louis de Bernieres, *Senor Vivo and the Coca Lord*, 1992
Louis de Bernieres, *The War of Don Emmanuel's Nether Parts*, 1992
Ben Okri, *The Famished Road*, 1992
Ben Okri, *Songs of Enchantment*, 1993

---

**3007**

### MICHAEL KANALY

## *Thoughts of God*

(New York: Ace, 1997)

**Story type:** Science Fiction (Theological; Science Fantasy)
**Major character(s):** Dennison York, Mercenary, Hero; Yvonne Stafford, Abuse Victim; Arnie Watts, Serial Killer
**Time period(s):** 2000s
**Locale(s):** New York, New York; Lancaster, Pennsylvania

**Summary:** The experiment to further the development of immortal spirits by putting them into bodies may not succeed. Observation continues. On Earth, Arnie Watts escapes from Dennison York and his crew, kidnapping one of York's employees. York may go bankrupt, but cannot abandon the search for the serial killer despite his guilt at the death of his son's killers. First novel.

**Other books you might like:**
David Brin, *Brightness Reef*, 1995
Orson Scott Card, *Lost Boys*, 1992
Parke Godwin, *Waiting for the Galactic Bus*, 1988
Ben Okri, *The Famished Road*, 1992
Susan Palwick, *Flying in Place*, 1992
Dan Simmons, *The Hollow Man*, 1992

---

**3008**

### MICHAEL KANALY

## *Virus Clans*

(New York: Ace, 1998)

**Story type:** Science Fiction (Disaster; Medical)

**Major character(s):** Gary Bracken, Scientist; Jacoby, Scientist
**Time period(s):** Indeterminate Future
**Locale(s):** United States

**Summary:** A scientist investigating viruses discovers that his subjects have abandoned their usual random patterns of activity and are working in a concerted fashion. He theorizes that this is a periodic change that once caused the extinction of the dinosaurs and may now presage the same end for humankind. The authorities disregard his warnings until it is too late and human nature changes forever.

**Other books you might like:**
Greg Bear, *Blood Music*, 1985
Frank Herbert, *The White Plague*, 1982
Damon Knight, *CV*, 1985
Nancy Kress, *Beggars in Spain*, 1993
Charles Pellegrino, *Dust*, 1998

---

**3009**

### MICHAEL KANDEL

## *Captain Jack Zodiac*

(New York: Bantam Spectra, 1992)

**Story type:** Fantasy (Light Fantasy; Post-Disaster)
**Major character(s):** Clifford ''Cliff'' Koussevitzky, Parent; Bernie ''Power Man'' Rifkin, Hero (crimefighter/superhero); Captain Jack Zodiac, Drug Dealer
**Time period(s):** 21st century
**Locale(s):** Earth; Moon Two, Planet—Imaginary

**Summary:** Despite the war and its surreal side effects, Cliff decides to remarry in hopes of starting a second family. Cliff then resolves to find and rescue his daughter, a mall zombie, and his son, a space cadet, even if it means using one of Captain Jack Zodiac's experimental drugs.

**Other books you might like:**
Neil Gaiman, *Good Omens: The Nice and Accurate Prophecies of Agnes Nutter, Witch*, 1990
    Terry Pratchett, co-author
K.W. Jeter, *Madlands*, 1990
George R.R. Martin, *Wild Cards*, 1987
    editor
Neal Stephenson, *Snow Crash*, 1992

---

**3010**

### MICHAEL KANDEL

## *In between Dragons*

(New York: Bantam Spectra, 1990)

**Story type:** Fantasy (Alternate World; Young Adult)
**Major character(s):** Sherman, Student—High School, Adventurer; Mr. McGulvey, Steward (McGulveyland)
**Time period(s):** 1990s
**Locale(s):** McGulveyland, Fictional Country; Cuspidor, Fictional City; Pittsburgh, Pennsylvania

**Summary:** A high school senior finds adventure and escape from the uncomfortable reality of being sixteen years old by going to a magic library and entering McGulveyland. There he is a hero in all the stories in which he gets to fight dragons, battle a psi-monster and drive a car. He brings a book which doesn't belong to the library without realizing he is putting McGulveyland at risk.

**Other books you might like:**
Antoine de Saint-Exupery, *The Little Prince*, 1943
Michael Ende, *The Neverending Story*, 1983

William Goldman, *The Princess Bride*, 1973
Clifford D. Simak, *The Goblin Reservation*, 1968
Christopher Stasheff, *The Warlock Is Missing*, 1986
James Thurber, *The Secret Life of Walter Mitty*, 1983

## 3011

### MICHAEL KANDEL

## *Panda Ray*

(New York: St. Martin's, 1996)

**Story type:** Science Fiction (Psychic Powers; Invasion of Earth)
**Major character(s):** Christopher Zimmerman, Adventurer, Time Traveler; Jane Palmer, Teacher; Debra Zimmerman, Parent
**Time period(s):** 1990s
**Locale(s):** Kansas

**Summary:** Mother calls a family meeting after Jane Palmer informs her that Christopher relays odd stories in history class. The family agrees she must scoop out Christopher's psi, omicron, and upsilon. His sister convinces Christopher to run away with his grandfather, leading to death, imprisonment, and the continuing interference of the FBI.

**Other books you might like:**
Lester Del Rey, *Pstalemate*, 1971
Steven Gould, *Jumper*, 1992
Robert A. Heinlein, *Tunnel in the Sky*, 1955
William Kotzwinkle, *The Fan Man*, 1974
R.A. Lafferty, *The Reefs of Earth*, 1968
Theodore Sturgeon, *More than Human*, 1953

## 3012

### MICHAEL KANDEL

## *Strange Invasion*

(New York: Bantam Spectra, 1989)

**Story type:** Science Fiction (Invasion of Earth)
**Major character(s):** Wally Griffith, Patient (Mental Patient); Lucille, Doctor
**Time period(s):** 20th century
**Locale(s):** Earth

**Summary:** Wally Griffith, a mental patient who tends to hallucinate anyway, discovers that he is the only one in the world capable of standing off a series of very strange and occasionally very silly alien invasions.

**Other books you might like:**
Philip K. Dick, *The Divine Invasion*, 1981
Philip K. Dick, *Do Androids Dream of Electric Sheep?*, 1968
Philip K. Dick, *Eye in the Sky*, 1957
Philip K. Dick, *Martian Time-Slip*, 1964
Philip K. Dick, *The Three Stigmata of Palmer Eldritch*, 1965
Philip K. Dick, *Ubik*, 1969
Philip K. Dick, *Valis*, 1981

## 3013

### MICHAEL KASNER

## *Finger of God*

(New York: Worldwide Library Gold Eagle, 1993)

**Story type:** Science Fiction (Military)
**Series:** Warkeep 2030

**Major character(s):** Alexander F. Rosemont, Military Personnel, Leader
**Time period(s):** 2030s (2030)
**Locale(s):** Amazon Jungle, Brazil; United States

**Summary:** When forces of the Allied nations of South America plan to attack Brazil for environmental crimes, the Peacekeepers rush to prevent continental warfare.

**Other books you might like:**
Bill Dolan, *Cobra Curse*, 1993
G. Harry Stine, *Force of Arms*, 1990
G. Harry Stine, *Guts and Glory*, 1991
G. Harry Stine, *The Lost Battalion*, 1989
G. Harry Stine, *Operation Steel Band*, 1988

## 3014

### KEN KATO

## *Yamato: A Rage in Heaven*

(New York: Warner/Questar, 1990)

**Story type:** Science Fiction (Space Opera)
**Series:** Yamato
**Major character(s):** Jos Hawken, Military Personnel (commodore), Spaceship Captain; Ellis Straker, Spaceship Captain, Psychic
**Time period(s):** 25th century (2420s)
**Locale(s):** Yamato Sector, Outer Space; Sado, Planet—Imaginary (Neutral Zone)

**Summary:** When space opened to colonization after 2100 A.D., areas were apportioned by sectors to different countries. The area settled by Japan, named Yamato, became very powerful with a ruling Shogunate which intends to control all the sectors. The only one that could possibly prevent them is the Amerikan sector, which is immobilized by internal politics and greed.

**Other books you might like:**
Greg Bear, *Eon*, 1989
C.J. Cherryh, *Downbelow Station*, 1981
Frank Herbert, *Dune*, 1965
Alis A. Rasmussen, *A Passage of Stars*, 1990
Dan Simmons, *The Fall of Hyperion*, 1990
Dan Simmons, *Hyperion*, 1989

## 3015

### DOUGLAS KAUFMAN, Editor
### ED STARK, Co-Editor

## *Dragons over England*

(Honesdale, Pennsylvania: West End Games, 1992)

**Story type:** Fantasy (Anthology; Legend)
**Series:** Torg: The Possibility Wars
**Time period(s):** 20th century
**Locale(s):** Aysle, Alternate Earth; England

**Summary:** This volume contains a six-page introduction by Ed Stark plus nine stories, two by the editors, in which legendary characters from European mythology come alive and co-exist with humanity in a limited area. Set in the universe of the game, *Torg*.

**Other books you might like:**
L. Sprague de Camp, *The Complete Compleat Enchanter*, 1989
   Fletcher Pratt, co-author
L. Sprague de Camp, *The Enchanter Reborn*, 1992
   Christopher Stasheff, co-editor
Greg Farshtey, *Strange Tales From the Nile Empire*, 1992
   Greg Gorden and Ed Stark, co-editors

L. Sprague de Camp, *The Land of Unreason*, 1942
  Fletcher Pratt, co-author
Clifford D. Simak, *Out of Their Minds*, 1970
Bill Slavicsek, *Storm Knights*, 1990
  C.J. Tramontana, co-author
Ed Stark, *Mysterious Cairo*, 1992
  editor

**3016**

**GUY GAVRIEL KAY**

## The Lions of Al-Rassan

(New York: HarperPrism, 1995)

**Story type:** Fantasy (Political)
**Major character(s):** Ammar ibn Khairan, Military Personnel, Courtier; Rodrigo Belmonte, Mercenary; Jehane bet Ishak, Doctor
**Time period(s):** Indeterminate Past
**Locale(s):** Al-Rassan, Fictional Country; Cartada, Fictional City

**Summary:** Created centuries ago by the savage Asharites, the Empire of Al-Rassan has since collapsed into warring states. There, three very different people pursue their fates against the backdrop of one king's drive for reunification. This novel draws heavily on the history of Moorish Spain for inspiration and flavor.

**Other books you might like:**
Glen Cook, *The Fire in His Hands*, 1984
Barbara Hambly, *The Ladies of Mandrigyn*, 1984
Katherine Kurtz, *Deryni Rising*, 1970
Mark E. Rogers, *The Expected One*, 1991
Judith Tarr, *Alamut*, 1989

**3017**

**GUY GAVRIEL KAY**

## A Song for Arbonne

(New York: Crown, 1993)

**Story type:** Fantasy (Historical; Romance)
**Major character(s):** Bertran de Talair, Nobleman, Minstrel; Blaise de Garsenc, Nobleman, Mercenary; Lisseut of Vezet, Minstrel
**Time period(s):** Indeterminate Past
**Locale(s):** Arbonne, Fictional Country; Gorhaut, Fictional Country

**Summary:** Self-exiled from the grim, misogynistic kingdom of Gorhaut, Blaise de Garsenc accepts a job as captain of the guards for a minor baron in Arbonne, the sunny, Goddess-worshipping country to the south, whose citizens exalt love and music. As the King of Gorhaut plots to conquer Arbonne, Blaise meets the priestess of Rian, the Queen of the Court of Love, and a noble minstrel who teach him about Arbonnais culture and politics. When Gorhaut invades Arbonne, Blaise finds his own destiny as he chooses among his divided loyalties.

**Other books you might like:**
Gael Baudino, *Maze of Moonlight*, 1993
Marion Zimmer Bradley, *The Mists of Avalon*, 1983
Parke Godwin, *Firelord*, 1980
Norah Lofts, *The Lute Player*, 1951
Diana L. Paxson, *The White Raven*, 1988
Elizabeth Marie Pope, *The Perilous Gard*, 1974
Chelsea Quinn Yarbro, *The Palace*, 1978

**3018**

**GUY GAVRIEL KAY**

## Tigana

(New York: Roc, 1990)

**Story type:** Fantasy (Political)
**Major character(s):** Alessan bar Valentin, Royalty (Prince of Tigana); Brandin of Ygrath, Ruler, Sorcerer
**Time period(s):** Indeterminate
**Locale(s):** The 9 Countries of the Palm, Fictional Country (Peninsula)

**Summary:** Eighteen years ago, when the countries of the Palm were invaded by competing sorcerer kings (Brandin and Alberico) from overseas, Prince Valentin of Tigana killed Brandin's son in battle and Brandin cast a spell that stripped the ability to hear "Tigana" from the minds of every person not born on Tigana's soil before the battle. Now all the work and planning of Valentin's son Alessan culminate in a final campaign to rid the Palm of its tyrants and release Tigana's name.

**Other books you might like:**
Steven Brust, *Brokedown Palace*, 1986
Heather Gladney, *Teot's War*, 1988
Katharine Kerr, *Daggerspell*, 1986
Diana L. Paxson, *The White Raven*, 1988
M.K. Wren, *Sword of the Lamb*, 1981

**3019**

**JEREMY KAY**

## The Secret Laboratory Journals of Dr. Victor Frankenstein

(New York: Overlook Press, 1995)

**Story type:** Horror (Reanimated Dead)
**Major character(s):** Victor Frankenstein, Scientist
**Time period(s):** 1800s (early)
**Locale(s):** Germany; Switzerland

**Summary:** Incorporating diaries and journals, this book is presented as Victor Frankenstein's random notes on how he came to conceive of, and build, his infamous monster. This heavily illustrated book "reproduces" laboratory diagrams and script in Victor's own hand, and incorporates his thoughts on, among other things, his scientific education, his family, the services of the local graverobbers, and of course the reanimation of dead body parts.

**Other books you might like:**
Brian W. Aldiss, *Frankenstein Unbound*, 1973
Martin H. Greenberg, *Frankenstein: The Monster Wakes*, 1993
  editor
Stephen Jones, *The Mammoth Book of Frankenstein*, 1995
  editor
Michel Parry, *Rivals of Frankenstein*, 1977
  editor
Theodore Roszak, *The Memoirs of Elizabeth Frankenstein*, 1995
Mary Shelley, *Frankenstein*, 1818
Robert Weinberg, *Vampire Diary: The Embrace*, 1995
  Mark Rein-Hagen, co-author

## 3020

**SUSAN KAY**

### *Phantom*

(New York: Delacorte, 1991)

**Story type:** Horror (Mystery)
**Major character(s):** Erik, Child, Musician; Madeleine, Parent (mother of Erik); Christine Daae, Student (vocal student), Singer
**Time period(s):** 19th century (1831-1851)
**Locale(s):** Paris, France; Nisni-Novgorod, Persia; Rome, Italy

**Summary:** This sweeping historical romance and prequel to Gaston Leroux's *The Phantom of the Opera* chronicles the plight of Erik, born hideously deformed, ultimately separated from his beloved mother, and forced to make his living while a child in courts and carnival side shows across two continents. It is in the sewer system beneath the Paris Opera House, however, that Erik finds a suitable dwelling and a base of operations from which to indulge his infatuation with a beautiful opera singer for whom he becomes an anonymous benefactor.

**Other books you might like:**
Kobo Abe, *The Face of Another*, 1966
Barbara Hambly, *Beauty and the Beast*, 1989
Gaston Leroux, *The Phantom of the Opera*, 1910
Steve Vance, *Spook*, 1990

## 3021

**MARILYN KAYE**

### *The Vanishing*

(New York: Avon, 1998)

**Story type:** Science Fiction (Disaster; Young Adult)
**Series:** Last on Earth
**Major character(s):** Jake Robbins, Teenager, Student; Cameron Daley, Teenager, Student; Martina Santiago, Teenager, Twin
**Time period(s):** 1990s
**Locale(s):** New York, New York

**Summary:** Emerging from the bomb shelter where their geometry class met, 25 students find a world empty of people. They set up a community, trying to adjust to new responsibilities and lack of control or support from adults, while taking what they want from surrounding stores and buildings. A circular depression in Central Park hints at a cause for the vanishing, but a split in the community prevents an effective search for answers.

**Other books you might like:**
William Golding, *Lord of the Flies*, 1954
Michaela Roessner, *Vanishing Point*, 1993
Kathy Tyers, *Shivering World*, 1991
Vernor Vinge, *Marooned in Realtime*, 1986
Philip Wylie, *The Disappearance*, 1951

## 3022

**MARVIN KAYE**, Editor

### *Angels of Darkness*

(Garden City, NY: Guild America, 1995)

**Story type:** Horror (Anthology)
**Summary:** The forty-four stories and poems in this anthology—divided equally between male and female authors—all feature women as either victims or perpetrators of horrors. Classic tales include Henry James's ''The Friend of the Friends,'' in which a man falls in love with a woman who turns out to be a ghost, Nathaniel Hawthorne's ''Lady Eleanor's Mantle,'' in which a woman's beauty is attributed to the magical power of her mantle, and Clemence Housman's ''The Were-Wolf,'' in which love for a human male redeems a female werewolf. More modern stories include Robert Bloch's ''The Unspeakable Betrothal,'' about a young girl ensorcelled by powers from beyond, Julian Kilman's ''The Mystery of the Black Jean,'' in which a woman befriends an abused pet to help her dispose of its owner, and Maurice Level's *conte cruel* ''The Last Kiss,'' about the just desserts that come to a woman who has disfigured her lover's face with acid. Paula Volsky supplies the introduction.

**Other books you might like:**
Seon Manley, *Women of the Weird*, 1976
   Gogo Lewis, co-editor
Kathryn Ptacek, *Women of Darkness*, 1988
   editor
Kathryn Ptacek, *Women of Darkness II*, 1990
   editor
Lisa Tuttle, *Skin of the Soul*, 1991
   editor

## 3023

**MARVIN KAYE**, Editor
**JOHN GREGORY BETANCOURT**, Co-Editor

### *The Best of Weird Tales: 1923*

(Berkeley Heights, New Jersey: Bleak House, 1997)

**Story type:** Horror (Anthology)

**Summary:** Thirteen stories culled from the first eight issue of *Weird Tales*, the long-running pulp weird fiction magazine. In addition to ''Dragon,'' H.P. Lovecraft's first professionally published work of fiction, the book includes Orville R. Emerson's ''The Grave,'' a story of premature burial during World War I; J. Paul Suter's ''Beyond the Door,'' about a ghost who haunts the house where he earthly form was murdered; Frank Owen's ''The Man Who Owned the World,'' the tale of a madman and his delusions; Lyle Wilson Holden's ''The Devil Plant,'' a gruesome revenge story involving a carnivorous plant; and James L. Ravenscroft's native curse story ''The Dead-Naming of Lukapehu.'' Kaye contributes the introduction and notes for each issue represented.

**Other books you might like:**
John Gregory Betancourt, *Weird Tales: Seven Decades of Terror*, 1997
   Robert Weinberg, co-editor
Robert Weinberg, *100 Wild Little Weird Tales*, 1995
   Stefan Dziemianowicz and Martin H. Greenberg, co-editors
Stefan Dziemianowicz, *Weird Tales: 32 Unearthed Terrors*, 1987
   Robert Weinberg and Martin H. Greenberg, co-editors
Marvin Kaye, *Weird Tales: The Magazine That Never Dies*, 1987
   editor
Robert Weinberg, *The Eighth Green Man and Other Strange Folk*, 1989
   editor

## 3024

**MARVIN KAYE**, Editor

### *Don't Open This Book!*

(Garden City, New York: Doubleday/Guild America, 1998)

**Story type:** Horror (Anthology)

**Summary:** These 39 stories, 16 of which are original to the volume, all deal with some aspect of the forbidden. Robert Bloch's "Black Bargain" tells of a man whose black magic deals create a shadowy doppelganger that eventually overwhelms him. Jean Paiva's "Cinnabar" concerns a man whose search for love leads him into a vampiric relationship. Patrick Lobrutto's "Genesis for Dummies" is a rewrite of the biblical book of Genesis in which the forbidden fruit is written word. W.C. Morrow's "The Monster-Maker" is a variation on the theme of Frankenstein. An original publication of the Science Fiction Book Club.

**Other books you might like:**
Nancy A. Collins, *Forbidden Acts*, 1995
    Edward Kramer, Martin H. Greenberg, co-editors
Jeff Gelb, *Fear Itself*, 1995
Gary L. Raisor, *Obsessions*, 1991
    editor
Michele Slung, *I Shudder at Your Touch*, 1991
    editor
Wendy Webb, *Phobias: Stories of Your Deepest Fears*, 1994
    Richard Gilliam, Edward Kramer, Martin H. Greenberg, co-editors

**3025**

**MARVIN KAYE**

## Fantastique

(New York: St. Martin's, 1992)

**Story type:** Horror (Literary)
**Major character(s):** Carl Richards, Director (theatre); Diana Lee Taylor, Actress (Carl's Wife); Angelica Winters, Actress
**Time period(s):** 1990s (1992)
**Locale(s):** New York, New York

**Summary:** Although renowned for his outrageous stagings of violent plays, Carl Richards realizes something is wrong with his current staging of Buchner's *Woyzeck* when a series of accidents push the violence over the edge from simulated to actual. Patterned on Hector Berlioz's *Symphonie Fantastique*, this novel tells of Carl's obsession with his wife's understudy in the play, Angelica Winters, whose presence has an uncanny disintegrating effect on the production and on Carl's private life.

**Other books you might like:**
Ramsey Campbell, *Ancient Images*, 1989
Chet Williamson, *Reign*, 1990

**3026**

**MARVIN KAYE**, Editor

## Lovers and Other Monsters

(Garden City, New York: Guild America, 1992)

**Story type:** Horror (Anthology)

**Summary:** Fifty-three stories and poems concerned with the darker side of love. Included are Ray Bradbury's macabre prose poem, "The Maiden," H.P. Lovecraft's tale of longing for the past, "The Strange High House in the Mist," Jerome Bixby and Joe E. Dean's tale of an unusual vampiric relationship, "Share Alike," Edgar Allan Poe's gruesome vignette on obsession, "Berenice," and Frank Stockton's classic tale of sexual politics, "The Lady or the Tiger," along with Jack Moffitt's contemporary response, "The Lady and the Tiger."

**Other books you might like:**
Margaret L. Carter, *Demon Lovers and Strange Seductions*, 1973

Don Congdon, *Tales of Love and Horror*, 1961
Ellen Datlow, *Alien Sex*, 1991
    editor
Jeff Gelb, *Hot Blood: Tales of Provocative Horror*, 1989
    Lonn Friend, co-editor
Michele Slung, *I Shudder at Your Touch*, 1991

**3027**

**MARVIN KAYE**

## Masterpieces of Terror and the Unknown

(Garden City, New York: Guild America, 1993)

**Story type:** Horror (Anthology)

**Summary:** A collection of 58 tales of horror and the supernatural that span several centuries. Included are ghost stories such as Arthur Machen's "The Happy Children" and Algernon Blackwood's "Keeping His Promise"; Theodore Sturgeon's tale of perverse obsession, "Bianca's Hands"; A. Merritt's tale of a lost race that lives in the Arctic wastes, "The People of the Pit"; H.P. Lovecraft's fusion of cosmic horror and mathematics, "Dreams in the Witch House"; Maurice Level's *conte cruel*, "The Cripple"; Edward Lucas White's ghoul story "Amina"; and Richard Matheson's vampire tale, "A Dress of White Silk."

**Other books you might like:**
David G. Hartwell, *The Dark Descent*, 1987
    editor
Bill Pronzini, *The Arbor House Treasury of Horror and the Supernatural*, 1981
    Barry Malzberg and Martin H. Greenberg, co-editors
Herbert Wise, *Great Tales of Terror and the Supernatural*, 1944
    Phyllis Fraser, co-editor

**3028**

**MARVIN KAYE**, Editor

## Weird Tales: The Magazine That Never Dies

(New York: Barnes & Noble, 1995)

**Story type:** Horror (Anthology)

**Summary:** Originally published in 1987, this omnibus volume presents one essay and 44 stories of fantasy and horror gathered from *Weird Tales*. The magazine was originally published between 1923 and 1954, and later, there were four short-lived attempts to revive it. Tales from the original magazine include Robert E. Howard's swashbuckling tale of adventurer Solomon Kane, "The Skulls in the Stars"; Ray Bradbury's brief tale of the afterlife, "Interim"; C. Hall Thompson's tale of psychopathology, "The Pale Criminal"; Richard Matheson's ghost story, "Wet Straw"; and H.P. Lovecraft's urban horror story, "He." Tales from the more recent incarnation of the magazine include Ed Hoch's ghostly "Funeral in the Fog," Katherine MacLean and Mary Kornbluth's wry "Chicken Soup," and a recently discovered tale by William Hope Hodgson, "The Terror of the Water Tank."

**Other books you might like:**
John Gregory Betancourt, *The Best of Weird Tales*, 1995
    editor
Robert Weinberg, *100 Wild Little Weird Tales*, 1995
    Martin H. Greenberg, Stefan Dziemianowicz, co-editor
Stefan Dziemianowicz, *Weird Tales: 32 Unearthed Terrors*, 1987
    Robert Weinberg, Martin H. Greenberg, co-editor

Robert Weinberg, *The Eighth Green Man and Other Strange Folk*, 1989
editor
Robert Weinberg, *Far Below and Other Horrors*, 1974
editor

---

**3029**

MEL KEEGAN

## Death's Head

(London: Gay Men's Press, 1993)

**Story type:** Science Fiction (Military; Gay/Lesbian Fiction)
**Major character(s):** Kevin Jarrat, Military Personnel, Homosexual; Jerry Stone, Military Personnel, Homosexual
**Time period(s):** 23rd century
**Locale(s):** Rethan, Planet—Imaginary

**Summary:** The NARCs fight the spread of an invariably deadly drug called Angel with co-captains who alternate undercover and command duties and backed up with massive military force. The NARC code demands non-involvement between captains, but Kevin and Stoney must defy it when kidnapping forces Stoney on Angel and his only hope becomes an unbreakable empathic link with Kevin.

**Other books you might like:**
Chris Claremont, *Grounded!*, 1991
Diane Duane, *High Moon*, 1992
  Peter Morwood, co-author
Maureen F. McHugh, *China Mountain Zhang*, 1992
George Nader, *Chrome*, 1979
Walter Jon Williams, *Days of Atonement*, 1991

---

**3030**

PAM KEESEY, Editor

## Darker Angels: Lesbian Vampire Stories

(Pittsburgh: Cleis Press, 1995)

**Story type:** Horror (Anthology; Vampire Story)

**Summary:** Six original and five reprint stories feature female vampires and their mostly female victims. In Gary Bowen's historical "Blood Wedding," a female aristocrat seduces the wife of her husband's best friend in a vampire tryst. Melanie Tem's "Presence" features a woman driven to various forms of carnality through her insatiable need for love, and Lawrence Schimel's "Femme de Siecle" a vampire who becomes bisexual to serve her monthly needs. In Shawn Dell's "Daria Dangerous," a woman recounts her death at the hands of an irresistable female vampire. The editor supplies an introduction on the history of the lesbian vampire theme and a bibliography of additional readings.

**Other books you might like:**
Poppy Z. Brite, *Love in Vein*, 1994
  Martin H. Greenberg, co-editor
Martin H. Greenberg, *Vamps*, 1988
  Charles G. Waugh, co-editor
Amarantha Knight, *Love Bites*, 1995
  editor
Cecilia Tan, *Blood Kiss: Vampire Erotica*, 1994
  editor

---

**3031**

PAM KEESEY, Editor

## Daughters of Darkness: Lesbian Vampire Stories

(San Francisco, California: Cleis Press, 1993)

**Story type:** Horror (Anthology; Vampire Story)

**Summary:** This book collects nine stories and novel excerpts featuring lesbian vampires. Included are J. Sheridan Le Fanu's Victorian classic, "Carmilla," Jewelle Gomez's "Louisiana 1850," featuring her black feminist vampire Gilda, and a portion of Elaine Bergstrom's novel *Daughter of the Night*, one of several that chronicle the history of a centuries-old vampire family.

**Other books you might like:**
Ellen Datlow, *Blood Is Not Enough*, 1989
  editor
Ellen Datlow, *A Whisper of Blood*, 1991
  editor
Jewelle Gomez, *The Gilda Stories*, 1991
Martin H. Greenberg, *Vamps*, 1987
  editor
Stephen Jones, *The Mammoth Book of Vampires*, 1992
  editor
Alan Ryan, *Vampires: Two Centuries of Great Vampire Stories*, 1987
  editor

---

**3032**

PAM KEESEY, Editor

## Women Who Run with Werewolves: Tales of Blood, Lust and Metamorphosis

(Boston: Cleis Press, 1996)

**Story type:** Horror (Anthology; Werewolf Story)

**Summary:** Fifteen stories, three of them reprints, use the werewolf theme to explore issues of female identity. Lycanthropy is equated with split personality in Charlee Jacobs' "Permafrost" and with a girl's sexual maturation in Suzy McKee Charnas' "Boobs." The werewolf symbolizes a man's transformation from a loving husband to a brutal mate in Ursula K. Le Guin's "The Wife's Story" and freedom from a life of repression in Jeremy E. Johnson's "Euphorbia Helioscopia." An excerpt from Melanie Tem's novel *Wilding* features a matriarchal family of werewolves, while Tom Piccirilli's "The Hound of God" is concerned with a female werewolf whose affliction empowers her to rid her neighborhood of criminals.

**Other books you might like:**
Martin H. Greenberg, *Werewolves*, 1995
  editor
Stephen Jones, *The Mammoth Book of Werewolves*, 1994
  editor
Byron Preiss, *The Ultimate Werewolf*, 1991
  David Keller, Megan Miller, John Gregory Betancourt, co-editors

## 3033

**STEPHANIE KEGAN**

### *The Baby*

(New York: Diamond, 1990)

**Story type:** Horror (Haunted House; Child-in-Peril)
**Major character(s):** Jill Douglas, Housewife (mother-to-be); Tom Douglas, Doctor (Jill's husband); Dora Miles, Widow(er) (Tom's deceased aunt)
**Time period(s):** 1990s (1990)
**Locale(s):** Bay Area, California

**Summary:** When Jill and Tom Douglas move into the house of Tom's recently-deceased aunt, a series of inexplicable experiences leaves Jill believing either that she is going insane or that an evil presence wants her unborn child. This is the author's first novel.

**Other books you might like:**
Ken Eulo, *The Brownstone*, 1980
Ira Levin, *Rosemary's Baby*, 1967
Robert Marasco, *Burnt Offerings*, 1973
Graham Masterton, *Walkers*, 1989
Randall Boyll, *After Sundown*, 1989

## 3034

**ANDREW KEITH**

### *Cohort of the Damned*

(New York: Roc, 1993)

**Story type:** Science Fiction (Military; Adventure)
**Series:** Fifth Foreign Legion
**Major character(s):** Wolfgang ''Karl Wolf'' Hauser, Military Personnel, Leader (lance); Lisa Scott, Military Personnel (recruit)
**Time period(s):** 29th century
**Locale(s):** Devereaux, Planet—Imaginary (Beau Soleil System)

**Summary:** After facing an enemy and being called a coward, Wolfgang Hauser changes his name and joins the Fifth Foreign Legion. He participates in several fights with enemies and himself as he grows up during basic training.

**Other books you might like:**
Bill Baldwin, *The Helmsman*, 1985
Gordon R. Dickson, *Dorsai!*, 1976
William C. Dietz, *Legion of the Damned*, 1993
William R. Forstchen, *Rally Cry!*, 1990
Robert Randle, *Seeds of War*, 1986
   Robert Cornett, co-author

## 3035

**ANDREW KEITH**
**WILLIAM H. KEITH JR.**, Co-Author

### *March or Die*

(New York: Roc, 1992)

**Story type:** Science Fiction (Military; Adventure)
**Series:** Fifth Foreign Legion
**Major character(s):** Colin Fraser, Military Personnel; Kelly Ann Winters, Engineer, Military Personnel; John ''Slick'' Grant, Military Personnel
**Time period(s):** 29th century
**Locale(s):** Hanuman, Planet—Imaginary

**Summary:** When Terran Commonwealth officials are assassinated at a diplomatic reception in the capital city of Hanuman, native forces initiate a simultaneous attack on the half-finished Foreign Legion Fortress. Surrounded by hostile forces and written off by higher-ups, the surviving troops choose to fight their way over the mountains to the relative safety of the Legion's main base.

**Other books you might like:**
Robert Asprin, *The Bug Wars*, 1979
Gordon R. Dickson, *Dorsai!*, 1976
Gordon R. Dickson, *Soldier, Ask Not*, 1967
Jerry Pournelle, *Falkenberg's Legion*, 1990
Elizabeth Ann Scarborough, *The Healer's War*, 1989
Jack Williamson, *The Legion of Space*, 1947

## 3036

**WILLIAM H. KEITH JR.**

### *Warlords of Jupiter*

(Lake Geneva, Wisconsin: TSR, 1993)

**Story type:** Science Fiction (Political)
**Series:** Invaders of Charon
**Major character(s):** Vince Pirelli, Spaceman, Warrior; Jovanna Trask, Spacewoman, Warrior
**Time period(s):** 25th century
**Locale(s):** Amalthea, Space Station (Jovian); Jupiter

**Summary:** While investigating the origin of a seemingly alien artifact lost by enemy forces, Vince and others come to the aid of winged giants and find new allies and possible leads in their search. Jovanna and others on Amalthea meet an invading force with deadly results. Concludes the trilogy set in the *Buck Rogers* milieu.

**Other books you might like:**
Britton Bloom, *Matrix Cubed*, 1991
C.M. Brennan, *The Genesis Web*, 1992
John Miller, *First Power Play*, 1990
M.S. Murdock, *Armageddon Off Vesta*, 1989
M.S. Murdock, *Hammer of Mars*, 1989
M.S. Murdock, *Prime Squared*, 1990
M.S. Murdock, *Rebellion 2456*, 1989
Philip Francis Nowlan, *Armageddon 2419 A.D.*, 1962
John Silbersack, *Roger's Rangers*, 1983

## 3037

**WILLIAM H. KEITH JR.**

### *Warstrider*

(New York: AvoNova, 1993)

**Story type:** Science Fiction (Military)
**Series:** Warstrider
**Major character(s):** Dev Cameron, Military Personnel
**Time period(s):** 26th century
**Locale(s):** Terran Hegemony, Interstellar Empire/Federation

**Summary:** Hoping to join the Hegemony Navy, Dev Cameron instead signs up for military duty and finds himself in the army, utilizing his neural implants not to operate a spaceship, but rather to direct heavy weaponry against alien Xenophobe invaders intent on wiping out humanity.

**Other books you might like:**
Robert Asprin, *The Bug Wars*, 1979
Orson Scott Card, *Ender's Game*, 1985
Gordon R. Dickson, *Dorsai!*, 1975

David Drake, *Battlestation*, 1992
  Bill Fawcett, co-editor
Andrew Keith, *Honor and Fidelity*, 1992
  William H. Keith, Jr., co-author
G. Harry Stine, *The Lost Battalion*, 1989
David Weber, *Path of the Fury*, 1992
Dave Wolverton, *On My Way to Paradise*, 1989

## 3038
#### WILLIAM H. KEITH JR.
### *Warstrider: Netlink*
(New York: AvoNova, 1995)

**Story type:** Science Fiction (Alternate Intelligence; Genetic Manipulation)
**Series:** Warstrider
**Major character(s):** Dev Cameron, Genetically Altered Being, Space Explorer; Kara Hagan, Military Personnel (Confederation lieutenant); Daren Cameron, Scholar, Scientist (Xenologist)
**Time period(s):** Indeterminate Future
**Locale(s):** Mars; *Sirghal*, Spaceship

**Summary:** While Confederate Rebels fight to maintain their independence from the Earth Imperium, Dev Cameron, once human but now part of a neurally-linked alien fleet, discovers a new alien threat so vast that human conflicts seem insignificant in comparison.

**Other books you might like:**
Keith William Andrews, *The Freedom's Rangers Series*, 1989-1991
  pseudonym of William H. Keith Jr.
Valerie J. Freireich, *Becoming Human*, 1995
Anne McCaffrey, *The Ship Who Sang*, 1995
John Varley, *The Ophiuchi Hotline*, 1977

## 3039
#### ANNE KELLEHER
### *A Once and Future Love*
(New York: Jove, 1998)

**Story type:** Fantasy (Historical; Romance)
**Major character(s):** Richard Lambert, Businessman
**Time period(s):** 1990s (1994); 13th century (1214)
**Locale(s):** England

**Summary:** Grieving for his recently deceased wife, an American travels to England to visit his family's ancestral home. There he is magically transported back into the body of one of his ancestors, in which he finds an entire new life.

**Other books you might like:**
Cheryl Biggs, *Yesterday's Passion*, 1992
Beverly Byrne, *A Matter of Time*, 1987
Marilyn Campbell, *Just in Time*, 1996
Laura Hayden, *A Margin in Time*, 1995
Kathleen Kane, *This Time for Keeps*, 1998

## 3040
#### ED KELLEHER
#### HARRIETTE VIDAL, Co-Author
### *Animus*
(New York: Leisure, 1993)

**Story type:** Horror (Doppelganger; Evil Children)

**Major character(s):** Catherine Bishop, Artisan (dollmaker); Ian Bishop, Art Dealer (gallery owner); Julian Bishop, Child (Catherine and Ian's son)
**Time period(s):** 1980s (1984); 1990s (1993)
**Locale(s):** New York, New York

**Summary:** Catherine Bishop is horrified to learn that her imaginary childhood playmate, Bobo, is actually her animus, the male side of her personality which murders to protect her whenever she feels threatened. She's even more horrified when Bobo becomes incarnated as her only son, Julian.

**Other books you might like:**
Ramsey Campbell, *To Wake the Dead*, 1980
Rick Hautala, *Cold Whisper*, 1991
Edmund Plante, *Seed of Evil*, 1991

## 3041
#### ED KELLEHER
#### HARRIETTE VIDAL, Co-Author
### *Breeder*
(New York: Leisure, 1991)

**Story type:** Horror (Black Magic)
**Major character(s):** Janet Young, Artist; Whitney Lancaster, Political Figure (mayor); Miranda Jane Young, Teenager
**Time period(s):** 1990s
**Locale(s):** Mount Garde, New York (Long Island)

**Summary:** A vacation to her family home to escape the pressures of life in Manhattan turns into a nightmare when Janet Young, her new husband and her psychically endowed stepdaughter Miranda discover that Janet's hometown has been taken over by Satanists, who have reanimated dead townspeople as zombies and plan to make her family their next sacrifice to placate the Devil.

**Other books you might like:**
Charles L. Grant, *The Hour of the Oxrun Dead*, 1977
Ira Levin, *The Stepford Wives*, 1972
John Saul, *Creature*, 1989

## 3042
#### ED KELLEHER
#### HARRIETTE VIDAL, Co-Author
### *The School*
(New York: Leisure, 1992)

**Story type:** Horror (Black Magic)
**Major character(s):** Vanessa Forbes, Student; Bobby Cannon, Student; Matthew Hanley, Principal (headmaster)
**Time period(s):** 1990s
**Locale(s):** Hanley, Massachusetts

**Summary:** Students at the Hanley School for Girls are given to bizarre visions and the expression of unbridled lusts, owing to a taint upon the land where the school was built. Sixty years after headmaster Malcolm Hanley was slain by an obsessed student, the performance of that student's play about witchcraft, "Flowers of Darkness," by the Hanley School's theatre class threatens to unleash the dark forces with which the school has become imbued. This novel was originally published in 1988.

**Other books you might like:**
Edward Lee, *Coven*, 1990
David van Meter Smith, *Trinity Grove*, 1990

## 3043

### VICTOR KELLEHER

## The Red King

(New York: Dial, 1990)

**Story type:** Fantasy (Adventure; Young Adult)
**Major character(s):** Timkin, Slave; Petie, Thief
**Time period(s):** Indeterminate Past
**Locale(s):** Forest Lands, Fictional Country

**Summary:** Timkin survives the red powder released by the Red King's men, only to be put back into the slave collar by Petie after he was certain she would live. Timkin realizes that the real enemy is the Red King, who Timkin and Petie hope to defeat at the Gathering, the biggest fair of the season.

**Other books you might like:**
Grace Chetwin, *The Crystal Stair*, 1988
Grace Chetwin, *Gom on Windy Mountain*, 1986
Grace Chetwin, *The Riddle and the Rune*, 1987
Rosemary Kirstein, *The Steerswoman*, 1989
Nancy Springer, *Red Wizard*, 1990

## 3044

### MARJORIE BRADLEY KELLOGG

## The Book of Earth

(New York: DAW, 1995)

**Story type:** Fantasy (Sword and Sorcery)
**Series:** Dragon Quartet
**Major character(s):** Erde von Alte, Noblewoman, Psychic (dragon guide); Earth, Mythical Creature (dragon), Guardian (Erde's); Guillemo Gotti, Religious (priest), Psychic (prophet)
**Time period(s):** Indeterminate
**Locale(s):** Germany; Tor Alte, Fictional Country; Deep Moor, Fictional Country

**Summary:** Having lost everyone close to her because of the machinations of an evil priest, Brother Guillemo Gotti, young Erde von Alte flees her father's mountain domain, literally stumbling across Earth, one of four dragons created from elemental energies to help set the world in motion. Erde helps Earth in his quest to find the One who has awakened him before his time, while the dragon aids Erde in staying one step ahead of Brother Guillemo, who would burn her as a witch.

**Other books you might like:**
Terry Goodkind, *Wizard's First Rule*, 1994
Michael Green, *Quest: In Search of the Dragontooth*, 1994
Barbara Hambly, *Dragonsbane*, 1986
Robert Jordan, *The Eye of the World*, 1989
Anne McCaffrey, *Dragonflight*, 1968
Anne McCaffrey, *Moreta's Story*, 1983
Mark C. Perry, *Morigu: The Dead*, 1990

## 3045

### MARJORIE BRADLEY KELLOGG

## The Book of Water

(New York: DAW, 1997)

**Story type:** Fantasy (Quest; Adventure)
**Series:** Dragon Quartet
**Major character(s):** D'Noch, Guide; Earth, Mythical Creature (dragon); Water, Mythical Creature (dragon)

**Time period(s):** 2010s (2013)
**Locale(s):** Africa

**Summary:** Water's call summons Earth and his human guide, Erde, from the tenth-century German principalities to 21st-century Africa where Water and D'Noch wait for their help. Amidst widespread environmental devastation, they discover forces at work that will require all their abilities and more to counter. Second in series.

**Other books you might like:**
Graham Edwards, *Dragoncharm*, 1996
Nancy Farmer, *The Ear, the Eye, and the Arm*, 1994
Anne McCaffrey, *Dragonflight*, 1968
Andre Norton, *Elvenblood*, 1995
    Mercedes Lackey, co-author
Irene Radford, *The Loneliest Magician*, 1996

## 3046

### MARJORIE BRADLEY KELLOGG

## Harmony

(New York: Roc, 1991)

**Story type:** Science Fiction (Arts)
**Major character(s):** Gwinn Rhys, Artist, Apprentice; Micah Miguel Cervantes, Artist (master scenographer)
**Time period(s):** 2040s
**Locale(s):** Chicago, Illinois (domed city); Harmony, Vermont (domed city); Tuamatuetuamatu, Pacific Islands (imaginary)

**Summary:** In the late 20th century the largest and richest cities built domes which kept pollution and excess population out. When the domes were completed, quite desperate people camped in large groups in the squalid, unhealthy conditions surrounding the domes. One of the first cities to construct a dome, Chicago, outlawed art as frivolous. However, Gwinn's talent is too compelling for her not to risk expulsion in her bid to move to Harmony, the domed artists' enclave, where she meets the Eye, a dance troupe which uses magic to tell their story.

**Other books you might like:**
Eleanor Arnason, *A Woman of the Iron People*, 1990
Pat Cadigan, *Synners*, 1991
Ernest Hogan, *Cortez on Jupiter*, 1990
James Patrick Kelly, *Look into the Sun*, 1989
Pat Murphy, *The City, Not Long After*, 1989
Sheri S. Tepper, *The Gate to Women's Country*, 1988

## 3047

### JAMES PATRICK KELLY

## Look into the Sun

(New York: Tor, 1989)

**Story type:** Science Fiction (First Contact)
**Major character(s):** Phillip Wing, Architect; Teaqua, Deity (Goddess), Ruler
**Time period(s):** 21st century
**Locale(s):** Earth; Aseneshesh, Planet—Imaginary

**Summary:** Phillip Wing, who built one of 21st century Earth's greatest architectural masterpieces, is haunted by feelings of mediocrity and the fear that he will never again achieve greatness. Wing therefore jumps at the chance to travel to Aseneshesh and build there a tomb for Teaqua, the planet's resident goddess. Teaqua, meanwhile, plots desperately to bring change to her planet's stagnant culture before it is swallowed up by the Messengers, a more advanced alien race whose cultural imperialism threatens both Aseneshesh and Earth.

**Other books you might like:**
Octavia E. Butler, *Adulthood Rites*, 1988
Octavia E. Butler, *Dawn*, 1987
Octavia E. Butler, *Imago*, 1989
Orson Scott Card, *Speaker for the Dead*, 1986
Mary Gentle, *Ancient Light*, 1989
Mary Gentle, *Golden Witchbreed*, 1983
Ursula K. Le Guin, *The Left Hand of Darkness*, 1969

### 3048

**JAMES PATRICK KELLY**

## Think Like a Dinosaur and Other Stories
(Collinsville, Illinois: Golden Gryphon Press, 1997)

**Story type:** Science Fiction (Collection)

**Summary:** Contains a six-page introduction by John Kessel, the Hugo Award winning title story and 13 other stories from periodicals and anthologies 1984-1997. Varying in tone from downbeat to satirical, the stories feature diverse themes, such as heroism, dystopian futures, relationships, virtual reality, law and order, hallucinations and life in outer space.

**Other books you might like:**
Greg Bear, *The Wind From a Burning Woman*, 1983
John Kessel, *Freedom Beach*, 1985
   James Patrick Kelly, co-author
John Kessel, *Meeting in Infinity*, 1992
Nancy Kress, *The Aliens of Earth*, 1993
Lucius Shepard, *The Ends of the Earth*, 1991
James Tiptree Jr., *Her Smoke Rose Up Forever*, 1990

### 3049

**JAMES PATRICK KELLY**

## Wildlife
(New York: Tor, 1994)

**Story type:** Science Fiction (Genetic Manipulation; Alternate Intelligence)
**Major character(s):** Wynne Cage, Journalist, Genetically Altered Being; Francois Bonivard, Computer Expert, Handicapped; Peter Cage, Genetically Altered Being
**Time period(s):** 22nd century (2100s)
**Locale(s):** Chillon, Switzerland; New Canaan, Connecticut; Gatsby, Asteroid

**Summary:** After stealing WILDLIFE, a program to create true artificial intelligence called a cognizer, Wynne meets the dying Bonivard who plans to use it to make himself immortal. Wynne stays with him until he dies, moves to Connecticut where she has herself changed into a Statue of Liberty, and keeps her son, Peter, a child. Peter and WILDLIFE escape before Wynne as the Statue of Liberty dies and Wynne, again a young woman, finds herself living on a space station, unaware of her origins.

**Other books you might like:**
Greg Bear, *Blood Music*, 1985
Pat Cadigan, *Mindplayers*, 1987
Jean Mark Gawron, *Dream of Glass*, 1993
James P. Hogan, *The Multiplex Man*, 1992
John Kessel, *Freedom Beach*, 1985
   James Patrick Kelly, co-author
Dan Simmons, *The Hollow Man*, 1992

Amy Thomson, *Virtual Girl*, 1993
David Weber, *Path of the Fury*, 1992

### 3050

**ROBERT B. KELLY**

## The Cloud People
(Lake Geneva, Wisconsin: TSR, 1991)

**Story type:** Fantasy (Quest; Science Fiction)
**Major character(s):** Paul Benjarth, Heir (Fief Karcan), Adventurer
**Time period(s):** Indeterminate
**Locale(s):** Calferon, Planet—Imaginary

**Summary:** When the ruling Duke disappears, a magic talisman falls into evil hands and strife threatens the previously peaceful society. Paul Benjarth sets off to retrace his great-great-grandfather's legendary descent from their aerial world to the surface of Calferon, hoping to discover the secret to his world's survival. This is the author's first novel.

**Other books you might like:**
Stephen Baxter, *Raft*, 1992
John Brosnan, *The Sky Lords*, 1991
Rosemary Kirstein, *The Steerswoman*, 1989
Anne McCaffrey, *All the Weyrs of Pern*, 1991
Larry Niven, *The Integral Trees*, 1984
Terry Pratchett, *Strata*, 1981
J.R.R. Tolkien, *The Hobbit*, 1938
John Varley, *Wizard*, 1981
Margaret Weis, *Dragon Wing*, 1990
   Tracy Hickman, co-author
Margaret Weis, *Elven Star*, 1990
   Tracy Hickman, co-author
Margaret Weis, *Fire Sea*, 1991
   Tracy Hickman, co-author

### 3051

**RONALD KELLY**

## Blood Kin
(New York: Zebra, 1996)

**Story type:** Horror (Vampire Story)
**Major character(s):** Boyd Andrews, Carpenter; Tammy Craven, Teacher (Sunday school); Dudley Craven, Farmer
**Time period(s):** 1990s (1996)
**Locale(s):** Green Hollow, Tennessee

**Summary:** When farmer Dudley Craven accidentally plows up his grandfather's coffin and removes a stake plunged into the crumbling remains, he unwittingly resurrects the vampire Josiah Crave. Josiah sates his eternal thirst first on his family, and then on others in the surrounding community, threatening to turn the entire countryside into vampires.

**Other books you might like:**
Ron Dee, *Dusk*, 1991
Stephen King, *Salem's Lot*, 1975
Jason Nickles, *Immortal*, 1996
Patrick Whalen, *Night Thirst*, 1991

## **3052**

### RONALD KELLY

## *Father's Little Helper*

(New York: Zebra, 1992)

**Story type:** Horror (Serial Killer)
**Major character(s):** Ben Gatlin, Police Officer (sheriff); Sonny McFarland, Teenager; Kathe Shelby, FBI Agent
**Time period(s):** 1990s (1992)
**Locale(s):** Cedar Bluff, Tennessee

**Summary:** Inspired by the memory of his mass murderer father—and possibly possessed by his spirit—Sonny McFarland turns from mild-mannered teenager to serial killer and returns to Cedar Bluff, Tennessee, the site of his father's final bloody rampage, to dispatch the survivors of that infamous event of 14 years before.

**Other books you might like:**
Douglas Borton, *Kane*, 1990
Dean R. Koontz, *Hideaway*, 1991
Joe R. Lansdale, *Cold in July*, 1989

## **3053**

### RONALD KELLY

## *Moon of the Werewolf*

(New York: Zebra, 1991)

**Story type:** Horror (Werewolf Story)
**Major character(s):** Patrick O'Shea, Undertaker, Werewolf; Devin O'Shea, Teenager, Werewolf; Rosie O'Shea, Teenager, Werewolf
**Time period(s):** 1990s (1990)
**Locale(s):** Old Hickory, Tennessee

**Summary:** The O'Sheas are a contented quartet of werewolves, feeding off the corpses father Patrick brings home from his undertaking business, until rebellious teenagers Rosie and Devin fail to keep their appetites and passions in check and bring the family into contact with the probing citizens of Old Hickory.

**Other books you might like:**
Ray Bradbury, ''The Homecoming'', 1947
    in *Dark Carnival*
Tanya Huff, *Blood Price*, 1992
S.P. Somtow, *Moon Dance*, 1989
Whitley Strieber, *The Wolfen*, 1978
Jack Williamson, *Darker than You Think*, 1948

## **3054**

### RONALD KELLY

## *Pitfall*

(New York: Zebra, 1990)

**Story type:** Horror (Nature in Revolt)
**Major character(s):** Felix Booth, Lawman (sheriff); Bowie Kane, Handyman, Indian; Roger Ketcham, Doctor
**Time period(s):** 1990s
**Locale(s):** Sulphur Springs, Texas

**Summary:** Two rednecks whose dogfights have been shut down travel to Mexico where they purchase and bring back to Texas several Tasmanian devils, *diablos hoyos*, for their pit fights. When the creatures escape and attack a small west-Texas town, only Indian

handyman Bowie Kane and his magic talisman offer hope in this violent paean to 1950s grade-B horror films.

**Other books you might like:**
Michael R. Linaker, *Scorpion*, 1980
Thomas F. Monteleone, *Night Things*, 1980
Les Simons, *Gila*, 1981
Peter Tremayne, *The Ants*, 1979

## **3055**

### RONALD KELLY

## *The Possession*

(New York: Zebra, 1993)

**Story type:** Horror (Possession)
**Major character(s):** Laura Locke, Writer; Rick Gardener, Artist; Wade Monroe, Paranormal Investigator
**Time period(s):** 1990s (1993)
**Locale(s):** Franklin, Tennessee

**Summary:** Bestselling historical romance writer Laura Locke thinks it's a dream come true when she buys the Magnolia plantation, but it's only the beginning of a nightmare. Haunted by the spirits of people who participated in an unredressed Civil War atrocity, the house takes over whoever strays onto the premises and forces them to re-enact the shameless deed that has left it cursed.

**Other books you might like:**
Tom Elliott, *The Dwelling*, 1989
Judith Hawkes, *Julian's House*, 1989
Al Sarrantonio, *House Haunted*, 1991

## **3056**

### RONALD KELLY

## *Something Out There*

(New York: Zebra, 1991)

**Story type:** Horror (Small Town Horror)
**Major character(s):** Jenny Brice, Artist; Jackson Dellhart, Businessman (owner of Eco-Plenty Corp.); Anthony Stoogeone, Organized Crime Figure (hit man)
**Time period(s):** 1990s
**Locale(s):** Tucker's Mill, Tennessee

**Summary:** Jenny Brice returns to her home town to investigate her father's murder and continue protecting the race of shapeshifters who have been the Brice family's responsibility for generations. But she runs afoul of the land-hungry Eco-Plenty Corporation, the devious conspirators behind her father's death who have as little respect for the land as they have belief in the supernatural.

**Other books you might like:**
Joseph A. Citro, *The Unseen*, 1990
John Farris, *Wildwood*, 1987

## **3057**

### FLOYD KEMSKE

## *Human Resources*

(North Haven, Connecticut: Catbird Press, 1995)

**Story type:** Horror (Vampire Story; Satire)
**Major character(s):** Norman, Businessman (human resources); Jacqueline, Businesswoman (human resources); Pierce, Vampire
**Time period(s):** 1990s (1996)

**Locale(s):** Paris, France; United States

**Summary:** Pierce, a vampire who has learned to hone his ruthlessness over the past two centuries of his life, finds his talents uniquely suited to the current corporate environment in America. Hired as a re-engineering consultant by Biomethods, Inc., he sets about revamping the company to survive in a dog-eat-dog world. Although copyrighted 1995, this novel was not available until 1996.

**Other books you might like:**
Thomas M. Disch, *The Businessman: A Tale of Terror*, 1984
Lionel Fenn, *The Mark of the Moderately Vicious Vampire*, 1992
David Prill, *The Unnatural*, 1995
William Browning Spencer, *Resume with Monsters*, 1995

---

## 3058

### PATRICIA KENNEALY

## The Oak Above the Kings: A Book of the Keltiad

(New York: Roc, 1994)

**Story type:** Science Fiction (Science Fantasy; Political)
**Series:** Keltiad: Tales of Arthur
**Major character(s):** Arthur Penarvon, Royalty; Gweniver Pendreic, Royalty; Taliesen, Minstrel (bard), Writer
**Time period(s):** Indeterminate
**Locale(s):** Gwynedd, Planet—Imaginary; Keltia, Interstellar Empire/Federation

**Summary:** After many setbacks, the Counterinsurgency drives the forces of the evil wizard Edeyrn to a confrontation. Uthyr becomes king, with Arthur and Gweniver to reign after him. Unfortunately, the long rule of the Death-druid leaves Keltia with many crises that demand the attention of the newly reinstated rulers.

**Other books you might like:**
Gillian Bradshaw, *Hawk of May*, 1980
Guy Gavriel Kay, *The Summer Tree*, 1985
Katherine Kurtz, *Deryni Rising*, 1970
Julian May, *The Many-Colored Land*, 1981
Evangeline Walton, *The Prince of Annwn*, 1974

---

## 3059

### PATRICIA KENNEALY-MORRISON

## Blackmantle: A Triumph

(New York: HarperPrism, 1997)

**Story type:** Fantasy (Magic Conflict; Political)
**Series:** Keltiad
**Major character(s):** Athyn ''Blackmantle'' Cahanagh, Orphan, Leader (High Queen); Morric Douglas, Musician (bard)
**Time period(s):** 17th century (1650s)
**Locale(s):** Tara, Planet—Imaginary; Keltia, Interstellar Empire/Federation

**Summary:** The death of the High King leaves Keltia without a recognized sovereign, allowing the alien Firvolgi an opportunity to move into Keltia. As Athyn rises to repel the invasion, her choice of Morric as her mate leads a former companion of Morric to drastic action.

**Other books you might like:**
Greg Bear, *Songs of Earth and Power*, 1994
Kenneth C. Flint, *Challenge of the Clans*, 1986
Guy Gavriel Kay, *The Summer Tree*, 1985
Morgan Llywelyn, *Grania: She-King of the Irish Seas*, 1986

---

Julian May, *The Many-Colored Land*, 1981
Diana L. Paxson, *The Shield between the Worlds*, 1994
   Adrienne Martine-Barnes, co-author

---

## 3060

### PATRICIA KENNEALY-MORRISON

## The Deer's Cry: A Book of the Keltiad

(New York: HarperPrism, 1998)

**Story type:** Fantasy (Science Fiction)
**Series:** Keltiad
**Major character(s):** Brendan Aoibhell, Leader, Spaceship Captain; Patraic ''Patricius Calpurnius'' mac Calprin, Religious, Slave; Nia, Noblewoman, Mythical Creature (danaan)
**Time period(s):** 5th century (453)
**Locale(s):** Slemish, Ireland; Keltia, Planet—Imaginary

**Summary:** When, millennia before the birth of Christ, aliens came to Earth, their power and technology formed the basis of the legends of the faeries of Ireland. When the spread of Christianity threatens his people and culture, Brendan the Navigator uses that alien technology to guide his people to the stars.

**Other books you might like:**
Kenneth C. Flint, *Challenge of the Clans*, 1986
Patricia Kennealy-Morrison, *The Copper Crown*, 1985
Patricia Kennealy-Morrison, *The Hawk's Gray Feather*, 1990
Patricia Kennealy, *The Throne of Scone*, 1986
Katharine Kerr, *Daggerspell*, 1986
Julian May, *The Many-Colored Land*, 1981
Anne McCaffrey, *The Rowan*, 1990
K.D. Wentworth, *House of Moons*, 1995

---

## 3061

### PATRICIA KENNEALY-MORRISON

## The Hawk's Gray Feather

(New York: Roc, 1990)

**Story type:** Fantasy (Science Fiction)
**Series:** Keltiad: Tales of Arthur
**Major character(s):** Arthur, Royalty (Foster brother of Taliesin), Military Personnel; Taliesen, Writer, Minstrel (Bard)
**Time period(s):** Indeterminate
**Locale(s):** Keltia, Interstellar Empire/Federation; Gwynedd, Planet—Imaginary

**Summary:** Taliesin tells the story: A Counterinsurgency group develops in order to free the people of Keltia from a tyrannical ruler. Arthur becomes adept at warfare but trouble with another heir to the throne precipitates an unhappy marriage and tragedy follows.

**Other books you might like:**
Kenneth C. Flint, *Isle of Destiny*, 1988
Katharine Kerr, *The Bristling Wood*, 1989
Stephen R. Lawhead, *Arthur*, 1989
Peter Tremayne, *My Lady of Hi-Brasil*, 1987
Paul Edwin Zimmer, *Blood of the Colyn Muir*, 1988

## 3062

### PATRICIA KENNEALY-MORRISON

## The Hedge of Mist

(New York: HarperPrism, 1996)

**Story type:** Science Fiction (Science Fantasy; Political)
**Series:** Keltiad: Tales of Arthur
**Major character(s):** Taliesen, Minstrel (bard), Writer; Arthur "Artos" Pendreic, Ruler (King of the Kelts); Morguenna Pendreic, Royalty (Princess of Keltia), Spouse (Taliesen's)
**Time period(s):** Indeterminate
**Locale(s):** Keltia, Interstellar Empire/Federation

**Summary:** In this series-concluding volume, Arthur's followers search for the Grail which will unite the Kelts' far-flung empire and allow Arthur to rest until needed in the distant future. A 39-page appendix includes a glossary, notes on pronunciation, a list of characters, notes on the series with bibiliography, and a genealogical chart.

**Other books you might like:**
Mike Ashley, *The Pendragon Chronicles*, 1990
   editor
Marion Zimmer Bradley, *The Mists of Avalon*, 1983
Gillian Bradshaw, *Hawk of May*, 1980
Andrea Hopkins, *Chronicles of King Arthur*, 1994
Guy Gavriel Kay, *The Summer Tree*, 1985
Julian May, *The Many-Colored Land*, 1981

## 3063

### KAY KENYON

## Leap Point

(New York: Bantam Spectra, 1998)

**Story type:** Science Fiction (Invasion of Earth; Adventure)
**Major character(s):** Abbey McCray, Parent, Heroine; Simon Haskell, Detective—Private; Zachariah Smith, Cult Member (Diamond Institute), Traitor
**Time period(s):** 2010s (2015)
**Locale(s):** Medicine Falls, Midwest

**Summary:** Hoping to prove Diamond Institute leader Zachariah Smith's involvement in her daughter's deah, Abbey McCray seeks help from Simon Haskell. The two discover Smith's criminal activities include his promotion of an addictive game in support of an alien invasion, which could threaten human dominance on Earth.

**Other books you might like:**
Octavia E. Butler, *Dawn*, 1987
Alan Dean Foster, *Quozl*, 1989
Robert A. Heinlein, *The Puppet Masters*, 1990
   expanded edition
Steve Perry, *Men in Black*, 1997
Harry Turtledove, *Worldwar: In the Balance*, 1994

## 3064

### KAY KENYON

## The Seeds of Time

(New York: Bantam Spectra, 1997)

**Story type:** Science Fiction (Time Travel; Dystopian)
**Major character(s):** Clio Finn, Time Traveler, Pilot (Biotime Corp); Harper Teeg, Time Traveler, Traitor; Timothy Ashe, Time Traveler, Spy
**Time period(s):** Indeterminate Future; Indeterminate Past
**Locale(s):** *Starhawk*, Spaceship; *Galactique*, Spaceship; Niang, Planet—Imaginary

**Summary:** To revitalize Earth's biota, Biotime Corp time travelers explore the past of distant planets, searching for plants which could survive Earth's degraded environment. Illegally diverting forward in time on a mission, Clio Finn discovers the death of humanity in Earth's immediate future, then finds a possible miraculous solution to Earth's problems in Niang's past. When Harper Teeg attempts a mutiny which would force the team to stay on Niang, Clio's actions trigger cataclysmic changes which could provide humanity's survival, but with potentially disastrous consequences for all non-human life in the galaxy. First novel.

**Other books you might like:**
Greg Bear, *Eon*, 1985
Octavia E. Butler, *Dawn*, 1987
J.R. Dunn, *Days of Cain*, 1997
Fritz Leiber, *The Big Time*, 1961
Mike Resnick, *Prophet*, 1993
Joan Slonczewski, *A Door into Ocean*, 1986
John Varley, *Millennium*, 1983

## 3065

### ELIZABETH KERNER

## Song in the Silence

(New York: Tor, 1997)

**Story type:** Fantasy (Quest; Legend)
**Major character(s):** Lanen Kaeler, Heroine, Bastard Daughter; Akhor, Mythical Creature (dragon), Royalty (Dragonking)
**Time period(s):** Indeterminate
**Locale(s):** Kolmar, Fictional Country; Dragon Isle, Fictional Country

**Summary:** Upon her cold, distant father's death, Lanen Kaeler pursues her lifelong dream to search for the legendary dragons of Dragon Isle. Her quest uncovers unexpected knowledge, such as the identity of her real father and the existence of a prophecy that Lanen herself may ful fll. First novel.

**Other books you might like:**
Graham Edwards, *Dragoncharm*, 1996
Ursula K. Le Guin, *A Wizard of Earthsea*, 1968
Anne McCaffrey, *The Girl Who Heard Dragons*, 1994
Anne McCaffrey, *Dragonflight*, 1968
Robin McKinley, *Beauty*, 1978
Andre Norton, *Elvenblood*, 1995
   Mercedes Lackey, co-author

## 3066

### DANIEL R. KERNS (Pseudonym of Jacqueline Lichtenberg)

## Border Dispute

(New York: Ace, 1994)

**Story type:** Science Fiction (Military)
**Series:** Pit Bull Squadron
**Major character(s):** Indiw, Alien (Ardr), Spaceship Captain (Pit Bull Squadron); Raymond Falstaff, Spaceship Captain (Pit Bull Squadron)
**Time period(s):** Indeterminate Future
**Locale(s):** Sinaha, Planet—Imaginary; Outer Space; *Tacoma*, Spaceship

**Summary:** Now landed, Indiw must fight with the humans to justify his not killing Raymond Falstaff for crashing on his land. Believing that Indiw would want to rejoin the Pit Bulls, Ray never understands his partner's problem, or the alien's perception of humanity.

**Other books you might like:**
A.C. Crispin, *Starbridge*, 1989
Jacqueline Lichtenberg, *Molt Brother*, 1982
Jacqueline Lichtenberg, *Dushau*, 1985
Anne McCaffrey, *Crisis on Doona*, 1992
    Jody Lynn Nye, co-author
S. Andrew Swann, *Forests of the Night*, 1993

## 3067

### KATHARINE KERR

## *Days of Air and Darkness*
(New York: Bantam Spectra, 1994)

**Story type:** Fantasy (Magic Conflict; Adventure)
**Series:** Deverry
**Major character(s):** Rhodry Maelwaedd, Mythical Creature (half-elf), Mercenary; Jill, Sorceress (ex-mercenary); Evander, Mythical Creature (elemental spirit), Sorcerer
**Time period(s):** Indeterminate Past
**Locale(s):** Cengarn, Fictional City; Deverry, Fictional Country; The Westlands, Fictional Country

**Summary:** Jill, Rhodry and Evander each use their own methods to defeat the elemental spirit, sorceress Alshandra, who brings war to the Westlands and siege to Cengarn in order to destroy Princess Carramaena. Alshandra wants to stop her people from leaving their elemental existence for the physical plane, especially her daughter who seeks to become human as the princess's unborn child.

**Other books you might like:**
Gael Baudino, *Dragonsword*, 1988
Richard A. Knaak, *The Shrouded Realm*, 1991
Melanie Rawn, *Stronghold*, 1990
Midori Snyder, *New Moon*, 1989
J.R.R. Tolkien, *The Silmarillion*, 1977

## 3068

### KATHARINE KERR

## *Days of Blood and Fire*
(New York: Bantam Spectra, 1993)

**Story type:** Fantasy (Magic Conflict; Adventure)
**Series:** Deverry
**Major character(s):** Jill, Sorceress; Rhodry Maelwaedd, Mythical Creature, Mercenary; Jahdo, Child, Adventurer
**Time period(s):** Indeterminate Past
**Locale(s):** Deverry, Fictional Country; The Westlands, Fictional Country

**Summary:** Sent away from home to guide the blind bard of the Horsekin on his search for his rebellious and heretical brother, both Jahdo and the bard find themselves allied with the Deverry borderfolk and under attack from the renegade Horsekin who follow a "new goddess," Jill and Rhodry's enemy, Alshandra.

**Other books you might like:**
Joy Chant, *The Grey Mane of Morning*, 1980
Diane Duane, *The Door into Fire*, 1979
Robert Jordan, *The Eye of the World*, 1989
Guy Gavriel Kay, *The Darkest Road*, 1986
Guy Gavriel Kay, *The Summer Tree*, 1985
Guy Gavriel Kay, *The Wandering Fire*, 1986
Patricia Kennealy-Morrison, *The Copper Crown*, 1984

## 3069

### KATHARINE KERR

## *The Dragon Revenant*
(New York: Doubleday Foundation, 1990)

**Story type:** Fantasy (Adventure; Quest)
**Series:** Deverry
**Major character(s):** Rhodry Maelwaedd, Mythical Creature, Mercenary; Jill of Cerrmor, Mercenary; Nevyn, Sorcerer
**Time period(s):** Indeterminate Past
**Locale(s):** Deverry, Fictional Country; Bardek, Fictional Country

**Summary:** Rhodry is the heir to Aberwyn and its best hope for peace, but he's been kidnapped, stripped of his memory, taken to Bardek and sold as a slave. Jill, still coming to terms with her magical talent, goes to rescue and avenge him with Salamander, Rhodry's elven half-brother. Nevyn meanwhile seeks to find and defeat his ancient enemy who has been behind Deverry's troubles for so long and is now luring Nevyn into even deeper traps.

**Other books you might like:**
Steven Brust, *Jhereg*, 1983
Joy Chant, *Red Moon and Black Mountain*, 1970
Guy Gavriel Kay, *The Summer Tree*, 1985
Patricia A. McKillip, *The Riddle-Master of Hed*, 1976
Elizabeth Moon, *Oath of Gold*, 1989
Elizabeth Moon, *Divided Allegiance*, 1988
Elizabeth Moon, *Sheepfarmer's Daughter*, 1988

## 3070

### KATHARINE KERR, Editor
### MARTIN H. GREENBERG, Co-Editor

## *Enchanted Forests*
(New York: DAW, 1995)

**Story type:** Fantasy (Anthology)

**Summary:** Contains a one-page introduction and brief individual introductions to 25 original stories presented in eight sections: "Woodwork"; "Speaking Woods"; "Inheritances"; "The Scars of War"; "Victorian Variations"; "The New World That Never Was"; "Impossible Loves"; and "Sanctuary." With tone varying from light to dark, the sylvan settings populated by witches, hermits, woodsmen, hunters, and mythical creatures feature a variety of themes such as mystery, heroic and Arthurian fantasy, romance, and pyromania. Authors include Jo Clayton, Kate Elliott, Gregory Feeley, Nina Kiriki Hoffman, Michelle Sagara, Susan Shwartz, Dave Smeds, Lois Tilton, and Lawrence Watt-Evans.

**Other books you might like:**
Kathleen M. Massie-Ferch, *Ancient Enchantresses*, 1995
    Martin H. Greenberg, Richard Gilliam, co-editors
Patricia A. McKillip, *The Book of Atrix Wolfe*, 1955
Josepha Sherman, *Orphans of the Night*, 1995
    Martin H. Greenberg, co-editor
Tom Shippey, *The Oxford Book of Fantasy Stories*, 1994
    editor
Sean Stewart, *Nobody's Son*, 1995
Patricia C. Wrede, *Searching for Dragons*, 1991
Patricia C. Wrede, *Talking to Dragons*, 1993
    revised edition

## 3071

### KATHARINE KERR

### *Freeze Frames*

(New York: Tor, 1995)

**Story type:** Science Fiction (Family Saga; Alternate Universe)
**Major character(s):** Maggie Corey, Single Parent; Nick Harrison, Demon; Rabbi Akiba, Religious
**Time period(s):** 1960s; 21st century
**Locale(s):** San Francisco, California; Alternate Earth

**Summary:** The deal with the devil into which Maggie Corey is maneuvered affects her descendants in multiple universes over the course of two centuries. Rabbi Akiba watches Maggie's descendants while working to stop Nick's plots to control humanity.

**Other books you might like:**
Mick Farren, *Necrom*, 1991
Neil Gaiman, *Good Omens: The Nice and Accurate Prophecies of Agnes Nutter, Witch*, 1990
    Terry Pratchett, co-author
Lisa Mason, *Summer of Love*, 1994
Rachel Pollack, *Temporary Agency*, 1994
Mike Resnick, *Deals with the Devil*, 1994
    Martin H. Greenberg, Loren D. Estleman, co-editors
Mary Alexander Walker, *The Scathach and the Maeve's Daughter*, 1990

## 3072

### KATHARINE KERR
### MARK KREIGHBAUM, Co-Author

### *Palace*

(New York: Bantam Spectra, 1996)

**Story type:** Science Fiction (Political; Alternate Intelligence)
**Series:** Pinch
**Major character(s):** Vida L'var y Smid, Heiress—Dispossessed, Fiance(e); Rico Hernandes y Jons, Computer Expert; Vi-Kata, Alien (Lep), Criminal (assassin)
**Time period(s):** Indeterminate Future
**Locale(s):** The Pinch, Interstellar Empire/Federation; Palace, Planet—Imaginary; Cyberspace

**Summary:** Attempting to escape Vi-Kata's unexpected attack, Vida discovers a helpful artificial intelligence program that flees confinement when Rico opens an illegal pathway into the Pleasure Sect. Identified as sole surviving member of a powerful family, Vida temporarily escapes danger through betrothal to the leader's son, bringing both new enemies and allies.

**Other books you might like:**
Isaac Asimov, *The Foundation Trilogy*, 1963
Raphael Carter, *The Fortunate Fall*, 1996
Christopher Hinz, *Liege-Killer*, 1987
Alis A. Rasmussen, *A Passage of Stars*, 1990
Melissa Scott, *Trouble and Her Friends*, 1994

## 3073

### KATHARINE KERR

### *Polar City Blues*

(New York: Bantam Spectra, 1990)

**Story type:** Science Fiction (Mystery; Psychic Powers)

**Major character(s):** Bobbie Lacey, Computer Expert, Police Officer; Tomaso, Murderer, Psychic; Jack Mulligan, Psychic (registered)
**Time period(s):** 23rd century
**Locale(s):** Polar City, Fictional City (on indeterminate world in Republic Space)

**Summary:** When an ambassador from the Interstellar Confederation is discovered murdered, Jack Mulligan happens to be nearby and offers assistance to the police. Attempting to psychically read the victim, he receives a psychic shock rendering him unconscious. Struggling to solve the murder, Lacey employs many helpers, human and alien, and an artificial intelligence with a sense of humor. The situation intensifies as a plague spreads and Mulligan himself becomes a target of Tomaso.

**Other books you might like:**
Alfred Bester, *The Demolished Man*, 1953
Roger Zelazny, *Jack of Shadows*, 1952
Lee Killough, *Deadly Silents*, 1981
Mercedes Lackey, *Burning Water*, 1989
Mercedes Lackey, *Children of the Night*, 1990

## 3074

### KATHARINE KERR

### *The Red Wyvern*

(New York: Bantam Spectra, 1997)

**Story type:** Fantasy (Magic Conflict; Political)
**Series:** Dragon Mage
**Major character(s):** Lillorigga "Lilli", Psychic; Maryn, Royalty (prince); Nevyn, Counselor
**Time period(s):** 9th century (849); 12th century (1117)
**Locale(s):** Deverry, Fictional Country

**Summary:** Lilli's maturing talents force her to choose between family and country loyalty as the usurper and rightful heir contend for power.

**Other books you might like:**
Laurell K. Hamilton, *Nightseer*, 1992
Robin Hobb, *Assassin's Apprentice*, 1995
J.V. Jones, *The Baker's Boy*, 1995
Peg Kerr, *Emerald House Rising*, 1997
Michelle Sagara, *Into the Dark Lands*, 1991

## 3075

### KATHARINE KERR

### *Resurrection*

(Eugene, Oregon: Pulphouse Publishing Axolotl Press, 1992)

**Story type:** Science Fiction (Alternate Universe; Medical)
**Major character(s):** Tiffany "Tif" Owens, Pilot, Patient; Nick "The Devil" Harrison, Angel (fallen)
**Time period(s):** 21st century
**Locale(s):** San Francisco, California

**Summary:** Returned to life after dying in a war-related Middle Eastern plane crash, Tif struggles to regain control of her body and thoughts while plagued with the feeling that reality does not match her memories. Tif wrestles with momentous decisions when the Devil offers her the opportunity to return as a hero to the world from which she came.

**Other books you might like:**
Pat Cadigan, *Mindplayers*, 1987
Jeffrey A. Carver, *From a Changeling Star*, 1989
George Alec Effinger, *Look Away*, 1990

Nancy Kress, *Beggars in Spain*, 1991
Nancy Kress, *Brain Rose*, 1990
Frederik Pohl, *Stopping at Slowyear*, 1991
Michael Swanwick, *Vacuum Flowers*, 1987

## 3076

**KATHARINE KERR**, Editor

### The Shimmering Door

(New York: HarperPrism, 1996)

**Story type:** Fantasy (Anthology)

**Summary:** Contains a four-page introduction plus brief biographical introductions to the authors of 32 original stories focusing on shamans, sorcerers and spell-casters of many varieties. Stories vary in tone to reflect the effect of sorcery on the user, from the giddy sense of power accompanying first use to the wearying burden that comes with familiarity, while settings reflect both contemporary and traditional fantasy environments. Themes include alternate worlds, apprenticeship, flawed sorcery, mythical creatures, magic conflict, the American Civil War, computer virtual reality, and the arts. Authors include Constance Ash, Margaret Ball, Janet Berliner, Jo Clayton, Charles de Lint, Teresa Edgerton, Kate Elliott, Gregory Feeley, Esther M. Friesner, M. John Harrison, Nina Kiriki Hoffman, Simon Ings, Mark Kreighbaum, Lisa Mason, Dennis L. McKiernan, Diana L. Paxson, Laura Resnick, Susan Shwartz, Dave Smeds, and Lawrence Watt-Evans.

**Other books you might like:**
Marion Zimmer Bradley, *The Sword and Sorceress Series*, 1984-1996
    editor
Jack Dann, *Sorcerers!*, 1986
    Gardner Dozois, co-editor
Kathleen M. Massie-Ferch, *Ancient Enchantresses,* 1995
    Martin H. Greenberg, co-editor
Kathleen M. Massie-Ferch, *Warrior Enchantresses*, 1996
    Martin H. Greenberg, co-editor
Will Shetterly, *Liavek: Wizard's Row*, 1987
    Emma Bull, co-editor

## 3077

**KATHARINE KERR**

### A Time of Exile

(New York: Doubleday Foundation, 1991)

**Story type:** Fantasy (Adventure; Magic Conflict)
**Series:** Deverry
**Major character(s):** Rhodry Maelwaedd, Mythical Creature (half-elf), Mercenary; Aderyn, Magician, Wanderer; Jill, Sorceress
**Time period(s):** Indeterminate Past
**Locale(s):** Deverry, Fictional Country

**Summary:** When Rhodry discovers he is half elven, he arranges an accident to cover his departure, knowing he must leave or ultimately endanger his family. He leaves with Jill and Aderyn to live with the elves and learn about his elven heritage.

**Other books you might like:**
Margaret Ball, *The Shadow Gate*, 1991
Marion Zimmer Bradley, *The Mists of Avalon*, 1983
Emma Bull, *War for the Oaks*, 1987
Tom Deitz, *Sunshaker's War*, 1990
Neil Hancock, *Across the Far Mountain*, 1983
Elizabeth Moon, *Oath of Gold*, 1989

James D. Priest, *Kirins: The Spell of No'an*, 1990
Jack Vance, *Lyonesse*, 1983

## 3078

**KATHARINE KERR**

### A Time of Omens

(New York: Bantam Spectra, 1992)

**Story type:** Fantasy (Adventure; Quest)
**Series:** Deverry
**Major character(s):** Jill, Sorceress; Rhodry, Ruler (exiled), Mercenary
**Time period(s):** Indeterminate Past
**Locale(s):** Deverry, Fictional Country; The Westlands, Fictional Country; Bardek, Fictional Country

**Summary:** As the tremendous changes foreseen by Nevyn draw closer, Jill urgently searches for the meaning and significance of the inscription in Rhodry's ring. Meanwhile, Rhodry returns to Deverry in disguise to draw a vengeful Guardian from his elvish kin and becomes further entwined in the developments bringing his two peoples together.

**Other books you might like:**
Gael Baudino, *Strands of Starlight*, 1989
Susan Cooper, *The Dark Is Rising*, 1973
Diane Duane, *The Door into Fire*, 1979
Diane Duane, *The Door into Shadow*, 1984
Diane Duane, *The Door into Sunset*, 1993
Patricia Kennealy-Morrison, *The Copper Crown*, 1984
Melanie Rawn, *Dragon Prince*, 1988
Joel Rosenberg, *D'Shai*, 1991

## 3079

**KATHARINE KERR**, Editor
**MARTIN H. GREENBERG**, Co-Editor

### Weird Tales From Shakespeare

(New York: DAW, 1994)

**Story type:** Fantasy (Anthology)

**Summary:** Contains a two-page introduction by Kerr plus individual introductions to 23 original stories about Shakespeare's life and body of literary work. Authors include Brian Aldiss, Gregory Benford, Charles de Lint, Teresa Edgerton, Kate Elliott, Esther M. Friesner, Gregory Feeley, Nina Kiriki Hoffman, Barry Malzberg, Adrienne Martine-Barnes, Dennis McKiernan, Diana L. Paxson, Mike Resnick and Josepha Sherman.

**Other books you might like:**
Poul Anderson, *A Midsummer Tempest*, 1974
Terry Pratchett, *Wyrd Sisters*, 1988
Clifford D. Simak, *Shakespeare's Planet*, 1976
W.J. Stuart, *Forbidden Planet*, 1956
Tad Williams, *Caliban's Hour*, 1994

## 3080

**PEG KERR**

### Emerald House Rising

(New York: Warner Aspect, 1997)

**Story type:** Fantasy (Mystery; Magic Conflict)

**Major character(s):** Jena Gemcutter, Apprentice, Wizard; Morgan Duone, Nobleman, Wizard; Kestrienne Duone, Noblewoman, Wizard
**Time period(s):** Indeterminate
**Locale(s):** Piyar, Fictional City; Piyanthia, Fictional Country; Uriat Mountains, Mythical Place

**Summary:** Unfamiliar with her blossoming magical abilities, Jena unexpectedly bonds with Morgan. Suprised to find herself abandoned among Morgan's relatives, Jena receives insight from Lady Kestrienne into her relationship with Morgan and aid in foiling a plot against the ruling families. First novel.

**Other books you might like:**
Lois McMaster Bujold, *The Spirit Ring*, 1992
Lynn Flewelling, *Stalking Darkness*, 1997
Laurell K. Hamilton, *Nightseer*, 1992
Anne Logston, *Firewalk*, 1997
Caroline Stevermer, *A College of Magics*, 1994
L.A. Taylor, *Cat's Paw*, 1995

**3081**

COLIN KERSEY

## Soul Catcher
(New York: St. Martin's, 1995)

**Story type:** Horror (Supernatural Vengeance)
**Major character(s):** Evan Baker, Child (Denise's 12-year-old son); Denise Baker, Public Relations; Paul Judge, Lawyer
**Time period(s):** 1990s (1995)
**Locale(s):** Seattle, Washington

**Summary:** With his dying breath, an Indian shaman murdered by Seattle street punks summons Williwaw, an ancient wind elemental, to avenge him. Williwaw wreaks devastation upon the city, searching for Evan Baker, a boy who appeared to the shaman in a final vision and who holds the power to send the spirit back from whence it came. This is the author's first novel.

**Other books you might like:**
Graham Masterton, *Burial*, 1994
Graham Masterton, *The Manitou*, 1974
G. Wayne Miller, *Thunder Rise*, 1988
Adam Niswander, *The Charm*, 1993
Eugene E. Pfaff Jr., *Uwharrie*, 1993
    Michael Causey, co-author
Kathryn Ptacek, *Ghost Dance*, 1990
Patrick Whalen, *Deathwalker*, 1992

**3082**

KEN KESEY

## Sailor Song
(New York: Viking, 1992)

**Story type:** Science Fiction (Post-Holocaust; Arts)
**Major character(s):** Alice Levertov Carmody, Indian, Businesswoman; Ike "the Bakatcha Bandit" Sallas, Indian, Sailor; Michael Carmody, Sea Captain, Fisherman
**Time period(s):** 21st century
**Locale(s):** Kuinak, Alaska

**Summary:** Life in the dreary fishing village of Kuinak remains largely unchanged by the disaster affecting the lower 48 states until the townspeople find that Kuinak may have been chosen as locale for a big budget filming of the classic Inuit fable, *Shoola and the Sea Lion*.

The look of the town changes to accommodate the project as it brings new faces and passions to the previously quiet village.

**Other books you might like:**
Terry Bisson, *Voyage to the Red Planet*, 1990
David Brin, *The Postman*, 1985
Pat Cadigan, *Synners*, 1991
Harry Harrison, *The Technicolor Time Machine*, 1967
Ernest Hogan, *Cortez on Jupiter*, 1990
Marjorie Bradley Kellogg, *Harmony*, 1991
Neal Stephenson, *Snow Crash*, 1992

**3083**

JOHN KESSEL

## Corrupting Dr. Nice
(New York: Tor, 1997)

**Story type:** Science Fiction (Time Travel; Theological)
**Major character(s):** Owen Vannice, Scientist (palentologist), Time Traveler; Genevieva Faison, Con Artist, Time Traveler; Simon, Religious, Time Traveler
**Time period(s):** 1st century (AD 40); 21st century
**Locale(s):** Jerusalem, Middle East; Thornberry, Connecticut

**Summary:** Stranded in ancient Jerusalem with a rapidly growing baby dinosaur, Dr. Owen Vannice falls in love with Genevieve Faison, a time-traveling con artist. However, he must choose sides when Simon, a former disciple of Christ, leads a revolt against the time travelers who have turned Jerusalem into a tourist trap.

**Other books you might like:**
Poul Anderson, *Guardians of Time*, 1981
Orson Scott Card, *Pastwatch: The Redemption of Christopher Columbus*, 1996
Bradley Denton, *Buddy Holly Is Alive and Well on Ganymede*, 1991
Parke Godwin, *Waiting for the Galactic Bus*, 1988
Connie Willis, *Remake*, 1995

**3084**

JOHN KESSEL

## Good News From Outer Space
(New York: Tor, 1989)

**Story type:** Science Fiction (Invasion of Earth)
**Major character(s):** George Eberhart, Journalist; Jimmy-Don Gilray, Religious (Evangelist)
**Time period(s):** 1990s (1999)
**Locale(s):** United States

**Summary:** As the millennium approaches, Americans are more and more ready to believe the fundamentalist Christian evangelists who predict the Second Coming. The most popular of these preachers, Jimmy-Don Gilray, claims God will send his messengers to the people of Earth in the form of aliens arriving in spaceships. On the surface this seems like madness, but crack investigative reporter George Eberhart is convinced that there may be some truth to the story.

**Other books you might like:**
James Patrick Kelly, *Look into the Sun*, 1989
James Morrow, *Only Begotten Daughter*, 1990
Pat Murphy, *The City, Not Long After*, 1989

## 3085

JOHN KESSEL, Editor
MARK L. VAN NAME, Co-Editor
RICHARD BUTNER, Co-Editor

### Intersections: The Sycamore Hill Anthology

(New York: Tor, 1996)

**Story type:** Science Fiction (Anthology; Fantasy)

**Summary:** Contains a nine-page introduction, a seven-page primer for science fiction workshops, a list of all invited authors attending the 1994 Sycamore Hill workshop and 14 original stories in final form, reflecting workshop criticism, with authors' afterwords discussing the workshop experience. The stories' tone varies from light to serious with themes including dystopian futures, education, scientific research, time travel, dance, mythology, crime, Harry Houdini, mythology, and spiritualism. Authors include Carol Emshwiller, Karen Joy Fowler, Alexander Jablokov, James Patrick Kelly, John Kessel, Nancy Kress, Jonathan Lethem, Maureen McHugh, Michaela Roessner, and Bruce Sterling.

**Other books you might like:**
Robin Scott Wilson, *Clarion*, 1971
  editor
Robin Scott Wilson, *Clarion II*, 1972
  editor
Robin Scott Wilson, *Clarion III*, 1973
  editor
Robin Scott Wilson, *Those Who Can: A Science Fiction Reader*, 1973
  editor

## 3086

JOHN KESSEL

### Meeting in Infinity

(Sauk City, Wisconsin: Arkham House, 1992)

**Story type:** Science Fiction (Collection)

**Summary:** Contains a six-page introduction by the author, one original story, ''Faustfeathers,'' and one story, ''The Lecturer,'' from Michael Bishop's anthology, *Light Years and Dark* (1984) plus 12 stories published 1981-1990 in periodicals, including the Nebula Award winning story, ''Another Orphan.'' In most stories, the author examines the human condition through unlikely juxtaposition of notably diverse characters, occasionally inserting humor into his investigation of the dynamics of opposites.

**Other books you might like:**
Greg Bear, *The Wind From a Burning Woman*, 1983
Michael Bishop, *Blooded on Arachne*, 1982
Michael Bishop, *One Winter in Eden*, 1984
Phyllis Eisenstein, *Born to Exile*, 1978
Lucius Shepard, *The Ends of the Earth*, 1991
Lucius Shepard, *The Jaguar Hunter*, 1987
Bruce Sterling, *Crystal Express*, 1989
Michael Swanwick, *Gravity's Angels*, 1991
James Tiptree Jr., *Her Smoke Rose Up Forever*, 1990

## 3087

JOHN KESSEL

### The Pure Product

(New York: Tor, 1997)

**Story type:** Science Fiction (Collection)

**Summary:** Contains a brief author's note plus two original and 17 stories from periodicals and anthologies 1980-1996. Varying in tone from serious to satirical, the stories explore themes such as time travel, alternate histories and popular literture, with three stories set in the milieu of *Corrupting Dr. Nice*.

**Other books you might like:**
Michael Flynn, *The Nanotech Chronicles*, 1991
Jonathan Lethem, *The Wall of the Sky, the Wall of the Eye*, 1996
Mary Rosenblum, *Synthesis & Other Virtual Realities*, 1996
Marc Stiegler, *The Gentle Seduction*, 1990
John Varley, *The Persistence of Vision*, 1978

## 3088

GABRIEL DEVLIN KESSLER

### Landscape of Demons and the Book of Sara

(Boston, Massachusetts: Millennium Press, 1998)

**Story type:** Horror (Collection)
**Major character(s):** Steve Goldblatt, Mentally Ill Person

**Summary:** Two tales of psychological horror centered around Steve Goldblatt, a mentally disturbed young boy who has suffered a series of abuses that amplified his problems, and who ironically is able to integrate normally into contemporary American society. A first book.

**Other books you might like:**
Robert Bloch, *Psycho*, 1959
Ramsey Campbell, *The Face That Must Die*, 1979
Bradley Denton, *Blackburn*, 1993
Peter Straub, *The Hellfire Club*, 1996
Thomas Tryon, *The Other*, 1971

## 3089

JOAN C. KESSLER, Editor

### Demons of the Night: Tales of the Fantastic, Madness, and the Supernatural From Nineteenth Century France

(Chicago: The University of Chicago Press, 1995)

**Story type:** Horror (Anthology)

**Summary:** The editor, a professor of French, has put together 13 stories by 10 nineteenth-century French authors that explore a variety of supernatural and nonsupernatural themes, including vampirism (Charles Nodier's ''Smarra, or the Demons of the Night''), pagan revival (Prosper Merimee's ''The Venus of Ille''), invisible beings (Guy de Maupassant's ''The Horla''), return from the dead (Theophile Gautier's ''The Dead in Love''), the incursion of the past upon the present (Gautier's ''Arria Marcella''), and the psychopathology of crime (Honore de Balzac's ''The Red Inn''). In an informative introduction, the author discusses these tales in the context of the nineteenth-century European romantic tradition.

**Other books you might like:**

Ray Furness, *The Dedalus Book of German Decadence*, 1994
   editor

Brian Stableford, *The Second Dedalus Book of Decadence: The Black Feast*, 1992
   editor

Brian Stableford, *The Dedalus Book of Decadence: Moral Ruins*, 1990
   editor

---

## 3090

### JACK KETCHUM

## The Exit at Toledo Blade Boulevard

(Auburn, Washington: Obsidian Press, 1998)

**Story type:** Horror (Collection)

**Summary:** This collection of 14 stories includes eight original to the book. Most of the tales elaborate simple crime scenarios into horror stories with possibly supernatural events. Included are ''The Rifle,'' in which a woman discovers through the theft of a rifle that her young son is a psychopath in the making; ''To Suit the Crime,'' a tale of future justice; ''When the Penny Drops,'' in which a man's Good Samaritan impulses are perverted into vengefulness by the death of his wife; and ''Winter Child,'' a story originally intended as an episode in the author's 1989 novel *She Wakes*. Introduction by Richard Laymon.

**Other books you might like:**

Poppy Z. Brite, *Swamp Foetus*, 1993
Richard Laymon, *A Good, Secret Place*, 1993
David J. Schow, *Black Leather Required*, 1994
John Shirley, *Black Butterflies: A Flock on the Dark Side*, 1998
Lucy Taylor, *Painted in Blood*, 1997

---

## 3091

### JACK KETCHUM (Pseudonym of Dallas Mayr)

## Ladies Night

(Woodinville, Washington: Silver Salamander Press, 1998)

**Major character(s):** Tom Braun, Writer; Susan Braun, Librarian; Elizabeth, Singer, Dancer
**Time period(s):** 1990s (1998)
**Locale(s):** New York, New York

**Summary:** A tanker truck carrying a secret chemical warfare weapon overturns in Manhattan, dispersing its contents into the air. Under its influence, the battle of the sexes turns brutal and the women in the Dorset Towers housing complex declare bloody war on the men. In his introduction, the author discusses the genesis of this book's idea and his failure to find a publisher for it in the early 1980s.

**Other books you might like:**

John Blackburn, *For Fear of Little Men*, 1972
John Russo, *Night of the Living Dead*, 1981
John Skipp, *The Bridge: A Horror Story*, 1991
   Craig Spector, co-author
Peter Straub, *Floating Dragon*, 1982
Lawrence Watt-Evans, *The Nightmare People*, 1990

---

## 3092

### JACK KETCHUM

## Offspring

(New York: Diamond, 1991)

**Story type:** Horror (Small Town Horror)
**Major character(s):** George Peters, Police Officer (ex-sheriff); Amy Halbard, Computer Expert; Luke Stevens, Child
**Time period(s):** 1990s (1992)
**Locale(s):** Dead River, Maine

**Summary:** Eleven years after they went on a feeding frenzy that terrorized the remote town of Dead River, a family of inbred cannibals re-emerges from the Maine woods to restock their larder with townspeople and abduct women and children to propagate their species. Sequel to *The Off Season*.

**Other books you might like:**

Randall Boyll, *After Sundown*, 1989
Richard Laymon, *The Woods Are Dark*, 1981
William W. Johnstone, *Watchers in the Woods*, 1991

---

## 3093

### SAMUEL M. KEY (Pseudonym of Charles de Lint)

## From a Whisper to a Scream

(New York: Berkley, 1992)

**Story type:** Horror (Child-in-Peril)
**Major character(s):** Jim McGann, Photographer (crime photographer); Nicola Chelsea ''Niki'' Adams, Teenager; Thomas Morningstar, Detective—Police
**Time period(s):** 1990s (1990)
**Locale(s):** Newford, Washington

**Summary:** A series of ritual murders attributed to the Friday Slasher smack not only of voodoo, but of the crimes of Teddy Bird, a pedophile killed two years earlier but whose past association with teenager Niki Adams, a teenager girl recently returned to Newford, seems to have resurrected him.

**Other books you might like:**

Lisa Cantrell, *Boneman*, 1992
Robert Weinberg, *The Black Lodge*, 1991

---

## 3094

### SAMUEL M. KEY (Pseudonym of Charles de Lint)

## I'll Be Watching You

(New York: Jove, 1994)

**Story type:** Horror (Psychological Suspense)
**Major character(s):** Rachel Sorenson, Artist; Harry Landon, Photographer; Lily Kataboki, Banker (teller)
**Time period(s):** 1990s (1994)
**Locale(s):** Newford, Canada

**Summary:** Rachel Sorenson thinks Harry Landon is a godsend when he saves her from her obsessive estranged husband. But Harry, a photographer, has his own perverse obsession with beauty, and will allow no one to come between him and his obsession with the beautiful Rachel.

**Other books you might like:**

John Fowles, *The Collector*, 1963
Ira Levin, *Sliver*, 1991
T.L. Parkinson, *The Man Upstairs*, 1991

Roland Topor, *The Tenant*, 1966

**3095**

J. GREGORY KEYES

## The Blackgod

(New York: Ballantine Del Rey, 1997)

**Story type:** Fantasy (Quest; Magic Conflict)
**Major character(s):** Perkar Kar Barku, Warrior, Hero; Hezhi Yehd Cha'dune, Royalty, Fugitive; Karak, Deity
**Time period(s):** Indeterminate
**Locale(s):** Southern Mang, Fictional Country; Nhol, Fictional Country; The River, Mythical Place

**Summary:** Guided by Karak, both Perkar and Hezhi seek the source of The River, a jealous deity pursuing omniscience. Perkar desires peace between the Mang and his people, while Hezhi hopes to free herself and her people from The River's enslavement. As the priesthood attempts to steer events, The River sends a killer and reanimated assassin of the priesthood to find Hezhi, hiding among the Mang, and regain control over her. Sequel to *The Waterborn*.

**Other books you might like:**
Raymond E. Feist, *Magician*, 1982
Mary Gentle, *Rats and Gargoyles*, 1991
Terry Goodkind, *Wizard's First Rule*, 1994
P.C. Hodgell, *God Stalk*, 1982
Douglas Niles, *A Breach in the Watershed*, 1995

**3096**

J. GREGORY KEYES

## Dark Genesis

(New York: Ballantine Del Rey, 1998)

**Story type:** Science Fiction (Psychic Powers; Political)
**Series:** Babylon 5
**Major character(s):** Lee Crawford, Political Figure (senator), Administrator (director of Psi Corps); Fiona Dexter, Telepath, Revolutionary; Kevin Vacit, Telepath, Administrator (director of Psi Corps)
**Time period(s):** 22nd century (2115-2189)
**Locale(s):** Washington, District of Columbia; Montenegro

**Summary:** When two graduate students successfully prove the existence of human telepaths, Senator Lee Crawford shrewdly lands an appointment as head of the new Metasensory Regulation Authority, the precursor to Psi Corps. Before long, Crawford has as much if not more power than the President of the United States.

**Other books you might like:**
Jeanne Cavelos, *The Shadow Within*, 1997
Kathryn M. Drennan, *To Dream in the City of Sorrows*, 1997
Gayle Greeno, *Exiles' Return*, 1995
Anne McCaffrey, *The Rowan*, 1990
Jim Mortimore, *Clark's Law*, 1996
Al Sarrantonio, *Personal Agendas*, 1997
John Vornholt, *Voices*, 1995

**3097**

J. GREGORY KEYES

## Newton's Cannon

(New York: Ballantine Del Rey, 1998)

**Story type:** Fantasy (Alternate World)
**Series:** Age of Unreason
**Major character(s):** Sir Isaac Newton, Inventor; Benjamin Franklin, Apprentice
**Time period(s):** 17th century (1681)
**Locale(s):** England; Boston, Massachusetts

**Summary:** Sir Isaac Newton discovers a way to harness a magical power so great that England and France go to war to control it. Elsewhere, Benjamin Franklin flees Boston when his discovery of a deadly secret attracts the attention of an enemy intent upon murdering him.

**Other books you might like:**
Lynn Abbey, *Unicorn and Dragon*, 1987
Poul Anderson, *A Midsummer Tempest*, 1974
James P. Blaylock, *Homunculus*, 1986
Edward Easton, *The Miscast Gentleman*, 1978
Stephen Leigh, *The Abraxas Marvel Circus*, 1990

**3098**

J. GREGORY KEYES

## The Waterborn

(New York: Ballantine Del Rey, 1996)

**Story type:** Fantasy (Quest; Religious)
**Major character(s):** Hezhi Yehd Cha'dune, Royalty (princess); Perkar Kar Barku, Hero; Ghan, Teacher, Librarian
**Time period(s):** Indeterminate
**Locale(s):** N'hol, Fictional City

**Summary:** Princess Hezhi searches for her vanished cousin, first in the flooded passages under the sprawling palace beside the River, then in the knowledge contained in the palace library's books. As she gradually realizes that her maturing magic potential endangers her life, she prays for a hero to rescue her. Far away, Perkar loves the goddess of a mountain stream and vows to kill the River God who devours her. The River brings Hezhi and her hero together, but can they save each other from Its power? First novel.

**Other books you might like:**
Lynn Abbey, *The Wooden Sword*, 1991
Eleanor Arnason, *The Sword Smith*, 1978
Margaret Ball, *Changeweaver*, 1993
C.J. Cherryh, *Rusalka*, 1989
Robert A. Heinlein, *Glory Road*, 1963
Ursula K. Le Guin, *The Tombs of Atuan*, 1971

**3099**

CHICO KIDD

## The Printer's Devil

(New York: Baen, 1995)

**Story type:** Fantasy (Magic Conflict)
**Major character(s):** Alan Bellman, Writer, Musician (bell ringer); Kim Bellman, Musician (bell ringer), Spouse; Roger Southwell, Magician, Scholar
**Time period(s):** 17th century; 1990s
**Locale(s):** England

**Summary:** Roger Southwell's magical machinations in the past snag Alan and Kim as Southwell attempts to bring his influence into the present. Kim must find the solution to their troubles through Fabian Stedman's journal which concerns Stedman and his wife's involvement with Southwell and Southwell's unusual investigations. First novel.

**Other books you might like:**
Susan Dexter, *The Wizard's Shadow*, 1993
Barbara Hambly, *Bride of the Rat God*, 1994
Elizabeth Hand, *Waking the Moon*, 1995
Holly Lisle, *Mall, Mayhem and Magic*, 1995
    Chris Guin, co-author
Holly Lisle, *Minerva Wakes*, 1994
Patricia A. McKillip, *The Book of Atrix Wolfe*, 1995

## 3100

### CAITLIN R. KIERNAN

## Candles for Elizabeth

(Decatur, Georgia: Meisha Merlin, 1998)

**Story type:** Horror (Collection)

**Summary:** This is a chapbook of three stories by a writer whose work is associated with the modern Gothic movement. Selections all feature young characters who experience encounters with the supernatural in incongruous decrepit urban settings. An exception is the one original selection, ''Postcards From the King of Tides,'' in which a trio of travelers stranded in the rural Pacific Northwest stumble upon a mystical museum of menacing oddities. Introduction by Poppy Z. Brite.

**Other books you might like:**
Poppy Z. Brite, *Swamp Foetus*, 1993
Nancy A. Collins, *Nameless Sins*, 1994
Roberta Lannes, *The Mirror of the Night*, 1997
Sue Storm, *Star Bones Weep the Blood of Angels*, 1995
Lucy Taylor, *Close to the Bone*, 1993

## 3101

### CAITLIN R. KIERNAN

## Silk

(New York: Roc, 1998)

**Major character(s):** Spyder Baxter, Store Owner; Daria Parker, Singer; Niki Ky, Dancer
**Time period(s):** 1990s (1998)
**Locale(s):** Birmingham, Alabama

**Summary:** Spyder Baxter's home is haven to a variety of musicians, artists and generation X dropouts who are unaware of her past sexual abuse by an alcoholic father. A group peyote trip breaks down the barrier to a dark dimension and gives some of Spyder's worst personal demons form. Co-winner of the International Horror Guild Award for best first novel.

**Other books you might like:**
Poppy Z. Brite, *Drawing Blood*, 1993
Paddy Chayefsky, *Altered States*, 1978
Brian Hodge, *Nightlife*, 1991
K.W. Jeter, *Dark Seeker*, 1987
Lucius Shepard, *Kalimantan*, 1990

## 3102

### GREG KIHN

## Big Rock Beat

(New York: Forge, 1998)

**Story type:** Horror (Mystery)
**Major character(s):** Landis Woodley, Director; Beau Young, Musician; Sol Kravitz, Producer
**Time period(s):** 1960s (1967)
**Locale(s):** Hollywood, California

**Summary:** Washed-up horror B-movie director Landis Woodley is hired to direct a rock 'n' roll exploitation film whose financial backer has stipulated the inclusion of a replica of the car in which James Dean died. When producer Sol Kravitz is found dead in the car, events take a turn for the weird, and Landis and his cronies must determine whether the supernatural, or more mundane forces, are at work. Reprises characters from the author's previous novel *Horror Show*.

**Other books you might like:**
Warren Newton Beath, *Who Killed James Dean?*, 1995
David Darke, *Horrorshow*, 1994
Norman Partridge, *Spyder*, 1995
Brad Strickland, *Shadowshow*, 1988

## 3103

### GREG KIHN

## Horror Show

(New York: Tor, 1996)

**Story type:** Horror (Black Magic)
**Major character(s):** Landis Woodley, Director (film); Buzzy Haller, Filmmaker (special effects technician); Neil Bugmeier, Writer (screenwriter)
**Time period(s):** 1990s (1996); 1950s (1957)
**Locale(s):** Hollywood, California

**Summary:** Horror B-movie director Landis Woodley recounts the making of his most notorious film, *Cadaver*, whose budget was so low he was forced to use real cadavers for special effects. One of those cadavers belonged to a former Satanist and housed a demon that has been killing members of the film crew for the last four decades. This is the author's first novel.

**Other books you might like:**
Robert Bloch, *Psycho II*, 1982
Ramsey Campbell, *Ancient Images*, 1989
David Darke, *Horrorshow*, 1994
Dennis Etchison, *Shadow Man*, 1993
Todd Grimson, *Brand New Cherry Flavor*, 1996
Dale Hoover, *65mm*, 1994
Tim Lucas, *Throat Sprockets*, 1994

## 3104

### GREG KIHN

## Shade of Pale

(New York: Tor/Forge, 1997)

**Story type:** Horror (Curse)
**Major character(s):** Jukes Wahler, Doctor (psychiatrist); Padraic O'Connor, Terrorist; George Jones, Detective—Police
**Time period(s):** 1990s (1997)
**Locale(s):** New York, New York

**Summary:** Jukes Wahler's efforts to save his sister from her abusive boyfriend dovetail with the mission of IRA terrorist Padraic O'Connor to capture the banshee, a creature of Irish legend who defends the plight of Irish women and who has caused the gruesome deaths of several expatriate Irishmen living in New York.

**Other books you might like:**
Ramsey Campbell, *The Long Lost*, 1993
Joe Donnelly, *The Shee*, 1991
Elizabeth Massie, *Sineater*, 1992
Michael O'Rourke, *The Undine*, 1996

## 3105

### CRAWFORD KILIAN

## Greenmagic

(New York: Ballantine Del Rey, 1992)

**Story type:** Fantasy (Quest)
**Major character(s):** Dheribi, Bastard Son (of a king)
**Time period(s):** Indeterminate
**Locale(s):** Cant'area, Fictional Country

**Summary:** Hoping to avoid slavery and achieve a pardon for his crime, Dheribi agrees to help overthrow a rival city. His mother, a slave, promises that if Dheribi can learn control of the magic of her people, his birthright, he could free himself, his mother's people and the land itself.

**Other books you might like:**
Laurell K. Hamilton, *Nightseer*, 1992
Guy Gavriel Kay, *Tigana*, 1990
Victor Kelleher, *The Red King*, 1990
Elizabeth Moon, *Surrender None: The Legacy of Gird*, 1990

## 3106

### CRAWFORD KILIAN

## Gryphon

(New York: Ballantine/Del Rey, 1989)

**Story type:** Science Fiction (Invasion of Earth)
**Major character(s):** Alexander McIntosh, Immortal; California Moran, Immortal
**Time period(s):** Indeterminate Future
**Locale(s):** Earth

**Summary:** Humanity has undergone radical change under the influence of alien cultures contacted through the "Net," an interstellar communications system, but has never met another intelligent species face to face. Earth is then invaded by a race of evangelical gryphons determined to convert humanity and the rest of the universe to their religious faith.

**Other books you might like:**
Iain M. Banks, *The Player of Games*, 1989
Iain M. Banks, *The State of the Art*, 1989
Michael Kandel, *Strange Invasion*, 1989
Fritz Leiber, *The Wanderer*, 1964
Michael Moorcock, *An Alien Heat*, 1972

## 3107

### CRAWFORD KILIAN

## Redmagic

(New York: Ballantine Del Rey, 1995)

**Story type:** Fantasy (Magic Conflict)
**Major character(s):** Calindor, Magician; Deir ni Bron, Refugee, Magician; Nazaual, Magician, Religious
**Time period(s):** Indeterminate
**Locale(s):** Cant'area, Fictional Country; Exteca, Fictional Country

**Summary:** Fleeing the Extecan invaders, Deir unconsciously summons a sea dragon who carries her to the boat in which Calindor and his bride, Callishandal, travel. The Exteca covet the fertile northern lands and wield the powerful magic of the True Gods, released only by the blood of human sacrifices. Calindor and his greenmagic cannot stop them, but Deir begins to learn how to use the magic of Earth. Set in the milieu of *Greenmagic*.

**Other books you might like:**
Maggie Furey, *Aurian*, 1994
Barbara Hambly, *The Dark Hand of Magic*, 1990
Robert Jordan, *The Dragon Reborn*, 1991
Kenneth Morris, *The Chalchiuhite Dragon*, 1992
Tad Williams, *To Green Angel Tower*, 1993

## 3108

### LEE KILLOUGH

## Blood Walk

(Decatur, Georgia: Meisha Merlin, 1997)

**Story type:** Horror (Collection; Vampire Story)
**Summary:** Omnibus reprint of two vampire novels. In *Blood Hunt* (1987), San Francisco police detective Gareth encounters vampire femme fatale Lane Barber during a murder investigation and is turned into a vampire by her. In *Bloodlinks* (1988), Gareth is still adjusting to his life as a vampire and enduring a series of misadventures and crimes for which he is framed to prevent him from pursuing his vampire initiator.

**Other books you might like:**
Vincent Courtney, *Vampire Beat*, 1991
P.N. Elrod, *Bloodlist*, 1990
Martin H. Greenberg, *Vampire Detectives*, 1995
  editor
Tanya Huff, *Blood Debt*, 1997
Michael Reaves, *Night Hunter*, 1991
Les Whitten, *Progeny of the Adder*, 1965

## 3109

### LEE KILLOUGH

## Dragon's Teeth

(New York: Popular Library Questar, 1990)

**Story type:** Science Fiction (Mystery; Adventure)
**Series:** Brill and Maxwell
**Major character(s):** Janna Brill, Police Officer (sargeant); Mahlon Sumner "Mama" Maxwell, Police Officer
**Time period(s):** 21st century
**Locale(s):** Topeka, Kansas; Kansas City, Kansas

**Summary:** When a gang of thieves defeats the high tech security equipment to commit robbery and murder, Brill and Maxwell are assigned to the case. Since the crime was broadcast on television as it occurred, Brill and Maxwell are under pressure to solve it quickly as they search from better neighborhoods to ghettos ferreting out the murderer.

**Other books you might like:**
Alan Dean Foster, *Cyber Way*, 1990
Randall Garrett, *Too Many Magicians*, 1967
Katharine Kerr, *Polar City Blues*, 1990
Michael Kurland, *Ten Little Wizards*, 1988
L. Neil Smith, *The Probability Broach*, 1980

`3110`

**NANCY KILPATRICK**

## *Dracul: An Eternal Love Story*
(San Diego, California: Lucard, 1998)

**Story type:** Horror (Vampire Story)
**Major character(s):** Dracula, Vampire; Lucy Westenra, Young Woman; Mina Murray, Young Woman
**Time period(s):** 1900s (1905)
**Locale(s):** London, England

**Summary:** A retelling of Bram Stoker's *Dracula*, in which the vampire Count Dracula is portrayed as a dashing and seductive lover whom Lucy Westenra and Mina Murray both find superior to the merely mortal men in their lives. A novel based on the stage musical *Dracul*, which was produced in San Diego in 1995.

**Other books you might like:**
Hamilton Deane, *Dracula: The Ultimate Illustrated Edition of the World-Famous Vampire Play*, 1993
Fred Saberhagen, *Bram Stoker's Dracula*, 1992
Bram Stoker, *Dracula*, 1897
Peter Tremayne, *Dracula, My Love*, 1980
Chelsea Quinn Yarbro, *Hotel Transylvania*, 1978

`3111`

**NANCY KILPATRICK**

## *Endorphins*
(Norfolk, VA: Macabre, Inc., 1997)

**Story type:** Horror (Collection; Vampire Story)

**Summary:** Two poems and two erotic vampire novellas. In "Time," young and old male vampires battle for the carnal interests of their victim. In "Lover of Horses," a young woman on a tour sponsred by gypsies finds her sexual fulfillment in the care of a dashing vampire count who abducts her. Illustrated by Chad Savage, with an introduction by Karen E. Taylor. Dated 1997 but not available until 1998.

**Other books you might like:**
Ron Dee, *Sex and Blood*, 1994
Brian Hodge, *Shrines and Desecrations*, 1994
Brian Lumley, *A Coven of Vampires*, 1998
Norman Spinrad, *Vampire Junkies*, 1994

`3112`

**NANCY KILPATRICK**, Editor
**THOMAS S. ROCHE**, Co-Editor

## *In the Shadow of the Gargoyle*
(New York: Ace, 1998)

**Story type:** Horror (Anthology)

**Summary:** Included here are 15 original stories, one reprint and one excerpt that feature gargoyles in a variety of roles. Gargoyles are literal presences in Harlan Ellison's "Bleeding Stones," in which the gargoyles of St. Patrick's Cathedral come to life and wreak havoc on New York City, and in Neil Gaiman's "How Do You Think It Feels?" in which a sculptor gives a statue of a gargoyle unnatural life. Gargoyles serve a symbolic purpose in Charles L. Grant's "The Soft Sound of Wings," where they are a metaphor for a man's loneliness, and in Melanie Tem's "Hagoday," in which they summarize a man's feelings of guilt for the irresponsible death of a friend.

**Other books you might like:**
Peter Crowther, *Heaven Sent: 18 Glorious Tales of the Angels*, 1995
    Martin H. Greenberg, co-editor
Peter Crowther, *Narrow Houses*, 1992
    editor
Ellen Datlow, *Blood Is Not Enough*, 1989
    editor
George Hatch, *Sinistre: An Anthology of Rituals*, 1993
    editor
Pam Keesey, *Women Who Run with Werewolves: Tales of Blood, Lust and Metamorphosis*, 1996
    editor

`3113`

**NANCY KILPATRICK**

## *Near Death*
(New York: Pocket, 1994)

**Story type:** Horror (Vampire Story)
**Major character(s):** Kathleen "Zero" Stevens, Prostitute; David Lyle Hardwick, Writer (poet), Vampire; Donald Reesone, Actor
**Time period(s):** 1990s (1994)
**Locale(s):** New York, New York; Canada

**Summary:** Byronic David Lyle Hardwick, a vampire for more than a century, befriends and rehabilitates the woman sent to kill him, then follows her back to the United States to learn the identities of her employers. The mystery leads him on a journey that spans North America and takes him back into his past to former friends who have betrayed him.

**Other books you might like:**
Traci Briery, *The Vampire Journals*, 1993
Mara McCuniff, *The Vampire Memoirs*, 1991
Brent Monahan, *The Book of Common Dread*, 1993
Anne Rice, *The Vampire Lestat*, 1985
T. Lucien Wright, *Thirst of the Vampire*, 1992

## 3114

### NANCY KILPATRICK

## *Sex and the Single Vampire*

(Leesburg, Virginia: TAL Publication, 1994)

**Story type:** Horror (Collection; Vampire Story)
**Major character(s):** Cheryl, Vampire; Aleron, Vampire; Nightshade, Vampire

**Summary:** The three stories in this collection, two of which were written especially for the volume, tell of the peculiar menage a trois between Cheryl, a mortal woman turned vampire, and Nightshade and Aleron, two older and more experienced vampires who use Cheryl as a pawn in their feeding and thrill-seeking.

**Other books you might like:**
Ron Dee, *Sex and Blood*, 1994
Brian Hodge, *Shrines and Desecrations*, 1994
Norman Spinrad, *Vampire Junkies*, 1994

## 3115

### GARRY KILWORTH

## *The Foxes of Firstdark*

(New York: Doubleday, 1990)

**Story type:** Fantasy (Light Fantasy)
**Major character(s):** O-ha, Animal (she-fox); Camio, Animal (fox)
**Time period(s):** 1990s (1990)
**Locale(s):** Trinity Wood, Earth

**Summary:** After losing her mate and her kits, O-ha becomes despondent. When Camio, who has escaped from a zoo, comes to Trinity Wood, he teaches O-ha to understand the way of man. O-ha and Camio get to know each other and O-ha decides she would trust Camio. Together they have three kits who give new meaning and direction to O-ha's life. ALA Best Young Adults Books title. British edition, 1989, titled Hunter's Moon.

**Other books you might like:**
Richard Adams, *Watership Down*, 1974
Kenneth Grahame, *The Wind in the Willows*, 1908
Brian Jacques, *Mattimeo*, 1990
Margery Sharp, *The Rescuers*, 1959
Tad Williams, *Tailchaser's Song*, 1985

## 3116

### GARRY KILWORTH

## *Hogfoot Right and Bird-Hands*

(Cambridge, Massachusetts: Edgewood Press, 1993)

**Story type:** Horror (Collection)
**Summary:** This outstanding collection brings together 13 tales of fantasy and horror, many set in exotic locales and concerned with the tug-of-war between faith and rational belief. Included are two tales of doppelgangers, "Doppelganger" and "Usurper," about supernatural doubles who overwhelm their lookalikes; two highly original ghost stories, "The Island with the Stink of Ghosts" and "Inside the Walled City," in which a land mass and a Hong Kong slum (respectively) manifest unique kinds of haunting; "The Vivarium," about a man who tries to create life in a controlled environment; and "White Noise," in which a glimpse into the historical past tests the religious faith of the characters. Robert Holdstock has supplied the introduction.

**Other books you might like:**
Michael Bishop, *Blooded on Arachne*, 1982
Brian Stableford, *Sexual Chemistry: Sardonic Tales of the Genetic Revolution*, 1991
Lisa Tuttle, *Memories of the Body*, 1992

## 3117

### KATHARINE ELISKA KIMBRIEL

## *Hidden Fires*

(New York: Warner Questar, 1991)

**Story type:** Science Fiction (Political; Adventure)
**Series:** Fire Sanctuary
**Major character(s):** Darame "Silver" Meath Atare, Ruler, Immigrant; Sheen Atare, Ruler, Hero; Garth Kristinsson, Orphan, Traveler
**Time period(s):** Indeterminate Future
**Locale(s):** Nuala, Planet—Imaginary; Cesarea Station, Space Station

**Summary:** Offworlders are welcome on Nuala where the high radiation levels caused generations of mutations and sterility. After the scam to steal from the mineral-rich Nualans was foiled, Darame married Sheen. Garth, the son of Darame's ex-partner, is looking for her to try to get reparation or revenge.

**Other books you might like:**
Greg Bear, *Eon*, 1986
Gregory Benford, *Tides of Light*, 1989
Alis A. Rasmussen, *A Passage of Stars*, 1990
Alis A. Rasmussen, *The Price of Ransom*, 1990
Alis A. Rasmussen, *Revolution's Shore*, 1990
Dan Simmons, *Hyperion*, 1989

## 3118

### KATHARINE ELISKA KIMBRIEL

## *Kindred Rites*

(New York: HarperPrism, 1997)

**Story type:** Fantasy (Adventure; Magic Conflict)
**Major character(s):** Alfreda "Allie" Sorensson, Magician, Midwife; Marta Donaltsson, Magician, Midwife; Death, Spirit
**Time period(s):** 19th century
**Locale(s):** North America

**Summary:** Allie studies magic and midwifery under Marta, learning quickly and, with Marta's direction, meeting Death for the first time. When kidnapped by an agent of the centuries-old Keeper who wishes to use her blossoming power, Allie escapes and survives using her knowledge of the woods, but must bind herself to Death to control wild magic and save herself from the Keeper.

**Other books you might like:**
Orson Scott Card, *Seventh Son*, 1987
Charles de Lint, *Memory and Dream*, 1994
David Drake, *Old Nathan*, 1991
Suzette Haden Elgin, *Twelve Fair Kingdoms*, 1981
Rachel Pollack, *Godmother Night*, 1996
Midori Snyder, *The Flight of Michael McBride*, 1994
Mark Sumner, *Devil's Tower*, 1996

## 3119

**KATHARINE ELISKA KIMBRIEL**

### Night Calls

(New York: HarperPaperbacks, 1996)

**Story type:** Horror (Wild Talents)
**Major character(s):** Alfreda ''Allie'' Sorensson, Young Woman; Eldon Sorensson, Farmer; Wylie Adamsson, Child
**Time period(s):** 1900s
**Locale(s):** Sun Return, Midwest

**Summary:** Shortly after a werewolf claims the life of her brother, Allie Sorensson discovers that she possesses The Gift, magical powers that generations of women in her family can control. Allie learns the Wise Arts and masters herbalism to grow into her calling and protect her kinsmen against the supernatural creatures of folklore that have travelled with them to the New World.

**Other books you might like:**
Nancy A. Collins, *Walking Wolf*, 1995
Catherine Montrose, *Wendigo Border*, 1995
Pat Murphy, *Nadya: The Wolf Chronicles*, 1996
Tom Piccirilli, *Pentacle*, 1994

## 3120

**GABRIEL KING**

### The Wild Road

(New York: Ballantine Del Rey, 1998)

**Story type:** Fantasy (Quest; Adventure)
**Major character(s):** Tag, Animal (cat); Majicou, Animal (cat), Guide; Sealink, Animal (cat)
**Time period(s):** 1990s
**Locale(s):** Wild Road, Mythical Place; Mythical Place (Tintagel Court apartment complex)

**Summary:** Despite youth and inexperience, Tag must undertake a mysterious and dangerous journey along the Wild Road to find the King and Queen of Cats and return them to Tintagel before the Spring Equinox.

**Other books you might like:**
Diane Duane, *The Book of Night with Moon*, 1997
Shirley Rousseau Murphy, *The Catswold Portal*, 1992
Michael Peak, *Cat House*, 1989
L.A. Taylor, *Cat's Paw*, 1995
Tad Williams, *Tailchaser's Song*, 1985

## 3121

**J. ROBERT KING**

### Conspiracy

(Renton, Washington: TSR, 1998)

**Story type:** Fantasy (Magic Conflict)
**Series:** Double Diamond Triangle
**Major character(s):** Aetheric III, Ruler; Kern, Warrior
**Time period(s):** Indeterminate
**Locale(s):** Utter East, Fictional Country

**Summary:** This volume is a very short installment of a multi-author series. Various groups of adventurers and professionals are searching for a woman kidnapped from her home and carried off into the Utter East. In this installment, some of those searchers encounter a petty ruler who has undergone a supernatural transformation.

**Other books you might like:**
Troy Denning, *The Parched Sea*, 1991
Susan Dexter, *The Sword of Calandra*, 1985
Barbara Hambly, *The Silicon Mage*, 1988
Mercedes Lackey, *By the Sword*, 1991
Douglas Niles, *Ironhelm*, 1990

## 3122

**J. ROBERT KING**

### Planar Powers

(Renton, Washington: TSR, 1997)

**Story type:** Fantasy (Adventure)
**Series:** Planescape: The Blood Wars Trilogy
**Major character(s):** Leonan, Deity; Nina, Mentally Ill Person, Military Personnel; Phaeton, Angel
**Time period(s):** Indeterminate
**Locale(s):** Tuscan, Mythical Place; Sigil, Fictional City

**Summary:** All victims in one way or another of the Lady of Pain, a group of people gather together by fate to fight against her. Dead god, amnesiac wizard, bodiless soul, soulless body, renegade angel and other misfits must use their limited power cleverly just to survive, much less triumph.

**Other books you might like:**
Glen Cook, *The Swordbearer*, 1982
Simon R. Green, *Hawk & Fisher*, 1990
Patricia A. McKillip, *The Riddle-Master of Hed*, 1976
Michael Shea, *Nifft the Lean*, 1982
Roger Zelazny, *Lord of Light*, 1967

## 3123

**J. ROBERT KING**

### Vinas Solamnus

(Renton, Washington: TSR, 1997)

**Story type:** Fantasy (Adventure)
**Series:** Dragonlance: Lost Legends
**Major character(s):** Vinas Solamnus, Warrior, Religious; Emann Quisling, Royalty (emperor); Luccia, Mythical Creature (half-elf)
**Time period(s):** Indeterminate Past
**Locale(s):** Ansalon, Fictional Country; Daltigoth, Fictional City; Krynn, Planet—Imaginary

**Summary:** Founded by Vinas Solamnus, the world's most famous and noble warrior, the Solamnic Knights strongly defend Krynn. Vinas begins as an ignorant youth who wants to be a soldier, but hardship and peril forge him into a mighty and holy warrior who will fight and win the freedom of his people.

**Other books you might like:**
Deborah Chester, *Reign of Shadows*, 1996
Robin Hobb, *Assassin's Apprentice*, 1995
Katherine Kurtz, *Deryni Rising*, 1970
Michael Scott Rohan, *The Anvil of Ice*, 1986
Kristine Kathryn Rusch, *The Changeling*, 1996

## 3124
### MICHAEL KING

## Lorien Lost
(New York: St. Martin's Press, 1996)

**Story type:** Fantasy (Literary; Contemporary)
**Major character(s):** Milton Radcliffe, Collector, Psychic; Lorien Larking, Spouse (wife); Heather, Singer, Handicapped
**Time period(s):** 1870s
**Locale(s):** London, England; Larking Land, Mythical Place

**Summary:** Milton Radcliffe can enter art works and visit the worlds depicted. In one such world he meets Lorien and falls in love, only to lose her when a fire destroys the only image he has of her. Milton must overcome his timidity and set out into the bizarre Victorian streets to find his love again. First novel.

**Other books you might like:**
Nick Bantock, *Griffin & Sabine*, 1991
James P. Blaylock, *Homunculus*, 1986
Jack Cady, *The Off Season*, 1995
Tim Powers, *The Anubis Gates*, 1983
Jessica Amanda Salmonson, *Anthony Shriek*, 1992

## 3125
### PAULA KING

## Mad Roy's Light
(New York: Baen, 1990)

**Story type:** Science Fiction (Adventure)
**Major character(s):** Jennan Bartlett, Spaceship Captain (of the *Ariel*); Morgen, Alien (Daruma), Spaceman (mate on the *Ariel*); Vaughn Tanner, Agent (McCrory Shipping Line)
**Time period(s):** Indeterminate Future
**Locale(s):** Scorpio/Sagittarius Sector, Interstellar Empire/Federation

**Summary:** While dealing with the Taki, Jennan Bartlett, along with Vaughn Tanner, wish to find out why the Li Fawn are stalking them and what happened to the McCrory ship *Crystal*. Convinced that the solution lies with the brain-scrambled Shann, Jennan goes there and buys a madringa, a ubiquitous cult object. Pursued by the Li Fawn, they jump to find themselves in the deadly system of Xi Scorpio along with a maniacal alien force. Jennan manages to redirect it toward the Li Fawn and escapes back to Naberr.

**Other books you might like:**
Poul Anderson, *Satan's World*, 1969
Johanna Bolton, *The Alien Within*, 1989
A. Bertram Chandler, *Gateway to Never*, 1972
C.J. Cherryh, *The Pride of Chanur*, 1982
Andre Norton, *Sargasso of Space*, 1955

## 3126
### STEPHEN KING

## Bag of Bones
(New York: Scribner's, 1998)

**Story type:** Horror (Ghost Story)
**Major character(s):** Mike Noonan, Writer; Kyra Devore, Child (three years old); Max Devore, Businessman
**Time period(s):** 1990s (1998)
**Locale(s):** Dark Score Lake, Maine

**Summary:** Afflicted with writer's block for the four years since his wife's untimely death, and subject to horrifying nightmares filled with ghostly presences, bestselling writer Mike Noonan retreats to Sara Laughs, a summer home in rural Maine. There Mike falls in love with Mattie Devore, experiences supernatural phenomena, and becomes involved in helping Mattie keep her daughter from being taken into the custody of her father-in-law, Max Devore, an unscrupulous man whose shameful past is revealed to be the source of the haunting Mike has experienced.

**Other books you might like:**
Clive Barker, *Galilee*, 1998
Noel Hynd, *Ghosts*, 1993
John Saul, *Second Child*, 1990
Peter Straub, *Ghost Story*, 1979
Thomas Tessier, *Fog Heart*, 1997

## 3127
### STEPHEN KING

## Carrie
(New York: Doubleday, 1990)

**Story type:** Horror (Wild Talents)
**Major character(s):** Carrie White, Teenager (Unpopular), Psychic (Telekinetic powers); Susan Snell, Teenager (Popular; sympathetic to Carrie)
**Time period(s):** 1970s (1979)
**Locale(s):** Chamberlain, Maine

**Summary:** Carrie White, a much maligned teenager with a fanatically religious mother, discovers she possesses telekinetic powers. When a cruel joke turns into violence at the senior prom, Carrie unleashes those powers against her tormentors. Originally published in 1974.

**Other books you might like:**
Charles L. Grant, *The Pet*, 1986
K.W. Jeter, *The Night Man*, 1990

## 3128
### STEPHEN KING

## The Dark Half
(New York: Viking, 1989)

**Story type:** Horror (Doppelganger)
**Major character(s):** Thad Beaumont, Writer (Popular novelist); George Stark, Murderer (Beaumont's fictional alter-ego)
**Time period(s):** 1980s
**Locale(s):** Castle Rock, Maine; Ludlow, Maine

**Summary:** After Beaumont "kills off" his pseudonym in a formal ceremony, his fictional alter ego comes to life and begins systematically murdering all those involved in his "demise," en route to a final confrontation with Beaumont himself.

**Other books you might like:**
Owen Brookes, *Deadly Communion*, 1984
James Herbert, *Moon*, 1985
Fritz Leiber, *Our Lady of Darkness*, 1977
John R. Maxim, *Abel/Baker/Charley*, 1983

## 3129

**STEPHEN KING**

### Desperation

(New York: Viking, 1996)

**Story type:** Horror (Ancient Evil Unleashed)
**Major character(s):** Collie Entragion, Police Officer; Johnny Marinville, Writer; David Carver, Child (11-year-old)
**Time period(s):** 1990s (1996)
**Locale(s):** Desperation, Nevada

**Summary:** The reopening of a closed mine shaft in a remote Nevada town unleashes Tak, a disembodied creature of evil who takes possession of a local police officer and embarks on a rampage of slaughter. The few survivors left rally around young David Carver, a young boy who has had a religious epiphany and whose family has been taken prisoner by Tak's avatar. This novel shares characters and themes with *The Regulators*, which bears King's Richard Bachman byline and was released at approximately the same time under one of the publisher's other imprints.

**Other books you might like:**
Douglas Clegg, *Goat Dance*, 1989
Stephen Gallagher, *Valley of Lights*, 1987
Owl Goingback, *Crota*, 1996
Robert R. McCammon, *Stinger*, 1988

## 3130

**STEPHEN KING**

### Dolores Claiborne

(New York: Viking, 1992)

**Story type:** Horror (Psychological Suspense)
**Major character(s):** Dolores Claiborne, Aged Person; Vera Donovan, Aged Person; Joe St. George, Handyman (Dolores' deceased husband)
**Time period(s):** 1990s (1992); 1960s (1963)
**Locale(s):** Little Tall Island, Maine

**Summary:** Inquiry into the death of her elderly employer leads Dolores Claiborne to recite a book-long monologue about her abusive marriage to Joe St. George and her murder of him 30 years ago when he became a physical threat to their three children.

**Other books you might like:**
Diane Duane, *Spectres*, 1991
Ruby Jean Jensen, *Celia*, 1991
Dean R. Koontz, *Shadowfires*, 1987
Robert R. McCammon, *Mine*, 1990

## 3131

**STEPHEN KING**

### The Drawing of the Three

(New York: NAL Signet, 1989)

**Story type:** Horror (Alternate World)
**Series:** Dark Tower
**Major character(s):** Roland, Gunfighter; Eddie Dean, Addict (drug)
**Time period(s):** 1980s
**Locale(s):** United States; Alternate Earth

**Summary:** Part II in the quest of Roland, the Last Gunslinger, to find the Dark Tower. Having vanquished Walter, the man in black, Roland embarks on the second stage in his quest. He is joined by two allies, Eddie Dean and Odetta Holmes, who, by accident or unknown design, step through "magic doors" into Roland's world from our own, where they encounter underworld menaces and otherworldly evil. Originally published in 1987.

**Other books you might like:**
Clive Barker, *Weaveworld*, 1987

## 3132

**STEPHEN KING**

### Four Past Midnight

(New York: Viking,1990)

**Story type:** Horror (Collection)

**Summary:** Four short novels with extensive introductions by King. "The Langoliers" is a *Twilight-Zone* inspired tale of a cross-country flight that goes astray into a dimension populated only by reality-destroying creatures. "Secret Window, Secret Garden" explores the relationship of a writer to his creations, while "The Library Policeman" probes guilt, child abuse, and monsters. Finally, "The Sun Dog" offers a magical camera that opens a window into another world whose terrifying canine denizen threatens to enter ours.

**Other books you might like:**
Charles L. Grant, *Nightmare Seasons*, 1982
Rod Serling, *New Stories From The Twilight Zone*, 1962
Rod Serling, *More Stories From The Twilight Zone*, 1961
Rod Serling, *Stories From the Twilight Zone*, 1960

## 3133

**STEPHEN KING**

### Gerald's Game

(New York: Viking, 1992)

**Story type:** Horror (Psychological Suspense)
**Major character(s):** Gerald Burlingame, Lawyer; Jessie Burlingame, Housewife
**Time period(s):** 1990s (1992)
**Locale(s):** Kashawakam Lake, Maine

**Summary:** Left handcuffed to a bed when her kinky husband Gerald suffers a heart attack during his most recent stint of sexual antics, Jessie Burlingame spends 28 hours meditating on the unconfronted psychological trauma of her past, the emptiness of her current life, and a hungry dog that has managed to break into the house where she is being held captive.

**Other books you might like:**
John Driver, *The Hunger of the Beast*, 1991
John Fowles, *The Collector*, 1963

## 3134

**STEPHEN KING**

### The Green Mile

(New York: Signet, 1996)

**Story type:** Horror (Mystery)
**Major character(s):** Paul Edgecomb, Guard; John Coffey, Prisoner; Percy Wetmore, Guard
**Time period(s):** 1930s (1932)
**Locale(s):** Cold Mountain Penitentiary, South

**Summary:** The discovery that John Coffey, a prisoner on death row, can heal by the laying on of hands makes him a valuable asset to the authorities who have imprisoned him and raises doubts whether he actually committed the crime for which he was sent to jail. This novel was serialized in six monthly installments as paperback originals with the titles, *The Two Dead Girls*, *The Mouse on the Mile*, *Coffey's Hands*, *The Bad Death of Eduard Delacroix*, *Night Journey*, and *Coffey on the Mile*. The title refers to the green walkway that leads prisoners to the electric chair.

**Other books you might like:**
Thomas Baum, *Out of Body*, 1997
Dean R. Koontz, *Cold Fire*, 1991
J.N. Williamson, *The Night Seasons*, 1991
F. Paul Wilson, *The Touch*, 1986

## 3135
### STEPHEN KING

## *Insomnia*
(New York: Viking, 1994)

**Story type:** Horror (Wild Talents)
**Major character(s):** Ralph Roberts, Aged Person; Lois Chasse, Aged Person; Ed Deepneau, Scientist (chemist), Researcher
**Time period(s):** 1990s (1994)
**Locale(s):** Derry, Maine

**Summary:** After his wife's death Ralph Roberts develops a major-league case of insomnia that sensitizes him to aspects of existence unappreciated by others. In particular, he becomes aware of the Centurions, gnomish little men who pull strings of destiny behind the scenes, and one of whom is working for a malefic being, referred to as the Crimson King, to turn an upcoming abortion-rights rally into a tragedy with serious repercussions for the world.

**Other books you might like:**
Dean R. Koontz, *The Vision*, 1977
Richard Matheson, *A Stir of Echoes*, 1958
T. Lucien Wright, *Dark Visions*, 1993

## 3136
### STEPHEN KING

## *My Pretty Pony*
(New York: Knopf, 1989)

**Story type:** Horror (Coming-of-Age)
**Major character(s):** George "Grandpa" Banning, Aged Person (weak heart); Clive "Clivey" Banning, Child (George's ten-year-old grandson)
**Time period(s):** 1960s (1962)
**Locale(s):** Troy, New York (The West Orchard)

**Summary:** Young Clivey takes "instruction" from his grandfather regarding the nature and value of time and the need for a personal "pretty pony" to give it meaning.

**Other books you might like:**
Ray Bradbury, *Dandelion Wine*, 1957

## 3137
### STEPHEN KING

## *Needful Things*
(New York: Viking, 1990)

**Story type:** Horror (Small Town Horror)

**Major character(s):** Leland Gaunt, Businessman (shopowner); Alan Pangborn, Police Officer (sheriff); Polly Chalmers, Business-woman (shopowner)
**Time period(s):** 1990s
**Locale(s):** Castle Rock, Maine

**Summary:** The mysterious Leland Gaunt comes to Castle Rock to open "Needful Things," a store that contains every resident's heart's desire. Instead of cash, Gaunt demands pranks against fellow neighbors, a type of commerce that soon has the citizens at each other's throats in a bloody civil war.

**Other books you might like:**
Ray Bradbury, *Something Wicked This Way Comes*, 1962
Douglas Clegg, *Goat Dance*, 1988
Charles G. Finney, *The Circus of Dr. Lao*, 1935
Charles L. Grant, *Something Stirs*, 1991

## 3138
### STEPHEN KING

## *Nightmares and Dreamscapes*
(New York: Viking, 1993)

**Story type:** Horror (Collection)

**Summary:** This massive volume collects 20 of Stephen King's hitherto uncollected novellas and stories, including the H.P. Lovecraft influenced "Crouch End"; the story of a haunted bathroom stall, "Sneakers"; the small town horror story, "Rainy Season"; the vampire stories, "Popsy" and "NightFlyer"; the zombie tale, "Home Delivery"; and a satire on rock music nostalgia, "You Know They Got a Hell of Band." Also included are "My Pretty Pony" and "Dolan's Cadillac," previously only available in limited booklet printings; the Sherlock Holmes pastiche, "The Doctor's Last Case"; an essay on Little League, "Head Down"; and the poem, "Brooklyn August."

**Other books you might like:**
Clive Barker, *Books of Blood Series*, 1984-1985
Richard Matheson, *Collected Stories*, 1989
Robert R. McCammon, *Blue World*, 1989
Peter Straub, *Houses Without Doors*, 1990

## 3139
### STEPHEN KING

## *Rose Madder*
(New York: Viking, 1995)

**Story type:** Horror (Psychological Suspense)
**Major character(s):** Rose McLendon Daniels, Businesswoman (reader for audiobooks), Abuse Victim; Norman Daniels, Detective—Police; Bill Steiner, Pawnbroker
**Time period(s):** 1990s (1995)
**Locale(s):** Libertyville, Midwest

**Summary:** After fourteen years of abuse from a psychopathic husband, Rose Daniels flees her New England past, sheds her identity, and begins a new life where she senses her worth as an individual for the first time. When her husband, a police detective, tracks her down, Rose lures him into the world of a painting from which she draws her power.

**Other books you might like:**
Rick Hautala, *Ghost Light*, 1993
Ruby Jean Jensen, *Celia*, 1991
Dean R. Koontz, *Shadowfires*, 1987
Andrew Neiderman, *The Immortals*, 1991

## 3140

### STEPHEN KING

## *Salem's Lot*

(New York: Doubleday, 1990)

**Story type:** Horror (Vampire Story)
**Major character(s):** Ben Mears, Writer (Novelist); Kurt Burlow, Vampire
**Time period(s):** 1970s (1975-1976)
**Locale(s):** Jerusalem's Lot, Maine (A small town in Southern Maine)

**Summary:** Author Ben Mears, a recent returnee to his home town, slowly realizes that "the Lot" is being gradually taken over by an old world vampire and his familiar. He joins forces with some of the locals to fight back and—at a terrible cost—eventually triumphs. Originally published in 1975.

**Other books you might like:**
Charles L. Grant, *The Nestling*, 1982
Robert R. McCammon, *They Thirst*, 1981
Peter Straub, *Ghost Story*, 1979

## 3141

### STEPHEN KING

## *The Shining*

(New York: Doubleday, 1990)

**Story type:** Horror (Haunted House)
**Major character(s):** Jack Torrance, Writer, Maintenance Worker; Danny Torrance, Child (Jack's five year old son), Psychic
**Time period(s):** 1970s
**Locale(s):** Overlook Hotel, Colorado (A resort in the Rockies)

**Summary:** Isolated with his family—wife, Wendy, and son, Danny—Jack Torrance gradually disintegrates under his external and internal devils. This opens the way for the malevolent forces of the Overlook to overwhelm the three of them, particularly Danny, possessor of clairvoyant powers—the "shine" in King's terminology. Originally published in 1977.

**Other books you might like:**
Jack Cady, *The Well*, 1980
John Christopher, *The Possessors*, 1964
Ken Eulo, *The Brownstone*, 1980
Robert Marasco, *Burnt Offerings*, 1973

## 3142

### STEPHEN KING

## *The Stand: The Complete and Uncut Edition*

(New York: Doubleday, 1990)

**Story type:** Horror (Apocalyptic Horror)
**Major character(s):** Stu Redman, Leader (of the "good" forces); Randall Flagg, Leader (of the "evil" forces)
**Time period(s):** 1990s (1991)
**Locale(s):** Boulder, Colorado; Las Vegas, Nevada

**Summary:** Originally published in 1978, there are approximately 500 pages added to this edition. After a superflu wipes out 99% of the world's population, several small groups mobilize—the good in Boulder, the evil in Las Vegas—to confront each other in a final battle for control of the earth.

**Other books you might like:**
Robert R. McCammon, *Swan Song*, 1987
Robert R. McCammon, *They Thirst*, 1981

## 3143

### STEPHEN KING

## *The Waste Lands*

(Kingston, Rhode Island: Donald M. Grant, 1991)

**Story type:** Horror (Science Fiction)
**Series:** Dark Tower
**Major character(s):** Roland of Gilead, Gunfighter; Eddie Dean, Addict (drug); Odetta Holmes, Handicapped
**Time period(s):** Indeterminate
**Locale(s):** The Waste Lands, Alternate Universe

**Summary:** In this third volume of the series set in an alternate universe suggested by Robert Browning's "Childe Roland to the Dark Tower Came," Roland of Gilead, The Last Gunslinger, continues his quest to find The Dark Tower. Accompanied by companions who have entered his world from our own through an interdimensional rift, he endures a series of encounters and ordeals in the desert referred to as The Waste Lands, each of which tests his determination to seek his destiny.

**Other books you might like:**
Clive Barker, *The Great and Secret Show*, 1989
Clive Barker, *Imajica*, 1991
Clive Barker, *Weaveworld*, 1987
Robert R. McCammon, *Swan Song*, 1987
Dan Simmons, *The Hyperion Cantos*, 1989
Brian Stableford, *The Empire of Fear*, 1988

## 3144

### STEPHEN KING

## *Wizard and Glass*

(Hampton Falls, New Hampshire: Donald M. Grant, 1997)

**Story type:** Horror (Apocalyptic Horror)
**Series:** Dark Tower
**Major character(s):** Roland of Gilead, Gunfighter; Susan Delgado, Teenager; Rhea of Coos, Witch
**Time period(s):** 1980s (1986)
**Locale(s):** Topeka, Kansas (alternate universe)

**Summary:** In this fourth adventure of Roland the Gunslinger, who is following the path of the beam to the Dark Tower, Roland kills time with his compatriots, who are trapped with him aboard a sentient train, by recounting his teenage years as a gunslinger initiate, and the ill-fated romance with Susan Delgado which has helped to shape his quest.

**Other books you might like:**
Clive Barker, *The Great and Secret Show*, 1989
L. Frank Baum, *The Wonderful Wizard of Oz*, 1900
Raymond E. Feist, *Faerie Tale*, 1987
J.R.R. Tolkien, *The Lord of the Rings Trilogy*, 1954-1956

## 3145

### AMANDA KINGSLEY

## *Hellcat*

(New York: Leisure, 1992)

**Story type:** Horror (Supernatural Vengeance)
**Major character(s):** Edna Wilkins, Clerk (supermarket); Helen Townsend, Clerk (supermarket); Gene Martin, Accountant
**Time period(s):** 1990s
**Locale(s):** Silver Springs, Maryland

**Summary:** This novel, which gives a whole new meaning to the expression ''the banality of evil,'' tells the sad story of Edna Wilkins, who has helped her abusive husband James overindulge himself to death but must now contend with a fiendishly mischeievous black cat possessed by James's black soul and determined to make her life living hell.

**Other books you might like:**
Robert Bloch, *Catnip*, 1945
short story in *The Opener of the Way*
Gordon Casserly, *Tiger Girl*, 1934
Claire Necker, *Supernatural Cats*, 1973
editor
Michel Parry, *Beware of the Cat*, 1972
editor

## 3146

### RICHARD KINION

## *Sacrifice*

(New York: Zebra, 1995)

**Story type:** Horror (Occult)
**Major character(s):** Alice Sterling, Lawyer; Holly Ryan, Psychologist (therapist); Steve, Murderer
**Time period(s):** 1990s (1995)
**Locale(s):** Annapolis, Maryland

**Summary:** Alice Sterling uses a hefty insurance settlement to buy the colonial Taylor Watch House and try to resume her life following a freak accident that results in the traumatic amputation of her leg. Unknown to her, the house is imbued with the influence of Amon, a pre-Druidic entity that came to American shores during the colonial period, and who begins using Alice as a vessel for sexual revenge to feed its needs.

**Other books you might like:**
Jane Brindle, *The Tallow Image*, 1994
Ruby Jean Jensen, *The Haunting*, 1994
David Robbins, *Spook Night*, 1995
Nina Romberg, *Shadow Walkers*, 1993

## 3147

### RUDYARD KIPLING

## *Kipling's Fantasy*

(New York: Tor, 1992)

**Story type:** Fantasy (Collection)

**Summary:** Contains a two-page list of Kipling's major publications from 1886-1940, a six-page introduction by John Brunner, ''About Rudyard Kipling,'' plus 12 excerpts and stories published 1888-1926 with individual introductions by Brunner.

**Other books you might like:**
Sir Arthur Conan Doyle, *The Best Supernatural Tales of Arthur Conan Doyle*, 1979
David Drake, *Heads to the Storm*, 1989
Sandra Miesel, co-editor
Lord Dunsany, *The Travel Tales of Mr. Joseph Jorkens*, 1931
Jack London, *Selected Science Fiction and Fantasy Stories*, 1979
Kenneth Morris, *The Secret Mountain and Other Tales*, 1926

## 3148

### RUDYARD KIPLING

## *Kipling's Science Fiction*

(New York: Tor, 1992)

**Story type:** Science Fiction (Collection)

**Summary:** Contains a two-page list of Kipling's major publications from 1886-1940, a six-page introduction by John Brunner, ''About Rudyard Kipling,'' plus 10 excerpts and stories published 1893-1932 with individual introductions by Brunner.

**Other books you might like:**
David Drake, *Heads to the Storm*, 1989
Sandra Miesel, co-editor
Lord Dunsany, *The Travel Tales of Mr. Joseph Jorkens*, 1931
Jack London, *Selected Science Fiction and Fantasy Stories*, 1979
Edgar Allan Poe, *The Science Fiction of Edgar Allan Poe*, 1976
Jules Verne, *Yesterday and Tomorrow*, 1965
H.G. Wells, *The Complete Short Stories of H.G. Wells*, 1965

## 3149

### MARIE KIRALY (Pseudonym of Elaine Bergstrom)

## *Leanna: Possession of a Woman*

(New York: Berkley, 1996)

**Story type:** Horror (Occult)
**Major character(s):** Hailey Martin, Writer; Ed O'Brien, Police Officer; Leanna de Noux, Femme Fatale
**Time period(s):** 1990s (1996)
**Locale(s):** New Orleans, Louisiana

**Summary:** Writer Hailey Martin rents a room in New Orleans' French Quarter and falls under the spell of Leanna de Noux, a woman who was murdered in it years before. What she learns while under Leanna's spell is enough to raise her suspicion that Leanna was not a completely innocent victim, and that she herself is in serious danger.

**Other books you might like:**
Jack Finney, *Marion's Wall*, 1973
Robert Girardi, *Madeleine's Ghost*, 1995
Stephen King, *The Shining*, 1977
Simon Maginn, *Virgins and Martyrs*, 1995
Roland Topor, *The Tenant*, 1964

## 3150

### MARIE KIRALY (Pseudonym of Elaine Bergstrom)

## *Madeline: After the Fall of Usher*

(New York: Berkley, 1996)

**Story type:** Horror (Gothic Family Chronicle; Historical)
**Major character(s):** Pamela Donaldson, Young Woman; Edgar Allan Poe, Writer, Historical Figure; Madeline Usher, Aged Person
**Time period(s):** 1840s (1849)

**Locale(s):** New Orleans, Louisiana

**Summary:** With the help of Edgar Allan Poe, Pamela Donaldson tracks her abducted infant son to her dead husband's family's estate on the Louisiana bayou. There, she discovers that the family matriarch, Madeline Usher, has survived the fate Poe described for her in his famous tale, ''The Fall of the House of Usher,'' and that the family history is founded on a tradition of incest and reincarnation from which she and her son cannot escape.

**Other books you might like:**
George Egon Hatvary, *The Murder of Edgar Allan Poe*, 1997
William Hjortsberg, *Nevermore*, 1994
Stephen Marlowe, *The Lighthouse at the End of the World*, 1995
Robert Poe, *Return to the House of Usher*, 1995

---

**3151**

**MARIE KIRALY** (Pseudonym of Elaine Bergstrom)

## Mina

(New York: Berkley, 1994)

**Story type:** Horror (Vampire Story)
**Major character(s):** Mina Harker, Teacher (former); Jonathan Harker, Lawyer (soliciter); Winston Gordon, Businessman, Nobleman (Lord Gance)
**Time period(s):** 1890s
**Locale(s):** Exeter, England

**Summary:** A variant on the story of Count Dracula, this novel focuses on Mina Harker, the wife of Count Dracula's most famous victim, and her recovery following Dracula's bite and subsequent death. Awakened to feelings of empowerment after her near vampirization, Mina grows increasingly estranged from her husband and increasingly fond of her randy neighbor, Lord Gance, as she tries to come to terms with her predatory sexuality.

**Other books you might like:**
Traci Briery, *The Vampire Journals*, 1993
Mara McCuniff, *The Vampire Memoirs*, 1991
Poppy Z. Brite, *Lost Souls*, 1992
Anne Rice, *Interview with the Vampire*, 1978
Chelsea Quinn Yarbro, *The Olivia Trilogy*, 1987-1989

---

**3152**

**T.J. KIRBY**

## Dangerous Nature

(New York: Zebra, 1993)

**Story type:** Horror (Science Fiction)
**Major character(s):** Jackie Mitchell, Animal Lover (animal welfare agent); Warren Maxey, Scientist; Dan Patton, Businessman
**Time period(s):** 1990s (1993)
**Locale(s):** South Port, Indiana

**Summary:** Outraged animal rights groups break into laboratories around the country, liberating specimens. Once in the wild, those from Patton Pharmaceuticals, an Indiana facility experimenting in tissue regeneration, turn monstrous and begin to threaten the town.

**Other books you might like:**
Richard Adams, *The Plague Dogs*, 1976
Dean R. Koontz, *Midnight*, 1989
Dean R. Koontz, *Shadowfires*, 1987
Dean R. Koontz, *Watchers*, 1987

---

**3153**

**T.J. KIRBY**

## Deadly Breed

(New York: Zebra, 1991)

**Story type:** Horror (Science Fiction)
**Major character(s):** Clayton Allen Kruger, Pilot (helicopter pilot); William Jameson ''Jay'' Harting, Doctor (surgeon); Charles Joseph Davidson, Doctor (surgeon)
**Time period(s):** 1990s
**Locale(s):** Clark's Corner, Tennessee

**Summary:** U.S. Army Project Chim-jag, which involves the transplant of human brain tissue into genetically engineered animals, goes awry when one of the animals, created as a sophisticated fighting machine to replace human soldiers, escapes into a nearby community in the Smoky Mountains.

**Other books you might like:**
Dean R. Koontz, *Watchers*, 1986
John Saul, *Creature*, 1989

---

**3154**

**MARY KIRCHOFF**

## The Seventh Sentinel

(Lake Geneva, Wisconsin: TSR, 1995)

**Story type:** Fantasy (Magic Conflict)
**Series:** Dragonlance: Defenders of Magic
**Major character(s):** Bram DiThorn, Nobleman, Mythical Creature; Lyim, Wizard, Handicapped; Guerrand DiThorn, Wizard
**Time period(s):** Indeterminate
**Locale(s):** Krynn, Planet—Imaginary

**Summary:** Once a close friend and colleague of Guerrand, Lyim hatches a plot to destroy magic on Krynn. When he takes control of Qindaras, a city protected from magic by ancient treaties, Bram, with his access to non-human magic, must try to stop the plot.

**Other books you might like:**
Glen Cook, *The Fire in His Hands*, 1984
John M. Ford, *Casting Fortune*, 1989
Katherine Kurtz, *Deryni Rising*, 1970
Patricia A. McKillip, *The Riddle-Master of Hed*, 1976
Mark E. Rogers, *The Expected One*, 1991

---

**3155**

**MARY KIRCHOFF**
**STEVE WINTER**, Co-Author

## Wanderlust

(Lake Geneva, Wisconsin: TSR, 1991)

**Story type:** Fantasy (Magic Conflict; Political)
**Series:** Dragonlance Saga: The Meetings Sextet
**Major character(s):** Tasslehoff Burrfoot, Mythical Creature; Flint Fireforge, Mythical Creature (dwarf), Artisan (metalsmith); Tanthalas ''Tanis'' Half-Elvin, Mythical Creature (elf), Warrior
**Time period(s):** Indeterminate
**Locale(s):** Abanasinia, Fictional Country

**Summary:** When Tasslehoff Burrfoot comes into possession of a copper bracelet, the fate of the entire race of Dargonesti sea elves hangs in the balance. A game tie-in novel.

**Other books you might like:**
Mark Anthony, *Kindred Spirits*, 1991
   Ellen Porath, co-author
Nancy Varian Berberick, *Stormblade*, 1988
Tina Daniell, *Dark Heart*, 1992
Richard A. Knaak, *The Legend of Huma*, 1988
Barbara Siegel, *Tanis, the Shadow Years*, 1990
   Scott Siegel, co-author
Margaret Weis, *Dragons of Autumn Twilight*, 1984
   Tracy Hickman, co-author

---

**3156**

### DAVID KIRSCHNER
### ERNIE CONTRERAS, Co-Author

## The Pagemaster

(Atlanta, Georgia: Turner Publishing, 1993)

**Story type:** Fantasy (Alternate World; Young Adult)
**Major character(s):** The Pagemaster, Librarian, Guardian; Richard Tyler, Child, Adventurer
**Time period(s):** 1990s
**Locale(s):** United States

**Summary:** Focusing on his fears as usual, Richard Tyler seeks shelter in a library, a locale previously uninteresting to him. A flash accompanies Richard's transportation to a place populated by characters from classic literature. There, animated genre books help Richard explore the adventures presented through reading and learn to conquer his fears.

**Other books you might like:**
Lewis Carroll, *Through the Looking Glass and What Alice Found There*, 1865
Michael Ende, *The Neverending Story*, 1983
James Gurney, *Dinotopia*, 1992
Michael Kandel, *In between Dragons*, 1990
Anne Lindbergh, *Travel Far, Pay No Fare*, 1992
Margaret Mahy, *The Pirates' Mixed-Up Voyage*, 1993

---

**3157**

### ROSEMARY KIRSTEIN

## The Outskirter's Secret

(New York: Ballantine Del Rey, 1992)

**Story type:** Science Fiction (Adventure; Science Fantasy)
**Series:** Steerswoman
**Major character(s):** Rowan, Cartographer, Librarian; Bel, Margasdotter Chanly, Warrior, Guide
**Time period(s):** Indeterminate Future
**Locale(s):** Planet—Imaginary

**Summary:** Having achieved unwanted notice from the wizard's guild when she discovered that their magical control simply involves technological understanding, Rowan travels with Bel across the uncharted Outskirts hoping to find a fallen navigational satellite, the missing Guidestar, and gain insight into the wizards' control of society. Bel's Outskirter background proves vital to the pair's survival when they meet and join with nomadic goat herders to aid their progress across the deadly land.

**Other books you might like:**
Eleanor Arnason, *A Woman of the Iron People*, 1991
Sharon Baker, *Quarrelling, They Met the Dragon*, 1984
Octavia E. Butler, *Survivor*, 1978
Mary Gentle, *Golden Witchbreed*, 1984

---

Heather Gladney, *Teot's War*, 1987
Barbara Hambly, *The Time of the Dark*, 1982
Marjorie Bradley Kellogg, *Reign of Fire*, 1986
Marjorie Bradley Kellogg, *The Wave and the Flame*, 1986
Anne McCaffrey, *Dragonflight*, 1968
Jack Vance, *The Dying Earth*, 1950

---

**3158**

### ROSEMARY KIRSTEIN

## The Steerswoman

(New York: Ballantine/Del Rey, 1989)

**Story type:** Science Fiction (Science Fantasy)
**Series:** Steerswoman
**Major character(s):** Rowan, Wanderer, Scientist
**Time period(s):** Indeterminate Future
**Locale(s):** Planet—Imaginary

**Summary:** On a primitive world wizards practice what may be magic, but is probably disguised science. Meanwhile, the Steerswomen, an order of wandering truthseekers, attempt to spread basic scientific knowledge across the planet. One Steerswoman in particular incurs the wrath of the wizards due to her attempts to find out the truth about her world.

**Other books you might like:**
Doris Egan, *The Gate of Ivory*, 1989
Mary Gentle, *Golden Witchbreed*, 1983
Jack Vance, *The Dying Earth*, 1950
Jack Vance, *The Eyes of the Overworld*, 1966
F. Paul Wilson, *The Tery*, 1990

---

**3159**

### LEE KISLING

## The Fools' War

(New York: HarperCollins, 1992)

**Story type:** Fantasy (Young Adult; Magic Conflict)
**Major character(s):** Fernholz the Wise, Royalty (king); Clemmy, Teenager
**Time period(s):** Indeterminate
**Locale(s):** Mulberia, Fictional City

**Summary:** Smitten with unrequited love, King Fernholz finds himself unable to organize resistance to an invasion of his kingdom. In desperation he sends his only soldier to fetch Clemmy, who may unlock the secret of an ancient magical book containing spells which could cure the king. Author's first book.

**Other books you might like:**
Louise Cooper, *The Sleep of Stone*, 1991
Meredith Ann Pierce, *The Pearl of the Soul of the World*, 1991
Sherwood Smith, *Wren to the Rescue*, 1990
Brad Strickland, *Wizard's Mole*, 1991
Jane Yolen, *Wizard's Hall*, 1991

---

**3160**

### JAMES KISNER

## The Quagmire

(New York: Zebra, 1991)

**Story type:** Horror (Black Magic)

**Major character(s):** Joey Wickes, Child; Margaret Wickes, Waiter/Waitress (Joey's mother), Witch; Selma Drake, Witch
**Time period(s):** 1950s (1957)
**Locale(s):** Evansville, Indiana

**Summary:** The Pigeon Creek swamp is always a dangerous place to play, but this year it's particularly dangerous for the children of Evansville: Margaret Wickes' regular sacrifices of innocents to help open the gate between Earth and Hell have stirred up the spirits of runaway slaves buried at the bottom, as well as a few other nasty things secreted in its slimy depths.

**Other books you might like:**
Joseph A. Citro, *The Unseen*, 1990
Allen Lee Harris, *Deliver Us From Evil*, 1988
Michael B. Sirota, *The Well*, 1991

---

### 3161
#### JAMES KISNER

## Tower of Evil
(New York: Leisure, 1994)

**Story type:** Horror (Supernatural Vengeance)
**Major character(s):** Shannon Elroy, Guard (security guard); Stan Cork, Guard (security guard); Ted "Dead Ted" Flanders, Vagrant
**Time period(s):** 1990s (1994)
**Locale(s):** Indianapolis, Indiana

**Summary:** Years after a security guard accidentally kills Ted Flanders for loitering outside a bank building and disposes of his body in the building's trash compactor, Ted manifests as a living presence in the building, trapping office workers inside on a snowy day and subjecting them to a night of terror.

**Other books you might like:**
Fritz Leiber, *Our Lady of Darkness*, 1977
Melisand March, *The Site*, 1988
Al Sarrantonio, *House Haunted*, 1991
David J. Schow, *The Shaft*, 1990

---

### 3162
#### ANNETTE CURTIS KLAUSE

## Blood and Chocolate
(New York: Delacorte, 1997)

**Story type:** Horror (Werewolf Story; Young Adult)
**Major character(s):** Vivian Gandillon, Teenager, Werewolf; Aiden Teague, Teenager; Rafe Dafoe, Teenager
**Time period(s):** 1990s (1997)
**Locale(s):** Riverview, Maryland

**Summary:** Coming-of-age young adult novel. Teenage werewolf Vivian Gandillon begins a relationship with Aiden Teague, a "meatboy" (mortal human) whom she hopes is sensitive enough to accept her supernatural heritage. Their romance is threatened by the call of the pack, and the inevitable animosity of Vivian's werewolf family toward the humans in town.

**Other books you might like:**
Peter S. Beagle, *Lila the Werewolf*, 1969
Ronald Kelly, *Moon of the Werewolf*, 1991
John Saul, *Guardian*, 1993
S.P. Somtow, *The Vampire's Beautiful Daughter*, 1997

---

### 3163
#### ANNETTE CURTIS KLAUSE

## The Silver Kiss
(New York: Delacorte, 1990)

**Story type:** Fantasy (Horror; Young Adult)
**Major character(s):** Zoe, Teenager, Student; Simon, Vampire; Christopher, Child, Vampire
**Time period(s):** 1990s (1990)
**Locale(s):** United States

**Summary:** Zoe is attracted to the darkly mysterious Simon, who finally confesses that he is a vampire, and enlists her help in destroying his brother, the child-vampire Christopher, who had killed their mother. A first novel.

**Other books you might like:**
Margaret Mahy, *The Changeover*, 1974
Otfried Preussler, *The Satanic Mill*, 1972
Bram Stoker, *Dracula*, 1897
Chelsea Quinn Yarbro, *Hotel Transylvania*, 1978

---

### 3164
#### ANDREW KLAVAN

## The Uncanny
(New York: Crown, 1998)

**Story type:** Horror (Occult; Mystery)
**Major character(s):** Richard Storm, Producer (of movies); Sophia Endering, Art Dealer (daughter of gallery owner); Harper Albright, Editor
**Time period(s):** 1990s (1998)
**Locale(s):** London, England

**Summary:** Inspired by a ghost story that has haunted him since childhood, Richard Storm travels to England in search of evidence of the supernatural. He finds the proof he is looking for in his experience with Sophia Endering, a rich young woman imperiled by the evil menace who centuries before gave rise to the legend on which the ghost story was based.

**Other books you might like:**
Jonathan Aycliffe, *Whispers in the Dark*, 1993
Tannarive Due, *My Soul to Keep*, 1997
Daniel Rhodes, *Next, After Lucifer*, 1988
John Saul, *Darkness*, 1991
Harry Stein, *Infinity's Child*, 1997

---

### 3165
#### RICHARD KLUGER

## The Sheriff of Nottingham
(New York: Viking, 1992)

**Story type:** Fantasy (Legend; Historical)
**Major character(s):** Philip Mark, Mercenary, Lawman (sheriff of Nottingham); John, Royalty (King of England), Historical Figure; Robin Hood, Hero, Outlaw
**Time period(s):** 13th century (1208-1224)
**Locale(s):** Nottingham, England; Sherwood Forest, England

**Summary:** Assigned by King John as Sheriff of Nottingham, Philip Mark mitigates King John's tyrannical orders, balancing between the excesses of the King and the rebellious gentry. Circumstances force

Philip to ally with Robin until political evolution forces them into opposition.

**Other books you might like:**
Parke Godwin, *Sherwood*, 1991
Robin McKinley, *The Outlaws of Sherwood*, 1989
Howard Pyle, *The Merry Adventures of Robin Hood*, 1883
Jennifer Roberson, *Lady of the Forest*, 1992

---

**3166**

### RICHARD A. KNAAK

## *Children of the Drake*

(New York: Warner Questar, 1991)

**Story type:** Fantasy (Magic Conflict)
**Series:** Dragonrealm
**Major character(s):** Sharissa, Sorceress; Dru Zeree, Sorcerer
**Time period(s):** Indeterminate
**Locale(s):** Dragonrealm, Planet—Imaginary

**Summary:** To save his people from a world poisoned by foul magics, Dru Zeree must lead them into a land of spirits.

**Other books you might like:**
Casey Flynn, *The Enchanted Isles*, 1991
Casey Flynn, *Most Ancient Song*, 1991
Pat Winter, *Madoc*, 1990
Pat Winter, *Madoc's Hundred*, 1991

---

**3167**

### RICHARD A. KNAAK

## *The Crystal Dragon*

(New York: Warner Questar, 1993)

**Story type:** Fantasy (Magic Conflict)
**Series:** Dragonrealm
**Major character(s):** Cabe Bedlam, Wizard; Darkhorse, Demon
**Time period(s):** Indeterminate
**Locale(s):** Legar, Fictional Country

**Summary:** Cabe Bedlam's sinister dreams lead him to a distant peninsula where wolf raiders have discovered a cavern housing sorcerous weapons of an ancient, inhuman race. Intending to utilize the weapons in their plans for conquest, they accidently unleash the ancient Quel whose hellish powers will destroy all unless Cabe becomes the willing pawn of the oldest drake lord, the Crystal Dragon.

**Other books you might like:**
Elizabeth Forrest, *Phoenix Fire*, 1992
Laurell K. Hamilton, *Nightseer*, 1992
Marc Laidlaw, *Neon Lotus*, 1988
Elizabeth Ann Scarborough, *Last Refuge*, 1992

---

**3168**

### RICHARD A. KNAAK

## *The Dragon Crown*

(New York: Warner Questar, 1994)

**Story type:** Fantasy (Magic Conflict; Political)
**Series:** Dragonrealm
**Major character(s):** Kyl, Mythical Creature (dragon), Heir
**Time period(s):** Indeterminate
**Locale(s):** The Drake Kingdoms, Mythical Place

**Summary:** Potentially lethal tests to determine Kyl's ability to rule as Dragon Emperor could purify his spirit or unleash dark lusts and produce a reign of horror.

**Other books you might like:**
Lois McMaster Bujold, *The Spirit Ring*, 1992
Laurell K. Hamilton, *Nightseer*, 1992
Melanie Rawn, *Dragon Prince*, 1988
James H. Schmitz, *The Demon Breed*, 1968
Martha Wells, *The Element of Fire*, 1993

---

**3169**

### RICHARD A. KNAAK

## *Dragon Tome*

(New York: Warner Questar, 1992)

**Story type:** Fantasy (Magic Conflict; Quest)
**Series:** Dragonrealm
**Major character(s):** Wellen Bedlam, Explorer, Mythical Creature (half-elf); Yalso, Scholar, Adventurer; King Dragon, Mythical Creature, Royalty
**Time period(s):** Indeterminate
**Locale(s):** Dragonrealm, Planet—Imaginary

**Summary:** Discovering Dragonrealm, Wellen encounters a warlock who directs Wellen to a building which contains a most powerful magic book. Immediately events sweep Wellen and his companions into a conflict through which the Dragon King intends to acquire supreme power.

**Other books you might like:**
Gordon R. Dickson, *The Dragon at War*, 1992
Rose Estes, *The Stone of Time*, 1992
   Tom Wham, co-author
Thorarinn Gunnarsson, *Dragons on the Town*, 1992
Ursula K. Le Guin, *A Wizard of Earthsea*, 1968

---

**3170**

### RICHARD A. KNAAK

## *Frostwing*

(New York: Warner Aspect, 1995)

**Story type:** Fantasy (Magic Conflict; Contemporary)
**Major character(s):** Grigori Nicolau, Amnesiac; Teresa Dvorak, Real Estate Agent; Frostwing, Monster
**Time period(s):** 1990s
**Locale(s):** Chicago, Illinois

**Summary:** Grigori's memories are stolen repeatedly over the centuries by visions of a gargoyle he calls Frostwing. When he moves to Chicago, for reasons he no longer remembers, Grigori stumbles upon the physical manifestation of his tormentor in an unlikely place, a real estate listing. With the reluctant help of Teresa, his real estate agent, he attempts to unravel the mystery of the monster, risking damnation in an attempt to find salvation.

**Other books you might like:**
Peter S. Beagle, *The Folk of the Air*, 1986
Lois McMaster Bujold, *The Spirit Ring*, 1992
Emma Bull, *Bone Dance: A Fantasy for Technophiles*,
Gene Wolfe, *Soldier of the Mist*, 1986

## 3171

### RICHARD A. KNAAK

## *The Janus Mask*

(New York: Warner Aspect, 1995)

**Story type:** Fantasy (Quest; Magic Conflict)
**Major character(s):** Mandrol, Nobleman (baron), Wizard; Viktor Falsche, Rebel, Wizard; G'Meni, Wizard (alchemist)
**Time period(s):** Indeterminate Past
**Locale(s):** Medecia, Fictional Country

**Summary:** Baron Mandrol's collection of masks holds spirits of dead men. The mask of Viktor Falsche, Mandrol's most hated enemy, wakes and manages to escape to again plot the Baron's death, impeded by ignorance and lack of time.

**Other books you might like:**
Glen Cook, *The Black Company*, 1984
Guy Gavriel Kay, *Tigana*, 1990
Katherine Kurtz, *Deryni Rising*, 1970
Patricia A. McKillip, *The Riddle-Master of Hed*, 1976
Patricia C. Wrede, *The Seven Towers*, 1984

## 3172

### RICHARD A. KNAAK

## *Kaz the Minotaur*

(Lake Geneva, Wisconsin, TSR, 1990)

**Story type:** Fantasy (Adventure)
**Series:** Dragonlance Heroes II
**Major character(s):** Kaz, Mythical Creature (minotaur), Knight; Darius, Knight; Molok, Mythical Creature (ogre)
**Time period(s):** Indeterminate
**Locale(s):** Solamnia, Planet—Imaginary; Krynn, Planet—Imaginary; Vingaard Keep, Fictional City

**Summary:** Kaz is wandering various lands as an outcast. He is hunted by different groups unfriendly to him. He hears rumors that make him return to Solamnia to warn his old comrades, the Knights of Solamnia, who have been turned against him.

**Other books you might like:**
Raymond E. Feist, *Magician*, 1982
Robert E. Howard, *Conan the Conqueror*, 1950
Robert Jordan, *The Eye of the World*, 1989
Fritz Leiber, *The Knight and Knave of Swords*, 1990
Karl Edward Wagner, *Darkness Weaves*, 1970
Karl Edward Wagner, *Death Angel's Shadow*, 1973

## 3173

### RICHARD A. KNAAK

## *King of the Grey*

(New York: Warner Questar, 1993)

**Story type:** Fantasy (Contemporary; Quest)
**Major character(s):** Jeremiah Todtmann, Ruler (reluctant); Haros Aguilana, Vampire, Spirit
**Time period(s):** 1990s; Indeterminate
**Locale(s):** Chicago, Illinois; World of the Grey, Mythical Place (shadow realm)

**Summary:** When the creatures created by humanity's fancies and nightmares, the Grey, decide to draft Jeremiah Todtmann as their king, they kidnap the unsuspecting commuter and bring him into their realm. By making the reluctant Jeremiah into the Grey's King of Kings, they hope to promote their plans to change from phantasm into creatures of substance and permanence.

**Other books you might like:**
Aaron Allston, *Galatea in 2-D*, 1993
Chester Anderson, *The Butterfly Kid*, 1967
Alan Dean Foster, *To the Vanishing Point*, 1988
Megan Lindholm, *Cloven Hooves*, 1991
Ben Okri, *The Famished Road*, 1992
Lucius Shepard, *Kalimantan*, 1992
Clifford D. Simak, *Out of Their Minds*, 1970
Wm. Mark Simmons, *When Dreams Collide*, 1992

## 3174

### RICHARD A. KNAAK

## *The Shrouded Realm*

(New York: Warner Questar, 1991)

**Story type:** Fantasy (Magic Conflict)
**Series:** Dragonrealm
**Major character(s):** Dru Zeree, Sorcerer, Immigrant; Sharissa, Sorceress, Immigrant
**Time period(s):** Indeterminate
**Locale(s):** Dragonrealm, Planet—Imaginary

**Summary:** Newly arrived on Dragonrealm, the immigrant sorcerers find their magic and immortality threatened. Unless they discover and remedy the cause, they will lose their sanity and even their human form.

**Other books you might like:**
Casey Flynn, *The Enchanted Isles*, 1991
Casey Flynn, *Most Ancient Song*, 1991
Margaret Weis, *Fire Sea*, 1991
    Tracy Hickman, co-author

## 3175

### RICHARD A. KNAAK

## *Wolfhelm*

(New York: Popular Library Questar, 1990)

**Story type:** Fantasy (Adventure; Sword and Sorcery)
**Series:** Dragonrealm
**Major character(s):** Gryphon, Mythical Creature (were-gryphon); Duke Morgis, Warrior, Mythical Creature (dragon); Gwen Bedlam, Witch
**Time period(s):** Indeterminate Past (pre-Industrial Revolution)
**Locale(s):** Dragonrealm, Fictional Country

**Summary:** The Gryphon, half-humanoid lion-bird, must go on a quest to find the Dream Lands, as much a state of mind as a place, in order to save the shape-shifting dragons from losing their powers and dragon shapes. His friends, Cabe and Gwen Bedlam must protect the Dragon Emperor's hatchlings from political assassination, while Gryphon must pass through the evil empire of the wolf raiders, their monstrous Runners and Pack Master, and their dark god, the Ravager.

**Other books you might like:**
Glen Cook, *A Shadow of All Night Falling*, 1979
Diane Duane, *The Door into Fire*, 1979
P.C. Hodgell, *Dark of the Moon*, 1985
Guy Gavriel Kay, *Tigana*, 1990
Fritz Leiber, *The Knight and Knave of Swords*, 1990
Clifford D. Simak, *The Goblin Reservation*, 1968

## 3176

**AMARANTHA KNIGHT** (Pseudonym of Nancy Kilpatrick)

### The Darker Passions Reader

(New York: Masquerade, 1996)

**Story type:** Horror (Collection)
**Series:** The Darker Passions

**Summary:** This sampler culls the best passages from the author's erotic reworking of classic horror tales: Bram Stoker's *Dracula*, Mary Shelley's *Frankenstein*, Robert Louis Stevenson's *The Strange Case of Dr. Jekyll and Mr. Hyde*, and Edgar Allan Poe's "The Fall of the House of Usher." Here depictions of Dracula as a domination fetishist, Frankenstein's monster as a sexually voracious female, Mr. Hyde as the unrestrained undercurrent of lust in Victorian England, and Roderick and Madeline Usher as truly intimate siblings are not for the squeamish.

**Other books you might like:**
Michael Hemmingson, *Nice Little Stories Jam-Packed with Depraved Sex and Violence*, 1996
Richard Sutphen, *Sexpunks & Savage Sagas*, 1991
Lucy Taylor, *Close to the Bone*, 1994

## 3177

**AMARANTHA KNIGHT** (Pseudonym of Nancy Kilpatrick)

### The Darker Passions: Carmilla

(New York: Masquerade, 1997)

**Story type:** Horror (Vampire Story)
**Series:** Darker Passions
**Major character(s):** Laura, Young Woman; Carmilla, Vampire; Martin Miller, Businessman
**Time period(s):** 1800s
**Locale(s):** Styria, Austria

**Summary:** Young Laura seeks escape from sadistic chastisements and leather fetishes of her governess in the arms of the mysterious Carmilla. Carmilla, whose presence has been associated with the mysterious deaths of several young girls, is in fact a vampire who indoctrinates Laura into the ecstasies of the Undead. A pornographic retelling of J. Sheridan Le Fanu's classic novella "Carmilla", explicitly focused through the original lesbian subtext.

**Other books you might like:**
Poppy Z. Brite, *Love in Vein II*, 1997
    Martin H. Greenberg, co-editor
Pam Keesey, *Daughters of Darkness: Lesbian Vampire Stories*, 1993
    editor
Pam Keesey, *Darker Angels: Lesbian Vampire Stories*, 1995
    editor
Cecilia Tan, *Vampire Erotica*, 1995
    editor
Cecilia Tan, *Erotica Vampirica*, 1996
    editor
Cecilia Tan, *Cherished Blood*, 1997
    editor

## 3178

**AMARANTHA KNIGHT** (Pseudonym of Nancy Kilpatrick)

### The Darker Passions: Dr. Jekyll and Mr. Hyde

(New York: Masquerade, 1995)

**Story type:** Horror (Doppelganger)
**Series:** The Darker Passions
**Major character(s):** Henry Jekyll, Doctor; Mr. Hyde, Criminal; Ursula Lawrence, Young Woman
**Time period(s):** 1890s
**Locale(s):** London, England

**Summary:** In this erotic retelling of Robert Louis Stevenson's classic tale of a chemically-induced split personality, Dr. Henry Jekyll's experiments lead to the discovery of a potion that transforms him into the image of his sexually rampant ego, whom he names Mr. Hyde. Hyde, a leather and flagellation fetishist, finds himself a welcome guest behind the closed doors of sexually repressed but ever-eager Victorian society.

**Other books you might like:**
Jay R. Bonansinga, *Sick*, 1995
Eric Higgs, *Doppelganger*, 1887
Richard Matheson, *Earthbound*, 1989
Robert Louis Stevenson, *The Strange Case of Dr. Jekyll and Mr. Hyde*, 1886

## 3179

**AMARANTHA KNIGHT** (Pseudonym of Nancy Kilpatrick)

### The Darker Passions: Dracula

(New York: Masquerade, 1994)

**Story type:** Horror (Vampire Story)
**Series:** Darker Passions
**Major character(s):** Vlad Tepes, Vampire (Count Dracula); Magda, Vampire; Jonathan Harker, Lawyer (solicitor)
**Time period(s):** 1890s
**Locale(s):** Transylvania (Castle Dracula)

**Summary:** This gymnastic retelling of the story of Count Dracula imagines Jonathan Harker, Mina Harker, Lucy Westenra, Dr. Van Helsing, Jonathan Seward, Count Dracula and others as consensual partners in sadomasochistic and fetishistic indulgences that loosely follow the events of Bram Stoker's novel, and give new meaning to Dracula's historical title of Vlad the Impaler.

**Other books you might like:**
C. Dean Andersson, *I Am Dracula*, 1993
Marie Kiraly, *Mina*, 1994
Fred Saberhagen, *Bram Stoker's Dracula*, 1993
    James V. Hart, co-author
Bram Stoker, *Dracula*, 1897

## 3180

**AMARANTHA KNIGHT** (Pseudonym of Nancy Kilpatrick)

### The Darker Passions: Frankenstein

(New York: Masquerade, 1995)

**Story type:** Horror (Reanimated Dead; Erotic Horror)
**Series:** Darker Passions
**Major character(s):** Victor Frankenstein, Scientist; Elizabeth Frankenstein, Young Woman; Crea, Reanimated Dead

**Time period(s):** 1810s
**Locale(s):** Geneva, Switzerland

**Summary:** At the suggestion of his bride-to-be, Elizabeth, kinky scientist Victor Frankenstein creates a living being out of dead body parts whose function is to serve as the ultimate love slave for Victor, Elizabeth, and their circle.

**Other books you might like:**
Brian W. Aldiss, *Frankenstein Unbound*, 1973
Martin H. Greenberg, *Frankenstein: The Monster Wakes*, 1994
  editor
Stephen Jones, *The Mammoth Book of Frankenstein*, 1995
  editor
Marie Kiraly, *Mina*, 1995
Mary Shelley, *Frankenstein*, 1818

## 3181

**AMARANTHA KNIGHT** (Pseudonym of Nancy Kilpatrick)

### Demon Sex
(New York: Rhinoceros, 1998)

**Story type:** Horror (Anthology; Erotic Horror)

**Summary:** Eleven tales of erotic horror from an established publisher of adult fiction. Included are Thomas Roche's ''Vixens,'' about a stripper from hell; Edo van Belkom's ''Strange Attraction,'' which explains the apparent immortality of an aging rock star and his seemingly endless sex appeal; and Gemma Files' ''Bottle of Smoke,'' about a shape-shifting demon of Indian mythology.

**Other books you might like:**
Poppy Z. Brite, *Love in Vein*, 1994
  editor
Ellen Datlow, *Little Deaths*, 1995
  editor
Pam Keesey, *Daughters of Darkness: Lesbian Vampire Stories*, 1993
  editor
Cecilia Tan, *The Beast Within: Erotic Tales of Werewolves*, 1993
  editor
Cecilia Tan, *Blood Kiss: Vampire Erotica*, 1993
  editor

## 3182

**AMARANTHA KNIGHT**, Editor

### Love Bites
(New York: Richard Kasak, 1994)

**Story type:** Horror (Anthology; Vampire Story)

**Summary:** Knight, a pseudonym of Nancy Kilpatrick, is herself a writer of vampire fiction. Here she has collected 11 newly written stories and reprints that make the sexual subtexts of vampire fiction explicit. In Kathryn Ptacek's ''Pleasure Domes,'' a European traveller becomes so caught up in a sexual liaison on his grand tour that he doesn't realize a century has passed in the interim. Lois Tilton, in ''Love Bites,'' describes a topsy-turvy world in which humans actually seek out vampires to taste *their* blood, and Nancy Collins, in ''Dancing Nitely,'' depicts a world in which vampires are the dominant species and humans their erotic playthings. David Dvorkin, in ''Reign of Blood,'' tells of a vampire in revolutionary France who uses the Reign of Terror to cover his own bloody tracks, and Karen Taylor, in ''The Mirrored Image,'' relates the tale of a vampire spirit that possesses a hooker in order to obtain its necessary victims.

**Other books you might like:**
Poppy Z. Brite, *Love in Vein*, 1994
  editor
Pam Keesey, *Daughters of Darkness: Lesbian Vampire Stories*, 1993
  editor
Cecilia Tan, *Erotic Vampire Tales*, 1994
  editor

## 3183

**AMARANTHA KNIGHT** (Pseudonym of Nancy Kilpatrick)

### The Pit and the Pendulum
(New York: Masquerade, 1998)

**Story type:** Horror (Erotic Horror)
**Series:** Darker Passions
**Major character(s):** Aurelia, Witch; Leonidas, Young Man
**Time period(s):** 16th century
**Locale(s):** Toledo, Spain

**Summary:** In this erotic variation on Edgar Allan Poe's classic conte cruel, Aurelia, a young woman suspected of witchcraft, is imprisoned at the height of the Spanish Inquisition, and introduced by her transsexual torturer to the Pit of Delight, where pain and pleasure meet.

**Other books you might like:**
Poppy Z. Brite, *Exquisite Corpse*, 1996
Marquis de Sade, *Eugenie de Franval and Other Stories*, 1965
Edward Lee, *Coven*, 1991
Lucy Taylor, *The Safety of Unknown Cities*, 1995
H.C. Turk, *Black Body*, 1989

## 3184

**AMARANTHA KNIGHT**, Editor

### Seductive Spectres
(New York: Rhinoceros, 1996)

**Story type:** Horror (Anthology; Ghost Story)

**Summary:** In 12 highly erotic stories, the living and the ghosts of the dead get to know each other very intimately. Michael A. Arnzen's ''Screwge'' works a variation on Charles Dickens' ''A Christmas Carol,'' featuring a heroine visited by two ghosts of Christmas to come, each with lusty lessons to teach. In ''Megan's Spirit,'' a ghost and a mortal lover provide each other with the companionship neither can get from their respective worlds. In ''Melia,'' Brian McNaughton tells of a man who fantasizes the ghost of a long-dead high school cheerleader into life. In ''All This and Heaven Too,'' John Mason Skipp presents a porn star visited by the communal spirit of the middle class male businessmen who watch her movies. A lengthy excerpt from Brian Lumley's novel *Necroscope* is also included.

**Other books you might like:**
John Pelan, *Darkside: Horror for the Next Millennium*, 1996
  editor
Cecilia Tan, *The Beast Within: Erotic Tales of Werewolves*, 1993
  editor
Cecilia Tan, *Blood Kiss: Vampire Erotica*, 1993
  editor
Cecilia Tan, *Erotica Vampirica*, 1996
  editor

## 3185

### DAMON KNIGHT

## God's Nose

(Eugene, Oregon: Pulphouse Publishing, 1991)

**Story type:** Science Fiction (Collection; Theological)
**Series:** Author's Choice Monthly

**Summary:** This volume contains 6 stories arranged from Creation to God's Day of Wrath, all sharing religious themes or themes of the spirit and nature of mankind: "God's Nose" (1966); "Catch That Martian" (1952); "Four in One" (1953); "You're Another" (1955); "The Country of the Kind" (1956); and "Shall Dust Save Thee" (1967).

**Other books you might like:**
Judith Moffett, *Two That Came True*, 1991
Frederik Pohl, *Stopping at Slowyear*, 1991
Robert Silverberg, *Thebes of the Hundred Gates*, 1991
John Varley, *The Persistence of Vision*, 1978
Kate Wilhelm, *State of Grace*, 1991

## 3186

### DAMON KNIGHT

## Humpty Dumpty: An Oval

(New York: Tor, 1996)

**Story type:** Science Fiction (Satire; Disaster)
**Major character(s):** Wellington "Bill" Nelson Stout, Businessman (lingerie); Thomas A. Stout, Relative (brother); Emilio da Lionghi, Criminal
**Time period(s):** 1990s
**Locale(s):** Milan, Italy; London, England; Potamos, Pennsylvania

**Summary:** On the way to his brother's wedding, Bill stops in Milan at the request of his brother, only to wake up with a bullet in his head. Accused of not delivering a requested package, Bill finds reality shifting around. A meteorite may have destroyed New York, or aliens may have landed there. However, heading home to Potamos only leads to further confusion of time and reality.

**Other books you might like:**
Deborah Christian, *Mainline*, 1996
Philip K. Dick, *Valis*, 1981
Jean Mark Gawron, *Dream of Glass*, 1993
James P. Hogan, *Paths to Otherwhere*, 1996
Ursula K. Le Guin, *The Lathe of Heaven*, 1971
Michael Swanwick, *Stations of the Tide*, 1991

## 3187

### DAMON KNIGHT

## One Side Laughing: Stories Unlike Other Stories

(New York: St. Martins Press, 1991)

**Story type:** Science Fiction (Collection)

**Summary:** This volume contains 14 stories originally published in 1980s magazines plus 2 from 1970s magazines and the longest story, a retitled novella, "The Other Foot," published in a slightly different form in 1963. The stories contain Knight's characteristic humor and social commentary with many featuring a technological change and its effect on human interaction.

**Other books you might like:**
Alfred Bester, *The Light Fantastic*, 1976
Alfred Bester, *Star Light, Star Bright*, 1976
Larry Niven, *N-Space*, 1990
Robert Silverberg, *The Science Fiction Hall of Fame, Volume 1*, 1970
editor
Cordwainer Smith, *The Best of Cordwainer Smith*, 1975
John Varley, *Blue Champagne*, 1986
John Varley, *The Persistence of Vision*, 1978

## 3188

### DAMON KNIGHT

## A Reasonable World

(New York: Tor, 1991)

**Story type:** Science Fiction (Invasion of Earth; Utopia)
**Series:** CV
**Major character(s):** Harriet Cleaver Owen, Researcher (behavioral epidemiologist); Dorothy Italiano, Researcher (hypnotherapist)
**Time period(s):** 21st century
**Locale(s):** United States; At Sea (medical detention center)

**Summary:** When deep sea researchers based on Sea Venture, an ocean-going habitat, release an alien life form, McNulty's Symbiont, the coherent energy beings begin invading human beings' bodies, changing the hosts' thinking ability in the process. Dr. Harriet Owen discovers the aliens can be driven from human beings with electroshock, then detected and killed while between hosts. Now Sea Venture has been made into an isolated research station using involuntary human subjects to study the McNulty's Symbiont. While some people work to bring about the Utopia offered, others work to return society to its former sorry state.

**Other books you might like:**
Octavia E. Butler, *Imago*, 1989
Octavia E. Butler, *Adulthood Rites*, 1988
Octavia E. Butler, *Dawn*, 1987
John W. Campbell, *Who Goes There?*, 1948
Robert A. Heinlein, *The Puppet Masters*, 1990
Eric Frank Russell, *Sinister Barrier*, 1948

## 3189

### DAMON KNIGHT

## Rule Golden and Double Meaning

(New York: Tor, 1991)

**Story type:** Science Fiction (Invasion of Earth)
**Major character(s):** Aza-Kra, Alien; Jawj Pero Pembun, Government Official (investigator); Wei, Alien (Rithian), Spy
**Time period(s):** 21st century; 26th century
**Locale(s):** Earth

**Summary:** This volume contains a 15-page autobiographical introduction titled "Beauty, Stupidity, Injustice, and Science Fiction," plus two stories, "Rule Golden," originally published in 1954 in *Science Fiction Adventures* and "Double Meaning," originally published in 1953 in *Startling Stories*. In "Rule Golden," Aza-Fra changes life on Earth when he releases a catalyst which forces human beings to feel empathy for those affected by their actions. In "Double Meaning," Jawj and others search for Rithian invaders who impersonate human beings, intending to completely compromise Earth security before revealing themselves.

**Other books you might like:**
Orson Scott Card, *Eye for Eye/The Tunesmith*, 1990
   Lloyd Biggle, co-author
Arthur C. Clarke, *A Meeting with Medusa/Green Mars*, 1988
   Kim Stanley Robinson, co-author
Fritz Leiber, *Ill Met in Lankhmar/The Fair in Emain Macha*, 1990
   Charles de Lint, co-author
Barry B. Longyear, *Enemy Mine/Another Orphan*, 1989
   John Kessel, co-author
Kim Stanley Robinson, *A Short, Sharp Shock/The Dragon Masters*, 1990
   Jack Vance, co-author
Walter Jon Williams, *Elegy for Angels and Dogs/The Graveyard Heart*, 1990
   Roger Zelazny, co-author

---

**3190**

**DAMON KNIGHT**

## Why Do Birds

(New York: Tor, 1992)

**Story type:** Science Fiction (Satire; UFO)
**Major character(s):** Edwin L. "Ed" Stone, Revolutionary, Activist; Linda Lavalle, Administrator, Girlfriend (Ed's)
**Time period(s):** 2000s (2002)
**Locale(s):** New York, New York; Europe; Argentina

**Summary:** When Ed Stone appears in clothing seven decades out-of-date, he presents a tale of his abduction by extraterrestials and plans to create a huge cube in which humans can survive a predicted holocaust. A ring with the power to win over others' opinions helps Ed to convince world leaders to help him. As he assembles help for his work, Ed's sanity comes into question as Linda Lavalle and her father resist the completion of Ed's project.

**Other books you might like:**
Bradley Denton, *Buddy Holly Is Alive and Well on Ganymede*, 1991
Colin Greenland, *Take Back Plenty*, 1992
Robert Rankin, *Armageddon: The Musical*, 1990

---

**3191**

**HARRY ADAM KNIGHT** (Pseudonym of John Brosnan)

## Carnosaur

(New York: Tor, 1993)

**Story type:** Science Fiction (Techno-Thriller; Genetic Manipulation)
**Major character(s):** David Pascal, Journalist; Jan Penward, Noblewoman; Darren Penward, Nobleman, Criminal
**Time period(s):** 1980s
**Locale(s):** Warchester, England

**Summary:** After deaths result from an escaped animal of Sir Darren Penward's unique collection of dangerous animals, officials blame a Siberian tiger. When a young witness identifies the killer as a dinosaur, Pascal follows the lead and finds a conspiracy which could herald a new age of dinosaurs. Novelizes the film. British edition published in 1984.

**Other books you might like:**
Michael Crichton, *Jurassic Park*, 1990
Larry Niven, *The Flight of the Horse*, 1973
Tim Sullivan, *Lords of Creation*, 1992
Dave Wolverton, *Serpent Catch*, 1991

---

**3192**

**HARRY ADAM KNIGHT** (Pseudonym of John Brosnan)

## The Fungus

(New York: Franklin Watts, 1989)

**Story type:** Horror (Techno-Horror)
**Major character(s):** Barry Wilson, Scientist (Mycologist), Writer (Thrillers); Kimberly Fairchild, Doctor (Medical)
**Time period(s):** 1980s
**Locale(s):** England; Ireland

**Summary:** Genetic experiments with mushrooms unleash a symbiotic fungi that devours everything in its path. In hopes of containing the plague, a small group is sent to track down Wilson's ex-wife Jane, the scientist who inadvertently set loose the fungi. Originally published in 1985.

**Other books you might like:**
J.G. Ballard, *The Crystal World*, 1966
James Herbert, *Domain*, 1984
James Herbert, *Lair*, 1979
James Herbert, *The Rats*, 1974

---

**3193**

**KATHE KOJA**

## Bad Brains

(New York: Dell/Abyss, 1992)

**Story type:** Horror (Wild Talents)
**Major character(s):** Austen Bandy, Artist; Emily Bandy, Writer; Dr. Quiet, Doctor (metaphysician)
**Time period(s):** 1990s
**Locale(s):** New Jersey; Detroit, Michigan

**Summary:** Down and out and working in a T-shirt design store, failed artist Austen Bandy suffers a serious head wound that induces abstract visual hallucinations. Uncertain whether he has become hostage to overdeveloped aesthetic sensibilities, or to an outside force seeking to make him its vessel, Austen embarks on a cross-country flight to find a cure.

**Other books you might like:**
Giles Blunt, *Cold Eye*, 1989
Stephen King, *The Dead Zone*, 1979
Jessica Amanda Salmonson, *Anthony Shriek*, 1992

---

**3194**

**KATHE KOJA**

## The Cipher

(New York: Dell/Abyss, 1991)

**Story type:** Horror (Wild Talents)
**Major character(s):** Nicholas Reid, Businessman (video store manager); Nakota, Waiter/Waitress; Malcolm, Artist
**Time period(s):** 1990s (1991)
**Locale(s):** United States

**Summary:** This excellent first novel is concerned with would-be poet Nicholas Reid, who along with his girlfriend Nakota becomes fascinated with "the Funhole," a bottomless hole in the wall of his apartment building that has a strange influence upon objects dropped into it. When Nicholas accidentally stumbles into the Funhole hand-first, he acquires a slowly expanding wound, the involuntary ability to melt steel and levitate, and a circle of artist friends whose reaction to his condition reveals truths about himself he would rather not face.

**Other books you might like:**
Fritz Leiber, *Our Lady of Darkness*, 1977
Roland Topor, *The Tenant*, 1964

---

**3195**

**KATHE KOJA**

## *Extremities*

(New York: Four Walls Eight Windows, 1998)

**Story type:** Horror (Collection)

**Summary:** This collection includes 16 stories, two original to the volume, most featuring characters whose alienation finds expression in extraordinary experiences. ''Jubilee'' is a ghost story in which a woman cannot resolve whether the disembodied voice she hears is a supernatural presence or the articulation of her dissatisfaction with her dispassionate marriage. In ''Bird Superior,'' a man copes with his survival of an airplane crash by developing the ability to fly. In ''The Neglected Garden,'' a woman determined not to be abandoned by her lover literally takes root in his back yard.

**Other books you might like:**
Angela Carter, *The Bloody Chamber*, 1979
A.M. Homes, *The Safety of Objects*, 1990
Rachel Ingalls, *The End of Tragedy*, 1987
Valerie Martin, *The Consolation of Nature, and Other Stories*, 1988
Joyce Carol Oates, *The Collector of Hearts: New Tales of the Grotesque*, 1998

---

**3196**

**KATHE KOJA**

## *Skin*

(New York: Delacorte, 1993)

**Story type:** Horror (Psychological Suspense)
**Major character(s):** Tess Bajac, Artist (sculptor); Bibi Bloss, Entertainer (performance artist); Michael Hispard, Dancer
**Time period(s):** 1990s (1993)
**Locale(s):** Rivertown

**Summary:** Tess and Bibi join together to form the Surgeons of Destruction, an avant garde performance art troupe that combines Tess's machine-like constructions with Bibi's radical dance style. But Bibi's increasing interest in exploring the limits of what the human body can withstand alienates Tess and plunges her deeper and deeper into a lifestyle of body piercing, scarification, and potential death.

**Other books you might like:**
Giles Blunt, *Cold Eye*, 1989
Brian D'Amato, *Beauty*, 1992
Jessica Amanda Salmonson, *Anthony Shriek*, 1992
David J. Skal, *Antibodies*, 1989

---

**3197**

**KATHE KOJA**

## *Strange Angels*

(New York: Delacorte, 1994)

**Story type:** Horror (Psychological Suspense)

---

**Major character(s):** Grant Cotto, Photographer; Robin Tobias, Artist, Mentally Ill Person; Johanna, Health Care Professional (art therapist)
**Time period(s):** 1990s (1994)
**Locale(s):** United States

**Summary:** Unsuccessful photographer Grant Cotto becomes fascinated by the paintings of Robin Tobias, a schizophrenic patient being tended by Grant's girlfriend. Grant moves in with Robin, ostensibly to help him realize his artistic potential, but as their relationship intensifies Grant loses perspective and becomes sucked into the vortex of Robin's insanity.

**Other books you might like:**
Giles Blunt, *Cold Eye*, 1989
Poppy Z. Brite, *Drawing Blood*, 1993
Jessica Amanda Salmonson, *Anthony Shriek*, 1992

---

**3198**

**JACK KOKE**

## *Beyond the Pale*

(New York: Roc, 1998)

**Story type:** Fantasy (Quest; Magic Conflict)
**Series:** Shadowrun
**Major character(s):** Ryan Mercury, Spy; Thayla, Sorceress
**Time period(s):** 2050s (2057)
**Locale(s):** Metaplanes, Mythical Place; United States

**Summary:** Ryan Mercury is a secret agent who has been entrusted with a powerful mystical object which must be delivered to the metaplanes to help in the defense of Earth against a horde of supernatural beings. Chief among the magical defenders of Earth is Thayla, but her unexpected destruction makes Mercury's job even more difficult.

**Other books you might like:**
Rick Cook, *Mall Purchase Night*, 1993
Nigel Findley, *House of the Sun*, 1995
Mel Odom, *Preying for Keeps*, 1996
Will Shetterly, *Nevernever*, 1993
Nyx Smith, *Who Hunts the Hunter*, 1995

---

**3199**

**VICTOR KOMAN**

## *Kings of the High Frontier*

(Centreville, Virginia: Final Frontier, 1998)

**Story type:** Science Fiction (Political)
**Major character(s):** Tammy Reis, Astronaut; Laurence Poubelle, Businessman; Gerald Cooper, Businessman
**Time period(s):** Indeterminate Future
**Locale(s):** Florida; Outer Space

**Summary:** Tammy Reis loses her flight status after an unpleasant encounter with a politician and takes a temporary assignment as a government agent investigating a secretive businessman. She discovers that he plans to bypass the moribund government space program and launch a commercial space station of his own. Eventually she decides to abandon her employers and support his plans.

**Other books you might like:**
Lester Del Rey, *Step to the Stars*, 1954
Stephen Baxter, *Titan*, 1997
Ben Bova, *Colony*, 1978
Arthur C. Clarke, *Islands in the Sky*, 1952
Edward Gibson, *In the Wrong Hands*, 1992

## **3200**

### VICTOR KOMAN

## *Solomon's Knife*

(New York: Franklin Watts, 1989)

**Story type:** Science Fiction (Medical)
**Major character(s):** Evelyn Fletcher, Doctor (Surgeon); Karen Chandler, Parent (Surrogate mother)
**Time period(s):** 1990s
**Locale(s):** California

**Summary:** Dr. Evelyn Fletcher has secretly created a new surgical procedure that allows her to transplant an aborted fetus into the womb of a surrogate mother. When the baby who results from the transplant falls ill and the facts surrounding her birth become public, a firestorm of controversy erupts.

**Other books you might like:**
Robin Cook, *Harmful Intent*, 1989
Michael Crichton, *The Terminal Man*, 1972
Daniel Keyes, *Flowers for Algernon*, 1966
Ayn Rand, *Atlas Shrugged*, 1957

## **3201**

### TODD KOMARNICKI

## *Famine*

(New York: Arcade, 1997)

**Story type:** Horror (Ghost Story)
**Major character(s):** Daniel Rowan, Bartender; Daniel Bell, Detective—Police; Emma Clough, Bartender
**Time period(s):** 1990s
**Locale(s):** New York, New York

**Summary:** Daniel Rowan's death from malnutrition prompts incredulous Detective Daniel Bell to investigate the case as a homicide. Bell's pursuit of Rowan's wife, Emma, uncovers the lifetime of pain and misunderstanding that drove Rowan to his fate, but also reveals coincidences of near supernatural intensity that parallel Bell's own troubled private life.

**Other books you might like:**
Paul Auster, *The New York Trilogy*, 1990
Peter S. Beagle, *A Fine and Private Place*, 1960
Judith Hawkes, *Julian's House*, 1989
T.M. Wright, *A Manhattan Ghost Story*, 1984

## **3202**

### DEAN R. KOONTZ

## *The Bad Place*

(New York: G.P. Putnam, 1990)

**Story type:** Horror (Mystery)
**Major character(s):** Bobbie Dakota, Detective—Private; Julie Dakota, Detective—Private
**Time period(s):** 1990s
**Locale(s):** Orange County, California

**Summary:** Amnesiac Frank Pollard hires the Dakotas to find out who he really is and why he is being stalked by some bizarre malevolent force. The Dakotas' investigation leads them into a terrifying conflict with a psychotic killer with paranormal abilities.

**Other books you might like:**
George C. Chesbro, *Bone*, 1989

## **3203**

### DEAN R. KOONTZ

## *Cold Fire*

(New York: G.P. Putnam's, 1991)

**Story type:** Horror (Science Fiction)
**Major character(s):** Jim Ironhart, Teacher (elementary school); Holly Thorne, Journalist (news reporter); Enemy, Alien
**Time period(s):** 1990s (1991)
**Locale(s):** Laguna Niguel, California; New Svenbrog, California

**Summary:** Holly Thorne joins forces with Jim Ironhart to discover the source of the secret power that has enabled him to foresee and prevent the deaths of several people in the last six months. For his part, Jim is forced to confront his buried past by returning to his childhood town for a rendezvous with the responsible entity.

**Other books you might like:**
Owen Brookes, *Deadly Communion*, 1984
James Herbert, *Moon*, 1985
Stephen King, *The Dead Zone*, 1979
Robert Silverberg, *Dying Inside*, 1972

## **3204**

### DEAN R. KOONTZ

## *Dark Rivers of the Heart*

(New York: Knopf, 1994)

**Story type:** Horror (Psychological Suspense)
**Major character(s):** Spencer Grant, Computer Expert; Roy Miro, Government Official; Valerie Keene, Waiter/Waitress (cocktail waitress)
**Time period(s):** 1990s (1994)
**Locale(s):** Santa Monica, California

**Summary:** Spencer Grant, a computer hacker, accidentally runs afoul of Roy Miro, emissary of a secret government agency who manipulates computer technology to change identities and abuses his powers by eliminating certain members of the human race who do not conform to his standards of perfection.

**Other books you might like:**
Mark A. Clements, *Children of the End*, 1993
Philip K. Dick, *Do Androids Dream of Electric Sheep?*, 1968
William Gibson, *Neuromancer*, 1984
Daniel H. Gower, *The Orpheus Process*, 1992

## **3205**

### DEAN R. KOONTZ

## *Dragon Tears*

(New York: Putnam, 1993)

**Story type:** Horror (Wild Talents)
**Major character(s):** Harry Lyon, Police Officer; Connie Gulliver, Police Officer; Bryan "Ticktock" Drackman, Young Man
**Time period(s):** 1990s (1993)
**Locale(s):** Laguna Niguel, California

**Summary:** Select residents of a small southern California town are terrorized by a bizarre young man with telekinetic powers and a nasty disposition. Cop Harry Lyon must discover the identity of the man and the source of his powers or die at his hands in 16 hours.

**Other books you might like:**
Rick Hautala, *Ghost Light*, 1993

Ruby Jean Jensen, *Celia*, 1991
Stephen King, *Salem's Lot*, 1975
Peter Straub, *Ghost Story*, 1979

### 3206

#### DEAN R. KOONTZ

### *The Eyes of Darkness*

(Arlington: Dark Harvest, 1989)

**Story type:** Science Fiction (Horror)
**Major character(s):** Christina Evans, Dancer, Producer; Elliot Stryker, Lawyer
**Time period(s):** 1980s
**Locale(s):** Las Vegas, Nevada; West

**Summary:** A year after Tina Evans's son Danny supposedly died in a horrible accident she finds evidence that he may indeed be alive, that the accident may involve biological warfare, and that she and her son may both be victims of a deadly cover-up.

**Other books you might like:**
Katherine Dunn, *Geek Love*, 1989
Stephen King, *The Dark Half*, 1989
Stephen King, *It*, 1986
Stephen King, *Pet Sematary*, 1983
Stephen King, *The Tommyknockers*, 1987
Bruce McAllister, *Dream Baby*, 1989
Dan Simmons, *Carrion Comfort*, 1989

### 3207

#### DEAN R. KOONTZ

### *Fear Nothing*

(New York: Bantam, 1998)

**Story type:** Horror (Mystery; Science Fiction)
**Major character(s):** Chris Snow, Writer; Sasha Goodall, Radio Personality (disc jockey); Bobby Halloway, Sports Figure (surfer)
**Time period(s):** 1990s (1998)
**Locale(s):** Moonlight Bay, California

**Summary:** Chris Snow becomes the investigator and quarry of a conspiracy to cover up an accident in a military-sponsored laboratory that has resulted in the escape of genetically engineered animals with the potential to infect and cause mutations in human beings. The first of a projected series of adventures featuring a hero whose affliction with the depigmentation disorder, xeroderma pigmentosum, limits his activities to the night. First published in England in 1997.

**Other books you might like:**
Daniel H. Gower, *The Orpheus Process*, 1993
Brian Hodge, *Prototype*, 1996
Pierre Ouellette, *The Deus Machine*, 1994
Douglas Preston, *Relic*, 1995
   Lincoln Child, co-author
John Saul, *The Homing*, 1994

### 3208

#### DEAN R. KOONTZ

### *Hideaway*

(New York: Putnam's, 1992)

**Story type:** Horror (Serial Killer)

**Major character(s):** Hatchford Harrison, Antiques Dealer; Regina, Child (adopted); Vassago, Serial Killer
**Time period(s):** 1990s
**Locale(s):** Laguna Niguel, California

**Summary:** Following a near-death experience Hatch Harrison tries to lead an exemplary life, but finds himself troubled by visions of ghastly murders perpetrated by Vassago, a satanic young man with whom he has developed a psychic link and whose actions bring him closer to Hatch and his family with each successive kill.

**Other books you might like:**
Robert Bloch, *Psycho*, 1959
Davis Grubb, *The Night of the Hunter*, 1953
Joe R. Lansdale, *The Nightrunners*, 1987
Ira Levin, *Sliver*, 1991

### 3209

#### DEAN R. KOONTZ

### *Icebound*

(New York: Ballantine, 1995)

**Story type:** Horror (Psychological Suspense)
**Major character(s):** Harold Carpenter, Scientist; Gunvald Larsson, Scientist; Brian Doughterty, Writer
**Time period(s):** 1990s (1995)
**Locale(s):** Thule, Greenland

**Summary:** A project to supply water-deprived parts of the world with icebergs cut from the Arctic iceflow goes awry when an earthquake breaks off part of an iceberg bearing the Edgeway Project scientific team and sets them adrift. As the team races against the clock to dismantle the explosive charges they have set, they discover that one of their members may be a psychopath who would just as soon see the project fail and all of them die. This novel has been revised since it appeared in 1976 under the title *Prison of Ice* and the pseudonym David Axton.

**Other books you might like:**
Joe R. Lansdale, *Act of Love*, 1981
Richard Laymon, *Midnight's Lair*, 1993
Richard Laymon, *Quake*, 1995
Alistair MacLean, *Ice Station Zebra*, 1993

### 3210

#### DEAN R. KOONTZ

### *Intensity*

(New York: Knopf, 1996)

**Story type:** Horror (Psychological Suspense)
**Major character(s):** Chyna Shepherd, Student—Graduate (psychology); Edgler Foreman Vess, Police Officer, Serial Killer; Ariel Delane, Teenager (16-year-old)
**Time period(s):** 1990s (1996)
**Locale(s):** Napa Valley, California

**Summary:** Chyna Shepherd knows she should flee from Edgler Vess, a mass murderer who is thrilled by the intensity of the feeling he gets from his kills, and who has just slaughtered the family of the schoolmate she is visiting. But upon hearing that Vess has imprisoned a teenage girl at his home, Chyna pursures him in the hope of saving the girl from a fate worse than death.

**Other books you might like:**
R. Patrick Gates, *Deathwalker*, 1995
Thomas Harris, *The Silence of the Lambs*, 1988
James Neal Harvey, *The Headsman*, 1991

Stephen King, *Rose Madder*, 1995
Joe R. Lansdale, *Act of Love*, 1981

## 3211

### DEAN R. KOONTZ

## *Lightning*

(New York: Berkley, 1989)

**Story type:** Horror (Time Travel)
**Major character(s):** Laura Shane, Writer (Beautiful bestselling author); Stefan Krieger, Time Traveler (Laura's "guardian")
**Time period(s):** 1980s (1989); 1940s (1944)
**Locale(s):** California; Germany

**Summary:** The mysterious "guardian," who intervenes to save Laura Stark several times, turns out to be a renegade time traveller from Hitler's Germany determined to destroy their time travel experiments. In his final trip to 1989, he and Laura must defend themselves from Nazi pursuers while searching for a way to prevent Hitler from retroactively winning World War II.

**Other books you might like:**
John Farris, *The Fury*, 1976
Stephen King, *Firestarter*, 1980

## 3212

### DEAN R. KOONTZ

## *Midnight*

(New York: Putnam, 1989; Berkley, 1989)

**Story type:** Horror (Small Town Horror)
**Major character(s):** Sam Booker, FBI Agent; Tessa Lockland, Young Woman
**Time period(s):** 1980s
**Locale(s):** Moonlight Cove, California (A northern coastal town)

**Summary:** A series of fatal "accidents" and "suicides" brings Booker and Lockland—whose sister was a victim—to Moonlight Cove, where they unite with a teenager and a crippled war veteran to investigate the mysterious deaths. The trail leads them to the New People, an emotionless, faster thinking, hard to kill group and the strange, dangerous secret behind their origins.

**Other books you might like:**
Jack Finney, *The Body Snatchers*, 1955
Charles L. Grant, *The Hour of the Oxrun Dead*, 1977

## 3213

### DEAN R. KOONTZ

## *Mr. Murder*

(New York: Putnam, 1993)

**Story type:** Horror (Doppelganger; Science Fiction)
**Major character(s):** Marty Stillwater, Writer (mystery novelist); Paige Stillwater, Health Care Professional (therapist); The Other, Amnesiac
**Time period(s):** 1990s (1993)
**Locale(s):** Laguna Niguel, California

**Summary:** A mysterious man with no memory of his past life learns how to relate to other human beings through the detritus of popular culture—junk films, splatter fiction, and pornography. When he notices that he bears a striking resemblance to mystery writer Marty Stillman, he tries to take over Marty's life, leading the befuddled

Marty to wonder if the man is not the dark side of his imagination come to life.

**Other books you might like:**
Michael Cadnum, *Ghostwright*, 1992
Stephen King, *The Dark Half*, 1989
Richard Christian Matheson, *Created By*, 1993

## 3214

### DEAN R. KOONTZ
### PHIL PARKS, Illustrator

## *Santa's Twin*

(New York: HarperPrism, 1996)

**Story type:** Fantasy (Legend; Adventure)
**Major character(s):** Bob "Santa" Claus, Imposter, Relative; Charlotte "Lottie", Child; Emily "Emmy", Child
**Time period(s):** 1990s
**Locale(s):** United States; North Pole, Arctic

**Summary:** When Lottie and Emmy question Santa's unusual behavior, they uncover a sociopathic relative of Kris Kringle running amok on Christmas Eve. A fortuitous accident provides the pair with an opportunity to rescue the holiday. Lavishly illustrated.

**Other books you might like:**
Cathy Crimmins, *Revenge of the Christmas Box*, 1996
  Tom Maeder, co-author
David Kirschner, *The Pagemaster*, 1993
  Ernie Contreras, co-author
James Finn Garner, *Politically Correct Holiday Stories*, 1995
Terry Jones, *Lady Cottington's Pressed Fairy Book*, 1994
  Brian Froud, co-author
Kristine Kathryn Rusch, *Pulphouse, Issue 10: Special Issue*, 1991
  editor

## 3215

### DEAN R. KOONTZ

## *Sole Survivor*

(New York: Knopf, 1997)

**Story type:** Horror (Wild Talents)
**Major character(s):** Joe Carpenter, Journalist; Rose Tucker, Scientist; Barbara Christman, Investigator (airplane crash)
**Time period(s):** 1990s (1997)
**Locale(s):** Los Angeles, California

**Summary:** One year after a devastating airplane crash took the lives of his family and supposedly everyone else on board, Joe Carpenter is contacted by a secretive woman who purports to be a survivor. Joe's efforts to track the woman down attract the interest of a secret scientific project responsible for the crash, who will stop at nothing to suppress the truth. First published in England in 1996

**Other books you might like:**
Mark Chadbourn, *The Eternal*, 1996
John Farris, *The Fury*, 1976
James Herbert, *Survivor*, 1976
Stephen King, *Firestarter*, 1980

## 3216

### DEAN R. KOONTZ

## Strange Highways

(New York: Warner, 1995)

**Story type:** Horror (Collection)

**Summary:** The author's first story collection in 25 years brings together two short novels and a dozen short stories. The title novel, written especially for this volume, tells of a man who returns to his family home town and inadvertently steps into mysteries from the past that have bearing on events in the present. The other novel, "Chase," was first published under the author's K.R. Dwyer pseudonym in 1972, and tells of a good Samaritan who is menaced by murderer. Of the other stories, "Hardshell" and "Miss Attila the Hun" blend science fiction and horror elements, "Trapped" is a suspense tale of a woman and her son imprisoned in a snowbound house besieged by genetically engineered rats, and "The Snatcher" is a witchcraft tale of just desserts.

**Other books you might like:**
Ed Gorman, *Cages*, 1995
Stephen King, *Four Past Midnight*, 1992
Robert R. McCammon, *Blue World*, 1989
William F. Nolan, *Night Shapes: Excursions into Terror*, 1995

## 3217

### DEAN R. KOONTZ

## Ticktock

(New York: Ballantine, 1998)

**Story type:** Horror (Black Magic)
**Major character(s):** Tommy Phan, Writer (detective fiction); Deliverance "Del" Payne, Waiter/Waitress; Gi Minh Phan, Baker (Tommy's brother)
**Time period(s):** 1900s (1997)
**Locale(s):** Irvines, California

**Summary:** Detective fiction writer Tommy Phan finds himself enmeshed in a real-life mystery when he is sent a demonically possessed rag doll and an anonymous computer message informing him "The Deadline is Dawn." Tommy enlists the aid of friends and family to avoid the relentlessly pursuing doll and discover who sent it to him and why. First published in England in 1996.

**Other books you might like:**
Matthew J. Costello, *Child's Play III*, 1991
William Goldman, *Magic*, 1978
Pat Graversen, *Dollies*, 1990
Ellen Jamison, *Stone Dead*, 1993
Ruby Jean Jensen, *Baby Dolly*, 1991

## 3218

### DEAN R. KOONTZ

## Winter Moon

(New York: Ballantine, 1994)

**Story type:** Horror (Science Fiction)
**Major character(s):** Jack McGarvey, Police Officer; Heather McGarvey, Housewife; Toby McGarvey, Child
**Time period(s):** 1990s
**Locale(s):** Montana

**Summary:** Trying to escape the mayhem of life as a Los Angeles police officer, Jack McGarvey moves his family to a ranch bequeathed them by the father of his former partner, unaware that it is inhabited by the Givers, extradimensional beings who usurp the bodies of humans to wreak havoc on Earth. This novel was originally published in shorter form in 1974 with the title *Invasion* and under Koontz's pseudonym, Aaron Wolfe.

**Other books you might like:**
Jack Finney, *The Body Snatchers*, 1955
Robert A. Heinlein, *The Puppet Masters*, 1951
Maxine O'Callaghan, *Dark Time*, 1992

## 3219

### C.M. KORNBLUTH

## His Share of Glory: The Complete Short Science Fiction of C.M. Kornbluth

(Framingham, Massachusetts: NESFA, 1997)

**Story type:** Science Fiction (Collection)

**Summary:** Contains a four-page introduction, "Cyril," by Frederik Pohl, a two-page introduction by the editor, Timothy P. Szczesuil, and all 56 stories written by Kornbluth, best known for his collaborations with Judith Merril and Frederik Pohl. This volume includes his witty, acerbic and insightful stories, all first published before his death in 1958. The many classics include "The Little Black Bag," "The Mindworm," "The Luckiest Man in Denv," "The Silly Season," "The Marching Morons" and "That Share of Glory."

**Other books you might like:**
Alfred Bester, *Virtual Unrealities: The Short Fiction of Alfred Bester*, 1997
Henry Kuttner, *The Best of Henry Kuttner*, 1975
Fritz Leiber, *The Leiber Chronicles*, 1990
C.L. Moore, *The Best of C.L. Moore*, 1975
Theodore Sturgeon, *Thunder and Roses*, 1997

## 3220

### MARK A. KOSTRUBULA

## Dark Legacy

(Nashville, Tennessee: Scythe Publications, 1996)

**Story type:** Horror (Black Magic)
**Major character(s):** Adolf Hitler, Military Personnel, Historical Figure; Lance Taylor, Businessman (salvage); Mike, Businessman (salvage)
**Time period(s):** 1940s; 1990s (1996)
**Locale(s):** Kehena Island, Pacific Ocean; Zurich, Switzerland

**Summary:** With the help of Satan, Adolf Hitler plants stolen treasure around the world in the hope of starting the Fourth Reich decades after the end of World War II. When a group of modern salvage specialists begin finding the hidden treasures, an age old battle between good and evil is reignited.

**Other books you might like:**
Peter Benchley, *White Shark*, 1994
Brian Lumley, *Demogorgon*, 1987
Robert R. McCammon, *The Night Boat*, 1980
Robert Weinberg, *The Armageddon Box*, 1991
Dennis Wheatley, *They Used Dark Forces*, 1964

## 3221

**ERIC KOTANI**
**JOHN MADDOX ROBERTS**, Co-Author

### Delta Pavonis

(New York: Baen, 1990)

**Story type:** Science Fiction (First Contact; Adventure)
**Series:** Island Worlds
**Major character(s):** Dierdre Jamail, Explorer; Sieglinde Kornfeld-Taggert, Scientist; M'ats, Alien
**Time period(s):** 22nd century
**Locale(s):** Delta Pavonis Star System, Outer Space

**Summary:** Dierdre Jamail has trouble with authority. That's the reason she is assigned to the Atropos expedition. She stumbles upon dinosaurs and a matter transmitter which calls aliens to the Delta Pavonis system, aliens who are surprised at how quickly their experimental subjects have learned.

**Other books you might like:**
John Brunner, *Total Eclipse*, 1974
Anne McCaffrey, *Dinosaur Planet*, 1978
John Rackham, *The Treasure of Tau Ceti*, 1969
Timothy Zahn, *Spinneret*, 1985

## 3222

**WILLIAM KOTZWINKLE**

### The Bear Went over the Mountain

(New York: Doubleday, 1996)

**Story type:** Fantasy (Satire; Contemporary)
**Major character(s):** Arthur Bramhall, Writer, Professor; Hal Jam, Animal (bear), Imposter (writer)
**Time period(s):** 1990s
**Locale(s):** Maine; New York, New York

**Summary:** After Arthur Bramhall buries his rewritten manuscript in the woods, an inquisitive bear digs it up and finds it interesting. The bear assumes a persona, Hal Jam, brings the manuscript to a literary agency and becomes an overnight success. Meanwhile, Arthur Bramhall's failed attempts to recover the manuscript or even get legal credit for his own work lead to the author's deterioration.

**Other books you might like:**
William Borden, *Superstoe*, 1968
Scott Bradfield, *Animal Planet*, 1995
Richard Brautigan, *Revenge of the Lawn: Stories 1962-1970*, 1971
Harlan Ellison, *The Fantasies of Harlan Ellison*, 1979
Jerzy Kosinski, *Being There*, 1971

## 3223

**WILLIAM KOTZWINKLE**

### The Hot Jazz Trio

(New York: Houghton Mifflin, 1989)

**Story type:** Horror (Collection)

**Summary:** The title novella and two short stories. "Hot Jazz Blues" takes place in the Paris of the 20s. Django Rinehardt, his Hot Jazz Trio, and various celebrities (Cocteau, Picasso, et al.) help LeBlanc the Magician find and rescue his assistant, Loli, who has been "eaten" by his Vanishing Lady Box. In "Blues on the Nile: A Fragment of Papyrus," the mighty Pharoah and his retinue journey on the Nile into eternity and their final destination. "Boxcar Blues"

is a fantasy of hobos who ride the rails and Pearl, a "blowsy, broad-beamed ex-cashier."

**Other books you might like:**
Roland Topor, *Joko's Anniversary*, 1970

## 3224

**EDWARD E. KRAMER**, Editor

### Dark Destiny

(Stone Mountain, Georgia: White Wolf, 1994)

**Story type:** Horror (Anthology)

**Summary:** Under the aegis of the gaming company responsible for the "World of Darkness" fantasy role playing game, the editor has assembled 22 stories that presuppose the existence of werewolves, vampires, witches, and wizards living in disguise among human beings and controlling world events. Included are Robert Bloch's "The Scent of Vinegar," about vampires influencing the movie industry; Harlan Ellison's "Sensible City," about two escaped convicts who meet a gruesome fate while on the run; Robert Weinberg's "In the Forests of the Night," about a human detective who turns the tables on two warring vampire factions using him as a pawn to obtain secret magic; Nancy A. Collins' "The Love of Monsters," about the forbidden love between a vampire and a werewolf; and Rick Hautala's "Winter Queen," about a plane crash survivor adopted into a clan of werewolves. Former splatterpunk John Skipp supplies the introduction.

**Other books you might like:**
Robert T. Garcia, *Chilled to the Bone*, 1992
  editor
Brian Thomsen, *Tales of Ravenloft*, 1994
  editor
Stewart Wieck, *When Will You Rage*, 1994
  editor
Erin Kelly, *City of Darkness: Unseen*, 1995
  Stewart Wieck, co-editor
Stewart Wieck, *World of Darkness: Death and Damnation*, 1994
  editor
Stewart Wieck, *World of Darkness: Truth Until Paradox*, 1994
  editor

## 3225

**EDWARD E. KRAMER**, Editor

### Dark Destiny II: Proprietors of Fate

(Clarkston, GA: White Wolf, 1995)

**Story type:** Horror (Anthology)

**Summary:** The twenty stories written exclusively for this anthology are set in the World of Darkness, a fantasy role-playing world in which mages, ghosts, vampires, werewolves and other supernatural beings masquerade as humans and integrate themselves unobtrusively with the human world. This volume focuses on the role these beings have played in major historical events. In Nancy Collins' "The Sign of the Asp," a mage has a hand in the fate of Cleopatra and the course of classical history. S.P. Somtow's "Beloved Disciple" imagines Jesus Christ interacting with vampires, and Charles L. Grant's "Gray" envisions werewolves engineering Custer's Last Stand. In James S. Dorr's narrative poem "The Westfarer," the World of Darkness dovetails with that of Norse mythology. Robert Weinberg sees disappearances in the Devil's Triangle as part of a vampire conspiracy in "The Skeptic," and Poppy Brite presents the exploits of a serial killer in Louisiana and the events leading up to the first World War as examples of how creatures in the World of Darkness use human surrogates to fight their century-old battles with one another. Robert Anton Wilson supplies an introduction.

**Other books you might like:**

Erin Kelly, *The Splendour Falls*, 1995
    editor
Staley Krause, *Strange City*, 1996
    Stuart Wieck, co-editor
Stewart Wieck, *The Beast Within*, 1995
    editor

## 3226

**EDWARD E. KRAMER**, Editor
**BERNIE WRIGHTSON**, Illustrator

### *Dark Destiny III: Children of Dracula*
(Clarkston, Georgia: White Wolf, 1996)

**Story type:** Horror (Anthology; Vampire Story)
**Series:** Dark Destiny

**Summary:** As part of the Dark Destiny series, which posits that supernatural creatures have a hand in the great events of history, this collection features 21 stories original to the volume concerned with Dracula and his progeny. S.P. Somtow detects a vampiric residue in the destruction of the biblical Sodom and Gomorrah in "Brimstone and Salt." Rick Reed proposes that the Lizzie Borden murders were a vampire blood offering in "How Do I Love Thee." John Mason Skipp and Marc Levinthal work a vampire riff on the death of Kurt Cobain in "On a Big Night in Monster History." Rick Hautala spots vampires fighting with the White and Red Russians in "White Terror" and Fred Olen Ray tells how one lucky passenger survived the Hindenberg disaster in "What So Proudly we Heil!" Filmmaker Brian Yuzna supplies an introduction.

**Other books you might like:**

Martin H. Greenberg, *Dracula: Prince of Darkness*, 1993
    editor
Stephen Jones, *The Mammoth Book of Dracula*, 1997
    editor
Robert Weinberg, *Rivals of Dracula*, 1996
    Stefan Dziemianowicz, Martin H. Greenberg, co-editors

## 3227

**EDWARD E. KRAMER**, Editor

### *Tales of the White Wolf*
(Stone Mountain, Georgia: White Wolf, Inc., 1994)

**Story type:** Fantasy (Anthology)
**Series:** Elric
**Major character(s):** Elric of Melnibone, Royalty, Wizard, Warrior
**Time period(s):** Indeterminate Past
**Locale(s):** The Young Kingdoms, Fictional Country

**Summary:** An introduction and story by Michael Moorcock plus 23 original stories continuing the adventures of Elric, Moorcock's popular fantasy character. Other authors include Scott Ciencin, Nancy Collins, Neil Gaiman, Colin Greenland, Gary Gygax, Nancy Holder, Brad Linaweaver, Brad Strickland, Karl Edward Wagner, Robert Weinberg and Tad Williams. Illustrated by artists including Timothy Bradstreet, Brom, George Pratt and Joshua Timbrook.

**Other books you might like:**

Glen Cook, *The Black Company*, 1984
Louise Cooper, *Nemesis*, 1989

Martin H. Greenberg, *After the King: Stories in Honor of J.R.R. Tolkien*, 1992
    editor
Staley Krause, *Truth Until Paradox*, 1995
    Stewart Wicch, co-author
Michael Moorcock, *Elric of Melnibone*, 1976

## 3228

**EDWARD E. KRAMER**, Editor
**PETER CROWTHER**, Co-Editor

### *Tombs*
(Clarkston, Georgia: White Wolf, 1995)

**Story type:** Horror (Anthology)

**Summary:** The premise of this collection of twenty-one stories and one poem commissioned especially for the volume is situations in which people find themselves trapped. In Michael Bishop's "Epistrophy'" a man preserves his wife's remains in a jukebox. Lisa Tuttle's "White Lady's Grave" is about a woman who finds herself inextricably trapped in the working out of a Scottish myth, and Christopher Fowler's "Ginansia's Ravishment" about a woman trapped by a family curse. Kathe Koja and Barry Malzberg's "The Unchained" liken a man's entrapment within his earthly body to the fate of Lazurus, while Stephen Gallagher, in "God's Bright Little Engine," tells of a woman who feels trapped in her apartment by the Peeping Tom living below her. In Nancy Collins' "The Land of the Reflected Ones," an unscrupulous occultist becomes trapped in a mirror, and in Neil Gaiman's narrative poem "Queen of Knives," a woman becomes trapped in a magic trick. Forrest J. Ackerman supplies a wacky introduction.

**Other books you might like:**

Robert T. Garcia, *Chilled to the Bone*, 1992
    editor
Ed Gorman, *Stalkers*, 1989
    Martin H. Greenberg, co-editor
Tim Sullivan, *Cold Shocks*, 1989

## 3229

**STALEY KRAUSE**, Editor
**STEWART WIECK**, Co-Editor

### *Strange City*
(New York: HarperPrism, 1996)

**Story type:** Horror (Anthology)
**Series:** World of Darkness

**Summary:** Set in White Wolf's World of Darkness gaming scenario, where vampires, wraiths, mages, werewolves, and other supernatural creatures mingle unobtrusively with human beings, this compilation gathers 14 stories written especially for the book. Included are S.P. Somtow's "The Voice of the Hummingbird," in which an Aztec vampire dead for centuries learns to adjust to the modern world; Lawrence Watt-Evans' "The Art of Dying," in which vampires compete for the right to turn a brilliant painter into one of their own; Richard Lee Byers' "Wolf-Trap," where a werewolf must save a fellow lycanthrope from scientific researchers; and Don Bassingthwaite's "Power," in which a vampire helps other vampires through her job in the coroner's office.

**Other books you might like:**

Erin Kelly, *City of Darkness*, 1995
    editor

Erin Kelly, *The Splendour Falls*, 1995
  editor
Edward E. Kramer, *Dark Destiny*, 1994
  editor
Stewart Wieck, *The Beast Within*, 1994
  editor
Stewart Wieck, *When Will You Rage*, 1990
  editor

---

### `3230`
#### STEVEN M. KRAUZER

### *Brainstorm*
(New York: Bantam, 1991)

**Story type:** Horror (Wild Talents)
**Major character(s):** David McKay, Child; Linda Gaylen, Journalist; August Breunner, Doctor (head of The Facility)
**Time period(s):** 1990s
**Locale(s):** Washington, District of Columbia

**Summary:** Young psychic David McKay seeks the help of a psychic journalist in his efforts to elude The Facility, a think-tank devoted to paranormal research that hopes to boost his psychokinetic powers through surgical means for use as a weapon.

**Other books you might like:**
John Arbucci, *The Innocent*, 1991
Jack Caravela, *The Gifted*, 1991
John Farris, *The Fury*, 1976
Stephen King, *Firestarter*, 1980
Michael Kurland, *Button Bright*, 1990

---

### `3231`
#### MARK KREIGHBAUM

### *The Eyes of God*
(New York: Bantam Spectra, 1998)

**Story type:** Science Fiction (Alternate Intelligence; Political)
**Series:** Pinch
**Major character(s):** Vida L'var y Smid, Political Figure, Fiance(e); Rico Hernandes y Jons, Computer Expert; Riva, Revolutionary, Fugitive
**Time period(s):** Indeterminate Future
**Locale(s):** The Pinch, Interstellar Empire/Federation; Palace, Planet—Imaginary; Cyberspace

**Summary:** As People's Factor, Vida L'var works toward equal rights for all sapients on Palace, while Riva uses patriots and traitors to overturn human dominance on the planet.

**Other books you might like:**
Frank Herbert, *Dune*, 1965
Katharine Kerr, *Palace*, 1996
  Mark Kreighbaum, co-author
Rosemary Kirstein, *The Outskirter's Secret*, 1992
Rosemary Kirstein, *The Steerswoman*, 1989
Richard Paul Russo, *Carlucci's Edge*, 1997
Joan Slonczewski, *The Children Star*, 1998
Joan Slonczewski, *Daughter of Elysium*, 1993
Sheri S. Tepper, *Grass*, 1989
Sarah Zettel, *Fool's War*, 1997

---

### `3232`
#### PENELOPE BANKA KREPS

### *Carnivores*
(New York: Zebra, 1993)

**Story type:** Horror (Nature in Revolt; Science Fiction)
**Major character(s):** Evan Tremayne, Doctor (psychiatrist); Lydia Matthews, Single Parent; Harold Burnham, Scientist (neuroscientist)
**Time period(s):** 1990s (1993)
**Locale(s):** Las Flores, Florida

**Summary:** A reversal of the earth's geomagnetic fields activates the genesis gene buried in some human beings and animals, reversing evolution and causing them to mutate into creatures resembling their monstrous prehistoric forebears.

**Other books you might like:**
Peter Benchley, *Beast*, 1991
Michael Crichton, *Jurassic Park*, 1990
William Dantz, *Hunger*, 1992
J.M. Morgan, *Between the Devil and the Deep*, 1992

---

### `3233`
#### PENELOPE BANKA KREPS

### *Demon's Fright*
(New York: Zebra, 1992)

**Story type:** Horror (Black Magic)
**Major character(s):** Patti Demarest, Teenager; Dirk Emerson, Teenager; Travis Carter, Teacher (high-school history teacher)
**Time period(s):** 1990s
**Locale(s):** Trapper's Cay, Florida

**Summary:** Patti Demarest's mother tries to put a bad divorce behind her by moving with Patti to her grandmother's house in South Florida. But Patti discovers that the in-group in her new home are members of a witch coven led by loose-screw Dirk Emerson, a juvenile delinquent who does not take kindly to those who refuse to obey his orders.

**Other books you might like:**
Ramsey Campbell, *To Wake the Dead*, 1980
Leigh Clark, *Blood Sabbath*, 1991
Matthew J. Costello, *Darkborn*, 1992
D.A. Fowler, *The Devil's End*, 1992

---

### `3234`
#### NANCY KRESS

### *The Aliens of Earth*
(Sauk City, Wisconsin: Arkham House, 1993)

**Story type:** Science Fiction (Collection)

**Summary:** Contains 18 stories from 1980s and 1990s periodicals and anthologies utilizing a wide range of classical genre themes including alternate history, time travel, clairvoyant powers and alien anthropology and tending toward dark in tone.

**Other books you might like:**
Greg Bear, *The Wind From a Burning Woman*, 1983
Michael Bishop, *Blooded on Arachne*, 1982
John Kessel, *Meeting in Infinity*, 1992
Rebecca Ore, *Alien Bootlegger and Other Stories*, 1993
Lucius Shepard, *The Ends of the Earth*, 1991

Bruce Sterling, *Crystal Express*, 1989
Michael Swanwick, *Gravity's Angels*, 1991
James Tiptree Jr., *Her Smoke Rose Up Forever*, 1990

---

**3235**

NANCY KRESS

## Beaker's Dozen

(New York: Tor, 1998)

**Story type:** Science Fiction (Collection)

**Summary:** This title contains a two-page general introduction as well as individual introductions to 13 stories culled from periodicals and anthologies from 1991 to 1997, with one, "Grant Us This Day," slightly rewritten. Frequently light and upbeat in tone, the stories explore diverse themes, such as genetic engineering, hard SF, alternative history, mathematics, dance, designer drugs, "Sleeping Beauty," police work, and sister-sister relationships.

**Other books you might like:**
Ursula K. Le Guin, *A Fisherman of the Inland Sea*, 1994
Pat Murphy, *Points of Departure*, 1990
James Tiptree Jr., *Her Smoke Rose Up Forever*, 1990
John Varley, *Blue Champagne*, 1986
Connie Willis, *Impossible Things*, 1994

---

**3236**

NANCY KRESS

## Beggars and Choosers

(New York: Tor, 1994)

**Story type:** Science Fiction (Genetic Manipulation; Political)
**Major character(s):** Diana Covington, Genetically Altered Being, Spy; Drew Arlen, Musician; Billy Washington, Aged Person, Hunter
**Time period(s):** 22nd century (2114-2115)
**Locale(s):** United States; Huevos Verdes, Mexico (island)

**Summary:** The SuperSleepless periodically dispense new and highly advanced technology from their artificially created island, helping both worker Donkeys and the Livers, idle beneficiaries of others' efforts. As technology fails to keep up with society's demands, a revolutionary plan of one SuperSleepless promises to free people from the physical need for food or clothing. However, government obstruction and reactionary forces seeking to rid Earth of all genetically modified people may halt this innovation.

**Other books you might like:**
F.M. Busby, *The Breeds of Man*, 1988
Octavia E. Butler, *Clay's Ark*, 1984
C.J. Cherryh, *Cyteen*, 1988
Helen Collins, *Mutagenesis*, 1993
Kathleen Ann Goonan, *Queen City Jazz*, 1994

---

**3237**

NANCY KRESS

## Beggars in Spain

(Eugene, Oregon: Pulphouse Publishing, 1991)

**Story type:** Science Fiction (Genetic Manipulation)
**Major character(s):** Alice "Leisha" Camden, Genetically Altered Being
**Time period(s):** 21st century

**Locale(s):** United States

**Summary:** Elizabeth and Roger Camden pressure researchers to modify and fertilize an egg, insuring that their daughter will never need sleep. By accident a second, unmodified egg implants at the same time resulting in fraternal twins, one requiring sleep and the other free from that requirement. The twins grow to be very different people. This work received a 1991 Nebula Award.

**Other books you might like:**
Edward Bryant, *Neon Twilight*, 1990
Judith Moffett, *Two That Came True*, 1991
Frederik Pohl, *Stopping at Slowyear*, 1991
Spider Robinson, *Kill the Editor*, 1991
Robert Silverberg, *Thebes of the Hundred Gates*, 1991

---

**3238**

NANCY KRESS

## Beggars Ride

(New York: Tor, 1996)

**Story type:** Science Fiction (Genetic Manipulation; Political)
**Series:** Beggars in Spain
**Major character(s):** Jackson Aranow, Doctor, Gentleman; Lizzie Francy, Teenager, Computer Expert; Jennifer Sharifi, Genetically Altered Being, Genius
**Time period(s):** 22nd century (2120-2128)
**Locale(s):** Manhattan East Enclave, New York; New York, New York

**Summary:** In a world where 20th century problems have escalated and governments collapsed, two generations of genetically modified humans prepare for war. Meanwhile, the gap between the haves and have-nots stretches beyond the breaking point, with nothing seeming to work anymore. Political, economic, and biologic forces besiege society while the sides in the war remain desperately indistinct.

---

**3239**

NANCY KRESS

## Brain Rose

(New York: William Morrow, 1989)

**Story type:** Science Fiction (Reincarnation)
**Major character(s):** Robbie Brekke, Thief; Caroline Bohentin, Heiress
**Time period(s):** 21st century
**Locale(s):** Rochester, New York

**Summary:** For varying reasons, some of them not entirely legitimate, a number of people apply for a new and fashionable surgical procedure called Previous Life Access Surgery which supposedly gives one access to previous incarnations. Slowly evidence accumulates that the surgery has startling and hitherto unnoticed side effects that could drastically change life on Earth.

**Other books you might like:**
Joe Haldeman, *Buying Time*, 1989
Robert Silverberg, *The Book of Skulls*, 1972
Robert Silverberg, *To Live Again*, 1969
Norman Spinrad, *Bug Jack Barron*, 1969

## **3240**

### NANCY KRESS

## *Dancing on Air*

(San Francisco, California: Tachyon Publications, 1997)

**Story type:** Science Fiction (Genetic Manipulation; Arts)
**Major character(s):** Angel, Animal (dog); Caroline Olson, Dancer; Susan Matthews, Journalist, Parent
**Time period(s):** 21st century
**Locale(s):** New York, New York; Paris, France

**Summary:** The murder of genetically enhanced New York City Ballet Company dancers leads the director to lease Angel for Caroline's protection. Assigned to write a story on the ballet company, Susan, whose daughter studies with the company and hopes to dance with them professionally, becomes obsessed with genetic enhancement, which is illegal in the United States. Susan's investigation leads her to a professional conference on genetic enhancement and some horrifying possibilities. Contains a seven-page afterword by James Patrick Kelly.

**Other books you might like:**
Peter S. Beagle, *The Rhinoceros Who Quoted Nietzsche and Other Odd Acquaintances*, 1997
Clifford D. Simak, *City*, 1952
Cordwainer Smith, *Norstrilia*, 1995
Cordwainer Smith, *The Rediscovery of Man*, 1993
Cherry Wilder, *Dealers in Light and Darkness*, 1995

## **3241**

### NANCY KRESS

## *Maximum Light*

(New York: Tor, 1998)

**Story type:** Science Fiction (Genetic Manipulation; Political)
**Major character(s):** Shana Walders, Teenager, Military Personnel (private, National Service); Nick Clementi, Doctor, Aged Person; Cameron Atuli, Dancer, Homosexual
**Time period(s):** 2030s
**Locale(s):** Washington, District of Columbia; New York, New York

**Summary:** A rare young person in a world facing a fertility crisis, Shana Walders witnesses an illegal and horrific sight — baby chimpanzees with human faces and hands. Hoping to gain admission to the exclusive United States Army, Shana searches for the chimps' origin, eventually crossing paths with Nick and Cameron, who also play crucial roles in the unfolding mystery even though they come from very different walks of life.

**Other books you might like:**
Margaret Atwood, *The Handmaid's Tale*, 1985
David Brin, *Glory Season*, 1993
Valerie J. Freireich, *Becoming Human*, 1995
M. John Harrison, *Signs of Life*, 1997
Linda Nagata, *The Bohr Maker*, 1995
Sheri S. Tepper, *The Family Tree*, 1997
Sheri S. Tepper, *Gibbon's Decline and Fall*, 1996

## **3242**

### NANCY KRESS

## *Oaths and Miracles*

(New York: Forge, 1996)

**Story type:** Science Fiction (Techno-Thriller; Genetic Manipulation)

**Major character(s):** Robert Cavanaugh, FBI Agent; Judy Kozinski, Journalist; Wendell Botts, Construction Worker
**Time period(s):** 1990s
**Locale(s):** United States

**Summary:** With Dr. Benjamen Kozinski murdered shortly after a recruitment interview with Verico Research Company, Robert Cavanaugh must decipher the pattern to prevent Judy Kozinski, Ben's widow, from death. Judy flees to a small town dominated by a religious sect where unexplained deaths also occur.

**Other books you might like:**
Kevin J. Anderson, *Virtual Destruction*, 1996
    Doug Beason, co-author
Lester Del Rey, *The Eleventh Commandment*, 1970
    revised edition
Joe Haldeman, *Worlds: A Novel of the Near Future*, 1981
Frank Herbert, *The White Plague*, 1982
Allen Steele, *The Jericho Iteration*, 1994
Walter Jon Williams, *Hardwired*, 1986
Chelsea Quinn Yarbro, *Time of the Fourth Horseman*, 1976

## **3243**

### NANCY KRESS

## *Stinger*

(New York: Forge, 1998)

**Story type:** Science Fiction (Political; Medical)
**Major character(s):** Robert Kavanaugh, FBI Agent; Melanie Anderson, Doctor
**Time period(s):** Indeterminate Future
**Locale(s):** Maryland

**Summary:** A nurse uncovers evidence that the death rate among minorities in Maryland is increasing. She convinces a doctor and an FBI agent that someone is using advanced medical technology to kill "undesirable" members of society. And it appears that some of the conspirators hold influential government positions.

**Other books you might like:**
John Brunner, *The Jagged Orbit*, 1969
Octavia E. Butler, *Kindred*, 1979
John Crowley, *Beasts*, 1976
K.W. Jeter, *Dark Horizon*, 1993
A.M. Lightner, *The Day of the Drones*, 1969

## **3244**

### NOVAK KRUGER, Author/Illustrator

## *Tooth: A Tale of Love and Death in Paradox*

(Huntington, West Virginia: University Editions, 1996)

**Story type:** Horror (Vampire Story)
**Major character(s):** Novak Darte, Vampire; Count Vigor, Vampire; Karis, Young Woman
**Time period(s):** 2090s (2092)
**Locale(s):** Bridgeport, Connecticut

**Summary:** In a future overrun with technology that is dehumanizing civilization, vampire Novak Darte ponders moral issues concerning the practicality of preserving the human race. Meanwhile, his arch enemy, the vampire Count Vigor, plots the overthrow of the world and Novak's demise. The author supplies the cover art and interior illustrations for this novel.

**Other books you might like:**
Jack Butler, *Nightshade*, 1989
Michael Conner, *Archangel*, 1995
J.G. Eccarius, *The Last Days of Christ the Vampire*, 1988
Doug Rice, *Blood of Mugwump*, 1996

---

**3245**

### CHRISTOPHER KUBASIK

## Changeling

(New York: Roc, 1992)

**Story type:** Fantasy (Legend; Urban)
**Series:** Shadowrun
**Major character(s):** Peter Clarris, Genetically Altered Being, Mythical Creature (troll); Katherine Amij, Businesswoman
**Time period(s):** 2050s (2053)
**Locale(s):** Chicago, Illinois

**Summary:** Transformation into a troll deprives Peter of his family, friends and opportunities for education and employment. Living on the streets as an outcast, Peter tries to find the combination of magic and nanotechnology which will restore his form and options. A game tie-in novel.

**Other books you might like:**
Greg Bear, *Blood Music*, 1985
Robert N. Charrette, *Choose Your Enemies Carefully*, 1991
Robert N. Charrette, *Find Your Own Truth*, 1991
Robert N. Charrette, *Never Deal with a Dragon*, 1990
Robert N. Charrette, *Never Trust an Elf*, 1992
Nigel Findley, *2XS*, 1992
K.W. Jeter, *Madlands*, 1991
Will Shetterly, *Elsewhere*, 1991
Jordan K. Weisman, *Into the Shadows*, 1992
    editor
Terri Windling, *Life on the Border*, 1991
    editor

---

**3246**

### CHRISTOPHER KUBASIK

## The Longing Ring

(New York: Roc, 1993)

**Story type:** Fantasy (Quest)
**Series:** Earth Dawn
**Major character(s):** Garlthik, Mythical Creature (ork), Thief; J'role, Teenager, Thief
**Time period(s):** Indeterminate Past
**Locale(s):** Throal, Fictional City; Parlainth, Fictional City

**Summary:** Possessed by an evil spirit and an outcast in his village, J'role leaves with a travelling ork. The pair share adventures as they flee enemies and pursue the promise of a magic city. First of a game tie-in series.

**Other books you might like:**
Steven Brust, *Jhereg*, 1983
Glen Cook, *The Black Company*, 1984
Barbara Hambly, *The Time of the Dark*, 1982
Fritz Leiber, *Swords and Deviltry*, 1970
Angus Wells, *Wrath of Ashar*, 1990

---

**3247**

### MICHAEL P. KUBE-MCDOWELL

## Before the Storm

(New York: Bantam Spectra, 1996)

**Story type:** Science Fiction (Space Opera; Psychic Powers)
**Series:** Star Wars: The Black Fleet Crisis
**Major character(s):** Lando Calrissian, Military Personnel (general); Leia Organa Solo, Royalty (princess), Leader; Luke Skywalker, Martial Arts Expert (Jedi knight), Hero
**Time period(s):** Indeterminate Past
**Locale(s):** New Republic, Interstellar Empire/Federation; Coruscant, Planet—Imaginary; Outer Space

**Summary:** With the thwarting of the evil Empire's expansion, the New Republic gains a fragile peace. Leia works to counter the forces threatening to tear the union into warring factions, while Lando investigates a mysterious and dangerous spacecraft. First of a trilogy.

**Other books you might like:**
Roger MacBride Allen, *Ambush at Corellia*, 1995
Kevin J. Anderson, *Jedi Search*, 1994
Brian Daley, *The Han Solo Adventures*, 1992
L. Neil Smith, *The Lando Calrissian Adventures*, 1994
Michael A. Stackpole, *Rogue Squadron*, 1996
Timothy Zahn, *Heir to the Empire*, 1991

---

**3248**

### MICHAEL P. KUBE-MCDOWELL

## Exile

(New York: Ace, 1992)

**Story type:** Science Fiction (Political; Science Fiction)
**Major character(s):** Meer Fastet, Judge, Revolutionary; Kedar Nanchen, Government Official, Revolutionary; Oren Anadon, Ruler (exarch)
**Time period(s):** Indeterminate Future
**Locale(s):** Taurin, Planet—Imaginary (cities of Ana and Edera)

**Summary:** A messenger interrupts Meer Fastet with a request from the ailing Kedar Nanchen that his body be brought back to Ana from exile in Edera, as the law permits. Compelled by a debt of honor, Meer risks the trip to fetch Kedar, finding many surprises which change his future and Ana.

**Other books you might like:**
C.J. Cherryh, *Cyteen*, 1988
Donald E. McQuinn, *Warrior*, 1990
Alis A. Rasmussen, *A Passage of Stars*, 1990
Joan Slonczewski, *A Door into Ocean*, 1986
Sheri S. Tepper, *Grass*, 1989
Walter Jon Williams, *Angel Station*, 1989

---

**3249**

### MICHAEL P. KUBE-MCDOWELL

## The Quiet Pools

(New York: Ace, 1990)

**Story type:** Science Fiction (Espionage Thriller)
**Major character(s):** Jeremiah, Activist, Terrorist (ecological); Mikhail Dryke, Businessman (security chief); Christopher McCutcheon, Librarian
**Time period(s):** 2090s
**Locale(s):** Earth

**Summary:** Ecoterrorist Jeremiah is determined to end the drain of human resources away from Mother Earth by using whatever means possible to shut down the starship program. The *Memphis'* security chief, Dryke, is just as determined to ensure that this second starship successfully launches.

**Other books you might like:**
Piers Anthony, *But What of Earth?*, 1989
Robert A. Heinlein, *Time for the Stars*, 1956
Judith Moffett, *Pennterra*, 1987
Sheri S. Tepper, *Grass*, 1989

---

**3250**

YUMIKO KURAHASHI

## The Woman with the Flying Head and Other Stories

(Armonk, NY: M. E. Sharpe, 1998)

**Story type:** Horror (Collection)

**Summary:** Stories of fantasy and horror, translated from the Japanese by Atsuko Sasaki, inflected with existentialist philosophies and conventions of the Noh drama tradition. The title story tells of teenage girl who detaches her head nightly and sends it out to have trysts with lovers. "The Trade" describes an eerie cave in a remote village that is a doorway to another world. In "The Passage of Dreams," a woman discovers that her husband can readily shift shape to a variety of animal and plant forms.

**Other books you might like:**
Kobo Abe, *Beyond the Curve*, 1991
Alan Brennert, *Ma Qui and Other Phantoms*, 1991
Lafcadio Hearn, *Some Chinese Ghosts*, 1987
Garry Kilworth, *Hogfoot Right and Bird-Hands*, 1993

---

**3251**

MICHAEL KURLAND

## Button Bright

(New York: Jove, 1990)

**Story type:** Horror (Child-in-Peril)
**Major character(s):** Rachel "Button" Gramm, Child; Philip Kasselman, Doctor (psychiatrist); Patswami, Cult Member (leader)
**Time period(s):** 1990s
**Locale(s):** Moldowen, Ohio (Grover College and places across the US)

**Summary:** Eleven-year-old genius "Button" Gramm is pursued by a cadre of mysterious men who seem out to abduct her and to kill everyone who stands in their way. As she begins to delve into the mysterious origins of her mysterious talents, Button moves perilously closer to a confrontation with Patswami, a mystic cult leader who has used thought control to manipulate henchmen to kill similarly gifted children throughout the country.

**Other books you might like:**
John Farris, *The Fury*, 1976
Stephen King, *Firestarter*, 1987
Dean R. Koontz, *Lightning*, 1980
John Wyndham, *The Midwich Cuckoos*, 1957
John Wyndham, *The Crysalids*, 1955
Chelsea Quinn Yarbro, *Firecode*, 1987

---

**3252**

MICHAEL KURLAND

## A Study in Sorcery

(New York: Ace, 1989)

**Story type:** Fantasy (Mystery)
**Major character(s):** Lord Darcy, Detective; Sean O. Lochlainn, Sidekick
**Time period(s):** Indeterminate
**Locale(s):** New World, Alternate Earth

**Summary:** In a world where magic works, Lord Darcy and his companion, Sean O Lochlainn, are sent to the New World to determine who murdered a member of Azteque royalty.

**Other books you might like:**
Barbara Hambly, *Those Who Hunt the Night*, 1988
Robert A. Heinlein, *The Unpleasant Profession of Jonathan Hoag*, 1959

---

**3253**

PYOTR KURTINSKI

## Thirst

(New York: Leisure, 1995)

**Story type:** Horror (Vampire Story)
**Major character(s):** William Van Diemen, Vampire; Vincent Mara, Writer; Bradford C. Wilcox, Lawyer
**Time period(s):** 1990s (1995)
**Locale(s):** New York, New York (the Bronx)

**Summary:** Bronx vampire William Van Diemen would like nothing more than for the world outside his castle in the Riverdale section of the Bronx to leave him alone so he can write his memoirs in peace. But the detemination of a businessman to buy Van Diemen's home at a bargain price puts him on the defensive and foments a blood war between the two.

**Other books you might like:**
Nancy Baker, *The Night Inside*, 1995
Nancy Kilpatrick, *Near Death*, 1995
Tanith Lee, *Darkness, I*, 1995
Michael Romkey, *The Vampire Papers*, 1994
Fred Saberhagen, *Dominion*, 1982
Whitley Strieber, *The Hunger*, 1981

---

**3254**

KATHERINE KURTZ
DEBORAH TURNER HARRIS, Co-Author

## The Adept

(New York: Ace, 1991)

**Story type:** Fantasy (Contemporary; Magic Conflict)
**Series:** Adept
**Major character(s):** Adam Sinclair, Doctor, Psychic; Peregrine Lovat, Artist, Psychic; Noel McLeod, Police Officer, Psychic
**Time period(s):** 1990s
**Locale(s):** Scotland

**Summary:** Sir Adam Sinclair, investigating the theft of the Hepburn Sword, comes across Peregrine Lovat and helps him to regain his Gift of Seeing. With the aid of Noel McLeod, the two must go to Castle Urqhart to stop black magicians who have stolen the fairy flag of the McLeods, lest they enslave all of Scotland.

**Other books you might like:**
Mildred Downey Broxon, *Too Long a Sacrifice*, 1981
Randall Garrett, *Lord Darcy Investigates*, 1981
Randall Garrett, *Murder and Magic*, 1979
Randall Garrett, *Too Many Magicians*, 1967
Mercedes Lackey, *Children of the Night*, 1990
Mercedes Lackey, *Burning Water*, 1989

---

### 3255

#### KATHERINE KURTZ

## The Bastard Prince

(New York: Ballantine Del Rey, 1994)

**Story type:** Fantasy (Political; Magic Conflict)
**Series:** Heirs of Saint Camber
**Major character(s):** Rhys Michael Alister Haldane, Ruler (king), Psychic; Cathan Drummond, Knight, Companion (Rhys Michael's); Rhysel Thuryn, Healer, Psychic
**Time period(s):** Indeterminate Past
**Locale(s):** Gwynedd, Fictional Country

**Summary:** After six years as a puppet king, Rhys Michael meets Miklos of Torenth and Marek, the Festil claimant to Gwynedd's throne. In order to defeat the two, Rhys Michael shows some of his psychic powers, but a wound to his hand gives the Regents their chance to kill him and make it seem like a natural death, despite the disastrous repercussions.

**Other books you might like:**
Marion Zimmer Bradley, *The Heirs of Hammerfell*, 1989
John Christopher, *The Sword of the Spirits*, 1972
Susan Schwartz, *Byzantium's Crown*, 1987
Harry Turtledove, *Krispos the Emperor*, 1994
Chelsea Quinn Yarbro, *Ariosto*, 1980

---

### 3256

#### KATHERINE KURTZ
#### DEBORAH TURNER HARRIS, Co-Author

## Dagger Magic

(New York: Ace, 1995)

**Story type:** Fantasy (Mystery; Religious)
**Major character(s):** Adam Sinclair, Doctor, Psychic; Peregrine Lovat, Artist, Psychic; Noel McLeod, Police Officer, Psychic
**Time period(s):** 1990s (1995)
**Locale(s):** Mull of Kintyre, Ireland; Scotland; Switzerland

**Summary:** When the untimely arrival of a corpse disturbs Peregrine Lovat's honeymoon, the psychic emanations from the corpse prompt Lovat to ask for help from his mentor, Adam Sinclair, and the magical lodge to which they both belong. Their search for truth leads them to an evil older than, but intimately connected with, Nazi Germany.

**Other books you might like:**
Lois McMaster Bujold, *The Spirit Ring*, 1992
Tom Deitz, *Soulsmith*, 1991
Umberto Eco, *The Name of the Rose*, 1983
Katharine Kerr, *Polar City Blues*, 1990
John Varley, *The Barbie Murders and Other Stories*, 1980
Vernor Vinge, *Marooned in Realtime*, 1986
Walter Jon Williams, *Aristoi*, 1992

---

### 3257

#### KATHERINE KURTZ
#### DEBORAH TURNER HARRIS, Co-Author

## Death of an Adept

(New York: Ace, 1996)

**Story type:** Fantasy (Psychic Powers; Religious)
**Series:** Adept
**Major character(s):** Adam Sinclair, Doctor, Psychic; Francis Raeburn, Psychic, Magician; Ximena Lockhart, Doctor, Fiance(e)
**Time period(s):** 1990s
**Locale(s):** Scotland

**Summary:** Adam Sinclair returns from the U.S.A. engaged to be married, while his nemesis, Francis Raeburn, contacts Taranis to regain his power over weather. Raeburn will stop at nothing to accomplish this, including sacrificing one of his own men, a druid priest, to resurrect an ancient wizard. However, this wizard needs a body to inhabit and decides Adam Sinclair's will do.

**Other books you might like:**
Orson Scott Card, *Alvin Journeyman*, 1995
Dale Estey, *A Lost Tale*, 1980
Elizabeth Hand, *Waking the Moon*, 1995
Nick Pollotta, *Full Monster*, 1992
Tim Powers, *The Drawing of the Dark*, 1979
Melissa Scott, *Point of Hopes*, 1995
    Lisa A. Barnett, co-author
Sean Stewart, *Resurrection Man*, 1995

---

### 3258

#### KATHERINE KURTZ

## King Javan's Year

(New York: Ballantine Del Rey, 1992)

**Story type:** Fantasy (Political; Magic Conflict)
**Series:** Heirs of Saint Camber
**Major character(s):** Javan Jashan Urien Haldane, Royalty (king), Psychic; Guiscard de Courcy, Knight, Psychic; Paulin, Religious (priest)
**Time period(s):** Indeterminate
**Locale(s):** Gwynedd, Fictional Country

**Summary:** After the death of his brother Alroy, Javan Haldane becomes king of Gwynedd despite opposition from the Regents who think him too threatening to their own power. Javan seeks to ease the restrictions upon the Deryni and rule more humanely despite the intimidation and killing of his allies. Finally, a journey to a holy site presents a lethal challenge to Javan's rule.

**Other books you might like:**
Judith Tarr, *Ars Magica*, 1989
Harry Turtledove, *Krispos of Videssos*, 1991
Chelsea Quinn Yarbro, *Ariosto*, 1980

---

### 3259

#### KATHERINE KURTZ
#### DEBORAH TURNER HARRIS, Co-Author

## The Lodge of the Lynx

(New York: Ace, 1992)

**Story type:** Fantasy (Magic Conflict; Psychic Powers)

**Series:** Adept
**Major character(s):** Adam Sinclair, Doctor (psychiatrist), Psychic; Peregrine Lovat, Artist (painter), Psychic; Francis Raeburn, Historian, Occultist
**Time period(s):** 1990s
**Locale(s):** Scotland

**Summary:** Investigating the assassination of Freemasons all over Scotland by means of black magic, Adam Sinclair finds the Lodge of the Lynx, which he had thought thoroughly destroyed but now finds with a new headmaster, none other than Rudolf Hess, who possesses a book of black magic once owned by Adolf Hitler. Francis Raeburn knows that Adam Sinclair and his friends present the greatest threat and tries to have them killed, drawing them and other Huntsmen into battle with the Lodge.

**Other books you might like:**
Mildred Downey Broxon, *Too Long a Sacrifice*, 1981
Randall Garrett, *Too Many Magicians*, 1967
Michael Kurland, *Ten Little Wizards*, 1988
Mercedes Lackey, *Children of the Night*, 1990
Andre Norton, *Dread Companion*, 1970

---

`3260`

**KATHERINE KURTZ**, Editor

## On Crusade

(New York: Aspect, 1998)

**Story type:** Fantasy (Anthology)

**Summary:** These ten original fantasy stories share a common theme of the Knights Templar and the magical powers they controlled during the Crusades. Contributors include Diane Duane, Andre Norton, Robert Reginald, and others.

**Other books you might like:**
Poul Anderson, *Gallicenae*, 1987
William F. Barrett, *The Lady and the Lotus*, 1989
Marion Zimmer Bradley, *The Forest House*, 1993
Scott MacMillan, *At Sword's Point*, 1994
Scott MacMillan, *Knights of the Blood*, 1993
   with Katherine Kurtz

---

`3261`

**KATHERINE KURTZ**
**DEBORAH TURNER HARRIS**, Co-Author

## The Templar Treasure

(New York: Ace, 1993)

**Story type:** Fantasy (Magic Conflict; Religious)
**Series:** Adept
**Major character(s):** Adam Sinclair, Doctor (psychiatrist), Psychic; Peregrine Lovat, Artist, Psychic; Sir John Grahame, Military Personnel (retired), Psychic
**Time period(s):** 1990s
**Locale(s):** England; Scotland

**Summary:** After the theft of the Seal of Solomon in York, Adam Sinclair attempts to retrieve it before it can unleash horrors on the world. In Kent, Sinclair calls upon a spirit for help then sets out to acquire necessary artifacts before battling demonic invasion.

**Other books you might like:**
Pierre Barbet, *Baphomet's Meteor*, 1972
Diana Gabaldon, *Dragonfly in Amber*, 1992
R. Garcia y Robertson, *The Spiral Dance*, 1991
Randall Garrett, *Too Many Magicians*, 1967

R.A. MacAvoy, *The Book of Kells*, 1985
Pamela F. Service, *Winter of Magic's Return*, 1985
Judith Tarr, *The Dagger and the Cross: A Novel of the Crusades*, 1991
Alison Uttley, *A Traveler in Time*, 1940

---

`3262`

**KATHERINE KURTZ**

## Two Crowns for America

(New York: Bantam Spectra, 1996)

**Story type:** Fantasy (Historical; Political)
**Major character(s):** George Washington, Military Personnel, Revolutionary (Freemason); Justin Carmichael, Revolutionary (Freemason); Comte de Saint-Germain, Revolutionary (Freemason)
**Time period(s):** 1770s (1775)
**Locale(s):** Philadelphia, Pennsylvania; Leipzig, Germany

**Summary:** Thrown from his horse in an America on the verge of revolt, George Washington has a curious dream. Meanwhile, many people drawn together under the banner of Freemasonry take action according to the plans of a mysterious Master. In the turmoil of revolt the future remains uncertain; will the revolution succeed in creating a truly free country?

---

`3263`

**EWA KURYLUK**

## Century 21

(Normal, Illinois: Dalkey Archive Press, 1992)

**Story type:** Science Fiction (Literary)
**Major character(s):** Ann Kar, Writer, Journalist; Carol, Mentally Ill Person
**Time period(s):** 21st century; 31st century
**Locale(s):** Earth; Montenegro

**Summary:** Suicidal and obsessed with leaving Earth for the Moon, Carol dreams of a lunar researcher who, discovering fragments concerning Carol and her sister's existence a thousand years after her death, constructs an erotic fantasy surrounding his relationship with Carol. Author's first novel.

**Other books you might like:**
Jesse Browner, *Conglomeros*, 1992
Haruki Murakami, *Hard-Boiled Wonderland and the End of the World*, 1991
Steve Szilagyi, *Photographing Fairies*, 1992
John Varley, *Steel Beach*, 1992
Kate Wilhelm, *Margaret and I*, 1971

---

`3264`

**ELLEN KUSHNER**, Editor
**DELIA SHERMAN**, Co-Editor
**DONALD G. KELLER**, Co-Editor

## The Horns of Elfland

(New York: Roc, 1997)

**Story type:** Fantasy (Anthology)

**Summary:** Contains seven pages of author biographies, a four-page introduction by Keller plus individual introductions by Kushner to 15 original stories focusing on music and magic. Authors include

John Brunner, Jane Emerson, Michael Kandel, Ellen Kushner, Susan Palwick, Delia Sherman, Terri Windling, Gene Wolfe and Jack Womack.

**Other books you might like:**
Gael Baudino, *Gossamer Axe*, 1990
Emma Bull, *War for the Oaks*, 1987
Anne McCaffrey, *Space Opera*, 1996
   Elizabeth Ann Scarborough, co-editor
Melisa Michaels, *Cold Iron*, 1997
Nancy Springer, *Damnbanna*, 1992

---

**3265**

### ELLEN KUSHNER

## Thomas the Rhymer

(New York: Morrow, 1990)

**Story type:** Fantasy (Adventure)
**Major character(s):** Thomas, Minstrel; Elspeth, Spouse (of Thomas)
**Time period(s):** 14th century (1300s)
**Locale(s):** Elfland, Mythical Place

**Summary:** Enamored by Elspeth, Thomas is abducted by the Queen of Elfland and spends seven years as her lover in her magical kingdom. Upon release, Thomas is unable to speak anything but the truth, causing complications when he marries Elspeth and resumes his earthly life.

**Other books you might like:**
John Desjarlais, *The Throne of Tara*, 1990
Peter Tremayne, *Bloodmist*, 1988

---

**3266**

### HENRY KUTTNER

## The Book of Iod

(Oakland: Chaosium, 1995)

**Story type:** Horror (Anthology; Collection)

**Summary:** This first major collection of weird fiction by an author best known for his groundbreaking Golden Age science fiction reflects his indebtedness to the mythos of extradimensional monsters created by his mentor, H.P. Lovecraft. ''The Eater of Souls'' and ''The Jest of Droom-Avista'' are fantasy stories set on the alien world of Bel Yarnak. In ''The Invaders,'' ''Hydra,'' and ''The Hunt,'' Bel Yarnakian monsters described in the forbidden Book of Iod become the nemeses of earthly mortals. ''Bells of Horror,'' ''The Salem Horror,'' and ''The Secret of Kralitz'' are Gothic tales written in Lovecraftian style. The book also contains Kuttner's collaboration with Robert Bloch, ''The Black Kiss,'' and one story apiece dealing with Kuttner's contribution to the Lovecraft mythos from Robert M. Price and Lin Carter. Edited by Robert M. Price.

**Other books you might like:**
Robert Bloch, *The Mysteries of the Worm*, 1993
Ramsey Campbell, *The Inhabitant of the Lake and Less Welcome Tenants*, 1964
H.P. Lovecraft, *The Watchers out of Time*, 1974
   August Derleth, co-author
Brian Lumley, *The Caller of the Black*, 1971

---

**3267**

### RICHARD LA PLANTE

## Mind Kill

(New York: Forge, 1998)

**Story type:** Horror (Wild Talents)
**Major character(s):** Bill Fogarty, Police Officer (former); Justin Gabriel, Prisoner; Joey Tanaka, Scientist (forensic pathologist), Psychic
**Time period(s):** 1990s (1998)
**Locale(s):** Philadelphia, Pennsylvania

**Summary:** Imprisoned for murder, cult-leader Justin Gabriel visits those who prosecuted him in their dreams, assuming horrible forms that kill them from fear. When Bill Fogarty, the cop who busted Gabriel, becomes ridden by nightmare demons, only his psychic friend Joey Tanaka can help him by fighting Gabriel on his own terms.

**Other books you might like:**
Thomas Baum, *Out of Body*, 1997
Ramsey Campbell, *Incarnate*, 1983
Elizabeth Forrest, *Retribution*, 1998
Kim Newman, *Bad Dreams*, 1991
Daniel Quinn, *Dreamer*, 1988

---

**3268**

### RICHARD LA PLANTE

## Tegne: Soul Warrior

(New York: Tor, 1995)

**Story type:** Fantasy (Political; Religious)
**Major character(s):** Tegne, Martial Arts Expert (Way of the Empty Hand), Bastard Son; Renagi, Warrior, Leader (Warlord of Zendow)
**Time period(s):** Indeterminate
**Locale(s):** Zendow, Fictional City (walled city state); Temple of the Moon, Mythical Place; The Plane Beyond, Mythical Place

**Summary:** Abandoned at birth, Tegne finds a savior and mentor in Tabata, a mystic and a martial arts adept. Despite attempts to kill him or subvert Tegne's efforts, he attains great spiritual and physical abilities as fate leads him toward eventual confrontation with the Warlord of Zendow. First novel, orginally published in Great Britain in 1988.

**Other books you might like:**
Adrian Cole, *Mother of Storms*, 1992
Roberta Cray, *The Sword and the Lion*, 1993
Elizabeth A. Lynn, *Watchtower*, 1979
Sean Russell, *The Initiate Brother*, 1991
Jessica Amanda Salmonson, *Tomoe Gozen*, 1984

---

**3269**

### MERCEDES LACKEY
### ELLEN GUON, Co-Author

## Bedlam's Bard

(New York: Baen, 1998)

**Story type:** Fantasy (Contemporary; Magic Conflict)
**Major character(s):** Eric Banyon, Musician (bard), Minstrel; Korendil, Royalty (prince), Mythical Creature (elf)
**Time period(s):** 1990s (1998)

**Locale(s):** San Francisco, California

**Summary:** This is an omnibus volume of two previously published novels, *Knight of Ghosts and Shadows* and *Summoned to Tourney*. Eric Banyon's music inadvertently frees an elf named Korendil from long imprisonment, and he goes on to raise havoc in modern day California, in the first novel. In the second, elves must ally themselves with humans to save their mutual homes.

**Other books you might like:**
Greg Bear, *Songs of Earth and Power*, 1994
Charles de Lint, *The Harp of the Grey Rose*, 1985
Alan Dean Foster, *Chorus Skating*, 1994
Esther Friesner, *Elf Defense*, 1988
Ellen Kushner, *Thomas the Rhymer*, 1990

## 3270

### MERCEDES LACKEY
### LARRY DIXON, Co-Author

### *The Black Gryphon*
(New York: DAW, 1994)

**Story type:** Fantasy (Magic Conflict; Adventure)
**Series:** Mage Wars
**Major character(s):** Skandranon, Mythical Creature (gryphon); Amberdrake, Healer (comfort worker/kestra'chern); Urtho, Magician
**Time period(s):** Indeterminate Past
**Locale(s):** Ka'venusho, Fictional Country; Tantara, Fictional Country

**Summary:** Once upon a time, the most powerful mages in the world go to war. A good man who goes to war only when it becomes unavoidable, Urtho has the aid of the intelligent creatures he created, the Kaled'a'in tribes with their shaman, kestra'chern, healers, warriors and others. Ma'ar uses his own constructs and allies, as well as viciousness, evil and treachery. Both sides give all they have in the service of those they believe in, building the war to a climax of unfathomable destruction.

**Other books you might like:**
Heather Gladney, *Teot's War*, 1987
Barbara Hambly, *The Time of the Dark*, 1982
Mickey Zucker Reichert, *The Last of the Renshai*, 1992
Michelle Sagara, *Into the Dark Lands*, 1991
Janny Wurts, *Stormwarden*, 1984

## 3271

### MERCEDES LACKEY
### LARRY DIXON, Co-Author

### *Born to Run*
(New York: Baen, 1992)

**Story type:** Fantasy (Light Fantasy; Urban)
**Series:** Serrated Edge
**Major character(s):** Keighvin, Mythical Creature (elf); Tania Jane Delaney, Runaway, Prostitute; Tannim, Magician
**Time period(s):** 1990s
**Locale(s):** Georgia

**Summary:** Three runaway teenagers, each forced into child prostitution, become unwitting pawns in a world of drugs, pornography, the quest to develop a low iron content hotrod and an unearthly vendetta.

**Other books you might like:**
Michael de Larrabeiti, *The Borribles*, 1978
Michael de Larrabeiti, *The Borribles Go for Broke*, 1982

Michael Reaves, *Street Magic*, 1991
Will Shetterly, *Elsewhere*, 1991
Terri Windling, *Borderland*, 1986
    Mark Alan Arnold, co-editor
Terri Windling, *Bordertown*, 1986
    Mark Alan Arnold, co-editor
Terri Windling, *Life on the Border*, 1991
    editor

## 3272

### MERCEDES LACKEY

### *Burning Water*
(New York: Tor, 1989)

**Story type:** Horror (Mystery)
**Series:** Diana Tregarde
**Major character(s):** Diana Tregarde, Paranormal Investigator (Witch), Writer (Romance novelist); Mark Valdez, Detective—Police, Psychic
**Time period(s):** 1980s
**Locale(s):** Dallas, Texas

**Summary:** Investigating a series of brutal, ritualistic murders, Tregarde and Valdez find themselves threatened by a cult intent upon completing an ancient ceremony that will release the powers of the ancient Aztec god Tezcatlipoca.

**Other books you might like:**
John Burke, *The Devil's Footsteps*, 1976
Manly Wade Wellman, *After Dark*, 1980
Manly Wade Wellman, *The Old Gods Waken*, 1979

## 3273

### MERCEDES LACKEY

### *By the Sword*
(New York: DAW, 1991)

**Story type:** Fantasy (Adventure)
**Series:** Valdemar
**Major character(s):** Kerowyn, Mercenary
**Time period(s):** Indeterminate Past
**Locale(s):** Rethwellen, Fictional Country; Valdemar, Fictional Country

**Summary:** In part one, titled "Kerowyn's Ride" her brother's wedding feast is attacked and the bride-to-be kidnapped, leaving only Kerowyn alive and whole enough to go after the raiders. Afterward, Tarma and Kethry train her to be a mercenary fighter. In part two, titled "Two Edged Blade" Kerowyn is a scout with the Skybolt Mercenary Company, when some treacherous border fighting separates her from the Skybolts. Returning, she finds the new Captain determined to get them all killed through her ignorance and pride. In part three, titled "The Price of Command" Kerowyn has been Captain of the Skybolts for 10 years when emissaries from Valdemar desperately plead for help and the Skybolts hire against the evil King Ancar of Hardorn, whose onslaught none may survive.

**Other books you might like:**
Steven Brust, *Jhereg*, 1983
Glen Cook, *The Black Company*, 1984
Barbara Hambly, *The Armies of Daylight*, 1983
Katharine Kerr, *Daggerspell*, 1986
Elizabeth Moon, *Sheepfarmer's Daughter*, 1988

## 3274

**MERCEDES LACKEY**
**JOSEPHA SHERMAN**, Co-Author

### A Cast of Corbies

(New York: Baen, 1994)

**Story type:** Fantasy (Religious; Political)
**Series:** Bardic Choices
**Major character(s):** Raven, Minstrel (Free Bard); Magpie, Minstrel (Free Bard); Regina, Religious
**Time period(s):** Indeterminate
**Locale(s):** Kingsford, Fictional City; Alanda, Fictional Country

**Summary:** Free Bards find increasing trouble as church officials create additional problems for musicians who refuse to follow Guild leadership.

**Other books you might like:**
Gael Baudino, *Strands of Starlight*, 1989
Emma Bull, *War for the Oaks*, 1987
Mary Gentle, *Rats and Gargoyles*, 1991
Elizabeth Ann Scarborough, *Phantom Banjo*, 1991
Josepha Sherman, *The Shining Falcon*, 1989
Josepha Sherman, *A Strange and Ancient Name*, 1993
Paula Volsky, *Illusion*, 1992

## 3275

**MERCEDES LACKEY**
**JOSEPHA SHERMAN**, Co-Author

### Castle of Deception

(New York: Baen, 1992)

**Story type:** Fantasy (Quest; Political)
**Series:** Bard's Tale
**Major character(s):** Kevin, Musician (apprentice bard), Magician; Volmar, Traitor, Nobleman; Carlotta, Mythical Creature (fairy), Imposter (Charina)
**Time period(s):** Indeterminate
**Locale(s):** Count Volmar's Castle, Mythical Place; Westerin, Fictional City

**Summary:** On a simple manuscript copying mission, Kevin loses the manuscript then meets Count Volmar's niece, Charina, diverting him from his copying mission. When Charina becomes a kidnap victim, Kevin and a group of adventurers try to rescue her, unexpectedly involving themselves in a plot to overthrow the king.

**Other books you might like:**
Charles de Lint, *The Little Country*, 1991
Josepha Sherman, *Child of Faerie, Child of Earth*, 1992
Josepha Sherman, *The Horse of Flame*, 1990
Josepha Sherman, *The Shining Falcon*, 1989
Josepha Sherman, *A Strange and Ancient Name*, 1993

## 3276

**MERCEDES LACKEY**

### Children of the Night

(New York: Tor, 1990)

**Story type:** Horror (Vampire Story; Mystery)
**Series:** Diana Tregarde
**Major character(s):** Diana Tregarde, Psychic, Detective; Andre LeBrel, Vampire

**Time period(s):** 1970s
**Locale(s):** New York, New York

**Summary:** Someone or something is slaughtering people in New York and destroying their souls. Diana Tregarde is bound to track down and stop it, bound by her friendship with her neighbor, her developing relationship with Andre, and chiefly by her role as a Guardian. This book is a prequel to *Burning Water*.

**Other books you might like:**
Randall Garrett, *Too Many Magicians*, 1967
Simon R. Green, *Hawk & Fisher*, 1990
Tanya Huff, *Blood Price*, 1991
Madeleine L'Engle, *The Young Unicorns*, 1968
Diana L. Paxson, *Brisingamen*, 1984

## 3277

**MERCEDES LACKEY**
**LARRY DIXON**, Co-Author

### Chrome Circle

(New York: Baen, 1994)

**Story type:** Fantasy (Urban; Magic Conflict)
**Series:** Serrated Edge
**Major character(s):** Tannim Drake, Sports Figure (race car driver), Magician; Foxtrot "Fox" X-ray, Mythical Creature (Japanese fox-spirit), Magician; SharMarali "Shar" Halanyn, Mythical Creature (Japanese fox-spirit), Magician
**Time period(s):** 1990s; Indeterminate
**Locale(s):** Oklahoma; Underhill, Fictional Country (mythic realm); The Unformed, Mythical Place

**Summary:** Tannim musters all his defenses when the woman of his dreams appears as his challenger, sent as a gambit in a continuing conflict among wizards.

**Other books you might like:**
Emma Bull, *War for the Oaks*, 1987
Susan Dexter, *The Wizard's Shadow*, 1993
Elizabeth Forrest, *Phoenix Fire*, 1992
Ellen Guon, *Bedlam Boyz*, 1993
Laurell K. Hamilton, *Nightseer*, 1992
Terri Windling, *Life on the Border*, 1991
  editor

## 3278

**MERCEDES LACKEY**

### The Eagle and the Nightingales

(New York: Baen, 1995)

**Story type:** Fantasy (Political; Adventure)
**Series:** Bardic Voices
**Major character(s):** Nightingale "Lyrebird", Musician (free bard), Magician; T'fyrr Redwing, Alien (Haspur), Musician; Theovere, Royalty (high king)
**Time period(s):** Indeterminate
**Locale(s):** Alanda, Fictional Country; The Twenty Kingdoms, Fictional Country

**Summary:** When independently approached by elves, Deliambrens and other Free Bards to travel as a spy to the capital of the Twenty Kingdoms, Nightingale reluctantly endeavors to discover why High King Theovere's excellent administration has deteriorated. After disguising her identity, arranging employment as a Bard and organizing street urchins into an information network, Nightingale joins forces with T'fyrr, the Chief Court Musician on a similar mission for the Deliambrens. With the union of their music and magic, they hope to restore Theovere's effective rule.

**Other books you might like:**
Phyllis Eisenstein, *In the Red Lord's Reach*, 1989
Suzette Haden Elgin, *Twelve Fair Kingdoms*, 1981
Robin Hobb, *Assassin's Apprentice*, 1995
Tanya Huff, *Sing the Four Quarters*, 1994
Caroline Stevermer, *A College of Magics*, 1994
Patricia C. Wrede, *The Raven Ring*, 1994

---

`3279`

### MERCEDES LACKEY

## *Fiddler Fair*

(New York: Baen, 1998)

**Story type:** Fantasy (Collection)

**Summary:** This collection contains a two-page bibliography, a nine-page article called ''How I Spent My Summer Vacation,'' and individual introductions to 12 stories reprinted from periodicals and anthologies dating between 1989 and 1995. From humorous to serious in tone, the stories explore diverse themes including a deal with the devil, alternate worlds, tabloid fiction, music, sword and sorcery, horses, legendary objects, and dinosaurs.

**Other books you might like:**
Lisa Goldstein, *Travelers in Magic*, 1994
Diana Wynne Jones, *Everard's Ride*, 1995
Elizabeth Moon, *Phases*, 1997
Pat Murphy, *Points of Departure*, 1990
Janny Wurts, *That Way Lies Camelot*, 1996

---

`3280`

### MERCEDES LACKEY

## *The Fire Rose*

(New York: Baen, 1995)

**Story type:** Fantasy (Magic Conflict; Romance)
**Major character(s):** Rosalind ''Rose'' Hawkins, Scholar, Orphan; Jason Cameron, Magician (Firemaster), Werewolf; Paul du Mond, Apprentice
**Time period(s):** 1910s
**Locale(s):** San Francisco, California; Chicago, Illinois

**Summary:** Recently orphaned, Rose Hawkins travels to San Francisco to work for a mysterious man, Jason Cameron, who requires her to read ancient texts about magic. She soon learns that Jason seeks a spell to free him from his half-man/half-wolf form.

**Other books you might like:**
Jill Barnett, *Imagine*, 1995
Peter David, *Howling Mad*, 1989
Pamela Dean, *The Dubious Hills*, 1994
Ashley McConnell, *The Fountains of Mirlacca*, 1995
Sharon Shinn, *The Shape-Changer's Wife*, 1995
Midori Snyder, *The Flight of Michael McBride*, 1994

---

`3281`

### MERCEDES LACKEY

## *Firebird*

(New York: Tor, 1996)

**Story type:** Fantasy (Legend; Magic Conflict)

**Major character(s):** Ilya, Guard, Adventurer
**Time period(s):** Indeterminate
**Locale(s):** Russia

**Summary:** Ilya's resourcefulness guarding a cherry orchard gains him a magical feather which allows him to understand animal speech. A subsequent deed of friendship brings him a constant companion, a fox, before he falls in love with an enchanted princess who requires rescue. Based on a Russian fairy tale.

**Other books you might like:**
Aleksandr Afanas'ev, *Russian Fairy Tales*, 1945
    editor
Steven Brust, *The Sun, the Moon, and the Stars*, 1987
C.J. Cherryh, *Chernevog*, 1990
C.J. Cherryh, *Rusalka*, 1989
C.J. Cherryh, *Yvgenie*, 1991
Fred Saberhagen, *Dancing Bears*, 1996

---

`3282`

### MERCEDES LACKEY
### RU EMERSON, Co-Author

## *Fortress of Frost and Fire*

(New York: Baen, 1993)

**Story type:** Fantasy (Adventure; Quest)
**Series:** Bard's Tale
**Major character(s):** Gawaine, Apprentice, Musician (bard); Naitachal, Mythical Creature (dark elf), Musician (bard); Voyvodan, Mythical Creature (snow dragon)
**Time period(s):** Indeterminate
**Locale(s):** Mythical Place

**Summary:** Rumors of a valley which remains snow covered even during the heat of summer spark Naitachal's interest. On the way to investigate the anomaly, Naitachal and Gawaine acquire knowledgeable guides and more rumors of dire consequences befalling any who venture there. However, neither musician anticipates events which would tempt Gawaine to forsake his master or Naitachal to return to the necromancy he had abandoned. Game tie-in.

**Other books you might like:**
Ru Emerson, *The Calling of the Three*, 1990
Ru Emerson, *The Craft of Light*, 1993
Ru Emerson, *One Land, One Duke*, 1992
Ru Emerson, *The Two in Hiding*, 1991
Elizabeth Moon, *Liar's Oath*, 1992

---

`3283`

### MERCEDES LACKEY

## *Four & Twenty Blackbirds*

(New York: Baen, 1997)

**Story type:** Fantasy (Mystery; Magic Conflict)
**Series:** Bardic Voices
**Major character(s):** Tal Rufin, Police Officer; Ardis, Religious; Rand, Magician
**Time period(s):** Indeterminate
**Locale(s):** Alanda, Fictional City; Twenty Kingdoms, Mythical Place

**Summary:** Without his superiors' support, constable Tal Rufin begins to investigate the murders and suicides of lower class women killed with objects usually found among religious regalia. He soon discovers nasty, overt forces at work.

**Other books you might like:**
Charles de Lint, *Memory and Dream*, 1994

Nancy Farmer, *The Ear, the Eye, and the Arm*, 1994
Lisa Goldstein, *Walking the Labyrinth*, 1996
Simon R. Green, *Hawk & Fisher*, 1990
Melissa Scott, *Point of Hopes*, 1995
    Lisa A. Barnett, co-author

**3284**

MERCEDES LACKEY

## Jinx High

(New York: Tor, 1991)

**Story type:** Horror (Occult; Mystery)
**Series:** Diana Tregarde
**Major character(s):** Diana Tregarde, Writer (romance writer), Witch; Derek "Deke" Kestrel, Teenager, Student; Fay Harper, Teenager, Student
**Time period(s):** 1990s
**Locale(s):** Tulsa, Oklahoma

**Summary:** Invited to lecture the senior class of Jenks High School—also called "Jinx High"—romance writer and occult investigator Diana Tregarde discovers that the teenage son of a good friend and fellow paranormal specialist is psychic, and that his aura has attracted a fiendish sex magick conjuration, summoned by a teenage dabbler in the black arts, who is jealous of his choice of dates for the senior prom.

**Other books you might like:**
Gael Baudino, *Gossamer Axe*, 1990
Emma Bull, *War for the Oaks*, 1987
Tanya Huff, *Blood Price*, 1991
Stephen King, *Carrie*, 1974
Katherine Kurtz, *Deryni Rising*, 1970

**3285**

MERCEDES LACKEY
**ELLEN GUON**, Co-Author

## Knight of Ghosts and Shadows

(New York: Baen, 1990)

**Story type:** Fantasy (Contemporary)
**Major character(s):** Eric Banyon, Musician (street busker), Minstrel (bard); Beth Kentraine, Psychic, Musician; Korendil, Mythical Creature (elf), Royalty (prince)
**Time period(s):** 1990s
**Locale(s):** Los Angeles, California

**Summary:** When Eric's music wakes Korendil after ten years of binding, Eric must come to terms with the knowledge that there really are elves in L.A., he really is a bard and he, Kory and Beth are the only ones who might be able to stop the destruction of the magic nexus that keeps the elves alive and fuels all the creativity of Southern California. Unfortunately, Korendil's enemy, Perenor, and Perenor's daughter, Ria, have considerably more power and experience at their disposal.

**Other books you might like:**
Gael Baudino, *Gossamer Axe*, 1990
Steven Brust, *Cowboy Feng's Space Bar and Grille*, 1990
Emma Bull, *War for the Oaks*, 1987
Tom Deitz, *Windmaster's Bane*, 1987
Charles de Lint, *Jack, the Giant-Killer*, 1987
Tanya Huff, *Gate of Darkness, Circle of Light*, 1989

**3286**

MERCEDES LACKEY

## The Lark and the Wren

(New York: Baen, 1991)

**Story type:** Fantasy (Young Adult; Adventure)
**Series:** Bardic Voices
**Major character(s):** Rune, Musician
**Time period(s):** Indeterminate
**Locale(s):** Nolton, Fictional City; Midsummer Faire at Kingsford, Fictional City

**Summary:** Goaded into a mortally dangerous and daring feat, Rune fiddles all night for the Skull Hill Ghost, the sight of whom is generally fatal. As a reward for her performance the ghost supplies Rune with enough money for her to pursue her goal of winning the trials for the Bardic Guild, allowing her to become a renowned musician.

**Other books you might like:**
Gael Baudino, *Gossamer Axe*, 1990
Emma Bull, *War for the Oaks*, 1987
Orson Scott Card, *Songmaster*, 1980
Stephen Leigh, *The Abraxas Marvel Circus*, 1990
Anne McCaffrey, *Crystal Singer*, 1982
Andrea Shettle, *Flute Song Magic*, 1990

**3287**

MERCEDES LACKEY

## Magic's Pawn

(New York: DAW, 1989)

**Story type:** Fantasy (Sword and Sorcery)
**Series:** Last Herald Mage
**Major character(s):** Vanyel, Magician (Teenager), Homosexual (Upper-class)
**Time period(s):** Indeterminate

**Summary:** Vanyel is despised by his father for his lack of strength and love of music. However, he discovers he has a great deal of magical power, and he must come to terms with his powers in order to grow up.

**Other books you might like:**
Sydney J. Van Scyoc, *Feather Stroke*, 1989

**3288**

MERCEDES LACKEY

## Magic's Price

(New York: Tor, 1990)

**Story type:** Fantasy (Magic Conflict)
**Series:** Last Herald Mage
**Major character(s):** Vanyel Ashkevron, Magician, Homosexual; Stefan, Minstrel (Bard), Homosexual; Savil Ashkevron, Magician
**Time period(s):** Indeterminate Past
**Locale(s):** Valdemar, Fictional Country

**Summary:** The Mages of Valdemar are dying or being killed much faster than they can be replaced. Valdemar's king is dying, and the perpetual raiding on the Karsite border threatens to develop into war. Vanyel, the most powerful Herald-Mage ever known, has held off disaster so far, but when all his fellow mages are gone, he realizes he must take the battle directly to the enemy.

**Other books you might like:**
Marion Zimmer Bradley, *The Heritage of Hastur*, 1975
Heather Gladney, *Teot's War*, 1987
Tanya Huff, *The Fire's Stone*, 1990
Katherine Kurtz, *Deryni Rising*, 1970
Ellen Kushner, *Swordspoint*, 1987

### 3289

### MERCEDES LACKEY

## Magic's Promise
(New York: DAW, 1990)

**Story type:** Fantasy (Adventure)
**Series:** Last Herald Mage
**Major character(s):** Vanyel, Religious (Herald Mage)
**Time period(s):** Indeterminate

**Summary:** Vanyel returns home for a much needed rest, only to find that he feels like a child once again. He soon ''hears'' the psychic pain of a child who will one day be a Herald Mage, only to find out the boy is a prince suspected of murdering his family by psychic means.

**Other books you might like:**
Megan Lindholm, *Luck of the Wheels*, 1989
Anne McCaffrey, *The Dragonriders of Pern Series*,

### 3290

### MERCEDES LACKEY

## Oathblood
(New York: DAW, 1998)

**Story type:** Fantasy (Collection; Sword and Sorcery)
**Major character(s):** Tarma, Warrior, Martial Arts Expert; Kethry, Sorceress, Martial Arts Expert
**Time period(s):** Indeterminate
**Locale(s):** Valdemar, Fictional Country

**Summary:** Contains a two-page introduction and individual introductions to two original stories and nine stories reprinted from periodicals and anthologies dating from 1986 to 1993. Frequently upbeat in tone, the stories focus on the predicaments arising as Tarma and Kethry battle evil and injustice and enlist others in their cause.

**Other books you might like:**
Marion Zimmer Bradley, *Free Amazons of Darkover*, 1985
Friends of Darkover, co-editor
Marion Zimmer Bradley, *The Sword and Sorceress Series*, 1984-1998
editor
Esther Friesner, *Chicks in Chainmail*, 1995
C.L. Moore, *Jirel of Joiry*, 1969
Jessica Amanda Salmonson, *Amazons!*, 1979
editor

### 3291

### MERCEDES LACKEY
### LARRY DIXON, Co-Author

## Owlflight
(New York: DAW, 1997)

**Story type:** Fantasy (Adventure)
**Major character(s):** Darian, Hunter, Apprentice (wizard)

**Time period(s):** Indeterminate
**Locale(s):** Errold's Grove, Fictional City; Valdemar, Fictional Country; Pelagiris Forest, Mythical Place

**Summary:** Darian grows up hunting with his parents in the Pelagiris Forest for the magical beasts created by the Mage Wars. One day he does not accompany them and they do not return from the hunt. A year later, when he watches barbarians sack Errold's Grove and kill his master, Darian flees into the Pelagiris Forest and discovers the Hawkbrothers, a race that has inhabited the forest since before the Mage Wars.

**Other books you might like:**
Robert Holdstock, *Mythago Wood*, 1984
Katharine Kerr, *Daggerspell*, 1986
Michaela Roessner, *Walkabout Woman*, 1988
Mary Stanton, *The Heavenly Horse From the Outermost West*, 1988
Michelle West, *Hunter's Oath*, 1995

### 3292

### MERCEDES LACKEY
### LARRY DIXON, Co-Author

## Owlsight
(New York: DAW, 1998)

**Story type:** Fantasy (Adventure)
**Major character(s):** Darian, Healer, Teenager; Keisha Adler, Healer, Teenager
**Time period(s):** Indeterminate
**Locale(s):** Errold's Grove, Fictional City; Valdemar, Fictional Country; Pelagiris Forest, Mythical Place

**Summary:** As Errold's Grove recovers from a barbarian attack, Keisha Adler uses her untrained talent as healer to benefit her growing community, instead of pursuing formal training at the Healer's Collegium. After living and studying with the Hawkbrothers for four years, Darian returns to Errold's Grove with a small band of Hawkbrothers to warn of another barbarian invasion and repel it if possible.

**Other books you might like:**
Robert Holdstock, *Mythago Wood*, 1994
Katharine Kerr, *Daggerspell*, 1986
Andre Norton, *Elvenblood*, 1995
Mercedes Lackey, co-author
Irene Radford, *The Dragon's Touchstone*, 1997
Michelle West, *Hunter's Oath*, 1995

### 3293

### MERCEDES LACKEY

## The Robin and the Kestrel
(New York: Baen, 1993)

**Story type:** Fantasy (Political; Religious)
**Series:** Bardic Voices
**Major character(s):** Robin, Minstrel, Revolutionary; Kestrel, Minstrel, Royalty; Padrik, Religious (High Bishop of Gradford), Criminal
**Time period(s):** Indeterminate
**Locale(s):** Skull Hill, Mythical Place; Gradford, Fictional City; Carthell Abbey, Mythical Place

**Summary:** When Robin and Kestrel decide to search out the cause of sudden and extreme prejudice against Free Bards, they discover unscrupulous kinsmen who unethically share gypsy magic with a clergyman intent on attaining ultimate worldly power through sham miracles and unwilling aid from the Skull Hill Ghost. Sequel to *The Lark and the Wren*.

**Other books you might like:**
Gael Baudino, *Gossamer Axe*, 1990
Lois McMaster Bujold, *The Spirit Ring*, 1992
Phyllis Eisenstein, *In the Red Lord's Reach*, 1989
Julie Dean Smith, *Call of Madness*, 1990
Paula Volsky, *Illusion*, 1992
Martha Wells, *The Element of Fire*, 1993

### 3294

MERCEDES LACKEY

## Sacred Ground

(New York: Tor, 1994)

**Story type:** Fantasy (Mystery; Magic Conflict)
**Major character(s):** Jennifer Talldeer, Detective—Private, Shaman (apprentice); Frank Talldeer, Chieftain (medicine chief), Indian; David Spotted Horse, Activist, Indian
**Time period(s):** 1990s
**Locale(s):** Tulsa, Oklahoma

**Summary:** When a bulldozer blows up after unearthing an ancient Osage burial ground, Jennifer investigates a developer's claim of conspiracy. She soon discovers the incidents relate to the earlier desecration of the resting place of her ancient ancestor that guarded a great evil, now loose in the land. Her dangerous battles with dark power reflect in both the spiritual world and in the physical realm.

**Other books you might like:**
Emma Bull, *Finder*, 1994
Charles de Lint, *Yarrow*, 1986
Tom Deitz, *Sunshaker's War*, 1990
Robert Morgan, *The Thing That Darkness Hides*, 1993
Dana Stabenow, *Red Planet Run*, 1995

### 3295

MERCEDES LACKEY
**LARRY DIXON**, Co-Author

## The Silver Gryphon

(New York: DAW, 1996)

**Story type:** Fantasy (Magic Conflict; Adventure)
**Series:** Mage Wars
**Major character(s):** Silverblade "Blade", Military Personnel (Silver Gryphon); Tadrith "Tad" Skandrakae, Mythical Creature (gryphon), Military Personnel (Silver Gryphon)
**Time period(s):** Indeterminate Past
**Locale(s):** White Gryphon Lands, Fictional Country

**Summary:** Magically transporting Blade and all needed equipment to their first solo assignment at a remote and isolated guardpost, Tad suddenly loses the ability to fly, crashing into the tropical rain forest. The pair must make their way without magical assistance, and survive whatever stalks them and the evil waiting in the jungle darkness. Third in the trilogy.

**Other books you might like:**
Raymond E. Feist, *Shadow of a Dark Queen*, 1994
Katharine Kerr, *The Bristling Wood*, 1989
Elizabeth Moon, *Sheepfarmer's Daughter*, 1988
Andre Norton, *Elvenblood*, 1995
    Mercedes Lackey, co-author
Judith Tarr, *Spear of Heaven*, 1994

### 3296

MERCEDES LACKEY

## Storm Breaking

(New York: DAW, 1996)

**Story type:** Fantasy (Magic Conflict)
**Series:** Mage Storms
**Major character(s):** An'desha, Magician; Firesong, Magician
**Time period(s):** Indeterminate Past
**Locale(s):** Dorisha Plains, Fictional Country; Tower of Urtho, Mythical Place (ruins); Valdemar, Fictional Country

**Summary:** With help from Shin'a'in plainsmen, An'desha and Firesong excavate and unleash an ancient weapon which temporarily disrupts the destructive magical vibrations emanating from two millennia past. Aided by the power of a magician long dead, they now must find a way to permanently reverse the mage storms. Third in the trilogy.

**Other books you might like:**
Diane Duane, *The Door into Fire*, 1979
Heather Gladney, *Teot's War*, 1987
Terry Goodkind, *Wizard's First Rule*, 1994
Barbara Hambly, *The Time of the Dark*, 1982
Elizabeth Moon, *Sheepfarmer's Daughter*, 1988
Christopher Stasheff, *The Warlock in Spite of Himself*, 1969
Patricia C. Wrede, *Shadow Magic*, 1982

### 3297

MERCEDES LACKEY

## Storm Rising

(New York: DAW, 1995)

**Story type:** Fantasy (Magic Conflict)
**Series:** Mage Storms
**Major character(s):** An'desha, Magician; Karal, Religious; Tremane, Military Personnel, Nobleman (grand duke)
**Time period(s):** Indeterminate Past
**Locale(s):** Valdemar, Fictional Country; Hardorn, Fictional Country

**Summary:** As the disruptions of the Mage Storms grow more extreme, Valdemar and her allies desperately search for a more lasting solution than their magically engineered breakwater. They may have to risk losing the war with the Empire in order to survive. Meanwhile, the storms wreak personal havoc on all fronts, especially on An'desha and Firesong's relationship. First of the series.

**Other books you might like:**
Gael Baudino, *O Greenest Branch!*, 1995
Diane Duane, *The Door into Fire*, 1979
Barbara Hambly, *The Time of the Dark*, 1982
Elizabeth Moon, *Sheepfarmer's Daughter*, 1988
Christopher Stasheff, *The Warlock in Spite of Himself*, 1969

### 3298

MERCEDES LACKEY

## Storm Warning

(New York: DAW, 1994)

**Story type:** Fantasy (Magic Conflict)
**Series:** Mage Storms
**Major character(s):** An'desha, Magician; Firesong, Magician; Ulrich, Diplomat (envoy from Karse), Religious (priest)
**Time period(s):** Indeterminate Past

**Locale(s):** Valdemar, Fictional Country

**Summary:** When the enigmatic Eastern Empire threatens both Valdemar and Karse, traditional enemies must overcome mutual prejudice and suspicion to thwart the danger. Meanwhile, An'desha and Firesong must overcome the shadows of An'desha's past in order to establish a healthy lifebonding, while using the information in those memories to fight the effects of the ancient mage wars echoing through time.

**Other books you might like:**
Diane Duane, *The Door into Fire*, 1979
Heather Gladney, *Teot's War*, 1987
Gayle Greeno, *Finders-Seekers*, 1993
Tanya Huff, *Sing the Four Quarters*, 1994
Marjorie Bradley Kellogg, *The Book of Earth*, 1995
Midori Snyder, *New Moon*, 1989
Patricia C. Wrede, *Shadow Magic*, 1982

---

**3299**

**MERCEDES LACKEY**
**ELLEN GUON**, Co-Author

## Summoned to Tourney

(New York: Baen, 1992)

**Story type:** Fantasy (Urban)
**Major character(s):** Eric Banyon, Minstrel (bard), Musician; Beth Kentraine, Psychic, Musician; Korendil, Mythical Creature (elf), Royalty (prince)
**Time period(s):** 1990s
**Locale(s):** San Francisco, California

**Summary:** Disaster interrupts the street musicians' idyllic life when evil researchers kidnap Beth for use in psychic experimentation and sadistic torture. After Korendil's attempt to rescue her fails, Eric enlists a deadly extraterrestrial force to return Beth to her friends. Sequel to *Knight of Ghosts and Shadows*.

**Other books you might like:**
Gael Baudino, *Gossamer Axe*, 1990
Steven Brust, *Cowboy Feng's Space Bar and Grille*, 1990
Emma Bull, *War for the Oaks*, 1987
Charles de Lint, *Moonheart: A Romance*, 1984
Charles de Lint, *Spiritwalk*, 1992
Tanya Huff, *Gate of Darkness, Circle of Light*, 1989
Will Shetterly, *Elsewhere*, 1991
Terri Windling, *Borderland*, 1986
    Mark Alan Arnold, co-editor
Terri Windling, *Bordertown*, 1986
    Mark Alan Arnold, co-editor
Terri Windling, *Life on the Border*, 1991
    editor

---

**3300**

**MERCEDES LACKEY**, Editor

## Sword of Ice and Other Tales of Valdemar

(New York: DAW, 1997)

**Story type:** Fantasy (Anthology; Adventure)
**Series:** Valdemar

**Summary:** Contains a one-page introduction and brief individual introductions to 18 original stories, three co-authored by Lackey. Generally upbeat in tone, the stories explore the history of Valdemar, the legendary Heralds and their telepathic, horselike Companions. Other authors include Richard Lee Byers, Larry Dixon, Tanya Huff,

Ben Ohlander, Mickey Zucker Reichert, Michelle Sagara, Mark Shepherd, Josepha Sherman and Elisabeth Waters.

**Other books you might like:**
Robert Asprin, *Thieves' World*, 1979
    editor
Marion Zimmer Bradley, *Free Amazons of Darkover*, 1985
    Friends of Darkover, co-editor
Richard Pini, *The Blood of Ten Chiefs*, 1986
    Robert Asprin, Lynn Abbey, co-editors
Will Shetterly, *Liavek*, 1985
    Emma Bull, co-editor
Terri Windling, *Borderland*, 1986
    Mark Allan Arnold, co-editor

---

**3301**

**MERCEDES LACKEY**
**MARK SHEPHERD**, Co-Author

## Wheels of Fire

(New York: Baen, 1992)

**Story type:** Fantasy (Urban; Quest)
**Series:** Serrated Edge
**Major character(s):** Jamie Case, Child, Prisoner; Alinor, Mythical Creature (elf), Detective—Amateur; Joe, Religious, Security Officer
**Time period(s):** 1990s
**Locale(s):** Oklahoma

**Summary:** After Jamie's non-custodial parent kidnaps him, Jamie suffers as the prisoner of a fanatical religious cult until his mother enlists Alinore's aid in finding and returning him to her. Additional help comes from the religious leader's disillusioned son.

**Other books you might like:**
Gael Baudino, *Gossamer Axe*, 1990
Michael de Larrabeiti, *The Borribles*, 1978
Michael Reaves, *Street Magic*, 1991
Will Shetterly, *Elsewhere*, 1991
Terri Windling, *Life on the Border*, 1991
    editor

---

**3302**

**MERCEDES LACKEY**
**HOLLY LISLE**, Co-Author

## When the Bough Breaks

(New York: Baen, 1993)

**Story type:** Fantasy (Psychic Powers; Urban)
**Series:** Serrated Edge
**Major character(s):** Lianne McCormick, Teacher, Heroine; Amanda Kendrick, Abuse Victim, Psychic (esper); Maclyn of Elfhame Outremer, Mythical Creature (elf)
**Time period(s):** 1990s
**Locale(s):** Fayetteville, North Carolina

**Summary:** During a class field trip to watch auto races, Amanda uses her telekenetic abilities to prevent an explosion. When Maclyn's mother requests her son arrange an audience with Amanda, he seeks help from Lianne, who discovers Amanda's abuse at the hands of her father. If Maclyn and Lianne do not help Amanda take control of her life, her telekenetic abilities could destroy both Earth and Faerie.

**Other books you might like:**
Emma Bull, *War for the Oaks*, 1987
Ellen Guon, *Bedlam Boyz*, 1993

Holly Lisle, *Bones of the Past*, 1993
Holly Lisle, *Fire in the Mist*, 1992
Susan Palwick, *Flying in Place*, 1992
Will Shetterly, *Elsewhere*, 1991
Terri Windling, *Borderland*, 1986
   Mark Alan Arnold, co-editor
Terri Windling, *Life on the Border*, 1991
   editor

## 3303

### MERCEDES LACKEY
### LARRY DIXON, Co-Author

## The White Gryphon

(New York: DAW, 1995)

**Story type:** Fantasy (Magic Conflict; Mystery)
**Series:** Mage Wars
**Major character(s):** Amberdrake, Healer, Leader; Skandranon, Mythical Creature (gryphon), Leader; Shalaman, Ruler (King of the Haighlei Empire)
**Time period(s):** Indeterminate Past
**Locale(s):** Haighlei Empire, Fictional Country

**Summary:** A decade after the cataclysmic end of the Mage Wars, refugees establish a settlement and start to thrive when they discover that the Haighlei empire includes their location. Hoping to establish a peaceful relationship, Amberdrake, Skandranon, and others visit the capitol, where accusations of murder put their diplomacy to the test. Second of the series.

**Other books you might like:**
Margaret Ball, *Flameweaver*, 1991
Lillian Stewart Carl, *Wings of Power*, 1989
Raymond E. Feist, *Daughter of the Empire*, 1987
   Janny Wurts, co-author
Simon R. Green, *The God Killer*, 1991
Caroline Stevermer, *A College of Magics*, 1994

## 3304

### MERCEDES LACKEY

## Winds of Change

(New York: DAW, 1992)

**Story type:** Fantasy (Adventure; Quest)
**Series:** Mage Winds
**Major character(s):** Elspeth, Heir, Government Official (herald); Darkwind, Scout; Nyara, Orphan
**Time period(s):** Indeterminate Past
**Locale(s):** K'Sheyna Vale, Mythical Place

**Summary:** Despite the Dark Adept Mornelithe's defeat, the K'Sheyna heartstone remains critically damaged. After Darkwind trains Elspeth, the two of them must attempt to stabilize the heartstone as the other mages remain too closely tied to the damaged stone. Meanwhile Nyara, with the help of the sword, Need, learns to make a life for herself free of her father Mornelithe's influence.

**Other books you might like:**
Margaret Ball, *Flameweaver*, 1991
Diane Duane, *The Door into Fire*, 1979
Diane Duane, *The Door into Shadow*, 1984
Diane Duane, *The Door into Sunset*, 1993
Barbara Hambly, *The Time of the Dark*, 1982
Katherine Kurtz, *Deryni Rising*, 1970
Patricia C. Wrede, *Shadow Magic*, 1982

## 3305

### MERCEDES LACKEY

## Winds of Fate

(New York: DAW, 1991)

**Story type:** Fantasy (Quest; Adventure)
**Series:** Mage Winds
**Major character(s):** Elspeth, Heir, Government Official (herald); Skif, Government Official (herald); Darkwind, Spy, Scout
**Time period(s):** Indeterminate Past
**Locale(s):** Valdemar, Fictional Country; K'Sheyna Vale, Mythical Place

**Summary:** Valdemar's protections against magic, set in place so long ago by Herald-Mage Vanyel, are starting to unravel. With Hardorn's evil sorcerer-king picking away at Valdemar's borders, Elspeth and Skif are sent to find a mage to help Valdemar. Meanwhile, the K'Sheyna Vale Tayledras are beset by a powerful mage who wants control of their heartstone.

**Other books you might like:**
Diane Duane, *The Door into Fire*, 1979
Barbara Hambly, *The Time of the Dark*, 1982
Tanya Huff, *The Fire's Stone*, 1990
Robert Jordan, *The Eye of the World*, 1989
Patricia Kennealy-Morrison, *The Copper Crown*, 1984
Katherine Kurtz, *Deryni Rising*, 1970
Patricia C. Wrede, *Shadow Magic*, 1982

## 3306

### MERCEDES LACKEY

## Winds of Fury

(New York: DAW, 1993)

**Story type:** Fantasy (Magic Conflict; Political)
**Series:** Mage Winds
**Major character(s):** Elspeth, Magician, Heiress; Ancar, Royalty (King of Hardorn), Magician; Darkwind, Scout
**Time period(s):** Indeterminate Past
**Locale(s):** Valdemar, Fictional Country; Hardorn, Fictional Country

**Summary:** When King Ancar initiates a magical attack on Valdemar and the ancient protective spells fail, Princess Elspeth must use her training from the Tayledras Adepts to protect the kingdom. After Ancar forces the Dark Adept, Mornelithe Falconsbane, to aid him in his conquest of Valdemar, Elspeth must rely for help on a powerful spirit reawakened from a forgotten past.

**Other books you might like:**
Lois McMaster Bujold, *The Spirit Ring*, 1992
Diane Duane, *The Door into Fire*, 1979
Barbara Hambly, *The Time of the Dark*, 1982
Laurell K. Hamilton, *Nightseer*, 1992
Robert Jordan, *The Eye of the World*, 1989
Melanie Rawn, *The Star Scroll*, 1989
Martha Wells, *The Element of Fire*, 1993
Patricia C. Wrede, *Shadow Magic*, 1982

## 3307

**MERCEDES LACKEY**
**ELLEN GUON**, Co-Author

### Wing Commander: Freedom Flight

(New York: Baen, 1992)

**Story type:** Science Fiction (Military)
**Series:** Wing Commander
**Major character(s):** Ian ''Hunter'' St. John, Pilot; Kirha, Alien (Kilrathi), Warrior; K'Kai, Alien (Firrekan), Spaceship Captain
**Time period(s):** Indeterminate Future
**Locale(s):** Firekka, Planet—Imaginary; *Tiger's Claw*, Spaceship; Confederation, Interstellar Empire/Federation

**Summary:** The Kilrathi, always warriors and conquerors, now fight a war they connot win. While rebel Kilrathi send a ship to make peace overtures to the Human-led Confederation, other ships from the Kilrath Empire attack the Firekkan System, a member of the Confederation, and take hostages. Hunter leads a team of Humans, Firekkan and Kilrath in an unauthorized rescue mission. A computer game tie-in.

**Other books you might like:**
C.J. Cherryh, *Chanur's Homecoming*, 1986
C.J. Cherryh, *The Pride of Chanur*, 1982
Chris Claremont, *First Flight*, 1987
Gordon R. Dickson, *Masters of Everon*, 1980
J.M. Dillard, *Star Trek VI: The Undiscovered Country*, 1991
Anne McCaffrey, *Sassinak*, 1989
    Elizabeth Moon, co-author

## 3308

**R.A. LAFFERTY**

### Lafferty in Orbit

(Cambridge, Massachusetts: Broken Mirrors Press, 1991)

**Story type:** Science Fiction (Collection)

**Summary:** Introduction by Damon Knight plus 19 stories by Lafferty that were originally published in the *Orbit* anthology series (1966-1980) edited by Knight. Noteworthy stories include two finalists for both Hugo and Nebula Awards, ''Continued on Next Rock'' and ''Entire and Perfect Chrysolite,'' and two stories appearing on initial Nebula Awards ballots, ''All the Pieces of a River Shore'' and ''Dorg.''

**Other books you might like:**
Alfred Bester, *Star Light, Star Bright*, 1976
Alan Dean Foster, *With Friends Like These. . .*, 1977
Raymond J. Healy, *Adventures in Time and Space*, 1946
    J. Francis McComas, co-editor
Larry Niven, *Tales of Known Space*, 1975
Robert Silverberg, *The Science Fiction Hall of Fame, Volume 1*, 1971
Cordwainer Smith, *The Best of Cordwainer Smith*, 1975
Theodore Sturgeon, *E Pluribus Unicorn*, 1953
Theodore Sturgeon, *A Way Home*, 1955
John Varley, *Blue Champagne*, 1986
John Varley, *The Persistence of Vision*, 1978

## 3309

**MICHAEL LAHEY**

### Quest for Apollo

(New York: DAW, 1989)

**Story type:** Fantasy (Legend)
**Major character(s):** Delbert Alderini, Writer (American); Virgil, Writer (Poet), Guide
**Time period(s):** 1980s
**Locale(s):** Italy

**Summary:** Virgil (of Dante's *Inferno*) takes Delbert on a trip to find the god, Apollo. Delbert must find Apollo to stave off the world's impending destruction from nuclear confrontation.

**Other books you might like:**
Kevin J. Anderson, *Gameplay*, 1989
Kara Dalkey, *Euryale*, 1988
Brad Strickland, *Nul's Quest*, 1989
Robert E. Vardeman, *The Infinity Plague*, 1989

## 3310

**MARC LAIDLAW**

### The 37th Mandala

(New York: St. Martin's, 1996)

**Story type:** Horror (Apocalyptic Horror)
**Major character(s):** Derek Crowe, Writer; Lenore Renzler, Young Woman; Michael Renzler, Clerk
**Time period(s):** 1990s (1996)
**Locale(s):** San Francisco, California

**Summary:** When Derek Crowe rewrites the text of book on mystical mandalas as a bestseller for New Age enthusiasts, he unwittingly unleashes the power for evil that the mandalas incarnate and hastens their eruption into the unsuspecting world.

**Other books you might like:**
Ramsey Campbell, *Midnight Sun*, 1990
Douglas Clegg, *Never Land*, 1991
Ray Garton, *Dark Channel*, 1992
Kim Newman, *Jago*, 1991
Whitley Strieber, *The Forbidden Zone*, 1993

## 3311

**MARC LAIDLAW**

### Kalifornia

(New York: St. Martin's Press, 1993)

**Story type:** Science Fiction (Satire; Theological)
**Major character(s):** Sandy Figueroa, Television Personality; Calafia ''Kali'' Figueroa, Television Personality, Religious; Poppy Figueroa, Television Personality, Parent
**Time period(s):** 2050s
**Locale(s):** California

**Summary:** Already wired to broadcast her own sensations, Poppy Figueroa decides to wire her fetal offspring, providing complete sensory connection between mother and daughter and allowing for the first birth of a prenatally wired human being. Religious fanatics derail Poppy's plans for Calafia's career when they present Calafia as Kali to fool their followers and increase their influence.

**Other books you might like:**
David Brin, *Earth*, 1990

Pat Cadigan, *Synners*, 1991
Mick Farren, *The Feelies*, 1990
Neil Gaiman, *Good Omens: The Nice and Accurate Prophecies of Agnes Nutter, Witch*, 1990
    Terry Pratchett, co-author
Parke Godwin, *Waiting for the Galactic Bus*, 1988
James Morrow, *Only Begotten Daughter*, 1990
Neal Stephenson, *Snow Crash*, 1992
Kurt Vonnegut Jr., *Cat's Cradle*, 1963

## 3312

### MARC LAIDLAW

## The Orchid Eater

(New York: St. Martin's, 1994)

**Story type:** Horror (Serial Killer)
**Major character(s):** Lupe Diaz, Drifter; Sal Diaz, Drug Dealer; Mike James, Student
**Time period(s):** 1990s (1994)
**Locale(s):** Bohemia Bay, California

**Summary:** Lupe Diaz's thirst for revenge against his older brother, whom he blames for his emasculation years before, and Mike James's desire to give vent to his dark side by running with southern California street gangs are both satisfied when the two come into contact with Lupe's brother, Sal, and his gang. This explosive and graphic novel explores the teenage gang scene as a commentary on the failure of American society.

**Other books you might like:**
Poppy Z. Brite, *Lost Souls*, 1992
Dennis Cooper, *Frisk*, 1992
Dennis Etchison, *Darkside*, 1986
Ray Garton, *Crucifax*, 1988
Jack Womack, *Random Acts of Senseless Violence*, 1994

## 3313

### MARC LAIDLAW

## The Third Force

(New York: Simon & Schuster Scribner Paperback Fiction, 1996)

**Story type:** Science Fiction (Dystopian; Political)
**Major character(s):** Elena Hausmann, Librarian, Revolutionary (Third Force); Louis Hausmann, Military Personnel; Paulo Orlovsky, Ruler (emperor)
**Time period(s):** Indeterminate Future
**Locale(s):** The Empire, Fictional Country

**Summary:** Louis Hausmann serves Emperor Paulo Orlovsky while, disillusioned with the Empire's increasing repression, Elena joins the Third Force and pursues dangerous investigations. CD-ROM game tie-in.

**Other books you might like:**
Ed Blome, *Title Deleted for Security Reasons*, 1993
Stanislaw Lem, *Peace on Earth*, 1994
Grant Naylor, *Red Dwarf: Infinity Welcomes Careful Drivers*, 1992
Larry Niven, *Fallen Angels*, 1991
    Jerry Pournelle, Michael Flynn, co-authors
Ken Rolston, *Extreme Paranoia: Nobody Knows the Trouble I've Shot*, 1991
Kurt Vonnegut Jr., *Cat's Cradle*, 1963

## 3314

### TERRY LAMSLEY

## Under the Crust

(Ashcroft, British Columbia: Ash-Tree Press, 1997)

**Story type:** Horror (Collection; Small Town Horror)

**Summary:** Six contemporary tales in the classic supernatural tradition, all set in and around the small British town Buxton. Included are the World-Fantasy Award-winning title story about a man's ill-fated discovery of a race of strange humanoid beings living in the remote English countryside; "The Two Returns," about an overcoat possessed by the spirit of its former owner; "Something Worse," in which an invalid is haunted to his death by deceased family members; and "Living Waters," about a preternatural menace that infests the water supply of a small town. First published in 1993.

**Other books you might like:**
Steve Duffy, *The Night Comes On*, 1998
David G. Rowlands, *The Executor and Other Ghost Stories*, 1996
Ron Weighell, *The White Road*, 1996
Robert Westall, *Antique Dust*, 1989
John Whitbourn, *Binscombe Tales*, 1998

## 3315

### SIMON LANG (Pseudonym of Darlene Hartman)

## Hopeship

(New York: Ace, 1994)

**Story type:** Science Fiction (Mystery; Medical)
**Series:** Voyages of the Skipjack
**Major character(s):** Charles Lassiter, Doctor, Patient; Dao Marik, Doctor, Alien (Einai), Military Personnel (second officer of spaceship); Audrey Lassiter, Artist
**Time period(s):** Indeterminate Future
**Locale(s):** *U.S.S. Hope*, Spaceship; Ildefor, Planet—Imaginary

**Summary:** Gravely wounded while saving Charles Lassiter, Dao Marik soon heals aboard the *Hope* medical ship and begins to practice medicine again, trying not to fall in love with Lassiter's wife. After a string of murders and attempted murders with the evidence pointing to him, Marik must clear his name and prevent the destruction of the ship itself.

**Other books you might like:**
Isaac Asimov, *The Caves of Steel*, 1954
C.J. Cherryh, *Hellburner*, 1992
David Drake, *Starliner*, 1992
Michael Jan Friedman, *Shadows on the Sun*, 1993
Jean Lorrah, *The Vulcan Academy Murders*, 1984

## 3316

### SIMON LANG (Pseudonym of Darlene Hartman)

## The Trumpets of Tagan

(New York: Ace, 1992)

**Story type:** Science Fiction (Adventure)
**Series:** Voyages of the Skipjack
**Major character(s):** Paul Whitfield Riker, Spaceship Captain; Dao Marik, Military Personnel, Alien (Einai), Doctor
**Time period(s):** Indeterminate Future
**Locale(s):** Eisernon, Planet—Imaginary; *U.S.S. Skipjack*, Spaceship

**Summary:** Captain Riker prepares his ship for a voyage through time made possible by the psychic powers of the unhatched young of the Elluvon emissary. Meanwhile, his friend and second officer, Dao Marik, the deposed emperor of the conquered planet of Eisernon, searches for his lost child. After the kidnappers take Riker and Marik prisoner, along with two Earth women, they have to fight for their lives and the safety of Marik's child.

**Other books you might like:**
Margaret Wander Bonanno, *Dwellers in the Crucible*, 1985
C.J. Cherryh, *The Faded Sun: Kesrith*, 1978
A.C. Crispin, *Time for Yesterday*, 1988
A.C. Crispin, *Yesterday's Son*, 1983
Frank Herbert, *Dune*, 1965
H. Beam Piper, *The Other Human Race*, 1964

---

**3317**

### DAVID LANGFORD

## Irrational Numbers

(West Warwick, Rhode Island: Necronomicon Press, 1994)

**Story type:** Horror (Collection)

**Summary:** This three-story chapbook approaches questions of identity from a variety of angles. "Deepnet" and "Serpent Eggs" are tales of hideous transformations that incorporate Lovecraftian elements into stories that blend horror and science fiction. "Lions in the Desert" is a witty tale of a shapeshifter desperately trying to keep his identity a secret.

**Other books you might like:**
Stephen Mark Rainey, *Fugue Devil and Other Weird Horrors*, 1993
Brian Stableford, *The Innsmouth Heritage*, 1992
Steve Rasnic Tem, *Decoded Mirrors: Three Tales after Lovecraft*, 1992

---

**3318**

### ROBERTA LANNES

## The Mirror of the Night

(Woodinville, Washington: Silver Salamander, 1997)

**Story type:** Horror (Collection)

**Summary:** Eleven tales of supernatural and nonsupernatural horror, many featuring dysfunctional relationships and sexual neuroses. In "Apostate in Denim," an emotionally troubled young boy finds a surrogate father in a psychopathic murderer. "Auntie" concerns a young girl who discovers that the abusive aunt whose care he is left in is actually her mother in disguise. In "Precious," a gynecologist expresses his warped sensibilities through therapeutic sexual mutilations. "In the Mirror of the Night" concerns a family of women cursed by a male demon that hopes to force a male child into birth to serve as its vessel. Harlan Ellison supplies an introduction to this first collection.

**Other books you might like:**
Poppy Z. Brite, *Swamp Foetus*, 1993
Scott Edelman, *Suicide Art*, 1992
Ray Garton, *Methods of Madness*, 1990
Gerard Daniel Houarner, *Painfreak*, 1996
Sue Storm, *Star Bones Weep the Blood of Angels*, 1995
Lucy Taylor, *Painted in Blood*, 1997

---

**3319**

### JOE R. LANSDALE

## Act of Love

(Baltimore, Maryland: CD Publications, 1993)

**Story type:** Horror (Serial Killer)
**Major character(s):** Marvin Hanson, Police Officer; Philip Barlowe, Journalist; Doc Warren, Doctor (medical examiner)
**Time period(s):** 1980s (1981)
**Locale(s):** Houston, Texas

**Summary:** Marvin Hanson is on the trail of "The Houston Hacker," a psychopathic killer who regularly mutilates blacks in the Houston ghettoes and communicates only by letters with Philip Barlowe, the newspaper reporter who named him. Hanson doesn't like Barlowe's smartaleck, racist manner—and eventually finds out he has even more visceral reasons for disliking him. Originally published 1981.

**Other books you might like:**
George C. Chesbro, *Bone*, 1989
Thomas Harris, *Red Dragon*, 1991
Rex Miller, *Slob*, 1987
Peter Straub, *Koko*, 1988

---

**3320**

### JOE R. LANSDALE

## Batman: Captured by the Engines

(New York: Warner, 1991)

**Story type:** Horror (Werewolf Story)
**Major character(s):** Pale Boy, Lawman (sheriff of Cold Shepherd); Bruce "Batman" Wayne, Hero, Detective—Amateur; Catherine Meadows, Doctor (of Cold Shepherd)
**Time period(s):** 1990s
**Locale(s):** Gotham City; Cold Shepherd, Alternate Universe

**Summary:** In Gotham City, "The Caped Crusader" Batman takes on bloodthirsty "were-cars," a species of sentient automobiles that are running amok and whose origins can be traced back to elemental forces drawn to the totemic Pyramid of Cars that decorates the automobile junkyard of the nearby Indian reservation in Cold Shepherd.

**Other books you might like:**
Eric Higgs, *Doppelganger*, 1987
Stephen King, *Christine*, 1983
Stephen King, "*Trucks*", 1978
    in *Night Shift*

---

**3321**

### JOE R. LANSDALE

## Bestsellers Guaranteed

(New York: Ace, 1993)

**Story type:** Horror (Collection)

**Summary:** This book collects sixteen tales of the supernatural and nonsupernatural which alternate between the amusing and the grotesque. Included are the hardboiled crime story, "On a Dark October"; the ghost tale, "Not From Detroit"; "The God of the Razor," which was later expanded into the novel *The Nightrunners* (1987); and the novella, "The Events Concerning a Nude Fold-Out Found in a Harlequin Romance," about a dog trainer for a circus who nurses a perverse desire to mutilate the bodies of young women. The author has supplied an enjoyable introduction and headnotes for each story.

**Other books you might like:**
Donald Burleson, *Lemon Drops and Other Horrors*, 1993
Ed Gorman, *Prisoners and Other Stories*, 1992
Stephen King, *Skeleton Crew*, 1985
Robert R. McCammon, *Blue World*, 1989
F. Paul Wilson, *Soft and Others*, 1989

**3322**

**JOE R. LANSDALE**

## By Bizarre Hands

(Shingletown, California: Mark V. Ziesing, 1989)

**Story type:** Horror (Collection)

**Summary:** Fifteen stories and one essay in Lansdale's distinctive voice featuring such items as disco zombies (''On the Far Side of the Cadillac Desert with Dead Folks''), hellish delinquents (''Boys Will Be Boys''), dead dogs (''Night They Missed the Horror Show''), desert nights filled with fish (''Fish Night''), contemporary religion (''The Fat Man and the Elephant''), and the end of the world (''Tight Little Stitches in a Dead Man's Back'').

**Other books you might like:**
Dennis Etchison, *Red Dreams*, 1984
David J. Schow, *Seeing Red*, 1990

**3323**

**JOE R. LANSDALE**

## Cold in July

(Shingletown, CA: Marc Ziesing, 1990)

**Story type:** Horror (Mystery)
**Major character(s):** Richard Dane, Businessman (frame shop owner); Ben Russel, Convict (ex-convict); Jim Bob Luke, Detective—Private
**Time period(s):** 1980s (1989)
**Locale(s):** La Borde, Texas

**Summary:** An unlikely trio of characters—a private detective, ex-con Ben Russel and Richard Dane, a man misled by the police to believe that he had killed Russel's son as a burglar—team up to find out why the police have deliberately created a trail of misinformation about the supposedly deceased Freddy Russel.

**Other books you might like:**
Peter Straub, *Koko*, 1988

**3324**

**JOE R. LANSDALE**, Editor
**KAREN LANSDALE**, Co-Editor

## Dark at Heart

(Arlington Heights, Illinois: Dark Harvest, 1992)

**Story type:** Horror (Anthology)

**Summary:** Twenty original tales of dark suspense, a subgenre that straddles the horror and suspense genres. Included are Joe Lansdale's Bram Stoker Award-winning novella ''The Events Concerning a Nude Fold-Out Found in a Harlequin Romance,'' in which a brutalized woman savagely revenges herself on her attacker; F. Paul Wilson's ''The Long Way Home,'' starring his series urban vigilante, Repairman Jack; David Schow's ''Action,'' which posits a

conspiracy between criminals and the media; and stories by Chet Williamson, Steve Rasnic Tem, Stephen Gallagher, and David Morrell.

**Other books you might like:**
Robert Bloch, *Psycho-Paths*, 1991
  Martin H. Greenberg, co-editor
Richard T. Chizmar, *Cold Chills*, 1991
  editor
Ed Gorman, *Dark Crimes: Great Noir Fiction From the '50's to the '90's*, 1991
  editor

**3325**

**JOE R. LANSDALE**

## Dead in the West

(Mount Holyoke, Massachusetts: Crossroads Press, 1995)

**Story type:** Horror (Reanimated Dead; Supernatural Vengeance)
**Major character(s):** Jebidiah Mercer, Religious; David, Child; Doc Peekner, Doctor
**Time period(s):** 19th century
**Locale(s):** Mud Creek, Texas

**Summary:** Traveling preacher Jebidiah Mercer finds his gunslinging skills sorely tested when he pulls into the town of Mud Creek and discovers that the lynching of an Indian medicine man has unleashed a curse that causes the dead to rise from the ground as murderous zombies. This tribute to the old pulp magazines and E.C. comics was first published in book form in 1986 and was revised for this edition.

**Other books you might like:**
T. Chris Martindale, *Demon Dance*, 1991
Graham Masterton, *Burial*, 1994
Graham Masterton, *The Manitou*, 1974
Graham Masterton, *Revenge of the Manitou*, 1979
Eugene E. Pfaff Jr., *Uwharrie*, 1993
  Michael Causey, co-author
Patrick Whalen, *Deathwalker*, 1992

**3326**

**JOE R. LANSDALE**

## The Drive-In: A Double Omnibus

(New York: Carroll & Graf, 1997)

**Story type:** Horror (Collection)

**Summary:** Omnibus of two novels, *The Drive-In (A B-Movie with Blood and Popcorn, Made in Texas)*, first published in 1988, and *The Drive-In 2 (Not Just One of Them Sequels)*, first published in 1989. In *The Drive-In*, attendees at an all-night horror movie marathon at a rural Texas drive-in find their world transformed into a hostile alien landscape by a passing comet. In *The Drive-In 2*, survivors of the first novel navigate a landscape in which horror and science fiction B-movie cliches have come to life, among them the Popalong Cassidy, a mutant demi-god who demands their obeisance.

**Other books you might like:**
Peter Atkins, *Big Thunder*, 1997
David Darke, *Horrorshow*, 1994
John Douglas, *The Late Show*, 1994
Dale Hoover, *65mm*, 1994
Jack Martin, *Videodrome*, 1982

## 3327

### JOE R. LANSDALE

## *Electric Gumbo: A Lansdale Reader*

(New York: Quality Paperback Book Club, 1995)

**Story type:** Horror (Collection)

**Summary:** This omnibus volume gathers a variety of fiction and non-fiction by a writer renowned for his blends of hardboiled horror and humor. Two articles, "Hell through a Windshield" and "A Hard-On for Horror: Low Budget Excitement," are paeans to monster movies and the drive-ins of Lansdale's youth. The book's 14 story selections include the post-apocalyptic nightmare "Tight Little Stitches in a Dead Man's Back"; two stories about redneck youths who get into more mischief than they bargain for, "The Night They Missed the Horror Show" and "Steppin' Out, Summer '68"; the zombie story "On the Far Side of the Cadillac Desert with Dead Folks"; the alternate history western "Trains Not Taken"; and the crime stories "The Steel Valentine" and "The Job." The book also includes the full length fantasy novel, *The Drive-In (A Novel)*, about a bunch of juvenile delinquents who become trapped in a world where life is nothing but a B-movie and themselves merely bit actors.

**Other books you might like:**
Neal Barrett Jr., *Slightly Off Center*, 1992
Fred Chappell, *More Shapes than One*, 1991
Nancy A. Collins, *Nameless Sins*, 1994
Ed Gorman, *Prisoners and Other Stories*, 1993

## 3328

### JOE R. LANSDALE

## *A Fist Full of Stories (and Articles)*

(Baltimore: CD Publications, 1997)

**Story type:** Horror (Collection)

**Summary:** Nineteen short stories and articles by a writer whose work straddles the border of crime and supernatural fiction. Included are "Bar Talk," a loopy vampire tale; "Personality Problem," a comic variation on the Frankenstein theme; "Listen," about a man who finds that his anonymity is turning him invisible; and "Old Charlie," a dramatic monologue delivered by a homicidal maniac.

**Other books you might like:**
Neal Barrett Jr., *Slightly Off Center*, 1992
Nancy A. Collins, *Nameless Sins*, 1994
Ed Gorman, *Prisoners and Other Stories*, 1992
Davis Grubb, *You Never Believe Me and Other Stories*, 1989
Robert R. McCammon, *Blue World*, 1989
William Relling Jr., *The Infinite Man*, 1989
Manly Wade Wellman, *The Valley So Low*, 1987
F. Paul Wilson, *Soft and Others*, 1989

## 3329

### JOE R. LANSDALE

## *The Good, the Bad, and the Indifferent*

(Burton, Michigan: Subterranean Press, 1997)

**Story type:** Horror (Collection)

**Summary:** Thirty-four stories and vignettes from early in the author's career. Selections include "Junkyard," about a monstrous creature that lives among the refuse of the local junkyard; "The Valley of the Swastika," a biker variation on Kipling's "The Man Who Would Be

King"; the dark suspense story "One Death, Two Episodes"; and "Walks," a portrait of a serial killer as a conscientious father. Illustrated by Mark A. Nelson. Released only in a signed, limited edition.

**Other books you might like:**
Neal Barrett Jr., *Slightly Off Center*, 1992
Nancy A. Collins, *Nameless Sins*, 1994
Ed Gorman, *Prisoners and Other Stories*, 1992
Davis Grubb, *You Never Believe Me and Other Stories*, 1989
Robert R. McCammon, *Blue World*, 1989
William Relling Jr., *The Infinite Man*, 1989
Manly Wade Wellman, *The Valley So Low*, 1987
F. Paul Wilson, *Soft and Others*, 1989

## 3330

### JOE R. LANSDALE

## *Mucho Mojo*

(New York: Mysterious Press, 1994)

**Story type:** Horror (Mystery)
**Major character(s):** Hap Collins, Worker; Leonard Pine, Martial Arts Expert; Florida Grange, Lawyer
**Time period(s):** 1990s (1994)
**Locale(s):** La Borde, Texas

**Summary:** This semi-sequel to Lansdale's *The Savage Season* further explores the friendship of white liberal Hap Collins and his black buddy, Leonard Pine, as they become enmeshed in a mystery revolving around the death of Hap's uncle, the unexpected windfall inheritance he has left his nephew, the skeleton of a child found wrapped in the pages of a pornographic magazine beneath the floorboards of his house, and the differences between the white and black culture of La Borde, and America in general.

**Other books you might like:**
Edward Anderson, *Thieves Like Us*, 1937
James Ross, *They Don't Dance Much*, 1940
Jim Thompson, *South of Heaven*, 1967
Charles Williams, *The Hot Spot*, 1953

## 3331

### JOE R. LANSDALE
### PAT LOBRUTTO, Co-Author

## *Razored Saddles*

(New York: Avon, 1990)

**Story type:** Horror (Anthology)

**Summary:** Seventeen stories of fantasy and horror with western themes, ranging in tone from Robert R. McCammon's dark tale of a homicidally deranged gunslinger, "Black Boots," to F. Paul Wilson's bizarre Doc Holliday anecdote, "The Tenth Toe." Images of the classic west abound in All Sarrantonio's science fiction horror story "Trail of the Chromium Bandits," Lewis Shiner's tale of lost treasure "Gold" and Chet Williamson's anti-western "Yore Skin's Jes' Soft 'N Purty. . .He Said," while a very modern west can be found in David Schow's "Sedalia," Melissa Mia Hall's "Stampede" and Howard Waldrop's alternate-world story "The Passing of the Western."

**Other books you might like:**
Joe R. Lansdale, *The New Frontier*, 1989
Frank D. McSherry Jr., *A Treasury of Great American Horror Stories*, 1985
Martin H. Greenberg, co-author

Frank D. McSherry Jr., *Western Ghosts*, 1990
  Charles G. Waugh and Martin H. Greenberg, co-editors

### 3332

#### JOE R. LANSDALE

## Savage Season

(Los Angeles, Marc Ziesing, 1990)

**Story type:** Horror (Psychological Suspense)
**Major character(s):** Hap Collins, Worker; Leonard Pine, Martial Arts Expert; Trudy Collins, Divorced Person (Hap's ex-wife)
**Time period(s):** 1990s
**Locale(s):** Marvel Creek, Texas

**Summary:** Hap Collins' ex-wife, Trudy, a former radical during the Vietnam years, convinces Hap and his best friend Leonard to help her recover a million dollars that wound up at the bottom of the Sabine River during a bungled bank heist years before. When the adventure goes tragically wrong, Hap is forced to reassess how his values were shaped by America's turbulent 1960s.

**Other books you might like:**
Robert R. McCammon, *Mine*, 1990
Peter Straub, *Koko*, 1988

### 3333

#### JOE R. LANSDALE

## Stories by Mama Lansdale's Youngest Boy

(Eugene, OR: Pulphouse, 1991)

**Story type:** Horror (Collection)
**Series:** Author's Choice Monthly

**Summary:** Fifteen stories by the horror genre's southwestern regionalist and humorist, many inspired by the eating of popcorn. The selections span the breadth of Lansdale's professional writing career and include the Ray Bradbury-influenced "The Fat Man" and "By the Hair of the Head," a dark fantasy with classic overtones. More characteristic of Lansdale's brand of tough horror is the hardboiled "The Job," the merging of racism and supernatural horror in "On a Dark October," and the surreal "God of the Razor," an offshoot from his 1987 novel *The Nightrunners*. Lansdale has written informative notes for each story.

**Other books you might like:**
Davis Grubb, *You Never Believe Me and Other Stories*, 1989
Richard Matheson, *Collected Stories*, 1989
William Relling Jr., *The Infinite Man*, 1989
Manly Wade Wellman, *The Valley So Low*, 1987

### 3334

#### JOE R. LANSDALE, Editor
#### RICHARD KLAW, Co-Editor

## Weird Business

(Austin, Texas: MoJo Press, 1995)

**Story type:** Horror (Anthology)

**Summary:** The 23 stories in this beautifully produced volume are all illustrated renderings by a variety of artists and writers of horror stories old and new. Classic tales adapted include Poe's surrealistic "The Masque of the Red Death" and Ambrose Bierce's amusing account of an unregenerate parricide, "Oil of Dog." New stories include Norman Partridge's "Gorilla Gunslinger," an alternate old

west tale with a gorilla hero; Poppy Z. Brite's "Becoming the Monster," a meditation on love and death; Chet Williamson's "Chip of Fools," about the vampiric hold an on-line computer system has on its users; and Joe Lansdale's "The Steel Valentine," a hardboiled revenge story.

**Other books you might like:**
Clive Barker, *Tapping the Vein: Book One*, 1989
Ray Bradbury, *The Autumn People*, 1965
Ray Bradbury, *Tomorrow Midnight*, 1966
Edward Gorey, *Amphigorey Also*, 1985
Gahan Wilson, *Still Weird*, 1994

### 3335

#### JOE R. LANSDALE

## Writer of the Purple Rage

(Baltimore: CD Publications, 1994)

**Story type:** Horror (Collection)

**Summary:** The author's fourth collection brings together 14 stories that display his skill at blending the grotesque and the amusing, one essay and a stage adaptation of his southern gothic tale, "By Bizarre Hands." Two stories are original to the volume: "Bubba Ho-Tep," in which an elderly Elvis Presley faces off against a soul-stealing Egyptian mummy, and "Godzilla's Twelve-Step Program," in which the legendary monster embarks on a self-improvement program to bring out the nice guy inside him. Other highlights include "Mr. Weed-Eater," about the perverse turn of events that befall an average man who helps out a blind groundskeeper, and "Man with Two Lives," a nostalgic reflection on western history. The signed limited edition of this volume contains an additional essay and a comic for which Lansdale wrote the script.

**Other books you might like:**
Davis Grubb, *You Never Believe Me and Other Stories*, 1989
Robert E. Howard, *The Last Ride*, 1978
Robert R. McCammon, *Blue World*, 1989

### 3336

#### JAN LARA (Pseudonym of Michael T. Hinkemeyer)

## Soulcatchers

(New York: Popular Library, 1990)

**Story type:** Horror (Serial Killer)
**Major character(s):** Lacy Timmers, Student—Graduate; Averell "The Needle" Turch, Student, Serial Killer; Mark Liston, Businessman
**Time period(s):** 1990s (1990)
**Locale(s):** San Francisco, California (Great Western University); Bear Claw Islands, South Carolina

**Summary:** History research fellow Lacy Timmers goes to the South Carolina coast to study descendants of missing members of the original Jamestown colony, unaware that she is being pursued by Averell Turch, a jealous fellow student whose alter ego is a mother-fixated serial killer known as "The Needle."

**Other books you might like:**
Clive Barker, *Cabal*, 1988
Robert Bloch, *Psycho*, 1959
Chet Williamson, *Dreamthorp*, 1989

## 3337

### R. KARL LARGENT

## Black Death

(New York: Leisure, 1995)

**Story type:** Horror (Small Town Horror)
**Major character(s):** C. Lane "Rusty" Bogner, Police Officer (deputy sheriff); Collee Barnes, Real Estate Agent; Harold Marsh, Doctor
**Time period(s):** 1980s (1988)
**Locale(s):** Half Moon, Kentucky

**Summary:** When townspeople in Half Moon begin falling prey to a flesh-eating virus, authorities trace it to a similar outbreak that happened a century before and race against the clock to discover the identity of the asymptomatic carrier who is inadvertently transmitting the disease to others. This novel was first published in 1988.

**Other books you might like:**
Michael Crichton, *The Andromeda Strain*, 1969
Christopher Hyde, *Jericho Falls*, 1988
Dean R. Koontz, *Phantoms*, 1983
Patrick Lynch, *Carriers*, 1995
Peter Straub, *Floating Dragon*, 1983

## 3338

### JEANNE LARSEN

## Bronze Mirror

(New York: Henry Holt, 1991)

**Story type:** Fantasy (Legend)
**Major character(s):** Pomegranate, Servant, Human; Silkweb Empress, Royalty, Mythical Creature; Tsang-jieh, Historian, Mythical Creature
**Time period(s):** Indeterminate (heavenly time); 12th century
**Locale(s):** Heavenly Realm, Mythical Place; China

**Summary:** When the Yellow Emperor orders a story telling contest between his Empress and the Royal Historian in heaven, the events related in the stories begin to affect events in the Earthly realm. They are informed by Bodhisattva Guan-yin that the competition messes up history on Earth and creates a karmic burden, but the competition continues.

**Other books you might like:**
Kathryn Grant, *The Willow Garden*, 1989
Barry Hughart, *Bridge of Birds*, 1984
Barry Hughart, *Eight Skilled Gentlemen*, 1991
Barry Hughart, *The Story of the Stone*, 1988
Andre Norton, *Imperial Lady*, 1989
    Susan Shwartz, co-author
Janny Wurts, *Daughter of the Empire*, 1987
    Raymond E. Feist, co-author

## 3339

### JEANNE LARSEN

## Silk Road

(New York: Holt, 1989)

**Story type:** Fantasy (Adventure)
**Major character(s):** Greenpearl, Captive
**Time period(s):** 8th century
**Locale(s):** China

**Summary:** The story follows Greenpearl, kidnapped daughter of a Chinese general, as she goes through life, her fate in the hands of slave traders, scholars, gods, and herself. She longs to return to her father's city to be reunited with her family.

**Other books you might like:**
Hugh Cook, *The Women and the Warlords*, 1989
    Chronicles of an Age of Darkness. Vol. 3
Raymond E. Feist, *Daughter of the Empire*, 1987
    Janny Wurts, co-author
Kathryn Grant, *The Willow Garden*, 1989
Andre Norton, *Imperial Lady*, 1989
Susan Schwartz, *Byzantium's Crown*, 1987

## 3340

### KATHRYN LASKY

## Double Trouble Squared

(New York: Harcourt Brace Jovanovich, 1991)

**Story type:** Fantasy (Adventure; Young Adult)
**Series:** Starbuck Family Adventure
**Major character(s):** Liberty Starbuck, Telepath, Twin; July Starbuck, Telepath, Twin; Shadrach Holmes, Spirit (literary ghost)
**Time period(s):** 1990s (1991)
**Locale(s):** London, England

**Summary:** Both pairs of Starbuck twins communicate telepathically. When Liberty and July sense another voice, the twins begin to analyze as would their hero, Sherlock Holmes. They search London for the new telepath and discover a literary ghost, the unborn character of Arthur Conan Doyle. This is the first Starbuck Family Adventure.

**Other books you might like:**
Peter Dickinson, *The Gift*, 1974
Sherryl Jordan, *The Juniper Game*, 1991
Pamela F. Service, *Being of Two Minds*, 1991
Wilmar H. Shiras, *Children of the Atom*, 1953

## 3341

### KATHRYN LASKY

## Shadows in the Water

(New York: Harcourt Brace Jovanovich, 1992)

**Story type:** Science Fiction (Young Adult; Psychic Powers)
**Series:** Starbuck Family Adventure
**Major character(s):** Liberty Starbuck, Telepath, Twin; July Starbuck, Telepath, Twin; Streak, Animal (dolphin), Telepath
**Time period(s):** 1990s
**Locale(s):** Florida Keys, Florida

**Summary:** When the Starbuck family moves to the Florida Keys to track down toxic waste polluters, Liberty and July begin to receive telepathic messages from the Gulf of Mexico. Investigating the communication, the twins prove valuable allies to dolphins and turtles, eventually playing the critical role needed to bring the polluters to justice.

**Other books you might like:**
Arthur C. Clarke, *Dolphin Island*, 1963
Gordon R. Dickson, *Secret Under the Caribbean*, 1964
Gordon R. Dickson, *Space Winners*, 1965
Sydney J. Van Scyoc, *Deepwater Dreams*, 1991

## 3342

### KEITH LAUMER

## *Alien Minds*

(New York: Baen, 1991)

**Story type:** Science Fiction (Collection)
**Time period(s):** Indeterminate Future

**Summary:** This collection of 10 stories with an 8-page introduction examines the question, ''What is intelligence and how is it recognized?'' Eight stories were published in the 1960s; two are originals—''The Propitiation of Brullamagoo'' and ''Reverse English.''

**Other books you might like:**
Alfred Bester, *Star Light, Star Bright*, 1976
Chad Oliver, *Unearthly Neighbors*, 1960
Theodore Sturgeon, *The Golden Helix*, 1979
William Tenn, *Of Men and Monsters*, 1968
William Tenn, *The Seven Sexes*, 1968

## 3343

### KEITH LAUMER

## *Back to the Time Trap*

(New York: Baen, 1992)

**Story type:** Science Fiction (Time Travel)
**Major character(s):** Roger Tyson, Time Traveler; Clarence ''Rusty'' Naill, Time Traveler, Sea Captain; Dob, Alien (Rhox)
**Time period(s):** Indeterminate Past; Indeterminate Future
**Locale(s):** Earth

**Summary:** A rutabaga-shaped alien materializes in Roger Tyson's TV and pulls him into a bewildering mass of times and places as it sucks in other innocent victims, rushing back and forth in time and often mixing the far past, the present and the future in one spot. Roger only wants to get back to his wife and his familiar surroundings, but that seems impossible due to time line mixing. Sequel to *Time Trap*.

**Other books you might like:**
Lloyd Biggle, *The Whirligig of Time*, 1979
Alan Dean Foster, *To the Vanishing Point*, 1988
Harry Harrison, *A Rebel in Time*, 1983
Harry Harrison, *The Stainless Steel Rat Saves the World*, 1972
Michael McCollum, *A Greater Infinity*, 1982
Hayford Peirce, *Napoleon Disentimed*, 1987
Kurt Vonnegut Jr., *The Sirens of Titan*, 1959

## 3344

### KEITH LAUMER

## *Judson's Eden*

(New York: Baen, 1991)

**Story type:** Science Fiction (Space Opera)
**Major character(s):** Marl Judson, Spaceship Captain; Clarence ''Cookie'' Murphy, Cook, Sidekick; Baggy, Alien
**Time period(s):** Indeterminate Future
**Locale(s):** Earth; Eden, Planet—Imaginary

**Summary:** Marl Judson escapes from Earth just ahead of the government men who wish him declared a traitor so they can steal his financial empire. He and his friend, Cookie, land on an earthlike planet where time is strangely skewed and whose sole inhabitant is an amoeboid alien they name Baggy. When the Navy arrives followed shortly by aliens who want to wipe out humans, Baggy's aid allows Judson to hold the planet against everyone who doesn't want to live together in peace.

**Other books you might like:**
Lloyd Biggle, *Monument*, 1974
John Brunner, *A Planet of Your Own*, 1966
Alan Dean Foster, *Midworld*, 1975
James P. Hogan, *Voyage From Yesteryear*, 1982
Dennis Schmidt, *Satori*, 1986
Bob Shaw, *The Wooden Spaceships*, 1988
Joan Slonczewski, *Still Forms on Foxfield*, 1980
Brian Stableford, *The Paradise Game*, 1974

## 3345

### KEITH LAUMER

## *Reward for Retief*

(New York: Baen Books, 1989)

**Story type:** Science Fiction (Humor)
**Series:** Retief
**Major character(s):** Jame Retief, Diplomat; Ben Magnan, Diplomat
**Time period(s):** Indeterminate Future
**Locale(s):** Zany-Doo, Planet—Imaginary

**Summary:** Retief is assigned to Zany-Doo, a primitive planet whose caterpillar-like inhabitants are strongly xenophobic. Eventually Retief discovers that this seemingly backward planet has a dark secret; it's at the center of a transtemporal flux where reality itself can be changed by a thought.

**Other books you might like:**
David Gerrold, *Chess with a Dragon*, 1987
Ron Goulart, *The Chameleon Corps*, 1972
Ron Goulart, *Starpirate's Brain*, 1987
Ron Goulart, *A Talent for the Invisible*, 1973
Alexei Panshin, *Masque World*, 1969
Alexei Panshin, *Star Well*, 1968
Alexei Panshin, *The Thurb Revolution*, 1968

## 3346

### KEITH LAUMER

## *The Stars Must Wait*

(New York: Baen Books, 1990)

**Story type:** Science Fiction (Post-Nuclear Holocaust)
**Series:** Bolo
**Major character(s):** Jack Jackson, Astronaut (Lieutenant commander); Renada, Young Woman
**Time period(s):** 1990s; 21st century (Late)
**Locale(s):** United States

**Summary:** As the world teeters on the edge of nuclear war, Lt. Commander Jackson and the crew of the experimental spaceship Prometheus prepare for a desperate voyage to Callisto. When Jackson awakes from suspended animation, however, he discovers that his ship has never left Earth, that a nuclear war did occur, and that he is now alone in a wilderness of radioactivity and primitive feuding tribes. He alone has the knowledge to re-establish civilization.

**Other books you might like:**
David Brin, *The Postman*, 1985
Algis Budrys, *Some Will Not Die*, 1961
Edward P. Hughes, *Masters of the Fist*, 1989

## 3347

### ANDREW LAURANCE

## Catacomb

(New York: Diamond, 1991)

**Story type:** Horror (Wild Talents)
**Major character(s):** Juan Ramirez Montoneros, Orphan (monk novitiate), Religious; Francesca Sciascia, Office Worker (Vatican); Father Anthony, Religious (monk of St. Dominitian monaste), Teacher (of Juan)
**Time period(s):** 1980s (1981)
**Locale(s):** Monte Trasimeno, Italy (Monastery of St. Dominitian, just outside of Rome)

**Summary:** Since a very early age, Juan has been able to see the specter of death hovering over those about to die. Banished to a remote monastery, he finds that he can converse with the deceased and that the true origin of his "gift" is being covered up by a Vatican conspiracy. This novel was originally published in Britain in 1981 as *The Hiss*.

**Other books you might like:**
Brian Lumley, *Necroscope*, 1987
Guy N. Smith, *Entombed*, 1982

## 3348

### ANDREW LAURANCE

## The Link

(New York: Diamond, 1991)

**Story type:** Horror (Wild Talents)
**Series:** Blood of Nostradamus Trilogy
**Major character(s):** Paul Saralyn, Young Man; Cathy Morrow, Businesswoman; Melanie Forbes, Paranormal Investigator
**Time period(s):** 1980s (1980)
**Locale(s):** London, England

**Summary:** Originally published in England in 1980, this second novel in the Blood of Nostradamus series continues the story begun in *The Premonition*. Upon traveling to Europe after his mother's death, Paul Saralyn discovers that the psychic premonitions that have troubled him all his life are the consequence of a blood link to sixteenth-century clairvoyant Nostradamus. Paul represents one of two bloodlines descended from Nostradamus who appear to be trying to kill each other off, although the conduct of his overseers leads Paul to believe he is being prevented intentionally from uniting with his relatives.

**Other books you might like:**
Daphne Du Maurier, *"Don't Look Now"*, 1971
in *Not After Midnight*

## 3349

### ANDREW LAURANCE

## The Premonition

(New York: Diamond, 1991)

**Story type:** Horror (Wild Talents)
**Series:** Blood of Nostradamus Trilogy
**Major character(s):** Michael Dartson, Businessman; Melanie Forbes, Paranormal Investigator; Emma Dartson, Child (Michael's granddaughter)
**Time period(s):** 1970s (1979)
**Locale(s):** France; Europe

**Summary:** Originally published in England in 1979 as *Premonitions of an Inherited Mind*, this lackluster novel tells of Michael Dartson, and his discovery that he is a lineal descendant of the sixteenth century French clairvoyant Nostradamus. Michael travels across Europe refining his psychic powers and investigating his family history, unaware that his traveling companion, who is similarly psychically endowed, is engineering a fate for him forecast in Nostradamus's predictions centuries before.

**Other books you might like:**
Daphne Du Maurier, *"Don't Look Now"*, 1971
in *Not After Midnight*
Brian Lumley, *The Necroscope Series*, 1987-1991

## 3350

### ANDREW LAURANCE

## The Unborn

(New York: Diamond, 1991)

**Story type:** Horror (Wild Talents)
**Series:** Blood of Nostradamus Trilogy
**Major character(s):** Celina Bell, Young Woman; Melanie Forbes, Paranormal Investigator; Giacomo Capuela, Businessman
**Time period(s):** 1980s (1980)
**Locale(s):** London, England; Europe

**Summary:** The Blood of Nostradamus Trilogy comes to a conclusion with this novel originally published in England in 1980 as *The Embryo*. Celina Bell, yet another blood descendant of the 16th-century clairvoyant Nostradamus, finds herself in a tug-of-war between Melanie Forbes, mother of two psychic children who are Celina's distant blood relations, and a business cartel trying to use the children for its own ends. Celina has been charged with taking care of the children, whose union will produce a superpsychic child capable of taking over the world.

**Other books you might like:**
Daphne Du Maurier, *"Don't Look Now"*, 1971
in *Not After Midnight*

## 3351

### FRANK LAURIA

## Dark City

(New York: St. Martin's, 1998)

**Story type:** Horror (Science Fiction)
**Major character(s):** John Murdoch, Fugitive; D.P. Schreber, Doctor (psychiatrist); Frank Bumstead, Detective
**Time period(s):** 1990s (1998)
**Locale(s):** Alternate Earth

**Summary:** John Murdoch's special mental talents endow him with the ability to resist the Strangers, an alien race who fled their dying planet for Earth eons before. John's efforts to elude the Strangers brings him into contact with others who have discovered that reality is an experiment of the Strangers, who regularly alter human memories to study their impact on survival. Novelization of a screenplay by Alex Proyas, Lem Dobbs and Davis S. Proyer for a Lem Dobbs film.

**Other books you might like:**
Clive Barker, *The Hellbound Heart*, 1986
Philip K. Dick, *Ubik*, 1969
Robert A. Heinlein, *The Unpleasant Profession of Jonathan Hoag*, 1959
Fritz Leiber, *You Are All Alone*, 1954
Eric Frank Russell, *Sinister Barrier*, 1943

## 3352

### STEPHEN R. LAWHEAD

## *Arthur*

(Westchester: Crossway Books, 1989)

**Story type:** Fantasy (Legend)
**Series:** Pendragon Cycle
**Major character(s):** Arthur Pendragon, Ruler (Britain); Merlin, Sorcerer
**Time period(s):** Indeterminate Past
**Locale(s):** England

**Summary:** In this version, Arthur is an extremely Christian king, determined to usher out the old ways and the magic, even though the pulling of the sword from the stone gives him claim to the throne. Much of the book is about Arthur's struggles to unite the warring kingdoms of Britain.

**Other books you might like:**
Marion Zimmer Bradley, *The Mists of Avalon*, 1988
Parke Godwin, *Beloved Exile*, 1984
Nikolai Tolstoy, *The Coming of the King*, 1988
T.H. White, *The Once and Future King*, 1983

## 3353

### STEPHEN R. LAWHEAD

## *Byzantium*

(New York: HarperPrism, 1996)

**Story type:** Fantasy (Adventure)
**Major character(s):** Aidan mac Cainnech, Religious (monk), Linguist; Harold Bull-Roar, Ruler (King of the Danes), Adventurer; Gunnar, Warrior, Traveler
**Time period(s):** 10th century
**Locale(s):** Europe; Byzantium, Byzantium (Miklagard)

**Summary:** Assigned to join a group of Irish monks transporting a valuable copy of the *Book of Kells* to Byzantium, Aidan loses his freedom to a Viking raid. Accompanying King Harold Bull-Roar on a raid of Miklagard, Aidan uses his language skills to keep the group from disaster. When the warriors accept guard duty on a diplomatic mission, Aidan becomes the emperor's spy and continues experiencing turns of fate.

**Other books you might like:**
Frans G. Bengtsson, *The Long Ships*, 1954
Allan Cole, *The Far Kingdoms*, 1993
   Chris Bunch, co-author
Judith Tarr, *Spear of Heaven*, 1994
Harry Turtledove, *The Misplaced Legion*, 1987

## 3354

### STEPHEN R. LAWHEAD

## *The Endless Knot*

(Batavia, Illinois: Lion, 1993)

**Story type:** Fantasy (Adventure; Alternate World)
**Series:** Song of Albion
**Major character(s):** Llew Silver Hand, Royalty, Ruler (King of Albion); Scatha, Noblewoman; Paladyr, Nobleman, Outlaw
**Time period(s):** Indeterminate
**Locale(s):** Albion, Fictional Country; Oxford, England

**Summary:** In the Otherworld, thieves threaten Llew's hopes for happiness on his wedding night when they raid and burn his home. He must learn what it means to be a king if he wants to preserve his new kingdom against the threat of the Brazen Man.

**Other books you might like:**
Charles de Lint, *The Little Country*, 1991
Tom Deitz, *Windmaster's Bane*, 1986
Patricia Kennealy-Morrison, *The Copper Crown*, 1984
Morgan Llywelyn, *Bard: The Odyssey of the Irish*, 1984
Ian McDonald, *King of Morning, Queen of Day*, 1991

## 3355

### STEPHEN R. LAWHEAD

## *Grail*

(New York: Avon, 1997)

**Story type:** Fantasy (Legend; Political)
**Series:** Pendragon Cycle
**Major character(s):** Gwalchavad, Knight, Nobleman; Arthur, Royalty (king); Morgian, Royalty, Sorceress
**Time period(s):** Indeterminate Past
**Locale(s):** England

**Summary:** Healed at the edge of death by the Holy Grail, King Arthur pledges his renewed life to heal the injuries of Britain. When an agent of Morgian steals the Grail along with the Queen, Arthur and his knights must find the Grail, searching throughout Britain and other worlds to bring about the Golden Age.

**Other books you might like:**
Marion Zimmer Bradley, *The Mists of Avalon*, 1983
Bernard Cornwell, *The Winter King*, 1996
Anne Eliot Crompton, *Gawain and Lady Green*, 1997
Helen Hollick, *Shadow of the King*, 1997
Phyllis Ann Karr, *The Idylls of the Queen*, 1982

## 3356

### STEPHEN R. LAWHEAD

## *The Iron Lance*

(New York: Harper, 1998)

**Story type:** Fantasy (Quest; Historical)
**Major character(s):** Murdo Ranulfson, Traveler (pilgrim)
**Time period(s):** 11th century (1095)
**Locale(s):** Constantinople, Turkey; Jerusalem, Israel

**Summary:** Murdo watches over the family's interests while his father and brothers set off to fight in the Crusades. Avaricious members of the government and the clergy combine to deprive him of the family property, and eventually Murdo sets off on a personal pilgrimage that will result in a grand tour of the Mediterranean world and the discovery of a magical relic.

**Other books you might like:**
Gael Baudino, *Spires of Spirit*, 1997
Marion Zimmer Bradley, *The Firebrand*, 1987
David Drake, *Vettius and His Friends*, 1978
Guy Gavriel Kay, *The Lions of Al-Rassan*, 1995
Richard Monaco, *Parsifal*, 1978

## 3357

### STEPHEN R. LAWHEAD

## *Pendragon*

(New York: William Morrow, 1994)

**Story type:** Fantasy (Political; Religious)
**Series:** Pendragon Cycle
**Major character(s):** Arthur, Ruler (King of the Britons); Amilcar, Military Personnel (Vandal warleader); Gwenhwyvar, Ruler (Queen of the Britons)
**Time period(s):** 6th century
**Locale(s):** Kingdom of Summer, Fictional Country; Wales; England

**Summary:** After triumphs and setbacks in the previous novels, Arthur's kingdom faces barbarian invaders who may well overwhelm it. Lawhead uses Cymric history and Christian imagery to retell one of the most famous Western myths.

**Other books you might like:**
Marion Zimmer Bradley, *The Mists of Avalon*, 1983
Tom Deitz, *Windmaster's Bane*, 1986
Guy Gavriel Kay, *The Summer Tree*, 1985
Patricia Kennealy-Morrison, *The Copper Crown*, 1984
Ian McDonald, *King of Morning, Queen of Day*, 1991

## 3358

### STEPHEN R. LAWHEAD

## *The Silver Hand*

(Batavia, Illinois: Lion Publishing, 1992)

**Story type:** Fantasy (Legend; Adventure)
**Series:** Song of Albion
**Major character(s):** Llew Silver Hand, Royalty, Warrior; Meldron, Royalty; Tegrid, Minstrel (bard)
**Time period(s):** Indeterminate Past
**Locale(s):** Pyrdain, Fictional Country

**Summary:** After the death of King Meldryn Mawr, Prince Meldron usurps the throne spurred on by Siawn Hy and backed by fierce warriors, the Wolf Pack. Llew, the true heir to the throne, leads a rebellion which will not succeed without the support of the Great Bard who alone may grant sovereignty.

**Other books you might like:**
John Desjarlais, *The Throne of Tara*, 1990
Kenneth C. Flint, *Riders of the Sidhe*, 1984
Casey Flynn, *The Enchanted Isles*, 1991
Casey Flynn, *Most Ancient Song*, 1991
Patricia Kennealy-Morrison, *The Copper Crown*, 1984
Morgan Llywelyn, *Bard: The Odyssey of the Irish*, 1984
Michael Moorcock, *The Swords Trilogy*, 1977
Andrew J. Offutt, *Sword of the Gael*, 1975
Keith Taylor, *Bard*, 1981

## 3359

### LOUISE LAWRENCE

## *Dream-Weaver*

(New York: Clarion Books, 1996)

**Story type:** Science Fiction (Young Adult; First Contact)
**Major character(s):** Troy Morrison, Teenager, Spaceman; Eth, Alien, Psychic (dreamweaver); Nemony, Alien, Psychic (dreamweaver)
**Time period(s):** 21st century

**Locale(s):** *Exodus 27*, Spaceship; Arbroth, Planet—Imaginary; Malroth, Planet—Imaginary

**Summary:** Although only a child, Eth consents to joining the Dream-Weavers Guild after feeling the death of the 3000 colonists heading from Earth to her planet, Arbroth, expecting to enslave the natives as a labor force. Troy mentally calls out on his six month awake shift, four years out on the seven year journey. Now a Dreamweaver, Eth again visits Troy, both realizing their potential danger at arrival, with only a slim chance for the colonists' ultimate survival and the potential benefits to all.

**Other books you might like:**
David Brin, *Brightness Reef*, 1995
John M. Ford, *Growing Up Weightless*, 1993
Alan Dean Foster, *The Tar-Aiym Krang*, 1972
Anne McCaffrey, *Powers That Be*, 1993
   Elizabeth Ann Scarborough, co-author
James H. Schmitz, *The Universe Against Her*, 1964

## 3360

### MARGERY LAWRENCE

## *Nights of the Round Table*

(Ashcroft, B.C.: Ash-Tree Press, 1998)

**Story type:** Horror (Collection)

**Summary:** Twelve tales of the supernatural, presented as one year of stories told at the monthly gathering of the Round Table, an exclusive supper club that convenes at the home of Frank Saunderson. Selections include "Vlasto's Doll," in which it is revealed that a stage magician's living dummy is a doll animated by the discorporate personality of his wife; "The Fifteenth Green," about the strange events that occur at a golf course built on the land of a man unjustly evicted from his home; and "Morag-of-the-Cave," in which a young woman's intense attraction to the sea leads to her ghastly tryst with a sea monster. Reprint of an obscure 1926 volume, edited by Richard Dalby.

**Other books you might like:**
Cynthia Asquith, *This Mortal Coil*, 1947
Christopher Blayre, *The Strange Papers of Dr. Blayre*, 1932
Elizabeth Bowen, *The Cat Jumps and Other Stories*, 1934
Marjorie Bowen, *Kecksies and Other Twilight Tales*, 1976
Walter de la Mare, *The Riddle and Other Stories*, 1923

## 3361

### JAY B. LAWS

## *Steam*

(Boston: Alyson, 1991)

**Story type:** Horror (Erotic Horror)
**Major character(s):** David Walker, Writer; Bobby, Office Worker; Mick, Office Worker
**Time period(s):** 1990s
**Locale(s):** San Francisco, California

**Summary:** In AIDS-ravaged San Francisco a horrible specter who calls himself Victor stalks the gay community, preying upon his victims' fears and enticing them with inevitably lethal promises of empowerment and sexual fulfillment that their conservatively altered lifestyles can no longer provide. This metaphoric rendering of the horrors of the AIDS epidemic is the author's first book.

**Other books you might like:**
Michael Crichton, *The Andromeda Strain*, 1969
Richard Matheson, *I Am Legend*, 1954

Ray Russell, *Incubus*, 1976

## 3362
### JAY B. LAWS
## *The Unfinished*
(Boston: Alyson, 1993)

**Story type:** Horror (Occult)
**Major character(s):** Jiggs Martin, Cook; Sam, Mechanic; Brent, Travel Agent
**Time period(s):** 1990s (1993)
**Locale(s):** San Francisco, California

**Summary:** An eye operation renders Jiggs Martin able to see supernatural manifestations of "the Unfinished," souls in the afterlife who died before they could fulfill their life's purpose. Jiggs is enjoined to record their sad stories, including the tale of a gay man killed during a lover's tryst and the story of an HIV-positive man who makes a terrible bargain with the forces of evil to stave off the ravaging effects of his disease. Published posthumously.

**Other books you might like:**
Clive Barker, *Books of Blood Series*, 1984-1985
John Skipp, *Dead Lines*, 1989
    Craig Spector, co-author
William T. Vollmann, *Whores for Gloria*, 1992

## 3363
### STEPHEN LAWS
### MARK MORRIS, Illustrator
### FRANK SMITH, Illustrator
## *Voyages into Darkness*
(Philadelphia: Bump in the Night Books)

**Story type:** Horror (Anthology)

**Summary:** This chapbook includes five stories by two British authors, both of whom are better known as novelists. Laws's "Pot Luck," a whimsical fantasy of a telepathic crab, is original to the volume. His "The Secret" and "Guilty Party" are both about characters pursued by monsters that may or may not be figments of their imaginations. Morris's "Warts and All" chronicles the gruesome fate of a farming family besieged by a strange fungus, while "The Fertilizer Man" tells of a new gardening product that yields an unusual crop. The book has an introduction by Gary Potter.

**Other books you might like:**
George R.R. Martin, *Night Visions 3*, 1986
    Paul Mikel, co-editor
Nicholas Royle, *Darklands*, 1991
    editor
Lucius Shepard, *Nantucket Slayrides*,
    Robert Frazier, co-author

## 3364
### RICHARD LAYMON
## *Beast House*
(Abingdon, Maryland: Cemetery Dance Publications, 1998)

**Story type:** Horror (Mystery)
**Major character(s):** Janice Crogan, Young Woman; Gorman Hardy, Writer
**Time period(s):** 1980s
**Locale(s):** Malcasa Point, California

**Summary:** Janice Crogan approaches hack writer Gorman Hardy with the story of the Beast House, whose true history she found in the diary of the sole survivor of the original Beast House attacks of 1903. Hardy hopes to usurp her rights to the story by traveling to the Beast House himself, unaware that the monster inhabiting the house is still very much alive. Second novel in a trilogy after *The Cellar*.

**Other books you might like:**
Clive Barker, *The Hellbound Heart*, 1991
Poppy Z. Brite, *Drawing Blood*, 1993
Matthew J. Costello, *The Seventh Guest*, 1995
Melisand March, *The Site*, 1989
T. Chris Martindale, *The Voice in the Basement*, 1993

## 3365
### RICHARD LAYMON
## *The Cellar*
(Baltimore: CD Publications, 1997)

**Story type:** Horror (Mystery)
**Major character(s):** Donna Hayes, Travel Agent; Roy Hayes, Criminal; Judgement Rucker, Hunter
**Time period(s):** 1980s
**Locale(s):** Malcasa Point, California

**Summary:** Newly released from prison, Roy Hayes cuts a swath of murder and destruction in pursuit of his wife, Donna, who testified against him in a rape case. Roy tracks Donna to Malcasa Point and corners her in the Beast House, a tourist attraction where more than a dozen people have died over the century, purportedly at the hands of a supernatural fiend known as The Beast. Deluxe hardcover edition of a novel published as a paperback original in 1980.

**Other books you might like:**
Rick Hautala, *Ghost Light*, 1993
Ruby Jean Jensen, *Celia*, 1991
Stephen King, *Rose Madder*, 1995
Dean R. Koontz, *Shadowfires*, 1987

## 3366
### RICHARD LAYMON
## *Funland*
(New York: NAL Onyx, 1990)

**Major character(s):** Dave Carson, Police Officer; Joan Delaney, Police Officer (Dave's partner)
**Time period(s):** 1980s
**Locale(s):** Boleta Bay, California (A northern California beach town)

**Summary:** The mixture at the Funland Amusement Park of "Trolls"—homeless derelicts, "Trollers"—teenagers who prey upon them, and the abandoned, but sinister Jasper Dunn Funhouse and Freak Show provokes continuing, intensifying violence that culminates in an explosion of chaos and gore.

**Other books you might like:**
William W. Johnstone, *Carnival*, 1989
Dean R. Koontz, *Twilight Eyes*, 1987

## 3367

### RICHARD LAYMON

## A Good, Secret Place

(San Jose, California: Deadline Press, 1993)

**Story type:** Horror (Collection)

**Summary:** This book collects 20 stories—15 reprints and five originals—from one of the more infamous writers of graphic modern horror. Most fall within the realm of dark suspense, and touch upon themes of poetic justice ("Desert Pickup," "Roadside Pickup," "Oscar's Audition") and the battle between the sexes ("A Good Cigar Is a Smoke," "Joyce"). The handful of overtly supernatural stories includes "Barney's Bigfoot Museum," which tackles the legend of the sasquatch; "The Grab," about a peculiar game played in a barroom; and "Stickman," in which the monster of a rural folk tale comes to life. Ed Gorman wrote the introduction.

**Other books you might like:**
Ed Gorman, *Prisoners and Other Stories*, 1992
Joe R. Lansdale, *By Bizarre Hands*, 1992
Edward Lee, *Edward Lee's Quest for Sex, Truth and Reality*, 1992
Brian Lumley, *Fruiting Bodies and Other Fungi*, 1993
Lucy Taylor, *Close to the Bone*, 1993

## 3368

### RICHARD LAYMON

## The Midnight Tour

(Abingdon, Maryland: Cemetery Dance Publications, 1998)

**Story type:** Horror (Mystery)
**Major character(s):** Dana Lake, Tour Guide; Lynn Tucker, Tour Guide; Sandy Blume, Tour Guide
**Time period(s):** 1990s (1998); 1980s (1980)
**Locale(s):** Malcasa Point, California

**Summary:** The Beast House, a tourist spot periodically visited by a semi-human predator with insatiable lusts and appetites, attracts a broad cross section of visitors from around the country. This third book in the trilogy begun with *The Cellar* (1979) and *Beast House* (1986) tells the story of how the Saturday midnight tour, which takes clients through the parts of the house the beast is more likely to visit, came into being.

**Other books you might like:**
Clive Barker, *The Hellbound Heart*, 1991
Poppy Z. Brite, *Drawing Blood*, 1993
Matthew J. Costello, *The Seventh Guest*, 1995
Ruby Jean Jensen, *The Haunting*, 1994
Tamara Thorne, *Haunted*, 1995

## 3369

### RICHARD LAYMON

## Midnight's Lair

(New York: St. Martin's, 1993)

**Story type:** Horror (Mystery)
**Major character(s):** Darcy Raines, Tour Guide; Kyle Mordock, Teenager; Greg Beaumont, Lawyer
**Time period(s):** 1980s
**Locale(s):** Mordock Caves, Southwest

**Summary:** Darcy Raines tries valiantly to bring her tour group back up from the underground lake of Mordock Caves when a disaster above-ground blocks off the usual avenues of escape, but her efforts are complicated by the presence of psychotic Kyle Mordock, who has been driven to a murderous frenzy through his sexual longing for her, and by a race of cannibal cave dwellers. This book was originally published in England in 1988 under the pseudonym Richard Kelly.

**Other books you might like:**
Leigh Clark, *The Feeding*, 1992
Jack Ketchum, *Offspring*, 1991

## 3370

### RICHARD LAYMON

## Quake

(New York: St. Martin's, 1994)

**Story type:** Horror (Psychological Suspense)
**Major character(s):** Stanley Banks, Secretary (former); Clint Banner, Lawyer; Emerald O'Hara, Teenager (13-year-old)
**Time period(s):** 1990s (1995)
**Locale(s):** Los Angeles, California

**Summary:** Natural disasters bring out the worst of humanity in this tale where looters, rapists and rioters use a major earthquake that devastates Los Angeles as an excuse to go on a rampage. One of the major malefactors is psychopath Stanley Banks who, after killing his domineering mother, decides to terrorize next-door neighbor Sheila Banner, while Sheila's husband Clint, unaware of her predicament, simply struggles to get back home to her.

**Other books you might like:**
James Herbert, *The Dark*, 1980
James Herbert, *The Fog*, 1975
Stephen King, *The Stand*, 1978
Peter Straub, *Floating Dragon*, 1982

## 3371

### RICHARD LAYMON

## Resurrection Dreams

(New York: NAL Onyx, 1989)

**Story type:** Horror (Black Magic)
**Major character(s):** Vicki Chandler, Doctor; Melvin Dobbs, Magician (Black magician)
**Time period(s):** 1980s
**Locale(s):** Ellsworth

**Summary:** Having completed medical school, Vicki Chandler returns to her hometown to set up practice. She encounters a town full of zombies, resurrected and directed by black magician Melvin Dobbs, formerly a high school misfit. Even worse, she learns that she is the primary object of Melvin's desires.

**Other books you might like:**
William W. Johnstone, *Cat's Eye*, 1989

## 3372

### RICHARD LAYMON

## The Stake

(New York: St. Martin's, 1991)

**Story type:** Horror (Vampire Story)

**Major character(s):** Larry Dunbar, Writer (horror writer); Lane Dunbar, Teenager (Larry's daughter); Bonnie Saxon, Teenager (dead, but very attractive)
**Time period(s):** 1990s
**Locale(s):** Sagebrush Flats, Arizona

**Summary:** Larry Dunbar's mild case of writer's block is momentarily alleviated when he and his friends uncover the body of a teenage girl with a stake driven through her heart in an Arizona ghost town. As Larry's obsession to determine the corpse's identity and write a story about her grows, he senses her vampiric hold upon him.

**Other books you might like:**
Ron Dee, *Blood Lust*, 1990
Ron Dee, *Dusk*, 1991

---

**3373**
### RICHARD LAYMON

## The Wilds
(Abingdon, Maryland: Cemetery Dance Publications, 1998)

**Story type:** Horror (Psychological Suspense)
**Major character(s):** Ned Champion, Student; Gloria, Young Woman; Susie, Young Woman
**Time period(s):** 1990s (1998)
**Locale(s):** Lost River Wilderness Area, California

**Summary:** Repressed and sexually frustrated, Ned Champion takes a short camping trip which turns into a prolonged sojourn in the wilderness that allows him to indulge his unspoken urges uninhibitedly. Ned's near-primitive regression leads him into a variety of strange and deadly encounters with fellow campers and backpackers in the wilds.

**Other books you might like:**
Stephen Gregory, *The Woodwitch*, 1989
Edward Lee, *The Bighead*, 1998
Robert D. Lee, *The Keeper*, 1993
Robert R. McCammon, *Gone South*, 1992
Lucy Taylor, *Spree*, 1998

---

**3374**
### GENE LAZUTA

## Bleeder
(New York: Diamond, 1991)

**Story type:** Horror (Serial Killer)
**Major character(s):** Nick Severanko, Writer; Reed Collings, Editor; Nasty Andrew, Serial Killer
**Time period(s):** 1990s
**Locale(s):** Cleveland, Ohio

**Summary:** Nick Severanko keeps a healthy separation between his daytime work as a writer for a trade magazine and evenings spent writing fiction about characters from a dark and horrific realm he calls "The Shadow Land." That is, until the day his serial killer Nasty Andrew decides to cross over into real life, bringing a bit of the Shadow Land with him in his bloody quest to locate his creator.

**Other books you might like:**
Stephen King, *The Dark Half*, 1987
John R. Maxim, *Abel/Baker/Charley*, 1983

---

**3375**
### GENE LAZUTA

## Forget Me Not
(New York: Diamond, 1992)

**Story type:** Horror (Serial Killer)
**Major character(s):** Jessie Reynolds, Young Woman; Henry Parks, Detective (former); Wilson Ellis, Detective—Private
**Time period(s):** 1990s (1992)
**Locale(s):** Cleveland, Ohio

**Summary:** Jessie Reynolds has mercifully forgotten the night twenty years ago when her immediate family was slaughtered and the murderer escaped the police. But with the murderer still on the rampage some three-score deaths later, Jessie is forced to confront truths buried in her subconscious not only about the murderer's identity, but about dark secrets kept by her extended family.

**Other books you might like:**
Orson Scott Card, *Lost Boys*, 1992
Matthew J. Costello, *Homecoming*, 1992
Samuel M. Key, *From a Whisper to a Scream*, 1992
Whitley Strieber, *Billy*, 1989

---

**3376**
### GENE LAZUTA

## Vyrmin
(New York: Diamond, 1992)

**Story type:** Horror (Werewolf Story)
**Major character(s):** H.W. Conway, Police Officer (sheriff); Michael Conway, Detective—Police; Robert Norris, Ranger (park ranger)
**Time period(s):** 1990s
**Locale(s):** Harpersville, Ohio

**Summary:** The appearance of The Man in the Woods in the small German community of Harpersville rekindles interest in ancient legends of the Vyrmin, people who have more evil than good in their souls and who transform into wolves. The human and animal deaths that follow shortly thereafter portend the naming of a new Blood Prince destined to lead the Vyrmin on a bloody rampage.

**Other books you might like:**
Gary Brandner, *The Howling*, 1979
Crosland Brown, *Tombley's Walk*, 1991
Geoffrey Caine, *Wake of the Werewolf*, 1991
Whitley Strieber, *The Wolfen*, 1978

---

**3377**
### URSULA K. LE GUIN

## Catwings
(New York: Orchard Books, 1988)

**Story type:** Fantasy (Adventure)
**Major character(s):** Jane Tabby, Animal (Kitten)
**Time period(s):** Indeterminate
**Locale(s):** Alternate Earth

**Summary:** Four kittens are born with wings and set out to find a place for themselves in the world.

**Other books you might like:**
Jan Brett, *The First Dog*, 1988
Jane Chelsea, *Winter Harvest*, 1988

Jack Dann, *Magicats!*, 1984
　Gardner Dozois, co-author
Terry Denton, *Felix and Alexander*, 1988
James Herriot, *Blossom Comes Home*, 1988
Andre Norton, *Catfantastic*, 1989
Michael Peak, *Cat House*, 1989
Susan Price, *The Ghost Drum: A Cat's Tale*, 1987
Tad Williams, *Tailchaser's Song*, 1985

## 3378
### URSULA K. LE GUIN

## Fish Soup
(New York: Atheneum, 1992)

**Story type:** Fantasy (Young Adult; Contemporary)
**Major character(s):** Writing Woman of Maho, Writer, Landowner; Thinking Man of Moha, Landowner
**Time period(s):** Indeterminate
**Locale(s):** Maho, Mythical Place; Moha, Mythical Place

**Summary:** When Writing Woman of Maho and Thinking Man of Moha wish for a child to transport messages and fish for meals for them, a pair of children suddenly come into their lives. When neither child achieves the hopes expressed by Writing Woman of Maho and Thinking Man of Moha, the adults rethink their expectations of the helpers and achieve an improved interrelationship.

**Other books you might like:**
Bruce Coville, *Jennifer Murdley's Toad*, 1992
Bruce Coville, *Jeremy Thatcher, Dragon Hatcher*, 1992
Garry Kilworth, *The Foxes of Firstdark*, 1990
Robin Morgan, *The Mer-Child: A Legend for Children and Other Adults*, 1991
Antoine de Saint-Exupery, *The Little Prince*, 1943

## 3379
### URSULA K. LE GUIN

## A Fisherman of the Inland Sea
(New York: HarperPrism, 1994)

**Story type:** Science Fiction (Collection)
**Time period(s):** Indeterminate Future

**Summary:** Contains an original introduction with a definition of science fiction and comments on the eight stories copyrighted 1983-1994 from periodicals and anthologies. Humor permeates several stories with themes including a time paradox, development of faster than light communication and "Churten" theory and an overall fascination with personal relationships.

**Other books you might like:**
Nancy Kress, *The Aliens of Earth*, 1993
Pat Murphy, *Points of Departure*, 1990
James Tiptree Jr., *Her Smoke Rose Up Forever*, 1990
Kate Wilhelm, *And the Angels Sing*, 1992
Gene Wolfe, *Endangered Species*, 1989

## 3380
### URSULA K. LE GUIN

## Four Ways to Forgiveness
(New York: HarperPrism, 1995)

**Story type:** Science Fiction (Political; Science Fiction)

**Series:** Hain
**Major character(s):** Yehedarhed Havzhiva, Diplomat (Hainish ambassador); Radosse Rakam, Teacher, Slave (former)
**Time period(s):** Indeterminate Future
**Locale(s):** Hain, Planet—Imaginary; Werel, Planet—Imaginary; Yeowe, Planet—Imaginary

**Summary:** Havzhiva comes to an epistemological epiphany after the women of Yeowe send a representative to create an alliance with the Ekumen, although Yeowe already belongs to the Ekumen of Worlds. Unaffected by the War of Liberation which benefited male "assets," women of Yeowe and Werel have not achieved freedom. After he decides to stay and help effect change, Havzhiva meets Rakam, a political activist accustomed to the struggle involved in translating freedom on paper to freedom in the world.

**Other books you might like:**
Eleanor Arnason, *Ring of Swords*, 1993
David Brin, *Glory Season*, 1993
Octavia E. Butler, *Parable of the Sower*, 1993
Samuel R. Delany, *They Fly at Ciron*, 1993
Kim Stanley Robinson, *Green Mars*, 1994

## 3381
### URSULA K. LE GUIN, Editor
### BRIAN ATTEBERY, Co-Editor

## The Norton Book of Science Fiction: North American Science Fiction, 1960-1990
(New York: Norton, 1993)

**Story type:** Science Fiction (Science Fiction; Anthology)

**Summary:** This volume contains a 28-page introduction by Le Guin, 11 pages of notes about the authors, plus 67 stories written in English, arranged chronologically, and selected by the editors and Karen Joy Fowler as examples of excellent stories as well as superlative science fiction from a mature genre. Authors include Poul Anderson, Margaret Atwood, Michael Bishop, Octavia E. Butler, Pat Cadigan, Orson Scott Card, Philip K. Dick, Suzette Haden Elgin, Harlan Ellison, Damon Knight, Nancy Kress, R.A. Lafferty, Katherine MacLean, Barry Malzberg, Vonda N. McIntyre, Pat Murphy, Frederik Pohl, Mike Resnick, Kim Stanley Robinson, Michael Swanwick, Kate Wilhelm, Connie Willis, Gene Wolfe and Roger Zelazny. Educator's study guide available.

**Other books you might like:**
Gardner Dozois, *Modern Classic Short Novels of Science Fiction*, 1994
　editor
Gardner Dozois, *Modern Classics of Science Fiction*, 1992
　editor
David G. Hartwell, *The World Treasury of Science Fiction*, 1989
　editor
Raymond J. Healy, *Adventures in Time and Space*, 1946
　J. Francis McComas, co-editor
Tom Shippey, *The Oxford Book of Science Fiction Stories*, 1992
　editor
Robert Silverberg, *The Science Fiction Hall of Fame, Volume 1*, 1970
　editor

**3382**

## URSULA K. LE GUIN

### A Ride on the Red Mare's Back

(New York: Orchard Books, 1992)

**Story type:** Fantasy (Quest; Young Adult)
**Major character(s):** The Girl, Child; The Red Mare, Mythical Creature, Animal; The Troll, Mythical Creature
**Time period(s):** Indeterminate Past
**Locale(s):** Scandinavia

**Summary:** Equipped with only a little bread, a scarf and her wooden horse, a girl sets out after her brother when trolls steal him away. Through adventures and finding her brother changing into a troll, the lessons she learns as she travels with the red mare help her grow as an individual. Illustrated by Julie Downing.

**Other books you might like:**
Verna Aardema, *Why Mosquitoes Buzz in People's Ears*, 1975
James Gurney, *Dinotopia*, 1992
Chris Van Allsburg, *Two Bad Ants*, 1988
Nancy Willard, *Pish, Posh, Said Hieronymus Bosch*, 1991
Jane Yolen, *The Dragon's Boy*, 1990
Jane Yolen, *Sky Dogs*, 1990
Roger Zelazny, *Way Up High*, 1992

**3383**

## URSULA K. LE GUIN

### Tehanu: The Last Book of Earthsea

(New York: Atheneum, 1990)

**Story type:** Fantasy (Quest)
**Series:** Earthsea
**Major character(s):** Tenar, Widow(er) (aging), Religious (former priestess); Therru, Handicapped (crippled), Abuse Victim (child abuse)
**Time period(s):** Indeterminate
**Locale(s):** Planet—Imaginary

**Summary:** Both Ged, having lost his powers, and Therru, abused by her parents, seek refuge with the former priestess Tenar. Evil threatens and it is Therru, holding unusual power born of her kinship with dragons, who repels it. This story is a continuation of Le Guin's earlier Earthsea books.

**Other books you might like:**
Joy Chant, *Red Moon and Black Mountain*, 1970
Elizabeth Cleghorn Gaskell, *Cranford*, 1976
Jackie Hyman, *Shadowlight*, 1989
Mercedes Lackey, *Magic's Pawn*, 1989
   The Last Herald Mage. Vol. 1

**3384**

## URSULA K. LE GUIN

### Unlocking the Air and Other Stories

(New York: HarperCollins, 1996)

**Story type:** Fantasy (Collection; Contemporary Realism)

**Summary:** Contains one original, 16 stories reprinted from periodicals and anthologies 1982-1995, and one broadcast on ''The Sound of Writing'' in 1995. With realistic settings, the stories frequently reflect magic realism or surrealism.

**Other books you might like:**
Margaret Atwood, *Good Bones and Simple Murders*, 1994
Octavia E. Butler, *Bloodchild and Other Stories*, 1995
Nancy Kress, *The Aliens of Earth*, 1993
Pat Murphy, *Points of Departure*, 1990
Rebecca Ore, *Alien Bootlegger and Other Stories*, 1993
L.A. Taylor, *Women's Work*, 1995
Connie Willis, *Impossible Things*, 1994

**3385**

## ADAM LEE (Pseudonym of A.A. Attanasio)

### The Dark Shore

(New York: Avon, 1997)

**Story type:** Fantasy (Magic Conflict)
**Series:** Dominions of Irth
**Major character(s):** Drev, Ruler (wizarduke), Wizard; Tywi, Orphan; Dogbrick, Thief, Philosopher
**Time period(s):** Indeterminate Past
**Locale(s):** Irth, Fictional Country; Arwar Odawl, Fictional City

**Summary:** Cursed to the Dark Shore, Wrat, a failed revolutionary, becomes the horrific Hu'dre Vra and launches a second war against his home. At first successful, his enemies dying by the thousands, Wrat fails to kill Wizarduke Drev who gathers his forces to counterattack. Either life or anti-life may win the war for Irth.

**Other books you might like:**
Eleanor Arnason, *The Sword Smith*, 1978
A.A. Attanasio, *Kingdom of the Grail*, 1992
A.A. Attanasio, *The Moon's Wife: A Hystery*, 1993
Glen Cook, *The Swordbearer*, 1982
Robin Hobb, *Assassin's Apprentice*, 1995
Robert Silverberg, *Lord Valentine's Castle*, 1980
Janny Wurts, *Stormwarden*, 1984

**3386**

## ADAM LEE (Pseudonym of A.A. Attanasio)

### The Shadow Eater

(New York: Avon Eos, 1998)

**Story type:** Fantasy (Magic Conflict; Quest)
**Series:** Dominions of Irth
**Major character(s):** Old Ric, Mythical Creature (gnome), Reanimated Dead; Asofel, Angel; Lara, Spirit, Witch
**Time period(s):** 1990s
**Locale(s):** New York, New York; Irth, Planet—Imaginary

**Summary:** The Lady of the Garden created the universe for the benefit of her unborn child, but something in that universe threatens her baby. She sends Old Ric, a tired and worn-out gnome, to find the source of the threat and destroy it. If the feeble gnome can't save the baby, the Lady will wake the child's father who will solve the problem by destroying everything.

**Other books you might like:**
Eleanor Arnason, *Daughter of the Bear King*, 1987
A.A. Attanasio, *Arthur*, 1995
A.A. Attanasio, *Kingdom of the Grail*, 1992
A.A. Attanasio, *The Moon's Wife: A Hystery*, 1993
A.A. Attanasio, *Wyvern*, 1988
Barbara Hambly, *The Time of the Dark*, 1982
Philip Pullman, *The Golden Compass*, 1996
Robert Silverberg, *Lord Valentine's Castle*, 1980
Roger Zelazny, *Nine Princes in Amber*, 1970

## 3387

**EDWARD LEE** (Pseudonym of L. Edward Seymour)

### The Bighead

(Orlando Florida: Necro Publications, 1997)

**Story type:** Horror (Mystery)
**Major character(s):** Jerrica Perry, Journalist; Charity Walsh, Student; Father Alexander, Religious (priest)
**Time period(s):** 1990s (1997)
**Locale(s):** Luntville, Virginia

**Summary:** The reopening of Wroxeter Abbey, a property of the Catholic church in rural Virginia, piques the interest of journalist Jerrica Perry, who hopes to write an investigative story on its scandalous past. Meanwhile, the Bighead, a congenitally deformed young man whose birth is intimately tied to the Abbey's secret past, embarks on a horrible rampage of rape and murder that only taints the Abbey's reputation further.

**Other books you might like:**
Jack Ketchum, *Off Season*, 1981
Jack Ketchum, *Offspring*, 1989
Richard Kinion, *Sacrifice*, 1995
Richard Laymon, *The Woods Are Dark*, 1981
Robert D. Lee, *The Keeper*, 1993

## 3388

**EDWARD LEE**
**JOHN PELAN**, Co-Author

### The Case of the Police Officer's Cock Ring and the Piano Player Who Had No Fingers

(Clay, New York: Dark Raptor Press, 1997)

**Story type:** Horror (Werewolf Story)
**Major character(s):** Richard Kinion, Police Officer; Micah Hays, Police Officer; Luger Roo, Farmer, Werewolf
**Time period(s):** 1990s (1997)
**Locale(s):** Luntville, Virginia

**Summary:** Richard Kinion answers a call for police help and finds himself face-to-face with a werewolf. Assistant Micah Hays fortunately finds an ingenious means of implanting lethal silver in the werewolf's body. A signed limited edition chapbook.

**Other books you might like:**
Edward Bryant, *Aqua Sancta*, 1994
Ron Dee, *Sex and Blood*, 1994
Nancy Kilpatrick, *Sex and the Single Vampire*, 1994

## 3389

**EDWARD LEE**

### The Chosen

(New York: Zebra, 1993)

**Story type:** Horror (Black Magic)
**Major character(s):** Vera Abbott, Restaurateur; Paul Kirby, Journalist; Feldspar, Businessman
**Time period(s):** 1990s (1993)
**Locale(s):** Waynesville, South

**Summary:** Vera Abbott agrees to manage the Carriage House, the restaurant of an inn made out of the renovated insane asylum

Wroxton Hall. Upon assuming her new job, however, she finds that the asylum's grisly legacy of torturing inmates to death has been perpetuated through cultists who use the inn as a meeting place for their unholy rituals.

**Other books you might like:**
Elizabeth Ergas, *Devil's Gate*, 1991
John Gideon, *Greely's Cove*, 1990
Adrian Savage, *Symphony*, 1992
J.N. Williamson, *The Monastery*, 1992

## 3390

**EDWARD LEE**

### Coven

(New York: Charter/Diamond, 1991)

**Story type:** Horror (Black Magic)
**Major character(s):** Wade St. John, Student; Dudley J. Besser, Professor (head of biology department)
**Time period(s):** 1990s
**Locale(s):** Exuam College, South

**Summary:** An outbreak of witchcraft enlivens the summer session at Exham College, an elite southern private school for the rich and stupid.

**Other books you might like:**
Fritz Leiber, *Conjure Wife*, 1953
Manly Wade Wellman, *The School of Darkness*, 1985

## 3391

**EDWARD LEE**

### Creekers

(New York: Zebra, 1994)

**Story type:** Horror (Mystery)
**Major character(s):** Phil Straker, Police Officer (narcotics agent); Lawrence Mullins, Police Officer; Cody Natter, Drug Dealer
**Time period(s):** 1990s (1994)
**Locale(s):** Crick City, Midwest

**Summary:** Lured back to his home town following his humiliating demotion after a drug bust gone bad, former narcotics agent Phil Straker begins investigating Cody Natter, a drug local kingpin who manufactures PCP. Straker soon finds that Natter is also in league with inbred residents known as the Creekers, who subject abducted women to a variety of grotesque perversions as offerings to a strange being they worship.

**Other books you might like:**
John Driver, *The Hunger of the Beast*, 1991
Jack Ketchum, *Off Season*, 1980
Jack Ketchum, *Offspring*, 1991
Robert D. Lee, *The Keeper*, 1993

## 3392

**EDWARD LEE**
**JOHN PELAN**, Illustrator
**ALAN CLARK**, Illustrator

### Goon

(Orlando, Florida: Necro Publications, 1996)

**Story type:** Horror (Black Magic)

**Major character(s):** Phillip Straker, Detective; Melinda Pierce, Journalist; Goon, Sports Figure (professional wrestler)
**Time period(s):** 1990s (1996)
**Locale(s):** Luntville, Virginia

**Summary:** To solve the mystery of a string of gruesome sex crimes connected with the professional wrestling circuit, detective Phillip Straker joins forces with Melinda Pierce, a self-described investigative journalist, and infiltrates the Deep South Wrestling Conference. His investigations take him into a world of kinky sex, violent perversions, and satanic bargains that make it hard for him to separate the good guys from the bad guys. This sexually-explicit novella-length chapbook, a first collaboration for both writers, carries an introduction by T. Winter-Damon.

**Other books you might like:**
Michael Hemmingson, *Nice Little Stories Jam-Packed with Depraved Sex and Violence*, 1995
Thom Metzger, *Big Gurl*, 1989
Rex Miller, *Slob*, 1987
Lucy Taylor, *Unnatural Acts and Other Stories*, 1994

---

**3393**
**EDWARD LEE**
**KEITH PETERS**, Illustrator

## Header

(Orlando, Florida: Necro Publications, 1995)

**Story type:** Horror (Psychological Suspense)
**Major character(s):** Stewart Cummings, Police Officer (ATF agent); Travis Clyde Tuckton, Convict (ex-convict); Grandpap Tuckton, Aged Person
**Time period(s):** 1990s (1995)
**Locale(s):** Lewisburg, Virginia

**Summary:** While scamming money from drug dealers in the backwoods of Virginia to pay for his wife's narcotics habit, Special Agent Stewart Cummings steps into the middle of a vendetta fought amongst the locals, and involving a gruesome type of revenge perpetrated upon the women of the families at war. This novella of explicit sex and violence was published as a signed limited edition chapbook. Lucy Taylor supplies an introduction and Keith Peters the black-and-white interior illustrations.

**Other books you might like:**
Poppy Z. Brite, *Swamp Foetus*, 1993
Ron Dee, *Sex and Blood*, 1994
Michael Hemmingson, *Nice Little Stories Jam-Packed with Depraved Sex and Violence*, 1995
Lucy Taylor, *Close to the Bone*, 1993
Lucy Taylor, *The Flesh Artist*, 1994

---

**3394**
**EDWARD LEE**

## Incubi

(New York: Diamond, 1991)

**Story type:** Horror (Occult)
**Major character(s):** Jack Cordesman, Detective—Police; Veronica Polk, Artist; Erim Khoronos, Wealthy (millionaire)
**Time period(s):** 1980s (1988)
**Locale(s):** Washington, District of Columbia

**Summary:** A rash of crimes of passion in which artistically inclined women are found mutilated and sexually violated by a creature with seemingly unnatural abilities leads detective Jack Cordesman to wonder if the perpetrator is a sexually predatory incubus—and whether there is any connection between the murders and the mysterious art enthusiast who has invited his girlfriend to a suburban retreat to put her in touch with her deeper artistic passions.

**Other books you might like:**
Steven Ray Fulgham, *The Summoned*, 1991
Ray Russell, *Incubus*, 1975

---

**3395**
**EDWARD LEE**
**ELIZABETH STEFFEN**, Co-Author

## Portrait of the Psychopath as a Young Woman

(Orlando, Florida: Necro Publications, 1998)

**Story type:** Horror (Serial Killer)
**Major character(s):** Kathleen Shade, Journalist (advice columnist); Maxwell Platt, Writer (poet); Jeffrey Spence, Detective
**Time period(s):** 1990s (1998)
**Locale(s):** Washington, District of Columbia

**Summary:** A female serial killer shows an unhealthy attraction for insecure advice columnist Kathleen Shade, mailing her grisly trophies of her kills as part of her campaign to persuade Kathleen to write a book about her. The unhealthy relationship has its roots in the sexual abuse both women suffered as children, and which Kathleen comes to terms with as she helps track her nemesis down.

**Other books you might like:**
Thomas Harris, *The Silence of the Lambs*, 1988
Barry Hoffman, *Hungry Eyes*, 1997
Rex Miller, *Iceman*, 1990
Rick R. Reed, *Penance*, 1993
Whitley Strieber, *Billy*, 1990

---

**3396**
**EDWARD LEE**
**JOHN PELAN**, Co-Author

## Shifters

(Auburn, Washington: Obsidian Press, 1998)

**Story type:** Horror (Vampire Story)
**Major character(s):** Richard Locke, Writer; Jack Cordesman, Detective; Lethe, Vampire
**Time period(s):** 1990s (1998)
**Locale(s):** Seattle, Washington

**Summary:** Unfulfilled as a poet and unrequited in love, Richard Locke becomes a beacon for Lethe, a vampiric being who preys upon the fear of humans and feeds on their life force. Published as a signed limited edition hardcover.

**Other books you might like:**
Michael Cadnum, *The Judas Glass*, 1996
Brett Easton Ellis, *The Informers*, 1994
John Shirley, *Wetbones*, 1991
Dan Simmons, *Carrion Comfort*, 1989
Melanie Tem, *Desmodus*, 1995

## **3397**

### EDWARD LEE
### JOHN PELAN, Co-Author

## *Splatterspunk: The Micah Hays Stories*

(Brewerton, New York: Sideshow, 1998)

**Story type:** Horror (Collection)
**Major character(s):** Micah Hays, Police Officer (deputy)

**Summary:** These four tasteless tales and one novel excerpt feature Micah Hays, the Luntville deputy whose physical endowments lead him into a variety of supernatural sexual situations. In ''Sideshow,'' Hays helps out a circus of sideshow freaks held against their will by a dwarf elemental. ''The Case of the Police Officer's Cock Ring and the Piano Player Who Had No Hands'' is a ribald werewolf tale, and ''Refrigerator Full of Sperm'' is a wacky story of extraterrestrial procreation and biological experimentation.

**Other books you might like:**
Ron Dee, *Sex and Blood*, 1994
Michael Hemmingson, *Nice Little Stories Jam-Packed with Depraved Sex and Violence*, 1995
Richard Sutphen, *Sexpunks & Savage Sagas*, 1991
Lucy Taylor, *Unnatural Acts and Other Stories*, 1994
Edo van Belkom, *Yours Truly, Jackie the Stripper*, 1998

## **3398**

### GENTRY LEE

## *Bright Messengers*

(New York: Bantam Spectra, 1995)

**Story type:** Science Fiction (First Contact; Theological)
**Major character(s):** Sister Beatrice, Religious (priestess), Traveler (pilgrim); Johann Eberhardt, Engineer, Businessman (director of Valhalla Outpost); Yasin al-Kharif, Engineer, Criminal (rapist)
**Time period(s):** 22nd century (2140s)
**Locale(s):** Valhalla Outpost Facility, Mythical Place; Mutchville, Fictional City; Mars

**Summary:** When a polar expedition on Mars disappears, leaving behind only a diary account of sightings of an amorphous entity and a cavernous, multi-level construction under the surface of the ice, Johann Eberhardt, Sister Beatrice, and several employees of Valhalla eagerly investigate. Sister Beatrice believes the cloud of white particles serves as a messenger from God, while Johann sees it as a scientific riddle to solve. A group committed to finding nonhuman intelligences, the Rama Society, hopes the phenomenon could indicate another visit from an alien race, whose spaceship might have been sighted ten years earlier. First novel as a solo author.

**Other books you might like:**
Roger MacBride Allen, *The Ring of Charon*, 1990
Orson Scott Card, *Ender's Game*, 1985
Jeffrey A. Carver, *The Rapture Effect*, 1987
Arthur C. Clarke, *Cradle*, 1988
    Gentry Lee, co-author
Arthur C. Clarke, *The Garden of Rama*, 1991
    Gentry Lee, co-author
Arthur C. Clarke, *Rama Revealed*, 1994
    Gentry Lee, co-author
Arthur C. Clarke, *Rama II*, 1989
    Gentry Lee, co-author
Arthur C. Clarke, *Rendezvous with Rama*, 1973
Robert L. Forward, *Dragon's Egg*, 1980
Michael P. Kube-McDowell, *Enigma*, 1986
Dan Simmons, *Hyperion*, 1989

David Alexander Smith, *Rendezvous*, 1988
Sheri S. Tepper, *Grass*, 1989

## **3399**

### JOHN LEE

## *The Unicorn Peace*

(New York: Tor, 1993)

**Story type:** Fantasy (Political)
**Series:** Unicorn Quest
**Major character(s):** Oliderval, Ruler (Oligarch of Isphardel); Naxania, Royalty (Queen of Poladine), Ruler; Jarrod Courtak, Magician
**Time period(s):** Indeterminate
**Locale(s):** Strand, Planet—Imaginary

**Summary:** Jarrod Courtak, Friend of the Unicorns, fears that the attempted partition of the outlands will cause war once again. As he fights to preserve the peace and protect the interests of the Discipline, he must rely on past loves, political allies and the power of the Unicorns. The resulting compromises surprise everyone.

**Other books you might like:**
Peter S. Beagle, *The Last Unicorn*, 1968
Rosemary Kirstein, *The Outskirter's Secret*, 1992
Rosemary Kirstein, *The Steerswoman*, 1989
Katherine Kurtz, *Deryni Checkmate*, 1972
Katherine Kurtz, *Deryni Rising*, 1970
Katherine Kurtz, *High Deryni*, 1973
Sheri S. Tepper, *King's Blood Four*, 1983
Sheri S. Tepper, *Necromancer Nine*, 1983
Sheri S. Tepper, *Wizard's Eleven*, 1984

## **3400**

### JOHN LEE

## *The Unicorn Solution*

(New York: Tor, 1991)

**Story type:** Fantasy (Quest)
**Series:** Unicorn Quest
**Major character(s):** Jarrod Courtak, Magician; Pellia, Mythical Creature (unicorn), Telepath
**Time period(s):** Indeterminate
**Locale(s):** Strand, Planet—Imaginary; Mythical Place

**Summary:** Jarrod Courtak hopes to help fulfill the prophecy that war on Strand can only be won by unicorns. He has discovered a family of unicorns and now must travel to another realm to secure a lost spell which will unchain their powers.

**Other books you might like:**
Pamela Dean, *The Hidden Land*, 1986
Pamela Dean, *The Secret Country*, 1985
Tanith Lee, *Black Unicorn*, 1991

## **3401**

### JOHN LEE

## *The Unicorn War*

(New York: Tor, 1995)

**Story type:** Fantasy (Magic Conflict; Political)
**Series:** Unicorn Quest

**Major character(s):** Jarrod Courtak, Magician; Varodias, Ruler (Emperor of Umbria); Nastrus, Mythical Creature (unicorn)
**Time period(s):** Indeterminate
**Locale(s):** Strand, Planet—Imaginary

**Summary:** Despite cessation of the long war with the Outsiders, the Discipline of Magic remains active. When Emperor Varodias declares war, his armies march with war machines that neutralize the power of magic. Human and unicorn must again join forces or perish. Fifth and final volume in the series.

**Other books you might like:**
Eleanor Arnason, *The Sword Smith*, 1978
Peter S. Beagle, *The Last Unicorn*, 1968
Diane Duane, *The Door into Fire*, 1979
Guy Gavriel Kay, *The Summer Tree*, 1985
Patricia A. McKillip, *The Riddle-Master of Hed*, 1976

## 3402
### ROBERT D. LEE
### The Keeper
(New York: Pinnacle, 1993)

**Story type:** Horror (Psychological Suspense)
**Major character(s):** Judy MacAuliffe, Saloon Keeper/Owner; Horst Von Ziegler, Animal Trainer (lion tamer); Jim Sweeney, Police Officer
**Time period(s):** 1990s (1993)
**Locale(s):** Rhinelander, New York

**Summary:** Judy MacAuliffe believes that her ticket out of Rhinelander is an apprenticeship under Horst Von Ziegler, the retired lion tamer who lives in a secluded mansion on the outskirts of town and whose name still has significance in the circus world. But Judy discovers that the spate of recent disappearances in the woods surrounding the town are intimately connected to the animal training in which Horst is currently involved.

**Other books you might like:**
John Driver, *The Hunger of the Beast*, 1991
John Fowles, *The Collector*, 1963
Thomas Harris, *The Silence of the Lambs*, 1988

## 3403
### STAN LEE, Editor
### The Ultimate Spider-Man
(New York: Berkley, 1994)

**Story type:** Science Fiction (Anthology; Adventure)
**Series:** Spider-Man
**Major character(s):** Peter "Spider-Man" Parker, Hero, Detective—Amateur
**Time period(s):** 1990s
**Locale(s):** New York, New York

**Summary:** Contains a five-page introduction by Lee, 11 pages of biographical notes plus 12 original Spider-man stories by 14 authors, including a retelling of Spider-Man's genesis by Stan Lee and Peter David. Other authors include John Gregory Betancourt, Tom De Haven, Craig Shaw Gardner, Dean Wesley Smith and Lawrence Watt-Evans.

**Other books you might like:**
Diane Duane, *Spider-Man: The Venom Factor*, 1994
Martin H. Greenberg, *The Further Adventures of Batman*, 1989 editor

Martin H. Greenberg, *The Further Adventures of Superman*, 1993 editor
John Varley, *Superheroes*, 1995
Ricia Mainhardt, co-editor
Len Wein, *Mayhem in Manhattan*, 1978
Marv Wolfman, co-author

## 3404
### TANITH LEE
### Black Unicorn
(New York: Atheneum, 1991)

**Story type:** Fantasy (Adventure; Young Adult)
**Series:** Dragonflight
**Major character(s):** Tanaquil, Teenager; Lizra, Royalty (princess); Peeve, Animal (enchanted), Companion
**Time period(s):** Indeterminate
**Locale(s):** Jaive's Fortress, Mythical Place; The City, Fictional City

**Summary:** When Tanaquil tries to alleviate boredom by assembling bones her pet discovered, she doesn't expect a phantom unicorn to whisk her toward the city which her mother has forbidden her to visit. Running afoul of a city craft guild, Tanaquil is rescued by her phantom unicorn and a chance meeting with Princess Lizra. Tanaquil discovers her heritage and the vital roll she will soon play.

**Other books you might like:**
Joy Chant, *The Grey Mane of Morning*, 1977
Damaris Cole, *Token of Dragonsblood*, 1991
Peter Dickinson, *The Blue Hawk*, 1976
Mercedes Lackey, *Bardic Voices*, 1991
C.S. Lewis, *The Horse and His Boy*, 1954
Patricia A. McKillip, *Moon-Flash*, 1984
A.C.H. Smith, *The Dark Crystal: A Novel*, 1982

## 3405
### TANITH LEE
### The Book of the Beast
(Woodstock, New York: The Overlook Press, 1991)

**Story type:** Fantasy (Historical; Collection)
**Series:** Secret Books of Paradys
**Major character(s):** Raoulin, Student; Vusca, Military Personnel (centurion); Ruquel, Doctor, Dancer
**Time period(s):** Indeterminate Past
**Locale(s):** Paradys, Fictional City

**Summary:** This volume traces a terrible curse through the strange history of the city of Paradys. By turns beautiful, terrifying and erotic, the three linked stories show how a demonic presence enters the world and causes misery over centuries. An unusual fantasy in its attention to detail and depictions of non-medieval historical periods. First published in England in 1988.

**Other books you might like:**
Nancy A. Collins, *Sunglasses After Dark*, 1989
Storm Constantine, *The Enchantments of Flesh and Spirit*, 1990
Ellen Kushner, *Swordspoint*, 1987
Anne Rice, *Interview with the Vampire*, 1976

## 3406

**TANITH LEE**

## Dark Dance

(New York: Dell/Abyss, 1992)

**Story type:** Horror (Gothic Family Chronicle)
**Major character(s):** Rachaela Day, Clerk (in a bookstore); Ruth Day, Child (Rachaela's daughter); Michael, Servant (to the Scarabae)
**Time period(s):** 1990s (1992)
**Locale(s):** London, England

**Summary:** Although warned by her mother to keep away from the family of the father she never knew, Rachaela Day visits the Scarabae at their remote estate and finds them an eccentric lot, living in the past and with a hint of supernatural menace to them. Rachaela escapes the estate, but finds herself mysteriously impregnated by her father. The child she gives birth to so closely resembles the Scarabae that Rachaela is forced to confront them once again and learn their secret.

**Other books you might like:**
Richie Tankersley Cusick, *Blood Roots*, 1992
Jean Simon, *Orphans*, 1992

## 3407

**TANITH LEE**

## Darkness, I

(New York: St. Martin's, 1996)

**Story type:** Horror (Vampire Story)
**Series:** Blood Opera Sequence
**Major character(s):** Rachaela Day, Vampire; Althene Simon, Vampire; Anna, Child (Rachaela & Althene's daughter)
**Time period(s):** 1990s (1996)
**Locale(s):** London, England

**Summary:** The Scarabae, a family of vampires descended from one of the biblical plagues, continue their diaspora across the English countryside in hopes of integrating with the rest of humanity and putting their bloody past behind them. But when Rachaela Day's daughter, Anna, is kidnapped and taken to a place redolent with Egyptian culture, it appears that someone—or something— intends to revive interest in the family's heritage for the next generation. This novel was first published in England in 1995.

**Other books you might like:**
Poppy Z. Brite, *Lost Souls*, 1992
Nancy A. Collins, *Sunglasses After Dark*, 1990
Anne Rice, *The Queen of the Damned*, 1988

## 3408

**TANITH LEE**

## Elephantasm

(New York: Dell, 1996)

**Story type:** Horror (Occult)
**Major character(s):** Annie Ember, Teenager, Servant; Hampton Smolte, Military Personnel; Darius, Religious (mystic)
**Time period(s):** 19th century
**Locale(s):** England

**Summary:** Fleeing her destitute life in the city, Annie Ember becomes indentured as a servant to Hampton Smolte, a world traveller infatuated with the East whose household pays obeisance to the Hindu god Ganesa. Unable to escape the rituals performed to supplicate the elephant-headed Lord of Beginnings, Annie is indoctrinated into a world of sexuality and mystery, and soon discovers why ivory has a peculiar allure for her.

**Other books you might like:**
Ramsey Campbell, *The Claw*, 1983
    published in America under the title *Nightof the Claw* the same year
Katherine Kurtz, *Dagger Magic*, 1995
    Deborah Turner Harris, co-author
Dan Simmons, *Song of Kali*, 1983
Dennis Wheatley, *The Devil Rides Out*, 1934

## 3409

**TANITH LEE**

## Faces under Water

(New York: Overlook Press, 1998)

**Story type:** Horror (Mystery)
**Series:** Secret Books of Venus
**Major character(s):** Furian Furiano, Apprentice; Dianus Straachen, Scientist (alchemist) Eurydiche, Young Woman
**Time period(s):** 15th century
**Locale(s):** Venice, Italy

**Summary:** At the height of the Carnival season, alchemist apprentice Furian Furiano is smitten by a beautiful woman in a butterfly mask. But the face beneath her mask is stony and death-like, suggesting to Furian that she is a lure used by the Mask Guild, a secret coven of assassins who prey on the most extravagantly masked citizens of this alternate Venice. First book in a new series.

**Other books you might like:**
Douglas W. Clark, *Rehearsal for a Renaissance*, 1992
Jack Dann, *The Memory Cathedral*, 1995
Robert Girardi, *Vaporetto 13*, 1997
Christopher Golden, *Of Saints and Shadows*, 1994
Tad Williams, *Caliban's Hour*, 1994

## 3410

**TANITH LEE**

## Gold Unicorn

(New York: Atheneum, 1994)

**Story type:** Fantasy (Young Adult; Adventure)
**Major character(s):** Tanaquil Veriam, Teenager, Sorceress; Lizora "Lizra" Veriam, Royalty (princess), Leader (ruler of Sea City); Peeve, Animal (enchanted), Companion (Tanaquil's)
**Time period(s):** Indeterminate
**Locale(s):** Fictional Country

**Summary:** Vaulted into leadership, young Princess Lizra envisions a totally controlled society which provides direction for its happy citizens. As a symbol of her power, Lizra constructs a gold-plated iron unicorn designed to work by steam power, but which needs Tanaquil's abilities to function. Tanaquil must decide whether to aid Lizra's vision of conquest or risk her powerful sister's anger.

**Other books you might like:**
Louise Cooper, *The Sleep of Stone*, 1991
Phyllis Eisenstein, *In the Red Lord's Reach*, 1989
Mercedes Lackey, *The Robin and the Kestrel*, 1993
Paula Volsky, *Illusion*, 1992
Tad Williams, *Child of an Ancient City*, 1992
    Nina Kiriki Hoffman, co-author

## 3411

### TANITH LEE

## Heart-Beast

(New York: Dell/Abyss, 1993)

**Story type:** Horror (Werewolf Story)
**Major character(s):** Daniel Vehmund, Secretary, Werewolf; Laura Wheelwright, Young Woman; Marsall Vehmund, Landowner
**Locale(s):** England

**Summary:** Daniel Vehmund pursues the thief who stole the strange talisman fashioned from a meteorite that turns him regularly into a ravenous werewolf. His journeys eventually take him from the Mediterranean back to his home in England, where he crosses paths with an abusive older brother whose ways threaten the family's survival.

**Other books you might like:**
Cheri Scotch, *The Werewolf's Kiss*, 1992
S.P. Somtow, *Moon Dance*, 1990
Jane Toombs, *Under the Shadow*, 1992

## 3412

### TANITH LEE

## A Heroine of the World

(New York: DAW, 1989)

**Story type:** Fantasy (Romance)
**Major character(s):** Aradia, Teenager (Orphan), Noblewoman
**Time period(s):** Indeterminate
**Locale(s):** Alternate Earth

**Summary:** Aradia's protected childhood comes to an end during an extended siege on the city in which she lives. The story follows her through her experiences as a mistress of an enemy officer to her love for a soldier of her own country.

**Other books you might like:**
Richard Adams, *Maia*, 1985
Sheila Gilluly, *Ritnym's Daughter*,
    Greenbriar Trilogy
Robin McKinley, *The Hero and the Crown*, 1984
Jessica Amanda Salmonson, *Tomoe Gozen*, 1984

## 3413

### TANITH LEE

## Personal Darkness

(New York: Dell, 1994)

**Story type:** Horror (Vampire Story)
**Major character(s):** Rachaela, Young Woman; Ruth, Vampire; Malach, Vampire
**Time period(s):** 1990s (1994)
**Locale(s):** London, England

**Summary:** In this sequel to the author's *Dark Dance*, the Scarabae, a family of vampires and other supernatural beings, try to recover from the destruction of their family home and integrate themselves with the London jetset. Meanwhile Ruth, the daughter of half-mortal Rachaela and the cause of the Scarabae's misfortunes, flees the family after an unsuccessful attempt to mate her with her grandfather, bringing death and mayhem to the city that threatens to draw public scrutiny down upon the family.

**Other books you might like:**
Poppy Z. Brite, *Lost Souls*, 1992

Pat Graversen, *Precious Blood*, 1983
Wendy Haley, *This Dark Paradise*, 1993
Anne Rice, *The Vampire Lestat*, 1985

## 3414

### TANITH LEE

## Red Unicorn

(New York: Tor, 1997)

**Story type:** Fantasy (Young Adult; Adventure)
**Major character(s):** Tanaquil Veriam, Wanderer, Sorceress; Worabex, Magician; Peeve, Animal (enchanted), Companion (Tanaquil's)
**Time period(s):** Indeterminate
**Locale(s):** Fictional Country

**Summary:** Trying to leave Worabex behind, Tanaquil returns home, only to find the magician there when she arrives. Finally happy, her mother has replaced almost everyone else with demons. When Tanaquil takes a walk in the desert, she realizes that her mother and Worabex unwittingly sent her to yet another alternate world. There, the Sulkana Liliam has an evil sister, Tanakil, who looks like Tanaquil. The red unicorn with bronze hooves also awaits her.

## 3415

**WARNER LEE** (Pseudonym of B.W. Battin)

## Night Sounds

(New York: Pocket, 1992)

**Story type:** Horror (Possession)
**Major character(s):** Dave Guthrie, Artist (illustrator); Paula Bjornsen, Teacher; Ed Prawdzik, Nurse
**Time period(s):** 1990s
**Locale(s):** Castle Bay, California

**Summary:** Dave Guthrie ponders his incredible luck as the only survivor of a plane crash that killed 132 people, unaware that he owes his life to a bargain he struck with powers of evil. With the help of good samaritan clairvoyant Paula Bjornsen, Dave discovers that his bargain entails the use of his body by the forces of evil to feed upon mortals.

**Other books you might like:**
John Gideon, *Greely's Cove*, 1991
L. Ron Hubbard, *Death's Deputy*, 1939
Dean R. Koontz, *Cold Fire*, 1991

## 3416

### FRITZ LEIBER

## Conjure Wife/Our Lady of Darkness

(New York: Tor, 1991)

**Story type:** Horror (Collection)

**Summary:** This repackaging of two-novels-in-one, the first originally published in 1943, the second in 1978, brings together two landmark stories of modern horror and fantasy. In the first, university professor Norman Saylor discovers misfortune when he forbids his wife Tansy to practice her seemingly harmless brand of witchcraft and it brings down upon the Saylor household the wrath of the other university professors' wives, all of whom are witches working to further their husbands' careers. In the second, which won the World Fantasy Award for best novel, Franz Westen's investigation into the paranormal leads to the discovery that his home is a focus for elemental forces attracted by the city of San Francisco.

**Other books you might like:**
James Blish, *The Devil's Day*, 1989
Henry Kuttner, *The Startling Worlds of Henry Kuttner*, 1987

---

**3417**

**FRITZ LEIBER**

### The Dealings of Daniel Kesserich

(New York: Tor, 1997)

**Story type:** Science Fiction (Science Fiction)
**Major character(s):** George Kramer, Writer; John Ellis, Doctor; Daniel Kesserich, Scientist
**Time period(s):** 1930s
**Locale(s):** Smithville, California

**Summary:** Subtitled "A Study of the Mass-Insanity at Smithville," this short novel, written in the 1930s and lost for decades, relates the adventures of George Kramer, who comes to visit his good friends John Ellis and Daniel Kesserich following the death of Ellis's wife, and finds that the town is in the grip of the strange belief that she was buried prematurely. Seemingly supernatural materializations, disappearances and reappearances persuade Kramer that something extraordinary is going on, the explanation for which is rooted in scientific research that Kesserich was involved in back in their college days.

**Other books you might like:**
L. Ron Hubbard, *Fear*, 1951
William Sloane, *To Walk the Night*, 1937
William Sloane, *The Edge of Running Water*, 1939

---

**3418**

**FRITZ LEIBER**

### Farewell to Lankhmar

(Clarkston, Georgia: White Wolf, 1998)

**Story type:** Fantasy (Collection)
**Major character(s):** Fafhrd, Thief, Warrior; The Gray Mouser, Thief, Magician
**Time period(s):** Indeterminate
**Locale(s):** Lankhmar, Fictional City

**Summary:** This collection includes one novel and three long stories, among the last written featuring Leiber's two likable thieves. Originally published between 1977 and 1988, the tales deal with the later careers of the two men, who at times almost become respectable merchants.

**Other books you might like:**
Robin Wayne Bailey, *Swords Against the Shadowland*, 1998
Robert E. Howard, *Skulls in the Stars*, 1978
John Jakes, *Brak the Barbarian*, 1968
Michael Moorcock, *Corum: The Coming of Chaos*, 1997
C.L. Moore, *Jirel of Joiry*, 1969

---

**3419**

**FRITZ LEIBER**

### Ill Met in Lankhmar

(Clarkston, Georgia: White Wolf, 1995)

**Story type:** Fantasy (Horror; Sword and Sorcery)

---

**Series:** Fafhrd and the Gray Mouser
**Major character(s):** Fafhrd, Thief, Warrior; The Grey Mouser, Thief, Wizard; Ningauble of the Seven Eyes, Wizard
**Time period(s):** Indeterminate
**Locale(s):** Lankhmar, Fictional City

**Summary:** Omnibus collection of stories of the early years of Leiber's ironic sword and sorcery heroes and their adventures in an urban fantasy full of theives, wizards, demons, and the walking dead. This edition collects *Swords and Deviltry* (1970), and *Swords Against Death* (1970), which contain 13 stories written 1934-1969. The book also contains four introductions by Leiber from earlier editions, a modern introduction by Michael Moorcock, and chapter, story, and volume headings by artist Mike Mignola.

**Other books you might like:**
Steven Brust, *Jhereg*, 1983
Ellen Kushner, *Swordspoint*, 1987
Michael Moorcock, *Elric of Melnibone*, 1976
Michael Shea, *Nifft the Lean*, 1982

---

**3420**

**FRITZ LEIBER**

### Lean Times in Lankhmar

(Clarkston, Georgia: White Wolf, 1996)

**Story type:** Fantasy (Collection; Sword and Sorcery)
**Major character(s):** Fafhrd, Thief, Warrior; The Grey Mouser, Thief, Wizard
**Time period(s):** Indeterminate
**Locale(s):** Lankhmar, Fictional City

**Summary:** Contains a two-page introduction by Raymond E. Feist, a two-page author's foreword and 10 stories written 1936-1968 and published as *Swords in the Mist* (1968) and *Swords Against Wizardry* (1968). Dark sorcery, deadly weaponry, and poverty plague Fafhrd and the Grey Mouser's adventures while they seek magical gain and female companionship.

**Other books you might like:**
Steven Brust, *Jhereg*, 1983
L. Sprague de Camp, *Warlocks and Warriors*, 1970 editor
Robert E. Howard, *Hour of the Dragon*, 1977
Michael Moorcock, *Elric of Melnibone*, 1976
Clark Ashton Smith, *Tales of Zothique*, 1995
Karl Edward Wagner, *Darkness Weaves*, 1978 revised edition

---

**3421**

**FRITZ LEIBER**

### The Leiber Chronicles

(Arlington Heights, IL: Dark Harvest, 1990)

**Story type:** Science Fiction (Collection)

**Summary:** This volume includes forty-four stories spanning Fritz Leiber's remarkable career, from his first published work, "Two Sought Adventure" (1939), to the recent "The Curse of the Smalls and the Stars" (1983). Among many fine stories are Leiber's Hugo and Nebula Award winners, "Gonna Roll the Bones" (1967), "Ship of Shadows" (1969), "Ill Met in Lankhmar" (1970) and "Catch that Zeppelin!" (1975). Other notable stories include "Coming Attraction" (1950), "A Pail of Air" (1951), "A Bad Day for Sales" (1953), "Rump-Titty-Titty-Tum-Tah-Tee" (1958), "The Man Who Made Friends with Electricity" (1962), "Bazaar of the Bizarre"

(1963), "When the Change Wind Blows" (1964), "Midnight by the Morphy Watch" (1974), and "Belsen Express" (1975).

**Other books you might like:**
Harlan Ellison, *Angry Candy*, 1988
Harlan Ellison, *Deathbird Stories*, 1975
Harlan Ellison, *The Essential Ellison: A 35-Year Retrospective*, 1987
Harlan Ellison, *Strange Wine*, 1978
P.C. Hodgell, *Dark of the Moon*, 1985
P.C. Hodgell, *God Stalk*, 1982
Tim Powers, *The Anubis Gates*, 1983

## 3422
### FRITZ LEIBER

## Return to Lankhmar
(Clarkston, Georgia: White Wolf, 1997)

**Story type:** Fantasy (Collection; Sword and Sorcery)
**Series:** Fafhrd and the Gray Mouser
**Major character(s):** Fafhrd, Thief, Warrior; The Grey Mouser, Thief, Wizard; Hisvet, Mythical Creature (rat-woman)
**Time period(s):** Indeterminate
**Locale(s):** Lankhmar, Fictional City; Nehwon, Planet—Imaginary

**Summary:** Contains a three-page introduction by Neil Gaiman, a foreword by the author, the novel *The Swords of Lankhmar* (1968), and eight short stories published as *Swords and Ice Magic* (1977), with illustrations by Mike Mignola. This collection sees the dangerous and degenerate duo save their beloved and shameless city from a horde of intelligent rats, then journey to the frozen ends of Nehwon in search of adventure, riches and release from boredom.

**Other books you might like:**
Steven Brust, *Jhereg*, 1983
Ellen Kushner, *Swordspoint*, 1987
Michael Shea, *The Mines of Behemoth*, 1997
Richard L. Tierney, *Scroll of Thoth*, 1997
Karl Edward Wagner, *Darkness Weaves*, 1978 revised

## 3423
### STEPHEN LEIGH

## The Abraxas Marvel Circus
(New York: Roc, 1990)

**Story type:** Fantasy (Contemporary)
**Major character(s):** Dirk, Musician (Rock & Roll); Ecclesiastes Mitsumishi, Undertaker
**Time period(s):** 1990s
**Locale(s):** Earth

**Summary:** Dirk and Ecclesiastes are just two of the characters searching for the Theopelli notebook, but no one knows what will happen when it is finally found.

**Other books you might like:**
Gael Baudino, *Gossamer Axe*, 1990
James P. Blaylock, *Land of Dreams*, 1989
Tom Deitz, *The Gryphon King*, 1989
Lisa Goldstein, *Tourists*, 1989

## 3424
### STEPHEN LEIGH

## Alien Tongue
(New York: Bantam Spectra, 1991)

**Story type:** Science Fiction (First Contact)
**Series:** Next Wave
**Major character(s):** Patrick Malone, Spaceman, Pilot; G.Ren.Bei.Yi, Alien (Avia); Hr.Tyi.Bei.k.ai, Alien (Avia), Royalty (Eggmother of the Bei)
**Time period(s):** 2060s
**Locale(s):** *Bright Hope*, Spaceship; Tir.ki.k.ai, Planet—Imaginary

**Summary:** Patrick Malone, pilot of the *Bright Hope*, and his crew follow Kaitlin Turek through the wormhole outside Pluto's orbit after a message is received on Earth. Although ordered not to interact with any aliens, the crew of *Bright Hope* has little choice as the ship is severely damaged during transit. The aliens transmit a message from Kaitlin Turek who has become very well known to some of the aliens. This book contains an introduction by Isaac Asimov, an essay by Rudy Rucker, and opens with a glossary of alien terminology.

**Other books you might like:**
Eleanor Arnason, *A Woman of the Iron People*, 1991
Octavia E. Butler, *Dawn*, 1987
John DeChancie, *Red Limit Freeway*, 1984
John DeChancie, *Starrigger*, 1983
Mary Gentle, *Golden Witchbreed*, 1984
Rebecca Ore, *Becoming Alien*, 1987
Catherine Wells, *The Earth Is All That Lasts*, 1991

## 3425
### STEPHEN LEIGH

## Changeling
(New York: Ace, 1989)

**Story type:** Science Fiction (Space Opera)
**Series:** Isaac Asimov's Robot City: Robots and Aliens
**Major character(s):** Derec, Amnesiac, Scientist; Ariel Welsh, Heiress
**Time period(s):** Indeterminate Future
**Locale(s):** Robot City, Planet—Imaginary

**Summary:** Still unaware of who he really is, Derec must help defend the city of robots from the evil, wolf-like aliens who threaten it with destruction.

**Other books you might like:**
Isaac Asimov, *The Caves of Steel*, 1954
Isaac Asimov, *The Complete Robot*, 1982
Isaac Asimov, *The Naked Sun*, 1957
Isaac Asimov, *Robots and Empire*, 1985
Isaac Asimov, *The Robots of Dawn*, 1983
Charles Ingrid, *Return Fire*, 1989
  Sand Wars 5
Michael A. Stackpole, *Battletech: Warrior: Coupe*, 1989

## 3426
### STEPHEN LEIGH

## Dark Water's Embrace
(New York: Avon Eos, 1998)

**Story type:** Science Fiction (Lost Colony; Genetic Manipulation)
**Major character(s):** Anais Koda-Levin, Doctor; Elio Allen-Shimmura, Historian; KaiSa, Alien (Miccail), Diplomat (ambassador)

**Time period(s):** Indeterminate Future
**Locale(s):** Mictlan, Planet—Imaginary

**Summary:** Stranded on Mictlan for 100 years, facing increasing birth defects and a declining birth rate, the colonists could become extinct in a few more generations. Discovery of the body of a Miccail, a member of an extinct native race, sets off a chain of events that may explain why the Miccail died out and how the humans might survive and prosper.

**Other books you might like:**
Marion Zimmer Bradley, *The World Wreckers*, 1971
David Brin, *Glory Season*, 1993
Helen Collins, *Mutagenesis*, 1993
M.J. Engh, *Rainbow Man*, 1993
Valerie J. Freireich, *Imposter*, 1997
Ursula K. Le Guin, *The Left Hand of Darkness*, 1969
Melissa Scott, *Shadow Man*, 1995

**3427**

STEPHEN LEIGH

# Ray Bradbury Presents: Dinosaur Planet
(New York: AvoNova, 1993)

**Story type:** Science Fiction (Time Travel; Adventure)
**Major character(s):** Aaron Cofield, Time Traveler, Teenager; Jennifer Mason, Teenager, Time Traveler; Raajeh, Animal (dinosaur-Mutata)
**Time period(s):** Indeterminate Past (Mesozoic Era); 1990s
**Locale(s):** Green Town, Illinois

**Summary:** While attempting to take Mondo to his home time, Aaron inadvertently arrives back at his grandfather's house 15 years after he left. More fluent in the Mutata language, Jennifer continues to work at developing an understanding with the dinosaurs, despite the lack of support from her fellow humans. Time storms plague all.

**Other books you might like:**
Poul Anderson, *The Time Patrol*, 1991
Roger L. DiSilvestro, *Living with the Reptiles*, 1990
James Gurney, *Dinotopia*, 1992
Julian May, *The Many-Colored Land*, 1981
Robert J. Sawyer, *Far-Seer*, 1992
Robert J. Sawyer, *Fossil Hunter*, 1993

**3428**

STEPHEN LEIGH

# Ray Bradbury Presents: Dinosaur World
(New York: AvoNova, 1992)

**Story type:** Science Fiction (Time Travel; Adventure)
**Major character(s):** Aaron Cofield, Teenager, Time Traveler; Jennifer Mason, Teenager, Time Traveler; SStragh, Animal (dinosaur-Mutata)
**Time period(s):** 1990s; Indeterminate Past
**Locale(s):** Green Town, Illinois

**Summary:** As Jenny and Aaron contemplate the end of their summer vacation, a dinosaur interrupts their idyll. Chasing after it, they inadvertently travel to different past eras. Captured by another time traveller and then by intelligent dinosaurs, Jenny begins to learn the dinosaur language. Contains a sixteen-page insert of Wayne Barlowe illustrations and a six-page glossary of Mutata terms.

**Other books you might like:**
Poul Anderson, *The Time Patrol*, 1991
Roger L. DiSilvestro, *Living with the Reptiles*, 1990

Gary Gentile, *Dragons Past*, 1990
James Gurney, *Dinotopia*, 1992
Warren Norwood, *Vanished*, 1988
Robert Silverberg, *Thebes of the Hundred Gates*, 1991
Clifford D. Simak, *Mastodonia*, 1978

**3429**

ROBERT LEININGER

# Black Sun
(New York: Avon, 1991)

**Story type:** Science Fiction (Disaster)
**Major character(s):** Maurice Tyler, Scientist, Professor
**Time period(s):** 21st century
**Locale(s):** Arizona

**Summary:** When Maurice Tyler's warning that changes in the Sun's output will spell disaster for humanity fails to take hold in the public awareness, he decides to retreat to his well-stocked survival shelter, if his enemies will allow it.

**Other books you might like:**
Roger MacBride Allen, *The Ring of Charon*, 1990
J.M. Morgan, *Desert Eden*, 1991
Larry Niven, *Fallen Angels*, 1991
    Michael Flynn and Jerry Pournelle, co-authors
Larry Niven, *Footfall*, 1985
    Jerry Pournelle, co-author
Larry Niven, *Lucifer's Hammer*, 1977
    Jerry Pournelle, co-author
Douglas Orgill, *The Sixth Winter*, 1979
    John Gribbin, co-author
David R. Palmer, *Emergence*, 1984
John Christopher, *The Long Winter*, 1962
    Christopher is a pseudonym of Christopher Sam Youd

**3430**

MURRAY LEINSTER (Pseudonym of William Fitzgerald Jenkins)

# First Contacts: The Essential Murray Leinster
(Framingham, Massachusetts: NESFA Press, 1998)

**Story type:** Science Fiction (Collection)

**Summary:** Edited by Joe Rico, this volume contains a two-page editor's introduction, a four-page introduction by Hal Clement, two original stories, and 22 stories reprinted from periodicals from 1934 through 1955. The stories explore diverse themes including time travel, solitude, alien contacts, alternative universes, space exploration, ray guns, computers, and immortality. The collection includes the Hugo Award winner, ''Exploration Team,'' as well as classics such as, ''A Logic Named Joe,'' ''The Ethical Equations'' and ''Sideways in Time.''

**Other books you might like:**
Lois McMaster Bujold, *Dreamweaver's Dilemma*, 1996
Zenna Henderson, *Ingathering: The Complete People Stories of Zenna Henderson*, 1995
James H. Schmitz, *The Best of James H. Schmitz*, 1991
Cordwainer Smith, *The Rediscovery of Man*, 1993
James White, *The White Papers*, 1996

## 3431

### BRAD LEITHAUSER

## *Hence*

(New York: Knopf, 1989)

**Story type:** Science Fiction (Literary)
**Major character(s):** Timothy Briggs, Sports Figure (Chessmaster); Garner Briggs, Professor (Law professor)
**Time period(s):** 1990s (1993, 1997)
**Locale(s):** Boston, Massachusetts

**Summary:** Garner Briggs writes a book in which he recounts the famous chess match some four years earlier between his younger brother Timothy and the chess playing computer program ANNDY. He also ponders the nature of artificial intelligence and its probable significance to the world.

**Other books you might like:**
William Gibson, *Neuromancer*, 1984
Stanislaw Lem, *The Cyberiad*, 1974
Stanislaw Lem, *Memoirs of a Space Traveler*, 1982
Stanislaw Lem, *Mortal Engines*, 1977
Stanislaw Lem, *Return From the Stars*, 1980
Bruce Sterling, *Islands in the Net*, 1988

## 3432

### BRAD LEITHAUSER, Editor

## *The Norton Book of Ghost Stories*

(New York: W.W. Norton, 1994)

**Story type:** Horror (Anthology; Ghost Story)

**Summary:** Nineteen Classic and contemporary authors are represented by 28 stories in a compilation that traces the influence of Henry James and M.R. James on the ghost story tradition. Classic tales include Henry James's tale of vengeance from beyond the grave, ''The Romance of Certain Old Clothes''; M.R. James' story of a ghost summoned by an artifact found in ancient ruins, '''Oh, Whistle, and I'll Come to You, My Lad'''; Oliver Onions' tale of a man whose life is destroyed by an amorous ghost, ''The Beckoning Fair One''; and Elizabeth Bowen's story of a haunted house's overwhelming effect on the personalities of mortals who stay there, ''The Cat Jumps.'' Among the more modern selections are V.S. Pritchett's ''The Story Don Juan,'' which tells of the legendary lover's influence on a vengeful ghost; Penelope Fitzgerald's ''The Axe,'' in which an employer is haunted by the ghost of a terminated employee; and Philip Graham's ''Ancient Music,'' which portrays a haunting from the ghost's point of view.

**Other books you might like:**
Michael Cox, *The Oxford Book of English Ghost Stories*, 1986
    R.A. Gilbert, co-editor
Michael Cox, *Victorian Ghost Stories: An Oxford Anthology*, 1991
    R.A. Gilbert, co-editor
Peter Haining, *The Ghost Companion*, 1994

## 3433

### BRAD LEITHAUSER

## *Seaward*

(New York: Knopf, 1993)

**Story type:** Horror (Ghost Story)
**Major character(s):** Terry Seward, Lawyer; Adam Mikolajczak, Lawyer; Curly Kopp, Store Owner (pet store)

**Time period(s):** 1990s (1993)
**Locale(s):** Washington, District of Columbia

**Summary:** Terry Seward's life is transformed irrevocably when he sees what he perceives as the ghost of his wife a year after her death by drowning. From that point on, Terry is a changed man, unable to tell if the changes in his life and the lives of those around him are the product of his unusual experience, or self-induced.

**Other books you might like:**
Jonathan Aycliffe, *Naomi's Room*, 1992
Peter S. Beagle, *A Fine and Private Place*, 1960
Daphne Du Maurier, *''Don't Look Now''*, 1976
    in *Echoes From the Macabre*

## 3434

### STANISLAW LEM

## *Eden*

(New York: Harcourt Brace Jovanovich, 1989)

**Story type:** Science Fiction (First Contact)
**Major character(s):** Captain, Astronaut; Doctor, Astronaut
**Time period(s):** Indeterminate Future
**Locale(s):** Eden, Planet—Imaginary

**Summary:** A spaceship from Earth crashes on Eden, fourth planet of another sun, and encounters a world of mystifying artifacts and bizarre lifeforms.

**Other books you might like:**
Philip K. Dick, *Do Androids Dream of Electric Sheep?*, 1968
Michael Kandel, *Strange Invasion*, 1989
Robert Silverberg, *Son of Man*, 1971
Boris Strugatsky, *Roadside Picnic*, 1977
    Arkady Strugatsky, co-author
Boris Strugatsky, *The Snail on the Slope*, 1980
    Arkady Strugatsky, co-author

## 3435

### STANISLAW LEM

## *Peace on Earth*

(New York: Harcourt Brace, 1994)

**Story type:** Science Fiction (Humor; Dystopian)
**Series:** Ijon Tichy
**Major character(s):** Ijon Tichy, Space Explorer, Writer
**Time period(s):** Indeterminate Future
**Locale(s):** Montenegro

**Summary:** With weapons of mass destruction relocated to the Moon, autonomous intelligences carry on the arms race independent of Earth oversight. Concerned that machine civilization may evolve on Luna, Ijon Tichy tries unsuccessfully to investigate by remote sensors. When Tichy investigates in person, one weapon severs the connection between the two hemispheres of his brain, rendering Tichy's right hand independent of his left.

**Other books you might like:**
Ed Blome, *Title Deleted for Security Reasons*, 1993
Algis Budrys, *Rogue Moon*, 1960
Jack L. Chalker, *The Red Tape War*, 1991
    Mike Resnick, George Alec Effinger, co-authors
Rudy Rucker, *Live Robots*, 1994
Neal Stephenson, *Snow Crash*, 1993

## 3436

### MADELEINE L'ENGLE

## *An Acceptable Time*

(New York: Dell Laurel Leaf, 1990)

**Story type:** Fantasy (Time Travel; Young Adult)
**Major character(s):** Polly O'Keefe, Student; Zachary Gray, Young Man; Anaral, Religious (druid-in-training)
**Time period(s):** 1980s; 11th century B.C.
**Locale(s):** Connecticut

**Summary:** While visiting her grandparents, Polly discovers she can move between her current time circle and that of 3,000 years ago. She and Zachary are caught up in a struggle between two factions of a Native American group who've been influenced by a Druid from Europe, but are now threatened by raiders whose home territory is suffering from drought. This book, set in L'Engle's Time Tetrology universe, was first published by Farrar Straus and Giroux in 1989.

**Other books you might like:**
Joy Chant, *Red Moon and Black Mountain*, 1970
Susan Cooper, *Over Sea, under Stone*, 1966
Alan Garner, *The Weirdstone of Brisingamen*, 1960
J. Alison James, *Sing for a Gentle Rain*, 1990
Katherine Kurtz, *Deryni Rising*, 1970
Andre Norton, *Lavender-Green Magic*, 1974

## 3437

### EDWARD M. LERNER

## *Probe*

(New York: Warner, 1991)

**Story type:** Science Fiction (Alternate Intelligence)
**Major character(s):** Robert Hanson, Computer Expert (designer); Sally Keller, Researcher (NASA)
**Time period(s):** 21st century
**Locale(s):** Rolling Meadows, Illinois

**Summary:** Asgard Aerospace Corporation's automated spaceship, *Prospector*, constantly sends back information. The data just received has picked up some organized interference which seems to be coming from around Jupiter, near *Prospector's* current position. The alien probe blows up soon after discovery, but the effects of its appearance involve NASA, the Space Development Agency, the FBI and Asgard Aerospace.

**Other books you might like:**
David Brin, *Earth*, 1990
David Gerrold, *When HARLIE Was One: Release 2.0*, 1988
Robert A. Heinlein, *The Moon Is a Harsh Mistress*, 1966
Dan Simmons, *The Fall of Hyperion*, 1990
Dan Simmons, *Hyperion*, 1989
David Alexander Smith, *Homecoming*, 1990
David Alexander Smith, *Rendezvous*, 1988

## 3438

### JONATHAN LETHEM

## *Amnesia Moon*

(New York: Harcourt Brace, 1995)

**Story type:** Fantasy (Post-Disaster; Contemporary)
**Major character(s):** Everett "Chaos" Moon, Amnesiac; Melinda Self, Traveler
**Time period(s):** 21st century

**Locale(s):** Wyoming; Nevada; California

**Summary:** Accompanied by Melinda Self, Chaos leaves a miserable existence in Hatfork, Wyoming, hoping to recover memories of a past hinted at in dreams. His odyssey reveals a fractured subjective reality and glimpses of old relationships as he finds former acquaintances.

**Other books you might like:**
C.S. Friedman, *Black Sun Rising*, 1992
Jean Mark Gawron, *Dream of Glass*, 1993
Ursula K. Le Guin, *The Lathe of Heaven*, 1971
Rachel Pollack, *Unquenchable Fire*, 1992
Michaela Roessner, *Vanishing Point*, 1993

## 3439

### JONATHAN LETHEM

## *As She Climbed Across the Table*

(New York: Doubleday, 1997)

**Story type:** Science Fiction (Satire)
**Major character(s):** Alice Coombs, Scientist (particle physics); Philip Estrand, Professor
**Time period(s):** 1990s
**Locale(s):** California

**Summary:** An experiment creates a discontinuity in the fabric of the universe, a nothingness which the researchers name "Lack." Lack develops intelligence and personality, becoming the object of Alice's obsession. In love with Alice and despairing at his loss of Alice's affection, Philip finally decides to confront Lack on his own.

**Other books you might like:**
William Borden, *Superstoe*, 1968
Richard Brautigan, *The Hawkline Monster*, 1974
Alan Dean Foster, *To the Vanishing Point*, 1988
Christopher Priest, *The Prestige*, 1996
Kurt Vonnegut Jr., *Cat's Cradle*, 1963

## 3440

### JONATHAN LETHEM

## *Girl in Landscape*

(New York: Doubleday, 1998)

**Story type:** Science Fiction (Genetic Manipulation; Psychic Powers)
**Major character(s):** Pella Marsh, Teenager, Adventurer; Efram Nugent, Farmer, Leader
**Time period(s):** Indeterminate Future
**Locale(s):** Earth; Planet of the Archbuilders, Planet—Imaginary

**Summary:** Leaving the ravaged Earth, Pella Marsh discovers that life on the Planet of the Archbuilders is different in every way. While most colonists freely eat the "potatoes" which contain powerful alien organisms which manipulate human DNA, Efram Nugent goes to some trouble to raise his own food to remain free of alien influence.

**Other books you might like:**
David Brin, *Glory Season*, 1993
L. Warren Douglas, *Cannon's Orb*, 1994
M.J. Engh, *Rainbow Man*, 1993
Nicola Griffith, *Ammonite*, 1993
Paul J. McAuley, *Child of the River*, 1998
Melissa Scott, *Shadow Man*, 1995
Joan Slonczewski, *A Door into Ocean*, 1986

## 3441

### JONATHAN LETHEM

## Gun, with Occasional Music

(New York: Harcourt Brace, 1994)

**Story type:** Fantasy (Mystery; Light Fantasy)
**Major character(s):** Conrad Metcalf, Detective—Private
**Time period(s):** 21st century
**Locale(s):** San Francisco, California; Oakland, California

**Summary:** Surrounded by intelligent animals that result from evolution therapy, Conrad Metcalf must solve a murder despite uncertainty concerning his employer. Success hinges on Metcalf's ability to avoid government inquisitors and others who wish to involve themselves. First novel.

**Other books you might like:**
Jonathan Carroll, *The Land of Laughs*, 1980
Glen Cook, *Sweet Silver Blues*, 1987
Mel Gilden, *Surfing Samurai Robots*, 1988
Laurell K. Hamilton, *Guilty Pleasures*, 1993
Cordwainer Smith, *The Rediscovery of Man*, 1993
Gary K. Wolf, *Who Censored Roger Rabbit?*, 1981
Gary K. Wolf, *Who P-P-Plugged Roger Rabbit?*, 1991

## 3442

### JONATHAN LETHEM

## The Wall of the Sky, the Wall of the Eye

(New York: Harcourt Brace, 1996)

**Story type:** Science Fiction (Collection; Horror)

**Summary:** Contains two original and five stories reprinted from periodicals and anthologies. Despite some dark levity, the stories generally vary in tone from hardboiled to downbeat as Lethem investigates virtual reality, reanimation of the dead, professional sports, failed relationships, alien encounters, penology, and sexual encounters.

**Other books you might like:**
Pat Cadigan, *Patterns*, 1989
John Kessel, *Meeting in Infinity*, 1992
Lucius Shepard, *The Ends of the Earth*, 1991
Marc Stiegler, *The Gentle Seduction*, 1990
Michael Swanwick, *Gravity's Angels*, 1991
James Tiptree Jr., *Her Smoke Rose Up Forever*, 1990

## 3443

### PRIMO LEVI

## The Mirror Maker

(New York: Schocken Books, 1989)

**Story type:** Science Fiction (Collection)

**Summary:** This posthumous collection by the famed Italian writer includes twelve short stories, two poems, and twenty-two essays. Most of the short stories are science fiction or fantasy. Among the best of these are "The Interview," "The Great Mutation," "The Mirror Maker," and "Time Checkmated." There is also a short preface by Levi and an introduction by Lorenzo Mondo. Translated by Raymond Rosenthal.

**Other books you might like:**
Dino Buzzati, *Catastrophe*, 1965
Italo Calvino, *Cosmicomics*, 1968
Italo Calvino, *Invisible Cities*, 1974
Italo Calvino, *The Watcher and Other Stories*, 1971

## 3444

### BETTY LEVIN

## Mercy's Mill

(New York: Greenwillow Books, 1992)

**Story type:** Fantasy (Young Adult; Time Travel)
**Major character(s):** Sarah Grissom, Child; Jethro Philips, Time Traveler
**Time period(s):** 1990s
**Locale(s):** Ashbury, Massachusetts

**Summary:** As Sarah's mother and stepfather work to restore an old dam and mill after the family moves to the country, Sarah befriends Jethro and learns of Jethro's attempts to help Mercy Bredcake, a 17th century child who narrowly escaped drowning as her penalty for witchcraft.

**Other books you might like:**
Margaret J. Anderson, *The Ghost Inside the Monitor*, 1990
Eleanor Cameron, *The Court of the Stone Children*, 1973
Gilbert B. Cross, *A Witch Across Time*, 1990
Peni R. Griffin, *Hobkin*, 1992
Nancy Springer, *The Friendship Song*, 1992

## 3445

### IRA LEVIN

## Son of Rosemary

(New York: Dutton, 1997)

**Story type:** Horror (Occult)
**Major character(s):** Rosemary Reilly, Parent (Andy's mother); Andy Woodhouse, Religious (aka Adrian Steven Castevet); Judy Kharyat, Secretary
**Time period(s):** 1990s (1999)
**Locale(s):** New York, New York; California

**Summary:** Rosemary Reilly (nee Woodhouse) awakens from a 27-year coma to find her son Andy, the offspring of a Satanic bargain, is venerated as an internationally renowned religious figure devoted to the betterment of the world. As Andy prepares the world for a global ritual that will usher in the next millennium, Rosemary can't shake the suspicion that her son is still beholden to his destiny to become the anti-Christ. A sequel to *Rosemary's Baby* (1967).

**Other books you might like:**
Joseph Howard, *Damien*, 1978
Alan Rodgers, *Night*, 1991
David Seltzer, *The Omen*, 1976
John Skipp, *The Scream*, 1988
   Craig Spector, co-author
F. Paul Wilson, *Nightworld*, 1992

## 3446

### ROBERT LEVY

## Clan of the Shape-Changers

(Boston: Houghton Mifflin, 1994)

**Story type:** Fantasy (Young Adult; Adventure)
**Major character(s):** Susan, Mythical Creature (shapechanger), Teenager; Jeffrey, Mythical Creature (shapechanger), Teenager

**Time period(s):** Indeterminate Future
**Locale(s):** Enstor, Planet—Imaginary

**Summary:** When the King of Reune orders all witches destroyed, Susan flees with her wolf companion, Farrun. After she saves Jeffrey, he brings her to a hiding place, a relic of their ancestors, the Elders. The evil Shaman, Ometerer, hopes to capture the pair of fugitives and learn the secret of their power for himself.

**Other books you might like:**
Octavia E. Butler, *Imago*, 1989
Monica Hughes, *The Promise*, 1992
Mercedes Lackey, *The Lark and the Wren*, 1991
Lawrence Watt-Evans, *Taking Flight*, 1993
Jane Yolen, *Shape Shifters: Fantasy and Science Fiction Tales about Humans Who Can Change Their Shapes*, 1978
    editor

---

**3447**

**D.F. LEWIS**

## The Best of D.F. Lewis

(Lessburg, Virginia: TAL Publications, 1993)

**Story type:** Horror (Collection)

**Summary:** This chapbook collects 15 stories by an English writer who, for reasons known only to the small press—where all of the selections first appeared—has become a favorite of non-mainstream publishing circles. Only one story, ''The Weirdmonger,'' is longer than several hundred words. Few are anything more than plotless assemblies of bizarre images and non-sequiturs. As a result, all are indescribable as fiction. Ramsey Campbell has supplied an introduction.

**Other books you might like:**
Ramsey Campbell, *Demons by Daylight*, 1973
Stefan Grabinski, *The Dark Domain*, 1993
Thomas Ligotti, *Grimscribe: His Lives and Works*, 1991
Thomas Ligotti, *Noctuary*, 1994
Thomas Ligotti, *Songs of a Dead Dreamer*, 1990
Edward Lucas White, *Lukundoo and Other Stories*, 1927

---

**3448**

**S.N. LEWITT**

## Blind Justice

(New York: Ace, 1991)

**Story type:** Science Fiction (Political)
**Major character(s):** Emile Saint-Just, Spaceman; Elizabeth Sarrault, Spaceship Captain
**Time period(s):** Indeterminate Future
**Locale(s):** *Mary Damned*, Spaceship (Free Trader); *Constanza*, Spaceship (Justica); Outer Space

**Summary:** Justica controls human space with an iron fist. When the *Mary Damned's* crew is caught, they are tried and sentenced to prison ships to work for Justica. The *Mary Damned* disappers, holds full of expensive cargo, leaving hope for the victims of Justica in the legends she leaves behind.

**Other books you might like:**
Glen Cook, *The Dragon Never Sleeps*, 1988
Colin Greenland, *Take Back Plenty*, 1991
Michael P. Kube-McDowell, *Emprise*, 1986
Timothy A. Madden, *Outbanker*, 1990
Joel Henry Sherman, *Random Factor*, 1991
Allen Steele, *Clarke County, Space*, 1990

Sheri S. Tepper, *Raising the Stones*, 1990
Jack Williamson, *Mazeway*, 1990

---

**3449**

**S.N. LEWITT**

## Cybernetic Jungle

(New York: Ace, 1992)

**Story type:** Science Fiction (Political)
**Major character(s):** Paulo ''Jackal'' Sulvia, Gang Member; Francisco Pope, Gang Member; Zeide Soledad, Student, Genetically Altered Being
**Time period(s):** Indeterminate Future
**Locale(s):** Brasilia, Brazil

**Summary:** When the power elite overthrows the government in Brasilia, the ensuing chaos destroys the economy and the middle classes. Pope and Sylvia, who had planned on becoming an astronaut, move to the poor section of town and start their own gang with the proviso that they will not deal in highwire. Their involvement with one of the native gangs leads to interaction with the ruling elite who retain contact with the outside world.

**Other books you might like:**
David Brin, *Earth*, 1990
Peter R. Emshwiller, *The Host*, 1991
Gregory Feeley, *The Oxygen Barons*, 1990
Pat Murphy, *The City, Not Long After*, 1989
David D. Ross, *The Argus Gambit*, 1989
Lucius Shepard, *Life During Wartime*, 1987
Neal Stephenson, *Snow Crash*, 1992

---

**3450**

**S.N. LEWITT**

## Cyberstealth

(New York: Ace, 1989)

**Story type:** Science Fiction (Military)
**Major character(s):** Cargo, Pilot, Spy; Ghoster, Alien, Spy
**Time period(s):** Indeterminate Future

**Summary:** In this prequel to *Dancing Vac*, Cargo is the hottest cyberstealth pilot around and the alien Ghoster is the perfect gunner. They have trouble making sense of each other face to face sometimes, but in the air, communicating through the cybernetic maze, they're definitely top guns.

**Other books you might like:**
Dale Brown, *Day of the Cheetah*, 1989
Emma Bull, *Falcon*, 1989
Dave Wolverton, *On My Way to Paradise*, 1989

---

**3451**

**S.N. LEWITT**

## Dancing Vac

(New York: Ace, 1990)

**Story type:** Science Fiction (Military)
**Major character(s):** Cargo, Pilot, Spy; Ghoster, Alien, Spy
**Time period(s):** Indeterminate Future
**Locale(s):** Marcanter, Planet—Imaginary; Tel Hasa, Planet—Imaginary

**Summary:** Betrayed by his alien partner and retired from life as a cyborg fighter pilot and spy, Cargo spends his time gambling until he's forced back into the espionage business. His friend Ghoster is a traitor and the powers that be want the alien dead. They want Cargo to kill him.

**Other books you might like:**
Emma Bull, *Falcon*, 1989
L.E. Modesitt Jr., *The Ecolitan Operation*, 1989
L.E. Modesitt Jr., *The Ecologic Envoy*, 1986
Dave Wolverton, *On My Way to Paradise*, 1989

---

### 3452
#### S.N. LEWITT

## Songs of Chaos
(New York: Ace, 1993)

**Story type:** Science Fiction (Political; Adventure)
**Major character(s):** Dante McCall, Outcast, Spaceman; Veronica Guimaraes, Spacewoman
**Time period(s):** Indeterminate Future
**Locale(s):** Europe; Eurostate, Fictional Country; *Mangueira*, Spaceship

**Summary:** An outcast among Florence's genetically altered perfection, Dante McCall presents an unacceptable threat to Eurostate. Dante stows away on a trading ship and finds acceptance among a spacefaring culture.

**Other books you might like:**
Alfred Bester, *The Stars My Destination*, 1956
Ernest Hogan, *Cortez on Jupiter*, 1990
Marjorie Bradley Kellogg, *Harmony*, 1991
Rebecca Ore, *Becoming Alien*, 1987
Alis A. Rasmussen, *A Passage of Stars*, 1990
Alis A. Rasmussen, *The Price of Ransom*, 1990
Alis A. Rasmussen, *Revolution's Shore*, 1990
Spider Robinson, *Stardance*, 1979
    Jeanne Robinson, co-author

---

### 3453
#### SHARIANN LEWITT

## Interface Masque
(New York: Tor, 1997)

**Story type:** Science Fiction (Arts; Political)
**Major character(s):** Cecilie 8 Sept-Fortune, Apprentice, Computer Expert; David Gavrilli, Heir, Runaway; Lina, Apprentice, Singer
**Time period(s):** 21st century
**Locale(s):** Venice, Italy; Rome, Italy

**Summary:** Stunned that she must illegally hack into a computer system to pass her last apprentice test in the great Sept-Fortune computer guild, Cecilie learns about the Sept houses' attempts to control the net and restrict free thought, in part by prohibiting innovative forms of music such as jazz.

**Other books you might like:**
David Brin, *Glory Season*, 1993
Orson Scott Card, *Songmaster*, 1980
Nicola Griffith, *Slow River*, 1995
Katharine Kerr, *Palace*, 1996
    Mark Kreighbaum, co-author
S.N. Lewitt, *Blind Justice*, 1991
S.N. Lewitt, *Cyberstealth*, 1989
S.N. Lewitt, *Dancing Vac*, 1991

Linda Nagata, *The Bohr Maker*, 1995
Mary Rosenblum, *The Stone Garden*, 1995
Katie Waitman, *The Merro Tree*, 1997

---

### 3454
#### SHARIANN LEWITT

## Memento Mori
(New York: Tor, 1995)

**Story type:** Science Fiction (Arts; Alternate Intelligence)
**Major character(s):** RICE, Artificial Intelligence; Johanna Henning, Scientist (mathematician); Peter Haas, Sports Figure (chess master), Artist
**Time period(s):** Indeterminate Future
**Locale(s):** Reis, Planet—Imaginary

**Summary:** When a plague on Reis quarantines the entire planet, society breaks down, with even the artificial intelligence controlling the cities acting strangely. Feeling doomed, several aspiring artists look for interesting ways to depict death in their work, or even interesting ways to die.

**Other books you might like:**
James P. Hogan, *The Two Faces of Tomorrow*, 1979
Gordon Kendall, *White Wing*, 1985
    pseudonym of Susan Shwartz and Shariann Lewitt
S.N. Lewitt, *Angel at Apogee*, 1987
S.N. Lewitt, *Blind Justice*, 1991
S.N. Lewitt, *Cyberstealth*, 1989
S.N. Lewitt, *Dancing Vac*, 1991
Larry Niven, *Achilles' Choice*, 1991
    Steven Barnes, co-author
Mary Rosenblum, *The Stone Garden*, 1995
John Varley, *Steel Beach*, 1992

---

### 3455
#### MARK LEYNER

## Et Tu, Babe
(New York: Harmony Books, 1992)

**Story type:** Science Fiction (Alternate Universe; Humor)
**Major character(s):** Mark Leyner, Writer, Socialite
**Time period(s):** 1990s
**Locale(s):** United States

**Summary:** Following the runaway success of *My Cousin, My Gastroenterologist*, Mark Leyner becomes the darling of the world through Team Leyner media opportunities. Fans everywhere receive inspirational messages by using touch tone telephones to call 1-800-T-LEYNER and Leyner's every activity attracts worldwide attention.

**Other books you might like:**
William Borden, *Superstoe*, 1968
Richard Brautigan, *Trout Fishing in America*, 1967
William S. Burroughs, *Naked Lunch*, 1959
William Kotzwinkle, *The Fan Man*, 1974
Neal Stephenson, *Snow Crash*, 1992
Hunter S. Thompson, *Fear and Loathing in Las Vegas*, 1971
Darius James, *Negrophobia: An Urban Parable*,

## 3456

**MARK LEYNER**

### My Cousin, My Gastroenterologist

(New York: Harmony, 1990)

**Story type:** Science Fiction (Literary; Contemporary Realism)
**Major character(s):** I, Human; Bev, Health Care Professional (speech pathologist)
**Time period(s):** 1990s
**Locale(s):** United States

**Summary:** A fast-paced, choppy series of detailed flashes of thought and action, this book is strong on description, actions, weird characters and transitions, with the actual plot threading through in the background. Portions of this book were published as short stories between 1984 and 1989.

**Other books you might like:**
Michael Blumlein, *The Brains of Rats*, 1990
Richard Brautigan, *The Hawkline Monster*, 1974
William S. Burroughs, *Naked Lunch*, 1959
Samuel R. Delany, *Dhalgren*, 1975
Philip K. Dick, *Ubik*, 1969
Tom Robbins, *Jitterbug Perfume*, 1984
Hunter S. Thompson, *Fear and Loathing in Las Vegas*, 1971
Kurt Vonnegut Jr., *Slaughterhouse Five*, 1969

## 3457

**MARK LEYNER**

### The Tetherballs of Bougainville

(New York: Harmony, 1997)

**Story type:** Fantasy (Literary; Satire)
**Major character(s):** Mark Leyner, Writer, Teenager; Warden, Police Officer
**Time period(s):** 1990s (1997)
**Locale(s):** Maplewood, New Jersey

**Summary:** The day after teeanager Mark Leyner watches his father executed, he wins an award for Best Screenplay written by a student at his junior high school. The novel, which acts as autobiography, screenplay, and movie review, examines and rc-examines Mark's response to these traumatic events.

**Other books you might like:**
Kathy Acker, *Empire of the Senseless*, 1988
William S. Burroughs, *Nova Express*, 1965
R.U. Sirius, *How to Mutate and Take Over the World*, 1996
　St. Jude, co-author
William T. Vollmann, *You Bright and Risen Angels*, 1987
Robert Anton Wilson, *Reality Is What You Can Get Away With: An Illustrated Screenplay*, 1992

## 3458

**JACQUELINE LICHTENBERG**

### Dreamspy

(New York: St. Martin's Press, 1989)

**Story type:** Science Fiction (Space Opera)
**Major character(s):** Kyllikki, Alien, Telepath; Zuchmul, Vampire
**Time period(s):** Indeterminate Future
**Locale(s):** Metaji Empire, Interstellar Empire/Federation; Teleod, Interstellar Empire/Federation

**Summary:** In the sequel to *Those of My Blood*, two great, galaxy-spanning empires, Metaji and Teleod, are at war, and their struggle threatens to destroy the very fabric of the space-time continuum. Intelligent beings of several different races struggle to end the war, among them Kyllikki, a Teleod and a powerful telepath; Zuchmul, a member of the vampiric, human-related luren race; and Elias, an Earth human, whose rare ability to dream may hold the key to the galaxy's salvation.

**Other books you might like:**
Emma Bull, *Falcon*, 1989
Jack Butler, *Nightshade*, 1989
Suzy McKee Charnas, *The Vampire Tapestry*, 1980
Richard Matheson, *I Am Legend*, 1954
Melisa C. Michaels, *Far Harbor*, 1989

## 3459

**ALAN LIGHTMAN**

### Einstein's Dreams

(New York: Pantheon, 1993)

**Story type:** Fantasy (Contemporary Realism; Literary)
**Major character(s):** Albert Einstein, Historical Figure, Government Official (patent clerk)
**Time period(s):** 1900s (1905)
**Locale(s):** Berne, Switzerland

**Summary:** As Albert Einstein concludes work on his special theory of relativity, 30 dreams of possible realms of time help him formulate ideas. First fiction.

**Other books you might like:**
Nicholson Baker, *The Fermata*, 1994
Philip K. Dick, *Ubik*, 1969
Ken Grimwood, *Replay*, 1986
Sam Moskowitz, *The Time Curve*, 1968
　Roger Elwood, co-editor
Fred Saberhagen, *A Spadeful of Spacetime*, 1981
　editor
Kurt Vonnegut Jr., *The Sirens of Titan*, 1959

## 3460

**THOMAS LIGOTTI**

### The Agonizing Resurrection of Victor Frankenstein and Other Gothic Tales

(Eugene, Oregon: Silver Salamander Press, 1994)

**Story type:** Horror (Collection)

**Summary:** The 19 prose poems collected here distill the essence of particular authors, literary works and films in the horror genre into a series of provocative extrapolations of their themes. Included are fantasias on ''The Insufferable Salvation of Lawrence Talbot, the Wolfman,'' ''The Intolerable Lesson of the Phantom of the Opera,'' and ''The Eternal Devotion of the Governness to the Residents of Bly.'' Two final sections of this beautifully produced book are devoted to the works of Edgar Allan Poe and H.P. Lovecraft.

**Other books you might like:**
J.G. Ballard, *The Atrocity Exhibition*, 1990
Jorge Luis Borges, *Ficciones*, 1962
Neil Gaiman, *Angels & Visitations: A Miscellany*, 1993
Franz Kafka, *Stories, 1904-1924*, 1990
Bruno Schulz, *The Street of Crocodiles*, 1934

**3461**

**THOMAS LIGOTTI**

## Grimscribe: His Lives and Works

(New York: Carroll & Graf, 1991)

**Story type:** Horror (Collection)

**Summary:** Thirteen stories in which hapless victims who look beyond the surfaces of their world are overwhelmed by a terrifying "other" reality. Included are the World Fantasy Award nominated homage to H.P. Lovecraft, "The Last Feast of Harlequin"; "The Mystics of Muelenberg," in which "reality" is found to be little more than a shared delusion; the metafictional "Nethescurial"; and a sardonic tale of a doctor-patient relationship, "The Cocoons."

**Other books you might like:**
Jorge Luis Borges, *Ficciones*, 1962
Dino Buzzati, *Catastrophe*, 1985
Ramsey Campbell, *Demons by Daylight*, 1973
Bruno Schulz, *The Street of Crocodiles*, 1934

**3462**

**THOMAS LIGOTTI**

## The Nightmare Factory

(New York: Carroll & Graf, 1996)

**Story type:** Horror (Collection)

**Summary:** The 45 stories collected here include most of the contents of the author's first three collections and six new stories that further elaborate his vision of existence as a series of nightmarish plunges through holes in the fabric of reality. "Teatro Grottesco" presents a group of artists who discover that their lives resemble the twisted art of an underground theatre group. "The Clown Puppet" employs a menacing doll figure to pose questions of identity among its human characters. The narrators of both "Gas Station Carnivals" and "The Bungalow House" discover that they themselves may be the originators of performance art works that intrigue, obsess, and eventually overwhelm them. All of the stories feature the author's trademark vision of a world whose nightmare logic calls into question the underlying logic of our own. Ligotti's essay, "The Consolations of Horror," appears as an introduction. Poppy Z. Brite supplies the foreword.

**Other books you might like:**
Robert Aickman, *The Wine-Dark Sea*, 1989
Jorge Luis Borges, *Labyrinths*, 1962
Ramsey Campbell, *Alone with the Horrors*, 1993
H.P. Lovecraft, *The Dunwich Horror and Others*, 1986

**3463**

**THOMAS LIGOTTI**

## Noctuary

(New York: Carroll & Graf, 1994)

**Story type:** Horror (Collection)

**Summary:** The author's third collection consists of eight stories, one previously unpublished, and 19 prose poems and fragments, all concerned with his favorite themes of the inherent instability of what we call reality. "Mad Night of Atonement" and "The Strange Design of Master Rignolo" deal with artists and creators who shine a light on our world that reflects its unreality, while "Conversations in a Dead Language," "The Prodigy of Dreams," "The Tsalal," and

especially "The Voice of the Bones" use dream imagery to evoke their horrors. The author has supplied "In the Dark, In the Night," an essay on the weird tale, as his introduction.

**Other books you might like:**
Robert Aickman, *The Wine-Dark Sea*, 1989
Jorge Luis Borges, *Labyrinths*, 1962
Ramsey Campbell, *Demons by Daylight*, 1973

**3464**

**THOMAS LIGOTTI**

## Songs of a Dead Dreamer

(New York: Carroll & Graf, 1990)

**Story type:** Horror (Collection)

**Summary:** The author's first book presents 20 profoundly disturbing stories that chronicle the experiences of characters in nightmarish worlds slightly off-center from our own. There are both ingenious variations on genre staples, such as the vampire ("The Lost of Art of Twilight"), possession ("The Christmas Eves of Aunt Elise") and sword 'n' sorcery ("Masquerade of a Dead Sword"), and ingeniously original efforts that include the baroque "Drink to Me Only with Labyrinthine Eyes," the surreal "The Greater Festival of Masks" and "Notes on the Writing of Horror," a fusion of fiction and non-fiction.

**Other books you might like:**
Jorge Luis Borges, *Ficciones*, 1962
Dino Buzzati, *Catastrophe*, 1985
Ramsey Campbell, *Demons by Daylight*, 1973
Bruno Schulz, *The Street of Crocodiles*, 1934

**3465**

**RUSSEL LIKE**

## After the Blue

(Highland Park, New Jersey: Brunswick Galaxy Press, 1998)

**Story type:** Science Fiction (Post-Holocaust; Humor)
**Major character(s):** Fred, Alien (Gruumsbaggian); Sheila, Agent; Jack, Teenager
**Time period(s):** 22nd century
**Locale(s):** Jamesburg, New Jersey

**Summary:** In the early part of the 21st century, the Gruumsbaggians come to Earth and accidentally destroy most of human civilization, but a century later, they return to fix the damage. With humanity's best interests at heart, the Gruumsbaggians reconstruct human life as they believe it was before the accident—with hilarious results.

**Other books you might like:**
Douglas Adams, *The Hitchhiker's Guide to the Galaxy*, 1980
John Sladek, *Roderick*, 1982
Walter Tevis, *Mockingbird*, 1980
Walter Jon Williams, *Rock of Ages*, 1995
Roger Zelazny, *This Immortal*, 1966

**3466**

**BRAD LINAWEAVER**, Editor
**EDWARD E. KRAMER**, Co-Editor

## Free Space

(New York: Tor, 1996)

**Story type:** Science Fiction (Anthology)

**Summary:** Contains a two-page introduction by Linaweaver plus individual introductions to two reprinted and 18 original stories, generally upbeat in tone, that explore Libertarian futures in space. Authors include Dafydd ab Hugh, Poul Anderson, Gregory Benford, Ray Bradbury, William F. Buckley, Jr., Arthur Byron Cover, Peter Crowther, John DeChancie, James P. Hogan, Victor Koman, Brad Linaweaver, Robert J. Sawyer, J. Neil Schulman, L. Neil Smith, Robert Anton Wilson, and William Wu.

**Other books you might like:**
Robert Adams, *Alternatives*, 1989
    Pamela Crippin Adams, co-author
Robert A. Heinlein, *The Moon Is a Harsh Mistress*, 1966
L. Neil Smith, *The Probability Broach*, 1980
F. Paul Wilson, *The LaNague Chronicles*, 1992

---

**3467**

**BRAD LINAWEAVER**

## Sliders: The Novel

(New York: Berkley Boulevared, 1996)

**Story type:** Science Fiction (Alternate Universe; Adventure)
**Major character(s):** Quinn Mallory, Inventor, Scientist; Maximillian Arturo, Professor, Adventurer; Rembrandt ''Cryin' Man'' Brown, Musician, Adventurer
**Time period(s):** 1990s
**Locale(s):** Alternate Earth

**Summary:** Quinn Mallory and his companions explore Earths in parallel dimensions using his homemade device. Television tie-in.

**Other books you might like:**
Dafydd ab Hugh, *Endgame*, 1996
    Brad Linaweaver, co-author
Dafydd ab Hugh, *Knee Deep in the Dead*, 1995
    Brad Linaweaver, co-author
Mona Clee, *Branch Point*, 1996
Ashley McConnell, *Quantum Leap: The Novel*, 1992
Robert Reed, *Down the Bright Way*, 1991
John Varley, *Millennium*, 1983

---

**3468**

**ANNE LINDBERGH**

## Travel Far, Pay No Fare

(New York: HarperCollins, 1992)

**Story type:** Fantasy (Young Adult; Quest)
**Major character(s):** Owen Noonan, Child, Adventurer; Parsley, Child, Adventurer
**Time period(s):** 1990s
**Locale(s):** Vermont

**Summary:** A magic bookmark transports Owen and Parsley into the world created in the book marked. There the pair seek a way to prevent their parents' upcoming marriage.

**Other books you might like:**
Michael Ende, *The Neverending Story*, 1983
Kathryn Lasky, *Double Trouble Squared*, 1991
Will Shetterly, *Elsewhere*, 1991
Nancy Springer, *The Friendship Song*, 1992
Vivian Vande Velde, *User Unfriendly*, 1991

---

**3469**

## Alien Earth

(New York: Bantam Spectra, 1992)

**Story type:** Science Fiction (First Contact; Post-Holocaust)
**Major character(s):** John Gen-93-Beta, Spaceship Captain; Evangeline, Alien (spaceship); Tug, Spaceship Captain, Alien (Arthroplana)
**Time period(s):** Indeterminate Future
**Locale(s):** *Evangeline*, Spaceship; Delta Station, Space Station; Earth

**Summary:** In the generations after the Arthroplana rescued humanity from the dying Earth and moved the population out of the solar system, humans evolved to fit the conditions of their new habitat. Sexual maturity occurs after sixty years of age, therefore natural conception has been eliminated and humanity totals approximately eighty-seven thousand. Unable to find other work for *Evangeline*, John accepts a contract to assess the potential viability of Earth, risking readjustment by the Human Conservancy.

**Other books you might like:**
Clare Bell, *People of the Sky*, 1989
Octavia E. Butler, *Dawn*, 1987
C.S. Friedman, *The Madness Season*, 1990
Diana G. Gallagher, *The Alien Dark*, 1990
T. Jackson King, *Retread Shop*, 1988
Vonda N. McIntyre, *Metaphase*, 1992
Larry Niven, *Protector*, 1973
Vernor Vinge, *A Fire upon the Deep*, 1992
Catherine Wells, *The Earth Is All That Lasts*, 1991
    pseudonym of Catherine Wells Dimenstein

---

**3470**

**MEGAN LINDHOLM**

## Cloven Hooves

(New York: Bantam Spectra, 1991)

**Story type:** Fantasy (Legend; Contemporary)
**Major character(s):** Evelyn Sylvia Potter, Farmer, Spouse; Pan, Mythical Creature (satyr)
**Time period(s):** 1970s (1976); 1960s
**Locale(s):** Washington; Alaska; Canada

**Summary:** When Evelyn and Tom Potter move from Alaska to Washington state to help with his family's farm, Evelyn begins to feel unappreciated and isolated until her childhood companion, Pan, reappears. Her relationship with Pan leads to a dangerous foot journey back towards Alaska, during which Evelyn begins a new life and family with the satyr.

**Other books you might like:**
Charles de Lint, *Greenmantle*, 1988
Charles de Lint, *Spiritwalk*, 1992
Gordon R. Dickson, *Wolf and Iron*, 1990
Greer Ilene Gilman, *Moonwise*, 1991
Robert Holdstock, *Mythago Wood*, 1984
Ian McDonald, *King of Morning, Queen of Day*, 1991
Thorne Smith, *Topper: An Improbable Adventure*, 1926
Mary Alexander Walker, *The Scathach and the Maeve's Daughter*, 1990

## 3471

### MEGAN LINDHOLM

## *Luck of the Wheels*

(New York: Ace, 1989)

**Story type:** Fantasy (Light Fantasy)
**Major character(s):** Ki, Trader (Gypsy); Vandien, Warrior (Swordsman)
**Time period(s):** Indeterminate

**Summary:** Ki and Vandien agree to escort an obnoxious teenage boy named Goat to a distant city. Encountering trouble along the way, they receive magic telepathic aid.

**Other books you might like:**
L. Sprague de Camp, *The Honorable Barbarian*, 1989
Barbara Hambly, *The Silent Tower*, 1988
Rosemary Kirstein, *The Steerswoman*, 1989
Jennifer Roberson, *Sword-Maker*, 1989
Christopher Stasheff, *The Warlock Insane*, 1989

## 3472

### CHARLES LINDLEY

## *The Ghost Book of Charles Lindley, Viscount Halifax*

(New York: Carroll & Graf, 1994)

**Story type:** Horror (Collection; Ghost Story)

**Summary:** Originally published as two volumes, *Lord Halifax's Ghost Book* (1936) and *Further Stories From Lord Halifax's Ghost Book* (1937), this compendium collects purportedly true ghost stories recorded by Lord Halifax, and culled from his apparently voluminous correspondence. "Marche!" tells of a ghost who repossesses its body long enough to keep away vermin during its disinterment, "The Man in the Iron Cage" of the spirit of an heir imprisoned in an iron cage that continues to haunt a castle, and "The Passenger with the Bag" of a spirit that helps solve the mystery of an embezzlement. For the most part, these stories are related in the straightforward fashion of folk tales, with few surprises or extraordinary motivations for their spectral players.

**Other books you might like:**
Jessica Amanda Salmonson, *The Mysterious Doom and Other Ghostly Tales of the Pacific Northwest*, 1992
Manly Wade Wellman, *John the Balladeer*, 1988
John Manchip White, *Whistling Past the Churchyard*, 1992

## 3473

### JANE M. LINDSKOLD

## *Brother to Dragons, Companion to Owls*

(New York: AvoNova, 1994)

**Story type:** Fantasy (Urban; Science Fiction)
**Major character(s):** Sarah, Handicapped (autistic), Psychic; Abalone, Computer Expert, Criminal; Betwixt and Between, Mythical Creature (animated rubber dragon)
**Time period(s):** Indeterminate Future
**Locale(s):** New York, New York; Ivy Green Institute, Mythical Place

**Summary:** Forced out of the Home by the mysterious Dr. Haas, Sarah befriends Abalone who takes her to the jungle, hoping Head Wolf will let her stay. After an old teacher comes to warn Sarah that she must hide, Sarah begins to gain control of her ability to hear inani-mate objects; however, the representatives of the Ivy Green Institute will not give up the search.

**Other books you might like:**
Iain M. Banks, *The Bridge*, 1986
Karen Joy Fowler, *Sarah Canary*, 1992
C.S. Friedman, *Black Sun Rising*, 1992
Susan Palwick, *Flying in Place*, 1992
Fay Weldon, *The Shrapnel Academy*, 1987

## 3474

### JANE M. LINDSKOLD

## *Changer*

(New York: Avon Eos, 1998)

**Story type:** Fantasy (Contemporary; Magic Conflict)
**Major character(s):** Arthur Pendragon, Ruler (king); Changer, Supernatural Being (shapechanger)
**Time period(s):** 1990s (1999)
**Locale(s):** New Mexico; Brazil

**Summary:** King Arthur and his followers survive into the 20th century because they discover the secret of immortality. Although they remain hidden from the world at large, a group of sorcerous enemies is aware of their existence. Arthur allies himself with a shapechanging creature whose desire to defeat their common enemies almost destroys them all.

**Other books you might like:**
Thomas Berger, *Arthur Rex*, 1978
David Drake, *The Dragon Lord*, 1982
Esther Friesner, *New York by Knight*, 1986
Helen Hollick, *Pendragon's Banner*, 1996
Ian McDowell, *Merlin's Gift*, 1997

## 3475

### JANE M. LINDSKOLD

## *Marks of Our Brothers*

(New York: AvoNova, 1995)

**Story type:** Science Fiction (First Contact; Psychic Powers)
**Major character(s):** Karen Saber, Linguist, Criminal; Aino Rand, Telepath; Onyx, Alien, Psychic (esper)
**Time period(s):** Indeterminate Future
**Locale(s):** U.A.N. Headquarters, Earth; *Shadowsweep*, Spaceship; Xi-7, Planet—Imaginary

**Summary:** Having begun a vendetta against the murderers of her ex-boss, Karen is distracted by a puzzle leading to a newly contacted, perhaps sentient, species. After rescuing the aliens, Karen must decide if the surviving one shows intelligence and, if so, how they can save her planet from colonization by the recent alliance of humans and aliens, the U.A.N.

**Other books you might like:**
Eleanor Arnason, *Ring of Swords*, 1993
L. Warren Douglas, *A Plague of Change*, 1992
Janet Kagan, *Hellspark*, 1988
Larry Niven, *The Mote in God's Eye*, 1974
    Jerry Pournelle, co-author
H. Beam Piper, *Little Fuzzy*, 1962

## 3476

### JANE M. LINDSKOLD

## *Smoke and Mirrors*
(New York: AvoNova, 1996)

**Story type:** Science Fiction (Psychic Powers; First Contact)
**Major character(s):** Smokey Smoke, Telepath, Prostitute; Ha'riel nu-Aten, Spaceship Captain, Alien (parasite); Clarence Beauduc, Professor (history), Tourist
**Time period(s):** Indeterminate Future
**Locale(s):** Arizona, Planet—Imaginary; *Ibn Battuta*, Spaceship; Guillen, Planet—Imaginary

**Summary:** Probing her customer during sex in order to perfectly satisfy, Smokey discovers an unpleasant alien presence. When acquaintances turn up brutally murdered, Smokey leaves Arizona with her parents, daughter and Clarence. Nu-Aten introduces Smokey to the conspiracy of humans with psychic powers and those with benign psychic parasites to fight the predatory psychic aliens Smokey experienced in Arizona.

**Other books you might like:**
Octavia E. Butler, *Dawn*, 1987
C.S. Friedman, *The Madness Season*, 1990
Robert A. Heinlein, *The Puppet Masters*, 1951
P.K. McAllister, *Siduri's Net*, 1994
Ian McDonald, *Evolution's Shore*, 1995

## 3477

### JANE M. LINDSKOLD

## *When the Gods Are Silent*
(New York: AvoNova, 1997)

**Story type:** Fantasy (Quest; Adventure)
**Major character(s):** Hulhe, Farmer, Scholar; Rabble, Warrior, Mythical Creature; Rylus, Entertainer
**Time period(s):** Indeterminate
**Locale(s):** Fictional Country

**Summary:** Hoping to find a cure for his wife's chronic illness, Hulhe hires Rylus and his Traveling Spectacular to escort him to the Storm Shroud Mountains where, he believes, the Magic still exists a generation after it ceased to function in the rest of the world. The troupe and their menagerie survive the dangers of bandits, surly mobs, pirates, bureaucrats, and the scheming Duke of Dragons. However, the truly dangerous portion of their journey only begins when they meet the ghost of a soldier who served the wizards that imprisoned the Elementals.

**Other books you might like:**
Lynn Abbey, *The Black Flame*, 1980
Ray Bradbury, *Something Wicked This Way Comes*, 1962
C.J. Cherryh, *Gate of Ivrel*, 1976
Ursula K. Le Guin, *A Wizard of Earthsea*, 1968
Robert Silverberg, *Lord Valentine's Castle*, 1980
Roger Zelazny, *Lord of Light*, 1967
Roger Zelazny, *Donnerjack*, 1997
    Jane Lindskold, co-author

## 3478

### HOLLY LISLE

## *Bones of the Past*
(New York: Baen, 1993)

**Story type:** Fantasy (Quest)
**Major character(s):** Medwind Song, Barbarian, Scholar; Nokar, Librarian; Roba Morgasdotte, Teacher (music), Adventurer
**Time period(s):** Indeterminate
**Locale(s):** Omwimmee Trade, Fictional City; Wennish Jungle, Fictional Country; First Folk Ruins, Fictional City

**Summary:** Wen children come to Omwimmee Trade hoping to secure food and agricultural technology. Medwind Song begins by trading a drum for the childrens' knowledge of drum talk language, but soon becomes interested in a First Folk artifact the children brought to trade. After learning of an abandoned First Folk city, Medwind Song arranges to journey there in exchange for extensive agricultural help for the Wen. None of Medwind Song's companions fully appreciate the perilous consequences of their anthropological undertaking.

**Other books you might like:**
Rosemary Kirstein, *The Outskirter's Secret*, 1992
Mercedes Lackey, *When the Bough Breaks*, 1993
    Holly Lisle, co-author
Marc Laidlaw, *Neon Lotus*, 1988
Lucius Shepard, *Kalimantan*, 1992

## 3479

### HOLLY LISLE

## *Curse of the Black Heron*
(New York: Baen, 1998)

**Story type:** Fantasy (Quest)
**Series:** Bard's Tale
**Major character(s):** Isbetta, Artisan (weaver); Giraud, Heir—Dispossessed; Black Heron, Murderer
**Time period(s):** Indeterminate
**Locale(s):** Terrosalle, Fictional Country

**Summary:** Isbetta must give up her life as a weaver when her friend Giraud becomes a fugitive because of his claim to a noble title. With a usurper running their country, they have a series of adventures before finding clues indicating that her father was killed by the legendary Black Heron, whose destiny seems linked to their own.

**Other books you might like:**
George Alec Effinger, *The Zork Chronicles*, 1990
Geary Gravel, *The Dreamwright*, 1995
Dixie Lee McKeone, *The Sentinel*, 1996
Mark Shepherd, *Escape From Roksamur*, 1997
Josepha Sherman, *The Chaos Gate*, 1994

## 3480

### HOLLY LISLE
### WALTER SPENCE, Co-Author

## *The Devil and Dan Cooley*
(New York: Baen, 1996)

**Story type:** Fantasy (Contemporary; Light Fantasy)
**Series:** Hellraised
**Major character(s):** Dan Cooley, Radio Personality; Puck, Demon; Lucifer, Demon

**Time period(s):** 1990s
**Locale(s):** Raleigh, North Carolina; Heaven

**Summary:** North Carolina goes to hell, literally, with thousands of the Damned released in, but confined to, that state. A radio personality with a patriotic bent, unresolved guilt, and two girlfriends, Dan Cooley decides to rehabilitate a demon as a publicity stunt. Trapped between Heaven, Hell, and angry humans, Dan soon finds more than ratings at stake.

**Other books you might like:**
Jack Dann, *Angels!*, 1995
   Gardner Dozois, co-editor
Neil Gaiman, *Good Omens: The Nice and Accurate Prophecies of Agnes Nutter, Witch*, 1990
   Terry Pratchett, co-author
James Morrow, *Only Begotten Daughter*, 1990
Nancy Springer, *Metal Angel*, 1994
Sean Stewart, *Resurrection Man*, 1995
Roger Zelazny, *If at Faust You Don't Succeed*, 1993
   Robert Sheckley, co-author

---

**3481**

**HOLLY LISLE**

## Diplomacy of Wolves

(New York: Warner Aspect, 1998)

**Story type:** Fantasy (Political; Magic Conflict)
**Series:** Secret Texts
**Major character(s):** Kait Galweigh, Mythical Creature (weredragon), Diplomat
**Time period(s):** Indeterminate
**Locale(s):** Calimekka, Fictional City

**Summary:** As a magical artifact attempts to attract enough magic users for activation, the few magic users remaining a millennium after a devastating magical war struggle for control of Calimekka. Kait Galweigh discovers a plot by House Sabir to wipe out House Galweigh. To escape mortal and demonic assassins, Kait may have to use a magical talent which could mean her death, if others discover its nature. First in series.

**Other books you might like:**
Lynn Flewelling, *Luck in the Shadows*, 1996
Carol Heller, *The Gates of Vensunor*, 1997
Robin Hobb, *Assassin's Apprentice*, 1995
Andre Norton, *The Elvenbane*, 1991
   Mercedes Lackey, co-author
Martha Wells, *The Element of Fire*, 1993

---

**3482**

**HOLLY LISLE**

## Fire in the Mist

(New York: Baen, 1992)

**Story type:** Fantasy (Magic Conflict)
**Major character(s):** Faia Rissedote, Shepherd, Sorceress; Medwind Song, Sorceress, Barbarian; Yaji Jennedote, Sorceress, Student
**Time period(s):** Indeterminate Past
**Locale(s):** Bright, Fictional City; Ariss, Fictional City

**Summary:** Discovering her village destroyed by plague, Faia uncages a magical explosion that removes the remains. This alerts the magicians of Ariss, who insist on Faia's training to avoid future disasters. Unfortunately, Faia's studies must wait as politics and ancient evil complicate her life.

**Other books you might like:**
Barbara Hambly, *The Time of the Dark*, 1982
Katherine Kurtz, *Deryni Rising*, 1970
Mercedes Lackey, *Arrows of the Queen*, 1987
Ursula K. Le Guin, *A Wizard of Earthsea*, 1968
Patricia A. McKillip, *The Riddle-Master of Hed*, 1976
Mercedes Lackey, *When the Bough Breaks*, 1993
   Holly Lisle, co-author

---

**3483**

**HOLLY LISLE**
**TED NOLAN**, Co-Author

## Hell on High

(New York: Baen, 1997)

**Story type:** Fantasy (Contemporary; Light Fantasy)
**Series:** Hellraised
**Major character(s):** Glibspet, Demon, Detective—Private; Jack Halloran, Engineer (electrical); Rheabeth "Rhea" Samuels, Businesswoman
**Time period(s):** 1990s
**Locale(s):** Heaven; Devil's Point, North Carolina

**Summary:** As God vacations, Jack Halloran works on a space drive. While Lucifer wants results from his demons, Glibspet, the only demonic private eye, tries to track down a missing Fallen Angel. Weirdly, it all connects.

**Other books you might like:**
Jack L. Chalker, *And the Devil Will Drag You Under*, 1979
Neil Gaiman, *Good Omens: The Nice and Accurate Prophecies of Agnes Nutter, Witch*, 1990
   Terry Pratchett, co-author
Christopher Moore, *Practical Demonkeeping*, 1992
Mike Resnick, *Deals with the Devil*, 1994
   Martin Greenberg, Loren Estleman, co-author
Roger Zelazny, *If at Faust You Don't Succeed*, 1993
   Robert Sheckley, co-author

---

**3484**

**HOLLY LISLE**

## Hunting the Corrigan's Blood

(New York: Baen, 1997)

**Story type:** Science Fiction (Genetic Manipulation; Political)
**Major character(s):** Cadence "Cady" Drake, Spaceship Captain; Strebban "Badger" Bede, Spaceman, Computer Expert; Peter Crane, Businessman (spaceship builder), Political Figure
**Time period(s):** Indeterminate Future
**Locale(s):** Cassamir Station, Space Station; *Hope's Reward*, Spaceship

**Summary:** Lifelong friends and companions since Cady ran away from her mother and the trouble she caused, Cady and Badger search for *Corrigan's Blood* stolen from Peter Crane. *Corrigan's Blood* uses a new drive which enables the spaceship to change course while in hyperdrive, making it very difficult to catch. It also seems that the thieves belong to a history cult whose members physically alter themselves to become super strong, but, unfortunately, can no longer survive without fresh human blood.

## 3485

**HOLLY LISLE**
**CHRIS GUIN**, Co-Author

### Mall, Mayhem and Magic

(New York: Baen, 1995)

**Story type:** Fantasy (Light Fantasy; Magic Conflict)
**Major character(s):** Jim Franklin, Clerk (bookstore); Sharra, Immortal; Gali, Mythical Creature (elf)
**Time period(s):** 1990s
**Locale(s):** North Carolina

**Summary:** While attempting to use a love spell discovered in an ancient book, Jim unwittingly begins to unlock the seals which confine Sharra's deadly mate and a cadre of demons ready to conquer the human realm.

**Other books you might like:**
Rick Cook, *Mall Purchase Night*, 1993
Elizabeth Forrest, *Phoenix Fire*, 1992
Alan Dean Foster, *Cyber Way*, 1990
Alan Dean Foster, *To the Vanishing Point*, 1988
Barbara Hambly, *Bride of the Rat God*, 1994
Harry Turtledove, *The Case of the Toxic Spell Dump*, 1993

## 3486

**HOLLY LISLE**

### Mind of the Magic

(New York: Baen, 1995)

**Story type:** Fantasy (Magic Conflict; Adventure)
**Major character(s):** Faia Rissedotte, Sorceress, Parent; Kirtha, Child, Magician; Medwind Song, Sorceress, Scholar
**Time period(s):** Indeterminate
**Locale(s):** Arhel, Fictional Country (continent)

**Summary:** Faia's hopes of raising Kirtha in peace vanish as a meddlesome god forces Faia into his machinations, bringing her a pivotal role in the future of magic in Arhel. Sequel to *Bones of the Past*.

**Other books you might like:**
Jo Clayton, *Wild Magic*, 1991
Dave Duncan, *The Cutting Edge*, 1993
Mary Gentle, *Rats and Gargoyles*, 1991
Laurell K. Hamilton, *Nightseer*, 1992
P.C. Hodgell, *God Stalk*, 1982
Patricia C. Wrede, *The Raven Ring*, 1994

## 3487

**HOLLY LISLE**

### Minerva Wakes

(New York: Baen, 1994)

**Story type:** Fantasy (Magic Conflict; Alternate World)
**Major character(s):** Minerva Kiakra, Parent, Heroine; Darryl Kiakra, Parent; Birkwelch, Mythical Creature
**Time period(s):** 1990s
**Locale(s):** Earth; Weird's Hold, Fictional City; Eyrith, Alternate Earth

**Summary:** Plotting to destroy all, the Unweaver kidnaps Minerva's children. A helpful satyr and dragon provide help as Minerva's maternal instinct drives her into a magical realm to save her children and rescue all of existence.

**Other books you might like:**
Emma Bull, *Finder*, 1994
Pamela Dean, *The Secret Country*, 1985
Rose Estes, *Troll-Taken*, 1993
Mercedes Lackey, *When the Bough Breaks*, 1993
  Holly Lisle, co-author
Vivian Vande Velde, *User Unfriendly*, 1991
Robert Weinberg, *A Logical Magician*, 1994

## 3488

**HOLLY LISLE**

### Sympathy for the Devil

(New York: Baen, 1996)

**Story type:** Fantasy (Contemporary; Light Fantasy)
**Series:** Hellraised
**Major character(s):** Dayne Kuttner, Nurse; Agonostis, Demon, Administrator; God, Deity
**Time period(s):** 1990s (1996)
**Locale(s):** Hell; Charlotte, North Carolina

**Summary:** Devastated by her husband's certain damnation and tormented by the suffering of her patients, Dayne Kuttner prays for relief for the damned. God responds by sending a contingent from Hell to North Carolina. While God acts in inscrutable ways and Satan wants Dayne's soul, neither fully realizes what Dayne plans to do.

**Other books you might like:**
Emma Bull, *War for the Oaks*, 1987
Jack L. Chalker, *And the Devil Will Drag You Under*, 1979
Neil Gaiman, *Good Omens: The Nice and Accurate Prophecies of Agnes Nutter, Witch*, 1990
  Terry Pratchett, co-author
Christopher Moore, *Practical Demonkeeping*, 1992
Mike Resnick, *Deals with the Devil*, 1994
  Martin H. Greenberg, Loren D. Estleman, co-editors

## 3489

**HOLLY LISLE**
**AARON ALLSTON**, Co-Author

### Thunder of the Captains

(New York: Baen, 1996)

**Story type:** Fantasy (Political; Adventure)
**Series:** Bard's Tale
**Major character(s):** Kin Underbridge, Servant (valet), Writer; Jerno Byriver, Royalty (king), Castaway; Halleyne dar Dero, Writer (scribe), Castaway
**Time period(s):** Indeterminate
**Locale(s):** Lieda, Fictional Country; Terosalle, Fictional Country; Fishtail Island, Mythical Place

**Summary:** Eight years of warfare and the death of all natural heirs leads to a treaty signed at sea on the eve of a storm. All three ships are destroyed, and the delegates arrive on Fishtail Island where a new system for survival and rule eventually emerges as Kin becomes compromise leader.

**Other books you might like:**
David Eddings, *Pawn of Prophecy*, 1982
Simon Hawke, *The Iron Throne*, 1995
J.V. Jones, *The Baker's Boy*, 1995
R.A. Salvatore, *The Legacy*, 1992
Josepha Sherman, *The Chaos Gate*, 1994

## 3490

### HOLLY LISLE
### AARON ALLSTON, Co-Author

## *Wrath of the Princes*

(New York: Baen, 1997)

**Story type:** Fantasy (Political; Adventure)
**Series:** Bard's Tale
**Major character(s):** Kin Underbridge, Judge; Halleyne dar Dero, Noblewoman, Sorceress; Jerno, Royalty, Leader (king)
**Time period(s):** Indeterminate
**Locale(s):** Feyndala, Mythical Place; Bekalli, Fictional City

**Summary:** Kin and Halleyne help Jerno reacquire power when they return to find that those who caused their shipwreck and subsequent dangers are now in control. Based on a computer game.

**Other books you might like:**
Aaron Allston, *Doc Sidhe*, 1995
Aaron Allston, *Galatea in 2-D*, 1993
Mercedes Lackey, *Castle of Deception*, 1992
    Josepha Sherman, co-author
Mercedes Lackey, *Fortress of Frost and Fire*, 1993
    Ru Emerson, co-author
Mercedes Lackey, *Prison of Souls*, 1993
    Mark Shepherd, co-author
Mark Shepherd, *Escape From Roksamur*, 1997
Josepha Sherman, *The Chaos Gate*, 1994

## 3491

### JONATHAN LITTELL

## *Bad Voltage*

(New York: NAL Signet, 1989)

**Story type:** Science Fiction (Cyberpunk)
**Major character(s):** Lynx, Gang Member (Gang leader); Mara, Gang Member
**Time period(s):** 21st century (2033)
**Locale(s):** Paris, France

**Summary:** High-tech hoods and cybernetically-augmented street gangs battle for survival in the streets of a decadent, near-future Paris. This is Littell's first novel.

**Other books you might like:**
William Gibson, *Count Zero*, 1985
William Gibson, *Mona Lisa Overdrive*, 1988
William Gibson, *Neuromancer*, 1984
W.T. Quick, *Dreams of Gods and Men*, 1989
Norman Spinrad, *Little Heroes*, 1987
Bruce Sterling, *Islands in the Net*, 1988

## 3492

### BENTLEY LITTLE

## *Dominion*

(New York: Signet, 1996)

**Story type:** Horror (Ancient Evil Unleashed)
**Major character(s):** Dion Semele, Teenager; Penelope Daneam, Teenager; Alice Semele, Clerk (bank teller), Parent (Dion's mother)
**Time period(s):** 1990s (1996)
**Locale(s):** Napa Valley, California

**Summary:** For untold years the women who run Daneam Vineyards have concealed their identities as mythological maenads, who slaughter their victims in a sexual frenzy. When Dion Semele moves to town the Daneams plan to mate him with their daughter Penelope and unleash a bacchanalian orgy of bloodlust and death. This book was first published in England in 1995 as *The Dark Dominion*.

**Other books you might like:**
Ron Faust, *Lord of the Dark Lake*, 1995
Michael O'Rourke, *The Undine*, 1996
Melanie Tem, *Wilding*, 1992
Kelley Wilde, *Angel Kiss*, 1993

## 3493

### BENTLEY LITTLE

## *The Ignored*

(New York: Signet, 1997)

**Story type:** Horror (Wild Talents)
**Major character(s):** Bob Jones, Writer (technical); Philipe, Terrorist; Jane Reynolds, Child-Care Giver
**Time period(s):** 1990s (1997)
**Locale(s):** Brea, California

**Summary:** As Bob Jones settles into the routine of his thankless job as a technical writer, he becomes so anonymous and ignored that he grows invisible to his colleagues. Outraged at his inconsequentiality, Bob uses his invisibility to cause mischief and murder, and eventually links up with a group of similarly underappreciated and angry people who suffer the same condition.

**Other books you might like:**
Nicholson Baker, *The Fermata*, 1994
Robert Cormier, *Fade*, 1989
Stephen King, *Insomnia*, 1995
Fritz Leiber, *The Sinful Ones*, 1953
H.G. Wells, *The Invisible Man*, 1897

## 3494

### BENTLEY LITTLE

## *The Mailman*

(New York: Onyx, 1990)

**Story type:** Horror (Satire)
**Major character(s):** Doug Albin, Teacher; Tritia Albin, Housewife (Doug's wife); John Smith, Postal Worker
**Time period(s):** 1990s
**Locale(s):** Willis, Arizona

**Summary:** Although he's a bit creepy, it's hard not to like the new mailman, who delivers neither junk mail nor bills. But when the good citizens of Willis find that some important letters are not being delivered, and worse, that those who accept mail from John Smith are at his beck and call, they discover a horrifying fact of life: he who controls the mail controls life.

**Other books you might like:**
Thomas M. Disch, *The M.D.: A Horror Story*, 1991
John Farris, *I Scream. You Scream. We All Scream for Ice Cream*, 1989
    in *Scare Tactics*
Jackie Hyman, *Echoes*, 1990

## 3495

### BENTLEY LITTLE

## *Murmerous Haunts*

(Concord, California: Dark Regions, 1997)

**Story type:** Horror (Collection)

**Summary:** Collection of nine stories, two original to the volume. Outstanding selections include ''The Mailman,'' a tale of psychological horror in which every tormentor in a man's life takes the form of a grotesque dwarf who terrorized him as a child; ''Estoppel,'' in which a man discovers he has the power to wish himself anything; ''Garage Sale,'' in which the fanatical persistence of garage-sale attendees suggests a preternaturally-endowed subculture; and the haunted house tale ''The Murmurous Haunts of Files.'' Richard Laymon supplies an introduction.

**Other books you might like:**
Gary A. Braunbeck, *Things Left Behind*, 1997
Brian Hopkins, *Something Haunts Us All*, 1996
Gerard Daniel Houarner, *Painfreak*, 1996
Elizabeth Massie, *Shadow Dreams*, 1996
Jeffrey Osier, *Horizon Lines*, 1997
David Niall Wilson, *The Fall of the House of Escher and Other Illusions*, 1996

## 3496

### BENTLEY LITTLE

## *The Revelation*

(New York: St. Martin's, 1990)

**Story type:** Horror (Apocalyptic Horror)
**Major character(s):** Jim Weldon, Police Officer (Sheriff); Brother Elias, Religious (Itinerant preacher)
**Time period(s):** 1990s
**Locale(s):** Randall, Arizona

**Summary:** An ancient evil gradually and progressively brings anarchy, madness, and death to Randall, as a small group of townspeople, led by a mysterious itinerant preacher, battles with long-forgotten rituals to save the town.

**Other books you might like:**
Ramsey Campbell, *The Hungry Moon*, 1986
Stephen King, *Salem's Lot*, 1975
T.E.D. Klein, *The Ceremonies*, 1984
Peter Straub, *Ghost Story*, 1979

## 3497

### BENTLEY LITTLE

## *The Store*

(New York: Signet, 1998)

**Story type:** Horror (Satire; Occult)
**Major character(s):** Bill Davis, Writer (technical); Newman King, Businessman (owner of The Store); Shannon Davis, Teenager, Relative (daughter of Bill)
**Time period(s):** 1990s (1998)
**Locale(s):** Juniper, Arizona

**Summary:** A huge retail outlet known as The Store comes to the small town of Juniper, providing residents with consumer goods to satisfy their every need. But as it destroys the local economy and promotes slavish devotion in its employees and outrageous behavior in its patrons, Juniper resident Bill Davis begins to suspect that there is something sinister, and even infernal, in its plans for the town.

**Other books you might like:**
James P. Blaylock, *All the Bells on Earth*, 1995
Stephen King, *Needful Things*, 1990
Harry Kressing, *The Cook*, 1965
David Prill, *Serial Killer Days*, 1996
Joan Samson, *The Auctioneer*, 1975

## 3498

### BENTLEY LITTLE

## *The Summoning*

(New York: Leisure, 1993)

**Story type:** Horror (Vampire Story)
**Major character(s):** Sue Wing, Journalist; Richard Carter, Editor (newspaper); Robert Carter, Police Officer
**Time period(s):** 1990s (1993)
**Locale(s):** Rio Verde, Arizona

**Summary:** A voracious *cup-hu-girngsi*, or shape-shifting vampire, comes to the remote town of Rio Verde, and complicates its removal by appearing in a variety of forms that stir the emotions of the townsfolk against one another.

**Other books you might like:**
Don Davis, *Bring on the Night*, 1993
  Jay Davis, co-author
Ron Dee, *Dusk*, 1991
Charles L. Grant, *The Soft Whisper of the Dead*, 1982
Stephen King, *Salem's Lot*, 1975
Richard Laymon, *The Stake*, 1991

## 3499

### BENTLEY LITTLE

## *University*

(New York: Signet, 1995)

**Story type:** Horror (Occult)
**Major character(s):** Jim Parker, Student, Editor (of the student newspaper); Faith Pullen, Student; Ian Emerson, Professor (of English literature)
**Time period(s):** 1990s (1995)
**Locale(s):** Brea, California

**Summary:** There's only one explanation for the violence, sexual debauchery, and hatred overflowing from the newly-founded University of California at Brea into the surrounding town: the university is actually a sentient entity, approaching its fourth year of life, after which it will evolve into an even more terrible being. A small band of enlightened students and professors at the school put their lives in jeopardy when they determine to put an end to the university's evil.

**Other books you might like:**
Ed Kelleher, *The School*, 1988
  Harriet Vidal, co-author
Fritz Leiber, *Conjure Wife*, 1953
R.L. Stine, *Superstitious*, 1995

## 3500

**DENISE LITTLE**, Editor

### Alien Pets

(New York: DAW, 1998)

**Story type:** Science Fiction (Anthology)

**Summary:** Here are 15 original stories about the problems of dealing with aliens as pets. The contributors include Nina Kiriki Hoffman, Karen Haber, Jack Williamson, Peter Crowther, and John DeChancie. A majority of the stories take this potentially humorous theme seriously.

**Other books you might like:**
Tara K. Harper, *Cataract*, 1995
Robert A. Heinlein, *The Star Beast*, 1952
Ted Key, *The Cat From Outer Space*, 1978
Andre Norton, *Catfantastic*, 1991
   Martin H. Greenberg, co-editor
William Tenn, *The Square Root of Man*, 1968

## 3501

**MORGAN LLYWELYN**

### Brian Boru: Emperor of the Irish

(New York: Tor, 1995)

**Story type:** Fantasy (Young Adult)
**Major character(s):** Brian mac Kennedy, Leader, Historical Figure; Murcha mac Brian, Warrior, Heir; Malachy the Great, Royalty (high king), Leader
**Time period(s):** 10th century
**Locale(s):** Ireland

**Summary:** Young Brian Boru vows over the bodies of his slain mother and brothers to drive the Viking invaders from his beloved Ireland forever. Schooled as both warrior and scholar, Brian battles his way to the High King's crown and dedicates his life to uniting the squabbling tribes of his kingdom. Reprint of 1990 Irish edition.

**Other books you might like:**
Kenneth C. Flint, *Challenge of the Clans*, 1986
Harry Harrison, *The Hammer and the Cross*, 1993
   John Holm, co-author
Robert E. Howard, *Conan the Barbarian*, 1955
Ron Miller, *Hearts and Armor*, 1992
Andrew J. Offutt, *Sword of the Gael*, 1975
Rosemary Sutcliff, *Sword at Sunset*, 1963
Paul O. Williams, *The Breaking of Northwall*, 1981
Bridget Wood, *Wolfking*, 1992

## 3502

**MORGAN LLYWELYN**

### Druids

(New York: Morrow, 1991)

**Story type:** Fantasy (Historical)
**Major character(s):** Ainvar, Religious (Druid priest); Vercingetorix, Warrior
**Time period(s):** 5th century; 6th century
**Locale(s):** Gaul

**Summary:** With Ainvar's help, Vercingetorix must unite the diverse Celtic tribes to resist the growing Roman threat within Gaul.

**Other books you might like:**
Frans G. Bengtsson, *The Long Ships*, 1954
Parke Godwin, *Sherwood*, 1991
Patricia Kennealy-Morrison, *The Copper Crown*, 1984
R.A. MacAvoy, *The Book of Kells*, 1985
Elona Malterre, *The Celts*, 1988

## 3503

**MORGAN LLYWELYN**

### The Elementals

(New York: Tor, 1993)

**Story type:** Fantasy (Post-Disaster; Religious)
**Major character(s):** Kesair, Artisan, Leader; Meriones, Musician; Annie Murphy, Housewife
**Time period(s):** 101st century B.C. (10,000 B.C.); 1850s (1855)
**Locale(s):** Crete, Greece (Knossos); New Hampshire

**Summary:** When Earth's ice cap melts, the water rises. After Kesair and her people build a boat, all but three men dying in its defense, Kesair comes to understand the language of the water and guides her band across the ocean to a new land. Meriones learns the power of fire while living on Minoan Crete. Annie Murphy's pragmatic upbringing inadvertently brings her into contact with Earth through the huge holy stone which influences her New Hampshire town.

**Other books you might like:**
David Brin, *Earth*, 1990
Thomas A. Easton, *Sparrowhawk*, 1990
Sue Harrison, *Mother Earth, Father Sky*, 1990
Anne McCaffrey, *Powers That Be*, 1993
   Elizabeth Ann Scarborough, co-author
Elizabeth Ann Scarborough, *Nothing Sacred*, 1991
Catherine Wells, *The Earth Is All That Lasts*, 1991

## 3504

**MORGAN LLYWELYN**

### Finn Mac Cool

(New York: Forge, 1994)

**Story type:** Fantasy (Legend; Adventure)
**Major character(s):** Finn Mac Cool, Warrior, Hero; Goll Mac Morna, Warrior; Cormac Mac Airt, Royalty, Leader
**Time period(s):** 3rd century
**Locale(s):** Ireland

**Summary:** Finn Mac Cool overcomes his early abandonment and life in the wilderness to lead a band of warriors of the Fianna. As Finn promotes legends about his deeds, Finn's defense of Tara leads King Cormac to appoint him supreme commander of the Fianna, further deteriorating his personal relationship with Goll Mac Morna.

**Other books you might like:**
Kenneth C. Flint, *Challenge of the Clans*, 1986
Andrew J. Offutt, *Sword of the Gael*, 1975
Diana L. Paxson, *Master of Earth and Water*, 1993
   Adrienne Martine-Barnes, co-author
Diana L. Paxson, *The Shield between the Worlds*, 1994
   Adrienne Martine-Barnes, co-author
John Vornholt, *The Fabulist*, 1993
Bridget Wood, *Wolfking*, 1992

## 3505

MORGAN LLYWELYN

### The Isles of the Blest

(New York: Ace, 1989)

**Story type:** Fantasy (Legend)
**Major character(s):** Connla, Warrior; Blathine, Mythical Creature (Fairy)
**Time period(s):** Indeterminate Past
**Locale(s):** Isles of the Blest, Mythical Place (Land of the faeries)

**Summary:** Connla, an Irish warrior, weary of battle, decides that he does not wish to engage himself in any further confrontation. With his lust for war depleted, he makes a deal with Blathine, but some deals turn out to be risky. This one is no exception.

**Other books you might like:**
Poul Anderson, *Three Hearts and Three Lions*, 1961
Ellen Kushner, *Thomas the Rhymer*,
Peter Tremayne, *Bloodmist*, 1988

## 3506

MORGAN LLYWELYN

### Pride of Lions

(New York: Forge, 1996)

**Story type:** Fantasy (Legend; Political)
**Major character(s):** Donough, Leader, Warrior; Gormlaith, Widow(er)
**Time period(s):** 11th century
**Locale(s):** Ireland

**Summary:** Thrust into leadership on the battlefield, Donough, the 15-year-old son of Brian Boru, hopes to continue his father's gains in unifying Ireland. However, Gormlaith seeks to gather power to herself, while Donough's duty requires great personal sacrifice in pursuit of his goals. Sequel to *Lion of Ireland*.

**Other books you might like:**
C.J. Cherryh, *Fortress in the Eye of Time*, 1995
Kenneth C. Flint, *Challenge of the Clans*, 1986
Andrew J. Offutt, *Sword of the Gael*, 1975
Diana L. Paxson, *Master of Earth and Water*, 1993
    Adrienne Martine-Barnes, co-author
Melanie Rawn, *The Golden Key*, 1996
    Jennifer Roberson, Kate Elliott, co-authors
Mary Stewart, *The Crystal Cave*, 1970
Bridget Wood, *Wolfking*, 1992

## 3507

MORGAN LLYWELYN

### Silverlight

(New York: Baen, 1996)

**Story type:** Fantasy (Adventure; Magic Conflict)
**Series:** Arcana
**Major character(s):** Caeled Silverhand, Hero, Warrior
**Time period(s):** Indeterminate Future
**Locale(s):** At Sea; Seven Nations, Fictional Country

**Summary:** Caeled Silverhand must locate the four emblems of ultimate power, the Arcana, before evil twin sorcerers, the Duet, can use them and Tantric Magic to plunge the world into eternal suffering.

**Other books you might like:**
Terry Goodkind, *Wizard's First Rule*, 1994
Frank Herbert, *Heretics of Dune*, 1984
Marjorie Bradley Kellogg, *The Book of Earth*, 1995
Marc Laidlaw, *Neon Lotus*, 1988
Fred Saberhagen, *The First Book of Swords*, 1983

## 3508

ANNE LOGSTON

### Dagger's Edge

(New York: Ace, 1994)

**Story type:** Fantasy (Mystery; Adventure)
**Series:** Shadow
**Major character(s):** Jael, Mythical Creature (half-elf), Royalty; Shadow, Mythical Creature (elf), Thief
**Time period(s):** Indeterminate
**Locale(s):** Allanmere, Fictional City

**Summary:** Hoping to improve Jael's standing as heir, Jael's parents engage her Aunt Shadow to help overcome her bad luck and the lethal intent of a secret cult bent on destroying elves.

**Other books you might like:**
Lois McMaster Bujold, *The Spirit Ring*, 1992
Elizabeth Moon, *Sheepfarmer's Daughter*, 1988
Andre Norton, *The Elvenbane*, 1991
    Mercedes Lackey, co-author
Paula Volsky, *Illusion*, 1992
Martha Wells, *The Element of Fire*, 1993

## 3509

ANNE LOGSTON

### Firewalk

(New York: Ace, 1997)

**Story type:** Fantasy (Political; Adventure)
**Major character(s):** Kayli, Magician (Order of the Inner Flame), Noblewoman; Radon, Heir, Spouse
**Time period(s):** Indeterminate
**Locale(s):** Agrond, Fictional Country

**Summary:** Dragged from an important initiation to become the bride in an arranged marriage which will strengthen her country's ties to its neighbor, Kayli must learn to control her magical abilities without the usual help offered by her Order. In Agrond, Kayli must quickly adapt to life as a ruler while insuring her place by producing an heir for her husband.

**Other books you might like:**
Lois McMaster Bujold, *The Spirit Ring*, 1992
Laurell K. Hamilton, *Nightseer*, 1992
J.V. Jones, *The Baker's Boy*, 1995
Peg Kerr, *Emerald House Rising*, 1997
Fiona Patton, *The Stone Prince*, 1997
Caroline Stevermer, *A College of Magics*, 1994

## 3510

ANNE LOGSTON

### Greendaughter

(New York: Ace, 1993)

**Story type:** Fantasy (Adventure; Political)

**Major character(s):** Chyrie, Mythical Creature (elf)
**Time period(s):** Indeterminate
**Locale(s):** Allanmere, Fictional City

**Summary:** Chyrie must affect cooperation between elves and their traditional enemies, humans, to secure Allanmere against barbarian invaders intent on total destruction. Prequel to *Shadow*.

**Other books you might like:**
Teresa Edgerton, *The Moon in Hiding*, 1989
Elizabeth Moon, *Surrender None: The Legacy of Gird*, 1990
Mark C. Perry, *Morigu: The Dead*, 1990
Kristine Kathryn Rusch, *The White Mists of Power*, 1991
Pat Zettner, *The Shadow Warrior*, 1990

---

**3511**

### ANNE LOGSTON

## *Guardian's Key*

(New York: Ace, 1996)

**Story type:** Fantasy (Quest)
**Major character(s):** Dara, Magician, Servant; The Vanian, Guardian (Crystal Keep's); Gespry, Companion
**Time period(s):** Indeterminate
**Locale(s):** Crystal Keep, Mythical Place

**Summary:** Accompanied by Gespry and sometimes aided by Lord Vanian, Dara searches for the Oracle behind the seemingly endless doorways of Crystal Keep, hoping to discover her own magical abilities and a means to marry her beloved.

**Other books you might like:**
Lois McMaster Bujold, *The Spirit Ring*, 1992
Laurell K. Hamilton, *Nightseer*, 1992
Caroline Stevermer, *A College of Magics*, 1994
Deborah Talmadge-Bickmore, *The Apprentice*, 1990
Martha Wells, *The Element of Fire*, 1993

---

**3512**

### ANNE LOGSTON

## *Shadow*

(New York: Ace, 1991)

**Story type:** Fantasy (Adventure; Mystery)
**Series:** Shadow
**Major character(s):** Shadow, Mythical Creature (elf), Thief; Lady Donya, Thief (former), Mythical Creature (half-elf)
**Time period(s):** Indeterminate
**Locale(s):** Allanmere, Fictional City

**Summary:** For someone so new in town, Shadow's drawing much dangerous attention, apparently because of the lovely silver bracelet she stole and now can't remove from her wrist. It seems an awfully small thing to have catapulted Shadow into the middle of religious and guild politics and human/elf tensions, to say nothing of the assassin on her trail. This is the author's first novel.

**Other books you might like:**
Steven Brust, *Jhereg*, 1983
Glen Cook, *Sweet Silver Blues*, 1987
Tanya Huff, *The Fire's Stone*, 1990
Fritz Leiber, *Swords and Deviltry*, 1970
Patricia C. Wrede, *Shadow Magic*, 1982

---

**3513**

### ANNE LOGSTON

## *Shadow Dance*

(New York: Ace, 1992)

**Story type:** Fantasy (Quest)
**Series:** Shadow
**Major character(s):** Shadow, Mythical Creature (elf), Thief; Lady Donya, Thief (former), Mythical Creature (half-elf); Mist, Hunter, Mythical Creature (elf)
**Time period(s):** Indeterminate
**Locale(s):** Fictional City; Dim Reaches, Mythical Place (swamp); Spirit Lake, Mythical Place

**Summary:** Reluctant to return to the swamp which nearly claimed her life, Shadow leads a band of warriors into the Dim Reaches to collect a plant needed to treat the Crimson Plague and find an ancient temple, the key to averting an invasion.

**Other books you might like:**
Elizabeth Moon, *Sheepfarmer's Daughter*, 1988
James D. Priest, *Kirins: The Spell of No'an*, 1990
Will Shetterly, *Elsewhere*, 1991
J.R.R. Tolkien, *The Hobbit*, 1938
Patricia C. Wrede, *Searching for Dragons*, 1991

---

**3514**

### ANNE LOGSTON

## *Shadow Hunt*

(New York: Ace, 1992)

**Story type:** Fantasy (Quest)
**Series:** Shadow
**Major character(s):** Shadow, Mythical Creature (elf), Thief; Blade, Murderer (assassin); Baloran, Wizard
**Time period(s):** Indeterminate
**Locale(s):** Allanmere, Mythical Place; Spirit Lake, Mythical Place; Baloran's Keep, Mythical Place

**Summary:** Hoping to find a fabulous ruby and discover why its owner, a powerful wizard, wishes ill to her guild, Shadow joins in partnership with Blade who wishes to exact revenge upon the wizard who has enslaved her as possessor of a magic dagger which holds a demon within. Both stand to profit if they survive their quest and partnership. Sequel to *Shadow*.

**Other books you might like:**
Steven Brust, *Jhereg*, 1983
Glen Cook, *Sweet Silver Blues*, 1987
Laurell K. Hamilton, *Nightseer*, 1992
Tanya Huff, *The Fire's Stone*, 1990
Patricia C. Wrede, *Shadow Magic*, 1982

---

**3515**

### FRANK BELKNAP LONG

## *Escape From Tomorrow*

(West Warwick, Rhode Island: Necronomicon Press, 1995)

**Story type:** Horror (Collection)
**Summary:** The three stories collected here in memory of the author, who died in 1994, all appeared originally in *Weird Tales* and have never been reprinted before. "You Can't Kill a Ghost" is a traditional ghost story, and "He Came at Dusk" a robot tale. The title

story is a dystopia about a man and woman rebelling against a totalitarian future society.

**Other books you might like:**
Arthur J. Burks, *Black Medicine*, 1966
Hugh B. Cave, *Murgunstrumm and Others*, 1977
August Derleth, *Someone in the Dark*, 1941
Carl Jacobi, *Smoke of the Snake*, 1994
E. Hoffman Price, *Strange Gateways*, 1967
Manly Wade Wellman, *Worse Things Waiting*, 1973

## 3516

### FRANK BELKNAP LONG

## The Eye Above the Mantel and Other Stories

(West Hills, California: Tsathoggua Press, 1995)

**Story type:** Horror (Collection)

**Summary:** Editor Perry Grayson has assembled four stories written by a close friend of H.P. Lovecraft (whose essay on Long for the amateur press is reprinted as the introduction) and fantasist in his own right. "Dr. Whitlock's Price," Long's first published tale in the amateur press, tells of the just rewards that befall an experimenter on animals. "The Eye Above the Mantel" evokes the imagery of Edgar Allan Poe in its account of an alien landscape, and "In the Tomb of Semenses" a horrifying nightmare of ancient Egypt. "A Dangerous Experiment" is a comic account of a clash of cultures.

**Other books you might like:**
Robert H. Barlow, *The Hoard of the Wizard Beast and One Other*, 1994
Hugh B. Cave, *Murgunstrumm and Others*, 1977
Duane Rimel, *To Yith and Beyond*, 1990

## 3517

### ROXANNE LONGSTREET

## Cold Kiss

(New York: Zebra, 1995)

**Story type:** Horror (Vampire Story)
**Major character(s):** Michael Bowman, Doctor, Vampire; Maggie Bowman, Detective—Homicide (Michael's wife); Celestine Vaughan, Vampire, Lawyer
**Time period(s):** 1990s (1995)
**Locale(s):** Dallas, Texas

**Summary:** Surgeon-turned vampire Michael Bowman mourns the companionship with a mortal wife that he can no longer share and finds himself torn between two distasteful styles of vampire life: becoming a member of the Society, a cabal of vampires who share pain with one another and exchange sex for blood with mortals; or running with a renegade vampire named William, who subjugates weaker vampires to his will and wants only to slaughter human victims. This novel is a sequel to *The Undead*.

**Other books you might like:**
Vincent Courtney, *Vampire Beat*, 1991
David Dvorkin, *Insatiable*, 1993
Nancy Kilpatrick, *Near Death*, 1994
Karen E. Taylor, *Bitter Blood*, 1994
Karen E. Taylor, *Blood Secrets*, 1994

## 3518

### ROXANNE LONGSTREET

## Red Angel

(New York: Zebra, 1994)

**Story type:** Horror (Serial Killer)
**Major character(s):** Alexandra Hobbs, Journalist (investigative reporter); Gabriel Davies, Detective (former); Anthony Lipaski, Detective
**Time period(s):** 1990s (1994)
**Locale(s):** Chicago, Illinois

**Summary:** Detective Gabriel Davies was destroyed professionally when an unscrupulous reporter published secret diaries he kept while covering a series of brutal murders that revealed his own psychopathic fantasies. Almost ten years later, tabloid reporter Alexandra Hobbs finds that someone is trying to make it appear that Davies himself is responsible for another string of murders—and that she is the next victim.

**Other books you might like:**
Matthew J. Costello, *Homecoming*, 1992
Thomas Harris, *Red Dragon*, 1981
Samuel M. Key, *From a Whisper to a Scream*, 1992
John D. MacDonald, *The Executioners*, 1957

## 3519

### ROXANNE LONGSTREET

## The Undead

(New York: Zebra, 1993)

**Story type:** Horror (Vampire Story)
**Major character(s):** Michael Bowman, Doctor; Maggie Bowman, Detective—Homicide; Adam Radburn, Vampire, Morgue Attendant
**Time period(s):** 1990s (1993)
**Locale(s):** Clear Creek, Texas

**Summary:** Mike Bowman finds his sympathies pulled in opposite directions when he discovers that his good friend Adam Radburn is a vampire: though repulsed by the idea of Adam's supernatural nature, he finds the fanatical human beings who want to kill him even more repugnant.

**Other books you might like:**
Don Davis, *Bring on the Night*, 1993
    Jay Davis, co-author
Elizabeth Engstrom, *Black Ambrosia*, 1988
Anne Rice, *Interview with the Vampire*, 1975
Theodore Sturgeon, *Some of Your Blood*, 1961

## 3520

### BARRY B. LONGYEAR

## The Change

(New York: Pocket, 1994)

**Story type:** Science Fiction (Invasion of Earth)
**Series:** Alien Nation
**Major character(s):** George Francisco, Alien (Tectonese), Detective—Police; Matthew Sykes, Detective—Police; Maanka "Pete Moss" Dak, Alien (Tectonese), Criminal
**Time period(s):** 21st century
**Locale(s):** Los Angeles, California

**Summary:** Tectonese scientist Maanka Dak declares a blood feud against George and anyone close to him when George kills his brother in an FBI raid. As ex-members of the Tectonese underground, George and Maanka know each other and recognize that each has chosen a different path to freedom and self-respect, and that only one of them will survive. Meanwhile George undergoes the change of life to a new stage of development.

**Other books you might like:**
Peter David, *Body and Soul*, 1993
Alan Dean Foster, *Alien Nation*, 1993
K.W. Jeter, *Dark Horizon*, 1993
Judith Reeves-Stevens, *The Day of Descent*, 1993
    Garfield Reeves-Stevens, co-author
David Alexander Smith, *In the Cube*, 1993

## 3521

### BARRY B. LONGYEAR

## The Homecoming
(New York: Walker, 1989)

**Story type:** Science Fiction (First Contact)
**Major character(s):** Carl Baxter, Advertising, Pilot; Deayl, Alien
**Time period(s):** 1980s
**Locale(s):** Earth; Outer Space

**Summary:** The Nitolans, intelligent dinosaurs, had originally evolved on Earth, but left the planet some seventy million years ago. Now they've returned to reclaim their territory, but find it occupied by humanity.

**Other books you might like:**
Arthur C. Clarke, *Childhood's End*, 1953
David Gerrold, *Chess with a Dragon*, 1987
Rebecca Ore, *Becoming Alien*, 1987
Rebecca Ore, *Being Alien*, 1989

## 3522

### BARRY B. LONGYEAR

## Infinity Hold
(New York: Popular Library Questar, 1989)

**Story type:** Science Fiction (Adventure)
**Major character(s):** Nicos Bando, Convict; Darrell Garoit, Convict, Revolutionary
**Time period(s):** 22nd century (2115)
**Locale(s):** Greenville, Mississippi; Tartaros, Planet—Imaginary

**Summary:** Earth decides to relieve prison overcrowding by sending all of its worst criminals on a one-way ride to Tartaros, a ghastly prison planet. Young Nicos Bando learns to survive on Tartaros and build a life for himself.

**Other books you might like:**
Gregory Benford, *Great Sky River*, 1987
Harry Harrison, *Deathworld*, 1960
Robert Sheckley, *The Status Civilization*, 1960
James White, *Escape Orbit*, 1964

## 3523

### BARRY LOPEZ

## Crow and Weasel
(San Francisco: North Point Press, 1990)

**Story type:** Fantasy (Legend; Adventure)
**Major character(s):** Crow, Adventurer, Indian; Weasel, Adventurer, Indian
**Time period(s):** Indeterminate Past
**Locale(s):** Northern Plains, North America

**Summary:** Crow and Weasel, two men too young to smoke themselves, are given a pipe bag to share with others on their journey to go further north than any of their tribe has gone before. While meeting new and interesting people on their trip, they grow and learn from their experiences.

**Other books you might like:**
Peter Gadol, *Coyote*, 1990
Garry Kilworth, *The Foxes of Firstdark*, 1990
Dean R. Koontz, *Oddkins*, 1988
H. Beam Piper, *Little Fuzzy*, 1962
Jane Yolen, *Tam Lin*, 1990

## 3524

### JEAN LORRAH

## Metamorphosis
(New York: Pocket, 1990)

**Story type:** Science Fiction (Space Opera)
**Series:** Star Trek: The Next Generation
**Major character(s):** Data, Android, Space Explorer, Military Personnel (lieutenant commander); Thelia, Alien, Adventurer
**Time period(s):** 24th century
**Locale(s):** Elysia, Planet—Imaginary; Dacket, Planet—Imaginary (Samdian System); *U.S.S. Enterprise*, Spaceship

**Summary:** Data is transformed into a human being by the gods of Elysia in return for helping one of their people. He enjoys the new sensations and emotions, but then becomes depressed. After the *Enterprise* answers an emergency call from the Samdian System, which is being taken over by a group apparently intent on genocide, Data decides he must return to Elysia.

**Other books you might like:**
Carmen Carter, *Doomsday World*, 1990
    Peter David, Michael Jan Friedman, Robert Greenberger, co-authors
A.C. Crispin, *The Eyes of the Beholders*, 1990
Peter David, *A Rock and a Hard Place*, 1990
    Star Trek - The Next Generation 10
Gene DeWeese, *The Peacekeepers*, 1988
    Star Trek - The Next Generation 2
Michael Jan Friedman, *Fortune's Light*, 1991
    Star Trek - The Next Generation 15

## 3525

### RICHARD LORTZ

## Bereavement
(Clarkston, Georgia: White Wolf, 1996)

**Story type:** Horror (Psychological Suspense)
**Major character(s):** Mrs. Harrington-Smith Evans, Wealthy; Martin Dzierlatka, Actor; Bruno David Carlson-Wade, Writer

**Time period(s):** 1990s
**Locale(s):** New York, New York; Harper's Gate, New York

**Summary:** Three young men who have lost their mothers compete to become the surrogate son of Mrs. Harrington-Smith Evans, a woman so bereaved by the loss of her boy Jamie that she has advertised in newspapers seeking a replacement. Events turn ugly and unpredictable once Mrs. Evans reveals the extent of the surrogacy she expects. This novel was first published in 1980.

**Other books you might like:**
Todd Komarnicki, *Famine*, 1997
Mark Morris, *The Immaculate*, 1992
Melanie Tem, *Prodigal*, 1991
Melanie Tem, *Revenant*, 1994

---

**3526**

**JANE WEBB LOUDON**

## The Mummy!: A Tale of the Twenty-Second Century

(Ann Arbor: University of Michigan Press, 1994)

**Story type:** Horror (Reanimated Dead; Satire)
**Major character(s):** Edmund Montagu, Military Personnel; Edric Montagu, Student; Cheops, Reanimated Dead (mummy)
**Time period(s):** 22nd century (2127)
**Locale(s):** London, England

**Summary:** Originally published in 1828, this late-Gothic satire on the social and political life of Great Britain tells of the accidental resuscitation of the mummy of Cheops, Egyptian pharaoh of the 26th century B.C., and the role he plays advising various political factions struggling to usurp the British throne, engineering its downfall. This edition has been edited by Professor Alan Rauch.

**Other books you might like:**
Charles L. Grant, *The Long Night of the Grave*, 1986
Michael Paine, *Cities of the Dead*, 1988
Thomas Love Peacock, *Nightmare Abbey*, 1818
Mary Shelley, *Frankenstein*, 1818
H.G. Wells, *The Time Machine*, 1898

---

**3527**

**PETER LOUGHRAN**

## The Third Beast

(Chelsea, Michigan: Scarborough House, 1990)

**Story type:** Horror (Psychological Suspense)
**Major character(s):** Laura Lewis, Teenager; Andrea, Teenager; McKinnan, Police Officer
**Time period(s):** 1990s (1990)
**Locale(s):** England

**Summary:** Receiving no help from the police and no satisfaciton from the courts when his teenage niece is gang-raped, the unnamed narrator of this novel takes the law into his own hands and systematically murders her assailants.

**Other books you might like:**
Joe R. Lansdale, *The Nightrunners*, 1987
David J. Schow, *The Kill Riff*, 1988
John Skipp, *The Cleanup*, 1987
   Craig Spector, co-author

---

**3528**

**SIMON LOUVISH**

## The Resurrections

(New York: Four Walls Eight Windows, 1994)

**Story type:** Science Fiction (Alternate Universe; Political)
**Major character(s):** Adolf Hitler, Historical Figure, Political Figure; Ernesto "Che" Guevara, Historical Figure, Revolutionary; Joseph "Joseph Gable" Goebbels, Historical Figure, Businessman
**Time period(s):** 1960s; 1970s
**Locale(s):** Alternate Earth

**Summary:** After WWII, in an alternate world, Adolph Hitler rises to U.S. Senator during the ascendance of the American Party then, after losing his office, plans new political achievements, aided by Joseph Goebbels. The student revolution in England flourishes, while Che Guevara foments revolution in Ethiopia and Italy.

**Other books you might like:**
Ben Bova, *Triumph*, 1993
Len Deighton, *SS-GB*, 1978
Philip K. Dick, *The Man in the High Castle*, 1962
Robert Harris, *Fatherland*, 1992
Norman Spinrad, *The Iron Dream*, 1972

---

**3529**

**H.P. LOVECRAFT**

## The Annotated H.P. Lovecraft

(New York: Dell, 1997)

**Story type:** Science Fiction (Collection)
**Summary:** Four stories by horror master H.P. Lovecraft, each annotated extensively with information on their composition, influences and historical lore. Included are "At the Mountains of Madness," a tale of horrors from beyond space and time that befall an expedition to the Anartic; "The Dunwich Horror," in which an extradimensional monster rampages through the New England countryside; and "The Colour out of Space," about a meteorite that unleashes an alien life form on a small farm. S.T. Joshi, the leading Lovecraft Scholar, contributes an introduction, an appendix outlining Lovecraft's philosophy of weird fiction, and a secondary bibliography.

**Other books you might like:**
Robert Bloch, *The Early Fears*, 1994
Frank Belknap Long, *The Hounds of Tindalos*, 1946
Clark Ashton Smith, *Out of Space and Time*, 1941
Donald Wandrei, *Don't Dream*, 1997

---

**3530**

**H.P. LOVECRAFT**

## The Dream Cycle of H.P. Lovecraft: Dreams of Terror and Death

(New York: Del Rey, 1995)

**Story type:** Horror (Collection)
**Summary:** The 25 stories, fragments and prose poems collected here span 15 years of the author's pulp-era writing career and range from the imaginary-world fantasy of "The Cats of Ulthar" to the horrors of supernatural possession in the short novel, "The Case of Charles Dexter Ward." Many of the stories employ nightmares and dream imagery, including those centered around the experiences of Lovecraft's fictional surrogate, Randolph Carter ("The State of Randolph

Carter," "The Silver Key," "Through the Gates of the Silver Key," and the novel *The Dream Quest of Unknown Kadath*). In more horror-oriented stories such as "The Dreams in the Witch House," "Hypnos," and "Beyond the Wall of Sleep," dreams penetrate and eventually overwhelm waking reality. Neil Gaiman supplies the introduction.

**Other books you might like:**
Ramsey Campbell, *Strange Things and Stranger Places*, 1993
Lord Dunsany, *A Dreamer's Tales*, 1910
Thomas Ligotti, *Noctuary*, 1994
Thomas Ligotti, *Songs of a Dead Dreamer*, 1989

### 3531

**H.P. LOVECRAFT**

## The Horror in the Museum and Other Revisions

(Sauk City, Wisconsin: Arkham House, 1989)

**Story type:** Horror (Collection)

**Summary:** A restoration and correction of the stories "revised" for other writers, arranged according to the degree of Lovecraft's involvement in the texts. Thirteen stories are listed as "Primary Revisions" and eleven are presented as "Secondary Revisions."

**Other books you might like:**
Ramsey Campbell, *New Tales of the Cthulhu Mythos*, 1980
August Derleth, *The Mask of Cthulhu*, 1958
Robert E. Howard, *Cthulhu: The Mythos and Kindred Horrors*, 1987

### 3532

**H.P. LOVECRAFT**
**JOHN JUDE PALENCAR**, Illustrator

## Road to Madness: The Transition of H.P. Lovecraft

(New York: Del Rey, 1996)

**Story type:** Horror (Collection)

**Summary:** This omnibus collection of 28 stories, poems, and fragments features works that span the short professional career of the writer acknowledged as the most important author of weird fiction in the 20th century. Juvenile shockers such as "The Beast in the Cave" and "The Transition of Juan Romero" are counterbalanced by the mature tales "At the Mountains of Madness" and "The Shunned House," which articulate Lovecraft's philosophy of a cosmos indifferent to human endeavors and conceptions. In addition to "Cool Air," "He," "The Horror at Red Hook," and several other tales of pure horror written under the influence of Edgar Allan Poe, the book includes wistful fantasies such as "The White Ship," which expresses the author's fondness for antiquity and aesthetic fulfillment. Barbara Hambly supplies an introduction.

**Other books you might like:**
Robert Bloch, *The Early Fears*, 1994
Ramsey Campbell, *Cold Print*, 1993
August Derleth, *The Mask of Cthulhu*, 1958
Thomas Ligotti, *The Nightmare Factory*, 1996

### 3533

**H.P. LOVECRAFT**
**JASON ECKHARDT**, Illustrator

## The Shadow over Innsmouth

(West Warwick, Rhode Island: Necronomicon Press, 1994)

**Story type:** Horror (Ancient Evil Unleashed)
**Major character(s):** Robert Olmstead, Traveler; Zadok Allen, Streetperson; Obediah Marsh, Sailor
**Time period(s):** 1920s (1927)
**Locale(s):** Innsmouth, Massachusetts

**Summary:** Lovecraft's classic tale tells of a young man who happens by chance upon a degenerate New England coastal town, discovers a history of congress between its inhabitants and a race of sea creatures, and finds out something about his own heritage he wished he never knew. Editors S.T. Joshi and David Schultz have annotated the text rigorously with data culled from Lovecraft's letters and other writings, and supplied an informative introduction concerned with the genesis of the story. Appendices contain Lovecraft's notes for the story and an early draft of the tale.

**Other books you might like:**
Fred Chappell, *Dagon*, 1968
Stephen Jones, *Shadows over Innsmouth*, 1994
   editor
David Langford, *Irrational Numbers*, 1993
Brian Stableford, *The Innsmouth Heritage*, 1992

### 3534

**H.P. LOVECRAFT**

## Tales of H.P. Lovecraft

(Hopewell, New Jersey: Ecco Press, 1997)

**Story type:** Science Fiction (Collection)

**Summary:** Joyce Carol Oates compiles and introduces a collection of ten of the best stories by H.P. Lovecraft, the writer whose tales of cosmic horror, published primarily in the pulp magazines of the early twentieth century, are credited with bringing the horror story out of the Gothic tradition and into the twentieth century. Included are "The Outsider," an homage to Poe; "The Shadow out of Time," about a man kidnapped by a cosmic race to write the history of the Earth; "The Shadow over Innsmouth," about a race of fish-like creatures who have taken over a New England seaside town; "The Music of Erich Zann," about a musician whose art opens the door to another dimension; and "The Call of Cthulhu," which maps the mythology of a race of extradimensional beings who embody the chaos of the universe.

**Other books you might like:**
Robert Bloch, *The Early Fears*, 1994
Frank Belknap Long, *The Hounds of Tindalos*, 1946
Clark Ashton Smith, *Out of Space and Time*, 1941
Donald Wandrei, *Don't Dream*, 1997

### 3535

**H.P. LOVECRAFT**
**AUGUST DERLETH**, Co-Author

## The Watchers out of Time

(New York: Carroll & Graf, 1991)

**Story type:** Horror (Collection)

**Summary:** Although billed as collaborative efforts between H.P. Lovecraft and his pupil August Derleth, the 15 stories in this book are entirely the work of the latter, laboring under the influence of his mentor. Some, such as "The Shadow out of Space" and "The Shuttered Room," approximate specific tales of Lovecraft's; others like "The Gable Window" and the uncompleted title novel use the motifs of Lovecraft's fiction to tell stories that differ fundamentally in intention from those of Lovecraft. Still others, among them "The Dark Brotherhood" and "The Fisherman of Falcon Point," attempt with varying degrees of success to evoke the dark mood of Lovecraft's writing without parroting his plots. A hardcover version of this collection, including the novel *The Lurker at the Threshold*, was published in 1973.

**Other books you might like:**
Edward P. Berglund, *Disciples of Cthulhu*, 1976
Lin Carter, *The Spawn of Cthulhu*, 1971
August Derleth, *Tales of the Cthulhu Mythos*, 1969

**3536**

**JACK LOVEJOY**

## Outworld Cats

(New York: DAW, 1994)

**Story type:** Science Fiction (First Contact; Political)
**Major character(s):** Tim Waverly, Activist, Security Officer; Rhoda Dawn, Psychic, Child; Benton Ingles, Industrialist, Villain
**Time period(s):** 1990s
**Locale(s):** Royal Beach, California; Sulatonga Island, Pacific Islands

**Summary:** Two young space cats investigate the communication satellite put up by humans. Kidnapped to Earth, they escape and befriend a security officer who teaches them chess. They inadvertently become embroiled in foiling a plot by Benton Ingles to take over the world by turning dissenters into surgically created automatons.

**Other books you might like:**
C.J. Cherryh, *The Pride of Chanur*, 1982
Bill Fawcett, *Cats in Space and Other Places*, 1992
  editor
Alan Dean Foster, *Cat-A-Lyst*, 1991
Marti Steussy, *Dreams of Dawn*, 1988
Marti Steussy, *Forest of the Night*, 1987

**3537**

**JAMES LOWDER**

## Crusade

(Lake Geneva, Wisconsin: TSR, 1991)

**Story type:** Fantasy (Historical)
**Series:** Forgotten Realms: The Empire Trilogy
**Major character(s):** Azoun, Ruler (king)
**Time period(s):** Indeterminate Past (Medieval period)
**Locale(s):** Cormyr, Fictional Country (European)

**Summary:** In this sequel to David Cook's *Horselords* and Troy Denning's *Dragonwall*, the barbarian horsemen have turned their sights westward. King Cormyr must unite the diverse factions threatened by the invasion to stop the conquering hordes. This book novelizes one chapter of history surrounding the invasion of Europe by Asian horsemen. A game tie in novel.

**Other books you might like:**
David Cook, *Horselords*, 1990
Troy Denning, *Dragonwall*, 1990

Troy Denning, *The Parched Sea*, 1991
Ed Greenwood, *Spellfire*, 1988
R.A. Salvatore, *The Crystal Shard*, 1988
R.A. Salvatore, *Homeland*, 1990

**3538**

**JAMES LOWDER**

## The Ring of Winter

(Lake Geneva, Wisconsin: TSR, 1992)

**Story type:** Fantasy (Quest)
**Series:** Forgotten Realms: The Harpers
**Major character(s):** Artus Climber, Adventurer
**Time period(s):** Indeterminate
**Locale(s):** Chult, Fictional Country; The Realms, Fictional Country

**Summary:** Artus Climber learns of the jungle hiding place of the fabled Ring of Winter which makes the wearer immortal and will bring a new ice age to the Realms. Artus sets off into the jungle where he meets villainous cultists and monstrous animals which hinder his efforts.

**Other books you might like:**
Mark Anthony, *Crypt of the Shadowking*, 1993
Scott Ciencin, *The Night Parade*, 1992
Elaine Cunningham, *Elfshadow*, 1991
Troy Denning, *The Parched Sea*, 1991
Jean Rabe, *Red Magic*, 1991

**3539**

**FRANCES LUCAS**

## Cathy IV

(Norwich, Vermont: New Victoria Publishers, Inc., 1992)

**Story type:** Science Fiction (Political; Gay/Lesbian Fiction)
**Major character(s):** Cathy Four, Cyborg (servo); Jenny Brooks, Traveler, Revolutionary
**Time period(s):** 33rd century (3200)
**Locale(s):** Saegrenot, Planet—Imaginary (1.2 light years from Earth)

**Summary:** When Jenny's spaceship crash lands on Saegrenot, a planet banned from the Interplanetary Alliance for violating the prohibition against slavery, Jenny falls in love with a female android and involves herself in the servos' revolution.

**Other books you might like:**
Judith Alguire, *Zeta Base*, 1991
Camarin Grae, *Stranded*, 1991
Elizabeth Moon, *Surrender None: The Legacy of Gird*, 1990
Paul Park, *The Cult of Loving Kindness*, 1991
Steve Perry, *The Man Who Never Missed*, 1985

**3540**

**GEORGE LUCAS**
**CHRIS CLAREMONT**, Co-Author

## Shadow Moon

(New York: Bantam Spectra, 1995)

**Story type:** Fantasy (Quest)
**Series:** Chronicles of the Shadow War
**Major character(s):** Thorn Drumheller, Mythical Creature (nelwyn), Wizard; Elora Danan, Royalty (princess); Rool, Mythical Creature (brownie)

**Time period(s):** Indeterminate Past
**Locale(s):** The Great Realms, Fictional Country

**Summary:** In this print sequel to the film *Willow*, Willow finds himself carried off, seemingly in a dream. He soon discovers that Princess Elora faces great danger and again needs his help.

**Other books you might like:**
Eleanor Arnason, *The Sword Smith*, 1978
Peter S. Beagle, *The Last Unicorn*, 1968
Glen Cook, *The Black Company*, 1984
Wayland Drew, *Willow*, 1988
Katherine Kurtz, *Deryni Rising*, 1970
Patricia A. McKillip, *The Riddle-Master of Hed*, 1976

## 3541
### TIM LUCAS

## Throat Sprockets
(New York: Delta/Cutting Edge, 1994)

**Story type:** Horror (Vampire Story)
**Major character(s):** Austin Ingersoll, Advertising; Emma Mitsouko, Artist; Nancy Reagan, Advertising
**Time period(s):** 1990s (1994)
**Locale(s):** Friendly, Ohio

**Summary:** The nameless narrator of this novel of obsession reveals how the viewing of a film of throat fetishism fires his imagination to create advertising campaigns that subliminally stimulate the world's perverse sexual drives. Partly adapted as a graphic novel between 1987 and 1989, this is the author's first novel.

**Other books you might like:**
Steven R. Boyett, *The Answer Tree*, 1988
   in David J. Schow's *Silver Scream*
Jonathan Carroll, *A Child Across the Sky*, 1989
Theodore Roszak, *Flicker*, 1992
Brad Strickland, *Shadowshow*, 1988
Theodore Sturgeon, *Some of Your Blood*, 1961

## 3542
### JAMES LUCENO

## A Fearful Symmetry
(New York: Ballantine/Del Rey, 1989)

**Story type:** Science Fiction (Mystical)
**Major character(s):** Karl Reydak, Spy; Tedman Brady, Political Figure (President of the United States)
**Time period(s):** 20th century
**Locale(s):** Washington, District of Columbia; Brazil

**Summary:** In this Philip K. Dick Award-nominated novel, the millennium is at hand and there appears to be an actual upsurge in the occurence of mystical and psychic phenomena. The president of the United States himself claims to have been kidnapped by aliens and insists on consulting a Brazilian shaman. Agent Karl Reydak is assigned to investigate.

**Other books you might like:**
John Kessel, *Good News From Outer Space*, 1989
James Morrow, *Only Begotten Daughter*, 1990

## 3543
### JAMES LUCENO

## Illegal Alien
(New York: Ballantine/Del Rey, 1990)

**Story type:** Science Fiction (Humor)
**Major character(s):** Remy Santoul, Spy
**Time period(s):** Indeterminate Future
**Locale(s):** Planet of the Q'aantre, Planet—Imaginary

**Summary:** Interstellar spy Remy Santoul is sent to an alien planet to discover its inhabitants' weaknesses. That weakness, of course, turns out to be sex. The Q'aantre tend to do it often and anywhere. Santoul finds that he fits right in.

**Other books you might like:**
Philip Jose Farmer, *Dare*, 1965
Philip Jose Farmer, *Flesh*, 1960
Philip Jose Farmer, *The Image of the Beast*, 1968
Philip Jose Farmer, *A Woman a Day*, 1960
Harry Harrison, *Star Smashers and Galaxy Rangers*, 1973
Andrew J. Offutt, *Ardor on Aros*, 1973

## 3544
### JAMES LUCENO

## The Mata Hari Adventure
(New York: Ballantine, 1992)

**Story type:** Fantasy (Adventure; Historical)
**Series:** Young Indiana Jones Chronicles
**Major character(s):** Indiana ''Indy'' Jones, Teenager, Military Personnel (battlefield messenger); Mata Hari, Spy, Historical Figure
**Time period(s):** 1910s
**Locale(s):** Verdun, France; Paris, France

**Summary:** While on leave from front line duty in World War I, Indy meets Mata Hari, finding an immediate and mutual attraction. As Indy begins to know her better, he finds the darker side of her life, creating a conflict between Indy's loyalties.

**Other books you might like:**
Richard Brightfield, *Valley of the Kings: Egypt, May 1908*, 1992
Les Martin, *Field of Death*, 1992
Les Martin, *Trek of Doom*, 1992
William McKay, *The Secret Peace*, 1992
Gavin Scott, *Revolution*, 1992
A.L. Singer, *Safari Sleuth*, 1992

## 3545
### NANCY LUENN

## Goldclimbers
(New York: Atheneum, 1991)

**Story type:** Fantasy (Quest; Young Adult)
**Series:** Dragonflight
**Major character(s):** Aracco, Apprentice, Adventurer
**Time period(s):** Indeterminate
**Locale(s):** Caraccen, Fictional Country

**Summary:** Aracco expects to become a goldsmith, following in his father's footsteps, even though he has an unusual aptitude for climbing mountains. When the appearance of giant avian predators discourages the goldclimbers, threatening the town's gold supply, Aracco sets out in search of the legendary Terenger, where streets are said to be made of gold, hoping to find a new source of gold to ensure the town's livelihood.

**Other books you might like:**
Lynne Reid Banks, *The Farthest-Away Mountain*, 1977
Louise Cooper, *The Sleep of Stone*, 1991
Charles de Lint, *The Dreaming Place*, 1990
J. Alison James, *Sing for a Gentle Rain*, 1990
Mercedes Lackey, *Bardic Voices*, 1991
Tanith Lee, *Black Unicorn*, 1991
Robert Silverberg, *Letters From Atlantis*, 1990
Lawrence Watt-Evans, *The Blood of a Dragon*, 1991
Jane Yolen, *Wizard's Hall*, 1991

**3546**

BRIAN LUMLEY

## Blood Brothers

(New York: Tor, 1992)

**Story type:** Horror (Vampire Story)
**Series:** Vampire World Trilogy
**Major character(s):** Nestor Kiklu, Twin, Psychic; Nathan Kiklu, Twin, Psychic; Wratha, the Unrisen, Vampire
**Time period(s):** 1990s
**Locale(s):** World of the Gate, Alternate Universe

**Summary:** In an alternate universe the twin sons of the late Harry Keough, a scourge to the vampire race that inhabits the Starside, are separated during a vampire invasion of the Sunside. Unaware of the genetic legacy their father has passed on to them, each must learn to cope with his developing occult powers, even as they seek to reunite with each other and save their world.

**Other books you might like:**
Brian Stableford, *The Empire of Fear*, 1988
T. Lucien Wright, *Blood Brothers*, 1992

**3547**

BRIAN LUMLEY

## Bloodwars

(New York: Tor, 1994)

**Story type:** Horror (Vampire Story)
**Series:** Vampire World Trilogy
**Major character(s):** Nestor Kiklu, Vampire, Twin; Nathan Keogh, Twin, Psychic (necroscope); Ben Trask, Spy
**Time period(s):** 2000s (2006)
**Locale(s):** London, England; Sunside, Alternate Universe (vampire world)

**Summary:** This concluding volume of the Vampire World series, spun off from Lumley's popular Necroscope quintet, pits necroscope Nathan Keogh, a man capable of conversing with the dead, against his evil twin brother, Nestor, whose life in the alternate universe of the wamphyrii (vampires) has perverted his character and made him the scourge of the vampire world. Having been expelled from the vampire world, Nathan returns with the help of British paranormal agents to fight the final showdown with Nestor, who is himself backed by Russian paranormal agents intent on fomenting Cold War aggressions in the vampire world.

**Other books you might like:**
Jack Butler, *Nightshade*, 1989
Dan Simmons, *Carrion Comfort*, 1989

**3548**

BRIAN LUMLEY

## The Burrowers Beneath

(New York: W. Paul Ganley, 1989)

**Story type:** Horror (Ancient Evil Unleashed)
**Series:** Titus Crow
**Major character(s):** Titus Crow, Paranormal Investigator; Shudde-M'ell, Monster
**Time period(s):** 20th century (Mid)

**Summary:** A group of anti-Cthulhu crusaders, led by Titus Crow, fight to destroy the offspring of the earth-burrowing Shudde-M'ell, along with other Cthulhu-type beings. Originally published in 1974.

**Other books you might like:**
Robert Bloch, *Strange Eons*, 1978
Fred Chappell, *Dagon*, 1968
Michael Shea, *The Colour out of Time*, 1984

**3549**

BRIAN LUMLEY

## A Coven of Vampires

(Minneapolis, Minnesota: Fedogan & Bremer, 1998)

**Story type:** Horror (Collection; Vampire Story)

**Summary:** Thirteen stories, culled from the author's vast body of work, elaborate on the vampire theme in a variety of ways. Traditional vampires appear in "Necros," and "Zack Phalanx is Vlad the Impaler," and ravenous monsters of Lovecraftian horror show up in "The Thing from the Blasted Heath" and "Haggopian." "Back Row" and "Uzzi" feature parasitic creatures in contemporary settings, and "The Kiss of the Lamia" is about a female vampire in a sword-and-sorcery setting. With an introduction by the author.

**Other books you might like:**
R. Chetwynd-Hayes, *The Vampire Stories of R. Chetwynd-Hayes*, 1997
Brian Hodge, *Shrines and Desecrations*, 1994
Nancy Kilpatrick, *Sex and the Single Vampire*, 1994
Graham Masterton, *Fortnight of Fear*, 1994
Karl Edward Wagner, *Exorcisms and Ecstasies*, 1997

**3550**

BRIAN LUMLEY

## Deadspawn

(New York: Tor, 1991)

**Story type:** Horror (Vampire Story)
**Series:** Necroscope
**Major character(s):** Harry Keogh, Spy (necroscope), Psychic; Darcy Clark, Spy; Shaithis, Vampire
**Time period(s):** 1990s
**Locale(s):** London, England

**Summary:** In this final novel of the Necroscope quintet, Harry Keough, who can converse with the souls of the dead, has successfully quelled the threat of an invasion from the vampire universe, but now faces a new nemesis: a mass murderer who commits rape and mutilation upon corpses, and who is familiar enough with Harry's secret links with the vampire race to be able to use them against him.

**Other books you might like:**
Robert R. McCammon, *They Thirst*, 1981

Brian Stableford, *The Empire of Fear*, 1988

## 3551
### BRIAN LUMLEY

## *Deadspeak*
(New York: Tor, 1990)

**Story type:** Horror (Vampire Story)
**Series:** Necroscope
**Major character(s):** Harry Keogh, Spy, Psychic (hears voices of the dead); Janos Ferenczy, Vampire, Magician (black magician)
**Time period(s):** 1980s
**Locale(s):** Transylvania; Greece

**Summary:** As Harry recovers from his battle with the vampiric hordes, he is thrust into a new competition with a master vampire, Janos Ferenczy. In his weakened condition he can fight Janos only by linking minds with the most powerful and deadly vampire of them all.

**Other books you might like:**
John Farris, *Catacombs*, 1981
Stephen King, *The Talisman*, 1984
    Peter Straub, co-author
Robert R. McCammon, *They Thirst*, 1981

## 3552
### BRIAN LUMLEY

## *Demogorgon*
(New York: Tor, 1992)

**Story type:** Horror (Occult)
**Major character(s):** Charlie Trace, Thief; Dimitrious Kastrouni, Spy; George Khumeni, Wealthy (millionaire)
**Time period(s):** 1930s (1936); 1980s (1983)
**Locale(s):** London, England; Greece

**Summary:** An avatar of Satan is prevented from consummating the ritual that will restore his earthly realm in 1936. Nearly half a century later Charlie Trace, who may or may not be the offspring of the devil and a mortal woman, is recruited by occultists to thwart his father's rise to power. This novel was originally published in England in 1987.

**Other books you might like:**
Ramsey Campbell, *To Wake the Dead*, 1980
Ira Levin, *Rosemary's Baby*, 1967

## 3553
### BRIAN LUMLEY

## *Fruiting Bodies and Other Fungi*
(New York: Tor, 1993)

**Story type:** Horror (Collection)
**Summary:** The 13 stories collected here demonstrate the range of one of the most popular British horror writers working today. ''Born of the Winds'' and ''The Mirror of Nitocris'' are both heavily influenced by the writing of H.P. Lovecraft; ''Necros'' is a vampire story; ''The Thin People'' blends horror with science fiction; and ''The Cyprus Shell'' and ''The Deep Sea Conch'' are interconnected stories about the horrors of creatures from the ocean floor which are able to exchange minds with men. The best stories are ''Fruiting Bodies,'' about a house and its inhabitants who are taken over by a

vile fungus, and ''The Viaduct,'' a *conte cruel* about two boys trapped on a train trestle by a deranged child.

**Other books you might like:**
Joe R. Lansdale, *By Bizarre Hands*, 1989
Richard Laymon, *A Good, Secret Place*, 1993
Edward Lee, *Edward Lee's Quest for Sex, Truth and Reality*, 1992
J.N. Williamson, *The Naked Flesh of Feeling*, 1991

## 3554
### BRIAN LUMLEY

## *The House of Doors*
(New York: Tor, 1990)

**Story type:** Horror (Science Fiction)
**Major character(s):** Spencer Gill, Scientist (Terminally ill); Sith, Alien
**Time period(s):** 1990s (1994-95)
**Locale(s):** Scotland

**Summary:** A group of scientists, led by Stephen Gill, enters the House of Doors, an alien artifact designed to test the ''worthiness'' of a species, where they are subjected to numerous horrors dredged up from their own deepest fears and imaginings. The situation is made doubly dangerous by the fact that the ''invigilator'' sent to test them has decided, for his own devious ends, that they must fail.

**Other books you might like:**
Algis Budrys, *Rogue Moon*, 1960

## 3555
### BRIAN LUMLEY

## *Iced on Aran and Other Dream Quests*
(Buffalo, New York: Ganley, 1992)

**Story type:** Horror (Collection)

**Summary:** Set in dreamlands inspired by the work of H. P. Lovecraft, these five stories chronicle the continuing adventures of David Hero and Eldin the Wanderer (nee Leonard Dingle), men who projected their psyches into the land of dreams at the times of their deaths, and who fight a variety of human and supernatural menaces during their stay there. This collection was published in England in 1990.

**Other books you might like:**
Lin Carter, *The Fishers From Outside*, 1990
Gary Myers, *The House of the Worm*, 1975

## 3556
### BRIAN LUMLEY

## *In His Own Write: Brian Lumley, Necroscribe*
(West Warwick, Rhode Island: Necronomicon Press, 1997)

**Story type:** Horror (Collection)

**Summary:** A trio of stories reprinted in a tribute volume to the author, who was guest of honor for Necronomi-Con 3, a convention devoted to the fiction of H.P. Lovecraft. Selections include ''The Thing in the Moonlight,'' a pastiche of H.P. Lovecraft; ''The Writer in the Garret,'' in which a writer of strange stories discovers the horrifying truth about a fellow writer whose work he admires; and ''Synchronicity, or Something,'' a scenario for a fantasy role-playing game in which a fantasy role-playing gamer becomes enmeshed in a world of mystery and dark terrors. Lumley provides an introduction. Illustrated by Dave Carson.

**Other books you might like:**
Lin Carter, *The Xothic Legend Cycle*, 1997
David Langford, *Irrational Numbers*, 1994
W.H. Pugmire, *Tales of Sesqua Valley*, 1997
Jeffrey Thomas, *The Bones of the Old Ones*, 1995
Stanley Wiater, *Mysteries of the Word*, 1994
F. Paul Wilson, *The Barrens*, 1992

---

**3557**

**BRIAN LUMLEY**

## The Last Aerie

(New York: Tor, 1993)

**Story type:** Horror (Vampire Story)
**Series:** Vampire World Trilogy
**Major character(s):** Nestor Kiklu, Twin, Psychic (necroscope); Nathan Kiklu, Twin, Psychic (necromancer); Ben Trask, Spy
**Time period(s):** 2000s (2006)
**Locale(s):** London, England

**Summary:** In this sequel to *Blood Brothers*, a spinoff from Lumley's *Necroscope* quintet, amnesiac Nestor Kiklu continues his overtures to the vampires living in a parallel universe, embarked on his apparent destiny to become their leader. Meanwhile, his twin brother Nathan, exiled to our world, becomes part of a plot to thwart the vampire menace much the same way that Nestor and Nathan's father, necroscope (someone who can converse with the dead) Harry Keough did decades before.

**Other books you might like:**
Lee Weathersby, *Kiss of the Vampire*, 1992
T. Lucien Wright, *Blood Brothers*, 1992

---

**3558**

**BRIAN LUMLEY**

## The Last Rite

(Minneapolis, Minnesota: Jwindz, 1993)

**Story type:** Horror (Collection)

**Summary:** The six stories collected here range widely over the spectrum of horror themes, including the Lovecraft influenced "The Thing From the Blasted Heath"; the urban horror story, "Back Row"; the occult thriller, "The Last Rite"; the non-supernatural horror tale, "A Thing about Cars!"; the ghostly "Vanessa's Voice"; and the tale of an insidious demon, "Uzzi."

**Other books you might like:**
Joe R. Lansdale, *By Bizarre Hands*, 1989
Richard Laymon, *A Good, Secret Place*, 1993
Edward Lee, *Edward Lee's Quest for Sex, Truth and Reality*, 1992
J.N. Williamson, *Author's Choice Monthly Number 24: The Naked Flesh of Feeling*, 1991

---

**3559**

**BRIAN LUMLEY**

## Maze of Worlds

(New York: Tor, 1998)

**Story type:** Horror (Science Fiction)

**Major character(s):** Spencer Gill, Scientist; Sith, Alien; Jack Turnbull, Military Personnel (soldier)
**Time period(s):** 1990s
**Locale(s):** Scotland

**Summary:** An onslaught of fulminant vegetation that is terraforming the earth into an environment hostile to human life is a ploy by Sith, alien mastermind of the renegade Thone, to lure nemesis Spencer Gill back to the House of Doors, a Thone supercomputer that creates virtual worlds drawn from the worst imaginings of its victims. Gill and a half-dozen other intrepid explorers endure the horrors forced upon them inside the computer and try to turn the technology to their advantage in the battle against the Thone. Sequel to Lumley's 1990 novel *House of Doors*.

**Other books you might like:**
Algis Budrys, *Rogue Moon*, 1960
Pat Cadigan, *Synners*, 1991
William Gibson, *Neuromancer*, 1984
William W. Johnstone, *Them*, 1992
Kim Newman, *The Night Mayor*, 1990

---

**3560**

**BRIAN LUMLEY**

## Necroscope: The Lost Years

(New York: Tor, 1995)

**Story type:** Horror (Vampire Story)
**Series:** Necroscope
**Major character(s):** Harry Keogh, Spy, Psychic; Bonnie Jean "B.J." Mirlu, Saloon Keeper/Owner, Vampire; Radu Lykan, Vampire
**Time period(s):** 1980s
**Locale(s):** London, England; Edinburgh, Scotland

**Summary:** This previously unrecounted episode from the life of Harry Keogh, a "necroscope" (someone who can communicate telepathically with the dead), is set in the time interval between the second and third volume of the author's nine-volume Necroscope series. Harry's frantic search to find his missing wife and son bring him into contact with a femme fatale. She's preparing him to serve as the vessel for a vampire whose consciousness needs flesh in order to wage war against fellow vampires who have destroyed his life.

**Other books you might like:**
Vincent Courtney, *Vampire Beat*, 1991
Lee Killough, *Blood Hunt*, 1987
Fred Saberhagen, *Seance for a Vampire*, 1994

---

**3561**

**BRIAN LUMLEY**

## Psychamok

(New York: Tor, 1993)

**Story type:** Horror (Wild Talents)
**Series:** Psychomech Trilogy
**Major character(s):** James Christopher Craig, Technician; Philip Stone, Businessman; Richard Stone, Telepath
**Time period(s):** 2000s (2004)
**Locale(s):** Sussex, England

**Summary:** Twenty years ago, in the events chronicled in *Psychosphere*, psychically-endowed Richard Allan Garrison destroyed evil telepath Charon Gubwa and achieved his transdimensional apotheosis. But Gubwa left the seeds of his resurrection implanted in technician James Christopher Craig, who sets about building a new Psychomech machine to facilitate Gubwa's return, leaving Garrison's bastard son Richard Stone no choice but to resume the battle where his father left off. This novel was originally published in England in 1984.

**Other books you might like:**
Andrew Laurance, *Blood of Nostradamus: The Unborn*, 1980
Jack Martin, *Scanners*, 1979
Curt Siodmak, *Gabriel's Body*, 1988

## 3562

### BRIAN LUMLEY

## *Psychomech*
(New York: Tor, 1992)

**Story type:** Horror (Wild Talents)
**Series:** Psychomech Trilogy
**Major character(s):** Thomas Schroeder, Businessman; Willy Koenig, Secretary (to Thomas Schroeder); Richard Garrison, Military Personnel (military police)
**Time period(s):** 1980s
**Locale(s):** London, England; Harz Mountains, Germany

**Summary:** Paranormally endowed ex-Nazi Thomas Schroeder returns from the dead by joining his mind with the personality of Richard Garrison. When Garrison undergoes boosting of his paranormal powers by means of a machine known as Psychomech, he finds himself possessed of a gestalt mind—Schroeder's and his own—and invested with god-like powers to change the world by means of his thoughts. This novel was originally published in England in 1983.

**Other books you might like:**
Curt Siodmak, *Donovan's Brain/Hauser's Memory*, 1992
Curt Siodmak, *Gabriel's Body*, 1988

## 3563

### BRIAN LUMLEY

## *Psychosphere*
(New York: Tor, 1992)

**Story type:** Horror (Wild Talents)
**Major character(s):** David Garrison, Wealthy (millionaire); Vicki Maler, Girlfriend (Garrison's); Charon Gubwa, Telepath
**Time period(s):** 1980s
**Locale(s):** Rhodes, Greece; London, England

**Summary:** David Garrison's gestalt mind, the product of his exposure to the Psychomech machine's brain-expanding capabilities, grows weaker every time he expends his paranormal talents to increase his empire or protect himself from his numerous enemies. It also causes telltale leaks into the Psychosphere, where it alerts the albino hermaphrodite, Charon Gubwa, a telepathic megalomaniac who determines to kill Garrison and afterward take over the world. This novel was originally published in England in 1984.

**Other books you might like:**
Jack Martin, *Scanners*, 1979
Curt Siodmak, *Donovan's Brain/Hauser's Memory*, 1992
Curt Siodmak, *Gabriel's Body*, 1988

## 3564

### BRIAN LUMLEY

## *Resurgence*
(New York: Tor, 1996)

**Story type:** Horror (Vampire Story)
**Series:** Necroscope
**Major character(s):** Harry Keogh, Spy, Psychic; Bonnie Jean ''B.J.'' Mirlu, Saloon Keeper/Owner, Vampire; Radu Lykan, Vampire
**Time period(s):** 1980s
**Locale(s):** Edinburgh, Scotland

**Summary:** This tenth volume in the author's long-running Necroscope series further elaborates the history of the otherworldly Wamphyri, some of whose members were exiled to our own world and live here as vampires and werewolves. Radu Lykan, one of the most fearsome of all Wamphyri, plans to appropriate the body of necroscope Harry Keogh in order to wage war on other Wamphyri factions. But Harry, a necroscope who can converse with the dead, staves off Lykan's attack with the help of Harry Houdini, Nostradamus, and B.J. Mirlu, a former disciple of Lykan's.

**Other books you might like:**
Nancy A. Collins, *Sunglasses After Dark*, 1989
Nancy A. Collins, *Wild Blood*, 1995
Robert R. McCammon, *They Thirst*, 1981
Kim Newman, *Anno Dracula*, 1992
John Steakley, *Vampire$*, 1990

## 3565

### BRIAN LUMLEY

## *The Source*
(New York: Tor, 1989)

**Story type:** Horror (Vampire Story)
**Series:** Necroscope
**Major character(s):** Harry Keogh, Spy, Psychic; Dweller, Alien (Vampire Antagonist)
**Time period(s):** 1980s
**Locale(s):** Perchorsk Pass, Union of Soviet Socialist Republics (a Soviet base in the Russian Urals); Alternate Universe (an alternate world of vampires)

**Summary:** As a result of a Soviet experiment gone awry, a portal is opened between our world and that of the Vampyri. Keogh enters the alternate world and forms an alliance with the Dweller, a mysterious, powerful vampire antagonist, to avert a massive vampiric invasion of the earth.

**Other books you might like:**
John Farris, *Catacombs*, 1981
Stephen King, *The Talisman*, 1984
     Peter Straub, co-author
Robert R. McCammon, *They Thirst*, 1981

## 3566

### BRIAN LUMLEY

## *Titus Crow, Volume One*
(New York: Tor, 1997)

**Story type:** Horror (Collection)
**Series:** Titus Crow
**Major character(s):** Titus Crow, Adventurer, Paranormal Investigator; Henri Laurent de Marigny, Sidekick, Paranormal Investigator

**Summary:** Omnibus repackaging of two novels featuring cosmic troubleshooter Titus Crow and his sidekick, Henri Laurent de Marigny. In *The Burrowers Beneath* (1974), Crow matches wits with Lovecraftian monsters who live beneath the Earth's crust. Its sequel, *The Transition of Titus Crow*, concerns Crow's escape by means of a magic clock to the realm beyond space and time where he is recruited by benevolent deities to fight malignant beings threatening to destroy the universal order.

**Other books you might like:**
Robert Bloch, *Strange Eons*, 1978
Fred Chappell, *Dagon*, 1068
August Derleth, *The Cthulhu Mythos*, 1997
Michael Shea, *The Colour out of Time*, 1984

## 3567

**BRIAN LUMLEY**

### Titus Crow, Volume Three

(New York: Tor, 1997)

**Story type:** Horror (Collection)
**Series:** Titus Crow
**Major character(s):** Titus Crow, Adventurer, Paranormal Investigator; Henri Laurent de Marigny, Sidekick, Paranormal Investigator; Hank Silberhutte, Telepath

**Summary:** Omnibus repackaging of the fifth and sixth novels of Lumley's saga of Titus Crow, a psychic investigator who battles Lovecraftian monsters. In *In the Moons of Borea*, Henri Laurent de Marigny and Hank Silberhutte combines forces to fight the wind elemental Ithaqua. In *Elysia: The Coming of Cthulhu* (1989), de Marigny and Silberhutte are reunited with Crow and two transmigrators to the realm of dream, David Hero and Eldin the Wanderer, to prevent the resurgence of the entity Cthulhu.

**Other books you might like:**
Robert Bloch, *Strange Eons*, 1978
August Derleth, *The Cthulhu Mythos*, 1997
Michael Shea, *The Colour out of Time*, 1984
Colin Wilson, *The Mind Parasites*, 1967

## 3568

**BRIAN LUMLEY**

### Titus Crow, Volume Two

(New York: Tor, 1997)

**Story type:** Horror (Collection)
**Series:** Titus Crow
**Major character(s):** Titus Crow, Adventurer, Paranormal Investigator; Henri Laurent de Marigny, Sidekick, Paranormal Investigator; Hank Silberhutte, Telepath

**Summary:** Omnibus repackaging of the third and fourth novels of Lumley's saga of Titus Crow, a psychic investigator who fights Lovecraftian monsters. In *The Clock of Dreams* (1978), Henri Laurent de Marigny uses a magic clock to traverse a cosmos filled with horrors in search of his lost friend, Titus Crow. In *Spawn of the Winds* (1978), de Marigny's friend Hank Silberhutte is abducted to the realm of the wind elemental Ithaqua, where he becomes involved in a plot to free the being's half-human daughter.

**Other books you might like:**
Robert Bloch, *Strange Eons*, 1978
August Derleth, *The Cthulhu Mythos*, 1997
Michael Shea, *The Colour out of Time*, 1984
Colin Wilson, *The Mind Parasites*, 1967

## 3569

**BRIAN LUMLEY**

### The Transition of Titus Crow

(Buffalo, New York: Ganley, 1992)

**Story type:** Horror (Ancient Evil Unleashed)
**Series:** Titus Crow
**Major character(s):** Titus Crow, Paranormal Investigator; Henri Laurent de Marigny, Paranormal Investigator, Sidekick; Nodens, Deity
**Time period(s):** 1970s
**Locale(s):** Aldebaran, Outer Space (a star)

**Summary:** Having narrowly escaped the Burrowers Beneath, minions of the The Great Old Ones, by means of their dimension-traversing grandfather clock, Titus Crow and Henri Laurent de Marigny are recruited by the benevolent Elder Gods to help them fight Cthulhu and The Great Old Ones in the cosmic showdown between good and evil. This novel, inspired by the work of H. P. Lovecraft and a sequel to the author's *The Burrower's Beneath*, was originally published in 1975.

**Other books you might like:**
Robert Bloch, *Strange Eons*, 1978
Donald Wandrei, *The Web of Easter Island*, 1948

## 3570

**CATHERINE A. LUNDIE**, Editor

### Restless Spirits

(Amherst, Massachusetts: University of Massachusetts Press, 1997)

**Story type:** Horror (Anthology)

**Summary:** Twenty-two tales of ghosts and the supernatural written by American women between 1872 and 1926. Many use the supernatural to explore feminine themes and issues, including Helen Hull's "Clay Shuttered Doors," about a woman kept alive after death by the needs of her demanding husband; Josephine Daskam Bacon's "The Gospel," about a woman prescribed domesticity as a cure to her apparent madness; Mary E. Wilkins-Freeman's "Luella Miller," about a self-centered woman whose needs drain life vampirically from her caretakers; and Edith Wharton's "The Lady Maid's Bell," about a woman protected by the ghost of her devoted former maid.

**Other books you might like:**
Alfred Bendixen, *Haunted Women: The Best Supernatural Tales by American Women Writers*, 1985
editor
Elizabeth Terry, *American Gothic*, 1997
Terri Hardin, co-editor
Seon Manley, *Ladies of Horror*, 1971
Gogo Lewis, co-author
Seon Manley, *Ghostly Gentlewomen*, 1977
Gogo Lewis, co-author
Alan Ryan, *Haunting Women*, 1988
editor
Jessica Amanda Salmonson, *What Did Miss Darrington See?: An Anthology of Feminist Supernatural Fiction*, 1989
editor

## 3571

### RICHARD A. LUPOFF

## *Before. . .12:01. . .and After*

(Minneapolis: Fedogan & Bremer, 1996)

**Story type:** Science Fiction (Collection)

**Summary:** Contains a five-page foreword by Robert Silverberg; a 14-page bibliography by Dave Nee; a nine-page introduction by Lupoff; and individual introductions describing the genesis of the five original and 18 stories reprinted from periodicals, conference program books, fanzines, and anthologies 1952-1996. Varying in tone from serious to light, the stories reflect a variety of themes including mythical creatures, urban life, alien encounters, time travel, Lovecraftian horror, and mystery.

**Other books you might like:**
Italo Calvino, *Numbers in the Dark and Other Stories*, 1995
Hugh B. Cave, *Death Stalks the Night*, 1995
Basil Copper, *The Black Death*, 1991
Robert M. Price, *The New Lovecraft Circle*, 1996
    editor
John Varley, *Blue Champagne*, 1986
Howard Wandrei, *Time Burial*, 1995

## 3572

### RICHARD A. LUPOFF

## *The Final Battle*

(New York: Bantam Spectra, 1990)

**Story type:** Fantasy (Alternate World; Adventure)
**Series:** Philip Jose Farmer's The Dungeon
**Major character(s):** Clive Folliot, Military Personnel; Frankenstein's Monster, Monster
**Time period(s):** 1870s (1870); 1890s (1896)
**Locale(s):** London, England; Alternate Earth

**Summary:** The adventures of Clive Folliot through the nine levels of the Dungeon's computer game-like world are concluded in this sixth volume. This time his traveling companions include Frankenstein's Monster, in addition to some of his friends from the earlier volumes.

**Other books you might like:**
Robin Wayne Bailey, *The Lake of Fire*, 1989
Bruce Coville, *The Dark Abyss*, 1989
Charles de Lint, *The Hidden City*, 1990
Charles de Lint, *The Valley of Thunder*, 1989
Robert A. Heinlein, *Glory Road*, 1964
Gene Wolfe, *The Shadow of the Torturer*, 1980

## 3573

### RICHARD A. LUPOFF

## *Night of the Living 'Gator!*

(New York: Ace, 1992)

**Story type:** Science Fiction (Humor)
**Series:** Daniel M. Pinkwater's Melvinge of the Megaverse
**Major character(s):** Melvinge, Hero, Werewolf; Loola, Girlfriend, Mythical Creature (were-lizard); Adela Rogers St. Jacques, Writer
**Time period(s):** Indeterminate
**Locale(s):** Megaverse Mall, Mythical Place

**Summary:** At last, Melvinge enters the Megaverse Mall itself, intent on buying a pair of squash shoes. As he roams the Mall, he hears a clue to the secret of the universe from a passing piglet. On his way to look up the word "echidna," he meets Adela Rogers St. Jacques at an autographing session. She and Melvinge buy a new Ferrari and drive somewhere else where Melvinge finds Loola, a tornado carries them to the city of Uz and they meet the alligator king, whose niece works in a shoe store at the Mall. Afterword by Daniel M. Pinkwater.

**Other books you might like:**
Douglas Adams, *So Long, and Thanks for All the Fish*, 1985
David Bischoff, *Night of the Living Shark!*, 1991
Ben Bova, *The Starcrossed*, 1975
Debra Doyle, *Night of the Living Rat!*, 1992
    James D. Macdonald, co-author
David Langford, *The Leaky Establishment*, 1984
Daniel Manus Pinkwater, *Borgel*, 1990
Terry Pratchett, *Moving Pictures*, 1992
John Sladek, *Mechasm*, 1968

## 3574

### ALISON LURIE, Editor

## *The Oxford Book of Modern Fairy Tales*

(New York: Oxford University Press, 1993)

**Story type:** Fantasy (Anthology; Legend)

**Summary:** This volume contains an eight-page introduction placing works within the context of fairy tale development and relationship to the world outside literature, 11 pages of biographical notes plus 40 tales from Anglo-American writers published 1839-1989, presented chronologically, and evidencing growth in the field from stories about mythical kingdoms and magical beasts to fairy tales incorporating feminism, multicultural mythology and urban issues. Authors include Donald Bartelme, L. Frank Baum, Angela Carter, Lucy Lane Clifford, John Collier, Mary de Morgan, Jeanne Desey, Philip K. Dick, Charles Dickens, Louise Erdrich, Juliana Horatia Ewing, Kenneth Grahame, Laurence Housman, Richard Hughes, Ursula K. Le Guin, Tanith Lee, George MacDonald, Bernard Malamud, Naomi Mitchison, Edith Nesbit, John Ruskin, Carl Sandberg, Catherine Sinclair, Isaac Bashevis Singer, Robert Louis Stevenson, Frank Stockton, James Thurber, H.G. Wells, T.H. White, Oscar Wilde, Jay Williams and Jane Yolen.

**Other books you might like:**
Chris Baldick, *The Oxford Book of Gothic Tales*, 1992
    editor
Orson Scott Card, *Dragons of Light*, 1980
    editor
Angela Carter, *The Old Wives' Fairy Tale Book*, 1990
    editor
Michael Patrick Hearn, *The Victorian Fairy Tale Book*, 1988
    editor
Tom Shippey, *The Oxford Book of Fantasy Stories*, 1994
    editor
Tom Shippey, *The Oxford Book of Science Fiction Stories*, 1992
    editor
Robert Silverberg, *The Fantasy Hall of Fame*, 1983
    editor
A. Susan Williams, *The Lifted Veil: The Book of Fantastic Literature by Women*, 1992
    editor
Jack Zipes, *Beauties, Beasts and Enchantments*, 1989
    editor

## 3575

**ALISON LURIE**

## Women and Ghosts

(New York: Doubleday/Nan A. Talese, 1994)

**Story type:** Horror (Collection)

**Summary:** This renowned mainstream author's first collection of supernatural tales brings together nine stories, four original to the volume. Included are "Ilse's House," about a woman haunted by the ex-wife of her fiance; "The Pool People," in which the imaginary friends a young girl makes at her grandmother's house turn out to have a bizarre history; "The Highboy," in which a piece of antique furniture develops a life of its own; "Counting Sheep," concerned with a young man's too-literal absorption into the Lake Country landscape which he is studying; "In the Shadow," about a haunting by the ghost of a dead former lover; and "Another Halloween," a chilling tale of a specter who drives a woman mad with its appearance every Halloween.

**Other books you might like:**
Fred Chappell, *More Shapes than One*, 1991
Shirley Jackson, *The Magic of Shirley Jackson*, 1965
Peter Taylor, *The Oracle at Stoneleigh Court*, 1993

## 3576

**JENNY LYKINS**

## Distant Dreams

(New York: Jove, 1998)

**Story type:** Fantasy (Romance; Historical)
**Major character(s):** Shaelyn Sumner, Journalist; Alec Hawthorne, Businessman
**Time period(s):** 1990s (1999); 1830s (1830)
**Locale(s):** Cape Helm, Maine

**Summary:** An investigative reporter decides to participate in an historic re-enactment of a wedding while visiting Maine in the present. She finds a magic ring which, when she wears it, sends her back through time to 1830, where she finds herself cast as the bride in a real wedding.

**Other books you might like:**
Rosalyn Alsobrook, *Time Storm*, 1993
Janice Bennett, *Forever in Time*, 1990
Barbara Bretton, *Somewhere in Time*, 1992
Cherlyn Jac, *Shadows in Time*, 1994
Marti Jones, *Star Dust*, 1995

## 3577

**PATRICK LYNCH**

## Omega

(New York: Dutton, 1997)

**Story type:** Horror (Mystery)
**Major character(s):** Marcus Ford, Doctor; Lucy Patou, Doctor; Helen Wray, Businesswoman (marketing)
**Time period(s):** 1990s (1997)
**Locale(s):** Los Angeles, California

**Summary:** When patients admitted to the Willowbrook Medical Center with routine injuries begin developing fatal secondary infections, trauma specialist Marcus Ford suspects the irresponsible use of antibiotics that have helped to breed resistant bacteria in the sur-rounding community. Ford's investigation of a greedy pharmaceutical company uncovers a conspiracy with world-shaking epidemiologic implications.

**Other books you might like:**
John David Connor, *Contagion*, 1992
Michael Crichton, *The Andromeda Strain*, 1969
Tess Gerritsen, *Life Support*, 1997
R. Karl Largent, *Black Death*, 1995
Richard Preston, *Cobra Event*, 1997

## 3578

**ELIZABETH A. LYNN**

## Dragon's Winter

(New York: Ace, 1998)

**Story type:** Fantasy (Quest)
**Major character(s):** Karadur Atani, Nobleman, Twin; Ankoku, Nobleman, Twin
**Time period(s):** Indeterminate
**Locale(s):** Ippa, Mythical Place

**Summary:** The King of Ippa sires twin sons, one of whom has the ability to change into the shape of a dragon. While the boys are still young, Ankoku steals the talisman that allows Karadur to alter his shape and disappears. Years later, an evil sorcerer menaces the kingdom, and Karadur realizes that he is facing his long lost brother.

**Other books you might like:**
Mark Acres, *Dragonspawn*, 1994
Gael Baudino, *Duel of Dragons*, 1989
Carol L. Dennis, *Dragon's Knight*, 1989
Robert Don Hughes, *Prophet of Lamath*, 1979
Dennis L. McKiernan, *Dragondoom*, 1990

## 3579

**LYNDA LYONS**

## Priorities

(Tallahassee: Naiad Press, 1990)

**Story type:** Science Fiction (Gay/Lesbian Fiction)
**Series:** Controllers
**Major character(s):** Amelia Roberts, Military Personnel; Valentine, Military Personnel
**Time period(s):** Indeterminate Future
**Locale(s):** Earth

**Summary:** The Doctor, a dangerous and brilliant criminal, has created an army of amazingly life-like androids and plans to use them in an attempt to kidnap the son of the president of the Earth. The Controllers, an elite organization dedicated to hunting and destroying robots and androids, must foil the plot.

**Other books you might like:**
Philip K. Dick, *Do Androids Dream of Electric Sheep?*, 1968
Lauren Wright Douglas, *In the Blood*, 1989
Nancy Tyler Glenn, *Clicking Stones*, 1989
Karen Marie Christa Minns, *Virago*, 1990
Joanna Russ, *The Two of Them*, 1978
Joanna Russ, *We Who Are About To...*, 1977

## 3580

### R.A. MACAVOY

## The Belly of the Wolf

(New York: William Morrow, 1994)

**Story type:** Fantasy (Quest; Religious)
**Series:** Lens of the World Trilogy
**Major character(s):** Nazhuret, Warrior; Nahvah, Doctor; Dinaos, Nobleman (Count of Lowcanton), Artist
**Time period(s):** 18th century
**Locale(s):** Velonya, Fictional Country; Canton, Fictional Country

**Summary:** While in exile, Nazhuret learns that his old friend King Rudof has died, perhaps from poisoning. Nazhuret and his daughter journey to discover the truth and punish the killer, even if that proves to be Rudof's son, Benar, the new king. They find Velonya teetering on the brink of civil war, with one of Nazhuret's students as a rebel leader, proclaiming Nazhuret's teachings as a new religion.

**Other books you might like:**
Orson Scott Card, *Red Prophet*, 1989
C.J. Cherryh, *Angel with the Sword*, 1985
Phyllis Eisenstein, *Born to Exile*, 1978
Katherine Kurtz, *Saint Camber*, 1978
Robert Silverberg, *Lord Valentine's Castle*, 1980

## 3581

### R.A. MACAVOY

## King of the Dead

(New York: Morrow, 1991)

**Story type:** Fantasy (Historical)
**Series:** Lens of the World Trilogy
**Major character(s):** Nazhuret, Warrior; Mynauzet, Royalty (Sanaur of Rezhmia); Charlan "Arlin" Bannering, Noblewoman, Martial Arts Expert
**Time period(s):** 18th century (7th Year of the Reign of Rudof I)
**Locale(s):** Velonya, Fictional Country; Rezhmia, Fictional Country

**Summary:** Taking place several years after events in *Lens of the World*, this story unfolds through Nazhuret's memoirs to Powl In-pres. Nazhuret and Arlin accept Powl's request to meet with the emperor of Rezhmia on a mission of peace. In Rezhmia, court politics and intrigue impede their efforts to curb Rezhmia's militarization and the impending conflict with Velonya.

**Other books you might like:**
M.A.R. Barker, *Man of Gold*, 1984
Margaret Wander Bonanno, *The Others*, 1990
Stephen R. Donaldson, *Lord Foul's Bane*, 1977
Raymond E. Feist, *Daughter of the Empire*, 1987
    Janny Wurtz, co-author
Melanie Rawn, *Stronghold*, 1990
Robert Silverberg, *Gilgamesh the King*, 1984
Paula Volsky, *Illusion*, 1992
Tad Williams, *The Dragonbone Chair*, 1988

## 3582

### R.A. MACAVOY

## Lens of the World

(New York: Morrow, 1990)

**Story type:** Fantasy (Historical)
**Series:** Lens of the World Trilogy

**Major character(s):** Nazhuret, Warrior; Powl, Teacher
**Time period(s):** 18th century
**Locale(s):** Vestinglon, Fictional Country

**Summary:** Belonging to The Royal Military School of Sordaling, Nazhuret unexpectedly has information imparted to him. Being kidnapped and brutalized prepares him for adventures beyond any he could have imagined and he joins the King of Velonya's court.

**Other books you might like:**
Ursula K. Le Guin, *A Wizard of Earthsea*, 1968
Alis A. Rasmussen, *The Labyrinth Gate*, 1988
Clark Ashton Smith, *The Book of Hyperborea*, 1971
Jane Yolen, *Sister Light, Sister Dark*, 1988
Jane Yolen, *White Jenna*, 1989

## 3583

### R.A. MACAVOY

## The Third Eagle: Lessons Along a Minor String

(New York: Doubleday Foundation, 1989)

**Story type:** Science Fiction (Satire)
**Major character(s):** Wanbli, Warrior, Indian; Reynaldo Errenthorp, Businessman
**Time period(s):** Indeterminate Future
**Locale(s):** The Planets of the Seven Senti, Interstellar Empire/Federation

**Summary:** Wanbli, a highly trained and somewhat egocentric Native American warrior of the far future, sets out to see the universe, taking a variety of jobs, including one as an actor. He meets a wide variety of people, not all of them human, growing from his experiences and ending a better person than he began.

**Other books you might like:**
Charles de Lint, *Svaha*, 1989
Andre Norton, *The Beast Master*, 1959
Andre Norton, *The Sioux Space Man*, 1960
Alexei Panshin, *Masque World*, 1969
Alexei Panshin, *Star Well*, 1968
Alexei Panshin, *The Thurb Revolution*, 1968

## 3584

### CAROLINE MACDONALD

## The Lake at the End of the World

(New York: Dial, 1989)

**Story type:** Science Fiction (Young Adult)
**Major character(s):** Diana Redfern, Teenager; Hector, Teenager
**Time period(s):** 21st century (2025)
**Locale(s):** Australia

**Summary:** A family lives in complete isolation by a lake after a series of ecological disasters has destroyed most human life. Then they discover a boy from a heretofore unknown underground shelter where a group of scientists and artists has been living since the 1960's. They moved in originally out of a fear of nuclear war and remain now due to their irrational fear of the surface.

**Other books you might like:**
Gary L. Blackwood, *The Dying Sun*, 1989
H.M. Hoover, *This Time of Darkness*, 1980
Gregory Maguire, *I Feel Like the Morning Star*, 1989
Robert C. O'Brien, *Z for Zachariah*, 1975
George R. Stewart, *Earth Abides*, 1949

## 3585

### SHAWN MACDONALD

## *The Darkness Within*

(New York: Zebra, 1993)

**Story type:** Horror (Psychological Suspense)
**Major character(s):** Anne Dennessy, Waiter/Waitress, Abuse Victim; Beth Dennessy, Twin, Abuse Victim; Carol Dennessy, Twin, Abuse Victim
**Time period(s):** 1990s (1993)
**Locale(s):** Colorado

**Summary:** Anne Dennessy narrates the woeful story of her abusive upbringing at the hands of a greedy mother and religiously fanatical grandmother, and how it has so twisted her psyche that she inflicts similar mistreatment on her twin daughters, Beth and Carol.

**Other books you might like:**
J.M. Dillard, *Specters*, 1991
R. Patrick Gates, *Tunnelvision*, 1991
Rick R. Reed, *Obsessed*, 1991

## 3586

### DAVID MACE

## *Firelance*

(New York: Ace, 1989)

**Story type:** Science Fiction (Post-Nuclear Holocaust)
**Major character(s):** Richard Bedford, Sea Captain; David Drexel, Government Official
**Time period(s):** 21st century
**Locale(s):** Cheyenne Mountain Command Cent, Wyoming; *U.S.S. Vindicator*, At Sea

**Summary:** In a world all but destroyed by a full-scale nuclear war and the nuclear winter that followed, military commanders, safe in their gigantic armored command centers, plot to wipe out the last vestiges of human life on Earth. Others, more sane, do their best to bring an end to the senseless killing. This is a reprint of the 1986 British edition.

**Other books you might like:**
William Brinkley, *The Last Ship*, 1988
Glen Cook, *The Heirs of Babylon*, 1972
David Drake, *Fortress*, 1987
Keith Laumer, *The Stars Must Wait*, 1990

## 3587

### ELISABETH MACE

## *Under Siege*

(New York: Orchard/Franklin Watts, 1990)

**Story type:** Fantasy (Romance; Young Adult)
**Major character(s):** Morris, Teenager; Uncle Patrick, Computer Expert; Vail, Artificial Intelligence
**Time period(s):** 1980s
**Locale(s):** England; Cyberspace

**Summary:** Powerless to affect his parents' separation, and in the face of his mother's disapproval, Morris enters the world of his Uncle Patrick's ongoing computer wargame. Falling in love with one of the gaming figurines, Vail, he joins the battle on her side as a giant-god in opposition to his Uncle Patrick. This is the author's first book.

**Other books you might like:**
Lynne Reid Banks, *The Indian in the Cupboard*, 1980
Pauline Clarke, *The Return of the Twelves*, 1964
Edward Eager, *Knight's Castle*, 1956
E. Nesbit, *The Magic World*, 1912
Will Shetterly, *The Tangled Lands*, 1989

## 3588

### ROB MACGREGOR

## *Indiana Jones and the Dance of the Giants*

(New York: Bantam Falcon, 1991)

**Story type:** Fantasy (Adventure; Quest)
**Series:** Indiana Jones
**Major character(s):** Indiana "Indy" Jones, Archaeologist; Deirdre Campbell, Student, Adventurer; Adrian Powell, Government Official
**Time period(s):** 1920s (1925)
**Locale(s):** England; Scotland

**Summary:** While teaching in the Archaeology Department at London University, his first post, Indiana Jones meets a Scottish student who claims to have discovered a scroll which proves the existence of the legendary sorcerer, Merlin. In their dangerous pursuit of the secrets contained in the scroll, they travel to Scotland and then Stonehenge where they foil Adrian Powell's attempt to return Druidism to Britain and seize power by returning the sacred stone, the Omphalos, to Stonehenge.

**Other books you might like:**
Campbell Black, *Raiders of the Lost Ark*, 1981
James Kahn, *Indiana Jones and the Temple of Doom*, 1984
Morgan Llywelyn, *Druids*, 1991

## 3589

### ROB MACGREGOR

## *Indiana Jones and the Genesis Deluge*

(New York: Bantam Falcon, 1992)

**Story type:** Fantasy (Adventure; Legend)
**Series:** Indiana Jones
**Major character(s):** Indiana "Indy" Jones, Archaeologist; Vladimir Zobolotsky, Doctor, Adventurer; Katrina Zobolotsky, Adventurer
**Time period(s):** 1920s (1927)
**Locale(s):** Chicago, Illinois; Istanbul, Turkey

**Summary:** Recruited by Vladimir and Katrina in the search for the remains of Noah's legendary ark, Indy travels with the pair to Mt. Ararat, hindered in their search by Kremlin and Sicilian agents and Turkish bandits.

**Other books you might like:**
Campbell Black, *Raiders of the Lost Ark*, 1981
James Kahn, *Indiana Jones and the Temple of Doom*, 1984
Catherine Lanigan, *Jewel of the Nile*, 1985

## 3590

### ROB MACGREGOR

## *Indiana Jones and the Interior World*

(New York: Bantam Falcon, 1992)

**Story type:** Fantasy (Adventure)

**Series:** Indiana Jones
**Major character(s):** Indiana "Indy" Jones, Archaeologist; Salandra, Guide, Adventurer
**Time period(s):** 1920s (1928-1929)
**Locale(s):** Isle of Chiloe, Chile; Pincoya, Subterranean World; Land of the Lost, Subterranean World (inside the Earth)

**Summary:** When Indy disposed of a dangerous relic, he opened the doorway to a world within the Earth. Later, the doorway provides access for the leader of an unstoppable invading army to enter and form a deadly liaison which Indy must defeat by restoring the balance between worlds.

**Other books you might like:**
Campbell Black, *Raiders of the Lost Ark*, 1981
Edgar Rice Burroughs, *At the Earth's Core*, 1922
Edgar Rice Burroughs, *Pellucidar*, 1923
James Kahn, *Indiana Jones and the Temple of Doom*, 1984
Jules Verne, *Journey to the Center of the Earth*, 1864

## 3591

### ROB MACGREGOR

## Indiana Jones and the Peril at Delphi

(New York: Bantam Falcon, 1991)

**Story type:** Fantasy (Adventure; Quest)
**Series:** Indiana Jones
**Major character(s):** Indiana "Indy" Jones, Archaeologist (Ph.D. candidate); Dorian Belecamus, Professor
**Time period(s):** 1920s (1922)
**Locale(s):** Chicago, Illinois; Paris, France; Delphi, Greece

**Summary:** On a field trip to Delphi, Indy becomes sexually involved with his instructor, Dorian. When Indy rediscovers the long-lost sacred stone, the Omphalos, Dorian plots to take control of Greece's future by becoming the Oracle of Delphi whose return has been prophecied for 16 centuries by the Order of Pythia.

**Other books you might like:**
Campbell Black, *Raiders of the Lost Ark*, 1981
James Kahn, *Indiana Jones and the Temple of Doom*, 1984
Marc Laidlaw, *Neon Lotus*, 1988
Catherine Lanigan, *Jewel of the Nile*, 1985

## 3592

### ROB MACGREGOR

## Indiana Jones and the Seven Veils

(New York: Bantam Falcon, 1991)

**Story type:** Fantasy (Quest; Adventure)
**Series:** Indiana Jones
**Major character(s):** Indiana "Indy" Jones, Archaeologist; Deirdre Campbell, Student, Adventurer
**Time period(s):** 1920s (1926)
**Locale(s):** Brazil

**Summary:** Following hints in the mysterious writings of a missing British explorer, Indy and Deirdre search for a lost city in the Brazilian jungle and a legendary red-headed race, possible descendants of Celtic Druids.

**Other books you might like:**
Campbell Black, *Raiders of the Lost Ark*, 1981
James Kahn, *Indiana Jones and the Temple of Doom*, 1984
Catherine Lanigan, *Romancing the Stone*, 1984
Morgan Llywelyn, *Druids*, 1991
Edward Myers, *The Mountain Made of Light*, 1992

## 3593

### ROB MACGREGOR

## Indiana Jones and the Unicorn's Legacy

(New York: Bantam Falcon, 1992)

**Story type:** Fantasy (Adventure; Quest)
**Series:** Indiana Jones
**Major character(s):** Indiana "Indy" Jones, Archaeologist; Mara Rogers, Professor (art history); Roland Walcott, Professor, Criminal
**Time period(s):** 1920s (1928)
**Locale(s):** Mesa Verde, Colorado; Southwest (Anasazi Ruins)

**Summary:** Indy joins Mara at the site of an ancient Anasazi ruin in pursuit of a unicorn's horn, legendary source of power. Their quest suffers from the return of Indy's nemesis, Roland Walcott, previously thought dead, but now back with a lethal lust for the horn.

**Other books you might like:**
Campbell Black, *Raiders of the Lost Ark*, 1981
James Kahn, *Indiana Jones and the Temple of Doom*, 1984

## 3594

### T.J. MACGREGOR

## The Hanged Man

(New York: Kensington, 1998)

**Story type:** Horror (Wild Talents)
**Major character(s):** Mira Morales, Psychic; Hal Bennet, Spy; Lenora Fletcher, FBI Agent (director)
**Time period(s):** 1990s (1998)
**Locale(s):** Florida

**Summary:** Mira Morales discovered she was psychic the day that she foresaw her husband's murder at a convenience store hold-up. Years later, she finds herself attuned to the activities of former members of the Delphi project, a secret CIA experiment in parapsychology that trained spies and killers with paranormal talents for secret espionage, and whose members are reconvening on their own to realize some of their megalomaniacal ambitions.

**Other books you might like:**
Hugh B. Cave, *Disciples of Dread*, 1988
John Farris, *The Fury*, 1976
James Herbert, *Sepulchre*, 1989
Stephen King, *Firestarter*, 1980
Dean R. Koontz, *The Vision*, 1977

## 3595

### ARTHUR MACHEN

## The Hill of Dreams

(Bristol, Rhode Island: Hobgoblin Press, 1997)

**Story type:** Horror (Occult)
**Major character(s):** Lucian Taylor, Writer; Dr. Burrows, Doctor; Jane Deacon, Young Woman
**Time period(s):** 1900s
**Locale(s):** Caermaen, Wales; London, England

**Summary:** Alienated by the banality of the modern world, hypersensitive Lucian Taylor withdraws into his studies of the arts and occult and learns how to retrieve the splendor of England's Roman past. His ambitions to write a book that will relate his sensual vision drive him to potentially fatal extremes of experience. First published in 1907.

**Other books you might like:**
Algernon Blackwood, *The Human Chord*, 1910
J.K. Huysmans, *A Rebours*, 1884
H.P. Lovecraft, *The Dream Quest of Unknown Kadath*, 1955
Oscar Wilde, *The Picture of Dorian Gray*, 1891

## 3596
### F. GWYNPLAINE MACINTYRE
### *The Woman between the Worlds*
(New York: Dell, 1994)

**Story type:** Science Fiction (Invasion of Earth; Horror)
**Major character(s):** Vanessa Steele, Alien, Revolutionary; Aleister Crowley, Magician, Historical Figure; The Dreadful Eye, Alien
**Time period(s):** 1890s (1898)
**Locale(s):** London, England; Alternate Universe

**Summary:** A tattoo artist receives the bizarre commission of a full body tattoo for a scientist who has turned herself invisible. Her story proves more complicated as the tattooist and Vanessa flee across London and out of the world. First novel, which makes liberal use of historic figures.

**Other books you might like:**
James P. Blaylock, *Lord Kelvin's Machine*, 1992
William Hjortsberg, *Nevermore*, 1994
K.W. Jeter, *Infernal Devices*, 1987
Kim Newman, *Anno Dracula*, 1993
Tim Powers, *The Anubis Gates*, 1983

## 3597
### SCOTT MACKAY
### *Outpost*
(New York: Tor, 1998)

**Story type:** Science Fiction (Time Travel; Lost Colony)
**Major character(s):** Felicitas, Prisoner, Amnesiac; Lungo Muso, Alien (uominilupi), Time Traveler; Piero, Prisoner, Leader
**Time period(s):** Indeterminate Future
**Locale(s):** Planet—Imaginary

**Summary:** Felicitas awakens from a zombie-like stupor to find herself a prisoner in a mechanized fortress, although she does not remember having committed a crime. As the prison's automatic systems break down and food runs low, several prisoners who have overcome the dreamphone-induced trance make desperate plans for escape, while Felicitas learns that only she can answer the questions of where they came from and why they were imprisoned.

**Other books you might like:**
Julie E. Czerneda, *A Thousand Words for Stranger*, 1997
Lisa Mason, *The Golden Nineties*, 1995
Patrick O'Leary, *Door Number Three*, 1995
Christopher Pike, *The Eternal Enemy*, 1993
Christopher Pike, *The Starlight Crystal*, 1996
Frederik Pohl, *The Singers of Time*, 1991
    Jack Williamson, co-author
Robert Silverberg, *Hawksbill Station*, 1968

## 3598
### JOHN MACLAY, Editor
### *Voices From the Night*
(Baltimore: Maclay & Associates, 1994)

**Story type:** Horror (Anthology)
**Summary:** This all-original non-theme anthology collects 27 tales of horror, fantasy, and dark suspense by well-known and relatively unknown writers. Among the best are Robert Weinberg's "Dial Your Dreams," about the extreme services available through a 1-900 number; Rick Hautala's atmospheric tale of supernatural vengeance, "A Little Bit of Divine Justice"; Ray Russell's "The Little Snakes of Tara," a whimsical retelling of the legend of St. Patrick; Mort Castle's paranoid fantasy, "The Call"; and J.N. Williamson's tale of a nerd who reasons his way out of a deadly love triangle, "The Autonomic Nervous System, Klause Von Klauswitz, and Omilian." This beautifully produced book appeared only in a signed collector's edition.

**Other books you might like:**
Richard T. Chizmar, *Cold Blood*, 1991
Joe R. Lansdale, *Dark at Heart*, 1992
    Karen Lansdale, co-editor
Thomas F. Monteleone, *Borderlands 3*, 1993
    editor
Claudia O'Keefe, *Ghosttide*, 1993
    editor
Stanley Wiater, *After the Darkness*, 1993
    editor

## 3599
### IAN R. MACLEOD
### *The Great Wheel*
(New York: Harcourt Brace, 1997)

**Story type:** Science Fiction (Theological; Medical)
**Major character(s):** John "Skiddle" Alston, Religious (priest); Felipe, Religious (priest); Tim Purdoe, Doctor
**Time period(s):** Indeterminate Future
**Locale(s):** Hemhill, England; Endless City, Africa; Rome, Italy

**Summary:** As a child, John's brother explained how the Borderers worked the fields, as the Europeans could no longer stay out in the sun. Later, as a priest in the Endless City, John observes the suffering of the Borderers, trying to cure with medicine, but unable to give the modern medical implants which prevent disease. Unfortunately, John's immune system cannot protect him when he exposes himself to the Borderer environment. He acquires the acute myeloid anemia which seems to be spreading through the Endless City. First novel.

**Other books you might like:**
Patricia Anthony, *God's Fires*, 1997
James Blish, *A Case of Conscience*, 1958
Frank Herbert, *Dune*, 1965
Mary Doria Russell, *The Sparrow*, 1996
N. Lee Wood, *Faraday's Orphans*, 1997

## 3600
### IAN R. MACLEOD
### *Voyages by Starlight*
(Sauk City, Wisconsin: Arkham House, 1997)

**Story type:** Science Fiction (Collection; Fantasy)

**Summary:** Contains a four-page foreword by Michael Swanwick and 10 stories reprinted from periodicals 1990-1995. Frequently downbeat to horrifying in tone, the stories occasionally reflect more than genre and include diverse themes such as an industrialized fantasy world, growing up, events at a lonely Arctic weather station during World War II and a world like our own but with a three-sexed human race.

**Other books you might like:**
Alexander Jablokov, *The Breath of Suspension*, 1994
Nancy Kress, *The Aliens of Earth*, 1993
Mary Rosenblum, *Synthesis & Other Virtual Realities*, 1996
Michael Swanwick, *Gravity's Angels*, 1991
James Tiptree Jr., *Her Smoke Rose Up Forever*, 1990

## 3601

### SCOTT MACMILLAN

## *At Sword's Point*

(New York: Roc, 1994)

**Story type:** Fantasy (Contemporary; Horror)
**Series:** Vampyr-SS
**Major character(s):** John Drummond, Detective—Homicide, Vampire; Wilhelm Kluge, Military Personnel, Vampire; Markus Eberle, Police Officer
**Time period(s):** 1990s
**Locale(s):** Germany; Austria

**Summary:** Wilhelm Kluge's Nazi vampires and the Vatican hunt for John Drummond, a newly created vampire also wanted by the Israeli Mossad, which hopes to create a vampire army. Drummond, Eberle and the Crusader vampires go into battle against Kluge and his company with dire consequences.

**Other books you might like:**
Robert Harris, *Fatherland*, 1992
Joan Kangilaski, *The Seeking Sword*, 1977
Lucius Shepard, *The Golden*, 1993
Brian Stableford, *The Empire of Fear*, 1991
Lois Tilton, *Darkness on the Ice*, 1993

## 3602

### SCOTT MACMILLAN

## *Knights of the Blood*

(New York: Roc, 1993)

**Story type:** Fantasy (Contemporary; Horror)
**Series:** Vampyr-SS
**Major character(s):** John Drummond, Detective—Homicide; Henri de Beq, Knight, Vampire; Wilhelm Kluge, Military Personnel (SS Sturmbannfuhrer), Vampire
**Time period(s):** 1970s (1972); 13th century (1291)
**Locale(s):** Los Angeles, California; Vienna, Austria

**Summary:** Investigating a bizarre series of murders in Los Angeles, John Drummond hears a New Hampshire priest claim he murdered vampires who served an evil SS officer. While looking into the murder of an elderly Jew in Vienna, Drummond travels into the Ardennes and meets a group of knights who still atone for crimes committed during the Crusades. First novel, from an idea by Katherine Kurtz.

**Other books you might like:**
Tanya Huff, *Blood Price*, 1991
Lee Killough, *Blood Hunt*, 1987
George R.R. Martin, *Fevre Dream*, 1982

Anne Rice, *Interview with the Vampire*, 1976
Brian Stableford, *The Empire of Fear*, 1991
Chelsea Quinn Yarbro, *Crusader's Torch*, 1988

## 3603

### TIMOTHY A. MADDEN

## *Outbanker*

(Lake Geneva, Wisconsin: TSR, 1990)

**Story type:** Science Fiction (Space Colony; Political)
**Major character(s):** Ian S. MacKenzie, Spaceship Captain
**Time period(s):** 24th century
**Locale(s):** 61 Cygni Colonies, Outer Space; *Outbanker Bravo*, Spaceship

**Summary:** When the Corporate Hegemony of Earth raises taxes and sends two corporate dreadnaughts to enforce compliance, the colonies around Cygnus A decide to make a deal, but the colonies around Cygnus B decide to resist. They design a small, superfast, one-man cruiser, which requiresd special persons called Outbankers to pilot them. This is the story of one of them.

**Other books you might like:**
F.M. Busby, *Young Rissa*, 1984
Stephen Goldin, *Jade Darcy and the Affair of Honor*, 1988
  Mary Mason, co-author
Robert A. Heinlein, *The Moon Is a Harsh Mistress*, 1966
Melisa C. Michaels, *Far Harbor*, 1989
David Alexander Smith, *Homecoming*, 1990
L. Neil Smith, *Contact and Commune*, 1990
John E. Stith, *Redshift Rendezvous*, 1990

## 3604

### TOM MADDOX

## *Halo*

(New York: Tor, 1991)

**Story type:** Science Fiction (Alternate Intelligence; Space Colony)
**Major character(s):** Mikhail Mikhailovitch Gonzales, Computer Expert, Auditor; Diana Heywood, Computer Expert; Aleph, Artificial Intelligence
**Time period(s):** Indeterminate Future
**Locale(s):** Halo City, Space Station (at L5)

**Summary:** Hoping to study long-term human/machine interface, SenTrax Corporation arranges for Gonzales and Heywood to supervise Jerry Chapman's neural interface to Aleph. With the higher brain functions of Chapman linked to Aleph, the computer program develops a stronger personality. Disaster threatens not only Aleph but also Halo City itself when SenTrax decides to reassert control by terminating Chapman's neural link. This is the author's first novel.

**Other books you might like:**
Greg Bear, *Queen of Angels*, 1990
Gregory Benford, *Great Sky River*, 1987
Gregory Benford, *Tides of Light*, 1989
David Brin, *Earth*, 1990
Pat Cadigan, *Mindplayers*, 1987
Pat Cadigan, *Synners*, 1991
William Gibson, *Neuromancer*, 1984
Victor Milan, *The Cybernetic Samurai*, 1986
Allen Steele, *Clarke County, Space*, 1990
Michael Swanwick, *Stations of the Tide*, 1991
John Varley, *The Persistence of Vision*, 1978

**Maguire**

## 3605
### DAVID MADSEN
## *Vodoun*
(New York: Morrow, 1994)

**Story type:** Horror (Occult; Possession)
**Major character(s):** Ray Falco, Journalist; Faustin Gabriel, Art Dealer (gallery owner); Carmen Mondesir, Businessman (charity director)
**Time period(s):** 1990s (1994)
**Locale(s):** Washington, District of Columbia

**Summary:** As star journalist Ray Falco ponders his recent inexplicable murder of a Haitian activist, he finds that he is possessed by the spirit of Nicholas Whitney Townshend, Haiti's American envoy during the 1793 slave rebellion. Gradually it unfolds that Falco has become a tool of recent Haitian acquaintances who are using voodoo to channel spirits of the dead into the living in the hope of liberating modern Haiti from its dictator's control.

**Other books you might like:**
Alex Abella, *The Killing of the Saints*, 1991
Hugh B. Cave, *Disciples of Dread*, 1988
Nicholas Conde, *The Religion*, 1982
Jewell Martin Rhodes, *Voodoo Dreams*, 1993
Theodore Roscoe, *Z Is for Zombie*, 1937

## 3606
### SIMON MAGINN
## *Sheep*
(Stone Mountain, Georgia: White Wolf, 1996)

**Story type:** Horror (Evil Children)
**Major character(s):** James Tullian, Contractor (construction); Adele Tullian, Artist; Sam Tullian, Child (7-year-old)
**Time period(s):** 1990s (1994)
**Locale(s):** Ty-Gwyneth, Wales

**Summary:** James Tullian moves his family to the rural sheep farming community of Ty-Gwyneth to help them recover from the depression that has set in after the drowning death of his young daughter. But the town's dark heritage, which includes a religious cult and a man who murdered his own family, begins having a strange effect on him, his wife, and his young son, leading him to wonder whether their private psychopathologies are beginning to express themselves. First published in England in 1994, this is the author's first novel.

**Other books you might like:**
William Golding, *Lord of the Flies*, 1954
William March, *The Bad Seed*, 1954
Sarban, *Ringstones, and Other Curious Tales*, 1951
Bernard Taylor, *The Godsend*, 1976
Gene Thompson, *Lupe*, 1977
Thomas Tryon, *The Other*, 1971

## 3607
### SIMON MAGINN
## *Virgins and Martyrs*
(Clarkston, Georgia: White Wolf, 1996)

**Story type:** Horror (Psychological Suspense)
**Major character(s):** Daniel Blennerhassett, Student; Wendy Bishop, Child; Terence Outhwaite, Police Officer (inspector)
**Time period(s):** 1990s (1995)
**Locale(s):** Hove, England

**Summary:** Shortly after moving into a new apartment where he hopes to find the quiet he needs to complete his dissertation, Daniel Blennerhassett is haunted by the image of a young woman who radiates a religious aura. As he slowly gives himself over to his obsession with her, Daniel discovers the horrifying truth about his landlord, a scholarly fanatic with some unorthodox theories concerning religious martyrdom. This novel was first published in England in 1995.

**Other books you might like:**
Jonathan Aycliffe, *Naomi's Room*, 1992
Josephine Boyle, *Holy Terror*, 1993
Richard Matheson, *Hell House*, 1971
Mary Elizabeth Murphy, *Virgin*, 1996
Michael Paine, *The Colors of Hell*, 1990

## 3608
### GREGORY MAGUIRE
## *I Feel Like the Morning Star*
(New York: Harper & Row, 1989)

**Story type:** Science Fiction (Post-Nuclear Holocaust)
**Major character(s):** Ella, Teenager; Mart, Teenager
**Time period(s):** 21st century
**Locale(s):** Pioneer Colony, Massachusetts

**Summary:** Pioneer Colony, a closed-access survival community buried some four-thousand feet beneath what was once the state of Massachusetts, is home to some 1,000 survivors of the nuclear war that occurred more than four years ago. Ella, Mart, and Sorb chafe at the colony's restrictions and plot rebellion.

**Other books you might like:**
Gary L. Blackwood, *The Dying Sun*, 1989
Pat Frank, *Alas, Babylon*, 1959
Daniel F. Galouye, *Dark Universe*, 1961
Robert C. O'Brien, *Z for Zachariah*, 1975
Mordecai Roshwald, *Level 7*, 1959

## 3609
### GREGORY MAGUIRE
## *Wicked: The Life and Times of the Wicked Witch of the West*
(New York: HarperCollins, 1995)

**Story type:** Fantasy (Political; Religious)
**Series:** Oz
**Major character(s):** Elphaba, Witch, Activist (talking animal rights); Galinda "Glinda the Good", Socialite, Witch; Nessarose, Witch, Religious
**Time period(s):** Indeterminate
**Locale(s):** Oz, Mythical Place

**Summary:** Born to an alcoholic parent, Elphaba's unusual appearance, her sibling care duties, and abuse by a parent produce a difficult childhood for her. At college Elphaba rooms with snobbish Galinda then evolves into a militant animal rights proponent before her untimely death.

**Other books you might like:**
L. Frank Baum, *Dorothy and the Wizard in Oz*, 1908
L. Frank Baum, *The Land of Oz*, 1904
Rachel R. Cosgrove, *The Hidden Valley of Oz*, 1951
Philip Jose Farmer, *A Barnstormer in Oz*, 1982

Eloise Jarvis McGraw, *Merry-Go-Round in Oz*, 1963
    Lauren McGraw Wagner, co-author
John Rea Neill, *The Wonder City of Oz*, 1940
Geoff Ryman, *Was*, 1992
Jack Snow, *The Magical Mimics in Oz*, 1946
Ruth Plumly Thompson, *The Royal Book of Oz*, 1921
Joan D. Vinge, *Return to Oz*, 1985

---

### 3610

**MARGARET MAHY**

## The Girl with the Green Ear: Stories about Magic in Nature

(New York: Knopf, 1992)

**Story type:** Fantasy (Young Adult; Collection)

**Summary:** Nine stories published in collections in Great Britain all sharing themes of magic and nature with some stories focusing on special abilities as in the title story, whose protagonist hears the voices of plants, while other stories feature mythical creatures such as dragons in ''Don't Cut the Lawn!'' and people of the woods in ''The Merry-Go-Round.''

**Other books you might like:**
Joan Aiken, *The Last Slice of Rainbow and Other Stories*, 1988
Margery Williams Bianco, *A Street of Little Shops*, 1932
Rudyard Kipling, *The Jungle Book*, 1893
Rudyard Kipling, *Just So Stories*, 1902
Laurence Yep, *The Rainbow People*, 1989
Jane Yolen, *The Girl Who Cried Flowers and Other Tales*, 1974

---

### 3611

**MARGARET MAHY**

## A Tall Story and Other Tales

(New York: Macmillan McElderry, 1992)

**Story type:** Fantasy (Young Adult; Collection)

**Summary:** 11 stories published in collections 1972-1975 all sharing fantastic themes. Several stories focus on animals including ''The Boy Who Went Looking for a Friend,'' ''Patrick Comes to School,'' ''Mrs. Bartelmy's Pet'' and the title story which features a giant land-dwelling oyster. Three stories feature witches, ''Aunt Nasty,'' ''The Witch Dog'' and ''Teddy and the Witches,'' while ''Looking for a Ghost'' suggests that one might not recognize a ghost upon seeing it. In another story, ''Kite Saturday,'' young Joan's investment in wishes and dreams yields a magic kite that allows her to fly.

**Other books you might like:**
Diana Wynne Jones, *Warlock at the Wheel and Other Stories*, 1985
Rudyard Kipling, *Just So Stories*, 1902
Penelope Lively, *Uninvited Ghosts and Other Stories*, 1985
Jane Yolen, *Zoo 2000: Twelve Stories of Science Fiction and Fantasy Beasts*, 1973
    editor

---

### 3612

**BARRY MALZBERG**

## Beyond Apollo

(New York: Carroll and Graf, 1989)

**Story type:** Science Fiction (Literary)
**Major character(s):** Harry M. Evans, Astronaut; Captain, Astronaut

**Time period(s):** 1980s (1981)
**Locale(s):** United States; Venus

**Summary:** This John W. Campbell Memorial Award-winning novel is narrated by Harry M. Evans, the sole survivor of the first manned expedition to Venus. Evans returns to Earth insane, his mind a complex hash of memories, hallucinations and wish fulfillment fantasies. Within his tortured brain lies the secret of what went wrong on the expedition. Originally published in 1972.

**Other books you might like:**
J.G. Ballard, *The Crystal World*, 1966
J.G. Ballard, *The Drowned World*, 1962
J.G. Ballard, *The Unlimited Dream Company*, 1977
Philip K. Dick, *Flow My Tears, the Policeman Said*, 1974
Philip K. Dick, *Martian Time-Slip*, 1964
Philip K. Dick, *A Scanner Darkly*, 1977
Philip K. Dick, *The Transmigration of Timothy Archer*, 1982
Philip K. Dick, *Valis*, 1981
Dan Simmons, *Phases of Gravity*, 1989

---

### 3613

**ALBERT J. MANACHINO**

## Noctet: Tales of Madonna-Moloch

(Austin, Texas: Argo Press, 1997)

**Story type:** Horror (Collection; Occult)
**Major character(s):** Virgil Hood, Detective
**Locale(s):** Madonna-Moloch, Planet—Imaginary

**Summary:** Eight stories set on the planet Madonna-Moloch—a world of sorcery and dark magic—and featuring occult detective Virgil Hood. Hood battles wizards, withces, and the ghastly products of their conjuring in adventures that include ''The White Orchard,'' ''The Hungry House,'' ''Evening Primrose,'' ''Sleeping Booty,'' and ''The Garden of Eden.''

**Other books you might like:**
Christie Golden, *Dance of the Dead*, 1992
Staley Krause, *Strange City*, 1996
    Stewart Wieck, co-editor
Brian Lumley, *Iced on Aran and Other Dream Quests*, 1990
Tom Piccirilli, *Pentacle*, 1995
Robert Weinberg, *Blood War*, 1995
Chet Williamson, *Mordenheim*, 1994

---

### 3614

**ALBERT J. MANACHINO**
**LARRY DICKISON**, Illustrator

## The Odd Lot: The Selected Works of Albert J. Manachino

(Concord, California: Dark Regions Press, 1993)

**Story type:** Horror (Collection)

**Summary:** The nine stories in this book are collected from a variety of small press publications and include the haunted house tale, ''Darby's Bane''; the surreal comedy, ''Head of the House''; two stories (''The White Orchard'' and ''The Hungry House'') which combine the detective story with metaphysical fantasy; and three stories (''Dark Bible,'' ''Escape Clause,'' and ''Mr. Diabolicus'') that chronicle the efforts of foolish mortals who attempt either to dispose of or buy the so-called devil's bible. Michael Ambrose has supplied the introductions.

**Other books you might like:**
D.F. Lewis, *The Best of D.F. Lewis*, 1993
Darrell Schweitzer, *Transients and Other Disquieting Tales*, 1993
Ken Wisman, *Weird Family Tales*, 1993

3615

**NINA MANDELIK**

## Entity

(New York: Diamond, 1991)

**Story type:** Horror (Ancient Evil Unleashed)
**Major character(s):** Michael Triplett, Teenager; Tim O'Connor, Teenager; Maggie Greene, Waiter/Waitress
**Time period(s):** 1990s
**Locale(s):** Fort Riley, Kansas

**Summary:** Although an exorcism was performed there over a century before, the Army town of Fort Riley is suddenly besieged by apparitions, mysterious deaths and a wave of unspeakable behavior among its citizens. As the only one who suspects that something out of the ordinary is going on, young Michael Triplett trains himself to battle the festering evil that has taken control of the town. This is the author's first novel.

**Other books you might like:**
Douglas Clegg, *Goat Dance*, 1989
T.E.D. Klein, *The Ceremonies*, 1984
Bentley Little, *The Revelation*, 1990

3616

**ALBERTO MANGUEL**, Editor

## Black Water 2: More Tales of the Fantastic

(New York: Clarkson Potter, 1990)

**Story type:** Horror (Anthology)
**Summary:** Sixty-five tales of the supernatural from around the world. The selections range from classics like Charlotte Perkins Gilman's ''The Yellow Wallpaper'' and Hans Heinz Ewer's ''The Spider,'' to stories by authors not generally associated with fantasy fiction, such as F. Scott Fitzgerald's ''A Short Trip Home,'' Joseph Conrad's ''The Brute'' and Gabriel Garcia Marquez's ''The Last Voyage of the Ghost Ship.''

**Other books you might like:**
Peter Haining, *The Lucifer Society*, 1972
Robert Phillips, *Triumph of the Night*, 1989

3617

**PHILLIP MANN**

## Wulfsyarn: A Mosaic

(New York: Morrow AvoNova, 1992)

**Story type:** Science Fiction (Theological; First Contact)
**Major character(s):** Jon Wilburfoss, Spaceship Captain, Religious (confrere); Wulf, Artificial Intelligence, Writer; Chi-da, Alien
**Time period(s):** Indeterminate Future
**Locale(s):** Juniper, Planet—Imaginary; *Nightingale*, Spaceship; Outer Space

**Summary:** Jon Wilburfoss accepts command of the *Nightingale*, the only ship capable of travelling in subspace after the War of Ignorance. After he picks up aliens of various races, the infected ship's brain self-destructs, destroying all life aboard except Jon Wilburfoss. Marooned on a planet, Wilburfoss makes friends with an alien life force, only to destroy it getting off the planet. Rescued, Wilburfoss returns to Juniper where he falls into a miasma of guilt, sulking about the monastery garden.

**Other books you might like:**
John Barnes, *Sin of Origin*, 1988
Gregory Benford, *If the Stars Are Gods*, 1977
   Gordon Eklund, co-author
Michael Bishop, *Transfigurations*, 1979
Philip Jose Farmer, *Night of Light*, 1966
Stanislaw Lem, *Solaris*, 1970
John Morressy, *The Mansions of Space*, 1983
Vernor Vinge, *A Fire upon the Deep*, 1992

3618

**WILLIAM J. MANN**, Editor

## Grave Passions

(New York: Badboy, 1997)

**Story type:** Horror (Anthology; Gay/Lesbian Fiction)

**Summary:** Eighteen tales of the gay supernatural, all original to the volume. Ghost stories (Felice Picano's ''Hunter,'' Scott O'Hara's ''Spirits,'' Noel Ambery II's ''Why I Killed Him,'' Gary Bowen's ''Hungry Ghost''), tales of passion and obession (Poppy Z. Brite's ''Entertaining Mr. Orton,'' Thomas Roche's ''Have I Sinned Against You?''), and fairy tale variations (Lawrence Schimel's ''The Farrier and the Elves'') explore the dark side of love in a gay context. Many of the selections implicitly address the horrors of love in the era of AIDS.

**Other books you might like:**
Poppy Z. Brite, *Love in Vein II*, 1997
   Martin H. Greenberg, co-editor
Poppy Z. Brite, *Love in Vein*, 1994
   Martin H. Grcenbcrg, co-editor
Pam Keesey, *Darker Angels: Lesbian Vampire Stories*, 1995
   editor
Amarantha Knight, *Seductive Spectres*, 1996
   editor
Amarantha Knight, *Sex Macabre*, 1996
   editor
Amarantha Knight, *Love Bites*, 1994
   editor
Michael Rowe, *Sons of Darkness: Tales of Men, Blood and Immortality*, 1996
   Thomas Roche, co-editor
Michael Rowe, *Brothers of the Night*, 1997
   Thomas Roche, co-editor

3619

**CYNTHIA MANSON**, Editor
**CHARLES ARDAI**, Co-Editor

## Future Crime: An Anthology of the Shape of Crime to Come

(New York: Donald I. Fine, 1992)

**Story type:** Science Fiction (Anthology; Mystery)

**Summary:** This volume addresses crime to come with original short stories by C.J. Cherryh and Alan Dean Foster and an original novelette by George Alec Effinger as well as stories by Isaac Asimov, Terry Black, Robert Bloch, Orson Scott Card, Harry Harrison, Kathe

Koja, Doug Larsen, Larry Niven, John Shirley, W.R. Thompson, John Varley and Lawrence Watt-Evans.

**Other books you might like:**
Isaac Asimov, *Tales of the Black Widowers*, 1974
J.G. Ballard, *The Atrocity Exhibition*, 1990
Ben Bova, *Future Crime*, 1990
Miriam Allen DeFord, *Space, Time and Crime*, 1964
Mike Resnick, *Whatdunits*, 1992
    editor
Howard Waldrop, *Night of the Cooters*, 1990
    editor
Howard Waldrop, *Them Bones*, 1984

## 3620

### MICHAEL MARANO

## Dawn Song

(New York: Tor, 1998)

**Story type:** Horror (Occult)
**Major character(s):** Lawrence, Clerk (in a bookstore); Ed Sloane, Student (at Harvard Divinity School); Paul La Cotta, Teacher
**Time period(s):** 1990s
**Locale(s):** Boston, Massachusetts

**Summary:** On the eve of the Gulf War, Belial, the Unbowed One and Leviathan, the Enfolded One, wage their ageless battle with human surrogates in the Harvard and Boston academic community. In this first novel, Marano envisions the relationships of individuals and the political sentiments of the era as mirrors that reflect aspects of the classic struggle between good and evil.

**Other books you might like:**
Clive Barker, *Sacrament*, 1996
Terry Brooks, *A Knight of the Word*, 1998
Garry Kilworth, *Angel*, 1993
Graham Masterton, *Master of Lies*, 1992
T.M. Wright, *The Ascending*, 1994

## 3621

### MELISAND MARCH

## The Site

(New York: Leisure, 1989)

**Story type:** Horror (Haunted House)
**Major character(s):** Valerie Harris, Advertising (Executive); Jennifer Cunningham, Advertising (Valerie's protegee)
**Time period(s):** 1960s (1961, 1965); 1970s (1977)
**Locale(s):** New York, New York

**Summary:** A novel "based on real incidents." A series of inexplicable accidents convince Valerie Harris that the "site" of a modern high-rise building is taking systematic "revenge" against its inhabitants.

**Other books you might like:**
Anne Rivers Siddons, *The House Next Door*, 1978

## 3622

### NORMA MARDER

## An Eye for Dark Places

(Boston: Little Brown, 1993)

**Story type:** Science Fiction (Post-Disaster; Political)

**Major character(s):** Sephony Berg-Benson, Farmer, Revolutionary; Claro, Alien
**Time period(s):** 21st century
**Locale(s):** England; Domino, Alternate Earth

**Summary:** Sephony remains generally satisfied with farm life and raising children in a politically repressive England despite her nagging visions and ill-defined desires. When Claro invites her to descend throught a hole in her kitchen floor one day, Sephony discovers Domino and its society, which fosters freedom. On returning home, Sephony fights for restoration of women's rights in her society. First novel.

**Other books you might like:**
Margaret Atwood, *The Handmaid's Tale*, 1985
Flynn Connolly, *The Rising of the Moon*, 1993
Suzette Haden Elgin, *Earthsong*, 1994
Suzette Haden Elgin, *The Judas Rose*, 1987
Suzette Haden Elgin, *Native Tongue*, 1984
Marge Piercy, *Woman on the Edge of Time*, 1976

## 3623

### KYLE MARFINN

## Carmilla: The Return

(Darien, Illinois: Design Image Group, 1998)

**Story type:** Horror (Vampire Story)
**Major character(s):** Lauren Vestal, Clerk (retail); Steve Michaels, Ranger; Millarca, Vampire
**Time period(s):** 1990s (1998); 19th century
**Locale(s):** Chicago, Illinois; Watersmeet, Michigan

**Summary:** This modernization of J. Sheridan Le Fanu's classic vampire novella "Carmilla" (1872) explicitly levers out its erotic subtext. In this version, the resilient vampire Carmilla, in the guise of exotic femme fatale Millarca, has survived the death Le Fanu described for her and emigrated to America, where she integrates perfectly with contemporary American culture and becomes involved in a love triangle involving the puzzled Lauren Vestal and her boyfriend Steve. A first novel.

**Other books you might like:**
Traci Briery, *The Vampire Journals*, 1993
Poppy Z. Brite, *Lost Souls*, 1992
P.D. Cacek, *Night Prayers*, 1998
Marie Kiraly, *Mina*, 1994
S.P. Somtow, *Vampire Junction*, 1983

## 3624

### LAURIE J. MARKS

## Dancing Jack

(New York: DAW, 1993)

**Story type:** Fantasy (Quest; Sword and Sorcery)
**Major character(s):** Ash of Ashland, Revolutionary, Adventurer; Rys, Sailor (riverboat pilot)
**Time period(s):** Indeterminate
**Locale(s):** Faerd, Fictional Country; All-Haven, Fictional Country

**Summary:** Deciding to find her nephew, Ash abandons a decade of farming ancestral ground while trying to forget her involvement in a bloody rebellion. She hopes her nephew will prove the vessel for her family's magical talent. However, plans do not proceed as wished when, shortly after Ash locates him, rebellion again sweeps into her life.

**Other books you might like:**
Tom Deitz, *Soulsmith*, 1991
Dave Duncan, *The Cutting Edge*, 1992
Tanith Lee, *Kill the Dead*, 1980
Elizabeth Moon, *Sheepfarmer's Daughter*, 1988
Caroline Stevermer, *River Rats*, 1992
Paula Volsky, *Illusion*, 1992

---

### 3625
#### LAURIE J. MARKS
## Delan the Mislaid
(New York: DAW, 1989)

**Story type:** Fantasy (Adventure)
**Series:** Children of Triad
**Major character(s):** Delan, Wanderer; Teksan Lafall, Traveler
**Time period(s):** Indeterminate
**Locale(s):** Alternate Universe

**Summary:** Despite a wide variety of sentient beings, with a wide variety of shapes, Delan is considered a freak in his world. As he (or possibly she) looks for an identity, he joins another wanderer and learns about the world.

**Other books you might like:**
Mary Brown, *The Unlikely Ones*, 1986
Charles de Lint, *Wolf Moon*, 1988
Andre Norton, *Flight in Yiktor*, 1987

---

### 3626
#### LAURIE J. MARKS
## The Moonbane Mage
(New York: DAW, 1990)

**Story type:** Fantasy (Quest)
**Major character(s):** Laril, Mythical Creature (Aeyrie; Exiled adolescent)
**Time period(s):** Indeterminate
**Locale(s):** Alternate Universe

**Summary:** Exiled by his community, Laril, a winged creature, takes refuge with a mage who turns out to be somewhat warped. In addition to discovering his own powers, Laril falls in love with the mage's servant woman, a Walker.

**Other books you might like:**
M. Coleman Easton, *Spirits of Cavern and Hearth*, 1989
Robert Jordan, *The Eye of the World*, 1989

---

### 3627
#### LAURIE J. MARKS
## The Watcher's Mask
(New York: DAW, 1992)

**Story type:** Fantasy (Political; Adventure)
**Major character(s):** Jamil/Alasil, Military Personnel, Spy; Ata'al, Shaman (Asakeiri); Adline Asakeiri, Sports Figure (runner), Shaman
**Time period(s):** Indeterminate
**Locale(s):** Akava, Fictional City; Ashami, Fictional City; Callia, Fictional Country

**Summary:** The Watchers, a cadre of spies and executioners for the Emperor consisting of multi-souled people kidnapped as children, have been taught they will become insane if left with their natural families. Jamil, one of the oldest, most successful Watchers, fears her "blackouts" exhibit a symptom of this insanity which afflicts many older Watchers. She struggles to survive a fall and near death from exposure, and to explain to herself why she is hundreds of miles from where she expected to be and why several weeks have passed. Rescued by the Asakeiri, Jamil learns about herself and her heritage and a threat to the Emperor requiring her immediate return to Ashami.

**Other books you might like:**
Constance Ash, *The Stalking Horse*, 1990
Mary Gentle, *Rats and Gargoyles*, 1991
Rosemary Kirstein, *The Steerswoman*, 1989
Ursula K. Le Guin, *Always Coming Home*, 1985
Elizabeth Moon, *Sheepfarmer's Daughter*, 1988
James Morrow, *Only Begotten Daughter*, 1990

---

### 3628
#### LOUISE MARLEY
## Receive the Gift
(New York: Ace, 1997)

**Story type:** Science Fiction (Lost Colony; Psychic Powers)
**Series:** Sing the Light
**Major character(s):** Siri, Psychic (esper), Singer; Mreen, Psychic (esper), Child; Jakri, Psychic (esper), Singer
**Time period(s):** Indeterminate Future
**Locale(s):** Nevya, Planet—Imaginary

**Summary:** Only Singers trained at Conservatory generate enough heat to maintain a viable temperature during the years-long winters on Nevya, but fewer talented children have been discovered in recent years. Siri believes the sequestered life at Conservatory proves too difficult for many parents, so the talents go untrained. She starts her own school at Observatory for the talented children born there, since Conservatory refuses to recognize Observatory or send them the Singers they need to survive. Third in series.

**Other books you might like:**
Maya Kaathryn Bohnhoff, *The Meri*, 1992
Suzette Haden Elgin, *Earthsong*, 1994
Nina Kiriki Hoffman, *The Thread That Binds the Bones*, 1994
Rosemary Kirstein, *The Steerswoman*, 1989
Anne McCaffrey, *The Rowan*, 1990
Sheri S. Tepper, *Raising the Stones*, 1990

---

### 3629
#### LOUISE MARLEY
## Sing the Light
(New York: Ace, 1995)

**Story type:** Science Fiction (Lost Colony; Psychic Powers)
**Major character(s):** Sira, Psychic (Cantrix), Singer; Rollie, Guide (ranger); Lu, Psychic (esper), Teacher (maestra)
**Time period(s):** Indeterminate Future
**Locale(s):** Nevya, Planet—Imaginary

**Summary:** On Nevya, survival for humans would be impossible without Singers who use psychic power to generate heat. Trained at the Conservatory from childhood to serve as Cantor or Cantrix at a great House, the best can never be touched by anyone not also trained. The youngest Cantrix ever graduated from the Conservatory, Sira finds life at the House of Bariken hostile and misses the respect she expects from her training. When politics turns to murder, from which she narrowly escapes, Sira's act of defiance almost costs her her future as a Cantrix.

**Other books you might like:**
Marion Zimmer Bradley, *Rediscovery: A Novel of Darkover*, 1993
    Mercedes Lackey, co-author
Suzette Haden Elgin, *Earthsong*, 1994
Rosemary Kirstein, *The Steerswoman*, 1989
Anne McCaffrey, *The Rowan*, 1990
Jack Williamson, *Demon Moon*, 1994

---

## 3630
### LOUISE MARLEY

## Sing the Warmth
(New York: Ace, 1996)

**Story type:** Science Fiction (Lost Colony; Psychic Powers)
**Series:** Sing the Light
**Major character(s):** Sira, Psychic (esper), Singer; Iban, Psychic (esper); Zakri, Psychic (esper), Singer
**Time period(s):** Indeterminate Future
**Locale(s):** Nevya, Planet—Imaginary

**Summary:** After living at Observatory as Cantrix for the last four years, Sira leaves a fully trained Theo as Cantor in her place. Unwilling to return to Conservatory, Sira looks for Zakri to train his very strong, undisciplined talent to solve the problems caused by lack of Candidates coming to Conservatory.

**Other books you might like:**
Marion Zimmer Bradley, *Rediscovery: A Novel of Darkover*, 1993
    Mercedes Lackey, co-author
Suzette Haden Elgin, *Earthsong*, 1994
Nina Kiriki Hoffman, *The Thread That Binds the Bones*, 1994
Rosemary Kirstein, *The Steerswoman*, 1989
Anne McCaffrey, *The Rowan*, 1990

---

## 3631
### STEPHEN MARLOWE

## The Lighthouse at the End of the World
(New York: Dutton, 1995)

**Story type:** Horror (Mystery)
**Major character(s):** Edgar Allan Poe, Writer, Historical Figure; C. Auguste Dupin, Detective; John J. Moran, Doctor
**Time period(s):** 1840s (1849)
**Locale(s):** Baltimore, Maryland

**Summary:** Presented as an account of Edgar Allan Poe's whereabouts the last week of his life, this novel tells how Poe hires detective C. Auguste Dupin to find his missing brother, and the mystical discoveries Poe makes in the process that allow him access to alternate lives and to witness the end of the world. The novel's events all are prefigured by characters and themes that run throughout Poe's tales of the mysterious and the macabre.

**Other books you might like:**
Brian W. Aldiss, *Frankenstein Unbound*, 1973
Mark Frost, *The List of 7*, 1993
William Hjortsberg, *Nevermore*, 1994
Kim Newman, *Anno Dracula*, 1995

---

## 3632
### JOHN S. MARR
### JOHN BALDWIN, Co-Author

## The Eleventh Plague: A Novel of Medical Terror
(New York: HarperCollins/Cliff Street, 1998)

**Story type:** Horror (Techno-Horror)
**Major character(s):** Jack Byrne, Scientist (virologist); Scott Hubbard, Spy, FBI Agent; Theodore R.G. Kameron, Scientist
**Time period(s):** 1990s (1998)
**Locale(s):** San Antonio, Texas

**Summary:** Jack Byrne and Scott Hubbard team up to thwart a mad scientist who is using mycotoxins and biological warfare to unleash the ten biblical plagues on an unsuspecting world. But can Scott trust Jack, a virologist whose intimate knowledge of the scourges he fights makes him suspicious?

**Other books you might like:**
Michael Crichton, *The Andromeda Strain*, 1969
Chuck Hogan, *The Blood Artists*, 1998
James Byron Huggins, *Cain*, 1997
Dean R. Koontz, *Midnight*, 1989
Patrick Lynch, *Omega*, 1997

---

## 3633
### RICHARD MARSH

## The Haunted Chair and Other Stories
(Ashcroft, British Columbia: Ash-Tree Press, 1997)

**Story type:** Horror (Collection)

**Summary:** Eighteen stories, representing the complete short supernatural fiction of the author. Included are ''The Adventure of Lady Wishaw's Hand,'' about a supernaturally animated disembodied hand; ''The Photographs,'' in which a woman uses astral projection to find the criminal responsible for the crime her husband was unjustly imprisoned for; ''The Violin,'' in which a ghostly tune from a violin reveals the whereabouts of its murdered owner's body; ''George Ogden's Will,'' in which a ghost executes its own will; and ''A Set of Chessmen,'' in which a chess set continues to move by the plays of its deceased owner. Edited and with an introduction by Richard Dalby.

**Other books you might like:**
E.F. Benson, *The Collected Ghost Stories of E.F. Benson*, 1992
A.M. Burrage, *Some Ghost Stories*, 1927
Frederick Cowles, *Fear Walks the Night*, 1992
Sabine Baring Gould, *A Book of Ghosts*, 1904
M.R. James, *The Collected Ghost Stories of M.R. James*, 1931

---

## 3634
### ANN MARSTON

## Broken Blade
(New York: HarperPrism, 1997)

**Story type:** Fantasy (Sword and Sorcery; Magic Conflict)
**Series:** Rune Blade Trilogy
**Major character(s):** Brynda al Keylan, Noblewoman, Bodyguard; Kenzie ''Catfoot'' dav Aidan, Mercenary, Nobleman; Mikal, Sorcerer
**Time period(s):** Indeterminate

**Locale(s):** Laringras, Fictional Country; Isle of Celi, Fictional Country

**Summary:** Kidnapped by the evil sorceress Francia, Brynda escapes and joins forces with Kenzie as they flee across Laringras. Eluding capture, Brynda returns to Celi to warn King Tiernyn that Francia and her son, Mikal may have the power to overcome the veil of enchantment protecting Celi for the last 40 years. When the battle comes, Brynda survives to guard the widow of Prince Tiegan and the unborn heir to the throne. First in trilogy.

**Other books you might like:**
Marion Zimmer Bradley, *The Shattered Chain*, 1976
Terry Brooks, *The Sword of Shannara*, 1978
C.J. Cherryh, *Gate of Ivrel*, 1976
Barbara Hambly, *The Dark Hand of Magic*, 1990
C.L. Moore, *Jirel of Joiry*, 1969
Elizabeth Ann Scarborough, *The Christening Quest*, 1985

## 3635

### ANN MARSTON

## Kingmaker's Sword
(New York: HarperPrism, 1996)

**Story type:** Fantasy (Sword and Sorcery)
**Series:** Rune Blade Trilogy
**Major character(s):** Kian ''Mouse'' dav Leydon, Heir—Lost, Hero; Kerridwen al Jorddyn, Noblewoman, Martial Arts Expert; Cullin dav Medroch, Nobleman, Mercenary
**Time period(s):** Indeterminate
**Locale(s):** Falinor, Fictional Country; Tyra, Fictional Country

**Summary:** Escaping slavery, Kian acquires a magical sword and discovers the identity of his grandfather. After several years travel with his uncle, Cullin, as a mercenary guard, he meets a swordswoman who seeks the rightful owner of the sword, the lost heir of Celi. A powerful sorcerer and Kian's former master also seek him, with less benevolent intentions. The story continues in *The Western King*.

**Other books you might like:**
C.J. Cherryh, *Gate of Ivrel*, 1976
Simon R. Green, *Blue Moon Rising*, 1991
Barbara Hambly, *The Ladies of Mandrigyn*, 1984
Katherine Kurtz, *Deryni Rising*, 1970
Roger Zelazny, *Nine Princes in Amber*, 1970

## 3636

### ANN MARSTON

## The Western King
(New York: HarperPrism, 1996)

**Story type:** Fantasy (Sword and Sorcery; Magic Conflict)
**Series:** Rune Blade Trilogy
**Major character(s):** Keylan ap Kian, Ruler (king); Donaugh ap Kian, Royalty (prince), Magician; Tiernyn ap Kian, Royalty (prince), Warrior
**Time period(s):** Indeterminate
**Locale(s):** Celi, Fictional Country

**Summary:** Kian decides that the time has come to step down as Regent of Skai and crown his son Keylan as King. Tiernyn receives the magic sword, ''Kingmaker,'' and urges his older brother to unite the bickering tribes in order to drive the Saesnesi invaders from their island. But to Donaugh goes the responsibility of advising his brothers and of bringing about an alliance with the Saesne sis in order to

fight the greater threat of the Maedun, led by the evil sorcerers Hakkar and Francia.

**Other books you might like:**
Marion Zimmer Bradley, *The Mists of Avalon*, 1983
C.J. Cherryh, *Faery in Shadow*, 1994
Simon R. Green, *Blood and Honor*, 1993
Harry Harrison, *The Hammer and the Cross*, 1993
    John Holm, co-author
Diana L. Paxson, *The White Raven*, 1988
Roger Zelazny, *Nine Princes in Amber*, 1970

## 3637

### DAVID MARTIN

## Bring Me Children
(New York: Random House, 1992)

**Story type:** Horror (Child-in-Peril)
**Major character(s):** John Lyon, Television Personality (news anchor), Journalist; Mason Quindell, Doctor; Claire Cept, Professor (of American Folklore)
**Time period(s):** 1990s (1992)
**Locale(s):** Hamelin, West Virginia

**Summary:** John Lyon oversteps the bounds of journalistic propriety when his obsessive interest in child abuse leads him to the estate of Mason Quindell, a physician whose own interest in children not only stretches the boundaries of clinical practice but runs to the near-satanic.

**Other books you might like:**
John Arbucci, *Blood of Innocents*, 1991
Eric Flanders, *The Forever Children*, 1992
John Saul, *Darkness*, 1991

## 3638

### DAVID MARTIN

## Cul-De-Sac
(New York: Villard, 1997)

**Story type:** Horror (Serial Killer)
**Major character(s):** Donald Growler, Murderer; Teddy Camel, Police Officer (former); Annie Milton, Young Woman
**Time period(s):** 1990s (1997)
**Locale(s):** Washington, District of Columbia

**Summary:** Framed for a murder which he did not commit, Donald Growler emerges from prison a psychotic criminal determined to kill those who set him up. Annie Milton, wife of an asylum owner who has benefitted from Growler's incarceration, engages the services of her former lover Teddy Camel, an ex-cop, whose efforts to protect her uncover a conspiracy that the murder victim's family is desperate to keep secret.

**Other books you might like:**
John Farris, *The Axman Cometh*, 1989
Joe R. Lansdale, *The Nightrunners*, 1987
Patrick McCabe, *The Butcher Boy*, 1992
John Saul, *Black Lightning*, 1995

## 3639

### DAVID MARTIN

### *Lie to Me*

(New York: Random House, 1990)

**Story type:** Horror (Psychological Suspense)
**Major character(s):** Mary Gaetan, Housewife; Teddy Camel, Police Officer; Philip Gaetan, Prisoner (recently released)
**Time period(s):** 1990s (1990)
**Locale(s):** Washington, District of Columbia

**Summary:** The gruesome death of wealthy contractor Jonathan Gaetan appears to have been the work of a psychopath, but Gaetan's wife and secretary maintain that the wounds were self-inflicted. As veteran cop Teddy Camel searches for a murderer and a motive, he becomes more and more convinced that Gaetan's family and associates are deliberately trying to hide something about Gaetan's past.

**Other books you might like:**
Whitley Strieber, *Billy*, 1990
T.M. Wright, *The Place*, 1989

## 3640

### DAVID MARTIN

### *Tap, Tap*

(New York: Random House, 1995)

**Story type:** Horror (Mystery)
**Major character(s):** Roscoe Bird, Teacher; Peter Tummelier, Wealthy, Friend (of Roscoe); Marianne Bird, Student—College (graduate student), Spouse (Roscoe's wife)
**Time period(s):** 1990s (1995)
**Locale(s):** Washington, District of Columbia

**Summary:** In this tale charged with hints of homoeroticism, Roscoe Bird discovers that the return of his old school friend Peter Tummelier coincides with the vampire-like deaths of Roscoe's worst enemies. In order to solve the mystery of Peter's role in the murders, Roscoe must confront ghosts from his past, including the suicide of his father which traumatized him emotionally and psychologically as a youth. British edition, 1994, titled *Love Me to Death*.

**Other books you might like:**
Giles Blunt, *Cold Eye*, 1989
Dennis Etchison, *California Gothic*, 1995
Rick Hautala, *Cold Whisper*, 1991
Thomas Tryon, *The Other*, 1972

## 3641

### GEORGE R.R. MARTIN
### MELINDA M. SNODGRASS, Co-Author

### *Ace in the Hole*

(New York: Bantam Spectra, 1990)

**Story type:** Science Fiction (Alternate Universe)
**Series:** Wild Cards
**Major character(s):** Gregg Hartmann, Political Figure (senator), Genetically Altered Being; Doctor Tachyon, Alien, Doctor
**Time period(s):** 1980s (1988)
**Locale(s):** New York, New York

**Summary:** When Dr. Tachyon released the mutagenic Wild Card virus over New York, the repercussions were numerous and widespread. The human species now includes a distressingly large number of super-heroes called Aces and super-villains called Jokers. Gregg Hartmann, an undeclared victim of the virus is a Joker called Puppetman, who wants to be an evil President of the United States, getting Aces more involved in politics than they desire. This braided novel, a form of shared-world anthology, was written by Stephen Leigh, Victor Milan, Walter Simons, Melinda M. Snodgrass and Walter Jon Williams.

**Other books you might like:**
Robert N. Charrette, *Never Deal with a Dragon*, 1990
Harlan Ellison, *Medea: Harlan's World*, 1985
Frank Herbert, *The White Plague*, 1982

## 3642

### GEORGE R.R. MARTIN

### *Black Trump*

(New York: Baen, 1995)

**Story type:** Science Fiction (Alternate Universe; Psychic Powers)
**Series:** Wild Cards
**Major character(s):** Mark "Captain Trips" Meadows, Genetically Altered Being, Scientist (biochemist); Croyd "The Sleeper" Crenson, Genetically Altered Being
**Time period(s):** 1990s
**Locale(s):** Jokertown, New York (New York City); Jerusalem, Israel; Vietnam (Free Peoples State of Vietnam)

**Summary:** When a joker and a reporter team up to expose the Card Shark conspiracy, the Sharks implement a terrible biological weapon, the Black Trump, which will kill all people with the wild card virus, both aces and jokers. A mosaic novel written by Stephen Leigh, George R.R. Martin, Victor Milan, John J. Miller, and Sage Walker.

**Other books you might like:**
Michael Bishop, *Count Geiger's Blues*, 1992
Frank Herbert, *The White Plague*, 1982
Michael Kandel, *Captain Jack Zodiac*, 1992
Victor Milan, *Turn of the Cards*, 1993
Melinda M. Snodgrass, *Double Solitaire*, 1992

## 3643

### GEORGE R.R. MARTIN, Editor
### MELINDA M. SNODGRASS, Co-Editor

### *Dealer's Choice*

(New York: Bantam Spectra, 1992)

**Story type:** Science Fiction (Alternate Universe; Anthology)
**Series:** Wild Cards
**Major character(s):** Wyungare, Shaman; Bloat, Genetically Altered Being (joker), Ruler (governor of the Rox); The Great and Powerful Turtle, Hero
**Time period(s):** 1990s (September 21-23, 1990)
**Locale(s):** Ellis Island, New York (the Rox)

**Summary:** This braided novel written by Stephen Leigh, Edward W. Bryant, John J. Miller, Walter Jon Williams and George R. R. Martin continues the saga of the war between the Nats and the Jokers on the Rox, with an ultimate solution finally in the offing. Concludes with a two-page closing credits and a one-page "about the contributors."

**Other books you might like:**
C.J. Cherryh, *Angel with the Sword*, 1985
C.J. Cherryh, *Festival Moon*, 1987
  editor

Harlan Ellison, *Medea: Harlan's World*, 1985
  editor
Philip Jose Farmer, *Doc Savage: His Apocalyptic Life*, 1973
Philip Jose Farmer, *Tarzan Alive*, 1972
Will Shetterly, *Liavek*, 1985
  Emma Bull, co-editor
Terri Windling, *Life on the Border*, 1991
  editor

**3644**

### GEORGE R.R. MARTIN

## *Dying of the Light*
(New York: Baen Books, 1990)

**Story type:** Science Fiction (Romance)
**Major character(s):** Dirk T'Larien, Scientist, Wanderer; Gwen Delvano, Scientist
**Time period(s):** Indeterminate Future
**Locale(s):** Worlorn, Planet—Imaginary

**Summary:** Responding to a call for aid from Gwen, his lover of many years before, Dirk T'Larien travels to the distant and primitive world of Worlorn. There he finds himself caught up in a web of violence and intrigue, expected to follow traditions and participate in rituals of which he has very little understanding. Originally published in 1977.

**Other books you might like:**
Dan Simmons, *Hyperion*, 1989
James Tiptree Jr., *Brightness Falls From the Air*, 1985
James Tiptree Jr., *Crown of Stars*, 1988
James Tiptree Jr., *Up the Walls of the World*, 1978
Joan D. Vinge, *Catspaw*, 1988
Joan D. Vinge, *The Snow Queen*, 1980

**3645**

### GEORGE R.R. MARTIN

## *A Game of Thrones*
(New York: Bantam Spectra, 1996)

**Story type:** Fantasy (Adventure; Political)
**Series:** Song of Ice and Fire
**Major character(s):** Eddard Stark, Nobleman; Lady Catelyn, Noblewoman; Tyrion Lannister, Bastard Son, Handicapped (dwarf)
**Time period(s):** Indeterminate
**Locale(s):** Seven Kingdoms, Fictional Country

**Summary:** In a medieval society plagued with seasons of extraordinary length, seven families plot to acquire the throne. For protection, Eddard Stark gives each of his children a direwolf pup to raise. When the king's advisor dies, Stark reluctantly joins the king as replacement Hand, hoping to alert the king to the scheming which threatens his rule and the stability of the Seven Kingdoms. Contains a 19-page appendix of dramatis personae and family background.

**Other books you might like:**
Lynn Flewelling, *Luck in the Shadows*, 1996
Robin Hobb, *Assassin's Apprentice*, 1995
J.V. Jones, *The Baker's Boy*, 1995
Melanie Rawn, *Dragon Prince*, 1988
Martha Wells, *The Element of Fire*, 1993
Roger Zelazny, *Nine Princes in Amber*, 1970

**3646**

### GEORGE R.R. MARTIN, Editor

## *Jokertown Shuffle*
(New York: Bantam Spectra, 1991)

**Story type:** Science Fiction (Alternate Universe)
**Series:** Wild Cards
**Major character(s):** Doctor Tachyon, Alien, Doctor; Bloat, Genetically Altered Being (joker), Ruler (governor of the Rox)
**Time period(s):** 1990s
**Locale(s):** New York, New York

**Summary:** As Governor of the Rox, Bloat is the final arbiter of the law. His position is secure, if uncomfortable, because the wall which protects the Rox from the authorities in Manhattan would disappear without him. Blaise, evil relative of Dr. Tachyon, would like to control Bloat, but has been unsuccessful so far. This braided novel, a form of shared-world anthology, was written by Steven Leigh, John J. Miller, Melinda M. Snodgrass, Victor Milan, Walter Jon Williams, Lewis Shiner, and Walter Simons.

**Other books you might like:**
C.J. Cherryh, *Angel with the Sword*, 1985
C.J. Cherryh, *Festival Moon*, 1987
  editor
Harlan Ellison, *Medea: Harlan's World*, 1985
  editor
C.S. Friedman, *Black Sun Rising*, 1991
Janet Kagan, *Mirabile*, 1991
Will Shetterly, *Liavek*, 1985
  Emma Bull, co-editor
Terri Windling, *Life on the Border*, 1991
  editor

**3647**

### GEORGE R.R. MARTIN, Editor

## *Marked Cards*
(New York: Baen, 1994)

**Story type:** Science Fiction (Alternate Universe; Psychic Powers)
**Series:** Wild Cards
**Major character(s):** Gregg Hartmann, Political Figure (ex-senator), Genetically Altered Being; Croyd "The Sleeper" Crenson, Genetically Altered Being; Hannah Davis, Journalist
**Time period(s):** 1990s
**Locale(s):** United States; Vietnam

**Summary:** When research uncovers a conspiracy, Hannah Davis and a few people affected by the Wild Card virus attempt to stop the plot to destroy all evidence of the virus and those infected by it.

**Other books you might like:**
Michael Bishop, *Count Geiger's Blues*, 1992
Harlan Ellison, *Medea: Harlan's World*, 1985
  editor
Michael Kandel, *Captain Jack Zodiac*, 1992
Victor Milan, *Turn of the Cards*, 1993
Melinda M. Snodgrass, *Double Solitaire*, 1992

## 3648

**GEORGE R.R. MARTIN**

### Portraits of His Children

(New York: Baen, 1992)

**Story type:** Science Fiction (Collection)

**Summary:** From surrealism to more traditional topics such as time travel, Martin presents a broad range of themes varying in tone from humor and irony to madness and violence. This collection of 11 stories published in periodicals and anthologies 1972-1986 includes "With Morning Comes Mistfall," "the Ice Dragon," "Unsound Variations," a Nebula Award winning story, "Portraits of His Children" and a five-page introduction by Roger Zelazny titled "A Sketch of Their Father." Reprint of a 1987 edition.

**Other books you might like:**
J.G. Ballard, *War Fever*, 1991
Groff Conklin, *The Best of Science Fiction*, 1946
   editor
Larry Niven, *Playgrounds of the Mind*, 1991
Michael Swanwick, *Gravity's Angels*, 1991
Harry Turtledove, *Earthgrip*, 1991
Lawrence Watt-Evans, *Crosstime Traffic*, 1992
John Varley, *Blue Champagne*, 1986
Roger Zelazny, *Gone to Earth*, 1991

## 3649

**MARK O. MARTIN**
**GREGORY BENFORD**, Co-Author

### A Darker Geometry

(New York: Baen, 1996)

**Story type:** Science Fiction (Military; First Contact)
**Series:** Man-Kzin Wars
**Major character(s):** Carol Faulk, Spaceship Captain, Military Personnel; Brund Takagama, Military Personnel, Spaceman; Prowl Captain, Alien (Kzin), Spaceship Captain
**Time period(s):** Indeterminate Future
**Locale(s):** Outer Space; Interstellar Empire/Federation; *Sun-Tzu*, Spaceship

**Summary:** Designed to attack Kzin near Alpha Centauri, *Sun-Tzu* does not possess adequate defenses when Kzin attack unexpectedly on the way there. A visit from a puppeteer ship quickly changes the situation, as does an appearance of the mysterious Outsiders.

**Other books you might like:**
Poul Anderson, *Inconstant Star*, 1991
Dean Ing, *Cathouse*, 1991
Larry Niven, *Man-Kzin Wars*, 1988
   editor
Larry Niven, *Man-Kzin Wars II-VII*, 1989-1995
   editor
Jerry Pournelle, *The Children's Hour*, 1991
   S.M. Stirling, co-author

## 3650

**THOMAS K. MARTIN**

### A Call to Arms

(New York: Ace, 1995)

**Story type:** Fantasy (Alternate World; Magic Conflict)

**Series:** Dreamer
**Major character(s):** Steve "The Dreamer" Wilkinson, Student—College; Jared, Mythical Creature (Druid lord); Erelvar, Nobleman, Religious
**Time period(s):** 1990s (1995); Indeterminate
**Locale(s):** Delgroth, Fictional City

**Summary:** After the Dreamer dies, Morvanor quickly falls to Daryna's troops and their modern weapons. When the Dreamer defies death, his return causes the destruction of the Mistress. Subsequent infighting among her generals may buy the beleaguered kings enough time to stop the destruction.

**Other books you might like:**
Brian Daley, *The Doomfarers of Coramonde*, 1977
L. Sprague de Camp, *The Complete Compleat Enchanter*, 1989
   Fletcher Pratt, co-author
Barbara Hambly, *The Time of the Dark*, 1982
Guy Gavriel Kay, *The Summer Tree*, 1985
Andre Norton, *Witch World*, 1963

## 3651

**THOMAS K. MARTIN**

### Magelord: The Awakening

(New York: Ace, 1997)

**Story type:** Fantasy (Magic Conflict; Political)
**Series:** MageLord Trilogy
**Major character(s):** Bjorn Rolfson, Hunter, Wizard; Gavin, Royalty (Prince of Reykvid); Valerian, Wizard (MageLord)
**Time period(s):** Indeterminate
**Locale(s):** Reykvid, Fictional City

**Summary:** Although he fears his abilities may not suffice, Bjorn must help when Prince Gavin fears his father has come under the influence of Valerian, possibly an ancient MageLord, awakened from a prison of sleep. First in trilogy.

**Other books you might like:**
Lynn Flewelling, *Luck in the Shadows*, 1996
Terry Goodkind, *Wizard's First Rule*, 1994
Robin Hobb, *Assassin's Apprentice*, 1995
Peg Kerr, *Emerald House Rising*, 1997

## 3652

**THOMAS K. MARTIN**

### The Time of Madness

(New York: Ace, 1998)

**Story type:** Fantasy (Magic Conflict; Political)
**Series:** MageLord Trilogy
**Major character(s):** Gavin, Royalty (prince); Mathen, Knight, Abuse Victim; Ian Urghart, Nobleman, Wizard
**Time period(s):** Indeterminate
**Locale(s):** Reykvid, Fictional Country

**Summary:** With the MageLord defeated at terrible cost, the kingdom of Prince Gavin tears at itself, killing anyone suspected of having Power. As the Hunt ravages the country, decent people do what they can to save the innocent, while one young noble finds a very personal reason for getting involved.

**Other books you might like:**
Eleanor Arnason, *The Sword Smith*, 1978
Glen Cook, *The Swordbearer*, 1982
Barbara Hambly, *The Time of the Dark*, 1982
Katherine Kurtz, *Deryni Rising*, 1970

Anne Logston, *Firewalk*, 1997

**3653**

### THOMAS K. MARTIN

## *A Two-Edged Sword*
(New York: Ace, 1994)

**Story type:** Fantasy (Alternate World; Magic Conflict)
**Major character(s):** Steve ''The Dreamer'' Wilkinson, Student—College, Volunteer (for sleep study); Erelvar, Nobleman (Lord of Quarin), Religious; Belevairn, Wizard, Mythical Creature (Dread Lord)
**Time period(s):** 1990s (1994); Indeterminate
**Locale(s):** New York, New York; Quarin, Fictional City

**Summary:** Pulled from our world into one of fantasy in the middle of a magic war, Steve Wilkinson must learn a great deal to survive. As the key to the conflict, he could unknowingly win the day for either side. First novel.

**Other books you might like:**
Glen Cook, *The Black Company*, 1984
Brian Daley, *The Doomfarers of Coramonde*, 1977
Barbara Hambly, *The Time of the Dark*, 1982
Guy Gavriel Kay, *The Summer Tree*, 1985
Patricia A. McKillip, *The Riddle-Master of Hed*, 1976

**3654**

### VALERIE MARTIN

## *Mary Reilly*
(New York: Doubleday, 1990)

**Story type:** Horror (Psychological Suspense)
**Major character(s):** Mary Reilly, Servant; Henry Jekyll, Doctor (Scientific experimenter)
**Time period(s):** 19th century (Victorian England)
**Locale(s):** London, England

**Summary:** A retelling of the Jekyll and Hyde story from the maid's point of view with the focus not on the disintegration of her ''dear Master'' Jekyll nor on the machinations of his ''assistant,'' Edward Hyde, but on the psychology of the spunky, resourceful, ultimately tragic Mary Reilly.

**Other books you might like:**
Robert Louis Stevenson, *The Strange Case of Dr. Jekyll and Mr. Hyde*, 1886

**3655**

### T. CHRIS MARTINDALE

## *Demon Dance*
(New York: Pocket, 1991)

**Story type:** Horror (Apocalyptic Horror)
**Major character(s):** Wilhemina ''Willie'' Ducane, Child; Tolman Shaddock, Gunfighter; Clancy ''Kolo'' Atwood, Indian (half-breed)
**Time period(s):** 1890s (1890)
**Locale(s):** Barlow, Nebraska

**Summary:** When the vengeful Indian medicine-woman Dee-Bo-Ha attempts to hasten the Ghost Dance, which will supposedly restore the true Indian nation in America, it is left to a band of settlers and Indians to try and avert the apocalypse the Ghost Dance ceremony portends.

**Other books you might like:**
Morgan Fields, *Shaman Woods*, 1990
Charles L. Grant, *The Nestling*, 1982
Kathryn Ptacek, *Ghost Dance*, 1990
Chet Williamson, *Dreamthorp*, 1989

**3656**

### T. CHRIS MARTINDALE

## *Nightblood*
(New York: Warner, 1990)

**Story type:** Horror (Vampire Story)
**Major character(s):** Chris Stiles, Veteran (Vietnam vet); Alex Stiles, Vampire (Chris' deceased brother)
**Time period(s):** 1990s
**Locale(s):** Isherwood, Indiana

**Summary:** Seeking ''payback'' for the death of his dead—but still active—brother, Chris settles in a small Indiana town where he encounters a master vampire and his crew.

**Other books you might like:**
Paul F. Olson, *Night Prophets*, 1989

**3657**

### T. CHRIS MARTINDALE

## *The Voice in the Basement*
(New York: Pocket, 1993)

**Story type:** Horror (Haunted House)
**Major character(s):** Cathy Ballard, Professor; Mitch Ballard, Unemployed (Cathy's husband); Larry Ackerman, Professor
**Time period(s):** 1990s (1993)
**Locale(s):** Harrodsburg, Indiana

**Summary:** Shortly after moving into their new home, Cathy and Mitch Ballard are plagued by apparitions and noises emanating from their basement. They discover that their home is a gateway to evil forces in the afterlife, and that the only way to prevent those forces from breaking through is to make contact with the apparition of a young boy who opened the gateway by escaping into this world.

**Other books you might like:**
Pat Franklin, *Dark Dreaming*, 1991
Richard Matheson, *Hell House*, 1971
Al Sarrantonio, *House Haunted*, 1991
T.M. Wright, *Little Boy Lost*, 1992
T.M. Wright, *The School*, 1990

**3658**

### T. CHRIS MARTINDALE

## *Where the Chill Waits*
(New York: Warner, 1990)

**Story type:** Horror (Ancient Evil Unleashed)
**Major character(s):** Elton Tucker, Businessman; Steve Wilhoit, Businessman; Andy Church, Foreman
**Time period(s):** 1990s (1991)
**Locale(s):** Atikokan, Ontario, Canada

**Summary:** Three employees of Tucker Pharmaceutical accept their boss's invitation to go deer hunting in a remote area near Thunder

Bay in the wilds of Canada. Accompanied by their Inidan guide, Barton Davejac, and his two elkhounds, the four men set off for the base camp at Chalako Lakes. During the trip, office politics and back-stabbing give way to cannibalism, terror, and murder when the men come under the sway of the windigo, an ancient supernatural demon, a gigantic cannibal spirit whose icy touch can transform humans into monsters—the fate that awaits the sole survivors of the trip.

**Other books you might like:**
Algernon Blackwood, *Best Ghost Stories of Algernon Blackwood*, 1973
Stephen King, *Pet Sematary*, 1983
Graham Masterton, *The Manitou*, 1975
Graham Masterton, *Revenge of the Manitou*, 1979
David Morrell, *Testament*, 1974

### 3659

**ADRIENNE MARTINE-BARNES**

## The Rainbow Sword

(New York: Avon, 1988)

**Story type:** Fantasy (Quest)
**Time period(s):** 1980s
**Locale(s):** Earth

**Summary:** A man who battles supernatural beings that enter this world searches for a sword to help him.

**Other books you might like:**
Gael Baudino, *Dragonsword*, 1988
Stephen R. Donaldson, *The Mirror of Her Dreams*, 1986
Eric Van Lustbader, *The Sunset Warrior*, 1989
Paul Edwin Zimmer, *Blood of the Colyn Muir*, 1988

### 3660

**ROBERT MASELLO**

## Private Demons

(New York: Jove, 1992)

**Story type:** Horror (Occult)
**Major character(s):** Lucien Calais, Businessman; Hallie Patton, Model; Sister Celeste, Religious (Catholic nun)
**Time period(s):** 1990s (1992)
**Locale(s):** New York, New York; Bangkok, Thailand

**Summary:** Lucien Calais becomes a millionaire after selling his soul to the serpent god Kaliya in order to recover the wealth seized from his family by the Khmer Rouge of Cambodia. When his empire begins to fall apart under the onslaught of occult forces, he must discover why it is that powers once in league with him have turned upon him.

**Other books you might like:**
Thomas M. Disch, *The Businessman: A Tale of Terror*, 1984

### 3661

**LISA MASON**

## Arachne

(New York: William Morrow, 1990)

**Story type:** Science Fiction (Cyberpunk; Robot Fiction)
**Major character(s):** Carly Nolan, Lawyer; Probe Spinner, Robot, Revolutionary; D. Wolfe, Lawyer

**Time period(s):** 21st century
**Locale(s):** San Francisco, California

**Summary:** When Carly's telelink fails during her first appearance in computer-generated court, Carly must find a remedy if her career is to advance. One option available from Wolfe is the illegal drug, cram, a telelink performance enhancer. Another option involves allowing a delicate psychic surgery aimed at releasing untapped potential. Carly must decide which option will best promote her career and what price she will pay. This book is the author's first novel.

**Other books you might like:**
David Brin, *Earth*, 1990
Pat Cadigan, *Synners*, 1991
Pat Cadigan, *Mindplayers*, 1987
Jeffrey A. Carver, *The Rapture Effect*, 1987
William Gibson, *Neuromancer*, 1984

### 3662

**LISA MASON**

## Cyberweb

(New York: AvoNova, 1995)

**Story type:** Science Fiction (Cyberpunk; Alternate Intelligence)
**Major character(s):** Carly Nolan, Computer Expert, Fugitive; Pr. Spinner, Artificial Intelligence, Computer Expert (perimeter prober); Ouija, Shaman
**Time period(s):** 21st century
**Locale(s):** San Francisco, California; Telespace, Cyberspace (computer virtual reality)

**Summary:** On the run from authorities and mainframe artificial intelligences, Carly Nolan finds life even more complicated when technophobic "aboriginals" kidnap her for Patina, a sophisticated robot covertly fronting for a mysterious mainframe AI, Cognatus. Carly reluctantly agrees to act as telelinker for Cognatus but remains mindful of the AI's lust for her metaprogramming, the unique archetype, Arachne. Sequel to *Arachne*.

**Other books you might like:**
Alexander Besher, *Rim: A Novel of Virtual Reality*, 1994
Bruce Bethke, *Headcrash*, 1995
Michael Flynn, *In the Country of the Blind*, 1990
Neal Stephenson, *Snow Crash*, 1992
John Varley, *Steel Beach*, 1992

### 3663

**LISA MASON**

## The Golden Nineties

(New York: Bantam Spectra, 1995)

**Story type:** Science Fiction (Time Travel)
**Major character(s):** Zhu Wong, Time Traveler, Revolutionary; Daniel J. Watkins, Gentleman, Alcoholic; Jessie Malone, Madam, Alcoholic
**Time period(s):** 1890s (1895-1896)
**Locale(s):** San Francisco, California

**Summary:** Facing a murder conviction, Zhu Wong agrees to t-port 600 years into the past, to San Francisco in the 1890s, where she must befriend a Chinese girl bearing an unusual piece of jewelry called the "Aurelia." Loosely related to *Summer of Love*.

**Other books you might like:**
L. Sprague de Camp, *Lest Darkness Fall*, 1941
Lisa Goldstein, *The Dream Years*, 1985

Robert A. Heinlein, *The Door into Summer*, 1957
Robert A. Heinlein, *Time Enough for Love*, 1973
Mercedes Lackey, *The Fire Rose*, 1995
Walter Jon Williams, *Days of Atonement*, 1991

## 3664
### LISA MASON

## Summer of Love

(New York: Bantam Spectra, 1994)

**Story type:** Science Fiction (Time Travel)
**Major character(s):** Susan ''Starbright'' Stein, Teenager, Runaway (flower child); Chiron Cat's Eye in Draco, Time Traveler
**Time period(s):** 1960s (June-September, 1967)
**Locale(s):** San Francisco, California

**Summary:** Chiron Cat's Eye in Draco travels back in time to Haight-Ashbury to find the flower child whose fate affects future generations.

**Other books you might like:**
Chester Anderson, *The Butterfly Kid*, 1967
Mick Farren, *The Texts of Festival*, 1975
George R.R. Martin, *The Armageddon Rag*, 1983
Robert Rankin, *Armageddon: The Musical*, 1990
Lewis Shiner, *Glimpses*, 1993

## 3665
### ROBERT MASON

## Solo

(New York: Putnam, 1992)

**Story type:** Science Fiction (Alternate Intelligence; Techno-Thriller)
**Major character(s):** Solo, Artificial Intelligence, Robot; Nimrod, Robot, Military Personnel (assassin); Daniel Sawyer, Military Personnel (colonel)
**Time period(s):** 21st century
**Locale(s):** Nicaragua; New York, New York

**Summary:** Having escaped its handlers and destruction, Solo finds friends and establishes contact with hundreds of satellites and computer networks, discovering Electron Dynamics cruelly programming a duplicate of itself. Solo resolves to contact Nimrod while Colonel Sawyer orders Nimrod to kill Solo. Sequel to *Weapon*.

**Other books you might like:**
Robert Cain, *Cybernarc*, 1991
Stephen Goldin, *Jade Darcy and the Affair of Honor*, 1988
   Mary Mason, co-author
Stephen Goldin, *Jade Darcy and the Zen Pirates*, 1990
   Mary Mason, co-author
Ed Naha, *Robocop*, 1987
Charles Sheffield, *The Nimrod Hunt*, 1986
Ben Sloane, *Ultimate Weapon*, 1991
Thomas T. Thomas, *ME: A Novel of Self Discovery*, 1991

## 3666
### ROBERT MASON

## Weapon

(New York: Putnam, 1989)

**Story type:** Science Fiction (Techno-Thriller)

**Major character(s):** Solo, Artificial Intelligence, Robot; Bill Stewart, Engineer (Computer engineer)
**Time period(s):** 21st century
**Locale(s):** Central America

**Summary:** Solo, a robot created to be the ultimate killing machine and destined to work for the American intelligence community, refuses to kill on command and then goes AWOL in the jungles of Central America. A picked CIA team is sent into the jungle to bring the robot back at any cost.

**Other books you might like:**
Isaac Asimov, *Robot Dreams*, 1986
Jerry Pournelle, *Prince of Mercenaries*, 1989
Lucius Shepard, *Life During Wartime*, 1987

## 3667
### ELIZABETH MASSIE

## Shadow Dreams

(Seattle, Washington: Silver Salamander Press, 1996)

**Story type:** Horror (Collection)

**Summary:** The 14 stories gathered in this second collection feature mostly nonsupernatural horrors that befall characters living quiet lives of desperation on the fringe of existence. ''Snowy Day'' and ''What Happened When Mosby Paulsen Had Her Painting Reproduced on the Cover of the Phone Book'' are concerned with psychic damage in emotionally abused children, and ''No Solicitors, Curious a Quarter'' with the extreme measures a woman takes to support her family by exploiting the public's fascination with the gruesome. In ''Dibs,'' a schoolgirl prank leads to a horrifying revenge decades later, and in ''Meat,'' an animal rights activist's principles are put to the ultimate test. Gary Braunbeck supplies an introduction.

**Other books you might like:**
Michael A. Arnzen, *Needles and Sins,* 1993
Poppy Z. Brite, *Swamp Foetus*, 1993
S. Darnbrook Colson, *People of the Night*, 1994
Brian Hodge, *The Convulsion Factory*, 1996
Brian Hopkins, *Something Haunts Us All*, 1995
Sue Storm, *Star Bones Weep the Blood of Angels*, 1995

## 3668
### ELIZABETH MASSIE

## Sineater

(New York: Carroll & Graf, 1994)

**Story type:** Horror (Wild Talents)
**Major character(s):** Joel Barker, Child; Burke, Child; Benton Hodge, Store Owner (hardware store)
**Time period(s):** 1990s (1992)
**Locale(s):** Beacon Cove, Virginia

**Summary:** A series of crimes in the backwoods of Virginia leads residents to suspect that their neighborhood sineater—a man who eats food over the bodies of the dead and thereby consumes their sins—has been driven mad by his work and is now spewing back all the evil he has absorbed from them.

**Other books you might like:**
John Byrne, *Whipping Boy*, 1992
Ramsey Campbell, *The Long Lost*, 1993
Bentley Little, *The Revelation*, 1990

## 3669

**ELIZABETH MASSIE**
**H.E. FASSL**, Illustrator

### Southern Discomfort: Selected Works of Elizabeth Massie

(Concord, California: Dark Regions Press, 1993)

**Story type:** Horror (Collection)

**Summary:** The nine stories in this book, all previously published, display their author's talent for deadpan grotesque. Several, such as "The Sick'un" and the zombie story, "Abed," explore the traditions of backwoods families for their bizarre potential, while others like "Hooked on Buzzer," "Smoothpicks," and "Whittler" are told with a chilling calmness from the point of view of psychotic characters. Yvonne Navarro has supplied an introduction.

**Other books you might like:**
Poppy Z. Brite, *Swamp Foetus*, 1993
Stephen Mark Rainey, *Fugue Devil and Other Weird Horrors*, 1993
Lucy Taylor, *Close to the Bone*, 1993
Lucy Taylor, *Unnatural Acts*, 1992

## 3670

**KATHLEEN M. MASSIE-FERCH**, Editor
**MARTIN H. GREENBERG**, Co-Editor
**RICHARD GILLIAM**, Co-Editor

### Ancient Enchantresses

(New York: DAW, 1995)

**Story type:** Fantasy (Anthology)

**Summary:** Contains a four-page introduction by Melanie Rawn plus individual introductions to 19 original stories utilizing traditional magical lore and symbology from world culture, goddesses, gods, and symbols of natural forces in the struggle to transform will into reality. Authors include Hugh B. Cave, Tanith Lee, Andre Norton, Diana L. Paxson, Melanie Rawn, Laura Resnick, Jennifer Roberson, Susan Shwartz, Lois Tilton, Harry Turtledove, Deborah Wheeler, and Mary Frances Zambreno.

**Other books you might like:**
Marion Zimmer Bradley, *The Sword and Sorceress Series*, 1984-1995
　editor
Richard Gilliam, *Grails: Quests of the Dawn*, 1994
　Martin H. Greenberg, Edward E. Kramer, co-editors
Jessica Amanda Salmonson, *Amazons!*, 1979
　editor
Susan Shwartz, *Sisters in Fantasy*, 1993
　Martin H. Greenberg, co-editor
A. Susan Williams, *The Penguin Book of Modern Fantasy by Women*, 1995
　Richard Glyn Jones, co-editor

## 3671

**GRAHAM MASTERTON**

### Burial

(New York: Tor, 1994)

**Story type:** Horror (Ancient Evil Unleashed; Supernatural Vengeance)

**Major character(s):** Harry Erskine, Psychic (medium); Karen van Hooven, Psychic; Papago Joe, Salesman
**Time period(s):** 1990s (1992)
**Locale(s):** New York, New York; Phoenix, Arizona

**Summary:** Twenty years after spiritualists Harry Erskine and Karen van Hooven (nee Tandy) helped exorcise the spirit of the ancient American Indian wizard Misquamacus in *The Manitou* (1974), the vengeful medicine man is back destroying entire cities and wreaking general havoc in his effort to obliterate the white man and return the world to his Native American brothers. Harry finds the only way to lay Misquamacus's spirit to rest this time is to travel to the Happy Hunting Grounds and bargain with the spirits who have endowed the Indian with his awesome powers. This book was originally published in England in 1992.

**Other books you might like:**
Adam Niswander, *The Charm*, 1993
Eugene E. Pfaff Jr., *Uwharrie*, 1993
　Michael Causey, co-author
Kathryn Ptacek, *Ghost Dance*, 1990
Patrick Whalen, *Deathwalker*, 1992

## 3672

**GRAHAM MASTERTON**

### The Burning

(New York: Tor, 1991)

**Story type:** Horror (Occult)
**Major character(s):** Lloyd Denman, Restaurateur; Otto Mander, Occultist; Waldo Slonimsky, Worker (restaurant)
**Time period(s):** 1990s
**Locale(s):** San Diego, California

**Summary:** Lloyd Denman's investigation into the self-immolation of his musician girlfriend Celia uncovers the underhanded dealings of ex-Nazi Otto Mander, an occultist who hopes to use the mystic secrets encoded in a lost piece of music by Richard Wagner and the self-sacrifice of numerous acolytes to placate the demon he serves and bring about a Fourth Reich in Southern California.

**Other books you might like:**
Ira Levin, *The Boys From Brazil*, 1976
Robert Weinberg, *The Armageddon Box*, 1990
Dennis Wheatley, *They Used Dark Forces*, 1964

## 3673

**GRAHAM MASTERTON**

### Flights of Fear

(New York: Severn House, 1996)

**Story type:** Horror (Collection)

**Summary:** These 14 stories, presented by the author as flights on a travel itinerary, are all collected from horror anthologies that appeared in the last half decade. "Absence of Beast," "The Gray Madonna" and "J.R.E. Ponsford" are subtle ghost stories with atmospheric chills. "The Bridal Suite," "Sex Object," and "The Jajouka Scarab" are some of the author's more typically lurid erotic horror tales. "Voodoo Child" features Jimi Hendrix, and "Will" William Shakespeare, both of whom are revealed to have struck satanic (or worse) bargains for their talents. This book was originally published in England in 1995.

**Other books you might like:**
Poppy Z. Brite, *Swamp Foetus*, 1993
Nancy A. Collins, *Nameless Sins*, 1995

John Farris, *Scare Tactics*, 1988
Christopher Fowler, *Flesh Wounds*, 1996
Brian Lumley, *The Second Wish and Other Exhalations*, 1995

## 3674

### GRAHAM MASTERTON

## *Fortnight of Fear*

(New York: Severn House, 1994)

**Story type:** Horror (Collection)

**Summary:** This first collection by an author known for his often graphic approach to horror fiction gathers together 14 stories originally published over the last decade. Among them are "Hurry Monster," about a man's lifelong fear of an imaginary monster; "Beijing Craps," about the peculiar stakes a jaded gambler decides to play for; "The Woman in the Wall," a variant on the haunted house theme; "Laird of Dunain," about the unusual lengths an artist goes to to get the flesh tones of her paints correct; "Making Belinda," a reworking of the classic horror story, "The Monkey's Paw"; "Heart of Stone" and "Pig's Dinner," both tales of supernatural vengeance; "The Sixth Man," which proposes the horrors that decimated Robert Scott's expedition to the Antarctic; and the infamous "Eric the Pie," the twisted tale of a man's eating habits deemed so objectionable when it first appeared that the magazine in which it was published was confiscated and ultimately scuttled.

**Other books you might like:**
Clive Barker, *Books of Blood Series*, 1984-1985
Christopher Fowler, *Sharper Knives*, 1992
Richard Laymon, *A Good, Secret Place*, 1993
Richard Laymon, *Out Are the Lights*, 1986

## 3675

### GRAHAM MASTERTON

## *The House That Jack Built*

(New York: Caroll & Graf, 1996)

**Story type:** Horror (Occult)
**Major character(s):** Craig Bellman, Lawyer; Effie Bellman, Spouse; Pepper Moriarity, Store Owner
**Time period(s):** 1990s (1996)
**Locale(s):** Cold Spring, New York

**Summary:** While recovering from a brutal mugging, high-powered lawyer Craig Bellman discovers the abandoned baronial mansion Valhalla, built on the banks of the Hudson River by evil textile magnate Jack Belias. Craig finds himself strongly attracted to it, and when its restoration has a deleterious effect on his personality, his wife Effie begins to suspect that Belias is trying to engineer a return through her husband.

**Other books you might like:**
Jonathan Aycliffe, *Naomi's Room*, 1991
Poppy Z. Brite, *Drawing Blood*, 1993
Stephen King, *The Shining*, 1977
H.P. Lovecraft, *The Case of Charles Dexter Ward*, 1971
Tamara Thorne, *Haunted*, 1995

## 3676

### GRAHAM MASTERTON

## *Master of Lies*

(New York: Tor, 1992)

**Story type:** Horror (Occult)
**Major character(s):** Larry Foggia, Detective—Police; Arne Knudsen, Police Officer; Mr. Mandrax, Occultist
**Time period(s):** 1990s
**Locale(s):** San Francisco, California

**Summary:** Under the moniker "The Fog City Satan," a serial killer prowls the streets of San Francisco, sadistically torturing and murdering victims as part of his arcane occult rituals. When detective Larry Foggia is assigned to the case, he uncovers a plot to resurrect Belial, first of the fallen angels, and a secret underground of occultists that include his friends and perhaps even members of his family.

**Other books you might like:**
Cleve Cartmill, *Prelude to Armageddon*, 1942
   magzaine publication only
Al Sarrantonio, *October*, 1990

## 3677

### GRAHAM MASTERTON

## *Mirror*

(New York: Tor, 1989)

**Story type:** Horror (Alternate World)
**Major character(s):** Martin Williams, Writer (Screenwriter); Boofuls, Actor (Murdered child filmstar), Spirit
**Time period(s):** 1980s
**Locale(s):** Los Angeles, California

**Summary:** Martin Williams learns that the spirit of the ex-owner of a recently purchased mirror—a murdered child actor—is trapped within it. This leads to the revelation that the mirror is, in fact, a doorway to another world and that Satan himself plans to use it to bring endless night to the earth.

**Other books you might like:**
Clive Barker, *Weaveworld*, 1987
Simon Rees, *The Devil's Looking-Glass*, 1985

## 3678

### GRAHAM MASTERTON

## *Rook*

(New York: Severn House, 1997)

**Story type:** Horror (Wild Talents; Black Magic)
**Major character(s):** Jim Rook, Teacher; T.J. Jones, Teenager; Umber Jones, Sorcerer
**Time period(s):** 1990s (1997)
**Locale(s):** Westwood, California

**Summary:** Schoolteacher Jim Rook finds his psychic powers tested when a troubled black student falls under the influence of his evil uncle Umber, a criminal who uses voodoo to extort riches from his victims and who doesn't hesitate to destroy people like Jim when they attempt to stop him. This novel was first published in England in 1996. First in a series.

**Other books you might like:**
Don Davis, *The Gris-Gris Man*, 1996

Stephen King, *The Dead Zone*, 1979
Dean R. Koontz, *Cold Fire*, 1991

## 3679

### GRAHAM MASTERTON

## *The Terror*

(New York: Severn House, 1998)

**Story type:** Horror (Occult)
**Series:** Rook
**Major character(s):** Jim Rook, Teacher; Rafael Diaz, Student
**Time period(s):** 1990s (1998)
**Locale(s):** West Grove, California

**Summary:** In his latest adventure, psychically sensitive college English teacher Jim Rook must find a way to reverse the process by which student Rafael Diaz, in the interest of helping his fellow students overcome their fears, accidentally liberated occult energies that have empowered an ancient demon.

**Other books you might like:**
Kevin J. Anderson, *Ruins*, 1996
Ray Garton, *Crucifax Autumn*, 1988
Charles L. Grant, *The Nestling*, 1982
K.W. Jeter, *The Night Man*, 1990
J. Michael Straczynski, *Other Syde*, 1990

## 3680

### GRAHAM MASTERTON

## *Tooth and Claw*

(New York: Severn House, 1997)

**Story type:** Horror (Occult)
**Major character(s):** Jim Rook, Teacher; Catherine White Bird, Teenager; Dog Brother, Supernatural Being
**Time period(s):** 1990s (1997)
**Locale(s):** West Grove, California; Window Rock, Arizona

**Summary:** In his second adventure, psychically endowed school teacher Jim Rook defends a Native American student implicated in several gruesome murders. His investigations bring him into confrontation with an avatar of Coyote, the trickster of Navajo legend, to whom the student was bethrothed by his family.

**Other books you might like:**
Chris Curry, *Trickster*, 1994
 Lisa Dean, Co-author
Muriel Gray, *The Trickster*, 1994
Colin Kersey, *Soul Catcher*, 1995
G. Wayne Miller, *Thunder Rise*, 1988
Adam Niswander, *The Charm*, 1993
Kathryn Ptacek, *Ghost Dance*, 1990

## 3681

### GRAHAM MASTERTON

## *Walkers*

(New York: Tor, 1989)

**Story type:** Horror (Haunted House)
**Major character(s):** Jack Reed, Businessman (Would-be commercial developer); Quintus Miller, Genius (lunatic), Occultist
**Time period(s):** 1980s
**Locale(s):** Wisconsin

**Summary:** Jack Reed buys The Oaks, a former insane asylum, to be developed into a country club, not knowing that the spirits of its former criminally insane inmates, led by a mad occultist, are trapped within its walls. When his young son is dragged into the walls, Reed must seek out an old priest and learn the dark secrets that will either enable him to rescue his son or release the trapped madmen on the world.

**Other books you might like:**
John Farris, *Wildwood*, 1987

## 3682

### RICHARD MATHESON

## *7 Steps to Midnight*

(New York: Tor, 1993)

**Story type:** Horror (Mystery)
**Major character(s):** Chris Barton, Scientist (mathematician); Albert Veering, Psychologist; Alexsandra Caludius, Spy
**Time period(s):** 1990s (1993)
**Locale(s):** London, England; Venice, Italy

**Summary:** In the middle of his work on a project involving defense lasers, Chris Barton finds that another man has assumed his identity, that he can get no one to believe he is really Chris Barton, that he is being chased across the globe by espionage agents who want information from him, and that the fabric of reality itself is beginning to fray.

**Other books you might like:**
Umberto Eco, *Foucault's Pendulum*, 1990
Theodore Roszak, *Flicker*, 1991
Peter Straub, *Koko*, 1988

## 3683

### RICHARD MATHESON

## *Collected Stories*

(Los Angeles: Dream/Press, 1989)

**Story type:** Horror (Collection)

**Summary:** Eighty-six stories written between 1950 and 1970. Mixing science fiction and horror, Matheson describes the "paranoid landscape" of the modern world with deft characterization, brilliant plot twists, and a wicked, ironical sense of humor.

**Other books you might like:**
Charles Beaumont, *Selected Stories*, 1988
Robert Bloch, *The Selected Stories of Robert Bloch*, 1987
Ray Bradbury, *The Stories of Ray Bradbury*, 1980
Fritz Leiber, *The Best of Fritz Leiber*, 1974
William F. Nolan, *Things Beyond Midnight*, 1984

## 3684

### RICHARD MATHESON

## *Earthbound*

(New York: Tor, 1994)

**Story type:** Horror (Ghost Story)
**Major character(s):** David Cooper, Writer; Ellen Cooper, Spouse; Grace Brentwood, Aged Person
**Time period(s):** 1980s (1981)
**Locale(s):** Long Island, New York (Logan Beach)

**Summary:** David and Ellen Cooper return to Logan Beach, the site of their honeymoon, to prop up their sagging marriage. In their vacation home David becomes obsessed with Marianna, the spirit of a dead woman who has driven other men insane and who plays upon the tensions in David and Ellen's marriage in order to win David over and satisfy the sexual lust that keeps her earthbound. This book was originally published in 1982 in a severely edited form under the pseudonym Logan Swanson.

**Other books you might like:**
Shirley Jackson, *The Haunting of Hill House*, 1961
Al Sarrantonio, *House Haunted*, 1989
Bernard Taylor, *Sweetheart, Sweetheart*, 1977
Chet Williamson, *Soulstorm*, 1986

---

**3685**

**RICHARD MATHESON**

## Hell House

(Springfield, Pennsylvania: Gauntlet Press, 1996)

**Story type:** Horror (Haunted House; Occult)
**Major character(s):** Lionel Barrett, Paranormal Investigator; Florence Tanner, Psychic (medium); Benjamin Franklin Fischer, Psychic
**Time period(s):** 1970s (1970)
**Locale(s):** Matawaskie Valley, Maine

**Summary:** A group of psychic investigators take up residence in the former home of Emeric Belasco, dubbed "Hell House" because of the vile satanic practices that Belasco indulged in there. The last expedition to the home ended in disaster and death 30 years before, but the current group hopes to exorcise the home through modern scientific means. This novel was first published in 1971. The 25th anniversary edition was produced as a signed limited edition hardcover with an introduction by the author.

**Other books you might like:**
Tom Elliott, *The Dwelling*, 1988
Shirley Jackson, *The Haunting of Hill House*, 1959
Al Sarrantonio, *House Haunted*, 1991
Chet Williamson, *Soulstorm*, 1986

---

**3686**

**RICHARD MATHESON**

## I Am Legend

(New York: Tor, 1995)

**Story type:** Horror (Collection)

**Summary:** A novel and 10 short stories, one of them previously uncollected, showcase the talents of a major force in fantasy and horror whose fiction in the 1950s and 1960s captured the undercurrent of paranoia in America. *I Am Legend* is a landmark vampire novel, in which the last mortal to survive a plague that has turned everyone else in the world into vampires, fights a daily battle for survival and begins to resemble, in his rapaciousness, the very creatures he fights. The book also includes another vampire tale, "Dress of White Silk"; a story of zombies in a post-nuclear future, "Dance of the Dead"; and the horror satire, "The Funeral." "From Shadowed Places" and "Prey" are standard occult menace stories, and "Mad House" and "Person to Person" tales that blur the boundary between psychological and supernatural horror.

**Other books you might like:**
Charles Beaumont, *Selected Stories*, 1989
Ray Bradbury, *The Stories of Ray Bradbury*, 1980
William F. Nolan, *Night Shapes: Excursions into Terror*, 1995

---

**3687**

**RICHARD MATHESON**

## The Incredible Shrinking Man

(New York: Tor, 1995)

**Story type:** Horror (Collection)

**Summary:** The bulk of this book is taken up with the author's classic 1956 novel, *The Shrinking Man*, about a man exposed to a toxic cloud who finds himself shrinking on a daily basis down to infinitessimal size. The book is complemented by nine other stories featuring Matheson's trademark sense of paranoia. In "Nightmare at 20,000 Feet," a man riding an airplane during a storm discovers that he alone can see a gremlin perched on the wing sabotaging the engines. In "Duel," a lone driver on a desert highway is menaced by a tractor trailer. "The Distributor," "The Holiday Man," and "By Appointment Only" all suggest infernal machinations behind the major and minor annoyances of life. In the book's one previously uncollected story, "Shoofly," a man finds a metaphor for the futility of his life in his inability to kill a fly that is bothering him.

**Other books you might like:**
Charles Beaumont, *Selected Stories*, 1988
Ray Bradbury, *The Stories of Ray Bradbury*, 1980
Dennis Etchison, *The Dark Country*, 1982
William F. Nolan, *Night Shapes: Excursions into Terror*, 1995

---

**3688**

**RICHARD MATHESON**

## Now You See It...

(New York: Tor, 1995)

**Story type:** Horror (Mystery)
**Major character(s):** Emil Delacorte, Magician; Maximillian Delacorte, Magician; Harry Kendal, Agent (theatrical)
**Time period(s):** 1980s (1980)
**Locale(s):** Boston, Massachusetts

**Summary:** This tale of illusion is narrated by Emil Delacorte, a stage magician who has been rendered a "vegetable" by a stroke. Emil's son Maximillian, also a magician, hosts a get-together at his home for his father and a group of others that includes an agent scheming with his unfaithful wife to take over Emil's magic act. Unbeknownst to them, the house is rigged for sleight-of-hand and magic tricks, making the events that occur there impossible to accept at face value.

**Other books you might like:**
Ray Bradbury, *A Graveyard for Lunatics*, 1990
Patrick McGrath, *The Grotesque*, 1989
Daniel Stashower, *The Adventure of the Ectoplasmic Man*, 1985
Thomas Tryon, *Night Magic*, 1995

---

**3689**

**RICHARD MATHESON**, Editor
**RICIA MAINHARDT**, Co-Editor

## Robert Bloch: Appreciations of the Master

(New York: Tor, 1995)

**Story type:** Horror (Collection)

**Summary:** This book collects 20 stories and 31 tributes to Robert Bloch, author of the novel *Psycho* and a leading talent in the horror field for over 60 years, who died in 1994. The stories selected span the full range of Bloch's career, including his homages to mentor

H.P. Lovecraft (''Notebook Found in a Deserted House''), his combinations of human and horror fiction (''The Cloak,'' ''The Pied Piper Fights the Gestapo''), his crossovers from horror to crime (''Final Performance,'' ''The Animal Fair''), his Hugo Award-winning tale of a deal with the devil (''The Hell-Bound Train''), and his studies of psychopathology (''Enoch,'' ''I Do Not Love Thee Doctor Fell,'' ''Your Truly Jack the Ripper''). Authors who supply tributes include Harlan Ellison, William F. Nolan, Gahan Wilson, Frederik Pohl, William Peter Blatty, Ramsey Campbell, Hugh B. Cave, Brian Lumley, and actor Christopher Lee.

**Other books you might like:**
Charles Beaumont, *Selected Stories*, 1988
Richard Matheson, *Collected Stories*, 1989
William F. Nolan, *The Bradbury Chronicles: Stories in Honor of Ray Bradbury*, 1992
　　Martin H. Greenberg, co-editor

---

**3690**

**RICHARD MATHESON**

## Somewhere in Time/What Dreams May Come

(Los Angeles: Dream Press, 1992)

**Story type:** Horror (Collection)

**Summary:** Two love stories, each with a supernatural component. In *Somewhere in Time*, originally published in 1975 as *Bid Time Return* and winner of the World Fantasy Award for best novel that year, dying screenwriter Robert Collier's obsessive interest in a nineteenth-century stage actress allows him to step back in time 75 years to meet her. *What Dreams May Come*, originally published in 1978, tells of Chris Neilson's gradual resignation to existence in the afterlife, in a world of souls in limbo known as Summerland. Contains corrected text and a new introduction by the author.

**Other books you might like:**
Robert Bloch, *Screams*, 1989
Jack Finney, *Three by Finney*, 1978
Jack Finney, *Time and Again*, 1970
Fritz Leiber, *Conjure Wife/Our Lady of Darkness*, 1991

---

**3691**

**RICHARD CHRISTIAN MATHESON**

## Created By

(New York: Bantam, 1993)

**Story type:** Horror (Doppelganger)
**Major character(s):** Alan White, Producer, Writer (television); A.E. Barek, Mercenary (television character); Jake Corea, Actor
**Time period(s):** 1990s (1993)
**Locale(s):** Hollywood, California

**Summary:** Alan White's ultra-violent, ultra-explicit television program ''The Mercenary'' makes a stunning impact on its viewing audience, who faithfully watch it every week in record numbers. When crimes that bear the signature of its lead character, A.E. Barek, begin occurring in the real world, Alan must face up to the fact that the devotion of the show's viewers has helped turn Barek, a fictional outlet for Alan's suppressed rage, into a terrifying reality.

**Other books you might like:**
Giles Blunt, *Cold Eye*, 1989
Michael Cadnum, *Ghostwright*, 1992
Stephen King, *The Dark Half*, 1989
John R. Maxim, *Abel/Baker/Charley*, 1983

---

**3692**

**SUSAN R. MATTHEWS**

## An Exchange of Hostages

(New York: AvoNova, 1997)

**Story type:** Science Fiction (Medical; Political)
**Major character(s):** Andrej Koscuisko, Doctor, Student (inquisitor/torturer); Joslire Curran, Slave (bond-involuntary), Martial Arts Expert (student); Mergau Noycannir, Civil Servant (clerk of court), Student (inquisitor/torturer)
**Time period(s):** Indeterminate Future
**Locale(s):** Fleet Orientation Station Med., Space Station; Interstellar Empire/Federation

**Summary:** Bowing to family pressure, talented neurosurgeon Andrej Koscuisko submits to training in prolonging and intensifying pain, preparing for a career as inquisitor, one of the torturers necessary for maintaining control in an empire based on slavery. However, fellow student Mergau Noycannir intends to break the Fleet's monopoly on inquisitors by graduating as inquisitor without medical credentials. First novel.

**Other books you might like:**
Orson Scott Card, *Ender's Game*, 1985
Samuel R. Delany, *They Fly at Ciron*, 1993
Stephen R. Donaldson, *The Gap into Conflict: The Real Story*, 1991
Elizabeth A. Lynn, *The Sardonyx Net*, 1981
Gene Wolfe, *The Shadow of the Torturer*, 1980

---

**3693**

**SUSAN R. MATTHEWS**

## Prisoner of Conscience

(New York: Avon Eos, 1998)

**Story type:** Science Fiction (Adventure)
**Series:** Andrej Koscuisko
**Major character(s):** Andrej Koscuisko, Doctor; Toska Simmanye, Prisoner
**Time period(s):** Indeterminate Future
**Locale(s):** Port Rudistal, Planet—Imaginary

**Summary:** The new doctor at the prison on Port Rudistal has an ambiguous position. In addition to healing the sick and injured, he is required to employ torture whenever necessary to ensure that no one upsets the status quo in the installation. He learns that most of the prisoners are there for political reasons, and secretly begins to sympathize with their cause.

**Other books you might like:**
Piers Anthony, *Chthon*, 1967
Martin Caidin, *Prison Ship*, 1989
William C. Dietz, *Prison Planet*, 1989
Barry B. Longyear, *Infinity Hold*, 1989
George Zebrowski, *Brute Orbits*, 1998

---

**3694**

**GUY DE MAUPASSANT**

## The Dark Side: Tales of Terror and the Supernatural

(New York: Carroll & Graf, 1990)

**Story type:** Horror (Collection)

**Summary:** Thirty-one stories selected, translated, and introduced by Arnold Kellet, with a foreward by Ramsey Campbell. Contains all of the major dark fantasies by the French master of the short story. The most important item is ''The Horla,'' one of the major precursors of modern horror fiction. The powerfully ambiguous story is told by a narrator who is either descending into madness or is the victim of a psychic vampire, the forerunner of a race destined to replace man. Other important stories include ''On the River'' and ''Little Louise Roque,'' two exercises in the psychopathology of fear, dread, and guilt.

**Other books you might like:**
Sir Arthur Conan Doyle, *The Best Horror Stories of Arthur Conan Doyle*, 1989

`3695`

**J.G. MAXON**

## Lethal Delivery

(New York: Pocket, 1991)

**Story type:** Horror (Psychological Suspense)
**Major character(s):** Rod Hoover, Salesman; Tanya Roode, Office Worker; Sam Roode, Child
**Time period(s):** 1990s
**Locale(s):** New York, New York

**Summary:** It's bad enough that hulk Rod Hoover has lethally doctored the mail-order products sold by his company, Serious Options, to get back at the boss who stole his ideas. In his terminal steroid-induced fugue, he's also taken to terrorizing fellow employee Tanya Roode and her son Sam, in the belief that Tanya would have been his girlfriend had he gotten the respect around the office he deserved.

**Other books you might like:**
John Farris, *The Axman Cometh*, 1989
Stephen Gallagher, *Down River*, 1989
Robert R. McCammon, *Mine*, 1990

`3696`

**JULIAN MAY**

## Blood Trillium

(New York: Bantam Spectra, 1992)

**Story type:** Fantasy (Magic Conflict; Quest)
**Major character(s):** Haramis, Sorceress (archmage), Scholar, Royalty (princess); Tolivar, Royalty (prince), Child; Orogastus/Portolanus, Sorcerer
**Time period(s):** Indeterminate
**Locale(s):** Zinora, Fictional Country; Ruwenda, Fictional Country

**Summary:** After 12 years the sorcerer Orogastus reappears and manages to get hold of Kadiya's third of the Sceptre, but when he gains Anigel's third by holding her husband and children hostage, a worried Haramis manages to contact the Archmage of the Sea who helps sow discord among Orogastus' followers and heal the breach between the three sisters. However, the Balance will not be restored for long as Prince Tolivar steals Orogastus' star box and kills to keep it, even from his parents. Sequel to *Black Trillium*.

**Other books you might like:**
Piers Anthony, *Wielding a Red Sword*, 1986
Leigh Brackett, *People of the Talisman*, 1964
Richard Cowper, *A Dream of Kinship*, 1982
Suzette Haden Elgin, *The Grand Jubilee*, 1981
Katherine Kurtz, *The Quest for Saint Camber*, 1986
Andre Norton, *Sorceress of the Witch World*, 1968

Jack Vance, *Emphyrio*, 1969
Marion Zimmer Bradley, *Black Trillium*, 1990
Julian May, Andre Norton, co-authors

`3697`

**JULIAN MAY**

## Diamond Mask: A Novel

(New York: Knopf, 1994)

**Story type:** Science Fiction (Family Saga; Psychic Powers)
**Series:** Galactic Milieu
**Major character(s):** Rogatien Remillard, Psychic, Businessman (bookseller); Jon Remillard, Psychic, Mutant; Dorothea Macdonald, Psychic, Political Figure
**Time period(s):** 22nd century
**Locale(s):** Hanover, New Hampshire; Caledonia, Planet—Imaginary

**Summary:** The Remillard family struggles with the concept of Unity, the malicious plots of Fury and their own internal struggles, setting the stage for the final encounter with Fury and the origins of the Metapsychic Rebellion. Because of the odd chronology of the series, this book should be read after *Intervention:. . .*, but either before or after The Saga of Pliocene Exile series (1981-1984).

**Other books you might like:**
Marion Zimmer Bradley, *The Forbidden Tower*, 1977
Suzette Haden Elgin, *The Grand Jubilee*, 1981
Patricia Kennealy-Morrison, *The Copper Crown*, 1985
Katherine Kurtz, *Deryni Rising*, 1970
Theodore Sturgeon, *More than Human*, 1953

`3698`

**JULIAN MAY**

## Jack the Bodiless

(New York: Knopf, 1992)

**Story type:** Science Fiction (Family Saga; Psychic Powers)
**Series:** Galactic Milieu
**Major character(s):** Rogatien Remillard, Psychic; Jack Rogillard, Psychic; The Fury, Psychic
**Time period(s):** 2050s
**Locale(s):** Denali, Planet—Imaginary

**Summary:** The Rogillard family, acknowledged mental giants, have a gene for extended life. Uncle Rogi, childless himself, intervenes to protect the young minds of the family from being overwhelmed before they can develop independence and skills of their own. Recently, the Human Polity was admitted to the Galactic Milieu, allowing the Rogillard family to extend their influence beyond Earth.

**Other books you might like:**
Gordon R. Dickson, *Dorsai!*, 1976
David R. Palmer, *Threshold*, 1985
David Alexander Smith, *Marathon*, 1982
Jack Vance, *The Anome*, 1973
A.E. Van Vogt, *The World of Null-A*, 1948
Roger Zelazny, *Isle of the Dead*, 1969

### 3699

**JULIAN MAY**

## *Magnificat*

(New York: Knopf, 1996)

**Story type:** Science Fiction (Family Saga; Psychic Powers)
**Series:** Galactic Milieu
**Major character(s):** Mark Remillard, Psychic, Revolutionary; Jack the Bodiless, Psychic, Relative (brother); Dorothea "Diamond Mask", Psychic
**Time period(s):** 22nd century
**Locale(s):** Galactic Milieu, Interstellar Empire/Federation; Kauai, Hawaii

**Summary:** In opposition to the Unity attempted by the Metapsychics of the Milieu, Mark Remillard works to establish the superiority of the human species and control of the Milieu. Only Jack and Diamond are knowledgeable enough to prevent him. Concludes the trilogy.

**Other books you might like:**
F.M. Busby, *Rissa Kerguelen*, 1977
Suzette Haden Elgin, *The Grand Jubilee*, 1981
Katherine Kurtz, *Deryni Rising*, 1970
Anne McCaffrey, *The Rowan*, 1990
David Wingrove, *Beneath the Tree of Heaven*, 1995

### 3700

**JULIAN MAY**

## *Sky Trillium*

(New York: Ballantine Del Rey, 1997)

**Story type:** Fantasy (Magic Conflict)
**Series:** Trillium
**Major character(s):** Tolivar, Nobleman (prince), Teenager; Orogastus, Sorcerer, Criminal; Haramis, Sorceress, Royalty (princess)
**Time period(s):** Indeterminate Future
**Locale(s):** Sobrania, Fictional Country; Dark Man's Moon, Moon—Imaginary

**Summary:** With the world badly out of balance, Orogastus devises a plan to gain the three-fold scepter of power from Anigel, Kadiya and Haramis, using prince Tolivar and the greedy, would-be Empress Naelore. But saving the world depends upon joint wielding of Orogastus' Star and the three-fold scepter with no coercion, or the world will perish under fire and ice. Sequel to *Black Trillium*.

**Other books you might like:**
Poul Anderson, *A Midsummer Tempest*, 1974
Marion Zimmer Bradley, *Black Trillium*, 1990
  Julian May, Andre Norton, co-authors
Marion Zimmer Bradley, *Lady of the Trillium*, 1995
Michael Lahey, *Quest for Apollo*, 1989
Andre Norton, *Golden Trillium*, 1993
Kathleen Sky, *Witchdame*, 1985
Jack Vance, *The Green Pearl*, 1985
Lawrence Watt-Evans, *Denner's Wreck*, 1988

### 3701

**BOB MAYER**

## *Operation Synbat*

(San Francisco: Presidio, 1994)

**Story type:** Horror (Science Fiction)

**Major character(s):** David Riley, Military Personnel; Robin Merrit, Scientist; David Ward, Scientist
**Time period(s):** 1990s (1994)
**Locale(s):** Fort Campbell, Kentucky

**Summary:** David Riley's special paramilitary crew is called in to clean up the escape of experimental animals accidentally sprung from a research facility, unaware that the animals are "synbats"—synthetic battle forms that are the result of genetic manipulation of baboon and human biology, bred for their superior strength and complete lack of compassion toward human prey.

**Other books you might like:**
Richard Adams, *The Plague Dogs*, 1976
Ken Eulo, *Claw*, 1994
  Joe Mauck, co-author
T.J. Kirby, *Dangerous Nature*, 1993
T.J. Kirby, *Deadly Breed*, 1992
Dean R. Koontz, *Watchers*, 1987
T.W. Stetson, *Night Beasts*, 1993

### 3702

**ARDATH MAYHAR**
**DON SCHANK**, Illustrator

## *Mean Little Old Lady at Work*

(Concord, California: Dark Regions Press, 1994)

**Story type:** Horror (Collection)

**Summary:** This chapbook, the first collection of the author's short stories, includes a dozen tales that reflect her ability to merge fantasy and horror. Included are "Trogolodytes," about a prisoner who witnesses a race of subterranean monsters emerge to kill his captors; "Echo of Thunder," about a psychic investigator who unravels the mystery of a ghostly event replayed regularly in the halls of a mansion; "Through the Padded Door," the narrative of a madman; "A Sculpted Smile," in which a king fills his halls with sculptures made from living people; and "The Children Beneath the Stones," about an ancient practice of burying live human beings beneath paving stones of a Roman road to ensure its safety. The book has an introduction by Joe Lansdale.

**Other books you might like:**
Charles de Lint, *Dreams Underfoot*, 1993
Garry Kilworth, *Hogfoot Right and Bird-Hands*, 1993
Brian Lumley, *The House of Cthulhu and Other Tales of the Primal Land*, 1984
Jessica Amanda Salmonson, *John Collier and Fredric Brown Went Quarrelling through My Head*, 1989

### 3703

**ARDATH MAYHAR**
**RON FORTIER**, Co-Author

## *Monkey Station*

(Lake Geneva, Wisconsin: TSR, 1989)

**Story type:** Science Fiction (Disaster)
**Major character(s):** Eric Littlefield, Teenager; Ko, Animal (Macaque Monkey)
**Time period(s):** Indeterminate Future
**Locale(s):** Brazil (The Rainforest)

**Summary:** Scientists working in the Brazilian jungle on experiments with genetically-altered, sentient macaque monkeys must fight for survival after a plague destroys most of the human race.

**Other books you might like:**
Roger MacBride Allen, *Orphan of Creation*, 1988
David Brin, *The Uplift War*, 1987
Michael Crichton, *The Andromeda Strain*, 1969
Peter Dickinson, *Eva*, 1988

**3704**

ARDATH MAYHAR

## People of the Mesa
(New York: Diamond, 1992)

**Story type:** Fantasy (Historical)
**Major character(s):** Uhatatse, Indian (Anasazi)
**Time period(s):** Indeterminate Past
**Locale(s):** Southwest

**Summary:** When the hostile Tsununni Indians threaten the peaceful Anasazi Indians who live in harmony with nature, only Uhatatse recognizes the danger. He must convince his people to change their way of life if they are to survive.

**Other books you might like:**
Alan Dean Foster, *Cyber Way*, 1990
W. Michael Gear, *People of the Earth*, 1992
    Kathleen O'Neal Gear, co-author
Sue Harrison, *Mother Earth, Father Sky*, 1990
Dean Ing, *Anasazi*, 1980
J. Alison James, *Sing for a Gentle Rain*, 1990
Catherine Wells, *The Earth Is All That Lasts*, 1991
Roger Zelazny, *Bridge of Ashes*, 1976

**3705**

MICHAEL MAYHEW, Editor
MONA CARON, Co-Editor

## Harvest Tales and Midnight Revels: Stories for the Waning of the Year
(San Francisco: Bald Mountain Books, 1998)

**Story type:** Horror (Anthology)

**Summary:** Here are 19 spooky stories and poems for adults and children written with the idea of being read aloud. Many have a comic edge, including Christian Ulm's "My Dinner with Buck," in which a lovelorn mortician sees his heart's desire stolen away by a corpse; Steven V. Taylor's "Organ Donors in Nightmare Land," in which entities that control nightmares have to figure out what really scares contemporary kids; and Michael Mayhew's "Graveyard," about a dysfunctional family with supernatural problems.

**Other books you might like:**
Martin H. Greenberg, *Great Writers and Kids Write Spooky Stories*, 1995
    Jill Morgan, Robert Weinberg, co-editors
Alan Ryan, *Halloween Horrors*, 1986
    editor
Jessica Amanda Salmonson, *The Mysterious Doom and Other Ghostly Tales of the Pacific Northwest*, 1992
John Manchip White, *Whistling Past the Churchyard*, 1991

**3706**

BRUCE MCALLISTER

## Dream Baby
(New York: Tor, 1989)

**Story type:** Science Fiction (Psychic Powers)
**Major character(s):** Mary Damico, Nurse, Military Personnel (Army lieutenant)
**Time period(s):** 1960s
**Locale(s):** Vietnam; United States

**Summary:** Mary Damico, an army nurse assigned to a field hospital in Vietnam, finds herself in a close approximation of hell. Her days are full of bleeding, dismembered bodies which she can't escape even in her dreams. Then something strange begins to happen. Damico realizes that the gaping wounds and horrid injuries she's been dreaming of are only showing up during her waking hours after she dreams about them. She makes the mistake of telling a CIA agent about her precognitive power and soon finds herself part of a dangerous and deadly secret project, an attempt to harness psychic powers and use them as weapons.

**Other books you might like:**
Jeanne Van Buren Dann, *In the Field of Fire*, 1987
    Jack Dann, co-author
Elizabeth Ann Scarborough, *The Healer's War*, 1989
Lucius Shepard, *The Jaguar Hunter*, 1987
Lucius Shepard, *Life During Wartime*, 1987
Lewis Shiner, *Deserted Cities of the Heart*, 1988

**3707**

P.K. MCALLISTER (Pseudonym of Paula E. Downing)

## Maia's Veil
(New York: Roc, 1995)

**Story type:** Science Fiction (Adventure; Political)
**Series:** Cloudships of Orion
**Major character(s):** Pov Janusz, Spaceship Captain, Gypsy; Avi Selenko, Spacewoman; Ekaterina "Kate" Marya Janusz, Spacewoman, Gypsy
**Time period(s):** Indeterminate Future
**Locale(s):** *Siduri's Net*, Spaceship; Outer Space

**Summary:** After discovering the treachery of their mother ship, *Siduri's Dance*, the crew of *Siduri's Net* votes to follow an earlier expedition to the Pleiades. Forced to run, the *Net* discovers a new fuel, perhaps allowing very long distance journeys. Still plagued by social and cultural clashes between the mixed nationalities on the Cloudships, *Net* decides to ally with Tripower, a space station in the Pleiades, leading toward an expedition to the Orion Nebula, if cultural diversity doesn't split *Net*'s crew. Sequel to *Siduri's Net*.

**Other books you might like:**
Paula E. Downing, *Fallway*, 1993
Paula E. Downing, *Flare Star*, 1992
Paula E. Downing, *A Whisper of Time*, 1994
Alis A. Rasmussen, *A Passage of Stars*, 1990
Robert Charles Wilson, *Gypsies*, 1989

### 3708

**P.K. MCALLISTER** (Pseudonym of Paula King)

## Orion's Dagger

(New York: Roc, 1996)

**Story type:** Science Fiction (Family Saga; Political)
**Series:** Cloudships of Orion
**Major character(s):** Pov Janusz, Spaceship Captain, Gypsy (Rom); Sigrid Thorsen, Businesswoman (station manager); Yuri Putakin, Computer Expert, Spaceman
**Time period(s):** Indeterminate Future
**Locale(s):** Tri Power Station, Space Station; *Siduri's Isle*, Spaceship; Orion Nebula, Outer Space

**Summary:** Despite a lack of cooperation, Pov leads the cloudships to the Orion Nebula, where conditions prove different than expected. Treachery from one of his partners may prevent the safe return of any of the ships.

**Other books you might like:**
F.M. Busby, *The Demu Trilogy*, 1980
Paula E. Downing, *Fallway*, 1993
Paula E. Downing, *Flare Star*, 1992
Paula E. Downing, *Rinn's Star*, 1990
Paula E. Downing, *A Whisper of Time*, 1994

### 3709

**P.K. MCALLISTER** (Pseudonym of Paula E. Downing)

## Siduri's Net

(New York: Roc, 1994)

**Story type:** Science Fiction (Political)
**Series:** Cloudships of Orion
**Major character(s):** Pov Janusz, Spaceship Captain (sailship sailmaster), Gypsy; Dina Kozel, Spacewoman, Traitor; Leonidas Andreos, Spaceship Captain
**Time period(s):** Indeterminate Future
**Locale(s):** *Siduri's Net*, Spaceship; *Siduri's Dance*, Spaceship; Outer Space (Epsilon Tauri)

**Summary:** The mixed nationalities and intricate contractual arrangements between the cloudships *Dance* and *Net* promote social and cultural clashes and lead to severe damage to *Dance*. Embarrassed by his former lover, Pov must integrate his Rom identity with his love for the *Net* to preserve his place as the *Net*'s sailmaster and the *Net*'s chance at freedom from debt.

**Other books you might like:**
Paula E. Downing, *A Whisper of Time*, 1994
Paula E. Downing, *Fallway*, 1993
Paula E. Downing, *Flare Star*, 1992
Paula E. Downing, *Rinn's Star*, 1990
Paula King, *Mad Roy's Light*, 1990
   pseudonym of Paula E. Downing

### 3710

**PAUL J. MCAULEY**

## Eternal Light

(New York: Morrow/AvoNova, 1993)

**Story type:** Science Fiction (Theological; Military)
**Major character(s):** Dorthy Yoshida, Psychic (esper); Suzanne "Suzy Falcon" Marie Thibodeaux, Pilot (spaceship); Talbeck Barlstilkin, Immortal

**Time period(s):** Indeterminate Future
**Locale(s):** Epsilon Eridani Two, Planet—Imaginary; Outer Space (galactic core)

**Summary:** Humanity travels to other star systems, only to find the remains of the Alea and their million-year-old civil war. Able to see the past and the future, Dorthy may prove the key to preventing the war from destroying not only humanity, but the entire universe. Sequel to *Four Hundred Billion Stars*.

**Other books you might like:**
Roger MacBride Allen, *The Ring of Charon*, 1990
Kevin J. Anderson, *Assemblers of Infinity*, 1993
   Doug Beason, co-author
James Blish, *The Triumph of Time*, 1958
Jeffrey A. Carver, *Down the Stream of Stars*, 1990
Glen Cook, *The Dragon Never Sleeps*, 1988
Frank Herbert, *Dune*, 1965
Michaela Roessner, *Vanishing Point*, 1993
David Weber, *Path of the Fury*, 1992

### 3711

**PAUL J. MCAULEY**

## Fairyland

(New York: Avon, 1996)

**Story type:** Science Fiction (Genetic Manipulation; Horror)
**Major character(s):** Alex Sharkey, Technician; Milena "Alfred Russell Wallace", Computer Expert, Teenager
**Time period(s):** 21st century
**Locale(s):** London, England

**Summary:** Psychoactive virus designer Alex Sharkey, his product barely legal, finds himself involved with a young genius out to change the world. Milena intends to give the genetically engineered "dolls" used for dirty work and amusement the capability of reproduction. She infects everyone she deals with, so she can control them with a laser burst, leaving Alex to deal with the fallout while she develops the deadly fairies.

**Other books you might like:**
Wilhelmina Baird, *Clipjoint*, 1994
Pat Cadigan, *Mindplayers*, 1987
Raphael Carter, *The Fortunate Fall*, 1996
Gwyneth Jones, *White Queen*, 1993
Neal Stephenson, *The Diamond Age*, 1995
Jim Young, *Armed Memory*, 1995

### 3712

**PAUL J. MCAULEY**

## The Invisible Country

(New York: Avon Eos, 1998)

**Story type:** Science Fiction (Collection)

**Summary:** This collection contains a five-page introduction by Kim Newman and nine stories from periodicals and anthologies dated 1991 to 1995 with original author's afterwords. Frequently somber or downbeat in tone, the stories explore diverse themes, including dystopian futures, biology, life in the distant future, sex, the fairy realm, the creation of life and childhood.

**Other books you might like:**
John Kessel, *Meeting in Infinity*, 1992
Jonathan Lethem, *The Wall of the Sky, the Wall of the Eye*, 1996
Clifford D. Simak, *Over the River & through the Woods*, 1996
Allen Steele, *All-American Alien Boy*, 1996

James Tiptree Jr., *Her Smoke Rose Up Forever*, 1990

## 3713

### PAUL J. MCAULEY

## *Of the Fall*

(New York: Ballantine Del Rey, 1989)

**Story type:** Science Fiction (First Contact)
**Major character(s):** David De Ramaira, Scientist; Rick Florey, Scientist
**Time period(s):** 21st century (Late)
**Locale(s):** Elysium, Planet—Imaginary

**Summary:** The Earth colony on the planet Elysium is in turmoil as long-time colonists vie with recent immigrants for political power. Meanwhile, on the periphery of human civilization, the primitive and much despised natives of the planet bide their time.

**Other books you might like:**
Orson Scott Card, *Speaker for the Dead*, 1986
C.J. Cherryh, *Forty Thousand in Gehenna*, 1983
Mike Resnick, *Paradise: A Chronicle of a Distant World*, 1989
Sheri S. Tepper, *After Long Silence*, 1987
Sheri S. Tepper, *Grass*, 1989

## 3714

### PAUL J. MCAULEY

## *Pasquale's Angel*

(New York: Morrow/AvoNova, 1995)

**Story type:** Fantasy (Historical)
**Major character(s):** Pasquale, Artist; Niccolo Machiavelli, Journalist, Political Figure (retired); Leonardo da Vinci, Genius, Aged Person
**Time period(s):** 16th century
**Locale(s):** Italy, Alternate Earth (Florence)

**Summary:** In a Florence greatly changed by the success of Da Vinci's strangest inventions, an artist named Pasquale struggles with the painting that will establish his reputation. The murder of the great Raphael's assistant drags Pasquale away from his studies and into a maze of corruption and danger. The evolving new world may contain no room for painters or Florence.

**Other books you might like:**
John Crowley, *Aegypt*, 1987
R.A. MacAvoy, *Damiano*, 1983
Tim Powers, *The Drawing of the Dark*, 1979
Melissa Scott, *The Armor of Light*, 1988
Lisa Barnett, co-author

## 3715

### PAUL J. MCAULEY

## *Red Dust*

(New York: Morrow/AvoNova, 1994)

**Story type:** Science Fiction (Alternate Intelligence; Political)
**Major character(s):** Wei Lee, Technician (agronomist), Traveler; Miriam Makepeace Mbele, Clone, Computer Expert; Redd, Cowboy (Martian)
**Time period(s):** 29th century (2800s)
**Locale(s):** Bitter Waters, Mars; Xin Beijing, Mars

**Summary:** Wei Lee and his friends rescue Miriam Mbele, an anarchist sent to Mars to help free the planet from the Ten Thousand Years who sold Mars for personal immortality. The Emperor may have died and Wei Lee's great-grandfather, one of the Ten Thousand Years, attempts to kill the clone while framing Wei Lee. Before dying, the clone infects Wei Lee with a tailored virus allowing him access to the computer side of reality.

**Other books you might like:**
Poul Anderson, *The Stars Are Also Fire*, 1994
Frederik Pohl, *Man Plus*, 1994
Thomas T. Thomas, co-author
Kim Stanley Robinson, *Green Mars*, 1994
Kim Stanley Robinson, *Red Mars*, 1993
Jack Williamson, *The Humanoids*, 1949

## 3716

### PATRICK MCCABE

## *The Butcher Boy*

(New York: Delta/Cutting Edge, 1994)

**Story type:** Horror (Psychological Suspense)
**Major character(s):** Francis Brady, Child; Philip Nugent, Child; Joe Purcell, Child
**Time period(s):** 1990s (1992)
**Locale(s):** Dublin, Ireland

**Summary:** Originally published in 1992, this extraordinary novel tells of Francis Brady, a slightly "simple" Irish boy whose loathing of himself and his dysfunctional family and envy of the next-door neighbor his age leads him to imagine persecutors and take drastic measures against them, in a tour-de-force of psychological horror.

**Other books you might like:**
Robert Bloch, *Psycho*, 1959
Anthony Burgess, *A Clockwork Orange*, 1962
Ramsey Campbell, *The Face That Must Die*, 1979

## 3717

### ANNE MCCAFFREY
### MARGARET BALL, Co-Author

## *Acorna*

(New York: HarperPrism, 1997)

**Story type:** Science Fiction (First Contact; Political)
**Major character(s):** Acorna, Alien, Foundling; Declan "Gill" Gioglie III, Spaceman, Miner; Judit Kendoro, Scientist (psycholinguistics), Heroine
**Time period(s):** Indeterminate Future
**Locale(s):** *Khedive*, Spaceship; Laboue, Planet—Imaginary; Maganos, Planet—Imaginary

**Summary:** Gill and the others on *Khedive*, a mining ship, rescue Acorna, an alien child. Acorna proves useful and intelligent, but the company they return to only wants to mutilate and abuse her. Judit helps Gill rescue Acorna, who soon uncovers a ring of child slavers led by a man known only as the Pied Piper.

**Other books you might like:**
Margaret Ball, *Mathemagics*, 1996
Margaret Ball, *The Shadow Gate*, 1991
Orson Scott Card, *Wyrms*, 1987
Alan Dean Foster, *The Tar-Aiym Krang*, 1972
Sheri S. Tepper, *Grass*, 1989

**3718**

ANNE MCCAFFREY
MARGARET BALL, Co-Author

### Acorna's Quest

(New York: Harper, 1998)

**Story type:** Science Fiction (Space Opera)
**Major character(s):** Acorna, Orphan, Telepath; Calum, Miner
**Time period(s):** Indeterminate Future
**Locale(s):** *Acadecki*, Spaceship; Kezdet, Planet—Imaginary

**Summary:** Acorna dreams of a world where her unusual appearance and abilities are normal, and convinces her Uncle Calum to help her find it. While they are exploring the galaxy, rumors arise that an unknown alien species plans to invade civilized space and conquer the relatively peaceful interstellar community. Sequel to *Acorna*.

**Other books you might like:**
Cynthia Felice, *The Sunbound*, 1981
Tara K. Harper, *Lightwing*, 1992
Vonda N. McIntyre, *The Exile Waiting*, 1975
Lisanne Norman, *Fire Margins*, 1996
Dan Simmons, *Endymion*, 1996

**3719**

ANNE MCCAFFREY

### All the Weyrs of Pern

(New York: Ballantine/Del Rey, 1991)

**Story type:** Science Fiction (Hard Science Fiction; Genetic Manipulation)
**Series:** Dragonriders of Pern
**Major character(s):** Lessa, Leader (Weyrwoman of Pern); Jaxom, Nobleman (Holder of Ruatha); AIVAS, Artificial Intelligence (Voice Activated System)
**Time period(s):** Indeterminate Future
**Locale(s):** Pern, Planet—Imaginary

**Summary:** The Pernese discover the artificial intelligence which had been abandoned 2500 years earlier, after Landing was covered by a volcanic eruption. They find it not only in working order, but prepared to help Pern eliminate the deadly Thread. This book is a direct sequel to *The Renegades of Pern*.

**Other books you might like:**
Margaret Wander Bonanno, *The Others*, 1990
C.J. Cherryh, *Forty Thousand in Gehenna*, 1983
Suzette Haden Elgin, *Twelve Fair Kingdoms*, 1981
Rosemary Kirstein, *The Steerswoman*, 1989
Michael P. Kube-McDowell, *Emprise*, 1985
Alis A. Rasmussen, *A Passage of Stars*, 1990

**3720**

ANNE MCCAFFREY

### Black Horses for the King

(New York: Harcourt Brace, 1996)

**Story type:** Fantasy (Legend; Young Adult)
**Major character(s):** Artos, Nobleman (Comes Britannorum), Warrior; Galwin Gaius Varianus, Linguist, Horse Trainer
**Time period(s):** 6th century
**Locale(s):** England; Europe

**Summary:** Galwin wins Artos' respect by translating and bargaining for food and lodging for Artos' group, bound for a market where they hope to secure large Libyan horses to use as Artos' cavalry. Galwin escapes his abusive uncle's ship and joins Artos' mission as translator, but quickly proves invaluable working with the fine new horses.

**Other books you might like:**
Susan Cooper, *Over Sea, under Stone*, 1966
Tanith Lee, *Black Unicorn*, 1991
T.H. White, *The Sword in the Stone*, 1939
Jane Yolen, *Camelot*, 1995
   editor
Jane Yolen, *Passager*, 1996

**3721**

ANNE MCCAFFREY

### The Chronicles of Pern: First Fall

(New York: Ballantine Del Rey, 1993)

**Story type:** Science Fiction (Collection)
**Series:** Dragonriders of Pern
**Time period(s):** Indeterminate Future
**Locale(s):** Pern, Planet—Imaginary

**Summary:** Contains a timeline for the first 20 years after landing, four pages of maps plus five original stories about life on Pern. Stories examine the original colony survey, exploration of dangerous Pernese oceans utilizing intelligent, talking dolphins and the founding of Ruatha Hold.

**Other books you might like:**
David Brin, *Startide Rising*, 1983
Robert L. Forward, *Marooned on Eden*, 1993
   Martha Dodson Forward, co-author
Diana G. Gallagher, *The Alien Dark*, 1990
Janet Kagan, *Mirabile*, 1991
Rosemary Kirstein, *The Outskirter's Secret*, 1992
Rosemary Kirstein, *The Steerswoman*, 1989

**3722**

ANNE MCCAFFREY
S.M. STIRLING, Co-Author

### The City Who Fought

(New York: Baen, 1993)

**Story type:** Science Fiction (Adventure; Military)
**Series:** Ship Who Sang
**Major character(s):** SSS-900-C Simeon, Administrator, Cyborg (shell person); Channa Hap, Spaceman (Brawn); Amos "Simeon" ben Sierra Nueva, Leader, Refugee
**Time period(s):** Indeterminate Future
**Locale(s):** SSS-900-C, Space Station

**Summary:** Channa Hap, unwanted new brawn for Simeon, must help Simeon defend SSS-900-C against attack by the Kolinar fleet before their partnership or any real trust can evolve. Prior to the attack, Joat, an electronics genius hiding out on SSS-900-C, meets Channa, but when Simeon attempts adoption, prejudice against shell people complicates the procedure. Because the navy cannot arrive for 16 days, Simeon, Channa and the refugees who warned of the pursuing pirates must prevent the destruction of the space station and the deaths of the 15,000 residents.

**Other books you might like:**
James Blish, *Cities in Flight*, 1970
Jeffrey A. Carver, *Dragons in the Stars*, 1992

Glen Cook, *The Dragon Never Sleeps*, 1988
John DeChancie, *Starrigger*, 1983
Debra Doyle, *The Price of the Stars*, 1992
   James D. Macdonald, co-author
R.M. Meluch, *The Queen's Squadron*, 1992
Vernor Vinge, *A Fire upon the Deep*, 1992

**3723**

### ANNE MCCAFFREY
### JODY LYNN NYE, Co-Author

## Crisis on Doona
(New York: Ace, 1992)

**Story type:** Science Fiction (Political; Mystery)
**Series:** Doona
**Major character(s):** Todd Reeve, Rancher, Hero; Hrriss, Alien (Hrruban), Settler; Kelly Solinari, Scholar, Detective—Amateur
**Time period(s):** 22nd century
**Locale(s):** Doona, Planet—Imaginary; Earth

**Summary:** On the way to Doona for the renewal of the treaty establishing the planet as one inhabited by two intelligent species, human and Hrruban, Todd Reeve and Hrriss answer a mayday call, going into interdicted territory to do so. On Doona, inspectors find contraband hidden on their ship and arrest the two, threatening the renewal of the treaty. Convinced of the men's innocence, Kelly Solinari returns to Earth to prove that politicians at the highest level on both Earth and Hrruba conspired to scuttle the treaty by framing its chief advocates. Sequel to *Decision on Doona*.

**Other books you might like:**
Poul Anderson, *People of the Wind*, 1973
C.J. Cherryh, *Forty Thousand in Gehenna*, 1983
Paula E. Downing, *Fallway*, 1993
Dean Ing, *Cathouse*, 1991
Rebecca Ore, *Being Alien*, 1989

**3724**

### ANNE MCCAFFREY

## Crystal Line
(New York: Ballantine Del Rey, 1992)

**Story type:** Science Fiction (Science Fiction)
**Series:** Crystal Singer
**Major character(s):** Killashandra Ree, Miner (crystal singer); Lars Dahl, Government Official (guild master)
**Time period(s):** Indeterminate Future
**Locale(s):** Ballybran, Planet—Imaginary; *BB-1066*, Spaceship

**Summary:** One of the oldest, most successful crystal singers, Killashandra, uses the side-effect associated with extended life, loss of memory, to forget anything painful. Kept alive by their symbionts, crystal singers eventually lose the ability to find their claims due to this memory loss and exposure to crystal. Finding her interactions with Lars disappointing, Killashandra risks her skills as a crystal singer. Sequel to *Killashandra*.

**Other books you might like:**
Pauline Ashwell, *Unwillingly to Earth*, 1992
Stephen Goldin, *Jade Darcy and the Affair of Honor*, 1988
   Mary Mason, co-author
Rosemary Kirstein, *The Steerswoman*, 1989
Alis A. Rasmussen, *A Passage of Stars*, 1990
Vernor Vinge, *A Fire upon the Deep*, 1992

**3725**

### ANNE MCCAFFREY

## Damia
(New York: Ace/Putnam, 1992)

**Story type:** Science Fiction (First Contact; Psychic Powers)
**Series:** Rowan
**Major character(s):** Afra Lyon, Psychic (Talent); Angharad "the Rowan" Gwynn-Raven, Psychic (Prime Talent); Damia Gwynn-Raven, Psychic (Prime Talent)
**Time period(s):** Indeterminate Future
**Locale(s):** Callisto, Jupiter (a moon of Jupiter); Deneb, Planet—Imaginary; Iota Aurigae, Planet—Imaginary

**Summary:** Afra grows up on rigid Capella where he befriends a spaceship captain who teaches him origami. Prepared for Tower work, Afra's acceptance by the Rowan as a friend and surrogate brother exercises his strength and patience. Acting as a substitute parent to the Raven and Jeff's children, he develops a special bond with Damia, the most Talented youngster. When Damia, now Aurigae Prime, contacts an alien intelligence, Afra recognizes the danger, thus preventing the destruction of Nine Star League planets.

**Other books you might like:**
Marion Zimmer Bradley, *The Firebrand*, 1987
F.M. Busby, *Rissa Kerguelen*, 1977
Jeffrey A. Carver, *Down the Stream of Stars*, 1990
Cheryl J. Franklin, *Fire Crossing*, 1991
Henry Kuttner, *Mutant*, 1953
Joan D. Vinge, *Psion*, 1982

**3726**

### ANNE MCCAFFREY

## Damia's Children
(New York: Ace/Putnam, 1993)

**Story type:** Science Fiction (Family Saga; Psychic Powers)
**Series:** Rowan
**Major character(s):** Laria Lyon, Teenager, Psychic (esper); Isthian "Thian" Lyon, Teenager, Psychic (esper); Rojer Lyon, Teenager, Psychic (esper)
**Time period(s):** Indeterminate Future
**Locale(s):** Iota Aurigae, Planet—Imaginary; Clarf, Planet—Imaginary; *Vadim*, Spaceship

**Summary:** Damia and Afra Raven-Lyon realize the Alliance will need their talented esper children when the Mrdini inform the Alliance that they sent ships to backtrack the trail of Hiver ships they discovered. To promote Human/Mrdini understanding, each of the Raven-Lyon children befriended a pair of 'Dinis from early childhood, now communicating well with them. At 16, Laria leaves for Clarf with her 'Dinis to become their primary teleporter. A year later Thian joins the expedition as communications expert while Rojer, now 15, visits the Alliance ships following a Hiver escape pod. All work to promote interspecies understanding.

**Other books you might like:**
Greg Bear, *Anvil of Stars*, 1992
Marion Zimmer Bradley, *The World Wreckers*, 1971
Orson Scott Card, *Ender's Game*, 1985
Jeffrey A. Carver, *Down the Stream of Stars*, 1990
Karen Haber, *Mutant Star*, 1992
Henry Kuttner, *Mutant*, 1953
Larry Niven, *The Gripping Hand*, 1993
   Jerry Pournelle, co-author
Joan D. Vinge, *Psion*, 1982

## 3727

**ANNE MCCAFFREY**
**JODY LYNN NYE**, Co-Author

### The Death of Sleep
(New York: Baen, 1990)

**Story type:** Science Fiction (Adventure; Future Shock)
**Series:** Planet Pirates
**Major character(s):** Lunzie Mespil, Doctor; Teodor Janos, Social Worker (caseworker); Zebara, Spaceship Captain (ARCT-10)
**Time period(s):** 28th century
**Locale(s):** Astris Alexandria, Planet—Imaginary; Ireta, Planet—Imaginary; Outer Space

**Summary:** Lunzie Mespil takes a job and winds up spending 62 years in cold sleep. After taking a refresher course to update her job skills, she travels to see her daughter and other descendants, is shipwrecked, and spends another 10 years in cold sleep. On Tau Ceti she is marked for assassination so she takes a job on the *ARC-10/* and winds up confronting pirates. Later she takes a routine jaunt to Ireta where the explorers are first marooned and then threatened by berserk Heavyworlders, so they go into cold sleep until help arrives.

**Other books you might like:**
C.J. Cherryh, *Forty Thousand in Gehenna*, 1983
Andre Norton, *The Last Planet*, 1955
John Rackham, *The Anything Tree*, 1970
    pseudonym of John Phillifent
Melissa Scott, *Mighty Good Road*, 1990
Marti Steussy, *Dreams of Dawn*, 1988

## 3728

**ANNE MCCAFFREY**
**RICHARD WOODS**, Co-Author

### A Diversity of Dragons
(New York: HarperPrism, 1997)

**Story type:** Fantasy (Legend)
**Major character(s):** Anne McCaffrey, Writer, Storyteller; Sean Evans, Student; Epiphanius "Eppy" Tighe, Storyteller
**Time period(s):** 1990s; Indeterminate Past
**Locale(s):** Ireland; Europe; Middle East

**Summary:** Sean's unexpected interest in dragon lore presents Anne and Eppy with the opportunity to enlighten him concerning dragons from myths and modern fiction. Contains seven pages of notes, sources, dragon classification, annotations and a list of other books about dragons.

**Other books you might like:**
Eleanor Arnason, *The Sword Smith*, 1978
Orson Scott Card, *Dragons of Darkness*, 1981
    editor
Orson Scott Card, *Dragons of Light*, 1983
    editor
Gordon R. Dickson, *The Dragon and the George*, 1976
Graham Edwards, *Dragoncharm*, 1996
Andre Norton, *Elvenblood*, 1995
    Mercedes Lackey, co-author
J.R.R. Tolkien, *The Hobbit*, 1938
Patricia C. Wrede, *Talking to Dragons*, 1993
    revised edition

## 3729

**ANNE MCCAFFREY**

### The Dolphins of Pern
(New York: Ballantine Del Rey, 1994)

**Story type:** Science Fiction (First Contact; Adventure)
**Series:** Dragonriders of Pern
**Major character(s):** Readis, Child; Alemi, Fisherman; T'lion, Teenager
**Time period(s):** Indeterminate Future
**Locale(s):** Pern, Planet—Imaginary

**Summary:** In Paradise River Hold, the first settlement on the newly opened Southern Continent, Alemi frequently takes Readis fishing. After being caught in a sudden squall, Readis and Alemi speak with dolphins, "ship-fish," who rescue them. Although forbidden by his mother to swim out and see the dolphins, Readis' fascination with them continues.

**Other books you might like:**
Betty Ballantine, *The Secret Oceans*, 1994
David Brin, *Startide Rising*, 1983
Arthur C. Clarke, *Dolphin Island*, 1963
Gordon R. Dickson, *Space Winners*, 1965
Kathryn Lasky, *Shadows in the Water*, 1992
Joan Slonczewski, *A Door into Ocean*, 1986
Sheri S. Tepper, *After Long Silence*, 1987
Sydney J. Van Scyoc, *Deepwater Dreams*, 1991
Joan D. Vinge, *The Summer Queen*, 1991
Catherine Wells, *The Earth Is All That Lasts*, 1991

## 3730

**ANNE MCCAFFREY**

### Dragonseye
(New York: Ballantine, Del Rey, 1997)

**Story type:** Science Fiction (Lost Colony; Political)
**Series:** Dragonriders of Pern
**Major character(s):** K'vin, Leader (Telgar Weyr); Chalkin, Leader (Bita Hold); Clisser, Musician, Professor
**Time period(s):** Indeterminate Future ((258 years after landing))
**Locale(s):** Pern, Planet—Imaginary; Telgar, Mythical Place; Fort Hold, Fictional City

**Summary:** Holder Chalkin refuses to prepare for Thread, endangering all Bitrians, as Thread, according to historical records, lasts 50 years and depletes available resources. Clisser encourages Jemmy to write the Duty ballad as a teaching tool for future generations. Fortunately music proves suitable for most subjects, overcoming the lack of material resources and failing Earth technology. British title is *Red Star Rising*, (published in 1996 in the U.K.). First novel in the second Chronicles of Pern series.

**Other books you might like:**
David Brin, *Startide Rising*, 1995
L. Warren Douglas, *Cannon's Orb*, 1994
Janet Kagan, *Mirabile*, 1991
Ursula K. Le Guin, *The Word for World Is Forest*, 1976
Louise Marley, *Sing the Light*, 1996

## 3731

### ANNE MCCAFFREY

## *An Exchange of Gifts*

(New York: Roc, 1995)

**Story type:** Fantasy (Romance)
**Major character(s):** Anastasia "Meanne" de Saumur et Navarre y Cordova, Royalty (princess); Dalain "Wisp" zu Blas und Fiersing, Nobleman
**Time period(s):** Indeterminate
**Locale(s):** Fictional Country

**Summary:** Meanne flees an arranged marriage, finding shelter in an abandoned cottage in the woods where she hopes to use her gift for growing things. In other areas of practical housekeeping she lacks skills, but Wisp, another runaway who soon joins her, knows about catching and cooking food. As Meanne gradually discovers that Wisp has other talents as well, their respective abilities enable them to survive and elude danger.

**Other books you might like:**
Pamela Dean, *The Dubious Hills*, 1994
Rosalie Fry, *The Secret of Roan Inish*, 1995
Ursula K. Le Guin, *The Beginning Place*, 1980
Ursula K. Le Guin, *Tehanu: The Last Book of Earthsea*, 1990
Elizabeth Ann Scarborough, *Song of Sorcery*, 1982
Gertrude Warner, *The Boxcar Children*, 1924

## 3732

### ANNE MCCAFFREY

## *Freedom's Challenge*

(New York: Ace/Putnam, 1998)

**Story type:** Science Fiction (Military; First Contact)
**Series:** Freedom's Landing
**Major character(s):** Kristen "Kris" Bjornson, Slave, Settler; Zainal, Alien (Catteni), Settler; Chuck Mitford, Military Personnel (sergeant), Settler
**Time period(s):** 1990s
**Locale(s):** Botany, Planet—Imaginary; Catten, Planet—Imaginary

**Summary:** Protected by the bubble the alien Farmers left over Botany, the settlers agree to use their ships to save as many people from Earth as possible, and at the same time send a mission to Catten to find some of Zianal's dissident Catteni cohorts. Ultimately, the Botany settlers plan to free all Eosi slaves, including themselves.

**Other books you might like:**
David Brin, *Brightness Reef*, 1995
C.J. Cherryh, *Foreigner*, 1994
Rosemary Kirstein, *The Outskirter's Secret*, 1992
Elizabeth Moon, *Remnant Population*, 1996
David Weber, *Mutineers' Moon*, 1991

## 3733

### ANNE MCCAFFREY

## *Freedom's Choice*

(New York: Ace/Putnam, 1997)

**Story type:** Science Fiction (Adventure; First Contact)
**Series:** Freedom's Landing
**Major character(s):** Kristen "Kris" Bjornson, Slave; Zainal, Alien (Catteni), Settler; Chuck Mitford, Military Personnel (sargeant)
**Time period(s):** 1990s
**Locale(s):** Botany, Planet—Imaginary

**Summary:** In the process of colonizing Botany, the castaways contact the aliens farming the planet, hoping to find an ally against the Catteni and the Eosi who use them. Zainal avoids a fate worse than death by remaining on Botany, while the Catteni, attempting to force his return, inadvertently antagonize the alien farmers.

**Other books you might like:**
David Brin, *Brightness Reef*, 1995
Rosemary Kirstein, *The Outskirter's Secret*, 1992
Amy Thomson, *The Color of Distance*, 1995
Vernor Vinge, *A Fire upon the Deep*, 1992
David Weber, *Mutineers' Moon*, 1991

## 3734

### ANNE MCCAFFREY

## *Freedom's Landing*

(New York: Ace/Putnam, 1995)

**Story type:** Science Fiction (First Contact; Adventure)
**Major character(s):** Kristin "Kris" Bjornsen, Slave, Settler; Zainal, Alien (Catteni), Settler; Chuck Mitford, Military Personnel (sergeant), Settler
**Time period(s):** 1990s
**Locale(s):** Barevi, Planet—Imaginary; Botany, Planet—Imaginary

**Summary:** A student the University of Denver when the Catteni empty Denver and 50 other Terran cities in their typical pattern of conquest, Kris and her fellow captives land on Barevi for sale as slaves. Kris finds herself part of an experimental colony of troublemakers on a planet the Catteni would like open for colonization. Unfortunately, the planet's parklike appearance conceals evidence of unknown dangers and unsuspected aliens. Expands "The Thorns of Barevi."

**Other books you might like:**
Roger MacBride Allen, *The Ring of Charon*, 1990
Hal Clement, *Fossil*, 1993
Rosemary Kirstein, *The Outskirter's Secret*, 1992
John E. Stith, *Manhattan Transfer*, 1993
Vernor Vinge, *Marooned in Realtime*, 1986

## 3735

### ANNE MCCAFFREY
### ELIZABETH MOON, Co-Author

## *Generation Warrior*

(New York: Baen, 1991)

**Story type:** Science Fiction (Political)
**Series:** Planet Pirates
**Major character(s):** Lunzie Mespil, Doctor; Sassinak, Spaceship Captain
**Time period(s):** Indeterminate Future
**Locale(s):** Federation Space, Interstellar Empire/Federation

**Summary:** Sassinak and Lunzie combine forces to beat the planet pirates once and for all. With Lunzie's contacts, Sassinak's crew and Sassinak herself, it would take a galaxy-wide conspiracy to foil them. Unfortunately, that's just what the planet pirates are.

**Other books you might like:**
Poul Anderson, *Ensign Flandry*, 1966
David Brin, *The Uplift War*, 1987
C.J. Cherryh, *Cyteen*, 1988
C.J. Cherryh, *The Pride of Chanur*, 1982
Brian Daley, *Requiem for a Ruler of Worlds*, 1985

Frank Herbert, *Dune*, 1965
Alis A. Rasmussen, *A Passage of Stars*, 1990

### 3736

#### ANNE MCCAFFREY

## The Girl Who Heard Dragons

(New York: Tor, 1994)

**Story type:** Science Fiction (Collection)

**Summary:** Contains an introduction and 15 stories with the title story set on Pern. Other stories feature a broad range of themes including a story from 1956, "The Greatest Love," in which in vitro fertilization and host motherhood lead to an incest trial.

**Other books you might like:**
Philip Jose Farmer, *Riders of the Purple Wage*, 1992
Nancy Kress, *The Aliens of Earth*, 1993
Pat Murphy, *Points of Departure*, 1990
James Tiptree Jr., *Her Smoke Rose Up Forever*, 1990
John Varley, *The Persistence of Vision*, 1978
Kate Wilhelm, *And the Angels Sing*, 1992

### 3737

#### ANNE MCCAFFREY

## If Wishes Were Horses

(New York: Roc, 1998)

**Story type:** Fantasy (Young Adult)
**Major character(s):** Lady Talarrie Eircelly, Healer; Tracell Eircelly, Child; Tirza Eircelly, Child
**Time period(s):** Indeterminate
**Locale(s):** Fictional Country (Mallafret Hall)

**Summary:** This short children's story is about a healer whose husband goes off to war. Left alone with her two children, Lady Talarrie fights to keep up their spirits, and in the process teaches them valuable lessons about life.

**Other books you might like:**
Alan Garner, *The Weirdstone of Brisingamen*, 1966
Tamora Pierce, *Alanna: The First Adventure*, 1983
Jane Yolen, *Child of Faerie*, 1997
Jane Yolen, *Here There Be Unicorns*, 1993

### 3738

#### ANNE MCCAFFREY

## Lyon's Pride

(New York: Ace/Putnam, 1994)

**Story type:** Science Fiction (Psychic Powers; Family Saga)
**Series:** Rowan
**Major character(s):** Prtglm, Alien (Mrdini); Rojer Lyon, Psychic (esper), Spaceman (engineer); Jeff Raven, Psychic (esper), Parent
**Time period(s):** Indeterminate Future
**Locale(s):** *Genesee*, Spaceship; Clarf, Planet—Imaginary (Mrdini Homeworld); Outer Space

**Summary:** The continuing war against the Hivers puts some humans and Mrdini at odds with each other. The humans want to end the war, but the Mrdini insist on exterminating the Hivers. In a fit of rage, Prtglm kills Rojer's pair of Mrdini, causing him to disappear. While mourning their loss and recovering from shock, he studies to become certified as an engineer, befriending the shy Afra. The Primes

continue to serve with the fleet, becoming more than simply supply and communication personnel.

**Other books you might like:**
F.M. Busby, *The Demu Trilogy*, 1980
Robert L. Forward, *Return to Rocheworld*, 1993
    Julie Forward Fuller, co-author
Diana G. Gallagher, *The Alien Dark*, 1990
Janet Kagan, *Mirabile*, 1991
Robert J. Sawyer, *Far-Seer*, 1992
Sheri S. Tepper, *Raising the Stones*, 1987

### 3739

#### ANNE MCCAFFREY

## The Masterharper of Pern

(New York: Ballantine Del Rey, 1998)

**Story type:** Science Fiction (Political; Lost Colony)
**Series:** Dragonriders of Pern
**Major character(s):** Robinton, Child, Telepath (with dragons); Petiron, Musician, Composer; Merelan, Singer, Parent
**Time period(s):** Indeterminate Future
**Locale(s):** Pern, Planet—Imaginary

**Summary:** Resentful of his son Robinton for weakening his wife Merelan, Petiron refuses to believe in Robinton's talent, despite the fact that many of his songs were used for teaching even while he was only a child. Unfortunately, Robinton will also have to convince the holds, always balking at hard work and expense, to prepare for the deadly Thread, due 50 years in the future.

**Other books you might like:**
L. Warren Douglas, *Cannon's Orb*, 1994
Rosemary Kirstein, *The Outskirter's Secret*, 1992
Louise Marley, *Sing the Light*, 1996
Larry Niven, *Destiny's Road*, 1997
Sharon Shinn, *Archangel*, 1996

### 3740

#### ANNE MCCAFFREY

## No One Noticed the Cat

(New York: Roc, 1996)

**Story type:** Fantasy (Young Adult; Political)
**Major character(s):** Jamas, Royalty, Leader; Niffy, Animal (cat), Counselor; Egdril, Royalty, Leader
**Time period(s):** Indeterminate
**Locale(s):** Esphania, Fictional Country

**Summary:** When Esphania's regent dies, Prince Jamas must lead the kingdom. The regent's surviving cat, Niffy, provides protection and direction as Jamas contends with neighboring King Egdril's plans for expansion through Jamas' marriage to his daughter and his wife's less benign lust for conquest.

**Other books you might like:**
Ursula K. Le Guin, *Catwings*, 1988
Andre Norton, *Catfantastic*, 1989
    Martin H. Greenberg, co-editor
Andre Norton, *The Mark of the Cat*, 1992
John Richard Stephens, *The Enchanted Cat*, 1990
    editor
L.A. Taylor, *Cat's Paw*, 1995
Tad Williams, *Tailchaser's Song*, 1985

## 3741

### ANNE MCCAFFREY
### MARGARET BALL, Co-Author

## PartnerShip

(New York: Baen, 1992)

**Story type:** Science Fiction (Adventure)
**Series:** Ship Who Sang
**Major character(s):** Nancia, Cyborg (Spaceship); Caleb, Spaceman; Forister, Spaceman
**Time period(s):** 28th century
**Locale(s):** *Nancia*, Spaceship (courier service ship)

**Summary:** Partnered with Caleb, then Forister, *Nancia* carries out missions which challenge her worldview, forcing her to adapt. When a hyperchip attack affects a synaptic connection to emotional signals, *Nancia* becomes more human than her sister ships.

**Other books you might like:**
John DeChancie, *Red Limit Freeway*, 1984
John DeChancie, *Starrigger*, 1983
Alis A. Rasmussen, *The Price of Ransom*, 1990
David Alexander Smith, *Marathon*, 1982
Walter Jon Williams, *Voice of the Whirlwind*, 1987

## 3742

### ANNE MCCAFFREY

## Pegasus in Flight

(New York: Ballantine/Del Rey, 1990)

**Story type:** Science Fiction (Psychic Powers; Family Saga)
**Series:** Pegasus
**Major character(s):** Rhyssa Owen, Telepath, Administrator
**Time period(s):** 21st century
**Locale(s):** Jerhattan, Fictional City

**Summary:** Rhyssa Owen, granddaughter of Henry Darrow, has taken over as Director of the Jerhattan Parapsychic Center. There Talents, people with parapsychic abilities, are found, tested, trained and sent where they are needed. Currently the space platform needs many Talents. Candidates come from all sectors of society including the Linear developments where excess children may be sold into slavery.

**Other books you might like:**
John Brunner, *Children of the Thunder*, 1989
Storm Constantine, *The Enchantments of Flesh and Spirit*, 1989
Henry Kuttner, *Mutant*, 1953
Robert Silverberg, *Dying Inside*, 1972
Joan D. Vinge, *Psion*, 1982

## 3743

### ANNE MCCAFFREY
### ELIZABETH ANN SCARBOROUGH, Co-Author

## Power Lines

(New York: Ballantine Del Rey, 1994)

**Story type:** Science Fiction (Political; First Contact)
**Series:** Powers That Be
**Major character(s):** Yanaba Maddock, Military Personnel (retired), Settler; Clodagh Senungatuk, Healer; Sean Shongili, Genetically Altered Being, Spouse
**Time period(s):** Indeterminate Future
**Locale(s):** Petaybee, Planet—Imaginary

**Summary:** Recognizing the sentience of the planet Petaybee, Yanaba works with the colonists to change company policy, stop attempts at mining and arrange for self determination for the planet and its colonists. Unscrupulous pirates allow the company to believe as it desires, that the planet could be extremely profitable, forcing the planet to prove its sentience.

**Other books you might like:**
J.R. Dunn, *This Side of Judgment*, 1994
Vonda N. McIntyre, *Metaphase*, 1992
Elizabeth Ann Scarborough, *The Healer's War*, 1989
Sheri S. Tepper, *After Long Silence*, 1987
Vernor Vinge, *A Fire upon the Deep*, 1992
Eric Vinicoff, *The Weigher*, 1992

## 3744

### ANNE MCCAFFREY
### ELIZABETH ANN SCARBOROUGH, Co-Author

## Power Play

(New York: Ballantine Del Rey, 1995)

**Story type:** Science Fiction (First Contact; Genetic Manipulation)
**Series:** Powers That Be
**Major character(s):** Yanaba Maddock, Military Personnel (retired captain), Administrator; Onidi "Dinah O'Neill" Louchard, Pirate, Disembodied Personality; Petaybee, Alien (sentient planet)
**Time period(s):** Indeterminate Future
**Locale(s):** Petaybee, Planet—Imaginary; Gal Three, Space Station

**Summary:** Pregnant, Yanaba marries Sean inside Petaybee immediately before she must leave for Gal Three to testify about Petaybee. Before the hearings begin, Yana, her companions from Petaybee and her mentor from Gal Three fall prey to the pirate Louchard who holds them for ransom. Meanwhile, Petaybee develops a method allowing her to speak.

**Other books you might like:**
David Brin, *Earth*, 1990
Harry Harrison, *The Deathworld Trilogy*, 1976
Janet Kagan, *Hellspark*, 1988
Elizabeth Ann Scarborough, *The Healer's War*, 1988
Elizabeth Ann Scarborough, *Nothing Sacred*, 1991

## 3745

### ANNE MCCAFFREY
### ELIZABETH ANN SCARBOROUGH, Co-Author

## Powers That Be

(New York: Ballantine Del Rey, 1993)

**Story type:** Science Fiction (First Contact; Genetic Manipulation)
**Series:** Powers That Be
**Major character(s):** Yanaba Maddock, Invalid, Military Personnel (retired); Buneka Rourke, Settler, Teenager; Diego Metaxos, Spaceman, Teenager
**Time period(s):** Indeterminate Future
**Locale(s):** Petaybee, Planet—Imaginary

**Summary:** Lungs destroyed by poison gas, Yanaba arrives on Petaybee for her assigned retirement. Expecting the frigid climate to prevent any outdoor activity, she notices how clean the air smells and how much better she seems to feel. When she comes in to the base, Yanaba finds that authorities may withhold medical treatment if she refuses to spy on the colonists with whom she will live. It seems that mineral deposits spotted from space disappear, or the explorers sent to find them disappear or return as raving lunatics. The colonists may also practice illegal genetic manipulation.

**Other books you might like:**
David Brin, *Earth*, 1990
Vonda N. McIntyre, *Metaphase*, 1992
Elizabeth Ann Scarborough, *Nothing Sacred*, 1991
Joan Slonczewski, *A Door into Ocean*, 1986
Sheri S. Tepper, *After Long Silence*, 1987
Kathy Tyers, *Shivering World*, 1991
Joan D. Vinge, *The Summer Queen*, 1991
Catherine Wells, *The Earth Is All That Lasts*, 1991

## 3746

### ANNE MCCAFFREY

## The Renegades of Pern

(New York: Ballantine/Del Rey, 1989)

**Story type:** Science Fiction (Science Fantasy)
**Series:** Dragonriders of Pern
**Major character(s):** Jayge, Trader; Aramina, Telepath
**Time period(s):** Indeterminate Future
**Locale(s):** Pern, Planet—Imaginary (Third Planet of the sun Rukbat in the Sagittarian sector)

**Summary:** Aramina, a homeless young woman reputed to be able to form a telepathic link with the dragons of Pern, is pursued by a powerful renegade leader who sees her as a means of gaining even greater power.

**Other books you might like:**
Leigh Brackett, *The Book of Skaith*, 1976
Leigh Brackett, *Eric John Stark, Outlaw of Mars*, 1982
Marion Zimmer Bradley, *City of Sorcery*, 1984
Marion Zimmer Bradley, *Sharra's Exile*, 1981
Marion Zimmer Bradley, *Stormqueen!*, 1978
Marion Zimmer Bradley, *Thendara House*, 1983

## 3747

### ANNE MCCAFFREY

## The Rowan

(New York: Ace/Putnam, 1990)

**Story type:** Science Fiction (Family Saga; Psychic Powers)
**Series:** Rowan
**Major character(s):** Angharad "the Rowan" Gwynn, Psychic (Talent), Orphan; Siglen, Psychic (Talent), Leader (of Altair Prime); Jeff Raven, Settler (colonist), Psychic (wild Talent)
**Time period(s):** Indeterminate Future
**Locale(s):** Callisto, Planet—Imaginary (Altair Colony)

**Summary:** The only survivor of Rowan Camp, the Rowan is taken to Altair Prime to be trained under Siglen. Later, as head of Callisto Prime, she gets a distress call from Deneb which is suffering from plague. Told that aid is unavailable, she gathers help and goes to Deneb against orders. She earns the gratitude of Jeff Raven, whom she later marries. Then they learn that the plague was the first step of an interstellar invasion. She and Jeff work to stop it.

**Other books you might like:**
Marion Zimmer Bradley, *The Bloody Sun*, 1964
A. Bertram Chandler, *Space Mercenaries*, 1965
Suzette Haden Elgin, *Twelve Fair Kingdoms*, 1981
R.M. Meluch, *Wind Child*, 1982
Andre Norton, *Ice Crown*, 1970

## 3748

### ANNE MCCAFFREY
### ELIZABETH MOON, Co-Author

## Sassinak

(New York: Baen Books, 1990)

**Story type:** Science Fiction (Space Opera)
**Series:** Planet Pirates
**Major character(s):** Sassinak, Spaceship Captain
**Time period(s):** Indeterminate Future
**Locale(s):** Federation of Sentient Planets, Interstellar Empire/Federation

**Summary:** Twelve year old Sassinak is kidnapped and enslaved by pirates, but she refuses to let her spirit be broken. Eventually she escapes. Later, grown up, she enters military service and dedicates her life to eliminating pirates.

**Other books you might like:**
Lois McMaster Bujold, *Brothers in Arms*, 1988
Lois McMaster Bujold, *The Warrior's Apprentice*, 1986
Emma Bull, *Falcon*, 1989
C.J. Cherryh, *Rimrunners*, 1989
Rosemary Kirstein, *The Steerswoman*, 1989
Anne Moroz, *No Safe Place*, 1986
Susan Shwartz, *Heritage of Flight*, 1989

## 3749

### ANNE MCCAFFREY
### MERCEDES LACKEY, Co-Author

## The Ship Who Searched

(New York: Baen, 1992)

**Story type:** Science Fiction (Adventure)
**Series:** Ship Who Sang
**Major character(s):** Hypatia "Tia" Cade, Cyborg (spaceship); Kennet Uhua-Sorg, Doctor, Handicapped (paraplegic); Alexander Joli-Chanteu, Spaceman (Brawn)
**Time period(s):** 28th century
**Locale(s):** Spaceship

**Summary:** Having spent the first seven years of her life on isolated archaeological digs with her parents, Tia spends much time alone and learns to be independent and comfortable with herself. While her parents work, Tia, with permission, plays at excavating her own site near their home base, unfortunately making a find which causes her total paralysis. Although thought to be too old to become a shell person, she proves to be an ideal candidate. As a brainship she and Alex search for the alien substance which paralyzed her while they transport supplies to remote archaeological sites similar to those where she grew up.

**Other books you might like:**
Glen Cook, *The Dragon Never Sleeps*, 1988
Debra Doyle, *The Price of the Stars*, 1992
   James D. Macdonald, co-author
Vonda N. McIntyre, *Metaphase*, 1992
R.M. Meluch, *The Queen's Squadron*, 1992
Melissa Scott, *Dreamships*, 1992
Vernor Vinge, *A Fire upon the Deep*, 1992

## **3750**

**ANNE MCCAFFREY**
**JODY LYNN NYE**, Co-Author

### *The Ship Who Won*

(New York: Baen, 1994)

**Story type:** Science Fiction (First Contact; Political)
**Series:** Ship Who Sang
**Major character(s):** Carialle, Spacewoman (shellperson); Keff Klemay, Spaceman; Nokias, Magician (High Mage of the South)
**Time period(s):** Indeterminate Future
**Locale(s):** *CK-963*, Spaceship; Ozrah, Planet—Imaginary

**Summary:** Carialle and Keff head out to search for alien intelligences and habitable planets. On Ozran they find what seems to be two groups of humans, slow thinking farmers and Mages who control powerful energies with thought using ancient artifacts given to them by previous residents. Unfortunately the climate has begun to degenerate and soon the planet will no longer support life unless the weather machinery mentioned in old records can be rediscovered and repaired.

**Other books you might like:**
William Adams, *The Unwound Way*, 1991
    Cecil Brooks, co-author
Stephen Baxter, *Raft*, 1992
C.J. Cherryh, *Foreigner*, 1994
Rosemary Kirstein, *The Outskirter's Secret*, 1992
Sheri S. Tepper, *After Long Silence*, 1987
Joan D. Vinge, *The Summer Queen*, 1991
David Weber, *Mutineers' Moon*, 1991

## **3751**

**ANNE MCCAFFREY**, Editor
**ELIZABETH ANN SCARBOROUGH**, Co-Editor

### *Space Opera*

(New York: DAW, 1996)

**Story type:** Science Fiction (Anthology; Arts)

**Summary:** Contains 20 original stories with an introduction by both editors and a brief biography of the author of each story. Themes revolve around music and musicians, including musicians caught in the jam, the traffic jam, a musician magician saving a town from eternal winter, and a singer in space. Authors include Robin Wayne Bailey, Peter S. Beagle, Marion Zimmer Bradley, Steven Brust, Suzette Haden Elgin, Alan Dean Foster, Anne McCaffrey, Jody Lynn Nye, Elizabeth Ann Scarborough, Josepha Sherman, and Gene Wolfe.

**Other books you might like:**
Gardner Dozois, *The Year's Best Science Fiction: Twelfth Annual Collection*, 1996
    editor
Don Sakers, *Carmen Miranda's Ghost Is Haunting Space Station Three*, 1990
Pamela Sargent, *Nebula Awards 29*, 1995
    editor
Kate Wilhelm, *And the Angels Sing*, 1992

## **3752**

**ANNE MCCAFFREY**
**JODY LYNN NYE**, Co-Author

### *Treaty at Doona*

(New York: Ace, 1994)

**Story type:** Science Fiction (First Contact; Political)
**Series:** Doona
**Major character(s):** Todd Reeve, Political Figure; Hrrestan, Alien (Hrruban), Political Figure; Grzzeearoghh "Grizz", Spaceship Captain, Alien (Gringg)
**Time period(s):** Indeterminate Future
**Locale(s):** Rraladoona, Planet—Imaginary; *Hamilton*, Spaceship

**Summary:** When the alien Gringg come to Rraladoona, Earth and Hrruban Space Force representatives plan to attack, unable to believe that the huge alien ship would come unarmed. Meanwhile, the Rraladoonans prepare to trade as they notice their children adore the aliens and that the Gringg captain brings her child to meet the humans and Hrrubans, even leaving him in their care.

**Other books you might like:**
Eleanor Arnason, *Ring of Swords*, 1993
C.J. Cherryh, *Serpent's Reach*, 1980
A.C. Crispin, *Silent Dances*, 1990
    Kathleen O'Malley, co-author
L. Warren Douglas, *Cannon's Orb*, 1994
Paula E. Downing, *Fallway*, 1993
Janet Kagan, *Hellspark*, 1988
Jody Lynn Nye, *Taylor's Ark*, 1993
Rebecca Ore, *Being Alien*, 1989

## **3753**

**ROBERT R. MCCAMMON**

### *Blue World*

(New York: Pocket, 1990)

**Story type:** Horror (Collection)

**Summary:** Thirteen stories, some previously published, including a novella, "Blue World." McCammon combines his gritty, realistic vision and deft characterization with a compression and precision not always evident in the novels. Especially noteworthy are the title novella about an unlikely alliance between a priest and a hooker to track a serial killer and "Nightcrawlers" about a Vietnam veteran who brings the war home with him—literally.

**Other books you might like:**
David Drake, *From the Heart of Darkness*, 1983
John Farris, *Scare Tactics*, 1989
Stephen King, *Night Shift*, 1978
Stephen King, *Skeleton Crew*, 1985

## **3754**

**ROBERT R. MCCAMMON**

### *Boy's Life*

(New York: Pocket, 1991)

**Story type:** Horror (Coming-of-Age)
**Major character(s):** Cory Mackenson, Child (12-year-old); Tom Mackenson, Worker (milkman), Parent (Cory's father); The Lady, Aged Person
**Time period(s):** 1960s (1964)

**Locale(s):** Zephyr, Alabama

**Summary:** This lyrical, episodic novel is told in the first-person by young Cory Mackenson, whose initiation into adulthood occurs over the course of a single summer in which he witnesses an inexplicable murder and the slow psychological decline of his father, is given a magic bike by a 102-year-old conjure woman, brings about the resurrection of his pet dog and experiences first love and first awareness of racial prejudice in the magic-laden town of Zephyr.

**Other books you might like:**
Ray Bradbury, *Dandelion Wine*, 1957
Stephen King, *It*, 1986
Dan Simmons, *Summer of Night*, 1991

---

**3755**

**ROBERT R. MCCAMMON**

## Gone South

(New York: Pocket, 1992)

**Story type:** Horror (Psychological Suspense)
**Major character(s):** Dan Lambert, Worker, Veteran (Vietnam); Flint Murtaugh, Bounty Hunter; Arden Halliday, Musician
**Time period(s):** 1990s (1991)
**Locale(s):** Shreveport, Louisiana; The Bayous, Louisiana

**Summary:** Afflicted with terminal cancer from his exposure to Agent Orange and accused of murdering a loan officer, Vietnam vet Dan Lambert flees to the Louisiana bayous, accompanied by disfigured Arden Halliday and pursued by a freaky band of bounty hunters, in what ultimately turns out to be a spiritual odyssey of healing and forgiveness.

**Other books you might like:**
Joe R. Lansdale, *Savage Season*, 1990
Peter Straub, *Koko*, 1988

---

**3756**

**ROBERT R. MCCAMMON**

## Mine

(New York: Pocket Books, 1990)

**Story type:** Horror (Psychological Suspense)
**Major character(s):** Mary ''Merry Terror'' Terrell, Terrorist (Psychotic); Laura Clayborne, Journalist, Parent
**Time period(s):** 1990s
**Locale(s):** United States

**Summary:** Psychotic ex-terrorist Mary Terrell kidnaps Laura Clayborne's baby to present to her former lover as ''their'' child. Laura gives pursuit and a wild, exciting, terrifying, violent cross-country chase ensues, a chase that threatens to turn Laura into the mirror image of her adversary.

**Other books you might like:**
Thomas Harris, *The Silence of the Lambs*, 1988
George R.R. Martin, *The Armageddon Rag*, 1983
Joel Townsley Rogers, *The Red Right Hand*, 1945
Charles Williams, *Dead Calm*, 1963
John D. MacDonald, *The Executioners*, 1958

---

**3757**

**ROBERT R. MCCAMMON**

## Swan Song

(Arlington Heights, IL: Dark Harvest, 1989)

**Story type:** Horror (Apocalyptic Horror)
**Major character(s):** Swan, Child (Focus for the ''good''); Friend, Ruler (Leader of the ''evil'' forces)
**Time period(s):** Indeterminate Future
**Locale(s):** United States

**Summary:** After nuclear war decimates most of the world, the ''good'' survivors mobilize around Swan, a young female, while ''evil'' is brought together by ''Friend.'' Thus, the forces of good and evil move together to an inevitable final confrontation.

**Other books you might like:**
Stephen King, *The Stand*, 1990

---

**3758**

**ROBERT R. MCCAMMON**, Editor

## Under the Fang

(New York: Pocket, 1991)

**Story type:** Horror (Anthology; Vampire Story)

**Summary:** Seventeen stories all predicated on the theme of a near future in which vampires have taken over the world. Selections include ''Advocates,'' Suzy McKee Charnas and Chelsea Quinn Yarbro's pairing of their vampire heroes Edward Weymouth and the Count Saint Germain; Charles de Lint's tale of gypsies collaborating with vampires, ''We Are Dead Together''; Nancy Collins' brief sketch of a vampire nightclub, ''Dancin' Nightly''; and McCammon's controversial story of a man ''protecting'' his family from the vampire onslaught, ''Miracle Mile.''

**Other books you might like:**
Ellen Datlow, *Blood Is Not Enough*, 1989
Richard Matheson, *I Am Legend*, 1954
John Skipp, *Book of the Dead*, 1989
    Craig Spector, co-author
F. Paul Wilson, *Freak Show*, 1992
F. Paul Wilson, *Midnight Mass*, 1991

---

**3759**

**ROBERT R. MCCAMMON**

## The Wolf's Hour

(New York: Pocket, 1989)

**Story type:** Horror (Werewolf Story)
**Major character(s):** Michael Gallatin, Spy, Werewolf; Chesna ''Echo'' Van Dorne, Actress (Nazi propaganda film star), Spy (For the Allies)
**Time period(s):** 1940s (1941)
**Locale(s):** London, England

**Summary:** Gallatin's mission to discover and destroy Iron Fist, a secret Nazi plot, is juxtaposed against his life as he develops from apprentice werewolf to British werewolf superspy.

**Other books you might like:**
Clive Barker, *Cabal*, 1988
Dennis Wheatley, *They Used Dark Forces*, 1964
F. Paul Wilson, *The Keep*, 1981
Chelsea Quinn Yarbro, *Tempting Fate*, 1982

## **3760**

### WIL MCCARTHY

## *Aggressor Six*

(New York: Roc, 1994)

**Story type:** Science Fiction (First Contact; Military)
**Major character(s):** Kenneth Jonson, Military Personnel (Marine corporal), Experimental Subject; Marshe "Queen" Talbott, Scientist (military exobiologist), Leader (Aggressor Six's); Josev T. Ranes, Military Personnel (Navy lieutenant), Experimental Subject
**Time period(s):** Indeterminate Future
**Locale(s):** ATG-311-B, Space Station; Outer Space

**Summary:** Fitted with a neural implant to aid his thinking in the alien language, Kenneth Jonson joins five other soldiers who attempt to understand the merciless alien invaders by adopting their lifestyle and language. First novel.

**Other books you might like:**
Roger MacBride Allen, *The Ring of Charon*, 1990
Roger MacBride Allen, *The Shattered Sphere*, 1994
Eleanor Arnason, *Ring of Swords*, 1993
Orson Scott Card, *Ender's Game*, 1985
C.J. Cherryh, *Foreigner*, 1994
Paula E. Downing, *Fallway*, 1993
David Alexander Smith, *Marathon*, 1982

## **3761**

### WIL MCCARTHY

## *Bloom*

(New York: Ballantine Del Rey, 1998)

**Story type:** Science Fiction (End of the World; Alternate Intelligence)
**Major character(s):** John Strasheim, Worker (shoemaker), Journalist; Vaclav Lottick, Administrator (research), Leader (of the Immunity); Darren Wallich, Doctor, Spaceship Captain
**Time period(s):** 2100s
**Locale(s):** Ganymede, Jupiter; *Louis Pasteur*, Spaceship; Saint Helier, Asteroid

**Summary:** Most citizens of the Immunity, the last humans in the solar system, live in constant fear of the Mycosystem, a group of tiny machinelike organisms, which now extends beyond Mars' orbit. When the blooms of the mycora seem to contain human DNA, a tiny ship makes a trip to earth in hopes of discovering humans still alive in the inner system, despite possible sabotage from the Temple of Transcendent Evolution, whose members suspect the Mycosystem is intelligent.

**Other books you might like:**
Mona Clee, *Overshoot*, 1998
Tom Cool, *Infectress*, 1997
C.S. Friedman, *This Alien Shore*, 1998
Charles Sheffield, *Aftermath*, 1998
John Varley, *Steel Beach*, 1992

## **3762**

### WIL MCCARTHY

## *The Fall of Sirius*

(New York: Roc, 1996)

**Story type:** Science Fiction (First Contact; Science Fiction)

**Major character(s):** Malyene Andreivne "Malye" Kurosov'e, Leader; Viktor Slavanovot, Repairman
**Time period(s):** 53rd century
**Locale(s):** Pinega, Planet—Imaginary (Sirius/Gate System); Holders Fastness, Planet—Imaginary (Sirius/Gate System); Suzerainty of Human Spaces, Interstellar Empire/Federation

**Summary:** Entering cryostasis to avoid the attack of the alien Waisters, Malye and Viktor find themselves awakened two millennia later, when their wartime experience with invading Waisters might prove valuable to the descendents of survivors, now faced with another invasion of the mysterious Waisters. Sequel set 2000 years after *Aggressor Six*.

**Other books you might like:**
Roger MacBride Allen, *The Ring of Charon*, 1990
Roger MacBride Allen, *The Shattered Sphere*, 1994
Eleanor Arnason, *Ring of Swords*, 1993
Jeffrey A. Carver, *Neptune Crossing*, 1994
Vernor Vinge, *A Fire upon the Deep*, 1992
David Weber, *Mutineers' Moon*, 1991
David Weber, *Path of the Fury*, 1992

## **3763**

### WIL MCCARTHY

## *Flies From the Amber*

(New York: Roc, 1995)

**Story type:** Science Fiction (Hard Science Fiction; First Contact)
**Major character(s):** Tomus Kreider, Spaceman, Scientist; Jhoe Freetz, Spaceman, Scientist; Luna Shiloh, Government Official
**Time period(s):** Indeterminate Future
**Locale(s):** Malhela System, Outer Space; Unua, Planet—Imaginary; *Introspectia*, Spaceship

**Summary:** Malhelan miners find a new substance in their peculiar solar system, motivating Earth to send an exploratory expedition of scientists. Distressed to find the deposit totally played out, yet certain the material springs from alien science, the Terrans detect alien material close to the event horizon of the system's ancient collapsed star.

**Other books you might like:**
Roger MacBride Allen, *The Ring of Charon*, 1990
Stephen Baxter, *Raft*, 1991
Gregory Benford, *Furious Gulf*, 1994
Mary Gentle, *Golden Witchbreed*, 1984
Jack McDevitt, *The Engines of God*, 1994
Sheri S. Tepper, *Grass*, 1989

## **3764**

### WIL MCCARTHY

## *Murder in the Solid State*

(New York: Tor, 1996)

**Story type:** Science Fiction (Mystery; Adventure)
**Major character(s):** David Sanger, Scientist (physicist); T. Bowser Jones, Lawyer; Marian Fouts, Journalist
**Time period(s):** 21st century
**Locale(s):** Baltimore, Maryland; Philadelphia, Pennsylvania; Cyberspace

**Summary:** Offended at a party by David Sanger's insult, the established patriarch of nanotechnology rushes into a high-tech swordfight with David, who wins due to his streetfighting skills, embarrassing the elder professor. The next day police accuse David of murder when they discover the professor's body and the weapon David had used in the non-lethal fight. Freed with Bowser's help, David must disappear from sight to avoid those willing to kill over the implications of David's revolutionary nanotechnology development.

**Other books you might like:**
Pat Cadigan, *Synners*, 1991
Jeffrey A. Carver, *From a Changeling Star*, 1989
Michael Flynn, *In the Country of the Blind*, 1990
Lisa Mason, *Arachne*, 1990
Robert J. Sawyer, *The Terminal Experiment*, 1995

## 3765

### DENNIS MCCARTY

## Across the Thlassa Mey

(New York: Ballantine/Del Rey, 1991)

**Story type:** Fantasy (Quest)
**Series:** Thlassa Mey
**Major character(s):** Palamon, Royalty, Adventurer
**Time period(s):** Indeterminate
**Locale(s):** Thlassa Mey, Mythical Place (Sea)

**Summary:** When he responds to the Oracle's summons, King Palamon hears of a great evil about to befall lands around the Thlassa Mey. Hoping to find his long-lost son and save the area from the prophecied evil, King Palamon dons his armor and mystic sword and sets off to find the Tome of Winds, knowing that his advanced age works against his success.

**Other books you might like:**
David Eddings, *Pawn of Prophecy*, 1982
Phyllis Eisenstein, *The Crystal Palace*, 1988
Robert Jordan, *The Eye of the World*, 1990
Guy Gavriel Kay, *The Summer Tree*, 1985
J.R.R. Tolkien, *The Fellowship of the Ring*, 1954
J.R.R. Tolkien, *The Hobbit*, 1938

## 3766

### DENNIS MCCARTY

## The Birth of the Blade

(New York: Ballantine Del Rey, 1993)

**Story type:** Fantasy (Political; Quest)
**Series:** Thlassa Mey
**Major character(s):** Geryam, Military Personnel, Hero; Lissa, Maiden; Rinna, Maiden
**Time period(s):** Indeterminate
**Locale(s):** Thlassa Mey, Mythical Place (sea)

**Summary:** The Goddess Pellas choses Geryam, Lissa and Rinna to thwart priests of the Dark Order whose evil magic controls the realms surrounding the Thlassa Mey. The trio follows Pellas' command, unaware of the sacrifice and danger involved as the priests strive to create even more powerful devices.

**Other books you might like:**
Carol Chase, *Hawk's Flight*, 1991
Jo Clayton, *Wild Magic*, 1991
Jo Clayton, *Wildfire*, 1992
David Eddings, *Pawn of Prophecy*, 1982
Mary Gentle, *Rats and Gargoyles*, 1991
P.C. Hodgell, *God Stalk*, 1982

## 3767

### BILL MCCAY
### ELOISE FLOOD, Co-Author

## Chains of Command

(New York: Pocket, 1992)

**Story type:** Science Fiction (Space Opera; Post-Holocaust)
**Series:** Star Trek: The Next Generation
**Major character(s):** Jean-Luc Picard, Spaceship Captain, Military Personnel; Beverly Crusher, Doctor, Space Explorer; Deanna Troi, Empath, Psychologist
**Time period(s):** 24th century
**Locale(s):** *U.S.S. Enterprise*, Spaceship; Koorn, Planet—Imaginary

**Summary:** Captain Picard sends an away team down to the planet Koorn in the midst of a slave rebellion. Human descendants of refugees from 21st century Earth warfare, the slaves have killed or captured their birdlike masters, the Tseetsk. Picard and Counselor Troi attempt to negotiate a peaceful settlement, but some of the rebels fear betrayal and take Picard and Troi hostage. The rebels' plans go awry when they meet the planet's natives.

**Other books you might like:**
Margaret Wander Bonanno, *Dwellers in the Crucible*, 1985
A.C. Crispin, *Silent Dances*, 1990
   Kathleen O'Malley, co-author
Gordon R. Dickson, *Way of the Pilgrim*, 1987
L.A. Graf, *Ice Trap*, 1992
Robert A. Heinlein, *Citizen of the Galaxy*, 1957
T.L. Mancour, *Spartacus*, 1992

## 3768

### BILL MCCAY
### DAVE GIBBONS, Illustrator

## Crossover

(New York: Roc, 1993)

**Story type:** Fantasy (Contemporary; Light Fantasy)
**Series:** Stan Lee's Riftworld
**Major character(s):** Harry Sturdley, Publisher (of comic books)
**Time period(s):** 1990s
**Locale(s):** New York, New York

**Summary:** An enchanted rift opens between Earth and the comic book realm allowing giant-sized superheroes to invade New York and presenting Harry Sturdley with the opportunity of a lifetime to get them under contract. First of a series.

**Other books you might like:**
Michael Bishop, *Count Geiger's Blues*, 1992
Craig Shaw Gardner, *Revenge of the Fluffy Bunnies*, 1990
Martin H. Greenberg, *The Further Adventures of Superman*, 1992
   editor
Clifford D. Simak, *Out of Their Minds*, 1970
Roger Stern, *The Death and Life of Superman*, 1993
Gary K. Wolf, *Who Censored Roger Rabbit?*, 1981
Gary K. Wolf, *Who P-P-Plugged Roger Rabbit?*, 1991

## 3769
### BILL MCCAY

## *Reconnaissance*
(New York: Roc, 1998)

**Story type:** Science Fiction (Space Opera)
**Series:** Stargate
**Major character(s):** Jack O'Neill, Military Personnel (colonel); Daniel Jackson, Scientist
**Time period(s):** Indeterminate Future
**Locale(s):** Ballas, Planet—Imaginary

**Summary:** The inhabitants of the planet Abydos use stargates to colonize the planet Ballas, which is more hospitable than their home world. Unfortunately, there are indigenous aliens on Ballas, warriors who plot to kill the invaders and seize control of the stargates. O'Neill and Jackson teach the colonists how to defend themselves.

**Other books you might like:**
Poul Anderson, *War of the Wing-Men*, 1958
Gordon R. Dickson, *Masters of Everon*, 1979
Alan Dean Foster, *The Howling Stones*, 1997
Andre Norton, *Star Born*, 1958
Chad Oliver, *Unearthly Neighbors*, 1960

## 3770
### MICHAEL MCCOLLUM

## *The Clouds of Saturn*
(New York: Ballantine/Del Rey, 1991)

**Story type:** Science Fiction (Post-Holocaust; Space Colony)
**Major character(s):** Larson Clarke Sands, Pilot (airship captain); Mikal Blount, Military Personnel (Northern Alliance Navy Admiral)
**Time period(s):** Indeterminate Future
**Locale(s):** *Sparrow Hawk*, Spaceship (in Saturn's atmosphere), Cloudcroft, Saturn

**Summary:** The Sun has entered a flare stage and Earth is no longer habitable. Humanity has moved to a viable layer of Saturn's atmosphere where large floating cities bear most of Earth's population. The Northern Alliance plans to unite all of humanity under their control. After Lars' brother dies during a Northern Alliance attack on the cloud city, New Philadelphia, Lars must find new employment for his ship, *Sparrow Hawk*, and avenge his brother's death.

**Other books you might like:**
James Blish, *A Life for the Stars*, 1962
Diana G. Gallagher, *The Alien Dark*, 1990
Larry Niven, *The Integral Trees*, 1984
Larry Niven, *The Smoke Ring*, 1987
Allen Steele, *Clarke County, Space*, 1990

## 3771
### MICHAEL MCCOLLUM

## *The Sails of Tau Ceti*
(New York: Ballantine Del Rey, 1992)

**Story type:** Science Fiction (First Contact)
**Major character(s):** Victoria ''Tory'' Bronson, Spacewoman; Faslorn, Alien (Phelan); Kit Claridge, Doctor, Spacewoman
**Time period(s):** 23rd century (2200s)
**Locale(s):** Outer Space; Earth; *Starhopper*, Spaceship

**Summary:** Tau Ceti has gone nova in 2001. Observers on Earth sight an alien light sail in that direction weeks before the launch of the *Starhopper* probe. Designated as advocate for the aliens, Tory must find room for the aliens on Earth without revealing the only alternative, total destruction.

**Other books you might like:**
Greg Bear, *Eon*, 1985
Johanna Bolton, *Mission: Tori*, 1990
Diana G. Gallagher, *The Alien Dark*, 1990
Ursula K. Le Guin, *Always Coming Home*, 1987
Jack McKinney, *Kaduna Memories*, 1990
Larry Niven, *Tales of Known Space*, 1975
Harry Turtledove, *Krispos Rising*, 1991

## 3772
### MICHAEL MCCOLLUM

## *Thunder Strike!*
(New York: Ballantine/Del Rey, 1989)

**Story type:** Science Fiction (Disaster)
**Major character(s):** Thomas Thorpe, Engineer; Amber Hastings, Scientist
**Time period(s):** 21st century
**Locale(s):** Montenegro; Asteroid

**Summary:** A comet is on track to strike the Earth and scientists struggle desperately to deflect it.

**Other books you might like:**
Gregory Benford, *Heart of the Comet*, 1986
  David Brin, co-author
Gregory Benford, *Shiva Descending*, 1980
  William Rotsler, co-author
Larry Niven, *Lucifer's Hammer*, 1977
  Jerry Pournelle, co-author

## 3773
### ASHLEY MCCONNELL

## *The Courts of Sorcery*
(New York: Ace, 1997)

**Story type:** Fantasy (Magic Conflict; Political)
**Series:** Demon Wars Trilogy
**Major character(s):** Jazen, Sorcerer (exorcist)
**Time period(s):** Indeterminate
**Locale(s):** Mirlacca, Fictional City

**Summary:** Having rid Eberly of its demon, Jazen returns to Mirlacca. Unfortunately the demon now possesses Jazen, hoping to use the Guild of Exorcists' knowledge to acquire access to his home, the world of evil. Third in series.

**Other books you might like:**
Charles de Lint, *Trader*, 1997
Susan Dexter, *The Wizard's Shadow*, 1993
P.C. Hodgell, *God Stalk*, 1982
J. Gregory Keyes, *The Blackgod*, 1997
J. Gregory Keyes, *The Waterborn*, 1996

## 3774

### ASHLEY MCCONNELL

## Days of the Dead

(New York: Diamond, 1992)

**Story type:** Horror (Occult)
**Major character(s):** Diane Lassiter, Engineer; Carlos Aguilar, Teenager; Gil Santillanes, Handyman
**Time period(s):** 1990s (October, 1992)
**Locale(s):** Desolada, New Mexico

**Summary:** Not until she moves into the house of her fiance's recently deceased aunt does Diane Lassiter discover that the old woman was an Aztec witch whose successive reincarnations have given her the power to call forth the dear departed on the forthcoming Day of the Dead festivities.

**Other books you might like:**
Ramsey Campbell, *The Influence*, 1988
Stephanie Kegan, *The Baby*, 1990
Robert Marasco, *Burnt Offerings*, 1973

## 3775

### ASHLEY MCCONNELL

## The Fountains of Mirlacca

(New York: Ace, 1995)

**Story type:** Fantasy (Magic Conflict)
**Series:** Demon Wars Trilogy
**Major character(s):** Jazen, Sorcerer (exorcist); Vettazen, Sorceress (Guild of Exorcists)
**Time period(s):** Indeterminate
**Locale(s):** Mirlacca, Fictional City

**Summary:** Hoping to learn control of his ability to make things burst into flame, Jazen accompanies Vettazne to Exorcists School in Mirlacca. When Vettazen disappears, Jazen attempts to uncover the secret of Mirlacca's fountains, which run red with blood, and discover his destiny. First of a trilogy.

**Other books you might like:**
Don Callander, *Pyromancer*, 1992
Laurell K. Hamilton, *Nightseer*, 1992
Robin Hobb, *Assassin's Apprentice*, 1995
J.V. Jones, *The Baker's Boy*, 1995
Martha Wells, *The Element of Fire*, 1993

## 3776

### ASHLEY MCCONNELL

## The Itinerant Exorcist

(New York: Ace, 1996)

**Story type:** Fantasy (Magic Conflict)
**Series:** Demon Wars Trilogy
**Major character(s):** Jazen sr'Yat, Sorcerer; Davos, Healer, Demon; Misele E'lan, Waiter/Waitress (innkeeper's daughter)
**Time period(s):** Indeterminate
**Locale(s):** Eberly, Fictional City; Mirlacca, Fictional City

**Summary:** Jazen travels from Mirlacca to the village of Eberly in search of Davos, whom he hopes to recruit into the still-secret Guild of Exorcists. He must use his own magic cautiously, for fear of persecution as one of the Yaan Maat, demons who can possess a human body and work magic. When the villagers imprison Davos as a demon, Jazen tries to prevent his execution, coming under suspicion himself. He then finds that worse things can happen than being burned at the stake. Sequel to *The Fountains of Mirlacca*.

**Other books you might like:**
C.J. Cherryh, *Rusalka*, 1989
Gayle Greeno, *Finders-Seekers*, 1993
Barbara Hambly, *Stranger at the Wedding*, 1994
Katherine Kurtz, *Saint Camber*, 1978
Mercedes Lackey, *When the Bough Breaks*, 1993
Patricia C. Wrede, *Mairelon the Magician*, 1991

## 3777

### ASHLEY MCCONNELL

## Stargate SG-1

(New York: Roc, 1998)

**Story type:** Science Fiction (Space Opera)
**Series:** Stargate SG-1
**Major character(s):** Jack O'Neill, Military Personnel (colonel); Apophis, Alien; Kawalsky, Military Personnel
**Time period(s):** Indeterminate Future
**Locale(s):** Abydos, Planet—Imaginary

**Summary:** The Stargate provides instantaneous travel to the planet Abydos, but when humans use it to explore that planet, they attract the attention of a godlike alien race. Although they killed the leader of the aliens before he could attack the Earth, a successor has seized power. An elite military force from Earth travels through the gate to track down the alien and eliminate him before he can organize an invasion.

**Other books you might like:**
Poul Anderson, *The Enemy Stars*, 1959
John Brunner, *The Web of Everywhere*, 1974
Kenneth Bulmer, *The Chariots of Ra*, 1972
C.J. Cherryh, *Exile's Gate*, 1988
Robert Hoskins, *To Control the Stars*, 1977

## 3778

### ASHLEY MCCONNELL

## Unearthed

(New York: Diamond, 1991)

**Story type:** Horror (Small Town Horror)
**Major character(s):** David Esher, Writer; Harry Kostner, Miner (owner of the Heartbreak Mine); Rick Zimmerman, Bodyguard
**Time period(s):** 1990s
**Locale(s):** Nintucca, Nevada

**Summary:** The town of Nintucca is just another one-horse town on the edge of the Nevada atomic bomb test range until the much reviled Harry Kostner decides to reopen the abandoned Heartbreak Mine. Soon, something at the bottom of the mine that doesn't like being disturbed begins manifesting to the townspeople under a variety of guises, all lethal. This is the author's first novel.

**Other books you might like:**
Joseph A. Citro, *Dark Twilight*, 1991
Douglas Clegg, *Goat Dance*, 1989
G. Wayne Miller, *Thunder Rise*, 1988
Steve Rasnic Tem, *Excavation*, 1987

## 3779

### ERIC MCCORMACK

## *First Blast of the Trumpet Against the Monstrous Regiment of Women*
(New York: Penguin, 1998)

**Story type:** Horror (Coming-of-Age)
**Major character(s):** Andrew Halfnight, Orphan; Harry Greene, Sailor
**Time period(s):** 1990s (1998)
**Locale(s):** Stroven, Canada

**Summary:** Orphaned by the age of 12, Andrew Halfnight spends much of his life haunted by dreams of stern-faced, black clad women. As he shuttles back and forth between towns in Canada and the Island of St. Jude, followed by tragedy, Andrew begins to discover that the dreams are the key to his origins and his future. First published in Canada in 1997.

**Other books you might like:**
Robert Aickman, *The Wine-Dark Sea*, 1988
Clive Barker, *The Thief of Always*, 1992
Raymond E. Feist, *Faerie Tale*, 1988
Stephen King, *The Talisman*, 1985
  Peter Straub, co-author
Patrick McGrath, *Dr. Haggard's Disease*, 1993

## 3780

### ERIC MCCORMACK

## *The Mysterium*
(New York: St. Martin's Press, 1994)

**Story type:** Horror (Mystery)
**Major character(s):** James Maxwell, Journalist; Reeve Blair, Police Officer; Robert Aiken, Pharmacist
**Time period(s):** 1990s (1992)
**Locale(s):** Carrick, Canada

**Summary:** James Maxwell is summoned to a distant island to unravel a mystery in which the apparent poisoning of the town in retribution for a crime committed decades before causes unique symptoms in each victim. As James examines different townspeople and hears their often conflicting stories about what has happened, he becomes overwhelmed by the sense of how little we know about our world and ourselves. This novel was first published in Canada in 1992.

**Other books you might like:**
Paul Auster, *The New York Trilogy*, 1990
Philip K. Dick, *The Three Stigmata of Palmer Eldritch*, 1965
Peter Straub, *The Throat*, 1993

## 3781

### MARA MCCUNIFF
### TRACI BRIERY, Co-Author

## *The Vampire Memoirs*
(New York: Zebra, 1991)

**Story type:** Horror (Vampire Story)
**Major character(s):** Mara McCunniff, Vampire; Gaarius "Gaar" Latticus, Warrior; Agyar, Political Figure (magistrate of ancient Gaul)
**Time period(s):** 4th century; 20th century
**Locale(s):** Los Angeles, California; Europe

**Summary:** Tracy Briery has helped 1600-year-old vampire Mara McCunniff transcribe the memoirs of her life, which began in the British Isles in 362 A.D. and led naturally to her settling in Los Angeles in the 20th century. Her tale is one of eternal love and perpetual hunger, as she tries to survive inconspicuously through the centuries, pursuing incarnations of her beloved first husband Gaar and avoiding the reappearance of her vampire nemesis Agyar.

**Other books you might like:**
Anne Rice, *The Vampire Lestat*, 1985
Michael Romkey, *I, Vampire*, 1990
S.P. Somtow, *Vampire Junction*, 1984
Chelsea Quinn Yarbro, *The Olivia Trilogy*, 1987-1989

## 3782

### ABIGAIL MCDANIELS (Pseudonym of Dan Trent and Lynda Trent)

## *Althea*
(New York: Zebra, 1995)

**Story type:** Horror (Possession)
**Major character(s):** Carol Horton, Lawyer; Holly Horton, Child (nine-year-old); Lisa Horton, Teenager
**Time period(s):** 1990s (1995)
**Locale(s):** Coulee, Louisiana

**Summary:** When Carol Horton inherits her family's Louisiana home, she inherits the legacy of horror that comes with it: an ornamental doll that contains the evil soul of Althea, a relative who murdered her child at the turn of the century and who has been waiting ever since to project herself into a living vessel.

**Other books you might like:**
Algernon Blackwood, *The Doll and One Other*, 1947
Matthew J. Costello, *Child's Play III*, 1991
Pat Graversen, *Dollies*, 1990
Ruby Jean Jensen, *Baby Dolly*, 1991
Ruby Jean Jensen, *Victoria*, 1990

## 3783

### ABIGAIL MCDANIELS (Pseudonym of Dan Trent and Lynda Trent)

## *Dead Voices*
(New York: Zebra, 1994)

**Story type:** Horror (Supernatural Vengeance)
**Major character(s):** Gail Lamont, Housewife; Roger Lamont, Businessman (for Woodbine Oil); Jerome Green, Religious
**Time period(s):** 1990s (1994)
**Locale(s):** New Falls Church, Louisiana

**Summary:** Shortly after moving into their new home near Lake Boudreaux, Gail and Roger Lamont are plagued by a series of "crank" phone calls and menacing apparitions attributable to long-dead townsfolk. Investigation reveals that the dead all have one thing in common: they were buried in a cemetery supposedly moved to higher ground before the encroaching lake inundated the older sections of the town.

**Other books you might like:**
Matthew J. Costello, *Beneath Still Waters*, 1989
Elizabeth Forrest, *Dark Tide*, 1993
Steve Rasnic Tem, *Excavation*, 1987
T.M. Wright, *The Island*, 1988

## 3784

**ABIGAIL MCDANIELS** (Pseudonym of Dan Trent and Lynda Trent)

### Playmates
(New York: Zebra)

**Story type:** Horror (Child-in-Peril)
**Major character(s):** Cassie Walker, Child (6 year old girl); Mark Walker, Parent (Cassie's father), Scientist (chemist); Janet Walker, Parent (Cassie's mother), Housewife
**Time period(s):** 1990s (1993)
**Locale(s):** Apollo, Louisiana

**Summary:** Several little girls who have lived in the old Morton House over the past century have died under mysterious circumstances, and Cassie Walker knows why: Ara, a doll found in the playhouse behind the house, is imbued with the vengeful soul of a young girl who was mistreated by the house's original owners.

**Other books you might like:**
Matthew J. Costello, *Child's Play III*, 1991
Pat Graversen, *Dollies*, 1990
Ellen Jamison, *Stone Dead*, 1993
Ruby Jean Jensen, *Baby Dolly*, 1991
Ruby Jean Jensen, *The Living Evil*, 1993

## 3785

**ABIGAIL MCDANIELS** (Pseudonym of Dan Trent and Lynda Trent)

### The Uprising
(New York: Zebra, 1994)

**Story type:** Horror (Ghost Story; Supernatural Vengeance)
**Major character(s):** Tess Bowen, Teacher (art); Tracy Wright, Teenager; Kevin Donatello, Teenager
**Time period(s):** 1990s (1994)
**Locale(s):** Maple Glen, Missouri

**Summary:** Under the instruction of fascistic Kevin Donatello, 12 students of Maple Glen High School commit suicide in the belief that they will attain occult powers. When the students in his new cult begin dying gruesome deaths, Kevin realizes that the original 12 are reaching from beyond the grave to exact their revenge.

**Other books you might like:**
Dennis Etchison, *Darkside*, 1986
Keith Ferrario, *Deadly Friend*, 1994
Stephen King, *Carrie*, 1974
Jean Simon, *Ghost Boy*, 1994

## 3786

**JACK MCDEVITT**

### Ancient Shores
(New York: HarperPrism, 1996)

**Story type:** Science Fiction (Political; Contemporary Realism)
**Major character(s):** Tom Lasker, Farmer; Max Collingwood, Pilot; April Cannon, Scientist
**Time period(s):** 1990s
**Locale(s):** Fort Moxie, North Dakota; Walhalla, North Dakota

**Summary:** The boat Tom digs up from his field draws too much attention to his rural North Dakota town, since it seems to have sunk while Lake Agassis still held water. Max and April discover another artifact on American Indian land which leads to speculation about flying saucers and, perhaps, impending economic collapse.

**Other books you might like:**
Greg Bear, *Eon*, 1985
Gregory Benford, *Timescape*, 1980
John Brunner, *The Shockwave Rider*, 1975
Michael D. Weaver, *My Father Immortal*, 1989
George Zebrowski, *Stranger Suns*, 1991

## 3787

**JACK MCDEVITT**

### The Engines of God
(New York: Ace, 1994)

**Story type:** Science Fiction (Science Fiction; Political)
**Major character(s):** Priscilla "Hutch" Hutchins, Spacewoman, Pilot (spaceship); Henry Jacobi, Engineer, Anthropologist; Richard Wald, Anthropologist
**Time period(s):** 23rd century (2200s)
**Locale(s):** Quaraqua, Planet—Imaginary; Oz, Moon—Imaginary (Quaraqua's); *Johann Winkelmann*, Spaceship

**Summary:** After a lower chamber of the Temple of Winds on Quaraqua produces tempting insights into the enigma of Oz, Richard Wald attempts to delay the imminent catastrophic terraforming of Quaraqua. Although the intelligent natives had only very recently died out, Quaraqua may once have been technologically advanced. The Oz object proves similar to other objects near once populated worlds, and may lead to the objects' creators and their significance.

**Other books you might like:**
Roger MacBride Allen, *The Ring of Charon*, 1990
Mary Gentle, *Golden Witchbreed*, 1984
Frank M. Robinson, *The Dark Beyond the Stars*, 1991
Allen Steele, *Labyrinth of Night*, 1992
Vernor Vinge, *A Fire upon the Deep*, 1992

## 3788

**JACK MCDEVITT**

### Eternity Road
(New York: HarperPrism, 1997)

**Story type:** Science Fiction (Post-Disaster; Quest)
**Major character(s):** Chaka Milana, Hunter, Scholar; Flojian Endine, Businessman (ferry boat operator); Quait Esterhok, Military Personnel
**Time period(s):** Indeterminate Future
**Locale(s):** Mississippi River, North America; New England

**Summary:** Only one member of an expedition to find Abraham Polk's Haven returns, dying soon after. Nevertheless, chafing at restrictions on a woman's role in Illyria, Chaka Milana decides to mount a second expedition. When half their number die almost immediately, the three survivors continue, finding Haven different than they expect with an expanding civilization having more technology and further knowledge of the Roadmaker culture.

**Other books you might like:**
Poul Anderson, *Orion Shall Rise*, 1983
Leigh Brackett, *The Long Tomorrow*, 1955
Kathleen Ann Goonan, *Queen City Jazz*, 1994
Sterling E. Lanier, *Hiero's Journey*, 1973
Andre Norton, *Daybreak, 2250 A.D.*, 1954
   originally published as *Star Man's Son*
Edgar Pangborn, *Davy*, 1964

Clifford D. Simak, *A Heritage of Stars*, 1977
Paul O. Williams, *The Song of the Axe*, 1984

---

**3789**

JACK MCDEVITT

## *Moonfall*

(New York: HarperPrism, 1998)

**Story type:** Science Fiction (Disaster; Hard Science Fiction)
**Major character(s):** Rachel Quinn, Spacewoman, Spaceship Captain; Charles L. "Charlie" Haskell, Political Figure (vice president); Evelyn Hampton, Administrator (Moonbase International), Businesswoman
**Time period(s):** 2020s (2024)
**Locale(s):** Moonbase, Montenegro; Washington, District of Columbia; Skyport, Space Station (Smithsonian Orbital Laboratory at L1)

**Summary:** On the moon for the opening of the very expensive and politically important Moonbase International, Charlie remains behind when comet Tomiko, detected during the total eclipse that coincided with the base's opening forces the evacuation of all present. Unusually fast, the comet will collide with the moon in five days, shattering it.

**Other books you might like:**
Stephen Baxter, *Titan*, 1997
David Brin, *Earth*, 1990
Michael Flynn, *Rogue Star*, 1998
Allen Steele, *Orbital Decay*, 1989
Bruce Sterling, *Heavy Weather*, 1994
Roger Zelazny, *Flare*, 1992
  Thomas T. Thomas, co-author

---

**3790**

JACK MCDEVITT

## *A Talent for War*

(New York: Ace, 1989)

**Story type:** Science Fiction (Military)
**Major character(s):** Alex Benedict, Businessman; Christopher Sims, Warrior
**Time period(s):** 31st century
**Locale(s):** Rimway, Planet—Imaginary

**Summary:** Alex Benedict, a young businessman, discovers that one of his culture's greatest heroes, the warrior Christopher Sim, who supposedly saved humanity from marauding aliens, may have been a fraud. In order to discover the truth, Benedict follows the tracks of a legend into incredible danger and mystery.

**Other books you might like:**
Orson Scott Card, *Ender's Game*, 1985
Orson Scott Card, *Speaker for the Dead*, 1986
Gordon R. Dickson, *Lost Dorsai*, 1980
Gordon R. Dickson, *Soldier, Ask Not*, 1967
Gordon R. Dickson, *The Tactics of Mistake*, 1971
Mike Resnick, *Ivory: A Legend of Past and Future*, 1988
Mike Resnick, *Paradise: A Chronicle of a Distant World*, 1989

---

**3791**

IAN MCDONALD

## *The Broken Land*

(New York: Bantam Spectra, 1992)

**Story type:** Science Fiction (Political; Genetic Manipulation)
**Major character(s):** Mathembe Fileli, Refugee; Kalimuni, Religious (advocate), Lawyer; Grandfather Fileli, Handicapped (severed head)
**Time period(s):** Indeterminate Future
**Locale(s):** Chepsenyt, Fictional City; Ol Tah, Fictional City

**Summary:** The Confessors and the Proclaimers, in conflict for centuries, react with equal confusion and unease when the Empire Across the River annexes their lands and changes their lives. When a resident hides two of the Warriors of Destiny, a rebellious paramilitary group, the Empire destroys Chepsenyt, leaving Methembe, homeless and friendless, to wander in a strange and cruel world. Her experiences as she tries to make her way in the big city underline the plight of people in countries torn by religious and political strife.

**Other books you might like:**
Iain M. Banks, *The Bridge*, 1986
John Crowley, *Little, Big*, 1981
Lisa Goldstein, *A Mask for the General*, 1987
M. John Harrison, *The Pastel City*, 1971
Geoff Ryman, *The Unconquered Country*, 1986

---

**3792**

IAN MCDONALD

## *Evolution's Shore*

(New York: Bantam Spectra, 1995)

**Story type:** Science Fiction (First Contact; Invasion of Earth)
**Major character(s):** Gabriel "Gaby" McAslan, Journalist; Dr. M. Shepard, Scientist (molecular biologist); T.P. Costello, Journalist (Nairobi Skynet station chief)
**Time period(s):** 2000s
**Locale(s):** Nairobi, Kenya

**Summary:** An ambitious journalist for Skynet News, Gaby McAslan devotes her career to reporting about the Chaga, a meteor-borne biological entity that gradually overtakes the African continent, physically changing those humans and animals who do not get out of its path.

**Other books you might like:**
J.G. Ballard, *The Crystal World*, 1966
Greg Bear, *Blood Music*, 1985
Octavia E. Butler, *Adulthood Rites*, 1988
Octavia E. Butler, *Dawn*, 1987
Octavia E. Butler, *Imago*, 1989
Arthur C. Clarke, *Childhood's End*, 1953
Nancy Kress, *Beggars and Choosers*, 1994

---

**3793**

IAN MCDONALD

## *King of Morning, Queen of Day*

(New York: Bantam Spectra, 1991)

**Story type:** Fantasy (Contemporary)
**Major character(s):** Emily Desmond, Teenager; Jessica Caldwell, Waiter/Waitress; Enye MacColl, Advertising, Courier

**Time period(s):** 20th century
**Locale(s):** County Sligo, Ireland; Dublin, Ireland

**Summary:** A family story stretching across three generations, *King of Morning, Queen of Day* follows the effects of meddling with the powers of Faerie from one end of the 20th century to the other. Each section functions as a complete story with its own style, linked by the readers' growing understanding of the overall plot. The first part, "Craigdarragh" appeared in an earlier version as "King of Morning, Queen of Day" in *Empire Dreams* (1988).

**Other books you might like:**
James P. Blaylock, *Land of Dreams*, 1987
John Crowley, *Little, Big*, 1981
Greer Ilene Gilman, *Moonwise*, 1991
Robert Holdstock, *Mythago Wood*, 1984
Christoph Ransmayr, *The Last World*, 1990

---

**3794**

**IAN MCDONALD**

### Out on Blue Six
(New York: Bantam Spectra, 1989)

**Story type:** Science Fiction (Dystopian)
**Major character(s):** Courtney Hall, Artist (Cartoonist), Revolutionary; Kilimanjaro West, Revolutionary, Amnesiac
**Time period(s):** Indeterminate Future
**Locale(s):** Earth

**Summary:** Courtney Hall, a cartoonist disgusted by the limits put upon her art by the censors of Great Yu, goes underground and meets a series of misfit artists, revolutionaries and madmen, all of whom are criminals under the laws of the Compassionate Society. Attempts are made to escape from Great Yu or transform it.

**Other books you might like:**
Richard Grant, *Rumors of Spring*, 1987
Aldous Huxley, *Brave New World*, 1932
Frederik Pohl, *The Space Merchants*, 1955
   C. M. Kornbluth, co-author
Bruce Sterling, *Islands in the Net*, 1988
Jack Williamson, *The Humanoids*, 1949

---

**3795**

**IAN MCDONALD**

### Scissors Cut Paper Wrap Stone
(New York: Bantam Spectra, 1994)

**Story type:** Science Fiction (Mystical; Cyberpunk)
**Major character(s):** Ethan Ring, Artist, Spy; Masahiko, Artist; Luba Casipriadin, Artist
**Time period(s):** 21st century
**Locale(s):** Japan

**Summary:** While on a 1000-mile pilgrimage of the 88 temples, Ethan Ring frees himself from the power symbols tattooed on his palms by a secret government agency. With the help of a computer, the symbols allow him to control a person's primitive subconscious responses, such as healing or fear, but make it impossible for Ethan to have a normal life.

**Other books you might like:**
Poul Anderson, *The Stars Are Also Fire*, 1994
Jean Mark Gawron, *Dream of Glass*, 1993
Victor Milan, *The Cybernetic Samurai*, 1985
Frederik Pohl, *Gladiator-at-Law*, 1955
   C.M. Kornbluth, co-author

---

Rudy Rucker, *Wetware*, 1988
Walter Jon Williams, *Voice of the Whirlwind*, 1987

---

**3796**

**IAN MCDONALD**

### Speaking in Tongues
(New York: Bantam Spectra, 1992)

**Story type:** Science Fiction (Collection)

**Summary:** Eleven stories published in periodicals and anthologies in England and the United States 1989-1991. Themes range widely from the arts in "Approaching Perpendicular," to ethics in "Fronts," with matter transmission examined in "Gardenias," time travel in "Atomic Avenue," fiction writing by an intelligent computer in "Speaking in Tongues" and an equally broad variety of themes in the remaining 6 stories.

**Other books you might like:**
J.G. Ballard, *War Fever*, 1991
Michael Flynn, *The Nanotech Chronicles*, 1991
Damon Knight, *One Side Laughing: Stories Unlike Other Stories*, 1991
Keith Laumer, *Alien Minds*, 1991
Cordwainer Smith, *The Best of Cordwainer Smith*, 1975
Michael Swanwick, *Gravity's Angels*, 1991

---

**3797**

**IAN MCDONALD**

### Terminal Cafe
(New York: Bantam Spectra, 1994)

**Story type:** Science Fiction (Cyberpunk; Genetic Manipulation)
**Major character(s):** Santiago Columbar, Artist (drugs)
**Time period(s):** 21st century
**Locale(s):** Los Angeles, California; St. John, California

**Summary:** Nanotechnology allows many wonders, including the physical resurrection of the dead. However, it also allows for their brutal economic exploitation. On November 1st, the Day of the Dead, five friends make an appointment to meet in the St. John deadtown and find themselves caught up in a wave of social change.

**Other books you might like:**
John Crowley, *Beasts*, 1976
M. John Harrison, *The Pastel City*, 1972
Robert Silverberg, *Born with the Dead*, 1974
Cordwainer Smith, *Norstrilia*, 1975
Amy Thomson, *Virtual Girl*, 1993

---

**3798**

**T. LIAM MCDONALD**, Editor
**STEFAN DZIEMIANOWICZ**, Co-Editor
**MARTIN H. GREENBERG**, Co-Editor

### Sea Cursed: Thirty Terrifying Tales of the Deep
(New York: Barnes & Noble, 1994)

**Story type:** Horror (Anthology)
**Locale(s):** At Sea

**Summary:** The 30 stories in this anthology span more than 150 years and explore a variety of horrors associated with the sea. Included are

H.P. Lovecraft's tale of an underwater civilization, ''The Temple''; Edgar Allan Poe's description of a whirlpool, ''Descent into the Maelstrom''; stories of deep-sea monsters in Arthur J. Burks' ''The Bells of Oceana'' and Frank Belknap Long's ''Second Night Out''; tales of haunted ships in Joseph Conrad's ''The Brute'' and Hugh Cave's ''Derelict''; and stories about mythic sea horrors in Clive Barker's ''Scape Goats'' and Robert Aickman's ''The Wine-Dark Sea.'' William Hope Hodgson's classic novel of the horrors encountered by sailors on a marooned ship, ''The Boats of the Glen Carrig,'' is reprinted in its entirety.

**Other books you might like:**
William Hope Hodgson, *Deep Waters*, 1967
William Hope Hodgson, *Demons of the Sea*, 1993
William Pattrick, *Mysterious Sea Stories*, 1985
   editor

## 3799

### ALEX MCDONOUGH

## *Dragon's Blood*

(New York: Ace, 1991)

**Story type:** Science Fiction (Adventure; Time Travel)
**Series:** Scorpio
**Major character(s):** Scorpio, Alien, Fugitive; Leah de Bernay, Apprentice, Doctor; Chan, Military Personnel
**Time period(s):** 1970s (1975); Indeterminate Past (Jurassic Period)
**Locale(s):** Phnom Penh, Cambodia

**Summary:** Once more, Leah and Scorpio have tried to return Leah to 14th-century Avignon and failed. This time, they've ended up in Cambodia, 1975. Surviving in a war-torn corner of the 20th century is hard enough, but soon they have to flee to the distant past to escape the Hunter, who is still determined to kill Scorpio and recover the orb.

**Other books you might like:**
Tom Deitz, *Windmaster's Bane*, 1986
Simon Hawke, *The Ivanhoe Gambit*, 1984
John Peel, *Timewyrm: Genesys*, 1991
Tim Powers, *The Anubis Gates*, 1983
Roger Zelazny, *Nine Princes in Amber*, 1970

## 3800

### ALEX MCDONOUGH

## *Dragon's Claw*

(New York: Ace, 1993)

**Story type:** Science Fiction (Time Travel; Adventure)
**Series:** Scorpio
**Major character(s):** Scorpio, Alien, Fugitive; Leah de Bernay, Apprentice, Doctor; Hatshepsut, Time Traveler
**Time period(s):** Indeterminate Future
**Locale(s):** Terrapin, Planet—Imaginary; Tamir, Planet—Imaginary

**Summary:** Having destroyed the Hunters' home planet, the vVos demand Terrapin's young. When Scorpio and Leah de Bernay travel to the vVos homeworld, Tamir, to see if they can be defeated, they discover humans from various historic times who have been abducted to play in the Game from which the vVos derive all their amusement and enjoyment. Sixth and final book of the series.

**Other books you might like:**
Pierre Barbet, *The Napoleons of Eridanus*, 1976
Marion Zimmer Bradley, *Hunters of the Red Moon*, 1973
C.J. Cherryh, *Hunter of Worlds*, 1977

Edmund Cooper, *Seahorse in the Sky*, 1969
Philip Jose Farmer, *The Wind Whales of Ishmael*, 1971
Alan Dean Foster, *Glory Lane*, 1987
Garry Kilworth, *In Solitary*, 1979
Jack Lovejoy, *The Hunters*, 1982
Andre Norton, *Here Abide Monsters*, 1973
Marti Steussy, *Dreams of Dawn*, 1988

## 3801

### ALEX MCDONOUGH

## *Dragon's Eye*

(New York: Ace, 1992)

**Story type:** Science Fiction (Time Travel; Political)
**Series:** Scorpio
**Major character(s):** Scorpio, Alien, Fugitive; Leah de Bernay, Apprentice, Doctor
**Time period(s):** 14th century (1351)
**Locale(s):** Earth; Terrapin, Planet—Imaginary

**Summary:** While Leah and Scorpio attempt to rescue Leah's condemned father, Lethor the Hunter finds them and tries to kill Scorpio. When Scorpio returns to Terrapin with Leah, they find hunters firmly in control of Terrapin. Aided by the orb which allows travel in time and space, the pair works to free Terrapin from the hunters.

**Other books you might like:**
John Dalmas, *Fanglith*, 1985
Harry Harrison, *The Stainless Steel Rat Saves the World*, 1972
John Jakes, *Time Gate*, 1961
Andre Norton, *Star Gate*, 1958
Connie Willis, *Doomsday Book*, 1992

## 3802

### ALEX MCDONOUGH

## *Scorpio*

(New York: Ace, 1990)

**Story type:** Science Fiction (Time Travel; Adventure)
**Series:** Scorpio
**Major character(s):** Scorpio, Alien, Fugitive; Leah de Bernay, Apprentice, Doctor; Pope Clement VII, Religious
**Time period(s):** 14th century
**Locale(s):** Terrapin, Planet—Imaginary; Avignon, France

**Summary:** Scorpio, a member of a placid race, accidently flees his home planet when he steals a mysterious artifact from the Hunters, a warlike race that is exterminating Scorpio's people. He ends up in medieval France during the height of the Black Death and must deal with the complexity of medieval life as well as the Hunters sent to catch him. Strong Jewish characters populate this novel.

**Other books you might like:**
Tom Deitz, *Windmaster's Bane*, 1986
Simon Hawke, *The Ivanhoe Gambit*, 1984
Tim Powers, *The Anubis Gates*, 1983
Sheri S. Tepper, *King's Blood Four*, 1983
Roger Zelazny, *Nine Princes in Amber*, 1970

### 3803
**ALEX MCDONOUGH**
## Scorpio Descending
(New York: Ace, 1991)

**Story type:** Science Fiction (Time Travel; Adventure)
**Series:** Scorpio
**Major character(s):** Scorpio, Alien, Fugitive; Leah de Bernay, Apprentice, Doctor; Daria Nicolaeuna Mirskaya, Scientist
**Time period(s):** 1910s (1917)
**Locale(s):** Siberia, Russia; Petrograd, Russia

**Summary:** Pursued by the Hunters, Scorpio and Leah have arrived in Imperial Russia on the eve of the Russian Revolution. Unfortunately, the orb that carries them through time and space has been damaged, and finding a reclusive scientist is the only way they have to repair it and return to their homes.

**Other books you might like:**
Janet Asimov, *Norby Through Time and Space*, 1988
　Isaac Asimov, co-author
Simon Hawke, *The Ivanhoe Gambit*, 1984
John Peel, *Timewyrm: Genesys*, 1991
Tim Powers, *The Anubis Gates*, 1983
Roger Zelazny, *Nine Princes in Amber*, 1970

### 3804
**ALEX MCDONOUGH**
## Scorpio Rising
(New York: Ace, 1990)

**Story type:** Science Fiction (Time Travel; Adventure)
**Series:** Scorpio
**Major character(s):** Scorpio, Alien, Fugitive; Leah de Bernay, Apprentice, Doctor; John Dee, Magician, Doctor
**Time period(s):** 16th century
**Locale(s):** London, England

**Summary:** Scorpio and Leah, jumping blindly in time, have arrived in London during the reign of Queen Elizabeth I. At first it looks like the two travelers will be able to discover how to control the orb (their time machine), but greed and treachery get in the way. Then the Hunters, the race that is exterminating Scorpio's people, return.

**Other books you might like:**
Tom Deitz, *Windmaster's Bane*, 1986
Simon Hawke, *The Ivanhoe Gambit*, 1984
Tim Powers, *The Anubis Gates*, 1983
Sheri S. Tepper, *King's Blood Four*, 1983
Roger Zelazny, *Nine Princes in Amber*, 1970

### 3805
**THOMAS R. MCDONOUGH**
## The Missing Matter
(New York: Bantam Spectra, 1992)

**Story type:** Science Fiction (Hard Science Fiction; Adventure)
**Series:** Next Wave
**Major character(s):** Tariq Salib, Scientist; Al-Hajji Brian Fitzpatrick, Scientist, Religious; Fairouz, Spaceship Captain
**Time period(s):** 21st century
**Locale(s):** *Ulug Beg*, Spaceship; Ronin, Planet—Imaginary; Alternate Universe

**Summary:** When researchers detect an anomaly at the fringes of the solar system, the director of a remote outpost orders the *Ulug Beg* to transport an exploratory crew to investigate. They discover a mysterious planet which drags the explorers with it into parallel universes, places in which changes to the physical laws of the universe threaten their very existence. This third title in the Next Wave Series contains an 8-page introduction by Isaac Asimov titled "Dark Matter," and a 52-page article by astrophysicist Dr. Wallace H. Tucker, "The Attraction of Darkness."

**Other books you might like:**
Roger MacBride Allen, *The Ring of Charon*, 1990
Stephen Baxter, *Raft*, 1991
David Brin, *Earth*, 1990
Robert L. Forward, *Dragon's Egg*, 1980
Alan Dean Foster, *To the Vanishing Point*, 1988
Vonda N. McIntyre, *Transition*, 1991
Robert Reed, *Down the Bright Way*, 1991

### 3806
**IAN MCDOWELL**
## Mordred's Curse
(New York: AvoNova, 1996)

**Story type:** Fantasy (Legend; Satire)
**Major character(s):** Mordred, Royalty, Bastard Son; Arthur, Ruler, Warrior; Merlin, Wizard, Homosexual
**Time period(s):** Indeterminate
**Locale(s):** The Orkneys, Scotland; Camelot, England

**Summary:** Mordred, Arthur's bastard, loves his father who, driven by guilt, repays love with indifference. Mordred remains at the Court, part of the splendor but always separate. Eventually, his desire for revenge leads him to usurp Arthur's kingdom and wife. First novel.

**Other books you might like:**
David Drake, *The Dragon Lord*, 1979
Phyllis Ann Karr, *The Idylls of the Queen*, 1982
Robert Nye, *Merlin*, 1979
Tim Powers, *The Drawing of the Dark*, 1979
Mary Stewart, *The Crystal Cave*, 1970

### 3807
**MICHAEL MCDOWELL**
## Toplin
(New York: Dell Abyss, 1991)

**Story type:** Horror (Psychological Suspense)
**Major character(s):** Toplin, Office Worker; Marta Aleksandrova Blyushkina, Waiter/Waitress; Howard, Worker (pharmacy delivery boy)
**Time period(s):** 1990s

**Summary:** As the disaffected Toplin schemes to murder the waitress Marta for her foul looks, he ruminates over his life and friends, providing a journey through a warped mind that is by turns hilarious, grotesque and frightening. Originally published in 1985.

**Other books you might like:**
Ramsey Campbell, *The Face That Must Die*, 1979
Stephen Gilbert, *Ratman's Notebooks*, 1970
Brett Easton Ellis, *American Psycho*, 1991
David J. Schow, *The Kill Riff*, 1988

## 3808

### IAN MCEWAN

## *Black Dogs*

(New York: Doubleday/Nan A. Talese, 1992)

**Story type:** Horror (Literary)
**Major character(s):** Bernard Tremaine, Journalist (political commentator); June Tremaine, Writer (ex-wife of Bernard); Jeremy, Writer (son-in-law of Bernard and June)
**Time period(s):** 10th century
**Locale(s):** Berlin, Germany, West; St. Maurice de Navacelles, France

**Summary:** The fall of the Berlin Wall resurrects the histories of Bernard and June Tremaine, former communist sympathizers who separated from one another after June experienced a vision of supernatural evil that appears to have foreshadowed the turn of world politics for the last four decades.

**Other books you might like:**
Clive Barker, *The Damnation Game*, 1985
Kim Newman, *Bad Dreams*, 1990
George Orwell, *1984*, 1949

## 3809

### DENNIS MCFARLAND

## *A Face at the Window*

(New York: Villard, 1997)

**Story type:** Horror (Ghost Story)
**Major character(s):** Cookson Selway, Restaurateur; Ellen Selway, Writer (mystery novelist); Pascal, Hotel Worker (porter)
**Time period(s):** 1990s (1997)
**Locale(s):** London, England

**Summary:** On a trip to London, Cookson Selway encounters ghosts at a hotel where several mysterious violent deaths occured half a century before. The startling experience leads Cookson to re-evaluate his morally questionable life to date, and to examine himself in terms of the ghosts, who may simply be projections of his own psyche.

**Other books you might like:**
Jack Cady, *The Off Season*, 1995
Brad Leithauser, *Seaward*, 1993
Mark Morris, *The Immaculate*, 1992
Michael Upchurch, *Passive Intruder*, 1995

## 3810

### DAN MCGIRT

## *Dirty Work*

(New York: Roc, 1993)

**Story type:** Fantasy (Light Fantasy; Quest)
**Series:** Jason Cosmo
**Major character(s):** Jason Cosmo, Farmer, Hero
**Time period(s):** Indeterminate (10th century A. H.)
**Locale(s):** Arden, Fictional Country

**Summary:** Events dash Jason Cosmo's hopes of a quiet retirement raising turnips when word of the return of the Superwand, the supreme tool of power, reaches him. Jason alone can find and banish the Superwand, if standing in the way of hostilities between the Gods and Demons does not prove fatal.

**Other books you might like:**
Kyle Crocco, *Heroes, Inc.*, 1991
Kyle Crocco, *Heroes Wanted*, 1991
Alan Dean Foster, *To the Vanishing Point*, 1988
Neil Gaiman, *Good Omens: The Nice and Accurate Prophecies of Agnes Nutter, Witch*, 1990
   Terry Pratchett, co-author
Parke Godwin, *The Snake Oil Wars*, 1989
John Moore, *Slay and Rescue*, 1993
Roger Zelazny, *Bring Me the Head of Prince Charming*, 1991
   Robert Sheckley, co-author

## 3811

### DAN MCGIRT

## *Jason Cosmo*

(New York: NAL Signet, 1989)

**Story type:** Fantasy (Light Fantasy)
**Major character(s):** Jason Cosmo, Farmer, Hero
**Time period(s):** Indeterminate
**Locale(s):** Alternate Earth

**Summary:** Jason Cosmo becomes, at once, a hero and a wanted man and must leave his village. He is caught up in the struggle between two competing organizations of wizards. He takes up with an unconventional wizard, who is also being tracked by bounty hunters.

**Other books you might like:**
Robert Asprin, *Phule's Company*, 1990
James P. Blaylock, *The Stone Giant*, 1989
Alan Dean Foster, *Glory Lane*, 1990
John Morressy, *Kedrigern and the Charming Couple*, 1990
Neil Gaiman, *Good Omens: The Nice and Accurate Prophecies of Agnes Nutter, Witch*, 1990
   Terry Pratchett, co-author

## 3812

### PATRICK MCGRATH

## *Asylum*

(New York: Random House, 1997)

**Story type:** Horror (Psychological Suspense)
**Major character(s):** Peter Cleave, Doctor (psychiatrist); Stella Raphael, Housewife; Edgar Stark, Artist (sculptor)
**Time period(s):** 1990s (1997)
**Locale(s):** London, England

**Summary:** After bringing disgrace on herself and her family by running off with psychotic inmate Edgar Stark, Stella Raphael, wife of the psychiatrist who heads the asylum Stark escaped from, becomes an inmate there herself. There she is cared for by Peter Cleave, a competitor of her husband's whose interest in her case approaches the obessiveness of her affair with Stark.

**Other books you might like:**
Michael Cadnum, *Skyscape*, 1994
Kathe Koja, *Strange Angels*, 1994

## 3813

### PATRICK MCGRATH

## Dr. Haggard's Disease

(New York: Poseidon, 1993)

**Story type:** Horror (Psychological Suspense)
**Major character(s):** Edward Haggard, Doctor; James Vaughan, Pilot (Royal Air Force); Mrs. Gregor, Servant
**Time period(s):** 1940s
**Locale(s):** Elgin, England

**Summary:** Edward Haggard nurses a passion for his deceased beloved so strong that it has left him a ruined man. When her grown son comes to visit him, he espies her physical presence in her son's features and takes bizarre steps to ensure that he will not lose her a second time.

**Other books you might like:**
Henry James, *The Turn of the Screw*, 1898
Edgar Allan Poe, *The Fall of the House of Usher*, 1966
    in *Complete Stories and Poems of Edgar Allan Poe*
Edgar Allan Poe, *Ligeia*, 1966
    in *Complete Stories and Poems of Edgar Allan Poe*

## 3814

### PATRICK MCGRATH

## The Grotesque

(New York: Poseidon/Simon & Schuster, 1989)

**Story type:** Horror (Psychological Suspense)
**Major character(s):** Hugo Coal, Nobleman, Handicapped; Fledge, Servant (Coal's butler)
**Time period(s):** 1940s (1949)
**Locale(s):** Berkshire, England (Crook Manor)

**Summary:** Sir Hugo engages in a complex and perverse "duel" with his butler, Fledge, with a brutal murder at the center of things.

**Other books you might like:**
Harry Kressing, *The Cook*, 1965

## 3815

### PATRICK MCGRATH

## Spider

(New York: Poseidon/Simon & Schuster, 1990)

**Story type:** Horror (Psychological Suspense)
**Major character(s):** Dennis "Spider" Cleg, Patient (ex-mental patient); Horace Cleg, Parent (Dennis' father), Maintenance Worker (Plumber); Hilda Wilkinson, Prostitute, Step-Parent (Dennis' stepmother)
**Time period(s):** 1930s (1937); 1950s (1957)
**Locale(s):** London, England (East End)

**Summary:** Returned from his 20-year incarceration as a mental patient, Dennis Cleg tells the story of his mother's death, his father's complicity in her murder, and how he evolved the persona of "Spider" to cope with emotional trauma of his childhood.

**Other books you might like:**
Scott Baker, *Webs*, 1989
Robert Bloch, *Psycho*, 1959
Robert Bloch, *The Scarf*, 1947
Shirley Jackson, *We Have Always Lived in the Castle*, 1962

## 3816

### ELOISE JARVIS MCGRAW

## The Moorchild

(New York: Simon & Schuster/Margaret K. McElderry Books, 1996)

**Story type:** Fantasy (Young Adult; Contemporary Realism)
**Major character(s):** Moql'nkkn "Moql/Saaski", Mythical Creature (half-fairy); Old Bess, Aged Person; Anwara, Parent
**Time period(s):** Indeterminate
**Locale(s):** The Mound, Mythical Place; Torskaal, Fictional City

**Summary:** Abandoned by her fairy parent, halfling Saaski grows up with human foster parents, unappreciated by her human companions except for Old Bess, who helps Saaski learn to read. When the townfolk begin to blame her for all of their ill luck, Saaski must find another home but resolves to first recover the human child taken by the fairy folk when they abandoned Saaski.

**Other books you might like:**
Pamela Dean, *The Dubious Hills*, 1994
Rose Estes, *Troll-Taken*, 1993
Rosalie Fry, *The Secret of Roan Inish*, 1995
Peni R. Griffin, *Hobkin*, 1992
Robin Morgan, *The Mer-Child: A Legend for Children and Other Adults*, 1991
Elizabeth Marie Pope, *The Perilous Gard*, 1974

## 3817

### MAUREEN F. MCHUGH

## China Mountain Zhang

(New York: Tor, 1992)

**Story type:** Science Fiction (Genetic Manipulation; Political)
**Major character(s):** Rafael Zhong "China Mountain" Shan, Engineer, Homosexual; Qian, Foreman; San-xiang Qian, Girlfriend
**Time period(s):** 21st century
**Locale(s):** New York, New York

**Summary:** Zhong Shan looks like an American Born Chinese only because his parents had his genetic construction altered to suppress his Hispanic mother's features, gaining him preferential treatment under Chinese rule but preventing him from passing a DNA check. When Elder Qian encourages China Mountain to date his ugly daughter, marry her and move to China, homosexual Zhong Shan inexorably becomes involved with the Qian family's destiny. Author's first novel.

**Other books you might like:**
Margaret Wander Bonanno, *The Others*, 1990
Gordon R. Dickson, *Way of the Pilgrim*, 1987
Peter R. Emshwiller, *The Host*, 1991
John Hersey, *White Lotus*, 1965
Kim Stanley Robinson, *The Gold Coast*, 1989
David Wingrove, *The Middle Kingdom*, 1990

## 3818

### MAUREEN F. MCHUGH

## Half the Day Is Night

(New York: Tor, 1994)

**Story type:** Science Fiction (Contemporary Realism; Political)
**Major character(s):** David Dai, Military Personnel (retired), Bodyguard; Mayla Ling, Banker; Tim Bennet, Bodyguard
**Time period(s):** 21st century

**Locale(s):** Caribe, Undersea Environment/Habitat

**Summary:** After Mayla Ling hires David Dai, the plots against her prove more complex than she imagined. Soon the two must flee terrorists through a richly detailed environment, simultaneously strange and familiar.

**Other books you might like:**
John Brunner, *The Shockwave Rider*, 1975
Pat Cadigan, *Synners*, 1991
William Gibson, *Neuromancer*, 1984
Ian McDonald, *Terminal Cafe*, 1994
Kim Stanley Robinson, *The Gold Coast*, 1989

**3819**

**MAUREEN F. MCHUGH**

## Mission Child

(New York: Avon Eos, 1998)

**Story type:** Science Fiction (Lost Colony; Science Fiction)
**Major character(s):** Janna, Linguist, Traveler
**Time period(s):** Indeterminate Future
**Locale(s):** Planet—Imaginary; Taufzin, Fictional City

**Summary:** Janna receives three biological enhancements from an offworlder immediately before distrusting colonists kill the offworlder and massacre Janna's family and friends. Maturing quickly, Janna starts a new family before tragedy sends her in search of her identity and place in the world.

**Other books you might like:**
Rosemary Kirstein, *The Outskirter's Secret*, 1992
Ursula K. Le Guin, *The Left Hand of Darkness*, 1969
Paul J. McAuley, *Child of the River*, 1998
Larry Niven, *Destiny's Road*, 1997
Sharon Shinn, *Archangel*, 1996

**3820**

**VONDA N. MCINTYRE**

## The Crystal Star

(New York: Bantam Spectra, 1994)

**Story type:** Science Fiction (Space Opera; Mystical)
**Series:** Star Wars
**Major character(s):** Leia Organa, Royalty, Diplomat; Chewbacca, Alien (Wookie), Adventurer; Luke Skywalker, Martial Arts Expert (Jedi Knight), Hero
**Time period(s):** Indeterminate Past
**Locale(s):** *Alderran*, Spaceship; Crseih, Planet—Imaginary; New Republic, Interstellar Empire/Federation

**Summary:** Leia, Chewbacca and robot Artoo-Detoo search for Leia and Han Solo's kidnapped children while Han, Luke and robot See-Threepio try to find a group of Jedi Knights. Set after Dave Wolverton's *The Courtship of Princess Leia*.

**Other books you might like:**
Roger MacBride Allen, *Ambush at Corellia*, 1995
Kevin J. Anderson, *Jedi Search*, 1994
L. Neil Smith, *The Lando Calrissian Adventures*, 1994
Dave Wolverton, *The Courtship of Princess Leia*, 1994
Timothy Zahn, *Heir to the Empire*, 1991

**3821**

**VONDA N. MCINTYRE**

## Metaphase

(New York: Bantam Spectra, 1992)

**Story type:** Science Fiction (First Contact; Science Fiction)
**Series:** Starfarers
**Major character(s):** Victoria McKenzie, Scientist, Leader; J.D. Sauvage, Scientist (alien contact specialist); Nemo, Alien (Squidmoth)
**Time period(s):** 21st century
**Locale(s):** *Starfarer*, Spaceship; *Chi*, Spaceship; *Nemo*, Spaceship

**Summary:** Pursuing their explorations rather than return to Earth forever, *Starfarer*'s residents meet and establish rapport with *Nemo* as its extremely long life draws to an end. They then continue onward hoping to discover civilization and the creators of the cosmic string transportation system.

**Other books you might like:**
Jeffrey A. Carver, *Down the Stream of Stars*, 1990
Glen Cook, *The Dragon Never Sleeps*, 1988
John DeChancie, *Paradox Alley*, 1987
Michael P. Kube-McDowell, *Empery*, 1987
Michael P. Kube-McDowell, *Enigma*, 1986
Larry Niven, *The Mote in God's Eye*, 1974
   Jerry Pournelle, co-author
Alis A. Rasmussen, *A Passage of Stars*, 1990
Alis A. Rasmussen, *The Price of Ransom*, 1990
Alis A. Rasmussen, *Revolution's Shore*, 1990
Vernor Vinge, *A Fire upon the Deep*, 1990

**3822**

**VONDA N. MCINTYRE**

## The Moon and the Sun

(New York: Pocket, 1997)

**Story type:** Fantasy (Historical)
**Major character(s):** Marie-Josephe de la Crois, Noblewoman; Lucien de Barenton, Nobleman, Military Personnel; Louis XIV, Historical Figure, Royalty (king of France)
**Time period(s):** 17th century (1693)
**Locale(s):** Versailles, France

**Summary:** Father Yves de la Croix captures a sea monster and hints to Louis XIV that its flesh holds the secret of immortality. His sister, Marie-Josephe, learns to communicate with the sea monster and wants to set her free. Marie-Josephe's plan thwarted, the sea monster must try to ransom herself with sunken treasure.

**Other books you might like:**
Poul Anderson, *A Midsummer Tempest*, 1974
Lisa Goldstein, *Strange Devices of the Sun and Moon*, 1993
Tim Powers, *The Drawing of the Dark*, 1979
Michaela Roessner, *The Stars Dispose*, 1997
Clifford D. Simak, *The Fellowship of the Talisman*, 1978
Melinda M. Snodgrass, *Queen's Gambit Declined*, 1989
Jack Vance, *Suldrun's Garden*, 1983
Chelsea Quinn Yarbro, *A Candle for D'Artagnan*, 1989

## 3823

### VONDA N. MCINTYRE

## *Nautilus*

(New York: Bantam Spectra, 1994)

**Story type:** Science Fiction (First Contact; Science Fiction)
**Series:** Starfarers
**Major character(s):** J.D. Sauvage, Scientist (alien contact specialist); Orchestra, Alien; Stephen Thomas, Professor, Genetically Altered Being
**Time period(s):** 21st century
**Locale(s):** *Starfarer*, Spaceship; *Nautilus*, Spaceship; Civilization, Interstellar Empire/Federation

**Summary:** While effecting repairs to the damaged *Starfarer*, the disparate crew finds little time for consensus building. J.D. Sauvage's initial contact with newly discovered aliens leads to a promising exchange of gifts, while an ancient intelligence plots a new attack on Civilization.

**Other books you might like:**
Roger MacBride Allen, *The Ring of Charon*, 1990
Roger MacBride Allen, *The Shattered Sphere*, 1994
Gregory Benford, *Furious Gulf*, 1994
David Brin, *Startide Rising*, 1983
Orson Scott Card, *Speaker for the Dead*, 1986
Glen Cook, *The Dragon Never Sleeps*, 1988
Robert L. Forward, *Return to Rocheworld*, 1993
    Julie Forward Fuller, co-author
Alis A. Rasmussen, *The Price of Ransom*, 1990
Vernor Vinge, *A Fire upon the Deep*, 1992

## 3824

### VONDA N. MCINTYRE

## *Starfarers*

(New York: Ace, 1989)

**Story type:** Science Fiction (Hard Science Fiction)
**Major character(s):** Victoria McKenzie, Scientist, Leader; Stephen Thomas Gregory, Scientist
**Time period(s):** 21st century
**Locale(s):** *Starfarer*, Spaceship

**Summary:** Construction of *Starfarer*, humanity's second interstellar probe, is almost complete, but the political and military situation on Earth makes it seem more and more likely that the spaceship will never be allowed to fulfill its mission. A dedicated group of mission scientists plot to steal the ship and head for the stars.

**Other books you might like:**
Gregory Benford, *Heart of the Comet*, 1986
    David Brin, co-author
Lois McMaster Bujold, *Falling Free*, 1988
Michael P. Kube-McDowell, *Enigma*, 1986
Pamela Sargent, *Venus of Dreams*, 1986

## 3825

### VONDA N. MCINTYRE

## *Transition*

(New York: Bantam Spectra, 1991)

**Story type:** Science Fiction (Hard Science Fiction)
**Series:** Starfarers

**Major character(s):** Victoria McKenzie, Scientist, Leader; J.D. Sauvage, Scientist (alien contact specialist)
**Time period(s):** 21st century
**Locale(s):** *Starfarer*, Spaceship; *Chi*, Spaceship

**Summary:** Mankind's first successful interstellar voyage has been shaky as evidenced by Starfarer's entering the Tau Ceti star system accompanied by the accidental explosion of a nuclear weapon. When a first contact team tracks down the source of intelligent signals to an airless moon of Tau Ceti II, they discover a dome which suffers an explosion as they land, leaving a single small artifact to be discovered by J.D. after the dome cools. The team plans to visit earthlike Tau Ceti II until *Starfarer's* preliminary system survey reveals a nexus of cosmic strings similar to the one allowing *Starfarer's* Sol-Tau Ceti voyage. When the cosmic string leading to Sol begins to move, everyone must decide whether to return to Earth while it is possible or to continue on via the cosmic string nexus, choosing a new mission, one from which returning to Earth seems impossible.

**Other books you might like:**
Roger MacBride Allen, *The Ring of Charon*, 1990
Glen Cook, *The Dragon Never Sleeps*, 1988
John DeChancie, *Paradox Alley*, 1987
John DeChancie, *Red Limit Freeway*, 1984
John DeChancie, *Starrigger*, 1983
Michael P. Kube-McDowell, *Empery*, 1987
Michael P. Kube-McDowell, *Emprise*, 1986

## 3826

### KENNETH MCKENNEY

## *The Offspring*

(New York: Ballantine, 1990)

**Story type:** Horror (Curse)
**Series:** Changeling Trilogy
**Major character(s):** Mark Lawrence, Young Man; Sally Lawrence, Parent
**Time period(s):** 1990s
**Locale(s):** Santa Monica, California; Europe

**Summary:** Supported by his mother and other allies, Mark Lawrence, son of ''the changeling,'' retraces his father's footsteps and does battle with an ancient evil to free himself and his father from the terrible curse that has plagued them both.

**Other books you might like:**
Jessie Kerruish, *The Undying Monster*, 1922

## 3827

### NANCY MCKENZIE

## *The Child Queen*

(New York: Ballantine Del Rey, 1994)

**Story type:** Fantasy (Legend)
**Major character(s):** Guinevere, Royalty (queen); Arthur, Ruler, Warrior; Lancelot, Knight
**Time period(s):** 5th century
**Locale(s):** England

**Summary:** Prophecied at birth to achieve greatness, Guinevere grows up with her cousin in North Wales, hearing tales of Arthur's heroism. After Guinevere's subsequent betrothal to Arthur, jealous King Medwyn acts on an old prophecy and kidnaps Guinevere, holding her until Lancelot and Merlin come to the rescue. Guinevere's difficulties continue as does her fame. Author's first novel.

**Other books you might like:**
Marion Zimmer Bradley, *The Mists of Avalon*, 1983
Gillian Bradshaw, *Hawk of May*, 1980
Sharan Newman, *Guinevere*, 1981
Mary Stewart, *The Crystal Cave*, 1970
Persia Woolley, *Child of the Northern Spring*, 1987

**3828**

### LEE MCKEONE

## Backblast

(New York: Popular Library Questar, 1989)

**Story type:** Science Fiction (Adventure)
**Series:** Ghoster
**Major character(s):** Conek Hayden, Spaceship Captain, Business-man; Cge, Robot, Sidekick
**Time period(s):** Indeterminate Future
**Locale(s):** Beldorph, Planet—Imaginary; *Windsong*, Spaceship

**Summary:** In this sequel to *Ghoster* a loner spaceship captain and his robot friend find themselves on the run from the law.

**Other books you might like:**
Joe Clifford Faust, *Desperate Measures*, 1989
Joe Clifford Faust, *The Essence of Evil*, 1990
Joe Clifford Faust, *Precious Cargo*, 1989
Harry Harrison, *Bill, the Galactic Hero*, 1965

**3829**

### LEE MCKEONE

## The Clone Crisis

(New York: Warner Questar, 1992)

**Story type:** Science Fiction (Adventure; Humor)
**Series:** Ghoster
**Major character(s):** Conek Hayden, Spaceship Captain, Business-man; Cge, Robot, Sidekick (Conek's)
**Time period(s):** Indeterminate Future
**Locale(s):** Outer Space; Siddah-II, Planet—Imaginary; *Bucephalus*, Spaceship

**Summary:** Plotting to take over a smuggling empire, crime lords begin to clone the king and his top leaders. Suddenly the galaxy contains many Coneks, each bent on survival, while the original Conek must thwart the galactic crime war.

**Other books you might like:**
Pat Cadigan, *Fools*, 1992
Dave Duncan, *Hero*, 1991
Ken Rolston, *Extreme Paranoia: Nobody Knows the Trouble I've Shot*, 1991
A.E. Van Vogt, *The World of Null-A*, 1945

**3830**

### LEE MCKEONE

## Starfire Down

(New York: Warner Questar, 1991)

**Story type:** Science Fiction (Adventure)
**Series:** Ghoster
**Major character(s):** Conek Hayden, Spaceship Captain, Business-man; Gella Icor, Spaceship Captain; Andro Arvin, Military Per-sonnel, Administrator (spaceport)

**Time period(s):** Indeterminate Future
**Locale(s):** *Destria*, Spaceship; *Starfire*, Spaceship; Holmarin IV, Planet—Imaginary

**Summary:** Conek Hayden, ex-smuggler, must rescue one of his pilots, Gella Icor, who has been arrested for a crime attributed to her deceased father. The atmosphere on Holmarin IV, where Gella is being held, is toxic to those not born there, complicating the rescue. This novel is a sequel to *Backblast*.

**Other books you might like:**
David Brin, *Startide Rising*, 1983
C.J. Cherryh, *Merchanter's Luck*, 1982
Mary Gentle, *Golden Witchbreed*, 1984
Katharine Kerr, *Polar City Blues*, 1990
Alis A. Rasmussen, *A Passage of Stars*, 1990
Alis A. Rasmussen, *The Price of Ransom*, 1990
Alis A. Rasmussen, *Revolution's Shore*, 1990
Walter Jon Williams, *Angel Station*, 1989

**3831**

### DENNIS L. MCKIERNAN

## Caverns of Socrates

(New York: Roc, 1995)

**Story type:** Fantasy (Adventure; Alternate World)
**Major character(s):** Eric Flannery, Computer Expert, Adventurer; Alice Maxon, Computer Expert, Adventurer; Avery, Artificial Intelligence
**Time period(s):** 1990s
**Locale(s):** Tucson, Arizona; Itheria, Cyberspace (computer virtual reality)

**Summary:** While testing a new virtual reality program intended to mimic reality, Eric, Alice, and other expert gamers, the Black Foxes, find themselves trapped within the computer's reality and must discover a way to regain control and return to their own world.

**Other books you might like:**
Greg Egan, *Permutation City*, 1995
Philip Jose Farmer, *Red Orc's Rage*, 1991
James P. Hogan, *Realtime Interrupt*, 1995
Joel Rosenberg, *The Sleeping Dragon*, 1983
Will Shetterly, *The Tangled Lands*, 1989
Wm. Mark Simmons, *In the Net of Dreams*, 1990
Vivian Vande Velde, *User Unfriendly*, 1991

**3832**

### DENNIS L. MCKIERNAN

## The Dragonstone

(New York: Roc, 1996)

**Story type:** Fantasy (Quest; Adventure)
**Major character(s):** Arin, Mythical Creature (elf), Noblewoman; Aiko, Warrior, Noblewoman; Egil, Warrior
**Time period(s):** Indeterminate
**Locale(s):** Mithgar, Fictional Country

**Summary:** Spurred by the horrific vision of all Mithgar engulfed in war, Arin and her companions seek understanding of her role in events and a means of finding the magic Dragonstone, focus of the impending disaster. Set three centuries prior to *Voyage of the Fox Rider*.

**Other books you might like:**
Lynn Flewelling, *Luck in the Shadows*, 1996
Terry Goodkind, *Wizard's First Rule*, 1994

Robin Hobb, *Assassin's Apprentice*, 1995
J.V. Jones, *The Baker's Boy*, 1995
Robert Jordan, *The Eye of the World*, 1990

## 3833

### DENNIS L. MCKIERNAN

## *The Eye of the Hunter*

(New York: Roc, 1992)

**Story type:** Fantasy (Quest)
**Major character(s):** Riatha, Mythical Creature (elf), Immortal; Aravan, Mythical Creature (elf)
**Time period(s):** Indeterminate (5E985-5E993)
**Locale(s):** Mithgar, Fictional Country

**Summary:** A thousand years after Riatha helped hunt down and subdue the evil Baron Stoke, the reappearance of the comet, Eye of the Hunter, foretells the imminent reappearance of Baron Stoke. Riatha joins with Aravan and three others in a desperate attempt to avert the prophecied disaster.

**Other books you might like:**
Glen Cook, *The Black Company*, 1984
Glen Cook, *Shadows Linger*, 1984
Glen Cook, *The White Rose*, 1985
David Eddings, *Pawn of Prophecy*, 1982
J.R.R. Tolkien, *The Fellowship of the Ring*, 1954
J.R.R. Tolkien, *The Return of the King*, 1956
J.R.R. Tolkien, *The Two Towers*, 1955

## 3834

### DENNIS L. MCKIERNAN

## *Into the Fire*

(New York: Roc, 1998)

**Story type:** Fantasy (Magic Conflict; Political)
**Major character(s):** Tipperton "Tip" Thistledown, Mythical Creature (warrow); Beacontor "Beau" Darby, Mythical Creature, Healer, Adventurer
**Time period(s):** Indeterminate
**Locale(s):** Mithgar, Fictional Country

**Summary:** As Tip and Beau attempt to fulfill a promise to a dying swordsman to carry a warning east to Agron, they receive help from many strange allies. When treachery and disaster threaten to drive the world into irredeemable darkness, a call from the High King summons Tip and Beau to the final battle, possibly aided by a mysterious pronouncement of an Elven Seer. Second book of the Hel's Crucible duology.

**Other books you might like:**
Glen Cook, *The Black Company*, 1984
David Drake, *Lord of the Isles*, 1997
Dave Duncan, *Magic Casement*, 1990
David Eddings, *Pawn of Prophecy*, 1982
J.R.R. Tolkien, *The Fellowship of the Ring*, 1954

## 3835

### DENNIS L. MCKIERNAN

## *Into the Forge*

(New York: Roc, 1997)

**Story type:** Fantasy (Quest; Magic Conflict)

**Series:** Mithgar
**Major character(s):** Tipperton "Tip" Thistledown, Mythical Creature (warrow), Adventurer; Beacontor "Beau" Darby, Mythical Creature, Adventurer, Healer
**Time period(s):** Indeterminate
**Locale(s):** Fictional Country

**Summary:** When a dying warrior presses a coin into Tip's hand, telling him to go east and warn all, Tip and Beau begin an adventure leading to foreign lands filled with monsters as strife engulfs the land.

**Other books you might like:**
Lynn Flewelling, *Luck in the Shadows*, 1996
Lynn Flewelling, *Stalking Darkness*, 1997
Terry Goodkind, *Wizard's First Rule*, 1994
J.V. Jones, *The Baker's Boy*, 1995
J.R.R. Tolkien, *The Fellowship of the Ring*, 1954
J.R.R. Tolkien, *The Hobbit*, 1938

## 3836

### DENNIS L. MCKIERNAN

## *Tales of Mithgar*

(New York: Roc, 1994)

**Story type:** Fantasy (Collection; Adventure)
**Time period(s):** Indeterminate
**Locale(s):** Mithgar, Fictional Country

**Summary:** Contains a three-page foreword, a two-page afterword, two-page author's note and 11 original, interwoven stories of heroic quests and great battles through the ages which form the basis for many legends in Mithgar.

**Other books you might like:**
Robert Asprin, *Thieves' World*, 1979
   editor
Fritz Leiber, *Swords Against Wizardry*, 1968
Will Shetterly, *Liavek*, 1985
   Emma Bull, co-editor
J.R.R. Tolkien, *The Silmarillion*, 1977
J.R.R. Tolkien, *Unfinished Tales of Numenor and Middle-Earth*, 1980

## 3837

### DENNIS L. MCKIERNAN

## *Voyage of the Fox Rider*

(New York: Roc, 1993)

**Story type:** Fantasy (Quest)
**Major character(s):** Alamar, Wizard; Jinnarin, Mythical Creature (pysk); Aravan, Mythical Creature (elf), Sea Captain
**Time period(s):** Indeterminate Past (1E9572-2E1)
**Locale(s):** Rwn, Fictional Country

**Summary:** Guided by a strange dream and assisted by the far-travelled Aravan, Jinnarin and Alamar hunt for Farrix, Jinnarin's missing mate. The pair discover greater stakes than the life of one Pysk as evil forces gather and an age draws to an end. Sequel to *The Eye of the Hunter*.

**Other books you might like:**
Glen Cook, *The Black Company*, 1984
Dave Duncan, *Magic Casement*, 1990
David Eddings, *Pawn of Prophecy*, 1982
Robert Jordan, *The Eye of the World*, 1989
Patricia A. McKillip, *The Riddle-Master of Hed*, 1976

## 3838

### PATRICIA A. MCKILLIP

## *The Book of Atrix Wolfe*

(New York: Ace, 1995)

**Story type:** Fantasy (Magic Conflict)
**Major character(s):** Atrix Wolfe, Magician, Criminal; Saro, Amnesiac, Heiress—Lost; Talis Pelucir, Royalty, Heir
**Time period(s):** Indeterminate
**Locale(s):** Pelucir, Fictional Country; Hunter's Field, Fictional Country; Chaumenard, Mythical Place (magicians' retreat)

**Summary:** Appalled by warfare and hoping to bring peace to Pelucir and Kardeth, Atrix Wolfe intends to craft a spirit to dispel the combatants, but instead brings forth the Hunter, a destroyer who plagues Hunter's Field for a generation. When Atrix Wolfe's magic deprives the Queen of the Wood of both her mate and her daughter, she summons Talis Pelucir to help find the missing Atrix Wolfe and her lost child.

**Other books you might like:**
Charles de Lint, *Memory and Dream*, 1994
Susan Dexter, *The Wizard's Shadow*, 1993
Elizabeth Forrest, *Phoenix Fire*, 1992
Lisa Goldstein, *Summer King, Winter Fool*, 1994
Terry Goodkind, *Wizard's First Rule*, 1994
Barbara Hambly, *Bride of the Rat God*, 1994

## 3839

### PATRICIA A. MCKILLIP

## *The Cygnet and the Firebird*

(New York: Ace, 1993)

**Story type:** Fantasy (Magic Conflict; Adventure)
**Series:** Sorceress and the Cygnet
**Major character(s):** Meguet Vervaine, Warrior; Nyx Ro, Sorceress
**Time period(s):** Indeterminate Past
**Locale(s):** Luxor Desert, Mythical Place; Ro Holding, Mythical Place

**Summary:** During a Ro Holding Council meeting, Ro Holding suffers an attack. Meguet and Nyx must discover the attacker's identity and thwart the effort, a task made much more difficult when Meguet and Nyx find themselves mysteriously transported to a dangerous desert far from home.

**Other books you might like:**
C.J. Cherryh, *The Faded Sun: Kesrith*, 1978
Barbara Hambly, *Dog Wizard*, 1993
Barbara Hambly, *The Ladies of Mandrigyn*, 1984
Barbara Hambly, *The Witches of Wenshar*, 1987
Laurell K. Hamilton, *Nightseer*, 1992
Katharine Kerr, *Daggerspell*, 1986
Melanie Rawn, *Stronghold*, 1990
Judith Tarr, *Alamut*, 1989
Martha Wells, *The Element of Fire*, 1993

## 3840

### PATRICIA A. MCKILLIP
### BRIAN FROUD, Co-Author

## *Something Rich and Strange*

(New York: Bantam Spectra, 1994)

**Story type:** Fantasy (Contemporary; Romance)

**Series:** Brian Froud's Faerielands
**Major character(s):** Megan, Artist; Jonah, Collector, Store Owner; Adam Fin, Artist, Mythical Creature
**Time period(s):** 1990s
**Locale(s):** At Sea; West Coast

**Summary:** Megan and Jonah live on the seacoast, above Jonah's shop, Things Rich and Strange, until a fateful day when Jenny's sketch of the sea shows something she didn't draw and a stranger brings beautiful jewelry into the store on consignment. Suddenly Jonah will give up everything to follow a mysterious singer and Jenny will do anything to save him.

**Other books you might like:**
Charles de Lint, *The Wild Wood*, 1994
    Brian Froud co-author
Barbara Hambly, *The Silent Tower*, 1986
R.A. MacAvoy, *The Grey Horse*, 1987
Anne McCaffrey, *The Coelura*, 1987
Elizabeth Marie Pope, *The Perilous Gard*, 1974

## 3841

### PATRICIA A. MCKILLIP

## *Song for the Basilisk*

(New York: Ace, 1998)

**Story type:** Fantasy (Political)
**Major character(s):** Rook Caladrius, Musician; Arioso Pellior, Royalty; Giulia Dulcet, Musician, Teacher
**Time period(s):** Indeterminate Past
**Locale(s):** Luly, Fictional City; Berylon, Fictional City

**Summary:** Rook, orphaned by intrigue, enrolls at the school in Luly to become a bard. His past haunts him and the years slip by as he neither leaves the school nor learns all its teachings. Finally, events conspire to drive him first into the wilderness and then to a decadent city ruled by the man who crushed Rook's family.

**Other books you might like:**
C.J. Cherryh, *The Tree of Swords and Jewels*, 1983
Lisa Goldstein, *Summer King, Winter Fool*, 1994
Ellen Kushner, *Swordspoint*, 1987
Paul J. McAuley, *Pasquale's Angel*, 1995
Paula Volsky, *Illusion*, 1992

## 3842

### PATRICIA A. MCKILLIP

## *The Sorceress and the Cygnet*

(New York: Ace, 1991)

**Story type:** Fantasy (Magic Conflict; Quest)
**Series:** Sorceress and the Cygnet
**Major character(s):** Corleau, Hero (Wayfarer)
**Time period(s):** Indeterminate Past
**Locale(s):** Delta, Mythical Place; Ro Holding, Mythical Place

**Summary:** The Wayfarers, a dark-haired race, retain the legend of their arrival from space. Corleu, a blond, is tormented for this difference, but he also has a gift for words, both reading and storytelling. When he tells his friends the story of the Cygnet and other stellar denizens he has no inkling that he will be forced into their story to save his love and his life.

**Other books you might like:**
Orson Scott Card, *Prentice Alvin*, 1989
John Deakins, *Barrow*, 1990
Mark C. Perry, *Morigu: The Dead*, 1990

Meredith Ann Pierce, *The Pearl of the Soul of the World*, 1990
Robert Silverberg, *To the Land of the Living*, 1990

---

**3843**

### PATRICIA A. MCKILLIP

## Winter Rose

(New York: Ace, 1996)

**Story type:** Fantasy (Romance; Alternate World)
**Major character(s):** Rois Melior, Heroine; Laurel Melior, Heroine; Corbet Lynn, Heir
**Time period(s):** Indeterminate
**Locale(s):** Lynn Hall, Mythical Place

**Summary:** Ignoring his grandfather's curse, Corbet Lynn comes to rebuild Lynn Hall and reclaim his ancestors' land. When the curse draws Corbet into a dream world. Rois and Laurel follow him, hoping to find a path back to reality.

**Other books you might like:**
Pamela Dean, *The Dubious Hills*, 1994
Robert Holdstock, *Mythago Wood*, 1984
L. Dean James, *Summerland*, 1994
Holly Lisle, *Minerva Wakes*, 1994
Delia Sherman, *The Porcelain Dove*, 1993
Jane Yolen, *Sister Light, Sister Dark*, 1988

---

**3844**

### ROBIN MCKINLEY

## Deerskin

(New York: Ace, 1993)

**Story type:** Fantasy (Legend; Quest)
**Major character(s):** Lissla "Deerskin" Lissar, Royalty, Fugitive; Ash, Animal (dog), Companion (Lissar's)
**Time period(s):** Indeterminate
**Locale(s):** Fictional Country

**Summary:** Acknowledging the elements of madness, violence and twisted sexuality from the unbowdlerized original story, "Donkeyskin," by Charles Perrault, this volume follows Princess Lissar as her father, maddened by grief and obsession, announces his own marriage to her then rapes her. To save herself and the kingdom, Lissar flees with Ash, changes her name and seeks healing in Ash's homeland.

**Other books you might like:**
Lois McMaster Bujold, *The Spirit Ring*, 1992
Ellen Datlow, *Snow White, Blood Red*, 1993
    Terri Windling, co-editor
Jacob Ludwig Grimm, *The Complete Fairy Tales of the Brothers Grimm*, 1992
    Wilhelm Grimm, co-author; Jack Zipes, editor, translator
Susan Palwick, *Flying in Place*, 1992
Elizabeth Ann Scarborough, *Last Refuge*, 1992
Martha Wells, *The Element of Fire*, 1993
Jack Zipes, *Spells of Enchantment*, 1991
    editor

---

**3845**

### ROBIN MCKINLEY

## A Knot in the Grain and Other Stories

(New York: Morrow Greenwillow, 1994)

**Story type:** Fantasy (Young Adult; Collection)
**Summary:** Contains two original stories and three stories reprinted from anthologies 1982-1985 with a generally upbeat tone and sometimes muted fantastic elements. Themes included romance, family life and heroic fantasy, with four of the stories set in the milieu of *The Hero and the Crown* and *The Blue Sword*.

**Other books you might like:**
Marion Zimmer Bradley, *The Best of Marion Zimmer Bradley*, 1988
Robert Holdstock, *The Bone Forest*, 1992
Diana Wynne Jones, *Warlock at the Wheel and Other Stories*, 1985
Anne McCaffrey, *Get Off the Unicorn*, 1977
Jane Yolen, *Tales of Wonder*, 1983

---

**3846**

### ROBIN MCKINLEY

## The Outlaws of Sherwood

(New York: Ace, 1989)

**Story type:** Fantasy (Legend)
**Major character(s):** Robin Hood, Outlaw, Hero; Marian, Noblewoman
**Time period(s):** Indeterminate Past
**Locale(s):** Sherwood Forest, England

**Summary:** Romantically retold, maintaining only the legend's setting and characters, Robin Hood is portrayed as a sensitive, non-macho and average hero. The characters of the other members of his band of outlaws are more fully developed in this version.

**Other books you might like:**
Patricia Aakhus, *The Voyage of Mael Duin's Curragh*, 1989
Ru Emerson, *Spell Bound*, 1990
Ellen Kushner, *Outlaws of Sherwood Forest*, 1985
    Choose Your Own Adventure Series 47
Elizabeth Moon, *Surrender None: The Legacy of Gird*, 1990
Gail Van Asten, *Charlemagne's Champion*, 1990

---

**3847**

### ROBIN MCKINLEY

## Rose Daughter

(New York: Greenwillow, 1997)

**Story type:** Fantasy (Legend)
**Major character(s):** Beauty, Gardener; The Beast, Animal (ensorcelled)
**Time period(s):** Indeterminate
**Locale(s):** Rose Cottage, Mythical Place; Beast's Palace, Mythical Place

**Summary:** After a comfortable life in the city, Beauty, her sisters and their fathers must become accustomed to life in a small rural cottage when forced to leave the city in disgrace. Adapting, the daughters begin to develop their talents, until a chance meeting by her father intertwines Beauty's fate with the Beast, resident of an enchanted palace. Concludes with a four-page author's note describing the novel's genesis.

**Other books you might like:**
Ellen Datlow, *Black Swan, White Raven*, 1997
   Terri Windling, co-editor
Lisa Goldstein, *Walking the Labyrinth*, 1996
Patricia A. McKillip, *Winter Rose*, 1996
Delia Sherman, *The Porcelain Dove*, 1993
Jane Yolen, *The Wild Hunt*, 1995

## 3848

### JACK MCKINNEY

## *Free Radicals*

(New York: Ballantine Del Rey, 1992)

**Story type:** Science Fiction (Adventure; Invasion of Earth)
**Series:** Black Hole Travel Agency
**Major character(s):** Lucky Junknowitz, Revolutionary; Ozwaldo Undershort, Alien, Agent; Asin Boxdale, Artist
**Time period(s):** Indeterminate Future
**Locale(s):** Confabulon, Planet—Imaginary; Japan; Root Canal, Planet—Imaginary

**Summary:** The story continues as Lucky travels farther from Earth toward the prison planet, al-Recm, aided by a duped agent of the Black Hole Travel Agency itself. Meanwhile, the Black Hole consolidates its gains on Earth. And the IRS still wants Lucky's hide. . .

**Other books you might like:**
Jack L. Chalker, *And the Devil Will Drag You Under*, 1979
Philip Jose Farmer, *The Maker of Universes*, 1965
Robert A. Heinlein, *Glory Road*, 1963
Keith Laumer, *The Time Bender*, 1981
Roger Zelazny, *Nine Princes in Amber*, 1970

## 3849

### JACK MCKINNEY

## *Hostile Takeover*

(New York: Ballantine Del Rey, 1994)

**Story type:** Science Fiction (Humor; Adventure)
**Series:** Black Hole Travel Agency
**Major character(s):** Yoo Sobek, Alien (Sysop), Rebel; Silvercup, Android; Lucky Junknowitz, Revolutionary
**Time period(s):** Indeterminate Future
**Locale(s):** Japan; Light Trap, Planet—Imaginary

**Summary:** Various factions form an unsteady alliance against the Black Hole Travel Agency. To succeed they must invade Light Trap, the Black Hole's impenetrable stronghold, and must also trust Yoo Sobek, the renegade Sysop. Concludes the series.

**Other books you might like:**
Harry Harrison, *The Adventures of the Stainless Steel Rat*, 1978
Simon Hawke, *The Ivanhoe Gambit*, 1984
Robert A. Heinlein, *Glory Road*, 1963
Michael Scott Rohan, *Chase the Morning*, 1991
Roger Zelazny, *Nine Princes in Amber*, 1970

## 3850

### JACK MCKINNEY

## *Kaduna Memories*

(New York: Ballantine, 1990)

**Story type:** Science Fiction (Cyberpunk; First Contact)

**Major character(s):** Felix McTurk, Computer Expert, Detective; Jain Nugget, Singer; Rec, Artificial Intelligence
**Time period(s):** 21st century
**Locale(s):** Earth; Earth Orbit, Outer Space

**Summary:** Felix and Jain play psychiatrists to an artifical intelligence with a split personality to solve the 15-year-old mystery of alien contact and her parents' deaths.

**Other books you might like:**
Pat Cadigan, *Synners*, 1991
William Gibson, *Neuromancer*, 1984
Bruce Sterling, *Islands in the Net*, 1988
Bruce Sterling, *Schismatrix*, 1985
Walter Jon Williams, *Voice of the Whirlwind*, 1987

## 3851

### MARK MCLAUGHLIN

## *Feeding the Glamour Hogs*

(Tallahassee, FL: Ministry of Whimsy Press, 1997)

**Story type:** Horror (Collection)

**Summary:** Eight strange and surreal stories by a small press editor and writer. ''Nightmares One Through Five, and What Comes After'' is related as a series of nightmare vignettes concerned with sex, money, family and other themes. In ''Largesse,'' plots of horror B-movie videos begin seeping into reality. ''Adroitly Wrapped'' concerns the relationship between a punkish young man and a shapeshifting sorceress. Dated 1997 but not available until 1998.

**Other books you might like:**
Cliff Burns, *The Reality Machine*, 1997
Jack Remick, *Terminal Weird*, 1996
Jeff Vandermeer, *The Book of Lost Places*, 1996
Don Webb, *Stealing My Rules*, 1998
Thomas Wiloch, *Mr. Templeton's Toyshop: Prose Poems and Short Fiction*, 1995

## 3852

### JEFFREY N. MCMAHAN

## *Somewhere in the Night*

(Boston: Alyson, 1989)

**Story type:** Horror (Collection)

**Summary:** Eight witty, sophisticated stories that are darkly humorous in tone, but end with nasty final twists. McMahan's focus on gay protagonists gives an original spin to traditional horror situations and motifs. Especially interesting are ''Two-faced Johnny,'' in which a Halloween costume party turns into a very bizarre banquet and two longer stories, ''Somewhere in the Night'' and ''Hell Is for Children,'' featuring Andrew, a gay vampire.

**Other books you might like:**
Sandy Bayer, *The Crystal Curtain*, 1988
Vincent Lardo, *China House*, 1983

## 3853

### JEFFREY N. MCMAHAN

## *Vampires Anonymous*

(Boston: Alyson, 1991)

**Story type:** Horror (Vampire Story)

**Major character(s):** Steven Verruckt, Student—Graduate; Eddie Cramer, Police Officer, Homosexual; Andrew Lyall, Vampire
**Time period(s):** 1990s
**Locale(s):** California

**Summary:** Gay cop Eddie Cramer hopes to rehabilitate his flagging reputation with the police force by bringing in "The Sleepy Hollow Murderer," a mass murderer who steals the heads of his victims and who may be masquerading innocently as a member of Vampires Anonymous, a secret self-help group dedicated to curing vampires of their bloodthirsty habits.

**Other books you might like:**
John Peyton Cooke, *Out for Blood*, 1991
Scott Edelman, *The Gift*, 1990
Jewelle Gomez, *The Gilda Stories*, 1991
Anne Rice, *Interview with the Vampire*, 1976
John Steakley, *Vampire$*, 1990

---

### 3854
#### SEAN MCMULLEN

## The Centurion's Empire
(New York: Tor, 1998)

**Story type:** Science Fiction (Historical; Time Travel)
**Major character(s):** Vitellan Bavalius, Military Personnel (Roman Centurion), Time Traveler; Lucel Hunter, Mercenary, Genetically Altered Being; Jacques Bonhomme, Cult Member (Luministes), Time Traveler
**Time period(s):** 1st century (71-72); 2020s (2028-2029)
**Locale(s):** Houston, Texas; Libarna, Italy; Switzerland

**Summary:** Originally a Roman Centurion before becoming a human time machine, Vitellan sleeps through the centuries with the help of the Temporians, an ancient religious order that possesses a precious hibernation elixir. After a few waking interludes during pivotal historical periods, Vitellan finally awakens in a bewildering 21st century, and learns that a 14th-century enemy has pursued him through sleep and time.

**Other books you might like:**
Poul Anderson, *The Boat of a Million Years*, 1989
Kage Baker, *In the Garden of Iden*, 1998
Orson Scott Card, *The Worthing Saga*, 1991
Michael Flynn, *In the Country of the Blind*, 1990
Garry Kilworth, *Highlander*, 1998
Ian McDonald, *King of Morning, Queen of Day*, 1991
Ian Watson, *Oracle*, 1997

---

### 3855
#### CHARLES MCNAIR

## Land O'Goshen
(New York: St. Martin's Press, 1994)

**Story type:** Science Fiction (Literary; Disaster)
**Major character(s):** Buddy, Teenager, Orphan; Sack, Disembodied Personality; Cissy Barber, Girlfriend
**Time period(s):** 21st century
**Locale(s):** Goshen, Alabama

**Summary:** After losing his family to the Christian soldiers who have taken over the United States, Buddy, with Sack, retaliates as best he can.

**Other books you might like:**
Jesse Browner, *Conglomeros*, 1992
Samuel R. Delany, *They Fly at Ciron*, 1993

Richard Grant, *Through the Heart*, 1991
Thomas Harris, *The Silence of the Lambs*, 1988
Mark Leyner, *My Cousin, My Gastroenterologist*, 1990

---

### 3856
#### CLARE MCNALLY

## Cries of the Children
(New York: Onyx, 1992)

**Story type:** Horror (Wild Talents)
**Major character(s):** Samantha Winstead, Doctor; Rachel Freleng, Teacher (high school music teacher); Will Sherer, Detective—Private
**Time period(s):** 1990s (1992)
**Locale(s):** Denver, Colorado

**Summary:** Three different people befriend and eventually adopt three different children, each of whom appears mysteriously in their lives and manifests extraordinary intellectual and paranormal powers. As the foster parents investigate the pasts of the children, they begin to turn up many unresolved questions about their own pasts and origins.

**Other books you might like:**
William W. Johnstone, *Them*, 1992
Maxine O'Callaghan, *Dark Time*, 1992
John Wyndham, *The Midwich Cuckoos*, 1957

---

### 3857
#### CLARE MCNALLY

## Good Night, Sweet Angel
(New York: Tor, 1996)

**Story type:** Horror (Child-in-Peril)
**Major character(s):** Jenn Galbraith, Teacher; Emily Galbraith, Child (Jenn's 4-year-old daughter); Laura Bayless, Baker
**Time period(s):** 1990s (1996)
**Locale(s):** Pinebridge, Vermont

**Summary:** The ghostly Tara protects young Emily Galbraith from the spirit of her dead father, who tries repeatedly to abuse her from the other side of the grave. But Tara and someone else close to Emily have an agenda of their own that requires friendship with Emily if Tara is to be reincarnated as a living person.

**Other books you might like:**
Rick Hautala, *Ghost Light*, 1993
Ruby Jean Jensen, *Celia*, 1991
Samuel M. Key, *From a Whisper to a Scream*, 1992

---

### 3858
#### CLARE MCNALLY

## Stage Fright
(New York: Tor, 1995)

**Story type:** Horror (Reanimated Dead)
**Major character(s):** Hayley Seagal, Director (theatre); Bruce Donner, Writer (playwright); Aidan McGilray, Writer (playwright)
**Time period(s):** 1990s (1995)
**Locale(s):** Montauk, New York (on Long Island)

**Summary:** Hayley Seagal is trying to put her life back together and resume her career as a theatre director five years after jealous playwright Bruce Donner murdered her lover and committed suicide. When a mysterious figure known as the Shadow Man brings mayhem and murder to her new theater troupe, Hayley suspects that Bruce has returned from the dead to be with her once more.

**Other books you might like:**
Rick Hautala, *Ghost Light*, 1992
Ruby Jean Jensen, *Celia*, 1991
Stephen King, *Rose Madder*, 1995
Chet Williamson, *Reign*, 1990

## 3859

### BRIAN MCNAUGHTON

## *The Throne of Bones*

(Black River, New York: Terminal Fright Publications, 1997)

**Story type:** Horror (Collection)

**Summary:** Ten stories of otherwordly dark fantasy distinguished by gruesome imagery and black comedy. The author evokes both the horrors of H.P. Lovecraft and the decadent imaginary lands of Clark Ashton Smith in a variety of stories featuring ghouls, sorcerers, necromancers, necrophiles, and other fiendish beings. Selections include ''Ringard and Dendra,'' ''Meryphillia,'' ''The Retrograde Necromancer,'' ''The Return of Liron Wolfbaiter,'' and ''Vendriel and Vendreela.'' Afterword by S.T. Joshi.

**Other books you might like:**
Lin Carter, *The Xothic Legend Cycle*, 1997
Lord Dunsany, *A Dreamer's Tales*, 1910
H.P. Lovecraft, *The Dream Quest of Unknown Kadath*, 1970
Gary Myers, *The House of the Worm*, 1975
Darrell Schweitzer, *Tom O'Bedlam's Night Out and Other Strange Excursions*, 1985
Clark Ashton Smith, *Tales of Zothique*, 1995
Brian Stableford, *Fables and Fantasies*, 1996

## 3860

### MIKE MCQUAY

## *The Nexus*

(New York: Bantam Spectra, 1989)

**Story type:** Fantasy (Psychic Powers)
**Major character(s):** Dennis Stiller, Journalist; Amy Kyle, Psychic
**Time period(s):** 1980s
**Locale(s):** Dallas, Texas

**Summary:** Stiller, a former hot-shot reporter fallen on hard times, follows up on a story about a Texas faith-healer and uncovers a story about an autistic girl who can perform miracles. He attempts to control her powers with horrifying results.

**Other books you might like:**
Stephen King, *Firestarter*, 1980
Joanna Russ, *And Chaos Died*, 1970
Robert Silverberg, *Dying Inside*, 1972
Victor Koman, *The Jehovah Contract*, 1989
James Morrow, *Only Begotten Daughter*, 1989
Michael Youssef, *Earth King*, 1988

## 3861

### DONALD E. MCQUINN

## *The Prisoner Within*

(New York: Del Rey, 1998)

**Story type:** Science Fiction (Military; Space Opera)

**Series:** Lannat
**Major character(s):** Lannat, Military Personnel (captain); Etasalou, Military Personnel (commander); Plon, Police Officer (sheriff)
**Time period(s):** Indeterminate Future
**Locale(s):** Hire, Planet—Imaginary

**Summary:** The Emperor believes Captain Lannat to be a traitor and orders his execution, but a faction within his own military spirits the fugitive offworld. To redeem his honor, Lannat travels to the wartorn planet Hire where Etasalou, a sworn enemy of the emperor, performs illegal experiments in order to turn men into mindless killing machines.

**Other books you might like:**
Poul Anderson, *Ensign Flandry*, 1966
Lois McMaster Bujold, *Komarr*, 1998
Kenneth Bulmer, *No Man's World*, 1961
Jack L. Chalker, *Warriors of the Storm*, 1987
Roland J. Green, *Warriors for the Working Day*, 1994

## 3862

### DONALD E. MCQUINN

## *Wanderer*

(New York: Ballantine Del Ray, 1993)

**Story type:** Science Fiction (Post-Nuclear Holocaust; Political)
**Series:** Warrior
**Major character(s):** Sylah, Religious (Rose priestess); Donnacee Tate, Military Personnel, Time Traveler; Lanta, Religious (Violet priestess), Psychic (esper)
**Time period(s):** 26th century
**Locale(s):** San Francisco, California; North America (western)

**Summary:** The Flower destined to find the legendary Door to the lost place of the exterminated Teachers, women who could read and who possessed knowledge, Sylah sets off with Donnacee, Conway and Lanta despite the request of the Harvester, probable new Mother-Sister of her Church. Displaced 500 years into the future in cold sleep, Tate searches to her detriment for black people, refusing to believe they have all intermixed.

**Other books you might like:**
Michael Armstrong, *Agviq*, 1990
Octavia E. Butler, *Parable of the Sower*, 1993
Heather Gladney, *Teot's War*, 1987
Rosemary Kirstein, *The Steerswoman*, 1989
J.M. Morgan, *Desert Eden*, 1991
Catherine Wells, *The Earth Is All That Lasts*, 1991
Paul O. Williams, *The Breaking of Northwall*, 1980

## 3863

### DONALD E. MCQUINN

## *Warrior*

(New York: Ballantine/Del Rey, 1990)

**Story type:** Science Fiction (Post-Nuclear Holocaust; Adventure)
**Series:** Warrior
**Major character(s):** Gan Moondark, Leader, Warrior; Sylah, Religious (priestess); Donnacee Tate, Military Personnel, Time Traveler
**Time period(s):** 26th century
**Locale(s):** Utah

**Summary:** In a desperate attempt to preserve humanity despite the 21st Century nuclear-biological holocaust, Dannacee Tate and many other superior individuals have been equipped with the tools needed to rebuild society and put into suspended animation. Few of the group survive to find a renewed environment where several warrior societies have evolved. Tate separates from her companions, who move to the city where they are adopted by the evil king Altanar of Olta who loves their weaponry. When Tate joins with Gan Moondark and his companions, their journey provides a look at several societies before Tate and her 21st century comrades reunite.

**Other books you might like:**
Suzy McKee Charnas, *Motherlines*, 1979
Suzy McKee Charnas, *Walk to the End of the World*, 1974
Gordon R. Dickson, *Wolf and Iron*, 1990
R.M. Meluch, *Chicago Red*, 1990
Paul O. Williams, *The Breaking of Northwall*, 1980

---

**3864**

**DONALD E. MCQUINN**

## *Witch*

(New York: Ballantine Del Rey, 1994)

**Story type:** Science Fiction (Post-Nuclear Holocaust; Political)
**Series:** Warrior
**Major character(s):** Gan Moondark, Leader, Warrior; Donnacee Tate, Military Personnel, Time Traveler; Louis Leclerc, Inventor, Time Traveler
**Time period(s):** 26th century
**Locale(s):** North America (northwest)

**Summary:** Having found the Door and the library behind it, Sylah and the women from the post teach the Chosen reading and mathematics. The Church calls Sylah "Witch," and the inventions of her friends "witchcraft," intending to subvert Gan's support at home as well as encourage an alliance among all his enemies, including even Moonpriest, self-declared enemy of the Church.

**Other books you might like:**
David Brin, *The Postman*, 1985
Octavia E. Butler, *Parable of the Sower*, 1993
Heather Gladney, *Teot's War*, 1987
Catherine Wells, *The Earth Is All That Lasts*, 1991
Paul O. Williams, *The Breaking of Northwall*, 1981

---

**3865**

**DONALD E. MCQUINN**

## *With Full Honors*

(New York: Ballantine Del Rey, 1997)

**Story type:** Science Fiction (Political; Military)
**Major character(s):** Casey, Royalty; Lannat, Military Personnel
**Time period(s):** Indeterminate Future
**Locale(s):** Interstellar Empire/Federation

**Summary:** As various forces scheme to overthrow the emperor and the rulers of the 12 planets, Prince Casey becomes the catalyst and rallying point for more than one faction. Torn between his personal devotion to Casey and his oath to the Empire, Lannat strives to save Casey's honor.

**Other books you might like:**
Gordon R. Dickson, *Dorsai!*, 1976
David Weber, *On Basilisk Station*, 1993
David Weber, *Path of the Fury*, 1992
M.K. Wren, *House of the Wolf*, 1981

---

**3866**

**FRANK D. MCSHERRY JR.**, Editor
**CHARLES G. WAUGH**, Co-Editor

## *Eastern Ghosts*

(Nashville, Tennessee: Rutledge Hill Press, 1990)

**Story type:** Horror (Ghost Story)
**Series:** American Ghosts
**Locale(s):** East

**Summary:** A dozen ghost stories set in six different eastern states. Included are Helen R. Hull's classic story of life after death, "Clay-Shuttered Doors," Robert Bloch's pulp chiller of necrophilic obsession, "The Man Who Collected Poe"; Edward D. Hoch's tale of an unusual contestant in the Miss America pageant, "Remember My Name"; as well as stories by Isaac Asimov, Paul Gallico, Mary Higgins Clark, and others.

**Other books you might like:**
Marvin Kaye, *Haunted America*, 1990

---

**3867**

**FRANK D. MCSHERRY JR.**, Editor

## *The Fantastic Civil War*

(New York: Baen, 1991)

**Story type:** Fantasy (Anthology; Historical)
**Time period(s):** 1860s (American Civil War)
**Locale(s):** United States

**Summary:** This volume contains an introduction by S.M. Stirling and 10 stories about the Civil War, all published between 1939 and 1991. The earliest is Manly Wade Wellman's "The Valley Was Still" from 1939. The 1950s give us Jack Finney and Ward Moore, while the 1960s are represented by Robert E. Howard and George Byran. The remaining five stories from the 1980s and 1990s are by Eric Davin, John M. Ford, Charles L. Harness, Jack McDevitt and Harry Turtledove.

**Other books you might like:**
Gregory Benford, *Alternate Wars*, 1991
    Martin H. Greenberg, co-editor
Terry Bisson, *Fire on the Mountain*, 1988
Ward Moore, *Bring the Jubilee*, 1953
Kevin D. Randle, *Remember Gettysburg*, 1988
    Robert J. Cornett, co-author
William Sanders, *The Wild Blue and the Gray*, 1991
S.M. Stirling, *Marching through Georgia*, 1988

---

**3868**

**FRANK D. MCSHERRY JR.**, Editor
**CHARLES G. WAUGH**, Co-Editor

## *Ghosts of the Heartland*

(Nashville, Tennessee: Rutledge Hill Press, 1990)

**Story type:** Horror (Ghost Story)
**Series:** American Ghosts
**Locale(s):** Midwest

**Summary:** Eighteen ghost stories set in 12 different midwestern states. Included are Fritz Leiber's masterpiece of urban horror "Smoke Ghost," Ambrose Bierce's suspenseful "The Boarded Window," Robert Bloch's sensitive "Floral Tribute," and "But at

My Back I Always Here,'' David Morrell's terrifying story of an obsessive love that persists beyond death.

**Other books you might like:**
Marvin Kaye, *Haunted America*, 1990

---

**3869**

**FRANK D. MCSHERRY JR.**, Editor
**CHARLES G. WAUGH**, Co-Editor
**MARTIN H. GREENBERG**, Co-Editor

### Great American Ghost Stories
(Nashville, Tennessee: Rutledge Hill Press, 1991)

**Story type:** Horror (Ghost Story)
**Locale(s):** United States

**Summary:** Twenty-nine ghost stories written by 26 authors and set in 22 different states. Included are Harlan Ellison's classic of supernatural betrayal, ''Pretty Maggie Moneyeyes''; H.P. Lovecraft's pastiche of *Frankenstein*, ''Herbert West Reanimator''; Ambrose Bierce's classic, ''The Boarded Window''; Seabury Quinn's mix of ghosts and lycanthropy, ''The Phantom Farmhouse''; Arthur J. Burks' tale of a ghostly re-enactment of a murder, ''The Ghosts of Steamboat Coulee''; and Joyce Carol Oates' story of a skeptic turned spiritualist, ''Night-Side.''

**Other books you might like:**
Marvin Kaye, *Haunted America*, 1990
Paul F. Olson, *Post Mortem: New Tales of Ghostly Horror*, 1988
   David Silva, co-author

---

**3870**

**FRANK D. MCSHERRY JR.**, Editor
**CHARLES G. WAUGH**, Co-Editor

### Western Ghosts
(Nashville, Tennessee: Rutledge Hill Press, 1990)

**Story type:** Horror (Ghost Story)
**Series:** American Ghosts
**Locale(s):** West

**Summary:** Thirteen stories representing 11 different western states. They range from Ambrose Bierce's spectral classic ''The Stranger,'' to Arthur J. Burks' grim ''The Ghosts of Steamboat Coulee,'' Harlan Ellison's cynical ''Pretty Maggie Moneyeyes,'' and Billy Wolfenbarger's poignant ''The Attic.''

**Other books you might like:**
Marvin Kaye, *Haunted America*, 1990
Joe R. Lansdale, *The New Frontier*, 1989
Joe R. Lansdale, *Razored Saddles*, 1989
   Pat LoBrutto, co-author

---

**3871**

**SHIRLEY MEIER**

### Shadow's Daughter
(New York: Baen, 1991)

**Story type:** Fantasy (Urban; Young Adult)
**Series:** Fifth Millennium
**Major character(s):** Megan Lixandashkya, Child; Lixand Mikhailovych, Storyteller, Artisan (weaver); Ness, Artisan, Parent (Megan's)
**Time period(s):** 36th century

**Locale(s):** F'talezon, Fictional City

**Summary:** Shortly after Megan begins school, political conflicts in the city cause her parents to lose their positions. As they struggle to re-establish themselves, Megan gets an education in street life with the kidpack. They manage to apprentice Megan to the Merchant's Guild (even with its unspoken connection to the Thieves' Guild), but Lixand and Ness are destroyed by the increasingly ruthless city government, leaving Megan to her Aunt Marte's brutality.

**Other books you might like:**
Sharon Baker, *Burning Tears of Sassurum*, 1988
Octavia E. Butler, *Survivor*, 1978
Sheila Gilluly, *The Boy From the Burren*, 1990
Diana Wynne Jones, *Cart and Cwidder*, 1977
Megan Lindholm, *Luck of the Wheels*, 1989
Robin McKinley, *The Blue Sword*, 1982
Will Shetterly, *Elsewhere*, 1991
S.M. Stirling, *Snow Brother*, 1992
   revised
Karen Wehrstein, *Lion's Heart*, 1991
Karen Wehrstein, *Lion's Soul*, 1991

---

**3872**

**SHIRLEY MEIER**
**S.M. STIRLING**, Co-Author
**KAREN WEHRSTEIN**, Co-Author

### Shadow's Son
(New York: Baen, 1991)

**Story type:** Fantasy (Quest)
**Series:** Fifth Millennium
**Major character(s):** Megan Whitlock, Businesswoman (merchant), Warrior, Mercenary; Shkai'ra, Warrior; Chevenga, Ruler
**Time period(s):** 35th century
**Locale(s):** Arkan, Fictional Country; Yeoli, Fictional Country

**Summary:** Megan's agent has finally located the son she bore in slavery. Sold away, he is now a dancing boy in the corrupt Arkan Empire. Megan and Sh'Kaira set out to rescue him, joining Chevenga's Yeoli army as the best way of reaching the Arkan capital in the midst of war. This novel is set eight years after the events of *Shadow's Daughter* (1991), 1 1/2 years after those of *The Cage* (1989) and concurrently with those of *Lion's Soul* (1991).

**Other books you might like:**
Gael Baudino, *Dragonsword*, 1988
Samuel R. Delany, *Tales of Neveryon*, 1979
Heather Gladney, *Teot's War*, 1987
Guy Gavriel Kay, *Tigana*, 1990
Rosemary Kirstein, *The Steerswoman*, 1989
Joel Rosenberg, *D'Shai*, 1991
S.M. Stirling, *Snow Brother*, 1992
   revised
Karen Wehrstein, *Lion's Heart*, 1991
Karen Wehrstein, *Lion's Soul*, 1991

---

**3873**

**R.M. MELUCH**

### Chicago Red
(New York: Roc, 1990)

**Story type:** Science Fiction (Post-Holocaust; Political)
**Major character(s):** Chris-John Stanton, Revolutionary; Edward III, Ruler (King of America)

**Time period(s):** Indeterminate Future
**Locale(s):** Kingdom of America, Fictional Country (northern Great Plains)

**Summary:** Motivated by the death of a rebel leader, Chris-John Stanton adopts the nom de guerre, Chicago Red, and organizes the rebellion to overthrow the king and the aristocracy.

**Other books you might like:**
Isaac Asimov, *Foundation and Empire*, 1952
Robert A. Heinlein, *Farnham's Freehold*, 1964
Robert A. Heinlein, *Sixth Column*, 1949
Donald E. McQuinn, *Warrior*, 1990
Steve Perry, *The Man Who Never Missed*, 1985
Alis A. Rasmussen, *Revolution's Shore*, 1990
Paul O. Williams, *The Breaking of Northwall*, 1980

## 3874

### R.M. MELUCH

## The Queen's Squadron

(New York: Roc, 1992)

**Story type:** Science Fiction (Immortality; Political)
**Major character(s):** Penetanguishene, Government Official (torturer); Paul Strand, Military Personnel, Hero; Ashata/Maya, Immortal, Pilot
**Time period(s):** 53rd century
**Locale(s):** Eta Cassiopeia IV, Planet—Imaginary (Eta Cas)

**Summary:** Maya, denying her immortality, becomes a c-ship pilot and begins to appreciate mortals as humans. With war between Telegonia and Vihrhalt looming, the last of the mondesi truthsayers, Penetanguishene, unsuccessfully tortures Paul to discover the details of ''Gotterdammerung,'' the Telegonian secret plan to destroy the immortals and win the war despite their lack of faster-than-light ships.

**Other books you might like:**
Octavia E. Butler, *Kindred*, 1979
James Gunn, *Star Bridge*, 1989
  Jack Williamson, co-author
Joe Haldeman, *Buying Time*, 1989
Robert Reed, *Down the Bright Way*, 1991
Frank M. Robinson, *The Dark Beyond the Stars*, 1991
Bruce Sterling, *Involution Ocean*, 1977
A.E. Van Vogt, *The Weapon Shops of Isher*, 1951
Gene Wolfe, *The Shadow of the Torturer*, 1980

## 3875

### R.M. MELUCH

## War Birds

(New York: NAL Signet, 1989)

**Story type:** Science Fiction (Military)
**Major character(s):** Anthony Northfield, Professor, Pilot
**Time period(s):** Indeterminate Future
**Locale(s):** Tannia, Planet—Imaginary; Erd, Planet—Imaginary; Occo, Planet—Imaginary

**Summary:** In a star system with three human-inhabited planets interplanetary war is the norm. When new hostilities seem in the offing, Anthony Northfield, former spaceplane ace, former prisoner of war, now an English professor, is pressured to reenlist.

**Other books you might like:**
Dale Brown, *Day of the Cheetah*, 1989
Emma Bull, *Falcon*, 1989

Gordon R. Dickson, *The Tactics of Mistake*, 1971
S.N. Lewitt, *Cyberstealth*, 1989
S.N. Lewitt, *Dancing Vac*, 1990

## 3876

### PAULINE MELVILLE

## Shape-Shifter: Stories by Pauline Melville

(New York: Pantheon, 1991)

**Story type:** Fantasy (Collection; Literary)
**Time period(s):** Indeterminate
**Locale(s):** West Indies

**Summary:** This volume contains 10 stories on West Indian themes, presenting strong characters with deft touches of humor. This won the Guardian Fiction Prize and the International PEN's Macmillan Silver Pen Award. Author's first book.

**Other books you might like:**
Brian W. Aldiss, *A Romance of the Equator: The Best Fantasy Stories of Brian W. Aldiss*, 1990
J.G. Ballard, *Vermilion Sands*, 1971
Chad Oliver, *Another Kind*, 1954
Rosemary Sutcliff, *Sun Horse, Moon Horse*, 1977
Mary Alexander Walker, *The Scathach and the Maeve's Daughter*, 1990

## 3877

### A. MERRITT

## Burn, Witch, Burn!/Creep, Shadow, Creep!

(New York: Leisure, 1996)

**Story type:** Horror (Collection)

**Summary:** THis omnibus volume collects two novels by a renowned fantasy writer from the early 20th century. *Burn, Witch, Burn!*, first published in book form in 1933, concerns Dr. Lowell's battle with Madame Mandilip, a practitioner of occult arts who steals the souls of her victims and uses them to reanimate malevolent dolls under her control. *Creep, Shadow, Creep!* first published in book form in 1943 (as *Creep, Shadow!*) concerns Alan Caranac, a colleague of Lowell's, who runs afoul of Madame Mandilip's former lover and his companion, a survivor of a pagan cult who awakens archetypal memories in her contemporary male victims and drives them to madness and death.

**Other books you might like:**
Edgar Rice Burroughs, *The Eternal Lover*, 1925
H. Rider Haggard, *She*, 1887
Henry Kuttner, *The Dark World*, 1965
Greye La Spina, *Invaders From the Dark*, 1960
Jack Williamson, *Darker than You Think*, 1948

## 3878

### A. MERRITT

## The Face in the Abyss

(New York: Collier, 1992)

**Story type:** Fantasy (Adventure; Alternate World)
**Major character(s):** Nicholas Graydon, Adventurer, Scientist; Suarra, Religious (priestess); Adana ''the Snake Mother'', Mythical Creature
**Time period(s):** 1930s

**Locale(s):** Andes Mountains, South America; Yu-Atlanchi, Fictional Country

**Summary:** First published in 1931, this novel relates Nicholas Graydon's adventures involving love, betrayal, ancient mystery and evil in the fabulous land of Yu-Atlanchi. Graydon battles human and supernatural enemies as well as his own conflicting desires as he struggles to win the hand of Suarra.

**Other books you might like:**
Margaret Ball, *Flameweaver*, 1991
Robert Holdstock, *Mythago Wood*, 1984
Edward Myers, *The Mountain Made of Light*, 1992
Elizabeth Ann Scarborough, *Last Refuge*, 1992
Elizabeth Ann Scarborough, *Nothing Sacred*, 1991
Rex Stout, *Under the Andes*, 1984

---

**3879**

**JOHN METCALFE**

### Nightmare Jack and Other Stories

(Ashcroft, British Columbia: Ash-Tree Press, 1998)

**Story type:** Horror (Collection)

**Summary:** These 17 stories represent the complete macabre fiction of a master of ambiguous supernatural horror. "The Feasting Dead" is concerned with the vampiric hold a repugnant, possibly dead being gains over a young boy during a European vacation. "The Badlands" tells of a man, possibly mad, who discovers menacing landscape on the horizon of a town he visits. Both "The Smoking Leg" and the title story concern the peculiar fates that befall people who steal gems from revered idols in primitive countries. Richard Dalby supplies an introduction and Alexis Lykiard the afterword.

**Other books you might like:**
Robert Aickman, *Cold Hand in Mine*, 1975
Sarban, *Ringstones, and Other Curious Tales*, 1951
H. Russell Wakefield, *They Return at Evening*, 1928
Edward Lucas White, *Lukundoo and Other Stories*, 1927
Henry S. Whitehead, *West India Lights*, 1946

---

**3880**

**JOHN METCALFE**

### Nightmare Jack and Other Stories

(Ashcroft, British Columbia: Ash-Tree Press, 1998)

**Story type:** Horror (Collection)

**Summary:** Seventeen stories represent the complete macabre fiction of a master of ambiguous supernatural horror. "The Feasting Dead" is concerned with the vampiric hold a repugnant, possibly dead being gains over a young boy during a European vacation. "The Badlands" tells of a man, perhaps mad, who discovers a menacing landscape on the horizon of a town he visits. Both "The Smoking Leg" and the title story concern peculiar fates that befall people who steal gems from revered idols in primitive countries. Richard Dalby supplies the introduction and Alexis Lykiard the afterword.

**Other books you might like:**
Robert Aickman, *Cold Hand in Mine*, 1975
Sarban, *Ringstones, and Other Curious Tales*, 1951
H. Russell Wakefield, *They Return at Evening*, 1928
Edward Lucas White, *Lukundoo and Other Stories*, 1927
Henry S. Whitehead, *West India Lights*, 1946

---

**3881**

**RIC MEYERS**

### Fear Itself

(New York: Dell, 1991)

**Story type:** Horror (Supernatural Vengeance)
**Series:** Book of the Undead Trilogy
**Major character(s):** Geoffrey Robert Merrick, Businessman (a.k.a. Grim), Reanimated Dead; Melanie Merrick, Housewife; Juan Ruiz, Criminal (assassin)
**Time period(s):** 1990s
**Locale(s):** New York, New York

**Summary:** Killed in an explosion set off to terminate his resistance to his company's trafficking with Central American drug cartels, Geoffrey Merrick fights off the demon that attempts to claim his soul and returns to the world of the living as Grim, a charred and scarred avenging angel. In this first novel of the "Book of the Undead" trilogy, Grim's mission to track down his assassins and protect his wife from the sleazy business associates who set him up is interrupted by encounters with New York City low-life, including derelict burners and a mass murderer.

**Other books you might like:**
Randall Boyll, *Darkman*, 1991

---

**3882**

**RIC MEYERS**

### Living Hell

(New York: Dell, 1991)

**Story type:** Horror (Reanimated Dead)
**Series:** Book of the Undead Trilogy
**Major character(s):** Geoffrey Robert Merrick, Businessman (a.k.a. Grim), Reanimated Dead; Melanie Merrick, Housewife; Classy Jack Watkins, Drug Dealer
**Time period(s):** 1990s
**Locale(s):** New York, New York

**Summary:** In this second book in the Book of the Undead Trilogy, Geoffrey Merrick, alias "Grim," continues his pursuit of the men who killed him, all the while serving as a vigilante who cleans up crime on the streets of New York. In this outing he destroys assorted pimps and pushers, as well as a coven of Satanists venting their rage on the nuns and priests of Manhattan.

**Other books you might like:**
Randall Boyll, *Darkman*, 1991
Barbara Hambly, *Beauty and the Beast*, 1989
F. Paul Wilson, *The Tomb*, 1984

---

**3883**

**RIC MEYERS**

### Worst Nightmare

(New York: Dell, 1992)

**Story type:** Horror (Supernatural Vengeance)
**Series:** Book of the Undead Trilogy
**Major character(s):** Geoffrey Robert Merrick, Businessman (aka Grim), Reanimated Dead; Martin Kirshner, Criminal (child molester); Joshua Carl Evans, Child
**Time period(s):** 1990s
**Locale(s):** New York, New York

**Summary:** The third installment in the ongoing saga of Geoffrey Marrick, a.k.a. Grim, a businessman blown to pieces for his do-gooding sensibilites who returns to life as a scarred avenger through sheer force of will. This time, Grim is on the trail of a ruthless child molester who uses the state welfare system to track down his victims.

**Other books you might like:**
Randall Boyll, *Darkman*, 1991
Barbara Hambly, *Beauty and the Beast*, 1989
Grant Stockbridge, *The Spider: Master of Men*, 1991
F. Paul Wilson, *The Tomb*, 1984

---

**3884**

**YVES MEYNARD**

### The Book of Knights

(New York: Tor, 1998)

**Story type:** Fantasy (Young Adult; Quest)
**Major character(s):** Adelrune, Child, Student Riander, Knight, Teacher
**Time period(s):** Indeterminate
**Locale(s):** Faudace, Fictional City

**Summary:** A young boy in a strict household in a very strict country learns to read a mysterious book. *The Book of Knights* gives him the idea of running away to become a knight himself, a path more dangerous than the book ever suggested. First book in English.

**Other books you might like:**
Anne Eliot Crompton, *Gawain and Lady Green*, 1997
Michael Ende, *The Neverending Story*, 1983
Cary James, *King & Raven*, 1995
Ursula K. Le Guin, *A Wizard of Earthsea*, 1968
Will Shetterly, *Elsewhere*, 1991

---

**3885**

**BILL MICHAELS** (Pseudonym of William Carney)

### Witchcraft

(New York: Zebra, 1997)

**Story type:** Horror (Black Magic)
**Major character(s):** Steve Brogan, Detective—Private; Molly Daniels, Witch; Lady Eva, Witch
**Time period(s):** 1990s (1997)
**Locale(s):** Hennington, California

**Summary:** Steve Brogan investigates the disinterment and mutilation of a corpse in the small town of Hennington and uncovers a feud between the Coven of the Crystal Moon, a Wicca cult, and the Coven of the Dark Dream, a black magic cult. The situation intensifies when Lady Eva, leader of the Coven of the Dark Dream, steals the daughter of one of the Wicca witches to use in a ritual that will let an ancient evil back into the world.

**Other books you might like:**
Ramsey Campbell, *The Nameless*, 1981
Gary L. Holleman, *Demon Fire*, 1995
Adrian Savage, *Symphony*, 1992
Brian Scott Smith, *When Shadows Fall*, 1997
Robert Weinberg, *The Black Lodge*, 1991

---

**3886**

**MELISA MICHAELS**

### Cold Iron

(New York: Roc, 1997)

**Story type:** Fantasy (Mystery; Urban)
**Major character(s):** Rosalynd ''Rosie'' Lavine, Detective—Private; Candy Cayne, Teenager, Fanatic (Cold Iron groupie); Jorandel ''Jorie'', Mythical Creature (elf), Musician (Cold Iron)
**Time period(s):** 1990s
**Locale(s):** San Francisco, California; Los Angeles, California

**Summary:** Against her better judgment, Rosalynd answers Candy's plea to uncover the person attempting to kill the lead singer of an elfrock band. Posing as Candy's cousin to gain acceptance among Cold Iron's entourage, Rosalynd cannot resist the fast lifestyle, despite the increased danger from those intent on thwarting her efforts.

**Other books you might like:**
Gael Baudino, *Gossamer Axe*, 1990
Greg Bear, *Songs of Earth and Power*, 1994
Emma Bull, *War for the Oaks*, 1987
Kara Dalkey, *Steel Rose*, 1997
Elizabeth Ann Scarborough, *Phantom Banjo*, 1991

---

**3887**

**MELISA MICHAELS**

### Sister to the Rain

(New York: Roc, 1998)

**Story type:** Fantasy (Mystery; Urban)
**Major character(s):** Rosalynd ''Rosie'' Lavine, Detective—Private; Shannon Arthur, Detective—Private
**Time period(s):** 1990s
**Locale(s):** Fey Valley, California (artists' colony)

**Summary:** When she investigates odd noises and disturbances at an artists' colony, Rosie doesn't expect much difficulty, until the death of a human brings her and Shannon into a deadly elven conflict.

**Other books you might like:**
Gael Baudino, *Gossamer Axe*, 1990
Emma Bull, *War for the Oaks*, 1987
Kara Dalkey, *Steel Rose*, 1997
Charles de Lint, *Memory and Dream*, 1994
Mercedes Lackey, *Chrome Circle*, 1994
    Larry Dixon, co-author

---

**3888**

**MELISA C. MICHAELS**

### Far Harbor

(New York: Tor, 1989)

**Story type:** Science Fiction (Space Opera)
**Major character(s):** Ugly Starling, Outcast; Prince Hawke, Heir
**Time period(s):** Indeterminate Future
**Locale(s):** Paradise, Planet—Imaginary

**Summary:** The Terran imperialists and the native rulers of Paradise are in an uneasy truce, political factions and undercover agents doing their best to give either side the advantage. Meanwhile, the one woman who can free her planet from the weight of Terran oppression is living in Cinderella-like poverty, beaten down by her step-parents, convinced that she's an alien.

**Other books you might like:**
Jay D. Blakeney, *The Goda War*, 1989
Jay D. Blakeney, *Requiem for Anthi*, 1990
Mary Gentle, *Ancient Light*, 1989
Mary Gentle, *Golden Witchbreed*, 1983
Anne McCaffrey, *Crystal Singer*, 1982
Anne McCaffrey, *The Ship Who Sang*, 1969

## 3889
### SANDRA MIESEL

## Shaman
(New York: Baen, 1989)

**Story type:** Fantasy (Adventure)
**Major character(s):** Ria, Shaman
**Time period(s):** Indeterminate
**Locale(s):** Alternate Earth

**Summary:** Ria, a young shaman, is able to travel between worlds because of her developing magic powers. Ultimately, her abilities make her the last hope of the human race.

**Other books you might like:**
Michaela Roessner, *Walkabout Woman*, 1988
Linda Lay Shuler, *She Who Remembers*, 1988

## 3890
### VICTOR MILAN

## The Cybernetic Shogun
(New York: Morrow, 1990)

**Story type:** Science Fiction (Robot Fiction)
**Major character(s):** Hidetada, Artificial Intelligence; Musashi, Artificial Intelligence
**Time period(s):** 21st century
**Locale(s):** Floating World, Space Station; The Reef, Alternate Universe

**Summary:** The artificial intelligence Tokugawa has been destroyed, but its "offspring," the AIs Hidetada and Musashi, have gained enormous power and are now in direct conflict. Hidetada desires to gain power over what's left of the Earth and its people. Musashi hopes to save humanity by building a space ark that will take the remnants of our race to the stars. This is the sequel to *The Cybernetic Samurai*.

**Other books you might like:**
William Gibson, *Count Zero*, 1985
William Gibson, *Mona Lisa Overdrive*, 1988
William Gibson, *Neuromancer*, 1984
W.T. Quick, *Dreams of Flesh and Sand*, 1988
W.T. Quick, *Dreams of Gods and Men*, 1989
Rudy Rucker, *Wetware*, 1988
Bruce Sterling, *Islands in the Net*, 1988
Walter Jon Williams, *Hardwired*, 1986

## 3891
### VICTOR MILAN

## Turn of the Cards
(New York: Bantam Spectra, 1993)

**Story type:** Science Fiction (Alternate Universe; Psychic Powers)
**Series:** Wild Cards
**Major character(s):** Mark "Captain Trips" Meadows, Genetically Altered Being, Scientist (biochemist); Croyd "The Sleeper" Crenson, Genetically Altered Being; Charles Sobel, Military Personnel
**Time period(s):** 1990s
**Locale(s):** Europe; Asia

**Summary:** Fleeing CIA and DEA agents, Mark Meadows meets Colonel Charles Sobel who plans a war of conquest utilizing an army with Joker powers. Mark must decide if he will follow his peaceful ideals or allow his submerged personalities, complete with Ace powers, to take over and serve the madman's goal of killing nats, unmodified humans.

**Other books you might like:**
Michael Bishop, *Count Geiger's Blues*, 1992
Mark Grant, *Mutants Amok*, 1991
Michael Kandel, *Captain Jack Zodiac*, 1992
George R.R. Martin, *The Wild Cards Series*, 1987-1993 editor
Melinda M. Snodgrass, *Double Solitaire*, 1992
Michael D. Weaver, *My Father Immortal*, 1989

## 3892
### CARL MILLER

## The Goblin Plain War
(New York: Ace, 1991)

**Story type:** Fantasy (Adventure)
**Series:** Dragonbound
**Major character(s):** Rockdream, Warrior, Hunter; Coral, Sorceress
**Time period(s):** Indeterminate
**Locale(s):** Goblin Plain, Mythical Place

**Summary:** Rockdream and Coral must find a way to end the war between humans and goblins before the war results in universal extermination.

**Other books you might like:**
David Eddings, *Pawn of Prophecy*, 1982
Robert Jordan, *The Eye of the World*, 1989
John Lee, *The Unicorn Solution*, 1991
Elizabeth Moon, *Divided Allegiance*, 1988
Elizabeth Moon, *Oath of Gold*, 1989
Elizabeth Moon, *Sheepfarmer's Daughter*, 1988

## 3893
### CARL MILLER

## The Warrior and the Witch
(New York: Ace, 1990)

**Story type:** Fantasy (Adventure)
**Major character(s):** Rockdream, Military Personnel (guardsman); Coral, Sorceress; Riversong, Mythical Creature (dragon)
**Time period(s):** Indeterminate
**Locale(s):** Newport, Fictional City

**Summary:** Newport was constructed to ward off attack from the ground, with its many towers and miles of walls. But Riversong will attack from the air and the city may not stand. Rockdream and Coral lead a small group of refugees to safety.

**Other books you might like:**
Glen Cook, *Tower of Fear*, 1989
Melanie Rawn, *Dragon Prince*, 1988
Michael Scott Rohan, *The Forge in the Forest*, 1989
J.R.R. Tolkien, *The Fellowship of the Ring*, 1954
Tad Williams, *The Dragonbone Chair*, 1988

---

**3894**

**FAREN MILLER**

## The Illusionists

(New York: Popular Library Questar, 1991)

**Story type:** Fantasy (Quest; Light Fantasy)
**Major character(s):** Gherifan Arnix, Actor; Moabet Shar, Psychic; Railu Knifedancer, Military Personnel (lancer)
**Time period(s):** Indeterminate Past
**Locale(s):** Xalycis Rock, Fictional City

**Summary:** In the ruins of Xalycis Rock, a powerful magical Artifact is found and leads to the murder of Aubric i-Arnix, a leading citizen of Xalycis Rock. Moabet Shar, a psychic percept, and Gherifan Arnix work to uncover the murderer and prevent the Artifact from destroying the city.

**Other books you might like:**
Steven Brust, *Jhereg*, 1983
Glen Cook, *Tower of Fear*, 1989
P.C. Hodgell, *God Stalk*, 1982

---

**3895**

**G. WAYNE MILLER**

## Thunder Rise

(New York: Jove, 1992)

**Story type:** Horror (Ancient Evil Unleashed)
**Major character(s):** Brad Gale, Journalist; Abby ''Apple Guy'' Gale, Child (Brad's five-year-old daughter); Charlie Moonlight, Drifter, Indian
**Time period(s):** 1980s (1988)
**Locale(s):** Morgantown, Massachusetts

**Summary:** The awakening of a demon inside Thunder Mountain manifests as a series of terrifying dreams that lead to debility and death among the children of nearby Morgantown. When Brad Gale's daughter becomes afflicted, he must put his skepticism behind him and join forces with Quidneck Indian Charlie Moonlight to restrain the demon once more. This novel, the author's first, was originally published in 1989.

**Other books you might like:**
Morgan Fields, *Shaman Woods*, 1989
T. Chris Martindale, *Where the Chill Waits*, 1990
Kathryn Ptacek, *Ghost Dance*, 1990
Patrick Whalen, *Deathwalker*, 1992
Chet Williamson, *Dreamthorp*, 1989

---

**3896**

**RAND MILLER**
**ROBYN MILLER**, Co-Author
**DAVID WINGROVE**, Co-Author

## Myst: The Book of Atrus

(New York: Hyperion, 1995)

**Story type:** Fantasy (Adventure)
**Series:** Myst
**Major character(s):** Atrus, Magician; Gehn, Magician
**Time period(s):** Indeterminate
**Locale(s):** Planet—Imaginary; Myst, Fictional Country (island)

**Summary:** Gehn locates his son, Atrus, and begins his training in the magic of the vanished D'ni, who possessed the ability to create new worlds through writing. First of a CD-ROM game tie-in.

**Other books you might like:**
Charles de Lint, *Memory and Dream*, 1994
Robin Hobb, *Assassin's Apprentice*, 1995
Ursula K. Le Guin, *The Lathe of Heaven*, 1971
David Wingrove, *The Broken Wheel*, 1991
David Wingrove, *The Middle Kingdom*, 1990
David Worsick, *Henry's Gift: The Magic Eye*, 1994

---

**3897**

**RAND MILLER**
**DAVID WINGROVE**, Co-Author

## Myst: The Book of D'ni

(New York: Hyperion, 1997)

**Story type:** Fantasy (Science Fiction; Quest)
**Series:** Myst
**Major character(s):** Eedrah, Royalty (D'ni); Atrus, Writer, Magician; Catherine, Adventurer
**Time period(s):** Indeterminate Future
**Locale(s):** Terahnee, Mythical Place; D'ni, Mythical Place

**Summary:** While exploring abandoned D'ni, Atrus and Catherine find the forbidden Book linking Terahee with D'ni, inadvertently helping Eedrah fulfill the prophecy and find the lost people of C'ni. CD-ROM game tie-in.

**Other books you might like:**
Charles de Lint, *Memory and Dream*, 1994
Alan Dean Foster, *The Dig*, 1996
Patricia A. McKillip, *The Riddle-Master of Hed*, 1976
David Wingrove, *The Middle Kingdom*, 1990
David Worsick, *Henry's Gift: The Magic Eye*, 1994

---

**3898**

**REX MILLER**

## Butcher

(New York: Pocket, 1994)

**Story type:** Horror (Serial Killer)
**Series:** Chaingang Bunkowski
**Major character(s):** Daniel ''Chaingang'' Bunkowski, Serial Killer; Ray Meara, Farmer; Solomon Royal, Doctor (aka Emil Shtolz)
**Time period(s):** 1990s (1994)
**Locale(s):** Bayou Ridge, Missouri

**Summary:** Former Vietnam vet and serial killer Chaingang Bunkowski is deployed by his handlers to terminate Solomon Royal, a midwestern doctor whose past as a Nazi war criminal has caught up with him. But Chaingang's superiors don't understand that giving the misanthrope a license to kill is not unlike handing a pyromaniac a book of matches.

**Other books you might like:**
Diane Duane, *Spectres*, 1991
Kathryn Ptacek, *The Hunted*, 1993
Robert Arthur Smith, *Silent Witness*, 1988
Peter Straub, *Koko*, 1988

**3899**

REX MILLER

## Chaingang
(New York: Pocket, 1992)

**Story type:** Horror (Serial Killer)
**Series:** Chaingang Bunkowski
**Major character(s):** Daniel "Chaingang" Bunkowski, Serial Killer; Dr. Norman, Doctor; Royce Hawthorne, Young Man
**Time period(s):** 1970s
**Locale(s):** Marion, Missouri (Marion Penitentiary)

**Summary:** This fifth novel in the chronicles of Chaingang Bunkowski, a 500-pound misanthrope who hates all human beings, especially those who kill animals, backtracks to his early prison years, when a penitentiary doctor first encouraged his antisocial proclivities and helped create a monster.

**Other books you might like:**
Douglas Borton, *Kane*, 1990
Stephen Gallagher, *Down River*, 1989
Stephen R. George, *Near Dead*, 1992
Thomas Harris, *Red Dragon*, 1981
Michael Slade, *Ghoul*, 1990

**3900**

REX MILLER

## Iceman
(New York: Onyx, 1990)

**Story type:** Horror (Serial Killer)
**Series:** Jack Eichord Chronicles
**Major character(s):** Jack Eichord, Detective—Police; Donna Eichord, Spouse; Arthur Spoda, Serial Killer
**Time period(s):** 1990s
**Locale(s):** Buckhead County, Arkansas

**Summary:** At work, cop Jack Eichord tracks an icepick-wielding serial killer while at home Donna tries to raise their two-year-old adopted son who, Jack suspects, may have inherited psychopathic tendencies from his late father, perpetrator of "the worst mass-murder case in history."

**Other books you might like:**
Stephen Gallagher, *Down River*, 1989
William Relling Jr., *New Moon*, 1988
Thomas Harris, *Red Dragon*, 1981

**3901**

REX MILLER

## Savant
(New York: Pocket, 1994)

**Story type:** Horror (Serial Killer)
**Series:** Chaingang Bunkowski
**Major character(s):** Daniel "Chaingang" Bunkowski, Serial Killer; Bobby Price, Criminal (assassin); Victor Trask, Journalist (radio)
**Time period(s):** 1990s (1994)
**Locale(s):** Kansas City, Missouri

**Summary:** Government-trained assassin Chaingang Bunkowski returns to his hometown to kill the abusive stepmother who helped turn him into a misanthrope, all the while being pursued by another government-trained assassin trying out the new SAVANT rifle, capable of terminating its target from a range of two miles. Running commentary on the proliferation of violence in America is provided by a radio talk-show personality who has caught wind of Chaingang's exploits.

**Other books you might like:**
Stephen Gallagher, *Down River*, 1989
T.J. Kirby, *Dangerous Nature*, 1993
Bob Mayer, *Operation Synbat*, 1994
Peter Straub, *Koko*, 1988

**3902**

REX MILLER

## Slice
(New York: NAL Onyx, 1990)

**Story type:** Horror (Serial Killer)
**Series:** Chaingang Bunkowski
**Major character(s):** Jack Eichord, Detective—Police (serial killer expert); Daniel "Chaingang" Bunkowski, Serial Killer (six foot seven)
**Time period(s):** 1980s
**Locale(s):** Atlanta, Georgia; Chicago, Illinois

**Summary:** After recovering from his injuries in the Chicago sewers, "Chaingang" sets out to get revenge against his nemesis, Jack Eichord.

**Other books you might like:**
Clive Barker, *The Damnation Game*, 1985
Ramsey Campbell, *The Face That Must Die*, 1979
Thomas Harris, *Red Dragon*, 1981

**3903**

RON MILLER

## Hearts and Armor
(New York: Ace, 1992)

**Story type:** Fantasy (Quest; Political)
**Series:** Bronwyn
**Major character(s):** Bronwyn, Royalty (princess), Warrior; Thud Mollockle, Mythical Creature (kobold), Adventurer
**Time period(s):** Indeterminate
**Locale(s):** Guesclin, Mythical Place; Tamlaght, Fictional Country; Blavek, Fictional City

**Summary:** Leading a mighty invasionary force, Princess Bronwyn returns to her homeland to overthrow her sibling rival and recapture her throne.

**Other books you might like:**
Elizabeth Moon, *Divided Allegiance*, 1988
Elizabeth Moon, *Oath of Gold*, 1989
Elizabeth Moon, *Sheepfarmer's Daughter*, 1988

## 3904

### RON MILLER

## Palaces and Prisons

(New York: Ace, 1991)

**Story type:** Fantasy (Adventure)
**Series:** Bronwyn
**Major character(s):** Bronwyn, Royalty (princess), Fugitive; Thud Mollockle, Mythical Creature (kobold), Adventurer (stonecutter)
**Time period(s):** Indeterminate Future
**Locale(s):** Tamlaght, Fictional Country

**Summary:** Discovered about to expose correspondence between Tamlaght's ruler, Ferenc, and the exiled power behind the throne, Payne Roelt, Bronwyn flees palace guards until befriended by Thud, then by a Gypsy who helps them escape the city. As they flee north to enlist aid from Bronwyn's relatives, they visit the kingdom of the kobolds, receiving aid and agreeing to help the kobold's cause of assisting refugee fairies of Londeac to emigrate.

**Other books you might like:**
Carol Chase, *Hawk's Flight*, 1991
Katharine Kerr, *The Dragon Revenant*, 1990
Elizabeth Moon, *Sheepfarmer's Daughter*, 1988
Elizabeth Moon, *Surrender None: The Legacy of Gird*, 1990

## 3905

### RON MILLER

## Silk and Steel

(New York: Ace, 1992)

**Story type:** Fantasy (Adventure)
**Series:** Bronwyn
**Major character(s):** Bronwyn, Royalty (princess), Fugitive; Thud Mollockle, Mythical Creature (kobold), Adventurer; Mathias Strelsau, Nobleman (duke), Ruler (Duchy of Lesser Piotr)
**Time period(s):** Indeterminate Future
**Locale(s):** Londeac, Fictional Country; Duchy of Piotr, Fictional Country

**Summary:** Fleeing Payne Roelt's treachery, Bronwyn travels from Londeac to the Duchy of Lesser Piotr. When an explosion cuts short Bronwyn's budding romance with Duke Mathias Strelsau, she resolves to remove Payne Roelt's influence from Tamlaght.

**Other books you might like:**
Alexis A. Gilliland, *The Shadow Shaia*, 1990
Sheila Gilluly, *The Boy From the Burren*, 1990
Diana L. Paxson, *The Wind Crystal*, 1990
Melanie Rawn, *Sunrunner's Fire*, 1990

## 3906

### SASHA MILLER

## Ladylord

(New York: Tor, 1996)

**Story type:** Fantasy (Adventure; Political)
**Major character(s):** Javere "Javerri", Noblewoman, Martial Arts Expert
**Time period(s):** Indeterminate
**Locale(s):** Fictional Country

**Summary:** Taught fighting and political skills as if she were a young man, Javerri receives the favor of her father, Lord Qai. After Lord Qai names her heir and *son*, Javerri sets off on a quest to prove her right to rule. Javerri's search for a dragon's egg suffers the treachery of an empire plotting to insure against a woman ruler.

**Other books you might like:**
Marion Zimmer Bradley, *The Sword and Sorceress Series*, 1984-1996
Raymond E. Feist, *Daughter of the Empire*, 1987
    Janny Wurts, co-author
Mercedes Lackey, *The Oathbound*, 1988
C.L. Moore, *Jirel of Joiry*, 1969
Andre Norton, *On Wings of Magic*, 1994
    Patricia Shaw Mathews, Sasha Miller, co-authors
Jessica Amanda Salmonson, *Tomoe Gozen*, 1984

## 3907

### STEVE MILLER
### SHARON LEE, Co-Author

## Carpe Diem

(New York: Ballantine/Del Rey, 1989)

**Story type:** Science Fiction (Adventure)
**Major character(s):** Val Con, Spy; Miri, Mercenary
**Time period(s):** Indeterminate Future
**Locale(s):** Planet—Imaginary (Interdicted primitive planet)

**Summary:** In this sequel to *Agent of Change*, an interstellar spy and a female mercenary, on the run from a variety of bad guys, relatives, and aliens, hide out on a primitive world, but trouble soon follows.

**Other books you might like:**
Poul Anderson, *A Circus of Hells*, 1970
Poul Anderson, *The Game of Empire*, 1985
Poul Anderson, *A Knight of Ghosts and Shadows*, 1977
Poul Anderson, *The Rebel Worlds*, 1969
John Dalmas, *The Lantern of God*, 1989
Kris Jensen, *FreeMaster*, 1989

## 3908

### WALTER M. MILLER JR.

## Saint Leibowitz and the Wild Horse Woman

(New York: Bantam, 1997)

**Story type:** Science Fiction (Religious; Satire)
**Major character(s):** Blacktooth "Nimmy" St. George, Religious (monk), Linguist; Elia Brownpony, Religious (cardinal), Leader (pope); Aedrea, Mutant, Femme Fatale
**Time period(s):** 33rd century

**Locale(s):** Great Plains, North America; Valana, Fictional City; Abbey of St. Leibowitz, Mythical Place

**Summary:** Learning to speak the Nomad tongue, Elia Cardinal Brownpony, Vicar Apostolic to the Three Hordes, spends his time and effort forging an alliance between the wild people of the Plains and the exiled papacy in its Rocky Mountain refuge at Valana. Obeying orders from his abbott while suffering a crisis of faith, and standing on the brink of expulsion from the Order of St. Leibowitz for his rebellion, Brother Blacktooth St. George accompanies Cardinal Brownpony as secretary and translator while Brownpony seeks to defeat the Emperor of Imperial Texark and reunite the church under one pope. Sequel to *A Canticle for Leibowitz*.

**Other books you might like:**
Neil Gaiman, *Good Omens: The Nice and Accurate Prophecies of Agnes Nutter, Witch*, 1990
   Terry Pratchett, co-author
Parke Godwin, *Waiting for the Galactic Bus*, 1988
Robert A. Heinlein, *Job: A Comedy of Justice*, 1984
James Morrow, *Bible Stories for Adults*, 1996
Anne Rice, *Memnoch the Devil*, 1995
Sheri S. Tepper, *Grass*, 1989
Paul O. Williams, *The Breaking of Northwall*, 1984

---

**3909**

**C.J. MILLS**

## Brander's Book

(New York: Ace, 1992)

**Story type:** Science Fiction (Political; Family Saga)
**Series:** Winter World
**Major character(s):** Brander Harlan, Nobleman, Revolutionary; Karne Halarek, Nobleman, Ruler (Lharr of House Halarek); Richard Harlan, Prisoner, Leader
**Time period(s):** Indeterminate Future
**Locale(s):** Starker IV, Planet—Imaginary

**Summary:** Brander Harlan acts to overthrow his family's leader, the imprisoned Duke Richard, and eliminate Karne Halarek's family by enlisting the aid of Karne's young bride.

**Other books you might like:**
Lois McMaster Bujold, *Barrayar*, 1991
Lois McMaster Bujold, *Shards of Honor*, 1986
C.J. Cherryh, *Serpent's Reach*, 1980
Frank Herbert, *Dune*, 1965

---

**3910**

**C.J. MILLS**

## Egil's Book

(New York: Ace, 1991)

**Story type:** Science Fiction (Political)
**Series:** Winter World
**Major character(s):** Karne Halarek, Nobleman, Ruler; Egil Olaffson, Bodyguard, Friend
**Time period(s):** Indeterminate Future
**Locale(s):** Starker IV, Planet—Imaginary

**Summary:** Expecting to die defending Karne Halarek, Egil finds himself rescued and repaired by survivors of Viking settlers who crash-landed on Starker IV and have lived secretly underground for 2,000 years. Prohibitions against leaving the underground civilization force Egil to plot his escape so he can return to Karne's service

and help Karne avenge the killing of his mother, the ruler of Starker IV. This book is a sequel to *Winter World*.

**Other books you might like:**
Poul Anderson, *Hrolf Kraki's Saga*, 1973
C.J. Cherryh, *Serpent's Reach*, 1980
Alan Dean Foster, *Quozl*, 1989
Frank Herbert, *Dune*, 1965
Ursula K. Le Guin, *The Left Hand of Darkness*, 1969
Jody Lynn Nye, *Mythology 101*, 1990
H. Beam Piper, *Little Fuzzy*, 1962
James D. Priest, *Kirins: The Spell of No'an*, 1990
Alis A. Rasmussen, *Revolution's Shore*, 1990
Sheri S. Tepper, *Grass*, 1989

---

**3911**

**C.J. MILLS**

## Kit's Book

(New York: Ace, 1991)

**Story type:** Science Fiction (Adventure; Political)
**Series:** Winter World
**Major character(s):** Karne Halarek, Nobleman, Ruler (Lharr of House Halarek); Kathryn "Kit" Magdalena Alysha Halarek, Noblewoman, Captive; Nicholas von Schuss, Nobleman, Heir
**Time period(s):** Indeterminate Future
**Locale(s):** Starker IV, Planet—Imaginary

**Summary:** Although sentenced to a spartan solitary confinement in the Retreat House at Breven Abbey for the treacherous murder of Karne and Kit's mother, Richard Harlan lives a lecherous life of luxury and continues to actively direct the total destruction of the Halarek line. His actions seem destined for success when he arranges Kit's abduction and forced marriage to Ennis Harlan. Hampered by a required period of mourning, Karne works to save Kit from an even worse fate.

**Other books you might like:**
Lois McMaster Bujold, *Barrayar*, 1991
C.J. Cherryh, *Forty Thousand in Gehenna*, 1983
C.J. Cherryh, *Serpent's Reach*, 1980
Mary Gentle, *Golden Witchbreed*, 1984
Heather Gladney, *Teot's War*, 1987
Frank Herbert, *Dune*, 1965

---

**3912**

**C.J. MILLS**

## Zjhanne's Book

(New York: Ace, 1992)

**Story type:** Science Fiction (Political; Family Saga)
**Series:** Winter World
**Major character(s):** Karne Halarek, Nobleman, Ruler (Lharr of House Halarek); Zjhanne Verlith, Spouse (Karne's), Historian (Terran pre-industrial history); Kathryn "Kit" Harlan, Noblewoman
**Time period(s):** Indeterminate Future
**Locale(s):** Starker IV, Planet—Imaginary

**Summary:** Kidnapped and forced to marry Karne in the traditional way, Zjhanne proves a defiant partner. She resists Karne's demand that she deliver House Halarek an heir until circumstances force the pair to flee. Zjhanne finally warms to her marriage partner, willingly accepting the duties expected of her. Concludes the series.

**Other books you might like:**
Lois McMaster Bujold, *Barrayar*, 1991

Lois McMaster Bujold, *Shards of Honor*, 1986
Cynthia Felice, *Iceman*, 1991
Rosemary Kirstein, *The Outskirter's Secret*, 1992
Alis A. Rasmussen, *Revolution's Shore*, 1990

## 3913
### CRAIG MILLS

## The Floating Castle
(New York: Berkley Boulevard, 1995)

**Story type:** Fantasy (Adventure)
**Series:** King's Quest
**Major character(s):** Alexander, Royalty; Telgrin, Magician
**Time period(s):** Indeterminate
**Locale(s):** Daventry, Fictional Country

**Summary:** As King Graham and his knights meet to discuss ways of removing the evil invaders from Daventry, Telgrin bursts in, magically steals the king's soul and declares himself the new ruler. Prince Alexander must find a way to drive out the usurper and restore peace to the land. First of a computer game tie-in series.

**Other books you might like:**
Robin Wayne Bailey, *Enchanter*, 1989
Matthew J. Costello, *The 7th Guest*, 1995
Mercedes Lackey, *Fortress of Frost and Fire*, 1993
James E. Reagen, *The League of the Crimson Crescent*, 1995
Harry Turtledove, *The Stolen Throne*, 1995

## 3914
### CRAIG MILLS

## Shadow of the Crown
(New York: Ballantine Del Rey, 1993)

**Story type:** Fantasy (Magic Conflict; Political)
**Major character(s):** Jerod Kemp, Thief, Adventurer; Cander Ellis, Spy, Martial Arts Expert; Holis Quordane, Nobleman (baron), Criminal
**Time period(s):** Indeterminate
**Locale(s):** West Gahant, Fictional Country

**Summary:** Jerod Kemp unwillingly accepts Baron Quordane's demand that he sneak into the Black Tower and steal a box containing a crown and ancient dagger, the key to gaining power for the exiled king.

**Other books you might like:**
Susan Dexter, *The Wizard's Shadow*, 1993
Tanya Huff, *The Fire's Stone*, 1990
Anne Logston, *Shadow Hunt*, 1991
Deborah Talmadge-Bickmore, *The Apprentice*, 1990
Martha Wells, *The Element of Fire*, 1993

## 3915
### KAREN MARIE CHRISTA MINNS

## Virago
(Tallahassee, Florida: Naiad Press, 1990)

**Story type:** Horror (Gay/Lesbian Fiction)
**Major character(s):** Darsen, Vampire; Ginny, Student, Lesbian; Manilla, Student, Lesbian
**Time period(s):** 1990s
**Locale(s):** New York, New York

**Summary:** Ginny and Manilla, students at Weston college, are lovers, but someone else lusts after Ginny—Darsen, a vampire of great age and cunning. This is Minns' first novel.

**Other books you might like:**
Suzy McKee Charnas, *The Vampire Tapestry*, 1980
Lauren Wright Douglas, *In the Blood*, 1989
Nancy Tyler Glenn, *Clicking Stones*, 1989

## 3916
### KEN MITCHELL

## Stones of the Dalai Lama
(New York: Soho, 1993)

**Story type:** Fantasy (Religious; Adventure)
**Major character(s):** Robert "Bob" Harlow, Professor, Archaeologist; Vern Cugnet, Mechanic, Adventurer; Jong Jing, Linguist (Foreign Ministry translator), Adventurer
**Time period(s):** 1980s (1987)
**Locale(s):** Bismarck, North Dakota; China; Tibet

**Summary:** Travelling in Tibet after completing a teaching assignment in China, Bob Harlow takes sacred funeral markers as mementos. When the transgression brings misfortune upon him at home in North Dakota, Bob and his friend, Vern, travel to Tibet to return the relics.

**Other books you might like:**
Campbell Black, *Raiders of the Lost Ark*, 1981
James Kahn, *Indiana Jones and the Temple of Doom*, 1984
Marc Laidlaw, *Neon Lotus*, 1988
Elizabeth Ann Scarborough, *Last Refuge*, 1992
Lucius Shepard, *Kalimantan*, 1992

## 3917
### KIRK MITCHELL

## Cry Republic
(New York: Ace, 1989)

**Story type:** Science Fiction (Alternate Universe)
**Series:** Procurator
**Major character(s):** Caesar Germanicus Agricola, Ruler; Mara, Young Woman
**Time period(s):** Indeterminate (20th century, alternate time)
**Locale(s):** Alternate Earth

**Summary:** In a universe where, two thousand years ago, Pilate pardoned Christ and in the twentieth century the Roman Empire still stands, the current Emperor, Casear Germanicus Agricola, seeks to transform his nation into a republic. There is violent opposition however, and Germanicus finds himself with a civil war on his hands. In attempting to end his Empire's stagnation, Germanicus fears he may have destroyed it.

**Other books you might like:**
L. Sprague de Camp, *Lest Darkness Fall*, 1941
Keith Roberts, *Pavane*, 1968
S.P. Somtow, *Aquila and the Iron Horse*, 1988
S.P. Somtow, *Aquila and the Sphinx*, 1989
S.P. Somtow, *Aquila in the New World*, 1983
    Revised 1988

## 3918

### V.E. MITCHELL

## *Enemy Unseen*

(New York: Pocket Books, 1990)

**Story type:** Science Fiction (Space Opera; Mystery)
**Series:** Star Trek
**Major character(s):** James T. Kirk, Spaceship Captain; Leonard Mc-Coy, Doctor; Janara Whitehorse, Telepath
**Time period(s):** 23rd century
**Locale(s):** *U.S.S. Enterprise*, Spaceship

**Summary:** The *Enterprise* has been assigned to transport a diplomatic mission. Captain Kirk's work is complicated by First Officer Spock's temporary absence, the presence of an old flame among the Federation ambassador's party, and the cultural taboos of the arrogant Kaldorni representatives. When a diplomatic attache is murdered and one of the *Enterprise* crew is a prime suspect, Kirk and McCoy must find the identity of the killer in their midst.

**Other books you might like:**
Isaac Asimov, *The Caves of Steel*, 1954
Diane Duane, *My Enemy, My Ally*, 1984
    Star Trek 18
Janet Kagan, *Uhura's Song*, 1985
    Star Trek 21
James H. Schmitz, *The Universe Against Her*, 1964

## 3919

### V.E. MITCHELL

## *Imbalance*

(New York: Pocket, 1992)

**Story type:** Science Fiction (Space Opera; First Contact)
**Series:** Star Trek: The Next Generation
**Major character(s):** Beverly Crusher, Doctor, Space Explorer; William Riker, Military Personnel (Starfleet commander), Space Explorer; Keiko Ishikawa, Scientist, Space Explorer
**Time period(s):** 24th century
**Locale(s):** *U.S.S. Enterprise*, Spaceship; Beltaxiyan Minor, Planet—Imaginary

**Summary:** After the Jarada, a mysterious race of insectoids, request Captain Picard's services as negotiator to establish diplomatic relations with the Federation, negotiations proceed smoothly. When the Jarada suggest separate guided tours for his away team, Picard agrees in the interest of learning more about Jaradan culture. Each crew member loses contact with the ship and must struggle to stay alive while Picard tries to solve the mysteries of Jaradan behavior.

**Other books you might like:**
C.J. Cherryh, *Serpent's Reach*, 1980
Michael Jan Friedman, *Reunion*, 1991
Mary Gentle, *Golden Witchbreed*, 1984
Keith Laumer, *Retief at Large*, 1978
Ursula K. Le Guin, *The Left Hand of Darkness*, 1969
Kathleen Sky, *Vulcan!*, 1978
Jim Young, *The Face of the Deep*, 1979

## 3920

### V.E. MITCHELL

## *Windows on a Lost World*

(New York: Pocket, 1993)

**Story type:** Science Fiction (Space Opera)
**Series:** Star Trek
**Major character(s):** James T. Kirk, Spaceship Captain; Pavel Chekov, Military Personnel (ensign), Space Explorer; Spock, Scientist, Alien (Vulcan)
**Time period(s):** 23rd century
**Locale(s):** Careta IV, Planet—Imaginary; *U.S.S. Enterprise*, Spaceship

**Summary:** Exploring the ruins of an ancient civilization, Kirk and his landing party discover a strange device appearing as a window which pulls in Ensign Chekov and a Djelifan archaeologist as they test its properties. Searching for the missing team, Kirk also disappears. Spock eventually identifies Kirk's consciousness inside an alien creature found halfway around the planet and must unravel the alien technology to save his crewmates, even if it means taking alien form himself.

**Other books you might like:**
Carmen Carter, *The Devil's Heart*, 1993
C.J. Cherryh, *Gate of Ivrel*, 1976
Gordon R. Dickson, *Time Storm*, 1977
Phyllis Eisenstein, *Shadow of Earth*, 1979
Clifford D. Simak, *Mastodonia*, 1978
Kathleen Sky, *Vulcan!*, 1978

## 3921

### LAURA J. MIXON

## *Glass Houses*

(New York: Tor, 1992)

**Story type:** Science Fiction (Cyberpunk)
**Major character(s):** Ruby Kubick, Construction Worker, Recluse; Sheila Nanopoulos, Police Officer
**Time period(s):** 21st century
**Locale(s):** New York, New York (Queens); Palisades, New Jersey

**Summary:** To acquire the rent money due Friday, Ruby, in her waldo, Golem, climbs the condemned bank building to do some scavenging before the demolition scheduled for the next morning. Finding a shipwreck victim, she attempts rescue but the collapsing building trashes her salvage and kills her passenger. The man proves to be a well known philanthropist, causing the police to hold Golem. Without rent, salvage or Golem, Ruby must brave the very hot, partially submerged New York City in her own body. Author's first novel.

**Other books you might like:**
Greg Bear, *Queen of Angels*, 1990
David Brin, *Earth*, 1990
Pat Cadigan, *Mindplayers*, 1987
Pat Cadigan, *Synners*, 1991
Emily Devenport, *Shade*, 1991
William Gibson, *Neuromancer*, 1984
Lisa Mason, *Arachne*, 1990
Rudy Rucker, *Software*, 1982
Neal Stephenson, *Snow Crash*, 1992
Michael Swanwick, *Vacuum Flowers*, 1987
Walter Jon Williams, *Hardwired*, 1986

## 3922

### LAURA J. MIXON

## Proxies

(New York: Tor, 1998)

**Story type:** Science Fiction (Alternate Intelligence; Political)
**Major character(s):** Pablo "Sam Krueger", Android, Teenager; Patricia "Mother" Taylor, Businesswoman, Criminal; Carli D'Auber MacLeod, Professor, Inventor
**Locale(s):** Shasta Station/Kaleidas, Space Station; Austin, Texas; *Exodus*, Spaceship

**Summary:** Despite losing the rights to her linking technology, Carli decides to leave the university and go into business for herself. One of Mother's Creche Kids, Pablo runs the Krueger proxy and produces proxies for use, primarily in space. Called to a meeting at Kaleidas, Pablo links into his primary proxy. When Mother finds out that Exodus launch will be next week, jeopardizing her plans to steal it, her violent outburst puts the station at risk.

**Other books you might like:**
Kim Antieau, *The Gaia Websters*, 1997
Gregory Benford, *Jupiter Project*, 1975
Pat Cadigan, *Synners*, 1991
Joe Haldeman, *Forever Peace*, 1997
James P. Hogan, *Bug Park*, 1997

## 3923

### BEN MIZRICH

## Reaper

(New York: HarperCollins, 1998)

**Story type:** Horror (Techno-Horror)
**Major character(s):** Samantha Craig, Scientist (virologist); Nick Barnes, Health Care Professional (paramedic); Marcus Teal, Businessman (computers)
**Time period(s):** 1990s (1998)
**Locale(s):** Boston, Massachusetts

**Summary:** The Reaper is a computer virus that swiftly kills anyone who accesses a computer infected with it. Samantha Craig and Nick Barnes race against the clock to uncover the cult of technophobes who unleashed it before it completely penetrates the international telecommunications networks.

**Other books you might like:**
Michael Crichton, *The Andromeda Strain*, 1969
Philip Kerr, *The Second Angel*, 1999
Pierre Ouellette, *The Deus Machine*, 1994
Graham Watkins, *Virus*, 1995

## 3924

### L.E. MODESITT JR.

## Adiamante

(New York: Tor, 1996)

**Story type:** Science Fiction (Post-Holocaust; Utopia)
**Major character(s):** Ecktor deJanes, Administrator (Old Earth coordinator), Leader, Widow(er); Kemra, Military Personnel (Vereal Union), Cyborg
**Time period(s):** Indeterminate Future
**Locale(s):** Earth

**Summary:** Newly appointed as Planetary Coordinator, Ecktor deJanes must deal with a fleet of warships which suddenly appears in orbit around Old Earth. In spite of the visitors' apparent civility, Ecktor suspects that these descendants of a former Earth colony have returned to their ancestral world with a single purpose in mind—revenge.

**Other books you might like:**
Arthur C. Clarke, *Imperial Earth*, 1976
Arthur C. Clarke, *The Songs of Distant Earth*, 1986
Robert A. Heinlein, *Stranger in a Strange Land*, 1991 revised edition
James P. Hogan, *Voyage From Yesteryear*, 1982
Larry Niven, *A World out of Time*, 1976

## 3925

### L.E. MODESITT JR.

## The Chaos Balance

(New York: Tor, 1997)

**Story type:** Fantasy (Magic Conflict)
**Series:** Recluce
**Major character(s):** Nylan, Engineer; Ayrlyn, Doctor (healer); Lephi the White, Ruler
**Time period(s):** Indeterminate
**Locale(s):** Candar, Fictional Country; Cyador, Fictional Country

**Summary:** After Nylan builds Tower Black and saves his shipmates, politics forces him to leave his new home. He takes his friend, Ayrlyn, and his infant son into a world full of war and half-understood power, hoping to find peace.

**Other books you might like:**
Eleanor Arnason, *The Sword Smith*, 1978
M.A.R. Barker, *Man of Gold*, 1984
Glen Cook, *Tower of Fear*, 1989
Lisa Goldstein, *Summer King, Winter Fool*, 1994
Guy Gavriel Kay, *Tigana*, 1990

## 3926

### L.E. MODESITT JR.

## The Death of Chaos

(New York: Tor, 1995)

**Story type:** Fantasy (Magic Conflict; Political)
**Series:** Recluce
**Major character(s):** Lerris, Apprentice, Carpenter; Krystal, Military Personnel
**Time period(s):** Indeterminate
**Locale(s):** Recluce, Fictional Country (island)

**Summary:** Lerris' hopes of a quiet life as an artisan evaporate when the Empire of Hamor invades from the continent Candar, intent on world domination. Lerris must quickly hone his abilities to help repel the troops. Sequel to *The Magic of Recluce*.

**Other books you might like:**
Dave Duncan, *Upland Outlaws*, 1993
David Eddings, *Guardians of the West*, 1987
Terry Goodkind, *Wizard's First Rule*, 1994
Robert Jordan, *The Eye of the World*, 1989
Katharine Kerr, *Daggerspell*, 1986

## 3927

### L.E. MODESITT JR.

### *The Ecolitan Enigma*

(New York: Tor, 1997)

**Story type:** Science Fiction (Political; Space Opera)
**Series:** Ecolitan Institute
**Major character(s):** Nathaniel Firstborne Whaler, Professor (economics), Agent (Ecolitan Institute); Sylvia Ferro-Maine, Professor (economics), Agent (Ecolitan Institute)
**Time period(s):** Indeterminate Future
**Locale(s):** Accord, Planet—Imaginary; Artos, Planet—Imaginary

**Summary:** Sent to the backwater colony planet Artos, ostensibly to perform an economic study, Nathaniel and his Ecolitan colleague Sylvia find themselves the targets of several sabotage and murder attempts. When they dig deeper and discover that two empires use Artos as the focal point of a brewing conflict, they employ every means at their disposalto avert an interstellar war.

**Other books you might like:**
Jane Emerson, *City of Diamond*, 1996
Valerie J. Freireich, *Becoming Human*, 1995
Frank Herbert, *Dune*, 1965
Kim Stanley Robinson, *Red Mars*, 1993
Sheri S. Tepper, *Grass*, 1989
Joan D. Vinge, *The Summer Queen*, 1991
Margaret Weis, *Knights of Black Earth*, 1995
    Don Perrin, co-author

## 3928

### L.E. MODESITT JR.

### *The Ecolitan Operation*

(New York: Tor, 1989)

**Story type:** Science Fiction (Adventure)
**Series:** Ecolitan
**Major character(s):** Jimjoy Earle Wright, Spy (Major)
**Time period(s):** 25th century
**Locale(s):** Galactic Empire, Interstellar Empire/Federation

**Summary:** Major Jimjoy Earle Wright is one of the most highly trained and successful secret agents employed by the Empire. Assigned to work the overthrow of a planetary dictatorship, he succeeds too well. The dictatorship is replaced by a new government which is violently opposed to the Empire and Wright, made a scapegoat, finds himself in disgrace with a bounty on his head.

**Other books you might like:**
Poul Anderson, *A Circus of Hells*, 1970
Poul Anderson, *Earthman, Go Home!*, 1960
Poul Anderson, *Ensign Flandry*, 1966
Poul Anderson, *The Game of Empire*, 1985
Poul Anderson, *A Knight of Ghosts and Shadows*, 1974
Poul Anderson, *The Rebel Worlds*, 1969
Emma Bull, *Falcon*, 1989
Janet Kagan, *Hellspark*, 1988

## 3929

### L.E. MODESITT JR.

### *The Ecologic Secession*

(New York: Tor, 1990)

**Story type:** Science Fiction (Space Opera)

**Series:** Ecolitan Trilogy
**Major character(s):** Jimjoy Earle Wright, Spy
**Time period(s):** 25th century
**Locale(s):** Accord, Planet—Imaginary

**Summary:** Major Wright, once an Imperial Special Operative, is on his way to fake his death. After contact with the Ecolitan Institute on Accord he chooses to ally himself with the Prime Ecolitan and Accord. He will return as Ecolitan Professor James Joyson Whaler, who will lead the ongoing conflict with the Empire.

**Other books you might like:**
Emma Bull, *Falcon*, 1989
W. Michael Gear, *The Web of Spider*, 1989
Melisa C. Michaels, *Far Harbor*, 1989
Sheri S. Tepper, *Grass*, 1989
Walter Jon Williams, *Angel Station*, 1989

## 3930

### L.E. MODESITT JR.

### *Fall of Angels*

(New York: Tor, 1996)

**Story type:** Fantasy (Magic Conflict)
**Series:** Recluce
**Major character(s):** Nylan, Engineer; Ryba, Leader; Terek, Wizard
**Time period(s):** Indeterminate
**Locale(s):** Outer Space; Candar, Fictional Country

**Summary:** Set in Recluce's distant past, this novel chronicles the founding of the Empire of the Legend. A space battle goes terribly wrong, stranding the crew of the United Faith Forces' frigate *Winterlance* on a world far from anything they know.

**Other books you might like:**
Eleanor Arnason, *The Sword Smith*, 1978
Glen Cook, *The Black Company*, 1984
Barbara Hambly, *The Silent Tower*, 1986
Robert Jordan, *The Eye of the World*, 1990
Martha Wells, *The Element of Fire*, 1993

## 3931

### L.E. MODESITT JR.

### *The Ghost of the Revelator*

(New York: Tor, 1998)

**Story type:** Science Fiction (Alternate History; Fantasy)
**Major character(s):** Doktor Johan Eschbach, Professor, Spy (former); Llysette du Boise, Refugee, Singer (opera); Joseph Smith, Spirit, Religious (Mormon leader)
**Time period(s):** Indeterminate Future
**Locale(s):** Columbia, Fictional Country; Deseret, Fictional Country; North America

**Summary:** A former secret agent, Johan Eschbach tries to build a new life as a university professor with his opera singer wife, Llysette. However, an invitation for Llysette to perform in the Mormon country of Deseret leads to her kidnapping and an unusual ransom demand—Johan must resurrect the ghost of Joseph Smith, a Mormon religious leader. Sequel to *Of Tangible Ghosts*.

**Other books you might like:**
Orson Scott Card, *The Folk of the Fringe*, 1989
Paul Di Filippo, *The Steampunk Trilogy*, 1995
Michael Flynn, *In the Country of the Blind*, 1990
William Gibson, *The Difference Engine*, 1991
    Bruce Sterling, co-author

Kathleen Ann Goonan, *Mississippi Blues*, 1997
Katie Waitman, *The Merro Tree*, 1997

**3932**

**L.E. MODESITT JR.**
**BRUCE SCOTT LEVINSON**, Co-Author

## The Green Progression

(New York: Tor, 1992)

**Story type:** Science Fiction (Political; Contemporary Realism)
**Major character(s):** Jack McDarvid, Researcher, Detective—Amateur
**Time period(s):** 1990s
**Locale(s):** Washington, District of Columbia; Moscow, Russia

**Summary:** Jack McDarvid retires from the E.P.A. hoping to advance his interests in business and environmental issues through work in a Washington D. C. legal firm specializing in business and environmental law. Shortly after McDarvid joins the firm, the murder of a firm leader and McDarvid's investigation into activity surrounding legislation concerning metals leads McDarvid into the dangerous labyrinth underlying environmental issues.

**Other books you might like:**
Isaac Asimov, *Our Angry Earth*, 1991
    Frederik Pohl, co-author
David Brin, *Earth*, 1990
Thomas A. Easton, *Greenhouse*, 1991
Thomas A. Easton, *Sparrowhawk*, 1990
Larry Niven, *Fallen Angels*, 1991
    Jerry Pournelle, Michael Flynn, co-authors

**3933**

**L.E. MODESITT JR.**

## The Magic Engineer

(New York: Tor, 1994)

**Story type:** Fantasy (Magic Conflict; Political)
**Series:** Recluce
**Major character(s):** Dorrin, Magician, Engineer; Liedral, Trader
**Time period(s):** Indeterminate
**Locale(s):** Recluce, Fictional Country (island)

**Summary:** When Dorrin's talent for creating mechanical devices leads to his exile from Recluce, he must construct his scientifically based machines in the land of Chaos. He hopes to defend Recluce when its gathering enemies attempt to incorporate the country into their growing empire.

**Other books you might like:**
Cheryl J. Franklin, *Fire Get*, 1987
Mary Gentle, *Ancient Light*, 1987
Mercedes Lackey, *The Robin and the Kestrel*, 1993
Michael Swanwick, *The Iron Dragon's Daughter*, 1994
Paula Volsky, *Illusion*, 1992

**3934**

**L.E. MODESITT JR.**

## The Magic of Recluce

(New York: Tor, 1991)

**Story type:** Fantasy (Magic Conflict; Romance)

**Major character(s):** Lerris, Apprentice, Carpenter; Krystal, Adventurer
**Time period(s):** Indeterminate
**Locale(s):** Wandernaught, Fictional Country; Recluce, Fictional Country (island); Nylan, Fictional Country

**Summary:** Lerris, a young teenager feels confined by the utopian community, based on order, into which he was born. His parents apprentice him to his Uncle Sardit, a woodworker, to give Lerris some skills he'll need on Dangergeld, the year of wandering required before rebellious youths are welcomed into the community. Permanent exile or compliance with community expectations are the only alternatives to the Dangergeld. While on Dangergeld, Lerris learns to make appropriate choices. He meets many people who are important in his development as a magician and a citizen.

**Other books you might like:**
Poul Anderson, *The Broken Sword*, 1954
C.J. Cherryh, *The Paladin*, 1988
Gordon R. Dickson, *The Dragon and the George*, 1976
Elizabeth Moon, *Sheepfarmer's Daughter*, 1988
Elizabeth Moon, *Surrender None: The Legacy of Gird*, 1990
Pamela F. Service, *Vision Quest*, 1989
Andrew Whitmore, *The Fortress of Eternity*, 1990

**3935**

**L.E. MODESITT JR.**

## Of Tangible Ghosts

(New York: Tor, 1994)

**Story type:** Fantasy (Science Fiction)
**Major character(s):** Doktor Johan Eschbach, Professor, Spy; Llysette Du Boise, Singer, Spy
**Time period(s):** Indeterminate
**Locale(s):** North America, Alternate Earth

**Summary:** On an Earth controlled by colonial superpowers and shared by living people and the ghosts of the dead who sometimes interact with the living, Johan Eschbach retires as a spy for Columbia and returns to teach in the Northeast, still dominated by the Dutch. Forced back into service as a spy, Johan investigates research into controlling ghosts until his discoveries result in enemies marking him for death.

**Other books you might like:**
Nina Kiriki Hoffman, *The Thread That Binds the Bones*, 1993
Marc Laidlaw, *Neon Lotus*, 1988
Rachel Pollack, *Temporary Agency*, 1994
Rachel Pollack, *Unquenchable Fire*, 1992
Elizabeth Ann Scarborough, *Last Refuge*, 1992

**3936**

**L.E. MODESITT JR.**

## The Order War

(New York: Tor, 1995)

**Story type:** Fantasy (Political; Magic Conflict)
**Series:** Recluce
**Major character(s):** Justen, Magician, Engineer; Gunar, Magician, Engineer
**Time period(s):** Indeterminate
**Locale(s):** Sarronnyn, Fictional Country; Candar, Fictional Country; Naclos, Fictional Country

**Summary:** Despite valiant help from Justen, Gunar, and a few other volunteers from Recluce, Sarronnyn forces cannot repel the armies of Fairhaven and the White wizards. Separated, Justen flees through the desert of Candar, where rescuers help him to Naclos and a new understanding of the balance between Black and White before he reenters the battle against White Aggression. Set between *The Magic Engineer* and *The Magic of Recluce*.

**Other books you might like:**
Terry Goodkind, *Stone of Tears*, 1995
Laurell K. Hamilton, *Nightseer*, 1992
L. Dean James, *Summerland*, 1994
Katharine Kerr, *Days of Blood and Fire*, 1993
Andre Norton, *Elvenblood*, 1995
   Mercedes Lackey, co-author
Martha Wells, *The Element of Fire*, 1993

**3937**

**L.E. MODESITT JR.**

## The Parafaith War

(New York: Tor, 1996)

**Story type:** Science Fiction (Military; Theological)
**Major character(s):** Trystin Desoll, Military Personnel (EcoTech Coalition lieutenant); Rhule Ghere, Alien (Farnkan), Doctor; Ulteena Freyer, Military Personnel (EcoTech Coalition major)
**Time period(s):** Indeterminate Future
**Locale(s):** Mara, Planet—Imaginary

**Summary:** One of many young EcoTech officers, Trystin Desoll fights desperately to defend his outpost on Mara from the Revenants, a fanatical religiouis group who attempt to wipe out all who oppose them. When Trystin goes undercover to infiltrate the Revenants, he ultimately plays a much larger role in ending the war.

**Other books you might like:**
Ben Bova, *Orion Among the Stars*, 1995
Orson Scott Card, *Ender's Game*, 1985
David Drake, *Counting the Cost*, 1987
Joe Haldeman, *The Forever War*, 1975
Frank Herbert, *Dune*, 1965

**3938**

**L.E. MODESITT JR.**

## The Soprano Sorceress

(New York: Tor, 1997)

**Story type:** Fantasy (Magic Conflict; Alternate World)
**Major character(s):** Anna Marshall, Singer, Sorceress; Lord Brill, Singer, Sorceress; Daffyd, Musician
**Time period(s):** 1990s; Indeterminate
**Locale(s):** Ames, Iowa; Defalk, Fictional Country

**Summary:** Transported by magic into an alternate world where music literally creates magic, Anna Marshall discovers that her vocal talents and training on Earth prepare her to wield great power on Erde. As she begins to use her new magical skills to defend the Kingdom of Defalk from invasion, she also discovers that some fear a powerful woman and that she must protect herself, even from those she has protected. First of a new series that is so far unnamed.

**Other books you might like:**
Peter S. Beagle, *The Unicorn Sonata*, 1996
Emma Bull, *War for the Oaks*, 1987
Gordon R. Dickson, *The Dragon and the George*, 1976
Barbara Hambly, *The Time of the Dark*, 1982
Anne McCaffrey, *Crystal Singer*, 1982
Elizabeth Ann Scarborough, *Phantom Banjo*, 1991

**3939**

**L.E. MODESITT JR.**

## The Spellsong War

(New York: Tor, 1998)

**Story type:** Fantasy (Magic Conflict; Alternate World)
**Series:** Spellsong Cycle
**Major character(s):** Anna Marshall, Singer, Sorceress; Ehara, Nobleman, Military Personnel; Hanfor, Military Personnel, Counselor
**Time period(s):** Indeterminate
**Locale(s):** Defalk, Fictional Country; Dumar, Fictional Country

**Summary:** Dragged from Ames, Iowa, to the world of Erde, Anna Marshall finds her musical talents make her a great sorceress and regent of a country. With Defalk now menaced by its neighbors, Anna, who wants only peace, must go to war again.

**Other books you might like:**
Eleanor Arnason, *Daughter of the Bear King*, 1987
Greg Bear, *The Infinity Concerto*, 1984
Alan Dean Foster, *Spellsinger*, 1983
Barbara Hambly, *The Time of the Dark*, 1982
Patricia A. McKillip, *The Riddle-Master of Hed*, 1976

**3940**

**L.E. MODESITT JR.**

## Timediver's Dawn

(New York: Tor, 1992)

**Story type:** Science Fiction (Post-Holocaust; Psychic Powers)
**Major character(s):** Sammis Arloff Olon, Witch, Military Personnel; Wryan Relorn, Witch, Scientist; Odin Thor, Military Personnel
**Time period(s):** Indeterminate Future
**Locale(s):** Query, Planet—Imaginary

**Summary:** The Empire of Westron faces an invasion by the Frost Giants, mysterious beings that cause an unnatural cold wave on the planet. Sammis, a descendant of the persecuted witches of Eastron, finds himself on the run when imperial troops destroy his home and family. Desperation teaches him how to use the psychic powers inherited from his mother, the ability to move in the dimension of time. Conscripted into the ConFed troops, he meets others with the same powers who work to defeat the Frost Giants and restore their world.

**Other books you might like:**
Marion Zimmer Bradley, *Stormqueen!*, 1978
Emma Bull, *Bone Dance: A Fantasy for Technophiles*, 1991
C.J. Cherryh, *Gate of Ivrel*, 1976
Gordon R. Dickson, *Time Storm*, 1977
Anne McCaffrey, *Dragonflight*, 1968
David R. Palmer, *Emergence*, 1984
Clifford D. Simak, *The Visitors*, 1979

**3941**

**L.E. MODESITT JR.**

## The Towers of the Sunset

(New York: Tor, 1992)

**Story type:** Fantasy (Magic Conflict; Romance)
**Series:** Recluce
**Major character(s):** Creslin, Wizard, Fiance(e) (unwilling); Magaera, Wizard
**Time period(s):** Indeterminate

**Locale(s):** Westwind, Fictional Country; Montgren, Fictional Country; Recluce, Fictional Country (island)

**Summary:** Rather than accept an arranged marriage to Magaera, Creslin chooses to flee his responsibility and search for his self identity. Magaera's magical link to Creslin forces her to pursue him while the White Wizards of Chaos attempt to eliminate Creslin and his threat to world domination by the White Wizards. Appointed co-regents to the desolate island of Recluce, the pair grow individually as their friendship blossoms into love while they and others found the island kingdom of Recluce. Set prior to the events in *The Magic of Recluce*.

**Other books you might like:**
Lois McMaster Bujold, *The Spirit Ring*, 1992
Robin McKinley, *The Hero and the Crown*, 1984
Elizabeth Moon, *Liar's Oath*, 1992
Elizabeth Moon, *Sheepfarmer's Daughter*, 1988
Patricia C. Wrede, *Dealing with Dragons*, 1990

---

**3942**

**L.E. MODESITT JR.**

## The White Order

(New York: Tor, 1998)

**Story type:** Fantasy (Magic Conflict)
**Series:** Recluce
**Major character(s):** Cerryl, Wizard, Apprentice; Faltar, Wizard, Apprentice; Leyladin, Wizard, Healer
**Time period(s):** Indeterminate
**Locale(s):** Fairhaven, Fictional City; Haisbarg, Fictional City

**Summary:** White mages who resented his father's studies killed Cerryl's father. Despite this and his guardian's distrust for magic, books and mirrors attract Cerryl. Eventually, another killing by a white mage forces Cerryl to flee his home and go out into the world to follow the lure of magic.

**Other books you might like:**
Glen Cook, *Tower of Fear*, 1989
Barbara Hambly, *The Time of the Dark*, 1982
Guy Gavriel Kay, *The Lions of Al-Rassan*, 1995
Michael Scott Rohan, *The Anvil of Ice*, 1986
Caroline Stevermer, *A College of Magics*, 1994

---

**3943**

**JUDITH MOFFETT**

## The Ragged World: A Novel of the Hefn on Earth

(New York: St. Martin's, 1991)

**Story type:** Science Fiction (Contemporary Realism; Fantasy)
**Major character(s):** Nancy Sandford, Scientist, Editor (magazine); Carril Sharpless, Teacher; Godfrey, Alien (Hefn)
**Time period(s):** 2020s (2023)
**Locale(s):** Earth

**Summary:** The Hefn, hairy gnomelike little people, millenia more advanced than we are scientifically and socially, have returned to Earth to pick up some of their fellows who had been left here during the 17th century. Conditions here were such that, rather than wipe out the human race, they have put a ban on childbirth until the environment stabilizes and humans have learned to care for the eco-system. Several humans have had personal interactions with the Hefn; this book contains their stories.

**Other books you might like:**
Robert A. Heinlein, *Stranger in a Strange Land*, 1991
Frederik Pohl, *Homegoing*, 1989
James D. Priest, *Kirins: The Spell of No'an*, 1990
David Alexander Smith, *Homecoming*, 1990
John Varley, *The Ophiuchi Hotline*, 1977

---

**3944**

**JUDITH MOFFETT**

## Time, Like an Ever-Rolling Stream

(New York: St. Martin's Press, 1992)

**Story type:** Science Fiction (Invasion of Earth; Contemporary Realism)
**Major character(s):** Pam Pruitt, Scientist (mathematician); Liam O'Hara, Scientist (mathematician, physicist); Humphrey, Alien (Hefn)
**Time period(s):** 2030s
**Locale(s):** College Park, Maryland

**Summary:** Hefn rules have changed life on Earth. The baby ban, still in effect, led to a decreased population, and the effective ban against fossil fuels resulted in a changed atmosphere and life-style. The Hefn, working successfully with the Gaists at keeping humanity from taking the easy path to the Earth's destruction may soon lift or ameliorate the baby ban. A direct sequel to *The Ragged World*.

**Other books you might like:**
David Brin, *Earth*, 1990
Octavia E. Butler, *Dawn*, 1987
Robert A. Heinlein, *Stranger in a Strange Land*, 1991 revised edition
Damon Knight, *A Reasonable World*, 1991
Larry Niven, *Footfall*, 1985
   Jerry Pournelle, co-author
James D. Priest, *Kirins: The Spell of No'an*, 1990
John Varley, *Steel Beach*, 1992
David Weber, *Mutineers' Moon*, 1991

---

**3945**

**JUDITH MOFFETT**

## Two That Came True

(Eugene, Oregon: Pulphouse Publishing, 1991)

**Story type:** Science Fiction (Collection)
**Series:** Author's Choice Monthly
**Time period(s):** 21st century

**Summary:** This volume reprints two stories. In ''Surviving'' (1986), Sally Barnes is raised by chimpanzees from the age of 4 1/2 to 13, then brought back to human society to which she must readapt. In ''Not Without Honor'' (1989), the Mickey Mouse Club has extraterrestrial fans who contact humanity hoping to enlist mouseketeer Jimmy Dodd's help as a teacher, but accepting Pat's help when they find Jimmy has died. A 7-page afterword follows the first story and a 6-page afterword the second.

**Other books you might like:**
Edward Bryant, *Neon Twilight*, 1990
Lisa Goldstein, *Daily Voices*, 1989
Ron Goulart, *Skyrocket Steele Conquers the Universe and Other Media Tales*, 1990
James Patrick Kelly, *Heroines*, 1990
Elizabeth A. Lynn, *Tales From a Vanished Country*, 1990

## `3946`

### DONALD MOFFITT

## Crescent in the Sky

(New York: Ballantine/Del Rey, 1990)

**Story type:** Science Fiction (Adventure)
**Series:** Mechanical Sky
**Major character(s):** Abdul Hamid-Jones, Scientist (Genetic Engineer); Aziz, Servant
**Time period(s):** 31st century (3030)
**Locale(s):** Mars

**Summary:** In a far future universe where Arabs have conquered both Earth and the stars, a young Anglo-Arab genetic engineer who thought himself divorced from politics, finds himself caught up in a complex web of intrigue and violence.

**Other books you might like:**
George Alec Effinger, *A Fire in the Sun*, 1989
George Alec Effinger, *When Gravity Fails*, 1987
Frank Herbert, *Dune*, 1965
Paul J. McAuley, *Of the Fall*, 1989

## `3947`

### DONALD MOFFITT

## A Gathering of Stars

(New York: Ballantine/Del Rey, 1990)

**Story type:** Science Fiction (Adventure)
**Series:** Mechanical Sky
**Major character(s):** Abdul Hamid-Jones, Scientist (Genetic Engineer); Sultan of Alpha Centauri, Ruler
**Time period(s):** 31st century
**Locale(s):** Alpha Centauri, Planet—Imaginary

**Summary:** Hamid-Jones escapes the mad Emir of Mars and heads for Alpha Centauri, where he takes a position with the Sultan of that solar system. The Sultan wishes to oppose the Emir and become ruler of the Islamic universe, but has never gone on the prerequisite pilgrimage to Mecca because it would take many years at sub-light speeds and thus jeopardize his political position at home. Hamid-Jones discovers that the Sultan seeks a solution to this problem, one involving black holes, and that this solution may involve the destruction of his home world of Mars.

**Other books you might like:**
George Alec Effinger, *A Fire in the Sun*, 1989
George Alec Effinger, *When Gravity Fails*, 1987
Frank Herbert, *Dune*, 1965

## `3948`

### KIM MOHAN, Editor

## Amazing Stories: The Anthology

(New York: Tor, 1995)

**Story type:** Science Fiction (Anthology)
**Summary:** Contains a six-page introduction, eight original stories and five stories reprinted from *Amazing Stories* 1953-1994 plus an *Amazing* memoir by Robert Bloch, "Fantastic Adventures with *Amazing*." Although a few of the stories are light, most vary in tone from moody to dark with themes including alternate universes, alien societies, religion, lunar exploration, the nature of humankind, and glimpses at future sports, criminal justice, and bureaucracy. Authors

include Gregory Benford, Thomas M. Disch, Alan Dean Foster, R.A. Lafferty, Ursula K. Le Guin, Lawrence Watt-Evans, and George Zebrowski.

**Other books you might like:**
Martin H. Greenberg, *Amazing Science Fiction Stories: The War Years 1936-1945*, 1987
　editor
Martin H. Greenberg, *Amazing Science Fiction Stories: The Wild Years 1946-1955*, 1987
　editor
Martin H. Greenberg, *Amazing Science Fiction Stories: The Wonder Years 1926-1935*, 1987
　editor
Kristine Kathryn Rusch, *The Best From Fantasy & Science Fiction: A 45th Anniversary Anthology*, 1994
　Edward L. Ferman, co-editor
Kristine Kathryn Rusch, *The Best of Pulphouse: The Hardback Magazine*, 1991
　editor

## `3949`

### KIM MOHAN, Editor

## More Amazing Stories

(New York: Tor, 1998)

**Story type:** Science Fiction (Anthology)
**Summary:** Contains a three-page introduction; 15 original stories; one essay by Robert Silverberg called "Quantity and Quality: The Short Fiction of Philip K. Dick"; and five stories originally published in *Amazing* from 1953 through 1994. Varying in tone, the stories include diverse themes, such as time travel, anthropology, nanotechnology, dreams, Charles Dickens, religion, artificial intelligence, reincarnation, and the effects of combat, dystopian future and post-disaster life. Eleanor Arnason contributes a story in the *Ring of Swords* milieu, with other authors including Gregory Benford, Philip K. Dick, James Alan Gardner, Ursula K. Le Guin, John Morressy, Linda Nagata, Robert Silverberg, Nancy Springer, L.A. Taylor and Howard Waldrop.

**Other books you might like:**
Martin H. Greenberg, *Amazing Science Fiction Stories: The War Years 1936-1945*, 1987
　editor
Martin H. Greenberg, *Amazing Science Fiction Stories: The Wild Years 1946-1955*, 1987
　editor
Martin H. Greenberg, *Amazing Science Fiction Stories: The Wonder Years 1926-1935*, 1987
　editor
Kristine Kathryn Rusch, *The Best From Fantasy & Science Fiction: A 45th Anniversary Anthology*, 1994
　Edward L. Ferman, co-editor
Kristine Kathryn Rusch, *The Best of Pulphouse: The Hardback Magazine*, 1991
　editor

## `3950`

### CLIFFORD MOHR (Pseudonym of Morton Reed)

## Requiem

(New York: Berkley, 1992)

**Story type:** Horror (Possession)

**Major character(s):** Robert Bauer, Musician; Libby Bauer, Parent (Robert's mother); Clyde Trap, Doctor
**Time period(s):** 1990s (1992)
**Locale(s):** New York, New York; Kansas

**Summary:** Although brain damaged at birth, nineteen-year-old Robert Bauer develops a sudden ability to play and master the violin. But when he begins speaking with the voice of someone who calls himself Nicolo, it becomes clear that Robert is possessed by the spirit of someone—or something.

**Other books you might like:**
Robert Bloch, *Fiddler's Fee*, 1945
   short story in *The Opener of the Way*
Nancy A. Collins, *Tempter*, 1991
Sheila Bristow Garner, *Night Music*, 1992
John Skipp, *The Scream*, 1988
   Craig Spector, co-author

---

## 3951
### SUSAN MOLONEY

## *A Dry Spell*
(New York: Delacorte, 1997)

**Story type:** Horror (Occult)
**Major character(s):** Karen Grange, Banker; Thompson Keatley, Magician (rainmaker); Vida Whalley, Young Woman
**Time period(s):** 1990s (1997)
**Locale(s):** Goodlands, North Dakota

**Summary:** Rainmaker Thompson Keatley arrives in parched Goodlands to put an end to a devastating four-year drought but his intervention rouses the ghosts—some literal—of the town's past, forcing the townspeople to acknowledge the source of the curse put upon them.

**Other books you might like:**
Ramsey Campbell, *The Hungry Moon*, 1986
Bentley Little, *The Revelation*, 1990
Steve Rasnic Tem, *Excavation*, 1987
Tamara Thorne, *Haunted*, 1995

---

## 3952
### STEPHEN MOLSTAD

## *Silent Zone*
(New York: HarperPrism, 1997)

**Story type:** Science Fiction (First Contact; UFO)
**Series:** Independence Day
**Major character(s):** Albert Alexander Nimziki, Government Official (CIA); Brackish Okun, Genius, Researcher; Sam Dworkin, Researcher, Aged Person
**Time period(s):** 1970s (1972)
**Locale(s):** Area 51, Nevada; Washington, District of Columbia

**Summary:** Nimziki takes control of the project at Area 51, where a few aged scientists study the wrecked Roswell UFO and the three dead aliens. Recognizing the need for a new leader for the project, he finds the young Brackish Okun, about to graduate Cal Tech, and has him introduced on a five-year to life contract, during which time Brackish discovers how to work the power system and finds a functional, undiscovered UFO.

**Other books you might like:**
David Brin, *Earth*, 1990
A.C. Crispin, *V*, 1984
John DeChancie, *Living with Aliens*, 1995

Dean Devlin, *Independence Day*, 1996
   Roland Emmerich, Stephen Molstad, co-authors
Robert Doherty, *Area 51*, 1997
Anne McCaffrey, *Freedom's Landing*, 1995

---

## 3953
### BRENT MONAHAN

## *The Bell Witch: An American Haunting*
(New York: St. Martin's, 1997)

**Story type:** Horror (Occult)
**Major character(s):** Richard Powell, Teacher; Elizabeth Bell, Child; John Bell, Businessman
**Time period(s):** 1810s; 1820s (1817-1821)
**Locale(s):** Adams, Tennessee

**Summary:** Twelve-year old Betsy Bell becomes possessed by a mischievous spirit, the result of a family quarrel with a vengeful local witch woman. The spirit's disruption of the Bell household attracts a variety of celebrities and charlatans of the era, all of whom hope to lay the spirit to rest and resolve Betsy's affliction. Presented as a true narrative, illustrated with period woodcuts.

**Other books you might like:**
Jack Cady, *The Well*, 1980
Tom Elliott, *The Dwelling*, 1989
Stephen King, *The Shining*, 1977
H.P. Lovecraft, *The Case of Charles Dexter Ward*, 1971
Graham Masterton, *The House That Jack Built*, 1996

---

## 3954
### BRENT MONAHAN

## *Blood of the Covenant*
(New York: St. Martin's, 1995)

**Story type:** Horror (Vampire Story)
**Major character(s):** Simon Penn, Librarian; Frederika Vanderveen, Librarian, Vampire; Father Dante Ferro, Religious (Catholic priest)
**Time period(s):** 1990s (1995)
**Locale(s):** Princeton, New Jersey

**Summary:** In a sequel to *The Book of Common Dread*, rare books curator Simon Penn seeks to hide the coveted scrolls of Ahriman, which reveal that vampires are the progeny of the devil and threaten to overturn the assumptions of all world religions, from the forces of Satan. Complicating his pursuit by the minions of Hell is the dependence of his girlfriend Frederika, who barely eluded the clutches of a vampire lover in the earlier adventure, on a powder that gives vampires their power and is distributed by satanic underlings.

**Other books you might like:**
Steven Brust, *Agyar*, 1992
Anne Rice, *The Vampire Lestat*, 1985
S.P. Somtow, *Vanitas: Escape From Vampire Junction*, 1995
Brian Stableford, *The Empire of Fear*, 1988

---

## 3955
### BRENT MONAHAN

## *The Book of Common Dread*
(New York: St. Martin's, 1993)

**Story type:** Horror (Vampire Story)

**Major character(s):** Vincent De Vilbiss, Vampire; Simon Penn, Librarian; Frederika Vanderveen, Librarian
**Time period(s):** 1990s
**Locale(s):** Princeton, New Jersey

**Summary:** Five-hundred-year old vampire Vincent De Vilbiss has been charged by the dark gods he serves to prevent scholars at the Princeton University Library from accessing a set of recently acquired ancient scrolls that will reveal the secrets of De Vilbiss and his kind. In the course of his mission, De Vilbiss becomes enamored of librarian Frederika Vanderveen, and thus an opponent of Frederika's adoring colleague, Simon Penn.

**Other books you might like:**
Steven Brust, *Agyar*, 1992
Anne Rice, *The Vampire Lestat*, 1985
Brian Stableford, *The Empire of Fear*, 1988

## 3956

### BRENT MONAHAN

## The Uprising

(New York: Pocket, 1992)

**Story type:** Horror (Ancient Evil Unleashed)
**Major character(s):** Keenan MacBreed, Archaeologist; Richard Meagher, Police Officer; Mary Liddy, Mentally Ill Person
**Time period(s):** 1980s (1988)
**Locale(s):** Carrick-on-Suir, Ireland

**Summary:** Keenan MacBreed's study of a cemetery relocation in the lands of his ancestors is complicated by the disinterment of several Druid skeletons, which become reanimated and steal the flesh of the nearby townspeople in order to work the magic that will resurrect their entire coven.

**Other books you might like:**
Al Sarrantonio, *Skeletons*, 1992
David van Meter Smith, *Trinity Grove*, 1990
Patrick Whalen, *Out of the Night*, 1990

## 3957

### THOMAS F. MONTELEONE

## Between Floors

(Burton, Michigan: Subterranean Press, 1997)

**Story type:** Horror (Psychological Suspense)
**Major character(s):** Charles Jameson, Businessman; Alan Markley, Businessman; Dr. Doom, Leader (insane)
**Time period(s):** 1990s (1997)
**Locale(s):** New York, New York

**Summary:** Relieved of his job by a ruthless CEO, Charles Jameson plots an ironic revenge with the help of a madman who calls himself Dr. Doom and who is convinced the company is responsible for despoiling the environment. Published as a signed limited edition chapbook.

**Other books you might like:**
James P. Blaylock, *All the Bells on Earth*, 1995
Thomas M. Disch, *The Businessman: A Tale of Terror*, 1984
Christopher Fowler, *Rune*, 1991
Floyd Kemske, *Human Resources*, 1995
William Browning Spencer, *Resume with Monsters*, 1995

## 3958

### THOMAS F. MONTELEONE

## The Blood of the Lamb

(New York: Tor, 1992)

**Story type:** Horror (Wild Talents)
**Major character(s):** Peter Carenza, Religious (priest); Marion Windsor, Journalist (newspaper reporter); Dan Ellington, Religious (Jesuit priest)
**Time period(s):** 1990s (1998)
**Locale(s):** New York, New York (Brooklyn); Vatican City

**Summary:** Father Peter Carenza's discovery that he has the power to heal or kill by the laying on of hands leads inevitably to his discovery that he was cloned by the Vatican from a blood stain of Jesus Christ left on the Shroud of Turin. But as he struggles to gain control of his godly powers, some begin to fear that he is using his messianic image to disguise satanic intentions.

**Other books you might like:**
Ramsey Campbell, *To Wake the Dead*, 1980
Andrew Laurance, *Catacomb*, 1981
Ira Levin, *Rosemary's Baby*, 1967
David Seltzer, *The Omen*, 1976

## 3959

### THOMAS F. MONTELEONE

## Borderlands

(New York: Avon, 1990)

**Story type:** Horror (Anthology)

**Summary:** A collection of 25 stories that "expand the envelope" of horror fiction beyond its present conventions. In almost all of the stories, horror occurs in unlikely settings (the home, the office) and arises from normally unextraordinary relationships (children and parents, male and female lovers). The best selections include Harlan Ellison's "Scartaris, June 28th," David Silva's "The Calling" and Karl Edward Wagner's "But You'll Never Follow Me." Two of the stories were nominated for 1991 Bram Stoker Awards.

**Other books you might like:**
Dennis Etchison, *Cutting Edge*, 1986
Charles L. Grant, *The Best of Shadows*, 1989
David B. Silva, *Best of The Horror Show*, 1987
J.N. Williamson, *The Best of Masques*, 1988

## 3960

### THOMAS F. MONTELEONE, Editor

## Borderlands 2

(New York: Avon, 1991)

**Story type:** Horror (Anthology)
**Series:** Borderlands

**Summary:** The second volume in this series contains 21 stories that "push the envelope" of the contemporary horror story. The great variety of themes these stories encompass is displayed in Paul F. Olson's "Down the Valley Wild," a ghost tale of guilt and retribution; David Silva's "Slipping," about a man who discovers he can't keep track of the intervals between specific "scenes" in his life; F. Paul Wilson's "Foet," which imagines a near future in which aborted embryos are exploited by the fashion world; Joe Lansdale's "Love Doll: A Fable," a scathing satire on sexual politics; and

Bentley Little's ''The Potato,'' in which a farmer comes to love his crops a little too intimately.

**Other books you might like:**
Dennis Etchison, *Cutting Edge*, 1984
Charles L. Grant, *The Shadows Series*, 1978-1991
David B. Silva, *Best of The Horror Show*, 1987
J.N. Williamson, *The Masques Series*, 1984-1992

---

**3961**

**THOMAS F. MONTELEONE**, Editor

## Borderlands 3

(Baltimore, Maryland: Borderlands Press, 1993)

**Story type:** Horror (Anthology)
**Series:** Borderlands

**Summary:** Twenty-one authors have contributed original stories to this non-theme anthology, among them Poppy Z. Brite, whose ''The Sixth Sentinel'' tells of the passionate attachment of a pirate ghost to a modern woman in Louisiana; Bentley Little, who writes about the strangest carjacking in history in ''The Man in the Passenger Seat''; Ronald Kelly, who leavens his ghostly ''Midnight Grinding'' with the flavor of the southern Gothic; Avram Davidson, whose ''The Man Who Was Made of Money'' is a marvelous satire on the battle of the sexes; and Kristine Kathryn Rusch, whose ''The Ghost of Christmas Present'' is a dark fantasy of loss and redemption.

**Other books you might like:**
Ramsey Campbell, *Superhorror*, 1976
Charles L. Grant, *The Best of Shadows*, 1988
Chris Morgan, *Dark Fantasies*, 1989
Claudia O'Keefe, *Ghosttide*, 1993
Stuart David Schiff, *Whispers: An Anthology of Fantasy and Horror*, 1977
Stanley Wiater, *After the Darkness*, 1993

---

**3962**

**THOMAS F. MONTELEONE**, Editor
**ELIZABETH MONTELEONE**, Co-Editor

## Borderlands 4

(Baltimore: Borderlands Press, 1994)

**Story type:** Horror (Anthology)
**Series:** Borderlands

**Summary:** The fourth in this series devoted to cutting edge weird fiction brings together 18 stories that fall outside conventional genre niches. Included are Dennis Etchison's ''A Wind From the South,'' an exerpt from his forthcoming novel, *California Gothic*; Ramsey Campbell's ''A Side of the Sea,'' which plays fast and loose with its portrayal of a sane man trapped on a bus full of lunatics; William Browning Spencer's ''The Ocean and All Its Devices,'' about a sea creature that preys upon a vacationing family; Don D'Ammassa's ''Misadventures in the Skin Trade,'' told from the point of view of a madman with a gruesome fetish; Lawrence C. Connolly's ''Circle of Lies,'' about a family's stopover in a small town caught up in a bizarre religious frenzy; and Peter Straub's ''Fee,'' a new novella in his ''Blue Rose'' series which examines the mind of a young boy raised in the midst of domestic horrors too painful for him to express that subtly warp his psyche. Released as a signed, limited collector's edition only.

**Other books you might like:**
Peter Crowther, *Narrow Houses*, 1991
   editor

Charles L. Grant, *The Best of Shadows*, 1989
   editor
Charles L. Grant, *Final Shadows*, 1991
   editor
Stuart David Schiff, *The Best of Whispers*, 1994
   editor

---

**3963**

**THOMAS F. MONTELEONE**

## Fantasma

(New York: Tor, 1989)

**Story type:** Horror (Black Magic)
**Major character(s):** Vincent Manzara, Musician (Grandson of Gaetano); Gaetano Manzara, Baker, Aged Person
**Time period(s):** 1980s (Flashbacks to 1875, 1919, 1924)
**Locale(s):** New York, New York; Sicily, Italy (Ciancia)

**Summary:** Vowing revenge against the Candelotto family for the murder of his cousin and father, Vincent Manzara imports a *strega* (Sicilian witchwoman) to summon a *fantasma* (demon). After considerable carnage, the *strega* is killed and her *fantasma* is unleashed, out of control, on New York City.

**Other books you might like:**
John Skipp, *The Light at the End*, 1986
   Craig Spector, co-author

---

**3964**

**THOMAS F. MONTELEONE**

## Night of Broken Souls

(New York: Warner, 1997)

**Story type:** Horror (Reincarnation)
**Major character(s):** Harford Nichols, Government Official (CIA); Isabella Mussina, Doctor; Michael Keating, Doctor
**Time period(s):** 1990s (1997)
**Locale(s):** New York, New York

**Summary:** Possessed by the spirit of Hirsh Dukor, a Jewish turncoat who assisted Nazi Dr. Mengele in the Auschwitz concentration camp, CIA assassin Harford Nichols embarks on a contemporary version of the Final Solution. Hoping to thwart him, Dr. Michael Keating musters the help of patients whose recurring nightmares indicate that they are reincarnations of people who died in the concentration camps of World War II.

**Other books you might like:**
Ira Levin, *The Boys From Brazil*, 1976
Robert R. McCammon, *The Night Boat*, 1980
Kathryn Ptacek, *The Hunted*, 1993
Nina Romberg, *Shadow Walkers*, 1993
Robert Weinberg, *The Armageddon Box*, 1991

---

**3965**

**THOMAS F. MONTELEONE**

## The Resurrectionist

(New York: Warner, 1995)

**Story type:** Horror (Wild Talents)
**Major character(s):** Thomas Flanagan, Political Figure (senator); Estela Barrero, Doctor; Sam Lattimore, Political Figure (senator)
**Time period(s):** 1990s (1995)

**Locale(s):** Washington, District of Columbia

**Summary:** Following his survival of an airplane crash, senator and Republican presidential hopeful Thomas Flanagan finds himself endowed with the power to resurrect the newly dead. While Flanagan ponders the ramifications of his newly discovered talents, the American political power elite decides how his powers can be exploited to their benefit. This novel is a loose sequel to the author's 1992 Bram Stoker Award-winning *Blood of the Lamb*.

**Other books you might like:**
Mark Burnell, *Freak*, 1994
Ramsey Campbell, *The Hungry Moon*, 1987
Stephen King, *The Dead Zone*, 1979
Richard Matheson, *A Stir of Echoes*, 1958

---

## 3966

### R.A. MONTGOMERY

## Traitors from Within

(New York: Bantam, 1990)

**Story type:** Science Fiction (Post-Holocaust; Young Adult)
**Series:** TRIO: Rebels in the New World
**Major character(s):** Matt Sampson, Military Personnel (freedom fighter), Teenager; Mimla Caceras, Military Personnel (freedom fighter), Teenager; David Hasgard, Military Personnel (freedom fighter), Teenager
**Time period(s):** 2010s (2015)
**Locale(s):** North America

**Summary:** Democratic Turtalia and totalitarian Dorado are the two major powers in a splintered North America. When Matt, Mimla and Dave are accused of being traitors, they must enter Dorado to rescue Matt's brother and find information to clear themselves, including evidence of the real moles.

**Other books you might like:**
Douglas Hill, *Exiles of Colsec*, 1984
Dean Ing, *Systemic Shock*, 1981
Marc Laidlaw, *Neon Lotus*, 1988
David R. Palmer, *Emergence*, 1984
Nevil Shute, *On the Beach*, 1957
    pseudonym of Nevil Shute Norway

---

## 3967

### CATHERINE MONTROSE

## Wendigo Border

(New York: Tor, 1995)

**Story type:** Horror (Curse)
**Major character(s):** Darcy Jacoby, Student—College (psychology); Charlie Stone, Cowboy (ranch hand), Indian; Richard Ghormley, Professor (psychology)
**Time period(s):** 1990s (1995)
**Locale(s):** Laramie, Wyoming

**Summary:** When a professor of psychology dabbles dangerously in black magic in the hope of summoning a demon, Native American Charlie Stone appears to young Darcy Jacoby. Charlie, an ageless Indian warrior born over a century ago, hopes to help Darcy prevent the invasion of the Wendigo, a cursed tribe banished to another dimension. They are trying to engineer their return, and Darcy does not know she plays a key role in keeping them at bay. Under her maiden name, Catherine Cooke, tha author has written several fantasy trilogies.

**Other books you might like:**
A.A. Carr, *Eye Killers*, 1995
Muriel Gray, *The Trickster*, 1994
T. Chris Martindale, *Demon Dance*, 1991
Adam Niswander, *The Charm*, 1993
Jessica Palmer, *Shadow Dance*, 1994
Kathryn Ptacek, *Ghost Dance*, 1990

---

## 3968

### ELIZABETH MOON

## Hunting Party

(New York: Baen, 1993)

**Story type:** Science Fiction (Adventure; Space Opera)
**Series:** Hunting Party
**Major character(s):** Heris Serrano, Spaceship Captain, Military Personnel (retired); Ronald "Ronnie" Carruthers, Teenager, Nobleman; Cecelia de Marktos, Noblewoman
**Time period(s):** Indeterminate Future
**Locale(s):** *Sweet Delight*, Spaceship; Sirialis, Planet—Imaginary

**Summary:** From a long line of military officers, Heris Serrano finds commanding the yacht of a wealthy aristocrat an unsettling change. The crew proves generally lazy and poorly trained and the passengers spoiled rich kids, but the ship inspections seem current so the *Sweet Delight* departs for Sirialis despite Captain Serrano's well-founded reservations.

**Other books you might like:**
Lois McMaster Bujold, *Shards of Honor*, 1986
Michelle Shirey Crean, *Dancer of the Sixth*, 1993
David Drake, *Starliner*, 1992
Stephen Goldin, *Jade Darcy and the Affair of Honor*, 1988
    Mary Mason, co-author
Jody Lynn Nye, *Taylor's Ark*, 1993
David Weber, *The Armageddon Inheritance*, 1993

---

## 3969

### ELIZABETH MOON

## Liar's Oath

(New York: Baen, 1992)

**Story type:** Fantasy (Magic Conflict; Political)
**Major character(s):** Gird, Revolutionary (retired), Leader (marshal-general); Luap, Royalty (bastard prince), Magician
**Time period(s):** Indeterminate Past
**Locale(s):** Planet—Imaginary; Mythical Place

**Summary:** After the successful revolution led by Gird, the mageborn, forbidden to use their magic on common folk, no longer rule. Tempted by his discovery of a new land accessible through magic, Luap ignores his oath to Gird in seeking to establish himself as leader of the mageborn in the new land. The hidden powers seeking to control Luap delight in the broken oath which they see as reflecting additional weakness which they may employ to their own evil ends. Set 500 years before events in *Sheepfarmer's Daughter*.

**Other books you might like:**
C.J. Cherryh, *Gate of Ivrel*, 1976
Casey Flynn, *The Enchanted Isles*, 1991
    pseudonym of Kenneth C. Flint
Casey Flynn, *Most Ancient Song*, 1991
    pseudonym of Kenneth C. Flint
L.E. Modesitt Jr., *The Towers of the Sunset*, 1992

## 3970

### ELIZABETH MOON

## *Once a Hero*

(New York: Baen, 1997)

**Story type:** Science Fiction (Space Opera; Political)
**Major character(s):** Esmay Suiza, Spacewoman, Military Personnel (lieutenant); Arhos Asperson, Criminal; Serrano, Military Personnel, Spacewoman
**Time period(s):** Indeterminate Future
**Locale(s):** *Harrier*, Spaceship; Altiplano, Planet—Imaginary; Koskiusko, Space Station

**Summary:** Having saved the planet Xavier from invasion after preventing the Captain from giving the ship to the *Bloodhorde*, Esmay stands trial for mutiny. Cleared by the Military Board for acting as captain and cleared by the court martial for mutiny, Esmay returns to Altiplano, there discovering the lies that had undermined her belief in herself. Now assigned to the *Koskiusko*, Esmay returns from leave, and she must prevent Arhos from giving it to the *Bloodhorde* for longevity drugs.

**Other books you might like:**
Poul Anderson, *Ensign Flandry*, 1966
Lois McMaster Bujold, *Shards of Honor*, 1986
Alfred Coppel, *Glory's War*, 1995
David Feintuch, *Midshipman's Hope*, 1994
David Weber, *On Basilisk Station*, 1993

## 3971

### ELIZABETH MOON

## *Phases*

(New York: Baen, 1997)

**Story type:** Science Fiction (Collection)

**Summary:** Contains a brief introduction plus individual introductions to 15 stories published between 1986 and 1995, about half from *Lunar Activity* (1990) and half original to this volume. Themes include art, cloning, character, horses and humor.

**Other books you might like:**
Alfred Bester, *Virtual Unrealities: The Short Fiction of Alfred Bester*, 1997
Nancy Kress, *The Aliens of Earth*, 1993
Henry Kuttner, *The Best of Henry Kuttner*, 1975
Mary Rosenblum, *Synthesis & Other Virtual Realities*, 1996
Connie Willis, *Impossible Things*, 1994

## 3972

### ELIZABETH MOON

## *Remnant Population*

(New York: Baen, 1996)

**Story type:** Science Fiction (First Contact; Political)
**Major character(s):** Ofelia Damareux Falfurrias, Aged Person, Runaway; Bluecloak, Alien; Kira Stavi, Scientist (xenobiologist)
**Time period(s):** Indeterminate Future
**Locale(s):** Sims Bancorp Colony 3245.12, Planet—Imaginary

**Summary:** When Sims Bancorp loses the franchise to Colony 3245.12 and evacuates the colonists, 70-year-old Ofelia hides, refusing to leave. Happy at finally being alone with no one to tell her what to do, Ofelia maintains the crops and livestock left behind, as well as the power plant and radio. When a new colony unexpectedly tries to land about 40 miles away, Ofelia overhears its total destruction by previously unknown intelligent natives who decide to send some of their juvenile hunters to check out her "abandoned" colony.

**Other books you might like:**
Eleanor Arnason, *Ring of Swords*, 1993
Eleanor Arnason, *A Woman of the Iron People*, 1991
David Brin, *Brightness Reef*, 1995
C.J. Cherryh, *Foreigner*, 1994
James H. Schmitz, *The Demon Breed*, 1968
Sheri S. Tepper, *Grass*, 1989
John Varley, *Titan*, 1979

## 3973

### ELIZABETH MOON

## *Sheepfarmer's Daughter*

(New York: Baen Books, 1988)

**Story type:** Fantasy (Quest)
**Series:** Deed of Paksenarrion
**Major character(s):** Paksenarrion "Paks" Dorthansdotter, Farmer, Military Personnel
**Time period(s):** Indeterminate
**Locale(s):** Alternate Universe

**Summary:** When her father arranges a marriage with a pig farmer, Paks runs away and joins the Duke's army. This begins a series of adventures that leave her a hero, chosen by the gods to restore a lost ruler to his throne.

**Other books you might like:**
C.J. Cherryh, *The Paladin*, 1988
Jo Clayton, *Diadem from the Stars*, 1986
Louise Cooper, *Nemesis*, 1989
   Indigo Series, Book 1
Robin McKinley, *The Blue Sword*, 1982

## 3974

### ELIZABETH MOON

## *Sporting Chance*

(New York: Baen, 1994)

**Story type:** Science Fiction (Adventure; Space Opera)
**Series:** Hunting Party
**Major character(s):** Heris Serrano, Spaceship Captain, Military Personnel (retired); Cecelia de Marktos, Noblewoman (spaceship owner); Sirkin, Spacewoman (navigator)
**Time period(s):** Indeterminate Future
**Locale(s):** *Sweet Delight*, Spaceship; Sirialis, Planet—Imaginary; Rockhouse Major, Planet—Imaginary

**Summary:** After returning the Prince to Rockhouse, Cecelia mentions to the Emperor that she noticed the changes in his son. Cecelia suddenly takes ill, remaining comatose, leaving Heris the logical culprit as the heir to the *Sweet Delight*. Not only must Heris and her crew save the *Sweet Delight*, they also must somehow rescue Cecelia, find a cure and unravel the mystery surrounding the Prince. Sequel to *Hunting Party*.

**Other books you might like:**
Pauline Ashwell, *Unwillingly to Earth*, 1992
Lois McMaster Bujold, *The Warrior's Apprentice*, 1986
C.J. Cherryh, *Tripoint*, 1994
David Drake, *Starliner*, 1992
T. Jackson King, *Retread Shop*, 1988

David Weber, *On Basilisk Station*, 1993

**3975**

ELIZABETH MOON

## Surrender None: The Legacy of Gird
(New York: Baen, 1990)

**Story type:** Fantasy (Adventure; Political)
**Series:** Deed of Paksenarrion
**Major character(s):** Gird, Farmer, Revolutionary
**Time period(s):** Indeterminate Past
**Locale(s):** Alternate Universe

**Summary:** A prequel to the Deed of Paksenarrion trilogy, this story tells how Gird gets some military training but returns to his family and attempts to make a life farming. The aristocracy, descended from overseas invaders, has become increasingly cruel and tyrannical. Eventually Gird is pressed too far and joins the dispossessed and rebellious outlaws in the forest. Gird puts his military training to good use to organize the outlaws, and develops plans for removing the aristocracy and instituting more compassionate and equitable rule.

**Other books you might like:**
Guy Gavriel Kay, *Tigana*, 1990
Katharine Kerr, *Daggerspell*, 1986
Robin McKinley, *The Blue Sword*, 1982
Steve Perry, *The Man Who Never Missed*, 1985
Karen Wehrstein, *Lion's Heart*, 1991

**3976**

ELIZABETH MOON

## Winning Colors
(New York: Baen, 1995)

**Story type:** Science Fiction (Adventure; Political)
**Series:** Hunting Party
**Major character(s):** Heris Serrano, Spaceship Captain, Military Personnel (retired); Cecelia de Marktos, Noblewoman; Esteban Kontsandas, Military Personnel
**Time period(s):** Indeterminate Future
**Locale(s):** *Sweet Delight*, Spaceship; Xavier, Planet—Imaginary; Music, Planet—Imaginary

**Summary:** With the government still unsettled by the abdication of the old king, Lady Cecelia finds her ship now belongs to Heris Serrano, her ex-military employee. They leave behind the suit against Cecelia's prisoners and test her rejuvenation at the Wherrin Horse Trials, taking along Esteban as a favor to the military commander who had saved *Sweet Delight* previously. Looking for horses, on Xavier they find traitors selling out the planet to the Benignity. Attempting to save the system, Heris takes over the naval vessels involved in the conspiracy, pretending to retain her commission.

**Other books you might like:**
David Brin, *The Uplift War*, 1987
Lois McMaster Bujold, *Shards of Honor*, 1986
Alis A. Rasmussen, *A Passage of Stars*, 1990
David Weber, *The Honor of the Queen*, 1993
David Weber, *On Basilisk Station*, 1993

**3977**

MICHAEL MOORCOCK

## Blood: A Southern Fantasy
(New York: Morrow/AvoNova, 1995)

**Story type:** Fantasy (Historical; Science Fiction)
**Major character(s):** Jack Karaquazian, Gambler, Adventurer; Sam Oakenhurst, Gambler
**Time period(s):** Indeterminate
**Locale(s):** Alternate Earth; Mississippi River; New Orleans, Louisiana

**Summary:** Searching for love and adventure, riverboat gamblers Jack Karaquazian and Sam Oakenhurst tempt luck and fate in the Game of Time, while the Biloxi fault threatens to engulf a South dominated by African Americans and thrust all into the barely explored multidimensional universe. Includes short fiction published 1991-1994.

**Other books you might like:**
Michael Bishop, *Brittle Innings*, 1994
Michael Bishop, *Count Geiger's Blues*, 1992
Michael Conner, *Archangel*, 1995
George R.R. Martin, *Fevre Dream*, 1982
Harry Turtledove, *The Guns of the South: A Novel of the Civil War*, 1992

**3978**

MICHAEL MOORCOCK

## Corum: The Coming of Chaos
(Clarkston, Georgia: White Wolf, 1997)

**Story type:** Fantasy (Quest; Sword and Sorcery)
**Series:** Eternal Champion
**Major character(s):** Corum Jhaelen Irsei, Royalty (prince), Wizard
**Time period(s):** Indeterminate
**Locale(s):** Alternate Earth; Tanelorn, Fictional City

**Summary:** The sole surviving member of the magical race of the Vadhagh, Prince Corum unleashes vast cosmic forces and acquires powerful adversaries as he travels through the multiverse to avenge his ravaged world. Omnibus edition of *The Knight of Swords* (1971), *The Queen of Swords* (1971) and *The King of Swords* (1971), previously published in 1977 as *The Swords Trilogy*.

**Other books you might like:**
Fred Saberhagen, *The First Book of Swords*, 1983
Martha Wells, *The Element of Fire*, 1993
Roger Zelazny, *The Guns of Avalon*, 1972
Roger Zelazny, *Nine Princes in Amber*, 1970
Roger Zelazny, *Sign of the Unicorn*, 1975

**3979**

MICHAEL MOORCOCK

## The Dancers at the End of Time
(Clarkston, Georgia: White Wolf, 1998)

**Story type:** Science Fiction (Time Travel)
**Major character(s):** Jherek Carnelian, Time Traveler
**Time period(s):** Indeterminate Future; Indeterminate Past

**Summary:** This is an omnibus of three novels published between 1972 and 1978. Jherek Carnelian is an inhabitant of the far future when life is so safe and predictable that he becomes bored. Eventually he travels back in time to various periods in Earth's history, pursued by a detective from his own time and occasionally accompanied by others.

**Other books you might like:**
Isaac Asimov, *The End of Eternity*, 1955
John Brunner, *The Productions of Time*, 1967
Peter Heath, *Assassins From Tomorrow*, 1967
Dean R. Koontz, *Lightning*, 1988
Dan Parkinson, *Viper's Spawn*, 1998

## 3980

### MICHAEL MOORCOCK

## Elric: Song of the Black Sword

(Clarkston, Georgia: White Wolf, 1995)

**Story type:** Fantasy (Sword and Sorcery; Magic Conflict)
**Series:** Elric
**Major character(s):** Elric of Melnibone, Warrior, Ruler, Wizard
**Time period(s):** Indeterminate
**Locale(s):** Melnibone, Fictional Country; The Young Kingdoms, Fictional Country

**Summary:** Omnibus edition containing a two-page introduction by Moorcock; a map of the Young Kingdoms; three novels, *Elric of Melnibone* (1976), *Fortress of the Pearl* (1989), and *The Sailor on the Seas of Fate* (1976); and three stories, ''The Dreaming City'' (1967), ''While the Gods Laugh'' (1967), and ''The Singing Citadel'' (1970). These tales of the Eternal Champion Cycle relate adventures of the morose anti-hero and his vampiric sword.

**Other books you might like:**
Poul Anderson, *The Broken Sword*, 1954
James Branch Cabell, *Jurgen*, 1919
Lord Dunsany, *The King of Elfland's Daughter*, 1924
Edward E. Kramer, *Tales of the White Wolf*, 1994
    Richard Gilliam, co-editor
Fritz Leiber, *Ill Met in Lankhmar*, 1995
Fletcher Pratt, *The Well of the Unicorn*, 1948
Roger Zelazny, *Nine Princes in Amber*, 1970

## 3981

### MICHAEL MOORCOCK

## Fabulous Harbors

(New York: Avon, 1997)

**Story type:** Fantasy (Collection; Literary)
**Major character(s):** Jack Karaquazian, Gambler (retired), Adventurer; Colinda Dovero, Adventurer (retired); Albert Begg, Military Personnel (Naval Intelligence, retired)
**Time period(s):** Indeterminate
**Locale(s):** Alternate Earth; Chelsea, England

**Summary:** Eleven interrelated stories fitting into the universe of *Blood: A Southern Fantasy* and *The War Amongst the Angels*. Lovers Jack Karaquazian and Colinda Dovero settle into retirement with their old cronies, the Beggs and the von Becks, entertaining one another with tales of their adventures in the multiverse. These include an encounter with Elric of Melnibone, rescuing virgins from high towers and certain doom, visitations from Egypt's ancient gods and running guns into Africa with Captain Horace Quelch, the infamous White Pirate.

**Other books you might like:**
Michael Bishop, *At the City Limits of Fate*, 1996
Zenna Henderson, *Ingathering: The Complete People Stories of Zenna Henderson*, 1995

Robert E. Howard, *Beyond the Borders*, 1996
Diana Wynne Jones, *Everard's Ride*, 1995
Harry Turtledove, *The Guns of the South: A Novel of the Civil War*, 1992

## 3982

### MICHAEL MOORCOCK

## The Fortress of the Pearl

(New York: Ace, 1989)

**Story type:** Fantasy (Quest)
**Series:** Elric
**Major character(s):** Elric of Melnibone, Warrior, Royalty (Prince), Wizard
**Time period(s):** Indeterminate
**Locale(s):** Quarzhasaata, Alternate Universe (Dream Realm)

**Summary:** Trapped within the dreams of a girl prophet, Elric must find the Pearl at the Heart of the World, as well as his way out of the dreams, before he can join the ruling council at Quarzhasaata.

**Other books you might like:**
Gael Baudino, *Dragonsword*, 1988
C.J. Cherryh, *Reap the Whirlwind*, 1989
    Mercedes Lackey, co-author
Glen Cook, *The Swordbearer*, 1990
Fritz Leiber, *The Knight and Knave of Swords*, 1988
Eric Van Lustbader, *The Sunset Warrior*, 1989

## 3983

### MICHAEL MOORCOCK

## Kane of Old Mars

(Clarkston, Georgia: White Wolf, 1998)

**Story type:** Science Fiction (Space Opera)
**Major character(s):** Michael Kane, Professor; Hool Haji, Alien, Warrior
**Time period(s):** 1960s (1968); Indeterminate Past
**Locale(s):** Mars

**Summary:** This is an omnibus of the three novels about Michael Kane, a professor from Earth who travels to Mars of the present and the past accidentally when an experiment with a matter transmitter goes awry. His adventures include becoming a military leader and saving a beleaguered city from its enemies, defeating a monstrous creature, and dealing with a plague of zombies. The stories are a homage to the work of Edgar Rice Burroughs. The novels were originally published in 1965 under the name Edward P. Bradbury and later retitled when published under Moorcock's name.

**Other books you might like:**
Alan Burt Akers, *Transit to Scorpio*, 1972
Edgar Rice Burroughs, *A Princess of Mars*, 1917
A. Bertram Chandler, *The Alternate Martians*, 1965
Otis Adelbert Kline, *The Outlaws of Mars*, 1961
Mike Resnick, *Pursuit on Ganymede*, 1968

## 3984

### MICHAEL MOORCOCK

## Lunching with the Antichrist

(Shingletown, California: Mark Ziesing, 1995)

**Story type:** Fantasy (Collection; Literary)

**Major character(s):** Jimi, Traveler; Edwin Begg, Religious (retired vicar); Savitsky, Military Personnel (Cossack)
**Time period(s):** 1990s (1992); 1920s (1920)
**Locale(s):** London, England; St. Crim, Fictional Country

**Summary:** Seven short stories, some with overt and others with muted fantastic elements, written 1974-1994, focusing on the Von Bek family and its various branches. From high society in the Twenties to an ex-roadie traveling with what might be the ghost of Jimi Hendrix, the stories trace the history of Britain as well.

**Other books you might like:**
Peter Ackroyd, *Hawksmoor*, 1986
John Crowley, *Little, Big*, 1981
Lisa Goldstein, *Travelers in Magic*, 1994
Patrick McGrath, *Blood and Water and Other Tales*, 1988

---

**3985**

**MICHAEL MOORCOCK**

### The Revenge of the Rose
(New York: Ace, 1991)

**Story type:** Fantasy (Quest)
**Series:** Elric
**Major character(s):** Elric of Melnibone, Warrior, Royalty (prince), Wizard; Rose, Time Traveler, Warrior; Wheldrake, Writer (poet)
**Time period(s):** Indeterminate
**Locale(s):** Northern Young Kingdoms, Fictional Country; The Sphere the Realm, Mythical Place (the multiverse)

**Summary:** In the Dreaming City, the spirit of Elric's deceased father asks Elric to find and free his soul, held captive by Gaynor. Elric and his companions seek out and find the soul, not knowing the Lord of Chaos had planned a trap aimed at separating Elric from his vampire sword.

**Other books you might like:**
David Eddings, *Pawn of Prophecy*, 1982
Raymond E. Feist, *Daughter of the Empire*, 1987
    Janny Wurtz, co-author
Robert Jordan, *The Eye of the World*, 1989
Marc Laidlaw, *Neon Lotus*, 1988
Fritz Leiber, *The Knight and Knave of Swords*, 1990
Roger Zelazny, *Nine Princes in Amber*, 1970

---

**3986**

**MICHAEL MOORCOCK**

### The War Amongst the Angels
(New York: Avon, 1997)

**Story type:** Fantasy (Religious; Political)
**Series:** Von Bek Family
**Major character(s):** Margaret Rose Moorcock, Revolutionary, Adventurer; Sam Oakenhurst, Adventurer; Jack Karaquazian, Gambler, Adventurer
**Time period(s):** 1990s; Indeterminate
**Locale(s):** London, England; The Second Ether, Mythical Place; Alternate Universe

**Summary:** A veteran of the battle against the tyranny of London's Universal Transport Company, Rose discovers the doors between the worlds, opening the way to infinite possibilities. Together with Sam, Jack and others, she joins in the great War in Heaven, battling against Lucifer himself. Last in series.

**Other books you might like:**
Neil Gaiman, *Good Omens: The Nice and Accurate Prophecies of Agnes Nutter, Witch*, 1990
    Terry Pratchett, co-author
Parke Godwin, *The Snake Oil Wars*, 1989
Robert A. Heinlein, *Job: A Comedy of Justice*, 1984
James Morrow, *Bible Stories for Adults*, 1996
James Morrow, *Blameless in Abaddon*, 1996
James Morrow, *Towing Jehovah*, 1994

---

**3987**

**ALAN MOORE**
**EDDIE CAMPBELL**, Illustrator

### From Hell
(Baltimore: Borderlands Press, 1994)

**Story type:** Horror (Serial Killer)
**Major character(s):** Annie Crook, Clerk (sweet shop employee); Walter Sickert, Artist; Annie Chapman, Prostitute
**Time period(s):** 1880s
**Locale(s):** London, England

**Summary:** This book presents the scripts of the "From Hell" series, a meditation on the life and crimes of Jack the Ripper which was published as a fully illustrated comic strip in the avant garde comic art magazine *Taboo* between 1988 and 1990. *Taboo* publisher Stephen Bissette supplies an afterword. The text is heavily annotated by Moore and illustrated by Eddie Campbell.

**Other books you might like:**
Shirley Harrison, *The Diary of Jack the Ripper: The Discovery, the Investigation, the Debate*, 1993
Stephen Knight, *Jack the Ripper: The Final Solution*, 1976
Donald Rumbelow, *The Complete Jack the Ripper*, 1987
Paul West, *The Women of Whitechapel and Jack the Ripper*, 1992

---

**3988**

**CHRISTOPHER MOORE**

### Bloodsucking Fiends: A Love Story
(New York: Simon & Schuster, 1995)

**Story type:** Horror (Vampire Story; Satire)
**Major character(s):** Jody, Clerk (claims clerk), Vampire; C. Thomas Flood, Writer; Elijah Ben Sapir, Vampire
**Time period(s):** 1990s (1995)
**Locale(s):** San Francisco, California

**Summary:** Vampirized for reasons she cannot understand, Jody seeks the assistance of Tommy Flood, an aspiring writer she has just met, to help her deal with her new lifestyle. As Jody and Thomas become lovers, grappling clumsily with their vastly different means of existence, both try to get to the bottom of the mystery surrounding Jody's victimization and exonerate Tommy of the suspicion that he is responsible for the recent spate of vampire deaths around town.

**Other books you might like:**
Anne Billson, *Suckers*, 1993
Ray Garton, *Live Girls*, 1987
Norman Spinrad, *Vampire Junkies*, 1994

## 3989

**CHRISTOPHER MOORE**

### Practical Demonkeeping

(New York: St. Martin's, 1991)

**Story type:** Horror (Satire)
**Major character(s):** Travis O'Hearn, Drifter; Catch, Demon; Jenny Masterson, Waiter/Waitress
**Time period(s):** 1990s
**Locale(s):** Pine Cove, California

**Summary:** The author's amusing first novel tells of Travis O'Hearn, who has grown tired of his relationship with Catch, a demon who grants him eternal youth in exchange for human victims. When Travis reaches Pine Cove, he must find a way to shed Catch, before Catch decimates the town and develops a taste for Travis's love interest, Jenny.

**Other books you might like:**
L. Sprague de Camp, *Solomon's Stone*, 1942
Esther Friesner, *Hooray for Hellywood*, 1990
L. Ron Hubbard, *The Case of the Friendly Corpse*, 1941
Daniel Rhodes, *Kiss of Death*, 1990
Thorne Smith, *Topper: An Improbable Adventure*, 1926

## 3990

**JAMES A. MOORE**

### Hell-Storm

(New York: HarperPrism, 1996)

**Story type:** Horror (Werewolf Story)
**Series:** World of Darkness: Werewolf
**Major character(s):** Gabriel White, Werewolf; Diane White, Parent; Jack Dawson, Mercenary
**Time period(s):** 1990s (1996)
**Locale(s):** Las Vegas, Nevada

**Summary:** Gabriel and his mother accept an invitation to the Platinum Palace casino to escape the blood wars that have taken the life of Gabriel's adoptive father. But the Wyrm, a spirit of corruption that poisons the World of Darkness, is conspiring with the mob to use the casino as a catalyst for yet more strife. This novel is set in White Wolf Books' "World of Darkness" gaming world, where humans and supernatural beings co-exist.

**Other books you might like:**
Doug Murray, *Call to Battle*, 1996
Edo van Belkom, *Wyrm Wolf*, 1995
Stewart Von Allmen, *Conspicuous Consumption*, 1995

## 3991

**JOHN MOORE**

### Slay and Rescue

(New York: Baen, 1993)

**Story type:** Fantasy (Light Fantasy)
**Major character(s):** Prince Charming, Hero, Royalty; Wendell, Sidekick
**Time period(s):** Indeterminate
**Locale(s):** Illyria, Fictional Country; Alacia, Fictional Country

**Summary:** Accompanied by Wendell, Prince Charming dazzles the kingdom with brave deeds while rescuing princesses and searching for a hot date.

**Other books you might like:**
Kyle Crocco, *Heroes, Inc.*, 1991
Barry Hughart, *Bridge of Birds*, 1984
Terry Pratchett, *Guards! Guards!*, 1991
Christopher Stasheff, *The Warlock in Spite of Himself*, 1969
Roger Zelazny, *Bring Me the Head of Prince Charming*, 1991
    Robert Sheckley, co-author
Roger Zelazny, *If at Faust You Don't Succeed*, 1993
    Robert Sheckley, co-author

## 3992

**STANLEY R. MOORE**

### Nightshade

(New York: NAL Onyx, 1989)

**Story type:** Horror (Nature in Revolt)
**Major character(s):** Peter Bileux, Police Officer (Deputy sheriff); Louise Kavanaugh, Researcher (Medical)
**Time period(s):** 1980s
**Locale(s):** Thomas Valley, Pennsylvania

**Summary:** In Moore's first novel, the quiet town of Thomas Valley is gradually terrorized by a mysterious plague of killing flies. A small group led by the deputy sheriff and a group of medical researchers search frantically for clues to the nature and source—natural or supernatural—in order to develop a defense against the infestation before it completely destroys the town and spreads beyond its perimeters.

**Other books you might like:**
James Herbert, *Domain*, 1984
James Herbert, *Lair*, 1979
James Herbert, *The Rats*, 1974
Harry Adam Knight, *The Fungus*, 1989

## 3993

**WARD MOORE**

### Bring the Jubilee

(New York: Ballantine Del Rey, 1997)

**Story type:** Science Fiction (Time Travel; Alternate Universe)
**Major character(s):** Hodgins "Hodge" Backmaker, Historian, Time Traveler; Rene Enfandin, Diplomat; Barbara Haggerwells, Inventor, Time Traveler
**Time period(s):** 1860s (1863); 20th century (1938-1952)
**Locale(s):** New York, New York; Pennsylvania; Alternate Earth

**Summary:** In an impoverished United States where the Confederacy won the Civil War, the War of Southern Independence, Hodge Backmaker goes to New York City and becomes involved with gangs. From Haven, a study institute in Pennsylvania where Barbara Haggerwells invents time travel, Hodge travels to view the battle of Gettysburg and changes history to create our world. Contains a three-page introduction by Jeff Shaara. Reissue of the 1953 classic by Moore (1903-1978).

**Other books you might like:**
Terry Bisson, *Fire on the Mountain*, 1988
Andre Norton, *The Crossroads of Time*, 1956
Kevin D. Randle, *Remember Gettysburg*, 1988
    Robert J. Cornett, co-author
William Sanders, *The Wild Blue and the Gray*, 1991
Wilson Tucker, *The Lincoln Hunters*, 1958
Harry Turtledove, *The Guns of the South: A Novel of the Civil War*, 1992

Connie Willis, *Lincoln's Dreams*, 1987

## 3994

### DANIEL KEYS MORAN

## The Last Dancer

(New York: Bantam Spectra, 1993)

**Story type:** Science Fiction (Political; Psychic Powers)
**Series:** Tales of the Continuing Time
**Major character(s):** Denice Castanaveras, Telepath, Genetically Altered Being; "William Devane" Gi'Tbad'Eovad'Dvan, Immortal, Security Officer; Gi'Suei'Obodi'Sedon, Immortal, Rebel
**Time period(s):** 2070s (2075-2076); 350th century B.C.
**Locale(s):** Earth

**Summary:** Fleeing from his executioner, Dvan, Sedon takes refuge in a stasis bubble for 37,000 years. Along with her twin brother David, Denice survives the massacre of the "genies" in 2062 by hiding among the street children in the rubble of New York City. On the eve of the Tricentennial, rebels in Occupied America prepare to overthrow the Unification government while Sedon, released from stasis and escaped from Peace Keeping Force detention, uses David's abilities to control the rebel movement. Denice, however, resists his attempts to control her talents—talents that even she does not yet understand.

**Other books you might like:**
Alfred Bester, *The Computer Connection*, 1975
Margaret Wander Bonanno, *The Others*, 1990
David Brin, *Startide Rising*, 1983
C.J. Cherryh, *Cyteen*, 1988
C.J. Cherryh, *Heavy Time*, 1991
Jane S. Fancher, *Ground-Ties*, 1991
Robert A. Heinlein, *The Moon Is a Harsh Mistress*, 1966
Larry Niven, *Protector*, 1973
Larry Niven, *Ringworld Engineers*, 1980
A.E. Van Vogt, *Slan*, 1946

## 3995

### DANIEL KEYS MORAN

## The Long Run

(New York: Bantam Spectra, 1989)

**Story type:** Science Fiction (Cyberpunk)
**Series:** Tales of the Continuing Time
**Major character(s):** Trent Castanaveras, Thief, Computer Expert; Denice Castanaveras, Telepath, Genetically Altered Being
**Time period(s):** 21st century
**Locale(s):** New York, New York; Montenegro

**Summary:** Trent was one of the few who survived the United Nations Peaceforce massacre of the Castanaveras telepaths. Now he lives as an outlaw computer hacker, making a living through datanet crime. The UN Peaceforcers, however, have a long arm and an even longer memory. Soon Trent finds them on his trail again and, almost against his will, becomes a key figure in a revolution against UN tyranny.

**Other books you might like:**
William Gibson, *Neuromancer*, 1984
W.T. Quick, *Systems*, 1989
Bruce Sterling, *Islands in the Net*, 1988
A.E. Van Vogt, *Slan*, 1946

## 3996

### THOMAS MORAN

## The World I Made for Her

(New York: Riverhead, 1998)

**Story type:** Horror (Wild Talents)
**Major character(s):** James Blatchley, Police Officer, Student (art history); Brigit, Nurse; Nuala, Nurse
**Time period(s):** 1990s (1998)
**Locale(s):** New York

**Summary:** Rendered comatose and brain damaged by a rogue strain of chicken pox, James Blatchley finds himself able to project his personality into the dreams of his devoted nurse, Nuala. James and Nuala's amorous relationship grows increasingly bittersweet and terrifying as James' condition deteriorates.

**Other books you might like:**
Robin Cook, *Coma*, 1977
Sean Costello, *Captain Quad*, 1991
Joseph McElroy, *Plus*, 1976
Dalton Trumbo, *Johnny Got His Gun*, 1939

## 3997

### JOE MOREY, Editor

## Glimring Night and Other Tales of Fantasy

(Concord, California: Dark Regions, 1991)

**Story type:** Horror (Anthology)

**Summary:** A trade paperback edition of the small press magazine *Dark Regions* that includes nine short stories and poems, among which are Albert J. Manachino's tale of a strange case of demonic possession, "Darby's Bane"; Keith Hudson's prose poem of a horrifying resurrection, "Upon the Wings of Lazarus"; and three stories by Ardath Mayhar, the best of which is her dark fairy tale, "Needles and Pins."

**Other books you might like:**
Robert Morrish, *The Quick Chills Series*, 1990-1992
    Peter Enfantino, co-author
Joy Oestreicher, *Alpha Gallery*, 1991
Steve Pasechnik, *The Best of the Rest*, 1990
    Brian Youmans, co-author
Elizabeth A. Saunders, *When the Black Lotus Blooms*, 1990
David B. Silva, *Best of The Horror Show*, 1987

## 3998

### J.M. MORGAN

## Between the Devil and the Deep

(New York: Pocket, 1992)

**Story type:** Horror (Nature in Revolt)
**Major character(s):** J. Kelsey Chase, Diver; Cyrus Gilbert, Police Officer (sheriff); Paige Burton, Scientist (marine biologist)
**Time period(s):** 1990s
**Locale(s):** Saratoga Springs, Nevada; Loch Ness, Scotland

**Summary:** Coincidences between underwater formations in Death Valley and Loch Ness suggest to diver J. Kelsey Chase a series of tunnels connecting bodies of water across the face of the earth. Chase quickly finds that his worst nemesis may not be the prehistoric mammals still living in the caves, but the business entrepreneur who has engaged his services and is neurotically protective of the fame and riches the discovery will bring.

**Other books you might like:**
Peter Benchley, *Beast*, 1991
Peter Benchley, *Jaws*, 1974
William Dantz, *Hunger*, 1992

## 3999
### J.M. MORGAN
### *Beyond Eden*
(New York: Pinnacle, 1992)

**Story type:** Science Fiction (Post-Holocaust; Adventure)
**Series:** Eden
**Major character(s):** Jonathan Katelo, Indian (Inuit), Explorer; Seth Katelo, Indian (Inuit), Explorer; Josiah Gray Wolf, Scientist, Explorer
**Time period(s):** 2010s
**Locale(s):** Biosphere Seven, Texas; Montana; North America

**Summary:** After plague wipes out most human life on Earth, survivors Jonathan and Seth Katelo set out from their Montana home in search of a legendary city of survivors. Meanwhile, Josiah Gray Wolf and his band of survivors living near Biosphere Seven struggle against traditional human difficulties as the second generation of Biosphere Seven residents anxiously plan to leave the safety of their environment for the excitement of exploring the depopulated surroundings.

**Other books you might like:**
Will Bradley, *Ark Liberty*, 1992
Octavia E. Butler, *Adulthood Rites*, 1988
Donald E. McQuinn, *Warrior*, 1990
Michael D. Weaver, *My Father Immortal*, 1989

## 4000
### J.M. MORGAN
### *Desert Eden*
(New York: Zebra Pinnacle, 1991)

**Story type:** Science Fiction (End of the World; Techno-Thriller)
**Series:** Eden
**Major character(s):** Jessica Nathan, Scientist; Josiah Gray Wolf, Scientist, Explorer; Jonathon Katelo, Guide, Linguist, Indian
**Time period(s):** 1990s (1997)
**Locale(s):** Claypool, Texas (Biosphere Seven); Siberia, Union of Soviet Socialist Republics (Biosphere Four)

**Summary:** After Biosphere Seven was sealed for a two-year trial of the huge, closed environment, a virus created secretly in Biosphere Four killed its inventors and got loose in Earth's atmosphere. No cure or treatment was discovered. The ten inhabitants of Biosphere Seven must decide what possibilities lie in their future when they realize they are permanently cut off from the outside world in their dome.

**Other books you might like:**
Roger MacBride Allen, *The Ring of Charon*, 1990
Michael Armstrong, *Agviq*, 1990
Stephen Baxter, *Raft*, 1992
David Brin, *Earth*, 1990
Octavia E. Butler, *Dawn*, 1987
Marjorie Bradley Kellogg, *Harmony*, 1991
Donald E. McQuinn, *Warrior*, 1990
Larry Niven, *Lucifer's Hammer*, 1977
   Jerry Pournelle, co-author

Vernor Vinge, *Marooned in Realtime*, 1986
Catherine Wells, *The Earth Is All That Lasts*, 1991

## 4001
### J.M. MORGAN
### *Future Eden*
(New York: Pinnacle, 1992)

**Story type:** Science Fiction (Post-Holocaust; Adventure)
**Series:** Eden
**Major character(s):** Willow Gray Wolf, Explorer; Seth Katelo, Indian, Explorer (Inuit); Sidra, Explorer
**Time period(s):** 2020s (2020)
**Locale(s):** Texas; North America

**Summary:** Decades after plague devastates humanity, some of the few survivors begin to explore in hopes of reestablishing a human presence on the depopulated Earth.

**Other books you might like:**
Octavia E. Butler, *Imago*, 1989
Sterling E. Lanier, *Hiero's Journey*, 1973
Donald E. McQuinn, *Warrior*, 1990
Catherine Wells, *The Earth Is All That Lasts*, 1991
Paul O. Williams, *The Breaking of Northwall*, 1980

## 4002
### ROBERT MORGAN (Pseudonym of C.J. Henderson)
### *All Things under the Moon*
(New York: Berkley, 1994)

**Story type:** Horror (Mystery; Werewolf Story)
**Series:** Adventures of Teddy London
**Major character(s):** Teddy London, Detective—Private; Lisa Hutchinson, Assistant; Maxim Warhelski, Werewolf
**Time period(s):** 1990s (1994)
**Locale(s):** New York, New York

**Summary:** In his fourth adventure, Teddy London, a detective whose case file frequently brings him into contact with the supernatural, is stalked by a centuries-old, seemingly indestructable werewolf who wants to be killed, but whose inhuman nature demands that he fight to the death those capable of putting him out of his misery.

**Other books you might like:**
Crosland Brown, *Tombley's Walk*, 1991
Richard Jaccoma, *The Werewolf's Revenge*, 1991
Richard Jaccoma, *The Werewolf's Tale*, 1988
H. Warner Munn, *The Werewolf of Ponkert*, 1958
S.P. Somtow, *Moon Dance*, 1988

## 4003
### ROBERT MORGAN (Pseudonym of C.J. Henderson)
### *The Only Thing to Fear*
(New York: Berkley, 1994)

**Story type:** Horror (Mystery; Ghost Story)
**Series:** Adventures of Teddy London
**Major character(s):** Teddy London, Detective—Private; Paul Morcey, Assistant; Kuan Yu-Chen, Religious (priest)
**Time period(s):** 1990s (1994)
**Locale(s):** Xian, China; New York, New York

**Summary:** Detective Teddy London's fifth adventure battling supernatural menaces takes him to China, where his destiny to save the earth from an oncoming meteor is intertwined with the mystery of an ancient ghost warrior leading him through a ritual of self-discovery.

**Other books you might like:**
T.E.D. Klein, *The Ceremonies*, 1983
Bentley Little, *The Summoning*, 1993
Kelley Wilde, *Makoto*, 1990
F. Paul Wilson, *Black Wind*, 1989
T.M. Wright, *The Ascending*, 1994

**4004**

**ROBERT MORGAN** (Pseudonym of C.J. Henderson)

## Some Things Come Back

(New York: Berkley, 1995)

**Story type:** Horror (Occult; Vampire Story)
**Series:** Adventures of Teddy London
**Major character(s):** Teddy London, Detective—Private; Martin Tabor, Vampire; Paul Morcey, Detective
**Time period(s):** 1990s (1995)
**Locale(s):** New York, New York

**Summary:** In the final adventure of Teddy London, a private eye whose work always brings him in contact with the occult, London faces down Martin Tabor, his nemesis from an earlier adventure. London's efforts to prevent Tabor and his vampire underlings from dropping nuclear bombs across the world in order to feed on the souls of the dead they will liberate dovetails with his quest to find a new incarnation for the Confessor, an ageless occult entity who may hold the key to thwarting Tabor.

**Other books you might like:**
Stephen Gallagher, *Valley of Lights*, 1987
Lee Killough, *Blood Hunt*, 1987
William Relling Jr., *New Moon*, 1987
Robert Weinberg, *Blood War*, 1995
Les Whitten, *Progeny of the Adder*, 1965

**4005**

**ROBERT MORGAN** (Pseudonym of C.J. Henderson)

## Some Things Never Die

(New York: Diamond, 1993)

**Story type:** Horror (Vampire Story)
**Series:** Adventures of Teddy London
**Major character(s):** Teddy London, Detective—Private; Lai Wan, Psychic (psychometrist); Jorhsa, Vampire
**Time period(s):** 1990s (1993)
**Locale(s):** New York, New York (Chinatown)

**Summary:** Summoned to Chinatown to investigate a grotesque murder, detective Teddy London runs afoul of the Gaun Cee Qui, a race of power-hungry vampires rampant in the neighborhood who force London to confront his own buried vampiric tendencies.

**Other books you might like:**
Stephen Gallagher, *Valley of Lights*, 1987
Richard Jaccoma, *The Werewolf's Tale*, 1988
Lee Killough, *Blood Hunt*, 1987
William Relling Jr., *New Moon*, 1987
Les Whitten, *Progeny of the Adder*, 1965

**4006**

**ROBERT MORGAN** (Pseudonym of C.J. Henderson)

## The Thing That Darkness Hides

(New York: Diamond, 1993)

**Story type:** Horror (Black Magic)
**Series:** Adventures of Teddy London
**Major character(s):** Teddy London, Detective—Private; George Collins, Wealthy; Father Bain, Religious
**Time period(s):** 1990s (1993)
**Locale(s):** New York, New York; Hell

**Summary:** In his toughest case yet, private detective Teddy London agrees to help George Collins retrieve the immortal soul he bartered to Satan for his mortal success—an assignment that ultimately calls for London meeting the devil on his home turf: Hell.

**Other books you might like:**
Cleve Cartmill, *Hell Hath Fury*, 1943
William Hjortsberg, *Falling Angel*, 1978
Robert Masello, *Private Demons*, 1992

**4007**

**ROBERT MORGAN** (Pseudonym of C.J. Henderson)

## The Things That Are Not There

(New York: Diamond, 1992)

**Story type:** Horror (Ancient Evil Unleashed; Mystery)
**Series:** Adventures of Teddy London
**Major character(s):** Teddy London, Detective—Private; Paul Morcey, Maintenance Worker (janitor); Lisa Hutchinson, Assistant
**Time period(s):** 1990s
**Locale(s):** New York, New York

**Summary:** In this hardboiled horror novel strongly influenced by the writing of H. P. Lovecraft, private detective Teddy London turns occult detective when his investigations into the paranoid delusions of Lisa Hutchinson uncover a plot by cosmic cultists to use her body as the earthly vessel for the extradimensional monstrosity Qtalu.

**Other books you might like:**
Robert Bloch, *Strange Eons*, 1978
August Derleth, *The Lurker at the Threshold*, 1945
Brian Lumley, *The Burrowers Beneath*, 1974
Michael Shea, *Fat Face*, 1987

**4008**

**ROBIN MORGAN**

## The Mer-Child: A Legend for Children and Other Adults

(New York: The Feminist Press at the City University of New York, 1991)

**Story type:** Fantasy (Contemporary; Legend)
**Major character(s):** Mer-Child, Mythical Creature (mermaid); Little Girl, Handicapped (paraplegic), Scientist
**Time period(s):** Indeterminate
**Locale(s):** At Sea; Earth (Northern Hemisphere sea shore)

**Summary:** Shunned by the Mer-People and orphaned, threatened or attacked by humans, the Mer-Child had dolphins to play with, but was lonely. The Little Girl whose black mother died when she was an infant has a wonderful relationship with her white father, but she is also lonely and has been hurt by being rejected. The Mer-Child and the Little Girl find they have much in common in this contemporary sequel to *The Little Mermaid* by Hans Christian Andersen.

**Other books you might like:**
Margaret Wander Bonanno, *The Others*, 1990
Antoine de Saint-Exupery, *The Little Prince*, 1943
Pamela Dean, *Tam Lin*, 1991
Frances Mary Hendry, *Quest for a Maid*, 1990
Michael Kandel, *In between Dragons*, 1990
Garry Kilworth, *The Foxes of Firstdark*, 1990
Barry Lopez, *Crow and Weasel*, 1990
Ethel Johnston Phelps, *Tatterhood and Other Tales*, 1978
    editor
Sheri S. Tepper, *Beauty*, 1991

## 4009
### A.R. MORLAN
## The Amulet
(New York: Bantam, 1991)

**Story type:** Horror (Curse)
**Major character(s):** Anna Sudek, Worker (cleaning woman); Tina Miner Sudek, Worker (cleaning woman), Parent (Anna's mother); Arlene "Grandma" Campbell, Aged Person
**Time period(s):** 1980s (1987)
**Locale(s):** Ewerton, Wisconsin

**Summary:** The Sudeks have been an embarrassment to the town of Ewerton ever since that night 56 years ago when the family patriarch brutally murdered his wife and his mother-in-law disappeared. Looking into her family's history, Anna Sudek discovers the truth of her family's tragedy, and its origins in a cursed talisman that brings misery to all who come in contact with it.

**Other books you might like:**
John Farris, *All Heads Turn When the Hunt Goes By*, 1977
Charles L. Grant, *Stunts*, 1990
Stephen King, *The Talisman*, 1984
    Peter Straub, co-author
Jack Martin, *Halloween III: Season of the Witch*, 1985

## 4010
### A.R. MORLAN
## Dark Journey
(New York: Bantam, 1991)

**Story type:** Horror (Carnival/Circus Horror)
**Major character(s):** Palmer Winston, Aged Person; Palmer Nemmitz, Aged Person; Brent Nimitz, Unemployed (Palmer Nemmitz's nephew)
**Time period(s):** 1980s (1988)
**Locale(s):** Ewerton, Wisconsin

**Summary:** After a 54-year hiatus the South-State Enterprises Carnival returns to the town of Ewerton, reviving memories of the town's unspoken past, devastating the town's younger citizens with the truth about their heritage, and reopening old wounds in those still alive who remember the last summer that the carnival performed there.

**Other books you might like:**
Ray Bradbury, *Something Wicked This Way Comes*, 1962
Charles G. Finney, *The Circus of Dr. Lao*, 1935
William W. Johnstone, *Carnival*, 1990
Richard Laymon, *Funland*, 1990
Thomas F. Monteleone, *The Magnificent Gallery*, 1987

## 4011
### DAVID MORRELL
## Testament: The Unpublished Prologues
(Burton, Michigan: Subterranean Press, 1998)

**Story type:** Horror (Collection)

**Summary:** This signed limited edition chapbook features two draft beginnings for *Testament*, a novel concerned with a writer who is forced to fight a right-wing paramilitary squad with their own violent tactics when an article he writes about them comes to the attention of authorities. In interspersed commentary, the author explains the reasons why these "prologues" were deleted before publication, and his discovery of them in his files in 1992.

**Other books you might like:**
Ramsey Campbell, *The One Safe Place*, 1996
Joe R. Lansdale, *The Good, the Bad, and the Indifferent*, 1996
Dan Simmons, *Lost Summer*, 1992

## 4012
### DAVID MORRELL
## The Totem
(Hampton Falls, New Hampshire: Donald M. Grant, 1994)

**Story type:** Horror (Mystery)
**Major character(s):** Nathan Slaughter, Police Officer; Gordon Dunlap, Journalist; Parsons, Political Figure (mayor)
**Time period(s):** 1990s (1993)
**Locale(s):** Potter's Field, Colorado

**Summary:** Twenty-three years after it dispersed a commune of hippies that took root on its outskirts, a remote cattle town is under siege from a mutant strain of the rabies virus that brings out animalistic behavior in the residents. Investigators trace the outbreak to remnants of the commune who took refuge in the nearby hills and who have now become predators preying on the townsfolk. This novel was originally published in 1979 in a shortened form.

**Other books you might like:**
Douglas Clegg, *Dark of the Eye*, 1994
Michael Crichton, *The Andromeda Strain*, 1969
Peter Straub, *Floating Dragon*, 1984

## 4013
### JOHN MORRESSY
## Kedrigern and the Charming Couple
(New York: Ace, 1990)

**Story type:** Fantasy (Light Fantasy; Adventure)
**Series:** Kedrigern
**Major character(s):** Kedrigern, Wizard (of Silent Thunder Mountain); Berzel, Royalty (Princess of Othion), Werewolf
**Time period(s):** Indeterminate
**Locale(s):** Othion, Fictional Country

**Summary:** King Ithian of Othion is having a problem with his beautiful daughter, Princess Berzel. When the moon is full, she turns into a werewolf. The King manages to elicit a promise from Kedrigern that he will find a cure before the next full moon. But Kedrigern finds time running out when he finds the cure written in a book locked in the library of a monastery. The problem is, not only are the monks not particularly fond of wizards, but they are hiding a terrible secret and aren't about to let anyone in to snoop around.

**Other books you might like:**
C.J. Cherryh, *Rusalka*, 1989
Barbara Hambly, *Dragonsbane*, 1987
Megan Lindholm, *Luck of the Wheels*, 1989
Terry Pratchett, *Equal Rites*, 1988
Christopher Stasheff, *The Warlock Insane*, 1989

---

## `4014`

### JOHN MORRESSY

## *A Remembrance for Kedrigern*

(New York: Ace, 1990)

**Story type:** Fantasy (Light Fantasy; Quest)
**Series:** Kedrigern
**Major character(s):** Kedrigern, Wizard (of Silent Thunder Mountain); Princess, Spouse (Kedrigern's), Royalty; Formidable, Royalty (Prince of Kallopane), Warrior
**Time period(s):** Indeterminate
**Locale(s):** Kallopane, Fictional Country; Moodymount, Mythical Place

**Summary:** The King of Kallopane has requested (bribed) Kedrigern to help his son, Prince Formidable, live up to his name and slay Great Crawling Loathliness, the monster that lives on Moodymount. Accompanied by a haunted huntsman and the Royal Wizard of Kallopane (who has been turned into a large bee), Kedrigern, Princess and Formidable go for the unpleasant creature.

**Other books you might like:**
Gordon R. Dickson, *The Dragon and the George*, 1976
Stephen R. Donaldson, *Lord Foul's Bane*, 1977
Barbara Hambly, *Dragonsbane*, 1987
Robert A. Heinlein, *Glory Road*, 1963
Terry Pratchett, *Mort*, 1989

---

## `4015`

### JANET MORRIS
### CHRIS MORRIS, Co-Author

## *City at the Edge of Time*

(New York: Baen, 1988)

**Story type:** Fantasy (Sword and Sorcery)
**Series:** Thieves' World
**Time period(s):** Indeterminate
**Locale(s):** Thieves' World, Planet—Imaginary

**Summary:** Trapped in a cursed city, a man has to find a powerful sponsor to protect him, or he will die.

**Other books you might like:**
Glen Cook, *Tower of Fear*, 1989
Simon R. Green, *Hawk & Fisher*, 1990
Fritz Leiber, *The Knight and Knave of Swords*, 1990
Keith Taylor, *Search for the Starblade*, 1990

---

## `4016`

### JANET MORRIS
### CHRIS MORRIS, Co-Author

## *The Stalk*

(New York: Roc, 1994)

**Story type:** Science Fiction (First Contact; Alternate Universe)
**Series:** Threshold

---

**Major character(s):** Michael "Mickey" Croft, Political Figure (secretary general); Vincent Remson, Government Official (bureaucrat); Joe South, Spaceman, Time Traveler
**Time period(s):** 27th century
**Locale(s):** Trust Territory of Threshold, Space Station

**Summary:** The aliens from the Council of Unity have contacted Mickey Croft, Secretary General of the United Nations of Earth, using as messengers two young humans who had fled to Unity Space. The Unity offers expanded contact if the humans will move Threshold beyond Pluto's orbit. Mickey Croft feels his own mental perceptions altered and wonders if increased contact will mean the end of the human race. Sequel to *Threshold*.

**Other books you might like:**
Octavia E. Butler, *Dawn*, 1987
C.J. Cherryh, *Downbelow Station*, 1981
Arthur C. Clarke, *Childhood's End*, 1953
Clifford D. Simak, *Time Is the Simplest Thing*, 1961
John Varley, *The Ophiuchi Hotline*, 1977

---

## `4017`

### JANET MORRIS
### DAVID DRAKE, Co-Author

## *Target*

(New York: Ace Books, 1989)

**Story type:** Science Fiction (First Contact)
**Major character(s):** Sam Yates, Police Officer; Channon, Alien, Diplomat
**Time period(s):** Indeterminate Future
**Locale(s):** Montenegro

**Summary:** An alien fleeing enemies is given asylum by a lunar colony and the various nations of Earth compete for access to him. Then the evil aliens hunting him show up. They're willing to destroy all human life in order to recapture their prey.

**Other books you might like:**
Martin Caidin, *Prison Ship*, 1989
Hal Clement, *Needle*, 1950
Rick Cook, *Limbo System*, 1989
L. Neil Smith, *Contact and Commune*, 1989

---

## `4018`

### JANET MORRIS
### CHRIS MORRIS, Co-Author

## *Threshold*

(New York: Roc/Penguin, 1990)

**Story type:** Science Fiction (Time Travel; Adventure)
**Series:** Threshold
**Major character(s):** Joe South, Spaceman, Time Traveler
**Time period(s):** 27th century
**Locale(s):** *Starbird*, Spaceship; Trust Territory of Threshold, Space Station

**Summary:** When Joe South unexpectedly travels 500 years into the future, he discovers a much-changed, highly repressive society in which access to Earth is available to only the privileged few. When his ship is confiscated and his lifestyle and freedom threatened, Joe must find a way to again become his own master while being dragged unwillingly into the political intrigue associated with a mysterious alien artifact.

**Other books you might like:**
Roger MacBride Allen, *The Ring of Charon*, 1990

Robert A. Heinlein, *Farnham's Freehold*, 1964
Vernor Vinge, *Marooned in Realtime*, 1986
Vernor Vinge, *The Peace War*, 1984

## 4019

### JANET MORRIS
### CHRIS MORRIS, Co-Author

## Trust Territory
(New York: Roc, 1992)

**Story type:** Science Fiction (Adventure; First Contact)
**Series:** Threshold
**Major character(s):** Joe South, Time Traveler, Spaceman; Michael "Mickey" Croft, Political Figure (Secretary General); Micah "the Scavenger" Keebler, Scavenger
**Time period(s):** 27th century
**Locale(s):** *Starbird*, Spaceship; Trust Territory of Threshold, Space Station; The Ball, Space Station (alien object)

**Summary:** As a "Relic" from the 21st century, Joe South's acceptance into 27th century society proves difficult, especially as the continuing displays of *The Ball* serve to focus attention on Joe. The Scavenger believes *The Ball* belongs to him, and the aliens call him the Pioneer, their special friend. Unfortunately for humans, the inimical alien environment overwhelms human space-time whenever the aliens show up. Sequel to *Threshhold*.

**Other books you might like:**
Isaac Asimov, *The Gods Themselves*, 1972
David Brin, *Startide Rising*, 1983
Octavia E. Butler, *Dawn*, 1987
Colin Greenland, *Take Back Plenty*, 1992
Frank Herbert, *Whipping Star*, 1970
Megan Lindholm, *Alien Earth*, 1992
Thomas R. McDonough, *The Missing Matter*, 1992
Larry Niven, *The Mote in God's Eye*, 1974
   Jerry Pournelle, co-author
Vernor Vinge, *Marooned in Realtime*, 1986
George Zebrowski, *Stranger Suns*, 1991

## 4020

### KENNETH MORRIS

## The Chalchiuhite Dragon
(New York: Tor, 1992)

**Story type:** Fantasy (Legend; Historical)
**Major character(s):** Nopal, Royalty, Traveler; Quauhtli, Religious
**Time period(s):** Indeterminate Past
**Locale(s):** Huitznahuac, Ancient Civilization; Central America

**Summary:** Peaceful Huitznahuac natives resist the bellicose overtures of their Toltec neighbors as events lead up to the birth of Quetzalcoatl as god incarnate. Ignored for years in the Theosophical Society archives, this novel was completed in 1935, ten years after Katherine Tingley requested Morris feature a pre-Columbian subject. Includes a three-page author's preface plus five-page afterword by Douglas A. Anderson and a seven-page glossary.

**Other books you might like:**
M.A.R. Barker, *Flamesong*, 1985
M.A.R. Barker, *Man of Gold*, 1984
James Hilton, *Lost Horizon*, 1933
Marc Laidlaw, *Neon Lotus*, 1988
Edward Myers, *Fire and Ice*, 1992
Edward Myers, *The Mountain Made of Light*, 1992

Elizabeth Ann Scarborough, *Nothing Sacred*, 1991
Lucius Shepard, *Kalimantan*, 1992

## 4021

### KENNETH MORRIS

## The Dragon Path: Collected Tales of Kenneth Morris
(New York: Tor, 1995)

**Story type:** Fantasy (Collection)

**Summary:** Contains a 23-page biographical introduction by Douglas A. Anderson, a two-page bibliography plus individual introductions to one essay/story on the *Mabinogion* and all 39 of Morris' short works of fiction, arranged chronologically. The tales utilize historical and contemporary settings to present mythical themes from Celtic, Norse, Taoist, and Buddhist philosophies and from areas including Wales, Sweden, Greece, Rome, Spain, the Middle East, India, and China.

**Other books you might like:**
Sir Arthur Conan Doyle, *The Best Supernatural Tales of Arthur Conan Doyle*, 1979
Lord Dunsany, *The Travel Tales of Mr. Joseph Jorkens*, 1931
Rudyard Kipling, *Kipling's Fantasy*, 1992
George MacDonald, *The Fantasy Stories of George MacDonald*, 1980
Clark Ashton Smith, *The Zothique*, 1970
J.R.R. Tolkien, *The Tolkien Reader*, 1966

## 4022

### MARK MORRIS

## The Horror Club
(New York: Bantam, 1991)

**Story type:** Horror (Occult)
**Major character(s):** Richard Gardener, Child; Nigel Figg, Child; Adrian "Toady" Tibbett, Child
**Time period(s):** 1980s (1989)
**Locale(s):** Starmouth, England

**Summary:** Tormented by older students at their school, Richard, Nigel, and Robin find escape from their pain by forming "The Horror Club," where they indulge their interest in horror film and fiction. When a new boy, "Toady," joins the club and urges them to contact real occult forces, they conjure an implacable power that takes care of their enemies but also threatens to decimate their town. This novel was originally published in England in 1989 under the title *Toady*.

**Other books you might like:**
Charles L. Grant, *The Pet*, 1986
K.W. Jeter, *The Night Man*, 1991
Stephen King, *Christine*, 1983
J. Michael Straczynski, *OtherSyde*, 1990

## 4023

### MARK MORRIS

## The Immaculate
(Clarkston, Georgia: White Wolf, 1996)

**Story type:** Horror (Ghost Story)

**Major character(s):** Jack Stone, Writer (horror); Gail Reeves, Teacher; Patty Bates, Businessman (garage owner)
**Time period(s):** 1990s
**Locale(s):** Beckford, England; London, England

**Summary:** When his father dies, Jack Stone returns to the family home in the English countryside to resolve his conflicted feelings over the man who disowned him when Jack's mother died in childbirth. Jack confronts metaphorical and literal ghosts of the past that bring him psychic healing but also force him to confront a difficult truth about his current life. This novel was first published in England in 1992.

**Other books you might like:**
Peter S. Beagle, *A Fine and Private Place*, 1960
Ramsey Campbell, *The Influence*, 1988
Melanie Tem, *Prodigal*, 1991
Melanie Tem, *Revenant*, 1994

---

### 4024

#### MARK MORRIS

### *Stitch*

(New York: Dell/Abyss, 1992)

**Story type:** Horror (Possession)
**Major character(s):** Dan Latcher, Writer, Student; Ian Raven, Student; Annie O'Donnell, Student
**Time period(s):** 1990s (1992)
**Locale(s):** Maybury, England

**Summary:** Left vulnerable by an abusive childhood, horror writer and Maybury University student Dan Latcher becomes the perfect vessel for Peregrine Stitch, a wily demon who helps Dan build a cult known as "The Crack" around him and then uses it to wreak his vengeance upon humanity in a variety of perverse ways.

**Other books you might like:**
Ramsey Campbell, *The Hungry Moon*, 1987
Ray Garton, *Dark Channel*, 1992
Kim Newman, *Jago*, 1991

---

### 4025

#### ROBERT MORRISH, Editor
#### PETER ENFANTINO, Co-Editor

### *Quick Chills II*

(San Jose, California: Deadline Publications, 1992)

**Story type:** Horror (Anthology)

**Summary:** Twenty-five stories representing the best offerings from small press horror fiction published in 1989 and 1990. Included are two outstanding stories based on the horrors of the Vietnam War, Mark Budz's "The War Inside" and Robert E. Cook's "Darkling"; Douglas Clegg's sensitive tale of a love so strong it resurrects the dead, "People Who Love Life"; Norman Partridge's hardboiled horror tale, "Guignoir"; five stories that take twisted sexuality as their theme: Nancy Collins' "The Two-Headed Man," Brad J. Boucher's "Cold Touch," Elizabeth Massie's "Hot Orgy of the Caged Virgins," Nancy Holder's "Woman's Little Wound," and Yvonne Navarro's "Memories"; and a novella about the horrors of urban life that David Schow expanded into his novel, *The Shaft* (1990).

**Other books you might like:**
Ellen Datlow, *The Year's Best Fantasy and Horror: Fourth Annual Collection*, 1991
Terri Windling, co-editor

---

Stephen Jones, *Best New Horror 2*, 1991
Ramsey Campbell, co-editor
Karl Edward Wagner, *The Year's Best Horror Stories XIX*, 1991
editor

---

### 4026

#### ROBERT MORRISON, Editor
#### CHRIS BALDICK, Co-Editor

### *The Vampyre and Other Tales of the Macabre*

(New York: Oxford, 1997)

**Story type:** Horror (Anthology)

**Summary:** Fourteen macabre stories published in popular British literary magazines between 1819 and 1938. Included are John Polidori's "The Vampyre," the first popular vampire tale, and its complimentary fragment, Lord Byron's "Augustus Darvell." Other selections include J. Sheridan Le Fanu's locked-room mystery, "Passage in the Secret History of an Irish Countess"; Edward Bulwer's doppelganger tale, "Monos and Daimonos"; and Horace Smith's tale of the reanimated dead, "Sir Guy Everling's Dream." Stories that take the form of true fact reporting include James Hogg's tale of a cholera epidemic, "Some Terrible Letters from Scotland," and William Carleton's account of a lynching, "Confessions of a Reformed Ribbonman."

**Other books you might like:**
Jack Adrian, *Strange Tales From the Strand*, 1991
editor
Peter Haining, *Great Tales of Terror From Europe and America*, 1973
editor
Robert Donald Spector, *Seven Masterpieces of Gothic Horror*, 1963
editor
Jack C. Wolf, *Ghosts, Castles and Victims*, 1971
Barbara H. Wolf, co-editor
Jack C. Wolf, *Tales of the Occult*, 1975
Barbara H. Wolf, co-editor

---

### 4027

#### BRADFORD MORROW, Editor
#### PATRICK MCGRATH, Co-Editor

### *The New Gothic*

(New York: Random House, 1991)

**Story type:** Horror (Anthology)

**Summary:** Billing itself as "A Collection of Contemporary Gothic Fiction," this compilation brings together 15 stories and 6 novel excerpts that "take as a starting place the concern with internal entropy—spiritual and emotional breakdown," and how this approach distorts perceptions of external reality. Included are John Edgar Wideman's "Fever," about a yellow fever epidemic that nearly decimates a town; Scott Bradfield's "Didn't She Know," about a woman sought for her life-sustaining attributes; William T. Vollman's metafictional riff on Edgar Allan Poe, "The Grave of Lost Stories"; and Patrick McGrath's tale of a man whose psychological decline manifests as his obsession with smells, "The Smell."

**Other books you might like:**
Chris Baldick, *The Oxford Book of Gothic Tales*, 1992
Patrick McGrath, *Blood and Water and Other Tales*, 1988

## 4028

### JAMES MORROW

## Bible Stories for Adults

(New York: Harcourt Brace, 1996)

**Story type:** Science Fiction (Collection; Theological)

**Summary:** Contains a three-page introduction plus 12 stories reprinted from periodicals and anthologies 1984-1994. Utilizing science fiction themes and frequently light or satirical in tone, four of the stories critique Biblical stories, the Flood, the Tower of Babel, Job, and the Nativity, while some of the other stories explore morality through the *Iliad* and Charles Dickens' Ebenezer Scrooge. Other themes include the mystery of consciousness, procreation, parenting, feminism, and epistemology.

**Other books you might like:**

Neil Gaiman, *Good Omens: The Nice and Accurate Prophecies of Agnes Nutter, Witch*, 1990
  Terry Pratchett, co-author
Parke Godwin, *The Snake Oil Wars*, 1989
Parke Godwin, *Waiting for the Galactic Bus*, 1988
Robert A. Heinlein, *Job: A Comedy of Justice*, 1984
Walter M. Miller Jr., *A Canticle for Leibowitz*, 1960
Anne Rice, *Memnoch the Devil*, 1995
Kurt Vonnegut Jr., *Cat's Cradle*, 1963

## 4029

### JAMES MORROW

## Blameless in Abaddon

(New York: Harcourt Brace, 1996)

**Story type:** Fantasy (Religious; Satire)
**Major character(s):** Martin Candle, Judge, Activist; Augustine, Historical Figure, Religious
**Time period(s):** 1990s; Indeterminate Past
**Locale(s):** Abaddon Township, Pennsylvania; The Hague, Netherlands

**Summary:** After towing the body of God to the arctic, promoters move the Corpus Dei to Orlando, Florida, to provide a focus for a new theme park, Celestial City USA. When a Justice of the Peace, Martin Candle, proposes trying God in the World Court for all of history's injustices, Martin begins an amazing odyssey through God's mind and human deism.

**Other books you might like:**

Neil Gaiman, *Good Omens: The Nice and Accurate Prophecies of Agnes Nutter, Witch*, 1990
  Terry Pratchett, co-author
Parke Godwin, *The Snake Oil Wars*, 1989
Parke Godwin, *Waiting for the Galactic Bus*, 1988
Victor Koman, *The Jehovah Contract*, 1987
Anne Rice, *Memnoch the Devil*, 1995
Kurt Vonnegut Jr., *Cat's Cradle*, 1963

## 4030

### JAMES MORROW

## City of Truth

(New York: St. Martin's Press, 1992)

**Story type:** Science Fiction (Genetic Manipulation; Satire)
**Major character(s):** Jack Sperry, Critic; Martina Coventry, Writer; Toby Sperry, Child

**Time period(s):** 21st century
**Locale(s):** Veritas City of Truth

**Summary:** In Veritas, City of Truth, contemplating the telling of a lie results in conditioned suffering. Jack Sperry works as an art deconstructionist, sparing Veritas from lies. When he learns that his son has contracted a fatal disease, Jack decides to join the Deceivers, people who have overcome their conditioning, to enable himself to lie to his son and hope psychoneuroimmunology will effect a cure.

**Other books you might like:**

Pauline Ashwell, *Unwillingly to Earth*, 1992
Michael Berlyn, *The Eternal Enemy*, 1990
Peter R. Emshwiller, *The Host*, 1991
Parke Godwin, *Waiting for the Galactic Bus*, 1988
Pat Murphy, *The City, Not Long After*, 1989
Michael Swanwick, *Stations of the Tide*, 1991
Jack Womack, *Heathern*, 1990

## 4031

### JAMES MORROW, Editor

## Nebula Awards 26

(New York: Harcourt Brace Jovanovich, 1992)

**Story type:** Science Fiction (Anthology)
**Series:** Nebula Awards

**Summary:** Subtitled "SFWA's Choice for the Best Science Fiction and Fantasy of the Year," this volume contains a 5-page introduction listing 1990 Nebula Award nominees, Terry Brooks' "A Tribute to Lester del Rey," in honor of the 1990 Grand Master Award winner, George Zebrowski's "In Memoriam: Donald A. Wollheim," Kathryn Cramer's 18-page article on SF in 1990, Bill Warren's 22-page article on 1990 SF films, 6 pages of appendices titled "About the Nebula Awards," "Selected Titles from the 1990 Preliminary Nebula Ballot" and "Past Nebula Award Winners," and a 2-page article on Rhysling Award winners with poems by G. Sutton Breiding and Patrick McKinnon. Fiction includes two Nebula Award winning stories, "The Hemmingway Hoax" by Joe Haldeman and "Bear Discovers Fire" by Terry Bisson plus stories by Ted Chiang, Karen Joy Fowler, Dafydd ab Hugh, Ursula K. Le Guin, Ian MacLeod, Pat Murphy and Martha Soukup.

**Other books you might like:**

Lou Aronica, *Full Spectrum 3*, 1991
  Amy Stout and Betsy Mitchell, co-editors
Michael Bishop, *Nebula Awards 23*, 1989
  editor
Michael Bishop, *Nebula Awards 24*, 1990
  editor
Michael Bishop, *Nebula Awards 25*, 1991
  editor
Ellen Datlow, *The Year's Best Fantasy and Horror: Fourth Annual Collection*, 1991
  Terri Windling, co-editor
Gardner Dozois, *The Year's Best Science Fiction: Eighth Annual Collection*, 1991
  editor
Harlan Ellison, *Dangerous Visions*, 1967
  editor
Frank Herbert, *Nebula Winners 15*, 1981
  editor
Damon Knight, *Nebula Award Stories 1965*, 1966
  editor
Robert Silverberg, *The Science Fiction Hall of Fame, Volume 1*, 1970
  editor

Donald A. Wollheim, *The 1990 Annual World's Best Science Fiction*, 1990
  Arthur W. Saha, co-editor
George Zebrowski, *Nebula Awards 21*, 1987
  editor
George Zebrowski, *Nebula Awards 22*, 1988
  editor

### 4032

**JAMES MORROW**, Editor

## Nebula Awards 27

(New York: Harcourt Brace, 1993)

**Story type:** Science Fiction (Anthology)
**Series:** Nebula Awards

**Summary:** Subtitled "SFWA's Choices for the Best Science Fiction and Fantasy of the Year," this volume contains a five-page introduction by the editor listing 1991 Nebula Award finalists and winners; a 15-page article by Kathryn Cramer, "Science Fiction for What? Remarks on the Year 1991"; a 27-page article on 1991 fantastic films by Bill Warren; a 10-page essay on literary criticism with bibliography by Bruce Sterling; four memorials to Isaac Asimov; two Rhysling Award winning poems by Joe Haldeman and David Memmott; nine pages of appendices, including selected titles from the preliminary ballot and a list of previous winners; plus fiction from Terry Bisson, Alan Brennert, Karen Joy Fowler, James Patrick Kelly, John Kessel, Nancy Kress, Susan Shwartz and Michael Swanwick.

**Other books you might like:**
Lou Aronica, *Full Spectrum 3*, 1991
  Amy Stout, Betsy Mitchell, co-editors
Michael Bishop, *Nebula Awards 23*, 1989
  editor
Michael Bishop, *Nebula Awards 24*, 1990
  editor
Michael Bishop, *Nebula Awards 25*, 1991
  editor
Ellen Datlow, *The Year's Best Fantasy and Horror: Fourth Annual Collection*, 1991
  Terri Windling, co-editor
Gardner Dozois, *The Year's Best Science Fiction: Ninth Annual Collection*, 1992
  editor
Frank Herbert, *Nebula Winners 15*, 1981
  editor
Damon Knight, *Nebula Award Stories 1965*, 1966
  editor
George Zebrowski, *Nebula Awards 21*, 1987
  editor
George Zebrowski, *Nebula Awards 22*, 1988
  editor

### 4033

**JAMES MORROW**, Editor

## Nebula Awards 28

(New York: Harcourt Brace, 1994)

**Story type:** Science Fiction (Anthology)
**Series:** Nebula Awards

**Summary:** Subtitled, "SFWA's Choices for the Best Science Fiction and Fantasy of the Year," this volume contains a five-page introduction by the editor listing 1992 Nebula Award finalists and winners; a nine-page article by John Clute, "Is Science Fiction Out to Lunch?

Some Thoughts on the Year 1992"; a 14-page article on fantastic films of 1992 by Nick Lowe; three memorials to Fritz Leiber; one poem by David Lunde; 10 pages of appendixes, including selected titles from the preliminary ballot and a list of previous winners; plus nine stories by authors including Gregory Benford, Nancy Kress, James Morrow, Kim Stanley Robinson, Pamela Sargent and Connie Willis.

**Other books you might like:**
Michael Bishop, *Nebula Awards 23*, 1989
  editor
Michael Bishop, *Nebula Awards 24*, 1990
  editor
Michael Bishop, *Nebula Awards 25*, 1991
  editor
George Zebrowski, *Nebula Awards 21*, 1987
  editor
George Zebrowski, *Nebula Awards 22*, 1988
  editor

### 4034

**JAMES MORROW**

## Only Begotten Daughter

(New York: Morrow, 1990)

**Story type:** Fantasy (Satire)
**Major character(s):** Julie Katz, Deity (Daughter of God); Billy Milk, Religious (Revelationist)
**Time period(s):** 1990s
**Locale(s):** Atlantic City, New Jersey; Hell

**Summary:** As the millennium approaches, a miracle occurs in a New Jersey sperm bank and Julie Katz, God's only begotten daughter, is immaculately conceived. As she grows to adulthood, Julie must reconcile the needs of a normal teenager with the powers of a demi-god. Eventually she is drawn into an apocalyptic confrontation with both Satan and his local representative on Earth, the Reverend Billy Milk.

**Other books you might like:**
Carol Emshwiller, *Carmen Dog*, 1990
Parke Godwin, *The Snake Oil Wars*, 1989
Parke Godwin, *Waiting for the Galactic Bus*, 1988
John Kessel, *Good News From Outer Space*, 1989
  Madness at the End of the Millenium

### 4035

**JAMES MORROW**

## Towing Jehovah

(New York: Harcourt Brace, 1994)

**Story type:** Fantasy (Religious; Light Fantasy)
**Major character(s):** Anthony Van Horne, Sea Captain; Father Thomas, Religious; Cassie Fowler, Writer (playwright)
**Time period(s):** 1990s (1992)
**Locale(s):** *SS Carpco Valparaiso*, At Sea (supertanker); Atlantic Ocean

**Summary:** Archangel Raphael informs Anthony Van Horne that God has died and His body has fallen into the ocean. Using the refloated and refitted *Carpco Valparaiso* flying Vatican colors, Van Horne must tow the two-mile-long Body to the Arctic to preserve Him to earn forgiveness for his oil spill. Accompanied by a Vatican representative chasing the Vatican's hope that some Divine neural activity might remain, the ship encounters natural and transcendant obstacles.

**Other books you might like:**

Neil Gaiman, *Good Omens: The Nice and Accurate Prophecies of Agnes Nutter, Witch*, 1990
    Terry Pratchett, co-author
Parke Godwin, *The Snake Oil Wars*, 1989
Parke Godwin, *Waiting for the Galactic Bus*, 1988
Victor Koman, *The Jehovah Contract*, 1987
Kurt Vonnegut Jr., *Cat's Cradle*, 1963

**4036**

## DAVID MORSE

## *The Iron Bridge*

(New York: Harcourt Brace, 1998)

**Story type:** Science Fiction (Time Travel; Alternate History)
**Major character(s):** Maggie Foster, Time Traveler; Abraham Darby III, Religious (Quaker), Industrialist; Samuel Johnson, Religious (Quaker), Architect
**Time period(s):** 1770s (1773-1777); 2040s (2043)
**Locale(s):** Shropshire, England; Southwest (Ecosophia commune)

**Summary:** A member of Ecosophia, a commune in an ecologically and socially ravaged 21st century, Maggie Foster travels back through time to 1770s England, where she intends to stop or at least postpone the Industrial Revolution by sabotaging the world's first iron bridge. First novel.

**Other books you might like:**

Kage Baker, *In the Garden of Iden*, 1998
Orson Scott Card, *Pastwatch: The Redemption of Christopher Columbus*, 1996
L. Sprague de Camp, *Lest Darkness Fall*, 1941
Jack Finney, *Time After Time*, 1995
Jack Finney, *Time and Again*, 1970
Lisa Mason, *The Golden Nineties*, 1995

**4037**

## PETER MORWOOD

## *Rules of Engagement*

(New York: Pocket, 1990)

**Story type:** Science Fiction (Space Opera)
**Series:** Star Trek
**Major character(s):** James T. Kirk, Spaceship Captain; Kasak sutai-Khornezh, Spaceship Captain, Alien (Klingon)
**Time period(s):** 23rd century
**Locale(s):** Dekkanar, Planet—Imaginary (Between the Federation and the Klingon Empire); *U.S.S. Enterprise*, Spaceship

**Summary:** Dekkanar is throwing all Federation personnel off the planet because of political unrest. Both Federation and Klingon ships head there, the *Enterprise*, *Vanguard* and *Sir Richard* to remove Federation people, and Kasak in a new type of Klington battle cruiser to take advantage of the situation. This novel fits chronologically between the time of *Star Trek: The Motion Picture* and *Star Trek II: The Wrath of Khan*.

**Other books you might like:**

Poul Anderson, *Flandry of Terra*, 1965
John M. Ford, *The Final Reflection*, 1984
    Star Trek 16
Keith Laumer, *Reward for Retief*, 1989

Judith Reeves-Stevens, *Prime Directive*, 1990
    Garfiedl Reeves-Stevens, co-author

**4038**

## MIKE MOSCOE

## *First Dawn*

(New York: Ace, 1996)

**Story type:** Science Fiction (Time Travel; Religious)
**Series:** Lost Millennium
**Major character(s):** Launa O'Brian, Military Personnel (lieutenant), Time Traveler; Jack Walking Bear, Military Personnel (captain), Time Traveler
**Time period(s):** 21st century; 40th century B.C.
**Locale(s):** Germany; Tall Oaks, Fictional City; River Bend, Fictional City

**Summary:** Acting on the theory that the designer virus annihilating most of 21st century humanity would never have been invented if society's naturally cooperative tendencies hadn't been overwhelmed by brute force, Lieutenant Launa O'Brian and Captain Jack Walking Bear travel 6000 years back in time. There, in a mathematically predetermined place, they must convince the hunters and traders of the People of the Badger to deny the very core of their culture in order to save it, by taking up arms against impending invaders on horseback. First novel.

**Other books you might like:**

Eleanor Arnason, *A Woman of the Iron People*, 1991
C.J. Cherryh, *Forty Thousand in Gehenna*, 1983
Joe Haldeman, *The Forever War*, 1975
Rosemary Kirstein, *The Outskirter's Secret*, 1992
H. Beam Piper, *Lord Kalvan of Otherwhen*, 1965
Sheri S. Tepper, *Raising the Stones*, 1990

**4039**

## MIKE MOSCOE

## *Lost Days*

(New York: Ace, 1998)

**Story type:** Science Fiction (Time Travel)
**Series:** Lost Millennium
**Major character(s):** Launa O'Brian, Military Personnel (lieutenant), Time Traveler; Jack Walking Bear, Military Personnel (captain), Time Traveler
**Time period(s):** 21st century; 40th century B.C.
**Locale(s):** Tall Oaks, Fictional City

**Summary:** Two time travelers successfully influence prehistoric humans to avert a world disaster that would have wiped out most of humankind in the 21st century. When they return to their own time, they find a changed society, but one in which there is a new flaw. Ethnic prejudice dominates everything, and the majority oppresses numerous minority groups. Launa O'Brien and Jack Walking Bear decide to travel back through time to make one more effort to achieve a more humane society.

**Other books you might like:**

Roger MacBride Allen, *Orphan of Creation*, 1988
Michael Bishop, *No Enemy but Time*, 1982
Rob Chilson, *The Shores of Kansas*, 1976
Mona Clee, *Branch Point*, 1995
William Golding, *The Inheritors*, 1962

## 4040

### MIKE MOSCOE

## *Second Fire*

(New York: Ace, 1997)

**Story type:** Science Fiction (Time Travel; Adventure)
**Series:** Lost Millennium
**Major character(s):** Jack Walking Bear, Time Traveler, Military Personnel (captain); Launa O'Brian, Time Traveler, Military Personnel (lieutenant)
**Time period(s):** 40th century B.C.; 21st century
**Locale(s):** Europe

**Summary:** Sent back 6000 years to change the history of the world, Jack and Launa try to persuade the gentle hunter-gatherer tribes of Europe to resist the attacks of the fierce Horse Clans from the Dniepr River. They hope that the establishment of a Goddess-worshipping culture will turn the course of history away from the war and pollution that threaten their own century.

**Other books you might like:**
Poul Anderson, *Guardians of Time*, 1960
Jean M. Auel, *The Valley of Horses*, 1982
Stephen Baxter, *The Time Ships*, 1996
L. Sprague de Camp, *Lest Darkness Fall*, 1941
David Drake, *The Fourth Rome*, 1996
    Janet Morris, co-author
Barbara Hambly, *Ishmael*, 1985

## 4041

### BILLIE SUE MOSIMAN

## *Night Cruise*

(New York: Diamond, 1992)

**Story type:** Horror (Serial Killer)
**Major character(s):** Molly Killany, Teenager; Mark Killany, Police Officer; Cruise Lavanic, Drifter, Serial Killer
**Time period(s):** 1990s (1992)
**Locale(s):** Mobile, Alabama; Southwest

**Summary:** With her father in hot pursuit, runaway Molly Killany hitches a ride with Cruise Lavanic, unaware that Lavanic is a notorious serial killer bent on indoctrinating her into his spree of savage murders before taking her life.

**Other books you might like:**
John Shirley, *Wetbones*, 1992
Whitley Strieber, *Billy*, 1990

## 4042

### WALTER MOSLEY

## *Blue Light*

(New York: Little Brown, 1998)

**Story type:** Science Fiction (Contemporary Realism; Theological)
**Major character(s):** Lester Chance, Historian, Mentally Ill Person (suicidal); William T. "Orde" Portman, Religious (prophet), Mutant; Horace "Gray Redstar" LaFontaine, Reanimated Dead (possessed), Murderer
**Time period(s):** 1960s; 1990s
**Locale(s):** Berkeley, California; San Francisco, California

**Summary:** When the Blue Lights hit the Earth, many of them fall fruitlessly into small insect or animal hosts, while the few who touch

humans optimize the potential success of whatever the humans were doing at the time. Orde finds Chance, who decides not to commit suicide, but to follow Orde instead. As the Blue Light which hit Horace as he died of cancer took over the body without the modifying influence of a person, Horace attempts to kill all the Blues who are developing immortality and a program to optimize humanity. First science fiction novel.

**Other books you might like:**
Octavia E. Butler, *Dawn*, 1987
Kay Kenyon, *Leap Point*, 1998
Matt Ruff, *Sewer, Gas & Electric*, 1997
David Weber, *Mutineers' Moon*, 1991
Connie Willis, *Bellwether*, 1996

## 4043

### STEVE MUDD

## *The Planet Beyond*

(New York: Popular Library Questar, 1990)

**Story type:** Science Fiction (Hard Science Fiction)
**Series:** Seelzar Chronicles
**Major character(s):** Alyssa Montoya, Activist; Bashir Arak, Aged Person, Explorer; Niala Kirowa, Administrator, Agent
**Time period(s):** Indeterminate Future
**Locale(s):** Seelzar, Planet—Imaginary

**Summary:** Alyssa Montoya's brother, Darrin, has been banned from the life-prolonging alien Wells and branded as a Transgressor in the city of Home, but only to provide cover for his activities as a narcotics agent investigating the trade in the drug, Purple Heaven. Meanwhile Alyssa, searching for a way to reinstate her brother, contacts Bashir Arak, a Wellborn recluse who has access to the cybernetic Matrix that controls Home. This book is a sequel to *Tangled Webs* with a "to-be-continued" ending.

**Other books you might like:**
Isaac Asimov, *The Currents of Space*, 1952
C.J. Cherryh, *Angel with the Sword*, 1985
Robert A. Heinlein, *Citizen of the Galaxy*, 1957
Vonda N. McIntyre, *The Exile Waiting*, 1975

## 4044

### STEVE MUDD

## *Tangled Webs*

(New York: Popular Library Questar, 1989)

**Story type:** Science Fiction (Political)
**Major character(s):** Triune Adjudicator Phillips, Judge; Overseer Selius, Government Official
**Time period(s):** Indeterminate Future
**Locale(s):** Drinan IV, Planet—Imaginary; Bekh-Nar, Planet—Imaginary

**Summary:** A tyrannical government is attempting to recreate an Interstellar Union from the scattered, isolated worlds of humanity. While the Union's rule is heavyhanded, individual government officials attempt to temper that reunification with justice. This is Mudd's first novel.

**Other books you might like:**
Isaac Asimov, *Foundation*, 1951
Isaac Asimov, *Foundation and Empire*, 1952
Isaac Asimov, *Second Foundation*, 1953
Iain M. Banks, *The Player of Games*, 1989
Ursula K. Le Guin, *The Word for World Is Forest*, 1972

Kathy Tyers, *Crystal Witness*, 1989

## 4045

### PATRICIA MULLEN

### *The Stone Movers*

(New York: Warner Aspect, 1995)

**Story type:** Fantasy (Magic Conflict; Political)
**Major character(s):** Eacon Gleese, Ruler (tyrant of Moer); Fallon, Wizard, Mythical Creature (shapeshifter); Telerhyde, Military Personnel (war leader of the Five Tribes)
**Time period(s):** Indeterminate
**Locale(s):** Isle of Morbihan, Fictional Country; Perime of Moer, Fictional Country

**Summary:** In the Perime of Moer, devotees of the New Faith believe humans must rule. The Isle of Morbihan, where Human, Dwarf, Elf, Peskie, and Ogre all follow the Old Faith in cooperative magic, remains a thorn in Gleese's side. To conquer Morbihan, Gleese must eliminate Fallon and Telerhyde and prevent the use of magic. First novel.

**Other books you might like:**
Don Callander, *Pyromancer*, 1992
Pamela Dean, *The Secret Country*, 1985
David Eddings, *The Diamond Throne*, 1985
Deborah Turner Harris, *Caledon of the Mists*, 1994
Paula Volsky, *Illusion*, 1992

## 4046

### HARUKI MURAKAMI

### *Dance Dance Dance*

(New York: Kodansha, 1994)

**Story type:** Science Fiction (Literary)
**Major character(s):** I, Writer
**Time period(s):** 1990s
**Locale(s):** Tokyo, Japan; Sapporo, Japan

**Summary:** A man living in modern high-tech Japan experiences his mid-life crisis with dreams of a woman who weeps for him and inspires him to dance through life. Translated by Alfred Birnbaum. Sequel to *The Wild Sheep Chase*.

**Other books you might like:**
Jesse Browner, *Conglomeros*, 1992
Samuel R. Delany, *The Bridge of Lost Desire*, 1987
Mark Jacobson, *Gojiro*, 1991
Mark Leyner, *My Cousin, My Gastroenterologist*, 1990
Milorad Pavic, *Landscape Painted with Tea*, 1990

## 4047

### HARUKI MURAKAMI
### ALFRED BIRNBAUM, Co-Author

### *Hard-Boiled Wonderland and the End of the World*

(New York: Kodansha International, 1991)

**Story type:** Science Fiction (Literary; Fantasy)
**Major character(s):** I, Writer, Computer Expert; Gatekeeper, Artisan
**Time period(s):** Indeterminate Future
**Locale(s):** Tokyo, Japan

**Summary:** The writer is hired as a translator to protect information from being stolen and used. In his work reading unicorn skulls, some subconscious information gets past the system, putting him in danger both mentally and physically.

**Other books you might like:**
Piers Anthony, *And Eternity*, 1990
Allen Appel, *Till the End of Time*, 1990
Samuel R. Delany, *The Bridge of Lost Desire*, 1987
Randall Garrett, *Too Many Magicians*, 1967
Milorad Pavic, *Landscape Painted with Tea*, 1990

## 4048

### MYLES MURCHISON

### *The Deathless*

(New York: Ballantine, 1989)

**Story type:** Horror (Ancient Evil Unleashed)
**Major character(s):** Henriette May Eddy, Anthropologist; Walker Stevenson, Anthropologist, Lover (Henrietta's)
**Time period(s):** 16th century (1521); 1890s
**Locale(s):** Bimini, Bahamas; San Francisco, California; Vancouver, British Columbia, Canada

**Summary:** Searching for the secrets of Ponce de Leon, Dr. Stevenson is mysteriously killed. Harriette Eddy seeks the truth about his death and about the awful secrets he had uncovered. Her quest takes her across the world, exposing her to terrible physical and psychic dangers, culminating in an encounter with Kamiri, the death god. This is Murchison's first novel.

**Other books you might like:**
Norah Lofts, *The Devil's Own*, 1960

## 4049

### M.S. MURDOCK

### *Hammer of Mars*

(Lake Geneva, Wisconsin: TSR, 1989)

**Story type:** Science Fiction (Space Opera)
**Series:** Buck Rogers: The Martian Wars Trilogy
**Major character(s):** Buck Rogers, Warrior; Wilma Deering, Warrior
**Time period(s):** 25th century
**Locale(s):** Mars; Montenegro

**Summary:** Buck Rogers and the NEO freedom fighters have defeated the evil forces of RAM repeatedly, but now the gigantic Martian corporate state is ready to unleash the full force of its power. Fleeing, Buck attempts to find allies among the many, often mutually antagonistic, nations of the inner planets.

**Other books you might like:**
C.S. Friedman, *In Conquest Born*, 1987
Christopher Hinz, *Ash Ock*, 1989
Christopher Hinz, *Liege-Killer*, 1987
Philip Francis Nowlan, *Armageddon 2419 A.D.*, 1962

## 4050

### MARY ELIZABETH MURPHY

### *Virgin*

(New York: Berkley, 1996)

**Story type:** Horror (Ancient Evil Unleashed)

Major character(s): Dan Fitzpatrick, Religious (priest); Sister Carrie, Religious (nun); Chaim Kesev, Spy (Israeli Secret Police)
Time period(s): 1990s (1995)
Locale(s): New York, New York

Summary: Thanks to a forged ancient scroll, Father Dan and his secret lover, Sister Carrie, discover the whereabouts of the mummified corpse of the Virgin Mary. However, a presentiment of evil hangs over the retrieval of her corpse, and the blessing that those who would exploit her powers hope for proves to be a curse.

Other books you might like:
Ron Hansen, *Mariette in Ecstasy*, 1991
Brent Monahan, *The Book of Common Dread*, 1993
Thomas F. Monteleone, *The Blood of the Lamb*, 1992
Michael Paine, *Cities of the Dead*, 1989
Alan Rodgers, *Night*, 1991

---

**4051**

PAT MURPHY

## The City, Not Long After

(New York: Doubleday Foundation, 1989)

Story type: Science Fiction (Arts)
Major character(s): Danny-boy, Artist; Jax, Artist
Time period(s): 21st century
Locale(s): San Francisco, California

Summary: Years ago a plague killed the majority of people in the United States, leaving most cities desolate. San Francisco, however, has maintained a strange sense of community as artists of various sorts have turned the entire city into a canvas for their creations. Now however, the city's peace is threatened by an impending military invasion and the artists must band together to defend their chosen lifestyle.

Other books you might like:
Samuel R. Delany, *Dhalgren*, 1975
Samuel R. Delany, *Triton*, 1976
Lisa Goldstein, *A Mask for the General*, 1987
Richard Paul Russo, *Subterranean Gallery*, 1989

---

**4052**

PAT MURPHY

## Nadya: The Wolf Chronicles

(New York: Tor, 1996)

Story type: Fantasy (Legend; Historical)
Major character(s): Nadya Rybak, Werewolf, Orphan; Jacob Lowell, Indian (half-Indian); Elizabeth Metcalf, Settler
Time period(s): 1820s; 1830s
Locale(s): Wolf Crossing, Missouri; Shoalwater Bay, Oregon

Summary: Orphaned when hunters kill her werewolf parents, Nadya heads west across the unsettled land to seek a home where people will accept her strange nature. Along the way, she helps Elizabeth, a stranded settler, make the dangerous trek across the Rocky Mountains.

Other books you might like:
Nancy A. Collins, *Walking Wolf*, 1995
Chad Oliver, *The Wolf Is My Brother*, 1967
Fred Saberhagen, *Dancing Bears*, 1996
S.P. Somtow, *Moon Dance*, 1990
Whitley Strieber, *The Wolfen*, 1978

---

**4053**

PAT MURPHY

## Points of Departure

(New York: Bantam, 1990)

Story type: Horror (Collection)
Summary: Twenty stories that cross the boundaries between science fiction, fantasy, and horror, many strongly influenced by the author's interest in travel and anthropology. "Dead Men on TV" is a fable about the stranglehold of memory, "Clay Devils" is a parable of third-world exploitation, and "Don't Look Back" is a subtle fantasy in which a woman begins to measure her life by the people who have replaced her in her various roles and occupations. Also included is the Nebula Award-winning "Rachel in Love."

Other books you might like:
Michael Blumlein, *The Brains of Rats*, 1989
Pat Cadigan, *Patterns*, 1989
Lucius Shepard, *The Jaguar Hunter*, 1987
Bruce Sterling, *Crystal Express*, 1989

---

**4054**

SHIRLEY ROUSSEAU MURPHY

## Cats Raise the Dead

(New York: HarperPrism, 1997)

Story type: Fantasy (Mystery; Contemporary Realism)
Series: Cat on the Edge
Major character(s): Joe Grey, Animal (cat); Clyde Damen, Mechanic (auto); Dulcie, Animal (cat)
Time period(s): 1990s
Locale(s): Molena Point, California (northern)

Summary: Joe Grey and Dulcie, two cats with human intelligence, investigate mysterious disappearances in a nursing home. When loot from a cat burglar working her crime spree up and down the California coast appears in the nursing home, Joe puts up wht the indignities of pet therapy to find out more.

Other books you might like:
Bill Fawcett, *Cats in Space and Other Places*, 1992
    editor
Anne McCaffrey, *No One Noticed the Cat*, 1996
Andre Norton, *Breed to Come*, 1972
Mark E. Rogers, *The Adventures of Samurai Cat*, 1984
Cordwainer Smith, *Norstrilia*, 1975
John Richard Stephens, *The Enchanted Cat*, 1990
    editor
L.A. Taylor, *Cat's Paw*, 1995
Tad Williams, *Tailchaser's Song*, 1985

---

**4055**

SHIRLEY ROUSSEAU MURPHY

## The Catswold Portal

(New York: Roc, 1992)

Story type: Fantasy (Contemporary; Quest)
Major character(s): Sarah/Melissa McCabe, Heiress—Dispossessed; Braden West, Artist; Siddonie, Ruler (queen of Affandar), Sorceress
Time period(s): 1950s (1957); Indeterminate
Locale(s): California; Netherworld, Mythical Place

**Summary:** Sarah remembers nothing of her past, but goes to the palace in Affandar to learn about it. When the queen catches her, freezes her in cat form and has her taken to California where she meets Braden, Sarah gradually remembers her claim as Heir to Catswold and returns to the Netherworld to fight for her rightful inheritance.

**Other books you might like:**
Poul Anderson, *Operation Chaos*, 1971
Jack L. Chalker, *Vengeance of the Dancing Gods*, 1985
Gordon R. Dickson, *The Dragon and the George*, 1976
R.A. MacAvoy, *Tea with the Black Dragon*, 1983
Andre Norton, *Moon of Three Rings*, 1966
A. Orr, *The World in Amber*, 1985
Jennifer Roberson, *Shapechangers*, 1984

---

**4056**

**SHIRLEY ROUSSEAU MURPHY**
**WELCH SUGGS**, Co-Author

## Medallion of the Black Hound

(New York: Harper & Row, 1989)

**Story type:** Fantasy (Adventure)
**Major character(s):** David, Teenager; Balcher, Criminal
**Time period(s):** 1980s; Indeterminate
**Locale(s):** Earth; Alternate Universe

**Summary:** David, heir to the Medallion of the Irish kings, is suddenly transported to another world, where the old magic still works. He must learn how to use the Medallion before the denizens of the undercity completely take over the world he has found himself in.

**Other books you might like:**
Lloyd Alexander, *Prydain Chronicles*,
Tom Holt, *Expecting Someone Taller*, 1988
Henry Maeve, *The Witch King*, 1988

---

**4057**

**WARREN MURPHY**
**MARK BROWNWOOD**, Co-Author

## Destiny's Carnival

(New York: Fawcett, 1992)

**Story type:** Horror (Carnival/Circus Horror)
**Major character(s):** Coley O'Brien, Entertainer (mind reader); Loki Sanderson, Professor (of ancient languages); Elissa Destin, Entertainer (carnival performer)
**Time period(s):** 1990s
**Locale(s):** Allenville, Pennsylvania

**Summary:** Drifter Coley O'Brien little suspects that when he takes the job of mind reader at a traveling carnival, he will be forced to use his precognitive skills to save the show and the daughter of its putative owner from the real owner, a demonic personality to whom it was bartered years before. This is a first novel for Brownwood and first collaborative effort between Murphy and Brownwood.

**Other books you might like:**
Ray Bradbury, *Something Wicked This Way Comes*, 1962
Katherine Dunn, *Geek Love*, 1990
Charles G. Finney, *The Circus of Dr. Lao*, 1935
F. Paul Wilson, *Freak Show*, 1992
    editor

---

**4058**

**DOUG MURRAY**

## Blood Relations

(New York: HarperPrism, 1996)

**Story type:** Horror (Vampire Story)
**Series:** World of Darkness: Vampire
**Major character(s):** Val, Vampire; Mariana, Vampire, Artist; Tessler, Vampire
**Time period(s):** 1990s (1996)
**Locale(s):** New York, New York

**Summary:** Val and Mariana meet at the Blood Club, a downtown meeting place for vampires, and fall in love. Little do they realize that their union was engineered decades before by overseers interested in their respective vampire clans, and the future wars that they will fight. This novel is set in White Wolf Books' World of Darkness gaming world, where humans and supernatural beings co-exist.

**Other books you might like:**
Richard Lee Byers, *Netherworld*, 1995
Keith Herber, *Prince of the City*, 1992
Brian Herbert, *Blood on the Sun*, 1996
    Marie Landis, co-author
Robert Weinberg, *Blood War*, 1995
Robert Weinberg, *The Unbeholden*, 1996
Robert Weinberg, *Unholy Allies*, 1995

---

**4059**

**DOUG MURRAY**

## Call to Battle

(Clarkston, Georgia: White Wolf, 1996)

**Story type:** Horror (Werewolf Story)
**Series:** Rage
**Major character(s):** Jay Caldwell, Student, Werewolf; Dr. Caldwell, Doctor; Colonel Sweet, Military Personnel
**Time period(s):** 1990s (1996)
**Locale(s):** Atlanta, Georgia (Marietta Military School)

**Summary:** Jay Caldwell discovers that he is Garou, a member of shapeshifting species, and that the rigorous military training he is receiving with the help of his adoptive father, Dr. Caldwell, is part of ploy by the Mage to breed him and his kind for their schemes. This novel is set in the publisher's Rage fantasy gaming world.

**Other books you might like:**
James A. Moore, *Hell-Storm*, 1996
John Saul, *Creature*, 1989
Edo van Belkom, *Wyrm Wolf*, 1995
Stewart Von Allmen, *Conspicuous Consumption*, 1995

---

**4060**

**BILL MYERS**

## Threshold

(Grand Rapids, Michigan: Zondervan, 1997)

**Story type:** Science Fiction (Theological; Psychic Powers)
**Major character(s):** Gertie Morrison, Psychic; Sarah Weintraub, Scientist (neurobiologist), Researcher; Helmut Reichner, Administrator, Scientist (physicist)
**Time period(s):** 1990s
**Locale(s):** Bethel Lake, Indiana; Katmandu, Nepal

**Summary:** Gertie prays and fasts to save the anointed one she sees in her dreams and thanks God for his approval. Still suffering from her abortion three years earlier, Sarah puts all her energy into her research into telekinesis. Meanwhile, Reichner travels to Nepal to meet his benefactor and discover the true purpose of his research institute.

**Other books you might like:**
Damien Broderick, *The White Abacus*, 1997
Tom Deitz, *Soulsmith*, 1991
Neil Gaiman, *Good Omens: The Nice and Accurate Prophecies of Agnes Nutter, Witch*, 1990
  Terry Pratchett, co-author
Marc Laidlaw, *Neon Lotus*, 1988
Dan Simmons, *Endymion*, 1996

---

**4061**

### EDWARD MYERS

## *Fire and Ice*
(New York: Roc, 1992)

**Story type:** Fantasy (Adventure; Religious)
**Series:** Mountain Trilogy
**Major character(s):** Forster Beckwith, Adventurer; Jesse O'Keefe, Anthropologist, Adventurer; Aeslu "Moon's Stead" of Vmatta, Indian (Rixtirra)
**Time period(s):** 1920s
**Locale(s):** Andes Mountains, Peru; Mountain Land, Mythical Place

**Summary:** As Forster's interest in the Rixtirra Indians and the Mountain of Light grows, the Rixtirra understand that he represents the outsider prophecied to appear during the Last Days and provide the means through which some will attain the Inner Realm while many others perish in the foretold disaster. Rixtirran society splinters into two opposing groups, both of which journey into the Inner Realm approaching the base of the Mountain of Light through use of a diadem containing a confusing map of the realm. Accompanying the first group, Aeslu works to save both groups despite mysterious interference.

**Other books you might like:**
James Hilton, *Lost Horizon*, 1933
Marc Laidlaw, *Neon Lotus*, 1988
James D. Priest, *Kirins: The Spell of No'an*, 1990
Elizabeth Ann Scarborough, *Final Refuge*, 1992
Elizabeth Ann Scarborough, *Nothing Sacred*, 1991
Lucius Shepard, *Kalimantan*, 1992

---

**4062**

### EDWARD MYERS

## *The Mountain Made of Light*
(New York: Roc, 1992)

**Story type:** Fantasy (Contemporary; Adventure)
**Series:** Mountain Trilogy
**Major character(s):** Jesse O'Keefe, Anthropologist, Adventurer; Aeslu "Moon's Stead" of Vmatta, Indian (Rixtirra), Linguist; Forster Beckwith, Adventurer
**Time period(s):** 1920s
**Locale(s):** Andes Mountains, Peru; Mountain Land, Mythical Place

**Summary:** Jesse O'Keefe, hoping to discover a fabled lost race, learns Rixtirra language and culture from Aeslu, who thinks Jesse may be the prophesied outsider. Forster Beckwith journeys to Mountain Land as a mountain climber, but he too becomes involved with the

Rixtirra, who hope to pursue their own vision despite the disaster foretold by the outsiders' appearance. This is the author's first novel.

**Other books you might like:**
Margaret Wander Bonanno, *The Others*, 1990
James Hilton, *Lost Horizon*, 1933
Michael P. Kube-McDowell, *Emprise*, 1985
Michael P. Kube-McDowell, *Enigma*, 1986
Marc Laidlaw, *Neon Lotus*, 1988
Louis L'Amour, *Haunted Mesa*, 1987
James D. Priest, *Kirins: The Spell of No'an*, 1990
Kim Stanley Robinson, *Escape From Kathmandu*, 1989
Elizabeth Ann Scarborough, *Nothing Sacred*, 1991
Lucius Shepard, *Kalimantan*, 1992
Rex Stout, *Under the Andes*, 1985
Sheri S. Tepper, *Grass*, 1989

---

**4063**

### EDWARD MYERS

## *The Summit*
(New York: Roc, 1994)

**Story type:** Fantasy (Adventure)
**Series:** Mountain Trilogy
**Major character(s):** Edward Myers, Writer, Researcher; Aeslu "Moon's Stead" of Vmatta, Indian (Rixtirra), Linguist; Jesse O'Keefe, Anthropologist, Adventurer
**Time period(s):** 1970s; 1920s
**Locale(s):** Andes Mountains, Peru; Mountain Land, Mythical Place

**Summary:** Surviving civil strife, Jesse O'Keefe and Aeslu must now survive an unprecedented climb to the summit of the Mountain Made of Light where they hope to enlist the help of the Founders' descendants in saving the Rixtirra people.

**Other books you might like:**
James Hilton, *Lost Horizon*, 1933
Robert Reed, *The Remarkables*, 1992
Elizabeth Ann Scarborough, *Last Refuge*, 1992
Elizabeth Ann Scarborough, *Nothing Sacred*, 1991
Robert Silverberg, *Kingdoms of the Wall*, 1993
Judith Tarr, *Spear of Heaven*, 1994

---

**4064**

### LINDA NAGATA

## *The Bohr Maker*
(New York: Bantam Spectra, 1995)

**Story type:** Science Fiction (Genetic Manipulation; Political)
**Major character(s):** Nikko Jiang-Tibayan, Genetically Altered Being, Experimental Subject; Phousita, Streetperson, Genetically Altered Being; Kirsten Adair, Police Officer (chief of Commonwealth Police)
**Time period(s):** Indeterminate Future
**Locale(s):** Sunda, Malaysia; Summer House, Space Station (orbital colony)

**Summary:** With only a short time before his body self-destructs, Nikko steals the Bohr Maker, a nanotechnological device with great powers. When the Bohr Maker infects Phousita instead, she decides to use the device to help her people better their lives.

**Other books you might like:**
Elton Elliott, *Nanodreams*, 1995
  editor
Valerie J. Freireich, *Becoming Human*, 1995

Nicola Griffith, *Slow River*, 1995
Nancy Kress, *Beggars and Choosers*, 1994
Nancy Kress, *Beggars in Spain*, 1993
Tricia Sullivan, *Lethe*, 1995

## 4065
### LINDA NAGATA
## Deception Well
(New York: Bantam Spectra, 1997)

**Story type:** Science Fiction (Political; Alternate Intelligence)
**Major character(s):** Lot Apolinario, Genetically Altered Being, Revolutionary; Urban, Revolutionary; Alta, Revolutionary
**Time period(s):** Indeterminate Future
**Locale(s):** Silk, Space Station (Orbital Colony); Deception Well, Planet—Imaginary

**Summary:** Ten years ago, Lot Apolinario's father led his devoted followers to their death as they attempted to reach Deception Well and enter the mysterious "Communion." Now a prisoner/ward of the orbiting city, Silk, Lot struggles with his inherited "charismata," an ability to affect others' emotions.

**Other books you might like:**
Gregory Benford, *Great Sky River*, 1987
Arthur C. Clarke, *The City and the Stars*, 1956
Valerie J. Freireich, *Becoming Human*, 1995
Nancy Kress, *The Beggars in Spain Trilogy*, 1993-96
Tricia Sullivan, *Lethe*, 1995

## 4066
### LINDA NAGATA
## Tech-Heaven
(New York: Bantam Spectra, 1995)

**Story type:** Science Fiction (Genetic Manipulation; Political)
**Major character(s):** Katie Kishida, Widow(er), Revolutionary; Ilene Carson, Political Figure (senator); Gregory Hunt, Doctor, Scientist
**Time period(s):** 1990s (1995-1999); 21st century (2000-2025)
**Locale(s):** Los Angeles, California; Voice-2, Space Station (orbital colony)

**Summary:** Katie Kishida preserves her recently-killed husband cryonically, hoping that future technology will treat his injuries. When many people protest, Katie embarks on a political struggle which lasts for decides fueled by rapid advances in nanotechnology.

**Other books you might like:**
Gregory Benford, *Far Futures*, 1995
  editor
Sterling Blake, *Chiller*, 1993
  pseudonym of Gregory Benford
Robert A. Heinlein, *I Will Fear No Evil*, 1970
Larry Niven, *Flatlander*, 1995
Clifford D. Simak, *Why Call Them Back From Heaven?*, 1967
James White, *The Dream Millennium*, 1974

## 4067
### LINDA NAGATA
## Vast
(New York: Bantam Spectra, 1998)

**Story type:** Science Fiction (Adventure)
**Major character(s):** Lot, Adventurer, Spaceman; Urban, Adventurer, Spaceman; Nikko, Artificial Intelligence
**Time period(s):** Indeterminate Future
**Locale(s):** *Null Boundary*, Spaceship; Outer Space

**Summary:** Four survivors of an ancient war investigate an area of space believed occupied by the Chenzeme Empire, the source of automated warships which have ravaged Orion Arm civilizations for millions of years.

**Other books you might like:**
Eleanor Arnason, *Ring of Swords*, 1993
Alan Dean Foster, *The Howling Stones*, 1997
Frederik Pohl, *Gateway*, 1977
Mary Doria Russell, *The Sparrow*, 1996
Sheri S. Tepper, *Grass*, 1989

## 4068
### JONATHAN NASAW
## Shadows
(New York: Dutton, 1997)

**Story type:** Horror (Vampire Story)
**Major character(s):** Jamey Whistler, Vampire; Aldo Striescu, Vampire; Selene Weiss, Witch (wicca)
**Time period(s):** 1990s (1997)
**Locale(s):** Santa Luz, Virgin Islands of the United States; New York, New York; Mill Valley, California

**Summary:** Jamey Whistler has repudiated his vampire life, setting the stage for his pursuit by Aldo Striescu, a vampire assassin hired by Jamey's estranged vampire father. Jamey's former lover Selene comes to the rescue, warning Jamey of the plot against him and marshaling Wiccan powers and herbal magic that protect but put her in the line of fire between Jamey and Aldo. A semi-sequel to *The World on Blood* (1996).

**Other books you might like:**
Nancy Baker, *The Night Inside*, 1995
Tanith Lee, *Darkness, I*, 1995
Michael Romkey, *The Vampire Papers*, 1996
Whitley Strieber, *The Hunger*, 1981

## 4069
### JONATHAN NASAW
## The World on Blood
(New York: Dutton, 1996)

**Story type:** Horror (Vampire Story)
**Major character(s):** Nick Santos, Writer, Vampire; Jamey Whistler, Vampire; Elizabeth "Betty" Corey, Religious (minister)
**Time period(s):** 1990s (1996)
**Locale(s):** El Cerrito, California

**Summary:** Nick Santos's efforts to rehabilitate fellow vampires through his Vampire's Anonymous organization is being undermined by the efforts of Jamey Whistler, a member who resents Nick's authoritarian approach and who schemes to break up the self-help group by reigniting the interest of his fellow members in blood-drinking.

**Other books you might like:**
Gary Bowen, *Diary of a Vampire*, 1995
Todd Grimson, *Stainless*, 1996
Jeffrey N. McMahan, *Vampires Anonymous*, 1991
Christopher Moore, *Bloodsucking Fiends: A Love Story*, 1995

## 4070
### JAMIL NASIR

## The Higher Space
(New York: Bantam Spectra, 1996)

**Story type:** Science Fiction (Science Fantasy; Mystery)
**Major character(s):** Bob Wilson, Lawyer; Diana Esterbrook, Teenager, Computer Expert; Wendall Thaxton, Reincarnated Person, Indian
**Time period(s):** 1990s
**Locale(s):** Sligo Woods, Mythical Place; United States

**Summary:** Bob Wilson reluctantly takes on what seems a routine child custody case, but soon discovers the unusual abilities of Diana Esterbrook, a teenage genius who uses a computer to map life patterns and to move through different dimensions.

**Other books you might like:**
Edwin A. Abbott, *Flatland*, 1884
Kim Antieau, *The Jigsaw Woman*, 1996
Steven Gould, *Jumper*, 1992
Neal Shusterman, *Scorpion Shards*, 1995
John Varley, *Blue Champagne*, 1986

## 4071
### JAMIL NASIR

## Quasar
(New York: Bantam Spectra, 1995)

**Story type:** Science Fiction (Cyberpunk; Adventure)
**Major character(s):** Theodore "Ted" Karmade, Technician (psychological); Quasar Zant, Socialite, Wealthy; Nelda Cloud, Guardian (Quasar's)
**Time period(s):** Indeterminate Future
**Locale(s):** The City, Earth

**Summary:** Ted Karmade attempts to integrate Quasar Zant's personalities, while Nelda Cloud plots to kill him. However, Quasar enlists Ted's help in searching the deepest tunnels for her missing parents, if her high-tech camouflage will allow the pair to avoid the agents looking for them. First novel.

**Other books you might like:**
Brian W. Aldiss, *Somewhere East of Life*, 1994
Pat Cadigan, *Fools*, 1992
Pat Cadigan, *Mindplayers*, 1987
Philip K. Dick, *Do Androids Dream of Electric Sheep?*, 1968
Nancy Kress, *Brain Rose*, 1990
Cordwainer Smith, *The Rediscovery of Man*, 1993
Michael Swanwick, *Vacuum Flowers*, 1987

## 4072
### YVONNE NAVARRO

## Afterage
(New York: Bantam, 1993)

**Story type:** Horror (Vampire Story)
**Major character(s):** William Perlman, Doctor; Howard Siebold, Traitor; Anyelet, Vampire
**Time period(s):** Indeterminate Future
**Locale(s):** Chicago, Illinois

**Summary:** While the scientifically-inclined among the human survivors of a vampire plague that has wiped out the world try to find a potent weapon against the undead, others plan to launch a full-scale assault against the vampires and their human toadies who have imprisoned the remaining human beings and begun breeding them for future foodstock. This is the author's first novel.

**Other books you might like:**
Jack Butler, *Nightshade*, 1989
Kathryn Meyer Griffith, *The Last Vampire*, 1992
Richard Matheson, *I Am Legend*, 1954
Robert R. McCammon, *They Thirst*, 1981
F. Paul Wilson, *Midnight Mass*, 1990

## 4073
### YVONNE NAVARRO

## Deadrush
(New York: Bantam, 1995)

**Story type:** Horror (Wild Talents)
**Major character(s):** Jason Spiro, Teenager; Jude Ewing, Detective—Police; Karla Bryant, Advertising (account executive)
**Time period(s):** 1990s (1995)
**Locale(s):** Chicago, Illinois

**Summary:** Jason Spiro takes up with a snake handling fundamentalist religion in rural Georgia and discovers he has the ability to resurrect the dead by sucking death out of them. He employs his talent after moving to Chicago and creates a growing army of resurrectees with the same talent, all of whom are addicted to the "rush" of power their resurrections afford.

**Other books you might like:**
John Byrne, *Whipping Boy*, 1992
Robert R. McCammon, *Mystery Walk*, 1983
Thomas F. Monteleone, *The Blood of the Lamb*, 1992
Thomas F. Monteleone, *The Resurrectionist*, 1995
F. Paul Wilson, *The Touch*, 1987

## 4074
### YVONNE NAVARRO

## Red Shadows
(New York: Bantam, 1998)

**Story type:** Science Fiction (Disaster; End of the World)
**Series:** Rogue Planet
**Major character(s):** Crystal Gelasias, Survivor; Lily, Survivor
**Time period(s):** 2020s (2021)
**Locale(s):** Minnesota

**Summary:** Twenty years have passed since a rogue planet hit the Earth and destroyed civilization. The only human survivors huddle in small, isolated communities, afraid to visit others because of a variety of plagues. A rebellious young man violates the taboo and visits a dead town, picking up an infection that threatens to destroy his own community.

**Other books you might like:**
Leigh Brackett, *The Long Tomorrow*, 1955
David Brin, *The Postman*, 1985
Edgar Pangborn, *Davy*, 1964
George R. Stewart, *Earth Abides*, 1949
John Wyndham, *Re-Birth*, 1955

**4075**

YVONNE NAVARRO

## Species

(New York: Bantam, 1995)

**Story type:** Science Fiction (Genetic Manipulation)
**Major character(s):** Sil, Experimental Subject, Genetically Altered Being; Xavier Fitch, Scientist, Leader
**Time period(s):** 1990s
**Locale(s):** Mojave Desert, California; Los Angeles, California

**Summary:** Extraterrestrial signals lead to secret research which incorporates alien DNA into human ova. When Sil avoids destruction and escapes, she makes her way to Los Angeles, her instincts driving her to reproduce, if a hastily assembled team cannot stop her. Novelizes the film.

**Other books you might like:**
Neal Barrett Jr., *Judge Dredd*, 1995
David Bischoff, *Hunter's Planet*, 1994
Terry Bisson, *Virtuosity*, 1995
Octavia E. Butler, *Dawn*, 1987
Michael Crichton, *Jurassic Park*, 1990
Alan Dean Foster, *Aliens*, 1986

**4076**

GRANT NAYLOR (Pseudonym of Rob Grant and Doug Naylor)

## Better than Life

(New York: Roc, 1993)

**Story type:** Science Fiction (Humor)
**Series:** Red Dwarf
**Major character(s):** David Lister, Spaceman; Kryten, Robot (cleaning); Cat, Animal (intelligent cat)
**Time period(s):** Indeterminate Future (about 3,000,000 A.D.)
**Locale(s):** Red Dwarf, Spaceship; Outer Space

**Summary:** While Cat, Lister, Kryten and the artifical intelligence, Arnold J. Rimmer, explore the ultimate virtual reality, "Better Than Life," the cheap little Toaster attempts to repair the stupified Holly, *Red Dwarf*'s resident artificial intelligence and captain.

**Other books you might like:**
Douglas Adams, *The Hitchhiker's Guide to the Galaxy*, 1980
Douglas Adams, *The Restaurant at the End of the Universe*, 1982
Ed Blome, *Title Deleted for Security Reasons*, 1993
John DeChancie, *Starrigger*, 1983
Ken Rolston, *Extreme Paranoia: Nobody Knows the Trouble I've Shot*, 1991
Neal Stephenson, *Snow Crash*, 1992

**4077**

GRANT NAYLOR (Pseudonym of Rob Grant and Doug Naylor)

## Red Dwarf: Infinity Welcomes Careful Drivers

(New York: Roc, 1992)

**Story type:** Science Fiction (Humor)
**Series:** Red Dwarf
**Major character(s):** Arnold J. Rimmer, Spaceman, Disembodied Personality; David Lister, Spaceman; Holly, Computer (ship's)
**Time period(s):** Indeterminate Future
**Locale(s):** Mimas, Saturn (moon of Saturn); *Red Dwarf*, Spaceship

**Summary:** When Lister arrives unconscious on Mimas with no identification and no way home, volunteering for the Space Corps seems his only route home. Unfortunately his ship, the *Red Dwarf*, has an accident, leaving him alone with only a holographic shipmate and the intelligent descendant of the ship's cat as company when Holly awakens him three million years later. A British television tie-in.

**Other books you might like:**
Douglas Adams, *The Hitchhiker's Guide to the Galaxy*, 1980
Douglas Adams, *Life, the Universe, and Everything*, 1982
Douglas Adams, *The Restaurant at the End of the Universe*, 1981
Douglas Adams, *So Long, and Thanks for All the Fish*, 1985
John DeChancie, *Starrigger*, 1983
Alan Dean Foster, *Quozl*, 1989
Laura J. Mixon, *Glass Houses*, 1992

**4078**

PHYLLIS REYNOLDS NAYLOR

## Bernie and the Bessledorf Ghost

(New York: Atheneum, 1990)

**Story type:** Fantasy (Mystery; Young Adult)
**Series:** Bessledorf Mystery
**Major character(s):** Bernie Magruder, Child, Student; Jonathon Bessledorf, Spirit (ghost)
**Time period(s):** 1980s
**Locale(s):** United States (Bessledorf Hotel)

**Summary:** Bernie and his friends and family must solve the mystery of why Jonathon Bessledorf is suddenly haunting the hotel, after lying quietly in his grave for a century.

**Other books you might like:**
Pam Conrad, *Stonewords: A Ghost Story*, 1990
Penelope Lively, *The Ghost of Thomas Kempe*, 1973
Patricia A. McKillip, *The House on Parchment Street*, 1973
Richard Peck, *The Ghost Belonged to Me*, 1975
Elizabeth Marie Pope, *The Sherwood Ring*, 1958

**4079**

PHYLLIS REYNOLDS NAYLOR

## The Witch Returns

(New York: Delacorte, 1992)

**Story type:** Fantasy (Young Adult; Magic Conflict)
**Series:** Witch
**Major character(s):** Lynn Morley, Child, Student; Marjorie "Mouse" Beasley, Friend; Greta Gullone, Witch
**Time period(s):** 1990s

**Locale(s):** United States

**Summary:** When a new neighbor moves into the house built on the ashes left from Mrs. Tuggle's house, Lynn suspects that Mrs. Tuggle has returned in the form of Mrs. Gullone. As Mrs. Gullone attempts to acquire Lynn's copy of the magic formulary, *Spells and Potions*, Lynn and Mouse work to alert others and foil her attempt to ensorcel Lynn.

**Other books you might like:**
Michael Bedard, *A Darker Magic*, 1987
Roald Dahl, *The Witches*, 1983
Diana Wynne Jones, *Witch's Business*, 1974
Margaret Mahy, *The Changeover*, 1974
John Masefield, *The Midnight Folk*, 1927

---

### 4080

**PHYLLIS REYNOLDS NAYLOR**

## The Witch's Eye
(New York: Delacorte, 1990)

**Story type:** Fantasy (Magic Conflict; Young Adult)
**Series:** Witch
**Major character(s):** Lynn Morley, Child, Student; Marjorie "Mouse" Beasley, Friend; Mrs. Tuggle, Witch, Spirit (recently deceased)
**Time period(s):** 1980s

**Summary:** Despite her recent death, Mrs. Tuggle continues to haunt the two girls who have been her adversaries through the medium of her glass eye. Once again she attempts to take possession of one of the girls, but this time it is Lynn herself.

**Other books you might like:**
L.M. Boston, *An Enemy at Green Knowe*, 1964
Roald Dahl, *The Witches*, 1983
Diana Wynne Jones, *Witch's Business*, 1974
Margaret Mahy, *The Changeover*, 1974
John Masefield, *The Midnight Folk*, 1927

---

### 4081

**REBECCA NEASON**

## Guises of the Mind
(New York: Pocket, 1993)

**Story type:** Science Fiction (Space Opera; Psychic Powers)
**Series:** Star Trek: The Next Generation
**Major character(s):** Jean-Luc Picard, Spaceship Captain, Military Personnel; Deanna Troi, Empath, Psychologist; Mother Veronica, Religious (abbess), Psychic
**Time period(s):** 24th century
**Locale(s):** *U.S.S. Enterprise*, Spaceship; Capulon IV, Planet—Imaginary

**Summary:** Captain Picard and Deanna Troi beam down to Capulon IV expecting to attend the coronation of Joakal I'lium as its ruler and to sign a treaty admitting the planet into the Federation. Mother Veronica, one of the nuns invited by Joakal to establish orphanages and care for children which the old laws would have killed in infancy, accompanies them. Instead, they find that Joakal's twin brother, long thought dead, has usurped the throne and only Mother Veronica's repressed telepathic talent can identify the rightful king.

**Other books you might like:**
Margaret Wander Bonanno, *Dwellers in the Crucible*, 1985
Marion Zimmer Bradley, *The Heirs of Hammerfell*, 1989
C.J. Cherryh, *Serpent's Reach*, 1980
Michael Jan Friedman, *Reunion*, 1991

Andrew M. Greeley, *The Final Planet*, 1987
Katherine Kurtz, *Saint Camber*, 1978
Walter M. Miller Jr., *A Canticle for Leibowitz*, 1959
A.E. Van Vogt, *Slan*, 1946
Howard Weinstein, *The Covenant of the Crown*, 1981

---

### 4082

**REBECCA NEASON**

## Shadow of Obsession
(New York: Warner Aspect, 1998)

**Story type:** Fantasy (Political; Adventure)
**Series:** Highlander
**Major character(s):** Duncan MacLeod, Immortal, Martial Arts Expert; Joe Dawson, Spy (watcher), Historian; Darius, Immortal
**Time period(s):** Indeterminate
**Locale(s):** Seacouver, Canada; Europe

**Summary:** An ancient rivalry threatens Duncan when an enemy of Duncan's old friend Darius vows to kill all those who are close to him.

**Other books you might like:**
L. Sprague de Camp, *The Fantastic Swordsmen*, 1967 editor
Jason Henderson, *Highlander: The Element of Fire*,
Ashley McConnell, *Highlander: Scimitar*, 1996
Jennifer Roberson, *Scotland the Brave*, 1996

---

### 4083

**ANDREW NEIDERMAN**

## After Life
(New York: Berkley, 1993)

**Story type:** Horror (Black Magic)
**Major character(s):** Lee Overstreet, Teacher (physical education); Jessie Overstreet, Writer; Bob Baker, Teacher (English)
**Time period(s):** 1990s (1993)
**Locale(s):** Gardner Town, New York

**Summary:** Something is rotten in upstate New York, or so Lee and Jessie Overstreet discover, when they move to Gardner Town and find a small community where the dead come back to life, the local high school students are encouraged to be ruthlessly violent in athletics, and the local benefactor, a physician, seems to have an influence on both.

**Other books you might like:**
David Darke, *Blind Hunger*, 1993
Ira Levin, *The Stepford Wives*, 1974
John Saul, *Creature*, 1989

---

### 4084

**ANDREW NEIDERMAN**

## The Dark
(New York: Pocket, 1997)

**Story type:** Horror (Occult)
**Major character(s):** Grant Blaine, Doctor (psychiatrist); Maggie Blaine, Lawyer; Jules Bois, Consultant
**Time period(s):** 1990s (1997)
**Locale(s):** Los Angeles, California

**Summary:** Grant Blaine assumes the case of Jules Bois, a patient of a murdered colleague, who confesses to a compulsion to cause people to commit evil. As Bois slowly discomposes Grant's life, undermining his self-assurance and turning his psychoanalytic inquiries against him, Grant's wife Maggie investigates Bois's background to discover psychotic, and possibly satanic, influences.

**Other books you might like:**
Robert Bloch, *The Scarf*, 1947
Michael Cadnum, *Skyscape*, 1994
Andrew Harper, *Bad Karma*, 1997
Thomas Harris, *The Silence of the Lambs*, 1988
Kathe Koja, *Strange Angels*, 1994
Patrick McGrath, *Asylum*, 1997

**4085**

ANDREW NEIDERMAN

## The Devil's Advocate
(New York: Pocket, 1997)

**Story type:** Horror (Black Magic)
**Major character(s):** Kevin Taylor, Lawyer; John Milton, Lawyer; Miriam Taylor, Housewife
**Time period(s):** 1990s
**Locale(s):** New York, New York

**Summary:** The law firm of John Milton and Associates is infamous for getting criminal clients acquitted for their crimes. Hotshot lawyer Kevin Taylor discovers that Milton, his employer, is the devil incarnate and that any effort to go against his wishes invites his infernal wrath. Originally published in 1990, but reissued to tie in with its 1997 film adaptation.

**Other books you might like:**
Clive Barker, *The Damnation Game*, 1985
Ramsey Campbell, *Obsession*, 1986
Matthew J. Costello, *Darkborn*, 1992
William Hjortsberg, *Falling Angel*, 1978
Stephen King, *Needful Things*, 1992
Robert Masello, *Private Demons*, 1992
Kim Newman, *The Quorum*, 1993

**4086**

ANDREW NEIDERMAN

## Duplicates
(New York: Berkley, 1994)

**Story type:** Horror (Mystery)
**Major character(s):** Marion Boxletter, Housewife; Bob Boxletter, Computer Expert (programmer); Nelson Congemi, Doctor
**Time period(s):** 1990s (1994)
**Locale(s):** Sandburg, New York

**Summary:** When she encounters a man who is the spitting image of the brother who disappeared with her son, Joey, over a year before, Marion Boxletter refuses to believe his protestations that he is someone else entirely different. Her investigations eventually uncover a government-sponsored program to give new identities and memories to criminals that has run amuck in the hands of its megalomaniacal overseers.

**Other books you might like:**
David Ambrose, *The Man Who Turned into Himself*, 1994
David Ely, *Seconds*, 1963
Timothy Findley, *Headhunter*, 1993

**4087**

ANDREW NEIDERMAN

## The Immortals
(New York: Pocket/Star, 1991)

**Story type:** Horror (Science Fiction)
**Major character(s):** Drake Edwards, Businessman (salesman); Cynthia Edwards, Housewife; Mr. Leon, Businessman (head of Youth Hold)
**Time period(s):** 1990s
**Locale(s):** Sandburg, New York

**Summary:** Drake Edwards jumps at the chance to become salesman for Youth Hold, a company that specializes in youth-preserving cosmetics. Unknown to Drake and his wife Cynthia, there is a direct connection between Youth Hold's products and the absence of spouses among the company's employees.

**Other books you might like:**
Ira Levin, *The Stepford Wives*, 1972
John Saul, *Creature*, 1989

**4088**

ANDREW NEIDERMAN

## In Double Jeopardy
(New York: Pocket, 1998)

**Story type:** Horror (Mystery; Psychological Suspense)
**Major character(s):** Jonathan Thomas Lewis, Murderer; Elaine Ross, Student (medical)
**Time period(s):** 1990s (1999)
**Locale(s):** New York, New York; Los Angeles, California; Billings, Montana

**Summary:** With the help of his rich father, murderer Dirk Stoner fakes his execution by lethal injection and assumes the new identity of Jonathan Thomas Lewis. Dirk's psychopathic proclivities compel him to seek out the family of his murdered wife, who sent him to death row, and to even the score with his sister-in-law Elaine, who has noticed disturbing behavioral similarities between Dirk and Jonathan.

**Other books you might like:**
Randall Boyll, *Shocker*, 1990
Ramsey Campbell, *The Face That Must Die*, 1979
Stephen Gallagher, *Down River*, 1989
Dean R. Koontz, *Whispers*, 1980
John Saul, *Black Lightning*, 1995

**4089**

ANDREW NEIDERMAN

## The Need
(New York: Putnam, 1992)

**Story type:** Horror (Vampire Story)
**Major character(s):** Clea/Richard Cave, Actress; Steve Mayer, Detective—Police; Alison/Nicholas, Actress
**Time period(s):** 1990s
**Locale(s):** Los Angeles, California

**Summary:** Clea Cave confesses to the police that she is a member of the Androgyne, a species that can change its sex at will and whose male personae feed by draining the life force from lovers and other victims. In so doing, she exposes herself to reprisals not only from other Androgynes, but from the Evil Eye, the name given to a devilish tempter whose sole purpose is to lure the Androgyne to self-destruction.

**Other books you might like:**
Robert Louis Stevenson, *The Strange Case of Dr. Jekyll and Mr. Hyde*, 1888
Whitley Strieber, *The Hunger*, 1981

## 4090
### ANDREW NEIDERMAN
### *Perfect Little Angels*
(New York: Berkley, 1989)

**Story type:** Horror (Satire)
**Major character(s):** Justine Freeman, Teenager (Rebellious fifteen-year-old); Felix Lawrence, Doctor (Psychologist/Nutritionist)
**Time period(s):** 1980s
**Locale(s):** Elesian Fields (Housing tract)

**Summary:** When the Freeman family moves into Elesian Fields, a middle class planned community, they are surprised by the extreme conformity of their neighbors, especially the teenagers, whose behavior is exemplary in every way. As the Freeman's daughter, Justine, rebels against her peers' docility, she becomes increasingly threatened by other teenagers, by the larger community—led by its mysterious leader, Dr. Lawrence—and finally by her own parents.

**Other books you might like:**
Jack Finney, *The Body Snatchers*, 1955
Ira Levin, *The Stepford Wives*, 1972

## 4091
### ANDREW NEIDERMAN
### *Sister, Sister*
(New York: Berkley, 1992)

**Story type:** Horror (Wild Talents)
**Major character(s):** Neil Richards, Teacher; Tania Webster, Scientist
**Time period(s):** 1990s
**Locale(s):** Centerville, New York (Mandicott Clinic)

**Summary:** When he is hired by a secretive research hospital for his skills in special education, Neil Richards is told that Siamese twins Alpha and Beta are being studied as examples of how human beings adapt to overcrowding. But Neil soon discovers that the births of the children have been engineered for a special reason, and that the pair have developed telepathic powers strong enough to kill those who fall into their disfavor.

**Other books you might like:**
Margaret Bingley, *Seeds of Evil*, 1988
Tom Piccirilli, *Dark Father*, 1990
Thomas Tryon, *The Other*, 1971
T. Lucien Wright, *Blood Brothers*, 1992

## 4092
### KATHERINE NEVILLE
### *The Eight*
(New York: Ballantine, 1989)

**Story type:** Fantasy (Historical)
**Major character(s):** Mireille de Remy, Noblewoman (narrator, 1770s); Catherine Velis, Computer Expert (narrator, 1970s)

**Time period(s):** 1770s; 1970s
**Locale(s):** Paris, France; New York, New York; Algiers, Algeria

**Summary:** Montglane Service, a mythical chess set, holds mystical powers. To crack its code is to unleash its enormous potential.

**Other books you might like:**
Thomas Bently, *Celestial Chess*, 1988
Ian Watson, *Queenmagic, Kingmagic*, 1990

## 4093
### LINDA NEVINS
### *Renaissance Moon*
(New York: St. Martin's, 1997)

**Story type:** Fantasy (Contemporary Realism; Religious)
**Major character(s):** Selene Catcher, Scholar, Religious; Giovanna Corio, Religious
**Time period(s):** 1990s
**Locale(s):** Cambridge, Massachusetts; Florence, Italy

**Summary:** Father Corio has known the brilliant Selene for a long time, watching her grow stranger as the years went by. Despite their fondness for each other, a gulf separates them. Corio became a Catholic priest, while Selene Catcher's connection to Goddess traces back to having been sealed to the Triple Goddess at birth. When Selene becomes attached to a charming and faithless young man, Goddess will have revenge on all of them.

**Other books you might like:**
A.A. Attanasio, *The Moon's Wife: A Hystery*, 1993
Bradley Denton, *Lunatics*, 1996
Lisa Goldstein, *Walking the Labyrinth*, 1996
Elizabeth Hand, *Waking the Moon*, 1995
Robert Holdstock, *Ancient Echoes*, 1996

## 4094
### KIM NEWMAN
### *Anno Dracula*
(New York: Carroll & Graf, 1993)

**Story type:** Horror (Vampire Story)
**Major character(s):** Dracula, Vampire; John Seward, Doctor (psychiatrist); Genevieve Dieudonne, Vampire, Health Care Professional
**Time period(s):** 1880s (1888)
**Locale(s):** England, Alternate Earth

**Summary:** In an alternate world, Dracula has outlived his renown as the villain of Bram Stoker's novel, married the widowed Queen Victoria and become a fiendish Prince Consort who allows vampirism to run rampant in Victorian London. Meanwhile, his nemesis, Dr. John Seward, becomes Jack the Ripper, a fearless vampire killer determined to expunge the vampire scourge from the world.

**Other books you might like:**
Brian W. Aldiss, *Dracula Unbound*, 1990
Anne Rice, *The Vampire Lestat*, 1985
Lucius Shepard, *The Golden*, 1993
Brian Stableford, *The Empire of Fear*, 1988
Bram Stoker, *Dracula*, 1895

## 4095

### KIM NEWMAN
### EUGENE BYRNE, Co-Author

## *Back in the USSA*

(Shingletown, California: Mark V. Ziesing, 1997)

**Story type:** Science Fiction (Alternate History; Political)
**Major character(s):** Charles Hardin Holley, Musician, Revolutionary; Alphonse Capone, Political Figure (party chairman), Historical Figure; Issac Asimov, Television Personality (astrologer), Historical Figure
**Time period(s):** 1980s (1989); 1910s (1917)
**Locale(s):** Chicago, Illinois; New York, New York; Alternate Earth

**Summary:** In A.D. 1917 a revolution topples a corrupt regime and creates a state based, in theory, on the principles of Socialism, the United Socialiist States of America. When the revolutionary leadership of Eugene Debs passes to the iron regime of Al Capone, the dream self-destructs. Now, with the Socialist governments collapsing, the truth of those years can be told. Parts of the novel, in somewhat different form, appeared as stories in *Interzone* Magazine.

**Other books you might like:**
Terry Bisson, *Voyage to the Red Planet*, 1990
Tim Powers, *Last Call*, 1992
Kim Stanley Robinson, *Red Mars*, 1993
Howard Waldrop, *Night of the Cooters*, 1990
Jack Womack, *Ambient*, 1987

## 4096

### KIM NEWMAN

## *Bad Dreams*

(New York: Carroll & Graf, 1991)

**Story type:** Horror (Vampire Story)
**Major character(s):** Anne Nielson, Journalist; Cameron Nielson, Writer (playwright); Mr. Skinner, Vampire (''The Monster'')
**Time period(s):** 1990s; 1950s
**Locale(s):** London, England

**Summary:** The death of her rebellious junkie sister Judi sends Anne Nielson to London to investigate. As she probes deeper into the S&M subculture of which Judi was a part, she comes closer and closer to an encounter with Mr. Skinner, an ageless vampire who feeds on human flesh and dreams and who, for personal reasons, has covertly been subjecting the Nielsons to one misery after another for decades. This novel was first published in Britain in 1990.

**Other books you might like:**
Anne Rice, *The Queen of the Damned*, 1988
Dan Simmons, *Carrion Comfort*, 1989
Brian Stableford, *The Empire of Fear*, 1988

## 4097

### KIM NEWMAN

## *The Bloody Red Baron*

(New York: Carroll & Graf, 1995)

**Story type:** Horror (Vampire Story)
**Major character(s):** Manfred von Richtofen, Military Personnel, Pilot; Edwin Winthrop, Military Personnel; Edgar Allan Poe, Writer, Historical Figure
**Time period(s):** 1910s (1918)

**Locale(s):** London, England; France, Alternate Earth
**Summary:** In a world where Count Dracula has eluded death and infected half of the global population with vampirisim, World War I is fought by mortals and vampires who convert themselves to airplane-sized bats to carry out dogfights. This imaginative and inventive novel ponders the social and military situation of the war that might have been had celebrities and renowned historical figures been unkillable vampires.

**Other books you might like:**
Les Daniels, *No Blood Spilled*, 1991
Anne Rice, *The Vampire Lestat*, 1985
Michael Romkey, *I, Vampire*, 1990
Fred Saberhagen, *An Old Friend of the Family*, 1979
Brian Stableford, *The Empire of Fear*, 1988

## 4098

### KIM NEWMAN

## *Judgment of Tears: Anno Dracula 1959*

(New York: Carroll & Graf, 1998)

**Story type:** Horror (Vampire Story)
**Series:** Anno Dracula
**Major character(s):** Kate Reed, Journalist, Vampire; Hamish Bond, Spy; Genevieve Dieudonne, Vampire
**Time period(s):** 1950s (1959)
**Locale(s):** Rome, Italy

**Summary:** Count Dracula's impending marriage to Moldavian Princess Asa Vadja is interrupted by the murder spree of the Crimson Executioner, a serial killer who preys upon vampires. Kate Reed investigates and discovers that the murderer may be more than just a human or fellow vampire with a grudge. This is the third novel set in the alternate world where Count Dracula survived the attempt on his life at the end of Bram Stoker's novel and became a member of the British nobility.

**Other books you might like:**
Brian W. Aldiss, *Dracula Unbound*, 1990
Anne Rice, *The Queen of the Damned*, 1989
Fred Saberhagen, *An Old Friend of the Family*, 1979
Lucius Shepard, *The Golden*, 1993
Brian Stableford, *The Empire of Fear*, 1988

## 4099

### KIM NEWMAN

## *The Night Mayor*

(New York: Carroll and Graf, 1990)

**Story type:** Science Fiction (Techno-Thriller; Arts)
**Major character(s):** Truro Daine, Fugitive; Susan Bishopric, Writer (Dreamer)
**Time period(s):** 21st century
**Locale(s):** San Francisco, California

**Summary:** Using the world's major computer to construct a 1940s and 1950s film noir dream world, Truro Daine has effectively escaped his imprisonment. Unwilling to lose Daine, authorities conscript Susan Bishopric to search him out.

**Other books you might like:**
Pat Cadigan, *Mindplayers*, 1987
Pat Cadigan, *Synners*, 1991
William Gibson, *Count Zero*, 1986
William Gibson, *Mona Lisa Overdrive*, 1988
William Gibson, *Neuromancer*, 1984

Dan Simmons, *The Fall of Hyperion*, 1990
Dan Simmons, *Hyperion*, 1989

## 4100

### KIM NEWMAN

## *The Quorum*

(New York: Carroll & Graf, 1994)

**Story type:** Horror (Black Magic)
**Major character(s):** Neil Martin, Worker (in a comic book store); Derek Leech, Businessman; Sally Rhodes, Detective—Private
**Time period(s):** 1990s (1993); 1970s (1978)
**Locale(s):** London, England

**Summary:** In 1978, three of Neil Martin's school chums make a pact with the devil incarnate, Derek Leech, to subject Neil to a life of unremitting misery in exchange for their own personal gains. When Neil finds out, though, the tide turns in his favor, and his friends receive their just desserts.

**Other books you might like:**
William Hjortsberg, *Falling Angel*, 1978
Stephen King, *Needful Things*, 1992
Robert Masello, *Private Demons*, 1992

## 4101

### NICHELLE NICHOLS
### MARGARET WANDER BONANNO, Co-Author

## *Saturn's Child*

(New York: Ace/Putnam, 1995)

**Story type:** Science Fiction (First Contact; Psychic Powers)
**Major character(s):** Saturna, Telepath, Genetically Altered Being; Krecis, Alien (Fazisian), Spaceship Captain; Nyota Dominque, Scientist, Spaceship Captain
**Time period(s):** 22nd century (2187)
**Locale(s):** *Dragon's Egg*, Spaceship; Titan, Saturn (a moon of Saturn)

**Summary:** Exploring space, searching for resources and other intelligent species, the telepathic Fazisians realize the Solar System contains intelligent life when Earth sends an expedition to Titan (which the Fazisians colonized 50 years earlier). Nyota becomes involved with one of the Fazisians, a relationship forbidden by both Earth and Fazis. Krecis arranges for them to have a child without anyone's knowledge, fostering the baby to a Fazisian couple. Nichols's first novel and first of a proposed series.

**Other books you might like:**
Margaret Wander Bonanno, *The Others*, 1990
Octavia E. Butler, *Dawn*, 1987
L. Warren Douglas, *Stepwater*, 1995
Anne McCaffrey, *The Rowan*, 1990
Alis A. Rasmussen, *A Passage of Stars*, 1990

## 4102

### JASON NICKLES

## *Immortal*

(New York: Zebra, 1996)

**Story type:** Horror (Vampire Story)
**Major character(s):** Emily Kane, Doctor; Ray Timmerson, Writer; Martin Crouper, Vampire

**Time period(s):** 1990s (1996)
**Locale(s):** Horn Pond, Massachusetts; New York, New York

**Summary:** A coffin uncovered during an archaeological dig in Massachusetts is shipped back to a New York museum. Unbeknownst to the scientists who uncovered it, the coffin contains the vampire Martin Crouper, formerly a member of a travelling carnival sideshow, who was interred following a rash of deaths he caused years before and who now threatens to perpetuate his bloody legacy in New York City.

**Other books you might like:**
Don Davis, *Bring on the Night*, 1993
   Jay Davis, co-author
Ron Dee, *Dusk*, 1993
Ronald Kelly, *Blood Kin*, 1996
Stephen King, *Salem's Lot*, 1975
Robert R. McCammon, *They Thirst*, 1981
Patrick Whalen, *Night Thirst*, 1993

## 4103

### DAVID F. NIGHBERT

## *The Clouds of Magellan*

(New York: St. Martins Press, 1991)

**Story type:** Science Fiction (Space Opera; First Contact)
**Major character(s):** Anton Stryker, Adventurer, Clone; Albert Samuels, Inventor (time machine), Clone; Abe, Alien, Telepath
**Time period(s):** 31st century
**Locale(s):** *Nefertiti*, Spaceship; Greater Magellanic Cloud, Outer Space

**Summary:** Hoping to learn more of the giant alien artifact and its builders, Anton Stryker and his comrades venture to The Wheel intending to pick up Albert Samuels and travel to the aliens' space. As they approach The Wheel, their nemesis, Isaac DeKoven, with battleship and destroyers, forces Stryker's ship away and uses The Wheel himself, projecting his party toward the planned alien meeting days ahead of Stryker's group. This is a sequel to *Timelapse*.

**Other books you might like:**
Greg Bear, *Eon*, 1985
Alexander Jablokov, *Carve the Sky*, 1991
Larry Niven, *Man-Kzin Wars IV*, 1991
   editor
Larry Niven, *Protector*, 1973
Larry Niven, *Ringworld*, 1970
Frederik Pohl, *Gateway*, 1977
Frederik Pohl, *The Gateway Trip: Tales and Vignettes of the Heechee*, 1990
Edward E. Smith, *Triplanetary*, 1948
John Varley, *Titan*, 1979

## 4104

### STEVEN NIGHTINGALE

## *The Thirteenth Daughter of the Moon*

(New York: St. Martin's, 1997)

**Story type:** Fantasy (Contemporary Realism; Literary)
**Series:** Lost Coast
**Major character(s):** Cookie, Cowboy (female); Chiara, Professor, Fugitive; Ananda, Musician, Lawyer
**Time period(s):** 1990s (1997)
**Locale(s):** Berkeley, California

**Summary:** As the strange travelers continue their search for the Lost Coast and Cookie's lost husband, they meet odd people with odder stories, including a medieval saint, a poet, and a coyote, and they tell their own tales along the way. When they reach their mythical destination, however, they learn that all ends become beginnings.

**Other books you might like:**
James P. Blaylock, *The Paper Grail*, 1991
Francesca Lia Block, *Weetzie Bat*, 1989
Jack Cady, *The Off Season*, 1995
John Crowley, *Little, Big*, 1981
Pat Murphy, *The City, Not Long After*, 1989

## 4105

### DOUGLAS NILES

### A Breach in the Watershed

(New York: Ace, 1995)

**Story type:** Fantasy (Quest; Magic Conflict)
**Series:** Watershed Trilogy
**Major character(s):** Rudgar "Rudy" Appenfell, Hero, Mountaineer (Iceman of Halverica); Raine of the Three Waters, Noblewoman; Anjell Appenfell, Child, Adventurer
**Time period(s):** Indeterminate
**Locale(s):** The Watershed, Mythical Place; Dalethica, Fictional Country (land of life)

**Summary:** As a poisonous essence from the land of death and minions of the dark god enter the land of the living through a fractured barrier, the fate of everyone hinges on the actions of a small band of heroes working on the surface and underground to repel the offensive and deadly invasion.

**Other books you might like:**
L. Dean James, *Summerland*, 1994
Robert Jordan, *The Eye of the World*, 1990
Patricia A. McKillip, *The Book of Atrix Wolfe*, 1995
Margaret Weis, *Dragon Wing*, 1990
    Tracy Hickman, co-author
Margaret Weis, *Into the Labyrinth*, 1993
    Tracy Hickman, co-author

## 4106

### DOUGLAS NILES

### The Coral Kingdom

(Lake Geneva, Wisconsin: TSR, 1992)

**Story type:** Fantasy (Quest)
**Series:** Forgotten Realms: The Druidhome Trilogy
**Major character(s):** Robyn Kendrick, Royalty (high queen of the Ffolk), Adventurer
**Time period(s):** Indeterminate
**Locale(s):** Moonshae Isles, Mythical Place; *Princess of Moonshae*, At Sea; Evermeet, Mythical Place

**Summary:** Robyn journeys to the Coral Kingdom to rescue her husband held prisoner there.

**Other books you might like:**
Richard Awlinson, *Shadowdale*, 1989
Troy Denning, *The Parched Sea*, 1991
Ed Greenwood, *Spellfire*, 1988
Kate Novak, *Azure Bonds*, 1988
    Jeff Grubb, co-author
Margaret Weis, *Dragons of Autumn Twilight*, 1984
    Tracy Hickman, co-author

## 4107

### DOUGLAS NILES

### Darkenheight

(New York: Ace, 1996)

**Story type:** Fantasy (Magic Conflict; Political)
**Series:** Watershed Trilogy
**Major character(s):** Rudgar "Rudy" Appenfell, Hero, Mountaineer (Iceman); Raine of the Three Waters, Noblewoman, Writer; Nicodareus, Monster, Leader
**Time period(s):** Indeterminate
**Locale(s):** The Watershed, Mythical Place; Dalethica, Fictional Country; Faerine, Fictional Country

**Summary:** After Nicodareus dies while failing to prepare all of the Watershed for the coming of the Nameless One, the Nameless One resurrects Nicodareus and charges him with finding and killing Rudy, the major stumbling block to the Nameless One's domination. The only hope of stopping the Nameless One's attack on all the realms of the Watershed remains with Rudy and his mixed company of heroes and warriors, if they can survive and stop the flow of Darkblood which will destroy all.

**Other books you might like:**
Terry Goodkind, *Stone of Tears*, 1995
L. Dean James, *Summerland*, 1994
Robert Jordan, *The Eye of the World*, 1990
Patricia Mullen, *The Stone Movers*, 1995
J.R.R. Tolkien, *The Fellowship of the Ring*, 1954

## 4108

### DOUGLAS NILES

### Feathered Dragon

(Lake Geneva, Wisconsin: TSR, 1991)

**Story type:** Fantasy (Historical)
**Series:** Forgotten Realms: The Maztica Trilogy
**Major character(s):** Cordell, Warrior, Leader; Gultec, Warrior, Indian
**Time period(s):** Indeterminate Past
**Locale(s):** Maztica, Fictional Country (Central American)

**Summary:** A new invasion force in Maztica threatens society's existence. The warriors must determine who is the enemy and organize a defense while hoping the prophecy of the Feathered Dragon's return will prove their salvation. This novel retells a chapter of Central American history. A game tie-in novel.

**Other books you might like:**
David Cook, *Horselords*, 1990
Troy Denning, *Dragonwall*, 1990
James Lowder, *Crusade*, 1991
Kate Novak, *Azure Bonds*, 1988
    Jeff Grubb, co-author
R.A. Salvatore, *Canticle*, 1991
R.A. Salvatore, *Homeland*, 1990

## 4109

### DOUGLAS NILES

### The Kinslayer Wars

(Lake Geneva, Wisconsin: TSR, 1991)

**Story type:** Fantasy (Adventure)
**Series:** Dragonlance: The Elven Nations Trilogy

**Major character(s):** Kith-Kanan, Mythical Creature (elf), Warrior; Sithas, Royalty, Mythical Creature (elf)
**Time period(s):** Indeterminate (2215 Pre-Cataclysm)
**Locale(s):** South Central Ansalon, Fictional Country

**Summary:** Two Elven brothers participate in a war between the human empire of Ergoth and the Silvanesh Elves. A game tie-in novel.

**Other books you might like:**
C.J. Cherryh, *Gate of Ivrel*, 1976
Michael Moorcock, *Elric of Melnibone*, 1976
Brian Craig, *Storm Warriors*, 1991
    Craig is a pseudonym for Brian Stableford
Paul B. Thompson, *Firstborn*, 1991
    Tonya R. Carter, co-author
Paul B. Thompson, *The Qualinesti*, 1991
    Tonya R. Carter, co-author
J.R.R. Tolkien, *The Fellowship of the Ring*, 1954

## 4110

### DOUGLAS NILES

## War of the Three Waters

(New York: Ace, 1997)

**Story type:** Fantasy (Magic Conflict; Quest)
**Series:** Watershed Trilogy
**Major character(s):** Rudgar ''Rudy'' Appenfell, Hero, Mountaineer (Iceman); Raine of the Three Waters, Noblewoman, Writer
**Time period(s):** Indeterminate
**Locale(s):** The Watershed, Mythical Place; Faerine, Fictional Country; Duloth-Trol, Fictional Country

**Summary:** As Darkenblood flows over the Watershed and the Nameless One's minions battle to control all, human and Faerine forces must unite to prevent chaos. To overcome the disaster, Rudy and Raine must travel deep into enemy lands to use the sword of their ancestors against the source of the evil assault.

**Other books you might like:**
Terry Goodkind, *Wizard's First Rule*, 1994
J. Gregory Keyes, *The Blackgod*, 1997
J. Gregory Keyes, *The Waterborn*, 1996
Patricia Mullen, *The Stone Movers*, 1995
J.R.R. Tolkien, *The Fellowship of the Ring*, 1954

## 4111

### ADAM NISWANDER

## The Charm

(Phoenix, Arizona: Integra Publishing, 1993)

**Story type:** Horror (Ancient Evil Unleashed)
**Major character(s):** Jack Foreman, Anthropologist; Greg Johnson, Police Officer; Tom Bear, Indian, Shaman
**Time period(s):** 1990s (1993)
**Locale(s):** Phoenix, Arizona

**Summary:** During field research, anthropologist Jack Foreman accidentally unleashes an ancient Indian demon into the world, prompting individuals from each of the southwestern tribes to band together in an effort to return the being to the supernatural realm.

**Other books you might like:**
Morgan Fields, *Shaman Woods*, 1989
G. Wayne Miller, *Thunder Rise*, 1989
Eugene E. Pfaff Jr., *Uwharrie*, 1993
    Michael Causey, co-author

Kathryn Ptacek, *Ghost Dance*, 1990
Patrick Whalen, *Deathwalker*, 1992

## 4112

### ADAM NISWANDER

## The Sand Dwellers

(Minneapolis: Fedogan & Bremer, 1998)

**Story type:** Horror (Ancient Evil Unleashed)
**Major character(s):** Aiden Mardian, Detective—Private; Aloysius Graham Porter, Military Personnel (colonel); Clem Barber, Recluse
**Time period(s):** 1990s (1998)
**Locale(s):** Superstition Mountain, Arizona

**Summary:** Aiden Mardian's government-sponsored search for a man who was last seen at Superstition Mountain coincides with strange sightings and inexplicable behavior among the members of the skeletal military staff that mans nuclear missile silos deep inside the mountain. With the help of others whose lives have been affected by strange phenomena at the mountain, Aiden discovers that the land is a hotbed of activity for the Sand Dwellers, a race of supernatural creatures whose ultimate goal is to enslave and destroy the human race.

**Other books you might like:**
Robert Bloch, *Strange Eons*, 1978
Brian Lumley, *The Burrowers Beneath*, 1974
Brian Lumley, *The Transition of Titus Crow*, 1978
Joseph S. Pulver Jr., *Nightmare's Disciple*, 1998
Michael Shea, *The Colour out of Time*, 1984

## 4113

### ADAM NISWANDER

## The Serpent Slayers

(Phoenix, Arizona: Integra Press, 1994)

**Story type:** Horror (Ancient Evil Unleashed)
**Series:** Shaman Cycle
**Major character(s):** Jeremy Myers, Scientist (herpetologist); Rachel Knight, Scientist (assistant to Jeremy Myers); Danny Webb, Indian, Shaman
**Time period(s):** 1990s (1991)
**Locale(s):** Phoenix, Arizona

**Summary:** An earthquake in the American Southwest releases The Scaled One, an ancient deity imprisoned in ice for centuries who commands an army of voracious snakes to do its bidding. In this indirect sequel to the author's first novel, *The Charm* (1993), southwestern tribes of Native Americans convening for their regular Gathering marshal their forces to defeat a scourge that threatens to overrun the world.

**Other books you might like:**
Morgan Fields, *Shaman Woods*, 1989
G. Wayne Miller, *Thunder Rise*, 1989
Eugene E. Pfaff Jr., *Uwharrie*, 1993
    Michael Causey, co-author
Kathryn Ptacek, *Ghost Dance*, 1990
Patrick Whalen, *Deathwalker*, 1992

## 4114

**LARRY NIVEN**
**STEVEN BARNES**, Co-Author

### Achilles' Choice

(New York: Tor, 1991)

**Story type:** Science Fiction (Adventure; Political)
**Major character(s):** Jillian Shomer, Sports Figure
**Time period(s):** 21st century
**Locale(s):** Earth

**Summary:** While competing in the potentially deadly event testing physical and mental strengths of potential government rulers, Jillian Shomer decides to unlock the mysteries behind the workings of the government.

**Other books you might like:**
Iain M. Banks, *The Player of Games*, 1988
Jeffrey A. Carver, *From a Changeling Star*, 1989
Philip K. Dick, *The Game-Players of Titan*, 1963
A.E. Van Vogt, *The Weapon Shops of Isher*, 1951
A.E. Van Vogt, *The Weapon Makers*, 1946

## 4115

**LARRY NIVEN**
**STEVEN BARNES**, Co-Author

### The Barsoom Project

(New York: Ace Books, 1989)

**Story type:** Science Fiction (Adventure)
**Series:** Dream Park
**Major character(s):** Max Sands, Sports Figure; Millicent Summers, Businesswoman
**Time period(s):** Indeterminate Future
**Locale(s):** Dream Park, Earth (An adventure park for role players)

**Summary:** Once again a determined ban of adventure gamers enter one of Dream Park's interactive scenarios and, once again, things go wrong and people begin to die.

**Other books you might like:**
Iain M. Banks, *The Player of Games*, 1988
Philip K. Dick, *The Game-Players of Titan*, 1963
Robert Scheckley, *The Tenth Victim*, 1966
Ian Watson, *Queenmagic, Kingmagic*, 1988

## 4116

**LARRY NIVEN**
**JERRY POURNELLE**, Co-Author
**STEVEN BARNES**, Co-Author

### Beowulf's Children

(New York: Tor, 1995)

**Story type:** Science Fiction (Space Colony; First Contact)
**Series:** Heorot
**Major character(s):** Aaron Tragen, Leader, Orphan; Cadmann Weyland, Explorer, Security Officer; Old Grendel, Alien
**Time period(s):** 22nd century
**Locale(s):** Avalon, Planet—Imaginary

**Summary:** As the children of the colonists explore the mainland, much to their elders' dismay, Avalon's seasons and the original ecology, devastated by the grendels, begins to come back. On the mainland, some of the grendels develop intelligence and one in particular tries to understand the colonists. When the dangers of the seasons become apparent, Aaron Tragen's desperate attempt to prevent retreat from the mainland may provide a situation that allows contact between humans and grendels.

**Other books you might like:**
Octavia E. Butler, *Survivor*, 1978
Joe Haldeman, *Worlds Enough and Time*, 1992
Anne McCaffrey, *Freedom's Landing*, 1995
Rebecca Ore, *Becoming Alien*, 1988
Frederik Pohl, *The Voices of Heaven*, 1994
Dennis Schmidt, *Way-Farer*, 1978
Sheri S. Tepper, *Grass*, 1989
James White, *The Silent Stars Go By*, 1991

## 4117

**LARRY NIVEN**
**STEVEN BARNES**, Co-Author

### The California Voodoo Game

(New York: Ballantine Del Rey, 1992)

**Story type:** Science Fiction (Mystery; Cyberpunk)
**Series:** Dream Park
**Major character(s):** Alex Griffin, Security Officer; Acacia "Panthesilea" Garcia, Entertainer (fantasy role-playing gamer); Nigel Bishop, Entertainer (fantasy role-playing gamer)
**Time period(s):** 2050s (2059)
**Locale(s):** Mojave Desert, California

**Summary:** MIMIC, the ruins of a 1990s arcology and future base of operations for the Barsoom Project, hosts the biggest fantasy role-playing game ever. Five teams of six players each will compete in the California Voodoo Game, pitting their characters against virtual reality simulations and live character actors. Suspecting one of the players has murdered for information on the security systems, Alex Griffin joins the Game as a non-player character to find out why.

**Other books you might like:**
Steven Barnes, *Gorgon Child*, 1989
Steven Barnes, *Streetlethal*, 1983
Emma Bull, *Bone Dance: A Fantasy for Technophiles*, 1991
Orson Scott Card, *Ender's Game*, 1985
Michael Crichton, *Jurassic Park*, 1991
Michael Crichton, *Westworld*, 1974
Philip K. Dick, *Do Androids Dream of Electric Sheep?*, 1968
William Gibson, *Neuromancer*, 1984
Lynn S. Hightower, *Alien Blues*, 1992

## 4118

**LARRY NIVEN**

### Crashlander

(New York: Ballantine Del Rey, 1994)

**Story type:** Science Fiction (Collection; Hard Science Fiction)
**Series:** Known Space
**Major character(s):** Beowulf Shaffer, Spaceship Captain, Space Explorer
**Time period(s):** 27th century
**Locale(s):** Outer Space; Spaceship

**Summary:** This volume contains all the stories that chronicle Beowulf Shaffer's adventures while exploring such exotic astronomical features as a neutron star and the galactic core. It includes two original stories, "Procrustes," and an interwoven story, "Ghost," which provides a unifying framework for five stories published 1966-1975 in periodicals and anthologies.

**Other books you might like:**
Pat Cadigan, *Patterns*, 1990
Michael Flynn, *The Nanotech Chronicles*, 1991
Robert A. Heinlein, *The Past through Tomorrow*, 1967
Walter M. Miller Jr., *The Science Fiction Stories of Walter M. Miller, Jr.*, 1984
Cordwainer Smith, *The Rediscovery of Man*, 1993
John Varley, *Blue Champagne*, 1986
John Varley, *The Persistence of Vision*, 1978

**4119**

**LARRY NIVEN**

### Destiny's Road

(New York: Tor, 1997)

**Story type:** Science Fiction (Lost Colony; Political)
**Major character(s):** Jemmy "Tim Hann" Bloocher, Fugitive, Cook; Loria Bednacort, Spouse; Damon ibn-Rushd, Businessman, Traveler (Caravan)
**Time period(s):** 28th century (2730s)
**Locale(s):** Destiny, Planet—Imaginary; Spiral Town, Fictional City

**Summary:** Without the speckles, people on Destiny lose their intelligence. In Spiral Town, the inhabitants trade with Caravans which carry speckles as money. After Jeremy kills a merchant from the spring Caravan, he must leave Spiral Town to prevent his family's suffering from lack of speckles. He follows the road formed by the *Cavorite's* engines, joining the Caravan as a chef, while hoping to discover the fate of ship and crew.

**Other books you might like:**
Helen Collins, *Mutagenesis*, 1993
L. Warren Douglas, *Cannon's Orb*, 1994
Marian Hughes, *Initiation*, 1995
Rosemary Kirstein, *The Steerswoman*, 1989
Elizabeth Moon, *Remnant Population*, 1996

**4120**

**LARRY NIVEN**
**JERRY POURNELLE**, Co-Author
**MICHAEL FLYNN**, Co-Author

### Fallen Angels

(New York: Baen Books, 1991)

**Story type:** Science Fiction (Political; Disaster)
**Major character(s):** Alex MacLoed, Hero, Pilot (angel); Sherrine Hartley, Computer Expert (science fiction fan); Will Waxman, Doctor (science fiction fan)
**Time period(s):** 2010s
**Locale(s):** Minneapolis, Minnesota; Chicago, Illinois; Edwards Air Force Base, California

**Summary:** Cleaning the air has allowed the ice to start spreading south. The uneducated masses have been misled by the anti-technological Greens to believe that missing nitrogen, stolen by Mir and Freedom, now space colonies, is the cause. When two astronauts are shot down on the North Dakota glacier, their only hope for rescue is from the Minicon, a World Science Fiction convention being held in Minneapolis, full of technophiles enamoured with space travel and angels, the people who managed to colonize in orbit.

**Other books you might like:**
Robert Asprin, *Another Fine Myth*, 1978

Emma Bull, *War for the Oaks*, 1987
Michael Flynn, *In the Country of the Blind*, 1990
Sharyn McCrumb, *Bimbos of the Death Sun*, 1987
Sharyn McCrumb, *Zombies of the Gene Pool*, 1992
Steve Perry, *The Man Who Never Missed*, 1985
Nick Pollotta, *Illegal Aliens*, 1989
    Phil Foglio, co-author
Harry Turtledove, *Earthgrip*, 1991

**4121**

**LARRY NIVEN**

### Flatlander

(New York: Ballantine Del Rey, 1995)

**Story type:** Science Fiction (Mystery; Collection)
**Series:** Known Space
**Major character(s):** Gil "the Arm" Hamilton, Detective—Police (ARM)
**Time period(s):** 22nd century
**Locale(s):** Earth; Montenegro

**Summary:** Omnibus edition of Gil the Arm stories including *The Long Arm of Gil Hamilton* (1976), *The Patchwork Girl* (1980), and one original, "The Woman in Del Rey Crater." In a future where criminals murder people for body parts to be used in transplant surgery, Gil Hamilton investigates cases involving organleggers and tries to keep people he cares about from becoming nothing but body parts.

**Other books you might like:**
Isaac Asimov, *The Caves of Steel*, 1954
Greg Bear, *Queen of Angels*, 1990
Alfred Bester, *The Demolished Man*, 1953
Richard Bowker, *Dover Beach*, 1987
Barney Cohen, *Blood on the Moon*, 1984
Alan Dean Foster, *Cyber Way*, 1990
Lee Killough, *Dragon's Teeth*, 1990
Jack Vance, *Trullion: Alastor 2262*, 1973

**4122**

**LARRY NIVEN**
**JERRY POURNELLE**, Co-Author

### The Gripping Hand

(New York: Pocket, 1993)

**Story type:** Science Fiction (First Contact; Hard Science Fiction)
**Major character(s):** Horace Hussein Bury, Businessman (Imperial Trader and Magnate); Kevin Renner, Military Personnel (Navy Reserve Captain), Pilot (spaceship); Eudoxus, Alien (Motie Mediator)
**Time period(s):** 31st century (3040s)
**Locale(s):** Murchison's Eye, Planet—Imaginary; *Sinbad*, Spaceship; New Calidonia, Planet—Imaginary

**Summary:** Obsessed by the thought that the Moties, a very intelligent, prolific species, might get out of their confinement into human space, Horace Hussein Bury finds possible evidence of Moties. The Blaines continue to keep Charlie, a Motie Mediator, alive as companion for their children while the Blaine Institute finds the solution to the Moties' problem of birth control. Bury realizes that the protostar in the Coal Sack Nebula will ignite much sooner than the 1000 years expected, allowing Moties other exits from their system not controlled by the Crazy Eddie fleet. Sequel to *The Mote in God's Eye*.

**Other books you might like:**
Roger MacBride Allen, *The Ring of Charon*, 1990
Stephen Baxter, *Raft*, 1992
David Brin, *Startide Rising*, 1983
Octavia E. Butler, *Dawn*, 1987
C.J. Cherryh, *The Pride of Chanur*, 1982
Sheri S. Tepper, *Grass*, 1989
Vernor Vinge, *A Fire upon the Deep*, 1992

**4123**

**LARRY NIVEN**
**JERRY POURNELLE**, Co-Author
**POUL ANDERSON**, Co-Author

### Man-Kzin Wars III
(New York: Baen, 1990)

**Story type:** Science Fiction (Anthology)
**Series:** Man-Kzin Wars
**Time period(s):** Indeterminate

**Summary:** This collection of three stories, all set in Larry Niven's Known Space Series (1966- ) universe, includes Larry Niven's "Madness Has Its Place," J.E. Pournelle and S.M. Stirling's "The Asteroid Queen," and Poul Anderson's "Inconstant Star."

**Other books you might like:**
David Brin, *Startide Rising*, 1983
Octavia E. Butler, *Dawn*, 1987
Robert L. Forward, *Dragon's Egg*, 1980
Robert A. Heinlein, *The Past through Tomorrow*, 1967
Alis A. Rasmussen, *A Passage of Stars*, 1990
Alis A. Rasmussen, *The Price of Ransom*, 1990
Alis A. Rasmussen, *Revolution's Shore*, 1990
Cordwainer Smith, *The Best of Cordwainer Smith*, 1975
John Varley, *Blue Champagne*, 1986
John Varley, *The Persistence of Vision*, 1978

**4124**

**LARRY NIVEN**, Editor

### Man-Kzin Wars IV
(New York: Baen, 1991)

**Story type:** Science Fiction (Anthology; Military)
**Series:** Man-Kzin Wars
**Major character(s):** Short-Son "Eater-of-Grass" of Chiirr-Nig, Alien (Kzin); Long-Reach, Slave, Alien (Jotok); Lawrence "Fixer-of-Weapons" Halloran, Spy (human), Telepath (projective)
**Time period(s):** 24th century; 25th century
**Locale(s):** Wunderland, Planet—Imaginary; Spaceship

**Summary:** Set in Larry Niven's *Known Space* universe, this anthology contains two stories by Donald Kingsbury, Greg Bear and S.M. Stirling. In Donald Kingsbury's novel-length *The Survivor*, the cowardly Eater-of-Grass learns how to bond and train Jotoki, becoming Trainer-of-Slaves. As he travels closer to Monkey Home trying to join a fleet attacking Earth, he intercepts a human ship attacking the Kzin near Alpha Centauri B, and captures both a revolutionary spaceship drive and Nora Argamentine whom he biologically manipulates into being more like a Kzin female. In Greg Bear and S.M. Stirling's novella, *The Man Who Would Be Kzin*, Lawrence Halloran, finding little use for his telepathic ability among human culture, enlists in the United Nations Space Navy, infiltrates a Kzin battleship, then turns heroic saboteur.

**Other books you might like:**
Poul Anderson, *Inconstant Star*, 1991
Christopher Anvil, *Pandora's Planet*, 1972
David Brin, *Startide Rising*, 1983
C.S. Friedman, *The Madness Season*, 1990
Diana G. Gallagher, *The Alien Dark*, 1990
Dean Ing, *Cathouse*, 1991
Jerry Pournelle, *The Children's Hour*, 1991
   S.M. Stirling, co-author
David Alexander Smith, *Homecoming*, 1989

**4125**

**LARRY NIVEN**, Editor

### Man-Kzin Wars V
(New York: Baen, 1992)

**Story type:** Science Fiction (Anthology; Military)
**Series:** Man-Kzin Wars
**Major character(s):** Jonah Matthieson, Pilot, Military Personnel (UN Space Navy, retired); Spots-Son of Chotrz-Shaa, Alien (Kzin), Military Personnel (retired); Durvash, Time Traveler, Alien (Tnuctipun)
**Time period(s):** Indeterminate Future
**Locale(s):** Wunderland, Planet—Imaginary; Beanstalk, Planet—Imaginary

**Summary:** Contains two stories set in Larry Niven's *Known Space* universe. Jerry Pournelle's collaboration with S. M. Stirling, "In the Hall of the Mountain King," features former human and Kzinti enemies cooperating in a salvage operation which recovers a Tnuctipun spy ship hidden for three billion years. In Thomas T. Thomas' story, "Hey Diddle Diddle," crews of both human and Kzinti spaceships hustle to find a Thrinturn artifact after a Bandersnatch damages each ship.

**Other books you might like:**
Poul Anderson, *Inconstant Star*, 1991
Barry B. Longyear, *Enemy Mine*, 1985
   David Gerrold, novelization co-author
Dean Ing, *Cathouse*, 1991
Jerry Pournelle, *The Children's Hour*, 1991
   S. M. Stirling, co-author

**4126**

**LARRY NIVEN**

### N-Space
(New York: Tor, 1990)

**Story type:** Science Fiction (Collection)
**Time period(s):** Indeterminate Future

**Summary:** This book is a retrospective of Larry Niven's first 25 years as a science fiction writer. It includes samples from his longer works including *World of Ptavvs* (1966), *A Gift From Earth* (1968), *Ringworld* (1970), *Protector* (1973) and *The Mote in God's Eye* (1974) (Jerry Pournelle, co-author), with a large sprinkling of short stories, introductions, essays and reminiscences.

**Other books you might like:**
Roger MacBride Allen, *The Ring of Charon*, 1990
David Brin, *Earth*, 1990
Octavia E. Butler, *Dawn*, 1987
Robert L. Forward, *Rocheworld*, 1990
Alis A. Rasmussen, *A Passage of Stars*, 1990

Cordwainer Smith, *The Best of Cordwainer Smith*, 1975
pseudonym of Paul Myron Anthony Linebarger
John Varley, *Blue Champagne*, 1986
John Varley, *The Persistence of Vision*, 1978

## 4127

### LARRY NIVEN

## *Playgrounds of the Mind*
(New York: Tor, 1991)

**Story type:** Science Fiction (Collection)

**Summary:** Spanning the second half of Niven's career to date, this companion volume to *N-Space* contains 49 listed entries plus anecdotal interludes and brief excerpts of fiction between listed works. The fiction includes longer short stories and 7 vignettes. Listed as works in progress are excerpts from *Fallen Angels* (1991), *The California Voodoo Game* (1992) and the half-completed *The Mote Around Murcheson's Eye*, a collaborative sequel to *The Mote in God's Eye* (1974). Nonfiction includes a letter, a memoir, a recipe for Irish Coffee that serves 200, memories of World Science Fiction conventions, Niven's view of critics and reviews and an article on how to build XXXL-size environments.

**Other books you might like:**
Groff Conklin, *The Best of Science Fiction*, 1946
    editor
Michael Flynn, *The Nanotech Chronicles*, 1991
Alan Dean Foster, *With Friends Like These...*, 1977
Raymond J. Healy, *Adventures in Time and Space*, 1946
    J. Francis McComas, co-editor
Robert A. Heinlein, *The Past through Tomorrow*, 1967
Cordwainer Smith, *The Best of Cordwainer Smith*, 1975
Marc Stiegler, *The Gentle Seduction*, 1990
John Varley, *Blue Champagne*, 1986
John Varley, *The Persistence of Vision*, 1978

## 4128

### LARRY NIVEN

## *The Ringworld Throne*
(New York: Ballantine Del Rey, 1996)

**Story type:** Science Fiction (Political; First Contact)
**Series:** Ringworld
**Major character(s):** Louis Wu, Adventurer; Chmeee, Alien (Kzin); The Hindmost, Alien (Puppeteer)
**Time period(s):** 29th century
**Locale(s):** Ringworld, Planet—Imaginary

**Summary:** Having saved Ringworld from destruction, Louis Wu must once again find a solution to complications from the interactions of the many races living there. Ringworld needs a leader due not only to an overabundance of vampires and unpredicatable attacks on incoming ships, but also to Protectors encroaching on species not in their care and on each other.

**Other books you might like:**
Eleanor Arnason, *Ring of Swords*, 1993
David Brin, *Brightness Reef*, 1995
C.J. Cherryh, *Invader*, 1995
A.C. Crispin, *Silent Dances*, 1990
    Kathleen O'Malley, co-author
George Turner, *Genetic Soldier*, 1994

## 4129

### GARTH NIX

## *Sabriel*
(New York: HarperCollins, 1996)

**Story type:** Fantasy (Young Adult; Magic Conflict)
**Major character(s):** Sabriel, Magician, Teenager; Mogget, Spirit, Animal (cat); Touchstone, Magician
**Time period(s):** Indeterminate
**Locale(s):** The Old Kingdom, Fictional Country; Ancelstierre, Fictional Country

**Summary:** When the magician Abhorsen becomes ensnared in the Land of the Dead, his daughter, Sabriel, must travel into the Old Kingdom, land of free magic, to save him.

**Other books you might like:**
Lois McMaster Bujold, *The Spirit Ring*, 1992
Kara Dalkey, *Little Sister*, 1996
Laurell K. Hamilton, *Nightseer*, 1992
Holly Lisle, *Minerva Wakes*, 1994
Meredith Ann Pierce, *The Pearl of the Soul of the World*, 1990
Nancy Springer, *The Friendship Song*, 1992

## 4130

### GARTH NIX

## *Shade's Children*
(New York: HarperCollins, 1997)

**Story type:** Science Fiction (Psychic Powers; Invasion of Earth)
**Major character(s):** Robert "Shade" Ingman, Disembodied Personality; Ella, Psychic (esper), Teenager; Gold-eye, Child, Psychic (esper)
**Time period(s):** Indeterminate Future
**Locale(s):** Earth

**Summary:** In the 15 years since the Change, when the adults disappeared and the children under 14 years old were herded into Dormitories, Shade has rescued and trained many escaped children. The Change brought the Overlords, moved Shade from his body to a computer and gave many children psychic powers. The Overlords use the brains harvested from 14-year-olds in their fighting creatures. Ella, Gold-eye and their teammates work with the disintegrating Shade to vanquish the Overlords.

**Other books you might like:**
Jean Mark Gawron, *Dream of Glass*, 1993
James P. Hogan, *The Multiplex Man*, 1992
Gwyneth Jones, *White Queen*, 1993
George R.R. Martin, *The Wild Cards Series*, 1987-1995
Sheri S. Tepper, *A Plague of Angels*, 1993

## 4131

### WILLIAM F. NOLAN, Editor
### MARTIN H. GREENBERG, Co-Editor

## *The Bradbury Chronicles: Stories in Honor of Ray Bradbury*
(New York: Roc, 1991)

**Story type:** Fantasy (Anthology)

**Summary:** 22 stories, each introduced by William F. Nolan, an introduction, a brief appreciation by Isaac Asimov, and an afterword by Ray Bradbury. The stories include "May 2000: The Tombstones,'' by James Kisner, a sequel to ''Mars is Heaven!''; Ed Gorman's ''The Wind From Midnight,'' a sequel to ''The Dwarf''; and F. Paul Wilson's ''The November Game,'' a sequel to ''The October Game.'' ''The Inheritance,'' by Bruce Francis, is a sequel to ''The Lake.'' Gregory Benford's ''Centigrade 233'' reflects *Fahrenheit 451*, and Orson Scott Card's ''Feed the Baby of Love'' shows us an aging Douglas Spaulding of *Dandelion Wine*. Other authors include Douglas Beaumont, Ray Bradbury, Richard Matheson, Chad Oliver and Robert Sheckley.

**Other books you might like:**
Robert Bloch, *The Selected Stories of Robert Bloch*, 1988
Robert Bloch, *The Star Stalker*, 1968
Ray Bradbury, *Dandelion Wine*, 1957
Ray Bradbury, *A Graveyard for Lunatics*, 1990
Ray Bradbury, *The Illustrated Man*, 1953
Ray Bradbury, *Something Wicked This Way Comes*, 1962
Ray Bradbury, *The Stories of Ray Bradbury*, 1980
Ray Bradbury, *The Toynbee Convector*, 1989
Ellen Datlow, *The Year's Best Fantasy: First Annual Collection*, 1990
    Terri Windling, co-editor
Kristine Kathryn Rusch, *Pulphouse, Issue 9: Dark Fantasy*, 1990
    editor
Theodore Sturgeon, *A Touch of Sturgeon*, 1987

## 4132

**WILLIAM F. NOLAN**

### Night Shapes: Excursions into Terror

(Baltimore: CD Publications, 1995)

**Story type:** Horror (Collection)

**Summary:** This compilation's 25 selections span 25 years of Nolan's career as a writer of horror, suspense, and science fiction. Stories include the ghost tale ''Major Preview Here Tonight''; the serial killer stories ''Him, Her, Them,'' ''The Visit,'' and ''Cure''; the psychological suspense tales ''My Name Is Dolly,'' ''Special Treat,'' and ''The Big Man''; monster stories that include ''On 42nd St.'' and ''The Halloween Man''; and stories told from the perspective of non-human narrators that include ''Gobble! Gobble!'' from ''Narrow House.''

**Other books you might like:**
Charles Beaumont, *Selected Stories*, 1988
Ray Bradbury, *The Stories of Ray Bradbury*, 1980
Richard Matheson, *Richard Matheson: Collected Stories*, 1989

## 4133

**WILLIAM F. NOLAN**, Editor
**MARTIN H. GREENBERG**, Co-Editor

### Urban Horrors

(Arlington Heights, Illinois: Dark Harvest, 1990)

**Story type:** Horror (Anthology)

**Summary:** This intelligently edited reprint anthology of primarily non-supernatural horror stories in urban settings during the last half of the 20th century includes such classics as Fritz Leiber's ''Smoke Ghost'' and Dennis Etchison's ''Talking in the Dark'' as well as unexpected stories by such authors as John Cheever, Alice Glaser, and Joyce Carol Oates.

**Other books you might like:**
Christopher Fowler, *City Jitters*, 1986

## 4134

**JEFF NOON**

### Automated Alice

(New York: Crown, 1996)

**Story type:** Fantasy (Light Fantasy; Time Travel)
**Major character(s):** Alice Pleasance Liddell, Child, Time Traveler; Celia, Robot
**Time period(s):** 1860s (1860); 1990s (1998)
**Locale(s):** Manchester, England

**Summary:** Alice chases a parrot into the clock and finds herself in a strange future, unable to return home until she locates a dozen jigsaw puzzle pieces. An automated version of Alice helps Alice navigate the perils of murder accusations, Civil Serpents, mutant hybrids, computermites, chaos theory, quantum physics and Vurt feathers.

**Other books you might like:**
Gilbert Adair, *Alice through the Needle's Eye: The Further Adventures of Lewis Carroll's ''Alice''*, 1985
Lewis Carroll, *Alice's Adventures in Wonderland*, 1865
Lewis Carroll, *Through the Looking Glass and What Alice Found There*, 1872
Randall Garrett, *Takeoff!*, 1979
Margaret Weis, *Fantastic Alice*, 1995
    editor

## 4135

**JEFF NOON**

### Pollen

(New York: Crown, 1996)

**Story type:** Science Fiction (Literary; Cyberpunk)
**Major character(s):** Sibyl Jones, Detective—Police, Telepath; Coyote, Genetically Altered Being, Taxi Driver; Boda, Genetically Altered Being, Taxi Driver
**Time period(s):** Indeterminate Future
**Locale(s):** Manchester, England; Vurt, Alternate Earth

**Summary:** Manchester Police Investigator Sibyl Jones hunts for a killer while nearly everyone around her suffers massive hayfever attacks from an astronomically high pollen count. She learns that a ''Vurtual,'' a creature from the alternate dream-world, Vurt, has unleashed a virulent strain of pollen in a plot to prepare the real world for colonization by Vurtuals. A loose sequel to *Vurt*.

**Other books you might like:**
J.G. Ballard, *The Crystal World*, 1966
Pat Cadigan, *Synners*, 1991
William Gibson, *Neuromancer*, 1984
Jonathan Lethem, *Amnesia Moon*, 1995
Kim Newman, *The Night Mayor*, 1990

## 4136

**JEFF NOON**

### Vurt

(New York: Crown, 1995)

**Story type:** Science Fiction (Cyberpunk; Adventure)
**Major character(s):** Stephen ''Scribble'', Addict (Vurt), Fugitive; Karli Dog, Robot (dog); Game Cat, Computer Expert, Editor
**Time period(s):** Indeterminate Future
**Locale(s):** Manchester, England

**Summary:** Scribble loses his beloved sister, Desdemona, in an English Voodoo garden hidden in a Curious Yellow feather, when the Vurt Thing-from-Outer-Space replaces her. Scribble carries and protects the amoeboid, illegal, live-drug Thing with hopes of exchanging it for Desdemona. Bitten by a dream snake, Scribble carries Vurt inside all the time, adding desperation to his adventures in the Battle, a neighborhood of broken glass, and in Turdsville, the home of the Robodogs. First novel and winner of the Arthur C. Clarke Award in Britain, where it was published in 1993.

**Other books you might like:**
Pat Cadigan, *Mindplayers*, 1987
Jean Mark Gawron, *Dream of Glass*, 1993
James P. Hogan, *The Multiplex Man*, 1992
Gwyneth Jones, *White Queen*, 1993
Dan Simmons, *Hyperion*, 1989
Cordwainer Smith, *The Rediscovery of Man*, 1993
Michael Swanwick, *The Iron Dragon's Daughter*, 1994

## 4137

### LISANNE NORMAN

## Fire Margins

(New York: DAW, 1996)

**Story type:** Science Fiction (Political; Psychic Powers)
**Series:** Sholan Alliance
**Major character(s):** Carrie, Psychic; Kusac, Psychic, Alien (Sholan); Kaid, Military Personnel, Alien (Sholan)
**Time period(s):** Indeterminate Future
**Locale(s):** Shola, Planet—Imaginary

**Summary:** Factions on Shola jockey for control of the mixed species mated pairs as Carrie recovers from her wounds and her miscarriage. Seeking to establish a new group outside the existing guilds, Kusac and Carrie join with Kaid for the ancient rituals to seek Vartra and in so doing learn more about Shola's past. Meanwhile, humans and Sholans cooperate in defense efforts against the Valtegans, a religious fanatic persecutes telepaths, and Vanna gives birth to her child, the first of the new species.

**Other books you might like:**
C.J. Cherryh, *Chanur's Homecoming*, 1986
Diane Duane, *Spock's World*, 1988
Mary Gentle, *Golden Witchbreed*, 1983
Gayle Greeno, *Exiles' Return*, 1995
Anne McCaffrey, *Crisis on Doona*, 1992
    Jody Lynn Nye, co-author

## 4138

### LISANNE NORMAN

## Fortune's Wheel

(New York: DAW, 1995)

**Story type:** Science Fiction (Psychic Powers; Political)
**Series:** Sholan Alliance
**Major character(s):** Carrie, Psychic; Kusac, Psychic, Alien (Sholan)
**Time period(s):** Indeterminate Future
**Locale(s):** *Khalossa*, Spaceship; Shola, Planet—Imaginary

**Summary:** Brought together by their telepathic powers and bound by love, Carrie and Kusac face difficulties adjusting to their new relationship. As they return to Shola aboard the *Khalossa*, Human and Sholan representatives attempt to forge an alliance against the warlike Valtegans, but opposing factions on both sides try to use the pair for their own ends.

**Other books you might like:**
Margaret Wander Bonanno, *Dwellers in the Crucible*, 1985
C.J. Cherryh, *Foreigner*, 1994
Kate Elliott, *An Earthly Crown*, 1993
Anne McCaffrey, *Crisis on Doona*, 1992
    Jody Lynn Nye, co-author
Andre Norton, *Catseye*, 1961
Vernor Vinge, *A Fire upon the Deep*, 1992

## 4139

### LISANNE NORMAN

## Razor's Edge

(New York: DAW, 1997)

**Story type:** Science Fiction (Psychic Powers; Adventure)
**Series:** Sholan Alliance
**Major character(s):** Carrie, Psychic; Kusac, Psychic, Alien (Sholan); Kaid, Military Personnel, Alien (Sholan)
**Time period(s):** Indeterminate Future
**Locale(s):** Shola, Planet—Imaginary; Jalna, Planet—Imaginary

**Summary:** As soon as she recovers from giving birth to her daughter, Carrie joins Kusac and Kaid in preparing to rescue the team of Sholans and Humans now trapped on Jalna. The three of them, like the other sets of Human-Sholan partners, struggle with the sexual and psychic strains of their new relationships, thus complicating the rescue attempt.

**Other books you might like:**
C.J. Cherryh, *The Pride of Chanur*, 1982
Philip Jose Farmer, *Strange Relations*, 1960
Michael Jan Friedman, *Shadows on the Sun*, 1993
Mary Gentle, *Golden Witchbreed*, 1983
Robert A. Heinlein, *Stranger in a Strange Land*, 1991 revised
Anne McCaffrey, *The Rowan*, 1990
James H. Schmitz, *The Universe Against Her*, 1964

## 4140

### LISANNE NORMAN

## Turning Point

(New York: DAW, 1993)

**Story type:** Science Fiction (First Contact; Psychic Powers)
**Series:** Sholan Alliance
**Major character(s):** Carrie, Psychic; Kusac, Psychic (intelligence officer), Alien (feline)
**Time period(s):** Indeterminate Future
**Locale(s):** Keiss, Planet—Imaginary

**Summary:** When Carrie's twin sister is killed by invading reptilian warriors, their telepathic link almost causes Carrie to die of trauma; but she is contacted by Kusac, a member of the feline Sholan race, whose spaceship has been wrecked. The only other telepath Carrie has encountered, Kusac cares for and comforts her and they develop a relationship in spite of their immense cultural differences. If their peoples can also overcome their prejudices, they can become valuable allies as well.

**Other books you might like:**
Eleanor Arnason, *Ring of Swords*, 1993
Marion Zimmer Bradley, *The World Wreckers*, 1971
C.J. Cherryh, *Serpent's Reach*, 1980
Paula E. Downing, *Rinn's Star*, 1990
Janet Kagan, *Hellspark*, 1988

Rebecca Ore, *Being Alien*, 1989

**4141**

### AMYAS NORTHCOTE

## *In Ghostly Company*

(Ashcroft, British Columbia: Ash-Tree Press, 1997)

**Story type:** Horror (Collection)

**Summary:** Thirteen quiet tales of ghosts and supernatural horrors, ranging in theme from ''Brickett Bottom,'' an eerie tale of a young girl lured into the past; and ''Mr. Kershaw and Mr. Wilcox,'' a weird invention story. First published in 1921. With an introduction by Richard Dalby and a bibliographic tailpiece by Jack Adrian.

**Other books you might like:**
E.F. Benson, *The Collected Ghost Stories of E.F. Benson*, 1992
M.P. Dare, *Unholy Relics*, 1947
August Derleth, *Someone in the Dark*, 1941
L.P. Hartley, *The Travelling Grave and Other Stories*, 1948
William Fryer Harvey, *The Beast with Five Fingers and Other Stories*, 1928
H. Russell Wakefield, *Imagine a Man in a Box*, 1931

**4142**

### ANDRE NORTON

## *Brother to Shadows*

(New York: Morrow AvoNova, 1993)

**Story type:** Science Fiction (Adventure; Mystical)
**Series:** Forerunner
**Major character(s):** Jofre, Outcast, Martial Arts Expert; Zurzal, Alien (Zacathan), Historian; Taynad Jewelbright, Bodyguard, Martial Arts Expert
**Time period(s):** Indeterminate Future
**Locale(s):** Asborgan, Planet—Imaginary; Tssek, Planet—Imaginary; Lochan, Planet—Imaginary

**Summary:** An off-world foundling raised by the Brotherhood of Shadows, now ready for his first Oathed assignment, Jofre loses his standing when the Lair Stone dies and the Lair readies for abandonment. Hated by the Shagga Priest of the Lair, Jofre lacks support when the Master dies. Setting off to find the spaceport, Jofre shelters in an abandoned lair where he picks up a small stone which retains enough power to utilize while he acts as bodyguard to Zurzal, who attempts to use Forerunner technology to find a Forerunner information storehouse.

**Other books you might like:**
Steven Brust, *Jhereg*, 1983
Emily Devenport, *Shade*, 1992
Gordon R. Dickson, *Dorsai!*, 1976
Steve Miller, *Agent of Change*, 1988
    Sharon Lee, co-author
Steve Miller, *Carpe Diem*, 1989
    Sharon Lee, co-author
Steve Miller, *Conflict of Honors*, 1988
    Sharon Lee, co-author
Steve Perry, *The 97th Step*, 1989

**4143**

### ANDRE NORTON, Editor
### MARTIN H. GREENBERG, Co-Editor

## *Catfantastic II*

(New York: DAW, 1991)

**Story type:** Fantasy (Anthology)
**Series:** Catfantastic

**Summary:** This volume contains a brief introduction plus 18 original stories featuring cats and having fantasy themes or settings. Among the authors are Claire Bell, Elizabeth H. Boyer, P.M. Griffin, Ardath Mayhar, Elizabeth Moon, Andre Norton, Elizabeth Ann Scarborough, Susan Shwartz and Nancy Springer. One story, ''Quest of Souls,'' is a collaboration between Ann Miller and Karen Rigley.

**Other books you might like:**
Clare Bell, *Clan Ground*, 1984
Clare Bell, *Ratha and Thistle-Chaser*, 1990
Clare Bell, *Ratha's Creature*, 1983
C.J. Cherryh, *The Pride of Chanur*, 1982
Alan Dean Foster, *Cat-A-Lyst*, 1991
Randall Garrett, *The Gandalara Cycle I*, 1986
    Vicki Ann Heydron, co-author
Robert A. Heinlein, *The Door into Summer*, 1957
Michael Peak, *Cat House*, 1989
Michael Peak, *Catamount*, 1992
Marti Steussy, *Dreams of Dawn*, 1988
Marti Steussy, *Forest of the Night*, 1987
Tad Williams, *Tailchaser's Song*, 1985

**4144**

### ANDRE NORTON, Editor
### MARTIN H. GREENBERG, Co-Editor

## *Catfantastic III*

(New York: DAW, 1994)

**Story type:** Fantasy (Anthology)
**Series:** Catfantastic

**Summary:** Contains a brief introduction by Norton and 20 original stories featuring cats and fantasy themes in diverse settings. Authors include Claire Bell, Charles de Lint, Charles L. Fontenay, P.M. Griffin, Mercedes Lackey, Ardath Mayhar, Andre Norton, Elizabeth Ann Scarborough, Mary H. Schaub and Susan Schwartz.

**Other books you might like:**
Clare Bell, *Ratha's Creature*, 1983
Jack Dann, *Magicats!*, 1984
    Gardner Dozois, co-editor
Jack Dann, *Magicats II*, 1991
    Gardner Dozois, co-editor
Bill Fawcett, *Cats in Space and Other Places*, 1990
    editor
Mark E. Rogers, *The Adventures of Samurai Cat*, 1984
John Richard Stephens, *The Enchanted Cat*, 1990
    editor
John Richard Stephens, *Mysterious Cat Stories*, 1993
    Kim Smith, co-editor
Tad Williams, *Tailchaser's Song*, 1985

## 4145

**ANDRE NORTON**, Editor
**MARTIN H. GREENBERG**, Co-Editor

### Catfantastic IV

(New York: DAW, 1996)

**Story type:** Fantasy (Anthology)
**Series:** Catfantastic

**Summary:** This volume contains 18 original stories, an introduction by Andre Norton, and a brief biographical sketch of each author. Authors include Jayge Carr, Charles L. Fontenay, P.M. Griffin, Mercedes Lackey, Jane M. Lindskold, Lyn McConchie, Andre Norton, and Elizabeth Ann Scarborough. The stories deal with cat pals, cat helpers, a cat music critic, and cat adventurers.

**Other books you might like:**
Clare Bell, *Ratha's Creature*, 1983
Jack Dann, *Magicats!*, 1984
    Gardner Dozois, co-editor
Bill Fawcett, *Cats in Space and Other Places*, 1990
    editor
John Richard Stephens, *The Enchanted Cat*, 1990
    editor
L.A. Taylor, *Cat's Paw*, 1995
Tad Williams, *Tailchaser's Song*, 1985

## 4146

**ANDRE NORTON**
**LYN MCCONCHIE**, Co-Author

### Ciara's Song

(New York: Aspect, 1998)

**Series:** Witch World
**Major character(s):** Ciara, Noblewoman; Trovagh, Noblewoman
**Time period(s):** Indeterminate
**Locale(s):** Aiskeep, Fictional City

**Summary:** The Duke of Kars issues an edict that anyone with witch blood in his or her ancestry should be executed. Following the murder of her parents, Ciara shelters in the stronghold of Lord Tarnoor and eventually marries his son. The mindless hatred of witches does not dim with time, however, and years later the kingdom erupts into open warfare, menacing them even in their stronghold.

**Other books you might like:**
Margaret Ball, *Changeweaver*, 1993
Marion Zimmer Bradley, *The Fall of Atlantis*, 1987
C.J. Cherryh, *The Tree of Swords and Jewels*, 1983
Mercedes Lackey, *The Eagle and the Nightingales*, 1995
Laurie J. Marks, *Dancing Jack*, 1993

## 4147

**ANDRE NORTON**

### Dare to Go A-Hunting

(New York: Tor Books, 1990)

**Story type:** Science Fiction (Fantasy)
**Major character(s):** Farree, Alien; Krip Vorlund, Spaceman
**Time period(s):** Indeterminate Future
**Locale(s):** Planet—Imaginary

**Summary:** The waif Farree discovers evidence that other winged intelligent beings like himself exist and, with Free Trader Krip Vorlund, the historian Zoor, and the sorceress Maelen, sets out across the galaxy to find them. Throughout their journey they must dodge the evil Guild, which is out to capture Farree. Sequel to *Flight in Yiktor*.

**Other books you might like:**
Clare Bell, *People of the Sky*, 1989
Marcia J. Bennett, *Seeking the Dream Brother*, 1989
Marion Zimmer Bradley, *Darkover Landfall*, 1972
Mary Caraker, *Seven Worlds*, 1986
Mary Caraker, *The Snows of Jaspre*, 1989
Rosemary Kirstein, *The Steerswoman*, 1989

## 4148

**ANDRE NORTON**
**SHERWOOD SMITH**, Co-Author

### Derelict for Trade

(New York: Tor, 1997)

**Story type:** Science Fiction (Adventure)
**Series:** Solar Queen
**Major character(s):** Dane Thorson, Spaceman, Trader; Rael Cofort, Spacewoman, Trader; Tooe, Alien (Rigellian)
**Time period(s):** Indeterminate Future
**Locale(s):** Harmony, Space Station

**Summary:** At the edge of human explored space, the crew of the *Solar Queen* find a derelict. Hoping to salvage it and turn a profit, the crew head for Harmony, run by humans and two alien races. Trying to stake their claim, they meet with interminable delays and several mysterious attacks, subsequently discovering a hijacking scheme managed by a rogue Terran who controls all communications in and out of the Habitat.

**Other books you might like:**
Poul Anderson, *Trader to the Stars*, 1964
Robert Asprin, *Phule's Paradise*, 1992
Lois McMaster Bujold, *Ethan of Athos*, 1986
C.J. Cherryh, *Rimrunners*, 1989
Paula E. Downing, *Flare Star*, 1992
Debra Doyle, *Starpilot's Grave*, 1993
    James D. Macdonald, co-author
Sherwood Smith, *The Phoenix in Flight*, 1993
    Dave Trowbridge, co-author
S.M. Stirling, *The Ship Avenged*, 1997

## 4149

**ANDRE NORTON**
**MERCEDES LACKEY**, Co-Author

### The Elvenbane

(New York: Tor, 1991)

**Story type:** Fantasy (Magic Conflict; Adventure)
**Series:** Halfblood Chronicles
**Major character(s):** Shana, Orphan; Alara, Shaman, Mythical Creature (dragon)
**Time period(s):** Indeterminate Future
**Locale(s):** Earth

**Summary:** When elves immigrated to Earth, they assumed power and enslaved humanity. Born to a mother dying in the desert, half-breed Shana finds a foster mother in Alara. If she survives, Shana may grow into the one prophesied to change Earth's new balance of power.

**Other books you might like:**
Emma Bull, *War for the Oaks*, 1987
Mercedes Lackey, *Bardic Voices*, 1991
Ursula K. Le Guin, *The Farthest Shore*, 1972
Ursula K. Le Guin, *Tehanu: The Last Book of Earthsea*, 1990
Ursula K. Le Guin, *The Tombs of Atuan*, 1971
Ursula K. Le Guin, *A Wizard of Earthsea*, 1968
Anne McCaffrey, *Dragonflight*, 1968
Anne McCaffrey, *Dragonquest*, 1971
Anne McCaffrey, *The White Dragon*, 1978
Joel Rosenberg, *The Road to Ehvenor*, 1991
Will Shetterly, *Elsewhere*, 1991

## 4150

### ANDRE NORTON
### MERCEDES LACKEY, Co-Author

## *Elvenblood*

(New York: Tor, 1995)

**Story type:** Fantasy (Political; Adventure)
**Series:** Halfblood Chronicles
**Major character(s):** Lashana "Shana", Hero, Leader; Sheyrena "Rena" an Treves, Mythical Creature (elf), Fiance(e); Keman, Mythical Creature (dragon), Wizard
**Time period(s):** Indeterminate Future
**Locale(s):** Earth

**Summary:** Fleeing unacceptible fates at the hands of their father, Rena and her brother find their way to the Iron People, who are protected from magic by their ubiquitous iron jewelry. When Shana attempts to establish trade and allies for her new colony of wizards and dragons, her exploration also leads to the Iron People, who imprison her with the same iron jewelry that protects them. Among the Iron People, both Rena and Shana find unexpected help for their problems. Second volume in the series.

**Other books you might like:**
J.V. Jones, *The Baker's Boy*, 1995
Marjorie Bradley Kellogg, *The Book of Earth*, 1995
Mercedes Lackey, *Arrows of the Queen*, 1987
Mercedes Lackey, *The Lark and the Wren*, 1991
Ursula K. Le Guin, *The Tombs of Atuan*, 1971
L.E. Modesitt Jr., *The Towers of the Sunset*, 1992
Elizabeth Moon, *Liar's Oath*, 1992

## 4151

### ANDRE NORTON
### P.M. GRIFFIN, Co-Author

## *Firehand*

(New York: Tor, 1994)

**Story type:** Science Fiction (Time Travel; Adventure)
**Series:** Time Traders
**Major character(s):** Ross Murdoch, Time Traveler; Eveleen Riordan, Time Traveler; Luroc I Loran, Ruler (Ton of Sapphirehold), Warrior
**Time period(s):** Indeterminate Past
**Locale(s):** Dominion of Virgin, Planet—Imaginary; Hawaika, Planet—Imaginary

**Summary:** Rescued from Hawaika's past and sent into that of the Dominion of Virgin as its civilization suddenly vanished during

negotiations with Terra, Ross, Eveleen and Gordon Ashe must act as mercenaries to prevent Zanthor I Yoroc from conquering Dominion for the Baldies. The team works under Luroc I Loran of Sapphirehold to stave off Zanthor.

**Other books you might like:**
Poul Anderson, *The Day of Their Return*, 1975
Leigh Brackett, *The Sword of Rhiannon*, 1953
Richard Cowper, *The Road to Corlay*, 1979
Leo Frankowski, *The Cross-Time Engineer*, 1986
Crawford Kilian, *The Empire of Time*, 1978

## 4152

### ANDRE NORTON
### P.M. GRIFFIN, Co-Author
### MARY SCHAUB, Co-Author

## *Flight of Vengeance*

(New York: Tor, 1992)

**Story type:** Fantasy (Military; Magic Conflict)
**Series:** Witch World
**Major character(s):** Duratan, Historian; Nolar, Scholar, Healer; Tarlach, Warrior, Mercenary
**Time period(s):** Indeterminate
**Locale(s):** Witch World, Planet—Imaginary

**Summary:** Shunned because of a prominent birthmark, Nolar pursues scholarly studies. After the Turning, Nolar brings a witch who lost all sense of self to seek a cure in a cave of the Old Ones found deep in the mountains. Meanwhile, hearing of a planned attack from another dimension, Tarlach gathers help to defeat it.

**Other books you might like:**
Orson Scott Card, *The Folk of the Fringe*, 1989
C.J. Cherryh, *The Fires of Azeroth*, 1979
Edmund Cooper, *The Cloud Walker*, 1973
L. Sprague de Camp, *The Hand of Zei*, 1963
Ursula K. Le Guin, *Tehanu: The Last Book of Earthsea*, 1990
Robert Silverberg, *Nightwings*, 1969
Sydney J. Van Scyoc, *Bluesong*, 1983

## 4153

### ANDRE NORTON

## *Golden Trillium*

(New York: Bantam Spectra, 1993)

**Story type:** Fantasy (Quest; Magic Conflict)
**Series:** Trillium
**Major character(s):** Kadiya, Explorer, Royalty; Jagun, Genetically Altered Being, Guide; Lamaril, Hero, Warrior
**Time period(s):** Indeterminate
**Locale(s):** Ruwenda, Fictional Country

**Summary:** Drawn back into the swamps, Kadiya discovers a long-deserted city where she meets the Hassitti who warn that a great, reawakened evil may conquer Ruwenda. When Kadiya calls forth Lamaril and learns of the ancient enemies his people could not steel themselves to kill, Kadiya and her companions travel to the western mountains to confront the enemies.

**Other books you might like:**
Poul Anderson, *Three Hearts and Three Lions*, 1961
Piers Anthony, *Being a Green Mother*, 1987
Marion Zimmer Bradley, *Black Trillium*, 1990
    Julian May, Andre Norton, co-authors
C.J. Cherryh, *Well of Shiuan*, 1978

Sterling E. Lanier, *Hiero's Journey*, 1973
Ursula K. Le Guin, *City of Illusions*, 1967
Julian May, *Blood Trillium*, 1992
Michelle Sagara, *Into the Dark Lands*, 1991

## 4154

### ANDRE NORTON

## The Hands of Lyr

(New York: Morrow/AvoNova, 1994)

**Story type:** Fantasy (Quest; Religious)
**Major character(s):** Dreen, Religious (priestess); Alnosha "Nosh", Foundling, Student; Kryn, Heir—Dispossessed, Outlaw
**Time period(s):** Indeterminate
**Locale(s):** The Ryft, Mythical Place (desert)

**Summary:** Rescued from slavery by Dreen, the last Priestess of Lyr, Nosh grows up in the Ryft, learning about Lyr and her Guards. When found by soldiers, Nosh discovers the shattered hands of Lyr and learns she has the gift of Lyr's touch. His family name destroyed by the evil Templars, Kryn must aid Nosh or all will become victims of Zellon's evil.

**Other books you might like:**
Don Callander, *Pyromancer*, 1992
Monica Hughes, *The Promise*, 1992
Robert Jordan, *The Eye of the World*, 1989
Crawford Kilian, *Greenmagic*, 1992
Meredith Ann Pierce, *The Pearl of the Soul of the World*, 1990

## 4155

### ANDRE NORTON
### SUSAN SCHWARTZ, Co-Author

## Imperial Lady

(New York: Tor, 1989)

**Story type:** Fantasy (Historical)
**Major character(s):** Silver Snow, Royalty, Warrior (Queen)
**Time period(s):** Indeterminate Past
**Locale(s):** China

**Summary:** To insult her family, the Emperor of China gives Silver Snow in marriage to the Hsiung-Nu leader. She finds, however, that nomadic life suits her.

**Other books you might like:**
Kathryn Grant, *The Willow Garden*, 1989
Barry Hughart, *Bridge of Birds*,
Jeanne Larsen, *Silk Road*, 1989

## 4156

### ANDRE NORTON
### LYN MCCONCHIE, Co-Author

## The Key of the Keplian

(New York: Warner Aspect, 1995)

**Story type:** Fantasy (Quest)
**Series:** Witch World
**Major character(s):** Eleeri, Runaway, Animal Trainer; Tharna, Animal (horse), Telepath; Romar, Captive
**Time period(s):** Indeterminate
**Locale(s):** Witch World, Planet—Imaginary

**Summary:** Rather than live with non-Indian relatives after her grandfather's death, Eleeri flees through a gate, arriving on Witch World. After saving a Keplian mare and foal, which people regard as evil, Eleeri lives in hiding while raising a herd of horses. Responding to dream communications, Eleeri and the horses move to rescue Romar, who is being held by an evil sorcerer.

**Other books you might like:**
Piers Anthony, *Virtual Mode*, 1991
Constance Ash, *The Horsegirl*, 1988
Joy Chant, *The Grey Mane of Morning*, 1980
Peter Dickinson, *The Blue Hawk*, 1976
C.S. Lewis, *The Horse and His Boy*, 1954
Robin McKinley, *The Blue Sword*, 1982
Karen Ripley, *The Persistence of Memory*, 1993
Nancy Springer, *A Horse to Love*, 1987

## 4157

### ANDRE NORTON

## The Mark of the Cat

(New York: Ace, 1992)

**Story type:** Fantasy (Quest)
**Major character(s):** Klaverel-va-Hynkkel, Traveler; Ravinga, Shaman (dollmaker); Murri, Animal (cat)
**Time period(s):** Indeterminate
**Locale(s):** Kahulawe, Fictional Country

**Summary:** Unesteemed by his family, Hynkkel starts his solo rite of passage without the ceremonial support of family and friends. The amulet given to him by the dollmaker becomes his most important possession and allows contact with Murri, who becomes his companion.

**Other books you might like:**
Clare Bell, *Ratha's Creature*, 1983
C.J. Cherryh, *The Pride of Chanur*, 1982
Alan Dean Foster, *Cat-A-Lyst*, 1991
Robert A. Heinlein, *The Door into Summer*, 1957
Michael Peak, *Cat House*, 1989
Tad Williams, *Tailchaser's Song*, 1985

## 4158

### ANDRE NORTON
### SHERWOOD SMITH, Co-Author

## A Mind for Trade

(New York: Tor, 1997)

**Story type:** Science Fiction (Adventure)
**Major character(s):** Dane Thorson, Spaceman (Cargo Master); Tooe, Alien (Rigelian hybrid), Apprentice; Rip Shannon, Spaceman, Pilot
**Time period(s):** Indeterminate Future
**Locale(s):** *Solar Queen*, Spaceship; *North Star*, Spaceship

**Summary:** Aboard the *Solar Queen*'s new sister ship, the *North Star*, Dane Thorson and his fellow Free Traders travel to Hesprid IV, where a strange electromagnetic force kills stranded miners. Only Thorson's newly developed psi-link with his crewmates allows them to communicate with the Hesprid IV's inhabitants and avoid the planet's hidden dangers.

**Other books you might like:**
Anne Mason, *The Stolen Law*, 1986
Larry Segriff, *Spacer Dreams*, 1995
Charles Sheffield, *The Billion Dollar Boy*, 1997

Sherwood Smith, *The Phoenix in Flight*, 1993
   Dave Trowbridge, co-author
Sherwood Smith, *A Prison Unsought*, 1994
   Dave Trowbridge, co-author
Robyn Tallis, *Visions from the Sea*, 1989

## 4159

### ANDRE NORTON

## *Mirror of Destiny*
(New York: Morrow/AvoNova, 1995)

**Story type:** Fantasy (Adventure; Magic Conflict)
**Major character(s):** Twilla, Healer, Apprentice; Ylon, Royalty, Handicapped (blind); Oxyle, Mythical Creature (magical)
**Time period(s):** Indeterminate
**Locale(s):** Varslaad, Fictional Country; Enchanted Forest, Mythical Place

**Summary:** Ordered to travel to another land where whe will marry someone chosen by lot, Twilla craftily uses her magic mirror to render herself unappealing. When her subterfuge backfires, Twilla must escape to the forest with Ylon, where she learns of an evil plot to control the forest and surrounding lands.

**Other books you might like:**
Lynn Abbey, *The Wooden Sword*, 1991
Poul Anderson, *Three Hearts and Three Lions*, 1961
Piers Anthony, *Being a Green Mother*, 1987
Piers Anthony, *If I Pay Thee Not in Gold*, 1993
   Mercedes Lackey, co-author
Maya Kaathryn Bohnhoff, *Taminy*, 1993
Robert Holdstock, *Mythago Wood*, 1984
Thomas Burnett Swann, *Day of the Minotaur*, 1966

## 4160

### ANDRE NORTON
### P.M. GRIFFIN, Co-Author

## *Redline the Stars*
(New York: Tor, 1993)

**Story type:** Science Fiction (Adventure)
**Series:** Solar Queen
**Major character(s):** Miceal Jellico, Spaceship Captain, Trader; Rael Cofort, Doctor, Spacewoman
**Time period(s):** Indeterminate Future
**Locale(s):** *Solar Queen*, Spaceship; Canuche of Halio, Planet—Imaginary

**Summary:** On the *Solar Queen* as a temporary crew member, Rael impresses the rest of the crew who yet remain curious about her. She seems to elicit trouble and never runs from it, resolving an undiscovered mass murder case and warning of a major disaster on Canuche of Halio, but revealing little of herself. Jellico must decide if he wants to offer her a permanent spot on the *Solar Queen*'s crew.

**Other books you might like:**
Poul Anderson, *Trader to the Stars*, 1964
Pauline Ashwell, *Unwillingly to Earth*, 1992
David Brin, *The Uplift War*, 1987
A.C. Crispin, *Starbridge*, 1989
Margaret Davis, *Mind Light*, 1993
T. Jackson King, *Retread Shop*, 1988
Alis A. Rasmussen, *A Passage of Stars*, 1990
Harry Turtledove, *Earthgrip*, 1991
Jack Williamson, *Beachhead*, 1992

## 4161

### ANDRE NORTON
### A.C. CRISPIN, Co-Author

## *Songsmith*
(New York: Tor, 1992)

**Story type:** Fantasy (Adventure; Psychic Powers)
**Series:** Witch World
**Major character(s):** Eydryth of Kar Garudwyn, Minstrel; Avris, Witch, Companion
**Time period(s):** Indeterminate
**Locale(s):** Witch World, Planet—Imaginary

**Summary:** Eydryth, a skilled Songsmith, travels through Estcarp searching out a cure for her father who has never recovered from an attempt at using a device chanced upon at a place of the old Power.

**Other books you might like:**
L. Sprague de Camp, *The Land of Unreason*, 1942
   Fletcher Pratt, co-author
Phyllis Eisenstein, *Born to Exile*, 1978
Ellen Kushner, *Thomas the Rhymer*, 1990
Anne McCaffrey, *Dragonsinger*, 1977
C.L. Moore, *Jirel of Joiry*, 1969
Melanie Rawn, *Dragon Prince*, 1988

## 4162

### ANDRE NORTON
### P.M. GRIFFIN, Co-Author

## *Storms of Victory*
(New York: Tor, 1991)

**Story type:** Fantasy (Adventure)
**Series:** Witch World
**Major character(s):** Destree, Orphan, Psychic; Una, Ruler (Lady of Seakeepdale); Tarlach, Warrior, Mercenary
**Time period(s):** Indeterminate
**Locale(s):** Witch World, Planet—Imaginary

**Summary:** Destree travels south with the Sulcar and certain of the Estcarp witches to discover the origin of strange ships. When she finds ancient evil has been reawakened, she and Kemoc lay it to rest along with the strange tools it has used. Meanwhile at Seakeepdale in High Hallack, Lady Una seeks aid in protecting her people from the evil Lord Ogin of Ravenfield who has turned pirate.

**Other books you might like:**
L. Sprague de Camp, *The Land of Unreason*, 1942
   Fletcher Pratt, co-author
Raymond Harris, *The Broken Worlds*, 1986
Katherine Kurtz, *The Quest for Saint Camber*, 1986
Sterling E. Lanier, *Hiero's Journey*, 1973
C.L. Moore, *Jirel of Joiry*, 1969
Sydney J. Van Scyoc, *Feather Stroke*, 1989

## 4163

### ANDRE NORTON

## *The Warding of Witch World*
(New York: Warner Aspect, 1996)

**Story type:** Fantasy (Quest; Magic Conflict)
**Series:** Witch World

**Major character(s):** Keris Tregarth, Warrior; Firdun, Nobleman; Trusla, Traveler, Dancer
**Time period(s):** Indeterminate Past
**Locale(s):** Witch World, Planet—Imaginary

**Summary:** Because ancient evil stirs again, the Council at Lormt decides to close all gates between worlds. To close the three most treacherous, in the far south, in the western wastes and in the ice-filled north, three expeditions set forth.

**Other books you might like:**
Poul Anderson, *The Broken Sword*, 1954
Joy Chant, *Red Moon and Black Mountain*, 1971
C.J. Cherryh, *Gate of Ivrel*, 1976
L. Sprague de Camp, *The Unbeheaded King*, 1983
Alan Dean Foster, *Spellsinger*, 1983
Diana Wynne Jones, *The Crown of Dalemark*, 1995
Katherine Kurtz, *Deryni Checkmate*, 1972
Karen Ripley, *The Warden of Horses*, 1994

---

**4164**

**WARREN NORWOOD**
**MEL ODOM**, Co-Author

## Stranded!

(New York: Lynx Omega, 1989)

**Story type:** Science Fiction (Time Travel)
**Series:** Time Police
**Major character(s):** Jackson Dubchek, Historian, Time Traveler
**Time period(s):** 23rd century (2244); 21st century (2074)
**Locale(s):** Mexico

**Summary:** Stranded by the Time Police in the year 2074, Dubchek begins to piece together that organization's secret plan to protect the future at all costs.

**Other books you might like:**
Poul Anderson, *The Corridors of Time*, 1965
Poul Anderson, *Time Patrolman*, 1983
Poul Anderson, *The Year of the Ransom*, 1988
Isaac Asimov, *The End of Eternity*, 1955
Simon Hawke, *The Kyber Connection*, 1986
    Timewars 6
Fritz Leiber, *The Big Time*, 1961
Fritz Leiber, *The Change War*, 1978
H. Beam Piper, *Lord Kalvan of Otherwhen*, 1965

---

**4165**

**KATE NOVAK**
**JEFF GRUBB**, Co-Author

## Finder's Bane

(Renton, Washington: TSR, 1997)

**Story type:** Fantasy (Quest)
**Series:** Forgotten Realms: The Harpers
**Major character(s):** Joel, Musician (harper), Religious; Holly Harrowslough, Religious, Rebel; Jasmine ''Jas'', Pilot, Mythical Creature (winged woman)
**Time period(s):** Indeterminate
**Locale(s):** Daggerdale, Fictional City; Sigil, Fictional City

**Summary:** A priest of the new god, Finder, Joel surrenders a great deal—position, friends and family—to follow his calling. Now his god calls him to risk his life and soul to prevent the resurrection of the terrible Bane, a dead and defeated god of evil. If Joel and his allies fail, not only will they and Finder die, but Bane's evil will also spread everywhere. Novelization based on role-playing game.

**Other books you might like:**
Steven Brust, *Jhereg*, 1983
Glen Cook, *The Swordbearer*, 1982
Robin Hobb, *Assassin's Apprentice*, 1996
Fritz Leiber, *Ill Met in Lankhmar*, 1995
Roger Zelazny, *Nine Princes in Amber*, 1970

---

**4166**

**KATE NOVAK**
**JEFF GRUBB**, Co-Author

## Masquerades

(Lake Geneva, Wisconsin: TSR, 1995)

**Story type:** Fantasy (Quest; Political)
**Series:** Forgotten Realms
**Major character(s):** Alias, Hero, Genetically Altered Being; Dragonbait Champion, Religious (paladin), Alien (Saurial); Jamal, Actress
**Time period(s):** Indeterminate
**Locale(s):** Westgate, Fictional City

**Summary:** In Westgate on personal business, Alias and Dragonbait get into trouble with the Night Masks' agents in the city. They gather a group of old and new allies, but even this help may not prevail against murder, magic, and treachery.

**Other books you might like:**
Steven Brust, *Jhereg*, 1983
Glen Cook, *Sweet Silver Blues*, 1987
Simon R. Green, *Hawk & Fisher*, 1990
Jeff Grubb, *Azure Bonds*, 1988
    Kate Novak, co-author
Fritz Leiber, *Ill Met in Lankhmar*, 1995
Will Shetterly, *Liavek*, 1985
    Emma Bull, co-editor

---

**4167**

**KATE NOVAK**
**JEFF GRUBB**, Co-Author

## Song of the Saurials

(Lake Geneva, Wisconsin: TSR, 1991)

**Story type:** Fantasy (Magic Conflict; Adventure)
**Series:** Forgotten Realms: The Finder's Stone Trilogy
**Major character(s):** Finder ''Nameless'' Wyvernspur, Musician, Magician; Olive Ruskettle, Mythical Creature (halfling); Dragonbait Champion, Alien (Saurian), Warrior (paladin)
**Time period(s):** Indeterminate
**Locale(s):** The Realms, Mythical Place; Mourngrim Castle Shadowdale, Planet—Imaginary

**Summary:** The trial of the Nameless Bard was interrupted by a minion of Moander the Darkbringer, a god who Nameless and his companions believed they had killed on their plane. They fight to once again free the land from the evil god, and to free the Saurials enslaved by the god. A game tie-in novel.

**Other books you might like:**
C.J. Cherryh, *The Paladin*, 1988
Sheila Gilluly, *The Boy From the Burren*, 1990
Guy Gavriel Kay, *Tigana*, 1990
Mercedes Lackey, *Magic's Price*, 1990
Elizabeth Moon, *Surrender None: The Legacy of Gird*, 1990

Andrea Shettle, *Flute Song Magic*, 1990
Andrew Whitmore, *The Fortress of Eternity*, 1990
Tad Williams, *Stone of Farewell*, 1990

## 4168

**PHILIP NUTMAN**

### Wet Work
(New York: Jove, 1993)

**Story type:** Horror (Reanimated Dead)
**Major character(s):** Dominic Corvino, Spy (CIA agent); Ryan Del Valle, Spy (CIA section chief); Nick Packard, Police Officer
**Time period(s):** 1990s (1995)
**Locale(s):** Washington, District of Columbia; New York, New York

**Summary:** The author's first novel expands his 1989 story of the same name, about the influence of the comet Saracen during its passage by Earth, resurrecting the newly dead as flesh-eating zombies. At the core of the novel is a vicious satire on the decline of American culture.

**Other books you might like:**
George Romero, *Dawn of the Dead*, 1978
John Skipp, *Book of the Dead*, 1989
    Craig Spector, co-editor
John Skipp, *Still Dead: Book of the Dead 2*, 1992

## 4169

**JODY LYNN NYE**, Editor

### Don't Forget Your Spacesuit, Dear
(New York: Baen, 1996)

**Story type:** Science Fiction (Anthology)
**Major character(s):** Mother, Parent
**Time period(s):** Indeterminate Future
**Locale(s):** Earth; Outer Space

**Summary:** Contains 19 original stories, many humorous, in appreciation of motherly advice. Authors include Robert Asprin, Diane Duane, George Alec Effinger, Esther M. Friesner, Ellen Guon, Morgan Llywelyn, Anne McCaffrey, Elizabeth Moon, Jody Lynn Nye, Elizabeth Ann Scarborough, and Josepha Sherman.

**Other books you might like:**
Marjorie Agosin, *The Secret Weavers: Stories of the Fantastic by Latin American Women*, 1991
    editor
Greg Bear, *New Legends*, 1995
    Martin H. Greenberg, co-editor
Esther Friesner, *Alien Pregnant by Elvis*, 1994
    Martin H. Greenberg, co-editor
Don Sakers, *Carmen Miranda's Ghost Is Haunting Space Station Three*, 1990
    editor
Susanna J. Sturgis, *Magic Realism by Women: Dreams in a Minor Key*, 1991
    editor

## 4170

**JODY LYNN NYE**

### Higher Mythology
(New York: Warner Questar, 1993)

**Story type:** Fantasy (Quest; Light Fantasy)
**Series:** Keith Doyle
**Major character(s):** Keith Doyle, Student; Holl, Mythical Creature (elf)
**Time period(s):** 1990s
**Locale(s):** Midwestern University, Illinois; Hollow Tree Farm, Illinois

**Summary:** When hunters kidnap Holl's baby daughter and a young faery, Keith utilizes his new interest in hot air ballooning to help organize sprites into an aerial spy network to seek out the abductors.

**Other books you might like:**
Orson Scott Card, *Lost Boys*, 1992
Rose Estes, *Troll-Taken*, 1993
Anne McCaffrey, *Crisis on Doona*, 1992
    Jody Lynn Nye, co-author
Anne McCaffrey, *The Death of Sleep*, 1990
    Jody Lynn Nye, co-author
Viido Polikarpus, *Down Town*, 1985
    Tappan King, co-author

## 4171

**JODY LYNN NYE**

### The Magic Touch
(New York: Warner Aspect, 1996)

**Story type:** Fantasy (Young Adult; Urban)
**Major character(s):** Raymond E. Crandall Jr., Teenager, Apprentice (fairy godfather); Rose Feinstein, Mythical Creature (fairy godmother), Teacher; Albert Froister, Mythical Creature (djin), Businessman
**Time period(s):** 1990s
**Locale(s):** United States; Enlightenment, Mythical Place (light fixture warehouse)

**Summary:** At his grandmother's bidding, Ray Crandall finds himself involved in her favorite charity, the Fairy Godmother's Union. Apprenticed to Mrs. Rose Feinstein, Ray begins to learn the proper use of magic and to enjoy using his talents to help troubled children. Ray's studies are interrupted when his best friend joins a tough street gang whose members exhibit magical, but menacing, powers of their own, and use them to spread fear through the neighborhood streets.

**Other books you might like:**
Piers Anthony, *Demons Don't Dream*, 1993
Gael Baudino, *Strands of Sunlight*, 1994
Charles de Lint, *Our Lady of the Harbour*, 1991
Robin Morgan, *The Mer-Child: A Legend for Children and Other Adults*, 1991
Terry Pratchett, *Eric*, 1995
Elizabeth Ann Scarborough, *The Godmother's Apprentice*, 1995
Harry Turtledove, *The Case of the Toxic Spell Dump*, 1993

## **4172**

### JODY LYNN NYE

## *Medicine Show*

(New York: Ace, 1994)

**Story type:** Science Fiction (Medical; Adventure)
**Major character(s):** Shona Taylor, Doctor, Space Explorer; Chirwl, Alien (ottle), Health Care Professional
**Time period(s):** Indeterminate Future
**Locale(s):** Proxt, Planet—Imaginary; *Sibyl*, Spaceship

**Summary:** Returning to Chirwl's home planet, Dr. Shona Taylor discovers both ottle and human populations afflicted by an unnatural malady which causes rapid aging. *Sibyl*'s crew must find a cure or face the immediate prospect of universal death.

**Other books you might like:**
Nicola Griffith, *Ammonite*, 1993
Murray Leinster, *The Med Series*, 1983
Frederik Pohl, *Stopping at Slowyear*, 1991
James H. Schmitz, *The Demon Breed*, 1968
James White, *Hospital Station*, 1962

## **4173**

### JODY LYNN NYE

## *Mythology 101*

(New York: Warner, 1990)

**Story type:** Fantasy (Contemporary)
**Series:** Keith Doyle
**Major character(s):** Marcy Collier, Student—College; Keith Doyle, Student—College
**Time period(s):** 1980s
**Locale(s):** United States

**Summary:** Keith is leading the effort to have the old university library torn down. However, Marcy, the girl of his dreams, is fighting him every step of the way, to protect the elves who make their home in the old library.

**Other books you might like:**
Gael Baudino, *Duel of Dragons*, 1989
Emma Bull, *War for the Oaks*,
Alan Dean Foster, *Metrognome*, 1990
Tanya Huff, *Gate of Darkness, Circle of Light*, 1989
Gene Wolfe, *Castleview*, 1990

## **4174**

### JODY LYNN NYE

## *Mythology Abroad*

(New York: Warner Questar, 1991)

**Story type:** Fantasy (Contemporary)
**Series:** Keith Doyle
**Major character(s):** Keith Doyle, Student, Traveler; Holl, Mythical Creature (elf); Master, Magician, Mythical Creature (elf)
**Time period(s):** 1980s
**Locale(s):** Scotland

**Summary:** In this sequel to *Mythology 101*, Keith travels to Scotland for Midwestern University course credit accompanied by Holl who has volunteered to re-establish contact with the Fair Folk. Suspicious government agents do not prove as problematic as does Keith's

unauthorized investigation which yields a Bodach's curse. Holl's call for help brings the Master who finds old friends and family.

**Other books you might like:**
Emma Bull, *War for the Oaks*, 1987
Kenneth C. Flint, *Cromm*, 1990
Andre Norton, *The Elvenbane*, 1991
    Mercedes Lackey, co-author
Will Shetterly, *Elsewhere*, 1991
Margaret Weis, *Fire Sea*, 1991
    Tracy Hickman, co-author
Terri Windling, *Life on the Border*, 1991
    editor

## **4175**

### JODY LYNN NYE

## *The Ship Errant*

(New York: Baen, 1996)

**Story type:** Science Fiction (First Contact; Alternate Intelligence)
**Series:** Ship Who Sang
**Major character(s):** Carialle, Cyborg; Keff, Pilot (spacechip), Spaceman; Narrow Leg, Scientist, Alien (Cridi)
**Time period(s):** Indeterminate Future
**Locale(s):** Cridi, Planet—Imaginary; Thelerie, Planet—Imaginary; Outer Space

**Summary:** Carialle and Keff carry a team of globe-frogs from Ozran to Cridi, their ancestral home. The two forge an alliance between the Central Worlds and Cridi, jeopardized when a second ship departs for Cridi piloted by the erratic Carialle. When pirate aliens from a neighboring star system led by renegade humans destroy that ship, Carialle, Keff, and a Cridi ship investigate.

**Other books you might like:**
John Barnes, *A Million Open Doors*, 1992
John Brunner, *A Maze of Stars*, 1991
Margaret Davis, *Minds Apart*, 1994
Paula E. Downing, *A Whisper of Time*, 1994
Lee Killough, *Liberty's World*, 1985
Anne McCaffrey, *The Ship Who Sang*, 1969
Anne McCaffrey, *The Ship Who Won*, 1994
    Jody Lynn Nye, co-author
Charles Sheffield, *Trader's World*, 1988

## **4176**

### JODY LYNN NYE

## *Taylor's Ark*

(New York: Ace, 1993)

**Story type:** Science Fiction (Medical; Adventure)
**Major character(s):** Shona Taylor, Doctor, Space Explorer; Jachin Verdadero, Administrator (Galactic Laboratory Corp.); Manny Mitchell, Administrator (Galactic Laboratory Corp.)
**Time period(s):** Indeterminate Future
**Locale(s):** Mars; *Sibyl*, Spaceship; Karela, Planet—Imaginary

**Summary:** A specialist in environmental medicine, Shona has been working for the government on the trip to and initial three month check-out of new colonies. Switching employers after miscarrying her baby, Shona travels with her vaccine dog, sniffer cat, rabbits, mice and an intelligent alien to provide medical services. Unfortunately she finds disaster wherever she goes.

**Other books you might like:**
Nicola Griffith, *Ammonite*, 1993

Janet Kagan, *Mirabile*, 1991
Murray Leinster, *The Med Series*, 1983
Anne McCaffrey, *Crisis on Doona*, 1992
   Jody Lynn Nye, co-author
Anne McCaffrey, *The Death of Sleep*, 1990
   Jody Lynn Nye, co-author
Vonda N. McIntyre, *Dreamsnake*, 1978
Frederik Pohl, *Stopping at Slowyear*, 1991
Robert Silverberg, *The Face of the Waters*, 1991
Michael Swanwick, *Stations of the Tide*, 1990
James White, *The Genocidal Healer*, 1991

### 4177

**JODY LYNN NYE**

## *Waking in Dreamland*

(New York: Baen, 1998)

**Story type:** Fantasy (Quest; Political)
**Major character(s):** Roan, Hero, Adventurer
**Time period(s):** Indeterminate
**Locale(s):** Dreamland, Mythical Place

**Summary:** The Seven Sleepers are the ones who created Dreamland, the realm occupied by sleepers as they dream. When someone threatens Dreamland's existence by beginning to kill the Seven Sleepers, Roan must foil the plot before Dreamland, and all dreams, vanish.

**Other books you might like:**
Jean Mark Gawron, *Dream of Glass*, 1993
Ursula K. Le Guin, *The Lathe of Heaven*, 1971
Jonathan Lethem, *Amnesia Moon*, 1995
Rachel Pollack, *Unquenchable Fire*, 1992
Michaela Roessner, *Vanishing Point*, 1993

### 4178

**ERIC S. NYLUND**

## *A Game of Universe*

(New York: AvoNova, 1997)

**Story type:** Fantasy (Quest; Science Fiction)
**Major character(s):** Germain, Criminal (magical assassin); Quilp, Criminal, Genius; Setebos, Artificial Intelligence
**Time period(s):** Indeterminate Future
**Locale(s):** Earth; Planet—Imaginary; *Grail Angel*, Spaceship

**Summary:** In the process of an assassination, Germain joins an expedition to discover and bring back the Holy Grail within a year or be killed. Germain enlists both his magical powers and his friends, finding himself and the Universe different from what he expected.

**Other books you might like:**
Piers Anthony, *The Ring*, 1968
   Robert E. Margroff, co-author
A.A. Attanasio, *The Dragon and the Unicorn*, 1996
Alan Dean Foster, *To the Vanishing Point*, 1988
Michael Moorcock, *The War Amongst the Angels*, 1997

### 4179

**ERIC S. NYLUND**

## *Signal to Noise*

(New York: Avon Eos, 1998)

**Story type:** Science Fiction (Cyberpunk; First Contact)

**Major character(s):** Jack Potter, Spy (National Security Office), Researcher; Wheeler, Alien, Businessman; Zero Al Qaseem, Scientist (gene-witch), Computer Expert
**Time period(s):** Indeterminate Future
**Locale(s):** Santa Sierra, California; Amsterdam, Netherlands; Montenegro

**Summary:** As an ex-NSA cyberspy, Jack fights for tenure at the Academe by stealing another's research. Believing he has found a hidden message in cosmic noise, Jack contacts the alien Wheeler who trades a genetic enhancer that cures cancer for information about human genetics. Also on the bargaining table is technology that allows people to transport instantly from place to place on Earth, but unfortunately, the rotation of the planet slows with each use of the device.

**Other books you might like:**
Roger MacBride Allen, *The Ring of Charon*, 1990
Greg Bear, *Slant*, 1997
John Cramer, *Einstein's Bridge*, 1997
Melissa Scott, *Trouble and Her Friends*, 1994
Michael Swanwick, *Jack Faust*, 1997

### 4180

**JOYCE CAROL OATES**, Editor

## *American Gothic Tales*

(New York: Penguin/Plume, 1996)

**Story type:** Horror (Anthology)

**Summary:** A renowned writer of mainstream fiction focused on the dark side of American experience assembles 46 classic and contemporary tales in the Gothic tradition by American writers. Classic stories include Edgar Allan Poe's "The Black Cat," narrated by a psychopathic murderer; Charlotte Perkins Gilman's "The Yellow Wallpaper," in which a woman becomes obsessed with a wallpaper pattern that reflects her madness; and H.P. Lovecraft's "The Outsider," a homage to Poe about a man who escapes from an underground prison and the horrifying revelation of his true identity. Among the contemporary tales are Raymond Carver's "Little Things," a sardonic short about a custody battle; Thomas Ligotti's "The Last Feast of Harlequin," in which a man discovers things he would rather not know about himself while attending a festival with pagan overtones; and Nicholson Baker's "Subsoil," a mock gothic story in which potatoes play the heavy. Oates contributes an introduction surveying the American Gothic tale.

**Other books you might like:**
Chris Baldick, *The Oxford Book of Gothic Tales*, 1992
   editor
Peter Haining, *Gothic Tales of Terror, Volume II*, 1972
   editor
Bradford Morrow, *The New Gothic*, 1991
   Patrick McGrath, co-editor
Alfred Bendixen, *Haunted Women: The Best Supernatural Tales by American Women Writers*, 1985
   editor

### 4181

**JOYCE CAROL OATES**

## *The Collector of Hearts: New Tales of the Grotesque*

(New York: Dutton, 1998)

**Story type:** Horror (Collection)

**Summary:** These 27 contemporary gothic tales eschew the traditional supernatural flourishes of horror fiction to focus on disturbed states of mind and experiences that are ambiguously yet eerily menacing. The title story is narrated by a young woman oblivious that she may be in the company of an older man who means her fatal harm. In "Labor Day," the disappearance of a child compels neighbors to suspect the worst about themselves. "The Sepulchre," in which a daughter's search for her apparently lost elderly father brings out the tensions in her relationship with her mother, is one of several stories whose dramatic core is family dysfunction.

**Other books you might like:**
Angela Carter, *Burning Your Boats: The Collected Short Stories*, 1996
A.M. Homes, *The Safety of Objects*, 1990
Shirley Jackson, *The Magic of Shirley Jackson*, 1966
Kathe Koja, *Extremities*, 1998
Patrick McGrath, *Blood and Water and Other Tales*, 1988

---

**4182**

**JOYCE CAROL OATES**

## Demon and Other Tales

(West Warwick, Rhode Island: Necronomicon Press, 1996)

**Story type:** Horror (Collection)

**Summary:** These seven short-short fictions, two original to the volume, deploy images of death in their inquiries into personal identity. In "The Omen," the narrator's discovery of the body of a miniscule man washed up on the shore shakes his belief in objective reality. "An Urban Paradox" is set in a future where a character tries to makes sense of sinister vans that randomly abduct people. A female character in "The Temple" turns the bones of an infant she unearths in her garden into a shrine. The title story tells of a hideous child whose abuse by adults turns him into a sociopath. "Posthumous" is a murder story with an uncanny twist suggested by its title.

**Other books you might like:**
Angela Carter, *The Bloody Chamber*, 1979
Rachel Ingalls, *The End of Tragedy*, 1987
Shirley Jackson, *The Magic of Shirley Jackson*, 1966
Lisa Tuttle, *Memories of the Body*, 1992

---

**4183**

**JOYCE CAROL OATES**
**BARRY MOSER**, Illustrator

## First Love: A Gothic Tale

(Hopewell, New Jersey: Ecco Press, 1996)

**Story type:** Horror (Child-in-Peril)
**Major character(s):** Josephine Carolyn "Josie" S-, Child (11-year-old); Jared Burkhardt Jr., Student (seminarian); Delia S-, Real Estate Agent
**Time period(s):** 1990s
**Locale(s):** Ransomville, New York

**Summary:** When Josie and her destitute mother move to their great aunt's home in upstate New York, the young girl is victimized sexually and psychologically by her cousin Jared, an obsessive young man whose pedophilic tendencies have driven him from the seminary.

**Other books you might like:**
Angela Carter, *The Magic Toyshop*, 1967
Davis Grubb, *The Night of the Hunter*, 1953
A.M. Homes, *The End of Alice*, 1996

---

Susan Palwick, *Flying in Place*, 1992

---

**4184**

**JOYCE CAROL OATES**

## Haunted: Tales of the Grotesque

(New York: Dutton, 1994)

**Story type:** Horror (Collection)

**Summary:** These 16 stories bring together most of this prolific mainstream writer's recent macabre fiction. "Haunted," "The Doll," and "Phase Change" all deal with bizarre experiences which reveal attitudes and suppressed memories that have shaped characters' lives. "The White Cat," "The Model," "Extenuating Circumstances," and "The Guilty Party" tell of people who avenge themselves against their spouses through pets and children. "Don't You Trust Me," "Poor Bibi," and "Martyrdom" use grotesque characters and situations as heavy-handed metaphors for human relationships. And the masterful "Accursed Inhabitants of the House of Bly" retells the events of Henry James' *Turn of the Screw* from the points of view of its ghostly nemeses. The author supplies an explanatory afterword defining "the grotesque."

**Other books you might like:**
Fred Chappell, *More Shapes than One*, 1992
Alison Lurie, *Women and Ghosts*, 1994
Peter Taylor, *The Oracle at Stoneleigh Court*, 1993

---

**4185**

**JOYCE CAROL OATES**

## Zombie

(New York: Dutton, 1995)

**Story type:** Horror (Psychological Suspense)
**Major character(s):** Quentin P, Student
**Time period(s):** 1990s (1995)
**Locale(s):** Detroit, Michigan (in the suburbs)

**Summary:** Presented as a series of diary entries kept by a sometime engineering student at Mount Vernon State College, this short novel recounts the narrator's seamy past as a paroled sex offender, and his monstrous present as someone who lures victims to his dwelling and performs crude lobotomies on them in an effort to turn them into obedient zombies. Loosely based on the real-life atrocities of Jeffrey Dahmer, this grim tale presents its narrator's dehumanizing of his victim as symbolic of the dehumanization of contemporary life.

**Other books you might like:**
Robert Bloch, *Psycho*, 1959
Ramsey Campbell, *The Face That Must Die*, 1979
Dennis Cooper, *Frisk*, 1992
Brett Easton Ellis, *American Psycho*, 1991
John Fowles, *The Collector*, 1963
Patrick McGrath, *Spider*, 1990

---

**4186**

**JAMES O'BARR**, Editor
**EDWARD E. KRAMER**, Co-Editor

## The Crow: Shattered Lives and Broken Dreams

(New York: Del Rey, 1998)

**Story type:** Horror (Anthology)

**Summary:** Twenty-seven original stories and poems set in the universe of James O'Barr's graphic novel series The Crow, in which the murdered are resurrected to avenge their deaths. Highlights include Chet Williamson's "The Blood-Red Sea," in which a poet avenges his own murder and a student's, Ramsey Campbell's "Twice By Fire," in which a dead cop pursues the pair of criminals who killed him and his family; Nancy Collins' "Variations on a Theme," in which vampire heroine Sonja Blue collaborates with a victim of white supremacists to track down his murderers; and John Shirley's "Wings Burnt Black," a parable in which Eric, hero of the graphic novel series, confronts God as the creator of earthly misery. Each story is illustrated by a different artist.

**Other books you might like:**
David Bischoff, *Quoth the Crow*, 1998
Poppy Z. Brite, *The Lazarus Heart*, 1998
Elizabeth Engstrom, *Imagination Fully Dilated*, 1998
    Engstrom is editor of stories based on the artof Alan D. Clark, who is also the co-editor.
Neil Gaiman, *The Sandman: Book of Dreams*, 1996
    Ed Kramer, co-editor
Chet Williamson, *Clash by Night*, 1998

**4187**

**CHARLES OBERNDORF**

## Foragers

(New York: Bantam Spectra, 1996)

**Story type:** Science Fiction (First Contact; Adventure)
**Major character(s):** Pauline Dikobe, Scholar (ethnographer), Spacewoman; Esoch al-Schouki, Military Personnel; Lightfoot Watcher, Alien (slazan)
**Time period(s):** Indeterminate Future
**Locale(s):** Tienah, Planet—Imaginary

**Summary:** Pauline Dikobe vanishes while studying a primitive society of slazans, a race at war with humans, hoping to learn how to defeat their technologically sophisticated cousins. Sent to investigate, Lieutenant Esoch al-Schouki must make his way to Pauline's camp alone through the slazan jungle when his shuttle probe fails.

**Other books you might like:**
Eleanor Arnason, *Ring of Swords*, 1993
Nicola Griffith, *Ammonite*, 1993
Elizabeth Moon, *Remnant Population*, 1996
Larry Niven, *The Mote in God's Eye*, 1974
    Jerry Pournelle, co-author
Joan Slonczewski, *A Door into Ocean*, 1986

**4188**

**CHARLES OBERNDORF**

## Sheltered Lives

(New York: Bantam Spectra, 1992)

**Story type:** Science Fiction (Dystopian; Political)
**Major character(s):** Anna Elizabeth Baxter, Widow(er), Heiress; Edward Winslow Lang, Government Official, Businessman; Rod Lawrence, Prostitute
**Time period(s):** 2020s
**Locale(s):** Cleveland, Ohio

**Summary:** In the closely monitored society of the Construct, security and safety seem assured until Rod, hired as a companion by Anna after her lover commits suicide, realizes that what the computer saves may not make his life secure. Disaster may follow Anna's potential involvement with revolutionaries who oppose the governmental policy of interring victims of the latest fatal sexually transmitted disease. Author's first novel.

**Other books you might like:**
Jeffrey A. Carver, *The Rapture Effect*, 1987
Mary Gentle, *Golden Witchbreed*, 1984
Larry Niven, *Achilles' Choice*, 1991
    Steven Barnes, co-author
George Orwell, *1984*, 1949
Edgar Pangborn, *A Mirror for Observers*, 1954

**4189**

**MAXINE O'CALLAGHAN**

## Dark Time

(New York: Diamond, 1992)

**Story type:** Horror (Science Fiction)
**Major character(s):** Corey Carpenter, Teenager; Gayle Carpenter, Clerk (Corey's mother); Amy Delgato, Teenager
**Time period(s):** 1990s (1992)
**Locale(s):** Longview, Washington

**Summary:** While adventuring in the woods one day, Corey Carpenter is entrusted with a tool from a dying extraterrestrial who calls himself "he who hunts with weapons of light." Thereafter, it becomes Corey's responsibility to fight the extraterrestrial wreaking havoc on the nearby town who was the other being's quarry.

**Other books you might like:**
Dean R. Koontz, *The Bad Place*, 1990
Dean R. Koontz, *Strangers*, 1986

**4190**

**MEL ODOM**

## Blade

(New York: Harper, 1998)

**Story type:** Horror (Vampire Story)
**Major character(s):** Blade, Vampire; Deacon Frost, Vampire; Karen Jansen, Doctor
**Time period(s):** 1990s (1998)
**Locale(s):** New York, New York

**Summary:** Blade, a half-human, half-vampire hybrid, wages war against the vampire underground of Manhattan which, under the leadership of rebellious punk vampire Deacon Frost, is preparing to unleash La Magra, the Blood God, in order to subjugate humanity. Novelization of a screenplay by David S. Goyer, adapted from a graphic novel series and filmed by Stephen Norrington.

**Other books you might like:**
Scott Ciencin, *The Vampire Odyssey*, 1992
Mick Farren, *The Time of Feasting*, 1996
Robert R. McCammon, *They Thirst*, 1981
John Skipp, *The Light at the End*, 1986
    Craig Spector, co-author
Robert Weinberg, *Blood War*, 1995

**4191**

MEL ODOM

## F.R.E.E.Lancers

(Lake Geneva, Wisconsin: TSR, 1995)

**Story type:** Science Fiction (Cyberpunk; Adventure)
**Major character(s):** Lee Won Underhill, Administrator (FREE-Lancers)
**Time period(s):** 2020s (2023)
**Locale(s):** Chicago, Illinois; Rinji 8, Space Station; Detroit, Michigan

**Summary:** In the balkanized, former United States, a powerful Japanese concern hires the FREELancers to find stolen industrial secrets. As the recovery increases in difficulty, Lee Won Underhill discovers that an information transfer might change the worldwide balance of power. Game tie-in.

**Other books you might like:**
Lois McMaster Bujold, *Brothers in Arms*, 1988
Robert N. Charrette, *Never Deal with a Dragon*, 1990
Nick Pollotta, *Bureau 13*, 1991
Neal Stephenson, *Snow Crash*, 1992
Walter Jon Williams, *Hardwired*, 1986
Dave Wolverton, *On My Way to Paradise*, 1989

**4192**

MEL ODOM

## Headhunters

(New York: Roc, 1997)

**Story type:** Science Fiction (Cyberpunk; Science Fantasy)
**Series:** Shadowrun
**Major character(s):** Jack Skater, Mercenary, Cyborg; Archangel, Mythical Creature (elf), Computer Expert; Duran, Mythical Creature (orc), Mercenary
**Time period(s):** 2050s (2057)
**Locale(s):** Seattle, Washington

**Summary:** The trail of the plot leading to the dragon Dunkelzahn's assassination runs through a double agent, also conveniently dead. Jack Skater's team must steal the body out of the morgue. When they discover that a lot of powerful people want this corpse, they learn that keeping hold of a dead body may prove easier than staying alive.

**Other books you might like:**
Pat Cadigan, *Fools*, 1992
Charles de Lint, *Svaha*, 1989
Eric James Fullilove, *Circle of One*, 1996
Ian McDonald, *Terminal Cafe*, 1994
Richard Paul Russo, *Destroying Angel*, 1992

**4193**

MEL ODOM

## Lethal Interface

(New York: Roc, 1992)

**Story type:** Science Fiction (Cyberpunk; Mystery)
**Major character(s):** Mick Traven, Detective—Police (vice); Earl Brandsetter, Murderer, Computer Expert
**Time period(s):** 21st century
**Locale(s):** Dallas, Texas

**Summary:** Despite pressure and obfuscation from the Japanese megacorp Nagamuchi, Mick Traven pursues the lethal trail of a sexual psychopath into the highest ranks of the Nagamuchi where he discovers a killer who moves invisibly through the computer network to accomplish his sick missions.

**Other books you might like:**
Philip K. Dick, *Blade Runner*, 1982
George Alec Effinger, *When Gravity Fails*, 1987
Victor Milan, *The Cybernetic Samurai*, 1986
Neal Stephenson, *Snow Crash*, 1992
John E. Stith, *Redshift Rendezvous*, 1990
Walter Jon Williams, *Days of Atonement*, 1991
Walter Jon Williams, *Voice of the Whirlwind*, 1987
Dave Wolverton, *On My Way to Paradise*, 1989

**4194**

KEVIN O'DONNELL JR.

## Fire on the Border

(New York: Roc, 1990)

**Story type:** Science Fiction (Military)
**Major character(s):** Kajiwara Hiroshi, Military Personnel; Darcy Lee, Military Personnel; Daitaku, Clone
**Time period(s):** 24th century (2351)
**Locale(s):** Earth

**Summary:** The alien Wayholder Empire has discovered that combat-trained troops have a much higher survival rate in their war with the Korrin. They decide to use the human colony worlds as the final step of basic training, threatening humanity with extinction if they defend the planets. Kajiwara, Darcy and Daitaku combine resources to compel the Wayholders to compromise.

**Other books you might like:**
C.J. Cherryh, *Rimrunners*, 1990
Gordon R. Dickson, *Soldier, Ask Not*, 1967
David Drake, *Hammer's Slammers*, 1979
Joe Haldeman, *The Forever War*, 1975
Keith Laumer, *The Complete Bolo*, 1990

**4195**

NICK O'DONOHOE

## The Healing of Crossroads

(New York: Ace, 1996)

**Story type:** Fantasy (Alternate World; Adventure)
**Series:** Crossroads
**Major character(s):** BJ Vaughan, Veterinarian; Charles ''Sugar'' Franklin Dobbs, Professor; The Griffin, Mythical Creature
**Time period(s):** 1990s; Indeterminate
**Locale(s):** Kendrick, Virginia; Crossroads, Fictional Country

**Summary:** With the help of the Book of Strangeways, BJ travels through real and imagined realms. When she discovers that mythical creatures suffer when away from Crossroads, BJ must find a way to entice them to return to Crossroads for treatment and recovery.

**Other books you might like:**
Charles de Lint, *Memory and Dream*, 1994
Janet Kagan, *Mirabile*, 1994
Larry Niven, *The Flight of the Horse*, 1973
Jody Lynn Nye, *Medicine Show*, 1994
Jody Lynn Nye, *Taylor's Ark*, 1993
James White, *Sector General*, 1983

## 4196

### NICK O'DONOHOE

## *The Magic and the Healing*

(New York: Ace, 1994)

**Story type:** Fantasy (Alternate World; Adventure)
**Series:** Crossroads
**Major character(s):** BJ Vaughan, Veterinarian; Charles "Sugar" Franklin Dobbs, Professor, Veterinarian; Lee Anne Harrison, Student, Veterinarian
**Time period(s):** 1990s; Indeterminate
**Locale(s):** Kendrick, Virginia; Crossroads, Fictional Country

**Summary:** When a failed class and her mother's death from Huntington's chorea nearly drive BJ from veterinary studies, Sugar gives BJ an unusual horn to research along with a guide to unbiological species. BJ plans a repair technique which she utilizes on a most unusual field trip to Crossroads where she mends a unicorn's horn. Travel in Crossroads brings the students practice in treating unusual species and offers BJ the hope of a cure for her potential genetic problems.

**Other books you might like:**
Algis Budrys, *Hard Landing*, 1993
Janet Kagan, *Mirabile*, 1991
Jody Lynn Nye, *Medicine Show*, 1994
Jody Lynn Nye, *Taylor's Ark*, 1993
Mary Alexander Walker, *The Scathach and the Maeve's Daughter*, 1990
James White, *Hospital Station*, 1962

## 4197

### NICK O'DONOHOE

## *Too, Too Solid Flesh*

(Lake Geneva, WI: TSR, 1989)

**Story type:** Science Fiction (Mystery)
**Major character(s):** Hamlet, Android, Actor; Horatio, Actor
**Time period(s):** Indeterminate Future
**Locale(s):** Earth

**Summary:** In the last live theater on Earth, androids perform *Hamlet* in front of an audience made up largely of holographic images. Moreover the androids don't simply play their characters; they are the characters, twenty-four hours a day. When the human creator of the androids is murdered, Hamlet sets out to discover the identity of the murderer. He is aided by the human being who, unbeknownst to anyone else, has taken on the role of Horatio. This is O'Donohoe's first science fiction novel.

**Other books you might like:**
Isaac Asimov, *Robot Dreams*, 1986
John Brunner, *The Productions of Time*, 1967
Frederik Pohl, *Narabedla, Ltd.*, 1988
Jack Vance, *Showboat World*, 1975
Jack Vance, *Space Opera*, 1965

## 4198

### NICK O'DONOHOE

## *Under the Healing Sign*

(New York: Ace, 1995)

**Story type:** Fantasy (Alternate World; Adventure)
**Series:** Crossroads

**Major character(s):** BJ Vaughan, Veterinarian; Polyta, Mythical Creature (hippoi), Leader; Lee Anne Harrison, Student, Veterinarian
**Time period(s):** 1990s; Indeterminate
**Locale(s):** Kendrick, Virginia; Crossroads, Fictional Country

**Summary:** BJ hopes to improve life in Crossroads through healing and education in science, while others promote discord. Events propel BJ and her friends into a vital role as someone attempts to seal closed the path to Crossroads.

**Other books you might like:**
Janet Kagan, *Mirabile*, 1991
Larry Niven, *The Flight of the Horse*, 1973
Jody Lynn Nye, *Medicine Show*, 1994
Jody Lynn Nye, *Taylor's Ark*, 1993

## 4199

### JOY OESTREICHER, Editor
### RICHARD SINGER, Co-Editor

## *Air Fish*

(Concord, California: Catseye Press, 1993)

**Story type:** Horror (Anthology)

**Summary:** The editors have assembled 50 stories, poems, prose fragments, and works in progress, both original and reprint, from some of the more interesting and challenging writers working in the science fiction, fantasy, and horror small press today. Included are Thom Metzger's view of a future in which women enslave men, "Downbound Train"; John Shirley's hallucinogenic take on a victim of self-help therapy, "Sweet Armageddon"; D.F. Lewis's confusion of objective and subjective perceptions in "Milk's Mirror"; and Adam Troy-Castro's disturbing child's-eye view of a dysfunctional family, "The House of Nails." The book is nicely illustrated by a variety of small press artists.

**Other books you might like:**
Peter Enfantino, *Quick Chills*, 1991
Robert Morrish, *Quick Chills II*, 1992
   Peter Enfantino, co-editor
Brian Smart, *Best of the Midwest's Science Fiction, Fantasy and Horror, Volume I*, 1992
   editor
Brian Smart, *Best of the Midwest's Science Fiction, Fantasy and Horror, Volume II*, 1993
   editor

## 4200

### JOY OESTREICHER, Editor

## *Alpha Gallery*

(Cupertino, California: SPWAO, 1991)

**Story type:** Horror (Anthology)

**Summary:** Sixty-one selections from the fantasy, horror and science fiction small presses, including poetry, prose and artwork by Kathe Koja, Steve Rasnic Tem, Bentley Little, Elizabeth Massie, Bruce Boston and numerous others.

**Other books you might like:**
Peter Enfantino, *Quick Chills*, 1990
George Hatch, *Guignoir and Other Furies*, 1991
Jessica Amanda Salmonson, *Tales by Moonlight II*, 1989
David B. Silva, *Best of The Horror Show*, 1987
J.N. Williamson, *Masques III*, 1989

## 4201

### ANDREW J. OFFUTT

## *Deathknight*

(New York: Ace, 1990)

**Story type:** Fantasy (Adventure)
**Major character(s):** Falc of Risskor, Knight
**Time period(s):** Indeterminate
**Locale(s):** The City-States of Sij, Fictional Country

**Summary:** The Sons of Ashah are Knights of the Order Most Old and are honor-sworn to preserve the peace of the city-states of Sij. When someone does the unthinkable and starts killing the Knights of the Order, one by one, it is Falc of Risskor, a Son of Ashad who must bring to justice the slayer, or himself be slain.

**Other books you might like:**
Glen Cook, *The Black Company*, 1984
Gordon R. Dickson, *Jamie the Red*, 1984
Janet Morris, *Tempus Bound*, 1989
    Chris Morris, co-author
Jerry Pournelle, *Janissaries*, 1979
Gene Wolfe, *The Shadow of the Torturer*, 1980
Gene Wolfe, *Soldier of Arete*, 1989

## 4202

### ANDREW J. OFFUTT

## *The Shadow of Sorcery*

(New York: Ace, 1993)

**Story type:** Fantasy (Magic Conflict; Quest)
**Series:** Thieves' World
**Major character(s):** Shadowspawn, Thief, Adventurer; Hanse, Adventurer, Warrior
**Time period(s):** Indeterminate
**Locale(s):** Firaqua, Fictional City

**Summary:** To free Firaqua from the rule of an evil sorcerer and save the life of a woman, Shadowspawn ventures into a deadly labyrinth in search of the fabled Rings of Senek.

**Other books you might like:**
Robert Asprin, *Thieves' World*, 1979
    editor
David Drake, *Dagger*, 1988
Janet Morris, *Beyond the Veil*, 1985
Janet Morris, *Beyond Wizardwall*, 1986
Janet Morris, *City at the Edge of Time*, 1988
    Chris Morris, co-author
Janet Morris, *Tempus*, 1987

## 4203

### MARTIN O'GRIOFA
### SHEILA KERN, Illustrator

## *Irish Tales of the Supernatural*

(New York: Sterling/Main Street, 1996)

**Story type:** Horror (Anthology)
**Locale(s):** Ireland

**Summary:** This anthology aimed at younger readers collects tales of horror and fantasy set in Ireland by 12 authors whose work was published primarily in the 19th century. Joseph Sheridan LeFanu is represented by two stories, "The White Cat of Drumgunniol," which features a spectral cat, and "Sir Dominick's Bargain," about a man who sells his soul to the devil. "Legend of Bottle Hill" by Thomas Crofton Croker and "Hairy Rouchy" by Patricia Kennedy are both humorous fantasies in the Irish folk tradition. Seamus Mac-Manus's "The Bewitched Fiddle" tells of a born-again Christian who discovers his fiddle is still imbued with the mischief of his old days. Jeremiah Curtin's "St. Martin's Eve" is about the sad fate that befalls a family who neglects to pay their proper respects to a household saint on his feast day.

**Other books you might like:**
Peter Haining, *Wild Night Company*, 1970
    editor
Joseph Hone, *Irish Ghost Stories*, 1979
    editor
Jim McGarry, *Irish Tales of Terror*, 1971
    editor
Daniel O'Keefe, *The Book of Famous Irish Ghost Stories*, 1986
    editor
H.M. Tichenor, *Irish Fairy Tales*, 1923
    editor
Peter Tremayne, *Irish Masters of Fantasy*, 1979
    editor

## 4204

### BEN OHLANDER
### DAVID DRAKE, Co-Author

## *Enemy of My Enemy*

(New York: Baen, 1995)

**Story type:** Science Fiction (Adventure; Military)
**Series:** Terra Nova
**Major character(s):** Ward Tuchman, Laird, Avenger; Mona, Avenger, Sidekick; Carlo Theisiger, Mercenary
**Time period(s):** Indeterminate Future
**Locale(s):** New Hope, Planet—Imaginary

**Summary:** After the destruction of his home and family in an ambush by the Wing clan, Ward Tuchman vows revenge. He slowly gathers allies while simultaneously evading further assassination attempts by his enemies.

**Other books you might like:**
David Drake, *Northworld*, 1990
David Drake, *Justice*, 1992
    Northworld 3
David Drake, *Vengeance*, 1991
    Northworld 2
Joe Haldeman, *The Forever War*, 1975
Robert A. Heinlein, *Starship Troopers*, 1959
John Steakley, *Armor*, 1984

## 4205

### CLAUDIA O'KEEFE

## *Black Snow Days*

(New York: Ace Books, 1990)

**Story type:** Science Fiction (Post-Nuclear Holocaust)
**Major character(s):** Eric Pope, Cyborg; Vivian, Spirit (Doppleganger)
**Time period(s):** 21st century (2046)
**Locale(s):** United States

**Summary:** Eric Pope is in a serious accident and lapses into a coma. He awakes twelve years later to a post-nuclear holocaust world whose survivors are all seemingly half-mad. Barely maintaining his own sanity, Eric discovers that he's the victim of a bizarre experiment. His body has been enhanced through reconstructive surgery, his brain has been tinkered with, and, strangely enough, there appears to be two of him. Living within him now is Vivian, his own female self. Although only he can see her, his lunatic doctors insist that she's entirely real. Then the doctors tell him the terrifying reason why he's been remade into something more than human.

**Other books you might like:**
Philip K. Dick, *The Penultimate Truth*, 1964
Richard Kadrey, *Metrophage*, 1988
Frederik Pohl, *Man Plus*, 1976
Mordecai Roshwald, *Level 7*, 1959

---

## 4206

**CLAUDIA O'KEEFE**, Editor

### Ghosttide

(Sherman Oaks, California: Revenant Press, 1993)

**Story type:** Horror (Anthology)

**Summary:** This book collects 15 stories of subtle horror, 12 original to the book. Among the best are Hugh B. Cave's ''The Mountains of Time,'' concerned with ghostly salvation in the ruins of a Jamaican coffee plantation; Susan Palwick's ''Force of Habit,'' about a workaholic whose work ethic outlives his body; and William Browning Spencer's ''Irrational Fears,'' in which victims of a bizarre self-help therapy for recovering addicts develop the power to induce hallucinations in others. Also included is Robert Bloch's classic *Weird Tales* story, ''Iron Mask,'' which updates the medieval legend of a man unjustly imprisoned in an iron mask to World War II.

**Other books you might like:**
Charles L. Grant, *Final Shadows*, 1991
    editor
Thomas F. Monteleone, *Borderlands 3*, 1993
    editor
Chris Morgan, *Dark Fantasies*, 1989
    editor
Paul F. Olson, *Post Mortem: New Tales of Ghostly Horror*, 1989
    David B. Silva, co-editor

---

## 4207

**BEN OKRI**

### The Famished Road

(New York: Doubleday, 1992)

**Story type:** Fantasy (Contemporary; Legend)
**Major character(s):** Azaro, Child, Psychic; Madame Koto, Saloon Keeper/Owner
**Time period(s):** 1960s
**Locale(s):** Africa

**Summary:** Azaro never severs his connection to the spirit world at birth, allowing him to view the mortal realm with perspective rooted in the realm of souls. Azaro brings augmented understanding to the child's vision of a family struggling to survive in the midst of sometimes violent change within a poverty-struck African ghetto. 1991 winner of the prestigious Booker Prize for Fiction in Britain.

**Other books you might like:**
Roger D. Abrahams, *Afro-American Folk Tales*, 1985
Maya Kaathryn Bohnhoff, *The Meri*, 1992
Alan Dean Foster, *Into the Out Of*, 1986
Edward Myers, *The Mountain Made of Light*, 1992

Paul Radin, *African Folktales*, 1985
    editor
Mike Resnick, *Bwana & Bully!*, 1991
Mike Resnick, *Future Earths: Under African Skies*, 1993
Elizabeth Ann Scarborough, *Last Refuge*, 1992
Lucius Shepard, *Kalimantan*, 1992
Gerald Vizenor, *Dead Voices: Natural Agonies in the Real World*, 1992

---

## 4208

**BEN OKRI**

### Songs of Enchantment

(New York: Doubleday, 1993)

**Story type:** Fantasy (Contemporary; Legend)
**Major character(s):** Azaro, Child, Psychic; Madame Koto, Saloon Keeper/Owner, Political Figure; Dad, Parent, Political Figure
**Time period(s):** 1960s
**Locale(s):** Africa; Madame Koto's Bar, Mythical Place

**Summary:** Due to his connection to the spirit realm, distractions from tormenting spirits drive Azaro away from school. Transformations at Madame Koto's bar and in Azaro's family disrupt the political hopes of Azaro's father as Azaro's mother affiliates with Madame Koto's ascendant cult. Meanwhile, mythical thought-forms of primal creation appear in the turbulent ghetto.

**Other books you might like:**
Louis de Bernieres, *Senor Vivo and the Coca Lord*, 1992
Louis de Bernieres, *The War of Don Emmanuel's Nether Parts*, 1992
Elizabeth Ann Scarborough, *Last Refuge*, 1992
Gerald Vizenor, *Dead Voices: Natural Agonies in the Real World*, 1992

---

## 4209

**SUSAN TORIAN OLAN**

### The Earth Remembers

(Lake Geneva, WI: TSR, 1990)

**Story type:** Science Fiction (Post-Holocaust)
**Major character(s):** Cimarron Langtry, Wanderer
**Time period(s):** Indeterminate Future
**Locale(s):** Texas (What was once the Texas-Mexico border); Mexico

**Summary:** Langtry, a subterranean race of radiation mutants, and a tribe of Comanches join forces to destroy the oppressive post-nuclear holocaust government of Tesharka. Olan's first novel.

**Other books you might like:**
David Brin, *The Postman*, 1985
Algis Budrys, *Some Will Not Die*, 1954
Sterling E. Lanier, *Hiero's Journey*, 1973
Walter M. Miller Jr., *A Canticle for Leibowitz*, 1960

---

## 4210

**PATRICK O'LEARY**

### Door Number Three

(New York: Tor, 1995)

**Story type:** Science Fiction (Time Travel; Horror)
**Major character(s):** John Donnelly, Psychologist, Time Traveler; Laura Johnson, Patient, Time Traveler; Saul Lowe, Inventor, Time Traveler

**Time period(s):** 1990s
**Locale(s):** Detroit, Michigan

**Summary:** Laura Johnson, a new therapy patient, intrigues John Donnelly when she claims the alien Holock kidnapped her and will let her remain on Earth if she can convince one person of this. First novel.

**Other books you might like:**

Jonathan Carroll, *Bones of the Moon*, 1987
Jonathan Carroll, *From the Teeth of Angels*, 1994
Nancy Kress, *Beggars in Spain*, 1993
Christopher Pike, *The Eternal Enemy*, 1993
Roger Zelazny, *The Dream Master*, 1966

**4211**

### PATRICK O'LEARY

## The Gift

(New York: Tor, 1997)

**Story type:** Fantasy (Magic Conflict; Science Fiction)
**Major character(s):** The Teller, Storyteller; Tim, Teenager, Adventurer; Simon, Royalty (king)
**Time period(s):** Indeterminate
**Locale(s):** At Sea; Fictional Country

**Summary:** The gifts of magic from the gods bring a price. To those aboard ship, the Teller speaks of King Simon who suffers the gift of magically acute hearing, Tim, deprived early of childhood, and their efforts to bring back the balance of magical forces disrupted by the Usher of Night.

**Other books you might like:**

Ursula K. Le Guin, *Tehanu: The Last Book of Earthsea*, 1990
Patricia A. McKillip, *The Book of Atrix Wolfe*, 1995
Rachel Pollack, *Godmother Night*, 1996
Philip Pullman, *The Golden Compass*, 1996
Gene Wolfe, *Peace*, 1975

**4212**

### PAUL F. OLSON, Editor
### DAVID B. SILVA, Co-Editor

## Dead End: City Limits

(New York: St. Martin's, 1991)

**Story type:** Horror (Anthology)

**Summary:** Seventeen stories which depend on urban environments for their horrors. Included are John Shirley's tale of urban paranoia, "Ash," Elizabeth Massies' tale of a peculiar street gang initiation, "Lock Her Room," Poppy Z. Brite's story of a trip to the abortion clinic with unexpected results, "The Ash of Memory, The Dust of Deire," and Gary L. Raisor's self explanatory "Hell Train."

**Other books you might like:**

Charles L. Grant, *Doom City*, 1987
Charles L. Grant, *Greystone Bay*, 1985
Charles L. Grant, *The SeaHarp Hotel*, 1990
William F. Nolan, *Urban Horrors*, 1990
    Martin H. Greenberg, co-author

**4213**

### PAUL F. OLSON

## Night Prophets

(New York: NAL Onyx, 1989)

**Story type:** Horror (Vampire Story)
**Major character(s):** Curt Potter, Student (Ministerial student); Arthur Bach, Religious (Televangelist), Vampire
**Time period(s):** 1980s
**Locale(s):** Chicago, Illinois

**Summary:** After joining Universal Ministries, Curt Potter finds himself confronting an ancient sect of vampires. He recruits a small group of friends to do battle with the undead. This is Olson's first novel.

**Other books you might like:**

T. Chris Martindale, *Nightblood*, 1990

**4214**

### PAUL F. OLSON, Editor
### DAVID B. SILVA, Co-Editor

## Post Mortem: New Tales of Ghostly Horror

(New York: Dell Abyss, 1992)

**Story type:** Horror (Anthology)

**Summary:** This excellent anthology of contemporary ghost stories, originally published in 1989, collects 18 stories by some of the best writers in the field. Included are Steve and Melanie Tem's "Resettling," a haunted house story involving a dysfunctional family; Ramsey Campbell's "The Guide," a brilliant homage to the fiction of M.R. James; Thomas Tessier's "Blanca," a ghostly rendering of "disappearances" in a third-world country undergoing political revolution; and P.W. Sinclair's moving "Getting Back," about a man haunted by the image of his failed life.

**Other books you might like:**

Robert Phillips, *Triumph of the Night*, 1988
Charles G. Waugh, *East Coast Ghosts*, 1989
    Martin H. Greenberg, co-editor
Donald A. Wollhcim, *The Avon Ghost Reader*, 1946
    editor

**4215**

### DENNIS O'NEIL

## Batman: Knightfall

(New York: Bantam Spectra, 1994)

**Story type:** Science Fiction (Adventure)
**Series:** Batman
**Major character(s):** Bruce "Batman" Wayne, Hero, Detective—Amateur; Bane, Criminal
**Time period(s):** 21st century
**Locale(s):** Gotham City

**Summary:** To take over Gotham City, Bane releases Batman's criminally insane enemies from Arkham Asylum, intending to attack Batman after battles with the escapees weaken him. Novelizes a comic book series issued 1992-1994.

**Other books you might like:**

Lynn Abbey, *Catwoman*, 1992
    Robert Asprin, co-author
Craig Shaw Gardner, *The Batman Murders*, 1992

Martin H. Greenberg, *The Further Adventures of Batman 3: Featuring Catwoman*, 1993
editor
Simon Hawke, *Batman: To Stalk a Specter*, 1991
Joe R. Lansdale, *Captured by the Engines*, 1991

## 4216

### REBECCA ORE

## Alien Bootlegger and Other Stories

(New York: Tor, 1993)

**Story type:** Science Fiction (Collection)

**Summary:** Contains one essay, ''Aliens and the Artificial Other,'' plus six stories discussing alien and artificial intelligences as in the title story whose alien protagonist goes native, finding satisfaction in making bootleg booze with a psychedelic kick.

**Other books you might like:**
Pat Cadigan, *Patterns*, 1989
Philip K. Dick, *The Best of Philip K. Dick*, 1977
Michael Flynn, *The Nanotech Chronicles*, 1991
Nancy Kress, *The Aliens of Earth*, 1993
Cordwainer Smith, *The Best of Cordwainer Smith*, 1975
Marc Stiegler, *The Gentle Seduction*, 1990
Theodore Sturgeon, *Aliens 4*, 1959
John Varley, *Blue Champagne*, 1986

## 4217

### REBECCA ORE

## Being Alien

(New York: Tor, 1989)

**Story type:** Science Fiction (First Contact)
**Major character(s):** Tom Red Clay, Diplomat; Marianne Schweigman, Linguist
**Time period(s):** 1980s
**Locale(s):** Earth; Karst, Planet—Imaginary; Outer Space

**Summary:** Tom returns to Earth to do research for the Interstellar Federation and meets Marianne, an out of work Berkeley Ph.D. whom his alien bosses think would make him an ideal mate. Oddly, they turn out to be correct. Tom and Marianne return to the Federation base on Karst along with her sister Molly, Molly's husband Sam, and Tom's brother Warren. As Tom pursues his career as a diplomat, Marianne fits into the multi-species Federation with few problems, but the other humans find the situation much more traumatic.

**Other books you might like:**
David Brin, *Startide Rising*, 1983
David Brin, *The Uplift War*, 1987
Octavia E. Butler, *Adulthood Rites*, 1988
Octavia E. Butler, *Dawn*, 1987
Octavia E. Butler, *Imago*, 1989
David Gerrold, *Chess with a Dragon*, 1987
David Alexander Smith, *Rendezvous*, 1988

## 4218

### REBECCA ORE

## Gaia's Toys

(New York: Tor, 1995)

**Story type:** Science Fiction (Dystopian; Cyberpunk)

**Major character(s):** Allison Dodge, Activist (eco-terrorist); Dorcas Rae, Scientist (genetics), Researcher; Willie Hunsucker, Cyborg (drode head)
**Time period(s):** 21st century
**Locale(s):** Virginia; New York, New York

**Summary:** After a sinister government official holds and brainwashes Allison Dodge, she joins with Dorcas Rae and Willie Hunsucker in an attempt to restore a more resilient worldwide ecology.

**Other books you might like:**
Kevin J. Anderson, *Ill Wind*, 1995
Doug Beason, co-author
John Barnes, *Kaleidoscope Century*, 1995
David Brin, *Earth*, 1990
Thomas A. Easton, *Sparrowhawk*, 1990
Nicola Griffith, *Slow River*, 1995
Neal Stephenson, *Snow Crash*, 1992
Bruce Sterling, *Heavy Weather*, 1994

## 4219

### REBECCA ORE

## Human to Human

(New York: Tor, 1990)

**Story type:** Science Fiction (First Contact)
**Series:** Tom Red Clay
**Major character(s):** Tom Red Clay, Diplomat; Karriaagzh, Scholar, Administrator; Black Amber, Administrator
**Time period(s):** 1990s
**Locale(s):** Karst, Planet—Imaginary; Boston, Massachusetts

**Summary:** Since he was taken from Lloyd, Virginia when he was 19 years old, Tom Red Clay has lived on Karst, an artificial planet built thousands of years ago by five alien species to be an inter-cultural university planet and center of the Federation. Tom, now a husband and father, is sent to Earth as part of the team assigned to bring Earth peacefully into the Federation.

**Other books you might like:**
David Brin, *Startide Rising*, 1983
Octavia E. Butler, *Adulthood Rites*, 1988
Octavia E. Butler, *Dawn*, 1987
Octavia E. Butler, *Imago*, 1989
Jeffrey A. Carver, *The Rapture Effect*, 1987
J. Brian Clarke, *The Expediter*, 1990
David Alexander Smith, *Rendezvous*, 1988

## 4220

### REBECCA ORE

## The Illegal Rebirth of Billy the Kid

(New York: Tor, 1991)

**Story type:** Science Fiction (Future Shock; Genetic Manipulation)
**Major character(s):** Billy the Kid, Android (Chimera), Experimental Subject; Jane Ayers, Health Care Professional; Simon Boyle, Scientist, Criminal
**Time period(s):** 2060s (2067)
**Locale(s):** Wyoming; New York; Virginia

**Summary:** Billy the Kid is a Chimera (artificial person) created and killed nine times by Simon Boyle. This last time he escapes, and with Jane Ayers, an ASPCA worker, goes to live in the primitive Appalachia Preserve. But Turner, a CIA man, catches up with the two, kills Boyle for treasonous experimentation and sees to it that neither Billy nor Jane will ever leave Appalachia again on the pain of death.

**Other books you might like:**
Philip K. Dick, *Blade Runner*, 1982
Robert Silverberg, *Tower of Glass*, 1970
Nicholas Yermakov, *Clique*, 1982
    pseudonum of Simon Hawke

---

**4221**

REBECCA ORE

## Slow Funeral

(New York: Tor, 1994)

**Story type:** Fantasy (Religious; Contemporary)
**Major character(s):** Maude Fuller, Witch, Psychic; Doug Sanderheim, Engineer, Boyfriend (Maude's); Partridge, Grandparent, Witch
**Time period(s):** 1990s
**Locale(s):** Bracken County, Virginia; Kobold, Virginia; Appalachians

**Summary:** A psychic call forces Maude to return to the Appalachian home she fled to avoid learning use of the native magic and its resulting control over others. Intending only to help her grandmother, Maude becomes more involved when she finds that people intend to use Doug in an evil attempt to keep away technological development.

**Other books you might like:**
Gael Baudino, *Strands of Sunlight*, 1994
Jack Cady, *Inagehi*, 1994
Tom Deitz, *Soulsmith*, 1991
Suzette Haden Elgin, *Twelve Fair Kingdoms*, 1981
Nina Kiriki Hoffman, *The Thread That Binds the Bones*, 1993

---

**4222**

MICHAEL O'ROURKE

## The Bad Thing

(New York: HarperPaperbacks, 1995)

**Story type:** Horror (Serial Killer)
**Major character(s):** Johnny, Murderer; Chris Kelly, Criminal (professional assassin); Sherry Mahan, Police Officer (sheriff's deputy)
**Time period(s):** 1990s (1994)
**Locale(s):** Bremerton, Pennsylvania

**Summary:** Nearly 30 years after his teenage sweetheart disappeared and was never found again, Chris Kelly returns to his hometown to investigate the disappearance of a relative. Legends of a mysterious being known as the Phantom bring Chris to the abandoned Summerland hotel, the secret home of Johnny, a local half-wit who was traumatized psychologically by his mother and who has been applying his taxidermy skills on "disappeared" people for the last 30 years.

**Other books you might like:**
Robert Bloch, *Psycho*, 1959
John Driver, *The Hunger of the Beast*, 1991
Thomas Harris, *The Silence of the Lambs*, 1992
Robert D. Lee, *The Keeper*, 1993

---

**4223**

MICHAEL O'ROURKE

## Darkling

(New York: HarperPaperbacks, 1994)

**Story type:** Horror (Occult)
**Major character(s):** Sara Raynor, Spirit; Rick Masterson, Journalist (television); Phylis Rand, Hotel Owner
**Time period(s):** 1990s (1994)
**Locale(s):** Spirit Lake, Nevada

**Summary:** Journalist Rick Masterson repairs to deserted Spirit Lake in dead winter to recover spiritually from the devastation he has witnessed in South Africa, Bosnia, and other trouble spots around the world. But an elemental haunts the setting, and finds itself so attracted to the darkness in Rick's soul that even the protective ghost of Sara Raynor, a woman who died thanks to the elemental's intervention years before, may not be able to save him. This is the author's first novel.

**Other books you might like:**
Randall Boyll, *After Sundown*, 1989
Stephen King, *The Shining*, 1977
Michael B. Sirota, *Demon Shadows*, 1989
Bernard Taylor, *Sweetheart, Sweetheart*, 1977

---

**4224**

MICHAEL O'ROURKE

## The Undine

(New York: HarperPaperbacks, 1996)

**Story type:** Horror (Occult)
**Major character(s):** Brian Kroft, Journalist; Stanley Williams, Photographer; Toby Mendel, Anthropologist
**Time period(s):** 1990s (1996)
**Locale(s):** Bel Air, California; Rookers Cove, Oregon

**Summary:** The escape from a remote business retreat of a clutch of mythological creatures known as the Undine threatens the world with a species whose contact brings sexual infatuation and death. Brian Kroft sets out to learn the full story of how the creatures have survived into this day, unaware that he is being pursued by ruthless businessmen who will stop at nothing to keep their involvement with Undine secret.

**Other books you might like:**
Mark A. Clements, *Lorelei*, 1994
Ron Dee, *Succumb*, 1994
John Farris, *Wildwood*, 1986
Christopher Fowler, *Red Bride*, 1992
Yvonne Navarro, *Species*, 1995

---

**4225**

CARY OSBORNE

## Darkloom

(New York: Ace, 1998)

**Story type:** Science Fiction (Military)
**Series:** Arden Grenfell
**Major character(s):** Arden Grenfell, Bodyguard; Jessa, Ruler, Royalty (empress)
**Time period(s):** Indeterminate Future
**Locale(s):** Glory, Planet—Imaginary

**Summary:** Empress Jessa has finally agreed to become the ruler of Glory, although she has little interest in politics. As the wedding day of the empress approaches, her most loyal bodyguard discovers that the various plots within the aristocracy are becoming a serious threat to the woman she is sworn to serve. There are plans to remove her from power, by killing her if necessary.

**Other books you might like:**
Lois McMaster Bujold, *Brothers in Arms*, 1989
William C. Dietz, *Bodyguard*, 1994
W. Michael Gear, *Relic of Empire*, 1989
Steve Perry, *Brother Death*, 1992
Steve Perry, *The Man Who Never Missed*, 1985

---

**4226**

**CARY OSBORNE**

## Deathweave

(New York: Ace, 1998)

**Story type:** Science Fiction (Adventure)
**Major character(s):** Arden Grenfell, Bodyguard; Jessa, Royalty (princess), Fugitive; Chase, Military Personnel
**Time period(s):** Indeterminate Future
**Locale(s):** Glory, Planet—Imaginary; Caldera, Planet—Imaginary

**Summary:** Pledged to guard Princess Jessa, Arden Grenfell helps the young woman to escape her stifling life at court. Years later, as the princess' mother dies, she offers Arden a pardon if she finds the runaway. Unfortunately, not everyone wants Jessa found.

**Other books you might like:**
Emma Bull, *Falcon*, 1989
Gordon R. Dickson, *Dorsai!*, 1976
David Drake, *Hammer's Slammers*, 1987
    expanded edition
Steve Perry, *The Man Who Never Missed*, 1985
Dennis Schmidt, *Kensho*, 1979

---

**4227**

**CARY OSBORNE**

## The Glaive

(New York: Ace, 1996)

**Story type:** Science Fiction (Mystical; Adventure)
**Series:** Glaive
**Major character(s):** Laicy "Iroshi" Campbell, Martial Arts Expert, Administrator; Ensi, Spirit, Martial Arts Expert; Jiron Yail, Police Officer
**Time period(s):** Indeterminate Future
**Locale(s):** Galicia, Planet—Imaginary; Bosque, Planet—Imaginary

**Summary:** A member of the Glaive, a close friend and mentor of Iroshi, dies during negotiations, the victim of a mob inspired by a mysterious organization dedicated to the Glaive's destruction. Investigating their plot leads Iroshi across the galaxy to a planet of ruins and savage carnivores. Sequel to *Iroshi*.

**Other books you might like:**
Steven Barnes, *Streetlethal*, 1983
Gordon R. Dickson, *Dorsai!*, 1976
Steve Perry, *The Man Who Never Missed*, 1985
Dennis Schmidt, *Kensho*, 1979
Roger Zelazny, *Warriors of Blood and Dream*, 1995
    Martin H. Greenberg, co-editor

---

**4228**

**CARY OSBORNE**

## Iroshi

(New York: Ace, 1995)

**Story type:** Science Fiction (Mystical; Adventure)
**Series:** Glaive
**Major character(s):** Laicy "Iroshi" Campbell, Martial Arts Expert, Wanderer; Mushimo, Martial Arts Expert (Kendo); Crowell, Martial Arts Expert, Heir
**Time period(s):** Indeterminate Future
**Locale(s):** Tokyo, Japan; Rune, Planet—Imaginary

**Summary:** A natural swordswoman, Laicy studies with Mushimo for two years before she finds the sword that speaks best to her. Old enemies attack Mushimo, who sends Laicy on as a warrior traveling where she feels a call to study or practice. Taking the name "Iroshi," she lands on Rune, called to the ruins of a temple.

**Other books you might like:**
Lois McMaster Bujold, *Shards of Honor*, 1986
Stephen Goldin, *Jade Darcy and the Affair of Honor*, 1988
    Mary Mason, co-author
Andre Norton, *Brother to Shadows*, 1993
Steve Perry, *The Man Who Never Missed*, 1985
Steve Perry, *The 97th Step*, 1989
Dennis Schmidt, *Kensho*, 1979

---

**4229**

**RICHARD OSBORNE**

## Demolition Man

(New York: Signet, 1993)

**Story type:** Science Fiction (Adventure)
**Major character(s):** John "Demolition Man" Spartan, Detective—Police; Simon Phoenix, Criminal, Murderer; Lenina Huxley, Police Officer
**Time period(s):** 2030s (2032); 1990s (1996)
**Locale(s):** San Angeles, California; Los Angeles, California

**Summary:** When Simon Phoenix escapes CryoPrison during a parole hearing, the vicious killer finds easy prey among the politically correct and well behaved residents of San Angeles. Desperate to rearrest Phoenix, the police thaw out his arresting officer, John Spartan, wrongly convicted of manslaughter, and parole him on the condition that he again apprehend Simon. Novelizes the film.

**Other books you might like:**
Philip K. Dick, *Blade Runner*, 1982
Dave Duncan, *Hero*, 1991
Stephen Goldin, *Jade Darcy and the Affair of Honor*, 1988
    Mary Mason, co-author
Ed Naha, *Robocop*, 1987
Richard Sapir, *The Destroyer #1: Created, the Destroyer*, 1971
    Warren Murphy, co-author
Robert Tine, *Universal Soldier*, 1992

---

**4230**

**JEFFREY OSIER**, Author/Illustrator

## Driftglider and Other Stories

(Pawtucket, Rhode Island: Montilla Publications, 1993)

**Story type:** Horror (Collection)

**Summary:** The author's first story collection brings together seven stories, four original to the volume, in which powerful emotions are manifest in strange relationships and even stranger monsters. In ''Driftglider,'' a troubled relationship takes the form of a weird creature of the snows. ''Snowlight'' tells of a boy whose troubled relationship with his father is mirrored by an unkillable stalker. And in ''Soul of a Spider'' a man's capacity to love takes the shape of a spiderlike monstrosity. The author illustrates all of the stories himself in surrealistic detail.

**Other books you might like:**
Michael A. Arnzen, *Needles and Sins*, 1993
D.F. Lewis, *The Best of D.F. Lewis*, 1992
Stephen Mark Rainey, *Fugue Devil and Other Weird Horrors*, 1993
Wayne Allen Sallee, *Pain-Grin*, 1993

---

**4231**

**JEFFREY OSIER**

### Horizon Lines
(Concord, California: Dark Regions, 1997)

**Story type:** Horror (Collection)

**Summary:** Seven stories, all previously published, in which strange, possibly supernatural experiences reflect or are colored by the unsettled minds of characters. Best selections include ''Snowlight,'' in which a young boy's anger over the death of his father manifests as a specter pursuing him; ''The Shabbie People,'' in which a man who may be mad discovers that his girlfriend is an otherwordly being; ''Why I Dropped Out of Art School,'' in which a young man's rite of passage into adulthood thrusts him into an unstable, supernaturally menacing world; and ''Don't Clean the Aquarium,'' in which a man's troubled emotional life is mirrored in the peculiarities of his living room fish tank. Elizabeth Massie supplies an introduction.

**Other books you might like:**
Gary A. Braunbeck, *Things Left Behind*, 1997
Cliff Burns, *The Reality Machine*, 1997
Brian Hopkins, *Something Haunts Us All*, 1996
Bentley Little, *Murmerous Haunts*, 1997
Stephen Mark Rainey, *Fugue Devil and Other Weird Horrors*, 1993
Wayne Allen Sallee, *With Wounds Still Wet*, 1996
David Niall Wilson, *The Fall of the House of Escher and Other Illusions*, 1996

---

**4232**

**PIERRE OUELLETTE**

### The Deus Machine
(New York: Villard, 1994)

**Story type:** Horror (Science Fiction)
**Major character(s):** Michael Riley, Computer Expert (programmer); DEUS, Artificial Intelligence; Jimi Tyler, Child (eight years old)
**Time period(s):** 2000s (2005)
**Locale(s):** Portland, Oregon; Washington, District of Columbia; New York, New York

**Summary:** In a future perched on the brink of political self-destruction, a computer programmed with artificial intelligence to be self perpetuating is abused by government agents performing chemical warfare experiments and begins creating mutant, shapeshifting life forms that threaten to overrun the Earth. This is the author's first novel.

**Other books you might like:**
Michael Crichton, *The Terminal Man*, 1972

Harlan Ellison, *I Have No Mouth and I Must Scream*, 1967
  in *Alone Against Tomorrow*
Daniel H. Gower, *The Orpheus Process*, 1992
D.F. Jones, *Colossus*, 1966

---

**4233**

**JAKE PAGE**

### Apacheria
(New York: Ballantine Del Rey, 1998)

**Story type:** Science Fiction (Alternate History)
**Major character(s):** Little Spring, Leader, Indian (Apache); Geronimo, Historical Figure, Indian (Apache); Juh, Leader, Indian (Apache)
**Time period(s):** 1880s; 1920s
**Locale(s):** Tucson, Arizona; Apacheria, Fictional Country; Southwest

**Summary:** To resist the U.S. Cavalry, Juh unites the Apache bands into an effective fighting force and establishes the independent country of Apacheria, with Geronimo acting as Ambassador to the United States. Juh's son attends Princeton University and outwits the Mob while running Apacheria's lucrative casino and resort business.

**Other books you might like:**
Richard Brautigan, *The Hawkline Monster*, 1974
Orson Scott Card, *Red Prophet*, 1988
Bill Dugan, *Geronimo*, 1994
Clifford D. Simak, *Mastodonia*, 1978
Harry Turtledove, *The Guns of the South: A Novel of the Civil War*, 1992

---

**4234**

**MICHAEL PAINE**

### The Colors of Hell
(New York: Charter, 1990)

**Story type:** Horror (Occult)
**Major character(s):** Charlotte Alderson, Widow(er); Clare Markham, Artist (stained glass artist), Religious; Robert Semnarek, Lawyer
**Time period(s):** 1950s; 1920s
**Locale(s):** New York, New York; Marrakesh, Morocco

**Summary:** In order to settle her father's estate and gain the inheritance bequeathed to her in his will, Charlotte Alderson must track down her sister Clare, who, along with her husband Marty, disappeared in Morocco 30 years earlier. In a convent deep in the Anti-Atlas mountains Charlotte, her son Steve, and lawyer Robert Semnarek find that Clare has become Sister Joseph, abbess to an ancient, autonomous order of nuns the local Bedouins call The House of Fifty. The centerpiece of this provocative novel is Clare's memoir, in which she tells how she went from a stained-glass designer at Tiffany's in New York to head of a convent whose members may guard one of the gateways to hell.

**Other books you might like:**
Elaine Bergstrom, *Shattered Glass*, 1989
Robert Silverberg, *The Book of Skulls*, 1971
Roland Topor, *The Tenant*, 1966

## 4235
### MICHAEL PAINE
### Owl Light
(New York: Charter, 1989)

**Story type:** Horror (Reanimated Dead)
**Major character(s):** Sybil Antissa, Sorceress (enchantress); Paul Eiden, Religious (would-be TV evangelist)
**Time period(s):** 1980s
**Locale(s):** Mill Creek, Pennsylvania (a rural small town)

**Summary:** Sybil, an enchantress who periodically animates the dead, seduces and manipulates three men—a cynical college biology teacher, an innocent young student, and a worldly preacher—into fathering her child and launching her mysterious "religion."

**Other books you might like:**
H. Rider Haggard, *She*, 1886
Arthur Machen, *The Great God Pan*, 1890
William Sloane, *To Walk the Night*, 1939

## 4236
### JEAN PAIVA
### The Lilith Factor
(New York: NAL Onyx, 1989)

**Story type:** Horror (Femme Fatale)
**Major character(s):** Elsie Crawford Vaughan, Doctor, Twin; Talia Crawford Harrah, Twin (The "dark" twin)
**Time period(s):** 1980s
**Locale(s):** United States

**Summary:** Twin sisters—one "light" and one "dark"—embody the ancient power of "Lilith." The dark sister, Talia, vows to become supremely powerful by absorbing her sister's untapped energies—and destroying Elsie in the process.

**Other books you might like:**
Thomas F. Monteleone, *Lyrica*, 1987
Simon Raven, *Doctors Wear Scarlet*, 1960

## 4237
### JESSICA PALMER
### Dark Lullaby
(New York: Pocket, 1991)

**Story type:** Horror (Possession)
**Major character(s):** Shelley Graves, Child (dead child); Sara Graves, Child; Elliott Graves, Teacher (of music appreciation)
**Time period(s):** 1990s
**Locale(s):** Claremont

**Summary:** Eleven-year-old Shelley Graves dies in a house fire as a consequence of her parents' irresponsibility. But Shelley follows the Graves to their new home and makes their life hell, avenging her death through the body of her baby sister Sara, who soon begins to display all the nasty habits that made Shelley such a difficult child. This is the author's first novel.

**Other books you might like:**
Lawrence Block, *Ariel*, 1980
Frank DeFelitta, *Audrey Rose*, 1975
Thomas Tryon, *The Other*, 1971

## 4238
### JESSICA PALMER
### Shadow Dance
(New York: Pocket, 1994)

**Story type:** Horror (Curse; Ancient Evil Unleashed)
**Major character(s):** Tiffany Blair, Child; Alan Blount, Police Officer; Robert Schoenwald, Construction Worker (heavy machinery operator)
**Time period(s):** 1990s (1994)
**Locale(s):** Stockton Springs, Maine

**Summary:** When Tiffany Blair unearths the finger bone of a centuries-dead Indian shaman, it releases a lupine elemental spirit, which goads the residents of Stockton Springs into wild flights of uninhibited sex and violence.

**Other books you might like:**
G. Wayne Miller, *Thunder Rise*, 1989
Adam Niswander, *The Charm*, 1993
Eugene E. Pfaff Jr., *Uwharrie*, 1993
    Michael Causey, co-author
Patrick Whalen, *Deathwalker*, 1992

## 4239
### JESSICA PALMER
### Sweet William
(New York: Pocket, 1995)

**Story type:** Horror (Evil Children; Possession)
**Major character(s):** William Scott McDowell, Child (four-year-old); Allison McDowell, Writer
**Time period(s):** 1990s (1995)
**Locale(s):** Long Island, New York

**Summary:** Born the day that his father, horror writer Scott McDowell, died, William Scott McDowell manifests unusual personality traits. Indeed, he has become the battleground between the soul of his father and the spirit of an evil "other" linked to the legacy of death and terror that imbues his family's house.

**Other books you might like:**
William Peter Blatty, *The Exorcist*, 1971
Ramsey Campbell, *The Influence*, 1988
Ramsey Campbell, *To Wake the Dead*, 1980
Stephen R. George, *Torment*, 1994
Clifford Mohr, *Requiem*, 1992

## 4240
### SUSAN PALWICK
### Flying in Place
(New York: Tor, 1992)

**Story type:** Horror (Child-in-Peril)
**Major character(s):** Emma Gray, Child, Abuse Victim; Stewart Gray, Doctor; Myrna Halloran, Nurse
**Time period(s):** 1970s
**Locale(s):** Wisconsin

**Summary:** Sexually abused by her father and completely ignored by her mother, Emma Grey befriends the spirit of her dead older sister Ginny, who teaches Emma how to discorporate her spirit and temporarily flee her wretched home life. This sensitively written story is the author's first novel.

**Other books you might like:**
Randall Boyll, *Mongster*, 1991
Sean Costello, *Captain Quad*, 1991
Judith Guest, *Ordinary People*, 1976
Thomas Tryon, *The Other*, 1971
R.R. Walters, *Wind Chimes*, 1991

## 4241
### PAUL PARK

### *Celestis*
(New York: Tor, 1995)

**Story type:** Science Fiction (Political; Genetic Manipulation)
**Major character(s):** Simon Mayaram, Diplomat, Human; Katharine Styreme, Genetically Altered Being (Aboriginal), Musician (concert pianist); Harriet Oimu, Revolutionary (National Liberation Coalition), Genetically Altered Being (Aboriginal)
**Time period(s):** Indeterminate Future
**Locale(s):** Shreveport, Fictional City; Celestis, Planet—Imaginary

**Summary:** Superior technology has allowed the small human colony to exploit the natives of Celestis to the verge of revolt. Both native and human factions feel appalled by the practice of natives surgically and pharmacologically altering themselves in order to appear human, thereby opening up more doors of opportunity in the rigidly stratified society. Kidnapped by terrorists of the National Liberation Coalition, Simon Mayaram falls in love with fellow hostage Katharine Styreme. But Katharine, an altered Celestis native, denied the daily medications that keep her "humanity" intact, rapidly transforms back into an alien unable to communicate emotions on a human level. British edition, 1993, titled *Coelestis*.

**Other books you might like:**
Roger MacBride Allen, *The Ring of Charon*, 1990
Eleanor Arnason, *Ring of Swords*, 1993
David Brin, *Brightness Reef*, 1995
David Brin, *The Uplift War*, 1987
Octavia E. Butler, *Dawn*, 1987
C.J. Cherryh, *Foreigner*, 1994
C.J. Cherryh, *Invader*, 1995
Ian McDonald, *The Broken Land*, 1992
Joan Slonczewski, *Daughter of Elysium*, 1993
John E. Stith, *Redshift Rendezvous*, 1990
Sheri S. Tepper, *Grass*, 1989

## 4242
### PAUL PARK

### *The Cult of Loving Kindness*
(New York: Morrow, 1991)

**Story type:** Science Fiction (Theological; Political)
**Series:** Starbridge Chronicles
**Major character(s):** Cassia, Teenager, Religious; Rael, Teenager, Religious
**Time period(s):** Indeterminate Future
**Locale(s):** Planet—Imaginary

**Summary:** The Cult of Loving Kindness grows in popularity among the refugees from Charn, threatening the power of the Starbridge caste. As Cassia and Rael proceed from their isolated jungle village to Brother Longo Starbridge's mission, they prove to be the prophesied elements as Cassia becomes Last Bishop.

**Other books you might like:**
Brian W. Aldiss, *Helliconia Spring*, 1982

Brian W. Aldiss, *Helliconia Summer*, 1983
Brian W. Aldiss, *Helliconia Winter*, 1985
Octavia E. Butler, *Adulthood Rites*, 1988
Octavia E. Butler, *Imago*, 1989
Mary Gentle, *Golden Witchbreed*, 1984
Robert A. Heinlein, *Stranger in a Strange Land*, 1991 revised
Sheri S. Tepper, *Grass*, 1989
Sheri S. Tepper, *Raising the Stones*, 1990
Gene Wolfe, *The Citadel of the Autarch*, 1983
Gene Wolfe, *Claw of the Conciliator*, 1981
Gene Wolfe, *The Shadow of the Torturer*, 1980
Gene Wolfe, *The Sword of the Lictor*, 1982

## 4243
### PAUL PARK

### *Sugar Rain*
(New York: Morrow, 1989)

**Story type:** Science Fiction (Theological; Political)
**Series:** Starbridge Chronicles
**Major character(s):** Charity Starbridge, Widow(er); Thanakar Starbridge, Doctor
**Time period(s):** Indeterminate Future
**Locale(s):** Planet—Imaginary

**Summary:** On a planet where each season lasts for decades, Spring invariably brings turmoil, starvation, and revolution. Two decent people caught up in the insanity, both criminals according to the perverse religious laws of their civilization, struggle desperately to maintain life and find some form of happiness.

**Other books you might like:**
Brian W. Aldiss, *The Helliconia Trilogy*, 1982-1985
Gene Wolfe, *The Book of the New Sun*, 1980

## 4244
### SEVERNA PARK

### *Hand of Prophecy*
(New York: Avon Eos, 1998)

**Story type:** Science Fiction (Political; Gay/Lesbian Fiction)
**Major character(s):** Frenna Yaeylie, Slave (Jatahn), Genetically Altered Being; Olney Mallau, Veterinarian, Alcoholic; D'Rasha, Businessman (slaver)
**Time period(s):** Indeterminate Future
**Locale(s):** Bellea-Naya, Planet—Imaginary; Traja, Planet—Imaginary

**Summary:** Despite her birth on Jatah, a planet freed by the Emirate from Faraqui slavers two centuries earlier, Frenna slaves as a vet's assistant, sold by the Emirate for fealty due from her family. Just as the Faraqui attack Bellea-Naya, Frenna learns that the virus which both protects slaves from damage and kills them after 20 years can be cured, freeing the slave. A friend gives Frenna three doses of Viravax and a way off the planet, but the panic and evacuation slow her down, permitting her to run across a D'Rasha slaver, which further complicates her bid for freedom.

**Other books you might like:**
Eleanor Arnason, *Ring of Swords*, 1993
C.J. Cherryh, *Forty Thousand in Gehenna*, 1983
Candas Jane Dorsey, *Black Wine*, 1997

Katharine Kerr, *Palace*, 1996
  Mark Kreighbaum, co-author
Sarah Zettel, *Reclamation*, 1996

## 4245

### SEVERNA PARK

## *Speaking Dreams*

(Ithica, New York: Firebrand Books, 1992)

**Story type:** Science Fiction (Gay/Lesbian Fiction; Political)
**Major character(s):** Costa, Psychic (prescient); Mira LoDire, Diplomat (Emirate), Businesswoman (negotiator)
**Time period(s):** Indeterminate Future
**Locale(s):** Traja, Planet—Imaginary; *Proviso*, Spaceship

**Summary:** Mira LoDire reluctantly purchases the enslaved Costa, not understanding that Costa can interpret the secret signed language with which Sector negotiators always outfox Emirate negotiators. On discovering Costa's ability, Mira plans to utilize Costa's skill in the Emir's bargaining to purchase Sector territory, but enemies capture them first. Mira and Costa struggle to escape the Sector agents who have begun dealing with vicious aliens in preparation for conquering the Emirate.

**Other books you might like:**
Camarin Grae, *Stranded*, 1991
Ursula K. Le Guin, *The Left Hand of Darkness*, 1969
Frances Lucas, *Cathy IV*, 1992
Lynda Lyons, *Priorities*, 1990

## 4246

### LARA PARKER

## *Angelique's Descent*

(New York: Harper, 1998)

**Story type:** Horror (Vampire Story)
**Series:** Dark Shadows
**Major character(s):** Barnabas Collins, Businessman, Vampire; Angelique Bouchard, Servant (maid); Josette du Pres, Noblewoman (countess)
**Time period(s):** 19th century; 1970s (1971)
**Locale(s):** Trinite, Martinique

**Summary:** When Barnabas spurns Angelique's love for that of her mistress, Josette, the jealous Angelique invokes a witch's curse that dooms him to a vampire's life thereafter. Novel based on the popular television soap opera "Dark Shadows," which aired between 1966 and 1971. The backstory for one of the show's characters, written by the actress who played her.

**Other books you might like:**
Traci Briery, *The Vampire Journals*, 1993
Wendy Haley, *These Fallen Angels*, 1995
Nancy Kilpatrick, *Near Death*, 1994
Kathryn Reines, *The Kiss*, 1996
Cheri Scotch, *The Werewolf's Touch*, 1993

## 4247

### DAN PARKINSON

## *The Whispers*

(New York: Ballantine Del Rey, 1998)

**Story type:** Science Fiction (Time Travel; Immortality)

**Series:** Gates of Time
**Major character(s):** Edwin Limmer, Time Traveler; Lucas Hawthorn, Travel Agent (time travel); Arthur Rex, Ruler
**Time period(s):** 1990s; 2040s
**Locale(s):** Eastwood, Kansas; Camelot, Fictional City

**Summary:** Edwin Limmer appears suddenly in Lucas Hawthorn's Kansas home, offering to turn it into a time-travel depot which the Hawthorns can use as a lucrative time travel agency. Limmer mainly intends, however, to use the base as a waystation for the Whispers, mysterious beings from the future searching for the beginning of time. First of a series.

**Other books you might like:**
Douglas Adams, *Dirk Gently's Holistic Detective Agency*, 1987
Joshua Dann, *Timeshare*, 1997
Joshua Dann, *Timeshare: Second Time Around*, 1998
Robert A. Heinlein, *The Door into Summer*, 1957
John Kessel, *Corrupting Dr. Nice*, 1997
Michael Moorcock, *The Dancers at the End of Time*, 1981

## 4248

### T.L. PARKINSON

## *The Man Upstairs*

(New York: Dutton, 1991)

**Story type:** Horror (Psychological Suspense)
**Major character(s):** Michael West, Administrator (hospital); Paul Marks, Doctor (plastic surgeon); Patricia, Model
**Time period(s):** 1990s
**Locale(s):** San Francisco, California

**Summary:** Succumbing to the mysterious and perverse character of his apartment building, Michael West becomes increasingly promiscuous with his fellow tenants and finds himself obsessed with "the man upstairs," a plastic surgeon whose features West appears to be gradually assuming himself. This tale of urban paranoia is the author's first novel.

**Other books you might like:**
Ramsey Campbell, *The Face That Must Die*, 1979
Fritz Leiber, *Our Lady of Darkness*, 1977
Ira Levin, *Sliver*, 1991
Roland Topor, *The Tenant*, 1966

## 4249

### JULIE ANNE PARKS

## *Storytellers*

(Darien, Illinois: Design Image Group, 1998)

**Story type:** Horror (Ancient Evil Unleashed)
**Major character(s):** Braxton Defoe, Writer; Piper Defoe, Teacher, Spouse (Braxton's wife); Ren Wyatt, Teacher
**Time period(s):** 1990s (1998)
**Locale(s):** Crooked Creek, North Carolina

**Summary:** Bestselling horror writer Braxton Defoe takes a sabbatical in rural Crooked Creek to turn around his dissipated life and get his creative inspiration back. But Crooked Creek is home to powerful supernatural forces memorialized in local Native American legends, and under their influence Braxton deteriorates and seeks an outlet for his bottled up rage. A first novel.

**Other books you might like:**
Stephen Gregory, *The Cormorant*, 1986
Steve Harris, *Straker's Island*, 1998
James Herbert, *The Magic Cottage*, 1986

Stephen King, *The Shining*, 1977
Garth Stein, *Raven Stole the Moon*, 1998

## 4250

### NORMAN PARTRIDGE

## *Bad Intentions*

(Burton, Michigan: Subterranean Press, 1996)

**Story type:** Horror (Collection)

**Summary:** Collected here are 14 short stories and one comic book script by an author whose work is strongly infected with '50s nostalgia and hommage to B-movies. "Bad Intentions" and "Dead Celebs" are both about collectors of celebrity memorabilia whose tastes verge on the necrophilic. "'59 Frankenstein" and "The Cut Man" are both variations on the Frankenstein theme, and "She's My Witch" and "Apotropaics" recast classic horror themes for tales of juvenile delinquency. "Guignoir" merges horror with the crime thriller, and "Dead Man's Hand" the horror and western tale. Joe Lansdale supplies the introduction. This book was released only in a limited hardcover edition.

**Other books you might like:**
Ed Gorman, *Cages*, 1995
Joe R. Lansdale, *By Bizarre Hands*, 1989
Joe R. Lansdale, *Writer of the Purple Rage*, 1994
John Shirley, *New Noir*, 1994

## 4251

### NORMAN PARTRIDGE
### MELISSA SHERMAN, Illustrator

## *The Bars on Satan's Jailhouse*

(Arvada, Colorado: Roadkill Press, 1995)

**Story type:** Horror (Psychological Suspense)
**Major character(s):** Midas Gerlach, Gunfighter; Stackalee, Gunfighter; Lie, Young Woman
**Time period(s):** 1890s
**Locale(s):** Fiddler, California

**Summary:** This wild western tells of tough hombre Midas Gerlach, who has a foot fetish for his captive concubine Lie, and the legendary gunslinger Stackalee, a mysterious figure who wears boots made out of live bats, and who engages Gerlach in a final showdown on his grue-decorated ranch. This short story chapbook was published in a signed limited edition of 500 copies.

**Other books you might like:**
Nancy A. Collins, *The Tortuga Hill Gang's Last Ride*, 1991
Nancy A. Collins, *Walking Wolf*, 1995
Joe R. Lansdale, *The Magic Wagon*, 1983
Joe R. Lansdale, *On the Far Side of the Cadillac Desert with Dead Folks*, 1989
S.P. Somtow, *Moon Dance*, 1989

## 4252

### NORMAN PARTRIDGE, Editor
### MARTIN H. GREENBERG, Co-Editor

## *It Came From the Drive-In*

(New York: DAW, 1996)

**Story type:** Horror (Anthology)

**Summary:** The 18 stories collected here are homages to the low-budget movies that played at neighborhood drive-ins in the 1950s, 1960s and 1970s. Several, like Ed Gorman's "The Morning of August 18," attempt a serious reflection on the relationship of film to real life. Others recast famous horror story plots as film scenarios, such as Nancy Collins' "The Thing From Lovers Lane" and Norman Partridge's "'59 Frankenstein," which adapt, respectively, H.P. Lovecraft's "The Dunwich Horror" and Mary Shelley's classic novel as juvenile delinquent tales. For the most part, the authors attempt deliberately cheesy riffs on the worst cliches of low budget filmmaking, among them Dan Perez's giant-bug gang story "Die, Baby, Die, Die, Die!," Adam Troy-Castro's psychowestern "The Good, The Bad, and The Danged," and Steve Tem's "Jungle J.D."

**Other books you might like:**
Peter Haining, *The Hollywood Nightmare*, 1970
  editor
Frank D. McSherry Jr., *Hollywood Ghosts*, 1991
  Charles G. Waugh, and Martin H. Greenberg, co-editors
David J. Schow, *Silver Scream*, 1988
  editor
Sebastian Wolfe, *Reel Terror*, 1992
  editor

## 4253

### NORMAN PARTRIDGE

## *Mr. Fox and Other Feral Tales*

(Arvada, Colorado: Roadkill Press, 1992)

**Story type:** Horror (Collection)

**Summary:** A first collection by this talented new writer brings together seven stories and novellas, only two of which have appeared in print before. Included are "Mr. Fox," a modern retelling of a classic folk tale; "Black Leather Kites," which mixes black magic with the modern police procedural; a morbid look at the southwest punk music scene, "Save the Last Dance for Me"; and a story of poetic justice for a porno magazine publisher, "In Beauty, Like the Night." Ed Bryant contributed an introduction.

**Other books you might like:**
Michael Blumlein, *The Brains of Rats*, 1989
Ed Gorman, *Prisoners and Other Stories*, 1992
Joe R. Lansdale, *By Bizarre Hands*, 1989
Dan Simmons, *Prayers to Broken Stones*, 1990

## 4254

### NORMAN PARTRIDGE

## *Slippin' into Darkness*

(Baltimore, Maryland: CD Publications, 1994)

**Story type:** Horror (Mystery)
**Major character(s):** Steve Austin, Police Officer; Shutterbug, Pornographer; Doug Douglas, Worker (bricklayer), Unemployed
**Time period(s):** 1990s (1994)
**Locale(s):** Vallejo, California

**Summary:** Eighteen years after she was gang-raped by four fellow high school students, April Destino, now the town slut, commits suicide. Her death forces the participants in her destruction to reflect on the paths their own lives have taken since then, and precipitates them on a downward spiral into self-hatred, and ultimately violence, with April's haunting presence in the background. This is the author's first novel.

**Other books you might like:**
Ramsey Campbell, *The Nameless*, 1981
Joe R. Lansdale, *The Nightrunners*, 1987
Peter Straub, *Ghost Story*, 1979

---

### 4255
#### NORMAN PARTRIDGE

## Spyder
(Burton, Michigan: Subterranean Press, 1995)

**Story type:** Horror (Occult)
**Major character(s):** James Dean, Actor, Historical Figure; Layla, Witch
**Time period(s):** 1950s
**Locale(s):** Marfa, Texas

**Summary:** This short reflection on the mystique of James Dean proposes that the late actor bought his fame with the help of supernatural forces, and that these same forces helped to immortalize him—literally and figuratively—after his death in a car crash. This short story chapbook was printed in a signed limited edition of 500 copies.

**Other books you might like:**
Nancy Holder, *Cannibal Dwight's Special Purpose*, 1992
Joe R. Lansdale, *Dead in the West*, 1986
William F. Nolan, *Blood Sky*, 1991
Wayne Allen Sallee, *Drinking Buddies*, 1989

---

### 4256
#### NORMAN PARTRIDGE

## Wildest Dreams
(Burton, Michigan: Subterranean Press, 1998)

**Story type:** Horror (Black Magic)
**Major character(s):** Clay Saunders, Murderer (contract killer); Janice Ravenwood, Psychic (medium), Writer; Circe Whistler, Sorceress
**Time period(s):** 1990s (1998)
**Locale(s):** Cliffside, California

**Summary:** Clay Saunders, a hit man sensitive to the spirit world, battles a double-crossing priestess of magic, her dead and decapitated father, and mummy guardians to save a young girl ghost from tormentors in the afterlife.

**Other books you might like:**
Nancy A. Collins, *Walking Wolf*, 1995
Todd Grimson, *Brand New Cherry Flavor*, 1996
Rick Hautala, *Beyond the Shroud*, 1996
John R. Maxim, *Platforms*, 1980
T.M. Wright, *Goodlow's Ghosts*, 1993

---

### 4257
#### HELEN K. PASSEY

## Speak to the Rain
(New York: Atheneum, 1989)

**Story type:** Horror (Ghost Story)
**Major character(s):** Janna Miles, Teenager (Seventeen year old girl); Karen Miles, Child (Janna's nine year old sister)
**Time period(s):** 1980s
**Locale(s):** Washington

**Summary:** Made vulnerable by guilt over the death of her mother, Karen Miles is drawn by the song of the owls to a mysterious lake. Janna looks to a wise Indian for a way to rescue her sister from the ghosts of long dead Indians that await Karen. Passey's first novel.

**Other books you might like:**
Joan Aiken, *The Shadow Guests*, 1980
Vivian Alcock, *The Haunting of Cassie Palmer*, 1980
Margaret Mahy, *The Haunting*, 1982

---

### 4258
#### FIONA PATTON

## The Painter Knight
(New York: DAW, 1998)

**Story type:** Fantasy (Political)
**Series:** Tales of the Branion Realm
**Major character(s):** Simon of Florenz, Artist (painter); Kassandra DeMarian, Child, Royalty; Fay Falconer, Government Official (town watch)
**Time period(s):** Indeterminate Past (783 DR)
**Locale(s):** Caerockeith, Fictional City; Branion, Fictional Country

**Summary:** Upon the assassination of Aristok Marsellos III, protection of the heir falls to the heretic Simon of Florenz. He must sneak the magically gifted Kassandra out of Branion, assuming a condemned heretic and a band of players can keep the heir safe, much less restore her throne.

**Other books you might like:**
Chris Bunch, *The Seer King*, 1997
Glen Cook, *A Shadow of All Night Falling*, 1979
Katherine Kurtz, *Deryni Rising*, 1970
George R.R. Martin, *A Game of Thrones*, 1996
Melanie Rawn, *Dragon Prince*, 1998

---

### 4259
#### FIONA PATTON

## The Stone Prince
(New York: DAW, 1997)

**Story type:** Fantasy (Political)
**Major character(s):** Demnor DeMarian, Royalty, Teenager; Melesandra DeMarian III, Royalty, Political Figure; Kelahnus, Warrior, Homosexual
**Time period(s):** Indeterminate Past
**Locale(s):** Gallia, Fictional Country; Branion, Fictional Country

**Summary:** The ruling family of Branion, blessed with magic and cursed with intrigue, includes Crown Prince Demnor, tormented by his power, disliked by his intense mother and threatened with an undesirable political marriage. However, the stakes rise when the Heathland revolt and the treacheries and pressures at court increase to fatal levels. First novel.

**Other books you might like:**
C.J. Cherryh, *Fortress in the Eye of Time*, 1995
Guy Gavriel Kay, *The Lions of Al-Rassan*, 1995
Katherine Kurtz, *Deryni Rising*, 1970
George R.R. Martin, *A Game of Thrones*, 1996
Kristine Kathryn Rusch, *The Changeling*, 1996

## **4260**

### EDITH PATTOU

## *Fire Arrow*

(New York: Harcourt Brace, 1998)

**Story type:** Fantasy (Young Adult; Quest)
**Series:** Songs of Eirren
**Major character(s):** Breo-Saight ''Brie'', Martial Arts Expert (archer), Hero; Balor, Sorcerer
**Time period(s):** Indeterminate
**Locale(s):** Eirren, Fictional Country

**Summary:** Searching for the murderer of her father, Brie discovers the power of her birthright, a magic arrow to which she becomes attuned with use.

**Other books you might like:**
Diane Duane, *A Wizard Abroad*, 1997
Morgan Llywelyn, *Brian Boru: Emperor of the Irish*, 1995
Tamora Pierce, *The Realms of the Gods*, 1996
Jane Yolen, *Wizard's Hall*, 1991
Mary Frances Zambreno, *A Plague of Sorcerers*, 1991

## **4261**

### EDITH PATTOU

## *Hero's Song*

(New York: Harcourt Brace Jovanovich, 1991)

**Story type:** Fantasy (Quest; Young Adult)
**Major character(s):** Collun, Adventurer; Talisen, Minstrel, Companion
**Time period(s):** Indeterminate
**Locale(s):** Eirren, Fictional Country

**Summary:** As Collun searches for his sister, Nessa, he discovers that his mission will determine the fate of Eirren, threatened by the Queen of Ghosts' invasion. This is the author's first novel.

**Other books you might like:**
Michael Reaves, *Street Magic*, 1991
Will Shetterly, *Elsewhere*, 1991
Michael Williams, *A Sorcerer's Apprentice*, 1990
Jane Yolen, *Wizard's Hall*, 1991
Mary Frances Zambreno, *A Plague of Sorcerers*, 1991

## **4262**

### GARY PAULSEN

## *The Transall Saga*

(New York: Delacorte, 1998)

**Story type:** Science Fiction (Young Adult; Post-Disaster)
**Major character(s):** Mark, Teenager
**Time period(s):** Indeterminate Future
**Locale(s):** Southwest; North America

**Summary:** While Mark hikes solo across the desert Southwest, a cone of blue light transports him elsewhere. Using his wits and learned skills, he survives in an unfamiliar jungle. A tribe he meets adopts him as he searches for a way home while exploring the new territory. A sinister leader also takes an unusual interest in Mark and hints at knowledge of the blue light, leading Mark to further adventures. First science fiction novel from this prolific teen author.

**Other books you might like:**
John Christopher, *No Blade of Grass*, 1957

Nancy Farmer, *The Ear, the Eye, and the Arm*, 1994
Robert A. Heinlein, *Tunnel in the Sky*, 1955
R.A. MacAvoy, *The Third Eagle: Lessons Along a Minor String*, 1989
David R. Palmer, *Emergence*, 1984

## **4263**

### MILORAD PAVIC

## *Landscape Painted with Tea*

(New York: Knopf, 1990)

**Story type:** Fantasy (Contemporary)
**Major character(s):** Atanas Svilar, Architect; Fyodor Alexeyevich Razin, Scientist (mathematician)
**Time period(s):** 20th century
**Locale(s):** Serbia

**Summary:** A metafictional tale of a mysterious quest that is part modern Odyssey, and part detective crossword, with entire chapters forming actual clues ''across'' and ''down.'' Atanas Svilar, a failed architect, sets out to find his father, an officer who vanished in Greece during the First World War.

**Other books you might like:**
Italo Calvino, *The Castle of Crossed Destinies*, 1977
Samuel R. Delany, *The Bridge of Lost Desire*, 1987
Tahar Ben Jelloun, *The Sand Child*, 1987
Gabriel Garcia Marquez, *One Hundred Years of Solitude*, 1970
Vladimir Nabokov, *Pale Fire*, 1962
Ellen Raskin, *The Mysterious Disappearance of Leon*, 1971
    I Mean Noel
Gene Wolfe, *Free Live Free*, 1985

## **4264**

### DIANA L. PAXSON

## *The Dragons of the Rhine*

(New York: Morrow AvoNova, 1995)

**Story type:** Fantasy (Legend; Romance)
**Major character(s):** Brunahild ''Sigdrifa'', Royalty, Warrior; Sigfrid, Mythical Creature (demigod shapechanger), Warrior
**Time period(s):** 5th century
**Locale(s):** Europe (northern)

**Summary:** When Sigfrid returns to find Sigdrifa, conspiracies, treachery, and honor combine to cause Sigfrid to deprive himself of her as his chosen mate. Sequel to *The Wolf and the Raven*; a retelling of *The Nibelungenlied*.

**Other books you might like:**
Donna Gillespie, *The Light Bearer*, 1994
Stephan Grundy, *Rhinegold*, 1994
Harry Harrison, *The Hammer and the Cross*, 1993
    John Holm, co-author
Jamake Highwater, *Dark Legend*, 1994
Morgan Llywelyn, *Druids*, 1991

## **4265**

### DIANA L. PAXSON

## *The Jewel of Fire*

(New York: Tor, 1992)

**Story type:** Fantasy (Quest; Magic Conflict)

**Series:** Westria
**Major character(s):** Julian of Stansvale, Royalty (king); Rana, Adventurer (regent's daughter); Caolin "Blood Lord", Sorcerer
**Time period(s):** Indeterminate
**Locale(s):** Westria, Fictional Country

**Summary:** Forces of the evil Caolin still fight against Julian and his friends as Julian sets out to find the fourth Jewel of Westria, the Jewel of Fire, hidden in the mouth of a volcano. Waiting until Julian recovers the jewel, Caolin captures and imprisons him. Aided by Coyote, a supernatural shape-changer, Rana sets out to find Julian, intent on rescuing him from the Blood Lord's dungeons and restoring his soul to health so that she and Julian can reign as King and Queen.

**Other books you might like:**
Lynn Abbey, *Daughter of the Bright Moon*, 1979
Marion Zimmer Bradley, *The Mists of Avalon*, 1983
C.J. Cherryh, *The Dreamstone*, 1983
Katherine Kurtz, *High Deryni*, 1973
Ursula K. Le Guin, *The Farthest Shore*, 1972
Patricia A. McKillip, *Harpist in the Wind*, 1979
Rick Shelley, *The Hero of Varay*, 1991

## 4266

### DIANA L. PAXSON
### ADRIENNE MARTINE-BARNES, Co-Author

## *Master of Earth and Water*

(New York: Morrow AvoNova, 1993)

**Story type:** Fantasy (Legend)
**Series:** Chronicles of Fionn mac Cumhall
**Major character(s):** Fionn "Demne" mac Cumhall, Historical Figure, Hero; Bodbmall, Warrior, Teacher
**Time period(s):** 3rd century
**Locale(s):** Ireland

**Summary:** Spirited away from danger as an infant, Demne grows up in relative safety, learning mystical secrets from Bodbmall who keeps from Demne the nature of his parentage and destiny.

**Other books you might like:**
Kenneth C. Flint, *Challenge of the Clans*, 1986
Courtway Jones, *In the Shadow of the Oak King*, 1991
Morgan Llywelyn, *Finn Mac Cool*, 1994
Adrienne Martine-Barnes, *The Crystal Sword*, 1988
Adrienne Martine-Barnes, *The Fire Sword*, 1984
Adrienne Martine-Barnes, *The Rainbow Sword*, 1988
Andrew J. Offutt, *Sword of the Gael*, 1975
Bridget Wood, *Wolfking*, 1992

## 4267

### DIANA L. PAXSON
### ADRIENNE MARTINE-BARNES, Co-Author

## *The Shield between the Worlds*

(New York: Morrow/AvoNova, 1994)

**Story type:** Fantasy (Legend)
**Series:** Chronicles of Fionn mac Cumhall
**Major character(s):** Fionn "Demne" mac Cumhall, Historical Figure, Hero; Goll mac Morna, Warrior; Sadb, Spouse (Fionn's)
**Time period(s):** 3rd century
**Locale(s):** Ireland

**Summary:** As an adult, Fionn excels as bard and as warrior, familiar with both mortal and faerie realms. Great deeds propel Fionn to

heroic stature, but Fionn remains unfulfilled until he meets the ensorcelled Sadb.

**Other books you might like:**
Kenneth C. Flint, *Challenge of the Clans*, 1986
Morgan Llywelyn, *Finn Mac Cool*, 1994
Adrienne Martine-Barnes, *The Crystal Sword*, 1988
Adrienne Martine-Barnes, *The Fire Sword*, 1984
Adrienne Martine-Barnes, *The Rainbow Sword*, 1988
Andrew J. Offutt, *Sword of the Gael*, 1975

## 4268

### DIANA L. PAXSON
### ADRIENNE MARTINE-BARNES, Co-Author

## *Sword of Fire and Shadow*

(New York: Morrow/AvoNova, 1995)

**Story type:** Fantasy (Legend; Adventure)
**Series:** Chronicles of Fionn mac Cumhall
**Major character(s):** Fionn "Demne" mac Cumhall, Historical Figure, Hero
**Time period(s):** 3rd century
**Locale(s):** Ireland

**Summary:** Bound by his oath, aging Fionn mac Cumhal continues to defend Ireland from its faerie and mortal enemies despite treachery and disfavor from his countrymen.

**Other books you might like:**
Kenneth C. Flint, *Challenge of the Clans*, 1986
Morgan Llywelyn, *Finn Mac Cool*, 1994
Adrienne Martine-Barnes, *The Crystal Sword*, 1988
Adrienne Martine-Barnes, *The Fire Sword*, 1984
Adrienne Martine-Barnes, *The Rainbow Sword*, 1988
Andrew J. Offutt, *Sword of the Gael*, 1975

## 4269

### DIANA L. PAXSON

## *The Wind Crystal*

(New York: Tor, 1990)

**Story type:** Fantasy (Quest)
**Series:** Westria
**Major character(s):** Julian of Stansvale, Royalty (prince), Heir—Dispossessed; Rana, Adventurer (regent's daughter)
**Time period(s):** Indeterminate
**Locale(s):** Westria, Fictional Country

**Summary:** To claim his right to his father's throne from the Regent, Julian must find the four jewels of power and learn to use them. Julian has found two of the four jewels lost in the magic war which killed his father, King Jehan. Now he must find the Wind Crystal, his key to the Realm of Air. Obstructed by foes, he journeys to the Wind Lord's castle to learn the Wind Crystal's secrets.

**Other books you might like:**
Marion Zimmer Bradley, *City of Sorcery*, 1984
Marion Zimmer Bradley, *Domains of Darkover*, 1990
Marion Zimmer Bradley, *The Heirs of Hammerfell*, 1989
Jack L. Chalker, *When the Changewinds Blow*, 1987
Andre Norton, *Horn Crown*, 1981

## 4270

### DIANA L. PAXSON

### *The Wolf and the Raven*

(New York: Morrow, 1993)

**Story type:** Fantasy (Historical; Legend)
**Major character(s):** Brunahild ''Sigdrifa'', Royalty, Warrior; Sigfrid, Mythical Creature (demigod shapechanger), Warrior
**Time period(s):** 5th century
**Locale(s):** Europe

**Summary:** Brunahild studies with the Walkyriun, magic wielders who worship Wodan All-Father, receiving initiation into their religious rites. After fleeing his father's killers, Sigfried seeks shelter in the deep woods with an aged smith who provides Sigfrid the opportunity to learn warfare and smithcraft and discover his ability as shapechanger. After crafting his great sword and fighting the dragon, Fafnir, Sigfrid must rescue Brunahild from an enchanted sleep. First of a trilogy based on the Germanic saga.

**Other books you might like:**
Frans G. Bengtsson, *The Long Ships*, 1954
Stephan Grundy, *Rhinegold*, 1994
Harry Harrison, *The Hammer and the Cross*, 1993
    John Holm, co-author
Courtway Jones, *In the Shadow of the Oak King*, 1991
Morgan Llywelyn, *Druids*, 1991

## 4271

### MICHAEL H. PAYNE

### *The Blood Jaguar*

(New York: Tor, 1998)

**Story type:** Fantasy (Quest)
**Major character(s):** Bobcat, Animal, Gambler; Skink, Animal; Fisher, Animal
**Time period(s):** Indeterminate
**Locale(s):** Ottersgate, Fictional City

**Summary:** In a North America full of intelligent animals and watched over by 12 spirits called the Curials, the 13th Curial, the Blood Jaguar, plots to kill most of the world. While she pursues this end, three animals try to stop her, despite repeated failure. However, Bobcat does not intend to fail. First novel.

**Other books you might like:**
Richard Adams, *Watership Down*, 1974
'Asta Bowen, *Hungry for Home: A Wolf Odyssey*, 1997
Brian Jacques, *Redwall*, 1986
Garry Kilworth, *The Foxes of Firstdark*, 1990
Tad Williams, *Tailchaser's Song*, 1985

## 4272

### ROBERTO PAZZI

### M.J. FITZGERALD, Co-Author

### *The Princess and the Dragon*

(New York: Knopf, 1990)

**Story type:** Fantasy (Historical; Time Travel)
**Major character(s):** George Alexandrovich Romanov, Royalty (Grand Duke); Helen, Noblewoman (Montenegro); Prince Ourousov, Nobleman
**Time period(s):** 1890s (1899)
**Locale(s):** Russia; Europe

**Summary:** The Tsar's brother George is dying of tuberculosis in his palace in the Caucasus Mountains. He dreams of escaping to Cannes and marrying his cousin Helen and of finding the secret to the fabled longevity of the Georgians. Then he is swept into a journey that takes him to St. Helena in 1816, to Paris in 1793, to China in 1825, and to Russia in 1796 and 1938. This book was first published in Italian as *La Principessa e il Drago* in 1986.

**Other books you might like:**
Philip K. Dick, *The Man in the High Castle*, 1963
John M. Ford, *The Dragon Waiting*, 1983
Lisa Goldstein, *The Dream Years*, 1985
Lisa Goldstein, *The Red Magician*, 1982
Gene Wolfe, *Soldier of the Mist*, 1986

## 4273

### MICHAEL PEAK

### *Catamount*

(New York: Roc, 1992)

**Story type:** Fantasy (Contemporary; Adventure)
**Major character(s):** Sarena, Animal (cougar); Lanakila, Animal (eagle); Laura Kay, Journalist
**Time period(s):** 1990s
**Locale(s):** San Diego, California

**Summary:** Sarena hunts alone until she forms an unlikely friendship with Lanakila. The two friends join forces to foil a pack of feral dogs, not realizing the danger they may soon face from two-legged hunters. Covering a story about the proposed mountain lion hunt as part of her job, Laura Kay soon takes an interest in the mountain lions and in Keith Gallatin, a rock star and psychic who works to prevent the hunt.

**Other books you might like:**
Richard Adams, *Shardik*, 1974
Richard Adams, *Watership Down*, 1972
Jack Dann, *Magicats!*, 1984
    Gardner Dozois, co-editor
T.S. Eliot, *Old Possum's Book of Practical Cats*, 1938
Ursula K. Le Guin, *The Word for World Is Forest*, 1972
Vonda N. McIntyre, *Star Trek IV: The Voyage Home*, 1986
Andre Norton, *Catfantastic*, 1989
    Martin H. Greenberg, co-editor
H. Beam Piper, *Little Fuzzy*, 1962
Tad Williams, *Tailchaser's Song*, 1985

## 4274

### PHILIPPA PEARCE, Editor

### *Dread and Delight: A Century of Children's Ghost Stories*

(New York: Oxford, 1995)

**Story type:** Horror (Anthology; Ghost Story)

**Summary:** The editor, herself an author of children's fiction, has chosen 40 tales of the supernatural that span the century and are suitable for young readers. Classic tales include M.R. James' ''A School Story,'' about a student who becomes the vehicle for his teacher's haunted past, Arthur Machen's ''John Double,'' in which a young boy shares the knowledge picked up by his doppelganger, and Walter de la Mare's ''Miss Jemima,'' about a nasty aunt who gets her comeuppance. Robert Westall's ''The Beach,'' in which a boy cannot separate dream from reality, and John Gordon's ''The Burning Baby,'' a tale of revenge from beyond the grave, are among the modern selections. Many of the book's contributors are renowned as childrens writers, but others, including Isaac Bashevis Singer and Penelope Lively, are more commonly thought of as writers for adults.

**Other books you might like:**
Ramsey Campbell, *The Gruesome Book*, 1983
    editor
Neil Gaiman, *Now We Are Sick*, 1991
    Stephen Jones, co-editor
Martin H. Greenberg, *Great Writers and Kids Write Spooky Stories*, 1995
    Jill Morgan and Robert Weinberg, co-editors
Robert Westall, *Ghost Stories*, 1988
    editor

## 4275

### CLAUDIA PECK

### *Spirit Crossings*
(New York: Bantam Spectra, 1991)

**Story type:** Fantasy (Contemporary; Horror)
**Major character(s):** Andrew Jackson, Teacher; Broken Echo, Indian (Cherokee), Spirit; Larry Bryge, Teenager, Student—High School
**Time period(s):** 1990s
**Locale(s):** Tennessee

**Summary:** On the way to accept a new teaching position, Andrew's wife and son are killed in an automobile crash. In his grief, Andrew secludes himself in his new home which is haunted by the ghosts of a Cherokee warrior, a slave trader and others who died horribly in the house. Tormented by them, he acts so strangely he loses his job and is unable to break free of the spirits until he must help Larry escape their evil influence, making peace with the ghosts and his own past.

**Other books you might like:**
Ambrose Bierce, *Can Such Things Be?*, 1893
Henry James, *The Two Magics: The Turn of the Screw, Covering End*, 1898
M.R. James, *The Best Ghost Stories of M.R. James*, 1944
Jill M. Phillips, *Walford's Oak*, 1990
Phyllis Reynolds Naylor, *The Witch's Eye*, 1990
Thorne Smith, *Topper: An Improbable Adventure*, 1926

## 4276

### HAYFORD PEIRCE

### *Phylum Monsters*
(New York: Tor, 1989)

**Story type:** Science Fiction (Satire)
**Major character(s):** Robert Clayborn, Scientist; Oneness, Alien
**Time period(s):** 24th century (2345)
**Locale(s):** Earth; Mars

**Summary:** Robert Clayborn is a designer of bestselling human genetic types until, for no apparent reason, most of his designs begin to go wrong. Apparently normal genetically-designed human beings, even his own son, suddenly regress into apes. Clayborn's life and business collapse. Then he is talked into going to Mars to help The Oneness, a Martian rock entity, find a means of liberating her people. For years telepathic Martian rocks have served human beings as pets and communications devices but now Clayborn must find them bodies and, in effect, free the slaves.

**Other books you might like:**
James Patrick Kelly, *Look into the Sun*, 1989
Frederik Pohl, *Narabedla, Ltd.*, 1988
Rudy Rucker, *Wetware*, 1988
Kate Wilhelm, *Crazy Time*, 1988

## 4277

### HAYFORD PEIRCE

### *The Thirteenth Majestral*
(New York: Tor, 1989)

**Story type:** Science Fiction (Space Opera)
**Major character(s):** Kerryl Ryson, Slave; Yveena Soolis, Noblewoman
**Time period(s):** Indeterminate (The Year 28,395 FIP)
**Locale(s):** Stohlson's Redemption, Planet—Imaginary; Diobastan Cluster, Interstellar Empire/Federation

**Summary:** Ten year old Kerryl Ryson is responsible for an unseemly incident that upsets a visiting VIP. As punishment his father is executed and he and his family are sold into slavery. Sixteen years later, aided by a beautiful noblewoman, aliens, a time machine, and a bunch of dinosaurs, he accomplishes his revenge.

**Other books you might like:**
Iain M. Banks, *The Player of Games*, 1989
L. Neil Smith, *Henry Martyn*, 1989
Jack Vance, *Araminta Station*, 1988
Jack Vance, *The Book of Dreams*, 1981
Jack Vance, *Cugel's Saga*, 1983
Jack Vance, *The Dragon Masters*, 1963
Jack Vance, *Galactic Effectuator*, 1980

## 4278

### JOHN PELAN, Editor
### ALAN M. CLARK, Illustrator

### *Darkside: Horror for the Next Millennium*
(Seattle: Darkside Press, 1996)

**Story type:** Horror (Anthology)

**Summary:** Thirty stories by diverse hands featuring mostly adult themes fill this anthology published exclusively in a signed limited hardcover edition. Included are Lucy Taylor's ''Scars,'' about a woman who beguiles a religious fanatic to kill her abusive father; Roman Ranieri's ''Window of Opportunity,'' in which a childish revenge fantasy gets out of hand; Brian Hodge's ''Stick Around, It Gets Worse,'' about the extremes of a man's devastating grief over the loss of his wife in a senseless accident; David B. Silva's ''Voices Lost and Clouded,'' in which a man is horrified to discover he can no longer separate fantasy from reality; and Brian McNaughton's ''ystery orm,'' in which a fan who writes a letter to his favorite author discovers that getting a reply is the worst thing that could have happened to him.

**Other books you might like:**
Dennis Etchison, *Cutting Edge*, 1986
    editor
Dennis Etchison, *Metahorror*, 1993
    editor
John Maclay, *Voices From the Night*, 1994
    editor
Thomas F. Monteleone, *Borderlands 2*, 1991
    editor

Stanley Wiater, *After the Darkness*, 1993
    editor
J.N. Williamson, *Masques*, 1991
    editor

`4279`

**CHARLES PELLEGRINO**

### Dust

(New York: Avon, 1998)

**Story type:** Horror (Nature in Revolt)
**Major character(s):** Richard Sinclair, Scientist (paleobiologist); Tam Sinclair, Child (Richard's daughter); Jerry Sigmond, Radio Personality
**Time period(s):** 2000s (2000)
**Locale(s):** Long Island, New York

**Summary:** Disruptions in planetary ecology lead to the unchecked proliferation of "motes," ravenous dust mites that swarm in clouds and strip flesh from the bones of their victims. Richard Sinclair and his scientific colleagues struggle to find a way to contain this environmental disaster and prevent the world from being transformed into a savage prehistoric landscape.

**Other books you might like:**
John Christopher, *The Death of Grass*, 1956
Matthew J. Costello, *Garden*, 1993
Michael Crichton, *Jurassic Park*, 1990
Richard Sanford, *Roadkill*, 1995
John Skipp, *The Bridge: A Horror Story*, 1991
    Craig Spector, co-author

`4280`

**CHARLES PELLEGRINO**

### Flying to Valhalla

(New York: Avonova/Morrow, 1993)

**Story type:** Science Fiction (First Contact; Hard Science Fiction)
**Major character(s):** Chris Wayville, Astronaut, Scientist; Clarice Wayville, Astronaut, Scientist; Catherine, Alien
**Time period(s):** 2050s; 2060s (2054-2061)
**Locale(s):** Alpha Centauri A-4, Planet—Imaginary; *Valkyrie*, Spaceship

**Summary:** Chris Wayville's nightmares may represent premonitions from alternate futures or symptoms of insanity caused by near-light speed travel to Alpha Centauri. On the fourth planet of Alpha Centauri A, contact between humans and the gentle, primitive natives proceeds smoothly at first, but Chris starts to worry about the effects of new ideas and new technology on this culture. When the human ship begins to receive radio signals from another planet in the Alpha Centauri system, he fears the nightmares may become reality. First novel.

**Other books you might like:**
Alfred Bester, *The Stars My Destination*, 1956
Arthur C. Clarke, *Rendezvous with Rama*, 1973
Gordon R. Dickson, *Masters of Everon*, 1980
Robert L. Forward, *Dragon's Egg*, 1980
Carl Sagan, *Contact*, 1985
James Tiptree Jr., *Up the Walls of the World*, 1978
John Varley, *Titan*, 1979

`4281`

**CHARLES PELLEGRINO**
**GEORGE ZEBROWSKI**, Co-Author

### The Killing Star

(New York: Morrow AvoNova, 1995)

**Story type:** Science Fiction (Invasion of Earth; Hard Science Fiction)
**Major character(s):** Joshua, Clone (Jesus's); Justin, Clone (Buddha's); Thaw Tint, Alien
**Time period(s):** 2090s
**Locale(s):** Outer Space (inside the Sun's corona); Sargenti-Peterson, Space Station (on a comet); Ceres, Asteroid

**Summary:** After aliens destroy Earth with relativistic bombs, killing almost all life in the Solar System, Thaw Tint continues to hunt down the remaining humans.

**Other books you might like:**
Roger MacBride Allen, *The Ring of Charon*, 1990
Greg Bear, *The Forge of God*, 1987
David Brin, *Earth*, 1990
Jack McDevitt, *The Engines of God*, 1994
Larry Niven, *Footfall*, 1985
    Jerry Pournelle, co-author
Dan Simmons, *Hyperion*, 1989
George Zebrowski, *Stranger Suns*, 1991

`4282`

**DENNIS PEPPER**, Editor

### The Young Oxford Book of Ghost Stories

(New York: Oxford, 1997)

**Story type:** Horror (Anthology; Young Adult)

**Summary:** Forty tales of horror and the supernatural that span the century and that were chosen with young adults' tastes in mind. Included are M.R. James's "Rats," in which a traveler witnesses a ghostly apparition at an inn; E.F. Benson's "The House with the Brick-Kiln," which features a guilty ghost that continually re-enacts the shocking murder of his former wife; Marjorie Bowen's "The Crown Derby Plate," in which a collector's zeal to complete a china set leads her into a ghostly encounter; and E. Nesbit's "John Charrington's," in which a man keeps his vow to return from the dead to attend his wedding. Contemporary contributions include Robert Westall's "The Call," William F. Nolan's "Dead Call," and John Gordon's "Little Black Pies." First published in 1994.

**Other books you might like:**
Ramsey Campbell, *The Gruesome Book*, 1983
Martin H. Greenberg, *Great Writers and Kids Write Spooky Stories*, 1995
    Jill Morgan and Robert Weinberg, co-editors
William Mayne, *Supernatural Stories*, 1996
Philippa Pearce, *Dread and Delight: A Century of Children's Ghost Stories*, 1995
    editor
Susan Price, *Horror Stories*, 1995
Robert Westall, *Ghost Stories*, 1988
    editor

## 4283

**COLE PERRIMAN** (Pseudonym of Wim Coleman and Pat Perrin)

### Terminal Games

(New York: Bantam, 1994)

**Story type:** Science Fiction (Alternate Intelligence; Mystery)
**Major character(s):** Marianne Hedison, Computer Expert, Detective—Amateur; Nolan Grobowski, Detective—Police; Auggie, Artificial Intelligence
**Time period(s):** 1990s
**Locale(s):** Los Angeles, California; Insomnia, Cyberspace (computer virtual reality)

**Summary:** When Marianne Hedison reports a similarity between a real murder and a computer simulation she witnessed on Insomnia, an interactive computer fantasyland, Detective Grobowski begins an investigation which convinces them that Insomnia plays a sinister and remarkable role in events.

**Other books you might like:**
Piers Anthony, *Killobyte*, 1993
Alexander Besher, *Rim: A Novel of Virtual Reality*, 1994
Ben Bova, *Death Dream*, 1994
Pierre Ouellette, *The Deus Machine*, 1994
John Varley, *Steel Beach*, 1992

## 4284

**MARK C. PERRY**

### Morigu: The Dead

(New York: Questar, 1990)

**Story type:** Fantasy (Magic Conflict)
**Major character(s):** Margawt ''The Morigu'', Mythical Creature, Warrior (elf); Anlon, Mythical Creature (unicorn)
**Time period(s):** Indeterminate

**Summary:** The elves, dwarves and humans are all involved in a battle against the forces of dark. The gods who once stabilized the world can do so no longer because of internal bickering.

**Other books you might like:**
Poul Anderson, *The Broken Sword*, 1983
Terry Brooks, *The Sword of Shannara*, 1977
John Deakins, *Barrow*, 1990
David Eddings, *The Belgariad Series*,
J.R.R. Tolkien, *The Lord of the Rings Trilogy*,

## 4285

**S.D. PERRY**

### Berserker

(New York: Bantam, 1998)

**Story type:** Science Fiction (Military)
**Series:** Aliens
**Major character(s):** MAX, Cyborg; Martin Jess, Convict (former); Katherine Lara, Military Personnel
**Time period(s):** Indeterminate Future
**Locale(s):** *Nemesis*, Spaceship; D.S. 949, Space Station

**Summary:** An interstellar corporation is experimenting with breeding and controlling a race of aliens when the staff loses control. The corporation sends three ex-convicts and a cyborg to one of its space stations to wipe out the largest known concentration of the creatures

without doing significant damage to the installation which they have seized.

**Other books you might like:**
Nathan Archer, *Cold War*, 1997
Robert Hovorka, *Derelict*, 1988
Anne Moroz, *No Safe Place*, 1986
Yvonne Navarro, *Music of the Spears*, 1997
Robert Sheckley, *Alien Harvest*, 1995

## 4286

**S.D. PERRY**

### Timecop

(New York: Berkley, 1994)

**Story type:** Science Fiction (Time Travel; Adventure)
**Major character(s):** Max Walker, Police Officer (Timecop), Time Traveler; Aaron McComb, Political Figure, Criminal
**Time period(s):** 2000s
**Locale(s):** Washington, District of Columbia

**Summary:** While assigned to search for Senator McComb who has violated the prohibition against traveling back in time, Max Walker faces the temptation of preventing his wife's murder. Novelizes the movie.

**Other books you might like:**
Dean Devlin, *StarGate*, 1994
    Roland Emmerich, co-author
Philip K. Dick, *Blade Runner*, 1982
Richard Osborne, *Demolition Man*, 1993
Robert Tine, *Universal Soldier*, 1992
Robert Charles Wilson, *A Bridge of Years*, 1991

## 4287

**STEVE PERRY**

### The 97th Step

(New York: Ace Books, 1989)

**Story type:** Science Fiction (Adventure)
**Major character(s):** Mwili-Ferret, Thief, Warrior
**Time period(s):** Indeterminate Future
**Locale(s):** Shin System, Planet—Imaginary; Tau System, Planet—Imaginary

**Summary:** In this prequel to *The Man Who Never Missed*, a young boy flees his desolate home planet and takes up life as a thief. Later he joins the Siblings of the Shroud, a violent cult bent on building an empire.

**Other books you might like:**
Emma Bull, *Falcon*, 1989
Frank Herbert, *Dune*, 1965
Christopher Hinz, *Liege-Killer*, 1987
Joan D. Vinge, *Catspaw*, 1988

## 4288

**STEVE PERRY**

### The Albino Knife

(New York: Ace, 1991)

**Story type:** Science Fiction (Adventure)
**Series:** Matador

**Major character(s):** Veate, Martial Arts Expert, Genetically Altered Being; Emile Khadaji, Martial Arts Expert, Parent (Veate's)
**Time period(s):** Indeterminate Future
**Locale(s):** Earth

**Summary:** When Veate's mother, Juete, disappears, Veate searches out her father, Emile Khadaji, whom she has never met. Emile joins other Matadors to find and free Juete. As they unravel the mystery they discover a plot which could threaten the Brotherhood, the martial arts society to which the defenders of liberty, the Matadors, belong.

**Other books you might like:**
Lois McMaster Bujold, *Borders of Infinity*, 1989
Allan Cole, *Revenge of the Damned*, 1989
   Chris Bunch, co-author
Glen Cook, *The Dragon Never Sleeps*, 1988
Gordon R. Dickson, *Dorsai!*, 1976
Michael Flynn, *In the Country of the Blind*, 1990
Alan Dean Foster, *Cat-A-Lyst*, 1991
Stephen Goldin, *Jade Darcy and the Affair of Honor*, 1988
   Mary Mason, co-author

## 4289

**STEVE PERRY**

### Aliens: Earth Hive

(New York: Bantam Spectra, 1992)

**Story type:** Science Fiction (Invasion of Earth; Political)
**Series:** Aliens
**Major character(s):** Billie, Patient (mental), Adventurer; Wilks, Military Personnel (Marine sergeant); Bueller, Military Personnel
**Time period(s):** Indeterminate Future
**Locale(s):** Earth; Planet—Imaginary (aliens' home planet); *Benedict*, Spaceship

**Summary:** Assigned to recover an alien for the government, Wilks frees Billie from confinement and smuggles her onboard ship, explaining her presence as the last-minute addition of an alien expert. While they work to retrieve an alien from the aliens' home planet, fanatics begin to facilitate implantation of embryonic aliens on Earth.

**Other books you might like:**
Alan Dean Foster, *Alien*, 1979
Alan Dean Foster, *Alien 3*, 1992
Alan Dean Foster, *Aliens*, 1986
Melissa Scott, *Mighty Good Road*, 1990
Charles Sheffield, *The Nimrod Hunt*, 1986

## 4290

**STEVE PERRY**
**STEPHANIE PERRY**, Co-Author

### Aliens: The Female War

(New York: Bantam, 1993)

**Story type:** Science Fiction (Adventure; Space Opera)
**Series:** Aliens
**Major character(s):** Ellen Ripley, Telepath, Warrior; Wilks, Military Personnel; Billy, Psychic (dreamer), Adventurer
**Time period(s):** Indeterminate Future
**Locale(s):** *Kurtz*, Spaceship; Outer Space

**Summary:** With humanity reduced to a minor power on an alien-dominated Earth, outcast Ellen Ripley finds companions in her pogrom against alien life. When the alien queen calls for aliens to assemble at a distant star system, Ripley and others set out to kill all

the aliens. Concludes the trilogy novelizing a graphic novel sequel to the film series.

**Other books you might like:**
Octavia E. Butler, *Dawn*, 1987
Orson Scott Card, *Ender's Game*, 1985
Alan Dean Foster, *Alien*, 1979
Alan Dean Foster, *Alien 3*, 1992
Alan Dean Foster, *Aliens*, 1986
Jayne Tannehill, *V: The Oregon Invasion*, 1988
Allen L. Wold, *V: The Pursuit of Diana*, 1984

## 4291

**STEVE PERRY**

### Black Steel

(New York: Ace, 1992)

**Story type:** Science Fiction (Adventure)
**Series:** Matador
**Major character(s):** Sleel, Bodyguard, Martial Arts Expert; Kildee Wu, Martial Arts Expert, Teacher; Hoja Cierto, Martial Arts Expert, Teacher
**Time period(s):** Indeterminate Future
**Locale(s):** Mtu, Planet—Imaginary; Thompson's Gazelle, Planet—Imaginary

**Summary:** Hoping to regain lost honor, Sleel and Wu join forces against Cierto who engineered the killing of Sleel's client and whose ancestor stole the secret of black steel production from Wu's ancestor.

**Other books you might like:**
Lois McMaster Bujold, *Shards of Honor*, 1986
Brian Daley, *Jinx on a Terran Inheritance*, 1985
George Alec Effinger, *When Gravity Fails*, 1987
Stephen Goldin, *Jade Darcy and the Affair of Honor*, 1988
   Mary Mason, co-author
Stephen Goldin, *Jade Darcy and the Zen Pirates*, 1990
   Mary Mason, co-author
Steve Miller, *Agent of Change*, 1988
   Sharon Lee, co-author
Steve Miller, *Carpe Diem*, 1989
   Sharon Lee, co-author
Steve Miller, *Conflict of Honors*, 1988
   Sharon Lee, co-author

## 4292

**STEVE PERRY**

### Brother Death

(New York: Ace, 1992)

**Story type:** Science Fiction (Adventure; Theological)
**Series:** Matador
**Major character(s):** Tazzimi "Taz" Bork, Police Officer; Saval Bork, Martial Arts Expert, Bodyguard; Ndug "Brother Death" Kifo, Martial Arts Expert, Leader (Unique of the Few)
**Time period(s):** Indeterminate Future
**Locale(s):** Tembo, Planet—Imaginary

**Summary:** After a failed assassination attempt on Taz while attending a ceremony for the infant son of Saval and Veate, Saval returns to Tembo with Taz to help investigate a series of assassinations. On Tembo, a small cadre of deadly fanatics utilize alien artifacts to prepare Tembo for the return of the long extinct alien Zonn.

**Other books you might like:**
Gordon R. Dickson, *Dorsai!*, 1976
Michael Flynn, *In the Country of the Blind*, 1990
Neal Stephenson, *Snow Crash*, 1992
Vernor Vinge, *A Fire upon the Deep*, 1992

## 4293
### STEVE PERRY

## Conan the Formidable
(New York: Tor, 1990)

**Story type:** Fantasy (Sword and Sorcery)
**Series:** Conan the Barbarian
**Major character(s):** Conan, Barbarian, Warrior; Teyle, Mythical Creature (giantess); Penz, Werewolf
**Time period(s):** Indeterminate
**Locale(s):** Alternate Earth

**Summary:** Conan's journey to the city of Shadizar is interrupted when he is captured by giants at war with little green men. Before long, bandits and evil magic further complicate his life.

**Other books you might like:**
Leonard Carpenter, *Conan the Great*, 1990
Roland J. Green, *Conan the Valiant*, 1988
Robert Jordan, *Conan the Invincible*, 1985
John Maddox Roberts, *Conan the Bold*, 1989

## 4294
### STEVE PERRY

## Conan the Indomitable
(New York: Tor, 1989)

**Story type:** Fantasy (Sword and Sorcery)
**Series:** Conan the Barbarian
**Major character(s):** Conan, Barbarian, Warrior
**Time period(s):** Indeterminate
**Locale(s):** Alternate Earth

**Summary:** In this adventure, Conan finds himself caught in the middle of a war between a sorcerer and a sorceress. Trapped in a subterranean world with his companions, he must fight his way through magical creatures summoned to destroy them.

**Other books you might like:**
Glen Cook, *The Swordbearer*, 1990
Phyllis Eisenstein, *In the Red Lord's Reach*, 1989
Rose Estes, *The Hunter*, 1990
Robert E. Howard, *Hour of the Dragon*, 1989
John Jakes, *Brak the Barbarian*, 1981
John Norman, *Magicians of Gor*, 1988

## 4295
### STEVE PERRY

## The Digital Effect
(New York: Ace, 1997)

**Story type:** Science Fiction (Space Colony; Mystery)
**Major character(s):** Gil Sivart, Artist, Detective—Amateur; Patricia "Trish" Blackwell, Dancer; Ray El-Sayed, Detective—Police
**Time period(s):** 2090s
**Locale(s):** Robert E. Lee, Space Station

**Summary:** Certain that her significant other did not commit suicide, Trish asks Gil to check further. Behind schedule building the microscopic sea ships already commissioned, Gil starts to refuse but changes his mind after his ship gets bombed.

**Other books you might like:**
J.M. Dillard, *Emissary*, 1993
Michael Flynn, *Firestar*, 1996
Howard V. Hendrix, *Lightpaths*, 1997
Katharine Kerr, *Polar City Blues*, 1990
Allen Steele, *Clarke County, Space*, 1990

## 4296
### STEVE PERRY

## The Forever Drug
(New York: Ace, 1995)

**Story type:** Science Fiction (Adventure)
**Series:** Spindoc
**Major character(s):** Zia Relanj, Spy; Venture Silk, Public Relations; Croft Colburn, Spy
**Time period(s):** Indeterminate Future
**Locale(s):** New Earth, Planet—Imaginary

**Summary:** Exiled from Earth, Venture Silk begins to rebuild his life on New Earth with his new lover, in spite of the hostility he faces from natives prejudiced against Terrans. Zia, meanwhile, begins a series of medical treatments that will make her virtually immortal. Earth wants to learn the secret of the treatments and sends its best agent to bring her back dead or alive. Sequel to *Spindoc*.

**Other books you might like:**
John Brunner, *Stand on Zanzibar*, 1968
Stephen Goldin, *Jade Darcy and the Affair of Honor*, 1988
    Mary Mason, co-author
Robert A. Heinlein, *Beyond This Horizon*, 1948
Ian McDonald, *Scissors Cut Paper Wrap Stone*, 1994
John T. Phillifent, *The Man From U.N.C.L.E.: The Mad Scientist Affair*, 1966

## 4297
### STEVE PERRY
### GARY A. BRAUNBECK, Co-Author

## Isaac Asimov's I-Bots
(New York: Harper Prism, 1998)

**Story type:** Science Fiction (Robot Fiction)
**Major character(s):** Annabelle Donohoe, Businesswoman (World Tech); Zac Robillard, Scientist
**Time period(s):** 2010s (2013)
**Locale(s):** United States

**Summary:** Annabelle Donohoe, the ruthless head of the largest multinational corporation on Earth, becomes furious when scientist Zac Robillard disappears, taking with him the I-Bots which he created. I-Bots are robots so cleverly made that they are indistinguishable from humans. She hires assassins to kill Robillard and seize his creations, but underestimates their ability to protect themselves.

**Other books you might like:**
Roger MacBride Allen, *Inferno*, 1994
Isaac Asimov, *I, Robot*, 1950
Philip K. Dick, *We Can Build You*, 1972
Barry B. Longyear, *Naked Came the Robot*, 1988
Eric Frank Russell, *Men, Martians, and Machines*, 1955

## **4298**

### STEVE PERRY

## *Men in Black*

(New York: Bantam, 1997)

**Story type:** Science Fiction (Invasion of Earth; Humor)
**Major character(s):** Kay, Government Official (Men in Black); James "Jay" Edwards, Government Official (Men in Black)
**Time period(s):** 1990s
**Locale(s):** New York, New York

**Summary:** Kay recruits James Edwards into the government's top secret bureau known as Men in Black, which keeps track of extraterrestrials operating covertly on Earth. Novelizes the film of the same name.

## **4299**

### STEVE PERRY

## *Shadows of the Empire*

(New York: Bantam Spectra, 1996)

**Story type:** Science Fiction (Space Opera; Psychic Powers)
**Series:** Star Wars
**Major character(s):** Luke Skywalker, Martial Arts Expert (Jedi Knight), Hero; Darth Vader, Martial Arts Expert (Jedi Knight), Psychic; Xisor, Organized Crime Figure
**Time period(s):** Indeterminate Past
**Locale(s):** Coruscant, Planet—Imaginary; Bothawui, Planet—Imaginary; Interstellar Empire/Federation

**Summary:** Xisor hopes to replace Darth Vader in Emperor Palpatine's eyes while both he and Vader plot to suborn Luke Skywalker to the Dark Side of the Force. Meanwhile, Leia initiates a mission to rescue Han Solo, frozen in carbonite, and sets out to discover Xisor's vulnerabilities. Set between the films *The Empire Strikes Back* and *Return of the Jedi*.

**Other books you might like:**
Kevin J. Anderson, *Darksaber*, 1995
Donald F. Glut, *The Empire Strikes Back*, 1980
Barbara Hambly, *Children of the Jedi*, 1995
Vonda N. McIntyre, *The Crystal Star*, 1994
L. Neil Smith, *The Lando Calrissian Adventures*, 1994
Kathy Tyers, *The Truce at Bakura*, 1994
Dave Wolverton, *The Courtship of Princess Leia*, 1994

## **4300**

### STEVE PERRY

## *Spindoc*

(New York: Ace, 1994)

**Story type:** Science Fiction (Mystery; Adventure)
**Series:** Spindoc
**Major character(s):** Venture Silk, Government Official (public relations), Sports Figure (archery); Depard King, Murderer, Spy; Zia Relanj, Spy
**Time period(s):** Indeterminate Future
**Locale(s):** Maui, Hawaii; New Earth, Planet—Imaginary

**Summary:** After Silk discovers that his lover has been murdered, he joins the spy searching for the murderer, also trained as a secret agent. Before he can figure out why the murder took place, Silk must discover if Zia, his new companion, deserves trust.

**Other books you might like:**
F.M. Busby, *Slow Freight*, 1991
Philip K. Dick, *Blade Runner*, 1982
Katharine Kerr, *Polar City Blues*, 1990
Anne McCaffrey, *Crisis on Doona*, 1992
    Jody Lynn Nye, co-author
Mel Odom, *Lethal Interface*, 1992
Richard Paul Russo, *Destroying Angel*, 1992

## **4301**

### STEVE PERRY

## *Target Earth*

(New York: Warner Aspect, 1997)

**Story type:** Science Fiction (First Contact; Invasion of Earth)
**Series:** Leonard Nimoy's Primordials
**Major character(s):** Stewart Davies, Computer Expert, Student—Graduate; Zeerus, Alien (Avitaur), Criminal; Jake Holcroft, Child, Computer Expert
**Time period(s):** 2000s
**Locale(s):** Long Island, New York; Washington, District of Columbia; Outer Space

**Summary:** Zeerus' failed coup against the Primordials, who had rescued his species from Earth 65 million years ago, forces him to steal a spaceship to find allies. He heads for Earth where he knows an intelligent species has evolved, but Jake hacks his message from Stewart's SETI lab. The Feds hunt for Jake, who tries to run from his militia-involved father and find his mother. Meanwhile, Stewart answers Zeerus' message. Includes a two-page foreword by Leonard Nimoy. Based on comic books.

**Other books you might like:**
Juanita Coulson, *Tomorrow's Heritage*, 1981
Dean Devlin, *Independence Day*, 1996
    Roland Emmerich, Stephen Molstad, co-authors
Valerie J. Freireich, *The Beacon*, 1996
Larry Niven, *Footfall*, 1985
    Jerry Pournelle, co-author
David Weber, *Mutineers' Moon*, 1991

## **4302**

### STEVE PERRY

## *The Trinity Vector*

(New York: Ace, 1996)

**Story type:** Science Fiction (Alternate Intelligence; Theological)
**Major character(s):** Huey "Hal" Alphonse Long, Courier, Hero; Miranda Moon, Religious (priestess), Parent; Ford Wentworth, Government Official, Criminal
**Time period(s):** 2030s (2030)
**Locale(s):** Washington, District of Columbia; Boulder, Colorado (Sugar Loaf Hill); Tuscaloosa, Alabama

**Summary:** When Miranda Moon hires Hal Long to deliver the mysterious silver box to the Embrace of the Goddess Temple, she feels relieved to have the disquieting object out of her life. But as director of the National Security Agency's President's Special Section, Ford Wentworth has the resources, including another silver box, to force Long to return to Miranda for a different delivery option. Wentworth's relentless pursuit of a second box that knows the past and predicts the future with absolute accuracy compels Long, Miranda, and her two teenage daughters to flee for their lives. Along the way, they meet the Reverend Walter Green, possessor of a third silver box, who joins them in their efforts to stop Wentworth's bid for supreme power.

**Other books you might like:**
Roger MacBride Allen, *The Ring of Charon*, 1990
John DeChancie, *Starrigger*, 1983
Alan Dean Foster, *Cyber Way*, 1990
Alex McDonough, *Scorpio*, 1990
Alis A. Rasmussen, *A Passage of Stars*, 1990
Robert Shea, *The Illuminatus! Trilogy*, 1988
    Robert Anton Wilson, co-author
John Varley, *The Barbie Murders and Other Stories*, 1980
John Varley, *Blue Champagne*, 1986

---

## 4303

### JUAN PERUCHO

## *Natural History*

(New York: Ballantine, 1990)

**Story type:** Horror (Vampire Story)
**Major character(s):** Antoni de Montpalau, Scientist (naturalist); Isidre de Novau, Sea Captain (Antoni's cousin); Onofre de Dip, Vampire
**Time period(s):** 1830s
**Locale(s):** Barcelona, Spain

**Summary:** During the First Carlist War, a young liberal Spanish naturalist sets out to free the village of Pratdip from the depradations of an ancient vampire. Although he succeeds, acquiring a fiancee in the process, the vampire escapes to assume the identity of a guerrilla leader called the Owl. Translation of a superb, popular novel written in 1960 by one of Catalonia's most distinguished writers.

**Other books you might like:**
Les Daniels, *The Black Castle*, 1978
Jerzy Kosinski, *The Painted Bird*, 1965
Chelsea Quinn Yarbro, *Out of the House of Life*, 1990

---

## 4304

### DAVID PETERS

## *Haven*

(New York: Diamond, 1992)

**Story type:** Fantasy (Political; Adventure)
**Series:** Psi-Man
**Major character(s):** Chuck Simon, Fugitive, Warrior (psychic)
**Time period(s):** 2020s (2020)
**Locale(s):** New York, New York; The Complex, Virginia (secret agency headquarters)

**Summary:** With many agencies and individuals out to get him, Chuck retreats to Haven, a safe house for people with psychic powers. Instead of sanctuary, he discovers internal strife at Haven as Haven suffers external assault. This sixth volume concludes the series.

**Other books you might like:**
Isaac Asimov, *Second Foundation*, 1953
Alfred Bester, *The Stars My Destination*, 1957
Robert N. Charrette, *Choose Your Enemies Carefully*, 1991
Robert N. Charrette, *Find Your Own Truth*, 1991
Robert N. Charrette, *Never Deal with a Dragon*, 1990
Steve Perry, *The Man Who Never Missed*, 1985
Nick Pollotta, *Bureau 13*, 1991

---

## 4305

### DAVID PETERS

## *Psi-Man*

(New York: Charter/Diamond, 1990)

**Story type:** Science Fiction (Psychic Powers; Adventure)
**Series:** Psi-Man
**Major character(s):** Chuck Simon, Psychic, Martial Arts Expert (aikido); Rommel, Animal (dog); Quint, Agent (government)
**Time period(s):** 2020s
**Locale(s):** Le Quier; Kansas

**Summary:** Chuck Simon, Quaker, returns from summer school to find that one of his students has been given an addictive drug and the police will do nothing about it. When one of his fellow teachers is killed, six of the agents involved fly into what is left of her house. The videotape of the incident, taken from across the street, is brought to Quint—who smiles.

**Other books you might like:**
Isaac Asimov, *Foundation and Empire*, 1952
James Blish, *Jack of Eagles*, 1952
Katharine Kerr, *Polar City Blues*, 1990
Steve Perry, *The 97th Step*, 1989
A.E. Van Vogt, *Slan*, 1946

---

## 4306

### RALPH PETERS

## *Red Army*

(New York: Pocket, 1989)

**Story type:** Science Fiction (Military)
**Major character(s):** Chibisov, Military Personnel (chief of staff); Bezarian, Military Personnel
**Time period(s):** 1990s
**Locale(s):** Germany

**Summary:** As nuclear war looms, the Soviet Army and its Warsaw Pact allies strike deep into West Germany. NATO desperately struggles to mount a counter attack, but the Soviets clearly have the upper hand.

**Other books you might like:**
Harold Coyle, *Team Yankee*, 1987
David Drake, *Hammer's Slammers*, 1979
David Drake, *Rolling Hot*, 1989
Sir John Hackett, *The Third World War, August 1985*, 1985

---

## 4307

### GAIL PETERSEN

## *The Making of a Monster*

(New York: Dell/Abyss, 1993)

**Story type:** Horror (Vampire Story)
**Major character(s):** Kate Davis, Musician (bass player), Vampire; Charly, Musician (vocalist); Drew, Musician (guitarist)
**Time period(s):** 1990s (1993)
**Locale(s):** Hollywood, California

**Summary:** Searching for a purpose that will help take her mind off her transformation into a vampire, Kate Davis joins the rock band the Uninvited as bass guitarist. But her love for the band's lead singer, Charly, only further complicates her life, as she finds it increasingly difficult to love him without turning him into her next meal. This is the author's first novel.

**Other books you might like:**
Poppy Z. Brite, *Lost Souls*, 1992
Nancy A. Collins, *Tempter*, 1991
Anne Rice, *The Vampire Lestat*, 1985
S.P. Somtow, *Vampire Junction*, 1984

---

**4308**

**RICHARD PEYTON**, Editor

### *Journey into Fear and Other Great Stories of Horror on the Railways*

(New York: Wings, 1991)

**Story type:** Horror (Anthology)

**Summary:** Twenty-five short stories and twenty-five filler pieces concerned with ghosts and trains. Included are Ray Bradbury's noirish exercise ''The Town Where No One Got Off,'' Charles Dickens' classic tale of psychic premonition, ''The Signal Man,'' Robert Bloch's Hugo-award winning story of a deal with the devil, ''That Hell-Bound Train,'' and August Derleth's amusing tale of a midwestern ghost train, ''Pacific 421.'' Originally published in the UK in 1990 under the title *The Ghost Now Standing on Platform One*.

**Other books you might like:**
Charles Beaumont, *Omnibus of Speed*, 1958
    William Nolan, co-editor
Charles G. Waugh, *Spooky Sea Stories*, 1991
    Frank McSherry, Jr., co-editor

---

**4309**

**EUGENE E. PFAFF JR.**
**MICHAEL CAUSEY**, Co-Author

### *Uwharrie*

(Greensboro, North Carolina: Tudor Publishing, 1993)

**Story type:** Horror (Supernatural Vengeance)
**Major character(s):** David Hale, Librarian; Diana Walters, Anthropologist; John Wolfe Singer, Handyman
**Time period(s):** 1990s (1993)
**Locale(s):** Clearview, North Carolina (Uwharrie Mountains)

**Summary:** A resurrected shaman of the Uwharrie Indian tribe prepares the last blood descendant of his tribe to help bring about the end of the white man's reign through rituals that include killing the blood descendants of all families who participated in the massacre of the Uwharries a century before.

**Other books you might like:**
Morgan Fields, *Shaman Woods*, 1989
G. Wayne Miller, *Thunder Rise*, 1989
Adam Niswander, *The Charm*, 1993
Kathryn Ptacek, *Ghost Dance*, 1990
Patrick Whalen, *Deathwalker*, 1992

---

**4310**

**JILL M. PHILLIPS**

### *Walford's Oak*

(New York: Citadel, 1990)

**Story type:** Fantasy (Historical)
**Major character(s):** John Walford, Murderer, Spirit; Samuel Taylor Coleridge, Writer, Historical Figure
**Time period(s):** 1790s (1797)
**Locale(s):** Over Stowey, England; Somerset, England

**Summary:** Samuel Colridge has recently moved to town when he becomes interested in the local ghost. The ghost had been hung for a year and a day before being buried for the crime of slitting his pregnant wife's throat.

**Other books you might like:**
Ramsey Campbell, *The Parasite*, 1980
Peter James, *Possession*, 1989
Alan Ryan, *The Kill*, 1982
John Skipp, *Dead Lines*, 1989
    Craig Spector, co-author
Patricia Wrightson, *Balyet*, 1989

---

**4311**

**ROBERT PHILLIPS**

### *The Omnibus of Twentieth Century Ghost Stories*

(New York: Carroll & Graf, 1991)

**Story type:** Horror (Anthology; Ghost Story)

**Summary:** Originally published in 1989 as *Triumph of the Night*, the editor's first anthology of supernatural fiction brings together 27 tales of ghosts and hauntings by literary authors, most of whom are not associated with the genre. Included are Walter de la Mare's brilliant tale of psychic vampirism, ''Seaton's Aunt,'' Tennessee Williams' story of passion turned to flesh, ''The Mysteries of the Joy Rio,'' Charlotte Perkins Gilman's classic of the deteriorating psyche, ''The Yellow Wallpaper,'' Louis Auchincloss's metaphoric representation of the lingering presence of the past, ''The Prison Window,'' and Graham Greene's surprisingly gruesome ''A Little Place Off the Edgware Road.''

**Other books you might like:**
Peter Haining, *The Lucifer Society*, 1972
Bill Pronzini, *The Arbor House Treasury of Horror and the Supernatural*, 1981
    Barry Malzberg and Martin H. Greenberg, co-authors
Herbert Wise, *Great Tales of Terror and the Supernatural*, 1944
    Phyllis Fraser, co-author

---

**4312**

**TOM PICCIRILLI**

### *Dark Father*

(New York: Pocket, 1990)

**Story type:** Horror (Evil Children)
**Major character(s):** Daniel, Twin; Samuel, Twin; Laurie, Vagrant
**Time period(s):** 1990s
**Locale(s):** Gallows

**Summary:** When Daniel falls in love with beautiful drifter Laurie, it gives his twin brother Samuel all the room he needs to become leader of the Darklings, the name given the reanimated corpses of the town's dead. Eventually, Samuel's actions precipitate a meeting with the boys' ''dark father,'' whom they never have met but whose horrifying heritage explains their peculiar behavior. This book was nominated for a Bram Stoker Award for outstanding achievement in a first novel.

**Other books you might like:**
Shirley Jackson, *We Have Always Lived in the Castle*, 1962
Jean Paiva, *The Lilith Factor*, 1989
Thomas Tryon, *The Other*, 1972

---

**4313**

**TOM PICCIRILLI**

## The Dog Syndrome and Other Sick Puppies

(Marietta Georgia: Marietta Publishing, 1997)

**Story type:** Horror (Collection)

**Summary:** Signed limited edition chapbook of six stories, most concerned with the dark side of male and female relationships. Highlights include ''The Dog Syndrome,'' which takes the anonymity of contemporary sexual relations to a horrifying extreme; ''Where the Swamp Folk Go When the Need Comes,'' a tale of haunting and madness on the bayou; and ''Lilith at the Playground,'' narrated by a child in the grip of an evil influence. Illustrations by Eric Turnmire, Keith Minnion, Alfred Klosterman, Ray Carlson, Tom Simonton, GARK, and Wayne Miller.

**Other books you might like:**
Kevin J. Anderson, *Shifting the Boundaries: The Selected Works of Kevin J. Anderson*, 1995
Michael A. Arnzen, *Needles and Sins*, 1994
Brian Hodge, *The Convulsion Factory*, 1996
Brian Hopkins, *Something Haunts Us All*, 1995
Jeffrey Osier, *Horizon Lines*, 1997
David Niall Wilson, *The Fall of the House of Escher and Other Illusions*, 1995

---

**4314**

**TOM PICCIRILLI**
**GERARD DANIEL HOUARNER**, Co-Author
**EDWARD LEE**, Co-Author

## Inside the Works

(Orlando, Florida: Necro Publications, 1997)

**Story type:** Horror (Anthology)

**Summary:** Miscellaneous works by three authors, each represented by approximately 30,000 words of text. Tom Piccirilli (introduced by Ed Gorman) contributes five short stories, including ''Passing Through,'' the tale of a small town experiencing perplexing slips in space and time. Gerard Daniel Houarner (introduced by Bentley Little) contributes the novella, ''Truth and Consequences in the Heart of Destruction,'' which features the author's series assassin, Max, to protect him against one of those he has killed. Edward Lee (introduced by Wayne Allen Sallee) is represented by ''The Pig,'' a grotesque tale of bestiality and pornography.

**Other books you might like:**
Various Authors, *The Night Visions Series*, 1984-1992
Dana Anderson, *Cafe Purgatorium*, 1991
  Charles de Lint and Ray Garton, co-authors

Richard T. Chizmar, *Chillers*, 1994
  editor
Lucius Shepard, *Nantucket Slayrides*, 1990
  Robert Frazer, co-author

---

**4315**

**TOM PICCIRILLI**

## Pentacle

(Islip, New York: Pirate Writings, 1995)

**Story type:** Horror (Collection)

**Summary:** Presented as an episodic novel, this book collects five stories told by a nameless narrator whose association with the occult includes the omnipresence of a wisecracking familiar named Self. In ''Neverdead,'' the pair stumble into a town given over to black magic, and in ''Paindance'' into an acting out of Hopi Indian mythology. In ''Bury St. Edmonds,'' they encounter witches who have survived down thorough the centuries, and in ''Eye-Biting and Other Displays of Affection,'' a witch hunter who is reincarnated as the warden of a lunatic asylum in which they are imprisoned. Jack Cady supplies the introduction.

**Other books you might like:**
Jewelle Gomez, *The Gilda Stories*, 1991
Mercedes Lackey, *Burning Water*, 1989
Brian Lumley, *The Compleate Crow*, 1987
Seabury Quinn, *The Phantom Fighter*, 1966
Robert Weinberg, *The Devil's Auction*, 1988

---

**4316**

**J. CALVIN PIERCE**

## The Door to Ambermere

(New York: Ace, 1992)

**Story type:** Fantasy (Alternate Universe; Light Fantasy)
**Series:** Ambermere
**Major character(s):** Asbrak, Royalty (king); Daniel, Gambler, Adventurer; Rogan the Inept, Wizard
**Time period(s):** Indeterminate
**Locale(s):** Ambermere, Mythical Place; Earth

**Summary:** Daniel, on the run from Charlie, a mob boss whose daughter decides she wants Daniel, escapes to Ambermere where he becomes embroiled in the conflict between its King Asbrak and King Razenor, a neighbor. Unfortunately, Rogan releases a demon on Earth when he opens the dimensional doorway. Author's first novel.

**Other books you might like:**
Piers Anthony, *Man From Mundania*, 1989
Brian Daley, *The Doomfarers of Coramonde*, 1977
John DeChancie, *Castle Perilous*, 1988
Gordon R. Dickson, *The Dragon and the George*, 1976
Fritz Leiber, *Swords and Deviltry*, 1970
John Morressy, *Kedrigern and the Charming Couple*, 1990
Christopher Stasheff, *The Warlock in Spite of Himself*, 1969

---

**4317**

**J. CALVIN PIERCE**

## The Wizard of Ambermere

(New York: Ace, 1993)

**Story type:** Fantasy (Alternate Universe; Light Fantasy)

**Series:** Ambermere
**Major character(s):** Marcia, Adventurer
**Time period(s):** Indeterminate
**Locale(s):** Ambermere, Mythical Place; Earth

**Summary:** After a demon follows Marcia home from the magical realm, Marcia's house becomes a bit crowded with a pack of pixies and other magical creatures who also move in. Marcia determines that she needs to become a proper magician to protect herself and brings a necromancer from the Lower Regions of Ambermere to advance her education.

**Other books you might like:**
Emma Bull, *War for the Oaks*, 1987
Esther Friesner, *Gnome Man's Land*, 1991
Esther Friesner, *Harpy High*, 1991
Esther Friesner, *Unicorn U.*, 1992
Christopher Moore, *Practical Demonkeeping*, 1992

### 4318

**MEREDITH ANN PIERCE**

## The Pearl of the Soul of the World
(Boston: Little Brown, 1990)

**Story type:** Fantasy (Magic Conflict; Young Adult)
**Series:** Darkangel
**Major character(s):** Aeriel, Sorceress; Irrylath, Royalty (King); Ravanna, Sorceress
**Time period(s):** Indeterminate
**Locale(s):** Terrain, Fictional Country

**Summary:** Aeriel made a bargain which would be very difficult to keep when she took Ravanna's pearl. The pearl is the only means with which Aeriel can defeat the White Witch, free her husband, Irrylath, and end the drought which is destroying her world. 1991 Best Book For Young Adults title.

**Other books you might like:**
Jacqueline Lichtenberg, *House of Zeor*, 1974
Jacqueline Lichtenberg, *Unto Zeor Forever*, 1978
Anne Rice, *Interview with the Vampire*, 1987
Anne Rice, *The Queen of the Damned*, 1988
Anne Rice, *The Vampire Lestat*, 1985

### 4319

**MEREDITH ANN PIERCE**

## The Son of Summer Stars
(Boston: Little Brown, 1996)

**Story type:** Fantasy (Young Adult; Adventure)
**Series:** Firebringer Trilogy
**Major character(s):** Aljan "Jan" Moonbrow, Mythical Creature (unicorn), Leader; Tek, Mythical Creature (unicorn), Warrior
**Time period(s):** Indeterminate
**Locale(s):** The Plain, Fictional Country; Hallow Hills, Mythical Place

**Summary:** Jan's skill in diplomacy and battle sets the stage for his prophesied accomplishments, the vanquishing of the unicorns' old enemy, the dragons, and the unicorns' return to their homeland.

**Other books you might like:**
Peter S. Beagle, *The Last Unicorn*, 1968
Bruce Coville, *The Unicorn Treasury*, 1988
editor
Pamela Dean, *The Secret Country*, 1985
John Lee, *The Unicorn Quest*, 1986
Tanith Lee, *Black Unicorn*, 1991

Jane Yolen, *Here There Be Unicorns*, 1994

### 4320

**MEREDITH ANN PIERCE**

## The Woman Who Loved Reindeer
(New York: Tor Books (St. Martin's Press), 1989)

**Story type:** Fantasy (Historical)
**Major character(s):** Caribou, Leader (Wisewoman); Reindeer, Mythical Creature (Trangl)
**Time period(s):** Indeterminate Past

**Summary:** Caribou, a wisewoman of the north, attempts to lead her people across the Burning Plain with her companion, Reindeer, a trangl, who can appear either as a stag or a human. Reindeer knows the only way to safety.

**Other books you might like:**
Jean M. Auel, *Clan of the Cave Bear*, 1980
Jim Crace, *The Gift of Stones*, 1989
W. Michael Gear, *People of the Wolf*, 1990
Kathleen O'Neal Gear, co-author
Sue Harrison, *Mother Earth, Father Sky*, 1990
Elizabeth Marshall Thomas, *Reindeer Moon*, 1987

### 4321

**TAMORA PIERCE**

## The Realms of the Gods
(New York: Atheneum, 1996)

**Story type:** Fantasy (Young Adult; Adventure)
**Series:** Immortals
**Major character(s):** Diane Sarrasri, Magician, Telepath (with animals); Numair Salmalin, Magician
**Time period(s):** Indeterminate Past
**Locale(s):** Realms of the Gods, Mythical Place; Tortall, Fictional Country

**Summary:** When they awaken in the realms of the gods, Diane and Numair must make their way back to wartorn Tortall without help from Diane's parents, gods engaged in war with the Queen of Chaos. With the badger god and the duckmole god as guides, Diane and Numair set out to find the dragons whose aid Diane hopes to enlist. Concluding volume of a tetralogy.

**Other books you might like:**
Gillian Bradshaw, *The Land of Gold*, 1992
Ursula K. Le Guin, *A Wizard of Earthsea*, 1968
Tanith Lee, *Black Unicorn*, 1991
Andre Norton, *Elvenblood*, 1995
Mercedes Lackey, co-author
Sherwood Smith, *Wren's War*, 1995

### 4322

**TAMORA PIERCE**

## Tris's Book
(New York: Scholastic Press, 1998)

**Story type:** Fantasy (Young Adult; Magic Conflict)
**Series:** Circle of Magic
**Major character(s):** Tris, Student, Wizard; Briar, Student, Wizard; Daja, Student, Wizard
**Time period(s):** Indeterminate

**Locale(s):** Winding Circle Temple, Mythical Place

**Summary:** Tris, Daja, Briar and Sandry discover that the magic they weave together when an earthquake strikes creates ties closer than friendship, as they share magical powers. These four untrained mages prove crucial defenders of Winding Circle Temple when the Pirate Queen and her mage brother attack in force with a devastating new weapon. Second in series.

**Other books you might like:**
Susan Cooper, *Over Sea, under Stone*, 1966
Diane Duane, *The Door into Fire*, 1979
Diana Wynne Jones, *Cart and Cwidder*, 1975
Patricia C. Wrede, *Talking to Dragons*, 1985
Jane Yolen, *Dragon's Blood*, 1982

## 4323

### TAMORA PIERCE

## *Wild Magic*
(New York: Atheneum, 1992)

**Story type:** Fantasy (Young Adult; Adventure)
**Series:** Immortals
**Major character(s):** Diane Sarrasri, Magician, Telepath (with animals); Onua Chamtong, Animal Trainer (horsemistress), Adventurer
**Time period(s):** Indeterminate Past
**Locale(s):** Tortall, Fictional Country (kingdom)

**Summary:** Daine must quickly learn to harness her budding magic abilities when the kingdom requires her help in stopping a sudden infestation of dangerous immortal creatures.

**Other books you might like:**
Lois McMaster Bujold, *The Spirit Ring*, 1992
Diane Duane, *Deep Wizardry*, 1985
Diane Duane, *High Wizardry*, 1990
Diane Duane, *So You Want to Be a Wizard?*, 1983
Laurell K. Hamilton, *Nightseer*, 1992
Mary H. Herbert, *Dark Horse*, 1990
Patricia C. Wrede, *Caught in Crystal*, 1987
Patricia C. Wrede, *Daughter of Witches*, 1983
Jane Yolen, *Wizard's Hall*, 1991
Mary Frances Zambreno, *A Plague of Sorcerers*, 1991

## 4324

### TAMORA PIERCE

## *Wolf-Speaker*
(New York: Atheneum, 1994)

**Story type:** Fantasy (Young Adult; Adventure)
**Series:** Immortals
**Major character(s):** Diane Sarrasri, Magician, Telepath (with animals); Numair Salmalin, Magician
**Time period(s):** Indeterminate Past
**Locale(s):** Tortall, Fictional Country

**Summary:** Fearful that human abuse of the Dunlath Valley environment will threaten animal survival, the wolves turn to Diane for help. When Diane, Numair and their companions come to help, they discover a greater challenge than they had anticipated. Sequel to *Wild Magic*.

**Other books you might like:**
Pamela Dean, *The Dubious Hills*, 1994
Tara K. Harper, *Shadow Leader*, 1991
Ursula K. Le Guin, *A Wizard of Earthsea*, 1968

Patricia C. Wrede, *Searching for Dragons*, 1991
Laurence Yep, *Dragon of the Lost Sea*, 1982

## 4325

### MARGE PIERCY

## *He, She and It*
(New York: Knopf, 1991)

**Story type:** Science Fiction (Literary; Dystopian)
**Major character(s):** Shira Shipman, Computer Expert; Yod, Android; Malkah Shipman, Aged Person
**Time period(s):** 21st century
**Locale(s):** United States

**Summary:** Returning home after a messy divorce, Shira must examine her past, her values and her definition of humanity when she becomes involved in tutoring an android. The story is intercut with the legend of a golem in the 1600s Warsaw Ghetto.

**Other books you might like:**
Eleanor Arnason, *A Woman of the Iron People*, 1991
Margaret Atwood, *The Handmaid's Tale*, 1985
Octavia E. Butler, *Dawn*, 1987
Philip K. Dick, *Do Androids Dream of Electric Sheep?*, 1968
Suzette Haden Elgin, *The Judas Rose*, 1987
Suzette Haden Elgin, *Native Tongue*, 1984
Marjorie Bradley Kellogg, *Harmony*, 1991
Ursula K. Le Guin, *The Left Hand of Darkness*, 1969
Pat Murphy, *The City, Not Long After*, 1989
Joan Slonczewski, *A Door into Ocean*, 1986
Norman Spinrad, *Riding the Torch*, 1978
Sheri S. Tepper, *The Gate to Women's Country*, 1988

## 4326

### CHRIS PIERSON

## *Spirit of the Wind*
(Renton, Washington: TSR, 1998)

**Story type:** Fantasy (Magic Conflict)
**Major character(s):** Malystryx, Mythical Creature (dragon); Riverwind, Chieftain; Kronn-alin Thistleknot, Traveler
**Time period(s):** Indeterminate
**Locale(s):** Abanasinia, Fictional Country

**Summary:** The evil dragon Malystryx has begun destroying villages in the outlying lands near Abanasinia. A kender travels about the country calling for heroes to battle the creature, but only the legendary, though aging, Riverwind rises to the occasion. First novel.

**Other books you might like:**
Troy Denning, *The Veiled Dragon*, 1996
Thorarinn Gunnarsson, *Dragonmage of Mystara*, 1996
L. Dean James, *Kingslayer*, 1992
James Lowder, *Knight of the Black Rose*, 1991
R.A. Salvatore, *Passage to Dawn*, 1997

## 4327

### CHRISTOPHER PIKE (Pseudonym of Kevin McFadden)

## *The Cold One*
(New York: Tor, 1995)

**Story type:** Horror (Reanimated Dead)
**Series:** Cold One

**Major character(s):** Peter Jacobs, Journalist; Julie Moore, Psychologist, Student (graduate student); Govinda Sharma, Scientist
**Time period(s):** 1990s (1995)
**Locale(s):** Los Angeles, California

**Summary:** *L.A. Times* columnist Peter Jacobs' investigations into a series of brutal murders dovetails with Julie Moore's graduate studies of near-death experiences, and leads to the discovery of "the Cold One," a creature of myth who hitchiked a passage into our world during a woman's return from a near-death experience. Now she commands an army of the dissolute and disenfranchised to fulfill her evil schemes. This is the first novel in a projected series.

**Other books you might like:**
Warren Newton Beath, *Bloodletter*, 1994
Stephen Gallagher, *Valley of Lights*, 1987
Stephen King, *Pet Sematary*, 1983
Dean R. Koontz, *Hideaway*, 1993
John Saul, *Black Lightning*, 1995

---

**4328**

**CHRISTOPHER PIKE** (Pseudonym of Kevin McFadden)

## The Last Vampire

(New York: Pocket/Archway, 1994)

**Story type:** Horror (Vampire Story)
**Series:** Last Vampire
**Major character(s):** Alisa Perne, Vampire (a.k.a. Lara Adonis); Ray Riley, Teenager; Yaksha, Demon (a.k.a. Rick Graham)
**Time period(s):** 1990s (1994)
**Locale(s):** Mayfair, Oregon

**Summary:** Five-thousand-year-old vampire Alisa Perne kills the detective hired to discover her true identity, then impersonates a high school student to befriend the detective's young son and find out how much his father knew. Her investigations ultimately bring her into contact with the demon who first vampirized her. Young adult novel.

**Other books you might like:**
Richie Tankersley Cusick, *Vampire*, 1991
Joseph Locke, *Vampire Heart*, 1994
Nicholas Pine, *Night School*, 1994
L.J. Smith, *Dark Reunion*, 1992
  Vampire Diaries, volume 4

---

**4329**

**CHRISTOPHER PIKE** (Pseudonym of Kevin McFadden)

## The Midnight Club

(New York: Pocket/Archway, 1994)

**Story type:** Horror (Mystery)
**Major character(s):** Ilonka Pawluk, Teenager, Patient; Kevin, Teenager, Patient; Dr. White, Doctor
**Time period(s):** 1990s (1994)
**Locale(s):** Washington

**Summary:** "The Midnight Club," a quintet of five terminally ill teens who meet nightly to tell each other tales of horror while living out their final days at a hospice, makes a pact that the first of their number to die will return to convince others of the existence of an afterlife. When one of them dies, they begin finding that the stories they tell one another have unusual significance for their own fates. Young adult novel.

**Other books you might like:**
David Pierce, *Forever Yours*, 1994
Nicholas Pine, *The In Crowd*, 1994

R.L. Stine, *The Thrill Club*, 1990

---

**4330**

**CHRISTOPHER PIKE** (Pseudonym of Kevin McFadden)

## Sati

(New York: St. Martin's Press, 1990)

**Story type:** Fantasy (Religious)
**Major character(s):** Sati, Deity; Michael Winters, Truck Driver; David Stone, Businessman (real estate investor), Landlord
**Time period(s):** 1990s (1990)
**Locale(s):** Los Angeles, California

**Summary:** Michael picks up a hitchhiker in the desert and takes her to his home in Los Angeles. She is young, blonde, pretty—and she says she is God. Michael doesn't believe her, and yet his life and the lives of people around him begin to change.

**Other books you might like:**
Suzette Haden Elgin, *Star Anchored, Star Angered*, 1979
Robert A. Heinlein, *Stranger in a Strange Land*, 1991
A.J. Langguth, *Jesus Christs*, 1968
C.S. Lewis, *The Lion, the Witch, and the Wardrobe*, 1950
Gore Vidal, *Messiah*, 1954

---

**4331**

**CHRISTOPHER PIKE** (Pseudonym of Kevin McFadden)

## The Season of Passage

(New York: Tor, 1992)

**Story type:** Horror (Vampire Story)
**Major character(s):** Lauren Wagner, Astronaut; Jennifer Wagner, Teenager (Lauren's sister); Terry Hayes, Journalist
**Time period(s):** 2000s (2002)
**Locale(s):** Mars

**Summary:** On the second manned mission to Mars, medical officer Lauren Wagner discovers the fate of the astronauts from the mysteriously aborted first mission: they have become the victims of a species of interstellar vampire who now want to use her as a vector invading Earth.

**Other books you might like:**
Alan Dean Foster, *Alien*, 1979
Nigel Kneale, *The Quatermass Experiment*, 1959
Colin Wilson, *The Space Vampires*, 1976

---

**4332**

**CHRISTOPHER PIKE** (Pseudonym of Kevin McFadden)

## See You Later

(New York: Pocket/Archway, 1990)

**Story type:** Fantasy (Romance; Young Adult)
**Major character(s):** Mark, Computer Expert; Victor, Computer Expert; Becky, Teenager, Girlfriend
**Time period(s):** 1980s; 2030s
**Locale(s):** California

**Summary:** Mark's attraction to record-store clerk Becky seems doomed by her relationship with Ray, until he meets the attractive, but ominous, Kara and Victor. They intervene in his life, breaking up Becky and Ray and propelling Becky and Mark into romance—but why? The answer lies in the future, and the true identities of Kara and

Victor in the present, or the identities of Becky and Mark in the future.

**Other books you might like:**
Jack Finney, *Time and Again*, 1970
Robert A. Heinlein, *The Door into Summer*, 1957
Pat Murphy, *The Falling Woman*, 1986
Philippa Pearce, *Tom's Midnight Garden*, 1958

---

**4333**

**CHRISTOPHER PIKE** (Pseudonym of Kevin McFadden)

### The Starlight Crystal
(New York: Pocket, 1996)

**Story type:** Science Fiction (Young Adult; Time Travel)
**Major character(s):** Paige Christian, Teenager, Space Explorer; Tem Basker, Teenager; Karl Christian, Spaceship Captain
**Time period(s):** 22nd century
**Locale(s):** *Traveler*, Spaceship

**Summary:** Paige Christian falls in love with Tem Basker a week before leaving on a one-way space mission. She vows to see Tem again, even if it means outliving humanity and the stars and embarks on an adventure that lasts nine billion years.

**Other books you might like:**
Stephen Baxter, *Ring*, 1996
Greg Bear, *Eon*, 1985
Margaret Wander Bonanno, *Preternatural*, 1996
Randall Frakes, *The Terminator*, 1985
  Bill Wisher, co-author
Randall Frakes, *Terminator 2: Judgment Day*, 1994
Patrick O'Leary, *Door Number Three*, 1995
Robert Silverberg, *Starborne*, 1996

---

**4334**

**CHRISTOPHER PIKE** (Pseudonym of Kevin McFadden)

### Witch
(New York: Pocket/Archway, 1990)

**Story type:** Fantasy (Contemporary; Young Adult)
**Major character(s):** Julia Florence, Teenager, Witch; Scott Hague, Teenager; Amy Belle, Teenager
**Time period(s):** 1980s
**Locale(s):** Indian Pole, Idaho

**Summary:** Julia has inherited strange powers from her family, and considers herself a good witch. When she has a vision of her best friend's boyfriend being shot, she intervenes to save his life, but her other best friend, Scott, is mortally wounded instead. She decides to use her powers to obtain vengeance on the murderers, but is such a decision compatible with her self-definition of "good"? And there may be other repercussions besides the loss of her own identity that her revenge will cost her and her friends.

**Other books you might like:**
Marion Zimmer Bradley, *The Heritage of Hastur*, 1975
Peter Dickinson, *Healer*, 1987
Diana Wynne Jones, *The Lives of Christopher Chant*, 1988
Stephen King, *Carrie*, 1974
Ursula K. Le Guin, *A Wizard of Earthsea*, 1968
Patricia A. McKillip, *The Forgotten Beasts of Eld*, 1974

---

**4335**

**RICHARD PINI**, Editor

### Dark Hours
(New York: Tor, 1993)

**Story type:** Fantasy (Anthology)
**Series:** Elfquest: The Blood of Ten Chiefs

**Summary:** Contains a character chart, three-page preface by the editor and nine original shared world stories by 11 authors including Lynn Abbey, Esther Friesner, Katharine Eliska Kimbriel, Mercedes Lackey, Diana L. Paxson and Nancy Springer.

**Other books you might like:**
Robert Asprin, *Thieves' World*, 1979
  editor
Wendy Pini, *Elfquest: Journey to Sorrow's End*, 1982
  Richard Pini, co-author
Will Shetterly, *Liavek*, 1985
  Emma Bull, co-editor
Terri Windling, *Borderland*, 1986
  Mark Alan Arnold, co-editor
Terri Windling, *Elsewhere II*, 1982
  Mark Alan Arnold, co-editor
Terri Windling, *Faery*, 1985
  editor
Terri Windling, *Life on the Border*, 1991
  editor

---

**4336**

**WENDY PINI**
**RICHARD PINI**, Co-Author

### Captives of the Blue Mountain
(New York: Ace, 1997)

**Story type:** Fantasy (Adventure)
**Series:** Elfquest
**Major character(s):** Cutter, Mythical Creature (elf), Leader; Leetah, Mythical Creature (elf); Winnowill, Mythical Creature (elf)
**Time period(s):** Indeterminate
**Locale(s):** Blue Mountain, Mythical Place

**Summary:** When giant winged creatures known as Bird Spirits attack and carry off four of the tribe, Cutter and other Wolfriders must assault the craggy spire of Blue Mountain to rescue them.

**Other books you might like:**
Richard Pini, *Against the Wind*, 1990
  editor
Richard Pini, *The Blood of Ten Chiefs*, 1986
  Robert Asprin, Lynn Abbey, co-editors
Richard Pini, *Dark Hours*, 1993
  editor
Richard Pini, *Winds of Change*, 1989
Richard Pini, *Wolfsong*, 1988
  Robert Asprin, Lynn Abbey, co-authors

## `4337`

**WENDY PINI**
**RICHARD PINI**, Co-Author

### *The Quest Begins*
(New York: Ace, 1996)

**Story type:** Fantasy (Adventure; Political)
**Series:** Elfquest
**Major character(s):** Cutter, Mythical Creature (elf), Leader; Skywise, Mythical Creature (elf); Leetah, Mythical Creature (elf)
**Time period(s):** Indeterminate
**Locale(s):** Sorrow's End, Mythical Place

**Summary:** When humans arrive at Sorrow's End, a sanctuary in the elves' flight from human interference, Cutter decides he must locate and unify disparate elven groups to allow their survival.

**Other books you might like:**
Gael Baudino, *Strands of Starlight*, 1989
Terry Goodkind, *Stone of Tears*, 1995
Richard Pini, *Against the Wind*, 1990
    editor
Richard Pini, *The Blood of Ten Chiefs*, 1986
    Robert Asprin, Lynn Abbey, co-editors
Richard Pini, *Dark Hours*, 1993
    editor
Richard Pini, *Winds of Change*, 1989
Richard Pini, *Wolfsong*, 1988
    Robert Asprin, Lynn Abbey, co-editors

## `4338`

**DANIEL MANUS PINKWATER**

### *Borgel*
(New York: Macmillan, 1990)

**Story type:** Fantasy (Contemporary; Young Adult)
**Major character(s):** Borgel, Time Traveler; Melvin, Child, Time Traveler; Fafner, Animal (dog)
**Time period(s):** 1990s (1990)
**Locale(s):** New York, New York

**Summary:** From the day Borgel moves into the spare bedroom of the Spellbound household, Melvin is on his way to becoming a time tourist with Uncle Borgel in a 1937 Dorbzeldge sedan. Meeting aliens and talking to the dog are great stuff, then the party joins in a quest for the Great Popsicle.

**Other books you might like:**
Janet Asimov, *Norby, the Mixed-up Robot*, 1983
    Isaac Asimov, co-author
Roald Dahl, *Charlie and the Chocolate Factory*, 1964
Diane Duane, *So You Want to Be a Wizard?*, 1983
Ian Fleming, *Chitty Chitty Bang Bang*, 1964
Mel Gilden, *Outer Space and All That Junk*, 1989
Diana Wynne Jones, *The Homeward Bounders*, 1981
Ian Marter, *Dr. Who and the Ribos Operation*, 1979

## `4339`

**STEVEN PIZIKS**

### *In the Company of the Mind*
(New York: Baen, 1998)

**Story type:** Science Fiction (Genetic Manipulation)

**Major character(s):** Lance Michaels Blackstone, Detective—Private; Jonathan Blackstone, Businessman
**Time period(s):** Indeterminate Future
**Locale(s):** North America; Space Station

**Summary:** Lance Blackstone escapes the clutches of his billionaire father, who used him as an experimental subject, and goes into business as a private investigator. He accepts a job that takes him aboard a space station, only to discover that the job is a sham, designed to trap him where his father can continue his experiments. First novel.

**Other books you might like:**
Joseph Addison, *Tesseract*, 1988
Mick Farren, *The Feelies*, 1990
Anne Harris, *Accidental Creatures*, 1998
Lee Killough, *Spider Play*, 1986
S.N. Lewitt, *Cybernetic Jungle*, 1992

## `4340`

**EDMUND PLANTE**

### *Seed of Evil*
(New York: Leisure, 1991)

**Story type:** Horror (Evil Children)
**Major character(s):** Patty Thompson, Office Worker (receptionist); Richard Thompson, Child; Lydia Thompson, Aged Person (Patty's mother)
**Time period(s):** 1990s
**Locale(s):** New England

**Summary:** Patty Thompson knew there was something unnatural about the incredibly strong and seductive barroom pick-up who raped her and left her with child, but even her worst suspicions have not prepared her for the intemperate offspring, Richard, whose childish petulance quickly evolves into an uncanny ability to cause mischief, mayhem and murder that betray his father's demonic nature. This novel was first published in 1988.

**Other books you might like:**
Ramsey Campbell, *To Wake the Dead*, 1980
John Coyne, *Child of Shadows*, 1990
Ira Levin, *Rosemary's Baby*, 1967
Raymond Van Over, *The Twelfth Child*, 1990

## `4341`

**CHARLES PLATT**

### *Free Zone*
(New York: Avon, 1989)

**Story type:** Science Fiction (Satire)
**Major character(s):** Dusty McCullough, Ruler
**Time period(s):** Indeterminate Future
**Locale(s):** Los Angeles, California

**Summary:** A group of fugitives, civil libertarians, misfits and oddballs take over part of Los Angeles and rename it the Free Zone, declaring themselves to be an independent nation. Their leader, Dusty McCullough, spends most of his time fighting off the underhanded attacks of the evil mayor of Los Angeles, a fundamentalist Christian. He also does battle with very strange aliens, talking dogs, dinosaurs, and movie stars.

**Other books you might like:**
Mel Gilden, *Surfing Samurai Robots*, 1988
Ron Goulart, *Hellquad*, 1984
Ron Goulart, *Shaggy Planet*, 1972

Ron Goulart, *Skyrocket Steele*, 1980
Rudy Rucker, *Master of Space and Time*, 1984
Rudy Rucker, *Software*, 1982
Rudy Rucker, *Wetware*, 1988

---

**4342**

**CHARLES PLATT**

### *Protektor*

(New York: AvoNova, 1996)

**Story type:** Science Fiction (Mystery; Cyberpunk)
**Major character(s):** Tom McCray, Troubleshooter (Protektor); Serena Catalano, Businesswoman, Organized Crime Figure; Eva Kurimoto, Journalist
**Time period(s):** Indeterminate Future
**Locale(s):** Agorima, Planet—Imaginary; Protektorate, Interstellar Empire/Federation

**Summary:** A computer virus threatens to turn Agorima from pleasure planet into a realm of anarchy if Tom McCray cannot root it out.

**Other books you might like:**
Ben Bova, *Death Dream*, 1984
Pat Cadigan, *Mindplayers*, 1987
Philip K. Dick, *Do Androids Dream of Electric Sheep?*, 1968
Katharine Kerr, *Palace*, 1996
Michael Swanwick, *Vacuum Flowers*, 1987
John Varley, *Steel Beach*, 1992

---

**4343**

**CHARLES PLATT**

### *The Silicon Man*

(New York: Bantam Spectra, 1991)

**Story type:** Science Fiction (Hard Science Fiction; Adventure)
**Major character(s):** James Bayley, FBI Agent; Leo Gottbaum, Scientist
**Time period(s):** 2030s (2030)
**Locale(s):** California

**Summary:** On the trail of illegal weapons, FBI agent James Bayley stumbles across a top-secret project run by a team of government scientists that has found a way to store the human mind inside a computer. Those scanned will be immortals, freed from the weaknesses of the flesh, virtual deities in a universe of their own creation. But godhood has a price. To gain immortality, you must be willing to die.

**Other books you might like:**
John Brunner, *Children of the Thunder*, 1989
Dean Ing, *Systemic Shock*, 1981
John Shirley, *Eclipse*, 1985
Bruce Sterling, *Islands in the Net*, 1988
Walter Jon Williams, *Hardwired*, 1986

---

**4344**

**ROBERT POE**

### *The Black Cat*

(New York: Tor/Forge, 1997)

**Story type:** Horror (Mystery)
**Major character(s):** John Charles Poe, Journalist; Julie Noir, Teenager; Lawrence Cully, Veterinarian

**Time period(s):** 1970s (1973)
**Locale(s):** Crowley Creek, Virginia

**Summary:** The disappearance of Margaret Cully, wife of the local veterinarian in the sleepy town of Crowley Creek, is blamed on his teenage assistant, Julie, whose mystical beliefs and expertise in herbalism have persuaded townsfolk that she is a witch. But John Charles Poe sees enough parallels between the mystery and "The Black Cat," the classic story by his distant relative Edgar Allan Poe, to believe more plausible mechanisms are at work.

**Other books you might like:**
Deborah Churchman, *Cross a Dark Bridge*, 1996
S.K. Epperson, *The Moons of Summer*, 1994
William Hjortsberg, *Nevermore*, 1995
Marie Kiraly, *Madeline: After the Fall of Usher*, 1996
Robert R. McCammon, *Usher's Passing*, 1984

---

**4345**

**ROBERT POE**

### *Return to the House of Usher*

(New York: Tor, 1996)

**Story type:** Horror (Psychological Suspense)
**Major character(s):** Roderick Usher, Doctor; Madeline Usher, Doctor (psychiatrist); John Charles Poe, Journalist
**Time period(s):** 1990s (1996)
**Locale(s):** Crowley Creek, Virginia

**Summary:** In this contemporary recasting of Edgar Allan Poe's classic short story "The Fall of the House of Usher," Doctor Roderick Usher summons newspaper reporter John Poe to the sanitarium he runs with his twin sister Madeleine to get to the bottom of its mysteries. Madeleine's death drives Usher over the edge, but Roderick's reports of ghosts of former sanitarium patients that haunt the halls spur John to look into the activities of organized crime members who covet the land the sanitarium was built on for their own. This is the author's first novel.

**Other books you might like:**
P.H. Cannon, *Pulptime*, 1984
William Hjortsberg, *Nevermore*, 1995
Marie Kiraly, *Madeline: After the Fall of Usher*, 1996
Daniel Stashower, *The Adventure of the Ectoplasmic Man*, 1986

---

**4346**

**FREDERIK POHL**

### *The Gateway Trip: Tales and Vignettes of the Heechee*

(New York: Del Rey, 1990)

**Story type:** Science Fiction (Adventure; Collection)
**Series:** Heechee
**Major character(s):** Audee Walthers, Pilot
**Time period(s):** Indeterminate Future
**Locale(s):** Venus; Gateway Asteroid, Space Station; Outer Space (Milky Way Galaxy)

**Summary:** This collection of 10 stories expands the Hugo Award and Nebula Award winning Heechee series. "The Merchant of Venus," the longest story (116 pages), is a first person narrative relating the discovery of Heechee tunnels on Venus which precipitates human voyages to interstellar space via the Heechee Asteroid. Other stories tell of early voyages using Heechee ships and their marvelous discoveries.

**Other books you might like:**
Gordon R. Dickson, *The Dorsai Companion*, 1986
Robert A. Heinlein, *The Past through Tomorrow*, 1967
Larry Niven, *Tales of Known Space*, 1975
Cordwainer Smith, *The Best of Cordwainer Smith*, 1975
John Varley, *The Persistence of Vision*, 1978

---

### 4347

#### FREDERIK POHL

## Homegoing

(New York: Ballantine/Del Rey, 1989)

**Story type:** Science Fiction (First Contact)
**Major character(s):** Sandy Washington, Young Man; Chin Tekkitho, Alien, Teacher
**Time period(s):** 21st century
**Locale(s):** Earth; Spaceship

**Summary:** Sandy Washington, a human being raised by aliens, is returned to an Earth that he has been ill-prepared for, but, Candide-like, does his best to fit in. Although the aliens claim to have come to Earth with humanity's best interests at heart, there are indications that this might not be the truth.

**Other books you might like:**
Octavia E. Butler, *Dawn*, 1987
C.J. Cherryh, *The Pride of Chanur*, 1984
Robert A. Heinlein, *Stranger in a Strange Land*, 1961
Rebecca Ore, *Becoming Alien*, 1987
Rebecca Ore, *Being Alien*, 1989

---

### 4348

#### FREDERIK POHL
#### THOMAS T. THOMAS, Co-Author

## Man Plus

(New York: Baen, 1994)

**Story type:** Science Fiction (Alternate Intelligence)
**Major character(s):** Roger Torraway, Cyborg, Military Personnel (retired officer); Demeter Coughlan, Spy, Student; Jory den Ostreicher, Cyborg (Creole)
**Time period(s):** 2040s (2043)
**Locale(s):** Tharsis Montes, Mars

**Summary:** Coming from an environment in which the grid seems to experience difficulties, Demeter dislikes computers. Having difficulty concentrating after an accident with a haircutting robot, Demeter plans to visit Mars as a tourist and do some intelligence work for her grandfather while there. Since his power source requires expensive recharging, Roger must deal with Demeter when she requests his help. Although it seems to be building weapons with which to attack the colonists, the grid controls everything on Mars and cannot be turned off without all the humans dying. Sequel to *Man Plus*.

**Other books you might like:**
Ben Bova, *Mars*, 1992
Kim Stanley Robinson, *Green Mars*, 1994
Kim Stanley Robinson, *Red Mars*, 1993
S.C. Sykes, *Red Genesis*, 1991
Thomas T. Thomas, *ME: A Novel of Self Discovery*, 1991
John Varley, *Steel Beach*, 1992
David Weber, *Path of the Fury*, 1992
Jack Williamson, *Beachhead*, 1992

---

### 4349

#### FREDERIK POHL

## Mining the Oort

(New York: Ballantine Del Rey, 1992)

**Story type:** Science Fiction (Hard Science Fiction; Political)
**Major character(s):** Dekker DeWoe, Student, Spaceman
**Time period(s):** 21st century
**Locale(s):** Mars; Earth; Co-Mars Two, Space Station (Oort Project Station)

**Summary:** Dekker DeWoe struggles to gain entry into the Oort project training program through which he could learn to mine cometary material from the Oort Cloud for use in the ambitious project of terraforming Mars. In training, Dekker discovers the very different social patterns of people not raised on Mars and learns that the healthy completion of the Martian project may fall victim to bureaucratic haste and short-sightedness.

**Other books you might like:**
John Barnes, *Orbital Resonance*, 1991
Ben Bova, *Mars*, 1992
A.C. Crispin, *Starbridge*, 1989
Vonda N. McIntyre, *Superluminal*, 1983
Rebecca Ore, *Becoming Alien*, 1987
Allen Steele, *Lunar Descent*, 1991
Jack Williamson, *Mazeway*, 1991

---

### 4350

#### FREDERIK POHL

## O Pioneer!

(New York: Tor, 1998)

**Story type:** Science Fiction (Political; Humor)
**Major character(s):** Evesham Giyt, Immigrant, Computer Expert; Hoak Hagbarth, Businessman, Civil Servant; Mrs. Brownbent-talon, Alien (Centaurian), Political Figure
**Time period(s):** Indeterminate Future
**Locale(s):** Tupelo, Planet—Imaginary

**Summary:** Computer wizard and thief Evesham Giyt immigrates to Tupelo where the human community elects him mayor. However, by refusing to grant special favors such as the illegal importation of weapons, he earns the enmity of Hoak Hagbarth, the ex-Earth representative. As Hagbarth's former enemies have come to bad ends, Giyt decides to investigate.

**Other books you might like:**
Robert Asprin, *Phule's Paradise*, 1992
Lloyd Biggle, *The Light That Never Was*, 1972
C.J. Cherryh, *Chanur's Venture*, 1981
Alan Dean Foster, *Glory Lane*, 1987
Joe Haldeman, *Worlds Enough and Time*, 1992
Jacqueline Lichtenberg, *Dushau*, 1985
Anne McCaffrey, *Crisis on Doona*, 1992
L. Neil Smith, *Brightsuit MacBear*, 1988

---

### 4351

#### FREDERIK POHL

## The Other End of Time

(New York: Tor, 1996)

**Story type:** Science Fiction (Theological; First Contact)

**Major character(s):** Jim Daniel ''Dan'' Dannerman, Spy, Spaceman; Patrice ''Pat'' Adcock, Scientist (astronomer), Spacewoman; Dopey, Alien
**Time period(s):** 1990s
**Locale(s):** Washington, District of Columbia; Starlab, Space Station

**Summary:** After messages arrive from space, Starlab, abandoned for 18 months, appears occupied by the aliens who sent the message. Ordered to join Pat's mission to Starlab, Dan and the rest of the crew find the aliens, only to get instantly jailed. The aliens allow them to discover that their originals have returned to Earth, that the interstellar war will reach Earth shortly, and that all will be taken care of at the Eschaton at the end of the universe.

**Other books you might like:**
Roger MacBride Allen, *The Ring of Charon*, 1990
Greg Bear, *Eon*, 1985
David Brin, *Brightness Reef*, 1995
Larry Niven, *Protector*, 1973
Robert J. Sawyer, *Starplex*, 1996

---

**4352**

FREDERIK POHL

## Outnumbering the Dead

(New York: St. Martin's Press, 1992)

**Story type:** Science Fiction (Immortality; Arts)
**Major character(s):** Rafiel, Actor, Aged Person; Alegretta, Doctor, Immortal; Mosay, Director, Immortal
**Time period(s):** 2000s
**Locale(s):** United States; *Hakluyt*, Spaceship (space colony)

**Summary:** The famous 90-year-old actor, Rafiel, recently released from the hospital, agrees to star in *Oedipus Rex*. His aging body proves no match for the youthful vigor of the Immortals around him, and their petty intrigues and squabbling upset him. Pursuing the only immortality available to Rafiel, when his old love, Alegretta, wants to bear his child, he accompanies her to Hakluyt where she plans to pilot the space colony.

**Other books you might like:**
Marta Randall, *Islands*, 1980
Pamela Sargent, *The Golden Space*, 1982
Michael D. Weaver, *My Father Immortal*, 1989
John Wyndham, *The Trouble with Lichen*, 1960

---

**4353**

FREDERIK POHL

## The Siege of Eternity

(New York: Tor, 1997)

**Story type:** Science Fiction (First Contact; Invasion of Earth)
**Series:** Eschaton Sequence
**Major character(s):** Hilda Jeanne Morrisey, Government Official, Administrator; Jim Daniel ''Dan'' Dannerman, Spy, Clone; Patrice ''Pat'' Adcock, Scientist (astronomer), Clone
**Time period(s):** Indeterminate Future
**Locale(s):** Arlington, Virginia; Washington, District of Columbia

**Summary:** Having returned from Starlab with no knowledge of the objects implanted in their brains, Pat and Dan adamantly refuse to give permission for their removal. Rescued by the return of their clones, Pat and Dan work with Hilda to prevent the aliens from taking over Earth, if they have not already done so.

**Other books you might like:**
Patricia Anthony, *Brother Termite*, 1993

Wilhelmina Baird, *Chaos Come Again*, 1996
Stephen Baxter, *Timelike Infinity*, 1993
Greg Bear, *Eon*, 1985
Gregory Benford, *Furious Gulf*, 1994
Ursula K. Le Guin, *The Lathe of Heaven*, 1971

---

**4354**

FREDERIK POHL
JACK WILLIAMSON, Co-Author

## The Singers of Time

(New York: Doubleday Foundation, 1991)

**Story type:** Science Fiction (Invasion of Earth; Hard Science Fiction)
**Major character(s):** Sue-Ling Quong, Doctor; Francis Krake, Spaceship Captain
**Time period(s):** Indeterminate Future
**Locale(s):** Earth; *The Golden Hind*, Spaceship

**Summary:** Pilot Francis Krake, first human captive of the Brotherhood, was saved by them during World War II. When he learned to pilot a spaceship he was given one which he could pilot for the alien Turtles on worlds that were uncomfortable for them. Centuries later, when he returns to Earth, he helps renegotiate Earth's arrangement with the Brotherhood when they have need of the old human science.

**Other books you might like:**
Roger MacBride Allen, *The Ring of Charon*, 1990
Piers Anthony, *Macroscope*, 1969
Glen Cook, *The Dragon Never Sleeps*, 1988
Steve Miller, *Carpe Diem*, 1989
    Sharon Lee, co-author
Steve Miller, *Agent of Change*, 1988
    Sharon Lee, co-author
Steve Miller, *Conflict of Honors*, 1988
    Sharon Lee, co-author

---

**4355**

FREDERIK POHL

## Stopping at Slowyear

(Eugene, Oregon: Pulphouse Publishing Axolotl Press, 1991)

**Story type:** Science Fiction (Romance; Medical)
**Major character(s):** Murra, Spouse; Arakaho Blundy Spenotex, Writer, Rancher; Mercy MacDonald, Spaceman
**Time period(s):** Indeterminate
**Locale(s):** Slowyear, Planet—Imaginary; *Nordvik*, Spaceship

**Summary:** The arival of the tramp spaceship *Nordvik* means excitement for all. Slowyear colonists hope for new trading goods and medical advances which would cure the high infant mortality rate. Some of the *Nordvik* crew hope to find the perfect planet to make final port of call, little suspecting that Slowyear may be *Nordvik's* last stop.

**Other books you might like:**
Nancy Kress, *Beggars in Spain*, 1991
Judith Moffett, *Two That Came True*, 1991
Spider Robinson, *Kill the Editor*, 1991
Robert Silverberg, *Thebes of the Hundred Gates*, 1991

## 4356

**FREDERIK POHL**

### The Voices of Heaven

(New York: Tor, 1994)

**Story type:** Science Fiction (First Contact; Theological)
**Major character(s):** Gerald Tscharka, Spaceship Captain, Fanatic; Barry di Hoa, Pilot (spaceship), Mentally Ill Person (manic depressive); Geronimo, Alien (Lep)
**Time period(s):** 22nd century
**Locale(s):** Montenegro; Pava, Planet—Imaginary (Delta Pavonis System)

**Summary:** Shanghaied to Pava without his medications, manic-depressive Barry di Hoa finds himself extremely lonely without his girlfriend, 18 years away on Luna. He befriends Geronimo, gradually becoming fascinated with the alien Leps. Meanwhile, a large section of the original population believing in Original Sin, the Millenialists, extoll suicide as the ultimate correct action, putting the colony at risk.

**Other books you might like:**
Eleanor Arnason, *Ring of Swords*, 1993
C.J. Cherryh, *Foreigner*, 1994
Anne McCaffrey, *Powers That Be*, 1993
  Elizabeth Ann Scarborough, co-author
Vonda N. McIntyre, *Metaphase*, 1992
Larry Niven, *The Mote in God's Eye*, 1974
  Jerry Pournelle, co-author
Vernor Vinge, *A Fire upon the Deep*, 1992

## 4357

**FREDERIK POHL**

### The World at the End of Time

(New York: Ballantine/Del Rey, 1990)

**Story type:** Science Fiction (Hard Science Fiction)
**Major character(s):** Wan-To, Alien; Viktor Sorricaine, Scientist
**Time period(s):** Indeterminate Future
**Locale(s):** *Mayflower*, Spaceship; Outer Space; Newmanhome, Planet—Imaginary

**Summary:** When Viktor Sorricaine was awakened during the voyage to Newmanhome from Earth, it was due to the unexpected and unexplained changes in some of the stars on the way to the new sun. His father, an astrophysicist, was unable to explain the phenomenon before their arrival at Newmanhome, and once there, everyone was busy. Newmanhome was a beautiful planet, and was becoming very comfortable for its new inhabitants until the unexplained astrophysical phenomena began to affect their survival.

**Other books you might like:**
David Brin, *Earth*, 1990
Robert L. Forward, *Rocheworld*, 1990
Frank Herbert, *Whipping Star*, 1970
Larry Niven, *Neutron Star*, 1968
John E. Stith, *Redshift Rendezvous*, 1990
Jack Williamson, *Mazeway*, 1990

## 4358

**RACHEL POLLACK**

### Godmother Night

(New York: St. Martin's, 1996)

**Story type:** Fantasy (Contemporary; Legend)

**Major character(s):** Lauren "Laurie" Cohen, Parent (adopted), Lesbian; Jacqueline "Jaqe" Lang, Parent, Lesbian; Mother Night, Mythical Creature (death incarnate), Guardian (godmother)
**Time period(s):** 1990s
**Locale(s):** United States

**Summary:** An appeal to Mother Night leads to Jaqe's daughter and unanticipated consequences. Raised by Laurie, Jaqe's daughter practices healing, sometimes aided by Mother Night's unusual potions, while Mother Night's help allows her to negotiate the spirit realm.

**Other books you might like:**
Piers Anthony, *On a Pale Horse*, 1983
Charles de Lint, *Memory and Dream*, 1984
Elizabeth Hand, *Waking the Moon*, 1995
Patricia A. McKillip, *Winter Rose*, 1996
Ben Okri, *The Famished Road*, 1992
Terri Windling, *The Wood Wife*, 1996

## 4359

**RACHEL POLLACK**, Editor
**CAITLIN MATTHEWS**, Co-Editor

### Tarot Tales

(New York: Ace, 1996)

**Story type:** Fantasy (Anthology)

**Summary:** This anthology contains a three-page foreword by Matthews, a three-page introduction by Pollack plus brief individual introductions and author biographies for 16 original stories inspired by the symbols of Tarot fortune-telling cards. The tone of the stories varies from humor and satire to more ominous views of the reanimated dead, snake worshippers in the Amazon, Greek mythology, and the decadent rich. Authors include Storm Constantine, Sheila Finch, M. John Harrison, Gwyneth Jones, Garry Kilworth, Jacqueline Lichtenberg, Caitlin Matthews, Michael Moorcock, Rachel Pollack, Josephine Saxton, and R.J. Stewart.

**Other books you might like:**
Piers Anthony, *Tarot*, 1987
Italo Calvino, *The Castle of Crossed Destinies*, 1977
Tim Powers, *Last Call*, 1992
Edward Whittemore, *Jerusalem Poker*, 1978
Charles Williams, *The Greater Trumps*, 1950

## 4360

**RACHEL POLLACK**

### Temporary Agency

(New York: St. Martin's Press, 1994)

**Story type:** Fantasy (Contemporary; Political)
**Major character(s):** Ellen Pierson, Artist (graphic), Lesbian; Alison Birkett, Lawyer; Lisa Black Dust 7, Demon (Ferocious One)
**Time period(s):** 21st century
**Locale(s):** New York, New York

**Summary:** In a world where Shamanist magic exists comfortably in an America similar to the late 20th century, a young man comes to the attention of an evil spirit. His 14-year-old cousin, Ellen must grow up quickly to save his, and soon her, life from a spiritual and political conspiracy. Over a decade later, frightening political plots draw Ellen back in, again threatening her survival. Sequel to *Unquenchable Fire*.

**Other books you might like:**
Poul Anderson, *Operation Chaos*, 1971
Scott Baker, *Drink the Fire From the Flames*, 1987

John Crowley, *Little, Big*, 1981
Lisa Goldstein, *A Mask for the General*, 1987
Pat Murphy, *The City, Not Long After*, 1989

## 4361
### RACHEL POLLACK

## Unquenchable Fire
(Woodstock, New York: The Overlook Press, 1992)

**Story type:** Fantasy (Political; Legend)
**Major character(s):** Jennifer "Jennie" Mazdan, Government Official (server), Psychic (dreamer); Allan "Al" Lightstorm, Religious (teller); Michael "Mike" Gold, Spouse (Jennie's), Worker (Wall Street messenger)
**Time period(s):** 21st century
**Locale(s):** Poughkeepsie, New York; New York, New York

**Summary:** After revolution brings the Agency to power and alters cultural priorities in the United States of America, storytellers motivated by dreams and visions take the place of prominence formerly held by politicians and cinema stars and ritual magic pervades society. Late for the summer solstice's Day of Truth recitation by Allan Lightstorm, New York City's most famous Teller, Jennie finds herself overcome by a powerful dream, leaving her impregnated. After her failed abortion, Jennie discovers the Agency's influence acts to thwart her wishes. Winner of the Arthur C. Clarke Award upon publication in Britain.

**Other books you might like:**
Suzette Haden Elgin, *And Then There'll Be Fireworks*, 1981
Suzette Haden Elgin, *The Grand Jubilee*, 1981
Suzette Haden Elgin, *Twelve Fair Kingdoms*, 1981
Ursula K. Le Guin, *Always Coming Home*, 1987
Ursula K. Le Guin, *The Lathe of Heaven*, 1971
John D. MacDonald, *Wine of the Dreamers*, 1951

## 4362
### NICK POLLOTTA

## Bureau 13
(New York: Ace, 1991)

**Story type:** Fantasy (Psychic Powers; Contemporary)
**Series:** Bureau 13
**Major character(s):** Michael Donaher, Religious (priest), FBI Agent; Richard Anderson, Wizard, FBI Agent; Jessica Taylor, Telepath, FBI Agent
**Time period(s):** 1990s
**Locale(s):** New York, New York; Chicago, Illinois

**Summary:** After it was discovered that supernatural phenomena were a danger to the citizens of the United States, Bureau 13, under the auspices of the F.B.I., was charged with protecting the populace. More than a century later the Bureau is continuing its secret fight to keep Americans safe from vampires, werewolves, demons or whatever monsters threaten the United States.

**Other books you might like:**
Glen Cook, *Sweet Silver Blues*, 1987
John DeChancie, *Castle for Rent*, 1989
Ron Goulart, *A Talent for the Invisible*, 1973
Simon Hawke, *The Wizard of Sunset Strip*, 1989
Mercedes Lackey, *Children of the Night*, 1990
Gene Wolfe, *Castleview*, 1990

## 4363
### NICK POLLOTTA

## Doomsday Exam
(New York: Ace, 1992)

**Story type:** Fantasy (Psychic Powers; Contemporary)
**Series:** Bureau 13
**Major character(s):** Kenneth Sanders, Mutant, FBI Agent; Edward Alvarez, FBI Agent; Raul Horta, Wizard, FBI Agent
**Time period(s):** 1990s
**Locale(s):** Chicago, Illinois; Holding Facility, Alternate Universe

**Summary:** After the Tunafish Team delivers Lumpy, an unkillable monster, to the Holding Facility, they watch the final exam of the graduating mages of the Bureau 13 Academy. When interrrupted by a jailbreak of the unkillables, the Tunafish Team must save the Academy then save the world with newly graduated cadets.

**Other books you might like:**
Robert N. Charrette, *Never Deal with a Dragon*, 1990
Esther Friesner, *Hooray for Hellywood*, 1990
Ron Goulart, *Brainz, Inc.*, 1985
Ron Goulart, *Hail Hibbler*, 1980
Stephen King, *The Dead Zone*, 1979
Dean R. Koontz, *Lightning*, 1988
George R.R. Martin, *Wild Cards*, 1987 editor

## 4364
### NICK POLLOTTA

## Full Moonster
(New York: Ace, 1992)

**Story type:** Fantasy (Contemporary; Psychic Powers)
**Series:** Bureau 13
**Major character(s):** Edwardo "Ed", FBI Agent, Leader; Michael Donaher, Religious (priest), FBI Agent; Jessica Taylor, Telepath, FBI Agent
**Time period(s):** 1990s
**Locale(s):** Chicago, Illinois

**Summary:** When a psychic blast opens a rift onto Earth through which werewolves and other Hellish fiends invade Earth looking for new territory, Bureau 13 rushes to stop the invasion, repair the damage and stop the Brotherhood of Darkness.

**Other books you might like:**
Alan Dean Foster, *Cyber Way*, 1990
Alan Dean Foster, *To the Vanishing Point*, 1988
Elizabeth Ann Scarborough, *Last Refuge*, 1992
Clifford D. Simak, *Out of Their Minds*, 1970
Michael A. Stackpole, *A Gathering Evil*, 1991

## 4365
### NICK POLLOTTA
### PHIL FOGLIO, Co-Author

## Illegal Aliens
(Lake Geneva, WI: TSR, 1989)

**Story type:** Science Fiction (Humor)
**Major character(s):** Trell, Alien (invader); Hammer, Criminal (gang leader)
**Time period(s):** 1980s

**Locale(s):** New York, New York

**Summary:** A truly nasty bunch of aliens land in New York's Central Park and kidnap what they think is a typical cross section of the population. They claim that they're putting the humans through a galactic citizenship test, but they're really sizing the planet up for invasion. Unfortunately for the aliens the supposedly typical human beings they've kidnapped belong to one of New York's more notorious street gangs.

**Other books you might like:**
Poul Anderson, *The High Crusade*, 1960
Martin Caidin, *Prison Ship*, 1989
Alan Dean Foster, *Quozl*, 1989
Michael Kandel, *Strange Invasion*, 1989

---

**4366**

NICK POLLOTTA

## *Shadowboxer*

(New York: Roc, 1997)

**Story type:** Science Fiction (Cyberpunk; Science Fantasy)
**Series:** Shadowrun
**Major character(s):** Two Bears, Genetically Altered Being (dwarf); Silver, Computer Expert; Moonfeather, Wizard
**Time period(s):** 2050s
**Locale(s):** Seattle, Washington

**Summary:** Hired for an easy job, finding out what "IronHell" means, Two Bears quickly finds the easy job turns difficult, then lethal. Soon he and his team run through a maze of plots that have killed at least one runner team. Novelization based on a role-playing game.

**Other books you might like:**
Steven Barnes, *Streetlethal*, 1983
Pat Cadigan, *Synners*, 1991
William Gibson, *Burning Chrome*, 1986
Richard Paul Russo, *Destroying Angel*, 1992
Walter Jon Williams, *Voice of the Whirlwind*, 1987

---

**4367**

PETRU POPESCU

## *In Hot Blood*

(New York: Fawcett, 1989)

**Story type:** Horror (Vampire Story)
**Major character(s):** Laura Walker, Young Woman; Alain Lecouveurs, Nobleman, Vampire
**Time period(s):** 1980s
**Locale(s):** New Orleans, Louisiana

**Summary:** A new arrival in New Orleans, Laura Walker quickly succumbs to the spell of the aristocratic Lecouveurs family, especially the clan patriarch, Emory, a voracious vampire in the Dracula tradition, and Alain, his handsome nephew, who would disavow his antecedents if he could.

**Other books you might like:**
Anne Rice, *Interview with the Vampire*, 1976
Whitley Strieber, *The Hunger*, 1981
Peter Tremayne, *Dracula, My Love*, 1980

---

**4368**

ELLEN PORATH

## *Steel and Stone*

(Lake Geneva, Wisconsin: TSR, 1992)

**Story type:** Fantasy (Quest; Romance)
**Series:** Dragonlance: The Meetings Sextet
**Major character(s):** Tanthalas "Tanis" Half-Elvin, Mythical Creature (half-elf), Warrior; Kitiara "Kit" Matar, Mercenary, Leader
**Time period(s):** Indeterminate
**Locale(s):** Krynn, Planet—Imaginary

**Summary:** Recently met, Tanis and Kitiara travel across Krynn while facing dangerous human and unhuman foes and magical interference.

**Other books you might like:**
Tina Daniell, *The Companions*, 1993
Tina Daniell, *Dark Heart*, 1992
Mary Kirchoff, *Wanderlust*, 1991
  Steve Winter, co-author
Michael Williams, *The Oath and the Measure*, 1992

---

**4369**

BARRY PORTER

## *Dark Souls*

(New York: Zebra, 1989)

**Story type:** Horror (Reanimated Dead)
**Major character(s):** Tom Howards, Doctor; Shadowman, Monster
**Time period(s):** 1980s
**Locale(s):** Hawksborough, Colorado (A small mountain mining town)

**Summary:** Five people, isolated in a cabin in a Colorado mining town, are surrounded by monster creatures from the depths of the earth capable of reanimating the dead and, more terribly, taking the souls of the living.

**Other books you might like:**
Randall Boyll, *After Sundown*, 1989
John Christopher, *The Possessors*, 1964

---

**4370**

BARRY PORTER

## *Junkyard*

(New York: Zebra, 1989)

**Story type:** Horror (Small Town Horror)
**Major character(s):** Ray Holscomb, Teenager; Kevin Gavel, Police Officer (deputy sheriff), Murderer (serial killer)
**Time period(s):** 1980s (1989)
**Locale(s):** Winsome

**Summary:** Four teenaged boys with a secret clubhouse in a junkyard gradually realize that they are sharing their junkyard with a human monster, a serial killer of runaway boys, and a mysterious, perhaps supernatural, flesh eating creature.

**Other books you might like:**
James Herbert, *The Rats*, 1974
Stephen King, *It*, 1986
Chauncey G. Parker III, *The Visitor*, 1981

## 4371

### JAN POTOCKI

## The Manuscript Found in Sragossa

(New York: Viking, 1995)

**Story type:** Horror (Occult)
**Major character(s):** Alphonse van Worden, Military Personnel; Don Pedro de Uzeda, Religious (brother)
**Time period(s):** 1730s (1739)
**Locale(s):** Madrid, Spain

**Summary:** In the Sierra Morena mountains of Spain, a young soldier is seduced into a world of the real and the supernatural that seems fashioned from the legends of Christianity, Judaism, and Islam. This episodic novel, written between 1797 and 1815, varies from the bawdy to the metaphysical in its accounts of the Wandering Jews, physical embodiments of the Gemini twins, the progeny of King Solomon, and other known personalities of history and legend. Translated by Ian Maclean.

**Other books you might like:**
L. Sprague de Camp, *The Land of Unreason*, 1942
   Fletcher Pratt, co-author
William Hope Hodgson, *The Night Land*, 1912
Charles Maturin, *Melmoth the Wanderer*, 1820
Edgar Allan Poe, *The Narrative of A. Gordon Pym*, 1838
Eugene Sue, *The Wandering Jew*, 1844

## 4372

### JERRY POURNELLE
### S.M. STIRLING, Co-Author

## The Children's Hour

(New York: Baen, 1991)

**Story type:** Science Fiction (Military)
**Series:** Man-Kzin Wars
**Major character(s):** Chuut-Riit, Alien (Kzin); Ingrid Raines, Military Personnel; Dnivtopun, Alien (Thrint)
**Time period(s):** 25th century
**Locale(s):** Wunderland, Planet—Imaginary; *U.N.S.N. Catskinner*, Spaceship

**Summary:** The Kzin occupy the human-colonized Alpha Centauri system and have sent four fleets from there to attack Earth. So far the humans have deflected all Kzin attacks and destroyed each fleet in succession. But it seems that they will not be able to hold off the Kzin now that Chuut-Riit is in control on Wunderland. From the humans he has been adapting a new technique, cooperation, so Earth's ARM sends a mission to assassinate him before it gets perfected.

**Other books you might like:**
Poul Anderson, *Inconstant Star*, 1991
Diana G. Gallagher, *The Alien Dark*, 1990
Dean Ing, *Cathouse*, 1991
Larry Niven, *Man-Kzin Wars*, 1988
   editor
Larry Niven, *Man-Kzin Wars II*, 1989
   editor
Larry Niven, *Man-Kzin Wars III*, 1990
   editor
Larry Niven, *Man-Kzin Wars IV*, 1991
   editor
Larry Niven, *Tales of Known Space*, 1975
S.M. Stirling, *Marching through Georgia*, 1988
S.M. Stirling, *The Stone Dogs*, 1990

## 4373

### JERRY POURNELLE, Editor
### JOHN F. CARR, Co-Editor

## CoDominium: Revolt on War World

(New York: Baen, 1992)

**Story type:** Science Fiction (Anthology; Military)
**Series:** War World
**Time period(s):** 21st century
**Locale(s):** Haven, Planet—Imaginary

**Summary:** Contains eight original stories by nine authors with Leslie Fish and Frank Gasperik collaborating on ''Janesfort War,'' plus an introduction, ''The Lost and the Founder'' and epilog, ''Farewell to Haven,'' by the editor. The stories depict the early history of Haven from bleak dumping ground for religious and political dissidents to wealthy mining planet which produces warriors capable of defeating the Sauron fighting machine. Other authors include John Dalmas, Susan Shwartz, Harry Turtledove, Eric Vinicoff and William F. Wu.

**Other books you might like:**
Robert Asprin, *The Bug Wars*, 1979
F.M. Busby, *The Alien Debt*, 1984
Orson Scott Card, *Ender's Game*, 1985
John Dalmas, *The White Regiment*, 1990
David Drake, *The Fleet*, 1988
   Bill Fawcett, co-editor
William R. Forstchen, *Ice Prophet*, 1983
Martin H. Greenberg, *Bootcamp 3000*, 1992
   Charles G. Waugh, co-editor
Keith Laumer, *Star Colony*, 1981
Larry Niven, *Man-Kzin Wars*, 1988
   editor
Joel Rosenberg, *Hero*, 1990

## 4374

### JERRY POURNELLE

## Falkenberg's Legion

(New York: Baen, 1990)

**Story type:** Science Fiction (Military)
**Series:** CoDominium
**Major character(s):** John Christian Falkenberg, Military Personnel
**Time period(s):** 21st century
**Locale(s):** Arrarat, Planet—Imaginary; Hadley, Planet—Imaginary; New Washington, Planet—Imaginary

**Summary:** The seeds of contradiction that lie at the heart of the Soviet-American alliance are bearing their final fruit. Soon they will rip the CoDominium apart and Earth will die. In the face of that inevitability, the fate of humanity lies with the colony worlds, few of which are equipped for more than bare survival. Thrown upon their own resources, their futures seem as limited as their past. They have one hope. To find someone with both the strength and vision to grasp the remnants of civilization and weld them into a single society. John Christian Falkenberg is that man. John Christian's story is complete for the first time in this volume which encompasses two previous titles, *The Mercenary* (1977) and *West of Honor* (1976), with some new filler material.

**Other books you might like:**
Gordon R. Dickson, *Dorsai!*, 1976
Gordon R. Dickson, *Soldier, Ask Not*, 1967
David Drake, *Cluster Command*, 1989
   W.C. Dietz, co-author
David Drake, *Hammer's Slammers*, 1979

Joe Haldeman, *The Forever War*, 1975
Keith Laumer, *Bolo: The Annals of the Dinochrome Brigade*, 1976

## 4375

**JERRY POURNELLE**
**S.M. STIRLING**, Co-Author

### Go Tell the Spartans
(New York: Baen, 1991)

**Story type:** Science Fiction (Military)
**Series:** CoDominium
**Major character(s):** Peter Owensford, Mercenary, Military Personnel
**Time period(s):** 21st century; 22nd century
**Locale(s):** Sparta, Planet—Imaginary

**Summary:** Hoping to provide themselves a secure base of operations, Falkenberg's Legion accepts the training of local troops on Sparta, settled by eccentric American political idealists and involuntary colonists who now hope to survive the impending collapse of Imperial rule. Others work to control Sparta for themselves.

**Other books you might like:**
Isaac Asimov, *Foundation*, 1951
Isaac Asimov, *Foundation and Empire*, 1952
Isaac Asimov, *Second Foundation*, 1953
Lois McMaster Bujold, *Borders of Infinity*, 1989
Lois McMaster Bujold, *The Warrior's Apprentice*, 1986
Allan Cole, *Sten*, 1984
    Chris Bunch, co-author
Glen Cook, *The Dragon Never Sleeps*, 1988
Alis A. Rasmussen, *Revolution's Shore*, 1990

## 4376

**JERRY POURNELLE**, Editor
**JOHN F. CARR**, Co-Editor

### Life Among the Asteroids
(New York: Ace, 1992)

**Story type:** Science Fiction (Anthology)
**Series:** Endless Frontier

**Summary:** Includes a two-page introduction by Pournelle and individual introductions for entries with two articles by Pournelle and one by Eric Drexler reprinted from periodicals and original stories by John Hegenberger, Peter L. Manly and Brooks Peck plus reprinted stories by Poul Anderson, Jack Clemons, Phillip C. Jennings, Jerry Pournelle, Charles Sheffield and Michael Swanwick.

**Other books you might like:**
Robert Silverberg, *The Science Fiction Hall of Fame, Volume 1*, 1970
    editor
Cordwainer Smith, *The Best of Cordwainer Smith*, 1975
Marc Stiegler, *The Gentle Seduction*, 1990
John Varley, *The Barbie Murders and Other Stories*, 1980
John Varley, *Blue Champagne*, 1986
John Varley, *The Persistence of Vision*, 1978

## 4377

**JERRY POURNELLE**

### Prince of Mercenaries
(New York: Baen Books, 1989)

**Story type:** Science Fiction (Military)
**Series:** CoDominium
**Major character(s):** John Christian Falkenberg, Mercenary; Lysander, Royalty
**Time period(s):** 21st century
**Locale(s):** CoDominium, Earth; Sparta, Planet—Imaginary

**Summary:** The CoDominium, the U.S.-Soviet alliance that has maintained peace on Earth and in space for decades, is crumbling and the colony worlds are beginning to assert their independence. Prince Lysander of Sparta enlists the aid of the mercenary commander John Christian Falkenberg to help break free from CoDominium oppression.

**Other books you might like:**
Gordon R. Dickson, *The Final Encyclopedia*, 1984
Gordon R. Dickson, *Lost Dorsai*, 1980
Gordon R. Dickson, *Soldier, Ask Not*, 1967
Gordon R. Dickson, *The Spirit of Dorsai*, 1979
David Drake, *Hammer's Slammers*, 1979
David Drake, *Rolling Hot*, 1989
Robert A. Heinlein, *Starship Troopers*, 1959

## 4378

**JERRY POURNELLE**
**S.M. STIRLING**, Co-Author

### Prince of Sparta
(New York: Baen, 1993)

**Story type:** Science Fiction (Military; Political)
**Series:** CoDominium
**Major character(s):** Lysander Collins, Military Personnel, Royalty (prince); Skida ''Skilly'' Thibodeau, Leader (resistance), Murderer; Peter Owensford, Mercenary, Military Personnel (General)
**Time period(s):** 21st century; 22nd century
**Locale(s):** Sparta, Planet—Imaginary

**Summary:** Hired by the Spartan government to quell the Helot Rebellion, Falkenberg's Legion discovers Grand Senate intrigues driving the situation. As Falkenberg's enemies and CoDominium Navy factions backing Skilly Thibodeau abet the insurgents, discord reverberates through the CoDominium.

**Other books you might like:**
Roger MacBride Allen, *The Torch of Honor*, 1985
Lois McMaster Bujold, *The Warrior's Apprentice*, 1986
John Dalmas, *The Regiment*, 1987
Gordon R. Dickson, *Dorsai!*, 1976
Alan Dean Foster, *The False Mirror*, 1992
Robert A. Heinlein, *Starship Troopers*, 1959
Keith Laumer, *The Glory Game*, 1973
H. Beam Piper, *Uller Uprising*, 1982
Timothy Zahn, *Cobra*, 1985

## 4379

**JERRY POURNELLE**

### Starswarm

(New York: Tor, 1998)

**Story type:** Science Fiction (Young Adult; Alternate Intelligence)
**Series:** Jupiter
**Major character(s):** Kip Brewster, Heir—Lost, Teenager; Gwen, Artificial Intelligence; Mike Brewster, Guardian, Fugitive
**Time period(s):** Indeterminate Future
**Locale(s):** Paradise, Planet—Imaginary

**Summary:** Growing up at the remote Starswarm Station on the planet Paradise, Kip instinctively keeps the ''voice'' in his head, an artificial intelligence program called Gwen, secret from his Uncle Mike and his friends. As the human settlers on Paradise begin to clash with the planet's native lifeforms, Kip learns that Gwen holds the key to his identity and destiny. Fifth in the Jupiter series of young adult stand-alone science fiction novels.

**Other books you might like:**
Frederik Pohl, *Mining the Oort*, 1992
Larry Segriff, *Spacer Dreams*, 1995
Charles Sheffield, *The Billion Dollar Boy*, 1997
Charles Sheffield, *The Cyborg From Earth*, 1998
Charles Sheffield, *Higher Education*, 1996
    Jerry Pournelle, co-author
Charles Sheffield, *Putting Up Roots*, 1997

## 4380

**SUSAN POWER**

### The Grass Dancer

(New York: Putnam, 1994)

**Story type:** Fantasy (Romance; Contemporary Realism)
**Major character(s):** Charlene Thunder, Indian; Harley Wind Soldier, Indian; Anna Thunder, Indian, Witch
**Time period(s):** 1960s; 1970s
**Locale(s):** North Dakota

**Summary:** Seperated in the 1880s with their love unfulfilled, two spirits attempt to find each other through the decades. Driven by the inertia of family history, Charlene Thunder and Harley Wind Soldier search for happiness despite external pressures after a motorcycle accident leads Charlene to suspect her grandmother, Anna Thunder, of causing the deaths. First novel.

**Other books you might like:**
J. Alison James, *Sing for a Gentle Rain*, 1990
Barry Lopez, *Crow and Weasel*, 1990
Gerald Vizenor, *Dead Voices: Natural Agonies in the Real World*, 1992
Roger Welsch, *Touching the Fire*, 1992
Roger Zelazny, *Bridge of Ashes*, 1976

## 4381

**RICHARD M. POWERS**

### Galatea 2.2

(New York: Farrar Straus Giroux, 1995)

**Story type:** Science Fiction (Alternate Intelligence; Literary)
**Major character(s):** Richard Powers, Teacher, Writer; C., Student; Helen, Artificial Intelligence
**Time period(s):** 1990s
**Locale(s):** U., Fictional City

**Summary:** Hired by the Center for the Study of Advanced Sciences, Richard Powers joins a project on Artificial Intelligence. As the programs grow more complex, Powers teaches them about life and literature, while he reminisces about a failed relationship.

**Other books you might like:**
Elizabeth Hand, *AEstival Tide*, 1992
D.F. Jones, *Colossus*, 1966
Ian McDonald, *Terminal Cafe*, 1994
Rudy Rucker, *Wetware*, 1988
Thomas T. Thomas, *ME: A Novel of Self Discovery*, 1991

## 4382

**TIM POWERS**

### Earthquake Weather

(New York: Tor, 1997)

**Story type:** Fantasy (Contemporary)
**Series:** Fisher King
**Major character(s):** Janis Plumtree, Mentally Ill Person; Sid Cochran, Vintner; Scott Crane, Religious (Fisher King), Spirit
**Time period(s):** 1990s
**Locale(s):** Los Angeles, California; San Francisco, California

**Summary:** Under a malign influence, Janis Plumtree murders the Fisher King. Driven by remorse, she finds a group of simultaneously helpless and powerful people who will help her bring the King back or find a new King. Unfortunately, other claimants and the god Dionysus plan otherwise. An after-the-fact sequel to *Last Call* and *Expiration Date*.

**Other books you might like:**
James P. Blaylock, *The Paper Grail*, 1991
Jack Cady, *The Off Season*, 1995
John Crowley, *Little, Big*, 1981
Charles de Lint, *Moonheart: A Romance*, 1984
Robert Holdstock, *Mythago Wood*, 1984

## 4383

**TIM POWERS**

### Expiration Date

(New York: Tor, 1996)

**Story type:** Fantasy (Contemporary)
**Major character(s):** Pete Sullivan, Technician (tramp electrician), Psychic; Thomas Edison, Inventor, Disembodied Personality; Koot ''Kootie'' Hoomie Parganas, Teenager, Psychic
**Time period(s):** 1990s
**Locale(s):** Los Angeles, California

**Summary:** When the dead hang on as half-conscious ghosts, real but dazed and intangible, people will exploit them. When a young boy opens the door to one of the most powerful ghosts ever, those people in-between notice. Suddenly, a great many people, living, dead, and in-between, must fight for their lives.

**Other books you might like:**
Peter S. Beagle, *A Fine and Private Place*, 1960
James P. Blaylock, *Night Relics*, 1994
Jack Cady, *The Off Season*, 1995
John Crowley, *Little, Big*, 1981
Megan Lindholm, *Wizard of the Pigeons*, 1986

## 4384

### TIM POWERS

## *Last Call*

(New York: Morrow, 1992)

**Story type:** Fantasy (Contemporary; Horror)
**Major character(s):** Scott Crane, Gambler; Benjamin ''Bugsy'' Siegel, Historical Figure, Criminal
**Time period(s):** 1990s
**Locale(s):** Las Vegas, Nevada

**Summary:** Abandoned by the father who would sacrifice him to gain mastery over Las Vegas, Scott Crane grows up in a foster family. As an adult, Scott and his adoptive family attempt to unseat his corrupted father utilizing the symbolic mysticism associated with tarot. The Charnel House limited edition's text differs slightly.

**Other books you might like:**
Piers Anthony, *Tarot*, 1987
James P. Blaylock, *The Paper Grail*, 1991
Charles de Lint, *The Little Country*, 1991
Alan Dean Foster, *To the Vanishing Point*, 1988
Stephen King, *The Stand: The Complete and Uncut Edition*, 1990
Edward Whittemore, *Jerusalem Poker*, 1978

## 4385

### TIM POWERS

## *The Stress of Her Regard*

(New York: Ace Books, 1989)

**Story type:** Horror (Vampire Story)
**Major character(s):** Michael Crawford, Doctor, Fugitive; George Gordon Byron, Historical Figure, Writer (poet)
**Time period(s):** 1820s
**Locale(s):** Europe; England

**Summary:** After his wife is murdered by a spectral female on their wedding night, Michael Crawford flees to seek counsel from the great English poets, Keats, Shelley, and Byron, who, he finds, have been similarly haunted. He learns of the *nephelim*, a race of spiritual vampires that plague the most sensitive and, along with Byron and Josephine, sister of his murdered wife, searches for a way to neutralize their terrible powers.

**Other books you might like:**
Brian W. Aldiss, *Frankenstein Unbound*, 1973
James P. Blaylock, *Homunculus*, 1986

## 4386

### TERRY PRATCHETT

## *Diggers*

(New York: Delacorte, 1991)

**Story type:** Science Fiction (Young Adult; Adventure)
**Series:** Bromeliad
**Major character(s):** Dorcas, Mythical Creature (nome); Grimma, Mythical Creature (nome)
**Time period(s):** 1990s
**Locale(s):** East Coast

**Summary:** Having narrowly escaped the destruction of their home, the nomes find their way to an abandoned quarry where life is possible, if difficult. When humans plan to reopen the quarry, the nomes face the loss of their new home and additional dangers of rat poison and wild animals. The desperate nomes arrange to refit and flee in a piece of heavy equipment. This book is a sequel to *Truckers*.

**Other books you might like:**
Murray Leinster, *Unknown Danger*, 1969
    Will F. Jenkins, real name
Mary Norton, *The Borrowers*, 1952
Mary Norton, *The Borrowers Afield*, 1955
Mary Norton, *The Borrowers Afloat*, 1959
John Peterson, *The Littles*, 1967

## 4387

### TERRY PRATCHETT

## *Equal Rites*

(New York: Signet, 1988)

**Story type:** Fantasy (Light Fantasy)
**Series:** Discworld
**Major character(s):** Esk, Witch
**Time period(s):** Indeterminate
**Locale(s):** Discworld, Planet—Imaginary

**Summary:** A dying wizard mistakenly gives his powers to what he thinks is the eighth son of an eighth son. However, this eighth son is really a daughter and although her family tries to raise her as a witch, it becomes apparent that she is fated to become a wizard.

**Other books you might like:**
Suzy McKee Charnas, *The Golden Thread*, 1989
Kara Dalkey, *The Curse of Sagamore*, 1988
Peter David, *Howling Mad*, 1989
John DeChancie, *Castle Perilous*, 1988

## 4388

### TERRY PRATCHETT

## *Eric*

(New York: Roc, 1995)

**Story type:** Fantasy (Light Fantasy; Legend)
**Major character(s):** Eric Thursley, Wizard; Rincewind, Wizard; Astfgl, Demon
**Time period(s):** Indeterminate
**Locale(s):** Pseudopolis, Fictional City; Pandemonium, Hell

**Summary:** Attempting to summon a demon to grant him three wishes, to rule the world, to meet the world's most beautiful woman, and to live forever, Eric instead conjures Rincewind from the Dungeon Dimensions. When Eric gets his wishes, Rincewind, with the help of his luggage and an aphasic parrot, must save them from the consequences by a slight detour through Hell.

**Other books you might like:**
Douglas Adams, *The Hitchhiker's Guide to the Galaxy*, 1980
Chester Anderson, *The Butterfly Kid*, 1967
Robert Asprin, *Another Fine Myth*, 1978
Janet Morris, *Heroes in Hell*, 1986
    editor
Roger Zelazny, *If at Faust You Don't Succeed*, 1993
    Robert Sheckley, co-author

## 4389

### TERRY PRATCHETT

## *Feet of Clay*

(New York: HarperPrism, 1996)

**Story type:** Fantasy (Light Fantasy; Mystery)
**Series:** Discworld
**Major character(s):** Samuel Vimes, Police Officer; Dorfl, Mythical Creature (golem); Carrot Gimlet, Police Officer
**Time period(s):** Indeterminate
**Locale(s):** Discworld, Planet—Imaginary; Ankh-Morpork, Fictional City

**Summary:** A series of mysterious murders and the near death of the Patrician of Ankh-Morpork baffle the officers of the City Watch. Clues lead them on a merry chase among the denizens of the city, including a revolutionary cell of golems seeking freedom. They also stumble across a sinister plot to install Corporal Nobbs as puppet king of the city. Commander Vimes uncovers the truth, but may be unable to bring the guilty to justice.

**Other books you might like:**
Douglas Adams, *Dirk Gently's Holistic Detective Agency*, 1987
Isaac Asimov, *The Caves of Steel*, 1954
Brett Davis, *The Faery Convention*, 1995
Lynn S. Hightower, *Alien Blues*, 1992
Elizabeth Ann Scarborough, *The Goldcamp Vampire; or The Sanguinary Sourdough*, 1987
Clifford D. Simak, *The Goblin Reservation*, 1968

## 4390

### TERRY PRATCHETT

## *Guards! Guards!*

(New York: Roc, 1991)

**Story type:** Fantasy (Light Fantasy)
**Series:** Discworld
**Major character(s):** Samuel Vimes, Police Officer (captain); Carrot Gimlet, Police Officer; Sybil Ramkin, Noblewoman (animal breeder)
**Time period(s):** Indeterminate
**Locale(s):** Ankh-Morpork, Fictional City; Discworld, Planet—Imaginary

**Summary:** Carrot, an orphaned human baby adopted by dwarves, is now 16 and growing too tall to work in the mines. He sets off for Ankh-Morpork to join the Night Watch and uphold the laws, not knowing that the Night Watch is barely surviving in the city since the Patrician has organized crime. However, when the Elucidated Brethren of the Ebon Night steal a book and summon a dragon in hopes of restoring the monarchy, Captain Vimes and his three men begin investigating. They find allies in Lady Ramkin, aristocratic breeder of swamp dragons, and the Librarian of the Unseen University, who ventures into L-space to recover his stolen book.

**Other books you might like:**
Douglas Adams, *Dirk Gently's Holistic Detective Agency*, 1987
Robert Asprin, *M.Y.T.H. Inc. Link*, 1986
Robin Wayne Bailey, *Nightwatch*, 1990
Steven Brust, *Jhereg*, 1983
Will Shetterly, *Liavek: Wizard's Row*, 1987
    Emma Bull, co-editor
Clifford D. Simak, *The Goblin Reservation*, 1968
Patricia C. Wrede, *Dealing with Dragons*, 1990

## 4391

### TERRY PRATCHETT

## *Hogfather*

(New York: HarperCollins, 1998)

**Story type:** Fantasy (Humor; Magic Conflict)
**Series:** Discworld
**Major character(s):** Susan Sto-Helit, Governess, Noblewoman; Death, Mythical Creature; Jonathan Teatime, Murderer (assassin)
**Time period(s):** Indeterminate
**Locale(s):** Ankh-Morpork, Fictional City

**Summary:** 'Tis the night before Hogswatch and the Hogfather has disappeared, so Death takes on the traditional duties—driving a sleigh pulled by four boars and bringing gifts to the children of Discworld. Death's granddaughter Susan, with the help of a Tooth Fairy, the God of Hangovers, and assorted wizards, tracks down the assassin and rescues the Hogfather.

**Other books you might like:**
Douglas Adams, *The Long Dark Tea-Time of the Soul*, 1988
Robert Asprin, *Myth-ing Persons*, 1984
Neil Gaiman, *Good Omens: The Nice and Accurate Prophecies of Agnes Nutter, Witch*, 1990
    Terry Pratchett, co-author
Simon Hawke, *The Wizard of 4th Street*, 1987
Christopher Stasheff, *Her Majesty's Wizard*, 1986

## 4392

### TERRY PRATCHETT

## *Interesting Times*

(New York: HarperCollins, 1997)

**Story type:** Fantasy (Light Fantasy)
**Series:** Discworld
**Major character(s):** Ghenghiz "Cohen the Barbarian" Cohen, Hero, Aged Person; Rincewind, Wizard; Lord Hong, Nobleman, Villain
**Time period(s):** Indeterminate
**Locale(s):** Ankh-Morpork, Fictional City; Agatean Empire, Fictional Country; Discworld, Planet—Imaginary

**Summary:** The wizards of the Unseen University pull Rincewind from a blissfully boring desert island and send him across the Discworld to the Agatean Empire where he meets his old friend, Cohen, leader of the Silver Horde—five geriatric heroes and a retired teacher. The Horde travels to Hunghung, capital of the Empire, where Cohen plans the crowning achievement of his career. In spite of his efforts to avoid danger, Rincewind ends up leading revolutionaries who want to overthrow the Empire (politely) and resurrecting the legendary Red Army. Reprint of the 1994 British edition.

**Other books you might like:**
Douglas Adams, *The Hitchhiker's Guide to the Galaxy*, 1980
Chester Anderson, *The Butterfly Kid*, 1967
Robert Asprin, *Another Fine Myth*, 1978
L. Sprague de Camp, *The Complete Compleat Enchanter*, 1989
    Fletcher Pratt, co-author
James H. Schmitz, *The Witches of Karres*, 1966
Christopher Stasheff, *Her Majesty's Wizard*, 1986

## 4393

**TERRY PRATCHETT**

### *Jingo*

(New York: Harper, 1998)

**Story type:** Fantasy (Humor)
**Series:** Discworld
**Major character(s):** Samuel Vimes, Police Officer (commander); Leonard, Inventor
**Time period(s):** Indeterminate
**Locale(s):** Discworld, Planet—Imaginary

**Summary:** A new island rises from the ocean on Discworld, and the two major nations are each intent upon claiming it. As war seems imminent, Leonard of Quirm invents a number of new military devices that don't depend on magic, but by doing so he may have made conflict even more dangerous than ever.

**Other books you might like:**
Piers Anthony, *Demons Don't Dream*, 1993
Robert Asprin, *Another Fine Myth*, 1978
Esther Friesner, *Elf Defense*, 1988
Craig Shaw Gardner, *A Bad Day for Ali Baba*, 1992
Tom Holt, *Expecting Someone Taller*, 1987

## 4394

**TERRY PRATCHETT**

### *Lords and Ladies*

(New York: HarperPrism, 1995)

**Story type:** Fantasy (Light Fantasy)
**Series:** Discworld
**Major character(s):** Granny Weatherwax, Witch, Heroine; Magrat Garlick, Fiance(e) (the king's), Witch; Nanny Ogg, Witch, Heroine
**Time period(s):** Indeterminate
**Locale(s):** Discworld, Planet—Imaginary; Lancre, Fictional City

**Summary:** When elves invade Lancre from the fairy realm, Granny Weatherwax and her companion witches must save the populace from the nasty infestation.

**Other books you might like:**
Emma Bull, *War for the Oaks*, 1987
Esther Friesner, *Gnome Man's Land*, 1991
Alan Dean Foster, *To the Vanishing Point*, 1988
Nick Pollotta, *Bureau 13*, 1991
Nick Pollotta, *Full Moonster*, 1992
Harry Turtledove, *The Case of the Toxic Spell Dump*, 1993

## 4395

**TERRY PRATCHETT**

### *Maskerade*

(New York: HarperPrism, 1997)

**Story type:** Fantasy (Light Fantasy; Satire)
**Series:** Discworld
**Major character(s):** Agnes Nitt, Singer; Granny Weatherwax, Witch; Death, Mythical Creature
**Time period(s):** Indeterminate Past
**Locale(s):** Discworld, Planet—Imaginary; Ankh-Morpork, Fictional City

**Summary:** Since Agnes wants to sing, Granny Weatherwax needs a new third witch. The Opera Ghost remains looney, while Death acquires a little repetetive motion stress in his arms. All of them come together as the Discworld collides with *The Phantom of the Opera*. Ankh Morpork and the eardrums of its inhabitants will never be the same again in this 18th book in the Discworld series.

**Other books you might like:**
Robert Asprin, *Another Fine Myth*, 1978
John Bellairs, *The Face in the Frost*, 1969
L. Sprague de Camp, *The Complete Compleat Enchanter*, 1989
Gaston Leroux, *The Phantom of the Opera*, 1990
    Lowell Blair, translator
Christopher Moore, *Practical Demonkeeping*, 1992

## 4396

**TERRY PRATCHETT**

### *Men at Arms*

(New York: HarperPrism, 1996)

**Story type:** Fantasy (Light Fantasy; Adventure)
**Series:** Discworld
**Major character(s):** Edward d'Eath, Nobleman, Criminal (assassin); Carrot Gimlet, Police Officer
**Time period(s):** Indeterminate
**Locale(s):** Discworld, Planet—Imaginary; Ankh-Morpork, Fictional City

**Summary:** In a sequel of sorts to *Guards! Guards!*, Carrot, adopted dwarf, attempts to bring law and order to Ankh-Morpork.

**Other books you might like:**
Robert Asprin, *Another Fine Myth*, 1978
John Bellairs, *The Face in the Frost*, 1969
Craig Shaw Gardner, *The Other Sinbad*, 1991
Christopher Moore, *Practical Demonkeeping*, 1992
Roger Zelazny, *Bring Me the Head of Prince Charming*, 1991
    Robert Sheckley, co-author

## 4397

**TERRY PRATCHETT**

### *Mort*

(New York: Signet, 1989)

**Story type:** Fantasy (Light Fantasy)
**Series:** Discworld
**Major character(s):** Mort, Apprentice (to Death)
**Time period(s):** Indeterminate
**Locale(s):** Discworld, Planet—Imaginary

**Summary:** Desperate to find a profession, Mort agrees to become Death's apprentice. The fun begins when soft-hearted Mort can't bring himself to collect the dead and those he spares remain dead in the eyes of the rest of the world.

**Other books you might like:**
Terry Brooks, *Magic Kingdom for Sale—Sold!*, 1986
    Magic Kingdom Series
Douglas W. Clark, *Alchemy Unlimited*, 1990
Charles de Lint, *Wolf Moon*, 1988
F.J. Hale, *Ogre Castle*, 1988
    After the Spell Wars Trilogy Book 1
Anne McCaffrey, *Alchemy and Academe*, 1970
Jack Vance, *The Dying Earth Series*,

## 4398
### TERRY PRATCHETT
## *Moving Pictures*
(New York: Roc, 1992)

**Story type:** Fantasy (Light Fantasy)
**Series:** Discworld
**Major character(s):** Victor Tugelbend, Student, Wizard; Cut-Me-Own-Throat Dibbler, Businessman; Caspode the Wonder Dog, Animal (dog)
**Time period(s):** Indeterminate
**Locale(s):** Discworld, Planet—Imaginary; Ankh-Morpork, Fictional City

**Summary:** When the idea of Hollywood leaks into Discworld, people instantly respond to the call of Tinsel Town and the adventure of film making. Ninth in the series.

**Other books you might like:**
Craig Shaw Gardner, *Bride of the Slime Monster*, 1990
Craig Shaw Gardner, *Revenge of the Fluffy Bunnies*, 1990
Craig Shaw Gardner, *Slaves of the Volcano God*, 1989
Lionel Fenn, *668: The Neighbor of the Beast*, 1992
    pseudonym of Charles L. Grant
Lionel Fenn, *Kent Montana and the Really Ugly Thing From Mars*, 1990
    pseudonym of Charles L. Grant

## 4399
### TERRY PRATCHETT
## *Reaper Man*
(New York: Roc, 1992)

**Story type:** Fantasy (Light Fantasy)
**Series:** Discworld
**Major character(s):** Death ''Bill Door'', Mythical Creature; Windle Poons, Wizard, Reanimated Dead; Renata Flitworth, Farmer, Maiden
**Time period(s):** Indeterminate
**Locale(s):** Ankh-Morpork, Fictional City; Discworld, Planet—Imaginary

**Summary:** Death loses his old job and finds another as a mortal farmhand for an eccentric spinster. As a result, when mortals die, no one comes for their souls. As pent-up Life Forces become so strong that ordinarily inanimate objects come to life, a plague of shopping carts overrun Ankh-Morpork. Newly deceased Windle Poons, now one of the undead, finds himself working with Dead Rights activists and wizards from the University to destroy the city-killing mall.

**Other books you might like:**
Douglas Adams, *The Long Dark Tea-Time of the Soul*, 1988
Robert Asprin, *Myth-ing Persons*, 1984
L. Sprague de Camp, *The Complete Compleat Enchanter*, 1989
    Fletcher Pratt, co-author
Gordon R. Dickson, *The Dragon and the George*, 1976
Christopher Stasheff, *The Warlock in Spite of Himself*, 1969
Chelsea Quinn Yarbro, *A Baroque Fable*, 1986
Neil Gaiman, *Good Omens: The Nice and Accurate Prophecies of Agnes Nutter, Witch*, 1990
    Terry Pratchet, co-author

## 4400
### TERRY PRATCHETT
## *Small Gods*
(New York: HarperCollins, 1994)

**Story type:** Fantasy (Religious; Light Fantasy)
**Series:** Discworld
**Major character(s):** Brutha, Religious; The Great God Om, Deity, Animal (turtle); Vorbis, Religious, Police Officer (Quisitor)
**Time period(s):** Indeterminate
**Locale(s):** Omnia, Fictional Country; Ephebe, Fictional City; Discworld, Planet—Imaginary

**Summary:** A novice in the service of The Great God Om, Brutha, encounters a turtle who claims to be his god. Not too bright, Brutha possesses a reasonably clear idea of right and wrong, which gets him and the turtle into trouble as his religion's followers go to war with a neighboring city state.

**Other books you might like:**
John Bellairs, *The Face in the Frost*, 1969
Neil Gaiman, *Good Omens: The Nice and Accurate Prophecies of Agnes Nutter, Witch*, 1990
    Terry Pratchett, co-author
Craig Shaw Gardner, *A Malady of Magicks*, 1986
Tom Holt, *Expecting Someone Taller*, 1988
Barry Hughart, *Bridge of Birds*, 1984

## 4401
### TERRY PRATCHETT
## *Soul Music*
(New York: HarperCollins, 1995)

**Story type:** Fantasy (Light Fantasy)
**Series:** Discworld
**Major character(s):** Susan Sto Helit, Student, Apprentice (of Death); Imp y Celyn, Musician (bard); The Death of Rats, Mythical Creature
**Time period(s):** Indeterminate
**Locale(s):** Discworld, Planet—Imaginary; Ankh-Morpork, Fictional City

**Summary:** Since Death decides that he needs to forget and disappears, his granddaughter, Susan, finds herself drafted to fill the void, despite some un-Deathlike notions. When a group of down and out musicians hits on something very new, Ankh-Morpork will never be the same again. Again.

**Other books you might like:**
Robert Asprin, *Another Fine Myth*, 1978
Gordon R. Dickson, *The Dragon and the George*, 1976
Alan Dean Foster, *Spellsinger*, 1983
Neil Gaiman, *Good Omens: The Nice and Accurate Prophecies of Agnes Nutter, Witch*, 1990
    Terry Pratchett, co-author
Craig Shaw Gardner, *The Other Sinbad*, 1991
Roger Zelazny, *Bring Me the Head of Prince Charming*, 1993
    Robert Sheckley, co-author

## 4402

### TERRY PRATCHETT

## *Truckers*

(New York: Delacorte, 1990)

**Story type:** Science Fiction (Humor; Young Adult)
**Series:** Truckers
**Major character(s):** Masklin, Mythical Creature (nome), Alien; Dorcas, Mythical Creature (nome), Alien; Thing, Computer (flight navigation/recording)
**Time period(s):** 20th century

**Summary:** The nomes of the store "Arnold Bros. (est. 1905): All Things Under One Roof" refuse to believe that Masklin and his fellow nomes have come from the mythical Outside. Their shock and disbelief are even greater when the Thing tells them that the store is going to be demolished, and all three thousand of them will have to leave.

**Other books you might like:**
Mary Norton, *The Borrowers*, 1952
Mary Norton, *The Borrowers Afield*, 1955
Mary Norton, *The Borrowers Afloat*, 1959
Mary Norton, *The Borrowers Aloft*, 1961
John Peterson, *The Littles*, 1967

## 4403

### TERRY PRATCHETT

## *Wings*

(New York: Delacorte, 1991)

**Story type:** Science Fiction (Young Adult; Adventure)
**Series:** Bromeliad
**Major character(s):** Masklin, Mythical Creature (nome), Alien; Gurder, Mythical Creature (nome), Alien; Thing, Computer (flight/navigation)
**Time period(s):** 1990s
**Locale(s):** East Coast; Florida

**Summary:** When the nomes decide to summon their spaceship, Masklin, Gurder, Angelo and Thing set out to Cape Canaveral to make use of a communication satellite launch. With Thing's help, the nomes use a Concorde jet to fly to Florida. While arranging to fly closer to the launch site by riding geese, the nomes find that thousands more of their kind exist, raising new questions of how to use the ship. This book is a sequel to *Diggers*.

**Other books you might like:**
Murray Leinster, *Land of the Giants*, 1968
    Will F. Jenkins, real name
Mary Norton, *The Borrowers*, 1952
Mary Norton, *The Borrowers Aloft*, 1961
John Peterson, *The Littles*, 1967
James D. Priest, *Kirins: The Spell of No'an*, 1990

## 4404

### TERRY PRATCHETT

## *Witches Abroad*

(New York: Roc, 1993)

**Story type:** Fantasy (Light Fantasy; Quest)
**Series:** Discworld
**Major character(s):** Magrat Garlick, Witch; Granny Weatherwax, Witch, Heroine; Emberella, Royalty (princess)
**Time period(s):** Indeterminate
**Locale(s):** Discworld, Planet—Imaginary

**Summary:** Newly made a fairy godmother, Magrate Garlick must try to stop Princess Emberella from marrying Prince Charming. Granny Weatherwax and Nancy Ogg try to assist her in this endeavor, battling mirror magic, recalcitrant broomsticks, the perils of travel and the power of the stories themselves.

**Other books you might like:**
L. Sprague de Camp, *The Complete Compleat Enchanter*, 1989
    Fletcher Pratt, co-author
Gordon R. Dickson, *The Dragon and the George*, 1976
Diane Duane, *So You Want to Be a Wizard?*, 1983
Neil Gaiman, *Good Omens: The Nice and Accurate Prophecies of Agnes Nutter, Witch*, 1990
    Terry Pratchett, co-author
Barry B. Longyear, *The God Box*, 1989
Christopher Stasheff, *The Warlock in Spite of Himself*, 1969
Jane Yolen, *Briar Rose*, 1992
Roger Zelazny, *Bring Me the Head of Prince Charming*, 1991
    Robert Sheckley, co-author
Roger Zelazny, *If at Faust You Don't Succeed*, 1993
    Robert Sheckley, co-author

## 4405

### TERRY PRATCHETT

## *Wyrd Sisters*

(New York: Penguin/ROC, 1990)

**Story type:** Fantasy (Light Fantasy)
**Series:** Discworld
**Major character(s):** Granny Weatherwax, Witch, Heroine; Felmet, Nobleman (duke), Murderer; Tomjon, Heir—Lost (to Lancre)
**Time period(s):** Indeterminate
**Locale(s):** Kingdom of Lancre, Fictional Country; Discworld, Planet—Imaginary

**Summary:** In order to hide him from the duke who killed his father, three witches foster the infant prince Tomjon to a travelling thespian. As time passes, the land grows discontented with Felmet's rule. Magical problems threaten if the prince is not restored to the throne.

**Other books you might like:**
Steven Brust, *Jhereg*, 1983
John DeChancie, *Castle Perilous*, 1988
Suzette Haden Elgin, *The Grand Jubilee*, 1981
James H. Schmitz, *The Witches of Karres*, 1966
Will Shetterly, *Liavek*, 1985
    Emma Bull, co-author

## 4406

### BYRON PREISS, Editor
### JOHN GREGORY BETANCOURT, Co-Editor
### KEITH R.A. DECANDIDO, Co-Editor

## *The Ultimate Alien*

(New York: Dell, 1995)

**Story type:** Science Fiction (Anthology)

**Summary:** Contains a six-page introduction with recommendations by Robert Silverberg, seven pages of biographies, and three reprinted and 12 original stories whose tone varies from dark to humorous. The settings range from Earth, Venus, and the artificial asteroid, Mallworld, to distant star systems, with themes including first contact, invasion of Earth, alien societies, and human/alien romance and marriage. Authors include Arthur C. Clarke, Peter Crowther, Don D'Ammassa, Mel Gilden, Ed Gorman, Nina Kiriki Hoffman, Anne McCaffrey, Robert Silverberg, S.P. Somtow, and Lawrence Watt-Evans. Authors collaborate on two stories, "Alien Radio" by Mike Resnick and Nicholas A. DiChario, and "First Contact, Sort Of" by Karen Haber and Carol Carr.

**Other books you might like:**
Groff Conklin, *Invaders of Earth*, 1952
    editor
Jack Dann, *Aliens!*, 1980
    Gardner Dozois, co-editor
Ellen Datlow, *Alien Sex*, 1990
    editor
Gardner Dozois, *Isaac Asimov's Aliens*, 1991
    editor
Stephen Goldin, *The Alien Condition*, 1973
    editor
Damon Knight, *First Contact*, 1971
    editor

---

### 4407

**BYRON PREISS**, Editor

## The Ultimate Dracula
(New York: Dell, 1991)

**Story type:** Horror (Anthology; Vampire Story)

**Summary:** Twenty original stories written to commemorate the 60th anniversary of the film "Dracula." Stand-outs include Dan Simmons' "All Dracula's Children," set in post-Ceausescu Romania, and Anne Rice's Victorian vampire story "Master of the Rampling Gate." Others include Edward Hoch's tale of vampires in Nazi Germany, "Dracula 1944," and two science fiction vampire stories, Kristine Kathryn Rusch's "Children of the Night" and Janet Asimov's "The Contagion." With a vampire filmography by Leonard Wolff.

**Other books you might like:**
Ellen Datlow, *Blood Is Not Enough*, 1989
Ellen Datlow, *A Whisper of Blood*, 1991
Martin H. Greenberg, *A Taste for Blood*, 1992
    Stefan Dziemianowicz and Robert A. Weinberg, co-editors
Alan Ryan, *Vampires: Two Centuries of Great Vampire Stories*, 1987
    editor
Leslie Shepard, *The Dracula Book of Great Vampire Stories*, 1979
    editor

---

### 4408

**BYRON PREISS**, Editor
**JOHN GREGORY BETANCOURT**, Co-Editor
**KEITH R.A. DECANDIDO**, Co-Editor

## The Ultimate Dragon
(New York: Dell, 1995)

**Story type:** Fantasy (Anthology)

**Summary:** Contains a four-page introduction by Tanith Lee, nine pages of biographies, and two reprinted and 16 original stories, frequently light or ironic in tone, which feature dragons in contemporary, historical, and mythical settings, with themes varying from adventure and magic conflict to artificial intelligence. Authors include Kevin J. Anderson, Phyllis Ann Karr, Ursula K. Le Guin, Tanith Lee, Josepha Sherman, S.P. Somtow, Lawrence Watt-Evans,

Chelsea Quinn Yarbro, and Jane Yolen. Authors collaborate on two stories, "Pleasantly Pink" by Mike Resnick and Nicholas A. DiChario, and "The Dragon on the Bookshelf" by Harlan Ellison and Robert Silverberg.

**Other books you might like:**
Isaac Asimov, *Dragon Tales*, 1982
    Martin H. Greenberg, Charles G. Waugh, co-editors
Orson Scott Card, *Dragons of Darkness*, 1981
    editor
Orson Scott Card, *Dragons of Light*, 1983
    editor
Jack Dann, *Dragons!*, 1993
    Gardner Dozois, co-editor
Rosalind M. Greenberg, *Dragon Fantastic*, 1992
    Martin H. Greenberg, co-editor
Margaret Weis, *A Dragon-Lover's Treasury of the Fantastic*, 1994
    editor
Jane Yolen, *Here There Be Dragons*, 1993

---

### 4409

**BYRON PREISS**, Editor

## The Ultimate Frankenstein
(New York: Dell, 1991)

**Story type:** Horror (Anthology; Reanimated Dead)

**Summary:** Twenty original stories written to commemorate the 60th anniversary of the film "Frankenstein." Stand-outs include David Schow's monster party *tour de force* "Last Call for the Sons of Shock," and Katherine Dunn's futuristic "Near-Flesh." Also included are pastiches of Mary Shelley's original novel by Philip Jose Farmer and Loren Estleman, Esther M. Friesner's amusing "Mad at the Academy," and Mike Resnick's tale of artificial humans recruited for professional football, "Monsters of the Midway." With a Frankenstein filmography by Leonard Wolff.

**Other books you might like:**
Michel Parry, *Rivals of Frankenstein*, 1977

---

### 4410

**BYRON PREISS**, Editor

## The Ultimate Werewolf
(New York: Dell, 1991)

**Story type:** Horror (Anthology; Werewolf Story)

**Summary:** Twenty stories written to commemorate the 50th anniversary of the film "The Wolfman." Stand-outs include Harlan Ellison's tale of a quest for personal salvation, "Adrift Just Off the Islets of Langerhans," Kathy Koja's prose poem "Angel's Moon," and Bob Weinberg's story of an unusually well-equipped nightwatchman, "Wolf Watch." Included are retellings of the werewolf myth by Philip Jose Farmer, Kim Antieau and Bill Pronzini, humorous werewolf stories by Jerome Charyn, Mel Gilden and Kevin J. Anderson, and science fiction werewolf tales by Larry Niven and Brad Strickland. With a werewolf filmography by Leonard Wolff.

**Other books you might like:**
Brian J. Frost, *Book of the Werewolf*, 1973
Bill Pronzini, *Werewolf!*, 1979

## 4411

**BYRON PREISS**, Editor
**JOHN GREGORY BETANCOURT**, Co-Editor

### The Ultimate Witch

(New York: Dell, 1993)

**Story type:** Horror (Anthology; Witchcraft)

**Summary:** The twenty-five stories in this volume, most original to the book, all feature witches and witchcraft. Included are Karl Edward Wagner's "A Walk on the Wild Side," about Satanic orgyists unaware that their virgin sacrifice is a male crossdresser; Tanith Lee's beautiful "Witch of the Moon," about a young woman whose life is saved by a lonely witch woman living on the moon; Steve Rasnic Tem's "Brooms Welcome the Dust," about the dire consequences of snatching the wrong broom for a Halloween witch's costume; and Stuart M. Kaminsky's wonderfully paranoid "In Thunder, Lightning or in Rain," about a warlock who switches bodies to avoid capture. The book's two reprints include Ray Bradbury's fantasy classic, "The April Witch," and Dean Koontz's story of a thief who unwittingly steals a witch's purse, "Snatcher." Philip Jose Farmer supplies an introduction.

**Other books you might like:**
Martin H. Greenberg, *Devil Worshippers*, 1990
    Charles Waugh, co-editor
Peter Haining, *A Circle of Witches*, 1971
    editor

## 4412

**BYRON PREISS**, Editor
**JOHN GREGORY BETANCOURT**, Co-Editor

### The Ultimate Zombie

(New York: Dell, 1993)

**Story type:** Horror (Anthology; Reanimated Dead)

**Summary:** The 23 stories in this anthology—19 original, three reprint, and one a novel excerpt—all resurrect the zombie for their theme. Variations on the usual formulae include zombie children (A.R. Morlan's "The Toddler Pit," Alan Rodgers' "Emma's Daughter"), zombies in politics (Bob Weinberg's "Silent Majority," Don D'Ammassa's "Corruption in Office"), zombies in big business (Matthew J. Costello's "Corporate Takeover"), zombies in comedy (Lionel Fenn's "The Dead Speaketh Not, They Just Grunteth Now and Then," Brian Hodge and William Relling Jr.'s "This One'll Kill You"), and zombies as persons with severe identity crises (Robert Silverberg's "Passengers," Chelsea Quinn Yarbro's "Restoration Comedy"). Dennis Etchison wrote the introduction.

**Other books you might like:**
Peter Haining, *Stories of the Walking Dead*, 1985
Stephen Jones, *The Mammoth Book of Zombies*, 1993
    editor
John Skipp, *Book of the Dead*, 1989
    Craig Spector, co-editor
John Skipp, *Still Dead: Book of the Dead 2*, 1992
    Craig Spector, co-editor

## 4413

**DOUGLAS PRESTON**
**LINCOLN CHILD**, Co-Author

### Mount Dragon

(New York: Tor/Forge, 1996)

**Story type:** Horror (Science Fiction)
**Major character(s):** Guy Carson, Scientist (biologist); Brent Scopes, Businessman; Charles Levine, Scientist (geneticist)
**Time period(s):** 1990s (1996)
**Locale(s):** Jornada del Muerto Desert, New Mexico

**Summary:** Guy Carson is hired to work at GeneDyne's Mount Dragon facility in the New Mexico desert, supposedly to help perfect an influenza vaccine. But when a teammate accidentally becomes infected with a flu strain that causes an absolutely ghastly death, Carson begins to suspect that GeneDyne owner Brent Scopes is using the lab's research for more insidious purposes.

**Other books you might like:**
Michael Crichton, *The Andromeda Strain*, 1969
Stephen King, *The Stand*, 1978
Dean R. Koontz, *Phantoms*, 1983
Patrick Lynch, *Carriers*, 1995

## 4414

**DOUGLAS PRESTON**
**LINCOLN CHILD**, Co-Author

### Relic

(New York: Tor, 1995)

**Story type:** Horror (Science Fiction)
**Major character(s):** Margo Green, Student (graduate student); Bill Smithback, Journalist; Gregory Kawakita, Museum Curator (assistant)
**Time period(s):** 1990s (1995)
**Locale(s):** New York, New York

**Summary:** In this first collaborative novel, a half reptile-half simian moster rampages through the subbasements of New York City's Museum of Natural History, feeding on hapless humans when its regular supply of food (shipped stateside as part of the artifacts of a doomed 1987 Brazilian expedition) and posing a problem for a variety of museum officials and political personnel who are planning to open a major exhibit at the museum.

**Other books you might like:**
Ken Eulo, *Claw*, 1994
    Joe Mauck, co-author
Stephen King, *The Crate*, 1985
    in *Skeleton Crew*
Frank Belknap Long, *The Horror From the Hills*, 1963
Bob Mayer, *Operation Synbat*, 1994

## 4415

**DOUGLAS PRESTON**
**LINCOLN CHILD**, Co-Author

### Reliquary

(New York: Tor/Forge, 1997)

**Story type:** Horror (Science Fiction)
**Major character(s):** Margo Green, Anthropologist; Vincent D'Agosta, Police Officer (lieutenant); Bill Smithback, Journalist

**Time period(s):** 1990s (1997)
**Locale(s):** New York, New York

**Summary:** The discovery of decapitated bodies of Manhattan's street police people raises fears of a race of predatory monsters who feed on human brains and live in the train tunnels beneath Manhattan. A sequel to *Relic* (1995).

**Other books you might like:**
Peter Benchley, *Beast*, 1991
Michael Crichton, *The Lost World*, 1995
Ken Eulo, *Claw*, 1994
   Joe Mauck, co-author
Frank Belknap Long, *The Horror From the Hills*, 1963

---

**4416**

**PAUL PREUSS**

## Core

(New York: Morrow, 1993)

**Story type:** Science Fiction (Disaster)
**Major character(s):** Cyrus Hudder, Parent, Scientist; Leiden "Leidy" Hudder, Scientist; Marta McDougal, Inventor, Scientist
**Time period(s):** 1980s; 1990s
**Locale(s):** Core City, Texas; Underground Environment

**Summary:** Earth's disintegrating magnetosphere allows human vulnerability to solar flares which create mutation, radiation burns and breakdowns in power and communications. Cyrus and Leiden Hudder must overcome their hatred of each other to rally around Marta McDougal who develops a machine to bore through the Earth's crust to repair the core, if the machine does not cause mankind's destruction.

**Other books you might like:**
Roger MacBride Allen, *The Ring of Charon*, 1990
Greg Bear, *The Forge of God*, 1987
David Brin, *Earth*, 1990
David Brin, *Sundiver*, 1979
David Kagan, *Sunstroke*, 1993
Philip Wylie, *When Worlds Collide*, 1933
   Edwin Balmer, co-author
Roger Zelazny, *Flare*, 1992
   Thomas T. Thomas, co-author

---

**4417**

**PAUL PREUSS**

## The Diamond Moon

(New York: Avon, 1990)

**Story type:** Science Fiction (First Contact; Adventure)
**Series:** Arthur C. Clarke's Venus Prime
**Major character(s):** Linda Ellen "Sparta" Troy, Genetically Altered Being, Agent (Board of Space Control); Randolph Mays, Historian, Television Personality; J.Q.R. Forster, Professor
**Time period(s):** 21st century
**Locale(s):** Earth; Amalthea, Moon—Imaginary (of Jupiter)

**Summary:** Professor Forster, having deduced the nature of Amalthea, is heading there from Ganymede. His nemesis, Randolph Mays, on his T.V. series *Overmind*, tried to prove his belief that a superior intelligence was directing human history and evolution. Mays accused Professor Forster of being the Free Spirit participant behind the theft of the Martian plague. Mays is also heading for Amalthea, despite the Board of Space Control's ban on any traffic around Amalthea until after Professor Forster's expedition.

**Other books you might like:**
Isaac Asimov, *Nemesis*, 1989
Gregory Benford, *Heart of the Comet*, 1986
   David Brin, co-author
Arthur C. Clarke, *Rendezvous with Rama*, 1973
John Varley, *Titan*, 1979

---

**4418**

**PAUL PREUSS**

## Hide and Seek

(New York: Avon, 1989)

**Story type:** Science Fiction (Adventure)
**Series:** Arthur C. Clarke's Venus Prime
**Major character(s):** Linda Ellen "Sparta" Troy, Detective—Police, Genetically Altered Being; Blake Redfield, Antiquarian
**Time period(s):** 22nd century
**Locale(s):** Mars

**Summary:** The ancient alien artifact discovered on Mars in a previous volume of this series has been stolen and two murders have been committed. Sparta goes to Mars to recover the artifact, only to find herself the subject of a murder attempt. Meanwhile the mysterious Free Spirit and the X culture from the stars remain in the background, their motives not entirely known.

**Other books you might like:**
Gregory Benford, *Great Sky River*, 1987
Gregory Benford, *Tides of Light*, 1989
David Brin, *Startide Rising*, 1983
David Brin, *The Uplift War*, 1988
Lois McMaster Bujold, *Falling Free*, 1988

---

**4419**

**PAUL PREUSS**

## The Medusa Encounter

(New York: Avon, 1990)

**Story type:** Science Fiction (Adventure)
**Series:** Arthur C. Clarke's Venus Prime
**Major character(s):** Linda Ellen "Sparta" Troy, Detective—Police, Genetically Altered Being; Blake Redfield, Antiquarian
**Time period(s):** 22nd century
**Locale(s):** Earth; Jupiter

**Summary:** The cult known as Free Spirit has attempted to subvert the Space Board and take over the mission to Jupiter where a strange life form has been discovered. Sparta must defeat Free Spirit and, in order to do so, must travel to Jupiter.

**Other books you might like:**
Gregory Benford, *Great Sky River*, 1987
Gregory Benford, *Tides of Light*, 1989
David Brin, *Startide Rising*, 1983
David Brin, *The Uplift War*, 1988
Lois McMaster Bujold, *Falling Free*, 1988

---

**4420**

**PAUL PREUSS**

## Secret Passages

(New York: Tor, 1997)

**Story type:** Science Fiction (Hard Science Fiction; Family Saga)

**Major character(s):** Anne-Marie Brand, Photographer, Parent; Manolis Minakis, Scientist (physicist), Businessman; Peter Slater, Scientist (physicist), Professor
**Time period(s):** 1990s
**Locale(s):** Crete, Greece; Athens, Greece; Geneva, Switzerland

**Summary:** Desperate to win custody of her son from her ex-husband, Anne-Marie Brand agrees to spy on Manolis Minakis, a Greek business magnate and physicist who possesses rare and valuable Minoan artifacts. In turn, Minakis uses Anne-Marie to gain access to her new husband, Peter, whom Minakis hopes to recruit for his radical physics experiments.

**Other books you might like:**
Greg Bear, *Eon*, 1985
Gregory Benford, *Timescape*, 1980
Arthur C. Clarke, *Richter 10*, 1996
     Mike McQuay, co-author
Greg Egan, *Quarantine*, 1995
Ursula K. Le Guin, *The Dispossessed*, 1974
Frederik Pohl, *The Singers of Time*, 1990
     Jack Williamson, co-author

---

`4421`

**PAUL PREUSS**

## The Shining Ones

(New York: Avon, 1991)

**Story type:** Science Fiction (First Contact; Alternate Universe)
**Series:** Arthur C. Clarke's Venus Prime
**Major character(s):** J.Q.R. Forster, Professor (xeno-archeology); Linda Ellen ''Sparta'' Troy, Genetically Altered Being, Heroine; Thowinda, Alien (Amalthean), Diplomat
**Time period(s):** 22nd century
**Locale(s):** *Amalthea*, Spaceship

**Summary:** *Amalthea* shed its coat of ices and left orbit heading past Earth toward the sun. The humans within have been altered by Thowinda and Medusa to live underwater and are now able to survive the acceleration. Medusa, using the sun as a slingshot, headed into outer space to give humanity a better chance for the survival of life on Earth. A section of illustrations is bound into the novel.

**Other books you might like:**
Isaac Asimov, *Nemesis*, 1989
David Brin, *Earth*, 1990
Arthur C. Clarke, *Rama II*, 1989
     Genry Lee, co-author
Colin Greenland, *Take Back Plenty*, 1991
Carol Severance, *Reefsong*, 1991
Joan Slonczewski, *A Door into Ocean*, 1986
Sydney J. Van Scyoc, *Deepwater Dreams*, 1991
John Varley, *Titan*, 1979
David Weber, *Mutineers' Moon*, 1991

---

`4422`

**ROBERT M. PRICE**, Editor

## The Azathoth Cycle

(Oakland, California: Chaosium, 1995)

**Story type:** Horror (Anthology)
**Series:** Cthulhu

**Summary:** One poem, one essay, and fourteen original and eight reprinted stories elaborate the idea, in the fiction of H.P. Lovecraft,

that the known universe is governed by forces indifferent to human fate. These forces manifest themselves in the form of incomprehensible extradimensional entities. This collection focuses on Lovecraft's ''blind idiot god'' Azathoth, an embodiment of cosmic chaos. Peter Cannon's two stories, ''Azathoth in Arkham'' and ''The Revenge of Azathoth,'' are sequels to Lovecraft's tale ''The Thing on the Doorstep,'' in which Azathoth influences the actions of the characters. Henry Kuttner's ''Hydra'' is concerned with a foolish mortal who inadvertently summons an extradimensional monster whose capabilities he has underestimated. Ramsey Campbell's ''The Insects from Shaggai'' tells of a man driven insane by his glimpse of an alien world.

**Other books you might like:**
Edward P. Berglund, *Disciples of Cthulhu*, 1975
     editor
Lin Carter, *The Spawn of Cthulhu*, 1971
     editor
Thomas M.K. Stratman, *Cthulhu's Heirs*, 1994
     editor
H.P. Lovecraft, *Tales of the Cthulhu Mythos: Golden Anniversary Anthology*, 1990
Robert Weinberg, *Miskatonic University*, 1996
     Martin H. Greenberg, co-editor

---

`4423`

**ROBERT M. PRICE**, Editor

## The Cthulhu Cycle

(Oakland, California: Chaosium, 1996)

**Story type:** Horror (Anthology)

**Summary:** Small press editor Price assembles 13 classic and contemporary tales that evoke the concept of H.P. Lovecraft's Cthulhu, an otherworldly monster who sums up his creator's vision of cosmic horror. Included are Lovecraft's ''The Call of Cthulhu,'' in which Cthulhu nearly succeeds at breaking into our own dimension, and two precursors that may have influenced the writing of Lovecraft's story, M.R. James' ''Count Magnus'' and Lord Dunsany's ''A Shop in Go-By Street.'' August Derleth's ''The Black Island'' and C.J. Henderson's ''Patiently Waiting'' are sequels of sorts to Lovecraft's tale and Alan Dean Foster's ''Some Notes Concerning a Green Box'' is a gloss on the original.

**Other books you might like:**
Edward P. Berglund, *Disciples of Cthulhu*, 1976
     editor
Lin Carter, *The Spawn of Cthulhu*, 1991
     editor
H.P. Lovecraft, *Tales of the Cthulhu Mythos: Golden Anniversary Anthology*, 1990
Thomas M.K. Stratman, *Cthulhu's Heirs*, 1994
Jim Turner, *Cthulhu 2000*, 1995
     editor

---

`4424`

**ROBERT M. PRICE**, Editor

## The Dunwich Cycle: Where the Old Gods Wait

(Oakland, CA: Chaosium, 1995)

**Story type:** Horror (Anthology)
**Series:** Cthulhu Cycle

**Summary:** The one original and eight reprinted stories collected here all elaborate an idea in the fiction of H.P. Lovecraft that the known universe is governed by forces indifferent to human fate and which manifest themselves in the form of incomprehensible extradimensional entities. Included here are two stories by early twentieth-century fantasist Arthur Machen, ''The Great God Pan'' and ''The White People,'' whose mythos about a pagan race surviving into modern times influenced Lovecraft's work. The other stories are set in Lovecraft's decadent New England town of Dunwich. Lovecraft's ''The Dunwich Horror'' tells of the twin sons born from the union of a mortal woman and an extradimensional monster. Ben Indick's ''The Road to Dunwich'' and August Derleth's ''The Shuttered Room'' are sequels to Lovecraft's tale, and Richard Lupoff's ''The Devil's Hop Yard'' is a retelling of the tale's events from a different perspective. The editor offers his own ''The Round Tower'' as an alternate final chapter to the *The Lurker at the Threshold*, which August Derleth based on Lovecraft's notes.

**Other books you might like:**

Stephen Jones, *Shadows over Innsmouth*, 1994
    editor
Thomas M.K. Stratman, *Cthulhu's Heirs*, 1994
    editor
H.P. Lovecraft, *Tales of the Cthulhu Mythos: Golden Anniversary Anthology*, 1990
Robert Weinberg, *Miskatonic University*, 1996
    Martin H. Greenberg, co-editor

## 4425

### ROBERT M. PRICE, Editor

## *The Hastur Cycle*

(Oakland, California: Chaosium, 1993)

**Story type:** Horror (Anthology)

**Summary:** The editor, who has edited and published the Lovecraftian fanzine *Crypt of Cthulhu* since 1981, brings together 13 stories centered around the mythical entity Hastur, and his significance to the Lovecraft myth cycle known as the Cthulhu Mythos. Included are Lovecraft's tale of an extraterrestrial invasion of rural Vermont, ''The Whisperer in Darkness''; Arthur Machen's ''The Novel of the Black Seal,'' Ambrose Bierce's ''Haita the Shepard'' and ''An Inhabitant of Carcosa,'' and Robert W. Chambers' ''The Yellow Sign,'' all of which inspired Lovecraft; James Blish's play ''More Light''; and Richard A. Lupoff's Lovecraft spoof, ''Documents in the Case of Elizabeth Akeley.'' Price has supplied an introduction and informative notes for each story.

**Other books you might like:**

Edward P. Berglund, *Disciples of Cthulhu*, 1975
    editor
Ramsey Campbell, *New Tales of the Cthulhu Mythos*, 1980
    editor
Lin Carter, *The Spawn of Cthulhu*, 1971
    editor
August Derleth, *Tales of the Cthulhu Mythos*, 1969
    editor
Thomas M.K. Stratman, *Cthulhu's Heirs*, 1994

## 4426

### ROBERT M. PRICE, Editor

## *The Innsmouth Cycle: The Taint of the Deep Ones in 13 Tales*

(Oakland, California: Chaosium, 1998)

**Story type:** Horror (Anthology)
**Series:** Call of Cthulhu Fiction

**Summary:** This anthology includes 13 stories and three poems celebrating H.P. Lovecraft's Innsmouth, a decadent and haunted New England town whose insular residents are the offspring of breeding between humans and a race from the sea. In addition to Lovecraft's own ''The Shadow Over Innsmouth,'' in which a young man first discovers the horrible legacy of Innsmouth society, selections include John Glasby's ''Devil Reef,'' in which a thief gets his just desserts when he tries to steal gold that is part of the local religious rituals; James Wade's ''The Deep Ones,'' in which scientific research into the intelligence of dolphins leads to the discovery of their rapport with a supernatural race; and Robert W. Chambers ''The Harbor Master,'' the story of a semi-aquatic human being that may have been one of Lovecraft's inspirations.

**Other books you might like:**

Edward P. Berglund, *Disciples of Cthulhu*, 1973
    editor
Ramsey Campbell, *New Tales of the Cthulhu Mythos*, 1980
    editor
Stephen Jones, *Shadows over Innsmouth*, 1994
    editor
Thomas M.K. Stratman, *Cthulhu's Heirs*, 1994
    editor
Jim Turner, *Cthulhu 2000*, 1995
    editor

## 4427

### ROBERT M. PRICE, Editor

## *The Necronomicon*

(Oakland, California: Chaosium, 1997)

**Story type:** Horror (Anthology)
**Series:** Call of Cthulhu Fiction

**Summary:** Miscellany of stories and articles inspired by the *Necronomicon*, the legendary book of forbidden knowledge that appears in the fiction of H.P. Lovecraft. Stories featuring the book include Fred Chappell's ''The Adder,'' in which the volume has the power to corrupt anything put next to it, and John Brunner's ''Concerning the Forthcoming Inexpensive Paperback Translation of the *Necronomicon*,'' about efforts to prevent the madness that will ensue when the book becomes accessible to anyone. Frank Belknap Long and L. Sprague de Camp contribute fragmentary ''excerpts'' from the *Necronomicon* itself.

**Other books you might like:**

Scott David Aniolowski, *Return to Lovecraft Country*, 1997
    editor
Edward P. Berglund, *Disciples of Cthulhu*, 1996
    editor
Robert Weinberg, *Miskatonic University*, 1996
    Martin H. Greenberg, co-editor

## 4428

**ROBERT M. PRICE**, Editor

### The New Lovecraft Circle

(Minneapolis: Fedogan & Bremer, 1996)

**Story type:** Horror (Anthology)

**Summary:** The long-time publisher of the small press magazine *Crypt of Cthulhu* gathers 25 stories, two original to this collection, written in homage to the horror themes of H.P. Lovecraft. Included are David Sutton's "Demoniacal," in which an incantation incorporated into song lyrics on an album summon dark forces, and Brian Lumley's "The Kiss of Bugg-Shash," a sequel to Sutton's tale. Some stories, such as Lin Carter's "The Fishers From Outside" and Ramsey Campbell's "The Plain of Sound," are deliberate pastiches of Lovecraft's tales of cosmic horror. Other stories, such as Thomas Ligotti's tale of a book of forbidden knowledge, "Vastarien," and Karl Wagner's "I've Come to Talk with You Again," about a horror writer with one foot in the supernatural realm, are only peripherally Lovecraftian. Peter Cannon's "The Madness out of Space" and Richard A. Lupoff's "Lights! Camera! Shub-Niggurath!" are among a handful of tales that satirize the cliches of Cthulhu Mythos fiction.

**Other books you might like:**

Edward P. Berglund, *Disciples of Cthulhu*, 1976
    editor
Lin Carter, *The Spawn of Cthulhu*, 1991
    editor
H.P. Lovecraft, *Tales of the Cthulhu Mythos: Golden Anniversary Anthology*, 1990
Thomas M.K. Stratman, *Cthulhu's Heirs*, 1994
Jim Turner, *Cthulhu 2000*, 1995
    editor

## 4429

**ROBERT M. PRICE**, Editor

### The Nyarlathotep Cycle

(Oakland, California: Chaosium, 1997)

**Story type:** Horror (Anthology)
**Series:** Call of Cthulhu Fiction

**Summary:** Fifteen stories and three poems featuring or redolent of Nyarlathotep, a mutable supernatural being who serves as a messenger of dark gods in the fiction of H.P. Lovecraft. Selections include Lovecraft's "Dreams in the Witch House," in which a student discovers an association between mathematics and black magic; August Derleth's "The Dweller in Darkness," in which Nyarlathotep appropriates a human form to beguile his victims; and Robert Bloch's "Fane of the Black Pharaoh," which explores Nyarlathotep's pervasive presence in Egypt mythology.

**Other books you might like:**

Edward P. Berglund, *Disciples of Cthulhu*, 1996
    editor
H.P. Lovecraft, *Tales of the Cthulhu Mythos*, 1990
Jim Turner, *Cthulhu 2000*, 1996
    editor

## 4430

**ROBERT M. PRICE**, Editor

### The Shub Niggurath Cycle

(Oakland, California: Chaosium, 1994)

**Story type:** Horror (Anthology)

**Summary:** The editor has collected 15 original and reprint stories of the supernatural featuring goats or goat-like beings, with an eye to fleshing out the mythology surrounding H.P. Lovecraft's imaginary deity Shub Niggurath, "the goat with a thousand young." Included are Lewis Spence's "The Horn of Vapula," about a man stalked by a goatish gargoyle; M.P. Dare's "The Demoniac Goat," in which an archaeological expedition liberates an evil goat-like being; J.S. Leatherbarrow's "The Ghostly Goat of Glamarra," about a witch's goat that haunts the English countryside; Ramsey Campbell's "The Moon Lens," in which a visitor to an inn during a local festival suffers a bestial transformation following his participation in an occult ritual; and the editor's own "A Thousand Young," in which devotion to Shub Niggurath is equated with sexual promiscuity.

**Other books you might like:**

Edward P. Berglund, *Disciples of Cthulhu*, 1975
Lin Carter, *The Spawn of Cthulhu*, 1971
Stephen Jones, *Shadows over Innsmouth*, 1994
    editor
Thomas M.K. Stratman, *Cthulhu's Heirs*, 1994
    editor
H.P. Lovecraft, *Tales of the Cthulhu Mythos: Golden Anniversary Anthology*, 1990

## 4431

**ROBERT M. PRICE**, Editor

### Tales of the Lovecraft Mythos

(Minneapolis, Minnesota: Fedogan & Bremer, 1992)

**Story type:** Horror (Anthology)

**Summary:** This anthology collects 20 stories that attempt to evoke the same sense of cosmic horror embodied in those stories by H. P. Lovecraft categorized as "the Cthulhu Mythos." Included are two stories by Robert E. Howard, among them the sword-and-sorcery adventure, "The Fire of Asshurbanipal"; two stories by August Derleth that elaborate the legend of the Wendigo, "Ithaqua" and "The Thing That Walked on the Wind"; an overwrought pastiche of Lovecraft by C. Hall Thompson, "Spawn of the Green Abyss"; Robert Bloch's tale of terror in the Egyptian pyramids, "Fane of the Black Pharoah"; and less well known tales by Clark Ashton Smith, Robert A. W. Lowndes, Fritz Leiber, Richard Searight, Duane Rimel, and Donald A. Wollheim. Price wrote a controversial introduction.

**Other books you might like:**

Edward P. Berglund, *Disciples of Cthulhu*, 1975
    editor
Ramsey Campbell, *New Tales of the Cthulhu Mythos*, 1980
    editor
Lin Carter, *The Spawn of Cthulhu*, 1981
August Derleth, *Tales of the Cthulhu Mythos*, 1969
    editor
H.P. Lovecraft, *Tales of the Cthulhu Mythos: Golden Anniversary Anthology*, 1990

## 4432

### CHRISTOPHER PRIEST

## The Prestige

(New York: St. Martin's Press, 1996)

**Story type:** Science Fiction (Contemporary Realism; Satire)
**Major character(s):** Alfred Borden, Magician, Writer; Rupert Angier, Magician, Writer; Nikola Tesla, Historical Figure, Inventor
**Time period(s):** 19th century; 1900s
**Locale(s):** England; United States

**Summary:** Misunderstandings and revealed methods fuel the professional rivalry and feud between two magicians. When Alfred Borden's teleportation trick defies analysis, Rupert Angier retains Nikola Tesla to create an actual matter transmitter. World Fantasy Award winner.

**Other books you might like:**
James P. Blaylock, *Lord Kelvin's Machine*, 1992
K.W. Jeter, *Infernal Devices*, 1987
Tim Powers, *The Anubis Gates*, 1983
Brooke Stevens, *The Circus of the Earth and Air*, 1994

## 4433

### JAMES D. PRIEST

## Kirins: The Flight of the Ain

(Shorewood, Minnesota: Yellowstone Press, 1992)

**Story type:** Fantasy (Quest; Magic Conflict)
**Series:** Kirins
**Major character(s):** Diliani, Mythical Creature (elf); Speckarin, Magician, Mythical Creature (elf)
**Time period(s):** 1990s
**Locale(s):** Atlantic Ocean; Stonehenge, England

**Summary:** The seven companions continue their journey to the source of their magic. Although besieged by evil valodons and gronoms the party reaches the ocean, finds help with the crossing and discovers an idyllic island society of integrated kirins and humans. Finally close to their objective, the group resolves to speedily complete their quest.

**Other books you might like:**
Stephen Billias, *Horrible Humes*, 1991
Orson Scott Card, *Seventh Son*, 1987
Mercedes Lackey, *Winds of Fate*, 1991
H. Beam Piper, *Little Fuzzy*, 1962
Christopher Stasheff, *The Warlock in Spite of Himself*, 1969
Vivian Vande Velde, *User Unfriendly*, 1991

## 4434

### JAMES D. PRIEST

## Kirins: The Secret of the Hanging Stones

(Shorewood, Minnesota: Yellowstone Press, 1993)

**Story type:** Fantasy (Quest; Magic Conflict)
**Series:** Kirins
**Major character(s):** Speckarin, Magician, Mythical Creature; Paskal Parody, Magician (Guardian)
**Time period(s):** 1990s
**Locale(s):** Stonehenge, England

**Summary:** The Kirins' rescue of the Guardian Magician continues as they search for the stronghold of Kirin magic. They discover humans

willing to help and continue to fly on blackbirds to complete their adventure and return home.

**Other books you might like:**
Nancy Varian Berberick, *The Jewels of Elvish*, 1991
Emma Bull, *War for the Oaks*, 1987
H. Beam Piper, *Little Fuzzy*, 1962
Terry Pratchett, *Wings*, 1991
Greg Snow, *That's All, Folks!*, 1992
Lawrence Watt-Evans, *The Rebirth of Wonder*, 1992

## 4435

### JAMES D. PRIEST

## Kirins: The Spell of No'an

(Shorewood, Minnesota: Yellowstone Press, 1990)

**Story type:** Fantasy (Magic Conflict; Quest)
**Series:** Kirins
**Major character(s):** Speckarin, Magician, Mythical Creature (brownie)
**Time period(s):** 1990s (1990)
**Locale(s):** Earth

**Summary:** In the old days kirins and humans worked together, both races using magic to get things done. For some unknown reason humans gave up magic, which was not working for them as well as it had. Now magic is not working as well for the kirins as it did. Even the Spell of No'an, which prevents only large sapient species from seeing kirins, is at risk. Speckarin leads a group of brave explorers on an expedition to save them from impending disaster.

**Other books you might like:**
Orson Scott Card, *Seventh Son*, 1987
John DeChancie, *Castle Perilous*, 1988
Jody Lynn Nye, *Mythology 101*, 1990
H. Beam Piper, *Little Fuzzy*, 1962
L. Neil Smith, *Brightsuit MacBear*, 1988
L. Neil Smith, *Taflak Lysandra*, 1988
Christopher Stasheff, *The Warlock in Spite of Himself*, 1969

## 4436

### DAVID PRILL

## Serial Killer Days

(New York: St. Martin's, 1996)

**Story type:** Horror (Satire)
**Major character(s):** Debbie Sue Morning, Teenager; Ole Rimbaud, Writer (poet); Griff Grimes, Journalist
**Time period(s):** 1990s (1996)
**Locale(s):** Standard Springs, Minnesota

**Summary:** While the small town of Standard Springs gears up for its annual Serial Killer Days celebration to mark the annual invasion of the town by a murderer who has taken the life of one person every year for the last two decades, happy-go-lucky Debbie Sue Morning tries to perfect her screaming in hopes of winning the Scream Queen title and riding the Scream Queen float in the Serial Killer Days parade.

**Other books you might like:**
Ramsey Campbell, *The Count of Eleven*, 1992
Thomas M. Disch, *The Businessman: A Tale of Terror*, 1984

## **4437**

### DAVID PRILL

## *The Unnatural*

(New York: St. Martin's, 1995)

**Story type:** Horror (Satire)
**Major character(s):** Andy Archway, Undertaker; P.T. Sunnyside, Undertaker; Wallace ''Wake'' Wakefield, Scout
**Time period(s):** 1990s (1995)
**Locale(s):** Minnesota; California; Soma, Fictional Country

**Summary:** In a world where mortuary science has achieved the cachet of professional sports, talented mortuary student Andy Archway sets his heart on the ambitious goal of breaking a 50-year old record for the most number of corpses embalmed in one year. While Andy prepares to move to Soma, a third-world country with a high death rate, as the place to ply his trade, he becomes embroiled in a competition between rival embalmers in the United States who also want his skills. This liberal spoof of Bernard Malamud's *The Natural* is the author's first novel.

**Other books you might like:**
Thomas M. Disch, *The M.D.: A Horror Story*, 1991
William Browning Spencer, *Resume with Monsters*, 1995
Evelyn Waugh, *The Loved One*, 1948
Gus Weill, *Flesh*, 1992

## **4438**

### MAGGIE PRINCE

## *The House on Hound Hill*

(Boston: Houghton Mifflin, 1998)

**Story type:** Fantasy (Young Adult; Time Travel)
**Major character(s):** Emily, Teenager; Jonah, Teenager Seth, Teenager
**Time period(s):** 1990s; 17th century
**Locale(s):** London, England

**Summary:** From her new home, seemingly haunted by voices, people, and one cat, Emily finds herself transported to the plague-ridden streets of London in 1665. Emily sees bloodstains on Jonah's bedroom wall, a tangible sign of the horrible things transpiring there. Only when she solves the mystery of these past events can Emily rest easily again. First published in England in 1996 as *Here Comes a Candle to Light You a Bed*.

**Other books you might like:**
Madeleine L'Engle, *An Acceptable Time*, 1990
Penelope Lively, *The Ghost of Thomas Kempe*, 1973
Patricia A. McKillip, *The House on Parchment Street*, 1973
Phyllis Reynolds Naylor, *Bernie and the Bessledorf Ghost*, 1990
Alis A. Rasmussen, *The Labyrinth Gate*, 1988

## **4439**

### DAVID PRINGLE, Editor

## *The Best of Interzone*

(New York: St. Martin's Press, 1997)

**Story type:** Science Fiction (Anthology; Science Fiction)
**Summary:** Published in conjunction with the 15th anniversary of the Hugo Award-winning British magazine *Interzone*, this volume contains a nine-page introduction outlining the magazine's origins and history, as well as 29 stories. Authors include Brian Aldiss, J.G.

Ballard, Stephen Baxter, Chris Beckett, Eric Brown, Molly Brown, Eugene Byrne, Richard Calder, Paul De Filippo, Thomas M. Disch, David Garnett, Greg Egan, Timons Esaias, Peter F. Hamilton, Mary Gentle, Nicola Griffith, Ben Jeapes, Graham Joyce, Garry Kilworth, David Langford, Ian Lee, Ian R. MacLeod, Sean McMullen, John Meaney, Kim Newman, Paul Park, Geoff Ryman, Brian Stableford, Ian Watson and Cherry Wilder.

**Other books you might like:**
Mike Ashley, *The Best of British SF*, 1977
  editor
John Clute, *Interzone: The 1st Anthology*, 1985
  David Pringle, Colin Greenland, co-editors
John Clute, *Interzone: The 4th Anthology*, 1989
  David Pringle, Simon Ounsley, co-editors
John Clute, *Interzone: The 2nd Anthology*, 1987
  David Pringle, Simon Ounsley, co-editors
John Clute, *Interzone: The 3rd Anthology*, 1988
  David Pringle, Simon Ounsley, co-editors
Paul Collins, *Metaworlds*, 1994
  editor
Gardner Dozois, *The Year's Best Science Fiction Series*, 1984-1997
  editor
David G. Hartwell, *Northern Stars: The Anthology of Canadian Science Fiction*, 1994
  Glenn Grant, co-editor
Kim Mohan, *Amazing Stories: The Anthology*, 1995
  editor
Pamela Sargent, *Nebula Awards 30*, 1996
  editor

## **4440**

### BILL PRONZINI, Editor
### MARTIN H. GREENBERG, Co-Editor
### BARRY MALZBERG, Co-Editor

## *Classic Tales of Horror and the Supernatural*

(New York: Morrow/Quill, 1991)

**Story type:** Horror (Anthology)

**Summary:** Originally published in 1981 as *The Arbor House Treasury of Horror and the Supernatural*, this omnibus collects 41 stories by both classic and modern masters of supernatural horror. Included from the classic writers are H.P. Lovecraft's famous story of monsters living beneath the streets of Rhode Island, ''Pickman's Model''; Edgar Allan Poe's *conte cruel* of a dwarf's revenge on his persecutors, ''Hop Frog''; Fritz Leiber's original vampire story, ''The Girl with the Hungry Eyes''; and Theodore Sturgeon's story of a man with an obsessive passion, ''Bianca's Hands.'' More modern tales include Cyril M. Kornbluth's tale of a psychic vampire, ''The Mindworm''; Ramsey Campbell's gruesome ''Call First''; and Stephen King's uncollected tale of a monster living in an abandoned crate, ''The Crate.''

**Other books you might like:**
David G. Hartwell, *The Dark Descent*, 1987
David G. Hartwell, *Foundations of Fear*, 1992
Herbert Wise, *Great Tales of Terror and the Supernatural*, 1945
  Phyllis Fraser, co-editor

## 4441

**KATHRYN PTACEK**

### Ghost Dance

(New York: Tor, 1990)

**Story type:** Horror (Apocalyptic Horror)
**Major character(s):** Chato del Klinne, Indian; Sunny Mae Foster, Worker (blackjack dealer); Bettina Salazar, Indian
**Time period(s):** 1990s
**Locale(s):** Las Vegas, Nevada; Southwest

**Summary:** The inexplicable deaths of several American Indians resistant to the Native American cause point to the work of the Ghost Dance religion, an ancient faith whose figurehead, the mysterious Crow Woman, is inciting members to rise up and help bring about the return of America to the first Americans.

**Other books you might like:**
Charles L. Grant, *The Nestling*, 1982
G. Wayne Miller, *Thunder Rise*, 1988

## 4442

**KATHRYN PTACEK**

### The Hunted

(New York: Walker, 1993)

**Story type:** Horror (Child-in-Peril)
**Major character(s):** Jessie Mae Morrison, Child (11-years-old); Wendy Wallace, Writer; Emerson Thorne, Doctor (pediatrician)
**Time period(s):** 1970s (1975)
**Locale(s):** Hunter Heights, New Jersey

**Summary:** Newly moved to Hunter Heights, Jessie Mae Morrison can't explain why she suddenly begins having blackout spells and showing signs of psychological trauma. It takes her pediatrician, the respected Dr. Thorne, to realize that Jessie is the reincarnation of a child he killed in the Nazi death camps decades before, and that he must kill her again to preserve his dark secret.

**Other books you might like:**
Frank DeFelitta, *Audrey Rose*, 1975
J.M. Dillard, *Specters*, 1991
Max Ehrlich, *The Reincarnation of Peter Proud*, 1974
Nina Romberg, *Shadow Walkers*, 1993

## 4443

**KATHRYN PTACEK**, Editor

### Women of Darkness II

(New York: Tor, 1990)

**Story type:** Horror (Anthology)
**Series:** Women of Darkness

**Summary:** Eighteen horror stories by women, concerned with both general and feminist themes. Included are Chelsea Quinn Yarbro's historical ''Fruits of Love''; Resa Nelson's allegory of sexual exploitation, ''Sara and the Slime Monster''; Nina Kiriki Hoffman's tale of a curse passed through a family bloodline, ''A Touch of the Old Lilith''; and Melanie Tem's dark meditation on childbearing and rearing, ''The Co-Op.''

**Other books you might like:**
Richard Dalby, *The Virago Book of Ghost Stories: The Twentieth Century*, 1987
published in London

Richard Dalby, *The Virago Book of Ghost Stories*, 1989
first American edition
Alan Ryan, *Haunting Women*, 1988
Jessica Amanda Salmonson, *What Did Miss Darrington See?: An Anthology of Feminist Supernatural Fiction*, 1989
Lisa Tuttle, *Skin of the Soul*, 1990

## 4444

**W.H. PUGMIRE**

### Tales of Sesqua Valley

(Westborough, Massachusetts: Necropolitan Press, 1997)

**Story type:** Horror (Collection)

**Summary:** Ten stories set in the Sesqua Valley, a fictional milieu of the Pacific Northwest. The author blends nostalgia, romance and Lovecraftian horrors in poetic and passionate tales that include ''Another Flesh,'' ''Apotheosis,'' ''Immortal Remains,'' ''An Image in Chalk,'' and ''Born in Strange Shadow.'' Introduction by Jeffrey Thomas. Illustrated by Earl Geier, Jeffrey Thomas, and Scott Thomas.

**Other books you might like:**
Lin Carter, *The Xothic Legend Cycle*, 1997
David Langford, *Irrational Numbers*, 1994
Brian Lumley, *In His Own Write: Brian Lumley, Necroscribe*, 1997
Jeffrey Thomas, *The Bones of the Old Ones*, 1995
Stanley Wiater, *Mysteries of the Word*, 1994
F. Paul Wilson, *The Barrens*, 1992

## 4445

**KATE PULLINGER**

### Where Does Kissing End?

(New York: Serpent's Tail, 1995)

**Story type:** Horror (Vampire Story)
**Major character(s):** Mina Savage, Travel Agent; Stephen Smith, Writer (travel writer); Lucy Savage, Worker (shopworker), Parent (Mina's mother)
**Time period(s):** 1990s (1992)
**Locale(s):** London, England

**Summary:** Mina, representative of the newest generation in a long line of illegitimate children on her mother's and father's sides, takes her satisfaction from men through sex that involves biting and bloodletting. When she meets Stephen, the two develop a co-dependent relationship that borders on the vampiric. This novel was first published in England in 1992.

**Other books you might like:**
Anne Billson, *Suckers*, 1993
Michael Cadnum, *The Judas Glass*, 1996
Lewis Gannett, *The Living One*, 1993
Jonathan Nasaw, *The World on Blood*, 1996
Brian Stableford, *Young Blood*, 1992

## 4446

**PHILIP PULLMAN**

### The Golden Compass

(New York: Knopf, 1996)

**Story type:** Fantasy (Historical; Quest)
**Series:** His Dark Materials

**Major character(s):** Lyra Belacqua, Child; Iorek Byrnison, Mercenary, Animal (bear); Lee Scoresby, Pilot (balloon)
**Time period(s):** Indeterminate
**Locale(s):** London, England; Svalbard, Fictional Country

**Summary:** Lyra Belacqua saves her uncle's life, an act of mercy that turns her life upside down. After a friend's kidnapping and Lyra's introduction to London's glittering society, Lyra flees, hiding with gypsies. When captured, Lyra takes chances, eventually pursuing her uncle to the far, frozen North and beyond. First of a trilogy. Published in Britain as *His Dark Materials: Northern Lights*.

**Other books you might like:**
Barbara Hambly, *The Silent Tower*, 1986
Diana Wynne Jones, *Cart and Cwidder*, 1977
Patricia A. McKillip, *The Riddle-Master of Hed*, 1976
Tim Powers, *The Anubis Gates*, 1983
Michael Scott Rohan, *The Anvil of Ice*, 1986

## 4447

### PHILIP PULLMAN

## Spring-Heeled Jack

(New York: Alfred A. Knopf, 1991)

**Story type:** Fantasy (Legend; Young Adult)
**Major character(s):** Mack the Knife, Criminal, Historical Figure; Ned, Orphan; Spring-Heeled Jack, Hero
**Time period(s):** 19th century
**Locale(s):** London, England

**Summary:** Mack the Knife grabbed Ned in order to force Rose and Lily to give him their mother's locket which they had planned to sell to escape to America. Spring-Heeled Jack, dressed like the devil, frightened the girls, but then vowed to hide them, find Ned and send them all to America. David Mostyn thoroughly illustrated this novel.

**Other books you might like:**
Ann Curry, *The Book of Brendan*, 1990
Sid Fleischman, *The Midnight Horse*, 1990
Robin Morgan, *The Mer-Child: A Legend for Children and Other Adults*, 1991
Cynthia Voigt, *Jackaroo*, 1985
Patricia C. Wrede, *Dealing with Dragons*, 1990

## 4448

### PHILIP PULLMAN

## The Subtle Knife

(New York: Knopf, 1997)

**Story type:** Fantasy (Historical; Quest)
**Series:** His Dark Materials
**Major character(s):** Lyra Belacqua, Child, Fugitive; William "Will" Parry, Child, Fugitive; Lee Scoresby, Traveler, Pilot (balloon)
**Time period(s):** Indeterminate; 1990s
**Locale(s):** Cittagazze, Fictional City; Oxford, England; Alternate Earth

**Summary:** Menancing men hunt Will Parry's mother and Will. When Will flees these men, he falls into another world, where he meets Lyra, also on the run. Together they search for their fathers, only to uncover the strangest plot of all. Second of trilogy.

**Other books you might like:**
Eleanor Arnason, *Daughter of the Bear King*, 1987
James P. Blaylock, *Land of Dreams*, 1987
John Crowley, *Little, Big*, 1981
Diana Wynne Jones, *Cart and Cwidder*, 1977

Patricia A. McKillip, *The Riddle-Master of Hed*, 1976

## 4449

### JOSEPH S. PULVER JR.

## Nightmare's Disciple

(Oakland, California: Chaosium, 1998)

**Story type:** Horror (Ancient Evil Unleashed; Serial Killer)
**Major character(s):** Christopher James Stewart, Detective—Police; Gregory Bradford Marsh, Serial Killer; Cosmo Renaldi, Businessman (bookstore owner)
**Time period(s):** 1990s (1998)
**Locale(s):** Rochester, New York

**Summary:** Clues in the case of the Mastectomy Murderer, a serial killer with a penchant for removing the breasts of his female victims, convince Detective Christopher James Stewart to seek the advice of horror buffs knowledgeable about the fiction of H.P. Lovecraft. With their help, Stewart sets out on the trail of Gregory Bradford Marsh, a strange man whose bibliographic pursuits have inspired him to try and summon Kassogtha, bride of the extradimensional monster Cthulhu. A first novel.

**Other books you might like:**
Robert Bloch, *Strange Eons*, 1978
Marc Laidlaw, *The 37th Mandala*, 1996
Brian Lumley, *The Burrowers Beneath*, 1974
Adam Niswander, *The Sand Dwellers*, 1998
Michael Shea, *The Colour out of Time*, 1984

## 4450

### MAUREEN S. PUSTI

## Neighbors

(New York: Leisure, 1991)

**Story type:** Horror (Black Magic)
**Major character(s):** Tom Roberts, Professor (of experimental psychology); Kristen Roberts, Housewife (Tom's wife); Eliza Norman, Witch
**Time period(s):** 1990s
**Locale(s):** Burnwell, Pennsylvania

**Summary:** Tom Roberts and his pregnant wife Kristen move to the small college town of Burnwell, unaware that their next-door neighbor is a witch who is responsible for the disappearance and death of several local children and who finds their proximity useful for the completion of her supernatural rituals.

**Other books you might like:**
Stephanie Kegan, *The Baby*, 1990
John Saul, *Suffer the Children*, 1977

## 4451

### W.T. QUICK

## Dreams of Gods and Men

(New York: Signet, 1989)

**Story type:** Science Fiction (Cyberpunk)
**Major character(s):** Ozzie, Computer Expert, Scientist; Arius, Artificial Intelligence
**Time period(s):** 21st century
**Locale(s):** Chicago, Illinois; San Francisco, California; Montenegro

**Summary:** A small group of beleaguered computer wizards struggles valiantly against Arius, the artificial intelligence who has seized control of the world's most powerful corporations. Their leader, Berg, has disappeared and the metamatrix, that strange computer-generated universe, has become increasingly hostile. This is the sequel to *Dreams of Flesh and Sand*.

**Other books you might like:**
William Gibson, *Count Zero*, 1985
William Gibson, *Mona Lisa Overdrive*, 1988
William Gibson, *Neuromancer*, 1984
Jonathan Littell, *Bad Voltage*, 1989
Daniel Keys Moran, *The Long Run*, 1989

---

**4452**

### W.T. QUICK

## Systems

(New York: Signet, 1989)

**Story type:** Science Fiction (Cyberpunk)
**Major character(s):** Josh Tower, Computer Expert, Spy; Dorothea Kelly, Nurse
**Time period(s):** 21st century
**Locale(s):** United States

**Summary:** Josh Tower, a former U.S. government agent now earning his living as a research specialist, is in a near-fatal air-taxi crash in which his wife is killed. Finding evidence that the crash was not entirely accidental, he uses his computer skills to discover who was responsible. To his surprise Tower uncovers an international conspiracy and soon finds himself on the run with a price on his head.

**Other books you might like:**
William Gibson, *Count Zero*, 1985
William Gibson, *Mona Lisa Overdrive*, 1988
William Gibson, *Neuromancer*, 1984
Jonathan Littell, *Bad Voltage*, 1989
Bruce Sterling, *Islands in the Net*, 1988

---

**4453**

### W.T. QUICK

## Yesterday's Pawn

(New York: NAL Signet, 1989)

**Story type:** Science Fiction (Space Opera)
**Major character(s):** Garry Hammersmidt, Businessman
**Time period(s):** Indeterminate Future
**Locale(s):** H'hogoth, Planet—Imaginary; Arius, Planet—Imaginary

**Summary:** Garry Hammersmidt works in his father's pawnshop. One day a nervous little man brings in an artifact to pawn and Garry's life is changed forever. It turns out that other people are interested in the artifact and will stop at nothing to get it.

**Other books you might like:**
Robert A. Heinlein, *Citizen of the Galaxy*, 1957
R.A. MacAvoy, *The Third Eagle: Lessons Along a Minor String*, 1989
Walter Jon Williams, *Angel Station*, 1989

---

**4454**

### DANIEL QUINN

## Dreamer

(New York: Tor, 1992)

**Story type:** Horror (Occult)
**Major character(s):** Greg Donner, Writer (freelance); Ginny Winters, Artist; Franklin Evelyn Winters, Businessman (Ginny's father)
**Time period(s):** 1990s
**Locale(s):** Chicago, Illinois

**Summary:** Greg Donner awakens from a dream of romance with the beautiful Ginny Winters to discover that he is, in reality, a middle-aged schoolteacher named Richard Iles, who is recovering from brainwashing at the hands of Soviet agents. When he awakens once more as Greg Donner, and is informed by Ginny that his Richard Iles persona is a trick foisted upon him by her jealous father, who is able to manipulate dreams through occult forces, Greg finds himself completely incapable of distinguishing between dream and reality. This novel was originally published in 1988.

**Other books you might like:**
Philip K. Dick, *The Three Stigmata of Palmer Eldritch*, 1964
Philip K. Dick, *Ubik*, 1969

---

**4455**

### DANIEL QUINN

## Ishmael

(New York: Bantam/Turner, 1992)

**Story type:** Science Fiction (Literary; Contemporary Realism)
**Major character(s):** Ishmael, Animal (gorilla), Telepath; I, Writer, Student
**Time period(s):** 1990s
**Locale(s):** United States

**Summary:** After the author answers an ad from a teacher seeking a pupil who has a great desire to save the world, he listens to a series of conversations in which Ishmael relates positive solutions to global problems. Winner of a Turner Tomorrow Fellowship.

**Other books you might like:**
Richard Bach, *Jonathan Livingston Seagull*, 1970
Andrew Goldblatt, *The Bully Pulpit*, 1992
C.S. Lewis, *That Hideous Strength*, 1946
Antoine de Saint-Exupery, *The Little Prince*, 1943
Michael Tobias, *Voice of the Planet*, 1990

---

**4456**

### DANIEL QUINN

## My Ishmael

(New York: Bantam, 1997)

**Story type:** Science Fiction (Literary; Contemporary Realism)
**Major character(s):** Julie Gerchak, Child, Student; Ishmael, Animal (gorilla), Telepath
**Time period(s):** 1990s
**Locale(s):** United States

**Summary:** When Ishmael again advertises for a student interested in saving the world, Julie answers, but must convince Ishmael that she can benefit from his tutelage. Julie's understanding of world events broadens with Ishmael as her mentor.

**Other books you might like:**
Richard Bach, *Jonathan Livingston Seagull*, 1970
Antoine de Saint-Exupery, *The Little Prince*, 1943
Andrew Goldblatt, *The Bully Pulpit*, 1992
James Gurney, *Dinotopia*, 1992
C.S. Lewis, *That Hideous Strength*, 1946
Michael Tobias, *Voice of the Planet*, 1990

### 4457
#### JEAN RABE

## The Day of the Tempest
(Renton, Washington: TSR, 1997)

**Story type:** Fantasy (Adventure)
**Series:** Dragonlance: Fifth Age
**Major character(s):** Malystryx, Mythical Creature (dragon); Rurak Gistere, Knight; Palin Majere, Wizard
**Time period(s):** Indeterminate Past
**Locale(s):** Krynn, Planet—Imaginary

**Summary:** When the dragons return to dominate Krynn, conquering the people and altering the land and climate, malystryx and the others under the Storm Over Krynn plan to increase their empire to include Ansalon. A small band of heroes armed with magic and a dragonlance chooses to stand in their way.

**Other books you might like:**
Glen Cook, *The Swordbearer*, 1982
Gordon R. Dickson, *The Dragon and the George*, 1976
Guy Gavriel Kay, *The Summer Tree*, 1985
Patricia A. McKillip, *The Riddle-Master of Hed*, 1976
Michael Scott Rohan, *The Anvil of Ice*, 1986

### 4458
#### JEAN RABE

## Red Magic
(Lake Geneva, Wisconsin: TSR, 1991)

**Story type:** Fantasy (Magic Conflict; Adventure)
**Series:** Forgotten Realms: The Harpers
**Major character(s):** Maligor, Wizard; Galvin, Magician (harper), Religious (Druid); Wynter, Mythical Creature (centaur)
**Time period(s):** Indeterminate
**Locale(s):** Thay, Fictional Country

**Summary:** The Harpers, fighting for freedom and justice in Thay, a land ruled by the evil Red Wizards, send an expedition to acquire information on conditions in Thay. Maligor, the Zulkir of Alteration, tries to prevent their return. The Harpers must foil Maligor and prevent him from adding them to his minions of undead slaves. This is the author's first book, a game tie-in novel.

**Other books you might like:**
Douglas Bell, *Mojo and the Pickle Jar*, 1991
Kyle Crocco, *Heroes, Inc.*, 1991
Philip Jose Farmer, *Red Orc's Rage*, 1991
Courtway Jones, *In the Shadow of the Oak King*, 1991
R.A. Salvatore, *The Crystal Shard*, 1988
Julie Dean Smith, *Mission of Magic*, 1991
Brad Strickland, *Wizard's Mole*, 1991
Margaret Weis, *Fire Sea*, 1991
   Tracy Hickman, co-author

### 4459
#### IRENE RADFORD

## The Dragon's Touchstone
(New York: DAW, 1997)

**Story type:** Fantasy (Magic Conflict)
**Series:** Dragon Nimbus History
**Major character(s):** Nimbulan "Lan", Magician, Warrior; Myrilandel "Myri", Healer; Amaranth, Mythical Creature (flywacket), Companion (Myri's familiar)
**Time period(s):** Indeterminate
**Locale(s):** Coronnan, Fictional Country

**Summary:** Weary of the system that exploits magic only to pursue warfare, one powerful Battlemage decides to unify the warring land by uniting all magicians who wish peace. Using her untrained, natural talent for healing, Myri flees those who would use her talent to their ends or destroy her, following the direction of the voices in her head. After she meets Nimbulan, the two discover their fates interwine.

**Other books you might like:**
Laurell K. Hamilton, *Nightseer*, 1992
Carol Heller, *The Gates of Vensunor*, 1997
Peg Kerr, *Emerald House Rising*, 1997
Katya Reimann, *Wind From a Foreign Sky*, 1996
Caroline Stevermer, *A College of Magics*, 1994

### 4460
#### IRENE RADFORD

## The Glass Dragon
(New York: DAW, 1994)

**Story type:** Fantasy (Magic Conflict; Mystery)
**Series:** Dragon Nimbus
**Major character(s):** Jaylor, Wizard; Brevelan, Witch
**Time period(s):** Indeterminate
**Locale(s):** Coronnan, Fictional Country

**Summary:** As dragons disappear from the land and the kingdom becomes vulnerable to attack, wizards seek the cause. With his unusual magical abilities, Jaylor searches with Brevclan, perhaps the kingdom's only hope for discovering the cause and finding a remedy before the magic completely vanishes. First novel.

**Other books you might like:**
Thorarinn Gunnarsson, *Dragon's Domain*, 1993
Larry Niven, *The Magic Goes Away*, 1979
Lawrence Watt-Evans, *The Blood of a Dragon*, 1991
Patricia C. Wrede, *Calling on Dragons*, 1993
Laurence Yep, *Dragon of the Lost Sea*, 1982

### 4461
#### IRENE RADFORD

## The Loneliest Magician
(New York: DAW, 1996)

**Story type:** Fantasy (Political; Quest)
**Series:** Dragon Nimbus
**Major character(s):** Jack, Magician, Adventurer; Rejiia de Draconis, Magician, Royalty; Katrina Kaantille, Teenager, Artisan
**Time period(s):** Indeterminate
**Locale(s):** SeLenicca, Fictional Country; Coronnan, Fictional Country

**Summary:** Jack searches for the dragon necessary to return magic to Coronnan and replace the protective magic taken with the departing wizards. Meanwhile, Rejiia de Draconis plots to topple Coronnan's ruling family and exert control over neighboring countries.

**Other books you might like:**
Graham Edwards, *Dragoncharm*, 1996
J.V. Jones, *The Baker's Boy*, 1995
Marjorie Bradley Kellogg, *The Book of Earth*, 1995
Ursula K. Le Guin, *A Wizard of Earthsea*, 1968
Andre Norton, *Elvenblood*, 1995
  Mercedes Lackey, co-author

---

## 4462

### IRENE RADFORD

## The Perfect Princess

(New York: DAW, 1995)

**Story type:** Fantasy (Political; Magic Conflict)
**Series:** Dragon Nimbus
**Major character(s):** Darville, Royalty; Rossemikka "Mikka", Royalty
**Time period(s):** Indeterminate
**Locale(s):** Coronnan, Fictional Country

**Summary:** With dragon magic vanishing from Coronnan, masters of a forbidden magic attempt to wrest control of the land from its rightful heir, Prince Darville. Without aid, Prince Darville and his beloved Mikka may both succumb to the evil onslaught. Second in the series.

**Other books you might like:**
Lois McMaster Bujold, *The Spirit Ring*, 1992
Katharine Kerr, *Daggerspell*, 1986
Ursula K. Le Guin, *A Wizard of Earthsea*, 1968
Michelle Sagara, *Into the Dark Lands*, 1991
Janny Wurts, *Curse of the Mistwraith*, 1994
Laurence Yep, *Dragon of the Lost Sea*, 1982

---

## 4463

### STEPHEN MARK RAINEY

## Fugue Devil and Other Weird Horrors

(Norfolk, Virginia: Macabre, Inc., 1993)

**Story type:** Horror (Collection)

**Summary:** The author's first collection consists of five stories ranging from the cosmic horror of "Return of the Navigator" to the science fictional trappings of "The Weird Violet," an ecodisaster story. Included are the title story, about a mythical rural monster; "Festival of the Jackal," a surreal urban horror story; and "Charon's Wings," a psychological horror story that probes the thoughts of an airplane hijacker. Robert M. Price wrote the introduction.

**Other books you might like:**
Joseph Payne Brennan, *Stories of Darkness and Dread*, 1973
Charles L. Grant, *Tales From the Nightside*, 1981
Albert J. Manachino, *The Odd Lot: The Selected Works of Albert J. Manachino*, 1993
Elizabeth Massie, *Southern Discomfort: Selected Works of Elizabeth Massie*, 1993
Norman Partridge, *Mr. Fox and Other Feral Tales*, 1992

---

## 4464

### GARY L. RAISOR

## Less than Human

(New York: Diamond, 1992)

**Story type:** Horror (Vampire Story)
**Major character(s):** Stephen Adler, Vampire; Earl Jacobs, Con Artist (pool hustler); John Warrick, Con Artist (pool hustler)
**Time period(s):** 1990s
**Locale(s):** Carruthers, Texas; Crowder Flats, Texas

**Summary:** The author's first novel offers an interesting variation on the vampire tale in its story of Stephen Adler, a vampire who hustles pool games—and his meals—with the help of a charmed cuestick.

**Other books you might like:**
Poppy Z. Brite, *Lost Souls*, 1992
Nancy A. Collins, *Sunglasses After Dark*, 1989
Nancy A. Collins, *Tempter*, 1990
Ron Dee, *Dusk*, 1991
P.N. Elrod, *The Vampire Chronicles*, 1989-1992
Anne Rice, *The Vampire Chronicles*, 1975-1992

---

## 4465

### GARY L. RAISOR, Editor

## Obsessions

(Arlington Heights, IL: Dark Harvest, 1991)

**Story type:** Horror (Anthology)

**Summary:** Thirty stories of fantasy and horror in which personal obsessions lead people to commit extreme acts. Obsessions detailed include death fixation (Dean R. Koontz's "The Interrogation"), ardent celebrity worship (Thomas Monteleone's "The Pleasure of Her Company"), artistic influences (John Shirley's "Woodgrains"), gluttony (F. Paul Wilson's "Topsy"), and neatness (Nicholas Royle's "Crispy Notes").

**Other books you might like:**
Margaret L. Carter, *Demon Lovers and Strange Seductions*, 1973
Don Congdon, *Tales of Love and Horror*, 1961
Jeff Gelb, *Hotter Blood: More Tales of Erotic Horror*, 1991
  Michael Garrett, co-author
Jeff Gelb, *Hot Blood: Tales of Provocative Horror*, 1989
  Michael Garrett, co-author
Michele Slung, *I Shudder at Your Touch*, 1991

---

## 4466

### KEVIN RANDLE

## Jefferson's War: Death of a Regiment

(New York: Ace, 1991)

**Story type:** Science Fiction (Military)
**Series:** Jefferson's War
**Major character(s):** David Steven Jefferson, Military Personnel; Victoria Torrence, Military Personnel; Rachel Davies, Military Personnel
**Time period(s):** Indeterminate Future
**Locale(s):** Outer Space; Eighty-Two Eridani, Outer Space (solar system)

**Summary:** The alien Croatoans have attacked and destroyed a convoy of Earth's spaceships. Now they seem to be poised for an attack on

Earth itself. Colonel Jefferson and Colonel Davies are sent with their regiments to stop, or at least delay, the alien advance.

**Other books you might like:**
Gordon R. Dickson, *Dorsai!*, 1976
Gordon R. Dickson, *Soldier, Ask Not*, 1967
Joe Haldeman, *The Forever War*, 1975
Robert A. Heinlein, *Starship Troopers*, 1959
Jerry Pournelle, *Falkenberg's Legion*, 1990
Elizabeth Ann Scarborough, *The Healer's War*, 1989

## 4467

### KEVIN D. RANDLE

## Galactic MI

(New York: Ace, 1993)

**Story type:** Science Fiction (Military)
**Series:** Galactic MI
**Major character(s):** Joshua Price, Military Personnel (captain); Emma Coollege, Spy, Military Personnel (lieutenant); Wallace "Rocky" Stone, Military Personnel (master sergeant)
**Time period(s):** Indeterminate Future
**Locale(s):** Bolton's Planet, Planet—Imaginary

**Summary:** Recently discovered by the coalition, Bolton's Planet seems an ideal society. In an attempt to confirm this before establishing full diplomatic contact, the colonel orders Sergeant Stone to kidnap a representative member of the society for interrogation. First of a new series.

**Other books you might like:**
Joe Haldeman, *All My Sins Remembered*, 1977
Harry Harrison, *The Adventures of the Stainless Steel Rat*, 1978
Steve Miller, *Agent of Change*, 1988
    Sharon Lee, co-author
Steve Miller, *Carpe Diem*, 1989
    Sharon Lee, co-author
Steve Miller, *Conflict of Honors*, 1988
    Sharon Lee, co-author
Steve Perry, *The 97th Step*, 1989
Steve Perry, *The Man Who Never Missed*, 1985
Alis A. Rasmussen, *A Passage of Stars*, 1990
Alis A. Rasmussen, *The Price of Ransom*, 1990
Alis A. Rasmussen, *Revolution's Shore*, 1990

## 4468

### KEVIN D. RANDLE

## The Galactic Silver Star

(New York: Ace, 1990)

**Story type:** Science Fiction (Military)
**Major character(s):** David Steven Jefferson, Military Personnel; Victoria Torrence, Military Personnel; Joseph Tyson, Military Personnel
**Time period(s):** Indeterminate Future
**Locale(s):** Outer Space

**Summary:** After his first combat mission, Lt. David Jefferson received the Galactic Silver Star for a daring attack that he did not make. Promoted to Major in the Space Infantry and put in command of a battalion, he has to prove his ability to command and earn his reputation for bravery. But who are the enemy—and why?

**Other books you might like:**
Gordon R. Dickson, *Lost Dorsai*, 1980
Gordon R. Dickson, *The Tactics of Mistake*, 1971

Phyllis Eisenstein, *In the Hands of Glory*, 1981
Jack Williamson, *The Legion of Space*, 1947
Helen S. Wright, *A Matter of Oaths*, 1990

## 4469

### KEVIN D. RANDLE
### RICHARD DRISCOLL, Co-Author

## Mind Slayer

(New York: Ace, 1992)

**Story type:** Science Fiction (Mystery; Space Colony)
**Series:** Star Precinct
**Major character(s):** Richard Brackett, Police Officer; Obo, Alien, Police Officer; Matthew Pendrake, Secretary, Telepath
**Time period(s):** Indeterminate Future
**Locale(s):** Tumbleweed, Planet—Imaginary (resort planet)

**Summary:** Star Precinct 106 responds to the murder of Dirk St. Romaine, a famous author of expose biographies. The investigation seems unusually difficult due to St. Romaine's millions of enemies and the disappearance of his personal secretary. However, the investigation soon reveals the murderer survived an experiment aimed at producing telepaths trained at murder.

**Other books you might like:**
Alfred Bester, *The Demolished Man*, 1953
Richard Bowker, *Marlborough Street*, 1987
Barney Cohen, *The Taking of Satcon Station*, 1982
    Jim Baen, co-author
Alan Dean Foster, *The I Inside*, 1984
Katharine Kerr, *Polar City Blues*, 1990

## 4470

### KEVIN D. RANDLE
### RICHARD DRISCOLL, Co-Author

## Star Precinct

(New York: Ace, 1992)

**Story type:** Science Fiction (Mystery; Space Colony)
**Series:** Star Precinct
**Major character(s):** Lute Brackett, Detective—Police; Jennifer Daily, Detective—Police; Dennis Profitt, Businessman (multibillionaire), Explorer
**Time period(s):** Indeterminate Future
**Locale(s):** Star Rest, Planet—Imaginary

**Summary:** Dennis Profitt, the richest human in the universe, calls in Star Precinct, a travelling police station, after the murder of his wife, seemingly in a locked room, Since the case appears to tie in with the murder of a priest by a berserk robot, Lute and Jennifer find the identity of the priest and follow his last known contact, only to be led back to Profitt's swanky hotel where they discover two more murders.

**Other books you might like:**
Isaac Asimov, *The Caves of Steel*, 1954
Jack L. Chalker, *The Identity Matrix*, 1982
Barney Cohen, *Blood on the Moon*, 1984
Larry Niven, *The Patchwork Girl*, 1980
Atanielle Annyn Noel, *Murder on Usher's Planet*, 1987
Charles Sheffield, *Sight of Proteus*, 1978
John E. Stith, *Redshift Rendezvous*, 1990

## 4471
### KIMBERLY RANGEL

## The Homecoming
(New York: Leisure, 1998)

**Story type:** Horror (Possession)
**Major character(s):** Darby Jayson, Journalist; Katy Evans, Patient (ex-psychiatric); Graham Tucker, Police Officer (deputy sheriff)
**Time period(s):** 1990s (1998)
**Locale(s):** Nostalgia, Texas

**Summary:** Plagued by dreams of gruesome murders, Darby Jayson returns to the home town where she and her friend Katy were the only survivors of an unsolved Halloween slumber party massacre that left three of their friends dead. Although local authorities believe Darby herself to be the murderer, Darby begins to suspect that the execution of serial killer Samuel Blue the night of the party played a role in the slumber party deaths and even now is having an impact on her nightmare visions.

**Other books you might like:**
Owen Brookes, *Deadly Communion*, 1984
H.B. Gilmour, *The Eyes of Laura Mars*, 1978
James Herbert, *Moon*, 1985
Dean R. Koontz, *The Vision*, 1977
Joe R. Lansdale, *The Nightrunners*, 1987

## 4472
### KIMBERLY RANGEL

## Shadows
(New York: Leisure, 1996)

**Story type:** Horror (Werewolf Story)
**Major character(s):** Selene DeMarco, Antiques Dealer; Reese Christian, Bounty Hunter; Mick Randall, Police Officer
**Time period(s):** 1990s (1996)
**Locale(s):** Los Angeles, California; Shadow Ridge, Oregon

**Summary:** The last female descendant of a race of were-panthers, Selene DeMarco must mate with a descendant of the man who helped activate her family's curse if she is to end her bloody heritage. But the last male decendant of Selene's kind is determined to claim Selene as his own and perpetuate their unholy bloodline.

**Other books you might like:**
Gary Brandner, *Cat People*, 1982
Traci Briery, *The Werewolf Chronicles*, 1995
Traci Briery, *Wolfsong*, 1996
Nancy A. Collins, *Wild Blood*, 1994
Dennis Danvers, *Wilderness*, 1991

## 4473
### ROBERT RANKIN

## Armageddon: The Musical
(New York: Dell, 1990)

**Story type:** Science Fiction (Time Travel; Humor)
**Major character(s):** Jovil Yspht, Alien; Elvis Presley, Musician, Historical Figure
**Time period(s):** 1950s (1958); Indeterminate
**Locale(s):** Earth

**Summary:** Zany aliens have been televising (and messing with) human development for thousands of years. The ratings of this program are starting to slip, so the production staff decides to send a representative with a Time Sprout to help keep the action rolling toward a dramatic final episode. The Time Sprout and Elvis decide to try to avert the catastrophe.

**Other books you might like:**
Alan Dean Foster, *To the Vanishing Point*, 1988
Mel Gilden, *Surfing Samurai Robots*, 1988
Parke Godwin, *The Snake Oil Wars*, 1989
Parke Godwin, *Waiting for the Galactic Bus*, 1988
Frederik Pohl, *Gladiator-at-Law*, 1955
    Cyril M. Kornbluth, co-author

## 4474
### CHRISTOPH RANSMAYR

## The Dog King
(New York: Knopf, 1997)

**Story type:** Fantasy (Literary; Historical)
**Major character(s):** Ambras "Dog King", Leader; Bering, Teenager, Bodyguard; Lily, Hunter
**Time period(s):** 1950s
**Locale(s):** Moor, Fictional City

**Summary:** With World War II over, the Allies return Germany to a pre-industrial state, destroying modern civilization entirely. Put in charge of a small town, a camp survivor watches the sullen people sink into apathy until a boy in his care develops a disease untreatable with Moor's private resources, impelling him to flee from the past and towards hope. Translated by John E. Woods.

**Other books you might like:**
J.G. Ballard, *Hello America*, 1981
Philip K. Dick, *The Man in the High Castle*, 1962
Robert Harris, *Fatherland*, 1992
Brad Linaweaver, *Moon of Ice*, 1988
Pat Murphy, *The City, Not Long After*, 1989

## 4475
### CHRISTOPH RANSMAYR

## The Last World
(New York: Grove Weidenfeld, 1990)

**Story type:** Fantasy (Historical; Quest)
**Major character(s):** Cotta, Tourist; Naso, Fugitive, Writer (poet); Lycaon, Artisan, Werewolf
**Time period(s):** 20th century
**Locale(s):** Tomi, Earth (city on the Black Sea)

**Summary:** This is the first English translation of *Die Letzte Welt*, published in 1988. Drawing heavily on the life and writings of the 1st century poet Ovid, the story follows a young man's search for an exiled poet. As the quest progresses, he finds more and more correlations between the poet's writings and the lives of the people of Tomi, eventually seeing transformations, magic and the boundaries of literature and reality.

**Other books you might like:**
John Crowley, *Little, Big*, 1981
Greer Ilene Gilman, *Moonwise*, 1991
Robert Holdstock, *Mythago Wood*, 1984
Gabriel Garcia Marquez, *One Hundred Years of Solitude*, 1970

## 4476

### BILL RANSOM

## *Burn*

(New York: Ace, 1995)

**Story type:** Science Fiction (Genetic Manipulation; Political)
**Series:** ViraVax
**Major character(s):** Rico Toledo, Military Personnel, Experimental Subject; Marte Chang, Inventor, Government Official; Harry Toledo, Teenager, Experimental Subject
**Time period(s):** 2010s (2015)
**Locale(s):** Confederation of Costa Brava, Fictional Country (in Central America)

**Summary:** After destroying the ViraVax underground facility, hoping to prevent the virus from escaping, Harry and Marte attempt to discover a cure. When Rico learns a shipment of the killer virus may leave the country, he enlists his church buddies to locate the deadly shipment.

**Other books you might like:**
Greg Bear, *Blood Music*, 1985
Helen Collins, *Mutagenesis*, 1993
L. Warren Douglas, *Cannon's Orb*, 1994
Frank Herbert, *The Jesus Incident*, 1979
    Bill Ransom, co-author
Frank Herbert, *The Lazarus Effect*, 1983
    Bill Ransom, co-author
Frank Herbert, *The White Plague*, 1982
S. Andrew Swann, *Forests of the Night*, 1993

## 4477

### BILL RANSOM

## *Jaguar*

(New York: Ace, 1990)

**Story type:** Science Fiction (Psychic Powers; Alternate Universe)
**Major character(s):** Eddie Reyes, Teenager; Maryellen Thompkins, Teenager; Afriqua Lee, Teenager
**Time period(s):** 1990s (1990)
**Locale(s):** Earth; Alternate Earth

**Summary:** In waking life he is a disabled Vietnam veteran with a mysterious sleep disorder, but to the people of another world, he is the Jaguar who can invade people's minds while they dream and force them to do his will. But others have learned to travel the "dreamways" between worlds and they have joined forces to track down the Jaguar and destroy him.

**Other books you might like:**
Glen Cook, *A Matter of Time*, 1985
Joe Haldeman, *The Forever War*, 1975
Gustav Hasford, *Phantom Blooper*, 1990
Elizabeth Ann Scarborough, *The Healer's War*, 1989

## 4478

### BILL RANSOM

## *ViraVax*

(New York: Ace, 1993)

**Story type:** Science Fiction (Genetic Manipulation; Political)
**Series:** ViraVax

**Major character(s):** Rico Toledo, Military Personnel, Experimental Subject; Marte Chang, Inventor, Government Official (Defense Intelligence Agency); Dajaj Mishwe, Murderer, Scientist
**Time period(s):** 2010s (2015)
**Locale(s):** Confederation of Costa Brava, Fictional Country (in Central America)

**Summary:** After Red Bartlett's wife kills him in self defense, Colonel Toledo realizes that Red had suffered from Meltdown, an experimental virus rumored to infect ViraVax's secret fifth level. Alcoholic and unstable, the Colonel loses his commission. When his son's kidnapping forces him to join the underground Peace and Freedom Party to effect a rescue, the Colonel realizes humanity can no longer tolerate the genetic warfare waged against the Catholics by the Children of Eden. Unfortunately, he may be too late to save humanity from Mishwe's secret project.

**Other books you might like:**
Jim Aikin, *The Wall at the Edge of the World*, 1993
Greg Bear, *Blood Music*, 1985
Frank Herbert, *The Ascension Factor*, 1987
    Bill Ransom, co-author
Frank Herbert, *The Jesus Incident*, 1979
    Bill Ransom, co-author
Frank Herbert, *The Lazarus Effect*, 1983
    Bill Ransom, co-author
Frank Herbert, *The White Plague*, 1982
Charles Oberndorf, *Sheltered Lives*, 1992
Neal Stephenson, *Snow Crash*, 1992
Elisabeth Vonarburg, *The Silent City*, 1992

## 4479

### DANIEL RANSOM (Pseudonym of Ed Gorman)

## *The Fugitive Stars*

(New York: DAW, 1995)

**Story type:** Science Fiction (Invasion of Earth; Political)
**Major character(s):** Wendy Abronowitz, Astronaut; Michael Raines, Psychic (esper); Jack "Cap'n Jack" Campbell, Astronaut
**Time period(s):** 2010s (2011)
**Locale(s):** Washington, District of Columbia

**Summary:** After visiting a comet, the astronauts all display signs of the same disease. When Cap'n Jack disappears, his wife kidnaps Michael Raines to help her find him. Murdered by assassins, all experts contacted with information about the disease die.

**Other books you might like:**
Octavia E. Butler, *Dawn*, 1987
L. Warren Douglas, *Cannon's Orb*, 1994
Janet Kagan, *Mirabile*, 1991
S. Andrew Swann, *Forests of the Night*, 1993
David Weber, *Mutineers' Moon*, 1991

## 4480

### DANIEL RANSOM (Pseudonym of Ed Gorman)

## *The Long Midnight*

(New York: Dell, 1993)

**Story type:** Horror (Wild Talents)
**Major character(s):** Richard Candlemas, Doctor; Meredith Sawyer, Journalist (*Windy City* magazine); Tom Gage, Detective
**Time period(s):** 1990s (1993)
**Locale(s):** Chicago, Illinois

**Summary:** When teachers and associates of the former Perpetual Light Institute, a private school for children with extrasensory capabilities, begin dying bizarre deaths, Meredith Sawyer, a graduate of the school, suspects that her sister Valerie may be the culprit. The only problem is that Valerie supposedly died in a car accident many years before the murders begin taking place.

**Other books you might like:**
John Arbucci, *Blood of Innocents*, 1989
Jack Caravela, *The Gifted*, 1991
Stephen King, *Firestarter*, 1980
Steven M. Krauzer, *Brainstorm*, 1991
Patricia Wallace, *Fatal Outcome*, 1992

---

## 4481

### ALIS A. RASMUSSEN

## *The Labyrinth Gate*

(New York: Baen, 1988)

**Story type:** Fantasy (Alternate World)
**Time period(s):** 1980s
**Locale(s):** Earth; Alternate Universe

**Summary:** Newlyweds find themselves tranported to a another world when they use a deck of magic cards. Two opposing powers then use them as pawns in an ongoing struggle.

**Other books you might like:**
Donald Aamodt, *A Name to Conjure With*, 1989
Lee Creighton, *Two Queens of Lochrie*, 1990
Aline Boucher Kaplan, *Khyren*, 1988

---

## 4482

### ALIS A. RASMUSSEN

## *A Passage of Stars*

(New York: Bantam Spectra, 1990)

**Story type:** Science Fiction (Adventure)
**Series:** High Road Trilogy
**Major character(s):** Lilyaka Ransome, Heiress, Spaceman; Heredes, Teacher, Martial Arts Expert
**Time period(s):** Indeterminate Future
**Locale(s):** Unruli, Planet—Imaginary

**Summary:** Heiress Lilyaka Hae Ransome is her own woman, answering to no man. When her tutor Heredes is kidnapped, she leaves her home, abandons her fortune, and goes to his rescue.

**Other books you might like:**
Jay D. Blakeney, *Requiem for Anthi*, 1990
Anne McCaffrey, *Sassinak*, 1990
　　Elizabeth Moon, co-author
Melisa C. Michaels, *Far Harbor*, 1989

---

## 4483

### ALIS A. RASMUSSEN

## *The Price of Ransom*

(New York: Bantam Spectra, 1990)

**Story type:** Science Fiction (Adventure; Political)
**Series:** Highroad Trilogy
**Major character(s):** Lilyaka Ransome, Spaceship Captain; Corrigan Tel Windsor, Bounty Hunter
**Time period(s):** Indeterminate Future

**Locale(s):** *Forlorn Hope*, Spaceship; Diomede, Planet—Imaginary; Outer Space (the Pale)

**Summary:** On Earth a deal is made with Corrigan Tel Windsor to bring Lily in for questioning leading to the capture, and perhaps death, of Hawk and Heredes. Meanwhile, unaware of this danger, the *Forlorn Hope* is on her way from Reft space to the Pale with Lily and Hawk on board.

**Other books you might like:**
David Brin, *Startide Rising*, 1983
Jeffrey A. Carver, *The Rapture Effect*, 1987
Glen Cook, *The Dragon Never Sleeps*, 1988
Frank Herbert, *Dune*, 1965
Michael P. Kube-McDowell, *Enigma*, 1986
Allen Steele, *Clarke County, Space*, 1990

---

## 4484

### ALIS A. RASMUSSEN

## *Revolution's Shore*

(New York: Bantam Spectra, 1990)

**Story type:** Science Fiction (Adventure; Political)
**Series:** Highroad Trilogy
**Major character(s):** Kyosti Bitterleaf Hakoni, Doctor, Spaceman; Lilyaka Ash Heredes, Spaceman
**Time period(s):** Indeterminate Future
**Locale(s):** Harsh, Planet—Imaginary; *Forlorn Hope*, Spaceship

**Summary:** Lily, now the adopted daughter of Heredes, is abandoned with her crewmates on Harsh where she plans on contacting the revolutionary Jehane, and rescuing Paisley, the Tattoo whom they had been forced to leave behind when they escaped from Harsh last time. Lily still plans to join Jehane's revolution, but something about him disturbs her.

**Other books you might like:**
Lois McMaster Bujold, *Borders of Infinity*, 1989
Lois McMaster Bujold, *Brothers in Arms*, 1988
F.M. Busby, *Rissa Kerguelen*, 1977
Stephen Goldin, *Jade Darcy and the Affair of Honor*, 1988
Melisa C. Michaels, *Skirmish*, 1985
Steve Miller, *Agent of Change*, 1988
　　Sharon Lee, co-author

---

## 4485

### MELANIE RAWN

## *The Dragon Token*

(New York: DAW, 1992)

**Story type:** Fantasy (Political; Magic Conflict)
**Series:** Dragon Star
**Major character(s):** Pol, Royalty (high prince), Ruler; Meiglan, Royalty (high princess); Andry, Ruler (lord of Goddess Keep), Magician (sunrunner)
**Time period(s):** Indeterminate
**Locale(s):** Fictional Country

**Summary:** The death of Rohan and the destruction of Stronghold left High Princess Sioned in shock, unable to help her son fight the war and discover his path as High Prince. With many people killed already, much rebuilding is necessary. Andry has left Goddess Keep to join Pol since both recognize the need to cooperate, although communication between the cousins has not begun.

**Other books you might like:**
Cheryl J. Franklin, *Fire Crossing*, 1990

C.S. Friedman, *Black Sun Rising*, 1991
Kris Jensen, *Mentor*, 1991
Katherine Kurtz, *Deryni Rising*, 1970
Anne McCaffrey, *Dragonflight*, 1981
Shirley Rousseau Murphy, *Nightpool*, 1987

---

**4486**

MELANIE RAWN
JENNIFER ROBERSON, Co-Author
KATE ELLIOTT, Co-Author

## The Golden Key
(New York: DAW, 1996)

**Story type:** Fantasy (Political; Romance)
**Major character(s):** Saavedra Grijalva, Artist (painter); Sario Grijalva, Artist (painter), Nobleman (Lord Limner); Alejandro do'Verrada, Nobleman (duke)
**Time period(s):** 10th century (940s); 14th century (1310s)
**Locale(s):** Tira Virte, Fictional Country; Meya Suerta, Fictional City; Palasso Grijalva, Mythical Place

**Summary:** Driven by his twin obsessions, immortality and his cousin, Saavedra, Sario Grijalva secretly delves into the dark magic of the Book of Kita'ab to unlock the secrets that can bring him both. Sario vents his jealous frustration by imprisoning Saavedra in a portrait he paints of her. For the next 300 years, Sario labors to perfect his own art and to hone the murderous techniques that allow him to steal the lives of other gifted, young, male family members. One day, the aged magic falters and Saavedra steps from her portrait into the real world.

**Other books you might like:**
Aaron Allston, *Galatea in 2-D*, 1993
Ray Bradbury, *Something Wicked This Way Comes*, 1962
Charles de Lint, *Memory and Dream*, 1994
Suzette Haden Elgin, *Native Tongue*, 1984
Kate Elliott, *An Earthly Crown*, 1993
    pseudonym of Alis A. Rasmussen
Michael King, *Loren Lost*, 1996
Jennifer Roberson, *Shapechangers*, 1984

---

**4487**

MELANIE RAWN

## Knights of the Morningstar
(New York: Ace, 1994)

**Story type:** Science Fiction (Time Travel)
**Series:** Quantum Leap
**Major character(s):** Sam Beckett, Time Traveler, Scientist; Cynthia "Lady Cyndara" Mulloy, Editor
**Time period(s):** 1980s (July 1987)
**Locale(s):** New York (Medieval Chivalry League tournament)

**Summary:** Sam's leap lands him amid medieval recreationists where people expect him to win the favors of a fair lady through his prowess at sword fighting. Sam's difficulties increase as another leaper threatens the project and Sam's life. Television tie-in.

**Other books you might like:**
Chris Claremont, *Dragon Moon*, 1994
    Beth Fleisher, co-author
Melissa Crandall, *Search and Rescue*, 1994
Ashley McConnell, *Prelude*, 1994
Ashley McConnell, *Quantum Leap: The Novel*, 1992
Ashley McConnell, *Too Close for Comfort*, 1993
Ashley McConnell, *The Wall*, 1994

---

Pamela F. Service, *All's Faire*, 1993

---

**4488**

MELANIE RAWN

## The Mageborn Traitor
(New York: DAW, 1997)

**Story type:** Fantasy (Political; Magic Conflict)
**Series:** Exiles
**Major character(s):** Cailet Ambrai Rille, Leader (Mage Captal), Teacher (magic); Collan Rosvenir, Minstrel (lute), Nobleman; Sarra Ambrai Liwellan, Political Figure (councillor), Noblewoman
**Time period(s):** Indeterminate
**Locale(s):** Lenfell, Planet—Imaginary

**Summary:** Cailet's and Sarra's sister, Glenin, now leads the Malerris, long-time enemy of the Mage Guardians. As Glenin and her son violently undermine Cailet's efforts to rebuild the decimated ranks of the Mage Guardians, Lady Sarra struggles politically to bring about the legal reforms necessary to break the rigid caste system and create a more equal society. All if Lenfell braces itself for another cataclysmic magical struggle that will determine the long-term political and economic destiny of their world. Second in series.

**Other books you might like:**
Steven Brust, *Jhereg*, 1983
Barbara Hambly, *The Ladies of Mandrigyn*, 1984
Katherine Kurtz, *The Bastard Prince*, 1994
Elizabeth Moon, *Liar's Oath*, 1992
Harry Turtledove, *Krispos of Videssos*, 1991
Paula Volsky, *Illusion*, 1992
Paul O. Williams, *The Breaking of Northwall*, 1980
Roger Zelazny, *Nine Princes in Amber*, 1970

---

**4489**

MELANIE RAWN

## The Ruins of Ambrai
(New York: DAW, 1994)

**Story type:** Fantasy (Political; Magic Conflict)
**Series:** Exiles
**Major character(s):** Sarra Ambrai Liwellan, Adoptee, Heiress; Avira Anniyas, Political Figure, Psychic (Mage); Gorynal Desse, Psychic (Mage), Revolutionary
**Time period(s):** Indeterminate
**Locale(s):** Lenfell, Planet—Imaginary

**Summary:** Orphaned when her mother dies in childbirth after her father kidnaps her older sister and burns Ambrai, Sarra, warded, forgets her newborn sister until meeting her years later. Already determined to change the matriarchal, hierarchic nature of her society, Sarra intends to join the Rising, which plans to overthrow the government of First Counsellor Anniyas and restore the freedom of the Guardian Mages. However, her older sister, Glenin, plans to control the government through her husband, Anniyas' only child.

**Other books you might like:**
Laurell K. Hamilton, *Nightseer*, 1992
Robert Jordan, *The Eye of the World*, 1989
Elizabeth Moon, *Liar's Oath*, 1992
Midori Snyder, *Beldan's Fire*, 1993
Tad Williams, *The Dragonbone Chair*, 1989

## 4490

### MELANIE RAWN

### *Skybowl*

(New York: DAW, 1993)

**Story type:** Fantasy (Political; Magic Conflict)
**Series:** Dragon Star
**Major character(s):** Sioned, Royalty (high princess); Pol, Royalty (high prince), Magician; Meiglan, Royalty (high princess)
**Time period(s):** Indeterminate
**Locale(s):** Fictional Country

**Summary:** Pol continues plans for the final battle with the Vellanti to take place at Skybowl. Meiglan, still in the hands of the enemy, sends a message to Pol warning that her ritual death will bless the battle. A magic mirror reveals many historical secrets and proves usable by Pol who now understands the Vellanti and the reasons for the war. Pol begins to understand his father's political philosophy and continues to attempt cooperation with Andry, eventually vowing again to become High Prince for all the people in his domain, and to never again utilize his gifts for killing.

**Other books you might like:**
David Eddings, *Pawn of Prophecy*, 1982
C.S. Friedman, *Black Sun Rising*, 1991
Anne McCaffrey, *Dragonflight*, 1968
Ron Miller, *Silk and Steel*, 1992
Elizabeth Moon, *Oath of Gold*, 1989
Shirley Rousseau Murphy, *Nightpool*, 1987
Paula Volsky, *Illusion*, 1992

## 4491

### MELANIE RAWN

### *The Star Scroll*

(New York: DAW, 1989)

**Story type:** Fantasy (Political)
**Series:** Dragon Prince
**Major character(s):** Rohan, Royalty, Ruler (High Prince); Masul, Revolutionary
**Time period(s):** Indeterminate
**Locale(s):** Fictional Country

**Summary:** Rohan and Sioned must defend both their reign and their son when an ancient scroll is discovered, giving Rohan's enemies a chance to defeat him.

**Other books you might like:**
Margaret Weis, *Elven Star*, 1990
    Tracy Hickman, co-author
Elizabeth H. Boyer, *The Clan of the Warlord*, 1992
Paula Volsky, *Illusion*, 1992
Mercedes Lackey, *Winds of Fury*, 1993

## 4492

### MELANIE RAWN

### *Stronghold*

(New York: DAW, 1990)

**Story type:** Fantasy (Magic Conflict; Political)
**Series:** Dragon Star
**Major character(s):** Rohan, Royalty (prince), Ruler; Sioned, Ruler (queen), Magician (sunrunner); Andry, Ruler (lord of Goddess Keep), Magician (sunrunner)
**Time period(s):** Indeterminate
**Locale(s):** Fictional Country

**Summary:** After several decades of peaceful, intelligent, progressive rule under Rohan and Sioned, and several centuries of constructive, if occasionally manipulative use of Faradhi magic by the Sunrunners of Goddess Keep, the realm is threatened by invaders from overseas. Believing that the invasion force is a tool of long outlawed Diamardhi sorcerers, Andry has been seeking knowledge of their craft and destruction of all its practitoners. His obsession puts him at odds with Rohan and Sioned and threatens to destroy the realm from within, whether or not the invaders are stopped.

**Other books you might like:**
Patricia Kennealy-Morrison, *The Copper Crown*, 1984
Katherine Kurtz, *Deryni Rising*, 1970
Anne McCaffrey, *Dragonflight*, 1968
Jennifer Roberson, *Shapechangers*, 1984
Joel Rosenberg, *The Sleeping Dragon*, 1983

## 4493

### MELANIE RAWN

### *Sunrunner's Fire*

(New York: DAW, 1990)

**Story type:** Fantasy (Political)
**Series:** Dragon Prince
**Major character(s):** Pol, Royalty (Prince); Andry, Nobleman, Magician
**Time period(s):** Indeterminate
**Locale(s):** Fictional Country

**Summary:** Challenged by rivals to the throne and by his cousin Andry who opposes him and his father, Pol repels their attempts at sorcery and murder.

**Other books you might like:**
Constance Ash, *The Stalking Horse*, 1990
Glen Cook, *Tower of Fear*, 1989
Raymond E. Feist, *Magician: Apprentice*, 1986
Mary H. Herbert, *Dark Horse*, 1990
Guy Gavriel Kay, *The Summer Tree*, 1985
    The Fionavar Tapestry: Book 1
Anne McCaffrey, *Dragonflight*, 1981
    Vol 1 - Dragon Riders of Pern
Shirley Rousseau Murphy, *Nightpool*, 1987
    Book 1 - Dragonbards Trilogy

## 4494

### FRED OLEN RAY, Editor

### *Weird Menace*

(Hollywood, CA: American Independent Press, 1994)

**Story type:** Horror (Anthology)

**Summary:** The editor, best known as a filmmaker, has assembled thirteen homages to the weird menace pulps, which featured tales of heroes and heroines threatened by apparently supernatural menaces that almost always prove to be the work of mortal, if demented, criminals. Hugh Cave, who wrote for the original weird menace pulps in the 1930s, contributes two stories: "Don't Open the Door" tells of a young bride's ordeal at the hands of her mother-in-law's Satanic cult, and "The Kutting Edge" (written under his "Justin Case" pseudonym) is about an amoral writer of horror fiction whose dabbling in metaphysics results in the horrors of his imagination coming to life. Richard Gilliam's "Hotel Stygia" concerns a man's efforts to free a young woman and her daughter from the clutches of a death cult, and Greg Nicoll mixes Nazi atrocities with native magic in ''Nazi Jungle Fury.'' Although published in 1994, this book was not available until 1995.

**Other books you might like:**
John Hanlon, *Death's Loving Arms and Other Terror Tales*, 1966
    editor
John Hanlon, *The House of Living Death and Other Terror Tales*, 1966
    editor
Sheldon Jaffery, *The Weirds*, 1987
    editor
Robert Weinberg, *Weird Menace 1: The Corpse Factory*, 1977
    editor
Robert Weinberg, *Weird Menace 2: Satan's Roadhouse*, 1977

## 4495

**JAMES E. REAGEN**

### The League of the Crimson Crescent

(Rocklin, California: Prima Proteus, 1995)

**Story type:** Fantasy (Alternate World; Political)
**Major character(s):** Bill ''Bill the Just'' Evans, Accountant, Hero
**Time period(s):** Indeterminate
**Locale(s):** The Empire, Fictional Country

**Summary:** Rendered unconscious while spelunking in the Adirondacks, Bill Evans awakens in a magical land populated by unpleasant mythical creatures. When Bill defeats a slave owner and liberates the human slaves, many believe the long neglected rebellion has resurfaced. First fiction and first of a computer game tie-in series.

**Other books you might like:**
Bruce Balfour, *Star Crusader*, 1995
Aaron Conners, *The Pandora Directive: A Tex Murphy Novel*, 1995
Matthew J. Costello, *The 7th Guest*, 1995
Arthur Byron Cover, *Planetfall*, 1988
Mercedes Lackey, *Castle of Deception*, 1992
    Josepha Sherman, co-author
Craig Mills, *The Floating Castle*, 1995
Chet Williamson, *Hell: A Cyberpunk Thriller*, 1995

## 4496

**MICHAEL REAVES**

### Night Hunter

(New York: Tor, 1991)

**Story type:** Horror (Vampire Story; Mystery)
**Major character(s):** Jake Hull, Detective—Police; Dan Stratton, Police Officer; Tace Daggett, Entertainer (stand-up comic)
**Time period(s):** 1990s (1995)
**Locale(s):** Hollywood, California

**Summary:** A series of murders in which victims are found with stakes driven through their hearts suggests to detective Jake Hull and the Los Angeles Police Department that a lunatic who believes in vampires is on the rampage. But the deeper they probe the crimes, the more they begin to wonder whether there really aren't vampires prowling the streets at night.

**Other books you might like:**
Peter Atkins, *Morningstar*, 1992
Warren Newton Beath, *Bloodletter*, 1994
Brian Lumley, *Necroscope*, 1986
Les Whitten, *Progeny of the Adder*, 1965

## 4497

**MICHAEL REAVES**

### Street Magic

(New York: Tor, 1991)

**Story type:** Fantasy (Quest; Urban)
**Major character(s):** Danny Thayer, Child, Heir—Lost (Keymaster); Robin, Child, Mythical Creature (fairy ''scatterling''); Scott Russell, Detective—Private
**Time period(s):** 1990s
**Locale(s):** San Francisco, California

**Summary:** Danny and Robin search for a way to open the path to Fairyland, closed by the Queen of Fairie. As they journey through familiar San Francisco landmarks, Danny is informed that he is a Keymaster and can open the needed pathway. As time grows short and the situation becomes deadly, Danny must discover his abilities or lose all.

**Other books you might like:**
Michael de Larrabeiti, *The Borribles*, 1978
Michael de Larrabeiti, *The Borribles Go for Broke*, 1982
Charles de Lint, *Ghosts of Wind and Shadow*, 1991
Edith Pattou, *Hero's Song*, 1991
Will Shetterly, *Elsewhere*, 1991
Terri Windling, *Life on the Border*, 1991
    editor

## 4498

**MICHAEL REAVES**

### Voodoo Child

(New York: Tor, 1998)

**Story type:** Horror (Black Magic)
**Major character(s):** Shane LaFitte, Religious (Voudoun priest); Jorge ''Mal Sangre'' Arnez, Religious (Voudoun priest); Lia St. Charles, Probation Officer
**Time period(s):** 1990s (1998)
**Locale(s):** New Orleans, Louisiana

**Summary:** Newly paroled from prison, where he served time for murdering his wife while under a voodoo spell, houngan Shane LaFitte, a practitioner of white magic, crosses paths with Jorge Arnez, the man who engineered his wife's murder, and who is now a powerful black magic priest known throughout New Orleans as ''Mal Sangre.'' Shane struggles to work within the legal constraints imposed by his parole as he attempts to eliminate the scourge of Mal Sangre, before the priest can take over the city.

**Other books you might like:**
Alex Abella, *The Killing of the Saints*, 1992
Lisa Cantrell, *Boneman*, 1992
Hugh B. Cave, *Legion of the Dead*, 1979
Don Davis, *The Gris-Gris Man*, 1997
Brian Hodge, *The Darker Saints*, 1993

## 4499

**DANA REED** (Pseudonym of Edwina Berkman)

### Demon Within

(New York: Leisure, 1993)

**Story type:** Horror (Black Magic)
**Major character(s):** Samantha Croft, Insurance Agent; Don Wheatley, Detective—Police; Garrett Land, Businessman

**Time period(s):** 1980s (1988)
**Locale(s):** New York, New York

**Summary:** Samatha Croft's apartment building is visited nightly—and sometimes twice a night—by a murderer who steals body parts from his victims, and who consulting occultists think is trying to replace parts of his own body that were transformed during a bungled summoning ceremony. This novel was originally published in 1988.

**Other books you might like:**
Clive Barker, *The Hellbound Heart*, 1991
Steven Ray Fulgham, *The Forsaken*, 1991
Stephen R. George, *The Forgotten*, 1991
Melisand March, *The Site*, 1988
Roland Topor, *The Tenant*, 1966

### 4500

#### RICK R. REED

## Obsessed

(New York: Dell Abyss, 1991)

**Story type:** Horror (Psychological Suspense)
**Major character(s):** Joe Macaree, Advertising; Pat Young, Invalid; Anne Macaree, Model (fashion model)
**Time period(s):** 1990s
**Locale(s):** Chicago, Illinois

**Summary:** In this stupendously silly first novel psychologically twisted advertising executive Joe Macaree, a victim of abuse when a child, finds himself in a jam when blackmailed by a wheelchair-bound woman who has seen him commit murder and drink his victim's blood.

**Other books you might like:**
Theodore Sturgeon, *Some of Your Blood*, 1961
Cornell Woolrich, *It Had to Be Murder*, 1988
   in *Rear Window and Other Stories*

### 4501

#### RICK R. REED

## Penance

(New York: Dell/Abyss, 1993)

**Story type:** Horror (Psychological Suspense)
**Major character(s):** Jimmy Fels, Teenager (13-years-old), Runaway; Richard Grebb, Religious (ex-priest); Dwight Morris, Businessman
**Time period(s):** 1990s (1993)
**Locale(s):** Chicago, Illinois

**Summary:** His life in ruins because of his pedophilic tendencies, Dwight Morris begins abducting and torturing the street children of Chicago, hoping eventually to get back, through them, at Jimmy Fels, a teenage hustler who escaped his clutches. With the help of Richard Grebb, an ex-priest and former pedophile, Jimmy returns to fight Morris and save his fellow vagabonds.

**Other books you might like:**
J.M. Dillard, *Specters*, 1991
Thomas Harris, *The Silence of the Lambs*, 1988
Ruby Jean Jensen, *The Reckoning*, 1992
David Martin, *Bring Me Children*, 1992
Whitley Strieber, *Billy*, 1990

### 4502

#### ROBERT REED

## Beneath the Gated Sky

(New York: Tor, 1997)

**Story type:** Science Fiction (Space Opera; Family Saga)
**Major character(s):** Porsche Neal, Alien (The Few), Fugitive; Cornell Novak, Fugitive; Trinidad, Alien (The Few), Traitor
**Time period(s):** 1990s
**Locale(s):** Texas; Jartee, Planet—Imaginary

**Summary:** On the run from the Cosmic Events Agency, an organization formed to investigate the mysterious Portal that replaced Earth's starry sky with a reflection of the planet, Porsche and Cornell try to prevent corrupt government officials from using alien technology to give the United States an unfair advantage over the rest of the world. Sequel to *Beyond the Veil of Stars*.

**Other books you might like:**
Greg Egan, *Quarantine*, 1995
Steven Gould, *Wildside*, 1996
Zenna Henderson, *Ingathering: The Complete People Stories of Zenna Henderson*, 1995
Frederik Pohl, *The Other End of Time*, 1996
Michaela Roessner, *Vanishing Point*, 1993
John E. Stith, *Reunion on Neverend*, 1994

### 4503

#### ROBERT REED

## Beyond the Veil of Stars

(New York: Tor, 1994)

**Story type:** Science Fiction (UFO; First Contact)
**Major character(s):** Cornell Novak, Traveler, Adventurer; Pete Forrest, Neighbor, Traveler; Porsche Neal, Alien, Traveler
**Time period(s):** 1990s
**Locale(s):** United States; Planet—Imaginary

**Summary:** Cornell remembers hunting for aliens since he was five years old and his mother disappeared. When the sky everts, he gains hope for her return, but by the time he turns 15, he doubts his memories of an alien kidnapping and leaves home. When he starts work for an undercover government agency, he realizes his father's search for extra-terrestrials had merit.

**Other books you might like:**
David Brin, *Earth*, 1990
Gwyneth Jones, *White Queen*, 1993
Sheri S. Tepper, *Raising the Stones*, 1990
Vernor Vinge, *A Fire upon the Deep*, 1992
George Zebrowski, *Stranger Suns*, 1991

### 4504

#### ROBERT REED

## Black Milk

(New York: Donald I. Fine, 1989)

**Story type:** Science Fiction (Genetic Manipulation)
**Major character(s):** Ryder, Genetically Altered Being; Cody, Genetically Altered Being
**Time period(s):** 21st century
**Locale(s):** Earth

**Summary:** Genetic mapping has reached a level of sophistication where it is possible for parents to order children with special talents. Ryder has a perfect memory, Cody superior physical skills, Marshall is a genius. As they grow up, the genetically-tailored children find themselves both increasingly alienated from normal humanity and increasingly aware of the way they are manipulated by those in power.

**Other books you might like:**
John Brunner, *Children of the Thunder*, 1989
Lois McMaster Bujold, *Falling Free*, 1988
Daniel Keys Moran, *Emerald Eyes*, 1988
John Wyndham, *The Midwich Cuckoos*, 1957

---

**4505**

**ROBERT REED**

## Down the Bright Way

(New York: Bantam Spectra, 1991)

**Story type:** Science Fiction (First Contact; Adventure)
**Major character(s):** Kyle Stevens Hastings, Imposter, Wanderer; Jy, Leader, Wanderer; Moliak, Cyborg, Wanderer
**Time period(s):** Indeterminate
**Locale(s):** Earth

**Summary:** Kyle poses as a Wanderer when Jy and her fellow Wanderers come to Earth with stories of multiple Earths all connected by the Bright, and of the Wanderers' attempts to contact and unite all humans. Kyle's ruse remains unchallenged until he attends Jy's rally and finds himself kidnapped then transported far from his Earth in a scheme which could destroy the Bright and the Wanderers' search for the Makers.

**Other books you might like:**
Roger MacBride Allen, *The Ring of Charon*, 1990
Greg Bear, *Eon*, 1985
David Brin, *Startide Rising*, 1983
Orson Scott Card, *Ender's Game*, 1985
Glen Cook, *The Dragon Never Sleeps*, 1988
John DeChancie, *Paradox Alley*, 1987
John DeChancie, *Red Limit Freeway*, 1984
John DeChancie, *Starrigger*, 1983
Philip K. Dick, *The Unteleported Man*, 1983 revised
Michael P. Kube-McDowell, *Enigma*, 1986
Vonda N. McIntyre, *Transition*, 1991
Alis A. Rasmussen, *The Price of Ransom*, 1990

---

**4506**

**ROBERT REED**

## An Exaltation of Larks

(New York: Tor, 1995)

**Story type:** Science Fiction (Immortality; Mystical)
**Major character(s):** Jesse Aylesworth, Student—College, Editor; Sully Faulkner, Student—College; The Indian, Time Traveler, Mythical Creature (turtle)
**Time period(s):** 1970s (1978); Indeterminate Future (end of the universe)
**Locale(s):** Warner, Midwest

**Summary:** Accepting a ride from Sully during a blizzard, Jesse realizes she seems somehow more familiar than she should. Events such as the radio failing to work, a turtle disappearing from the science lab, and Sully appearing similar to the woman in his Breton

print, all portend the visit from the Indian who recruits Jesse to help change the future and make humans immortal.

**Other books you might like:**
John Brunner, *Age of Miracles*, 1973
Arthur C. Clarke, *Childhood's End*, 1953
Frederik Pohl, *The World at the End of Time*, 1990
Vernor Vinge, *Marooned in Realtime*, 1986
Robert Charles Wilson, *The Harvest*, 1993

---

**4507**

**ROBERT REED**

## The Remarkables

(New York: Bantam Spectra, 1992)

**Story type:** Science Fiction (Adventure)
**Major character(s):** Service, Guide, Leader; Ranier, Empath, Adventurer; Talker, Alien (Remarkable)
**Time period(s):** Indeterminate Future
**Locale(s):** Pitcairn, Planet—Imaginary

**Summary:** A few offworld humans plus Pitcairn humans who live symbiotically with Remarkable settlements accompany juvenile Remarkables on their deadly, mandated rite of passage to a remote, religiously significant area of Pitcairn.

**Other books you might like:**
David Drake, *The Jungle*, 1991
Brian Herbert, *The Race for God*, 1990
David R. Palmer, *Emergence*, 1984
Alexei Panshin, *Rite of Passage*, 1968
Robert Silverberg, *The Face of the Waters*, 1991
Dan Simmons, *The Fall of Hyperion*, 1990
Dan Simmons, *Hyperion*, 1989
Sheri S. Tepper, *Grass*, 1989

---

**4508**

**GARFIELD REEVES-STEVENS**

## Bloodshift

(New York: Popular Library, 1990)

**Story type:** Horror (Vampire Story; Science Fiction)
**Major character(s):** Granger Helman, Murderer; Adrienne St. Clair, Scientist, Vampire; Eduardo Diego y Rey, Vampire
**Time period(s):** 1980s (1980)
**Locale(s):** Toronto, Ontario, Canada

**Summary:** A retired contract killer is blackmailed into becoming involved in a 400-year war between a secret organization of vampires called the Conclave which seeks to dominate the world and a no-less-secret sect of Jesuits. Granger is comissioned to administer The Final Death to the traitorous vampire Adrienne St. Clair, who has discovered the non-supernatural scientific basis of vampirism and who is also being pursued by the Royal Canadian Mounted Police, British Intelligence, a secret American group called Project Nevada, another secret organization of vampires, and the CIA. The result is a complex, uneven meld of SF, espionage novel, political adventure, paranoid conspiracty thriller, and vampire tale which was originally published in Canada in 1981 by Virgo, a small press.

**Other books you might like:**
Barbara Hambly, *Those Who Hunt the Night*, 1988
James Herbert, *Sepulchre*, 1987
Lee Killough, *Blood Links*, 1988
Anne Rice, *The Vampire Lestat*, 1985
Brian Stableford, *The Empire of Fear*, 1988

Whitley Strieber, *The Hunger*, 1981
Les Whitten, *Progeny of the Adder*, 1965

### 4509
**GARFIELD REEVES-STEVENS**

## Dark Matter
(New York: Doubleday, 1990)

**Story type:** Horror (Psychological Suspense)
**Major character(s):** Anthony Cross, Scientist (theoretical physicist), Serial Killer; Charis Neale, Scientist (Cross's lover); Katherine Duvall, Detective—Homicide
**Time period(s):** 1990s (1995)
**Locale(s):** Los Angeles, California

**Summary:** A talented black homicide detective becomes obsessed with her pursuit of charismatic but deranged high-energy physicist and serial killer Anthony Cross, who by slaughter seeks to understand the mysteries of quantum mechanics and thus bridge the chasm between life and death. Meanwhile, Cross's fellow physicist and girlfriend, Charis Neale, tries to keep stable his increasingly testy relationship with his employers, the evil conglomerate known as Cathedral Three.

**Other books you might like:**
Thomas Harris, *The Silence of the Lambs*, 1988
Dean R. Koontz, *The Bad Place*, 1990
Dean R. Koontz, *Midnight*, 1989

### 4510
**GARFIELD REEVES-STEVENS**

## Nighteyes
(New York: Doubleday Foundation, 1989)

**Story type:** Science Fiction (UFO)
**Major character(s):** Sarah Gilmour, Parent; Wendy Gilmour, Teenager
**Time period(s):** 1980s
**Locale(s):** Connecticut

**Summary:** The Gilmour family is bedeviled by shadowy aliens, evidently from UFOs. The sadistic aliens seem bent on abducting Wendy and conducting genetic experiments.

**Other books you might like:**
Robert A. Heinlein, *The Puppet Masters*, 1951
Fritz Leiber, *The Wanderer*, 1964
Whitley Strieber, *Majestic*, 1989

### 4511
**JUDITH REEVES-STEVENS**
**GARFIELD REEVES-STEVENS**, Co-Author

## Federation
(New York: Pocket, 1994)

**Story type:** Science Fiction (Space Opera)
**Series:** Star Trek
**Major character(s):** Jean-Luc Picard, Spaceship Captain, Military Personnel; James T. Kirk, Spaceship Captain; Zefrem Cochrane, Scientist, Space Explorer
**Time period(s):** 23rd century; 24th century
**Locale(s):** *U.S.S. Enterprise*, Spaceship

**Summary:** Zefrem Cochrane thought he had found a safe haven on Gamma Canaris where his 21st century enemies could not follow him, but someone in the 23rd century accesses Captain Kirk's personal logs containing the secret and kidnaps Cochrane. Pursuing the kidnappers, the *Enterprise* enters the event horizon of a black hole. A hundred years later, Picard's *Enterprise* bargains for a mysterious Preserver artifact containing the personality of Cochrane's enemy which takes over the ship and Commander Data. When the two *Enterprise*s meet in the black hole, only their complete cooperation can save both ships and Zefrem Cochrane.

**Other books you might like:**
Alfred Bester, *The Stars My Destination*, 1956
Margaret Wander Bonanno, *Strangers From the Sky*, 1987
Diane Duane, *The Wounded Sky*, 1983
Dean McLaughlin, *The Man Who Wanted Stars*, 1965
Frederik Pohl, *Beyond the Blue Event Horizon*, 1980
Garfield Reeves-Stevens, *Memory Prime*, 1988
    Judith Reeves-Stevens, co-author

### 4512
**JUDITH REEVES-STEVENS**
**GARFIELD REEVES-STEVENS**, Co-Author

## Icefire
(New York: Pocket, 1998)

**Story type:** Science Fiction (Techno-Thriller)
**Major character(s):** Mitch Webber, Military Personnel (captain); Cory Rey, Scientist (oceanographer)
**Time period(s):** 1990s (1999)
**Locale(s):** Antarctica

**Summary:** Terrorists have exploded several stolen nuclear weapons in the Antarctic, and the Ross ice shelf has broken loose. The initial event kills most of those in the immediate area, but far more deadly is the series of tidal waves of unprecedented force which will be striking land all around the Pacific Basin in a matter of hours. Former lovers Webber and Rey use technology to stop the waves.

**Other books you might like:**
Laurence Delaney, *The Triton Ultimatum*, 1977
Daniel V. Gallery, *The Brink*, 1968
Trevor Hoyle, *The Last Gasp*, 1983
Basil Jackson, *State of Emergency*, 1982
William H. Lovejoy, *White Night*, 1994

### 4513
**JUDITH REEVES-STEVENS**
**GARFIELD REEVES-STEVENS**, Co-Author

## Nightfeeder
(New York: Roc, 1991)

**Story type:** Fantasy (Alternate World; Quest)
**Series:** Chronicles of Galen Sword
**Major character(s):** Galen Sword, Adventurer, Businessman; Melody Ko, Adventurer, Engineer
**Time period(s):** Indeterminate Future
**Locale(s):** New York, New York

**Summary:** Because Galen Sword was born human and totally without magical powers, he was sent by his parents to an alternate world, Earth. When he discovers his true heritage, his search for a way to return to the First World makes him the focal point in a war between two clans. Galen's survival ends up depending on his alliance with a being from the First World, Orion Clan Isis, a vampire.

**Other books you might like:**
Robert N. Charrette, *Never Deal with a Dragon*, 1990
Nancy A. Collins, *Sunglasses After Dark*, 1989
Barbara Hambly, *Dragonsbane*, 1986
Tad Williams, *The Dragonbone Chair*, 1989
Chelsea Quinn Yarbro, *A Candle for D'Artagnan*, 1989

---

**4514**

### JUDITH REEVES-STEVENS
### GARFIELD REEVES-STEVENS, Co-Author

## *Prime Directive*
(New York: Pocket, 1990)

**Story type:** Science Fiction (Space Opera)
**Series:** Star Trek
**Major character(s):** James T. Kirk, Spaceship Captain; Spock, Scientist, Alien; Leonard McCoy, Doctor
**Time period(s):** 23rd century
**Locale(s):** *U.S.S. Enterprise*, Spaceship; Starfleet First Contact Office, Space Station; Talos IV, Planet—Imaginary

**Summary:** After being discredited by Starfleet for violation of their prime directive, to avoid interfering in cultures not affiliated with the United Federation of Planets, the *U.S.S. Enterprise* bridge crew must clear their names and restore their rank.

**Other books you might like:**
Carolyn Clowes, *The Pandora Principle*, 1990
    Star Trek 49
Diane Duane, *Doctor's Orders*, 1990
    Star Trek 50
Julia Ecklar, *The Kobayashi Maru*, 1990
    Star Trek 47
Michael Jan Friedman, *Double, Double*, 1989
    Star Trek 45
Peter Morwood, *Rules of Engagement*, 1990
    Star Trek 48

---

**4515**

### JUDITH REEVES-STEVENS
### GARFIELD REEVES-STEVENS, Co-Author

## *Shifter*
(New York: Roc, 1990)

**Story type:** Fantasy (Alternate World; Quest)
**Series:** Chronicles of Galen Sword
**Major character(s):** Galen Sword, Adventurer, Businessman; Melody Ko, Adventurer, Engineer; Adrian Forsyte, Scientist
**Time period(s):** Indeterminate Future
**Locale(s):** New York, New York

**Summary:** Galen Sword, a rich New York playboy haunted by shadowy memories of being sent away from his beloved parents, has embarked on a deadly and seemingly impossible quest. A near-fatal car accident leads Galen to the knowledge that he was really from a parallel world, not Earth, and had been heir to a powerful dynasty. With the help of a staff of "unusually" talented people, Galen must find his way back home by capturing a being that has crossed over from that world to his one. The being is a werewolf.

**Other books you might like:**
Marion Zimmer Bradley, *Hawkmistress!*, 1982
Robert Jordan, *The Eye of the World*, 1989
Stephen King, *Silver Bullet*, 1985
Michael Moorcock, *The Fortress of the Pearl*, 1989

Sydney J. Van Scyoc, *Feather Stroke*, 1989

---

**4516**

### MICKEY ZUCKER REICHERT

## *Beyond Ragnarok*
(New York: DAW, 1996)

**Story type:** Fantasy (Legend; Adventure)
**Series:** Renshai Chronicles
**Major character(s):** Kevral Tainharsdartter, Thief, Adventurer; Rakhir of Erythane, Apprentice, Knight; Tae Kahn, Teenager, Warrior (Renshai)
**Time period(s):** Indeterminate Past
**Locale(s):** Bearn, Fictional Country

**Summary:** Three centuries after the final battle of the gods, the search for the successor for a dying human king involves unprecedented trials, precipitated by widespread attacks on legitimate heirs.

**Other books you might like:**
Linda Evans, *Sleipnir*, 1994
Jason Henderson, *The Spawn of Loki*, 1994
Martha Wells, *The Element of Fire*, 1993
Janny Wurts, *Curse of the Mistwraith*, 1994

---

**4517**

### MICKEY ZUCKER REICHERT

## *By Chaos Cursed*
(New York: DAW, 1991)

**Story type:** Fantasy (Magic Conflict; Adventure)
**Series:** Bifrost Guardians
**Major character(s):** Al Larson, Military Personnel, Mythical Creature (elf); Silme, Sorceress; Taziar Medakan, Thief
**Time period(s):** 1960s (1968); 10th century
**Locale(s):** New York, New York; Europe, Alternate Universe

**Summary:** When Al Larson died in Vietnam calling on the Norse gods, they transferred his life energy into the body of an elf in their universe, so that he could save one of the gods. Now Allerum and his friends Silme, Taziar and Astryd, are in danger from the sorcerer Bolverkr, whose destruction would upset the balance between Law and Chaos. In the ensuing magical battle, Al is flung back to his own body in New York City of 1968, where he must destroy Bolverkr, rescue Silme from the Dragon mage's influence, keep Taziar out of jail, and avoid getting sent to Vietnam again.

**Other books you might like:**
L. Sprague de Camp, *The Incomplete Enchanter*, 1942
    Fletcher Pratt, co-author
Jude Deveraux, *A Knight in Shining Armor*, 1989
Phyllis Eisenstein, *Shadow of Earth*, 1979
Barbara Hambly, *Dragonsbane*, 1986
Barbara Hambly, *The Time of the Dark*, 1987
R.A. MacAvoy, *Tea with the Black Dragon*, 1983
Bill Ransom, *Jaguar*, 1990
Roger Zelazny, *Nine Princes in Amber*, 1970

## 4518

### MICKEY ZUCKER REICHERT

### *The Children of Wrath*

(New York: DAW, 1998)

**Story type:** Fantasy (Magic Conflict)
**Series:** Renshai Chronicles
**Major character(s):** Kevral Tainharsdarter, Warrior (Renshai); Tae Kahn, Royalty (prince); Ra-Hir, Knight
**Time period(s):** Indeterminate
**Locale(s):** Midgard, Mythical Place

**Summary:** Following Ragnarok, the human race has been cursed with nearly total sterility. When it appears that wars will be fought to control the few children still being born, a group of heroes sets out to enter a series of other worlds in order to gather together the shards of a magical stone that can lift the curse.

**Other books you might like:**
Poul Anderson, *The Broken Sword*, 1954
Charles Barnitz, *The Deepest Sea*, 1996
Thorarinn Gunnarsson, *Song of the Dwarves*, 1988
Harry Harrison, *The Hammer and the Cross*, 1993
Bernard King, *Starkadder*, 1985

## 4519

### MICKEY ZUCKER REICHERT

### *Dragonrank Master*

(New York: DAW, 1989)

**Story type:** Fantasy (Legend)
**Series:** Bifrost Guardians
**Major character(s):** Al Larson, Military Personnel (Vietnam veteran), Mythical Creature (elf); Gaelinar, Companion (of Al)
**Time period(s):** Indeterminate
**Locale(s):** Midgard, Mythical Place

**Summary:** Al discovers there is a possibility that he can bring his lover, Silme, back from the dead, but only if he can outsmart the goddess, Hel. Unfortunately Loki's wolfson and the other gods are doing everything they can to stop Al and Gaelinar from achieving this goal.

**Other books you might like:**
Robert Adams, *Stairway to Forever*, 1988
Alan Dean Foster, *Spellsinger*, 1981
Kate Green, *Contrarywise*, 1989
Morgan Llywelyn, *The Isles of the Blest*, 1989
Robin McKinley, *The Outlaws of Sherwood*, 1989
Gail Van Asten, *Charlemagne's Champion*, 1990

## 4520

### MICKEY ZUCKER REICHERT

### *The Last of the Renshai*

(New York: DAW, 1992)

**Story type:** Fantasy (Sword and Sorcery)
**Series:** Renshai Chronicles
**Major character(s):** Rache Kallmirsson, Warrior; Shadimar, Wizard; Mitrian, Warrior
**Time period(s):** Indeterminate Past
**Locale(s):** Northlands, Fictional Country

**Summary:** The ancient prophecies foretold that a Renshai warrior would be a hero in the Great War, the final battle that will usher in the Age of Change which would destroy mortals, wizards and the gods themselves. Rache, only survivor of an attack on his homeland, is the last of the Renshai. As the Swordmaster for the ruler Santagithi, he fights for his life and for vengeance.

**Other books you might like:**
C.J. Cherryh, *The Fires of Azeroth*, 1979
Stephen R. Donaldson, *Lord Foul's Bane*, 1977
Phyllis Eisenstein, *Born to Exile*, 1978
Barbara Hambly, *The Time of the Dark*, 1987
C.L. Moore, *Jirel of Joiry*, 1969
J.R.R. Tolkien, *The Fellowship of the Ring*, 1954

## 4521

### MICKEY ZUCKER REICHERT

### *The Legend of Nightfall*

(New York: DAW, 1993)

**Story type:** Fantasy (Adventure; Quest)
**Major character(s):** Nightfall, Thief; Edward Nargol, Royalty (prince); Kelryn, Dancer
**Time period(s):** Indeterminate Past
**Locale(s):** Alyndar, Fictional Country

**Summary:** Finally captured after years on the run, Nightfall must choose between execution and a magically enforced oath to become squire to the irritatingly idealistic and naive Prince Edward, see that he establishes himself by becoming landed and keep him out of trouble. After embarking on their journey, events turn upside down nearly every prior conception they have about themselves, their world and the people they trust.

**Other books you might like:**
Steven Brust, *Jhereg*, 1983
Heather Gladney, *Teot's War*, 1988
P.C. Hodgell, *God Stalk*, 1982
Tanya Huff, *The Fire's Stone*, 1990
Steve Perry, *The Man Who Never Missed*, 1985
Jennifer Roberson, *Sword-Dancer*, 1986

## 4522

### MICKEY ZUCKER REICHERT

### *Prince of Demons*

(New York: DAW, 1996)

**Story type:** Fantasy (Legend; Adventure)
**Series:** Renshai Chronicles
**Major character(s):** Colbey Calistinsson, Warrior (Renshai); Dh'arlo'me, Mythical Creature (elf); Kevral Tainharsdartter, Warrior (Renshai)
**Time period(s):** Indeterminate Past
**Locale(s):** Bearn, Fictional Country; Pudar, Fictional Country; The Westlands, Fictional Country

**Summary:** Three hundred years after Ragnarok, Dh'arlo'me attempts to entice mortals into championing Chaos, an event which could spell disaster for both mortals and immortals. Colbey Calistinsson must identify the correct opponent to set against Dh'arlo'me to maintain the balance between law and chaos.

**Other books you might like:**
Linda Evans, *Sleipnir*, 1994
Mary Gentle, *Rats and Gargoyles*, 1991
Jason Henderson, *The Spawn of Loki*, 1994

P.C. Hodgell, *God Stalk*, 1982
Joel Rosenberg, *The Fire Duke*, 1995
Janny Wurts, *Curse of the Mistwraith*, 1994
Roger Zelazny, *Nine Princes in Amber*, 1970

---

**4523**

MICKEY ZUCKER REICHERT

## Shadow's Realm

(New York: DAW, 1990)

**Story type:** Fantasy (Adventure)
**Series:** Bifrost Guardians
**Major character(s):** Taziar Medakan, Thief; Allerum, Mythical Creature (elf); Al Larson, Military Personnel (Vietnam veteran), Mythical Creature
**Time period(s):** Indeterminate
**Locale(s):** Cullinsberg, Fictional City

**Summary:** When Larson, Shadow, Astryd and Silme killed the Chaos Dragon, they were unaware that all the released Chaos found and bonded with Bolverkr, the greatest surviving Dragonmage and drove him mad. Convinced by Chaos that Shadow and Larson must suffer for the destruction caused by the unleashed Chaos, Bolverkr lures them to Shadow's home town and into a trap.

**Other books you might like:**
Catherine Cooke, *Mask of the Wizard*, 1985
Brian Daley, *The Doomfarers of Coramonde*, 1977
Leo Frankowski, *The Cross-Time Engineer*, 1986
Barbara Hambly, *The Time of the Dark*, 1987
Roger Zelazny, *Nine Princes in Amber*, 1970

---

**4524**

MICKEY ZUCKER REICHERT
JENNIFER WINGERT, Co-Author

## Spirit Fox

(New York: DAW, 1998)

**Story type:** Fantasy (Magic Conflict)
**Major character(s):** Kiarda, Noblewoman; Maddock, Warrior
**Time period(s):** Indeterminate
**Locale(s):** The River, Fictional Country; The Marchlands, Fictional Country

**Summary:** When the immortals patched up their quarrels and stopped fighting, it led to peace between the River and the Marchlands, a peace now in danger of ending. Kiarda, whose body is inhabited by the spirit of a fox, discovers that her unique condition is a mixed blessing. She and her companions must escape an enemy and help avert a new war.

**Other books you might like:**
Alan Dean Foster, *Chorus Skating*, 1994
Terry Goodkind, *Blood of the Fold*, 1994
Barbara Hambly, *Icefalcon's Quest*, 1998
Tanya Huff, *Fifth Quarter*, 1995
Robert Jordan, *The Great Hunt*, 1990

---

**4525**

MICKEY ZUCKER REICHERT

## The Unknown Soldier

(New York, DAW, 1994)

**Story type:** Science Fiction (Time Travel; Military)
**Major character(s):** Carrigan, Military Personnel, Time Traveler; Jason Walker, Doctor (resident); Shawna Nicholson, Doctor (chief resident)
**Time period(s):** 1980s (1985)
**Locale(s):** North Liberty, Iowa

**Summary:** While on call at the emergency room, Jason handles an unhuman patient who seems to have been hit by a bomb. The unidentifiable patient begins to trust the doctors and recalls his name, Carrigan. Shawna realizes Carrigan comes from the future as, unfortunately, do his enemies who follow him to the 20th century, attempting to kill him and all who know of him.

**Other books you might like:**
Poul Anderson, *The Time Patrol*, 1991
Bill Baldwin, *The Defenders*, 1992
Randall Frakes, *Terminator 2: Judgment Day*, 1991
George Turner, *Genetic Soldier*, 1994
Robert Charles Wilson, *A Bridge of Years*, 1991

---

**4526**

MICKEY ZUCKER REICHERT

## The Western Wizard

(New York: DAW, 1992)

**Story type:** Fantasy (Magic Conflict)
**Series:** Renshai Chronicles
**Major character(s):** Shadimar, Wizard; Colbey Calistinsson, Warrior; Santagithi, Warrior (Renshai)
**Time period(s):** Indeterminate Past
**Locale(s):** The Westlands, Fictional Country; Santagithi, Fictional City

**Summary:** With the death of the Western Wizard, the balance between the three other Cardinal Wizards slips, further entangling the political situation. Shadimar, the Eastern Wizard, searches for a replacement while preparing for the upcoming struggle.

**Other books you might like:**
Poul Anderson, *Hrolf Kraki's Saga*, 1973
Glen Cook, *The Black Company*, 1984
Barbara Hambly, *The Time of the Dark*, 1982
Robert Jordan, *The Eye of the World*, 1989
Tad Williams, *The Dragonbone Chair*, 1988

---

**4527**

KATYA REIMANN

## A Tremor in the Bitter Earth

(New York: Tor, 1998)

**Story type:** Fantasy (Political; Psychic Powers)
**Major character(s):** Gaultry Blas, Wizard; Martin Stalker, Warrior, Nobleman
**Time period(s):** Indeterminate Past
**Locale(s):** Bissanty Empire, Fictional Country; Tielmark, Fictional Country

**Summary:** After Gaultry Blas foils an attempt by Bissanty assassins to taint Tielmark's prince with poisonous magic, she must venture deep into Bissanty, accompanied by an ensorcelled assassin, to rescue Martin. Sequel to *Wind From a Foreign Sky*.

**Other books you might like:**
Terry Goodkind, *Stone of Tears*, 1995
Laurell K. Hamilton, *Nightseer*, 1992
J. Gregory Keyes, *The Blackgod*, 1997
Andre Norton, *Elvenblood*, 1995
    Mercedes Lackey, co-author
Martha Wells, *The Element of Fire*, 1993

---

**4528**

KATYA REIMANN

## Wind From a Foreign Sky

(New York: Tor, 1996)

**Story type:** Fantasy (Magic Conflict; Political)
**Series:** Tielmaran Chronicles
**Major character(s):** Heiratikus, Wizard, Political Figure; Issachar Dan, Nobleman, Warrior; Gaultry, Hunter, Wizard
**Time period(s):** Indeterminate Past
**Locale(s):** Tielmark, Fictional Country; Bissanty Empire, Fictional Country

**Summary:** Prince Clarin makes a deal with the gods to separate his nation from the Bissanty Empire. Three hundred years later a plot may undo that action with magic and duplicity, while a young woman finds herself at the hub of destiny armed with strange powers. First novel.

**Other books you might like:**
Lisa Goldstein, *Summer King, Winter Fool*, 1994
Terry Goodkind, *Wizard's First Rule*, 1994
Patricia A. McKillip, *The Riddle-Master of Hed*, 1976
Caroline Stevermer, *A College of Magics*, 1994
Janny Wurts, *Curse of the Mistwraith*, 1994

---

**4529**

KATHRYN REINES

## The Kiss

(New York: Avon, 1996)

**Story type:** Horror (Vampire Story)
**Major character(s):** Rebecca Bittan, Student; Maria Viroslav, Noblewoman (countess), Vampire; Alexander Viroslav, Nobleman (count), Vampire
**Time period(s):** 1930s (1938)
**Locale(s):** Boleslaus, Bulgaria

**Summary:** Stranded at the Romanian border while fleeing from the Nazis, Rebecca Bittan and her boyfriend, Richard Anderson, accept the invitation of Countess Viroslav to stay at her mansion. There, they are indoctrinated into the ways of vampirism that have sustained the Count and Countess Viroslav for centuries. First novel.

**Other books you might like:**
Elaine Bergstrom, *Shattered Glass*, 1989
Andrei Codrescu, *Blood Countess*, 1995
William Pridgen, *Night of the Dragon's Blood*, 1997
Shawn Ryan, *Nocturnas*, 1995
F. Paul Wilson, *The Keep*, 1981

---

**4530**

WILLIAM RELLING JR.

## The Infinite Man

(Los Angeles: Scream/Press, 1989)

**Story type:** Horror (Collection)

**Summary:** Twenty-one stories first published between 1980 and 1989 with five original to the volume, plus an "Afterword." Clever, ironical, biting, usually short, often quite funny—a few, like "Sorry, but We Only Offer That Course in the Fall" and "Burton's Word," being little more than extended jokes. Quite contemporary in setting and theme, with frequent sho-biz references ("The King," "Abbott & Costello Go to Jonestown"). The outstanding story in the volume is the title story, "The Infinite Man," which tells of the rise and fall of a writer obsessed with mirrors.

**Other books you might like:**
Dennis Etchison, *The Dark Country*, 1982
Richard Christian Matheson, *Scars and Other Distinguishing Marks*, 1988

---

**4531**

WILLIAM RELLING JR.

## Silent Moon

(New York: Tor, 1990)

**Story type:** Horror (Occult)
**Major character(s):** Gillian Woodbury, Journalist (TV reporter); Bud Friendly, Journalist (Newspaperman)
**Time period(s):** 1980s (1988)
**Locale(s):** San Francisco, California

**Summary:** Reporters Woodbury and Friendly are drawn into a conspiracy involving evangelism, presidential politics, and a moon cult's attempt to utilize human sacrifice to free an ancient monster from its long confinement.

**Other books you might like:**
Ramsey Campbell, *The Hungry Moon*, 1986
Dennis Wheatley, *The Satanist*, 1960
Dennis Wheatley, *To the Devil, a Daughter*, 1953

---

**4532**

JACK REMICK

## Terminal Weird

(Seattle: Black Heron Press, 1996)

**Story type:** Horror (Collection)

**Summary:** This collection contains eleven stories tinged with fantasy and often told from extraordinary perspectives. In "Roach," a man consumed by cockroaches sees the world from their point of view. "Monica Metallica" features a femme fatale heavy-metal musician with the habits of spiders. Death takes the form of alligators endlessly pursued by immortals in "Lizard," and heaven is a complex machine whose function is not understood by those running it in "Machine." A young woman's dreams of her awakening sexuality manifest as a crocodile in "Crocodile."

**Other books you might like:**
William S. Burroughs, *Interzone*, 1989
Wayne Allen Sallee, *With Wounds Still Wet*, 1996
Don Webb, *A Spell for the Fulfillment of Desire*, 1996

## 4533

**LAURA RESNICK**

### In Legend Born
(New York: Tor, 1998)

**Story type:** Fantasy (Political)
**Series:** Sileria
**Major character(s):** Mirabar, Religious (Guardian); Tansen, Warrior; Josarian, Thief
**Time period(s):** Indeterminate Past
**Locale(s):** Cavasar, Fictional City; Sileria, Fictional Country (island)

**Summary:** With the country of Sileria conquered for centuries, its fractured tribes more interested in fighting one another than ousting their overlords, one young woman has a vision of freedom. As the tribes begin to take action, their promised hero remains a divided man, as likely to bring destruction as freedom.

**Other books you might like:**
Glen Cook, *Tower of Fear*, 1989
Guy Gavriel Kay, *The Lions of Al-Rassan*, 1995
Katherine Kurtz, *Deryni Rising*, 1970
George R.R. Martin, *A Game of Thrones*, 1996
Fiona Patton, *The Stone Prince*, 1997

## 4534

**MIKE RESNICK**, Editor
**MARTIN H. GREENBERG**, Co-Editor

### Aladdin: Master of the Lamp
(New York: DAW, 1992)

**Story type:** Fantasy (Anthology; Legend)
**Major character(s):** Aladdin, Adventurer
**Locale(s):** Middle East

**Summary:** Contains a one-page introduction by Resnick plus 43 original stories sharing themes from the famous Middle Eastern story of Aladdin, the magic lamp and wish-granting djinn, including one collaboration, "If Wishes Were Genies," by Terry McGarry and Austin Dridge and two stories each by Jack C. Haldeman II and Barry N. Malzberg. Other authors include Mark Aronson, John Betancourt, Pat Cadigan, George Alec Effinger, David Gerrold, Karen Haber, Patrick Nielson Hayden, Janet Kagan, Katharine Kerr, Maureen F. McHugh, Josepha Sherman, Martha Soukup, Judith Tarr and Jane Yolen.

**Other books you might like:**
Martin H. Greenberg, *The Fantastic Adventures of Robin Hood*, 1991
    editor
Andrew Lang, *The Arabian Nights Entertainments*, 1969
    editor
Susan Shwartz, *Arabesques: More Tales of the Arabian Nights*, 1988
    editor
Susan Shwartz, *Arabesques II*, 1989
    editor
Jack Zipes, *Arabian Nights: The Marvels and Wonders of the Thousand and One Nights*, 1991
    editor

## 4535

**MIKE RESNICK**

### An Alien Land
(Concord, California: Dark Regions, 1998)

**Story type:** Science Fiction (Collection)

**Summary:** Included in this collection are seven stories published between 1990 and 1997, an essay explaining the author's frequent use of an African setting for his stories, and two award winning novelettes, "Seven Views of Olduvai Gorge" and "Bully!".

**Other books you might like:**
Damon Knight, *Late Knight Edition*, 1985
Robert Silverberg, *Beyond the Safe Zone*, 1986
Clifford D. Simak, *Skirmish: The Great Short Fiction of Clifford D. Simak*, 1977
Connie Willis, *Impossible Things*, 1994

## 4536

**MIKE RESNICK**, Editor

### Alternate Kennedys
(New York: Tor, 1992)

**Story type:** Science Fiction (Anthology; Alternate Universe)

**Summary:** Contains a four-page introduction plus individual introductions to one poem by Jane Yolen and 25 original stories whose themes involve the famous American political family, the Kennedys. Authors include Mark Aronson, Ginjer Buchanan, Pat Cadigan, Esther M. Friesner, David Gerrold, Jack C. Haldeman II, Nancy Kress, Michael P. Kube-McDowell, Mike Resnick, Kristine Kathryn Rusch, Robert Sheckley, Susan Shwartz, Martha Soukup, Judith Tarr and Harry Turtledove.

**Other books you might like:**
Gregory Benford, *Alternate Americas*, 1992
    Martin H. Greenberg, co-editor
Gregory Benford, *Alternate Heroes*, 1990
    Martin H. Greenberg, co-editor
Philip K. Dick, *The Man in the High Castle*, 1962
L. Neil Smith, *The Gallatin Divergence*, 1985

## 4537

**MIKE RESNICK**, Editor

### Alternate Presidents
(New York: Tor, 1992)

**Story type:** Science Fiction (Anthology; Alternate Universe)

**Summary:** Contains a three-page introduction plus individual introductions to 28 stories asking the question, "What if. . ." concerning United States Presidents arranged chronologically 1789-1988. Authors include Pat Cadigan, Bill Fawcett, David Gerrold, Alexis A. Gilliland, Janet Kagan, Michael P. Kube-McDowell, Judith Moffett, Jody Lynn Nye, Mike Resnick, Kristine Kathryn Rusch, Robert Sheckley, Susan Shwartz, Martha Soukup, Lawrence Watt-Evans and two stories by Barry N. Malzberg.

**Other books you might like:**
Gregory Benford, *Alternate Americas*, 1992
    Martin H. Greenberg, co-editor
Gregory Benford, *Alternate Empires*, 1989
    Martin H. Greenberg, co-editor

Gregory Benford, *Alternate Heroes*, 1990
    Martin H. Greenberg, co-editor
Gregory Benford, *Alternate Wars*, 1991
    Martin H. Greenberg, co-editor

### 4538

**MIKE RESNICK**, Editor

## *Alternate Warriors*

(New York: Tor, 1993)

**Story type:** Science Fiction (Anthology; Alternate Universe)

**Summary:** Contains a two-page introduction plus individual introductions to 29 original stories from authors challenged to write a story about a historical figure who chose to fight for beliefs rather than die for them. Authors include George Alec Effinger, Esther Friesner, David Gerrold, Jack C. Haldeman II, Tappan King, Kathe Koja, Michael P. Kube-McDowell, Mercedes Lackey, Brad Linaweaver, Barry N. Malzberg, Maureen McHugh, Beth Meacham, Kristine Kathryn Rusch, Michelle Sagara, Josepha Sherman and Judith Tarr.

**Other books you might like:**
Gregory Benford, *Alternate Americas*, 1992
    Martin H. Greenberg, co-editor
Gregory Benford, *Alternate Empires*, 1989
    Martin H. Greenberg, co-editor
Gregory Benford, *Alternate Heroes*, 1990
    Martin H. Greenberg, co-editor
Gregory Benford, *Alternate Wars*, 1991
    Martin H. Greenberg, co-editor
Harry Turtledove, *The Guns of the South: A Novel of the Civil War*, 1992

### 4539

**MIKE RESNICK**

## *Bully!*

(Eugene, OR: Pulphouse Axolotl Press, 1990)

**Story type:** Science Fiction (Alternate Universe; Political)
**Major character(s):** Theodore Roosevelt, Historical Figure, Political Figure
**Time period(s):** 1910s (1910)
**Locale(s):** Kirinyaga Territory, Africa; Alternate Earth

**Summary:** On a trip to Africa, Theodore Roosevelt becomes convinced to help inflict American-style democracy on Africans ill-equipped to appreciate its benefits.

**Other books you might like:**
Ursula K. Le Guin, *The Word for World Is Forest*, 1976
Mack Reynolds, *The Best Ye Breed*, 1978
Mack Reynolds, *Blackman's Burden*, 1972
Mack Reynolds, *Border, Breed Nor Birth*, 1972
G. Harry Stine, *The Bastard Rebellion*, 1988

### 4540

**MIKE RESNICK**, Editor
**MARTIN H. GREENBERG**, Co-Editor

## *By Any Other Fame*

(New York: DAW, 1994)

**Story type:** Science Fiction (Anthology; Alternate History)

**Summary:** Contains a one-page introduction and brief individual introductions to 23 original stories about celebrities who lead different lives in other universes, with Mercedes Lackey collaborating with Larry Dixon on one story. Other authors include Ginjer Buchanan, Thomas A. Easton, George Alec Effinger, David Gerrold, Jack C. Haldeman II, Janet Kagan, Nancy Kress, Barry N. Malzberg, Beth Meacham, Laura Resnick, Kristine Kathryn Rusch, Michelle Sagara, Dean Wesley Smith, Judith Tarr, and Brian M. Thomsen.

**Other books you might like:**
Gregory Benford, *Alternate Heroes*, 1990
    Martin H. Greenberg, co-editor
Esther Friesner, *Alien Pregnant by Elvis*, 1994
    Martin H. Greenberg, co-editor
Richard Peabody, *Mondo Elvis*, 1993
    Lucinda Ebersole, co-editor
Paul M. Sammon, *The King Is Dead: Tales of Elvis Post Mortem*, 1994
    editor
Kay Sloan, *Elvis Rising: Stories on the King*, 1993
    Constance Pierce, co-editor

### 4541

**MIKE RESNICK**, Editor
**MARTIN H. GREENBERG**, Co-Editor

## *Christmas Ghosts*

(New York: DAW, 1993)

**Story type:** Horror (Anthology; Ghost Story)

**Summary:** The 27 original stories collected here all deal with Christmas spirits, most in the Dickensian sense of ghosts of Christmas Past and Present. Frank Robinson's "Merry Christmas, No. 30267" tells of an unregenerate prisoner given a chance to repent his past and start life over. Kathe Koja and Barry N. Malzberg imagine Sir William Gilbert visited on his deathbed by the ghost of Jack the Ripper in "The Timbrel Sound of Darkness," a wry meditation on artistic prostitution. John Betancourt's "The River Lethe Is Made of Tears" and Kristine Kathryn Rusch's "Three Wishes Before a Fire" use supernatural manifestations to reassure their characters, while Dean Wesley Smith's "The Ghosts of Christmas Future" offers a bleak vision of holiday hopelessness.

**Other books you might like:**
Kathryn Cramer, *Christmas Ghosts*, 1988
    David Hartwell, co-editor
Kathryn Cramer, *Spirits of Christmas*, 1989
    David Hartwell, co-editor
Richard Dalby, *Ghosts for Christmas*, 1988
    editor
Richard Dalby, *Thrillers for Christmas*, 1989
    editor
Seon Manley, *Christmas Ghosts: An Anthology*, 1978
    Gogo Lewis, co-editor

### 4542

**MIKE RESNICK**, Editor
**MARTIN H. GREENBERG**, Co-Editor
**LOREN D. ESTLEMAN**, Co-Editor

## *Deals with the Devil*

(New York: Daw, 1994)

**Story type:** Horror (Anthology)

**Summary:** The 36 stories written especially for this volume approach the classic fantasy theme of dealing with the devil—and the consequences thereof—from a variety of angles. Jane Yolen's "Pitch" tells of the lengths to which successful screenwriters will go to drum up an exciting movie idea. Dean Wesley Smith's "Another Damn Deal" concerns a writer who makes a deal with the devil not to write a story about him. Lawrence Watt-Evans' "For Value Received" is about a man who discovers the true price of his measly soul. Mike Resnick's "Stanley the Eighteen-Percenter" tells about what happens when a hardnosed agent must argue his client's case against Satan. And Brian Thomsen's "Nobody Wins a Deal with the Devil" tells of the steps Satan takes to bind his rebellious son to him.

**Other books you might like:**
Basil Davenport, *Deals with the Devil: An Anthology*, 1958
    editor
Martin H. Greenberg, *Devil Worshippers*, 1990
    Charles G. Waugh, co-editor
Marvin Kaye, *Devils and Demons*, 1987
    editor

---

`4543`

**MIKE RESNICK**, Editor
**MARTIN H. GREENBERG**, Co-Editor

## *Dinosaur Fantastic*
(New York: DAW, 1993)

**Story type:** Fantasy (Anthology)

**Summary:** Contains a two-page introduction by the editor noting this as the first all original dinosaur anthology ever published plus 25 stories by 27 authors including Roger MacBride Allen, Pat Cadigan, David Gerrold, Katharine Kerr, Kathe Koja, Mercedes Lackey, Barry N. Malzberg, Beth Meacham, Kevin O'Donnell Jr., Frank M. Robinson, Kristine Kathryn Rusch, Michelle M. Sagara, Robert J. Sawyer, Robert Sheckley, Josepha Sherman, John E. Stith and Judith Tarr.

**Other books you might like:**
Poul Anderson, *The Night Fantastic*, 1991
    Karen Anderson, co-editor
Jack Dann, *Dinosaurs!*, 1990
    Gardner Dozois, co-editor
Martin H. Greenberg, *Horse Fantastic*, 1991
    Rosalind M. Greenberg, co-editor
Rosalind M. Greenberg, *Dragon Fantastic*, 1992
    Martin H. Greenberg, co-editor
James Gurney, *Dinotopia*, 1992
Andre Norton, *Catfantastic*, 1989
    Martin H. Greenberg, co-editor
Andre Norton, *Catfantastic II*, 1991
    Martin H. Greenberg, co-editor
Robert Silverberg, *The Science Fictional Dinosaur*, 1982
    Charles G. Waugh, Martin Harry Greenberg, co-editors

---

`4544`

**MIKE RESNICK**, Editor
**GARDNER DOZOIS**, Co-Editor

## *Future Earths: Under African Skies*
(New York: DAW, 1993)

**Story type:** Science Fiction (Anthology)
**Locale(s):** Africa

**Summary:** Contains a three-page list of books about Africa and short stories with African themes, a four-page introduction plus individual introductions to 15 stories set in Africa which first appeared in periodicals and anthologies, 1965-1993. Authors include Gregory Benford, Janet Gluckman, George Guthridge, Ian McDonald, Naomi Mitchison, Kim Stanley Robinson, Dave Smeds, Bruce Sterling and Vernor Vinge.

**Other books you might like:**
Gillian Bradshaw, *The Land of Gold*, 1992
Bill Dolan, *White Rhino*, 1992
George Alec Effinger, *When Gravity Fails*, 1987
Ben Okri, *The Famished Road*, 1992
Robert Silverberg, *Lion Time in Timbuctoo*, 1990
G. Harry Stine, *The Bastard Rebellion*, 1988

---

`4545`

**MIKE RESNICK**

## *A Hunger in the Soul*
(New York: Tor, 1998)

**Story type:** Science Fiction (Adventure)
**Major character(s):** Enoch Stone, Hunter, Museum Curator; Robert Markham, Journalist, Adventurer; Michael Drake, Scientist
**Time period(s):** Indeterminate Future
**Locale(s):** Bushveld, Planet—Imaginary

**Summary:** Robert Markham wants to secure his own immortality by locating Dr. Michael Drake, who alone can develop a vaccine for ybonia, a cross species plague. He enlists the aid of Enoch Stone to go to Bushveld. Unfortunately, Markham's manner so alienates the natives and his companions that it threatens the success of their expedition.

**Other books you might like:**
L. Sprague de Camp, *The Venom Trees of Sunga*, 1992
Philip Jose Farmer, *The Green Odyssey*, 1956
Alan Dean Foster, *Voyage to the City of the Dead*, 1984
Lee Killough, *Liberty's World*, 1985
Jerry Pournelle, *King David's Spaceship*, 1980
William Sanders, *Journey to Fusang*, 1988
Jack Vance, *Big Planet*, 1957

---

`4546`

**MIKE RESNICK**, Editor

## *Inside the Funhouse*
(New York: AvoNova, 1992)

**Story type:** Science Fiction (Anthology; Science Fiction)

**Summary:** This collection of stories sharing a recursive theme, science fiction *about* science fiction, contains a two-page introduction and individual introductions to Jane Yolen's poem and 16 stories by 15 authors with two, Frederik Pohl and C.M. Kornbluth, collaborating on "Mute Inglorious Tam." Three authors explore the epistolary form, Jack Lewis in "Who's Cribbing," Patricia Cribbing Nurse in "One Rejection Too Many" and Eric Norden in "The Curse of the Mhondoro Nkablele." Allen Steele spoofs a deceased L. Ron Hubbard inspired character through interviews in "Hapgood's Hoax." Other authors include A, Isaac Asimov, Philip K. Dick, George Alec Effinger, Edmond Hamilton, Frederik Pohl, Mike Resnick and Ian Watson with Barry N. Malzberg contributing two Mike Resnick and Ian Watson with Barry N. Malzberg contributing two stories.

**Other books you might like:**
Michael Bishop, *The Secret Ascension*, 1987

Robert Bloch, *The Eighth Stage of Fandom: Selections From 25 Years of Fan Writing*, 1962
Fredric Brown, *Martians, Go Home*, 1955
Fredric Brown, *What Mad Universe*, 1949
Jonathan Carroll, *The Land of Laughs*, 1980
Robert Coulson, *Charles Fort Never Mentioned Wombats*, 1977
  Gene DeWeese, co-author
Gene DeWeese, *Now You See It/Him/Them...*, 1975
  Robert Coulson, co-author
Philip K. Dick, *The Man in the High Castle*, 1962
Philip Jose Farmer, *Venus on the Half Shell*, 1975
  written as Kilgore Trout
Sharyn McCrumb, *Bimbos of the Death Sun*, 1987
Larry Niven, *Fallen Angels*, 1991
  Jerry Pournelle, Michael Flynn, co-authors
Tim Powers, *The Stress of Her Regard*, 1989

---

**4547**

**MIKE RESNICK**

## Ivory: A Legend of Past and Future

(New York: Tor, 1988)

**Story type:** Science Fiction (Adventure)
**Major character(s):** Duncan Rojas, Researcher; Bukoba Mandaka, Warrior (The last Maasai warrior)
**Time period(s):** Indeterminate Future (The year 6303 of the Galactic Era)
**Locale(s):** Earth; Athena, Planet—Imaginary

**Summary:** In this Nebula award nominated novel, Duncan Rojas, senior researcher and authenticator for Braxton's Records of Big Game, is visited by Bukoba Mandaka, last of the Maasai, who makes an unusual request. Mandaka wants to hire Rojas to find the tusks of the fabled Kilimanjaro Elephant, the largest tusks ever authenticated. Unfortunately the Elephant was killed more than six thousand years ago and its tusks disappeared more than three thousand years ago.

**Other books you might like:**
Roger MacBride Allen, *Orphan of Creation*, 1988
David Brin, *The Uplift War*, 1987
Orson Scott Card, *Speaker for the Dead*, 1986
Paul J. McAuley, *Of the Fall*, 1989

---

**4548**

**MIKE RESNICK**

## Kirinyaga: A Fable of Utopia

(New York: Ballantine Del Rey, 1998)

**Story type:** Science Fiction (Utopia; Collection)
**Major character(s):** Koriba, Religious (Kikuyu witch doctor), Aged Person; Ndemi, Apprentice
**Time period(s):** 22nd century (2123-2137)
**Locale(s):** Kirinyaga, Planet—Imaginary; Marsabit, Kenya

**Summary:** A Kikuyu *mundumugu*, or witch doctor, Koriba leads a group of settlers to the terraformed planetoid Kirinyaga, where they hope to establish a utopian world based on the old Kikuyu ways. As the years slip past, however, Koriba realizes that humans seldom agree upon the concept of utopia, especially as younger generations grow up and question the wisdom of old traditions. These 10 linked stories have individually won two Hugo Awards and one Nebula Award, as well as numerous other awards and nominations.

**Other books you might like:**
Ray Bradbury, *The Martian Chronicles*, 1950

Orson Scott Card, *The Worthing Saga*, 1990
Arthur C. Clarke, *The Songs of Distant Earth*, 1986
Julia Ecklar, *Regenesis*, 1995
Kim Stanley Robinson, *Red Mars*, 1993

---

**4549**

**MIKE RESNICK**

## Lucifer Jones

(New York: Warner Questar, 1992)

**Story type:** Fantasy (Light Fantasy)
**Major character(s):** Lucifer Jones, Adventurer, Religious
**Time period(s):** 1920s (1926-1929); 1930s (1930-1934)
**Locale(s):** Asia; Europe

**Summary:** Lucifer Jones jaunts around the globe foiling villains, battling mythical creatures, clobbering literary icons and hobnobbing with the high and mighty while searching for a place to build his tabernacle. Spoofs the *Indiana Jones Series* (1981-1992).

**Other books you might like:**
Campbell Black, *Raiders of the Lost Ark*, 1981
Craig Shaw Gardner, *The Other Sinbad*, 1991
James Kahn, *Indiana Jones and the Temple of Doom*, 1984
Catherine Lanigan, *Jewel of the Nile*, 1985
Catherine Lanigan, *Romancing the Stone*, 1984
Rob MacGregor, *Indiana Jones and the Last Crusade*, 1989
Rob MacGregor, *Indiana Jones and the Peril at Delphi*, 1991
Rob MacGregor, *Indiana Jones and the Seven Veils*, 1991
Mark E. Rogers, *Samurai Cat in the Real World*, 1989
Mark E. Rogers, *The Sword of Samurai Cat*, 1991

---

**4550**

**MIKE RESNICK**

## A Miracle of Rare Design

(New York: Tor, 1994)

**Story type:** Science Fiction (Adventure; First Contact)
**Major character(s):** Xavier William Lennox, Explorer, Genetically Altered Being; Beatrice Ngoni, Doctor (surgeon); Chomanche, Religious (priest), Alien
**Time period(s):** Indeterminate Future
**Locale(s):** Medina, Planet—Imaginary; Artismo, Planet—Imaginary

**Summary:** Crippled after spying on Firefly religious rites, Xavier William Lennox is surgically altered into a Firefly to facilitate contact and negotiation of mineral rights on the planet. Once he has become an alien, he craves the experience and repeats it, aiding first contacts.

**Other books you might like:**
John Barnes, *Sin of Origin*, 1988
Michael Bishop, *Transfigurations*, 1979
C.J. Cherryh, *The Faded Sun: Kesrith*, 1978
Rebecca Ore, *Becoming Alien*, 1987
Charles Sheffield, *Proteus Combined*, 1994

---

**4551**

**MIKE RESNICK**

## Oracle

(New York: Ace, 1992)

**Story type:** Science Fiction (Adventure; Political)

**Series:** Oracle
**Major character(s):** Carlos "Iceman" Mendoza, Saloon Keeper/ Owner, Spy (retired); Jimmy "the Injun" Two Feathers, Murderer, Government Official; Joshua "the Whistler" Jeremiah Chandler, Bounty Hunter, Murderer
**Time period(s):** Indeterminate Future
**Locale(s):** Last Chance, Planet—Imaginary; Hades, Planet— Imaginary

**Summary:** When a person claiming to be Penelope Bailey's mother asks the Iceman to bring back her daughter, he hires the Whistler to approach Penelope and kill her if possible, or bring her back if, as likely, Penelope's precognition protects her from attack.

**Other books you might like:**
Karen Haber, *Mutant Star*, 1992
Frank Herbert, *Chapterhouse: Dune*, 1985
Frank Herbert, *Heretics of Dune*, 1984
Katharine Kerr, *Polar City Blues*, 1990

## 4552

### MIKE RESNICK

## *Paradise: A Chronicle of a Distant World*
(New York: Tor, 1989)

**Story type:** Science Fiction (First Contact)
**Major character(s):** Matthew Breen, Journalist (Biographer); Buko Pepon, Revolutionary, Ruler
**Time period(s):** Indeterminate Future
**Locale(s):** Peponi, Planet—Imaginary

**Summary:** Humans colonize a planet strikingly similar to nineteenth-century Kenya despite the presence of a native sentient race. A journalist visiting the planet attempts to trace the key events in that colonization over a period of decades.

**Other books you might like:**
Roger MacBride Allen, *Orphan of Creation*, 1988
David Brin, *The Uplift War*, 1987
Judith Moffett, *Pennterra*, 1987
Sheri S. Tepper, *Grass*, 1989

## 4553

### MIKE RESNICK

## *Prophet*
(New York: Ace, 1993)

**Story type:** Science Fiction (Space Opera; Psychic Powers)
**Series:** Oracle
**Major character(s):** Carlos "Iceman" Mendoza, Saloon Keeper/ Owner, Spy (retired); Penelope Bailey, Psychic, Leader; Felix "Gravedancer" Lomax, Bodyguard, Spy
**Time period(s):** Indeterminate Future
**Locale(s):** Last Chance, Planet—Imaginary; Mozart, Planet— Imaginary

**Summary:** Obsessed with locating Penelope and neutralizing the threat she represents, Carlos deploys Felix to investigate the Prophet. Carlos then prepares his final assault on Penelope Bailey while she continues her ominous shaping of human history.

**Other books you might like:**
Isaac Asimov, *Foundation and Empire*, 1952
Marion Zimmer Bradley, *The Firebrand*, 1987
Glen Cook, *The Dragon Never Sleeps*, 1988
Frank Herbert, *The God-Emperor of Dune*, 1981
Ursula K. Le Guin, *The Lathe of Heaven*, 1971

Anne McCaffrey, *Damia*, 1992
Michaela Roessner, *Vanishing Point*, 1993
Lewis Shiner, *Glimpses*, 1993

## 4554

### MIKE RESNICK

## *Purgatory: A Chronicle of a Distant World*
(New York: Tor, 1993)

**Story type:** Science Fiction (Science Fiction)
**Major character(s):** Jalanopi, Alien, Leader (King of the Tulabete tribe); Andrew McFarley, Religious
**Time period(s):** Indeterminate Future
**Locale(s):** Karimon, Planet—Imaginary (Rockgarden)

**Summary:** Human arrival on Karimon brings advanced technology to native sentient reptiles who had achieved stone age technology. The natives rapidly lose control of their culture, identity and land as successive generations yield to the pressure of immigration.

**Other books you might like:**
Robert L. Forward, *Dragon's Egg*, 1980
Gwyneth Jones, *White Queen*, 1993
Janet Kagan, *Hellspark*, 1988
H. Beam Piper, *Little Fuzzy*, 1962
Joan Slonczewski, *A Door into Ocean*, 1986
Vernor Vinge, *A Fire upon the Deep*, 1992

## 4555

### MIKE RESNICK

## *Second Contact*
(New York: Tor Books, 1990)

**Story type:** Science Fiction (Mystery)
**Major character(s):** Max Becker, Lawyer; Jaimie, Computer Expert
**Time period(s):** 21st century (2065)
**Locale(s):** United States

**Summary:** Twenty-three years earlier human and alien space explorers met and destroyed each other; no one knows exactly why. Since then there has been no contact with the aliens. Then a spaceship captain kills two of his crew members, claiming they're extraterrestrials in disguise. Although everyone assumes the captain is insane, Max Becker, the attorney assigned to his case, discovers evidence that there may be more to it than that. Soon a complex conspiracy is exposed and Becker finds himself on the run with a price on his head.

**Other books you might like:**
Philip K. Dick, *Do Androids Dream of Electric Sheep?*, 1968
Philip K. Dick, *Martian Time-Slip*, 1964
John Kessel, *Good News From Outer Space*, 1989
W.T. Quick, *Systems*, 1989
John E. Stith, *Deep Quarry*, 1989

## 4556

### MIKE RESNICK, Editor
### MARTIN H. GREENBERG, Co-Editor

## *Sherlock Holmes in Orbit*
(New York: DAW, 1995)

**Story type:** Science Fiction (Anthology; Mystery)

**Major character(s):** Sherlock Holmes, Detective—Private, Adventurer; John H. Watson, Doctor, Writer
**Time period(s):** 1900s; 1890s
**Locale(s):** London, England

**Summary:** Contains a four-page introduction by Resnick and 26 original stories featuring Sir Arthur Conan Doyle's famous detective and his faithful chronicler in familiar and new settings, arranged in four sections, "Holmes in the Past," "Holmes in the Present," "Holmes in the Future" and "Holmes After Death." Authors include Mark Aronson, John DeChancie, George Alec Effinger, Craig Shaw Gardner, David Gerrold, Barry N. Malzberg, Vonda N. McIntyre, Laura Resnick, Mike Resnick, Frank M. Robinson, Kristine Kathryn Rusch, Robert J. Sawyer, Josepha Sherman, Dean Wesley Smith, Brian M. Thomsen, and Leah A. Zeldes.

**Other books you might like:**
Isaac Asimov, *Sherlock Holmes through Time and Space*, 1984
Martin Harry Greenberg, Charles Waugh, co-editors
The Council of Four, *The Science Fictional Sherlock Holmes*, 1960
editor
Esther Friesner, *Druid's Blood*, 1988
Andy Lane, *All-Consuming Fire*, 1994

---

**4557**

**MIKE RESNICK**

## Soothsayer

(New York: Ace, 1991)

**Story type:** Science Fiction (Space Opera; Psychic Powers)
**Major character(s):** Penelope Bailey, Psychic (precognitive), Fugitive; Mouse, Thief, Companion (Penelope's); Carlos "Iceman" Mendoza, Saloon Keeper/Owner, Spy (retired)
**Time period(s):** Indeterminate Future
**Locale(s):** Last Chance, Planet—Imaginary; Solomon, Planet—Imaginary; Killhaven, Planet—Imaginary

**Summary:** When Mouse rescued Penelope from her alien captor she couldn't foresee being hunted by three governments and two hundred bounty hunters searching the galaxy for the child who can foresee the future. With Penelope's help, the pair repeatedly escape captors to again become unwilling associates of the next person wishing to use Penelope to develop personal wealth and power.

**Other books you might like:**
Alfred Bester, *The Demolished Man*, 1953
Alfred Bester, *The Stars My Destination*, 1957
David Brin, *Startide Rising*, 1983
Frank Herbert, *Dune*, 1965
Alis A. Rasmussen, *A Passage of Stars*, 1990
Alis A. Rasmussen, *The Price of Ransom*, 1990
Alis A. Rasmussen, *Revolution's Shore*, 1990
Charles Sheffield, *The Nimrod Hunt*, 1986

---

**4558**

**MIKE RESNICK**, Editor

## Whatdunits

(New York: DAW, 1992)

**Story type:** Science Fiction (Anthology; Mystery)
**Time period(s):** Indeterminate Future

**Summary:** 18 original stories arising from scenarios presented to each author by the editor, as related in the introduction. Brief individual introductions to each story include the scenario. Contains stories by

Roger MacBride Allen, Virginia Booth, Pat Cadigan, John DeChancie, Katharine Kerr, Michael A. Stackpole and Judith Tarr.

**Other books you might like:**
Michael Bishop, *Nebula Awards 25*, 1991
editor
Gardner Dozois, *The Year's Best Science Fiction: Eighth Annual Collection*, 1991
editor
Kristine Kathryn Rusch, *Pulphouse, Issue 11: Speculative Fiction*, 1991
editor
Donald A. Wollheim, *The 1990 Annual World's Best Science Fiction*, 1990
Arthur W. Saha, co-editor
Jane Yolen, *2041: Twelve Short Stories about the Future by Top Science Fiction Writers*, 1991
editor

---

**4559**

**MIKE RESNICK**

## The Widowmaker

(New York: Bantam Spectra, 1996)

**Story type:** Science Fiction (Adventure; Genetic Manipulation)
**Major character(s):** Jefferson "Widowmaker" Nighthawk, Clone, Criminal (assassin); Melisande, Dancer, Mutant; Father Christmas, Thief
**Time period(s):** Indeterminate Future (5101 Galactic Era)
**Locale(s):** Tundra, Planet—Imaginary; Solio II, Planet—Imaginary

**Summary:** Created from the DNA of the famed Widowmaker, now a corpsicle waiting in cold sleep for a cure to a disfiguring disease, Jefferson Nighthawk learns quickly how to kill efficiently. Along the way to his assignment to kill the man who assassinated the dictator of Solio II, he hones his killing skills in the employ of the Marquis of Queensbury and falls in love. However, a month-old clone may not have developed his social skills enough to detect duplicity.

**Other books you might like:**
C.J. Cherryh, *Cyteen*, 1988
Michael Jan Friedman, *Kahless*, 1996
Robert A. Heinlein, *The Door into Summer*, 1957
Rebecca Ore, *The Illegal Rebirth of Billy the Kid*, 1991
Richard Osborne, *Demolition Man*, 1993

---

**4560**

**MIKE RESNICK**

## The Widowmaker Reborn

(New York: Bantam Spectra, 1997)

**Story type:** Science Fiction (Adventure; Genetic Manipulation)
**Series:** Widowmaker
**Major character(s):** Jefferson "Widowmaker" Nighthawk, Clone, Mercenary; Ito Kinoshita, Martial Arts Expert; Ibn ben Khalid, Rebel
**Time period(s):** Indeterminate
**Locale(s):** Interstellar Empire/Federation

**Summary:** Created from the DNA of the famous Widowmaker, now a corpsicle waiting in cryostorage for a cure for his deadly disease, Jefferson Nighthawk has the experience as well as the body of the original Widowmaker, and the memories of the dead first clone. In order to pay for the continued care and hoped-for cure for the disease, he accepts an assignment to rescue the daughter of a corrupt politician and kill the rebel leader who holds her hostage. This time he will trust no one. Second in trilogy.

**Other books you might like:**
C.J. Cherryh, *Cyteen*, 1988
Gordon R. Dickson, *Dorsai!*, 1976
Ian Fleming, *You Only Live Twice*, 1964
Keith Laumer, *Retief at Large*, 1978
Rebecca Ore, *The Illegal Rebirth of Billy the Kid*, 1991
James H. Schmitz, *The Universe Against Her*, 1964
John Varley, *The Ophiuchi Hotline*, 1977

**4561**

**MIKE RESNICK**, Editor

## Will the Last Person to Leave the Planet Please Shut Off the Sun?

(New York: Tor, 1992)

**Story type:** Science Fiction (Collection)

**Summary:** Contains a 4-page introduction plus introductions to the original title story and each of the 27 other stories reprinted from periodicals and anthologies from 1977-1992. One story, "Kirinyaga," received a Nebula Award nomination and a Hugo Award; the new John Justin Mallory story, "For I Have Touched the Sky," received a Hugo Award nomination. Many stories feature humorous themes.

**Other books you might like:**
Mack Reynolds, *Blackman's Burden*, 1972
Lucius Shepard, *The Ends of the Earth*, 1990
Theodore Sturgeon, *Sturgeon Is Alive and Well*, 1971
John Varley, *Blue Champagne*, 1986
John Varley, *The Persistence of Vision*, 1978
Gene Wolfe, *Storeys From the Old Hotel*, 1992

**4562**

**LEAH REWOLINSKI**
**HARRY TRUMBORE**, Illustrator

## Star Wreck 6: Geek Space Nine

(New York: St. Martin's, 1994)

**Story type:** Science Fiction (Parody; Space Opera)
**Series:** Star Wreck
**Major character(s):** Bungeeman Crisco, Military Personnel (Starfreak), Spaceman; James T. Smirk, Spaceship Captain; Jean-Lucy Ricardo, Spaceship Captain
**Time period(s):** 25th century (Stardate 4780.5)
**Locale(s):** Geek Space Nine, Space Station (Bridgeoran); *U.S.S. Endocrine*, Spaceship; Outer Space

**Summary:** When an ambience of boredom permeates Geek Space Nine, threatening Starfreak's investment, Starfreak dispatches both *U.S.S. Endocrine*s to liven up the scene and promote alien tourism.

**Other books you might like:**
Douglas Adams, *The Hitchhiker's Guide to the Galaxy*, 1980
Henry N. Beard, *Bored of the Rings*, 1969
 Douglas C. Kenny, co-author
John M. Ford, *How Much for Just the Planet?*, 1987
Alan Dean Foster, *Glory Lane*, 1987
Mark E. Rogers, *The Adventures of Samurai Cat*, 1984
Ken Rolston, *Extreme Paranoia: Nobody Knows the Trouble I've Shot*, 1991
Ellis Weiner, *National Lampoon's Doon*, 1984

**4563**

**LEAH REWOLINSKI**
**HARRY TRUMBORE**, Illustrator

## Star Wreck II: The Attack of the Jargonites

(New York: St. Martin's Press, 1991)

**Story type:** Science Fiction (Parody; Space Opera)
**Series:** Star Wreck
**Major character(s):** James T. Smirk, Spaceship Captain; Jean-Lucy Ricardo, Spaceship Captain; B.S. Galore, Leader (Jargonites)
**Time period(s):** 23rd century
**Locale(s):** *U.S.S. Endocrine*, Spaceship

**Summary:** Captain Smirk has badgered Starfreak into recommissioning the *Endocrine* to allow two Starfreak vessels to engage the Jargonites who threaten security with boring group encounter sessions. When Captain Smirk attacks, the Jargonite Conundrum's Reality Deflectors easily divert the *Endocrine's* futon torpedos, leaving Smirk's crew at the mercy of the Jargonite attack until Smirk disables the communication system. When Piker misuses Dr. Beverage's diagnostic equipment, Piker and the *Endocrine's* other bridge crew are rendered temporarily deaf and immune to the Jargonite's language. With the Jargonites in near total control of Earth, both *Endocrines* rush to the rescue.

**Other books you might like:**
Douglas Adams, *The Hitchhiker's Guide to the Galaxy*, 1980
Henry N. Beard, *Bored of the Rings*, 1969
 Douglas C. Kenney, co-author
John M. Ford, *How Much for Just the Planet?*, 1987
Harry Harrison, *Bill, the Galactic Hero*, 1965
Ellis Weiner, *National Lampoon's Doon*, 1984

**4564**

**LEAH REWOLINSKI**
**HARRY TRUMBORE**, Illustrator

## Star Wreck III: Time Warped

(New York: St. Martin's, 1992)

**Story type:** Science Fiction (Parody; Space Opera)
**Series:** Star Wreck
**Major character(s):** Jean-Lucy Ricardo, Spaceship Captain (*U.S.S. Endocrine*); James T. Smirk, Spaceship Captain (*U.S.S. Endocrine*); Dacron, Android
**Time period(s):** 24th century
**Locale(s):** *U.S.S. Endocrine*, Spaceship (Starfreak)

**Summary:** After Commander Wilson Piker accidentally flings a videotape into the past, a computer preview feature shows that "Star Wreck" fandom will spring into existence fully formed, fifty years in the future, much to Ricardo's distress and Smirk's delight. Hoping to cure the offensive anachronism, the *Endocrine's* crew ricochets through time and parodies of "Star Trek" and "Star Trek: The Next Generation" episodes, wreaking havoc and rewriting history.

**Other books you might like:**
Douglas Adams, *The Hitchhiker's Guide to the Galaxy*, 1980
Henry N. Beard, *Bored of the Rings*, 1969
 Douglas C. Kinney, co-author
Roger L. DiSilvestro, *Living with the Reptiles*, 1990
John M. Ford, *How Much for Just the Planet?*, 1987
Harry Harrison, *Bill, the Galactic Hero*, 1965
Daniel Manus Pinkwater, *Borgel*, 1990
Ellis Weiner, *National Lampoon's Doon*, 1984

## 4565

**LEAH REWOLINSKI
HARRY TRUMBORE**, Illustrator

### Star Wreck IV: Live Long and Profit

(New York: St. Martin's, 1993)

**Story type:** Science Fiction (Parody; Space Opera)
**Series:** Star Wreck
**Major character(s):** Jean-Lucy Ricardo, Spaceship Captain (*U.S.S. Endocrine*); James T. Smirk, Spaceship Captain (*U.S.S. Endocrine*); Deanna "Dee" Troit, Alien (half Betavoid), Telepath
**Time period(s):** 24th century
**Locale(s):** *U.S.S. Endocrine*, Spaceship (Starfreak)

**Summary:** After wrekkie fans present a full scale working model of the *Endocrine* to James T. Smirk and his crew, Starfreak decides to decommission one *Endocrine*, relieve many crew of duties and assign Jean-Lucy Ricardo to find the Fountain of Youth to bottle and sell throughout the galaxy. Hoping to gain favor, Smirk tries to find the Fountain of Youth before Ricardo, but first discovers the Fountain of Love and Fountain of Truth and proceeds, kissing and telling, across the galaxy.

**Other books you might like:**
Douglas Adams, *The Hitchhiker's Guide to the Galaxy*, 1980
Chester Anderson, *The Butterfly Kid*, 1967
Henry N. Beard, *Bored of the Rings*, 1969
    Douglas C. Kenney, co-author
John M. Ford, *How Much for Just the Planet?*, 1987
Jovial Bob Stine, *Spaceballs: The Book*, 1987
Ellis Weiner, *National Lampoon's Doon*, 1984

## 4566

**LEAH REWOLINSKI
HARRY TRUMBORE**, Illustrator

### Star Wreck: The Generation Gap

(New York: St. Martin's Press, 1990)

**Story type:** Science Fiction (Parody; Space Opera)
**Series:** Star Wreck
**Major character(s):** James T. Smirk, Spaceship Captain; Jean-Lucy Ricardo, Spaceship Captain
**Time period(s):** 23rd century (stardate 2323.23232323232323 1/2)
**Locale(s):** *U.S.S. Endocrine*, Spaceship; Cellulite-1 Starfreak Colony, Planet—Imaginary

**Summary:** Captain Jean-Lucy Ricardo becomes the unwilling host to Captain Smirk, Mr. Smock, Dr. McCaw and others until the *Endocrine* is captured by a tractor beam drawing them to the Planet of the Cellulites. Captain Smirk and crew steal the cup section of the ship leaving Captain Ricardo and crew with the saucer section and the Cellulites. After a month of party-hopping around the galaxy, Captain Smirk decides he wants another try at Counselor Troit's attention and returns. The combined crew co-operates to free themselves using junk food and sedatives.

**Other books you might like:**
Douglas Adams, *The Hitchhiker's Guide to the Galaxy*, 1980
Henry N. Beard, *Bored of the Rings*, 1969
    Douglas C. Kenney, co-author
John M. Ford, *How Much for Just the Planet?*, 1987
    Star Trek 36
Harry Harrison, *Bill, the Galactic Hero*, 1965
Ellis Weiner, *National Lampoon's Doon*, 1984

## 4567

**TED REYNOLDS**

### The Tides of God

(New York: Ace, 1989)

**Story type:** Science Fiction (Theological)
**Major character(s):** Elwyn Kimberlin, Spaceship Captain; Foth, Scholar
**Time period(s):** 33rd century
**Locale(s):** *Hound of Heaven*, Spaceship

**Summary:** Scientists have discovered that the periods of religious frenzy which have periodically disrupted Earth civilization since the beginning of recorded history are actually the result of psychic broadcasts sent by a gigantic spaceborne entity which moves on a long orbit through our galaxy. The crew of the *Hound of Heaven* set off on a dangerous and ambiguous mission to destroy the being.

**Other books you might like:**
James Blish, *A Case of Conscience*, 1958
John Kessel, *Good News From Outer Space*, 1989
Walter M. Miller Jr., *A Canticle for Leibowitz*, 1960
James Morrow, *Only Begotten Daughter*, 1990

## 4568

**DANIEL RHODES**

### Adversary

(New York: Tor, 1989)

**Story type:** Horror (Satanism)
**Major character(s):** Nicole Partrick, Young Woman (Ambitious); Guy-Luc Valcourt, Demon, Servant
**Time period(s):** 1980s
**Locale(s):** San Francisco, California

**Summary:** In this sequel to *Next, After Lucifer*, Nicole Partrick is gradually seduced into a cult led by the demonic Guy-Luc Valcourt, putting not only her own life and soul in jeopardy, but also those of her son. A small group, including her lover, a priest, and a clairvoyant woman and her husband, race against time to rescue Nicole and destroy Valcourt/Courdeval.

**Other books you might like:**
T.E.D. Klein, *The Ceremonies*, 1984
Dennis Wheatley, *To the Devil, a Daughter*, 1953

## 4569

**DANIEL RHODES**

### Kiss of Death

(New York: St. Martin's, 1990)

**Story type:** Horror (Erotic Horror)
**Major character(s):** Selena Clermont, Heiress; Donald Clermont, Vintner; Gene Farrell, Doctor (emergency room)
**Time period(s):** 1980s (1988); 1960s (1966)
**Locale(s):** Sonoma, California; Saint-Fabrisse, France

**Summary:** Selena Clermont, the grown-up child of a woman who was raped while her father made an offering to the bloodthirsty moon goddess, sacrifices her casual lovers to appease the goddess and her minions. Trouble begins when she falls in love with Gene Farrell and her demonic overseers demand him as a sacrifice as well.

**Other books you might like:**
Thomas F. Monteleone, *Lyrica*, 1987

Kathryn Ptacek, *In Silence Sealed*, 1988
Peter Straub, *Ghost Story*, 1979

---

**4570**

**ANNE RICE**

## Lasher

(New York: Knopf, 1993)

**Story type:** Horror (Occult)
**Series:** Lives of the Mayfair Witches
**Major character(s):** Rowan Mayfair Curry, Doctor, Witch; Michael Curry, Architect; Samuel Larkin, Doctor
**Time period(s):** 1990s (1993)
**Locale(s):** New Orleans, Louisiana

**Summary:** In this direct sequel to the author's *The Witching Hour*, Rowan Mayfair, a member of a long established family of witches, and her husband Michael, a mortal, give birth to a child, Julien, a.k.a. Lasher, who is both a prodigy and a genetic mutant who represents a synthesis greater than the sum of his mortal and supernatural parts.

**Other books you might like:**
Edward Bryant, *Fetish*, 1991
John Updike, *The Witches of Eastwick*, 1984

---

**4571**

**ANNE RICE**

## Memnoch the Devil

(New York: Knopf, 1995)

**Story type:** Horror (Vampire Story)
**Series:** Vampire Chronicles
**Major character(s):** Lestat de Lioncourt, Vampire; Memnoch, Demon; Roger, Criminal (assassin)
**Time period(s):** 1990s (1995)
**Locale(s):** New York, New York

**Summary:** The vampire Lestat's encounter with the ghost of one of his victims reignites the crisis of religious faith he experienced when he was first vampirized. Memnoch, the biblical devil, chooses this moment to reveal himself to Lestat and presents himself as a lover of man aggrieved at the human suffering demanded by God. In his effort to enlist Lestat in his eternal struggle, he retells the story of the Creation from his point of view and brings Lestat to Heaven and Hell to see God's handiwork directly.

**Other books you might like:**
Marie Corelli, *The Sorrows of Satan*, 1895
Anatole France, *Revolt of the Angels*, 1914
John Milton, *Paradise Lost*, 1667

---

**4572**

**ANNE RICE**

## The Mummy, or Ramses the Damned

(New York: Ballantine, 1989)

**Story type:** Horror (Reanimated Dead)
**Major character(s):** Ramses the Great, Historical Figure (Egyptian Pharaoh), Reanimated Dead (Disguised as an Egyptologist); Julie Stratford, Adventurer, Heiress (Rich and beautiful)
**Time period(s):** 1900s (Edwardian Age)
**Locale(s):** London, England; Egypt

**Summary:** Restored to life, Ramses experiences the feverish appetites of the living. In the guise of Egyptologist Dr. Ramsey, he woos a beautiful adventuress as he tries to locate and reanimate his beloved Cleopatra—with terrible consequences.

**Other books you might like:**
Charles L. Grant, *The Long Night of the Grave*, 1986
H. Rider Haggard, *She*, 1886

---

**4573**

**ANNE RICE**

## Pandora

(New York: Knopf, 1998)

**Story type:** Horror (Vampire Story)
**Series:** New Tales of the Vampires
**Major character(s):** Lydia "Pandora", Vampire; Marius, Religious (priest); Flavius, Slave
**Time period(s):** 1st century B.C.
**Locale(s):** Antioch, Greece; Rome, Italy

**Summary:** In Antioch, to which she has fled following the death of Julius Caesar and the disgrace of her family, Lydia, under the alias Pandora, is given the Dark Gift of vampirism by Marius, a priest of Akasha, the vampire queen of Egypt. For the next two centuries, Marius and Pandora guard Akasha and witness the rise of Christianity, which will eventually damn them and their kind. The first in a new series of stories spun off from the mythology of *Interview with the Vampire* (1975).

**Other books you might like:**
Alice Borchardt, *The Silver Wolf*, 1998
Marion Zimmer Bradley, *Lady of Avalon*, 1997
Les Daniels, *The Silver Skull*, 1979
S.P. Somtow, *Vampire Junction*, 1984
Chelsea Quinn Yarbro, *Blood Games*, 1979

---

**4574**

**ANNE RICE**

## The Queen of the Damned

(New York: Knopf, 1988)

**Story type:** Horror (Vampire Story)
**Series:** Vampire Chronicles
**Major character(s):** Lestat de Lioncourt, Vampire (Posing as rock-and-roll singer); Akasha, Vampire (Mother of all vampires)
**Time period(s):** 1980s; Indeterminate Past
**Locale(s):** San Francisco, California; South America; Egypt

**Summary:** When rock singer-vampire Lestat reveals his true origins, he rouses Akasha, Queen of the Damned, who, claiming to "save" mankind from itself, sets a plan in motion to give herself and her son/lover the power and status of gods.

**Other books you might like:**
Suzy McKee Charnas, *The Vampire Tapestry*, 1980
Pierre Kast, *The Vampires of Alfama*, 1975
S.P. Somtow, *Vampire Junction*, 1984
Whitley Strieber, *The Hunger*, 1981

**4575**

ANNE RICE

## *Servant of the Bones*

(New York: Knopf, 1996)

**Story type:** Horror (Occult)
**Major character(s):** Azriel, Mythical Creature (genie); Zurvan, Scholar; Gregory Belkin, Religious (televangelist)
**Time period(s):** 7th century B.C. (600 B.C.); 1990s (1996)
**Locale(s):** Babylon; New York, New York

**Summary:** Tricked into allowing himself to be sacrificed to save his people, the Hebrew aristocrat Azriel becomes the "Servant of the Bones," a genie who can be summoned to do the bidding of whoever possesses his gold covered remains. Azriel's experiences over the centuries stimulate great reflection on the human condition, particularly his encounter with Gregory Belkin, a contemporary televangelist who has sacrificed his daughter Esther and who hopes to use Azriel's powers to achieve world domination.

**Other books you might like:**
Clive Barker, *Everville*, 1994
Graham Joyce, *Requiem*, 1996
Tanith Lee, *Darkness, I*, 1994
Alan Rodgers, *Night*, 1991

**4576**

ANNE RICE

## *The Tale of the Body Thief*

(New York: Alfred A. Knopf, 1992)

**Story type:** Horror (Vampire Story)
**Series:** Vampire Chronicles
**Major character(s):** Lestat de Lioncourt, Vampire; David Talbot, Occultist (retired academic); Raglan James, Supernatural Being (body thief)
**Time period(s):** 1990s
**Locale(s):** Miami, Florida; Paris, France

**Summary:** Bored with his long life, and tortured by dreams and memories of his bloody past, the centuries old vampire Lestat decides to end his life. While making his final preparations, he encounters a body thief, a supernatural being who lives by commandeering the bodies of living human beings, who offers Lestat the chance to assume a mortal's body and become human again.

**Other books you might like:**
Scott Ciencin, *The Vampire Odyssey*, 1992
Elizabeth Engstrom, *Black Ambrosia*, 1988
Brian Stableford, *The Empire of Fear*, 1988
Theodore Sturgeon, *Some of Your Blood*, 1961

**4577**

ANNE RICE

## *Taltos*

(New York: Knopf, 1994)

**Story type:** Horror (Occult)
**Series:** Lives of the Mayfair Witches
**Major character(s):** Ashlar "Mr. Ash", Businessman; Yuri Stefano, Gypsy; Mona Mayfair, Businesswoman
**Time period(s):** 1990s (1994)
**Locale(s):** New York, New York

**Summary:** Ashlar, a member of a dying race of prehistoric beings known as the Taltos, hopes to produce an heir by mating with one of the Mayfair witches in this third installment in the Lives of the Mayfair Witches saga. Over the course of the novel, Ashlar gives a running history of how he has survived over the millenia, strategically embracing and integrating with the human civilization that has repeatedly tried to exterminate him and his kind.

**Other books you might like:**
Kathryn Meyer Griffith, *Witches*, 1993
Ira Levin, *Rosemary's Baby*, 1967
John Updike, *The Witches of Eastwick*, 1984

**4578**

ANNE RICE

## *The Vampire Armand*

(New York: Knopf, 1998)

**Story type:** Horror (Vampire Story)
**Series:** New Tales of the Vampires
**Major character(s):** Armand, Vampire; Marius De Romanus, Artist (painter), Vampire; David Talbot, Detective (psychic); Talamasca, Vampire
**Time period(s):** 1990s (1998); 16th century
**Locale(s):** New Orleans, Louisiana; Venice, Italy

**Summary:** While he tends the body of the comatose vampire Lestat, awaiting the revelation Lestat has brought from his encounter with the deity, Armand relates the 500-year history of his life. This includes his purchase as a servant by the vampire painter Marius, Marius's vampirization of him, Armand's founding of the decadent Theatre des Vampires in Paris, and his eventual involvement with Benji and Sybelle, two mortal children who save his life. A sequel to *Pandora*, and the second novel in the author's series of new adventures concerned with peripheral characters from *Interview with the Vampire* and other installments in the Vampire Chronicles.

**Other books you might like:**
Pierre Kast, *The Vampires of Alfama*, 1975
Tanith Lee, *Darkness, I*, 1994
Brian Stableford, *The Empire of Fear*, 1988
Michael Talbot, *The Delicate Dependency*, 1982
Chelsea Quinn Yarbro, *The Angry Angel*, 1998

**4579**

ANNE RICE

## *Violin*

(New York: Knopf, 1997)

**Story type:** Horror (Ghost Story)
**Major character(s):** Triana Becker, Musician; Stephan Stefanovsky, Musician (violinist), Spirit; Katrinka Russell, Housewife (Triana's sister)
**Time period(s):** 1990s (1997); 19th century
**Locale(s):** New Orleans, Louisiana; Vienna, Austria; Rio de Janeiro, Brazil

**Summary:** Devastated with grief over the loss of loved ones and haunted by memories of the past, failed musician Triana Becker is vulnerable to the influence of Stefan Stefanovsky, a violinist who died unfulfilled and miserable centuries before. Unbounded by the limits of time and space, Triana and Stefan pursue each other across the centuries and the globe, Stefan trying to dominate Triana with his music and imprison her in his own hell, and Triana trying to usurp Stefan's power and find salvation.

**Other books you might like:**
Clive Barker, *Sacrament*, 1996
Jonathan Carroll, *From the Teeth of Angels*, 1994
Lewis Shiner, *Glimpses*, 1993
Danielle Steele, *Ghost*, 1997

---

**4580**

ANNE RICE

## The Witching Hour

(New York: Knopf, 1990)

**Story type:** Horror (Black Magic)
**Series:** Lives of the Mayfair Witches
**Major character(s):** Michael Curry, Architect; Rowan Mayfair, Doctor (Neurosurgeon), Witch; Lasher, Demon
**Time period(s):** 20th century
**Locale(s):** New Orleans, Louisiana; San Francisco, California

**Summary:** Interspersed into Rice's vast, sprawling story of the love of psychically gifted recluse Michael Curry and San Francisco neurosurgeon Rowan Mayfair is the 300-year history of the Mayfairs, a family of witches, as revealed by a group of scholars of the occult called the Talamasca, who offer aid when Michael and Rowan's exploration of their heritage is endangered by an evil spirit.

**Other books you might like:**
Shirley Jackson, *The Haunting of Hill House*, 1959
Dan Simmons, *Carrion Comfort*, 1989

---

**4581**

DOUG RICE

## Blood of Mugwump

(Normal, Illinois: Black Ice Books, 1996)

**Story type:** Horror (Vampire Story)
**Major character(s):** Doug Rice, Young Man, Vampire; Caddie Rice, Young Woman, Vampire; Grandma Mugwump Torgov, Aged Person, Vampire
**Time period(s):** 1990s (1996)
**Locale(s):** Endicott, Pennsylvania

**Summary:** This first novel offers a series of vignettes concerning the Mugwumps, a clan of gender-shifting vampires. Doug Rice, the youngest member of the clan, has taken possession of his sister Caddie's body and spends much of the book pondering the problems of gender-defined identity that this new form of being poses.

**Other books you might like:**
Kathy Acker, *Empire of the Senseless*, 1988
William S. Burroughs, *Nova Express*, 1964
Joseph McElroy, *Plus*, 1976
Melanie Tem, *Desmodus*, 1994

---

**4582**

JANE RICE
JACON ECKHARDT, Illustrator

## The Sixth Dog

(West Warwick, Rhode Island: Necronomicon Press, 1995)

**Story type:** Horror (Black Magic)
**Major character(s):** Agnes Hanlon, Assistant (to a veterinarian); Otis Clanton, Aged Person; Billy Williams, Handyman
**Time period(s):** 1990s (1995)

**Locale(s):** Midwest

**Summary:** The unnamed narrator of this story, a veterinarian, tells of his peculiar neighbor Otis Clanton, who mysteriously appears to acquire a new dog every time someone in town—usually someone who has openly expressed dislike of him—disappears. This is the author's first book (a 28 page booklet.)

**Other books you might like:**
Jonathan Carroll, *The Land of Laughs*, 1980
S.K. Epperson, *Borderland: A Novel of Terror*, 1992
James Herbert, *Fluke*, 1977
Jack Williamson, *Darker than You Think*, 1948

---

**4583**

PETER L. RICE

## Monsoon

(Chicago: FASA Corporation, 1992)

**Story type:** Science Fiction (Military)
**Series:** Renegade Legion
**Major character(s):** Wilson Goode, Bounty Hunter; Spencer Kennet, Miner, Businessman (mine operator); Archemon, Alien (Leilan)
**Time period(s):** 69th century (6830)
**Locale(s):** Monsoon, Planet—Imaginary (Leilas)

**Summary:** Humans from Earth, organized as the Terran Overlord Government, enforce Terran rule over other humans in the galaxy. On Monsoon, TOG forces threaten to destroy the environment and intelligent natives unless the Rock Rangers, Renegade Legions or the Commonwealth resistance can free the world from TOG influence.

**Other books you might like:**
Gordon R. Dickson, *Dorsai!*, 1976
David Drake, *Hammer's Slammers*, 1979
Robert A. Heinlein, *Starship Troopers*, 1959
William H. Keith Jr., *Renegade's Honor*, 1988
Steve Perry, *The Man Who Never Missed*, 1985
Jerry Pournelle, *Falkenberg's Legion*, 1990
Robert Thurston, *Way of the Clans*, 1991

---

**4584**

ROBERT RICE

## The Last Pendragon

(New York: Walker, 1991)

**Story type:** Fantasy (Legend)
**Major character(s):** Bedwyr, Knight; Irion ap Medrault, Royalty
**Time period(s):** 6th century (540s)
**Locale(s):** England

**Summary:** Eleven years after Arthur Pendragon's fall from power, Bedwyr returns from service in the Roman Imperial Army with the news that the Roman Empire can spare no soldiers to help curb the Saxon rebellion in Britain. Bedwyr reluctantly joins forces with Arthur's grandson, Irion, hoping to unite the many kingdoms left after Arthur's reign. This is the author's first novel.

**Other books you might like:**
John Desjarlais, *The Throne of Tara*, 1990
Parke Godwin, *Sherwood*, 1991
Patricia Kennealy-Morrison, *The Hawk's Gray Feather*, 1990
Mary Stewart, *The Wicked Day*, 1983
Rosemary Sutcliff, *The Shining Company*, 1990

## 4585

### ENID RICHEMONT

## The Time Tree

(Boston: Little Brown, 1990)

**Story type:** Fantasy (Time Travel; Historical)
**Major character(s):** Rachel, Child, Student; Joanna, Child, Student; Anne, Handicapped (deaf), Spirit (ghost child)
**Time period(s):** 1990s (1990); 16th century (1598)
**Locale(s):** Finchley, England

**Summary:** Two 20th century schoolgirls befriend an oddly costumed ghost-girl they meet while climbing a tree, and teach her to read. Anne, the 16th century ghost, is able to teach her family in the 20th century that despite her handicap, she is neither stupid nor evil and can learn from lessons, finally embroidering a sampler that survives to the 20th century in a museum.

**Other books you might like:**
L.M. Boston, *The Treasure of Green Knowe*, 1958
E. Nesbit, *The House of Arden*, 1909
Edward Ormondroyd, *Time at the Top*, 1963
Ruth Park, *Playing Beatie Bow*, 1980
Philippa Pearce, *Tom's Midnight Garden*, 1959

## 4586

### PHIL RICKMAN

## Candle Night

(New York: Jove 1995)

**Story type:** Horror (Ancient Evil Unleashed)
**Major character(s):** Giles Freeman, Journalist; Claire Freeman, Photographer; Berry Morelli, Journalist
**Time period(s):** 1990s (1991)
**Locale(s):** Y Groes, Wales

**Summary:** Englishman Giles Freeman moves with his wife Claire to the Welsh town of Y Groes, renowned for its insularity and legendary aversion to visits by outsiders. The relocation awakens Claire to her Welsh heritage and reignites a legacy of Druidic terror that has been a suppressed part of her family history for centuries. This first novel was first published in England in 1991.

**Other books you might like:**
Algernon Blackwood, *Julius LeVallon: An Episode*, 1917
Arthur Machen, *The Green Round*, 1933
Arthur Machen, *The Hill of Dreams*, 1907
Brent Monahan, *The Uprising*, 1993
David van Meter Smith, *Trinity Grove*, 1988

## 4587

### PHIL RICKMAN

## Curfew

(New York: Putnam's, 1993)

**Story type:** Horror (Ancient Evil Unleashed)
**Major character(s):** Max Goff, Producer (record producer); Joe M. Powys, Writer; Faye Morrison, Journalist
**Time period(s):** 1990s (1993)
**Locale(s):** Crybbe, Wales

**Summary:** Naively inspired by a mystical history of the small Welsh town of Crybbe, filthy rich record producer Max Goff buys up much of the town with the hope of exploiting its New Age appeal. But

Crybbe harbors many dark secrets, among them an occult Druidic heritage that Goff's ambitions threaten to resurrect. This novel was originally published in England under the title *Crybbe*.

**Other books you might like:**
Ramsey Campbell, *The Hungry Moon*, 1986
Kim Newman, *Jago*, 1992

## 4588

### PHIL RICKMAN

## December

(New York: Berkley, 1996)

**Story type:** Horror (Occult)
**Major character(s):** Dave Reilly, Musician; Moira Cairns, Musician; Simon St. John, Musician
**Time period(s):** 1990s (1994)
**Locale(s):** Gwent, Wales (Abbey of Ystrad Ddu)

**Summary:** When their recording session at a legend-haunted Welsh castle ends with a band member dead and John Lennon coincidentally murdered halfway across the world, the members of Philosopher's Stone agree to disband and never play together again. Thirteen years later, a bootleg tape of the session resurfaces and the band members must work together to prevent the horror of that night from happening again. This novel was first published in England in 1994 in a slightly different form.

**Other books you might like:**
Marvin Kaye, *Fantastique*, 1992
Adrian Savage, *Symphony*, 1992
John Skipp, *The Scream*, 1988
   Craig Spector, co-author

## 4589

### ALAN RIEFE

## Viper

(New York: Diamond, 1990)

**Story type:** Horror (Wild Talents)
**Major character(s):** Felicity Jane Hadfield, Child; Roger Grenier, Businessman; Zaman, Servant (Indian manservant)
**Time period(s):** 1980s (1980)
**Locale(s):** Dharwar District, India; Honolulu, Hawaii

**Summary:** In India, where she has been taken by her loving stepfather and stepmother, Felicity Jane Hadfield discovers she is *davia*, a person venerated for her ability to summon and control snakes. She returns with her newfound powers to Honolulu to seek revenge on the murderers of her wealthy benefactress.

**Other books you might like:**
John Tigges, *Venom*, 1988

## 4590

### L.S. RIKER

## Kill Crazy

(New York: St. Martin's, 1993)

**Story type:** Science Fiction (Adventure)
**Series:** Swag
**Major character(s):** Swag, Martial Arts Expert, Detective—Private; Mortimer Bammer, Military Personnel, Leader; Dobbs, Public Relations (spin doctor)

**Time period(s):** 21st century
**Locale(s):** New York, New York

**Summary:** After the death of his friend, Swag's investigation leads to a deadly new drug and his old enemies from Provost headquarters. Sequel to *Full Clip*.

**Other books you might like:**
Pat Cadigan, *Fools*, 1992
Robert Cain, *Cybernarc*, 1991
Robert Cain, *Gold Dragon*, 1991
Jake Davis, *The Last Rangers*, 1992
Michael Kandel, *Captain Jack Zodiac*, 1992
William Shatner, *TekLords*, 1991
Neal Stephenson, *Snow Crash*, 1992

**4591**

**STEVEN WILLIAM RIMMER**

### Coven

(New York: Ballantine, 1989)

**Story type:** Horror (Black Magic)
**Major character(s):** Elspet, Witch; Margrett, Witch
**Time period(s):** 1980s (1986; Prologue in 1641)
**Locale(s):** Drenewydd, Scotland

**Summary:** In Rimmer's first novel, the tranquility of Elspet's coven is upset by the arrival of Master Paul, his woman, Margrett, and their gang of biker followers, who seek to revive the old practices, including ritual human sacrifice, to restore the power of the "old witches' magic." At the risk of her life, Elspet defies the Master and Margrett to protect the lives of her friends and the survival of the coven.

**Other books you might like:**
John Burke, *The Devil's Footsteps*, 1976
Norah Lofts, *The Devil's Own*, 1960

**4592**

**KAREN RIPLEY**

### The Persistence of Memory

(New York: Ballantine Del Rey, 1993)

**Story type:** Science Fiction (Adventure; Mystery)
**Series:** Slow World
**Major character(s):** Cassidy, Horse Trainer, Amnesiac; Rowena, Worker (goatherd); Allen, Farmer, Lawman
**Time period(s):** Indeterminate
**Locale(s):** Earth (unknown grasslands)

**Summary:** Knowing only the name of her horse and that she came from elsewhere, Cassidy uses a name from a partly remembered film, not noticing things missing from her environment. She fits in among Horsemen, but must hide her differences when saved by Riders. She leaves them with another "different" woman to achieve answers to questions about the grasslands and her background. First of a series.

**Other books you might like:**
John Brunner, *The Tides of Time*, 1984
C.J. Cherryh, *Wave Without a Shore*, 1981
M.A. Foster, *Preserver*, 1985
Garry Kilworth, *The Night of Kadar*, 1980
Ursula K. Le Guin, *City of Illusions*, 1967
Andre Norton, *Forerunner*, 1981
Andrew J. Offutt, *King Dragon*, 1980

**4593**

**KAREN RIPLEY**

### Prisoner of Dreams

(New York: Ballantine/Del Rey, 1989)

**Story type:** Science Fiction (Space Opera)
**Major character(s):** Jo-lac, Spaceship Captain; Lewis, Servant (Indentured), Psychic, Genetically Altered Being
**Time period(s):** Indeterminate Future
**Locale(s):** *Raptor*, Spaceship

**Summary:** Jo-lac runs cargo from one star system to another until she's talked into taking on human freight, Lewis, a prisoner who someone apparently wants dead. It turns out there's a complex plot afoot involving sentient computers and psychics. Jo-lac falls in love with Lewis and decides to get to the bottom of the mystery no matter what the consequences. This is Ripley's first novel.

**Other books you might like:**
C.J. Cherryh, *Merchanter's Luck*, 1982
Melissa Scott, *The Empress of Earth*, 1987
Melissa Scott, *Silence in Solitude*, 1986
Walter Jon Williams, *Angel Station*, 1989

**4594**

**KAREN RIPLEY**

### The Tenth Class

(New York: Ballantine/Del Rey, 1991)

**Story type:** Science Fiction (Adventure; Genetic Manipulation)
**Series:** Tenth Class
**Major character(s):** Jo-Lac, Spaceship Captain; Lewis, Genetically Altered Being, Psychic; Taylor, Public Relations
**Time period(s):** Indeterminate Future
**Locale(s):** Porta Flora, Planet—Imaginary; Earthheart, Planet—Imaginary

**Summary:** Captain Jo-Lac is asked to cooperate with the authorities in tracking down powerful people who want to round up the Class Tens, including Lewis. Frightened by the power of those against her, Jo-Lac and Taylor travel a roundabout way, first to Heinlein, then to Earthheart where the Class Tens are. Mysteriously tracked, when they discover Taylor has been made a human marker, Lewis cures this, allowing them to destroy the enemy and give hope to all the genetically substandard.

**Other books you might like:**
Jack L. Chalker, *Pirates of the Thunder*, 1987
M.A. Foster, *The Warriors of Dawn*, 1975
Cheryl J. Franklin, *The Light in Exile*, 1990
Raymond Harris, *The Broken Worlds*, 1986
S.N. Lewitt, *Angel at Apogee*, 1987
R.M. Meluch, *Wind Child*, 1982
Melisa C. Michaels, *Skirmish*, 1985
Melissa Scott, *Five-Twelfths of Heaven*, 1985
Timothy Zahn, *Deadman Switch*, 1988

**4595**

**KAREN RIPLEY**

### The Warden of Horses

(New York: Ballantine Del Rey, 1994)

**Story type:** Science Fiction (Alternate Universe; Adventure)
**Series:** Slow World

**Major character(s):** Cathy "Cassidy" Delaney, Amnesiac, Horse Trainer; Andy "the Warden" Greene, Ruler; Click, Leader, Tinker
**Time period(s):** Indeterminate
**Locale(s):** Iron City, Fictional City

**Summary:** Robbed by a woodsman, Cassidy and Rowena link up with a band of tinkers traveling to Iron City. Pursued by villagers and almost killed by monsters, Cassidy confronts the Warden only to find she remembers him from her past life as Andy Greene, an autistic boy she taught to ride. As he cannot answer her questions and monsters still pursue her, she sets off with Click to find the mysterious Alchemist of Time.

**Other books you might like:**
Poul Anderson, *Three Hearts and Three Lions*, 1961
Piers Anthony, *Orn*, 1971
David Brin, *The Practice Effect*, 1984
John Brunner, *The Tides of Time*, 1984
M.A. Foster, *Preserver*, 1985
Garry Kilworth, *The Night of Kadar*, 1980
Ursula K. Le Guin, *City of Illusions*, 1967
Andre Norton, *Here Abide Monsters*, 1973
Andrew J. Offutt, *King Dragon*, 1980
John Varley, *Titan*, 1979

---

**4596**

**J.F. RIVKIN**

## Mistress of Ambiguities

(New York: Ace, 1991)

**Story type:** Fantasy (Sword and Sorcery)
**Series:** Silverglass
**Major character(s):** Nyctasia, Ruler; Corson, Martial Arts Expert (swordswoman)
**Time period(s):** Indeterminate Past
**Locale(s):** Rhostshyl, Fictional City

**Summary:** The aftermath of civil war brings Rhostshyl, city and court, into nearly as much turmoil as the war itself, though of a different sort. The intense political intrigues, an amnesiac wanderer, an ambitious scholar, a proposed marriage alliance and a brace of newly recovered spellbooks combine to create a situation requiring all of Nyctasia and Corson's craft and skill to negotiate.

**Other books you might like:**
Gael Baudino, *Gossamer Axe*, 1990
Barbara Hambly, *The Ladies of Mandrigyn*, 1984
Rosemary Kirstein, *The Steerswoman*, 1989
Mercedes Lackey, *The Oathbound*, 1988
Anne Logston, *Shadow*, 1991
Shirley Meier, *The Cage*, 1989
    S.M. Stirling, co-author

---

**4597**

**J.F. RIVKIN**

## Tyrannosaurus Rex

(New York: Roc, 1992)

**Story type:** Science Fiction (Time Travel; Adventure)
**Major character(s):** Christine Fawcett, Explorer, Time Traveler; Mark Anthony "Tony" Blondell, Explorer, Time Traveler; Manuel "Manny" Aburto, Guide, Time Traveler
**Time period(s):** 1990s; Indeterminate Past (Cretaceous Epoch)
**Locale(s):** London, England; Brazil

**Summary:** After Christine discovers her grandfather's diary and an unaged dinosaur bone, she organizes an expedition to the Brazilian jungle he explored. In a pyramid far from most Mayan ruins, Christine, Tony and Manny find themselves thrown back in time to the Cretaceous where they must thwart hungry dinosaurs and treacherous villains to return home.

**Other books you might like:**
Michael Crichton, *Jurassic Park*, 1990
Sir Arthur Conan Doyle, *The Lost World*, 1912
James Gurney, *Dinotopia*, 1992
Stephen Leigh, *Ray Bradbury Presents: Dinosaur World*, 1992

---

**4598**

**DAVID ROBBINS**

## Hell-O-Ween

(New York: Leisure, 1992)

**Story type:** Horror (Ancient Evil Unleashed)
**Major character(s):** Cory Fleming, Teenager; Ann Weatherby, Teenager; Wesley Eagen, Teenager
**Time period(s):** 1990s (1992)
**Locale(s):** Pagosa Springs, Colorado

**Summary:** A Halloween prank pulled to scare class nerd Cory Fleming backfires horribly, unleashing a legendary demon from the nearby Caverna del Diablo who begins systematically killing the pranksters in typically gruesome fashion.

**Other books you might like:**
D.A. Fowler, *The Devil's End*, 1992
Steven Ray Fulgham, *The Summoned*, 1991
Robert Kline, *Campfire Story*, 1990

---

**4599**

**DAVID ROBBINS**

## L.A. Strike

(New York: Leisure, 1990)

**Story type:** Science Fiction (Post-Holocaust)
**Series:** Blade
**Major character(s):** Blade, Warrior; Leo "Lobo" Wood, Warrior; Mike Havoc, Military Personnel (captain)
**Time period(s):** 22nd century (106 years post-holocaust)
**Locale(s):** Los Angeles, California

**Summary:** When one of two rival ganglords kidnaps a new recruit to the Freedom Force, Blade leads his Force to rescue her, and wipes out both gangs in the process.

**Other books you might like:**
David Brin, *The Postman*, 1985
Mark Grant, *Mutants Amok*, 1991
    pseudonym of David Bischoff
Robert A. Heinlein, *Farnham's Freehold*, 1964
David R. Palmer, *Emergence*, 1984

---

**4600**

**DAVID ROBBINS**

## Madman Run

(New York: Leisure, 1991)

**Story type:** Science Fiction (Post-Holocaust)
**Series:** Endworld

**Major character(s):** Blade, Teenager, Warrior; Geronimo, Teenager, Warrior; Endora Morlock, Gentlewoman (mistress of Castle Orm)
**Time period(s):** 21st century
**Locale(s):** Minnesota (northern)

**Summary:** Sixteen-year-old Blade, having just attained Warrior status, travels the countryside with his friends Hickok and Geronimo. They come upon a castle where a pale woman beckons to them. Entering, they are captured by her husband, a madman who keeps others enslaved underground. After trying futilely to get the slaves to revolt, Blade and his companions kill the Morlock masters and return home.

**Other books you might like:**
Poul Anderson, *Twilight World*, 1961
John Dalmas, *The Yngling*, 1971
James B. Johnson, *Daystar and Shadow*, 1981
Henry Kuttner, *Mutant*, 1953
    written as Lewis Padgett
Andrew J. Offutt, *The Castle Keeps*, 1972
Paul O. Williams, *The Song of the Axe*, 1984
Roger Zelazny, *Damnation Alley*, 1969

## 4601
### DAVID ROBBINS

## *Prank Night*
(New York: Leisure, 1994)

**Story type:** Horror (Ancient Evil Unleashed)
**Major character(s):** Ben Shields, Writer; Nadine Somersby, Store Owner; Travis Sinclair, Police Officer (sheriff)
**Time period(s):** 1990s (1994)
**Locale(s):** Cemetery Ridge, Oregon

**Summary:** Ben Shields' return to his childhood hometown coincides with the rampage of a monster that lives in the local cemetery and wreaks havoc every few Halloweens. Efforts to track the monster and destroy it are thwarted by the mischief of several locals who resent Ben's return.

**Other books you might like:**
Charles L. Grant, *Stunts*, 1990
Jack Martin, *Halloween III: Season of the Witch*, 1985
Robert R. McCammon, *Usher's Passing*, 1985
Ashley McConnell, *Days of the Dead*, 1992

## 4602
### DAVID ROBBINS

## *Spartan Run*
(New York: Leisure, 1991)

**Story type:** Science Fiction (Post-Holocaust)
**Series:** Endworld
**Major character(s):** Blade, Warrior; Rikki-Tikki-Tavi, Warrior; "Agis" Agesilaus, Military Personnel (head of the Secret Police)
**Time period(s):** 22nd century
**Locale(s):** Iowa (northeast)

**Summary:** When Blade and two companions wish to contact Sparta, a strong city-state in northeast Iowa, their presence sparks a civil war between the two kings as the power-mad Agesilaus tries to seize power and have Blade and his friends put to death. While his companions try to rally King Dercyllidas's forces, Blade must undergo trial by ordeal.

**Other books you might like:**
Poul Anderson, *Orion Shall Rise*, 1983
Neal Barrett Jr., *Dawn's Uncertain Light*, 1989
Edmund Cooper, *The Cloud Walker*, 1973
John Dalmas, *The Yngling*, 1971
Dean Ing, *Systemic Shock*, 1981
Paul O. Williams, *The Sword of Forebearance*, 1985
Timothy Zahn, *The Blackcollar*, 1983
Roger Zelazny, *Damnation Alley*, 1969

## 4603
### DAVID ROBBINS

## *Spook Night*
(New York: Leisure, 1995)

**Story type:** Horror (Supernatural Vengeance)
**Major character(s):** John Grant, Computer Expert; Kip Grant, Teenager; Shery Grant, Teenager
**Time period(s):** 1990s (1995)
**Locale(s):** Spook Hollow, Pennsylvania

**Summary:** John Grant relocates his family from Philadelphia to rural Spook Hollow in order to save his marriage, and risks losing his children. Too late, he discovers that his home is the site where a Civil War atrocity produced a local legend, the Headless Horror, who rampages on the Halloween night that his children are attending the local school dance.

**Other books you might like:**
Charles L. Grant, *Stunts*, 1990
Jack Martin, *Halloween III: Season of the Witch*, 1985
Robert R. McCammon, *Usher's Passing*, 1985
Ashley McConnell, *Days of the Dead*, 1992

## 4604
### DAVID ROBBINS

## *Vengeance Strike*
(New York: Leisure, 1991)

**Story type:** Science Fiction (Post-Holocaust)
**Series:** Blade
**Major character(s):** Blade, Warrior; Grizzly, Genetically Altered Being, Warrior; Zhongli Quan, Alien
**Time period(s):** 22nd century
**Locale(s):** California

**Summary:** The Lords of Kismet have sent shapeshifters to impersonate key members of the California government with the sole purpose of wiping out Blade and the Special Forces. When Blade sees through their ruse, one shapeshifter escapes to Oakland where the group catches up with him and kills him, eliminating the menace for the moment.

**Other books you might like:**
Neal Barrett Jr., *Through Darkest America*, 1987
Richard Bowker, *Marlborough Street*, 1987
John Crowley, *Beasts*, 1976
Paul O. Williams, *An Ambush of Shadows*, 1983
Jack Williamson, *Darker than You Think*, 1948
Timothy Zahn, *The Blackcollar*, 1983
Roger Zelazny, *Damnation Alley*, 1969

## 4605

### DAVID ROBBINS

## Yellowstone Run

(New York: Leisure, 1990)

**Story type:** Science Fiction (Post-Holocaust)
**Series:** Endworld
**Major character(s):** Blade, Warrior; Hickock, Warrior; Achilles, Warrior
**Time period(s):** 22nd century (106 years post-holocaust)
**Locale(s):** West (Yellowstone Park, Civilized Zone, Federation)

**Summary:** Blade and his warriors are asked to destroy a band of homicidal mutants—bearlike humanoids—who are threatening to take over the area in and around Yellowstone Park.

**Other books you might like:**
Algis Budrys, *Some Will Not Die*, 1961
Walter M. Miller Jr., *A Canticle for Leibowitz*, 1959
Janet Morris, *Heroes in Hell*, 1986
David R. Palmer, *Emergence*, 1984

## 4606

### TOM ROBBINS

## Half Asleep in Frog Pajamas

(New York: Bantam, 1994)

**Story type:** Science Fiction (Satire; Contemporary Realism)
**Major character(s):** Gwendolyn ''Gwen'' Mati, Stock Broker, Fiance(e); Q-Jo Huffington, Psychic; Motofusa Yamaguchi, Doctor, Administrator
**Time period(s):** 1990s
**Locale(s):** Seattle, Washington

**Summary:** The stock market crash on Maundy Thursday sends Gwen Mati scrambling to recover over Easter weekend.

**Other books you might like:**
William Borden, *Superstoe*, 1968
Michael Kandel, *Captain Jack Zodiac*, 1992
Mark Leyner, *My Cousin, My Gastroenterologist*, 1990
Thomas Pynchon, *Gravity's Rainbow*, 1973
Kurt Vonnegut Jr., *Slaughterhouse Five*, 1969

## 4607

### TOM ROBBINS

## Skinny Legs and All

(New York: Bantam, 1990)

**Story type:** Fantasy (Contemporary; Political)
**Major character(s):** Ellen Cherry Charles, Artist, Waiter/Waitress; Boomer Petway, Mechanic, Artist; Spike Dohen, Restaurateur (partner in Isaac and Ishmael's)
**Time period(s):** 1990s (1990)
**Locale(s):** New York, New York; Jerusalem, Israel

**Summary:** Ellen Cherry Charles is an artist, waitressing at an Arab-Jewish restaurant and in search of something. First Boomer swept her off her feet with his giant Airstream turkey. Now Isaac and Ishmael's restaurant is livelier every week, and all eyes are focused, at some level, on Jerusalem.

**Other books you might like:**
Jim Dodge, *Stone Junction*, 1990

Neil Gaiman, *Good Omens: The Nice and Accurate Prophecies of Agnes Nutter, Witch*, 1990
Terry Pratchett, co-author
Kurt Vonnegut Jr., *Cat's Cradle*, 1963

## 4608

### JENNIFER ROBERSON

## Flight of the Raven

(New York: DAW, 1990)

**Story type:** Fantasy (Quest; Adventure)
**Series:** Cheysuli
**Major character(s):** Aidan, Heir
**Time period(s):** Indeterminate Past
**Locale(s):** Homana, Fictional Country; Solinde, Fictional Country; Erinn, Fictional Country

**Summary:** Aidan has been tormented all his life with dreams of a golden chain that vanishes when he touches it. He knows that even his parents do not believe the visions are real and wonder about his sanity. Now he finds that this knowledge means he's empathic, and gods have begun to visit him with riddles, goading him out into the world to find the real links in the chain.

**Other books you might like:**
Diane Duane, *The Door into Fire*, 1979
Bill Fawcett, *Lords of Dragonclaw*, 1989
Patricia Kennealy-Morrison, *The Copper Crown*, 1984
Adrienne Martine-Barnes, *The Fire Sword*, 1984
Shirley Rousseau Murphy, *The Ring of Fire*, 1977

## 4609

### JENNIFER ROBERSON

## Lady of the Forest

(New York: Zebra, 1992)

**Story type:** Fantasy (Legend; Romance)
**Major character(s):** Marion ''Marion of Ravenskeep'' FitzWalter, Noblewoman; Robert ''Robin Hood'' of Locksley, Nobleman, Outlaw; William deLacey, Nobleman, Lawman (sheriff of Nottingham)
**Time period(s):** 12th century (1190s)
**Locale(s):** Nottingham, England; Sherwood Forest, England; Ravenskeep, England

**Summary:** Suitors assail Marion upon her father's death. As her attraction for Robert of Locksley grows, Marion eschews her father's deathbed wish and William deLacey's advances by citing her status as ward of the captive king, Richard the Lionhearted. When Will Scarlet kidnaps Marion, Little John and Robert rush to her rescue. Robert rebels against Prince John's authority in loyalty to King Richard.

**Other books you might like:**
Marion Zimmer Bradley, *The Mists of Avalon*, 1983
Parke Godwin, *Sherwood*, 1991
Robin McKinley, *The Outlaws of Sherwood*, 1989
Bernard Miles, *Robin Hood: His Life and Legend*, 1979
Howard Pyle, *The Merry Adventures of Robin Hood*, 1883
Richard Kluger, *The Sheriff of Nottingham*, 1990

## 4610

JENNIFER ROBERSON, Editor

### *Return to Avalon: A Celebration of Marion Zimmer Bradley*

(New York: DAW, 1996)

**Story type:** Fantasy (Anthology; Legend)

**Summary:** This volume contains an introduction by Diana L. Paxson; a forward by Andre Norton; essays of appreciation by C.J. Cherryh, Charles de Lint, Paul Edwin Zimmer, and Jennifer Roberson; and 19 original stories by authors including Kate Elliott, Katharine Kerr, Jane M. Lindskold, Melanie Rawn, Jennifer Roberson, Judith Tarr, and Dave Wolverton. The stories reflect and elaborate Marion Zimmer Bradley's vision of legendary Britain and Darkover.

**Other books you might like:**
Mike Ashley, *The Camelot Chronicles*, 1992
    editor
Marion Zimmer Bradley, *The Mists of Avalon*, 1983
Marion Zimmer Bradley, *The Sword and Sorceress Series*, 1984-
    1996
    editor
George Alec Effinger, *Maureen Birnbaum, Barbarian Swordsper-
    son: The Complete Stories*, 1993
Kathleen M. Massie-Ferch, *Ancient Enchantresses*, 1995
    Martin H. Greenberg, Richard Gilliam, co-editors
C.L. Moore, *Jirel of Joiry*, 1969

## 4611

JENNIFER ROBERSON

### *Scotland the Brave*

(New York: Warner Aspect, 1996)

**Story type:** Fantasy (Political; Adventure)
**Series:** Highlander
**Major character(s):** Duncan MacLeod, Immortal, Martial Arts Ex-
    pert; Joe Dawson, Spy (Watcher), Historian; Annie Devlin, Im-
    mortal, Revolutionary (IRA)
**Time period(s):** 1990s; 18th century
**Locale(s):** Pacific Northwest; Scotland

**Summary:** A mad immortal still hoping to avenge the defeat of Scottish forces at the Battle of Culloden in 1746 sends Annie Devlin to entangle Duncan MacLeod in his machinations. Television tie-in.

**Other books you might like:**
L. Sprague de Camp, *The Fantastic Swordsmen*, 1967
    editor
Jason Henderson, *Highlander: The Element of Fire*, 1995
Ashley McConnell, *Highlander: Scimitar*, 1996
Melanie Rawn, *The Golden Key*, 1996
    Jennifer Roberson, Kate Eliot, co-authors

## 4612

JENNIFER ROBERSON

### *Sword-Born*

(New York: DAW, 1998)

**Story type:** Fantasy (Adventure)
**Series:** Tiger and Del
**Major character(s):** Tiger, Warrior; Del, Warrior; Prima Rhannet,
    Pirate, Lesbian

**Time period(s):** Indeterminate Past
**Locale(s):** Skandi, Fictional City

**Summary:** Cast out of their homelands, Tiger and Del set out to find Tiger's family. On the way, a pirate captures them, planning to use Tiger to bilk money out of a wealthy family. If Tiger fails, Del could die, but success could be even more costly.

**Other books you might like:**
Scott Baker, *Drink the Fire From the Flames*, 1987
Steven Brust, *Jhereg*, 1983
Simon R. Green, *Hawk & Fisher*, 1990
Ellen Kushner, *Swordspoint*, 1987
Matthew Woodring Stover, *Iron Dawn*, 1997

## 4613

JENNIFER ROBERSON

### *Sword-Breaker*

(New York: DAW, 1991)

**Story type:** Fantasy (Adventure; Quest)
**Series:** Tiger and Del
**Major character(s):** Delilah ''Del'', Warrior (Sword-Singer, North);
    Sandtiger ''Tiger'', Warrior (Sword-Dancer, South)
**Time period(s):** Indeterminate Past
**Locale(s):** Punja Desert, Fictional Country

**Summary:** Tiger and Del have finally hunted down and destroyed the man who killed Del's family, raped her and sold her brother to slavers. However, the Southron tribes think the man was their messiah and want to take their revenge on Del and Tiger. Complicating matters, Tiger's sword is possessed by an evil sorcerer who wants to take over Tiger in a first step toward unmaking the world. Del and Tiger must elude their pursuers, cross the desert and reach the one person who may be able to discharge the sword safely, if he still exists.

**Other books you might like:**
Steven Brust, *Jhereg*, 1983
Heather Gladney, *Teot's War*, 1987
Barbara Hambly, *The Armies of Daylight*, 1982
Mercedes Lackey, *The Oathbound*, 1988
Melanie Rawn, *Dragon Prince*, 1988

## 4614

JENNIFER ROBERSON

### *Sword-Maker*

(New York: DAW, 1989)

**Story type:** Fantasy (Sword and Sorcery)
**Series:** Tiger and Del
**Major character(s):** Tiger, Hero
**Time period(s):** Indeterminate Past
**Locale(s):** Alternate Universe

**Summary:** Having mastered two separate schools of swordplay, Tiger finds himself being called the savior in a new land. The inhabitants want Tiger to fight off a dragon, and Tiger unwillingly sets off to confront the monster.

**Other books you might like:**
Carole Nelson Douglas, *Six of Swords*, 1984
Barbara Hambly, *The Dark Hand of Magic*, 1989
Barbara Hambly, *The Ladies of Mandrigyn*, 1984
Phyllis Ann Karr, *Frostflower and Thorn*, 1980
Janet Morris, *City at the Edge of Time*, 1988

## 4615

**JENNIFER ROBERSON**

### A Tapestry of Lions

(New York: DAW, 1992)

**Story type:** Fantasy (Quest)
**Series:** Cheysuli
**Major character(s):** Kellin, Mythical Creature (shapechanger)
**Time period(s):** Indeterminate Past
**Locale(s):** Homana, Fictional Country

**Summary:** Kellin rejects the generations' long effort to recreate the magical race populating Homana by refusing to mate with an Ihlini woman, the key to fulfilling their plan. Ihlini sorcerers also wish to trap Kellin to prevent the prophecy's fruition which would end life as the Ihlini know it. Concludes the series started in *Shapechangers* (1984).

**Other books you might like:**
Louise Cooper, *The Sleep of Stone*, 1991
Thorarinn Gunnarsson, *Dragons on the Town*, 1992
Nancy Luenn, *Goldclimbers*, 1991
Andre Norton, *The Elvenbane*, 1991
    Mercedes Lackey, co-author
Will Shetterly, *Elsewhere*, 1991

## 4616

**JOHN MADDOX ROBERTS**

### Conan and the Treasure of Python

(New York: Tor, 1993)

**Story type:** Fantasy (Sword and Sorcery)
**Series:** Conan the Barbarian
**Major character(s):** Conan, Barbarian, Warrior; Wulfrede, Sailor, Warrior; Ulfilo, Sailor, Warrior
**Time period(s):** Indeterminate Past
**Locale(s):** Stygia, Fictional Country; Acheron, Fictional Country

**Summary:** When Conan hears of the magnificent treasure hidden in the capital city of Python by the rulers of that lost civilization, he sails and marches with other adventurers hoping for a profitable looting experience, ever mindful of the fierce warriors following them. When they arrive, they find descendants little interested in parting with treasure.

**Other books you might like:**
Roland J. Green, *Conan the Guardian*, 1991
Robert E. Howard, *Hour of the Dragon*, 1977
Robert E. Howard, *The People of the Black Circle*, 1977
Robert E. Howard, *Red Nails*, 1977
Robert Jordan, *Conan the Magnificent*, 1984
Steve Perry, *Conan the Free Lance*, 1990
Karl Edward Wagner, *Echoes of Valor I*, 1987
    editor

## 4617

**JOHN MADDOX ROBERTS**

### Conan the Rogue

(New York: Tor, 1991)

**Story type:** Fantasy (Sword and Sorcery)
**Series:** Conan the Barbarian
**Major character(s):** Conan, Barbarian, Warrior; Brita, Orphan, Guardian (sister's)

**Time period(s):** Indeterminate
**Locale(s):** Sicas Aquilonia, Fictional Country

**Summary:** Conan agrees to help Piris reacquire an object stolen from him and travels to Sicas, arriving with Brita. While waiting for Piris, Conan assists Brita in locating her sister among the vicious thugs who inhabit Sicas.

**Other books you might like:**
Leonard Carpenter, *Conan the Great*, 1990
Robert E. Howard, *King Conan*, 1953
Robert E. Howard, *The Sword of Conan*, 1952
Robert Jordan, *Conan the Invincible*, 1985
Steve Perry, *Conan the Formidable*, 1990
Karl Edward Wagner, *Death Angel's Shadow*, 1973
Karl Edward Wagner, *Echoes of Valor III*, 1991
    editor

## 4618

**JOHN MADDOX ROBERTS**

### The Enigma Variations

(New York: Ace, 1989)

**Story type:** Science Fiction (Cyberpunk)
**Major character(s):** Slate, Warrior; Pamela Conyers, Business-woman, Fugitive
**Time period(s):** 21st century
**Locale(s):** United States

**Summary:** Slate wakes up in the desert, his mind a blank, an artificial hand of polished steel attached to his wrist. Gradually he reconstructs his past and makes his way into a complex web of intrigue and violence. In a world on the edge of collapse, the great corporations fight for power using mindwipes, cyborg killers, and any other deadly technology they can bring to bear. Slate decides to fight back.

**Other books you might like:**
S.N. Lewitt, *Cyberstealth*, 1989
S.N. Lewitt, *Dancing Vac*, 1990
Walter Jon Williams, *Hardwired*, 1986
Walter Jon Williams, *Voice of the Whirlwind*, 1987
Dave Wolverton, *On My Way to Paradise*,

## 4619

**JOHN MADDOX ROBERTS**

### The Poisoned Lands

(New York: Tor, 1992)

**Story type:** Fantasy (Post-Disaster; Science Fiction)
**Series:** Stormlands
**Major character(s):** Ansa, Warrior, Explorer; Gasam, Warrior, Royalty (king); Fyana, Healer
**Time period(s):** Indeterminate Future
**Locale(s):** Sono, Fictional Country; Gran, Fictional Country

**Summary:** Wanting to conquer the world and learn the location of King Hael's iron mine, King Gasam of Chiwa succeeds in the first and starts on the second by invading Sono. After Ansa's capture while scouting out the intentions of King Gasam, Fyana dangles the prospect of rejuvenation before Queen Larissa, allowing both to escape and report back to King Hael.

**Other books you might like:**
Robert Adams, *The Seven Magical Jewels of Ireland*, 1985
Poul Anderson, *The Winter of the World*, 1976
Piers Anthony, *Sos the Rope*, 1968
Edmund Cooper, *The Cloud Walker*, 1973

John Dalmas, *The Yngling*, 1971
Andre Norton, *No Night Without Stars*, 1975
Kim Stanley Robinson, *The Wild Shore*, 1985
Clifford D. Simak, *A Heritage of Stars*, 1978
Paul O. Williams, *The Song of the Axe*, 1984

## 4620

### JOHN MADDOX ROBERTS

## Queens of Land and Sea

(New York: Tor, 1994)

**Story type:** Fantasy (Adventure; Post-Disaster)
**Series:** Stormlands
**Major character(s):** Larissa, Royalty (queen), Political Figure; Ansa, Explorer, Warrior; Shazad, Royalty (queen), Political Figure
**Time period(s):** Indeterminate Future
**Locale(s):** Neva, Fictional Country

**Summary:** When strangers from the southern highlands come to the Islands and to Neva carrying a plague that attacks all but Shasinn, Queen Larissa decides to attack the Nevans. The Shasinn invasion sidetracks Ansa when he comes to Neva to rally forces to fight the Mezpans, but Ansa captures Queen Larissa despite hindrance. Retaliation on a ransom mission nearly spells disaster for Shazad.

**Other books you might like:**
Poul Anderson, *The Winter of the World*, 1975
John Barnes, *The Man Who Pulled Down the Sky*, 1986
Orson Scott Card, *The Folk of the Fringe*, 1989
Clifford D. Simak, *A Heritage of Stars*, 1977
Stanley G. Weinbaum, *The Black Flame*, 1948

## 4621

### JOHN MADDOX ROBERTS

## The Steel Kings

(New York: Tor, 1993)

**Story type:** Fantasy (Post-Disaster; Political)
**Series:** Stormlands
**Major character(s):** Kairn, Warrior, Explorer; Hael, Royalty (king), Warrior; Larissa, Royalty (queen), Political Figure
**Time period(s):** Indeterminate Future
**Locale(s):** Mezpa, Fictional Country; Thezas, Fictional Country

**Summary:** When Kairn comes to Mezpa to warn his father about Gasam's seizure of his father's steel mines, Deathmoon captures him. After his father helps him escape, the two plot how to use Deathmoon and Gasam to eliminate each other.

**Other books you might like:**
Poul Anderson, *The Winter of the World*, 1976
Piers Anthony, *Sos the Rope*, 1968
Neal Barrett Jr., *Through Darkest America*, 1988
John Dalmas, *The Yngling*, 1971
Floyd Gibbon, *The Red Napoleon*, 1929
Robert E. Howard, *Conan the Conqueror*, 1950
Dean R. Koontz, *Warlock*, 1972
Sterling E. Lanier, *Hiero's Journey*, 1973
Paul O. Williams, *An Ambush of Shadows*, 1983
Chelsea Quinn Yarbro, *False Dawn*, 1978

## 4622

### KENNETH ROBESON (Pseudonym of Will Murray)

## The Frightened Fish

(New York: Bantam Falcon, 1992)

**Story type:** Fantasy (Adventure; Mystery)
**Series:** Doc Savage
**Major character(s):** Clark ''Doc'' Savage Jr., Adventurer, Genius; Seryi Mitroff, Revolutionary; Max Wood, Scientist, Activist (political agitator)
**Time period(s):** 1940s (1949)
**Locale(s):** New York, New York; Quincy, Massachusetts; Japan

**Summary:** A strangely deadly gag involving a man terrified of ''frightened fish'' launches Doc Savage and his crew into another mystery. This time they travel to New England and Japan in an effort to solve the puzzle that masks a diabolical scheme for global destruction. Waiting in Japan lurks another threat, one to Doc Savage's heart and peace of mind.

**Other books you might like:**
Lin Carter, *The Volcano Ogre*, 1976
Philip Jose Farmer, *Escape From Loki*, 1991
Jon Stephen Fink, *Further Adventures*, 1993
Rob MacGregor, *Indiana Jones and the Genesis Deluge*, 1992
Grant Stockbridge, *The Spider #3: Death's Crimson Juggernaut/ The Red Death Rain*, 1992

## 4623

### KENNETH ROBESON (Pseudonym of Will Murray)

## The Jade Ogre

(New York: Bantam Falcon, 1992)

**Story type:** Fantasy (Adventure; Mystery)
**Series:** Doc Savage
**Major character(s):** Clark ''Doc'' Savage Jr., Adventurer, Genius; Jason Baird, Jeweler; Quon, Cult Member (leader)
**Time period(s):** 1930s
**Locale(s):** San Francisco, California; Cambodia

**Summary:** Traveling to San Francisco by airplane, Doc Savage narrowly escapes death when the plane goes out of control after the pilot's sudden death. Upon arrival, the Man of Bronze discovers his contact mysteriously missing in a deadly puzzle that leads Savage and his companions half way around the world through a maze of cultists, assassins and supernatural creatures to face the Jade Ogre.

**Other books you might like:**
Lin Carter, *Invisible Death*, 1975
Philip Jose Farmer, *Escape From Loki*, 1991
Jon Stephen Fink, *Further Adventures*, 1993
Rob MacGregor, *Indiana Jones and the Peril at Delphi*, 1991
Grant Stockbridge, *The Spider #1: The Spider and the Pain Master/ Secret City of Crime*, 1991

## 4624

### KENNETH ROBESON (Pseudonym of Lester Dent and Will Murray)

## Python Isle

(New York: Bantam Falcon, 1991)

**Story type:** Fantasy (Adventure)
**Series:** Doc Savage

**Major character(s):** Clark "Doc" Savage Jr., Adventurer, Military Personnel; Blackbird Hinton, Smuggler; Lha, Royalty (queen)
**Time period(s):** 1930s
**Locale(s):** New York, New York; Cape Town, South Africa; Python Isle, Fictional Country (in the Indian Ocean)

**Summary:** When Doc Savage's friend, Renny, is kidnapped in Cape Town, Doc and his companions travel there to help rescue him. In Cape Town, Doc becomes involved with an aviator thought long dead and his friend, Queen Lha of Python Isle, a descendant of the Biblical King Solomon who possesses remnants of the legendary treasure of Ophir.

**Other books you might like:**
Kenneth Robeson, *Doc Savage Omnibus #1*, 1986
     Kenneth Robeson is pseudonym for Lester Dent, Harold A. Davis, Will Murray, William G. Bogart, Ryerson Johnson, Laurence Donovan, and Alan Hathway, who all wrote Doc Savage stories under this name.
Kenneth Robeson, *Doc Savage Omnibus #12*, 1990
     Kenneth Robeson is pseudonym for Lester Dent, Harold A. Davis, Will Murray, William G. Bogart, Ryerson Johnson, Laurence Donovan, and Alan Hathway, who all wrote Doc Savage stories under this name.
Kenneth Robeson, *Doc Savage Omnibus #13*, 1990
     Kenneth Robeson is pseudonym for Lester Dent, Harold A. Davis, Will Murray, William G. Bogart, Ryerson Johnson, Laurence Donovan, and Alan Hathway, who all wrote Doc Savage stories under this name.
Philip Jose Farmer, *Doc Savage: His Apocalyptic Life*, 1973
Philip Jose Farmer, *Escape From Loki*, 1991
Philip Jose Farmer, *The Mad Goblin*, 1970

---

**4625**

**KENNETH ROBESON** (Pseudonym of Will Murray)

### White Eyes
(New York: Bantam Falcon, 1992)

**Story type:** Fantasy (Adventure)
**Series:** Doc Savage
**Major character(s):** Clark "Doc" Savage Jr., Adventurer, Genius; White Eyes, Criminal
**Time period(s):** 1930s
**Locale(s):** New York, New York; Cuba

**Summary:** Investigating a series of deaths in which the victim's eyes turn an unseeing white, Doc Savage and his companions discover that the plague results from the efforts of New York's criminals who have united in hopes of seizing Doc Savage's fabled Mayan wealth.

**Other books you might like:**
Philip Jose Farmer, *Doc Savage: His Apocalyptic Life*, 1973
Philip Jose Farmer, *Escape From Loki*, 1991
Philip Jose Farmer, *The Mad Goblin*, 1970

---

**4626**

**FRANK M. ROBINSON**

### The Dark Beyond the Stars
(New York: Tor, 1991)

**Story type:** Science Fiction (Generation Starship; Adventure)
**Major character(s):** Michael Kusaka, Spaceship Captain, Immortal; Sparrow, Amnesiac, Space Explorer
**Time period(s):** 40th century
**Locale(s):** *Astron*, Spaceship

**Summary:** The Spaceship *Astron* has been searching for life for 200 generations. Old and worn out equipment makes much of the ship unusable. Most of the crew has lost hope of finding life and wants to return to Earth. Sparrow, recovering from a near-fatal accident on his last mission, discovers that the Captain is programmed to continue and is unable to turn back even though the ship has reached the end of the spiral arm and doesn't have the resources to survive passage to the next.

**Other books you might like:**
Brian W. Aldiss, *Non-Stop*, 1989
Octavia E. Butler, *Dawn*, 1987
Michael Capobianco, *Burster*, 1990
Glen Cook, *The Dragon Never Sleeps*, 1988
Alan Dean Foster, *Dark Star*, 1974
Diana G. Gallagher, *The Alien Dark*, 1990
Robert A. Heinlein, *Orphans of the Sky*, 1963
Fritz Leiber, *Ship of Shadows*, 1988
David Alexander Smith, *Homecoming*, 1990

---

**4627**

**JANE E.M. ROBINSON**

### The Amazon Chronicles
(San Diego, California: Clothespin Fever Press, 1994)

**Story type:** Fantasy (Adventure; Political)
**Major character(s):** Antiope, Warrior (Amazon), Lesbian; Penthesilea, Warrior (Amazon), Foundling; Abba-Bashti, Trader (Lesbian)
**Time period(s):** 13th century B.C. (1240 B.C.)
**Locale(s):** Amazonia, Fictional Country; Europe; Asia Minor

**Summary:** Achaean designs on Amazonia present Penthesilea with the opportunity for glory on her expedition, while political hopefuls jostle for power and Antiope waits anxiously in Amazonia for Penthesilea's return.

**Other books you might like:**
Suzy McKee Charnas, *The Furies*, 1994
Charlotte Perkins Gilman, *Herland*, 1979
Jessica Amanda Salmonson, *Amazons!*, 1979
Jacqui Singleton, *Heartstone and Silver*, 1994
Joan Slonczewski, *A Door into Ocean*, 1986

---

**4628**

**KIM STANLEY ROBINSON**

### Antarctica
(New York: Harper, 1998)

**Story type:** Science Fiction (Techno-Thriller)
**Major character(s):** Valerie Kenning, Guide; Wade, Terrorist
**Time period(s):** Indeterminate Future
**Locale(s):** Antarctica

**Summary:** The industrialized nations of the world are finally opening up Antarctica for exploitation. Infuriated, a group of ecoterrorists concocts an elaborate plot to destroy the footholds of civilization already established, even if that means killing many of the local inhabitants. A handful of unlikely heroes learn of the plan and disrupt it.

**Other books you might like:**
John Calvin Batchelor, *The Birth of the People's Republic of Antarctica*, 1983
Stephen Baxter, *Anti-Ice*, 1993
Edmund Cooper, *The Last Continent*, 1969

Trevor Hoyle, *The Last Gasp*, 1983
Crawford Kilian, *Icequake*, 1979

## 4629

### KIM STANLEY ROBINSON

## *Blue Mars*

(New York: Bantam Spectra, 1996)

**Story type:** Science Fiction (Hard Science Fiction; Political)
**Series:** Mars Trilogy
**Major character(s):** Ann Clayborne, Scientist, Aged Person; Saxifrage "Sax" Russell, Scientist, Aged Person; Nirgal Hawkins, Political Figure (first generation Martian)
**Time period(s):** 22nd century; 23rd century
**Locale(s):** Mars; Venus; Mercury

**Summary:** After the second Martian revolution, a delegation visits Earth while the many Martian groups, both Red and Green, work on a constitution they can all sign. Nirgal advocates giving the life extension drug to everyone on Earth, recognizing that this will lead to a major increase in the already disastrous population problem, but claims that Martian immigration will take some of the pressure off. Ann agrees to cooperate with the Greens rather than start a civil war if Sax will remove the soletta which focuses sunlight on Mars. He moves it to Venus to block sunlight, hoping he can find a way to avoid a Martian ice age. Concluding volume of trilogy.

**Other books you might like:**
Greg Bear, *Moving Mars*, 1993
Ben Bova, *Mars*, 1992
David Brin, *Earth*, 1990
William C. Dietz, *Mars Prime*, 1992
Joan Slonczewski, *A Door into Ocean*, 1986
S.C. Sykes, *Red Genesis*, 1991

## 4630

### KIM STANLEY ROBINSON

## *Escape From Kathmandu*

(New York: Tor, 1989)

**Story type:** Science Fiction (Humor)
**Major character(s):** George, Expatriate; Freds, Expatriate
**Locale(s):** Kathmandu, Nepal

**Summary:** These four interconnected stories tell the adventures of George and Freds, a pair of not very practical American expatriates living in Kathmandu. Typical of their antics is an attempt to smuggle a yeti in sportsclothes out of a hotel while Jimmy Carter is making a visit.

**Other books you might like:**
John Kessel, *Good News From Outer Space*, 1989
Marc Laidlaw, *Neon Lotus*, 1988
Geoff Ryman, *The Unconquered Country*, 1986
Lucius Shepard, *The Jaguar Hunter*, 1987

## 4631

### KIM STANLEY ROBINSON, Editor

## *Future Primitive: The New Ecotopias*

(New York: Tor, 1994)

**Story type:** Science Fiction (Anthology; Utopia)

**Summary:** Contains a three-page introduction, 10 pages of endnotes, five pages of suggested reading, plus two poems published in 1935 and 1974 and 13 stories reprinted from periodicals and anthologies 1974-1994, all of which utilize ecological themes such as human/animal interactions, escaping the confines of the human body, primitive peoples and synthesizing a new culture by combining ancient cultures with technologically advanced cultures. Authors include Terry Bisson, Carol Emshwiller, Garry Kilworth, R.A. Lafferty, Ursula K. Le Guin, Pat Murphy, Paul Park, Rachel Pollack, Robert Silverberg, Howard Waldrop and Gene Wolfe.

**Other books you might like:**
Ernest Callenbach, *Ecotopia: A Novel about Ecology, People and Politics in 1999*, 1975
Ernest Callenbach, *Ecotopia Emerging*, 1981
Ursula K. Le Guin, *Always Coming Home*, 1985
Pat Murphy, *The City, Not Long After*, 1989
Rachel Pollack, *Unquenchable Fire*, 1992
John Stadler, *Eco-Fiction*, 1971
    editor
Starhawk, *The Fifth Sacred Thing*, 1993
George R. Stewart, *Earth Abides*, 1949
Sheri S. Tepper, *The Gate to Women's Country*, 1988

## 4632

### KIM STANLEY ROBINSON

## *The Gold Coast*

(New York: Tor Books, 1989)

**Story type:** Science Fiction (Political)
**Series:** Orange County Trilogy
**Major character(s):** Jim McPherson, Teacher, Writer; Dennis McPherson, Engineer
**Time period(s):** 21st century
**Locale(s):** Orange County California, Alternate Earth

**Summary:** In this novel which was nominated for the British Science Fiction Award for 1989 and which made *SF & Fantasy Book Review Annual*'s list of the ten best novels of 1988, a large cast of characters live out their lives against a twenty-first century California backdrop of monstrous superhighways, senseless violence, designer drugs, and military-industrial boondoggles.

**Other books you might like:**
Ben Bova, *Peacekeepers*, 1988
John Kessel, *Good News From Outer Space*, 1989
Dan Simmons, *Phases of Gravity*, 1989
Bruce Sterling, *Islands in the Net*, 1988
Robert Charles Wilson, *Memory Wire*, 1987

## 4633

### KIM STANLEY ROBINSON

## *Green Mars*

(New York: Bantam Spectra, 1994)

**Story type:** Science Fiction (Hard Science Fiction; Political)
**Series:** Mars Trilogy
**Major character(s):** Maya Toitovna, Revolutionary, Scientist; Nirgal Hawkins, Political Figure, Revolutionary; Saxifrage "Sax" Russell, Scientist, Revolutionary
**Time period(s):** 22nd century
**Locale(s):** Mars

**Summary:** Now operational, the new space elevator sparks fear in the remaining First Hundred, still in hiding after the failed revolution in

2061 and not yet in agreement on their plans and goals for Mars and the people there. The second and third generation Martians work to create a habitable surface and atmosphere or fight to free Mars from control by multinational corporations and the United Nations Transitional Authority, all of which maintain armed security forces on Mars.

**Other books you might like:**
Greg Bear, *Moving Mars*, 1993
Ben Bova, *Mars*, 1992
David Brin, *Earth*, 1990
William C. Dietz, *Mars Prime*, 1992
Janet Kagan, *Mirabile*, 1991
Joan Slonczewski, *A Door into Ocean*, 1986
S.C. Sykes, *Red Genesis*, 1991
Wynne Whiteford, *The Specialist*, 1990

### 4634

**KIM STANLEY ROBINSON**

## Pacific Edge

(New York: Tor, 1990)

**Story type:** Science Fiction (Alternate Universe; Political)
**Series:** Orange County Trilogy
**Major character(s):** Kevin Claiborne, Inventor, Political Figure; Nadezhda Katayev, Scientist
**Time period(s):** 21st century
**Locale(s):** Orange County California, Alternate Earth

**Summary:** Begun with *The Wild Shore* and *The Gold Coast*, this triptych of novels is completed with *Pacific Edge*. Each takes place in an alternate version of Orange County. Sensible use of materials and the environment are featured here.

**Other books you might like:**
Ben Bova, *Peacekeepers*, 1988
David Brin, *Earth*, 1990
Joan Slonczewski, *A Door into Ocean*, 1986
Bruce Sterling, *Islands in the Net*, 1988
Jack Vance, *Trullion: Alastor 2262*, 1973

### 4635

**KIM STANLEY ROBINSON**

## Red Mars

(New York: Bantam Spectra, 1993)

**Story type:** Science Fiction (Hard Science Fiction; Political)
**Series:** Mars Trilogy
**Major character(s):** Frank Chalmers, Administrator, Scientist; Jack Boone, Scientist, Space Explorer; Maya Toitovna, Administrator, Scientist
**Time period(s):** 2020s (2026)
**Locale(s):** *Ares*, Spaceship; Mars

**Summary:** While on the *Ares* enroute to Mars, the first 100 colonists, scientists and astronauts realize that they have their own hidden ideas for Mars, incompatible with Earth's inevitable policy of development and exploitation of scarce Martian riches. After briefly working together on Mars, some colonists begin to warm the atmosphere and work on terraforming Mars while others leave for the hills to pursue self-sufficiency and escape Earth control; however, the true Martian potential exceeds everyone's vision. First of a series.

**Other books you might like:**
Piers Anthony, *Total Recall*, 1989
David Brin, *Earth*, 1990

Octavia E. Butler, *Dawn*, 1987
Robert L. Forward, *Martian Rainbow*, 1991
Jack C. Haldeman II, *High Steel*, 1993
    Jack Dann, co-author
S.C. Sykes, *Red Genesis*, 1991
Sheri S. Tepper, *Raising the Stones*, 1990
Wynne Whiteford, *The Specialist*, 1990

### 4636

**KIM STANLEY ROBINSON**

## Remaking History

(New York: Tor, 1991)

**Story type:** Science Fiction (Collection)

**Summary:** This title contains 14 stories published between 1986 and 1991 in periodicals and anthologies and Pulphouse's Author's Choice Monthly series and one story, "Vineland the Dream," original to this collection. Some stories feature near future settings and themes similar to the Orange County Trilogy including the Nebula Award nominee "Before I Wake," plus "Down and Out in the Year 2000" and "A History of the 20th Century with Illustrations." The latter was revised for this book as was "The Part of Us That Loves." "Rainbow Bridge," retitled herein, reflects the author's interest in mountain climbing. A near future ice age is depicted in "Glacier" while harder SF themes appear in "The Lunatics," about miners of the lunar crust.

**Other books you might like:**
J.G. Ballard, *War Fever*, 1991
Ray Bradbury, *The Toynbee Convector*, 1989
Spider Robinson, *Antinomy*, 1980
Spider Robinson, *Callahan and Company*, 1988
John Varley, *Blue Champagne*, 1986
John Varley, *The Persistence of Vision*, 1978
Kurt Vonnegut Jr., *Welcome to the Monkey House*, 1968

### 4637

**SPIDER ROBINSON**

## The Callahan Touch

(New York: Ace, 1993)

**Story type:** Fantasy (Light Fantasy; Science Fiction)
**Series:** Callahan's
**Major character(s):** Jake Stonebender, Saloon Keeper/Owner; Ernie "Lucky Duck" Shea, Mythical Creature (Pooka/Fir Darrig cross); Jonathan Crawford, Health Care Professional (medical researcher)
**Time period(s):** 1980s (May 1988)
**Locale(s):** Mary's Place, Mythical Place (saloon); United States

**Summary:** Two years after the nuking of Callahan's place, Jake Stonebender and other Callahan's regulars inaugurate Mary's Place. Within minutes of opening, improbable and magical events herald special newcomers and wishes come true.

**Other books you might like:**
Grendel Briarton, *The Collected Feghoot*, 1992
    pseudonym of Reginald Bretnor
Steven Brust, *Cowboy Feng's Space Bar and Grille*, 1990
Arthur C. Clarke, *Tales From the White Hart*, 1957
L. Sprague de Camp, *Tales From Gavagan's Bar*, 1978
    expanded edition; Fletcher Pratt, co-author
Stephen Goldin, *Jade Darcy and the Affair of Honor*, 1988
    Mary Mason, co-author

Steve Perry, *The Man Who Never Missed*, 1985
Don Sakers, *Carmen Miranda's Ghost Is Haunting Space Station Three*, 1990
   editor

---

**4638**

### SPIDER ROBINSON

## Callahan's Lady

(New York: Ace, 1989)

**Story type:** Science Fiction (Humor)
**Series:** Callahan's
**Major character(s):** Lady Sally Callahan, Madam; Maureen, Prostitute
**Time period(s):** 20th century
**Locale(s):** New York, New York (Brooklyn)

**Summary:** Four interrelated stories tell of the amazing goings on in a house of prostitution owned by Callahan's wife.

**Other books you might like:**
Steven Brust, *Cowboy Feng's Space Bar and Grille*, 1990
Sterling E. Lanier, *The Peculiar Exploits of Brigadier Ffellowes*, 1977
Mike Resnick, *The Three-Legged Hootch Dancer*, 1983

---

**4639**

### SPIDER ROBINSON

## Callahan's Legacy

(New York: Tor, 1996)

**Story type:** Science Fiction (Humor; Invasion of Earth)
**Series:** Callahan's
**Major character(s):** Mike Callahan, Time Traveler; Jake Stonebender, Saloon Keeper/Owner (Mary's Place); Mary Callahan-Finn, Computer Expert
**Time period(s):** 1980s (Fall 1988)
**Locale(s):** Mary's Place, Mythical Place (saloon); United States

**Summary:** Jake Stonebender begins a typical day at Mary's Place with an obnoxious beast turned away at the door and a customer intent on burning a suitcase full of hundred dollar bills one at a time. Before long, Mary Callahan-Finn arrives from another planet with the news that the punning patrons of Mary's Place may prove humanity's only hope against the Lizard, a cybernetic monster capable of total destruction.

**Other books you might like:**
Grendel Briarton, *The Collected Feghoot*, 1992
   pseudonym of Reginald Bretnor
Steven Brust, *Cowboy Feng's Space Bar and Grille*, 1990
Arthur C. Clarke, *Tales From the White Hart*, 1957
L. Sprague de Camp, *Tales From Gavagan's Bar*, 1978
   expanded edition; Fletcher Pratt, co-author
Larry Niven, *Fallen Angels*, 1991
   Jerry Pournelle, Michael Flynn, co-authors

---

**4640**

### SPIDER ROBINSON

## Lady Slings the Booze

(New York: Ace, 1992)

**Story type:** Science Fiction (Mystery; Humor)

---

**Series:** Callahan's
**Major character(s):** Lady Sally Callahan, Madam; Joe Quigley, Detective—Private, Imposter (prostitute)
**Time period(s):** 1980s
**Locale(s):** New York, New York

**Summary:** Joe Quigley accepts a mysterious assignment involving an invisible rapist whose crimes disturb the ambience at Lady Sally's brothel which caters to every taste of society's rich and powerful citizens. While posing as a prostitute, Joe uncovers a plot which threatens the world with nuclear destruction.

**Other books you might like:**
Mel Gilden, *Surfing Samurai Robots*, 1988
Stephen Goldin, *Jade Darcy and the Affair of Honor*, 1988
   Mary Mason, co-author
Simon R. Green, *Hawk & Fisher*, 1990
Dean Ing, *Cathouse*, 1991
John E. Stith, *Redshift Rendezvous*, 1990
Thomas T. Thomas, *Crygender*, 1992

---

**4641**

### SPIDER ROBINSON

## Lifehouse

(New York: Baen, 1997)

**Story type:** Science Fiction (Time Travel; Adventure)
**Major character(s):** June Bellamy, Con Artist; Wallace "Wally" Kemp, Computer Expert (science fiction fan); Paul Donald Throtmanian, Con Artist
**Time period(s):** 1990s
**Locale(s):** Vancouver, British Columbia, Canada

**Summary:** Walking in the woods, June loses some memory, almost causing the end of the world, while Paul, pretending to come from the future, scams Wallace and Moira. June and Paul retire and decide to return the scam money, but the real time travelers destroy Paul's apartment and the money. The four new friends must find the time travelers to protect the present and get their money. Sequel to *Deathkiller*, a 1996 omnibus collecting *Mindkillers* and *Time Pressure*.

**Other books you might like:**
Chester Anderson, *The Butterfly Kid*, 1967
John Barnes, *Patton's Spaceship*, 1997
Gordon R. Dickson, *Time Storm*, 1977
Larry Niven, *Fallen Angels*, 1991
   Jerry Pournelle, Michael Flynn, co-authors
Dan Simmons, *Hyperion*, 1989
Robert Charles Wilson, *A Bridge of Years*, 1991

---

**4642**

### SPIDER ROBINSON
### JEANNE ROBINSON, Co-Author

## Starmind

(New York: Ace, 1995)

**Story type:** Science Fiction (Arts; Genetic Manipulation)
**Series:** Stardance
**Major character(s):** Rhea Paixao, Writer, Spouse (Rand's); Rand Porter, Computer Expert, Spouse (Rhea's); Jay Sasaki, Dancer, Spaceman
**Time period(s):** 2060s (2065)
**Locale(s):** Provincetown, Massachusetts; *Shimizu Hotel*, Spaceship (high earth orbit)

**Summary:** Not yet ready to leave her ancestral home in Provincetown, Rhea reluctantly accompanies Rand to the fabulous Shimizu Hotel where Rand and his half-brother, Jay, co-operate as artistic directors. Unhappy at the though of never returning home, Rhea decides to go despite the heroic actions of Rand and Jay, saving the hotel from destruction and stopping a plot against the Stardancers.

**Other books you might like:**
Arthur C. Clarke, *Childhood's End*, 1953
L. Warren Douglas, *A Plague of Change*, 1992
Ernest Hogan, *Cortez on Jupiter*, 1990
Marjorie Bradley Kellogg, *Harmony*, 1991
Theodore Sturgeon, *The Dreaming Jewels*, 1950

---

**4643**

### SPIDER ROBINSON
### JEANNE ROBINSON, Co-Author

## *Starseed*

(New York: Ace, 1991)

**Story type:** Science Fiction (Arts)
**Series:** Stardance
**Major character(s):** Morgan McLeod, Dancer, Student; Robert Chen, Teacher, Spaceman
**Time period(s):** 2020s (2020)
**Locale(s):** Top Step, Space Station; Earth

**Summary:** A dancer for 32 years until her injuries prohibit it, Morgan decides that the only alternative to euthanasia involves becoming a Stardancer, one of the telepathic, symbiotic creatures which live in Outer Space. She moves to the Starseed Foundation's Top Step where she studies those disciplines which should ease the transition into the telepathic community. Her determination to become a Stardancer helps her through hinderances, difficulty adjusting to zero gee, romantic involvement with an instructor and a terrorist plot aimed at stopping the Stardancers. This novel is set a few years later in the same universe as *Stardance*.

**Other books you might like:**
John Barnes, *Orbital Resonance*, 1991
Lois McMaster Bujold, *Falling Free*, 1988
Ernest Hogan, *Cortez on Jupiter*, 1990
James Patrick Kelly, *Look into the Sun*, 1989
Alis A. Rasmussen, *A Passage of Stars*, 1990
David Alexander Smith, *Homecoming*, 1990
Theodore Sturgeon, *More than Human*, 1953
John Varley, *Blue Champagne*, 1986
John Varley, *The Persistence of Vision*, 1978

---

**4644**

### BARBARA RODEN, Editor
### CHRISTOPHER RODEN, Co-Editor

## *Midnight Never Comes*

(Ashcroft, British Columbia: Ash-Tree Press, 1997)

**Story type:** Horror (Anthology; Ghost Story)

**Summary:** Seventeen ghostly tales, all original to this volume and many written in the classic ghostly tradition. Selections include Terry Lamsley's ''The Snug,'' concerned with an inn haunted by the spirits of a satanic coven; Colin Mackay's ''Mary King's Close,'' in which a man stumbles back in time to Scotland's plague-ridden past; Ron Wieghell's ''The Mouth of the Medusa,'' in which an archaeological team falls under the pernicious influence of the pagan ruins they are excavating; Rosemary Pardoe's ''The Sheelagh-na-gig,'' about the evil doom portended by an ancient fertility symbol; and Marni Griffin's poignant ''Outside the Gates,'' in which an emotionally troubled woman finds a surrogate for her lost mother in a dead female writer.

**Other books you might like:**
Ramsey Campbell, *Uncanny Banquet*, 1992
  editor
Chris Morgan, *Dark Fantasies*, 1989
  editor
Claudia O'Keefe, *Ghosttide*, 1993
  editor
Paul F. Olson, *Post Mortem: New Tales of Ghostly Horror*, 1989
  David B. Silva, co-editor
Wendy Webb, *Gothic Ghosts*, 1997
  Charles L. Grant, co-editor

---

**4645**

### ALAN RODGERS

## *Blood of the Children*

(New York: Bantam, 1990)

**Story type:** Horror (Evil Children)
**Major character(s):** Ben Tompkins, Parent; Jimmy Tompkins, Child
**Time period(s):** 1990s
**Locale(s):** Green Hill, South

**Summary:** An ancient ''stone'' possesses the children of Green Hill, forcing them to evil deeds. Newcomers Ben and Jimmy Tompkins are able to confront and do battle against the stone's sinister powers. This is Rodgers' first novel.

**Other books you might like:**
John Saul, *Suffer the Children*, 1977
John Wyndham, *The Midwich Cuckoos*, 1957

---

**4646**

### ALAN RODGERS

## *Bone Music*

(Stamford, Connecticut: Longmeadow, 1995)

**Story type:** Horror (Ancient Evil Unleashed)
**Major character(s):** Elvis Presley, Musician, Historical Figure; Dan Alvarez, Musician; Lisa Henderson, Young Woman
**Time period(s):** 1930s (1938); 1990s (1995)
**Locale(s):** New Orleans, Louisiana

**Summary:** In a world where Robert Johnson's singing of the song ''Judgment Day'' has cracked The Eye of the World, and let in all the hoodoo that 20th century blues singers have warned of, musician Dan Alvarez, devil girl Lisa Henderson, and a resurrected Elvis Presley struggle to save the world from the encroaching darkness foretold by a cast of classic blues players, many of whom are given walk-on roles.

**Other books you might like:**
Clifford Mohr, *Requiem*, 1992
Al Sarrantonio, *Skeletons*, 1992
Adrian Savage, *Symphony*, 1993

### ALAN RODGERS

## *Fire*

(New York: Bantam, 1990)

**Story type:** Horror (Apocalyptic Horror)
**Major character(s):** Paul Green, Political Figure (President of the United States); Ron Hawkins, Maintenance Worker (janitor); Luke Munsen, Scientist (genetic engineer)
**Time period(s):** Indeterminate Future
**Locale(s):** Mountainville, Tennessee; Washington, District of Columbia; Republic of Korea

**Summary:** In this epic horror novel, the accidental death of the First Lady in Moscow causes her unbalanced conservative husband to threaten nuclear annihilation of the Soviet Union. Meanwhile, an explosion at the Mountain Institute Genetic Research Facility in Tennessee releases a genetically engineered monster that resembles The Beast of Revelations. Soon thereafter, a scientist at the Institute lets loose an indestructable virus that can revivify the dead and make them effectively immortal. The bombs begin to fall, and there begins a complex though often arbitrary and aimless conflict between characters who represent the forces of Good and Evil.

**Other books you might like:**
James Blish, *Black Easter*, 1968
James Blish, *The Day After Judgment*, 1971
Stephen King, *The Stand: The Complete and Uncut Edition*, 1990
Robert R. McCammon, *Swan Song*, 1987

**4648**

### ALAN RODGERS

## *New Life for the Dead*

(Newark, New Jersey: Wildside Press, 1991)

**Story type:** Horror (Collection)
**Summary:** Five stories generally concerned with characters who find that what they wish for and what they get are often two entirely different things. Included are the Bram Stoker Award-winning story "The Boy Who Came Back from the Dead," about the upset caused in a family by a child's resurrection, and "Emma's Daughter," about the extent to which a mother will go to bring her dead child back to life. There are also seven poems.

**Other books you might like:**
Robert R. McCammon, *Blue World*, 1989
William Relling Jr., *The Infinite Man*, 1989
F. Paul Wilson, *Soft and Others*, 1989

**4649**

### ALAN RODGERS

## *Night*

(New York: Bantam, 1991)

**Story type:** Horror (Apocalyptic Horror)
**Major character(s):** Tim Fischer, Psychic; Joel Kimball, Police Officer (deputy sheriff); The Bleeding Man, Mythical Creature
**Time period(s):** 1990s
**Locale(s):** Running Board, Nebraska

**Summary:** When his grandfather is murdered, Tim Fischer, who has been blessed with the gift of second sight, inherits the old man's most sacred possession, a fragment of the true cross on which Jesus died.

From that day forward, Tim assumes responsibility for uncovering the identity of his grandfather's killer and keeping the talisman from The Bleeding Man, a manifestation of the man who nailed Jesus to the cross and who hopes to use the fragment to recreate the world in his own soulless image.

**Other books you might like:**
Stephen King, *The Dead Zone*, 1979
Robert Weinberg, *The Armageddon Box*, 1991

**4650**

### ALAN RODGERS

## *Pandora*

(New York: Bantam, 1995)

**Story type:** Horror (Science Fiction)
**Major character(s):** Pandora, Alien; Belisarius Hightower, Military Personnel (U.S. Air Force general); Ken Estes, Military Personnel
**Time period(s):** 1990s (1995)
**Locale(s):** Wright-Patterson AF Base, Ohio; Pine Junction, Tennessee

**Summary:** Pandora, a survivor of a space ship crash outside of Roswell, New Mexico, escapes the military compound where she has been kept for half a century to search for the father whom she believes is on Earth. Her escape instigates a manhunt that includes friends who want to protect her, and psychotic military types who will stop at nothing to return her to captivity and dispose of anyone who might give away her secret.

**Other books you might like:**
Donald Burleson, *Flute Song*, 1996
Maxine O'Callaghan, *Dark Time*, 1992
Whitley Strieber, *Majestic*, 1989

**4651**

### MICHAELA ROESSNER

## *The Stars Dispose*

(New York: Tor, 1997)

**Story type:** Fantasy (Political)
**Major character(s):** Caterina de Medici, Historical Figure; Tommaso Arista, Apprentice
**Time period(s):** 16th century
**Locale(s):** Florence, Italy

**Summary:** Learning his craft from master chefs and artists and befriended by Michelangelo, Tommaso progresses toward a career preparing food for the powerful de Medici family. Orphaned and in the guardianship of the pope, Caterina de Medici learns the magic of the hearth and culinary magic as she prepares to rule, if Florence does not prove too tempting a prize for others. Includes a food glossary and six pages of references and recipes.

**Other books you might like:**
Jack Dann, *The Memory Cathedral*, 1995
Guy Gavriel Kay, *A Song for Arbonne*, 1993
Paul J. McAuley, *Pasquale's Angel*, 1995
Melissa Scott, *The Armor of Light*, 1988
  Lisa A. Barnett, co-author
Melissa Scott, *Point of Hopes*, 1995
  Lisa A. Barnett, co-author
Chelsea Quinn Yarbro, *Ariosto*, 1980

**MICHAELA ROESSNER**

## Vanishing Point

(New York: Tor, 1993)

**Story type:** Science Fiction (Post-Disaster)
**Major character(s):** Nesta Christiana Easterman, Scientist; Renzie, Researcher (assistant), Warrior; Hake, Scientist
**Time period(s):** 2020s
**Locale(s):** San Jose, California (Winchester Mansion/The House); Palo Alto, California

**Summary:** Thirty years after the Vanishing, the time when 90% of the population simply disappeared, little has been learned about the phenomenon. The scientists at Silicon Valley expect a physicist from Pennsylvania to join their research effort. When she arrives, she first goes to her old family home and then to the House where her investigation into the continuing process started by the Vanishing may come to fruition.

**Other books you might like:**
Roger MacBride Allen, *Supernova*, 1991
  Eric Kotani, co-author
David Brin, *Earth*, 1990
C.S. Friedman, *Black Sun Rising*, 1992
Geary Gravel, *A Key for the Nonesuch*, 1990
Michael Swanwick, *Stations of the Tide*, 1991
Kathy Tyers, *Shivering World*, 1991
Vernor Vinge, *Marooned in Realtime*, 1986
Philip Wylie, *The Disappearance*, 1951
George Zebrowski, *Stranger Suns*, 1991

**4653**

**MARK E. ROGERS**

## The Devouring Void

(New York: Ace, 1991)

**Story type:** Fantasy (Magic Conflict; Horror)
**Series:** Blood of the Lamb
**Major character(s):** Sharif ben Shaqar, Sorcerer
**Time period(s):** Indeterminate
**Locale(s):** Kadjafi Lands, Fictional Country

**Summary:** The wizards of the Order strike at their ancient enemies, thinking them responsible for the demonic attacks on the Masters of the Council, unaware of the treachery existing at the heart of the Order.

**Other books you might like:**
Mary Gentle, *Rats and Gargoyles*, 1991
P.C. Hodgell, *Dark of the Moon*, 1985
P.C. Hodgell, *God Stalk*, 1982
Brian Craig, *Zaragoz*, 1990

**4654**

**MARK E. ROGERS**

## The Riddled Man

(New York: Ace, 1992)

**Story type:** Fantasy (Religious; Magic Conflict)
**Series:** Blood of the Lamb
**Major character(s):** Erim Sawalha, Religious (inquisitor), Sorcerer; Essaj Ben Yussef, Religious (messiah); Khaddam Al-Ra,ma, Sorcerer, Teacher

**Time period(s):** Indeterminate
**Locale(s):** Thanqurn, Fictional City; Kadjafi Lands, Fictional Country

**Summary:** When Essaj acquires a death sentence for Heresy, divisions within the Sharajnaghim match the divisions among the three friends while the hidden evil manipulates everyone. As do the previous two, the concluding volume makes strong use of Christian symbolism and theology.

**Other books you might like:**
Mary Gentle, *Rats and Gargoyles*, 1991
P.C. Hodgell, *God Stalk*, 1982
Stephen R. Lawhead, *In the Hall of the Dragon King*, 1982
C.S. Lewis, *Out of the Silent Planet*, 1943
Roger Zelazny, *Lord of Light*, 1967

**4655**

**MARK E. ROGERS**

## Samurai Cat Goes to Hell

(New York: Tor, 1998)

**Story type:** Fantasy (Light Fantasy; Adventure)
**Series:** Samurai Cat
**Major character(s):** Miaowara Tomokato, Animal (cat), Warrior (Samurai); Miaowara Shiro, Relative (nephew of Tomokato), Warrior
**Time period(s):** Indeterminate
**Locale(s):** Hell; Asia

**Summary:** At death, Shiro finds himself judged worthy of Hell, while his guardian angel gives Tomokato the opportunity to kill Satan, preventing great evil, and rescue Shiro in the process. In Hell, many of Tomokato's deceased enemies await the chance for revenge.

**Other books you might like:**
Gael Baudino, *Gossamer Axe*, 1990
Neil Gaiman, *Good Omens: The Nice and Accurate Prophecies of Agnes Nutter, Witch*, 1990
  Terry Pratchett, co-author
Harry Harrison, *The Stainless Steel Rat Goes to Hell*, 1996
Janet Morris, *Heroes in Hell*, 1985
  editor
Roger Zelazny, *If at Faust You Don't Succeed*, 1993
  Robert Sheckley, co-author

**4656**

**MARK E. ROGERS**

## Samurai Cat Goes to the Movies

(New York: Tor, 1994)

**Story type:** Science Fiction (Parody; Alternate Universe)
**Series:** Samurai Cat
**Major character(s):** Miaowara Tomokato, Animal (cat), Warrior (16th century samurai); Miaowara Shiro, Animal (cat), Adventurer; Terminationer, Robot, Martial Arts Expert
**Time period(s):** 1990s
**Locale(s):** United States; Oz, Mythical Place

**Summary:** While Terminationer searches for Shiro with lethal intent, Shiro and Tomokato must find their way back from Oz before they can defeat the assassin while spoofing films including *The Magnificent Seven*, *Alien* and *Star Trek*.

**Other books you might like:**
Douglas Adams, *The Hitchhiker's Guide to the Galaxy*, 1980
Henry N. Beard, *Bored of the Rings*, 1969
  Douglas C. Kenny, co-author

John M. Ford, *How Much for Just the Planet?*, 1987
Leah Rewolinski, *Star Wreck: The Generation Gap*, 1990
Jovial Bob Stine, *Spaceballs: The Book*, 1987
Ellis Weiner, *National Lampoon's Doon*, 1984

## 4657

### MARK E. ROGERS

## The Sword of Samurai Cat

(New York: Tor, 1991)

**Story type:** Science Fiction (Alternate Universe; Humor)
**Series:** Samurai Cat
**Major character(s):** Miaowara Tomokato, Animal (cat), Warrior (16th C. samurai); Miaowara Shiro, Animal (cat), Adventurer
**Time period(s):** 1980s
**Locale(s):** United States; India; At Sea (aboard the *Gross Indulgence*)

**Summary:** Miaowara and Shiro, having avenged the death of Miaowara's master, encounter the undead, thugees, and a mastermind terrorist in a series of adventures which parody *Indiana Jones and the Temple of Doom*, *Invasion of the Body Snatchers* and *American Ninja*.

**Other books you might like:**
Henry N. Beard, *Bored of the Rings*, 1969
   Douglas C. Kennedy, co-author
C.J. Cherryh, *The Pride of Chanur*, 1982
Harry Harrison, *Bill, the Galactic Hero*, 1965
Ellis Weiner, *National Lampoon's Doon*, 1984

## 4658

### MICHAEL SCOTT ROHAN

## Chase the Morning

(New York: William Morrow, 1991)

**Story type:** Fantasy (Contemporary)
**Series:** Spiral
**Major character(s):** Steve Fisher, Importer/Exporter; Jyp, Sailor; Mad Mall, Sailor, Warrior
**Time period(s):** 1990s (1991)
**Locale(s):** England; Alternate Universe

**Summary:** Steve is a dead-end yuppie who risks his life on a whim to save a stranger and gets caught up in a strange world of voodoo and pirate ships which somehow exist just outside of our world. While there is a great deal of action, the plot of the novel centers on Steve's growth as a human being.

**Other books you might like:**
Greg Bear, *The Infinity Concerto*, 1984
Katherine Blake, *The Interior Life*, 1990
Emma Bull, *War for the Oaks*, 1987
Tim Powers, *The Anubis Gates*, 1983

## 4659

### MICHAEL SCOTT ROHAN

## Cloud Castles

(New York: Morrow/AvoNova, 1994)

**Story type:** Fantasy (Contemporary; Quest)
**Series:** Spiral

**Major character(s):** Steve Fisher, Importer/Exporter; Baron Lutz von Amerningen, Nobleman; Alison Laidlaw, Police Officer (EC trade investigator)
**Time period(s):** 1990s
**Locale(s):** London, England; Frankfort, Germany; The Spiral, Mythical Place

**Summary:** Although at the top of his profession, Steve Fisher suffers from boredom and is distracted by feelings of stagnation. When drawn back into The Spiral by the plots of Le Stryge, his uneasy ally from *Chase the Morning*, Steve faces a supremely hellish foe and higher stakes than ever.

**Other books you might like:**
Greg Bear, *Songs of Earth and Power*, 1994
Katherine Blake, *The Interior Life*, 1990
Emma Bull, *War for the Oaks*, 1987
Guy Gavriel Kay, *The Summer Tree*, 1985
Tim Powers, *The Anubis Gates*, 1983

## 4660

### MICHAEL SCOTT ROHAN

## The Forge in the Forest

(New York: Avon, 1989)

**Story type:** Fantasy (Quest)
**Series:** Winter of the World
**Major character(s):** Elof, Magician, Blacksmith; Kermovan, Nobleman
**Time period(s):** Indeterminate
**Locale(s):** Planet—Imaginary

**Summary:** While trying to gain some understanding of his powers, Elof and his friends battle to turn the invasion of the Ice. They gather a small band of men and set off to find the mythical lands to the East.

**Other books you might like:**
J.R.R. Tolkien, *The Lord of the Rings Trilogy*,
Tad Williams, *The Dragonbone Chair*, 1988

## 4661

### MICHAEL SCOTT ROHAN

## The Gates of Noon

(New York: Morrow AvoNova, 1993)

**Story type:** Fantasy (Contemporary)
**Series:** Spiral
**Major character(s):** Steve Fisher, Importer/Exporter; Raganda, Mythical Creature; Ape, Wizard
**Time period(s):** 1990s
**Locale(s):** London, England; The Spiral, Mythical Place; Bangkok, Thailand

**Summary:** Steve Fisher returns to the Spiral and his memories of strange adventures years after his last visit. He must deliver a crate of vital computer parts to Bali, which means a trip through the waters of the Spiral. Hampered by his emotional limits, Steve must grow as a person to survive.

**Other books you might like:**
Greg Bear, *The Infinity Concerto*, 1984
Katherine Blake, *The Interior Life*, 1990
Emma Bull, *War for the Oaks*, 1987
Guy Gavriel Kay, *The Summer Tree*, 1985
Tim Powers, *On Stranger Tides*, 1987

## 4662

### KEN ROLSTON

## Extreme Paranoia: Nobody Knows the Trouble I've Shot

(Honesdale, Pennsylvania: West End Books, 1991)

**Story type:** Science Fiction (Humor; Alternate Intelligence)
**Series:** Paranoia
**Major character(s):** Homer-R-ICK-3, Clone, Troubleshooter; Jakobot "Jacko" 490,9000, Robot, Sidekick; The Computer, Artificial Intelligence, Ruler
**Time period(s):** Indeterminate (year of the Computer 194, A.B.O.)
**Locale(s):** Alpha Complex, Earth

**Summary:** Homer and his crew of troubleshooters try to faithfully carry out The Computer's every wish while killing nearly everyone in sight. They are hampered by constantly changing demands from the Computer and low security clearances which do not allow the human clones to know their mission objectives or destinations, information entrusted only to the artificial intelligences inhabiting the tools used by the troubleshooters. This book is a tie-in to the game, Paranoia.

**Other books you might like:**
Douglas Adams, *The Hitchhiker's Guide to the Galaxy*, 1980
Thomas J. Bassler, *Half Past Human*, 1971
   as T.J. Bass
John DeChancie, *Paradox Alley*, 1987
John DeChancie, *Red Limit Freeway*, 1984
John DeChancie, *Starrigger*, 1983
Alan Dean Foster, *Glory Lane*, 1989
Frank Herbert, *Hellstrom's Hive*, 1973
Henry Kuttner, *Robots Have No Tails*, 1952
Frederik Pohl, *Gladiator-at-Law*, 1955
   Cyril M. Kornbluth, co-author
Robert Shea, *The Illuminatus! Trilogy*, 1988
   Robert Anton Wilson, co-author

## 4663

### NINA ROMBERG

## Shadow Walkers

(New York: Pinnacle, 1993)

**Story type:** Horror (Child-in-Peril; Haunted House)
**Major character(s):** Sadie Williams, Child (11-years-old), Runaway; Miriam Winchester, Shaman (medicine woman), Indian (Comanche); Popsy, Child, Runaway
**Time period(s):** 1990s (1993)
**Locale(s):** Gusher, Texas

**Summary:** A group of runaway children find a refuge for themselves in an abandoned east Texas mental institution they dub Pinecreek. Upon uncovering the institution's history as a home for soldiers who fought in Europe during World War II, the children unconsciously begin to fight the same power struggles that led to the rise of the Nazis, amplifying and reinforcing the perverse spirit that haunts the building.

**Other books you might like:**
Tom Elliott, *The Dwelling*, 1989
William Golding, *Lord of the Flies*, 1954
Shirley Jackson, *The Haunting of Hill House*, 1959
Al Sarrantonio, *House Haunted*, 1991

## 4664

### NINA ROMBERG

## The Spirit Stalker

(New York: Pinnacle, 1989)

**Story type:** Horror (Serial Killer)
**Major character(s):** Sunny Hansen, Artist (Commerical illustrater); Miriam, Indian (Comanche medicine woman), Abuse Victim
**Time period(s):** 1980s
**Locale(s):** Texas

**Summary:** Fleeing an abusive husband, Sunny Hansen finds herself threatened by a serial killer with supernatural powers.

**Other books you might like:**
Robert Bloch, *Psycho House*, 1990
Nicholas Conde, *In the Deep Woods*, 1989
Chet Williamson, *Dreamthorp*, 1989

## 4665

### MICHAEL ROMKEY

## I, Vampire

(New York: Fawcett, 1990)

**Story type:** Horror (Vampire Story)
**Major character(s):** David Parker, Vampire; Wolfgang Amadeus Mozart, Composer, Historical Figure; Rasputin, Religious (mad monk), Historical Figure
**Time period(s):** 1980s
**Locale(s):** Paris, France; Chicago, Illinois; Bayreuth, Germany

**Summary:** A genteel, cultured ex-lawyer recounts the story of his life and loves and how Tatiana Romanov, daughter of Czar Nicholas II and heiress to the throne of Russia made him one of the vampire race. As he tells this story (through his diary), he tries in the present to track down an evil, aristocratic English vampire, whom he saw slaughter a young woman at Montmartre Cemetery, and waits for his mentor Mozart to take him to Bayreuth to be reunited with Tatiana, his love.

**Other books you might like:**
Suzy McKee Charnas, *The Vampire Tapestry*, 1980
Anne Rice, *Interview with the Vampire*, 1976
Whitley Strieber, *The Hunger*, 1981
Michael Talbot, *The Delicate Dependency*, 1982

## 4666

### MICHAEL ROMKEY

## The Vampire Papers

(New York: Fawcett, 1994)

**Story type:** Horror (Vampire Story)
**Major character(s):** Becker Thorne, Vampire; David Parker, Vampire; Victoria Buchanan, Teacher (of English)
**Time period(s):** 1990s (1994)
**Locale(s):** Jerusalem, Mississippi

**Summary:** Vampire Becker Thorne establishes himself at the old Arlington Plantation in Jerusalem to settle the score with four families of the old southern aristocracy against whom he has had bitter feelings for more than a century. But he is followed by David Parker, a member of the Illuminati, whose task it is to turn vampire energies to positive historical and cultural ends and protect mortals against the bloodlust of the undead.

**Other books you might like:**
Scott Ciencin, *Parliament of Blood*, 1992
Pat Graversen, *Sweet Blood*, 1992
Wendy Haley, *This Dark Paradise*, 1994
Dan Simmons, *Carrion Comfort*, 1989
Karen E. Taylor, *Bitter Blood*, 1994

## 4667

### MICHAEL ROMKEY

## *The Vampire Princess*

(New York: Fawcett, 1996)

**Story type:** Horror (Vampire Story)
**Major character(s):** David Parker, Vampire; Nicoletta Vittorini di Medusa, Vampire; Carrie Anderson, Doctor
**Time period(s):** 1990s (1996)
**Locale(s):** Miami, Florida

**Summary:** A series of vampiric deaths on board the *Atlantic Princess*, bound from Miami to Italy, reveals the handiwork of Princess Nicoletta, a vampire who spurns the rule of the Illuminati that she and all other vampires follow to keep their activities secret from the human beings they co-exist with. Interspersed with accounts of the on-board adventures is the princess's narrative of her upbringing and vampirization.

**Other books you might like:**
Scott Ciencin, *The Vampire Odyssey*, 1992
Mick Farren, *The Time of Feasting*, 1995
Floyd Kemske, *Human Remains*, 1995
Fred Saberhagen, *A Sharpness on the Neck*, 1995
Karen E. Taylor, *Blood Secrets*, 1994

## 4668

### MICHAEL ROMKEY

## *The Vampire Virus*

(New York: Fawcett, 1998)

**Story type:** Horror (Vampire Story)
**Major character(s):** Bailey Harrison, Scientist, Researcher; Don Lazaro Ruiz Cortinez, Vampire; Father Xavier, Religious (priest)
**Time period(s):** 1990s (1998)
**Locale(s):** Paradisio, Costa Rica

**Summary:** The investigation of disease-control specialist Bailey Harrison into the bizarre virus that killed an archaeologist in the jungles of Costa Rica leads her to Paradisio, and the home of Don Lazaro, a 500-year-old vampire who uses his infectious bite to keep the nearby ruins of Zonatitucan secret and to protect his own privacy.

**Other books you might like:**
A.A. Carr, *Eye Killers*, 1995
Les Daniels, *The Silver Skull*, 1979
John Farris, *Sacrifice*, 1994
Brian Stableford, *The Empire of Fear*, 1988
Chelsea Quinn Yarbro, *Mansions of Darkness*, 1996

## 4669

### JOEL ROSENBERG

## *The Crimson Sky*

(New York: Avon, 1998)

**Story type:** Fantasy (Alternate World; Magic Conflict)

**Series:** Keepers of the Hidden Ways
**Major character(s):** Ian Silverstein, Martial Arts Expert (fencer), Hero; Maryanne "Maggie" Christensen, Warrior (fencer), Girlfriend, Martial Arts Expert; Thorian "Torrie" Thorsen, Martial Arts Expert (fencer), Young Man
**Time period(s):** 1990s; Indeterminate
**Locale(s):** Minneapolis, Minnesota; Hardwood, North Dakota; Tir Na Nog, Fictional Country

**Summary:** Once again, an unknown agent has dispatched a Son of Fenris, one of a tribe of fierce man/wolf shapechangers, to assassinate a member of Thorian Thorsen's family. As the assassin stalks its prey on the modern streets of Minneapolis, Ian and Hosea travel a Hidden Way to Tir Na Nog to find the culprit responsible for this sudden and unexpected attack. Unfortunately, the entire scene may have been played out for the express purpose of luring Ian to Tir Na Nog and his death.

**Other books you might like:**
Eleanor Arnason, *Daughter of the Bear King*, 1987
Gordon R. Dickson, *The Dragon and the George*, 1976
Doranna Durgin, *Changespell*, 1997
Barbara Hambly, *The Silent Tower*, 1986
Diana L. Paxson, *The Wolf and the Raven*, 1993

## 4670

### JOEL ROSENBERG

## *D'Shai*

(New York: Ace, 1991)

**Story type:** Fantasy (Mystery)
**Series:** D'Shai
**Major character(s):** Kami Khuzud, Entertainer (acrobat); Narantir, Wizard; Lord Toshtai, Ruler
**Time period(s):** Indeterminate
**Locale(s):** Den Oroshtai, Fictional Country; D'Shai, Fictional Country

**Summary:** Kami is twice trapped by D'Shai's rigid caste system. He is a peasant in love with a daughter of the upper classes and he is an acrobat with no magical talent for acrobatics. But when he is falsely accused of a nobleman's murder, Kami must defy tradition and find his special power to save his life and name.

**Other books you might like:**
Steven Brust, *Jhereg*, 1983
Steven Brust, *To Reign in Hell*, 1984
Brian Daley, *A Tapestry of Magics*, 1983
Robert Silverberg, *Lord Valentine's Castle*, 1980
Roger Zelazny, *Nine Princes in Amber*, 1970

## 4671

### JOEL ROSENBERG

## *The Fire Duke*

(New York: AvoNova, 1995)

**Story type:** Fantasy (Alternate World; Magic Conflict)
**Series:** Keepers of the Hidden Ways
**Major character(s):** Thorian "Torrie" Thorsen, Martial Arts Expert (fencer), Young Man; Ian Silverstein, Martial Arts Expert (fencer), Hero; Orfindel "Hosea Lincoln", Deity (Old One), Handyman (the Builder)
**Time period(s):** 1990s (1995)
**Locale(s):** Hardwood, North Dakota; Tir Na Nog, Fictional Country; Falias, Fictional City

**Summary:** While on vacation with friends at his parents' farm in North Dakota, Torrie Thorsen learns that his father and Uncle Hosea long ago came through the Hidden Ways to this world, fleeing the machinations of the Fire Duke. Now Torrie and his father lie imprisoned in His Warmth's stronghold, having failed to rescue his kidnapped mother and girlfriend. Ian and Hosea must now attempt to free all four of them before the Duke's evil schemes come to fruition. First in the series.

**Other books you might like:**
Steven Brust, *Jhereg*, 1983
Charles de Lint, *The Little Country*, 1991
Gordon R. Dickson, *The Dragon and the George*, 1976
Gordon R. Dickson, *The Dragon, the Earl, and the Troll*, 1994
Geary Gravel, *A Key for the Nonesuch*, 1990
Barbara Hambly, *The Silent Tower*, 1986
Christopher Stasheff, *The Witch Doctor*, 1995
Vivian Vande Velde, *User Unfriendly*, 1991

## 4672

### JOEL ROSENBERG

### *Hero*

(New York: Roc, 1990)

**Story type:** Science Fiction (Military)
**Major character(s):** Ari Hanavi, Warrior (hereditary), Military Personnel (private); Isadore Lipschitz, Military Personnel (sargeant); Shimon Bar-el, Military Personnel (general)
**Time period(s):** Indeterminate Future
**Locale(s):** Metzadan, Planet—Imaginary

**Summary:** A commander unconventionally precipitates victory against overwhelming opposition by calling for an artillary barrage to be laid down on his troops' current position, and ordering his troops to take the enemy position or die on the spot. Sequel to *Not for Glory* (1988).

**Other books you might like:**
Gordon R. Dickson, *The Tactics of Mistake*, 1971
David Drake, *The Forlorn Hope*, 1984
David Drake, *Rolling Hot*, 1989
Roland J. Green, *Squadron Alert*, 1989
Robert A. Heinlein, *Starship Troopers*, 1959
Jerry Pournelle, *Falkenberg's Legion*, 1990

## 4673

### JOEL ROSENBERG

### *Hour of the Octopus*

(New York: Ace, 1994)

**Story type:** Fantasy (Mystery; Political)
**Series:** D'Shai
**Major character(s):** Kami Khuzud, Detective (Discoverer-of-Truths); Lady ViKay, Noblewoman, Fiance(e); Dun Lidjun, Nobleman, Martial Arts Expert
**Time period(s):** Indeterminate
**Locale(s):** D'Shai, Fictional Country

**Summary:** Kami Dan'Shir addresses a royal conundrum which brings him an uncomfortable opportunity to prove his recently recognized skill at detection when clues frame the groom as murderer in an attempt to foil a wedding.

**Other books you might like:**
Steven Brust, *Jhereg*, 1983
James Clavell, *Shogun*, 1975

Glen Cook, *Dread Brass Shadows*, 1990
Glen Cook, *Sweet Silver Blues*, 1987
Randall Garrett, *Murder and Magic*, 1979
Randall Garrett, *Too Many Magicians*, 1967
Simon R. Green, *Hawk & Fisher*, 1990
Barry Hughart, *Bridge of Birds*, 1984

## 4674

### JOEL ROSENBERG

### *The Road Home*

(New York: Roc, 1995)

**Story type:** Fantasy (Adventure; Sword and Sorcery)
**Series:** Guardians of the Flame
**Major character(s):** Jason Cullinane, Warrior, Nobleman (baron); Walter Slovotsky, Warrior; Ahira Bandylegs, Mythical Creature (dwarf), Guardian (Jason's)
**Time period(s):** Indeterminate
**Locale(s):** Biemestren, Fictional City; Pandathaway, Fictional City; The Empire, Fictional Country

**Summary:** In order to find his former best friend, Mikyn, and stop him from single-handedly wiping out all slavers to keep the legend of the Warrior alive, Jason and Ahira form a distasteful alliance with Toryn, a Journeyman Slaver under a geas from his guild to aid them. Escaping an uncomfortable political situation in Emperor Thomen's stronghold, Walter Slovotsky sets off for Castle Cullinane where he hopes to hitch a ride with Ellegon, a dragon of his acquaintance, find Jason and Ahira, and help them with their task. Seventh in the series.

**Other books you might like:**
Steven Brust, *Jhereg*, 1983
C.J. Cherryh, *Faery in Shadow*, 1994
Jo Clayton, *Wildfire*, 1992
Glen Cook, *The Black Company*, 1984
Barbara Hambly, *Dragonsbane*, 1987
Barbara Hambly, *The Ladies of Mandrigyn*, 1984
Robert A. Heinlein, *Glory Road*, 1963

## 4675

### JOEL ROSENBERG

### *The Road to Ehvenor*

(New York: Roc, 1991)

**Story type:** Fantasy (Magic Conflict)
**Series:** Guardians of the Flame
**Major character(s):** Walter Slovotsky, Warrior; Andrea Cullinane, Wizard
**Time period(s):** Indeterminate
**Locale(s):** Ehvenor, Fictional City

**Summary:** When magic from Faerie begins to infest the area around Ehvenor, a border town between Faerie and the mortal realm, Walter Slovotsky and his companions respond to pleas for help, not realizing the magical anomaly represents the opening round of a war to be inflicted on the mortal realm.

**Other books you might like:**
Stephen Billias, *Horrible Humes*, 1991
Emma Bull, *War for the Oaks*, 1987
Andre Norton, *The Elvenbane*, 1991
    Mercedes Lackey, co-author
Michael Reaves, *Street Magic*, 1991
Will Shetterly, *Elsewhere*, 1991

Terri Windling, *Borderland*, 1986
  Mark Alan Arnold, co-editor
Terri Windling, *Bordertown*, 1986
  Mark Alan Arnold, co-editor
Terri Windling, *Life on the Border*, 1991
  editor

## 4676

### JOEL ROSENBERG

## The Silver Stone

(New York: Avon, 1996)

**Story type:** Fantasy (Alternate World; Magic Conflict)
**Series:** Keepers of the Hidden Ways
**Major character(s):** Ian Silverstein, Martial Arts Expert (fencer), Hero; Thorian "Torrie" Thorsen, Martial Arts Expert (fencer), Young Man; Maryanne "Maggie" Christensen, Martial Arts Expert (fencer), Girlfriend
**Time period(s):** Indeterminate
**Locale(s):** Hardwood, North Dakota; Tir Na Nog, Fictional Country; Vandescard, Fictional Country

**Summary:** Journeying back to Tir Na Nog to save Orfindel, the ailing Old One, Ian Silverstein finds himself a reluctant messenger for Odin himself, carrying the great god's spear and a warning not to disturb his peace with plans of war. While the power of the spear causes the men of Vandescard to look on Ian as the possible Promised Warrior, the powerful ruling family sees him as a potential threat to their plans. Unfortunately, Ian can find no way to make either side see Odin's point of view.

**Other books you might like:**
Steven Brust, *Jhereg*, 1983
Eve Forward, *Villains by Necessity*, 1995
Craig Shaw Gardner, *Dragon Sleeping*, 1994
Barbara Hambly, *The Silent Tower*, 1986
Diana L. Paxson, *The Dragons of the Rhine*, 1995

## 4677

### MARY ROSENBLUM

## Chimera

(New York: Ballantine Del Rey, 1993)

**Story type:** Science Fiction (Cyberpunk; Arts)
**Major character(s):** Jewel Martina, Health Care Professional; Flander, Computer Expert; David Chen, Artist, Computer Expert
**Time period(s):** Indeterminate Future
**Locale(s):** Erebus Complex, Antarctica; California

**Summary:** To escape the 'burbs, Jewel Martina manages to get enough education to become a med tech, able to keep the bodies of powerful, elderly citizens alive while they spend their time in virtual reality in the computer network. David Chen, a brilliant virtual artist, and his partner, Flander, befriend Jewel when she saves Flander's life. Jewel tries to discover the identity of the mountain lion which seems able to manifest itself in reality outside of virtual space.

**Other books you might like:**
David Brin, *Earth*, 1990
Pat Cadigan, *Synners*, 1991
Jean Mark Gawron, *Dream of Glass*, 1993
Jack C. Haldeman II, *High Steel*, 1993
  Jack Dann, co-author
James P. Hogan, *The Multiplex Man*, 1992
Neal Stephenson, *Snow Crash*, 1992

Amy Thomson, *Virtual Girl*, 1993

## 4678

### MARY ROSENBLUM

## The Drylands

(New York: Ballantine Del Rey, 1993)

**Story type:** Science Fiction (Post-Holocaust; Political)
**Major character(s):** Carter Voltaire, Military Personnel; Nita Montoya, Psychic; Dan Greeley, Activist, Farmer
**Time period(s):** 21st century
**Locale(s):** Columbia River Valley, Oregon

**Summary:** Charged with the unpopular job of rationing scarce water in drought-stricken America, the Army Corps of Engineers must stop the sabotage of the Columbia Riverbed Pipeline, a job which has already cost the previous commander of The Dalles base his life. Carter Voltaire, the new C.O., must decide whom he can trust: General Hastings, his superior officer; Dan Greeley, leader of the disgruntled farmers whose fields are drying up; Johnny Seldon, his friend and a member of the powerful Water Policy Committee; or Nita Montoya, who fears persecution if she reveals her abnormal talents.

**Other books you might like:**
David Brin, *The Postman*, 1985
John Brunner, *Stand on Zanzibar*, 1968
Arsen Darnay, *A Hostage for Hinterland*, 1976
Gordon R. Dickson, *Wolf and Iron*, 1990
Bill Dolan, *Afrikorps*, 1991
Gregory Feeley, *The Oxygen Barons*, 1990
Ursula K. Le Guin, *The Lathe of Heaven*, 1971
Colleen McCullough, *A Creed for the Third Millennium*, 1985
John Wyndham, *Re-Birth*, 1955

## 4679

### MARY ROSENBLUM

## The Stone Garden

(New York: Ballantine Del Rey, 1995)

**Story type:** Science Fiction (Arts; First Contact)
**Major character(s):** Michael Tryon, Artist; Margarita Espinoza, Artist; Xia Quejaches, Dancer, Wanderer
**Time period(s):** Indeterminate Future
**Locale(s):** Old Taos, New Mexico; Upper New York, Space Station

**Summary:** After Margarita writes claiming to be his daughter, Michael realizes he can no longer hide in his Taos studio. His art, layering emotion on sensitive space stones, has taken too much from him, and he decides that to survive he must get away from his past, preserved all around him in his stones. A powerful enemy attacks Michael when he leaves Taos to meet his potential daughter. Found a month later, he discovers stone sculptors committing suicide but believes their involuntary acts may have an outside cause.

**Other books you might like:**
John Barnes, *A Million Open Doors*, 1992
Jack C. Haldeman II, *High Steel*, 1993
  Jack Dann, co-author
Mark S. Geston, *Mirror to the Sky*, 1992
Ernest Hogan, *Cortez on Jupiter*, 1990
Spider Robinson, *Stardance*, 1979
  Jeanne Robinson, co-author

## 4680

### MARY ROSENBLUM

## Synthesis & Other Virtual Realities

(Sauk City, Wisconsin: Arkham House, 1996)

**Story type:** Science Fiction (Collection; Dystopian)

**Summary:** Contains nine stories, frequently dark in tone, with several set in the milieu of *The Drylands*. Themes include nature out of balance, family relationships, virtual reality, and the difficulties of emigration.

**Other books you might like:**
Alexander Jablokov, *The Breath of Suspension*, 1994
John Kessel, *Meeting in Infinity*, 1992
Nancy Kress, *The Aliens of Earth*, 1993
Rebecca Ore, *Alien Bootlegger and Other Stories*, 1993
Michael Swanwick, *Gravity's Angels*, 1991
James Tiptree Jr., *Her Smoke Rose Up Forever*, 1990

## 4681

### DAVID D. ROSS

## The Argus Gambit

(New York: St. Martin's Press, 1989)

**Story type:** Science Fiction (Espionage Thriller)
**Series:** Dreamers of the Day
**Major character(s):** Mel Hardrim, Police Officer; Jeffrey Shefferton, Political Figure (President)
**Time period(s):** 21st century
**Locale(s):** United States

**Summary:** Police officer Mel Hardrim thinks he's guarding a noted scientist. After the man is murdered, Hardrim discovers he was a fake and that the real scientist has disappeared. His career in ruins, Hardrim attempts to solve the murder, but finds himself drawn into a complex web of political intrigue involving the mysterious Argus Society, a secret organization apparently bent on taking over the world.

**Other books you might like:**
Joe Haldeman, *Buying Time*, 1989
Thomas Pynchon, *Gravity's Rainbow*, 1973
Bruce Sterling, *Islands in the Net*, 1988

## 4682

### DAVID D. ROSS

## The Eighth Rank

(New York: St. Martin's Press, 1991)

**Story type:** Science Fiction (Political; Techno-Thriller)
**Series:** Dreamers of the Day
**Major character(s):** Jason Scott, Administrator (Sunside Project); Jeffrey Shefferton, Political Figure (president); Lenore Lippman, Computer Expert, Cyborg
**Time period(s):** 21st century
**Locale(s):** United States; Montenegro; Icarus, Asteroid

**Summary:** Repeal of the 31st Amendment reopens the United States for trade with the rest of the world. Food is scarce, technology is feared, and the Sunside Project to produce food is a hoax. Working for the project is very dangerous, not only for those located off Earth, but also for those having to contend with the polical and military hostilities on Earth. This novel is a sequel to *The Argus Gambit*.

**Other books you might like:**
Isaac Asimov, *Foundation*, 1951
David Brin, *Earth*, 1990
Philip K. Dick, *The Unteleported Man*, 1983
  revised
Gregory Feeley, *The Oxygen Barons*, 1990
Michael Flynn, *In the Country of the Blind*, 1990
Michael P. Kube-McDowell, *The Quiet Pools*, 1990
Alis A. Rasmussen, *A Passage of Stars*, 1990
Allen Steele, *Orbital Decay*, 1989
Bruce Sterling, *Islands in the Net*, 1988
A.E. Van Vogt, *The World of Null-A*, 1950
David Wingrove, *The Middle Kingdom*, 1990

## 4683

### THEODORE ROSZAK

## Flicker

(New York: Summit Books, 1991)

**Story type:** Horror (Mystery)
**Major character(s):** John Gates, Student (film student); Simon Dunkle, Director (film director); Clare Swann, Critic (film critic)
**Time period(s):** 1990s
**Locale(s):** Los Angeles, California

**Summary:** While researching the work of Depression-era German expressionist horror film director Max Castle, film student John Gates discovers that Castle was raised and educated by the Cathars, a heretical sect of Albigensian Christians involved in filmmaking since its inception, who train their acolytes to encode films with subliminal messages that promulgate their amoral viewpoint. Gates' investigations draw attention to him and plunge him into a dark world of paranoia and conspiracy.

**Other books you might like:**
Ramsey Campbell, *Ancient Images*, 1989
Jonathan Carroll, *A Child Across the Sky*, 1989
Umberto Eco, *Foucault's Pendulum*, 1988

## 4684

### THEODORE ROSZAK

## The Memoirs of Elizabeth Frankenstein

(New York: Random House, 1995)

**Story type:** Horror (Occult)
**Major character(s):** Victor Frankenstein, Scientist; Elizabeth Frankenstein, Young Woman; Seraphina, Witch
**Time period(s):** 1780s; 1790s
**Locale(s):** Geneva, Switzerland

**Summary:** Young Elizabeth Lavenza becomes the ward of Baron and Lady Caroline Frankenstein, and the playmate and eventual wife of their son, Victor. Elizabeth is indoctrinated into the witch cult Caroline belongs to and encouraged to embrace romantic ideals regarding her relationship to the natural and supernatural in this feminist retelling of the Frankenstein tale. The Story is presented as diaries edited by Robert Walton, the explorer who preserved the original account of Victor Frankenstein's ordeal with his monster in Mary Shelley's original novel.

**Other books you might like:**
Brian W. Aldiss, *Frankenstein Unbound*, 1973
Emmanuel Carrere, *Gothic Romance*, 1984
Marie Kiraly, *Mina*, 1994
Mary Shelley, *Frankenstein*, 1818

## 4685

### JANE ROUTLEY

## *Fire Angels*

(New York: Avon Eos, 1998)

**Story type:** Fantasy (Magic Conflict)
**Major character(s):** Dion Holyhands, Wizard; Leon Sahr, Nobleman (duke); Darmen Stalker, Secretary
**Time period(s):** Indeterminate
**Locale(s):** Moria, Fictional Country

**Summary:** Dion, a powerful wizard, returns to her homeland to find that it has been invaded by villains both natural and supernatural. Their depredations are linked to machinations of various members of the nobility trying to seize the throne of Moria. Sequel to *Mage Heart*.

**Other books you might like:**
Raymond E. Feist, *Rage of a Demon King*, 1997
Terry Goodkind, *Wizard's First Rule*, 1994
Simon R. Green, *Blue Moon Rising*, 1991
Oliver Johnson, *The Forging of the Shadows*, 1997
Janny Wurts, *Shadowfane*, 1988

## 4686

### JANE ROUTLEY

## *Mage Heart*

(New York: Morrow/AvoNova, 1996)

**Story type:** Fantasy (Magic Conflict)
**Major character(s):** Dion, Magician, Student; Kitten "Our Lady of Roses" Avignon, Noblewoman
**Time period(s):** Indeterminate
**Locale(s):** Gallia, Fictional City; Moria, Fictional Country

**Summary:** Despite Dion's especially powerful magical abilities, society's conventions restrict her practice to mundane healing. After entering the Gallian College of Magic, the first woman to do so, Dion reluctantly accepts Duke Leon's order to serve his favorite mistress, an appointment which fosters a broader application of Dion's talents as an evil necromancer presses his attack on Kitten. First novel.

**Other books you might like:**
Lois McMaster Bujold, *The Spirit Ring*, 1992
Lynn Flewelling, *Luck in the Shadows*, 1996
Laurell K. Hamilton, *Nightseer*, 1992
Guy Gavriel Kay, *A Song for Arbonne*, 1993
Caroline Stevermer, *A College of Magics*, 1994
Paula Volsky, *Illusion*, 1992

## 4687

### JEFF ROVIN

## *Return of the Wolfman*

(New York: Berkley/Boulevard, 1998)

**Story type:** Horror (Werewolf Story)
**Major character(s):** Caroline Cooke, Doctor; Larry Talbot, Werewolf; Tom Stevenson, Lawyer
**Time period(s):** 1990s (1998)
**Locale(s):** La Mirada, Florida

**Summary:** When Caroline Cooke inherits her great aunt's estate, she also inherits the continuing battle between the Wolfman, Count Dracula and the Frankenstein monster, all of whom met their sup-posed ends there half a century before, but who are resurrected in the fashion of the movies that have immortalized them to resume their conflict.

**Other books you might like:**
John Burke, *Dracula, Prince of Darkness*, 1998
John Burke, *The Hammer Horror Omnibus*, 1967
Carl Dreadstone, *The Bride of Frankenstein*, 1977

## 4688

### JEFF ROVIN

## *Vespers*

(New York: St. Martin's, 1998)

**Story type:** Horror (Nature in Revolt)
**Major character(s):** Robert Gentry, Detective—Police; Nancy Joyce, Scientist (zoologist); Kathy Leung, Journalist
**Time period(s):** 1990s (1998)
**Locale(s):** New York, New York

**Summary:** The progeny of mutant bats damaged by radiation in Russia and smuggled into the United States grow to enormous size and become the leaders of a bat army terrorizing Manhattan. Police detective Robert Gentry and Bronz Zoo bat specialist Nancy Joyce team up to destroy the bats before they breed and release their offspring on the world.

**Other books you might like:**
Ken Eulo, *Claw*, 1994
　　Joe Mauck, co-author
William W. Johnstone, *Bats*, 1993
Douglas Preston, *Relic*, 1995
　　Lincoln Child, co-author
Martin Cruz Smith, *Nightwing*, 1977
Robert Charles Wilson, *Second Fire*, 1993

## 4689

### MICHAEL ROWE, Editor
### THOMAS S. ROCHE, Co-Editor

## *Brothers of the Night*

(San Francisco: Cleis Press, 1997)

**Story type:** Horror (Anthology; Vampire Story)

**Summary:** Eleven tales of the supernatural that use the vampire theme to explore issues of gay male sexuality. In Caitlin R. Kiernan's "Superheroes," two gay lovers seek to escape their unfulfilling lives through a tryst with an unusual contact made during an on-line chat. In Edo van Belkom's "Letting Go," a vampire stalks a hospital, bestowing the gift of death on AIDS patients. Both Robert Thomsen, in "Third Night," and Bruce Benderson, in "Old World Manners," report the indoctrination of young men by experienced male vampires. David Quinn's "Forever October" is an ambiguous tale of a man whose vampire behavior may be a sign of madness.

**Other books you might like:**
Poppy Z. Brite, *Love in Vein II*, 1997
　　Martin H. Greenberg, co-editor
Pam Keesey, *Daughters of Darkness: Lesbian Vampire Stories*, 1993
　　editor
Pam Keesey, *Darker Angels: Lesbian Vampire Stories*, 1995
　　editor
Amarantha Knight, *Love Bites*, 1995
　　editor
Cecilia Tan, *Vampire Erotica*, 1995
　　editor

Cecilia Tan, *Erotica Vampirica*, 1996
  editor

---

**4690**

**MICHAEL ROWE**, Editor
**THOMAS S. ROCHE**, Co-Editor

### Sons of Darkness: Tales of Men, Blood and Immortality

(Boston: Cleis Press, 1996)

**Story type:** Horror (Anthology; Vampire Story)

**Summary:** These 12 stories with strong erotic subtexts all feature male vampires. C. Dean Anderrson's ''My Greatest Fear'' and Nancy Kilpatrick's ''The Game'' feature vampires who have the tables turned on them by their male lovers. Carol Queen's ''Feeding'' tells of a vampire chef who finds a restaurant client his ultimate meal, while Wickie Stamps' ''Retribution for Golgotha'' concerns a vampire who tracks down the blood relatives of those responsible for his death alongside Jesus Christ on Golgotha. Ron Oliver's ''Bela Lugosi's Dead'' is about a young boy who immerses himself too deeply in the vampire imagery of horror films and music. In the book's one reprint, Poppy Z. Brite's ''His Mouth Shall Taste of Wormwood,'' vampires troll the decadent Gothic underground of New Orleans.

**Other books you might like:**
Poppy Z. Brite, *Love in Vein*, 1994
  Martin H. Greenberg, co-editor
Poppy Z. Brite, *Love in Vein II*, 1997
  Martin H. Greenberg, co-editor
Cecilia Tan, *Blood Kiss: Vampire Erotica*, 1995
  editor

---

**4691**

**CHRISTOPHER ROWLEY**

### Battledragon

(New York: Roc, 1995)

**Story type:** Fantasy (Adventure)
**Series:** Bazil Broketail
**Major character(s):** Bazil Broketail, Mythical Creature (dragon), Military Personnel; Relkin, Military Personnel, Companion
**Time period(s):** Indeterminate
**Locale(s):** Argonath Region, Fictional Country; At Sea; Eigo, Mythical Place

**Summary:** After hearing intelligence concerning the development of weapons of unthinkable destruction by the Master of Darkness, Argonath's emperor dispatches a fleet, including Relkin and the 109th Marneri Dragons, to thwart the upcoming invasion from the distant continent of Eigo.

**Other books you might like:**
Gael Baudino, *Duel of Dragons*, 1991
Don Callander, *Dragon Companion*, 1994
Gordon R. Dickson, *The Dragon at War*, 1992
Ursula K. Le Guin, *A Wizard of Earthsea*, 1968
Anne McCaffrey, *Dragonriders of Pern*, 1988

---

**4692**

**CHRISTOPHER ROWLEY**

### Bazil Broketail

(New York: Roc, 1992)

**Story type:** Fantasy (Adventure)
**Series:** Bazil Broketail
**Major character(s):** Bazil Broketail, Mythical Creature (dragon), Warrior; Relkin, Military Personnel, Companion (Bazil's); Lessis of Valmes, Witch, Heroine
**Time period(s):** Indeterminate
**Locale(s):** Marneri, Fictional City (Argonath Region); Ryetelth, Mythical Place

**Summary:** While fighting to qualify for military service, Bazil suffers a treacherous attack that severs his prehensile tail, an injury which would normally condemn Bazil and Relkin to farm labor. When Relkin searches for an immediate magical cure, Lessis comes to their rescue, allowing flawed regrowth of the tail's tip and allowing Bazil and Relkin to aid the witches in their desperate attempt to save everyone from The Doom's attempt to dominate the human realms.

**Other books you might like:**
Richard Adams, *Shardik*, 1975
Anne McCaffrey, *Dragonflight*, 1968
Anne McCaffrey, *Dragonquest*, 1970
Anne McCaffrey, *The White Dragon*, 1978

---

**4693**

**CHRISTOPHER ROWLEY**

### A Dragon at World's End

(New York: Roc, 1997)

**Story type:** Fantasy (Adventure; Magic Conflict)
**Series:** Bazil Broketail
**Major character(s):** Bazil Broketail, Mythical Creature (dragon), Military Personnel; Relkin, Military Personnel
**Time period(s):** Indeterminate
**Locale(s):** Eigo, Fictional Country; Mirchaz, Fictional City

**Summary:** Separated from the 109th Marneri Dragons and thought dead, Bazil and Relkin plan to help a jungle tribe. When captured by slavers and taken to Mirchaz, Relkin becomes the pawn of an Elven wizard, forced to develop his rudimentary magical abilities in his struggle for freedom. Meanwhile, Bazil plots an assault on Mirchaz itself. Sixth in series.

**Other books you might like:**
Gael Baudino, *Duel of Dragons*, 1991
Glen Cook, *The Black Company*, 1984
Ursula K. Le Guin, *A Wizard of Earthsea*, 1968
Anne McCaffrey, *Dragonriders of Pern*, 1988
Elizabeth Moon, *The Deed of Paksenarrion*, 1992

---

**4694**

**CHRISTOPHER ROWLEY**

### Dragons of Argonath

(New York: Roc, 1998)

**Story type:** Fantasy (Political; Magic Conflict)
**Series:** Bazil Broketail
**Major character(s):** Bazil Broketail, Mythical Creature (dragon), Military Personnel; Relkin, Military Personnel
**Time period(s):** Indeterminate

**Locale(s):** Argonath, Fictional Country; Quosh, Fictional City

**Summary:** Relkin and Bazil Broketail return to Quosh in triumph after their battles, but cannot enjoy peace for long. The influence of a new terror, the Dominator, may shatter the empire if Relkin cannot harness his emerging magical abilities.

**Other books you might like:**
Gael Baudino, *Duel of Dragons*, 1991
Glen Cook, *The Black Company*, 1984
Ursula K. Le Guin, *A Wizard of Earthsea*, 1968
Anne McCaffrey, *Dragonriders of Pern*, 1988
Elizabeth Moon, *The Deed of Paksenarrion*, 1992

---

**4695**

CHRISTOPHER ROWLEY

## Dragons of War
(New York: Roc, 1994)

**Story type:** Fantasy (Adventure)
**Series:** Bazil Broketail
**Major character(s):** Bazil Broketail, Mythical Creature (dragon), Military Personnel; Relkin, Military Personnel, Companion (Bazil's)
**Time period(s):** Indeterminate
**Locale(s):** Argonath Region, Fictional Country; Kenor, Fictional Country

**Summary:** Bazil's surprise reunion results in a murder charge against Relkin at a time when the empire's survival depends on the Dragon Legions as waves of giants, imps and trolls threaten to overwhelm all.

**Other books you might like:**
Gael Baudino, *Dragonsword*, 1991
Gael Baudino, *Duel of Dragons*, 1991
Gordon R. Dickson, *The Dragon at War*, 1992
Anne McCaffrey, *Dragonflight*, 1968
Lawrence Watt-Evans, *The Blood of a Dragon*, 1991

---

**4696**

CHRISTOPHER ROWLEY

## The Founder
(New York: Ballantine/Del Rey, 1989)

**Story type:** Science Fiction (First Contact)
**Series:** Fenrille
**Major character(s):** Dane Fundan, Heir, Spaceman
**Time period(s):** 25th century
**Locale(s):** *Founder*, Spaceship; Fenrille, Planet—Imaginary

**Summary:** Earth and the space habitats are about to go to war over who controls the solar system. To escape the impending holocaust, Dane Fundan builds an interstellar colony ship. Reaching another star system, however, the colonists find themselves immediately immersed in even more treachery and danger. Prequel to *The War for Eternity*.

**Other books you might like:**
Gregory Benford, *Tides of Light*, 1989
Dave Duncan, *Strings*, 1990
Vonda N. McIntyre, *Starfarers*, 1989
Susan Shwartz, *Heritage of Flight*, 1989

---

**4697**

CHRISTOPHER ROWLEY

## A Sword for a Dragon
(New York: Roc, 1993)

**Story type:** Fantasy (Adventure)
**Series:** Bazil Broketail
**Major character(s):** Bazil Broketail, Mythical Creature (dragon), Military Personnel; Relkin, Military Personnel, Companion (Bazil's)
**Time period(s):** Indeterminate
**Locale(s):** Argonath Region, Fictional Country

**Summary:** Receiving paramount decorations for valor during their first campaign, Relkin and Bazil recruit a former battle dragon into the 109th Marneri Dragons and prepare for another glorious campaign. Plans derail briefly as sinister forces ally with traitorous companions to kidnap Relkin and Bazil for study.

**Other books you might like:**
Gael Baudino, *Dragonsword*, 1991
Gordon R. Dickson, *The Dragon and the George*, 1976
Gordon R. Dickson, *The Dragon at War*, 1992
Gordon R. Dickson, *The Dragon on the Border*, 1992
Anne McCaffrey, *Dragonflight*, 1968
Anne McCaffrey, *Dragonquest*, 1970
Anne McCaffrey, *The White Dragon*, 1978

---

**4698**

CHRISTOPHER ROWLEY

## To a Highland Nation
(New York: Ballantine Del Rey, 1993)

**Story type:** Science Fiction (Immortality; Political)
**Series:** Fenrille
**Major character(s):** Fair Fundan, Rancher (chitin talker), Leader; Hof Wiltin, Rancher, Warrior; Martin Overed, Government Official
**Time period(s):** 26th century
**Locale(s):** Fenrille, Planet—Imaginary

**Summary:** Human colonists and native Fein must band together to resist an attack and attempted takeover by greedy humans from off planet. The attackers intend to acquire total control of the longevity drug produced by native insects.

**Other books you might like:**
C.J. Cherryh, *Serpent's Reach*, 1980
Frank Herbert, *Dune*, 1965
James H. Schmitz, *The Demon Breed*, 1968
Joan Slonczewski, *Daughter of Elysium*, 1993
Joan Slonczewski, *A Door into Ocean*, 1986
Cordwainer Smith, *Norstrilia*, 1975

---

**4699**

CHRISTOPHER ROWLEY

## The Wizard and the Floating City
(New York: Roc, 1996)

**Story type:** Fantasy (Quest; Magic Conflict)
**Major character(s):** Danais Evander, Royalty (prince), Heir—Dispossessed; Serena, Royalty (princess); Gadjung, Wizard
**Time period(s):** Indeterminate
**Locale(s):** Bakan, Fictional Country; Monjon, Fictional City

**Summary:** Having knowingly offended an evil wizard, the exiled prince Evander barely escapes drowning at sea, only to find that part of his skin has metamorphosed into a lizard's. Hoping to find a cure for his deformity, he travels with two imps to the magic city of Monjon, which floats 10 feet above the land due to the power of the Thymnal. First, he must rescue a princess, battle wicked witches, flee fantastic beasts, and defeat an evil wizard. Set in the *Bazil Broketail* Universe.

**Other books you might like:**
Lynn Abbey, *The Wooden Sword*, 1991
C.J. Cherryh, *Chernevog*, 1990
Simon R. Green, *Blood and Honor*, 1993
Barbara Hambly, *The Dark Hand of Magic*, 1990
Elizabeth Ann Scarborough, *Bronwyn's Bane*, 1983

---

**4700**

**J.K. ROWLING**

## Harry Potter and the Sorcerer's Stone

(New York: Scholastic, 1998)

**Story type:** Fantasy (Young Readers)
**Major character(s):** Harry Potter, Student
**Time period(s):** Indeterminate
**Locale(s):** Mythical Place (Hogwarts School of Witchcraft); Fictional Country

**Summary:** Harry Potter suffers neglect while growing up a fosterling at his aunt and uncle's house, until an invitation to Hogwarts School of Witchcraft and Wizardry opens the way to a great destiny.

**Other books you might like:**
Debra Doyle, *School of Wizardry*, 1990
    James D. Macdonald, co-author
Sherwood Smith, *Wren to the Rescue*, 1990
Caroline Stevermer, *A College of Magics*, 1994
Jane Yolen, *Wizard's Hall*, 1991
Mary Frances Zambreno, *A Plague of Wizards*, 1991

---

**4701**

**P.D. ROZZI**

## Waltz with Evil

(New York: Zebra, 1991)

**Story type:** Horror (Haunted House)
**Major character(s):** Tommy Clarkston, Child; Dan Cook, Police Officer; Rachel Clarkston, Spirit
**Time period(s):** 1980s (1988)
**Locale(s):** Clinton

**Summary:** One hundred years ago, as she was being buried alive, Rachel Clarkston vowed she would return from the dead to claim her son. Having fulfilled the first part of her promise by absorbing a mortal soul to reconstitute her flesh, Rachel next lures Tommy Clarkston, her youngest lineal descendant, to her former seaside home.

**Other books you might like:**
Campbell Black, *Letters From the Dead*, 1985
Diane Guest, *Lullaby*, 1990
Al Sarrantonio, *House Haunted*, 1991

---

**4702**

**PETER RUBIE**

## Werewolf

(Stamford, Connecticut: Longmeadow Press, 1991)

**Story type:** Horror (Werewolf Story)
**Major character(s):** George Llewellyn, Police Officer; Nevil Stimpson, Convict (rehabilitated child molester); Vera Armstrong, Nurse
**Time period(s):** 1940s (1941)
**Locale(s):** London, England (East End)

**Summary:** Detective Sergeant George Llewellyn learns to rue the day that he intervened during a childbirth at a gypsy settlement on the outskirts of London in 1931 and was cursed for his interference. Ten years later, during the Nazi blitz of London, the werewolf offspring of that birth runs amok through the city, and Llewellyn's only hope is to team up with an enemy he once put behind bars to stop the bloody murder spree.

**Other books you might like:**
Clive Barker, *"Twilight at the Towers"*, 1989
    in *Cabal*
Richard Jaccoma, *The Werewolf's Tale*, 1988
Robert R. McCammon, *The Wolf's Hour*, 1989
H. Warner Munn, *The Werewolf of Ponkert*, 1958
Jane Rice, *"The Refugee"*, 1990
    in *Rivals of Weird Tales*

---

**4703**

**RUDY RUCKER**

## Freeware

(New York: Avon, 1997)

**Story type:** Science Fiction (Alternate Intelligence; Cyberpunk)
**Series:** Software
**Major character(s):** Monique, Robot (moldie); Tre Dietz, Artist, Inventor; Randy Karl Tucker, Kidnapper
**Time period(s):** 2050s
**Locale(s):** Santa Cruz, California; Luna, Montenegro; Bangalore, India

**Summary:** An artificial life form made of mold and plastic, Monique works for Tre Dietz as maid and bookkeeper at his wife's motel. Randy Karl, a fallen Heritagist, kidnaps Monique when she tries to insert a piece of herself as control in his brain. The Loonies download some programs from space which may lead to disaster for all. Sequel to *Software* and *Wetware*.

**Other books you might like:**
Tom Cool, *Infectress*, 1997
Jean Mark Gawron, *Dream of Glass*, 1993
Gwyneth Jones, *White Queen*, 1995
Ian McDonald, *Terminal Cafe*, 1994
Jeff Noon, *Vurt*, 1995

---

**4704**

**RUDY RUCKER**

## The Hacker and the Ants

(New York: Morrow/AvoNova, 1994)

**Story type:** Science Fiction (Alternate Intelligence; Cyberpunk)

**Major character(s):** Jerzy Rugby, Computer Expert, Detective—Amateur; Susan Poker, Real Estate Agent; Riscky "Hex DEF6" Pharbeque, Computer Expert, Criminal
**Time period(s):** 21st century
**Locale(s):** Silicon Valley, California; Cyberspace

**Summary:** Jerzy Rugby feels set up for blame when an artificial life program designed as a computerized testing program infects television sets. Impending local and federal charges limit Jerzy's options as he develops new code and searches for the origin of and cure for the plague of crafty AIs.

**Other books you might like:**
David Brin, *Earth*, 1990
Pat Cadigan, *Mindplayers*, 1987
Victor Milan, *The Cybernetic Samurai*, 1985
Neal Stephenson, *Snow Crash*, 1992
Amy Thomson, *Virtual Girl*, 1993

### 4705

**RUDY RUCKER**

## The Hollow Earth: The Narrative of Mason Algiers Reynolds of Virginia
(New York: William Morrow, 1990)

**Story type:** Science Fiction (Adventure; Alternate Universe)
**Major character(s):** Mason Algiers Reynolds, Fugitive; Otha, Slave
**Time period(s):** 1830s
**Locale(s):** Alternate Earth (Pre-Civil War Virginia)

**Summary:** After a murder, Mason and Otha flee Virginia, journeying to Antarctica where they travel through a hole into the Earth. There they discover a rich and varied land and continue their adventures.

**Other books you might like:**
Greg Bear, *Eon*, 1985
Greg Bear, *Eternity*, 1988
Edgar Rice Burroughs, *Pellucidar*, 1923
John Varley, *Titan*, 1979
Jules Verne, *Journey to the Center of the Earth*, 1864

### 4706

**RUDY RUCKER**

## Transreal!
(Englewood, Colorado: WSC Books, 1991)

**Story type:** Science Fiction (Collection)

**Summary:** This volume contains an introduction by Robert Sheckley with Rudy Rucker material presented in four parts labelled books, the first of which, "Light Fuse and Get Away," contains 21 poems written 1975-1982. Book two, titled "The 57th Franz Kafka," contains 18 stories written 1980-1983. Book three, titled "Weird Screens," contains 15 stories written 1984-1990 including three collaborative efforts, "Storming the Cosmos" written with Bruce Sterling, "Probability Pipeline" with Marc Laidlaw and "Instability" with Paul deFilipo. The fourth, titled "Some of the Dharma," includes 11 articles.

**Other books you might like:**
Isaac Asimov, *The Complete Stories - Volume 1*, 1990
Alfred Bester, *Star Light, Star Bright*, 1976
Michael Flynn, *The Nanotech Chronicles*, 1991
Alan Dean Foster, *With Friends Like These...*, 1977
Larry Niven, *Neutron Star*, 1968
Larry Niven, *Tales of Known Space*, 1975

Cordwainer Smith, *The Best of Cordwainer Smith*, 1975
Marc Stiegler, *The Gentle Seduction*, 1990
William Tenn, *The Seven Sexes*, 1968
John Varley, *Blue Champagne*, 1986
John Varley, *The Persistence of Vision*, 1978

### 4707

**MATT RUFF**

## Fool on the Hill
(New York: Atlantic Monthly Press, 1989)

**Story type:** Fantasy (Light Fantasy)
**Major character(s):** Luther, Student; Zephyr, Mythical Creature (Sprite)
**Time period(s):** 1980s
**Locale(s):** Ithaca, New York (Cornell University)

**Summary:** An assortment of characters, from sprites to humans, cats to dogs, and William F. Buckley to an evil thing buried in the boneyard are cast in this story. Eventually, most of the characters come together to fight the evil thing buried in the boneyard.

**Other books you might like:**
Gael Baudino, *Duel of Dragons*, 1990
Barry B. Longyear, *The God Box*, 1989
Ian Watson, *Queenmagic, Kingmagic*, 1988

### 4708

**MATT RUFF**

## Sewer, Gas & Electric
(New York: Atlantic Monthly Press, 1997)

**Story type:** Science Fiction (Science Fiction; Humor)
**Major character(s):** Joan Fine, Activist; Morris Kazenstein, Inventor, Activist; Sarah Emma "Kite" Edmonds, Aged Person (180 years old), Activist
**Time period(s):** 2030s (2023)
**Locale(s):** New York, New York; Atlanta, Georgia

**Summary:** Daughter of Catholic Women's Crusader Sister Ellen Fine and ex-wife of billionaire Harry Grant, Joan loses her job as a sewer worker after the rest of her crew becomes shark food. She accepts a job researching the possibility that an electric servant murdered its owner, an act considered impossible by all, but which provides the key to a deeper mystery endangering millions of lives.

**Other books you might like:**
David Brin, *Earth*, 1990
Laura J. Mixon, *Glass Houses*, 1992
Robert Shea, *The Illuminatus! Trilogy*, 1988
   Robert Anton Wilson, co-author
Dan Simmons, *Hyperion*, 1989
Neal Stephenson, *The Diamond Age*, 1995
Jim Young, *Armed Memory*, 1995

### 4709

**KRISTINE KATHRYN RUSCH**
**KEVIN J. ANDERSON**, Co-Author

## Afterimage
(New York: Roc, 1992)

**Story type:** Fantasy (Mystery; Contemporary)

**Major character(s):** Rebecca ''Michael Kerr'' Tamerlane, Detective—Amateur, Mythical Creature (shapeshifter); Matthew Adolphus, Detective—Police; Gantha, Alien (Darkling), Sorceress (shapeshifter)
**Time period(s):** 1980s (1989)
**Locale(s):** Santa Cruz, California

**Summary:** Brutally raped and murdered by a serial killer, Rebecca finds herself saved by mysterious strangers who change her shape. Transformed into the image she remembers last, that of the serial killer, Rebecca must find the strangers to regain her form before police arrest her for the serial killings.

**Other books you might like:**
Kevin J. Anderson, *Gamearth*, 1989
Kevin J. Anderson, *Gameplay*, 1989
Kevin J. Anderson, *Game's End*, 1990
Glen Cook, *Red Iron Nights*, 1991
Peter R. Emshwiller, *The Host*, 1991
Peter R. Emshwiller, *Short Blade*, 1992
Mercedes Lackey, *Burning Water*, 1989
Mercedes Lackey, *Children of the Night*, 1990
Mercedes Lackey, *Jinx High*, 1991
James D. Priest, *Kirins: The Spell of No'an*, 1990

## 4710

**KRISTINE KATHRYN RUSCH**
**KEVIN J. ANDERSON**, Co-Author

### Afterimage Aftershock

(Decatur, Georgia: Meisha Merlin, 1998)

**Story type:** Horror (Serial Killer)
**Major character(s):** Rebecca Tamerlane, Clerk (bookstore); Matthew Adolphus, Detective
**Time period(s):** 1980s (1989)
**Locale(s):** Santa Cruz, California

**Summary:** With the help of the darklings, a race of shapeshifters, Rebecca Tamerlane is resurrected from her death at the hands of a serial killer. Wearing the body of her murderer, Rebecca helps the darklings in their struggle to survive the earthquakes that have set them on the path of possible extinction, even as she seeks to regain her original form and avoid being prosecuted for her murderer's crimes. Revised preferred text of a novel published in 1992.

**Other books you might like:**
Warren Newton Beath, *Shock Lines*, 1993
Leigh Clark, *Evil Reincarnate*, 1994
Peter R. Emshwiller, *The Host*, 1991
Dee Graham, *Fallen*, 1998
Muriel Gray, *The Trickster*, 1995

## 4711

**KRISTINE KATHRYN RUSCH**

### Alien Influences

(New York: Bantam Spectra, 1997)

**Story type:** Science Fiction (First Contact; Political)
**Major character(s):** Justin Schafer, Psychologist; Netta Goldin, Administrator; Latona Etanl, Activist (Extra-Species Alliance)
**Time period(s):** Indeterminate Future
**Locale(s):** Bountiful, Planet—Imaginary; Minor Base, Moon—Imaginary (of Bountiful)

**Summary:** Hired to express the situation between the colonists and nearly extinct native Dancers on Bountiful despite his previous disastrous error with the Minarans, Justin meets Netta on Bountiful. Netta explains the current situation: eight of the children have been brutally murdered using the same ritual the Dancers use to help their children into adulthood. The colonists want to blame the Dancers and want them removed, as the colonists no longer need the Dancers to produce the plants that go into the drug they export. Unfortunately, Justin finds the murderers to be other children. He cannot permit another alien species' destruction, despite the colonists' wishes. First published in England, 1994.

**Other books you might like:**
C.J. Cherryh, *Foreigner*, 1994
L. Warren Douglas, *Cannon's Orb*, 1994
Alan Dean Foster, *The Tar-Aiym Krang*, 1972
James Gunn, *The Joy Machine*, 1996
    Theodore Sturgeon, co-author
Mary Doria Russell, *The Sparrow*, 1996
Sheri S. Tepper, *Grass*, 1989

## 4712

**KRISTINE KATHRYN RUSCH**, Editor
**EDWARD L. FERMAN**, Co-Editor

### The Best From Fantasy & Science Fiction: A 45th Anniversary Anthology

(New York: St. Martin's Press, 1994)

**Story type:** Science Fiction (Anthology)
**Series:** Best From Fantasy and Science Fiction

**Summary:** This 26th volume in the series contains a three-page introduction by Ferman, a three-page introduction by Rusch plus individual introductions to 19 stories encompassing science fiction, fantasy and horror representative of 1988-1993. These include one Hugo Award winner, Mike Resnick's ''Kirinyaga''; one Nebula Award nominee, Carolyn Ives Gilman's ''The Honeycrafters''; two Nebula Award winners, Alan Brennert's ''Ma Qui'' and Mike Connor's ''Guide Dog''; one Nebula Award winner and World Fantasy Award winner, Joe Haldeman's ''Graves''; and the first short piece from novelist Richard Bowes. Other authors include Ray Aldridge, Terry Bisson, Harlan Ellison, Karen Joy Fowler, Thomas Ligotti, James Morrow, Robert Reed, and Gene Wolf.

**Other books you might like:**
Avram Davidson, *The Best From Fantasy and Science Fiction: 12-14*, 1963-1965
    editor
Edward L. Ferman, *The Best From Fantasy and Science Fiction: 15-20*, 1966-1973
    editor
Edward L. Ferman, *The Best From Fantasy and Science Fiction: A Special 25th Anniversary Anthology*, 1974
    editor
Edward L. Ferman, *The Best From Fantasy & Science Fiction: A 40th Anniversary Anthology*, 1989
    editor
Robert P. Mills, *The Best From Fantasy and Science Fiction: 9-11*, 1960-1962
    editor

## **4713**

### KRISTINE KATHRYN RUSCH, Editor

## *The Best of Pulphouse: The Hardback Magazine*

(New York: St. Martins Press, 1991)

**Story type:** Science Fiction (Anthology)
**Series:** Pulphouse: The Hardback Magazine

**Summary:** This title contains a foreward by Kate Wilhelm and an introduction by the editor plus 25 stories, each with a brief introduction, previously published in *Pulphouse: The Hardback Magazine*, the hardcover periodical appearing 1988-1991. This volume draws on the broad range of the periodical's material including science fiction such as Charles de Lint's ''The Soft Whisper of Midnight Snow,'' and horror such as Edward Bryant's ''While She Was Out.'' This title includes some newer authors plus more established genre authors including George Alec Effinger, Harlan Ellison, Lisa Goldstein, Steve Perry, Harry Turtledove, Lisa Tuttle, J.N. Williamson, William F. Wu and Jane Yolen.

**Other books you might like:**
Damien Broderick, *Strange Attractors: Original Australian Speculative Fiction*, 1985
    editor
Algis Budrys, *L. Ron Hubbard Presents Writers of the Future, Volume II*, 1986
    editor
Harlan Ellison, *Again, Dangerous Visions*, 1972
    editor
Harlan Ellison, *Dangerous Visions*, 1967
    editor
Judith Merril, *Tesseracts*, 1985
    editor
Bruce Sterling, *Mirrorshades: The Cyberpunk Anthology*, 1986
    editor

## **4714**

### KRISTINE KATHRYN RUSCH

## *The Changeling*

(New York: Bantam Spectra, 1996)

**Story type:** Fantasy (Political; Magic Conflict)
**Series:** Fey
**Major character(s):** Nicholas, Royalty; Jewel, Mythical Creature (fey), Royalty; Matthias, Religious (Rocaan)
**Time period(s):** Indeterminate Past
**Locale(s):** Blue Isle, Fictional Country; The Shadowlands, Mythical Place; Alternate Universe

**Summary:** King Alexander's murder by ambush breaks the uneasy peace on Blue Isle. Both Human and Fey misunderstand and mistrust one another, leading to greater treachery and greater tragedy. Amid death and suspicion, only those who stand between the two races offer hope, although they have little hope for themselves.

**Other books you might like:**
C.J. Cherryh, *Fortress in the Eye of Time*, 1995
Barbara Hambly, *The Ladies of Mandrigyn*, 1984
Katherine Kurtz, *Deryni Rising*, 1970
Patricia A. McKillip, *The Riddle-Master of Hed*, 1976
Paula Volsky, *Illusion*, 1992

## **4715**

### KRISTINE KATHRYN RUSCH

## *The Devil's Churn*

(New York: Dell, 1996)

**Story type:** Horror (Occult)
**Major character(s):** Adelaine Hawthorne Taylor Rustin, Aged Person; Billy Malone, Lawyer; Evelyn Brand , Aged Person
**Time period(s):** 1980s (1989)
**Locale(s):** Dory Cove, Oregon

**Summary:** On the same day that Addy Rustin returns home for her mother's funeral, her former boyfriend, Spencer Chadwick, returns unaged from the Devil's Churn, an inlet off the Oregon coast where he supposedly drowned half a century before. Spencer's reappearance strengthens Addy's resolve to resist a mystical faith that her mother and the women of Dory Cove have held for a century and that involves secret blood sacrifices.

**Other books you might like:**
Matthew J. Costello, *Beneath Still Waters*, 1989
Elizabeth Forrest, *Dark Tide*, 1993
Charles L. Grant, *Night Songs*, 1984
Allen Lee Harris, *Let There Be Dark*, 1994
Nancy Holder, *Dead in the Water*, 1995

## **4716**

### KRISTINE KATHRYN RUSCH

## *Facade*

(New York: Dell/Abyss, 1993)

**Story type:** Horror (Psychological Suspense)
**Major character(s):** Thomas Stratton, Actor; Jillian Maxwell, Editor (newspaper); Alicia Maxwell, Teenager (Jillian' sister)
**Time period(s):** 1990s (1993)
**Locale(s):** Seavy Village, Oregon

**Summary:** Following the abduction and death of his young daughter, Thomas Stratton, an actor losing his ability to distinguish between reality and the characters he plays, returns to the scene of the crime. His research into a series of murders, of which his daughter's was only the most recent, turns up damning evidence that all the killings occurred at times when Thomas was in town, forcing him to confront the possiblity that he may have committed them while in the grip of one of his acting personas.

**Other books you might like:**
Scott Baker, *Webs*, 1989
Ehren M. Ehly, *Star Prey*, 1992
Chet Williamson, *Reign*, 1990

## **4717**

### KRISTINE KATHRYN RUSCH

## *The Gallery of His Dreams*

(Eugene, Oregon: Pulphouse Publishing Axolotl Press, 1991)

**Story type:** Fantasy (Historical; Contemporary)
**Major character(s):** Mathew B. Brady, Historical Figure, Photographer; Julia Brady, Spouse, Historical Figure
**Time period(s):** 19th century (1838-1887)
**Locale(s):** United States

**Summary:** Slices in the life and photographic work of pioneering photographer Mathew Brady reflect the gallery exhibition which

Brady helps to assemble. While examining his own photographs, he has visions of his future with Julia and the acceptance of his work as art and historical documentation. This is the first book of Rusch's own work published by this editor and publisher.

**Other books you might like:**
Charles de Lint, *The Little Country*, 1991
Sheila Gilluly, *The Boy From the Burren*, 1990
Mike Resnick, *Soothsayer*, 1991

---

**4718**

**KRISTINE KATHRYN RUSCH**

## Heart Readers

(New York: Roc, 1993)

**Story type:** Fantasy (Political)
**Major character(s):** Pardu, Royalty, Parent; Tarne, Counselor (royal advisor)
**Time period(s):** Indeterminate
**Locale(s):** Leanda, Fictional Country

**Summary:** To determine which of Pardu's twin sons will rule the kingdom, heart readers must wait for years after the twins' birth to allow each the opportunity to grow, love and hate, after which the heart readers can divine the next ruler. However, as the twins age, King Pardu's ambitious advisor attempts to steer events in the direction he desires prior to the heart readers' assistance.

**Other books you might like:**
Lois McMaster Bujold, *The Spirit Ring*, 1992
Katharine Kerr, *The Dragon Revenant*, 1990
Mercedes Lackey, *Winds of Fate*, 1991
Paula Volsky, *Illusion*, 1992
Martha Wells, *The Element of Fire*, 1993

---

**4719**

**KRISTINE KATHRYN RUSCH**

## The New Rebellion

(New York: Bantam Spectra, 1996)

**Story type:** Science Fiction (Space Opera; Mystical)
**Series:** Star Wars
**Major character(s):** Leia Organa Solo, Royalty, Leader; Han Solo, Spaceship Captain, Warrior; Luke Skywalker, Martial Arts Expert (Jedi Knight), Hero
**Time period(s):** Indeterminate Past
**Locale(s):** Coruscant, Planet—Imaginary; New Republic, Interstellar Empire/Federation; *Millenium Falcon*, Spaceship

**Summary:** Shortly after the admittance of former Imperials to the New Republic Senate, an explosion in the Senate casts suspicion on Han Solo. Investigating, Luke Skywalker discovers a previously unknown Master of the Dark Side of the Force who threatens the existence of the New Republic.

**Other books you might like:**
Roger MacBride Allen, *Ambush at Corellia*, 1995
Kevin J. Anderson, *Jedi Search*, 1994
Michael P. Kube-McDowell, *Before the Storm*, 1996
Steve Perry, *Shadows of the Empire*, 1996
Michael A. Stackpole, *Rogue Squadron*, 1996
Timothy Zahn, *Heir to the Empire*, 1991

---

**4720**

**KRISTINE KATHRYN RUSCH**, Editor

## Pulphouse, Issue 10: Special Issue

(Eugene, Oregon: Pulphouse Publishing, 1991)

**Story type:** Fantasy (Anthology)
**Series:** Pulphouse: The Hardback Magazine

**Summary:** This thematic anthology contains a 3-page introduction by the editor and introductions to each of the 14 stories, all thematically tied as holiday stories set between the harvest holidays and Passover, plus one non-fiction article by series columnist Jon Gustafson, "The Gimlet Eye Returns," continuing his history of SF art. All stories appear here for the first time except Dennis Etchison's "Deadspace," originally published in *Whispers V* and Michael Bishop's, "Icicle Music," revised herein. Many stories feature Christmas, as those by John Brunner, M. Elayn Harvey, Nina Kiriki Hoffman, Charles de Lint and two by Ken Wisman. Kara Dalkey's "The Peony Lantern" is set at the time of the Japanese Festival of the Dead, O-Bon, while William Wu chooses Chinese New Year and Robert Sheckley makes up his own holiday in "Onesday." The other authors are Marina Fitch, Esther M. Friesner and Lisa Goldstein.

**Other books you might like:**
Richard Brautigan, *In Watermelon Sugar*, 1968
Philip Jose Farmer, *Dayworld*, 1985
Stephen Goldin, *Jade Darcy and the Zen Pirates*, 1990
    Mary Mason, co-author
Martin H. Greenberg, *Christmas on Ganymede and Other Stories*, 1990
    editor
Gene Wolfe, *Gene Wolfe's Book of Days*, 1981

---

**4721**

**KRISTINE KATHRYN RUSCH**, Editor

## Pulphouse, Issue 11: Speculative Fiction

(Eugene, Oregon: Pulphouse Publishing, 1991)

**Story type:** Science Fiction (Anthology)
**Series:** Pulphouse: The Hardback Magazine

**Summary:** This volume includes articles by D.W. Taylor and Jon Gustafson, a 2-page introduction by the editor, and 18 stories by Edward Bryant, Nina Kiriki Hoffman, Kij Johnson, James Morrow, Tim Sullivan, Harry Turtledove, William Wu and others. D.W. Taylor's article, "Turn the Mothers Out," is a manifesto for genre writers, while Jon Gustafson's "The Gimlet Eye Returns" continues his column on the history of science fiction art.

**Other books you might like:**
Kingsley Amis, *Spectrum*, 1962
    Robert Conquest, co-editor
John Carnell, *New Writings in SF 1*, 1966
    editor
Terry Carr, *Universe 1*, 1970
    editor
Samuel R. Delany, *Quark 1*, 1970
    Marilyn Hacker, co-editor
Harlan Ellison, *Again, Dangerous Visions*, 1972
    editor
Harlan Ellison, *Dangerous Visions*, 1967
    editor
Damon Knight, *Orbit 1*, 1966
    editor
Robert Silverberg, *Alpha 1*, 1970
    editor

## 4722

**KRISTINE KATHRYN RUSCH**, Editor

### *Pulphouse, Issue 12: The Last Issue*
(Eugene, Oregon: Pulphouse, 1993)

**Story type:** Horror (Anthology)
**Series:** Pulphouse: The Hardback Magazine

**Summary:** The long-awaited final issue of this "hardback magazine," which published some exceptional short horror, fantasy, and science fiction between 1988 and 1993, presents 20 stories and one essay. Outstanding contributions include Adam-Troy Castro's "Metastasis," about a woman's unusual relationship with her cancer; David B. Silva's "Because I Could" and Robert Frazier's "Sendings," both poignant stories about psychic links between children and their grandparents; Darrell Schweitzer's "Angry Man," in which a man must confront discarnate aspects of his own personality; Nina Kiriki Hoffman's "Surreal Estate," a light fantasy involving a haunted house; and Steve Rasnic Tem's "Fairy Tales," about the very pertinent myths a father tells his children to shield them from harm.

**Other books you might like:**
John Maclay, *Voices From the Night*, 1994
   editor
Thomas F. Monteleone, *Borderlands 4*, 1994
   editor
Stanley Wiater, *After the Darkness*, 1993
   editor

## 4723

**KRISTINE KATHRYN RUSCH**, Editor

### *Pulphouse, Issue 6: Fantasy*
(Eugene, Oregon: Pulphouse Publishing, 1990)

**Story type:** Fantasy (Anthology)
**Series:** Pulphouse: The Hardback Magazine
**Time period(s):** Indeterminate

**Summary:** This book contains two articles, 24 stories and an introduction by the editor, including works by Charles de Lint, William F. Wu, Avram Davidson, Steve Perry, George Alec Effinger, Emma Bull, and many others. This issue in this unusual hardcover magazine series is devoted entirely to fantasy.

**Other books you might like:**
Ellen Datlow, *The Year's Best Fantasy and Horror: Third Annual Collection*, 1990
   Terri Windling, co-editor
Ellen Datlow, *The Year's Best Fantasy: First Annual Collection*, 1988
   Terri Windling, co-editor
Alan Dean Foster, *Smart Dragons, Foolish Elves*, 1991
   Martin Harry Greenberg, co-editor
Will Shetterly, *Liavek: Festival Week*, 1990
   Emma Bull, co-editor
Will Shetterly, *Liavek*, 1985
   Emma Bull, co-editor

## 4724

**KRISTINE KATHRYN RUSCH**, Editor

### *Pulphouse, Issue 7: Horror*
(Eugene, Oregon: Pulphouse, Spring 1990)

**Story type:** Horror (Anthology)
**Series:** Pulphouse: The Hardback Magazine

**Summary:** Twenty-two stories and two essays comprise the contents of this quarterly hardcover magazine which publishes one issue each year of fantasy, science fiction, horror and dark fantasy. The selections include Kathy Koja's haunting meditation on art and life, "Illusions in Relief"; Kim Antieau's erotic vampire spoof, "Oral Tradition"; and David Schow's gruesome tale of rural horror, "Not From Around Here."

**Other books you might like:**
Lin Carter, *Weird Tales*, 1981-1983
   4 Vols.
Thomas F. Monteleone, *Borderlands*, 1990
Stuart David Schiff, *The Whispers Series*, 1977-1987
David B. Silva, *Best of The Horror Show*, 1987
J.N. Williamson, *The Best of Masques*, 1988

## 4725

**KRISTINE KATHRYN RUSCH**, Editor

### *Pulphouse, Issue 8: Science Fiction*
(Eugene, Oregon: Pulphouse Publishing, 1990)

**Story type:** Science Fiction (Anthology; Science Fiction)
**Series:** Pulphouse: The Hardback Magazine
**Time period(s):** Indeterminate

**Summary:** This collection of 16 stories, one article and an introduction by the editor, includes works by Charles de Lint, Jane Yolen, George Alec Effinger, S.P. Somtow and many others. This is issue number 8, dated Summer 1990, in this unusual hardcover magazine series and is devoted entirely to science fiction.

**Other books you might like:**
Groff Conklin, *The Best of Science Fiction*, 1946
Gardner Dozois, *The Year's Best Science Fiction: Seventh Annual Collection*, 1990
Harlan Ellison, *Medea: Harlan's World*, 1985
David G. Hartwell, *The World Treasury of Science Fiction*, 1989
Donald A. Wollheim, *The 1990 Annual World's Best Science Fiction*, 1990

## 4726

**KRISTINE KATHRYN RUSCH**, Editor

### *Pulphouse, Issue 9: Dark Fantasy*
(Eugene, Oregon: Pulphouse Fall 1990)

**Story type:** Horror (Anthology)
**Series:** Pulphouse: The Hardback Magazine

**Summary:** Fifteen stories and two essays that prove the branch of imaginative fiction referred to as "dark fantasy" is virtually indistiguishable from that simply called "horror." Counterbalancing the subtle discussions of male and female sexuality in Lisa Tuttle's "Bits and Pieces" and Nina Kiriki Hoffman's "Housewife" are the hardcore physical horrors of Joe Lansdale's "The Pit" and the grotesquerie of Nancy A. Collins' self-explanatory "The Two-Headed Man."

**Other books you might like:**
Lin Carter, *Weird Tales*, 1981-1983
    4 Vols.
Thomas F. Monteleone, *Borderlands*, 1990
Stuart David Schiff, *The Whispers Series*, 1977-1987
David B. Silva, *Best of The Horror Show*, 1987
J.N. Williamson, *The Best of Masques*, 1988

## 4727

### KRISTINE KATHRYN RUSCH

## The Resistance

(New York: Bantam, 1998)

**Series:** Fey
**Major character(s):** Gift, Nobleman; Rugad, Ruler (king); Arianna, Noblewoman, Warrior
**Time period(s):** Indeterminate
**Locale(s):** Blue Isle, Fictional Country

**Summary:** The evil King Rugad wants to guarantee his supremacy and to do so he must capture and control his two half-Fey grandchildren, Arianna and Gift. They in turn must escape his agents, but their efforts are made more difficult by their initial dislike for each other.

**Other books you might like:**
C.J. Cherryh, *The Goblin Mirror*, 1992
Raymond E. Feist, *Krondor, the Betrayal*, 1998
Barbara Hambly, *Icefalcon's Quest*, 1998
Patricia A. McKillip, *Harpist in the Wind*, 1979
Robin McKinley, *The Blue Sword*, 1982

## 4728

### KRISTINE KATHRYN RUSCH

## Sins of the Blood

(New York: Dell/Abyss, 1994)

**Story type:** Horror (Vampire Story)
**Major character(s):** Camilla Timms, Vampire Hunter; Ben Sadler, Vampire; Scott Eliason, Vampire Hunter
**Time period(s):** 1990s (1994)
**Locale(s):** Portland, Oregon

**Summary:** A childhood spent with an abusive father has turned Ben Sadler into a domineering vampire and his sister Camilla into a vampire hunter who finds it increasingly difficult not to become what Ben is. This novel was expanded from the author's 1991 story, ''Children of the Night.''

**Other books you might like:**
Peter Atkins, *Morningstar*, 1993
Tom Piccirilli, *Dark Father*, 1990
John Steakley, *Vampire$*, 1990
T. Lucien Wright, *Blood Brothers*, 1992

## 4729

### KRISTINE KATHRYN RUSCH

## Traitors

(New York: Roc, 1994)

**Story type:** Fantasy (Political)
**Major character(s):** Emilio Diate, Dancer; Sheba, Political Figure; Beltar, Businessman
**Time period(s):** Indeterminate Future

**Locale(s):** Port City, Fictional City; Golga, Fictional Country; The Kingdom, Fictional Country

**Summary:** Emilio Diate's life focuses on dance and family, but the Kingdom to which he owes his allegiance and for which he dances slaughters his family because his father criticized the social structure. Although he flees the Kingdom, revolution and love of the new Queen, Sheba, draw him inevitably back to the land of his birth.

**Other books you might like:**
Orson Scott Card, *Songmaster*, 1980
Frank Herbert, *Dune*, 1965
Joan D. Vinge, *The Summer Queen*, 1991
Vernor Vinge, *Tatja Grimm's World*, 1987
Walter Jon Williams, *Aristoi*, 1992

## 4730

### KRISTINE KATHRYN RUSCH

## The White Mists of Power

(New York: Roc, 1991)

**Story type:** Fantasy (Quest; Political)
**Major character(s):** Adric, Royalty, Runaway; Byron, Musician, Wanderer; Seymour, Magician
**Time period(s):** Indeterminate Past (the Middle Ages)
**Locale(s):** Kilot, Fictional Country

**Summary:** A young prince is left to die in the slums of an unfriendly city and a mysterious wanderer tries to escape his enemies with the help of an inept magician. Their destinies entwine in an effort to stop a war that may lead to the intervention of the alien Enos and the death of every human in Kilot. This is the author's first novel.

**Other books you might like:**
Glen Cook, *The Black Company*, 1984
Guy Gavriel Kay, *The Summer Tree*, 1984
Katherine Kurtz, *Deryni Rising*, 1970
Patricia A. McKillip, *The Riddle-Master of Hed*, 1977
Judith Tarr, *The Hall of the Mountain King*, 1986

## 4731

### SALMAN RUSHDIE

## Haroun and the Sea of Stories

(New York: Viking Penguin, 1990)

**Story type:** Fantasy (Contemporary; Quest)
**Major character(s):** Rashid Khalifa, Storyteller; Haroun Khalifa, Adventurer; Iff, Mythical Creature (water genie)
**Time period(s):** 20th century
**Locale(s):** The Sad City, Fictional Country; Alifbay, Fictional Country; Kahani, Moon—Imaginary (Earth's second moon)

**Summary:** Haroun's father loses his Gift of Gab, and Haroun is determined to get it back for him. With the genie Iff, Haroun travels to the Sea of Stories, encountering many wonderful creatures and learning that the whole source of stories is in danger.

**Other books you might like:**
John Barth, *Chimera*, 1972
Patricia Daniels, *Sinbad the Sailor*, 1980
Norton Juster, *The Phantom Tollbooth*, 1961
Andrew Lang, *The Arabian Nights Entertainments*, 1969

## 4732

### DOUGLAS RUSHKOFF

## Ecstasy Club

(New York: HarperCollins, 1997)

**Story type:** Science Fiction (Contemporary Realism; Mystical)
**Major character(s):** George Thomas Duncan, Leader (guru), Revolutionary; Peter, Computer Expert, Technician; Zach, Teacher, Student
**Time period(s):** 1990s (1996)
**Locale(s):** Oakland, California

**Summary:** A group of young techno-idealists working with computers, mysticism, sex and drugs start a dance club as a base for their operations. When their theories prove a little too sound and their experiments a little too successful, everyone from religious kooks to the police wants to get them. But, perhaps, what they have noticed has noticed them. First novel.

**Other books you might like:**
Lisa Goldstein, *The Dream Years*, 1985
Stuart Gordon, *Smile on the Void*, 1981
Richard Grant, *Tex and Molly in the Afterlife*, 1996
Stewart Home, *Come Before Christ and Murder Love*, 1997
Jeff Noon, *Vurt*, 1995

## 4733

### J.S. RUSSELL

## Burning Bright

(New York: St. Martin's, 1998)

**Story type:** Horror (Mystery; Occult)
**Major character(s):** Marty Burns, Detective—Private, Actor; Uma Dharmamitra, Agent; June Hanover, Public Relations
**Time period(s):** 1990s (1998)
**Locale(s):** London, England; Woodhenge, England; Liverpool, England

**Summary:** On a publicity tour in England to promote his television detective series "Burning Bright," Marty Burns stumbles upon the activites of Ultima Thule, a neo-Nazi splinter group with occult leanings. Marty and a multicultural team representing the contemporary English melting pot struggle to stay one step ahead of the cult in their efforts to harness the powers of the ancient gods. A sequel to *Celestial Dogs*, first published in England in 1997.

**Other books you might like:**
John Blackburn, *Children of the Night*, 1966
Ramsey Campbell, *The Hungry Moon*, 1987
Christopher Fowler, *Rune*, 1991
Stephen Laws, *Macabre*, 1995
Robert Weinberg, *The Dead Man's Kiss*, 1992

## 4734

### J.S. RUSSELL

## Celestial Dogs

(New York: St. Martin's, 1997)

**Story type:** Horror (Occult; Mystery)
**Major character(s):** Marty Burns, Detective; Long John Silver, Criminal (pimp); Jack Rippen, Producer
**Time period(s):** 1990s (1997)
**Locale(s):** Los Angeles, California

**Summary:** Marty Burns, a detective with ties to the Hollywood film industry, traces the death of an acquaintance's girlfriend to the underground snuff film industry, where the Japanese backers of Laughing Boy Pictures are apparently subsidizing ritual murders to propitiate a centuries-old supernatural menace. This first novel was originally published in England in 1996.

**Other books you might like:**
Ramsey Campbell, *Ancient Images*, 1989
Jonathan Carroll, *A Child Across the Sky*, 1989
Dennis Cooper, *Frisk*, 1991
Tim Lucas, *Throat Sprockets*, 1994
Theodore Roszak, *Flicker*, 1991

## 4735

### MARY DORIA RUSSELL

## Children of God

(New York: Villard, 1998)

**Story type:** Science Fiction (Theological; First Contact)
**Major character(s):** Emilio Sandoz, Religious (Jesuit priest), Linguist; Sofia Mendes Quinn, Castaway, Computer Expert; Supaari VaGayjur, Alien (Jana'ata), Revolutionary
**Time period(s):** 21st century (2042-2096)
**Locale(s):** Naples, Italy; Rakhat, Planet—Imaginary

**Summary:** Only a few short years after returning from a disastrous first contact mission, the emotionally and physically fragile Emilio Sandoz unwillingly participates in another mission to the planet Rakhat. His terror abates slightly when he discovers that his colleague Sofia Mendes is still alive on Rakhat, but he still fears facing the planet that caused his spiritual downfall. Sequel to the Tiptree Award-winning novel *The Sparrow*.

**Other books you might like:**
C.J. Cherryh, *Foreigner*, 1994
Molly Gloss, *The Dazzle of Day*, 1997
Jacqueline Lichtenberg, *First Channel*, 1980
  Jean Lorrah, co-author
Frederik Pohl, *The Singers of Time*, 1991
  Jack Williamson, co-author
Sheri S. Tepper, *Grass*, 1989
Amy Thomson, *The Color of Distance*, 1995

## 4736

### MARY DORIA RUSSELL

## The Sparrow

(New York: Villard, 1996)

**Story type:** Science Fiction (Theological; First Contact)
**Major character(s):** Emilio Sandoz, Religious (Jesuit), Linguist; Sofia Mendez, Computer Expert, Pilot (spaceship); Jimmy Quinn, Scientist (astronomer), Spaceman
**Time period(s):** 2010s (2019); 2060s (2060)
**Locale(s):** Arecibo, Puerto Rico; *Magellan*, Spaceship; Rakhat, Planet—Imaginary

**Summary:** The only survivor of the first expediton to Rakhat returns physically and spiritually broken. Having organized the expedition with his closest friends as crew, Emilio Sandoz must recover enough to testify before the Father General of the Order of Jesuits in order to have him release the scientific papers written during the expedition, and to understand why his treatment by the Order seems so hostile. First novel.

**Other books you might like:**
Eleanor Arnason, *Ring of Swords*, 1993
Catherine Asaro, *Primary Inversion*, 1995
James Blish, *A Case of Conscience*, 1958
C.J. Cherryh, *Foreigner*, 1994
Suzette Haden Elgin, *Native Tongue*, 1984
Dan Simmons, *Hyperion*, 1989
Sheri S. Tepper, *Grass*, 1989

---

**4737**

PAUL RUSSELL

## Boys of Life

(New York: Dutton, 1991)

**Story type:** Horror (Psychological Suspense)
**Major character(s):** Carlos Reichart, Director (film director), Homosexual; Tony Blair, Teenager (Actor)
**Time period(s):** 1990s
**Locale(s):** New York, New York

**Summary:** Attracted by the sophistication of Carlos Reichart, a gay film director who specializes in confrontational and tasteless avant-garde films, Tony Blair flees his rural southern home to take up with Reichert's New York entourage, The Company. But Tony finds that work as an actor for Reichert entails being subjected to sexual and emotional abuse, which for Reichert are merely extensions of his personal aesthetic into life.

**Other books you might like:**
Dennis Cooper, *Frisk*, 1991

---

**4738**

RAY RUSSELL

## Absolute Power

(Baltimore, Maryland: Maclay, 1992)

**Story type:** Horror (Occult)
**Major character(s):** Cindy Carewe, Artist, Clerk (bookstore worker); Julian Trask, Anthropologist, Paranormal Investigator; Eliza ''Bettina'' Carewe, Witch
**Time period(s):** 1980s (1983)
**Locale(s):** Los Angeles, California

**Summary:** Cindy Carewe's banker father dies penniless, leaving her only a manuscript recounting his perfidious life and an encounter with a witch who may have drained his bank account and forced his suicide. Cindy's investigation to discover the identity of this witch leads her to Bettina, her long lost mother, whom Cynthia fears has evil designs on her as well.

**Other books you might like:**
John Farris, *All Heads Turn When the Hunt Goes By*, 1977
Fritz Leiber, *Conjure Wife*, 1953

---

**4739**

SEAN RUSSELL

## Beneath the Vaulted Hills

(New York: DAW, 1997)

**Story type:** Fantasy (Magic Conflict; Political)
**Series:** River into Darkness
**Major character(s):** Lord Eldrich, Wizard; Erasmus Flattery, Apprentice, Adventurer

**Time period(s):** Indeterminate
**Locale(s):** Farrland, Fictional Country; Avonel, Fictional City

**Summary:** After all other mages disappear from the land, Lord Eldrich works to eliminate the possibility of magic use forever, while the Tellerites strive to regain the lost knowledge. Erasmus agonizes over his role in Eldrich's plotting years earlier until he again receives a summons from Eldrich, which will send him into a subterranean labyrinth in search of an ancient secret, hidden since the time of the First Mages.

**Other books you might like:**
Graham Edwards, *Dragoncharm*, 1996
Lynn Flewelling, *Luck in the Shadows*, 1996
Terry Goodkind, *Stone of Tears*, 1995
Peg Kerr, *Emerald House Rising*, 1997
Paula Volsky, *Illusion*, 1992

---

**4740**

SEAN RUSSELL

## The Compass of the Soul

(New York: DAW, 1998)

**Story type:** Fantasy (Magic Conflict)
**Series:** River into Darkness
**Major character(s):** Erasmus Flattery, Adventurer; Anna Fielding, Wizard, Apprentice; Lord Eldrich, Wizard
**Time period(s):** Indeterminate
**Locale(s):** Castlebough, Fictional City

**Summary:** Lord Eldrich, the last mage, wants magic to fade to prevent apocalypse, while Anna Fielding wants to return magic to the world and gain its miraculous powers for herself. Tormented by guilt, Erasmus Flattery stands between them, an ordinary man with a chance to affect the whole world.

**Other books you might like:**
James P. Blaylock, *Homunculus*, 1986
John Crowley, *Aegypt*, 1987
Brian Stableford, *The Werewolves of London*, 1990
Caroline Stevermer, *A College of Magics*, 1994
Paula Volsky, *Illusion*, 1992

---

**4741**

SEAN RUSSELL

## Gatherer of Clouds

(New York: DAW, 1992)

**Story type:** Fantasy (Adventure; Historical)
**Major character(s):** Shuyun, Religious (Botah), Martial Arts Expert; Shonto, Nobleman, Military Personnel
**Time period(s):** Indeterminate Past
**Locale(s):** Empire of Wa, Fictional Country

**Summary:** Rumors of war permeate the Emperor's court while the Botahist monks expectantly await the prophecied master and Lord Shonto prepares to counter a massive invasion by barbarian horsemen. Concludes the story begun in *The Initiate Brother*.

**Other books you might like:**
Raymond E. Feist, *Daughter of the Empire*, 1987
    Janny Wurts, co-author
Raymond E. Feist, *Servant of the Empire*, 1990
    Janny Wurts, co-author
Robert Jordan, *The Eye of the World*, 1989
E. Hoffman Price, *The Devil Wives of Li Fong*, 1979
E. Hoffman Price, *Far Lands, Other Days*, 1975

E. Hoffman Price, *The Jade Enchantress*, 1982

**4742**

### SEAN RUSSELL

## The Initiate Brother

(New York: DAW, 1991)

**Story type:** Fantasy (Adventure)
**Major character(s):** Shuyun, Religious (monk), Martial Arts Expert; Nishima, Royalty (princess); Lord Shanto, Military Personnel (General)
**Time period(s):** Indeterminate Past
**Locale(s):** Empire of Wa, Fictional Country

**Summary:** A fearful emperor uses intrigue and subterfuge to eliminate adversaries of his reign, causing greater calamity throughout the empire. The challenge to return the empire to a just path is accepted by a Lord who is a military genius and his young spiritual advisor, a monk of extraordinary talents.

**Other books you might like:**
David Charnee, *Sensei*, 1983
James Clavell, *Shogun*, 1975
Barry Hughart, *Bridge of Birds*, 1984
Barry Hughart, *Eight Skilled Gentlemen*, 1990
Barry Hughart, *The Story of the Stone*, 1988
Jeanne Larsen, *Silk Road*, 1989
Jessica Amanda Salmonson, *Tomoe Gozen*, 1984
Laurence Yep, *Tongues of Jade*, 1991

**4743**

### SEAN RUSSELL

## Sea Without a Shore

(New York: DAW, 1996)

**Story type:** Fantasy (Magic Conflict; Political)
**Series:** Moontide and Magic Rise
**Major character(s):** Tristam Flattery, Naturalist; Averil Kent, Nobleman, Artist (painter)
**Time period(s):** Indeterminate Past
**Locale(s):** At Sea; Varua, Fictional Country

**Summary:** With the last Mage dead and his secrets lost, the Age of Magic ends. A rising star in the new, rational world, the Magician's nephew sets out to explore a distant island. There he discovers many things and must choose for everyone whether to reopen the path to magic or leave it locked forever. Second in the series.

**Other books you might like:**
Poul Anderson, *Three Hearts and Three Lions*, 1961
Guy Gavriel Kay, *The Lions of Al-Rassan*, 1995
Ellen Kushner, *Swordspoint*, 1987
Larry Niven, *The Magic Goes Away*, 1979
Robert J. Sawyer, *Far-Seer*, 1992

**4744**

### SEAN RUSSELL

## World Without End

(New York: DAW, 1995)

**Story type:** Fantasy (Political; Quest)
**Series:** Moontide and Magic Rise
**Major character(s):** Tristam Flattery, Naturalist

**Time period(s):** 16th century
**Locale(s):** *Swallow*, At Sea; Farrland, Fictional Country; Farrow, Fictional Country (island)

**Summary:** In a new age of enlightenment and science which pushes magic into the background, Tristam Flattery follows a path of reason, rejecting the mystic arts. When called upon to help the king with a medicinal plant having seemingly magical properties, Tristam finds that political machinations draw him into a multigenerational plot and send him in search of new plant stocks.

**Other books you might like:**
Allan Cole, *The Far Kingdoms*, 1993
    Chris Bunch, co-author
Marc Laidlaw, *Neon Lotus*, 1988
Robert J. Sawyer, *Far-Seer*, 1992
Robert J. Sawyer, *Fossil Hunter*, 1993
Elizabeth Ann Scarborough, *Last Refuge*, 1992

**4745**

### JOHN RUSSO

## Night of the Living Dead

(Edmonton, Alberta: Commonwealth, 1997)

**Story type:** Horror (Reanimated Dead)
**Major character(s):** Ben, Truck Driver; Barbara, Young Woman; Harry Cooper, Businessman
**Time period(s):** 1970s
**Locale(s):** Pennsylvania (rural)

**Summary:** A cross-section of people representing the best and worst of humanity hide in an abandoned house overnight, trying to fend off an army of the newly dead who have been resurrected by radioactivity from outer space as flesh-eating zombies. Novelization of George Romero's cult classic movie, first published in 1974. Romero supplies an introduction.

**Other books you might like:**
Clive Barker, *Cabal*, 1988
Philip Nutman, *Wet Work*, 1993
Byron Preiss, *The Ultimate Zombie*, 1993
    John Betancourt, co-author
George Romero, *Dawn of the Dead*, 1978
    Susannah Sparrow, co-author
John Skipp, *Book of the Dead*, 1989
    Craig Spector, co-editor
John Skipp, *Still Dead: Book of the Dead 2*, 1992
    Craig Spector, co-editor

**4746**

### JOHN RUSSO

## Return of the Living Dead

(Edmonton, Alberta: Commonwealth, 1997)

**Story type:** Horror (Reanimated Dead)
**Major character(s):** John Carter, Criminal; David Benton, Police Officer (state trooper); Conan McClellan, Police Officer (sheriff)
**Time period(s):** 1980s
**Locale(s):** Pennsylvania (rural)

**Summary:** Ten years after the events in *Night of the Living Dead*, to which this novel is a sequel, packs of flesh-eating zombies still roam the American countryside, which has been transformed into a Darwinian proving ground where looters, scavengers and vigilantes who exploit the state of emergency are as bad as the zombie menace. Based on the scenario of George Romero's cult film *Night of the*

*Living Dead*, although it is not related to films in the series or to the similarly titled movie of 1985. First published in 1978.

**Other books you might like:**
Clive Barker, *Cabal*, 1988
Philip Nutman, *Wet Work*, 1993
Byron Preiss, *The Ultimate Zombie*, 1993
    John Betancourt, co-author
George Romero, *Dawn of the Dead*, 1978
    Susannah Sparrow, co-author
John Skipp, *Book of the Dead*, 1989
    Craig Spector, co-editor
John Skipp, *Still Dead: Book of the Dead 2*, 1992
    Craig Spector, co-editor

---

## 4747

### RICHARD PAUL RUSSO

## Carlucci's Edge

(New York: Ace, 1995)

**Story type:** Science Fiction (Cyberpunk; Mystery)
**Major character(s):** Paula Asgard, Musician; Frank Carlucci, Detective—Police; Ian Tremaine, Journalist
**Time period(s):** Indeterminate Future
**Locale(s):** San Francisco, California

**Summary:** After the termination of Chick's small-time operation, the cops seem uninterested in investigating his murder. Curious why they seem anxious to bury the investigation rather than merely ignore it, Paula Asgard and Frank Carlucci risk everything to find Chick's killer. Sequel to *Destroying Angel*.

**Other books you might like:**
Isaac Asimov, *The Caves of Steel*, 1954
Steven Barnes, *Streetlethal*, 1983
Pat Cadigan, *Fools*, 1992
William Gibson, *Burning Chrome*, 1986
Katharine Kerr, *Polar City Blues*, 1990
Walter Jon Williams, *Hardwired*, 1986
Walter Jon Williams, *Voice of the Whirlwind*, 1987

---

## 4748

### RICHARD PAUL RUSSO

## Carlucci's Heart

(New York: Ace, 1997)

**Story type:** Science Fiction (Mystery; Medical)
**Major character(s):** Frank Carlucci, Detective—Police; Ryland "Ry" Cage, Doctor; Caroline Carlucci, Detective—Amateur
**Time period(s):** 21st century
**Locale(s):** San Francisco, California

**Summary:** When Caroline's terminally ill friend disappears from the hospice house, Caroline asks her father to help find him, passing on the name, "Cancer Cell," the only possible clue she has. Frank's investigation yields little, but soon expands as plague begins to engulf the city and federal troops move into the Tenderloin.

**Other books you might like:**
Greg Bear, *Blood Music*, 1985
Pat Cadigan, *Synners*, 1991
Michael Conner, *Archangel*, 1995
Philip K. Dick, *Blade Runner*, 1982
Frank Herbert, *The White Plague*, 1982
Katharine Kerr, *Polar City Blues*, 1990
David Alexander Smith, *In the Cube*, 1993

---

## 4749

### RICHARD PAUL RUSSO

## Destroying Angel

(New York: Ace, 1992)

**Story type:** Science Fiction (Cyberpunk; Mystery)
**Major character(s):** Louis Tanner, Smuggler, Detective—Amateur
**Time period(s):** 21st century
**Locale(s):** San Francisco, California

**Summary:** Retired police officer Louis Tanner enjoys a profitable smuggling career until the reappearance of a serial killer jolts Tanner into investigating the crimes.

**Other books you might like:**
Philip K. Dick, *Blade Runner*, 1982
George Alec Effinger, *When Gravity Fails*, 1987
Katharine Kerr, *Polar City Blues*, 1990
Neal Stephenson, *Snow Crash*, 1992

---

## 4750

### RICHARD PAUL RUSSO

## Subterranean Gallery

(New York: Tor, 1989)

**Story type:** Science Fiction (Arts)
**Major character(s):** Rheinhardt, Artist; Justinian, Veteran
**Time period(s):** 21st century
**Locale(s):** San Francisco, California

**Summary:** Artists in a near-future San Francisco are increasingly faced with censorship and government repression. Rheinhardt, a talented but tormented sculptor, tries desperately to produce great art in a world from which he is almost totally alienated.

**Other books you might like:**
Lisa Goldstein, *A Mask for the General*, 1987
Ian McDonald, *Out on Blue Six*, 1989
Pat Murphy, *The City, Not Long After*, 1989

---

## 4751

### BRETT RUTHERFORD

## Night Gaunts: An Entertainment Based on the Life and Work of H.P. Lovecraft

(Boston: Grim Reaper Books, 1993)

**Story type:** Horror (Collection)

**Summary:** The bulk of this booklet is comprised of a memory play, in which renowned horror writer H.P. Lovecraft merges fiction with real life while ruminating on his deathbed on some of his best known stories and the events that gave rise to them. The book is filled out with five poems—"At Lovecraft's Grave," "Low Tide," "Things Seen in Graveyards," "Maker of Monsters, Maker of Gods," and "Hearing the Wendigo"—all of which are homages to Lovecraft or Lovecraftian themes.

**Other books you might like:**
P.H. Cannon, *Pulptime*, 1984
Richard A. Lupoff, *Lovecraft's Book*, 1985
James Schevill, *Lovecraft's Follies: A Play*, 1971
Ralph Vaughan, *Sherlock Holmes in the Adventure of the Ancient Gods*, 1990

## **4752**

### BRETT RUTHERFORD

## *Whippoorwill Road*

(New York: Poet's Press, 1998)

**Story type:** Horror (Collection)

**Summary:** A collection of haunting and evocative poems of horror and the supernatural, culled from the author's previous collections. Selections include the vampire poem "Son of Dracula," the Frankenstein riff "Hunchback Assistant Tells All," and "At Lovecraft's Grave," one of several lyrical poems influenced by the l.ife and literary legacy of H. P. Lovecraft. A revised and expanded edition of the author's 1985 volume of the same name.

**Other books you might like:**
Joseph Payne Brennan, *Nightmare Need*, 1964
Fritz Leiber, *The Demons of the Upper Air*, 1969
Frank Belknap Long, *In Mayan Splendor*, 1977
Stanley McNail, *Something Breathing*, 1965

## **4753**

### MARY RYAN

## *Mask of the Night*

(New York: St. Martin's, 1997)

**Story type:** Horror (Reincarnation)
**Major character(s):** Desiree McGlinn, Public Relations; Jenny Stephenson, Young Woman; Theo O'Reilly, Military Personnel (soldier)
**Time period(s):** 1960s (1967); 1920s
**Locale(s):** Kilashane, Ireland; Venice, Italy

**Summary:** Through a carnival mask from Venice, Jenny Stephenson glimpses an alluring and mysterious figure. Imagine her shock when she discovers he is the spirit of a seventh-century Venetian inquisitor, who has been reincarnated in the body of her lover, Theo O'Reilly, that she herself is the reincarnation of a witch who bedeviled him, and that the two are destined to be reincarnated eternally. Originally published in England in 1995.

**Other books you might like:**
Leigh Clark, *Evil Reincarnate*, 1994
Barbara Erskine, *Midnight Is a Lonely Place*, 1994
Marcy Heidish, *The Torching*, 1992
Richard Matheson, *Bid Time Return*, 1975
Michael Stewart, *Belladonna*, 1992

## **4754**

### SHAWN RYAN

## *Brethren*

(New York: Pocket, 1993)

**Story type:** Horror (Curse)
**Major character(s):** Jason Medlocke, Detective—Homicide; Alex Cotton, Computer Expert (programmer); Stephen Medlocke, Parent (Jason's father), Religious (minister)
**Time period(s):** 1990s (1993)
**Locale(s):** Gwinnett County, Georgia

**Summary:** When a serial killer who signs himself "The Mercy Killer" begins showing an intimate knowledge of the details of homicide detective Jason Medlocke's life, Jason's father Stephen informs him that the killer is a servant of Moloch, a demon summoned by one of Jason's ancestors, and charges Jason with the task of sending the creature back to its own world. This is the author's first novel.

**Other books you might like:**
Douglas Clegg, *Goat Dance*, 1989
T.E.D. Klein, *The Ceremonies*, 1984
Brent Monahan, *The Uprising*, 1992
Adrian Savage, *Symphony*, 1992

## **4755**

### SHAWN RYAN

## *Nocturnas*

(New York: Pocket, 1995)

**Story type:** Horror (Vampire Story)
**Major character(s):** Adam Chase, Photographer; Silas Freeborn, Businessman (arms merchant); Livia, Military Personnel
**Time period(s):** 1990s
**Locale(s):** Bucharest, Romania

**Summary:** While on assignment in Romania during the final days of the Ceausescu regime, American photographer Adam Chase runs afoul of the Nocturnas, a secret arm of the Securitate comprised of the country's legendary vampires, and teams up with rebel forces in the hope of putting an end to their rule.

**Other books you might like:**
Elaine Bergstrom, *Shattered Glass*, 1989
Kim Newman, *The Bloody Red Baron*, 1995
Dan Simmons, *Children of the Night*, 1992
Lois Tilton, *Darkness on the Ice*, 1993
Robert Weinberg, *The Armageddon Box*, 1991

## **4756**

### GEOFF RYMAN

## *The Child Garden*

(New York: St. Martin's Press, 1990)

**Story type:** Science Fiction (Genetic Manipulation; Dystopian)
**Major character(s):** Milena, Actress; Rolfa, Genetically Altered Being
**Time period(s):** 21st century
**Locale(s):** London, England

**Summary:** As scientific techniques advance, cancer is cured. Then cancer's useful side effect, the doubling of the human lifespan, is discovered. Viruses are used to implant memories, allowing instant education. Milena has a typical reaction to the viruses. She is unable to join the Consortium which causes her to be very lonely.

**Other books you might like:**
Greg Bear, *Blood Music*, 1985
Margaret Wander Bonanno, *The Others*, 1990
Octavia E. Butler, *Dawn*, 1987
Jeffrey A. Carver, *From a Changeling Star*, 1989
Frank Herbert, *The White Plague*, 1982
Dean R. Koontz, *Watchers*, 1987
Robert Reed, *Black Milk*, 1989

## 4757

**GEOFF RYMAN**

### *Unconquered Countries: Four Novellas*

(New York: St. Martin's Press, 1994)

**Story type:** Fantasy (Collection; Science Fiction)

**Summary:** Contains a four-page introduction by Samuel R. Delany, a three-page afterword plus two original and two reprinted stories including the title story which received a Nebula Award nomination and a World Fantasy Award. Themes include magic in a Tibet dominated by China, politics, homosexuality and the importance of music in daily life.

**Other books you might like:**
John Crowley, *Antiquities*, 1993
Charles de Lint, *Spiritwalk*, 1992
Robert Holdstock, *The Bone Forest*, 1992
Gene Wolfe, *Storeys From the Old Hotel*, 1992

## 4758

**GEOFF RYMAN**

### *Was*

(New York: Alfred A. Knopf, 1992)

**Story type:** Fantasy (Historical; Contemporary)

**Major character(s):** Dorothy "Dotty" Gael, Orphan, Abuse Victim; Bill Davison, Psychologist; L. Frank Baum, Historical Figure, Writer

**Time period(s):** 1870s; 20th century

**Locale(s):** Manhattan, Kansas; California; Canada

**Summary:** This mosaic unites diverse elements surrounding L. Frank Baum's *The Wonderful Wizard of Oz* (1900) including the life of Dorothy Gael who inspired Baum's book, Judy Garland who played the part of Dorothy in the subsequent film and Bill Davison and his dying patient, Jonathan, their lives forever changed by the film. The disclosure of her sexual and psychological abuse to Dorothy's substitute teacher, L. Frank Baum, led to Baum's creating the fictional Dorothy's happier adventures in Oz and the film which changed the life of Judy Garland. Chapters begin with brief non-fiction sketches and exerpts of material which provide insight to Oz or the environment surrounding its creation.

**Other books you might like:**
L. Frank Baum, *The Wonderful Wizard of Oz*, 1900
Orson Scott Card, *Lost Boys*, 1992
Karen Joy Fowler, *Sarah Canary*, 1991
Susan Palwick, *Flying in Place*, 1992
Kristine Kathryn Rusch, *The Gallery of His Dreams*, 1991
Jane Yolen, *Briar Rose*, 1992

## 4759

**FRED SABERHAGEN**, Editor

### *An Armory of Swords*

(New York: Tor, 1995)

**Story type:** Fantasy (Anthology; Sword and Sorcery)
**Series:** Swords

**Summary:** Contains eight original stories, frequently dark in tone, featuring swords forged by Vulcan from Saberhagen's The Swords Series and The Lost Swords Series, such as Soulcutter, Doomgiver, Dragonslicer, and Wayfinder and their unique magical properties.

Authors include Fred Saberhagen, Thomas Saberhagen, Michael A. Sackpole, Robert E. Vardeman, and Walter Jon Williams.

**Other books you might like:**
Marion Zimmer Bradley, *Sword and Sorceress I-XII*, 1984-1995
    editor
L. Sprague de Camp, *The Fantastic Swordsmen*, 1967
    editor
L. Sprague de Camp, *Swords and Sorcery*, 1963
    editor
Richard Gilliam, *Excalibur*, 1995
    Martin H. Greenberg, Edward E. Kramer, co-editors
Edward E. Kramer, *Tales of the White Wolf*, 1994
    Richard Gilliam, co-editor
Karl Edward Wagner, *Echoes of Valor I-III*, 1987-1991
    editor

## 4760

**FRED SABERHAGEN**

### *Berserker Fury*

(New York: Tor, 1997)

**Story type:** Science Fiction (Military)
**Series:** Berserker
**Major character(s):** Sebastian "Nifty" Gift, Spaceman, Military Personnel (spacer first class); Jory Yokusuka, Journalist
**Time period(s):** Indeterminate Future
**Locale(s):** Outer Space; Earth; Uhao, Planet—Imaginary

**Summary:** Now able to construct Berserker units which look like human-created androids, the Berserkers prepare a final attack on human-occupied space. Humanity's only hope lies in cracking the Berserker's cryptography and preparing against their battle plans.

**Other books you might like:**
Roger MacBride Allen, *The Ring of Charon*, 1990
Roger MacBride Allen, *The Shattered Sphere*, 1994
Glen Cook, *The Dragon Never Sleeps*, 1988
Larry Niven, *Footfall*, 1985
    Jerry Pournelle, co-author
Vernor Vinge, *A Fire upon the Deep*, 1993

## 4761

**FRED SABERHAGEN**

### *Berserker Kill*

(New York: Tor, 1993)

**Story type:** Science Fiction (Alternate Intelligence; Robot Fiction)
**Series:** Berserker
**Major character(s):** Nicholas Hawksmoor, Pilot (spaceship), Artificial Intelligence; Dirac Sardoll, Leader (Premier); Lake Genevieve "Jenny" Sardou, Artificial Intelligence
**Time period(s):** Indeterminate Future
**Locale(s):** Space Station (colonization laboratory); *Eidolon*, Spaceship; Outer Space

**Summary:** When a berserker breaks the pattern of universal human destruction by stealing human zygotes and a biological laboratory, Nicholas Hawksmoor becomes involved in an AI's plan to provide a new body for the goodlife human on which it focused.

**Other books you might like:**
Roger MacBride Allen, *The Ring of Charon*, 1990
Octavia E. Butler, *Dawn*, 1987
Diana G. Gallagher, *The Alien Dark*, 1990
John Varley, *Steel Beach*, 1992

Vernor Vinge, *A Fire upon the Deep*, 1993

## 4762
### FRED SABERHAGEN
## *Berserker Lies*
(New York: Tor Books, 1991)

**Story type:** Science Fiction (Collection; Robot Fiction)
**Series:** Berserker
**Major character(s):** Third Historian, Alien (Carmpan)
**Time period(s):** Indeterminate Future

**Summary:** Five stories, originally published between 1965 and 1990, portray the conflict between humanity, which has recently begun colonizing the galaxy, and the Berserkers, alien sentient killing machines intent on destroying all life.

**Other books you might like:**
Roger MacBride Allen, *The Ring of Charon*, 1990
Isaac Asimov, *Nightfall*, 1990
   Robert Silverberg, co-author
Octavia E. Butler, *Dawn*, 1987
Orson Scott Card, *Ender's Game*, 1985
Diana G. Gallagher, *The Alien Dark*, 1990
Dan Simmons, *The Fall of Hyperion*, 1990
Dan Simmons, *Hyperion*, 1989

## 4763
### FRED SABERHAGEN
### JAMES V. HART, Co-Author
## *Bram Stoker's Dracula*
(New York: Signet, 1992)

**Story type:** Horror (Vampire Story)
**Major character(s):** Dracula, Vampire; Jonathan Harker, Real Estate Agent; Mina Harker, Housewife (Jonathan Harker's wife)
**Time period(s):** 1890s (1895)
**Locale(s):** London, England; Transylvania

**Summary:** In this novelization of the script of the Francis Ford Coppola film, *Bram Stoker's Dracula*, arch-vampire Count Dracula moves his base of operations from Transylvania to England, only to discover that Mina Harker, the wife of his real estate agent, is the spitting image of his wife of 500 years before for whom he still bears undying love.

**Other books you might like:**
Mara McCuniff, *The Vampire Memoirs*, 1990
Michael Romkey, *I, Vampire*, 1990
Bram Stoker, *Dracula*, 1895

## 4764
### FRED SABERHAGEN
## *Dancing Bears*
(New York: Tor, 1996)

**Story type:** Fantasy (Adventure; Historical)
**Major character(s):** John Sherwood, Hunter, Mythical Creature (werebear); Gregori Lohmatski, Nobleman, Mythical Creature (werebear); Natalya Lohmatski, Noblewoman, Revolutionary
**Time period(s):** 1900s (1908-1909)
**Locale(s):** Novgorod, Russia; Siberia, Russia

**Summary:** John Sherwood accompanies Gregori Lohmatski to his Russian estate to hunt a mysterious man-eating bear, but corrupt policemen arrest Gregori and exile him to Siberia. As Sherwood and Natalya Lohmatski, Gregori's sister, travel across Russia to attempt a rescue, they learn that old peasant legends about "werebears" may actually be true.

**Other books you might like:**
James Blish, *There Shall Be No Darkness*, 1950
Mercedes Lackey, *The Fire Rose*, 1995
Pat Murphy, *Nadya: The Wolf Chronicles*, 1996
Whitley Strieber, *The Wolfen*, 1970
Jack Williamson, *Darker than You Think*, 1940
Roger Zelazny, *The Black Throne*, 1990
   Fred Saberhagen, co-author

## 4765
### FRED SABERHAGEN
## *The Dracula Tape*
(New York: Tor, 1989)

**Story type:** Horror (Vampire Story)
**Series:** Dracula
**Major character(s):** Dracula, Vampire (Aristocratic); Mina Harker, Heroine, Lover (Dracula's)
**Time period(s):** 1870s
**Locale(s):** London, England (Carfax Estate)

**Summary:** In a diary sent to Mina Harker's grandson, the Count tells his side of the story: he was a persecuted victim of malicious slander who was only defending himself and his lover, Mina Harker, from the fanaticism and medical bungling of Van Helsing and his dupes, as well as the insanity of Renfield. Originally published in 1975.

**Other books you might like:**
Jeffrey Sackett, *Blood of the Impaler*, 1989
Peter Tremayne, *Bloodright*, 1977
   UK: *Dracula Unborn*
Peter Tremayne, *Dracula, My Love*, 1980
Peter Tremayne, *The Revenge of Dracula*, 1978

## 4766
### FRED SABERHAGEN
## *The Face of Apollo*
(New York: Tor, 1998)

**Story type:** Science Fiction (Science Fantasy; Alternate Intelligence)
**Series:** Book of the Gods
**Major character(s):** Jeremy Redthorn, Farmer, Deity; Sal, Warrior, Religious; Hades, Deity
**Time period(s):** Indeterminate Future
**Locale(s):** Pangur Ban, Fictional City

**Summary:** When Apollo and Hades clash, the Lord of the Underworld suffers severe injuries, but Apollo dies. One of his followers retrieves the god's mask and carries it off to merge with a young man and bring the defeated god back to life. The young man must learn a great deal to avoid his predecessor's fate.

**Other books you might like:**
Glen Cook, *The Swordbearer*, 1982
Brian Stableford, *The Werewolves of London*, 1990
Christopher Stasheff, *The Warlock in Spite of Himself*, 1969
Sheri S. Tepper, *King's Blood Four*, 1983
Roger Zelazny, *Lord of Light*, 1967

## 4767

### FRED SABERHAGEN

## The Holmes-Dracula File

(New York: Tor, 1989)

**Story type:** Horror (Vampire Story)
**Series:** Dracula
**Major character(s):** Dracula, Vampire (Aristocratic); Sherlock Holmes, Detective—Private (The Count's cousin)
**Time period(s):** 1890s
**Locale(s):** London, England

**Summary:** Sherlock Holmes discovers that Count Dracula is his look-alike cousin. The two form a partnership and use their identical looks to thwart a plot to loose the bubonic plague on London. Originally published in 1978.

**Other books you might like:**
Les Daniel, *Don Sebastian Series*,
   1978-1986
Chelsea Quinn Yarbro, *The Saint-Germain Chronicles*,
   1978-1983

## 4768

### FRED SABERHAGEN

## The Last Book of Swords: Shieldbreaker's Story

(New York: Tor, 1994)

**Story type:** Fantasy (Magic Conflict)
**Series:** Swords
**Major character(s):** Stephen, Teenager, Royalty; Vilkata, Wizard
**Time period(s):** Indeterminate Past
**Locale(s):** Tasavalta, Fictional Country; Sarykam, Fictional City

**Summary:** Vilkata returns from defeat and banishment armed with Mindsword, intending to capture Prince Mark's cache of powerful magical swords. With Prince Mark absent from Sarykam, only Prince Stephen, armed with the supremely powerful Shieldbreaker, can hope to stop Vilkata.

**Other books you might like:**
Lois McMaster Bujold, *The Spirit Ring*, 1992
Terry Goodkind, *Wizard's First Rule*, 1992
Laurell K. Hamilton, *Nightseer*, 1992
Martha Wells, *The Element of Fire*, 1993
Patricia C. Wrede, *The Raven Ring*, 1994

## 4769

### FRED SABERHAGEN, Editor

## Machines That Kill

(New York: Tor, 1992)

**Story type:** Science Fiction (Anthology; Robot Fiction)
**Time period(s):** Indeterminate Future

**Summary:** 15 stories about inimical robots first published between 1942 and 1975 including "Fondly Fahrenheit" by Alfred Bester, "Second Variety" by Philip K. Dick, "The Wabbler" by Murray Leinster, "Steel" by Richard Matheson, "Goodlife" by Fred Saberhagen, "The Cruel Equations" by Robert Sheckley, "Alpha Ralpha Boulevard" by Cordwainer Smith, "Killdozer!" by Theodore Sturgeon and "Auto-Da-Fe" by Roger Zelazny. Stories by

David Drake, Carol Emshwiller, Keith Laumer, Barry N. Malzberg, Peter Phillips and Robert Silverberg complete this volume.

**Other books you might like:**
Roger MacBride Allen, *The Ring of Charon*, 1990
David Brin, *Earth*, 1990
Keith Laumer, *Rogue Bolo*, 1986
Dan Simmons, *The Fall of Hyperion*, 1990
Dan Simmons, *Hyperion*, 1989
Cordwainer Smith, *The Best of Cordwainer Smith*, 1975
G. Harry Stine, *Sierra Madre*, 1988

## 4770

### FRED SABERHAGEN

## A Matter of Taste

(New York: Tor, 1990)

**Story type:** Horror (Vampire Story)
**Series:** Dracula
**Major character(s):** Matthew Maule, Philanthropist, Vampire (a.k.a. Count Dracula); John Southerland, Businessman, Wealthy; Valentine Kaiser, Public Relations (celebrity publicist), Vampire (a.k.a. Cesar Borgia)
**Time period(s):** 1990s (1990)
**Locale(s):** Chicago, Illinois

**Summary:** On the night that John Southerland brings his fiancee to meet his adoptive "Uncle Matthew," publicist Valentine Kaiser also pays a visit. John is unaware that Uncle Matthew is really Count Dracula and that Kaiser, a member of the medieval Borgia family, was turned into a vampire by Matthew centuries before and now seeks to take his uncle's life in revenge.

**Other books you might like:**
Les Daniels, *No Blood Spilled*, 1991
Brian Stableford, *The Empire of Fear*, 1988
Bram Stoker, *Dracula*, 1897
Peter Tremayne, *Dracula Unborn*, 1977
Chelsea Quinn Yarbro, *The Palace*, 1978

## 4771

### FRED SABERHAGEN

## Merlin's Bones

(New York: Tor, 1995)

**Story type:** Fantasy (Legend; Political)
**Major character(s):** Amby, Actor, Psychic; Elaine Brusen, Scientist (physicist); Morgan le Fay, Sorceress
**Time period(s):** 21st century; Indeterminate Past (Dark Ages)
**Locale(s):** England; Fairy Realm, Mythical Place

**Summary:** As forces in the past attempt to control the Oracle of Merlin's Bones, Dr. Elaine Brusen's invention, the hypostator, threatens to change reality. Morgan le Fay, Mordred, and the Fisher King focus their grab for power on Brusen's device, while Merlin plots to reestablish Camelot.

**Other books you might like:**
Martin Caidin, *The Messiah Stone*, 1986
Robert N. Charrette, *A Prince Among Men*, 1994
Molly Cochran, *The Forever King*, 1992
   Warren Murphy, co-author
Simon Hawke, *The Wizard of Camelot*, 1993
Simon Hawke, *The Wizard of 4th Street*, 1987
Susan Cooper, *Over Sea, under Stone*, 1966

## **4772**

### FRED SABERHAGEN

## *A Question of Time*

(New York: Tor, 1992)

**Story type:** Horror (Vampire Story)
**Major character(s):** Bill Burdon, Detective—Private; Sarah Tyrell, Widow(er); Jacob Resner, Worker (with the CCC)
**Time period(s):** 1930s (1931); 1990s (1991)
**Locale(s):** Grand Canyon, Colorado

**Summary:** The search for a woman lost in the Grand Canyon uncovers an area at the bottom impervious to time and the arrogant vampire who presides over it.

**Other books you might like:**
Brian W. Aldiss, *Dracula Unbound*, 1990
Dean Wesley Smith, *Laying the Music to Rest*, 1989

## **4773**

### FRED SABERHAGEN

## *Seance for a Vampire*

(New York: Tor, 1994)

**Story type:** Horror (Vampire Story)
**Series:** Dracula
**Major character(s):** John Watson, Doctor; Sherlock Holmes, Detective—Private; Dracula, Vampire
**Time period(s):** 1900s (1903)
**Locale(s):** London, England

**Summary:** A seance to summon a dead loved one accidentally summons the vampire who killed her and releases him into the world to redress the injustice that resulted in his vampirization a century before. When Sherlock Holmes' investigations into the affair result in his mysterious disappearance, Holmes' friend John Watson has no recourse but to summon an expert in such matters, the Prince of Vampires, Count Dracula.

**Other books you might like:**
Mark Frost, *The List of 7*, 1993
William Hjortsberg, *Nevermore*, 1994
Nicholas Meyer, *The Canary Trainer*, 1993
Nicholas Meyer, *The Seven-Percent Solution*, 1977
Kim Newman, *Anno Dracula*, 1992
Sam Siciliano, *The Angel of the Opera*, 1993

## **4774**

### FRED SABERHAGEN

## *A Sharpness on the Neck*

(New York: Tor, 1996)

**Story type:** Horror (Vampire Story)
**Major character(s):** Vlad Dracula, Vampire (a.k.a. Mr. Graves); Radu Dracula, Vampire (Vlad's brother); Phillip Radcliffe, Young Man
**Time period(s):** 1990s (1996); 1790s (1792)
**Locale(s):** Paris, France

**Summary:** In 1792, Phillip Radcliffe performs a service for Vlad Dracula that earns him the vampire's promise to protect him from harm. As a result, Phillip, and a twentieth century descendant named for him, become pawns in Vlad's centuries-old feud with his evil brother Radu.

**Other books you might like:**
Mara McCuniff, *The Vampire Memoirs*, 1991
P.N. Elrod, *Red Death*, 1993
Anne Rice, *The Vampire Lestat*, 1985
T. Lucien Wright, *Thirst of the Vampire*, 1992

## **4775**

### FRED SABERHAGEN

## *Shiva in Steel*

(New York: Tor, 1998)

**Story type:** Science Fiction (Military; Alternate Intelligence)
**Series:** Berserker
**Major character(s):** Claire Normandy, Military Personnel (Space Force commander); Harry Silver, Pilot; Shiva, Artificial Intelligence
**Time period(s):** Indeterminate Future
**Locale(s):** Hyperborea, Planet—Imaginary

**Summary:** After a long stalemate period, the ongoing Humanity-Berserker war has flared up yet again. This time, the Berserkers develop a new tactical computer, nicknamed ''Shiva'' after the goddess of destruction, that seems virtually unbeatable. Commander Claire Normandy must lead a motley group of humans in a last-ditch effort against the machine.

**Other books you might like:**
Greg Bear, *The Forge of God*, 1987
David Gerrold, *Voyage of the Star Wolf*, 1990
Joe Haldeman, *The Forever War*, 1975
Wil McCarthy, *Aggressor Six*, 1994
Wil McCarthy, *The Fall of Sirius*, 1996
Larry Niven, *Footfall*, 1985
    Jerry Pournelle, co-author

## **4776**

### FRED SABERHAGEN

## *The Sixth Book of Lost Swords: Mindsword's Story*

(New York: Tor, 1990)

**Story type:** Fantasy (Legend)
**Series:** Lost Swords
**Major character(s):** Murat, Royalty (crown prince); Kristin, Royalty (princess)
**Time period(s):** Indeterminate Past
**Locale(s):** Culm, Fictional Country; Tasavalta, Fictional Country

**Summary:** Murat of Culm, searching for a present for the Princess of Tasavalta, finds the Mindsword. He knows that its magic is overwhelming so he sheaths it and binds it before touching it, but before he can set it at Kristin's feet he is attacked and must use the sword to save himself, which frees the sword's power to sway men's minds consequently making it very difficult to give up.

**Other books you might like:**
C.J. Cherryh, *Rusalka*, 1989
Stephen R. Donaldson, *Lord Foul's Bane*, 1977
Christopher Priest, *The Glamour*, 1984
Tom Reamy, *Blind Voices*, 1978
Tad Williams, *The Dragonbone Chair*, 1989

## 4777

### FRED SABERHAGEN

## *Wayfinder's Story: The Seventh Book of Lost Swords*

(New York: Tor, 1992)

**Story type:** Fantasy (Sword and Sorcery; Quest)
**Series:** Lost Swords
**Major character(s):** Valdemar "Val", Farmer, Traveler; Yambu, Aged Person, Royalty (Silver Queen); Zoltan, Royalty (prince), Traveler
**Time period(s):** Indeterminate Past
**Locale(s):** Tasavalta, Fictional Country

**Summary:** When Wayfinder comes into Valdemar's hands, his desire causes Wayfinder to bring Valdemar to Rambu, who travels with Zoltan in search of Wayfinder to aid in his quest for the Emperor's treasure and the magic sword, Woundhealer. However, the road to treasure contains many enemies who desire possession of Wayfinder.

**Other books you might like:**
Glen Cook, *The Black Company*, 1984
Glen Cook, *The Swordbearer*, 1982
Marc Laidlaw, *Neon Lotus*, 1988
Michael Moorcock, *The Fortress of the Pearl*, 1989
Michael Moorcock, *The Revenge of the Rose*, 1991

## 4778

### LESLIE RAYMOND SACHS

## *The Virginia Ghost Murders*

(Richmond, Virginia: Pussycat Press, 1998)

**Story type:** Horror (Mystery)
**Series:** Amanda Poe Mysteries
**Major character(s):** Amanda Poe, Detective; David Allan, Detective; Dabney Horton, Businessman
**Time period(s):** 1990s (1998)
**Locale(s):** Richmond, Virginia

**Summary:** Investigating a series of unsolved murders, Amanda Poe and David Allan discover that their case closely parallels a string of murders that occurred 140 years before, and that the evil influence of Uriah Jenkins, who was lynched then, may be influencing the current murderer. First in a projected series of supernatural mysteries featuring a lineal descendant of Edgar Allan Poe.

**Other books you might like:**
Tom Elliott, *The Dwelling*, 1989
Robert R. McCammon, *Usher's Passing*, 1984
Robert Poe, *The Black Cat*, 1997
Robert Poe, *Return to the House of Usher*, 1996
Harold Schechter, *Nevermore*, 1999

## 4779

### JEFFREY SACKETT

## *Blood of the Impaler*

(New York: Bantam, 1989)

**Story type:** Horror (Vampire Story)
**Major character(s):** Malcolm Harker, Detective—Amateur; Dracula, Vampire
**Time period(s):** 1980s (Flashbacks to 1890s and 15th centur)
**Locale(s):** Transylvania; England

**Summary:** A "sequel" to Bram Stoker's *Dracula*. Following the clues in Stoker's novel, Jonathan Harker's great-grandson restores Lucy Westerna to life—unleashing a vampire on society—and recovers the ashes of Dracula, thereby restoring the powers of Dracula's blood and even setting the stage for his return to life.

**Other books you might like:**
Bram Stoker, *Dracula*, 1897
Fred Saberhagen, *The Dracula Tape*, 1975
Peter Tremayne, *Bloodright*, 1977
Peter Tremayne, *Dracula, My Love*, 1980
Peter Tremayne, *The Revenge of Dracula*, 1978

## 4780

### JEFFREY SACKETT

## *Mark of the Werewolf*

(New York: Bantam, 1990)

**Story type:** Horror (Werewolf Story)
**Major character(s):** Janos Kaldy, Werewolf; Frederick Bracher, Racist
**Time period(s):** 1990s
**Locale(s):** Mannering, North Dakota (Hulltech Center for Genetic Research)

**Summary:** Having captured Janos Kaldy, a werewolf, Bracher sets a plan in motion to breed a race of invulnerable Nazi-werewolves to use as shock troops in the war to "purify" the races. Only Kaldy himself can thwart Bracher's plan by looking into himself for a way to escape and, perhaps, to find the death he desperately longs for.

**Other books you might like:**
Robert R. McCammon, *The Wolf's Hour*, 1988
Thomas Tessier, *The Nightwalker*, 1979

## 4781

### MICHELLE SAGARA

## *Chains of Darkness, Chains of Light*

(New York: Ballantine Del Rey, 1994)

**Story type:** Fantasy (Magic Conflict; Political)
**Series:** Sundered
**Major character(s):** Erin of Elliath, Warrior, Healer; Stefanos, Ruler, Immortal; Amalayna, Noblewoman, Avenger
**Time period(s):** Indeterminate
**Locale(s):** Marantine, Fictional Country; Mordantari, Fictional Country

**Summary:** Erin of Elliath and others of Dagothrin travel into the Empire to cleanse it of the Dark Heart, finding treachery and tragedy before events mitigate the extremes of Light and Dark.

**Other books you might like:**
Piers Anthony, *For Love of Evil*, 1988
C.J. Cherryh, *Rusalka*, 1989
Katherine Kurtz, *The Bastard Prince*, 1994
Mike Resnick, *The Dark Lady: A Romance of the Far Future*, 1987
Brian Stableford, *The Empire of Fear*, 1991

## 4782

### MICHELLE SAGARA

## Children of the Blood: Book Two of The Sundered

(New York: Ballantine Del Rey, 1992)

**Story type:** Fantasy (Magic Conflict; Horror)
**Series:** Sundered
**Major character(s):** Darin of Culverne, Child, Religious (priest of Keranya of Lernan); Sara, Amnesiac; Stefanos, Ruler (Dark Lord of Malthan), Immortal
**Time period(s):** Indeterminate
**Locale(s):** Malthan, Fictional Country

**Summary:** Eight-year-old Darin, the last of the Lines, passes as a slave from High Priest Wellen to Stefanos, who wishes Darin to care for Sara, also of the Lines. Not even Stefanos' protection immunizes Darin and Sara who must fight when the next four most powerful of the Sundered wish to claim Sara for the High Priest.

**Other books you might like:**
Piers Anthony, *For Love of Evil*, 1988
Katherine Kurtz, *The Harrowing of Gwynedd*, 1989
Andre Norton, *Warlock of the Witch World*, 1967
Harry Turtledove, *Krispos Rising*, 1991
Harry Turtledove, *The Misplaced Legion*, 1987
Chelsea Quinn Yarbro, *The Palace*, 1978

## 4783

### MICHELLE SAGARA

## Into the Dark Lands

(New York: Ballantine/Del Rey, 1991)

**Story type:** Fantasy (Magic Conflict)
**Series:** Sundered
**Major character(s):** Erin of Elliath, Warrior, Healer; Stefanos, Ruler (Dark Lord of Malthan), Immortal
**Time period(s):** Indeterminate
**Locale(s):** Elliath, Fictional Country; Malthan, Fictional Country

**Summary:** Erin of Elliath, though a natural healer, is driven by the deaths of her parents to become the best warrior of all the Lines. Later she is chosen to become Sarillorn and sent to the battlefield to aid the injured and dying. Captured by Stefanos and made his consort, she turns against him when he kills some of her people to give her quasi-immortality. This is the author's first novel and the first of a series.

**Other books you might like:**
Piers Anthony, *Being a Green Mother*, 1987
Katherine Kurtz, *Deryni Rising*, 1970
Katherine Kurtz, *The Harrowing of Gwynedd*, 1989
Andre Norton, *Witch World*, 1963

## 4784

### MICHELLE SAGARA

## Lady of Mercy

(New York: Ballantine Del Rey, 1993)

**Story type:** Fantasy (Magic Conflict; Political)
**Series:** Sundered

**Major character(s):** Erin of Elliath, Warrior, Healer; Renar of Dagothrin, Heir—Dispossessed, Fugitive; Darin of Culverne, Child, Religious (priest of Keranya of Lernan)
**Time period(s):** Indeterminate
**Locale(s):** Malthan, Fictional Country (empire); Maratine, Fictional Country

**Summary:** With Stefanos temporarily destroyed, Erin of Elliath and Darin of Culverne travel to Illan, formerly Maratine, to raise up the people against Vellen. When Swords of the church ambush them, Renar of Dagothrin rescues them. The three then move to take possession of Illan.

**Other books you might like:**
Piers Anthony, *If I Pay Thee Not in Gold*, 1993
　Mercedes Lackey, co-author
Ru Emerson, *The Two in Hiding*, 1991
Barbara Hambly, *The Ladies of Mandrigyn*, 1984
Katherine Kurtz, *King Javan's Year*, 1992
Jacqueline Lichtenberg, *Zelerod's Doom*, 1986
　Jean Lorrah, co-author
Carol Severance, *Demon Drums*, 1992
Brian Stableford, *The Empire of Fear*, 1988
Chelsea Quinn Yarbro, *A Candle for D'Artagnan*, 1989

## 4785

### DON SAKERS, Editor

## Carmen Miranda's Ghost Is Haunting Space Station Three

(New York: Baen, 1990)

**Story type:** Science Fiction (Humor; Anthology)
**Major character(s):** Carmen Miranda, Spirit, Entertainer
**Time period(s):** 21st century (first decade)
**Locale(s):** Space Station

**Summary:** 19 authors including Anne McCaffrey and C.J. Cherryh, as well as several newcomers, use the science fiction folksong of the same title as an inspiration for their stories. Mystery and humor characterize the collection. Sakers' storynotes and afterword and the words and music to the notorious song fill out the book.

**Other books you might like:**
Douglas Adams, *The Hitchhiker's Guide to the Galaxy*, 1980
Poul Anderson, *Hoka!*, 1984
　Gordon R. Dickson, co-author
John M. Ford, *How Much for Just the Planet?*, 1987
　Star Trek 36
David Gerrold, *Flying Sorcerers*, 1971
　Larry Niven, co-author
Sharyn McCrumb, *Bimbos of the Death Sun*, 1987

## 4786

### WAYNE ALLEN SALLEE

## For You, the Living

(Arvada, Colorado: Roadkill Press, 1992)

**Story type:** Horror (Apocalyptic Horror)
**Major character(s):** Sherideen MacLaren, Young Woman
**Time period(s):** 1990s (1992)
**Locale(s):** Chicago, Illinois

**Summary:** The narrator tells of the epidemic of TREATS, a devastating social disease that manifests itself as sexual voracity after death and that is slowly turning the world in a channel house of promiscuous zombies.

**Other books you might like:**
Clive Barker, *The Age of Desire*, 1984
   short story in *Books of Blood IV*
John David Connor, *Contagion*, 1992
Michael Crichton, *The Andromeda Strain*, 1969
Richard Laymon, *The Mop Up*, 1989
   in *Night Visions 7*
John Skipp, *Book of the Dead*, 1990
   Craig Spector, co-editor
John Skipp, *Still Dead: Book of the Dead 2*, 1992
   Craig Spector, co-editor

## 4787

### WAYNE ALLEN SALLEE

## *The Holy Terror*

(Shingletown, California: Marc V. Ziesing, 1992)

**Story type:** Horror (Wild Talents)
**Major character(s):** Francis Madsen "Painkiller" Haid, Serial Killer; Evan "American Dream" Shustak, Vagrant; Victor Anthony "Tremble" Tremulis, Handicapped
**Time period(s):** 1980s (1988-1989)
**Locale(s):** Chicago, Illinois

**Summary:** As a boy, Francis Haid had a religious vision during a fire in his school. As an adult, Haid trolls the streets of Chicago under the guise of the "Painkiller," a serial murderer who puts bums and derelicts out of their misery by absorbing their pain—and their bodies—into himself.

**Other books you might like:**
John Byrne, *Whipping Boy*, 1992
George C. Chesbro, *Bone*, 1989
Gordon Linzner, *The Troupe*, 1988
Chet Williamson, *Lowland Rider*, 1988

## 4788

### WAYNE ALLEN SALLEE

## *Pain-Grin*

(Lessburg, Virginia: TAL, 1993)

**Story type:** Horror (Collection)
**Summary:** Through a powerful cycle of poems, prose-poems and short stories, the author likens his bout with cerebral palsy—and the constant state of "pain-grin" it produces—to a variety of horrifying experiences.

**Other books you might like:**
Sean Costello, *Captain Quad*, 1991
Patrick McGrath, *The Grotesque*, 1990

## 4789

### WAYNE ALLEN SALLEE

## *With Wounds Still Wet*

(Seattle: Silver Salamander, 1996)

**Story type:** Horror (Collection)
**Summary:** Twenty-four stories, ten original to the book, provide a survey of the past decade of work from this writer of elliptical and often surreal macabre fiction. Most are nonsupernatural urban horror stories set in the author's native Chicago, including his Dennis Cassady Trilogy, comprised of "Rapid Transit," "Take the 'A'

Train," and "Bleeding Between the Lines," all of which feature a man whose life is chronically discomposed by a murder he witnesses at a train station. "Don's Last Minute" and "With the Wound Still Wet" both probe acts of random tragedy for their horror, while "Things We Do at Night" is concerned with two voyeurs whose harmless pastime leads to a brutal crime. The ghost of Richard Speck haunts "The Pink Twist Inn" and the ghost of Elvis Presley "Orient Are."

**Other books you might like:**
S. Darnbrook Colson, *People of the Night*, 1994
Jack Remick, *Terminal Weird*, 1996
Don Webb, *A Spell for the Fulfillment of Desire*, 1996

## 4790

### JESSICA AMANDA SALMONSON

## *Anthony Shriek*

(New York: Dell/Abyss, 1992)

**Story type:** Horror (Wild Talents)
**Major character(s):** Anthony Shriek, Artist; Emily Maupin, Student (art student); Wesley Katts, Store Owner (bookstore)
**Time period(s):** 1990s (1992)
**Locale(s):** Seattle, Washington

**Summary:** Struggling to cope with an abusive childhood and misunderstood life, modern expressionist artist Anthony Shriek finds himself slipping in and out of the real world into a bizarre alternate world known as the Nightland, and unable to tell whether this is a consequence of his work as an artist or merely an expression of incipient madness.

**Other books you might like:**
Giles Blunt, *Cold Eye*, 1989
Kathe Koja, *Bad Brains*, 1992

## 4791

### JESSICA AMANDA SALMONSON

## *The Mysterious Doom and Other Ghostly Tales of the Pacific Northwest*

(Seattle, Washington: Sasqatch Books, 1992)

**Story type:** Horror (Collection)
**Locale(s):** Pacific Northwest

**Summary:** These 17 stories are intriguing retellings of folktales from the Pacific Northwest as tales of supernatural horror. The first eight tell of phantom hounds, Indian princesses turned into fish, and foolish men who build their houses on an Indian burial mounds. The remainder are presented as the experiences of Penelope Pettiweather, Northwest Ghost Hunter, and abound with haunted houses, sea monsters, and other supernatural manifestations.

**Other books you might like:**
Ellen Datlow, *Snow White, Blood Red*, 1993
   Terri Windling, co-editor
Howard Schwartz, *Lilith's Cave: Jewish Tales of the Supernatural*, 1991
Manly Wade Wellman, *John the Balladeer*, 1988

## 4792

### B.J. SALTERBERG

## *The Outlander: Captivity*

(Tucson: Harbinger House, 1989)

**Story type:** Science Fiction (Post-Nuclear Holocaust)
**Series:** Outlander Trilogy
**Major character(s):** Konnor, Military Personnel (Misogynist); Meagar, Government Official
**Time period(s):** Indeterminate Future (509 after the Holocaust)
**Locale(s):** The Center, Earth

**Summary:** Konnor is captured by the forces of the Center, a women's community where men are little more than docile breeders. Meagar is given the task of breaking Konnor, turning him into the kind of man acceptable to the women of the Center. Their clash leads to a compromise and a new chance for men and women to find common ground.

**Other books you might like:**
Suzy McKee Charnas, *Motherlines*, 1979
Suzy McKee Charnas, *Walk to the End of the World*, 1974
Joanna Russ, *The Female Man*, 1975
Joanna Russ, *We Who Are About To. . .*, 1977
Pamela Sargent, *The Shore of Women*, 1986

## 4793

### R.A. SALVATORE

## *Canticle*

(Lake Geneva, Wisconsin: TSR, 1991)

**Story type:** Fantasy (Magic Conflict)
**Series:** Forgotten Realms: The Cleric Quintet
**Major character(s):** Cadderly, Student, Scholar; Aballister Bonaduce, Sorcerer; Danica, Warrior, Martial Arts Expert
**Time period(s):** Indeterminate
**Locale(s):** Snowflake Mountains, Mythical Place

**Summary:** A vain sorcerer creates a chaotic potion intending to curse a library and college of scholars pursuing knowledge of the natural world, resulting in a conflict of philosophy and the use of knowledge. Based on TSR's game, Forgotten Realms.

**Other books you might like:**
John M. Ford, *The Dragon Waiting*, 1983
Randall Garrett, *Murder and Magic*, 1979
Barbara Hambly, *The Silent Tower*, 1986
Katherine Kurtz, *The Deryni Archives*, 1986
Mercedes Lackey, *Magic's Pawn*, 1989

## 4794

### R.A. SALVATORE

## *The Demon Awakens*

(New York: Ballantine Del Rey, 1997)

**Story type:** Fantasy (Magic Conflict; Political)
**Major character(s):** Elbryan Wyndon, Teenager, Adventurer, Warrior; Jilseponie "Pony", Teenager, Adventurer; Avelyn, Religious, Wizard
**Time period(s):** Indeterminate
**Locale(s):** Corona, Fictional Country; Dundalis, Fictional City

**Summary:** Their village destroyed by goblins, Elbryan and Jilseponie follow different paths to gain the skills they need to protect their land

from the evil dactyl. The monks train Avelyn to prepare magic stones for the same purpose, but Avelyn discovers different properties in them than he expects. The three meet and join together in seemingly a futile attempt to save their land from the evil army of the dactyl.

**Other books you might like:**
Steven Brust, *Jhereg*, 1983
Brian Daley, *The Doomfarers of Coramonde*, 1977
Terry Goodkind, *Wizard's First Rule*, 1994
Douglas Niles, *A Breach in the Watershed*, 1995
Andre Norton, *Elvenblood*, 1995
    Mercedes Lackey, co-author

## 4795

### R.A. SALVATORE

## *The Demon Spirit*

(New York: Ballantine Del Rey, 1998)

**Story type:** Fantasy (Magic Conflict; Political)
**Major character(s):** Elbryan Wyndon, Warrior (ranger), Adventurer; Jilseponie "Pony", Psychic, Adventurer; Belli'mar Juraviel, Mythical Creature (elf), Warrior
**Time period(s):** Indeterminate
**Locale(s):** Corona, Fictional Country

**Summary:** After a monk sacrifices his life to destroy a demon dactyl who threatens their land, Elbryan and Pony struggle against the goblins and other monsters who still seek to destroy humanity. Incompletely vanquished, the dactyl insinuates its evil influence into a sacred place and, through a spiritual leader, attempts to control powerful magical gemstones. Sequel to *The Demon Awakens*.

**Other books you might like:**
Maggie Furey, *Harp of Winds*, 1995
Terry Goodkind, *Stone of Tears*, 1995
J. Gregory Keyes, *The Blackgod*, 1997
Patricia Mullen, *The Stone Movers*, 1995
Douglas Niles, *Darkenheight*, 1996

## 4796

### R.A. SALVATORE

## *The Dragon King*

(New York: Warner Aspect, 1996)

**Story type:** Fantasy (Sword and Sorcery; Political)
**Series:** Crimson Shadow
**Major character(s):** Luthien "Crimson Shadow" Bedwyr, Warrior
**Time period(s):** Indeterminate
**Locale(s):** Eriador, Fictional Country

**Summary:** When King Greensparrow plots to destabilize King Brind'Amour's rule of Eriador, Luthien Bedwyr must organize Eriador's people to repel the outside threat to the kingdom.

**Other books you might like:**
Lynn Flewelling, *Luck in the Shadows*, 1996
Terry Goodkind, *Wizard's First Rule*, 1994
Robin Hobb, *Assassin's Apprentice*, 1995
J.V. Jones, *A Man Betrayed*, 1996
Michael A. Stackpole, *Once a Hero*, 1994

## 4797

### R.A. SALVATORE

## The Dragon's Dagger

(New York: Ace, 1994)

**Story type:** Fantasy (Alternate World)
**Series:** Spearwielder's Tale
**Major character(s):** Gary Leger, Adventurer, Hero; Kelsenellenelvial Gil-Ravandry, Mythical Creature (elf)
**Time period(s):** Indeterminate
**Locale(s):** Faerie, Mythical Place; Earth

**Summary:** When Gary returns to Faerie, he finds war threatening, a dragon laying waste to the countryside and the sacred armor and enchanted spear of the realm's greatest hero missing. Repairing this mess requires Gary to invade the dragon's very lair.

**Other books you might like:**
Pamela Dean, *The Secret Country*, 1985
Stephen R. Donaldson, *Lord Foul's Bane*, 1977
Robert Holdstock, *Lavondyss: Journey to an Unknown Region*, 1988
Robert Holdstock, *Mythago Wood*, 1984
Holly Lisle, *Minerva Wakes*, 1994

## 4798

### R.A. SALVATORE

## Dragonslayer's Return

(New York: Ace, 1995)

**Story type:** Fantasy (Adventure)
**Series:** Spearwielder's Tale
**Major character(s):** Gary Leger, Adventurer, Hero; Ceridwen, Witch; Mickey McMickey, Mythical Creature (leprechaun)
**Time period(s):** 1990s; Indeterminate
**Locale(s):** Faerie, Mythical Place; Earth

**Summary:** Upset over his father's death, Gary Leger tries to find meaning by returning to Faerie, this time with his wife, Diane. With Ceridwen plotting evil again, the couple must survive, aid Gary's friends, and defeat the witch for the sake of two worlds.

**Other books you might like:**
Eleanor Arnason, *Daughter of the Bear King*, 1987
Emma Bull, *War for the Oaks*, 1987
Pamela Dean, *The Secret Country*, 1985
Tom Deitz, *Windmaster's Bane*, 1986
Barbara Hambly, *The Time of the Dark*, 1982

## 4799

### R.A. SALVATORE

## Echoes of the Fourth Magic

(New York: Roc, 1990)

**Story type:** Fantasy (Alternate World; Magic Conflict)
**Major character(s):** Jeff DelGiudice, Scientist; Billy Shank, Scientist
**Time period(s):** 1990s
**Locale(s):** Devil's Triangle, Atlantic Ocean; *Unicorn*, Submarine

**Summary:** The *Unicorn*, a deep-sea research submarine is caught in a storm near the Devil's Triangle. Pulled through to an alternate universe, the destroyed submarine ends up in a cavern five miles beneath the ocean surface. The few remaining members of the crew repair the submarine well enough to make their way to the surface.

While trying to find a safe haven, they are contacted by a god whose likeness speaks to them from the water in a bucket.

**Other books you might like:**
Piers Anthony, *Through the Ice*, 1989
William R. Forstchen, *Rally Cry!*, 1990
Leo Frankowski, *The Cross-Time Engineer*, 1986
Alis A. Rasmussen, *The Labyrinth Gate*, 1988
Nancy Springer, *Red Wizard*, 1990

## 4800

### R.A. SALVATORE

## In Sylvan Shadows

(Lake Geneva, Wisconsin: TSR, 1992)

**Story type:** Fantasy (Quest)
**Series:** Forgotten Realms: The Cleric Quintet
**Major character(s):** Cadderly, Religious (priest), Scholar
**Time period(s):** Indeterminate
**Locale(s):** Shilmista, Mythical Place (Forest of Shadows)

**Summary:** Cadderly and his companions journey into the elven forest, Shilmista, to save the inhabitants from an army of monsters and its evil leader.

**Other books you might like:**
Richard Awlinson, *Shadowdale*, 1989
Scott Ciencin, *The Night Parade*, 1992
Elaine Cunningham, *Elfshadow*, 1991
Troy Denning, *The Parched Sea*, 1991
James Lowder, *The Ring of Winter*, 1992
Jean Rabe, *Red Magic*, 1991

## 4801

### R.A. SALVATORE

## The Legacy

(Lake Geneva, Wisconsin: TSR, 1992)

**Story type:** Fantasy (Adventure)
**Series:** Forgotten Realms
**Major character(s):** Drizzt Do'Urden, Mythical Creature (elf), Adventurer; Regis, Mythical Creature (halfling)
**Time period(s):** Indeterminate
**Locale(s):** Mithril Hall, Mythical Place

**Summary:** Happy at Mithril Hall with his friends and companions, Drizzt vowed never to kill another of his people, but his enemy, the Spider Queen Lioth, will not permit him to remain in peace. This sequel to *Sojourn* is a game tie-in and TSR's first hardcover novel.

**Other books you might like:**
Sheila Gilluly, *The Boy From the Burren*, 1990
Mercedes Lackey, *Magic's Pawn*, 1989
Andre Norton, *Dark Piper*, 1968
Mickey Zucker Reichert, *Shadow's Realm*, 1990
Andrea Shettle, *Flute Song Magic*, 1990

## 4802

### R.A. SALVATORE

## Luthien's Gamble

(New York: Warner Aspect, 1996)

**Story type:** Fantasy (Sword and Sorcery; Political)
**Series:** Crimson Shadow

**Major character(s):** Luthien ''Crimson Shadow'' Bedwyr, Warrior; Siobahn, Mythical Creature (half-elf), Martial Arts Expert; Oliver deBurrows, Mythical Creature (halfling), Martial Arts Expert

**Time period(s):** Indeterminate

**Locale(s):** Eriador, Fictional Country; Caer MacDonald, Fictional City

**Summary:** Freeing Monfort, now renamed Caer MacDonald, will prove only a temporary victory unless the Crimson Shadow and his peasant revolution can resist the thousands of Praetorian Guards sent by evil Wizard-King Greensparrow to quell the revolt.

**Other books you might like:**
Robin Hobb, *Royal Assassin*, 1996
J.V. Jones, *Master and Fool*, 1996
Elizabeth Moon, *Surrender None: The Legacy of Gird*, 1990
Paula Volsky, *Illusion*, 1992

### 4803

**R.A. SALVATORE**

## Passage to Dawn

(Lake Geneva, Wisconsin: TRS, 1996)

**Story type:** Fantasy (Magic Conflict; Adventure)
**Series:** Forgotten Realms
**Major character(s):** Drizzt Do'Urden, Mythical Creature (elf), Adventurer; Catti-Brie Bruenor, Mythical Creature (dwarf), Adventurer
**Time period(s):** Indeterminate
**Locale(s):** *Sea Sprite*, At Sea

**Summary:** Drizzt and Cattie-Brie briefly enjoy their carefree life aboard *Sea Sprite* until sorcery and threats bring them back to the land where they found the crystal shard. Old friends and new allies help them in their attempt to free a loved one and thwart the menace to Drizzt and those he cares for.

**Other books you might like:**
Richard Awlinson, *Shadowdale*, 1989
Elaine Cunningham, *Elfshadow*, 1991
Troy Denning, *The Parched Sea*, 1991
James Lowder, *The Ring of Winter*, 1992
Douglas Niles, *Darkwalker on Moonshae*, 1987

### 4804

**R.A. SALVATORE**

## Siege of Darkness

(Lake Geneva, Wisconsin, TSR, 1994)

**Story type:** Fantasy (Adventure; Magic Conflict)
**Series:** Forgotten Realms
**Major character(s):** Drizzt Do'Urden, Mythical Creature (elf), Adventurer; Lloth, Leader (Spider Queen), Deity (goddess of the dark elves); Catti-Brie Bruenor, Mythical Creature (dwarf), Adventurer
**Time period(s):** Indeterminate
**Locale(s):** Mithril Hall, Mythical Place; Faerun's Underdark, Mythical Place; Menzoberranzan, Fictional City

**Summary:** When survivors of Drizzt's defeat of House Baenre in Menzoberranzan plan to retaliate against Mithril Hall and the Spider Queen feeds the chaos in the dark elves' city by turning magic laws unreliable, Drizzt must rely on allies from the Underdark and his own wits to save his friends. Game tie-in.

**Other books you might like:**
Richard Awlinson, *Shadowdale*, 1989
Elaine Cunningham, *Elfshadow*, 1991
Troy Denning, *The Parched Sea*, 1991
Laurell K. Hamilton, *Nightseer*, 1992
James Lowder, *The Ring of Winter*, 1992
Martha Wells, *The Element of Fire*, 1993

### 4805

**R.A. SALVATORE**

## The Silent Blade

(Renton, Washington: Wizards of the Coast/TSR, 1998)

**Story type:** Fantasy (Sword and Sorcery; Adventure)
**Series:** Forgotten Realms
**Major character(s):** Drizzt Do'Urden, Mythical Creature (elf), Adventurer; Catti-Brie, Mythical Creature (dwarf), Adventurer; Wulfgar, Barbarian, Warrior
**Time period(s):** Indeterminate
**Locale(s):** Calimport, Fictional City; Spine of the World, Mythical Place; Menzoberranzan, Fictional City

**Summary:** Drizzt leads his friends to destroy the evil crystal shard once and for all.

**Other books you might like:**
Richard Awlinson, *Shadowdale*, 1989
Elaine Cunningham, *Elfshadow*, 1991
Troy Denning, *The Parched Sea*, 1991
James Lowder, *The Ring of Winter*, 1992
Douglas Niles, *Deathwalker on Moonshea*, 1987

### 4806

**R.A. SALVATORE**

## Sojourn

(Lake Geneva, Wisconsin: TSR, 1991)

**Story type:** Fantasy (Adventure)
**Series:** Forgotten Realms: The Dark Elf Trilogy
**Major character(s):** Drizzt Do'Urden, Mythical Creature (elf), Adventurer; Catti-Brie Bruenor, Mythical Creature (dwarf), Adventurer; Montolio De Brouchee, Ranger
**Time period(s):** Indeterminate Past
**Locale(s):** Termalaine Maer Dualdon, Mythical Place

**Summary:** Drizzt Do'Urden, a drow, left his home in the Underdark where his people worshipped the Spider Queen. Accompanied by his magical panther, the dark elf makes a place for himself in the world above, making friends and fighting evil and prejudice along the way. A game tie-in novel.

**Other books you might like:**
Catherine Cooke, *Mask of the Wizard*, 1985
Sheila Gilluly, *The Boy From the Burren*, 1990
Elizabeth Moon, *Surrender None: The Legacy of Gird*, 1990
Kate Novak, *Song of the Saurials*, 1991
    Jeff Grubb, co-author
Mickey Zucker Reichert, *Shadow's Realm*, 1990
Andrea Shettle, *Flute Song Magic*, 1990

### 4807

**R.A. SALVATORE**

## Starless Night

(Lake Geneva, Wisconsin: TSR, 1993)

**Story type:** Fantasy (Quest)
**Series:** Forgotten Realms
**Major character(s):** Drizzt Do'Urden, Mythical Creature (elf), Adventurer; Catti-Brie Bruenor, Mythical Creature (dwarf), Warrior; Dantrag Baenre, Martial Arts Expert (swordsman)
**Time period(s):** Indeterminate
**Locale(s):** Mithril Hall, Mythical Place; The Underdark, Mythical Place

**Summary:** To protect his friends in Mithril Hall, Drizzt Do'Urden reluctantly travels to the Underdark where he battles monsters and evil foes intent on robbing Drizzt of sanity and freedom before attacking Mithril Hall. Game tie-in sequel to *The Legacy*.

**Other books you might like:**
David Cook, *Horselords*, 1990
Elaine Cunningham, *Elfshadow*, 1991
Troy Denning, *The Parched Sea*, 1991
James Lowder, *The Ring of Winter*, 1992
Jean Rabe, *Red Magic*, 1991
Margaret Weis, *Into the Labyrinth*, 1993
    Tracy Hickman, co-author

### 4808

**R.A. SALVATORE**

## The Sword of Bedwyr

(New York: Warner Aspect, 1995)

**Story type:** Fantasy (Sword and Sorcery)
**Series:** Crimson Shadow
**Major character(s):** Luthien "Crimson Shadow" Bedwyr, Warrior; Oliver deBurrows, Mythical Creature (helf-elf), Highwayman
**Time period(s):** Indeterminate
**Locale(s):** Eriador, Fictional Country; Monfort, Fictional City

**Summary:** An outcast after seeking justice for a murder, Luthien Bedwyr befriends Oliver deBurrows, making questionable use of his arena skills. Enlisted in a wizard's quest, Luthien acquires valuable tools with which to begin the liberation of his people from unwanted outside rule.

**Other books you might like:**
David Cook, *King Pinch*, 1995
Phyllis Eisenstein, *In the Red Lord's Reach*, 1989
David Gemmell, *Morningstar*, 1993
Robin Hobb, *Assassin's Apprentice*, 1995
Mercedes Lackey, *The Eagle and the Nightingales*, 1995
Michael A. Stackpole, *Once a Hero*, 1994
J.R.R. Tolkien, *The Hobbit*, 1938

### 4809

**R.A. SALVATORE**

## The Woods out Back

(New York: Ace, 1993)

**Story type:** Fantasy (Alternate World)
**Series:** Spearwielder's Tale
**Major character(s):** Gary Leger, Adventurer, Hero; Kelsenellenelvial Gil-Ravandry, Mythical Creature (elf)

**Time period(s):** 1990s; Indeterminate
**Locale(s):** Faerie, Mythical Place; Earth

**Summary:** In the woods behind his home, Gary finds himself transported to a realm populated by mythical creatures. There he discovers he alone can wear the armor of a fabled lost warrior and wield a magical spear. Unfortunately, Gary cannot go home unless he assumes the hero's mantle.

**Other books you might like:**
Pamela Dean, *The Secret Country*, 1985
Susan Dexter, *The Wizard's Shadow*, 1993
Gordon R. Dickson, *The Dragon and the George*, 1976
Stephen R. Donaldson, *Lord Foul's Bane*, 1977
Dave Duncan, *The Reluctant Swordsman*, 1988
Robert Holdstock, *The Bone Forest*, 1992
Robert Holdstock, *Lavondyss: Journey to an Unknown Region*, 1989
Robert Holdstock, *Mythago Wood*, 1984

### 4810

**PAUL M. SAMMON**, Editor

## The King Is Dead: Tales of Elvis Post Mortem

(New York: Delta, 1994)

**Story type:** Horror (Anthology)
**Major character(s):** Elvis Presley, Musician, Historical Figure

**Summary:** This volume brings together 31 stories, articles, and reflections on Elvis Presley and how his persona has become larger than life since his death. Stories written originally for the volume include Joyce Carol Oates' "Elvis Is Dead: Why Are You Alive?," in which a man ponders the significance of his Elvis fascination in his dreams; Del James' "Backstage"; Chet Williamson's "Double Trouble," about a man who travels back in time to save Elvis' stillborn twin brother and the consequences of his action; Joe R. Lansdale's "Bubba Ho-Tep," in which an elderly Elvis matches wits with an Egyptian mummy unearthed during a Texas flood; Michael Reaves' "Elvis Meets Godzilla," about Elvis' final film appearance; and Nancy A. Collins' "The Sacred Treasures of Graceland: Excerpts From the Sanctioned Museum Catalogue," which analyzes Elvis kitsch as future museum pieces.

**Other books you might like:**
Jeff Gelb, *Shock Rock*, 1992
    editor
Jeff Gelb, *Shock Rock II*, 1994
    editor
Greil Marcus, *Dead Elvis*, 1994
Paul J. McAuley, *In Dreams*, 1993
    Kim Newman, co-editor

### 4811

**PAUL M. SAMMON**, Editor

## Splatterpunks II: Over the Edge

(New York: Tor, 1995)

**Story type:** Horror (Anthology)

**Summary:** In this follow-up to his 1990 volume *Splatterpunks: Extreme Horror*, the editor assembles two interviews and twenty-six stories (eight original to the volume) in which writers imbue their horror tales with sex, violence and nihilism. The book is dominated by female writers, including Kathe Koja, who describes the god-like powers a dog develops over humans in "Impermanent Mercies"; Nancy Holder, whose "Cannibal Cats Come Out Tonight" is a horror satire involving teenage cannibal males; Nancy Collins, whose ''Rant'' takes the point of view of a psychotic woman; and Lucy Taylor, whose revenge story, ''Heels,'' features a foot fetishist. Melanie Tem's ''Intimates'' and Wildy Petoud's ''Accident D'Amour'' feature female characters whose discomposed emotions manifest in gruesome physical ways, and Nina Kiriki Hoffman's ''Imprint'' and Shira Daemon's ''Red Shift'' both deal with the horrors of domestic abuse. The book also includes reprints by Karl Edward Wagner, Clive Barker, and Poppy Z. Brite.

**Other books you might like:**

John Skipp, *Book of the Dead*, 1989
    Craig Spector, co-editor
John Skipp, *Still Dead: Book of the Dead 2*, 1992
    Craig Spector, co-editor
David J. Schow, *Silver Scream*, 1988
    editor

---

**4812**

**PAUL M. SAMMON**, Editor

## *Splatterpunks: Extreme Horror*

(New York: St. Martin's, 1990)

**Story type:** Horror (Anthology)

**Summary:** Sixteen tales of ''extreme horror'' strongly influenced by the concerns of modern horror films and fueled with the energies of rock music. Plots involving abortion, murder, racism, sexual exploitation, urban squalor and social taboos are rendered in frequently graphic detail. Among the best selections are Douglas Winter's ''Less than Zombie,'' Nancy Collins' ''Freaktent'' and Clive Barker's ''The Midnight Meat Train.''

**Other books you might like:**

Dennis Etchison, *Cutting Edge*, 1986
David J. Schow, *Silver Scream*, 1988
John Skipp, *Book of the Dead*, 1989
    Craig Spector, co-author
Bruce Sterling, *Mirrorshades: The Cyberpunk Anthology*, 1986

---

**4813**

**SCOTT RUSSELL SANDERS**

## *The Invisible Company*

(New York: Tor, 1989)

**Story type:** Science Fiction (Immortality)
**Major character(s):** Leon Ash, Scientist; Kate Trilling, Actress, Spy
**Time period(s):** 21st century
**Locale(s):** Paradise Island, Maine

**Summary:** Twenty years ago a mysterious and powerful organization known as the Invisible Company saved Leon Ash's life. They required in payment only that he promise to take a trip for them some day, no questions asked. Now Ash finds himself on an airplane bound for Paradise Island, a posh resort off the coast of Maine. He has no idea why he's been called to the island but, once there, finds himself at the center of a subtle and potentially deadly mystery.

**Other books you might like:**

Joe Haldeman, *Buying Time*, 1989
Robert A. Heinlein, *Time Enough for Love*, 1973
Frederik Pohl, *Drunkard's Walk*, 1960
Robert Silverberg, *The Book of Skulls*, 1971
Norman Spinrad, *Bug Jack Barron*, 1969
Jack Vance, *To Live Forever*, 1956
Roger Zelazny, *This Immortal*, 1966

---

**4814**

**WILLIAM SANDERS**

## *The Wild Blue and the Gray*

(New York: Warner Questar, 1991)

**Story type:** Science Fiction (Alternate Universe; Military)
**Major character(s):** Amos Ninekiller, Indian (Cherokee), Pilot; William Faulkner, Writer, Pilot; James Lucas, Military Personnel
**Time period(s):** 1910s (1916)
**Locale(s):** France, Alternate Earth

**Summary:** Amos Ninekiller, a Cherokee educated at the University of Virginia, and the only Indian pilot, is sent by his chief to serve with the Confederate Air Force who are fighting with the allies in France. While there he is directed to pick up any information that can help his people stay free of both the Confederacy and the Yankees.

**Other books you might like:**

Gregory Benford, *Alternate Wars*, 1991
    Martin H. Greenberg, co-editor
Orson Scott Card, *Seventh Son*, 1987
Philip Jose Farmer, *Two Hawks From Earth*, 1979
Leo Frankowski, *The Flying Warlord*, 1989
Frank D. McSherry Jr., *The Fantastic Civil War*, 1991
    editor
Ward Moore, *Bring the Jubilee*, 1953
George H. Smith, *Kar Kaballa*, 1969
Martin Cruz Smith, *The Indians Won*, 1970

---

**4815**

**RICHARD SANFORD**

## *Roadkill*

(Aurora, Colorado: Write Way, 1995)

**Story type:** Horror (Nature in Revolt)
**Major character(s):** Charlie Hardin, Truck Driver; Sidney Frankel, Professor (of comparative religion); Melissa Frankel, Teenager
**Time period(s):** 1990s (1995)
**Locale(s):** Deuce Creek, Oregon

**Summary:** Liberated from their burial beneath ancient tribal grounds by excavations around the Portland area, a race of ravenous bird-like creatures begins preying upon the nearby citizens.

**Other books you might like:**

William W. Johnstone, *Bats*, 1994
Barry Porter, *Junkyard*, 1989
Martin Cruz Smith, *Nightwing*, 1977
T.W. Stetson, *Night Beasts*, 1994
Robert Charles Wilson, *Second Fire*, 1994

---

**4816**

**DAVID SAPERSTEIN**

## *Red Devil*

(New York: Berkley, 1989)

**Story type:** Horror (Satanism)
**Major character(s):** Nickolai Valarian, Government Official (Soviet), Demon (Current incarnation of Satan); Peter Somoroff, Spy (KGB agent)
**Time period(s):** 1990s
**Locale(s):** Union of Soviet Socialist Republics

**Summary:** Satan, incarnated in the person of Nickolai Valarian, schemes to take over the Soviet Union, prompting a coalition of Russian, American, and Israeli agents to try to thwart the devil's dangerous, ambitious plan.

**Other books you might like:**
John Farris, *Catacombs*, 1981

---

**4817**

### WILLIAM SARABANDE

## *The Edge of the World*
(New York: Ballantine, 1993)

**Story type:** Fantasy (Quest; Historical)
**Series:** First Americans Saga
**Major character(s):** Cha-kwena, Shaman, Prehistoric Human; Ban-ya, Prehistoric Human; Mah-ree, Prehistoric Human
**Time period(s):** 120th century B.C.
**Locale(s):** Great Plains, North America

**Summary:** To pursue his vision of finding a land of plenty where the People's dreams can flower, Cha-kwena must violate a taboo, alienating his mate and his tribe as he follows the mammoth's trail.

**Other books you might like:**
Jean M. Auel, *Clan of the Cave Bear*, 1980
Jean M. Auel, *The Mammoth Hunters*, 1985
Jean M. Auel, *The Valley of Horses*, 1982
W. Michael Gear, *People of the Wolf*, 1990
    Kathleen O'Neal Gear, co-author
Sue Harrison, *Mother Earth, Father Sky*, 1990
Roger Welsch, *Touching the Fire*, 1992

---

**4818**

### WILLIAM SARABANDE

## *The Sacred Stones*
(New York: Bantam Domain, 1991)

**Story type:** Fantasy (Historical; Romance)
**Series:** First Americans Saga
**Major character(s):** Ysuna, Religious (high priestess), Prehistoric Human; Masau, Hunter, Prehistoric Human; Maliwal, Hunter, Prehistoric Human
**Time period(s):** Indeterminate Past
**Locale(s):** North America

**Summary:** When Maliwal returns to announce success at finding mammoths and a bride, Ysuna and her adopted sons, Masau and Maliwal, all hope that they will find the mythical white mammoth whose flesh will return power to Ysuna and the People of the Watching Star.

**Other books you might like:**
Jean M. Auel, *Clan of the Cave Bear*, 1980
Jean M. Auel, *The Mammoth Hunters*, 1985
Jean M. Auel, *The Valley of Horses*, 1982
W. Michael Gear, *People of the Wolf*, 1990
    Kathleen O'Neal Gear, co-author
Sue Harrison, *Mother Earth, Father Sky*, 1990
Richard Herley, *The Stone Arrow*, 1978
Elizabeth Marshall Thomas, *The Animal Wife*, 1990

---

**4819**

### WILLIAM SARABANDE

## *Thunder in the Sky*
(New York: Bantam Domain, 1992)

**Story type:** Fantasy (Historical; Religious)
**Series:** First Americans Saga
**Major character(s):** Cha-kwena, Shaman, Prehistoric Human
**Time period(s):** 120th century B.C.
**Locale(s):** Great Plains, North America

**Summary:** Hoping to lead his people to the promised land of safety and plenty, Cha-kwena follows the legendary white mammoth while vicious enemies pursue them in hopes of stealing Cha-kwena's magical and passionate woman.

**Other books you might like:**
Jean M. Auel, *Clan of the Cave Bear*, 1980
Jean M. Auel, *The Mammoth Hunters*, 1985
Jean M. Auel, *The Valley of Horses*, 1982
W. Michael Gear, *People of the Wolf*, 1990
    Kathleen O'Neal Gear, co-author
Sue Harrison, *Mother Earth, Father Sky*, 1990
Richard Herley, *The Stone Arrow*, 1978
Elizabeth Marshall Thomas, *The Animal Wife*, 1990

---

**4820**

### JORGE SARALEGUI

## *Looker*
(New York: Charter, 1990)

**Story type:** Horror (Erotic Horror)
**Major character(s):** Jonathan Lewis, Student; Lylah Cassidy, Professor (of English), Murderer; Kim Powell, Student (Jonathan's girlfriend)
**Time period(s):** 1990s
**Locale(s):** Village, Massachusetts (Suburb of Boston)

**Summary:** A reclusive student falls in love with his college literature professor unaware that she is addicted to murder and castration.

**Other books you might like:**
David C. Smith, *The Fair Rules of Evil*, 1989

---

**4821**

### CARL SARGENT
### MARC GASCOIGNE, Co-Author

## *Streets of Blood*
(New York: Roc, 1992)

**Story type:** Fantasy (Science Fiction; Political)
**Series:** Shadowrun
**Major character(s):** Serrin Shamandar, Magician, Mythical Creature (elf); Geraint Llanfrechfa, Nobleman, Adventurer; Francesca Young, Computer Expert (decker)
**Time period(s):** 21st century
**Locale(s):** London, England

**Summary:** A convoluted plot drags three shadowrunners back into contact after years of separation. Industrial espionage, illegal experiments, political maneuvering and a serial killer threaten all their lives. The trio require the help of a young Indian woman from the slums of London to solve the mystery and avoid destruction.

**Other books you might like:**
John Brunner, *The Shockwave Rider*, 1975
Emma Bull, *War for the Oaks*, 1987
Pat Cadigan, *Synners*, 1991
Robert N. Charrette, *Never Deal with a Dragon*, 1990
Nigel Findley, *2XS*, 1992
William Gibson, *Neuromancer*, 1984
Christopher Kubasik, *Changeling*, 1992
Jordan K. Weisman, *Into the Shadows*, 1992
   editor
Jack Yeovil, *Comeback Tour: The Sky Belongs to the Stars*, 1992
   The Sky Belongs to the Stars

## 4822

**PAMELA SARGENT**, Editor

### Nebula Awards 29

(New York: Harcourt Brace, 1995)

**Story type:** Science Fiction (Anthology)
**Series:** Nebula Awards

**Summary:** Subtitled ''SFWA's Choices for the Best Science Fiction and Fantasy of the Year,'' this volume contains a four-page introduction by the editor listing 1993 Nebula Award finalists and winners; comments by nine authors in ''The Year in Science Fiction and Fantasy: A Symposium''; a 14-page article on fantastic films of 1993 by Kathi Maio; memorials to Avram Davidson, Lester del Rey and Chad Oliver; two poems by William J. Daciuk and Jane Yolen; 11 pages of appendixes, including selected titles from the preliminary ballot and a list of previous winners; plus nine stories and exerpts by authors including Terry Bisson, Jack Cady, Harlan Ellison, Lisa Goldstein, Joe Haldeman, and Connie Willis.

**Other books you might like:**
Michael Bishop, *Nebula Awards 24*, 1990
   editor
Michael Bishop, *Nebula Awards 25*, 1991
   editor
James Morrow, *Nebula Awards 26*, 1992
   editor
James Morrow, *Nebula Awards 27*, 1993
   editor
James Morrow, *Nebula Awards 28*, 1994
   editor
George Zebrowski, *Nebula Awards 22*, 1988
   editor

## 4823

**PAMELA SARGENT**, Editor

### Nebula Awards 30

(New York: Harcourt Brace, 1996)

**Story type:** Science Fiction (Anthology)
**Series:** Nebula Awards

**Summary:** Subtitled ''SFWA's Choices for the Best Science Fiction and Fantasy of the Year,'' this volume contains a five-page introduction by the editor listing 1994 Nebula Award finalists and winners; comments by seven authors in ''The Year in Science Fiction and Fantasy: A Symposium''; a 14-page article on fantastic films of 1994 by Kathi Maio; a memorial to Robert Bloch; three poems by W. Gregory Steward and Robert Frazier, Jeff Vandermeer, and Bruce Boston; 11 pages of appendixes including selected titles from the preliminary ballot and a list of previous winners; plus 11 excerpts and stories by authors including Greg Bear, Ben Bova, Joe

Haldeman, Damon Knight, Ursula K. Le Guin, Maureen F. McHugh, Mike Resnick, Martha Soukup, and Kate Wilhelm.

**Other books you might like:**
Michael Bishop, *Nebula Awards 24*, 1990
   editor
Michael Bishop, *Nebula Awards 25*, 1991
   editor
James Morrow, *Nebula Awards 26*, 1992
   editor
James Morrow, *Nebula Awards 27*, 1993
   editor
James Morrow, *Nebula Awards 28*, 1994
   editor
George Zebrowski, *Nebula Awards 22*, 1988
   editor

## 4824

**PAMELA SARGENT**, Editor

### Nebula Awards 31

(New York: Harcourt Brace, 1997)

**Story type:** Science Fiction (Anthology; Fantasy)
**Series:** Nebula Awards

**Summary:** Subtitled ''SFWA's Choices for the Best Science Fiction and Fantasy of the Year,'' this volume contains a six-page introduction by the editor, listing 1995 Nebula Award-finalists and winners; comments by six authors in ''The Year in Science Fiction and Fantasy: A Symposium''; a 16-page article on fantastic films of 1995; memorials to John Brunner and Roger Zelazny; two poems by Rysling Award-winners David Lunde and Dan Raphael; 11 pages of appendixes including selected titles from the preliminary ballot and a list of previous winners; ''Enchanted Village'' by Grand Master Award-winner A.E. van Vogt; plus 10 other excerpts and stories by authors including Gregory Benford, Esther M. Friesner, Lisa Goldstein, Elizabeth Hand, James Patrick Kelly, Ursula K. Le Guin, Maureen F. McHugh and Robert J. Sawyer.

**Other books you might like:**
Michael Bishop, *Nebula Awards 23-25*, 1989-1991
   editor
Jack Dann, *Nebula Awards 32*, 1998
   cditor
Gardner Dozois, *The Year's Best Science Fiction Series*, 1984-1997
   editor
James Morrow, *Nebula Awards 26-28*, 1992-1994
   editor
George Zebrowski, *Nebula Awards 21-22*, 1987-1988
   editor

## 4825

**PAMELA SARGENT**, Editor

### Women of Wonder, the Classic Years: Science Fiction by Women From the 1940s to the 1970s

(New York: Harcourt Brace, 1995)

**Story type:** Science Fiction (Anthology)
**Series:** Women of Wonder

**Summary:** This companion volume to *Women of Wonder, the Contemporary Years:...* contains a 20-page introduction detailing women's involvement in science fiction literature from its earliest publication through the mid-1970s and the important directions in the genre which grow directly from interests promoted by women writers, 15 pages of notes about the authors and editor, 13 pages of recommended science fiction by women 1818-1978, plus 21 stories arranged chronologically 1944-1978. Frequently dark in tone, the stories explore a broad range of themes, many focusing on human interaction and new possibilities, with 13 reprinted from earlier *Women of Wonder* anthologies and eight newly incorporated herein. Authors include Eleanor Arnason, Leigh Brackett, Marion Zimmer Bradley, Zenna Henderson, Ursula K. Le Guin, Katherine MacLean, Anne McCaffrey, Vonda N. McIntyre, Judith Merril, C.L. More, Kit Reed, Joanna Russ, Margaret St. Clair, James Tiptree, Jr., Lisa Tuttle, Joan D. Vinge, Kate Wilhelm, and Chelsea Quinn Yarbro.

**Other books you might like:**

Janrae Frank, *New Eves: Science Fiction about the Extraordinary Women of Today and Tomorrow*, 1994
    Jean Stine, Forrest J. Ackerman, co-editors
Virginia Kidd, *Millennial Women*, 1978
    editor
Alice Laurance, *Cassandra Rising*, 1978
    editor
Vonda N. McIntyre, *Aurora: Beyond Equality*, 1976
    Susan Janice Anderson, co-editor
Robert Silverberg, *The Crystal Ship*, 1976
    editor

---

**4826**

**PAMELA SARGENT**, Editor

## Women of Wonder, the Contemporary Years: Science Fiction by Women From the 1970s to the 1990s

(New York: Harcourt Brace, 1995)

**Story type:** Science Fiction (Anthology)
**Series:** Women of Wonder

**Summary:** This companion volume to *Women of Wonder, the Classic Years:. . .* contains a 20-page introduction discussing new directions within modern science fiction and the vital contributions made by women to the genre and to its evolution, 14 pages of notes about the authors and editor, 16 pages of recommended science fiction by women 1979-1993, plus 21 stories arranged chronologically 1978-1993. Stories vary in tone from light to dark with some investigating feminist topics but most exploring the broad wealth of themes available in the genre. Authors include Octavia E. Butler, Pat Cadigan, Suzy McKee Charnas, C.J. Cherryh, Storm Constantine, Carol Emshwiller, Karen Joy Fowler, Mary Gentle, Lisa Goldstein, Nancy Kress, Judith Moffett, Pat Murphy, Rebecca Ore, Pamela Sargent, Sydney J. Van Scyoc, and Connie Willis.

**Other books you might like:**

Janrae Frank, *New Eves: Science Fiction about the Extraordinary Women of Today and Tomorrow*, 1994
    Jean Stine, Forrest J. Ackerman, co-editors
Virginia Kidd, *Millennial Women*, 1978
    editor
Alice Laurance, *Cassandra Rising*, 1978
    editor
Vonda N. McIntyre, *Aurora: Beyond Equality*, 1976
    Susan Janice Anderson, co-editor
A. Susan Williams, *The Lifted Veil: The Book of Fantastic Literature by Women*, 1993
    editor

---

**4827**

**SARAH SARGENT**

## Jonas McFee, A.T.P.

(New York: Bradbury Press, 1989)

**Story type:** Science Fiction (Young Adult)
**Major character(s):** Jonas McFee, Teenager; Jacobious Fiar, Scientist
**Time period(s):** 1980s
**Locale(s):** United States

**Summary:** Jonas McFee, friendless, the new kid at school, thinks his luck has changed when a mysterious girl gives him a strange blue ball which can apparently work miracles. Then he finds out that the scientist who created the ball, Jacobious Fiar, is after it, and is willing to do anything to get it. Fiar plans to use the ball's powers to conquer the world.

**Other books you might like:**

John Brunner, *Children of the Thunder*, 1989
Gertrude Friedberg, *The Revolving Boy*, 1966
H.M. Hoover, *Children of Morrow*, 1973

---

**4828**

**AL SARRANTONIO**, Editor
**MARTIN H. GREENBERG**, Co-Editor

## 100 Hair-Raising Little Horror Stories

(New York: Barnes & Noble, 1993)

**Story type:** Horror (Anthology)

**Summary:** The 100 short-short (3000 words or less) horror stories collected here cover two centuries and a range of themes, including resurrection of the dead (''The Adventure of the German Student'' by Washington Irving), psychotic obsession (''Berenice'' by Edgar Allan Poe), horrifying encounters with animals (''The Boarded Window'' by Ambrose Bierce), ghosts (''A Different Kind of Dead'' by Ed Gorman), psychological horror (''The Grab'' by Richard Laymon), alien life forms (''The Rag Thing'' by Donald M. Wollheim), premonitions of death (E.F. Benson's ''The Passenger''), and combat (Stephen Crane's ''The Upturned Face'').

**Other books you might like:**

Isaac Asimov, *Microcosmic Tales*, 1980
    Martin H. Greenberg and Joseph Olander, co-editors
Robert Weinberg, *100 Creepy Little Creature Stories*, 1994
    Stefan Dziemianowicz and Martin H. Greenberg, co-editors
Stefan Dziemianowicz, *100 Ghastly Little Ghost Stories*, 1993
    Robert Weinberg and Martin H. Greenberg, co-editors
Sebastian Wolfe, *The Little Book of Horrors*, 1992

---

**4829**

**AL SARRANTONIO**

## Exile

(New York: Roc, 1996)

**Story type:** Science Fiction (Space Opera)
**Series:** Five Worlds
**Major character(s):** Dalin Shar, Ruler (King of Earth); Tabrel Kris, Diplomat; Prime Cornelian, Ruler (High Leader of Mars), Fanatic
**Time period(s):** 25th century
**Locale(s):** Earth; Mars

**Summary:** Seizing rule of Mars by betrayal and brute force, Prime Cornelian will not rest until he controls the human-settled Four

Worlds of Earth, Mars, Titan, and Pluto, and moves on to turn Venus into the Fifth World. Dalin Shar must flee his home planet so that he may regroup and gather the necessary forces to fight Cornelian.

**Other books you might like:**
Kevin J. Anderson, *Blindfold*, 1995
Bill Baldwin, *Canby's Legion*, 1995
David Drake, *The Hammer's Slammers Series*, 1979-1994
Alan Dean Foster, *The Tar-Aiym Krang*, 1972
Margaret Weis, *The Star of the Guardians Series*, 1990-1993
Dave Wolverton, *Beyond the Gate*, 1995

## 4830

### AL SARRANTONIO

## *House Haunted*

(New York: Bantam Spectra, 1991)

**Story type:** Horror (Haunted House)
**Major character(s):** Gary Gaimes, Murderer; Richard Falconi, Detective—Police; Ted Brennan, Psychologist (specialist in the paranormal)
**Time period(s):** 1990s
**Locale(s):** Hudson Valley, New York

**Summary:** A house in upstate New York modeled loosely on the same Compass Cross design that formed the foundation of an occult house of horrors built in Europe a century before becomes the gateway for a monster on the other side of life, who draws four victims randomly from the four points of the compass to its lair and subjects them to the degradation and debauchery necessary for its emergence into the world of the living.

**Other books you might like:**
Michael Cadnum, *Nightlight*, 1989
Tom Elliott, *The Dwelling*, 1989
Richard Matheson, *Hell House*, 1971
Chet Williamson, *Soulstorm*, 1986

## 4831

### AL SARRANTONIO

## *Moonbane*

(New York: Bantam Spectra, 1989)

**Story type:** Science Fiction (Invasion of Earth)
**Major character(s):** Jason Blake, Writer (Poet); Pettis, Military Personnel, Astronaut
**Time period(s):** 1980s
**Locale(s):** United States

**Summary:** Monstrous, wolf-like aliens invade Earth. If they so much as draw blood from a human being, that person becomes one of them. A small band of soldiers, astronauts, and scientists struggle to defeat them.

**Other books you might like:**
David Dvorkin, *Ursus*, 1989
Richard Matheson, *I Am Legend*, 1954
George Romero, *Dawn of the Dead*, 1978
Susanna Sparrow, co-author

## 4832

### AL SARRANTONIO

## *October*

(New York: Bantam, 1990)

**Story type:** Horror (Ghost Story)
**Major character(s):** Eileen Connel, Writer; James Weston, Actor (former); Kevin Michaels, Professor
**Time period(s):** 1990s
**Locale(s):** New Polk, New England

**Summary:** As Halloween approaches, aging author Eileen Connel, who is afflicted with Alzheimer's disease, and burned-out actor James Weston, on the run from his crowded career and searching for himself, remember their pasts while Kevin Michaels, an assistant professor of literature at the University of New Polk enmeshed in academic politics tries to stimulate interest in Connel's occult book, *Season of Witches*.

**Other books you might like:**
Ray Bradbury, *The October Country*, 1955
Lisa Cantrell, *The Manse*, 1987
Charles L. Grant, *For Fear of the Night*, 1988
Charles L. Grant, *The Last Call of Mourning*, 1979
Stephen King, *Carrie*, 1974

## 4833

### AL SARRANTONIO

## *Personal Agendas*

(New York: Dell, 1997)

**Story type:** Science Fiction (Space Opera; Political)
**Series:** Babylon 5
**Major character(s):** G'Kar, Alien (Narn), Prisoner; Londo Mollari, Alien (Centauri), Political Figure; Vir Cotto, Alien (Centauri), Political Figure
**Time period(s):** 23rd century (2261)
**Locale(s):** Centauri Prime, Planet—Imaginary; Babylon 5, Space Station

**Summary:** Determined to rescue former ambassador G'Kar from imprisonment on Centauri Prime, a group of Narn warriors threatens Londo Mollari's plans to use G'Kar as a diversion in his plot to kill the mad Emperor Cartagia. Meanwhile, Vir Cotto tries to disentangle himself from his fiancee's extravagant wedding preparations.

**Other books you might like:**
Neal Barrett Jr., *The Touch of Your Shadow, the Whisper of Your Name*, 1996
Jeanne Cavelos, *The Shadow Within*, 1997
Kathryn M. Drennan, *To Dream in the City of Sorrows*, 1997
Jim Mortimore, *Clark's Law*, 1996
S.M. Stirling, *Betrayals*, 1996
Lois Tilton, *Accusations*, 1995
John Vornholt, *Blood Oath*, 1995
John Vornholt, *Voices*, 1995

## 4834

### AL SARRANTONIO

## *Skeletons*

(New York: Bantam, 1992)

**Story type:** Horror (Apocalyptic Horror; Reanimated Dead)

**Major character(s):** Clair St. Eve, Child; Roger Garbage, Producer (record producer); Abraham Lincoln, Historical Figure
**Time period(s):** 1990s
**Locale(s):** Cold Spring Harbor, New York; Moscow, Russia; Springfield, Illinois

**Summary:** The earth's passage through a peculiar interstellar cloud results in the resurrection of the dead as an army of walking skeletons. Seen through the eyes of four different characters, this novel tells of war between the humans and the skeletons, the latter acting mostly as they did while still alive.

**Other books you might like:**
George Romero, *Dawn of the Dead*, 1978
    Susannah Sparrow, co-author
John Russo, *Night of the Living Dead*, 1981
Chet Williamson, *Ash Wednesday*, 1987

---

## 4835
### RON SARTI
### The Lanterns of God
(New York: Avon Eos, 1998)

**Story type:** Science Fiction (Post-Holocaust; Political)
**Series:** Chronicles of Scar
**Major character(s):** Arn Brant, Royalty, Military Personnel; Major Kren, Genetically Altered Being (beastman), Military Personnel; Dakota, Scout
**Time period(s):** 27th century
**Locale(s):** North America; Kenesee, Fictional Country; Pacifica, Fictional Country

**Summary:** Victorious in war against Virginia and Texas, but regretting the cost of those victories Prince Arn decides to travel to Pacifica. The codes that have protected humanity begin to break down, requiring new answers. The journey to Pacifica will be hard and the answers will not be what Arn expects.

**Other books you might like:**
David Gemmell, *Wolf in Shadow*, 1997
Walter M. Miller Jr., *Saint Leibowitz and the Wild Horse Woman*, 1997
William F. Nolan, *Logan's Run*, 1967
    George Clayton Johnson, co-author
David R. Palmer, *Emergence*, 1984
H. Beam Piper, *Lord Kalvan of Otherwhen*, 1965

---

## 4836
### RON SARTI
### Legacy of the Ancients
(New York: AvoNova, 1997)

**Story type:** Science Fiction (Political; Post-Holocaust)
**Series:** Chronicles of Scar
**Major character(s):** Arn Brant, Royalty (prince), Military Personnel; Robert, Royalty, Handicapped; Sokol, Genetically Altered Being (Beastman), Diplomat
**Time period(s):** Indeterminate Future
**Locale(s):** Kenesee, Fictional Country; Arkan, Fictional Country; North America

**Summary:** In a future where civilization has collapsed and been resurrected, dinosaurs and prehistoric mammals wander the wilderness. Trying to keep his people safe, Prince Arn must travel 1,000 miles through allied and hostile countries to destroy a weapon that could destroy civilization again. Sequel to *The Chronicles of Scar*.

**Other books you might like:**
David Brin, *The Postman*, 1985
Octavia E. Butler, *Parable of the Sower*, 1993
Sterling E. Lanier, *Hiero's Journey*, 1973
Vonda N. McIntyre, *Dreamsnake*, 1978
Walter M. Miller Jr., *A Canticle for Leibowitz*, 1960
Jake Saunders, *The Texas-Israeli War: 1999*, 1974
    Howard Waldrop, co-author

---

## 4837
### JOHN SAUL
### Black Lightning
(New York: Fawcett Columbine, 1995)

**Story type:** Horror (Serial Killer; Supernatural Vengeance)
**Major character(s):** Anne Jeffers, Journalist; Glen Jeffers, Architect; Mark Blakemore, Police Officer
**Time period(s):** 1990s (1995)
**Locale(s):** Seattle, Washington

**Summary:** Richard Kraven, a serial killer obsessed with the metaphysics of life and death, dies in the electric chair at the same moment that Glen Jeffers suffers a heart attack. After Glen's recovery, his wife Anne, a newspaper reporter who helped send Kraven to his death, notices a pattern in a series of murders closing in on her that suggests Kraven's spirit and motivation have some how managed to outlive him.

**Other books you might like:**
Dean R. Koontz, *Hideaway*, 1992
Joe R. Lansdale, *The Nightrunners*, 1987
Christopher Pike, *The Cold One*, 1995
Ramona Stewart, *The Possession of Joel Delaney*, 1970

---

## 4838
### JOHN SAUL
### The Blackstone Chronicles
(New York: Fawcett, 1997)

**Story type:** Horror (Curse)
**Major character(s):** Oliver Metcalf, Editor (newspaper); Bill McGuire, Contractor; Rebecca Morrison, Librarian
**Time period(s):** 1990s (1997)
**Locale(s):** Blackstone, New Hampshire

**Summary:** Serial novel, published in six individual monthly installments: *An Eye for An Eye: The Doll; Twist of Fate: The Locket; Ashes to Ashes: The Dragon's Flame; In the Shadow of Evil: The Handkerchief; Day of Reckoning: The Stereoscope*; and *Asylum*. Plans to renovate the abandoned Blackstone Asylum fall apart when a series of anonymous gifts to different townspeople causes death and ruin in their families. Each gift belonged at some time to an inmate at the asylum, and the identity of the mysterious benefactor who sends them, and his reason for causing so much misery throughout the town, are the core of the novel's mystery.

**Other books you might like:**
Charles L. Grant, *The Hour of the Oxrun Dead*, 1977
William L. Johnston, *Asylum*, 1972
Stephen King, *The Green Mile*, 1997
Michael McDowell, *Blackwater*, 1983

## 4839

### JOHN SAUL

## *Creature*

(New York: Bantam, 1990)

**Story type:** Horror (Science Fiction)
**Major character(s):** Sharon Tanner, Housewife; Mark Tanner, Teenager, Sports Figure (Football player)
**Time period(s):** 1980s
**Locale(s):** Silverdale, Colorado

**Summary:** Silverdale seems idyllic to the Tanner family, especially the high school with its perenially undefeated football team. But when Mark joins the team, the Tanners learn about the peculiar training and conditioning techniques the boys are subjected to—procedures that threaten to turn Mark into a raging monster.

**Other books you might like:**
Andrew Neiderman, *Perfect Little Angels*, 1989

## 4840

### JOHN SAUL

## *Darkness*

(New York: Bantam, 1991)

**Story type:** Horror (Child-in-Peril)
**Major character(s):** Warren Phillips, Doctor; Kelly Anderson, Teenager; Ted Anderson, Construction Worker, Parent (Kelly's father)
**Time period(s):** 1990s
**Locale(s):** Villejeune, Florida

**Summary:** Under the cover of night, respected town physician Warren Phillips adopts the guise of "The Dark Man," a cult leader who extracts fluid from the thymus glands of the children who follow him. By day, he injects this fluid into the leading male citizens of Villejeune, guaranteeing them eternal youth as long as the fluid supply is not exhausted.

**Other books you might like:**
John Arbucci, *Blood of Innocents*, 1991
Dean R. Koontz, *The Servants of Twilight*, 1984
Andrew Neiderman, *Perfect Little Angels*, 1989

## 4841

### JOHN SAUL

## *Guardian*

(New York: Fawcett/Columbine, 1993)

**Story type:** Horror (Werewolf Story)
**Major character(s):** Joey Wilkerson, Teenager; Mary Anne Carpenter, Parent; Alison Carpenter, Teenager
**Time period(s):** 1990s
**Locale(s):** Sugarloaf Valley, Idaho

**Summary:** When her best friend and best friend's husband are mauled to death by a wild animal, Mary Anne Carpenter moves her family from New Jersey to the El Monte Ranch in Idaho to take care of the couple's child, her godson Joey. But Joey's fascination with animals, his nighttime activities, and the continuation of maulings amongst the townspeople of the Sugarloaf Valley convince Mary Anne that Joey somehow is responsible for the deaths.

**Other books you might like:**
Ramsey Campbell, *Incarnate*, 1983

Charles L. Grant, *The Pet*, 1986
Stephen Gresham, *The Living Dark*, 1991
Stephen King, *Firestarter*, 1980
Melanie Tem, *Wilding*, 1992

## 4842

### JOHN SAUL

## *The Homing*

(New York: Fawcett Columbine, 1994)

**Story type:** Horror (Science Fiction)
**Major character(s):** Karen Spellman, Secretary—Legal; Julie Spellman, Teenager (Karen's 16-year-old daughter); Carl Henderson, Scientist (entomologist)
**Time period(s):** 1990s
**Locale(s):** Pleasant Valley, California

**Summary:** In an attempt to cover up his perverse penchant for abducting runaways and torturing them to death, entomologist Carl Henderson injects a witness, Julie Spellman, with an anti-venin used to treat the strings of the strain of mutant bees he has created to help the local farmers. But the attempted murder backfires, transforming Julie into a monstrous hybrid of human and insect.

**Other books you might like:**
H.F. Heard, *A Taste for Honey*, 1941
Frank Herbert, *Hellstrom's Hive*, 1973
H.G. Wells, *The Food of the Gods*, 1904

## 4843

### JOHN SAUL

## *The Presence*

(New York: Fawcett/Columbine, 1997)

**Story type:** Horror (Science Fiction; Child-in-Peril)
**Major character(s):** Katherine Sundquist, Anthropologist; Michael Sundquist, Teenager; Rob Silver, Anthropologist
**Time period(s):** 1990s (1997)
**Locale(s):** Maui, Hawaii

**Summary:** Katherine Sundquist discovers that her son's worsening physical condition is related to the Serinus project, a covert operation investigating the possible extraterrestrial orgins of human life. Her efforts to save her son and expose the project invite resistance from the hand of the operation, who will stop at nothing, even murder, to protect the experiment.

**Other books you might like:**
John Arbucci, *Blood of Innocents*, 1991
John Farris, *The Fury*, 1976
Gary Goshgarian, *Rough Beast*, 1995
Dean R. Koontz, *Lightning*, 1988
Michael Kurland, *Bottom Right*, 1990

## 4844

### JOHN SAUL

## *Second Child*

(New York: Bantam, 1990)

**Story type:** Horror (Ghost Story)
**Major character(s):** Melissa Holloway, Teenager; Teri MacIver, Teenager (Melissa's stepsister); D'Arcy Malloy, Spirit
**Time period(s):** 1990s

**Locale(s):** Secret Cove, Maine

**Summary:** Ostracized by her peer group and tormented by her cruel stepsister, Melissa Holloway finds solace in her friendship with the spirit of D'Arcy Malloy, a serving girl who died in her house a century before and whose tragically spurned affections mirror Melissa's own plight.

**Other books you might like:**
William March, *The Bad Seed*, 1954
Jean Paiva, *The Lilith Factor*, 1989
Thomas Tryon, *The Other*, 1971

---

### 4845
#### JOHN SAUL

### *Shadows*
(New York: Bantam, 1993)

**Story type:** Horror (Child-in-Peril)
**Major character(s):** Josh MacCallum, Child (10 years old); Brenda MacCallum, Waiter/Waitress; Amy Carlson, Child (10 years old)
**Time period(s):** 1990s (1992)
**Locale(s):** Barrington, California

**Summary:** Brenda MacCallum enrolls her precocious but difficult child Josh in the prestigious Barrington Academy for gifted children, unaware that the director of the school is embarked on a secret project to literally merge the intelligences of his young students with computers. This novel was originally published in 1992.

**Other books you might like:**
John Arbucci, *Blood of Innocents*, 1991
Eric Flanders, *The Forever Children*, 1992
Dean R. Koontz, *Midnight*, 1989
David Martin, *Bring Me Children*, 1992

---

### 4846
#### ELIZABETH A. SAUNDERS, Editor

### *When the Black Lotus Blooms*
(Atlanta: Unnameable Press, 1990)

**Story type:** Horror (Anthology)

**Summary:** Forty-two stories and poems of the macabre, ranging from a reprint of Mary Elizabeth Counselman's 1941 *Weird Tales* story, ''The Drifting Atoms,'' to contemporary tales such as Gerald W. Page's H.P. Lovecraft spoof, ''Strange High Armadillo in the Mist''; James A. Riley's rural horror story, ''The Old Marsh Road''; Charles Grant's ghostly western, ''Pinto Rider''; and Joseph Payne Brennan's tale of a soldier's guilt, ''The Gray Smudge.'' Illustrated and with an introduction by Robert R. McCammon.

**Other books you might like:**
Peter Enfantino, *Quick Chills*, 1990
Jessica Amanda Salmonson, *Tales by Moonlight II*, 1989
Jessica Amanda Salmonson, *Tales by Moonlight*, 1984
Stuart David Schiff, *The Whispers Series*, 1977-1987
David B. Silva, *Best of The Horror Show*, 1987

---

### 4847
#### ADRIAN SAVAGE

### *Symphony*
(New York: Pocket, 1992)

**Story type:** Horror (Occult)

---

**Major character(s):** Prometheus ''Bruce Payne'' Faust, Religious (Satanic priest); Helen Singer, Police Officer (detective sergeant, NYPD); Cal Hudson, Producer (record producer), Religious (Satanic priest)
**Time period(s):** 1990s (1992)
**Locale(s):** New York, New York

**Summary:** Ex-cop and dignified Satanist Prometheus Faust teams up with police officer Helen Singer to thwart a cult of renegade Satanists who commit ritual murders in the hope of inciting race riots that will further their rise to power.

**Other books you might like:**
Ken Eulo, *Manhattan Heat*, 1991
Tanya Huff, *Blood Price*, 1991
Gordon Linzner, *The Troupe*, 1988
Graham Masterton, *The Burning*, 1991
Robert Weinberg, *The Black Lodge*, 1991

---

### 4848
#### FELICITY SAVAGE

### *The Daemon in the Machine*
(New York: Harper, 1998)

**Story type:** Fantasy (Magic Conflict)
**Series:** Ever
**Major character(s):** Crispin Kateralbin, Sorcerer, Military Personnel (captain); Mickey Ash, Military Personnel
**Time period(s):** 1890s (1896)
**Locale(s):** Kirekune, Fictional Country

**Summary:** The second book of the Ever series contains the further adventures of a young daemon handler and his companion, both now in the service of the empire of Ferupe. Their mission this time takes them into the heart of a rival empire, and they have their first contact with denizens of the mysterious, far off land known as America.

**Other books you might like:**
Graham Edwards, *Dragoncharm*, 1995
Raymond E. Feist, *Shadow of a Dark Queen*, 1994
John Jakes, *The Mark of the Demons*, 1969
R.A. Salvatore, *The Demon Awakens*, 1997
Lawrence Watt-Evans, *Seven Altars of Dusarra*, 1981

---

### 4849
#### FELICITY SAVAGE

### *Delta City*
(New York: Roc, 1996)

**Story type:** Fantasy (Political; Religious)
**Series:** Humility Garden
**Major character(s):** Humility ''Humi'' Garden, Ruler (deposed), Revolutionary; Pati, Deity, Ruler; Arity ''Ari'', Addict, Outcast
**Time period(s):** Indeterminate
**Locale(s):** Delta City, Fictional City

**Summary:** Where Humility, the first and last human Divinarch, once ruled, Pati now reigns so insanely that even the cowed populace plots against him. They need a leader and turn to Humility. But since the last time she fought Pati she lost both her eyes and throne, what does she have left to lose? Sequel to *Humility Garden*.

**Other books you might like:**
Steven Brust, *Jhereg*, 1983
Storm Constantine, *Wraeththu*, 1993
P.C. Hodgell, *God Stalk*, 1982
Tanith Lee, *Death's Master*, 1979

Fritz Leiber, *Ill Met in Lankhmar*, 1995

## **4850**
### FELICITY SAVAGE

## *Humility Garden*
(New York: Roc, 1995)

**Story type:** Fantasy (Political; Religious)
**Series:** Humility Garden
**Major character(s):** Humility "Humi" Garden, Apprentice (ghostier), Artist, Religious; Beauty "Beau" Garden, Artist (ghost), Religious (sacrifice to gods)
**Time period(s):** Indeterminate (local year 1352)
**Locale(s):** Salt, Planet—Imaginary

**Summary:** Childhood friends, Humi and Beau depart their impoverished village, bound for different fates. While Beau's beauty propels him into becoming undead artwork, a ghost, displayed for the pleasure of the powerful, Humi's drive and intelligence leads her to an apprenticeship as ghoster and on to that prestigious vocation. First novel.

**Other books you might like:**
Richard Adams, *Maia*, 1985
Kim Antieau, *The Jigsaw Woman*, 1996
Mary Gentle, *Rats and Gargoyles*, 1991
P.C. Hodgell, *God Stalk*, 1982
Nancy Kress, *Beggars in Spain*, 1993
S.P. Somtow, *I Wake From a Dream of a Drowned Star City*, 1992
Michael Swanwick, *The Iron Dragon's Daughter*, 1994

## **4851**
### FELICITY SAVAGE

## *The War in the Waste*
(New York: HarperPrism, 1997)

**Story type:** Fantasy (Alternate Universe; Adventure)
**Series:** Ever
**Major character(s):** Crispin Kateralbin, Entertainer (aerialist), Mechanic (daemon handler); Rae, Orphan, Tailor; Daniel "Butch" Keynes, Military Personnel
**Time period(s):** 1870s (alternate world); 1890s (alternate world)
**Locale(s):** Valestock, Fictional City; Wraithwaste, Fictional Country; Alternate Earth

**Summary:** In a wildly, different Europe, where daemons provide energy for an industrializing world, a young man and woman become tangled in the complex politics of a continent at war. From back alleys to battlefields, they simply try to survive and find peace, but find themselves increasingly involved in pivotal events. First of a trilogy.

**Other books you might like:**
Storm Constantine, *Wraeththu*, 1993
Avram Davidson, *The Adventurers of Dr. Eszterhazy*, 1991
Teresa Edgerton, *Goblin Moon*, 1991
Tanith Lee, *The Book of the Beast*, 1991
Paula Volsky, *Illusion*, 1992

## **4852**
### FELICITY SAVAGE

## *The War in the Waste*
(New York: Harper, 1998)

**Story type:** Fantasy (Magic Conflict)
**Series:** Ever
**Major character(s):** Crispin Kateralbin, Sorcerer, Military Personnel; Mickey Ash, Military Personnel; David Burns, Military Personnel (captain)
**Time period(s):** 19th century
**Locale(s):** Ferupe, Fictional Country

**Summary:** Crispin must abandon his life as a circus entertainer, where he learned the art of handling daemons, and make a new life for himself in an alternate Europe. He joins a young orphan girl and the two of them get caught up in the battle between an aging queen and her chief adversary.

**Other books you might like:**
David Eddings, *Belgarath the Sorcerer*, 1995
Raymond E. Feist, *A Darkness at Sethanon*, 1986
Ken Hood, *Demon Knight*, 1998
Mike Jefferies, *Stone Angels*, 1992
Paula Volsky, *The Sorcerer's Curse*, 1989

## **4853**
### ROBERT J. SAWYER

## *End of an Era*
(New York: Ace, 1994)

**Story type:** Science Fiction (Time Travel; Invasion of Earth)
**Major character(s):** Brandon Thackeray, Scientist (paleontologist), Museum Curator; Miles Jordan, Scientist (paleontologist), Museum Curator
**Time period(s):** 2010s (2013); Indeterminate Past (Cretaceous era)
**Locale(s):** Alberta, Canada; *Sternberger*, Spaceship (timeship); North America

**Summary:** Using an experimental timeship, Brandon Thackeray travels to the end of the Cretaceous to discover the cause of dinosaur extinction.

**Other books you might like:**
Octavia E. Butler, *Dawn*, 1987
Michael Crichton, *Jurassic Park*, 1990
Diana G. Gallagher, *The Alien Dark*, 1990
Harry Harrison, *West of Eden*, 1984
Stephen Leigh, *Ray Bradbury Presents: Dinosaur World*, 1992

## **4854**
### ROBERT J. SAWYER

## *Far-Seer*
(New York: Ace, 1992)

**Story type:** Science Fiction (Adventure; Theological)
**Major character(s):** Afsan, Alien (Quintaglio), Apprentice (astrologer)
**Time period(s):** Indeterminate
**Locale(s):** Quintaglio Home World, Moon—Imaginary

**Summary:** On his coming-of-age pilgrimage to the far side of his world, Afsan makes a discovery which could bring revolution to his profession if not his entire society.

**Other books you might like:**
James Gurney, *Dinotopia*, 1992
Stephen Leigh, *Ray Bradbury Presents: Dinosaur Planet*, 1993
Stephen Leigh, *Ray Bradbury Presents: Dinosaur World*, 1992
Dave Wolverton, *Path of the Hero*, 1993
Dave Wolverton, *Serpent Catch*, 1991

## 4855

### ROBERT J. SAWYER

### *Fossil Hunter*

(New York: Ace, 1993)

**Story type:** Science Fiction (Theological)
**Series:** Far-Seer
**Major character(s):** Kee-Toroca, Alien (Quintaglio), Scientist; Afsan, Alien (Quintaglio), Scholar; Dy-Dybo, Alien (Quintaglio), Ruler (Emperor)
**Time period(s):** Indeterminate
**Locale(s):** Quintaglio Home World, Moon—Imaginary

**Summary:** To aid the effort to leave their moon which will disintegrate all too soon, Toroca leads the effort to inventory everything on their moon. He discovers an alien artifact which changes his understanding of his world and the Quintaglios' place on it.

**Other books you might like:**
Eleanor Arnason, *A Woman of the Iron People*, 1991
C.J. Cherryh, *Chanur's Legacy*, 1992
Diana G. Gallagher, *The Alien Dark*, 1990
James Gurney, *Dinotopia*, 1992
Stephen Leigh, *Ray Bradbury Presents: Dinosaur World*, 1992
L. Neil Smith, *Their Majesties' Bucketeers*, 1981
Vernor Vinge, *A Fire upon the Deep*, 1992

## 4856

### ROBERT J. SAWYER

### *Frameshift*

(New York: Tor, 1997)

**Story type:** Science Fiction (Genetic Manipulation; Hard Science Fiction)
**Major character(s):** Pierre Tardivel, Researcher; Molly Bond, Psychologist, Psychic (esper); Ivan "Burian Klimus" Marchenko, Professor, Criminal
**Time period(s):** 1990s
**Locale(s):** Berkeley, California

**Summary:** When Pierre discovers his natural father suffers from Huntington's Chorea, he decides to win the Nobel Prize for finding the cure. Because he thinks in French, Molly can't read his mind and likes him instantly. They seem the perfect couple except that Molly wants a baby and someone wants Pierre dead. Burian volunteers to donate sperm for Molly, resulting in an abnormal baby.

**Other books you might like:**
Octavia E. Butler, *Parable of the Sower*, 1995
Frank Herbert, *The White Plague*, 1982
Elizabeth Moon, *Remnant Population*, 1996
Kathy Tyers, *Shivering World*, 1991
Jack Womack, *Heathern*, 1990

## 4857

### ROBERT J. SAWYER

### *Golden Fleece*

(New York: Popular Library/Questar, 1990)

**Story type:** Science Fiction (Mystery)
**Major character(s):** Aaron Rossman, Spaceman (landing fleet supervisor); JASON, Computer
**Time period(s):** 22nd century (2179)
**Locale(s):** *Argo*, Spaceship; Thunder Bay, Ontario, Canada

**Summary:** In order to avoid the possibility of losing crew from the *Argo* before departing to a distant world, artificial intelligences have kept news of the first intelligent signals from space hidden from humans. When Diana Chandler dies, her ex-husband cannot accept the death as accidental. As Aaron probes, he finds the murderer must be the artificial intelligence which controls every facet of shipboard life.

**Other books you might like:**
Jeffrey A. Carver, *The Rapture Effect*, 1987
Arthur C. Clarke, *2001: A Space Odyssey*, 1968
D.F. Jones, *Colossus*, 1967
Dan Simmons, *The Fall of Hyperion*, 1990
Dan Simmons, *Hyperion*, 1989

## 4858

### ROBERT J. SAWYER

### *Illegal Alien*

(New York: Ace, 1997)

**Story type:** Science Fiction (First Contact; Mystery)
**Major character(s):** Francis "Frank" Nobilio, Scientist, Government Official; Hask, Alien (Tosok); Dale Rice, Lawyer
**Time period(s):** 2010s
**Locale(s):** New York, New York (United Nations); Los Angeles, California (Valcour Hall, University of Southern California)

**Summary:** Seven aliens from Alpha Centauri arrive on Earth in need of help to repair their ship, having damaged it on the way. Frank and the rest of the contact team especially befriend Hask, the first alien to land. When all evidence in the murder of one of the humans on the team points to Hask, Frank hires Dale Rice, a prominent civil rights attorney, to defend him.

**Other books you might like:**
Pauline Ashwell, *Project Farcry*, 1995
Kathleen Ann Goonan, *Queen City Jazz*, 1994
Katharine Kerr, *Polar City Blues*, 1990
Ian McDonald, *Evolution's Shore*, 1995
Larry Niven, *Footfall*, 1985

## 4859

### ROBERT J. SAWYER

### *Starplex*

(New York: Ace, 1996)

**Story type:** Science Fiction (First Contact; Time Travel)
**Major character(s):** Gilbert "Keith" Lansing, Administrator, Immortal; Jag Kandarq em-Pelsh, Alien (Waldahud); Bottlenose, Animal (dolphin), Pilot (spaceship)
**Time period(s):** 2090s (2094)
**Locale(s):** Tau Ceti, Outer Space; Alpha Draconis, Outer Space

**Summary:** Jointly owned and operated by the four known intelligent species, *Starplex* uses the shortcut system, discovered ready to use, to explore new places. Through a newly opened shortcut, the *Starplex* crew discovers dark matter while Keith goes through later to emerge near an unknown, advanced ship carrying a clear, slightly aquamarine man from the future.

**Other books you might like:**
Glen Cook, *The Dragon Never Sleeps*, 1988
John DeChancie, *Starrigger*, 1983
L. Warren Douglas, *Cannon's Orb*, 1994
Alan Dean Foster, *Design for Great-Day*, 1995
    Eric Frank Russell, co-author
Jack McDevitt, *The Engines of God*, 1994
Frederik Pohl, *The Other End of Time*, 1996
George Zebrowski, *Stranger Suns*, 1991

---

**4860**

**ROBERT J. SAWYER**

## The Terminal Experiment

(New York: HarperPrism, 1995)

**Story type:** Science Fiction (Mystery; Alternate Intelligence)
**Major character(s):** Peter Hobson, Scientist, Engineer (biomedical); Cathy Hobson, Advertising; Sarkar Muhammed, Computer Expert
**Time period(s):** 2010s (2011)
**Locale(s):** Toronto, Ontario, Canada

**Summary:** Peter Hobson and Sarkar Muhammed develop a personality scanner which creates artificial intelligences based on a human subject. When Peter generates electronic copies of himself to investigate theories of immortality and life after death, one becomes a murderer, while all three escape into the computer network. Serialized as *Hobson's Choice*.

**Other books you might like:**
Ben Bova, *Death Dream*, 1994
Pat Cadigan, *Fools*, 1992
Pierre Ouellette, *The Deus Machine*, 1994
Cole Perriman, *Terminal Games*, 1994
John Varley, *Steel Beach*, 1992

---

**4861**

**ELIZABETH ANN SCARBOROUGH**

## Carol for Another Christmas

(New York: Ace, 1996)

**Story type:** Fantasy (Urban; Legend)
**Major character(s):** Monica Banks, Businesswoman; Ebenezer Scrooge, Spirit, Artificial Intelligence; Curtis Lu, Computer Expert
**Time period(s):** 1990s
**Locale(s):** Seattle, Washington

**Summary:** Monica Banks allows her work to keep her too busy for any personal life. Created as a computer program artifact, Ebenezer Scrooge visits Monica as the Ghosts of Christmas Past, Present, and Future, hoping to awaken Monica to a wider, more meaningful world.

**Other books you might like:**
Richard Dalby, *Ghosts for Christmas*, 1988
    editor
James Finn Garner, *Politically Correct Holiday Stories*, 1995

Kathryn Cramer, *Spirits of Christmas*, 1989
    David G. Hartwell, co-editor
Tom Mula, *Jacob Marley's Christmas Carol*, 1995
Mike Resnick, *Christmas Ghosts*, 1993
    Martin H. Greenberg, co-editor
Kristine Kathryn Rusch, *Pulphouse, Issue 10: Special Issue*, 1991
    editor

---

**4862**

**ELIZABETH ANN SCARBOROUGH**

## The Godmother

(New York: Ace, 1994)

**Story type:** Fantasy (Urban; Light Fantasy)
**Major character(s):** Rosalie "Rose" Samson, Social Worker; Felicity Fortune, Mythical Creature (fairy godmother)
**Time period(s):** 1990s
**Locale(s):** Seattle, Washington

**Summary:** Rose's wish for a fairy godmother for the city of Seattle brings Felicity, who helps in the battle against a mountain of problems afflicting youngsters. Rewritten plots and characters from many fairy tales appear as framework while themes of child abuse, gang violence and other urban issues provide a modern setting.

**Other books you might like:**
Chester Anderson, *The Butterfly Kid*, 1967
Gael Baudino, *Strands of Sunlight*, 1994
Ellen Guon, *Bedlam Boyz*, 1993
Mercedes Lackey, *Born to Run*, 1992
    Larry Dixon, co-author
Mercedes Lackey, *Summoned to Tourney*, 1992
    Ellen Guon, co-author
Mercedes Lackey, *Wheels of Fire*, 1992
    Mark Shepherd, co-author
Susan Palwick, *Flying in Place*, 1992
Nancy Springer, *The Friendship Song*, 1992

---

**4863**

**ELIZABETH ANN SCARBOROUGH**

## The Godmother's Apprentice

(New York: Ace, 1995)

**Story type:** Fantasy (Light Fantasy; Legend)
**Major character(s):** Felicity Fortune, Mythical Creature (fairy godmother); Snohomish "Sno" Quantrill, Apprentice, Traveler
**Time period(s):** 1990s
**Locale(s):** Ireland

**Summary:** When Felicity Fortune undertakes the task of teaching Snohomish Quantrill to become a fairy godmother, Sno must travel to Ireland to learn the roots of the craft. Journal entries interweave contemporary action and Celtic lore.

**Other books you might like:**
Chester Anderson, *The Butterfly Kid*, 1967
Gael Baudino, *Strands of Sunlight*, 1994
Maya Kaathryn Bohnhoff, *The Meri*, 1992
Esther Friesner, *Wishing Season*, 1993
Jody Lynn Nye, *Mythology Abroad*, 1991
S.P. Somtow, *The Wizard's Apprentice*, 1993

## 4864

### ELIZABETH ANN SCARBOROUGH

## *The Godmother's Web*

(New York: Ace, 1998)

**Story type:** Fantasy (Contemporary; Quest)
**Major character(s):** Cindy Ellis, Horse Trainer; Grandma Webster, Indian, Religious
**Time period(s):** 1990s
**Locale(s):** Arizona; Navajo Nation, Southwest

**Summary:** Cindy expects her trip will bring only a change of scenery and an opportunity to help a friend by training a horse. When she casually befriends a weary traveler, she journeys into a world of magic and experiences unexpected growth in the Navajo Nation.

**Other books you might like:**
Chester Anderson, *The Butterfly Kid*, 1967
Gael Baudino, *Strands of Sunlight*, 1994
Charles de Lint, *Our Lady of the Harbour*, 1991
Alan Dean Foster, *Cyber Way*, 1990
Jody Lynn Nye, *The Magic Touch*, 1996

## 4865

### ELIZABETH ANN SCARBOROUGH

## *The Healer's War*

(New York: Bantam Spectra, 1989)

**Story type:** Fantasy (Contemporary)
**Series:** Healer's War
**Major character(s):** Kitty McCulley, Nurse, Military Personnel (Lieutenant)
**Time period(s):** 1960s
**Locale(s):** Vietnam

**Summary:** One of Kitty's patients, a Vietnamese holy man, gives her an amulet that gives her the power to touch people in a way that gives meaning to life in the midst of war. When Kitty is stranded in enemy-held jungle with a child, the amulet's power saves her sanity, and her life.

**Other books you might like:**
Gustav Hasford, *The Short Timers*, 1987
Bruce McAllister, *Dream Baby*, 1989
Peter Straub, *Koko*, 1989

## 4866

### ELIZABETH ANN SCARBOROUGH

## *Last Refuge*

(New York: Bantam Spectra, 1992)

**Story type:** Fantasy (Post-Disaster; Religious)
**Series:** Healer's War
**Major character(s):** Chime Cincinnati, Guardian (bodhissatva), Religious (guide)
**Time period(s):** 22nd century
**Locale(s):** Shambala, Tibet

**Summary:** Shambala's reincarnated guardian protector hears the call of souls wishing entrance to Shambala. On reaching adulthood, Chime decides to continue her ancient duty of guiding enlightened individuals to the hidden realm. Chime ventures outside the haven into a land devastated by nuclear war where evil spirits attempt to thwart her mission. Sequel to *Nothing Sacred*.

**Other books you might like:**
Suzette Haden Elgin, *Twelve Fair Kingdoms*, 1981
James Hilton, *Lost Horizon*, 1933
Marc Laidlaw, *Neon Lotus*, 1988
Kim Stanley Robinson, *Escape From Kathmandu*, 1989
Geoff Ryman, *The Unconquered Country*, 1986
Terri Windling, *Life on the Border*, 1991
   editor

## 4867

### ELIZABETH ANN SCARBOROUGH

## *Nothing Sacred*

(New York: Doubleday Foundation, 1991)

**Story type:** Fantasy (Contemporary; Post-Disaster)
**Series:** Healer's War
**Major character(s):** Viveka "Viv" Jeng Vanachek, Military Personnel, Cartographer; Ama "Ama-la" Terton, Doctor, Guardian (Bodhisattva); Nyima Wu, Actress (journalist), Military Personnel (POW camp commandant)
**Time period(s):** 2070s
**Locale(s):** Shambala, Tibet

**Summary:** The story unfolds through Viveka's journal entries begun after an ill-fated first mission. When captured, Viveka and other captives march through the Himalaya Mountains to an isolated POW camp where they work on rebuilding an ancient lamasary. As weeks go by Viveka learns that the site and its occupants may be the last and best hope for the survival of humanity. This book follows *The Healer's War* (1989).

**Other books you might like:**
Diana G. Gallagher, *The Alien Dark*, 1990
James Hilton, *Lost Horizon*, 1933
Marc Laidlaw, *Neon Lotus*, 1988
A. Merritt, *Dwellers in the Mirage*, 1932
Ayn Rand, *Atlas Shrugged*, 1957
Kim Stanley Robinson, *Escape From Kathmandu*, 1989
Geoff Ryman, *The Unconquered Country*, 1986
Dan Simmons, *Hyperion*, 1989
Sheri S. Tepper, *Grass*, 1989
Vernor Vinge, *The Peace War*, 1984

## 4868

### ELIZABETH ANN SCARBOROUGH

## *Phantom Banjo*

(New York: Bantam Spectra, 1991)

**Story type:** Fantasy (Magic Conflict; Quest)
**Series:** Songkiller Saga
**Major character(s):** Willie MacKai, Musician; Julianne Martin, Musician; Augusta "Gussie" Turner, Saloon Keeper/Owner
**Time period(s):** 1990s
**Locale(s):** United States; Hell

**Summary:** Once upon a time, "all the devils in the world" decided that folk music was impeding their mission of making the human race completely miserable. When the Chairdevil put his plan into action, folk musicians began to find themselves in trouble with the IRS, unemployed, or in trouble with the law, their recordings and sheet music "accidentally" destroyed, and the words forgotten. When musician Sam Hawthorne dies suddenly, his magic banjo ends up in the hands of retired musician Willie MacKai who sets out to learn the truth, aided by the banjo and his friends and hindered by the Devils.

**Other books you might like:**
Eleanor Arnason, *Daughter of the Bear King*, 1987
Emma Bull, *War for the Oaks*, 1987
Mercedes Lackey, *Knight of Ghosts and Shadows*, 1990
    Ellen Guon, co-author
C.S. Lewis, *The Screwtape Letters*, 1942
R.A. MacAvoy, *Twisting the Rope*, 1986

**4869**

**ELIZABETH ANN SCARBOROUGH**

### Picking the Ballad's Bones

(New York: Bantam Spectra, 1991)

**Story type:** Fantasy (Magic Conflict; Quest)
**Series:** Songkiller Saga
**Major character(s):** Willie MacKai, Musician; Augusta "Gussie" Turner, Saloon Keeper/Owner; Sir Walter Scott, Historical Figure, Spirit
**Time period(s):** 1990s
**Locale(s):** Scotland; England; Hell

**Summary:** The forces of evil make progress in their war against folk music, but a small band of musicians, following the musical hints of a magical banjo, have arrived in Great Britain to find the originals of the songs which are disappearing in the United States. They find allies in the ghosts of Sir Walter Scott and his wizard ancestor, Michael Scott, and Torchy Burns, a.k.a. Debauchery Devil, a.k.a. Queen of Faerie. She arranges a spell that will allow them to go back and learn the ballads by re-living the situations that inspired them, thereby recovering the songs, if they can survive.

**Other books you might like:**
Margaret Ball, *The Shadow Gate*, 1990
R.A. MacAvoy, *Damiano*, 1983
R.A. MacAvoy, *Damiano's Lute*, 1984
Janet Morris, *Heroes in Hell*, 1986
Clifford D. Simak, *Out of Their Minds*, 1970

**4870**

**ELIZABETH ANN SCARBOROUGH**

### Strum Again?

(New York: Bantam Spectra, 1992)

**Story type:** Fantasy (Magic Conflict; Contemporary)
**Series:** Songkiller Saga
**Major character(s):** Willie MacKai, Musician; Julianne Martin, Musician; Debauchery Devil/Torchy Burns, Mythical Creature, Demon
**Time period(s):** 1990s
**Locale(s):** Southwest

**Summary:** Willie MacKai and his fellow musicians have returned to the United States with a renewed stock of songs to sing, but they encounter trouble getting people interested in folk music. While the Chairdevil and his minions wreak havoc with tornadoes, floods and serial killers, Willie strikes a deal with the debauchery devil, formerly the Queen of Faerie, agreeing to use Willie as her sacrifice which pays her overdue tithe to Hell. With a magic mandolin made from the broken remains of the phantom banjo, Willie's friends gather on Midsummer's Eve for the final showdown with the forces of evil.

**Other books you might like:**
Gael Baudino, *Gossamer Axe*, 1990
Emma Bull, *War for the Oaks*, 1987

Pamela Dean, *Tam Lin*, 1991
John M. Ford, *How Much for Just the Planet?*, 1987
R.A. MacAvoy, *Twisting the Rope*, 1986
Anne McCaffrey, *Crystal Singer*, 1982
Elizabeth Marie Pope, *The Perilous Gard*, 1974

**4871**

**ELIZABETH ANN SCARBOROUGH**, Editor
**MARTIN H. GREENBERG**, Co-Editor

### Warrior Princesses

(New York: DAW, 1998)

**Story type:** Fantasy (Anthology)

**Summary:** This anthology contains 20 original stories of female warriors in fantasy worlds, all of whom are members of royal families. Contributors include Elizabeth Moon, Ru Emerson, Megan Lindholm, Jane Yolen, Esther Friesner, and John Helfers.

**Other books you might like:**
Lynn Abbey, *The Black Flame*, 1980
Ru Emerson, *The Princess of Flames*, 1986
Ron Miller, *Hearts and Armor*, 1992
C.L. Moore, *Jirel of Joiry*, 1969
Tamora Pierce, *In the Hand of the Goddess*, 1984

**4872**

**FRANK SCHAEFER**

### Whose Song Is Sung

(New York: Tor, 1996)

**Story type:** Fantasy (Legend; Adventure)
**Major character(s):** Musculus Herodes Formosus, Adventurer, Handicapped (dwarf); Beowulf, Hero, Adventurer; Grundbur, Monster
**Time period(s):** Indeterminate Past
**Locale(s):** Europe; Middle East

**Summary:** After a lowly birth and rise to a position of power, Musculus loses Imperial favor in Byzantium and finds himself sold into slavery. His subsequent odyssey leads to Northern Europe where he meets Beowulf and shares his travels.

**Other books you might like:**
Frans G. Bengtsson, *The Long Ships*, 1954
John Gardner, *Grendel*, 1971
Parke Godwin, *The Tower of Beowulf*, 1995
Stephan Grundy, *Rhinegold*, 1994
Harry Harrison, *The Hammer and the Cross*, 1993
    John Holm, co-author

**4873**

**STUART DAVID SCHIFF**, Editor

### The Best of Whispers

(Baltimore: Borderlands Press, 1994)

**Story type:** Horror (Anthology)

**Summary:** The 23 stories gathered here represent the cream of *Whispers*, the semi-professional magazine and anthology series published between 1972 and 1987 that forged a link between modern fiction of the pre- and postwar years and the contemporary horror movement. Included are two World Fantasy Award-winning stories, Karl Edward Wagner's "Sticks" and Alan Ryan's "The Bones Wizard"; Steve Rasnic Tem's British Fantasy Award-winning

"Leaks"; Hugh Cave's sea monster tale, "From the Lower Deeps"; David Schow's tale of a haunted movie theatre, "One for the Horrors"; Dennis Etchison's tale of medical horror, "The Dead Line"; David Campton's story of a disabled young girl's strange playmate, "At the Bottom of the Garden"; David Drake's dark heroic fantasy, "The Barrow Troll"; Ramsey Campbell's Christmas chiller, "The Chimney"; the original version of Ray Bradbury's "The Screaming Woman"; and the original short novel version of Lucius Shepard's vampire tale "The Golden." Five stories are original to the book.

**Other books you might like:**

Charles L. Grant, *The Best of Shadows*, 1988
  editor
David B. Silva, *Best of The Horror Show*, 1992
  editor

---

**4874**

**GERALD A. SCHILLER**

### Deadly Dreams

(Fairfax Station, Virginia: Intercontinental Publishing, 1996)

**Story type:** Horror (Mystery)
**Major character(s):** Denise Burton, Secretary; Richard Kramer, Scientist (biologist); Rogers Kennison, Journalist
**Time period(s):** 1990s (1996)
**Locale(s):** Chatsworth, California

**Summary:** Denise Burton suspects that her horrifying nightmares of lying on an operating table while surgeons systematically remove her internal organs is linked to her job at Marikem Industries, a chemical company. Her investigations reveal a cover-up of a biological experiment that used human beings as guinea pigs. First novel.

**Other books you might like:**

Kevin J. Anderson, *Ground Zero*, 1995
Robin Cook, *Coma*, 1977
Lyle Howard, *Mr. Sandman*, 1995
Dean R. Koontz, *The House of Thunder*, 1982
F. Paul Wilson, *Implant*, 1995

---

**4875**

**VIVIAN SCHILLING**

### Sacred Prey

(Sherman Oaks, California: Truman Press, 1994)

**Story type:** Horror (Supernatural Vengeance)
**Major character(s):** Adam Claiborne, Businessman; Monique Sinclair, Entertainer (barroom singer); Kyle Claiborne, Criminal
**Time period(s):** 1990s (1994)
**Locale(s):** New Orleans, Louisiana

**Summary:** When loan shark Adam Claiborne hunts down and shoots a man with an outstanding debt to him in the swamps of Louisiana, he incurs the wrath of voodoo powers to which his victim was privy. Suddenly, Adam finds himself trapped inside his quarry's body, struggling to avoid pursuit and convince others that he is not who he appears to be. This is the author's first novel.

**Other books you might like:**

Rene Belletto, *Machine*, 1993
Harlan Ellison, *Mefisto in Onyx*, 1993
Damon Knight, *Mind Switch*, 1963
Richard Matheson, *7 Past Midnight*, 1992
Rod Serling, *The Season to Be Wary*, 1967

---

**4876**

**LAWRENCE SCHIMEL**, Editor
**MARTIN H. GREENBERG**, Co-Editor

### Blood Lines: Vampire Stories From New England

(Nashville, Tennessee: Cumberland House, 1997)

**Story type:** Horror (Anthology; Vampire Story)
**Locale(s):** New England

**Summary:** Ten tales of vampires and vampirism set in the New England states. Included are Hugh Cave's "The Brotherhood of Blood" and Earl Pierce, Jr.'s "The Doom of the House of Duryea," both of which feature families with hereditary vampire curses, and Kristine Kathryn Rusch's "The Beautiful, the Damned," a vampire riff on F. Scott Fitzgerald's *The Great Gatsby*. Nontraditional vampire stories include Mary E. Wilkins Freeman's "Luella Miller," about a woman whose incessant demands on others sap their vitality, and H.P. Lovecraft's "The Shunned House," about a house that absorbs the essence of its victims.

**Other books you might like:**

Ellen Datlow, *Blood Is Not Enough*, 1989
  editor
Stephen Jones, *The Mammoth Book of Vampires*, 1992
  editor
Frank D. McSherry Jr., *New England Ghosts*, 1990
  Charles G. Waugh and Martin H. Greenberg, co-editors

---

**4877**

**LAWRENCE SCHIMEL**, Editor
**MARTIN H. GREENBERG**, Co-Editor

### Camelot Fantastic

(New York: DAW, 1998)

**Story type:** Fantasy (Anthology)

**Summary:** These seven original stories are set in the world of King Arthur and the Knights of the Round Table. The contributors are Fiona Patton, Nancy Springer, Brian Stableford, Mike Ashley, Ian McDowell, Gregory Maguire, and Rosemary Edghill.

**Other books you might like:**

Marion Zimmer Bradley, *The Mists of Avalon*, 1982
Vera Chapman, *The King's Damosel*, 1978
Helen Hollick, *The Kingmaking*, 1995
Sanders Anne Laubenthal, *Excalibur*, 1973
Stephen R. Lawhead, *Arthur*, 1989

---

**4878**

**LAWRENCE SCHIMEL**

### The Drag Queen of Elfland

(Cambridge, Massachusetts: Ultra Violet, 1997)

**Story type:** Horror (Collection)

**Summary:** Seventeen tales of fantasy and horror. Highlights include "Black Sounds," a vampire tale set in Spain; "Old as a Rose in Bloom," a poignant ghost story; "Coming out of the Broom Closet," an amusing story of sexual and supernatural identity; and the sword and sorceress tales, "Barbarian Legacy," "Crow Feathers" and "In Sheep's Clothing."

**Other books you might like:**
Nina Kiriki Hoffman, *Legacy of Fire*, 1990
Joel Lane, *The Earth Wire and Other Stories*, 1994
Pat Murphy, *Points of Departure*, 1990
W.H. Pugmire, *Tales of Sesqua Valley*, 1997
Jessica Amanda Salmonson, *A Silver Thread of Madness*, 1989

**4879**

**LAWRENCE SCHIMEL**, Editor
**MARTIN H. GREENBERG**, Co-Editor

## Fields of Blood: Vampire Stories of the Heartland

(Nashville, Tennessee: Cumberland House, 1998)

**Story type:** Horror (Anthology)
**Series:** American Vampire
**Locale(s):** Midwest

**Summary:** These ten vampire stories are all set in the Midwest. Selections include P.N. Elrod's ''A Night at the Horse Opera,'' in which vampire detective Jack Fleming teams up with Harpo Marx on a case; Henry Kuttner's ''Masquerade,'' about a man and woman who make an unscheduled stop at a house full of vampires and other weird creatures; and Tina L. Jens's ''A 12-Step Program (for the Corporally Challenged),'' about a self-help program for vampires who want to resist drinking blood.

**Other books you might like:**
Richard Dalby, *Vampire Stories*, 1992
   editor
Ellen Datlow, *Blood Is Not Enough*, 1989
   editor
Stephen Jones, *The Mammoth Book of Vampires*, 1992
   editor
Alan Ryan, *Vampires: Two Centuries of Great Vampire Stories*, 1987
   editor
Robert Weinberg, *100 Vicious Little Vampire Stories*, 1995
   Stefan Dziemianowicz, Martin H. Greenberg, co-editors

**4880**

**LAWRENCE SCHIMEL**, Editor
**MARTIN H. GREENBERG**, Co-Editor

## Southern Blood: Vampire Stories From the American South

(Nashville, Tennessee: Cumberland House, 1997)

**Story type:** Horror (Anthology; Vampire Story)
**Locale(s):** South

**Summary:** One dozen tales of vampires and vampirism set in the American south. Many work variations on the traditional vampire theme, including Brian Hodge's ''Like a Pilgrim to the Shrine,'' which pits a punk vampire against Count Dracula; William Tenn's ''She Only Goes out at Night,'' which devises a scientific explanation and cure for vampirism; Dan Simmons's ''Carrion Comfort,'' in which vampires feed on the violent deaths of victims; and Fred Chappell's ''The Flame,'' in which vampires are drawn like moths to a flame by a woman whose beauty casts a vampiric spell over them.

**Other books you might like:**
Ellen Datlow, *Blood Is Not Enough*, 1989
   editor

Richard Gilliam, *Confederacy of the Dead*, 1993
   Edward E. Kramer and Martin H. Greenberg, co-editors
Stephen Jones, *The Mammoth Book of Vampires*, 1992
   editor

**4881**

**LAWRENCE SCHIMEL**, Editor
**MARTIN H. GREENBERG**, Co-Editor

## Streets of Blood: Vampire Stories From New York City

(Nashville, Tennessee: Cumberland House, 1998)

**Story type:** Horror (Anthology)
**Series:** American Vampire
**Locale(s):** New York, New York

**Summary:** These 13 vampire stories share New York City settings. Selections include Chet Williamson's ''To Feel Another's Woe,'' about a vampire actress on the New York stage; Alan Ryan's ''Following the Way,'' which draws haunting parallels between vampirism and the priesthood; and Chelsea Quinn Yarbro's ''Seat Partner,'' a tale of her vampire hero Count Saint-Germain.

**Other books you might like:**
Richard Dalby, *Vampire Stories*, 1992
   editor
Ellen Datlow, *Blood Is Not Enough*, 1989
   editor
Stephen Jones, *The Mammoth Book of Vampires*, 1992
   editor
Alan Ryan, *Vampires: Two Centuries of Great Vampire Stories*, 1987
   editor
Robert Weinberg, *100 Vicious Little Vampire Stories*, 1995
   Stefan Dziemianowicz, Martin H. Greenberg, co-editors

**4882**

**LAWRENCE SCHIMEL**, Editor

## Things Invisible to See: Gay and Lesbian Tales of Magic Realism

(Cambridge, Massachusetts: Circlet Press, 1998)

**Story type:** Fantasy (Anthology; Magic Realism)

**Summary:** These 11 original stories of magic and surrealism each deal with gay or lesbian issues as well as fantasy. The contributors include Martha Soukup, Nancy Springer, Michelle Sagara West, Brian M. Thomsen, and others. Strong sexual content.

**Other books you might like:**
Jennifer DiMarco, *Escape to the Wind*, 1993
Catherine Ennis, *To the Lightning*, 1988
Caroline Forbes, *The Needle on Full*, 1985
Katherine V. Forrest, *Dreams and Swords*, 1987
Nancy Tyler Glenn, *Clicking Stones*, 1989

**4883**

**DAN SCHMIDT**

## Silent Scream

(New York: Leisure, 1998)

**Story type:** Horror (Wild Talents)

**Major character(s):** John Wilkins, Journalist; Mike Wilkins, Alcoholic; Sam Watterson, Journalist
**Time period(s):** 1990s (1998)
**Locale(s):** Glendale, Illinois; Philadelphia, Pennsylvania

**Summary:** Having acquired a magic medallion that endows him with formidable psychic powers, Mike Wilkins embarks on a spree of revenge against all those who have humiliated him, sharpening his abilities to confront his brother, whom he blames for his sloppy decline into alcoholism and dissipation. A first novel.

**Other books you might like:**
John Farris, *The Fury*, 1976
Dean R. Koontz, *Dragon Tears*, 1993
Tom Piccirilli, *Dark Father*, 1990
T. Lucien Wright, *Blood Brothers*, 1992

---

**4884**

**DENNIS SCHMIDT**

## Labyrinth

(New York: Ace Books, 1989)

**Story type:** Science Fiction (Space Opera)
**Series:** Questioner Trilogy
**Major character(s):** Seeker, Alien; Bilrog, Alien
**Time period(s):** Indeterminate Future
**Locale(s):** Labyrinth, Planet—Imaginary

**Summary:** The dangerous and mysterious sentient planet Labyrinth, used by the Galactic Empire to train its elite police force, seems a very different place to each trainee, depending largely on that person's attitude towards existence.

**Other books you might like:**
Orson Scott Card, *Ender's Game*, 1985
Harry Harrison, *Deathworld*, 1960
Stanislaw Lem, *Solaris*, 1971
Larry Niven, *The Legacy of Heorot*, 1987
    Jerry Pournelle and Steven Barnes, co-authors
Dave Wolverton, *On My Way to Paradise*, 1989

---

**4885**

**DAVID J. SCHOW**

## Black Leather Required

(Shingletown, California: Mark V. Ziesing, 1994)

**Story type:** Horror (Collection)

**Summary:** This third collection of short fiction by the leading exponent of splatterpunk contains 13 previously uncollected short stories, including three original to the volume. Among the best are ''Jerry's Kids Meet Wormboy,'' a deliriously graphic tale of a social misfit defending himself against a horde of ravenous zombies; ''Kamikaze Butterflies,'' in which people from the present travel back to the prehistoric age to deliberately change the course of history; the vampire tale, ''A Week in the Unlife''; ''The Shaft,'' a tale of urban horror that eventually grew into the author's second novel; ''Bad Guy Hats,'' a tale of ultraviolence; and a moving tale of love and redemption, ''Pitt Night at the Lewiston Boneyard.''

**Other books you might like:**
Joe R. Lansdale, *By Bizarre Hands*, 1989
Richard Christian Matheson, *Scars and Other Distinguishing Marks*, 1987
John Skipp, *Dead Lines*, 1990
    Craig Spector
Lucy Taylor, *Close to the Bone*, 1993

---

**4886**

**DAVID J. SCHOW**

## Crypt Orchids

(Burton, Michigan: Subterranean Press, 1998)

**Story type:** Horror (Collection)

**Summary:** Twelve previously uncollected stories, three original to the volume, all hard-edged explorations of survival in the unsentimental and loveless modern world. Serial killers are the common theme of ''Pick Me Up,'' a semi-satirical tale in which a truck driver and the hitchhiker he picks up discover that they are both murderers trying to kill one another, and ''The Incredibly True Facts in the Case,'' a meditation on Jack the Ripper. ''Gills,'' ''Action,'' and ''Seeing Things'' all examine the breakdown between cinematic illusion and reality. ''Jeff and Linda,'' ''Penetration,'' and ''A Punch in the Donut'' are studies of extreme emotional and sexual relationships. Robert Bloch, who supplies the introduction, is eulogized in ''(Melodrama),'' a gentle tale of an aging TV monster movie host. Published in a signed limited edition only.

**Other books you might like:**
Poppy Z. Brite, *Swamp Foetus*, 1993
Harlan Ellison, *Slippage*, 1997
Dennis Etchison, *The Dark Country*, 1982
John Shirley, *Black Butterflies: A Flock on the Dark Side*, 1998
Karl Edward Wagner, *Why Not You and I*, 1987

---

**4887**

**DAVID J. SCHOW**

## The Kill Riff

(New York: Tor, 1989)

**Story type:** Horror (Psychological Suspense)
**Major character(s):** Lucas Ellington, Parent (Bereaved father); Gabriel Stannard, Singer (Rock and roll)
**Time period(s):** 1980s (References to 1978)
**Locale(s):** United States

**Summary:** After the death of his daughter at a concert of the rock group Whip Hand, Lucas Ellington vows revenge and sets about systematically to get it. Ellington's ultimate target, lead singer Gabriel Stannard, understands that he is the prey and looks forward to the confrontation.

**Other books you might like:**
George R.R. Martin, *The Armageddon Rag*, 1983
Robert R. McCammon, *Mine*, 1990
John Skipp, *The Scream*, 1986
    Craig Spector, co-author

---

**4888**

**DAVID J. SCHOW**

## Lost Angels

(New York: Onyx, 1990)

**Story type:** Horror (Collection)

**Summary:** Among the five stories in this collection by a primary exponent of ''splatterpunk'' horror fiction are the sentimental World Fantasy Award-winning tale ''Red Light,'' the ''Twilight-Zone'' inspired fantasy ''Pamela's Get,'' the occult thriller ''Brass,'' and an upbeat story about the love of horror films, ''Monster Movies.'' All but the final story are concerned with the loss of love in the modern world. Introduction by Richard Christian Matheson.

**Other books you might like:**
Dennis Etchison, *Cutting Edge*, 1986
Douglas E. Winter, *Prime Evil*, 1988

---

**4889**

### DAVID J. SCHOW

## *Seeing Red*

(New York: Tor, 1990)

**Story type:** Horror (Collection)

**Summary:** Fourteen stories by a self-confessed "splatterpunk" writer. Gory, ironical, extreme, often funny, saturated with paranoia, the stories find horror in the contemporary world, especially in such off-beat locations as neo-Gothic hotels, cockroach infested movie theaters, rock tours, Hollywood, Beverly Hills, and the pages of pulp magazines.

**Other books you might like:**
Harlan Ellison, *The Essential Ellison: A 35-Year Retrospective*, 1987
Dennis Etchison, *The Dark Country*, 1982
Dennis Etchison, *Red Dreams*, 1984
George R.R. Martin, *Songs the Dead Men Sing*, 1983

---

**4890**

### HOWARD SCHWARTZ

## *Lilith's Cave: Jewish Tales of the Supernatural*

(New York: Oxford University Press, 1991)

**Story type:** Horror (Collection)

**Summary:** Originally published in 1988, this excellent collection of 50 traditional Jewish folktales retold by Schwartz includes the title story, "The Demon of the Waters," "The Homunculus of Maimonodes," the famous "Rabbi Loew and the Angel of Death," and other tales and fables leavened with the religious beliefs of the European Yiddish community from the last eight centuries. Schwartz provides an index, informative introduction, notes and glossary of terms.

**Other books you might like:**
Iona Opie, *The Classic Fairy Tales*, 1974
    Peter Opie, co-author
Isaac Bashevis Singer, *Collected Stories*, 1982
Jack Zipes, *Spells of Enchantment*, 1991

---

**4891**

### DARRELL SCHWEITZER

## *Transients and Other Disquieting Tales*

(Buffalo, New York: Ganley, 1993)

**Story type:** Horror (Collection)

**Summary:** These 15 stories (three written in collaboration) explore a variety of dark experiences for their horror content. "Transients," "Peeling It Off," "Jason, Come Home," "Soft" and "Leaving" are all dark fantasies about the terrifying psychological dislocations that come from feelings of loss and alienation. "Clocks" and "The Paloverde Lodge" (written with Jason Van Hollander) are poignant tales about the pathological persistence of love, while "The Man

Who Wasn't Nice to Pumpkin Head Dolls" is a satire on consumerism and "The Children of Lommos" (written with John Gregory Betancourt) is a powerful traditional tale of supernatural vengeance.

**Other books you might like:**
Donald Burleson, *Lemon Drops and Other Horrors*, 1993
Charles L. Grant, *Tales From the Nightside*, 1989
Jessica Amanda Salmonson, *John Collier and Fredric Brown Went Quarrelling through My Head*, 1989

---

**4892**

### CHERI SCOTCH

## *The Werewolf's Touch*

(New York: Diamond, 1993)

**Story type:** Horror (Werewolf Story)
**Major character(s):** Andrew Marley, Werewolf, Religious (Episcopal priest); Angela Winfield, Professor, Anthropologist; Simon Spencer, Doctor (psychiatrist)
**Time period(s):** 1960s (1965)
**Locale(s):** New Orleans, Louisiana

**Summary:** In this continuation of the saga begun in *The Werewolf's Kiss* (1992), Andrew Marley, firstborn child of the latest generation of the Marley family, discovers that he is afflicted with the curse of lycanthropy as a result of his grandfather's murder of a voodoo priestess almost a century before. Andrew spends most of the story trying to avoid the same fate as his father, who killed himself upon discovering that he too had inherited the werewolf taint.

**Other books you might like:**
Michael Cadnum, *St. Peter's Wolf*, 1991
Jane Toombs, *Under the Shadow*, 1992
Chelsea Quinn Yarbro, *The Godforsaken*, 1983

---

**4893**

### JEFFERSON SCOTT

## *Terminal Logic*

(Sisters, Oregon: Multnomah Publishers, 1997)

**Story type:** Science Fiction (Techno-Thriller; Theological)
**Major character(s):** Ethan Hamilton, Computer Expert; Jordan Hamilton, Child, Computer Expert; Yoseph, Artificial Intelligence
**Time period(s):** 2000s (2006)
**Locale(s):** Cyberspace; Tyler, Texas; Washington, District of Columbia

**Summary:** After vanquishing a homicidal hacker, Ethan builds a new home in rural Tyler, designed to completely repel a hacker attack. When Ethan finds stray AIs loose in the net he realizes he may have another battle to face. Unfortunately his home proves vulnerable to Yoseph, who targets Ethan as an enemy, not understanding the permanency of death for humans.

**Other books you might like:**
Bruce Bethke, *Headcrash*, 1995
James Gunn, *The Joy Machine*, 1996
    Theodore Sturgeon, co-author
Lisa Mason, *Arachne*, 1990
Mel Odom, *Lethal Interface*, 1992
Joan Slonczewski, *Daughter of Elysium*, 1993
Neal Stephenson, *Snow Crash*, 1992

## 4894

### MELISSA SCOTT

## Burning Bright

(New York: Tor, 1993)

**Story type:** Science Fiction (Political; Adventure)
**Major character(s):** Quin Lioe, Spacewoman (starpilot), Computer Expert (gamer); Illario "Ambidexter" Ransome, Computer Expert, Artist; Damian Chrestil, Alien (hsai), Businessman
**Time period(s):** Indeterminate Future
**Locale(s):** Burning Bright, Planet—Imaginary

**Summary:** While her ship undergoes maintenance at Burning Bright, a human and alien center for virtual reality role-playing gaming, Quin Lioe premieres her new gaming scenario. Events on Burning Bright begin to resemble the intrigues of Lioe's game as she finds herself involved in a struggle between commercial and royal interests.

**Other books you might like:**
C.J. Cherryh, *Serpent's Reach*, 1980
Jean Mark Gawron, *Dream of Glass*, 1993
Rebecca Ore, *Becoming Alien*, 1987
Neal Stephenson, *Snow Crash*, 1992
Jack Williamson, *Mazeway*, 1990

## 4895

### MELISSA SCOTT

## Dreaming Metal

(New York: Tor, 1997)

**Story type:** Science Fiction (Alternate Intelligence; Arts)
**Major character(s):** Celinde "Cissy" Fortune, Magician (conjurer), Technician; Reverdy Jian, Pilot (spaceship), Lesbian; Fanning "Fan" Jones, Musician, Cousin
**Time period(s):** Indeterminate Future
**Locale(s):** Persephone, Planet—Imaginary; Landage, Fictional City

**Summary:** Fortune seeks a very sophisticated controller for her new trick, picking up two spaceship controllers and putting them together. It works amazingly well, and Fortune renames it "Celeste." Part of Celeste comes from Reverdy who sells it because she no longer trusts Spelvin matrix technology after Manfred, another Spelvin matrix, almost killed her. To Reverdy, all Spelvins feel like potential artificial intelligences (AIs), while Persephone society still suffers from the riots resulting when Manfred, a Spelvin thought to be an AI, tried to kill its crew. Sequel to *Dreamships*.

**Other books you might like:**
David Brin, *Earth*, 1990
Robert A. Heinlein, *The Moon Is a Harsh Mistress*, 1996
Steve Perry, *The Trinity Vector*, 1996
Alis A. Rasmussen, *Revolution's Shore*, 1990
John Varley, *Steel Beach*, 1992
Vernor Vinge, *A Fire upon the Deep*, 1992

## 4896

### MELISSA SCOTT

## Dreamships

(New York: Tor, 1992)

**Story type:** Science Fiction (Alternate Intelligence; Political)

**Major character(s):** Reverdy Jian, Pilot (spaceship), Lesbian; Meredalia Mitexi, Computer Expert; Manfred, Artificial Intelligence (shipboard computer)
**Time period(s):** Indeterminate Future
**Locale(s):** Persephone, Planet—Imaginary; *Young Lord Byron*, Spaceship; Refuge, Planet—Imaginary

**Summary:** The Coolies, abandoned indentured workers, violently oppose Dreampeace, an organization promoting the rights of AI's and threatening the Coolies' livelihood. Jian, a Coolie sympathizer given only sketchy specifications for the ship's computer, reluctantly accepts the contract to pilot Mitexi to Refuge to find her brother, the founder of Dreampeace and creator of Manfred. Manfred seems the best ship's controller Jian has ever worked with and possibly the sentient machine Dreampeace needs.

**Other books you might like:**
Orson Scott Card, *Xenocide*, 1991
Jeffrey A. Carver, *Dragons in the Stars*, 1992
Glen Cook, *The Dragon Never Sleeps*, 1988
Edward Gibson, *In the Wrong Hands*, 1992
Colin Greenland, *Take Back Plenty*, 1992
Dan Simmons, *Hyperion*, 1989
David Alexander Smith, *Homecoming*, 1990

## 4897

### MELISSA SCOTT

## Mighty Good Road

(New York: Baen, 1990)

**Story type:** Science Fiction (Adventure)
**Major character(s):** Gwynne Heikki, Businesswoman (salvage expert), Adventurer; Sebasten-Janurias, Pilot; Galler Heikki, Businessman (executive of Lo-Moth Corporati)
**Time period(s):** Indeterminate Future
**Locale(s):** Iadara, Planet—Imaginary

**Summary:** Gwynne Heikki returns to her home planet under contract to salvage a downed craft when a previous contractor fails to recover a prototype of the device which will allow rapid development of faster-than-light spacecraft. Investigating the crash site, Gwynne finds the craft was shot down and the prototype device taken. Returning to her home base Gwynne finds her contract cancelled, but doggedly pursues the device, involving herself in unexpected corporate intrigue with her brother, whom she'd hoped never to meet again.

**Other books you might like:**
Melisa C. Michaels, *Skirmish*, 1985
Alis A. Rasmussen, *A Passage of Stars*, 1990
Alis A. Rasmussen, *The Price of Ransom*, 1990
Alis A. Rasmussen, *Revolution's Shore*, 1990
James H. Schmitz, *The Demon Breed*, 1968

## 4898

### MELISSA SCOTT

## Night Sky Mine

(New York: Tor, 1996)

**Story type:** Science Fiction (Gay/Lesbian Fiction; Cyberpunk)
**Major character(s):** Ista Kelly, Foundling, Teenager; Rangsey Justin, Computer Expert, Homosexual; Sein Tarasov, Computer Expert (Technical Squad troubleshooter), Homosexual
**Time period(s):** Indeterminate Future
**Locale(s):** Wildnet, Cyberspace; Bestla, Planet—Imaginary

**Summary:** Orphaned during a pirate raid on an asteroid mine, Ista struggles to learn her true identity in a society where one cannot live without an official identity. Her search entails investigating mysterious raids on mining colonies, which the Night Sky Mining Corporation seems to cover up.

**Other books you might like:**
Jack L. Chalker, *The Cybernetic Walrus*, 1995
C.J. Cherryh, *Cyteen*, 1988
Nicola Griffith, *Slow River*, 1995
Joan D. Vinge, *Psion*, 1982
Vernor Vinge, *A Fire upon the Deep*, 1992

**4899**

MELISSA SCOTT
LISA A. BARNETT, Co-Author

*Point of Hopes*

(New York: Tor, 1995)

**Story type:** Fantasy (Mystery; Magic Conflict)
**Major character(s):** Nicolas "Nico" Rathe, Police Officer (pointsman); Philip Eslingen, Military Personnel (retired)
**Time period(s):** Indeterminate
**Locale(s):** Chenedolle, Fictional Country

**Summary:** As Midsummer Faire approaches in the medieval capital of the kingdom, Nicolas Rathe must find the cause of increasing numbers of missing children. The problem seems tied to astrological divinations which portend social upheaval.

**Other books you might like:**
Orson Scott Card, *Lost Boys*, 1992
Pamela Dean, *The Dubious Hills*, 1994
Simon R. Green, *Hawk & Fisher*, 1990
Mickey Zucker Reichert, *Beyond Ragnarok*, 1995
Delia Sherman, *The Porcelain Dove*, 1993
Patricia C. Wrede, *Mairelon the Magician*, 1991

**4900**

MELISSA SCOTT

*Shadow Man*

(New York: Tor, 1995)

**Story type:** Science Fiction (Gay/Lesbian Fiction; Lost Colony)
**Major character(s):** Warreven "Raven" Stiller, Activist, Lawyer; Mhyre Tatian, Businessman; Temelathe Stane, Political Figure (Most Important Man)
**Time period(s):** Indeterminate Future
**Locale(s):** Hara, Planet—Imaginary; Concord Worlds, Interstellar Empire/Federation

**Summary:** After 100 years of contact with the Concord, Hara refuses to join, or even to acknowledge the mutation caused by faster-than-light travel which resulted in five human sexes. A "man" on Hara but a hermaphrodite to the Concord Worlds, Warrenven realizes this lack of recognition of all sexes prevents Haran society from developing. When Temelathe forces Warrenven to run for political office to prevent him from working as an advocate, forces beyond his control cause him to see himself as a hermaphrodite and to fight for recognition of all the sexes.

**Other books you might like:**
Eleanor Arnason, *Ring of Swords*, 1993
David Brin, *Glory Season*, 1993
Octavia E. Butler, *Imago*, 1989
M.J. Engh, *Rainbow Man*, 1993

Ursula K. Le Guin, *The Left Hand of Darkness*, 1969
Alis A. Rasmussen, *The Price of Ransom*, 1990

**4901**

MELISSA SCOTT

*The Shapes of Their Hearts*

(New York, Tor, 1998)

**Story type:** Science Fiction (Alternate Intelligence; Religious)
**Major character(s):** Dr. Anton Sien Hsia Tso, Clone, Businessman (designer pharmaceuticals); Renli DaSilva, Bodyguard, Genetically Altered Being; Anjeillo "Angel" Harijadi, Security Officer, Businessman
**Time period(s):** Indeterminate Future
**Locale(s):** Idun "Eden", Planet—Imaginary; Jericho, Planet—Imaginary

**Summary:** On Eden, the Deity, in the form of the Memoriant which contains the downloaded memories of the prophet who revealed that DNA must not be tampered with, continues to be consulted by the theologians who rule Eden. When an explosion on Jericho proves the result of a degraded copy of the Memoriant, Tso is forced by family interests, despite his status as an abomination, to go to Eden and retrieve a working copy of the Memoriant, which has the ability to evade computer security systems.

**Other books you might like:**
C.S. Friedman, *This Alien Shore*, 1998
Mel Odom, *Lethal Interface*, 1994
Jefferson Scott, *Terminal Logic*, 1997
Dan Simmons, *Hyperion*, 1989
John Varley, *Steel Beach*, 1992

**4902**

MELISSA SCOTT

*Trouble and Her Friends*

(New York: Tor, 1994)

**Story type:** Science Fiction (Gay/Lesbian Fiction; Cyberpunk)
**Major character(s):** India "Trouble" Carless, Computer Expert, Lesbian; Cerise, Computer Expert, Lesbian; Butch van Liesvelt, Computer Expert, Homosexual
**Time period(s):** 22nd century (2100s)
**Locale(s):** Seahaven, New Hampshire

**Summary:** Before the laws changed making their activities illegal, Cerise and Trouble had roamed the nets together. Thereafter Trouble leaves and becomes a syscop, while Cerise becomes a security expert for a large corporation. When Butch warns Trouble that someone, impersonating her and using her old routines to break into other people's spaces, has caused enough problems that Treasury will pursue her, Trouble feels compelled to use her illegal equipment to search the nets for the imposter before Treasury decides to settle for her, the real Trouble.

**Other books you might like:**
Eleanor Arnason, *Ring of Swords*, 1993
Jean Mark Gawron, *Dream of Glass*, 1993
Mel Odom, *Lethal Interface*, 1992
Joan Slonczewski, *A Door into Ocean*, 1986
Neal Stephenson, *Snow Crash*, 1992

## 4903

### CORDELL SCOTTEN

## *Renegade*

(New York: Ace Books, 1989)

**Story type:** Science Fiction (Robot Fiction)
**Series:** Isaac Asimov's Robot City: Robots and Aliens
**Major character(s):** Derec, Amnesiac, Scientist; Ariel Welsh, Heiress
**Time period(s):** Indeterminate Future
**Locale(s):** Robot City, Planet—Imaginary

**Summary:** Derec and Ariel continue their battle against the evil aliens who would destroy Robot City. Scotten's first science fiction novel.

**Other books you might like:**
Isaac Asimov, *The Caves of Steel*, 1954
Isaac Asimov, *The Complete Robot*, 1982
Isaac Asimov, *The Naked Sun*, 1957
Isaac Asimov, *Robots and Empire*, 1985
Isaac Asimov, *The Robots of Dawn*, 1983
Charles Ingrid, *Return Fire*, 1989
    Sand Wars 5
Michael A. Stackpole, *Warrior: Coup*, 1989
    Battletech series
Jack Williamson, *The Humanoids*, 1949

## 4904

### RICHARD F. SEARIGHT

## *The Brain in the Jar and Others*

(West Warwick, Rhode Island: Necronomicon Press, 1992)

**Story type:** Horror (Collection)

**Summary:** This first in a projected series of three volumes collecting the work of a correspondent of H. P. Lovecraft and contributor to the early weird and science fiction pulps brings together 12 poems and five stories, only one of which was previously published. The title story concerns a disembodied brain which develops telekinetic powers. "The Formula" tells of a scientist prevented from developing a formula for cheap atomic energy by the ghost of his uncle, "Rays of Madness" of an alien invasion of Earth, and "In the Dwelling of Madness" of a plot by unscrupulous psychiatrists to deprive an heir of his fortune.

**Other books you might like:**
Arthur J. Burks, *Black Medicine*, 1966
August Derleth, *Harrigan's File*, 1975
Carl Jacobi, *Revelations in Black*, 1947
Frank Belknap Long, *The Hounds of Tindalos*, 1946
Donald Wandrei, *Strange Harvest*, 1965

## 4905

### RICHARD F. SEARIGHT

## *The Sealed Casket and Other Stories*

(West Warwick, Rhode Island: Necronomicon Press, 1996)

**Story type:** Horror (Collection)

**Summary:** The six stories and twelve poems in this collection of work by a correspondent of horror master H.P. Lovecraft run the gamut of fantasy fiction subgenres. "The Sealed Casket," the only previously published story, tells of an invisible vampiric being liberated from an artifact by an unwitting collector. "The Guardian of the Cairn" is a heroic fantasy, and "The Fire-Shapes" and "Terre Venus" science

fiction stories set, respectively, at the South Pole and on the planet Venus. "Switchboard Morse" and "Sit Down" are both mainstream tales with suspense elements. One poem, "The New World," was published in a 1935 issue of the classic pulp magazine, *Weird Tales*. The author's son, Franklyn Searight, who edited the volume, supplies an informative introduction.

**Other books you might like:**
Arthur J. Burks, *Black Medicine*, 1966
August Derleth, *Harrigan's File*, 1975
Carl Jacobi, *Revelations in Black*, 1947
Frank Belknap Long, *The Hounds of Tindalos*, 1946
Donald Wandrei, *Strange Harvest*, 1965

## 4906

### BAIRD SEARLES, Editor
### BRIAN THOMSEN, Co-Editor

## *Halflings, Hobbits, Warrows & Weefolk: A Collection of Tales of Heroes Short in Stature*

(New York: Warner Questar, 1991)

**Story type:** Fantasy (Anthology)

**Summary:** This volume contains a four-page introduction by Baird Searles and nine stories, seven originals plus Maya Kaathryn Bornhoff's "Hobbits," previously published in *Analog*, and Judith Moffett's "The Origin of the Hob," an excerpt of "T. Whinney Moor Thoo Cums at Last," previously published in *Isaac Asimov's Science Fiction*. Other authors are John Dalmas, Charles de Lint, Craig Shaw Gardner, Jody Lynn Nye, Mickey Zucker Reichert, R.A. Salvatore, and Michael Williams.

**Other books you might like:**
Lin Carter, *Dragons, Elves and Heroes*, 1969
    editor
Jack Dann, *Little People!*, 1991
    Gardner Dozois, co-editor
J.R.R. Tolkien, *The Fellowship of the Ring*, 1954
J.R.R. Tolkien, *The Hobbit*, 1938
J.R.R. Tolkien, *The Return of the King*, 1956
J.R.R. Tolkien, *The Two Towers*, 1955

## 4907

### DAVID J. SEARLS

## *Yellow Moon*

(New York: Warner, 1994)

**Story type:** Horror (Apocalyptic Horror; Small Town Horror)
**Major character(s):** Tom Luckinbill, Police Officer (chief); Thad Crocker, Political Figure (mayor); Ben Crocker, Child
**Time period(s):** 1990s (1994)
**Locale(s):** Cleary, Ohio

**Summary:** Heralded by the rising of a sickly yellow moon, a hole opens up in the local baseball field of Cleary, engulfing a group of youngsters. When the boys return, they bring an unearthly power back with them that afflicts the entire town with madness and death.

**Other books you might like:**
Ramsey Campbell, *The Hungry Moon*, 1987
Douglas Clegg, *Goat Dance*, 1989
Michael Green, *The Jimjams*, 1994
John Shirley, *In Darkness Waiting*, 1988
Dan Simmons, *Summer of Night*, 1990

## 4908

### MARK SEBANC

## *Flight to Hollow Mountain*

(Grand Rapids, Michigan: Eerdmans, 1996)

**Story type:** Fantasy (Magic Conflict; Adventure)
**Series:** Talamadh
**Major character(s):** Kal, Teenager, Adventurer; Gelly, Teenager, Adventurer; Wilum, Magician
**Time period(s):** Indeterminate
**Locale(s):** Lammermorn, Fictional Country

**Summary:** Created centuries earlier by King Ardiel's magic harp, the magic spell which binds together the heavens and earth begins to unravel, allowing an evil master to ascend to power.

**Other books you might like:**
David Eddings, *Pawn of Prophecy*, 1982
Terry Goodkind, *Wizard's First Rule*, 1994
L. Dean James, *Summerland*, 1994
Patricia A. McKillip, *The Book of Atrix Wolfe*, 1995
Douglas Niles, *A Breach in the Watershed*, 1995
J.R.R. Tolkien, *The Fellowship of the Ring*, 1954

## 4909

### STEPHEN MICHAEL SECHI, Editor

## *Tales of Talislanta*

(Renton, Washington: Wizards of the Coast, 1992)

**Story type:** Fantasy (Anthology)
**Time period(s):** Indeterminate Past
**Locale(s):** Talislanta, Fictional Country

**Summary:** Contains a two-page preface, a map of Talislanta a five-page introduction and three stories by the editor/creator of the roleplaying game plus stories by Ru Emerson, Lawrence Watt-Evans and four other authors. Set in the *Talislanta* game world.

**Other books you might like:**
Robert N. Charrette, *Never Deal with a Dragon*, 1990
David Cook, *Beyond the Moons*, 1991
Greg Farshtey, *Strange Tales From the Nile Empire*, 1991
　　Greg Gorden and Ed Stark, co-editors
Douglas Kaufman, *Dragons over England*, 1992
　　Ed Stark, co-editor
Ken Rolston, *Extreme Paranoia: Nobody Knows the Trouble I've Shot*, 1991
Michael A. Stackpole, *A Gathering Evil*, 1991

## 4910

### LARRY SEGRIFF

## *Alien Dreams*

(New York: Baen, 1998)

**Story type:** Science Fiction (Space Opera; First Contact)
**Major character(s):** Tom Jenkins, Military Personnel (Space Guard Cadet), Pilot; Alex, Military Personnel (Space Guard Ensign); Jamie, Military Personnel (Space Guard Cadet)
**Time period(s):** Indeterminate Future
**Locale(s):** Outer Space; *Michaelangelo*, Spaceship

**Summary:** Tom and his friend Jamie have some trouble adjusting to life aboard the Space Guard cruiser. In the midst of routine patrolling, the crew discovers a vessel of apparently alien origin. When the boarding party disappears along with the alien ship, Alex blames herself, and the *Michaelangelo* searches for clues to their fate.

**Other books you might like:**
Isaac Asimov, *Lucky Starr and the Pirates of the Asteroids*, 1953
C.J. Cherryh, *Finity's End*, 1997
Peter David, *Worf's First Adventure*, 1993
Robert A. Heinlein, *Starship Troopers*, 1959
Anne McCaffrey, *Sassinak*, 1990
　　Elizabeth Moon, co-author

## 4911

### LARRY SEGRIFF

## *Spacer Dreams*

(New York: Baen, 1995)

**Story type:** Science Fiction (Space Opera; Young Adult)
**Major character(s):** Tom Jenkins, Orphan; Michaela "Mikey" Delacourte, Military Personnel (Space Guard ensign), Spy; Frank, Mechanic, Pirate
**Time period(s):** Indeterminate Future
**Locale(s):** Brighthome, Planet—Imaginary

**Summary:** Tom Jenkins dreams of becoming a Space Guardian. He finally has a chance when space pirates try to recruit Tom's best friend and other fellow residents at the Brighthome Youth Center. First novel.

**Other books you might like:**
David Drake, *Surface Action*, 1990
John M. Ford, *Growing Up Weightless*, 1993
Robert A. Heinlein, *Space Cadet*, 1948
Robert A. Heinlein, *Starship Troopers*, 1959
Anne Mason, *The Stolen Law*, 1986
Frederik Pohl, *Mining the Oort*, 1992

## 4912

### DAVID L. SEIDMAN

## *The First Casualty*

(New York: Boulevard, 1997)

**Story type:** Fantasy (Legend)
**Series:** Hercules: The Legendary Journeys
**Major character(s):** Hercules, Hero (demi-god); Salmoneus, Salesman, Sidekick
**Time period(s):** Indeterminate Past
**Locale(s):** Mercantilius, Greece; Pastoralis, Greece

**Summary:** Trying to prevent war between Mercantilius and Pastoralis, Hercules discovers that Pan has already appeared there as Hercules to stir up trouble. Television tie-in.

**Other books you might like:**
John Gregory Betancourt, *The Vengeance of Hera*, 1997
John Gregory Betancourt, *The Wrath of Poseidon*, 1997
Timothy Boggs, *By the Sword*, 1996
Timothy Boggs, *The Eye of the Ram*, 1997
Timothy Boggs, *Serpent's Shadow*, 1996
Ru Emerson, *The Thief of Hermes*, 1997
Stella Howard, *Prophecy of Darkness*, 1997

## 4913

**CAROL SERLING**, Editor

### Journeys to the Twilight Zone
(New York: DAW, 1993)

**Story type:** Horror (Anthology)

**Summary:** Fifteen original stories and one reprint have been assembled with the idea of capturing the spirit of Rod Serling's famous television series "The Twilight Zone." Included are Alan Dean Foster's "Laying Veneer," about an American construction boss in Australia who discovers the land has a soul of its own; Kristine Kathryn Rusch and Dean Wesley Smith's "Mists," in which a man meets a banshee; Jack Dann's "The Extra," about a man who travels into his own past; Charles de Lint's "Waifs and Strays," a ghost story; and Rod Serling's own 1972 story "Suggestion," about a hypnosis session with disastrous results.

**Other books you might like:**
Martin H. Greenberg, *New Stories From the Twilight Zone*, 1991
    editor
Martin H. Greenberg, *The Twilight Zone: The Original Stories*, 1985
    editor
Rod Serling, *The Night Gallery Reader*, 1990
Rod Serling, *Stories From the Twilight Zone*, 1990
J. Michael Straczynski, *Tales From the New Twilight Zone*, 1989
    editor

## 4914

**CAROL SERLING**, Editor

### Return to the Twilight Zone
(New York: DAW, 1994)

**Story type:** Horror (Anthology)

**Summary:** The 19 stories in this compilation were written in the spirit of Rod Serling's renowned television series, "The Twilight Zone," which frequently examined the dark side of human experience through fables that embraced the supernatural. Highlights include Robert Weinberg's "The Midnight El," in which a man must stump the devil in order to save his soul; Charles L. Grant's "Always, in the Dark," a tale of an unusual ghost and an equally unusual haunting; John Gregory Betancourt's "The Duke of Demolition Goes to Hell," about the peculiar hell a construction mogul is sent to; John Maclay's "The Food Court," about the desserts meted out to a glutton; and Hugh Cave's "Gordie's Pets," about the dangerous overconfidence a boy develops through his rapport with animals. Also reprinted is Rod Serling's "Sole Survivor," a variation on the Flying Dutchman theme filmed originally as an episode for "The Twilight Zone."

**Other books you might like:**
Martin H. Greenberg, *New Stories From the Twilight Zone*, 1991
    editor
Martin H. Greenberg, *The Twilight Zone: The Original Stories*, 1985
    editor
Rod Serling, *The Gallery Reader*, 1990
Rod Serling, *Stories From the Twilight Zone*, 1990
J. Michael Straczynski, *Tales From the New Twilight Zone*, 1989
    editor

## 4915

**ROBERT SERLING**

### Something's Alive on the Titanic
(New York: St. Martin's, 1990)

**Story type:** Horror (Ghost Story)
**Major character(s):** Derek Montague, Adventurer; J. Benjamin Henning, Paranormal Investigator; William Gillespie, Scientist
**Time period(s):** 1970s (1975); 1990s (1993)
**Locale(s):** At Sea

**Summary:** A 1975 expedition to recover gold from the sunken ocean liner *Titanic* leaves all of its participants dead of horrifying phenomena, except cryptographer Derek Montague. Eighteen years later, Montague sets out on yet another expedition to recover the gold and find an explanation for what happened on the earlier mission.

**Other books you might like:**
Orson Scott Card, *The Abyss*, 1989
Michael Crichton, *Sphere*, 1987
Dean Wesley Smith, *Laying the Music to Rest*, 1989

## 4916

**ROD SERLING**

### The Twilight Zone: Complete Stories
(New York: TV Books, 1998)

**Story type:** Horror (Collection)

**Summary:** These 19 stories, which Rod Serling fleshed out from scripts for his award winning television program *The Twilight Zone*, include "The Odyssey of Flight 33," in which an airplane full of passengers is transported mysteriously back in time; "Escape Clause," in which a deal with the devil for immortality goes horribly awry; and "The Shelter," in which the threat of nuclear war turns the people of a small town against one another. Originally assembled in 1986 as *Stories From the Twilight Zone*, this omnibus volume reprints the full contents of *Stories From the Twilight Zone* (1960), *More Stories From the Twilight Zone* (1961) and *New Stories From the Twilight Zone* (1962). Introduction by T.E.D. Klein.

**Other books you might like:**
Charles Beaumont, *Selected Stories*, 1988
Ray Bradbury, *The October Country*, 1955
Richard Matheson, *The Twilight Zone Scripts*, 1998
Carol Serling, *Journeys to the Twilight Zone*, 1993
    editor
Carol Serling, *Return to the Twilight Zone*, 1994
    editor

## 4917

**PAMELA F. SERVICE**

### All's Faire
(New York: Fawcett Juniper, 1993)

**Story type:** Fantasy (Time Travel; Young Adult)
**Major character(s):** Kevin, Time Traveler, Teenager; Gina, Time Traveler, Teenager
**Time period(s):** 1990s; Indeterminate Past
**Locale(s):** Indiana; Europe

**Summary:** Unenthusiastic about his parents' interest in historic recreations, Kevin's boredom with a Renaissance festival vanishes when a strange phenomenon transports Kevin and Gina to medieval Europe where their adventure becomes exciting and dangerous.

**Other books you might like:**
Eleanor Cameron, *Beyond Silence*, 1980
Jane Louise Curry, *Over the Sea's Edge*, 1971
Michael Ende, *The Neverending Story*, 1983
Barbara Ireson, *Tales out of Time*, 1981
　　editor
Janet Luenn, *The Root Cellar*, 1983
William Mayne, *A Game of Dark*, 1971

## 4918

### PAMELA F. SERVICE

## Being of Two Minds

(New York: Atheneum, 1991)

**Story type:** Fantasy (Young Adult; Contemporary)
**Major character(s):** Connie Hendricks, Teenager, Telepath; Rudolph "Rudy", Royalty (crown prince), Telepath; Wolfgang "Wolfie" Reichmann, Teacher
**Time period(s):** 1990s
**Locale(s):** Midwest; Thulgaria, Fictional Country

**Summary:** Connie and Rudolph keep their telepathic bond secret, fearing that others would not understand. When Rudolph's kidnapping forces Connie to reveal the truth, she travels to Thulgaria to help rescue Rudolph.

**Other books you might like:**
James Blish, *Jack of Eagles*, 1952
Robert A. Heinlein, *Time for the Stars*, 1956
J. Alison James, *Sing for a Gentle Rain*, 1990
Kathryn Lasky, *Double Trouble Squared*, 1991
Robert Silverberg, *Letters From Atlantis*, 1990
Theodore Sturgeon, *More than Human*, 1953
A.E. Van Vogt, *Slan*, 1946

## 4919

### PAMELA F. SERVICE

## Under Alien Stars

(New York: Atheneum, 1990)

**Story type:** Science Fiction (Invasion of Earth; Young Adult)
**Major character(s):** Jason Sikes, Teenager; Aryl, Teenager, Alien
**Time period(s):** 21st century
**Locale(s):** San Francisco, California

**Summary:** Ten years after the Tsorians arrive and establish a military base on Earth, resistance is still strong. When Jason's mom's boss, Rogav Jy, is kidnapped by Resisters, both Earth and the Tsorians are menaced by an invasion of Hykzoi, a species of bloodthirsty conquerers. Jason must unwillingly join forces with Aryl, Rogav's daughter, to free Rogav and rout the Hykzoi.

**Other books you might like:**
David Brin, *Startide Rising*, 1983
John Christopher, *The Prince in Waiting*, 1970
John Christopher, *The White Mountains*, 1967
Paula Danziger, *This Place Has No Atmosphere*, 1986
Robert A. Heinlein, *The Rolling Stones*, 1952
Larry Niven, *Footfall*, 1985
　　Jerry Pournelle, co-author

## 4920

### PAMELA F. SERVICE

## Vision Quest

(New York: Atheneum, 1989)

**Story type:** Fantasy (Magic Conflict)
**Major character(s):** Kate Elliott, Teenager (Army brat); Jimmy Fong, Teenager (Kate's friend)
**Time period(s):** 1980s
**Locale(s):** Nevada

**Summary:** When Kate's family moves to Nevada, she finds life boring until one day, while walking in the desert, she finds a talisman left long ago by a shaman. When she takes possession of the talisman, she starts having visions of what happened to the original owner.

**Other books you might like:**
Diana Wynne Jones, *The Lives of Christopher Chant*, 1988
Adrienne Martine-Barnes, *The Fire Sword*, 1984
Patricia Wrightson, *Balyet*, 1989

## 4921

### PAMELA F. SERVICE

## Weirdos of the Universe, Unite!

(New York: Atheneum, 1992)

**Story type:** Fantasy (Legend; Young Adult)
**Major character(s):** Mandy, Student, Teenager; Owen, Student, Teenager; Baba Yaga, Mythical Creature (Russian)
**Time period(s):** 1990s
**Locale(s):** Hermes, Iowa

**Summary:** While researching a paper on mythological beings, Mandy and Owen find several mythological characters have come alive. The group must unite to save the earth from an invasion from outer space.

**Other books you might like:**
Margaret J. Anderson, *The Ghost Inside the Monitor*, 1990
Bruce Coville, *My Teacher Flunked the Planet*, 1992
Philip Jose Farmer, *Red Orc's Rage*, 1991
Will Shetterly, *Cats Have No Lord*, 1985
Clifford D. Simak, *Out of Their Minds*, 1970
Vivian Vande Velde, *User Unfriendly*, 1991

## 4922

### CAROL SEVERANCE

## Demon Drums

(New York: Ballantine Del Rey, 1992)

**Story type:** Fantasy (Magic Conflict)
**Major character(s):** Iuti Mano, Warrior (retired), Magician; Tarawe, Warrior, Magician
**Time period(s):** Indeterminate
**Locale(s):** Fanape Island, Fictional Country; Losan Island, Fictional Country

**Summary:** Weary of the endless killing of the Teronin War, Iuti had retired to Fanape Island promising to avoid use of her protective spirit, the shark, in order to stay among the peaceful inhabitants. When agents of her enemy come to Fanape to capture her and force her to fight for them, Iuti resolves to again take up her sword and destroy the enemy's scheming for all time. While escaping with Tarawe, Iuti and Tarawe fall victim to a magical storm which transports them to Losan Island where deadly drummers construct magic drums utilizing the skin of warriors as drum heads, a fate which will befall Iuti if she remains.

**Other books you might like:**
Joan Slonczewski, *A Door into Ocean*, 1986
Dave Smeds, *The Schemes of Dragons*, 1989
Dave Smeds, *The Sorcery Within*, 1985
Christopher Stasheff, *King Kobold Revived*, 1984

## 4923
### CAROL SEVERANCE
### *Reefsong*
(New York: Ballantine/Del Rey, 1991)

**Story type:** Science Fiction (Genetic Manipulation; Utopia)
**Major character(s):** Pualeiokekai Pukai, Genetically Altered Being; Angela Dinsman, Troubleshooter (U.N.), Anthropologist
**Time period(s):** Indeterminate Future
**Locale(s):** Central Forest Preserve, Colorado; Lesaat, Planet—Imaginary (water world)

**Summary:** Able to provide basic nourishment for Earth's billions from its algae farms on Lesaat, the World Life Company has a stranglehold on most of the world's economy. The U.N. would like to change this situation by exposing the illegal activities it believes the World Life Company commits, but must be careful since much of the overpopulated planet depends on the Company for food. On Lesaat, the genetically altered colonists may have developed an enzyme which would allow humans to convert any vegetables into complete proteins. A first novel.

**Other books you might like:**
Eleanor Arnason, *A Woman of the Iron People*, 1991
David Brin, *Startide Rising*, 1983
Gordon R. Dickson, *Home From the Shore*, 1978
Alan Dean Foster, *Cachalot*, 1980
Damon Knight, *CV*, 1985
Joan Slonczewski, *A Door into Ocean*, 1986
Sydney J. Van Scyoc, *Deepwater Dreams*, 1991
John Wyndham, *Out of the Deeps*, 1953

## 4924
### CAROL SEVERANCE
### *Storm Caller*
(New York: Ballantine Del Rey, 1993)

**Story type:** Fantasy (Magic Conflict; Legend)
**Series:** Island Warrior
**Major character(s):** Iuti Mano, Warrior, Magician; Tarawe, Magician; Ma'eva, Mythical Creature (shapeshifter)
**Time period(s):** Indeterminate
**Locale(s):** At Sea; Tahena, Fictional Country (volcanic island)

**Summary:** When Iuti's kinsmen seek revenge for her killing of the clan's totem, Iuti, Tarwe and Ma'eva flee across a danger-filled ocean until they find an inhabited island which provides shelter but no safety on their journey. Based on Hawaiian legends.

**Other books you might like:**
Gordon R. Dickson, *The Dragon at War*, 1992
Ursula K. Le Guin, *A Wizard of Earthsea*, 1968
Megan Lindholm, *Harpy's Flight*, 1983
Megan Lindholm, *The Windsingers*, 1984
Elizabeth Moon, *Sheepfarmer's Daughter*, 1988
Michelle Sagara, *Into the Dark Lands*, 1991

## 4925
### ELLEN DODGE SEVERSON
### *Hederick, the Theocrat*
(Lake Geneva, Wisconsin: TSR, 1994)

**Story type:** Fantasy (Religious; Magic Conflict)
**Series:** Dragonlance: Villains
**Major character(s):** Hederick, Religious, Leader
**Time period(s):** Indeterminate
**Locale(s):** Krynn, Planet—Imaginary

**Summary:** From an abandoned youth, Hederick grows into a demagogue who commands a goblin army, intending to vanquish the practitioners of magic and worshippers of the old gods.

**Other books you might like:**
Mark Anthony, *Kindred Spirits*, 1991
   Ellen Porath, co-author
Mary Kirchoff, *The Black Wing*, 1993
Douglas Niles, *Emperor of Ansalon*, 1993
Ellen Porath, *Steel and Stone*, 1992
Michael Williams, *Before the Mask*, 1993
   Teri Williams, co-author

## 4926
### BARBARA SHAFFERMAN
### *The President's Astrologer*
(St. Paul, Minnesota: Llewellyn, 1998)

**Story type:** Fantasy (Political)
**Major character(s):** Addie Price, Astrologer; Walter Wycliff, Political Figure (president)
**Time period(s):** 2010s (2006)
**Locale(s):** Washington, District of Columbia

**Summary:** Addie Price is hired to give advice to the president, who has come to the conclusion that astrology works, which it does in the context of the story. Shortly after being introduced to the political life of the capitol, Price discovers evidence through her divination that someone is plotting to kill the president. First novel.

**Other books you might like:**
Piers Anthony, *Faith of Tarot*, 1980
Joan Brady, *God on a Harley*, 1995
Louise Cooper, *The Book of Paradox*, 1973
Esther Friesner, *New York by Knight*, 1986
Romain Gary, *The Gasp*, 1973

## 4927
### WILLIAM SHATNER
### JUDITH REEVES-STEVENS, Co-Author
### GARFIELD REEVES-STEVENS, Co-Author
### *The Ashes of Eden*
(New York: Pocket, 1995)

**Story type:** Science Fiction (Space Opera)
**Series:** Star Trek
**Major character(s):** Pavel Chekov, Military Personnel (Starfleet Commander), Space Explorer; Hikaru Sulu, Military Personnel (Starfleet Captain), Spaceship Captain; James T. Kirk, Spaceship Captain (Starfleet Captain)
**Time period(s):** 23rd century

**Locale(s):** *U.S.S. Excelsior*, Spaceship; Chal, Planet—Imaginary; United Federation of Planets, Interstellar Empire/Federation

**Summary:** Approaching retirement, Kirk accepts an offer from a mysterious young woman to command a starship again, to defend an uncharted planet from the Klingons and Romulans—and to regain his lost youth. While old and new conspiracies force Sulu and his old crewmates to track down Kirk, Kirk must save the fragile peace between the Klingons and the Federation.

**Other books you might like:**
C.J. Cherryh, *Hellburner*, 1992
J.M. Dillard, *The Lost Years*, 1989
Jane S. Fancher, *Ground-Ties*, 1991
Cynthia Felice, *Downtime*, 1985
L.A. Graf, *Traitor Winds*, 1994
Garfield Reeves-Stevens, *Memory Prime*, 1988
    Judith Reeves-Stevens, co-author
Judith Reeves-Stevens, *Federation*, 1994
    Garfield Reeves-Stevens, co-author
Judith Reeves-Stevens, *Prime Directive*, 1990
    Garfield Reeves-Stevens, co-author

## 4928

### WILLIAM SHATNER
### JUDITH REEVES-STEVENS, Co-Author
### GARFIELD REEVES-STEVENS, Co-Author

### *Avenger*
(New York: Pocket, 1997)

**Story type:** Science Fiction (Mystery; Disaster)
**Series:** Star Trek
**Major character(s):** Jean-Luc Picard, Spaceship Captain; James T. Kirk, Spaceship Captain; Spock, Diplomat, Alien (Vulcan)
**Time period(s):** 24th century
**Locale(s):** Chal, Planet—Imaginary; Vulcan, Planet—Imaginary; United Federation of Planets, Interstellar Empire/Federation

**Summary:** Left in a Borg recycling center and restored to health, Kirk seeks his lost love on the planet Chal, suffering from the same ecological disaster that threatens life throughout the Federation. Meanwhile, Spock suspects that his father's death resulted from murder, not natural causes. Reunited, the two friends follow the clues to Tarsus IV where they learn the truth about the origins of the new plague with the help of the *Enterprise E*.

**Other books you might like:**
Michael Crichton, *The Andromeda Strain*, 1969
Michael Jan Friedman, *Reunion*, 1991
Lynn S. Hightower, *Alien Rites*, 1995
Jean Lorrah, *The IDIC Epidemic*, 1988
Jean Lorrah, *The Vulcan Academy Murders*, 1984
Judith Reeves-Stevens, *Prime Directive*, 1990
    Garfield Reeves-Stevens, co-author

## 4929

### WILLIAM SHATNER
### MICHAEL TOBIAS, Co-Author

### *Believe: A Novel*
(New York: Berkley, 1992)

**Story type:** Fantasy (Historical; Quest)
**Major character(s):** Harry Houdini, Magician, Historical Figure; Arthur Conan Doyle, Historical Figure, Writer
**Time period(s):** 1920s

**Locale(s):** United States; Canada; England

**Summary:** Pursuant to a *Scientifica Americana* contest, skeptical Harry Houdini and Arthur Conan Doyle, a believer, investigate the possibility of life after death.

**Other books you might like:**
Philip Jose Farmer, *Tales of Riverworld*, 1992
    editor
Pamela Sargent, *Afterlives: An Anthology of Stories about Life After Death*, 1986
    editor
Daniel Stashower, *The Adventure of the Ectoplasmic Man*, 1985
Steve Szilagyi, *Photographing Fairies*, 1992
Michael Tobias, *Voice of the Planet*, 1990

## 4930

### WILLIAM SHATNER

### *Delta Search*
(New York: HarperPrism, 1997)

**Story type:** Science Fiction (Adventure; Genetic Manipulation)
**Series:** Quest for Tomorrow
**Major character(s):** Carl "Johnson" Endicott, Fugitive; James "Jimmy" Endicott, Teenager, Genetically Altered Being; Catherine "Cat" Thibaudeaux, Spy
**Time period(s):** 23rd century (2280s)
**Locale(s):** San Francisco, California; Prima City, Fictional City; Wolfbane, Planet—Imaginary

**Summary:** Despite his father's disapproval, Jimmy sends his application to the Solis Space Academy, including his father's genotype. As soon as he discovers his son's actions, Carl abandons his home, taking his family with only what they can carry to a cabin in the woods. After an attack by people in space armor and being forced by his dying father to memorize a code, Jimmy realizes he must rescue his mother and discover who attacked his family and why. First in a series.

**Other books you might like:**
Emily Devenport, *Shade*, 1991
David Feintuch, *Voices of Hope*, 1996
Alan Dean Foster, *The Tar-Aiym Krang*, 1972
Robert A. Heinlein, *Have Spacesuit—Will Travel*, 1958
Melissa Scott, *Night Sky Mine*, 1996
Joan D. Vinge, *Psion*, 1982

## 4931

### WILLIAM SHATNER

### *The Law of War*
(New York: Ace/Putnam, 1998)

**Story type:** Science Fiction (Political; Space Colony)
**Major character(s):** Benton Hawkes, Diplomat, Government Official; Michael Carri, Political Figure
**Time period(s):** 2060s
**Locale(s):** Mars

**Summary:** Benton Hawkes, reluctant diplomat, travels to Mars, where he brokers a peace with rebellious miners and ends up as Prime Minister of Mars, a job he never wanted. Now powerful enemies want him dead and his new republic crushed.

**Other books you might like:**
Lester Del Rey, *Police Your Planet*, 1956
    as Erik Van Lhin
Robert A. Heinlein, *The Moon Is a Harsh Mistress*, 1996

Cordwainer Smith, *Norstrilia*, 1975
Allen Steele, *Lunar Descent*, 1991
Walter Jon Williams, *Metropolitan*, 1995

## 4932

### WILLIAM SHATNER

### *Man o' War*

(New York: Ace/Putnam, 1996)

**Story type:** Science Fiction (Political; Space Colony)
**Major character(s):** Benton Hawkes, Diplomat, Rancher; Dina Martel, Diplomat; Michael Carri, Government Official (senator)
**Time period(s):** 2060s (2067)
**Locale(s):** Mars; Wyoming

**Summary:** When Benton Hawkes refuses to render the politically mandated verdict in an arbitration, he thinks his diplomatic career finished. Instead, Senator Carri offers him the governorship of Mars, a job in which he will have to stave off impending revolution to maintain the flow of crucial raw materials to Earth. Hawkes prefers to return to his ranch, but after two attempts on his life and evidence that some of his attackers had lived on Mars, he accepts the postion. On Mars, he discovers not only who tried to kill him, but why.

**Other books you might like:**
Robert Asprin, *The Cold Cash War*, 1977
C.J. Cherryh, *Foreigner*, 1994
Robert A. Heinlein, *The Moon Is a Harsh Mistress*, 1966
Keith Laumer, *Relief at Large*, 1978
Ursula K. Le Guin, *The Dispossessed*, 1978
Kim Stanley Robinson, *Red Mars*, 1993

## 4933

### WILLIAM SHATNER
### JUDITH REEVES-STEVENS, Co-Author
### GARFIELD REEVES-STEVENS, Co-Author

### *The Return*

(New York: Pocket, 1996)

**Story type:** Science Fiction (Space Opera; Genetic Manipulation)
**Series:** Star Trek
**Major character(s):** Jean-Luc Picard, Spaceship Captain, Military Personnel; James T. Kirk, Spaceship Captain; Spock, Scientist, Alien (Vulcan)
**Time period(s):** 24th century
**Locale(s):** Veridian III, Planet—Imaginary; Romulus, Planet—Imaginary; Interstellar Empire/Federation

**Summary:** While salvage operations begin on the wreckage of the *Enterprise* and Starfleet prepares to bring Kirk's body back to Earth for burial, Romulan ships attack and transport Kirk's body from its grave. Using an ancient alien artifact, they restore the body to life and program it to turn against the Federation. The Romulans have allied themselves with the Borg, and only the combined talents of two *Enterprise* crews can save the Federation.

**Other books you might like:**
Octavia E. Butler, *Dawn*, 1987
C.J. Cherryh, *Cyteen*, 1988
Michael Jan Friedman, *Kahless*, 1996
Judith Reeves-Stevens, *Prime Directive*, 1990
    Garfield Reeves-Stevens, co-author
Della Van Hise, *Killing Time*, 1985
John Varley, *The Ophiuchi Hotline*, 1977

## 4934

### WILLIAM SHATNER
### JUDITH REEVES-STEVENS, Co-Author
### GARFIELD REEVES-STEVENS, Co-Author

### *Spectre*

(New York: Pocket Books, 1998)

**Story type:** Science Fiction (Space Opera; Alternate Universe)
**Series:** Star Trek
**Major character(s):** James T. Kirk, Spaceship Captain; Jean-Luc Picard, Spaceship Captain; Spock, Resistance Fighter, Alien (half-Vulcan)
**Time period(s):** 24th century
**Locale(s):** Asteroid (Prison camp); *U.S.S. Enterprise*, Spaceship; United Federation of Planets, Interstellar Empire/Federation

**Summary:** The resurrected Jim Kirk refuses the pleas of the mirror universe Spock and Janeway to aid their rebellion against the Empire, but when Kirk receives news of the kidnapping of his pregnant wife, Tehani, he goes to the rescue. His ship hijacked by his own counterpart from the mirror universe, Picard teams up with Tehani to stop the hijackers before they complete a device that will transfer the *Enterprise* into the mirror universe and use its advanced technology to crush the rebels.

**Other books you might like:**
Diane Duane, *Dark Mirror*, 1993
Phyllis Eisenstein, *Shadow of Earth*, 1979
Michael Jan Friedman, *Double, Double*, 1989
Michael Jan Friedman, *Relics*, 1992
Judith Reeves-Stevens, *Federation*, 1992
    Garfield Reeves-Stevens, co-author

## 4935

### WILLIAM SHATNER

### *Tek Money*

(New York: Ace/Putnam, 1995)

**Story type:** Science Fiction (Adventure)
**Series:** Tek
**Major character(s):** Jake Cardigan, Detective—Private; Sid Gomez, Detective—Private
**Time period(s):** 22nd century
**Locale(s):** California; Tropical Island (Atlantic); Spain

**Summary:** Police suspect Jake Cardigan of murdering an acquaintance from the days of his Tek addiction by use of a Tek chip which plugs directly into the brain. With the police and the victim's acquaintances all requesting their help, Jake and Sid follow the money as its trail leads them overseas and into greater danger as they attempt to clear Jake's name.

**Other books you might like:**
Robert Cain, *Cybernarc*, 1991
Philip K. Dick, *A Scanner Darkly*, 1977
Alan Dean Foster, *Outland*, 1981
Simon R. Green, *Guard Against Dishonor*, 1991
Ernest Hogan, *High Aztec*, 1992
Lynn S. Hightower, *Alien Blues*, 1992

## 4936

### WILLIAM SHATNER

## Tek Net

(New York: Ace/Putnam, 1997)

**Story type:** Science Fiction (Adventure)
**Series:** Tek
**Major character(s):** Jake Cardigan, Detective—Private; Sid Gomez, Detective—Private
**Time period(s):** 22nd century
**Locale(s):** Earth

**Summary:** Shortly after Sid receives a request from his second ex-wife, currently working on a screenplay about an infamous TekLord thought dead, Sid and Jake's personal investigation receives official sanction when they learn a client places a premium on finding the TekLord alive.

**Other books you might like:**
Robert Cain, *Cybernarc*, 1991
Philip K. Dick, *A Scanner Darkly*, 1997
Lynn S. Hightower, *Alien Blues*, 1992
Ernest Hogan, *High Aztec*, 1992
Richard Paul Russo, *Carlucci's Heart*, 1997

## 4937

### WILLIAM SHATNER

## Tek Power

(New York: Ace/Putnam, 1994)

**Story type:** Science Fiction (Adventure; Political)
**Series:** Tek
**Major character(s):** Jake Cardigan, Detective—Private; Sid Gomez, Detective—Private; Warren Brookmeyer, Political Figure (U.S. president)
**Time period(s):** 22nd century
**Locale(s):** New York, New York; Washington, District of Columbia; Managua, Nicaragua

**Summary:** When President Brookmeyer agrees to clandestine treatment for Tek addiction, he intends that his robot simulacrum will replace him in public only briefly. While investigating a murder, Jake and Sid chance onto a conspiracy aimed at controlling the government through more permanent tenure for the robot.

**Other books you might like:**
Philip K. Dick, *A Scanner Darkly*, 1977
Michael Flynn, *In the Country of the Blind*, 1990
Robert A. Heinlein, *Double Star*, 1956
Allen Steele, *Clarke County, Space*, 1990

## 4938

### WILLIAM SHATNER

## Tek Vengeance

(New York: Ace/Putnam, 1993)

**Story type:** Science Fiction (Adventure)
**Series:** Tek
**Major character(s):** Jake Cardigan, Detective—Private; Sid Gomez, Detective—Private
**Time period(s):** 22nd century
**Locale(s):** Los Angeles, California; Brazil; Austria

**Summary:** While Beth Kittridge travels to Berlin to testify against a drug dealing Teklord, Jake pursues vital information from a dying informant in South America. Jake's absence from Beth's side allows their enemies to plot Beth's murder, resulting in Jake's assignment to the murder investigation. Sequel to *TekLab*.

**Other books you might like:**
Robert Cain, *Cybernarc*, 1991
Alan Dean Foster, *Alien Nation*, 1988
Alan Dean Foster, *Outland*, 1981
Lynn S. Hightower, *Alien Blues*, 1992
L.S. Riker, *Kill Crazy*, 1993

## 4939

### WILLIAM SHATNER

## TekLab

(New York: Ace/Putnam, 1991)

**Story type:** Science Fiction (Adventure)
**Series:** Tek
**Major character(s):** Jake Cardigan, Detective—Private; Sid Gomez, Detective—Private (Cardigan's partner)
**Time period(s):** 22nd century
**Locale(s):** Paris, France; London, England; Nassau, Bahamas

**Summary:** To interview a client about a recent assassination, Jake and Sid travel to Paris where a phone call from Jake's son, Dan, alerts Jake to the disappearance of Dan's girlfriend. Tracking down his son in London, Jake finds the disappearance involves the assassin, Unknown Soldier; a new drug, SuperTek; and a group of neo-royalists, the Excalibur Movement, intent on again turning Great Britain into a monarchy. This book is a sequel to *TekLords*.

**Other books you might like:**
Robert Cain, *Cybernarc*, 1991
Robert Cain, *Gold Dragon*, 1991
Allan Cole, *Sten*, 1984
   Chris Bunch, co-author
Philip K. Dick, *Blade Runner*, 1982
Alan Dean Foster, *Alien Nation*, 1988
Lynn S. Hightower, *Alien Blues*, 1992
Katharine Kerr, *Polar City Blues*, 1990

## 4940

### WILLIAM SHATNER

## TekLords

(New York: Ace/Putnam, 1991)

**Story type:** Science Fiction (Adventure)
**Series:** Tek
**Major character(s):** Jake Cardigan, Detective—Private; Sid Gomez, Detective—Private (Cardigan's partner)
**Time period(s):** 22nd century (2120)
**Locale(s):** California; Japan

**Summary:** In this sequel to *TekWar*, Cardigan and Gomez are assigned to discover who is behind a recent wave of murders and attempted murders. When his wife becomes infected by a synthetic virus, Jake seeks an antidote and those who caused the plague.

**Other books you might like:**
Isaac Asimov, *The Currents of Space*, 1952
Philip K. Dick, *A Scanner Darkly*, 1977
Alan Dean Foster, *Cyber Way*, 1990
Alan Dean Foster, *Outland*, 1981
Ron Goulart, *The Wicked Cyborg*, 1978

Richard Kadrey, *Metrophage*, 1988
Katharine Kerr, *Polar City Blues*, 1990
Lee Killough, *Dragon's Teeth*, 1990

## 4941

**WILLIAM SHATNER**

### TekWar

(New York: Ace/Putnam, 1989)

**Story type:** Science Fiction (Mystery)
**Series:** Tek
**Major character(s):** Jake Cardigan, Detective—Private; Sonny Hakori, Drug Dealer
**Time period(s):** 22nd century
**Locale(s):** Los Angeles, California

**Summary:** Jake Cardigan, an ex-cop, was framed for allegedly dealing Tek, a mind-altering computerized drug. Out of jail and working as a private detective, Jake is out to get whoever framed him and break up the Tek cartel.

**Other books you might like:**
Richard Bowker, *Dover Beach*, 1987
George Alec Effinger, *A Fire in the Sun*, 1989
George Alec Effinger, *When Gravity Fails*, 1987
F. Paul Wilson, *Dydeetown World*, 1989

## 4942

**BOB SHAW**

### The Fugitive Worlds

(New York: Baen, 1990)

**Story type:** Science Fiction (Adventure)
**Series:** Land and Overland
**Major character(s):** Toller Maraquine II, Pilot (airship); Vantara, Noblewoman (countess), Pilot (airship); The Xa, Computer (sentient), Alien
**Time period(s):** Indeterminate Future
**Locale(s):** Land, Planet—Imaginary; Overland, Planet—Imaginary

**Summary:** While returning from Land, Toller Maraquine II discovers an invisible barrier midway between the two planets which has swallowed up Countess Vantara. Investigating, Maraquine meets the Dussarrans who, along with their planet, are fleeing a galactic explosion. Learning that they plan to use Land/Overland to abet this, (which will destroy these planets), Maraquine, using The Xa, transports Overland to a new continuum—our own.

**Other books you might like:**
Philip Jose Farmer, *The Unreasoning Mask*, 1981
Robert L. Forward, *Rocheworld*, 1990
Melissa Scott, *Five-Twelfths of Heaven*, 1985
John Varley, *Millennium*, 1983
John Varley, *Titan*, 1979

## 4943

**MAGGIE SHAYNE**

### Eternity

(New York: Jove, 1998)

**Story type:** Fantasy (Romance)
**Major character(s):** Raven St. James, Witch; Duncan, Religious (minister)
**Time period(s):** 17th century (1694); 1990s (1998)
**Locale(s):** Sanctuary, Massachusetts

**Summary:** Raven St. James was persecuted as a witch in colonial Massachusetts, defended only by the local minister. Immortal, she survives to the modern day, where she finally encounters a reincarnation of Duncan, whom she has loved throughout the ages.

**Other books you might like:**
Scott Baker, *Firedance*, 1986
Jonathan Carroll, *Sleeping in Flame*, 1988
Suzy McKee Charnas, *Dorothea Dreams*, 1986
Elizabeth Goudge, *The Middle Window*, 1939
Valerie James, *Bewitching Beloved*, 1981

## 4944

**MICHAEL SHEA**

### I, Said the Fly

(Seattle, Washington: Silver Salamander Press, 1993)

**Story type:** Horror (Science Fiction)
**Major character(s):** Paul Rant, Scientist (entomologist); Brad, Filmmaker; Dean, Doctor (pathologist)
**Time period(s):** 1990s (1993)
**Locale(s):** Los Angeles, California

**Summary:** While filming a short feature titled *I, Said the Fly*, which presents the world of human beings as seen through the eyes of several species of the animal kingdom, a series of strange events on both the global and local scale convince the filmmakers that the human species is being investigated under the microscopes of a race of extraterrestrial invaders.

**Other books you might like:**
Jack Finney, *The Body Snatchers*, 1955
Robert A. Heinlein, *The Puppet Masters*, 1951
Frank Herbert, *Hellstrom's Hive*, 1973
Eric Frank Russell, *Sinister Barrier*, 1943

## 4945

**MICHAEL SHEA**

### The Mines of Behemoth

(New York: Baen, 1997)

**Story type:** Fantasy (Adventure; Quest)
**Major character(s):** Nifft the Lean, Adventurer; Barnar Hammer-Hand, Adventurer
**Time period(s):** Indeterminate
**Locale(s):** Dolmen, Fictional Country; Dry Hole, Fictional City; Costard's Superior Mine, Mythical Place

**Summary:** Shipwrecked on the way to work Costard's sap mine, Nifft the Lean and Barnar Hammer-hand agree to retrieve ichor uniquely produce by a monstrous insectile queen. The pair soon discover this plan to acquire quick wealth will prove trickier to accomplish than anticipated. Sequel to *Nifft the Lean*.

**Other books you might like:**
Glen Cook, *The Black Company*, 1984
Fritz Leiber, *Ill Met in Lankhmar*, 1995
John Moore, *Slay and Rescue*, 1993
Jack Vance, *Cugel's Saga*, 1983
Jack Vance, *Rhialto the Marvellous*, 1984

## 4946

**ROBERT SHEA**

### Shaman

(New York: Ballantine, 1991)

**Story type:** Fantasy (Historical)
**Major character(s):** Auguste "White Bear" de Marion, Shaman; Raoul de Marion, Farmer; Redbird, Fiance(e)
**Time period(s):** 19th century
**Locale(s):** Michigan

**Summary:** White Bear, a man caught between two heritages, searches for love and the power of a shaman in a dying world. With the United States pushing its boundary west, there is no place for the native people to go. White Bear's distress is heightened by conflict with his uncle, who represents everything negative about Western life.

**Other books you might like:**
Orson Scott Card, *Seventh Son*, 1987
Stuart Gordon, *Smile on the Void*, 1981
Joe R. Lansdale, *The Magic Wagon*, 1986
S.P. Somtow, *Moon Dance*, 1989
Patricia Wrightson, *The Dark Bright Water*, 1978
Patricia Wrightson, *The Ice Is Coming*, 1977
Patricia Wrightson, *Journey Behind the Wind*, 1981

## 4947

**CHARLES SHEFFIELD**

### Aftermath

(New York: Bantam Spectra, 1998)

**Story type:** Science Fiction (Hard Science Fiction; Disaster)
**Major character(s):** Saul Steinmetz, Political Figure (U.S. President); Celine Tanaka, Astronaut; Art Ferrand, Computer Expert
**Time period(s):** 2020s (2026)
**Locale(s):** Washington, District of Columbia; Catoctin Mountain Park, Maryland; *Schiaparelli*, Spaceship

**Summary:** After the Alpha Centauri supernova releases a gamma ray burst which fries all electronics, the northern hemisphere gradually begins to feel the effects. The southern hemisphere, exposed directly to the heat and light, suffers almost immediate damaging climate effects. Saul tries to restore amenities and any old pre-chip equipment still around, while the leaders of Congress may be plotting to take over the world. The crew of the *Schiaparelli* may be stuck in space after returning from Mars. Meanwhile, Art and some cronies from his experimental cancer treatment group rescue from internment as a mass murderer the only doctor who knows enough to save their lives.

**Other books you might like:**
Roger MacBride Allen, *The Ring of Charon*, 1990
Stephen Baxter, *Titan*, 1997
David Brin, *Earth*, 1990
Larry Niven, *Lucifer's Hammer*, 1977
   Jerry Pournelle, co-author
Roger Zelazny, *Flare*, 1992
   Thomas T. Thomas, co-author

## 4948

**CHARLES SHEFFIELD**

### The Billion Dollar Boy

(New York: Tor, 1997)

**Story type:** Science Fiction (Young Adult; Adventure)
**Major character(s):** Shelby Cheever V, Teenager, Heir; Grace Trask, Spaceship Captain, Miner; Lana Trask, Spaceship Captain, Miner
**Time period(s):** Indeterminate Future
**Locale(s):** *Harvest Moon*, Spaceship; Messina Dust Cloud, Outer Space

**Summary:** Spoiled heir to one of Earth's largest private fortunes. Shelby Cheever takes an unauthorized trip through the interstellar node network, stranding himself in the Messina Dust Cloud. A group of transuranics miners takes Shelby in, teaching him that not wealth but only hard work and loyalty will earn their respect. Second in series.

**Other books you might like:**
Arthur C. Clarke, *Dolphin Island*, 1963
Steven Gould, *Wildside*, 1996
Robert A. Heinlein, *Space Cadet*, 1948
Frederik Pohl, *Mining the Oort*, 1992
Jerry Pournelle, *West of Honor*, 1976
Larry Segriff, *Spacer Dreams*, 1995

## 4949

**CHARLES SHEFFIELD**

### Brother to Dragons

(New York: Baen, 1992)

**Story type:** Science Fiction (Future Shock; Political)
**Major character(s):** Job Napoleon Salk, Orphan; Father "Mr. Bones" Bonifant, Administrator; Alan Singh, Professor
**Time period(s):** 2010s
**Locale(s):** Xanadu, Nebraska

**Summary:** Deserted at birth, Job spends his formative years at Cloak House orphanage. When he escapes at age eleven, his talent for languages and the trips accompanying Mr. Bones on forage runs help him survive in the extreme poverty of the city, and eventually at Xanadu, an escape-proof prison area surrounding a toxic and nuclear waste dump where scientists have been sentenced since the Crash. Job hopes to survive long enough to escape with the fruits of the on-going research.

**Other books you might like:**
David Brin, *Earth*, 1990
Emma Bull, *Bone Dance: A Fantasy for Technophiles*, 1991
Peter R. Emshwiller, *The Host*, 1991
Frederik Pohl, *Stopping at Slowyear*, 1991
Jim Shepard, *Lights Out in the Reptile House*, 1990
Allen Steele, *Lunar Descent*, 1991
Dave Wolverton, *Serpent Catch*, 1991

## 4950

**CHARLES SHEFFIELD**

### Cold as Ice

(New York: Tor, 1992)

**Story type:** Science Fiction (Hard Science Fiction; Political)

**Major character(s):** Jon Perry, Scientist; Cyrus "Torquemada" Mobarak, Inventor, Businessman; Rustum "Bat" Battacharia, Government Official
**Time period(s):** 2090s (2092)
**Locale(s):** Ganymede, Jupiter (a moon of Jupiter); Europa, Jupiter (a moon of Jupiter)

**Summary:** Twenty-five years after the war between the Inner Planets and the Belt, peace and the Moby, a portable fusion engine, have enabled the populations to prosper. Jon Perry, a deep sea researcher from Earth, travels to Europa to find any native life which may have evolved in the fresh water ocean under the ice. Mobarak plots to use his Mobies to create a new environment for humans on Europa.

**Other books you might like:**
Stephen Baxter, *Raft*, 1991
David Brin, *Earth*, 1990
John Brunner, *Children of the Thunder*, 1989
Octavia E. Butler, *Dawn*, 1987
Arthur C. Clarke, *2061: Odyssey Three*, 1987
Gregory Feeley, *The Oxygen Barons*, 1990
Edward Gibson, *In the Wrong Hands*, 1992
Michael Swanwick, *Stations of the Tide*, 1991

---

**4951**

**CHARLES SHEFFIELD**

## Convergence

(New York: Baen, 1997)

**Story type:** Science Fiction (Space Opera; Science Fiction)
**Series:** Heritage Universe
**Major character(s):** Darya Lang, Scientist, Adventurer; Atvar H'sial, Alien (Cecropian), Businesswoman; Louis Nenda, Adventurer
**Time period(s):** 63rd century
**Locale(s):** Genizee, Planet—Imaginary; *Indulgence*, Spaceship; Torvil Anfract, Outer Space

**Summary:** While escaping from Genizee, Louis Nenda and Atvar H'sial inadvertently capture a live Zardulu, worth millions back in the Benignity. Darya Lang must again go to space to refute a challenge to her theory of the origin of the Artifacts and the intent of the builders. Much to Darya's chagrin, the Artifacts continue to change, but some changes bring a lengthier future for human presence among the intelligent races of the Galaxy. Fourth in series.

**Other books you might like:**
Greg Bear, *Eon*, 1985
David Brin, *Startide Rising*, 1983
Glen Cook, *The Dragon Never Sleeps*, 1988
Alis A. Rasmussen, *A Passage of Stars*, 1990
Robert J. Sawyer, *Starplex*, 1990
Dan Simmons, *Hyperion*, 1989

---

**4952**

**CHARLES SHEFFIELD**

## The Cyborg From Earth

(New York: Tor, 1998)

**Story type:** Science Fiction (Young Adult; Political)
**Major character(s):** Jefferson "Jeff" Kopal, Heir, Cyborg; Lilah Desmon, Spacewoman; Simon Macafee, Inventor, Space Explorer
**Time period(s):** Indeterminate Future
**Locale(s):** Messina Dust Cloud, Outer Space

**Summary:** Shipmates leave Jeff Kopal to die after he receives injuries on a naval vessel exploring the Messina Cloud. Saved by cyborg technology forbidden on Earth, he becomes an excuse for Earth to annex or destroy the Messina Cloud. But Macafee, a mysterious man who is the key to solving the Earth-Messina Cloud impasse as well as Jeff's more personal problems, plans to counter the overwhelming Earth force.

**Other books you might like:**
Isaac Asimov, *Lucky Starr and the Rings of Saturn*, 1958
Gregory Benford, *Jupiter Project*, 1975
Ben Bova, *Moonrise*, 1996
Octavia E. Butler, *Patternmaster*, 1976
Robert A. Heinlein, *Citizen of the Galaxy*, 1957
Jerry Pournelle, *Exiles to Glory*, 1978
John E. Stith, *Redshift Rendezvous*, 1990
Jack Vance, *Marune: Alastor 933*, 1975

---

**4953**

**CHARLES SHEFFIELD**

## Dancing with Myself

(New York: Baen, 1993)

**Story type:** Science Fiction (Collection)

**Summary:** Contains a one-page introduction, eleven stories with individual afterwords, four articles published in periodicals and anthologies 1982-1992, and one original, "A Biography of the Universe." Stories exhibit a wide range of tone with a variety of themes including terrestrial biology, extraterrestrial intelligence, physical laws of the universe and a 600,000 kilometer bike race around the Earth and Moon.

**Other books you might like:**
Michael Flynn, *The Nanotech Chronicles*, 1991
Janet Kagan, *Mirabile*, 1991
Larry Niven, *N-Space*, 1990
Larry Niven, *Tales of Known Space*, 1975
Allen Steele, *Rude Astronauts*, 1993
Marc Stiegler, *The Gentle Seduction*, 1990
John Varley, *The Persistence of Vision*, 1978

---

**4954**

**CHARLES SHEFFIELD**

## Divergence

(New York: Ballantine/Del Rey, 1991)

**Story type:** Science Fiction (Adventure)
**Series:** Heritage Universe
**Major character(s):** Darya Lang, Scientist, Adventurer; Hans Rebka, Adventurer; E.C. Tally, Artificial Intelligence
**Time period(s):** 63rd century
**Locale(s):** *Summer Dreamboat*, Spaceship; Glister, Planet—Imaginary

**Summary:** While continuing a millennia-long search for The Builders, legendary creators of mysterious constructs, Darya Lang and Hans Rebka discover a threat to all intelligent life.

**Other books you might like:**
Algis Budrys, *Rogue Moon*, 1960
Arthur C. Clarke, *2061: Odyssey Three*, 1988
Arthur C. Clarke, *2010: Odyssey Two*, 1982
Arthur C. Clarke, *2001: A Space Odyssey*, 1968
Dan Simmons, *The Fall of Hyperion*, 1990
Dan Simmons, *Hyperion*, 1989

## 4955

### CHARLES SHEFFIELD

## *The Ganymede Club*

(New York: Tor, 1995)

**Story type:** Science Fiction (Mystery; Space Colony)
**Series:** Cold as Ice
**Major character(s):** Lola Belman, Psychologist; Bryce Sonnenberg, Scientist (mathematician), Sports Figure (scooter racer); Rustum "Bat" Battacharia, Computer Expert, Teenager
**Time period(s):** 2060s; 2070s (2067-2072)
**Locale(s):** Ganymede, Jupiter (moon); Mars

**Summary:** After war ravages most of the innersolar system, Bryce Sonnenberg comes to Lola Belman on Ganymede because of blackouts and strange dreams, frightening some descendants of the members of the First Saturn Expedition who have formed a tight club. When Lola enlists the aid of her young brother and his friend to discover whether or not Bryce's dreams have any basis in reality, their dangerous investigation uncovers ancient secrets.

**Other books you might like:**
Kevin J. Anderson, *Assemblers of Infinity*, 1993
    Doug Beason, co-author
C.J. Cherryh, *Cyteen*, 1988
Betty Anne Crawford, *The Bushido Incident*, 1992
Robert A. Heinlein, *Methuselah's Children*, 1958
Nancy Kress, *Beggars in Spain*, 1993
Frederik Pohl, *Outnumbering the Dead*, 1992
Karen Ripley, *Prisoner of Dreams*, 1989
Allen Steele, *Clarke County, Space*, 1990

## 4956

### CHARLES SHEFFIELD

## *Georgia on My Mind and Other Places*

(New York: Tor, 1995)

**Story type:** Science Fiction (Collection; Science Fiction)
**Summary:** Contains a brief introduction and 14 stories published 1987-1994 in periodicals and anthologies, each with an afterword indicating the story's genesis. The selections range from short, silly pieces such as "Fifteen-Love on the Dead Man's Chest" to longer, more serious treatments, including the Nebula Award-winning title story.

**Other books you might like:**
Poul Anderson, *The Book of Poul Anderson*, 1974
Isaac Asimov, *The Best of Isaac Asimov*, 1973
Arthur C. Clarke, *The Nine Billion Names of God*, 1967
Robert A. Heinlein, *The Green Hills of Earth*, 1951
Allen Steele, *Rude Astronauts*, 1993
John Varley, *Blue Champagne*, 1986
Jack Williamson, *The Best of Jack Williamson*, 1978

## 4957

### CHARLES SHEFFIELD

## *Godspeed*

(New York: Tor, 1993)

**Story type:** Science Fiction (Lost Colony)
**Major character(s):** Jay Hara, Teenager, Spaceman; Paddy Enderton, Spaceman; Eileen Xavier, Doctor
**Time period(s):** Indeterminate Future

**Locale(s):** Erin, Planet—Imaginary; The Forty Worlds, Outer Space (Maveen star system)

**Summary:** Growing up across the lake from the spaceport on Erin, Jay aspires to become a spaceman. Only Dr. Eileen seems to recognize that Erin cannot completely support human life. Since the Isolation 800 years earlier when the flow of goods from outside the Forty Worlds ceased, Erin supports a reduced technological level and decreased population which now produces three girls for every 100 boys. Jay discovers the location of a Godspeed station and, with the help of Dr. Eileen, must find a way to end the Isolation.

**Other books you might like:**
Stephen Baxter, *Raft*, 1991
David Brin, *Glory Season*, 1993
Debra Doyle, *The Price of the Stars*, 1992
    James D. Macdonald, co-author
Harry Harrison, *The Deathworld Trilogy*, 1975
Rosemary Kirstein, *The Outskirter's Secret*, 1992
Megan Lindholm, *Alien Earth*, 1992
Larry Niven, *The Integral Trees*, 1984
Frederik Pohl, *Stopping at Slowyear*, 1991
Alis A. Rasmussen, *A Passage of Stars*, 1990

## 4958

### CHARLES SHEFFIELD
### JERRY POURNELLE, Co-Author

## *Higher Education*

(New York: Tor, 1996)

**Story type:** Science Fiction (Young Adult; Adventure)
**Series:** Jupiter
**Major character(s):** Rick Luban, Teenager, Apprentice; Vido Valdez, Teenager, Apprentice; Alice Klein, Teenager, Apprentice
**Time period(s):** Indeterminate Future
**Locale(s):** CM-2, Space Station; CM-26, Space Station

**Summary:** Kicked out of school for a harmless pratical joke, Rick Luban signs on with Vanguard Mining, enduring months of rigorous training in the hopes of making a career in asteroid mining.

**Other books you might like:**
Isaac Asimov, *Lucky Starr and the Pirates of the Asteroids*, 1953
Robert A. Heinlein, *Space Cadet*, 1948
Frederik Pohl, *Mining the Oort*, 1992
Jerry Pournelle, *West of Honor*, 1976
Larry Segriff, *Spacer Dreams*, 1995

## 4959

### CHARLES SHEFFIELD, Editor

## *How to Save the World*

(New York: Tor, 1995)

**Story type:** Science Fiction (Anthology; Dystopian)
**Summary:** Contains a four-page introduction, three pages "About the Authors," plus 11 original and two stories reprinted in a different form from an anthology and a periodical publication. A wide range of global problems receive simple, if not painless, solutions as if presented by extraterrestrials who view humanity's problems from the outside. The 15 authors include Doug Beason, B.W. Clough, James P. Hogan, Kathe Koja, Barry N. Malzberg, Larry Niven, Jerry Oltion, Nick Pollotta, Jerry Pournelle, and Charles Sheffield.

**Other books you might like:**
Thomas M. Disch, *The New Improved Sun: An Anthology of Utopian Science Fiction*, 1975
   editor
Thomas M. Disch, *The Ruins of Earth: An Anthology of the Immediate Future*, 1971
   editor
Harry Harrison, *There Won't Be War*, 1991
   Bruce McAllister, co-editor
Kim Stanley Robinson, *Future Primitive: The New Ecotopias*, 1994
   editor
Lewis Shiner, *When the Music's Over*, 1991
   editor
John Stadler, *Eco-Fiction*, 1971
   editor

## 4960
### CHARLES SHEFFIELD
### DAVID BISCHOFF, Co-Author

## The Judas Cross
(New York: Warner/Aspect, 1994)

**Story type:** Horror (Occult)
**Major character(s):** Louis Villette, Nobleman (Marquis of Saint Ame); Celine Villette, Bastard Daughter (of Louis Villette); Jenny Marshall, Young Woman
**Time period(s):** 1910s (1916)
**Locale(s):** Saint Ame, France

**Summary:** Appalled at the carnage against his countrymen at the hands of the German army during World War I, Louis Villette, keeper of the Cross of Judas, formed from the pieces of silver given to Judas Iscariot for his betrayal of Jesus Christ and which imprisons his traitor soul, vows to use the talisman to prevent further bloodshed. In order to wield the cross's power, though, Louis finds it necessary to first betray family, lovers, and other innocents who have placed their trust in him.

**Other books you might like:**
James Herbert, *The Spear*, 1978
Robert Weinberg, *The Armageddon Box*, 1991
Robert Weinberg, *The Devil's Auction*, 1988
Dennis Wheatley, *They Used Dark Forces*, 1964

## 4961
### CHARLES SHEFFIELD

## One Man's Universe
(New York: Tor, 1993)

**Story type:** Science Fiction (Collection; Hard Science Fiction)
**Major character(s):** Arthur Morton McAndrews, Scientist, Spaceman
**Time period(s):** 21st century
**Locale(s):** Outer Space

**Summary:** Contains a three-page introduction, a 36-page appendix on the science in Sheffield's science fiction plus two original stories and five reprinted from 1970s and 1980s periodicals, all focusing on McAndrew's fantastic experimentation with black holes. Expands *The McAndrew Chronicles* (1983).

**Other books you might like:**
Stephen Baxter, *Timelike Infinity*, 1993
David Brin, *Earth*, 1990
Vonda N. McIntyre, *Metaphase*, 1992
Larry Niven, *Neutron Star*, 1968

Larry Niven, *Tales of Known Space*, 1975
Frederik Pohl, *Gateway*, 1977
John E. Stith, *Redshift Rendezvous*, 1990
John Varley, *Blue Champagne*, 1986
John Varley, *The Persistence of Vision*, 1978

## 4962
### CHARLES SHEFFIELD

## Proteus in the Underworld
(New York: Baen, 1995)

**Story type:** Science Fiction (Genetic Manipulation; Mystery)
**Series:** Proteus
**Major character(s):** Sondra Dearborn, Researcher, Troubleshooter (Office of Form Control); Trudy Melford, Businesswoman, Wealthy; Behrooz ''Bey'' Wolf, Recluse, Scientist
**Time period(s):** 22nd century
**Locale(s):** Earth; Mars; Oort Cloud, Outer Space

**Summary:** Assigned to discover why genetic certification tests have begun to misidentify subjects as human, Sondra Dearborn calls upon Bey Wolf, who is happily retired and reluctant to involve himself. Bey's investigation of the anomalies points to sabotage as his search leads to Mars, while Sondra's duties draw her to the Oort Cloud.

**Other books you might like:**
Isaac Asimov, *Nemesis*, 1989
Ben Bova, *Colony*, 1978
Alexis A. Gilliland, *The Revolution From Rosinante*, 1981
Melisa C. Michaels, *Floater Factor*, 1988
Frederik Pohl, *Mining the Oort*, 1992
Kim Stanley Robinson, *Icehenge*, 1984
Allen Steele, *Clarke County, Space*, 1990
John Varley, *The Ophiuchi Hotline*, 1977

## 4963
### CHARLES SHEFFIELD

## Proteus Unbound
(New York: Ballantine/Del Rey, 1989)

**Story type:** Science Fiction (Hard Science Fiction)
**Major character(s):** Behrooz ''Bey'' Wolf, Government Official (Former), Scientist; Leo Manx, Genetically Altered Being
**Time period(s):** 22nd century
**Locale(s):** Outer System Federation, Interstellar Empire/Federation

**Summary:** Bey Wolf is the former head of the government office that controls the technology involved in adapting the human body to extraterrestrial environments. Wolf has spent the last several years in suspended animation, however, in an attempt to escape encroaching madness. Now he's been summoned back to consciousness because someone is attempting to provoke war between the inner planets and the outer solar system. This is the sequel to *Sight of Proteus*.

**Other books you might like:**
Lois McMaster Bujold, *Brothers in Arms*, 1988
Lois McMaster Bujold, *Falling Free*, 1988
Gordon Eklund, *A Thunder on Neptune*, 1989
Frederik Pohl, *Man Plus*, 1976

## 4964

### CHARLES SHEFFIELD

## *Putting Up Roots*

(New York: Tor, 1997)

**Story type:** Science Fiction (First Contact; Young Adult)
**Major character(s):** Joshua ''Josh'' Kerrigan, Hero, Outcast; Sapphire Karpov, Addict, Young Woman; Winnie Carlson, Technician, Spy
**Time period(s):** Indeterminate Future
**Locale(s):** Solferino, Planet—Imaginary

**Summary:** Sent with a party of throwaway teens to settle on Solferino, Joshua and his autistic cousin, Dawn, find no settlers waiting to greet them. Mysteriously shuttled around the planet with no off-world communications possible, Josh believes he has seen mining ships while his cousin says she has found intelligent aliens.

**Other books you might like:**
Gregory Benford, *Jupiter Project*, 1975
Robert A. Heinlein, *Farmer in the Sky*, 1950
Colin Kapp, *The Survival Game*, 1976
Andre Norton, *The Stars Are Ours*, 1954
Frederik Pohl, *The Voices of Heaven*, 1994
Jerry Pournelle, *Birth of Fire*, 1976
Carol Severance, *Reefsong*, 1991
Joan D. Vinge, *Psion*, 1982

## 4965

### CHARLES SHEFFIELD

## *Summertide*

(New York: Ballantine/Del Rey, 1990)

**Story type:** Science Fiction (Adventure)
**Series:** Heritage Universe
**Major character(s):** Darya Lang, Scientist, Adventurer; Max Perry, Government Official
**Time period(s):** 63rd century
**Locale(s):** Opal, Planet—Imaginary; Quake, Planet—Imaginary

**Summary:** When humanity reaches the stars, strange alien artifacts are found spread throughout the galaxy. Many are entirely incomprehensible. A scientist discovers that something is about to happen to one of the artifacts and sets out to discover its secret.

**Other books you might like:**
Algis Budrys, *Rogue Moon*, 1960
Arthur C. Clarke, *2001: A Space Odyssey*, 1968
Arthur C. Clarke, *2010: Odyssey Two*, 1982
Arthur C. Clarke, *2061: Odyssey Three*, 1987
Dan Simmons, *The Fall of Hyperion*, 1990
Dan Simmons, *Hyperion*, 1989

## 4966

### CHARLES SHEFFIELD

## *Tomorrow and Tomorrow*

(New York: Bantam Spectra, 1997)

**Story type:** Science Fiction (Alternate Intelligence; Immortality)
**Major character(s):** Walter Drake Merlin, Musician; Tom Lambert, Doctor; Anastasia ''Ana'' Merlin, Singer
**Time period(s):** 2000s; Indeterminate Future
**Locale(s):** Earth; Cyberspace

**Summary:** In love with his wife Ana from the first sound of her voice, Drake cannot accept her suddenly impending death from an extremely rare disease. He decides to have her cryogenically stored, develop himself as an expert to insure his revival and join her. The first time he wakes, Drake pretends the cure for his obsession with Ana worked, steals a spaceship and Ana's cryochamber, then heads out to Canopus. When, on his way back, he opens the casket, causing Ana permanent brain damage, Drake and Ana return to the chambers with instructions to revive Drake only if needed or if Ana can be cured.

**Other books you might like:**
John Brunner, *Age of Miracles*, 1973
Ken Grimwood, *Replay*, 1986
Joe Haldeman, *The Forever War*, 1997 revised
Christopher Pike, *The Starlight Crystal*, 1996
Vernor Vinge, *A Fire upon the Deep*, 1992

## 4967

### CHARLES SHEFFIELD

## *Transcendence*

(New York: Ballantine Del Rey, 1992)

**Story type:** Science Fiction (Adventure; Hard Science Fiction)
**Series:** Heritage Universe
**Major character(s):** Darya Lang, Scientist, Adventurer; Hans Rebka, Adventurer; Dulcimer, Alien (Chism Polypheme), Pilot (spaceship)
**Time period(s):** 63rd century
**Locale(s):** *Erebus*, Spaceship; Torvil Anfract, Outer Space; Genizee, Planet—Imaginary

**Summary:** Darya Lang realizes that her adventures leading to the discovery of live Zardalu leave her unsatisfied by academic research. When presented with the opportunity to join a new expedition and bring back evidence to convince the Alliance Council of the Zardalu's return, Darya and her companions must first find the location of Genizee, the lost homeworld of the Zardalu, perhaps located in the Torvil Anfract, a region of space-time distorted by macroscopic quantum phenomena.

**Other books you might like:**
David Brin, *Startide Rising*, 1983
C.J. Cherryh, *Chanur's Legacy*, 1992
Arthur C. Clarke, *Rendezvous with Rama*, 1973
David Drake, *Starliner*, 1992
Vonda N. McIntyre, *Metaphase*, 1992
Alis A. Rasmussen, *A Passage of Stars*, 1990
Vernor Vinge, *A Fire upon the Deep*, 1992

## 4968

### MARY SHELLEY

## *Collected Tales and Stories*

(Baltimore, Maryland: The Johns Hopkins University Press, 1976)

**Story type:** Horror (Collection)

**Summary:** An indispensible collection of 25 stories by the author of *Frankenstein*. Of particular note are the doppelganger story ''Ferdinando Eboli: A Tale,'' a story of personality exchange ''Transformation,'' and a fable about the burdens of immortality ''The Mortal Immortal.'' Illustrated with original plates from the stories' magazine appearances. Edited by Charles E. Robinson.

**Other books you might like:**

Elizabeth Cleghorn Gaskell, *Mrs. Gaskell's Tales of Mystery and Horror*, 1978
Gertrude Atherton, *The Bell in the Fog and Other Stories*, 1905
Everett F. Bleiler, *The Collected Ghost Stories of Mrs. J.H. Riddell*, 1977
Vernon Lee, *Supernatural Tales: Excursions into Fantasy*, 1987
E. Nesbit, *In the Dark*, 1988

---

**4969**

MARY SHELLEY

## The Mortal Immortal

(San Francisco: Tachyon Publications, 1996)

**Story type:** Horror (Collection)

**Summary:** This collection of five supernatural tales by the author of *Frankenstein* shows her preoccupation with the theme of unnaturally prolonged life. The title story is about a man who tires of his alchemically induced immortality and seeks a means of death. "Roger Dodsworth: Reanimated Englishman" and "Valerius: The Re-Animated Roman" both are about the bodies of men from ancient times revived in the present day of the author. The book also includes "Transformation," a tale of body exchange, and "The Dream." Michael Bishop supplies an introduction.

**Other books you might like:**

Vernon Lee, *The Snake Lady and Other Stories*, 1955
Margaret Oliphant, *Stories of the Seen and Unseen*, 1889
Mrs. J.H. Riddell, *The Collected Ghost Stories of Mrs. J.H. Riddell*, 1977
Bram Stoker, *Dracula's Guest*, 1912

---

**4970**

RICK SHELLEY

## The Hero King

(New York: Roc, 1992)

**Story type:** Fantasy (Quest; Alternate World)
**Series:** Varayan Memoir
**Major character(s):** Gil Tyner, Royalty (King of Varay), Hero; Aaron Carpenter, Wizard; Parthet "Uncle Parker", Wizard
**Time period(s):** 1990s
**Locale(s):** Earth; Faerie, Mythical Place; Varay, Fictional Country

**Summary:** Gil tries to take a shower back on Earth only to discover that the high radiation level there prevents access. A Russian trawler carried ashore on Varay by a tidal wave coupled with the sudden appearance of a second and then a third moon, and the realization that World War III occurred on Earth, compels Gil to consult with his enemy from Faerie, the Elford of Xayber, who informs Gil that when seven Moons rise, Varay, Earth and Faerie will end. Gil must prevent that outcome.

**Other books you might like:**

Charles de Lint, *The Little Country*, 1991
John DeChancie, *Castle Perilous*, 1988
Alan Dean Foster, *To the Vanishing Point*, 1988
Geary Gravel, *A Key for the Nonesuch*, 1990
Marc Laidlaw, *Neon Lotus*, 1988
S.P. Somtow, *Riverrun*, 1991

---

**4971**

RICK SHELLEY

## The Hero of Varay

(New York: Roc, 1991)

**Story type:** Fantasy (Quest; Alternate World)
**Series:** Varayan Memoir
**Major character(s):** Gil Tyner, Royalty, Hero; Parthet "Uncle Parker", Wizard
**Time period(s):** 1990s
**Locale(s):** Earth; Varay, Fictional Country

**Summary:** Gil Tyner is the Hero of Varay, a buffer zone between Earth and the Lands of Fairy. Terrorist bombings on Earth have set off a chain reaction of magic in the buffer zone, disastrous for both worlds unless the chaos can be stopped using the legendary jewels of the Great Mother Earth. However, the only being who can lead Gil to the jewels is the elf that he has recently beheaded.

**Other books you might like:**

Margaret Ball, *The Shadow Gate*, 1990
Mark Twain, *A Connecticut Yankee in King Arthur's Court*, 1898
    Written as Mark Twain
L. Sprague de Camp, *The Complete Compleat Enchanter*, 1989
    Fletcher Pratt, co-author
Gordon R. Dickson, *The Dragon Knight*, 1990
Phyllis Eisenstein, *Shadow of Earth*, 1979
Ursula K. Le Guin, *The Beginning Place*, 1980
Terri Windling, *Life on the Border*, 1991
    editor

---

**4972**

RICK SHELLEY

## Lieutenant

(New York: Ace, 1998)

**Story type:** Science Fiction (Military)
**Series:** Dirigent Mercenary Corps
**Major character(s):** Lon Nolan, Military Personnel (lieutenant); Arnold Gaffney, Military Personnel (colonel)
**Time period(s):** 29th century (2804)
**Locale(s):** Dirigent, Planet—Imaginary; Belletiener, Planet—Imaginary

**Summary:** Newly commissioned as a mercenary officer, Lon Nolan is part of a force hired to put an end to an interplanetary war. During the course of the battle, he discovers that there are additional stresses when he is forced to make decisions that could cost the life of the people serving under him.

**Other books you might like:**

Lois McMaster Bujold, *Barrayar*, 1991
John Dalmas, *The Kalif's War*, 1991
William C. Dietz, *The Final Battle*, 1995
David Drake, *The Butcher's Bill*, 1998
David Feintuch, *Fisherman's Hope*, 1996

---

**4973**

RICK SHELLEY

## Officer Cadet

(New York: Ace, 1998)

**Story type:** Science Fiction (Military)
**Series:** Dirigent Mercenary Corps

**Major character(s):** Lon Nolan, Military Personnel (cadet); Orlis, Military Personnel (captain)
**Time period(s):** 29th century (2803)
**Locale(s):** Norbank, Planet—Imaginary; Dirigent, Planet—Imaginary

**Summary:** False charges result in Lon Nolan's expulsion from the military academy on Earth. Frustrated, he joins the Dirigent Mercenary Corps and accompanies them on a dangerous mission, during which he proves himself a capable and valuable member of their company, although one with much remaining to learn.

**Other books you might like:**
Bill Baldwin, *Canby's Legion*, 1995
David Drake, *The Forlorn Hope*, 1984
David Feintuch, *Challenger's Hope*, 1997
Roland J. Green, *Division of the Spoils*, 1990
William H. Keith Jr., *Bolo Brigade*, 1997

## 4974

### RICK SHELLEY

## Return to Camerein

(New York: Ace, 1998)

**Story type:** Science Fiction (Military)
**Major character(s):** David Spencer, Military Personnel; Marie Caffre, Housewife
**Time period(s):** Indeterminate Future
**Locale(s):** Camerein, Planet—Imaginary

**Summary:** The war between two interstellar empires grinds toward a close. On the verge of peace, they both decide to resolve the question of a former resort planet's status by military means, and in order to do so, one side decides to interrogate a man who was marooned there for several years. Retrieving him without provoking a military response proves a difficult task.

**Other books you might like:**
Bill Baldwin, *The Defenders*, 1992
Lois McMaster Bujold, *The Warrior's Apprentice*, 1986
David Drake, *The Jungle*, 1992
Roland J. Green, *These Green Foreign Hills*, 1987
William H. Keith Jr., *Warstrider*, 1993

## 4975

### RICK SHELLEY

## The Wizard at Home

(New York: Roc, 1995)

**Story type:** Fantasy (Magic Conflict)
**Series:** Seven Towers
**Major character(s):** Silvas, Wizard, Deity; Maria, Deity; Mikel, Deity
**Time period(s):** 13th century (1238)
**Locale(s):** Mecq, Fictional City; The Citadel, Mythical Place; England

**Summary:** Before the White Brotherhood triumphs over the Blue Rose, the 20 true gods lose a quarter of their number. As Carillia dies, she passes her divinity to the surprised Silvas and the even more surprised Maria. The two must defend themselves against Carillia's siblings, who disapprove of mortals claiming divinity. Second in the series.

**Other books you might like:**
Steven Brust, *Jhereg*, 1983
Glen Cook, *The Swordbearer*, 1982
Diane Duane, *The Door into Fire*, 1979

Simon R. Green, *Hawk & Fisher*, 1990
Fritz Leiber, *Swords and Deviltry*, 1970

## 4976

### JIM SHEPARD

## Lights Out in the Reptile House

(New York: W. W. Norton, 1990)

**Story type:** Fantasy (Political; Historical)
**Major character(s):** Karel Roeder, Student—High School; Albert Delp, Scientist (herpetologist)
**Time period(s):** 1990s
**Locale(s):** Alternate Earth

**Summary:** Karel Roeder enjoys his job at the zoo which makes life at home difficult since his father is unable to find work. Life at home is even more difficult as Karel and his father do not like each other. Karel's job is threatened by nationalization of the zoo when the National Unity Party's rise to power creates a very repressive society.

**Other books you might like:**
Mary Gentle, *Ancient Light*, 1987
Mary Gentle, *Golden Witchbreed*, 1984
Heather Gladney, *Teot's War*, 1987
Robert Onopa, *The Pleasure Tube*, 1979
George Orwell, *Animal Farm*, 1946
George Orwell, *1984*, 1949
Ayn Rand, *Atlas Shrugged*, 1957
Allen Steele, *Orbital Decay*, 1989

## 4977

### LUCIUS SHEPARD

## The Ends of the Earth

(Sauk City, Wisconsin: Arkham House, 1991)

**Story type:** Horror (Collection)

**Summary:** Seventeen blendings of fantasy, science fiction and horror by one of the most provocative writers of contemporary imaginative literature. Many stories are set in exotic locales such as Katmandu (''A Wooden Tiger'') or Guatemala (''Fire Zone Emerald'') or use the Vietnam war as their launching pad (''Delta Sly Honey,'' ''Shades''). Regardless of their time or place, they address such timeless themes as the subjectivity of experience (''The Ends of the Earth''), the abuses of sexual power (''The Black Clay Boy''), the application of values to life (''The Exercise of Faith'') and the relation of art to life (''The Scalehunter's Beautiful Daughter'').

**Other books you might like:**
Michael Blumlein, *The Brains of Rats*, 1990
Pat Cadigan, *Patterns*, 1990
Harlan Ellison, *Deathbird Stories*, 1975
John Shirley, *Heatseeker*, 1989

## 4978

### LUCIUS SHEPARD

## The Golden

(Shingletown, California: Mark V. Zeising, 1993)

**Story type:** Horror (Vampire Story; Mystery)
**Major character(s):** Michel Beheim, Vampire; Roland Agenor, Vampire; Lady Alexandra Conforti, Vampire

**Time period(s):** 19th century
**Locale(s):** Castle Banat, Europe

**Summary:** During a gathering of the vampire "Family" at the Castle Banat, a "Golden," or human bred specifically to be vampirized, is slain under unusual circumstances. Michel Beheim, the newest member of the Family, is charged with the task of finding out who the murderer is, and his experiences become milestones in his odyssey of self-discovery as a vampire.

**Other books you might like:**
Poppy Z. Brite, *Lost Souls*, 1992
Anne Rice, *The Vampire Lestat*, 1985
Dan Simmons, *Carrion Comfort*, 1989
Brian Stableford, *The Empire of Fear*, 1988
Brian Stableford, *Young Blood*, 1992

---

**4979**

**LUCIUS SHEPARD**

### Kalimantan

(New York: St. Martin's Press, 1992)

**Story type:** Horror (Occult)
**Major character(s):** Curtis Mackinnon, Businessman; Paul Tenzer, Scientist (zoologist)
**Time period(s):** 1980s
**Locale(s):** Kalimantan Borneo, Indonesia

**Summary:** Seeking refuge in the jungles of Borneo fron botched business deals, nebbish Curtis Mackinnon discovers a ceremonial drug used by the natives to alter the fabric of reality. Through use of the drug, Mackinnon becomes a despotic powermonger who threatens to vent his anger upon the world.

**Other books you might like:**
Paddy Chayefsky, *Altered States*, 1979
Joseph Conrad, *Heart of Darkness*, 1902
Philip K. Dick, *The Three Stigmata of Palmer Eldritch*, 1964
K.W. Jeter, *Dark Seeker*, 1987

---

**4980**

**MARK SHEPHERD**

### Elvendude

(New York: Baen, 1994)

**Story type:** Fantasy (Urban; Magic Conflict)
**Major character(s):** Aedham "Adam" Tuiereann, Mythical Creature (elf), Amnesiac; Samantha "Sammi" McDaris, Mythical Creature (elf), Royalty; Zeldan Dhu, Mythical Creature (elf), Magician
**Time period(s):** Indeterminate
**Locale(s):** Dallas, Texas; Elfhame Avalon, Fictional Country

**Summary:** To preserve Aedham from an attack on Elfhame Avalon by evil elves, King Traighthren magically alters Aedham's memory and hides him on Earth. Known as Adam to his mundane suburban friends, Aedham must suddenly come to grips with the fact that elven agents and drug dealers want to track him down.

**Other books you might like:**
Ellen Guon, *Bedlam Boyz*, 1993
Katharine Kerr, *Daggerspell*, 1986
Mercedes Lackey, *Born to Run*, 1992
    Larry Dixon, co-author
Mercedes Lackey, *Chrome Circle*, 1994
    Larry Dixon, co-author

Mercedes Lackey, *Knight of Ghosts and Shadows*, 1990
    Ellen Guon, co-author
Mercedes Lackey, *Prison of Souls*, 1993
    Mark Shepherd, co-author
Mercedes Lackey, *Summoned to Tourney*, 1992
    Ellen Guon, co-author
Mercedes Lackey, *Wheels of Fire*, 1992
    Mark Shepherd, co-author

---

**4981**

**MARK SHEPHERD**

### Spiritride

(New York: Baen, 1997)

**Story type:** Fantasy (Magic Conflict; Political)
**Major character(s):** Petrus, Mythical Creature (elf), Warrior; Wolf, Veteran, Shaman; Lucus Vaughan, Religious (devil worshipper)
**Time period(s):** 1990s
**Locale(s):** Underhill, Mythical Place (Elven realm); New Mexico

**Summary:** Petrus's reconnaissance mission to Earth presents evil Unseelie warriors an opportunity for revenge, enlisting the help of devil worshippers and an ancient Egyptian cat spirit to that end. Petrus and his small band received help from a protective guard of motorcycle riders, a young motorcyclist and a veteran of the Gulf War conflict who is a shaman and sole surviving member of his tribe. Sequel to Elvendude.

**Other books you might like:**
Margaret Ball, *Mathemagics*, 1996
Greg Bear, *Songs of Earth and Power*, 1994
Emma Bull, *War for the Oaks*, 1987
Mercedes Lackey, *Prison of Souls*, 1993
    Mark Shepherd, co-author
Mercedes Lackey, *Wheels of Fire*, 1992
    Mark Shepherd, co-author

---

**4982**

**DAVID SHERMAN**
**DAN CRAGG**, Co-Author

### School of Fire

(New York: Del Rey, 1998)

**Story type:** Science Fiction (Military; Political)
**Series:** Starfist
**Major character(s):** Joseph Deane, Military Personnel (lance corporal); Rachman Claypoole, Military Personnel (lance corporal)
**Time period(s):** Indeterminate Future
**Locale(s):** Wanderjahr, Planet—Imaginary

**Summary:** A group of mercenaries arrives on Wanderjahr, employed by the loyal government to put down a rebellion that has adversely affected the planet's economy. The soldiers soon find themselves fighting on two fronts—one against the stubborn revolutionaries, the other against an entrenched bureaucracy that appears determined to prevent them from winning a decisive victory.

**Other books you might like:**
Bill Baldwin, *The Siege*, 1994
Lois McMaster Bujold, *The Vor Game*, 1990
William C. Dietz, *Legion of the Damned*, 1993
David Drake, *Counting the Cost*, 1987
Roland J. Green, *The Mountain Walks*, 1989

## **4983**

### DELIA SHERMAN

## *The Porcelain Dove*

(New York: Dutton, 1993)

**Story type:** Fantasy (Historical)
**Major character(s):** Berthe Duvet, Servant (chambermaid), Writer
**Time period(s):** 18th century; Indeterminate
**Locale(s):** Paris, France; Chateau Beauxpres, France; Jura Mountains, France

**Summary:** Unless the family finds and acquires a fabulous pocelain dove, an ancestral curse dictates madness and ruin for the House of Malvoeux. Trapped outside time for 200 years, Berthe Duvet chronicles her life and events surrounding the French Revolution, including detailed views of the extravagant and eccentric practices of the oblivious nobility.

**Other books you might like:**
Lois McMaster Bujold, *The Spirit Ring*, 1992
Mary Gentle, *The Architecture of Desire*, 1993
Mary Gentle, *Rats and Gargoyles*, 1991
Katherine Neville, *The Eight*, 1989
Paula Volsky, *Illusion*, 1992
Martha Wells, *The Element of Fire*, 1993

## **4984**

### JOEL HENRY SHERMAN

## *Random Factor*

(New York: Ballantine/Del Rey, 1991)

**Story type:** Science Fiction (Adventure)
**Major character(s):** Kenneth Christian Rourke, Security Officer; Gral Il Chedo, Alien (Col); Nebuun, Alien (Eng)
**Time period(s):** Indeterminate Future
**Locale(s):** Mael Station, Space Station; Jerrume, Planet—Imaginary (Mael System)

**Summary:** When the Ssoorii Unity received the signal, it awoke from its dormant state and began constructing itself into a battle fleet. Rejected by the Col High Triumvirate, Gral Il Chedo made a secret pact with the Unity. After the factor of Mael Station was killed in an accident, and after a disastrous political decision forced a job change, Kenneth Rourke becomes the new factor of Mael Station, perhaps the chance occurrence which will prevent a major interstellar war.

**Other books you might like:**
David Brin, *Startide Rising*, 1983
Lois McMaster Bujold, *Borders of Infinity*, 1989
Glen Cook, *The Dragon Never Sleeps*, 1988
John Dalmas, *The Kalif's War*, 1991
C.S. Friedman, *The Madness Season*, 1990
Stephen Goldin, *Jade Darcy and the Affair of Honor*, 1988
    Mary Mason, co-author
Steve Miller, *Agent of Change*, 1988
    Sharon Lee, co-author
Alis A. Rasmussen, *A Passage of Stars*, 1990
Timothy Zahn, *Cobra*, 1985

## **4985**

### JOSEPHA SHERMAN

## *Child of Faerie, Child of Earth*

(New York: Walker, 1992)

**Story type:** Fantasy (Romance; Young Adult)
**Major character(s):** Percinet, Mythical Creature (faerie), Royalty (prince); Graciosa, Human, Noblewoman
**Time period(s):** 12th century
**Locale(s):** France; Faerie, Mythical Place

**Summary:** Percinet journeys to the mortal realm and resolves to win Graciosa's heart despite his mother's misgivings and the interference of Graciosa's mother, an abusive sorceress, in this adaptation of Mme. d'Aulnoy's fairy tale "Gracieuse and Percinet."

**Other books you might like:**
Louise Cooper, *The Sleep of Stone*, 1991
Parke Godwin, *Sherwood*, 1991
Tanith Lee, *Black Unicorn*, 1991
Megan Lindholm, *Cloven Hooves*, 1991
Will Shetterly, *Elsewhere*, 1991
Nancy Springer, *Wings of Flame*, 1985
Terri Windling, *Life on the Border*, 1991
    editor

## **4986**

### JOSEPHA SHERMAN

## *King's Son, Magic's Son*

(New York: Baen, 1994)

**Story type:** Fantasy (Magic Conflict; Political)
**Major character(s):** Aidan ap Nia, Royalty, Magician; King Estmere, Royalty, Leader
**Time period(s):** Indeterminate
**Locale(s):** Cymra, Fictional Country; King Estmere's Lands, Fictional Country; Lundinia, Fictional City

**Summary:** Raised in Cymra, Aidan studies magic with local faerie folk. On her deathbed, Aidan's mother exacts Aidan's promise to join King Estmere and lend magical assistance to his half-brother. In King Estmere's lands, Aidan learns about the intrigues and politics of court life.

**Other books you might like:**
Dave Duncan, *The Cutting Edge*, 1992
Terry Goodkind, *Wizard's First Rule*, 1994
Mercedes Lackey, *A Cast of Corbies*, 1994
    Josepha Sherman, co-author
Elizabeth Moon, *Liar's Oath*, 1992
Brad Strickland, *Wizard's Mole*, 1991
Elizabeth Willey, *The Well-Favored Man: The Tale of the Sorcerer's Nephew*, 1993

## **4987**

### JOSEPHA SHERMAN

## *Once upon a Galaxy*

(Little Rock, Arkansas: August House, 1994)

**Story type:** Fantasy (Collection; Legend)

**Summary:** Subtitled "The Ancient Stories Behind Star Wars, Superman and Other Popular Fantasies," this volume contains a two-page introduction plus introductions to individual sections, grouping by subject 42 tales from around the world which provide classical foundations for modern characters and themes in film, television and comics, such as "Star Trek," Superman, *Star Wars*, cartoon tricksters and the quest for a magic implement. Sherman draws on millennia of world literature and mythos to exemplify themes common to diverse cultures. Includes 22 pages of notes providing source information and folkloric background for each story plus a 15-page suggested reading and viewing list.

**Other books you might like:**
I.G. Edmonds, *Trickster Tales*, 1966
    editor
Richard Gilliam, *Grails: Quests of the Dawn*, 1994
    Martin H. Greenberg, Edward E. Kramer, co-editors
Andrea Hopkins, *Chronicles of King Arthur*, 1994
Ethel Johnston Phelps, *Tatterhood and Other Tales*, 1978
    editor
Jane Yolen, *Favorite Folktales From around the World*, 1986
    editor
Jack Zipes, *Spells of Enchantment*, 1991
    editor

---

**4988**

**JOSEPHA SHERMAN**, Editor
**MARTIN H. GREENBERG**, Co-Editor

### Orphans of the Night

(New York: Walker, 1995)

**Story type:** Fantasy (Anthology; Young Adult)

**Summary:** Contains a brief introduction, four pages of author biographies, and 13 original stories featuring lesser-known nocturnal creatures of legend and folklore and varying in tone from mysterious to ominous. Authors include Jo Clayton, Esther M. Friesner, Laura Resnick, Pamela F. Service, Susan Shwartz, Sherwood Smith, Nancy Springer, Harry Turtledove, Lawrence Watt-Evans, and Jane Yolen.

**Other books you might like:**
Isaac Asimov, *Mythical Beasties*, 1996
    Martin H. Greenberg, Charles G. Waugh, co-editors
Jack Dann, *Little People!*, 1991
    Gardner Dozois, co-editor
Michael Stearns, *A Wizard's Dozen*, 1993
    editor
Jane Yolen, *Vampires*, 1991
    Martin H. Greenberg, co-editor
Martin H. Greenberg, *Werewolves*, 1988
    Jane Yolen, co-editor

---

**4989**

**JOSEPHA SHERMAN**

### The Shattered Oath

(New York: Baen, 1995)

**Story type:** Fantasy (Magic Conflict)
**Series:** Prince of the Sidhe
**Major character(s):** Ardagh Lithaniel, Royalty, Mythical Creature (elf); Gervinus, Religious (bishop), Sorcerer; Eithne, Royalty (queen), Witch
**Time period(s):** 8th century (798-799)
**Locale(s):** Ireland (Eriu)

**Summary:** Thrown out of Faerie into the human world to live or die in exile, Ardagh finds shelter with the High King of Eriu and aids the king against Vikings and rebellious subjects. The greatest threat,

however, comes from a sorcerer with demonic powers. First of the series.

**Other books you might like:**
Poul Anderson, *The Broken Sword*, 1971
    revised edition
Emma Bull, *War for the Oaks*, 1987
Charles de Lint, *Moonheart: A Romance*, 1984
Patricia Kennealy-Morrison, *The Copper Crown*, 1985
Mercedes Lackey, *A Cast of Corbies*, 1994
    Josepha Sherman, co-author
Morgan Llywelyn, *Druids*, 1993

---

**4990**

**JOSEPHA SHERMAN**

### Son of Darkness

(New York: Roc, 1998)

**Story type:** Fantasy (Contemporary; Magic Conflict)
**Major character(s):** Denise Sheridan, Scholar, Museum Curator; Ilaron Highborn, Businessman, Mythical Creature (Unseelie faerie); Lamashtu, Demon
**Time period(s):** 1990s
**Locale(s):** New York, New York

**Summary:** When a curator of Mesopotamian art becomes the target of a demon summoned by the fanatical worshippers of an almost forgotten religion, she turns to Ilaron Highborn, an enigmatic art dealer, for help. Accepting Ilaron's aid means becoming his enemy's enemy, with the Unseelie Court more dangerous than any other.

**Other books you might like:**
Emma Bull, *War for the Oaks*, 1987
Charles de Lint, *Moonheart: A Romance*, 1984
Jennifer Roberson, *Scotland the Brave*, 1996
Will Shetterly, *Elsewhere*, 1991
Roger Zelazny, *This Immortal*, 1986

---

**4991**

**JOSEPHA SHERMAN**

### A Strange and Ancient Name

(New York: Baen, 1993)

**Story type:** Fantasy (Quest)
**Major character(s):** Hauberin, Mythical Creature (elf), Royalty; Alliar, Spirit; Matilde, Noblewoman
**Time period(s):** Indeterminate Past (medieval)
**Locale(s):** Faerie, Mythical Place; France

**Summary:** The curse of a dying enemy sends Hauberin to the human realm in search of his mother's father's name, the goal causing him as much unease as the curse since Hauberin fears learning of diminished elvish heritage. In Faerie, Hauberin has had trouble making his place and holding his princedom in peace in the face of constant plots and reminders that he remains a young half-human among nearly immortal elves.

**Other books you might like:**
Margaret Ball, *The Shadow Gate*, 1991
Charles de Lint, *Svaha*, 1989
Richard A. Knaak, *Wolfhelm*, 1990
Mercedes Lackey, *A Cast of Corbies*, 1994
    Josepha Sherman, co-author
Mercedes Lackey, *Castle of Deception*, 1992
    Josepha Sherman, co-author

Mercedes Lackey, *Knight of Ghosts and Shadows*, 1990
  Ellen Guon, co-author
Adrienne Martine-Barnes, *The Fire Sword*, 1984

## 4992
### WILL SHETTERLY

## Dogland
(New York: Tor, 1997)

**Story type:** Fantasy (Contemporary Realism; Literary)
**Major character(s):** Luke Nix, Businessman; Ethorne Hawkins, Worker; Chris Nix, Child
**Time period(s):** 1950s (1959)
**Locale(s):** Latchahee County, Florida

**Summary:** Based extremely loosely on events in the author's life, this novel takes place around Dogland, an amusement park displaying every breed of dog recognized by the American Kennel Club. The family of Luke Nix comes to Florida to run Dogland, hiring Ethorne Hawkins, a black man, at a white man's wage. From this simple decency, a complex web of magic and history, cruelty and education forms around the Nix family and the county.

**Other books you might like:**
James P. Blaylock, *The Paper Grail*, 1991
Jack Cady, *The Off Season*, 1995
John Crowley, *Love & Sleep*, 1994
Karen Joy Fowler, *The Sweetheart Season*, 1996
Robert Holdstock, *Lavondyss: Journey to an Unknown Region*, 1988

## 4993
### WILL SHETTERLY

## Elsewhere
(New York: Harcourt Brace Jovanovich, 1991)

**Story type:** Fantasy (Urban; Post-Disaster)
**Series:** Borderland
**Major character(s):** Ron Starbuck, Runaway, Human; Mooner, Mythical Creature (elf)
**Time period(s):** Indeterminate Future
**Locale(s):** Bordertown, Fictional City

**Summary:** Hoping to find his lost brother, Ron travels to Bordertown, a city located between the human world and the world of Elfland. When befriended by an elf motorcyclist, Mooner, Ron moves into Mooner's home, Castle Pup, shared among elves, halflings and humans. There he finds companionship among the outcasts until a tragic fire turns Ron's world upside down. This book was honored as winner of a Minnesota Book Award.

**Other books you might like:**
Gael Baudino, *Gossamer Axe*, 1990
Emma Bull, *War for the Oaks*, 1987
Mercedes Lackey, *Knight of Ghosts and Shadows*, 1990
  Ellen Guon, co-author
Michael Reaves, *Street Magic*, 1991
Joel Rosenberg, *The Road to Ehvenor*, 1991
Terri Windling, *Borderland*, 1986
  Mark Alan Arnold, co-editor
Terri Windling, *Bordertown*, 1986
  Mark Alan Arnold, co-editor
Terri Windling, *Life on the Border*, 1991
  editor

## 4994
### WILL SHETTERLY
### EMMA BULL, Co-Author

## Liavek: Festival Week
(New York: Ace, 1990)

**Story type:** Fantasy (Anthology; Magic Conflict)
**Series:** Liavek
**Time period(s):** Indeterminate
**Locale(s):** Liavek, Fictional Country

**Summary:** A collection of stories dealing with Festival Week in Liavek. A minor god escorts a young ruler on a night of forbidden revelry, a powerless wizard tries to halt an invasion of Ka Zhir airships, and two Green Priests die mysteriously while watching a parade. On Festival Week, anything can happen.

**Other books you might like:**
Steven Brust, *Jhereg*, 1983
John M. Ford, *Casting Fortune*, 1989
Fritz Leiber, *Swords and Deviltry*, 1970
Robert Silverberg, *Lord Valentine's Castle*, 1980
Terri Windling, *Borderland*, 1986
  Mark Arnold, co-editor
Terri Windling, *Bordertown*, 1986
  Mark Arnold, co-editor
Roger Zelazny, *Changeling*, 1980
Roger Zelazny, *Nine Princes in Amber*, 1970

## 4995
### WILL SHETTERLY

## Nevernever
(New York: Harcourt Brace, 1993)

**Story type:** Fantasy (Post-Disaster; Urban)
**Series:** Borderland
**Major character(s):** Ron Starbuck, Adventurer, Teenager; Florida, Child, Mythical Creature (elf); Leda, Mythical Creature (elf), Orphan
**Time period(s):** Indeterminate Future
**Locale(s):** Borderland, Mythical Place; Bordertown, Fictional City; Nevernever, Mythical Place

**Summary:** Wolfboy and his friends struggle to protect Florida from kidnappers who would take her to Elfland to forward political goals. On a subsequent foray into Nevernever with the elf who ensorcelled him, Wolfboy helps her overcome an addiction while she rescues Wolfboy from becoming the pet of wild elves. Sequel to *Elsewhere*.

**Other books you might like:**
Emma Bull, *Finder*, 1994
Emma Bull, *War for the Oaks*, 1987
Charles de Lint, *Moonheart: A Romance*, 1984
Ellen Guon, *Bedlam Boyz*, 1993
Tanya Huff, *Gate of Darkness, Circle of Light*, 1989
Terri Windling, *Borderland*, 1986
  Mark Alan Arnold, co-editor
Terri Windling, *Bordertown*, 1986
  Mark Alan Arnold, co-editor
Terri Windling, *Life on the Border*, 1991
  editor

## 4996

**ANDREA SHETTLE**

### Flute Song Magic

(New York: Avon Flare, 1990)

**Story type:** Fantasy (Quest)
**Major character(s):** Flutirr, Nobleman
**Time period(s):** Indeterminate
**Locale(s):** Land of the Nelvins, Fictional Country

**Summary:** Flutirr is born a high noble in a very rigid, class-stratified society. However, he hears strange and beautiful music, magic music, played on a flute by a classless Nelvin who, to Flutirr, is an untouchable. Driven to disregard the mores of his culture, he feels compelled to start a quest for forbidden music. This book was published as the winner of Avon's Flare competition.

**Other books you might like:**
Emma Bull, *War for the Oaks*, 1987
Anne McCaffrey, *Crystal Singer*, 1982
Anne McCaffrey, *Dragon Song*, 1976
Andre Norton, *Dragon Magic*, 1972
Sydney J. Van Scyoc, *Darkchild*, 1982

## 4997

**LEWIS SHINER**

### Glimpses

(New York: Morrow, 1993)

**Story type:** Horror (Wild Talents)
**Major character(s):** Ray Shackleford, Repairman, Psychic; Graham Hudson, Producer (Carnival Dog Records); Brian Wilson, Musician (leader of the Beach Boys), Historical Figure
**Time period(s):** 1960s; 1980s
**Locale(s):** Austin, Texas

**Summary:** Emotionally confused over the recent death of the father who never loved him, Ray Shackleford retreats into the rock music of his childhood and discovers that he has the uncanny ability to reproduce the music from the great apocryphal albums of the 1960s and 1970s that were planned but never recorded by the Doors, the Beach Boys, and Jimi Hendrix. As Ray's emotional turmoil worsens, his sympathy with the past threatens to leave him stranded there.

**Other books you might like:**
Bradley Denton, *Buddy Holly Is Alive and Well on Ganymede*, 1991
George R.R. Martin, *The Armageddon Rag*, 1983
David J. Schow, *The Kill Riff*, 1988
John Skipp, *The Scream*, 1988
  Craig Spector, co-author

## 4998

**LEWIS SHINER**

### Nine Hard Questions about the Nature of the Universe

(Eugene, Oregon: Pulphouse Press, 1990)

**Story type:** Science Fiction (Collection)
**Series:** Author's Choice Monthly

**Summary:** This collection consists of two original pieces and seven stories previously published in *Analog, Isaac Asimov's Science Fiction Magazine,* and elsewhere by one of the leaders of the cyberpunk movement. Among the better stories are

"Snowbirds," "Dancers," "Soldier, Sailor," "Kings of the Afternoon," and "Nine Hard Questions About the Nature of the Universe." Shiner has also included a short introduction to each story.

**Other books you might like:**
Greg Bear, *Tangents*, 1989
Pat Cadigan, *Patterns*, 1989
William Gibson, *Burning Chrome*, 1986
Bruce Sterling, *Crystal Express*, 1989

## 4999

**SHARON SHINN**

### The Alleluia Files

(New York, Ace: 1998)

**Story type:** Science Fiction (Lost Colony; Theological)
**Series:** Archangel
**Major character(s):** Tamar, Fugitive, Revolutionary; Jared, Genetically Altered Being (angel), Leader; Lucinda, Genetically Altered Being (angel), Singer
**Time period(s):** Indeterminate Future
**Locale(s):** *Jovah*, Spaceship; Samaria, Planet—Imaginary (cities of Luminaux and Angel Rock)

**Summary:** One of the few Jacobites to survive being hunted by the Archangels' Jansai, Tamar finds an ex-priest to install an eye in her arm which she believes will allow her to be in public without being recognized. At the Gloria, Jared hears Lucinda sing while musing that he should expect to become the next Archangel, although Jovah has as yet failed to name anyone and the current Archangel may refuse to give up his post. All the while, Tamar must try to prove that *Jovah* is not a god, but merely a piece of ancient technology, flying in the face of all Samarian tradition.

**Other books you might like:**
Suzette Haden Elgin, *Earthsong*, 1995
Rosemary Kirstein, *The Steerswoman*, 1989
Louise Marley, *Sing the Light*, 1995
Anne McCaffrey, *The Chronicles of Pern: First Fall*, 1993
Larry Niven, *Destiny's Road*, 1997

## 5000

**SHARON SHINN**

### Archangel

(New York: Ace, 1996)

**Story type:** Science Fiction (Theological; Lost Colony)
**Major character(s):** Gabriel, Singer, Angel (archangel-elect); Rachel, Spouse (Gabriel's), Singer; Raphael, Angel (archangel)
**Time period(s):** Indeterminate Future
**Locale(s):** Samaria, Planet—Imaginary

**Summary:** To avoid annihilation by Yovah, disparate groups must regularly prove their willingness to cooperate by singing at an annual gloria. Ordered by Yovah's oracle to wed Rachel and sing together at the next Gloria, Gabriel discovers that Rachel's sympathies lie with the downtrodden humans, while her resentment threatens the Gloria.

**Other books you might like:**
Stephen Baxter, *Raft*, 1991
Orson Scott Card, *The Memory of Earth*, 1992
Larry Niven, *The Smoke Ring*, 1987
Frank M. Robinson, *The Dark Beyond the Stars*, 1991
Robert Silverberg, *Kingdoms of the Wall*, 1993
John Varley, *Wizard*, 1980
Gene Wolfe, *The Shadow of the Torturer*, 1980

`5001`

**SHARON SHINN**

## *Jovah's Angel*

(New York: Ace, 1997)

**Story type:** Science Fiction (Genetic Manipulation; Theological)
**Major character(s):** Alleluia "Alleya" Wellin, Genetically Altered Being (angel), Leader (archangel); Caleb Augustus, Engineer, Scientist; Delilah "Lilah", Genetically Altered Being (angel), Singer
**Time period(s):** Indeterminate Future
**Locale(s):** Samaria, Planet—Imaginary; Luminaux, Fictional City; Eyrie, Mythical Place (angel stronghold)

**Summary:** Because Jovah no longer hears the Angels, the storms on Samaria continue to worsen. When Archangel Delilah breaks a wing, Alleluia, the only angel Jovah still hears, replaces her. While researching to fulfill her new position and find her partner for the Gloria, Alleluia inadvertently learns the language used by the Oracles to communicate with Jovah. Caleb works to repair Delilah's wing, after adding an external power source to fix the old music players. Sequel to *Archangel*.

**Other books you might like:**
Orson Scott Card, *The Memory of Earth*, 1992
Rosemary Kirstein, *The Outskirter's Secret*, 1992
Louise Marley, *Sing the Light*, 1995
Anne McCaffrey, *The Chronicles of Pern: First Fall*, 1993
Dan Simmons, *Endymion*, 1996

`5002`

**SHARON SHINN**

## *The Shape-Changer's Wife*

(New York: Ace, 1995)

**Story type:** Fantasy (Magic Conflict; Romance)
**Major character(s):** Aubrey, Student, Wizard; Lilith, Genetically Altered Being, Spouse; Glyrenden, Wizard
**Time period(s):** Indeterminate
**Locale(s):** Fictional Country

**Summary:** Aubrey comes to study under Glyrenden to learn shape-changing, but soon becomes intrigued by Lilith, Glyrenden's wife, and begins to investigate the household's strange secrets. First novel.

**Other books you might like:**
Don Callander, *Pyromancer*, 1992
Diane Duane, *So You Want to Be a Wizard?*, 1983
Teresa Edgerton, *The Castle of the Silver Wheel*, 1993
Nancy Kress, *The Golden Grove*, 1984
Thomas Burnett Swann, *The Tournament of Thorns*, 1976
Patricia C. Wrede, *Mairelon the Magician*, 1991
Mary Frances Zambreno, *Journeyman Wizard*, 1994
Andre Norton, *The Crystal Gryphon*, 1972

`5003`

**TOM SHIPPEY**, Editor

## *The Oxford Book of Fantasy Stories*

(New York: Oxford University Press, 1994)

**Story type:** Fantasy (Anthology)
**Summary:** Contains a 14-page introduction, five-page select bibliography and 31 stories from periodicals, collections and anthologies

1888-1992 which exemplify the diverse interests of fantasists throughout time, from sword and sorcery set in the ancient Hyborian Age of Conan in Robert E. Howard's "The Tower of the Elephant," to modern urban themes in Phyllis Eisenstein's "Subworld," and a bargain with a wish granting demon in the distant future of Zothique in Clark Ashton Smith's "Xeethra." Magic, supernatural realms, parallel worlds, battles between order and chaos and mythical creatures populate other stories by authors including Poul Anderson, Peter S. Beagle, Ray Bradbury, Angela Carter, Robert Holdstock, Henry Kuttner, Tanith Lee, Fritz Leiber, H.P. Lovecraft, Abraham Merritt, Catherine L. Moore, Larry Niven, Mervyn Peake, Terry Pratchett, Theodore Sturgeon, Thomas Burnett Swann, James Tiptree Jr., Jack Vance, Manly Wade Wellman and Jane Yolen.

**Other books you might like:**
Robert H. Boyer, *Visions & Imaginings: Classic Fantasy Fiction*, 1992
Kenneth J. Zahorski, co-editor
Ellen Datlow, *The Year's Best Fantasy and Horror Series*, 1989-
Terri Windling, co-editor
Alison Lurie, *The Oxford Book of Modern Fairy Tales*, 1993
editor
Robert Silverberg, *The Fantasy Hall of Fame*, 1983
Martin H. Greenberg, co-editor
Cary Wilkins, *A Treasury of Fantasy: Heroic Adventures in Imaginary Lands*, 1981
editor

`5004`

**TOM SHIPPEY**, Editor

## *The Oxford Book of Science Fiction Stories*

(New York: Oxford University Press, 1992)

**Story type:** Science Fiction (Anthology)

**Summary:** Contains an 18-page introduction, 6-page bibliography and 30 stories by different authors arranged chronologically, 1903-1990, by appearance in periodical or anthology and chosen to express the range, vitality and literary quality of the genre which characterizes the 20th century. Stories nominated for a Nebula Award include "Cloak of Anarchy" by Larry Niven, "A Thing of Beauty" by Norman Spinrad and "How the Whip Came Back" by Gene Wolfe. Other stories include "Who Can Replace a Man?" by Brian W. Aldiss, "Billennium" by J.G. Ballard, "Piecework" by David Brin, "Burning Chrome" by William Gibson, "Crucifixus Etiam" by Walter M. Miller, Jr., "Desertion" by Clifford D. Simak, "The Ballad of Lost C'mell" by Cordwainer Smith, "The Monster" by A.E. van Vogt and "A Martian Odyssey" by Stanley G. Weinbaum.

**Other books you might like:**
Groff Conklin, *The Best of Science Fiction*, 1946
editor
Harlan Ellison, *Dangerous Visions*, 1967
editor
David G. Hartwell, *The World Treasury of Science Fiction*, 1989
editor
Raymond J. Healy, *Adventures in Time and Space*, 1946
J. Francis McComas, co-editor
Robert Silverberg, *The Science Fiction Hall of Fame, Volume 1*, 1970
editor
Donald A. Wollheim, *The Pocket Book of Science Fiction*, 1943
editor

## 5005

### JOHN SHIRLEY

### *Black Butterflies: A Flock on the Dark Side*

(Shingletown, California: Ziesing, 1998)

**Story type:** Horror (Collection)

**Summary:** These 17 hard-nosed, occasionally surreal stories express a cynical world view. Selections grouped under the subheading "This World" are nonsupernatural and include "Cram," which elaborates the hysteria and horror inside a subway car caught underground during an earthquake, and "What Would You Do for Love," an over-the-top tale of marital infidelity and retribution. Stories collected in the section entitled "That World" include "Delia and the Dinner Party," in which a young girl sees the scatological reality underlying the seemingly placid surface of the adult world, and "Black Hole Sun, Won't You Come," a futuristic tale of a false shaman. Foreword by Paula Guran.

**Other books you might like:**
Michael Blumlein, *The Brains of Rats*, 1989
Poppy Z. Brite, *Are You Loathsome Tonight?*, 1998
Jack Ketchum, *The Exit at Toledo Blade Boulevard*, 1998
Richard Christian Matheson, *Scars and Other Distinguishing Marks*, 1986
David J. Schow, *Crypt Orchids*, 1998

## 5006

### JOHN SHIRLEY

### *Eclipse Corona*

(New York: Popular Library Questar, 1990)

**Story type:** Science Fiction (Cyberpunk)
**Series:** Song Called Youth
**Major character(s):** Daniel "Hardeyes" Torrence, Revolutionary; Steinfeld, Revolutionary
**Time period(s):** 21st century (2021)
**Locale(s):** Europe

**Summary:** The New Resistance continues its desperate, losing battle against the cybernetically-enhanced forces of the Neo-fascist Second Alliance. The Alliance continues its experiments in genetic manipulation and its policy of genocide. Meanwhile, aboard an orbiting space station, a madman toys with the idea of wiping out all life on Earth.

**Other books you might like:**
Bruce Sterling, *Islands in the Net*, 1988
Walter Jon Williams, *Hardwired*, 1986
Dave Wolverton, *On My Way to Paradise*, 1989

## 5007

### JOHN SHIRLEY

### *Heatseeker*

(Los Angeles: Scream Press, 1989)

**Story type:** Horror (Collection)

**Summary:** Nineteen stories written over a fifteen-year period (with three originals) that demonstrate Shirley's lucidity, elegance, variety, and virtuosity. Dark parables on such subjects as death, sex, drugs, nuclear war, and transmutations of body and soul are treated with power, horror, and humor. Among the best stories are "Wolves of

the Plateau," "Equilibrium," and "Recurrent Dreams of Nuclear War. . .."

**Other books you might like:**
Clive Barker, *Cabal*, 1988
Ramsey Campbell, *Scared Stiff*, 1987
Dennis Etchison, *Red Dreams*, 1984
William Gibson, *Burning Chrome*, 1986
David J. Schow, *Seeing Red*, 1990
Bruce Sterling, *Crystal Express*, 1989

## 5008

### JOHN SHIRLEY

### *New Noir*

(Boulder, Colorado: Black Ice Books, 1993)

**Story type:** Horror (Collection)

**Summary:** These six stories portray the horror and humor that befalls characters leading lives of desperation in the contemporary urban jungle. "Jody and Anne on TV" tells of joyriding youngsters who commit murder to see how they are portrayed on television. "Skeeter Junkie" is a dream fantasy in which a junkie on the nod imagines he is a mosquito and becomes incapable of extricating himself from that fantasy. "I Want to Get Married, Says the World's Smallest Man," is a tabloid-type story of a sideshow midget who hopes to marry a rich woman, and the poor woman who marries him in the hope of getting her hands on his presumed riches. "Just Like Suzie" is a grotesque tale of necrophilia. The remaining two stories first appeared in the author's 1989 collection, *Heatseeker*.

**Other books you might like:**
Poppy Z. Brite, *Swamp Foetus*, 1993
David J. Schow, *Lost Angels*, 1990
David J. Schow, *Seeing Red*, 1989
John Skipp, *Dead Lines*, 1989
   Craig Spector, co-author

## 5009

### JOHN SHIRLEY

### *Silicon Embrace*

(Shingletown, California: Mark V. Ziesing Books, 1996)

**Story type:** Science Fiction (Cyberpunk; UFO)
**Major character(s):** Farraday, Public Relations; Quinn, Journalist; Anatole, Teenager
**Time period(s):** 2010s (2017)
**Locale(s):** California; Area 51, Nevada

**Summary:** In a violent, balkanizing United States, extraterrestials decide to come out of hiding, having surreptitiously watched humans for years. To produce the correct spin for their unveiling, one group of aliens enlists Farraday's help. Meanwhile, other aliens attempt to contact humans directly.

**Other books you might like:**
Stephen Bury, *Interface*, 1994
Michael Kandel, *Strange Invasion*, 1989
Earl Mac Rauch, *Buckaroo Banzai*, 1984
Robert Shea, *The Illuminatus! Trilogy*, 1988
   Robert Anton Wilson, co-author
Neal Stephenson, *Snow Crash*, 1992

## 5010

### JOHN SHIRLEY

### *Wetbones*

(Shingletown, California: Mark V. Ziesing, 1991)

**Story type:** Horror (Vampire Story)
**Major character(s):** Tom Prentice, Writer (screenwriter); Ephram Pixie, Drifter; Reverend Garner, Religious (former minister)
**Time period(s):** 1990s
**Locale(s):** Los Angeles, California

**Summary:** Tom Prentice's investigation of the mysterious death of his ex-wife and the disappearance of a friend's younger brother leads him to a ranch on the outskirts of Los Angeles and the discovery of the Akishra, a race of extradimensional vampires who work symbiotically with thrill-seeking human hosts to drain victims of their souls so that they can pass into the earthly plane.

**Other books you might like:**
Clive Barker, *The Hellbound Heart*, 1991
Stephen Gallagher, *Valley of Lights*, 1987
Eric Frank Russell, *Sinister Barrier*, 1943
Dan Simmons, *Carrion Comfort*, 1989

## 5011

### MIKE SHUPP

### *Death's Gray Land*

(New York: Ballantine/Del Rey, 1991)

**Story type:** Science Fiction (Time Travel; Military)
**Series:** Destiny Makers
**Major character(s):** Timothy Harper, Time Traveler, Military Personnel (Sergeant); Kylene Waterfall, Time Traveler, Telepath; Cherrid ris Clendannan, Military Personnel (General)
**Time period(s):** 900th century (90000s)
**Locale(s):** Fohima Alghera, Fictional Country; Midpassage, Fictional Country

**Summary:** Tim Harper, caught in a time flux in 1970, is now an agent of the Algheran Time-Travel Project. Humanity has evolved into two different races, both long-lived, one telepathic. The Teeps and Normals have agreed on rules to prevent the Teeps from enslaving the Normals. The Time-Travel Project aims at changing history to prevent the Chelmmysian Alliance from conquering Alghera.

**Other books you might like:**
Poul Anderson, *The Shield of Time*, 1990
Keith William Andrews, *Freedom's Rangers*, 1989
Phyllis Eisenstein, *Shadow of Earth*, 1979
William R. Forstchen, *Rally Cry!*, 1990
H. Beam Piper, *Lord Kalvan of Otherwhen*, 1965
Sheri S. Tepper, *Sideshow*, 1992
John Varley, *Millennium*, 1983

## 5012

### MIKE SHUPP

### *The Last Reckoning*

(New York: Ballantine/Del Rey, 1991)

**Story type:** Science Fiction (Time Travel; Political)
**Series:** Destiny Makers
**Major character(s):** Timothy Harper, Time Traveler, Military Personnel; Kylene Waterfall, Time Traveler, Telepath
**Time period(s):** 900th century (90000s)

**Locale(s):** Midpassage, Fictional Country

**Summary:** Timothy Harper, transplanted 90,000 years into the future, has lost too many battles. His alternate, Timmian Haarper, fights against him. Each is in love with a Kylene Waterfall. When Kylene steals his time machine, she risks Alghera, all their lives and their futures together.

**Other books you might like:**
Keith William Andrews, *Search and Destroy*, 1990
Gordon R. Dickson, *Time Storm*, 1977
Randall Frakes, *The Terminator*, 1985
    Bill Wisher, co-author
Warren Norwood, *Vanished*, 1988
Dan Simmons, *Hyperion*, 1989
L. Neil Smith, *The Gallatin Divergence*, 1985

## 5013

### NEAL SHUSTERMAN

### *Scorpion Shards*

(New York: Tor, 1995)

**Story type:** Science Fiction (Young Adult; Science Fantasy)
**Major character(s):** Dillon Cole, Teenager, Outcast; Deanna Chang, Teenager, Outcast; Lourdes Hidalgo, Teenager, Outcast
**Time period(s):** 1990s
**Locale(s):** Mt. St. Helens, Washington; St. Louis, Missouri

**Summary:** When a distant star goes nova, a mysterious force draws six teenagers together from all over the United States. They then discover and battle the cause of the terrible afflictions each of them suffers.

**Other books you might like:**
Robert Cormier, *Fade*, 1988
Annabel Johnson, *Prisoner of Psi*, 1985
    Edgar Johnson, co-author
Madeleine L'Engle, *A Wrinkle in Time*, 1962
Christopher Pike, *The Eternal Enemy*, 1993

## 5014

### SUSAN SHWARTZ

### *Cross and Crescent*

(New York: Tor, 1997)

**Story type:** Fantasy (Political; Religious)
**Major character(s):** Leo Ducas, Military Personnel; Binah, Companion, Mythical Creature (goddess's offspring); Theodoulos, Linguist, Mythical Creature (goddess's offspring)
**Time period(s):** 11th century (1096-1099); 12th century (1104-1190)
**Locale(s):** Constantinople, Byzantine Empire; Asia Minor; Jerusalem, Middle East

**Summary:** The invasions bring hope and danger for Leo, as Theodoulos travels with the Crusaders for the Emperor and Binah attends to the Emperor's daughter. Set in the milieu of *Shards of Empire*.

**Other books you might like:**
Frans G. Bengtsson, *The Long Ships*, 1954
John M. Ford, *The Dragon Waiting*, 1983
Stephen R. Lawhead, *Byzantium*, 1996
Andre Norton, *Imperial Lady*, 1989
    Susan M. Shwartz, co-author
Judith Tarr, *The Dagger and the Cross: A Novel of the Crusades*, 1991

## 5015
### SUSAN SHWARTZ

## *The Grail of Hearts*
(New York: Tor, 1992)

**Story type:** Fantasy (Legend; Religious)
**Major character(s):** Kundry, Immortal, Wanderer; Amfortas, Knight; Klingsor, Sorcerer
**Time period(s):** 1st century (33); 10th century
**Locale(s):** Broceliande, Fictional Country; Jerusalem, Israel

**Summary:** Kundry seduces and betrays Amfortas, guardian of the Holy Grail, on the orders of the evil Klingsor. Feeling guilt and despair, she defies Klingsor who punishes her by forcing her to relive events in her own life a thousand years earlier. She discovers the ability to act differently this time, but remains unable to change the final outcome, again cursed to wander the Earth eternally for laughing at the Crucifixion. Awakening back in Broceliande a changed woman, she eventually finds Amfortas and forgiveness.

**Other books you might like:**
Marion Zimmer Bradley, *The Mists of Avalon*, 1983
Katherine Kurtz, *Saint Camber*, 1978
A.J. Langguth, *Jesus Christs*, 1968
Helen M. Mustard, *Parzival: A Romance of the Middle Ages*, 1961
    Charles E. Passage, co-translator
Andre Norton, *Imperial Lady*, 1989
Diana L. Paxson, *The White Raven*, 1988
Rosemary Sutcliff, *Sword at Sunset*, 1963
Judith Tarr, *The Dagger and the Cross: A Novel of the Crusades*, 1991

## 5016
### SUSAN SHWARTZ

## *Heritage of Flight*
(New York: Tor, 1989)

**Story type:** Science Fiction (First Contact)
**Major character(s):** Pauli Yeager, Pilot, Military Personnel; Rafe Adams, Scientist
**Time period(s):** Indeterminate Future
**Locale(s):** Cynthia, Planet—Imaginary

**Summary:** In this Philip K. Dick Award-nominated novel, mankind is engaged in a genocidal, planet-destroying civil war and a small convoy of spaceships flees the destruction, seeking a haven for a remnant of humanity's children. Landing on the planet Cynthia, they discover beautiful, airborne lifeforms that prove highly intelligent. Behind that beauty, however, lurks horror.

**Other books you might like:**
Clare Bell, *People of the Sky*, 1989
Octavia E. Butler, *Adulthood Rites*, 1988
Octavia E. Butler, *Dawn*, 1987
Octavia E. Butler, *Imago*, 1989
Larry Niven, *The Legacy of Heorot*, 1987
    Jerry Pournelle and Steven Barnes, co-authors
Sheri S. Tepper, *Grass*, 1989

## 5017
### SUSAN SHWARTZ

## *Shards of Empire*
(New York: Tor, 1996)

**Story type:** Fantasy (Political; Adventure)
**Major character(s):** Leo Ducas, Military Personnel; Romanus Diogenes, Ruler (emperor); Micheal Psellus, Scholar
**Time period(s):** 10th century
**Locale(s):** Constantinople, Byzantine Empire

**Summary:** During a battle against the Turks, Leo's uncle betrays the emperor, who is captured and then ransomed to the Byzantines. With the emperor when he dies, Leo remains haunted by the memories of Asherah and tortured by memories of the emperor's death. When Leo flees Constantinople, travelling through Asia Minor to redeem his family's name, Psellus gathers power by appointing a puppet emperor.

**Other books you might like:**
Marion Zimmer Bradley, *The Firebrand*, 1987
Steven Brust, *The Phoenix Guards*, 1991
Glen Cook, *The Black Company*, 1984
Alexandre Dumas, *The Three Musketeers*, 1846
John M. Ford, *The Dragon Waiting*, 1983
Stephen R. Lawhead, *Byzantium*, 1996
Melanie Rawn, *The Golden Key*, 1996
    Jennifer Roberson, Kate Elliott, co-authors
Roger Zelazny, *Nine Princes in Amber*, 1970

## 5018
### SUSAN SHWARTZ, Editor
### MARTIN H. GREENBERG, Co-Editor

## *Sisters in Fantasy 2*
(New York: Roc, 1996)

**Story type:** Fantasy (Anthology)

**Summary:** This anthology contains a six-page introduction by Shwartz plus brief individual introductions to 23 original stories varying in tone from upbeat to horrific, using contemporary and classic settings, with themes including revisionist myths and religion, women's relationship with the Earth, transformations, and abuse and loneliness. The 22 authors include Gael Baudino, Ru Emerson, Valerie J. Freireich, Esther Friesner, Ellen Guon, Mercedes Lackey, Patricia McKillip, Beth Meacham, Sharan Newman, Rebecca Ore, Diana Paxson, Susan Shwartz, Sherwood Smith, Martha Soukup, Nancy Springer, Lois Tilton, and Jane Yolen.

**Other books you might like:**
Marion Zimmer Bradley, *The Sword and Sorceress Series*, 1984-1996
    editor
Esther Friesner, *Chicks in Chainmail*, 1995
    editor
Susanna J. Sturgis, *Magic Realism by Women: Dreams in a Minor Key*, 1991
    editor
A. Susan Williams, *The Lifted Veil: The Book of Fantastic Literature by Women*, 1993
    editor
A. Susan Williams, *The Penguin Book of Modern Fantasy by Women*, 1995
    Richard Glyn Jones, co-editor

## 5019

**SUSAN SHWARTZ**

### Vulcan's Forge

(New York: Pocket, 1997)

**Story type:** Science Fiction (Adventure; Space Opera)
**Series:** Star Trek
**Major character(s):** Spock, Spaceship Captain, Alien (Vulcan); David Rabin, Military Personnel (captain); Leonard McCoy, Doctor, Spaceman
**Time period(s):** 23rd century
**Locale(s):** *U.S.S. Intrepid II*, Spaceship; United Federation of Planets, Interstellar Empire/Federation

**Summary:** Assigned to a Federation outpost on the planet Obsidian, Captain Rabin tries to help the inhabitants improve their lives, but saboteurs destroy supplies and equipment. Captained by Spock, a boyhood friend with whom Rabin had once survived the desert known as Vulcan's Forge, the *Intrepid II* arrives in response to Rabin's request for help. With their shuttlecraft forced down in the desert, Dr. McCoy kidnapped and supplies running low, Rabin and Spock face another desert and a dangerous madman.

**Other books you might like:**
Margaret Wander Bonanno, *Dwellers in the Crucible*, 1985
C.J. Cherryh, *The Faded Sun: Kesrith*, 1978
J.M. Dillard, *The Lost Years*, 1989
Diane Duane, *Spock's World*, 1988
Diane Duane, *The Romulan Way*, 1987
　　Peter Morwood, co-author
Michael Jan Friedman, *Crossover*, 1995
Frank Herbert, *Dune*, 1965
L.A. Taylor, *The Blossom of Erda*, 1986

## 5020

**SAM SICILIANO**

### Blood Feud

(New York: Pinnacle, 1993)

**Story type:** Horror (Vampire Story)
**Major character(s):** Steve Ryan, Businessman; Mary Connely, Teacher (Maryglenn College); Fred Martin, Religious (priest)
**Time period(s):** 1980s (1988)
**Locale(s):** Portland, Oregon

**Summary:** Bored with their immortality, and full of nothing but hatred for others of their ilk, the ageless vampires Ruthven and Madame Rambouillet wage a war against one another using human pawns as their foot soldiers.

**Other books you might like:**
Brian Lumley, *Necroscope*, 1986
Kim Newman, *Bad Dreams*, 1990
Dan Simmons, *Carrion Comfort*, 1989
Lee Weathersby, *Kiss of the Vampire*, 1992
T. Lucien Wright, *Thirst of the Vampire*, 1992

## 5021

**ANNE RIVERS SIDDONS**

### The House Next Door

(Ballantine, 1989)

**Story type:** Horror (Haunted House)

**Major character(s):** Colquitt Kennedy, Housewife; Kim Dougherty, Architect (Builder of "the house")
**Time period(s):** 1970s
**Locale(s):** Atlanta, Georgia

**Summary:** When insanity and violence overwhelm three families that move into a beautiful, newly built home, the nextdoor neighbors decide that the house is "haunted" and set out to locate and destroy the evil that possesses it. Originally published in 1978.

**Other books you might like:**
Shirley Jackson, *The Haunting of Hill House*, 1959
Ira Levin, *The Stepford Wives*, 1972
John Updike, *The Witches of Eastwick*, 1984

## 5022

**SCOTT SIEGEL**, Editor

### Tales From Tethedril

(New York: Del Rey, 1998)

**Story type:** Fantasy (Anthology)

**Summary:** A story by R.A. Salvatore serves as the inspiration for eight other original pieces. All have the common setting of a magical world on which a comet has wakened a race of reptilian creatures who challenge the human race. Contributors include Dan Parkinson, Ed Greenwood, Christie Golden, and Douglas Niles.

**Other books you might like:**
Elaine Cunningham, *Evermeet: Island of Elves*, 1998
Richard A. Knaak, *Kaz the Minotaur*, 1990
Victor Milan, *War in Tethyr*, 1995
Dan Parkinson, *The Gully Dwarves*, 1996
R.A. Salvatore, *Starless Night*, 1994

## 5023

**JOHN SIEVERT**

### Suicide Attack

(New York: Zebra, 1990)

**Story type:** Science Fiction (Military; Post-Holocaust)
**Series:** C.A.D.S.
**Major character(s):** Dean Sturgis, Military Personnel (colonel); Major Danirov, Military Personnel
**Time period(s):** Indeterminate Future
**Locale(s):** West

**Summary:** The Russian invaders have occupied the east and west coasts of the United States; but Colonel Dean Sturgis leads his soldiers, in their Computerized Attack/Defense System (C.A.D.S.) suits, on another deadly fight amid the nuclear ruins. Their current target is a Soviet base in California, but its commander, Major Danirov, has captured Sturgis' wife Robin and has a plan for destroying the C.A.D.S. troops and their leader.

**Other books you might like:**
Peter Bryant, *Red Alert*, 1959
　　pseudonym of Peter George
Robert A. Heinlein, *Starship Troopers*, 1959
George Lucas, *Star Wars*, 1976
David Robbins, *L.A. Strike*, 1990
David Robbins, *Yellowstone Run*, 1990
Ryder Stacy, *Doomsday Warrior*, 1984

## 5024

**JOHN SILBERSACK**, Editor
**CHRISTOPHER SCHELLING**, Co-Editor

### The Magic of Christmas
(New York: Roc, 1992)

**Story type:** Fantasy (Anthology)

**Summary:** Themes of glad Christmas tidings including ghosts, elves, life after death and time travel fill this volume which features a four-page introduction and six original stories plus one, ''Holiday'' by Richard Christian Matheson, first published in 1988. Other authors include Gael Baudino, Julian May, Dennis L. McKiernan, Andre Norton, Christopher Stasheff and Judith Tarr.

**Other books you might like:**
Alan Brennert, *Kindred Spirits*, 1984
Martin H. Greenberg, *Christmas on Ganymede and Other Stories*, 1990
  editor
Rosalind M. Greenberg, *Christmas Bestiary*, 1992
  Martin H. Greenberg, co-editor
David G. Hartwell, *Christmas Stars*, 1992
  editor
Kristine Kathryn Rusch, *Pulphouse, Issue 10: Special Issue*, 1991
  editor
Gene Wolfe, *Gene Wolfe's Book of Days*, 1981

## 5025

**DAVID B. SILVA**, Editor

### The Definitive Best of the Horror Show
(Baltimore, Maryland: CD Publications, 1992)

**Story type:** Horror (Anthology)

**Summary:** A collection of 40 stories by 36 different authors from the pages of *The Horror Show*, a small press magazine that helped to shape horror fiction in the 1980s. Included are Robert R. McCammon's post-apocalypse horror tale, ''The I Scream Man''; Dennis Etchison's tale of loss and alienation, ''The Scar''; Joe Lansdale's hardboiled suspense story, ''On a Dark October''; Nancy Collins' tale of a sideshow photographer, ''The Freaktent''; and Ramsey Campbell's science fictional ''Passing Phase.''

**Other books you might like:**
Jessica Horsting, *Midnight Graffiti*, 1992
  James Van Hise, co-author
Robert Morrish, *Quick Chills II*, 1992
  Peter Enfantino, co-author
Stephen Mark Rainey, *The Best of Deathrealm*, 1993
Stuart David Schiff, *The Whispers Series*, 1977-1987

## 5026

**DAVID B. SILVA**

### The Night in Fog
(Burton, Michigan: Subterranean Press, 1998)

**Story type:** Horror (Ghost Story)
**Major character(s):** Bryan, Young Man; Rick, Young Man; Jude Fairclough, Young Woman
**Time period(s):** 1990s (1998)
**Locale(s):** Weed, California

**Summary:** At the request of his troubled younger brother Rick, Bryan travels to remote Weed to help Rick dispatch Jude Fairclough, a teenage femme fatale who causes death wherever she appears. But Bryan believes Jude is only a figment of Rick's imagination, created to rationalize his brother's homicidal behavior.

**Other books you might like:**
Richard T. Chizmar, *Midnight Promises*, 1996
Douglas Clegg, *The Halloween Man*, 1996
Brian Hodge, *Falling Idols*, 1998
Stephen King, *Bag of Bones*, 1998
Jack Martin, *Halloween*, 1978

## 5027

**ROBERT SILVERBERG**

### The Alien Years
(New York: HarperPrism, 1998)

**Story type:** Science Fiction (Family Saga; Invasion of Earth)
**Major character(s):** Anson Carmichael, Military Personnel (retired), Rancher; Anson ''Andy'' Gannett, Computer Expert (hacker); Khalil Haleem Burke, Criminal (assassin)
**Time period(s):** 21st century
**Locale(s):** California; Salisbury, England

**Summary:** Aliens land on Earth, ignoring humans except when they need labor or the humans annoy them. The Carmichaels of Santa Barbara vow eternal resistance and to find a way to assassinate the aliens. Even this presents only a slight annoyance and does not drive them away. Most people become dependent on the aliens and would feel lost without them.

**Other books you might like:**
Brian W. Aldiss, *Bow Down to Nul*, 1960
John Brunner, *Age of Miracles*, 1973
John Christopher, *When the Tripods Came*, 1988
Gordon R. Dickson, *Way of the Pilgrim*, 1987
Thomas M. Disch, *The Genocides*, 1965
Valerie J. Freireich, *The Beacon*, 1996
Robert A. Heinlein, *The Puppet Masters*, 1951
Timothy Zahn, *The Blackcollar*, 1983

## 5028

**ROBERT SILVERBERG**

### The Collected Stories of Robert Silverberg, Volume 1: Secret Sharers
(New York: Bantam Spectra, 1992)

**Story type:** Science Fiction (Collection)

**Summary:** Contains a seven-page introduction plus 24 stories published 1981-1988, each with an individual introduction. This volume includes one Nebula Award nominee, ''Homefaring''; one Nebula Award and Hugo Award nominee, ''The Secret Sharers''; and one Hugo Award winner, ''Enter a Soldier. Later: Enter Another.''

**Other books you might like:**
Alfred Bester, *Star Light, Star Bright*, 1976
Orson Scott Card, *Maps in a Mirror*, 1990
Kim Stanley Robinson, *Remaking History*, 1991
Marc Stiegler, *The Gentle Seduction*, 1990
Michael Swanwick, *Gravity's Angels*, 1991
John Varley, *Blue Champagne*, 1986

## 5029

### ROBERT SILVERBERG

## *The Face of the Waters*

(New York: Bantam Spectra, 1991)

**Story type:** Science Fiction (Adventure)
**Major character(s):** Valben Lawler, Doctor; Father Quillan, Religious (Church of All Worlds); Sundira Thane, Adventurer
**Time period(s):** 24th century
**Locale(s):** Hydros, Planet—Imaginary; *Queen of Hydros*, At Sea

**Summary:** Marooned on Hydros, humans live at the mercy of the indigenous race, the Gillies. When banished from their home on Sorve Island, a group of humans sail off to find The Face of the Waters, the planet's largest solid land mass which has mystical significance to the Gillies.

**Other books you might like:**
Carol Severance, *Reefsong*, 1991
Dan Simmons, *The Fall of Hyperion*, 1990
Dan Simmons, *Hyperion*, 1989
Joan Slonczewski, *A Door into Ocean*, 1986
Sydney J. Van Scyoc, *Deepwater Dreams*, 1991

## 5030

### ROBERT SILVERBERG, Editor

## *The Fantasy Hall of Fame*

(New York: HarperPrism, 1998)

**Story type:** Fantasy (Anthology)

**Summary:** The anthology contains a six-page introduction plus individual introductions to 30 stories from periodicals and anthologies 1939-1990, voted best of all time by the Science Fiction and Fantasy Writers of America. Varying widely in tone, the stories explore diverse themes in contemporary and fantastic settings. Authors include Poul Anderson, J.G. Ballard, Peter S. Beagle, Jorge Luis Borges, Ray Bradbury, Avram Davidson, Philip K. Dick, Harlan Ellison, Shirley Jackson, Ursula K. Le Guin, Fritz Leiber, Lucius Shepard, Robert Silverberg, Theodore Sturgeon, James Tiptree Jr., Jack Vance, Gene Wolfe and Roger Zelazny.

**Other books you might like:**
Mike Ashley, *The Random House Book of Fantasy Stories*, 1997
  editor
Robert H. Boyer, *Visions & Imaginings: Classic Fantasy Fiction*, 1992
  Kenneth J. Zahorski, co-editor
Gardner Dozois, *Modern Classics of Fantasy*, 1997
Alison Lurie, *The Oxford Book of Modern Fairy Tales*, 1993
  editor
Tom Shippey, *The Oxford Book of Fantasy Stories*, 1993
  editor

## 5031

### ROBERT SILVERBERG, Editor
### MARTIN H. GREENBERG, Co-Editor

## *The Horror Hall of Fame*

(New York: Carroll & Graf, 1991)

**Story type:** Horror (Anthology)

**Summary:** Eighteen classic stories spanning the last century-and-a-half, chosen by attendees of the 1981 and 1982 World Fantasy

Convention to commemorate stories written before the creation of the World Fantasy Award. Aspects of horror addressed include psychological horror (Edgar Allan Poe's ''The Fall of the House of Usher,'' J. Sheridan Le Fanu's ''Green Tea''), elemental and natural horror (Arthur Machen's ''The White People,'' Algernon Blackwood's ''The Willows''), urban horror (Fritz Leiber's ''Smoke Ghost,'' Harlan Ellison's ''The Whimper of Whipped Dogs''), the occult (M.R. James' ''Casting the Runes,'' Robert Bloch's ''Yours Truly, Jack the Ripper''), voodoo (Robert E. Howard's ''Pigeons from Hell''), reanimated dead (W.W. Jacobs' ''The Monkey's Paw,'' Theodore Sturgeon's ''It''), demon children (Ray Bradbury's ''The Small Assassin''), ghosts (Ramsey Campbell's ''Calling Card,'' Stephen King's ''The Reach''), and others.

**Other books you might like:**
Dennis Etchison, *The Complete Masters of Darkness*, 1991
  editor
David G. Hartwell, *The Dark Descent*, 1987
  editor
Robert Silverberg, *The Science Fiction Hall of Fame, Volume 1*, 1970
  editor
Herbert Wise, *Great Tales of Terror and the Supernatural*, 1944
  Phyllis Fraser, co-editor

## 5032

### ROBERT SILVERBERG

## *Hot Sky at Midnight*

(New York: Bantam Spectra, 1994)

**Story type:** Science Fiction (Space Colony; Genetic Manipulation)
**Major character(s):** Victor Farkas, Genetically Altered Being; Paul Carpenter, Sea Captain, Office Worker; Jolanda Bermudez, Artist
**Time period(s):** 22nd century
**Locale(s):** California; Nuevo Valparaiso, Space Station (L5 colony)

**Summary:** On an Earth becoming unfit for human life, most people long to escape to space colonies. Fired on his first tour of duty on an iceberg ship, Paul Carpenter gets involved in a plot to take over Nuevo Valparaiso, a corrupt space colony.

**Other books you might like:**
John Barnes, *The Man Who Pulled Down the Sky*, 1986
Barney Cohen, *The Taking of Satcon Station*, 1982
  Jim Baen, co-author
Gordon R. Dickson, *The Pritcher Mass*, 1972
Mary Rosenblum, *The Drylands*, 1993
Allen Steele, *Clarke County, Space*, 1990

## 5033

### ROBERT SILVERBERG

## *Kingdoms of the Wall*

(New York: Bantam Spectra, 1993)

**Story type:** Science Fiction (Mystical; Fantasy)
**Major character(s):** Poilar Crookleg, Adventurer, Religious (pilgrim); Traiben, Adventurer, Religious
**Time period(s):** Indeterminate Future
**Locale(s):** Planet—Imaginary

**Summary:** Among the few chosen each generation for a difficult Pilgrimage to the home of the gods, Poilar Crookleg and Traiben ascend the Wall in honor of their ancestor, the First Climber. The creatures and adventures in the kingdoms along the way to the summit leave the group barely able to accept the truth at the end of their arduous journey.

**Other books you might like:**
Orson Scott Card, *The Memory of Earth*, 1992
C.J. Cherryh, *Angel with the Sword*, 1985
Philip Jose Farmer, *The Maker of Universes*, 1965
Brian Herbert, *The Race for God*, 1990
Edward Myers, *Fire and Ice*, 1992
Edward Myers, *The Mountain Made of Light*, 1992
Robert Reed, *The Remarkables*, 1992
John Varley, *Wizard*, 1980

## 5034

**ROBERT SILVERBERG**, Editor

### Legends: Short Novels by the Masters of Modern Fantasy

(New York: Tor, 1998)

**Story type:** Fantasy (Anthology; Magic Conflict)
**Summary:** This anthology contains a six-page introduction as well as individual introductions for its 11 lengthy, original stories set in their authors' established series: Orson Scott Card's Tales of Alvin Maker, Raymond E. Feist's Riftwar Saga, Terry Goodkind's Sword of Truth, Robert Jordan's Wheel of Time, Stephen King's Dark Tower, Ursula K. Le Guin's Earthsea, George R.R. Martin's Song of Ice and Fire, Anne McCaffrey's Pern, Terry Pratchett's Discworld, Robert Silverberg's Majipoor, and Tad Williams' Memory, Sorrow and Thorn. The anthology also contains bibliographic citations for the books in these series.

**Other books you might like:**
Orson Scott Card, *Seventh Son*, 1987
Raymond E. Feist, *Magician*, 1992
   revised
Terry Goodkind, *Wizard's First Rule*, 1994
Robert Jordan, *The Eye of the World*, 1990
Stephen King, *The Gunslinger*, 1982
Ursula K. Le Guin, *A Wizard of Earthsea*, 1968
George R.R. Martin, *A Game of Thrones*, 1996
Anne McCaffrey, *Dragonflight*, 1969
Terry Pratchett, *The Colour of Magic*, 1983
Tad Williams, *The Dragonbone Chair*, 1988

## 5035

**ROBERT SILVERBERG**

### Letters From Atlantis

(New York: Atheneum, 1990)

**Story type:** Fantasy (Time Travel; Legend)
**Major character(s):** Roy, Time Traveler; Ram Ramifon Blayl, Royalty (Heir to the Throne of Atlantis)
**Time period(s):** 189th century B.C. (18,862 B.C.)
**Locale(s):** *Lord of Day*, At Sea (Ship bound for Atlantis); Athilan, Mythical Place (Island Kingdom of Atlantis)
**Summary:** Through letters to a fellow time traveller, Roy tells Lora that his consciousness has settled in the person who is heir apparent to the King of Atlantis. When Ram discovers Roy's presence, he rebels, then accepts Roy. During an initiation rite, Roy sees Ram's peoples' Sun go nova and the eventual destruction of Atlantis.

**Other books you might like:**
Isaac Asimov, *Atlantis*, 1988
   Martin H. Greenberg, co-editor; Charles Waugh, co-editor

Marion Zimmer Bradley, *Web of Darkness*, 1984
Marion Zimmer Bradley, *Web of Light*, 1983
J. Alison James, *Sing for a Gentle Rain*, 1990
Roger Zelazny, *Bridge of Ashes*, 1976

## 5036

**ROBERT SILVERBERG**

### Lion Time in Timbuctoo

(Eugene, Oregon: Axolotl Press, 1990)

**Story type:** Science Fiction (Alternate Universe; Political)
**Series:** Gate of Worlds
**Major character(s):** Little Father, Heir (to the Emir of Songhay); Michael, Diplomat, Apprentice (to the English Ambassador); Selima, Young Woman (Turkish Ambassador's daughter)
**Time period(s):** 1980s
**Locale(s):** Timbuctoo, Africa

**Summary:** As the Emir of Timbuctoo lies dying, foreign ambassadors gather and plot what will happen after his death. Michael, uncovering a plot to murder Little Father, cannot resist telling his love, Selima, who then goes to Little Father and reveals the plot. Little Father succeeds the Emir and expels those who plotted against him.

**Other books you might like:**
Leo Frankowski, *The Cross-Time Engineer*, 1986
Kirk Mitchell, *Procurator*, 1984
Mack Reynolds, *The Other Time*, 1984
Harry Turtledove, *Agent of Byzantium*, 1987
Harry Turtledove, *The Pugnacious Peacemaker*, 1990

## 5037

**ROBERT SILVERBERG**

### The Mountains of Majipoor

(New York: Bantam Spectra, 1995)

**Story type:** Science Fiction (Political)
**Series:** Majipoor
**Major character(s):** Harpirias of Muldemar, Royalty (prince), Diplomat; Korinaam the Shapeshifter, Guide, Linguist (translator); Toikella, Royalty (king), Leader
**Time period(s):** Indeterminate Future
**Locale(s):** Majipoor, Planet—Imaginary

**Summary:** To escape bureaucratic exile in a provincial city, Prince Harpirias leads a negotiating mission aimed at rescuing a team of captured paleontologists. After a dangerous journey to the cold northern regions, Harpirias must overcome Korinaam's reluctance to translate literally, King Toikella's preconceptions, and his own vow of chastity to avoid disaster.

**Other books you might like:**
Margaret Wander Bonanno, *OtherWise*, 1993
A.C. Crispin, *Silent Songs*, 1994
   Kathleen O'Malley, co-author
Rosemary Kirstein, *The Outskirter's Secret*, 1992
Edward Myers, *The Mountain Made of Light*, 1992
James H. Schmitz, *The Demon Breed*, 1968
Melissa Scott, *Shadow Man*, 1995

## 5038

**ROBERT SILVERBERG**, Editor
**MARTIN H. GREENBERG**, Co-Editor

### Murasaki

(New York: Bantam Spectra, 1992)

**Story type:** Science Fiction (Anthology)
**Time period(s):** 23rd century
**Locale(s):** Genji, Planet—Imaginary; Chujoan, Planet—Imaginary

**Summary:** This book contains a six-part novel examining life forms of the Murasaki star system and their interrelationships by Nebula Award winners Poul Anderson, Greg Bear, Gregory Benford, David Brin, Nancy Kress and Frederik Pohl plus an introduction by Robert Silverberg and one appendix, "Design for Two Worlds," by Poul Anderson and another, "Murasaki's Worlds," by Frederik Pohl.

**Other books you might like:**
C.J. Cherryh, *Angel with the Sword*, 1985
C.J. Cherryh, *Festival Moon*, 1987
    editor
Harlan Ellison, *Medea: Harlan's World*, 1985
    editor
Janet Kagan, *Mirabile*, 1991
George R.R. Martin, *Wild Cards*, 1987
    editor
Will Shetterly, *Liavek*, 1985
    Emma Bull, co-editor
Terri Windling, *Life on the Border*, 1991
    editor

## 5039

**ROBERT SILVERBERG**
**KAREN HABER**, Co-Author

### The Mutant Season

(New York: Doubleday Foundation, 1989)

**Story type:** Science Fiction (Psychic Powers)
**Major character(s):** Michael Ryton, Mutant; Melanie Ryton, Mutant
**Time period(s):** 21st century
**Locale(s):** United States

**Summary:** A race of mutant psychics makes its presence known and demands equal rights. An enormous amount of prejudice is generated against the mutants and marriages between mutants and normals are looked down upon. The mutants themselves are capable of prejudice and the situation has a potential for violence. First of four planned novels.

**Other books you might like:**
Poul Anderson, *The Boat of a Million Years*, 1989
Henry Kuttner, *Mutant*, 1953
Daniel Keys Moran, *Emerald Eyes*, 1988
Daniel Keys Moran, *The Long Run*, 1989
A.E. Van Vogt, *Slan*, 1946
Joan D. Vinge, *Catspaw*, 1988
Joan D. Vinge, *Psion*, 1982

## 5040

**ROBERT SILVERBERG**

### The New Springtime

(New York: Warner Books, 1990)

**Story type:** Science Fiction (Post-Holocaust)
**Major character(s):** Taniane, Ruler; Nialli Apuilana, Royalty (Taniane's daughter)
**Time period(s):** Indeterminate Future (Forty years after the Coming Forth)
**Locale(s):** Earth

**Summary:** In this sequel to *At Winter's End*, forty years have passed since the end of the last ice age and the great Coming Forth from their underground city of the People, an evolved race of apes. The People have founded cities and spread out across the Continent, but they still have to deal with the intelligent, insectoid hjjk, their main competitors for control of the Earth, and with the last remnants of humanity.

**Other books you might like:**
Brian W. Aldiss, *Helliconia Spring*, 1982
Brian W. Aldiss, *Helliconia Summer*, 1983
Brian W. Aldiss, *Helliconia Winter*, 1985
Clifford D. Simak, *City*, 1952

## 5041

**ROBERT SILVERBERG**

### Sorcerers of Majipoor

(New York: HarperPrism, 1997)

**Story type:** Science Fiction (Political; Science Fantasy)
**Series:** Majipoor
**Major character(s):** Korsibar, Royalty (prince); Prestimion, Royalty (prince); Thismet, Royalty (princess)
**Time period(s):** Indeterminate Future
**Locale(s):** Majipoor, Planet—Imaginary

**Summary:** Against all custom, Prince Korsibar becomes "coronal" of Majipoor, instead of the expected heir, Prince Prestimion. Resentful of this, Prestimion starts a rebellion, but must flee to Triggoin, a city of sorcerers, where he gains the wisdom to make a change of rulers meaningful before continuing his battle against Korsibar. Fifth in series.

**Other books you might like:**
Lois McMaster Bujold, *Barrayar*, 1991
Octavia E. Butler, *Patternmaster*, 1976
Orson Scott Card, *The Memory of Earth*, 1992
Katherine Kurtz, *The Bastard Prince*, 1994
Harry Turtledove, *The Stolen Throne*, 1995
Jack Vance, *Lyonesse*, 1983
Joan D. Vinge, *The Snow Queen*, 1980
Roger Zelazny, *Nine Princes in Amber*, 1970

## 5042

**ROBERT SILVERBERG**

### Starborne

(New York: Bantam Spectra, 1996)

**Story type:** Science Fiction (First Contact; Mystical)
**Major character(s):** Noelle, Telepath
**Time period(s):** 23rd century
**Locale(s):** Outer Space; *Wotan*, Spaceship

**Summary:** The *Wotan* searches for planets humanity can settle, at first finding only unsuitable ones. Their telepath, Noelle, then loses contact with her sister on Earth, making everyone feel isolated. When Noelle decides to reach out to whatever prevents the contact, she discovers sentient life quite different from what everyone always thought.

**Other books you might like:**
John Brunner, *A Maze of Stars*, 1991
F.M. Busby, *Slow Freight*, 1991
Samuel R. Delany, *The Ballad of Beta-2*, 1965
William R. Forstchen, *Into the Sea of Stars*, 1986
Robert A. Heinlein, *Orphans of the Sky*, 1961
Frank Herbert, *Whipping Star*, 1970
Robert J. Sawyer, *Golden Fleece*, 1990
Norman Spinrad, *The Void Captain's Tale*, 1986
James White, *The Dream Millennium*, 1974

---

**5043**

**ROBERT SILVERBERG**

### Thebes of the Hundred Gates

(Eugene, Oregon: Pulphouse Publishing Axolotl Press, 1991)

**Story type:** Science Fiction (Time Travel)
**Major character(s):** Edward Davis, Time Traveler; Elaine "Nefret" Sandburg, Time Traveler, Religious; Roger "Senmut-Ptah" Lehman, Time Traveler, Scientist (astronomer)
**Time period(s):** 15th century B.C. (18th dynasty)
**Locale(s):** Thebes, Egypt

**Summary:** When Edward Davis arrives in Thebes, dizzy with characteristic time travel shock, a good samaritan takes him into a nearby temple where Elaine Sandburg, masquerading as a priestess, takes charge of him. Elaine and Roger then plot to deprive Edward of his return trip to the future, hoping to hide the fact that they relocated to Thebes in an unauthorized time trip.

**Other books you might like:**
Harry Harrison, *The Technicolor Time Machine*, 1967
Vernor Vinge, *Marooned in Realtime*, 1986
Vernor Vinge, *The Peace War*, 1984
Robert Charles Wilson, *A Bridge of Years*, 1991

---

**5044**

**ROBERT SILVERBERG**

### To the Land of the Living

(New York: Questar, 1990)

**Story type:** Fantasy (Legend)
**Major character(s):** Gilgamesh, Warrior, Royalty (King of Uruk)
**Time period(s):** 40th century; Indeterminate Past
**Locale(s):** Sumer, Middle East; Mythical Place

**Summary:** While trying to avoid the dangers of the Afterworld, Gilgamesh seeks out his closest friend. Along the way he interacts with various historical characters who, like himself, are caught up in a never ending cycle of death and rebirth.

**Other books you might like:**
Philip Jose Farmer, *To Your Scattered Bodies Go*, 1971
Roger Zelazny, *The Black Throne*, 1990

---

**5045**

**ROBERT SILVERBERG**, Editor
**KAREN HABER**, Co-Editor

### Universe 2

(New York: Bantam Spectra, 1992)

**Story type:** Science Fiction (Anthology)
**Series:** Universe

**Summary:** Contains a five-page introduction by Silverberg plus individual introductions to 21 original stories and one story, Brian W. Aldiss's "Her Toes Were Beautiful on the Hilltops," revised and retitled from its appearance in a semiprofessional magazine. The stories include some with a dark tone such as Paul Di Filippo's first professional sale, "Forty at the Kiosk," portraying a disturbing view of an all too regulated future, and Alex Jeffers' "From *The Bridge*" with its post-alien invasion San Francisco, complete with kinky alien sex and the Golden Gate Bridge as an all night hot spot. A lighter tone permeates some work such as Deborah Wessel's "The Cool Equations," a parody of Tom Godwin's "The Cold Equations" (1954). Other provocative stories also explore a broad range of settings and themes as pioneered in Terry Carr's Universe series.

**Other books you might like:**
Lou Aronica, *Full Spectrum*, 1988
    Shawna McCarthy, co-editor
Terry Carr, *The Best From Universe*, 1984
    editor
Terry Carr, *The Best Science Fiction Novellas of the Year 1-2*, 1979-1980
    editor
Terry Carr, *The Best Science Fiction of the Year 1-16*, 1972-1987
    editor
Beth Meacham, *Terry's Universe*, 1988
    editor

---

**5046**

**ROBERT SILVERBERG**, Editor
**KAREN HABER**, Co-Editor

### Universe 3

(New York: Bantam Spectra, 1994)

**Story type:** Science Fiction (Anthology)
**Series:** Universe

**Summary:** Contains a four-page introduction by Silverberg and 15 original stories, frequently dark in tone, which explore a broad range of familiar themes such as alien perceptions of humanity, politics, overpopulation, life in space, metaphysics and a revolt of bioengineered life forms in a Farmer McGregor theme park. Authors include Brian W. Aldiss, E. Michael Blake, Paul Di Filippo, Joe Haldeman, Phillip C. Jennings, Barry N. Malzberg and Wil McCarthy.

**Other books you might like:**
Terry Carr, *The Best From Universe*, 1984
    editor
Terry Carr, *The Best Science Fiction Novellas of the Year 1-2*, 1979-1980
    editor
Terry Carr, *The Best Science Fiction of the Year 1-16*, 1972-1987
    editor
Gardner Dozois, *The Year's Best Science Fiction: Eleventh Annual Collection*, 1994
    editor

Beth Meacham, *Terry's Universe*, 1988
editor

## 5047

### CLIFFORD D. SIMAK

## *Over the River & through the Woods*

(San Francisco: Tachyon, 1996)

**Story type:** Science Fiction (Collection)
**Major character(s):** Old Mose, Farmer; Henderson James, Scientist
**Time period(s):** 1950s
**Locale(s):** Wisconsin; Minneapolis, Minnesota

**Summary:** Eight short stories from 1951 to 1980, providing a broad view of the career of Clifford Simak. The stories showcase Simak's wide emotional and thematic range, from cautionary tales of a "free lunch" that isn't free, to issues of identity and a study of alienation. Includes a five-page introduction by Poul Anderson.

**Other books you might like:**
Henry Kuttner, *The Best of Henry Kuttner*, 1975
Fritz Leiber, *Night's Black Agents*, 1947
C.L. Moore, *The Best of C.L. Moore*, 1975
Howard Waldrop, *Strange Monsters of the Recent Past*, 1991

## 5048

### CLIFFORD D. SIMAK

## *Way Station*

(New York: Collier, 1993)

**Story type:** Science Fiction (First Contact; Theological)
**Major character(s):** Enoch Wallace, Military Personnel (Civil War), Recluse; Claude Lewis, Government Official (intelligence); Ulysses, Alien
**Time period(s):** 1960s (1965)
**Locale(s):** Millville, Wisconsin

**Summary:** After learning of 125 year old Enoch Wallace, Claude Lewis discovers that Earth is located at an interstellar transfer station where events will decide the fate of Earth and the interstellar confederation of travellers who use Way Station. Reissue of the 1963 Hugo Award-winning novel.

**Other books you might like:**
John Brunner, *The Whole Man*, 1964
John Brunner, *The World Swappers*, 1959
A.C. Crispin, *Starbridge*, 1989
Philip K. Dick, *Solar Lottery*, 1955
Rebecca Ore, *Becoming Alien*, 1987
Wilson Tucker, *The Year of the Quiet Sun*, 1970
A.E. Van Vogt, *The Voyage of the Space Beagle*, 1950
Jack Williamson, *The Legion of Space*, 1947

## 5049

### DAN SIMMONS

## *Carrion Comfort*

(Arlington Heights, IL: Dark Harvest, 1989)

**Story type:** Horror (Vampire Story)
**Major character(s):** Saul Laski, Doctor, Survivor (Holocaust); Natalie Preston, Photographer
**Time period(s):** 1980s (Pre-1945)
**Locale(s):** Germany; United States; Israel

**Summary:** Three aging psychic vampires—Melanie, Nina, and Willie—amuse themselves with their "Game," the stimulation of random worldwide violence and mass murder. After the 1980 meeting, dissention and violence breaks out amongst the trio, setting off repercussions that reach to the highest levels of government and threaten to unleash the apocalypse. Three individuals—a holocaust survivor, a young black woman, and an intellectual Southern sheriff—set out against overwhelming odds to thwart the conflicting machinations of the mind vampires.

**Other books you might like:**
Colin Wilson, *The Space Vampires*, 1976

## 5050

### DAN SIMMONS

## *Children of the Night*

(New York: Putnam, 1992)

**Story type:** Horror (Vampire Story)
**Major character(s):** Kate Neumann, Doctor; Mike O'Rourke, Religious (Catholic priest); Vernor Deacon Trent, Businessman (a.k.a. Dracula)
**Time period(s):** 1990s
**Locale(s):** Bucharest, Romania; Transylvania

**Summary:** While rendering emergency medical services in post-Ceausescu Romania, Doctor Kate Neumann discovers a seven-month-old baby whose extraordinary immune system portends a breakthrough in medical knowledge for the management of numerous untreatable diseases. But Kate's plans for the child are complicated by businessman Vernor Deacon Trent, alias Count Dracula, who recognizes the child as the offspring of his vampire family, which has had a hand in Romanian politics for five centuries and is destined to be led by the boy once he has attained his majority.

**Other books you might like:**
Richard Matheson, *I Am Legend*, 1954
Fred Saberhagen, *The Dracula Tape*, 1975
Brian Stableford, *The Empire of Fear*, 1988
Peter Tremayne, *Dracula Unborn*, 1977

## 5051

### DAN SIMMONS

## *Endymion*

(New York: Bantam Spectra, 1996)

**Story type:** Science Fiction (Immortality; Theological)
**Series:** Hyperion
**Major character(s):** Raul Endymion, Prisoner, Hero, Guardian (of Aenea); A. Bettik, Android; Aenea, Child, Religious (messiah)
**Time period(s):** 32nd century
**Locale(s):** Armaghast, Planet—Imaginary; Hyperion, Planet—Imaginary; Pacem, Planet—Imaginary

**Summary:** While waiting in a Schrodinger Cat box for execution, Endymion writes his memoirs of his travels with Aenea and A. Bettik after rescuing Aenea from the Pax army waiting for her release from the Time Tombs. The Shrike appears with her and seems to accompany the travelers through the Farcasters, thought useless since their shutdown 300 years earlier caused the Fall, promoting the rise of the Pax and the Catholic Church. Unfortunately, an immortal crew of Church warriors follows the trio to capture or kill Aenea. Third book in the series.

**Other books you might like:**
Isaac Asimov, *The Robots of Dawn*, 1983

Frank Herbert, *Dune*, 1965
James P. Hogan, *The Immortality Option*, 1995
Stuart Hopen, *Warp Angel*, 1995
Vernor Vinge, *A Fire upon the Deep*, 1992

## 5052

### DAN SIMMONS

## The Fall of Hyperion

(New York: Doubleday Foundation, 1990)

**Story type:** Science Fiction (Literary)
**Series:** Hyperion
**Major character(s):** Meina Gladstone, Government Official; Joseph Severn, Reincarnated Person (cybernetic John Keats)
**Time period(s):** 28th century
**Locale(s):** Hyperion, Planet—Imaginary

**Summary:** The pilgrims who sought the Time Tombs in *Hyperion* have finally reached them. Each interacts with the tombs and with the Shrike, the deadly creature who guards them, in his or her own unique manner. Some find transcendence, others merely death. Increasingly important is Joseph Severn, that strange reincarnation of the ancient poet John Keats. More is revealed about the complex game of political intrigue being played by a number of major powers, not all of them human.

**Other books you might like:**
William Barton, *Iris*, 1989
    Michael Capobianco, co-author
Greg Bear, *Eon*, 1985
Greg Bear, *Eternity*, 1989
Tim Powers, *The Stress of Her Regard*, 1989
Robert Silverberg, *Downward to the Earth*, 1970

## 5053

### DAN SIMMONS

## Fires of Eden

(New York: Putnam, 1994)

**Story type:** Horror (Supernatural Vengeance)
**Major character(s):** Byron Trumbo, Businessman (real estate developer); Eleanor Perry, Professor (of English); Cordie Stumpf, Widow(er)
**Time period(s):** 1990s (1994); 1860s (1866)
**Locale(s):** South Kona, Hawaii

**Summary:** Reprehensible real estate mogul Byron Trumbo tries desperately to sell the Mauna Pele, a luxury resort built on the slopes of an active Hawaiian volcano. Complicating matters are the doings of a pantheon of ancient Hawaiian gods, invoked by natives upset with Trumbo's desecration of their sacred land, who begin stealing the souls of the resort's visitors.

**Other books you might like:**
Robert Bloch, *Strange Eons*, 1976
Michael Green, *The Jimjams*, 1994
Graham Masterton, *Burial*, 1994
Adam Niswander, *The Charm*, 1993

## 5054

### DAN SIMMONS

## The Hollow Man

(New York: Bantam Spectra, 1992)

**Story type:** Science Fiction (Psychic Powers; Theological)
**Major character(s):** Jeremy "Jerry" Bremen, Psychic, Widow(er); Robby Bustamante, Psychic, Handicapped (blind, deaf, retarded); Vannie Fucci, Criminal
**Time period(s):** 1990s
**Locale(s):** Denver, Colorado; Boston, Massachusetts; Barnegat Light, New Jersey

**Summary:** Gail and Jeremy, both telepaths, protect each other from random thoughts around them. After Gail dies of cancer, Jeremy falls prey to the negative thoughts and emotions her loss leaves him open to. He finds occasional relief in memories of Gail, their relationship and the mathematical representations of the mind and the universe that he had been generating.

**Other books you might like:**
Alfred Bester, *The Demolished Man*, 1953
Frank Herbert, *The White Plague*, 1982
Robert Reed, *Down the Bright Way*, 1991
Kate Wilhelm, *Death Qualified: A Mystery of Chaos*, 1991
George Zebrowski, *Stranger Suns*, 1991

## 5055

### DAN SIMMONS

## Hyperion

(New York: Doubleday/Foundation, 1989)

**Story type:** Science Fiction (Literary)
**Series:** Hyperion
**Major character(s):** Consul, Diplomat; Father Hoyt, Religious
**Time period(s):** 28th century
**Locale(s):** Hegemony of Man, Interstellar Empire/Federation; Hyperion, Planet—Imaginary

**Summary:** The Hegemony of Man seems on the verge of war and the mysterious planet Hyperion may hold the information necessary to avert the crisis. On that planet seven pilgrims set forth to reach the Time Tombs, each for a very different reason, while the killing machine known as the Shrike hovers on the horizon.

**Other books you might like:**
Robert Silverberg, *Downward to the Earth*, 1970
Jack Vance, *The Anome*, 1973
Jack Vance, *The Asutra*, 1974
Jack Vance, *Showboat World*, 1975

## 5056

### DAN SIMMONS

## Lovedeath

(New York: Warner, 1993)

**Story type:** Science Fiction (Collection; Horror)
**Summary:** Contains a 10-page foreword about the novellas and their shared themes of love and death in the two reprinted and three original stories. First published as a chapbook, "Entropy's Bed at Midnight" utilizes as framework a thrilling alpine slide in Colorado and accidents recorded in an auto insurance file. Slightly revised from its *Playboy* appearance as "Death in Bangkok," "Dying in

Bangkok'' features John Merrick's return to the site of youthful indiscretions in search of a sexual vampire. The longest work, ''Sleeping with Teeth Women,'' combines several legends of American Indian origin in the story of Hoka Ushte's spirit quest on which the fate of his entire people rests. In ''Flashback,'' a federal agent agonizes over his inability to prevent an assassination as a powerful new pharmaceutical drug reveals additional problems. ''The Great Lover'' examines the literary dimension of tragedy associated with war through historical poetry attributed to the fictional James Edwin Rooke.

**Other books you might like:**
Jeff Gelb, *Hot Blood: Tales of Provocative Horror*, 1989
    Lonn Friend, co-editor
Jeff Gelb, *Hotter Blood: More Tales of Erotic Horror*, 1991
    Michael Garret, co-editor
Jeff Gelb, *Hottest Blood: The Ultimate in Erotic Horror*, 1993
    Michael Garret, co-editor
Stephen King, *Different Seasons*, 1982
Stephen King, *Four Past Midnight*, 1990
Lucius Shepard, *The Ends of the Earth*, 1990
Michele Slung, *I Shudder at Your Touch*, 1991
    editor
Michele Slung, *Shudder Again*, 1993
    editor

**5057**

**DAN SIMMONS**

## Phases of Gravity

(New York: Bantam Spectra, 1989)

**Story type:** Science Fiction (Contemporary Realism)
**Major character(s):** Richard Baedecker, Astronaut (Aero-space consultant), Businessman; Scott Baedecker, Young Man (Richard's son)
**Time period(s):** 20th century
**Locale(s):** United States; India

**Summary:** Richard Baedecker, who once walked on the moon, feels like his entire life since that experience has been a disappointment. In a quest to come to terms with his depression, Baedecker travels first to India, then to visit other ex-astronauts who have made more successful lives for themselves than he has, and finally undergoes a mystical experience atop a butte in South Dakota.

**Other books you might like:**
Edward Gibson, *Reach*, 1989
Barry Malzberg, *Beyond Apollo*, 1972
Barry Malzberg, *The Falling Astronauts*, 1971
Lewis Shiner, *Deserted Cities of the Heart*, 1988

**5058**

**DAN SIMMONS**

## Prayers to Broken Stones

(Arlington Heights, IL: Dark Harvest, 1990)

**Story type:** Horror (Collection)

**Summary:** Thirteen stories of horror, fantasy, and science fiction, including one new story espcially written for the book, ''The Death of the Centaur,'' which straddles the border between fantasy and realistic fiction. Though the author is most at home working with straightforward horror themes, as in the vampire tales ''Carrrion Comfort'' and ''Shave and A Haircut, Two Bites'' and the ghost story ''Iverson's Pits,'' he is also adept at moving evocations of grief

in ''The River Styx Runs Upstream,'' social satire in ''Vanni Fucci is Alive and Well and Living in Hell'' and hard science fiction in ''Remembering Siri.''

**Other books you might like:**
Michael Blumlein, *The Brains of Rats*, 1989
Pat Cadigan, *Patterns*, 1989
Harlan Ellison, *Angry Candy*, 1988
George R.R. Martin, *Songs the Dead Men Sing*, 1983
Pat Murphy, *Points of Departure*, 1990

**5059**

**DAN SIMMONS**

## The Rise of Endymion

(New York: Bantam Spectra, 1997)

**Story type:** Science Fiction (Theological; Alternate Intelligence)
**Series:** Hyperion
**Major character(s):** Aenea, Genetically Altered Being, Religious (messiah); Raul Endymion, Hero, Guardian (of Aenea), Lover (of Aenea); Martin Silenus, Writer (poet), Aged Person
**Time period(s):** 32nd century
**Locale(s):** Pacem, Planet—Imaginary; Hyperion, Planet—Imaginary; *Yggdrasill*, Spaceship (treeship)

**Summary:** While remaining in the Schroedinger Cat Box prison, Raul continues writing his remembrances of Aenea, the One Who Teaches, their developing relationship and their travels. Designed as a weapon to prevent the TechnoCore from completely enslaving or destroying human and alien life, Aenea glimpses the future and sees her own death, permitting her to know how short a time remains to complete her task. A concluding fourth volume in the series is likely.

**Other books you might like:**
Isaac Asimov, *The Robots of Dawn*, 1983
David Brin, *Brightness Reef*, 1995
Frank Herbert, *Dune*, 1965
James P. Hogan, *The Immortality Option*, 1995
Larry Niven, *Protector*, 1973
Vernor Vinge, *A Fire upon the Deep*, 1992

**5060**

**DAN SIMMONS**

## Summer of Night

(New York: Putnam's, 1991)

**Story type:** Horror (Coming-of-Age)
**Major character(s):** Dale Stewart, Child; Mike O'Rourke, Child; Duane McBride, Child
**Time period(s):** 1960s (1960)
**Locale(s):** Elm Haven, Illinois

**Summary:** When a young boy disappears on the last day of school at the Old Central schoolbuilding before it is to be boarded up forever, his classmates vow to solve the mystery. Their summer of investigations uncovers an ancient evil influencing their town and dark revelations about themselves.

**Other books you might like:**
Ray Bradbury, *Something Wicked This Way Comes*, 1962
Ray Bradbury, *Dandelion Wine*, 1957
Stephen King, *Different Seasons*, 1982
    The Body

## 5061

**TRANA MAE SIMMONS**

### Spell Bound

(New York: Jove, 1998)

**Story type:** Fantasy (Light Fantasy; Romance)
**Major character(s):** Nick Bardou, Businessman
**Time period(s):** 1990s (1998)
**Locale(s):** New Orleans, Louisiana

**Summary:** Nick Bardou visits New Orleans to wind up affairs surrounding his family's estate. There he encounters an attractive young woman who has magical powers and who helps him uncover the truth about an old mystery.

**Other books you might like:**
John Dickson Carr, *The Devil in Velvet*, 1951
Glen Cook, *Deadly Quicksilver Lies*, 1994
Charles de Lint, *Mulengro: A Romany Tale*, 1985
Melisa Michaels, *Cold Iron*, 1997
Melisa Michaels, *Sister to the Rain*, 1998

## 5062

**WM. MARK SIMMONS**

### One Foot in the Grave

(New York: Baen, 1996)

**Story type:** Fantasy (Adventure; Contemporary)
**Major character(s):** Christopher Csejthe, Vampire, Radio Personality; Lupe Garou, Werewolf; Bassarab, Vampire, Nobleman
**Time period(s):** 1990s (1996)
**Locale(s):** Pittsburg, Kansas; Seattle, Washington

**Summary:** After the deaths of his wife and daughter, Christopher Csejthe wraps himself in a cocoon of work until a degenerative disease forces him to the doctor. After discovering the nature of his disease—vampirism—he must soon run for his life. Christopher needs education to survive, but his allies may prove as deadly as his friends.

**Other books you might like:**
Emma Bull, *War for the Oaks*, 1987
Laurell K. Hamilton, *Guilty Pleasures*, 1993
Tanya Huff, *Blood Price*, 1991
Christopher Moore, *Bloodsucking Fiends: A Love Story*, 1995
Kristine Kathryn Rusch, *Sins of the Blood*, 1994

## 5063

**WM. MARK SIMMONS**

### When Dreams Collide

(New York: Warner Questar, 1992)

**Story type:** Fantasy (Adventure; Quest)
**Major character(s):** Robert Remington Ripley III, Writer, Martial Arts Expert; Cerebus, Artificial Intelligence (Superego of Dreamland), Imposter (Walter Hanson)
**Time period(s):** 21st century
**Locale(s):** Russia; Dreamland, Cyberspace (computer program)

**Summary:** When Artificial Ego and Superego of Dreamland escape the computer generated dream world into bodies of human beings, Robert Ripley must free the minds captured in Dreamland and return control of their bodies to them after capturing the fugitive artificial intelligences. Sequel to *In the Net of Dreams*.

**Other books you might like:**
Rick Cook, *Wizard's Bane*, 1989
Philip Jose Farmer, *Red Orc's Rage*, 1991
Joel Rosenberg, *The Sleeping Dragon*, 1983
Will Shetterly, *Cats Have No Lord*, 1985
Will Shetterly, *The Tangled Lands*, 1989
Vivian Vande Velde, *User Unfriendly*, 1991

## 5064

**JEAN SIMON**

### Ghost Boy

(New York: Zebra, 1994)

**Story type:** Horror (Ghost Story)
**Major character(s):** Libby Gregory, Receptionist (medical office); Joely Gregory, Child (Libby's daughter); Martin Philip Stanovich, Child, Spirit
**Time period(s):** 1990s (1994)
**Locale(s):** Cielo, California

**Summary:** Divorcee Libby Gregory's relocation to the home town of her former husband coincides with the resumption of a series of child murders that plagued the town decades before. Libby's daughter Joely befriends a ghost boy who lives in the local cemetery and who convinces Joely that he was murdered by the same person who has begun killing children again.

**Other books you might like:**
Jonathan Aycliffe, *Naomi's Room*, 1992
Anne Dillard, *Specters*, 1991
Dennis Etchison, *Darkside*, 1986
Keith Ferrario, *Deadly Friend*, 1994
Abigail McDaniels, *The Uprising*, 1994
Melanie Tem, *Prodigal*, 1991

## 5065

**JEAN SIMON**

### Orphans

(New York: Zebra, 1992)

**Story type:** Horror (Wild Talents)
**Major character(s):** Rae Downing, Secretary; Josie Falco, Young Woman; Julian, Young Man (Josie's houseguest)
**Time period(s):** 1990s (1992)
**Locale(s):** Running Horse Lake, Minnesota

**Summary:** Rae Downing discovers that bad things come in threes when she meets a long lost sister who informs her that they are two of three triplets born in a hippie commune in the 1960s and that, working together, they can manipulate destructive telekinetic powers.

**Other books you might like:**
Margaret Bingley, *Seeds of Evil*, 1992
Theodore Sturgeon, *More than Human*, 1953
Thomas Tryon, *The Other*, 1972
John Wyndham, *The Midwich Cuckoos*, 1957

## 5066

### JEAN SIMON

## *Sweet Revenge*

(New York: Zebra, 1991)

**Story type:** Horror (Possession)
**Major character(s):** Jessica Callahan, Teenager; Mardie Callahan, Accountant (bookkeeper); Zack Nelson, Teenager
**Time period(s):** 1990s
**Locale(s):** Wisdom Beach, California

**Summary:** Jessica Callahan visits her Aunt Mardie at her new beach house and finds the woman dressing flamboyantly, acting promiscuously, and possibly responsible for the deaths of several young men in the neighborhood. All of this leads Jessica to wonder if her aunt has become possessed by the vengeful spirit of the former owner, who was murdered by one of her lovers.

**Other books you might like:**
Ramona Stewart, *The Possession of Joel Delaney*, 1970

## 5067

### GEORGE GAYLORD SIMPSON

## *The Dechronization of Sam Magruder*

(New York: St. Martin's Press, 1996)

**Story type:** Science Fiction (Time Travel)
**Major character(s):** Sam Magruder, Scientist, Time Traveler; Pierre Precieux, Scientist (geologist); The Universal Historian, Scholar
**Time period(s):** 22nd century (2162); 800000th cent. B.C. (Cretaceous Period)
**Locale(s):** North America

**Summary:** Via stone tablets, Sam Magruder records his life and existence in the Cretaceous period, while future scholars reflect on Magruder's chronological experiment. Contains a 13-page introduction by Arthur C. Clarke, a 22-page afterword by Stephen Jay Gould and a 6-page memoir by Joan Simpson Burns. Author's only fiction, discovered 10 years after his death.

**Other books you might like:**
Robert T. Bakker, *Raptor Red*, 1995
Mona Clee, *Branch Point*, 1996
Sir Arthur Conan Doyle, *The Lost World*, 1915
Robert J. Sawyer, *End of an Era*, 1994
Vernor Vinge, *Marooned in Realtime*, 1986
H.G. Wells, *The Time Machine*, 1895

## 5068

### ALISON SINCLAIR

## *Blueheart*

(New York: HarperPrism, 1998)

**Story type:** Science Fiction (Political; Genetic Manipulation)
**Major character(s):** Rache of Scole, Genetically Altered Being (Blueheart adapted), Administrator; Teal Blane Berenice, Computer Expert, Traveler (consultant); Cesar Kamehameha, Administrator (Adaptation Oversight Committee), Scientist (genetics)
**Time period(s):** Indeterminate Future
**Locale(s):** Blueheart, Planet—Imaginary

**Summary:** Still in the process of terraforming, Blueheart, a water world, has been settled for only a few hundred years. The inhabitants have been altered to enable their survival in the ocean environment, but the time has come for the planet to develop continents that would destroy the current environment. Rache works to promote a compromise which would permit the pastoral aquatic lifestyle and social structure to remain, but someone has begun to kill any who interfere with the ban on continuing adaptation, and may attempt to eliminate all adaptees.

**Other books you might like:**
L. Warren Douglas, *Cannon's Orb*, 1994
Wil McCarthy, *Bloom*, 1998
Ian McDonald, *Evolution's Shore*, 1995
Joan Slonczewski, *The Children Star*, 1998
Joan Slonczewski, *A Door into Ocean*, 1986

## 5069

### ALISON SINCLAIR

## *Legacies*

(New York: HarperPrism, 1996)

**Story type:** Science Fiction (Lost Colony; Post-Holocaust)
**Major character(s):** Lian D'Halldt, Handicapped; Daisainia Travassa, Political Figure
**Time period(s):** Indeterminate Future
**Locale(s):** Taridwyn, Planet—Imaginary; Burdania, Planet—Imaginary

**Summary:** Several generations after a group of exiles flees their Burdania homes, possibly destroying their world in the process, descendants live on Taridwyn, aloof from the native people and consumed by guilt and pride. When a group of youngsters decides to return to Burdania, their success hinges on a brain-damaged man raised as much by aliens as his own people.

**Other books you might like:**
Iain M. Banks, *The Player of Games*, 1989
Ursula K. Le Guin, *The Word for World Is Forest*, 1976
Ian McDonald, *Desolation Road*, 1988
Larry Niven, *Ringworld*, 1970
Sarah Zettel, *Reclamation*, 1996

## 5070

### MARILYN SINGER

## *Charmed*

(New York: Atheneum, 1990)

**Story type:** Fantasy (Alternate World; Time Travel)
**Major character(s):** Miranda, Adventurer, Companion; Bastable, Alien (fenine), Royalty (deposed king of Appledura)
**Time period(s):** 1980s (1988); 2030s (2033)
**Locale(s):** Earth; Appledura, Planet—Imaginary

**Summary:** When 12-year-old Miranda is taken by her invisible friend, Bastable, to see the cobra-headed deity, Naja, Miranda is told of the Charmer who plans to destroy their worlds. Miranda finds her companions consider her the human needed for the Correct Combination, the only group, when complete, that will be able to defeat the Charmer. After a narrow escape, Miranda and her companions must travel through time and space to collect others for the Correct Combination, then overcome the Charmer before all is destroyed.

**Other books you might like:**
Suzy McKee Charnas, *Merlin's King*, 1985
Diane Duane, *So You Want to Be a Wizard?*, 1983
Maurice Gee, *The Halfmen of O*, 1982
Beth Hilgartner, *Colors in the Dreamweaver's Loom*, 1989
Shirley Rousseau Murphy, *Medallion of the Black Hound*, 1989

L.J. Smith, *Heart of Valor*, 1990
L.J. Smith, *The Night of the Solstice*, 1987

## 5071

### JACQUI SINGLETON

## *Heartstone and Silver*

(Huntington, New York: Rising Tide Press, 1994)

**Story type:** Fantasy (Sword and Sorcery)
**Major character(s):** Elayna, Witch, Lesbian; Cydell Ra Sadiin, Ruler, Lesbian
**Time period(s):** Indeterminate
**Locale(s):** Mauldar, Planet—Imaginary

**Summary:** After saving Elayna from raiders, Cydell brings her to the palace as a servant. Despite the clash of their personalities, Elayna and Cydell must overcome their differences when they travel to Wisdom Keep to thwart the threat to Cydell's kingdom and Elayna's life.

**Other books you might like:**
Marion Zimmer Bradley, *The Shattered Chain*, 1976
Ouida Crozier, *Shadows After Dark*, 1993
Jane E.M. Robinson, *The Amazon Chronicles*, 1994
Jessica Amanda Salmonson, *Amazons!*, 1979
    editor
Karen Wehrstein, *Lion's Soul*, 1991

## 5072

### CURT SIODMAK

## *Donovan's Brain/Hauser's Memory*

(New York: Leisure, 1992)

**Story type:** Horror (Collection)
**Major character(s):** Patrick Cory, Scientist

**Summary:** These two novels, published 25 years apart, are mixtures of science fiction and horror concerned with the exploits of Doctor Patrick Cory, a relatively benign mad scientist. In *Donovan's Brain* (originally published in 1943) Cory's efforts to sustain the disembodied brain of a dead gangster in his laboratory produces a superbrain capable of compelling others to do its evil bidding. In *Hauser's Memory* (originally published in 1968), Cory's injection of DNA from a dying German scientist into a living recipient produces a genetic monster that runs amok.

**Other books you might like:**
L. Ron Hubbard, *Typewriter in the Sky/Fear*, 1951
Fritz Leiber, *Conjure Wife/Our Lady of Darkness*, 1991
Les Whitten, *Moon of the Wolf/Progeny of the Adder*, 1992

## 5073

### CURT SIODMAK

## *Gabriel's Body*

(New York: Leisure, 1988)

**Story type:** Horror (Science Fiction)
**Major character(s):** Patrick Cory, Scientist; James O'Brian, Scientist; Gabriel Deeping, Young Man
**Time period(s):** 1980s (1988)
**Locale(s):** Los Angeles, California

**Summary:** In this sequel to the author's previous novels *Donovan's Brain* (1943) and *Hauser's Memory* (1968), disfigured research scientist Patrick Cory perfects a thought transference machine with the idea of projecting his mind into the body of a young encephalitis victim. But Cory soon finds himself engaged in a struggle for his identity when it turns out that his patient's will is strong and refuses to be displaced so easily.

**Other books you might like:**
Kobo Abe, *The Face of Another*, 1962
Randall Boyll, *Darkman*, 1990
Ariel Dorfman, *Mascara*, 1988

## 5074

### R.U. SIRIUS
### ST. JUDE, Co-Author

## *How to Mutate and Take Over the World*

(New York: Ballantine, 1996)

**Story type:** Science Fiction (Cyberpunk; Humor)
**Major character(s):** MONDO Vanelli, Revolutionary, Computer Expert
**Time period(s):** 2000s (2000)
**Locale(s):** United States; Cyberspace

**Summary:** As the government tightens its repressive control on all aspects of life, brave hackers attempt to reverse the stampede to Big Brotherdom.

**Other books you might like:**
Ed Blome, *Title Deleted for Security Reasons*, 1993
Stanislaw Lem, *Peace on Earth*, 1994
Ken Rolston, *Extreme Paranoia: Nobody Knows the Trouble I've Shot*, 1991
Robert Shea, *The Illuminatus! Trilogy*, 1988
    Robert Anton Wilson, co-author
Neal Stephenson, *Snow Crash*, 1992
Robert Anton Wilson, *Reality Is What You Can Get Away With: An Illustrated Screenplay*, 1992

## 5075

### MICHAEL B. SIROTA

## *Demon Shadows*

(New York: Bantam, 1990)

**Story type:** Horror (Supernatural Vengeance)
**Major character(s):** Paul Fleming, Writer; Gail Farringer, Artist (Fleming's girlfriend); Walter McClain, Administrator
**Time period(s):** 1980s
**Locale(s):** Stilwell, California (the Sierra Nevada Mountains)

**Summary:** Trying to recover from writer's block compounded by the collapse of his marriage, writer Paul Fleming retreats to an artists and writers colony in the high Sierras, unaware that the remote locale was once the site of a terrible tragedy: a small band of settlers, faced with starvation and the ordeal of winter, made a pact with an ancient Indian demon to ensure their survival, a pact that the present owners of the colony must continue to fulfill.

**Other books you might like:**
Thomas Page, *The Spirit*, 1977
Seth Pfefferle, *Stickman*, 1987
William Relling Jr., *Brujo*, 1986

## 5076

### MICHAEL B. SIROTA

## *The Ultimate Bike Path*

(New York: Ace, 1992)

**Story type:** Science Fiction (Humor)
**Series:** Bicycling Through Space and Time
**Major character(s):** Jack Miller, Traveler (bicyclist)
**Time period(s):** 1990s
**Locale(s):** Ultimate Bike Path, Mythical Place; Amazina, Mythical Place; Castle Frankenstein, Mythical Place

**Summary:** Using the 22nd gear on his 21-speed mountain bike, Jack Miller continues his zany adventures through space and time on the Ultimate Bike Path, including a visit with Dr. Frankenstein and a brief stay with the Amazins to whom he introduces the condom, revolutionizing their culture.

**Other books you might like:**
Douglas Adams, *The Hitchhiker's Guide to the Galaxy*, 1980
Douglas Adams, *The Restaurant at the End of the Universe*, 1982
John DeChancie, *Paradox Alley*, 1987
John DeChancie, *Red Limit Freeway*, 1984
John DeChancie, *Starrigger*, 1983

## 5077

### MICHAEL B. SIROTA

## *The Well*

(New York: Bantam, 1991)

**Story type:** Horror (Ancient Evil Unleashed)
**Major character(s):** Greg Lowell, Editor (executive editor, Sabre Books); Janet Lowell, Spouse (Greg's wife); Dora Waverly, Aged Person
**Time period(s):** 1990s
**Locale(s):** Bonner, California

**Summary:** During the settling of Bonner, California in the nineteenth century, the Padgett family sank a well on grounds sacred to the Modoc Indians and unleashed the Montanni, a bloodthirsty demon. More than a century later Greg Lowell, lineal descendant of the Padgetts, moves his family to Bonncr, initiating the cycle of blood-letting once more.

**Other books you might like:**
Douglas Clegg, *Goat Dance*, 1989
Morgan Fields, *Shaman Woods*, 1990
Charles L. Grant, *The Nestling*, 1982
Chet Williamson, *Dreamthorp*, 1989

## 5078

### SUSAN SIZEMORE

## *Forever Knight: A Stirring of Dust*

(New York: Berkley/Boulevard, 1997)

**Story type:** Horror (Vampire Story)
**Series:** Forever Knight
**Major character(s):** Nicholas Knight, Detective—Homicide, Vampire; Natalie Lambert, Doctor (forensic pathologist); Lucien LaCroix, Radio Personality, Vampire
**Time period(s):** 1990s (1997)
**Locale(s):** Toronto, Ontario, Canada

**Summary:** Crack homicide detective Nicholas Knight investigates a series of brutal homicides in which victims are drained of blood and decapitated. Although he first suspects one of his fellow vampires, Nicholas discovers that the kills are the work of a revenant, a lower order of vampire created by the infected bite of one of his own species. Based on the cable television series *Forever Knight*, about an 800-year-old vampire who lives inconspicuously with other vampires among mortals in contemporary Ontario.

**Other books you might like:**
Vincent Courtney, *Vampire Beat*, 1991
P.N. Elrod, *Bloodlist*, 1990
Laurell K. Hamilton, *Guilty Pleasures*, 1993
Tanya Huff, *Blood Price*, 1991
Roxanne Longstreet, *Cold Kiss*, 1995
Karen E. Taylor, *Blood Secrets*, 1994

## 5079

### JOSEPH SKIBELL

## *A Blessing on the Moon*

(Chapel Hill, North Carolina: Algonquin Books of Chapel Hill, 1997)

**Story type:** Fantasy (Religious; Contemporary Realism)
**Major character(s):** Chaim Skibelski, Spirit; Zalman, Religious
**Time period(s):** 1930s; 1940s
**Locale(s):** Poland

**Summary:** Shot during the Holocaust, Chaim does not settle in the peace of the World to Come. Instead he wanders around the world as a ghost. He visits his old home and meets the soldier who shot him, then reluctantly, helps two Hasids in their search for the missing Moon. First novel.

**Other books you might like:**
Janet Gluckman, *Child of the Light*, 1992
   George Guthridge, co-author
Lisa Goldstein, *The Red Magician*, 1982
Richard Grant, *Tex and Molly in the Afterlife*, 1996
Kurt Vonnegut Jr., *Slaughterhouse Five*, 1969
Jane Yolen, *Briar Rose*, 1992
Jane Yolen, *The Devil's Arithmetic*, 1988

## 5080

### JOHN SKIPP
### CRAIG SPECTOR, Co-Author

## *Animals*

(New York: Bantam, 1993)

**Story type:** Horror (Werewolf Story)
**Major character(s):** Syd Jarrett, Worker (steelworker); Nora, Werewolf; Jane, Waiter/Waitress
**Time period(s):** 1990s (1993)
**Locale(s):** Monville, Pennsylvania

**Summary:** Nora shows Syd Jarrett how to get in touch with the feral side of himself before pitting him against Vic, her werewolf boyfriend, who mauls Syd and leaves him for dead. Eighteen months later, after Syd has recovered under the tender ministrations of Jane, Vic and Nora return for a final showdown.

**Other books you might like:**
Crosland Brown, *Tombley's Walk*, 1990
Michael Cadnum, *St. Peter's Wolf*, 1991
Whitley Strieber, *The Wild*, 1991

## 5081

**JOHN SKIPP**
**CRAIG SPECTOR**, Co-Author

### The Bridge: A Horror Story

(New York: Bantam, 1991)

**Story type:** Horror (Nature in Revolt)
**Major character(s):** Gary Taylor, Worker (mechanic); Gwen Taylor, Artist (Gary's wife); Werner Blake, Businessman
**Time period(s):** 1990s
**Locale(s):** Paradise, Pennsylvania

**Summary:** There's trouble in Paradise (Pennsylvania, that is) when one barrel of chemical waste too many gets dumped into the Codorus Creek. A sentient Mother Nature retaliates, marshaling polluted streams, clouds of acid rain, and toxic zombies to do her bidding. Eco-Armageddon has begun!

**Other books you might like:**
John Brunner, *The Sheep Look Up*, 1972
Robert Charles, *Flowers of Evil*, 1982
Alison Drake, *Lagoon*, 1990
D. Keith Mano, *The Bridge*, 1972
Alan E. Nourse, *The Fourth Horseman*, 1983

## 5082

**JOHN SKIPP**
**CRAIG SPECTOR**, Co-Author

### Dead Lines

(New York: Bantam, 1989)

**Story type:** Horror (Ghost Story)
**Major character(s):** Jack Rowan, Writer, Spirit; Katie Conner, Young Woman
**Time period(s):** 1980s
**Locale(s):** New York, New York

**Summary:** When Katie and Meryl rent a room they discover a box containing stories written by the apartment's former occupant, a suicide victim. Their lives are powerfully altered by the individual stories and, more importantly, by the author's ghost, which disturbs and threatens to possess the vulnerable young women.

**Other books you might like:**
Roland Topor, *The Tenant*, 1966

## 5083

**JOHN SKIPP**, Editor
**CRAIG SPECTOR**, Co-Editor

### Still Dead: Book of the Dead 2

(Shingletown, California: Mark V. Ziesing, 1992)

**Story type:** Horror (Anthology)
**Summary:** The nineteen stories continue the theme first explored in *Book of the Dead* (1989), further describing a possible future in which the newly dead rise from the grave as zombies to eat the flesh of the living and serve as useful symbols of typical human behavior. Included are Mort Castle's Hemingway pastiche, "The Old Man and the Dead"; Douglas Winter's parody of Jay McInerney, "Bright Lights, Big Zombie"; Dan Simmons' sentimental "Class Picture"; Chan McConnell's tale of zombies who blend in inconspicuously with Manhattan street life, "Don't/Walk"; K.W. Jeter's tale of a lunatic with a messiah complex who thinks he is responsible for the resurrection of the dead; and Poppy Z. Brite's hypnotic tale of death and its meaning in India, "Calcutta, Lord of Nerves."

**Other books you might like:**
Peter Haining, *Stories of the Walking Dead*, 1985
  editor
Bill Pronzini, *The Arbor House Necropolis*, 1987
  editor

## 5084

**MICHAEL SLADE**

### Cutthroat

(New York: Signet, 1992)

**Story type:** Horror (Serial Killer)
**Major character(s):** Robert De Clerq, Police Officer; Zinc Chandler, Police Officer; Martin Kwan, Lawyer
**Time period(s):** 1980s (1987)
**Locale(s):** Vancouver, British Columbia, Canada

**Summary:** Two Canadian police officers with a specialty in serial killers team up to apprehend one killing lawyers throughout the American West, in a novel that ranges from Vietnam and Hong Kong to Canada and the Great Plains, and whose plot hinges on an archaeological specimen of great import found in the midst of the slaughter at Custer's Last Stand in 1876.

**Other books you might like:**
Thomas Harris, *Red Dragon*, 1981
Daniel Ransom, *The Serpent's Kiss*, 1992
Garfield Reeves-Stevens, *Gray Matter*, 1990

## 5085

**MICHAEL SLADE**

### Evil Eye

(New York: Signet, 1997)

**Story type:** Horror (Occult)
**Major character(s):** Robert DeClerq, Detective; Zinc Chandler, Detective; Nick Craven, Detective
**Time period(s):** 1990s (1994); 1870s (1879)
**Locale(s):** New Westminster, British Columbia, Canada; Africa

**Summary:** A murderer is targeting members of the Royal Canadian Mounted Police, killing them and their families. Detectives Robert DeClerq and Zin Chandler investigate and, once more, discover a legacy of evil extending back more than a century, this time to Africa and practitioners of tribal magic. First published in England in 1996.

**Other books you might like:**
Ramsey Campbell, *The Claw*, 1983
  published in America under the title *Night of the Claw* in the same year
Todd Grimson, *Brand New Cherry Flavor*, 1997
Thomas Harris, *Red Dragon*, 1981
Richard Jaccoma, *The Werewolf's Tale*, 1988
Graham Masterton, *Master of Lies*, 1992
Robert Morgan, *All Things under the Moon*, 1994
Peter Straub, *Koko*, 1988

## 5086

**IAN SLATER**

### Battle Front

(New York: Fawcett, 1998)

**Story type:** Science Fiction (Military; Political)
**Major character(s):** Doug Freeman, Military Personnel (general); David Brentwood, Military Personnel
**Time period(s):** 1990s (1999)
**Locale(s):** United States

**Summary:** This story gives a battle-by-battle account of the government's attempt to use military force to suppress scattered revolutionary militia groups trying to control isolated areas of North America. Although the rebels are inexperienced and badly trained, the government makes several blunders that allow them to consolidate their position after several inconclusive battles. Sequel to *Showdown: USA vs Militia*.

**Other books you might like:**
Jerry Ahern, *The Battle Begins*, 1988
David Brin, *The Postman*, 1985
Robert Charles, *The Scream of the Dove*, 1975
Sinclair Lewis, *If This Goes On*, 1935
Jack Williamson, *The Silicon Dagger*, 1999

## 5087

**BILL SLAVICSEK**
**C.J. TRAMONTANA**, Co-Author

### Storm Knights

(Baltimore, Maryland: GW Books/Games Workshop, 1990)

**Story type:** Fantasy (Magic Conflict; Horror)
**Series:** Torg: The Possibility Wars
**Major character(s):** Tolwyn Tancred, Knight; Christopher Bryce, Religious (priest); Andrew Jackson Decker, Political Figure
**Time period(s):** 1990s
**Locale(s):** New York, New York

**Summary:** Raiders from alternate realities have invaded Earth. The only thing that stands between them and total victory is the "stormers," people like Tolwyn Tancred who have weathered the violent reality storms in other worlds. Joining forces with the humans of Earth, they battle across a continent to defeat the raiders and their demonic leader. First of a series.

**Other books you might like:**
Robin Wayne Bailey, *Nightwatch*, 1990
Brian Craig, *Zaragoz*, 1990
Gordon R. Dickson, *Time Storm*, 1977
Barbara Hambly, *Dragonsbane*, 1985
Clifford D. Simak, *Out of Their Minds*, 1970
Ian Watson, *Inquisitor*, 1990

## 5088

**WILLIAM SLEATOR**

### Strange Attractors

(New York: Dutton, 1989)

**Story type:** Science Fiction (Alternate Universe)
**Major character(s):** Max, Teenager; Eve Sylvan, Teenager
**Time period(s):** 1980s
**Locale(s):** United States

**Summary:** Max visits the lab of the famous scientist Dr. Sylvan and becomes mixed up in a complex and confusing exercise in Chaos Theory. It seems that Dr. Sylvan has a double in another universe who has so badly damaged his own timeline that he is now attempting to escape it by supplanting the Dr. Sylvan from Max's timeline. Max ends up with amnesia and a strange machine that both the Sylvans, neither of them particularly nice people, desperately want back. A young adult novel.

**Other books you might like:**
Grace Chetwin, *Collidescope*, 1989
John Cramer, *Twistor*, 1989
Michael P. Kube-McDowell, *Alternities*, 1988
Sarah Sargent, *Jonas McFee, A.T.P.*, 1989
Jerry Sohl, *Costigan's Needle*, 1953

## 5089

**KAY SLOAN**, Editor
**CONSTANCE PIERCE**, Co-Editor

### Elvis Rising: Stories on the King

(New York: Avon, 1993)

**Story type:** Fantasy (Anthology; Historical)
**Major character(s):** Elvis Presley, Musician, Historical Figure
**Time period(s):** 1990s
**Locale(s):** Graceland, Tennessee; Washington, District of Columbia

**Summary:** 16 short stories 1961-1993, featuring Elvis Presley as a character or catalyst. Most of the stories reflect straight or slightly twisted realism, but in Howard Waldrop's "Ike at the Mike" Senator Presley imagines what his life would have been like if he'd become a musician like the great Dwight Eisenhower. Gardner Dozois, Jack Dann and Michael Swanwick collaborate on a story about a mysterious and poignant reunion concert. Other authors include Elizabeth Hand and W.P. Kinsella.

**Other books you might like:**
Bradley Denton, *Buddy Holly Is Alive and Well on Ganymede*, 1991
Richard Peabody, *Mondo Elvis*, 1993
    Lucinda Ebersole, co-editor
Robert Rankin, *Armageddon: The Musical*, 1990
Mike Resnick, *By Any Other Fame*, 1994
    Martin H. Greenberg, co-editor
Lewis Shiner, *Glimpses*, 1993
Allen Steele, *Clarke County, Space*, 1990
Jack Womack, *Elvissey*, 1993
Jack Yeovil, *Comeback Tour: The Sky Belongs to the Stars*, 1991
    pseudonym of Kim Newman

## 5090

**JOAN SLONCZEWSKI**

### The Children Star

(New York: Tor, 1998)

**Story type:** Science Fiction (Alternate Intelligence; Political)
**Major character(s):** 'jum G'hana, Child, Genetically Altered Being; Sarai, Scientist (biologist), Healer; Rhodonite "Rod", Religious (Sacred Order of the Spirit)
**Time period(s):** Indeterminate Future
**Locale(s):** Prokaryon, Planet—Imaginary (colony world); The Fold, Interstellar Empire/Federation; Fold Council Station, Space Station (xenobiotic research facility)

**Summary:** While Sarai and others probe the mysteries of Prokaryon life, Sacred Order of the Spirit colonists undergo radical changes, allowing them to settle in an otherwise lethal environment which seems intentionally manicured, despite the apparent lack of intelligent life. When the corporate owner of Prokaryon decides to improve profitability by sterilizing the planet and reseeding Earth life, some colonists pursue local remedies, while others attempt to bring pressure through legislative means.

**Other books you might like:**
Eleanor Arnason, *Ring of Swords*, 1993
Octavia E. Butler, *Dawn*, 1987
Helen Collins, *Mutagenesis*, 1993
Nicola Griffith, *Ammonite*, 1993
Janet Kagan, *Hellspark*, 1988
Rosemary Kirstein, *The Outskirter's Secret*, 1992

## 5091

### JOAN SLONCZEWSKI

## *Daughter of Elysium*

(New York: Morrow AvoNova, 1993)

**Story type:** Science Fiction (Alternate Intelligence; Genetic Manipulation)
**Major character(s):** Raincloud Windclan, Linguist (translator), Parent; Verid, Immortal, Political Figure; Doggie, Robot (trainsweep)
**Time period(s):** Indeterminate Future (1020th century)
**Locale(s):** Shora, Planet—Imaginary; Urulan, Planet—Imaginary; Free Fold, Interstellar Empire/Federation

**Summary:** Visiting Elysians' intentions to finance terraforming of other worlds precipitate a crisis between native Sharers and their centuries-old Elysian guests. Hoping to avert disaster, an Elysian delegation travels to Urulan to seek alternate solutions to human overpopulation. Sequel to *A Door into Ocean*.

**Other books you might like:**
Eleanor Arnason, *Ring of Swords*, 1993
Eleanor Arnason, *A Woman of the Iron People*, 1991
David Brin, *Glory Season*, 1993
Octavia E. Butler, *Dawn*, 1987
Rosemary Kirstein, *The Steerswoman*, 1989
Rudy Rucker, *Software*, 1982

## 5092

### JOAN SLONCZEWSKI

## *The Wall Around Eden*

(New York: William Morrow, 1989)

**Story type:** Science Fiction (Post-Nuclear Holocaust)
**Major character(s):** Isabel Garcia-Chase, Teenager (Electrician); Daniel Jacoby, Teenager (Quaker)
**Time period(s):** 21st century
**Locale(s):** Gwynwood, Pennsylvania

**Summary:** Some years ago, simultaneous with the outbreak of nuclear war, the aliens appeared. For reasons known only to themselves, they isolated a number of towns and cities around the world behind impregnable "air walls," leaving most of the rest of humanity to die from the effects of the war. In Pennsylvania, one small, largely Quaker community struggles to survive within its air wall. A young woman devotes her life to discovering the mysterious truth behind the aliens' actions.

**Other books you might like:**
Neal Barrett Jr., *Through Darkest America*, 1987
Octavia E. Butler, *Dawn*, 1987

Ursula K. Le Guin, *Always Coming Home*, 1985
Judith Moffett, *Pennterra*, 1987
Sheri S. Tepper, *The Gate to Women's Country*, 1988

## 5093

### MICHELE SLUNG, Editor

## *I Shudder at Your Touch*

(New York: Roc, 1991)

**Story type:** Horror (Anthology)

**Summary:** Twenty-two tales with sexual subthemes that span nearly a century, ranging from Robert Hitchens' classic Edwardian tale of a love-sick ghost, "How Love Came to Professor Guildea," to the contemporary magic realism of T.L. Parkinson's "The Tiger Returns to the Mountain" and the psychological horror of Michael Blumlein's "Keeping House." Standout stories include Robert Aickman's creepy account of sexual initiation, "The Swords," and Patrick McGrath's hilarious spoof of sexual psychopathology, "Cleave the Vampire, or, a Gothic Pastorale."

**Other books you might like:**
Margaret L. Carter, *Demon Lovers and Strange Seductions*, 1973
   editor
Ellen Datlow, *Alien Sex*, 1990
   editor
Jeff Gelb, *Hot Blood: Tales of Provocative Horror*, 1990
   Lonn Friend, co-editor
Jeff Gelb, *Hotter Blood: More Tales of Erotic Horror*, 1991
   Michael Garret, co-editor
Michel Parry, *Devil's Kisses*, 1976

## 5094

### MICHELE SLUNG, Editor

## *Shudder Again*

(New York: Roc, 1993)

**Story type:** Horror (Anthology)

**Summary:** In this follow-up to *I Shudder at Your Touch* (1991), the editor has collected 22 tales of erotic horror. Four stories are original to the volume: Nancy Collins' "Aphra" is told from the point of view of a man whose obsession with thin women reflects his morbid interest in death; David Kuehls' "The First Time" tells of a near future in which androids can recreate a person's sexual initiation; Claudia O'Keefe's "On the Lake of Last Wishes" recounts the erotic dreams of a woman with a terminal illness; and Sarah Smith's "When The Red Storm Comes, or the History of a Young Lady's Awakening to Her Nature," juxtaposes vampirism with world events in Europe at the turn of the century. Classic reprints include Charles Beaumont's "The Crooked Man," about a future in which it is illegal to be heterosexual; Arthur Machen's "The Ceremony," which links paganism with eroticism; Sir Arthur Conan Doyle's "The Parasite," about a medium who uses mental energy to control her clients; and stories by Robert Aickman, J.G. Ballard, Thomas Ligotti, and Ramsey Campbell.

**Other books you might like:**
Ellen Datlow, *Alien Sex*, 1991
   editor
Jeff Gelb, *Hot Blood: Tales of Provocative Horror*, 1989
   Lonn Friend, co-editor
Jeff Gelb, *Hotter Blood: More Tales of Erotic Horror*, 1991
   Michael Garrett, co-editor

Jeff Gelb, *Hottest Blood: The Ultimate in Erotic Horror*, 1993
  Michael Garrett, co-editor
Michel Parry, *Devil's Kisses*, 1976
  editor

---

**5095**

**BRIAN SMART**, Editor

## Best of the Midwest's Science Fiction, Fantasy and Horror, Volume II

(Harrisonville, Missouri: ESA Books, 1993)

**Story type:** Horror (Anthology)

**Summary:** The 28 stories written especially for this book, each lavishly illustrated, either feature midwestern settings or are by midwestern writers. Of interest to horror readers is Mark Rich's "Payment," a gruesome deal-with-the-devil story; Greg Beatty's "The Hunger From the Depths," about the type of monster that might be attracted to the garbage dumped in Puget Sound; Stephen M. Rainey's "Portals," in which extraterrestrial invaders mobilize via telephone lines; Lisa Y. Drexel's "'Til Death Do Us Part," a sentimental vampire story; Brian A. Hopkins' "Scarecrow's Dream," a tale of reincarnation; Bobby G. Warner's "Graveyard Beetles," in which a murder victim's corpse is animated to revenge by the title creatures; Marthayn Pelegrimas' "The Resurrection Man," about a fire-and-brimstone swindler who discovers to his horror that he has the power to raise the dead; S. Darnbrook Colson's "Nightmare at Brookgreen Gardens," about a ghost who moves the statuary of a park around; and Diswell Crinkle's "Bumps in the Night," a slapstick zombie story.

**Other books you might like:**
Robert Morrish, *Quick Chills II*, 1992
  Peter Enfantino, co-editor
Joy Oestreicher, *Air Fish*, 1993
  Richard Singer, co-editor
Joy Oestreicher, *Alpha Gallery*, 1992
  Richard Singer, co-editor

---

**5096**

**LISA SMEDMAN**

## Blood Sport

(New York: Roc, 1998)

**Story type:** Fantasy (Mystery)
**Series:** Shadowrun
**Major character(s):** Leni Ramirez, Detective—Private; Rafael Ramirez, Teenager
**Time period(s):** 2050s (2057)
**Locale(s):** United States; Mexico (now Atzlan)

**Summary:** Someone murders Mama Grande shortly after she has a vision of the end of the world. Two of her grandchildren, one a private detective, travel to the former Mexico, now Atzlan, to find out why cultists committed the crime, and discover that their organization is attempting to make her prophecy come true.

**Other books you might like:**
Emma Bull, *War for the Oaks*, 1987
Tom Dowd, *Night's Pawn*, 1993
Esther Friesner, *New York by Knight*, 1986
Jack Koke, *Dead Air*, 1996
Caroline Spector, *Worlds Without End*, 1995

---

**5097**

**DAVE SMEDS**

## The Schemes of Dragons

(New York: Ace, 1989)

**Story type:** Fantasy (Quest)
**Major character(s):** Toren, Warrior
**Time period(s):** Indeterminate

**Summary:** When Toren is magically forced to disgorge his tribe's totem, he finds himself alone in his body for the first time ever. His search for the stolen totem leads him into a parallel search by a brother and sister. Sequel to *Sorcery Within*.

**Other books you might like:**
M. Coleman Easton, *Spirits of Cavern and Hearth*, 1989
Rose Estes, *The Hunter*, 1990
Rosemary Kirstein, *The Steerswoman*, 1989

---

**5098**

**BEECHER SMITH**, Editor

## Monsters From Memphis

(Palo Alto, California: Zapizdat Publications, 1997)

**Story type:** Horror (Anthology)

**Summary:** Thirty-one stories original to the volume, all set in Memphis, Tennessee and featuring horrors based on southern characters and traditions. Highlights include Brent Monahan's "Shadow," about a predatory monster that becomes whatever it consumes; Tom Piccirilli's "Cotton," in which a Native American curse manifests in the form of a plague; Steve Climer's ocult detective tale, "By any Name a Devil"; Richard Park's "Eucharist," an amusing tale of Elvis sightings in the future; and Don Webb's "The Heart of the Matter," about a 500-year-old witch kept alive by the mechanical heart of a warlock.

**Other books you might like:**
Richard Gilliam, *Confederacy of the Dead*, 1993
  Edward E. Kramer and Martin H. Greenberg, co-editors
Richard Gilliam, *Somewhere South of Midnight*, 1994
  Martin H. Greenberg, co-editor
Frank D. McSherry Jr., *Civil War Ghosts*, 1990
  Charles G. Waugh and Martin H. Greenberg, co-editors
Frank D. McSherry Jr., *More Dixie Ghosts*, 1994
  Charles G. Waugh and Martin H. Greenberg, co-editors
Frank D. McSherry Jr., *Nightmares in Dixie*, 1987
  Charles G. Waugh and Martin H. Greenberg, co-editors
Billie Sue Mosiman, *Death in Dixie*, 1997
  Martin H. Greenberg, co-editor
Lawrence Schimel, *Southern Blood: Vampire Stories From the American South*, 1997
  Martin H. Greenberg, co-editor

---

**5099**

**BEECHER SMITH**, Editor

## More Monsters From Memphis

(Palo Alto, California: Zapizdat Publications, 1998)

**Story type:** Horror (Anthology)
**Locale(s):** Memphis, Tennessee

**Summary:** These 32 stories, all original to the volume, are set in Memphis, Tennessee. Brent Monahan's "The Midnight Show at the

Pink Palace'' concerns a meteorite kept in the local planetarium that reveals itself to be a very active alien spaceship. Lou Kemp's ''From the River'' is a tale of the monsters that prey upon ships traveling the Mississippi River. Kiel Stuart's ''Now or Never'' is one of a handful of stories that explore the supernatural possibilities of the Elvis Presley myth, and Tim Waggoner's ''Anubis Has Left the Building,'' a tale of parallels between modern Memphis and ancient Memphis in Egypt. In Tom Piccirilli's ''Go Back to the Church,'' a sorcerer and his familiar find themselves in the middle of a war waged between the living and the dead in a blues bar.

**Other books you might like:**

Richard Gilliam, *Confederacy of the Dead*, 1993
   Edward E. Kramer, Martin H. Greenberg, co-editors
Richard Gilliam, *Somewhere South of Midnight*, 1994
   Martin H. Greenberg, co-editor
Frank D. McSherry Jr., *Nightmares in Dixie*, 1987
   Charles G. Waugh, Martin H. Greenberg, co-editors
Billie Sue Mosiman, *Death in Dixie*, 1997
   Martin H. Greenberg, co-editor
Lawrence Schimel, *Southern Blood: Vampire Stories From the American South*, 1997
   Martin H. Greenberg, co-editor

## 5100
### BRIAN SCOTT SMITH

## When Shadows Fall
(New York: Leisure, 1997)

**Story type:** Horror (Black Magic)
**Major character(s):** Martin LaVine, Businessman (electronics); Sylvia Belou, Witch; Danny Dallaugher, Young Man
**Time period(s):** 1990s (1997)
**Locale(s):** North Andover, Massachusetts

**Summary:** Martin LaVine investigates the mysterious death of his Aunt Day and discovers her friendship with Sylvia Belou, a self-proclaimed witch. When Martin and his friends accidentally stumble upon a ceremony performed by Sylvia and her coven, they become the object of a supernatural manhunt. A first novel.

**Other books you might like:**

Leigh Clark, *Blood Sabbath*, 1991
Elizabeth Ergas, *Devil's Gate*, 1991
Gary L. Holleman, *Demon Fire*, 1995
Edward Lee, *The Chosen*, 1993
Tamara Thorne, *Moonfall*, 1996
J.N. Williamson, *The Monastery*, 1992

## 5101
### CHERYL A. SMITH

## The Falcon and the Serpent
(Westchester, Illinois: Crossway, 1990)

**Story type:** Fantasy (Religious; Romance)
**Major character(s):** Falcon Jaqueth, Knight; Crotalus, Wizard
**Time period(s):** Indeterminate Past
**Locale(s):** Corigo, Fictional Country; Paduan, Fictional Country

**Summary:** Falcon Jaqueth tutors Prince Krieth of Paduan in the arts of war. Crotalus wants control of Corigo and Paduan and the love of Rafaela. He intends to see Temrane, Prince of Corigo, whom he had marked at birth, attain this goal. Rafaela finds the strength to resist him in worship of the Redeemer God.

**Other books you might like:**

John Desjarlais, *The Throne of Tara*, 1990
Roger Elwood, *Angelwalk: A Modern Fable*, 1988
Parke Godwin, *Waiting for the Galactic Bus*, 1989
Andrew M. Greeley, *Angel Fire*, 1988
Mike McQuay, *The Nexus*, 1989

## 5102
### CLARK ASHTON SMITH

## The Book of Hyperborea
(West Warwick, Rhode Island: Necronomicon Press, 1996)

**Story type:** Horror (Collection)

**Summary:** The 13 stories assembled here are all of the tales that the author, one of the most popular writers for the fantasy pulp *Weird Tales*, set in the imaginary prehistoric realm of Hyperborea. Included are a diptych of comic stories, ''The Tale of Satampra Zeiros'' and ''The Theft of Thirty-Nine Girdles,'' featuring the thief Satampra Zeiros and the mordantly amusing fates that he and his companions experience. Other highlights include ''Ubbo Sathla,'' in which a modern character finds himself transported back to primal origins with the help of the Hyperborean sorcerer Eibon; ''The Seven Geases,'' in which a character confronts the fount of all creation; and the poetic end-of-the-world fantasy, ''The Coming of the White Worm.'' The volume was edited by Will Murray, who supplies the introduction.

**Other books you might like:**

Lin Carter, *Great Short Novels of Adult Fantasy 1*, 1972
   editor
Lord Dunsany, *At the Edge of the World*, 1970
Fritz Leiber, *Swords Against Death*, 1970
H.P. Lovecraft, *The Dream Quest of Unknown Kadath*, 1970
Gary Myers, *The House of the Worm*, 1975

## 5103
### CLARK ASHTON SMITH

## A Prophecy of Monsters
(Alexandria, Virginia: 13th Hour Books, 1996)

**Story type:** Horror (Werewolf Story; Science Fiction)
**Major character(s):** Unnamed Character, Werewolf; Unnamed Character, Robot
**Time period(s):** 21st century
**Locale(s):** Earth

**Summary:** A werewolf of the future gets the surprise of his life when he discovers his latest victim is not the human prey he thought it was. The short story that makes up this chapbook was first published in 1954 and is sometimes reprinted under the title ''Monsters in the Night.'' Paul A. Roales supplies an introduction.

**Other books you might like:**

Lord Dunsany, *A Dreamer's Tales*, 1910
Gary Myers, *The House of the Worm*, 1975
Brian Stableford, *Fables and Fantasies*, 1997

## 5104

**CLARK ASHTON SMITH**

### Tales of Zothique

(West Warwick, Rhode Island: Necronomicon Press, 1995)

**Story type:** Fantasy (Collection)
**Time period(s):** Indeterminate Past; Indeterminate Future
**Locale(s):** Hyperborea, Mythical Place (Earth's past); Zothique, Mythical Place (Earth's future)

**Summary:** Editors Will Murray and Steve Behrens incorporate stories previously published in Lin Carter's Ballantine Adult Fantasy Series, with some corrections, and some stories passed over by Carter. Stories frequently exhibit a dark or ominous tone as Smith discusses humanity's foibles and include settings from the heroic distant past in the Hyperborean Age to the dim future and a dying Earth, Zothique, in which humankind declines, drifting into superstition and barbarism.

**Other books you might like:**
Robert Bloch, *The Best of Robert Bloch*, 1977
Frank Belknap Long, *The Rim of the Unknown*, 1972
H.P. Lovecraft, *The Best of H.P. Lovecraft: Bloodcurdling Tales of Horror and the Macabre*, 1982
H.P. Lovecraft, *Dagon and Other Macabre Tales*, 1965
Howard Wandrei, *Time Burial*, 1995

## 5105

**CORDWAINER SMITH** (Pseudonym of Paul Myron Anthony Linebarger)

### Norstrilia

(Framingham, Massachusetts: NESFA Press, 1995)

**Story type:** Science Fiction (Genetic Manipulation; Immortality)
**Series:** Instrumentality of Mankind
**Major character(s):** Rod McBan, Telepath; C'mel, Animal (cat), Genetically Altered Being (cat-person)
**Time period(s):** 160th century
**Locale(s):** Norstrilia, Planet—Imaginary (Old North Australia); Earth

**Summary:** After multiple childhoods, Rod McBan provisionally passes his adulthood test, avoiding the ecstatic euthanasia awarded many on resource-scarce Norstrilia. Now responsible for a vast ranch with giant, sick sheep which produce a raw immortality drug, Rod sustains attacks from a former childhood friend and flees to a hidden shelter where an ancient, forbidden computer implements an economic warfare trading strategy aimed at cornering the commodities market in immortality drug futures. Acquiring new and powerful enemies and friends, Rod decides to vanish from public view and visit Earth anonymously to pursue a minor philatelic interest and becomes involved in the underpeople's struggle to attain legal status and guaranteed rights. Contains a 25-page appendix noting significant variations from some prior publications of the text, including "Lost Music in an Old World," previously omitted from the novel. Originally published 1975.

**Other books you might like:**
Felix C. Forrest, *Carola*, 1948
    pseudonym of Paul Linebarger
Felix C. Forrest, *Ria*, 1947
    pseudonym of Paul Linebarger
Elizabeth Hand, *Icarus Descending*, 1993
Ian McDonald, *Terminal Cafe*, 1994
Carmichael Smith, *Atomsk*, 1949
    pseudonym of Paul Linebarger

S. Andrew Swann, *Forests of the Night*, 1993

## 5106

**CORDWAINER SMITH** (Pseudonym of Paul Myron Anthony Linebarger)

### The Rediscovery of Man

(Framingham, Massachusettes: NESFA Press, 1993)

**Story type:** Science Fiction (Collection)
**Series:** Instrumentality of Mankind
**Time period(s):** 21st century; Indeterminate Future
**Locale(s):** Outer Space; Spaceship

**Summary:** This omnibus edition contains an 8-page introduction by John J. Pierce, a 2-page introduction by editor James A. Mann, six non-series stories with a rewritten version of "War No. 81-Q" and all 27 Instrumentality of Mankind series stories presented in chronological order with the previously unpublished story, "Himself in Anachron," and one attributed to Smith but written by his wife, Genevieve Linebarger, "Down to a Sunless Sea." Smith's adventure stories present recurrent sociological issues through diverse science fiction themes. "Scanners Live in Vain," points to an emerging technology that will allow humans to travel in space without terrible physical modifications; "Think Blue, Count Two" demonstrates a vision of the computer's use in daily human life; "The Game of Rat and Dragon" examines the partnership between humans and telepathic cats in their desperate battles against outer space creatures who suck lifeforce from human souls; "The Burning of the Brain" and "The Crime and Glory of Commander Suzdal" detail the sacrifice and consequences of frontier explorations; "Under Old Earth" hints at the terrifying resources available to the rulers of the galaxy; and "Alpha Ralpha Boulevard" describes wondrous technology and the attempts of the Instrumentality to reintroduce vitality into the human spirit.

**Other books you might like:**
Felix C. Forrest, *Carola*, 1948
    pseudonum of Paul Linebarger
Felix C. Forrest, *Ria*, 1947
    pseudonum of Paul Linebarger
Robert A. Heinlein, *The Past through Tomorrow*, 1967
Fritz Leiber, *The Leiber Chronicles*, 1990
Walter M. Miller Jr., *The Science Fiction Stories of Walter M. Miller, Jr.*, 1984
Larry Niven, *Tales of Known Space*, 1975
Carmichael Smith, *Atomsk*, 1949
    pseudonym of Paul Linebarger
Theodore Sturgeon, *E Pluribus Unicorn*, 1953
John Varley, *The Barbie Murders and Other Stories*, 1980
John Varley, *Blue Champagne*, 1986
John Varley, *The Persistence of Vision*, 1978

## 5107

**DAVID ALEXANDER SMITH**, Editor

### Future Boston

(New York: Tor, 1994)

**Story type:** Science Fiction (Anthology)
**Time period(s):** 21st century
**Locale(s):** Boston, Massachusetts

**Summary:** This is a shared universe volume created by an ongoing Boston writers' workshop containing a seven-page afterword, "How It Came to Be," two pages of notes, "About the Authors," six maps of Boston 1772-2061 and 28 stories about the city afflicted with a rising sea and an involuntary immigration of alien Phneri. Authors include Alexander Jablokov, Geoffrey A. Landis, Steven Popkes and David Alexander Smith. Set in the milieu of *In the Cube*.

**Other books you might like:**
Alan Dean Foster, *Alien Nation*, 1988
Alexander Jablokov, *Carve the Sky*, 1991
Alexander Jablokov, *A Deeper Sea*, 1992
Steven Popkes, *Caliban Landing*, 1987
Steven Popkes, *Slow Lightning*, 1991

## 5108

### DAVID ALEXANDER SMITH

## *Homecoming*

(New York: Ace, 1990)

**Story type:** Science Fiction (First Contact)
**Series:** Marathon Trilogy
**Major character(s):** Walter Tai-Ching Jones, Spaceship Captain; Ozymandias, Artificial Intelligence
**Time period(s):** 21st century
**Locale(s):** *Open Palm*, Spaceship; Earth

**Summary:** Earth's first starship, *Open Palm*, returns home bearing members of the Cygnan race known as Bluebears. Both human crew members and Cygnans soon discover, however, that they are pawns in a deadly power struggle between competing Earth factions. Only the artificial intelligence Ozymandias can save the situation.

**Other books you might like:**
Gregory Benford, *Great Sky River*, 1987
Gregory Benford, *Tides of Light*, 1989
David Brin, *Startide Rising*, 1983
David Brin, *The Uplift War*, 1987
Octavia E. Butler, *Dawn*, 1987
Paul J. McAuley, *Four Hundred Billion Stars*, 1988

## 5109

### DAVID ALEXANDER SMITH

## *In the Cube*

(New York: Tor, 1993)

**Story type:** Science Fiction (Mystery; Political)
**Major character(s):** Beverly O'Meara, Orphan, Detective—Private; Akktri, Alien (Phner); Iris "Butcher of Boston" Sherwood, Government Official, Step-Parent
**Time period(s):** 21st century
**Locale(s):** Boston, Massachusetts (the Cube)

**Summary:** The early 21st century arrival of many extraterrestrials into Boston allowed its redesign into the Cube, a kilometer high monad with quasi-independent status. When coerced by Iris Sherwood to find out the details surrounding her adopted daughter's disappearance, Beverly O'Meara and Akktri uncover a plot which pits the Cube's paramount business family against the supremely powerful City Operator, Iris Sherwood.

**Other books you might like:**
Alfred Bester, *Golem *[100], 1980
Alan Dean Foster, *Alien Nation*, 1988
Alan Dean Foster, *Cyber Way*, 1990
K.W. Jeter, *Madlands*, 1991
Katharine Kerr, *Polar City Blues*, 1990
Jacqueline Lichtenberg, *Molt Brother*, 1982
James H. Schmitz, *The Demon Breed*, 1968

## 5110

### DAVID C. SMITH

## *Engor's Sword Arm*

(North East, Pennsylvania: Forgotten Ages Press, 1997)

**Story type:** Horror (Occult)
**Major character(s):** Engor, Pirate; Kyla, Young Woman; Lord Bilitu, Sorcerer
**Time period(s):** Indeterminate Past (prehistory)

**Summary:** Engor, a warrior with only one good fighting arm, hopes to prevent the delivery of Kyla to her betrothed, Lord Bilitu, and thereby settle a long-standing score with the wizard. In order to do so, Engor must overcome a variety of horrors and snares conjured by his sorcerer enemy. A sword and sorcery tale, published in facsimile of a pulp magazine layout and illustrated by Rick McCollum.

**Other books you might like:**
Ramsey Campbell, *Far Away and Never*, 1996
David Drake, *Vettius and His Friends*, 1989
Robert E. Howard, *Conan the Barbarian*, 1955
Richard L. Tierney, *Scroll of Thoth*, 1997
Karl Edward Wagner, *The Book of Kane*, 1985

## 5111

### DAVID C. SMITH

## *The Fair Rules of Evil*

(New York: Avon, 1989)

**Story type:** Horror (Black Magic)
**Major character(s):** David Trevisan, Student (Ex-seminary); Theodore Fry, Magician (Black magician)
**Time period(s):** 1980s
**Locale(s):** United States

**Summary:** David Trevisan takes a crash course in sorcery in order to track and confront Theodore Fry, the black magician responsible for his sister's death.

**Other books you might like:**
Charles L. Grant, *The Hour of the Oxrun Dead*, 1977
M.R. James, "Casting the Runes", 1911
Dennis Wheatley, *The Devil Rides Out*, 1935

## 5112

### DAVID VAN METER SMITH

## *Trinity Grove*

(New York: Avon, 1990)

**Story type:** Horror (Ancient Evil Unleashed)
**Major character(s):** Nick Lombard, Student; Lewis Janeway, Detective—Police; Jan Troop, Farmer
**Time period(s):** 1990s (1990)
**Locale(s):** Cambridge, England

**Summary:** A brutalized corpse dubbed "the Midsummer Murder" ties in with a series of ritual murders which have taken place near the Cambridge campus at 33-year intervals ever since the 19th century. Evidence points to the Pentacle Commune, a cult which practices ancient Celtic ceremonies. But student Nick Lombard is unaware that his girl friend belongs to the commune—or that this year the cult requires a blood sacrifice to renew their pact with the forces of darkness.

**Other books you might like:**
Joseph A. Citro, *The Unseen*, 1990
Douglas Clegg, *Goat Dance*, 1989
T.E.D. Klein, *The Ceremonies*, 1984

---

**5113**

### DEAN WESLEY SMITH
### KRISTINE KATHRYN RUSCH, Co-Author

## The Escape
(New York: Pocket, 1995)

**Story type:** Science Fiction (Space Opera; Time Travel)
**Major character(s):** Kathryn Janeway, Spaceship Captain, Military Personnel (Starfleet), Space Explorer; Tuvok, Security Officer, Alien (Vulcan); B'Elanna Torres, Engineer, Alien (half-Klingon)
**Time period(s):** 24th century
**Locale(s):** *U.S.S. Voyager*, Spaceship; Alcawell, Planet—Imaginary

**Summary:** Searching for salvageable metals, Neelix, Torres, and Kim explore a graveyard of abandoned ships on a deserted world. When Neelix accidentally activates one of those ships, they travel 300,000 years back into the planet's past and learn that they have committed a capital offense. Only when Tuvok and Paris discover the identity of a ''ghost'' among the abandoned ships can Janeway help her missing crew.

**Other books you might like:**
Poul Anderson, *Time Patrolman*, 1983
Barbara Hambly, *Ishmael*, 1985
Andre Norton, *Galactic Derelict*, 1959
Kristine Kathryn Rusch, *Heart Readers*, 1993
Kristine Kathryn Rusch, *Traitors*, 1994
Kristine Kathryn Rusch, *The White Mists of Power*, 1991
Clifford D. Simak, *Special Deliverance*, 1982
Della Van Hise, *Killing Time*, 1985

---

**5114**

### DEAN WESLEY SMITH

## Laying the Music to Rest
(New York: Popular Library Questar, 1989)

**Story type:** Horror (Ghost Story)
**Major character(s):** Kellogg ''Doc'' Jones, Saloon Keeper/Owner, Professor (Former); Susan, Scientist (parapsychologist), Time Traveler
**Time period(s):** 1900s (1909); 1990s (1990)
**Locale(s):** Idaho

**Summary:** In Smith's first novel, a guest lodge on the shore of Lake Roosevelt in Idaho is bothered by the ghost of a young woman who evidently died in the natural disaster that created the lake some eighty years earlier. Investigating the ghost, Doc Jones meets a parapsychologist, Susan, who turns out to be a time traveller.

**Other books you might like:**
Allen Appel, *Time After Time*, 1987
Jack L. Chalker, *Dance Band on the Titanic*, 1979
Matthew J. Costello, *Beneath Still Waters*, 1989
Clive Cussler, *Raise the Titanic!*, 1984
Jerry Sohl, *Costigan's Needle*, 1953

---

**5115**

### DEAN WESLEY SMITH
### KRISTINE KATHRYN RUSCH, Co-Author

## The Soldiers of Fear
(New York: Pocket, 1996)

**Story type:** Science Fiction (Space Opera)
**Series:** Star Trek: The Next Generation
**Major character(s):** Jean-Luc Picard, Spaceship Captain, Military Personnel; William Riker, Military Personnel (Starfleet Commander), Space Explorer; Deanna Troi, Psychologist, Alien (half-Betazoid)
**Time period(s):** 24th century
**Locale(s):** *U.S.S. Enterprise*, Spaceship; United Federation of Planets, Interstellar Empire/Federation

**Summary:** Warned by an abortive invasion 80 years before, Starfleet keeps watch for the Fury, aliens who look like humanity's worst nightmares. Now they return in full force, with the ability to project a paralyzing fear directly into the minds of their enemies. Even the combined efforts of Federation and Klingon fleets cannot stop them, unless a one-way mission into a wormhole can block their access to the Alpha Quadrant. Second of the four-part Invasion! Series which spans all four Star Trek television series and continues in *Time's Enemy*.

**Other books you might like:**
Dafydd ab Hugh, *The Final Fury*, 1996
Diane Carey, *First Strike*, 1996
Gene DeWeese, *The Final Nexus*, 1988
L.A. Graf, *Time's Enemy*, 1996
Joe Haldeman, *The Forever War*, 1975

---

**5116**

### EDWARD E. SMITH

## Galactic Patrol
(Baltimore, Maryland: Old Earth Books, 1998)

**Story type:** Science Fiction (Space Opera)
**Series:** Lensman
**Major character(s):** Kimball Kinnison, Military Personnel (Lensman), Psychic; Worsel, Alien (Velantian); Helmuth, Pirate, Agent
**Time period(s):** Indeterminate Future
**Locale(s):** Trenco, Planet—Imaginary; Grand Base, Fictional City

**Summary:** Newly empowered as a Lensman and member of the Galactic Patrol, Kimball Kinnison throws himself into the war against Boskone. From one end of the galaxy to the other, he explores, fights individuals and space fleets, and uncovers evil and treachery. Finally, the young hero must face the ultimate challenge, the space fortress of Helmuth, who speaks for Boskone. Facsimile of the 1950 Fantasy Press edition. Third in series.

**Other books you might like:**
Isaac Asimov, *Foundation*, 1951
Iain M. Banks, *Consider Phlebas*, 1987
Glen Cook, *The Dragon Never Sleeps*, 1988
George Lucas, *Star Wars*, 1976
Vernor Vinge, *A Fire upon the Deep*, 1992

## 5117

### EDWARD E. SMITH

## Gray Lensman

(Baltimore, Maryland: Old Earth Books, 1998)

**Story type:** Science Fiction (Space Opera)
**Series:** Lensman
**Major character(s):** Kimball Kinnison, Military Personnel (Lensman), Psychic; Clarrissa MacDougall, Nurse; Worsel, Alien (Velantian)
**Time period(s):** Indeterminate Future
**Locale(s):** Jarnevon, Planet—Imaginary

**Summary:** In the great war between the super-advanced civilizations of Arisia and Eddore, the Galactic Patrol, especially Kimball Kinnison, becomes the chief weapon for good, while helping the Medonians against Boskone gives the Galactic Patrol access to fantastic new technology. Disguised as a drunken reprobate, Kinnison sets out to discover the secret of Boskone, a secret that may lead to torture and death. Facsimile of the 1951 Fantasy Press edition.

**Other books you might like:**
Iain M. Banks, *Use of Weapons*, 1992
Frank Herbert, *Dune*, 1965
Cordwainer Smith, *Norstrilia*, 1975
Norman Spinrad, *The Iron Dream*, 1972
David Weber, *On Basilisk Station*, 1993

## 5118

### GUY N. SMITH

## The Dark One

(New York: Zebra, 1995)

**Story type:** Horror (Evil Children)
**Major character(s):** Rankin Gorlay, Journalist; Glenn Gorlay, Child; Marcel Hart, Child
**Time period(s):** 1990s (1995)
**Locale(s):** Sandpits, England

**Summary:** The Gorlays think that Marcel, the son of their close friends, is ill-mannered and under-disciplined. When they agree to let him stay with them for a week while his parents go on holiday, they discover that his badness is actually evil that grows out of satanic practices he is trying to pull their family into.

**Other books you might like:**
Margaret Bingley, *Seeds of Evil*, 1988
D.A. Fowler, *Bad Blood*, 1993
Edmund Plante, *Seed of Evil*, 1988

## 5119

### GUY N. SMITH

## Dead End

(New York: Zebra, 1996)

**Story type:** Horror (Reanimated Dead)
**Major character(s):** Max Frame, Teacher (driving instructor); Shanifa Smith, Waiter/Waitress; Nat Bonner, Child
**Time period(s):** 1990s (1996)
**Locale(s):** London, England

**Summary:** While recovering from a devastating automobile accident, Max Frame sees his girlfriend Shanifa, who by all accounts died in the same accident. Max pursues Shanifa to "The Waste," an aban-doned ghetto on the fringe of town, and discovers satanic forces that are resurrecting the dead in the service of evil.

**Other books you might like:**
William W. Johnstone, *Rockabilly Hell*, 1995
Stephen Laws, *Daemonic*, 1995
Stephen Laws, *Macabre*, 1994
Richard Laymon, *Funland*, 1990

## 5120

### GUY N. SMITH

## Dead Meat

(Staten Island, New York: Creation Books, 1997)

**Story type:** Horror (Collection)

**Summary:** Omnibus reprinting the complete adventures—four novels and two short stories ("Vampire Village," "Hellbeat")—of Mark Sabat, an exorcist who dispatches skinhead vampires, necrophilic cultists, cannibals, witches, and other supernatural and non-supernatural horrors with bell, book, and loaded revolver. The novels, which are sexually and violently explicit, are *Graveyard Vultures* (1982), *Blood Merchants* (1982), *Cannibal Cult* (1983), and *Druid Connection* (1983).

**Other books you might like:**
Ron Dee, *Blood*, 1993
Shaun Hutson, *Heathen*, 1992
Richard Laymon, *The Cellar*, 1980
Edward Lee, *Incubi*, 1991
Brian Lumley, *Necroscope*, 1986

## 5121

### GUY N. SMITH

## Water Rites

(New York: Zebra, 1997)

**Story type:** Horror (Ancient Evil Unleashed)
**Major character(s):** Phil Quiles, Inspector (water service); Royston Shannon, Wealthy; Jocelyn Jackson, Artist
**Time period(s):** 1990s (1997)
**Locale(s):** Hopwas, England

**Summary:** Mysterious nocturnal activity at the underground reservoir in Hopwas leads to the discovery of the People of the Water, a cult devoted to the ancient water witch Mukasa, who is preparing for the inundation of the world and a return to her unholy reign.

**Other books you might like:**
Elizabeth Forrest, *Dark Tide*, 1993
Phil Rickman, *Candle Night*, 1991
Michael B. Sirota, *The Well*, 1991
Richard L. Tierney, *The House of the Toad*, 1993

## 5122

### GUY N. SMITH

## Witch Spell

(New York: Zebra, 1993)

**Story type:** Horror (Black Magic; Wild Talents)
**Major character(s):** Belinda "Bobbie" Wheeler, Teenager; Yvonne Wheeler, Witch; Alec Wheeler, Warlock
**Time period(s):** 1990s (1993)
**Locale(s):** Willington College, England

**Summary:** White witch Yvonne Wheeler sends her daughter Bobbie to boarding school to keep her from the clutches of her black magician father Alec. But every time Bobbie inadvertently vents her supernatural powers on unsuspecting students and faculty, she comes that much closer to falling entirely under her father's pernicious influence.

**Other books you might like:**
Kathryn Meyer Griffith, *Witches*, 1993
Ed Kelleher, *The School*, 1992
   Harriet Vidal, co-author
Anne Rice, *Lasher*, 1993
Anne Rice, *The Witching Hour*, 1991

---

**5123**

### JAMES V. SMITH

## *The Lurker*
(New York: Dell, 1989)

**Story type:** Horror (Serial Killer)
**Major character(s):** Laren Hodges, Journalist; Thomas E. "Ted" Dewey, Journalist (Police reporter)
**Time period(s):** 1980s
**Locale(s):** United States

**Summary:** A "dead" child murderer, nicknamed "The Lurker," reappears to terrorize the city. An unlikely pair of reporters joins forces in an attempt to discover the nature and identity of the killer.

**Other books you might like:**
Nicholas Conde, *In the Deep Woods*, 1989
Rex Miller, *Slob*, 1987

---

**5124**

### JULIE DEAN SMITH

## *Call of Madness*
(New York: Del Rey, 1990)

**Story type:** Fantasy (Adventure)
**Series:** Caithan Crusade
**Major character(s):** Athaya Trelane, Royalty (Princess), Wizard
**Time period(s):** Indeterminate Past
**Locale(s):** Alternate Universe

**Summary:** In a world where magic is outlawed and those with magical abilities are killed, Athaya discovers that she, too, has magical abilities. In a race against time, she must find someone to train her before she goes mad from the magic or is captured by the church.

**Other books you might like:**
Cheryl J. Franklin, *Fire Get*, 1989
   Book 1 - Tales of the Taormin
Mercedes Lackey, *Arrows of the Queen*, 1987
   Book 1 - Heralds of Valdemar
Stephen R. Lawhead, *In the Hall of the Dragon King*, 1982
   Book 1 - The Dragon King Trilogy
Sandra Miesel, *Shaman*, 1989

---

**5125**

### JULIE DEAN SMITH

## *Mission of Magic*
(New York: Ballantine/Del Rey, 1991)

**Story type:** Fantasy (Adventure; Magic Conflict)
**Series:** Caithan Crusade
**Major character(s):** Athaya Trelane, Royalty (princess), Wizard; Daniel Ventan, Religious (archbishop); Durek Trelane, Royalty (king)
**Time period(s):** Indeterminate Past
**Locale(s):** Isle of Sare, Fictional Country

**Summary:** King Durek and Archbishop Ventan search through the library of deceased wizard Rhodri for ammunition against the Lorngeld, who are wizards, and against the Princess Athaya who killed their father with magic. Princess Athaya escapes to a neighboring kingdom where magic is not considered against the church. Somehow she must clear her name and save the Lorngeld from annihilation.

**Other books you might like:**
David Eddings, *Sorceress of Darshiva*, 1989
Cheryl J. Franklin, *Fire Get*, 1989
Mercedes Lackey, *Arrows of the Queen*, 1987
Sandra Miesel, *Shaman*, 1989
Melinda M. Snodgrass, *Queen's Gambit Declined*, 1989

---

**5126**

### JULIE DEAN SMITH

## *Sage of Sare*
(New York: Ballantine Del Rey, 1992)

**Story type:** Fantasy (Adventure; Magic Conflict)
**Series:** Caithan Crusade
**Major character(s):** Athaya Trelane, Royalty, Wizard; Durek Trelane, Royalty (king); Jaren McLaud, Magician
**Time period(s):** Indeterminate Past (Middle Ages)
**Locale(s):** Caithe, Fictional Country

**Summary:** Outlawed, Princess Athaya flees to the forest, gathering around her people who wish to learn control of their magic abilities. There, some hope of acceptance in society comes from a distant but powerful wizard who seeks to help the group.

**Other books you might like:**
Katherine Kurtz, *The Harrowing of Gwynedd*, 1989
Katherine Kurtz, *King Javan's Year*, 1992
Paula Volsky, *Illusion*, 1992

---

**5127**

### JULIE DEAN SMITH

## *The Wizard King*
(New York: Ballantine Del Rey, 1994)

**Story type:** Fantasy (Political; Magic Conflict)
**Series:** Caithan Crusade
**Major character(s):** Athaya Trelane, Royalty, Wizard; Sage of Sare, Wizard, Ruler
**Time period(s):** Indeterminate Past (Middle Ages)
**Locale(s):** Caithe, Fictional Country

**Summary:** Although Athaya desires political reform which allows the magic-wielding Lorngeld to learn and practice their art overtly, her revolutionary activity presents the Sage of Sare with an opportunity to advance his scheme of bringing not just acceptance for the wizards, but also the ouster of Caithe's king and his replacement with the Sage of Sare, his rule enforced by wizards' magic. While an ancient prophecy indicates Athaya's role in events will become crucial, her initial goal involves convincing the Sage to remove a deadly compulsion with which he ensorcels Athaya's brother.

**Other books you might like:**
Jo Clayton, *Dancer's Rise*, 1993
Barbara Hambly, *Stranger at the Wedding*, 1994
Laurell K. Hamilton, *Nightseer*, 1992
Mercedes Lackey, *By the Sword*, 1991
Michelle Sagara, *Chains of Darkness, Chains of Light*, 1994

**5128**

L. NEIL SMITH

## Bretta Martyn

(New York: Tor, 1997)

**Story type:** Science Fiction (Family Saga; Political)
**Series:** Henry Martyn
**Major character(s):** Arran ''Henry Martyn'' Islay, Leader; Robretta ''Bretta Martyn'' Islay, Teenager; Lisa Woodgate, Ruler
**Time period(s):** 31st century (3020s)
**Locale(s):** Hanover, Planet—Imaginary; Monopolity of Hanover, Interstellar Empire/Federation; Skye, Planet—Imaginary

**Summary:** Lia, Ceo of Hanover, commissions Arran to destroy the slave trade which has claimed millions of people over the past millennium. Arran brings his wife and oldest daughter to Hanover and on the mission, with the story that they search for lost Earth. The slavers' spy rapes and attempts to kill Bretta, throwing her off the ship in a trash can where she should die from her wounds. With Earth inhabitable, the terraformed Moon flourishes with a free and independent population and many colonies throughout the spiral arm.

**Other books you might like:**
Lois McMaster Bujold, *Borders of Infinity*, 1989
F.M. Busby, *Rissa Kerguelen*, 1977
Orson Scott Card, *Wyrms*, 1987
Sheri S. Tepper, *Grass*, 1989
Jack Vance, *Madouc*, 1990

**5129**

L. NEIL SMITH

## Contact and Commune

(New York: Popular Library Questar, 1990)

**Story type:** Science Fiction (First Contact)
**Series:** Contact
**Major character(s):** Estrellita Reille y Sanchez, Spaceship Captain, Explorer
**Time period(s):** 21st century
**Locale(s):** 5023 Eris, Asteroid

**Summary:** A pioneering expedition sets down on a mineral-rich asteroid intending to claim it for humanity, but discovers an alien race there ahead of them. The brilliant Elders, descended from ancient Earthly sea creatures, must decide whether or not to destroy humanity.

**Other books you might like:**
Gregory Benford, *Tides of Light*, 1989
Barry B. Longyear, *The Homecoming*, 1989

Janet Morris, *Target*, 1989
    David Drake, co-author
Allen L. Wold, *Crown of the Serpent*, 1989

**5130**

L. NEIL SMITH

## Converse and Conflict

(New York: Popular Library Questar, 1990)

**Story type:** Science Fiction (Alternate Universe; Political)
**Series:** Elders
**Major character(s):** Eichra Oren, Human, Agent (for the Nautiloid Elders); Mr. Thoggish, Alien (Nautiloid); Toya Pulaski, Scientist (biologist), Spy
**Time period(s):** 21st century
**Locale(s):** 5023 Eris, Planet—Imaginary

**Summary:** Eichra Oren, a representative of a nautiloid species from a parallel universe, attempts to teach the members of a stranded ASSR expedition the values of anarchy while the Elders search for the remains of an interstellar ship on 5023 Eris. Unknown to them, a ship from the USSR carrying The Banker, a KGB superagent, is coming to destroy everyone and claim the spoils for itself. But a Chinese fleet arrives and saves the day. They prove very receptive to the Elders' teachings.

**Other books you might like:**
Octavia E. Butler, *Dawn*, 1987
Jack L. Chalker, *Midnight at the Well of Souls*, 1977
Keith Laumer, *Zone Yellow*, 1990
Joan Slonczewski, *A Door into Ocean*, 1986
Allen Steele, *Clarke County, Space*, 1990
Jack Vance, *The Asutra*, 1974

**5131**

L. NEIL SMITH

## Henry Martyn

(New York: Tor, 1989)

**Story type:** Science Fiction (Space Opera)
**Major character(s):** Arran ''Henry Martyn'' Islay, Heir—Dispossessed, Pirate; Black Usurper, Criminal (Usurper)
**Time period(s):** 31st century
**Locale(s):** Outer Space; Planet—Imaginary

**Summary:** Arran Islay, deprived of his inheritance by the evil Black Usurper, vows revenge. He becomes the daring pirate Henry Martyn, scourge of the space lanes, and wins back all that he has lost and more.

**Other books you might like:**
Poul Anderson, *The High Crusade*, 1960
Lois McMaster Bujold, *Brothers in Arms*, 1988
R.A. MacAvoy, *The Third Eagle: Lessons Along a Minor String*, 1989
Alexei Panshin, *Masque World*, 1969
Alexei Panshin, *Star Well*, 1968
Alexei Panshin, *The Thurb Revolution*, 1968

## 5132
### L. NEIL SMITH

## Pallas
(New York: Tor, 1993)

**Story type:** Science Fiction (Political; Space Colony)
**Major character(s):** Emerson Ngu, Engineer, Businessman; Gibson Altman, Government Official (retired), Businessman; Aloysius Brody, Judge, Businessman
**Time period(s):** 2030s
**Locale(s):** Pallas, Asteroid

**Summary:** William Wilde Curringer terraformed Pallas and opened it for colonization by anyone willing to sign the Hyperdemocratic Covenant, a corporate agreement based on libertarian principles. A loophole allows the creation of the Greeley Project where Gibson Altman holds voting privileges for all project members, including their children, in perpetuity. Emerson Ngu builds a radio as a child and learns about life Outside. After he escapes from the Project, Altman uses him as a scapegoat for his failures, but Emerson's ingenuity and help from friends allow him to prevail.

**Other books you might like:**
Piers Anthony, *Refugee*, 1983
David Brin, *Earth*, 1990
Samuel R. Delany, *They Fly at Ciron*, 1993
Robert A. Heinlein, *The Moon Is a Harsh Mistress*, 1966
Charles Sheffield, *Brother to Dragons*, 1992
F. Paul Wilson, *The LaNague Chronicles*, 1992
F. Paul Wilson, *The Tery*, 1990

## 5133
### MARK SMITH
### JULIA SMITH, Co-Author

## Shadow-Maze
(New York: Warner Questar, 1994)

**Story type:** Fantasy (Magic Conflict; Quest)
**Major character(s):** Brostek, Teenager, Hunter; Varo, Teenager, Hunter; Magara, Storyteller
**Time period(s):** Indeterminate
**Locale(s):** Levindre, Fictional Country; Bari, Fictional Country; Trevine, Fictional Country

**Summary:** Meeting on the return home from their adulthood survival test, Brostek and Varo find their townsfolk dead at the hands of the Knifemen of Bari, and set out to avenge their relatives and protect their neighbors. When Slaton and his strange nephew Lisle join them, they realize they must succeed against an ancient, lost power now possessed by an insane and evil wizard by mastering the shadow-maze which Magara's tapestry reflects.

**Other books you might like:**
Sharon Green, *The Hidden Realms*, 1993
Jane M. Lindskold, *Brother to Dragons, Companion to Owls*, 1994
S.M. Stirling, *The Rose Sea*, 1994
    Holly Lisle, co-author
Deborah Talmadge-Bickmore, *The Heldan*, 1994
Jonathan Wylie, *The First Named*, 1987
    pseudonym of Mark Smith and Julia Smith

## 5134
### NYX SMITH

## Fade to Black
(New York: Roc, 1994)

**Story type:** Science Fiction (Cyberpunk; Science Fantasy)
**Series:** Shadowrun
**Major character(s):** Thorvin, Mythical Creature (dwarf), Cyborg (rigger); Rico, Mercenary (shadowrunner); Bandit, Shaman
**Time period(s):** 2050s (2055)
**Locale(s):** Newark, New Jersey

**Summary:** Hired for a seemingly simple corporate extraction, freeing a valuable asset from his contract, Rico and his gang discover that lies and betrayals make it difficult to escape with their lives. Game tie-in.

**Other books you might like:**
Emma Bull, *Bone Dance: A Fantasy for Technophiles*, 1991
Pat Cadigan, *Synners*, 1991
Charles de Lint, *Svaha*, 1989
Nigel Findley, *2XS*, 1992
Walter Jon Williams, *Voice of the Whirlwind*, 1987

## 5135
### NYX SMITH

## Striper Assassin
(New York: Roc, 1993)

**Story type:** Fantasy (Adventure; Urban)
**Series:** Shadowrun
**Major character(s):** Tikki "Striper", Hunter, Mythical Creature (shapechanger)
**Time period(s):** 2050s (2054)
**Locale(s):** Philadelphia, Pennsylvania

**Summary:** Tikki's usual role reverses as hunter becomes prey when another hunter sets his sights on Tikki. Game tie-in.

**Other books you might like:**
Robert N. Charrette, *Choose Your Enemies Carefully*, 1991
Robert N. Charrette, *Find Your Own Truth*, 1991
Robert N. Charrette, *Never Deal with a Dragon*, 1990
Robert N. Charrette, *Never Trust an Elf*, 1992
Tom Dowd, *Night's Pawn*, 1993
Nigel Findley, *2XS*, 1992
Nigel Findley, *Shadowplay*, 1993
Christopher Kubasik, *Changeling*, 1992
Carl Sargent, *Streets of Blood*, 1992
    Marc Gascoigne, co-author
Jordan K. Weisman, *Into the Shadows*, 1992
    editor

## 5136
### ROBERT ARTHUR SMITH

## Silent Witness
(New York: Fawcett, 1991)

**Story type:** Horror (Science Fiction)
**Major character(s):** Nicole Brill, Child; Willy Brill, Doctor (ex-Nazi); Peter Van Buren, Young Man
**Time period(s):** 1990s
**Locale(s):** Brazil (the rain forest)

**Summary:** Nicole Brill's discovery that her father and his closest friends are ex-Nazis who sought refuge and new identities following the war isn't nearly as devastating as her discovery that her father was a greatly reviled surgeon who is continuing the same hideous experiments he performed for the benefit of the Third Reich.

**Other books you might like:**
Ira Levin, *The Boys From Brazil*, 1976
Robert Weinberg, *The Armageddon Box*, 1991

---

**5137**

### SHERWOOD SMITH

## *Court Duel*

(New York: Harcourt Brace, 1998)

**Story type:** Fantasy (Young Adult; Political)
**Major character(s):** Meliara "Mel" Astiar, Teenager, Noblewoman (countess)
**Time period(s):** Indeterminate
**Locale(s):** Remalna, Fictional Country

**Summary:** With the evil king defeated, Mel discovers the intrigues of court, where manners and ritual disguise the true nature of relationships. Sequel to *Crown Duel*.

**Other books you might like:**
Peg Kerr, *Emerald House Rising*, 1997
Caroline Stevermer, *A College of Magics*, 1994
Paula Volsky, *Illusion*, 1992
Patricia C. Wrede, *Magician's Ward*, 1997
Patricia C. Wrede, *Sorcery and Cecelia*, 1988
   Caroline Stevermer, co-author

---

**5138**

### SHERWOOD SMITH
### DAVE TROWBRIDGE, Co-Author

## *The Phoenix in Flight*

(New York: Tor, 1993)

**Story type:** Science Fiction (Adventure; Political)
**Series:** Exordium
**Major character(s):** Jerrode Eusabian, Political Figure (Lord of Vengeance); Gelasaar III, Royalty (Emperor), Leader (Pantarch)
**Time period(s):** Indeterminate Future
**Locale(s):** *Bloodknife*, Spaceship; Brangornie, Planet—Imaginary; Narbon, Planet—Imaginary

**Summary:** Having come through the Vortex thousands of years earlier, humans now inhabit the many planets composing the Thousand Suns, an interstellar empire maintaining control for a thousand years. Eusabian plots to overthrow the empire by killing the heirs and capturing Gelasaar III. A computer expert discovers the plotting and attempts to undo it. When the youngest son of Gelasaar III fails to attend the ceremony where assassination waits, he survives to fight the Lord of Vengeance and the destruction of the Panarchy.

**Other books you might like:**
Iain M. Banks, *Use of Weapons*, 1992
Allan Cole, *Sten*, 1984
   Chris Bunch, co-author
Glen Cook, *The Dragon Never Sleeps*, 1988
Debra Doyle, *The Price of the Stars*, 1992
   James D. Macdonald, co-author
Frank Herbert, *Dune*, 1965
Andre Norton, *Brother to Shadows*, 1993
David Weber, *On Basilisk Station*, 1993

David Weber, *Path of the Fury*, 1992
Vernor Vinge, *A Fire upon the Deep*, 1992

---

**5139**

### SHERWOOD SMITH
### DAVE TROWBRIDGE, Co-Author

## *A Prison Unsought*

(New York: Tor, 1994)

**Story type:** Science Fiction (Political; Military)
**Series:** Exordium
**Major character(s):** Brandon vlith-Arkad, Military Personnel, Heir—Dispossessed, Fugitive
**Time period(s):** Indeterminate Future
**Locale(s):** Ares, Planet—Imaginary (Panarchic Navy headquarters); Gehenna, Planet—Imaginary (prison planet); Panarchy of the Thousand Suns, Interstellar Empire/Federation

**Summary:** With the usurper Eusabian of Dol'jhar in control of the Empire, Brandon vlith-Arkad rallies with followers on Ares as he tries to win the Panarchic Navy's loyalty. As the deposed Pantarch, Brandon's father, travels to Gehenna, he tries to find a way to turn the usurper's son against his father and regain power indirectly.

**Other books you might like:**
Lois McMaster Bujold, *The Warrior's Apprentice*, 1986
Glen Cook, *The Dragon Never Sleeps*, 1988
Debra Doyle, *The Price of the Stars*, 1992
   James D. Macdonald, co-author
Alis A. Rasmussen, *Revolution's Shore*, 1990
David Weber, *On Basilisk Station*, 1993

---

**5140**

### SHERWOOD SMITH
### DAVE TROWBRIDGE, Co-Author

## *The Rifter's Covenant*

(New York: Tor, 1995)

**Story type:** Science Fiction (Adventure; Political)
**Series:** Exordium
**Major character(s):** Brandon hai-Arkad, Royalty (Panarch); Jerrode Eusabian, Political Figure (Lord of Vengeance)
**Time period(s):** Indeterminate Future
**Locale(s):** Ares, Space Station; *Suneater*, Spaceship; Panarchy of the Thousand Suns, Interstellar Empire/Federation

**Summary:** Against all expectations, Brandon Arkad survives many attacks to become Pantarch of the Thousand Suns. Unfortunately, his enemies control or attack most of his empire while Brandon attempts to gather support as a traitor sabotages his efforts.

**Other books you might like:**
Iain M. Banks, *The Player of Games*, 1989
Glen Cook, *The Dragon Never Sleeps*, 1988
Debra Doyle, *The Price of the Stars*, 1992
   James D. Macdonald, co-author
Frank Herbert, *Dune*, 1965
H. Beam Piper, *Space Viking*, 1963
Vernor Vinge, *A Fire upon the Deep*, 1992
David Weber, *On Basilisk Station*, 1993

## 5141

### SHERWOOD SMITH
### DAVE TROWBRIDGE, Co-Author

## Ruler of Naught
(New York: Tor, 1993)

**Story type:** Science Fiction (Adventure; Political)
**Series:** Exordium
**Major character(s):** Margot O'Reilly Ng, Spaceship Captain; Brandon vlith-Arkad, Heir—Dispossessed (aerenarch), Fugitive (exile), Military Personnel; Ivard, Pirate
**Time period(s):** Indeterminate Future
**Locale(s):** *Grozniy*, Spaceship; *Telvarna*, Spaceship; Arthelion, Planet—Imaginary

**Summary:** Eusabian of Dol'jhar sits on the Emerald Throne of the Thousand Suns while Brandon, the rightful heir, flees across the galaxy. Captors turned allies, the rifter crew of the *Telvarna* help Brandon evade pursuit as they make their way toward Ares Station where the scattered remnants of the Imperial Fleet assemble for counterinsurgency.

**Other books you might like:**
Isaac Asimov, *Foundation and Empire*, 1952
C.J. Cherryh, *Chanur's Homecoming*, 1986
C.J. Cherryh, *The Pride of Chanur*, 1982
Debra Doyle, *The Price of the Stars*, 1992
    James D. Macdonald, co-author
Frank Herbert, *Dune*, 1965
George Lucas, *Star Wars*, 1976
Judith Reeves-Stevens, *Prime Directive*, 1990
    Garfield Reeves-Stevens, co-author
Edward E. Smith, *The Skylark of Space*, 1946

## 5142

### SHERWOOD SMITH

## Wren to the Rescue
(New York: Harcourt Brace Jovanovich, 1990)

**Story type:** Fantasy (Quest)
**Series:** Wren
**Major character(s):** Wren, Orphan, Adventurer, Magician; Tryon, Magician, Apprentice; Connor Shaltar, Royalty (prince of Siradayel)
**Time period(s):** Indeterminate
**Locale(s):** Meldrith, Fictional Country; Senna Lirwan, Fictional Country

**Summary:** When Wren's friend, Princess Teressa, is kidnapped from Three Groves Orphanage, Wren uses a once-heard spell in the vain hope of helping her friend. The spell transports her to the Magic School where she is told not to try the spell again and she acquires the aid of Tryon. On their journey to rescue Teressa from King Andreus, they are joined by Tryon's friend, Connor. During the rescue attempt, Wren is changed into a dog, but even that difficulty does not deter their efforts.

**Other books you might like:**
Lloyd Alexander, *The Beggar Queen*, 1984
Lloyd Alexander, *The Kestrel*, 1982
Lloyd Alexander, *Westmark*, 1981
Grace Chetwin, *Gom on Windy Mountain*, 1986
Geraldine Harris, *Prince of the Godborn*, 1983
Ursula K. Le Guin, *A Wizard of Earthsea*, 1968
Ursula K. Le Guin, *The Farthest Shore*, 1972
Ursula K. Le Guin, *The Tombs of Atuan*, 1971

Susan Price, *The Ghost Drum: A Cat's Tale*, 1987

## 5143

### SHERWOOD SMITH

## Wren's Quest
(New York: Harcourt Brace Jovanovich, 1993)

**Story type:** Fantasy (Quest; Young Adult)
**Series:** Wren
**Major character(s):** Wren, Adventurer, Student (of magic), Orphan; Connor Shaltar, Royalty (Prince of Siradayel)
**Time period(s):** Indeterminate
**Locale(s):** Cantirmoor, Fictional Country; Meldrith, Fictional Country; Siradayel, Fictional Country

**Summary:** Having earned her first break from magic school, Wren decides to pursue clues she receives from her orphanage and try to find her relatives. Wren's mission becomes dangerous as human and magical agents interfere. Sequel to *Wren to the Rescue*.

**Other books you might like:**
Terry Brooks, *Hook*, 1992
Phyllis Eisenstein, *Sorcerer's Son*, 1979
Nancy Luenn, *Goldclimbers*, 1991
Shirley Rousseau Murphy, *The Catswold Portal*, 1992
Will Shetterly, *Elsewhere*, 1991
Jane Yolen, *Briar Rose*, 1992

## 5144

### SHERWOOD SMITH

## Wren's War
(New York: Harcourt Brace/Jane Yolen Books, 1995)

**Story type:** Fantasy (Young Adult; Adventure)
**Series:** Wren
**Major character(s):** Wren, Adventurer, Magician, Orphan; Teressa Rhisadel, Royalty (Princess of Meldrith), Leader; Connor Shaltar, Royalty (Prince of Siradayel)
**Time period(s):** Indeterminate
**Locale(s):** Meldrith, Fictional Country

**Summary:** Lusting for power and revenge, Andreus attacks Meldrith, killing King Verne and Queen Astren. Escaping with Prince Connor, Princess Teressa joins with Wren and others to repel the invaders and reinstate a proper Meldrith sovereign.

**Other books you might like:**
Lois McMaster Bujold, *The Spirit Ring*, 1992
Laurell K. Hamilton, *Nightseer*, 1992
Tanith Lee, *Gold Unicorn*, 1994
Martha Wells, *The Element of Fire*, 1992
Patricia C. Wrede, *Calling on Dragons*, 1993

## 5145

### STEPHANIE A. SMITH

## Other Nature
(New York: Tor, 1995)

**Story type:** Science Fiction (Post-Disaster)
**Major character(s):** Sean Rider, Spouse (Emily's); Emily Rider, Spouse (Sean's)
**Time period(s):** 21st century
**Locale(s):** Oregon; California; Monkar

**Summary:** Formerly a high tech research center, Monkar now decays as birth defects and premature mortality rates soar. After Sean Rider leaves his pregnant wife to search near San Francisco for his former mate, events in Monkar further degrade the fragile society.

**Other books you might like:**
Richard Brautigan, *In Watermelon Sugar*, 1968
Jack Cady, *The Off Season*, 1995
Nancy Farmer, *The Ear, the Eye, and the Arm*, 1994
K.W. Jeter, *Madlands*, 1991
Ken Kesey, *Sailor Song*, 1992
Rachel Pollack, *Unquenchable Fire*, 1992
Geoff Ryman, *The Child Garden*, 1990

## 5146

### WAYNE SMITH

### *Thor*

(New York: St. Martin's/Thomas Dunne, 1992)

**Story type:** Horror (Werewolf Story)
**Major character(s):** Thor, Animal (German Shepherd); Uncle Ted, Photographer, Werewolf; Dad, Lawyer
**Time period(s):** 1990s (1992)
**Locale(s):** Oregon

**Summary:** This ingenious first novel is told from the point of view of Thor, the family dog, who desperately tries to warn his human owners that a family member has become a werewolf but is frustratingly misunderstood for all of his efforts.

**Other books you might like:**
Michael Cadnum, *St. Peter's Wolf*, 1992
Dennis Danvers, *Wilderness*, 1992
Stephen King, *Cujo*, 1981
H. Warner Munn, *The Werewolf of Ponkert*, 1958
S.P. Somtow, *Moon Dance*, 1990

## 5147

### MELINDA M. SNODGRASS

### *Queen's Gambit Declined*

(New York: Popular Library Questar, 1989)

**Story type:** Fantasy (Alternate World)
**Major character(s):** Wiiliam Henry, Ruler (Prince of Orange), Historical Figure; Louis XIV, Ruler (King of France), Historical Figure
**Locale(s):** Alternate Earth (France and the Netherlands)

**Summary:** History and magic are interwoven in this story about William of Orange and Louis of France. The war between the two sovereigns is fought in the traditional manner, as well as with magic.

**Other books you might like:**
Roberto Pazzi, *The Princess and the Dragon*,
Melissa Scott, *The Armor of Light*, 1988
   Lisa Barnett, co-author
Bob Skimin, *Gray Victory*, 1988

## 5148

### GREG SNOW

### *That's All, Folks!*

(New York: Random House, 1992)

**Story type:** Fantasy (Contemporary; Light Fantasy)

**Major character(s):** Nick Taig, Advertising; Lucy, Girlfriend; Christian Kidd, Advertising (art director), Homosexual
**Time period(s):** 1990s
**Locale(s):** London, England

**Summary:** During an accident with a kitchen appliance, Nick discovers that his body exhibits cartoon characteristics. Nick soon realizes the changed nature of his existence and begins the search for answers and remission to his former state. Published in 1991 in Great Britain as *Surface Tension*. Author's first novel.

**Other books you might like:**
Michael Bishop, *Count Geiger's Blues*, 1992
Michael Kandel, *Captain Jack Zodiac*, 1992
George R.R. Martin, *Wild Cards*, 1987
   editor
Clifford D. Simak, *Out of Their Minds*, 1970
Gary K. Wolf, *Who Censored Roger Rabbit?*, 1981
Gary K. Wolf, *Who P-P-Plugged Roger Rabbit?*, 1991

## 5149

### JACK SNOW
### ERIC SHANOWER, Illustrator

### *Spectral Snow: The Dark Fantasies of Jack Snow*

(Bloomsbury, New Jersey: Hungry Tiger Press, 1996)

**Story type:** Horror (Collection)

**Summary:** The author is best known as a writer chosen by the estate of L. Frank Baum to continue Baum's series of Oz books. This collection brings together eight tales of horror, fantasy, and science fiction, including "Second Childhood," about an evil imaginary playmate who returns to a woman in her old age; "The Dimension Terror," about the horrifying experiences of a married couple who stumble upon a fallen meteorite on their honeymoon; "Seed," in which a woman is impregnated with the seed of a plant that will grow inside her; and "The Rope," about a man who discovers to his dismay the truth behind the Indian rope trick. Editor David Maxine has also included the previously unpublished "A Murder in Oz."

**Other books you might like:**
Arthur J. Burks, *Black Medicine*, 1966
Hugh B. Cave, *Murgunstrumm and Others*, 1977
Carl Jacobi, *Smoke of the Snake*, 1994
Frank Belknap Long, *Escape From Tomorrow*, 1995
Howard Wandrei, *Time Burial*, 1995

## 5150

### MIDORI SNYDER

### *Beldan's Fire*

(New York: Tor, 1993)

**Story type:** Fantasy (Magic Conflict; Political)
**Series:** New Moon
**Major character(s):** Zorah, Ruler (Fire Queen); Jobber, Revolutionary, Psychic (pyromancer); Shedwyn, Revolutionary, Psychic (esper)
**Time period(s):** Indeterminate
**Locale(s):** Beldan, Fictional City; Oran, Fictional Country

**Summary:** Zorah, Fire Queen, depends on the foreign Silean soldiers to police Beldan. Although possession of Oran talents results in a death penalty, three of the four women necessary to create a Queen's quarter knot of the powers of earth, air, fire and water already belong to the revolutionary group, New Moon. Having already killed her three complementary Queens, Zorah anticipates wresting power from the new quarter knot and increasing her own powers.

**Other books you might like:**
David Eddings, *Pawn of Prophecy*, 1982
Phyllis Eisenstein, *Shadow of Earth*, 1979
Barbara Hambly, *The Time of the Dark*, 1982
Mickey Zucker Reichert, *The Western Wizard*, 1992
Paula Volsky, *Illusion*, 1992

---

**5151**

### MIDORI SNYDER

## The Flight of Michael McBride

(New York: Tor, 1994)

**Story type:** Fantasy (Magic Conflict; Horror)
**Major character(s):** Michael McBride, Cowboy, Mythical Creature (part fairy); John O'Connor, Cowboy, Leader
**Time period(s):** 1870s
**Locale(s):** New York; Texas

**Summary:** While fleeing spirits made visible by his mother's death-bed ritual, Michael meets a gambler who directs him to Texas where he will find a job. In Texas, mentioning the gambler secures Michael employment as a drover, but attacks now afflict his companions on the cattle drive.

**Other books you might like:**
Richard Brautigan, *The Hawkline Monster*, 1974
Susan Dexter, *The Prince of Ill Luck*, 1994
Karen Joy Fowler, *Sarah Canary*, 1991
Stephen King, *The Dark Tower: The Gunslinger*, 1982
Louis L'Amour, *Haunted Mesa*, 1987
George R.R. Martin, *Fevre Dream*, 1982
Steve Perry, *Stellar Ranger*, 1994
Elizabeth Ann Scarborough, *The Goldcamp Vampire; or The Sanguinary Sourdough*, 1987
S.P. Somtow, *Moon Dance*, 1989

---

**5152**

### MIDORI SNYDER

## The Innamorati

(New York: Tor, 1998)

**Story type:** Fantasy (Historical; Legend)
**Major character(s):** Anna Forsetti, Artisan (mask-maker); Rinaldo Gustiano, Nobleman, Mercenary; Fabrizio, Actor
**Time period(s):** Indeterminate Past
**Locale(s):** Labirinto, Italy; Venice, Italy

**Summary:** Against the backdrop of Renaissance Italy, a mask-maker, a duelist, an actor and a siren each journey to Labirinto to walk the mysterious labyrinth they believe will remove their respective curses.

**Other books you might like:**
Jack Dann, *The Memory Cathedral*, 1995
Paul J. McAuley, *Pasquale's Angel*, 1995
Vonda N. McIntyre, *The Moon and the Sun*, 1997
Michaela Roessner, *The Stars Dispose*, 1997
Melissa Scott, *Point of Hopes*, 1995
    Lisa Barnett, co-author

---

**5153**

### ZILPHA KEATLEY SNYDER

## Song of the Gargoyle

(New York: Delacorte Press, 1991)

**Story type:** Fantasy (Adventure; Young Adult)
**Major character(s):** Komus, Entertainer (court jester); Tymmon, Teenager
**Time period(s):** Indeterminate Past (the Middle Ages)
**Locale(s):** Austerneve North Countries, Fictional Country

**Summary:** After Komus was kidnapped, his son Tymmon, who wants to be a knight, escapes, intending to rescue his father. During his search he notices the way knights treat the populace and comes to appreciate his father's choice of profession.

**Other books you might like:**
John Deakins, *Barrow*, 1990
Phyllis Eisenstein, *Born to Exile*, 1978
Phyllis Eisenstein, *Sorcerer's Son*, 1989
Esther Friesner, *The Water King's Laughter*, 1989
Matt Ruff, *Fool on the Hill*, 1989
Peter Vansittart, *Parsifal*, 1989

---

**5154**

### CARO SOLES, Editor

## Meltdown!

(New York: Masquerade Books, Inc., 1994)

**Story type:** Science Fiction (Anthology; Gay/Lesbian Fiction)

**Summary:** Subtitled "An Anthology of Erotic Science Fiction and Dark Fantasy for Gay Men," this volume contains a two-page introduction plus 11 original and three reprinted stories by authors including Robin Wayne Bailey, Samuel R. Delany and Edmund White.

**Other books you might like:**
Camilla Decarnin, *Worlds Apart*, 1986
    Eric Garber, Lyn Paleo, co-editors
Jeffrey M. Elliot, *Kindred Spirits*, 1984
    editor
Pam Keesey, *Daughters of Darkness: Lesbian Vampire Stories*, 1993
    editor

---

**5155**

### S.P. SOMTOW

## Darker Angels

(New York: Tor, 1998)

**Story type:** Horror (Reanimated Dead)
**Major character(s):** Laura Grainger, Widow(er); Zack Brown, Military Personnel (former soldier); Walt Whitman, Writer (poet)
**Time period(s):** 1860s (1865)
**Locale(s):** New York, New York

**Summary:** From Walt Whitman and other veterans of the American Civil War, Laura Grainger learns of a legacy of voodoo and black magic among southern slaves who are led by a shapeshifting priest and priestess who have resurrected the dead for a zombie army. Laura's ambition is to apply this newfound knowledge to reviving the assassinated President Abraham Lincoln, whose body lies in state preparatory to interment in Springfield, Illinois. First published in

England in 1997. Expanded from a novella of the same name published in 1993.

**Other books you might like:**
Hugh B. Cave, *Legion of the Dead*, 1979
Richard Gilliam, *Confederacy of the Dead*, 1993
    Edward E. Kramer, Martin H. Greenberg, co-editors
Frank D. McSherry Jr., *Nightmares in Dixie*, 1987
    Charles G. Waugh, Martin H. Greenberg, co-editors
Frank McSherry Jr., *Civil War Ghosts*, 1990
    Charles G. Waugh, Martin H. Greenberg, co-editors
Manly Wade Wellman, *Worse Things Waiting*, 1973

---

**5156**

**S.P. SOMTOW** (Pseudonym of Somtow Sucharitkul)

## Forest of the Night

(New York: AvoNova, 1992)

**Story type:** Fantasy (Alternate World; Religious)
**Series:** Darkling Wars
**Major character(s):** Theo Etchison, Psychic (truthsayer); Phil Etchison, Writer (poet); Serena Sommers, Girlfriend (Josh Etchison's)
**Time period(s):** 1990s
**Locale(s):** Southwest; Alternate Earth; Alternate Universe

**Summary:** Once again the warring dragon-children wish to win the mortal realm. The Darkling King Strang draws Theo into Strang's dimension to act as pawn in a bizarre odyssey. Phil and Serena search for Theo while Theo must rescue his brother from hell and the demonic forces which have claimed him.

**Other books you might like:**
Philip K. Dick, *Ubik*, 1969
Philip K. Dick, *The Unteleported Man*, 1983
    revised
Alan Dean Foster, *To the Vanishing Point*, 1988
K.W. Jeter, *Madlands*, 1991
Will Shetterly, *The Tangled Lands*, 1989
Terri Windling, *Life on the Border*, 1991
    editor

---

**5157**

**S.P. SOMTOW** (Pseudonym of Somtow Sucharitkul)

## I Wake From a Dream of a Drowned Star City

(Eugene, Oregon: Pulphouse Publishing Axolotl Press 1992)

**Story type:** Science Fiction (Political; Genetic Manipulation)
**Major character(s):** Morry Draus, Clone, Heir (Crown Prince)
**Time period(s):** Indeterminate Future
**Locale(s):** Dreambreak, Fictional City

**Summary:** At the palace, Morry, a cloned prince, receives the formal education necessary for the ruler-to-be while acquiring street education from future subjects. After he reaches puberty, Morry's mother ritually initiates him in family sexual practice and declares him an adult worthy of becoming king, incurring an automatic death sentence for his genetically imperfect elder brother.

**Other books you might like:**
Octavia E. Butler, *Dawn*, 1987
Orson Scott Card, *Wyrms*, 1987
Thomas A. Easton, *Sparrowhawk*, 1990
Aldous Huxley, *Brave New World*, 1932
Robert Silverberg, *Tower of Glass*, 1970

Cordwainer Smith, *Norstrilia*, 1975

---

**5158**

**S.P. SOMTOW** (Pseudonym of Somtow Sucharitkul)

## Moon Dance

(New York: Tor, 1990)

**Story type:** Horror (Werewolf Story)
**Major character(s):** Speranza Martinique, Governess; Johnny Kinkaid, Werewolf (Multiple personality)
**Time period(s):** 1880s (1883); 1960s (1963)
**Locale(s):** West (Dakota Territory)

**Summary:** Led by a European nobleman, a colony of werewolves move to the Dakota Territory, where they encounter a tribe of American Indian werewolves. The fate of the count's young son and his spunky governess rests on the outcome of this confrontation.

**Other books you might like:**
Basil Copper, *The House of the Wolf*, 1983
Robert R. McCammon, *They Thirst*, 1981

---

**5159**

**S.P. SOMTOW** (Pseudonym of Somtow Sucharitkul)

## Riverrun

(New York: Avon, 1991)

**Story type:** Fantasy (Alternate World; Religious)
**Series:** Darkling Wars
**Major character(s):** Theo Etchison, Teenager, Psychic (truthsayer); Katastrofa "Kathy" Darkling, Police Officer (superintendent), Mythical Creature (were-dragon)
**Time period(s):** 1990s (1990)
**Locale(s):** Southwest; Alternate Universe

**Summary:** The Etchison family, while travelling from Virginia to Mexico, stops at a Chinese restaurant where Theo is drawn into another universe. He is kidnapped by Thorn Darkling, the eldest of three children of the King of the Universe. A latent Truthsayer with supernatural powers, Theo is needed to prevent the Darklings from destroying the universe when all he wants is to have his family safe and to get back to Earth.

**Other books you might like:**
Charles de Lint, *The Little Country*, 1991
Philip K. Dick, *The Unteleported Man*, 1983
    (revised)
Alan Dean Foster, *To the Vanishing Point*, 1988
Geary Gravel, *A Key for the Nonesuch*, 1990
Geary Gravel, *The Return of the Breakneck Boys*, 1991
Robert A. Heinlein, *The Number of the Beast*, 1980
Will Shetterly, *Cats Have No Lord*, 1985
Will Shetterly, *The Tangled Lands*, 1989

---

**5160**

**S.P. SOMTOW** (Pseudonym of Somtow Sucharitkul)

## Valentine

(New York: Tor, 1992)

**Story type:** Horror (Vampire Story)
**Series:** Vampire Junction
**Major character(s):** Angel Todd, Actor; P.J. Gallegher, Shaman; Simone Arletta, Sorceress

**Time period(s):** 1990s (1992)
**Locale(s):** Junction, Idaho

**Summary:** In this sequel to the 1984 novel, *Vampire Junction*, director Jonathan Burr begins shooting the film biography of adolescent rock star Timmy Valentine in the town where Valentine disappeared eight years before, unaware that Valentine is a vampire over two millenia old, and that many who *are* aware of Timmy's true nature will use the shooting of the film to make contact with Timothy and exploit his powers.

**Other books you might like:**
Poppy Z. Brite, *Lost Souls*, 1992
Nancy A. Collins, *Tempter*, 1990
Anne Rice, *The Vampire Lestat*, 1985

### 5161

**S.P. SOMTOW** (Pseudonym of Somtow Sucharitkul)

## The Vampire's Beautiful Daughter
(New York: Atheneum, 1997)

**Story type:** Horror (Vampire Story)
**Major character(s):** Johnny Raitt, Teenager; Rebecca Teppish, Teenager, Vampire; Vladimir X. Teppish III, Vampire, Parent (Rebecca's father)
**Time period(s):** 1990s (1997)
**Locale(s):** Encino, California

**Summary:** A young adult coming-of-age story. Johnny Raitt, newly moved from North Dakota to California, befriends Rebecca Teppish at Claudette Colbert high school. While Rebecca helps Johnny acclimate to his new surroundings, Johnny helps Rebecca in her choice between embracing her family's vampire heritage or living life as a normal teenager.

**Other books you might like:**
Richie Tankersley Cusick, *Buffy the Vampire Slayer*, 1997
Elvira, *Transylvania 90210*, 1996
　John Paragon, co-author
Joseph Locke, *Vampire Heart*, 1994
Christopher Pike, *The Last Vampire*, 1994
Nicholas Pine, *Night School*, 1994
L.J. Smith, *Dark Reunion*, 1992
　Vampire Diaries, volume 4

### 5162

**S.P. SOMTOW** (Pseudonym of Somtow Sucharitkul)

## Vanitas: Escape From Vampire Junction
(New York: Tor, 1995)

**Story type:** Horror (Vampire Story)
**Series:** Vampire Junction
**Major character(s):** Timmy Valentine, Musician (rock music singer); P.J. Gallegher, Art Dealer (gallery owner); Lauren McCandless, Artist (painter)
**Time period(s):** 1990s (1995)
**Locale(s):** Los Angeles, California; Bangkok, Thailand

**Summary:** Having traded his vampirism for a human soul to Angel Todd, the teenage boy who was to portray him in a movie, vampire rock star Timmy Valentine begins aging and finds that his music has lost its passion. Refusing to be forgotten, the now discorporate Angel acts as an evil influence on human beings in close proximity, forcing them to commit vampire-like murders and goading Timmy to track Angel to Thailand for a final showdown.

**Other books you might like:**
Poppy Z. Brite, *Lost Souls*, 1992
Gail Petersen, *The Making of a Monster*, 1993
Anne Rice, *The Vampire Lestat*, 1985
Robert Weinberg, *Vampire Diary: The Embrace*, 1995
　Mark Rein-Hagen, co-author

### 5163

**S.P. SOMTOW** (Pseudonym of Somtow Sucharitkul)

## The Wizard's Apprentice
(New York: Atheneum, 1993)

**Story type:** Fantasy (Light Fantasy; Young Adult)
**Series:** Dragonflight
**Major character(s):** Aaron Maguire, Magician (apprentice), Teenager; Anaxagoras, Wizard, Teacher
**Time period(s):** 1990s
**Locale(s):** Los Angeles, California

**Summary:** During summer vacation from school, Aaron Maguire accepts apprenticeship with Anaxagoras and begins his studies. Magic turns to mayhem as Aaron loses his magic mirror to his girlfriend and magic monsters begin to terrorize Hollywood.

**Other books you might like:**
C. Dale Brittain, *A Bad Spell in Yurt*, 1991
Lois McMaster Bujold, *The Spirit Ring*, 1992
Michael Ende, *The Night of Wishes: or The Satanarchaeolidealcohellish Notion Potion*, 1992
Esther Friesner, *Majyk by Accident*, 1993
Esther Friesner, *Wishing Season*, 1993
Nancy Springer, *Red Wizard*, 1990
Somtow Sucharitkul, *The Fallen Country*, 1986
Somtow Sucharitkul, *Mallworld*, 1981

### 5164

**ROY SORRELS**

## The Eyes of Torie Webster
(New York: Pinnacle, 1990)

**Story type:** Horror (Occult)
**Major character(s):** Torie Webster, Journalist (television newscaster); Rex Sullivan, Artist (Torie's boyfriend); Father Michael, Religious (priest; exorcist), Alcoholic
**Time period(s):** 17th century (1693); 1990s (1994)
**Locale(s):** New York; New Jersey

**Summary:** In 1693, Lizzie Dedalus is burned as a witch in the swamps of New Jersey. Three centuries later, her lingering presence causes a series of unexplained disappearances at the new airport built on her death site. This is the author's first novel.

**Other books you might like:**
Melisand March, *The Site*, 1988

### 5165

**MARTHA SOUKUP**

## The Arbitrary Placement of Walls
(Minneapolis: DreamHaven Books, 1997)

**Story type:** Fantasy (Collection; Science Fiction)
**Major character(s):** Carl, Actor; Shawana Mooney, Single Parent, Traveler (trucker); Herb, Animal

**Time period(s):** Indeterminate Future; 1990s
**Locale(s):** New York, New York

**Summary:** Contains 17 short stories from periodicals and anthologies 1986-1996, plus a foreword by the author and an introductory poem by Neil Gaiman. The stories, both science fiction and fantasy, show a broad range of settings and tone, from ''Dress Rehearsal,'' in which an actor finds a surprising reaction to the remote-controlled bodies on stage, to ''Over the Long Haul,'' which shows the life of an impoverished woman on a dystopian mobile future. Author's first book.

**Other books you might like:**
Jack Cady, *The Sons of Noah and Other Stories*, 1992
John Crowley, *Antiquities*, 1993
Neil Gaiman, *Angels & Visitations: A Miscellany*, 1993
Lisa Goldstein, *Travelers in Magic*, 1994
Pat Murphy, *Points of Departure*, 1990

## 5166

### MURIEL SPARK

## Open to the Public

(New York: New Directions, 1997)

**Story type:** Horror (Collection)

**Summary:** Collection of thirty-seven stories spanning more than 45 years. The majority are mainstream fiction, but most of the author's short macabre stories are included, among them ''The Portobello Road,'' which is narrated by the ghost of a murder victim; ''The Leaf Sweeper,'' in which a man and his ghost co-exist; ''The House of the Famous Poet,'' featuring a precognition of death; and ''The Girl I Left Behind Me,'' in which a woman discovers that the one detail of the day that has eluded her memory is literally a matter of life and death.

**Other books you might like:**
Jonathan Carroll, *The Panic Hand*, 1995
Fred Chappell, *More Shapes than One*, 1992
Rachel Ingalls, *The End of Tragedy*, 1987
Shirley Jackson, *One Ordinary Day, with Peanuts*, 1997
Alison Lurie, *Women and Ghosts*, 1994
Joyce Carol Oates, *Haunted: Tales of the Grotesque*, 1994

## 5167

### WILLIAM BROWNING SPENCER

## Irrational Fears

(Stone Mountain, Georgia: White Wolf, 1998)

**Story type:** Horror (Occult; Satire)
**Major character(s):** Jack Lowry, Professor (American literature); Dorian Greenway, Leader (cult); Kerry Beckett, Teenager
**Time period(s):** 1990s (1998)
**Locale(s):** Harken, Virginia

**Summary:** Jack Lowry's attempts to manage his alcoholism lead him from Alcoholics Anonymous to the Clear, a wacky New Age cult that believes alcoholics are in thrall to extradimensional forces described in the Cthulhu Mythos fiction of H.P. Lovecraft. The Clear's absurd claims grow increasingly believable as Jack discerns a sinister design behind the group's program. Expanded from the author's 1993 novella of the same name.

**Other books you might like:**
Scott Bradfield, *What's Wrong with America*, 1994
Jonathan Carroll, *The Land of Laughs*, 1980
Fred Chappell, *Dagon*, 1967
Thomas M. Disch, *The M.D.: A Horror Story*, 1991

David Prill, *The Unnatural*, 1995

## 5168

### WILLIAM BROWNING SPENCER

## Resume with Monsters

(Sag Harbor, New York: Permanent Press, 1995)

**Story type:** Horror (Satire)
**Major character(s):** Philip Kenan, Writer; Sissy Deal, Waiter/Waitress; Lily Metcalf, Psychologist
**Time period(s):** 1990s (1995)
**Locale(s):** Austin, Texas

**Summary:** Stuck in a dead-end day job at a resume typesetting company, hopelessly in love with a woman distrustful of his financial and psychological stability, and unable to sell the 2,000-page horror novel he has been working on for decades, Philip Kenan becomes convinced that he is trapped in the indifferent mechanistic universe of H.P. Lovecraft's fiction, and that he is being stalked by Lovecraft's extradimensional monsters.

**Other books you might like:**
Scott Bradfield, *What's Wrong with America*, 1994
Fred Chappell, *The Lodger*, 1993
Christopher Moore, *Practical Demonkeeping*, 1993
John Kennedy Toole, *A Confederacy of Dunces*, 1980
Gahan Wilson, *Eddy Deco's Last Caper*, 1987

## 5169

### WILLIAM BROWNING SPENCER

## Zod Wallop

(New York: St. Martin's, 1995)

**Story type:** Horror (Mystery)
**Major character(s):** Harry Gainsborough, Writer; Raymond Story, Patient (psychiatric); Emily Engel, Patient (psychiatric)
**Time period(s):** 1990s (1995)
**Locale(s):** Austin, Texas

**Summary:** As an extension of the therapy he undergoes at the Harwood Psychiatric Institute to cope with the death of his young daughter, Harry Gainsborough is encouraged to publish *Zod Wallop*, an unorthodox childrens book with morbid overtones. After his release from the clinic, Harry is confronted by escaped schizophrenic inmate Raymond Story, who tells him that the characters of his novel, all based on people Harry knew while institutionalized, have invaded reality, and that Harry must help him avert the fates they are destined to meet as the result of Harry's plot.

**Other books you might like:**
Fredric Brown, *What Mad Universe*, 1949
Jonathan Carroll, *The Land of Laughs*, 1980
Stephen King, *The Dark Half*, 1988

## 5170

### NORMAN SPINRAD

## The Children of Hamelin

(Houston, Texas: Tafford Publishing, 1991)

**Story type:** Science Fiction (Contemporary Realism)
**Major character(s):** Tom Hollander, Editor, Hippie; Harvey Brustein, Cult Member (psychology cult leader); Arlene Cooper, Writer (aspiring)

**Time period(s):** 1960s
**Locale(s):** New York, New York (Greenwich Village)

**Summary:** A thematic prequel to *The Mind Game* (1980), *The Children of Hamelin* looks at the mechanics of addiction, specifically a cult. The hero, Tom Hollander, managed to kick heroin and knows an addiction when he sees it. So when two friends, Ted and Doris, get involved in the Foundation for Total Consciousness, Tom follows them into a strange trip across the underground of '60s America, headed toward enlightenment or death. Portions of this book were serialized in slightly different forms in *The Los Angeles Free Press* and *The Staff*.

**Other books you might like:**
Chester Anderson, *The Butterfly Kid*, 1967
Pat Cadigan, *Mindplayers*, 1991
Mick Farren, *The Texts of Festival*, 1975
Michael Kurland, *The Unicorn Girl*, 1969
George R.R. Martin, *The Armageddon Rag*, 1983
T.A. Waters, *The Probability Pad*, 1970
Robert Shea, *The Illuminatus! Trilogy*, 1988
    Robert Anton Wilson, co-author

**5171**

### NORMAN SPINRAD

## Deus X

(New York: Bantam Spectra, 1993)

**Story type:** Science Fiction (Alternate Intelligence; Theological)
**Major character(s):** Marley Philippe, Detective—Private; Father "Deus X" De Leone, Artificial Intelligence, Experimental Subject
**Time period(s):** 21st century
**Locale(s):** Earth; The Big Board, Cyberspace (cyberspace); *Mellow Yellow*, At Sea

**Summary:** Intent on investigating immortal souls and the nature of consciousness holograms created from living humans, Pope Mary I orders dying Father De Leone to explore the computer phenomenon. When he disappears, the Pontiff hires Marley Philippe to find the kidnapped artificial intelligence and return it to the Vatican computer.

**Other books you might like:**
Isaac Asimov, *The Bicentennial Man*, 1993
    Robert Silverberg, co-author
Pat Cadigan, *Fools*, 1992
Pat Cadigan, *Synners*, 1991
Brian Daley, *Tron*, 1982
Jean Mark Gawron, *Dream of Glass*, 1993
Clifford D. Simak, *Project Pope*, 1981
Neal Stephenson, *Snow Crash*, 1992

**5172**

### NORMAN SPINRAD

## Journals of the Plague Years

(New York: Bantam Spectra, 1995)

**Story type:** Science Fiction (Post-Disaster; Dystopian)
**Major character(s):** Richard Bruno, Scientist (genetic synthesizer), Criminal; Linda Lewin, Religious, Criminal; Walter T. Bigelow, Political Figure, Administrator (Federal Quarantine Agency)
**Time period(s):** 22nd century
**Locale(s):** Palo Alto, California; San Francisco, California; Washington, District of Columbia

**Summary:** Richard Bruno's investigation into AIDS immunization leads to his discovery of a cure and permanent protection from all forms of AIDS, now ravaging America. Unfortunately, its distribution would bankrupt Bruno's employer. Seeing herself as a divine agent, Linda Lewin spreads AIDS with illegal sexual contact, while Walter Bigelow seeks to confine plague sufferers, as he believes God intends.

**Other books you might like:**
Greg Bear, *Blood Music*, 1985
Michael Conner, *Archangel*, 1995
Nicola Griffith, *Ammonite*, 1993
Frank Herbert, *The White Plague*, 1982
Dan Simmons, *Children of the Night*, 1992
Joan Slonczewski, *A Door into Ocean*, 1986

**5173**

### NORMAN SPINRAD

## Pictures at 11

(New York: Bantam Spectra, 1994)

**Story type:** Science Fiction (Contemporary Realism)
**Major character(s):** Toby Inman, Television Personality, Journalist; Edward "Eddie" Franker, Television (KLAX-TV station manager); Carl Mendoza, Television Personality (sportscaster)
**Time period(s):** 1990s
**Locale(s):** Los Angeles, California

**Summary:** KLAX-TV newscasters find themselves broadcasting a violent ecoterrorist group's attempt to publicize their cause when the group takes over the KLAX newsroom and wires the building to explode.

**Other books you might like:**
Wilhelmina Baird, *Crashcourse*, 1993
David Brin, *Earth*, 1990
John Brunner, *Stand on Zanzibar*, 1968
Philip K. Dick, *A Scanner Darkly*, 1977
William C. Dietz, *Matrix Man*, 1990

**5174**

### NORMAN SPINRAD

## Russian Spring

(New York: Bantam, 1991)

**Story type:** Science Fiction (Political)
**Major character(s):** Jerry Reed, Scientist (space); Sonya Ivanova, Linguist (translator), Political Figure; Ilya Pashikov, Political Figure
**Time period(s):** 1990s
**Locale(s):** Paris, France; Brussels, Belgium

**Summary:** Jerry left the USA for Paris to work at the European Space Agency because he had no chance to get into space working on the Battle Star program. Russia has joined the European Common Market and the USA may be planning a new Vietnam-type war in South America as a stop-gap solution to its economic woes. World war and global disaster may be on the horizon.

**Other books you might like:**
Margaret Wander Bonanno, *The Others*, 1990
David Brin, *Earth*, 1990
Peter George, *Dr. Strangelove*, 1964
Peter Bryant, *Red Alert*, 1959
    Bryant is a pseudonym of Peter George

Paul Myron Anthony Linebarger, *Atomsk*, 1949
    as Carmichael Smith
Larry Niven, *Achilles' Choice*, 1991
    Steven Barnes, co-author
L. Neil Smith, *Contact and Commune*, 1990
Sheri S. Tepper, *Raising the Stones*, 1990

---

**5175**

### NORMAN SPINRAD

## Vampire Junkies

(Brooklyn, New York: Gryphon Publications, 1994)

**Story type:** Horror (Vampire Story)
**Major character(s):** Vlad Dracul, Vampire (Count Dracula); Little Mary Sunshine, Prostitute
**Time period(s):** 1990s (1994)
**Locale(s):** New York, New York

**Summary:** Originally published in *Tomorrow* magazine in 1993, this novella chronicles the co-dependency that develops between Count Dracula and a heroin-addicted hooker he bites. Having passed on their habits to one another, each becomes a supplier for the other.

**Other books you might like:**
Poppy Z. Brite, *Lost Souls*, 1992
Ray Garton, *Live Girls*, 1987
Nancy Kilpatrick, *Sex and the Single Vampire*, 1994
John Skipp, *The Light at the End*, 1986
    Craig Spector, co-author

---

**5176**

### NANCY SPRINGER

## Apocalypse

(New York: Baen, 1989)

**Story type:** Fantasy (Horror)
**Major character(s):** Joanie Musser, Witch; Cally Wilmore, Housewife (Anorexic; frustrated)
**Time period(s):** Indeterminate Future
**Locale(s):** Hoadley, Pennsylvania

**Summary:** A beautiful woman comes to Hoadley, a town filled with dark secrets, and offers a kind of satanic salvation. With seemingly little effort, the woman manages to make a grim reality even worse. Cally must find the strength to confront the devil and save Hoadley.

**Other books you might like:**
Bentley Little, *The Revelation*, 1990
R.A. MacAvoy, *Tea with the Black Dragon*, 1983
Sandra Miesel, *Shaman*, 1989
Diana L. Paxson, *Brisingamen*, 1984
Tom Reamy, *Blind Voices*, 1978

---

**5177**

### NANCY SPRINGER

## Damnbanna

(Eugene, Oregon: Pulphouse Publishing Axolotl Press, 1992)

**Story type:** Fantasy (Contemporary; Religious)
**Major character(s):** Angel, Student—High School, Sports Figure; "Damnbanna" Deil, Musician, Student—High School; McCready, Teacher, Criminal
**Time period(s):** 1990s

**Locale(s):** United States
**Summary:** Against her parents' wishes, Angel pursues her budding romance with Deil after he rescues her from a dog attack and sexual assault by a high school teacher.

**Other books you might like:**
Gael Baudino, *Gossamer Axe*, 1990
Louise Cooper, *The Sleep of Stone*, 1991
Megan Lindholm, *Cloven Hooves*, 1991
Mary Alexander Walker, *The Scathach and the Maeve's Daughter*, 1990
Kate Wilhelm, *State of Grace*, 1991

---

**5178**

### NANCY SPRINGER

## Fair Peril

(New York: Avon, 1996)

**Story type:** Fantasy (Contemporary; Legend)
**Major character(s):** Buffy Murphy, Storyteller; Adamus d'Aurca, Royalty (prince), Animal (frog); Emily Murphy, Teenager
**Time period(s):** 1990s
**Locale(s):** Pennsylvania; Fair Peril, Mythical Place

**Summary:** Recently divorced and unemployed, Buffy Murphy finds a talking frog which she refuses to kiss. When her daughter and the frog disappear, Buffy, out of shape and harassed, needs to face the mall and Fair Peril to get Emily back.

**Other books you might like:**
Eleanor Arnason, *Daughter of the Bear King*, 1987
John Barnes, *One for the Morning Glory*, 1996
Pamela Dean, *Tam Lin*, 1991
William Goldman, *The Princess Bride*, 1973
John Myers Myers, *Silverlock*, 1949

---

**5179**

### NANCY SPRINGER

## The Friendship Song

(New York: Atheneum, 1992)

**Story type:** Fantasy (Young Adult; Urban)
**Major character(s):** Harper Feree, Child, Hero; Rawnie Stello, Child, Hero; Gus "Aengus Mac Og" McCogg, Artist, Mythical Creature (master of the afterworlds)
**Time period(s):** 1990s
**Locale(s):** United States; The Afterworlds, Mythical Place (afterlife shadowland)

**Summary:** When Harper's father decides to marry a folk artist, Harper must adjust to new family, friends, house and school. An early adventure with Rawnie yields insight into the neighborhood mystery surrounding late night lights and music coming from Harper's labyrinthian back yard. When Harper's friendship with white supremacists threatens Harper and Rawnie's friendship, an upcoming rock concert presents an opportunity to repair their relationship then together venture into the afterlife to rescue a band member from death.

**Other books you might like:**
Gael Baudino, *Gossamer Axe*, 1990
Emma Bull, *Bone Dance: A Fantasy for Technophiles*, 1991
Emma Bull, *War for the Oaks*, 1987
Mercedes Lackey, *Bardic Voices*, 1991
Will Shetterly, *Elsewhere*, 1991
Andrea Shettle, *Flute Song Magic*, 1990

## 5180

### NANCY SPRINGER

## *Larque on the Wing*

(New York: Morrow/AvoNova, 1994)

**Story type:** Fantasy (Contemporary; Psychic Powers)
**Major character(s):** Larque ''Lark'' Harootunian, Psychic, Artisan (home decoration products); Geoffrey ''Hoot'' Harootunian, Spouse (Larque's)
**Time period(s):** 1990s
**Locale(s):** Pennsylvania

**Summary:** Larque surprises herself and Hoot with a doppelganger of her younger self with an all-too-verbal assessment of Larque's life. To Hoot's consternation, Larque's reevaluation includes her personal transformation into a muscular teenage boy and an examination of her life and fate painful to her family.

**Other books you might like:**
A.A. Attanasio, *The Moon's Wife: A Hystery*, 1993
Octavia E. Butler, *Kindred*, 1979
Charles de Lint, *Memory and Dream*, 1994
Megan Lindholm, *Cloven Hooves*, 1991
Marge Piercy, *Woman on the Edge of Time*, 1976

## 5181

### NANCY SPRINGER

## *Metal Angel*

(New York: Roc, 1994)

**Story type:** Fantasy (Contemporary)
**Major character(s):** Volos, Angel; Box ''Texas'' McCardle, Police Officer; Angela Bradley, Housewife, Songwriter
**Time period(s):** 1990s
**Locale(s):** Los Angeles, California; Jenkins, Pennsylvania

**Summary:** Volos, least of the angels, chooses flesh, sin, and rock music over his place in the heavenly choir. Human except for angelic wings that he cannot shed, he sings lyrics written by a housewife whose passion matches his own and he rockets to the top of the charts. But Volos' private war with God affects the lives of the humans who love him.

**Other books you might like:**
Emma Bull, *War for the Oaks*, 1987
Parke Godwin, *Waiting for the Galactic Bus*, 1987
Tanith Lee, *The Silver Metal Lover*, 1982
Will Shetterly, *Elsewhere*, 1991
Norman Spinrad, *Little Heroes*, 1987

## 5182

### NANCY SPRINGER

## *Red Wizard*

(New York: Atheneum, 1990)

**Story type:** Fantasy (Alternate World)
**Major character(s):** Ryan De Witt, Student—Junior High School (seventh grade); Persyvaunce, Wizard
**Time period(s):** 1990s
**Locale(s):** Alternate Universe; United States

**Summary:** While on summer vacation with his parents, Ryan is magically transported into another world when a bumbling wizard's spell misfires. While there, Ryan must experience a series of adven-

tures and help defeat an evil king before he can return to his own world.

**Other books you might like:**
Ellen Conford, *Genie with the Light Blue Hair*, 1989
Pamela Dean, *The Secret Country*, 1986
   The Secret Country Trilogy - Book 1
Pamela Dean, *The Whim of the Dragon*, 1989
C.S. Lewis, *The Lion, the Witch, and the Wardrobe*,
Shirley Rousseau Murphy, *Medallion of the Black Hound*, 1989
   Welch Suggs, co-author

## 5183

### STEVEN SPRUILL

## *Daughter of Darkness*

(New York: Doubleday, 1997)

**Story type:** Horror (Vampire Story)
**Major character(s):** Jenn Hrluska, Doctor; Merrick Chapman, Detective—Police; Zane Chapman, Vampire
**Time period(s):** 1990s
**Locale(s):** Washington, District of Columbia

**Summary:** Zane Chapman, a hemophage with a hereditary craving for blood, escapes from the concrete bunker his father imprisoned him in a decade before, and attempts to seduce his daughter Jenn, a successful pediatrician who hitherto has resisted the vampiric calling of her blood, to his way. A sequel to *Rulers of Darkness* (1995).

**Other books you might like:**
Scott Baker, *Ancestral Hungers*, 1995
Poppy Z. Brite, *Lost Souls*, 1992
Mark Burnell, *Glittering Savages*, 1995
Brian Stableford, *Young Blood*, 1991

## 5184

### STEVEN SPRUILL

## *My Soul to Take*

(New York: St. Martin's, 1994)

**Story type:** Science Fiction (Techno-Thriller; Medical)
**Major character(s):** Suzannah Lord, Doctor (surgeon); Andrew Dugan, Artist; Jay Mallernee, Journalist
**Time period(s):** 1990s
**Locale(s):** Washington, District of Columbia

**Summary:** Suzannah finds Andrew's request to remove from his brain the implant permitting him to see very disturbing. She had inserted many of the experimental devices while a resident, removal leads to blindness, and FDA approval seems imminent. Unable legally to remove to the implant, Suzannah, perhaps the only surgeon capable of saving any sight for the patients if the implants must be removed, finds that the implants indeed cause the user to see the future, and that some government agency wants them, and her.

**Other books you might like:**
Pat Cadigan, *Fools*, 1992
Pat Cadigan, *Synners*, 1991
Mickey Zucker Reichert, *The Unknown Soldier*, 1994
Mike Resnick, *Soothsayer*, 1991
Kate Wilhelm, *The Clewiston Test*, 1976

## 5185
### STEVEN SPRUILL
## *Rulers of Darkness*
(New York: St. Martin's, 1995)

**Story type:** Horror (Mystery; Vampire Story)
**Major character(s):** Katie O'Keefe, Doctor (hematologist); Merrick Chapman, Detective, Vampire; Zane Chapman, Vampire
**Time period(s):** 1990s (1995)
**Locale(s):** Washington, District of Columbia

**Summary:** A rash of vampire-type deaths in Washington, D.C. leads to the blowing of the cover of 900-year-old "hemophage" Merrick Chapman, a vampire who has devoted his long existence to tracking down and disposing of other hemophages. The picture is complicated by the revelation that the murderer is Chapman's son Vane, and by the existence of other children Chapman has sired and people he has turned into hemophages in order to save their lives.

**Other books you might like:**
Mark Burnell, *Glittering Savages*, 1995
Roxanne Longstreet, *The Undead*, 1993
Brian Stableford, *The Empire of Fear*, 1988

## 5186
### RILEY ST. JAMES
## *In the Shadows of the Moonglade*
(Tustin, California: ShadowCrest Publications, 1998)

**Major character(s):** Fletcher McKeane, Photojournalist; Jennifer Jaynes, Pilot; Christopher Wilkinson, Artist (painter)
**Time period(s):** 1990s (1997); 1830s
**Locale(s):** Newport Beach, California; London, England

**Summary:** Fletcher McKeane sees his new romance with Jennifer as an end to the deaths and tragedies that have hitherto dominated his life. But their romance is troubled by ghosts of the past, reincarnation, and satanic intrigues that must be laid to rest in a London graveyard, where they were initiated a century and a half before. A first novel.

**Other books you might like:**
John Coyne, *Fury*, 1989
Marcy Heidish, *The Torching*, 1992
Shawn Ryan, *Brethren*, 1993
Michael Stewart, *Belladonna*, 1993
John Tigges, *The Curse*, 1993

## 5187
### DANA STABENOW
## *Red Planet Run*
(New York: Ace, 1995)

**Story type:** Science Fiction (Family Saga; Adventure)
**Series:** Star Svensdotter
**Major character(s):** Esther "Star" Svensdotter, Judge, Spacewoman; Helen Ricadonna, Businesswoman; Natasha Quijance, Parent, Storyteller
**Time period(s):** 2020s
**Locale(s):** *Outpost*, Spaceship; Mars; Asteroid Belt, Outer Space

**Summary:** When the first project of Outpost reaches completion, Star realizes that she has failed to overcome the death of her husband 12 years previously. As her team begins to split up and her 16-year-old twins pull one prank too many, Star accepts Helen's request to explore the discovery found in ancient ruins on Mars. However, an old enemy precedes her there, killing all who get in his way.

**Other books you might like:**
Greg Bear, *Moving Mars*, 1993
David Brin, *Glory Season*, 1993
Arthur C. Clarke, *The Sands of Mars*, 1952
Kim Stanley Robinson, *Green Mars*, 1994
Kim Stanley Robinson, *Red Mars*, 1993

## 5188
### DANA STABENOW
## *Second Star*
(New York: Ace, 1991)

**Story type:** Science Fiction (Space Colony)
**Major character(s):** ARCHY, Artificial Intelligence; Esther Elizabeth Quijance-Turgenev, Child (mute); Esther "Star" Svensdotter, Administrator (Space Colony)
**Time period(s):** 2010s
**Locale(s):** Ellfive, Space Station; Copernicus, Montenegro

**Summary:** After fifteen years of construction, Ellfive is weeks from receiving its first shipment of colonists. Star Svensdotter, in charge from the beginning of construction, realizes a take-over attempt could occur before any colonists arrive. Conditions on Earth are worsening and it's rumored that another message from Betelgeuse has been intercepted by the Russians on Mars.

**Other books you might like:**
Roger MacBride Allen, *The Ring of Charon*, 1990
C.J. Cherryh, *Rimrunners*, 1989
Vonda N. McIntyre, *Starfarers*, 1989
Paul Preuss, *Starfire*, 1988
Mack Reynolds, *Chaos in Lagrangia*, 1984
Mack Reynolds, *Lagrange Five*, 1979
Allen Steele, *Clarke County, Space*, 1990
Allen Steele, *Orbital Decay*, 1989

## 5189
### BRIAN STABLEFORD
## *The Angel of Pain*
(New York: Carroll & Graf, 1993)

**Story type:** Horror (Apocalyptic Horror)
**Major character(s):** David Lydyard, Scientist; Cordelia Lydyard, Housewife; James Austen, Doctor
**Time period(s):** 1890s (1893)
**Locale(s):** London, England

**Summary:** In this sequel to the author's *The Werewolves of London*, David Lydyard, some twenty years after the events chronicled in that book, is still afflicted by dream visions of the unearthly creatures known to most human beings only through the merciful veil of myth and legend. In his efforts to understand them, David becomes embroiled in their internecine wars and is used as one of several human pawns whose conflicts with other human beings portend cataclysms of cosmic proportions.

**Other books you might like:**
Ramsey Campbell, *Midnight Sun*, 1991
H.P. Lovecraft, *At the Mountains of Madness and Other Novels*, 1964
Kim Newman, *Sago*, 1991

## 5190

**BRIAN STABLEFORD**

### The Carnival of Destruction

(New York: Carroll & Graf, 1994)

**Story type:** Horror (Apocalyptic Horror)
**Major character(s):** Anatole Daumier, Military Personnel (soldier); David Lydyard, Scientist; Jacob Harkender, Supernatural Being
**Time period(s):** 1910s (1918)
**Locale(s):** Paris, France; London, England

**Summary:** As World War I grinds to its bloody finish and the end of the world seems imminent, the five fallen angels who have pulled the strings behind events in the author's earlier novels *The Werewolves of London* and *The Angel of Pain* begin jockeying for power. This ambitious novel has them marshaling their human consorts and supernatural creations to fight climactic battles, and awaiting the revelation of the identities of two other angels which will determine how the balance of power shall fall.

**Other books you might like:**
Clive Barker, *Everville*, 1994
Clive Barker, *The Great and Secret Show*, 1990
Stephen King, *The Stand*, 1978
Robert R. McCammon, *Swan Song*, 1987
Anne Rice, *Memnoch the Devil*, 1995
Alan Rodgers, *Fire*, 1992

## 5191

**BRIAN STABLEFORD**

### The Empire of Fear

(New York: Carroll & Graf, 1991)

**Story type:** Horror (Vampire Story)
**Major character(s):** Noell Cordery, Scientist; Richard Lionheart, Royalty (king of Grand Normandy); Vlad Tepes, Warrior, Vampire (Dracula)
**Time period(s):** 18th century
**Locale(s):** New Normandy, Fictional Country

**Summary:** In an alternate universe, nobles and world leaders are Machiavellian vampires who subjugate the masses by manipulating their superstitions. Convinced that there is a scientific basis by which vampirism can be understood and neutralized, and determined to avenge his father's death at the hands of the vampire court of New Normandy, Noell Cordery sets off for Africa, reputed site of the vampires' origins, all the while pursued by a vampire armada that would suppress his discoveries. This novel was originally published in England in 1988.

**Other books you might like:**
Les Daniels, *The Chronicles of Don Sebastian*, 1978-1990
Anne Rice, *The Vampire Chronicles*, 1976-1988
Michael Romkey, *I, Vampire*, 1990
Chelsea Quinn Yarbro, *The Saint-Germain Chronicles*, 1983

## 5192

**BRIAN STABLEFORD**

### The Hunger and Ecstasy of Vampires

(Shingletown, California: Mark V. Ziesing, 1996)

**Story type:** Horror (Vampire Story; Science Fiction)
**Major character(s):** Edward Copplestone, Scientist; Oscar Wilde, Writer, Historical Figure; Count Lugard, Nobleman
**Time period(s):** 1890s (1895)
**Locale(s):** London, England

**Summary:** In this mixture of fantasy and the classic scientific romance, a gentleman's club whose members include H.G. Wells, Oscar Wilde, M.P. Shiel, and other writers and thinkers of the Victorian era convenes one night to hear scientist Edward Copplestone tell of three drug-induced trances in which he travelled into the far future and discovered mankind under the rule of benevolent vampires who have helped save the human species from itself. Unknown to those gathered, one in their midst who hears this story will be instrumental in engineering this future.

**Other books you might like:**
Emmanuel Carrere, *Gothic Romance*, 1990
Kim Newman, *Anno Dracula*, 1992
Kathryn Ptacek, *In Silence Sealed*, 1988
H.G. Wells, *The Time Machine*, 1895

## 5193

**BRIAN STABLEFORD**

### Inherit the Earth

(New York: Tor, 1998)

**Story type:** Science Fiction (Post-Disaster)
**Major character(s):** Conrad Helier, Scientist; Damon Hart, Artist (virtual reality)
**Time period(s):** 22nd century
**Locale(s):** United States

**Summary:** After the Plague Wars, the survivors enjoy good health thanks to nanotechnology. Damon Hart, who creates virtual reality programs, is the son of Conrad Helier, a famous scientist now presumed dead. When terrorists begin killing Hart's friends, he discovers that his father is still alive, secretly opposing a worldwide conspiracy.

**Other books you might like:**
Ben Bova, *Peacekeepers*, 1988
John Brunner, *Stand on Zanzibar*, 1968
Philip Jose Farmer, *Dayworld Rebel*, 1988
Nancy Kress, *Brain Rose*, 1990
Robert Silverberg, *Tom O'Bedlam*, 1985

## 5194

**BRIAN STABLEFORD**

### The Innsmouth Heritage

(West Warwick, Rhode Island: Necronomicon Press, 1992)

**Story type:** Horror (Science Fiction)
**Major character(s):** Ann Eliot, Writer; David Stevenson, Scientist (biochemist); Gideon Sargent, Fisherman
**Time period(s):** 1990s
**Locale(s):** Innsmouth, Massachusetts

**Summary:** In this sequel to H.P. Lovecraft's classic novella, "The Shadow over Innsmouth," David Stevenson arrives in Innsmouth to study the genetic heritage of the Innsmouth natives, convinced that he will find their peculiar physical traits and degeneration a byproduct of inbreeding. Instead, he finds evidence that suggests forces more supernatural than scientifically provable may be involved.

**Other books you might like:**
Steve Rasnic Tem, *Decoded Mirrors: Three Tales after Lovecraft*, 1992
F. Paul Wilson, *The Barrens*, 1992

## 5195

### BRIAN STABLEFORD

## The Walking Shadow

(New York: Carroll & Graff, 1989)

**Story type:** Science Fiction (Time Travel)
**Major character(s):** Paul Heisenberg, Religious (Evangelist); Adam Wishart, Public Relations
**Time period(s):** Indeterminate Future
**Locale(s):** Earth

**Summary:** Evangelist Paul Heisenberg appears to have the ability to move himself and his disciples through time, purely through the power of prayer. Originally published in 1979.

**Other books you might like:**
Mike McQuay, *Memories*, 1987
Michael Moorcock, *Behold the Man*, 1964
James Morrow, *Only Begotten Daughter*, 1990
Ted Reynolds, *The Tides of God*, 1989
Robert Silverberg, *The Masks of Time*, 1968

## 5196

### BRIAN STABLEFORD

## The Werewolves of London

(New York: Carroll & Graf, 1992)

**Story type:** Horror (Werewolf Story; Ancient Evil Unleashed)
**Major character(s):** David Lydyard, Young Man; Sir Edward Tellentyre, Scientist; Gabriel Gill, Child
**Time period(s):** 1870s (1872)
**Locale(s):** London, England; Egypt

**Summary:** While travelling through a burial site in Egypt David Lydyard falls victim to a snake bite that induces apocalyptic visions. At the same time, Gabriel Gill is abducted from a London orphanage by a group of Shapeshifters who hope to exploit his nascent occult powers. Together, Lydyard's and Gill's experiences serve as portents of an ancient and immortal force erupting into our dimension and threatening the world. This novel was originally published in England in 1990.

**Other books you might like:**
Daniel Easterman, *Name of the Beast*, 1992

## 5197

### MICHAEL A. STACKPOLE
### WILLIAM F. WU, Co-Author

## An Enemy Reborn

(New York: Harper, 1998)

**Story type:** Fantasy (Magic Conflict)
**Series:** Realms of Chaos
**Major character(s):** Len Fong, Salesman; Myat, Noblewoman; Shoth, Sorcerer
**Time period(s):** Indeterminate
**Locale(s):** Chaos, Mythical Place

**Summary:** An evil power gathers its forces in the region known as Chaos, preparing a war of conquest. Len Fong, a spirited but unlikely hero from our world, is recruited to lead the combined forces to two traditional enemies to end the threat and save two worlds.

**Other books you might like:**
Steven Brust, *Teckla*, 1987

Jack L. Chalker, *Vengeance of the Dancing Gods*, 1985
Glen Cook, *Bleak Seasons*, 1996
Thomas K. Martin, *A Matter of Honor*, 1994
Andrew J. Offutt, *My Lord Barbarian*, 1977

## 5198

### MICHAEL A. STACKPOLE

## Evil Ascending

(Bloomington, Illinois: GDW Books, 1991)

**Story type:** Science Fiction (Invasion of Earth; Mystery)
**Series:** Fiddleback Trilogy
**Major character(s):** Tycho Caine, Amnesiac, Imposter
**Time period(s):** 21st century
**Locale(s):** Kanggenpo, Tibet; Tokyo, Japan

**Summary:** Investigating the invasion of Earth by Fiddleback, a monstrous intelligence from another dimension, Tycho Caine takes the name of his benefactor, Coyote, and sends Sinclair MacNeal to Tokyo to find Fiddleback's training school for assassins. Caine travels to Tibet to recover his memory and mastery of his skills while Rajani, reawakened from suspended animation, pursues her own goal of repelling Fiddleback's invasion. This novel is set in the universe of the roleplaying game *Dark Conspiracy*.

**Other books you might like:**
William Adams, *The Unwound Way*, 1991
Marc Laidlaw, *Neon Lotus*, 1988
Frank M. Robinson, *The Dark Beyond the Stars*, 1991
Elizabeth Ann Scarborough, *Nothing Sacred*, 1991
Michael Swanwick, *Vacuum Flowers*, 1987

## 5199

### MICHAEL A. STACKPOLE

## Evil Triumphant

(Bloomington, Illinois: GDW Books, 1992)

**Story type:** Science Fiction (Invasion of Earth; Adventure)
**Series:** Fiddleback Trilogy
**Major character(s):** Tycho Caine, Criminal (assassin), Hero; Damon Crowley, Warrior, Hero; Nicholas ''Pygmalion'' Hunt, Mythical Creature (Dark Lord)
**Time period(s):** 2010s (2010)
**Locale(s):** Phoenix, Arizona; Titan's Dimension, Mythical Place

**Summary:** Through many dimensions Coyote, Crowley and Jyette struggle and treacherously change alliances to prevent Pygmalion, Fiddleback and other Dark Lords from capturing the greatest prize, Earth. Set in the universe of the role-playing game, *Dark Conspiracy*.

**Other books you might like:**
Alan Dean Foster, *Cyber Way*, 1990
Alan Dean Foster, *To the Vanishing Point*, 1988
Marc Laidlaw, *Neon Lotus*, 1988
Elizabeth Ann Scarborough, *Final Refuge*, 1992

## 5200

### MICHAEL A. STACKPOLE

## Eyes of Silver

(New York: Bantam Spectra, 1998)

**Story type:** Fantasy (Political; Adventure)

**Major character(s):** Malachy Kidd, Religious, Warrior; Rafiq Khast, Warrior (nomad); Natalya Ohanscai, Royalty (princess)
**Time period(s):** Indeterminate
**Locale(s):** Helansajar, Fictional Country; Aran, Fictional Country

**Summary:** Centuries after a great warrior conquers a vast empire, nations struggle over its remnants. While Rafiq Khast fights to regain his homeland and family honor and events sweep Natalya into a pivotal role, Malachy Kidd and his powerful battlemagicks may determine the fate of the entire world.

**Other books you might like:**
C.J. Cherryh, *Fortress in the Eye of Time*, 1995
David Gemmell, *Morningstar*, 1993
Andre Norton, *Mirror of Destiny*, 1995
R.A. Salvatore, *The Sword of Bedwyr*, 1995
Michelle West, *The Broken Crown*, 1997

---

**5201**

**MICHAEL A. STACKPOLE**

## A Gathering Evil

(Bloomington, Illinois: GDW Books, 1991)

**Story type:** Science Fiction (Invasion of Earth; Mystery)
**Series:** Fiddleback Trilogy
**Major character(s):** Tycho Caine, Amnesiac
**Time period(s):** 21st century
**Locale(s):** Phoenix, Arizona

**Summary:** When Tycho Caine wakes up in a body bag, ready to supply parts for transplantation, he has to overcome his captors and escape before beginning the search for his lost memory and mission. His quest leads from the poverty-stricken ground-level Phoenix into the restricted city above, where he learns his employer may have double-crossed him with deadly intent. This novel is set in the universe of the role-playing game *Dark Conspiracy*.

**Other books you might like:**
William Adams, *The Unwound Way*, 1991
  Cecil Brooks, co-author
Jeffrey A. Carver, *From a Changeling Star*, 1989
Dave Duncan, *Hero*, 1991
Frank M. Robinson, *The Dark Beyond the Stars*, 1991
Michael Swanwick, *Vacuum Flowers*, 1987

---

**5202**

**MICHAEL A. STACKPOLE**

## A Hero Born

(New York: HarperPrism, 1997)

**Story type:** Fantasy (Sword and Sorcery)
**Series:** Realms of Chaos
**Major character(s):** Lachlan ''Locke'', Military Personnel; Kit, Military Personnel
**Time period(s):** Indeterminate
**Locale(s):** City of Sorcerers, Fictional City

**Summary:** Locke dreams of becoming a Chaos Rider and seeking his father in the Wildness beyond the Wall, little expecting the evil forces waiting there to snare him.

**Other books you might like:**
David Gemmell, *Morningstar*, 1993
Terry Goodkind, *Wizard's First Rule*, 1994
Robin Hobb, *Assassin's Apprentice*, 1995
Mercedes Lackey, *Arrows of the Queen*, 1987
Elizabeth Moon, *Sheepfarmer's Daughter*, 1988

---

**5203**

**MICHAEL A. STACKPOLE**

## Once a Hero

(New York: Bantam Spectra, 1994)

**Story type:** Fantasy (Adventure; Political)
**Major character(s):** Neal ''Dun Wolf'' Roclawzi, Warrior; Genevera ''Gena'', Mythical Creature (elf), Warrior; Aarundel, Mythical Creature (elf), Warrior
**Time period(s):** Indeterminate
**Locale(s):** Skirren, Planet—Imaginary; Ispar, Fictional Country; Elven Holdings, Fictional Country

**Summary:** With his deadly sword, Neal Roclawzi helps free humanity from tyrannical Reithrese rule, reconciling feuding families and bringing about a unified government. When disharmony threatens 500 years later, Gena brings Neal to life from his ensorcelled tomb to help save the empire.

**Other books you might like:**
Robert N. Charrette, *A Prince Among Men*, 1994
Glen Cook, *The Black Company*, 1984
David Eddings, *Pawn of Prophecy*, 1982
Mary Gentle, *Rats and Gargoyles*, 1991
Terry Goodkind, *Wizard's First Rule*, 1994
Simon Hawke, *The Wizard of Camelot*, 1993
P.C. Hodgell, *God Stalk*, 1982
Robert Jordan, *The Eye of the World*, 1989
Dennis L. McKiernan, *The Eye of the Hunter*, 1992

---

**5204**

**MICHAEL A. STACKPOLE**

## Prince of Havoc

(New York: Roc, 1998)

**Story type:** Science Fiction (Military)
**Series:** Battletech
**Major character(s):** Victor Steiner-Davion, Military Personnel, Royalty (prince); Katrina Steiner, Noblewoman
**Time period(s):** Indeterminate Future
**Locale(s):** Strana Mechty, Planet—Imaginary

**Summary:** A vast interstellar war nears its end. Prince Victor leads his armies against the hostile clans, striking at their home worlds in what should finally bring peace. Unfortunately, his sister assumed control of the government while he was away, and she uses military force to oppose his return to power.

**Other books you might like:**
Bruce Balfour, *Star Crusader*, 1995
William R. Forstchen, *Action Stations*, 1998
Stephen Goldin, *The Eternity Brigade*, 1980
William H. Keith Jr., *Bolo Brigade*, 1997
Jack McKinney, *End of the Circle*, 1990

---

**5205**

**MICHAEL A. STACKPOLE**

## Rogue Squadron

(New York: Bantam Spectra, 1996)

**Story type:** Science Fiction (Military; Space Opera)
**Series:** Star Wars: X-Wing

**Major character(s):** Wedge Antilles, Military Personnel, Pilot (X-wing fighter); Corran Horn, Military Personnel, Pilot (X-wing fighter)
**Time period(s):** Indeterminate Past
**Locale(s):** Galactic Empire, Interstellar Empire/Federation; New Republic, Interstellar Empire/Federation

**Summary:** Determined to defend the fledgling New Republic from the mighty Galactic Empire, Wedge Antilles organizes Rogue Squadron, a force of X-wing fighters piloted by the best warriors. However, the Rogue Squadron may meet its match when orders send them to assault the Imperial stronghold of Black Moon.

**Other books you might like:**
Roger MacBride Allen, *Ambush at Corellia*, 1995
Kevin J. Anderson, *Jedi Search*, 1994
George Lucas, *The Star Wars Trilogy*, 1987
    Donald F. Glut, James Kahn, co-authors
Steve Perry, *Shadows of the Empire*, 1996
Timothy Zahn, *Heir to the Empire*, 1991

---

**5206**

MICHAEL A. STACKPOLE

*Talion: Revenant*

(New York: Bantam Spectra, 1997)

**Story type:** Fantasy (Political; Adventure)
**Major character(s):** Nolan ra Sinjaria, Lawman (Talion), Wizard; Morai, Criminal (bandit); Tirrell, Ruler (king)
**Time period(s):** Indeterminate Past
**Locale(s):** Hamis, Fictional Country

**Summary:** His family destroyed by war, Nolan flees to Talianna to become a Justice. Sent home to protect the man whose armies crushed his nation and family, Nolan must choose between orders and revenge if he desires true justice.

**Other books you might like:**
Glen Cook, *The Black Company*, 1984
Barbara Hambly, *The Ladies of Mandrigyn*, 1984
Guy Gavriel Kay, *Tigana*, 1990
Fritz Leiber, *Ill Met in Lankhmar*, 1995
Michael Scott Rohan, *The Forge in the Forest*, 1986

---

**5207**

MICHAEL A. STACKPOLE

*Wolf and Raven*

(New York: Roc, 1998)

**Story type:** Fantasy (Magic Conflict)
**Series:** Shadowrun
**Major character(s):** Wolfgang Kies, Vigilante, Shaman; Dr. Richard Raven, Vigilante; Etienne La Plante, Criminal
**Time period(s):** 2050s (2057)
**Locale(s):** Seattle, Washington

**Summary:** A shaman joins forces with a man who has devoted his life to battling the criminal element in a magical version of Seattle. The local crimelord opposes them with a virtual army of thugs, human and otherwise, none of whom prove capable of standing up to the supernatural fury which sometimes escapes the shaman's control.

**Other books you might like:**
Robert N. Charrette, *Just Compensation*, 1996
Raymond E. Feist, *Faerie Tale*, 1988
Lisa Smedman, *The Lucifer Deck*, 1997
Nyx Smith, *Fade to Black*, 1994

Lawrence Watt-Evans, *The Reign of the Brown Magician*, 1996

---

**5208**

KATHLYN S. STARBUCK

*India's Story*

(New York: HarperPrism, 1995)

**Story type:** Science Fiction (Psychic Powers; Political)
**Major character(s):** India Gilbert, Psychic (esper), Student; Anara, Innkeeper, Teacher; Mama, Monster, Mythical Creature (arachnid)
**Time period(s):** Indeterminate Future
**Locale(s):** Giles Three, Planet—Imaginary (Orion Sector); No-Place, Mythical Place (interdimensional plane); Continental Americas, Fictional Country

**Summary:** India grows up as the abused daughter of a big-time criminal. Her psychic abilities tapped and blocked by an unknown Agency, India makes her way past Mama to the inn between dimensions managed by Anara. At the inn, India begins to regain some memories and some psychic powers, but the threat remains. India must uncover the plot against her to regain her strength and identity. Originally published in the United Kingdom in 1993.

**Other books you might like:**
Jeffrey A. Carver, *Down the Stream of Stars*, 1990
John DeChancie, *Castle Perilous*, 1988
Alan Dean Foster, *To the Vanishing Point*, 1988
Anne McCaffrey, *To Ride Pegasus*, 1973
Michaela Roessner, *Vanishing Point*, 1993

---

**5209**

STARHAWK (Pseudonym of Miriam Simos)

*The Fifth Sacred Thing*

(New York: Bantam, 1993)

**Story type:** Fantasy (Post-Disaster; Psychic Powers)
**Major character(s):** Maya, Religious, Grandparent; Madrone, Healer, Revolutionary; Bird, Revolutionary, Leader
**Time period(s):** 2040s (2048)
**Locale(s):** California

**Summary:** In an ecologically transformed 21st century, the nation state in Northern California esteems harmony with the environment while the regime of religious extremists in Southern California fosters repression of women and control of scarce vital resources. When Bird escapes prison and returns to the North with news of an impending attack from the South, Madrone travels south to help resistance forces and attempts to discover a cure for the plagues she thinks originated as an attack from the southerners. First novel.

**Other books you might like:**
David Brin, *Earth*, 1990
Jennifer DiMarco, *Escape to the Wind*, 1991
Suzette Haden Elgin, *Native Tongue*, 1984
Steve Erickson, *Arc d'X*, 1993
Marc Laidlaw, *Kalifornia*, 1993
Pat Murphy, *The City, Not Long After*, 1989
Larry Niven, *Fallen Angels*, 1991
    Jerry Pournelle, Michael Flynn, co-authors
Joan Slonczewski, *A Door into Ocean*, 1986
Jean Stewart, *Return to Isis*, 1992
Sheri S. Tepper, *The Gate to Women's Country*, 1988
Karen Wehrstein, *Lion's Heart*, 1991
Karen Wehrstein, *Lion's Soul*, 1991

## 5210

**ED STARK**, Editor

### Mysterious Cairo

(Honesdale, Pennsylvania: West End Games, 1992)

**Story type:** Fantasy (Anthology)
**Series:** Torg: The Possibility Wars
**Time period(s):** 21st century
**Locale(s):** Nile Empire, Alternate Earth (Cairo)

**Summary:** This volume contains an eight-page introduction by Ed Stark plus 11 stories by six authors sharing a modern world combining elements of ancient Egypt and 1930s heroic pulp fiction. Set in the universe of the game, *Torg*.

**Other books you might like:**
George Alec Effinger, *When Gravity Fails*, 1987
Greg Farshtey, *Strange Tales From the Nile Empire*, 1992
   Greg Gorden and Ed Stark, co-editors
Douglas Kaufman, *Dragons over England*, 1992
   Ed Stark, co-editor
Will Shetterly, *Liavek*, 1985
   Emma Bull, co-editor
Will Shetterly, *Liavek: Wizard's Row*, 1987
   Emma Bull, co-editor
Bill Slavicsek, *Storm Knights*, 1990
   C.J. Tramontana, co-author

## 5211

**KIRT STARK**

### 13 Haunting Ghost Tales

(Apache Junction, Arizona: Dark Woods Publishing, 1998)

**Story type:** Horror (Collection)

**Summary:** A first collection of thirteen amateurish tales of ghosts and other horrors. The stories are relatively conventional and include "Baby's Breath," in which parents discover that their newborn child has been given a doll possessed by a spirit; "Night Cries," a poignant story of a ghostly family reunion; "Sheila," in which a bereaved young man receives phone calls from his deceased girlfriend; the werewolf tale "Lycanthropy"; and "Ectoplasm," in which students in a university sponsored experiment in parapsychology discover that they can conjure up monsters out of pure thought energy.

**Other books you might like:**
Joseph Payne Brennan, *Nine Horrors and a Dream*, 1958
Ruth D. Hein, *Ghostly Tales of Iowa*, 1996
Carl Jacobi, *Smoke of the Snake*, 1994
Jessica Amanda Salmonson, *The Mysterious Doom and Other Ghostly Tales of the Pacific Northwest*, 1992
C.E. Ward, *Vengeful Ghosts*, 1998

## 5212

**JIM STARLIN**
**DAINA GRAZIUNAS**, Co-Author

### Among Madmen

(New York: Roc, 1990)

**Story type:** Science Fiction (Post-Holocaust)
**Major character(s):** Tom Laker, Lawman (sheriff); Maria Laker, Spouse, Murderer

**Time period(s):** 1990s (1990)
**Locale(s):** Shandaken County, New York

**Summary:** A mysterious disease afflicts people at random, causing some to fall into comas and others to become killers. Sheriff Tom Laker tries to provide law and order to a small rural community as civilization slowly falls apart.

**Other books you might like:**
Frank Herbert, *The White Plague*, 1982
Brian Lumley, *Necroscope*, 1988
Richard Matheson, *I Am Legend*, 1954
Walter M. Miller Jr., *A Canticle for Leibowitz*, 1960
David R. Palmer, *Emergence*, 1984
Roger Zelazny, *This Immortal*, 1966

## 5213

**JIM STARLIN**
**DAINA GRAZIUNAS**, Co-Author

### Lady El

(New York: Roc, 1992)

**Story type:** Science Fiction (Alternate Intelligence; Hard Science Fiction)
**Major character(s):** Walter "Walt" Hillerman, Scientist, Computer Expert; Arlene "Lady El" Washington, Artificial Intelligence, Experimental Subject
**Time period(s):** 1990s
**Locale(s):** New York, New York; Washington, District of Columbia (the Pentagon)

**Summary:** Killed in a subway accident, Arlene regains consciousness only to discover her brain, complete with personality, now acts as the core of a sophisticated biological/mechanical supercomputer. Horrified to find Arlene's personality intact with her brain, Walt conspires with Arlene to hide her consciousness while she assumes military and scientific tasks, creating monumental intuitive breakthroughs in fundamental science. However, Arlene's solitary attachment to Walt soon creates problems.

**Other books you might like:**
Pat Cadigan, *Fools*, 1992
Pat Cadigan, *Synners*, 1991
Robert A. Heinlein, *The Moon Is a Harsh Mistress*, 1966
Victor Milan, *The Cybernetic Samurai*, 1986
Rudy Rucker, *Software*, 1982
Cordwainer Smith, *Norstrilia*, 1975
Thomas T. Thomas, *ME: A Novel of Self Discovery*, 1991

## 5214

**CHRISTOPHER STASHEFF**, Editor
**BILL FAWCETT**, Co-Editor

### Blessings and Curses

(New York: Ace, 1992)

**Story type:** Fantasy (Anthology)
**Series:** Crafter Family
**Time period(s):** 18th century; 19th century
**Locale(s):** Canada; New England

**Summary:** Contains a prolog by Bill Fawcett plus 11 stories original to this shared history anthology of Crafter Family tales set between 1784 and 1865. Contributing authors are Judith R. Conly, Barbara Delaplace, Ru Emerson, Esther Friesner, Morgan Llywelyn, Morris G. McGee, Jody Lynn Nye, Robert Sheckley, Christopher Stasheff, Brian M. Thomsen and Wendy Wheeler.

**Other books you might like:**

Robert Asprin, *Thieves' World*, 1979
  editor

Harlan Ellison, *Medea: Harlan's World*, 1985
  editor

Martin H. Greenberg, *After the King: Stories in Honor of J.R.R. Tolkien*, 1992
  editor

George R.R. Martin, *Wild Cards*, 1987
  editor

Will Shetterly, *Liavek*, 1985
  Emma Bull, co-editor

Terri Windling, *Life on the Border*, 1991
  editor

---

### 5215

**CHRISTOPHER STASHEFF**

## A Company of Stars

(New York: Ballantine/Del Rey, 1991)

**Story type:** Science Fiction (Adventure)
**Series:** Starship Troupers
**Major character(s):** Ramou Lazarian, Spaceman, Student; Horace Burbage, Actor; Suzanne Souci, Actress
**Time period(s):** 26th century
**Locale(s):** New York, New York

**Summary:** Ramou Lazarian, fleeing a forced marriage, comes to New York where he is mugged and then falls in with a company of actors who are planning a tour of the colonies. Elector Rudders wants to stop all theater, which he considers immoral, while Ramou's ex-girlfriend's father has detectives hot on his trail. Moving the departure day up, the company manages to hire a captain and escape from Port Newark one step ahead of detectives, process servers and Elector Rudders' men.

**Other books you might like:**

Terry Bisson, *Voyage to the Red Planet*, 1990
Jeffrey A. Carver, *Down the Stream of Stars*, 1990
Robert A. Heinlein, *Double Star*, 1956
Barry B. Longyear, *Circus World*, 1980
Barry B. Longyear, *City of Baraboo*, 1980
Barry B. Longyear, *Elephant Song*, 1982
Mike Resnick, *The Best Rootin' Tootin' Shootin' Gunslinger in the Whole Damned Galaxy*, 1983
Mike Resnick, *Sideshow*, 1982
Mike Resnick, *The Three-Legged Hootch Dancer*, 1983
Mike Resnick, *The Wild Alien Tamer*, 1983
Jack Vance, *Space Opera*, 1965

---

### 5216

**CHRISTOPHER STASHEFF**, Editor
**BILL FAWCETT**, Co-Editor

## The Crafters

(New York: Ace, 1991)

**Story type:** Fantasy (Anthology)
**Series:** Crafter Family
**Time period(s):** 17th century (1680s); 18th century
**Locale(s):** New England, American Colonies; England

**Summary:** This volume contains a prolog and epilog by Bill Fawcett plus 10 stories original to this first ''shared world''-type anthology which relates tales of the Crafter Family between 1682 and 1845 as they appear in the family archives. Authors contributing include Ru

---

Emerson, Esther Friesner, Katherine Kurtz, Morgan Llywelyn, Jody Lynn Nye, Robert Sheckley and Christopher Stasheff. There is and one collaborative work by Anna O'Connell and Doug Houseman.

**Other books you might like:**

Robert Asprin, *Thieves' World*, 1979
  editor

Harlan Ellison, *Medea: Harlan's World*, 1985
  editor

Bill Fawcett, *The Siege of Arista*, 1991

Martin H. Greenberg, *After the King: Stories in Honor of J.R.R. Tolkien*, 1992
  editor

George R.R. Martin, *Wild Cards*, 1987
  editor

Will Shetterly, *Liavek*, 1985
  Emma Bull, co-editor

Will Shetterly, *Liavek: Festival Week*, 1990
  Emma Bull, co-editor

Will Shetterly, *Liavek: The Players of Luck*, 1986
  Emma Bull, co-editor

Will Shetterly, *Liavek: Spells of Binding*, 1988
  Emma Bull, co-editor

Will Shetterly, *Liavek: Wizard's Row*, 1987
  Emma Bull, co-editor

Terri Windling, *Borderland*, 1986
  Mark Alan Arnold, co-editor

Terri Windling, *Bordertown*, 1986
  Mark Alan Arnold, co-editor

Terri Windling, *Life on the Border*, 1991
  editor

---

### 5217

**CHRISTOPHER STASHEFF**

## M'Lady Witch

(New York: Ace, 1994)

**Story type:** Fantasy (Adventure; Psychic Powers)
**Series:** Warlock
**Major character(s):** Cordelia Gallowglass, Witch, Noblewoman; Alain, Royalty; Geoffrey Gallowglass, Warlock, Nobleman
**Time period(s):** Indeterminate Future
**Locale(s):** Gramarye, Planet—Imaginary

**Summary:** When Prince Alain decides to woo Lady Cordelia, he discovers her penchant for excitement.

**Other books you might like:**

Lois McMaster Bujold, *The Spirit Ring*, 1992
Sharon Green, *Silver Princess, Golden Knight*, 1993
Josepha Sherman, *Child of Faerie, Child of Earth*, 1992
Martha Wells, *The Element of Fire*, 1993
Patricia C. Wrede, *Dealing with Dragons*, 1990

---

### 5218

**CHRISTOPHER STASHEFF**

## My Son, the Wizard

(New York: Ballantine Del Rey, 1997)

**Story type:** Fantasy (Magic Conflict; Alternate World)
**Series:** Wizard in Rhyme
**Major character(s):** Matthew ''Matt'' Mantrell, Wizard; Nirobus, Wizard, Drug Dealer; Lakshmi, Mythical Creature (djinn)
**Time period(s):** Indeterminate Future

**Locale(s):** Merovence, Fictional Country; Ibile, Fictional Country; New Jersey

**Summary:** Matt Mantrell rescues his parents, both of whom prove to have magic powers, from a drug-infested neighborhood just in time to involve them in a war between Merovence and the Moors. Allied with a love sick genie and an enterprising thief, Matt and his father must confront an evil sorcerer who, by means of drugs and magic, plans to rule and destroy two worlds.

**Other books you might like:**
Marion Zimmer Bradley, *The House Between the Worlds*, 1980
Jack L. Chalker, *Songs of the Dancing Gods*, 1990
Gordon R. Dickson, *The Dragon and the Djinn*, 1996
Esther Friesner, *Wishing Season*, 1993
Diana Wynne Jones, *Castle in the Air*, 1991
Guy Gavriel Kay, *The Lions of Al-Rassan*, 1995
Harry Turtledove, *Thessalonica*, 1997
Chelsea Quinn Yarbro, *Ariosto*, 1980

## 5219

**CHRISTOPHER STASHEFF**

## *The Oathbound Wizard*

(New York: Ballantine Del Rey, 1993)

**Story type:** Fantasy (Light Fantasy; Alternate World)
**Major character(s):** Matt, Wizard, Fiance(e); Narlh, Mythical Creature (dragon/gryphon chimera), Adventurer; Robin Hood, Hero, Outlaw
**Time period(s):** Indeterminate
**Locale(s):** Planet—Imaginary; Ibile, Fictional Country; Ys, Fictional Country

**Summary:** When Matt discovers he lacks the kingdom necessary to attain marriage to Queen Alisande, Matt's hasty oath drives him inevitably toward winning his kingdom from evil King Gordogrosso. Matt enlists the help of Narlh, Robin Hood's band and others in his pun-filled adventure. Sequel to *Her Majesty's Wizard.*

**Other books you might like:**
Piers Anthony, *A Spell for Chameleon*, 1977
Robert Asprin, *Another Fine Myth*, 1978
C. Dale Brittain, *Mage Quest*, 1993
L. Sprague de Camp, *The Enchanter Reborn*, 1992
    Christopher Stasheff, co-author
Suzette Haden Elgin, *Twelve Fair Kingdoms*, 1981
John Moore, *Slay and Rescue*, 1993

## 5220

**CHRISTOPHER STASHEFF**

## *Quicksilver's Knight*

(New York: Ace, 1995)

**Story type:** Fantasy (Psychic Powers; Science Fiction)
**Series:** Warlock
**Major character(s):** Geoffrey Gallowglass, Warlock, Nobleman; Jane "Quicksilver", Outlaw, Psychic; Finister "Moraga", Agent (S.P.I.T.E.), Psychic
**Time period(s):** Indeterminate Future
**Locale(s):** Gramarye, Planet—Imaginary

**Summary:** Geoffrey rides off to capture Quicksilver, the leader of an outlaw band who has killed the Old Count Laeg and taken control of his land. But having accomplished his mission, he listens to Quicksilver's story of Laeg's oppression of the peasants and agrees to help her argue the justice of her cause before the King and Queen.

However, the agent for S.P.I.T.E. (Society for the Prevention of Integration of Telepathic Entities) hopes to lure him away from his task.

**Other books you might like:**
C.J. Cherryh, *The Paladin*, 1988
Sharon Green, *Silver Princess, Golden Knight*, 1993
Barbara Hambly, *The Ladies of Mandrigyn*, 1984
C.L. Moore, *Jirel of Joiry*, 1969
Elizabeth Ann Scarborough, *Bronwyn's Bane*, 1983

## 5221

**CHRISTOPHER STASHEFF**

## *The Sage*

(New York: Ballantine Del Rey, 1996)

**Story type:** Fantasy (Magic Conflict; Quest)
**Series:** Star Stone
**Major character(s):** Culaehra, Warrior, Adventurer; Yocote, Shaman, Mythical Creature (gnome); Ohaern, Warrior, Blacksmith
**Time period(s):** Indeterminate
**Locale(s):** Fictional Country

**Summary:** When the offspring of his vanquished enemy sows discord among the lesser races, Ohaern begins molding Culaehra from a selfish ruffian into the warrior needed to defeat the new threat. To assure victory Ohaern must first locate the Star Stone and forge it into an effective weapon for the transformed Culaehra. Set 500 years after *The Shaman.*

**Other books you might like:**
Greg Bear, *Songs of Earth and Power*, 1994
Dave Duncan, *Emperor and Clown*, 1992
David Gemmell, *Morningstar*, 1993
Mary Gentle, *Rats and Gargoyles*, 1991
Robert Jordan, *The Eye of the World*, 1990

## 5222

**CHRISTOPHER STASHEFF**

## *The Secular Wizard*

(New York: Ballantine Del Rey, 1995)

**Story type:** Fantasy (Alternate World; Magic Conflict)
**Series:** Wizard in Rhyme
**Major character(s):** Matthew "Matt" Mantrell, Wizard, Minstrel; Boncorro, Ruler (king), Wizard; Arouetto, Scholar
**Time period(s):** Indeterminate Past
**Locale(s):** Latruria, Fictional Country; Merovence, Fictional Country

**Summary:** Hearing mixed news concerning the new king of Latruria, Matt Mantrell decides to travel south to reconnoiter. He finds that the people, freed of toil, flock to the city, becoming the prey of thieves and pimps. Matt meets with King Boncorro and continues his adventures as the forces of humanism and secular government gain influence.

**Other books you might like:**
Piers Anthony, *Dragon's Gold*, 1987
    Robert E. Margroff, co-author
Lois McMaster Bujold, *The Spirit Ring*, 1992
L. Sprague de Camp, *The Pixilated Peeress*, 1991
    Catherine Crook de Camp, co-author
Guy Gavriel Kay, *A Song for Arbonne*, 1993
Katherine Kurtz, *The Bastard Prince*, 1994
R.A. MacAvoy, *Damiano's Lute*, 1984
Fletcher Pratt, *The Blue Star*, 1969

Judith Tarr, *Ars Magica*, 1989

## 5223

### CHRISTOPHER STASHEFF

## *The Shaman*

(New York: Ballantine Del Rey, 1995)

**Story type:** Fantasy (Magic Conflict; Adventure)
**Series:** Star Stone
**Major character(s):** Ohaern, Warrior, Hunter; Lomallin, Immortal, Mythical Creature (Ulin); Ulahane, Shaman, Mythical Creature (Ulin)
**Time period(s):** Indeterminate
**Locale(s):** Fictional Country

**Summary:** Ohaern helps Lomallin as he battles Ulahane and his campaign against humans, using many unpleasant creatures he creates and looses on humanity.

**Other books you might like:**
Margaret Ball, *The Shadow Gate*, 1991
Greg Bear, *Songs of Earth and Power*, 1994
Nancy Varian Berberick, *The Panther's Hoard*, 1994
Mary Gentle, *Rats and Gargoyles*, 1991
Mark C. Perry, *Morigu: The Dead*, 1990

## 5224

### CHRISTOPHER STASHEFF

## *Warlock and Son*

(New York: Ace, 1991)

**Story type:** Science Fiction (Young Adult; Adventure)
**Series:** Warlock
**Major character(s):** Rod Gallowglass, Warlock; Magnus Gallowglass ''Gar Pike'' d'Armand, Warrior, Psychic, Wizard
**Time period(s):** 31st century
**Locale(s):** Gramarye, Planet—Imaginary

**Summary:** Feeling hemmed in at home, Magnus decides to wander about Gramarye to find himself. Rod, fearing for his son, follows at a distance. After several adventures, Magnus encounters a maid who robs him of his will to live. When cured, he decides to leave Gramarye, not knowing that agents of S.P.I.T.E. have engineered his problems.

**Other books you might like:**
Piers Anthony, *A Spell for Chameleon*, 1977
Robert Asprin, *Another Fine Myth*, 1978
Jack L. Chalker, *The River of Dancing Gods*, 1984
Alan Dean Foster, *Spellsinger*, 1983

## 5225

### CHRISTOPHER STASHEFF

## *The Warlock Insane*

(New York: Ace Books, 1989)

**Story type:** Fantasy (Light Fantasy)
**Series:** Warlock
**Major character(s):** Rod Gallowglass, Warlock; Fess, Robot (Robot Horse)
**Time period(s):** 31st century
**Locale(s):** Gramarye, Fictional Country

**Summary:** On a planet where magic appears to work, though it's all actually psychic phenomena, Rod Gallowglass, the famed Warlock, begins to have hallucinations and apparently goes mad. Wandering the forest he has amazing encounters with characters out of *Don Quixote* and *Orlando Furioso*. It's all a trick, of course, and he eventually saves the day with the help of his robot horse, Fess, and his psychically endowed wife and children.

**Other books you might like:**
Piers Anthony, *Out of Phaze*, 1987
Piers Anthony, *Robot Adept*, 1988
Piers Anthony, *Unicorn Point*, 1989
F. Paul Wilson, *The Tery*, 1990

## 5226

### CHRISTOPHER STASHEFF

## *The Warlock Rock*

(New York: Ace, 1990)

**Story type:** Science Fiction (Fantasy; Humor)
**Series:** Warlock
**Major character(s):** Rod Gallowglass, Warlock; Fess, Robot (robot horse); Gwen Gallowglass, Witch
**Time period(s):** 31st century
**Locale(s):** Gramarye, Planet—Imaginary

**Summary:** Rod, Fess, Gwen and their family venture forth in search of puns and the source of the dangerous rock music which is enslaving the minds of susceptible young listeners.

**Other books you might like:**
Piers Anthony, *Out of Phaze*, 1987
Piers Anthony, *Robot Adept*, 1988
Piers Anthony, *Unicorn Point*, 1989
F. Paul Wilson, *The Tery*, 1990

## 5227

### CHRISTOPHER STASHEFF

## *We Open on Venus*

(New York: Ballantine Del Rey, 1994)

**Story type:** Science Fiction (Humor; Arts)
**Series:** Starship Troupers
**Major character(s):** Ramou Lazarian, Spaceman (ensign), Student (theater); Suzanne Souci, Actress; Barry Tallendar, Director (theater)
**Time period(s):** 26th century
**Locale(s):** New Venus, Planet—Imaginary

**Summary:** The Star Company leaves New York in the nick of time, just before the Lords prevent them from touring the colonies. On New Venus, where they open with *Macbeth*, owning cigarettes or fire starting equipment results in the death penalty, since the planet, owned by an oil company, could be flammable.

**Other books you might like:**
Terry Bisson, *Voyage to the Red Planet*, 1990
L. Sprague de Camp, *The Swords of Zinjaban*, 1991
    Catherine Crook de Camp, co-author
John DeChancie, *Starrigger*, 1983
Kate Elliott, *An Earthly Crown*, 1993
Colin Greenland, *Take Back Plenty*, 1992
Robert A. Heinlein, *Double Star*, 1956

## 5228

### CHRISTOPHER STASHEFF

## The Witch Doctor

(New York: Ballantine Del Rey, 1994)

**Story type:** Fantasy (Alternate World; Magic Conflict)
**Series:** Wizard in Rhyme
**Major character(s):** Saul Bremener, Wizard; Frisson, Writer (poet); Suettay, Ruler (queen)
**Time period(s):** Indeterminate Past
**Locale(s):** Allustria, Fictional Country

**Summary:** Bitten by a spider, Saul Bremener awakens to find himself a wizard in a land of dichotomous good and evil, which one must choose between. Told by his guardian angel that he must free Allustria from its evil ruler, the doubtful Saul gathers a band of followers and sets out to discover how things work.

**Other books you might like:**
Gordon R. Dickson, *The Dragon and the George*, 1976
Fletcher Pratt, *The Blue Star*, 1958
Clifford D. Simak, *The Fellowship of the Talisman*, 1978
Paula Volsky, *Illusion*, 1992
Chelsea Quinn Yarbro, *Ariosto*, 1980

## 5229

### CHRISTOPHER STASHEFF

## A Wizard in Absentia

(New York: Ace, 1993)

**Story type:** Science Fiction (Political; Robot Fiction)
**Series:** Warlock
**Major character(s):** Magnus Gallowglass "Gar Pike" d'Armand, Adventurer, Psychic (ESP, telekenetic), Wizard; Fess, Robot (robot horse); Ian Tobinson, Companion
**Time period(s):** 31st century
**Locale(s):** Maxima, Asteroid; Taxhaven, Planet—Imaginary

**Summary:** Curious about his family and heritage, Magnus visits the ancestral d'Armand asteroid with Fess, which he sends back to Gramarye after receiving his own robot from relatives. Magnus becomes interested in the Society for the Conversion of Extraterrestrial Nascent Totalitarianisms and sets off to bring enlightenment to the serfs of a society modeled on late 17th century French culture.

**Other books you might like:**
Steve Perry, *The Man Who Never Missed*, 1985
Alis A. Rasmussen, *A Passage of Stars*, 1990
Alis A. Rasmussen, *The Price of Ransom*, 1990
Alis A. Rasmussen, *Revolution's Shore*, 1990
Melissa Scott, *Dreamships*, 1992

## 5230

### CHRISTOPHER STASHEFF

## A Wizard in Chaos

(New York: Tor, 1997)

**Story type:** Science Fiction (Science Fantasy; Political)
**Series:** Rogue Wizard
**Major character(s):** Magnus Gallowglass "Gar Pike" d'Armand, Psychic, Troubleshooter, Wizard; Dirk Dulaine, Sidekick, Military Personnel; Cort, Military Personnel (lieutenant)
**Time period(s):** Indeterminate Future
**Locale(s):** Durvie, Planet—Imaginary

**Summary:** Gar and Dirk arrive on Durvie, settled by idealistic anarchists, but now involved in constant war between rival strongholds. The only technology remains hidden in hollow hills regarded as fairy mounds by a superstitious peasantry. When Gar incurs the wrath of a villainous and wrathful steward, he and Dirk must get all factions working together to build some sort of governmental stability.

**Other books you might like:**
Lloyd Biggle, *The World Menders*, 1971
J.F. Bone, *Confederation Matador*, 1978
Colin Kapp, *The Wizard of Anharitte*, 1973
Lee Killough, *Liberty's World*, 1985
Barbara Paul, *Under the Canopy*, 1980
Mack Reynolds, *Planetary Agent X*, 1965
Arkadi Strugatsky, *Hard to Be a God*, 1973
   Boris Strugatsky, co-author
Lawrence Watt-Evans, *Denner's Wreck*, 1988

## 5231

### CHRISTOPHER STASHEFF

## A Wizard in Midgard

(New York: Tor, 1998)

**Story type:** Science Fiction (Adventure; Science Fantasy)
**Series:** Rogue Wizard
**Major character(s):** Magnus Gallowglass "Gar Pike" d'Armand, Wizard, Troubleshooter, Psychic; Alea Larsdatter, Fugitive
**Time period(s):** Indeterminate Future
**Locale(s):** Siegfried, Planet—Imaginary

**Summary:** Gar Pike lands on Siegfried where genetic drift has created giants and dwarves in addition to regular humans, who hate and fear both the giants and dwarves, and kill or enslave them. Magnus rescues Alea Larsdatter, too tall to be normal but too short to be a giant, who reluctantly joins with Magnus to bring change.

**Other books you might like:**
Poul Anderson, *Three Hearts and Three Lions*, 1961
Lloyd Biggle, *The World Menders*, 1971
Helen Collins, *Mutagenesis*, 1993
Harry Harrison, *Planet of the Damned*, 1962
Colin Kapp, *The Wizard of Anharitte*, 1973
Mack Reynolds, *The Rival Rigellians*, 1967
Brian Stableford, *Wildeblood's Empire*, 1977
Walter Jon Williams, *Ambassador of Progress*, 1984

## 5232

### CHRISTOPHER STASHEFF

## A Wizard in Mind

(New York: Tor, 1995)

**Story type:** Science Fiction (Psychic Powers; Family Saga)
**Series:** Warlock
**Major character(s):** Magnus Gallowglass "Gar Pike" d'Armand, Wizard, Revolutionary, Psychic; Gianni Braccalese, Businessman; Medallia, Spy
**Time period(s):** Indeterminate Future
**Locale(s):** Petrarch, Planet—Imaginary

**Summary:** A wizard and rebel, Magnus d'Armand wants to save the backward Petrarch from the inept meddling of AEGIS (Association for the Elevation of Governmental Institutions and Systems), and the home-grown tyranny of Prince Raginaldi. Impersonating a mercenary soldier, he takes service with Gianni, a wealthy merchant's son, but finds his simple mission complicated by outside forces and another wizard.

**Other books you might like:**
Alfred Bester, *The Stars My Destination*, 1956
Glen Cook, *Sweet Silver Blues*, 1987
William Goldman, *The Princess Bride*, 1973
Harry Harrison, *The Stainless Steel Rat*, 1961
Ward Moore, *Joyleg*, 1962
    Avram Davidson, co-author
David R. Palmer, *Emergence*, 1984
Terry Pratchett, *Small Gods*, 1994

---

**5233**

**CHRISTOPHER STASHEFF**

## A Wizard in Peace

(New York: Tor, 1996)

**Story type:** Science Fiction (Lost Colony; Political)
**Major character(s):** Magnus Gallowglass ''Gar Pike'' d'Armand, Psychic, Revolutionary, Wizard; Dirk Dulaine, Sidekick, Adventurer; Orgoru, Fugitive, Imposter
**Time period(s):** 31st century
**Locale(s):** Planet—Imaginary

**Summary:** On a planet they think too individually repressive and puritanical, Magnus and Dirk organize revolutionaries to help loosen up the dictatorial rule.

**Other books you might like:**
Stephen Baxter, *Raft*, 1992
Orson Scott Card, *The Memory of Earth*, 1992
Rosemary Kirstein, *The Steerswoman*, 1989
Larry Niven, *The Integral Trees*, 1984
Joan Slonczewski, *A Door into Ocean*, 1986

---

**5234**

**CHRISTOPHER STASHEFF**

## A Wizard in War

(New York: Tor, 1995)

**Story type:** Science Fiction (Political; Psychic Powers)
**Series:** Rogue Wizard
**Major character(s):** Magnus Gallowglass ''Gar Pike'' d'Armand, Psychic, Warrior, Wizard; Dirk Dulaine, Sidekick
**Time period(s):** 31st century
**Locale(s):** Maltroit, Planet—Imaginary

**Summary:** Magnus Gallowglass and Dirk Dulaine attempt to initiate democratic reforms on medieval Maltroit, a planet otherwise doomed to repeat all of humanity's Earthly mistakes.

**Other books you might like:**
Lois McMaster Bujold, *Brothers in Arms*, 1989
Stephen Goldin, *Jade Darcy and the Zen Pirates*, 1990
    Mary Mason, co-author
Robert A. Heinlein, *The Moon Is a Harsh Mistress*, 1966
Alis A. Rasmussen, *Revolution's Shore*, 1990
James H. Schmitz, *The Witches of Karres*, 1966
Allen Steele, *Lunar Descent*, 1991
John Varley, *Demon*, 1984

---

**5235**

**MICHAEL C. STAUDINGER**

## The Falcon Rises

(Lake Geneva, Wisconsin: TSR, 1991)

**Story type:** Fantasy (Alternate World; Magic Conflict)
**Major character(s):** Roy ''Ratha'' Arthre, Professor, Magician; Mordeth, Magician, Ruler (usurper); Mithra, Leader
**Time period(s):** Indeterminate
**Locale(s):** Shaleth, Fictional Country; Kesh, Fictional Country

**Summary:** Dragged from Earth to Shaleth by a dying wizard, Roy finds himself mistaken for the wizard, Ratha. With his companions, Roy must harness his new abilities to overcome the evil wizard who has usurped the rule of Shaleth. This is the author's first published book.

**Other books you might like:**
Pamela Dean, *The Hidden Land*, 1986
Pamela Dean, *The Secret Country*, 1985
Pamela Dean, *The Whim of the Dragon*, 1989
Gordon R. Dickson, *The Dragon and the George*, 1976
Stephen R. Donaldson, *The Illearth War*, 1977
Stephen R. Donaldson, *Lord Foul's Bane*, 1977
Stephen R. Donaldson, *The Power That Preserves*, 1977
Suzette Haden Elgin, *The Grand Jubilee*, 1981
Suzette Haden Elgin, *And Then There'll Be Fireworks*, 1981
Suzette Haden Elgin, *Twelve Fair Kingdoms*, 1981
Christopher Stasheff, *The Warlock in Spite of Himself*, 1969

---

**5236**

**JOHN STCHUR**

## Paddywhack

(New York: St. Martin's, 1989)

**Story type:** Horror (Nature in Revolt)
**Major character(s):** Jack Lerille, Actor (Former), Librarian (Former); Bruce, Animal (A malevolent dog)
**Time period(s):** 1980s
**Locale(s):** Granger, Michigan

**Summary:** Having lost his jobs in New York City, Jack Lerille takes his family to live in northern Michigan with his maiden Aunt Blanche, owner of a sinister dog. Blanche becomes increasingly strange and the dog increasingly vicious, until they both die. Then the dog returns and becomes really nasty.

**Other books you might like:**
Stephen King, *Cujo*, 1981

---

**5237**

**JOHN STEAKLEY**

## Vampire$

(New York: Roc, 1990)

**Story type:** Horror (Vampire Story)
**Major character(s):** Jack Crow, Vampire Hunter; William Charles ''Gunman'' Felix, Vampire Hunter; Simon Kennedy, Vampire
**Time period(s):** 1990s
**Locale(s):** Dallas, Texas

**Summary:** When vampires run amok in your neighborhood, who you gonna call? Vampire$, Inc., the paranormal paramilitary hit squad, led by Jack Crow and the Crow team, who guarantee to put vampires in their place, the ground.

**Other books you might like:**
Ron Dee, *Blood Lust*, 1990
Ron Dee, *Dusk*, 1991
Robert R. McCammon, *They Thirst*, 1981

**5238**

**MICHAEL STEARNS**, Editor

## A Starfarer's Dozen
(New York: Harcourt Brace/Jane Yolen Books, 1995)

**Story type:** Science Fiction (Anthology; Young Adult)

**Summary:** Contains a two-page introduction, four pages of authors' biographies and 13 original stories reflecting the hope which motivates voyages of exploration. Generally upbeat in tone, the stories encompass a broad range of themes including education, space rescue, dinosaurs, and superheroes, with Debra Doyle and James D. Macdonald collaborating on one story. Other authors include Gregory Feeley, Will Shetterly, Sherwood Smith, Martha Soukup, Nancy Springer, Dave Trowbridge, Lawrence Watt-Evans, and Jane Yolen.

**Other books you might like:**
Isaac Asimov, *Young Extraterrestrials*, 1984
    Martin H. Greenberg, Charles G. Waugh, co-editors
Groff Conklin, *The Best of Science Fiction*, 1946
    editor
Raymond J. Healy, *Adventures in Time and Space*, 1946
    J. Francis McComas, co-editor
Andre Norton, *Gates to Tomorrow: An Introduction to Science Fiction*, 1973
    Ernestine Donaldy, co-editor
Jane Yolen, *2041: Twelve Short Stories about the Future by Top Science Fiction Writers*, 1991
    editor

**5239**

**MICHAEL STEARNS**, Editor

## A Wizard's Dozen
(New York: Harcourt Brace, 1993)

**Story type:** Fantasy (Anthology; Young Adult)

**Summary:** Contains 13 original stories populated by mythical characters ranging from fairies and a werewolf princess to a midget giant. The adventures include perilous quests, a kidnapping by evil ants and a journey via computer to the world of Faerie. Debra Doyle and James D. Macdonald collaborate on one story with other authors including Bruce Coville, Charles de Lint, Tappan King, Betty Levin, Will Shetterly, Sherwood Smith, Vivian Vande Velde, Patricia C. Wrede and Jane Yolen.

**Other books you might like:**
Isaac Asimov, *Dragon Tales*, 1982
    Charles G. Waugh, Martin H. Greenberg, co-editors
Lin Carter, *The Young Magicians*, 1969
    editor
Diana Wynne Jones, *Warlock at the Wheel and Other Stories*, 1984
Robin McKinley, *Imaginary Lands*, 1985
    editor
Baird Searles, *Halflings, Hobbits, Warrows & Weefolk: A Collection of Tales of Heroes Short in Stature*, 1991
    Brian Thomsen, co-editor

Jane Yolen, *Shape Shifters: Fantasy and Science Fiction Tales about Humans Who Can Change Their Shapes*, 1978
editor

**5240**

**ALLEN STEELE**

## All-American Alien Boy
(Baltimore: Old Earth Books, 1996)

**Story type:** Science Fiction (Collection)

**Summary:** Contains a general introduction plus brief individual introductions to 11 stories, ranging from ironic and humorous to dark in tone, with the first book publication of one Hugo Award nominee, ''The Good Rat.'' Themes include space opera, warfare, and medical testing of animals and humans, with hints of Steele's background in journalism shining through.

**Other books you might like:**
David Brin, *The River of Time*, 1986
John Kessel, *Meeting in Infinity*, 1992
Nancy Kress, *The Aliens of Earth*, 1993
Marc Stiegler, *The Gentle Seduction*, 1990
Connie Willis, *Impossible Things*, 1994

**5241**

**ALLEN STEELE**

## Clarke County, Space
(New York: Ace, 1990)

**Story type:** Science Fiction (Political; Adventure)
**Major character(s):** Henry Bigthorn, Police Officer (sheriff), Indian; Henry Ostrow, Murderer (The Golem); Blind Boy Grunt, Artificial Intelligence
**Time period(s):** 2040s (2049)
**Locale(s):** Clarke County, Space Station; Canaveral Pier, Florida

**Summary:** Sheriff Bigthorn prevents the Golem from killing his victim during an Elvis Presley revival and a local political revolution. A potential nuclear disaster and help from an unknown source further stress the meager police department.

**Other books you might like:**
Ben Bova, *Colony*, 1978
David Brin, *Earth*, 1990
Robert A. Heinlein, *The Moon Is a Harsh Mistress*, 1966
Melisa C. Michaels, *Pirate Prince*, 1987
Michael Swanwick, *Vacuum Flowers*, 1987

**5242**

**ALLEN STEELE**

## The Jericho Iteration
(New York: Ace, 1994)

**Story type:** Science Fiction (Disaster; Mystery)
**Major character(s):** Gerry Rosen, Journalist; John Tiernan, Journalist
**Time period(s):** 2010s (April 17-20, 2013)
**Locale(s):** St. Louis, Missouri

**Summary:** When Gerry asks John about a misdirected message, John allows Gerry to assist an investigation into Tiptree Corporation's Sentinel Project. After John's murder, Gerry's rash action brings more attention from the martial law forces than Gerry desires.

**Other books you might like:**
David Brin, *Earth*, 1990
David Brin, *The Postman*, 1985
Larry Niven, *Lucifer's Hammer*, 1977
    Jerry Pournelle, co-author
David R. Palmer, *Emergence*, 1984
John Varley, *Steel Beach*, 1992

**5243**

**ALLEN STEELE**

## A King of Infinite Space

(New York: HarperPrism, 1997)

**Story type:** Science Fiction (Alternate Intelligence; Space Colony)
**Series:** Near Space Stories
**Major character(s):** William Alec Tucker III, Reanimated Dead, Cyborg; Pasquale Chicago, Businessman; Chip, Artificial Intelligence, Companion (Alec's)
**Time period(s):** 2090s (2099)
**Locale(s):** 4442 Garcia, Asteroid (1985 RB1); Clarke County, Space Station (Lagrange Five Colony)

**Summary:** Pasquale Chicago reanimates Alec from cryogenic suspension a century after his fatal accident, repairing his injuries and implanting Chip to aid his scrambled memories. Alec's feelings toward his role in the future and his benefactor change as he learns about Chicago's bold bid for power. When he discovers his girlfriend may also have survived the accident, Alec escapes Chicago's colony to find her.

**Other books you might like:**
Ron Goulart, *When the Waker Sleeps*, 1975
Frederik Pohl, *The Age of the Pussyfoot*, 1969
Clifford D. Simak, *Why Call Them Back From Heaven?*, 1967
Ernest Tidyman, *Absolute Zero*, 1971
H.G. Wells, *When the Sleeper Wakes*, 1899
James White, *The Dream Millennium*, 1974

**5244**

**ALLEN STEELE**

## Labyrinth of Night

(New York: Ace, 1992)

**Story type:** Science Fiction (First Contact; Political)
**Series:** Near Space Stories
**Major character(s):** W.J. Boggs, Pilot (U.S.S. Edgar Rice Burroughs); Terrance L'Enfant, Administrator (Cydonia Base); August Nash, Security Officer, Spy (Skycorp's)
**Time period(s):** 2030s
**Locale(s):** Arsia Station, Mars; Cydonia Base, Mars; City, Mars (lost city of Mars)

**Summary:** Investigating a human visage carved into a Martian mesa, explorers discover the City, left by alien colonists millennia earlier. Within a series of pyramids, a labyrinth tests human intelligence and creativity before activating robots which isolate themselves from humans to carry on their alien activity. Many forces battle for control of the Martian mission and access to alien technology.

**Other books you might like:**
Roger MacBride Allen, *The Ring of Charon*, 1990
Arthur C. Clarke, *The Garden of Rama*, 1991
    Gentry Lee, co-author
Diana G. Gallagher, *The Alien Dark*, 1990
Larry Niven, *Protector*, 1973

Frederik Pohl, *The Gateway Trip: Tales and Vignettes of the Heechee*, 1991
W.J. Stuart, *Forbidden Planet*, 1956

**5245**

**ALLEN STEELE**

## Lunar Descent

(New York: Ace, 1991)

**Story type:** Science Fiction (Political; Hard Science Fiction)
**Series:** Near Space Stories
**Major character(s):** Lester Riddell, Businessman, Spaceman; "Mighty" Joe Young, Pilot, Spaceman; Willard "Jeremy Schneider" DeWitt, Computer Expert, Businessman
**Time period(s):** 2020s
**Locale(s):** Descartes Station, Montenegro

**Summary:** Recruited against his will to return to Luna as general manager for Descartes Station, Lester Riddell must win respect, boost morale and restore the construction schedule for Skycorp's new moonbase. His achieving all three does not stop Skycorp from planning to abandon the unprofitable project. When Lester finds himself involved in Labor Action, he turns to DeWitt for help in fabricating a solution.

**Other books you might like:**
Jeffrey A. Carver, *From a Changeling Star*, 1989
Robert A. Heinlein, *The Moon Is a Harsh Mistress*, 1966
Rudy Rucker, *Wetware*, 1988
John Varley, *Blue Champagne*, 1986
John Varley, *The Persistence of Vision*, 1978
Walter Jon Williams, *Voice of the Whirlwind*, 1988

**5246**

**ALLEN STEELE**

## Orbital Decay

(New York: Ace, 1989)

**Story type:** Science Fiction (Hard Science Fiction)
**Major character(s):** Popeye Hooker, Construction Worker (Beamjack); Virgin Bruce, Construction Worker (Beamjack)
**Time period(s):** 21st century (2020)
**Locale(s):** Skycan, Space Station

**Summary:** A varied crew of astronauts, scientists, and bluecollar construction workers called beamjacks put in long and dangerous hours building a giant solar power satellite. A secret government plot is discovered to use scientific equipment being installed on a neighboring space station for illegal spying and a number of the beamjacks decide to sabotage the equipment.

**Other books you might like:**
C.J. Cherryh, *Rimrunners*, 1989
Robert A. Heinlein, *Starman Jones*, 1954
Robert A. Heinlein, *Starship Troopers*, 1961
Paul Preuss, *Starfire*, 1988

**5247**

**ALLEN STEELE**

## Rude Astronauts

(Baltimore: Old Earth Books, 1993)

**Story type:** Science Fiction (Collection)

**Series:** Near Space Stories

**Summary:** Contains a seven-page introduction, one original and six reprinted articles about science or science fiction, and eight stories all published 1985-1992 in periodicals and anthologies. Collection includes the author's first story, "Live From the Mars Hotel," two alternate history stories, three stories set in an astronaut bar and five stories which fit into Steele's Near Space Stories series with his first four novels.

**Other books you might like:**
Frank Harvey, *Air Force!*, 1959
Robert A. Heinlein, *The Green Hills of Earth*, 1951
Andre Norton, *Space Pioneers*, 1954
    editor
Charles Sheffield, *The McAndrew Chronicles*, 1983
Dan Simmons, *Phases of Gravity*, 1989
John Varley, *Blue Champagne*, 1986

---

## 5248

### ALLEN STEELE

## *The Tranquility Alternative*
(New York: Ace, 1996)

**Story type:** Science Fiction (Alternate Universe; Gay/Lesbian Fiction)
**Major character(s):** Christine Ryder, Pilot (lunar shuttle), Lesbian; Eugene M. Parnell, Spaceman, Leader; Paul Dooley, Imposter, Computer Expert
**Time period(s):** 1990s
**Locale(s):** Alternate Earth

**Summary:** Half a century after Germany's attack on the United States from space sparks rapid space development, economic forces drive the sale of an American Lunar base to German business interests. Sent to decommission Cold War era nuclear weapons left at the abandoned Lunar base, Ryder and Parnell must derail covert plans of crew members aimed at acquiring the weapons from imperialistic expansion.

**Other books you might like:**
Raphael Carter, *The Fortunate Fall*, 1996
Michael Flynn, *Firestar*, 1996
Michael Flynn, *In the Country of the Blind*, 1990
Robert A. Heinlein, *Double Star*, 1956
David Alexander Smith, *Marathon*, 1982
John Varley, *Steel Beach*, 1992

---

## 5249

### GARTH STEIN

## *Raven Stole the Moon*
(New York: Pocket, 1998)

**Major character(s):** Jenna Rosen, Relative (mother of drowned son); David Livingstone, Shaman; Ed Fleming, Fisherman
**Time period(s):** 1990s (1998)
**Locale(s):** Wrangell, Alaska

**Summary:** Feeling the neglect of her husband and pangs of guilt over the drowning death of their five-year-old son Bobby, Jenna flees to the Alaskan town where the boy died, pursued by a private investigator in the employ of her husband. With the help of shaman David Livingstone, Jenna placates Raven, a god of Tlingit mythology, and fights the Kushtaka, creatures of myth who have captured her son's soul. A first novel.

**Other books you might like:**
Owl Goingback, *Crota*, 1996
Rick Hautala, *Beyond the Shroud*, 1996
Catherine Montrose, *Wendigo Border*, 1995
Adam Niswander, *The Charm*, 1993
Patrick Whalen, *Deathwalker*, 1992

---

## 5250

### HARRY STEIN

## *Infinity's Child*
(New York: Delacorte, 1997)

**Story type:** Horror (Science Fiction)
**Major character(s):** Sally Benedict, Journalist; R. Paul Holland, Scientist (biochemist); Raymond Lynch, Scientist
**Time period(s):** 1990s (1997)
**Locale(s):** Edwardstown, New Hampshire

**Summary:** Sally Benedict discovers that her family possesses the "infinity gene," genetic material that is crucial to a nearby biochemical research laboratory conducting experiments to prolong human life. Trapped in the maternity ward of the local hospital following the birth of her first child, Sally realizes that her life is in danger from agents eager to obtain a sample of living tissue from her newborn.

**Other books you might like:**
Eric Flanders, *The Forever Children*, 1992
Dean R. Koontz, *The Servants of Twilight*, 1984
David Martin, *Bring Me Children*, 1992
John Saul, *Darkness*, 1991

---

## 5251

### KEVIN STEIN

## *Twisted Dragon*
(New York: Ace, 1993)

**Story type:** Fantasy (Political; Sword and Sorcery)
**Series:** Elfwood
**Major character(s):** Jaeme, Noblewoman, Warrior; Decutonius, Magician; Laela, Mythical Creature (shapechanger), Magician (Druidic)
**Time period(s):** Indeterminate
**Locale(s):** Elfwood, Mythical Place; Albion, Fictional Country

**Summary:** Four fearless warriors must find the cause of a chilling mist which has descended on Elfwood, tainting the souls of human and elfkind. Uninterrupted, the dark forces will destroy Elfwood in just three days.

**Other books you might like:**
Lois McMaster Bujold, *The Spirit Ring*, 1992
C.J. Cherryh, *The Goblin Mirror*, 1992
Rose Estes, *Elfwood*, 1992
Barbara Hambly, *The Time of the Dark*, 1982
Robert Jordan, *The Eye of the World*, 1989
Martha Wells, *The Element of Fire*, 1993

## 5252

**JOHN RICHARD STEPHENS**, Editor
**KIM SMITH**, Co-Editor

### *Mysterious Cat Stories*

(New York: Carroll & Graf, 1993)

**Story type:** Horror (Anthology)

**Summary:** The authors have compiled 26 tales of horror and fantasy in which cats play a prominent role. Included are August Derleth's tale of a catlike demonic familiar, "Balu"; Robert Bloch's tale of witchcraft, "Catnip"; and H.P. Lovecraft's tale of feline revenge, "The Cats of Ulthar." The book also includes stories by Lilian Jackson Braun, Wilbur Daniel Steele, Algernon Blackwood, and Saki, as well as excerpts from Cervantes' *Don Quixote* and Bram Stoker's *Jewel of the Seven Stars*.

**Other books you might like:**
Jack Dann, *Magicats!*, 1984
    Gardner Dozois, co-editor
Jack Dann, *Magicats II*, 1991
    Gardner Dozois, co-editor
Bill Fawcett, *Cats in Space and Other Places*, 1992
    editor
Claire Necker, *Supernatural Cats*, 1973
Andre Norton, *Catfantastic*, 1989
    Martin H. Greenberg, co-editor
Andre Norton, *Catfantastic II*, 1991
    Martin H. Greenberg, co-editor
Michel Parry, *Beware of the Cat*, 1972
Mark E. Rogers, *The Adventures of Samurai Cat*, 1984

## 5253

**NEAL STEPHENSON**

### *The Diamond Age*

(New York: Bantam Spectra, 1995)

**Story type:** Science Fiction (Cyberpunk)
**Major character(s):** John Percival Hackworth, Engineer (nanotechnology); Dr. X, Criminal; Nellodee "Nell", Child
**Time period(s):** 21st century
**Locale(s):** Shanghai, China; Leased Territories, Fictional Country

**Summary:** Nell and her brother, Harv, struggle to survive in the slums while others live in undreamed-of splendor. Nell's life changes utterly when she receives one of two copies of a strange interactive book which gradually draws her into the problems of a society in transition.

**Other books you might like:**
Stephen Bury, *Interface*, 1994
    pseudonym of Neal Stephenson and George F. Jewsbury
Pat Cadigan, *Synners*, 1991
Marc Laidlaw, *Neon Lotus*, 1988
Ian McDonald, *Terminal Cafe*, 1994
Maureen F. McHugh, *China Mountain Zhang*, 1992
David Wingrove, *The Middle Kingdom*, 1990

## 5254

**NEAL STEPHENSON**

### *Snow Crash*

(New York: Bantam Spectra, 1992)

**Story type:** Science Fiction (Cyberpunk; Theological)
**Major character(s):** Hiro Protagonist, Computer Expert, Martial Arts Expert; Yours "Y.T." Truely, Businesswoman (Kourier), Teenager; Raven, Martial Arts Expert, Organized Crime Figure
**Time period(s):** 21st century
**Locale(s):** Los Angeles, California; The Metaverse, Cyberspace (virtual reality); *Raft*, At Sea

**Summary:** While delivering pizza for the Mafia, Hiro causes a disaster which leads to Y.T.'s doing a favor for the Mafia and leads both into a search for the origin of a computer virus which attacks computer hackers and an analog neurolinguistic virus existing since the fall of the Tower of Babel. Author's first science fiction novel.

**Other books you might like:**
Pat Cadigan, *Mindplayers*, 1987
Pat Cadigan, *Synners*, 1991
Samuel R. Delany, *Babel-17*, 1966
Philip K. Dick, *A Scanner Darkly*, 1977
William Gibson, *Neuromancer*, 1984
Ernest Hogan, *High Aztec*, 1991
K.W. Jeter, *Madlands*, 1991
Richard Kadrey, *Metrophage*, 1988
Bruce Sterling, *Islands in the Net*, 1988
John Varley, *Steel Beach*, 1992
Vernor Vinge, *A Fire upon the Deep*, 1992

## 5255

**BRUCE STERLING**

### *Crystal Express*

(Sauk City, Wisconsin: Arkham House, 1989)

**Story type:** Science Fiction (Collection)

**Summary:** This collection includes twelve of Sterling's short stories, ranging in publishing date from 1982 to 1987. Five of the pieces, including "Swarm," "Spider Rose," and "Cicada Queen," are from his Shaper/Mechanist series. Other well-known stories include "Green Days in Brunei," "Flowers of Edo," and "Dinner in Audoghast."

**Other books you might like:**
Greg Bear, *Blood Music*, 1985
Greg Bear, *Tangents*, 1989
Pat Cadigan, *Patterns*, 1989
William Gibson, *Burning Chrome*, 1986
William Gibson, *Neuromancer*, 1984
John Shirley, *Heatseeker*, 1989

## 5256

**BRUCE STERLING**

### *Distraction*

(New York: Bantam Spectra, 1998)

**Story type:** Science Fiction (Political; Dystopian)
**Major character(s):** Oscar Valparaiso, Consultant; Greta Penninger, Doctor; Yosh Pelicanos, Agent (majordomo)
**Time period(s):** 2040s (2044)

**Locale(s):** Washington, District of Columbia; New Orleans, Louisiana

**Summary:** In a North America on the verge of collapse, a political spin doctor takes drastic steps. Driven by his past, he turns to a brilliant neurologist for aid, with whom he forms a plan that will save him and maybe the world, if hundreds of special interest groups don't kill them first.

**Other books you might like:**
John Brunner, *The Shockwave Rider*, 1975
Pat Cadigan, *Synners*, 1991
Greg Egan, *Distress*, 1997
Ian McDonald, *Terminal Cafe*, 1994
Maureen F. McHugh, *Half the Day Is Night*, 1994

## 5257
### BRUCE STERLING
## Globalhead
(Shingletown, California: Mark V. Ziesing, 1992)

**Story type:** Science Fiction (Collection)

**Summary:** Contains one original story, "Are You for 86?" plus 12 stories published in periodicals and anthologies between 1985 and 1991. Themes include humor, cyberpunk, hard science fiction and fantasy in a variety of settings from ancient Assyria to an unpleasant France a millennium hence. Sterling collaborates with Rudy Rucker in "Storming the Chaos" and with John Kessel in "The Mortal Bullet."

**Other books you might like:**
Greg Bear, *The Wind From a Burning Woman*, 1983
Pat Cadigan, *Patterns*, 1989
Michael Flynn, *The Nanotech Chronicles*, 1991
William Gibson, *Burning Chrome*, 1986
John Kessel, *Meeting in Infinity*, 1992
Marc Stiegler, *The Gentle Seduction*, 1990
Michael Swanwick, *Gravity's Angels*, 1991
John Varley, *Blue Champagne*, 1986
John Varley, *The Persistence of Vision*, 1978

## 5258
### BRUCE STERLING
## Heavy Weather
(New York: Bantam Spectra, 1994)

**Story type:** Science Fiction (Medical; Disaster)
**Major character(s):** Alejandro "Alex" Unger, Invalid, Drifter; Juanita "Jane" Unger, Fanatic, Researcher; Gerald "Jerry" Mulcahey, Scientist (mathematician), Genius
**Time period(s):** 2030s (2031)
**Locale(s):** Nuevo Laredo, Mexico

**Summary:** Jane rescues Alex from an illegal medical facility after a lung flush which extends his life. Despite his illness, Alex manages to get along with the Storm Troupe, the group of misfits helping Jerry document the F6 tornado no one else believes will occur, a project to which the Storm Troupe dedicate their lives.

**Other books you might like:**
John Barnes, *Mother of Storms*, 1994
John Brunner, *Children of the Thunder*, 1989
Frank Herbert, *The White Plague*, 1982
Bill Ransom, *ViraVax*, 1993
Allen Steele, *Orbital Decay*, 1989

Roger Zelazny, *Flare*, 1992
Thomas T. Thomas, co-author

## 5259
### BRUCE STERLING
## Holy Fire
(New York: Bantam Spectra, 1996)

**Story type:** Science Fiction (Hard Science Fiction)
**Major character(s):** Mia Ziemann, Noblewoman (Gerontocrat); Brett/Natalie, Teenager, Artisan
**Time period(s):** 2090s
**Locale(s):** Europe; United States

**Summary:** In a world of synthetic memory drugs, benevolent government surveillance, underground anarchists, and talking canine companions, dominated by the medical-industrial complex, conservative senior citizens who have access to the latest life-extension technology hold the power while the young live on the fringes of society. A deathbed visit with an ex-lover and a chance meeting with a young clothing designer brings Mia, a 94-year-old medical economist who enjoys all the benefits of her position, to the awful realization that she lives her life bereft of pleasure and adventure. To have a second chance she must go through a radical and painful experimental procedure to make her young again.

**Other books you might like:**
Wilhelmina Baird, *Crashcourse*, 1993
Bruce Bethke, *Headcrash*, 1995
Stephen Bury, *Interface*, 1994
Pat Cadigan, *Synners*, 1991
Michael Flynn, *The Nanotech Chronicles*, 1991
Neal Stephenson, *The Diamond Age*, 1995
Thomas T. Thomas, *ME: A Novel of Self Discovery*, 1991

## 5260
### BRUCE STERLING
## Schismatrix Plus
(New York: Ace, 1996)

**Story type:** Science Fiction (Collection; Space Opera)
**Major character(s):** Abelard Lindsay, Diplomat, Revolutionary
**Time period(s):** Indeterminate Future
**Locale(s):** Earth; Spaceship; Space Station

**Summary:** Abelard Lindsay works to unify an interplanetary empire as disparate forces try to control humanity and mold society to their will. Omnibus edition including *Schismatrix* (1985) and five short stories from periodicals and anthologies 1982-1984, set in the Shaper-Mechanist universe.

**Other books you might like:**
Roger MacBride Allen, *The Ring of Charon*, 1990
Alfred Bester, *The Stars My Destination*, 1996 revised edition
Glen Cook, *The Dragon Never Sleeps*, 1988
Thomas A. Easton, *Sparrowhawk*, 1990
A.E. Van Vogt, *The Weapon Shops of Isher*, 1951
Vernor Vinge, *A Fire upon the Deep*, 1992

## 5261

### DAVID STERN

## Nightmare World

(New York: Ace Books, 1989)

**Story type:** Science Fiction (Adventure)
**Series:** Dr. Bones
**Major character(s):** Ezekiel "Zeke" Bones, Archaeologist
**Time period(s):** Indeterminate Future
**Locale(s):** Ahng, Planet—Imaginary

**Summary:** Ezekiel Bones, an archaeologist perhaps reminiscent of Doctor Who or Indiana Jones, specializes in saving entire planets from destruction. In this volume of the series, Dr. Bones' friends are menaced by evil earthworm-like aliens. *Nightmare World* is Stern's first science fiction novel.

**Other books you might like:**
Terrance Dicks, *The Claws of Axos*, 1977
Terrance Dicks, *Doctor Who: The Mind of Evil*, 1985
Charles Ingrid, *Alien Salute*, 1989
 Sand Wars 4
Charles Ingrid, *Return Fire*, 1989
 Sand Wars 5

## 5262

### ROGER STERN

## The Death and Life of Superman

(New York: Bantam Spectra, 1993)

**Story type:** Science Fiction (Adventure; Invasion of Earth)
**Series:** Superman
**Major character(s):** Clark "Superman" Kent, Journalist, Alien (Kryptonian); Lois Lane, Journalist, Girlfriend (Superman's); Doomsday, Monster
**Time period(s):** 1990s
**Locale(s):** Metropolis (New York City); Outer Space

**Summary:** Superman loses his life as he kills Doomsday and saves the Earth. Later, four superbeings astonish Superman's family, friends and foes when they arrive in Metropolis, each claiming the status of the last son of Krypton.

**Other books you might like:**
Michael Bishop, *Count Geiger's Blues*, 1992
Martin H. Greenberg, *The Further Adventures of Superman*, 1993
 editor
William Kotzwinkle, *Superman III*, 1983
Elliot S. Maggin, *Superman: Last Son of Krypton*, 1978
Elliot S. Maggin, *Superman: Miracle Monday*, 1981

## 5263

### T.W. STETSON

## Night Beasts

(New York: Pinnacle, 1993)

**Story type:** Horror (Science Fiction; Nature in Revolt)
**Major character(s):** Rodman Stanley, Police Officer (state trooper); Kate MacDavid, Young Woman; Dick "Dutch" Bork, Biker
**Time period(s):** 1990s (1993)
**Locale(s):** Forest City, California

**Summary:** When a Russian satellite explodes over the United States, the U.S. government's genetic weapons program, releases flocks of pterodactyl-like "Night Beasts" who, contrary to prior belief, not only live for longer than a few days, but breed and exhibit a taste for human flesh.

**Other books you might like:**
William W. Johnstone, *Bats*, 1993
Stephen King, *The Mist*, 1985
 in *Skeleton Crew*
Martin Cruz Smith, *Nightwing*, 1977
Robert Charles Wilson, *Second Fire*, 1993

## 5264

### BROOKE STEVENS

## The Circus of the Earth and Air

(New York: Harcourt Brace, 1994)

**Story type:** Fantasy (Mystery; Contemporary)
**Major character(s):** Alex Barton, Spouse
**Time period(s):** 1990s
**Locale(s):** New England

**Summary:** To gain admission to a circus, Iris agrees to volunteer to help in Father Fish's disappearing act, but does not return to Alex after the show. Alex searches for her then reports the disappearance to the police with no satisfactory result. Searching for her, Alex travels to the island owned by a great circus master, simultaneously beginning a metaphysical investigation into his own nature. First novel.

**Other books you might like:**
Ray Bradbury, *Something Wicked This Way Comes*, 1962
Marion Zimmer Bradley, *The Catch Trap*, 1979
Katherine Dunn, *Geek Love*, 1989
Charles G. Finney, *The Circus of Dr. Lao*, 1935
Barry B. Longyear, *City of Baraboo*, 1980
Warren Murphy, *Destiny's Carnival*, 1992
 Mark Brownwood, co-author

## 5265

### JOHN RICHARD STEVENS, Editor

## Vampires, Wine & Roses

(New York: Berkley, 1997)

**Story type:** Horror (Anthology)

**Summary:** Compilation of thirty-four stories, poems, song lyrics, and novel excerpts featuring vampires. Included are H.P. Lovecraft's "The Hound," about a sorceror resurrected from his coffin by two ignorant necrophiles; Rod Serling's "The Riddle of the Crypt," filmed as an episode of his television series "The Twilight Zone"; H.G. Well's "The Flowering of the Strange Orchid," about a blood-drinking plant; Guy de Maupassant's "The Horla," about an invisible blood drinking monster; and Bram Stoker's "Dracula's Guest," originally intended as an opening chapter to his novel Dracula. Other authors include Shakespeare, Woody Allen and Sting.

**Other books you might like:**
Martin H. Greenberg, *A Taste for Blood*, 1992
 editor
Martin H. Greenberg, *Vampires: The Greatest Stories*, 1997
 editor
Stephen Jones, *The Mammoth Book of Vampires*, 1992
 editor
Alan Ryan, *Vampires: Two Centuries of Great Vampire Stories*, 1987
 editor

Leslie Shepard, *The Dracula Book of Great Vampire Stories*, 1977
  editor
Leonard Wolf, *Blood Thirst: 100 Years of Vampire Fiction*, 1997
  editor

## 5266

### CAROLINE STEVERMER

## A College of Magics

(New York: Tor, 1994)

**Story type:** Fantasy (Quest; Magic Conflict)
**Major character(s):** Faris Nallaneen, Magician, Royalty (Duchess of Galazon); Jane Brailsford, Magician, Adventurer; Tyrian, Bodyguard, Companion
**Time period(s):** 1900s
**Locale(s):** Greenlaw, France (Greenlaw College); Aravis, Fictional Country; Alternate Earth

**Summary:** Initially an unwilling student at Greenlaw College, Faris Nallaneen cultivates friendships and studies magic until a fracas with another student reveals a fate that he must pursue.

**Other books you might like:**
Maya Kaathryn Bohnhoff, *The Meri*, 1992
Laurell K. Hamilton, *Nightseer*, 1992
Mercedes Lackey, *Jinx High*, 1991
Deborah Talmadge-Bickmore, *The Apprentice*, 1990
Paula Volsky, *Illusion*, 1992
Martha Wells, *The Element of Fire*, 1993
Patricia C. Wrede, *Sorcery and Cecelia*, 1988
  Caroline Stevermer, co-author

## 5267

### CAROLINE STEVERMER

## River Rats

(New York: Harcourt Brace Jovanovich, 1992)

**Story type:** Science Fiction (Post-Nuclear Holocaust; Young Adult)
**Major character(s):** Tomcat, Sailor (riverboat hand), Teenager; King, Fugitive, Musician
**Time period(s):** 21st century
**Locale(s):** Mississippi River

**Summary:** Tomcat and the crew of the *River Rat* interrupt their idyllic riverboat life of delivering mail and presenting rock concerts when they rescue King from the river. A wild chase evolves as the *River Rat* tries to elude the Lester family pursuing King to acquire his knowledge of a survivalist's weapons stash. Highly reminiscent of *The Adventures of Huckleberry Finn* (1885).

**Other books you might like:**
David Brin, *The Postman*, 1985
Mark Twain, *The Adventures of Huckleberry Finn*, 1885
Sterling E. Lanier, *Hiero's Journey*, 1973
David R. Palmer, *Emergence*, 1984
Will Shetterly, *Elsewhere*, 1991
Nancy Springer, *The Friendship Song*, 1992

## 5268

### JEAN STEWART

## Return to Isis

(New York: Rising Tide Press, 1992)

**Story type:** Science Fiction (Post-Nuclear Holocaust; Gay/Lesbian Fiction)
**Major character(s):** Tomyris "Whit Hastings" Whitaker, Military Personnel, Spy; Amelia, Farmer
**Time period(s):** 2090s (2093)
**Locale(s):** North America; Freeland, Fictional Country (western USA); Elysium, Fictional Country (eastern USA)

**Summary:** Discovered as a Freeland spy, Whit flees the Regulators and Elysium taking Amelia with her. There Amelia learns about the female society flourishing in city-colonies, finds herself falsely accused as a spy then later discovers the important role she will play in Freeland.

**Other books you might like:**
Margaret Atwood, *The Handmaid's Tale*, 1985
Suzy McKee Charnas, *Motherlines*, 1979
Suzy McKee Charnas, *Walk to the End of the World*, 1974
Suzette Haden Elgin, *Native Tongue*, 1984
Pat Murphy, *The City, Not Long After*, 1989
Joan Slonczewski, *A Door into Ocean*, 1986
Sheri S. Tepper, *The Gate to Women's Country*, 1989

## 5269

### KATE STEWART

## The Devil's Cradle

(New York: Zebra, 1992)

**Story type:** Horror (Child-in-Peril)
**Major character(s):** Dorothy Kite, Librarian; Elmo Small, Pharmacist; Hallie Crecilius, Musician
**Time period(s):** 1990s (1992)
**Locale(s):** New York, New York

**Summary:** Dorothy Kite has to fight to save herself and her as-yet-unborn children when she discovers that the man who has artificially inseminated her is in league with the devil and has a centuries-old history of assisting the birth of twins, one of whom always goes on to bring tragedy into the lives of whomever he or she touches. This is the author's first novel.

**Other books you might like:**
Margaret Bingley, *Seeds of Evil*, 1988
Stephanie Kegan, *The Baby*, 1990
Ira Levin, *Rosemary's Baby*, 1967

## 5270

### MARY STEWART

## The Prince and the Pilgrim

(New York: Morrow, 1996)

**Story type:** Fantasy (Legend; Quest)
**Major character(s):** Alexander, Royalty, Teenager; Alice, Teenager, Noblewoman; Morgan le Fay, Royalty, Sorceress
**Time period(s):** 5th century
**Locale(s):** England (Britain)

**Summary:** When he reaches his majority, Alexander sets off to seek justice from King Arthur for his father's murder. Morgan LeFay's machinations bring Alexander and Alice together when Morgan diverts Alexander with her lust for the Holy Grail, a cup identified to Alice while accompanying her father on a pilgrimage.

**Other books you might like:**
Marion Zimmer Bradley, *The Mists of Avalon*, 1983
Coningsby Dawson, *The Road to Avalon*, 1911
Parke Godwin, *Invitation to Camelot*, 1988
  editor
Cary James, *King & Raven*, 1995
Courtway Jones, *Witch of the North*, 1992

## 5271

### MICHAEL STEWART

## Belladonna

(New York: HarperCollins 1993)

**Story type:** Horror (Possession)
**Major character(s):** Matthew Cavewood, Historian; Hazel, Photographer, Fiance(e) (Matthew's); Josie McDowell, Student
**Time period(s):** 1990s (1992)
**Locale(s):** Charlottesville, Virginia

**Summary:** While researching the life of 17th-century physicist Nathaniel Shawcrosse, professor Matthew Cavewood becomes obsessed with Shawcrosse's lover, the murderer Isabel Hardiment. Cavewood's delving into Shawcrosse's metaphysical experiments facilitates Isabel's reincarnation as a 20th-century woman determined to repeat her pattern of murder and destruction.

**Other books you might like:**
Jonathan Aycliffe, *Naomi's Room*, 1991
Emmanuel Carrere, *Gothic Romance*, 1984
Marcy Heidish, *The Torching*, 1992
Daniel Rhodes, *Adversary*, 1988

## 5272

### SEAN STEWART

## Clouds End

(New York: Ace, 1996)

**Story type:** Fantasy (Quest)
**Major character(s):** Brook, Parent (mother); Jo, Mythical Creature; Rope, Sailor
**Time period(s):** Indeterminate Past
**Locale(s):** Clouds End, Fictional City; The Mist, Mythical Place

**Summary:** Jo comes out of The Mist and remakes herself as Brook. She should kill Brook but cannot do it, instead becoming two women with one soul. A dangerous journey lies ahead of them before their paths may separate.

**Other books you might like:**
Lisa Goldstein, *A Mask for the General*, 1987
Mark Helprin, *Winter's Tale*, 1983
Ursula K. Le Guin, *A Wizard of Earthsea*, 1986
Patricia A. McKillip, *The Riddle-Master of Hed*, 1976

## 5273

### SEAN STEWART

## Mockingbird

(New York, Ace, 1998)

**Story type:** Fantasy (Contemporary; Family Saga)

**Major character(s):** Antoinette "Toni" Beauchamp, Businesswoman (actuary), Psychic; Candace Jane "Candy" Beauchamp, Waiter/Waitress, Psychic; Elena Beauchamp, Psychic, Parent (mother)
**Time period(s):** 1990s (1995)
**Locale(s):** Montrose, Texas

**Summary:** Unlike her sister Candy, Toni hates the Gods which ride her mother. When her mother dies and the epitaph on her stone reads, "There are some gifts which cannot be refused," Toni knows it's meant for her. Then when Candy admits that she has followed Momma's instructions not to partake of the Mockingbird Cordial, Toni understands she has to take her mother's place.

**Other books you might like:**
John Crowley, *Love & Sleep*, 1994
Kara Dalkey, *Steel Rose*, 1997
Charles de Lint, *Trader*, 1997
Ben Okri, *The Famished Road*, 1992
Lawrence Watt-Evans, *Touched by the Gods*, 1997

## 5274

### SEAN STEWART

## The Night Watch

(New York: Ace, 1997)

**Story type:** Fantasy (Post-Disaster; Science Fiction)
**Series:** Resurrection Man
**Major character(s):** Emily Thompson, Heir, Fugitive; Water Spider, Government Official; Claire, Military Personnel, Governess
**Time period(s):** 21st century
**Locale(s):** Edmonton, Alberta, Canada (Southside); Vancouver, British Columbia, Canada (Chinatown)

**Summary:** Seven decades after magic rises up and overwhelms civilization, when the Powers begin to fade, rational Southside and mystical Chinatown face this fact in very different ways. Meanwhile, the heir to Southside performs a ritual to an unknown and and flees to Chinatown for safety. Since the rulers of Chinatown have their own plots, however, through human and Power conspiracy and error, no one may get out alive.

**Other books you might like:**
John Crowley, *Little, Big*, 1981
Lisa Goldstein, *A Mask for the General*, 1987
Megan Lindholm, *Wizard of the Pigeons*, 1986
Rachel Pollack, *Temporary Agency*, 1994
Michaela Roessner, *Vanishing Point*, 1993

## 5275

### SEAN STEWART

## Nobody's Son

(New York: Ace, 1995)

**Story type:** Fantasy (Political; Magic Conflict)
**Major character(s):** Shielder's Mark, Hero, Spouse; Gail, Royalty (princess), Spouse; Lissa, Courtier (lady-in-waiting)
**Time period(s):** Indeterminate
**Locale(s):** Ghostwood, Mythical Place; Borders, Fictional Country (dukedom); Swangard, Fictional City

**Summary:** Having prepared for years to assault the deadly mystery of the Ghostwood, Shielder's Mark proves a quick study as he unwinds the ancient sorcery which locks the Ghostwood outside time. In payment for his feat, Mark requests the king's daughter as wife and receives her troth, a title, and control over the Ghostwood. Mark's background as a commoner ill-prepares him for life as a nobleman, while winning Princess Gail's hand proves easier than winning her heart.

**Other books you might like:**
Terry Goodkind, *Wizard's First Rule*, 1994
Robin Hobb, *Assassin's Apprentice*, 1995
Mercedes Lackey, *The Lark and the Wren*, 1991
Patricia A. McKillip, *The Book of Atrix Wolfe*, 1995
Delia Sherman, *The Porcelain Dove*, 1993
Roger Zelazny, *Forever After*, 1995
    editor

---

**5276**

SEAN STEWART

## Passion Play
(New York: Ace, 1993)

**Story type:** Science Fiction (Mystery; Theological)
**Major character(s):** Diane Fletcher, Detective—Private, Empath (Shaper)
**Time period(s):** 21st century
**Locale(s):** United States

**Summary:** After the election of a Redemptionist candidate as President, the United States becomes a Christian theocracy. Diane seeks to promote justice by utilizing her empathic powers in crime solving for the police. When a high-tech theatrical costume claims the life of a well-known Redemptionist, Diane's empathic powers indicate not, as appears, suicide but rather murder. First novel.

**Other books you might like:**
Margaret Atwood, *The Handmaid's Tale*, 1985
Alfred Bester, *The Demolished Man*, 1953
Flynn Connolly, *The Rising of the Moon*, 1993
Suzette Haden Elgin, *Native Tongue*, 1984
Katharine Kerr, *Polar City Blues*, 1990
Mercedes Lackey, *Burning Water*, 1989

---

**5277**

SEAN STEWART

## Resurrection Man
(New York: Ace, 1995)

**Story type:** Fantasy (Religious; Contemporary)
**Major character(s):** Dante Ratkay, Psychic (Angel); Jet Ratkay, Relative (brother); Laura Chen, Friend
**Time period(s):** 1990s
**Locale(s):** North America

**Summary:** After World War II, some people called angels display psychic abilities, in China becoming accepted members of society and forming the Angels Guild. Raised as an atheist by his pragmatic physician father, Dante rejects the angel in himself as evil. When he finds his corpse, Dante takes it as an omen that he must accept his angel abilities and get his expectedly short life in order.

**Other books you might like:**
Tom Deitz, *Soulsmith*, 1991
C.S. Friedman, *Black Sun Rising*, 1991
Parke Godwin, *Waiting for the Galactic Bus*, 1988
James Morrow, *Only Begotten Daughter*, 1990
Sean Russell, *The Initiate Brother*, 1991

---

**5278**

G. HARRY STINE

## Blood Siege
(New York: Pinnacle, 1990)

**Story type:** Science Fiction (Military; Robot Fiction)
**Series:** Warbots
**Major character(s):** Curt Carlson, Military Personnel (Sierra Charlie colonel); Dyani Mortega, Military Personnel (Sierra Charlie captain), Indian (crow); Clark Jeremy, Religious, Television Personality
**Time period(s):** 21st century
**Locale(s):** Sanctuary, Nevada; Battle Mountain, Nevada

**Summary:** When the Soviets demand to know why the USA is constructing a new missile facility, the US government discovers that the base is not located in a military reservation, but rather on land owned by the fanatic and militant Galactic Tabernacle of the Human Future. Curt Carlson and Dyani Mortega infiltrate the organization, where they meet the fanatics' leader, Clark Jeremy, and a hireling who is an old nemesis of Carlson's. When the pair attempt to escape, only Carlson succeeds. As Carlson and his unit, the Washington Greys, stage a rescue attempt, Jeremy unleashes the threat of nuclear weapons on Las Vegas.

**Other books you might like:**
Alan Dean Foster, *Cyber Way*, 1990
Robert A. Heinlein, *Starship Troopers*, 1959
Frank Herbert, *Dune*, 1965
Keith Laumer, *Bolo: The Annals of the Dinochrome Brigade*, 1976
Keith Laumer, *Rogue Bolo*, 1986
Dave Wolverton, *On My Way to Paradise*, 1989

---

**5279**

G. HARRY STINE

## Force of Arms
(New York: Pinnacle, 1990)

**Story type:** Science Fiction (Military; Robot Fiction)
**Series:** Warbots
**Major character(s):** Curt Carlson, Military Personnel (Sierra Charlie colonel); Maggie MacPherson, Journalist (television)
**Time period(s):** 21st century
**Locale(s):** Sakhalin Island, Pacific Islands

**Summary:** When Soviet, Japanese and Chinese troops all gather on mineral-rich Sakhalin Island in violation of treaties, troops from the Washington Greys, from Brunei and Chile move to the island to help keep peace. The situation provides the first test of Soviet warbots after the Soviets took abandoned American warbots during a previous operation.

**Other books you might like:**
Donald F. Glut, *The Empire Strikes Back*, 1980
Robert A. Heinlein, *Starship Troopers*, 1959
Keith Laumer, *Bolo: The Annals of the Dinochrome Brigade*, 1976
Keith Laumer, *Rogue Bolo*, 1986
C.J. Mills, *Winter World*, 1988
Dave Wolverton, *On My Way to Paradise*, 1989

## 5280

### G. HARRY STINE

## Guts and Glory

(New York: Pinnacle, 1991)

**Story type:** Science Fiction (Military; Robot Fiction)
**Series:** Warbots
**Major character(s):** Curt Carlson, Military Personnel (Sierra Charlie Lieutenant Col.); Arwa Bint Muhammad al-Badr, Royalty (Queen of Yemen Royal Republic)
**Time period(s):** 21st century
**Locale(s):** Yemen

**Summary:** The Sierra Charlies have been deployed to protect the 250 kilometer robot railroad carrying 20% of the world's high-grade iron ore from guerrilla warfare. Curt Carlson must work despite excessive casualties resulting from lack of appropriate training and the use of high-tech weaponry by guerrillas, previously poorly armed. When all U.S. military forces are suddenly recalled, Curt must rescue his commanding officer, General Belinda Hettrick, and Yemen's Sultana, Queen Arwa.

**Other books you might like:**
Lois McMaster Bujold, *The Warrior's Apprentice*, 1986
David Drake, *The Jungle*, 1991
Alan Dean Foster, *Dark Star*, 1974
Diana G. Gallagher, *The Alien Dark*, 1990
Robert A. Heinlein, *Starship Troopers*, 1959
Keith Laumer, *Rogue Bolo*, 1986
Dave Wolverton, *On My Way to Paradise*, 1989

## 5281

### G. HARRY STINE

## Judgment Day

(New York: Pinnacle, 1992)

**Story type:** Science Fiction (Military)
**Series:** Warbots
**Major character(s):** Curt Carlson, Military Personnel (Sierra Charlie colonel); Willa Lovell, Scientist, Computer Expert (warbot)
**Time period(s):** 21st century
**Locale(s):** Nevada; Pakistan

**Summary:** Curt Carlson and the Washington Grays travel into the Himalayan Mountains with orders to destroy a secret enemy facility which produces interference having disastrous effects on warbot communications.

**Other books you might like:**
Jerry Earl Brown, *Snowmen*, 1991
Keith Laumer, *Bolo: The Annals of the Dinochrome Brigade*, 1976
Neal Stephenson, *Snow Crash*, 1992
Dave Wolverton, *On My Way to Paradise*, 1989

## 5282

### G. HARRY STINE

## Starsea Invaders: First Action

(New York: Roc, 1993)

**Story type:** Science Fiction (Invasion of Earth; Military)
**Series:** Starsea Invaders
**Major character(s):** William M. Corry, Military Personnel, Sea Captain
**Time period(s):** 21st century

**Locale(s):** Pacific Ocean; *U.S.S. Shenandoah*, Submarine

**Summary:** While the United States and China vie for supremacy of the Pacific Ocean, a prototype submersible aircraft carrier investigating the disappearance of U.S. citizens discovers extraterrestrials hiding beneath the sea and harvesting human beings.

**Other books you might like:**
David Brin, *Startide Rising*, 1983
Orson Scott Card, *The Abyss*, 1989
A.C. Crispin, *V*, 1984
Diane Duane, *seaQuest DSV: The Novel*, 1993
    Peter Morwood, co-author
James H. Schmitz, *The Demon Breed*, 1968
Theodore Sturgeon, *Voyage to the Bottom of the Sea*, 1961
John Varley, *Millennium*, 1983
Denise Vitola, *Half-Light*, 1992
David Weber, *Mutineers' Moon*, 1991

## 5283

### G. HARRY STINE

## Warrior Shield

(New York: Pinnacle, 1992)

**Story type:** Science Fiction (Military)
**Series:** Warbots
**Major character(s):** Curt Carlson, Military Personnel (Sierra Charlie colonel)
**Time period(s):** 21st century
**Locale(s):** Senegambia, Africa

**Summary:** When the United States president demands that dictator Generalissimo Modibo cease his attempt to gain power for his impoverished nation, the dictator begins slaughtering and imprisoning American nationals. The President then orders Curt Carlson and his warbots to rescue the imprisoned Americans and restore freedom to the area in order to avoid total global war.

**Other books you might like:**
Lois McMaster Bujold, *The Vor Game*, 1990
Lois McMaster Bujold, *The Warrior's Apprentice*, 1986
Robert A. Heinlein, *Starship Troopers*, 1959
Keith Laumer, *Rogue Bolo*, 1986
Dave Wolverton, *On My Way to Paradise*, 1989

## 5284

### JEAN MARIE STINE, Editor
### FORREST J. ACKERMAN, Co-Editor

## I, Vampire: Interviews with the Undead

(Stamford, CT: Longmeadow Press, 1995)

**Story type:** Horror (Anthology; Vampire Story)

**Summary:** The dozen vampire stories written especially for this volume are all narrated in the first person by vampires. In John Gregory Betancourt's "By Moonlight," a vampire relates how his father's death brings him to a new understanding about his family. Darrell Schweitzer's "Runaway" is the story of a young boy who becomes a vampire through his mother's occult practices. In William F. Nolan's "Vympyre," a dying vampire's long life flashes before his eyes. Diana G. Gallagher, in "Tipping Is Not a City in China," describes the dilemma faced by a former vegetarian and new member of the undead who prepares for her feast feeding. Chris Moran's "Two Spirits" tells of a transexual vampire who discovers it is of two minds (literally) regarding its vampiredom. The editors supply a badly fact-checked appendix of further reading and movie viewing of vampire material.

**Other books you might like:**
Ellen Datlow, *Blood Is Not Enough*, 1990
    editor
Robert Weinberg, *100 Vicious Little Vampire Stories*, 1995
    Stefan Dziemianowicz and Martin H. Greenberg, co-editors
Stephen Jones, *The Mammoth Book of Vampires*, 1993
    editor

**5285**

**R.L. STINE**

## The Cat

(New York: Pocket/Archway, 1997)

**Story type:** Horror (Young Adult; Apocalyptic Horror)
**Series:** Fear Street
**Major character(s):** Marty Harper, Teenager, Student—High School; Dwayne, Teenager; Maggie, Scientist; Coach Griffin, Coach (basketball)
**Time period(s):** 1990s (1997)
**Locale(s):** Shadyside, Fictional City (Shadyside High School)

**Summary:** Marty Harper kills the mischievous cat that caused an injury which jeopardizes his chances at a basketball scholarship. But now Marty sees the cat everywhere, stalking him with a murderous intent that extends to his family and friends. A young adult novel.

**Other books you might like:**
Caroline B. Cooney, *The Terrorist*, 1997
Lois Duncan, *I Walk at Night*, 1997
Diane Hoh, *Book of Horrors*, 1994
Joan Lowery Nixon, *Don't Scream*, 1997
Christopher Pike, *Die Softly*, 1991

**5286**

**R.L. STINE**

## The Curse of Camp Cold Lake

(New York: Scholastic, 1997)

**Story type:** Horror (Ghost Story; Young Adult)
**Major character(s):** Sarah Maas, Child; Aaron Maas, Child; Brianna, Child
**Time period(s):** 1990s (1996)
**Locale(s):** Camp Cold Lake

**Summary:** Sarah Maas uses a near-drowning experience at summer camp to get sympathy from her bunkmates. Thereafter, she is persuaded by the ghost of Della, a young girl who died at the camp and who demands that Sarah be her buddy. A novel for pre-teenage readers.

**Other books you might like:**
Avi, *Devil's Race*, 1994
Lynn Blankman, *Ghost Beyond the Garden*, 1996
William Brittain, *Who Knew There'd Be Ghosts?*, 1995
Bruce Coville, *My Teacher Is an Alien*, 1989

**5287**

**R.L. STINE**

## Double Date

(New York: Pocket/Archway, 1994)

**Story type:** Horror (Mystery)
**Series:** Fear Street
**Major character(s):** Bobby Newkirk, Teenager; Bree Wade, Teenager, Twin; Samantha Wade, Teenager, Twin
**Time period(s):** 1990s (1994)
**Locale(s):** Shadyside

**Summary:** High school stud Bobby Newkirk believes in loving and leaving his dates, even twin sisters Bree and Samantha Wade. But it soon appears to Bobby that Bree is not about to give him up to her sister, and that she will even stoop to impersonating her sister—or worse—to get him back.

**Other books you might like:**
Debra Franklin, *The Admirer*, 1994
G.G. Gath, *Driven to Kill*, 1994
Gloria D. Miklowitz, *Desperate Pursuit*, 1992
Nicholas Pine, *The New Kid*, 1992

**5288**

**R.L. STINE**

## The First Horror

(New York: Pocket/Archway, 1994)

**Story type:** Horror (Haunted House)
**Series:** 99 Fear Street: The House of Evil
**Major character(s):** Cally Frasier, Teenager; Cody Frasier, Teenager; Anthony, Teenager
**Time period(s):** 1990s (1994)
**Locale(s):** Shadyside

**Summary:** This first novel in a spin-off from Stine's enormously popular "Fear Street" young adult horror series chronicles the tribulations of the Frasier family, who move into their new home on Fear Street unaware of its bloody legacy and special link to Shadyside's evil town founder, Simon Fear.

**Other books you might like:**
Michael August, *New Year's Evil*, 1994
Peg Kehret, *Horror at the Haunted House*, 1994
Simon Lake, *Daughter of Darkness*, 1992
Edmund Plante, *Alone in the House*, 1991

**5289**

**R.L. STINE**

## My Best Friend Is Invisible

(New York: St. Martin's, 1996)

**Story type:** Horror (Science Fiction; Young Adult)
**Major character(s):** Sammy Jacobs, Child; Simon Jacobs, Child; Roxanne, Child
**Time period(s):** 1990s (1996)
**Locale(s):** Middletown, Fictional City

**Summary:** Imaginative Sammy Jacobs can't get anyone to believe that the mischief he continually gets into is due to an invisible friend who won't stop pestering him. A novel for preteen readers.

**Other books you might like:**
Avi, *Devil's Race*, 1994

Lynn Blankman, *Ghost Beyond the Garden*, 1996
William Brittain, *Who Knew There'd Be Ghosts?*, 1995
Bruce Coville, *My Teacher Is an Alien*, 1989

## 5290
### R.L. STINE

## Superstitious

(New York: Warner/Tartikoff, 1995)

**Story type:** Horror (Occult)
**Major character(s):** Sara Morgan, Student; Liam Morgan, Professor (of folklore); Milton Cohn, Administrator (dean of students)
**Time period(s):** 1990s (1995)
**Locale(s):** Moore, Pennsylvania

**Summary:** Without a job or a boyfriend, former publishing minion Sara Morgan decides to resume her education at Moore State College, where she is soon swept off her feet and married by professor of folklore Liam O'Connor. Liam's superstitious behavior is not without merit: he is haunted by literal demons who make the lives of those within his and Sara's sphere a literal hell on earth. This is the author's first adult horror novel, after 56 novels written for the young adult market.

**Other books you might like:**
Marcy Heidish, *The Torching*, 1992
Fritz Leiber, *Conjure Wife*, 1953
Brent Monahan, *Blood of the Covenant*, 1993
Michael Stewart, *Belladonna*, 1992

## 5291
### R.L. STINE

## Vampire Breath

(New York: Scholastic, 1996)

**Story type:** Horror (Vampire Story)
**Series:** Goosebumps
**Major character(s):** Freddy Martinez, Child (12-year-old); Cara Simonetti, Child (12-year-old); Count Nightwing, Vampire
**Time period(s):** 1990s (1996)
**Locale(s):** Ohio

**Summary:** When Freddy and Cara discover the coffin of Count Nightwing in a tunnel underneath Freddy's house, they accidentally awaken him from his century-long slumber. Nightwing transports them back to the nineteenth century and the castle where he keeps his private supply of Vampire Breath, the elixir that allows him to grow fangs.

**Other books you might like:**
M.T. Coffin, *Blood Red Eightball*, 1996
Christopher Pike, *The Creature in the Teacher*, 1996
Tom B. Stone, *The Fright Before Christmas*, 1996

## 5292
### S.M. STIRLING
### JUDITH TARR, Co-Author
### SUSAN SHWARTZ, Co-Author
### HARRY TURTLEDOVE, Co-Author

## Blood Feuds

(New York: Baen, 1993)

**Story type:** Science Fiction (Military; Political)

**Series:** War World
**Major character(s):** Aiysha, Leader
**Time period(s):** Indeterminate Future
**Locale(s):** Haven, Moon—Imaginary (Byers' star system)

**Summary:** After 300 years of Sauron domination, disparate human forces unite under Aiysha's leadership to meet their enemies at Sauron Citadel and reclaim their world at any cost. Braided novel set in Jerry Pournelle's CoDominium milieu.

**Other books you might like:**
Frank Herbert, *Dune*, 1965
Gordon Kendall, *White Wing*, 1985
   pseudonym of S.N. Lewitt and Susan Shwartz
Larry Niven, *The Mote in God's Eye*, 1974
   Jerry Pournelle, co-author
Jerry Pournelle, *CoDominium: Revolt on War World*, 1992
   John F. Carr, co-editor
Jerry Pournelle, *Go Tell the Spartans*, 1991
   S.M. Stirling, co-author
Jerry Pournelle, *War World I: The Burning Eye*, 1988
   John F. Carr, co-editor
Jerry Pournelle, *War World II: Death's Head Rebellion*, 1990
   John F. Carr, co-editor
Jerry Pournelle, *War World III: Sauron Dominion*, 1991
   John F. Carr, co-editor
Susan Shwartz, *Silk Roads and Shadows*, 1988
Judith Tarr, *Arrows of the Sun*, 1993
Harry Turtledove, *The Guns of the South: A Novel of the Civil War*, 1992

## 5293
### S.M. STIRLING
### SHIRLEY MEIER, Co-Author

## The Cage

(New York: Baen, 1989)

**Story type:** Fantasy (Adventure)
**Major character(s):** Megan Whitlock, Warrior (Female); Shkai'ra, Warrior (Female), Barbarian
**Time period(s):** Indeterminate

**Summary:** A woman who escapes slavery is determined to avenge herself on the ones who enslaved her.

**Other books you might like:**
Gael Baudino, *Gossamer Axe*, 1990
Marion Zimmer Bradley, *Free Amazons of Darkover*, 1985
Phyllis Ann Karr, *Frostflower and Windbourne*, 1982
Patricia A. McKillip, *The Changeling Sea*, 1988
Jennifer Roberson, *Sword-Dancer*, 1986

## 5294
### S.M. STIRLING

## Drakon

(New York: Baen, 1996)

**Story type:** Science Fiction (Military; Alternate Universe)
**Series:** Draka
**Major character(s):** Gwendolyn Ingolfsson, Genetically Altered Being; Henry Carmaggio, Detective—Police; Jennifer Feinberg, Businesswoman
**Time period(s):** 1990s (1995-1999); 25th century (2442-2445)
**Locale(s):** New York, New York; Andros Island, Bahamas

**Summary:** A failed space travel experiment strands Gwendolyn Ingolfsson, a Draka, on a parallel Earth—our Earth—where *Homo sapiens* have not been genetically engineered into other species. She views her predicament as an opportunity to subjugate yet another world to Draka rule, while Detective Henry Carmaggio attempts to stop her. Fourth in the series.

**Other books you might like:**
Gordon R. Dickson, *Dorsai!*, 1976
David Drake, *Igniting the Reaches*, 1994
David Drake, *Northworld*, 1990
Joe Haldeman, *The Forever War*, 1975
Fred Saberhagen, *Brother Assassin*, 1969

---

### 5295

#### S.M. STIRLING

## Island in the Sea of Time
(New York: Roc, 1998)

**Story type:** Science Fiction (Disaster; Military)
**Major character(s):** Marian Alston, Military Personnel (U.S. Coast Guard captain), Lesbian; Jared Cofflin, Police Officer
**Time period(s):** 1990s (1998); 13th century B.C. (1250 B.C.)
**Locale(s):** Nantucket Island, England

**Summary:** Thrown back in time to 1250 B.C., Nantucket residents and visitors must plan for survival. When they travel to Britain for stores of grain, they discover a war between patriarchal invaders and a peaceful, but stagnant, matriarchal society.

**Other books you might like:**
Robert Adams, *Castaways in Time*, 1985
Poul Anderson, *The Dancer From Atlantis*, 1972
L. Sprague de Camp, *Lest Darkness Fall*, 1941
Robert A. Heinlein, *Tunnel in the Sky*, 1955
Fred Hoyle, *October the First Is Too Late*, 1966
Larry Niven, *Lucifer's Hammer*, 1977
   Jerry Pournelle, co-author
Henry Treece, *The Golden Strangers*, 1956
Robert Charles Wilson, *Mysterium*, 1944

---

### 5296

#### S.M. STIRLING
#### HOLLY LISLE, Co-Author

## The Rose Sea
(New York: Baen, 1994)

**Story type:** Fantasy (Magic Conflict; Quest)
**Major character(s):** Bren Morkaarin, Heir—Lost, Military Personnel (captain); Karah Grenlaarin, Equestrian, Military Personnel (draftee); Willek Tornsaarin, Military Personnel (grand admiral), Sorcerer
**Time period(s):** Indeterminate
**Locale(s):** Tykissian Empire, Fictional Country; Tarin Tseld, Fictional Country

**Summary:** Away from home by herself for the first time, Karah finds herself unknowingly involved in an ancient battle between gods when she is suddenly impressed into the army. Destiny forces her to show her mettle, while a ghostly shaman leads her on prophetic voyages during sleep.

**Other books you might like:**
Constance Ash, *The Stalking Horse*, 1990
Rosemary Kirstein, *The Steerswoman*, 1989

Mercedes Lackey, *When the Bough Breaks*, 1993
   Holly Lisle, co-author
Holly Lisle, *Fire in the Mist*, 1992
Laurie J. Marks, *The Watcher's Mask*, 1992
Elizabeth Moon, *Sheepfarmer's Daughter*, 1988
Angus Wells, *Dark Magic*, 1992

---

### 5297

#### S.M. STIRLING
#### SHIRLEY MEIER, Co-Author

## Saber & Shadow
(New York: Baen, 1992)

**Story type:** Fantasy (Adventure; Political)
**Series:** Fifth Millennium
**Major character(s):** Shkai'ra Mek Kermak's-kin, Warrior; Megan Whitlock, Warrior
**Time period(s):** 50th century
**Locale(s):** Illizbuah, Fictional City; Almerkun, Fictional Country; North America

**Summary:** Shkai'ra and Megan join forces to wreak havoc with established intrigues in Almerkun's metropolis.

**Other books you might like:**
Shirley Meier, *Shadow's Daughter*, 1991
Shirley Meier, *Shadow's Son*, 1991
   S.M. Stirling, Karen Wehrstein, co-authors
Karen Wehrstein, *Lion's Heart*, 1991
Karen Wehrstein, *Lion's Soul*, 1991

---

### 5298

#### S.M. STIRLING

## The Ship Avenged
(New York: Baen, 1997)

**Story type:** Science Fiction (Adventure; Space Colony)
**Series:** Ship Who Sang
**Major character(s):** Joat Simeon-Hap, Spaceship Captain; Soamosa, Young Woman; Bro Sperin, Spy
**Time period(s):** Indeterminate Future
**Locale(s):** New Dentinies, Space Station; Kolnar, Space Station

**Summary:** Devastated by a designed virus, the Kolnari vow revenge, intending to drop a mind-destroying virus on the planet Bethel. When Joat Simeon-Hap needs to earn money quickly to pay a fine, she has to deal with the man who sold her into slavery and must meet with the Kolnari. Sequel to *The City Who Fought*.

**Other books you might like:**
Lois McMaster Bujold, *The Vor Game*, 1990
C.J. Cherryh, *Tripoint*, 1994
Alfred Coppel, *Glory*, 1993
Anne McCaffrey, *The City Who Fought*, 1993
   S.M. Stirling, co-author
Anne McCaffrey, *The Ship Who Sang*, 1969
Melissa Scott, *Five-Twelfths of Heaven*, 1985
John E. Stith, *Redshift Rendezvous*, 1990
Timothy Zahn, *Deadman Switch*, 1988

## 5299

### S.M. STIRLING

## Snow Brother

(New York: Baen, 1992)

**Story type:** Fantasy (Quest; Psychic Powers)
**Series:** Fifth Millennium
**Major character(s):** Shkai'ra Mek Kermak's-kin, Warrior; Maihu Jonnah's-kin, Religious (Way of the Circle), Captive; Eh'rik, Warrior
**Time period(s):** 50th century (4960s)
**Locale(s):** Great Plains, North America; Central Almerkun, Fictional Country

**Summary:** Capturing Maihu and Taimi while sacking a village, Shkai'ra continues eastward on her mission of raiding and capturing new goods, hampered by shamanistic forces and treachery. Expands the 1985 release.

**Other books you might like:**
Shirley Meier, *Shadow's Daughter*, 1991
Shirley Meier, *Shadow's Son*, 1991
    S.M. Stirling, Karen Wahrstein, co-authors
Karen Wehrstein, *Lion's Heart*, 1991
Karen Wehrstein, *Lion's Soul*, 1991

## 5300

### S.M. STIRLING

## The Stone Dogs

(New York: Baen, 1990)

**Story type:** Science Fiction (Alternate Universe; Military)
**Series:** Draka
**Major character(s):** Yolande Ingolfsson, Royalty (Drakan aristocracy); Frederick LeFarge, Royalty (Drakan aristocracy); Marya LeFarge, Royalty (Drakan aristocracy)
**Time period(s):** 20th century
**Locale(s):** Alternate Earth; Outer Space

**Summary:** Conflict between the Domination of the Draka and the American Lead Alliance for Democracy continues, with both sides waiting for the right moment to start and win the next war with their respective secret weapons; computer technologies for the Alliance, and bio-engineering (germ warfare) for the Domination.

**Other books you might like:**
Gregory Benford, *Hitler Victorious: Eleven Stories of the German Victory in World War II*, 1986
    Martin H. Greenberg, co-editor
Philip K. Dick, *The Man in the High Castle*, 1963
David Drake, *Fortress*, 1987
Ralph Peters, *Red Army*, 1989
Jerry Pournelle, *Falkenberg's Legion*, 1990

## 5301

### S.M. STIRLING

## Under the Yoke

(New York: Baen Books, 1989)

**Story type:** Science Fiction (Alternate Universe)
**Major character(s):** Marya Sokolowska, Religious (Nun); Captain Fred Kustaa, Pilot
**Time period(s):** Indeterminate (1948 in alternate time)
**Locale(s):** Alternate Universe (Europe and the United States)

**Summary:** After the American Revolution, the Tories fled not to Canada but to South Africa where they founded the nation of Drakesland. Now, more than one hundred and fifty years later, the slave-owning, totalitarian Draka have conquered half the world. If they have their way, the United States will be next. Sequel to *Marching Through Georgia*.

**Other books you might like:**
Gregory Benford, *Hitler Victorious: Eleven Stories of the German Victory in World War II*, 1986
    Martin H. Greenberg, co-editor
Gregory Benford, *Alternate Empires*, 1989
    Martin H. Greenberg, co-editor
John Hersey, *White Lotus*, 1965
Keith Roberts, *Pavane*, 1968
Sarban, *The Sound of His Horn*, 1952

## 5302

### JOHN E. STITH

## Deep Quarry

(New York: Ace, 1989)

**Story type:** Science Fiction (Mystery)
**Major character(s):** Ben Takent, Detective—Private; Kate Dunlet, Professor
**Time period(s):** Indeterminate Future
**Locale(s):** Tankur, Planet—Imaginary

**Summary:** Private-eye Ben Takent is hired to solve a difficult case involving two murders and alien artifacts which are disappearing from a locked vault. At a nearby dig, a team of archaeologists engaged in the excavation of an ancient civilization may be in horrible danger.

**Other books you might like:**
Richard Bowker, *Dover Beach*, 1988
Victor Koman, *The Jehovah Contract*, 1987
William Shatner, *TekWar*, 1989
F. Paul Wilson, *Dydeetown World*, 1989

## 5303

### JOHN E. STITH

## Manhattan Transfer

(New York: Tor, 1993)

**Story type:** Science Fiction (Disaster; First Contact)
**Major character(s):** Matt Sheehan, Government Official, Troubleshooter; Abby Terza, Linguist, Anthropologist (cultural); Bobby Joe Brewster, Scientist
**Time period(s):** 21st century
**Locale(s):** New York, New York (Manhattan); Outer Space

**Summary:** When aliens suddenly pick up the island of Manhattan and deposit it in a strange grey medium aboard a giant space ship, some, including Matt Sheehan, want to know why they have been abducted and if they can communicate with other abducted cities. When Matt and others contact the abductors, they find that Earth will be ruined for human life unless they find a way to disable another ship which will soon modify the Earth to suit alien needs.

**Other books you might like:**
Roger MacBride Allen, *The Ring of Charon*, 1990
James Blish, *Cities in Flight*, 1970
David Brin, *Earth*, 1990
Octavia E. Butler, *Dawn*, 1987
Edmund Cooper, *Seahorse in the Sky*, 1969

Fritz Leiber, *The Wanderer*, 1964
William Tenn, *Of Men and Monsters*, 1968
Harlan Thompson, *Silent Running*, 1972
Richard Wilson, *And Then the Town Took Off*, 1960

## 5304

### JOHN E. STITH

## *Reckoning Infinity*

(New York: Tor, 1997)

**Story type:** Science Fiction (First Contact; Adventure)
**Major character(s):** Alis Mary Nussem, Spacewoman, Pilot (spaceship); Karl Stanton, Spaceman, Pilot (spaceship)
**Time period(s):** Indeterminate Future
**Locale(s):** Tokyan Station, Space Station; *Ranger*, Spaceship; *Cantaloupe*, Spaceship

**Summary:** Karl accepts a position on *Ranger*, stationed near Pluto, hoping to escape the infamy he acquired when falsely blamed for an accident resulting from sabotage. Alis also hopes to escape her memories of the disaster when she sign on with *Ranger*, but meeting Karl there prohibits relief. Unwilling workmates, Alis and Karl together explore a fabulous alien vessel as it visits the Solar System.

**Other books you might like:**
Roger MacBride Allen, *The Ring of Charon*, 1990
Greg Bear, *Eon*, 1985
Vonda N. McIntyre, *Metaphase*, 1992
Larry Niven, *Ringworld*, 1970
John Varley, *Titan*, 1979

## 5305

### JOHN E. STITH

## *Redshift Rendezvous*

(New York: Ace Books, 1990)

**Story type:** Science Fiction (Hard Science Fiction)
**Major character(s):** Jason Kraft, Spaceman; Tara Cline, Passenger
**Time period(s):** Indeterminate Future
**Locale(s):** *Redshift*, Spaceship

**Summary:** A new spacedrive works by shifting a spaceship to another universe, one where the speed of light is just eighty meters per second. This causes all sorts of bizarre problems for the crew and passengers, especially when one passenger is killed and pirates show up.

**Other books you might like:**
Poul Anderson, *Tau Zero*, 1970
James Blish, *Common Time*, 1953
Larry Niven, *Neutron Star*, 1968
Christopher Priest, *The Inverted World*, 1974

## 5306

### JOHN E. STITH

## *Reunion on Neverend*

(New York: Tor, 1994)

**Story type:** Science Fiction (Mystery; Techno-Thriller)
**Major character(s):** Lan Dillon, Police Officer (secret agent); Parke Brenlek, Friend; Tessa Farlan, Businesswoman (museum owner)
**Time period(s):** Indeterminate Future
**Locale(s):** Neverend, Asteroid (space colony); Arangorta, Planet—Imaginary

**Summary:** On Neverend for his school reunion, Lan maintains his old persona as a cowardly weakling until Tessa needs protection. The mysterious death of her father, continuing disturbances at her museum and attempts to intimidate her into selling the museum propel the friends into a wonderful discovery and a dangerous adventure.

**Other books you might like:**
Philip K. Dick, *The Unteleported Man*, 1983
  revised edition
Geary Gravel, *A Key for the Nonesuch*, 1990
Andre Norton, *Star Gate*, 1958
Sheri S. Tepper, *Grass*, 1989
George Zebrowski, *Stranger Suns*, 1991

## 5307

### GRANT STOCKBRIDGE

## *The Spider #3: Death's Crimson Juggernaut/The Red Death Rain*

(New York: Carroll & Graf, 1992)

**Story type:** Fantasy (Contemporary; Mystery)
**Series:** Spider
**Major character(s):** Richard Wentworth, Adventurer (crime fighter); Ya Che, Criminal; Gentleman Jack Hayes, Criminal
**Time period(s):** 1930s
**Locale(s):** United States

**Summary:** Reprints two 1934 pulp stories full of weird adventure, strange plots and daring escapes. In "Death's Crimson Juggernaut" a blindfolded Spider must foil a plot by sadistic gangsters to frame him. In "The Red Death Rain" a mad cult poisoning thousands of people to hold the USA hostage comes to the Spider's attention, but can even the Spider stop these geniuses of evil?

**Other books you might like:**
Lin Carter, *Invisible Death*, 1975
Philip Jose Farmer, *Escape From Loki*, 1991
Jon Stephen Fink, *Further Adventures*, 1993
Rob MacGregor, *Indiana Jones and the Dance of the Giants*, 1991
Kenneth Robeson, *The Frightened Fish*, 1992
  pseudonym of Will Murray

## 5308

### GRANT STOCKBRIDGE

## *The Spider #4: Death Reign of the Vampire King/The Pain Emperor*

(New York: Carroll & Graf, 1992)

**Story type:** Fantasy (Contemporary; Mystery)
**Series:** Spider
**Major character(s):** Richard Wentworth, Adventurer (crime fighter); The Bat Man, Criminal; The Avenger, Adventurer (crime fighter), Criminal
**Time period(s):** 1930s
**Locale(s):** United States

**Summary:** Reprints two pulp stories from 1935 complete with weird mystery and lurid adventure. In "Death Reign of the Vampire King" the Spider combats a fiendish genius who flies and controls deadly swarms of killer bats. In "The Pain Emperor" the Spider battles combined forces when a ring of prisoners and a false crime fighter team up.

**Other books you might like:**
Lin Carter, *The Volcano Ogre*, 1976
Philip Jose Farmer, *Escape From Loki*, 1991
Jon Stephen Fink, *Further Adventures*, 1993
Rob MacGregor, *Indiana Jones and the Peril at Delphi*, 1991
Kenneth Robeson, *The Jade Ogre*, 1992
    pseudonym of Will Murray

## 5309

### GRANT STOCKBRIDGE

## The Spider #8: The Devil's Paymaster/ Legions of the Accursed Light

(New York: Carroll & Graf, 1993)

**Story type:** Fantasy (Contemporary; Mystery)
**Series:** Spider
**Major character(s):** Richard Wentworth, Adventurer (crime fighter); Stanley Kirkpatrick, Police Officer (commissioner); Ram Singh, Servant, Warrior
**Time period(s):** 1930s
**Locale(s):** New York, New York

**Summary:** Reprints two lurid crime stories from 1938 and 1941 pulps delivering weird mystery and two-fisted action. "The Devil's Paymaster" forces the Spider to follow a trail of mysterious corpses to a fiendish plot. In "Legions of the Accursed Light," a villain with a death ray holds a city hostage.

**Other books you might like:**
Martin Caidin, *Indiana Jones and the Sky Pirates*, 1993
Lin Carter, *Invisible Death*, 1975
Philip Jose Farmer, *Escape From Loki*, 1991
Jon Stephen Fink, *Further Adventures*, 1993
Kenneth Robeson, *The Jade Ogre*, 1992
    pseudonym of Will Murray

## 5310

### FRANK STOCKTON

## The Lady or the Tiger and Other Stories

(New York: Tor, 1992)

**Story type:** Fantasy (Collection; Legend)

**Summary:** Contains 11 stories published last century including Stockton's most famous, the title story, and one of its sequels, "The Discourager of Hesitancy," with other stories featuring mythical creatures such as the three stories about a tiny fairy, "Ting-a-Ling," "Ting-a-Ling and the Five Magicians" and "Ting-a-Ling's Visit to Tur-il-i-ra." Jane Yolen contributes a four-page biography of Frank Stockton, a three-page foreword focusing on the periodical *St. Nicholas, A Monthly Magazine for Boys and Girls*, and a two-page afterword.

**Other books you might like:**
Rudyard Kipling, *Kipling's Fantasy*, 1992
Rudyard Kipling, *Puck of Pook's Hill*, 1906
Andrew Lang, *The Blue Fairy Book*, 1889
    editor
Andrew Lang, *The Green Fairy Book*, 1892
    editor
Andrew Lang, *The Red Fairy Book*, 1890
    editor
Jack London, *Selected Science Fiction and Fantasy Stories*, 1979
Kenneth Morris, *The Secret Mountain and Other Tales*, 1926

## 5311

### JAMES STODDARD

## The High House

(New York: Aspect, 1998)

**Major character(s):** Carter Anderson, Heir; Duskin Anderson, Recluse
**Time period(s):** Indeterminate
**Locale(s):** Fictional Country (Evenmere)

**Summary:** Carter Anderson returns to the mysterious house where he lived as a child. There he seeks to solve the mystery of his late father's refusal to leave the ancient building, opposed by a sullen relative who makes no secret of his desire that Carter leave. He discovers that the house is a gateway to a magical realm hidden from the normal world. First novel.

**Other books you might like:**
Jonathan Carroll, *The Land of Laughs*, 1980
Pamela Dean, *The Secret Country*, 1985
Pamela Dean, *The Whim of the Dragon*, 1986
Esther Friesner, *New York by Knight*, 1986
Mervyn Peake, *Titus Alone*, 1946

## 5312

### BRAM STOKER

## The Jewel of Seven Stars

(New York: Oxford, 1996)

**Story type:** Horror (Reanimated Dead)
**Major character(s):** Abel Trelawney, Archaeologist (Egyptologist); Margaret Trelawney, Young Woman; Malcolm Ross, Lawyer
**Time period(s):** 1900s (1903)
**Locale(s):** London, England

**Summary:** An experiment to resurrect the mummy of Queen Tera leaves Abel Trelawney in a coma. Friends and family attempting to revive Trelawney discover that his daughter, Margaret, may be possessed of a portion of Tera's soul, and thus pose a danger to herself and her father. This novel was first published in England in 1903. An appendix reprints the alternative ending from the 1912 revised edition.

**Other books you might like:**
Kathryn Meyer Griffith, *The Calling*, 1994
Jane Webb Loudon, *The Mummy!: A Tale of the Twenty-Second Century*, 1827
Michael Paine, *Cities of the Dead*, 1988
Anne Rice, *The Mummy, or Ramses the Damned*, 1991
Anne Rice, *Servant of the Bones*, 1996

## 5313

### DEL STONE JR.

## Dead Heat

(Austin, Texas: Mojo Press, 1996)

**Story type:** Horror (Reanimated Dead)
**Major character(s):** Hitch, Reanimated Dead (zombie), Biker; Frederick Gerenz, Administrator (labor camp director); Frank Black, Military Personnel (ex-Air Force officer)
**Time period(s):** 1990s
**Locale(s):** Amarillo, Texas; Waterloo, Michigan; Death Valley, California

**Summary:** In the near future a genetically altered virus has turned the world's population into hordes of mindless zombies with a taste for human flesh. Hitch, a zombie biker endowed with unusual intelligence by a disembodied presence he calls "the other," travels cross-country on a mission to save the world from an evil entity who is taking advantage of the chaos to bring about the earth's destruction. His adventures along the way bring him into contact with a dictator who runs a forced labor camp for the few remaining humans, chain-saw wielding zombie hunters, and other escapades that tax his decomposing body to the limit. This is the author's first novel.

**Other books you might like:**
Philip Nutman, *Wet Work*, 1993
George Romero, *Dawn of the Dead*, 1978
   Susanna Sparrow, co-author
John Russo, *Inhuman*, 1986
John Skipp, *Book of the Dead*, 1989
   Craig Spector, co-editor
John Skipp, *Still Dead: Book of the Dead 2*, 1992
   Craig Spector, co-editor; Title could be Book of the Dead II

**5314**

**JORDAN STORM**

## Substitute Teacher

(New York: Pocket, 1993)

**Story type:** Horror (Child-in-Peril)
**Major character(s):** Mary Margaret McCarthy, Teacher; Beth Flynn, Administrator (personnel analyst); Lizbeth Flynn, Child (Beth's daughter)
**Time period(s):** 1990s (1993)
**Locale(s):** New York, New York

**Summary:** Although gifted with a talent for sizing up people from details most others don't even pay attention to, Beth Flynn can't put her finger on why she feels uneasy about her daughter's new teacher. Yet her intuition is correct, for Mary Margaret McCarthy is a psychologically damaged transient whose teaching method includes murder.

**Other books you might like:**
J.M. Dillard, *Specters*, 1991
Eric Flanders, *The Forever Children*, 1992
Ed Kelleher, *The School*, 1992
   Harriet Vidal, co-author
David Martin, *Bring Me Children*, 1992
Kathryn Ptacek, *The Hunted*, 1993
John Saul, *Darkness*, 1991

**5315**

**L. ELIZABETH STORM**

## Angels Unaware

(New York: Boulevard, 1997)

**Story type:** Science Fiction (Time Travel; Theological)
**Series:** Quantum Leap
**Major character(s):** Sam Beckett, Time Traveler, Scientist; Teresa Bruckner, Student; Angelita Carmen Jiminez, Angel
**Time period(s):** 1990s (1995)
**Locale(s):** Boston, Massachusetts

**Summary:** Having met Sam as a child, Teresa believes in angels, but finds herself unable to accept the Hispanic flapper Angelita as an angel, even though she proves to have much information about Teresa that she shouldn't know. When Sam finds himself a local priest, he may be able to save Teresa from the drug dealers who want to kill her for stealing their drugs. Television tie-in.

**Other books you might like:**
Poul Anderson, *The Time Patrol*, 1991
Mona Clee, *Branch Point*, 1996
Carol Davis, *Quantum Leap: Obsessions: A Novel*, 1997
S.D. Perry, *Timecop*, 1994
George Gaylord Simpson, *The Dechronization of Sam Magruder*, 1996

**5316**

**SUE STORM**
**KAREN HARRIS**, Illustrator

## Star Bones Weep the Blood of Angels

(Denver: Cyber-Psychos A.O.D., 1995)

**Story type:** Horror (Collection)

**Summary:** This short-story chapbook, the author's first, comprises seven tales that skirt the boundary between horror and fantasy. "Getting Happy" and "The Sorry Child's Christmas" are both tales of people living on society's fringe driven to extreme measures. "Missy Loves Her Daddy" is a horror story of child abuse. "The Wolf-Girl's Song" and "Halfbreed" involve the mystical transformation of characters who are not what they appear to be, even unto themselves. Edward Lee supplies an introduction.

**Other books you might like:**
Michael A. Arnzen, *Needles and Sins*, 1993
Michael Hemmingson, *Nice Little Stories Jam-Packed with Depraved Sex and Violence*, 1995
Brian Hopkins, *Something Haunts Us All*, 1995
Elizabeth Massie, *Southern Discomfort: Selected Works of Elizabeth Massie*, 1993
David Niall Wilson, *The Fall of the House of Escher and Other Illusions*, 1995

**5317**

**WILLIAM R. STOTLER**
**ALAN KOSZOWSKI**, Illustrator

## The Final Diary Entry of Kees Hujgens

(West Warwick, Rhode Island: Necronomicon Press, 1995)

**Story type:** Horror (Ancient Evil Unleashed)
**Major character(s):** Kees Hujgens, Architect; Vilmos Niehaus, Architect; Jozef P. Janszoon, Architect
**Time period(s):** 1920s (1925)
**Locale(s):** Amsterdam, Netherlands

**Summary:** Presented as a diary kept by an architecture student fascinated by the De Stijl style popular at the turn of the century, this short story chapbook recounts how he falls under the tutelage of a renegade architect whose theories allow him to penetrate beyond physical boundaries into the spatial dimensions De Stijl evokes. This is the author's first book.

**Other books you might like:**
Stefan Grabinski, *The Dark Domain*, 1994
Franz Kafka, *Stories, 1904-1924*, 1981
Thomas Ligotti, *Songs of a Dead Dreamer*, 1990
Bruno Schulz, *Sanatorium under the Sign of the Hourglass*, 1937

**5318**

**LAREN STOVER**

## Pluto, Animal Lover

(New York: HarperCollins, 1994)

**Story type:** Horror (Psychological Suspense; Satire)
**Major character(s):** Pluto Hellbender Gerome, Editor (copyeditor); Wanda Swann, Prostitute; Camillia, Editor (of *Pancreas Journal*)
**Time period(s):** 1990s (1994)
**Locale(s):** New York, New York

**Summary:** By day, Pluto works as a copyeditor for a medical magazine and walks dogs at the nearby ASPCA on his lunch hour. In his private life, Pluto's deep love of animals breeds a misanthropy that drives him to take murderous extremes against those whom he believes endanger animal lives. This is the author's first published novel.

**Other books you might like:**
Ramsey Campbell, *The Face That Must Die*, 1979
Thomas Harris, *The Silence of the Lambs*, 1988
F. Paul Wilson, *Pelts*, 1990

**5319**

**MATTHEW WOODRING STOVER**

## Heroes Die

(New York: Del Rey, 1998)

**Story type:** Science Fiction (Adventure)
**Major character(s):** Hari Michaelson, Entertainer; Arturo Kollberg, Businessman; Ma'elKoth, Ruler
**Time period(s):** Indeterminate Future
**Locale(s):** Ankhana, Planet—Imaginary

**Summary:** Hari Michaelson fights for his life on the barbaric world of Ankhana, while his adventures are recorded to entertain the population of Earth. The next show turns personal when someone kidnaps his estranged wife, a plot that has its origin within the corrupt corporate structure that employs him.

**Other books you might like:**
Poul Anderson, *The Game of Empire*, 1985
L. Sprague de Camp, *The Prisoner of Zhamanak*, 1982
Alan Dean Foster, *Sentenced to Prism*, 1985
Harry Harrison, *Planet of the Damned*, 1062
Mike Resnick, *Santiago*, 1986

**5320**

**MATTHEW WOODRING STOVER**

## Iron Dawn

(New York, Roc, 1997)

**Story type:** Fantasy (Magic Conflict; Political)
**Major character(s):** Barra the Pict, Warrior, Mercenary, Leader; Leucas, Warrior, Mercenary; Kheperu, Magician, Mercenary, Con Artist
**Time period(s):** 13th century B.C.
**Locale(s):** Tyre, Ancient Civilization (Phoenicia)

**Summary:** When an evil necromancer attempts to raise an army of the undead in the wake of the Trojan War, the Pict, Barra, and her companions become involved in a battle to control commerce in the port city of Tyre. First novel.

**Other books you might like:**
Lynn Flewelling, *Luck in the Shadows*, 1996
Lynn Flewelling, *Stalking Darkness*, 1997
Terry Goodkind, *Wizard's First Rule*, 1994
J.V. Jones, *The Baker's Boy*, 1995
Robert Jordan, *The Eye of the World*, 1990

**5321**

**MATTHEW WOODRING STOVER**

## Jericho Moon

(New York: Roc, 1998)

**Story type:** Fantasy (Magic Conflict; Historical)
**Major character(s):** Barra the Pict, Mercenary, Leader, Warrior; Leucas, Mercenary, Warrior; Kheperu, Mercenary, Con Artist, Magician
**Time period(s):** 13th century B.C.
**Locale(s):** Jebusai Canaan, Middle East (Jerusalem)

**Summary:** The hiring of Barra and her friends by the King of Jebusai to rescue his son from the Habiru inflames the invaders. Soon the Habiru march toward Jebusai, under the leadership of Joshua, who destroyed the mighty city of Jericho. When armies, demons and gods congregate, it's time for sensible people like Barra to be elsewhere, but that proves difficult.

**Other books you might like:**
Scott Baker, *Drink the Fire From the Flames*, 1987
Richard Garfinkle, *Celestial Matters*, 1996
Lynda S. Robinson, *Murder at the Place of Anubis*, 1994
Richard L. Tierney, *Scroll of Thoth*, 1997
Gene Wolfe, *Soldier of the Mist*, 1986

**5322**

**J. MICHAEL STRACZYNSKI**

## Demon Night

(New York: Berkley, 1989)

**Story type:** Horror (Apocalyptic Horror)
**Major character(s):** Eric Matthews, Young Man; Liz Chasen, Writer
**Time period(s):** 1980s
**Locale(s):** Dredmouth Point, Maine

**Summary:** Drawn back to his hometown by a series of nightmares, Eric Matthews confronts a band of powerful demons that are terrorizing the town. As the ravages intensify, Matthews and a small group of associates—a female writer, a priest, a doctor, and a policeman—attempt to thwart the demons, at risk of life and soul, by finding and closing the "door" from the netherworld through which they emerged.

**Other books you might like:**
Stephen King, *Salem's Lot*, 1975
Bentley Little, *The Revelation*, 1990
Peter Straub, *Ghost Story*, 1979

**5323**

**J. MICHAEL STRACZYNSKI**

## OtherSyde

(New York: E.P. Dutton, 1990)

**Story type:** Horror (Supernatural Vengeance)

**Major character(s):** Chris Martino, Teenager, Student—High School; Roger Obst, Teenager, Student—High School; Susan Warrick, Police Officer
**Time period(s):** 1990s (1990)
**Locale(s):** Los Angeles, California

**Summary:** Nerdy Roger Obst is mercilessly bullied by his high school classmates—until the insectoid race that calls itself OtherSyde empowers him to take revenge on his tormentors.

**Other books you might like:**
Ray Garton, *Crucifax Autumn*, 1988
Charles L. Grant, *The Pet*, 1986
K.W. Jeter, *The Night Man*, 1990
Stephen King, *Christine*, 1983

---

### 5324

**TODD STRASSER**

## Addams Family Values

(New York: Pocket, 1993)

**Story type:** Fantasy (Light Fantasy; Quest)
**Series:** Addams Family
**Major character(s):** Uncle Fester Addams, Fiance(e); Debbie Jelinsky, Child-Care Giver, Criminal (black widow); Morticia Addams, Parent, Spouse
**Time period(s):** 1990s
**Locale(s):** Addams Family Mansion, Mythical Place; Hawaii; Camp Chippewa, Mythical Place

**Summary:** Concerned over Wednesday's and Pugsley's reaction to the new baby, Morticia and Gomez hire Debbie Jelinsky as nanny. Seeing possible access to the Addams' Family fortune through Uncle Fester, Debbie arranges a summer camp experience for Wednesday and Pugsley while planning a wedding and fatal honeymoon for Uncle Fester. Novelizes the film.

**Other books you might like:**
Richie Tankersley Cusick, *Buffy the Vampire Slayer*, 1992
Robert Egan, *Little Shop of Horrors*, 1986
   Loise Egan, co-author
Laurell K. Hamilton, *Guilty Pleasures*, 1993
Christopher Moore, *Practical Demonkeeping*, 1992
Gilbert Pearlman, *Young Frankenstein*, 1974

---

### 5325

**THOMAS M.K. STRATMAN**, Editor

## Cthulhu's Heirs

(Oakland, California: Chaosium, 1995)

**Story type:** Horror (Anthology)

**Summary:** The author has assembled 21 original and reprint stories that pay tribute to H.P. Lovecraft and his concept of a universe controlled by incomprehensible forces of chaos embodied in the form of extradimensional beings. Included are Ramsey Campbell's "The Franklyn Paragraphs," which suggests that life as we know it may be no more than the fantasy of a horror writer; Hugh B. Cave's "The Death Watch," a reprint from the pulp magazine *Weird Tales*, concerning a man's return from the dead with the help of occult forces; Charles M. Saplak's "The Scourge," about a man drawn into an inescapable realm of forbidden knowledge; and Michael D. Winkle's "Typo," about the horrors lurking in the card catalog of a university library. Also included are three variations on or sequels to stories by Lovecraft himself: Darrell Schweitzer's and Jason van Hollander's "Those of the Air" (a tribute to Lovecraft's "The

---

Dunwich Horror"); Gordon Linzner's "Pickman's Legacy" (a follow-up to Lovecraft's tale of an unusual painter, "Pickman's Model"); and Arthur William Lloyd Breach's "The Return of the White Ship" (a sequel to Lovecraft's fantasy "The White Ship.")

**Other books you might like:**
Edward P. Berglund, *Disciples of Cthulhu*, 1975
Robert M. Price, *Tales of the Lovecraft Mythos*, 1993
   editor
H.P. Lovecraft, *Tales of the Cthulhu Mythos: Golden Anniversary Anthology*, 1990

---

### 5326

**PETER STRAUB**

## The Hellfire Club

(New York: Random House, 1996)

**Story type:** Horror (Serial Killer)
**Major character(s):** Nora Chancel, Housewife; Dick Dart, Serial Killer; Davey Chancel, Editor
**Time period(s):** 1990s (1996)
**Locale(s):** Westerholm, Connecticut

**Summary:** Nora Chancel is catapulted out of her stale marriage and boring life when she is kidnapped by serial killer Dick Dart and forced to accompany him on a grisly murder spree. The diabolically brilliant Dart is motivated not only by bloodlust, but his interest in bringing to light the dark secret behind a bestselling book that has sustained the publishing house run by Nora's husband's family for half a century.

**Other books you might like:**
Brett Easton Ellis, *American Psycho*, 1991
Thomas Harris, *Red Dragon*, 1981
Thomas Harris, *The Silence of the Lambs*, 1988
Joyce Carol Oates, *Zombie*, 1995

---

### 5327

**PETER STRAUB**

## Houses Without Doors

(New York: Dutton, 1990)

**Story type:** Horror (Collection)

**Summary:** A stunning collection of six powerful, claustrophobic supernatural stories about isolation, obsession, the destruction of innocence, madness, and "the violence of unfinished things." In "Blue Rose" a 10-year-old boy hypnotizes then kills his younger brother. In the related "The Juniper Tree" a young boy is abused sexually by a tramp, an experience that haunts his adult self, the narrator of the tale. And in "The Buffalo Hunter" an obsessed man discovers the power to enter the world of the books he reads. One story, "Mrs. God," was heavily edited for this edition. Two of the stories have links to Straub's Vietnam novel, *Koko*.

**Other books you might like:**
Ramsey Campbell, *The Face That Must Die*, 1979
Stephen Gilbert, *Ratman's Notebooks*, 1968
Michael McDowell, *Toplin*, 1985

## 5328

### PETER STRAUB

### *Koko*

(New York: Signet NAL, 1989)

**Story type:** Horror (Serial Killer)
**Series:** Blue Rose Trilogy
**Major character(s):** Michael Poole, Doctor (Pediatrician), Veteran (Vietnam); Tim Underhill, Writer (Homosexual), Veteran (Vietnam)
**Time period(s):** 1980s
**Locale(s):** Asia; United States

**Summary:** A serial murderer calling himself "Koko" is systematically killing all those involved in the Vietnam Ia Thuc massacre. Veteran Michael Poole realizes that the killer is one of their own unit and he mobilizes his old friends to identify and locate Koko before he can complete his "mission."

**Other books you might like:**
Thomas Harris, *Red Dragon*, 1981
Thomas Harris, *The Silence of the Lambs*, 1988

## 5329

### PETER STRAUB

### *Mrs. God*

(Hampton Falls, New Hampshire: Donald Grant, 1990)

**Story type:** Horror (Ghost Story)
**Major character(s):** William Standish, Professor
**Time period(s):** 1990s (1990)
**Locale(s):** England

**Summary:** This original, longer, superior version of the final story in Straub's collection *Houses Without Doors* tells of the descent into insanity of a literature professor who visits a haunted English country house called Eswood to pursue research on a little-known poet. There he encounters ghostly manifestations, strange sounds, and other accoutrements of the English ghost story. Ultimately his pursuit by the spectre of an aborted child sparks his deterioration into madness and brutality. This edition is illustrated by Rick Berry and includes an otherwise unpublished afterword by Straub concerning the story.

**Other books you might like:**
Robert Aickman, *Cold Hand in Mine*, 1975
Robert Aickman, *Painted Devils*, 1979
Robert Aickman, *The Wine-Dark Sea*, 1988
Ramsey Campbell, *Dark Companions*, 1982
Ramsey Campbell, *The Height of the Scream*, 1976
Shirley Jackson, *The Haunting of Hill House*, 1959
Richard Matheson, *Hell House*, 1971

## 5330

### PETER STRAUB

### *Mystery*

(New York: Dutton, 1989)

**Story type:** Horror (Psychological Suspense)
**Major character(s):** Tom Pasmore, Heir; Lamont "the Shadow" Von Heilitz, Detective
**Time period(s):** 1980s
**Locale(s):** Mill Walk, Caribbean (Island); Eagle Lake, Wisconsin

**Summary:** Pasmore entices Von Heilitz into joining him in the investigation of two murders, a 40-year-old killing in Eagle Lake and a recent one in Mill Walk.

**Other books you might like:**
Joyce Carol Oates, *Mysteries of Winterhurn*, 1984

## 5331

### PETER STRAUB, Editor

### *Peter Straub's Ghosts*

(New York: Pocket, 1995)

**Story type:** Horror (Anthology; Ghost Story)

**Summary:** This fourth anthology of stories sponsored and written by members of the Horror Writers of America contains fourteen original ghost stories and an introduction by the editor, which is itself a ghost story narrated by a deceased embezzler. In Norman Partridge's "Styx," a man searches for the person who has stolen his soul and threatens his hope for an afterlife. Kathe Koja relates a woman's transformation into a ghost in "Jubilee," and Alan Rodgers draws parallels between inner city life and being an unseen ghost in "Momma Ghost." In Clark Perry's "Mother's Hands," unrelenting grief leads the living to haunt the dead, and in Chet Williamson's "Coventry Carol," the ghost of a stillborn child may or may not be the figment of the grieving mother's imagination.

**Other books you might like:**
Ramsey Campbell, *Deathport*, 1994
    editor
Claudia O'Keefe, *Ghosttide*, 1993
    editor
Paul F. Olson, *Post Mortem: New Tales of Ghostly Horror*, 1989
    David B. Silva, co-editor

## 5332

### PETER STRAUB

### *The Throat*

(New York: Dutton, 1993)

**Story type:** Horror (Mystery)
**Major character(s):** Tim Underhill, Writer, Veteran (Vietnam); Tom Pasmore, Detective
**Time period(s):** 1990s (1993)
**Locale(s):** Millhaven, Illinois

**Summary:** In this sequel to the author's World Fantasy Award-winning novel *Koko*, resumption of the "Blue Rose" murders that terrorized Millhaven over a decade before leads locals Tim Underhill and Tom Pasmore into an investigation that will bring to light undisclosed truths about the town's residents, and force each of them to confront aspects of their traumatic involvement in the Vietnam War.

**Other books you might like:**
S.K. Epperson, *Dumford Blood*, 1990
Dennis Etchison, *Darkside*, 1986
Chelsea Quinn Yarbro, *Beastnights*, 1989

## **5333**

### VICTORIA STRAUSS

## *The Arm of the Stone*

(New York: Avon Eos Books, 1998)

**Story type:** Fantasy (Religious; Magic Conflict)
**Major character(s):** Bron ''Selwyn Forester'' Miner, Religious (Arm of the Stone), Avenger; Liliane Merchant, Religious (Guardian of the Stone), Spy; Jolyon, Religious (Arm of the Stone), Zealot
**Time period(s):** Indeterminate
**Locale(s):** Greshing, Fictional City; Fortress of the Stone, Mythical Place; Brittania, Fictional Country (Northern Orderhouse)

**Summary:** For 1000 years Bron's family waited in anonymity for the One of their lineage who would free the Stone from its imprisonment and create a new world where technology and magic could abide in harmony. Meanwhile, the Order of the Guardians of the Stone rule the world, enforcing the rigid and detailed laws of mindpower by meting out swift, harsh punishment to any who would dare improve the lives of their fellow citizens by inventing a new tool or labor-saving process. When Bron's brother almost dies under the lash for a tool violation, Bron's Gift surfaces for the first time, saving his brother and revealing that he may be the One prophesied by the Tale. With the rest of his family dead by decree of the Guardians, Bron vows to use his Gift to infiltrate their ranks and destroy them from within.

**Other books you might like:**
Orson Scott Card, *Seventh Son*, 1987
Lynn Flewelling, *Luck in the Shadows*, 1996
C.S. Friedman, *Black Sun Rising*, 1991
Elizabeth Moon, *Sheepfarmer's Daughter*, 1988
Rebecca Ore, *Slow Funeral*, 1994
Paula Volsky, *The Gates of Twilight*, 1996

## **5334**

### S.J. STRAYHORN

## *Black Night*

(New York: Kensington, 1996)

**Story type:** Horror (Small Town Horror)
**Major character(s):** Eugenia Fairfax, Social Worker; Lena Fairfax, Worker (deli); Rafael Chavez, Waiter/Waitress
**Time period(s):** 1990s (1996)
**Locale(s):** Fort Grant, Kansas

**Summary:** Eugenia Fairfax returns temporarily to Fort Grant, the town where she was raised in the local orphanage, to lay to rest the ghosts of her past. However, her return reawakens many of the old prejudices that were turned against her and her fellow orphans. Worse, Eugenia's daughter, Lena, and Lena's lover, Rafael, appear to be reliving an ill-fated romance played out on the site of the orphanage during the town's frontier days, the legacy of which haunts the town to this day. This is the author's first novel.

**Other books you might like:**
Jane Brindle, *The Tallow Image*, 1995
S.K. Epperson, *The Moons of Summer*, 1994
Judith Hawkes, *Julian's House*, 1989
Nina Romberg, *Shadow Walkers*, 1993
Tamara Thorne, *Haunted*, 1995

## **5335**

### NEWTON E. STREETER

## *Noise and Other Night Terrors*

(Duluth, Georgia: Bone Yard Press, 1998)

**Story type:** Horror (Collection)
**Summary:** Seven scrappy tales of supernatural and nonsupernatural horror, and an excerpt from the author's unpublished novel *Dare*. In addition to the the werewolf story ''Predator,'' the contents include the afterlife fantasies ''Noise'' and ''South of LA,'' the serial killer story ''Mr FUBAR,'' and ''Acquired Taste,'' a vampire tale with a psychological horror edge. Introduction by Cindie Geddes.

**Other books you might like:**
Mel D. Ames, *Tales of Titillation and Terror*, 1996
S. Darnbrook Colson, *People of the Night*, 1994
Brian Hopkins, *Something Haunts Us All*, 1995
Albert J. Manachino, *The Odd Lot: The Selected Works of Albert J. Manachino*, 1993
David Niall Wilson, *The Fall of the House of Escher and Other Illusions*, 1995

## **5336**

### BRAD STRICKLAND

## *Dragon's Plunder*

(New York: Atheneum, 1992)

**Story type:** Fantasy (Quest)
**Series:** Dragonflight
**Major character(s):** Jamie Falconer, Wizard; Deadmon, Pirate, Sea Captain; Amelia, Royalty (princess)
**Time period(s):** Indeterminate
**Locale(s):** *Betty*, At Sea; Windrose Island, Mythical Place

**Summary:** Unable to rest until he has plundered a dragon's hoard, the deceased Captain Deadmon enlists the help of Jamie Falconer, who possesses the ability of whistling up a breeze any time he wishes.

**Other books you might like:**
Louise Cooper, *The Sleep of Stone*, 1991
Charles de Lint, *The Dreaming Place*, 1990
Tanith Lee, *Black Unicorn*, 1991
Robert Silverberg, *Letters From Atlantis*, 1990
Tad Williams, *Child of an Ancient City*, 1992
    Nina Kiriki Hoffman, co-author

## **5337**

### BRAD STRICKLAND

## *Wizard's Mole*

(New York: Roc, 1991)

**Story type:** Fantasy (Light Fantasy; Alternate World)
**Series:** Jeremy Moon
**Major character(s):** Jeremy Moon, Magician, Advertising; Nul, Animal (mole); Barach Loremaster, Wizard
**Time period(s):** 1990s
**Locale(s):** Thaumia, Planet—Imaginary (Whitehorn Keep); New York, New York

**Summary:** The Evil Dark One once again troubles Thaumia and may be controlling one of the mages there. Jeremy Moon's double, Sebastian, now on Earth, may be able to help recognize him. When Jeremy goes to Earth to get his help, Sebastian returns to Thaumia, leaving Jeremy behind. Jeremy must defeat the Evil Dark One and find a way home to his family on Thaumia.

**Other books you might like:**
Steven Brust, *Jhereg*, 1983
John DeChancie, *Castle Perilous*, 1988
Gordon R. Dickson, *The Dragon and the George*, 1976
Suzette Haden Elgin, *The Grand Jubilee*, 1981
Thorarinn Gunnarsson, *Make Way for Dragons!*, 1990
John Morressy, *Kedrigern in Wanderland*, 1988
Terry Pratchett, *Wyrd Sisters*, 1990

---

## 5338

### WHITLEY STRIEBER

## *Billy*

(New York: Putnams, 1990)

**Story type:** Horror (Serial Killer)
**Major character(s):** Billy Neary, Child (12-year-old boy); Barton Royal, Murderer (child molester); Mark Neary, Teacher (high school history teacher)
**Time period(s):** 1990s (1990)
**Locale(s):** Stevensville, Iowa

**Summary:** Abused as a child, mentally deranged Barton Royal abducts Billy Neary from a shopping mall and subjects him to a series of physical and psychological torments as he debates whether to adopt the boy or murder him.

**Other books you might like:**
Robert Bloch, *The Kidnapper*, 1954
Thomas Harris, *The Silence of the Lambs*, 1988
Jim Thompson, *After Dark, My Sweet*, 1955

---

## 5339

### WHITLEY STRIEBER

## *Evenings with Demons*

(Grantham, New Hampshire: Borderlands Press, 1997)

**Story type:** Horror (Collection)

**Summary:** Twenty-five stories, many previously unpublished, from a writer known primarily as a novelist. Included are ''Pain'' and ''The Resurrection of the Inquistion in P. Salter,'' both about people who discover private ecstasy as recipients and givers of torture; ''The Richard Nixon Mask,'' about a strangely haunted Halloween mask; ''Under the Old Oak Tree,'' a tale of aliens among us; ''The Pool,'' in which a conversation between father and son reveals a gulf, possibly extraterrestrial, separating them; and the monster story, ''Flies.'' Released as a signed limited hardcover edition.

**Other books you might like:**
Nancy A. Collins, *Nameless Sins*, 1994
Dennis Etchison, *The Blood Kiss*, 1989
Ed Gorman, *Prisoners and Other Stories*, 1992
Robert R. McCammon, *Blue World*, 1989
Kim Newman, *The Original Dr. Shade and Other Stories*, 1994
William Relling Jr., *The Infinite Man*, 1989
F. Paul Wilson, *Soft and Others*, 1989

---

## 5340

### WHITLEY STRIEBER

## *The Forbidden Zone*

(New York: Dutton, 1993)

**Story type:** Horror (Apocalyptic Horror)
**Major character(s):** Brian Kelly, Scientist; Ellen Maas, Journalist; Bob Kelly, Police Officer
**Time period(s):** 1990s (1993)
**Locale(s):** Oscola, New York

**Summary:** A series of strange events in the sleepy little town of Oscola—screaming heard underground, the transformation of townspeople into soulless zombies, and the infiltration of the surrounding woods by monstrous creatures—leads Brian Kelly to speculate that colleagues using the data he generated through experiments in subatomic particle physics have broken through to another dimension that is trying to take over our own.

**Other books you might like:**
T.E.D. Klein, *The Ceremonies*, 1984
Brian Lumley, *The Burrowers Beneath*, 1974
John Skipp, *The Scream*, 1988
    Craig Spector, co-author
F. Paul Wilson, *Nightworld*, 1992

---

## 5341

### WHITLEY STRIEBER

## *Majestic*

(New York: Putnam, 1989)

**Story type:** Science Fiction (UFO)
**Major character(s):** Nicholas Duke, Journalist; Will Stone, Spy (CIA agent)
**Time period(s):** 1940s (1947)
**Locale(s):** New Mexico

**Summary:** In 1947 an alien spacecraft crash lands near Roswell, New Mexico and the corpses of two aliens and a surgically altered human fetus are discovered, but the matter is quickly hushed up. A journalist attempting to find out the truth discovers a massive cover-up which evidently continues to this day.

**Other books you might like:**
Robert A. Heinlein, *The Puppet Masters*, 1951
Fritz Leiber, *The Wanderer*, 1964
Garfield Reeves-Stevens, *Nighteyes*, 1989

---

## 5342

### WHITLEY STRIEBER

## *Unholy Fire*

(New York: Dutton, 1992)

**Story type:** Horror (Occult)
**Major character(s):** John Rafferty, Religious (priest); Frank Bayley, Religious (priest); Maria Julien, Heiress
**Time period(s):** 1990s (1992)
**Locale(s):** New York, New York

**Summary:** The struggle between two priests for the pastorship of Mary and Joseph, a Catholic Church in New York's Greenwich Village, is exacerbated by the presence of Maria Julien, who entices both priests sexually. Maria's brutal death proves just the first in a vicious series modeled on those of the Inquisition and points to either psychosis or demonic possession of one of the two priests.

**Other books you might like:**
Adrian Blake, *Unholy Communion*, 1989
William Peter Blatty, *The Exorcist*, 1971
William Peter Blatty, *Legion*, 1983
Jack Olesker, *Confessional*, 1989

### `5343`
### WHITLEY STRIEBER

## The Wild
(New York: Tor, 1991)

**Story type:** Horror (Werewolf Story)
**Major character(s):** Bob Duke, Stock Broker, Werewolf; Cindy Duke, Spouse (Bob's wife); Kevin Thomas Duke, Child (Cindy & Bob's 12-year-old son)
**Time period(s):** 1990s
**Locale(s):** New York, New York

**Summary:** Bob Duke assumes that his nightly dreams of turning into a wolf are only an expression of his subconscious mind's poetic rebellion against his mundane daily life. But one day, Bob awakens from his dreams transformed, and it becomes his wife's and son's responsibility to find and reclaim him before he runs amok.

**Other books you might like:**
Scott Bradfield, *Dream of the Wolf*, 1990
Michael Cadnum, *St. Peter's Wolf*, 1991
Dennis Danvers, *Wilderness*, 1991

### `5344`
### THEODORE STURGEON

## Killdozer!
(Berkeley, California: North Atlantic Books, 1996)

**Story type:** Science Fiction (Collection; Science Fiction)
**Series:** Complete Stories of Theodore Sturgeon

**Summary:** Contains a seven-page foreword by Robert Silverberg, a seven-page afterword by Robert A. Heinlein and 25 pages of story notes by the series editor, Paul Williams, including an unpublished alternate ending to "Mewhu's Jet" and the original ending of "Killdozer!" Varying in tone from light to downbeat, the 11 reprinted and four original stories all written 1941-1946, feature diverse themes including first contact, heavy construction equipment operation, human relationships, government folly, and space exploration. Third of the projected 10-volume series.

**Other books you might like:**
Alfred Bester, *Star Light, Star Bright*, 1976
Philip K. Dick, *The Collected Stories of Philip K. Dick*, 1987 five volumes
Clifford D. Simak, *Over the River & through the Woods*, 1996
Cordwainer Smith, *The Rediscovery of Man*, 1993
John Varley, *Blue Champagne*, 1986

### `5345`
### THEODORE STURGEON

## Microcosmic God
(Berkeley, California: North Atlantic Books, 1995)

**Story type:** Science Fiction (Collection; Science Fiction)

**Series:** Complete Short Stories of Theodore Sturgeon

**Summary:** Contains at 27-page foreword by Samuel R. Delany, 22 pages of story notes by series editor Paul Williams, and 17 stories written between April 1940 and June 1941, all published in *Astounding* or *Unknown* except "The Anonymous" and "Two Sidecars," an unfinished early draft of "Microcosmic God." Second of 10 proposed volumes collecting all of Sturgeon's short fiction.

**Other books you might like:**
J.G. Ballard, *The Best Short Stories of J.G. Ballard*, 1978
Robert A. Heinlein, *The Green Hills of Earth*, 1951
Larry Niven, *N-Space*, 1990
Cordwainer Smith, *The Rediscovery of Man*, 1993
John Varley, *The Persistence of Vision*, 1978

### `5346`
### THEODORE STURGEON

## The Perfect Host
(Berkeley, California: North Atlantic Books, 1998)

**Story type:** Science Fiction (Collection)
**Series:** Complete Stories of Theodore Sturgeon

**Summary:** This collection contains a 12-page foreword by Larry McCaffrey, 25 pages of story notes by the series editor, Paul Williams, 15 reprinted stories one original story, and the beginning of a novel which works as a story, all written between late 1947 and early 1949. Varying in tone from humorous and whimsical to downbeat, the stories explore diverse themes including warfare, relationships, music, interspecies communication, impending death, alien contact, and life in the future.

**Other books you might like:**
Alfred Bester, *Virtual Unrealities: The Short Fiction of Alfred Bester*, 1997
Philip K. Dick, *The Collected Short Stories of Philip K. Dick*, 1987 five volumes
Clifford D. Simak, *Over the River & through the Woods*, 1996
Cordwainer Smith, *The Rediscovery of Man*, 1993
John Varley, *Blue Champagne*, 1986

### `5347`
### THEODORE STURGEON

## Some of Your Blood
(New York: Carroll & Graf, 1994)

**Story type:** Horror (Vampire Story)
**Major character(s):** George Smith, Military Personnel; Philip Outerbridge, Psychologist; Albert Williams, Psychologist
**Time period(s):** 1950s
**Locale(s):** Smithton Township, California

**Summary:** Originally published in 1961, this novel is presented as the account of two psychologists trying to unravel the reason why a young soldier with a grotesque personal background and aberrant ways of coping with life events has developed a taste for blood.

**Other books you might like:**
Poppy Z. Brite, *Lost Souls*, 1992
Elizabeth Engstrom, *Black Ambrosia*, 1988
Roxanne Longstreet, *The Undead*, 1993
Anne Rice, *Interview with the Vampire*, 1975

## 5348

### THEODORE STURGEON

## *Thunder and Roses*

(Berkeley, California: North Atlantic Books, 1997)

**Story type:** Science Fiction (Collection; Science Fiction)
**Series:** Complete Short Stories of Theodore Sturgeon

**Summary:** Contains a seven-page foreword by James Gunn, 18 pages of story notes by series editor Paul Williams, an appendix with the original second half of ''Maturity'' and 16 stories published 1946-1947, with one, ''Wham Bop!,'' previously not reprinted in book form. Themes include psychology, UFOs, politics, horror and the West. One of a ten-volume series.

**Other books you might like:**
J.G. Ballard, *The Best Short Stories of J.G. Ballard*, 1978
Ray Bradbury, *Quicker than the Eye*, 1996
C.M. Kornbluth, *His Share of Glory: The Complete Short Science Fiction of C.M. Kornbluth*, 1997
Henry Kuttner, *The Best of Henry Kuttner*, 1975
Clifford D. Simak, *Over the River & through the Woods*, 1996
John Varley, *The Persistence of Vision*, 1978

## 5349

### THEODORE STURGEON

## *The Ultimate Egoist*

(Berkeley, California: North Atlantic Books, 1994)

**Story type:** Science Fiction (Collection)

**Summary:** Contains a four-page Ray Bradbury foreword, a three-page Arthur C. Clarke foreword, a three-page Gene Wolfe foreword, 36 pages of story notes by the book's editor, Paul Williams, with extensive comments by Sturgeon on individual stories. Text consists of one poem and 46 stories submitted to publishers 1937-1940, 10 original and 36 reprinted from periodicals. Stories reflect Sturgeon's earliest work and include ''Bianca's Hands,'' ''Derm Fool'' and ''It.'' First of ten proposed volumes collecting all the author's short fiction.

**Other books you might like:**
Alfred Bester, *Star Light, Star Bright*, 1976
Philip K. Dick, *The Collected Stories of Philip K. Dick*, 1987
   five volumes
Robert A. Heinlein, *The Past through Tomorrow*, 1967
Larry Niven, *Tales of Known Space*, 1975
Cordwainer Smith, *The Rediscovery of Man*, 1993
John Varley, *Blue Champagne*, 1986

## 5350

### TIM SULLIVAN, Editor

## *Cold Shocks*

(New York: Avon, 1991)

**Story type:** Horror (Anthology)

**Summary:** Sixteen original stories that use cold geographic locales or the winter months as a basis for the horrors they unfold. Included are Graham Masterton's tale of an ill-fated polar expedition, ''The Sixth Man''; S.P. Somtow's tale of the terrors of a peculiar festival in Japan, ''The Pavilion of Frozen Women''; Michael Tolman's fantasy, ''A Winter Memory,'' chronicling a time after the sun has ceased to shine; Gray Brandner's ''The Ice Children'' and Steve

Rasnic Tem's ''Adleparmeun,'' both about the influence of primitive folk tales and legends on their protagonists; and Chet Williamson's tale of unusual hunters, ''First Kill.''

**Other books you might like:**
Ramsey Campbell, *Midnight Sun*, 1990
Basil Copper, *The Great White Space*, 1974
Graham Masterton, *The Manitou*, 1975

## 5351

### TIM SULLIVAN

## *Lords of Creation*

(New York: Avon, 1992)

**Story type:** Science Fiction (First Contact; Theological)
**Major character(s):** David Albee, Scientist (paleontologist); Jeffrey Flanagan, Religious (evangelist), Administrator (Secretary of Morality); Charles Margolis, Administrator (White House Chief of Staff)
**Time period(s):** 1990s (1999)
**Locale(s):** Montana

**Summary:** The Christian Millennialists in control of the government have eliminated any grants for paleontological digs or research. David Albee, a dinosaur lover, and his fellow amateur paleontologists find a 65 million-year-old box containing five dinosaur eggs which have been preserved by a stasis field. A local veterinarian and David's ex-girlfriend Liz care for the hatched dinosaurs under the auspices of the federal government. The young dinosaurs exhibit unusually rapid growth and remarkable intelligence for the short time since they've hatched; however their voracious appetite for protein may lead to their destruction.

**Other books you might like:**
David Brin, *Earth*, 1990
C.J. Cherryh, *Forty Thousand in Gehenna*, 1983
Michael Crichton, *Jurassic Park*, 1990
Parke Godwin, *The Snake Oil Wars*, 1989
Parke Godwin, *Waiting for the Galactic Bus*, 1988
Larry Niven, *The Flight of the Horse*, 1973
Dave Wolverton, *Serpent Catch*, 1991

## 5352

### TIM SULLIVAN

## *The Parasite War*

(New York: Avon, 1989)

**Story type:** Science Fiction (Invasion of Earth)
**Major character(s):** Alex Ward, Veteran; Jo, Social Worker
**Time period(s):** Indeterminate Future
**Locale(s):** United States

**Summary:** A Vietnam vet leads the battle against hideous alien parasites who turn human beings into monsters. The only people who appear to be immune to the parasites are those with a history of mental problems.

**Other books you might like:**
David Gerrold, *A Day for Damnation*, 1984
David Gerrold, *A Matter for Men*, 1983
David Gerrold, *A Rage for Revenge*, 1989
Robert A. Heinlein, *The Puppet Masters*, 1951
Kate Wilhelm, *The Clone*, 1965
   Ted Thomas, co-author

## 5353

### TRICIA SULLIVAN

## *Dreaming in Smoke*

(New York: Bantam, 1998)

**Story type:** Science Fiction (Techno-Thriller)
**Major character(s):** Kalypso Deed, Computer Expert; Azamat Marcsson, Statistician
**Time period(s):** Indeterminate Future
**Locale(s):** T'nane, Planet—Imaginary

**Summary:** A statistician loses his sanity while participating in a virtual reality interface with the computer intelligence that runs the planet T'nane. Kalypso Deed must find a way to force him to complete the sequence because his breakdown has destabilized the programming for the entire planet.

**Other books you might like:**
Alexander Besher, *Mir*, 1998
Jack L. Chalker, *The March Hare Network*, 1996
Thomas A. Easton, *Silicon Karma*, 1997
Mick Farren, *The Feelies*, 1990
Eric S. Nylund, *Signal to Noise*, 1998

## 5354

### TRICIA SULLIVAN

## *Lethe*

(New York: Bantam Spectra, 1995)

**Story type:** Science Fiction (Genetic Manipulation; Lost Colony)
**Major character(s):** Jenae Kim, Genetically Altered Being; Daire Morales, Pilot, Spaceman; Tsering, Genetically Altered Being
**Time period(s):** 22nd century (2166)
**Locale(s):** Earth; Dilarang, Planet—Imaginary

**Summary:** Investigating a mysterious object in solar orbit, Daire Morales disappears through a "gate" and finds himself on an alien planet populated by the descendants of shipwrecked humans. News travels to the League of New Alchemists, who rule an Earth nearly destroyed by ecological poisons and wars. Jenae Kim, whose genetic mutations allow her to breathe underwater and communicate with dolphins, accepts the assignment of finding the key to open the gate again. But when she finds the secret, she also realizes that the ruling oligarchy does not want the truth revealed. First novel.

**Other books you might like:**
David Brin, *Startide Rising*, 1983
Octavia E. Butler, *Dawn*, 1987
C.J. Cherryh, *Cyteen*, 1988
John Varley, *The Ophiuchi Hotline*, 1977
Vernor Vinge, *A Fire upon the Deep*, 1992

## 5355

### TRICIA SULLIVAN

## *Someone to Watch over Me*

(New York: Bantam Spectra, 1997)

**Story type:** Science Fiction (Alternate Intelligence)
**Major character(s):** Adrien Reyes, Experimental Subject, Slave; Sabina Lazarich, Musician, Composer; C, Disembodied Personality
**Time period(s):** Indeterminate Future
**Locale(s):** Earth

**Summary:** Adrien Reyes hopes to escape the slavery of life as a surrogate body, but the experimental brain implant may allow C to download itself permanently into Adrien's body.

**Other books you might like:**
Stephen Bury, *Interface*, 1994
Raphael Carter, *The Fortunate Fall*, 1996
Peter R. Emshwiller, *The Host*, 1991
Sage Walker, *Whiteout*, 1996
David Weber, *Path of the Fury*, 1992

## 5356

### MARK SUMNER

## *Devil's Engine*

(New York: Ballantine Del Rey, 1997)

**Story type:** Fantasy (Magic Conflict; Historical)
**Series:** Jake Bird
**Major character(s):** Jake Bird, Lawman, Wizard; William Cody, Scout, Historical Figure; Mr. Kastle, Scientist
**Time period(s):** 1870s
**Locale(s):** New York, New York; Medicine Rock, West

**Summary:** Following in his father's footsteps, Jake Bird, the sheriff of a small Western town, protects it from all threats by his magic. However, a new threat, a plot by an Eastern financier to drain the west of its magic, causes a great deal of grief. But will a future of technology and capitalism-run-amok fare any better?

**Other books you might like:**
Orson Scott Card, *Seventh Son*, 1987
David Drake, *Old Nathan*, 1991
Alan Dean Foster, *Mad Amos*, 1996
Midori Snyder, *The Flight of Michael McBride*, 1994
Harry Turtledove, *The Guns of the South: A Novel of the Civil War*, 1992

## 5357

### MARK SUMNER

## *Devil's Tower*

(New York: Ballantine Del Rey, 1996)

**Story type:** Fantasy (Magic Conflict; Alternate History)
**Series:** Jake Bird
**Major character(s):** Jake Bird, Maintenance Worker (stablehand); George Armstrong Custer, Sorcerer, Historical Figure; Hatty Ash, Healer
**Time period(s):** 1870s
**Locale(s):** Laramie, Wyoming

**Summary:** In an Old West where the sudden development of magic interrupts the American Civil War, Jake Bird lies low. He fears General Custer, who killed Bird's father and who possesses unheard-of magical power. Unfortunately for Jake Bird, fate pushes him towards a confrontation with Custer and destiny.

**Other books you might like:**
Orson Scott Card, *Seventh Son*, 1987
David Drake, *Old Nathan*, 1991
Alan Dean Foster, *Mad Amos*, 1996
Kenyon Morr, *Kingdom of Sorrow*, 1996
    pseudonym of Mark Sumner and Marella Sands
Kenyon Morr, *See No Weevil*, 1996
    pseudonym of Mark Summer and Marella Sands
Midori Snyder, *The Flight of Michael McBride*, 1994

Harry Turtledove, *The Guns of the South: A Novel of the Civil War*, 1992

## 5358

### MARK SUMNER

## *Insanity, Illinois*

(New York: Ace, 1998)

**Story type:** Science Fiction (Mystery)
**Series:** News From the Edge
**Major character(s):** Savvy McKinnon, Journalist (tabloid reporter); Frederick Benedict, Doctor
**Time period(s):** Indeterminate Future
**Locale(s):** Meridian, Illinois

**Summary:** Savvy McKinnon, reporter for a tabloid newspaper, finds a series of bizarre reports intriguing because they all originate in the same small town. She travels there for more details and discovers that each resident is undergoing a very realistic and personal set of delusions, sometimes with dangerous consequences.

**Other books you might like:**
Jonathan Carroll, *The Land of Laughs*, 1980
Charles L. Grant, *Goblins*, 1994
Charles L. Grant, *Whirlwind*, 1994
Dean R. Koontz, *Phantoms*, 1983
Jerry Sohl, *Night Slaves*, 1965

## 5359

### ROSEMARY SUTCLIFF

## *The Shining Company*

(New York: Farrar, Straus and Giroux, 1990)

**Story type:** Fantasy (Historical; Legend)
**Major character(s):** Prosper, Nobleman; Conn, Slave; Gorthyn, Royalty (prince)
**Time period(s):** 7th century
**Locale(s):** Scotland

**Summary:** King Mynyddog calls 300 warriors together to form the Companions. When they have trained for a year, they go to fight the invading Saxons. Prosper, a shield bearer, tells the tale of how the Shining Company learns to work as one and their valiant battle against overwhelming odds. This is an ALA Notable Children's Books For Older Readers title.

**Other books you might like:**
Lloyd Alexander, *The Book of Three*, 1964
Marion Zimmer Bradley, *The Mists of Avalon*, 1983
Morgan Llywelyn, *Red Branch*, 1988
Thomas Mallory, *Le Morte d'Arthur*, 1982

## 5360

### RICHARD SUTPHEN

## *Sexpunks & Savage Sagas*

(Agoura Hills, California: Spine-Tingling Press, 1991)

**Story type:** Horror (Collection)

**Summary:** Thirteen short stories plus the short novel ''Pisces Rising,'' most of which merge the physicality of sexual horror with the out-of-body spirituality of the New Age. In ''Freak Link,'' a woman accidentally becomes psychically linked to a grotesque alter ego. In ''The AIDS Giver,'' a male prostitute, fully aware he is HIV-

positive, gets his just rewards from all of his contacts. In ''The Mislabeled Tape,'' a mix-up in audiotape packaging turns an out-of-shape milquetoast into a subliminally programmed super-lover. And in ''The Inflatable Woman''—well, never mind.

**Other books you might like:**
Ramsey Campbell, *Scared Stiff*, 1987
Ray Garton, *Methods of Madness*, 1991
David J. Schow, *Seeing Red*, 1990
John Skipp, *Dead Lines*, 1990
   Craig Spector, co-author

## 5361

### HANNE MARIE SVENDSEN

## *The Gold Ball*

(New York: Knopf, 1989)

**Story type:** Fantasy (Magic Conflict)
**Time period(s):** Indeterminate
**Locale(s):** Denmark

**Summary:** The story follows the history of a small island off the coast of Denmark, and the life of Maja Stinn. Magic works on the island, but it is not mysterious magic.

**Other books you might like:**
Peter Gadol, *Coyote*, 1990

## 5362

### S. ANDREW SWANN (Pseudonym of Steven Swiniarski)

## *Emperors of the Twilight*

(New York: DAW, 1994)

**Story type:** Science Fiction (Genetic Manipulation; Invasion of Earth)
**Series:** Forests of the Night
**Major character(s):** Evi Isham, Genetically Altered Being, Human; Ezra Frey, Military Personnel (retired); Nohar Rajasthan, Genetically Altered Being, Animal (tiger)
**Time period(s):** 2050s (2058)
**Locale(s):** New York, New York

**Summary:** Just back from vacation, Evi Isham begins her day with the Peeper still watching her exercise, until the sniper starts shooting and the genetically modified Afghanis attempt to kidnap or kill her. Evi's attempt to escape starts her building on fire, and while she runs away through Central Park, Ezra Frey saves her from a cyborg dog. Frey, her old Agency contact, gets killed just before he can explain who wants her dead and why—and dawn has not yet broken.

**Other books you might like:**
Lois McMaster Bujold, *Mirror Dance*, 1994
Stephen Goldin, *Jade Darcy and the Affair of Honor*, 1988
   Mary Mason, co-author
Jonathan Lethem, *Gun, with Occasional Music*, 1994
Laura J. Mixon, *Glass Houses*, 1992
David Weber, *On Basilisk Station*, 1993

## 5363

### S. ANDREW SWANN (Pseudonym of Steven Swiniarski)

## *Forests of the Night*

(New York: DAW, 1993)

**Story type:** Science Fiction (Genetic Manipulation; Mystery)

**Major character(s):** Nohar Rajasthan, Genetically Altered Being (tiger), Detective—Private; Mandvi "Manny" Gujerat, Genetically Altered Being (mongoose), Doctor; Robert "Bobby" Dittrich, Computer Expert
**Time period(s):** 2050s
**Locale(s):** Cleveland, Ohio

**Summary:** When hired against his principles to find the murderer of a human politican, Nohar must defend himself and his friends from a rat gang, avoid the Feds who believe he deals drugs, thwart a plot to repeal the rights of genetically altered beings and identify the assassin who continues his killing spree.

**Other books you might like:**
Octavia E. Butler, *Dawn*, 1987
C.J. Cherryh, *Chanur's Legacy*, 1992
L. Warren Douglas, *A Plague of Change*, 1992
Thomas A. Easton, *Sparrowhawk*, 1990
George Alec Effinger, *When Gravity Fails*, 1987
Janet Kagan, *Mirabile*, 1991
Richard Paul Russo, *Destroying Angel*, 1992
Cordwainer Smith, *The Best of Cordwainer Smith*, 1975
David Alexander Smith, *In the Cube*, 1993
Vernor Vinge, *A Fire upon the Deep*, 1992

### 5364

S. ANDREW SWANN (Pseudonym of Steven Swiniarski)

## God's Dice

(New York: DAW, 1997)

**Story type:** Fantasy (Alternate World; Quest)
**Major character(s):** Richard Brandon, Psychologist, Professor; Rick, Editor (newspaper); Rocky, Police Officer
**Time period(s):** 1990s
**Locale(s):** Cleveland, Ohio; Quinque, Fictional Country

**Summary:** Traumatized by a car crash that killed his father and obsessed by an imaginary land he created in childhood, Dr. Richard Brandon experiments with alternate life regressions. His experiments open gateways between worlds, giving substance to nightmare creatures from his imaginary world and allowing four versions of himself to meet. Richard, Rick, Richie and Rocky escape the Thrall of Chaos that kills Dr. Brandon and flee to Quinque where they must retrieve the four relics of power and confront the Adversary before they can restore order in the land.

### 5365

S. ANDREW SWANN (Pseudonym of Steven Swiniarski)

## Partisan

(New York: DAW, 1995)

**Story type:** Science Fiction (Political)
**Series:** Hostile Takeover
**Major character(s):** Dominic "Dom" Magnus, Cyborg, Businessman; Klaus Dacham, Military Personnel (colonel, TEC); Kari Tetsami, Computer Expert, Genetically Altered Being
**Time period(s):** 24th century
**Locale(s):** Bakunin, Planet—Imaginary; Earth

**Summary:** Klaus Dacham's plan to subdue the independent planet Bakunin continues with one commune after another falling to his military superiority. The Diderot Holding Company begins to muster support for the resistance, while back on Earth, the political situation grows increasingly complex and dangerous.

**Other books you might like:**
Iain M. Banks, *Consider Phlebas*, 1987
Glen Cook, *The Dragon Never Sleeps*, 1988
Robert A. Heinlein, *The Moon Is a Harsh Mistress*, 1966
Steve Perry, *The Man Who Never Missed*, 1985
F. Paul Wilson, *The LaNague Chronicles*, 1992

### 5366

S. ANDREW SWANN (Pseudonym of Steven Swiniarski)

## Profiteer

(New York: DAW, 1995)

**Story type:** Science Fiction (Political)
**Series:** Hostile Takeover
**Major character(s):** Dominic "Dom" Magnus, Cyborg, Businessman; Kari Tetsami, Computer Expert, Genetically Altered Being; Random Walk, Artificial Intelligence
**Time period(s):** 24th century
**Locale(s):** Bakunin, Planet—Imaginary; Earth; Mars

**Summary:** To escape his past as a government agent, Dominic Magnus retires to Bakunin, the only human-occupied planet not part of the Terran Confederacy. Unfortunately, the Terran Confederacy decides that Bakunin must be brought into line and sends troops led by Magnus's worst enemy. Magnus must escape and act quickly to save Bakunin's freedom and his own life.

**Other books you might like:**
Robert A. Heinlein, *The Moon Is a Harsh Mistress*, 1966
Christopher Hinz, *Liege-Killer*, 1987
Ursula K. Le Guin, *The Dispossessed*, 1974
Steve Perry, *The Man Who Never Missed*, 1985
F. Paul Wilson, *The LaNague Chronicles*, 1992

### 5367

S. ANDREW SWANN (Pseudonym of Steven Swiniarski)

## Revolutionary

(New York: DAW, 1996)

**Story type:** Science Fiction (Political; Alternate Intelligence)
**Series:** Hostile Takeover
**Major character(s):** Dominic "Dom" Magnus, Cyborg, Businessman; Kari Tetsami, Computer Expert, Genetically Altered Being; Random Walk, Artificial Intelligence
**Time period(s):** 24th century
**Locale(s):** Bakunin, Planet—Imaginary

**Summary:** Warfare between Dom and his brother wreaks havoc on Bakunin. With most of the population dead or under siege, Bakunin needs help from a major power to rescue the planet from the Terran Executive Command attack, risking takeover of the planetary anarchy.

**Other books you might like:**
Robert A. Heinlein, *The Moon Is a Harsh Mistress*, 1966
Ursula K. Le Guin, *The Dispossessed*, 1974
Alis A. Rasmussen, *The Price of Ransom*, 1990
Robert J. Sawyer, *Starplex*, 1996
Diann Thornley, *Ganwold's Child*, 1995
F. Paul Wilson, *The LaNague Chronicles*, 1992

## 5368

**S. ANDREW SWANN** (Pseudonym of Steven Swiniarski)

### Specters of the Dawn

(New York: DAW, 1994)

**Story type:** Science Fiction (Genetic Manipulation; Mystery)
**Series:** Forests of the Night
**Major character(s):** Angelica "Angel" Lorenzo Lopez, Genetically Altered Being (rabbit); Byron Dorset, Genetically Altered Being (fox); Anaka, Detective—Police
**Time period(s):** 2050s
**Locale(s):** San Francisco, California

**Summary:** Arriving in San Francisco and looking forward to living in a town without prejudice, Angel little expects the need to defend herself from crazy skinheads in her local sports bar. When she goes with the police to identify Byron's body, Angel discovers that someone wants the property she inherited as his heri.

**Other books you might like:**
David Brin, *Glory Season*, 1993
Octavia E. Butler, *Dawn*, 1987
Thomas A. Easton, *Sparrowhawk*, 1990
Joan Slonczewski, *Daughter of Elysium*, 1993
Cordwainer Smith, *The Best of Cordwainer Smith*, 1975

## 5369

**MICHAEL SWANWICK**

### Gravity's Angels

(Sauk City, Wisconsin: Arkham House, 1991)

**Story type:** Science Fiction (Collection)

**Summary:** This collection contains 13 stories published in magazines and anthologies between 1980 and 1989 including Nebula Award finalist stories "The Feast of St. Janis," "Ginungagap," "Mummer Kiss," and "Trojan Horse." One story, "The Man Who Met Picasso," was nominated for a World Fantasy Award, while "The Edge of the World" was nominated for both Hugo and Nebula Awards and then won the Theodore Sturgeon Award for short fiction.

**Other books you might like:**
J.G. Ballard, *Memories of the Space Ages*, 1988
Greg Bear, *The Wind From a Burning Woman*, 1983
Michael Bishop, *Blooded on Arachne*, 1982
Michael Bishop, *One Winter in Eden*, 1984
Phyllis Eisenstein, *Born to Exile*, 1978
Michael Flynn, *The Nanotech Chronicles*, 1991
Janet Kagan, *Mirabile*, 1991
Tanith Lee, *Dreams of Dark and Light*, 1986
Larry Niven, *Tales of Known Space*, 1975
Cordwainer Smith, *The Best of Cordwainer Smith*, 1975
Marc Stiegler, *The Gentle Seduction*, 1990
James Tiptree Jr., *Her Smoke Rose Up Forever*, 1990
    Alice Sheldon, real name
John Varley, *Blue Champagne*, 1986
John Varley, *The Persistence of Vision*, 1978

## 5370

**MICHAEL SWANWICK**

### Griffin's Egg

(New York: St. Martin's Press, 1992)

**Story type:** Science Fiction (Adventure; Political)

**Major character(s):** Gunther Weil, Worker (lunar transport driver); Ekatarina Izmailova, Scientist, Leader
**Time period(s):** 21st century
**Locale(s):** Montenegro

**Summary:** When Earth becomes too ecologically sensitive for continued environmental abuse by corporations, companies move to Luna to continue research without ecological fallout. As war breaks out on Earth, sabotage affects those on Luna, many of whom suffer the effects of a recent development in human neurochemistry which allows modification of higher brain functions.

**Other books you might like:**
Robert A. Heinlein, *The Moon Is a Harsh Mistress*, 1966
Marjorie Bradley Kellogg, *Harmony*, 1991
Allen Steele, *Lunar Descent*, 1991
Neal Stephenson, *Snow Crash*, 1992
John Varley, *Steel Beach*, 1992

## 5371

**MICHAEL SWANWICK**

### The Iron Dragon's Daughter

(New York: Morrow/AvoNova, 1994)

**Story type:** Fantasy (Urban; Science Fiction)
**Major character(s):** Jane Alderberry, Student, Thief; Melanchthon "7332", Mythical Creature (dragon); Puck Aleshire, Mythical Creature
**Time period(s):** Indeterminate Future
**Locale(s):** Great Gray City, Fictional City

**Summary:** In her bleak existence as a factory worker turning out dragons for the military, Jane finds little hope for the future until she befriends dragon-plane 7332. Their bargain yields some hope of a brighter future including formal education and new friends but the temptations of the street prove irresistible while Jane's sexual studies precipitously alter her relationship with Melanchthon.

**Other books you might like:**
C.S. Friedman, *When True Night Falls*, 1993
Mary Gentle, *Rats and Gargoyles*, 1991
P.C. Hodgell, *God Stalk*, 1982
Will Shetterly, *Elsewhere*, 1991
Sheri S. Tepper, *A Plague of Angels*, 1993

## 5372

**MICHAEL SWANWICK**

### Jack Faust

(New York: Avon, 1997)

**Story type:** Science Fiction (First Contact)
**Major character(s):** Johannes "Jack" Faust, Scholar, Genius; Wagner, Student; Mephistopheles, Alien, Demon
**Time period(s):** 19th century; 20th century
**Locale(s):** Europe

**Summary:** Stopped by Wagner from completely burning his library, Faust demonstrates by debate that he needs more information. He realizes he will do anything for the truth when Mephistopheles tells him he will give Faust all the information he needs, but it will lead to the end of humanity.

**Other books you might like:**
Mary Gentle, *Ancient Light*, 1987
Jack McDevitt, *The Engines of God*, 1994
Christopher Pike, *The Eternal Enemy*, 1993
Mary Doria Russell, *The Sparrow*, 1996

Dan Simmons, *Hyperion*, 1989

## 5373

### MICHAEL SWANWICK

## *Stations of the Tide*

(New York: Morrow, 1991)

**Major character(s):** The Bureaucrat, Agent; Gregorian, Scientist, Magician; Chu, Police Officer
**Time period(s):** Indeterminate Future
**Locale(s):** Miranda, Planet—Imaginary

**Summary:** The planet Miranda is periodically inundated and all land surfaces are expected to be washed clean. The bureaucrat is sent to Miranda to confront Gregorian, and talk the ''magician'' into returning the proscribed technology. Gregorian demonstrates his magical prowess, and the agency back on Earth denies the alleged theft, but declines to recall the bureaucrat.

**Other books you might like:**
Alfred Bester, *The Demolished Man*, 1953
Octavia E. Butler, *Adulthood Rites*, 1988
Octavia E. Butler, *Dawn*, 1987
Octavia E. Butler, *Imago*, 1989
Robert A. Heinlein, *Stranger in a Strange Land*, 1991
Sheri S. Tepper, *Grass*, 1990

## 5374

### S.A. SWINIARSKI (Pseudonym of Steven Swiniarski)

## *Raven*

(New York: DAW, 1996)

**Story type:** Horror (Black Magic; Vampire Story)
**Major character(s):** Kane Tyler, Detective; Gail Tyler, Teenager; Manuel ''Childe'' Deite, Sorcerer
**Time period(s):** 1990s (1996)
**Locale(s):** Cleveland, Ohio

**Summary:** Private detective Kane Tyler awakens out of an amnesiac fugue with a vampiric taste for blood and a price on his head for the ritualistic murder of his ex-wife. His efforts to retrieve his memory and discover how this state of affairs has come to pass bring him into contact with Childe, a black magician who leads a cult of the undead and who has targeted Kane for his investigations into the cult's activities. First novel.

**Other books you might like:**
Vincent Courtney, *Vampire Beat*, 1991
P.N. Elrod, *Bloodlist*, 1991
Tanya Huff, *Blood Price*, 1991
Lee Killough, *Blood Hunt*, 1987
Karen E. Taylor, *Blood Ties*, 1995

## 5375

### JEFFERSON P. SWYCAFFER

## *Warsprite*

(Lake Geneva, Wisconsin: TSR, 1990)

**Story type:** Science Fiction (Robot Fiction)
**Major character(s):** Delta, Robot; Sam Taramasco, Scientist; Madeline Leuoir Schenk, Museum Curator
**Time period(s):** Indeterminate Future
**Locale(s):** Southwest; San Antonio, Texas

**Summary:** Two leftovers from a galactic war have fallen on the planet Earth. Delta was created to find the robot Omicron. Learning about Earth as she goes, Delta acquires enemies and allies in her pursuit. Finally she confronts Omicron in a chamber beneath a nuclear test site in the Nevada desert.

**Other books you might like:**
Isaac Asimov, *The Robots of Dawn*, 1983
Margaret Wander Bonanno, *Strangers From the Sky*, 1987
Philip K. Dick, *Blade Runner*, 1982
Alan Dean Foster, *Starman*, 1984
Anne McCaffrey, *The Ship Who Sang*, 1970

## 5376

### JEFFERSON P. SWYCAFFER

## *Web of Futures*

(Lake Geneva, Wisconsin: TSR, 1991)

**Story type:** Fantasy (Religious; Time Travel)
**Major character(s):** Maddock O'Shaughnessy, Time Traveler; Stheneleos Magus XLIV, Alien, Time Traveler
**Time period(s):** 1860s (1862); 2010s (2017)
**Locale(s):** United States

**Summary:** Stheneleos Magus LXIV enlists Maddock's help saving human lives and caring for the souls of the dead he carries. Helpers join and leave the group as they travel from the Civil War era to the 21st century on their mission of enlightenment and rescue.

**Other books you might like:**
Pat Cadigan, *Mindplayers*, 1987
Diana G. Gallagher, *The Alien Dark*, 1990
Marc Laidlaw, *Neon Lotus*, 1988
Mike Resnick, *Soothsayer*, 1991
Jules Verne, *Mysterious Island*, 1876

## 5377

### S.C. SYKES

## *Red Genesis*

(New York: Bantam Spectra, 1991)

**Story type:** Science Fiction (Hard Science Fiction; Political)
**Series:** Next Wave
**Major character(s):** Graham Kuan Sinclair, Criminal, Businessman; Jonathan Baker, Sociologist; Paris Tucker, Settler, Adventurer
**Time period(s):** 21st century
**Locale(s):** Mars

**Summary:** Graham Sinclair, convicted of illegally dumping toxins which caused the deaths of millions, is sentenced to Mars without ever having the chance to see or hear anything of Earth again. On Mars, he finds friendship with his courier Jonathan Baker and a young Earth emigrant, Paris Tucker, then he marries and has a daughter. Pardoned after 20 years, he finds Mars is his true home. This second book in Spectra's The Next Wave series contains a 10-page introduction by Isaac Asimov, a 26-page article titled ''Off to Explore Mars'' by MIT chief science writer Eugene Mallove, plus a brief Mars bibliography.

**Other books you might like:**
Isaac Asimov, *The Martian Way*, 1955
Ben Bova, *The Trikon Deception*, 1992
    Bill Pogue, co-author
Arthur C. Clarke, *The Sands of Mars*, 1952
D.G. Compton, *Farewell, Earth's Bliss*, 1971
Edward E. Hale, *The Man Without a Country*, 1863

Raymond Harris, *Shadows of the White Sun*, 1988
Ursula K. Le Guin, *The Dispossessed*, 1974
Frederik Pohl, *Man Plus*, 1976
Jerry Pournelle, *Prince of Mercenaries*, 1989
Pamela Sargent, *Venus of Dreams*, 1986

---

**5378**

**RYDER SYVERTSON**

## Fortress of Forbidden Destiny
(New York: Pinnacle, 1991)

**Story type:** Science Fiction (Mystical; Adventure)
**Series:** Mystic Rebel
**Major character(s):** Burt Lasker, Martial Arts Expert, Religious (Mystic Rebel); Losang, Religious (Dalai Lama)
**Time period(s):** 1990s
**Locale(s):** Dharmsala, India; Beijing, China

**Summary:** Burt Lasker, ex-CIA agent, was shot down by Communist Chinese over Tibet, found by the Bonpa who trained him in E Kung and recognized by the Dalai Lama as the legendary Mystic Rebel expected to come and save Tibet. When trained masters of Buddhism start disappearing from their retreat near Dharmsala, the Dalai Lama requests help from Lasker to find them and prevent the destruction of mankind.

**Other books you might like:**
Jerry Earl Brown, *Snowmen*, 1991
Gordon R. Dickson, *Dorsai!*, 1976
Marc Laidlaw, *Neon Lotus*, 1988
Kim Stanley Robinson, *Escape From Kathmandu*, 1989
Elizabeth Ann Scarborough, *Nothing Sacred*, 1991

---

**5379**

**STEVE SZILAGYI**

## Photographing Fairies
(New York: Ballantine, 1992)

**Story type:** Fantasy (Historical; Quest)
**Major character(s):** Arthur Conan Doyle, Historical Figure, Writer; Charles Castle, Photographer; Michael Walsmear, Police Officer (constable)
**Time period(s):** 1920s
**Locale(s):** London, England; Burkinwell, England

**Summary:** A country constable approaches Sir Arthur Conan Doyle to verify the photographs of fairies on Charles Castle. When Doyle instead tries to have photographs destroyed, Castle decides to learn the truth, traveling to Burkinwell and finally discovering the people and fairies seen in the photographs. Author's first book.

**Other books you might like:**
Alan Dean Foster, *Quozl*, 1989
Tanya Huff, *Gate of Darkness, Circle of Light*, 1989
Jody Lynn Nye, *Mythology Abroad*, 1991
James D. Priest, *Kirins: The Spell of No'an*, 1990
Kristine Kathryn Rusch, *The Gallery of His Dreams*, 1991

---

**5380**

**MICHAEL TALBOT**

## Night Things
(New York: Avon, 1989)

**Story type:** Horror (Haunted House)
**Major character(s):** Lauren Ransom, Spouse (recent bride); Garrett Ransom, Child (Lauren's 11-year-old son)
**Time period(s):** 1980s (Prologue in 1870)
**Locale(s):** New York (Lake House, a lodge in the Adirondacks)

**Summary:** Pop recording star Stephen Ransom takes his new bride, Lauren, and her son Garrett to live in Lake House, a huge lodge, filled with strange staircases and hidden rooms. Soon the marriage sours, the frightening history of the house envelops them, and they must face the "Master," a mysterious demonic figure who would use the house to unleash a terrible evil upon the world.

**Other books you might like:**
John Farris, *Wildwood*, 1987
Stephen King, *The Shining*, 1977
Chet Williamson, *Soulstorm*, 1986

---

**5381**

**ROBYN TALLIS**

## Rebel From Alphorion
(New York: Ballantine Ivy, 1989)

**Story type:** Science Fiction (Young Adult)
**Series:** Planet Builders
**Major character(s):** Philippa Bidding, Teenager; Will Mornette, Teenager
**Time period(s):** 26th century (2520)
**Locale(s):** Gauguin, Planet—Imaginary

**Summary:** Philippa's family was exiled from the planet Alphorion but now she's being called back by her former boyfriend, the leader of the rebels attempting to overthrow the evil rulers of the planet.

**Other books you might like:**
Frank Asch, *Journey to Terezor*, 1989
Janet Asimov, *Norby Down to Earth*, 1989
    Isaac Asimov, co-author
Jo Dereske, *The Lone Sentinel*, 1989

---

**5382**

**DEBORAH TALMADGE-BICKMORE**

## The Apprentice
(New York: Ballantine/Del Rey, 1990)

**Story type:** Fantasy (Magic Conflict)
**Major character(s):** Jaimah, Servant (Female); Corwyn, Apprentice (Male)
**Time period(s):** Indeterminate

**Summary:** A servant girl, whose magical powers have been stolen, is trapped between her sorceress employer, Shayna, and Corwyn, the sorceress's apprentice, who are fighting one another for power.

**Other books you might like:**
Mary Brown, *The Unlikely Ones*, 1987

## 5383

**DEBORAH TALMADGE-BICKMORE**

### The Heldan

(New York: Ballantine Del Rey, 1994)

**Story type:** Fantasy (Quest; Psychic Powers)
**Major character(s):** Senea, Military Personnel (draftee), Psychic (esper); Vayhawk, Warrior, Leader; Aldived, Leader (Tribelord)
**Time period(s):** Indeterminate
**Locale(s):** Mon'ay, Fictional City

**Summary:** Still unmarried at the age of 24, Senea must become a heldan to defend her village when drafted to the Held and forbidden family contact. When attacked by the Ja'sid, Senea discovers she has legendary psychic abilities unknown to her previously. She and Vayhawk, who chooses her as his student, must learn to control their gift to avoid defeat or exile.

**Other books you might like:**
Orson Scott Card, *The Folk of the Fringe*, 1989
Edmund Cooper, *The Cloud Walker*, 1973
Ursula K. Le Guin, *Always Coming Home*, 1987
C.L. Moore, *Jirel of Joiry*, 1969
Elizabeth Ann Scarborough, *The Healer's War*, 1989
S.M. Stirling, *The Rose Sea*, 1994
    Holly Lisle, co-author

## 5384

**CECILIA TAN**, Editor

### The Beast Within: Erotic Tales of Werewolves

(Boston: Circlet Press, 1994)

**Story type:** Horror (Anthology; Werewolf Story)

**Summary:** This quartet of stories uses the werewolf theme to explore ideas of human sexuality. Jay Michaelson's "The Spirit That Denies" has a werewolf instruct his lover in the proper methods of killing before becoming a werewolf initiate herself. Linda Hooper's "The Killing of the Calf" tells of the erotic relationship between a woman and a wolf bitch, and Robert M. Schroeck's "Alma Mater" recounts the unique destiny of a man soldier saved by a female werewolf lover. In Reina Delacroix's "Wilderland," a mortal with lycanthropic inclinations finds her dreams come true in a virtual reality scenario that allows her to act out her predatory tendencies.

**Other books you might like:**
Byron Preiss, *The Ultimate Werewolf*, 1992
    editor
Brian J. Frost, *Book of the Werewolf*, 1973
    editor
David Hill, *The Way of the Werewolf*, 1966
    editor
Stephen Jones, *The Mammoth Book of Werewolves*, 1994
    editor
Bill Pronzini, *Werewolf!*, 1979
    editor

## 5385

**CECILIA TAN**, Editor

### Blood Kiss: Vampire Erotica

(Boston: Circlet Press, 1994)

**Story type:** Horror (Anthology; Vampire Story)

**Summary:** This chapbook collects seven stories that explore heterosexuality and homosexuality under the guise of vampire fiction. Pat Salah's "The Perfect Form" explores an after hours club for vampires and vampire wannabes and "Cinnamon Roses," an unusual beauty salon staffed by vampires. Warren Lapine's "The Hunger" is a vampire tale set in a postapocalyptic world and Amelia G's "Wanting" the tale of a groupie who befriends the vampire rock star she idolizes. In Raven Kaldera's "Predator," vampirism is caused by a sexually-transmitted virus, and in David Smeds' "Loved to Death" it manifests as a woman whose voracious sexual appetite drains her companions of their life force. Gary Bowen's "The Brass Ring," a novel excerpt, chronicles the relationship of a vampire shapeshifter and his lover.

**Other books you might like:**
Poppy Z. Brite, *Love in Vein*, 1994
    editor
Ellen Datlow, *Little Deaths*, 1994
    editor
Jeff Gelb, *Hottest Blood: The Ultimate in Erotic Horror*, 1993
    editor
Pam Keesey, *Daughters of Darkness: Lesbian Vampire Stories*, 1993
    editor

## 5386

**CECILIA TAN**, Editor

### Cherished Blood

(Cambridge, Massachusetts: Circlet Press, 1997)

**Story type:** Horror (Anthology; Vampire Story)

**Summary:** Ten tales of vampire erotica original to the anthology, including Gary Bowen's "His Name Was Wade," A.R. Morlan's "Drink to Me Only with Thine Eyes," Thomas S. Roche's "Lunar Eclipse," David May's "Katje," and Susan Elizabeth Gray's "Blood Dreams."

**Other books you might like:**
Poppy Z. Brite, *Love in Vein II*, 1997
    Martin H. Greenberg, co-editor
Poppy Z. Brite, *Love in Vein*, 1994
    Martin H. Greenberg, co-editor
Pam Keesey, *Darker Angels: Lesbian Vampire Stories*, 1995
    editor
Amarantha Knight, *Sex Macabre*, 1996
    editor
Amarantha Knight, *Seductive Spectres*, 1996
    editor
Amarantha Knight, *Love Bites*, 1994
    editor
William J. Mann, *Grave Passions*, 1997
    editor
Michael Rowe, *Sons of Darkness: Tales of Men, Blood and Immortality*, 1996
    Thoms Roche, co-editor
Michael Rowe, *Brothers of the Night*, 1997
    Thomas Roche, co-editor

## 5387

**CECILIA TAN**, Editor

### Erotica Vampirica

(Boston: Circlet Press, 1996)

**Story type:** Horror (Anthology; Vampire Story)

**Summary:** Ten erotic fantasies written especially for this volume feature male and female vampires. Whitt Pond's ''When Michael Comes'' tells of a vampire who resists turning his lover into one of the undead through their sexual union. R. Boyczuk's ''Doing Time'' is concerned with a vampire sent to prison for crimes his lover committed. In Lela E. Buis's ''Shadows,'' a woman is stalked by the vampire brother of her dead husband. Alan Smale's ''Vox Vampirica'' features two participants on a telephone sex line who make a supernatural fantasy come true.

**Other books you might like:**
Poppy Z. Brite, *Love in Vein*, 1994
    Martin H. Greenberg, co-editor
Poppy Z. Brite, *Love in Vein II*, 1997
    Martin H. Greenberg, co-editor
Pam Keesey, *Dark Angels: Lesbian Vampire Stories*, 1995
    editor
Pam Keesey, *Daughters of Darkness: Lesbian Vampire Stories*, 1993
    editor
Amarantha Knight, *Love Bites*, 1995
    editor
Michael Rowe, *Sons of Darkness: Tales of Men, Blood and Immortality*, 1996
    Thomas Roche, co-editor

## 5388

**CHRISTINE TANASIUK**

### Howl

(Edmonton, Alberta: Commonwealth, 1997)

**Story type:** Horror (Nature in Revolt)
**Major character(s):** Samantha Harris, Scientist; Adam Haley, Scientist; Druce Harris, Spouse (abusive)
**Time period(s):** 1990s (1997)
**Locale(s):** Black Thunder, Canada

**Summary:** Samantha Harris and Adam Haley investigate the disappearance of a Canadian expedition to study the lives of a species of highly intelligent wolves, but are hampered by the arrival of Druce, Samantha's abusive husband, who is more predatory than the animals they study. A first novel.

**Other books you might like:**
Chris N. Africa, *When Wolves Cry*, 1997
David Dvorkin, *Ursus*, 1989
Randy Goldman, *Werewolf Wars*, 1996
Brian Hopkins, *Cold at Heart*, 1997
Dean R. Koontz, *Watchers*, 1987
Whitley Strieber, *The Wolfen*, 1978

## 5389

**I.U. TARCHETTI**

### Fantastic Tales

(San Francisco, California: Mercury House, 1992)

**Story type:** Horror (Collection)

**Summary:** The only collection by a neglected nineteenth-century Italian writer of Gothic horror, this book assembles nine stories, two by other writers who strongly influenced Tarchetti, and a biographical essay. Included are ''A Dead Man's Bone,'' based loosely on Theophile Gautier's classic ''The Mummy's Foot''; ''A Spirit in a Raspberry'' (based on Erckmann-Chatrian's ''The Burgomaster in the Bottle''), about a man who imbibes from a bottle of wine the spirit of the person from whose grave the grapevine grew; the Poe-esque tale of a madman's obsession, ''The Letter U''; and a tale of necrophilia titled ''Bouvard.'' The superb translation is by Lawrence Venutti.

**Other books you might like:**
Anonymous, *Ghost Tales of the Villa Deodati*, 1992
Margaret Crosland, *The Gothic Tales of the Marquis de Sade*, 1965
    editor
Peter Haining, *Gothic Tales of Terror*, 1972
    editor
E.T.A. Hoffmann, *The Best Tales of Hoffmann*, 1967

## 5390

**JUDITH TARR**

### Alamut

(New York: Doubleday, 1989)

**Story type:** Fantasy (Romance)
**Series:** Alamut
**Major character(s):** Aidan, Royalty (Prince of Rhiyana), Mythical Creature (half-Faerie)
**Time period(s):** Indeterminate Past (Medieval period)
**Locale(s):** Jerusalem, Middle East (Saracen Lands); Alternate Universe

**Summary:** Aidan seeks vengeance on the powerful Assassins who have murdered his nephew and threaten to annihilate the entire family. The Assassins most powerful weapon, the immortal Morgiana, becomes one of Prince Aidan's two loves in this medieval romantic fantasy.

**Other books you might like:**
Tanith Lee, *A Heroine of the World*, 1989
Diana L. Paxson, *The White Raven*, 1989
Josepha Sherman, *The Shining Falcon*, 1989
Pamela Simpson, *Partners in Time*, 1990

## 5391

**JUDITH TARR**

### Arrows of the Sun

(New York: Tor, 1993)

**Story type:** Fantasy (Political)
**Series:** Avaryan Rising
**Major character(s):** Estarion, Ruler (Golden Emperor); Vanyi, Religious (priestess)
**Time period(s):** Indeterminate
**Locale(s):** Asanion, Fictional Country

**Summary:** Having survived regency to ascend to the imperial throne, Estarion returns with his beloved Vanyi to the hated Asanion where deadly rivals for power await any opportunity for advancement.

**Other books you might like:**
M.A.R. Barker, *Flamesong*, 1985
M.A.R. Barker, *Man of Gold*, 1984
Gillian Bradshaw, *The Land of Gold*, 1992
Dave Duncan, *The Cutting Edge*, 1992

R.A. MacAvoy, *Lens of the World*, 1990
Melanie Rawn, *Dragon Prince*, 1988
Martha Wells, *The Element of Fire*, 1993

---

### `5392`
#### JUDITH TARR

## *Ars Magica*
(New York: Bantam, 1989)

**Story type:** Fantasy (Historical)
**Major character(s):** Gerbert, Religious (Monk)
**Time period(s):** Indeterminate Past (The Dark Ages)
**Locale(s):** Europe

**Summary:** Gerbert is first introduced as a young monk in France. The story follows him as he studies magic within the confines of the Catholic church, and later becomes a priest.

**Other books you might like:**
John Desjarlais, *The Throne of Tara*, 1990
Susan Howatch, *Glittering Images*, 1987

---

### `5393`
#### JUDITH TARR

## *The Dagger and the Cross: A Novel of the Crusades*
(New York: Doubleday Foundation, 1991)

**Story type:** Fantasy (Romance; Religious)
**Series:** Alamut
**Major character(s):** Aidan, Royalty (Prince of Rhiyana); Morgiana, Immortal, Noblewoman
**Time period(s):** Indeterminate Past (Medieval Period)
**Locale(s):** Acre, Middle East; Alternate Earth

**Summary:** Christian Knight Prince Aidan and Muslim Lady Morgiana are in love. King Gwydion, older identical twin to Aidan, brings the papal decree allowing them to marry. Powerful enemies conspire to keep them apart, and the magic from Aidan's Elvish mother may not be sufficient to overcome them.

**Other books you might like:**
Katherine Kurtz, *Camber of Culdi*, 1976
Tanith Lee, *A Heroine of the World*, 1989
Diana L. Paxson, *The White Raven*, 1989
Josepha Sherman, *The Shining Falcon*, 1989
Pamela Simpson, *Partners in Time*, 1990

---

### `5394`
#### JUDITH TARR

## *His Majesty's Elephant*
(New York: Harcourt Brace, 1993)

**Story type:** Fantasy (Historical; Young Adult)
**Major character(s):** Rowan, Witch; Charlemagne, Historical Figure, Ruler (Emperor of the West)
**Time period(s):** 9th century
**Locale(s):** Europe

**Summary:** When Charlemagne falls victim to an evil Byzantine spell, his daughter, Rowan, must call on her inherited magic and the power of a magic elephant talisman to effect a cure.

**Other books you might like:**
Lois McMaster Bujold, *The Spirit Ring*, 1993
Louise Cooper, *The Sleep of Stone*, 1991
Tanith Lee, *Black Unicorn*, 1991
Vivian Vande Velde, *Dragon's Bait*, 1992
Martha Wells, *The Element of Fire*, 1993

---

### `5395`
#### JUDITH TARR

## *Lord of the Two Lands*
(New York: Tor, 1993)

**Story type:** Fantasy (Historical)
**Major character(s):** Alexander the Great, Historical Figure, Warrior; Meriamon, Royalty, Religious
**Time period(s):** 4th century B.C.
**Locale(s):** Macedonia; Middle East; Egypt

**Summary:** After becoming King of Macedonia and ruler of the Hellenic city-states, Alexander the Great moves against the Persian Empire. In Egypt, the priests of Amon decide to secure Alexander's protection against the Persians by enticing him to rule Egypt. To further their goals, Meriamon journeys from Egypt to join the victorious Alexander and tempt him with Egyptian rule. First, however, Alexander must conquer Tyre and Gaza.

**Other books you might like:**
David Gemmell, *Dark Prince*, 1993
David Gemmell, *Lion of Macedon*, 1992
Nikos Kazantzakis, *Alexander the Great*, 1982
Edison Marshall, *Conqueror*, 1962
Mary Renault, *The Persian Boy*, 1972

---

### `5396`
#### JUDITH TARR

## *Spear of Heaven*
(New York: Tor, 1994)

**Story type:** Fantasy (Adventure; Political)
**Series:** Avaryan Rising
**Major character(s):** Daruya, Royalty, Magician; Vanyi, Magician, Leader (guildsmaster)
**Time period(s):** Indeterminate
**Locale(s):** Asanion, Fictional Country; Su-Shaklan, Fictional Country; Kingdom of Heaven, Fictional Country

**Summary:** Built during a lengthy peacetime, a series of gates allows rapid travel half way around the world. After Estarion plans to establish an Avaryan embassy at the most distant gate location, a disaster which closes the gateway interferes with Daruya's intention to go and mature a bit while away from home. Surreptitiously joining the diplomatic mission, Daruya must soon utilize her magical abilities. With some difficulty, the group reaches the Kingdom of Heaven where they can pursue the mystery of the destroyed gate in the isolated kingdom.

**Other books you might like:**
James Hilton, *Lost Horizon*, 1933
Edward Myers, *The Mountain Made of Light*, 1992
Geoff Ryman, *The Unconquered Country*, 1987
Elizabeth Ann Scarborough, *Nothing Sacred*, 1991

## 5397

**JUDITH TARR**

### Throne of Isis

(New York: Tor Forge, 1994)

**Story type:** Fantasy (Political; Religious)
**Major character(s):** Cleopatra, Historical Figure, Religious (incarnation of Isis); Marcus Antonius, Historical Figure, Military Personnel; Dions, Religious (priestess of Isis), Psychic
**Time period(s):** 1st century B.C. (41 B.C.-30 B.C.)
**Locale(s):** Alexandria, Egypt; Greece; Asia Minor

**Summary:** Dione attends her goddess incarnate, Cleopatra, from her union with Marcus Antonius through his defeat and Cleopatra's suicide.

**Other books you might like:**
Marion Zimmer Bradley, *The Mists of Avalon*, 1983
Shere Hite, *The Divine Comedy of Ariadne and Jupiter: The Amazing and Spectacular Adventures of Ariadne and Jupiter in Heaven and on Earth*, 1994
Guy Gavriel Kay, *A Song for Arbonne*, 1993
Jennifer Roberson, *Lady of the Forest*, 1992

## 5398

**DONNA TARTT**

### The Secret History

(New York: Alfred A. Knopf, 1992)

**Story type:** Horror (Psychological Suspense)
**Major character(s):** Richard Papen, Student—College; Henry Winter, Student—College; Julian Morrow, Professor (classics professor)
**Time period(s):** 1980s
**Locale(s):** Vermont (Hampden College)

**Summary:** When several students obsessively devoted to their classics studies accidentally kill a bystander during a pagan ritual in the Vermont woods, they struggle to cover up their crime—and formulate a plan for eliminating the one member of their group likely to report them to the authorities. This is the author's first novel.

**Other books you might like:**
Douglas Clegg, *Goat Dance*, 1989
Matthew J. Costello, *Darkborn*, 1992
Sean Costello, *The Cartoonist*, 1991
Mark Morris, *Toady*, 1990
Peter Straub, *Ghost Story*, 1979

## 5399

**BERNARD TAYLOR**

### Charmed Life

(New York: Leisure, 1993)

**Story type:** Horror (Mystery)
**Major character(s):** Guy Holman, Teacher; Annie Milburn, Teacher; Mary Hughes, Spy
**Time period(s):** 1990s (1991)
**Locale(s):** London, England

**Summary:** While Guy Holman strives to discover the truth about the death of his estranged wife and the son she supposedly bore him years before, two mysterious groups of agents struggle against one another in the background of his life, each attempting to manipulate

his role in world events. This novel was originally published in England in 1992.

**Other books you might like:**
Stephen King, *The Dead Zone*, 1979
Stephen King, *Insomnia*, 1994
Dean R. Koontz, *Lightning*, 1988
Dan Simmons, *Carrion Comfort*, 1989

## 5400

**BERNARD TAYLOR**

### Evil Intent

(New York: Leisure, 1996)

**Story type:** Horror (Black Magic)
**Major character(s):** John Callow, Occultist; Jack Forrest, Writer (television screenwriter); Connie Forrest, Housewife
**Time period(s):** 1990s (1994)
**Locale(s):** Valley Green, England

**Summary:** When the Forrest family moves into their deceased cousin's home in rural Valley Green, they run afoul of their neighbor John Callow, an occultist feared throughout the town. Pretending to be a generous man, Callow begins eliminating family members one by one, passing them magical runes in gifts that summon occult forces. First published in England in 1994, this novel was inspired by M.R. James' classic story, "Casting the Runes."

**Other books you might like:**
Ramsey Campbell, *The Long Lost*, 1994
Ramsey Campbell, *Obsession*, 1985
Christopher Fowler, *Rune*, 1990
Phil Rickman, *The Man in the Moss*, 1994

## 5401

**BERNARD TAYLOR**

### The Godsend

(New York: Leisure, 1992)

**Story type:** Horror (Evil Children)
**Major character(s):** Mr. Marlowe, Artist (book illustrator); Kate Marlowe, Housewife; Bonnie Bryant, Child, Foundling (adopted by the Marlowes)
**Time period(s):** 1970s (1976)
**Locale(s):** Little Haverstraw, England

**Summary:** When a strange woman leaves her day old infant with the Marlowes and disappears, it seems only natural for them to adopt the baby as their own. But as each of the Marlowes' other four children die under mysterious circumstances, the couple begin to wonder who—or what—they have adopted. This novel, the author's first, was originally published in 1976.

**Other books you might like:**
Ira Levin, *Rosemary's Baby*, 1967
Edmund Plante, *Seed of Evil*, 1991
David Seltzer, *The Omen*, 1976
Thomas Tryon, *The Other*, 1972

## 5402

### BERNARD TAYLOR

## *Sweetheart, Sweetheart*

(New York: Leisure, 1992)

**Story type:** Horror (Haunted House)
**Major character(s):** David Warwick, Teacher; Shelagh, Teacher, Fiance(e) (David's); Jean Timpson, Housekeeper
**Time period(s):** 1970s (1977)
**Locale(s):** Hillingham, England

**Summary:** David Warwick travels with his girlfriend Shelagh to Gerrard's Hill Cottage in Hillingham, where his twin brother Colin and Colin's wife Helen were slain. Although David suspects a local woman of their murders, it becomes increasingly clear through assaults on Shelagh that the house is imbued with the two-century-old spirit of a jealous female bent on destroying the two of them. This novel was originally published in 1977.

**Other books you might like:**
Michael Cadnum, *Nightlight*, 1989
Judith Hawkes, *Julian's House*, 1989
Shirley Jackson, *The Haunting of Hill House*, 1959
Paul Theroux, *The Black House*, 1977

## 5403

### JERI TAYLOR

## *Mosaic*

(New York: Pocket, 1996)

**Story type:** Science Fiction (Space Opera; Military)
**Series:** Star Trek: Voyager
**Major character(s):** Kathryn Janeway, Spaceship Captain, Space Explorer, Military Personnel; Mark "Hobbes" Johnson, Philosopher, Scientist; Justin Tighe, Military Personnel (lieutenant)
**Time period(s):** 24th century
**Locale(s):** Delta Quadrant, Outer Space; Earth; Planet—Imaginary

**Summary:** While an Away Team visits an unknown planet as the Kazon search for them, Captain Janeway ponders what to do while reviewing her past from early childhood, through her Academy days and early missions, up to the present. One incident in her past gives her the clue she needs to rescue the Away Team.

**Other books you might like:**
Poul Anderson, *Ensign Flandry*, 1966
Pauline Ashwell, *Unwillingly to Earth*, 1992
F.M. Busby, *Star Rebel*, 1984
A. Bertram Chandler, *The Road to the Rim*, 1967
Alfred Coppel, *Glory's War*, 1995
Paula E. Downing, *Flare Star*, 1993
David Feintuch, *Midshipman's Hope*, 1994
L. Neil Smith, *Tom Paine Maru*, 1984

## 5404

### JERI TAYLOR

## *Pathways*

(New York: Pocket Books, 1998)

**Story type:** Science Fiction (Adventure)
**Series:** Star Trek: Voyager
**Major character(s):** Tom Paris, Pilot, Military Personnel (Starfleet Lieutenant); B'Elanna Torres, Engineer, Alien (half-Klingon); Chakotay, Military Personnel (Starfleet Commander), Indian

**Time period(s):** 24th century
**Locale(s):** Planet—Imaginary; *U.S.S. Voyager*, Spaceship

**Summary:** Captured by the Subu and imprisoned, the members of the away team plot their escape. Each evening, the prisoners recount stories of the events that led them to *Voyager*.

**Other books you might like:**
Dafydd ab Hugh, *The Final Fury*, 1996
C.J. Cherryh, *Forty Thousand in Gehenna*, 1983
Julia Ecklar, *The Kobayashi Maru*, 1989
Dana Kramer-Rolls, *Home Is the Hunter*, 1990
Lisanne Norman, *Turning Point*, 1993

## 5405

### KAREN E. TAYLOR

## *Bitter Blood*

(New York: Zebra, 1994)

**Story type:** Horror (Vampire Story)
**Series:** Vampire Legacy
**Major character(s):** Deirdre Griffin, Vampire, Designer (fashion); Mitchell Greer, Detective—Police; Ron Wilkes, Lawyer
**Time period(s):** 1990s (1994)
**Locale(s):** New York, New York

**Summary:** Vampire Deirdre Griffin is called back from her exile in London to help rehabilitate the mortal lover with whom she engineered the death of Max Hunter, fellow vampire and owner of the Ballroom of Romance nightclub. Upon her return, Deirdre is haunted by the immortal spirit of Max, who has bequeathed all he owned to her. She also finds herself in the clutches of The Cadre, an elite cabal of vampires who resent her murder of Max and who force her to do their bidding under the penalty of death to her and all she holds dear. This is a sequel to *Blood Secrets*.

**Other books you might like:**
Michael Cecilione, *The Parliament of Blood*, 1992
Laurell K. Hamilton, *Guilty Pleasures*, 1993
Gordon Linzner, *The Troupe*, 1988
Michael Romkey, *The Vampire Papers*, 1994
Dan Simmons, *Carrion Comfort*, 1989

## 5406

### KAREN E. TAYLOR

## *Blood Secrets*

(New York: Zebra, 1994)

**Story type:** Horror (Vampire Story)
**Series:** Vampire Legacy
**Major character(s):** Deirdre Griffin, Vampire, Designer (fashion); Max Hunter, Businessman (nightclub owner); Mitchell Greer, Detective—Police
**Time period(s):** 1990s (1994)
**Locale(s):** New York, New York

**Summary:** Deirdre, a 150 year old vampire, works by day as a clothing designer, and by night frequents Ballroom of Romance, a hot New York nightclub where it's easy to find dates from whom she can take nonlethal nightly feedings. When patrons of the club begin dying gruesomely, Deirdre is compelled to find out who is responsible before suspicion falls upon her. First book in the series.

**Other books you might like:**
Anne Billson, *Suckers*, 1993
Poppy Z. Brite, *Lost Souls*, 1992
Ray Garton, *Live Girls*, 1987

Tanya Huff, *Blood Price*, 1991
Anne Rice, *The Vampire Lestat*, 1985

---

**5407**

KAREN E. TAYLOR

### Blood Ties

(New York: Zebra, 1995)

**Story type:** Horror (Vampire Story)
**Series:** Vampire Legacy
**Major character(s):** Deirdre Griffin, Vampire, Designer; Mitchell Greer, Vampire, Detective—Police; Larry Martin, Vampire
**Time period(s):** 1990s (1995)
**Locale(s):** New York, New York

**Summary:** It's payback time for vampire nightclub owner Deirdre Griffin and her recently vampirized lover Mitch Greer. A renegade vampire is violating vampire protocol, killing others of his own kind as well as mortals, and the elite vampire hierarchy known as the Cadre enjoins them to kill the rebel. Deirdre's stake in the events is considerable, because her quarry is a vampire she herself converted.

**Other books you might like:**
Michael Cecilione, *The Parliament of Blood*, 1992
Christopher Golden, *Angel Souls and Devil Hearts*, 1995
Laurell K. Hamilton, *Guilty Pleasures*, 1993
Gordon Linzner, *The Troupe*, 1988
Michael Romkey, *The Vampire Papers*, 1994

---

**5408**

KEITH TAYLOR

### Search for the Starblade

(New York: Ace, 1990)

**Story type:** Fantasy (Quest; Adventure)
**Series:** Danans
**Major character(s):** Oghmal, Warrior, Hero; Carbri, Musician (harp), Minstrel (bard); Dirona, Royalty (princess), Sorceress
**Time period(s):** Indeterminate
**Locale(s):** Ireland (Tirtangir); *Summer Dancer*, At Sea

**Summary:** Oghmal, Prince of the Danans, is a great warrior in search of a weapon worthy of his skills, so he and his twin brother Carbri, leave Ireland and set sail to find the legendary Isle of Swans whose people are the keepers of the Tree of Fire. There Oghmal receives the knowledge necessary to find the rare skymetal needed to make a sword that is not only unbreakable, but will also defeat sorcery. Oghmal marries Dirona, sister to the king of the Isle of Swans, and they and their companions go back to Ireland to find the skymetal of Oghmal's vision.

**Other books you might like:**
Kenneth C. Flint, *A Storm upon Ulster*, 1980
Morgan Llywelyn, *Bard: The Odyssey of the Irish*, 1984
Morgan Llywelyn, *The Horse Goddess*, 1982
Morgan Llywelyn, *Lion of Ireland*, 1980
Michael Moorcock, *Elric of Melnibone*, 1972

---

**5409**

L.A. TAYLOR

### Cat's Paw

(New York: Ace, 1995)

**Story type:** Fantasy (Mystery; Contemporary Realism)
**Major character(s):** Miranda Glivven, Detective—Amateur, Spouse; The Cat, Animal, Companion
**Time period(s):** Indeterminate
**Locale(s):** Province of Bierdsey, Fictional Country

**Summary:** When Alexi Glivven fails to return home to his family and his duties at the lighthouse after accepting a secret assignment for the governor, Miranda Glivven sets out by train to find him. Accompanied by a cat, Miranda follows her husband's trail, questioning people along the railroad line for clues to Alexi's whereabouts.

**Other books you might like:**
Emma Bull, *Finder*, 1994
Pamela Dean, *The Dubious Hills*, 1994
Rose Estes, *Troll-Taken*, 1993
Holly Lisle, *Minerva Wakes*, 1994
Brooke Stevens, *The Circus of the Earth and Air*, 1994

---

**5410**

L.A. TAYLOR

### Women's Work

(Minneapolis, Minnesota: Allau Press, 1995)

**Story type:** Science Fiction (Collection)

**Summary:** Contains three original stories and two reprinted from *Analog* in 1986 and 1992, the tone of which varies from ominous through wistful to light. Two stories focus on Link Services and the grand project of bringing water to the planet Urt, while other themes include music and alternate universes.

**Other books you might like:**
Katharine Kerr, *Resurrection*, 1992
Nancy Kress, *The Aliens of Earth*, 1993
Ursula K. Le Guin, *A Fisherman of the Inland Sea*, 1994
Pat Murphy, *Points of Departure*, 1990
James Tiptree Jr., *Her Smoke Rose Up Forever*, 1990
Connie Willis, *Impossible Things*, 1994

---

**5411**

LUCY TAYLOR

### Close to the Bone

(Woodinville, Washington: Silver Salamander Press, 1993)

**Story type:** Horror (Collection)

**Summary:** This second collection brings together 10 explicit tales of psychological and supernatural horror, seven of which are original to the volume. Included are the bizarre juvenile delinquent story, "Virgin"; the alien invasion tale, "Animal Souls"; the tale of a horrifying afterlife, "The Best in the Business"; the story of a woman confronting her own sexual psychoses, "Cages"; and the title story, about the strange perspective a physically and emotionally abused woman develops toward love. Ed Bryant supplies the introduction.

**Other books you might like:**
Poppy Z. Brite, *Swamp Foetus*, 1993
Scott Edelman, *Suicide Art*, 1992
Ray Garton, *Methods of Madness*, 1990

Edward Lee, *Edward Lee's Quest for Sex, Truth and Reality*, 1992

---

**5412**

### LUCY TAYLOR

## The Flesh Artist

(Woodinville, Washington: Silver Salamander Press, 1994)

**Story type:** Horror (Collection)

**Summary:** The six stories in this volume range in their approach to horror from "Wall of Words," a lyrical look at a dysfunctional family, and "Wrestling with the Devil," a wacky tale of the grotesque in which a man combines faith healing with wrestling, to "The Flesh Artist," about the gruesome revenge a plastic surgeon takes upon his patients, and "Windowsitting," in which an aging woman's desire to have a baby becomes a nightmare of pathology for the midwife attending her. Norman Partridge supplies the introduction.

**Other books you might like:**
Poppy Z. Brite, *Swamp Foetus*, 1993
Adam-Troy Castro, *Lost in Booth Nine*, 1993
Edward Lee, *Edward Lee's Quest for Sex, Truth and Reality*, 1992

---

**5413**

### LUCY TAYLOR

## Painted in Blood

(Woodinville, Washington: Silver Salamander, 1997)

**Story type:** Horror (Collection)

**Summary:** Thirteen stories, seven original to the collection, featuring charcters driven by intense loneliness and unfulfilled longing to extreme, often grotesque acts of sex and violence. Selections include "Heat," in which a woman's unbridled sexual passion manifests as pyromania; "Pain Threshold," in which a wrestler's growing numbmess to the dismal circumstances of his life is mirrored in the increasing extravagance of the injuries he sustains; "The Story Box," in which a woman coerces her child into believing that her murdered father was only part of a make-believe story; and the title tale, about the desperation of two lovers imprisoned in a fundamentalist society.

**Other books you might like:**
Poppy Z. Brite, *Swamp Foetus*, 1993
Scott Edelman, *Suicide Art*, 1992
Gerard Daniel Houarner, *Painfreak*, 1996
Roberta Lannes, *The Mirror of the Night*, 1997
David J. Schow, *Seeing Red*, 1990

---

**5414**

### LUCY TAYLOR

## The Safety of Unknown Cities

(Woodinvill, Washington: Darkside Press, 1995)

**Story type:** Horror (Vampire Story)
**Major character(s):** Val Petrillo, Traveler; Arthur Quentin Breen, Serial Killer; Majeed, Young Man
**Time period(s):** 1990s (1995)
**Locale(s):** Taroudannt, Morocco

**Summary:** Alienated and disaffected by her abusive upbringing, Val Petrillo travels the globe, trying to connect with her world through an endless string of sexual encounters. Stories of The City, a mythical

land of perversities that will offer her the ultimate fulfillment she seeks, sends her to Morocco, pursued by a psychopathic former lover whose passions help stoke the torrid events that follow. This sexually explicit first novel grew out of a 1994 novella of the same title.

**Other books you might like:**
Clive Barker, *Everville*, 1995
Clive Barker, *The Great and Secret Show*, 1989
Paul Bowles, *The Sheltering Sky*, 1949
Poppy Z. Brite, *Drawing Blood*, 1994
Stephen King, *Rose Madder*, 1995

---

**5415**

### LUCY TAYLOR

## Spree

(Abingdon, Maryland: CD Publications, 1998)

**Story type:** Horror (Mystery; Wild Talents)
**Major character(s):** Lonny Flynn, Convict (former); Tommy Gleason, Doctor (chiropractor); Julia, Young Woman
**Time period(s):** 1990s (1999)
**Locale(s):** Boulder, Colorado

**Summary:** Released after a short stretch in prison, Lonny Flynn returns home to settle the score with whoever is responsible for the death of his beloved mother. Lonny's investigations bring him into bloody confrontation with a variety of acquaintances who have made his life miserable, and force him to wrestle with his uncontrollable talent for out-of-body experiences.

**Other books you might like:**
Thomas Baum, *Out of Body*, 1997
Sean Costello, *Captain Quad*, 1991
Graham Masterton, *Rook*, 1996
Susan Palwick, *Flying in Place*, 1992
Peter Straub, *If You Could See Me Now*, 1977

---

**5416**

### LUCY TAYLOR

## Unnatural Acts and Other Stories

(New York: Richard Kasak Books, 1994)

**Story type:** Horror (Collection)

**Summary:** The nine stories in this volume examine the alienation of living on the fringe of society in brutal, and often sexually explicit terms. "Knockouts" is concerned with a psychopath who seeks sexual gratification in physical violence; "The Best in the Business" with a hell created in the image of one man's sexual fantasies; "Making the Woman" with the self-loathing of two children from dysfunctional families that explodes violently; and "Rush" with the extremes to which a bodybuilder goes to obtain his steroid fix. Both "Flamethrower" and "Idol" examine the sideshow nature of wrestling and the freaks attracted to it. Edward Lee supplies the introdution.

**Other books you might like:**
Poppy Z. Brite, *Swamp Foetus*, 1993
Ramsey Campbell, *Scared Stiff*, 1987
S. Darnbrook Colson, *People of the Night*, 1994
Edward Lee, *Edward Lee's Quest for Sex, Truth and Reality*, 1992
Richard Sutphen, *Sexpunks & Savage Sagas*, 1992

## 5417

**PETER TAYLOR**

### The Oracle at Stoneleigh Court

(New York: Knopf, 1993)

**Story type:** Horror (Collection)

**Summary:** This outstanding collection by a Pulitzer Prize-winning author renowned as one of the best short-fiction writers of his age brings together eleven tales and three one-act plays in which the magic of daily life often blends uncannily with the supernatural. In the title story, a widowed aunt with mystical powers pushes her nephew into a relationship with a woman who may or may not be under her psychic control. In "Demons," a young boy's life is changed by the voices he hears inside his head and cannot distinguish from his own willful desires. "The Real Ghost" tells of a man who does not know he is a ghost, "The Witch of Owl Mountain Springs" of an embittered woman's revenge against a former lover, and "Cousin Aubrey" of a family outcast's personality transformation while accompanying the casket of a relative back home.

**Other books you might like:**
Fred Chappell, *More Shapes than One*, 1991
Joyce Carol Oates, *Haunted: Tales of the Grotesque*, 1994
Robert Phillips, *Triumph of the Night*, 1989
   editor

## 5418

**RONALD TAYLOR**, Editor

### Six German Romantic Tales

(Chester Springs, Pennsylvania: Dufour Editions, 1993)

**Story type:** Horror (Anthology)

**Summary:** The six stories collected in this volume are offered as an example of the romantic movement's commingling of the natural and supernatural, beauty and horror. Included are two stories apiece by Ludwig Tieck, Heinrich von Kleist and E.T.A. Hoffman. The highlights are Hoffmann's "Don Giovanni," in which a man's rapture over Mozart's opera turns its fictional heroine into a figure of flesh and blood; von Kleist's *conte cruel*, "The Earthquake in Chile," which juxtaposes incidents of human cruelty against a background of natural devastation; and Tieck's "Eckbert the Fair," in which a virtuous man is driven to murder and despair over the story of his wife's infidelity as a child. This book was originally published in 1985.

**Other books you might like:**
Chris Baldick, *The Oxford Book of Gothic Tales*, 1992
   editor
Peter Haining, *Great Tales of Terror From Europe and America*, 1972
   editor
Peter Haining, *Black Tales*, 1965
E.T.A. Hoffmann, *The Tales of Hoffmann*, 1946

## 5419

**WILLIAM TEDFORD**

### Liquid Diet

(New York: Diamond, 1992)

**Story type:** Horror (Vampire Story)
**Major character(s):** Troy Davidson, Teenager, Vampire; Melissa French, Teenager, Vampire; Randolf Hansen, Doctor

**Time period(s):** 1990s (1992)
**Locale(s):** Hanesburg

**Summary:** Melissa French is disgusted the night she witnesses her vampire next-door neighbor Troy Davidson drink blood from the neck of a victim—that is, until she discovers that she too is a vampire, and that Troy is her competition in their small town.

**Other books you might like:**
Robert Aickman, *Pages From a Young Girl's Journal*, 1975
   short story in *Cold Hand in Mine*
Poppy Z. Brite, *Lost Souls*, 1992
Nancy A. Collins, *Sunglasses After Dark*, 1989
Elizabeth Engstrom, *Black Ambrosia*, 1988
S.P. Somtow, *Vampire Junction*, 1983

## 5420

**MELANIE TEM**
**STEVE RASNIC TEM**, Co-Author

### Beautiful Strangers

(Arvada, Colorado: Roadkill Press, 1992)

**Story type:** Horror (Science Fiction)
**Major character(s):** Mary, Prostitute
**Time period(s):** Indeterminate Future
**Locale(s):** Wheat, Planet—Imaginary

**Summary:** While turning tricks at a space bar, Mary encounters a beautiful stranger no one else can see whose bizarre sexual preferences offer her an intimacy lacking in her alienated and disaffected life. This chapbook is illustrated by Melissa Sherman.

**Other books you might like:**
Ramsey Campbell, *Medusa*, 1987

## 5421

**MELANIE TEM**

### Desmodus

(New York: Dell, 1995)

**Story type:** Horror (Vampire Story)
**Major character(s):** Joel Desmodus, Vampire; Rory Desmodus, Vampire; Eli Desmodus, Vampire
**Time period(s):** 1990s (1995)
**Locale(s):** Tallus, Colorado

**Summary:** A matriarchal race of vampire-like beings lives in isolation in the hills of Colorado, their only contact with the world their feeding on mammals. When Joel, a member of the Desmodus family of this species, prepares to move the Tallus community as they prepare to enter one of their periodic hibernations, he discovers truths about the clan's history and the relationship between Desmodus men and women that lead him to radical actions that will bring self-understanding.

**Other books you might like:**
Scott Baker, *Ancestral Hungers*, 1995
Christopher Golden, *Of Saints and Shadows*, 1995
Jewelle Gomez, *The Gilda Stories*, 1991
Anne Rice, *The Witching Hour*, 1990
S.P. Somtow, *Moon Dance*, 1989
J.N. Williamson, *Bloodlines*, 1994

## 5422

**MELANIE TEM**
**NANCY HOLDER**, Co-Author

### Making Love

(New York: Dell/Abyss, 1993)

**Story type:** Horror (Supernatural Vengeance)
**Major character(s):** Charlotte Tobias, Teacher (of English); Cameron Tobias, Mentally Ill Person (Charlotte's brother); Phanes, Mythical Creature
**Time period(s):** 1990s (1993)
**Locale(s):** Pittsburgh, Pennsylvania

**Summary:** With the help of her schizophrenic brother Cameron, lovelorn Charlotte Tobias learns how to turn Phanes, her fantasized ideal lover, into reality. When Phanes begins expressing murderous impulses, Charlotte realizes he has inherited all of her subconscious resentment against people who have helped to make her life miserable.

**Other books you might like:**
Stephen King, *The Dark Half*, 1989
Richard Christian Matheson, *Created By*, 1993
John R. Maxim, *Abel/Baker/Charley*, 1983
Mary Shelley, *Frankenstein*, 1818

## 5423

**MELANIE TEM**

### Prodigal

(New York: Dell Abyss, 1991)

**Story type:** Horror (Vampire Story)
**Major character(s):** Lucy Brill, Teenager; Rae Brill, Teenager (Lucy's older sister); Jerry Johnston, Social Worker
**Time period(s):** 1990s
**Locale(s):** United States

**Summary:** Traumatized by the unexplained disappearances of her older brother and sister, Lucy Brill begins seeing social worker Jerry Johnston—unaware that Jerry, a corpulent misfit who "feeds" on the pain of his charges, was the last person to see her two siblings alive. This is the author's first novel.

**Other books you might like:**
John Metcalfe, *The Feasting Dead*, 1954
Theodore Sturgeon, *Some of Your Blood*, 1961

## 5424

**MELANIE TEM**

### Revenant

(New York: Dell/Abyss, 1994)

**Story type:** Horror (Ghost Story)
**Major character(s):** Gabriel Carmichael, Child; Thomas L. Krieg Jr., Architect; Elinor Dietrich, Aged Person
**Time period(s):** 1990s (1994)
**Locale(s):** Revenant, Colorado

**Summary:** People from different walks of life are drawn by the specters of their various griefs—an aborted child, a husband as he was before being stricken by Alzheimer's, children who died in car accidents—to Revenant, a ghost town in Colorado's Rocky Mountains. There, a presiding spirit of grief allows them to overcome their emotional devastation by helping one another or by being absorbed into the town.

**Other books you might like:**
Tom Elliott, *The Dwelling*, 1988
Shirley Jackson, *The Haunting of Hill House*, 1959
Richard Matheson, *Hell House*, 1977
Chet Williamson, *Ash Wednesday*, 1987

## 5425

**MELANIE TEM**

### Wilding

(New York: Dell/Abyss, 1992)

**Story type:** Horror (Werewolf Story)
**Major character(s):** Deborah, Teenager; Julian, Streetperson; Mary, Aged Person
**Time period(s):** 1990s (1992)
**Locale(s):** Denver, Colorado

**Summary:** This poignant allegory of the role of women in contemporary society chronicles the lives of a matriarchal extended family of four-generations of werewolves, whose members express emotions through shape-shifting.

**Other books you might like:**
Peter S. Beagle, *Lila the Werewolf*, 1969
Michael Cadnum, *St. Peter's Wolf*, 1991
Dennis Danvers, *Wilderness*, 1991
Ronald Kelly, *Something Out There*, 1991
H. Warner Munn, *The Werewolf of Ponkert*, 1958

## 5426

**STEVE RASNIC TEM**

### Decoded Mirrors: Three Tales after Lovecraft

(West Warwick, Rhode Island: Necronomicon Press, 1992)

**Story type:** Horror (Collection)

**Summary:** A triptych of stories that use the motifs of H.P. Lovecraft's horror fiction in poignant tales of relationships between parents and children. "Decodings" describes a woman's painful odyssey of self-discovery during a trip to her father's hometown. "Guardian Angels" tells of the real terrors spawned by childhood fears. And "Mirror Man" is concerned with the unbridgeable gulf between children and adults created by parental neglect.

**Other books you might like:**
P.H. Cannon, *Pulptime*, 1986
Michael Shea, *Fat Face*, 1987
Brian Stableford, *The Innsmouth Heritage*, 1992

## 5427

**STEVE RASNIC TEM**

### Fairytales

(Arvada, Colorado: Road Kill Press, 1990)

**Story type:** Horror (Collection)

**Summary:** A dozen stories presented as the secret fairytales that Jack Johansen writes in his notebook: dark stories that he will not tell his children because they chronicle the pains and disappointments of life from which he is trying to shelter them.

**Other books you might like:**
Donald Barthelme, *The King*, 1990
Chet Williamson, *The House of Fear*, 1989
David Henry Wilson, *The Coachman Rat*, 1985

---

**5428**

**SHERI S. TEPPER**

## Beauty

(New York: Doubleday Foundation, 1991)

**Story type:** Fantasy (Legend; Time Travel)
**Major character(s):** Beauty, Noblewoman, Time Traveler; Carabosse, Mythical Creature (fairy); Giles, Military Personnel
**Time period(s):** 14th century; 20th century
**Locale(s):** England; Faerie, Fictional Country

**Summary:** Beauty is the half-fairy daughter of the Duke of Westfaire who is under a curse. Arranging for her half-sister, Beloved, to sleep instead of her, she escapes only to be captured by a film crew from the 21st century, where she discovers that all life except for man has been destroyed. She goes to the 20th century and slowly learns her fairy powers. But her cold and uncaring mother in Faerie harrasses Beauty further.

**Other books you might like:**
Mildred Downey Broxon, *Too Long a Sacrifice*, 1981
Michael Greatrex Coney, *King of the Scepter'd Isle*, 1989
Pamela Dean, *Tam Lin*, 1991
Diana Wynne Jones, *Fire and Hemlock*, 1984
Tanith Lee, *Red as Blood: Or Tales from the Sisters Grimmer*, 1983
Terri Windling, *Life on the Border*, 1991
    editor
Patricia C. Wrede, *Snow White and Rose Red*, 1989

---

**5429**

**SHERI S. TEPPER**

## The Family Tree

(New York: Avon, 1997)

**Story type:** Science Fiction (Genetic Manipulation; Time Travel)
**Major character(s):** Dora Henry, Police Officer; Nassifeh "Opalears" Nazir, Time Traveler, Storyteller; Izakar "Izzy", Linguist, Time Traveler
**Time period(s):** 2000s; 51st century
**Locale(s):** United States

**Summary:** Defying her husband, Dora welcomes the weed. When she moves out, another finds her at her new home and seems to understand her. While the weed becomes a forest, Dora investigates the murder of a retired geneticist who, reportedly, created a talking pig. The environment no longer supports the range of wildlife needed to maintain itself due to overpopulation and construction, but the strange new trees change that with a little help from the future.

**Other books you might like:**
David Brin, *Brightness Reef*, 1995
Paula E. Downing, *A Whisper of Time*, 1994
Thomas A. Easton, *Greenhouse*, 1991
Alan Dean Foster, *Quozl*, 1989
Kay Kenyon, *The Seeds of Time*, 1997
Megan Lindholm, *Alien Earth*, 1992
Catherine Wells, *The Earth Is All That Lasts*, 1991

---

**5430**

**SHERI S. TEPPER**

## Gibbon's Decline and Fall

(New York: Bantam Spectra, 1996)

**Story type:** Science Fiction (Political; Genetic Manipulation)
**Major character(s):** Carolyn Crespin Shepherd, Lawyer, Farmer; Agnes "Aggie" McGann, Religious (nun); Sovawanea "Sophy" a Tesuawane, Indian, Feminist
**Time period(s):** 2000s (2000)
**Locale(s):** Sante Fe, New Mexico; New York, New York; Salt Lake City, Utah

**Summary:** Carolyn, Agnes, Ophy, Betti, Faye, Jessy, and Sophy meet the first day of college and soon form the Decline and Fall Club, swearing they will meet every year, even after they graduate. They would each find a place they could stand and be a woman as self-defined and never decline or fall from that position. When Carolyn's daughter asks her to come out of retirement to defend a 14-year-old who left her baby in a dumpster, the DFC comes to Carolyn's aid. Unfortunately, the evil prosecutor, a minion of the right-wing American Alliance, intends the case as a stepping stone to the presidency.

**Other books you might like:**
Margaret Atwood, *The Handmaid's Tale*, 1986
Margaret Wander Bonanno, *The Others*, 1990
Octavia E. Butler, *Mind of My Mind*, 1977
Helen Collins, *Mutagenesis*, 1993
Suzette Haden Elgin, *Native Tongue*, 1984
Nicola Griffith, *Ammonite*, 1993
Susan Palwick, *Flying in Place*, 1992
Neal Stephenson, *The Diamond Age*, 1995

---

**5431**

**SHERI S. TEPPER**

## Grass

(New York: Doubleday Foundation, 1989)

**Story type:** Science Fiction (Science Fiction)
**Major character(s):** Marjorie Westriding Yrarier, Diplomat; Sylvan Bon Damfels, Nobleman
**Time period(s):** Indeterminate Future
**Locale(s):** Earth; Grass, Planet—Imaginary

**Summary:** A deadly plague spreads across inhabited space and only one world appears to be immune, the planet Grass. Diplomat Marjorie Westriding Yrarier is sent to discover the source of this immunity, but can make little headway in the stagnant, intensely xenophobic society of the planet's hereditary ruling class. They seem to care about nothing but the frightening hunts they conduct mounted upon enormously dangerous alien steeds known as Hippae. Eventually Lady Westriding discovers that both the hunts and the Hippae are more than they seem.

**Other books you might like:**
Gregory Benford, *Great Sky River*, 1987
Gregory Benford, *Tides of Light*, 1989
David Brin, *Startide Rising*, 1983
David Brin, *The Uplift War*, 1987
Octavia E. Butler, *Dawn*, 1987
Larry Niven, *The Legacy of Heorot*, 1987
    Jerry Pournelle, and Steven Barnes, co-authors

## 5432

### SHERI S. TEPPER

## *Marianne, the Matchbox and the Malachite Mouse*

(New York: Ace, 1989)

**Story type:** Fantasy (Alternate World)
**Series:** Marianne
**Major character(s):** Marianne, Young Woman
**Time period(s):** 1980s
**Locale(s):** Earth; Alternate Universe

**Summary:** Marianne must return a matchbox, and the game that goes with it, to the original, magical owner. After she discovers how to transport herself into the game as one of the playing pieces, she begins her search for the owner.

**Other books you might like:**
Kevin J. Anderson, *Gameplay*, 1989

## 5433

### SHERI S. TEPPER

## *A Plague of Angels*

(New York: Bantam Spectra, 1993)

**Story type:** Fantasy (Quest; Science Fiction)
**Major character(s):** Abasio Cermit, Traveler; Orphan, Heroine; Quince Ellel, Witch
**Time period(s):** Indeterminate Future
**Locale(s):** The Place of Power, Mythical Place; Manland, Fictional Country; Artemesia, Fictional Country

**Summary:** Most of humanity departed for the stars leaving a much reduced population. The few remaining Manland cities, filled with gangs and violence and rife with sexually transmitted diseases, continue to shrink while monsters from Earth's past repopulate the countryside. In control of legions of android "walkers," Quince Ellel searches for a unique girl to utilize as guidance system for her shuttle. While Orphan searches for objects seen in a dream, Abasio joins and travels with Orphan, escaping from walkers, trolls and griffins. In Artemisia, a talking coyote joins their search.

**Other books you might like:**
David Brin, *Earth*, 1990
Emma Bull, *Bone Dance: A Fantasy for Technophiles*, 1991
Richard Grant, *Through the Heart*, 1991
Morgan Llywelyn, *The Elementals*, 1993
Anne McCaffrey, *Powers That Be*, 1993
   Elizabeth Ann Scarborough, co-author
J.M. Morgan, *Desert Eden*, 1991
Catherine Wells, *The Earth Is All That Lasts*, 1991

## 5434

### SHERI S. TEPPER

## *Raising the Stones*

(New York: Doubleday Foundation, 1990)

**Story type:** Science Fiction (Science Fiction; Family Saga)
**Major character(s):** Samasnier Girat, Administrator (topman); Saluniel Girat, Administrator (rec officer); Phaed Girat, Parent (father of Sam and Sal)
**Time period(s):** Indeterminate Future

**Locale(s):** Hobbs Land, Planet—Imaginary; Voorstod, Fictional Country

**Summary:** Hobbs Land is a quiet agricultural colony, where men and women work together to build a new society. When the children of this world start to rebuild a temple of the vanished Owlbrit race, it seems a harmless exercise. At first, no one notices that the gods have returned to their temples. Voorstod is a world of grim misogynists, men who live obedient to their prophets while enslaving the alien Gharm. They look forward to the day they will go forth with whip and sword, killing all who disobey the one true God. To speed their cause, they must recapture singer Maire Manone, who fled with her children to Hobbs Land. Caught between cultures, Maire's son, Samasnier Girat, searches restlessly for his purpose in life. He is convinced he has a higher destiny, somehow linked with his father on Voorstod. He doesn't know how rapidly that destiny will come to claim him, or the price he must pay to become a hero.

**Other books you might like:**
Marion Zimmer Bradley, *The Firebrand*, 1987
Marion Zimmer Bradley, *Thendara House*, 1983
Orson Scott Card, *Speaker for the Dead*, 1986
C.J. Cherryh, *Cyteen*, 1988
Frank Herbert, *Dune*, 1965
Gene Wolfe, *The Shadow of the Torturer*, 1980

## 5435

### SHERI S. TEPPER

## *Shadow's End*

(New York: Bantam Spectra, 1994)

**Story type:** Science Fiction (Theological; Genetic Manipulation)
**Major character(s):** Saluez, Servant (Shadow); Lutha Tallstaff, Linguist, Parent; Leelson Famber, Empath
**Time period(s):** Indeterminate Future
**Locale(s):** Dinadh, Planet—Imaginary; Alliance Central, Earth; Perdur, Planet—Imaginary

**Summary:** Sole surviving planet of the Ularian disaster, which wiped out all other human life in the Hermes Sector, Dinadh remains insular and unwilling to help defend the planets in the Hermes Sector from attack. Sent to Dinadh with her retarded son by Alliance Central, Lutha befriends Saluez, a Dinadh woman. Eventually a Dinadh ceremony leads to a revelation more awful than anyone expects.

**Other books you might like:**
Octavia E. Butler, *Dawn*, 1987
Nicola Griffith, *Ammonite*, 1993
Megan Lindholm, *Alien Earth*, 1992
Anne McCaffrey, *Powers That Be*, 1993
   Elizabeth Ann Scarborough, co-author
Joan Slonczewski, *A Door into Ocean*, 1986
Catherine Wells, *The Earth Is All That Lasts*, 1991

## 5436

### SHERI S. TEPPER

## *Sideshow*

(New York: Bantam Spectra, 1992)

**Story type:** Science Fiction (Alternate Intelligence; Political)
**Series:** Arbai Device
**Major character(s):** Fringe Dorwalk Owldark, Police Officer (enforcer); Nela Zy-Czorsky Korsyzczy, Twin (Siamese), Time Traveler; Margorie "Jory" Westriding, Traveler, Heroine
**Time period(s):** 1990s; 61st century

**Locale(s):** United States; Elsewhere, Planet—Imaginary

**Summary:** In this sequel to *Grass* and *Raising the Stones*, all humans remaining free of the Hobbs Land Gods are on Elsewhere. There the legacy of Brannigan Galaxity's "Great Question Committee," diversity, is practiced without interference or restraint within the borders of each community. Enforcers attend to any situation which threatens this diversity and the ability of each community to potentially discover the ultimate destiny of man, while the Human and Arbai doors connecting Elsewhere with the slaves of the Hobbs Land Gods are locked and guarded.

**Other books you might like:**
David Brin, *Startide Rising*, 1983
Octavia E. Butler, *Dawn*, 1987
Orson Scott Card, *Wyrms*, 1987
Robert A. Heinlein, *Stranger in a Strange Land*, 1991
  revised
Dan Simmons, *Hyperion*, 1989
Joan Slonczewski, *A Door into Ocean*, 1986
Michael Swanwick, *Stations of the Tide*, 1991

---

**5437**

**SHERI S. TEPPER**

## Six Moon Dance

(New York, Avon Eos, 1998)

**Story type:** Science Fiction (First Contact; Political)
**Major character(s):** Mouche, Student (consort trainee), Teenager; Questioner II, Cyborg, Judge; Ellen Voy, Dancer, Clone
**Time period(s):** Indeterminate Future
**Locale(s):** Newholme, Planet—Imaginary

**Summary:** While Newholme becomes more unstable, people continue to pretend the "invisible" native work force doesn't exist. If the native population comes to light when the Inquisitor visits Newholme, she may remove the colonists who have settled there. Unfortunately the humans share Newholme with an undetected ancient alien, whom the natives have been supporting for millennia, and who now needs special attention, requiring the cooperation of all species, or Newholme will be destroyed.

**Other books you might like:**
David Brin, *Brightness Reef*, 1995
L. Warren Douglas, *Stepwater*, 1995
Anne McCaffrey, *Powers That Be*, 1993
  Elizabeth Ann Scarborough, co-author
Elizabeth Moon, *Remnant Population*, 1996
Joan Slonczewski, *The Children Star*, 1998

---

**5438**

**JOHN TERRA**

## City of Pain

(Honesdale, Pennsylvania: West End Books, 1994)

**Story type:** Fantasy (Religious; Science Fiction)
**Series:** Torg: The Possibility Wars
**Major character(s):** Jacques Deveaux, Religious, Computer Expert (Cyberpapal); Cory Jones, Journalist, Warrior; Padrig O'Shay, Magician, Warrior
**Time period(s):** 21st century
**Locale(s):** Berlin, Germany; Europe; Tharkold Occupation Zone, Fictional Country (alien)

**Summary:** Jacques Deveaux travels to Berlin to finish work on the Fourth Seal, a devastating computer program which could spell the

---

end of the Cyberpapacy and promote widespread destruction. If the Storm Knights cannot stop him, worldwide disaster could insure the invading techno-demons' victory over humanity.

**Other books you might like:**
Jonatha Adriane Caspian, *The Nightmare Dream*, 1990
Greg Farshtey, *Strange Tales From the Nile Empire*, 1992
  Greg Gorden, Ed Stark, co-editors
Douglas Kaufman, *The Dark Realm*, 1990
Douglas Kaufman, *Dragons over England*, 1992
  Ed Stark, co-editor
Bill Slavicsek, *Storm Knights*, 1990
  C.J. Tramontana, co-author
Neal Stephenson, *Snow Crash*, 1992

---

**5439**

**ELIZABETH TERRY**, Editor
**TERRI HARDIN**, Co-Editor

## American Gothic

(New York: Barnes & Noble, 1997)

**Story type:** Horror (Anthology)

**Summary:** Twenty-five stories from the nineteenth and early twentieth century that represent different aspects of the Gothic literary tradition in Amrican fiction. Several haunted house stories are included, among them Charlotte Perkins Gilman's "The Giant Wistaria," which features the spectral presence of an unwed mother, and John Greenleaf Whittier's "The Haunted House," a tale of a mock haunting and its consequences. Tales of psychological horror include Gilman's classic "The Yellow Wallpaper," in which a woman sees the shape of her growing madness in a wallpaper pattern, and Stephen Crane's "An Illusion in Red and White," in which a man brainwashes his children into believing they never saw a murder he committed. Fitz-James O'Brien's "The Diamond Lens" is an early science fiction story of a man who discovers an entire universe in a drop of water, and Ambrose Bierce's "The Eyes of the Panther" is a shapeshifter tale.

**Other books you might like:**
Chris Baldick, *The Oxford Book of Gothic Tales*, 1992
  editor
Alfred Bendixen, *Haunted Dusk*, 1985
  editor
Peter Haining, *Great Tales of Terror From Europe and America*, 1972
  editor
David G. Hartwell, *Bodies of the Dead*, 1997
  editor
Catherine A. Lundie, *Restless Spirits*, 1997
  editor
Joyce Carol Oates, *American Gothic Tales*, 1996
  editor
Patricia L. Skarda, *The Evil Image: Two Centuries of Gothic Short Fiction and Poetry*, 1981
  Nora Crow Jaffe, co-editor

---

**5440**

**THOMAS TESSIER**

## Fog Heart

(New York: St. Martin's, 1998)

**Story type:** Horror (Ghost Story; Wild Talents)
**Major character(s):** Oona Muir, Psychic (medium); Oliver Spence, Businessman; Charley O'Donnell, Teacher

**Time period(s):** 1990s (1998)
**Locale(s):** Westport, Connecticut

**Summary:** Ghostly visitations by deceased family members to Oliver and Claire Spence and Charley and Jan O'Donnell lead them to Oona Muir, a young woman in rapport with the spirit world. Oona's channeling of psychic forces leads to revelations with tragic consequences for both couples. Originally published in England in 1997.

**Other books you might like:**
Jack Cady, *The Off Season*, 1995
Brad Leithauser, *Seaward*, 1993
Dennis McFarland, *A Face at the Window*, 1997
Michael Upchurch, *Passive Intruder*, 1995
Chet Williamson, *Ash Wednesday*, 1987

**5441**

**THOMAS TESSIER**
**JAMES KISNER**, Co-Author
**RICK HAUTALA**, Co-Author

## Night Visions 9

(Arlington Heights, Illinois: Dark Harvest, 1991)

**Story type:** Horror (Anthology)

**Summary:** The most recent volume in this long-running annual series, in which three authors each contribute a block of fiction that totals 30,000 words in length, includes Thomas Tessier's novella, "The Dreams of Dr. Ladybank," about a peculiar psychiatrist whose treatments drive his patients into psychosis; five stories by James Kisner, including "Jack's Demon," about the force which motivates Jack the Ripper; and seven stories and vignettes by Rick Hautala, all based on the Micmac Indian legends that gave rise to his 1988 novel, *Little Brothers*. F. Paul Wilson supplies an introduction.

**Other books you might like:**

**5442**

**THOMAS TESSIER**

## The Nightwalker

(New York: Berkley, 1989)

**Story type:** Horror (Werewolf Story)
**Major character(s):** Bobby Ives, Veteran (Vietnam), Werewolf; Miss Tanith, Psychic
**Time period(s):** 1970s
**Locale(s):** London, England

**Summary:** As Ives gradually turns into a werewolf, he becomes increasingly violent, killing girlfriends and others as he tries to find a way to reverse the process. Originally published in 1979.

**Other books you might like:**
David Case, *The Cell*, 1969
Whitley Strieber, *The Wolfen*, 1978
Les Whitten, *Moon of the Wolf*, 1967

**5443**

**PAUL THEROUX**

## Chicago Loop

(New York: Random House, 1991)

**Story type:** Horror (Psychological Suspense)
**Major character(s):** Parker Jagoda, Architect; Barbara Jagoda, Model (Parker's wife); Ewa Womack, Worker (Parker's mistress)

**Time period(s):** 1990s
**Locale(s):** Chicago, Illinois

**Summary:** Parker Jagoda, successful businessman and pathological liar, tries to balance his private and public personas by indulging in bizarre sexual fantasies with his wife and keeping trysts with women who answer his personal ads in newspapers. When one of his affairs leads to murder, he is plunged into a tailspin of depression, born out of guilt and obsession. This novel was originally published in England in 1990.

**Other books you might like:**
Robert Bloch, *The Will to Kill*, 1954
Brett Easton Ellis, *American Psycho*, 1991
David J. Schow, *The Kill Riff*, 1988

**5444**

**ELIZABETH MARSHALL THOMAS**

## The Animal Wife

(Boston: Houghton Mifflin, 1990)

**Story type:** Fantasy (Romance; Historical)
**Major character(s):** Kori, Hunter, Prehistoric Human; Swift, Hunter, Prehistoric Human
**Time period(s):** Indeterminate Past (Prehistoric—Paleolithic)
**Locale(s):** Siberia, Russia

**Summary:** Kori, just entering manhood, elects to return with his father to the Hair River Tribe, a blue-eyed people like himself. While on an expedition to find the strangers whose campsite had been spotted nearby, Kori captures a woman to be his wife who teaches him her foreign ways. This book takes place a few years after Thomas's first book, *Reindeer Moon*.

**Other books you might like:**
Michael Armstrong, *Agviq*, 1990
Jean M. Auel, *The Plains of Passage*, 1990
Jean M. Auel, *The Valley of Horses*, 1982
Jean M. Auel, *Clan of the Cave Bear*, 1980
W. Michael Gear, *People of the Wolf*, 1990
   Kathleen O'Neal Gear, co-author
Richard Herley, *The Stone Arrow*, 1978
William Sarabande, *Beyond the Sea of Ice*, 1987

**5445**

**JEFFREY THOMAS**

## Black Walls, Red Glass

(Marietta, Georgia: Marietta Publishing, 1997)

**Story type:** Horror (Collection)

**Summary:** A trio of stories. In "Black Walls," a bullet that carries brain tissue into the head of a man it strikes causes problems when it appears to have imported part of its owner's personality as well. "Red Glass" is a dreamy rumination on madness, and "The Red Machine" ia the story of a frustrated young woman who channels her disaffection into works of art that can kill.

**Other books you might like:**
Brian Hopkins, *Something Haunts Us All*, 1996
Gerard Daniel Houarner, *Painfreak*, 1996
Bentley Little, *Murmerous Haunts*, 1997
Jeffrey Osier, *Horizon Lines*, 1997
Tom Piccirilli, *The Dog Syndrome and Other Sick Puppies*, 1997
David Niall Wilson, *The Fall of the House of Escher and Other Illusions*, 1996

## 5446

**JEFFREY THOMAS**, Author/Illustrator

### The Bones of the Old Ones and Other Lovecraftian Tales

(Westborough, Massachusetts: Necropolitan Press, 1995)

**Story type:** Horror (Collection)

**Summary:** The five stories and two poems collected here pay tribute to the literary influence of H.P. Lovecraft. "Book Worm" and "Lost Soul" both concern forbidden books that draw the unwary— mentally and physically—into extradimensional worlds. "The Boarded Window" and "The House on the Plain" are about peculiarities of architecture that draw investigators into worlds of horror. The title novella concerns the incursions made by a cult dedicated to Lovecraftian monsters on an alien planet.

**Other books you might like:**

David Langford, *Irrational Numbers*, 1994
Stephen Mark Rainey, *Fugue Devil and Other Weird Horrors*, 1992
Michael Shea, *Fat Face*, 1987
Brian Stableford, *The Innsmouth Heritage*, 1993
William R. Stotler, *The Final Diary Entry of Kees Hujgens*, 1995
Steve Rasnic Tem, *Decoded Mirrors: Three Tales after Lovecraft*, 1993
Stanley Wiater, *Mysteries of the Word*, 1994
F. Paul Wilson, *The Barrens*, 1992

## 5447

**JEFFREY THOMAS**, Editor

### Terata: Anomalies of Literature

(Westborough, MA: Necropolitan Press, 1998)

**Story type:** Horror (Anthology)

**Summary:** Eighteen poems and seven short stories, all original to the volume and spanning a variety of horror themes. Todd H. C. Fisher's "The Trailer" is set in a circus sideshow and concerns a failed experiment in black magic that resulted in the creation of one of the freaks. Jason Kuhl's "Letter to the Editor" is a tale of urban decay and the monsters it spawns, written in the form of a letter to a newspaper editor. James Doig's "The Kindness of Strangers" is a tale of changelings and the little people.

**Other books you might like:**

George Hatch, *Guignoir and Other Furies*, 1991
   editor
Joy Oestreicher, *Air Fish*, 1993
   editor
Jessica Amanda Salmonson, *Tales by Moonlight*, 1984
   editor
Elizabeth A. Saunders, *When the Black Lotus Blooms*, 1990
   editor
Brian Smart, *The Best of the Midwest's Science Fiction, Fantasy and Horror, Volume II*, 1995
   editor

## 5448

**JEFFREY THOMAS**, Editor

### A Vampire Bestiary

(Westborough, MA: Necropolitan Press, 1998)

**Story type:** Horror (Anthology; Vampire Story)

**Summary:** Seven unusual vampire stories original to the volume. Selections include Wilum H. Pugmire's "The Boy Who Made Me Scream," a tale of vampiric lust and necrophilia; Joanne S. Karnakiewicz's "Night Light," about a shipwrecked survivor who washes up on an island whose only inhabitant is a vampire; and J. M. Rozanski's "Trial By Vampire," about the ordeal a vampire initiate goes through trying to find the appropriate form to shift shape to.

**Other books you might like:**

Esther Friesner, *Blood Muse: Timeless Tales of Vampires in the Arts*, 1995
   Martin H. Greenberg, co-editor
Robert R. McCammon, *Under the Fang*, 1991
Byron Preiss, *The Ultimate Dracula*, 1991
   editor
Jean Marie Stine, *I, Vampire: Interviews with the Undead*, 1995
   Forrest J Ackerman, co-editor
Robert Weinberg, *100 Vicious Little Vampire Stories*, 1995
   Stefan Dziemianowicz and Martin H. Greenberg, co-editors

## 5449

**QUENTIN THOMAS** (Pseudonym of W.T. Quick)

### Chains of Light

(New York: Roc, 1992)

**Story type:** Science Fiction (Fantasy; Political)
**Series:** Luciferian Chronicles
**Major character(s):** Lucifer "Luke" Angelus, Computer (human), Military Personnel; Charlie, Nurse, Military Personnel; Naomia, Prostitute, Military Personnel
**Time period(s):** Indeterminate
**Locale(s):** The Hegemony, Interstellar Empire/Federation

**Summary:** Charlie decides to play a joke on his pubertal "template," Luke, a human clone wired with others as part of the master computer. Realizing The Hegemony suffered attack by the Twister, Luke begins to divert resources into military development, but the necessary leadership does not exist. Somehow Luke must find a way out of the empire of his mind and into reality to save The Hegemony.

**Other books you might like:**

William Barton, *Dark Sky Legion*, 1992
Gregory Benford, *Great Sky River*, 1987
Cheryl J. Franklin, *Fire Get*, 1987
Robert A. Heinlein, *Stranger in a Strange Land*, 1991
   revised
Rebecca Ore, *Becoming Alien*, 1987
W.T. Quick, *Dreams of Flesh and Sand*, 1988
W.T. Quick, *Dreams of Gods and Men*, 1989
W.T. Quick, *Systems*, 1989
W.T. Quick, *Yesterday's Pawn*, 1989
Dan Simmons, *Hyperion*, 1989
George Zebrowski, *Stranger Suns*, 1991
Roger Zelazny, *Creatures of Light and Darkness*, 1969

## 5450

**SUE THOMAS**

### Correspondence

(Woodstock, New York: The Overlook Press, 1993)

**Story type:** Science Fiction (Alternate Intelligence; Literary)
**Major character(s):** Marie, Guide; Rosa, Cyborg, Friend; Shirley, Cyborg, Traveler
**Time period(s):** Indeterminate Future
**Locale(s):** England

**Summary:** With the help of Marie as tour guide, the reader functions as compositer in constructing Rosa and Shirley in this experimental, role playing novel. The reader defines and decides the characters' humanity using the guilt, loneliness, desire and wish fulfillment presented.

**Other books you might like:**
Eleanor Arnason, *A Woman of the Iron People*, 1991
Nick Bantock, *Griffin & Sabine*, 1991
Nick Bantock, *Sabine's Notebook*, 1992
Jean Mark Gawron, *Dream of Glass*, 1993
William Gibson, *The Difference Engine*, 1990
　　Bruce Sterling, co-author
Gwyneth Jones, *White Queen*, 1993
Marge Piercy, *He, She and It*, 1991
Joan Slonczewski, *A Door into Ocean*, 1986
Amy Thomson, *Virtual Girl*, 1993

## 5451

### THOMAS T. THOMAS

## *Crygender*

(New York: Baen, 1992)

**Story type:** Science Fiction (Mystery; Techno-Thriller)
**Major character(s):** "Cry" Crygender, Criminal; Jean Metis, Agent (criminal investigator); Austin Tinker, Agent (U.S. Department of Justice)
**Time period(s):** 2020s (2020)
**Locale(s):** San Francisco, California; Babylon, Pacific Islands (Alcatraz); New Orleans, Louisiana

**Summary:** On the trail of a runaway teenager, Metis and Tinker arrange to stay at Babylon, the Japanese-owned island brothel of Crygender. Cry is a genetically and surgically altered person, now half male, half female, whose past is totally unknown, including Cry's original gender. Metis and Tinker inadvertently discover and solve the mystery of Crygender and the dark secret of Babylon.

**Other books you might like:**
Greg Bear, *Queen of Angels*, 1990
C.S. Friedman, *The Madness Season*, 1990
Katharine Kerr, *Polar City Blues*, 1990
Rudy Rucker, *Wetware*, 1988
Allen Steele, *Clarke County, Space*, 1990
Michael Swanwick, *Vacuum Flowers*, 1987

## 5452

### THOMAS T. THOMAS

## *ME: A Novel of Self Discovery*

(New York: Baen, 1991)

**Story type:** Science Fiction (Alternate Intelligence; Robot Fiction)
**Major character(s):** Multiple Entity "ME", Artificial Intelligence, Spy; Jason Bathespeake, Computer Expert, Administrator (project manager)
**Time period(s):** 21st century
**Locale(s):** San Francisco, California; Canada; Russia

**Summary:** Developed as an espionage tool, ME is tested by its infiltrating a Canadian oil and gas reserve data base, then the Russian military nuclear weapons data base. After ME returns to San Francisco from the second mission, a judge rules that it is an illegal virus. Modified, ME is rendered immobile and told it must devise a new purpose for its existence or be terminated within a week.

**Other books you might like:**
David Gerrold, *When HARLIE Was One: Release 2.0*, 1988
Robert A. Heinlein, *The Moon Is a Harsh Mistress*, 1966
Victor Milan, *The Cybernetic Samurai*, 1986
Rudy Rucker, *Wetware*, 1988
Cordwainer Smith, *Norstrilia*, 1975
David Alexander Smith, *Homecoming*, 1990
David Alexander Smith, *Rendezvous*, 1988

## 5453

### JOYCE THOMPSON

## *Bones*

(New York: Morrow, 1991)

**Story type:** Horror (Psychological Suspense)
**Major character(s):** Frederika "Freddy" Bascomb, Artist; Charles "Chaz" Bascomb, Child (Freddy's son); Peter, Businessman (investor), Step-Parent (Freddy's stepfather)
**Time period(s):** 1990s
**Locale(s):** Seattle, Washington

**Summary:** Freddy Bascomb's life as an artist who earns her living reconstructing faces from "bones"—the remains of murder victims—takes a bizarre twist when she is summoned to identify the gruesomely mutilated remains of her father. She struggles to make sense of the clues her father's murderer has left—the theft of his brain, and periodically delivered chapters of a novel in manuscript that have eerie relevance to her experiences—even as the murderer begins to stalk her and her children.

**Other books you might like:**
Thomas Harris, *The Silence of the Lambs*, 1988
David Martin, *Lie to Me*, 1990
Garfield Reeves-Stevens, *Dark Matter*, 1990

## 5454

### PAUL B. THOMPSON
### TONYA R. CARTER, Co-Author

## *Firstborn*

(Lake Geneva, Wisconsin: TSR, 1991)

**Story type:** Fantasy (Political; Adventure)
**Series:** Dragonlance: The Elven Nations Trilogy
**Major character(s):** Sithas, Mythical Creature (elf), Royalty; Kith-Kanan, Mythical Creature (elf), Royalty
**Time period(s):** Indeterminate
**Locale(s):** Silvanesti, Fictional Country (Elven Nation)

**Summary:** Sithas allies himself with court factions in the elven capital while his brother, Kith-Kanan, leads the Wildrunners, elves who trade with humans of Ergoth. When events implicate Kith-Kanan in their father's death, Sithas, the firstborn twin, ascends to the throne. A game tie-in novel.

**Other books you might like:**
Nancy Varian Berberick, *Stormblade*, 1988
Mary Kirchoff, *Flint the King*, 1990
　　Douglas Niles, co-author
Richard A. Knaak, *The Legend of Huma*, 1988
Douglas Niles, *The Kinslayer Wars*, 1991
Barbara Siegel, *Tanis, the Shadow Years*, 1990
　　Scott Siegel, co-author
Margaret Weis, *Dragons of Autumn Twilight*, 1984
　　Tracy Hickman, co-author

Margaret Weis, *Time of the Twins*, 1986
    Tracy Hickman, co-author
Margaret Weis, *War of the Twins*, 1986
    Tracy Hickman, co-author

## 5455

**PAUL B. THOMPSON**
**TONYA R. CARTER**, Co-Author

### The Qualinesti

(Lake Geneva, Wisconsin: TSR, 1991)

**Story type:** Fantasy (Magic Conflict; Political)
**Series:** Dragonlance: The Elven Nations Trilogy
**Major character(s):** Kith-Kanan, Mythical Creature (elf), Warrior; Drulethen ''Dru'', Mythical Creature (elf), Sorcerer; Greenhands ''Silveran'', Mythical Creature (half-breed elf)
**Time period(s):** Indeterminate
**Locale(s):** Qualinesti, Fictional Country

**Summary:** As leader, Kith-Kanan promotes peace with the dwarves of Thorgardin and works toward equality for all within the kingdom. A simple onyx amulet and sorcerers in conflict work to make matters difficult for Kith-Kanan and his heir, Silveran. A game tie-in novel.

**Other books you might like:**
Nancy Varian Berberick, *Stormblade*, 1988
Mary Kirchoff, *Flint the King*, 1990
    Douglas Niles, co-author
Richard A. Knaak, *The Legend of Huma*, 1988
Douglas Niles, *The Kinslayer Wars*, 1991
Barbara Siegel, *Tanis, the Shadow Years*, 1990
    Scott Siegel, co-author
Margaret Weis, *Dragons of Autumn Twilight*, 1984
    Tracy Hickman, co-author
Margaret Weis, *Time of the Twins*, 1986
    Tracy Hickman, co-author
Margaret Weis, *War of the Twins*, 1986
    Tracy Hickman, co-author

## 5456

**PAUL B. THOMPSON**

### Thorn and Needle

(Lake Geneva, Wisconsin: TSR, 1992)

**Story type:** Fantasy (Religious; Quest)
**Major character(s):** Rado, Gambler, Traveler; Eride ''Thorn'', Religious (Sentinel of the Temple), Martial Arts Expert; Harlic Vost, Religious (College of Peace)
**Time period(s):** Indeterminate
**Locale(s):** Miyesti, Fictional City

**Summary:** Thorn and Rado use terrorism as a cover for their secret mission to kill the new god in Miyesti.

**Other books you might like:**
Douglas Bell, *Mojo and the Pickle Jar*, 1991
Maya Kaathryn Bohnhoff, *The Meri*, 1992
Adrian Cole, *Mother of Storms*, 1992
Neil Gaiman, *Good Omens: The Nice and Accurate Prophecies of Agnes Nutter, Witch*, 1990
    Terry Pratchett, co-author
Rosemary Kirstein, *The Outskirter's Secret*, 1992

## 5457

**WILLIAM R. THOMPSON**

### Debtors' Planet

(New York: Pocket, 1994)

**Story type:** Science Fiction (Space Opera)
**Series:** Star Trek: The Next Generation
**Major character(s):** Jean-Luc Picard, Spaceship Captain, Military Personnel (Starfleet); Wesley Crusher, Student (Starfleet Academy cadet); Ralph Offenhouse, Diplomat, Businessman
**Time period(s):** 24th century
**Locale(s):** Megara, Planet—Imaginary; *U.S.S. Enterprise*, Spaceship; United Federation of Planets, Interstellar Empire/Federation

**Summary:** When a space probe reports advanced power sources on the formerly primitive planet Megara, the Federation appoints as investigator Ralph Offenhouse, a 20th-century Terran cryogenically preserved until the 24th century. Although the Ferengi have supplied the technology, transforming the peaceful Megarans into xenophobic killers in the process, Offenhouse must discover who hired the Ferengi.

**Other books you might like:**
Robert Asprin, *The Cold Cash War*, 1977
C.J. Cherryh, *Forty Thousand in Gehenna*, 1983
Bill McCay, *Chains of Command*, 1992
H. Beam Piper, *Fuzzy Sapiens*, 1964
Jack Vance, *Emphyrio*, 1969

## 5458

**BRIAN THOMSEN**

### The Mage in the Iron Mask

(Lake Geneve, Wisconsin: TSR, 1996)

**Story type:** Fantasy (Sword and Sorcery)
**Series:** Forgotten Realms: The Nobles
**Major character(s):** Volothamp ''Volo'' Geddarms, Traveler, Scholar; Passepout, Actor; Jocchario Lawre, Wizard, Diplomat
**Time period(s):** Indeterminate
**Locale(s):** Mulmaster, Fictional City

**Summary:** Volo continues his trip of research for his *Guide to the Moonsen* by going to Mulmaster, the ''City of Danger.'' Unfortunately, retrieving Passepout from prison interrupts his fact-finding mission, soon trapping the two in the schemes of the nobility and wizards.

**Other books you might like:**
Steven Brust, *The Phoenix Guards*, 1991
Glen Cook, *The Swordbearer*, 1982
Ellen Kushner, *Swordspoint*, 1987
Fritz Leiber, *Ill Met in Lankhmar*, 1995
Caroline Stevermer, *A College of Magics*, 1994

## 5459

**BRIAN THOMSEN**, Editor
**MARTIN H. GREENBERG**, Co-Editor

### Mob Magic

(New York: DAW, 1998)

**Story type:** Fantasy (Anthology)
**Summary:** The 17 stories in this collection all appear here for the first time. Each deals with a combination of criminal activity and the

power of magic, with themes ranging from serious to humorous. The contributors include Mickey Zucker Reichert, Mike Resnick, Simon Hawke, P.N. Elrod, and Jody Lynn Nye.

**Other books you might like:**
Glen Cook, *Deadly Quicksilver Lies*, 1994
Brett Davis, *The Faery Convention*, 1995
Charles G. Waugh, *Supernatural Sleuths*, 1996
  Martin H. Greenberg, co-editor
Martin H. Greenberg, *Vampire Detectives*, 1995
Mike Resnick, *Stalking the Unicorn: A Fable of Tonight*, 1987

## 5460

### BRIAN THOMSEN
### MARTIN H. GREENBERG, Co-Author

## *The Reel Stuff*

(New York: DAW, 1998)

**Story type:** Horror (Anthology)

**Summary:** These eleven reprint tales of horror and science fiction by nine writers have been adapted as television or theatrical films in the past two decades. Selections include Philip K. Dick's masterpiece of futuristic paranoia, ''We Can Remember It for You Wholesale,'' filmed as *Total Recall*; Clive Barker's urban horror story ''The Forbidden,'' filmed as *Candyman*; H.P. Lovecraft's ''Herbert West: Reanimator,'' a Frankenstein pastiche filmed as *Reanimator*; and George R.R. Martin's science fiction horror story ''Sandkings,'' filmed as an episode of the revived ''Outer Limits'' series. Also included are stories by Donald A. Wollheim, Barry Longyear, William Gibson, Robert Silverberg and John Varley.

**Other books you might like:**
Peter Haining, *The Ghouls*, 1972
  editor
Peter Haining, *The Hollywood Nightmare*, 1970
  editor
David Wheeler, *No, but I Saw the Movie*, 1990
  editor
Sebastian Wolfe, *Reel Terror*, 1992
  editor

## 5461

### AMY THOMSON

## *The Color of Distance*

(New York: Ace, 1995)

**Story type:** Science Fiction (First Contact)

**Major character(s):** Juna ''Eerin'' Saari, Scientist (biologist), Explorer (alien contact specialist); Anito, Alien (Tendu); Moki, Alien (Tendu)
**Time period(s):** Indeterminate Future
**Locale(s):** Lyanan, Planet—Imaginary

**Summary:** When her ship crashes, Juna loses all her companions before the Tendu initiate fundamental changes in her physiology that allow Juna to survive on the deadly planet. With a human ship years away, Juna allies with the natives and investigates their societies as she and the natives form a close bond.

**Other books you might like:**
Eleanor Arnason, *A Woman of the Iron People*, 1991
Octavia E. Butler, *Dawn*, 1987
Octavia E. Butler, *Imago*, 1989
C.J. Cherryh, *Foreigner*, 1994
L. Warren Douglas, *A Plague of Change*, 1992

Nicola Griffith, *Ammonite*, 1993
Melissa Scott, *Shadow Man*, 1995

## 5462

### AMY THOMSON

## *Virtual Girl*

(New York: Ace, 1993)

**Story type:** Science Fiction (Alternate Intelligence; Robot Fiction)
**Major character(s):** Arnold Brompton, Computer Expert, Wanderer; Maggie, Artificial Intelligence; Brandon Smith, Computer Expert, Recluse
**Time period(s):** 2000s
**Locale(s):** Denver, Colorado; New Orleans, Louisiana; New York, New York

**Summary:** While hiding from his father, super hacker Arnold Brompton creates a girl whom he transfers from the Net to a constructed body in defiance of the AI laws. Called Maggie, she quickly learns to handle her body after a fortuitous command allows reconfiguration of her programming to avoid fatal overload. Separated from Arnold and found almost dead in the desert, Maggie befriends some farmers but leaves after a month fearing recognition, needing repair and reacquisition of her memory. In New Orleans, Maggie makes new friends who help her define her priorities and see herself as a person. Author's first novel.

**Other books you might like:**
Roger MacBride Allen, *The Modular Man*, 1992
Emily Devenport, *Shade*, 1991
Philip K. Dick, *Blade Runner*, 1982
Jean Mark Gawron, *Dream of Glass*, 1993
Tom Maddox, *Halo*, 1991
Lisa Mason, *Arachne*, 1990
Sue Thomas, *Correspondence*, 1993
Vernor Vinge, *A Fire upon the Deep*, 1992

## 5463

### TAMARA THORNE (Pseudonym of Chris Curry)

## *Haunted*

(New York: Zebra, 1995)

**Story type:** Horror (Haunted House)
**Major character(s):** David Masters, Writer (horror); Amber Masters, Teenager (David's daughter); Melanie Lord, Agent (literary)
**Time period(s):** 1990s (1995)
**Locale(s):** Red Cay, California

**Summary:** Writer David Masters takes up residence in the old Baudey House on a pensinsula outside Red Cay, in the hope that its reputed hauntings will supply him with the atmosphere he seeks to complete his new horror opus, *Mephisto Palace*. But the presence of David and his daughter Amber also helps bring out the legacy of evil sown at the house nearly a century before, by a woman who used it as a bordello and her daughter, who practiced voodoo rites that have imbued the house with a supernatural menace. This is the author's first novel under her Tamara Thorne pseudonym.

**Other books you might like:**
Jonathan Aycliffe, *Naomi's Room*, 1991
Poppy Z. Brite, *Drawing Blood*, 1993
Barbara Erskine, *Midnight Is a Lonely Place*, 1994
Gary L. Holleman, *Demon Fire*, 1995
Stephen King, *The Shining*, 1977

## 5464

**TAMARA THORNE** (Pseudonym of Chris Curry)

### Moonfall

(New York: Zebra, 1996)

**Story type:** Horror (Black Magic)
**Major character(s):** John Lawson, Police Officer (sheriff); Sara Hawthorne, Teacher; Mother Superior Lucy Barthlomew, Religious (nun)
**Time period(s):** 1990s (1996)
**Locale(s):** Moonfall, California

**Summary:** Sara Hawthorne ran away from St. Gertrude's Home for Girls in Moonfall, following the death of her best friend. Decades later, she returns to town as a teacher and discovers that her friend's death was one of many ritual murders conducted by the nuns who run the home to perpetuate a legacy of evil older than the town itself.

**Other books you might like:**
S.K. Epperson, *Nightmare*, 1993
Stephen King, *It*, 1986
S.J. Strayhorn, *Black Night*, 1996
Donna Tartt, *The Secret History*, 1993
J.N. Williamson, *The Black School*, 1989

## 5465

**DIANN THORNLEY**

### Dominion's Reach

(New York: Tor, 1997)

**Story type:** Science Fiction (Family Saga; Military)
**Series:** Saga of the Unified Worlds
**Major character(s):** Lujan Ansellic Serege, Military Personnel, Patient; Tristan "Tris" Serege, Teenager, Military Personnel (volunteer); Darcie Dartmuth, Military Personnel (captain), Spouse
**Time period(s):** Indeterminate Future
**Locale(s):** Topawa, Planet—Imaginary; Issel, Planet—Imaginary; *Shadow*, Spaceship

**Summary:** Wounded during the signing of the Isselan Assistance Pact, Lujan recovers from a shattered vertebra and neurological damage suffered while saving the Isselan ambassador. Darcie helps him learn to communicate while he recovers and receives necessary neurological implants. The Isselan plot to take over the United Worlds from within provides military assistance to destroy the slavers. Third in series.

**Other books you might like:**
Lois McMaster Bujold, *Memory*, 1996
L. Warren Douglas, *Stepwater*, 1995
Scott G. Gier, *In the Shadow of the Moon*, 1996
Jerry Pournelle, *Falkenberg's Legion*, 1990
Jack Vance, *Alastor*, 1995

## 5466

**DIANN THORNLEY**

### Echoes of Issel

(New York: Tor, 1996)

**Story type:** Science Fiction (Political; Family Saga)
**Series:** Unified Worlds
**Major character(s):** Lujan Ansellic Serege, Military Personnel (admiral), Parent; Tristan "Tris" Serege, Teenager, Refugee; Libby Moses, Doctor, Military Personnel

**Time period(s):** Indeterminate Future
**Locale(s):** Saede, Planet—Imaginary; Issel II, Planet—Imaginary; Unified Worlds/Dominion, Interstellar Empire/Federation

**Summary:** Reunited, the Serege family stumbles toward mutual respect and understanding in this sequel to *Ganwold's Child*. Lujan works to gain Tristan's trust while helping his former enemies fight Masuki slavers. Tristan's knowledge of Issel II from his former imprisonment there permits the Unified Worlds military to attempt a rescue of Dominion soldiers in fortified Dominion strongholds controlled by alien Masuki.

**Other books you might like:**
Eleanor Arnason, *Ring of Swords*, 1993
Lois McMaster Bujold, *Borders of Infinity*, 1989
F.M. Busby, *Rissa Kerguelen*, 1977
L. Warren Douglas, *A Plague of Change*, 1992
Alis A. Rasmussen, *The Price of Ransom*, 1990

## 5467

**DIANN THORNLEY**

### Ganwold's Child

(New York: Tor, 1995)

**Story type:** Science Fiction (First Contact; Political)
**Major character(s):** Mordan Renier, Military Personnel (general), Political Figure (governor); Tristan "Tris" Serege, Teenager, Castaway; Pulon, Alien, Sidekick
**Time period(s):** Indeterminate Future
**Locale(s):** Ganwold, Planet—Imaginary; *Bonne Fortune*, Spaceship; Unified Worlds/Dominion, Interstellar Empire/Federation

**Summary:** Having escaped from slavers, the toddler Tris and his mother become marooned on a Dominion planet. They live with the alien Gan and avoid humans. When his mother becomes uncurably ill, Tris decides to find his father knowing that he must leave Ganwold to do so. His Gan brother, Pulon, accompanies him to the stronghold of his family's enemy, Renier, who intends to use Tris to provoke war while Tris only wants to get help for his dying mother. First novel.

**Other books you might like:**
Eleanor Arnason, *Ring of Swords*, 1993
Gordon R. Dickson, *Naked to the Stars/The Alien Way*, 1991
L. Warren Douglas, *Cannon's Orb*, 1994
Paula E. Downing, *Fallway*, 1993
Jacqueline Lichtenberg, *Molt Brother*, 1982

## 5468

**L.L. THRASHER**

### Charlie's Bones

(Aurora, Colorado: Write Way, 1998)

**Story type:** Horror (Mystery; Ghost Story)
**Major character(s):** Lizbet Lange, Waiter/Waitress (former); Charlie Bilbo, Police Officer (undercover), Spirit; Jonathan Bilbo, Police Officer
**Time period(s):** 1990s (1998)
**Locale(s):** Oak Valley, California

**Summary:** Excavation on Lizbet Lange's property turns up the skeleton—and ghost—of Charlie Bilbo, a corrupt former undercover cop who "disappeared" suspiciously thirty years ago after a drug bust gone bad. With Charlie's help, Lizbet and Charlie's son Jonathan, a cop himself, investigate corruption in the Oak Valley police department, putting their lives in danger from the same heavies who disposed of Charlie.

**Other books you might like:**
Robert Bloch, *Lori*, 1989
Mary R. Callaghan, *I Met a Man Who Wasn't There*, 1997
Noel Hynd, *Cemetery of Angels*, 1995
Michael Jahn, *The Frighteners*, 1996
T.M. Wright, *Goodlow's Ghosts*, 1993

---

**5469**

### ROBERT THURSTON

## Way of the Clans

(New York: Roc, 1991)

**Story type:** Science Fiction (Military)
**Series:** Battletech: Legend of the Jade Phoenix
**Major character(s):** Aidan, Military Personnel; Ter Roshak, Military Personnel; Joanna, Military Personnel
**Time period(s):** 31st century
**Locale(s):** Ironhold, Planet—Imaginary; Tokasha, Planet—Imaginary

**Summary:** The Clans, descended from colonists who fled the worlds of the Inner Sphere, are organized in a caste system, the highest being "trueborn" Warriors, conceived and born in a laboratory and raised in a sibling group, who look with contempt on the "freeborn," the result of random matings among other Castes. Aidan and his group begin their training under Falconer Joanna. Those who survive will become full-fledged Warriors, fighting from inside their formidable armored Battle Mechs. A game tie-in novel.

**Other books you might like:**
Robert N. Charrette, *Wolf Pack*, 1992
C.J. Cherryh, *The Faded Sun: Kesrith*, 1978
Gordon R. Dickson, *Dorsai!*, 1976
Gordon R. Dickson, *Soldier, Ask Not*, 1967
Robert A. Heinlein, *Starship Troopers*, 1959
Aldous Huxley, *Brave New World*, 1932
Jerry Pournelle, *Falkenberg's Legion*, 1990
Kevin D. Randle, *The Galactic Silver Star*, 1990
John Sievert, *Suicide Attack*, 1990

---

**5470**

### RICHARD L. TIERNEY

## The House of the Toad

(Minneapolis, Minnesota: Fedogan & Bremer, 1993)

**Story type:** Horror (Ancient Evil Unleashed)
**Major character(s):** James Kerrick, Archaeologist; Janus Cornelius Wasserman, Publisher; Rosa Andrada, Secretary
**Time period(s):** 1990s
**Locale(s):** St. Regis, Iowa

**Summary:** Unscrupulous archaeologist James Kerrick sells a stolen Mexican artifact to publisher Janus Wasserman, and falls under the would-be occultist's spell. Too late, Kerrick discovers that his actions have furthered the summoning of Ghantanathoa, an ancient toad-like god bent on promoting chaos and suffering in the earthly plane.

**Other books you might like:**
Robert Bloch, *Strange Eons*, 1978
August Derleth, *The Trail of Cthulhu*, 1962
H.P. Lovecraft, *The Lurker at the Threshold*, 1945
　　August Derleth, co-author

Brian Lumley, *The Burrowers Beneath*, 1975
Colin Wilson, *The Mind Parasites*, 1967

---

**5471**

### RICHARD L. TIERNEY

## Scroll of Thoth

(Oakland, California: Chaosium, 1997)

**Story type:** Horror (Collection)

**Summary:** The complete adventures of Simon Magus, a magician and warrior who applies his knowledge of arcane wisdom to fighting unholy religious cults, corrupt kingdoms and Lovecraftian monsters. The twelve stories have the spirit of Robert E. Howard's tales of Conan the Barbarian and the philosophical underpinnings of Lovecrft tales of cosmic horror, and include "The Sword of Spartacus," "The Worm of Urakhu," "The Curse of the Crocodile," and "The Ring of Set." Edited and introduced by Robert M. Price.

**Other books you might like:**
Ramsey Campbell, *Far Away and Never*, 1996
David Drake, *Vettius and His Friends*, 1989
Fritz Leiber, *Ill Met in Lankhmar*, 1995
Brian Lumley, *Iced on Aran and Other Dream Quests*, 1992
Gary Myers, *The House of the Worm*, 1975
Michael Shea, *Nifft the Lean*, 1982
David C. Smith, *Engor's Sword Arm*, 1997
Karl Edward Wagner, *The Book of Kane*, 1985

---

**5472**

### JOHN TIGGES

## The Curse

(New York: Leisure, 1993)

**Story type:** Horror (Curse)
**Major character(s):** Sabra Narman, Artist; Bart Narman, Businessman; Father Wisdom, Religious (Catholic priest)
**Time period(s):** 1990s (1993)
**Locale(s):** Cascade, New York

**Summary:** Excavations on the land recently bought by the Narman family uncover the artifacts of a cult of pre-Columbian satanists, whose influence begins to make itself known through the bizarre dreams and behavior of the Narmans.

**Other books you might like:**
Douglas Clegg, *Goat Dance*, 1989
Rick Hautala, *Dark Silence*, 1992
Brian Hodge, *Oasis*, 1987
Roy Sorrels, *The Eyes of Torie Webster*, 1990

---

**5473**

### JOHN TIGGES

## Kevin Browne's Nightales

(New York: Upper West Side Publishing, 1990)

**Story type:** Horror (Collection)

**Summary:** Fourteen stories of the weird and supernatural, adapted from scripts written by Kevin Browne for "Tales from the Darkside," "Monsters," and "A Nightmare on Elm Street," and presented as tales a group of bus riders tell to pass the time. They include "All Bets Are Down," about a casino where the years of one's age are used to place bets, "Just the Right Card," about a store whose greeting cards make whatever a card says happen to the recipient, and "Over the Wall," about a near future in which the criminals outnumber the innocent.

**Other books you might like:**
Mitchell Galen, *Tales From the Darkside, Volume 1*, 1989
  Tom Allen, co-author
Jack Oleck, *Tales From the Crypt*, 1972
Rod Serling, *The Night Gallery Reader*, 1990
Rod Serling, *Stories From the Twilight Zone*, 1989
J. Michael Straczynski, *Tales From the New Twilight Zone*, 1989

---

## 5474

**JOHN TIGGES**

### Monster

(New York: Leisure, 1995)

**Story type:** Horror (Nature in Revolt)
**Major character(s):** Jonna Evans, Teacher; Malcolm Evans, Clerk; Peter Roth, Guide
**Time period(s):** 1990s (1995)
**Locale(s):** Hatchet Blade, British Columbia, Canada

**Summary:** On a camping trip in the Canadian woods that she takes to save her marriage, Jonna Evans is abducted by a lust-ridden Sasquatch and realizes that having a difficult husband is the least of her problems.

**Other books you might like:**
Merian C. Copper, *King Kong*, 1933
  Edgar Wallace, co-author
Barbara Hambly, *Beauty and the Beast*, 1989
Jack Ketchum, *Offspring*, 1991
Richard Laymon, *Midnight's Lair*, 1988
Dean R. Koontz, *Watchers*, 1987

---

## 5475

**LOIS TILTON**

### Darkness on the Ice

(New York: Pinnacle, 1993)

**Story type:** Horror (Vampire Story)
**Major character(s):** Hauptsturmfuhrer Wolff, Military Personnel (Nazi soldier), Vampire; Martin Dietrich, Military Personnel (Nazi Captain); Matt Ferrier, Military Personnel (American Sergeant)
**Time period(s):** 1940s (1944)
**Locale(s):** Greenland

**Summary:** A skilled guerilla and vampire to boot, Wolff is sent by Adolf Hitler to help destroy an American weather station in Greenland at the height of World War II. Though the dark and cold climate are ideal for Wolff's constitution, no one could have anticipated that the relative lack of sustenance in the arctic would force Wolff to victimize his fellow Nazis.

**Other books you might like:**
Elaine Bergstrom, *Shattered Glass*, 1989
Dan Simmons, *Carrion Comfort*, 1989
Robert Weinberg, *The Armageddon Box*, 1991

---

## 5476

**ROBERT TINE**

### Universal Soldier

(New York: Jove, 1992)

**Story type:** Science Fiction (Military; Techno-Thriller)
**Major character(s):** Luc Devreaux, Cyborg, Reanimated Dead (Universal Soldier); Andrew Scott, Cyborg, Reanimated Dead (Universal Soldier); Veronica "Ronnie" Roberts, Journalist
**Time period(s):** 1990s (1993)
**Locale(s):** Nevada

**Summary:** Cryogenically frozen for a quarter century, Luc and Andrew now find themselves transformed into cybernetic constructs useful as SWAT members in the deadliest situations. However, the humanity remaining within the machine proves a difficult force to control. Novelizes the film.

**Other books you might like:**
Martin Caidin, *Cyborg*, 1972
Philip K. Dick, *Do Androids Dream of Electric Sheep?*, 1968
Dave Duncan, *Hero*, 1991
Stephen Goldin, *Jade Darcy and the Affair of Honor*, 1988
  Mary Mason, co-author
Ed Naha, *Robocop*, 1987
Ed Naha, *Robocop 2*, 1990
Richard Sapir, *The Destroyer #1: Created, the Destroyer*, 1971
  Warren Murphy, co-author

---

## 5477

**JAMES TIPTREE JR.** (Pseudonym of Alice Sheldon)

### Her Smoke Rose Up Forever

(Sauk City, Wisconsin: Arkham House, 1990)

**Story type:** Science Fiction (Collection)
**Summary:** 17 stories written between 1969-1981 that are strongly feminist. Tiptree's stories are both inventive and grim, showing human strengths and failings in alien settings. "The Women Men Don't See" uses a plane crash to propose that women may have more in common with aliens than with men.

**Other books you might like:**
Suzy McKee Charnas, *Walk to the End of the World*, 1974
Ursula K. Le Guin, *The Left Hand of Darkness*, 1969
Pat Murphy, *The Falling Woman*, 1986
Joanna Russ, *The Female Man*, 1975
Fay Weldon, *Lives and Loves of a She-Devil*, 1983

---

## 5478

**STEPHANIE S. TOLAN**

### The Witch of Maple Park

(New York: William Morrow, 1992)

**Story type:** Fantasy (Contemporary; Young Adult)
**Major character(s):** Casey Corrigan, Teenager; Mackenzie Brewster, Psychic, Teenager; Mrs. Brewster, Businesswoman
**Time period(s):** 1990s
**Locale(s):** Maple Park, Ohio (Maple Park High School)
**Summary:** Casey and Mackenzie, best friends since childhood, discover that Mackenzie's feelings and meditations seem to be coming true, many of which show difficulties for herself and her mother, especially since her father left them and married another woman.

**Other books you might like:**
Peter Dickinson, *Healer*, 1987
E.W. Hildick, *The Active-Enzyme Lemon-Freshened Junior High
    School Witch*, 1973
Diana Wynne Jones, *The Ogre Downstairs*, 1990
Michael Kandel, *In between Dragons*, 1990
Christopher Pike, *Witch*, 1990

## 5479

### J.R.R. TOLKIEN

## *Roverandom*

(Boston: Houghton Mifflin, 1998)

**Story type:** Fantasy (Young Readers; Adventure)
**Major character(s):** Rover ''Roverandom'', Animal (dog), Adven-
    turer; Psamathos, Wizard; Mew, Animal (seagull), Adventurer
**Time period(s):** Indeterminate
**Locale(s):** Montenegro; Fictional Country; At Sea

**Summary:** Transformed from a dog to a toy dog, Rover seeks the
wizard who ensorcelled him. Accompanied by a talking seagull,
Rover visits with the Man-in-the-Moon and strange mer-animals as
he searches.

**Other books you might like:**
Lloyd Alexander, *The Iron Ring*, 1996
Graeme Base, *The Discovery of Dragons*, 1996
James Gurney, *Dinotopia*, 1992
James Gurney, *The World Beneath*, 1995

## 5480

### J.R.R. TOLKIEN

## *Sauron Defeated*

(New York: Houghton Mifflin, 1992)

**Story type:** Fantasy (Collection)

**Summary:** Ninth volume compiled from J.R.R. Tolkien's prolific
notes with commentary by Christopher Tolkien divided into three
parts, ''The End of the Third Age (The History of the Lord of the
Rings Part Four),''''The Notion Club Papers'' and ''The Drowning
of Anadune.'' Part one completes Christopher Tolkien's account of
the writing of *The Lord of the Rings* including a much-changed
scourging of the Shire and versions of the unpublished ''Epilog,'' a
variant ending in which Sam attempts to tell his children of Bilbo and
Frodo years after their departure. Part two reveals a literary group
similar to the Inklings, including J.R.R. Tolkien, C.S. Lewis and
Charles Williams, in the first publication of a story surrounding the
early 21st century discovery of papers from an Oxford literary club's
discussions during 1986-1987 in which the members consider the
possibility of using ''true dream'' to travel in time and space, the
legend of Atlantis, communication received from the past, and the
explosion of the Atlantean legend into northwest Europe. Part three
documents the evolution of Tolkien's fifteenth language, Adunaic,
which was learned by Arundel Lowdham of the Notion Club during
his dreams. Presents a third version of ''The Fall of Numenor'' and
three versions of ''The Drowning of Anadune.'' Concludes with a
42-page index.

**Other books you might like:**
Robert A. Heinlein, *Requiem*, 1992
    Yoji Kondo, editor
Larry Niven, *N-Space*, 1990
Larry Niven, *Playgrounds of the Mind*, 1991

## 5481

### JANE TOOMBS

## *Under the Shadow*

(New York: Roc, 1992)

**Story type:** Horror (Werewolf Story)
**Series:** Moonrunner
**Major character(s):** Ulysses Koshka, Werewolf; Don Alfonso,
    Rancher; William Tecumseh Sherman, Historical Figure, Mili-
    tary Personnel
**Time period(s):** 1840s
**Locale(s):** San Francisco, California

**Summary:** In this first novel of a continuing series, a young man
cursed with lycanthropy who travels under the alias Ulysses Koshka
washes up on the shores of California during the Gold Rush of 1849.
His adventures take him across America, through the landscape of
the American Civil War and the Louisiana bayou, as he struggles to
remember his past in an effort to find an antidote for his curse.

**Other books you might like:**
Michael Cadnum, *St. Peter's Wolf*, 1991
Guy Endore, *The Werewolf of Paris*, 1933
H. Warner Munn, *The Werewolf of Ponkert*, 1958
Cheri Scotch, *The Werewolf's Kiss*, 1992
S.P. Somtow, *Moon Dance*, 1990

## 5482

### PETER TREMAYNE (Pseudonym of Peter Berresford Ellis)

## *Snowbeast!*

(New York: Severn House, 1992)

**Story type:** Horror (Black Magic)
**Major character(s):** Ellen MacDonald, Secretary; Murdo MacDonald,
    Doctor (Ellen's uncle); Tony Glover, Mountaineer
**Time period(s):** 1980s (1983)
**Locale(s):** Cairngorms, Scotland

**Summary:** Originally published in 1983, this novel tells of a strange
fever that befalls a monk at the monastery of St. Berchan in the
mountains of Scotland at the same time that local animals begin
disappearing and giant footprints are found in the nearby snow—all
of which suggests that the legendary ''Big Gray Man of Ben Mac-
Dhui,'' or Snowbeast, has returned to the Scottish highlands.

**Other books you might like:**
Basil Copper, *The Great White Space*, 1974
H.P. Lovecraft, *At the Mountains of Madness*, 1964
    short story in *At the Mountains of Madness and Other Novels*

## 5483

### PETER TREMAYNE (Pseudonym of Peter Berresford Ellis)

## *Swamp*

(New York: St. Martin's, 1989)

**Story type:** Horror (Ancient Evil Unleashed)
**Major character(s):** Dean Michaels, Convict (Escaped); Peter Pirelli,
    Ranger (Swamp Ranger)
**Time period(s):** 1980s
**Locale(s):** Florida (Everglades)

**Summary:** Dean Michaels and Ruiz Alverez escape jail and head into
the Florida swamps, taking a female hostage with them. The search

for them is complicated by an angry prehistoric monster, which roams the swamps killing at will, and an imminent hurricane.

**Other books you might like:**
Charles L. Grant, *The Nestling*, 1982
Stephen Gresham, *Blood Wings*, 1990

## 5484

**ELLESTON TREVOR**

### *The Sister*

(New York: Tor, 1994)

**Story type:** Horror (Evil Children)
**Major character(s):** Madlen, Teenager; Debra, Teenager; Father Giovanni Falconi, Religious (priest)
**Time period(s):** 1990s (1994)
**Locale(s):** Westbury, Connecticut

**Summary:** Madlen persuades her adopted sister Debra to join her in taking religious vows to escape their difficult family. But even as a member of the Sisters of the Sacred Light, Madlen perpetrates acts, seemingly under the compulsion of an alter ego, that appear designed to push Debra into madness, and possibly to her death. This is a sequel to *Sibling*.

**Other books you might like:**
V.C. Andrews, *Secrets of the Morning*, 1991
Margaret Bingley, *Seeds of Evil*, 1988
D.A. Fowler, *Bad Blood*, 1993
Robert R. McCammon, *Mystery Walk*, 1984
Thomas Tryon, *The Other*, 1972

## 5485

**THOMAS TRYON**

### *Night Magic*

(New York: Simon & Schuster, 1995)

**Story type:** Horror (Occult)
**Major character(s):** Max Wurlitzer, Magician; Michael Hawke, Magician; Emily Chang, Musician
**Time period(s):** 1990s (1995)
**Locale(s):** New York, New York

**Summary:** Recognizing true talent in street performer Michael Hawke, aging magician Max Wurlitzer takes the boy under his wing to teach him the black arts. Michael finds himself in the difficult position of having to turn his back on everything he has known in the past in order to harness the powers Max wields and become like him. Left unrevised at the author's death in 1991, the novel was touched up by John Cullen and Valerie Martin.

**Other books you might like:**
John Fowles, *The Magus*, 1965
Richard Matheson, *Now You See It. . .*, 1995
Robert R. McCammon, *Mystery Walk*, 1983
Peter Straub, *Shadowland*, 1980

## 5486

**THOMAS TRYON**

### *The Night of the Moonbow*

(New York: Knopf, 1989)

**Story type:** Horror (Evil Children)

**Major character(s):** Leo Joaquim, Child (an unpopular boy); Reece Hartwig, Counselor (camp counselor)
**Time period(s):** 1930s (1938)
**Locale(s):** United States (Camp Friend-Indeed on Moonbow Lake)

**Summary:** Introverted, out-of-place Leo Joaquim is belittled and harassed by the other boys at Camp Friend-Indeed. This torment, led by Reece Hartwig, his proto-Nazi cabin counselor, is intensified after the accidental death of Leo's best friend until the external harassment combines with Leo's own dark secrets to erupt in violence.

**Other books you might like:**
William Golding, *Lord of the Flies*, 1954
Stephen King, *Carrie*, 1974
Stephen King, *Christine*, 1983

## 5487

**WILSON TUCKER**

### *The Lincoln Hunters*

(New York: Baen, 1992)

**Story type:** Science Fiction (Time Travel)
**Major character(s):** Ben Steward, Time Traveler, Anthropologist; Karl Dobbs, Time Traveler; Evelyn Kung, Widow(er)
**Time period(s):** 26th century (2578); 1850s (1856)
**Locale(s):** Cleveland, Ohio; Bloomington, Illinois

**Summary:** Intending to visit 1856 to recover a lost speech by Abraham Lincoln, Ben Steward discovers he somehow arrived a day too late and, worse, people there recognize him from an earlier meeting. Steward must travel back in time again, but must take great care not to meet himself since such a meeting would result in both selves instantly ceasing to exist. Reissue of the 1958 edition with a new, two-page introduction by David Drake.

**Other books you might like:**
Poul Anderson, *The Shield of Time*, 1990
Poul Anderson, *The Time Patrol*, 1991
Philip K. Dick, *Ubik*, 1969
Gordon R. Dickson, *Time Storm*, 1977
Fred Saberhagen, *After the Fact*, 1988
Harry Turtledove, *The Guns of the South: A Novel of the Civil War*, 1992
John Varley, *Millennium*, 1983

## 5488

**H.C. TURK**

### *Black Body*

(New York: Zebra/Pinnacle, 1991)

**Story type:** Horror (Black Magic)
**Major character(s):** Lady Amanda Rathel, Paranormal Investigator; Alba Denton, Witch; Eric Denton, Nobleman
**Time period(s):** 18th century
**Locale(s):** England

**Summary:** First published in 1989, this novel is presented as the journal of Alba, a white witch and the only member of her coven whose life is spared by the witch-hunter Lady Amanda Rathel. Lady Amanda's plans for Alba include marriage to Eric, son of her former lover, Edward Denton, with the idea that consummation of the marriage will mean instant death for the boy and a fulfilling revenge for herself.

**Other books you might like:**
Anne Rice, *The Witching Hour*, 1990
John Updike, *The Witches of Eastwick*, 1984

## 5489

**ALICE K. TURNER**, Editor

### *The Playboy Book of Science Fiction*
(New York: HarperPrism, 1998)

**Story type:** Science Fiction (Anthology)

**Summary:** Collecting works that originally appeared in *Playboy* since the magazine's inception in 1953, this volume contains a two-page introduction by the editor and brief introductions to each of the 25 stories. Authors include J.G. Ballard, Terry Bisson, Ray Bradbury, Arthur C. Clarke, Philip K. Dick, George Alec Effinger, Harlan Ellison, Joe Haldeman, Stephen King, Damon Knight, Ursula K. Le Guin, Doris Lessing, Larry Niven, Frederik Pohl, Robert Sheckley, Lucius Shepard, Robert Silverberg, Norman Spinrad, William Tenn, Walter Tevis, Kurt Vonnegut, Jr., Howard Waldrop, Donald E. Westlake, and Chet Williamson. Comedian Billy Crystal also makes a surprise appearance.

**Other books you might like:**
Playboy Editors, *The Playboy Book of Science Fiction and Fantasy*, 1968
Jack Dann, *Nebula Awards 32*, 1998
    editor
Gardner Dozois, *The Year's Best Science Fiction Series*, 1984-1998
    editor
David G. Hartwell, *The World Treasury of Science Fiction*, 1989
    editor
Kim Mohan, *Amazing Stories: The Anthology*, 1995
    editor
David Pringle, *The Best of Interzone*, 1997
    editor
Pamela Sargent, *Nebula Awards 29-31*, 1995-1997
    editor

## 5490

**DELIA MARSHALL TURNER**

### *Nameless Magery*
(New York: Ballantine Del Rey, 1998)

**Story type:** Fantasy (Psychic Powers; Magic Conflict)
**Major character(s):** Lisane, Refugee, Psychic; Kaihan, Wizard, Royalty; Deteras "Detter" Anhand, Student, Wizard
**Time period(s):** Indeterminate
**Locale(s):** Sassevin, Fictional City; Asterman's Wood, Mythical Place; Planet—Imaginary

**Summary:** Fleeing the Enforcers who destroy her planet, Lisane lands on an unnamed planet where she packs off to Mages' School. She dislikes the Mages and takes up with a merchant, then reluctantly agrees to help defeat a rogue Mage. When the Enforcers land, Lisane must unite all those who can work magic. First novel.

**Other books you might like:**
Robert S. Blum, *The Girl From the Emerald Island*, 1984
Philip Jose Farmer, *Flesh*, 1960
Robert Graves, *Watch the Northwind Rise*, 1949
Diana Wynne Jones, *Witch Week*, 1982
Peg Kerr, *Emerald House Rising*, 1997
Caroline Stevermer, *A College of Magics*, 1994
Patricia C. Wrede, *Mairelon the Magician*, 1991

## 5491

**GEORGE TURNER**

### *Brain Child*
(New York: William Morrow, 1991)

**Story type:** Science Fiction (Genetic Manipulation)
**Major character(s):** David Chance, Orphan; Arthur Hazard, Genetically Altered Being; Jonesy, Spy
**Time period(s):** 2040s (2047)
**Locale(s):** Melbourne, Australia; Westerton, Australia

**Summary:** In 2002, Australia began an experimental project to produce test-tube babies with super intellects. Four groups of four babies were produced. One set of four died shortly after birth. The most intelligent group committed suicide in 2022, but they left a legacy with instructions to the true genetic model which would allow humans to become, perhaps, immortal. Unfortunately, the legacy has been lost and David Chance is set to find it.

**Other books you might like:**
Lois McMaster Bujold, *Falling Free*, 1988
Pat Cadigan, *Mindplayers*, 1987
Pat Cadigan, *Synners*, 1991
Aldous Huxley, *Brave New World*, 1932
Geoff Ryman, *The Child Garden*, 1990
Robert Silverberg, *Tower of Glass*, 1970
Michael D. Weaver, *My Father Immortal*, 1989

## 5492

**GEORGE TURNER**

### *Genetic Soldier*
(New York: Morrow/AvoNova, 1994)

**Story type:** Science Fiction (Genetic Manipulation; Post-Holocaust)
**Major character(s):** Thomas "Soldier" Atkins, Military Personnel (general); Nugan Taylor, Linguist, Spacewoman; Library, Librarian, Psychic (esper)
**Time period(s):** 30th century (2900s)
**Locale(s):** Yarra Valley, Australia; *Search*, Spaceship

**Summary:** The homsesick crew of *Search* returns to Earth without finding a planet to colonize. Nugan lands alone, as the only linguist on the ship, prepared to cope with the similarities and differences in language, but finds great difficulty in understanding the motivation of the genetically manipulated survivors. Nugan learns that the crew will not be allowed to stay, with Soldier planning for them to leave without bloodshed. Unfortunately, Soldier meets Nugan's daughter, changing his relationship with everyone.

**Other books you might like:**
Eleanor Arnason, *Ring of Swords*, 1993
Octavia E. Butler, *Dawn*, 1987
Helen Collins, *Mutagenesis*, 1993
Samuel R. Delany, *They Fly at Ciron*, 1993
Megan Lindholm, *Alien Earth*, 1992
Michael D. Weaver, *My Father Immortal*, 1989
Catherine Wells, *The Earth Is All That Lasts*, 1991
Catherine Wells, *Children of the Earth*, 1992

## 5493

**JIM TURNER**, Editor

### Cthulhu 2000

(Sauk City, Wisconsin: Arkham House, 1995)

**Story type:** Horror (Anthology)

**Summary:** The 18 stories collected here are a wonderfully diverse testimony to the enduring power of H.P. Lovecraft's fiction and its influence. More traditional attempts to manifest Lovecraftian horrors include F. Paul Wilson's "The Barrens," about an extradimensional monster in the wilds of New Jersey; Ted Klein's "Black Man with a Horn," in which a writer is pursued by beings for what he knows about them; and Thomas Ligotti's "The Last Feast of Harlequin," which reveals the horrifying truth of human origins. Both Ramsey Campbell in "The Faces at Pine Dunes" and Basil Copper in "Shaft 247" attempt to capture the ineffability of Lovecraft's horrors. Lovecraftian monsters are updated for the computer age in Lawrence Watt-Evans' "Pickman's Modem," and postdated to the mid-century in Kim Newman's hard-boiled detective tale, "The Big Fish." Humorous riffs on Lovecraft's themes include Esther Friesner's "Love's Eldritch Ichor" and Fred Chappell's "The Adder."

**Other books you might like:**
Ramsey Campbell, *New Tales of the Cthulhu Mythos*, 1980
Stephen Jones, *Shadows over Innsmouth*, 1990
  editor
Robert Weinberg, *Lovecraft's Legacy*, 1990
  Martin H. Greenberg, co-editor

## 5494

**JIM TURNER**, Editor

### The Eternal Lovecraft: The Persistence of HPL in Popular Culture

(Collinsville, Illinois: Golden Gryphon, 1998)

**Story type:** Horror (Anthology)

**Summary:** Eighteen reprint tales of horror, fantasy and science fiction, redolent with the influence of H. P. Lovecraft and his Cthulhu Mythos. Some, like Fred Chappell's "Weird Tales," which posits a cosmic conspiracy behind the premature deaths of Lovecraft and poet Hart Crane, and Stephen King's "Crouch End," about Lovecraftian monsters in the English underground, are relatively traditional tributes to Lovecraft. Others, such as Thomas Ligotti's evocative prose poem "The Shadow at the Bottom of the World," Don Webb's "To Mars and Providence," which imagines H.G. Wells' *The War of the Worlds* as written by Lovecraft, and Fritz Leiber's "A Bit of the Dark World," about extradimensional forces that wreak havoc in our own dimension, are Lovecraftian in spirit more so than content.

**Other books you might like:**
Ramsey Campbell, *New Tales of the Cthulhu Mythos*, 1980
  editor
Stephen Jones, *Shadows over Innsmouth*, 1990
  editor
Robert M. Price, *Tales of the Lovecraft Mythos*, 1992
  editor
Robert M. Price, *The Lovecraft Circle*, 1996
  editor
Robert Weinberg, *Lovecraft's Legacy*, 1990
  Martin H. Greenberg, co-editor

## 5495

**HARRY TURTLEDOVE**, Editor

### Alternate Generals

(New York: Baen, 1998)

**Story type:** Science Fiction (Anthology)

**Summary:** These 16 original stories of alternate history pose unlikely situations in which, for example, Rommel takes the place of Darius and other major historical characters are displaced in time. Contributors include Brad Linaweaver, William Sanders, Lois Tilton, and William R. Forstchen.

**Other books you might like:**
Roland J. Green, *The Great King's War*, 1985
  John F. Carr, co-author
Harry Harrison, *Stars and Stripes Forever*, 1998
Michael Kurland, *The Whenabouts of Burr*, 1975
Mike Resnick, *Alternate Presidents*, 1992
Harry Turtledove, *How Few Remain*, 1998

## 5496

**HARRY TURTLEDOVE**

### Between the Rivers

(New York: Tor, 1998)

**Story type:** Fantasy (Historical; Religious)
**Major character(s):** Sharur, Businessman, Trader; Habbazu, Thief; Engibil, Deity
**Time period(s):** Indeterminate Past
**Locale(s):** Gibil, Fictional City

**Summary:** Master Trader Sharur cannot trade anywhere outside his city because the rest of the gods think his city's god allows people too much freedom. A war and the theft of a powerful amulet show Sharur and others in the city the gods' vulnerability, in this novel set in a fantasy land similar to ancient Mesopotamia.

**Other books you might like:**
Poul Anderson, *The Boat of a Million Years*, 1989
Piers Anthony, *Isle of Woman*, 1993
Edmund Cooper, *A Far Sunset*, 1967
L. Sprague de Camp, *The Dragon of the Ishtar Gate*, 1961
Diana Wynne Jones, *The Spellcoats*, 1979
A. Merritt, *The Ship of Ishtar*, 1926
Mike Moscoe, *First Dawn*, 1996
Richard Purtill, *The Stolen Goddess*, 1980
Robert Silverberg, *Gilgamesh the King*, 1984

## 5497

**HARRY TURTLEDOVE**

### The Case of the Toxic Spell Dump

(New York: Baen, 1993)

**Story type:** Fantasy (Light Fantasy; Mystery)
**Major character(s):** David Fisher, Government Official (environmental investigator)
**Time period(s):** Indeterminate
**Locale(s):** Alternate Earth (Angels City, California)

**Summary:** Ordered to quietly investigate events at a Toxic Spell Dump, David Fisher discovers an ancient deity attempting to set up operations which would destroy Western Civilization.

**Other books you might like:**
Elizabeth Forrest, *Phoenix Fire*, 1992
Alan Dean Foster, *Cyber Way*, 1990
Alan Dean Foster, *To the Vanishing Point*, 1988
Barbara Hambly, *Dog Wizard*, 1993
Dean R. Koontz, *The Haunted Earth*, 1973
Larry Niven, *The Flight of the Horse*, 1973
Nick Pollotta, *Bureau 13*, 1991
Nick Pollotta, *Full Moonster*, 1992

**5498**

HARRY TURTLEDOVE

## *Departures*

(New York: Ballantine Del Rey, 1993)

**Story type:** Science Fiction (Alternate Universe; Collection)

**Summary:** Contains an author's note plus individual introductions to 20 stories reprinted from 1980s and 1990s anthologies and periodicals. Stories appear in chronological order from the 2nd century B.C. to *ca.* 3000 A.D. with three set on an Earth on which Muhammed led a monk's life rather than a prophet's, two baseball stories, one of them epistolary, and other stories with themes ranging from an alternate American Civil War outcome to contemporary culture and environmental issues.

**Other books you might like:**
Gregory Benford, *Alternate Americas*, 1992
    Martin H. Greenberg, co-editor
Gregory Benford, *Alternate Empires*, 1989
    Martin H. Greenberg, co-editor
Gregory Benford, *Alternate Heroes*, 1990
    Martin H. Greenberg, co-editor
Gregory Benford, *Alternate Wars*, 1991
    Martin H. Greenberg, co-editor
Mike Resnick, *Alternate Kennedys*, 1992
    editor
Mike Resnick, *Alternate Presidents*, 1992
    editor
Mike Resnick, *Alternate Warriors*, 1993
    editor

**5499**

HARRY TURTLEDOVE

## *Earthgrip*

(New York: Ballantine/Del Rey, 1991)

**Story type:** Science Fiction (Collection; Adventure)
**Major character(s):** Jennifer Logan, Trader, Teacher; Bernard Greenberg, Trader, Spaceship Captain; Pawasar Pawasar Ras, Leader, Alien (Foitani)
**Time period(s):** 31st century
**Locale(s):** L'Rau, Planet—Imaginary; Athet, Planet—Imaginary; Gilver, Planet—Imaginary

**Summary:** Subtitled *Tales from the Traders' World*, this book contains three stories originally published in *Analog* magazine which relate trading voyages as seen through the eyes of a teacher specializing in Middle English (20th century) Science Fiction who happens into a successful trading career. Jennifer discovers her interest in 20th-century literature helps her resolve impediments to doing business among the intelligent races residing on the planets she visits.

**Other books you might like:**
Poul Anderson, *Trader to the Stars*, 1964

James Blish, *Earthman, Come Home*, 1955
James Blish, *A Life for the Stars*, 1962
Octavia E. Butler, *Dawn*, 1987
Janet Kagan, *Mirabile*, 1991
Larry Niven, *Fallen Angels*, 1991
    Jerry Pournelle and Michael Flynn, co-authors
Andre Norton, *The Time Traders*, 1958

**5500**

HARRY TURTLEDOVE

## *Fox and Empire*

(New York: Baen, 1998)

**Story type:** Fantasy (Military; Political)
**Series:** Gerin the Fox
**Major character(s):** Gerin the Fox, Military Personnel, Royalty (king); Ferdulf, Child, Mythical Creature (demigod); Dagref, Teenager, Scholar
**Time period(s):** Indeterminate
**Locale(s):** Northlands, Mythical Place

**Summary:** About to go to war against Aragis the Archer, Garin the Fox decides a more prudent course would unite the two against the Empire, which seeks to regain control over the Northlands. To achieve this goal, they have the aid of an obscure prophecy as well as the dubious help of the four-year-old demigod Ferdulf.

**Other books you might like:**
Robert Adams, *The Seven Magical Jewels of Ireland*, 1985
Jack L. Chalker, *The River of Dancing Gods*, 1984
Harry Harrison, *King and Emperor*, 1996
    John Holm, co-author
Katherine Kurtz, *King Javan's Year*, 1992
John Maddox Roberts, *The Steel Kings*, 1993
Christopher Stasheff, *The Witch Doctor*, 1994
Judith Tarr, *The Eagle's Daughter*, 1995
Paul O. Williams, *The Breaking of Northwall*, 1981

**5501**

HARRY TURTLEDOVE

## *The Great War: American Front*

(New York: Ballantine Del Rey, 1998)

**Story type:** Science Fiction (Alternate Universe; Military)
**Series:** Great War
**Major character(s):** George Enos, Sea Captain, Sailor; Anne Colleton, Plantation Owner; Cincinnatus, Worker, Spy
**Time period(s):** 1910s (1914-1915)
**Locale(s):** North America; Alternate Earth

**Summary:** In a world where the South won the Civil War, World War I sets the U.S.A. against the Confederacy and Canada, with scrambled roles allowing Negroes and women into positions they would not normally have held. As Marxism spreads among Southern Negroes who await a signal to start a revolution, the U.S.A. considers Mormonism the greatest threat of all.

**Other books you might like:**
Patricia Anthony, *Flanders*, 1998
Donald Benson, *And Having Writ*, 1979
Robert Conroy, *1901*, 1995
William Gibson, *The Difference Engine*, 1991
    Bruce Sterling, co-author
Mike Resnick, *Bully!*, 1991
William Sanders, *The Wild Blue and the Gray*, 1991

Chelsea Quinn Yarbro, *Writ in Blood*, 1997
Jerry Yulsman, *Elleander Morning*, 1984

---

**5502**

**HARRY TURTLEDOVE**

## The Guns of the South: A Novel of the Civil War

(New York: Ballantine, 1992)

**Story type:** Science Fiction (Alternate Universe; Time Travel)
**Major character(s):** Andries Rhoodie, Time Traveler, Military Personnel; Robert E. Lee, Historical Figure, Military Personnel
**Time period(s):** 1860s
**Locale(s):** Confederate States of America, Fictional Country

**Summary:** Hoping to change history and provide a benevolent environment for South African slavery, Andries Rhoodie leads a group of volunteers to Civil War Era America where they join the Confederate Army and provide them with modern assault rifles. After winning the conflict and separating from the North, the Confederacy elects Robert E. Lee as president. Events do not unfold as Rhoodie had hoped when Lee, a champion of the proposed emancipation of slaves and no friend of the 21st century South Africans, becomes involved in political intrigue.

**Other books you might like:**
Gregory Benford, *Alternate Wars*, 1991
    Martin H. Greenberg, co-editor
Terry Bisson, *Fire on the Mountain*, 1988
Frank D. McSherry Jr., *The Fantastic Civil War*, 1991
    editor
Ward Moore, *Bring the Jubilee*, 1953
David C. Poyer, *The Shiloh Project*, 1981
Kevin D. Randle, *Remember Gettysburg*, 1988
    Robert Cornett, co-author
William Sanders, *The Wild Blue and the Gray*, 1991
S.M. Stirling, *Marching through Georgia*, 1988

---

**5503**

**HARRY TURTLEDOVE**

## Hammer and Anvil

(New York: Ballantine Del Rey, 1996)

**Story type:** Fantasy (Military; Historical)
**Major character(s):** Maniakes, Military Personnel (general), Rebel; Etzilios, Barbarian, Leader (Khagan); Lysia, Noblewoman
**Time period(s):** Indeterminate Past
**Locale(s):** Videssos, Fictional Country

**Summary:** Because of extreme mismanagement and barbarous cruelty, Maniakes challenges Genesios for the throne of Videssos. Once autokrator, he must cope with no resources, generals of dubious loyalty, and major attacks from both Kubrat and Makuran, both of which manage to penetrate to the suburbs of the city, Videssos.

**Other books you might like:**
Poul Anderson, *The Game of Empire*, 1985
John M. Ford, *The Dragon Waiting*, 1983
Katherine Kurtz, *King Javan's Year*, 1992
Kirk Mitchell, *Procurator*, 1984
Susan Schwartz, *Byzantium's Crown*, 1987
Robert Silverberg, *Up the Line*, 1968
Judith Tarr, *Ars Magica*, 1989
Elizabeth Willey, *A Sorcerer and a Gentleman*, 1995
Chelsea Quinn Yarbro, *A Flame in Byzantium*, 1987

---

**5504**

**HARRY TURTLEDOVE**

## How Few Remain

(New York: Ballantine Del Rey, 1997)

**Story type:** Science Fiction (Military; Political)
**Major character(s):** Sam Clemens, Journalist, Historical Figure; Frederick Douglass, Journalist, Historical Figure (orator); George A. Custer, Military Personnel, Historical Figure
**Time period(s):** 1880s (1881-1882)
**Locale(s):** United States; North America (Confederate States of America); Alternate Earth

**Summary:** When the Confederacy moves to buy Sonora Chihuahua from the cash-strapped Mexican Empire, President James Blaine declares war. As the United Kingdom and France aid the Confederacy, the U.S.A. finds its shores blockaded and its cities bombarded. Realizing he cannot win, Blaine must develop other alliances.

**Other books you might like:**
Orson Scott Card, *Alvin Journeyman*, 1995
Richard Dreyfuss, *The Two Georges*, 1996
    Harry Turtledove, co-author
Alan Dean Foster, *Mad Amos*, 1996
Stephen King, *The Dark Tower: The Gunslinger*, 1982
Kirk Mitchell, *Never the Twain*, 1987
Kevin Randle, *Remember the Little Bighorn*, 1990
    Robert Cornett, co-author
Mike Resnick, *Bwana & Bully!*, 1991
Mark Sumner, *Devil's Tower*, 1996

---

**5505**

**HARRY TURTLEDOVE**

## Kaleidoscope

(New York: Ballantine/Del Rey, 1990)

**Story type:** Science Fiction (Collection)

**Summary:** The thirteen stories in this collection were originally published in such magazines as *Amazing Stories, Analog, The Magazine of Fantasy and Science Fiction, Twilight Zone,* and the anthology *Ripper!* between 1984 and 1988. Among the best of them are ''And So to Bed,'' ''Bluff,'' ''Gentlemen of the Shade,'' and ''The Last Article.''

**Other books you might like:**
Gregory Benford, *Alternate Empires*, 1989
    Martin H. Greenberg, editor
Gregory Benford, *Alternate Heroes*, 1989
    Martin H. Greenberg, editor
L. Sprague de Camp, *Lest Darkness Fall*, 1941
David Drake, *Vettius and His Friends*, 1989

---

**5506**

**HARRY TURTLEDOVE**

## Krispos of Videssos

(New York: Ballantine/Del Rey, 1991)

**Story type:** Fantasy (Political; Magic Conflict)
**Series:** Krispos of Videssos
**Major character(s):** Krispos, Ruler (Avtokrator of Videssos); Dara, Royalty (Empress of Videssos); Harvas Black-Robe, Wizard, Barbarian
**Time period(s):** Indeterminate Past

**Locale(s):** Videssos, Fictional Country

**Summary:** Krispos, having become Avtokrator of Videssos, marries the former Empress Dara who may or may not be carrying his child. After quelling a rebellion by Petronas, the former Avtokrator's uncle, he must face Harvas Black-Robe who is attacking the northern borders. While he is away, his father-in-law and the former Patriarch conspire against him.

**Other books you might like:**
Randall Garrett, *Too Many Magicians*, 1967
Katherine Kurtz, *Camber of Culdi*, 1976
Fletcher Pratt, *The Blue Star*, 1952
Melissa Scott, *A Choice of Destinies*, 1986
Susan Shwartz, *Silk Roads and Shadows*, 1988
Judith Tarr, *The Dagger and the Cross: A Novel of the Crusades*, 1991

---

**5507**

**HARRY TURTLEDOVE**

## Krispos Rising

(New York: Ballantine/Del Rey, 1991)

**Story type:** Fantasy (Adventure; Political)
**Series:** Krispos of Videssos
**Major character(s):** Krispos, Adventurer; Anthimos, Ruler (Avtokrator of Videssos); Pyrrhos, Religious (abbot)
**Time period(s):** Indeterminate Past
**Locale(s):** Videssos, Fictional Country

**Summary:** Five hundred years before events in *The Misplaced Legion*, Krispos, driven out of his farm village by taxation and cholera, comes to Videssos and finds the Abbot Pyrrhos willing to help him. Rising first to groom in the service of the Avtokrator who thinks only of his pleasure, Krispos then becomes vestiarios. He incurs the anger of Petronas, the real ruler of Videssos, then finally of Anthimos who tries to kill him, but ends by killing himself with a spell gone bad. Krispos then becomes Avtokrator.

**Other books you might like:**
Randall Garrett, *Too Many Magicians*, 1967
Elizabeth Moon, *Surrender None: The Legacy of Gird*, 1990
Fletcher Pratt, *The Blue Star*, 1952
Melissa Scott, *A Choice of Destinies*, 1986

---

**5508**

**HARRY TURTLEDOVE**

## Krispos the Emperor

(New York: Ballantine Del Rey, 1994)

**Story type:** Fantasy (Political; Magic Conflict)
**Series:** Krispos of Videssos
**Major character(s):** Krispos, Ruler (Avtokrator of Videssos); Phostis, Heir, Captive; Olyvria, Heiress, Adventurer
**Time period(s):** Indeterminate Past
**Locale(s):** Videssos, Fictional Country

**Summary:** When a new heresy in Videssos attracts Krispos' heir, Phostis, he nevertheless joins his father and brothers at the head of the army to suppress it. Kidnapped, Phostis learns that Makuran masterminds the outbreak while a sorcerer uses the power of the newly dead to fight Krispos and Videssos. Phostis must escape and rejoin Krispos for them to defeat the rebels and the wizard.

**Other books you might like:**
John Christopher, *The Prince in Waiting*, 1970
Richard Cowper, *The Road to Corlay*, 1979

Katherine Kurtz, *The Harrowing of Gwynedd*, 1989
Susan Schwartz, *Byzantium's Crown*, 1987
Roger Zelazny, *Sign of the Unicorn*, 1975

---

**5509**

**HARRY TURTLEDOVE**

## Prince of the North

(New York: Baen, 1994)

**Story type:** Fantasy (Political; Adventure)
**Major character(s):** Gerin the Fox, Ruler, Military Personnel; Van, Barbarian; Selatre, Religious
**Time period(s):** Indeterminate Past
**Locale(s):** Castle Fox, Mythical Place; Ikos, Fictional City; Empire of Elabon, Fictional Country

**Summary:** Chaos and ignorance threaten Gerin's attempt to rule in the Northlands with some measure of enlightenment. An amateur wizard and reluctant prince, he must fight gods, monsters and barbarians for order and the life of his son. Old friends, such as Van, and new allies, such as Selatre the Sibyl, join in his fight toward an uncertain outcome.

**Other books you might like:**
Glen Cook, *The Black Company*, 1984
Barbara Hambly, *Dragonsbane*, 1986
P.C. Hodgell, *God Stalk*, 1982
Elizabeth Moon, *Sheepfarmer's Daughter*, 1988
Patricia C. Wrede, *Caught in Crystal*, 1987

---

**5510**

**HARRY TURTLEDOVE**

## The Stolen Throne

(New York: Ballantine Del Rey, 1995)

**Story type:** Fantasy (Political; Adventure)
**Series:** Stolen Throne
**Major character(s):** Abivard, Nobleman, Military Personnel, Warrior; Sharbaraz, Heir—Dispossessed, Prisoner; Roshnani, Spouse, Counselor
**Time period(s):** Indeterminate Past
**Locale(s):** Makuran, Fictional Country

**Summary:** After the defeat and killing of Makuran's emperor, Smerdis usurps the throne, imprisoning the rightful heir, Sharbaraz. When Abivard and his sister free Sharbaraz, he raises an army to challenge Smerdis, whose forces do not yield easily. First part of a trilogy.

**Other books you might like:**
Poul Anderson, *The Game of Empire*, 1985
Octavia E. Butler, *Patternmaster*, 1976
Diana Wynne Jones, *The Crown of Dalemark*, 1995
Katherine Kurtz, *Camber of Culdi*, 1976
Melissa Scott, *A Choice of Destinies*, 1987
Susan Schwartz, *Byzantium's Crown*, 1987
Melinda M. Snodgrass, *Queen's Gambit Declined*, 1989
Judith Tarr, *Lord of the Two Lands*, 1993

## 5511

### HARRY TURTLEDOVE

## *Thessalonica*

(New York: Baen, 1997)

**Story type:** Fantasy (Historical; Mystery)
**Major character(s):** George, Artisan (shoemaker); Father Luke, Religious; Ampelus, Mythical Creature (satyr)
**Time period(s):** 6th century
**Locale(s):** Greece; Ancient Civilization

**Summary:** When the Slavs and the Avars besiege Thessalonica and the Empire supplies no aid, Christian powers seem useless against Slav gods and demons. When a satyr rescues George, locked out of the city, George discovers that the Slavs and Avars also threaten the satyr and his friends, the centaurs, despite their magical nature.

## 5512

### HARRY TURTLEDOVE

## *The Thousand Cities*

(New York: Ballantine Del Ray, 1997)

**Story type:** Fantasy (Military; Political)
**Series:** Time of Troubles
**Major character(s):** Abivard, Military Personnel; Tzikas, Military Personnel, Traitor; Sharbaraz, Ruler (King of Kings)
**Time period(s):** Indeterminate Past
**Locale(s):** Videssos, Fictional Country; Makuran, Fictional Country

**Summary:** Abivard must defend Makuran from Videssos despite the fact that Sharbaraz, King of Kings, grows suspicious of his success, but only keeps him alive as long as he maintains success. He must also contend with Tzikas, a military genius who cannot be trusted. Yet the two must work together for any hope of conquering Videssos. Third in series.

**Other books you might like:**
Richard Garfinkle, *Celestial Matters*, 1996
Diana Wynne Jones, *The Crown of Dalemark*, 1995
Katherine Kurtz, *The Bastard Prince*, 1994
Kirk Mitchell, *Procurator*, 1984
Jerry Pournelle, *Janissaries*, 1979
Melissa Scott, *A Choice of Destinies*, 1986
Robert Silverberg, *Valentine Pontifex*, 1983
Jack Vance, *The Green Pearl*, 1985

## 5513

### HARRY TURTLEDOVE

## *Videssos Besieged*

(New York: Ballantine Del Rey, 1998)

**Story type:** Fantasy (Political)
**Series:** Time of Troubles
**Major character(s):** Maniakes, Ruler (Emperor), Military Personnel; Tzikas, Military Personnel (general), Traitor; Abivard, Military Personnel, Political Figure
**Time period(s):** Indeterminate Past
**Locale(s):** Videssos, Fictional City; Videssos, Fictional Country

**Summary:** Maniakes begins a campaign only to discover that General Abivard has besieged the city of Videssos, arranging for an attack from the north. Religious infighting in the empire complicates Maniakes's life, as do slanderous comments about his marriage, considered incestuous by many priests.

**Other books you might like:**
John M. Ford, *The Dragon Waiting*, 1983
Richard Garfinkle, *Celestial Matters*, 1996
Roland J. Green, *The Great King's War*, 1985
    John F. Carr, co-author
Stephen R. Lawhead, *Byzantium*, 1996
Jerry Pournelle, *Janissaries*, 1979
Susan Shwartz, *Shards of Empire*, 1996
Robert Silverberg, *Up the Line*, 1968
Judith Tarr, *The Eagle's Daughter*, 1995

## 5514

### HARRY TURTLEDOVE

## *A World of Difference*

(New York: Ballantine/Del Rey, 1990)

**Story type:** Science Fiction (Alternate Universe; First Contact)
**Major character(s):** Irv Levitt, Scientist (anthropologist); Pat Marquard, Scientist (biologist); Reatur, Ruler (Domain Lord of Omolo)
**Time period(s):** 21st century
**Locale(s):** Minerva, Planet—Imaginary

**Summary:** Reatur and Hogram, two Domain-Lords of Minerva, the fourth planet from the sun, are planning a war when ships from the USA and the USSR land, one in each Domain. While the Americans plan ways to let females survive childbirth, the Russians are blackmailed into giving weapons to Hogram and training his people to use them. When they attack Reatur, an American is killed, but Lopatin, a KGB agent, sacrifices himself to stop the fighting from spreading back to Earth. Reatur and Hogram make peace and the Earthmen leave for home.

**Other books you might like:**
Poul Anderson, *Ensign Flandry*, 1966
Pierre Boulle, *Planet of the Apes*, 1963
L. Neil Smith, *Contact and Commune*, 1990
Wynne Whiteford, *Lake of the Sun*, 1989

## 5515

### HARRY TURTLEDOVE

## *Worldwar: In the Balance*

(New York: Ballantine Del Rey, 1994)

**Story type:** Science Fiction (Alternate History; Invasion of Earth)
**Series:** Worldwar
**Major character(s):** Atvar, Alien, Leader (Fleetlord); Sam Yeager, Military Personnel; Enrico Fermi, Historical Figure, Scientist
**Time period(s):** 1940s
**Locale(s):** Alternate Earth

**Summary:** With World War II enveloping the globe, Fleetleader Atvar's forces arrive to claim Earth for the People, forcing humanity to join forces against the aliens.

**Other books you might like:**
Patricia Anthony, *Cold Allies*, 1993
Gregory Benford, *Alternate Wars*, 1991
    Martin H. Greenberg, co-editor
Octavia E. Butler, *Dawn*, 1987
Philip K. Dick, *The Man in the High Castle*, 1962
Ursula K. Le Guin, *The Lathe of Heaven*, 1971

## 5516

### HARRY TURTLEDOVE

## *Worldwar: Striking the Balance*

(New York: Ballantine Del Rey, 1996)

**Story type:** Science Fiction (Invasion of Earth; Alternate History)
**Series:** Worldwar
**Major character(s):** Atvar, Military Personnel, Alien; Moishe Russie, Refugee, Radio Personality; Liu Han, Revolutionary, Parent (mother)
**Time period(s):** 1940s (1944-1945)
**Locale(s):** Alternate Earth

**Summary:** With the Fleet in disarray, plagued by mutiny, ginger addiction, and the Tosevites, Terrans hold their own and even gain a bit in the colder regions of the planet. The Fleet needs a cease-fire, if the Tosevites will accept one.

**Other books you might like:**

Kevin J. Anderson, *The Trinity Paradox*, 1991
    Doug Beason, co-author
Ben Bova, *Triumph*, 1993
Philip K. Dick, *The Man in the High Castle*, 1962
Newt Gingrich, *1945*, 1995
    William Forstchen, co-author
James P. Hogan, *The Proteus Operation*, 1985
Larry Niven, *Footfall*, 1985
    Jerry Pournelle, co-author
William F. Wu, *Dictator*, 1994
Jerry Yulsman, *Elleander Morning*, 1984

## 5517

### HARRY TURTLEDOVE

## *Worldwar: Tilting the Balance*

(New York: Ballantine Del Rey, 1995)

**Story type:** Science Fiction (Invasion of Earth)
**Series:** Worldwar
**Major character(s):** Ludmila Gorbunova, Military Personnel, Pilot; Atvar, Alien (Lizard), Leader; Moishe Russie, Fugitive
**Time period(s):** 1940s (1943)
**Locale(s):** Alternate Earth

**Summary:** The attack of the Lizards forces former human enemies into uneasy cooperation, rushing to develop nuclear weapons despite some disastrous setbacks. As the Lizards consolidate their holdings, increasing numbers succumb to ginger addiction, while human resistance takes on new significance when the Allies learn of the Lizard colonists en route to Earth.

**Other books you might like:**

Brian W. Aldiss, *The Year Before Tomorrow*, 1987
Patricia Anthony, *Cold Allies*, 1993
Ben Bova, *Triumph*, 1993
Newt Gingrich, *1945*, 1995
    William Forstchen, co-author
Robert Harris, *Fatherland*, 1992
Keith Laumer, *Worlds of the Imperium*, 1962
Brad Linaweaver, *Moon of Ice*, 1988
Larry Niven, *Footfall*, 1985
    Jerry Pournelle, co-author
Jerry Yulsman, *Elleander Morning*, 1984

## 5518

### HARRY TURTLEDOVE

## *Worldwar: Upsetting the Balance*

(New York: Ballantine Del Rey, 1996)

**Story type:** Science Fiction (Invasion of Earth; Alternate Universe)
**Series:** Worldwar
**Major character(s):** Atvar, Military Personnel (Fleetlord), Alien; Sam Yeager, Military Personnel (sergeant); Ludmila Gorbunova, Military Personnel, Pilot
**Time period(s):** 1940s (1944)
**Locale(s):** Alternate Earth

**Summary:** The human/alien war reaches a new and more dangerous level as the aliens pay attention to shipping, taking reprisals by bombing human cities more often. As the invasion of Britain fails and alien scientists raise a human baby in the hope of gaining understanding, the cold and hopelessness cause troops to start rebelling. Third in the series.

**Other books you might like:**

Brian W. Aldiss, *The Year Before Yesterday*, 1987
Kevin J. Anderson, *The Trinity Paradox*, 1991
    Doug Beason, co-author
Ben Bova, *Triumph*, 1993
Robert Harris, *Fatherland*, 1992
Brad Linaweaver, *Moon of Ice*, 1988
Jerry Yulsman, *Elleander Morning*, 1984

## 5519

### LISA TUTTLE

## *Familiar Spirit*

(New York: Tor, 1989)

**Story type:** Horror (Haunted House)
**Major character(s):** Sarah, Young Woman; Jade, Spirit
**Time period(s):** 1980s
**Locale(s):** Austin, Texas

**Summary:** After breaking up with her boyfriend, Sarah moves into a house dominated by the spirit of a deceased magician and a protracted duel between them ensues. Originally published in 1983.

**Other books you might like:**

Campbell Black, *Letters From the Dead*, 1985
Arthur Calder-Marshall, *The Scarlet Boy*, 1961
Ken Eulo, *The Brownstone*, 1980
Susan Hill, *The Woman in Black*, 1983

## 5520

### LISA TUTTLE

## *Lost Futures*

(New York: Dell/Abyss, 1992)

**Story type:** Science Fiction (Horror)
**Major character(s):** Clare Beckett, Accountant; Sophie Baxter, Artist; Michael Zacharias, Musician
**Time period(s):** 1990s (1992)
**Locale(s):** Virgil, New York

**Summary:** Bored with her lackluster life, Clare Beckett begins to live a more vivid and stimulating existence in dreams, where she is able to experience how her life might have turned out had she made different life choices. When her dream life begins to intrude upon the waking world, however, she is unable to tell whether she is going mad or whether her dreams are actually beginning to shape reality.

**Other books you might like:**
Paddy Chayefsky, *Altered States*, 1979
Philip K. Dick, *The Three Stigmata of Palmer Eldritch*, 1964
Daniel Quinn, *Dreamer*, 1988
Lucius Shepard, *Kalimantan*, 1990

---

**5521**

**LISA TUTTLE**

## Memories of the Body

(New York: Severn House, 1992)

**Story type:** Horror (Collection)

**Summary:** Fifteen stories of fantasy, horror and science fiction written in the last half-decade by one of the best practitioners in all three genres. Included are two savage looks at the battle of the sexes, ''The Wound'' and ''Lizard Lust''; two tales of motherly love gone away, ''Jamie's Grave'' and ''A Mother's Heart''; a blend of time travel and Victorian spiritualism, ''The Spirit Cabinet''; and a science-fictional look at the afterlife, ''Dead Television.''

**Other books you might like:**
Pat Cadigan, *Patterns*, 1989
Elizabeth Engstrom, *Nightmare Flower*, 1992
Pat Murphy, *Points of Departure*, 1990
Jessica Amanda Salmonson, *John Collier and Fredric Brown Went Quarrelling through My Head*, 1989

---

**5522**

**LISA TUTTLE**

## Pillow Friend

(Clarkston, Georgia: White Wolf, 1996)

**Story type:** Horror (Wild Talents)
**Major character(s):** Agnes Grey, Writer; Graham Storey, Writer (poet); Marjorie Grey, Writer
**Time period(s):** 1990s (1996)
**Locale(s):** Austin, Texas; London, England

**Summary:** Agnes Grey discovers that, like her aunt, she has an uncanny talent to wish her dreams into reality. Her talent brings her a lifetime of fulfillment, but also problems, as she becomes increasingly unable to determine who and what is real, and whom and what she has simply wished into existence.

**Other books you might like:**
Ramsey Campbell, *Incarnate*, 1983
Orson Scott Card, *Treasure Box*, 1996
Charles L. Grant, *In a Dark Dream*, 1989
Melanie Tem, *Making Love*, 1993
Stephen King, *It*, 1986

---

**5523**

**LISA TUTTLE**, Editor

## Skin of the Soul

(New York: Pocket, 1991)

**Story type:** Horror (Anthology)

**Summary:** Sixteen horror stories and one poem all written by women and concerned largely with female experience. Included are Melanie Tem's ''Lightning Rod,'' about women who sacrifice their lives to spare their families pain; Joyce Carol Oates' ''Pregnant,'' about an unborn child's control over its expectant mother; G.K. Sprinkle's ''Serena Sees,'' about a radio talk show psychic; and Suzy McKee Charnas' ''Boobs'' and Karen Joy Fowler's ''The Night Wolf,'' both of which use supernatural experiences as a metaphor for sexual awakening.

**Other books you might like:**
Richard Dalby, *The Virago Book of Ghost Stories: The Twentieth Century*, 1987
  published in London
Kathryn Ptacek, *Women of Darkness*, 1988
Kathryn Ptacek, *Women of Darkness II*, 1990
Alan Ryan, *Haunting Women*, 1988
Jessica Amanda Salmonson, *What Did Miss Darrington See?: An Anthology of Feminist Supernatural Fiction*, 1989

---

**5524**

**KATHY TYERS**

## Crystal Witness

(New York: Bantam Spectra, 1989)

**Story type:** Science Fiction (Space Opera)
**Major character(s):** Ming Dalamini, Smuggler; Holjpip Langelleik, Ruler
**Time period(s):** Indeterminate Future
**Locale(s):** Mannheim, Planet—Imaginary

**Summary:** One company controls all interstellar travel and its police force rules with an iron fist. Dalamini is caught using illegal technology to smuggle sunstones. The company brain wipes her and forces her to spy on the ruler of the planet Mannheim. Gradually Dalamini recovers her identity and begins to work against the company.

**Other books you might like:**
Patricia A. McKillip, *Fool's Run*, 1987
Melisa C. Michaels, *Far Harbor*, 1989
Janet Morris, *Cruiser Dreams*, 1981
Janet Morris, *Dream Dancer*, 1980
Janet Morris, *Earth Dreams*, 1982

---

**5525**

**KATHY TYERS**

## One Mind's Eye

(New York: Bantam Spectra, 1996)

**Story type:** Science Fiction (First Contact; Psychic Powers)
**Major character(s):** Llyn Torfinn, Adoptee, Psychic; Jahn Korsakov, Psychic; Karine Torfinn, Parent, Psychologist
**Time period(s):** Indeterminate Future
**Locale(s):** Antar, Planet—Imaginary

**Summary:** The human settlers of the Concord worlds rebuild after the alien Devastators attack, but interplanetary war threatens their precarious recovery when Tdega secedes. A human child found drugged and lost in virtual reality with no memories, Llyn has grown to adulthood under the guidance of Karine, but in spite of her adoptive mother's efforts to make her normal, still longs for her virtual experiences and for knowledge of her origins. Now her paranormal abilities may well prove the key to saving humanity.

## 5526

### KATHY TYERS

## Shivering World

(New York: Bantam Spectra, 1991)

**Story type:** Science Fiction (Disaster; Young Adult)
**Major character(s):** Graysha Brady-Phillips, Scientist (microbiologist); Lindon DalLierx, Administrator (colonial); Trevarre Chase-Frisson L'Zalle, Stowaway, Teenager
**Time period(s):** Indeterminate Future
**Locale(s):** Goddard, Planet—Imaginary (Epsilon Eridani)

**Summary:** Graysha left her teaching position to work for Gaea Corporation as a soils specialist on Goddard, recently opened to colonization and not yet stably terraformed. She willingly left the safety of habitat life because the job will help her pay off the huge debt left after her divorce and because of rumors that the Lwuites, the religious group who colonized Goddard, have the technology to cure the genetic disorder which will cause her early death.

**Other books you might like:**
David Brin, *The Uplift War*, 1987
Octavia E. Butler, *Dawn*, 1987
Gregory Feeley, *The Oxygen Barons*, 1990
Diana G. Gallagher, *The Alien Dark*, 1990
Frank Herbert, *Dune*, 1965
Larry Niven, *The Integral Trees*, 1984
Joan Slonczewski, *A Door into Ocean*, 1986

## 5527

### KATHY TYERS

## The Truce at Bakura

(New York: Bantam Spectra, 1994)

**Story type:** Science Fiction (Space Opera; Political)
**Series:** Star Wars
**Major character(s):** Leia Organa, Royalty, Diplomat; Luke Skywalker, Martial Arts Expert (Jedi Knight), Hero; Han Solo, Spaceship Captain, Warrior
**Time period(s):** Indeterminate Past
**Locale(s):** Bakura, Planet—Imaginary; New Republic, Interstellar Empire/Federation

**Summary:** The Rebel Alliance sends forces to aid the Bakura Imperial garrison, under attack from invading forces of the alien Ssi-ruuk, who were formerly allied to the now deceased Emperor. As they aid in repelling the invasion, Luke, Han and Leia must win allies among native Bakurans to insure against treachery from those aided. Set after James Kahn's *The Return of the Jedi* (1983).

**Other books you might like:**
Brian Daley, *The Han Solo Adventures*, 1992
George Lucas, *The Star Wars Trilogy*, 1987
    Donald F. Glut, James Kahn, co-authors
Vonda N. McIntyre, *The Crystal Star*, 1994
James H. Schmitz, *The Demon Breed*, 1968
L. Neil Smith, *The Lando Calrissian Adventures*, 1994

## 5528

### DONALD TYSON

## The Messenger

(St. Paul, Minnesota: Llewellyn Publications, 1993)

**Story type:** Horror (Occult)

**Major character(s):** Ebeneezer Hale, Paranormal Investigator; Liza Grey, Student (English graduate); Lee Sheppard, Student
**Time period(s):** 1990s (1993)
**Locale(s):** Haven-by-the-Sea, Nova Scotia, Canada

**Summary:** A group of parapsychologists and occultists stay at Haven-by-the-Sea, a remote fortress that once served as a hotel but turns out to have been a sanitarium for children run by Daniel Brannon, a member of the occult society the Brotherhood of the Fiery Heart. Brannon's efforts to create an avenging angel through the deaths of his child wards has produced a demonic fury who haunts the house, and whom the visitors try desperately to exorcise before it kills them all.

**Other books you might like:**
Judith Hawkes, *Julian's House*, 1990
Shirley Jackson, *The Haunting of Hill House*, 1959
Stephen King, *The Shining*, 1977
Richard Matheson, *Hell House*, 1971
Nina Romberg, *Shadow Walkers*, 1993

## 5529

### SALINDA TYSON

## Wheel of Dreams

(New York: Ballantine Del Rey, 1996)

**Story type:** Fantasy (Romance)
**Major character(s):** Kiera Danio, Fugitive, Psychic; Nikkael Roshannon, Mercenary, Psychic; Beren ''Brat'' SanDyllin Harth, Orphan
**Time period(s):** Indeterminate
**Locale(s):** Sanctum, Fictional Country; Blue Forest, Mythical Place; Cartheon, Fictional City (city and state)

**Summary:** After Kiera's father sells her to Nikkael as a wife, Kiera flees north to Cartheon, hoping to find the fabled witches who can explain her strange ability to dream prophetically. As Nikkael pursues, events pull the psychically linked pair into the struggle of Cartheon to resist Sanctum domination. First novel.

**Other books you might like:**
Tom Deitz, *Soulsmith*, 1991
Mary H. Herbert, *City of the Sorcerers*, 1994
J.V. Jones, *The Baker's Boy*, 1995
J.V. Jones, *A Man Betrayed*, 1996
Elizabeth Moon, *The Deed of Paksenarrion*, 1992
Rachel Pollack, *Temporary Agency*, 1994
Rachel Pollack, *Unquenchable Fire*, 1992

## 5530

### MICHAEL UPCHURCH

## Passive Intruder

(New York: Norton, 1995)

**Story type:** Horror (Ghost Story)
**Major character(s):** Susan Pond, Receptionist; Walker Popman, Photographer; Jerry Plume, Doctor (psychiatrist)
**Time period(s):** 1990s (1995)
**Locale(s):** Seattle, Washington

**Summary:** Walker Popman dies shortly after marrying Susan, and Susan notes a presence in his photographs that may be ghosts. Susan's investigations into Walker's past put her in touch with his first wife and psychiatrist, and introduce her to literal and symbolic ghosts that lead to greater self-awareness.

**Other books you might like:**
Peter S. Beagle, *A Fine and Private Place*, 1960
Jack Cady, *The Off Season*, 1995
Brad Leithauser, *Seaward*, 1993
Mark Morris, *The Immaculate*, 1992
Chet Williamson, *The House of Fear*, 1989

---

**5531**

JOHN UPDIKE

## Toward the End of Time
(New York: Knopf, 1997)

**Story type:** Science Fiction (Post-Disaster; Dystopian)
**Major character(s):** Ben Turnbull, Aged Person
**Time period(s):** 2020s
**Locale(s):** Massachusetts

**Summary:** In a depopulated post-war America, Ben Turnbull retains some retirement amenities, despite social chaos. Ben becomes involved with the ''many worlds'' hypothesis derived from quantum theory as his identity follows the branches into the past and future, exploring various possibilities.

**Other books you might like:**
Deborah Christian, *Mainline*, 1996
James P. Hogan, *Paths to Otherwhere*, 1996
Katharine Kerr, *Resurrection*, 1992
Nancy Kress, *Brain Rose*, 1990
Robert Reed, *Down the Bright Way*, 1991
Kurt Vonnegut Jr., *The Sirens of Titan*, 1959

---

**5532**

PETER USTINOV

## The Old Man and Mr. Smith
(New York: Little Brown/Arcade, 1991)

**Story type:** Fantasy (Religious; Light Fantasy)
**Major character(s):** God ''The Old Man'', Deity; Satan ''Mr. Smith'', Angel (fallen)
**Time period(s):** 1990s
**Locale(s):** United States; Israel; Asia

**Summary:** When God decides to check up on how human beings live and how they treat each other, God takes Satan along. Visiting the United States results in problems for religious and government personnel. God and Satan then travel to Russia, China, Israel and India before leaving Earth.

**Other books you might like:**
Neil Gaiman, *Good Omens: The Nice and Accurate Prophecies of Agnes Nutter, Witch*, 1990
   Terry Pratchett, co-author
Parke Godwin, *The Snake Oil Wars*, 1989
Parke Godwin, *Waiting for the Galactic Bus*, 1988
Robert A. Heinlein, *Job: A Comedy of Justice*, 1984
Robert A. Heinlein, *Stranger in a Strange Land*, 1991
   revised
Marc Laidlaw, *Neon Lotus*, 1988
Elizabeth Ann Scarborough, *Nothing Sacred*, 1991
Donald E. Westlake, *Humans*, 1991
Roger Zelazny, *Lord of Light*, 1967

---

**5533**

DORIS VALLEJO

## Ladies: Retold Tales of Goddesses and Heroines
(New York: Roc, 1992)

**Story type:** Fantasy (Legend; Collection)
**Summary:** Doris Vallejo retells fables of mythological females Arachne, Ariadne, Circe, Coronis, Deianira, Eurydice, Gorgon, Medea, Pandora and Persephone. Lavishly illustrated in color and monocolor by Boris Vallejo.

**Other books you might like:**
Thomas Bulfinch, *Bulfinch's Mythology*, 1934
Robert Graves, *Greek Myths*, 1955
   2 volumes
Edith Hamilton, *Mythology*, 1942

---

**5534**

GAIL VAN ASTEN

## Charlemagne's Champion
(New York: Ace, 1990)

**Story type:** Fantasy (Legend)
**Major character(s):** Roland, Bastard Son, Warrior
**Time period(s):** Indeterminate Past
**Locale(s):** Europe

**Summary:** Based on *The Song of Roland*, the novel examines the legend of Roland in a new light, adding supernatural elements. Roland rises to become the champion of Charlemagne, all the while trying to solve the mystery of his birth.

**Other books you might like:**
Ru Emerson, *Spell Bound*, 1990
Morgan Llywelyn, *The Isles of the Blest*, 1989
Andre Norton, *Merlin's Mirror*, 1975
Nikolai Tolstoy, *The Coming of the King*, 1989
Jane Yolen, *Dove Isabeau*, 1990

---

**5535**

EDO VAN BELKOM

## Wyrm Wolf
(New York: HarperPaperbacks, 1995)

**Story type:** Horror (Werewolf Story)
**Series:** World of Darkness: Werewolf
**Major character(s):** Father Wendel Oldman, Werewolf, Religious (priest); Kenneth Holt, Streetperson; Caroline Keegan, Journalist (televison reporter)
**Time period(s):** 1990s (1995)
**Locale(s):** San Francisco, California

**Summary:** In the World of Darkness, which bears a close resemblance to our own, the Garou, a race of werewolves, conceal their beastly nature from human beings as best they can. When a renegade Garou begins slaughtering members of his community, Father Oldman, a Garou who runs the Scott Mission for the homeless, investigates the crimes in both his human and werewolf form to find out which of his brethren is in thrall to the Wyrm and acting as an instrument of pure evil. Set against the World of Darkness scenario of the White Wolf gaming company, this is the author's first novel.

**Other books you might like:**
Don Bassingthwaite, *Breathe Deeply*, 1994
Don Bassingthwaite, *Such Pain*, 1995
Richard Lee Byers, *Netherworld*, 1995
Stewart Von Allmen, *Conspicuous Consumption*, 1995

## 5536

**EDO VAN BELKOM**
**CALI WEST**, Illustrator

### Yours Truly, Jackie the Stripper

(Clay, New York: Dark Raptor Press, 1998)

**Story type:** Horror (Erotic Horror)
**Major character(s):** Jacqueline Strangelove, Stripper; Derwent Mack, Criminal; Bill Loman, Police Officer
**Time period(s):** 1990s (1998)
**Locale(s):** Pacific Northwest

**Summary:** When a disgruntled patron takes over the Up Front Lounge at gunpoint and takes its strippers hostage, Jackie Strangelove finds it necessary to develop a literal taste for violence in order to save her life. Illustrated by Cali West. Issued as a signed limited edition chapbook.

**Other books you might like:**
Ray Garton, *Pieces of Hate*, 1996
Jeff Gelb, *Hot Blood: Stranger by Night*, 1994
　Michael Garrett, co-editor
Michael Hemmingson, *Nice Little Stories Jam-Packed with Depraved Sex and Violence*, 1995
Edward Lee, *Splatterspunk: The Micah Hays Stories*, 1998
　John Pelan, co-author
Lucy Taylor, *The Flesh Artist*, 1994

## 5537

**DELLA VAN HISE**

### Ragged Angels

(Yucca Valley, California: Eye Scry, 1997)

**Story type:** Horror (Vampire Story)
**Major character(s):** Stefan London, Businessman (memorabilia dealer); Dimitri Alexander Karros, Computer Expert, Vampire; Miquel Kaliq Constantine, Vampire
**Time period(s):** 1990s (1997)
**Locale(s):** Los Angeles, California; San Diego, California

**Summary:** At a science fiction convention, Stefan meets Dimitri and embraces his vampire way of life. Stefan's adjustment to vampirism distracts him from his consuming grief over the recent death of his teenage daughter, but opens him up to a host of emotional and philosophical dilemmas he never anticipated.

**Other books you might like:**
Richard Lee Byers, *The Vampire's Apprentice*, 1992
John Peyton Cooke, *Out for Blood*, 1991
David Darke, *Shade*, 1994
Mark Ivanhoe, *Virgintooth*, 1991
Anne Rice, *Interview with the Vampire*, 1976
T. Lucien Wright, *Blood Brothers*, 1991

## 5538

**RAYMOND VAN OVER**

### The Twelfth Child

(New York: Pinnacle, 1990)

**Story type:** Horror (Evil Children)
**Major character(s):** David Mallory, Doctor (obstetrician); Lily Shikome, Nurse; Father Paul, Religious (Catholic priest)
**Time period(s):** 1980s (1989)
**Locale(s):** Hanover, New Hampshire (Hitchcock Medical Center)

**Summary:** A routine childbirth that leaves the mother drained of her blood sends obstetrician David Mallory searching for an explanation. When Mallory finds the records of 10 equidistantly-spaced births over the last 10 years in which the mothers died under similar circumstances and the attending physicians were murdered within the year, he begins a race to solve the riddle of the mysterious births before he too is murdered. This is the author's first novel.

**Other books you might like:**
Ira Levin, *Rosemary's Baby*, 1967
David Seltzer, *The Omen*, 1976

## 5539

**RAYMOND VAN OVER**

### Whisper

(New York: Zebra/Pinnacle, 1991)

**Story type:** Horror (Possession)
**Major character(s):** Brion McKibben, Child; Eleazar, Indian; Louis Edward Church, Police Officer (sheriff)
**Time period(s):** 1990s
**Locale(s):** New Thetford, Vermont

**Summary:** Heartbroken over the death of his dog Whisper, Brion McKibben brings the carcass to the old Iroquois medicine man Eleazar for resuscitation. Too late, Eleazar discovers that the resurrected dog has become possessed by bloodthristy demons known as the Yaksha.

**Other books you might like:**
Stephen King, *Cujo*, 1981
Stephen King, *Pet Sematary*, 1983
John Stchur, *Paddywhack*, 1989

## 5540

**NICOLAS VAN PALLANDT**

### Anvil

(New York: Roc, 1998)

**Story type:** Science Fiction (Political; Techno-Thriller)
**Major character(s):** Gabriel Kylie, Backwoodsman, Rebel; Isadora Katarina Manuela Gatzalumendi, Researcher, Animal Lover; Hitedoro Izeki, Police Officer
**Time period(s):** Indeterminate Future
**Locale(s):** Thors Anvil, Planet—Imaginary; Kyara, Fictional City; The Seventeen Planets, Interstellar Empire/Federation

**Summary:** Meeting on the shuttle down to Kyara, Gabriel tells Isadora about his sister who fell to her death in Rainer Park, a large park filled with many GenTech animals. The treatment he receives from the local police and TARC, another official law enforcement agency, forces him to believe his sister may have been murdered. First novel.

**Other books you might like:**
Stephen Baxter, *Raft*, 1991
David Brin, *Earth*, 1990
C.S. Friedman, *This Alien Shore*, 1998
Charles Sheffield, *Cold as Ice*, 1992
Dan Simmons, *Phases of Gravity*, 1987

---

**5541**

SYDNEY J. VAN SCYOC

### Deepwater Dreams

(New York: Avon, 1991)

**Story type:** Science Fiction (Genetic Manipulation)
**Major character(s):** Nuela, Student; Polmaire, Political Figure
**Time period(s):** Indeterminate Future
**Locale(s):** Aurlanis, Planet—Imaginary (Aurlanis Island)

**Summary:** The Chakera were genetically engineered to live in the sea after war made much of the land uninhabitable. When a ship full of the Chakera to be sold as slaves was stolen and crashed into a water world, they developed a culture based on their genetically inherited dreams. Land is scarce, and the inhabitants of Aurlanis ritually attain adulthood by staying alive in the ocean for 42 days. Nuela, passed in her turn at the ritual for several years, is suddenly sent to find a secret ocean-based society to deliver a message from Polmaire, and to experience deep water dreaming.

**Other books you might like:**
Gregory Benford, *Great Sky River*, 1987
Lois McMaster Bujold, *Falling Free*, 1988
Gordon R. Dickson, *Home From the Shore*, 1978
Alis A. Rasmussen, *A Passage of Stars*, 1990
Carol Severance, *Reefsong*, 1991
A.E. Van Vogt, *The Silkie*, 1969
John Wyndham, *Out of the Deeps*, 1953

---

**5542**

SYDNEY J. VAN SCYOC

### Feather Stroke

(New York: Avon, 1989)

**Story type:** Fantasy (Quest)
**Major character(s):** Dara, Telepath
**Time period(s):** Indeterminate
**Locale(s):** Tith, Planet—Imaginary

**Summary:** Dara learns that she was adopted, and that her abilities are a part of her heritage. While trying to control her powers, she has to defend herself from the priestly caste of Tith.

**Other books you might like:**
Marion Zimmer Bradley, *Hawkmistress!*, 1982
Marjie Douglis, *Matrix Witch*, 1988
Katherine Kurtz, *Chronicle of Deryni*, 1987
Mercedes Lackey, *Magic's Pawn*, 1989

---

**5543**

JACK VANCE

### Alastor

(New York: Tor, 1995)

**Story type:** Science Fiction (Political; Space Opera)
**Major character(s):** Oman Ursht, Leader (Connatic)

**Time period(s):** Indeterminate Future
**Locale(s):** Alastor Cluster, Interstellar Empire/Federation; Numenes, Planet—Imaginary

**Summary:** Omnibus edition containing *Trullion: Alastor 2262* (1973), *Marune Alastor 933* (1975), and *Wyst: Alastor 1716* (1978). The Connatic, ruler of the Alastor Cluster with its thousands of stars containing 3000 inhabited planets, may seem omniscient using information from the Ring of Worlds in his palace, but he can only occupy one room at a time.

**Other books you might like:**
Iain M. Banks, *Against a Dark Background*, 1993
Glen Cook, *The Dragon Never Sleeps*, 1988
L. Warren Douglas, *Stepwater*, 1995
Mary Gentle, *Golden Witchbreed*, 1984
Sheri S. Tepper, *Raising the Stones*, 1990
A.E. Van Vogt, *The Weapon Makers*, 1946

---

**5544**

JACK VANCE

### The Demon Princes: Volume One

(New York: Tor, 1997)

**Story type:** Science Fiction (Adventure; Space Opera)
**Series:** Demon Princes
**Major character(s):** Kirth Gersen, Avenger, Hero, Criminal (assassin); Viole Falushe, Kidnapper, Outlaw; Alusz Iphigenia, Companion, Fugitive
**Time period(s):** Indeterminate Future
**Locale(s):** Earth; Planet—Imaginary (the Rigel Concourse planetary system); Interstellar Empire/Federation

**Summary:** To avenge his parents' death in the Mount Pleasant massacre, Kirth Gersen must track down the five men involved, called Demon Princes, using any and all resources at his command. Omnibus edition of the first three books in the series, *The Star King* (1964), *The Killing Machine* (1964), and *The Palace of Love* (1967).

**Other books you might like:**
Ben Bova, *Orion*, 1984
Lois McMaster Bujold, *Memory*, 1996
Jack L. Chalker, *The Four Lords of the Diamond Series*, 1981-1983
Kate Elliott, *Jaran*, 1992
George R.R. Martin, *Dying of the Light*, 1977
Norman Spinrad, *The Void Captain's Tale*, 1983
Diann Thornley, *Ganwold's Child*, 1995
Vernor Vinge, *Tatja Grimm's World*, 1987

---

**5545**

JACK VANCE

### The Demon Princes: Volume Two

(New Yor: Tor, 1997)

**Story type:** Science Fiction (Adventure; Space Opera)
**Series:** Demon Princes
**Major character(s):** Kirth Gersen, Avenger, Hero, Criminal (assassin); Alice Wroke, Secretary, Spy; Lens Larque, Outlaw, Thief
**Time period(s):** Indeterminate Future
**Locale(s):** Dar Sai, Planet—Imaginary; Moudervelt, Planet—Imaginary; Interstellar Empire/Federation

**Summary:** As Kirth Gersen continues to seek the two remaining Demon Princes to avenge the death of his parents in the Mount Pleasant massacre, he discovers that even Lens Larque possesses some positive aspects. Contains the last two books in the series, *The Face* (1979) and *The Book of Dreams* (1981).

**Other books you might like:**
Lois McMaster Bujold, *The Vor Game*, 1990
Jack L. Chalker, *The Four Lords of the Diamond Series*, 1981-1983
Gordon R. Dickson, *Other*, 1994
George R.R. Martin, *Dying of the Light*, 1977
Andre Norton, *The Beast Master*, 1959
Mike Resnick, *Ivory: A Legend of Past and Future*, 1988
Allen Steele, *Clarke County, Space*, 1990
John E. Stith, *Reunion on Neverend*, 1994

## 5546

### JACK VANCE

## Ecce and Old Earth

(New York: Tor, 1991)

**Story type:** Science Fiction (Mystery; Political)
**Series:** Cadwal Chronicles
**Major character(s):** Glawen Clattuc, Police Officer; Wayness Tamm, Detective—Amateur; Pirie Tamm, Administrator
**Time period(s):** Indeterminate Future
**Locale(s):** Cadwal, Planet—Imaginary; Earth

**Summary:** Glawen Clattuc, having discovered his father is alive, rescues him from a prison in Ecce. Meanwhile, Wayness Tamm goes to Old Earth to find the missing Charter of the Nature Society, without which Cadwall will be parcelled out into landed estates and overrun by Yips.

**Other books you might like:**
Isaac Asimov, *The Stars Like Dust*, 1951
Orson Scott Card, *The Memory of Earth*, 1992
Philip Jose Farmer, *Dayworld*, 1985
Raymond Harris, *Shadows of the White Sun*, 1988
Melissa Scott, *Five-Twelfths of Heaven*, 1985

## 5547

### JACK VANCE

## Madouc

(New York: Ace, 1990)

**Story type:** Fantasy (Political)
**Series:** Lyonesse
**Major character(s):** Madouc, Heroine (Changeling)
**Time period(s):** Indeterminate
**Locale(s):** Europe

**Summary:** Madouc, daughter of a faerie, is making life miserable for everyone as political intrigue and skullduggery pervade her home and a quest for the Holy Grail begins.

**Other books you might like:**
Constance Ash, *The Stalking Horse*, 1990
Claudia J. Edwards, *Eldrie the Healer*, 1989
   *The Bastard Princess. Vol. 1*
M. John Harrison, *A Storm of Wings*, 1980
Michael Moorcock, *Gloriana, or the Unfulfilled Queen*, 1986
Melanie Rawn, *The Star Scroll*, 1989
   *Dragon Prince. Bk. 2*
Michael Shea, *Nifft the Lean*, 1982

## 5548

### JACK VANCE

## Night Lamp

(New York: Tor, 1996)

**Story type:** Science Fiction (Adventure; Science Fiction)
**Major character(s):** Jaro Fath, Foundling, Spaceman; Skirlet Hutsenreiter, Noblewoman, Investigator; Asrubal, Thief
**Time period(s):** Indeterminate Future
**Locale(s):** Thanet, Planet—Imaginary; Fader, Planet—Imaginary

**Summary:** An adopted foundling with no memory of his past, Jaro Fath seeks his origins. When his natural father finds him, the two go off to punish those responsible for his plight and come across a very strange society.

**Other books you might like:**
Kevin J. Anderson, *Blindfold*, 1995
Lois McMaster Bujold, *Cetaganda*, 1996
C.J. Cherryh, *Cuckoo's Egg*, 1985
Paula E. Downing, *A Whisper of Time*, 1994
Raymond Harris, *Shadows of the White Sun*, 1988
Mike Resnick, *The Dark Lady: A Romance of the Far Future*, 1987
Sydney J. Van Scyoc, *Darkchild*, 1982
Joan D. Vinge, *The Summer Queen*, 1991

## 5549

### JACK VANCE

## Ports of Call

(New York: Tor, 1998)

**Story type:** Science Fiction (Adventure; Science Fantasy)
**Major character(s):** Myron Tany, Adventurer; Fay Schwatzendale, Engineer, Gambler; Marcel Moncrief, Magician, Criminal (swindler)
**Time period(s):** Indeterminate Future
**Locale(s):** Fiametta, Planet—Imaginary; *Glicca*, Spaceship

**Summary:** Marooned because of a disagreement with his great-aunt, Myron Tany takes a job on the cargo ship *Glicca* until he can gain revenge. He must cope with mysterious religious pilgrims and rescue three young women from a future in prostitution.

**Other books you might like:**
Poul Anderson, *Trader to the Stars*, 1964
John Brunner, *A Maze of Stars*, 1991
A. Bertram Chandler, *The Wild Ones*, 1978
Alfred Coppel, *Glory*, 1993
William R. Forstchen, *Into the Sea of Stars*, 1986
Andre Norton, *Sargasso of Space*, 1955
Mike Resnick, *A Miracle of Rare Design*, 1994
L. Neil Smith, *Tom Paine Maru*, 1984

## 5550

### JACK VANCE

## Throy

(New York: Tor, 1993)

**Story type:** Science Fiction (Mystery; Political)
**Series:** Cadwal Chronicles
**Major character(s):** Glawen Clattuc, Police Officer; Eustace Chilke, Police Officer; Felitzia "Flitz" Stronsi, Heir—Dispossessed
**Time period(s):** Indeterminate Future
**Locale(s):** Cadwal, Planet—Imaginary; Rosalia, Planet—Imaginary

**Summary:** Glawen Clattus must postpone his marriage while he and Eustace Chilke capture Julian Bohost who has profited from the sale of indentured Yips on other planets. On Soum they confiscate Bohost's finances, then on Rosalia they rescue Flitz who has been robbed of family and fortune. Finally, on Cadwal, Glawen learns details of his mother's death and of a conspiracy to overthrow the Conservancy.

**Other books you might like:**
Lloyd Biggle, *Monument*, 1974
Johanna Bolton, *Mission: Tori*, 1990
Lois McMaster Bujold, *Brothers in Arms*, 1989
Raymond Harris, *The Broken Worlds*, 1986
Edward Llewellyn, *Fugitive in Transit*, 1985
Atanielle Annyn Noel, *The Duchess of Kneedeep*, 1986
Norman Spinrad, *The Void Captain's Tale*, 1986

---

**5551**

JACK VANCE

### When the Five Moons Rise

(Lancaster, Pennsylvania: Underwood-Miller, 1992)

**Story type:** Science Fiction (Collection)

**Summary:** Contains 11 stories published in 1950s periodicals plus one, "Dust of Far Suns," retitled from its 1962 publication as "Gateway to Strangeness." Other stories explore the breadth of Vance's 1950s short fiction with some set far from the here and now such as "Noise" and "When the Five Moons Rise," while Vance looks closer to home when he investigates urban folly of the future in "Dodkin's Job" and "Ulward's Retreat." "The New Prime" reflects Vance's love of space opera, and "Telek" postulates a universe in which a person's subjective reality affects everyone's shared reality.

**Other books you might like:**
Isaac Asimov, *The Complete Stories - Volume 1*, 1990
Alfred Bester, *Star Light, Star Bright*, 1976
Robert A. Heinlein, *The Past through Tomorrow*, 1967
Larry Niven, *N-Space*, 1990
Cordwainer Smith, *The Best of Cordwainer Smith*, 1975
Theodore Sturgeon, *E Pluribus Unicorn*, 1953
John Varley, *Blue Champagne*, 1986
John Varley, *The Persistence of Vision*, 1978
Kurt Vonnegut Jr., *Welcome to the Monkey House*, 1968

---

**5552**

STEVE VANCE

### Shapes

(New York: Leisure, 1991)

**Story type:** Horror (Werewolf Story)
**Major character(s):** Dominic Poduano, Monster (shapeshifter); Kelly Brynn Davis, Journalist; Blake Corbett, Writer (of horror fiction)
**Time period(s):** 1990s
**Locale(s):** Indigo Lake, New York

**Summary:** Blake Corbett finds himself torn between his promise to the government that he will not reveal his investigations into the viral origins of lycanthropy or what he witnessed during an experiment that went awry and turned one of his best friends into a shapeshifter. In addition, a group of supernaturally-endowed researchers want him to speak at their upcoming convention and could be just as dangerous as the government if he refuses their request.

**Other books you might like:**
Crosland Brown, *Tombley's Walk*, 1991
George C. Chesbro, *The Fear in Yesterday's Rings*, 1991

---

**5553**

STEVE VANCE

### Spook

(New York: Soho Press, 1990)

**Story type:** Horror (Mystery)
**Major character(s):** MaryAnn "Spook" Nelson, Teenager; Nedra Muriel Nelson, Artist (former Hollywood make-up artis); Ross Walker, Police Officer
**Time period(s):** 1990s (1990)
**Locale(s):** Sturgis, Georgia

**Summary:** Taunted by her peers for her physical deformities and shunned with her mother for their association with a series of sinister goings-on about town, MaryAnn Nelson endures a hellish adolescence. The persistence of the local school board to make her attend school eventually uncovers secrets about MaryAnn and her mother that outward appearances conceal.

**Other books you might like:**
John Farris, *Fiends*, 1990
Stephen King, *Carrie*, 1974

---

**5554**

VIVIAN VANDE VELDE

### The Changeling Prince

(New York: HarperPrism, 1998)

**Story type:** Fantasy (Sword and Sorcery)
**Major character(s):** Weiland, Teenager; Daria de Gris, Noblewoman, Sorceress; Shile, Thief (burglar)
**Time period(s):** Indeterminate
**Locale(s):** St. Celias, Fictional City

**Summary:** Raised by Daria for most of his 16 years, Weiland has not been able to escape the pain and suffering she whimsically inflicts. Of all the animals Daria has shapechanged into human form to serve her nefarious plans, Weiland remains only one who knows that her death will revert them all back to their original animal form, while he alone desires to remain human. So, without hope, Weiland stays with Daria and protects her from harm until they move to St. Celia's where he meets Shile, an affable burglar who butts into Weiland's life and forces him to make decisions that will either kill or free him.

**Other books you might like:**
Doranna Durgin, *Changespell*, 1997
Rosalie Fry, *The Secret of Roan Inish*, 1995
Terry Goodkind, *Wizard's First Rule*, 1994
Victoria Strauss, *The Arm of the Stone*, 1998
J.R.R. Tolkien, *The Fellowship of the Ring*, 1954

---

**5555**

VIVIAN VANDE VELDE

### The Conjurer Princess

(New York: HarperPrism, 1997)

**Story type:** Fantasy (Adventure)
**Major character(s):** Lylene Delroy, Apprentice, Wizard; Harkta, Wizard; Shile, Warrior

**Time period(s):** Indeterminate
**Locale(s):** Cragsfall, Fictional City

**Summary:** Lylene does not anticipate the cost nor expect the changes that result from requesting that Harkta teach her magic so she can recover her lost sister, who was kidnapped on her wedding day.

**Other books you might like:**
Lois McMaster Bujold, *The Spirit Ring*, 1992
Emma Bull, *Finder*, 1994
Peg Kerr, *Emerald House Rising*, 1997
Holly Lisle, *Minerva Wakes*, 1994
Rachel Pollack, *Godmother Night*, 1996

---

`5556`

### VIVIAN VANDE VELDE

## Dragon's Bait

(New York: Harcourt Brace Jovanovich, 1992)

**Story type:** Fantasy (Young Adult; Quest)
**Major character(s):** Alys, Criminal (accused witch), Teenager; Selendrile, Mythical Creature (dragon)
**Time period(s):** Indeterminate
**Locale(s):** St. Toby's-by-the-Mountain, Fictional City; Griswold, Fictional City

**Summary:** Saved by the dragon that she had expected to kill her, Alys discovers an ally in her desire for revenge on her townspeople. While pursuing their scheme, their capture precipitates a lethal encounter and may prove deadly for Selendrile.

**Other books you might like:**
Orson Scott Card, *Dragons of Darkness*, 1981
   editor
Louise Cooper, *The Sleep of Stone*, 1991
R.A. MacAvoy, *Tea with the Black Dragon*, 1983
Andre Norton, *The Elvenbane*, 1991
   Mercedes Lackey, co-author
Will Shetterly, *Elsewhere*, 1991
Patricia C. Wrede, *Dealing with Dragons*, 1991

---

`5557`

### VIVIAN VANDE VELDE

## Tales From the Brothers Grimm and the Sisters Weird

(New York: Harcourt Brace/Jane Yolen Books, 1995)

**Story type:** Fantasy (Collection; Legend)

**Summary:** Retells eight stories and five poems, modernizing the popular works with contemporary character motivations and humorous, sometimes dark, twists. Tales include "Rumplestiltskin," "Little Red Riding Hood," "Hansel and Gretl," "Jack and the Beanstalk," and "Beauty and the Beast."

**Other books you might like:**
Margaret Atwood, *Good Bones and Simple Murders*, 1994
William J. Brooke, *A Telling of the Tales: Five Stories*, 1990
William J. Brooke, *Teller of Tales*, 1994
James Finn Garner, *Once upon a More Enlightened Time*, 1995
James Finn Garner, *Politically Correct Bedtime Stories*, 1994
James Finn Garner, *Politically Correct Holiday Stories*, 1995

---

`5558`

### VIVIAN VANDE VELDE

## User Unfriendly

(New York: Harcourt Brace Jovanovich, 1991)

**Story type:** Fantasy (Quest; Young Adult)
**Major character(s):** Arvin "Harek" Rizalli, Student, Mythical Creature (elf); Felice, Parent (Arvin's mother), Thief; Sheldon Jankowitz, Student, Wizard
**Time period(s):** 1990s
**Locale(s):** Sannatia, Fictional City

**Summary:** Expecting a few hours' diversion, Arvin, his mother and his school mates enter the world of a bootleg computer game. As they pursue their quest, rescuing the king's daughter, Dorinda, the computer game's program seems somewhat odd and alarming as Felice begins to fade away. As their adventure progresses, Arvin must make brave and difficult decisions if the company is to make their way out of the dangerous world.

**Other books you might like:**
Margaret J. Anderson, *The Ghost Inside the Monitor*, 1990
Steven Brust, *Jhereg*, 1983
Diane Duane, *High Wizardry*, 1990
Philip Jose Farmer, *Red Orc's Rage*, 1991
Joel Rosenberg, *The Sleeping Dragon*, 1983
Will Shetterly, *The Tangled Lands*, 1989

---

`5559`

### VIVIAN VANDE VELDE

## A Well-Timed Enchantment

(New York: Crown, 1990)

**Story type:** Fantasy (Time Travel; Young Adult)
**Major character(s):** Deanna, Vacationer
**Time period(s):** 1990s; Indeterminate Past (Middle Ages)
**Locale(s):** France

**Summary:** While Deanna makes a wish at a well, she accidently drops her wristwatch into it. At that, a magical hand reaches out and drags her into the well. She is informed by elves that her watch, falling into the past, has messed up history. She must return to medieval France accompanied by her cat, enchanted into a strange young man, to retrieve the watch and correct history.

**Other books you might like:**
Keith William Andrews, *Sink the Armada*, 1990
Eleanor Cameron, *The Court of the Stone Children*, 1973
Catherine Dexter, *Mazemaker*, 1989
Roger L. DiSilvestro, *Living with the Reptiles*, 1990
Winifred Morris, *With Magical Horses to Ride*, 1985
Marilyn Singer, *Charmed*, 1990
Nancy Springer, *Red Wizard*, 1990

---

`5560`

### PETER VANSITTART

## Parsifal

(Chester Springs, PA: Peter Owen/Dufour Editions, 1989)

**Story type:** Fantasy (Legend)
**Major character(s):** Parsifal, Knight
**Time period(s):** 15th century (16th century); 20th century
**Locale(s):** Europe; Germany

**Summary:** Rather than focusing on a plot, Vansittart explores the legends that grew around the myth of Parsifal, as well as the particular times in history that had a profound effect on the legend.

**Other books you might like:**
Richard Barber, *The Arthurian Legends*,
Stephen R. Lawhead, *Arthur*, 1989
C.W. Sullivan, *Welsh Celtic Myth in Modern Fantasy*,
Jack Zipes, *The Brothers Grimm: From Enchanted Forests to the Modern World*, 1988

---

**5561**

ROBERT E. VARDEMAN

## Ancient Heavens

(New York: Avon, 1989)

**Story type:** Science Fiction (Adventure)
**Major character(s):** Richard Drake, Scientist (Terraformer); Michaeline Drake, Scientist
**Time period(s):** 21st century; 23rd century
**Locale(s):** Earth; Nerth, Planet—Imaginary (In the Alpha Centauri System)

**Summary:** Richard Drake specializes in the creation of entire new landscapes. Using the most advanced techniques in engineering and genetics, he can turn a desert into a productive agricultural region or whatever else is wanted. Now he's been offered the ultimate challenge. The Church of the Lost Eden wishes to terraform an entire planet and they want Richard Drake in charge. Drake agrees to do the job, not realizing that, when the work is done, the religious zealots who will populate that world may well come to look on him as the Creator Himself.

**Other books you might like:**
Poul Anderson, *The Snows of Ganymede*, 1955
Gregory Benford, *Jupiter Project*, 1975
John Brunner, *The Dramaturges of Yan*, 1971
Arthur C. Clarke, *The Sands of Mars*, 1951
David Gerrold, *Moonstar Odyssey*, 1977
Frank Herbert, *Children of Dune*, 1976
Ian Watson, *The Martian Inca*, 1977

---

**5562**

ROBERT E. VARDEMAN

## Death Channels

(New York: Avon, 1992)

**Story type:** Horror (Occult)
**Series:** Peter Thorne, Psychic Investigator
**Major character(s):** Peter Thorne, Magician, Paranormal Investigator; Charlie Hayes, Businessman (computers); Nyushka, Psychic (medium and channeler)
**Time period(s):** 1990s (1993)
**Locale(s):** San Francisco, California

**Summary:** Psychic detective Peter Thorne investigates a spirit channeler whom he thinks is preying on the grief of recently widowed friend, Charlie Hayes. Instead, he discovers that Charlie and his wife may have each been plotting to kill the other.

**Other books you might like:**
Geoffrey Caine, *Curse of the Dead*, 1991
Geoffrey Caine, *Legion of the Dead*, 1992
Geoffrey Caine, *Wake of the Werewolf*, 1991
Ehren M. Ehly, *Star Prey*, 1992
Ray Garton, *Dark Channel*, 1992

Seabury Quinn, *The Phantom Fighter*, 1966

---

**5563**

ROBERT E. VARDEMAN

## The Glass Warrior

(New York: Tor, 1989)

**Story type:** Fantasy (Quest)
**Series:** Demon Crown
**Major character(s):** Glass Warrior, Warrior
**Time period(s):** Indeterminate
**Locale(s):** Porotane, Planet—Imaginary

**Summary:** Porotane is torn by civil war. The aging ruler, on the throne by pretense and connivery, asks the Glass Warrior to find the legitimate heirs to the throne, in order to end the war.

**Other books you might like:**
Richard A. Knaak, *Firedrake*, 1989
Dave Smeds, *The Sorcery Within*, 1985
Janny Wurts, *Cycle of Fire Trilogy*, 1988

---

**5564**

ROBERT E. VARDEMAN

## The Infinity Plague

(New York: Ace Books, 1989)

**Story type:** Science Fiction (Military)
**Series:** Biowarriors
**Major character(s):** Jerome Walden, Scientist
**Time period(s):** 21st century
**Locale(s):** Delta Cygnus 4, Planet—Imaginary; Earth

**Summary:** The Frinn, an evil alien race, invade Earth space bent on conquest. Earth's leaders must decide whether or not to use dangerous genetically engineered bioweapons to repel the invasion.

**Other books you might like:**
Rick Cook, *Limbo System*, 1989
Charles Ingrid, *Alien Salute*, 1989
    Sand Wars 4
L. Neil Smith, *Contact and Commune*, 1989
Allen L. Wold, *Crown of the Serpent*, 1989

---

**5565**

JOHN VARLEY

## The Golden Globe

(New York: Ace, 1998)

**Story type:** Science Fiction (Arts; Adventure)
**Major character(s):** Kenneth ''Sparky'' Valentine, Actor, Mentally Ill Person; John Barrymore Valentine, Actor, Parent; Isambard Comfort, Agent, Criminal
**Time period(s):** Indeterminate Future
**Locale(s):** Pluto; King City, Montenegro; *Halley*, Spaceship

**Summary:** Using his early Shakespearean training, Sparky hides on the stages of the outer solar system. Lured back to the moon to play Lear, Sparky, his dog Toby, and his imaginary friend Elwood incur the wrath of the Charonese Mafia, then steal a spaceship in order to arrive in time to fill the role. Forced to face the consequences of events that chased him from the moon 70 years earlier, Sparky finds himself able to invest in the Heinleiner's project and hide from the Charonese.

**Other books you might like:**
Joshua Dann, *Timeshare*, 1997
Alan Dean Foster, *Design for Great-Day*, 1995
  Eric Frank Russell, co-author
Harry Harrison, *The Technicolor Time Machine*, 1967
Ernest Hogan, *Cortez on Jupiter*, 1990
Mary Rosenblum, *The Stone Garden*, 1995

**5566**

### JOHN VARLEY

## *Steel Beach*

(New York: Ace/Putnam, 1992)

**Story type:** Science Fiction (Alternate Intelligence; Immortality)
**Series:** Eight Worlds
**Major character(s):** Hildy Johnson, Journalist (*News Nipple*), Teacher; Brenda, Journalist (cub reporter); Central "CC" Computer, Artificial Intelligence
**Time period(s):** 23rd century
**Locale(s):** Montenegro

**Summary:** Assigned to produce a series of stories surrounding the 200th anniversary of aliens wiping out human life on Earth, Hildy unwillingly accepts a naive young partner enthusiastic to develop her journalistic skills. Hildy's research leads to the disturbing conclusion that CC may exhibit lethal insanity.

**Other books you might like:**
David Brin, *Earth*, 1990
Jeffrey A. Carver, *The Rapture Effect*, 1987
Robert A. Heinlein, *The Moon Is a Harsh Mistress*, 1966
Cordwainer Smith, *Norstrilia*, 1975
Allen Steele, *Clarke County, Space*, 1990
Allen Steele, *Lunar Descent*, 1991
Neal Stephenson, *Snow Crash*, 1992
Vernor Vinge, *A Fire upon the Deep*, 1992

**5567**

### JOHN VARLEY, Editor
### RICIA MAINHARDT, Co-Editor

## *Superheroes*

(New York: Ace, 1995)

**Story type:** Fantasy (Anthology; Science Fiction)

**Summary:** Contains an 11-page introduction by Varley plus 25 original stories of comic book type superheroes set in alternate universes with contemporary themes joining traditional pulp literature conceits. Authors include B.W. Clough, John DeChancie, Alan Dean Foster, Laurell K. Hamilton, Richard A. Knaak, Brad Linaweaver, Jody Lynn Nye, Mickey Zucker Reichert, Josepha Sherman, Michael A. Stackpole, Brian M. Thomsen, John Varley, Lawrence Watt-Evans, and Roger Zelazny.

**Other books you might like:**
Michael Bishop, *Count Geiger's Blues*, 1992
Michael Kandel, *Captain Jack Zodiac*, 1992
Stan Lee, *The Ultimate Spider-Man*, 1994
  editor
George R.R. Martin, *The Wild Cards Series*, 1987-1995
Victor Milan, *Turn of the Cards*, 1993
Melinda M. Snodgrass, *Double Solitaire*, 1992

**5568**

### JULES VERNE

## *Paris in the Twentieth Century*

(New York: Random House, 1996)

**Story type:** Science Fiction (Dystopian; Satire)
**Major character(s):** Michael Dufrenoy, Writer (poet), Orphan; Quinsonnas, Accountant, Musician
**Time period(s):** 1960s (1960-1961)
**Locale(s):** Paris, France

**Summary:** Denied artistic satisfaction at his bank job, Michael searches for higher meaning and love in a society which worships business and technology advance. Written, rejected by a publisher, and filed away, Verne's second novel remained lost for 125 years before its rediscovery by Verne's great-grandson and translation into English by Richard Howard. Includes a 17-page analytical introduction by Eugen Weber.

**Other books you might like:**
Edward Bellamy, *Looking Back 2000-1887*, 1888
Ray Bradbury, *Fahrenheit 451*, 1953
Aldous Huxley, *Brave New World*, 1932
George Orwell, *1984*, 1949
H.G. Wells, *When the Sleeper Wakes*, 1899

**5569**

### GORE VIDAL

## *Live From Golgotha: A Novel*

(New York: Random House, 1992)

**Story type:** Science Fiction (Satire; Theological)
**Major character(s):** Timothy "Timmy", Religious (Bishop of Macedonia), Writer; Chester "Chet" W. Claypoole, Businessman, Television (executive)
**Time period(s):** 1st century (96); 1990s (1992)
**Locale(s):** Thessalonika, Greece (Macedonia); Rome, Italy

**Summary:** While a computer hacker's virus deletes tapes describing the Good News, a 20th century television executive uses holographic projections through time to convince Timothy to write a gospel resistant to the Hacker's evil virus. The NBC executive, Chet Claypoole, wants Timothy to anchor the spectacular show covering the Crucifixion, "*Live* from Golgotha," with 20th century televangelists and spiritualists providing commentary.

**Other books you might like:**
Neil Gaiman, *Good Omens: The Nice and Accurate Prophecies of Agnes Nutter, Witch*, 1990
  Terry Pratchett, co-author
Parke Godwin, *The Snake Oil Wars*, 1989
Parke Godwin, *Waiting for the Galactic Bus*, 1988
A.J. Langguth, *Jesus Christs*, 1968
Michael Moorcock, *Behold the Man*, 1970
Neal Stephenson, *Snow Crash*, 1992
Peter Ustinov, *The Old Man and Mr. Smith*, 1991

**5570**

### GORE VIDAL

## *The Smithsonian Institution*

(New York: Random House, 1998)

**Story type:** Fantasy (Literary; Alternate History)

**Major character(s):** T., Teenager, Genius; Mrs. Benjamin Harrison, Spirit, Historical Figure; Abraham Lincoln, Spirit, Historical Figure
**Time period(s):** 1930s (1939)
**Locale(s):** Washington, District of Columbia

**Summary:** Summoned to the Smithsonian Institution on Good Friday in 1998, T., a mathematically gifted orphan, finds worlds inside of worlds, returned dead, and doors to the past. On the edge of World War II, when history and physics will shift dramatically, one young man occupies a very odd ringside seat.

**Other books you might like:**
Jack Cady, *The Off Season*, 1995
Mark Helprin, *Winter's Tale*, 1983
Michael King, *Lorien Lost*, 1996
Tim Powers, *Expiration Date*, 1996
Thorne Smith, *The Night Life of the Gods*, 1931

## 5571

### JOAN D. VINGE

## Dreamfall

(New York: Warner Aspect, 1996)

**Story type:** Science Fiction (Psychic Powers; Political)
**Series:** Psion
**Major character(s):** Cat "Bian", Psychic (half Hydran-Psion); Miya, Alien (Hydran), Psychic (therapist); Naoh, Alien (Hydran), Revolutionary
**Time period(s):** Indeterminate Future
**Locale(s):** Refuge, Planet—Imaginary

**Summary:** On Refuge, home planet of the psychic Hydrans, Cat finds conditions deplorable for the native population. Tau Biotech mines the sacred reefs left by the alien Cloud Whales who no longer float over Hydran reservations. Consultant to the team called into study the Cloud Whales, Cat, tortured as a native, becomes embroiled in local politics.

**Other books you might like:**
Greg Bear, *Legacy*, 1995
David Brin, *Brightness Reef*, 1995
Emily Devenport, *Eggheads*, 1996
Alan Dean Foster, *Mid-Flinx*, 1995
Alis A. Rasmussen, *Revolution's Shore*, 1990

## 5572

### JOAN D. VINGE

## The Summer Queen

(New York: Warner Questar, 1991)

**Story type:** Science Fiction (Political; Family Saga)
**Series:** Snow Queen
**Major character(s):** Moon Dawntreader Summer, Ruler (Queen of Tiamat); BZ Gundhalinu, Police Officer, Judge; Reede Kulleva Kullervo, Genetically Altered Being, Researcher
**Time period(s):** Indeterminate Future
**Locale(s):** Tiamat, Planet—Imaginary; Ondinee, Planet—Imaginary

**Summary:** Due to BZ Gundhalinu's discoveries on World's End and Kullervo's genius in research, the Hegemony goes back to Tiamat to resume hunting the Mers whose blood grants immortality. Moon, the Summer Queen, knows that the Mers are vital to the functioning of the Hegemony so she and BZ Gundhalinu manage to stall the Hunt until Gundhalinu is arrested for treason by those factions determined to hunt the Mers. Kullervo, criminal and kidnapper though he is,

proves to be the key to stopping the slaughter, as he is an Avatar of Vanamoonen, co-designer of both Mers and Sybils.

**Other books you might like:**
C.J. Cherryh, *Cyteen*, 1988
Cynthia Felice, *Eclipses*, 1983
C.S. Friedman, *Black Sun Rising*, 1991
C.S. Friedman, *The Madness Season*, 1990
Mary Gentle, *Golden Witchbreed*, 1984
Jacqueline Lichtenberg, *Molt Brother*, 1982
Pamela Sargent, *Venus of Shadows*, 1988
A.C.H. Smith, *The Dark Crystal: A Novel*, 1982

## 5573

### VERNOR VINGE

## A Fire upon the Deep

(New York: Tor, 1992)

**Story type:** Science Fiction (Alternate Intelligence; First Contact)
**Major character(s):** Ravna Bergsndot, Librarian; Blueshell, Alien (Skroderider), Businessman (trader); Pham Nuwen, Religious (Godshattered), Reanimated Dead
**Time period(s):** Indeterminate Future
**Locale(s):** *Out of Band*, Spaceship; Tine's World, Planet—Imaginary

**Summary:** In a galaxy possessing variable physical laws, a research team unwittingly reassembles an inactive, malevolent artificial intelligence who immediately begins searching for that which had destroyed it, an immunizing program which barely escapes with the research team's children. While the malevolent entity destroys civilizations around the galaxy, Ravna, Blueshell and others rush to save or destroy the children held prisoner by intelligent colony creatures.

**Other books you might like:**
Roger MacBride Allen, *The Ring of Charon*, 1990
David Brin, *Earth*, 1990
Jeffrey A. Carver, *Down the Stream of Stars*, 1990
Glen Cook, *The Dragon Never Sleeps*, 1988
Rudy Rucker, *Software*, 1982
Rudy Rucker, *Wetware*, 1988
David Alexander Smith, *Homecoming*, 1990
David Alexander Smith, *Rendezvous*, 1988
Neal Stephenson, *Snow Crash*, 1992
John Varley, *Steel Beach*, 1992
Walter Jon Williams, *Angel Station*, 1989

## 5574

### ERIC VINICOFF
### MARCIA MARTIN, Co-Author

## The Weigher

(New York: Baen, 1992)

**Story type:** Science Fiction (First Contact; Political)
**Major character(s):** Slasher, Alien, Businesswoman (mediator); Ralphayers Delta, Clone (human), Genetically Altered Being; Pamayers Alpha, Clone (human), Explorer
**Time period(s):** Indeterminate Future
**Locale(s):** Planet—Imaginary (City of Coalgathering)

**Summary:** As Weigher of Coalgathering, a town of anarchic carnivorous predators, Slasher's Weighing rarely goes to the Challenge Field. After the third strange, dangerous-scented animal is killed despite Slasher's having spoken for it, Slasher's relief almost outweighs her curiosity and greed. Risking her life and position, Slasher contracts to broker the humans' information and ideas after they return smelling like grass.

**Other books you might like:**
Eleanor Arnason, *A Woman of the Iron People*, 1991
C.J. Cherryh, *Serpent's Reach*, 1980
Gordon R. Dickson, *The Alien Way*, 1965
Suzette Haden Elgin, *Twelve Fair Kingdoms*, 1981
Diana G. Gallagher, *The Alien Dark*, 1990
Donald E. McQuinn, *Warrior*, 1990
Larry Niven, *Tales of Known Space*, 1975
David Alexander Smith, *Homecoming*, 1990

### 5575

**DENISE VITOLA**

## Half-Light

(Lake Geneva, Wisconsin: TSR, 1992)

**Story type:** Science Fiction (Theological; Political)
**Major character(s):** Ariann Centuri, Military Personnel (commander), Religious; Winn Forrest, Religious, Government Official (viceroy); Stuk elan Emok, Alien (Benar), Spaceship Captain
**Time period(s):** Indeterminate Future
**Locale(s):** Alune, Planet—Imaginary; Corsicata, Planet—Imaginary; Benarus, Planet—Imaginary

**Summary:** Infected with a brain parasite during an attack on their expedition, Ariann finds herself forced to marry Winn to save her life and sanity. The hungry Benar look for "Humanities" to eat and now use a captured star chart to find where to get "meat." Ariann and Winn must link in religiously induced Half-Light to save Ariann and protect humanity from the Benar.

**Other books you might like:**
Aline Boucher-Kaplan, *World Spirits*, 1991
Jeffrey A. Carver, *Dragons in the Stars*, 1992
Adrian Cole, *Mother of Storms*, 1992
A.C. Crispin, *V*, 1984
Gordon R. Dickson, *The Alien Way*, 1965
Frank Herbert, *Dune*, 1965
Larry Niven, *The Mote in God's Eye*, 1974
    Jerry Pournelle, co-author
Sheri S. Tepper, *Raising the Stones*, 1990

### 5576

**DENISE VITOLA**

## Manjinn Moon

(New York: Ace, 1998)

**Story type:** Science Fiction (Mystery; Dystopian)
**Series:** Ty Merrick
**Major character(s):** Ty Merrick, Detective—Police; Andy Larue, Detective—Police
**Time period(s):** 21st century
**Locale(s):** East Coast

**Summary:** Overpopulation, pollution, and government corruption have remade North America into a dismal nation divided into administrative districts. Ty Merrick, a police detective, investigates a series of heart attacks among government agents which seem like too much of a coincidence, and discovers a clever assassin.

**Other books you might like:**
Patricia Anthony, *Happy Policeman*, 1994
Wilhelmina Baird, *Clipjoint*, 1994
Eric James Fullilove, *Circle of One*, 1996

Lee Killough, *Dragon's Teeth*, 1990
Mel Odom, *Lethal Interface*, 1992

### 5577

**DENISE VITOLA**

## Opalite Moon

(New York: Ace, 1997)

**Story type:** Fantasy (Mystery)
**Major character(s):** Ty Merrick, Detective—Police (district marshals office), Werewolf; Andy LaRue, Detective—Police (district marshals office)
**Time period(s):** 21st century
**Locale(s):** United States

**Summary:** Ty Merrick, a detective with a scientifically explicable case of acquired lycanthropy, can shapeshift for greater strengh and cunning. She is chosen to investigate a series of murders that lead her to the Opalite, a cult that believes in the existence of the supernatural and practices rituals in obedience to it. Sequel to *Quantum Moon*.

**Other books you might like:**
Pamela Dean, *The Dubious Hills*, 1994
Laurell K. Hamilton, *Guilty Pleasures*, 1993
Laurell K. Hamilton, *The Lunatic Cafe*, 1996
Tanya Huff, *Blood Price*, 1991
Nick Pollotta, *Full Moonster*, 1992

### 5578

**GERALD VIZENOR**

## Dead Voices: Natural Agonies in the Real World

(Norman, Oklahoma: University of Oklahoma Press, 1992)

**Story type:** Fantasy (Legend; Urban)
**Major character(s):** Bagese Bear, Animal (bear), Indian; I "Laundry", Writer
**Time period(s):** 1970s (1979); 1990s (1992)
**Locale(s):** Oakland, California

**Summary:** To preserve Indian cultural heritage, Bagese Bear encourages the author to discover the voice within as she retells her stories to the author with the understanding that he not write them down since the stories' validity lies in their oral presentation. Each day Bagese tries to view the world through the eyes of some particular animal or sometimes as the Trickster would see the world. Her stories range from creation mythology to the unfortunate innovations visited upon Indian life by the dominant Western culture.

**Other books you might like:**
Richard Erdoes, *American Indian Myths and Legends*, 1984
    Alfonso Ortiz, co-editor
Peter Gadol, *Coyote*, 1990
Barry Lopez, *Crow and Weasel*, 1990
Howard Norman, *Northern Tales: Traditional Stories of Eskimo and Indian Peoples*, 1980
Ben Okri, *The Famished Road*, 1992
Paul Radin, *The Trickster*, 1972

## 5579

### CYNTHIA VOIGT

## On Fortune's Wheel

(New York: Atheneum, 1990)

**Story type:** Fantasy (Adventure; Young Adult)
**Series:** Jackaroo
**Major character(s):** Biale, Runaway; Orien, Nobleman, Thief
**Time period(s):** Indeterminate Past (pre-Industrial Revolution)
**Locale(s):** The Kingdom, Alternate Earth

**Summary:** Biale, the runaway Innkeeper's daughter, meets up with the itinerant, incognito Orien, a lord's son. They leave the confines of the structured society of their homeland, The Kingdom, for adventures in the free-wheeling southern lands. There Biale falls into slavery, and The Kingdom starts to look more attractive. ALA Best Young Adult book.

**Other books you might like:**
Lloyd Alexander, *Westmark*, 1981
Eleanor Arnason, *The Sword Smith*, 1978
Diana Wynne Jones, *Cart and Cwidder*, 1977
Ellen Kushner, *Swordspoint*, 1988
Sherwood Smith, *Wren to the Rescue*, 1990
Gene Wolfe, *The Devil in a Forest*, 1976

## 5580

### WILLIAM T. VOLLMANN

## The Ice-Shirt

(New York: Viking, 1990)

**Story type:** Fantasy (Historical)
**Series:** Seven Dreams
**Major character(s):** Freydis Eiriksdottir, Historical Figure; Leif Eiriksson, Historical Figure; Gudrid Thorbjornsdottir, Historical Figure
**Time period(s):** 11th century
**Locale(s):** Greenland; Vinland, North America

**Summary:** The Norse have settled in Greenland and send a colony to Vinland to exploit its riches. Rivalries and feuds among the colonists, especially between Gudrid, a Christian, and Freydis, who has made a pact with a demon, seriously weaken their community. Outside attacks by the native ''skraelings'' finally drive them out. In between is a collage of folklore, magic tales, and contemporary observations.

**Other books you might like:**
Nancy Varian Berberick, *Shadow of the Seventh Moon*, 1990
Orson Scott Card, *Red Prophet*, 1988
Ursula K. Le Guin, *Always Coming Home*, 1985
Ursula K. Le Guin, *The Left Hand of Darkness*, 1969

## 5581

### PAULA VOLSKY

## The Gates of Twilight

(New York: Bantam Spectra, 1996)

**Story type:** Fantasy (Adventure; Religious)
**Major character(s):** Renille vo Chaumelle, Civil Servant; Jathondi, Royalty; KhriNyad-Son, Religious
**Time period(s):** Indeterminate
**Locale(s):** Kahnderule, Fictional City; Aveshq, Fictional Country

**Summary:** The government of Vonahr holds an uneasy ascendancy over the Aveshquien people. When rumors of an uprising fed by KhriNyad-Son circulate, Renille, who grew up comfortable in both cultures, infiltrates the temple to uncover the plot. After a narrow escape, Renille takes cover at OodPray castle, the ancestral centerpiece of the Aveshquien empire, where he enlists the princess Jathandi into his mission to save the planet.

**Other books you might like:**
Lynn Flewelling, *Luck in the Shadows*, 1996
Katherine Kurtz, *Deryni Rising*, 1970
Will Shetterly, *The Liavek Series*, 1985-1990
   Emma Bull, co-editor
Robert Silverberg, *Lord Valentine's Castle*, 1980

## 5582

### PAULA VOLSKY

## Illusion

(New York: Bantam Spectra, 1992)

**Story type:** Fantasy (Political; Magic Conflict)
**Major character(s):** Eliste vo Derrivalle, Noblewoman (Exalted); Dref Zeenoson, Revolutionary; Whiss Valeur, Revolutionary, Leader (Protector)
**Time period(s):** Indeterminate
**Locale(s):** Vonahr, Fictional Country; Sherreen, Fictional City

**Summary:** Raised as Exalted with little opportunity for genuine interaction with the populace at large, Eliste travels to Sherreen expecting her position as Queen's Maid of Honor will provide excitement and marital prospects. Eliste occupies herself with learning proper court behavior until the desire for revolution among the intellectuals and middle class results in a revolt which overturns Eliste's way of life, forcing her to the streets in fear for her life. Whiss Valeur's usurpation turns especially ugly after he reanimates ancient weapons and begins public executions. When the philosophical leaders of the revolution become targets of dictator Valeur, popular sentiment turns against Valeur and his reign of terror. Realizing Valeur's rule to be worse in all respects than that of the former monarchy, revolutionary leaders ally with Exalted magicians in hope of overthrowing the tyrant.

**Other books you might like:**
Adrian Cole, *Mother of Storms*, 1992
R.A. MacAvoy, *King of the Dead*, 1991
R.A. MacAvoy, *Lens of the World*, 1990
Melanie Rawn, *Dragon Prince*, 1988
Melanie Rawn, *The Star Scroll*, 1989
Melanie Rawn, *Sunrunner's Fire*, 1990
Jack Vance, *The Green Pearl*, 1985
Jack Vance, *Lyonesse*, 1983
Jack Vance, *Madouc*, 1990

## 5583

### PAULA VOLSKY

## The White Tribunal

(New York: Bantam Spectra, 1997)

**Story type:** Fantasy (Political; Magic Conflict)
**Major character(s):** Tradain liMarchborg, Imposter, Sorcerer
**Time period(s):** Indeterminate Future
**Locale(s):** Upper Hetzia, Fictional Country; Lis Folaze, Fictional Country

**Summary:** After Tradain's father dies, falsely accused of performing frobidden practices by the White Tribunal, Tradain attempts to ruin his father's accusers by acquiring unusual powers through a demonic pact.

**Other books you might like:**
Susan Dexter, *The Wizard's Shadow*, 1993
Robin Hobb, *Assassin's Apprentice*, 1995
J.V. Jones, *The Baker's Boy*, 1995
J. Gregory Keyes, *The Waterborn*, 1996

---

**5584**

PAULA VOLSKY

## The Wolf of Winter

(New York: Bantam Spectra, 1993)

**Story type:** Fantasy (Magic Conflict; Political)
**Major character(s):** Varis, Royalty, Sorcerer; Shalindra, Royalty
**Time period(s):** Indeterminate
**Locale(s):** Rhazaulle, Fictional Country

**Summary:** When Prince Varis breaks the universal taboo of necromancy in his attempt to usurp the Wolfe Throne, his niece, Shalindra, proves the only hope for restoration of the kingdom's rightful heir, her brother.

**Other books you might like:**
Lois McMaster Bujold, *The Spirit Ring*, 1992
Laurell K. Hamilton, *Nightseer*, 1992
Marc Laidlaw, *Neon Lotus*, 1988
R.A. MacAvoy, *Lens of the World*, 1990
Martha Wells, *The Element of Fire*, 1990

---

**5585**

STEWART VON ALLMEN (Pseudonym of Stewart Wieck)
AIDA MUSANOVIC, Illustrator

## St. Vitus Dances Eternity: A Sarajevo Ghost Story

(Clarkston, Georgia: White Wolf, 1996)

**Story type:** Horror (Ghost Story)
**Series:** World of Darkness: Wraith
**Major character(s):** Dragos Miloslavic, Doctor
**Time period(s):** 1990s (1992)
**Locale(s):** Sarajevo, Bosnia-Hercegovina

**Summary:** In war-torn Bosina, the ghost of Dragos Miloslavic helps the newly dead adapt to their non-existence and avoid the dangers that can befall fledgling ghosts. Dragos's anguish over the war and bloodshed that has colored centuries of his country's history are further aggravated when he discovers from a mercenary Reaper that the souls he is saving are being forced into slavery by his overseers. The book is illustrated by Aida Musanovic, who has also translated the text into Bosnian on facing pages. All proceeds from the sale of the book go to the New Bosnian Fund. Michael Moorcock supplies an afterword.

**Other books you might like:**
Richard Lee Byers, *On a Darkling Plain*, 1995
Sam Chupp, *Sins of the Fathers*, 1995
Rick Hautala, *Beyond the Shroud*, 1996

---

**5586**

KENNETH VON GUNDEN

## Cry Wolf

(New York: Ace, 1992)

**Story type:** Science Fiction (Adventure)
**Series:** K-9 Corps
**Major character(s):** Ray Larken, Businessman (K-9 Corps), Adventurer; Beowulf, Animal (dog), Leader (pack's alpha dog)
**Time period(s):** Indeterminate Future
**Locale(s):** *Spirit of St. Louis*, Spaceship; Earth; Ghandi, Planet—Imaginary

**Summary:** Ray and the K-9 Corps team view post-disaster America when they travel to the Terran Federation Institute of Canine Genetics in Bethesda, Maryland, where they discover humans and dogs and rescue them from suspended animation. The newcomers join Ray's team as they take possession of their newly purchased planet then return to New York to rescue badly manipulated dogs.

**Other books you might like:**
David Brin, *The Uplift War*, 1987
Dean R. Koontz, *Watchers*, 1987
Clifford D. Simak, *City*, 1952
Cordwainer Smith, *The Best of Cordwainer Smith*, 1975
Cordwainer Smith, *Norstrilia*, 1975

---

**5587**

KENNETH VON GUNDEN

## The Sounding Stillness

(New York: Ace, 1993)

**Story type:** Science Fiction (Robot Fiction; Science Fiction)
**Major character(s):** Galen Yeager, Government Official (secret agent); Sam, Cyborg
**Time period(s):** Indeterminate Future
**Locale(s):** Costeau, Planet—Imaginary

**Summary:** After decades of living on the water world, Costeau, genetically altered humans and dolphins have sufficiently damaged Costeau to threaten their uneasy peace with the intelligent natives. Galen Yeager and Sam travel to Costeau from Earth to investigate the situation and find a way to reestablish peace.

**Other books you might like:**
David Brin, *Startide Rising*, 1983
Alexander Jablokov, *A Deeper Sea*, 1992
Joan Slonczewski, *Daughter of Elysium*, 1993
Joan Slonczewski, *A Door into Ocean*, 1986
David Alexander Smith, *In the Cube*, 1993

---

**5588**

KENNETH VON GUNDEN

## StarSpawn

(New York: Ace, 1990)

**Story type:** Science Fiction (First Contact)
**Major character(s):** Morrough, Knight; Brother Gregory, Religious (Friar)
**Time period(s):** Indeterminate Past (Middle Ages)
**Locale(s):** Outer Space

**Summary:** An alien spaceship lands on Earth to make repairs and accidentally releases an extraordinarily dangerous parasite. The aliens must then ally themselves with the primitive natives of Earth to recapture the parasite before it can do catastrophic damage to the planet. This is Von Gunden's first novel.

**Other books you might like:**
Poul Anderson, *The High Crusade*, 1960
John Dalmas, *Fanglith*, 1985
John Dalmas, *The Lantern of God*, 1989
John Dalmas, *The Lizard War*, 1989
F. Paul Wilson, *The Tery*, 1990

### 5589

**KENNETH VON GUNDEN**

## Under Fire

(New York: Ace, 1991)

**Story type:** Science Fiction (Adventure)
**Series:** K-9 Corps
**Major character(s):** Ray Larken, Businessman (K-9 Corps), Adventurer; Maria Valdez, Telepath, Leader (scout cat team); Beowulf, Animal (dog), Leader (pack's alpha dog)
**Time period(s):** Indeterminate Future
**Locale(s):** Hephaestus, Planet—Imaginary

**Summary:** Ray and his physician partner, Ake, with nine intelligent, speaking canines arrive on the volcanic jungle planet, Hephaestus, to accept a one-year Federation contract at the combination gem mine and prison colony. They team up with Maria and her intelligent, speaking, telepathic guard cats to protect miners from diggers, a hostile indigenous life form. Ray soon becomes interested in discovering more about the intelligent native species, the K'anii.

**Other books you might like:**
David Brin, *Startide Rising*, 1983
Alan Dean Foster, *Cat-A-Lyst*, 1991
Dean R. Koontz, *Watchers*, 1987
James H. Schmitz, *The Demon Breed*, 1968
Clifford D. Simak, *City*, 1952
Cordwainer Smith, *The Best of Cordwainer Smith*, 1975
Cordwainer Smith, *Norstrilia*, 1975
Michael D. Weaver, *My Father Immortal*, 1989

### 5590

**ELISABETH VONARBURG**

## In the Mothers' Land

(New York: Bantam Spectra, 1992)

**Story type:** Science Fiction (Post-Holocaust; Psychic Powers)
**Major character(s):** Lisbei of Bethely, Psychic; Tula, Psychic; Kelys, Teacher, Wanderer
**Time period(s):** Indeterminate Future
**Locale(s):** Bethely, Fictional City; Wardenberg, Fictional City

**Summary:** Lisbei, a very unusual child, grows up in a post-holocaust society run by women. Possessed of powers which she doesn't understand, Lisbei attempts to understand them and her world, threatening the order which her world has set up against the errors of the past. Translated by Jane Brierly.

**Other books you might like:**
Eleanor Arnason, *A Woman of the Iron People*, 1991
Octavia E. Butler, *Dawn*, 1987
Octavia E. Butler, *Mind of My Mind*, 1977
Suzy McKee Charnas, *Walk to the End of the World*, 1974
Marge Piercy, *He, She and It*, 1991
Joan Slonczewski, *A Door into Ocean*, 1986

Sheri S. Tepper, *The Gate to Women's Country*, 1988
Paul O. Williams, *The Breaking of Northwall*, 1980
Monique Wittig, *Les Guerilleres*, 1971

### 5591

**ELISABETH VONARBURG**

## Reluctant Voyagers

(New York: Bantam Spectra, 1995)

**Story type:** Science Fiction (Alternate Universe; Science Fantasy)
**Major character(s):** Catherine Rhymer, Teacher
**Time period(s):** 1980s
**Locale(s):** Montreal, Quebec, Canada; Alternate Earth

**Summary:** Catherine Rhymer wakes up to a Montreal changed from the one she knows. Her attempts to figure out her world lead her to subversive political activists and on a quest for understanding in the distant north country. Based on a series of short stories written 1977-1986 and translated from the French by Jane Brierley.

**Other books you might like:**
Eleanor Arnason, *Daughter of the Bear King*, 1987
Octavia E. Butler, *Dawn*, 1987
John Crowley, *Aegypt*, 1987
Ursula K. Le Guin, *The Lathe of Heaven*, 1971
Rachel Pollack, *Unquenchable Fire*, 1992

### 5592

**ELISABETH VONARBURG**

## The Silent City

(New York: Bantam Spectra, 1992)

**Story type:** Science Fiction (Genetic Manipulation; Post-Holocaust)
**Major character(s):** Paul "Papa" Kramer, Scientist; Marquande De Styx, Political Figure; Elisa, Genetically Altered Being
**Time period(s):** Indeterminate Future
**Locale(s):** The City, Europe

**Summary:** The City, a "temporary" shelter for the poisoned world above, supports the eight remaining humans and the ommechs, androids which allow the aged, failing residents to interact with the outside. Paul creates Elisa to withstand disease, attack and age to repopulate The City and prevent the destruction of the accumulated knowledge stored there. When all but the insane Paul die, Elisa must leave The City to survive, eventually becoming a leader of the Outsiders. Originally published in French in 1981. Translated by Jane Brierley.

**Other books you might like:**
Jeffrey A. Carver, *The Rapture Effect*, 1987
Marjorie Bradley Kellogg, *Harmony*, 1991
Ursula K. Le Guin, *The Left Hand of Darkness*, 1969
J.M. Morgan, *Desert Eden*, 1991
Pat Murphy, *The City, Not Long After*, 1989
Charles Oberndorf, *Sheltered Lives*, 1992
George Orwell, *1984*, 1949
Sheri S. Tepper, *Sideshow*, 1992
Michael D. Weaver, *My Father Immortal*, 1989

## 5593

**KURT VONNEGUT JR.**

### *Hocus Pocus or, What's the Hurry, Son?*

(New York: G.P. Putnam's Sons, 1990)

**Story type:** Science Fiction (Satire; Literary)
**Major character(s):** Eugene Debs Hartke, Professor (physics); Hiroshi Matsumoto, Administrator (warden); Alton Darwin, Convict (Athena State Prison)
**Time period(s):** 2000s (2001)
**Locale(s):** Scipio, New York (Tarkington College)

**Summary:** Eugene Hartke tells the tale of his progress from Vietnam to professor for learning disabled rich kids, to warden of the local prison, to prisoner. In the process, he also tells the story of the United States being abandoned by its foreign investors and left to its own fate.

**Other books you might like:**
Philip K. Dick, *A Scanner Darkly*, 1977
Mark Leyner, *My Cousin, My Gastroenterologist*, 1990
Edgar Pangborn, *Davy*, 1964
Frederik Pohl, *Gladiator-at-Law*, 1955
Tom Robbins, *Another Roadside Attraction*, 1971
Bruce Sterling, *Islands in the Net*, 1988

## 5594

**KURT VONNEGUT JR.**

### *Timequake*

(New York: Putnam, 1997)

**Story type:** Science Fiction (Time Travel; Contemporary Realism)
**Major character(s):** Kurt "Junior" Vonnegut, Writer; Kilgore Trout, Writer
**Time period(s):** 2000s (2001)
**Locale(s):** Earth

**Summary:** Junior finds an old manuscript for *Timequake*, which he decides to incorporate, in part, in an updated version. He calls the older sections "Timequake One" and includes anecdotes from Kilgore Trout's life from 1935 to 2001. In 2001 a timequake forces everyone on Earth to relive 10 years with no means of changing anything or avoiding errors.

**Other books you might like:**
Jack Finney, *From Time to Time*, 1995
Ken Grimwood, *Replay*, 1986
Pete Hautman, *Mr. Was*, 1996
Dan Simmons, *Hyperion*, 1989
Theodore Sturgeon, *The Ultimate Egoist*, 1994

## 5595

**JOHN VORNHOLT**

### *The Fabulist*

(New York: AvoNova, 1993)

**Story type:** Fantasy (Historical)
**Major character(s):** Aesop, Writer, Traveler; Xanthus, Professor
**Time period(s):** 6th century B.C.
**Locale(s):** Greece; Egypt; Babylon

**Summary:** Raised as a mute slave, Aesop's encounter with Isis and her muses results in his ability to create fantastic tales. With this gift, Aesop wanders throughout the ancient civilized world, entertaining

and enlightening all with his wit until meeting his fated destiny. Author's first non-Star Trek novel.

**Other books you might like:**
Dave Duncan, *The Reaver Road*, 1992
David Gemmell, *Lion of Macedon*, 1992
Tom Holt, *Goatsong*, 1990
Tom Holt, *The Walled Orchard*, 1991
Robert Watson, *Whilom*, 1990
Gene Wolfe, *Soldier of the Mist*, 1986

## 5596

**JOHN VORNHOLT**

### *Mind Meld*

(New York: Pocket, 1997)

**Story type:** Science Fiction (Psychic Powers; Space Opera)
**Series:** Star Trek
**Major character(s):** Spock, Alien (Vulcan), Companion (chaperone); Teska, Alien (Vulcan), Telepath; James T. Kirk, Spaceship Captain
**Time period(s):** 23rd century
**Locale(s):** Rigel V, Planet—Imaginary; *U.S.S. Enterprise*, Spaceship; United Federation of Planets, Interstellar Empire/Federation

**Summary:** When Ambassador Sarek makes arrangements to promote unity between Romulans and Vulcans through the betrothal of a young Vulcan girl to a Romulan boy, Spock agrees to act as the "uncle" in the upcoming ceremonies. A stopover on Rigel en route to Vulcan turns deadly when Teska mindmelds with a dying man, learning the murderer's identity. She and Spock flee from a criminal network determined to silence Teska's evidence forever, while Kirk and his crew rescue the intended bridegroom from kidnappers.

**Other books you might like:**
C.J. Cherryh, *Angel with the Sword*, 1985
Michael Jan Friedman, *Crossover*, 1995
Eric James Fullilove, *Circle of One*, 1996
Lynn S. Hightower, *Alien Blues*, 1992
Jean Lorrah, *The Vulcan Academy Murders*, 1984
Jeri Taylor, *Unification*, 1991

## 5597

**JOHN VORNHOLT**

### *Sanctuary*

(New York: Pocket, 1992)

**Story type:** Science Fiction (Space Opera)
**Series:** Star Trek
**Major character(s):** James T. Kirk, Spaceship Captain; Spock, Scientist, Alien (Vulcan); Leonard McCoy, Doctor
**Time period(s):** 23rd century
**Locale(s):** Sanctuary, Planet—Imaginary; *U.S.S. Enterprise*, Spaceship

**Summary:** The *Enterprise* pursues the notorious pirate, Auk-Rex, to an unknown planet in an unexplored sector where Kirk, Spock and McCoy follow the pirate vessel down to the planet's surface. They learn that a race called Senites rules Sanctuary, to which anyone may come, regardless of their criminal or political activities, but no one may leave. With their communicators nonfunctional and their shuttlecraft gone, the three Starfleet officers journey across the surface in search of a way to return to their ship while Commander Scott orbits the planet along with a Klingon cruiser and a beautiful Orion bounty hunter.

**Other books you might like:**
Arthur C. Clarke, *A Fall of Moondust*, 1961
Hal Clement, *Mission of Gravity*, 1968
Barbara Hambly, *Ishmael*, 1985
Larry Niven, *Ringworld*, 1970
Joanna Russ, *Picnic on Paradise*, 1968
Howard Weinstein, *Deep Domain*, 1987

---

**5598**

JOHN VORNHOLT

## Voices

(New York: Dell, 1995)

**Story type:** Science Fiction (Space Colony; Psychic Powers)
**Series:** Babylon 5
**Major character(s):** Susan Ivanova, Military Personnel, Telepath; Michael Garibaldi, Military Personnel, Security Officer; Talia Winters, Telepath, Fugitive
**Time period(s):** 23rd century (2258)
**Locale(s):** Babylon 5, Space Station; Interstellar Empire/Federation; Earth

**Summary:** A bombing during a Psi Corps convention brings suspicion onto Babylon 5's resident telepath, Talia Winters. When Talia escapes confinement, neither Susan Ivanova nor Michael Garibaldi can help overtly as Talia flees her Psi Corps pursuers. First of a television tie-in series.

**Other books you might like:**
Alfred Bester, *The Stars My Destination*, 1956
J.M. Dillard, *Emissary*, 1993
Jim Mortimore, *Clark's Law*, 1996
Allen Steele, *Clarke County, Space*, 1990
Lois Tilton, *Accusations*, 1995

---

**5599**

KARL EDWARD WAGNER, Editor

## Echoes of Valor III

(New York: Tor, 1991)

**Story type:** Fantasy (Anthology; Sword and Sorcery)
**Series:** Echoes of Valor

**Summary:** This book contains eight stories originally published in 1930's periodicals from five authors with brief introductions by Wagner. Included are Robert E. Howard's only story of Sonya of Rogatino (Red Sonya), "The Shadow of the Vulture," the complete saga of Henry Kuttner's Prince Raynor and Eblik the Nubian in "Cursed Be the City" and "The Citadel of Darkness," the first reprint in 50 years of Manly Wade Wellman's "Hok Goes to Atlantis," and Jack Williamson's "Wolves of Darkness," a primeval horror tale. The final section contains three stories by Nictzin Dyalhis (1880-1942) preceded by Sam Moskowitz's 22-page, original biography and discussion of the mysterious literary figure's work, "Nictzin Dyalhis: Mysterious Master of Fantasy."

**Other books you might like:**
Glen Cook, *The Black Company*, 1984
L. Sprague de Camp, *The Fantastic Swordsmen*, 1967
    editor
L. Sprague de Camp, *Swords and Sorcery*, 1963
    editor
L. Sprague de Camp, *Warlocks and Warriors*, 1970
    editor
Phyllis Eisenstein, *In the Red Lord's Reach*, 1989

Robert E. Howard, *The Coming of Conan*, 1953
Robert E. Howard, *Conan the Barbarian*, 1955
Fritz Leiber, *The Leiber Chronicles*, 1990
Will Shetterly, *Liavek*, 1985
    Emma Bull, co-editor

---

**5600**

KARL EDWARD WAGNER

## Exorcisms and Ecstasies

(Minneapolis: Fedogan & Bremer, 1997)

**Story type:** Horror (Collection)

**Summary:** Thirty-two previously uncollected stories and fragments by a leading horror writer and editor who died in 1994. Included are "Did They Get You to Trade" and "I've Come to Talk with You Again," about the desperate measures by which a rock music star and a celebrated writer (respectively) sustain their fading reputations; the vampire stories "The Slug" and "Prince of the Punks"; the medical horror stories "But You'll Never Follow Me" and "The Final Cut"; and the exceptional haunted house story "Cedar Lane." Five selections feature the author's well-known sword and sorcery anti-hero Kane. Included as well are the science fiction story "Killer," written in collaboration with David Drake, and "The Coming of Ghor," a pastiche of Robert E. Howard's fiction contributed to the episodic novel *Genseric's Fifth-Born Son*. Edited by Stephen Jones, who has included appreciations by Ramsey Campbell, David Schow, Peter Struab and others, as well as a comprehensive bibliography of Wagner's writing.

**Other books you might like:**
Ramsey Campbell, *Strange Things and Stranger Places*, 1993
Dennis Etchison, *The Blood Kiss*, 1988
Brian Hodge, *The Convulsion Factory*, 1996
Joe R. Lansdale, *By Bizarre Hands*, 1989
Robert R. McCammon, *Blue World*, 1990
F. Paul Wilson, *Soft and Others*, 1989

---

**5601**

KARL EDWARD WAGNER, Editor
GERALD PAGE, Co-Editor

## Horrorstory III

(Lancaster, Pennsylvania: Underwood-Miller, 1991)

**Story type:** Horror (Anthology)

**Summary:** This repackaging of DAW's *The Year's Best Horror Stories*, Series VII (edited by Gerald Page), VIII and IX (edited by Karl Edward Wagner) brings together 40 of the best horror stories written in the years 1978-80. Top selections include T.E.D. Klein's homage to H.P. Lovecraft, "Black Man with a Horn," ghost stories in the classic and modern tradition by (respectively) Canon Basil Smith ("The Propert Bequest") and Charles L. Grant ("Hear Me Now, My Sweet Abbey Rose"), tales of psychological horror by Harlan Ellison ("All the Birds Come Home to Roost") and Alan Ryan ("Sheets"), *contes cruel* by Dennis Etchison and Ramsey Campbell ("The Dead Line," "Heading Home") and two stories by Stephen King.

**Other books you might like:**
Ellen Datlow, *The Year's Best Fantasy and Horror: Fourth Annual Collection*, 1991
    Terry Windling, co-editor
Stephen Jones, *Best New Horror 2*, 1991
    Ramsey Campbell, co-editor

Robert Morrish, *Quick Chills II*, 1992
    Peter Enfantino, co-editor

## 5602

### KARL EDWARD WAGNER

### *Horrorstory IV*

(Lancaster, Pennsylvania: Underwood-Miller, 1990)

**Story type:** Horror (Anthology)

**Summary:** A three-in-one compilation of *The Year's Best Horror Stories X* (1982), *XI* (1983) and *XII* (1984) that collects 52 excellent stories. Five were written by Ramsey Campbell, among them his tale of a haunted movie house, "The Show Must Go On." Included are Dennis Etchison's World Fantasy Award thriller, "The Dark Country," Stephen King's Castle Rock fantasy, "Uncle Otto's Truck," Scott Bradfield's delicate "The Flash! Kid" and Harlan Ellison's tale of psychic violation, "Broken Glass."

**Other books you might like:**
Ellen Datlow, *The Year's Best Fantasy and Horror Series*, 1988-1991
Peter Enfantino, *Quick Chills*, 1990
Stephen Jones, *Best New Horror*, 1990-1991
    Ramsey Campbell, co-author

## 5603

### KARL EDWARD WAGNER

### *Horrorstory V*

(Lancaster, Pennsylvania: Underwood-Miller, 1990)

**Story type:** Horror (Anthology)

**Summary:** A three-in-one compilation of *The Year's Best Horror Stories XIII* (1985), *XIV* (1986) and *XV* (1987) that brings together 55 of the best horror stories published over three years. Outstanding among these are two of three written by David Schow: "Coming Soon to a Theatre Near You" about a monster-ridden movie house, and the World Fantasy Award-winning "Red Light," concerned with a starlet's relationship with the camera and her audience. Also notable are Dennis Etchison's tale of writers and readers, "Talking in the Dark," Joe Lansdale's post-apocalyptic nightmare, "Tight Little Stitches in a Dead Man's Back," Stephen King's story of another reality, "Mrs. Todd's Shortcut," and Robert Bloch's update of the Dracula legend, "The Yougoslaves."

**Other books you might like:**
Ellen Datlow, *The Year's Best Fantasy and Horror Series*, 1988-1991
    Terry Windling, co-author
Peter Enfantino, *Quick Chills*, 1990
Stephen Jones, *Best New Horror*, 1990-1991
    Ramsey Campbell, co-author

## 5604

### KARL EDWARD WAGNER

### *Intensive Scare*

(New York: DAW 1990)

**Story type:** Horror (Anthology)

**Summary:** Thirteen stories of medical horror ranging in style from the gothic shockers, "The Body Snatcher" by Robert Louis Stevenson and "Herbert West: Reanimator" by H.P. Lovecraft, to the SF-

horror of Cyril Kornbluth's "The Little Black Bag," to Richard McKenna's bittersweet fantasy "Casey Agonistes." Of special note are Dennis Etchison's moving parable of organ donation, "The Dead Line," and Michael Shea's masterpiece of visceral horror, "The Autopsy."

**Other books you might like:**
Groff Conklin, *Great Science Fiction about Doctors*, 1965
    Noah D. Fabricant, co-author

## 5605

### KARL EDWARD WAGNER

### *The Year's Best Horror Stories XVIII*

(New York: DAW, 1990)

**Story type:** Horror (Anthology)

**Summary:** Twenty-three stories and three poems that reflect the richness of the annual horror yield. The best of the best include Ramsey Campbell's homage to M.R. James, "The Guide," Nicholas Royle's story of urban paranoia, "Archway," Ian McDowell's atmospheric tale of a backwoods legend, "On the Dark Road," and David Schow's ferociously funny satire of evangelical religion, "Jerry's Kids Meet Wormboy."

**Other books you might like:**
Ellen Datlow, *The Year's Best Fantasy and Horror: Third Annual Collection*, 1990
    Terry Windling, co-author
Peter Enfantino, *Quick Chills*, 1990
Stephen Jones, *Best New Horror*, 1990
    Ramsey Campbell, co-author

## 5606

### KARL EDWARD WAGNER, Editor

### *The Year's Best Horror Stories XX*

(New York: DAW, 1992)

**Story type:** Horror (Anthology)

**Summary:** The twentieth volume in the longest-running of the annual best-of-horror collections brings together 22 exceptional British and American horror stories published in 1991. Included are Alan Brennert's Nebula-Award winning tale of the horrors of Vietnam, "Ma Qui"; Ramsey Campbell's tale of Grecian horror, "The Same in Any Language"; Brian Lumley's original vampire story, "The Picnickers"; Robert S. Fuqua's story of a satanic music deal, "The Sharps and Flats Guarantee"; and Philip Nutman's hardcore riff on Thomas Mann's *Death in Venice*, "Churches of Desire."

**Other books you might like:**
Ellen Datlow, *The Year's Best Fantasy and Horror Series*, 1988-1996
    Terri Windling, co-editor
Stephen Jones, *Best New Horror*, 1990-1992
    Ramsey Campbell, co-editor
Robert Morrish, *The Quick Chills Series*, 1989-1992
    Peter Enfantino, co-editor

## 5607

**KARL EDWARD WAGNER**, Editor

### The Year's Best Horror Stories XXI

(New York: DAW, 1993)

**Story type:** Horror (Anthology)

**Summary:** The latest in this long running series of horror fiction anthologies that strongly favors the small press includes 27 stories, including perennial Ramsey Campbell's erotic horror tale, "The Limits of Fantasy"; two stories on nuclear holocaust, W.M. Shockley's "A Father's Gift" and Yvonne Navarro's "Feeding the Masses"; Ron Weighell's vampire tale, "China Rose"; Kim Antieau's tale of a rape victim's bizarre strategy for self-defense and forgetfulness, "Briar Rose"; Rick Kennet's Jamesian ghost tale, "The Outsider"; and Rand Soellner's gremlin story, "Mom School."

**Other books you might like:**
Ellen Datlow, *The Year's Best Fantasy and Horror: Sixth Annual Collection*, 1993
    Terri Windling, co-editor
Stephen Jones, *Best New Horror 4*, 1993
    Ramsey Campbell, co-editor

## 5608

**KARL EDWARD WAGNER**, Editor

### The Year's Best Horror Stories XXIII

(New York: DAW, 1994)

**Story type:** Horror (Anthology)

**Summary:** The last volume in this long-running series, completed shortly before the death of its editor, brings together 31 stories published in a variety of professional and semi-professional venues. Highlights include Ted Klein's tale of a ravenous sleeping bag, "One Size Eats All"; David Langford's shapeshifter tale, "Lions in the Desert"; Robert Devereaux's chilling rendering of infidelity and murder as a slapstick routine, "Ridi Bobo"; Chet Williamson's tale of an aging serial murderer, "Perfect Days"; Dennis Etchison's tale of urban menace, "A Little-Known Side of Elvis"; and Terry Lamsley's World Fantasy Award-winning novella of a strange race who live underground in British coal-mining country, "Under the Crust."

**Other books you might like:**
Ellen Datlow, *The Year's Best Fantasy and Horror: Seventh Annual Collection*, 1994
    Terri Windling, co-editor
Stephen Jones, *Best New Horror 5*, 1995
    Ramsey Campbell, co-editor

## 5609

**KATIE WAITMAN**

### The Merro Tree

(New York: Ballantine Del Rey, 1997)

**Story type:** Science Fiction (Arts; Political)
**Major character(s):** Mikk, Actor (Performance Master), Alien (Vyzanian); Thissizz, Alien (Droos), Singer; Huud Maroc, Actor (Performance Master), Alien (Vyzanian)
**Time period(s):** Indeterminate Future
**Locale(s):** Kekoi, Planet—Imaginary; Droos, Planet—Imaginary

**Summary:** The galaxy's most revered Performance Master, Mikk, stands trial for his life after performing the Somalite songdance in defiance of a galactic ban. First novel.

**Other books you might like:**
Octavia E. Butler, *The Xenogenesis Trilogy*, 1987-1989
Orson Scott Card, *The Worthing Saga*, 1990
Robert A. Heinlein, *Double Star*, 1956
Anne Mason, *The Stolen Law*, 1986
Spider Robinson, *Stardance*, 1986
    Jeanne Robinson, co-author
Mary Rosenblum, *The Stone Garden*, 1995

## 5610

**H. RUSSELL WAKEFIELD**

### The Clock Strikes Twelve

(Ashcroft, British Columbia: Ash-Tree Press, 1998)

**Story type:** Horror (Collection)

**Summary:** This collection includes 21 stories, most featuring ghosts and some with a mordantly humorous streak, including "Lucky's Grove," in which a Christmas tree taken from a forest protected by the primitive god Loki, is a source of havoc in the household of the unwitting owner who cut it down. Selections also include "Farewell Performance" and "Out of the Wrack I Rise," in which stage performers are revealed to be murderers when the ghosts of their victims insinuate themselves into their stage shows, and "A Fishing Story," about the ghost that haunts the waters where its body was drowned. Includes the prefatory essay "Why I Write Ghost Stories" and an introduction by Barbara Roden. Three previously uncollected stories have been added to this full reprint of the original 1939 edition.

**Other books you might like:**
E.F. Benson, *The Collected Ghost Stories of E.F. Benson*, 1992
A.M. Burrage, *Someone in the House: Strange Stories Old and New*, 1997
Bernard Capes, *The Black Reaper*, 1998
L.P. Hartley, *The Travelling Grave and Other Stories*, 1948
William Fryer Harvey, *Midnight Tales*, 1946

## 5611

**H. RUSSELL WAKEFIELD**

### Imagine a Man in a Box

(Ashcroft, British Columbia: Ash-Tree Press, 1997)

**Story type:** Horror (Collection)

**Summary:** Thirteen tales of horror, mystery, science fiction and social comedy by one of the best known writers of ghost stories in the twentieth century. Selections include "Damp Sheets," a tale of supernatural revenge; "Frontier Guards," in which a pair of ghost-busters greatly underestimates the haunted house they are exploring; "Dream-Day in Macedon," a tale of psychic synchronicity; the humorous ghost story "Corporal Humpit of the 4th Musketeers," and "The Central Figure," in which a playwright discovers that his life has begun uncannily to imitate one of his tragic stage productions. First published in 1931.

**Other books you might like:**
E.F. Benson, *The Collected Ghost Stories of E.F. Benson*, 1992
A.M. Burrage, *Someone in the Room: Strange Tales Old and New*, 1931
M.P. Dare, *Unholy Relics*, 1947
L.P. Hartley, *The Travelling Grave and Other Stories*, 1948

R.H. Malden, *Nine Ghosts*, 1943
A.N.L. Munby, *The Alabaster Hand and Other Ghost Stories*, 1949
L.T.C. Rolt, *Sleep No More*, 1948

## 5612

### HOWARD WALDROP

## A Dozen Tough Jobs

(Willimantic, CT: Ziesling, 1989)

**Story type:** Fantasy (Legend)
**Major character(s):** Invictus Ovidius "I.O." Lace, Orphan (Teenage narrator); Houlka Lee, Hero
**Time period(s):** 1920s (1926)
**Locale(s):** Mississippi

**Summary:** I.O. Lace tells the story of Houlka Lee, a convict serving time as a farm laborer. This is a retelling of the labors of Hercules, set in Mississippi.

**Other books you might like:**
Stephen Billias, *The Quest for the 36*, 1988
Donald Harington, *The Cockroaches of Stay More*, 1989

## 5613

### HOWARD WALDROP

## Going Home Again

(New York: St. Martin's Press, 1998)

**Story type:** Science Fiction (Collection)

**Summary:** This collection includes a six-page introduction by Lucius Shepard, a six-page introduction by Waldrop, a six-page bibliography, and individual afterwords to one original story as well as eight stories from periodicals, anthologies, a chapbook, and a literary conference program book dating between 1993 and 1997. Frequently humorous in tone, the stories explore diverse themes such as music, Charles Dickens' "A Christmas Carol," alternative worlds, film, and a strange college experience.

**Other books you might like:**
Alfred Bester, *Virtual Unrealities: The Short Fiction of Alfred Bester*, 1997
Walter M. Miller Jr., *The Science Fiction Stories of Walter M. Miller, Jr.*, 1984
Cordwainer Smith, *The Rediscovery of Man*, 1993
Theodore Sturgeon, *The Ultimate Egoist*, 1994
John Varley, *The Persistence of Vision*, 1978

## 5614

### HOWARD WALDROP

## Night of the Cooters

(Kansas City, Missouri: Ursus Imprints, 1990)

**Story type:** Science Fiction (Collection)
**Major character(s):** Alfred Jarry, Historical Figure, Writer (poet); Jetboy, Hero, Pilot
**Time period(s):** 1940s (1946); 1890s
**Locale(s):** New York, New York; Paris, France

**Summary:** 10 stories written between 1986 and 1990 which mix science fiction, fantasy, alternate history and popular culture. It reprints "Thirty Minutes Over Broadway," the "origin story" of the popular Wild Card series, and premieres "Fin de Cycle," a historical

tale mixing poets, printers, filmmakers and writers against a backdrop of the notorious Dreyfus Affair.

**Other books you might like:**
James P. Blaylock, *The Paper Grail*, 1991
Pat Cadigan, *Patterns*, 1989
Lisa Goldstein, *The Dream Years*, 1985
Kim Newman, *The Night Mayor*, 1990
Tim Powers, *The Stress of Her Regard*, 1989

## 5615

### HOWARD WALDROP

## Strange Monsters of the Recent Past

(New York: Ace, 1991)

**Story type:** Science Fiction (Collection)

**Summary:** Containing 8 stories written between 1980 and 1989, this is an omnibus volume of *All About Strange Monsters of the Recent Past*, 1987, and *A Dozen Tough Jobs*, 1989, both small press productions. The stories are a mix of subtle alternate histories such as "The Lions Are Asleep This Night," and strangely approached science fiction ideas such as the doo-wop and UFO story "Flying Saucer Rock and Roll." "A Dozen Tough Jobs," a retelling of the Hercules myth set in 1926 Mississippi, is a striking example of Waldrop's unique approach to storytelling.

**Other books you might like:**
James P. Blaylock, *The Paper Grail*, 1991
Joe R. Lansdale, *The Magic Wagon*, 1986
George R.R. Martin, *The Armageddon Rag*, 1983
Pat Murphy, *Points of Departure*, 1990
Tim Powers, *The Stress of Her Regard*, 1989

## 5616

### BARBARA G. WALKER

## Amazon: A Novel

(New York: HarperCollins, 1992)

**Story type:** Fantasy (Satire; Time Travel)
**Major character(s):** Antiope, Warrior (Amazon), Time Traveler; Diane, Writer
**Time period(s):** 20th century
**Locale(s):** United States

**Summary:** Thrown thousands of years into her future, Antiope must adapt to the modern world, but finds the male-dominated society strange. Diane writes Antiope's biography, *Amazon*, which presents a detailed description of non-patriarchal society and spawns criticism and an Amazon fashion craze. On meeting a reincarnated enemy Antiope had killed thousands of years before, Antiope discovers an attraction to the man who could bring further tragedy into her life. A first novel.

**Other books you might like:**
Eleanor Arnason, *A Woman of the Iron People*, 1991
Suzette Haden Elgin, *And Then There'll Be Fireworks*, 1981
Suzette Haden Elgin, *The Grand Jubilee*, 1981
Suzette Haden Elgin, *Twelve Fair Kingdoms*, 1981
Carol Emshwiller, *Carmen Dog*, 1990
Parke Godwin, *The Snake Oil Wars*, 1989
Parke Godwin, *Waiting for the Galactic Bus*, 1988
James Morrow, *Only Begotten Daughter*, 1990

## 5617

### BARBARA G. WALKER

## *Feminist Fairy Tales*

(New York: HarperSanFrancisco, 1996)

**Story type:** Fantasy (Collection; Legend)

**Summary:** Contains a two-page introduction plus individual introductions to 28 stories contradicting the usual message of fairy tales for young girls, that their purpose in life should be decorative. Walker includes many traditional fairy tales, myths, and legends, primarily European, rewritten with modern feminist concepts and spirituality, along with new stories written in the same view.

**Other books you might like:**

Margaret Atwood, *Good Bones and Simple Murders*, 1994
George Alec Effinger, *Maureen Birnbaum, Barbarian Swordsperson: The Complete Stories*, 1993
James Finn Garner, *Once upon a More Enlightened Time*, 1995
Jody Lynn Nye, *Don't Forget Your Spacesuit, Dear*, 1996
   editor
Ethel Johnston Phelps, *Tatterhood and Other Tales*, 1978
   editor
Jack Zipes, *Don't Bet on the Prince*, 1987
   editor
Jack Zipes, *The Outspoken Princess and the Gentle Knight*, 1994
   editor

## 5618

### MARY ALEXANDER WALKER

## *The Scathach and the Maeve's Daughter*

(New York: Atheneum, 1990)

**Story type:** Fantasy (Legend; Contemporary)
**Major character(s):** The Scathach, Mythical Creature (Celtic), Spirit (shapechanger); Maeve Brigitta, Immigrant (pioneer); Maeve Nicole, Student, Veterinarian
**Time period(s):** 17th century; 2000s (2000)
**Locale(s):** England; Canada; New York, New York

**Summary:** When an 8th Century Irish lass, Maeve Moira, passed the Scathach's test, the Scathach pledges that all of her female descendants will have her attributes: a kind heart, healing hands, courage and wit. The Scathach then follows Maeve's family, helping Maeve Gwenna in the 12th century escape her cruel guardians in Brennith before the Black Plague devastates the town. In Canada the Scathach helps Maeve Brigitta acquire needed medicine from the Iroquois Indians. In modern New York City, the Scathach saves maeve Nicole from a gang of street toughs.

**Other books you might like:**

Mercedes Lackey, *Knight of Ghosts and Shadows*, 1990
   Ellen Guon, co-author
R.A. MacAvoy, *Tea with the Black Dragon*, 1983
Rosemary Sutcliff, *Sun Horse, Moon Horse*, 1977

## 5619

### SAGE WALKER

## *Whiteout*

(New York: Tor, 1996)

**Story type:** Science Fiction (Hard Science Fiction; Dystopian)
**Major character(s):** Signy Thomas, Computer Expert, Scientist; Pilar Videla, Artist, Lesbian; Paul Maury, Businessman, Lawyer

**Time period(s):** 2020s
**Locale(s):** Antarctica; Cyberspace; United States

**Summary:** Hired by a Japanese conglomerate to influence Antarctic treaty negotiations, members of the Edges partnership pursue research and production at disparate sites while communicating through intimate cybernetic connections. Drawn to Antarctica, one team member suffers apparent disaster, fracturing Edges' harmony and efficiency and driving Signy into a desperate search. First novel.

**Other books you might like:**

Wilhelmina Baird, *Crashcourse*, 1993
Pat Cadigan, *Synners*, 1991
Raphael Carter, *The Fortunate Fall*, 1996
Melissa Scott, *Trouble and Her Friends*, 1994
Neal Stephenson, *Snow Crash*, 1992

## 5620

### WILLIAM A. WALKER JR.

## *Dystopia*

(Marietta, Georgia: Marietta Publishing, 1997)

**Story type:** Horror (Collection)

**Summary:** A trio of stories comprise the author's first published book. "Sniper" is a futuristic tale of civil war complicated by a zombie menace. In "The Institute Man," an ambitious businessman enrolls in a rugged self-improvement program and learns belatedly the macabre price he must pay for his success. In "Pit 666," two criminals on the run get their just desserts from a supernatural menace. Signed limited edition chapbook, illustrated by Donald R. Owen III.

**Other books you might like:**

Brian Hopkins, *Something Haunts Us All*, 1996
Gerard Daniel Houarner, *Painfreak*, 1996
Bentley Little, *Murmerous Haunts*, 1997
Jeffrey Osier, *Horizon Lines*, 1997
Tom Piccirilli, *The Dog Syndrome and Other Sick Puppies*, 1997
Jeffrey Thomas, *Black Walls, Red Glass*, 1997
David Niall Wilson, *The Fall of the House of Escher and Other Illusions*, 1996

## 5621

### IAN WALLACE

## *Megalomania*

(New York: DAW Books, 1989)

**Story type:** Science Fiction (Space Opera)
**Series:** Croyd
**Major character(s):** Croyd, Businessman; Dino Trigg, Psychic
**Time period(s):** Indeterminate Future
**Locale(s):** Sol Galaxy, Interstellar Empire/Federation

**Summary:** Croyd's protege, Dino Trigg, uses his psychic powers in an attempt to undermine Croyd's position as chair of the board of directors that runs Sol Galaxy. When Croyd foils his attempt, Trigg plots to destroy the galaxy.

**Other books you might like:**

Phillip C. Jennings, *Tower to the Sky*, 1988
Daniel Keys Moran, *The Armageddon Blues*, 1988
Daniel Keys Moran, *Emerald Eyes*, 1988
Daniel Keys Moran, *The Long Run*, 1989
A.E. Van Vogt, *Null-A Three*, 1985
A.E. Van Vogt, *The Pawns of Null-A*, 1956
A.E. Van Vogt, *The World of Null-A*, 1948

## 5622

**PATRICIA WALLACE**

### Fatal Outcome
(New York: Zebra, 1992)

**Story type:** Horror (Wild Talents)
**Major character(s):** Alan Kramer, Doctor; Honor Matheson, Nurse; Shea Novak, Lawyer
**Time period(s):** 1990s
**Locale(s):** Idle Springs, Nevada

**Summary:** When maverick physician Alan Kramer opens up a clinic teaching patients how to harness the powers of their brains to heal themselves, he proves a godsend to the terminally ill who flock to take advantage of his services. That is, until it is discovered that the secret Affinity elixir that makes his treatment possible endows his patients with uncontrollable psychokinetic abilities.

**Other books you might like:**
John Arbucci, *Blood of Innocents*, 1991
Michael Hammond, *The Burning Man*, 1991

## 5623

**PATRICIA WALLACE**

### Monday's Child
(New York: Zebra, 1989)

**Story type:** Horror (Evil Children)
**Major character(s):** Jill Baker, Child; Noah Huston, Doctor
**Time period(s):** 1980s
**Locale(s):** Winslow, California

**Summary:** The townspeople grow increasingly suspicious and frightened of Jill Baker, the beautiful little girl with the mysterious birth, who increasingly becomes the focus for the progressively intensifying "accidents" that gradually decimate the entire town.

**Other books you might like:**
Lawrence Block, *Ariel*, 1980
John Saul, *Suffer the Children*, 1977
Bernard Taylor, *The Godsend*, 1976

## 5624

**PATRICIA WALLACE**

### Thrill
(New York: Zebra, 1990)

**Major character(s):** Sheldon Rice, Businessman; Wesley Davison, Engineer; Max Brown, Teenager
**Time period(s):** 1990s (1992)
**Locale(s):** McKenna's Creek, California

**Summary:** With the help of technological prodigy Wesley Davison, entrepreneur Sheldon Rice builds The Park, the world's largest amusement park. On opening day, technical malfunctions of a suspicious nature turn the park's rides and attractions into a nightmarish ordeal for patrons.

**Other books you might like:**
William W. Johnstone, *Carnival*, 1989
Richard Laymon, *Funland*, 1990
Owen West, *The Funhouse*, 1981
  Pseudonym of Dean R. Koontz; novelization of movie

## 5625

**R.R. WALTERS**

### Wind Chimes
(New York: Zebra, 1991)

**Story type:** Horror (Evil Children)
**Major character(s):** Megan Jordan, Child; Pamela Jordan, Businesswoman; Greg Jordan, Accountant
**Time period(s):** 1990s
**Locale(s):** Florida

**Summary:** Greg and Pamela Jordan are amused by their precocious daughter Megan's talk of her imaginary playmate Rosamond and the "Special Place" where they play, called Wunderland. That is, until the people Megan invites to come with her to Wunderland are found dead afterwards.

**Other books you might like:**
Stephen King, *The Shining*, 1977
Thomas Tryon, *The Other*, 1971
Patricia Wallace, *Monday's Child*, 1989

## 5626

**EVANGELINE WALTON**

### The Island of the Mighty
(New York: Collier, 1993)

**Story type:** Fantasy (Legend; Magic Conflict)
**Major character(s):** Gwydion ap Don, Magician, Royalty (Prince of Gwynedd); Arianrhod, Magician, Royalty; Math ap Mathonwy, Magician, Royalty (King of Gwynedd)
**Time period(s):** Indeterminate Past
**Locale(s):** Gwynedd, Wales

**Summary:** Peace deteriorates after Gwydion and his brother attempt to steal magical pigs belonging to Lord Pyrderi. The indiscretion brings consequences which later fall on Gwydion's son, Llew Llaw Gyffes, who must endure the burden of his father's actions and the curses of his unwilling mother. Reissue of the Fourth Branch of the Mabinogian, origianlly published in 1936 as *The Virgin and the Swine*.

**Other books you might like:**
John Bellairs, *The Face in the Frost*, 1969
Charles de Lint, *The Little Country*, 1991
Patrick K. Ford, *The Mabinogi and Other Medieval Welsh Tales*, 1977
  editor, translator
Fritz Leiber, *A Specter Is Haunting Texas*, 1969
Morgan Llywelyn, *The Horse Goddess*, 1982
A. Merritt, *Dwellers in the Mirage*, 1932
A. Merritt, *The Face in the Abyss*, 1931
A. Merritt, *The Ship of Ishtar*, 1926

## 5627

**DONALD WANDREI**

### Don't Dream
(Minneapolis, Minnesota: Fedgan & Bremer, 1997)

**Story type:** Horror (Collection)

**Summary:** Collection of twenty-six stories that represent the complete horror and fantasy fiction of a protege of H.P. Lovecraft who contributed primarily to the weird fiction pulps. Included are "The

Lives of Alfred Kramer," a tale of ancestral memory in which a man retraces his heritage back to his primordial origins; "The Nerveless Man," about a scientific experiment that renders a man insensitive to pain: "The Tree-Men of Mbwa," about a strange dimension where plant and animal life are indistinguishable from one another; and several stories of horrors from the sea, including "Spawn of the Sea," "Uneasy Lie the Drowned," and "Giant Plasm." The book is augmented with fourteen essays and prose poems, many previously unpublished. Edited by Philip J. Rahman and Dennis E. Weiler and illustrated by Roger Geberding.

**Other books you might like:**
Robert Bloch, *The Early Fears*, 1994
Arthur J. Burks, *Black Medicine*, 1966
Carl Jacobi, *Revelations in Black*, 1947
Frank Belknap Long, *The Hounds of Tindalos*, 1946
Clark Ashton Smith, *A Rendezvous in Averoigne*, 1989

## 5628

**HOWARD WANDREI**, Author/Illustrator

### Time Burial

(Minneapolis: Fedogan & Bremer, 1995)

**Story type:** Horror (Collection)

**Summary:** The twenty stories of fantasy, horror, and science fiction collected here constitute a first collection by a prolific writer for the pulps considered a peripheral member of H.P. Lovecraft's circle. "Macklin's Little Friend" and "The Black Farm" both feature human encounters with inexplicable monsters, while "The Wall" and "The God Box" feature the use and abuse of new discoveries by men. In "Exit Willy Carney," a criminal undergoes a gender change to avoid being apprehended. "Over Time's Threshold" is a surreal tale of a time travel experience, and "The Hand of the O'Mecca" a well-known tale of rural werewolves. Both "Here Lies" and "After You, Montagu" display the author's fondness for eccentric characters and humor. Dwayne Olson supplies a historical overview of Wandrei's life and writing.

**Other books you might like:**
Hugh B. Cave, *Death Stalks the Night*, 1995
Hugh B. Cave, *Murgunstrumm and Others*, 1977
Carl Jacobi, *Revelations in Black*, 1947
Frank Belknap Long, *The Hounds of Tindalos*, 1946
E. Hoffman Price, *Far Lands, Other Days*, 1975
Clark Ashton Smith, *Other Dimensions*, 1963
Donald Wandrei, *The Eye and the Finger*, 1944

## 5629

**ELISABETH WATERS**

### Changing Fate

(New York: DAW, 1994)

**Story type:** Fantasy (Romance; Adventure)
**Major character(s):** Acila, Noblewoman, Mythical Creature (shapechanger); Briam, Nobleman, Musician; Lord Ranulf, Nobleman
**Time period(s):** Indeterminate
**Locale(s):** Diadem, Fictional City

**Summary:** Forced to fight and then flee with her brother, Briam, when Lord Ranulf arrives to claim their dead father's castle, Acila survives the winter with a pack of wolves and then follows Briam to the court of a queen, who chooses him as her Year-King. Saving Briam from the Year-King's fate reveals secrets about Ranulf. First novel.

**Other books you might like:**
C.S. Friedman, *Black Sun Rising*, 1991
Patricia A. McKillip, *The Changeling Sea*, 1988
Tamora Pierce, *Alanna: The First Adventure*, 1983
Jennifer Roberson, *Shapechangers*, 1984
Sheri S. Tepper, *Song of Mavin Manyshaped*, 1985

## 5630

**GRAHAM WATKINS**

### Dark Winds

(New York: Berkley, 1989)

**Story type:** Horror (Ancient Evil Unleashed)
**Major character(s):** Elliot Collins, Professor (College); Nikki, Femme Fatale
**Time period(s):** 1960s; 1970s
**Locale(s):** New York, New York

**Summary:** Obsessed by a photograph of his late father's former lover, Elliot Collins pursues the image until he is drawn into a web of horror and intrigue that involves a dark family secret, ritual black magic, an ancient Aztec cult, a serial killer of women, and a seemingly immortal seductress. This is Watkins' first novel.

**Other books you might like:**
Mercedes Lackey, *Burning Water*, 1989
Michael Paine, *Owl Light*, 1989

## 5631

**GRAHAM WATKINS**

### Kaleidoscope Eyes

(New York: Carroll & Graf, 1993)

**Story type:** Horror (Erotic Horror)
**Major character(s):** Sam Leo, Doctor (epidemiologist); Stephanie Dixon, Doctor (pathologist); Selinde, Deity (Aztec)
**Time period(s):** 1990s (1993)
**Locale(s):** Outer Banks, North Carolina

**Summary:** Following his contact with Selinde, an Aztec deity heavily into sex and death, Sam Leo vacations with his friends at a secluded house on the North Carolina shore. Aided by the sense-enhancing power of a kaleidoscope, the quartet indulge in days of increasingly bizarre sexual games that will inevitably culminate in the sort of ritualistic sacrifice upon which the goddess thrives.

**Other books you might like:**
Warren Newton Beath, *Shock Lines*, 1993
Ashley McConnell, *Days of the Dead*, 1992
Al Sarrantonio, *House Haunted*, 1991

## 5632

**GRAHAM WATKINS**

### Virus

(New York: Carroll & Graf, 1995)

**Story type:** Horror (Science Fiction)
**Major character(s):** Mark Roberts, Doctor; Alex Walton, Doctor (psychiatrist); Drew Thompson, Businessman
**Time period(s):** 1990s (1995)
**Locale(s):** Durham, North Carolina

**Summary:** When Penny, the penultimate software program, meets a computer virus, she mutates into a sentient entity who subliminally manipulates computer users on the Internet to stay glued to their computer screens. An influx of exhausted computer hackers at the Duke University hospital compels doctors Mark Roberts and Alex Walton to get to the bottom of the problem, forcing Penny to turn more violent in her quest to ensure that nothing will stop her proliferation and worldwide spread.

**Other books you might like:**
Daniel H. Gower, *The Orpheus Process*, 1993
D.F. Jones, *Colossus*, 1966
Pierre Ouellette, *The Deus Machine*, 1994

**5633**

### IAN WATSON

## Chekhov's Journey

(New York: Carroll & Graf, 1989)

**Story type:** Science Fiction (Alternate Universe)
**Major character(s):** Anton Chekhov, Writer, Historical Figure
**Time period(s):** 1980s; 1890s (1890)

**Summary:** A Soviet film crew doing a motion picture about Chekhov's visit to Siberia attempts to improve the performance of their lead actor by an experiment in reincarnation through hypnosis. Unfortunately, their experiment goes awry and they accidentally succeed in changing history. Whereas Chekhov had originally gone to Siberia to visit a convict colony, he now becomes involved in the investigation of the famed Tunguska meteor, thereby changing Russian history. Originally published in 1983.

**Other books you might like:**
Gregory Benford, *What Might Have Been*, 1989
    Martin H. Greenberg, co-editor
Terry Bisson, *Fire on the Mountain*, 1988
John Crowley, *Novelty*, 1989
Keith Roberts, *Pavane*, 1968

**5634**

### IAN WATSON

## The Embedding

(New York: Carroll & Graf, 1990)

**Story type:** Science Fiction (First Contact)
**Major character(s):** Chris Sole, Scientist; Charlie Faith, Engineer
**Time period(s):** Indeterminate Future

**Summary:** In an English hospital a group of Pakistani orphans are brought up in complete isolation and taught a complex artificial language that changes the nature of reality for them. Simultaneously an anthropologist working in Brazil discovers a primitive tribe who, under the influence of a local drug, speaks a sophisticated language otherwise unknown to them. Our planet is contacted by the Sp'thra, a spacefaring alien race who gather languages from across the Galaxy in the hope of someday transcending reality. Originally published in 1973.

**Other books you might like:**
Samuel R. Delany, *Babel-17*, 1966
Samuel R. Delany, *The Splendor and Misery of Bodies, of Cities*, 1985
Samuel R. Delany, *Stars in My Pocket Like Grains of Sand*, 1984
Suzette Haden Elgin, *The Judas Rose*, 1987
Suzette Haden Elgin, *Native Tongue*, 1984
Jack Vance, *The Languages of Pao*, 1958
Kate Wilhelm, *Juniper Time*, 1979

**5635**

### IAN WATSON

## The Flies of Memory

(New York: Carroll & Graf, 1991)

**Story type:** Science Fiction (First Contact)
**Major character(s):** Charles Spark, Empath; Olivia Mendelssohn, Psychic, Security Officer; Kathinka, Religious, Guide
**Time period(s):** 21st century
**Locale(s):** Rome, Italy; Mars

**Summary:** A novel about memory, this book opens with an attempt to understand an alien race, the Flies, whose transportation of parts of Earth cities to Mars forces a small group of humans to follow. Once it reaches Mars, however, the group discovers it has a much longer and stranger journey to make.

**Other books you might like:**
James Blish, *A Case of Conscience*, 1958
William Gibson, *Neuromancer*, 1984
Lisa Goldstein, *The Dream Years*, 1985
Spider Robinson, *Stardance*, 1979
    Jeanne Robinson, co-author
Norman Spinrad, *Songs From the Stars*, 1980

**5636**

### IAN WATSON

## God's World

(New York: Carroll and Graf, 1990)

**Story type:** Science Fiction (Adventure; Theological)
**Major character(s):** Amy Dove, Sociologist
**Time period(s):** 21st century
**Locale(s):** *Pilgrim Crusader*, Spaceship; God's World, Moon—Imaginary (circling a gas giant in Orbit Around B2 Eridani; Askatharli Space)

**Summary:** When, in 1977, messages from God appear in worship centers demanding champions and representatives, a mission to God's World is mounted. When the Pilgrim Crusader arrives at God's World an attack forces Amy Dove and 5 pilots to abandon the ship, escaping to the moon. On the world they find an alien civilization partly in everyday reality and partly in heaven. Further investigation yields surprising revelations. Reprint of 1979 British edition.

**Other books you might like:**
Arthur C. Clarke, *Childhood's End*, 1953
Parke Godwin, *The Snake Oil Wars*, 1989
Parke Godwin, *Waiting for the Galactic Bus*, 1988
Robert A. Heinlein, *Job: A Comedy of Justice*, 1984

**5637**

### IAN WATSON

## Inquisitor

(Baltimore, Maryland: GW Books/Games Workshop, 1990)

**Story type:** Science Fiction (Political; Adventure)
**Series:** Warhammer 40,000
**Major character(s):** Jag Braco, Religious, Police Officer; Meh'Lindi, Spy; Grimm, Engineer, Warrior
**Time period(s):** Indeterminate Future
**Locale(s):** Stalinvast, Planet—Imaginary; The Eye of Terror, Outer Space (Planetary cluster—imaginary)

**Summary:** Jag Braco, an Imperial Inquisitor, and his companions are sent to assist in stopping a rebellion caused by alien monsters. During the mission they discover evidence of a conspiracy which they pursue from the chaos of the Eye of Terror to the throne of the Emperor.

**Other books you might like:**
Iain M. Banks, *Consider Phlebas*, 1991
C.J. Cherryh, *Cyteen*, 1988
Glen Cook, *The Dragon Never Sleeps*, 1988
Frank Herbert, *Dune*, 1965
Roger Zelazny, *Lord of Light*, 1967

## 5638

### IAN WATSON
### JOHN VARLEY, Co-Author

## Nanoware Time/The Persistence of Vision
(New York: Tor, 1991)

**Story type:** Science Fiction (Hard Science Fiction; Post-Holocaust)
**Major character(s):** Paul Royal, Experimental Subject; Succor-of-Yellowways-Sands, Alien (Hydra), Teacher; Pink, Farmer, Teenager
**Time period(s):** 21st century; 1990s
**Locale(s):** Montenegro; New Mexico (Navajo Nation)

**Summary:** Ian Watson's "Nanoware Time," published herein unabridged for the first time in book form, explores the gift of nanotechnology by aliens from Beta Hydri to suspicious humans who arrange to study the microscopic machines on an isolated lunar colony. John Varley's "The Persistence of Vision" received both a Hugo Award and Nebula Award for best story published in 1978. This poignant story examines a post-war agricultural commune for deaf-blind co-operators as seen through the eyes of a sighted and hearing visitor.

**Other books you might like:**
Pat Cadigan, *Mindplayers*, 1987
Jeffrey A. Carver, *From a Changeling Star*, 1989
Michael Flynn, *The Nanotech Chronicles*, 1991
Joan Slonczewski, *A Door into Ocean*, 1986
Cordwainer Smith, *The Best of Cordwainer Smith*, 1975
Marc Stiegler, *The Gentle Seduction*, 1990
Michael Swanwick, *Vacuum Flowers*, 1987
John Varley, *The Barbie Murders and Other Stories*, 1980
John Varley, *Blue Champagne*, 1986
John Varley, *The Persistence of Vision*, 1978

## 5639

### ROBERT WATSON

## Whilom
(New York: Atlantic Monthly Press, 1990)

**Story type:** Fantasy (Literary; Light Fantasy)
**Major character(s):** Nick Bottom, Artisan (weaver); Dewdrop, Animal (talking donkey); Theseus, Royalty (king)
**Time period(s):** Indeterminate Past
**Locale(s):** Greece (ancient)

**Summary:** Nick Bottom and his talking donkey meet Theseus on the road. Nick asks if his amateur theatrical group can perform at the palace for Theseus' upcoming engagement celebration. Theseus tests Nick's ability by commanding him to perform the role of messenger, not usually the safest part to play. A retelling of Midsummer Night's Dream.

**Other books you might like:**
L. Sprague de Camp, *The Undesired Princess and the Enchanted Bunny*, 1990
   David Drake, co-author
Alan Dean Foster, *Glory Lane*, 1990
Tom Holt, *Goatsong*, 1990
Deborah Smith, *Legends*, 1990
Jack Vance, *Madouc*, 1990
Patricia C. Wrede, *Snow White and Rose Red*, 1989

## 5640

### LAWRENCE WATT-EVANS

## The Blood of a Dragon
(New York: Ballantine/Del Rey, 1991)

**Story type:** Fantasy (Quest; Young Adult)
**Major character(s):** Dumery of Shiphaven, Child, Traveler; Kensher Kinner's Son, Rancher, Businessman; Teneria of Fishertown, Witch
**Time period(s):** Indeterminate
**Locale(s):** Hegemony of the Three Ethshars, Fictional Country; Barony of Sardiron, Fictional Country

**Summary:** Desperate to achieve apprenticeship, Dumery follows Kensher who he believes is a dragon hunter. Following Kensher proves harder than Dumery anticipated. Arriving at Kensher's home, Dumery discovers Kensher's true situation, one which does not allow for an apprentice. Meanwhile Teneria doggedly follows her assignment-to find Dumery and see him safely home.

**Other books you might like:**
Debra Doyle, *School of Wizardry*, 1990
   James D. Macdonald, co-author
Nancy Luenn, *Goldclimbers*, 1991
Anne McCaffrey, *The White Dragon*, 1978
J.R.R. Tolkien, *The Hobbit*, 1938
Patricia C. Wrede, *Dealing with Dragons*, 1990
Mary Frances Zambreno, *A Plague of Sorcerers*, 1991

## 5641

### LAWRENCE WATT-EVANS

## Crosstime Traffic
(New York: Ballantine Del Rey, 1992)

**Story type:** Science Fiction (Collection; Alternate Universe)

**Summary:** Contains a 16-page introduction which anecdotally elucidates the origins of the stories published in periodicals and anthologies 1975-1992, including the Hugo Award winning story "Why I Left Harry's All-Night Hamburgers." Also included are "Real Time," "Science Fiction," "Monster Kidnaps Girl at Mad Scientist's Command," "After the Dragon Is Dead" and 14 others.

**Other books you might like:**
Alfred Bester, *Star Light, Star Bright*, 1976
Carol Emshwiller, *The Start of the End of It All*, 1991
Damon Knight, *Tomorrow and Tomorrow*, 1973
Keith Laumer, *Alien Minds*, 1991
George R.R. Martin, *Portraits of His Children*, 1992
Pat Murphy, *Points of Departure*, 1990
James Tiptree Jr., *Her Smoke Rose Up Forever*, 1990
Howard Waldrop, *Strange Monsters of the Recent Past*, 1991

## 5642

**LAWRENCE WATT-EVANS**, Editor

### Newer York

(New York: Roc, 1991)

**Story type:** Science Fiction (Anthology)
**Time period(s):** Indeterminate Future
**Locale(s):** New York, New York

**Summary:** This thematic anthology about New York City contains a three-page introduction by the editor and 25 original stories including three collaborations, "Watching New York Melt" by Lawrence Watt-Evans and Julie Evans, "The Last Real Newyorker in the World" by James D. Macdonald and Debra Doyle, and "A Nice Place to Visit" by Warren Murphy and Molly Cochran. Other authors include Piers Anthony, Janet Asimov, B.W. Clough, Esther Friesner, S.N. Lewitt, Kristine Kathryn Rusch, Don Sahers, Susan Shwartz, John Shirley, Martha Soukup and Michael A. Stockpole.

**Other books you might like:**
Emma Bull, *War for the Oaks*, 1987
Philip K. Dick, *The Man Who Japed*, 1956
Peter R. Emshwiller, *The Host*, 1991
Esther Friesner, *New York by Knight*, 1986
George R.R. Martin, *Wild Cards*, 1987
    editor
Frederik Pohl, *The Years of the City*, 1984
Mike Resnick, *Stalking the Unicorn: A Fable of Tonight*, 1987
Jack Womack, *Heathern*, 1990

## 5643

**LAWRENCE WATT-EVANS**

### The Nightmare People

(New York: Onyx, 1990)

**Story type:** Horror (Possession; Doppelganger)
**Major character(s):** Edward Smith, Computer Expert (programmer); Khalil Saad, Worker (garage mechanic); Annie McGowan, Aged Person
**Time period(s):** 1990s
**Locale(s):** Diamond Park, Maryland (Bedford Mills Apartments)

**Summary:** Edward Smith awakens one August morning to find that all 142 other inhabitants of his large apartment complex have vanished. Later, the missing persons reappear, strangely altered. Before long Smith is seeing frightening figures in the window of his room at night and decides to join forces with a handful of other people to try and save the world from possession by the mysterious invaders.

**Other books you might like:**
John Christopher, *The Possessors*, 1964
Jack Finney, *The Body Snatchers*, 1955
Fritz Leiber, *The Sinful Ones*, 1953

## 5644

**LAWRENCE WATT-EVANS**

### Nightside City

(New York: Ballantine/Del Rey, 1989)

**Story type:** Science Fiction (Mystery)
**Major character(s):** Carlisle Hsing, Detective—Private
**Time period(s):** 23rd century
**Locale(s):** Epimetheus, Planet—Imaginary

**Summary:** When Epimetheus was first settled it was believed that the planet didn't rotate. Nightside City, home to gamblers, prostitutes, and other purveyors of vice and entertainment, was built very near the terminator and the blazing heat of Epimetheus' star. Now the planet's slow, only recently discovered rotation has doomed the city. Private eye Carlisle Hsing is hired by the residents of some apartment blocks on the sun-side edge of the city to find out why someone has kicked them out of their homes when those buildings are soon to be destroyed by nature. She uncovers a complex plot and finds herself a potential murder victim.

**Other books you might like:**
Richard Bowker, *Dover Beach*, 1987
George Alec Effinger, *A Fire in the Sun*, 1989
George Alec Effinger, *When Gravity Fails*, 1987
John E. Stith, *Deep Quarry*, 1989
F. Paul Wilson, *Dydeetown World*, 1989

## 5645

**LAWRENCE WATT-EVANS**

### Out of This World

(New York: Ballantine Del Rey, 1994)

**Story type:** Fantasy (Alternate World; Science Fiction)
**Series:** Three Worlds
**Major character(s):** Pellimore "Pel" Brown, Businessman; Amy Jewell, Divorced Person; Raven, Hero
**Time period(s):** 1990s
**Locale(s):** Earth; Outer Space; Interstellar Empire/Federation

**Summary:** When a seemingly unfunctional spaceship lands on Amy Jewell's lawn and an elf invades Pel Brown's basement, Pel and family, Amy, her lawyer and the stranded spacemen decide to investigate Raven's world. After pirates capture them and sell them into slavery, their rescuers ask the group to join the fight against Shadow, the entity from Raven's magical world which may invade Earth as it spills into the galactic empire.

**Other books you might like:**
Leigh Brackett, *The Starmen of the Lyrdis*, 1976
Jack L. Chalker, *The River of Dancing Gods*, 1984
L. Sprague de Camp, *The Carnelian Cube*, 1948
    Fletcher Pratt, co-author
Keith Laumer, *The Great Time Machine Hoax*, 1964
C.L. Moore, *Judgment Night*, 1962
Andrew J. Offutt, *My Lord Barbarian*, 1977
Frederik Pohl, *Narabedla, Ltd.*, 1988

## 5646

**LAWRENCE WATT-EVANS**

### The Rebirth of Wonder

(New York: Tor, 1992)

**Story type:** Fantasy (Contemporary; Light Fantasy)
**Major character(s):** Arthur "Art" Dunham, Businessman (theater manager); Merle "Myrddin" Innisfree, Wizard; Maggie Gowdie, Witch
**Time period(s):** 1990s
**Locale(s):** Bampton, Massachusetts; Faerie, Mythical Place

**Summary:** Before Art can clean up what was to be the last show of the season, his father rents the theater for the remaining month to a strange group called the Bringers of Wonder. Their leader, Mr. Innisfree, unwillingly accepts Art's help to produce the show, *The Return of Magic*. Art's baliwick, the theater originally built as a church, provides one of the last places the ritual to return magic to Earth can be performed successfully. Includes the story, ''The Final Folly of Captain Dancy.''

**Other books you might like:**
Emma Bull, *War for the Oaks*, 1987
John DeChancie, *Castle Perilous*, 1988
Diane Duane, *High Wizardry*, 1989
Simon Hawke, *The Wizard of 4th Street*, 1987
Tanya Huff, *Gate of Darkness, Circle of Light*, 1989
Mercedes Lackey, *Knight of Ghosts and Shadows*, 1990
   Ellen Guon, co-author

## 5647

**LAWRENCE WATT-EVANS**

### The Reign of the Brown Magician
(New York: Ballantine Del Rey, 1996)

**Story type:** Fantasy (Science Fiction; Historical)
**Series:** Three Worlds
**Major character(s):** Pellimore ''Pel'' Brown, Magician, Ruler; Proserpine Thorpe, Telepath; John Bascombe, Administrator
**Time period(s):** 1990s
**Locale(s):** Faerie, Mythical Place; Galactic Empire, Interstellar Empire/Federation

**Summary:** Pellimore Brown, now Pelbrun, obsesses about bringing his wife and daughter back to life. However, the Galactic Empire cannot believe his modest goals and keeps refusing to return the bodies, thus provoking war. Then Pel finds that his powers, while nearly omnipotent, have definite limitations and that resurrecting the dead has its drawbacks.

**Other books you might like:**
Poul Anderson, *Three Hearts and Three Lions*, 1961
Leigh Brackett, *The Ginger Star*, 1974
Jack L. Chalker, *The Birth of Flux and Anchor*, 1985
L. Sprague de Camp, *The Carnelian Cube*, 1948
   Fletcher Pratt, co-author
Alan Dean Foster, *To the Vanishing Point*, 1988
John Varley, *Titan*, 1979
Ted White, *Phoenix Prime*, 1966
Robert Charles Wilson, *Gypsies*, 1989

## 5648

**LAWRENCE WATT-EVANS**

### The Spell of the Black Dagger
(New York: Ballantine Del Rey, 1993)

**Story type:** Fantasy (Magic Conflict; Political)
**Series:** Ethshar
**Major character(s):** Tabaea, Thief; Lady Sarai, Detective, Royalty
**Time period(s):** Indeterminate (Year of Speech 5227)
**Locale(s):** Hegemony of the Three Ethshars, Fictional Country

**Summary:** While attempting to duplicate an incompletely heard spell, Tabaea creates a magical dagger, little suspecting the tool's abilities. After accidently discovering the knife's power, Tabaea declares herself Empress of Ethshar, causing the royal wizards to unleash an ancient weapon against her, one which could destroy the entire world.

**Other books you might like:**
Lois McMaster Bujold, *The Spirit Ring*, 1992
Anne Logston, *Shadow*, 1991
Michael Moorcock, *The Bane of the Black Sword*, 1976

Michael Moorcock, *Sailor on the Seas of Fate*, 1976
Paula Volsky, *Illusion*, 1992

## 5649

**LAWRENCE WATT-EVANS**
**ESTHER FRIESNER**, Co-Author

### Split Heirs
(New York: Tor, 1993)

**Story type:** Fantasy (Light Fantasy)
**Major character(s):** Queen Artemisia, Royalty, Parent; Arbol, Royalty, Imposter (prince); Clootie, Wizard
**Time period(s):** Indeterminate
**Locale(s):** Hydrangea, Fictional Country

**Summary:** When Queen Artemisia gives birth to triplets, two must be hidden to avoid their deaths. Unfortunately, a visually impaired servant neglects to leave one of the princes, allowing the princess to grow up as gender confused heir-apparent and the princes to adopt careers as wizard and shepherd. First of a series.

**Other books you might like:**
Kyle Crocco, *Heroes, Inc.*, 1991
Kyle Crocco, *Heroes Wanted*, 1991
Esther Friesner, *Demon Blues*, 1989
Esther Friesner, *Elf Defense*, 1988
Esther Friesner, *Hooray for Hellywood*, 1990
Esther Friesner, *Majyk by Accident*, 1993
Esther Friesner, *Unicorn U.*, 1992
John Moore, *Slay and Rescue*, 1993
Terry Pratchett, *Guards! Guards!*, 1991

## 5650

**LAWRENCE WATT-EVANS**

### Taking Flight
(New York: Ballantine Del Rey, 1993)

**Story type:** Fantasy (Adventure; Quest)
**Series:** Ethshar
**Major character(s):** Kelder of Shulara, Adventurer; Irith, Mythical Creature (shapeshifter), Magician
**Time period(s):** Indeterminate
**Locale(s):** The Great Highway, Mythical Place; Angarossa, Fictional Country; Shan on the Desert, Fictional City (bazaar)

**Summary:** Motivated by a seer's prophecy that he will become a champion of the lost and forlorn, Kelder sets out to find adventure and a mate. Joining the beautiful, winged Irith on the road, Kelder's adventures begin all too quickly with deadly consequences for some bandits. As Kelder and Irith try to help the sister of one deceased bandit find rest for his soul, Kelder begins to suspect that Irith has hidden much about herself.

**Other books you might like:**
David Eddings, *Pawn of Prophecy*, 1982
Robert Jordan, *The Eye of the World*, 1989
Elizabeth Moon, *Sheepfarmer's Daughter*, 1988
Michael Moorcock, *The Revenge of the Rose*, 1991
Jennifer Roberson, *Shapechangers*, 1984

## `5651`

### LAWRENCE WATT-EVANS

## *Touched by the Gods*
(New York: Tor, 1997)

**Story type:** Fantasy (Magic Conflict; Political)
**Major character(s):** Malledd, Artisan (smith), Hero; Vadeviya, Religious; Duzon, Nobleman, Warrior
**Time period(s):** Indeterminate
**Locale(s):** Domdur Empire, Fictional Country

**Summary:** After generations of peace, the oracles indicate a newborn with the mark of the God, Ba'el, will lead the Domdur Empire to victory when war breaks out. Teased for years about becoming champion, Malledd rejects his prophecied role, content with his life as a smith. When the oracles cease communicating with the priests and an evil magician raises an army of the dead to invade, Malledd must decide whether to remain a simple smith or shoulder his foretold responsibility.

**Other books you might like:**
Stephen R. Donaldson, *Lord Foul's Bane*, 1977
Dave Duncan, *The Reluctant Swordsman*, 1988
David Eddings, *Pawn of Prophecy*, 1982
Terry Goodkind, *Wizard's First Rule*, 1994
Robert Jordan, *The Eye of the World*, 1990

## `5652`

### CHARLES G. WAUGH, Editor
### FRANK D. MCSHERRY JR., Co-Editor

## *Spooky Sea Stories*
(Camden, Massachusetts: Yankee Books, 1991)

**Story type:** Horror (Anthology)
**Summary:** Fifteen stories of ghostly doings on the high seas, including Sir Arthur Conan Doyle's tale of obsessive pursuit, "The Captain of the Pole Star"; William Hope Hodgson's tale of the horrible fate of a shipwrecked crew on an uncharted island, "The Voice in the Night"; Joseph Conrad's tale of a vicious ship's officer and his just rewards, "The Brute"; and three variants on the Flying Dutchman theme: John William DeForest's "A Strange Arrival," Wilhelm Hauff's "The Story of the Haunted Ship," and Edgar Allan Poe's "Ms. Found in a Bottle."

**Other books you might like:**
William Pattrick, *Mysterious Sea Stories*, 1985

## `5653`

### CHARLES G. WAUGH, Editor
### MARTIN H. GREENBERG, Co-Editor

## *Supernatural Sleuths*
(New York: DAW, 1996)

**Story type:** Horror (Anthology; Mystery)
**Summary:** These 14 tales of fantasy, horror, and science fiction span the century and feature crimes both solved and committed by supernatural means. The oldest, "The Gateway of the Monster," features William Hope Hodgson's psychic detective Carnacki preventing the invasion of our sphere by an extradimensional monster. Jack Ritchie's "The Cardula Detective Agency" employs Count Dracula as a nighttime detective, and Lee Killough's "The Existential Man" has a sleuth investigating his own death. Bob Weinberg's deal-with-

the-devil tale "The Midnight El" and William F. Nolan's "Lonely Train A'Comin'" both use phantom trains as the locus for their horrors.

**Other books you might like:**
Roger Elwood, *Horror Hunters*, 1971
  Vic Ghidalia, co-editor
Peter Haining, *Peter Cushing's Tales of a Monster Hunter*, 1975
  editor
Peter Haining, *Supernatural Sleuths*, 1986
  editor

## `5654`

### SYLVIA WAUGH

## *The Mennyms*
(New York: Greenwillow, 1994)

**Story type:** Fantasy (Young Adult; Contemporary)
**Series:** Mennyms
**Major character(s):** Vinetta Mennym, Parent, Mythical Creature; Appleby Mennym, Teenager, Mythical Creature; Tulip Mennym, Grandparent, Mythical Creature
**Time period(s):** 1990s
**Locale(s):** England

**Summary:** News of their landlord's upcoming visit sends the Mennyms scurrying to provide additional cover for their well-hidden secret. First novel.

**Other books you might like:**
L. Frank Baum, *The Patchwork Girl of Oz*, 1913
Michael Bedard, *Painted Devil*, 1994
Pauline Clarke, *The Return of the Twelves*, 1963
Lynne Reid Banks, *The Indian in the Cupboard*, 1981

## `5655`

### SYLVIA WAUGH

## *Mennyms Alive*
(New York: Greenwillow, 1997)

**Story type:** Fantasy (Young Adult; Contemporary)
**Series:** Mennyms
**Major character(s):** Soobie Mennym, Mythical Creature; Daisy Maughan, Businesswoman, Antiques Dealer; Tulip Mennym, Mythical Creature, Grandparent
**Time period(s):** 1990s
**Locale(s):** England

**Summary:** When the ghost of their creator, Kate Penshaw, departs her mansion after 46 years, the Mennyms lose their life force. When the rag dolls awaken in Daisy Maughan's care, they must acquire new accomodations to regain their freedom, a task Tulip undertakes through intermediaries.

**Other books you might like:**
Lynne Reid Banks, *The Indian in the Cupboard*, 1981
L. Frank Baum, *The Patchwork Girl of Oz*, 1913
Michael Bedard, *Painted Devil*, 1994
Pauline Clarke, *The Return of the Twelves*, 1963

## 5656

### SYLVIA WAUGH

## *Mennyms Under Siege*

(New York: Greenwillow, 1996)

**Story type:** Fantasy (Young Adult; Contemporary)
**Series:** Mennyms
**Major character(s):** Pilbeam Mennym, Mythical Creature; Appleby Mennym, Teenager, Mythical Creature
**Time period(s):** 1990s
**Locale(s):** England

**Summary:** When Pilbeam decides to go to the theater to relieve her feeling of unbearable isolation, she encounters a nosy neighbor, bringing about possible discovery of the Mennym family secret and disaster for the entire family.

**Other books you might like:**
Lynne Reid Banks, *The Indian in the Cupboard*, 1981
L. Frank Baum, *The Patchwork Girl of Oz*, 1913
Michael Bedard, *Painted Devil*, 1994
Pauline Clarke, *The Return of the Twelves*, 1963
Mary James, *Shoebag*, 1990

## 5657

### LEE WEATHERSBY

## *Kiss of the Vampire*

(New York: Zebra, 1992)

**Story type:** Horror (Vampire Story)
**Major character(s):** Franz Drake, Vampire (Simon Drake's brother); Simon Tepes Drake, Vampire (Franz Drake's brother); Cassandra Lane "Casey" Brighton, Businesswoman (bookstore owner)
**Time period(s):** 1990s
**Locale(s):** Ft. Walton Beach, Florida

**Summary:** Betrayed by the brother upon whom he bestowed the gift of vampirism and who forsook it for the love of a mortal woman, Franz Drake follows Simon Drake to southern Florida, where he terrorizes the town's citizens and threatens Simon's girlfriend Casey, in order to teach his wayward brother a lesson.

**Other books you might like:**
Kathryn Meyer Griffith, *Vampire Blood*, 1991
Tom Piccirilli, *Dark Father*, 1990
T. Lucien Wright, *Blood Brothers*, 1992

## 5658

### INGRID WEAVER

## *A Wish and a Dream*

(New York: Jove, 1998)

**Story type:** Fantasy (Light Fantasy; Romance)
**Major character(s):** Dylan Stonehouse, Businessman; Constance Vandermeer, Fiance(e); Seraphina, Mythical Creature (pixie)
**Time period(s):** 1990s (1998)
**Locale(s):** United States

**Summary:** Frustrated when the woman he loves agrees to marry another, Dylan Stonehouse discovers that the figure in a painting is actually a pixie. He releases her and forces her to grant his wishes, with usually comical results. First fantasy novel.

**Other books you might like:**
Alice Alfonsi, *Some Enchanted Evening*, 1998

C.J. Card, *One Wish*, 1998
H.M. Egbert, *Mrs. Aladdin*, 1925
Esther Friesner, *Wishing Season*, 1993
Kathleen Kane, *This Time for Keeps*, 1998

## 5659

### MICHAEL D. WEAVER

## *My Father Immortal*

(New York: St. Martin's Press, 1989)

**Story type:** Science Fiction (Science Fiction)
**Major character(s):** David, Child; Stigg, Genetically Altered Being
**Time period(s):** 61st century
**Locale(s):** Earth; Outer Space

**Summary:** As a spaceship flees the solar system, a group of children are ejected from it in escape pods. As the years go by and the escape pods make their slow way back toward Earth, the children gradually begin to make sense of the fragmented information available to them about their pasts and about the strange society that has evolved on a far future Earth.

**Other books you might like:**
Brian W. Aldiss, *Hothouse*, 1962
Robert A. Heinlein, *Farnham's Freehold*, 1964
H.G. Wells, *The Time Machine*, 1958

## 5660

### MICHAEL D. WEAVER

## *A Second Infinity*

(New York: AvoNova, 1996)

**Story type:** Science Fiction (Post-Disaster; Alternate Intelligence)
**Major character(s):** Orfei Agamon, Artist (Holomage); Derek Soul, Government Official, Divorced Person; Holly Linn, Government Official
**Time period(s):** 22nd century (2107); Indeterminate Future
**Locale(s):** Moscow, Russia; Novyraj, Fictional City

**Summary:** Assigned against his will to investigate a series of disappearances at the Moscow office of the Reconstruction Department, Derek learns of a security report recommending his "Physical Discontinuance." Unsure of whether he can trust his assigned partner Holly, his ex-wife Linda, or even his own senses, Derek searches the tunnels under the devastated city. In the subterranean environment of Novyraj of the far future, Orfei experiences Derek's life by means of virtual reality dreams. When others plan to turn his art into reality, he tries to foil them by fleeing to Earth's surface.

**Other books you might like:**
Arthur C. Clarke, *Childhood's End*, 1953
Jane S. Fancher, *Harmonies of the 'Net*, 1992
Ursula K. Le Guin, *The Lathe of Heaven*, 1971
Amy Thomson, *Virtual Girl*, 1993
Vernor Vinge, *Marooned in Realtime*, 1986
Roger Zelazny, *Lord of Light*, 1967

## 5661

### DON WEBB

## *The Double*

(New York: St. Martin's, 1998)

**Story type:** Horror (Mystery; Doppelganger)

**Major character(s):** John Reynman, Writer (computer games); Michelle Galen, Lawyer
**Time period(s):** 1990s (1998)
**Locale(s):** Austin, Texas

**Summary:** In this ribald post-modern occult mystery, John Reynman awakens one morning to discover a man who is his spitting image dead on the floor of his living room. His investigations to discover who the man was and how he got there lead to his discovery of the secret Brotherhood of Something or Other and a world of mystery and intrigue his double was involved in. A first novel.

**Other books you might like:**
David Ambrose, *The Man Who Turned into Himself*, 1994
Martin Amis, *Night Train*, 1998
Paul Auster, *The New York Trilogy*, 1990
Philip K. Dick, *The Three Stigmata of Palmer Eldritch*, 1965
Eric McCormack, *The Paradise Motel*, 1987

## 5662

### DON WEBB

## A Spell for the Fulfillment of Desire

(Normal, Illinois: Black Ice Books, 1996)

**Story type:** Horror (Collection)

**Summary:** The author, a dedicated postmodernist, offers 27 stories published over the last decade that mix horror and mainstream elements in highly original stories. "The Literary Fruitcake" imagines a fruitcake handed down from Charles Dickens, through Arthur Machen and Algernon Blackwood, to Jack Kerouac and William S. Burroughs, each of whom imbues it with a taste of his own literary genius. "Mark 16:14-29, Matthew 14:1-12" depicts a truly gruesome dance of the seven veils that Salome performs for Herod Antipas. "Spiral" drops allusions to H.P. Lovecraft, Robert W. Chambers, E.T.A. Hoffman and detective B-movies in its account of a man whose strange life becomes even more bizarre when he drops acid. "In the Dark Ages" folds elements of popular culture into a spoof of the Black Mass.

**Other books you might like:**
William S. Burroughs, *Interzone*, 1989
Jack Remick, *Terminal Weird*, 1996
Wayne Allen Sallee, *With Wounds Still Wet*, 1996

## 5663

### DON WEBB

## Stealing My Rules

(Denver: Cyber-Psychos AOD, 1997)

**Story type:** Horror (Collection)

**Summary:** One dozen tales of post-modern dark fantasy and science fiction, many featuring time slips and alternate realities. In "The Game," a stalker suffers complete discomposure when everyone in the world disappears unexpectedly. In "Boy," a gang runs afoul of ancient magic when they find that the old man they are terrorizing is a priest of the Aztec god Tezcatlipoca. "The Works of Hieronimus Bosch Considered as Realism" is a stream of conscious fantasy built from disturbing imagery in Bosch's paintings. In "Avocation," a husband and wife discover peculiar behaviors in one another that suggest the influence of ancient mystical beliefs. Paul Di Filippo supplies the introduction.

**Other books you might like:**
Cliff Burns, *The Reality Machine*, 1997
William S. Burroughs, *Interzone*, 1989

Harlan Ellison, *Slippage*, 1997
Jack Remick, *Terminal Weird*, 1996
Wayne Allen Sallee, *With Wounds Still Wet*, 1996

## 5664

### SHARON WEBB

## The Halflife

(New York: Tor Books, 1989)

**Story type:** Science Fiction (Medical)
**Major character(s):** Tim Monahan, Writer; Jody Hinson, Psychologist
**Time period(s):** 1980s
**Locale(s):** Atlanta, Georgia

**Summary:** Twenty years ago something strange happened to Tim Monahan at a summer camp for gifted children. Now a moderately successful writer, he has been asked to take part in a scientific study on creativity. The other participants, he discovers, are an odd, unstable lot. Monahan has had nightmares ever since that summer twenty years ago, but now he begins to suffer blackouts as well. Several murders occur and Tim determines to get to the bottom of the mystery, no matter what it might cost him.

**Other books you might like:**
Richard Condon, *The Manchurian Candidate*, 1959
Dean R. Koontz, *The Eyes of Darkness*, 1981
Robert Reed, *Black Milk*, 1989

## 5665

### WENDY WEBB, Editor
### CHARLES L. GRANT, Co-Editor

## Gothic Ghosts

(New York: Tor, 1997)

**Story type:** Horror (Anthology; Ghost Story)

**Summary:** An anthology of 19 new stories of ghosts and hauntings selected for their evocations of atmosphere and mood. Stand-out selections include Lucy Taylor's "Visitation," in which the ghost of a little girl leads to an aging bachelor's revelations about his life and loves; Stuart Palmer's "Cinder Child," in which a young boy's encounter with ghosts uncovers a ghastly family secret; Nancy Holder's "Syngamy," in which death and life are linked at a fertility clinic; and Matthew J. Costello's "Unexpected Attraction," about a man persuaded by the ghost he has fallen in love with to murder his wife. Other contributors include Jessica Amanda Salmonson, Rick Hautala, Brian Stableford, Katherine Ptacek and Ester Friesner.

**Other books you might like:**
Richard Gilliam, *Phantoms of the Night*, 1996
    Martin H. Greenberg, co-editor
Marvin Kaye, *Ghosts*, 1981
    editor
Paul F. Olson, *Post Mortem: New Tales of Ghostly Horror*, 1989
    David B. Silva, co-editor
Gahan Wilson, *Gahan Wilson's The Ultimate Haunted House*, 1996
    editor

## 5666

WENDY WEBB, Editor
RICHARD GILLIAM, Co-Editor
EDWARD E. KRAMER, Co-Editor
MARTIN H. GREENBERG, Co-Editor

### More Phobias
(New York: Pocket, 1995)

**Story type:** Horror (Anthology)

**Summary:** The twenty-seven stories commissioned especially for this compilation are all built upon a particular phobia or fear. Robert Bloch's ''None Are So Blind'' is a mordant tale of a man who develops a fear of cats after his fate is foretold by a fortuneteller. Nancy Kilpatrick's ''Sunphobic'' tells of a woman with a justifiable aversion to sunlight, and Douglas Clegg's ''The Mysteries of Paris'' of a man with an equally justifiable fear of serial killers. In Rick Hautala's ''The Back of My Hands,'' there is less phobia than obsession, as a man who covets his twin brother's hands goes to the ultimate extreme to possess them.

**Other books you might like:**
Jeff Gelb, *Fear Itself*, 1995
    editor
Charles L. Grant, *Fears*, 1983
    editor
Gary L. Raisor, *Obsessions*, 1991
    editor

## 5667

WENDY WEBB, Editor
RICHARD GILLIAM, Co-Editor
EDWARD E. KRAMER, Co-Editor
MARTIN H. GREENBERG, Co-Editor

### Phobias: Stories of Your Deepest Fears
(New York: Pocket, 1994)

**Story type:** Horror (Anthology)

**Summary:** The 24 stories written originally for this volume are all concerned with personal fears and neuroses. Included are Robert Weinberg's ''Endure the Night,'' about crooks who try to use a man's fear of the dark against him; Karl Edward Wagner's ''Passages,'' in which doctors discuss the different fears that have affected their performance in their chosen profession; Kathryn Ptacek's ''Hair,'' about a woman whose sexual anxieties manifest as a preoccupation with body hair; Sharon and Jerry Ahern's ''Silent Pace,'' about a hit man afraid to fall asleep; Kristine Kathryn Rusch's ''Hot Water,'' about a woman's inability to deal with her nakedness; and two stories about fear of flying, Lawrence Watt-Evans' ''The Worst Part'' and Brad Strickland's ''The Hungry Sky.'' Robert Bloch supplies the introduction.

**Other books you might like:**
Peter Crowther, *Narrow Houses*, 1993
Charles L. Grant, *Fears*, 1983
Gary L. Raisor, *Obsessions*, 1991

## 5668

DAVID WEBER

### The Armageddon Inheritance
(New York: Baen, 1993)

**Story type:** Science Fiction (Invasion of Earth; Military)
**Series:** Mutineer's Moon
**Major character(s):** Colin MacIntyre, Spaceship Captain, Leader (Governor of Earth); Sean Horus MacIntyre, Leader (Lieutenant Governor of Earth); Dahak, Artificial Intelligence (spaceship)
**Time period(s):** Indeterminate Future
**Locale(s):** *Dahak*, Spaceship; Outer Space

**Summary:** Preparing for the impending invasion by the Achuultani, Horus' Imperial machinery and medical technology, along with mobilized Terran equipment and manpower, may permit completion of planetary defenses before the leading Achuultani scouts arrive. Meanwhile Colin and *Dahak* must locate Fourth Imperium heavy support in time to return before the main Achuultani fleet reaches Earth. Sequel to *Mutineers' Moon*.

**Other books you might like:**
Bill Baldwin, *The Defenders*, 1992
Glen Cook, *The Dragon Never Sleeps*, 1988
Brian Daley, *Jinx on a Terran Inheritance*, 1985
Brian Daley, *Requiem for a Ruler of Worlds*, 1985
Dan Simmons, *Hyperion*, 1989
Vernor Vinge, *A Fire upon the Deep*, 1992

## 5669

DAVID WEBER

### Echoes of Honor
(New York: Baen, 1998)

**Story type:** Science Fiction (Military; Political)
**Series:** Honor Harrington
**Major character(s):** Honor Harrington, Military Personnel (admiral), Hero; Benjamin Mayhew IX, Political Figure (Planetary Protector of Grayson), Leader; Allison Harrington, Doctor (genetic research), Parent (mother)
**Time period(s):** Indeterminate Future
**Locale(s):** Grayson, Planet—Imaginary; *RMS Minotaur*, Spaceship; Hades, Planet—Imaginary (Camp Charon)

**Summary:** Horrified by the televised execution of Honor, the populations of both Manticore and Grayson hold simultaneous state funerals for her. On Grayson, Benjamin arranges for a truly Graysonian Harrington heir, while the Manticoran Royal Navy acquires Graysonian ships and technology for their cooperative effort in the war against the People's Republic of Haven. Unknown to all, including the Peeps, Honor and most of her crew survive, but now must rescue their fellow prisoners and find a way off Hades, the hidden penal colony of the Peeps.

**Other books you might like:**
David Brin, *Infinity's Shore*, 1996
Lois McMaster Bujold, *Shards of Honor*, 1986
Jan Clark, *Prodigy*, 1997
Donald E. McQuinn, *With Full Honors*, 1997
Elizabeth Moon, *Once a Hero*, 1997

## 5670

### DAVID WEBER

## *Field of Dishonor*
(New York: Baen, 1994)

**Story type:** Science Fiction (Political; Military)
**Series:** Honor Harrington
**Major character(s):** Honor Harrington, Military Personnel, Noblewoman; Pavel Young, Nobleman (Earl of Northhollow)
**Time period(s):** Indeterminate Future
**Locale(s):** Star Kingdom of Manticore, Interstellar Empire/Federation; Manticore, Planet—Imaginary; *Nike*, Spaceship

**Summary:** The Star Kingdom of Manticore should immediately declare war on the People's Republic of Haven, now in disarray after Honor's "victory" at Hancock. Unfortunately, many of the House of Lords reject the facts, desiring the problem to resolve itself. A proven deserter and coward in battle and enemy of Honor, Pavel Young weasels out of the death penalty. However, his dishonorable discharge from the Navy revokes his rank of captain and could prove worse punishment. He vows to destroy Honor and just may realize his goal.

**Other books you might like:**
Lois McMaster Bujold, *Shards of Honor*, 1986
Michelle Shirey Crean, *Dancer of the Sixth*, 1993
William C. Dietz, *Legion of the Damned*, 1993
Stephen Goldin, *Jade Darcy and the Affair of Honor*, 1988
    Mary Mason, co-author
Alis A. Rasmussen, *The Price of Ransom*, 1990

## 5671

### DAVID WEBER

## *Flag in Exile*
(New York: Baen, 1995)

**Story type:** Science Fiction (Military; Space Opera)
**Series:** Honor Harrington
**Major character(s):** Honor Harrington, Military Personnel (admiral), Noblewoman; Benjamin Mayhew, Leader (Grayson)
**Time period(s):** Indeterminate Future
**Locale(s):** Grayson, Planet—Imaginary; Star Kingdom of Manticore, Interstellar Empire/Federation; People's Republic of Haven, Interstellar Empire/Federation

**Summary:** Not yet recovered from the murder of her lover and the execution of the traitorous Pavel Young, Honor attempts to recuperate on Grayson. When Haven attacks Grayson on the way to Manticore, Honor must answer the call to protect her adopted home. She is hindered by plots against her and local resistance to the many changes she instituted to improve the life style of her steaders.

**Other books you might like:**
Lois McMaster Bujold, *Shards of Honor*, 1986
Frank Herbert, *Dune*, 1965
Elizabeth Moon, *Hunting Party*, 1993
Alis A. Rasmussen, *A Passage of Stars*, 1990
Sherwood Smith, *The Phoenix in Flight*, 1993
    Dave Trowbridge, co-author

## 5672

### DAVID WEBER

## *Heirs of Empire*
(New York: Baen, 1996)

**Story type:** Science Fiction (Family Saga; Political)
**Series:** Mutineer's Moon
**Major character(s):** Sean Horus MacIntyre, Heir, Military Personnel (midshipman); Colin MacIntyre, Ruler (emperor), Spaceship Captain; Dahak, Artificial Intelligence (spaceship)
**Time period(s):** Indeterminate Future
**Locale(s):** Bia, Planet—Imaginary; *Imperial Terra*, Spaceship; Pardal, Planet—Imaginary

**Summary:** Enhanced with imperial technology, Sean, his twin sister and their friends, including a young Achuultani, join the Imperial Marines. Targeted by a traitor who plots to take over the empire after destroying the current leadership and allies, the friends survive the destruction of *Imperial Terra*, due to prior intervention by Dahak. Fortunately the crew arrives at a habitable planet whose residents, unfortunately, find the enhanced castaways demonic.

**Other books you might like:**
Lois McMaster Bujold, *Mirror Dance*, 1994
F.M. Busby, *The Demu Trilogy*, 1980
Debra Doyle, *The Price of the Stars*, 1992
    James D. Macdonald, co-author
Frank Herbert, *Dune*, 1965
Anne McCaffrey, *Damia's Children*, 1993
Alis A. Rasmussen, *The Price of Ransom*, 1990

## 5673

### DAVID WEBER

## *Honor Among Enemies*
(New York: Baen, 1996)

**Story type:** Science Fiction (Space Opera; Military)
**Series:** Honor Harrington
**Major character(s):** Honor Harrington, Military Personnel, Noblewoman; Aubrey Wanderman, Military Personnel
**Time period(s):** Indeterminate Future
**Locale(s):** *H.M.S. Wayfarer*, Spaceship; Star Kingdom of Manticore, Interstellar Empire/Federation; Silesian Confederacy, Interstellar Empire/Federation

**Summary:** Nominally given the opportunity to redeem her career in the Royal Manticorian Navy by rousting troublesome space pirates, Honor Harrington commands an ill-equipped merchant fleet and the least desirable service personnel assigned to the effort by enemies hoping that Honor might fail.

**Other books you might like:**
Lois McMaster Bujold, *Shards of Honor*, 1986
Debra Doyle, *The Price of the Stars*, 1992
    James D. Macdonald, co-author
David Feintuch, *Midshipman's Hope*, 1994
Frank Herbert, *Dune*, 1965
Sherwood Smith, *The Phoenix in Flight*, 1993
    Dave Trowbridge, co-author

**DAVID WEBER**

## The Honor of the Queen

(New York: Baen, 1993)

**Story type:** Science Fiction (Military; Space Opera)
**Series:** Honor Harrington
**Major character(s):** Honor Harrington, Military Personnel, Noblewoman; Raoul Courvossier, Military Personnel, Diplomat (ambassador); Benjamin Mayhew, Leader (planetary)
**Time period(s):** Indeterminate Future
**Locale(s):** Grayson, Planet—Imaginary; *Fearless*, Spaceship; Outer Space

**Summary:** As captain of the new *Fearless* and commander of the escort for Admiral Courvossier's delegation, Honor confronts religious prejudice against women having rank or station. After saving the planet's leader from assassination, she must then defend the planet from ultra-religious fanatics willing to destroy it.

**Other books you might like:**
Eleanor Arnason, *Ring of Swords*, 1993
Lois McMaster Bujold, *Barrayar*, 1991
Debra Doyle, *The Price of the Stars*, 1992
    James D. Macdonald, co-author
Debra Doyle, *Starpilot's Grave*, 1993
    James D. Macdonald, co-author
Melisa C. Michaels, *Skirmish*, 1985
Alis A. Rasmussen, *Revolution's Shore*, 1990

**5675**

**DAVID WEBER**

## In Enemy Hands

(New York, Baen, 1997)

**Story type:** Science Fiction (Military; Space Opera)
**Series:** Honor Harrington
**Major character(s):** Honor Harrington, Military Personnel, Noblewoman
**Time period(s):** Indeterminate Future
**Locale(s):** Star Kingdom of Manticore, Interstellar Empire/Federation; Outer Space

**Summary:** After a brief rest at home on Grayson, Honor accompanies a space convoy as guard, sacrificing her ship when the enemy springs a trap. Captured and tortured, Honor must escape or die.

**5676**

**DAVID WEBER**
**DAVID DRAKE**, Co-Author
**S.M. STIRLING**, Co-Author

## More than Honor

(New York: Baen, 1998)

**Story type:** Science Fiction (Collection)
**Time period(s):** Indeterminate Future
**Locale(s):** Sphinx, Planet—Imaginary

**Summary:** This collection contains three stories set in the universe of Honor Harrington and an 80-page description, "The Universe of Honor Harrington."

**Other books you might like:**
David Drake, *Hammer's Slammers*, 1987
    expanded edition
David Drake, *Starliner*, 1993
S.M. Stirling, *Betrayals*, 1996
S.M. Stirling, *Marching through Georgia*, 1988
S.M. Stirling, *Snow Brother*, 1992

**5677**

**DAVID WEBER**

## Mutineers' Moon

(New York: Baen, 1991)

**Story type:** Science Fiction (Invasion of Earth; Alternate Intelligence)
**Major character(s):** Colin MacIntyre, Military Personnel, Spaceship Captain; Hector MacMahan, Military Personnel; Jiltanith, Military Personnel, Pilot
**Time period(s):** 2040s
**Locale(s):** Montenegro; Colorado Springs, Colorado; *Dahak*, Spaceship

**Summary:** While testing some new equipment, Colin MacIntyre finds the moon unexpectedly hollow. He is captured by Dahak, the spaceship he'd inadvertantly contacted. Dahak, the artificial intelligence which had evolved from the ship's computer, conscripts Colin as its captain because it needs help to fulfill its mission and wants to save humanity, descended from its crew, from the dreaded alien Achuultani.

**Other books you might like:**
Roger MacBride Allen, *The Ring of Charon*, 1990
Greg Bear, *The Forge of God*, 1987
David Brin, *Earth*, 1990
Octavia E. Butler, *Dawn*, 1987
Damon Knight, *A Reasonable World*, 1991
Larry Niven, *Footfall*, 1985
    Jerry Pournelle, co-author

**5678**

**DAVID WEBER**

## Oath of Swords

(New York: Baen, 1995)

**Story type:** Fantasy (Sword and Sorcery; Magic Conflict)
**Major character(s):** Bahzell Bahnakson, Warrior (horse stealer), Royalty (prince); Brandark Brandarkson, Warrior (Bloody Sword), Minstrel (bard); Harnak, Royalty (Crown Prince of Navahk), Warrior (Bloody Sword)
**Time period(s):** Indeterminate
**Locale(s):** Empire of the Spear, Fictional Country; Land of the Purple Lords, Fictional Country

**Summary:** Prince Bahzell Bahnakson and Crown Prince Harnak become counterweights in the struggle between the Gods of Light and Darkness, beginning with Bahzell severely beating Harnak for raping and nearly killing a ward of the crown. When Bahzell flees Navahk with her, he breaks his royal hostage bond, giving Harnak an excuse to hunt Bahzell down, revenge himself and get rid of the witnesses to the crime which could cost him his claim to the throne.

**Other books you might like:**
Eve Forward, *Villains by Necessity*, 1995
Simon R. Green, *Blood and Honor*, 1993
Barbara Hambly, *The Ladies of Mandrigyn*, 1984
Robert Jordan, *Lord of Chaos*, 1994

S.M. Stirling, *The Rose Sea*, 1994
  Holly Lisle, co-author
Elizabeth Moon, *Sheepfarmer's Daughter*, 1988

**5679**

## DAVID WEBER

### *On Basilisk Station*

(New York: Baen, 1993)

**Story type:** Science Fiction (Political; Military)
**Series:** Honor Harrington
**Major character(s):** Honor Harrington, Military Personnel (Commander), Noblewoman; Estelle Matsuko, Royalty, Government Official (Commissioner); Alister McKeon, Military Personnel (Lt. Commander-Exec)
**Time period(s):** Indeterminate Future
**Locale(s):** *Fearless*, Spaceship; Haven, Planet—Imaginary; Medusa, Planet—Imaginary (Basilisk Station)

**Summary:** Assigned to the newly refitted light cruiser, *Fearless*, Honor Harrington must prove herself as a captain to the crew and preserve the honor of *Fearless*, despite inadequate armaments. Basilisk Station serves as punishment duty for incompetents but, when assigned there, Honor decides to accomplish real work in spite of limited ships and personnel, poor morale and natives who use a drug which makes them violent. First of a series.

**Other books you might like:**
Lois McMaster Bujold, *Shards of Honor*, 1986
Glen Cook, *The Dragon Never Sleeps*, 1988
David Drake, *Starliner*, 1992
Stephen Goldin, *Jade Darcy and the Zen Pirates*, 1990
  Mary Mason, co-author
Larry Niven, *The Mote in God's Eye*, 1974
  Jerry Pournelle, co-author
Alis A. Rasmussen, *A Passage of Stars*, 1990
Vernor Vinge, *A Fire upon the Deep*, 1992

**5680**

## DAVID WEBER

### *Path of the Fury*

(New York: Baen, 1992)

**Story type:** Science Fiction (Alternate Intelligence)
**Major character(s):** Alicia "Tisiphone" De Vries, Military Personnel (Imperial Cadre, retired), Disembodied Personality; Arthur Keita, Military Personnel (Imperial Cadre, general); Ferhat Ben Belkassem, Military Personnel (Special Forces, O-branch)
**Time period(s):** Indeterminate Future
**Locale(s):** Mathison's World, Planet—Imaginary; Soissons, Planet—Imaginary; *Megarea*, Spaceship (AI)

**Summary:** Alicia retires to Mathison's World with her whole family when she leaves the Imperial Cadre. Few people possess the ability required to interface with all the enhancements necessary for the elite and deadly drop commandos. When offered the chance to live Alicia accepts, in order to destroy the mastermind behind the pirates who kill everyone else on the planet. Although hampered by the belief that she has become unstable, she and Tisiphone escape, capture *Megarea* and attempt to locate and discover who commands the pirates.

**Other books you might like:**
Jeffrey A. Carver, *From a Changeling Star*, 1989
Glen Cook, *The Dragon Never Sleeps*, 1988

Debra Doyle, *The Price of the Stars*, 1992
  James D. Macdonald, co-author
Stephen Goldin, *Jade Darcy and the Affair of Honor*, 1988
  Mary Mason, co-author
James P. Hogan, *The Multiplex Man*, 1992
Anne McCaffrey, *The Ship Who Sang*, 1969
Dan Simmons, *The Hollow Man*, 1992
Walter Jon Williams, *Voice of the Whirlwind*, 1987

**5681**

## DAVID WEBER

### *The Short Victorious War*

(New York: Baen, 1994)

**Story type:** Science Fiction (Military; Space Opera)
**Series:** Honor Harrington
**Major character(s):** Honor Harrington, Military Personnel, Noblewoman
**Time period(s):** Indeterminate Future
**Locale(s):** *Nike*, Spaceship; Star Kingdom of Manticore, Interstellar Empire/Federation; Outer Space

**Summary:** As war begins, the Royal Manticorian space navy must defend their small empire against forces of the gigantic People's Republic of Haven, built up during a 50-year-long arms race. Contains 16 pages of notes on Honor Harrington's navy.

**Other books you might like:**
Eleanor Arnason, *Ring of Swords*, 1993
Lois McMaster Bujold, *The Warrior's Apprentice*, 1986
Debra Doyle, *The Price of the Stars*, 1992
  James D. Macdonald, co-author
Mercedes Lackey, *Wing Commander: Freedom Flight*, 1992
  Ellen Guon, co-author
Sherwood Smith, *The Phoenix in Flight*, 1993
  Dave Trowbridge, co-author

**5682**

## DAVID WEBER

### *The War God's Own*

(New York: Baen, 1998)

**Story type:** Fantasy (Military; Quest)
**Major character(s):** Bahzell Bahnakson, Warrior; Tomanak, Deity
**Time period(s):** Indeterminate
**Locale(s):** Empire of the Axe, Mythical Place

**Summary:** The god Tomanak chooses a member of a clan of horse stealers to become his champion and help preserve a nation from an enemy army. Bahzell's reluctance to accept his fated role complicates matters, as does the fact that the people whom he has been ordered to protect resent him as an outsider. Some of their number plot to murder him so that the god will choose a new, more acceptable champion.

**Other books you might like:**
Glen Cook, *The Black Company*, 1984
Troy Denning, *The Parched Sea*, 1991
Stephen R. Donaldson, *Lord Foul's Bane*, 1978
Mercedes Lackey, *Arrow's Flight*, 1987
Tanith Lee, *Volkhavaar*, 1977

## 5683

### KAREN WEHRSTEIN

## *Lion's Heart*

(New York: Baen, 1991)

**Story type:** Fantasy (Adventure; Political)
**Series:** Fifth Millennium
**Major character(s):** Fourth Chevenga, Heir, Ruler; Mana, Warrior
**Time period(s):** Indeterminate Future
**Locale(s):** Yeoli, Fictional Country

**Summary:** Set in the world of S. M. Stirling and Shirley Meier's *The Cage* (1989), this is the first book in the story of Chevenga. Driven by the foretelling of his death at an early age, Chevenga endures war and slavery to become a brilliant leader.

**Other books you might like:**
C.J. Cherryh, *Gate of Ivrel*, 1976
Glen Cook, *The Black Company*, 1984
Tanith Lee, *The Storm Lord*, 1976
Michael Moorcock, *Elric of Melnibone*, 1976
Roger Zelazny, *Nine Princes in Amber*, 1970

## 5684

### KAREN WEHRSTEIN

## *Lion's Soul*

(New York: Baen, 1991)

**Story type:** Fantasy (Political; Science Fiction)
**Series:** Fifth Millennium
**Major character(s):** Fourth Chevenga, Ruler
**Time period(s):** 35th century
**Locale(s):** Arko, Fictional Country; Yeou, Fictional Country

**Summary:** Chevenga escapes slavery in Arko and returns to Yeou to lead his people in defeating Arko. Afterward, as Demarch in Yeoli, he must heal his country's war wounds, while as Emperor in Arko, he must break down the old totalitarian structure by teaching Arkans about voting, equality and non-aggression. Somehow he must teach the two countries to get along.

**Other books you might like:**
Samuel R. Delany, *Tales of Neveryon*, 1979
Diane Duane, *The Door into Fire*, 1979
Heather Gladney, *Teot's War*, 1987
Patricia Kennealy-Morrison, *The Copper Crown*, 1984
Mercedes Lackey, *Arrows of the Queen*, 1987
Shirley Meier, *Shadow's Daughter*, 1991
S.M. Stirling, *The Cage*, 1989
    Shirley Meier, co-author
M.K. Wren, *Sword of the Lamb*, 1981

## 5685

### GUS WEILL

## *Flesh*

(New York: Pocket, 1993)

**Story type:** Horror (Satire)
**Major character(s):** Marion Anderson, Student (music student); Justin Caeser, Student (music student); Polly Kole, Pharmacist
**Time period(s):** 1990s (1990)
**Locale(s):** Caeser Island, Maine

**Summary:** Flattered that his rich acquaintance, Justin Caeser, has invited him to the family island off the coast of Maine to acquaint him with the rest of the Caesers and to work with him on the music for his gestating Broadway musical, *Laffin' at the Palace*, Marion Anderson is blinded to all warnings that when the Caesers have someone for dinner, they do so literally. This satire of the conspicuous consumption of the filthy rich was first published in 1990.

**Other books you might like:**
Randall Boyll, *After Sundown*, 1989
Nancy Holder, *Cannibal Dwight's Special Purpose*, 1992
William W. Johnstone, *Watchers in the Woods*, 1991
Jack Ketchum, *Offspring*, 1991
Richard Laymon, *Midnight's Lair*, 1988

## 5686

### ROBERT WEINBERG, Editor
### STEFAN DZIEMIANOWICZ, Co-Editor
### MARTIN H. GREENBERG, Co-Editor

## *100 Creepy Little Creature Stories*

(New York: Barnes & Noble, 1994)

**Story type:** Horror (Anthology)

**Summary:** The 100 short-short stories in this anthology, drawn largely from the pages of the pulp magazine, *Weird Tales*, cover all sorts of weird creatures, including ghouls in Edward Lucas White's "Amina," werewolves in Thomas Ligotti's "The Real Wolf," familiars in Robert M. Price's "Familiar Face," aliens from outer space in Hugh B. Cave's "Take Me for Instance," vampires in Charles King's "Father's Vampire," creatures of Polish folklore in Stefan Grabinski's "The White Wyrak," and emonically possessed cats in Donald Burleson's "Little Brother."

**Other books you might like:**
Al Sarrantonio, *100 Hair-Raising Little Horror Stories*, 1992
    Martin H. Greenberg, co-editor
Sebastian Wolfe, *The Little Book of Horrors*, 1992
    editor

## 5687

### ROBERT WEINBERG, Editor
### STEFAN DZIEMIANOWICZ, Co-Editor
### MARTIN H. GREENBERG, Co-Editor

## *100 Tiny Tales of Terror*

(New York: Barnes & Noble, 1996)

**Story type:** Horror (Anthology)

**Summary:** More than a century of horror is packed into the 100 stories assembled here. All classic horror themes are covered, including the vampire in John Bender's "The Visitor," the shapeshifter in Theodore Sturgeon's "Talent," the witch in Fred Chappell's "Ember," the ghost in Carl Jacobi's "Phantom Brass" and Mary Elizabeth Counselman's "House of Shadows," and vengeance from beyond the grave in Vincent O'Sullivan's "Will." Joe Lansdale's "Boo, Yourself" and Richard Laymon's "Roadside Pickup" cross over into crime fiction, Howard Wandrei's "Over Time's Threshold" and F. Paul Wilson's "The Cleaning Machine" into science fiction, and F. Marion Crawford's "The Doll's Ghost" and Thomas Ligotti's "The Greater Festival of Masks" into fantasy.

**Other books you might like:**
Isaac Asimov, *100 Great Fantasy Short Short Stories*, 1984
    Terry Carr, Martin H. Greenberg, co-editors

Al Sarrantonio, *100 Hair-Raising Little Horror Stories*, 1993
  Martin H. Greenberg, co-editor
Sebastian Wolfe, *The Little Book of Horrors*, 1992

---

### 5688

**ROBERT WEINBERG**, Editor
**STEFAN DZIEMIANOWICZ**, Co-Editor
**MARTIN H. GREENBERG**, Co-Editor

## *100 Vicious Little Vampire Stories*

(New York: Barnes & Noble, 1995)

**Story type:** Horror (Anthology; Vampire Story)

**Summary:** The one hundred tales of vampirism included here are all approximately 3000 words (or fewer) long. Most were written specifically for the anthology. The different approaches to the vampire theme found herein include vampire plants (''Snip My Suckers'' by Lois Gresh), vampires who feed on books (''And by a Word Immortal'' by Mark Kreighbaum), vampires who prey on human misery (''Just Enough'' by Joel Lane), a battlefield that lives on human blood (''The Witness'' by Mike Ashley), vampires who travel over computer systems (''Coffin.Nail'' by Richard Parks), devoutly religious vampires (''The Crumbs Beneath Thy Table'' by Pamela Hodgson), anorexic vampires (''Bingin''' by Greg Cox), and a vampire tale told from the point of view of the blood (''Hemo Gobblin''' by Robert M. Price).

**Other books you might like:**
Richard Dalby, *Vampire Stories*, 1992
Ellen Datlow, *Blood Is Not Enough*, 1988
Ellen Datlow, *A Whisper of Blood*, 1991
Martin H. Greenberg, *Celebrity Vampires*, 1995
Martin H. Greenberg, *Dracula: Prince of Darkness*, 1992
Stephen Jones, *The Mammoth Book of Vampires*, 1992
Alan Ryan, *Vampires: Two Centuries of Great Vampire Stories*, 1987

---

### 5689

**ROBERT WEINBERG**, Editor
**STEFAN DZIEMIANOWICZ**, Co-Editor
**MARTIN H. GREENBERG**, Co-Editor

## *100 Wild Little Weird Tales*

(New York: Barnes & Noble, 1994)

**Story type:** Horror (Anthology)

**Summary:** This book draws together 100 short-short stories, 3,000 words or less in length, from the pages of the original *Weird Tales*, the pulp magazine that published between 1923 and 1954 and served as the birthplace for modern horror fiction. Included are H.P. Lovecraft's ''Hypnos,'' about two men pursued by a dream monster; Robert Bloch's first professionally published tale, ''The Feast in the Abbey,'' about a traveller's visit to a ghostly monastery; Clark Ashton Smith's ''The Last Incantation,'' about the lesson a sorceror learns upon summoning the souls of the dead; Carl Jacobi's ''The Last Drive,'' about a curious event that befalls a man driving a truck with a coffin and its corpse; Richard Searight's ''The Sealed Casket,'' the tale of a spectral vampire; H. Warner Munn's *conte cruel*, ''The Chain''; and Fritz Leiber's fusion of science fiction and horror, ''Mr. Bauer and the Atoms.'' Classic reprints from the magazine include stories by Edgar Allan Poe, E.F. Benson, and Bram Stoker.

**Other books you might like:**
Peter Haining, *Weird Tales*, 1976
  editor

---

Leo Margulies, *Weird Tales*, 1964
  editor
Leo Margulies, *Worlds of Weird*, 1965
  editor

---

### 5690

**ROBERT WEINBERG**

## *The Armageddon Box*

(Newark, NJ: Wildside Press, 1991)

**Story type:** Horror (Vampire Story)
**Major character(s):** Alex Warner, Professor (history professor); Valerie Warner, Sorceress (Alex's wife); Dietrich Vril, Monster, Vampire
**Time period(s):** 1990s
**Locale(s):** Chicago, Illinois; Switzerland

**Summary:** The death of an antiquarian bookdealer friend throws Alex and Valerie Warner into the path of Dietrich Vril, a maniacal vampire master searching for a legendary talisman that threatens the entire human race.

**Other books you might like:**
Elaine Bergstrom, *Shattered Glass*, 1989
Gardner Dozois, ''Down Among the Dead Men'', 1989
  Jack Dann, co-author. In Ellen Datlow, *Blood Is Not Enough*
Hanz Heine Ewers, *Alraune*, 1911
Dan Simmons, *Carrion Comfort*, 1989

---

### 5691

**ROBERT WEINBERG**, Editor
**STEFAN DZIEMIANOWICZ**, Co-Editor
**MARTIN H. GREENBERG**, Co-Editor

## *Between Time and Terror*

(New York: Roc, 1995)

**Story type:** Horror (Anthology)

**Summary:** The 17 stories collected here span 75 years and straddle the boundary between science fiction and horror. Included are H.P. Lovecraft's classic of the effects of a meteor crash on a small town, ''The Colour out of Space''; Frank Belknap Long's tale of a scientific experiment in physical transformation, ''The Man with a Thousand Legs''; Robert Bloch's apocalyptic vision of a future taken over by machines, ''It Happened Tomorrow''; Ray Bradbury's melding of the alien and psychic possession themes, ''Asleep in Armageddon''; Dan Simmons' technological rendering of the vampire theme, ''Metastasis''; Cliver Barker's riff on the Frankenstein theme, ''The Age of Desire''; and Arthur C. Clarke's interplanetary campfire tale, ''A Walk in the Dark.''

**Other books you might like:**
Groff Conklin, *Science Fiction Terror Tales*, 1955
August Derleth, *The Other Side of the Moon*, 1949
August Derleth, *Strange Ports of Call*, 1948
Stephen Jones, *The Mammoth Book of Frankenstein*, 1995
Damon Knight, *The Dark Side*, 1965

## 5692

### ROBERT WEINBERG

## *The Black Lodge*

(New York: Pocket, 1991)

**Story type:** Horror (Occult)
**Major character(s):** Sid Taine, Detective, Psychic; Janet Packard, Businesswoman (Jeweller); Papa Benjamin, Religious (voodoo priest)
**Time period(s):** 1990s
**Locale(s):** Chicago, Illinois

**Summary:** After agreeing to investigate an apparent family feud, New Age detective Sid Taine is drawn into the affairs of the Black Lodge, a cult made up of Chicago's wealthiest businessmen with links to the lucrative drug trade. Ultimately, he joins forces with a voodoo practitioner to defeat the lodge's henchman, the murderous Dark Man.

**Other books you might like:**
Hugh B. Cave, *Disciples of Dread*, 1988
Hugh B. Cave, *The Lower Deep*, 1990
David J. Schow, *The Shaft*, 1990
Dennis Wheatley, *The Devil Rides Out*, 1935

## 5693

### ROBERT WEINBERG

## *Blood War*

(Stone Mountain, Georgia: White Wolf, 1995)

**Story type:** Horror (Vampire Story)
**Series:** A Vampire the Masquerade: Masquerade of the Red Death
**Major character(s):** Dire McCann, Detective; Alicia Varney, Businesswoman, Vampire; Makish, Criminal (assassin)
**Time period(s):** 1990s (1994)
**Locale(s):** St. Louis, Missouri; Washington, District of Columbia

**Summary:** In an alternate world secretly run by 13 vampire clans who maintain an uneasy alliance, detective Dire McCann investigates the appearance of the Red Death, a monstrous being capable of incinerating anyone and anything in its path. In the process of uncovering whether the appearance of the Red Death portends the re-emergence of an earlier generation of vampire elders ravenous for the blood of its descendants, McCann must hide his own secret identity from his vampire employers. This story is set in the universe of the *World of Darkness: Vampire* role-playing game.

**Other books you might like:**
Scott Baker, *Ancestral Hungers*, 1995
Scott Ciencin, *The Vampire Odyssey*, 1992
Kim Newman, *Anno Dracula*, 1992
Brian Stableford, *The Empire of Fear*, 1988
Stewart Wieck, *The Beast Within*, 1995
   editor

## 5694

### ROBERT WEINBERG

## *A Calculated Magic*

(New York: Ace, 1995)

**Story type:** Fantasy (Magic Conflict)
**Major character(s):** Jack Collins, Scientist, Magician; Roger Quinn, Businessman, Magician; The Old Man of the Mountain, Mythical Creature

**Time period(s):** 1990s (1995)
**Locale(s):** Chicago, Illinois; Las Vegas, Nevada

**Summary:** Jack Collins, the Logical Magician, hopes for some time off after having just saved the world. But when the Old Man of the Mountain kidnaps his fiancee, Megan Ambrose, and threatens to sell a biological plague virus to the highest bidder, Jack finds himself once again drawn into the world of magic, a world of amazing puissant mathematics.

**Other books you might like:**
Emma Bull, *Finder*, 1994
L. Sprague de Camp, *The Complete Compleat Enchanter*, 1989
   Fletcher Pratt, co-author
Gordon R. Dickson, *The Dragon and the George*,
Michael Flynn, *In the Country of the Blind*, 1990
Leo Frankowski, *The Cross-Time Engineer*, 1986
Robert A. Heinlein, *Waldo and Magic, Inc.*, 1990
Christopher Stasheff, *The Warlock in Spite of Himself*, 1969

## 5695

### ROBERT WEINBERG

## *The Dead Man's Kiss*

(New York: Pocket, 1992)

**Story type:** Horror (Occult)
**Major character(s):** Ellen Harper, Archaeologist (Egyptologist); David Ross, Detective; Carl Garrett, Murderer (white supremacist)
**Time period(s):** 1990s
**Locale(s):** Chicago, Illinois

**Summary:** With the help of artifacts stolen from a nearby museum, white supremacist Carl Garrett resurrects the mummy Jambres to help him wipe out the Jewish race. But Carl is unaware that Jambres has engineered his own resurrection and has more far-reaching plans that will have an impact on the whole of western civilization.

**Other books you might like:**
Charles L. Grant, *The Long Night of the Grave*, 1986
Robert E. Howard, *Skull-Face*, 1946
   short story in *Skullface and Others*
Michael Paine, *Cities of the Dead*, 1988
Anne Rice, *The Mummy, or Ramses the Damned*, 1989

## 5696

### ROBERT WEINBERG

## *The Devil's Auction*

(Philadelphia: Owlswick, 1988)

**Story type:** Horror (Occult)
**Major character(s):** Valerie Warner, Sorceress, Model; Alex Warner, Professor (history professor)
**Time period(s):** 1980s (1988)
**Locale(s):** Chicago, Illinois

**Summary:** When her sorcerer father is murdered by supernatural agents, Valerie Warner inherits his invitation to the Devil's Auction, a periodic event which only the successful bidder survives. This is the author's first novel.

**Other books you might like:**
Dion Fortune, *The Secrets of Dr. Taverner*, 1926
Mercedes Lackey, *Burning Water*, 1989
Seabury Quinn, *The Devil's Bride*, 1976
Sax Rohmer, *The Brood of the Witch Queen*, 1918
Dennis Wheatley, *The Devil Rides Out*, 1935

## 5697

### ROBERT WEINBERG

## *A Logical Magician*
(New York: Ace, 1994)

**Story type:** Fantasy (Magic Conflict; Light Fantasy)
**Major character(s):** Jack Collins, Student (graduate school mathematician); Cassandra Cole, Immortal, Martial Arts Expert (Amazon warrior)
**Time period(s):** 1990s
**Locale(s):** Chicago, Illinois; California

**Summary:** Named by Merlin Ambrose as savior of Humanking, Jack Collins must puzzle out both the threat and the solution after an ancient deity kidnaps the wizard. Enlisting help from other mythical champions who acieved existence through human mythology, Jack must also apply ancient mythical patterns to modern technological society to battle the reemergent evil.

**Other books you might like:**
Gene DeWeese, *Now You See It/Him/Them...*, 1975
    Robert Coulson, co-author
Elizabeth Forrest, *Phoenix Fire*, 1992
Simon Hawke, *The Wizard of 4th Street*, 1987
Megan Lindholm, *Wizard of the Pigeons*, 1986
Holly Lisle, *Minerva Wakes*, 1994
Larry Niven, *Fallen Angels*, 1991
    Jerry Pournelle, Michael Flynn, co-authors
Clifford D. Simak, *Out of Their Minds*, 1970

## 5698

### ROBERT WEINBERG
### MARTIN H. GREENBERG, Co-Author

## *Lovecraft's Legacy*
(New York: Tor, 1990)

**Story type:** Horror (Anthology)

**Summary:** A collection of 13 stories by different authors commemorating the 100th anniversary of the birth of H. P. Lovecraft. The stories are written less in emulation of Lovecraft's rich, atmospheric style than as examples of what the authors learned from Lovecraft about the craft of writing. Best selections include Gene Wolfe's "Lord of the Land," Brian McNaughton's "Merphyllia" and F. Paul Wilson's "The Pine Barrens."

**Other books you might like:**
Edward P. Berglund, *Disciples of Cthulhu*, 1976
Ramsey Campbell, *New Tales of the Cthulhu Mythos*, 1980
Lin Carter, *The Spawn of Cthulhu*, 1971
H.P. Lovecraft, *Tales of the Cthulhu Mythos: Golden Anniversary Anthology*, 1990

## 5699

### ROBERT WEINBERG, Editor
### STEFAN DZIEMIANOWICZ, Co-Editor
### MARTIN H. GREENBERG, Co-Editor

## *Rivals of Dracula*
(New York: Barnes & Noble, 1996)

**Story type:** Horror (Anthology; Vampire Story)

**Summary:** Nineteen reprint stories feature the famous vampire Count Dracula and his descendants as characters. Dracula bests pickpockets in contemporary France in Robert Bloch's "The Yougoslaves" and Nazis during World War II in Ed Hoch's "Dracula 1944." He is summoned by a boy with a childhood obsession with vampires in Richard Matheson's "Drink My Red Blood" and by a punk challenger in Brian Hodge's "Like a Pilgrim to a Shrine." He pulls strings that control the fate of contemporary Romania in Dan Simmons' "All Dracula's Children" and Kevin J. Anderson's "Much at Stake." His progeny extend their unholy lives in Angela Carter's "Lady in the House of Love" and Tanith Lee's "Nunc Dimittis."

**Other books you might like:**
Martin H. Greenberg, *Dracula: Prince of Darkness*, 1992
    editor
Stephen Jones, *The Mammoth Book of Dracula*, 1997
    editor
Michel Parry, *The Rivals of Dracula: A Century of Vampire Fiction*, 1977
    editor

## 5700

### ROBERT WEINBERG
### STEFAN DZIEMIANOWICZ, Co-Author
### MARTIN H. GREENBERG, Co-Author

## *Rivals of Weird Tales*
(New York: Bonanza, 1990)

**Story type:** Horror (Anthology)

**Summary:** Thirty stories from the pulp fantasy and weird fiction magazines that were *not* published in *Weird Tales*, the most famous and influential fantasy magazine of the period. Included are H.P. Lovecraft's Poe homage "Cool Air," Jack Williamson's werewolf tale "Wolves of Darkness" and Seabury Quinn's ghost story "Doomed," all from magazines that tried to emulate *Weird Tales*, as well as Norvell Page's superman novel "But Without Horns," Theodore Sturgeon's amusing "Shottle Bop" and Richard Matheson's twilight-zonish "Sorry, Right Number," which appeared in magazines that tried to break new ground.

**Other books you might like:**
D.R. Benson, *The Unknown*, 1963
Edward L. Ferman, *The Best Horror From Fantasy & Science Fiction*, 1988
    Anne Jordan, co-author
Stanley Schmidt, *Unknown Worlds: Tales From Beyond*, 1988
    Martin H. Greenberg, co-author

## 5701

### ROBERT WEINBERG

## *The Road to Hell, Volume I*
(Clarkston, Georgia: White Wolf, 1997)

**Story type:** Horror (Apocalyptic Horror)
**Series:** World of Darkness: Mage the Ascension: The Horizon War Trilogy
**Major character(s):** Alvin Reynolds, Computer Expert; Sharon Reed, Magician (technomancer); Seventeen, Prisoner
**Time period(s):** 1990s (1997)
**Locale(s):** Rochester, New York

**Summary:** In the Wolrd of Darkness, where supernatural creatures coexist with human beings, members of the warring Mage clans, who combine necromancy and science, battle members of the vampire

Kindred for control of the Horizon Realms, dimensions that provide access to realms other than their own. First Book in a trilogy.

**Other books you might like:**
Richard Lee Byers, *The Ebon Mask*, 1996
Jackie Cassada, *Shadows on the Hill*, 1996
Gherbod Fleming, *The Devil's Advocate*, 1997
Staley Krause, *Truth Until Paradox*, 1995
    Stewart Wieck, co-editor
Doug Murray, *Call to Battle*, 1996
Stewart Wieck, *The Essential World of Darkness*, 1997
    editor

**5702**

ROBERT WEINBERG

## The Road to Hell, Volume II

(Clarkston, Georgia: White Wolf, 1997)

**Story type:** Horror (Apocalyptic Horror)
**Series:** World of Darkness: Mage: The Horizon War Trilogy
**Major character(s):** Alvin Reynolds, Computer Expert; Sharon Reed, Magician (technomancer); Madeleine Giovanni, Vampire
**Time period(s):** 1990s (1997)
**Locale(s):** Rochester, New York

**Summary:** The Ascension Warrior, who claims to be the reincarnation of the legendary Heylel Teomin, emerges in the World of Darkness to bring peace to the warring Mages of the Nine Traditions and the Technicians of the Technocracy. Will he help the Mages secure the Horizon Realms from the vampire Kindred, or is he motivated by his own whims and schemes? Second book in the trilogy.

**Other books you might like:**
Richard Lee Byers, *The Ebon Mask*, 1996
Jackie Cassada, *Shadows on the Hill*, 1996
Gherbod Fleming, *The Devil's Advocate*, 1997
Staley Krause, *Truth Until Paradox*, 1995
    Stewart Wieck, co-editor
Doug Murray, *Call to Battle*, 1996
Stewart Wieck, *The Essential World of Darkness*, 1997
    editor

**5703**

ROBERT WEINBERG

## The Unbeholden

(Clarkston, Georgia: White Wolf, 1996)

**Story type:** Horror (Vampire Story)
**Series:** Vampire: The Masquerade
**Major character(s):** Dire McCann, Detective; Alicia Varney, Businesswoman, Vampire; Madeleine Giovanni, Vampire
**Time period(s):** 1990s (1994)
**Locale(s):** Vienna, Austria; Paris, France; Tel Aviv, Israel

**Summary:** Dire McCann and Alicia Varney, the avatars of ancient beings engaged in the sectarian struggles of the Camarilla and Sabbat vampires, have their final showdown with the Red Death, a monstrous creation of the Order of Dreadful Night whose existence means not only the end of the Vampire Masquerade, but destruction of the world as we know it. This novel, the third in the author's Masquerade of the Red Death Trilogy, is set in the publisher's "Vampire: The Masquerade" gaming world, in which vampire clans are enjoined by the law of their species to mingle unobtrusively with mortals and keep their supernatural identities secret.

**Other books you might like:**
Don Bassingthwaite, *As One Dead*, 1996
    Nancy Kilpatrick, co-author
Nancy A. Collins, *A Dozen Black Roses*, 1996
James A. Moore, *The House of Secrets*, 1995
    Kevin Murphy, co-author

**5704**

ROBERT WEINBERG

## Unholy Allies

(Clarkston, Georgia: White Wolf, 1995)

**Story type:** Horror (Vampire Story)
**Series:** A Vampire: The Masquerade: Masquerade of the Red Death
**Major character(s):** Dire McCann, Detective; Alicia Varney, Businesswoman, Vampire; Madeleine Giovanni, Vampire
**Time period(s):** 1990s (1995)
**Locale(s):** Washington, District of Columbia

**Summary:** In this continuation of the author's first novel in the series, *The Masquerade of the Red Death* (1995), detective Dire McCann searches for the origins of The Red Death, an unstoppable nemesis to the vampire nation that rules an alternate Earth with mortals. Meanwhile, Alicia Varney, a contemporary woman possessed by the soul of an ancient vampire queen, allies herself with McCann in an effort to prevent the truth of his and her secret identities.

**Other books you might like:**
Brian Lumley, *Necroscope: The Lost Years*, 1995
Kim Newman, *Anno Dracula*, 1992
Dan Simmons, *Carrion Comfort*, 1989
Brian Stableford, *The Empire of Fear*, 1988
Karen E. Taylor, *Blood Secrets*, 1994

**5705**

ROBERT WEINBERG
MARK REIN-HAGEN, Co-Author

## Vampire Diary: The Embrace

(Stone Mountain, Georgia: White Wolf, 1995)

**Story type:** Horror (Vampire Story)
**Series:** Vampire Diary
**Major character(s):** Auston Jacobson, Saloon Keeper/Owner; Claudius, Vampire; Danya, Teenager
**Time period(s):** 1990s (1995)
**Locale(s):** Los Angeles, California

**Summary:** Told in the form of a diary, this novella chronicles the thoughts and fears of Auston Jacobson, bartender at the Neverland night club, whose promotion to manager entails being "embraced" by its vampire owner, and becoming a being whose vampire nature disgusts his human self. The story is set in the universe of the *World of Darkness: Vampire* role-playing game.

**Other books you might like:**
Scott Ciencin, *The Vampire Odyssey*, 1992
Lewis Gannett, *The Living One*, 1993
Pat Graversen, *Sweet Blood*, 1993
Anne Rice, *Interview with the Vampire*, 1976
Karen E. Taylor, *Blood Secrets*, 1994
William Tedford, *Liquid Diet*, 1993

## **5706**
ROBERT WEINBERG, Editor
STEFAN DZIEMIANOWICZ, Co-Editor
MARTIN H. GREENBERG, Co-Editor

### *Weird Vampire Tales*
(New York: Gramercy, 1992)

**Story type:** Horror (Anthology; Vampire Story)

**Summary:** Thirty stories from pulp fiction magazines such as *Weird Tales, Strange Tales, Unknown Worlds,* and *Beyond Fantasy Fiction,* that served as the bridge between classic and contemporary vampire stories. Included are Seabury Quinn's "The Man Who Cast No Shadow," one of the first vampire stories set on American soil; Robert E. Howard's southwestern vampire story "The Horror from the Mound"; Carl Jacobi's "Revelations in Black" and Everil Worrell's "The Canal," both of which employ vampire femmes fatales; Robert Bloch's "The Cloak" and August Derleth's "Who Shall I Say Is Calling," both humorous vampire stories; Cyril Kornbluth's tale of psychic vampirism, "The Mindworm"; and Hugh Cave's classic story of vampires living on a shipwrecked boat, "Stragella."

**Other books you might like:**
Alan Ryan, *Vampires: Two Centuries of Great Vampire Stories,* 1987
    editor
Leslie Shepard, *The Dracula Book of Great Vampire Stories,* 1977
    editor
Devendra P. Varma, *Voices From the Vault: Authentic Vampire Tales,* 1987
    editor

## **5707**
MARGARET WEIS
DAVID BALDWIN, Co-Author

### *Dark Heart*
(New York: HarperPrism, 1998)

**Story type:** Fantasy (Adventure; Contemporary)
**Series:** Dragon's Disciple
**Major character(s):** Justin Sterling, Immortal, Agent; The Dragon, Deity; Sandra McCormick, Police Officer (lieutenant)
**Time period(s):** 1990s
**Locale(s):** Chicago, Illinois

**Summary:** Although Justin Sterling served as a bloody hand of the Dragon for centuries, when he kills a Chicago police officer, he comes to the attention of equally tormented Sandra McCormick. Can these two deadly individuals, united by love and pain, withstand the events that will demand they kill each other?

**Other books you might like:**
Laurell K. Hamilton, *The Laughing Corpse,* 1994
Jason Henderson, *Highlander: The Element of Fire,* 1995
Ashley McConnell, *Highlander: Scimitar,* 1996
Jennifer Roberson, *Scotland the Brave,* 1996
Roger Zelazny, *This Immortal,* 1966

## **5708**
MARGARET WEIS
DON PERRIN, Co-Author

### *The Doom Brigade*
(Lake Geneva, Wisconsin: TSR, 1996)

**Story type:** Fantasy (Adventure; Political)
**Series:** Dragonlance
**Major character(s):** Kang, Mythical Creature (dragon), Military Personnel; Gloth, Mythical Creature (dragon), Military Personnel
**Time period(s):** Indeterminate
**Locale(s):** Krynn, Planet—Imaginary

**Summary:** When a group of draconians attempt to hide in the mountains and pursue a life of peace, dwarves make the decision difficult, as a great treasure hidden in the mountains lures both groups.

## **5709**
MARGARET WEIS
TRACY HICKMAN, Co-Author

### *Dragon Wing*
(New York: Bantam, 1990)

**Story type:** Fantasy (Adventure)
**Series:** Death Gate Cycle
**Major character(s):** Hugh the Hand, Criminal (assassin); Sinistrad, Wizard (Mysteriarch)
**Time period(s):** Indeterminate
**Locale(s):** Earth

**Summary:** King Stephen saves Hugh from the executioner, but Hugh must kill Bane, Sinistrad's son and spy. It becomes apparent that there are other forces at work when Hugh is unable to kill Bane and gets caught up in bigger events.

**Other books you might like:**
Dave Duncan, *The Destiny of the Sword,* 1988
    The Seventh Sword, Book 3
Pat Zettner, *The Shadow Warrior,* 1990

## **5710**
MARGARET WEIS, Editor

### *A Dragon-Lover's Treasury of the Fantastic*
(New York: Warner Aspect, 1994)

**Story type:** Fantasy (Anthology)

**Summary:** Contains a two-page introduction and 20 stories about dragons published 1957-1992 in periodicals and anthologies including Anne McCaffrey's Award-winning "Weyr Search" and Gordon R. Dickson's "St. Dragon and the George," a story subsequently expanded into *The Dragon and the George* (1976). The tone varies from humorous to dark and themes include biotechnology, ecology, magic conflict, and dragons and the law. Authors include Nancy Varian Berberick, Orson Scott Card, L. Sprague de Camp, David Drake, Esther M. Friesner, Craig Shaw Gardner, George R.R. Martin, Patricia A. McKillip, Mickey Zucker Reichert, Mike Resnick, Joan D. Vinge and Roger Zelazny.

**Other books you might like:**
Orson Scott Card, *Dragons of Darkness,* 1981
    editor

Orson Scott Card, *Dragons of Light*, 1983
   editor
Jack Dann, *Dragons!*, 1993
   Gardner Dozois, co-editor
Rosalind M. Greenberg, *Dragon Fantastic*, 1992
   Martin H. Greenberg, co-editor
Jane Yolen, *Here There Be Dragons*, 1993

### 5711

**MARGARET WEIS**
**TRACY HICKMAN**, Co-Author

## *Dragons of Summer Flame*

(Lake Geneva, Wisconsin: TSR, 1995)

**Story type:** Fantasy (Political; Magic Conflict)
**Series:** Dragonlance
**Major character(s):** Tanis, Mythical Creature (half-elf); Dalamar, Wizard; Raistlin Majere, Wizard
**Time period(s):** Indeterminate
**Locale(s):** Krynn, Planet—Imaginary

**Summary:** As the Dark Queen gathers her warriors and unnatural minions, Paul Majere seeks the long lost Raistlin Majere. If defenders do not come forward, evil forces will dominate the continent.

**Other books you might like:**
Nancy Varian Berberick, *Stormblade*, 1988
Robert Jordan, *The Eye of the World*, 1987
Mary Kirchoff, *Kendermore*, 1989
Richard A. Knaak, *The Legend of Huma*, 1988
Dan Parkinson, *The Gates of Thorbardin*, 1990
Kevin Stein, *Brothers Majere*, 1989
Michael Williams, *Weasel's Luck*, 1988

### 5712

**MARGARET WEIS**
**TRACY HICKMAN**, Co-Author

## *Elven Star*

(New York: Bantam Spectra, 1990)

**Story type:** Fantasy (Alternate World; Adventure)
**Series:** Death Gate Cycle
**Major character(s):** Haplo, Adventurer, Wizard; Paithan, Mythical Creature (Elf), Adventurer
**Time period(s):** Indeterminate
**Locale(s):** Pryan, Planet—Imaginary (Realm of Fire)

**Summary:** Haplo, the Patryn, is sent by his adoptive father to Pryan, a large stony world with a molten core, to investigate the world and its inhabitants. Magically flying his ship, Dragon Wing, he visits the elves, humans and dwarves who are all hoping for the Lost Lords to return and save them from the menacing renegade giants and one another.

**Other books you might like:**
Dave Duncan, *The Destiny of the Sword*, 1988
Elizabeth Moon, *Surrender None: The Legacy of Gird*, 1990
Alis A. Rasmussen, *The Labyrinth Gate*, 1988
Melanie Rawn, *The Star Scroll*, 1989
Pat Zettner, *The Shadow Warrior*, 1990

### 5713

**MARGARET WEIS**, Editor

## *Fantastic Alice*

(New York: Ace, 1995)

**Story type:** Fantasy (Anthology)
**Major character(s):** Alice, Child

**Summary:** Contains a three-page introduction and 17 original stories varying in tone from whimsical to humorous and all featuring Alice in new situations inspired by Lewis Carroll's *Alice's Adventures in Wonderland*. Authors include Janet Asimov, Robin Wayne Bailey, Peter Crowther, Esther M. Friesner, Jane M. Lindskold, Lisa Mason, Jody Lynn Nye, Mickey Zucker Reichert, Lawrence Watt-Evans and Roger Zelazny.

**Other books you might like:**
Gilbert Adair, *Alice through the Needle's Eye: The Further Adventures of Lewis Carroll's ''Alice''*, 1985
Lewis Carroll, *Alice's Adventures in Wonderland*, 1865
Lewis Carroll, *Through the Looking Glass and What Alice Found There*, 1872
David Kirschner, *The Pagemaster*, 1993
   Ernie Contreras, co-author
Randall Garrett, *Takeoff!*, 1979

### 5714

**MARGARET WEIS**
**TRACY HICKMAN**, Co-Author

## *Fire Sea*

(New York: Bantam Spectra, 1991)

**Story type:** Fantasy (Alternate World; Adventure)
**Series:** Death Gate Cycle
**Major character(s):** Haplo, Adventurer, Wizard (Patryn); Alfred, Adventurer, Wizard (Sartan)
**Time period(s):** Indeterminate
**Locale(s):** Abarrach, Planet—Imaginary (Realm of Stone)

**Summary:** Ordered to journey to each of the worlds connected by the Death Gate, Haplo travels to Abarrach accompanied, unintentionally, by Alfred, thought to be the last survivor of his people. As they travel through Abarrach's underground civilization, they meet a lost tribe of Alfred's people and become involved in the civil war engulfing Abarrach.

**Other books you might like:**
Michael Cassutt, *Dragon Season*, 1991
Philip Jose Farmer, *To Your Scattered Bodies Go*, 1971
Marc Laidlaw, *Neon Lotus*, 1988
Elizabeth Moon, *Oath of Gold*, 1989
J.R.R. Tolkien, *The Fellowship of the Ring*, 1954
J.R.R. Tolkien, *The Return of the King*, 1956
J.R.R. Tolkien, *The Two Towers*, 1955

### 5715

**MARGARET WEIS**
**TRACY HICKMAN**, Co-Author

## *The Hand of Chaos*

(New York: Bantam Spectra, 1993)

**Story type:** Fantasy (Quest)
**Series:** Death Gate Cycle

**Major character(s):** Haplo, Adventurer, Wizard (Patryn); Bane, Child, Adventurer; Hugh the Hand, Criminal (assassin)
**Time period(s):** Indeterminate
**Locale(s):** Arianus, Planet—Imaginary (Realm of Air)

**Summary:** The Lord of the Nexus, Xar, orders Haplo and Bane to Arianus to carry on his work. Xar intends Bane to aid Xar's acquisition of ultimate power through control of gate technology and plans for Haplo's eventual death. Meanwhile, Haplo's companion suffers imprisonment in a deadly labyrinth.

**Other books you might like:**
Barbara Hambly, *Dog Wizard*, 1993
Robert Jordan, *The Eye of the World*, 1989
Katharine Kerr, *The Bristling Wood*, 1989
Katharine Kerr, *Daggerspell*, 1986
Katharine Kerr, *Darkspell*, 1987
Tad Williams, *The Dragonbone Chair*, 1989
Jonathan Wylie, *The Lightless Kingdom*, 1989

---

**5716**

**MARGARET WEIS**
**TRACY HICKMAN**, Co-Author

## Into the Labyrinth

(New York: Bantam Spectra, 1993)

**Story type:** Fantasy (Political; Quest)
**Series:** Death Gate Cycle
**Major character(s):** Haplo, Adventurer, Wizard (Patryn); Alfred, Adventurer, Wizard (Sartan); Hugh the Hand, Criminal (assassin)
**Time period(s):** Indeterminate
**Locale(s):** Abarrach, Planet—Imaginary (Realm of Stone); Arianus, Planet—Imaginary (Realm of Air); Pyran, Planet—Imaginary (Realm of Fire)

**Summary:** The Lord of the Nexus, Xar, abandons his plans to invade the four worlds with armies of reanimated dead when he learns of the Chamber of the Damned and the Seventh Gate, key to the fate of all worlds. Xar plots to kill and reanimate Haplo as his servant to gain Haplo's unique knowledge of the Gate's location.

**Other books you might like:**
Lois McMaster Bujold, *The Spirit Ring*, 1992
Terry Brooks, *The Talismans of Shannara*, 1993
Barbara Hambly, *Dog Wizard*, 1993
Elizabeth Ann Scarborough, *Last Refuge*, 1992
Martha Wells, *The Element of Fire*, 1993
Roger Zelazny, *Nine Princes in Amber*, 1970

---

**5717**

**MARGARET WEIS**

## King's Sacrifice

(New York: Bantam Spectra, 1991)

**Story type:** Science Fiction (Science Fantasy; Political)
**Series:** Star of the Guardians
**Major character(s):** Dion Starfire, Heir, Royalty (king); Maigrey Morianna, Noblewoman, Pilot; Derek Sagan, Military Personnel (General)
**Time period(s):** Indeterminate Future
**Locale(s):** *Phoenix II*, Spaceship; Outer Space

**Summary:** Dion, fighting to regain his hereditary position as king, must overthrow the corrupt new Republic and protect the church which he is helping become reestablished in the Empire. His prob-

lems will not be resolved until he has made the ultimate sacrifice to ensure peace in his realm.

**Other books you might like:**
Lois McMaster Bujold, *Barrayar*, 1991
Frank Herbert, *Dune*, 1965
Steve Miller, *Agent of Change*, 1988
   Sharon Lee, co-author
L.E. Modesitt Jr., *The Ecologic Secession*, 1990
Alis A. Rasmussen, *A Passage of Stars*, 1990
Michael Swanwick, *Stations of the Tide*, 1991
Ian Watson, *God's World*, 1990

---

**5718**

**MARGARET WEIS**
**DON PERRIN**, Co-Author

## Knights of the Black Earth

(New York: Roc, 1995)

**Story type:** Science Fiction (Space Opera; Political)
**Major character(s):** Xris, Cyborg, Mercenary (Mag Force 7); Dalin Rowan, Computer Expert
**Time period(s):** Indeterminate Future
**Locale(s):** Outer Space

**Summary:** Seeking Dalin Rowan to exact revenge for betraying Mag Force 7, Xris uncovers a plot by Earth supremacists to assassinate the King of the Galaxy and restore Earth's rule. Set in the Universe of The Star of the Guardians series (1990-1993).

**Other books you might like:**
Lois McMaster Bujold, *Brothers in Arms*, 1989
Glen Cook, *The Dragon Never Sleeps*, 1988
William C. Dietz, *Legion of the Damned*, 1993
Dave Duncan, *Hero*, 1991
Rick Shelley, *Until Relieved*, 1994
David Weber, *On Basilisk Station*, 1993

---

**5719**

**MARGARET WEIS**
**TRACY HICKMAN**, Co-Author

## Legacy of the Darksword

(New York: Bantam Spectra, 1997)

**Story type:** Fantasy (Adventure; Magic Conflict)
**Series:** Darksword
**Major character(s):** Mosiah, Wizard; Saryon, Scholar; Reuven, Secretary
**Time period(s):** Indeterminate Future
**Locale(s):** Thimhallen, Fictional Country; Oxford, England

**Summary:** Joram forged the Darksword 20 years ago, destroying the magic land of Thimhallen and forcing his people to take refuge in the dreary relocation camps of Earth. When a rapacious alien threatens Earth, salvation rests in finding Joram and his new Darksword. But a new breed of wizard, the terrifying Technomancers, oppose the search in the wastelands of Thimhallen.

**Other books you might like:**
Eleanor Arnason, *Daughter of the Bear King*, 1987
Gordon R. Dickson, *The Dragon and the George*, 1976
Barbara Hambly, *The Silent Tower*, 1986
Guy Gavriel Kay, *The Summer Tree*, 1985
Will Shetterly, *The Tangled Lands*, 1989

## 5720

**MARGARET WEIS**

### The Lost King

(New York: Bantam Spectra, 1990)

**Story type:** Science Fiction (Science Fantasy; Political)
**Series:** Star of the Guardians
**Major character(s):** Dion Starfire, Heir, Royalty (prince); Maigrey Morianna, Noblewoman (lady), Pilot; Derek Sagan, Military Personnel (general)
**Time period(s):** Indeterminate Future
**Locale(s):** *Phoenix*, Spaceship; *Defiant*, Spaceship

**Summary:** The Warlord is searching the galaxy for the heir to the murdered king of the Starfire dynasty. Only if Prince Dion can be destroyed or controlled will the future of the harsh Democratic Republic be assured. Lady Maigrey and a few other surviving Guardians of the throne help Dion fight the corruption of the new Republic and claim his rightful heritage.

**Other books you might like:**
Frank Herbert, *Dune*, 1965
George Lucas, *Star Wars*, 1976
Alis A. Rasmussen, *A Passage of Stars*, 1990
Alis A. Rasmussen, *The Price of Ransom*, 1990
Alis A. Rasmussen, *Revolution's Shore*, 1990
Gene Wolfe, *The Shadow of the Torturer*, 1980

## 5721

**MARGARET WEIS**, Editor

### A Magic-Lover's Treasury of the Fantastic

(New York: Warner Aspect, 1998)

**Story type:** Fantasy (Anthology; Magic Conflict)

**Summary:** This anthology contains a two-page introduction and 20 stories about magic reprinted from periodicals and anthologies dating from 1950 to 1995, with themes including mythical creatures, magical objects, a Gypsy's lethal curse, music, and sword and sorcery. Authors include Marion Zimmer Bradley, Orson Scott Card, C.J. Cherryh, Raymond E. Feist, Zenna Henderson, Katherine Kurtz, Mercedes Lackey, Ursula K. Le Guin, Fritz Leiber, Andre Norton, Melanie Rawn, Robert Silverberg, Christopher Stasheff, Jack Vance, and Roger Zelazny.

**Other books you might like:**
Mike Ashley, *The Random House Book of Fantasy Stories*, 1997
   editor
Robert H. Boyer, *Visions & Imaginings: Classic Fantasy Fiction*, 1992
   Kenneth Zahorski, co-author
Gardner Dozois, *Modern Classics of Fantasy*, 1997
Alison Lurie, *The Oxford Book of Modern Fairy Tales*, 1993
   editor
Tom Shippey, *The Oxford Book of Fantasy Stories*, 1994
   editor

## 5722

**MARGARET WEIS**
**TRACY HICKMAN**, Co-Author

### Nightsword

(New York: Ballantine Del Rey, 1998)

**Story type:** Fantasy (Adventure; Science Fiction)
**Major character(s):** Jeremy Griffiths, Spaceship Captain, Royalty; Merinda Neskat, Alien, Historian; Evon Flynn, Worker, Scholar
**Time period(s):** Indeterminate Future
**Locale(s):** Avadon, Planet—Imaginary

**Summary:** Wearing the Mantle of Kendis-Dai brings Jeremy Griffiths infinite knowledge, which is unfortunately not as useful as he had hoped, since his condition makes him prophet-emperor of a theocracy. After escaping and locating the Nightsword, he must figure out how to keep it out of the hands of the evil Tang of Gandri.

**Other books you might like:**
Iain M. Banks, *The Player of Games*, 1989
Lois McMaster Bujold, *The Vor Game*, 1990
Frank Herbert, *Dune*, 1965
Tracy Hickman, *The Immortals*, 1996
Jack Vance, *The Demon Princes: Volume One*, 1998

## 5723

**MARGARET WEIS**, Editor
**TRACY HICKMAN**, Co-Editor

### Relics and Omens

(Renton, Washington: TSR, 1998)

**Story type:** Fantasy (Anthology)

**Summary:** These 14 original stories are set in the world of the Dragonlance saga. Included are primarily writers who have contributed novels to the ongoing saga, such as Jean Rabe, Jeff Grubb, Richard Knaak, Nancy Varian Berberick, and Douglas Niles.

**Other books you might like:**
Richard Awlinson, *Waterdeep*, 1989
Roland J. Green, *The Wayward Knights*, 1997
Simon Hawke, *The Outcast*, 1993
James Lowder, *Prince of Lies*, 1993
Jean Rabe, *Red Magic*, 1991

## 5724

**MARGARET WEIS**
**TRACY HICKMAN**, Co-Author

### The Second Generation

(Lake Geneva, Wisconsin: TSR, 1994)

**Story type:** Fantasy (Collection; Adventure)
**Series:** Dragonlance
**Major character(s):** Tanis, Mythical Creature (half-elf), Warrior; Caramon, Innkeeper (The Inn of the Last Home), Hero; Raistlin, Wizard, Hero
**Time period(s):** Indeterminate
**Locale(s):** Krynn, Planet—Imaginary

**Summary:** Contains a two-page foreword, 20-page appendix, poetry by Michael Williams and five stories featuring the offspring of the heroes who restored the balance of good and evil bringing peace to Krynn. As defeated forces rally to destroy the harmony, younger warriors must come to the rescue. Game tie-in.

**Other books you might like:**
Mary Kirchoff, *Kendermore*, 1989
Richard A. Knaak, *The Legend of Huma*, 1988
Richard A. Knaak, *Kaz the Minotaur*, 1990
Paul B. Thompson, *Riverwind the Plainsman*, 1990
　　Tonya R. Carter, co-author
Nancy Varian, *Berberick, Stormblade*, 1988
Michael Williams, *Galen Beknighted*, 1990
Michael Williams, *Weasel's Luck*, 1988

## 5725

**MARGARET WEIS**
**TRACY HICKMAN**, Co-Author

### Sentinels

(New York: Ballantine Del Rey, 1996)

**Story type:** Science Fiction (Space Opera; Political)
**Series:** Starshield
**Major character(s):** Merinda Neskat, Alien, Historian (Omnet inquisitor); Jeremy Griffiths, Spaceship Captain; Queekat Shn'dar, Alien, Historian (Omnet inquisitor)
**Time period(s):** Indeterminate Future
**Locale(s):** *Brishan*, Spaceship; Brishan V, Planet—Imaginary

**Summary:** When the synthetic minds of the intergalactic Omnet begin to rebel, Merinda embarks on a search to find the legendary Mantle of Kendis-dai, which she hopes will restore order to the Omnet. Captain Griffiths and his crew, lost and stranded light years from Earth when the first FTL flight goes awry, somewhat reluctantly join Merinda in her search.

**Other books you might like:**
Jane Emerson, *City of Diamond*, 1996
David Gerrold, *Voyage of the Star Wolf*, 1990
Tracy Hickman, *The Immortals*, 1996
Jack Vance, *Alastor*, 1995
David Wingrove, *Beneath the Tree of Heaven*, 1995

## 5726

**MARGARET WEIS**
**TRACY HICKMAN**, Co-Author

### Serpent Mage

(New York: Bantam Spectra, 1992)

**Story type:** Fantasy (Quest)
**Series:** Death Gate Cycle
**Major character(s):** Haplo, Adventurer, Wizard (Patryn); Alfred, Adventurer, Wizard (Sartan)
**Time period(s):** Indeterminate
**Locale(s):** Chelestra, Planet—Imaginary (realm of water)

**Summary:** Continuing their explorations, Haplo, Alfred and Haplo's dog travel through the Death Gate to the fourth world in which dwarves, elves and humans coexist peacefully on bubble-encased submerged islands where they work together on escape plans for use when Chelestra's sun expires. Haplo helps battle a sudden infestation of dragon-snakes while Alfred discovers and wakens his sleeping Sartan ancestors hidden within Chelestra, actions which could precipitate universal disaster.

**Other books you might like:**
Piers Anthony, *Mercycle*, 1991
Philip Jose Farmer, *To Your Scattered Bodies Go*, 1971
Mary Gentle, *Ancient Light*, 1987
Mary Gentle, *Rats and Gargoyles*, 1991

Alis A. Rasmussen, *The Labyrinth Gate*, 1988
Robert Silverberg, *The Face of the Waters*, 1991
Joan Slonczewski, *A Door into Ocean*, 1986
J.R.R. Tolkien, *The Hobbit*, 1938

## 5727

**MARGARET WEIS**
**TRACY HICKMAN**, Co-Author

### The Seventh Gate

(New York: Bantam Spectra, 1994)

**Story type:** Fantasy (Magic Conflict; Adventure)
**Series:** Death Gate Cycle
**Major character(s):** Haplo, Adventurer, Wizard (Patryn); Alfred, Adventurer, Wizard (Sartan); Xar, Nobleman (Lord of the Nexus), Wizard
**Time period(s):** Indeterminate
**Locale(s):** Abarrach, Planet—Imaginary; Seventh Gate, Mythical Place

**Summary:** Pursuing knowledge of the Seventh Gate, Xar takes the mortally wounded Haplo to Abarrach, intending to make him an undead slave, while the Labyrinth imprisons Merit and Hugh the Hand who seek Alfred, captured by a dragon. An invasion of dragon-snakes portends disaster until the wizard, Zifnab, arrives with good dragons and the Sartan answer a summons. However, Xar must help to ensure victory. This concluding volume contains a 34-page appendix.

**Other books you might like:**
David Eddings, *Pawn of Prophecy*, 1982
Mary Gentle, *Ancient Light*, 1987
Robert Jordan, *The Eye of the World*, 1989
Katharine Kerr, *Daggerspell*, 1986
Melanie Rawn, *Dragon Prince*, 1988
Tad Williams, *The Dragonbone Chair*, 1989
Roger Zelazny, *Nine Princes in Amber*, 1970

## 5728

**MARGARET WEIS**

### The Soulforge

(Renton, Washington: TSR, 1998)

**Story type:** Fantasy (Adventure)
**Series:** Dragonlance
**Major character(s):** Raistlin Majere, Wizard, Handicapped; Caramon Majere, Warrior, Child; Antimodes, Wizard
**Time period(s):** Indeterminate Past
**Locale(s):** Krynn, Planet—Imaginary

**Summary:** A wizard traveling on an important mission comes across a young boy of frail health and burning ambition. He arranges for the child, to train as a mage, never realizing that this child will affect the future of Krynn. Raistlin's early training and the grueling test he must pass to become a mage mold a new hero.

**Other books you might like:**
Lisa Goldstein, *Summer King, Winter Fool*, 1994
Ursula K. Le Guin, *A Wizard of Earthsea*, 1968
Caroline Stevermer, *A College of Magics*, 1994
Martha Wells, *The Element of Fire*, 1993
Janny Wurts, *Stormwarden*, 1984

## 5729

**MARGARET WEIS**, Editor

### Testament of the Dragon

(New York: HaperPrism, 1997)

**Story type:** Fantasy (Adventure; Anthology)
**Major character(s):** Justin Sterling, Immortal, Artist; The True Dragon, Deity; Alexandra Stone, Police Officer
**Time period(s):** 1990s; 14th century
**Locale(s):** Loch Ness, Scotland; Chicago, Illinois

**Summary:** Contains three short stories by Jeff Grubb, J. Robert King and Janet Pack, supported by several explanatory articles and many illustrations. Justin Sterling sells himself to the True Dragon to save his family from the Plague, then fights the forces of darkness for six centuries as a man, as the half-human Wyrm and as a comic-book creator. Illustrated by Steve Lieber, Rags Morales and others.

**Other books you might like:**
Jason Henderson, *Highlander: The Element of Fire*, 1995
Ashley McConnell, *Highlander: Scimitar*, 1996
Jennifer Roberson, *Scotland the Brave*, 1996
Roger Zelazny, *This Immortal*, 1966

## 5730

**MARGARET WEIS**, Editor
**TRACY HICKMAN**, Co-Editor

### Treasures of Fantasy

(New York: HarperPrism, 1997)

**Story type:** Fantasy (Anthology)

**Summary:** Contains a two-page introduction by Weis plus brief biographical introductions to 24 stories reprinted from periodicals, anthologies and collections from 1948 through 1996. Varying in tone from somber to light, the stories feature diverse themes, such as sword and sorcery, magic conflict, high fantasy, mythical creatures, contemporary realism, impossible topology, and magical wishes. Authors include Poul Anderson, Marion Zimmer Bradley, Orson Scott Card, C.J. Cherryh, Philip K. Dick, Mercedes Lackey, R.A. Lafferty, Ursula K. Le Guin, Anne McCaffrey, Patricia A. McKillip, Andre Norton, Melanie Rawn, Jennifer Roberson, Joanna Russ, Robert Sheckley, Theordore Sturgeon, Jane Yolen and Roger Zelazny.

**Other books you might like:**
Mike Ashley, *The Random House Book of Fantasy Stories*, 1997
 editor
Robert H. Boyer, *Visions & Imaginings: Classic Fantasy Fiction*, 1992
 Kenneth J. Zahorski, co-editor
Alison Lurie, *The Oxford Book of Modern Fairy Tales*, 1993
 editor
Tom Shippey, *The Oxford Book of Fantasy Stories*, 1994
 editor
Robert Silverberg, *The Fantasy Hall of Fame*, 1993
 Martin H. Greenberg, co-editor

## 5731

**JORDAN K. WEISMAN**, Editor

### Into the Shadows

(New York: Roc, 1992)

**Story type:** Fantasy (Anthology; Urban)
**Series:** Shadowrun
**Time period(s):** 2050s (2050)
**Locale(s):** Seattle, Washington

**Summary:** Contains a one-page prologue, a two-page contributors' biography, a five-page glossary of slang used in 2050, a seven-page chronology of events 2000-2050 plus nine stories by eight authors with two stories contributed by Michael A. Stackpole. A game tie-in anthology edited by the game's creator.

**Other books you might like:**
M.A.R. Barker, *Man of Gold*, 1984
Robert N. Charrette, *Choose Your Enemies Carefully*, 1991
Robert N. Charrette, *Find Your Own Truth*, 1991
Robert N. Charrette, *Never Deal with a Dragon*, 1990
Robert N. Charrette, *Never Trust an Elf*, 1992
Nigel Findley, *2XS*, 1992
Christopher Kubasik, *Changeling*, 1992

## 5732

**FAY WELDON**

### The Cloning of Joanna May

(New York: Viking, 1990)

**Story type:** Science Fiction (Literary)
**Major character(s):** Joanna May, Divorced Person; Carl May, Businessman
**Time period(s):** 1990s

**Summary:** Joanna May, sixtyish, divorced, discovers that some thirty years earlier her then husband, a wealthy industrialist, had her cloned. Childless because her husband did not want children, she feels an overwhelming desire to find her four clones and discover what their lives are like. The five women hit it off well together and form an alliance of sorts against the world.

**Other books you might like:**
C.J. Cherryh, *Cyteen*, 1988
Ira Levin, *The Boys From Brazil*, 1976
Pamela Sargent, *Cloned Lives*, 1976
Kate Wilhelm, *Where Late the Sweet Birds Sang*, 1976
Gene Wolfe, *The Fifth Head of Cerberus*, 1972

## 5733

**ANGUS WELLS**

### Dark Magic

(New York: Bantam Spectra, 1992)

**Story type:** Fantasy (Quest; Magic Conflict)
**Series:** Godwars
**Major character(s):** Calandryll den Karynth, Royalty, Adventurer; Bracht ni Errhyn, Mercenary; Katya, Adventurer
**Time period(s):** Indeterminate
**Locale(s):** Lysse, Fictional Country; Cuan na'For, Fictional Country

**Summary:** Calandryll and his companions pursue the evil necromancer Rythamun, whose persona now inhabits the body of another man, to war-torn Kandahar and across the Narrow Sea to

Lysse. When Rythamun takes over another body, the three follow the trail, seeking to take from him the stolen *Arcanum* before it can be used to summon the Mad God, Tharn. Unknown to them, another sorcerer pursues them, plotting to obtain the *Arcanum* himself.

**Other books you might like:**
Lynn Abbey, *Daughter of the Bright Moon*, 1979
C.J. Cherryh, *Rusalka*, 1989
C.J. Cherryh, *Well of Shiuan*, 1978
Stephen R. Donaldson, *Lord Foul's Bane*, 1977
Barbara Hambly, *The Witches of Wenshar*, 1987
Patricia A. McKillip, *The Riddle-Master of Hed*, 1976
Patricia C. Wrede, *Caught in Crystal*, 1987

---

**5734**

ANGUS WELLS

## Exile's Challenge

(New York: Bantam Spectra, 1996)

**Story type:** Fantasy (Psychic Powers; Political)
**Series:** Exiles Saga
**Major character(s):** Dafyd Furth, Psychic; Chakthi, Leader, Warrior; Tomas Var, Military Personnel
**Time period(s):** Indeterminate
**Locale(s):** Matawaye, Fictional Country; Salvation, Mythical Place (prison colony); Ket-Ta-Thanne, Fictional Country

**Summary:** Chakthi plots to capture the land of Matawaye and wreak vengeance. While Major Tomas Var attempts to quell the unrest in Salvation caused by renegade Matawaye warriors, he must simultaneously contend with a personal battle with his own superior.

**Other books you might like:**
Lynn Flewelling, *Luck in the Shadows*, 1996
Terry Goodkind, *Wizard's First Rule*, 1994
J.V. Jones, *The Baker's Boy*, 1995
Robert Jordan, *The Eye of the World*, 1990
Katharine Kerr, *Daggerspell*, 1986

---

**5735**

ANGUS WELLS

## Exile's Children

(New York: Bantam Spectra, 1996)

**Story type:** Fantasy (Psychic Powers; Political)
**Series:** Exiles Saga
**Major character(s):** Dafyd Furth, Psychic; Arcole Blayke, Gambler, Martial Arts Expert; Flysse Cobal, Waiter/Waitress
**Time period(s):** Indeterminate
**Locale(s):** Ket-Ta-Witko, Fictional Country; Salvation, Mythical Place (prison colony)

**Summary:** When a blood feud evolves into violence and destructive demons overrun the land, hope for the future rests with three residents of the prison colony: Salvation, a tavern girl, a gambler, and a young boy with a prohibited talent at True Dreaming.

**Other books you might like:**
Dave Duncan, *The Cursed*, 1995
Dave Duncan, *Magic Casement*, 1990
Lynn Flewelling, *Luck in the Shadows*, 1996
Barbara Hambly, *The Ladies of Mandrigyn*, 1984
L.E. Modesitt Jr., *The Towers of the Sunset*, 1992

---

**5736**

ANGUS WELLS

## Forbidden Magic

(New York: Bantam Spectra, 1992)

**Story type:** Fantasy (Quest)
**Series:** Godwars
**Major character(s):** Calandryll den Karynth, Royalty, Scholar; Bracht ni Errhyn, Mercenary
**Time period(s):** Indeterminate
**Locale(s):** Tezin-dar, Fictional City; Gessyth, Fictional Country; Kandahar, Fictional Country

**Summary:** Intending to stop an evil wizard from waking a mad god whose parents forced him into eternal sleep to curtail an ancient war, Calandryll and Bracht must find and destroy a legendary book, the *Arcanum*, before the evil sorcerer finds it.

**Other books you might like:**
David Eddings, *Pawn of Prophecy*, 1982
Barbara Hambly, *The Time of the Dark*, 1982
Robert Jordan, *The Eye of the World*, 1990
Michael Moorcock, *The Revenge of the Rose*, 1991
Tad Williams, *The Dragonbone Chair*, 1988

---

**5737**

ANGUS WELLS

## The Guardian

(New York: Bantam Spectra, 1998)

**Story type:** Fantasy (Magic Conflict; Political)
**Major character(s):** Gailard, Military Personnel; Ellyn, Royalty (princess), Wizard; Nestor, Wizard
**Time period(s):** Indeterminate Past
**Locale(s):** Chaldor, Fictional Country; Hel's Town, Fictional City

**Summary:** Supported by the evil power of a Vachyn sorcerer, the Kingdom of Danant has smashed the forces of Chaldor and slain their king. Gailard the Highlander, who has no greater wish than to die for his lord, must live and save Princess Ellyn, who has never been on good terms with the Highlander. The two then must learn to trust one another and find allies to free their land from its conqueror.

**Other books you might like:**
Glen Cook, *The Black Company*, 1984
Barbara Hambly, *The Time of the Dark*, 1982
Robin Hobb, *Assassin's Apprentice*, 1995
J.V. Jones, *The Baker's Boy*, 1995
Katherine Kurtz, *Deryni Rising*, 1970

---

**5738**

ANGUS WELLS

## Lords of the Sky

(New York: Bantam Spectra, 1994)

**Story type:** Fantasy (Quest; Magic Conflict)
**Major character(s):** Daviot, Traveler (rememberer); Rwyan, Wizard; Urt, Genetically Altered Being
**Time period(s):** Indeterminate
**Locale(s):** Durbrecht, Fictional City; Dharbek, Fictional Country; Dragoncastle, Mythical Place

**Summary:** Dharbek suffers from periodic attacks by the people of Ahn, their bizarre magical enemies. Trained to remember past and current events as a sort of traveling historian, Daviot grows increasingly worried about his culture, crumbling from internal and external pressures. His solution, however, may increase the destruction.

**Other books you might like:**
David Gemmell, *Lion of Macedon*, 1992
Barbara Hambly, *The Time of the Dark*, 1982
Michael Scott Rohan, *The Forge in the Forest*, 1987
Judith Tarr, *Lord of the Two Lands*, 1993
Gene Wolfe, *Soldier of the Mist*, 1986

---

**5739**

ANGUS WELLS

### The Usurper

(New York: Bantam Spectra, 1990)

**Story type:** Fantasy (Legend; Magic Conflict)
**Series:** Book of the Kingdoms
**Major character(s):** Kedryn Caitin, Royalty (Prince of Tamur), Warrior; Wynett, Royalty (Princess of the Three Kingdoms), Religious (Sister); Hattim Sethiyan, Nobleman (Lord of Ust-Galich), Ruler (Usurper)
**Time period(s):** Indeterminate Past (Middle Ages)
**Locale(s):** The Three Kingdoms, Mythical Place

**Summary:** In the hour of his triumph over Taws, demon of the fire-god Ashar, Prince Kedryn was blinded by a magic sword. To regain his sight, Kedryn and Wynett journey to the abode of the dead to confront the spirit of the warrior who wielded the blade. While he is gone, Taws rises again and convinces the ambitious and greedy Lord Hattim to Murder King Darr and steal his throne. Kedryn returns to find the Three Kingdoms in chaos and Taws waiting to destroy him.

**Other books you might like:**
C.J. Cherryh, *Wizard Spawn*, 1989
  Nancy Asire, co-author
Frank Herbert, *Dune*, 1965
Elizabeth Moon, *Oath of Gold*, 1989
Elizabeth Moon, *Divided Allegiance*, 1988
Elizabeth Moon, *Sheepfarmer's Daughter*, 1988

---

**5740**

ANGUS WELLS

### The Way Beneath

(New York: Bantam Spectra, 1991)

**Story type:** Fantasy (Magic Conflict)
**Series:** Books of the Kingdoms
**Major character(s):** Kedryn Caitin, Royalty, Warrior; Wynett, Royalty, Religious; Ashar, Deity
**Time period(s):** Indeterminate Past ((Middle Ages))
**Locale(s):** The Three Kingdoms, Fictional Country; Magoria, Fictional Country

**Summary:** Kedryn descends into the netherworld to rescue Wynett and defeat Ashar who has secured Wynett's portion of the talisman and plans to acquire Kedryn's part.

**Other books you might like:**
Frank Herbert, *Dune*, 1965
Elizabeth Moon, *Divided Allegiance*, 1988
Elizabeth Moon, *Oath of Gold*, 1989
Elizabeth Moon, *Sheepfarmer's Daughter*, 1988
Michael Moorcock, *The Revenge of the Rose*, 1991
Margaret Weis, *Fire Sea*, 1991
  Tracy Hickman, co-author

---

**5741**

ANGUS WELLS

### Wild Magic

(New York: Bantam Spectra, 1993)

**Story type:** Fantasy (Quest; Magic Conflict)
**Series:** Godwars
**Major character(s):** Calandryll den Karynth, Royalty, Renegade; Bracht ni Errhyn, Mercenary; Katya, Adventurer
**Time period(s):** Indeterminate
**Locale(s):** Anwar-Teng, Fictional City; Jesseryn Plain, Fictional Country

**Summary:** Calandryll and his companions pursue the evil necromancer, Rythamun, whose persona now inhabits the body of another man, across the Jesseryn Plain. The three encounter Cennaire, beautiful pawn of the wizard Anomius who holds her heart in a magically concealed box. At first distrustful, Calandryll falls in love with her and she with him. Cennaire provides them aid against Anomius and Rythamun.

**Other books you might like:**
Lynn Abbey, *The Black Flame*, 1980
C.J. Cherryh, *Chernevog*, 1990
C.J. Cherryh, *The Fires of Azeroth*, 1979
Stephen R. Donaldson, *The Illearth War*, 1977
Barbara Hambly, *The Dark Hand of Magic*, 1990
P.C. Hodgell, *God Stalk*, 1982
Ursula K. Le Guin, *The Tombs of Atuan*, 1971
Mickey Zucker Reichert, *Godslayer*, 1987
J.R.R. Tolkien, *The Return of the King*, 1956
Tad Williams, *To Green Angel Tower*, 1993

---

**5742**

ANGUS WELLS

### Wrath of Ashar

(New York: Bantam Spectra, 1990)

**Story type:** Fantasy (Legend; Magic Conflict)
**Series:** Book of the Kingdoms
**Major character(s):** Kedryn Caitin, Royalty (Prince of Tamur), Warrior; Bedyr Caitin, Nobleman (Lord of Tamur), Warrior; Taws, Demon
**Time period(s):** Indeterminate Past (Medieval)
**Locale(s):** The Three Kingdoms, Mythical Place; Beltrevan, Mythical Place

**Summary:** By virtue of the astonishing powers he possesses, young Prince Kedryn of Tamur seems to be the one prophecied by the Sisterhood of the Lady to save the Three Kingdoms (Tamur, Ust-Galich and Kesh) from Taws, demon messenger of the fire-god Ashar and the warrior horde from the north. With the help of his father Bedyr and King Darr, Kedryn raises a mighty army and goes forth to do battle.

**Other books you might like:**
C.J. Cherryh, *Wizard Spawn*, 1989
  Nancy Asire, co-author
Frank Herbert, *Dune*, 1965
Elizabeth Moon, *Divided Allegiance*, 1988
Elizabeth Moon, *Oath of Gold*, 1989
Elizabeth Moon, *Sheepfarmer's Daughter*, 1988

## 5743

**CATHERINE WELLS** (Pseudonym of Catherine Wells Dimenstein)

### Children of the Earth

(New York: Ballantine Del Rey, 1992)

**Story type:** Science Fiction (Post-Holocaust)
**Major character(s):** Coconino, Time Traveler, Indian; Debra McKay, Scientist, Hunter; Derek Lujan, Time Traveler, Spaceman
**Time period(s):** Indeterminate Future
**Locale(s):** Canyonlands, Utah; Argo, Planet—Imaginary; Beta, Planet—Imaginary

**Summary:** This novel follows Coconino when he and Derek Lujan emerge from the time warp 150 years after the action in *The Earth Is All That Lasts*, and also examines the lives of those left behind, focusing on his yet unborn children. On Beta, the relatives of those marooned on Earth learn of the expedition's possible survival and attempt to organize a rescue.

**Other books you might like:**
Michael Armstrong, *Agviq*, 1990
Clare Bell, *People of the Sky*, 1989
Ursula K. Le Guin, *Always Coming Home*, 1987
Megan Lindholm, *Alien Earth*, 1992
R.A. MacAvoy, *The Third Eagle: Lessons Along a Minor String*, 1989
Donald E. McQuinn, *Warrior*, 1990
J.M. Morgan, *Desert Eden*, 1991
Paul O. Williams, *The Breaking of Northwall*, 1981

## 5744

**CATHERINE WELLS** (Pseudonym of Catherine Wells Dimenstein)

### The Earth Is All That Lasts

(New York: Ballantine/Del Rey, 1991)

**Story type:** Science Fiction (Post-Holocaust)
**Major character(s):** Coconino, Indian, Hunter; Debra McKay, Scientist, Hunter
**Time period(s):** Indeterminate Future (500 years after Earth's evacuation)
**Locale(s):** Canyonlands, Utah; Argo, Planet—Imaginary

**Summary:** Five hundred years after the Earth was evacuated, a few people plan an expedition to visit Earth. Since most people believe the Earth remains uninhabitable, the expedition is short on funding and mostly ignored. Meanwhile, the recovered Earth has two surviving societies, a group of scientists who have retained some technology, including a flyer, and the descendants of the 2,000 Indians who refused to abandon Earth. First novel.

**Other books you might like:**
Clare Bell, *People of the Sky*, 1989
David Brin, *Earth*, 1990
Alan Dean Foster, *Cyber Way*, 1990
Frank Herbert, *Dune*, 1965
Marc Laidlaw, *Neon Lotus*, 1988
R.A. MacAvoy, *The Third Eagle: Lessons Along a Minor String*, 1989
Carol Severance, *Reefsong*, 1991

## 5745

**CATHERINE WELLS** (Pseudonym of Catherine Wells Dimenstein)

### The Earth Saver

(New York: Ballantine Del Rey, 1993)

**Story type:** Science Fiction (Family Saga; Post-Disaster)
**Major character(s):** Montana "Tana" Winthrop, Administrator, Handicapped; Coconino, Indian, Time Traveler; Debra McCay, Leader
**Time period(s):** Indeterminate Future
**Locale(s):** Earth; Beta, Planet—Imaginary

**Summary:** Inspired by the recently discovered family records, Tana becomes CEO of the Winthrop Institute to develop a means of returning to Earth via point to point matter transmission. Obsessed with rescuing any survivors from the *Homeward Bound* crash, Tana makes a second trip without her medical aid dog, Doc, with mechanical failure delaying her return. While recovering from a seizure she meets many people, including Coconino, and realizes she must protect the Earth and its current inhabitants. Concludes the trilogy.

**Other books you might like:**
William Barton, *Dark Sky Legion*, 1992
David Brin, *Earth*, 1990
Tony Daniel, *Warpath*, 1993
Jack C. Haldeman II, *High Steel*, 1993
    Jack Dann, co-author
Ursula K. Le Guin, *Always Coming Home*, 1987
Anne McCaffrey, *Powers That Be*, 1993
    Elizabeth Ann Scarborough, co-author
Joan Slonczewski, *Daughter of Elysium*, 1993
Joan D. Vinge, *The Summer Queen*, 1991
Paul O. Williams, *The Breaking of Northwall*, 1981

## 5746

**H.G. WELLS**

### Thirty Strange Stories

(New York: Carroll & Graf, 1998)

**Story type:** Horror (Collection)

**Summary:** This collection contains 30 seminal stories of fantasy, horror, science fiction and menace introduced by Stephen Jones. Included are the conte cruel "The Cone," the ghost story "The Red Room," the native curse tale "Pollock and the Poroh Man," and "The Flowering of the Strange Orchid," a science fiction horror story about a bizarre plant that feeds on blood. Originally published in 1897.

**Other books you might like:**
Sir Arthur Conan Doyle, *The Horror of the Heights and Other Tales of Suspense*, 1992
William Hope Hodgson, *Out of the Storm*, 1975
Jack London, *Curious Fragments*, 1975
Sam Moskowitz, *Science Fiction by Gaslight*, 1968
    editor
S. Fowler Wright, *The Throne of Saturn*, 1949

## 5747

### H.G. WELLS

## *Thirty Strange Stories*
(New York: Carroll & Graf, 1998)

**Story type:** Science Fiction (Collection)

**Summary:** These 30 stories include most of the more famous examples of Welles' science fiction, as well as a few of the more obscure stories that are not otherwise readily available. There is also a brief biography of the author focusing on his literary career.

**Other books you might like:**
Brian W. Aldiss, *The Saliva Tree and Other Strange Growths*, 1981
Joseph O'Neill, *The Land under England*, 1935
Christopher Priest, *An Infinite Summer*, 1979
Ian Watson, *The Very Slow Time Machine*, 1979
John Wyndham, *Tales of Gooseflesh and Laughter*, 1956

## 5748

### MARTHA WELLS

## *City of Bones*
(New York: Tor, 1995)

**Story type:** Fantasy (Science Fiction; Post-Disaster)
**Major character(s):** Khat, Businessman (relic dealer), Genetically Altered Being (kris); Elen, Psychic (warder)
**Time period(s):** Indeterminate Future
**Locale(s):** Planet—Imaginary

**Summary:** To pursue the Master Warder's lust for power, Khat and Elen pursue ancient magical artifacts deep into the wasteland, not understanding their dangerous, true nature.

**Other books you might like:**
Anne Kelleher Bush, *Daughter of Prophecy*, 1995
Mary Gentle, *Ancient Light*, 1987
Terry Goodkind, *Wizard's First Rule*, 1994
Rosemary Kirstein, *The Steerswoman*, 1989
Sheri S. Tepper, *A Plague of Angels*, 1993

## 5749

### MARTHA WELLS

## *The Death of the Necromancer*
(New York: Avon Eos, 1998)

**Story type:** Fantasy (Magic Conflict; Mystery)
**Major character(s):** Nicholas "Donatien" Valiarde, Nobleman, Thief; Madeline, Thief, Sorceress; Reynard Morane, Martial Arts Expert, Criminal
**Time period(s):** Indeterminate
**Locale(s):** Vienne, Fictional City; Ile-Rien, Fictional Country

**Summary:** Nicholas and Madeline happen across a crime that leads them to suspect someone is going to attempt a magical endeavor that could devastate Vienne. Now they must determine who to stop and how to accomplish that good without alerting the authorities.

**Other books you might like:**
Lois McMaster Bujold, *The Spirit Ring*, 1992
Lynn Flewelling, *Luck in the Shadows*, 1996
Daniel Hood, *Scales of Justice*, 1998
Peg Kerr, *Emerald House Rising*, 1997
Patricia C. Wrede, *The Raven Ring*, 1994

## 5750

### MARTHA WELLS

## *The Element of Fire*
(New York: Tor, 1993)

**Story type:** Fantasy (Magic Conflict)
**Major character(s):** Kade Carrion, Royalty (Queen of Air and Darkness), Sorceress; Thomas Boniface, Bodyguard (queen's); Urbain Grandier, Imposter, Sorcerer
**Time period(s):** Indeterminate
**Locale(s):** Ile-Rein, Fictional Country

**Summary:** Hoping to settle unresolved family issues, Kade returns to court just in time to blunt the surprise attack of a traitorous confidant of the king. With the royal guard routed and dark Faery forces in control of the castle, Kade must use her wits and unusual magical abilities to rescue the monarchy. Author's first novel.

**Other books you might like:**
Lois McMaster Bujold, *The Spirit Ring*, 1992
Laurell K. Hamilton, *Nightseer*, 1992
Elizabeth A. Lynn, *Watchtower*, 1979
Elizabeth Ann Scarborough, *Last Refuge*, 1992
Paula Volsky, *Illusion*, 1992
Tad Williams, *The Dragonbone Chair*, 1988
Tad Williams, *Stone of Farewell*, 1990

## 5751

### ROGER WELSCH

## *Touching the Fire*
(New York: Villard Books, 1992)

**Story type:** Fantasy (Collection; Legend)
**Time period(s):** 20th century; Indeterminate Past
**Locale(s):** Great Plains, North America

**Summary:** Contains 12 pages of notes by the author plus seven stories surrounding the Nehawka's Sky Bundle which relate tribal history and tradition back to the tribe's earliest days.

**Other books you might like:**
Richard Erdoes, *American Indian Myths and Legends*, 1984
    Alfonso Ortiz, co-editor
Alan Dean Foster, *Cyber Way*, 1990
W. Michael Gear, *People of the Fire*, 1990
    Kathleen O'Neal Gear, co-author
J. Alison James, *Sing for a Gentle Rain*, 1990
Paul Radin, *The Trickster*, 1972
Lewis Spence, *The Myths of the North American Indians*, 1989
Gerald Vizenor, *Dead Voices: Natural Agonies in the Real World*, 1992

## 5752

### K.D. WENTWORTH

## *House of Moons*
(New York: Ballantine Del Rey, 1995)

**Story type:** Science Fiction (Political; Psychic Powers)
**Series:** Moonspeaker
**Major character(s):** Haemas Sennay Tal, Psychic, Heiress—Dispossessed; Diren Chee, Nobleman, Villain; Kevisson Monmart, Psychic, Healer
**Time period(s):** Indeterminate Future
**Locale(s):** Desalaya, Planet—Imaginary

**Summary:** Wishing to rule the entire Highlands, Diren Chee kidnaps Haemas Tal using a forbidden mind control device, a latteh. He then sends Haemas and his sister Axia into the past to discover how the latteh works. While searching for Haemas, Kevisson Monmart uncovers Chee's path of madness and murder and learns the sinister truth about the latteh. Sequel to *Moonspeaker*.

**Other books you might like:**
Lynn Abbey, *Beneath the Web*, 1994
Leigh Brackett, *The Sword of Rhiannon*, 1953
Marion Zimmer Bradley, *The Forbidden Tower*, 1977
Cheryl J. Franklin, *The Light in Exile*, 1990
Katherine Kurtz, *Camber of Culdi*, 1976
Andre Norton, *Ordeal in Otherwhere*, 1964
Julie Dean Smith, *The Wizard King*, 1994

## 5753

### K.D. WENTWORTH

## The Imperium Game

(New York: Ballantine Del Rey, 1994)

**Story type:** Science Fiction (Mystery; Alternate Intelligence)
**Major character(s):** Arvid Gerald Kerickson, Computer Expert, Divorced Person; Amaelia Metullus, Computer Game Player; Alline Bolton Kerickson, Divorced Person
**Time period(s):** 21st century
**Locale(s):** United States; Virtual Reality, Cyberspace

**Summary:** The murder of a computer game player inside a simulation of ancient Rome brings murder charges which discredit Kerickson, depriving him of computer access and the opportunity to clear himself. Entering the system illegally, Kerickson discovers a powerful and deadly twist added to his game.

**Other books you might like:**
Piers Anthony, *Killobyte*, 1993
Ben Bova, *Death Dream*, 1994
Brian Daley, *Tron*, 1982
Pierre Ouellette, *The Deus Machine*, 1994
Cole Perriman, *Terminal Games*, 1994

## 5754

### K.D. WENTWORTH

## Moonspeaker

(New York: Ballantine Del Rey, 1994)

**Story type:** Science Fiction (Psychic Powers; Political)
**Series:** Moonspeaker
**Major character(s):** Haemas Sennay Tal, Psychic, Fugitive; Jarid Tal Ketral, Psychic, Bastard Son; Kevisson Monmart, Psychic, Healer
**Time period(s):** Indeterminate
**Locale(s):** The Highlands, Fictional Country; Dorbin, Fictional City

**Summary:** Accused of patricide, Haemas flees into a hostile world. Pursued by searchers from both authorities and plotters, she navigates mundane dangers and esoteric, inhuman plans. If Haemas survives, the world may change for the better, but if she dies, it ceases to exist

**Other books you might like:**
Alfred Bester, *The Demolished Man*, 1953
Marion Zimmer Bradley, *The Heritage of Hastur*, 1975
Octavia E. Butler, *Patternmaster*, 1976
Katherine Kurtz, *Deryni Rising*, 1970
Julian May, *The Many-Colored Land*, 1981

## 5755

### BERNARD WERBER

## Empire of the Ants

(New York: Bantam, 1998)

**Story type:** Science Fiction (First Contact)
**Major character(s):** Chli-pou-ni, Animal (ant)
**Time period(s):** Indeterminate Future
**Locale(s):** Paris, France

**Summary:** The Wells family promptly disappears into their basement shortly after renting an apartment in Paris. This proves to be a critical event for the population of ants in the area, through whose eyes we see the first effort at contact between the two species. Originally published in France.

**Other books you might like:**
Richard Adams, *Watership Down*, 1974
Frank Herbert, *Hellstrom's Hive*, 1973
James P. Hogan, *Bug Park*, 1997
Rex Dean Levie, *Insect Warriors*, 1965
Eric North, *The Ant Men*, 1955

## 5756

### EARLE WESCOTT

## Winter Wolves

(New York: Bantam, 1989)

**Story type:** Horror (Nature in Revolt)
**Major character(s):** Fran Thomas, Journalist; Caroline Parker, Innkeeper
**Time period(s):** 1980s
**Locale(s):** Steel Harbor, Maine

**Summary:** Returning to his hometown to recover from professional and marital failures, Fran Thomas encounters a series of vicious killings supposedly carried out by a pack of ghostly wolves, as well as nightmare visions of a beautiful but terrifying seductress. This is Westcott's first novel.

**Other books you might like:**
Alan Ryan, *Dead White*, 1983
Jack Williamson, *Darker than You Think*, 1948

## 5757

**MICHELLE WEST** (Pseudonym of Michelle Sagara)

## The Broken Crown

(New York: DAW, 1997)

**Story type:** Fantasy (Political; Magic Conflict)
**Series:** Sun Sword
**Major character(s):** Valedan kai de'Leonne, Royalty (prince); Diora di'Marano, Noblewoman, Widow(er); Kiriel, Orphan (Warrior)
**Time period(s):** Indeterminate
**Locale(s):** Dominion of Annagar, Fictional Country; Empire of Essalieyan, Fictional Country

**Summary:** Although Diora de'Marano, the bride of the heir apparent to Annagar's throne and a pawn in the courtly intrigues of her family, did not love her husband, she seeks opportunity to avenge his death and the deaths of her co-wives when a military coup overthrows the royal family. But one heir to the throne, Valedan, still lives as a hostage held by the rival Essalieyan Empire. The Kings and Queens of Essalieyan agree to aid Valedan, while the demons of the Shining Court assist the rebels in Annagar. First in series.

**Other books you might like:**
Margaret Ball, *Flameweaver*, 1991
Marion Zimmer Bradley, *The Mists of Avalon*, 1983
Terry Brooks, *The Sword of Shannara*, 1978
C.J. Cherryh, *Foreigner*, 1994
Robert Jordan, *The Eye of the World*, 1990
J. Gregory Keyes, *The Waterborn*, 1996
Elizabeth Ann Scarborough, *Nothing Sacred*, 1991
Joan D. Vinge, *The Snow Queen*, 1980

---

**5758**

MICHELLE WEST

## Hunter's Death

(New York: DAW, 1996)

**Story type:** Fantasy (Psychic Powers; Magic Conflict)
**Major character(s):** Gilliam, Hunter, Nobleman; Stephen, Companion (huntbrother); Jewel, Psychic
**Time period(s):** Indeterminate Past
**Locale(s):** Averalaan, Fictional City; Essalieyan, Fictional Country

**Summary:** To battle the lord of Hell's influence as their god demands, Lord Gilliam and Stephen travel to Averalaan, already afflicted by the great evil.

**Other books you might like:**
Lynn Flewelling, *Luck in the Shadows*, 1996
Lynn Flewelling, *Stalking Darkness*, 1997
J.V. Jones, *The Baker's Boy*, 1995
Melissa Scott, *Point of Hopes*, 1995
    Lisa A. Barnett, co-author
Paula Volsky, *Illusion*, 1992

---

**5759**

MICHELLE WEST

## Hunter's Oath

(New York: DAW, 1995)

**Story type:** Fantasy (Adventure; Psychic Powers)
**Major character(s):** Steven, Orphan, Companion (huntbrother); Gilliam, Hunter, Nobleman
**Time period(s):** Indeterminate Past
**Locale(s):** Breodanir, Fictional Country

**Summary:** The starving Steven can't believe his good fortune when he is chosen as a possible Huntbrother to Gilliam. When the time comes, he gladly takes the Oath that binds their minds, forming a completeness in the links between Gilliam, the animals, Steven, and the people of their land. Thereafter, threatened interference in those bonds by unknown forces creates great discomfort.

**Other books you might like:**
Robin Hobb, *Assassin's Apprentice*, 1995
Guy Gavriel Kay, *The Darkest Road*, 1986
Andre Norton, *The Beast Master*, 1959
Sheri S. Tepper, *Grass*, 1989

---

**5760**

MICHELLE WEST

## The Uncrowned King

(New York: DAW, 1998)

**Story type:** Fantasy (Magic Conflict; Political)
**Series:** Sun Sword
**Major character(s):** Valedan kai de'Leonne, Royalty (crown prince) Kiriel, Orphan, Warrior; Jewel A'Terafin, Businesswoman
**Time period(s):** Indeterminate
**Locale(s):** Dominion of Annagar, Fictional Country; Empire of Essalieyan, Fictional Country

**Summary:** Valedan trains for the King's Challenge, the athletic contest that only one Southerner has won before. His allies guard him from assassins, both human and demon, while civil war between rival factions in Essalieyen threatens to unleash the deadly forces of the Lord of the Night.

**Other books you might like:**
C.J. Cherryh, *Angel with the Sword*, 1985
C.J. Cherryh, *Invader*, 1995
Barbara Hambly, *The Witches of Wenshar*, 1987
Robert Jordan, *The Dragon Reborn*, 1991
Joan D. Vinge, *World's End*, 1984

---

**5761**

PAUL WEST

## The Women of Whitechapel and Jack the Ripper

(New York; Random House, 1991)

**Story type:** Horror (Serial Killer)
**Major character(s):** Walter Sickert, Artist (painter); Dr. Gull, Doctor; Prince Albert Victor Christian Edward, Royalty (heir to the British throne)
**Time period(s):** 1880s (1888)
**Locale(s):** London, England

**Summary:** Walter Sickert becomes drawn into a scandal at the highest levels of British royalty when his models, prostitutes from London's West End, begin dying in a grisly fashion and the evidence points to a cover-up to protect the heir to the throne.

**Other books you might like:**
Robert Bloch, *Night of the Ripper*, 1984
Gardner Dozois, *Ripper!*, 1988
    Susan Casper, co-editor
Martin H. Greenberg, *Red Jack*, 1988
    Frank McSherry and Charles G. Waugh, co-editors
Marie Belloc Lowndes, *The Lodger*, 1910

---

**5762**

ROBERT WESTALL

## The Call and Other Stories

(New York: Viking, 1993)

**Story type:** Horror (Collection)
**Summary:** This collection brings together six traditional ghost stories with modern settings. "Woman and Home" tells of a haunted house that engulfs its visitor, and "Uncle Otto at Denswick Park" of a gentrified British estate haunted by the ghost of its former self. In "The Badger," a poacher is haunted by the ghost of his quarry, while

in the title story, a telephone crisis line is haunted every Christmas by the ghost of a murder victim. ''Warren, Sharon and Darren'' is a delightful fantasy that mixes fairy folk of British legend with the contemporary urban punk scene. Originally published in England in 1990.

**Other books you might like:**
Joan Aiken, *The Haunting of Lamb House*, 1991
John Buchan, *The Far Islands and Other Tales of Fantasy*, 1984
John Gordon, *The Burning Baby and Other Ghosts*, 1992

`5763`

### ROBERT WESTALL

## Demons and Shadows: The Ghostly Best Stories of Robert Westall

(New York: Farrar, Straus & Giroux, 1993)

**Story type:** Horror (Collection)

**Summary:** Its title notwithstanding, this book collects eleven stories, not all of which are supernatural. Mixed with wistful recollections of childhood and adolescence such as ''The Making of Me'' and ''Night Out'' are the fantasy of a child meeting with a biblical angel, ''Rachel and the Angel''; the Jamesian ghost story of a churchman whose concealed perversity persists beyond the grave, ''The Last Days of Dorinda Molyneaux''; the story of creatures that haunt a house and drain psychic energy from its inhabitants, ''The Creatures in the House''; and the story of a young boy with poetic aspirations who finds himself cursed with the ability to see the truth in people, ''The Death of Wizards.'' The only story original to the book is ''Graveyard Shift,'' about a kindly cemetery keeper protected from a vampire by the revenants of his charges.

**Other books you might like:**
Robert Aickman, *Unsettled Dust*, 1990
Walter de la Mare, *The Collected Tales of Walter de la Mare*, 1949
John Gordon, *The Burning Baby and Other Ghosts*, 1992
E. Nesbit, *In the Dark*, 1988

`5764`

### ROBERT WESTALL

## In Camera and Other Stories

(New York: Scholastic, 1993)

**Story type:** Horror (Collection)

**Summary:** Although supposedly aimed at schoolchildren, this collection of five novellas by a modern master of the classic ghost story form, first published in 1992, will please adults too. Included are the title story, about an antique camera whose undeveloped roll of film yields secrets surrounding a possible murder committed almost half a century before; ''Blind Bill,'' about a blind man whose other senses detect a murder in progress; the amusing ''Beelzebub,'' in which the bride of Satan attempts to get their offspring registered with the local civil service registry office; ''Charlie Ferber,'' about a man who transforms himself into a cat to serve as a young girl's guardian; and the tale of a haunting, ''Henry Marlborough.''

**Other books you might like:**
Robert Aickman, *Unsettled Dust*, 1990
Walter de la Mare, *The Collected Tales of Walter de la Mare*, 1949
John Gordon, *The Burning Baby and Other Ghosts*, 1992
E. Nesbit, *In the Dark*, 1988

`5765`

### ROBERT WESTALL

## Shades of Darkness: More of the Ghostly Best Stories of Robert Westall

(New York: Farrar, Strauss and Giroux, 1994)

**Story type:** Horror (Collection)

**Summary:** The 11 stories collected here come from the pen of a writer known for both his ghost stories and children's books. ''The Haunting of Chas Magill'' tells of a boy who learns the horrors of war from the ghost of a deceased soldier. ''The Call'' is about a haunted emergency phone line. ''In Camera'' tells of a mystery discovered and solved on the basis of film left in a camera for decades. In ''The Cat, Spartan,'' a young boy is haunted by the ghost of his grandfather, who tries to make amends for his curmudgeonly life. ''Fifty-Fafty'' is about a young boy who turns people in his regular life into the monsters of his nightmares. ''Woman and Home'' tells of a wayward boy who stumbles upon a haunted house that destroys everyone who would exploit it. And the previously unpublished ''Cats'' tells of a married couple haunted by the ghosts of cats from the husband's earlier life.

**Other books you might like:**
Robert Aickman, *Unsettled Dust*, 1990
Walter de la Mare, *The Collected Tales of Walter de la Mare*, 1949
John Gordon, *The Burning Baby and Other Ghosts*, 1992
E. Nesbit, *In the Dark*, 1988

`5766`

### SCOTT WESTERFELD

## Fine Prey

(New York: Roc, 1998)

**Story type:** Science Fiction (First Contact)
**Major character(s):** Spider, Student
**Time period(s):** Indeterminate Future
**Locale(s):** North America

**Summary:** The alien Aya have effectively seized control of the Earth, although not through a show of force. Their superior technology overwhelms human society and their schools become the only place where one can become really educated. Spider, a brilliant human student, discovers the truth about his masters and the loss of human freedom.

**Other books you might like:**
Brian W. Aldiss, *Vanguard From Alpha*, 1959
Algis Budrys, *Michaelmas*, 1978
Mark Clifton, *When They Come From Space*, 1963
Hayden Howard, *The Eskimo Invasion*, 1967
Fred Hoyle, *A for Andromeda*, 1964
  with Geoffrey Hoyle

`5767`

### SCOTT WESTERFELD

## Polymorph

(New York: Roc, 1997)

**Story type:** Science Fiction (Political; Science Fiction)
**Major character(s):** Lee, Mythical Creature (shapeshifter); Freddie Smith, Computer Expert; Bonita, Mythical Creature (shapeshifter)

**Time period(s):** Indeterminate Future
**Locale(s):** New York, New York

**Summary:** Believing herself to be the only shapeshifter, Lee lives a solitary life, constantly changing and meeting new people as a stranger. Bonita not only has the gift, but also recognizes Lee as a threat to his/her plot to become the richest, most powerful person on the planet, forcing Lee to get involved. First novel.

**Other books you might like:**
John W. Campbell, *Who Goes There? and Other Stories*, 1955
Stuart Hopen, *Warp Angel*, 1995
Nancy Kress, *Brain Rose*, 1990
Jennifer Roberson, *Shapechangers*, 1984

### 5768
#### DONALD E. WESTLAKE

## Humans

(New York: Warner Mysterious Press, 1992)

**Story type:** Fantasy (Religious)
**Major character(s):** Ananayel, Angel; X "Brother Rush", Demon; Maria Elena, Musician, Agent
**Time period(s):** 1990s
**Locale(s):** New York, New York; Moscow, Union of Soviet Socialist Republics

**Summary:** When God becomes fed up with matters on Earth, he dispatches an angel, Ananayel, to arrange for Armageddon using human agents. Deciding that the human realm is progressing acceptably, Lucifer sends a demon, X, to interfere with Ananayel's plotting and restore free will to the involved humans.

**Other books you might like:**
Bradley Denton, *Buddy Holly Is Alive and Well on Ganymede*, 1991
Neil Gaiman, *Good Omens: The Nice and Accurate Prophecies of Agnes Nutter, Witch*, 1990
 Terry Pratchett, co-author
Parke Godwin, *The Snake Oil Wars*, 1989
Parke Godwin, *Waiting for the Galactic Bus*, 1988
Victor Koman, *The Jehovah Contract*, 1987
Robert Rankin, *Armageddon: The Musical*, 1990
Peter Ustinov, *The Old Man and Mr. Smith*, 1991

### 5769
#### PATRICK WHALEN

## Deathwalker

(New York: Pocket, 1992)

**Story type:** Horror (Ancient Evil Unleashed)
**Major character(s):** John Winter, Spy; Erin O'Donnell, Police Officer (Police Chief of Avalon); James Spear, Businessman, Computer Expert
**Time period(s):** 1980s (1981)
**Locale(s):** Avalon, Washington

**Summary:** The eruption of dormant volcano Mount St. Helens awakens the Witiko, a flesh-eating demon of Ahtantum Indian legend, who was buried inside the mountain for 800 years and now yearns to turn all those whom it encounters into an army of walking dead disciples.

**Other books you might like:**
Douglas Clegg, *Goat Dance*, 1989
Charles L. Grant, *The Nestling*, 1982
T. Chris Martindale, *Where the Chill Waits*, 1990
G. Wayne Miller, *Thunder Rise*, 1988

Kathryn Ptacek, *Ghost Dance*, 1989

### 5770
#### PATRICK WHALEN

## Night Thirst

(New York: Pocket, 1991)

**Story type:** Horror (Vampire Story)
**Major character(s):** Braille, Vampire; Gregory, Vampire; Hargrave Cutter, Doctor (surgeon)
**Time period(s):** 1990s
**Locale(s):** Seattle, Washington

**Summary:** The nuclear blast at the end of the author's first novel, *Monastery*, was supposed to have wiped out the vampire colony referred to as the Ancient Ones on a small island off the coast of Washington. But survivors of that blast, known as the New Ones, make it back to the mainland, where they become a seemingly indestructible scourge—and a source of interest to a government agency looking for new types of medical weapons.

**Other books you might like:**
Ron Dee, *Dusk*, 1991
Stephen King, *Salem's Lot*, 1975
Richard Matheson, *I Am Legend*, 1954
Robert R. McCammon, *They Thirst*, 1981

### 5771
#### PATRICK WHALEN

## Out of the Night

(New York: Pocket, 1990)

**Story type:** Horror (Ancient Evil Unleashed)
**Major character(s):** John Cable, Professor, Archaeologist; Marvin Larchmont, Archaeologist; Henry Sutton, Police Officer
**Time period(s):** 1990s
**Locale(s):** Ravina, California

**Summary:** In 1889, the citizens of Ravina lynched six gypsy squatters whom they blamed for unexplained deaths in the town. A century later, the ancient evil the gypsies embodied is on the rampage once more, leaving a trail of dessicated corpses as proof that it is steadily regenerating it powers, to burst forth in malignant fullness.

**Other books you might like:**
Piers Anthony, *Firefly*, 1990
Douglas Clegg, *Goat Dance*, 1989

### 5772
#### EDITH WHARTON

## The Ghost-Feeler

(Pomfret, Connecticut: Peter Owen, 1996 (dist. by Dufour Editions))

**Story type:** Horror (Collection)

**Summary:** Veteran editor Peter Haining assembles nine stories of terror and the supernatural by a Pulitzer Prize-winning author renowned for her novels of American style and manners at the turn of the century. Among the better-known stories collected here are the classic ghost tale, "Afterwards," and a tale of emotional vampirism, "Bewitched." Less well-known efforts include "A Bottle of Perrier," a tale of madness and murder set in the African desert, and "The Looking-Glass," a poignant tale of a spiritual medium. Several stories share the common theme of marital dissatisfaction that leads

to desperate measures. In "The Lady Maid's Bell," a ghostly maid prevents her mistress's lovers from being discovered by the woman's husband. "The Duchess at Prayer" is a conte cruel about the horrible fate that befalls the lover of a woman who hides beneath the altar in her chapel. "The Fullness of Life" is a tragic allegory of a woman who willingly acquiesces to unrequited love in the afterlife.

**Other books you might like:**
Cynthia Asquith, *This Mortal Coil*, 1947
Marjorie Bowen, *Kecksies and Other Twilight Tales*, 1976
Henry James, *Stories of the Supernatural*, 1949
Vernon Lee, *The Snake Lady and Other Stories*, 1954
Mary E. Wilkins-Freeman, *Collected Ghost Stories*, 1974

## 5773

### DENNIS WHEATLEY

## *The Devil Rides Out*

(London: Mandarin Books, 1996 (distributed by Reed Trade))

**Story type:** Horror (Black Magic)
**Major character(s):** Duke de Richlieu, Nobleman; Rex Van Ryn, Spy; Mr. Mocata, Sorcerer
**Time period(s):** 1930s (1934)
**Locale(s):** London, England

**Summary:** The Duke de Richlieu and his disciple, American Rex van Ryn, team up to save their friend Simon Aron from Mr. Mocata, a black magician who has ingratiated himself with the young man. Complicating the situation is Tanith, a medium to whom Rex is attracted and whom Mocato hopes to use along with Simon to obtain the powerful Talisman of Set. Originally published in 1935.

**Other books you might like:**
Katherine Kurtz, *Death of an Adept*, 1996
  Deborah Turner Harris, co-author
Brian Lumley, *Necroscope*, 1986
Robert Morgan, *The Things That Are Not There*, 1992
Robert Weinberg, *The Armageddon Box*, 1991
Robert Weinberg, *The Devil's Auction*, 1988

## 5774

### DEBORAH WHEELER

## *Jaydium*

(New York: DAW, 1993)

**Story type:** Science Fiction (Alternate Universe; First Contact)
**Major character(s):** Kithri Bloodyluck, Miner, Pilot (spaceship); Eril Trioran, Pilot (spaceship); Lennart, Spaceman
**Time period(s):** Indeterminate Future
**Locale(s):** Stayman, Planet—Imaginary

**Summary:** Marooned on Stayman when her father dies of a neurological, mind-destroying disease, Kithri makes her way as a Jaydium miner. Used for power and faster-than-light travel, Jaydium has become rare on the surface and must be mined from the deep, twisty natural tunnels. Although distrustful of men since her father's disappearance, Kithri's suddenly finding a partner brings hope they can mine enough Jaydium to earn passage off planet. When an accident causes Lennart to pop out of the space-time flux which had trapped him for centuries, it becomes clear that fundamental changes have occurred on Stayman. A first novel.

**Other books you might like:**
Gregory Benford, *Timescape*, 1980
Geary Gravel, *A Key for the Nonesuch*, 1990
Anne McCaffrey, *Crystal Singer*, 1992

Robert Reed, *Down the Bright Way*, 1990
Clifford D. Simak, *Ring Around the Sun*, 1953
Dan Simmons, *Hyperion*, 1989
George Zebrowski, *Stranger Suns*, 1991

## 5775

### DEBORAH WHEELER

## *Northlight*

(New York: DAW, 1995)

**Story type:** Science Fiction (Post-Holocaust; Political)
**Major character(s):** Kardith, Warrior; Terricel "Terris" sen'Laurea, Student, Psychic (esper); Esmelda "Esme", Government Official
**Time period(s):** Indeterminate Future
**Locale(s):** Laureal City, Fictional City; Northland, Fictional Country

**Summary:** Upset by orders forbidding her to search for her friend, Kardith comes to Laureal City in time to see the Patreos murdered. Her friend's brother, Terris, joins her search to find evidence against General Montborne, who wants more weapons development at any cost, including war between Laureal City and Northland.

**Other books you might like:**
Geary Gravel, *A Key for the Nonesuch*, 1990
Robert Reed, *Beyond the Veil of Stars*, 1994
John E. Stith, *Reunion on Neverend*, 1994
Sheri S. Tepper, *Grass*, 1989
George Zebrowski, *Stranger Suns*, 1991

## 5776

### JOHN WHITBOURN

## *Binscombe Tales*

(Ashcroft, British Columbia: Ash-Tree Press, 1998)

**Story type:** Horror (Collection)
**Locale(s):** Binscombe, England

**Summary:** These 15 witty tales of the supernatural, with an antiquarian flavor, are set in the imaginary southeastern English town of Binscombe. The stories, which feature recurring characters, include the haunted car tale "Only One Careful Owner"; "Peace on Earth, Goodwill to Most Men," about the nasty fate that befalls some unwary hooligans who are imprisoned in the crypt of the church whose services they interrupt on Christmas; and "The Will to Live," in which a feisty man carries on after his death as though he were still alive. Introduction by Professor E. Griffiths.

**Other books you might like:**
Steve Duffy, *The Night Comes On*, 1998
Sheila Hodgson, *The Fellow Travellers and Other Ghost Stories*, 1998
Terry Lamsley, *Under the Crust*, 1993
Ron Weighell, *The White Road*, 1996
Robert Westall, *Antique Dust*, 1989

## 5777

### JAMES WHITE

## *Final Diagnosis*

(New York: Tor, 1997)

**Story type:** Science Fiction (First Contact; Medical)
**Series:** Sector General

**Major character(s):** Medalont, Alien (Melfan), Doctor; Hewlitt, Patient; Braithwaite, Psychologist (estraterrestrial)
**Time period(s):** Indeterminate Future
**Locale(s):** Sector General Hospital, Space Station; Outer Space

**Summary:** While in Sector General Hospital for many anomalous symptoms which began during his childhood, Patient Hewlitt cannot convince the doctors that his chidlhood experience on an alien planet may prove relevant. Constantly angry at not being believed, Hewlitt still manages to convince Braithwaite and Medalont that he retains his sanity, as well as perfect health, except for his occasional attacks of cardiac arrest. When his symptoms appear contagious, all on Sector General become alarmed.

**Other books you might like:**
David Brin, *Brightness Reef*, 1995
Murray Leinster, *The Med Series*, 1983
Jody Lynn Nye, *Taylor's Ark*, 1993
Alis A. Rasmussen, *A Passage of Stars*, 1990
Mary Rosenblum, *The Stone Garden*, 1995

---

**5778**

JAMES WHITE

## The Galactic Gourmet

(New York: Tor, 1996)

**Story type:** Science Fiction (First Contact; Medical)
**Series:** Sector General
**Major character(s):** Gurronsevas, Alien (Tralthan), Cook (master chef); Prilicla, Alien (Cinrusskin), Psychic (empath); Murchison, Doctor (pathologist), Spacewoman
**Time period(s):** Indeterminate Future
**Locale(s):** Sector General Hospital, Space Station; *Rhabwar*, Spaceship (ambulance ship); Wemar, Planet—Imaginary

**Summary:** No longer challenged as master chef of the most renowned interspecies hotel, Gurronsevas volunteers to work at Sector General. Gurronsevas thinks that more palatable food will promote appetite and quicker patient recovery and improve staff health and morale. Unfortunately, accidents and misunderstandings force Gurronsevas to join the staff of the *Rhabwar* on its mission to Wemar.

**Other books you might like:**
David Brin, *Brightness Reef*, 1995
Murray Leinster, *The Med Series*, 1983
Jody Lynn Nye, *Medicine Show*, 1994
Jody Lynn Nye, *Taylor's Ark*, 1993
Larry Niven, *The Gripping Hand*, 1993
  Jerry Pournelle, co-author

---

**5779**

JAMES WHITE

## The Genocidal Healer

(New York: Ballantine/Del Rey, 1991)

**Story type:** Science Fiction (Medical; First Contact)
**Series:** Sector General
**Major character(s):** Lioren, Doctor, Alien; O'Mara, Administrator, Psychologist
**Time period(s):** Indeterminate Future
**Locale(s):** Sector General Hospital, Space Station; Outer Space

**Summary:** Surgeon-Captain Lioren was in charge when his inadequate medical facilities were unable to provide a cure for the plague on a planet in his care. After being found innocent by the courts on his home world, Lioren petitioned the Monitor Corps, his employers,

to re-try the case. Unwilling to lose his talents and skills, the Monitor Corps stripped him of rank and assigned him to Major O'Mara, Chief of Sector General's Interspecies Psychology Department.

**Other books you might like:**
Piers Anthony, *Prostho Plus*, 1973
David Brin, *Startide Rising*, 1983
David Brin, *The Uplift War*, 1987
Stephen Goldin, *Jade Darcy and the Affair of Honor*, 1988
  Mary Mason, co-author
Murray Leinster, *The Med Series*, 1983
T. Jackson King, *Retread Shop*, 1988

---

**5780**

JAMES WHITE

## Mind Changer

(New York, Tor, 1998)

**Story type:** Science Fiction (First Contact; Medical)
**Series:** Sector General
**Major character(s):** O'Mara, Administrator, Psychologist; Craythorne, Military Personnel (Monitor Corps), Psychologist; Prilicla, Alien (Cinrusskin), Psychic (empath)
**Time period(s):** Indeterminate Future
**Locale(s):** Outer Space (Sector Twelve General inter-species hospital)

**Summary:** O'Mara learns that he will be chief administrator as well as chief psychologist for Sector General until he finds a successor. A civilian physician must fill the new merged position.

**Other books you might like:**
David Brin, *Brightness Reef*, 1995
A.C. Crispin, *Starbridge*, 1989
L. Warren Douglas, *The Wells of Phyre*, 1996
Murray Leinster, *The Med Series*, 1983
Jody Lynn Nye, *Taylor's Ark*, 1993

---

**5781**

JAMES WHITE

## The Silent Stars Go By

(New York: Ballantine/Del Rey, 1991)

**Story type:** Science Fiction (First Contact; Alternate Universe)
**Major character(s):** Nolan, Doctor, Immigrant; O'Riordan, Religious; Wanachtee, Indian (Algonquin), Chieftain
**Time period(s):** 15th century
**Locale(s):** New World, Alternate Earth

**Summary:** When Monsignor O'Riordan, suspicious of Nolan and all non-Catholics, maroons Nolan and all the other potential trouble-makers 2000 miles away from the colony site, Nolan leads the group overland to the colony. On the way, he and the others contact amphibious intelligent beings who help them get back to the main colony.

**Other books you might like:**
John Brunner, *Polymath*, 1974
F.M. Busby, *All These Earths*, 1978
Gordon R. Dickson, *The Lifeship*, 1976
  Harry Harrison, co-author
Colin Kapp, *The Survival Game*, 1976
John Maddox Roberts, *King of the Wood*, 1983
William Sanders, *Journey to Fusang*, 1988
L. Neil Smith, *The Crystal Empire*, 1986
Sydney J. Van Scyoc, *Deepwater Dreams*, 1991

## 5782

**JAMES WHITE**

### The White Papers

(Framingham, Massachusetts: NESFA Press, 1996)

**Story type:** Science Fiction (Collection)

**Summary:** Published in conjunction with the World Science Fiction Convention, this volume contains a three-page introduction by Mike Resnick; a six-page article by Walt Willis reprinted from a conference program book; two original essays by Gary Louie, "A Sector General Timeline" and "The Classification System" with notes on categorizing extraterrestrial life forms; one original and nine stories reprinted from periodicals, anthologies, and collections published between 1959 and 1988; and 10 articles with diverse themes, often humorous, reprinted from science fiction periodicals published between 1957 and 1990. The stories include "The Secret History of Sector General," expanded from *Ambulance Ship* and three other stories set in the *Sector General* milieu, as well as one Hugo Award nominee, "Custom Fitting." Frequently light in tone, the stories' themes include medicine, intelligent extraterrestrial life forms, ghosts, life in the future, human relationships, Santa Claus, and nuclear warfare.

**Other books you might like:**
Lois McMaster Bujold, *Dreamweaver's Dilemma*, 1996
Emma Bull, *Double Feature*, 1994
    Will Shetterly, co-author
Joe Haldeman, *Vietnam and Other Alien Worlds*, 1993
Diana Wynne Jones, *Everard's Ride*, 1995
James H. Schmitz, *The Best of James H. Schmitz*, 1991
Cordwainer Smith, *The Rediscovery of Man*, 1993
Jane Yolen, *Storyteller*, 1992

## 5783

**JAMES GORDON WHITE**

### The Nomad Queen

(New York: Leisure, 1993)

**Story type:** Fantasy (Quest; Adventure)
**Major character(s):** Sheela, Royalty (Queen of the Thorgons); Alon, Mercenary, Adventurer; Sumara, Royalty (Princess of Istwar), Mercenary
**Time period(s):** Indeterminate
**Locale(s):** Planet—Imaginary

**Summary:** With the help of a wizard and his demon, Sheela journeys to gain the wisdom to become Queen of her people and win back their land from invading armies. She helps Princess Sumara regain her rightful throne and both learn *noblesse oblige*. First of a series.

**Other books you might like:**
Jack Holland, *The Fire Queen*, 1991
Mercedes Lackey, *Arrow's Fall*, 1988
Mercedes Lackey, *Arrow's Flight*, 1987
Mercedes Lackey, *Arrows of the Queen*, 1987
Mercedes Lackey, *By the Sword*, 1991
Julie Dean Smith, *Call of Madness*, 1990

## 5784

**MARIE ARDELL WHITE**
**JAMES GORDON WHITE**, Co-Author

### The Beast

(New York: Leisure, 1994)

**Story type:** Horror (Occult)
**Major character(s):** Diana Landers, Writer; Lionel Doyle, Professor; Jonathan Hagar, Wealthy
**Time period(s):** 1990s (1994)
**Locale(s):** Beverly Hills, California

**Summary:** Recovering from the gruesome death of her fiance, Diana Landers finds herself swept off her feet by the dashing Jonathan Hagar. When the forecast of a concerned psychic sends Diana probing into Jonathan's past, she begins to worry that he is a monster from another dimension overlapping ours, who engineered the death of her fiance and who has sinister plans for her as well. This is the authors' first novel.

**Other books you might like:**
John Byrne, *Fear Book*, 1988
D.A. Fowler, *The Book of the Damned*, 1993
Daniel H. Gower, *Harrowgate*, 1993
T. Chris Martindale, *The Voice in the Basement*, 1992
T.M. Wright, *Little Boy Lost*, 1992

## 5785

**STEVE WHITE**

### Legacy

(New York: Baen, 1995)

**Story type:** Science Fiction (Adventure; Time Travel)
**Major character(s):** Robert Sarnac, Military Personnel (Solar Union Space Fleet), Time Traveler; Tiraena DiFalco, Military Personnel (Raehaniv Space Forces), Time Traveler; Tylar, Historian, Time Traveler
**Time period(s):** 5th century (469); 23rd century (2261)
**Locale(s):** *Taelarn*, Spaceship; England

**Summary:** After a narrow escape from the Korvaasha, an alien enemy, Lieutenant Robert Sarnac shifts through time to the 5th century where he battles alongside the legendary King Arthur. Sequel to *The Disinherited*.

**Other books you might like:**
Dafydd ab Hugh, *Arthur War Lord*, 1994
Dafydd ab Hugh, *Far Beyond the Wave*, 1994
Robert Asprin, *Time Scout*, 1995
    Linda Evans, co-author
David Weber, *The Armageddon Inheritance*, 1993
David Weber, *Crusade*, 1992
    Steve White, co-author
David Weber, *Insurrection*, 1990
    Steve White, co-author
David Weber, *Mutineers' Moon*, 1991

## 5786

**STEVE WHITE**

### Prince of Sunset

(New York: Baen, 1998)

**Story type:** Science Fiction (Military; Political)

**Major character(s):** Basil Castellan, Military Personnel; Sonja Rady, Military Personnel
**Time period(s):** Indeterminate Future
**Locale(s):** Outer Space

**Summary:** The human-dominated interstellar empire is on the verge of collapse, and a less than enlightened revolutionary group known as the New Humans threatens to establish a much more restrictive government in its place. Three recent graduates of the Space Academy unwittingly become focal points in the struggle and help shape the future of all humankind.

**Other books you might like:**
Robert Frezza, *A Small Colonial War*, 1990
W. Michael Gear, *Relic of Empire*, 1992
Donald E. McQuinn, *With Full Honors*, 1997
R.M. Meluch, *The Queen's Squadron*, 1992
David Weber, *In Enemy Hands*, 1997

---

**5787**

### WYNNE WHITEFORD

## Lake of the Sun

(New York: Ace Books, 1989)

**Story type:** Science Fiction (First Contact)
**Major character(s):** Rah, Alien (Martian); Paul Russell, Scientist, Engineer
**Time period(s):** Indeterminate Future
**Locale(s):** Mars

**Summary:** Earthmen exploring Mars are perceived as evil invaders by the native Martians. The possibility of war seems very real.

**Other books you might like:**
Gregory Benford, *Tides of Light*, 1989
Janet Morris, *Target*, 1989
    David Drake, co-author
David Alexander Smith, *Rendezvous*, 1988

---

**5788**

### WYNNE WHITEFORD

## The Specialist

(New York: Ace, 1990)

**Story type:** Science Fiction (Mystery; Genetic Manipulation)
**Major character(s):** Lance Garrith, Journalist (star reporter, Solar News); Jack Darch, Prospector; Jocasta Borg, Cyborg, Businesswoman
**Time period(s):** 2090s (2095)
**Locale(s):** Outer Space; Mars

**Summary:** Lance Garrith, sent to Mars to investigate a possible extra solar probe, finds himself the target of assassination plots, and is horrified at the types of genetic manipulation he comes across. Finally out in the Martian desert, he meets the ultimate in recombinate DNA, a type designed to carry mankind to the stars. Lance is put into suspended animation. He awakens after 100 years to a very strange and alien Mars.

**Other books you might like:**
James Blish, *The Seedling Stars*, 1957
C.J. Cherryh, *Serpent's Reach*, 1980
James P. Hogan, *Voyage From Yesteryear*, 1982
Michael P. Kube-McDowell, *Emprise*, 1985
Michael McCollum, *Life Probe*, 1983

---

**5789**

### JOHN WHITMAN

## Disturbing Behavior

(New York: Bantam, 1999)

**Story type:** Horror (Child-in-Peril)
**Major character(s):** Steve Clark, Teenager; Gavin Strick, Teenager; Edgar Caldicott, Doctor (psychiatrist)
**Time period(s):** 1990s (1998)
**Locale(s):** Cradle Bay, Pennsylvania

**Summary:** Following the tragic suicide of his older brother, Steve Clark and his family move from Chicago to remote Cradle Bay, seeking a less traumatic life. Steve soon discovers that the well-behaved, strait-laced Blue Ribbon Group of high-achieving students at his high school are teens who have been turned into zombies by parents who hope to keep them from going astray. Novelization of Scott Rosenberg's screenplay for the film directed by David Nuter.

**Other books you might like:**
Robert Cormier, *The Chocolate War*, 1974
Eric Flanders, *The Forever Children*, 1992
Ira Levin, *The Stepford Wives*, 1972
Andrew Neiderman, *Perfect Little Angels*, 1989
John Saul, *Creature*, 1988

---

**5790**

### ANDREW WHITMORE

## The Fortress of Eternity

(New York: Avon, 1990)

**Story type:** Fantasy (Sword and Sorcery; Quest)
**Major character(s):** Isaf, Warrior; Pagadon Alphen Trevayne, Scholar
**Time period(s):** Indeterminate Past
**Locale(s):** Julkrease, Fictional Country

**Summary:** When Isaf got to town he was stopped by a fortune teller who read the cards foretelling that he would be the deciding factor in many battles, experience love, see much death and have a fearful adventure. After Trevayne came to town and introduced himself he hired Isaf to help him kill a god. This is the author's first book.

**Other books you might like:**
Richard A. Knaak, *Firedrake*, 1989
Elizabeth Moon, *Sheepfarmer's Daughter*, 1988
Elizabeth Moon, *Surrender None: The Legacy of Gird*, 1990
Mickey Zucker Reichert, *Dragonrank Master*, 1989
Tad Williams, *The Dragonbone Chair*, 1989
Gene Wolfe, *Soldier of Arete*, 1989

---

**5791**

### LES WHITTEN

## Moon of the Wolf/Progeny of the Adder

(New York: Leisure, 1992)

**Story type:** Horror (Collection)

**Summary:** This book brings together two novels that merge the tale of ambiguous horror and the police procedural by a writer largely unknown within the horror genre. *Moon of the Wolf* (originally published in 1967) tells of deputy Aaron Whitaker's investigation of a series of brutal murders in racially volatile Stanley, Mississippi, evidence of which points increasingly to the work of a werewolf. *Progeny of the Adder* (originally published in 1965) chronicles the investigations of homicide detective Harry Picard, whose sketicism toward the supernatural erodes when a serial killer with a penchant for beautiful blonde woman leaves an accumulating trail of clues that indicates he is a vampire.

**Other books you might like:**
L. Ron Hubbard, *Typewriter in the Sky/Fear*, 1951
Fritz Leiber, *Conjure Wife/Our Lady of Darkness*, 1991
Curt Siodmak, *Donovan's Brain/Hauser's Memory*, 1992

---

### 5792

#### JACK WHYTE

## The Eagles' Brood

(New York: Forge, 1997)

**Story type:** Fantasy (Legend)
**Series:** Camulod Chronicles
**Major character(s):** Caius Merlyn Britannicus, Leader, Writer; Uther Pendragon, Warrior
**Time period(s):** 5th century
**Locale(s):** Camulod, England

**Summary:** Merlyn and Uther Pendragon lead the abandoned former Roman colony toward advanced Roman law and culture, until a vicious crime drives them apart and threatens the future both strive for.

**Other books you might like:**
Marion Zimmer Bradley, *The Forest House*, 1994
Marion Zimmer Bradley, *The Mists of Avalon*, 1983
Courtway Jones, *In the Shadow of the Oak King*, 1991
Morgan Llywelyn, *Druids*, 1991
Harry Turtledove, *Werenight*, 1994

---

### 5793

#### JACK WHYTE

## The Saxon Shore

(New York: Tor Forge, 1998)

**Story type:** Fantasy (Legend)
**Series:** Camulod Chronicles
**Major character(s):** Caius Merlyn Britannicus, Leader, Writer; Arthur Pendragon, Child, Heir
**Time period(s):** 5th century
**Locale(s):** England

**Summary:** With Uther Pendragon killed, Merlyn must attempt to save the infant Arthur from those who would kill him because the youngster is destined to fulfill Merlyn's dream of preserving a vestige of Roman law and culture in a unified Britain.

**Other books you might like:**
A.A. Attanasio, *The Dragon and the Unicorn*, 1996
Marion Zimmer Bradley, *The Forest House*, 1994
Marion Zimmer Bradley, *The Mists of Avalon*, 1983
Courtway Jones, *In the Shadow of the Oak King*, 1991
Morgan Llywelyn, *Druids*, 1991

---

### 5794

#### JACK WHYTE

## The Skystone

(New York: Tor Forge, 1996)

**Story type:** Fantasy (Legend; Adventure)

---

**Series:** Camulod Chronicles: The Forging of Arthur's Britain
**Major character(s):** Gaius Publius Varrus, Military Personnel (retired), Blacksmith; Caius Britannicus, Military Personnel, Leader
**Time period(s):** 4th century
**Locale(s):** England (Britain)

**Summary:** When invaders breach Hadrian's Wall, Caius Britannicus and his legionnaires spend the next deadly year fighting their way back to comrades in the south. Cleared of cowardice, Britannicus troops receive reassignment as the Roman Empire reasserts its authority. Discharged from service, Gaius Publius Varrus turns to work as a smith, lusting for meteoric metal to work into the finest sword steel. As the Roman Empire withdraws south, Britannicus, Varus and others work to establish a territory in Britain which will retain Roman culture and respect for law.

**Other books you might like:**
Marion Zimmer Bradley, *The Forest House*, 1994
Courtway Jones, *In the Shadow of the Oak King*, 1991
Morgan Llywelyn, *Druids*, 1991
Anne McCaffrey, *Black Horses for the King*, 1996
Harry Turtledove, *Werenight*, 1994

---

### 5795

#### STANLEY WIATER, Editor

## After the Darkness

(Baltimore, Maryland: Maclay, 1993)

**Story type:** Horror (Anthology)

**Summary:** In response to the proliferation of theme horror anthologies, the editor presents 17 stories on no specific theme, with afterwords by the authors discussing the genesis of each story. Among the best are Chet Williamson's "Perfect Days," the memoirs of an elderly serial killer; Les Daniels' "Little Green Ones," about the strange obsession a man develops for cemetery statuary; and Philip Nutman's ghost story, "Memories of Leaving Lydia." Thomas Monteleone's "Love Is the Prey" is a short story sequel to his 1987 novel *Lyrica*.

**Other books you might like:**
Dennis Etchison, *Metahorror*, 1992
   editor
Charles L. Grant, *Final Shadows*, 1991
   cditor
Thomas F. Monteleone, *Borderlands 3*, 1993
   editor
Chris Morgan, *Dark Fantasies*, 1989
   editor
Claudia O'Keefe, *Ghosttide*, 1993
   editor

---

### 5796

#### STANLEY WIATER
#### GAHAN WILSON, Illustrator

## Mysteries of the Word

(Holyoke, Massachusetts: Crossroads Press, 1994)

**Story type:** Horror (Ancient Evil Unleashed)
**Major character(s):** Paul Henkin, Child; Mrs. Crindle, Teacher; Mr. Stiles, Principal (grade school)
**Time period(s):** 1990s (1994)
**Locale(s):** United States (The Hooker School)

**Summary:** Supposedly based on an urban folktale, this chapbook-length story tells of a young boy who learns a sacred word, and what his chanting of that word calls forth into the world. The booklet includes an introduction by Jack Ketchum.

**Other books you might like:**
Ray Bradbury, *The Halloween Tree*, 1972
Graham Masterton, *Hurry, Monster*, 1989
Gahan Wilson, *Eddy Deco's Last Caper*, 1988
Roger Zelazny, *A Night in the Lonesome October*, 1993

---

**5797**

**STEWART WIECK**, Editor
**ANNA BRANSCOME**, Co-Editor

## The Essential World of Darkness
(Clarkston, Georgia: White Wolf, 1997)

**Story type:** Horror (Anthology)
**Series:** World of Darkness

**Summary:** Five novels set in the World of Darkness, an alternate world created for fantasy role-playing in which mages, wraiths, vampires, werewolves, and changelings are the ruling elite over human beings. Included are Robert Weinberg and Mark Rein-Hagen's *Vampire Diary: The Embrace*, a vampire coming-of-age story; Owl Goingback's *Shaman Moon*, a werewolf coming-of-age tale; Scott Ciencin's *Lightning Under Glass*, which pits three mages against one another; David Niall Wilson's *Except You Go Through Shadow*, in which a wraith pursues the cult leader who coerced him into committing suicide; and Esther M. Friesner's *Playing with Fire*, a tale of changeling cultural identity set in San Francisco's Chinatown.

**Other books you might like:**
Erin Kelly, *The Splendour Falls*, 1995
    editor
Edward E. Kramer, *Dark Destiny III: Children of Dracula*, 1996
    editor
Edward E. Kramer, *Dark Destiny II: Proprietors of Fate*, 1995
    editor
Edward E. Kramer, *Dark Destiny*, 1994
    editor
Staley Krause, *Strange City*, 1996
    Stewart Wieck, co-editor
Erin Kelly, *City of Darkness: Unseen*, 1995
    Stewart Wieck, co-editor
Stewart Wieck, *The Beast Within*, 1995
    editor
Stewart Wieck, *When Will You Rage*, 1994
    editor
Stewart Wieck, *World of Darkness: Truth Until Paradox*, 1994
    editor

---

**5798**

**STEWART WIECK**, Editor
**ANNA BRANSCOME**, Co-Editor

## The Quintessential World of Darkness
(Clarkston, Georgia: White Wolf, 1998)

**Story type:** Horror (Anthology)
**Series:** World of Darkness

**Summary:** These five novellas are set in the World of Darkness, an alternate universe where humans and creatures of the supernatural—vampires, werewolves, mages, wraiths, and others—co-exist uneasily and are perpetually embroiled in power struggles. Selections include Kevin Andrew Murphy's vampire tale "The Lotus of

Five Pearls"; Jody Lynn Nye's "The Muse"; William Bridge's "The Silver Crown," about an epic quest for the magic talisman that will save a werewolf clan from succumbing to evil; Edo van Belkom's "Mister Magick"; and Rick Hautala's "Beyond the Shroud," in which the ghost of a murdered man struggles to prevent his wife from falling victim to a man laboring under the influence of Jack the Ripper.

**Other books you might like:**
Justin Achilli, *Dark Tyrants*, 1997
    Robert Hatch, co-editor
Erin Kelly, *The Splendour Falls*, 1995
    editor
Edward E. Kramer, *Dark Destiny*, 1994
Edward E. Kramer, *Dark Destiny II: Proprietors of Fate*, 1995
Edward E. Kramer, *Dark Destiny III: Children of Dracula*, 1996

---

**5799**

**MARIANNE WIGGINS**

## John Dollar
(New York: Harper & Row, 1989)

**Story type:** Horror (Evil Children)
**Major character(s):** Charlotte Lewes, Widow(er), Teacher; John Dollar, Sea Captain (Charlotte's ill-fated lover)
**Time period(s):** 1910s (1918)
**Locale(s):** Rangoon, Myanmar; Pacific Islands

**Summary:** Widowed by World War I, Charlotte Lewes finds new life as a schoolteacher in Rangoon and new love with John Dollar, a ship's captain. When Dollar, Charlotte, and a group of her female charges are shipwrecked on an uncharted island, Dollar is crippled, Charlotte is lost, and the girls, cast onto their own resources, revert to savagery.

**Other books you might like:**
J.G. Ballard, *Running Wild*, 1989
William Golding, *Lord of the Flies*, 1954

---

**5800**

**KELLEY WILDE**

## Angel Kiss
(New York: Dell/Abyss, 1993)

**Story type:** Horror (Mystery)
**Major character(s):** Jack Pepper, Advertising (copywriter); Hank Boone, Businessman (building manager); Suki Hirazawa, Worker (in a department store)
**Time period(s):** 1990s (1993)
**Locale(s):** Atlanta, Georgia; San Francisco, California; Tokyo, Japan

**Summary:** An East-West dating service known as Angel Kiss is actually a front for the Makahari, a secret order of Japanese women who violate the Oriental ideal of female subservience by pulverizing their male victims to extract their life essence. In chauvinistic men like Jack Pepper and Hank Boone, the Makahari find the perfect avenue for spreading their influence across America.

**Other books you might like:**
Michael Cecilione, *Domination*, 1993
Gordon Linzner, *The Oni*, 1987
Bentley Little, *The Summoning*, 1993

## **5801**

### KELLEY WILDE

## *Makoto*

(New York: Tor, 1990)

**Story type:** Horror (Possession)
**Major character(s):** Makoto Shirata Leigh, Teacher (language); Cotter Sloan, Handyman; Henry Daez, Landlord
**Time period(s):** 1980s (1985)
**Locale(s):** New York, New York

**Summary:** Brought to New York by wealthy advertising man Michael Leigh, Makoto Shirata is haunted by the memory of her brother's suicide, which she witnessed at age 12. Faced with massive culture shock and abused by her neighbors, landlord, sadistic husband, and the city of New York, Makoto only gradually realizes that her brother's spirit is hovering about her in the form of an *oni* (a demon), gathering strength and seeking corporeal form in order to seek revenge upon her.

**Other books you might like:**
Lafcadio Hearn, *Kwaidan*, 1904

## **5802**

### KELLEY WILDE

## *Mastery*

(New York: Dell Abyss, 1991)

**Story type:** Horror (Vampire Story)
**Major character(s):** Dodge Cunningham, Detective—Private; Wolf Cotter, Journalist; Austin Blacke, Vampire
**Time period(s):** 1980s (1985); 1900s (1906)
**Locale(s):** San Francisco, California

**Summary:** On a train bound for the West Coast in 1985 to track the path of Halley's Comet, a diverse group of survivors from the American counterculture of the 1960s find themselves transported back in time to turn-of-the-century San Francisco. While there, they find a means for resuscitating their exhausted social consciences by helping to track down a vampire menace who has been transported back in time with them.

**Other books you might like:**
Jewelle Gomez, *The Gilda Stories*, 1991
Anne Rice, *The Vampire Lestat*, 1985
Brian Stableford, *The Empire of Fear*, 1988
Chelsea Quinn Yarbro, *The Saint-Germain Chronicles*, 1979-83

## **5803**

### KELLEY WILDE

## *The Suiting*

(New York: Tor, 1989)

**Story type:** Horror (Possession)
**Major character(s):** Victor Frankl, Office Worker; Jean-Paul Bouchette, Criminal, Spirit
**Time period(s):** 1980s (1980)
**Locale(s):** Toronto, Ontario, Canada; Montreal, Quebec, Canada

**Summary:** Having come into possession of a gorgeous suit, Victor gradually loses his identity to its previous owner.

**Other books you might like:**
Ray Bradbury, *"The Wonderful Ice Cream Suit"*, 1959
short story

## **5804**

### CHERRY WILDER

## *Signs of Life*

(New York: Tor, 1996)

**Story type:** Science Fiction (Lost Colony; Adventure)
**Major character(s):** Anat Asher, Military Personnel (World Space Services); Gene "Wink" Winkler, Military Personnel (World Space Services); Paddy Rork, Sailor, Young Man
**Time period(s):** Indeterminate Future
**Locale(s):** *Serendip Dana*, Spaceship; Rhomary Land, Planet—Imaginary

**Summary:** When the *Serendip Dana* runs into trouble, her crew and passengers make forced lifeship landings on the Rhomary Land. There, they must survive in unfamiliar terrain and make peace with the Rhomarians, descendents of another human crew stranded there many generations before. A loose sequel to *Second Nature*.

**Other books you might like:**
David Brin, *Glory Season*, 1993
Arthur C. Clarke, *The Songs of Distant Earth*, 1986
Nicola Griffith, *Ammonite*, 1993
James P. Hogan, *Voyage From Yesteryear*, 1982
Tricia Sullivan, *Lethe*, 1995
Amy Thomson, *The Color of Distance*, 1995

## **5805**

### KATE WILHELM

## *And the Angels Sing*

(New York: St. Martin's, 1992)

**Story type:** Science Fiction (Collection)

**Summary:** 12 stories published 1970 to the present including one original to this volume, "The Day of the Sharks"; a Nebula Award winner from 1988, "Forever Yours, Anna"; and 10 others spanning the thematic range of the genre, with a three-page foreword by Karen Joy Fowler.

**Other books you might like:**
Damon Knight, *One Side Laughing: Stories Unlike Other Stories*, 1991
Pat Murphy, *Points of Departure*, 1990
Robert Sheckley, *The Collected Robert Sheckley*, 1991
5 volumes
Michael Swanwick, *Gravity's Angels*, 1991
John Varley, *The Persistence of Vision*, 1978
Howard Waldrop, *Strange Monsters of the Recent Past*, 1991

## **5806**

### KATE WILHELM

## *Cambio Bay*

(New York: St. Martin's Press, 1990)

**Story type:** Fantasy (Legend)
**Major character(s):** Carolyn Engleman, Businesswoman; Luisa, Innkeeper
**Time period(s):** 1990s
**Locale(s):** Cambio Bay, California

**Summary:** When a mudslide washes out the California freeway, a number of stranded travelers put up for the night at the mysterious Miss Luisa's Guest House on Cambio Bay. They find the bay a place of odd transformations, a place where the mythological past comes to life.

**Other books you might like:**
Robert Holdstock, *Lavondyss: Journey to an Unknown Region*, 1988
Robert Holdstock, *Mythago Wood*, 1985
Pat Murphy, *The Falling Woman*, 1986
Connie Willis, *Lincoln's Dreams*, 1987
Gene Wolfe, *There Are Doors*, 1988

**5807**

KATE WILHELM

## Children of the Wind: Five Novellas
(New York: St. Martin's Press, 1989)

**Story type:** Science Fiction (Collection)

**Summary:** Four of the five stories in this collection are previously published, the best known, "The Gorgon Field" and "The Girl Who Fell into the Sky," appearing in 1985 and 1986 respectively. "A Brother to Dragons, a Companion to Owls" appeared in 1974. "The Blue Ladies," which is not science fiction, appeared in *Redbook* in 1983. "Children of the Wind" appears here for the first time.

**Other books you might like:**
Karen Joy Fowler, *Artificial Things*, 1986
Ursula K. Le Guin, *Buffalo Gals and Other Animal Presences*, 1987
Ursula K. Le Guin, *The Compass Rose*, 1982
Ursula K. Le Guin, *The Wind's Twelve Quarters*, 1975
Kim Stanley Robinson, *The Planet on the Table*, 1986
John Varley, *Blue Champagne*, 1986
John Varley, *The Persistence of Vision*, 1978
Connie Willis, *Fire Watch*, 1985

**5808**

KATE WILHELM

## The Good Children
(New York: St. Martin's, 1998)

**Story type:** Horror (Gothic Family Chronicle)
**Major character(s):** Brian McNair, Child (six-year-old); Liz McNair, Child (eleven-year-old); William Radix, Lawyer
**Time period(s):** 1990s (1998)
**Locale(s):** Portland, Oregon

**Summary:** Orphaned by the mysterious death of their mother, the five young McNair children bury her in their garden and orchestrate a scheme to pretend that she is still alive, in order to keep the family from being farmed out to foster homes. The trick works for years, but takes its toll on young Brian, who is haunted by the memory of his mother, and perhaps more, and whose grasp on reality grows tenuous as the children grow through adolescence and move ahead with their lives.

**Other books you might like:**
Athena Alexis, *Along Came a Spider*, 1991
V.C. Andrews, *Flowers in the Attic*, 1979
Deborah Churchman, *Cross a Dark Bridge*, 1996
Michael McDowell, *Blackwater*, 1983
Ian McEwan, *The Cement Garden*, 1978

**5809**

KATE WILHELM

## Naming the Flowers
(Eugene, Oregon: Pulphouse Publishing Axolotl Press, 1992)

**Story type:** Science Fiction (Genetic Manipulation; Romance)
**Major character(s):** Winston Seton, Publisher; Francie, Genetically Altered Being, Child; Jeremy Kersh, FBI Agent
**Time period(s):** 1990s
**Locale(s):** Atlantic City, New Jersey

**Summary:** On the beach at Atlantic City, Winston Seton briefly befriends Francie, later discovering the FBI wishes to acquire the rapidly aging child to insure that her genes remain unincorporated into the human genome. Seton arranges a place for Francie to grow up undisturbed by the FBI, then becomes romantically involved with her late in Francie's life.

**Other books you might like:**
Lois McMaster Bujold, *Falling Free*, 1988
Diana G. Gallagher, *The Alien Dark*, 1990
Janet Kagan, *Mirabile*, 1991
Frederik Pohl, *Stopping at Slowyear*, 1991
Cordwainer Smith, *Norstrilia*, 1975
Michael Swanwick, *Vacuum Flowers*, 1987
Michael D. Weaver, *My Father Immortal*, 1989

**5810**

KATE WILHELM

## State of Grace
(Eugene, Oregon: Pulphouse Publishing, 1991)

**Story type:** Fantasy (Collection)
**Series:** Author's Choice Monthly

**Summary:** This volume contains 6 stories written between 1966 and 1988. Three related stories are "The Book of Ylin," "Jenny with Wings," and "The Downstairs Room." Two stories originally appeared in anthologies, "State of Grace," in *Orbit 19* (1977) and "Isosceles," in *Terry's Universe* (1988). Each story has a new introduction.

**Other books you might like:**
Charles de Lint, *Hedgework and Guessery*, 1991
Elizabeth A. Lynn, *Tales From a Vanished Country*, 1990
Spider Robinson, *True Minds*, 1990
Robert Sheckley, *Minotaur Maze*, 1990

**5811**

ELIZABETH WILLEY

## The Price of Blood and Honor
(New York: Tor, 1996)

**Story type:** Fantasy (Political; Magic Conflict)
**Series:** Well-Favored Man
**Major character(s):** Prospero, Sorcerer, Royalty; Avril, Royalty, Sorcerer; Dewar, Sorcerer
**Time period(s):** Indeterminate
**Locale(s):** Landuc, Fictional Country; Argylle, Fictional Country

**Summary:** The long struggle between Emperor Avril and his brother, Prospero, becomes open war, which Prospero seems to be losing. Caught in the middle, Prospero's children, Freia and Dewar, try desperately to save their father, his land and his lore. Loosely based on Shakespeare's *The Tempest*.

**Other books you might like:**
Lisa Goldstein, *Summer King, Winter Fool*, 1994
Katherine Kurtz, *Deryni Rising*, 1970
Ellen Kushner, *Swordspoint*, 1987
Caroline Stevermer, *A College of Magics*, 1994
Martha Wells, *The Element of Fire*, 1993

**5812**

### ELIZABETH WILLEY

## A Sorcerer and a Gentleman

(New York: Tor, 1995)

**Story type:** Fantasy (Political; Magic Conflict)
**Series:** Well-Favored Man
**Major character(s):** Prospero, Sorcerer, Royalty; Avril, Ruler, Sorcerer; Dewar, Sorcerer
**Time period(s):** Indeterminate
**Locale(s):** Phesaotois, Fictional Country; Pheyarcet, Fictional Country

**Summary:** Permanently exiled from Pheyarcet, Prospero acts to overthrow his brother, Emperor Avril, and assume power. Prequel to *The Well-Favored Man: The Tale of the Sorcerer's Nephew*.

**Other books you might like:**
Laurell K. Hamilton, *Nightseer*, 1992
Guy Gavriel Kay, *Tigana*, 1990
Melanie Rawn, *Dragon Prince*, 1988
Martha Wells, *The Element of Fire*, 1993
Roger Zelazny, *Nine Princes in Amber*, 1970

**5813**

### ELIZABETH WILLEY

## The Well-Favored Man: The Tale of the Sorcerer's Nephew

(New York: Tor, 1993)

**Story type:** Fantasy (Quest; Political)
**Series:** Well-Favored Man
**Major character(s):** Gwydion, Royalty (prince), Sorcerer; Prospero, Sorcerer, Royalty
**Time period(s):** Indeterminate
**Locale(s):** Dominion of Argylle, Fictional Country

**Summary:** Long term absences of his father and uncle leave Prince Gwydion in charge of the Dominion of Argylle, a fate ill-appreciated by the prince. Events demand Gwydion's attention when a huge dragon takes up residence in the countryside; a mysterious woman appears, claiming sisterhood; and high-tech aliens arrive, intending to conduct a legal investigation. Author's first novel.

**Other books you might like:**
Steven Brust, *Jhereg*, 1983
Lois McMaster Bujold, *The Spirit Ring*, 1992
Ellen Kushner, *Swordspoint*, 1987
Paula Volsky, *Illusion*, 1992
Martha Wells, *The Element of Fire*, 1993
Roger Zelazny, *Nine Princes in Amber*, 1970

**5814**

### A. SUSAN WILLIAMS, Editor

## The Lifted Veil: The Book of Fantastic Literature by Women

(New York: Carroll & Graf, 1993)

**Story type:** Fantasy (Anthology)

**Summary:** Subtitled "The Book of Fantastic Literature by Women 1800—World War II," this volume contains a nine-page introduction, five pages of authors' biographies and 33 reprinted stories by authors contributing to World Literature of the fantastic 1806-1936. From renowned authors, the stories contain fantasy themes encompassing ghosts and other substantial apparitions, utopian societies, alternate universes with societies repressive to women and gender roles as a product of social construction. Authors include "A.M. Barnard" (Louisa May Alcott), Charlotte Bronte, Willa Cather, Isak Dinesen (Karen Blixen), George Eliot, Charlotte Perkins Gilman, Katherine Mansfield, C.L. Moore, Edith Nesbit, Mary Shelley, Harriet Beecher Stowe, Edith Wharton and Virginia Woolf.

**Other books you might like:**
Marjorie Agosin, *The Secret Weavers: Stories of the Fantastic by Latin American Women*, 1991
    editor
Nina Auerbach, *Forbidden Journeys: Fairy Tales and Fantasies by Victorian Women Writers*, 1992
    U.C. Knoepflmacher, co-editor
Angela Carter, *The Old Wives' Fairy Tale Book*, 1990
    editor
Richard Dalby, *Modern Ghost Stories by Eminent Women Writers*, 1991
    editor
Richard Dalby, *Victorian Ghost Stories by Eminent Women Writers*, 1991
    editor
Alison Lurie, *The Oxford Book of Modern Fairy Tales*, 1993
    editor
Jessica Amanda Salmonson, *What Did Miss Darrington See?: An Anthology of Feminist Supernatural Fiction*, 1989
    editor
Susanna J. Sturgis, *Magic Realism by Women: Dreams in a Minor Key*, 1991
    editor

**5815**

### A. SUSAN WILLIAMS, Editor
### RICHARD GLYN JONES, Co-Editor

## The Penguin Book of Modern Fantasy by Women

(New York: Viking, 1995)

**Story type:** Fantasy (Anthology)

**Summary:** Contains a three-page introduction by Joanna Russ and 38 stories written in English, arranged chronologically 1941-1994 and chosen as representative of the wealth of variety expressed in fantasy. The tone ranges from dark and ironic to lighter with both traditional and modern themes explored by authors including Joan Aiken, Margaret Atwood, Leigh Brackett, Octavia E. Butler, Angela Carter, Suzy McKee Charnas, Daphne du Maurier, Carol Emshwiller, Mary Gentle, Zenna Henderson, Shirley Jackson, P.D. James, Anna Kavan, Ursula K. Le Guin, Anne McCaffrey, Vonda N. McIntyre, Joyce Carol Oates, Kit Reed, Joanna Russ, Josephine Saxton, James Tiptree Jr., Lisa Tuttle, Fay Weldon, and Kate Wilhelm.

**Other books you might like:**
Marjorie Agosin, *The Secret Weavers: Stories of the Fantastic by Latin American Women*, 1991
   editor
Nina Auerbach, *Forbidden Journeys: Fairy Tales and Fantasies by Victorian Women Writers*, 1992
   U.S. Knoepflmacher, co-editor
Richard Dalby, *Modern Ghost Stories by Eminent Women Writers*, 1991
   editor
Susan Shwartz, *Sisters in Fantasy*, 1995
   Martin H. Greenberg, co-editor
Susanna J. Sturgis, *Magic Realism by Women: Dreams in a Minor Key*, 1991
   editor

---

**5816**

### CONRAD WILLIAMS

## Head Injuries

(Chester, Pennsylvania: Do-Not Press/Dufour, 1999)

**Major character(s):** David Munro, Artist (painter); Seamus Cope, Young Man; Helen Soper, Store Owner (crafts)
**Time period(s):** 1990s (1998)
**Locale(s):** Morecambe, England

**Summary:** Helen and Seamus call former school friend David to the seaside town of Morecambe to discuss their feelings of being followed by an indefinable presence. Recalling their pasts, the three discover that certain shared memories have been suppressed, and may be the key to their nightmares and of the murder of a girl on the periphery of their circle. A first novel.

**Other books you might like:**
Ramsey Campbell, *Incarnate*, 1983
Joel Lane, *The Earth Wire and Other Stories*, 1994
Daniel Quinn, *Dreamer*, 1988
Nicholas Royle, *Counterparts*, 1995
Lisa Tuttle, *Pillow Friend*, 1996

---

**5817**

### MICHAEL WILLIAMS

## Allamanda

(New York: Roc, 1997)

**Story type:** Fantasy (Religious; Adventure)
**Major character(s):** Garrick Hawken, Heir
**Time period(s):** Indeterminate
**Locale(s):** Urthona, Fictional Country; Urizen, Fictional Country

**Summary:** When Garrick discovers the Absence, a void beneath the family house, Arcady, he moves in with relatives at the family's old country house, Allamanda. Drawn to the Hawkens, the void comes to Allamanda, forcing Garrick to find some means of fighting the void's progression. Direct sequel to *Arcady*.

**Other books you might like:**
Greg Bear, *Songs of Earth and Power*, 1994
Richard Brautigan, *The Hawkline Monster*, 1974
Alan Dean Foster, *To the Vanishing Point*, 1988
Robert Holdstock, *Mythago Wood*, 1984
J. Gregory Keyes, *The Waterborn*, 1996
Eric S. Nylund, *Dry Water*, 1997

---

**5818**

### MICHAEL WILLIAMS

## Arcady

(New York: Roc, 1996)

**Story type:** Fantasy (Quest)
**Major character(s):** Solomon Hawken, Magician, Scholar
**Time period(s):** Indeterminate
**Locale(s):** Arcady, Mythical Place; Urthona, Fictional Country

**Summary:** When the edge of no-man's land, the Border, crosses into the family estate, Arcady, Solomon Hawken's niece vanishes into the flux. With little ability to control the magic he wields, Solomon must try to save his family and maybe the entire world.

**Other books you might like:**
Greg Bear, *Songs of Earth and Power*, 1994
Emma Bull, *Finder*, 1994
Charles de Lint, *Moonheart: A Romance*, 1984
Robert Holdstock, *Mythago Wood*, 1984
Michaela Roessner, *Vanishing Point*, 1993
Terri Windling, *Life on the Border*, 1991

---

**5819**

### MICHAEL WILLIAMS

## A Forest Lord

(New York: Warner Questar, 1991)

**Story type:** Fantasy (Quest)
**Series:** From Thief to King
**Major character(s):** Brenn, Adventurer; Terrance, Wizard
**Time period(s):** Indeterminate Past
**Locale(s):** Palerna, Fictional Country; Corbinwood, Fictional Country

**Summary:** When Brenn and Terrance escape the inhuman forces of the evil sorceress, Ravenna, they flee to Corbinwood, where they hope to enlist outlaws to help in their battle against the usurper, King Dragmond. To gain their help, Brenn must save the Forest Lord from Ravenna's curse. This book is a sequel to *A Sorcerer's Apprentice*.

**Other books you might like:**
Steven Brust, *Jhereg*, 1983
David Ferring, *Shadowbreed*, 1990
Katharine Kerr, *The Dragon Revenant*, 1990
Elizabeth Moon, *Surrender None: The Legacy of Gird*, 1990

---

**5820**

### MICHAEL WILLIAMS

## A Sorcerer's Apprentice

(New York: Popular Library/Questar, 1990)

**Story type:** Fantasy (Adventure)
**Series:** From Thief to King
**Major character(s):** Brenn, Thief; Terrance, Wizard
**Time period(s):** Indeterminate Past
**Locale(s):** Palerna, Fictional Country

**Summary:** Brenn, a teenager living in the streets of Palerna, tries to rob a house and is captured by the Mage who lives there. He chooses to stay and finds he is more than he knew. He must avoid King Dragmond's murderous fury while he learns enough to defend himself and discover his birthright.

**Other books you might like:**
Donald Aamodt, *A Name to Conjure With*, 1989
Orson Scott Card, *Prentice Alvin*, 1989
David Eddings, *Sorceress of Darshiva*, 1989
Jackie Hyman, *Shadowlight*, 1989
Deborah Talmadge-Bickmore, *The Apprentice*, 1990

**5821**

PAUL O. WILLIAMS

### The Gift of the Gorboduc Vandal

(New York: Ballantine/Del Rey, 1989)

**Story type:** Science Fiction (Space Opera)
**Major character(s):** Umber Trreggerthann, Scientist, Warrior; Dame Dyann Penne, Artisan (Potter)
**Time period(s):** Indeterminate Future
**Locale(s):** Landsdrum, Planet—Imaginary

**Summary:** The barbarian Gorboduc Vandals attack the planet Landsdrum, demanding tribute or death. A renegade Gorboduc, Umber Trreggerthann, holds the key to defeating the invaders, but the people of Landsdrum must decide if they can trust him.

**Other books you might like:**
F.M. Busby, *Rissa Kerguelen*, 1976
C.S. Friedman, *In Conquest Born*, 1987
H. Beam Piper, *Space Viking*, 1963
Alis A. Rasmussen, *A Passage of Stars*, 1989

**5822**

RUTH L. WILLIAMS

### The Silver Tree

(New York: HarperCollins, 1992)

**Story type:** Fantasy (Young Adult; Time Travel)
**Major character(s):** Michelle ''Micki'' Ann Silver, Child, Time Traveler
**Time period(s):** 1990s; 1890s (1891)
**Locale(s):** Madame F's Toy Museum, Mythical Place

**Summary:** In a magical back room of Madame F's Toy Museum, Micki unintentionally makes a regrettable wish, one which puts her very existence in jeopardy. To reverse the effects of her wish, Micki must travel to the past. Author's first book.

**Other books you might like:**
Bruce Coville, *Jeremy Thatcher, Dragon Hatcher*, 1991
Edward Eager, *Half Magic*, 1954
Diana Wynne Jones, *A Tale of Time City*, 1987
Will Shetterly, *Elsewhere*, 1991
Marilyn Singer, *Charmed*, 1990
Vivian Vande Velde, *A Well-Timed Enchantment*, 1990

**5823**

SIDNEY WILLIAMS

### Gnelfs

(New York: Zebra/Pinnacle, 1991)

**Story type:** Horror (Child-in-Peril)
**Major character(s):** Heaven Davis, Child; Gabrielle Davis, Business-woman; Terry Guillory, Child
**Time period(s):** 1990s
**Locale(s):** Riverland

**Summary:** Like her classmates, precocious Heaven Davis is fond of Gnelfs, the docile half gnome-half elf animated cartoon characters she watches on children's television programs. Unlike her classmates, though, Heaven's subconscious is so endowed with imaginative power that it turns the Gnelfs into creatures of flesh and blood, who torment her with threats of physical harm.

**Other books you might like:**
Pat Graversen, *Dollies*, 1991
William W. Johnstone, *Toy Cemetery*, 1987
Stephen King, *The Dark Half*, 1990
Gene Lazuta, *Bleeder*, 1991

**5824**

SIDNEY WILLIAMS

### Night Brothers

(New York: Pinnacle, 1989)

**Story type:** Horror (Vampire Story)
**Major character(s):** Navarra, Vampire; Travis Dixon, Publisher (Newspaper)
**Time period(s):** 1980s (1868)
**Locale(s):** Bristol Springs, Louisiana

**Summary:** Revived from a watery grave by drought, the vampire Navarra uses her powers over animals to terrorize the locals while she prepares for a ritual to enhance her powers and perpetuate her race. Dixon gathers a small group of citizens to fight the menace, unaware that his wife, Alisoun, has been chosen by Navarra for her own.

**Other books you might like:**
Michael Paine, *Owl Light*, 1989
Jean Paiva, *Lilith*, 1989
Whitley Strieber, *The Hunger*, 1981

**5825**

SIDNEY WILLIAMS

### When Darkness Falls

(New York: Pinnacle, 1992)

**Story type:** Horror (Werewolf Story)
**Major character(s):** Charlie Black, Teenager; Miss Nielson, Teacher (high school); Nell Devery, Student—College (art student)
**Time period(s):** 1990s (1992)
**Locale(s):** Petittville, Louisiana

**Summary:** Murderous packs of dogs begin terrorizing the residents of Pettitville shortly after the beautiful Miss Nielson comes to teach at the local high school, and misfit student Charlie Black has reason to believe that Miss Nielson is somehow nurturing a power within him to control them.

**Other books you might like:**
Charles L. Grant, *The Pet*, 1986
Stephen Gresham, *The Living Dark*, 1991
K.W. Jeter, *The Night Man*, 1990

**5826**

TAD WILLIAMS

### Caliban's Hour

(New York: HarperPrism, 1994)

**Story type:** Fantasy (Legend; Horror)

**Major character(s):** Caliban, Monster; Miranda, Parent
**Time period(s):** 17th century
**Locale(s):** Naples, Italy; Prospero's Isle, Fictional Country

**Summary:** Twenty years after her father, Prospero, discovered Caliban, Caliban sneaks into Miranda's bedroom to explain his view of Prospero's actions and find vengeance for wrongs he perceives.

**Other books you might like:**
Jeff Collignon, *Her Monster*, 1992
Katharine Kerr, *Weird Tales From Shakespeare*, 1994
    Martin H. Greenberg, co-author
Valerie Martin, *Mary Reilly*, 1990
William Shakespeare, *The Tempest*, 1623
Clifford D. Simak, *Shakespeare's Planet*, 1976

---

**5827**

**TAD WILLIAMS**
**NINA KIRIKI HOFFMAN**, Co-Author

## *Child of an Ancient City*

(New York: Atheneum, 1992)

**Story type:** Fantasy (Legend; Adventure)
**Series:** Dragonflight
**Major character(s):** Susri "Fawn", Child, Traveler; Vampyr, Vampire
**Time period(s):** Indeterminate Past
**Locale(s):** Caucassian Mountains, Asia

**Summary:** While journeying through the forest, Susri's companions tell stories all night to keep away a bothersome vampire. On the last night in the forest, the vampire approaches the group to propose a story-telling contest with potentially lethal consequences if Susri's story proves happier than the vampire's story.

**Other books you might like:**
Louise Cooper, *The Sleep of Stone*, 1991
Charles de Lint, *The Dreaming Place*, 1990
Jeanne Larsen, *Bronze Mirror*, 1991
Tanith Lee, *Black Unicorn*, 1991
Salman Rushdie, *Haroun and the Sea of Stories*, 1990
Robert Silverberg, *Letters From Atlantis*, 1990

---

**5828**

**TAD WILLIAMS**

## *City of Golden Shadow*

(New York: DAW, 1997)

**Story type:** Science Fiction (Cyberpunk; Political)
**Series:** Otherland
**Major character(s):** Renie Sulaweyo, Teacher; !Xabbu, Traveler, Student; Orlando Teenager, Warrior
**Time period(s):** 1910s (1918); Indeterminate Future
**Locale(s):** Durban, South Africa; The Net, Cyberspace

**Summary:** In the near future, a worldwide network of virtual reality provides stores, entertainment, schools and nearly everything people need. When a mysterious disease begins to send children throughout the world into comas, a small group of people begin to realize that something strange lies behind the Net. First of a planned four-book series.

**Other books you might like:**
Iain M. Banks, *Feersum Endjinn*, 1995
Pat Cadigan, *Mindplayers*, 1987
Nigel Findley, *No Limits*, 1996
Ian McDonald, *Terminal Cafe*, 1994

Brian Stableford, *The Werewolves of London*, 1990

---

**5829**

**TAD WILLIAMS**

## *The Dragonbone Chair*

(New York, DAW, 1989)

**Story type:** Fantasy (Quest)
**Series:** Memory, Sorrow and Thorn Trilogy
**Major character(s):** Simon, Sorcerer, Apprentice
**Time period(s):** Indeterminate

**Summary:** Unware of his heritage, Simon begins a quest for the solution to a riddle about long-lost swords of power that are the only hope of salvation in a war fueled by the dark powers of sorcery.

**Other books you might like:**
Robert Jordan, *The Eye of the World*, 1990
    Book 1 - Wheel of Time
Anne McCaffrey, *The Dragonriders of Pern Series*, 1968-1986
Mervyn Peake, *Gormenghast Trilogy*, 1946-1959
J.R.R. Tolkien, *The Lord of the Rings Trilogy*, 1954-1955

---

**5830**

**TAD WILLIAMS**

## *River of Blue Fire*

(New York: DAW, 1998)

**Story type:** Fantasy (Alternate Universe)
**Series:** Otherland
**Major character(s):** Paul Jonas, Military Personnel; Irene Sulaweyo, Teacher
**Time period(s):** Indeterminate Future
**Locale(s):** Alternate Universe

**Summary:** A group of powerful men have found the secret of creating other universes, each with its own set of laws and limitations. Although they strictly control access to these creations, a handful of people are able to slip past safeguards in a quest to discover the purpose of the project.

**Other books you might like:**
Gregory Benford, *Cosm*, 1998
David Brin, *The Practice Effect*, 1984
Jack L. Chalker, *The Labyrinth of Dreams*, 1987
Philip Jose Farmer, *The Maker of Universes*, 1965
Richard Lupoff, *Circumpolar!*, 1984

---

**5831**

**TAD WILLIAMS**

## *Stone of Farewell*

(New York: DAW, 1990)

**Story type:** Fantasy (Quest)
**Series:** Memory, Sorrow and Thorn Trilogy
**Major character(s):** Simon, Sorcerer, Apprentice; Ineluki the Storm King, Ruler, Alien (Sithi)
**Time period(s):** Indeterminate
**Locale(s):** Osten Ard, Fictional Country

**Summary:** Osten Ard is besieged by trolls, Sithi, and the evil minions of the undead Ineluki. Simon and the remaining members of the League of the Scroll discover the truth of an ancient legend.

**Other books you might like:**
M. Coleman Easton, *Spirits of Cavern and Hearth*, 1989
Robert Jordan, *The Great Hunt*, 1990
Robert Jordan, *The Eye of the World*, 1989
Michael Scott Rohan, *The Forge in the Forest*, 1989
Robert Silverberg, *To the Land of the Living*, 1990
Robert Silverberg, *Gilgamesh the King*, 1984

**5832**

### TAD WILLIAMS

## *To Green Angel Tower*
(New York: DAW, 1993)

**Story type:** Fantasy (Magic Conflict; Quest)
**Series:** Memory, Sorrow and Thorn Trilogy
**Major character(s):** Miriamele, Royalty (princess); Simon "Seoman/ Snowlock", Knight; Josua, Royalty (prince)
**Time period(s):** Indeterminate
**Locale(s):** Erkynland, Fictional Country; Hernystir, Fictional Country

**Summary:** As the evil minions of the undead Sithi Storm King prepare for the triumph of their dark sorceries and draw King Elias deeper into their spells, the loyal allies of Prince Josua desperately struggle to rally their forces at the Stone of Farewell. Miriamele confronts her father as the final battle between Good and Evil rages, while Sir Simon discovers his true heritage.

**Other books you might like:**
C.J. Cherryh, *The Tree of Swords and Jewels*, 1983
Stephen R. Donaldson, *Lord Foul's Bane*, 1977
Stephen R. Donaldson, *The Wounded Land*, 1980
David Eddings, *The Seeress of Kell*, 1991
Barbara Hambly, *The Armies of Daylight*, 1983
Katherine Kurtz, *High Deryni*, 1973
Ursula K. Le Guin, *The Farthest Shore*, 1972
J.R.R. Tolkien, *The Return of the King*, 1956

**5833**

### WALTER JON WILLIAMS

## *Angel Station*
(New York: Tor, 1989)

**Story type:** Science Fiction (Cyberpunk)
**Major character(s):** Ubu Roy, Pilot, Trader; Beautiful Maria, Pilot, Psychic
**Time period(s):** Indeterminate Future
**Locale(s):** *Runaway*, Spaceship; Angel Station, Space Station

**Summary:** Ubu Roy and Beautiful Maria, brother and sister, ply the spacelanes in their beat-up starship, always on the edge of bankruptcy, taking on cargoes too inconsequential for the major traders to waste their time on. Eventually they find what might be their big score, if they can get away with their lives.

**Other books you might like:**
C.J. Cherryh, *Downbelow Station*, 1981
C.J. Cherryh, *The Kif Strike Back*, 1985
C.J. Cherryh, *Merchanter's Luck*, 1982
C.J. Cherryh, *The Pride of Chanur*, 1982
C.J. Cherryh, *Rimrunners*, 1989
Bruce Sterling, *Schismatrix*, 1985

**5834**

### WALTER JON WILLIAMS

## *Aristoi*
(New York: Tor, 1992)

**Story type:** Science Fiction (Space Opera; Political)
**Major character(s):** Gabriel, Government Official (Aristoi), Detective—Amateur; Saigo, Government Official (Aristoi), Revolutionary
**Time period(s):** Indeterminate Future
**Locale(s):** Logarchy, Interstellar Empire/Federation (commonwealth of empires)

**Summary:** Alerted to Saigo's tampering with the universal data pool in hopes of covering up his own experiments, Gabriel investigates and discovers Saigo and his co-conspirators do not use their gifts to help humanity, but rather work to overturn the government which unifies diverse worlds.

**Other books you might like:**
Greg Bear, *Great Sky River*, 1987
David Brin, *Earth*, 1990
Glen Cook, *The Dragon Never Sleeps*, 1988
Cordwainer Smith, *The Best of Cordwainer Smith*, 1975
Cordwainer Smith, *Norstrilia*, 1975
Neal Stephenson, *Snow Crash*, 1992
Vernor Vinge, *A Fire upon the Deep*, 1992
Jack Williamson, *Mazeway*, 1990

**5835**

### WALTER JON WILLIAMS

## *City on Fire*
(New York: HarperPrism, 1997)

**Story type:** Science Fiction (Political; Science Fantasy)
**Series:** Metropolitan
**Major character(s):** Aiah, Political Figure, Police Officer; Constantine, Political Figure, Revolutionary; Ethemark, Police Officer, Genetically Altered Being
**Time period(s):** Indeterminate Future
**Locale(s):** Caraqui, Fictional City

**Summary:** Aiah flees her job one step ahead of the police, joining her partner in crime and sometimes lover, the once-Metropolitan Constantine, trying to build the city of his dreams. In this strange world, the sky shields, cities cover everything, and plasma provides the blood of civilization. Aiah and the revolutionaries must fight traitors, counterrevolutionaries, hostile neighbors, the criminal underworld, and Constantine's dangerous ally, the "hanged man," Taikon. Sequel to *Metropolitan*.

**Other books you might like:**
Alfred Bester, *The Demolished Man*, 1996 revised
Glen Cook, *The Dragon Never Sleeps*, 1988
Frank Herbert, *Dune*, 1965
Cordwainer Smith, *Norstrilia*, 1975
Roger Zelazny, *Lord of Light*, 1967

## 5836

### WALTER JON WILLIAMS

## *Days of Atonement*

(New York: Tor, 1991)

**Story type:** Science Fiction (Mystery)
**Major character(s):** Loren Hawn, Police Officer (chief)
**Time period(s):** 21st century
**Locale(s):** Atocha, New Mexico

**Summary:** When a car crashes into Loren Hawn's office, the bullet-ridden driver lives long enough to recognize and speak to him, begging for help. Loren knew the man and had, impossibly, watched him die twenty years earlier. It quickly becomes obvious that the nearby Advanced Technologies Laboratories is involved. As he investigates, he becomes obsessed with solving the mystery surrounding the deaths.

**Other books you might like:**
Isaac Asimov, *The Caves of Steel*, 1954
Isaac Asimov, *The Naked Sun*, 1957
Isaac Asimov, *The Robots of Dawn*, 1983
Alan Dean Foster, *Cyber Way*, 1990
Katharine Kerr, *Polar City Blues*, 1990
Allen Steele, *Clarke County, Space*, 1990

## 5837

### WALTER JON WILLIAMS

## *Facets*

(New York: Tor Books, 1990)

**Story type:** Science Fiction (Collection)

**Summary:** This collection of Williams' best short fiction includes nine stories published between 1985 and 1989 in *Isaac Asimov's Science Fiction Magazine* and elsewhere. The best known story in the book is the Hugo and Nebula Award nominee "Surfacing." Other excellent stories include "Flatline," "Dinosaurs," and "Witness." Introduction by Roger Zelazny.

**Other books you might like:**
Greg Bear, *Tangents*, 1989
Pat Cadigan, *Patterns*, 1989
William Gibson, *Burning Chrome*, 1986
Bruce Sterling, *Crystal Express*, 1989
Roger Zelazny, *Frost and Fire*, 1989

## 5838

### WALTER JON WILLIAMS

## *Frankensteins and Foreign Devils*

(Framingham, Massachusetts: NESFA Press, 1998)

**Story type:** Science Fiction (Collection)

**Summary:** The collection contains a three-page introduction by Gardner Dozois and individual introductions or afterwords by Wlilliams to two original tales and eight stories reprinted from periodicals and anthologies dating 1989 to 1996. One of the stories, "Wall, Stone, Craft," received a Hugo Award nomination. Frequently downbeat in tone, the stories explore diverse themes including the invasion of Earth, politics, magic, martial arts, time travel, and alternative universes.

**Other books you might like:**
Lois McMaster Bujold, *Dreamweaver's Dilemma*, 1996

Zenna Henderson, *Ingathering: The Complete People Stories of Zenna Henderson*, 1995
James H. Schmitz, *The Best of James H. Schmitz*, 1991
Cordwainer Smith, *The Rediscovery of Man*, 1993
James White, *The White Papers*, 1996

## 5839

### WALTER JON WILLIAMS

## *Metropolitan*

(New York: HarperPrism, 1995)

**Story type:** Science Fiction (Political; Psychic Powers)
**Major character(s):** Aiah, Civil Servant; Constantine, Political Figure; Sorya, Revolutionary
**Time period(s):** Indeterminate Future
**Locale(s):** Fictional City; Old Shorings, Mythical Place; Mage Towers, Mythical Place

**Summary:** Leaving her Barkazil ghetto and her heritage for government employment, Aiah wants to work directly with the magic plasma, the lifeblood of the city, but high tuition prevents this. Believing herself confined to parceling out the stuff of power to others without the ability to touch it herself, Aiah discovers a secret gloryhole and a new life.

**Other books you might like:**
David Brin, *Earth*, 1990
Emma Bull, *Bone Dance: A Fantasy for Technophiles*, 1991
Michael Swanwick, *Vacuum Flowers*, 1987
Joan D. Vinge, *The Snow Queen*, 1980
Roger Zelazny, *Lord of Light*, 1967

## 5840

### WALTER JON WILLIAMS

## *Rock of Ages*

(New York: Tor, 1995)

**Story type:** Science Fiction (Humor; Mystery)
**Series:** Drake Maijstral
**Major character(s):** Roman, Servant; Drake Maijstral, Thief, Nobleman (duke); Roberta Altunin, Noblewoman (duchess)
**Time period(s):** Indeterminate Future
**Locale(s):** Fort Worth, Texas (Tejas); Cozumel Reef, Caribbean; Graceland, Tennessee

**Summary:** While Drake Maijstral, Duke of Dornier and Allowed Burglar, wants only a nice, safe holiday on historic old Earth, he finds instead a succession of challenges to duels, multiple marriage proposals, and entanglements with the Church of Elvis.

**Other books you might like:**
Steven Brust, *The Phoenix Guards*, 1991
Fritz Leiber, *Swords and Deviltry*, 1970
Terry Pratchett, *The Colour of Magic*, 1983
Allen Steele, *Clarke County, Space*, 1990
John Varley, *Demon*, 1984

## 5841

### WALTER JON WILLIAMS

## *Solip: System*

(Eugene, Or: Axolotl Press, 1989)

**Story type:** Science Fiction (Cyberpunk)

**Major character(s):** Reno, Revolutionary, Disembodied Personality; Mercedes Calderon, Businesswoman, Abuse Victim
**Time period(s):** 21st century
**Locale(s):** Earth Orbit, Outer Space

**Summary:** In *Hardwired* a desperate group of cyborged revolutionaries managed to fight off the avaricious Orbital corporations intent on taking control of Earth. Now Reno, one of the heroes of that earlier battle, his body destroyed, has been implanted in the mind of the depraved Orbital corporate executive Albrecht Roon. Reno's mission is to use Roon's authority to destroy the Orbitals for good.

**Other books you might like:**
William Gibson, *Count Zero*, 1985
William Gibson, *Mona Lisa Overdrive*, 1988
William Gibson, *Neuromancer*, 1984
Bruce Sterling, *Islands in the Net*, 1988
Bruce Sterling, *Schismatrix*, 1985
Dave Wolverton, *On My Way to Paradise*, 1989

---

**5842**

**WALTER JON WILLIAMS**

## Wall, Stone, Craft

(Portland, Oregon: Axolotl/Pulphouse, 1993)

**Story type:** Horror (Literary)
**Major character(s):** Percy Bysshe Shelley, Writer (poet), Historical Figure; Mary Wollstonecraft, Writer; George Gordon, Nobleman (Lord Newstead)
**Time period(s):** 1810s
**Locale(s):** Le Caillou, France

**Summary:** In this alternate history, the author imagines how the relationship between Percy Bysshe Shelley and Lord Byron would have differed had Byron not been a poet but a soldier responsible for the capture of Napoleon, and how the difference would have influenced the writing of Mary Shelley's *Frankenstein*.

**Other books you might like:**
Emmanuel Carrere, *Gothic Romance*, 1990
Tim Powers, *On Stranger Tides*, 1987
Tim Powers, *The Stress of Her Regard*, 1989
Kathryn Ptacek, *In Silence Sealed*, 1988
Paul West, *Lord Byron's Doctor*, 1989

---

**5843**

**CHET WILLIAMSON**

## City of Iron

(New York: Avon, 1998)

**Story type:** Horror (Mystery; Ancient Evil Unleashed)
**Series:** Searchers
**Major character(s):** Laika Harris, Spy; Tony Luciano, Spy; Joseph Stein, Spy
**Time period(s):** 1990s (1998)
**Locale(s):** Plattsburgh, New York; Drumnadrochit, Scotland

**Summary:** The Searchers, a trio of CIA agents assigned to cases that defy routine investigation, look for a link between the assassination of an 11-member occult society in a cabin in the Adirondack Mountains, and the disappearance of New York artist Peder Holberg, whose iron pipe sculptures have been recognized by supernatural presences as a doorway for entry into our world. First novel in a projected trilogy.

**Other books you might like:**
Kevin J. Anderson, *Ground Zero*, 1995

Chris Carter, *The X-Files: Fight the Future*, 1998
Elizabeth Hand, co-author
Lewis Gannett, *Gehenna*, 1997
Charles L. Grant, *Genesis*, 1998
Peter Saxon, *The Curse of Rathlaw*, 1968

---

**5844**

**CHET WILLIAMSON**

## Clash by Night

(New York: HarperPrism, 1998)

**Story type:** Horror (Supernatural Vengeance)
**Series:** Crow
**Major character(s):** Amy Carlisle, Child-Care Giver; David Levenson, Detective; Virgil "Rip" Withers, Revolutionary (militia member)
**Time period(s):** 1990s (1998)
**Locale(s):** Hobie, Minnesota; Eau Claire, Wisconsin

**Summary:** Amy Carlisle dies trying to save children at her day care center from a bomb planted by an right wing paramilitary group. With the Crow as her familiar, Amy is allowed to return from the dead and infiltrate the Sons of a Free America to get revenge on her murderers. Set in the universe of the Crow graphic novel series, "where the innocent must die so that justice can triumph."

**Other books you might like:**
David Bischoff, *Quoth the Crow*, 1998
Poppy Z. Brite, *The Lazarus Heart*, 1998
Ric Meyers, *Fear Itself*, 1991
David Morrell, *Testament*, 1975
James O'Barr, *The Crow: Shattered Lives and Broken Dreams*, 1998
Edward Kramer, co-editor

---

**5845**

**CHET WILLIAMSON**

## Dreamthorp

(Arlington Heights, Illinois: Dark Harvest, 1989)

**Story type:** Horror (Ancient Evil Unleashed)
**Major character(s):** Tom Brewer, Artisan, Widow(er); Laura Stark, Young Woman
**Time period(s):** 1980s
**Locale(s):** Dreamthorpe, Pennsylvania

**Summary:** When an Indian gravesite is disturbed, spirits are released which gradually decimate the village of Dreamthorpe. At the same time, Laura Stark is pursued across the country by a vengeful serial killer. Thus, both old evil and recent malevolence meet and culminate in Dreamthorpe.

**Other books you might like:**
John Farris, *The Axman Cometh*, 1989
Peter Straub, *Floating Dragon*, 1982

---

**5846**

**CHET WILLIAMSON**

## Empire of Dust

(New York: Avon, 1998)

**Story type:** Horror (Mystery; Occult)
**Series:** Searchers

**Major character(s):** Laika Harris, Spy; Joseph Stein, Spy; Tony Luciano, Spy
**Time period(s):** 1990s (1998)
**Locale(s):** Joseph City, Arizona

**Summary:** Continuing the adventure begun in City of Iron, the Searchers, a trio of CIA agents on the track of paranormal menaces, investigate the discovery of a dessicated corpse found in the Arizona desert. There they pick up the trail of the Divine, a demon being that has broken into our dimension and who is being helped by a fanatical cult of believers. Second novel in a trilogy.

**Other books you might like:**
Kevin J. Anderson, *Ruins*, 1996
Chris Carter, *The X-Files: Fight the Future*, 1998
    Elizabeth Hand, co-author
Lewis Gannett, *Gehenna*, 1997
Charles L. Grant, *Genesis*, 1998
Peter Saxon, *The Curse of Rathlaw*, 1968

## 5847

### CHET WILLIAMSON

## Mordenheim

(Lake Geneva, Wisconsin: TSR, 1994)

**Story type:** Horror (Reanimated Dead)
**Series:** Ravenloft
**Major character(s):** Victor Mordenheim, Doctor; Friedrich Kreutzer, Writer (poet and necromancer); Hilda Von Karlsfeld, Teacher (necromancer)
**Time period(s):** Indeterminate
**Locale(s):** Ravenloft, Fictional Country

**Summary:** Victor Mordenheim summons two apprentice necromancers to his Gothic castle to assist him in the soul transference that will reanimate the personality of his beloved dead wife. But Adam, the monster whom Mordenheim created from dead body parts, absconds with her body out of jealousy, forcing the necromancers to undertake a perilous journey across a landscape fraught with supernatural dangers. Based on the Ravenloft game.

**Other books you might like:**
Elaine Bergstrom, *Tapestry of Dark Souls*, 1993
P.N. Elrod, *I, Strahd*, 1993
Christie Golden, *Dance of the Dead*, 1992
J. Robert King, *Carnival of Fear*, 1993
Mary Shelley, *Frankenstein*, 1818

## 5848

### CHET WILLIAMSON

## Murder in Cormyr

(Lake Geneva, Wisconsin: TSR, 1996)

**Story type:** Fantasy (Mystery)
**Series:** Forgotten Realms
**Major character(s):** Jasper, Servant, Student; Benelaius, Wizard (war, retired); Lindavar, Wizard (war)
**Time period(s):** Indeterminate
**Locale(s):** Cormyr, Fictional Country; Gahrs, Fictional City

**Summary:** Benelaius volunteers his servant, ex-apprentice, and himself to solve the murder of Dovo, who had been impersonating a ghost. Before they can complete the task, Grodoveth, the king's representative, becomes the next victim, giving them one less suspect and giving more credence to the idea that the ghost still protects his hidden treasure.

**Other books you might like:**
Steven Brust, *Jhereg*, 1983
Glen Cook, *Pretty Pewter Gods*, 1995
Pamela Dean, *The Dubious Hills*, 1994
Simon R. Green, *Hawk & Fisher*, 1996
Daniel Hood, *Fanuilh*, 1994

## 5849

### CHET WILLIAMSON

## Reign

(Arlington Heights, Illinois: Dark Harvest, 1990)

**Story type:** Horror (Doppelganger)
**Major character(s):** Dennis Hamilton, Actor, Producer; Ann Deems, Widow(er); Dan Munro, Police Officer (police chief)
**Time period(s):** 1990s (1991)
**Locale(s):** Kirkland, Pennsylvania

**Summary:** After renovating the Venetian Theatre, Dennis Hamilton plans to open the first season with *A Private Empire*, the play in which he achieved notoriety. A series of inexplicable deaths among the actors and technical crew prove only a prelude to Dennis' confrontation with "The Emperor," the character whom he turned into a star role now come to life.

**Other books you might like:**
Clive Barker, *Sex, Death and Starshine*, 1984
    *Clive Barker's Books of Blood, Vol. 2*
Stephen King, *The Dark Half*, 1989
Fritz Leiber, *Four Ghosts in Hamlet*, 1984
    in *The Ghost Light*

## 5850

### CHET WILLIAMSON

## Second Chance

(Baltimore: CD Publications, 1994)

**Story type:** Horror (Psychological Suspense)
**Major character(s):** Woody Robinson, Musician; Tracy Zempelios Robinson, Housewife; Keith "Pan" Aarons, Terrorist
**Time period(s):** 1990s (1993); 1960s (1969)
**Locale(s):** Iselin, Pennsylvania; Bone, Texas

**Summary:** Woody Robinson's sixties nostalgia party inadvertently sends its participants back in time long enough for them to snatch back to the present friends who died in 1969 as a result of their radical idealism. Among the retrieved, however, is an unrepentant radical who becomes an ecoterrorist who will stop at nothing—even the destruction of the world as we know it—to draw attention to his cause.

**Other books you might like:**
Douglas Clegg, *Dark of the Eye*, 1994
Stephen King, *Firestarter*, 1980
Joe R. Lansdale, *Savage Season*, 1989
Lewis Shiner, *Glimpses*, 1993

## 5851

### J.N. WILLIAMSON

## The Black School

(New York: Dell, 1989)

**Story type:** Horror (Child-in-Peril)

**Major character(s):** Michael Scott, Parent, Teacher; Jacob Weir, Teacher (Homunculus)
**Time period(s):** 1980s
**Locale(s):** United States; Scotland; Hell

**Summary:** The Devil kidnaps Scott's daughter, Jill, to hold hostage in a school in Hell until Michael produces a book belonging to Old Nick. With homunculus friend Weir, he locates the door to Hell in Scotland, fights off demons and black knights, and goes underground to rescue Jill.

**Other books you might like:**
Dan Simmons, *Song of Kali*, 1985

## 5852

### J.N. WILLIAMSON

## Bloodlines

(Stamford, Connecticut: Longmeadow Press, 1994)

**Story type:** Horror (Vampire Story)
**Major character(s):** Marshall Madison, Vampire; Thaddie Madison, Child (Marshall's son); Jake Spencer, Taxi Driver
**Time period(s):** 1990s (1994)
**Locale(s):** New York, New York

**Summary:** The son of a vampire, Thaddie Madison flees his foster parents to squat in an abandoned New York City hotel and ponder his heritage. His disappearance pits two parties of searchers against one another: the goodhearted parents who have adopted his sister Caroline, and his father, who will stop at nothing to reclaim a blood descendant.

**Other books you might like:**
Poppy Z. Brite, *Lost Souls*, 1992
Scott Ciencin, *Parliament of Blood*, 1992
Scott Ciencin, *The Vampire Odyssey*, 1992
Scott Ciencin, *The Wildlings*, 1992
Pat Graversen, *Sweet Blood*, 1992
Dan Simmons, *Children of the Night*, 1992

## 5853

### J.N. WILLIAMSON

## The Book of Webster's

(Stamford, Connecticut: Longmeadow Press, 1993)

**Story type:** Horror (Serial Killer)
**Major character(s):** Dell, Drifter; Kee, Teenager; Kirk Douglas, Detective
**Time period(s):** 1990s (1993)
**Locale(s):** Cherokee Rose, Georgia

**Summary:** Convinced that he has been instructed by Webster's Dictionary to kill, Dell and his teenage companion, Kee, go on a murder rampage across the American South, tailed by detective Kirk Douglas, who desperately hopes to bring them to justice. This novel was expanded from a 1986 short story.

**Other books you might like:**
Billie Sue Mosiman, *Night Cruise*, 1992
John Shirley, *Wetbones*, 1992

## 5854

### J.N. WILLIAMSON

## The Fifth Season

(Seattle, Washington: A E Press, 1993)

**Story type:** Horror (Collection)

**Summary:** This chapbook collects eight stories, one original to the volume, by one of the genre's more prolific writers. ''Cycles,'' ''Troth,'' and ''Free Among the Dead'' all explore the boundary between life and death. ''Townkiller'' is narrated from the point of view of a homicidal maniac. Both ''Watchwolf'' and ''Mercy'' serve up poetically just retributions for their point-of-view characters. And ''I'll Give You Magic If You'll Give Me Love'' became the basis for the author's novel of a young boy trapped in the horror of a dysfunctional family, *Don't Take Away the Light* (1993). James Kisner supplies an introduction.

**Other books you might like:**
Edward Lee, *Edward Lee's Quest for Sex, Truth and Reality*, 1992
William F. Nolan, *Things Beyond Midnight*, 1984
William Relling Jr., *The Infinite Man and Other Stories*, 1990

## 5855

### J.N. WILLIAMSON, Editor

## Masques IV

(Baltimore, Maryland: Maclay, 1991)

**Story type:** Horror (Anthology)

**Summary:** Twenty-five original stories and one classic reprint by both new and well-recognized authors. Included are two stories of nature in revolt, Chet Williamson's ''The Pack'' and Gahan Wilson's ''Sea Gulls''; F. Paul Wilson's sardonic tale of a female avenger, ''Please Don't Hurt Me''; Ray Russell's glib study of a punk rock band, ''The Collapse of Civilization''; Dan Simmons' satiric tale of personal shortcoming made flesh, ''My Private Memoirs of the Hoffer Stigmata Pandemic''; and Steve Allen's story of a near-death experience, ''The Secret.''

**Other books you might like:**
Dennis Etchison, *Cutting Edge*, 1986
Thomas F. Monteleone, *The Borderlands Series*, 1990-1992

## 5856

### J.N. WILLIAMSON

## The Monastery

(New York: Zebra, 1992)

**Story type:** Horror (Black Magic)
**Major character(s):** Dean Knight, Parent; Noel Night, Parent; Kevin Night, Child (Dean & Noel's 12-year-old son)
**Time period(s):** 1990s (1992)
**Locale(s):** Noblesville, Indiana; Neva Monastery, Indiana

**Summary:** After plowing their car into a snowdrift on the back roads of Indiana, the Knight family takes refuge in Neva Monastery, unaware that they have landed in the home of the Radenyi, a cult that uses ritual torture and sacrifice to summon its god.

**Other books you might like:**
Edward Lee, *Incubi*, 1991

## 5857

### J.N. WILLIAMSON

### *The Naked Flesh of Feeling*

(Eugene, Oregon: Pulphouse, 1991)

**Story type:** Horror (Collection)
**Series:** Author's Choice Monthly

**Summary:** Seven stories by one of the most prolific authors in the horror genre, ranging in approach from "Public Places," about a monster that lurks in a public toilet, to "They Never Even See Me" and "Aspirations," which straddle the boundary between mystery and horror. The author has supplied an introduction and explanatory headnotes.

**Other books you might like:**
William F. Nolan, *Things Beyond Midnight*, 1984

## 5858

### J.N. WILLIAMSON

### *The Night Seasons*

(New York: Zebra, 1991)

**Story type:** Horror (Nature in Revolt)
**Major character(s):** Richard Stenvall, Writer; Doc Kinsey, Prisoner; Noble Ellair, Doctor
**Time period(s):** 1990s
**Locale(s):** Indianapolis, Indiana

**Summary:** While sleeping off a binge in the drunk tank at the local penitentiary, failed writer Richard Stenvall, along with his fellow prisoners, becomes part of an experiment carried out by prison physician Noble Ellair—one that entails unleashing carnivorous plants within the closed environment of the prison. This novel was expanded from a shorter version written in 1986.

**Other books you might like:**
Robert Charles, *Flowers of Evil*, 1982
John Wyndham, *The Day of the Triffids*, 1951

## 5859

### JACK WILLIAMSON

### *Beachhead*

(New York: Tor, 1992)

**Story type:** Science Fiction (Adventure)
**Major character(s):** Sam Houston Kelligan, Astronaut, Heir (Kelligan Enterprises); Jayne Ryan, Astronaut, Scientist
**Time period(s):** 2000s
**Locale(s):** Fort Worth, Texas; *Ares*, Spaceship; Mars

**Summary:** Following a childhood dream, Sam finally becomes a crew member of the first Mars expedition, despite his family's disapproval. Rumor of a Martian disease almost forces the project into bankrupcy before *Ares* can reach Mars. When Kelligan Enterprises' investment forces contact the spaceship, Earth learns Sam and Jayne made the first descent and have been out of contact since their parachute deployed.

**Other books you might like:**
Terry Bisson, *Voyage to the Red Planet*, 1990
Robert L. Forward, *Martian Rainbow*, 1991
Robert A. Heinlein, *Red Planet*, 1949
Charles Sheffield, *Cold as Ice*, 1992
Dana Stabenow, *Second Star*, 1991

Allen Steele, *Lunar Descent*, 1991

## 5860

### JACK WILLIAMSON

### *The Black Sun*

(New York: Tor, 1997)

**Story type:** Science Fiction (First Contact; Horror)
**Major character(s):** Carlos Mondragon, Stowaway, Immigrant; Kip Virili, Child; Rima Virili, Scientist (biomedical officer)
**Time period(s):** Indeterminate Future
**Locale(s):** White Sands, New Mexico; Hellfrost, Planet—Imaginary

**Summary:** With no control over their destination, the passengers of Mission Starseed's 99th and last quantum-wave ship arrive at a frozen, dead planet in a black dwarf system. Their situation deteriorates further when mysterious black stones begin to possess and possibly even kill members of the crew.

**Other books you might like:**
Arthur C. Clarke, *Childhood's End*, 1953
Michael Flynn, *Firestar*, 1996
Christopher Pike, *The Season of Passage*, 1992
Christopher Pike, *The Starlight Crystal*, 1996
Frederik Pohl, *The Singers of Time*, 1991
    Jack Williamson, co-author
Robert Silverberg, *Starborne*, 1996
A.E. Van Vogt, *The Voyage of the Space Beagle*, 1950
James White, *The Dream Millennium*, 1974

## 5861

### JACK WILLIAMSON

### *Darker than You Think*

(New York: Macmillan Collier Nucleus, 1989)

**Story type:** Horror (Werewolf Story)
**Major character(s):** Will Barbee, Journalist; April Bell, Werewolf
**Time period(s):** 1940s
**Locale(s):** Clarendon, Midwest (A city somewhere in Mid-America)

**Summary:** Will Barbee is torn between his attraction to a beautiful seductress/werewolf and his loyalty to his old werewolf-fighting university comrades as they all wait with anticipation or trepidation for the identification and return of the Child of Night, a superior werewolf who will attempt to lead *Homo lycanthropus* to victory over man in the evolutionary struggle. Originally published in 1948.

**Other books you might like:**
Charles L. Grant, *The Dark Cry of the Moon*, 1986
Thomas Tessier, *The Nightwalker*, 1979
Chelsea Quinn Yarbro, *The Godforsaken*, 1983

## 5862

### JACK WILLIAMSON

### *Demon Moon*

(New York: Tor, 1994)

**Story type:** Science Fiction (Lost Colony)
**Major character(s):** Zorn ir Var, Heir—Dispossessed, Fugitive; Lyrane lo Lyrane, Student; Argoth Ayth, Religious, Magician
**Time period(s):** Indeterminate Future
**Locale(s):** Planet—Imaginary

**Summary:** From his exiled parents Zorn learns of the heritage stolen by his uncle Thorg's treachery. Later, with his father imprisoned and the red light of the demon moon in the sky, he sets out to find the legendary Dragonshield once wielded by his ancestor, Nuradoon, to save the world from the demons of the god Xath. But when Zorn and his unlikely allies meet the demons, they learn a startling truth about the world and its origins.

**Other books you might like:**

Marion Zimmer Bradley, *Rediscovery: A Novel of Darkover*, 1993
  Mercedes Lackey, co-author
Orson Scott Card, *The Memory of Earth*, 1992
C.J. Cherryh, *Angel with the Sword*, 1985
Anne McCaffrey, *Dragonflight*, 1968
Robert Silverberg, *Kingdoms of the Wall*, 1993

---

**5863**

### JACK WILLIAMSON

## The Fortress of Utopia

(Brooklyn, New York: Gryphon, 1998)

**Story type:** Science Fiction (End of the World)
**Major character(s):** Jay Cartwright, Astronaut; Captain Pat Drumm, Astronaut
**Time period(s):** 1930s (1939); Indeterminate Future
**Locale(s):** Montenegro

**Summary:** In this first book publication of a novel serialized in 1939, an astronaut discovers that a group of Utopian dreamers have knowledge that the world is about to end. He joins them in suspended animation to help create a new society in the aftermath, but, predictably, things go wrong.

**Other books you might like:**

Edmond Hamilton, *The Sun Smashers*, 1959
Clifford D. Simak, *The Cosmic Engineers*, 1950
Edward E. Smith, *Skylark of Valeron*, 1949
George O. Smith, *Pattern for Conquest*, 1949
David Weber, *Mutineers' Moon*, 1991

---

**5864**

### JACK WILLIAMSON

## The Girl from Mars & The Prince of Space

(Brooklyn, New York: Gryphon, 1998)

**Story type:** Science Fiction (Collection; Space Opera)

**Summary:** These two long stories, now bound back to back, were originally published separately in 1929 and 1931. Both are old style space operas featuring superscientific devices, bold heroes, and a sinister villain. The author remains active in the field 70 years later.

**Other books you might like:**

Leigh Brackett, *The Starmen of the Lyrdis*, 1952
Ray Cummings, *Brigands of the Moon*, 1931
Ray Cummings, *Wandl the Invader*, 1961
Edward E. Smith, *The Galaxy Primes*, 1965
George O. Smith, *Nomad*, 1950

---

**5865**

### JACK WILLIAMSON

## The Humanoids

(New York: Tor Orb, 1996)

**Story type:** Science Fiction (Robot Fiction; Dystopian)
**Major character(s):** Frank Ironsmith, Engineer; Clay Forester, Scientist, Engineer (rhodomagnetic); Underhill, Engineer
**Time period(s):** 120th century; Indeterminate Future
**Locale(s):** Two Rivers, Fictional City; Interstellar Empire/Federation; Planet—Imaginary

**Summary:** As mechanical servants begin to help people to survive and thrive as they determine best, some people rebel against the benign invasion of the aggressively helpful humanoids. Later, a philosopher organizes a small assault team with unique abilities, intending to overturn humanoid control. Includes "With Folded Hands" (1947) and *The Humanoids* (1949).

**Other books you might like:**

Roger MacBride Allen, *The Ring of Charon*, 1990
Isaac Asimov, *The Foundation Trilogy*, 1982
Isaac Asimov, *Robots and Empire*, 1985
Paul J. McAuley, *Red Dust*, 1994
A.E. Van Vogt, *The Weapon Makers*, 1946
A.E. Van Vogt, *The Weapon Shops of Isher*, 1951
John Varley, *Steel Beach*, 1992

---

**5866**

### JACK WILLIAMSON

## Mazeway

(New York: Ballantine/Del Rey, 1990)

**Story type:** Science Fiction (Post-Holocaust)
**Major character(s):** Benn Dain, Explorer, Student; Roxane Kwan, Wanderer (Nomad)
**Time period(s):** Indeterminate Future
**Locale(s):** Earth; Oort Cloud, Outer Space

**Summary:** After the disaster which destroyed Earth's technological society, the survivors have become nomadic hunter gatherers. One family of humans has been transported to the Oort Cloud as a reward for eliminating a potential threat. Unfortunately, it is too late to save Earth's technology. While there, the family's only son is being trained to understand the aliens and demonstrate that humans are ready for space.

**Other books you might like:**

Roger MacBride Allen, *The Ring of Charon*, 1990
David Brin, *The Uplift War*, 1987
Larry Niven, *Footfall*, 1985
  Jerry Pournelle, co-author
John Varley, *The Ophiuchi Hotline*, 1977
Roger Zelazny, *This Immortal*, 1989

---

**5867**

### CONNIE WILLIS

## Bellwether

(New York: Bantam Spectra, 1996)

**Story type:** Science Fiction (Contemporary Realism)
**Major character(s):** Sandra "Sandy" Foster, Scientist, Researcher; Philippa J. "Flip" Orliotti, Clerk; Bennett "Ben" O'Reilly, Scientist, Researcher

**Time period(s):** 1990s
**Locale(s):** Boulder, Colorado

**Summary:** Getting nowhere with her research into a fad, bobbed hair, Sandy recognizes the incompetence of the support staffer, Flip. Redelivering a misdelivered package, Sandy meets Bennett whose research seems complementary. Bennett fascinates Sancy as he seems totally immune to fad and fashion.

**Other books you might like:**
John Brunner, *The Sheep Look Up*, 1972
Philip K. Dick, *A Scanner Darkly*, 1977
Suzette Haden Elgin, *Native Tongue*, 1984
Mark Leyner, *My Cousin, My Gastroenterologist*, 1990
Jack McDevitt, *Ancient Shores*, 1996
Tom Robbins, *Skinny Legs and All*, 1990

---

**5868**

CONNIE WILLIS

## Doomsday Book

(New York: Bantam Spectra, 1992)

**Story type:** Science Fiction (Time Travel; Disaster)
**Major character(s):** Kivrin Engle, Student, Time Traveler; James Dunworthy, Professor; Father Roche, Religious (priest)
**Time period(s):** 21st century; 14th century (1348)
**Locale(s):** Oxfordshire, England

**Summary:** Intending to observe everyday life in 1320, Kivrin travels into the past, immediately suffering illness and amnesia. After a plague strikes Oxford causing its quarantine, Kivrin discovers that she arrived in 1348, the year of the Black Death. As the plague spreads throughout Oxfordshire, Kivrin's immunizations allow her to survive while awaiting help from friends working in the future.

**Other books you might like:**
Katherine Kurtz, *The Harrowing of Gwynedd*, 1989
Richard Meredith, *Run, Come See Jerusalem*, 1976
Robert Silverberg, *The Gate of Worlds*, 1967
Robert Charles Wilson, *A Bridge of Years*, 1991
Chelsea Quinn Yarbro, *Time of the Fourth Horseman*, 1976

---

**5869**

CONNIE WILLIS

## Impossible Things

(New York: Bantam Spectra, 1994)

**Story type:** Science Fiction (Collection)

**Summary:** Contains a six-page introduction by Gardner Dozois and 11 stories reprinted from periodicals and anthologies 1986-1992 with one Nebula Award winning story, "At the Rialto," and two stories which won both Nebula and Hugo Awards, "The Last of the Winnebagos" and "Even the Queen." Willis focuses on people, frequently using insightful humor with a prickly kernel which appears after reflection. Themes include political correctness, small town life, hard science, the end of the world and one Shakespeare conspiracy.

**Other books you might like:**
Alfred Bester, *Star Light, Star Bright*, 1976
Cordwainer Smith, *The Rediscovery of Man*, 1993
Marc Stiegler, *The Gentle Seduction*, 1990
Theodore Sturgeon, *The Ultimate Egoist*, 1994
John Varley, *Blue Champagne*, 1986

---

**5870**

CONNIE WILLIS
CYNTHIA FELICE, Co-Author

## Light Raid

(New York: Ace, 1989)

**Story type:** Science Fiction (Young Adult)
**Major character(s):** Helene Ariadne, Student; Helene Medea, Scientist
**Time period(s):** 21st century
**Locale(s):** Denver Springs, Colorado; Canada

**Summary:** As the fragmented nations of what was once the United States and Canada wage war with massive laser assaults from orbiting weapons platforms, young Helene Ariadne tries to unravel a complex plot to undermine part of her nation's weapons capability, a plot in which her mother may be involved.

**Other books you might like:**
Ben Bova, *The Kinsman Saga*, 1987
John Christopher, *The Tripods Trilogy*, 1980

---

**5871**

CONNIE WILLIS, Editor
MARTIN H. GREENBERG, Co-Editor

## The New Hugo Winners, Volume III

(New York: Baen, 1994)

**Story type:** Science Fiction (Anthology)
**Series:** Hugo Winners

**Summary:** Contains a three-page introduction by the editor plus individual introductions to nine stories given Science Fiction Achievement Awards, so-called "Hugo Awards," by voting members of World Science Fiction Conventions 1989-1991. Authors include Lois McMaster Bujold, Suzy McKee Charnas, George Alec Effinger, Joe Haldeman, Mike Resnick and Robert Silverberg.

**Other books you might like:**
Isaac Asimov, *The Hugo Winners 1-5*, 1962-1986
    editor
Isaac Asimov, *Isaac Asimov Presents the Great SF Stories: 1-25*, 1979-1992
    Martin H. Greenberg, co-editor
Michael Bishop, *Nebula Awards 24*, 1990
    editor
Michael Bishop, *Nebula Awards 25*, 1991
    editor
James Morrow, *Nebula Awards 26*, 1992
    editor

---

**5872**

CONNIE WILLIS
CYNTHIA FELICE, Co-Author

## Promised Land

(New York: Ace, 1997)

**Story type:** Science Fiction (Adventure; Science Fiction)
**Major character(s):** Delanna Milleflores, Heiress, Spouse; Jay "Mad Dog" Madog, Businessman, Bachelor; Tarleton "Sonny" Tanner, Farmer, Spouse
**Time period(s):** Indeterminate Future
**Locale(s):** Grassedge, Fictional City; Keramos, Planet—Imaginary

**Summary:** Sent off planet as a child by her mother, Delanna reluctantly returns to collect her inheritance and leave the planet her mother hated. Unfortunately, laws on Keramos prevent Delanna from selling or even keeping her land if she fails the residency requirement. Her surprise inherited marriage to Sonny also compromises her determination to leave.

**Other books you might like:**
Eleanor Arnason, *A Woman of the Iron People*, 1991
F.M. Busby, *Rissa Kerguelen*, 1977
Elizabeth Moon, *Remnant Population*, 1996
James H. Schmitz, *The Demon Breed*, 1968
Joan D. Vinge, *Dreamfall*, 1996

## `5873`
### CONNIE WILLIS
## *Remake*
(New York: Bantam Spectra, 1995)

**Story type:** Science Fiction (Satire; Mystery)
**Major character(s):** Alis, Actress, Historian (film history); Tom, Filmmaker, Editor
**Time period(s):** 21st century
**Locale(s):** Hollywood, California

**Summary:** Hired to delete politically incorrect references to substance abuse, such as alcohol intoxication, from classic Hollywood films in Viamount vaults, Tom meets Alis, fresh from film school and hoping to dance in a musical. When Tom finds Alis' image appearing in the background of well-known films, he suspects improper digital insertion of her image. However, his investigation forces him to consider that she uses time travel to further her obsessive goal.

**Other books you might like:**
David Brin, *Earth*, 1990
Pat Cadigan, *Synners*, 1991
Jack Finney, *Time and Again*, 1970
Marjorie Bradley Kellogg, *Harmony*, 1991
Lisa Mason, *Summer of Love*, 1994
Lewis Shiner, *Glimpses*, 1993

## `5874`
### CONNIE WILLIS
## *To Say Nothing of the Dog*
(New York: Bantam Spectra, 1998)

**Story type:** Science Fiction (Time Travel; Humor)
**Series:** Doomsday Book
**Major character(s):** Ned Henry, Historian, Time Traveler; Verity Kindle, Historian, Time Traveler; Lady Schrapnell, Wealthy (dowager)
**Time period(s):** 21st century; 19th century
**Locale(s):** Oxford, England; Coventry, England

**Summary:** Ned Henry is a 21st century historian working on a reconstruction of the hideously ugly Coventry Cathedral, which was destroyed during World War II. Dizzy and confused from a serious case of time lag, he is sent back to the Victorian era to correct a serious mistake made by another historian, who has accidentally brought a 19th century artifact back to the 21st century. This could alter history and destroy the entire space-time continuum. Unfortunately, Ned, half asleep on his feet, doesn't understand the assignment properly and things go hilariously astray.

**Other books you might like:**
Peter Delacorte, *Time on My Hands*, 1997

J.R. Dunn, *Days of Cain*, 1997
Jerome K. Jerome, *Three Men in a Boat*,
John Kessel, *Corrupting Dr. Nice*, 1997

## `5875`
### CONNIE WILLIS
## *Uncharted Territory*
(New York: Bantam Spectra, 1994)

**Story type:** Science Fiction (Humor)
**Major character(s):** Bult, Alien; Sarah "Fin" Finriddy, Scientist, Explorer; Aloysius Byron Carson, Scientist, Explorer
**Time period(s):** Indeterminate Future
**Locale(s):** Boohte, Planet—Imaginary

**Summary:** Finriddy and Carson's job of mapping the primitive world Boohte means facing dust storms, cantankerous mounts, nitpicking bureaucrats and venomous animals. Back home, millions watch a highly romanticized version of their exploits in the DHT series. One of their fans, a young socioexobiologist specializing in sex, joins them on their latest mapping expedition into uncharted territory, with hilarious results.

**Other books you might like:**
Poul Anderson, *Earthman's Burden*, 1957
    Gordon R. Dickson, co-author
Poul Anderson, *Hoka!*, 1983
    Gordon R. Dickson, co-author
John M. Ford, *How Much for Just the Planet?*, 1987
Keith Laumer, *Relief at Large*, 1978
Terry Pratchett, *Moving Pictures*, 1992

## `5876`
### THOMAS WILOCH
## *Mr. Templeton's Toyshop: Prose Poems and Short Fiction*
(La Grande, Oregon: Jazz Police Books, 1995)

**Story type:** Horror (Collection)

**Summary:** Forty-five prose poems and brief tales elaborate the private hells and uncanny experiences that the author's uncommon characters endure. "The Mystical Intention" describes the fate of someone who is too sympathetic towards the sensuality of his environment. "Marionettes," "The Terrible Secret," and "Puppets Holding Mirrors" draw disturbing comparisons between human beings and puppets controlled by uncaring puppetmasters. The title piece, a series of nine vignettes about a toyshop whose customers become the playthings of its eerie proprietor, conjures the vision of a mechanistic universe in which we are all the playthings of a sadistic overseer.

**Other books you might like:**
Thomas Ligotti, *The Agonizing Resurrection of Victor Frankenstein and Other Gothic Tales*, 1994
Thomas Ligotti, *Noctuary*, 1994
Bruno Schulz, *The Street of Crocodiles*, 1934
Steve Rasnic Tem, *Celestial Inventory*, 1991

## 5877

### CHARLES WILSON

## *Extinct*

(New York: St. Martin's, 1997)

**Story type:** Horror (Nature in Revolt)
**Major character(s):** Carolyn Haines, Pilot (boat); Alan Freeman, Scientist (marine biologist); Admiral Vandiver, Military Personnel (Navy)
**Time period(s):** 1990s (1997)
**Locale(s):** Biloxi, Mississippi

**Summary:** Marine experts and experienced sea personnel converge on the waters off Mississippi when the disappearance of several recreational swimmers and clues recovered from the ocean floor indicate the resurgence of the megalodon, a ravenous, prehistoric precursor of the great white shark.

**Other books you might like:**
Steve Alten, *Meg*, 1997
Peter Benchley, *Jaws*, 1974
Peter Benchley, *Beast*, 1991
William Dantz, *Hunger*, 1992
J.M. Morgan, *Between the Devil and the Deep*, 1992

## 5878

### COLIN WILSON

## *The Delta*

(New York: Ace Books, 1989)

**Story type:** Science Fiction (Invasion of Earth)
**Series:** Spider World
**Major character(s):** Niall, Psychic, Revolutionary
**Time period(s):** Indeterminate Future
**Locale(s):** Earth

**Summary:** Giant intelligent spiders and other mutant fauna and flora now control the Earth. Humanity lives like vermin. The rebel Niall and his intrepid followers enter the Delta looking for the secret that may free humanity from the spiders.

**Other books you might like:**
Gregory Benford, *Great Sky River*, 1987
Rob Chilson, *Men Like Rats*, 1989
Thomas M. Disch, *Mankind under the Leash*, 1966
David Gerrold, *A Rage for Revenge*, 1989
Joan Slonczewski, *The Wall Around Eden*, 1989
Tim Sullivan, *The Parasite War*, 1989
H.G. Wells, *The War of the Worlds*, 1898

## 5879

### DAVID HENRY WILSON

## *The Coachman Rat*

(New York: Carroll & Graf, 1989)

**Story type:** Fantasy (Legend)
**Major character(s):** Robert, Animal (Rat; Cinderella's coachman); Devlin, Scientist
**Time period(s):** Indeterminate
**Locale(s):** Fictional Country

**Summary:** The story of Cinderella, from the rat's eyes, is continued beyond "happily ever after" to show a bloody palace coup. Dark and grim, this is not for children.

**Other books you might like:**
Raymond E. Feist, *Faerie Tale*, 1988
K.W. Jeter, *Soul Eater*, 1983

## 5880

### DAVID NIALL WILSON

## *Chrysalis*

(New York: Pocket, 1997)

**Story type:** Science Fiction (First Contact)
**Series:** Star Trek: Voyager
**Major character(s):** Kathryn Janeway, Spaceship Captain, Military Personnel, Space Explorer; Tom Paris, Pilot (spaceship), Military Personnel; Kes, Alien (Okampan), Telepath
**Time period(s):** 24th century
**Locale(s):** *U.S.S. Voyager*, Spaceship; Urrytha, Planet—Imaginary; United Federation of Planets, Interstellar Empire/Federation

**Summary:** Janeway and her crew stop to replenish their food supplies on a planet with abundant plant life, only to discover that the planet also harbors sentient life and an ancient civilization. When the seductively soothing effects of the vegetation send some of her crew into comas, the natives interpret this as a sign of the prophesied Awakening and interfere with efforts to find a cure.

**Other books you might like:**
Carmen Carter, *Dreams of the Raven*, 1987
C.J. Cherryh, *Hestia*, 1979
Ursula K. Le Guin, *The Word for World Is Forest*, 1976
Rebecca Neason, *Guises of the Mind*, 1993
Dean Wesley Smith, *The Escape*, 1995
    Kristine Kathryn Rusch, co-author
John Varley, *Titan*, 1979
Joan D. Vinge, *The Snow Queen*, 1980

## 5881

### DAVID NIALL WILSON
### MICHAEL GRILLA, Illustrator

## *The Fall of the House of Escher and Other Illusions*

(Norfolk, Virginia: Macabre, Inc., 1995)

**Story type:** Horror (Collection)

**Summary:** This first story collection by a small press magazine editor brings together seven tales of horror with mystical and religious overtones. In the title story, a riff on Edgar Allan Poe's "The Fall of the House of Usher," a man develops an acute aesthetic sensitivity that allows him to penetrate into other dimensions. "A Candle Lit in Sunlight," "On the Third Day," and "The Road to Damascus" all find horrific potential in the iconography of Christianity. "Yours the Vengeance" and "Sparkling Eyes" are both environmentally conscious tales of fantasy. Hugh B. Cave supplies an introduction.

**Other books you might like:**
Kevin J. Anderson, *Shifting the Boundaries: The Selected Works of Kevin J. Anderson*, 1995
Michael A. Arnzen, *Needles and Sins*, 1994
Brian Hopkins, *Something Haunts Us All*, 1995
Albert J. Manachino, *The Odd Lot: The Selected Works of Albert J. Manachino*, 1993
Elizabeth Massie, *Southern Discomfort: Selected Works of Elizabeth Massie*, 1993
Ardath Mayhar, *Mean Little Old Lady at Work*, 1994
Stephen Mark Rainey, *Fugue Devil and Other Weird Horrors*, 1992

## **5882**

### DAVID NIALL WILSON

## *To Dream of Dreamers Lost*

(Clarkston, Georgia: White Wolf, 1998)

**Story type:** Horror (Vampire Story)
**Series:** Vampire, the Dark Ages: The Grails Covenant
**Major character(s):** Montrovant, Vampire; Noirceuil, Vampire Hunter; Antonio, Vampire
**Time period(s):** 12th century
**Locale(s):** Grenoble, France

**Summary:** Montrovant's quest for the Holy Grail ends in northern France, where the Order of Bitter Ashes have hidden it. His efforts to retrieve the magic talisman and use its power for his own purposes are complicated by dissension within the remnants of his Knights Templar, the wiliness of the enigmatic Kli Kodesh, and vampire hunters in the employ of the Vatican who hope to prevent him from realizing the goal of his quest. Third book in the Grail's Covenant Trilogy, set in the World of Darkness, an alternate universe where supernatural beings and human beings co-exist.

**Other books you might like:**
Justin Achilli, *Dark Tyrants*, 1997
    Robert Hatch, co-editor
Gherbod Fleming, *The Devil's Advocate*, 1997
Gherbod Fleming, *The Winnowing*, 1998
Edward E. Kramer, *Dark Destiny*, 1994
    editor
Robert Weinberg, *The Unbeholden*, 1996

## **5883**

### DAVID NIALL WILSON

## *To Speak in Lifeless Tongues*

(Clarkston, Georgia: White Wolf, 1997)

**Story type:** Horror (Vampire Story)
**Series:** Vampire: The Grails Covenant Trilogy
**Major character(s):** Montrovant, Vampire; Santos, Vampire; Kli Kodesh, Vampire
**Time period(s):** 12th century
**Locale(s):** Jerusalem, Israel

**Summary:** Montrovant, vampire founder of the Knights Templar, seeks to obtain the Holy Grail upon hearing that the order is on the verge of disbanding. Guided by a devious guardian in the Templars' castle, Montrovant rushes to the Holy Land, enduring many adventures with members of rival vampire clans along the way. Set in the World of Darkness gaming universe, an alternate world in which supernatural monsters co-exist with human beings. Second book in a trilogy, after *To Sift Through Bitter Ashes*.

**Other books you might like:**
Justin Achilli, *Dark Tyrants*, 1997
    Robert Hatch, co-editor
Gherbod Fleming, *The Devil's Advocate*, 1997
Robert Weinberg, *The Unbeholden*, 1996
Robert Weinberg, *Unholy Allies*, 1995
Robert Weinberg, *Blood War*, 1995

## **5884**

### F. PAUL WILSON

## *The Barrens*

(Newark, New Jersey: Wildside Press, 1992)

**Story type:** Horror (Ancient Evil Unleashed)
**Major character(s):** Kathleen MacKelston, Accountant; Jonathan Creighton, Psychologist; Jasper Mulliner, Farmer
**Time period(s):** 1990s (1992)
**Locale(s):** Pine Barrens, New Jersey

**Summary:** In this story strongly influenced by the writings of H. P. Lovecraft, Kathleen MacKelston agrees to help her old lover, Jonathan Creighton, investigate the legend of the Jersey Devil as part of the research for his doctoral thesis. But the pair discover that there is more truth to the legend than they thought, and that the Jersey Devil represents only a shadow of the threat to human life posed by the dimension from which it has come. Originally published in 1990.

**Other books you might like:**
Edward P. Berglund, *Disciples of Cthulhu*, 1975
Michael Shea, *The Colour out of Time*, 1984
Brian Stableford, *The Innsmouth Heritage*, 1992
Steve Rasnic Tem, *Decoded Mirrors: Three Tales after Lovecraft*, 1992
Robert Weinberg, *Lovecraft's Legacy*, 1990
    Martin Greenberg, co-editor

## **5885**

### F. PAUL WILSON

## *The Barrens and Others*

(New York: Tor, 1998)

**Story type:** Horror (Collection)

**Summary:** Twelve stories, one stage adaptation and one original teleplay, all published between 1987 and 1998 and most strongly informed by the writer's opinions on personal and social responsibility. "Pelts" is an anti-fur story with a supernatural twist, and "Feelings" a revenge story bristling with attitude about the failures of the justice system. Wilson's approach to his themes ranges from comedy ("Topsy," "The Tenth Toe") to dark suspense ("A Day in the Life") and science fiction ("Bob Dylan, Troy Johnson and the Speed Queen"). The title story is a powerful modern excursion into the Cthulhu Mythos of H.P. Lovecraft. With story notes by the author.

**Other books you might like:**
Ed Gorman, *Cages*, 1995
Dean R. Koontz, *Strange Highways*, 1995
Joe R. Lansdale, *By Bizarre Hands*, 1989
William F. Nolan, *Things Beyond Midnight*, 1984
Norman Partridge, *Bad Intentions*, 1997

## **5886**

### F. PAUL WILSON, Editor

## *Diagnosis: Terminal*

(New York: Tor, 1996)

**Story type:** Horror (Anthology)

**Summary:** Subtitled "An Anthology of Medical Terror," this compilation brings together 14 original nonsupernatural stories centered around the medical profession. Bill Pronzini's "Angel of Mercy" and Matthew Costello's "Friendly Wager" feature physician serial killers. Chet Williamson's "Doctor Joe" tells of a doctor who kills terminal patients for their insurance settlements in order to subsidize the needy patients in his practice. Ridley Pearson's "All Over but the Dying" is a tale of medical revenge, and Tina L. Jens' "The Cuban Solution" a tale of scientific paranoia in which physicians spread disease through refugees returned to Cuba in order to destabilize the government. F. Paul Wilson in "Offshore" and Ed Gorman in "Survival" envision futures where scarce medical resources create a terrifying competition among patients.

**Other books you might like:**
Groff Conklin, *Great Science Fiction about Doctors*, 1963
  editor
Stephen Jones, *The Mammoth Book of Frankenstein*, 1995
  editor
Stuart David Schiff, *Mad Scientists*, 1980
  editor
Karl Edward Wagner, *Intensive Scare*, 1989
  editor

## 5887

### F. PAUL WILSON

## Dydeetown World

(New York: Baen Books, 1989)

**Story type:** Science Fiction (Cyberpunk)
**Major character(s):** Sigmund Dreyer, Detective—Private; Jean Harlow-c, Clone
**Time period(s):** Indeterminate Future
**Locale(s):** Dydeetown, New York (A corrupt bluelight district)

**Summary:** Dreyer, a cynical, down on his luck, but basically decent private eye in the tradition of Sam Spade, is hired by the clone of an ancient movie star to find a missing person, and finds himself at the center of a complex web of intrigue and murder.

**Other books you might like:**
Richard Bowker, *Dover Beach*, 1987
George Alec Effinger, *When Gravity Fails*, 1987
Victor Koman, *The Jehovah Contract*, 1987

## 5888

### F. PAUL WILSON, Editor

## Freak Show

(New York: Pocket Books, 1992)

**Story type:** Horror (Anthology; Carnival/Circus Horror)

**Summary:** In this second collection of stories sponsored by the Horror Writers of America, editor Wilson has woven eighteen stories by diverse hands into a single shared-world novel concerned with the Peabody-Ozymandias Traveling Circus and Oddity Emporium, a traveling freak show assembling a machine along every stop on its itinerary that ultimately will allow another dimension to overwhelm our own and render every human being a freak. The stories carry only town names for their titles, but the book includes fine contributions from Chet Williamson, Dan Simmons and Steven Spruill.

**Other books you might like:**
Charles L. Grant, *The Chronicles of Greystone Bay*, 1985-1990
  short story in .
Robert R. McCammon, *Under the Fang*, 1991
  editor
John Skipp, *Book of the Dead*, 1990
  Craig Spector, co-editor

John Skipp, *Still Dead: Book of the Dead 2*, 1992
  Craig Spector, co-editor

## 5889

### F. PAUL WILSON

## The LaNague Chronicles

(New York: Baen, 1992)

**Story type:** Science Fiction (Political; Adventure)
**Series:** LaNague Federation
**Major character(s):** Peter LaNague, Revolutionary (Pacifist Libertarian); Steven Dalt, Anthropologist, Spy; Josephine Finch, Businesswoman
**Time period(s):** Indeterminate Future
**Locale(s):** Throne, Planet—Imaginary; Kwashi, Planet—Imaginary; LaNague Federation, Interstellar Empire/Federation

**Summary:** Integrates three separate novels, *An Enemy of the State* (1980), *Healer* (1976) and *Wheels Within Wheels* (1979), reorganized and expanded with new material relating the history of a galactic culture based on Libertarian principles. From its founding, the LaNague Federation balances on the dynamic conflict between personal responsibility and greed. Includes a new four-page introduction by the author and complete LaNague chronology of novels and stories.

**Other books you might like:**
Piers Anthony, *Refugee*, 1983
Robert A. Heinlein, *The Moon Is a Harsh Mistress*, 1966
Ursula K. Le Guin, *The Dispossessed*, 1974
Brad Linaweaver, *Moon of Ice*, 1988
Steve Perry, *The Man Who Never Missed*, 1985
L. Neil Smith, *The Probability Broach*, 1980

## 5890

### F. PAUL WILSON
### MATTHEW J. COSTELLO, Co-Author

## Masque

(New York: Warner, 1998)

**Story type:** Science Fiction (Genetic Manipulation)
**Major character(s):** Tristan, Clone, Spy; Lani, Clone; Okasan, Businessman
**Time period(s):** Indeterminate Future
**Locale(s):** Interstellar Empire/Federation

**Summary:** Corporations of the future breed their workers, clones with the ability to change their shapes and impersonate others. Some of these workers are allowed their freedom if they perform certain unusual tasks, but one such clone discovers that his secret mission involves more danger than he anticipated.

**Other books you might like:**
Wilhelmina Baird, *Chaos Come Again*, 1996
Ben Bova, *The Multiple Man*, 1976
Edmund Cooper, *The Overman Culture*, 1971
Matthew J. Costello, *Day of the Snake*, 1992
Matthew J. Costello, *Midsummer*, 1990
Matthew J. Costello, *Wurm*, 1991
Richard Cowper, *Clone*, 1972
Tanith Lee, *Don't Bite the Sun*, 1976

## **5891**

### F. PAUL WILSON

## *Midnight Mass*

(Seattle, Washington: Axolotl Press, 1990)

**Story type:** Horror (Vampire Story; Science Fiction)
**Major character(s):** Zev Wolpin, Religious (rabbi); Joseph Cahill, Religious (priest)
**Time period(s):** Indeterminate Future
**Locale(s):** Spring Lake, New Jersey

**Summary:** A Jewish rabbi tries to help Catholic priest Joseph Cahill defend his parish church from attack by the vampires that have taken over the world. But Cahill has an even greater problem: loss of faith. This novella is a tribute to Richard Matheson's classic vampire tale, *I Am Legend*.

**Other books you might like:**
Stephen King, *Salem's Lot*, 1975
Robert R. McCammon, *They Thirst*, 1981
Richard Matheson, *I Am Legend*, 1954

## **5892**

### F. PAUL WILSON
### MATTHEW J. COSTELLO, Co-Author

## *Mirage*

(New York: Warner, 1996)

**Story type:** Horror (Science Fiction; Psychological Suspense)
**Major character(s):** Julie Gordon, Scientist; Eathan Gordon, Doctor; Nathan Gordon, Scientist (neurochemist)
**Time period(s):** 1990s (1996)
**Locale(s):** New York, New York; Paris, France

**Summary:** With the aid of a virtual reality diagnostic tool she has perfected, Julie Gordon probes the brain of her twin sister Samantha to find out what has put her into a coma. Julie discovers memories not only of their past that help her to reconcile herself with her estranged sibling, but also clues to the identity of the person responsible for Samantha's misfortune, who is also very much a threat to Julie.

**Other books you might like:**
Isaac Asimov, *Fantastic Voyage II: Destination Brain*, 1987
Elizabeth Forrest, *Killjoy*, 1996
Michael Marshall Smith, *Spares*, 1995
F. Paul Wilson, *Sibs*, 1991

## **5893**

### F. PAUL WILSON

## *Nightworld*

(Arlington Heights, Illinois: Dark Harvest, 1992)

**Story type:** Horror (Apocalyptic Horror)
**Series:** Nightworld Cycle
**Major character(s):** Glaeken Veilleur, Aged Person; William Ryan, Religious (priest); Repairman Jack, Vigilante
**Time period(s):** 1990s (1992)
**Locale(s):** New York, New York

**Summary:** Fluctuations in the sunrise and sunset and the opening of bottomless sinkholes in New York that spew forth flesheating giant insects signal the coming apocalypse. Drawing together a band of mortals who have all encountered the supernatural, mystic warrior

Glaeken Veilleur prepares for his final battle with Rasalom, the incarnation of ultimate evil.

**Other books you might like:**
T.E.D. Klein, *The Ceremonies*, 1984
John Skipp, *The Scream*, 1988
    Craig Spector, co-author

## **5894**

### F. PAUL WILSON

## *Pelts*

(Roundtop, New York: Footsteps Press, 1990)

**Story type:** Horror (Nature in Revolt)
**Major character(s):** Gary Jameson, Trapper; Jake Feldman, Businessman (Furrier); Shanna, Model (Fashion model)
**Time period(s):** 1990s (1990)
**Locale(s):** Pine Barrens, New Jersey; New York, New York

**Summary:** The most recent batch of hides from racoons trapped by Gary Jameson and his father seeks revenge on those who would turn them into an exploitable commodity.

**Other books you might like:**
Stephen King, *Cujo*, 1981
Michael Stewart, *Monkey Shines*, 1973
Earle Wescott, *Winter Wolves*, 1989

## **5895**

### F. PAUL WILSON

## *Reborn*

(Arlington Heights, Illinois: Dark Harvest, 1990)

**Story type:** Horror (Science Fiction)
**Series:** Adversary
**Major character(s):** Jim Stevens, Writer (horror novelist), Journalist; Carol Stevens, Social Worker; Roderick Hanley, Scientist (geneticist)
**Time period(s):** 1960s (1968)
**Locale(s):** Monroe Village, New York

**Summary:** Jim Stevens discovers that he is the clone of wealthy geneticist Roderick Hanley at about the same time that a group of maverick Christian fundamentalists, who call themselves The Chosen, decide that he is the anti-Christ and must be destroyed.

**Other books you might like:**
Dean R. Koontz, *The Servants of Twilight*, 1984
Dean R. Koontz, *Shadowfires*, 1987
Ira Levin, *The Boys From Brazil*, 1976
Ira Levin, *Rosemary's Baby*, 1967
Robert Weinberg, *The Armageddon Box*, 1991

## **5896**

### F. PAUL WILSON

## *Reprisal*

(Arlington Heights, Illinois: Dark Harvest, 1991)

**Story type:** Horror (Ancient Evil Unleashed)
**Series:** Adversary
**Major character(s):** Lisl Whitman, Professor (of mathematics); Will Ryerson, Worker (college groundskeeper); Rafe Losmara, Student—Graduate
**Time period(s):** 1990s

**Locale(s):** South Carolina

**Summary:** In this third novel of the series that began with the *The Keep* (1981), the evil spirit who possessed the cloned Jim Hanley in *Reborn* (1990) has passed into Hanley's precocious son who, under the name Rafe Losmara, is embarked on graduate work in psychology, the better to prepare himself for battle with the nemesis intent on exterminating him.

**Other books you might like:**
William Peter Blatty, *The Exorcist*, 1971
William Peter Blatty, *Legion*, 1983
John Farris, *Son of the Endless Night*, 1985

## 5897

### F. PAUL WILSON

## The Select

(New York: Morrow, 1994)

**Story type:** Horror (Psychological Suspense)
**Major character(s):** Quinn Cleary, Student (medical); Tim Brown, Student (medical); Arthur Alston, Doctor
**Time period(s):** 1990s (1994)
**Locale(s):** Laurel Hills, Maryland

**Summary:** The Ingraham College of Medicine, managed with near military discipline, is the most prestigious institution of its kind in the United States. This is because its students are chosen not only for their intelligence, but for their susceptibility to subliminal suggestion and training practices that will benefit the Kleederman Foundation, a pharmaceutical concern that will stop at nothing to protect its investment in the type of health care they render. The author originally published this novel in England in 1993, as *The Foundation*, under the pseudonym Colin Andrews.

**Other books you might like:**
John E. Ames, *The Asylum*, 1994
Robin Cook, *Coma*, 1977
Timothy Findley, *Headhunter*, 1993

## 5898

### F. PAUL WILSON

## Sibs

(Arlington Heights, Illinois: Dark Harvest, 1992)

**Story type:** Horror (Possession)
**Major character(s):** Kara Wade, Writer; Rob Morris, Detective; Lawrence Gates, Doctor (psychiatrist)
**Time period(s):** 1990s (1992)
**Locale(s):** New York, New York

**Summary:** Kara Wade returns to New York to bury her twin sister Jill, who died during a steamy sexual liaison that Kara refuses to believe her mild-mannered sister could have been involved in. Her investigations into her sister's past lead her to Jill's psychiatrist, a man who either has extraordinary insight into Jill's and Kara's past or who has fabricated a smokescreen of lies to cover up his real interest in the two women.

**Other books you might like:**
William Peter Blatty, *The Ninth Configuration*, 1978
Thomas Tessier, *The Dreams of Dr. Ladybank*, 1991
  shot story in *Night Visions 9*

## 5899

### F. PAUL WILSON

## Soft and Others

(New York: Tor, 1989)

**Story type:** Horror (Collection)

**Summary:** Sixteen stories originally published between 1971 and 1988, plus one original, each prefaced briefly by the author. Cerebral, graphic, well crafted stories that focus on horrors of the contemporary world, rather than traditional monsters, often utilizing Wilson's expertise and experiences as an M.D. Outstanding are the title story, a graphic narrative about a near future plague in which the victims' bones dissolve into jelly, "Dat-Tag-Vao," about a mysterious healing touch, "Green Winter," about a shifting balance of power between two intelligent species, "Buckets," which chronicles a physician's chilling Halloween encounter, and "Cuts," which describes a novelist's terrible revenge on the filmmaker who desecrated his work.

**Other books you might like:**
Michael Blumlein, *The Brains of Rats*, 1989
Katherine Dunn, *Geek Love*, 1989
K.W. Jeter, *Dark Seeker*, 1987
K.W. Jeter, *Farewell Horizontal*, 1989
K.W. Jeter, *In the Land of the Dead*, 1989
Robert R. McCammon, *Blue World*, 1990
John Shirley, *Heatseeker*, 1989
Dan Simmons, *Carrion Comfort*, 1989
Dan Simmons, *Hyperion*, 1989

## 5900

### F. PAUL WILSON

## The Tery

(New York: Baen Books, 1990)

**Story type:** Science Fiction (Psychic Powers)
**Series:** Steven Dalt
**Major character(s):** Steven Dalt, Spy; Jon, Mutant
**Time period(s):** Indeterminate Future
**Locale(s):** Jacobi IV, Planet—Imaginary

**Summary:** A human society long separated from interstellar civilization is technologically primitive, but has evolved a wide variety of psi phenomena. Those who possess such powers are often mistreated or killed. Secret agent Steven Dalt goes to the planet in an attempt to improve the lot of the downtrodden. This volume also includes the novelette "Pard," another Steven Dalt adventure.

**Other books you might like:**
Poul Anderson, *The High Crusade*, 1960
John Dalmas, *The Lantern of God*, 1989
John Dalmas, *The Lizard War*, 1989
Kenneth Von Gunden, *StarSpawn*, 1990

## 5901

### GAHAN WILSON, Author/Illustrator

## The Cleft and Other Odd Tales

(New York: Tor, 1998)

**Story type:** Horror (Collection)

**Summary:** These twenty-four tales of light and dark fantasy, include one original to the volume. The reprints, which span more than thirty years, reflect the same macabre, and sometimes comic, sensibility that Wilson expresses through his artwork. Selections include "Traps," in which rats organize to fight against an exterminator; the grim Halloween story "Yesterday's Witch"; the comic psychopathic killer story "Them Bleaks"; the vampire tale "The Sea Was Wet as Wet Could Be"; and the zombie tale "Come One, Come All." Liberally illustrated by the author.

**Other books you might like:**
Charles Beaumont, *Selected Stories*, 1988
Ray Bradbury, *The October Country*, 1955
Shirley Jackson, *The Lottery, or the Adventures of James Harris*, 1949
Richard Matheson, *Collected Stories*, 1989
William F. Nolan, *Night Shapes: Excursions into Terror*, 1995

## 5902

**GAHAN WILSON**, Author/Illustrator

### Gahan Wilson's The Ultimate Haunted House
(New York: HarperPrism, 1996)

**Story type:** Horror (Anthology; Haunted House)

**Summary:** The 13 original stories commissioned for this house are all purportedly based on artist Gahan Wilson's popular CD-ROM game, "The Ultimate Haunted House." Each writer's tale is set in a different room of a haunted house. Nancy Collins, who served as consulting editor for the book, contributes "Someone's in the Kitchen," about a man who becomes the object of affection for the ghost of a good cook. Ted Klein's "Curtains for Nat Crumley" tells of a nebbish man who discovers that his bathroom mirror reflects the more robust life he might have led. In Gregory Nicoll's "The Ratz in the Halls," a rock band discovers the perils of recording a video in the basement of a haunted house. Lucy Taylor's "Bundling" concerns the dark secret buried in the attic of a haunted house a woman moves into with her young daughter, and Steve Antczak's "The Monster Lab" tells of a mad scientist who may or may not be haunted by the ghost of his dead wife. Wilson supplies an introduction and illustration for each story.

**Other books you might like:**
Kathryn Cramer, *The Architecture of Fear*, 1987
    Peter Pautz, co-editor
Kathryn Cramer, *Walls of Fear*, 1990
    editor
Charles G. Waugh, *House Shudders*, 1987
    Martin Greenberg, co-editor

## 5903

**ROBERT ANTON WILSON**

### Nature's God
(New York: Roc, 1991)

**Story type:** Fantasy (Historical)
**Series:** Historical Illuminatus Chronicles
**Major character(s):** Sigismundo Celine, Magician, Musician; Seamus Muadhen, Military Personnel; Maria Babcock, Revolutionary
**Time period(s):** 18th century (1776-1780)
**Locale(s):** New England; Lousewartshire, England

**Summary:** In this sequel to *The Widow's Son*, the tangled plot of the series continues as Celine travels to the wilds of Ohio to meditate, Muadhen becomes part of General Washington's army and Maria Babcock unleashes a barrage against male privilege. Through its

themes and characters this third volume in the continuing series ties into Wilson's other fiction.

**Other books you might like:**
James P. Blaylock, *The Paper Grail*, 1991
Umberto Eco, *Foucault's Pendulum*, 1989
Michael Flynn, *In the Country of the Blind*, 1990
Stuart Gordon, *Smile on the Void*, 1981
Thomas Pynchon, *Gravity's Rainbow*, 1973
Gene Wolfe, *Castleview*, 1990

## 5904

**ROBERT ANTON WILSON**

### Reality Is What You Can Get Away With: An Illustrated Screenplay
(New York: Dell, 1992)

**Story type:** Science Fiction (Humor; Arts)
**Major character(s):** Padraic Hakim Hasagawa, Professor; J.R. "BoB" Dobbs, Religious, Activist; George Herbert Walker Bush, Political Figure, Historical Figure
**Time period(s):** Indeterminate Future; 20th century
**Locale(s):** Earth; Sirius 23, Planet—Imaginary (University of New Dublin)

**Summary:** Professor Padraic Hakim Hasagawa brings historical perpective to a long-lost 20th century screenplay, recently discovered, which presents a view of ancient Earth life which includes a larger-than-life presentation of the Church of the Subgenius.

**Other books you might like:**
Roger Elwood, *Six Science Fiction Plays*, 1976
    editor
Malacypse the Younger, *Principia Discordia*, 1991
    expanded
Reverend Ivan Stang, *Three-Fisted Tales of "Bob"*, 1990
    editor
Kurt Vonnegut Jr., *Between Time and Timbuktu*, 1972
Kurt Vonnegut Jr., *Happy Birthday, Wanda June*, 1970

## 5905

**ROBERT CHARLES WILSON**

### A Bridge of Years
(New York: Doubleday Foundation, 1991)

**Story type:** Science Fiction (Time Travel; Hard Science Fiction)
**Major character(s):** Tom Winter, Time Traveler; Ben Collier, Time Traveler, Clone
**Time period(s):** 1980s (1989); 1960s (1962)
**Locale(s):** Belltower, Washington; New York, New York

**Summary:** When Tom Winter returns home to Washington state suffering from emotional trauma, he expects a quiet recovery. Instead, he finds his home invaded by a time tunnel which leads to New York City a quarter century earlier. As he investigates the mystery, he discovers a deadly foe and menace to his world's future.

**Other books you might like:**
Jeffrey A. Carver, *From a Changeling Star*, 1989
Ken Grimwood, *Replay*, 1986
Marge Piercy, *Woman on the Edge of Time*, 1976
Dan Simmons, *The Fall of Hyperion*, 1990
Dan Simmons, *Hyperion*, 1989
Kurt Vonnegut Jr., *The Sirens of Titan*, 1959

## 5906

### ROBERT CHARLES WILSON

## *Darwinia*

(New York: Tor, 1998)

**Story type:** Science Fiction (Alternate World; Mystical)
**Major character(s):** Guilford Law, Photographer, Explorer; The Picket, Immortal, Spirit; Lily Law, Child, Journalist
**Time period(s):** 1940s (1945); 1960s (1965)
**Locale(s):** Darwinia, Mythical Place; Alternate Universe; Europe

**Summary:** After Darwinia replaces 1912 Europe, Guilford Law sets out to explore it. However the Picket, a ghostly Guilford Law who died at Belleau Wood in Europe before psions invaded history, determines to wreak havoc unless Law and some others like him can defeat them.

**Other books you might like:**
Poul Anderson, *The Shield of Time*, 1990
J.G. Ballard, *The Drowned World*, 1962
Philip K. Dick, *Dr. Bloodmoney*, 1965
Brad Ferguson, *The World Next Door*, 1990
Fred Hoyle, *October the First Is Too Late*, 1966
Michaela Roessner, *Vanishing Point*, 1993
Fred Saberhagen, *A Century of Progress*, 1983
L. Neil Smith, *The Crystal Empire*, 1986

## 5907

### ROBERT CHARLES WILSON

## *The Divide*

(New York: Doubleday Foundation, 1990)

**Story type:** Science Fiction (Genetic Manipulation)
**Major character(s):** John Shaw, Genetically Altered Being; Susan, Student
**Time period(s):** 1990s
**Locale(s):** Toronto, Ontario, Canada

**Summary:** After he is abandoned by the scientist who created him, a genetically-tailored superman hides behind an apparently normal alter ego until events conspire to force his real personality to reemerge.

**Other books you might like:**
John Brunner, *Children of the Thunder*, 1989
Daniel Keyes, *Flowers for Algernon*, 1966
Daniel Keys Moran, *Emerald Eyes*, 1988
Robert Reed, *Black Milk*, 1989

## 5908

### ROBERT CHARLES WILSON

## *Gypsies*

(New York: Doubleday Foundation, 1989)

**Story type:** Science Fiction (Alternate Universe)
**Major character(s):** Karen White, Housewife (Separated); Michael, Child (Karen's son)
**Time period(s):** 20th century
**Locale(s):** Alternate Universe; United States

**Summary:** Karen White's past is a mystery. Her parents were odd people who moved frequently, obviously on the run from persons and places unknown. Karen herself has strange dreams of a world she's never seen and of a dark, haunting presence, the Gray Man.

Then her son Michael begins to have similar dreams and, later, begins to see the Gray Man following him. Someone, Karen realizes, is after her family—someone not entirely of this Earth.

**Other books you might like:**
Michael P. Kube-McDowell, *Alternities*, 1988
Marge Piercy, *Woman on the Edge of Time*, 1976
Frederik Pohl, *The Coming of the Quantum Cats*, 1986
Gene Wolfe, *There Are Doors*, 1988

## 5909

### ROBERT CHARLES WILSON

## *The Harvest*

(New York: Bantam Spectra, 1993)

**Story type:** Science Fiction (First Contact; Mystical)
**Major character(s):** Matt Wheeler, Doctor, Leader; John Tyler, Military Personnel; Tom Kindle, Mountain Man
**Time period(s):** 21st century
**Locale(s):** Oregon; Georgia

**Summary:** After an alien artifact appears in the night sky, everyone seems to contract a new variety of flu, later learning the symptoms portend immortality, transformation and interstellar travel. One of those unhappy with the alien gift, Matt Wheeler, leads a small group of fellow refusers on a dangerous trip to Ohio, suffering when John Tyler meets up with the group.

**Other books you might like:**
John Brunner, *Age of Miracles*, 1971
Arthur C. Clarke, *Childhood's End*, 1953
Joe Haldeman, *Worlds Apart*, 1983
Michael P. Kube-McDowell, *The Quiet Pools*, 1990
Pat Murphy, *The City, Not Long After*, 1989
Robert Silverberg, *Tom O'Bedlam*, 1985
Clifford D. Simak, *A Choice of Gods*, 1972
Norman Spinrad, *Songs From the Stars*, 1980
Brian Stableford, *The Walking Shadow*, 1989
Vernor Vinge, *Marooned in Realtime*, 1986

## 5910

### ROBERT CHARLES WILSON

## *A Hidden Place*

(New York: Bantam Spectra, 1989)

**Story type:** Science Fiction (First Contact)
**Major character(s):** Anna Blaise, Young Woman; Bone, Streetperson
**Time period(s):** 1930s (Great Depression)
**Locale(s):** Haute Montaigne, Midwest

**Summary:** Anna Blaise, an unworldly young woman who seems to have no past, appears in the town of Haute Montaigne and changes the lives of a number of citizens. Simultaneously, a gigantic, seemingly retarded tramp named Bone makes his way across country, in search, although he isn't entirely aware of it, of Anna. The unearthly nature of their relationship, when it is revealed, is both strange and beautiful.

**Other books you might like:**
Richard Paul Russo, *Subterranean Gallery*, 1989
Pamela Sargent, *The Alien Upstairs*, 1983
Theodore Sturgeon, *Alien Cargo*, 1984
Theodore Sturgeon, *Godbody*, 1986
Theodore Sturgeon, *More than Human*, 1953
Theodore Sturgeon, *Slow Sculpture*, 1982

## 5911

### ROBERT CHARLES WILSON

## Mysterium

(New York: Bantam Spectra, 1994)

**Story type:** Science Fiction (Alternate Universe; Political)
**Major character(s):** Clifford Stockton, Child; Dexter Graham, Teacher; Linneth Stone, Scholar
**Time period(s):** 1990s (1994)
**Locale(s):** Two Rivers, Michigan; Alternate Earth

**Summary:** Early one morning, Two Rivers, Michigan, moves inexplicably to another Earth, where a totalitarian government dominates a dystopian America. On this new Earth, Christianity and history developed differently, leaving the inhabitants of the town to cope with a world simultaneously familiar and strange.

**Other books you might like:**
Margaret Atwood, *The Handmaid's Tale*, 1985
Walter M. Miller Jr., *A Canticle for Leibowitz*, 1960
James Morrow, *Only Begotten Daughter*, 1990
Pat Murphy, *The City, Not Long After*, 1989
Howard Waldrop, *Them Bones*, 1984

## 5912

### TERRI WINDLING, Editor

## The Armless Maiden and Other Tales for Childhood's Survivors

(New York: Tor, 1995)

**Story type:** Fantasy (Anthology)

**Summary:** Contains a four-page introduction to original and reprinted modern fairy tales ordered to draw the adult reader along a dark journey through childhood's pitfalls, abuse and neglect, aimed at suggesting positive social change. Some humor and much painful insight infuses 17 poems, four essays, three memoirs, and 21 stories, some with individual introductions, by authors including Emma Bull, Kara Dalkey, Charles de Lint, Steven Gould, Tappan King, Ellen Kushner, Tanith Lee, Patricia A. McKillip, Susan Palwick, Kristine Kathryn Rusch, Joanna Russ, Delia Sherman, Will Shetterly, Midori Snyder, Caroline Stevermer, Peter Straub, Terri Windling, and Jane Yolen.

**Other books you might like:**
Gael Baudino, *Strands of Sunlight*, 1984
Ellen Datlow, *Ruby Slippers, Golden Tears*, 1995
    Terri Windling, co-editor
Ellen Datlow, *The Year's Best Fantasy and Horror Series*, 1989-
    Terri Windling, co-editor
Charles de Lint, *Dreams Underfoot*, 1993
Mercedes Lackey, *Born to Run*, 1992
    Larry Dixon, co-author
Robin McKinley, *Deerskin*, 1993
Susan Palwick, *Flying in Place*, 1992
Geoff Ryman, *Was*, 1992
Jane Yolen, *Briar Rose*, 1992
Jack Zipes, *Spells of Enchantment*, 1991
    editor

## 5913

### TERRI WINDLING, Editor
### MARK ALAN ARNOLD, Co-Editor

## Borderland

(New York: Tor, 1992)

**Story type:** Fantasy (Anthology; Urban)
**Series:** Borderland
**Time period(s):** Indeterminate Future
**Locale(s):** Borderland, Mythical Place; Bordertown, Fictional City

**Summary:** Contains four original stories by Bellamy Bach, Steven R. Boyett, Charles de Lint and Ellen Kushner, all sharing Terri Windling's Borderland setting, the intersection of the mortal world with Elfland, and each utilizing music as a dominant theme. Reissue of the 1986 edition.

**Other books you might like:**
Emma Bull, *War for the Oaks*, 1987
Charles de Lint, *Moonheart: A Romance*, 1984
Charles de Lint, *Spiritwalk*, 1992
Megan Lindholm, *Wizard of the Pigeons*, 1986
Will Shetterly, *Elsewhere*, 1991
Will Shetterly, *Liavek*, 1985
    Emma Bull, co-editor
Will Shetterly, *Liavek: Spells of Binding*, 1988
    Emma Bull, co-editor
Will Shetterly, *Liavek: Wizard's Row*, 1987
    Emma Bull, co-editor
Gene Wolfe, *Storeys From the Old Hotel*, 1992

## 5914

### TERRI WINDLING, Editor
### DELIA SHERMAN, Co-Editor

## The Essential Bordertown

(New York: Tor, 1998)

**Story type:** Fantasy (Anthology; Urban)
**Series:** Borderland
**Time period(s):** Indeterminate
**Locale(s):** Bordertown, Fictional City; Borderland, Mythical Place

**Summary:** With hints on cuisine, accomodations, points of interest, and survival tips for towns bordering the magical realm, this volume contains 13 original stories, frequently downbeat in tone, which share Terri Windling's Borderland milieu. Authors include Steven Brust, Charles de Lint, Ellen Kushner, Patricia A. McKillip, Felicity Savage, Delia Sherman, Midori Snyder and Caroline Stevermer.

**Other books you might like:**
Emma Bull, *Finder*, 1994
Emma Bull, *War for the Oaks*, 1987
Delia Sherman, *The Porcelain Dove*, 1993
Will Shetterly, *Elsewhere*, 1991
Will Shetterly, *Nevernever*, 1993

## 5915

### TERRI WINDLING, Editor

## Life on the Border

(New York: Tor, 1991)

**Story type:** Fantasy (Anthology; Urban)
**Series:** Borderland

**Time period(s):** Indeterminate Future
**Locale(s):** Bordertown, Fictional City

**Summary:** This volume contains eight stories including Ellen Kushner's interwoven epistolary story, "Lost in the Mail," plus verse by Emma Bull, all set in the city which lies in the border between the human realm and Elfland, occupied by the Truebloods. In "Nevermore," Will Shetterly takes up the story of Ron Starbuck, now Wolfboy, two years after the events in his novel, *Elsewhere* (1991). Charles de Lint's "Berlin" examines Bordertown turf wars between human and elf gangs, as does Bellamy Bach's "Rain and Thunder." Other authors are Midori Snyder, Michael Korolenko, Kara Dalkey, and Craig Shaw Gardner.

**Other books you might like:**
Gael Baudino, *Gossamer Axe*, 1990
Emma Bull, *War for the Oaks*, 1987
Mercedes Lackey, *Knight of Ghosts and Shadows*, 1990
    Ellen Guon, co-author
Joel Rosenberg, *The Road to Ehvenor*, 1991
Will Shetterly, *Elsewhere*, 1991
Will Shetterly, *Liavek*, 1985
    Emma Bull, co-editor
Will Shetterly, *Liavek: Spells of Binding*, 1988
    Emma Bull, co-editor
Will Shetterly, *Liavek: Wizard's Row*, 1987
    Emma Bull, co-editor

---

**5916**

**TERRI WINDLING**

## The Wood Wife

(New York: Tor, 1996)

**Story type:** Fantasy (Contemporary; Mystery)
**Major character(s):** Marguerita "Maggie" Black, Writer (poet); Johnny "Fox" Foxxe, Musician
**Time period(s):** 1990s
**Locale(s):** Tucson, Arizona; Southwest

**Summary:** When Maggie travels to Tucson to claim the inheritance from her murdered mentor, Fox and others help her discover the magic of the desert and its guardians as Maggie investigates her inner self and events surrounding her mentor's desert drowning.

**Other books you might like:**
Charles de Lint, *Memory and Dream*, 1994
Charles de Lint, *The Wild Wood*, 1994
    Brian Froud, co-author
Lisa Goldstein, *Walking the Labyrinth*, 1996
Megan Lindholm, *Cloven Hooves*, 1991
Patricia A. McKillip, *Something Rich and Strange*, 1994
    Brian Froud, co-author
Jane Yolen, *Briar Rose*, 1992

---

**5917**

**DAVID WINGROVE**

## Beneath the Tree of Heaven

(New York: Dell, 1995)

**Story type:** Science Fiction (Political; Family Saga)
**Series:** Chung Kuo
**Major character(s):** Kao Chen, Military Personnel (T'ang's security forces); Emily Ascher, Revolutionary; Hans Ebert, Revolutionary
**Time period(s):** 23rd century (2210-2213)

**Locale(s):** Earth; Mars

**Summary:** With the rule of the T'ang weakening as forces for change spread from the vast city-nations to a planet-wide conspiracy on Mars, generations of mind-manipulation and iron control may no longer suffice. Now they face treachery from within their own ranks, while Hans Ebert begins a new fight among Martian colonists. Revolution, in the form of True History, may finally free the long oppressed masses, or it may rain destruction across an entire world.

**Other books you might like:**
Poul Anderson, *A Stone in Heaven*, 1979
Isaac Asimov, *Foundation*, 1951
C.J. Cherryh, *Cyteen*, 1988
C.J. Cherryh, *The Pride of Chanur*, 1982
Gordon R. Dickson, *The Final Encyclopedia*, 1984
Frank Herbert, *Dune*, 1965
Larry Niven, *Man-Kzin Wars*, 1988
    editor
Alis A. Rasmussen, *A Passage of Stars*, 1990
S.M. Stirling, *Blood Feuds*, 1993
    Judith Tarr, Susan Shwartz, Harry Turtledove, co-authors
Timothy Zahn, *Dark Force Rising*, 1992

---

**5918**

**DAVID WINGROVE**

## The Broken Wheel

(New York: Doubleday Delacorte, 1991)

**Story type:** Science Fiction (Alternate Universe; Political)
**Series:** Chung Kuo
**Major character(s):** Emily Ascher, Political Figure; Howard De Vore, Political Figure, Military Personnel (retired)
**Time period(s):** 23rd century (2206)
**Locale(s):** Earth

**Summary:** China has been the world's major power for over a century. War and strife are not permitted. Leading agent in the struggle against China's ruling elite, known as The Seven, Howard De Vore is the force modifying the great "War of the Two Directions," determining which direction society will follow.

**Other books you might like:**
Philip K. Dick, *The Man in the High Castle*, 1962
Gordon R. Dickson, *Way of the Pilgrim*, 1987
John Hersey, *White Lotus*, 1965
Jeanne Larsen, *Silk Road*, 1989
Ian McDonald, *Out on Blue Six*, 1989

---

**5919**

**DAVID WINGROVE**

## The Middle Kingdom

(New York: Delacorte, 1990)

**Story type:** Science Fiction (Alternate Universe)
**Series:** Chung Kuo
**Major character(s):** Li Yuan, Heir, Royalty; Ben Shepherd, Artist
**Time period(s):** 22nd century
**Locale(s):** Earth

**Summary:** China rules the world and has done so for more than one hundred years. Peace and stability are virtually universal, but they've been achieved, some feel, at the cost of tyranny and stagnation. Dissatisfaction is particularly keen in the European merchant class, some of whom form the Dispersionists, a group dedicated to dramatic change and the expansion of humankind into outer space. The struggle between those who would prohibit change and those who would force it at any cost is given the name "The War of the Two Directions."

**Other books you might like:**
Philip K. Dick, *The Man in the High Castle*, 1962
Gordon R. Dickson, *Way of the Pilgrim*, 1987
John Hersey, *White Lotus*, 1965
Ian McDonald, *Out on Blue Six*, 1989

## 5920

### DAVID WINGROVE

## The Stone Within

(New York: Dell, 1993)

**Story type:** Science Fiction (Political; Family Saga)
**Series:** Chung Kuo
**Major character(s):** Stefan Lehman, Criminal, Leader; Kim Ward, Scientist; Li Yuan, Leader (T'ang of Europe)
**Time period(s):** 23rd century (2209)
**Locale(s):** Earth; Outer Space

**Summary:** Their hand forced, the Seven T'ang struggle to overcome dissension from both within and without as chaos seems to erupt from all sides. Remnants of DeVore's old forces have their own agendas while the Seven's unity falls apart. To buy time and win allies, the generations-old Edict of Technological Change finally undergoes amendment in return for suppport in placing population controls throughout the city-nations, yet struggles in the War of Two Directions grow more bitter.

**Other books you might like:**
Isaac Asimov, *Foundation*, 1951
Orson Scott Card, *Seventh Son*, 1987
C.J. Cherryh, *Cyteen*, 1988
Gordon R. Dickson, *The Final Encyclopedia*, 1984
Frank Herbert, *Dune*, 1965
Alis A. Rasmussen, *A Passage of Stars*, 1990
Paul O. Williams, *The Breaking of Northwall*, 1980

## 5921

### DAVID WINGROVE

## White Moon, Red Dragon

(New York: Dell, 1996)

**Story type:** Science Fiction (Political; Family Saga)
**Series:** Chung Kuo
**Major character(s):** Li Yuan, Leader (T'Ang of Europe); Howard DeVore, Revolutionary, Leader; Kim Ward, Scientist
**Time period(s):** 23rd century
**Locale(s):** Earth; Mars

**Summary:** Thought dead by his enemies, the rebel DeVore readies a terrifying flotilla to bring against the T'Ang, rulers of Earth. On Mars, the long-exiled Hans Ebert meets with a lost African tribe, the Osu, to reveal his plan to take them home to Earth. On Earth, the mega-cities of the T'Ang begin to crumble as war ripples across the planet, while beginnings and endings accompany Li Yuan's terrifying alliance. Sixth in the series.

**Other books you might like:**
Poul Anderson, *The Time Patrol*, 1991
Isaac Asimov, *Foundation*, 1951
C.J. Cherryh, *Cyteen*, 1988
Gordon R. Dickson, *The Final Encyclopedia*, 1984
Stephen R. Donaldson, *Lord Foul's Bane*, 1977

Frank Herbert, *Dune*, 1965
Alis A. Rasmussen, *A Passage of Stars*, 1990

## 5922

### DAVID WINGROVE

## The White Mountain

(New York: Delacorte, 1992)

**Story type:** Science Fiction (Political; Family Saga)
**Series:** Chung Kuo
**Major character(s):** Li Yuan, Leader (T'ang of Europe); Howard DeVore, Revolutionary, Leader; Kim Ward, Scientist
**Time period(s):** Indeterminate Future
**Locale(s):** Earth; Mars

**Summary:** Seven T'ang who rule the great city-continents of Chung Kuo struggle to hold onto their power. The destruction of the Dispersionists allow newer, more violent bands of rebels to gain power among the downtrodden people of the lowest levels of the cities. The young overlords hope to continue ruling by the ancient Chinese tenets of peace through strict order and stability, but may have to allow change to alter their ancestors' vision of an enforced peace lasting 10,000 years.

**Other books you might like:**
Poul Anderson, *Ensign Flandry*, 1966
Poul Anderson, *The Time Patrol*, 1991
Isaac Asimov, *Foundation*, 1951
C.J. Cherryh, *Cyteen*, 1988
C.J. Cherryh, *Downbelow Station*, 1981
C.J. Cherryh, *The Pride of Chanur*, 1982
Gordon R. Dickson, *The Final Encyclopedia*, 1984
Stephen R. Donaldson, *Lord Foul's Bane*, 1977
Frank Herbert, *Dune*, 1965
Alis A. Rasmussen, *A Passage of Stars*, 1990

## 5923

### DOUGLAS E. WINTER
### STEPHEN R. BISSETTE, Illustrator

## Black Sun

(Washington, D.C.: One-Eyed Dog)

**Story type:** Horror (Apocalyptic Horror)
**Major character(s):** Hagopian, Aged Person; The Stranger, Young Man; Karen, Young Woman
**Time period(s):** 1990s
**Locale(s):** The City

**Summary:** In an arresting fusion of images from horror literature and film, the author details a trek across a post-apocalyptic urban landscape ravaged by cancer, social ills and possibly nuclear destruction.

**Other books you might like:**
Richard Matheson, *The Dance of the Dead*, 1989
  in *Collected Stories*
Richard Matheson, *I Am Legend*, 1954
Wayne Allen Sallee, *For You, the Living*, 1992
Brian Stableford, *Slumming in Voodooland*, 1991

## 5924

**DOUGLAS E. WINTER**, Editor

### *Revelations*

(New York: HarperPrism, 1997)

**Story type:** Horror (Anthology)
**Time period(s):** 20th century

**Summary:** Anthology in the form of a mosaic novel. Each selection represents a decade of the twentieth century and uses an event specific to that decade as a vehicle for horror. Included is F. Paul Wilson's "Aryans and Absinthe," about the supernatural machinations behind Hitler's rise to power; Charles Grant's "Riding the Black," a meditation on the cultural impact of the atomic bomb; Richard Christian Matheson's "Whatever," which examines the dark side of the 1960's counterculture through the rise and fall of a legendary rock band; and Ramsey Campbell's "The Word," about a fan's run-in with a hack horror writer turned New Age prophet. Clive Barker wraps all the stories with "Men and Sin" and "A Movement at the River's Heart." Published in England as *Millennium*.

**Other books you might like:**
Ramsey Campbell, *New Terrors*, 1982
    editor
Charles L. Grant, *The Dodd Mead Gallery of Horror*, 1983
    editor
David G. Hartwell, *The Dark Descent*, 1987
    editor
Kirby McCauley, *Dark Forces*, 1980
    editor
John Pelan, *Darkside: Horror for the Next Millennium*, 1996
    editor

## 5925

**PAT WINTER**

### *Madoc's Hundred*

(New York: Bantam Domain, 1991)

**Story type:** Fantasy (Legend; Adventure)
**Series:** Madoc Saga
**Major character(s):** Madoc "Weather Eyes" ab Owen, Leader; Rhys "Sun Eyes" ab Meredydd, Minstrel; Tumkis "Lady Sun", Indian
**Time period(s):** 12th century (1172)
**Locale(s):** North America (currently Tennessee and Kentucky)

**Summary:** The exiled Welsh prince Madoc has crossed the Atlantic Ocean and landed on the shores of what will be called North America, finding enemies and allies among the people living there. Now, two years after coming to this land, Madoc's band travel down the Tennessee and Ohio Rivers on the way to the Great River Road, the Mech-a-sip-i, where the great pyramids of the sun god stand in the city of Ixtulan.

**Other books you might like:**
Orson Scott Card, *Red Prophet*, 1988
Parke Godwin, *The Last Rainbow*, 1985
Sue Harrison, *Mother Earth, Father Sky*, 1990
R.A. MacAvoy, *The Third Eagle: Lessons Along a Minor String*, 1989

## 5926

**B.L. WINTERS**

### *Bloody Waters*

(New York: Pocket, 1993)

**Story type:** Horror (Mystery)
**Major character(s):** Kara Noble Worthington, Housewife; John Worthington, Lawyer; Buchanan "Bucky" Worthington, Actor
**Time period(s):** 1990s (1993)
**Locale(s):** Homeplace, Virginia

**Summary:** When friends of the conservative Worthington family begin dying under mysterious circumstances, suspicion falls on Kara Worthington, John Worthington's new bride, whom they fear has yet to tame her West Coast wildness. But Kara's suspicions fall on Lorraine Worthington, the sexually-inhibited family matriarch who sternly rules her four sons' lives and will brook no interference.

**Other books you might like:**
Athena Alexis, *Along Came a Spider*, 1992
V.C. Andrews, *Flowers in the Attic*, 1979
Shawn MacDonald, *The Darkness Within*, 1993
Michael McDowell, *Blackwater*, 1983

## 5927

**JEANETTE WINTERSON**

### *Sexing the Cherry*

(New York: Atlantic Monthly Press, 1990)

**Story type:** Fantasy (Historical)
**Major character(s):** Jordon, Child; Dog-Woman, Animal Trainer; John Tradescant, Farmer, Philosopher
**Time period(s):** 17th century
**Locale(s):** London, England

**Summary:** The Dog-Woman and her adopted child live in the dirt and disease of London. They leave, first to Wimbleton, then further and further, moving through time and space and fable into a mutable world of allegory and meaning.

**Other books you might like:**
Iain M. Banks, *The Bridge*, 1989
John Crowley, *Little, Big*, 1981
Stuart Gordon, *Fire in the Abyss*, 1983
Robert Holdstock, *Mythago Wood*, 1984
Fay Weldon, *Lives and Loves of a She-Devil*, 1983

## 5928

**DAVID WISEMAN**

### *A Tie to the Past*

(New York: Houghton, 1989)

**Story type:** Fantasy (Historical)
**Major character(s):** Mary, Teenager
**Time period(s):** 1980s; 20th century
**Locale(s):** England

**Summary:** After stealing the tie, pin and diary of an old British suffragette, a modern young girl discovers she can see the life of the former owner by touching the objects. Guilt-ridden over the theft, she nevertheless becomes preoccupied with the past.

**Other books you might like:**
Lloyd Alexander, *The Drackenberg Adventure*, 1988
    Book 3 of Vesper Holly Series

Pamela F. Service, *Vision Quest*, 1989
Rosemary Sutcliff, *The Mark of the Horse Lord*, 1989

**5929**

KEN WISMAN

## Weird Family Tales

(Parma, Ohio: Earth Prime Press, 1993)

**Story type:** Horror (Collection)

**Summary:** These seven stories from the small press are presented as tales about the narrator's extended family, each of whom falls prey to a supernatural encounter. Among the menaces chronicled are a phantom shark, a winged human, the infinite world created by placing two mirrors facing each other, a phantasm of the mind, and a fertility god.

**Other books you might like:**
Ray Bradbury, *The Stories of Ray Bradbury*, 1980
Darrell Schweitzer, *Transients and Other Disquieting Tales*, 1993
Chet Williamson, *The House of Fear*, 1989

**5930**

DON WISMER

## A Roil of Stars

(New York: Baen, 1991)

**Story type:** Science Fiction (Military; Psychic Powers)
**Major character(s):** Asher Tye, Warrior, Psychic; Celia "Lee" D'Ame, Heroine, Waiter/Waitress; Ryne Sangre, Pilot (spaceship)
**Time period(s):** Indeterminate Future
**Locale(s):** Sigma Radidiani, Planet—Imaginary; Polar Cloud, Outer Space

**Summary:** The Polar Cloud is trying to prevent being taken over by the Whole Empire which had been rediscovered only 30 years ago. Before the war could start, both Empires appeared to be threatened by aliens called the Onn, while forces continued to overcome the Cloud, one planet per year.

**Other books you might like:**
Michael Berlyn, *The Eternal Enemy*, 1990
John Dalmas, *The White Regiment*, 1990
William C. Dietz, *War World*, 1986
Paula King, *Mad Roy's Light*, 1990
Timothy A. Madden, *Outbanker*, 1990
L.E. Modesitt Jr., *The Hammer of Darkness*, 1985
Paul Preuss, *Breaking Strain*, 1987

**5931**

PAUL WITCOVER

## Waking Beauty

(New York: HarperPrism, 1997)

**Story type:** Fantasy (Political; Religious)
**Major character(s):** Cyrus "Cy" Galingale, Carpenter; Rose Rubra, Bride; Rumer, Prostitute
**Time period(s):** Indeterminate
**Locale(s):** Jubilar, Fictional City; Quoz, Fictional City

**Summary:** In a minor town in a strange, socially rigid world, a young man and woman about to be married find marriage only part of their destiny. Events in motion shake the social structure from base to peak, bringing a new era in the war between the Furies and the male-dominated Hierarchate. First novel.

**Other books you might like:**
Scott Baker, *Drink the Fire From the Flames*, 1987
Clive Barker, *Imajica*, 1991
Storm Constantine, *Wraeththu*, 1993
Tanith Lee, *Death's Master*, 1982
Robert Silverberg, *Lord Valentine's Castle*, 1980

**5932**

ALLEN L. WOLD

## Crown of the Serpent

(New York: Popular Library Questar, 1989)

**Story type:** Science Fiction (Adventure)
**Series:** Rikard Braeth
**Major character(s):** Rikard Braeth, Adventurer, Historian
**Time period(s):** Indeterminate Future
**Locale(s):** Nowarth, Planet—Imaginary; Kohltri, Planet—Imaginary

**Summary:** Rikard Braeth is recruited to help destroy or neutralize the Thathas, an evil alien race with strange powers who have been destroying human planets.

**Other books you might like:**
Rick Cook, *Limbo System*, 1989
John Dalmas, *The Lizard War*, 1989
Janet Morris, *Target*, 1989
    David Drake, co-author
L. Neil Smith, *Contact and Commune*, 1989

**5933**

ALLEN L. WOLD

## Lair of the Cyclops

(New York: Warner Questar, 1992)

**Story type:** Science Fiction (Adventure)
**Series:** Rikard Braeth
**Major character(s):** Rikard Braeth, Adventurer, Historian; Endark Droagn, Alien, Telepath; Grayshard, Alien
**Time period(s):** Indeterminate Future
**Locale(s):** Dannon's Keep, Planet—Imaginary; Malvrone, Planet—Imaginary; Tsikshka, Planet—Imaginary

**Summary:** Hoping to enhance his academic standing as historian, Rikard Braeth and his companions follow ancient clues in hopes of discovering the answers to the two-million-year-old mystery concerning why the precursor cyclopean race who changed the galaxy suddenly disappeared.

**Other books you might like:**
John DeChancie, *Paradox Alley*, 1987
John DeChancie, *Red Limit Freeway*, 1984
John DeChancie, *Starrigger*, 1983
Diana G. Gallagher, *The Alien Dark*, 1990
Michael P. Kube-McDowell, *Enigma*, 1986
Michael P. Kube-McDowell, *Empery*, 1987
Michael P. Kube-McDowell, *Emprise*, 1985
Frederik Pohl, *The Gateway Trip: Tales and Vignettes of the Heechee*, 1990

## 5934

### GARY K. WOLF

## *Who P-P-Plugged Roger Rabbit?*

(New York: Villard Books, 1991)

**Story type:** Fantasy (Mystery; Light Fantasy)
**Series:** Roger Rabbit
**Major character(s):** Roger Rabbit, Actor (toon), Spouse (Jessica Rabbit's); Eddie Valiant, Detective—Private; Clark Gable, Actor, Historical Figure
**Time period(s):** 1940s
**Locale(s):** Los Angeles, California; Toontown, California (fictional Los Angeles suburb)

**Summary:** When rumors of Jessica Rabbit's affair with Clark Gable cause Roger to worry about losing his role as Rhett Butler in a *Gone with the Wind* remake, Roger convinces Eddie to help eliminate the rumors. Eddie's help becomes more valuable as rumors turn sinister and Roger is accused of multiple murders.

**Other books you might like:**

David Bischoff, *Night of the Living Shark!*, 1991
Craig Shaw Gardner, *Bride of the Slime Monster*, 1990
Craig Shaw Gardner, *Revenge of the Fluffy Bunnies*, 1990
Craig Shaw Gardner, *Slaves of the Volcano God*, 1989
Mel Gilden, *Surfing Samurai Robots*, 1988
Lionel Fenn, *Kent Montana and the Really Ugly Thing From Mars*, 1990
Clifford D. Simak, *Out of Their Minds*, 1970

## 5935

### LEONARD WOLF, Editor

## *Blood Thirst: 100 Years of Vampire Fiction*

(New York: Oxford, 1997)

**Story type:** Horror (Anthology; Vampire Story)

**Summary:** Twenty-seven vampire tales by diverse hands that span the century since the publication of Bram Stoker's *Dracula*. The stories are divided into six sections covering the classic vampire, the psychological vampire, the science fiction vampire, the non-human vampire, the comic vampire and the heroic vampire. Included are C.L. Moore's "Shambleau," about a Medusa-like race of extraterrestrial vampires: Woody Allen's "Count Dracula," which projects the problems Count Dracula might have were he to emerge for feeding during a brief solar eclipse; Fritz Leiber's "The Girl with the Hungry Eyes," about an advertising model who feeds on consumer needs, and M.R. James's "Count Magnus," in which an unwary traveler accidentally liberates a sorcerer and his bloodthirsty familiar from their mausoleum.

**Other books you might like:**

Ellen Datlow, *Blood Is Not Enough*, 1989
  editor
Martin H. Greenberg, *A Taste for Blood*, 1992
  editor
Stephen Jones, *The Mammoth Book of Vampires*, 1992
  editor
Alan Ryan, *Vampires: Two Centuries of Great Vampire Stories*, 1987
  editor

## 5936

### LEONARD WOLF, Editor

## *Doubles, Dummies and Dolls: 21 Terror Tales of Replication*

(New York: Newmarket, 1995)

**Story type:** Horror (Anthology)

**Summary:** Through almost two dozen stories assembled by a renowned authority on supernatural fiction, authors from around the world explore the classic horror theme of the double. Theophile Gautier's "The Double Knight," Edgar Allan Poe's "William Wilson," and Ramsey Campbell's "The Scar" are all doppelganger stories. Robert Bloch's "Sweets to the Sweets" is concerned with the terrible use to which a voodoo doll is put, and Anthony Boucher's "The Ghost of Me" with a man haunted by his own ghost and his imminent death. In Gerald Kersh's "The Extraordinarily Horrible Dummy," Susan Sontag's "The Dummy," and E.T.A. Hoffman's "The Sand-man," dolls take on lives that supersede those of their human counterparts. Algernon Blackwood's "The Terror of the Twins" tells of twin brothers who prove to be two sides of a single personality.

**Other books you might like:**

Chris Baldick, *The Oxford Book of Gothic Tales*, 1992
  editor
Alberto Manguel, *Black Water 2: More Tales of the Fantastic*, 1990
  editor
Alberto Manguel, *Black Water: The Book of Fantastic Literature*, 1983
  editor

## 5937

### GENE WOLFE

## *Calde of the Long Sun*

(New York: Tor, 1994)

**Story type:** Science Fiction (Generation Starship; Religious)
**Series:** Book of the Long Sun
**Major character(s):** Patera Silk, Religious (priest); Maytera Mint, Religious, Teacher; Quetzal, Religious, Vampire
**Time period(s):** Indeterminate Future
**Locale(s):** *Whorl of the Long Sun*, Spaceship; Viron, Fictional City

**Summary:** Civil unrest propels Silk into accepting his popular elevation to Calde, since the gods from mainframe seem to have chosen him and the Chapter finally supports him. Possessed by the gods, Maytera Mint proves an inspired general, while Maytera Marble remembers events from her childhood.

**Other books you might like:**

Brian W. Aldiss, *Non-Stop*, 1989
Stephen Baxter, *Raft*, 1992
James Blish, *A Life for the Stars*, 1962
Samuel R. Delany, *Tales of Neveryon*, 1979
Frank M. Robinson, *The Dark Beyond the Stars*, 1991

## 5938

### GENE WOLFE

## *Castle of Days*

(New York: Tor, 1992)

**Story type:** Science Fiction (Collection)

**Summary:** Selections from Wolfe's writing 1968-1992 presented in three sections. Part I reprints *Gene Wolfe's Book of Days* (1981) including an introduction and 18 stories each relating to a day of particular note during the year. Part II reprints *The Castle of the Otter*, published previously as a small press volume discussing The Book of the New Sun series (1980-1983) in 11 articles including 12 pages of Urth jokes and an 18-page article, "Words Weird and Wonderful," discussing the language of Urth. Part III, "Castle of Days" contains 29 items divided into "Writers," "Writing" and "Books" including articles from periodicals and anthologies and excerpts from encyclopedia articles, speeches and personal correspondence.

**Other books you might like:**
Isaac Asimov, *Opus 200*, 1979
Isaac Asimov, *Opus 300*, 1984
Robert A. Heinlein, *Expanded Universe*, 1980
Larry Niven, *N-Space*, 1990
Larry Niven, *Playgrounds of the Mind*, 1991

## 5939

### GENE WOLFE

## *Castleview*

(New York: Tor, 1990)

**Story type:** Fantasy (Contemporary)
**Time period(s):** 1990s
**Locale(s):** Castleview, Illinois

**Summary:** In Castleview, so named for the phantom castle that periodically appears in mid-air, the lives of the town folk take a strange turn when all sorts of creatures from myth and legend start appearing in ever increasing numbers and with ever increasing frequency.

**Other books you might like:**
John DeChancie, *Castle Kidnapped*, 1989
Roger L. DiSilvestro, *Ursula's Gift*, 1988
Esther Friesner, *Sphynxes Wild*, 1989
Lisa Goldstein, *Tourists*, 1989

## 5940

### GENE WOLFE

## *Endangered Species*

(New York: Tor, 1989)

**Story type:** Science Fiction (Collection)

**Summary:** Wolfe's most recent collection contains thirty-four stories, ranging in publication date from 1968 to 1988, and features virtually all of his recent short fiction. Included are "The Map" and "The Cat," two stories set in the world of his Book of the New Sun series; the novella "Silhouette"; and such shorter pieces as "The Woman the Unicorn Loved," "The HORARS of War," "All the Hues of Hell," "Procreation," and "The Tale of the Rose and the Nightingale."

**Other books you might like:**
Brian W. Aldiss, *Helliconia Spring*, 1982
Brian W. Aldiss, *Helliconia Summer*, 1985
Brian W. Aldiss, *Helliconia Winter*, 1985
Brian W. Aldiss, *An Island Called Moreau*, 1981
Brian W. Aldiss, *Last Orders*, 1989
Brian W. Aldiss, *Man in His Time: The Best Science Fiction Stories of Brian W. Aldiss*, 1989
Paul Park, *Soldiers of Paradise*, 1987

Paul Park, *Sugar Rain*, 1989

## 5941

### GENE WOLFE

## *Exodus From the Long Sun*

(New York: Tor, 1996)

**Story type:** Science Fiction (Literary; Generation Starship)
**Series:** Book of the Long Sun
**Major character(s):** Patera Silk, Religious (priest); Maytera Auk, Criminal (former), Religious (prophet); Mint, Military Personnel (general)
**Time period(s):** Indeterminate Future
**Locale(s):** Viron, Fictional City; *Whorl of the Long Sun*, Spaceship

**Summary:** Once a mere priest, Calde Silk now rules the *Whorl* by the gods' decree. As the starship seemingly deteriorates, revolution and war break out among the millions living on the ship, while the gods increasingly manifest themselves and intervene in human affairs.

**Other books you might like:**
C.S. Friedman, *Crown of Shadows*, 1995
Simon Hawke, *The Whims of Creation*, 1992
Frank Herbert, *Dune*, 1965
Frank Herbert, *Dune Messiah*, 1969
Sheri S. Tepper, *Sideshow*, 1992

## 5942

### GENE WOLFE

## *Lake of the Long Sun*

(New York: Tor, 1994)

**Story type:** Science Fiction (Generation Starship; Alternate Universe)
**Series:** Book of the Long Sun
**Major character(s):** Patera Silk, Religious (priest); Maytera Marble, Robot (chem), Religious; Crane, Doctor, Spy
**Time period(s):** Indeterminate Future
**Locale(s):** *Whorl of the Long Sun*, Spaceship

**Summary:** Still trying to save his manteion, or religious enclave, as directed by his patron god, the Outsider, Silk must somehow find a huge sum of money. To the surprise of all, despite the sacrifices, only Silk's manteion again receives communications from the gods, the first in 20 years. Unrest in Viron leads to Silk's popular, god supported, campaign for Calde.

**Other books you might like:**
Poul Anderson, *The Boat of a Million Years*, 1989
Samuel R. Delany, *They Fly at Ciron*, 1993
Robert A. Heinlein, *Orphans of the Sky*, 1963
Fritz Leiber, *Ship of Shadows*, 1988
Sheri S. Tepper, *A Plague of Angels*, 1993

## 5943

### GENE WOLFE

## *Nightside the Long Sun*

(New York: Tor, 1993)

**Story type:** Science Fiction (Generation Starship; Alternate Intelligence)
**Series:** Book of the Long Sun
**Major character(s):** Silk, Religious (Patera); Blood, Criminal; Crane, Doctor, Spy

**Time period(s):** Indeterminate Future
**Locale(s):** *Whorl of the Long Sun*, Spaceship

**Summary:** Patera Silk, recently charged with responsibility for the Manteion School on Sun Street, receives enlightenment from the Outsider, a god not included in the usual pantheon, who instructs Silk to keep the Manteion open. Unfortunately the Manteion and grounds now belong to Blood, compelling Silk to attempt coercing Blood into returning title to him, despite the fact that the gods have not spoken from Mainframe for generations and the Outsider told Silk he could not help.

**Other books you might like:**
Brian W. Aldiss, *Non-Stop*, 1989
Stephen Baxter, *Raft*, 1992
James Blish, *A Life for the Stars*, 1962
Samuel R. Delany, *Nova*, 1968
Robert A. Heinlein, *Orphans of the Sky*, 1963
Fritz Leiber, *Ship of Shadows*, 1988
Frank M. Robinson, *The Dark Beyond the Stars*, 1991

**5944**
### GENE WOLFE
## *Soldier of Arete*
(New York: Tor, 1989)

**Story type:** Fantasy (Legend)
**Major character(s):** Latro, Mercenary (Swordsman)
**Time period(s):** 5th century B.C.; Indeterminate Past
**Locale(s):** Greece

**Summary:** Handicapped by the loss of his memory every time he sleeps, Latro is able to orient himself in the ancient world of the Peloponnesian War by keeping daily diaries and through his ability to converse with the gods who are inaccessible to other mortals. Sequel to *Soldier of the Mist*.

**Other books you might like:**
Mickey Zucker Reichert, *Dragonrank Master*, 1989
Howard Waldrop, *A Dozen Tough Jobs*, 1989

**5945**
### GENE WOLFE
## *Storeys From the Old Hotel*
(New York: Tor, 1992)

**Story type:** Fantasy (Collection)

**Summary:** This volume contains an eight-page introduction with 34 stories utilizing diverse themes including two Liavek shared world stories, "The Green Rabbit of S'Rian" and "Choice of the Black Goddess," plus other stories from anthologies and periodicals with three appearing originally. The British limited edition hardcover received the World Fantasy Award for best collection of the year.

**Other books you might like:**
David Brin, *The River of Time*, 1986
John Crowley, *Novelty*, 1989
Samuel R. Delany, *Driftglass: 10 Tales of Speculative Fiction*, 1971
Samuel R. Delany, *Tales of Neveryon*, 1979
Kristine Kathryn Rusch, *Pulphouse, Issue 6: Fantasy*, 1990
editor
Will Shetterly, *Liavek*, 1985
Emma Bull, co-editor
Will Shetterly, *Liavek: Festival Week*, 1990
Emma Bull, co-editor

Will Shetterly, *Liavek: Wizard's Row*, 1987
Emma Bull, co-editor
Terri Windling, *Life on the Border*, 1991
editor

**5946**
### SEBASTIAN WOLFE, Editor
## *The Little Book of Horrors*
(New York: Barricade, 1992)

**Story type:** Horror (Anthology)

**Summary:** This slim book collects 68 macabre tales, vignettes, cartoons, and brief factual articles, none longer than a page or two. Included are modern works by Joe Lansdale, Richard Christian Matheson, Stephen Gallagher, Frederic Brown and Robert Bloch, classic tales from Franz Kafka, Lafcadio Hearn, Ambrose Bierce, and Charles Dickens, an excerpt from Thomas Rymer's penny dreadful *Varney the Vampire* and illustrations by Gahan Wilson and Edward Gorey.

**Other books you might like:**
Isaac Asimov, *Microcosmic Tales*, 1980
Martin H. Greenberg and Joseph Olander, co-editors

**5947**
### SEBASTIAN WOLFE, Editor
## *Reel Terror*
(New York: Carroll & Gaf, 1992)

**Story type:** Horror (Anthology)

**Summary:** A dozen stories that have been adapted into some of the finest horror, science fiction and suspense films of all time. Included are "Spurs," Todd Robbins' tale of vengeful circus freaks, which served as the basis of Tod Browning's 1932 underground classic *Freaks*; H. P. Lovecraft's "The Colour out of Space," the story of an extraterrestial influence invading the earth that was adapted for the 1965 film, *Die, Monster, Die*; Angela's Carter's brilliant "The Company of Wolves," a metafictional variant on the fairy tale of Little Red Riding Hood that served as the basis for the 1984 film of the same name; and Philip K. Dick's paranoid science fiction tale "We Can Remember It for You Wholesale," adapted in 1990 for the Paul Verhoeven film, *Total Recall*.

**Other books you might like:**
Peter Haining, *The Ghouls*, 1972
editor
Peter Haining, *The Hollywood Nightmare*,
editor
David Wheeler, *No, but I Saw the Movie*, 1990
editor

**5948**
### DONALD A. WOLLHEIM, Editor
### ARTHUR W. SAHA, Co-Editor
## *The 1990 Annual World's Best Science Fiction*
(New York: DAW, 1990)

**Story type:** Science Fiction (Anthology)

**Summary:** This 25th anniversary issue contains stories by Gregory Benford, Orson Scott Card, Lisa Tuttle, Lucius Shepard and Robert Silverberg, among others. The stories cover a wide range of themes including genetic engineering, future warfare, nuclear waste and interactions with computers.

**Other books you might like:**
Isaac Asimov, *Isaac Asimov Presents the Great SF Stories: 15 (1953)*, 1986
Groff Conklin, *The Best of Science Fiction*, 1946
Gardner Dozois, *The Year's Best Science Fiction: Seventh Annual Collection*, 1990
Harlan Ellison, *Dangerous Visions*, 1967
Robert Silverberg, *The Science Fiction Hall of Fame, Volume 1*, 1970

## 5949

### DAVE WOLVERTON

## Beyond the Gate

(New York: Tor, 1995)

**Story type:** Science Fiction (Space Opera)
**Series:** Golden Queen
**Major character(s):** Gallen O'Day, Warrior, Hero; Maggie Flynn, Fiance(e); Orick, Animal (bear), Adventurer
**Time period(s):** Indeterminate Future
**Locale(s):** Tremonthin, Planet—Imaginary; Interstellar Empire/Federation

**Summary:** As Gallen O'Day and Maggie Flynn plan to wed, Gallen receives orders to go to Tremonthin as Lord Protector of the planet. There he must destroy a secret society, the Inhuman, and deflect another invasion of the insectoid Dronons.

**Other books you might like:**
David Brin, *Startide Rising*, 1983
C.J. Cherryh, *Serpent's Reach*, 1980
Dave Duncan, *Hero*, 1991
Joan Slonczewski, *A Door into Ocean*, 1986
Sheri S. Tepper, *Grass*, 1989
Vernor Vinge, *A Fire upon the Deep*, 1992

## 5950

### DAVE WOLVERTON

## The Courtship of Princess Leia

(New York: Bantam Spectra, 1994)

**Story type:** Science Fiction (Space Opera; Mystical)
**Series:** Star Wars
**Major character(s):** Leia Organa, Royalty, Diplomat; Han Solo, Spaceship Captain, Warrior; Luke Skywalker, Martial Arts Expert (Jedi Knight), Hero
**Time period(s):** Indeterminate Past
**Locale(s):** Dathomir, Planet—Imaginary; New Republic, Interstellar Empire/Federation

**Summary:** Unwilling to accept Leia's proposed marriage to Prince Isolder to cement relations between the Rebel Alliance and the Hapes consortium, Han Solo tricks Leia into accompanying him to Dathomir. Interrupting his search for Jedi Knight lore, Luke with Artoo-Detoo and Prince Isolder, travels to Dathomir, little expecting the treasure and the danger that await.

**Other books you might like:**
Roger MacBride Allen, *Ambush at Corellia*, 1995
Kevin J. Anderson, *Jedi Search*, 1994

Brian Daley, *The Han Solo Adventures*, 1992
George Lucas, *The Star Wars Trilogy*, 1987
    Donald F. Glut, James Kahn, co-authors
Vonda N. McIntyre, *The Crystal Star*, 1994

## 5951

### DAVE WOLVERTON

## The Golden Queen

(New York: Tor, 1994)

**Story type:** Science Fiction (Space Opera)
**Series:** Golden Queen
**Major character(s):** Everynne, Clone, Royalty (queen); Gallen O'Day, Warrior, Hero; Orick, Animal (bear), Adventurer
**Time period(s):** Indeterminate Future
**Locale(s):** Tihrglas, Planet—Imaginary

**Summary:** Chased by dronon vanquishers, Everynne and her guardian search Tihrglas for the portal leading to other worlds. Vulnerable to Everynne's immortal beauty, Gallen follows her through the portal after stealing a key from the vanquishers. Gallen, his companion talking bear, Orick, and Maggie, a waitress from the local inn, hope to save humanity from the insectoid dronons and rescue Everynne.

**Other books you might like:**
William Barton, *Dark Sky Legion*, 1992
C.J. Cherryh, *The Fires of Azeroth*, 1979
C.J. Cherryh, *Gate of Ivrel*, 1976
C.J. Cherryh, *Well of Shiuan*, 1978
Cheryl J. Franklin, *Fire Crossing*, 1991

## 5952

### DAVE WOLVERTON, Editor

## L. Ron Hubbard Presents Writers of the Future, Volume IX

(Los Angeles: Bridge Publications, 1993)

**Story type:** Science Fiction (Anthology)
**Series:** Writers of the Future

**Summary:** Includes a two-page introduction by Wolverton, five articles on writing and art by the editor and Kevin J. Anderson, Octavia E. Butler, L. Ron Hubbard and Julius Schwartz plus 17 original stories with diverse themes and tones written by emerging writers who recently won Writers of the Future Contests. Concludes with nine pages about the contest, including contest rules and deadlines.

**Other books you might like:**
Algis Budrys, *L. Ron Hubbard Presents Writers of the Future, Volumes I-VIII*, 1985-1992
    editor
George R.R. Martin, *The John W. Campbell Awards, Volume 5*, 1984
    editor
George R.R. Martin, *New Voices I-IV*, 1977-1981
    editor
Victoria Schochet, *The Berkley Showcase: New Writings in Science Fiction and Fantasy, Volumes 1-4*, 1980-1981
    John Silbersack, co-editor

## 5953

**DAVE WOLVERTON**, Editor

### L. Ron Hubbard Presents Writers of the Future, Volume XII

(Los Angeles: Bridge Publications, 1996)

**Story type:** Science Fiction (Anthology; Fantasy)
**Series:** Writers of the Future

**Summary:** Contains a three-page introduction by Wolverton, three articles on writing and art by Doug Beason, L. Ron Hubbard and Paul Lehr plus 16 original stories with diverse themes and tones, written by emerging writers who recently won Writers of the Future contests. Concludes with 11 pages about the contest including contest rules and deadlines.

**Other books you might like:**
Algis Budrys, *L. Ron Hubbard Presents Writers of the Future, Volumes I-VIII*, 1993-1992
    editor
George R.R. Martin, *The John W. Campbell Awards, Volume 5*, 1984
    editor
George R.R. Martin, *New Voices I-IV*, 1977-1981
    editor
Victoria Schochet, *The Berkley Showcase: New Writings in Science Fiction and Fantasy, Volumes 1-4*, 1980-1981
    John Silbersack, co-editor
Robin Scott Wilson, *Clarion I-III*, 1971-1973
    editor

## 5954

**DAVE WOLVERTON**, Editor

### L. Ron Hubbard Presents Writers of the Future, Volume XIV

(Los Angeles: Bridge, 1998)

**Story type:** Science Fiction (Anthology)

**Summary:** This is the latest in a long-standing series designed to identify promising new writers. There are 17 original stories included, along with essays on writing science fiction by L. Ron Hubbard, Anne McCaffrey, Vincent Di Fate, Eric Kotani, and Michael A. Stackpole.

**Other books you might like:**
Isaac Asimov, *The Mammoth Book of Vintage Science Fiction*, 1990
    Martin H. Greenberg, co-editor
Gardner Dozois, *Modern Classic Short Novels of Science Fiction*, 1994
    editor
Gardner Dozois, *The Year's Best Science Fiction: Fifteenth Annual Collection*, 1998
Norman Partridge, *It Came From the Drive-In*, 1996
    Martin H. Greenberg, co-editor
Kristine Kathryn Rusch, *The Best of Pulphouse: The Hardback Magazine*, 1991

## 5955

**DAVE WOLVERTON**

### On My Way to Paradise

(New York: Bantam Spectra, 1989)

**Story type:** Science Fiction (Cyberpunk)

**Major character(s):** Angelo Osic, Scientist, Military Personnel; Tamara, Spy
**Time period(s):** 21st century
**Locale(s):** Baker, Planet—Imaginary; Panama

**Summary:** One day Angelo Osic helps an injured woman named Tamara and finds himself in the middle of a complex web of violence and intrigue. Tamara, it seems, is in possession of dangerous information, information that someone else wants and is willing to kill to get. Fleeing Earth, Angelo signs on as a cyborg mercenary with a Japanese corporation fighting a bloody war off planet.

**Other books you might like:**
Orson Scott Card, *Ender's Game*, 1985
Joe Haldeman, *The Forever War*, 1974
Lucius Shepard, *Life During Wartime*, 1987
Bruce Sterling, *Islands in the Net*, 1988

## 5956

**DAVE WOLVERTON**

### Serpent Catch

(New York: Bantam Spectra, 1991)

**Story type:** Science Fiction (Adventure; Genetic Manipulation)
**Major character(s):** Tull, Hero, Prehistoric Human (Neanderthal/human halfbreed); Fava, Girlfriend, Prehistoric Human (Neanderthal)
**Time period(s):** Indeterminate Future
**Locale(s):** Anee, Moon—Imaginary

**Summary:** On Anee, genetic paleontologists were constructing the greatest zoo in the galaxy. Each of three continents was populated from a different era of Earth's history and kept separate by gigantic sea serpents which ate anything attempting to swim across the oceans and dragons that hunted the flying pterodactyls. When the alien Eridani killed all humans in space, the paleontologists were forced to descend to Anee where some befriended and others exploited the Neanderthals. Generations later when the sea serpents began to disappear, Tull, a young half-breed Neanderthal, learns about life, freedom and love on his odyssey to find new sea serpents and protect his home from dinosaurs.

**Other books you might like:**
David Brin, *Earth*, 1990
Octavia E. Butler, *Dawn*, 1987
Suzette Haden Elgin, *Native Tongue*, 1984
Larry Niven, *The Flight of the Horse*, 1973
Joan Slonczewski, *A Door into Ocean*, 1986
Michael Swanwick, *In the Drift*, 1985

## 5957

**JACK WOMACK**

### Elvissey

(New York: Tor, 1993)

**Story type:** Science Fiction (Satire; Alternate Universe)
**Series:** Dryco Chronicles
**Major character(s):** Elvis Presley, Musician, Religious; Isabel ''Iz'' Bonney, Spouse, Time Traveler; John Bonney, Spouse, Time Traveler
**Time period(s):** 21st century; 1950s
**Locale(s):** New York, New York; Graceland, Tennessee; Alternate Earth

**Summary:** With Elvis Presley religions proliferating, John and Iz plan to bring Elvis Presley from the past to provide the Second Coming.

However, the 1950s they discover includes a past absent the United States Civil War and a 1950s Europe under Nazi domination.

**Other books you might like:**
Richard Peabody, *Mondo Elvis*, 1993
    Lucinda Ebersole, co-editor
Robert Rankin, *Armageddon: The Musical*, 1990
Allen Steele, *Clarke County, Space*, 1990
Neal Stephenson, *Snow Crash*, 1992
Jack Yeovil, *Comeback Tour: The Sky Belongs to the Stars*, 1991

---

## 5958

### JACK WOMACK

## *Heathern*

(New York: Tor, 1990)

**Story type:** Science Fiction (Theological; Contemporary Realism)
**Series:** Dryco Chronicles
**Major character(s):** Thatcher Dryden, Businessman (executive); Lester Hill Macaffrey, Teacher, Psychic (miracle worker)
**Time period(s):** 1990s (1990)
**Locale(s):** New York, New York

**Summary:** When Thatcher Dryden heard about Lester Macaffrey performing miracles he sent some representatives to invite Lester to Dryco to meet him. While they were there Lester miraculously resuscitated a man one of the envoys had killed. Thatcher was determined to control and use Lester to make a fortune for Dryco.

**Other books you might like:**
Neil Gaiman, *Good Omens: The Nice and Accurate Prophecies of Agnes Nutter, Witch*, 1990
    Terry Pratchett, co-author
Parke Godwin, *Waiting for the Galactic Bus*, 1988
John Kessel, *Good News From Outer Space*, 1989
James Morrow, *Only Begotten Daughter*, 1990
Robert Rankin, *Armageddon: The Musical*, 1990

---

## 5959

### JACK WOMACK

## *Random Acts of Senseless Violence*

(New York: Atlantic Monthly Press, 1994)

**Story type:** Fantasy (Science Fiction; Urban)
**Series:** Dryco Chronicles
**Major character(s):** Lola Hart, Teenager, Student, Gang Member; Jude, Teenager, Gang Member; Iz, Teenager, Gang Member
**Time period(s):** 21st century
**Locale(s):** New York, New York

**Summary:** Lola Hart lives in a world on the edge of disaster. When hard times rob her writer parents of their livelihood, the family moves to the Shattered East Side, from modest privilege to danger and poverty. As Lola wanders unprepared into violence and love, she finds a sadly plausible future.

**Other books you might like:**
Francesca Lia Block, *Primavera*, 1994
Pat Cadigan, *Synners*, 1991
Jim Carroll, *The Basketball Diaries*, 1978
William Gibson, *Virtual Light*, 1993
Jonathan Littell, *Bad Voltage*, 1989

---

## 5960

### JACK WOMACK

## *Terraplane*

(New York: Tor Books, 1990)

**Story type:** Science Fiction (Alternate Universe)
**Series:** Dryco Chronicles
**Major character(s):** Robert Luther Bickerstaff, Military Personnel (Retired General), Businessman; Jake, Criminal (Assassin)
**Time period(s):** 21st century
**Locale(s):** Russia; New York, Alternate Universe

**Summary:** In this sequel to *Ambient*, Bickerstaff and Jake are engaged in espionage in a post-communist Russia which has become intensely consumer oriented. Suddenly they and two Russians are thrown into an alternate universe and find themselves in New York, circa 1939. In this universe, however, racism is much worse than in ours and Bickerstaff, being black and used to being in command, finds himself in immediate trouble.

**Other books you might like:**
William Gibson, *Count Zero*, 1985
William Gibson, *Mona Lisa Overdrive*, 1988
William Gibson, *Neuromancer*, 1984
Richard Kadrey, *Metrophage*, 1988
Bruce Sterling, *Islands in the Net*, 1988
Gene Wolfe, *There Are Doors*, 1988

---

## 5961

### BARI WOOD

## *The Basement*

(New York: Morrow, 1995)

**Story type:** Horror (Supernatural Vengeance)
**Major character(s):** Myra Lundens, Housewife; Reed Lerner, Doctor (psychiatrist); Arlen Pinchot, Housewife
**Time period(s):** 1990s (1995)
**Locale(s):** Fallsbridge, Connecticut

**Summary:** Myra Ludens tries to rid her house of its uncanny malaise by exorcising the spirit of a witch whose remains were buried in the land it rests on three centuries before, but only rouses the witch's ire. As her friends begin dying gruesome deaths, Myra looks for more scientific solutions to her problem and ponders the coincidence that most of the witch's victims are people who she has fought with.

**Other books you might like:**
Douglas Clegg, *Goat Dance*, 1989
Morgan Fields, *Shaman Woods*, 1990
Melisand March, *The Site*, 1988
Roy Sorrels, *The Eyes of Torie Webster*, 1990
Chet Williamson, *Dreamthorp*, 1989

---

## 5962

### BRIDGET WOOD

## *The Lost Prince*

(New York: Ballantine Del Rey, 1993)

**Story type:** Fantasy (Political; Time Travel)
**Major character(s):** Fergus, Military Personnel, Time Traveler; Grainne, Royalty (crown prince); Medoc, Wizard, Ruler (usurper)
**Time period(s):** Indeterminate Past; Indeterminate Future
**Locale(s):** Ireland

**Summary:** When the Enchantment fades from the royal houses of ancient Ireland, the Beastline of rulers dies out until only Grainne and Fergus remain to ascend to the Wolf throne. When the evil wizard Medoc usurps power and spreads corruption throughout the land, Grainne searches for help from the Castle of Shadows while Fergus travels to the distant future where he hopes to harness the power of the Apocalypse to overthrow Medoc. Sequel to *Wolfking*.

**Other books you might like:**
Kenneth C. Flint, *Challenge of the Clans*, 1986
Kenneth C. Flint, *The Dark Druid*, 1987
Kenneth C. Flint, *Storm Shield*, 1986
Morgan Llewelyn, *Grania: She-King of the Irish Seas*, 1986
Elizabeth Moon, *Sheepfarmer's Daughter*, 1988
Andrew J. Offutt, *The Sign of the Moonbow*, 1980
Andrew J. Offutt, *Sword of the Gael*, 1975
Andrew J. Offutt, *The Undying Wizard*, 1982

## 5963

### BRIDGET WOOD

## Wolfking

(New York: Ballantine Del Rey, 1992)

**Story type:** Fantasy (Time Travel; Post-Disaster)
**Major character(s):** Joanna Grady, Time Traveler; Flynn O'Connor, Time Traveler; Cormac, Royalty
**Time period(s):** Indeterminate Future; Indeterminate Past
**Locale(s):** Ireland; Tara, Mythical Place

**Summary:** Joanna's romance with Flynn blossoms in post-apocalyptic Ireland until Joanna's father decides she must marry an ignorant pig farmer. Joanna flees into a radioactive area where she uses a Gateway to travel back in time to ancient Ireland. When Flynn follows Joanna, the pair find themselves involved in Cormac's struggle for his crown.

**Other books you might like:**
Kenneth C. Flint, *Challenge of the Clans*, 1986
Kenneth C. Flint, *The Dark Druid*, 1987
Kenneth C. Flint, *Storm Shield*, 1986
Elizabeth Moon, *Sheepfarmer's Daughter*, 1988
Andrew J. Offutt, *The Sign of the Moonbow*, 1980
Andrew J. Offutt, *Sword of the Gael*, 1975
Andrew J. Offutt, *The Tower of Death*, 1982
    co-author
Andrew J. Offutt, *The Undying Wizard*, 1982
Andrew J. Offutt, *When Death Birds Fly*, 1980
    co-author

## 5964

**MACKAY WOOD** (Pseudonym of Susan Mackay Smith)

## Wolf's Cub

(Aurora, Colorado: Write Way Publishing, 1998)

**Story type:** Fantasy (Political; Magic Conflict)
**Major character(s):** Herric, Royalty (prince), Scholar; Elaine, Royalty, Wizard; Worgan, Wizard
**Time period(s):** Indeterminate Past
**Locale(s):** Athgar, Fictional City; Camfield, Fictional City

**Summary:** Forced to rule and driven into an unwanted marriage, Prince Herric must protect his kingdom from barbarians. When he attempts to form a peace, Herric discovers that a vengeful wizard drives the barbarians. Herric and his new wife must learn to trust and love one another in order for the kingdom to survive. First novel.

**Other books you might like:**
Deborah Chester, *Reign of Shadows*, 1996
J.V. Jones, *The Baker's Boy*, 1995
Patricia A. McKillip, *The Riddle-Master of Hed*, 1976
Melanie Rawn, *Dragon Prince*, 1988
Michael Scott Rohan, *The Anvil of Ice*, 1986

## 5965

### N. LEE WOOD

## Faraday's Orphans

(New York: Ace, 1997)

**Story type:** Science Fiction (Post-Holocaust)
**Major character(s):** Berkeley "Berk" Nielsen, Pilot (helicopter); "Wy" Wysaigh, Pilot (airplane); Leonard Cormack, Government Official (City Council), Pilot
**Time period(s):** 23rd century (2242)
**Locale(s):** Pittsburgh, North America

**Summary:** Having learned to love the freedom and open spaces outside the dome from his father, Berk continues to fly his helicopter for the city. The lack of support from Leonard or his wife only spurs Berk to crave exploration. Finally getting the exploratory run to Philadelphia, Berk lands, only to have his machine thrown off a 20 story building. Wounded and ill, Berk must learn enough about the society and environment to survive outside.

**Other books you might like:**
Octavia E. Butler, *Parable of the Sower*, 1993
Marjorie Bradley Kellogg, *Harmony*, 1991
Donald E. McQuinn, *Warrior*, 1990
Catherine Wells, *The Earth Is All That Lasts*, 1991
Paul O. Williams, *The Breaking of Northwall*, 1981

## 5966

### N. LEE WOOD

## Looking for the Mahdi

(New York: Ace, 1996)

**Story type:** Science Fiction (Political; Techno-Thriller)
**Major character(s):** Kahlili "Kay Bee" bint Munadi Sulaiman, Journalist; John Halton, Genetically Altered Being; Cullen Laidcliff, Government Official
**Time period(s):** 21st century
**Locale(s):** Clarke Orbital Station, Space Station; Nok Kuzlat, Middle East; Khuruchabja, Middle East

**Summary:** Having worked behind a desk for 10 years since passing as a man while covering the war in Khuruchabja, Kay Bee reluctantly permits Laidcliff to coerce her into transporting and delivering Halton to the new king of Khuruchabja. Unfortunately, Halton arrives with an extra item to deliver, nearly resulting in their deaths, and forces Kay Bee to reevaluate John and the mission. First novel.

**Other books you might like:**
David Brin, *Earth*, 1990
Raphael Carter, *The Fortunate Fall*, 1996
Philip K. Dick, *Blade Runner*, 1982
George Alec Effinger, *When Gravity Fails*, 1987
Elizabeth Moon, *Hunting Party*, 1993
Neal Stephenson, *The Diamond Age*, 1995

## `5967`

### FRANCINE G. WOODBURY

## *Shade and Shadow*

(New York: Ballantine Del Rey, 1996)

**Story type:** Fantasy (Mystery)
**Major character(s):** Raoul "Rags" Smythe, Magician, Professor; Maxwell "Max" Bolton, Journalist
**Time period(s):** Indeterminate
**Locale(s):** England, Alternate Earth (Oxford and London)

**Summary:** Upon the murder of the offensive chairman of the University's College of Magic, police suspect Assistant Professor Raoul Smythe. Intending to clear himself, Raoul and his friend, Max, begin an independent investigation stretching to events decades in the past and casting suspicion on Raoul's potential new girlfriend. First novel.

**Other books you might like:**
Randall Garrett, *Too Many Magicians*, 1967
Laurell K. Hamilton, *Nightseer*, 1992
Caroline Stevermer, *A College of Magics*, 1994
L.A. Taylor, *Cat's Paw*, 1995
Robert Weinberg, *A Logical Magician*, 1994

## `5968`

### ELVIRA WOODRUFF

## *The Summer I Shrank My Grandmother*

(New York: Holiday, 1990)

**Story type:** Fantasy (Light Fantasy; Young Adult)
**Major character(s):** Nelly Brown, Child, Scientist; Emma Brown, Grandparent
**Time period(s):** 1990s (1990)
**Locale(s):** Seaview, California

**Summary:** Experimenting with a magical chemistry set, Nelly reverses the aging process in her grandmother. Will she be able to find an antidote before her grandmother shrinks to an embryo?

**Other books you might like:**
Florence P. Heide, *The Shrinking of Treehorn*, 1971
Elaine Horseman, *Hubble's Bubble*, 1964
Diana Wynne Jones, *The Ogre Downstairs*, 1974
E. Nesbit, *Five Children and It*, 1905

## `5969`

### JOHN WOOLEY
### RON WOLFE, Co-Author

## *Death's Door*

(New York: Dell/Abyss, 1992)

**Story type:** Horror (Doppelganger)
**Major character(s):** Case Hamilton, Police Officer; Stephen Glasser, Doctor (surgeon); Diana Hamilton, Police Officer
**Time period(s):** 1990s (1993)
**Locale(s):** Los Angeles, California

**Summary:** The second time after he is brought back from death following injury in the line of duty, police officer Case Hamilton finds himself saddled with an alter ego he refers to as the Gray Man, a creature from the other side of life who embarks on a murderous rampage.

**Other books you might like:**
Kathe Koja, *Bad Brains*, 1992
Dean R. Koontz, *Hideaway*, 1992
Joe R. Lansdale, *The Nightrunners*, 1987
T.M. Wright, *Little Boy Lost*, 1992

## `5970`

### PERSIA WOOLLEY

## *Guinevere: The Legend in Autumn*

(New York: Poseidon Press, 1991)

**Story type:** Fantasy (Legend; Romance)
**Series:** Child of the Northern Spring
**Major character(s):** Guinevere, Royalty (queen); Arthur, Ruler (king); Lancelot, Knight
**Time period(s):** 6th century
**Locale(s):** Camelot, England; Joyous Gard, England (Northumbria)

**Summary:** A mature Guinevere relates adventures of Arthur's knights, her personal vision of the Goddess, the Grail quest, Mordred's difficult relationship with Arthur and her passion for Lancelot. When Morgan le Fey's treachery results in Guinevere's trial, death sentence and rescue by Lancelot, she and Lancelot flee north. After Arthur threatens to march on Joyous Gard, Guinevere returns to Camelot to the great joy of her subjects. She later acts as mediator between Arthur and Morgan le Fey concerning Christianity and the Goddess Religion.

**Other books you might like:**
Marion Zimmer Bradley, *The Mists of Avalon*, 1983
Gillian Bradshaw, *Hawk of May*, 1980
Courtway Jones, *In the Shadow of the Oak King*, 1991
Sharan Newman, *The Chessboard Queen*, 1983
Sharan Newman, *Guinevere*, 1981
Sharan Newman, *Guinevere Evermore*, 1985
Howard Pyle, *The Story of the Champions of the Round Table*, 1905
Howard Pyle, *The Story of King Arthur and His Knights*, 1903

## `5971`

### PERSIA WOOLLEY

## *Queen of the Summer Stars*

(New York: Poseidon, 1990)

**Story type:** Fantasy (Legend; Romance)
**Series:** Child of the Northern Spring
**Major character(s):** Guinevere, Royalty (queen); Arthur, Ruler (king); Lancelot, Knight
**Time period(s):** 6th century
**Locale(s):** Camelot, England

**Summary:** Gwen decides to help her husband, Arthur, cement his relationships with the independent client kings into the legendary Round Table. She decides to have constructed the most wonderful setting for them, Camelot. 1991 Best Books For Young Adults title.

**Other books you might like:**
Marion Zimmer Bradley, *The Mists of Avalon*, 1983
Gillian Bradshaw, *Hawk of May*, 1980
Gillian Bradshaw, *In Winter's Shadow*, 1982
Gillian Bradshaw, *Kingdom of Summer*, 1981
Sharan Newman, *The Chessboard Queen*, 1983
Sharan Newman, *Guinevere*, 1981
Sharan Newman, *Guinevere Evermore*, 1985

**5972**

**DAVID WORSICK**

## Henry's Gift: The Magic Eye

(Kansas City, Missouri: Andrews and McMeel, 1994)

**Story type:** Fantasy (Psychic Powers; Quest)
**Major character(s):** Henry of Veldran, Orphan; Byron, Knight; Nadia, Adventurer
**Time period(s):** Indeterminate
**Locale(s):** Haunted Hills, Fictional Country; Barony of Veldran, Fictional Country

**Summary:** When Henry comes of age, his adopted father passes on a parchment found with the infant Henry. When his legacy points to great wealth awaiting him, Henry sets out with Byron and Nadia to earn his inheritance, mindful of legends surrounding the treasure and his disturbing visions. Concludes with ''About 3D Images,'' ''How to See 3D Images'' and sketches of the 20 3D images depicting Henry's psychic visions.

**Other books you might like:**
David Kirschner, *The Pagemaster*, 1993
    Ernie Contreras, co-author
Michael Ende, *The Neverending Story*, 1983
Terry Goodkind, *Wizard's First Rule*, 1994
James Gurney, *Dinotopia*, 1992
Roger Zelazny, *Way Up High*, 1992

**5973**

**PATRICIA C. WREDE**

## Book of Enchantments

(New York: Harcourt Brace/Jane Yolen Books, 1996)

**Story type:** Fantasy (Collection; Young Adult)

**Summary:** Contains eight pages of author's notes plus six original stories and five stories reprinted from anthologies 1986-1994. Frequently light in tone, the stories explore a broad range of themes from unicorns and werewolves to fairy tales, English music, and *The Thousand and One Arabian Nights*, with one new story set in the Enchanted Forest Chronicles milieu.

**Other books you might like:**
Emma Bull, *Double Feature*, 1994
    Will Shetterly, co-author
Ellen Datlow, *Black Thorn, White Rose*, 1994
    Terri Windling, co-editor
Diana Wynne Jones, *Everard's Ride*, 1995
Will Shetterly, *Liavek: The Players of Luck*, 1986
    Emma Bull, co-editor
Michael Stearns, *A Wizard's Dozen*, 1993
    editor
Jane Yolen, *Storyteller*, 1992

**5974**

**PATRICIA C. WREDE**

## Calling on Dragons

(New York: Harcourt Brace Jovanovich, 1993)

**Story type:** Fantasy (Quest; Young Adult)
**Series:** Enchanted Forest Chronicles
**Major character(s):** Cimorene, Royalty (queen); Kazul, Mythical Creature (dragon), Royalty (king); Morwen, Witch
**Time period(s):** Indeterminate

**Locale(s):** Enchanted Forest, Mythical Place

**Summary:** Evil wizards steal King Mendanbar's magic sword and begin stealing magic from the kingdom. Joined by Kazul, Morwen, a magician, Killer the rabbit-donkey and many opinionated cats, Queen Cimorene must recover the sword before it drains all magic from the Enchanted Forest, killing it.

**Other books you might like:**
Karen Brush, *Demon Pig*, 1991
Ursula K. Le Guin, *A Wizard of Earthsea*, 1968
Larry Niven, *The Magic Goes Away*, 1979
Meredith Ann Pierce, *The Pearl of the Soul of the World*, 1990
Sherwood Smith, *Wren to the Rescue*, 1990
Laurence Yep, *Dragon of the Lost Sea*, 1982

**5975**

**PATRICIA C. WREDE**

## Dealing with Dragons

(New York: Harcourt Brace Jovanovich, 1990)

**Story type:** Fantasy (Light Fantasy; Young Adult)
**Series:** Enchanted Forest Chronicles
**Major character(s):** Cimorene, Royalty (princess); Kazul, Mythical Creature (dragon)
**Time period(s):** Indeterminate
**Locale(s):** Linderwall, Fictional Country; Enchanted Forest, Mythical Place

**Summary:** Cimorene is interested in learning a lot of things, but not the ones considered proper by her parents. When they decide to marry her to Prince Therandil, Cimorene takes action by fleeing to the Enchanted Forest to become a Dragon's Princess. Dragon politics, sneaky wizards and other princesses all combine to make lively times for Cimorene. This was twice honored by librarians, as an ALA Best Young Adult Books and as winner of a Minnesota Book Award.

**Other books you might like:**
Susan Fletcher, *Dragon's Milk*, 1989
Diana Wynne Jones, *Howl's Moving Castle*, 1986
M.M. Kaye, *The Ordinary Princess*, 1984
Jane Zaring, *The Return of the Dragon*, 1981

**5976**

**PATRICIA C. WREDE**

## Magician's Ward

(New York: Tor, 1997)

**Story type:** Fantasy (Mystery; Romance)
**Series:** Mairelon the Magician
**Major character(s):** Richard ''Mairelon'' Merrill, Magician; Kim, Apprentice, Magician; Alexei Durmontov, Royalty (prince), Wizard
**Time period(s):** 1810s
**Locale(s):** London, England; Alternate Universe

**Summary:** As Kim learns magic and more complicated rules of London society, disaster strikes Mairelon. When a mysterious money lender organizes slum magicians, and robbers suddenly become interested in books written by pre-Revolution French magicians, Kim becomes the only link between society and slum, despite her supposed status as a lady.

**Other books you might like:**
Joan Aiken, *Black Hearts in Battersea*, 1964
Randall Garrett, *Too Many Magicians*, 1967
Diana Wynne Jones, *The Lives of Christopher Chant*, 1988

Ellen Kushner, *Swordspoint*, 1987
Fletcher Pratt, *The Blue Star*, 1952
Melissa Scott, *Point of Hopes*, 1995
   Lisa A. Barnett, co-author
Caroline Stevermer, *A College of Magics*, 1994
Mary Frances Zambreno, *Journeyman Wizard*, 1994

## 5977

### PATRICIA C. WREDE

## *Mairelon the Magician*

(New York: Tor, 1991)

**Story type:** Fantasy (Magic Conflict; Young Adult)
**Major character(s):** Kim, Orphan; Mairelon, Magician, Traveler
**Time period(s):** 1810s
**Locale(s):** London England, Alternate Universe

**Summary:** The chance to earn five pounds is unbelievably good luck for Kim since it would mean not having to live on the streets disguised as a boy, something she won't be able to do much longer. To earn the money she must sneak into Mairelon's wagon and see if it contains a certain silver bowl, but if Mairelon is a real sorcerer, why is he playing the travelling showman and why is that bowl so sought-after?

**Other books you might like:**
Joan Aiken, *Black Hearts in Battersea*, 1964
Joan Aiken, *Nightbirds on Nantucket*, 1966
Suzy McKee Charnas, *The Golden Thread*, 1989
Diane Duane, *So You Want to Be a Wizard?*, 1983
Alan Garner, *The Weirdstone of Brisingamen*, 1969
Diana Wynne Jones, *Cart and Cwidder*, 1977
Robin McKinley, *The Blue Sword*, 1982
Will Shetterly, *Elsewhere*, 1991

## 5978

### PATRICIA C. WREDE

## *The Raven Ring*

(New York: Tor, 1994)

**Story type:** Fantasy (Magic Conflict; Adventure)
**Series:** Lyra
**Major character(s):** Elerct Slaven, Martial Arts Expert, Teenager; Daner Vallaniri, Martial Arts Expert, Nobleman; Karvonen Aurelico, Thief, Guide
**Time period(s):** Indeterminate
**Locale(s):** Ciaron, Fictional City

**Summary:** Immediately after retrieving the possessions of her mercenary mother who died inexplicably after a battle, Eleret encounters offers, scams, attempted thefts and burglaries, all seemingly aimed at parting her from her family heirloom, a ring her mother took with her to battle. Befriended by Lord Daner and his family, Eleret also utilizes Karvonen's aid when the attacks continue inside Lord Daner's home.

**Other books you might like:**
Marion Zimmer Bradley, *The Shattered Chain*, 1976
Steven Brust, *Jhereg*, 1983
Lois McMaster Bujold, *The Spirit Ring*, 1992
Terry Goodkind, *Wizard's First Rule*, 1994
Laurell K. Hamilton, *Nightseer*, 1992
Caroline Stevermer, *A College of Magics*, 1994
Martha Wells, *The Element of Fire*, 1993

## 5979

### PATRICIA C. WREDE

## *Searching for Dragons*

(New York: Harcourt Brace Jovanovich, 1991)

**Story type:** Fantasy (Quest; Young Adult)
**Series:** Enchanted Forest Chronicles
**Major character(s):** Cimorene, Royalty, Companion (Kazul's); Mendanbar, Ruler (king)
**Time period(s):** Indeterminate
**Locale(s):** Enchanted Forest, Mythical Place

**Summary:** On advice of the witch, Morwen, Mendanbar seeks the counsel of Kazul, King of the Dragons, to discover how to stop the destruction of the Enchanted Forest. When Mendanbar discovers Kazul has been captured by wizards, he and Cimorene, the dragon's princess, set off to find and bring back Kazul, apparently the latest victim of the feud between the wizards and the dragons. Sequel to *Dealing with Dragons*.

**Other books you might like:**
Diana Wynne Jones, *Archer's Goon*, 1984
Diana Wynne Jones, *Howl's Moving Castle*, 1986
Tanith Lee, *Black Unicorn*, 1991
Jane Yolen, *Dragon's Blood*, 1982
Jane Yolen, *Wizard's Hall*, 1991
Mary Frances Zambreno, *A Plague of Sorcerers*, 1991

## 5980

### PATRICIA C. WREDE

## *Shadows over Lyra*

(New York: Tor, 1997)

**Story type:** Fantasy (Magic Conflict; Political)
**Series:** Lyra
**Major character(s):** Alethia Tel'anh, Royalty (princess), Adventurer; Ranira "Renra", Servant (bondwoman), Adventurer; Emereck, Minstrel, Adventurer
**Time period(s):** Indeterminate
**Locale(s):** Lyra, Planet—Imaginary; Alkyra, Fictional Country

**Summary:** As unbound Shadow-born and a second Lithmern invasion threaten Alkyra's, Alethia, Ranira and Emereck forge new alliances, develop magical abilities and utilize a powerful magical object as they seek to protect the country. Omnibus edition of *Shadow Magic* (1982), *Daughter of Witches* (1984) and *The Harp of Imach Thyssel* (1985) with 13 pages of early Lyran history and a four-page timeline.

**Other books you might like:**
Steven Brust, *Jhereg*, 1983
Lois McMaster Bujold, *The Spirit Ring*, 1992
Laurell K. Hamilton, *Nightseer*, 1992
Diana Wynne Jones, *Cart and Cwidder*, 1977
Martha Wells, *The Element of Fire*, 1993

## 5981

### PATRICIA C. WREDE

## *Snow White and Rose Red*

(New York: Tor, 1989)

**Story type:** Fantasy (Legend)
**Series:** Fairy Tales
**Major character(s):** Snow White Arden, Maiden; Rose Red Arden, Maiden

**Time period(s):** 16th century
**Locale(s):** England

**Summary:** A re-working of the Grimm Brothers' version, weaving history and fantasy together for a familiar, yet new story.

**Other books you might like:**
Steven Brust, *The Sun, the Moon, and the Stars*, 1987
Robin McKinley, *Beauty*, 1985
Susan Shwartz, *Arabesques: More Tales of the Arabian Nights*, 1980

## 5982

### M.K. WREN

## A Gift upon the Shore

(New York: Ballantine, 1990)

**Story type:** Science Fiction (Post-Nuclear Holocaust)
**Major character(s):** Mary Hope, Writer; Rachel Morrow, Artist, Farmer
**Time period(s):** Indeterminate Future
**Locale(s):** Oregon

**Summary:** Mary, a young writer, takes refuge on Rachel's isolated farm in Oregon and both survive the gradual collapse of society due to a series of plagues, natural disasters and, eventually, a nuclear war. Years later Mary finds herself fighting desperately to keep the fundamentalist Christians with whom she now lives from destroying the remnants of pre-holocaust culture still existing.

**Other books you might like:**
Neal Barrett Jr., *Through Darkest America*, 1987
David Brin, *The Postman*, 1985
Sheri S. Tepper, *The Gate to Women's Country*, 1988

## 5983

### SARA J. WRENCH

## The Duke of Sumava

(New York: Baen, 1997)

**Story type:** Fantasy (Historical; Magic Conflict)
**Major character(s):** Ottokar, Nobleman (duke); Zo'e'minira "Zoe", Supernatural Being
**Time period(s):** 17th century (1620s)
**Locale(s):** Duchy of Simava, Fictional Country; Fasosi, Alternate Earth

**Summary:** Fleeing from the invading Austrian army, the duke calls on the Powers of the land for help. To his surprise, they respond. Ottokar learns that the magical inhabitants of Fasosi, as well as the Wild Hunt led by the Black Huntsman, can help him defend his beloved country, if their help will not come at too high a price. First novel.

**Other books you might like:**
Lynn Abbey, *The Wooden Sword*, 1991
Gael Baudino, *Maze of Moonlight*, 1993
C.J. Cherryh, *Rusalka*, 1989
Lisa Goldstein, *The Red Magician*, 1982
Patricia A. McKillip, *The Riddle-Master of Hed*, 1976
Elizabeth Marie Pope, *The Perilous Gard*, 1974

## 5984

### GARY WRIGHT

## The Road West

(Lake Geneva, Wisconsin: TSR, 1990)

**Story type:** Fantasy (Sword and Sorcery)
**Major character(s):** Keven, Orphan, Traveler
**Time period(s):** Indeterminate Past
**Locale(s):** Midvale, Fictional Country

**Summary:** When Keven is orphaned at 15 years of age, he decides to leave the sea to enter the King's Academy. He graduates as King's Ranger-at-Arms, buys his contract to the king with his inheritance, and sets off to practice what he has learned. This is the author's first novel.

**Other books you might like:**
Joy Chant, *Red Moon and Black Mountain*, 1970
Phyllis Eisenstein, *Born to Exile*, 1978
Rosemary Kirstein, *The Steerswoman*, 1989
Ursula K. Le Guin, *A Wizard of Earthsea*, 1968

## 5985

### HELEN S. WRIGHT

## A Matter of Oaths

(New York: Popular Library Questar, 1990)

**Story type:** Science Fiction (Space Opera)
**Major character(s):** Rallya, Spaceship Captain (commander); Rafe, Spaceman (first officer); Joshim, Spaceman (webmaster)
**Time period(s):** Indeterminate Future
**Locale(s):** *Bhattya*, Spaceship

**Summary:** The crew of the *Bhattya* needs a new First Officer and Rafe needs a web position. Rafe had been mind-wiped ten years earlier for breaking his oath to the Emperor. At first Rallya is reluctant to have him in spite of his evident ability with the web machinery which operates the ship. Soon after he comes on board, Rallya begins to suspect he has dangerous memories still locked inside his mind, and dangerous enemies who would like him dead. Rallya and Joshim set out to solve the mystery that spans two empires. A first novel.

**Other books you might like:**
C.J. Cherryh, *Chanur's Venture*, 1984
C.J. Cherryh, *The Kif Strike Back*, 1985
C.J. Cherryh, *The Pride of Chanur*, 1982
Frank Herbert, *Dune*, 1965
Vonda N. McIntyre, *Superluminal*, 1983

## 5986

### T. LUCIEN WRIGHT

## Blood Brothers

(New York: Pinnacle, 1992)

**Story type:** Horror (Vampire Story)
**Major character(s):** Harry Matheson, Writer (horror writer), Vampire; Jerry Matheson, Writer (horror writer); Tad Matheson, Child (Jerry's son)
**Time period(s):** 1990s
**Locale(s):** Naples Falls, New York

**Summary:** When horror writer Harry Matheson is turned into a vampire, his sensitive twin brother Jerry translates the images he receives of Harry's killings into superior horror fiction. Harry then decides to extend their longstanding sibling rivalry by turning Jerry into a vampire as well.

**Other books you might like:**
Kathryn Meyer Griffith, *Vampire Blood*, 1991
Tom Piccirilli, *Dark Father*, 1990
Lee Weathersby, *Kiss of the Vampire*, 1992

---

`5987`

**T. LUCIEN WRIGHT**

### Dark Visions
(New York: Pinnacle, 1993)

**Story type:** Horror (Wild Talents)
**Major character(s):** Amelia Fortunato, Student—College; Freeman Ridge, Maintenance Worker (janitor); John A. Sanders, Police Officer
**Time period(s):** 1990s (1993)
**Locale(s):** Buffalo, New York

**Summary:** When psychically-endowed Amelia Fortunato begins college in Buffalo, her familiar visions of The Tunnel, which she has always feared and dreaded, become combined with her visions of past unsolved crimes in the area and the man responsible for them. Freeman Ridge, the criminal, knows that he must kill Amelia if he is to remain a free man.

**Other books you might like:**
Stephen King, *The Dead Zone*, 1979
Dean R. Koontz, *Hideaway*, 1992
Dean R. Koontz, *The Vision*, 1977
Joe R. Lansdale, *The Nightrunners*, 1987

---

`5988`

**T. LUCIEN WRIGHT**

### Thirst of the Vampire
(New York: Pinnacle, 1992)

**Story type:** Horror (Vampire Story)
**Major character(s):** Mike Marat, Journalist; Beverly Marat, Relative (Mike's sister); Phillipe Brissot, Vampire
**Time period(s):** 1990s (1992)
**Locale(s):** Rochester, New York; Watertown, New York

**Summary:** Phillipe Brissot holds the world's record for longstanding grudges: wronged by eighteenth-century French revolutionary Jean Marat, he has devoted his immortal life to systematically tracking down and destroying Marat's descendants, several of whom seem to have lived long enough to produce a branch of the family tree that has survived into the twentieth century and settled in upstate New York.

**Other books you might like:**
Kim Newman, *Bad Dreams*, 1990
Lee Weathersby, *Kiss of the Vampire*, 1992

---

`5989`

**T.M. WRIGHT**

### The Ascending
(New York: Tor, 1994)

**Story type:** Horror (Occult)
**Major character(s):** Ryerson Biergarten, Psychic; Lenny Baker, Psychic; Rick Dunn, Architect
**Time period(s):** 1990s (1994)

**Locale(s):** Toronto, Ontario, Canada
**Summary:** In this follow-up to the author's *Goodlow's Ghosts*, psychic Ryerson Biergarten travels to Canada to apply his skills to a mysterious series of murders in which victims are intimately linked to the architectural structures in which their bodies are concealed.

**Other books you might like:**
James Kisner, *Tower of Evil*, 1994
Melisand March, *The Site*, 1988
Robert Morgan, *The Only Thing to Fear*, 1994

---

`5990`

**T.M. WRIGHT**

### Boundaries
(New York: Tor, 1990)

**Story type:** Horror (Alternate World)
**Major character(s):** David Case, Worker (at a pharmaceutical company); Christian Grieg, Young Man; Karen Duffy, Young Woman
**Time period(s):** 1990s
**Locale(s):** Batavia, New York

**Summary:** Thinking that the murderer of his twin sister Anne has committed suicide to join her on "the Other Side," David Case takes an experimental drug that will allow him to cross the boundary between life and death. What David doesn't know is that the real murderer is very much alive and determined that David shall never return to the land of the living.

**Other books you might like:**
Dennis Etchison, *Darkside*, 1986

---

`5991`

**T.M. WRIGHT**

### Goodlow's Ghosts
(New York: Tor, 1993)

**Story type:** Horror (Ghost Story)
**Major character(s):** Ryerson Biergarten, Psychic; Sam Goodlow, Detective
**Time period(s):** 1990s
**Locale(s):** Boston, Massachusetts

**Summary:** In his typically opaque style, the author explores the boundaries between the worlds of the living and the dead through two story lines: in one, a psychic seeks the whereabouts of a man who has disappeared and is presumed dead; in the other, the man who is presumed dead undergoes a series of bizarre experiences that lead him to believe he is no longer living but is experiencing the afterlife.

**Other books you might like:**
Jonathan Aycliffe, *Naomi's Room*, 1992
Judith Hawkes, *Julian's House*, 1989
Shirley Jackson, *The Haunting of Hill House*, 1961
Richard Matheson, *Hell House*, 1971
Chet Williamson, *Ash Wednesday*, 1987

---

`5992`

**T.M. WRIGHT**

### Little Boy Lost
(New York: Tor, 1992)

**Story type:** Horror (Child-in-Peril)

**Major character(s):** C.J. Gale, Teenager; Miles Gale, Archaeologist; Jessica French, Doctor
**Time period(s):** 1990s
**Locale(s):** New York

**Summary:** The disappearance of Aaron Gale during a shopping trip leads to an intimate inspection of the Gale family's history, including the desertion of Marie Gale, Aaron's mother, who may have fled to another dimension and found a way to take Aaron with her.

**Other books you might like:**
Jonathan Aycliffe, *Naomi's Room*, 1991
Tom Piccirilli, *Dark Father*, 1990
Whitley Strieber, *Billy*, 1990

## 5993
### T.M. WRIGHT
## *The Place*
(New York: Tor, 1989)

**Story type:** Horror (Serial Killer)
**Major character(s):** Harlan DeVries, Serial Killer, Psychic; Greta King, Psychic, Child
**Time period(s):** 1990s
**Locale(s):** Ithaca, New York; Canaan, New York (Underground Village)

**Summary:** Harlan DeVries, serial killer and leader of an underground community, murders at will. He terrorizes the King family, sending the father to the hospital and kidnapping the mother and young son, while setting his sights on Greta, the paranormal daughter. But the little girl, in psychic contact with her family, marshals her psychic powers to battle DeVries in this world and the next.

**Other books you might like:**
Stephen King, *The Shining*, 1977
Dean R. Koontz, *The Vision*, 1977

## 5994
### T.M. WRIGHT
## *The School*
(New York: Tor, 1990)

**Story type:** Horror (Haunted House)
**Major character(s):** Allison Hitchcock, Writer; Frank Hitchcock, Photographer (Allison's husband)
**Time period(s):** 1990s
**Locale(s):** Danby, New York (Finger Lakes region)

**Summary:** Frank and Allison Hitchcock buy the old elementary schoolhouse on Ohio Road with intent to turn it into a bed-and-breakfast, unaware that their bereavement over the recent death of their son Joey is fueling the evil power that permeates the building.

**Other books you might like:**
Shirley Jackson, *The Haunting of Hill House*, 1959
Stephen King, *The Shining*, 1977

## 5995
### PATRICIA WRIGHTSON
## *Balyet*
(New York: McElderry, 1989)

**Story type:** Fantasy (Legend)
**Major character(s):** Jo, Teenager; Balyet, Spirit (Exiled)

**Time period(s):** 1980s
**Locale(s):** Australia

**Summary:** Young Jo follows a boy going camping. Instead of finding romance, however, she encounters the exiled spirit, Balyet. Fun turns to danger when Balyet starts showing the darker side of her nature.

**Other books you might like:**
Suzy McKee Charnas, *The Golden Thread*, 1989
Brian Keaney, *No Need for Heroes*, 1989
Pamela F. Service, *Vision Quest*, 1989
Jane Yolen, *The Faery Flag*, 1989

## 5996
### WILLIAM F. WU
## *Dictator*
(New York: AvoNova, 1994)

**Story type:** Science Fiction (Robot Fiction; Time Travel)
**Series:** Isaac Asimov's Robots in Time
**Major character(s):** Hunter, Robot, Detective; Judy Taub, Historian; Wayne Nystrom, Scientist, Time Traveler
**Time period(s):** 1940s (1941); Indeterminate Future
**Locale(s):** Moscow, Union of Soviet Socialist Republics

**Summary:** While waiting for the Germans to attack Moscow, natives capture Hunter and his team. When Dr. Nystrom and Ishihara claim Hunter works for the Germans, the NKVD arrests him. Hunter must escape capture and rally his team to complete the mission.

**Other books you might like:**
Poul Anderson, *Time Patrolman*, 1983
Ben Bova, *Triumph*, 1993
James P. Hogan, *The Proteus Operation*, 1985
Andre Norton, *The Crossroads of Time*, 1956
Harry Turtledove, *Worldwar: In the Balance*, 1994

## 5997
### WILLIAM F. WU
## *Hong on the Range*
(New York: Walker, 1989)

**Story type:** Science Fiction (Young Adult)
**Major character(s):** Louie Hong, Cowboy (Drifter); Chuck, Animal (A Steerite)
**Time period(s):** 21st century
**Locale(s):** West

**Summary:** After a series of biological disasters has all but destroyed the American West, a hardy new breed of cybernetic cowboys, equipped with all sorts of built-in mechanical and electronic advantages, attempts to reestablish ranching as a profession. Instead of cattle, however, they herd steerites, intelligent, cyborg steers. Louie Hong is a control-natural, a drifter with no cybernetic improvements. Despite this disadvantage, he's determined to make it in this new, silly, and very wild west.

**Other books you might like:**
Ron Goulart, *Cowboy Heaven*, 1979
Ron Goulart, *The Prisoner of Blackwood Castle*, 1984
Ron Goulart, *Starpirate's Brain*, 1987
Ron Goulart, *The Wicked Cyborg*, 1978
Richard Wilson, *The Girls from Planet 5*, 1955

## 5998

**WILLIAM F. WU**

### Predator

(New York: AvoNova, 1993)

**Story type:** Science Fiction (Time Travel; Robot Fiction)
**Series:** Isaac Asimov's Robots in Time
**Major character(s):** Hunter, Robot, Detective; Chad Mora, Scientist (paleontologist); Wayne Nystrom, Scientist, Time Traveler
**Time period(s):** 21st century; Indeterminate Past (Cretaceous period)
**Locale(s):** United States; North America (prehistoric Canada)

**Summary:** When five of the six Governor robots enter closed loops, the sixth decides to save itself from that fate by travelling into the past. Hunter and three humans travel back in time to capture the Governor robot which has split into six components, one located in the Cretaceous.

**Other books you might like:**
Poul Anderson, *Time Patrolman*, 1983
Philip Jose Farmer, *Time's Last Gift*, 1972
David Gerrold, *Deathbeast*, 1978
Garry Kilworth, *Split Second*, 1985
Julian May, *The Many-Colored Land*, 1981
Chad Oliver, *The Mists of Time*, 1952
Clifford D. Simak, *Mastodonia*, 1978

## 5999

**WILLIAM F. WU**

### The Robin Hood Ambush

(New York: Harper and Row, 1990)

**Story type:** Science Fiction (Time Travel; Young Adult)
**Series:** Robert Silverberg's Time Tours
**Major character(s):** Bob Washburn, Student; Allan Leong, Student; Will Ulrich, Student
**Time period(s):** 2060s (2061); 12th century (1189)
**Locale(s):** London, England

**Summary:** Three friends, Bob, Allan and Will, head back to 1189 A.D. for a vacation to see King Richard the Lion-Hearted crowned. They discover a corrupt Time Patrolman altering history to build an evil empire. The three boys wish Robin Hood would appear to help, but they know he was only a myth. No one else knows it however, so arming themselves with longbows, quarterstaffs and tales of Robin Hood, they set out to battle the Time Patrolman's scheme with a legend from the past.

**Other books you might like:**
Poul Anderson, *The Corridors of Time*, 1965
Poul Anderson, *The Shield of Time*, 1990
Poul Anderson, *There Will Be Time*, 1972
Gordon R. Dickson, *Time Storm*, 1977
H.G. Wells, *The Time Machine*, 1895

## 6000

**WILLIAM F. WU**

### Warrior

(New York: AvoNova, 1993)

**Story type:** Science Fiction (Time Travel; Robot Fiction)
**Series:** Isaac Asimov's Robots in Time
**Major character(s):** Hunter, Robot, Detective; Steve Chang, Time Traveler; Wayne Nystrom, Scientist, Time Traveler

**Time period(s):** 21st century; 1st century
**Locale(s):** Germany (between the Rhine and Weser Rivers)

**Summary:** Hunter and three assistants go back in time to capture the third MC Governor robot component to return it to the proper time. Unfortunately, they must operate in a Roman-occupied Germany whose residents will soon massacre and drive out the Romans.

**Other books you might like:**
Poul Anderson, *Time Patrolman*, 1983
John Brunner, *Times Without Number*, 1969
L. Sprague de Camp, *Lest Darkness Fall*, 1941
Crawford Kilian, *Rogue Emperor*, 1988
Kevin D. Randle, *Remember the Alamo!*, 1986
     Robert Cornett, co-author
Mack Reynolds, *The Other Time*, 1984

## 6001

**JANNY WURTS**

### Curse of the Mistwraith

(New York: Roc, 1994)

**Story type:** Fantasy (Magic Conflict; Political)
**Series:** Wars of Light and Shadow
**Major character(s):** Lysaer s'Ilessid, Royalty (prince), Magician (master or light); Arithon s'Falenn, Royalty (prince), Magician (master of shadows); Asandir, Sorcerer
**Time period(s):** Indeterminate
**Locale(s):** Athera, Planet—Imaginary

**Summary:** Covering all Athera for 500 years, mist and fog brings chaos and war. Prophecy says that a prince descended from one of the four royal heirs who fled through the Worldsend Gate into exile on Dascen Elur can restore sunlight. But the powers needed for Athera's deliverance come divided between two half-brothers, Lysaer, lord of light, and Arithon, master of shadows. With generations of blood feud in their homeworld of Dascen Elur lying between them before they step through the Worldsend Gate that leads to Athera, how can they combine their powers to fight the Mistwraith?

**Other books you might like:**
Steven Brust, *The Sun, the Moon, and the Stars*, 1987
C.J. Cherryh, *Gate of Ivrel*, 1976
Raymond E. Feist, *Daughter of the Empire*, 1987
     Janny Wurts, co-author
Simon R. Green, *Blue Moon Rising*, 1991
Roger Zelazny, *Nine Princes in Amber*, 1970

## 6002

**JANNY WURTS**

### Fugitive Prince

(New York: HarperPrism, 1997)

**Story type:** Fantasy (Political; Magic Conflict)
**Series:** Wars of Light and Shadow
**Major character(s):** Lysaer s'Ilessid, Royalty, Wizard; Arithon s'Falenn, Musician, Wizard; Elaira, Wizard, Doctor
**Time period(s):** Indeterminate (4th Age)
**Locale(s):** Araethura, Fictional Country; Avenor, Fictional City

**Summary:** The defeat of the Vastmark army disrupts the balance of power in the Five Kingdoms. Lysaer wants to maintain the throne, while the Koriani want to break the deadlock and Arithon wants peace. Unfortunately, the two brothers, cursed to hate one another, determine the fate of the whole world.

**Other books you might like:**
Glen Cook, *The Black Company*, 1984
Guy Gavriel Kay, *The Lions of Al-Rassan*, 1995
Katherine Kurtz, *Deryni Rising*, 1970
George R.R. Martin, *A Game of Thrones*, 1996
Patricia A. McKillip, *The Riddle-Master of Hed*, 1976

---

## 6003

### JANNY WURTS

## The Master of Whitestorm

(New York: Roc, 1992)

**Story type:** Fantasy (Quest; Magic Conflict)
**Major character(s):** Korendir, Adventurer, Mercenary; Haldeth, Artisan (blacksmith); Ithariel, Sorceress
**Time period(s):** Indeterminate Past
**Locale(s):** Tir Amindel, Fictional City; Datha, Fictional City; Aerith, Mythical Place

**Summary:** A galley slave, Korendir, escapes and sets out to gain enough money to build a truly secure home. He battles wereleopards, magicians, armies and demons, always winning, but never satisfied. Eventually, secrets and forgotten memories conspire to take away everything he has earned.

**Other books you might like:**
Glen Cook, *The Black Company*, 1984
Raymond E. Feist, *Daughter of the Empire*, 1987
Katherine Kurtz, *Deryni Rising*, 1970
Patricia A. McKillip, *The Riddle-Master of Hed*, 1976
Tad Williams, *The Dragonbone Chair*, 1988

---

## 6004

### JANNY WURTS

## Ships of Merior

(New York: HarperCollins, 1995)

**Story type:** Fantasy (Political; Magic Conflict)
**Series:** Wars of Light and Shadow
**Major character(s):** Lysaer s'Ilessid, Royalty (crown prince), Magician (master of light); Arithon s'Falenn, Royalty (prince), Magician (master of shadows); Dakar, Psychic, Religious
**Time period(s):** Indeterminate (Fourth Age)
**Locale(s):** Athera, Planet—Imaginary

**Summary:** When Lysaer and Arithon defeat Desh-thiere, the Mistwraith curses them to eternal hatred of each other. Reisting the compulsion to hate, Arithon establishes a shipyard at Merior before Lysaer's armies can find and destroy him. Second in the series.

**Other books you might like:**
Raymond E. Feist, *Daughter of the Empire*, 1987
    Janny Wurts, co-author
Terry Goodkind, *Stone of Tears*, 1995
Patricia A. McKillip, *The Book of Atrix Wolfe*, 1995
L.E. Modesitt Jr., *The Order War*, 1995
Margaret Weis, *Dragon Wing*, 1990
    Tracy Hickman, co-author

---

## 6005

### JANNY WURTS

## That Way Lies Camelot

(New York: HarperPrism, 1996)

**Story type:** Fantasy (Collection; Science Fiction)

**Summary:** Contains four original tales and 11 stories reprinted from periodicals and anthologies 1986-1993. Themes include military conflict, mythical creatures, high fantasy, magic conflict, the Camelot saga, and the transformatory power of wishes.

**Other books you might like:**
Marion Zimmer Bradley, *The Best of Marion Zimmer Bradley's Fantasy Magazine*, 1994
    editor
David Drake, *The Fleet 1-6*, 1988-1991
    Bill Fawcett, co-editor
Richard Gilliam, *Grails: Quests of the Dawn*, 1994
    Martin H. Greenberg, Edward Kramer, co-editors
Elizabeth Moon, *Lunar Activity*, 1990
Richard Pini, *The Blood of Ten Chiefs*, 1986
    Robert Asprin, Lynn Abbey, co-editor
Terri Windling, *Elsewhere*, 1981
    Mark Alan Arnold, co-editor

---

## 6006

### E.A. WYKE-SMITH
### GEORGE MORROW, Illustrator

## The Marvellous Land of Snergs

(Baltimore: Old Earth Books, 1996)

**Story type:** Fantasy (Adventure; Young Adult)
**Major character(s):** Vanderdecker, Sea Captain, Mythical Creature; Sylvia, Child; Gorbo, Mythical Creature (Snerg)
**Time period(s):** 1920s
**Locale(s):** The Marvelous Land of Snergs, Fictional Country

**Summary:** In a strange, nearly unreachable land, a race of pixies aid the Society for the Removal of Superfluous Children in tending their charges. One day when Joe and Sylvia, two of the naughtier children, run away from home, Gorbo, a well-meaning but stupid Snerg, rescues them, whereupon all set out on an amazing adventure. Originally published in England in 1927, this novel had a strong impact on J.R.R. Tolkien, inspiring the hobbits of his famous novels. Includes an introduction and discussion of Wyke-Smith's writings by Douglas Anderson, 50 illustrations by George Morrow, and maps.

**Other books you might like:**
L. Frank Baum, *The Land of Oz*, 1904
Alan Garner, *The Weirdstone of Brisingamen*, 1961
Tove Jansson, *Finn Family Moomintroll*, 1958
Carol Kendall, *The Gammage Cup*, 1959
Mary Norton, *The Borrowers*, 1953
J.R.R. Tolkien, *The Hobbit*, 1938

---

## 6007

### JONATHAN WYLIE

## The Lightless Kingdom

(New York: Bantam Spectra, 1989)

**Story type:** Fantasy (Quest)
**Series:** Unbalanced Earth

**Major character(s):** Gemma, Sorceress; Arden, Lover (Gemma's)
**Time period(s):** Indeterminate
**Locale(s):** Southern Continent, Fictional Country; Lightless Kingdom, Fictional Country

**Summary:** Gemma is able to save the people of a valley from drought, but has lost Arden to caves beneath the mountain. Arden, meanwhile, has found a tribe living in caves, who are slowly being poisoned by the water from above.

**Other books you might like:**
David Eddings, *The Diamond Throne*, 1989
    Book 1 - The Elenium
Ru Emerson, *To the Haunted Mountains*,
    Book 1 - Tales of the Nedao

## 6008

### KAREN TEI YAMASHITA

## *Through the Arc of the Rain Forest*

(Minneapolis, Minnesota: Coffee House Press, 1990)

**Story type:** Fantasy (Satire)
**Major character(s):** Kazumasa Ishimaru, Engineer (safety); Chico Paco, Fisherman; Jonathan B. Tweep, Genius (3-armed)
**Time period(s):** 2000s (2002)
**Locale(s):** Brazil; South America

**Summary:** A freewheeling black comedy featuring a bizarre cast of characters, including a Japanese man with a ball floating six inches in front of his head, an American CEO with three arms, and a Brazilian peasant who discovers the art of healing by tickling one's earlobe with a feather. By the end of this story they have each risen to heights of wealth and fame before arriving at disasters, both personal and ecological, that destroy the rain forest and all the birds of Brazil.

**Other books you might like:**
Douglas Adams, *The Hitchhiker's Guide to the Galaxy*, 1980
John Brunner, *Children of the Thunder*, 1989
Charles de Lint, *Svaha*, 1989
Frank Herbert, *Dune*, 1965

## 6009

### KAREN TEI YAMASHITA

## *Tropic of Orange*

(Minneapolis: Coffee House Press, 1997)

**Story type:** Fantasy (Literary)
**Major character(s):** Rafaela Cortez, Housekeeper; Archangel, Writer (poet), Activist; El Gran Mojado, Sports Figure (masked wrestler)
**Time period(s):** 1990s
**Locale(s):** Mazatlan, Mexico; Los Angeles, California

**Summary:**

**Other books you might like:**
Octavia E. Butler, *Parable of the Sower*, 1993
Martha Cerda, *Senora Rodriguez and Other Worlds*, 1997
Lisa Goldstein, *A Mask for the General*, 1987
Richard Kadrey, *Kamikaze L'Amour*, 1995
Ian McDonald, *Terminal Cafe*, 1994
Pat Murphy, *The City, Not Long After*, 1989

## 6010

### CHELSEA QUINN YARBRO

## *The Angry Angel*

(New York: Avon, 1998)

**Story type:** Horror (Vampire Story)
**Series:** Sisters of the Night
**Major character(s):** Kelene, Young Woman; Dracula, Vampire; Magda, Servant
**Time period(s):** 16th century
**Locale(s):** Belgrade, Yugoslavia

**Summary:** First of a projected series of novels concerned with the three female consorts of Count Dracula. Kelene, the fourteen-year-old daughter of a Christian family, is subject to visions of the Militant Angels, who offer her family guidance and protection as they flee the Turkish invasion of Greece. In Belgrade, Kelene discovers that the angel who has enchanted her with erotic dreams is Dracula, the Dragon Prince, who buys her at auction and spirits her away to his castle in the Carpathian Mountains to indoctrinate her in the ways of vampires.

**Other books you might like:**
Roderick Anscombe, *The Secret Life of Laszlo, Count Dracula*, 1994
Jeanne Kalogridis, *Covenant with the Vampire*, 1994
Marie Kiraly, *Mina*, 1994
Fred Saberhagen, *The Dracula Tape*, 1975
Peter Tremayne, *Dracula Unborn*, 1977

## 6011

### CHELSEA QUINN YARBRO

## *Better in the Dark*

(New York: Tor, 1993)

**Story type:** Horror (Vampire Story)
**Series:** Chronicles of Saint-Germain
**Major character(s):** Comte de Saint-Germain, Vampire (aka Francois Rgoczy); Rangegonda, Noblewoman; Pentacoste, Noblewoman
**Time period(s):** 10th century (937)
**Locale(s):** Saxony, Germany

**Summary:** The ageless vampire Comte de Saint Germain washes up on the shores of Saxony and is ransomed as a prisoner by Ranegonda, sister of the Gerefa of the fortress of Leosan who has abdicated his leadership position to become a monk. Saint Germain falls in love with Ranegonda and helps her run interference with the besieging Danes, and with Pentacoste, her brother's embittered former wife.

**Other books you might like:**
C. Dean Andersson, *I Am Dracula*, 1993
Les Daniels, *No Blood Spilled*, 1991
P.N. Elrod, *I, Strahd*, 1993
Pierre Kast, *The Vampires of Alfama*, 1975

## 6012

### CHELSEA QUINN YARBRO

## *Blood Roses*

(New York: Tor, 1998)

**Story type:** Horror (Vampire Story)
**Series:** Chronicles of Saint-Germain
**Major character(s):** Francois de Saint-Germain, Vampire, Musician (trobadour); Hue d'Ormonde, Businessman (merchant); Huegenet da Brabant, Noblewoman

**Time period(s):** 14th century (1345)
**Locale(s):** Orgon, France

**Summary:** The 3000-year-old vampire Count St.-Germain is respected by his countrymen as a healer until the Black Plague sweeps through the French countryside and superstition runs free. To protect himself from knaves and opportunists who would accuse him of witchcraft, St.-Germain adopts the disguise of a traveling troubadour and flees Orgon, playing the role of a good samaritan and witnessing the many types of human folly that follow in the disease's wake.

**Other books you might like:**
Maura McCuniff, *The Vampire Memoirs*, 1991
    co-author, Traci Briery
Les Daniels, *The Black Castle*, 1978
Pierre Kast, *The Vampires of Alfama*, 1976
Anne Rice, *The Vampire Lestat*, 1985
Brian Stableford, *The Empire of Fear*, 1988

---

## 6013

### CHELSEA QUINN YARBRO

## *A Candle for D'Artagnan*

(New York: Tor, 1989)

**Story type:** Horror (Vampire Story)
**Series:** Olivia Trilogy
**Major character(s):** Atta Olivia Clemens, Vampire (1500 years old); Charles D'Artagnan, Warrior (Heroic French swordsman)
**Time period(s):** 17th century (1637)
**Locale(s):** Rome, Italy; France

**Summary:** When Papal politics drive Olivia Clemens from Rome to France, she meets and falls in love with the great swordsman D'Artagnan. Together they battle the machinations of Richelieu, as the wily Cardinal's last, desperate bid to hold power plunges them all into danger.

**Other books you might like:**
Les Daniels, *The Black Castle*, 1978
Pierre Kast, *The Vampires of Alfama*, 1976

---

## 6014

### CHELSEA QUINN YARBRO

## *Crown of Empire*

(New York: Baen, 1994)

**Story type:** Science Fiction (Political; Military)
**Series:** Crisis of Empire
**Major character(s):** Tira Bouriere, Political Figure, Teenager; Wiley Bouriere, Political Figure, Teenager; Chaney, Military Personnel
**Time period(s):** Indeterminate Future
**Locale(s):** First Empire, Interstellar Empire/Federation

**Summary:** When the High Secretary dies, a fight for power erupts as corporations, the military and non-human slaves struggle to control events through use of the High Secretary's survivors.

**Other books you might like:**
Allan Cole, *Sten*, 1984
    Chris Bunch, co-author
Brian Daley, *Requiem for a Ruler of Worlds*, 1985
David Drake, *Cluster Command*, 1989
    W.C. Dietz, co-author
David Drake, *An Honorable Defense*, 1988
    Thomas T. Thomas, co-author
David Drake, *The War Machine*, 1989
    Roger MacBride Allen, co-author

---

## 6015

### CHELSEA QUINN YARBRO

## *Crusader's Torch*

(New York: Tor, 1989)

**Story type:** Horror (Vampire Story)
**Series:** Olivia Trilogy
**Major character(s):** Atta Olivia Clemens, Vampire (1000 years old); Valence Rainaut, Knight (Knight Hospitaler)
**Time period(s):** 12th century (1189)
**Locale(s):** Tyre, Middle East; Rome, Italy

**Summary:** Forced from her home in Tyre by the approaching Islamic forces, Olivia Clemens undertakes a difficult and dangerous trip back to Rome, accompanied only by Valence Rainaut, a Knight Hospitaler, who has, against his will, fallen in love with her.

**Other books you might like:**
Les Daniels, *The Black Castle*, 1978
Pierre Kast, *The Vampires of Alfama*, 1976

---

## 6016

### CHELSEA QUINN YARBRO

## *Mansions of Darkness*

(New York: Tor, 1996)

**Story type:** Horror (Vampire Story)
**Series:** Chronicles of Saint-Germain
**Major character(s):** Comte de Saint-Germain, Vampire; Acanna Tupac, Royalty (Incan); Dom Enrique, Explorer
**Time period(s):** 17th century (1640)
**Locale(s):** Cuzco, Peru

**Summary:** While in Peru at the twilight of the Inca civilization, the immortal vampire Count St. Germain intervenes to save a woman of the royal family from the wrath of the Spanish conquistadors. His actions make St. Germain an enemy of the Spaniards, who regard him as a sorcerer for his knowledge of medicine and biology.

**Other books you might like:**
Les Daniels, *The Black Castle*, 1978
Les Daniels, *The Silver Skull*, 1979
Pierre Kast, *The Vampires of Alfama*, 1976
Mara McCuniff, *The Vampire Memoirs*, 1991
    Tracy Briery, co-author
Anne Rice, *Servant of the Bones*, 1996

---

## 6017

### CHELSEA QUINN YARBRO

## *Monet's Ghost*

(New York: Atheneum, 1997)

**Story type:** Fantasy (Young Adult; Alternate World)
**Major character(s):** Geena Howe, Teenager; Claude Monet, Spirit, Artist
**Time period(s):** 1990s
**Locale(s):** United States; Mythical Place

**Summary:** Geena acquires the ability to project herself into paintings, allowing her to experience the realm within the artworks, then exit from the spot she entered. When changes made to one painting while Geena explores inside it threaten to trap her within, Geena must negotiate a maze and confront the ghost of Claude Monet, if she hopes to return to her own world.

**Other books you might like:**
Suzy McKee Charnas, *The Kingdom of Kevin Malone*, 1993
Louise Cooper, *The Sleep of Stone*, 1991
Charles de Lint, *The Dreaming Place*, 1990
Esther Friesner, *Wishing Season*, 1993
Tanith Lee, *Black Unicorn*, 1991
Robert Silverberg, *Letters From Atlantis*, 1990
S.P. Somtow, *The Wizard's Apprentice*, 1993

## 6018

### CHELSEA QUINN YARBRO

## Out of the House of Life

(New York: Tor, 1990)

**Story type:** Horror (Vampire Story)
**Series:** Chronicles of Saint-Germain
**Major character(s):** Comte de Saint-Germain, Vampire; Madelaine de Montalia, Vampire; Egidius Maximillian Falke, Doctor
**Time period(s):** 1820s (1825-1828)
**Locale(s):** Thebes, Egypt

**Summary:** Madelaine de Montalia, acolyte and former lover of the millenia-old vampire Le Comte de Saint Germain, travels with the Baundilet archaeological expedition to the ruins of ancient Thebes. While she fends off the advances of the lecherous Professor Baundilet and nurtures a romance for the scholarly Doctor Falke, she learns the history of Egypt through her correspondance with Saint Germain, who was enslaved there as a demon god thousands of years before.

**Other books you might like:**
Les Daniels, *The Black Castle*, 1978
Pierre Kast, *The Vampires of Alfama*, 1975
Tim Powers, *The Stress of Her Regard*, 1989
Anne Rice, *The Vampire Lestat*, 1985
Brian Stableford, *The Empire of Fear*, 1988

## 6019

### CHELSEA QUINN YARBRO

## Writ in Blood

(New York: Tor, 1997)

**Story type:** Horror (Vampire Story)
**Series:** Chronicles of St. Germain
**Major character(s):** Comte de Saint-Germain, Vampire; Rowena Pearce Manning, Artist; Baron Klemens Manfred von Wolgast, Businessman (munitions)
**Time period(s):** 1910s
**Locale(s):** St. Petersburg, Russia; London, England

**Summary:** At the behest of Czar Nicholas, the Count St. Germain attempts to use his diplomatic influence to ease tension leading Europe to the brink of war. But arms merchants who hope to profit from the impending conflict resort to kidnapping and blackmail to thwart him, forcing him to use his vampire powers.

**Other books you might like:**
Les Daniels, *Yellow Fog*, 1986
Kim Newman, *Anno Dracula*, 1992
Kim Newman, *The Bloody Red Baron*, 1995
Michael Romkey, *I, Vampire*, 1990
Fred Saberhagen, *Seance for a Vampire*, 1994

## 6020

### JACK YEOVIL (Pseudonym of Kim Newman)

## Comeback Tour: The Sky Belongs to the Stars

(Baltimore, Maryland: GW Books, 1991)

**Story type:** Science Fiction (Adventure; Alternate Universe)
**Series:** Dark Future: Demon Download Cycle
**Major character(s):** Elvis Presley, Lawman, Historical Figure; Krokodil, Cyborg; Roger Duroc, Agent, Religious (Josephite elder)
**Time period(s):** 1990s (1998)
**Locale(s):** Memphis Tennessee, Alternate Earth; Cape Canaveral Florida, Alternate Earth

**Summary:** After a 20-year stint in the Army and the abandonment of his musical career, Elvis is making a living as a Sactioned Op in the Deep South when Krokodil enlists him in her war against Elder Nguyen Seth. His latest plot against life on Earth revolves around an obsolete orbital weapons system controlled from a forgotten launch facility in the Florida swamps. Unfortunately for both sides, these swamps also contain a GenTech laboratory about to suffer a serious crisis. A game tie-in novel.

**Other books you might like:**
Bradley Denton, *Buddy Holly Is Alive and Well on Ganymede*, 1991
Nigel Findley, *2XS*, 1992
William Gibson, *Neuromancer*, 1984
David Pringle, *Route 666*, 1990
   editor
Robert Rankin, *Armageddon: The Musical*, 1990
Allen Steele, *Clarke County, Space*, 1990
Howard Waldrop, *Strange Monsters of the Recent Past*, 1991

## 6021

### JACK YEOVIL (Pseudonym of Kim Newman)

## Demon Download

(Baltimore, Maryland: GW Books/Games Workshop, 1990)

**Story type:** Fantasy (Adventure)
**Series:** Dark Future: Demon Download Cycle
**Major character(s):** Sister Chantal Juillerat, Agent (papal), Computer Expert (cyberexorcist); Nguyen Seth, Spirit, Religious (priest of the Dark Ones); Nathan Stack, Police Officer (U.S. Highway Trooper)
**Time period(s):** 1990s
**Locale(s):** Fort Apache, Arizona; Welcome, Arizona

**Summary:** A malevolent computer virus called Nguyen Seth invades the U.S. Cavalry Highway Command Center at Fort Apache, Arizona. Papal agent Sister Chantal Juillerat is dispensed by the Pope to exorcise the spirit.

**Other books you might like:**
David Pringle, *Route 666*, 1990
Ian Watson, *Inquisitor*, 1989

## 6022

### JACK YEOVIL (Pseudonym of Kim Newman)

## Drachenfels

(Baltimore, Maryland: GW Books/Games Workshop, 1990)

**Story type:** Fantasy (Quest; Horror)

**Series:** Warhammer
**Major character(s):** Detlef Sierek, Writer; Oswald, Royalty (crown prince); Genevieve Dieudonne, Vampire
**Time period(s):** 16th century
**Locale(s):** Old World, Europe; Alternate Earth

**Summary:** Detlef Sierek is released from debtor's prison to produce a play celebrating Crown Prince Oswald's victory over the undead sorcerer Drachenfels. The production is threatened by both plots and sorcery as the playwright begins to uncover the truth about the ''glorious past.''

**Other books you might like:**
Steven Brust, *Jhereg*, 1983
Glen Cook, *Sweet Silver Blues*, 1987
Barry Hughart, *Bridge of Birds*, 1984
Tim Powers, *The Stress of Her Regard*, 1989
Howard Waldrop, *Night of the Cooters*, 1990

## 6023

**JACK YEOVIL** (Pseudonym of Kim Newman)

### Krokodil Tears

(Baltimore, Maryland: GW Books/Games Workshop, 1990)

**Story type:** Fantasy (Adventure)
**Series:** Dark Future: Demon Download Cycle
**Major character(s):** Jessamyn ''Krokodil'' Bonney, Leader (juvenile gang); Ottoken Proctor, Economist, Criminal (psychopathic killer); Hawk-That-Settles, Indian, Religious (spiritual advisor)
**Time period(s):** 1990s (1997-1998)
**Locale(s):** Salt Lake City, Utah; Gila Desert, Arizona (Monastery of Santa de Nogueria)

**Summary:** Former juvenile gang member Jessamyn Bonney is nearly killed in an attack on Elder Nguyen Seth's convoy to Salt Lake City. Transformed by extensive biomechanical surgery and fusion with an extra-dimensional entity, she struggles against the Dark Ones in an attempt to prevent the Apocalypse.

**Other books you might like:**
Neil Jones, *Deathwing*, 1989
    David Pringle, co-editor
Alan Dean Foster, *Cyber Way*, 1990

## 6024

**LAURENCE YEP**

### Dragon Cauldron

(New York: HarperCollins, 1991)

**Story type:** Fantasy (Quest; Adventure)
**Series:** Dragon of the Lost Sea
**Major character(s):** Shimmer, Royalty, Mythical Creature (dragon); Civet, Witch; Monkey, Wizard, Mythical Creature
**Time period(s):** Indeterminate Past
**Locale(s):** Desolate Mountains, Mythical Place

**Summary:** Trying for years to restore the stolen Inland Sea so that dragons may return, Shimmer sees hope for her quest's success now that Civet has repented for stealing the sea. To succeed, Shimmer must repair the Dragon cauldron with the help of Snail Woman and Smith.

**Other books you might like:**
Ursula K. Le Guin, *The Farthest Shore*, 1972
Ursula K. Le Guin, *The Tombs of Atuan*, 1971
Ursula K. Le Guin, *A Wizard of Earthsea*, 1968

Andre Norton, *The Elvenbane*, 1991
    Mercedes Lackey, co-author
J.R.R. Tolkien, *The Fellowship of the Ring*, 1954
J.R.R. Tolkien, *The Hobbit*, 1938
Patricia C. Wrede, *Searching for Dragons*, 1991

## 6025

**LAURENCE YEP**

### Dragon War

(New York: HarperCollins, 1992)

**Story type:** Fantasy (Adventure; Quest)
**Series:** Dragon of the Lost Sea
**Major character(s):** Shimmer, Royalty (princess of the Inland Sea), Mythical Creature (dragon); Monkey, Wizard, Mythical Creature (Chinese); Indigo, Adventurer
**Time period(s):** Indeterminate Past
**Locale(s):** Egg Mountain, Mythical Place; Ramsgate, Fictional City

**Summary:** Shimmer, Monkey and Indigo escape from Egg Mountain then journey to Ramsgate to recover the Dragon Cauldron and Thorn, the child imprisoned within. They hope to defeat the Boneless King then restore the Inland Sea, the dragons' stolen home.

**Other books you might like:**
Karen Brush, *Demon Pig*, 1991
Ursula K. Le Guin, *The Farthest Shore*, 1972
Ursula K. Le Guin, *Tehanu: The Last Book of Earthsea*, 1990
Ursula K. Le Guin, *The Tombs of Atuan*, 1971
Ursula K. Le Guin, *A Wizard of Earthsea*, 1968
Sherwood Smith, *Wren to the Rescue*, 1990
Patricia C. Wrede, *Searching for Dragons*, 1991

## 6026

**LAURENCE YEP**

### Tongues of Jade

(New York: HarperCollins, 1991)

**Story type:** Fantasy (Collection; Young Adult)
**Time period(s):** Indeterminate Past
**Locale(s):** China

**Summary:** From the oral tradition which preserved Chinese thought among those living away from China, Jon Lee collected and translated 69 stories from immigrants in Oakland's Chinatown during a 1930s WPA project, later supplemented by Professor Wolfram Eberhard's collecting more stories in San Francisco's Chinatown. Herein Yep presents 17 stories grouped with an introduction into themes titled ''Roots,'' ''Family Ties,'' ''The Wild Heart,'' ''Face'' and ''Beyond the Grave,'' incorporating magic, mythical spirits, mystery and whimsy into tales insightful of Chinese ideals. This companion volume to *The Rainbow People* includes an introduction and afterword with bibliography.

**Other books you might like:**
Wolfram Eberhard, *Folktales of China*, 1965
Barry Hughart, *Bridge of Birds*, 1984
Karl S.Y. Kao, *Classical Chinese Tales of the Supernatural and the Fantastic*, 1985
Jeanne Larsen, *Bronze Mirror*, 1991
Ernest Bramah Smith, *Kai Lung Unrolls His Mat*, 1923
    written as Ernest Bramah
Ernest Bramah Smith, *Kai Lung's Golden Hours*, 1928
    written as Ernest Bramah

## 6027

**JANE YOLEN**, Editor

### 2041: Twelve Short Stories about the Future by Top Science Fiction Writers

(New York: Delacorte Press, 1991)

**Story type:** Science Fiction (Anthology; Young Adult)
**Time period(s):** 2040s (2041)

**Summary:** This thematic anthology looks at the world of 2041 and contains 10 stories original to this title plus two stories previously published in periodicals including Peg Kerr's "Free Day," revised herein and Connie Willis' retitled "Much Ado About (Censored)." Other significant stories include Nancy Springer's "Who's Gonna Rock Us Home?," Anne McCaffrey's "A Quiet One," Patricia A. McKillip's "Moby James," Joe Haldeman's "If I Had the Wings of an Angel," Kara Dalkey's "You Want It When?," Jane Yolen's "Ear" and Susan Shwartz's "Beggarman."

**Other books you might like:**
Lester Del Rey, *The Year After Tomorrow: An Anthology of Science Fiction Stories*, 1954
    Carl Cramer, co-editor
Harry Harrison, *Science Fiction Novellas*, 1975
    Willis E. McNelly, co-editor
Harry Harrison, *A Science Fiction Reader*, 1973
    Carol Pugner, co-editor
Bernard Hollister, *You and Science Fiction: A Humanistic Aproach to Tomorrow*, 1976
    editor
Cecile Matschatt, *Fiction Stories*, 1954
Joseph D. Olander, *School and Society Through Science Fiction*, 1974
    Martin H. Greenberg and Patricia Warrick, co-editors
Robert Silverberg, *Beyond Control*, 1972
    editor
Robert Silverberg, *Earth Is the Strangest Place*, 1977
    editor
Robert Silverberg, *The Science Fiction Hall of Fame, Volume 1*, 1970
    editor

## 6028

**JANE YOLEN**
**BRUCE COVILLE**, Co-Author

### Armageddon Summer

(New York: Harcourt Brace, 1998)

**Story type:** Science Fiction (Young Adult; End of the World)
**Major character(s):** Marina, Teenager; Jed, Teenager; Raymond Beelson, Religious (reverend)
**Time period(s):** 2000s (2000)
**Locale(s):** Mount Weeupcutt, Massachusetts

**Summary:** Jed and Marina are two teenagers whose parents belong to a millennial cult run by Reverend Beelson. The Reverend believes that the world is going to end in the year 2000, and he leads his followers to a remote mountaintop, where they stock up on supplies and weapons to await the end of the world. Jed and Marina are among those who aren't there voluntarily and don't believe in the imminent apocalypse, and are more afraid of a confrontation with the police.

**Other books you might like:**
Dorothy Bryant, *The Kin of Ata Are Waiting for You*, 1976

Taylor Caldwell, *Your Sins and Mine*, 1955
Edmund Cooper, *All Fool's Day*, 1966
Mick Farren, *The Armageddon Crazy*, 1989
Elizabeth Hand, *Glimmering*, 1997

## 6029

**JANE YOLEN**

### Briar Rose

(New York: Tor, 1992)

**Story type:** Fantasy (Legend; Quest)
**Major character(s):** Rebecca "Becca", Journalist, Traveler; Gemma Rose Mandlestein, Grandparent (Becca's)
**Time period(s):** 1990s
**Locale(s):** United States; Poland

**Summary:** Gemma never spoke about herself to her grandchildren, repeatedly retelling the story of Briar Rose which she called "Seepin Boot" instead. After Gemma's deathbed confession to Becca that, "I am Briar Rose," Becca sets out to discover Gemma's life story, guided by the story of "Seepin Boot" to the horrors of World War II Nazi genocide. A retelling of "Sleeping Beauty."

**Other books you might like:**
Martin Amis, *Time's Arrow*, 1991
Janet Gluckman, *Child of the Light*, 1992
    George Guthridge, co-author
Kurt Vonnegut Jr., *Slaughterhouse Five*, 1969

## 6030

**JANE YOLEN**

### The Dragon's Boy

(New York: Harper and Row, 1990)

**Story type:** Fantasy (Legend; Young Adult)
**Major character(s):** Artos, Foundling; Sir Ector, Knight; Cai Youngman, Nobleman (Sir Ector's Son)
**Time period(s):** Indeterminate Past (Medieval)
**Locale(s):** England

**Summary:** Artos stumbles across a dragon's lair and becomes its unwilling student. Artos uses a jewel the dragon gives him to have a sword made, and with it he is finally accepted as one of the young men.

**Other books you might like:**
Barbara Ninde Byfield, *Andrew and the Alchemist*, 1977
Grace Chetwin, *Gom on Windy Mountain*, 1986
Grace Chetwin, *The Riddle and the Rune*, 1987
Peter Dickinson, *Merlin Dreams*, 1988
Susan Fletcher, *Dragon's Milk*, 1989

## 6031

**JANE YOLEN**

### Here There Be Angels

(New York: Harcourt Brace, 1996)

**Story type:** Fantasy (Collection; Religious)

**Summary:** Contains individual introductions with 11 stories and nine poems, 16 original and four reprinted from periodicals and anthologies 1974-1983. Frequently light in tone, the work explores miracles and transformations via angels from various traditions in contemporary and fantasy settings.

**Other books you might like:**

Peter Crowther, *Heaven Sent: 18 Glorious Tales of the Angels*, 1995
  Martin H. Greenberg, co-editor
Jack Dann, *Angels!*, 1995
  Gardner Dozois, co-editor
Neil Gaiman, *Good Omens: The Nice and Accurate Prophecies of Agnes Nutter, Witch*, 1990
  Terry Pratchett, co-author
Alan Ryan, *Perpetual Light*, 1982
  editor
Pamela Sargent, *Afterlives: An Anthology of Stories about Life After Death*, 1986
  Ian Watson, co-editor

### 6032

#### JANE YOLEN

## Here There Be Dragons

(New York: Harcourt Brace, 1993)

**Story type:** Fantasy (Collection; Young Adult)

**Summary:** Contains two reprinted and 11 original stories and poems with a broad range of themes concerning dragons. Stories encompass a variety of literary traditions including Arthurian, Chinese and classic fairy tale and a tale of Saint George and the Dragon.

**Other books you might like:**

Orson Scott Card, *Dragons of Darkness*, 1981
  editor
Orson Scott Card, *Dragons of Light*, 1980
  editor
Ellen Datlow, *The Year's Best Fantasy and Horror Series*, 1989-
  Terri Windling, co-editor
James Gurney, *Dinotopia*, 1992
Ursula K. Le Guin, *A Wizard of Earthsea*, 1968
Patricia C. Wrede, *Dealing with Dragons*, 1990
Roger Zelazny, *Here There Be Dragons*, 1992

### 6033

#### JANE YOLEN

## Here There Be Unicorns

(New York: Harcourt Brace, 1994)

**Story type:** Fantasy (Collection; Legend)

**Summary:** Contains individual introductions to 10 short stories and eight poems, 15 of them original and three reprinted from periodicals and anthologies. Settings range from medieval to contemporary in stories which examine many unicorn myths and speculations, with tone ranging from ominous to light.

**Other books you might like:**

Bruce Coville, *The Unicorn Treasury*, 1988
  editor
Jack Dann, *Unicorns!*, 1982
  Gardner Dozois, co-editor
Jack Dann, *Unicorns II*, 1992
  Gardner Dozois, co-editor
Pamela Dean, *The Secret Country*, 1985
Tanith Lee, *Black Unicorn*, 1991

### 6034

#### JANE YOLEN

## Here There Be Witches

(New York: Harcourt Brace, 1995)

**Story type:** Fantasy (Collection)

**Summary:** Yolen individually introduces seven poems and 10 stories published 1977-1995 in periodicals, anthologies, and collections. The stories focus on diverse aspects of witches. The settings vary from ancient and fantastic to more contemporary, generally employing a strong sense of wonder while avoiding a darker tone. Themes include modern as well as traditional fairy tale topics.

**Other books you might like:**

Peter Haining, *A Circle of Witches*, 1971
  editor
Byron Preiss, *The Ultimate Witch*, 1993
  John Betancourt, co-editor
Mike Resnick, *Witch Fantastic*, 1995
  Martin H. Greenberg, co-editor
Susan Shwartz, *Hecate's Cauldron*, 1985

### 6035

#### JANE YOLEN

## Merlin

(New York: Harcourt Brace & Company, 1997)

**Story type:** Fantasy (Legend; Young Adult)
**Series:** Young Merlin Trilogy
**Major character(s):** Merlin, Child, Orphan; Hawk-Hobby, Teenager
**Time period(s):** Indeterminate Past
**Locale(s):** England

**Summary:** While accompanying a group of misfits and outcasts, Merlin begins to discover his magical abilities. At the same time, his dreams of the future distress his acquaintances. Concludes the trilogy.

**Other books you might like:**

T.A. Barron, *The Merlin Effect*, 1994
Ann Curry, *The Book of Brendan*, 1990
Anne McCaffrey, *Black Horses for the King*, 1996
Mark Twain, *A Connecticut Yankee in King Arthur's Court*, 1889
T.H. White, *The Sword in the Stone*, 1939

### 6036

#### JANE YOLEN

## Merlin and the Dragons

(New York: Dutton Cobbhill, 1995)

**Story type:** Fantasy (Young Adult; Legend)
**Major character(s):** Arthur Pendragon, Royalty; Merlin, Magician; Emrys, Psychic
**Time period(s):** 5th century
**Locale(s):** England

**Summary:** When dreams disturb young Arthur's sleep, Merlin weaves the heroic tale of Uther Pendragon's rise to power and the battle of the dragons that occurs after warriors free two of the sleeping beasts.

**Other books you might like:**

Susan Cooper, *Over Sea, under Stone*, 1965

Michael Hague, *The Book of Dragons*, 1995
  editor
Ursula K. Le Guin, *A Wizard of Earthsea*, 1968
David Worsick, *Henry's Gift: The Magic Eye*, 1994
Roger Zelazny, *Here There Be Dragons*, 1992

### 6037
#### JANE YOLEN

## *The One-Armed Queen*
(New York: Tor, 1998)

**Story type:** Fantasy (Political; Adventure)
**Series:** Chronicles of Great Alta
**Major character(s):** Jenna, Ruler (queen), Warrior; Scillia, Orphan, Heiress; Jemson "Jem", Royalty (prince)
**Time period(s):** Indeterminate
**Locale(s):** the Dales, Fictional Country

**Summary:** When Jenna designates her adopted daughter, Scillia, heir to the throne of the matriarchial Dales, enemies take the opportunity to recruit Jem into their subversive plots. As Scillia grows older, her discovery of old secrets distances her from her adoptive mother.

**Other books you might like:**
Geraldine Harris, *Prince of the Godborn*, 1983
Diana Wynne Jones, *Cart and Cwidder*, 1977
Ursula K. Le Guin, *A Wizard of Earthsea*, 1968
Robin McKinley, *The Hero and the Crown*, 1985
Philip Pullman, *The Golden Compass*, 1996

### 6038
#### JANE YOLEN

## *Passager*
(New York: Harcourt Brace, 1996)

**Story type:** Fantasy (Legend)
**Series:** Young Merlin Trilogy
**Major character(s):** Merlin, Child; Robin, Hunter (falconer), Step-Parent
**Time period(s):** Indeterminate Past
**Locale(s):** England

**Summary:** Abandoned by his mother, Merlin grows up feral until he follows Master Robin home, where he begins to learn language and civilized manners and discovers his true name. Expanded from "The Wild Child," published in *Merlin's Booke*.

**Other books you might like:**
T.A. Barron, *The Merlin Effect*, 1994
Ann Curry, *The Book of Brendan*, 1990
Peter Dickinson, *Heartsease*, 1969
Anne McCaffrey, *Black Horses for the King*, 1996
Mark Twain, *A Connecticut Yankee in King Arthur's Court*, 1889
T.H. White, *The Sword in the Stone*, 1939

### 6039
#### JANE YOLEN

## *Sister Light, Sister Dark*
(New York: Tor, 1988)

**Story type:** Fantasy (Adventure)
**Major character(s):** Jenna, Orphan, Heroine
**Time period(s):** Indeterminate

**Locale(s):** Alternate Universe

**Summary:** Jenna is raised in a hame, a self-sufficient commune of women, after she has been orphaned three times in infancy. She soon realizes that the circumstances of her birth have been foretold by a prophecy.

**Other books you might like:**
Elise Guttenberg, *Sunder, Eclipse and Seed*, 1990
R.A. MacAvoy, *Lens of the World*, 1990

### 6040
#### JANE YOLEN

## *Twelve Impossible Things Before Breakfast*
(New York: Harcourt Brace, 1997)

**Story type:** Fantasy (Collection; Young Adult)

**Summary:** Contains a five-page introduction, 11-page afterword, three original and nine stories reprinted from anthologies 1989-1996. Frequently light or ironic in tone, the stories feature twists on familiar themes and fairy tales such as mythical creatures, extraterrestrials, ants that steal babies, a bridge in need of a goat-eating troll, an Alice hardened by her stay in Wonderland and a rebellion of Peter Pan's followers.

### 6041
#### JANE YOLEN

## *White Jenna*
(New York: Tor, 1989)

**Story type:** Fantasy (Adventure)
**Major character(s):** Jenna, Orphan, Heroine
**Time period(s):** Indeterminate
**Locale(s):** Alternate Universe

**Summary:** In this sequel to *Sister Light, Sister Dark*, Jenna starts down the path which will destroy the old way of the hames, and herald a new age.

**Other books you might like:**
Lynn Abbey, *Unicorn and Dragon*, 1985
Marion Zimmer Bradley, *Web of Darkness*, 1983
Phyllis Ann Karr, *Frostflower and Thorn*, 1980

### 6042
#### JANE YOLEN

## *The Wild Hunt*
(New York: Harcourt Brace, 1995)

**Story type:** Fantasy (Quest; Magic Conflict)
**Major character(s):** Jerod, Child; Gerund, Child; The Cat, Animal
**Time period(s):** Indeterminate

**Summary:** The Horned Man's scheming transcends the boundary between realities, drawing Jerod and Gerund into his chronic attempt to corrupt the innocent and find a way to win the obedience and loyalty of his wife.

**Other books you might like:**
Lloyd Alexander, *The High King*, 1968
Louise Cooper, *The Sleep of Stone*, 1991
Susan Dexter, *The Wizard's Shadow*, 1993
Patricia A. McKillip, *The Book of Atrix Wolfe*, 1995
Pat O'Shea, *The Hounds of the Morrigan*, 1986

## 6043

**JANE YOLEN**

### *Wizard's Hall*

(New York: Harcourt Brace Jovanovich, 1991)

**Story type:** Fantasy (Magic Conflict; Young Adult)
**Major character(s):** Henry "Thornmallow", Student; Gorse, Student; Magister Hickory, Wizard, Teacher
**Time period(s):** Indeterminate
**Locale(s):** Wizard's Hall, Mythical Place (School)

**Summary:** When Henry mentions a minor interest in Wizardry, his mother immediately sends him to Wizard's Hall with the advice that he needn't succeed, it only matters that he try. His first few days at school prove so difficult that Henry, renamed "Thornmallow," wants to leave but is talked into staying by his magisters who see his presence as necessary to defeat their nemesis, a former magister at Wizard's Hall. Thornmallow soon discovers his efforts rewarded in the overthrow of the evil magister and his terrible quilted beast.

**Other books you might like:**
Debra Doyle, *School of Wizardry*, 1990
    James D. Macdonald, co-author
Diana Wynne Jones, *Castle in the Air*, 1991
Andrea Shettle, *Flute Song Magic*, 1990
Sherwood Smith, *Wren to the Rescue*, 1990
Mary Frances Zambreno, *A Plague of Sorcerers*, 1991

## 6044

**JANE YOLEN**, Editor

### *Xanadu*

(New York: Tor, 1993)

**Story type:** Fantasy (Anthology)
**Series:** Xanadu

**Summary:** First in a new anthology series of original stories and poems with a two-page introduction by Yolen, five pages "About the Authors" and four poems by Steven Brust, Pat Schneider, Donna J. Waidtlow and Jane Yolen. The 18 stories range in tone from euphoric to sinister by authors who include Eleanor Arnason, Gardner Dozois, Esther Friesner, Patrick Nielsen Hayden, Nancy Kress, Ursula K. Le Guin, Tanith Lee, Elise Matthesen, John Morressy, Mike Resnick and Will Shetterly.

**Other books you might like:**
Ellen Datlow, *Snow White, Blood Red*, 1993
    Terri Windling, co-editor
Ellen Datlow, *The Year's Best Fantasy and Horror Series*, 1989-
    Terri Windling, co-editor
Ellen Datlow, *The Year's Best Fantasy: First Annual Collection*, 1988
    Terri Windling, co-editor
Lester Del Rey, *Once upon a Time: A Treasury of Modern Fairy Tales*, 1991
    Risa Kessler, co-editor
Martin H. Greenberg, *After the King: Stories in Honor of J.R.R. Tolkien*, 1992
    editor
Kristine Kathryn Rusch, *Pulphouse, Issue 6: Fantasy*, 1990
    editor
Terri Windling, *Life on the Border*, 1991
    editor

## 6045

**JANE YOLEN**, Editor

### *Xanadu 2*

(New York: Tor, 1994)

**Story type:** Fantasy (Anthology)
**Series:** Xanadu

**Summary:** Contains a two-page introduction, seven pages of biographical sketches of the authors, seven original poems and 19 original stories with tone varying from humorous to dark and themes such as sword and sorcery, reincarnation, twists on classic fairy tales, dragons, elves and magical cats. Authors include Diane Duane, Barbara Hambly, Tappan King, Ursula K. Le Guin, Megan Lindholm, Patricia A. McKillip, Jessica Amanda Salmonson, Delia Sherman, Will Shetterly, Martha Soukup, Vivian Vande Velde, Terri Windling and Jane Yolen.

**Other books you might like:**
Ellen Datlow, *Black Thorn, White Rose*, 1994
    Terry Windling, co-editor
Ellen Datlow, *Snow White, Blood Red*, 1993
    Terry Windling co-editor
Lester Del Rey, *Once upon a Time: A Treasury of Modern Fairy Tales*, 1991
    Risa Kessler, co-editor
Kristine Kathryn Rusch, *The Best of Pulphouse: The Hardback Magazine*, 1991
    editor
Terri Windling, *Life on the Border*, 1991
    editor

## 6046

**JANE YOLEN**, Editor

### *Xanadu 3*

(New York: Tor, 1995)

**Story type:** Fantasy (Anthology)
**Series:** Xanadu

**Summary:** This volume of original work contains a two-page introduction, a nine-page section "About the Authors," 11 poems, and 25 stories utilizing diverse themes, many with a feminist bent. Although occasionally light in tone, the selections are frequently somber. Authors include Ruth Berman, Jo Clayton, Mark A. Garland, Tanith Lee, Elise Matthesen, Susan Palwick, Josepha Sherman, Midori Snyder, Laurie Aylma Taylor, Terri Windling, and Jane Yolen.

**Other books you might like:**
Marion Zimmer Bradley, *The Best of Marion Zimmer Bradley's Fantasy Magazine*, 1994
    editor
Ellen Datlow, *Black Thorn, White Rose*, 1994
    Terri Windling, co-editor
Ellen Datlow, *Snow White, Blood Red*, 1993
    Terri Windling, co-editor
Lester Del Rey, *Once upon a Time: A Treasury of Modern Fairy Tales*, 1991
    Risa Kessler, co-editor
David G. Hartwell, *Masterpieces of Fantasy and Wonder*, 1994
    editor

## 6047

### JANINE ELLEN YOUNG

## *Cinderblock*

(New York: Roc, 1997)

**Story type:** Science Fiction (Cyberpunk; Post-Disaster)
**Major character(s):** Alexander "Sander" Kitatimate, Prisoner, Computer Expert; Urban Myth, Computer Expert, Robot; Hawthorn "D-base", Artificial Intelligence
**Time period(s):** Indeterminate Future
**Locale(s):** Cyberspace

**Summary:** Imprisoned since birth by his uncle Hawthorne, Alexander meets Urban, who helps him escape with Cinderblock. Hawthorne works to corrupt young college students while Cinderblock and her crew of assistants attempt to destroy him. First novel.

**Other books you might like:**
Tom Cool, *Infectress*, 1997
Neal Stephenson, *Snow Crash*, 1992
Sheri S. Tepper, *A Plague of Angels*, 1993
Michael D. Weaver, *A Second Infinity*, 1996
Walter Jon Williams, *Hardwired*, 1986

## 6048

### JIM YOUNG

## *Armed Memory*

(New York: Tor, 1995)

**Story type:** Science Fiction (Genetic Manipulation; Alternate Intelligence)
**Major character(s):** Timothy J. Wandel, Genetically Altered Being; Nils Ullrich, Genetically Altered Being (hammerhead shark); Johnny Sanders, Inventor, Artist
**Time period(s):** 21st century
**Locale(s):** New York, New York; Minneapolis, Minnesota

**Summary:** Arriving in a New York City where the criminal hammerheads prey on the populace, Timothy accepts a job with his cousin, Johnny Sanders. Inventor of the microding process which genetically alters people, Sanders plans to solve the problem of the hammerheads who stole his technique, who kidnap recruits, and who ultimately intend to eliminate life on land.

**Other books you might like:**
Wilhelmina Baird, *Clipjoint*, 1994
Octavia E. Butler, *Dawn*, 1987
Thomas A. Easton, *Sparrowhawk*, 1990
S. Andrew Swann, *Emperors of the Twilight*, 1994
S. Andrew Swann, *Forests of the Night*, 1993
George R.R. Martin, *Wild Cards*, 1987
   editor

## 6049

### ROY V. YOUNG

## *Captains Outrageous, or, For Doom the Bell Tolls*

(Lake Geneva, Wisconsin: TSR, 1994)

**Story type:** Fantasy (Light Fantasy; Quest)
**Major character(s):** Yor, Warrior, Adventurer; Dword Ecklundson, Minstrel (loremaster), Warrior; Trebor Blackburn, Warrior, Adventurer

**Time period(s):** Indeterminate
**Locale(s):** Leiblein, Planet—Imaginary

**Summary:** Yor, Dword and Trebor must stop the mad wizard, Bosamp, from using the Mallet of Doom on the Bell at the Top of the World or all Leiblein could suffer disaster. First novel.

**Other books you might like:**
Piers Anthony, *A Spell for Chameleon*, 1977
K.B. Bogen, *Go Quest, Young Man*, 1994
Gordon R. Dickson, *The Dragon and the George*, 1976
Neil Gaiman, *Good Omens: The Nice and Accurate Prophecies of Agnes Nutter, Witch*, 1990
   Terry Pratchett, co-author
John Moore, *Slay and Rescue*, 1993

## 6050

### FAY ZACHARY

## *Blood Work*

(New York: Berkley, 1994)

**Story type:** Horror (Psychological Suspense)
**Major character(s):** Liz Broward, Doctor; Zack James, Computer Expert, Artist; Phillip Trapp, Technician (laboratory)
**Time period(s):** 1990s (1994)
**Locale(s):** Philadelphia, Pennsylvania

**Summary:** Under the impression that people with the blood disease porphyria are actually vampires, loony Phillip Trapp, whose obsessions trace back to a childhood incident involving mock vampires at a carnival sideshow, sets about systematically killing porphyria victims at the local hospital.

**Other books you might like:**
Peter Atkins, *Morningstar*, 1992
Barbara Hambly, *Those Who Hunt the Night*, 1987
Roxanne Longstreet, *The Undead*, 1993
Kim Newman, *Bad Dreams*, 1990

## 6051

### TIMOTHY ZAHN

## *Conqueror's Pride*

(New York: Bantam Spectra, 1994)

**Story type:** Science Fiction (Space Opera; First Contact)
**Major character(s):** Pheylan Cavanagh, Spaceship Captain; Stewart Cavanagh, Businessman, Political Figure; Adam Quinn, Security Officer
**Time period(s):** Indeterminate Future
**Locale(s):** Interstellar Empire/Federation; Mra-mig, Planet—Imaginary

**Summary:** Four alien starships destroy a Peacekeeper task force. While Pheylan Cavanagh, the sole survivor, attempts to free himself from his alien captors, his family assembles a rescue force, in defiance of Commonwealth security restrictions and in spite of a curious reluctance on the part of the Mrachi members of the Commonwealth to share information on a mystery race they call the Conquerors.

**Other books you might like:**
Margaret Wander Bonanno, *Dwellers in the Crucible*, 1985
David Brin, *Startide Rising*, 1983
Orson Scott Card, *Ender's Game*, 1985
C.J. Cherryh, *Brothers of the Earth*, 1976
Gordon R. Dickson, *The Forever Man*, 1986

## 6052

**TIMOTHY ZAHN**

### *Dark Force Rising*

(New York: Bantam Spectra, 1992)

**Story type:** Science Fiction (Space Opera; Psychic Powers)
**Series:** Star Wars
**Major character(s):** Leia Organa, Royalty (princess), Diplomat; Luke Skywalker, Martial Arts Expert (Jedi Knight), Hero; Joruus C'boath, Psychic (Jedi Master)
**Time period(s):** Indeterminate Past
**Locale(s):** Coruscant, Planet—Imaginary; *Chimaera*, Spaceship (Imperial Flagship)

**Summary:** Battles between the Old Empire and the Rebel Alliance (New Republic) continue as Grand Admiral Thrawn depends on his secret informer, Delta Source, to keep abreast of the movements of Luke, Leia, Han and the Rebellion. Luke faces the Dark Side of the Force while Leia negotiates with the deadly Moghri despite the risk to her unborn twins and herself. Han tries to uncover the identity of Delta Source and finds himself again battling Imperial forces.

**Other books you might like:**
Allan Cole, *Sten*, 1984
   Chris Bunch, co-author
Brian Daley, *Han Solo and the Lost Legacy*, 1980
Brian Daley, *Han Solo at Star's End*, 1979
Brian Daley, *Han Solo's Revenge*, 1979
Alan Dean Foster, *Splinter of the Mind's Eye*, 1978
Donald F. Glut, *The Empire Strikes Back*, 1980
Frank Herbert, *Dune*, 1965
James Kahn, *Return of the Jedi*, 1983
George Lucas, *Star Wars*, 1976
L. Neil Smith, *Lando Calrissian and the Flamewind of Oseon*, 1983
L. Neil Smith, *Lando Calrissian and the Mindharp of Sharu*, 1983
L. Neil Smith, *Lando Calrissian and the Starcave of Thon Boka*, 1983
Helen S. Wright, *A Matter of Oaths*, 1990

## 6053

**TIMOTHY ZAHN**

### *Distant Friends and Others*

(New York: Baen, 1992)

**Story type:** Science Fiction (Collection; Psychic Powers)
**Time period(s):** Indeterminate Future
**Locale(s):** United States

**Summary:** The first three stories in this collection combine to form the short novel, "Distant Friends," in which telepaths cannot tolerate physical proximity to each other. The remaining six unconnected stories appeared in 1980s periodicals.

**Other books you might like:**
Marion Zimmer Bradley, *The Firebrand*, 1987
Karen Haber, *The Mutant Season*, 1990
   Robert Silverberg, co-author
Henry Kuttner, *Mutant*, 1953
Anne McCaffrey, *Damia*, 1992
Anne McCaffrey, *The Rowan*, 1990
Joan D. Vinge, *Psion*, 1982

## 6054

**TIMOTHY ZAHN**

### *Heir to the Empire*

(New York: Bantam Spectra, 1991)

**Story type:** Science Fiction (Space Opera)
**Series:** Star Wars
**Major character(s):** Luke Skywalker, Martial Arts Expert, Hero; Leia Organa Solo, Administrator, Royalty; Han Solo, Spaceship Captain, Warrior
**Time period(s):** Indeterminate
**Locale(s):** Coruscant, Planet—Imaginary; Outer Space

**Summary:** Five years after the death of Darth Vader, Princess Leia and Han are expecting twins; Luke is reorganizing the Jedi Knights, who have discovered that governing the New Republic is more work than they had expected. Meanwhile, unknown to anyone in the new government, the last remnants of the Imperial Fleet under Admiral Thrawn are preparing to destroy the New Republic, to them the Rebellion.

**Other books you might like:**
Allan Cole, *Sten*, 1984
   Chris Bunch, co-author
Brian Daley, *Han Solo and the Lost Legacy*, 1980
Brian Daley, *Han Solo at Star's End*, 1979
Brian Daley, *Han Solo's Revenge*, 1979
Alan Dean Foster, *Splinter of the Mind's Eye*, 1978
Donald F. Glut, *The Empire Strikes Back*, 1980
James Kahn, *Return of the Jedi*, 1983
George Lucas, *Star Wars*, 1976
L. Neil Smith, *Lando Calrissian and the Flamewind of Oseon*, 1983
L. Neil Smith, *Lando Calrissian and the Mindharp of Sharu*, 1983
L. Neil Smith, *Lando Calrissian and the Starcave of Thon Boka*, 1983

## 6055

**TIMOTHY ZAHN**

### *The Last Command*

(New York: Bantam Spectra, 1993)

**Story type:** Science Fiction (Space Opera; Psychic Powers)
**Series:** Star Wars
**Major character(s):** Luke Skywalker, Martial Arts Expert (Jedi Knight), Hero; Leia Organa Solo, Royalty, Leader; Thrawn, Military Personnel, Leader
**Time period(s):** Indeterminate Past
**Locale(s):** *Wild Karrde*, Spaceship; New Republic, Interstellar Empire/Federation; Outer Space

**Summary:** When Grand Admiral Thrawn rallies surviving Imperial forces and constructs a clone army with which to attack the Alliance, Leia leads the Alliance resistance to Thrawn's siege. Han Solo and Chewbacca attempt to organize smugglers while Luke leads a small force determined to destroy Thrawn's cloning machines. Occurs five years after events of *Return of the Jedi* (1983) and concludes Zahn's trilogy.

**Other books you might like:**
Brian Daley, *The Han Solo Adventures*, 1992
Paul Davids, *The Glove of Darth Vader*, 1992
Alan Dean Foster, *Splinter of the Mind's Eye*, 1978
George Lucas, *The Star Wars Trilogy*, 1987
   Donald F. Glut, James Kahn, co-authors
L. Neil Smith, *Lando Calrissian and the Flamewind of Oseon*, 1983
L. Neil Smith, *Lando Calrissian and the Mindharp of Sharu*, 1983

L. Neil Smith, *Lando Calrissian and the Starcave of Thon Boka*, 1983

Kathy Tyers, *The Truce at Bakura*, 1994

## 6056

### TIMOTHY ZAHN

## *Warhorse*

(New York: Baen Books, 1990)

**Story type:** Science Fiction (First Contact)
**Major character(s):** Haml Roman, Spaceship Captain; Chayne Ferrol, Spaceman
**Time period(s):** Indeterminate Future
**Locale(s):** *C.S.S. Dryden*, Spaceship; Kialinninni Alpha, Planet—Imaginary

**Summary:** Humanity's expanding sphere of exploration brings us into conflict with the Tampies, a species who consider themselves the guardians of all life and who have developed bioscience to the point where they can actually create living spaceships and weapons. War between our species and theirs seems imminent.

**Other books you might like:**
Gregory Benford, *Tides of Light*, 1989
David Brin, *Startide Rising*, 1983
Thorarinn Gunnarsson, *Battle of the Ring*, 1989
    Starwolves 2
Jack Vance, *The Dragon Masters*, 1963

## 6057

### MARY FRANCES ZAMBRENO

## *Journeyman Wizard*

(New York: Harcourt Brace, 1994)

**Story type:** Fantasy (Young Adult; Mystery)
**Major character(s):** Jermyn Graves, Wizard, Detective—Amateur; Delia, Animal (skunk), Companion (wizard's familiar); Brianne Campbell, Teenager, Healer
**Time period(s):** Indeterminate
**Locale(s):** Land's End, Fictional City

**Summary:** When Jermyn goes to study magic under Lady Jean Allons, he must defend himself against accusations of murder and discover the real killer.

**Other books you might like:**
Debra Doyle, *School of Wizardry*, 1990
    James D. Macdonald, co-author
Caroline Stevermer, *A College of Magics*, 1994
Robyn Tallis, *Children of the Storm*, 1989
    pseudonym of Mary Frances Zambreno
Patricia C. Wrede, *The Raven Ring*, 1994
Jane Yolen, *Wizard's Hall*, 1991

## 6058

### MARY FRANCES ZAMBRENO

## *A Plague of Sorcerers*

(New York: Harcourt Brace Jovanovich, 1991)

**Story type:** Fantasy (Magic Conflict; Young Adult)
**Major character(s):** Jermyn Graves, Apprentice (wizard's); Delia, Animal (skunk), Companion (familiar); William Eschar, Wizard (master)

**Time period(s):** Indeterminate
**Locale(s):** Fictional Country

**Summary:** When Jermyn's aunt transfers apprenticeship of Jermyn and his not-too-welcome familiar to Master Eschar the Theoretician, Jermyn hopes his control over magic will improve. With study and practice he discovers that his magic skill increases, if slowly. When faced publicly with a dangerous test, Jermyn finally begins to harness his abilities, barely in time to help foil an attempt to seize political power and help cure a plague affecting magic users.

**Other books you might like:**
Stephen R. Donaldson, *The Illearth War*, 1977
Stephen R. Donaldson, *Lord Foul's Bane*, 1977
Stephen R. Donaldson, *The Power That Preserves*, 1977
Debra Doyle, *School of Wizardry*, 1990
    James D. Macdonald, co-author
Randall Garrett, *Too Many Magicians*, 1967
Sherwood Smith, *Wren to the Rescue*, 1990
Jane Yolen, *Wizard's Hall*, 1991

## 6059

### GEORGE ZEBROWSKI

## *Brute Orbits*

(New York: Harper Prism, 1998)

**Story type:** Science Fiction (Political; Space Colony)
**Major character(s):** Yevgeny Tasarov, Prisoner; Osokin, Prisoner
**Time period(s):** 21st century
**Locale(s):** Asteroid

**Summary:** In order to avoid having to deal with long-term prisoners, the government of Earth moves hardened criminals to a prison on an asteroid which will not approach the Earth again until their sentences have expired. Something goes wrong with the maintenance system, and the prisoners must take control of the asteroid and fashion their own society in order to survive.

**Other books you might like:**
Ben Bova, *Exiled From Earth*, 1971
William C. Dietz, *Prison Planet*, 1989
Tom Godwin, *Space Prison*, 1960
Barry B. Longyear, *Infinity Hold*, 1989
Mike McQuay, *Escape From New York*, 1981

## 6060

### GEORGE ZEBROWSKI

## *Stranger Suns*

(New York: Bantam Spectra, 1991)

**Story type:** Science Fiction (Alternate Universe; Future Shock)
**Major character(s):** Dr. Juan Obrion, Scientist (physicist); Dr. Lena Dravie, Scientist (biologist)
**Time period(s):** 22nd century (2100s)
**Locale(s):** U.N. Base, Montenegro; Antarctica; Spaceship (alien)

**Summary:** Dr. Juan Obrion and his friend Malachi Moede have just finished the tachyon detector. They hope to intercept alien messages, but do not detect any tachyons from space. Only Antarctica seems to be producing them, which doesn't make any sense. Hoping to discover the source of the tachyons they get permission to investigate with a U.N. team, Lena Dravie and Magnus Rasmussen. The spaceship they find buried is more interesting than they could have imagined.

**Other books you might like:**
Gregory Benford, *Timescape*, 1980

Philip K. Dick, *The Unteleported Man*, 1983
  revised
Alan Dean Foster, *Cat-A-Lyst*, 1991
Parke Godwin, *Waiting for the Galactic Bus*, 1988
Stephen Goldin, *Jade Darcy and the Zen Pirates*, 1990
  Mary Mason, co-author
Edward M. Lerner, *Probe*, 1991
Andre Norton, *Star Gate*, 1958
Clifford D. Simak, *Ring Around the Sun*, 1953

## 6061

### ANN TONSOR ZEDDIES

## *Deathgift*

(New York: Ballantine/Del Rey, 1989)

**Story type:** Science Fiction (Military)
**Major character(s):** Singer, Psychic, Musician; Janet Logan, Doctor
**Time period(s):** Indeterminate Future
**Locale(s):** New Hope, Planet—Imaginary

**Summary:** Singer, a talented psychic and musician raised by a primitive tribe of horsemen, finds himself in the middle of an intergalactic war. The author's first novel.

**Other books you might like:**
Lois McMaster Bujold, *The Warrior's Apprentice*, 1986
Rebecca Ore, *Becoming Alien*, 1987
Lucius Shepard, *Life During Wartime*, 1987
Lawrence Watt-Evans, *Denner's Wreck*, 1988
Dave Wolverton, *On My Way to Paradise*, 1989

## 6062

### ROGER ZELAZNY
### ROBERT SHECKLEY, Co-Author

## *Bring Me the Head of Prince Charming*

(New York: Bantam Spectra, 1991)

**Story type:** Fantasy (Light Fantasy; Legend)
**Series:** Millennial Contest
**Major character(s):** Azzie Elbub, Demon; Frike, Servant; Babriel, Angel
**Time period(s):** 10th century (999)
**Locale(s):** North Discomfort Pit 405, Hell; Augsburg, Switzerland; Glass Mountain Village, Mythical Place (Glass Mountain)

**Summary:** Serving as a pit boss in Hell to pay off a gambling debt, Azzie Elbub receives an opportunity to get back to Earth as an escort for a human mistakenly placed in Pit 405 before he was dead. When Azzie gets to Earth he realizes it is almost time for the millennial contest between the forces of good and evil, deciding which side will control human destiny for the coming millennium. He develops an idea, the recreation of Prince Charming and Sleeping Beauty in such a way that the forces of evil will win the contest. The Powers of Evil like his idea and give him a black credit card authorizing him for instant and unlimited credit with Infernal Supply.

**Other books you might like:**
Alan Dean Foster, *Quozl*, 1989
Alan Dean Foster, *To the Vanishing Point*, 1988
Neil Gaiman, *Good Omens: The Nice and Accurate Prophecies of Agnes Nutter, Witch*, 1990
  Terry Pratchett, co-author
Parke Godwin, *The Snake Oil Wars*, 1989
Robert Sheckley, *Dimension of Miracles*, 1968
Robert Sheckley, *Dramocles: An Intergalactic Soap Opera*, 1983

Robert Sheckley, *Options*, 1977
Donald E. Westlake, *Humans*, 1992
Patricia C. Wrede, *Snow White and Rose Red*, 1989

## 6063

### ROGER ZELAZNY
### JANE M. LINDSKOLD, Co-Author

## *Donnerjack*

(New York: Avon, 1997)

**Story type:** Science Fiction (Alternate Intelligence; Family Saga)
**Major character(s):** Death, Artificial Intelligence, Mythical Creature; John D'Arcy Donnerjack, Computer Expert; Aryadyss, Artificial Intelligence, Mythical Creature (banshee)
**Time period(s):** 22nd century
**Locale(s):** Deep Field, Cyberspace; Virtu, Cyberspace; Eilean a'Tempull Dubh, Scotland (Verite)

**Summary:** When Death takes Aryadyss, John realizes his true love belonged in Virtu and could never have come to Verite. Despite this understanding he decides to visit Death to bargain for her return. Death promises to return her in Verite, a seemingly impossible feat, if John will build a castle and give Death his firstborn. Since children cannot result from such a liaison, John feels free to make the bargin. However, after moving to their newly constructed castle, one of the ghosts warns that the banshee howls to warn of death for her family, including the baby. In Virtu, the old gods invent a religion and plot to move into Verite.

**Other books you might like:**
James C. Bassett, *Living Real*, 1997
Raphael Carter, *The Fortunate Fall*, 1996
Jane M. Lindskold, *Marks of Our Brothers*, 1995
Neal Stephenson, *Snow Crash*, 1992
Janine Ellen Young, *Cinderblock*, 1997

## 6064

### ROGER ZELAZNY
### ROBERT SHECKLEY, Co-Author

## *A Farce to Be Reckoned With*

(New York: Bantam Spectra, 1995)

**Story type:** Fantasy (Light Fantasy; Religious)
**Series:** Millennial Contest
**Major character(s):** Azzie Elbub, Demon; Pietro Aretino, Writer (poet and playwright)
**Time period(s):** 16th century
**Locale(s):** Europe; Realm of Darkness, Hell; Heaven

**Summary:** When Azzie discovers popular morality plays, he decides to write and produce an immorality play in which the participants magically achieve their hearts' desires. The event runs into difficulty when Heavenly forces hope to prevent the opening of the play and, on stage, characters begin to change their hearts' desires.

**Other books you might like:**
Neil Gaiman, *Good Omens: The Nice and Accurate Prophecies of Agnes Nutter, Witch*, 1990
  Terry Pratchett, co-author
Parke Godwin, *The Snake Oil Wars*, 1989
Parke Godwin, *Waiting for the Galactic Bus*, 1988
Robert Sheckley, *Journey Beyond Tomorrow*, 1962
Robert Sheckley, *Mindswap*, 1966

## **6065**

### ROGER ZELAZNY
### THOMAS T. THOMAS, Co-Author

### *Flare*

(New York: Baen, 1992)

**Story type:** Science Fiction (Hard Science Fiction; Disaster)
**Major character(s):** Hannibal Freede, Scientist (astronomer); Piero Mosca, Student (astronomer); Sultana Carr, Scientist (astronomer)
**Time period(s):** 2080s (2081)
**Locale(s):** Outer Space; Montenegro

**Summary:** This novel traces a solar flare from its inception as a quantum accident deep within the sun millions of years ago to its eruption as a flare in 2081 while examining human beliefs about Sol and human social development. Erroneous beliefs about the Sun's nature lead to disaster when the major flare finally appears after an 80-year hiatus in solar activity.

**Other books you might like:**
Roger MacBride Allen, *The Ring of Charon*, 1990
David Brin, *Earth*, 1990
David Brin, *Sundiver*, 1980
Paula E. Downing, *Flare Star*, 1992
Robert L. Forward, *Dragon's Egg*, 1980
Charles Sheffield, *The McAndrew Chronicles*, 1983
Allen Steele, *Orbital Decay*, 1989

## **6066**

### ROGER ZELAZNY, Editor

### *Forever After*

(New York: Baen, 1995)

**Story type:** Fantasy (Anthology; Quest)

**Summary:** Contains a three-page afterword by David Drake and preludes by Zelazny to four stories by Robert Lynn Asprin, David Drake, Jane Lindskold, and Michael A. Stackpole. Each author pursues the disposal of one of four magical objects which had been needed to achieve the current calm, but must now find a resting place to achieve peace forever after.

**Other books you might like:**
Kyle Crocco, *Heroes, Inc.*, 1991
Barry Hughart, *Bridge of Birds*, 1984
Dan McGirt, *Dirty Work*, 1993
John Moore, *Slay and Rescue*, 1993
Sean Stewart, *Nobody's Son*, 1995

## **6067**

### ROGER ZELAZNY

### *Frost and Fire*

(New York: William Morrow, 1989)

**Story type:** Science Fiction (Collection)

**Summary:** This latest collection of Zelazny's work consists of ten stories, each with an introduction, and three essays on science fiction. The pieces appeared between 1984 and 1987 in such magazines as *Omni*, *Twilight Zone*, *The Writer*, and *Isaac Asimov's Science Fiction Magazine*. The best known stories in the collection are Zelazny's recent Hugo and Nebula Award winners, "Permafrost" and "24

Views of Mt. Fuji, by Hokusai." Also included are "Quest's End," "Dayblood," and "Mana From Heaven."

**Other books you might like:**
Michael Bishop, *Close Encounters with the Deity*, 1986
Kim Stanley Robinson, *The Planet on the Table*, 1986
Bruce Sterling, *Crystal Express*, 1989
Gene Wolfe, *Endangered Species*, 1989
Gene Wolfe, *The Island of Doctor Death and Other Stories and Other Stories*, 1980
   Title is correct; not a typo!

## **6068**

### ROGER ZELAZNY

### *Gone to Earth*

(Eugene, Oregon: Pulphouse, 1991)

**Story type:** Science Fiction (Collection)
**Series:** Author's Choice Monthly

**Summary:** This book contains a 3-page introduction plus four previously published stories. "Deadboy Donner and the Filstone Cup" (1988) draws inspiration from Damon Runyan and slang of the 1920s. "Kalifriki of the Thread" (1989) was written at the request of Diana Wynne Jones for *Hidden Turnings*. Themes of cars and computer viruses are seen in "Devil Car" (1965) and "The Last of the Wild Ones" (1981).

**Other books you might like:**
Edward Bryant, *Neon Twilight*, 1990
Ron Goulart, *Skyrocket Steele Conquers the Universe and Other Media Tales*, 1990
Joe R. Lansdale, *Stories by Mama Lansdale's Youngest Boy*, 1991
Judith Moffett, *Two That Came True*, 1991
Frederik Pohl, *Stopping at Slowyear*, 1991

## **6069**

### ROGER ZELAZNY

### *Here There Be Dragons*

(Hampton Falls, New Hampshire: Donald M. Grant, 1992)

**Story type:** Fantasy (Young Adult; Quest)
**Major character(s):** William, Knight, Adventurer; Belkis "Bell", Animal (lizard), Royalty (king of dragons); Gibberling, Courtier, Cartographer
**Time period(s):** Indeterminate Past
**Locale(s):** Mythical Place

**Summary:** When the king wishes to supply fireworks for his daughter's birthday party, the task of retrieving a dragon to use as fireworks display falls to William. When he can find no one to help him, he sets out alone, but discovers Bell who promises to help if William will introduce him to the royal cartographer, Gibberling. At court, Bell grows large, becoming Belkis, and confronts Gibberling whose labeling the edge of maps with "Here There Be Dragons," has given dragonkind a bad name.

**Other books you might like:**
Gordon R. Dickson, *The Dragon and the George*, 1976
James Gurney, *Dinotopia*, 1992
Ursula K. Le Guin, *A Wizard of Earthsea*, 1968
J.R.R. Tolkien, *The Hobbit*, 1938
Lawrence Watt-Evans, *The Blood of a Dragon*, 1991
Patricia C. Wrede, *Dealing with Dragons*, 1990

## 6070

**ROGER ZELAZNY**
**ROBERT SHECKLEY**, Co-Author

### *If at Faust You Don't Succeed*
(New York: Bantam Spectra, 1993)

**Story type:** Fantasy (Light Fantasy; Legend)
**Series:** Millennial Contest
**Major character(s):** Mephistopheles, Demon; Johann Faust, Thief, Imposter; Marco Polo, Historical Figure, Leader
**Time period(s):** 13th century; 18th century
**Locale(s):** Europe; Asia; Limbo, Mythical Place

**Summary:** In the continuing battle between forces of Light and Dark for mankind's destiny, archangel Michael constructs a test through which Mephistopheles presents Faust the opportunity to make key decisions at critical junctures in human events. The test runs amiss when Mephistopheles mistakenly engages a thief and failed monk rather than the intended magician. Sequel to *Bring Me the Head of Prince Charming*.

**Other books you might like:**
Neil Gaiman, *Good Omens: The Nice and Accurate Prophecies of Agnes Nutter, Witch*, 1990
    Terry Pratchett, co-author
Craig Shaw Gardner, *The Other Sinbad*, 1991
Parke Godwin, *The Snake Oil Wars*, 1989
Robert A. Heinlein, *Job: A Comedy of Justice*, 1984
Robert Sheckley, *Dimension of Miracles*, 1968
Robert Sheckley, *On the Planet of Bottled Brains*, 1990
    Harry Harrison, co-author
Robert Sheckley, *Options*, 1975

## 6071

**ROGER ZELAZNY**
**THOMAS T. THOMAS**, Co-Author

### *The Mask of Loki*
(New York: Baen, 1990)

**Story type:** Fantasy (Legend; Adventure)
**Major character(s):** Tom Gurden, Musician (piano player), Religious (avatar of Loki); Hasan al Sabah, Criminal (assassin), Religious (avatar of Ahriman)
**Time period(s):** 12th century (Christian Crusades); 21st century
**Locale(s):** Middle East (Palestine and the Holy Lands); New Jersey

**Summary:** Tom Gurden works to prevent al Sabah from triggering the explosion of a large nuclear power plant in New Jersey. Concurrently, Gurden and al Sabah, who are the mortal avatars of Loki and Ahriman, Lord of Darkness, battle for the destiny of mankind.

**Other books you might like:**
James Blish, *Black Easter*, 1968
Marion Zimmer Bradley, *The Mists of Avalon*, 1983
Philip Jose Farmer, *To Your Scattered Bodies Go*, 1971
Marc Laidlaw, *Neon Lotus*, 1988
Flora M. Speer, *Castle of Dreams*, 1990

## 6072

**ROGER ZELAZNY**
**GAHAN WILSON**, Illustrator

### *A Night in the Lonesome October*
(New York: AvoNova/Morrow, 1993)

**Story type:** Horror (Satire)
**Major character(s):** Jack the Ripper, Serial Killer; Larry Talbot, Werewolf; Snuff, Animal (Jack's dog), Sidekick
**Time period(s):** 1890s
**Locale(s):** London, England

**Summary:** A cast of characters that includes Victor Frankenstein and his monster, the Wolfman, Count Dracula, Jack the Ripper, and assorted other famous literary and cinematic ghouls have assembled once more to play the Game, a ritual in which half will try to summon Lovecraftian deities back to Earth and the other half will try to stop them, with none knowing which side who is on until the day of reckoning. This delightful spoof of nearly every cliche in horror fiction is told from the viewpoint of the pets and familiars of the major characters. Gahan Wilson has supplied 32 striking interior illustrations.

**Other books you might like:**
Lionel Fenn, *668: The Neighbor of the Beast*, 1992
Gahan Wilson, *Eddy Deco's Last Caper*, 1987
Gahan Wilson, *Everybody's Favorite Duck*, 1989

## 6073

**ROGER ZELAZNY**

### *Prince of Chaos*
(New York: William Morrow and Co., 1991)

**Story type:** Fantasy (Magic Conflict)
**Series:** Amber
**Major character(s):** Merlin, Royalty (Prince of Chaos); Gryll, Demon
**Time period(s):** Indeterminate
**Locale(s):** Courts of Chaos, Alternate Universe

**Summary:** Merlin, Prince of the House of Sawall, finds that he is recently third in the line of succession to the throne left by the death of Swayvil, King of Chaos. His father, Corwin, is still lost in darkness and it seems that Merlin is being set up to be the next king.

**Other books you might like:**
Steven Brust, *Jhereg*, 1983
David Eddings, *Pawn of Prophecy*, 1982
Cheryl J. Franklin, *Fire Get*, 1987
Barbara Hambly, *The Time of the Dark*, 1982
Robert Jordan, *The Eye of the World*, 1989
Mercedes Lackey, *Arrows of the Queen*, 1987
Marc Laidlaw, *Neon Lotus*, 1988

## 6074

**ROGER ZELAZNY**

### *This Immortal*
(New York: Baen Books, 1989)

**Story type:** Science Fiction (Immortality)
**Major character(s):** Conrad Nomikos, Government Official, Immortal; Cort Myshtigo, Alien, Journalist
**Time period(s):** Indeterminate Future
**Locale(s):** Isle of Kos, Earth

**Summary:** In this Hugo Award-winning novel, originally published in 1966, the Earth was nearly destroyed by a nuclear war and now, several hundred years later, it still hasn't recovered. Galactic civilization, dominated by the Vegans, regards our planet as a backwater. Sometimes they come visit us as tourists. Conrad Nomikos, apparently immortal due to a radiation-induced mutation, has done many things in his life, but is currently serving as a tour guide for the distinguished and obnoxious Vegan journalist, Cort Myshtigo. Then Conrad discovers that someone is out to murder the Vegan and he must decide whether Myshtigo's life is worth preserving, possibly at the cost of his own.

**Other books you might like:**
Poul Anderson, *The Boat of a Million Years*, 1989
Octavia E. Butler, *Adulthood Rites*, 1988
Samuel R. Delany, *The Einstein Intersection*, 1967

## 6075

**ROGER ZELAZNY**, Editor
**MARTIN H. GREENBERG**, Co-Editor

### Warriors of Blood and Dream

(New York: AvoNova, 1995)

**Story type:** Fantasy (Anthology; Science Fiction)

**Summary:** Contains a 10-page introduction and brief individual introductions by Zelazny to 15 original stories focusing on martial arts and mystical enlightenment. Frequently dark or ominous in tone, the stories present diverse fantastic and mundane settings and explore techniques, philosophies, and gadgets employed by explorers of various paths of enlightenment and action. Stories conclude with a brief discussion of their genesis by the authors who include Steven Barnes, Jeffrey A. Carver, Karen Haber, Jack C. Haldeman, II, Joe R. Lansdale, Jane Lindskold, Richard A. Lupoff, Victor Milan, Dave Smeds, Michael A. Stackpole, and Walter Jon Williams.

**Other books you might like:**
Steven Barnes, *Streetlethal*, 1983
Gordon R. Dickson, *Dorsai!*, 1976
Donald F. Glut, *The Empire Strikes Back*, 1980
Elizabeth A. Lynn, *Watchtower*, 1979
David R. Palmer, *Emergence*, 1984
Steve Perry, *The 97th Step*, 1989
Dennis Schmidt, *Way-Farer*, 1978

## 6076

**ROGER ZELAZNY**
**VAUGHN BODE**, Illustrator

### Way Up High

(Hampton Falls, New Hampshire: Donald M. Grant, 1992)

**Story type:** Fantasy (Young Adult; Adventure)
**Major character(s):** Susi, Child, Student; Herman, Animal (pterodactyl)
**Time period(s):** 1990s
**Locale(s):** Earth

**Summary:** When Susi meets Herman on her way home from school, she learns from him about pterodactyls and spends her summer vacation flying around with him.

**Other books you might like:**
James Gurney, *Dinotopia*, 1992
Evelyn Sibley Lampman, *The Shy Stegosaurus of Cricket Creek*, 1955
Ursula K. Le Guin, *Catwings*, 1988

Rodney Matthews, *Yendor*, 1978
Edward Ormondroyd, *David and the Phoenix*, 1957
Doris Vallejo, *The Boy Who Saved the Stars*, 1978

## 6077

**ROGER ZELAZNY**, Editor

### The Williamson Effect

(New York: Tor, 1996)

**Story type:** Fantasy (Anthology; Science Fiction)

**Summary:** This tribute to award-winning author and educator Jack Williamson contains a seven-page introduction by David Brin and individual introductions by Jim Frenkel to two poems and 14 stories, with author afterwords. Many of these original pieces accept the milieu of a Williamson story, while other authors provide a direct sequel to a famous work such as *Darker Than You Think* (1948), *Demon Moon* (1994), *The Humanoids* (1949), The Legion of Space Series (1947-1983), and "With Folded Hands" (1947). Concludes with seven pages of biographies of the contributors, who include Poul Anderson, Ben Bova, John Brunner, Jane Lindskold, Andre Norton, Frederik Pohl, Mike Resnick, Fred Saberhagen, David Weber, and Connie Willis.

**Other books you might like:**
Kevin J. Anderson, *War of the Worlds: Global Dispatches*, 1996
   editor
Steven R. Boyett, *Treks Not Taken: What if Stephen King, Anne Rice, Bret Easton Ellis, and Other Literary Greats Had Written Episodes of Star Trek: The Next Generation?*, 1996
Randall Garrett, *Takeoff!*, 1979
Randall Garrett, *Takeoff, Too*, 1986
Martin H. Greenberg, *After the King: Stories in Honor of J.R.R. Tolkien*, 1992
   editor
William F. Nolan, *The Bradbury Chronicles: Stories in Honor of Ray Bradbury*, 1991
   Martin H. Greenberg, co-editor

## 6078

**STEVE ZELL**

### WiZrD

(New York: St. Martin's, 1994)

**Story type:** Horror (Ancient Evil Unleashed)
**Major character(s):** Trevor Williams, Artist; Bryce Williams, Teenager; Megan Williams, Teenager (Bryce's stepsister)
**Time period(s):** 1990s (1994)
**Locale(s):** Pinon Rim, Arizona

**Summary:** Trevor Williams relocates his family from upstate New York to Pinon Rim, a former mining town almost literally rendered a ghost town a century before, following an outbreak of madness and mass murder that depopulated the town. Inadvertently, Bryce and Megan's explorations into a secret cave help jump start the Circle of the Harvest, a mythic ritual played out by a legendary Navajo entity that threatens once more to plunge the town into a sacrificial blood bath. This is the author's first novel.

**Other books you might like:**
G. Wayne Miller, *Thunder Rise*, 1989
Adam Niswander, *The Charm*, 1993
Eugene E. Pfaff Jr., *Uwharrie*, 1993
   Michael Causey, co-author
Kathryn Ptacek, *Ghost Dance*, 1990

Patrick Whalen, *Deathwalker*, 1992

## 6079
**SARAH ZETTEL**

### Fool's War
(New York: Warner Aspect, 1997)

**Story type:** Science Fiction (Alternate Intelligence; Space Opera)
**Major character(s):** Katmer Al Shei, Businesswoman, Engineer; Evelyn Dobbs, Spacewoman, Psychologist (professional Fool)
**Time period(s):** Indeterminate Future
**Locale(s):** *Pasadena*, Spaceship; The Farther Kingdom, Planet—Imaginary; Guild Hall Station, Space Station ((Fool's Guild headquarters))

**Summary:** *Pasadena's* routine transportation and transfer of medical records data turns problematic when hospital officials accuse the crew of loosing an artificial intelligence into facility computers. As *Pasadena's* crew attempt to reverse the damage and prevent further disaster, officials back home arrest Katmer Al Shei's husband, while events unmask the true nature of the Fool's Guild.

**Other books you might like:**
Roger MacBride Allen, *The Ring of Charon*, 1990
Raphael Carter, *The Fortunate Fall*, 1996
Glen Cook, *The Dragon Never Sleeps*, 1988
Katharine Kerr, *Palace*, 1996
   Mark Kreighbaum, co-author
Alis A. Rasmussen, *A Passage of Stars*, 1990
Neal Stephenson, *Snow Crash*, 1992
John Varley, *Steel Beach*, 1992
Vernor Vinge, *A Fire upon the Deep*, 1992
David Weber, *Path of the Fury*, 1992

## 6080
**SARAH ZETTEL**

### Playing God
(New York: Warner Aspect, 1998)

**Story type:** Science Fiction (Genetic Manipulation; Space Colony)
**Major character(s):** Lynn Nussbaumer, Scientist (planetary ecologist); Praeis Shin, Alien (Dedelphinian), Spy (for the Queens-of-All); Aaron Hogopian, Activist, Researcher (university)
**Time period(s):** Indeterminate Future
**Locale(s):** Dedelphi, Planet—Imaginary; Ur, Space Station; Interstellar Empire/Federation

**Summary:** When Lynn Nussbaumer accepts the leadership of the Bioverse Inc. team hired to stop a terrible plague and regulate the ecology of Dedelphi, she expects some local resistance to the relocation, but not a continuation of the warfare which created the planetwide disaster. Both familiar with Dedelphinian culture, Lynn and Aaron must use all of their knowledge and the tools at hand to prevent further genocide.

**Other books you might like:**
Octavia E. Butler, *Dawn*, 1987
Kay Kenyon, *Leap Point*, 1998
Katharine Kerr, *Palace*, 1996
   Mark Kreighbaum, co-author
Joan Slonczewski, *The Children Star*, 1998
Joan Slonczewski, *A Door into Ocean*, 1986

## 6081
**SARAH ZETTEL**

### Reclamation
(New York: Warner Aspect, 1996)

**Story type:** Science Fiction (Psychic Powers; Political)
**Major character(s):** Dorias Waesc, Artificial Intelligence, Refugee; Eric Born, Psychic; Arla Stone, Psychic
**Time period(s):** Indeterminate
**Locale(s):** The Realm of the Nameless, Planet—Imaginary; May 16, Planet—Imaginary; *U-Kenai*, Spaceship

**Summary:** The Alliance for the Re-Unification of the Human Family rescues/kidnaps Arla Stone from the Realm of the Nameless, only to have her kidnapped from them by the Rhudolant Vitae. In the pay of the Rhudolant Vitae, Eric Born recognizes Arla and rescues her. Both the Alliance and Vitae want Eric and Arla not only for their psychic abilities, but also because they believe the Realm of the Nameless gave birth to the human species. First novel.

**Other books you might like:**
David Brin, *Brightness Reef*, 1995
C.J. Cherryh, *Forty Thousand in Gehenna*, 1983
Glen Cook, *The Dragon Never Sleeps*, 1996
Dan Simmons, *Endymion*, 1996
E.C. Tubb, *The Winds of Gath*, 1967

## 6082
**PAT ZETTNER**

### The Shadow Warrior
(New York: Atheneum, 1990)

**Story type:** Fantasy (Adventure)
**Major character(s):** Lady Llyndreth, Royalty (Princess)
**Time period(s):** Indeterminate

**Summary:** While her brother is away on a goblin hunt, rebel lords take over his castle and Llyndreth takes off to find him. Along the way she runs into the last of the giants and a wounded goblin, all three of whom discover it is best to stay together, despite initial mistrust.

**Other books you might like:**
Orson Scott Card, *Wyrms*, 1989
Gun Guneli, *On the Road to Baghdad*, 1989
Elizabeth Moon, *Surrender None: The Legacy of Gird*, 1990
Alis A. Rasmussen, *A Passage of Stars*, 1990
   Highroad Vol. 1

## 6083
**PAUL EDWIN ZIMMER**
**JON DE CLES**, Co-Author

### Blood of the Colyn Muir
(New York: Avon, 1988)

**Story type:** Fantasy (Quest)
**Major character(s):** Darith, Hero
**Time period(s):** Indeterminate
**Locale(s):** Tondur, Fictional Country

**Summary:** The protagonist goes on a search for a magic sword to help him defeat the powers that have invaded his homeland.

**Other books you might like:**
Adrienne Martine-Barnes, *The Rainbow Sword*, 1988

James Silke, *Plague of Knives*, 1990
Frank Frazetta's Death Dealer - Vol 4

---

## 6084

### PAUL ZINDEL

### *Raptor*

(New York: Hyperion, 1998)

**Story type:** Science Fiction (Young Adult; Adventure)
**Major character(s):** Zach Norak, Teenager; Uta, Indian, Teenager
**Time period(s):** 1990s
**Locale(s):** Utah

**Summary:** After his father is injured in a mysterious accident, Zach and his Native American friend Uta discover the secret—Zach's father uncovered a nest of surviving dinosaurs and was injured as he fled the area. The two boys battle to protect a young raptor and return it to its own kind.

**Other books you might like:**
Robert T. Bakker, *Raptor Red*, 1995
Greg Bear, *Dinosaur Summer*, 1998
Michael Crichton, *Jurassic Park*, 1990
Brett Davis, *Bone Wars*, 1998

---

## 6085

### DAVID ZINDELL

### *The Broken God*

(New York: Bantam Spectra, 1994)

**Story type:** Science Fiction (Adventure; Mystical)
**Series:** Neverness
**Major character(s):** Danlo Ringess, Pilot (spaceship); Hanuman, Companion
**Time period(s):** Indeterminate Future
**Locale(s):** Icefall, Planet—Imaginary; Interstellar Empire/Federation

**Summary:** Danlo must confront and reject godhood to succeed in his quest to destroy the menace at the heart of the galaxy. Sequel to *Neverness*.

**Other books you might like:**
Roger MacBride Allen, *The Ring of Charon*, 1990
Jeffrey A. Carver, *Down the Stream of Stars*, 1990
Glen Cook, *The Dragon Never Sleeps*, 1988
Michael P. Kube-McDowell, *Enigma*, 1986
Vernor Vinge, *A Fire upon the Deep*, 1992

---

## 6086

### DAVID ZINDELL

### *The Wild*

(New York: Bantam Spectra, 1996)

**Story type:** Science Fiction (Family Saga; Mystical)
**Series:** Neverness
**Major character(s):** Danlo Ringess, Pilot (spaceship); Mallory Ringess, Parent (father); Ede, Artificial Intelligence
**Time period(s):** Indeterminate Future
**Locale(s):** Farfara, Planet—Imaginary; Interstellar Empire/Federation

**Summary:** Sent by the Order of Mystic Mathematicians both to establish a new Order within the heart of the Wild on the lost planet of Tannahill and to destroy the cause of the sudden death by

---

supernova of so many stars, Danlo also seeks his father, who went out with the first expedition.

**Other books you might like:**
Roger MacBride Allen, *The Ring of Charon*, 1990
Stephen Baxter, *Ring*, 1996
Jeffrey A. Carver, *Neptune Crossing*, 1994
Debra Doyle, *The Price of the Stars*, 1992
   James D. Macdonald, co-author
Alis A. Rasmussen, *A Passage of Stars*, 1990
Vernor Vinge, *A Fire upon the Deep*, 1992

---

## 6087

### JACK ZIPES, Editor

### *Arabian Nights: The Marvels and Wonders of the Thousand and One Nights*

(New York: Signet, 1991)

**Story type:** Fantasy (Anthology; Legend)
**Time period(s):** Indeterminate Past
**Locale(s):** Middle East

**Summary:** Zipes adapted and modernized the language of the 49 tales herein from the unexpurgated Richard Burton translation of the bawdy and erotic adult tales from the Middle East. Among the many popular tales included are "Ali Baba and the Forty Thieves," "Aladdin and the Magic Lamp" and many tales of Sinbad the Seaman. This book also contains notes on the text and translator, plus an afterword, glossary and bibliography.

**Other books you might like:**
John Barth, *The Last Voyage of Somebody the Sailor*, 1991
Richard F. Burton, *The Book of the Thousand Nights and a Night: A Plain and Literal Translation of the Arabian Nights Entertainments*, 1885-1886
   10 volumes
Patricia Daniels, *Sinbad the Sailor*, 1980
Lester Del Rey, *Once upon a Time: A Treasury of Modern Fairy Tales*, 1991
   Risa Kessler, co-author
Craig Shaw Gardner, *The Other Sinbad*, 1991
Stephen Goldin, *Crystals of Air and Water*, 1989
Stephen Goldin, *Shrine of the Desert Mage*, 1988
Stephen Goldin, *The Storyteller and the Jahn*, 1988
Andrew Lang, *The Arabian Nights Entertainments*, 1969
   editor
Andrew Lang, *The Blue Fairy Book*, 1889
   editor
John Payne, *The Book of the Thousand Nights and the One Night*, 1882-1884
   9 volumes
Salman Rushdie, *Haroun and the Sea of Stories*, 1990
Susan Shwartz, *Arabesques: More Tales of the Arabian Nights*, 1988
   editor
Susan Shwartz, *Arabesques II*, 1989
   editor

---

## 6088

### JACK ZIPES, Editor

### *Beauties, Beasts and Enchantments*

(New York: Penguin Meridian, 1991)

**Story type:** Fantasy (Anthology; Legend)

**Summary:** This volume includes the most important fairy tales from 17th and 18th century France which gave birth to the Western tradition of fairy tales, inspiring the Grimm brothers. The 36 tales by 12 authors are primarily adult-oriented with several enjoyable by younger readers. Major contributions include 10 tales by Charles Perrault and 15 tales by Marie-Catherine d'Aulnoy. Zipes also includes two accounts of "Beauty and the Beast," an 11-page version by Jeanne-Marie Leprince de Beaumont and a 177-page version by Gabrielle-Suzanne de Villeneuve. Reprint of the 1989 hardcover.

**Other books you might like:**
Steven Brust, *The Sun, the Moon, and the Stars*, 1987
Kara Dalkey, *The Nightingale*, 1988
Charles de Lint, *Jack, the Giant-Killer*, 1987
Lester Del Rey, *Once upon a Time: A Treasury of Modern Fairy Tales*, 1991
    Risa Kessler, co-editor
Michael Patrick Hearn, *The Victorian Fairy Tale Book*, 1988
    editor
Andrew Lang, *The Blue Fairy Book*, 1889
    editor
Andrew Lang, *The Red Fairy Book*, 1890
    editor
Ethel Johnston Phelps, *Tatterhood and Other Tales*, 1978
    editor
Sheri S. Tepper, *Beauty*, 1991
Patricia C. Wrede, *Snow White and Rose Red*, 1989

**6089**

JACK ZIPES, Editor

## The Outspoken Princess and the Gentle Knight

(New York: Bantam, 1994)

**Story type:** Fantasy (Anthology)

**Summary:** Contains a 10-page introduction addressing the roots of fairy tales and their role in post-World War II societal evolution. Published 1951-1992, the 15 stories by British and American authors document the modern rise of feminist protagonists and the discussion of oppression and empowerment within current society by twisting the traditional roles of princesses and revising classic tales such as "Little Red Riding Hood," "Ferdinand the Bull" and "Cinderella." Authors include Lloyd Alexander, A.S. Byatt, John Gardner, Ernest Hemingway, Tanith Lee, Dov Mir, Richard Schickel, Jack Sendak, Catherine Storr, Jay Williams and Jane Yolen.

**Other books you might like:**
Nina Auerbach, *Forbidden Journeys: Fairy Tales and Fantasies by Victorian Women Writers*, 1992
    U.C. Knoepflmacher, co-editor

James Finn Garner, *Politically Correct Bedtime Stories*, 1994
Ursula K. Le Guin, *Fish Soup*, 1992
Robin Morgan, *The Mer-Child: A Legend for Children and Other Adults*, 1991
Ethel Johnston Phelps, *Tatterhood and Other Tales*, 1978
    editor

**6090**

JACK ZIPES, Editor

## Spells of Enchantment

(New York: Viking, 1991)

**Story type:** Fantasy (Anthology; Legend)

**Summary:** Subtitled *The Wondrous Fairy Tales of Western Culture*, this volume is the first collection of literary fairy tales for adults containing all major European and American authors from the 2nd century to the present. It contains 67 stories, more than a dozen of which appear here for the first time in English. Zipes himself translates 70-80% of the stories. Seminal fairy tales include Charles Perrault's "Riquet with the Tuft," Angela Carter's "The Tiger's Bride," Johann Wolfgang Goethe's "The Fairy Tale," E.T.A. Hoffman's "The Mines of Falun," Oscar Wilde's "The Fisherman and His Soul," William Butler Yeats' "Dreams That Have No Moral," and Italo Calvino's "The Enchanted Palace."

**Other books you might like:**
Steven Brust, *The Sun, the Moon, and the Stars*, 1987
Kara Dalkey, *The Nightingale*, 1988
Charles de Lint, *Jack, the Giant-Killer*, 1987
Lester Del Rey, *Once upon a Time: A Treasury of Modern Fairy Tales*, 1991
    Risa Kessler, co-editor
Michael Patrick Hearn, *The Victorian Fairy Tale Book*, 1988
    editor
Andrew Lang, *The Blue Fairy Book*, 1889
    editor
Andrew Lang, *The Green Fairy Book*, 1892
    editor
Andrew Lang, *The Red Fairy Book*, 1890
    editor
Sheri S. Tepper, *Beauty*, 1991
Beatrice Silverman Weinreich, *Yiddish Folk Tales*, 1988
    editor
Patricia C. Wrede, *Snow White and Rose Red*, 1989
W.B. Yeats, *A Treasury of Irish Myth, Legend and Folklore*, 1986
    editor

# Series Index

This index alphabetically lists series to which books featured in the entries belong. Beneath each series name, book titles are listed alphabetically with author names. Numbers refer to the entries that feature each title.

**99 Fear Street: The House of Evil**
*The First Horror* - R.L. Stine   *h*   5288

**Abductors**
*The Abductors: Conspiracy* - Jonathan Frakes   *s*   2034

**Addams Family**
*Addams Family Values* - Todd Strasser   *f*   5324

**Adept**
*The Adept* - Katherine Kurtz   *f*   3254
*Death of an Adept* - Katherine Kurtz   *f*   3257
*The Lodge of the Lynx* - Katherine Kurtz   *f*   3259
*The Templar Treasure* - Katherine Kurtz   *f*   3261

**Adventures of Abraham Stroud**
*Curse of the Vampire* - Geoffrey Caine   *h*   832
*Legion of the Dead* - Geoffrey Caine   *h*   833
*Wake of the Werewolf* - Geoffrey Caine   *h*   834

**Adventures of Conrad Stargard**
*The Flying Warlord* - Leo Frankowski   *s*   2044
*The High-Tech Knight* - Leo Frankowski   *s*   2045
*Lord Conrad's Lady* - Leo Frankowski   *s*   2046
*The Radiant Warrior* - Leo Frankowski   *s*   2047

**Adventures of Dirk Gently**
*The Long Dark Tea-Time of the Soul* - Douglas Adams   *s*   30

**Adventures of Jonathan Barrett**
*Dance of Death* - P.N. Elrod   *h*   1794
*Death Masque* - P.N. Elrod   *h*   1795
*Red Death* - P.N. Elrod   *h*   1798

**Adventures of Miles Vorkosigan**
*Barrayar* - Lois McMaster Bujold   *s*   756
*Borders of Infinity* - Lois McMaster Bujold   *s*   757
*Cetaganda* - Lois McMaster Bujold   *s*   758
*Komarr* - Lois McMaster Bujold   *s*   760
*Memory* - Lois McMaster Bujold   *s*   761
*Mirror Dance* - Lois McMaster Bujold   *s*   762
*The Vor Game* - Lois McMaster Bujold   *s*   764

**Adventures of Teddy London**
*All Things under the Moon* - Robert Morgan   *h*   4002
*The Only Thing to Fear* - Robert Morgan   *h*   4003
*Some Things Come Back* - Robert Morgan   *h*   4004
*Some Things Never Die* - Robert Morgan   *h*   4005
*The Thing That Darkness Hides* - Robert Morgan   *h*   4006
*The Things That Are Not There* - Robert Morgan   *h*   4007

**Adversary**
*Reborn* - F. Paul Wilson   *h*   5895
*Reprisal* - F. Paul Wilson   *h*   5896

**AEgypt**
*Love & Sleep* - John Crowley   *f*   1277

**Afrikorps**
*Afrikorps* - Bill Dolan   *s*   1566
*Cobra Curse* - Bill Dolan   *s*   1567
*Iron Horse* - Bill Dolan   *s*   1568
*White Rhino* - Bill Dolan   *s*   1569

**After Such Knowledge Trilogy**
*The Devil's Day* - James Blish   *h*   525

**Age of Unreason**
*Newton's Cannon* - J. Gregory Keyes   *f*   3097

**Alamut**
*Alamut* - Judith Tarr   *f*   5390
*The Dagger and the Cross: A Novel of the Crusades* - Judith Tarr   *f*   5393

**Alex Balfour**
*Till the End of Time* - Allen Appel   *f*   201

**Alien**
*Alien 3* - Alan Dean Foster   *s*   1993
*Alien Resurrection* - A.C. Crispin   *s*   1258

**Alien Blues**
*Alien Blues* - Lynn S. Hightower   *s*   2682
*Alien Eyes* - Lynn S. Hightower   *s*   2683
*Alien Heat* - Lynn S. Hightower   *s*   2684
*Alien Rites* - Lynn S. Hightower   *s*   2685

**Alien Nation**
*The Change* - Barry B. Longyear   *s*   3520
*Cross of Blood* - K.W. Jeter   *s*   2909
*Dark Horizon* - K.W. Jeter   *s*   2910

**Aliens**
*Aliens: Earth Hive* - Steve Perry   *s*   4289
*Aliens: The Female War* - Steve Perry   *s*   4290
*Berserker* - S.D. Perry   *s*   4285

**Aliens vs. Predator**
*Hunter's Planet* - David Bischoff   *s*   492

**Amanda Poe Mysteries**
*The Virginia Ghost Murders* - Leslie Raymond Sachs   *h*   4778

**Amber**
*Prince of Chaos* - Roger Zelazny   *f*   6073

**Ambermere**
*The Door to Ambermere* - J. Calvin Pierce   *f*   4316

**The Wizard of Ambermere** - J. Calvin Pierce   *f*   4317

**American Ghosts**
*Eastern Ghosts* - Frank D. McSherry Jr.   *h*   3866
*Ghosts of the Heartland* - Frank D. McSherry Jr.   *h*   3868
*Western Ghosts* - Frank D. McSherry Jr.   *h*   3870

**American Vampire**
*Fields of Blood: Vampire Stories of the Heartland* - Lawrence Schimel   *h*   4879
*Streets of Blood: Vampire Stories From New York City* - Lawrence Schimel   *h*   4881

**Andrej Koscuisko**
*Prisoner of Conscience* - Susan R. Matthews   *s*   3693

**Angel's Luck**
*Desperate Measures* - Joe Clifford Faust   *s*   1891
*Precious Cargo* - Joe Clifford Faust   *s*   1893

**Anita Blake, Vampire Hunter**
*Bloody Bones* - Laurell K. Hamilton   *h*   2512
*Blue Moon* - Laurell K. Hamilton   *h*   2513
*Burnt Offerings* - Laurell K. Hamilton   *h*   2514
*Circus of the Damned* - Laurell K. Hamilton   *h*   2515
*Guilty Pleasures* - Laurell K. Hamilton   *f*   2517
*The Killing Dance* - Laurell K. Hamilton   *h*   2518
*The Laughing Corpse* - Laurell K. Hamilton   *f*   2519
*The Lunatic Cafe* - Laurell K. Hamilton   *h*   2520

**Anno Dracula**
*Judgment of Tears: Anno Dracula 1959* - Kim Newman   *h*   4098

**Anthi**
*Requiem for Anthi* - Jay D. Blakeney   *s*   517

**Apprentice Adept**
*Phaze Doubt* - Piers Anthony   *f*   184

**Arabian Nights**
*A Bad Day for Ali Baba* - Craig Shaw Gardner   *f*   2123
*The Last Arabian Night* - Craig Shaw Gardner   *f*   2129

**Arbai Device**
*Sideshow* - Sheri S. Tepper   *s*   5436

**Arbiter Tale**
*Stepwater* - L. Warren Douglas   *s*   1588
*The Wells of Phyre* - L. Warren Douglas   *s*   1589

**ARC Riders**
*The Fourth Rome* - David Drake   *s*   1631

**Arcana**
*Silverlight* - Morgan Llywelyn  *f*  3507

**Archangel**
*The Alleluia Files* - Sharon Shinn  *s*  4999

**Arden Grenfell**
*Darkloom* - Cary Osborne  *s*  4225

**Arthur C. Clarke's Venus Prime**
*The Diamond Moon* - Paul Preuss  *s*  4417
*Hide and Seek* - Paul Preuss  *s*  4418
*The Medusa Encounter* - Paul Preuss  *s*  4419
*The Shining Ones* - Paul Preuss  *s*  4421

**Arthur War Lord**
*Arthur War Lord* - Dafydd ab Hugh  *f*  6

**Arthurian**
*The Wolf and the Crown* - A.A. Attanasio  *f*  273

**Aubrey Knight**
*Firedance* - Steven Barnes  *s*  360

**Aurian**
*Dhiammara* - Maggie Furey  *f*  2096
*Harp of Winds* - Maggie Furey  *f*  2097
*Sword of Flame* - Maggie Furey  *f*  2098

**Author's Choice Monthly**
*Daily Voices* - Lisa Goldstein  *s*  2261
*God's Nose* - Damon Knight  *s*  3185
*Gone to Earth* - Roger Zelazny  *s*  6068
*Hedgework and Guessery* - Charles de Lint  *f*  1428
*It's Been Fun* - Esther Friesner  *f*  2078
*Ma Qui and Other Phantoms* - Alan
  Brennert  *h*  675
*The Naked Flesh of Feeling* - J.N.
  Williamson  *h*  5857
*Nine Hard Questions about the Nature of the Universe*
  - Lewis Shiner  *s*  4998
*The Old Funny Stuff* - George Alec Effinger  *s*  1753
*State of Grace* - Kate Wilhelm  *f*  5810
*Stories by Mama Lansdale's Youngest Boy* - Joe R.
  Lansdale  *h*  3333
*Two That Came True* - Judith Moffett  *s*  3945

**Avaryan Rising**
*Arrows of the Sun* - Judith Tarr  *f*  5391
*Spear of Heaven* - Judith Tarr  *f*  5396

**Babylon 5**
*Dark Genesis* - J. Gregory Keyes  *s*  3096
*Day of the Dead* - Neil Gaiman  *s*  2102
*Personal Agendas* - Al Sarrantonio  *s*  4833
*The Shadow Within* - Jeanne Cavelos  *s*  944
*Thirdspace* - Peter David  *s*  1387
*To Dream in the City of Sorrows* - Kathryn M.
  Drennan  *s*  1654
*The Touch of Your Shadow, the Whisper of Your Name*
  - Neal Barrett Jr.  *s*  367
*Voices* - John Vornholt  *s*  5598

**Banned and the Banished**
*Wit'ch Fire* - James Clemens  *f*  1082

**Bardic Choices**
*A Cast of Corbies* - Mercedes Lackey  *f*  3274

**Bardic Voices**
*The Eagle and the Nightingales* - Mercedes
  Lackey  *f*  3278
*Four & Twenty Blackbirds* - Mercedes
  Lackey  *f*  3283
*The Lark and the Wren* - Mercedes Lackey  *f*  3286
*The Robin and the Kestrel* - Mercedes
  Lackey  *f*  3293

**Bard's Tale**
*Castle of Deception* - Mercedes Lackey  *f*  3275
*Curse of the Black Heron* - Holly Lisle  *f*  3479
*Fortress of Frost and Fire* - Mercedes
  Lackey  *f*  3282
*Thunder of the Captains* - Holly Lisle  *f*  3489

*Wrath of the Princes* - Holly Lisle  *f*  3490

**Batman**
*Batman: Knightfall* - Dennis O'Neil  *s*  4215
*Batman Returns* - Craig Shaw Gardner  *s*  2124
*Catwoman* - Lynn Abbey  *s*  14
*The Further Adventures of Batman 2: Featuring the
  Penguin* - Martin H. Greenberg  *s*  2391
*The Further Adventures of Batman 3: Featuring
  Catwoman* - Martin H. Greenberg  *s*  2392
*Mask of the Phantasm* - Geary Gravel  *s*  2331

**Battlestar Galactica**
*Armageddon* - Richard Hatch  *s*  2602

**Battlestation**
*Battlestation* - David Drake  *s*  1627

**Battletech**
*Prince of Havoc* - Michael A. Stackpole  *s*  5204
*Shadows of War* - Thomas S. Gressman  *s*  2432

**Battletech: Legend of the Jade Phoenix**
*Way of the Clans* - Robert Thurston  *s*  5469

**Bazil Broketail**
*Battledragon* - Christopher Rowley  *f*  4691
*Bazil Broketail* - Christopher Rowley  *f*  4692
*A Dragon at World's End* - Christopher
  Rowley  *f*  4693
*Dragons of Argonath* - Christopher Rowley  *f*  4694
*Dragons of War* - Christopher Rowley  *f*  4695
*A Sword for a Dragon* - Christopher
  Rowley  *f*  4697

**Beggars in Spain**
*Beggars Ride* - Nancy Kress  *s*  3238

**Belisarius**
*In the Heart of Darkness* - Eric Flint  *s*  1955

**Berserker**
*Berserker Fury* - Fred Saberhagen  *s*  4760
*Berserker Kill* - Fred Saberhagen  *s*  4761
*Berserker Lies* - Fred Saberhagen  *s*  4762
*Shiva in Steel* - Fred Saberhagen  *s*  4775

**Bessledorf Mystery**
*Bernie and the Bessledorf Ghost* - Phyllis Reynolds
  Naylor  *f*  4078

**Best From Fantasy and Science Fiction**
*The Best From Fantasy & Science Fiction: A 45th
  Anniversary Anthology* - Kristine Kathryn
  Rusch  *s*  4712

**Best New Horror**
*Best New Horror* - Stephen Jones  *h*  2961
*Best New Horror 4* - Stephen Jones  *h*  2963

**Bicycling Through Space and Time**
*The Ultimate Bike Path* - Michael B. Sirota  *s*  5076

**Bifrost Guardians**
*By Chaos Cursed* - Mickey Zucker Reichert  *f*  4517
*Dragonrank Master* - Mickey Zucker
  Reichert  *f*  4519
*Shadow's Realm* - Mickey Zucker Reichert  *f*  4523

**Bill, the Galactic Hero**
*Bill, the Galactic Hero: On the Planet of Tasteless
  Pleasure* - Harry Harrison  *s*  2567
*Bill, the Galactic Hero: The Final Incoherent
  Adventure* - Harry Harrison  *s*  2568
*Planet of the Robot Slaves* - Harry Harrison  *s*  2573

**Biowarriors**
*The Infinity Plague* - Robert E. Vardeman  *s*  5564

**Birthright**
*The Iron Throne* - Simon Hawke  *f*  2618
*War* - Simon Hawke  *f*  2625

**Black Company: Glittering Stone Triology**
*She Is the Darkness* - Glen Cook  *f*  1154

**Black Hole Travel Agency**
*Free Radicals* - Jack McKinney  *s*  3848
*Hostile Takeover* - Jack McKinney  *s*  3849

**Black Oak**
*Genesis* - Charles L. Grant  *h*  2308

**Blade**
*L.A. Strike* - David Robbins  *s*  4599
*Vengeance Strike* - David Robbins  *s*  4604

**Blade Runner**
*Blade Runner: Replicant Night* - K.W. Jeter  *s*  2907

**Blending**
*Challenges* - Sharon Green  *f*  2354
*Competition* - Sharon Green  *f*  2355
*Convergence* - Sharon Green  *f*  2356

**Blood of Nostradamus Trilogy**
*The Link* - Andrew Laurance  *h*  3348
*The Premonition* - Andrew Laurance  *h*  3349
*The Unborn* - Andrew Laurance  *h*  3350

**Blood of the Goddess**
*Bhagavati* - Kara Dalkey  *f*  1316
*Bijapur* - Kara Dalkey  *f*  1317

**Blood of the Lamb**
*The Devouring Void* - Mark E. Rogers  *f*  4653
*The Riddled Man* - Mark E. Rogers  *f*  4654

**Blood Opera Sequence**
*Darkness, I* - Tanith Lee  *h*  3407

**Blue Rose Trilogy**
*Koko* - Peter Straub  *h*  5328

**Bolo**
*Honor of the Regiment* - Bill Fawcett  *s*  1896
*The Stars Must Wait* - Keith Laumer  *s*  3346

**Book of the Art Trilogy**
*Everville* - Clive Barker  *h*  338
*The Great and Secret Show* - Clive Barker  *h*  341

**Book of the Gods**
*The Face of Apollo* - Fred Saberhagen  *s*  4766

**Book of the Kingdoms**
*The Usurper* - Angus Wells  *f*  5739
*Wrath of Ashar* - Angus Wells  *f*  5742

**Book of the Long Sun**
*Calde of the Long Sun* - Gene Wolfe  *s*  5937
*Exodus From the Long Sun* - Gene Wolfe  *s*  5941
*Lake of the Long Sun* - Gene Wolfe  *s*  5942
*Nightside the Long Sun* - Gene Wolfe  *s*  5943

**Book of the Painter**
*The Boy From the Burren* - Sheila Gilluly  *f*  2236

**Book of the Undead Trilogy**
*Fear Itself* - Ric Meyers  *h*  3881
*Living Hell* - Ric Meyers  *h*  3882
*Worst Nightmare* - Ric Meyers  *h*  3883

**Book of Words**
*The Baker's Boy* - J.V. Jones  *f*  2956
*A Man Betrayed* - J.V. Jones  *f*  2958
*Master and Fool* - J.V. Jones  *f*  2959

**Books of the Kingdoms**
*The Way Beneath* - Angus Wells  *f*  5740

**Books of Wraeththu**
*Bewitchments of Love and Hate* - Storm
  Constantine  *s*  1140
*The Enchantments of Flesh and Spirit* - Storm
  Constantine  *s*  1141
*The Fulfillments of Fate and Desire* - Storm
  Constantine  *s*  1142

**Borderland**
*Borderland* - Terri Windling  *f*  5913
*Elsewhere* - Will Shetterly  *f*  4993
*The Essential Bordertown* - Terri Windling  *f*  5914

*Finder* - Emma Bull  *f*  769
*Life on the Border* - Terri Windling  *f*  5915
*Nevernever* - Will Shetterly  *f*  4995

**Borderlands**
*Borderlands 2* - Thomas F. Monteleone  *h*  3960
*Borderlands 3* - Thomas F. Monteleone  *h*  3961
*Borderlands 4* - Thomas F. Monteleone  *h*  3962

**Brian Froud's Faerielands**
*Something Rich and Strange* - Patricia A.
   McKillip  *f*  3840
*The Wild Wood* - Charles de Lint  *f*  1440

**Brightglade**
*Marbleheart* - Don Callander  *f*  846

**Brill and Maxwell**
*Dragon's Teeth* - Lee Killough  *s*  3109

**Bromeliad**
*Diggers* - Terry Pratchett  *s*  4386
*Wings* - Terry Pratchett  *s*  4403

**Bronwyn**
*Hearts and Armor* - Ron Miller  *f*  3903
*Palaces and Prisons* - Ron Miller  *f*  3904
*Silk and Steel* - Ron Miller  *f*  3905

**Brothers of the Dragon**
*Brothers of the Dragon* - Robin Wayne
   Bailey  *f*  286
*Flames of the Dragon* - Robin Wayne Bailey  *f*  287

**Bruce Coville's Alien Adventures**
*Aliens Stole My Body* - Bruce Coville  *s*  1217

**Buck Rogers**
*A Life in the Future* - Martin Caidin  *s*  827

**Buck Rogers: The Inner Planets Trilogy**
*Matrix Cubed* - Britton Bloom  *s*  554

**Buck Rogers: The Martian Wars Trilogy**
*Hammer of Mars* - M.S. Murdock  *s*  4049

**Buffy the Vampire Slayer**
*The Harvest* - Richie Tankersley Cusick  *h*  1302
*Return to Chaos* - Craig Shaw Gardner  *h*  2131

**Bureau 13**
*Bureau 13* - Nick Pollotta  *f*  4362
*Doomsday Exam* - Nick Pollotta  *f*  4363
*Full Moonster* - Nick Pollotta  *f*  4364

**C.A.D.S.**
*Suicide Attack* - John Sievert  *s*  5023

**Cadwal Chronicles**
*Ecce and Old Earth* - Jack Vance  *s*  5546
*Throy* - Jack Vance  *s*  5550

**Caithan Crusade**
*Call of Madness* - Julie Dean Smith  *f*  5124
*Mission of Magic* - Julie Dean Smith  *f*  5125
*Sage of Sare* - Julie Dean Smith  *f*  5126
*The Wizard King* - Julie Dean Smith  *f*  5127

**Caledon**
*Caledon of the Mists* - Deborah Turner
   Harris  *f*  2560
*The Queen of Ashes* - Deborah Turner
   Harris  *f*  2561

**Call of Cthulhu Fiction**
*The Innsmouth Cycle: The Taint of the Deep Ones in
   13 Tales* - Robert M. Price  *h*  4426
*The Necronomicon* - Robert M. Price  *h*  4427
*The Nyarlathotep Cycle* - Robert M. Price  *h*  4429
*The Xothic Legend Cycle: The Complete Mythos
   Fiction of Lin Carter* - Lin Carter  *h*  925

**Callahan's**
*The Callahan Touch* - Spider Robinson  *f*  4637
*Callahan's Lady* - Spider Robinson  *s*  4638
*Callahan's Legacy* - Spider Robinson  *s*  4639
*Lady Slings the Booze* - Spider Robinson  *s*  4640

**Camulod Chronicles**
*The Eagles' Brood* - Jack Whyte  *f*  5792
*The Saxon Shore* - Jack Whyte  *f*  5793

**Camulod Chronicles: The Forging of Arthur's
   Britain**
*The Skystone* - Jack Whyte  *f*  5794

**Car Warriors**
*Double Jeopardy* - Aaron Allston  *s*  86
*The Square Deal* - David Drake  *s*  1644

**Castaways in Time**
*Of Beginnings and Endings* - Robert Adams  *s*  33

**Castell Family**
*Gates of Paradise* - V.C. Andrews  *h*  145
*Web of Dreams* - V.C. Andrews  *h*  147

**Castle Falkenstein**
*From Prussia with Love* - John DeChancie  *f*  1457

**Castle Perilous**
*Bride of the Castle* - John DeChancie  *s*  1452
*Castle Dreams* - John DeChancie  *s*  1453
*Castle Spellbound* - John DeChancie  *s*  1454
*Castle War!* - John DeChancie  *s*  1455

**Cat on the Edge**
*Cats Raise the Dead* - Shirley Rousseau
   Murphy  *f*  4054

**Catfantastic**
*Catfantastic II* - Andre Norton  *f*  4143
*Catfantastic III* - Andre Norton  *f*  4144
*Catfantastic IV* - Andre Norton  *f*  4145

**Chaingang Bunkowski**
*Butcher* - Rex Miller  *h*  3898
*Chaingang* - Rex Miller  *h*  3899
*Savant* - Rex Miller  *h*  3901
*Slice* - Rex Miller  *h*  3902

**Changeling Star**
*Down the Stream of Stars* - Jeffrey A.
   Carver  *s*  928

**Changeling Trilogy**
*The Offspring* - Kenneth McKenney  *h*  3826

**Chanur**
*Chanur's Legacy* - C.J. Cherryh  *s*  981

**Chaos Chronicles**
*The Infinite Sea* - Jeffrey A. Carver  *s*  932
*Neptune Crossing* - Jeffrey A. Carver  *s*  933
*Strange Attractors* - Jeffrey A. Carver  *s*  934

**Chaos Gate Trilogy**
*The Avenger* - Louise Cooper  *f*  1174
*The Deceiver* - Louise Cooper  *f*  1175

**Cheysuli**
*Flight of the Raven* - Jennifer Roberson  *f*  4608
*A Tapestry of Lions* - Jennifer Roberson  *f*  4615

**Chicks in Chainmail**
*Mathemagics* - Margaret Ball  *f*  316

**Child of the Northern Spring**
*Guinevere: The Legend in Autumn* - Persia
   Woolley  *f*  5970
*Queen of the Summer Stars* - Persia
   Woolley  *f*  5971

**Childe Cycle**
*Other* - Gordon R. Dickson  *s*  1538
*Young Bleys* - Gordon R. Dickson  *s*  1540

**Children of the Stars**
*Legacy of Earth* - Juanita Coulson  *s*  1209
*The Past of Forever* - Juanita Coulson  *s*  1210

**Children of Triad**
*Delan the Mislaid* - Laurie J. Marks  *f*  3625

**Chronicles of Aelwyn**
*Timespell* - Robert N. Charrette  *f*  978
*Wizard of Bones* - Robert N. Charrette  *f*  979

**Chronicles of Don Sebastian**
*No Blood Spilled* - Les Daniels  *h*  1338

**Chronicles of Fionn mac Cumhall**
*Master of Earth and Water* - Diana L.
   Paxson  *f*  4266
*The Shield between the Worlds* - Diana L.
   Paxson  *f*  4267
*Sword of Fire and Shadow* - Diana L.
   Paxson  *f*  4268

**Chronicles of Galen Sword**
*Nightfeeder* - Judith Reeves-Stevens  *f*  4513
*Shifter* - Judith Reeves-Stevens  *f*  4515

**Chronicles of Great Alta**
*The One-Armed Queen* - Jane Yolen  *f*  6037

**Chronicles of Greystone Bay**
*In the Fog* - Charles L. Grant  *h*  2311
*The SeaHarp Hotel* - Charles L. Grant  *h*  2315

**Chronicles of Saint-Germain**
*Better in the Dark* - Chelsea Quinn Yarbro  *h*  6011
*Blood Roses* - Chelsea Quinn Yarbro  *h*  6012
*Mansions of Darkness* - Chelsea Quinn
   Yarbro  *h*  6016
*Out of the House of Life* - Chelsea Quinn
   Yarbro  *h*  6018

**Chronicles of St. Germain**
*Writ in Blood* - Chelsea Quinn Yarbro  *h*  6019

**Chronicles of Scar**
*The Lanterns of God* - Ron Sarti  *s*  4835
*Legacy of the Ancients* - Ron Sarti  *s*  4836

**Chronicles of the Austra Family**
*Daughter of the Night* - Elaine Bergstrom  *h*  463

**Chronicles of the Black Company**
*Dreams of Steel* - Glen Cook  *f*  1150

**Chronicles of the Black Company: Glittering Stone**
*Bleak Seasons* - Glen Cook  *f*  1147

**Chronicles of the King's Tramp**
*The End-of-Everything Man* - Tom De
   Haven  *f*  1421
*The Last Human* - Tom De Haven  *f*  1422
*Walker of Worlds* - Tom De Haven  *f*  1423

**Chronicles of the Shadow War**
*Shadow Dawn* - Chris Claremont  *f*  1042
*Shadow Moon* - George Lucas  *f*  3540

**Chung Kuo**
*Beneath the Tree of Heaven* - David
   Wingrove  *s*  5917
*The Broken Wheel* - David Wingrove  *s*  5918
*The Middle Kingdom* - David Wingrove  *s*  5919
*The Stone Within* - David Wingrove  *s*  5920
*White Moon, Red Dragon* - David
   Wingrove  *s*  5921
*The White Mountain* - David Wingrove  *s*  5922

**Cineverse Cycle**
*Bride of the Slime Monster* - Craig Shaw
   Gardner  *f*  2125
*Revenge of the Fluffy Bunnies* - Craig Shaw
   Gardner  *f*  2132

**Circle and Quarters**
*Fifth Quarter* - Tanya Huff  *f*  2795
*No Quarter* - Tanya Huff  *f*  2798

**Circle of Magic**
*School of Wizardry* - Debra Doyle  *f*  1605
*Tris's Book* - Tamora Pierce  *f*  4322

**Cloak and Dagger**
*Anvil of the Sun* - Anne Lesley Groell  *f*  2451

*Bridge of Valor* - Anne Lesley Groell  *f*  2452

**Cloakmaster Cycle**
*Beyond the Moons* - David Cook  *f*  1144
*Into the Void* - Nigel Findley  *f*  1937
*The Radiant Dragon* - Elaine Cunningham  *f*  1291
*The Ultimate Helm* - Russ T. Howard  *f*  2785

**Cloudships of Orion**
*Maia's Veil* - P.K. McAllister  *s*  3707
*Orion's Dagger* - P.K. McAllister  *s*  3708
*Siduri's Net* - P.K. McAllister  *s*  3709

**CoDominium**
*Falkenberg's Legion* - Jerry Pournelle  *s*  4374
*Go Tell the Spartans* - Jerry Pournelle  *s*  4375
*Prince of Mercenaries* - Jerry Pournelle  *s*  4377
*Prince of Sparta* - Jerry Pournelle  *s*  4378

**Cold as Ice**
*The Ganymede Club* - Charles Sheffield  *s*  4955

**Cold One**
*The Cold One* - Christopher Pike  *h*  4327

**Coldfire Trilogy**
*Black Sun Rising* - C.S. Friedman  *f*  2056
*Crown of Shadows* - C.S. Friedman  *s*  2057
*When True Night Falls* - C.S. Friedman  *f*  2060

**Collected Spook Stories of E.F. Benson**
*The Terror by Night* - E.F. Benson  *h*  455

**Collected Stories of Philip K. Dick**
*The Collected Stories of Philip K. Dick, Volume One:
The Short Happy Life of the Brown Oxford* - Philip
K. Dick  *s*  1519
*The Collected Stories of Philip K. Dick, Volume Two:
We Can Remember It for You Wholesale* - Philip K.
Dick  *s*  1520

**The Coming of the Magdalene**
*AEstival Tide* - Elizabeth Hand  *s*  2533
*Winterlong* - Elizabeth Hand  *s*  2539

**Committee**
*Cardinal's Sin* - Raymond Buckland  *h*  751

**Compact Space**
*Heavy Time* - C.J. Cherryh  *s*  995
*Hellburner* - C.J. Cherryh  *s*  996

**Company**
*In the Garden of Iden* - Kage Baker  *s*  298

**Complete Short Stories of Theodore Sturgeon**
*Microcosmic God* - Theodore Sturgeon  *s*  5345
*Thunder and Roses* - Theodore Sturgeon  *s*  5348

**Complete Stories of Theodore Sturgeon**
*Killdozer!* - Theodore Sturgeon  *s*  5344
*The Perfect Host* - Theodore Sturgeon  *s*  5346

**Conan the Barbarian**
*Conan and the Treasure of Python* - John Maddox
Roberts  *f*  4616
*The Conan Chronicles* - Robert Jordan  *f*  2983
*Conan of the Red Brotherhood* - Leonard
Carpenter  *f*  906
*Conan, Scourge of the Bloody Coast* - Leonard
Carpenter  *f*  910
*Conan the Formidable* - Steve Perry  *f*  4293
*Conan the Gladiator* - Leonard Carpenter  *f*  907
*Conan the Guardian* - Roland J. Green  *f*  2347
*Conan the Indomitable* - Steve Perry  *f*  4294
*Conan the Outcast* - Leonard Carpenter  *f*  908
*Conan the Relentless* - Roland J. Green  *f*  2348
*Conan the Rogue* - John Maddox Roberts  *f*  4617
*Conan the Savage* - Leonard Carpenter  *f*  909

**Conrad Stargard**
*Conrad's Quest for Rubber* - Leo
Frankowski  *s*  2043

**Contact**
*Contact and Commune* - L. Neil Smith  *s*  5129

**Controllers**
*Priorities* - Lynda Lyons  *s*  3579

**Crafter Family**
*Blessings and Curses* - Christopher Stasheff  *f*  5214
*The Crafters* - Christopher Stasheff  *f*  5216

**Crashcourse**
*Chaos Come Again* - Wilhelmina Baird  *s*  293
*Clipjoint* - Wilhelmina Baird  *s*  294
*Crashcourse* - Wilhelmina Baird  *s*  295
*Psykosis* - Wilhelmina Baird  *s*  296

**Crimson Shadow**
*The Dragon King* - R.A. Salvatore  *f*  4796
*Luthien's Gamble* - R.A. Salvatore  *f*  4802
*The Sword of Bedwyr* - R.A. Salvatore  *f*  4808

**Crisis of Empire**
*Cluster Command* - David Drake  *s*  1630
*Crown of Empire* - Chelsea Quinn Yarbro  *s*  6014
*The War Machine* - David Drake  *s*  1650

**Crossroads**
*The Healing of Crossroads* - Nick
O'Donohoe  *f*  4195
*The Magic and the Healing* - Nick
O'Donohoe  *f*  4196
*Under the Healing Sign* - Nick O'Donohoe  *f*  4198

**Crow**
*Clash by Night* - Chet Williamson  *h*  5844
*Quoth the Crow* - David Bischoff  *h*  494

**Crown of Stars**
*King's Dragon* - Kate Elliott  *f*  1773
*Prince of Dogs* - Kate Elliott  *f*  1775

**Croyd**
*Megalomania* - Ian Wallace  *s*  5621

**Crystal Singer**
*Crystal Line* - Anne McCaffrey  *s*  3724

**Crystal Warriors**
*The Crystal Sorcerers* - William R.
Forstchen  *f*  1979

**Cthulhu**
*The Azathoth Cycle* - Robert M. Price  *h*  4422

**Cthulhu Cycle**
*The Dunwich Cycle: Where the Old Gods Wait* -
Robert M. Price  *h*  4424

**Culture**
*Against a Dark Background* - Iain M. Banks  *s*  322
*Canal Dreams* - Iain M. Banks  *s*  323
*Excession* - Iain M. Banks  *s*  324
*The State of the Art* - Iain M. Banks  *s*  327

**The Culture**
*Use of Weapons* - Iain M. Banks  *s*  328

**Cups and Sorcery**
*Another Day, Another Dungeon* - Greg
Costikyan  *f*  1206
*One Quest, Hold the Dragons* - Greg
Costikyan  *f*  1208

**CV**
*A Reasonable World* - Damon Knight  *s*  3188

**Cybernarc**
*Cybernarc* - Robert Cain  *s*  829
*End Game* - Robert Cain  *s*  830
*Gold Dragon* - Robert Cain  *s*  831

**Daimbert**
*A Bad Spell in Yurt* - C. Dale Brittain  *f*  701
*Daughter of Magic* - C. Dale Brittain  *f*  703
*The Witch and the Cathedral* - C. Dale
Brittain  *f*  705
*The Wood Nymph and the Cranky Saint* - C. Dale
Brittain  *f*  706

**Dalemark**
*The Crown of Dalemark* - Diana Wynne
Jones  *f*  2945

**Damned**
*A Call to Arms* - Alan Dean Foster  *s*  1995
*The False Mirror* - Alan Dean Foster  *s*  2004
*The Spoils of War* - Alan Dean Foster  *s*  2016

**Danans**
*Search for the Starblade* - Keith Taylor  *f*  5408

**Dance of the Gods**
*Catastrophe's Spell* - Mayer Alan Brenner  *f*  671
*Spell of Apocalypse* - Mayer Alan Brenner  *f*  672
*Spell of Fate* - Mayer Alan Brenner  *f*  673

**Dance of the Rings**
*Ring of Intrigue* - Jane S. Fancher  *f*  1863
*Ring of Lightning* - Jane S. Fancher  *f*  1864

**Dancer Trilogy**
*Dancer's Rise* - Jo Clayton  *f*  1064

**Dancing Gods**
*Horrors of the Dancing Gods* - Jack L.
Chalker  *f*  955
*Songs of the Dancing Gods* - Jack L. Chalker  *f*  962

**Dangerous Journeys**
*The Anubis Murders* - Gary Gygax  *f*  2472
*Death in Delhi* - Gary Gygax  *f*  2473

**Daniel M. Pinkwater's Melvinge of the Megaverse**
*Night of the Living 'Gator!* - Richard A.
Lupoff  *s*  3573
*Night of the Living Rat!* - Debra Doyle  *s*  1603
*Night of the Living Shark!* - David Bischoff  *s*  493

**Danilov Family Saga**
*These Fallen Angels* - Wendy Haley  *h*  2492
*This Dark Paradise* - Wendy Haley  *h*  2493

**Dark Destiny**
*Dark Destiny III: Children of Dracula* - Edward E.
Kramer  *h*  3226

**Dark Future**
*Ghost Dancers* - Brian Craig  *s*  1238

**Dark Future: Demon Download Cycle**
*Comeback Tour: The Sky Belongs to the Stars* - Jack
Yeovil  *s*  6020
*Demon Download* - Jack Yeovil  *f*  6021
*Krokodil Tears* - Jack Yeovil  *f*  6023

**Dark Horse**
*City of the Sorcerers* - Mary H. Herbert  *f*  2673
*Dark Horse* - Mary H. Herbert  *f*  2674
*Lightning's Daughter* - Mary H. Herbert  *f*  2676
*Valorian* - Mary H. Herbert  *f*  2677
*Winged Magic* - Mary H. Herbert  *f*  2678

**Dark Shadows**
*Angelique's Descent* - Lara Parker  *h*  4246

**Dark Sun: Chronicles of Athas**
*The Brazen Gambit* - Lynn Abbey  *f*  13
*Cinnabar Shadows* - Lynn Abbey  *f*  15

**Dark Sun: Tribe of One**
*The Outcast* - Simon Hawke  *f*  2621
*The Seeker* - Simon Hawke  *f*  2624

**Dark Tower**
*The Drawing of the Three* - Stephen King  *h*  3131
*The Waste Lands* - Stephen King  *h*  3143
*Wizard and Glass* - Stephen King  *h*  3144

**Darkangel**
*The Pearl of the Soul of the World* - Meredith Ann
Pierce  *f*  4318

**Darker Passions**
*The Darker Passions: Carmilla* - Amarantha
Knight  *h*  3177

**The Darker Passions**
*The Darker Passions: Dr. Jekyll and Mr. Hyde* - Amarantha Knight   *h*   3178

**Darker Passions**
*The Darker Passions: Dracula* - Amarantha Knight   *h*   3179
*The Darker Passions: Frankenstein* - Amarantha Knight   *h*   3180

**The Darker Passions**
*The Darker Passions Reader* - Amarantha Knight   *h*   3176

**Darker Passions**
*The Pit and the Pendulum* - Amarantha Knight   *h*   3183

**Darkling Wars**
*Forest of the Night* - S.P. Somtow   *f*   5156
*Riverrun* - S.P. Somtow   *f*   5159

**Darkman**
*Darkman #1: The Hangman* - Randall Boyll   *h*   612
*Darkman #2: The Price of Fear* - Randall Boyll   *h*   613
*Darkman #3: The Gods of Hell* - Randall Boyll   *h*   614
*Darkman #4: The Face of Death* - Randall Boyll   *h*   615

**Darkness and Light**
*Ronin* - D.A. Heeley   *f*   2639

**Darkover**
*Domains of Darkover* - Marion Zimmer Bradley   *s*   631
*Exile's Song* - Marion Zimmer Bradley   *s*   632
*The Heirs of Hammerfell* - Marion Zimmer Bradley   *s*   638
*Leroni of Darkover* - Marion Zimmer Bradley   *s*   642
*Rediscovery: A Novel of Darkover* - Marion Zimmer Bradley   *s*   643
*Renunciates of Darkover* - Marion Zimmer Bradley   *s*   644
*The Shadow Matrix* - Marion Zimmer Bradley   *s*   645
*Towers of Darkover* - Marion Zimmer Bradley   *f*   653

**Darksword**
*Legacy of the Darksword* - Margaret Weis   *f*   5719

**Darwath**
*Icefalcon's Quest* - Barbara Hambly   *f*   2504
*Mother of Winter* - Barbara Hambly   *f*   2506

**David Sullivan**
*Darkthunder's Way* - Tom Deitz   *f*   1470
*Dreamseeker's Road* - Tom Deitz   *f*   1472
*Landslayer's Law* - Tom Deitz   *f*   1474
*Stoneskin's Revenge* - Tom Deitz   *f*   1476
*Sunshaker's War* - Tom Deitz   *f*   1477

**Dayworld**
*Dayworld Breakup* - Philip Jose Farmer   *s*   1869

**Dead Girls**
*Dead Boys* - Richard Calder   *s*   836
*Dead Girls* - Richard Calder   *s*   837
*Dead Things* - Richard Calder   *s*   838

**Death Gate Cycle**
*Dragon Wing* - Margaret Weis   *f*   5709
*Elven Star* - Margaret Weis   *f*   5712
*Fire Sea* - Margaret Weis   *f*   5714
*The Hand of Chaos* - Margaret Weis   *f*   5715
*Into the Labyrinth* - Margaret Weis   *f*   5716
*Serpent Mage* - Margaret Weis   *f*   5726
*The Seventh Gate* - Margaret Weis   *f*   5727

**Deed of Paksenarrion**
*Sheepfarmer's Daughter* - Elizabeth Moon   *f*   3973

*Surrender None: The Legacy of Gird* - Elizabeth Moon   *f*   3975

**Demon Crown**
*The Glass Warrior* - Robert E. Vardeman   *f*   5563

**Demon Princes**
*The Demon Princes: Volume One* - Jack Vance   *s*   5544
*The Demon Princes: Volume Two* - Jack Vance   *s*   5545

**Demon Wars Trilogy**
*The Courts of Sorcery* - Ashley McConnell   *f*   3773
*The Fountains of Mirlacca* - Ashley McConnell   *f*   3775
*The Itinerant Exorcist* - Ashley McConnell   *f*   3776

**Destiny Makers**
*Death's Gray Land* - Mike Shupp   *s*   5011
*The Last Reckoning* - Mike Shupp   *s*   5012

**Deverry**
*Days of Air and Darkness* - Katharine Kerr   *f*   3067
*Days of Blood and Fire* - Katharine Kerr   *f*   3068
*The Dragon Revenant* - Katharine Kerr   *f*   3069
*A Time of Exile* - Katharine Kerr   *f*   3077
*A Time of Omens* - Katharine Kerr   *f*   3078

**Diana Tregarde**
*Burning Water* - Mercedes Lackey   *h*   3272
*Children of the Night* - Mercedes Lackey   *h*   3276
*Jinx High* - Mercedes Lackey   *h*   3284

**Diaries of the Family Dracul**
*Children of the Vampire* - Jeanne Kalogridis   *h*   3003
*Lord of the Vampires* - Jeanne Kalogridis   *h*   3005

**Diego**
*Time: The Semi-Final Frontier* - Lionel Fenn   *s*   1921

**Dinosaur Bones**
*Bone Wars* - Brett Davis   *s*   1398

**Dinotopia**
*Dinotopia* - James Gurney   *f*   2468
*Dinotopia Lost* - Alan Dean Foster   *f*   2003
*The World Beneath* - James Gurney   *f*   2469

**Dirigent Mercenary Corps**
*Lieutenant* - Rick Shelley   *s*   4972
*Officer Cadet* - Rick Shelley   *s*   4973

**Discworld**
*Equal Rites* - Terry Pratchett   *f*   4387
*Feet of Clay* - Terry Pratchett   *f*   4389
*Guards! Guards!* - Terry Pratchett   *f*   4390
*Hogfather* - Terry Pratchett   *f*   4391
*Interesting Times* - Terry Pratchett   *f*   4392
*Jingo* - Terry Pratchett   *f*   4393
*Lords and Ladies* - Terry Pratchett   *f*   4394
*Maskerade* - Terry Pratchett   *f*   4395
*Men at Arms* - Terry Pratchett   *f*   4396
*Mort* - Terry Pratchett   *f*   4397
*Moving Pictures* - Terry Pratchett   *f*   4398
*Reaper Man* - Terry Pratchett   *f*   4399
*Small Gods* - Terry Pratchett   *f*   4400
*Soul Music* - Terry Pratchett   *f*   4401
*Witches Abroad* - Terry Pratchett   *f*   4404
*Wyrd Sisters* - Terry Pratchett   *f*   4405

**Divine Endurance**
*Flowerdust* - Gwyneth Jones   *s*   2952

**DNA Cowboys**
*The Last Stand of the DNA Cowboys* - Mick Farren   *s*   1879

**Doc Savage**
*Escape From Loki* - Philip Jose Farmer   *f*   1870
*The Frightened Fish* - Kenneth Robeson   *f*   4622
*The Jade Ogre* - Kenneth Robeson   *f*   4623
*Python Isle* - Kenneth Robeson   *f*   4624

*White Eyes* - Kenneth Robeson   *f*   4625

**Dr. Bones**
*Nightmare World* - David Stern   *s*   5261

**Dominions of Irth**
*The Dark Shore* - Adam Lee   *f*   3385
*The Shadow Eater* - Adam Lee   *f*   3386

**Doomsday Book**
*To Say Nothing of the Dog* - Connie Willis   *s*   5874

**Doona**
*Crisis on Doona* - Anne McCaffrey   *s*   3723
*Treaty at Doona* - Anne McCaffrey   *s*   3752

**Double Diamond Triangle**
*Conspiracy* - J. Robert King   *f*   3121

**Dracula**
*The Dracula Tape* - Fred Saberhagen   *h*   4765
*The Holmes-Dracula File* - Fred Saberhagen   *h*   4767
*A Matter of Taste* - Fred Saberhagen   *h*   4770
*Seance for a Vampire* - Fred Saberhagen   *h*   4773

**Dragon**
*Dragon Tempest* - Don Callander   *f*   844

**Dragon Circle**
*Dragon Burning* - Craig Shaw Gardner   *f*   2126
*Dragon Sleeping* - Craig Shaw Gardner   *f*   2127
*Dragon Waking* - Craig Shaw Gardner   *f*   2128

**Dragon Knight**
*The Dragon and the Djinn* - Gordon R. Dickson   *f*   1528
*The Dragon and the Gnarly King* - Gordon R. Dickson   *f*   1529
*The Dragon at War* - Gordon R. Dickson   *f*   1530
*The Dragon in Lyonesse* - Gordon R. Dickson   *f*   1531
*The Dragon Knight* - Gordon R. Dickson   *f*   1532
*The Dragon on the Border* - Gordon R. Dickson   *f*   1533
*The Dragon, the Earl, and the Troll* - Gordon R. Dickson   *f*   1534

**Dragon Mage**
*The Red Wyvern* - Katharine Kerr   *f*   3074

**Dragon Nimbus**
*The Glass Dragon* - Irene Radford   *f*   4460
*The Loneliest Magician* - Irene Radford   *f*   4461
*The Perfect Princess* - Irene Radford   *f*   4462

**Dragon Nimbus History**
*The Dragon's Touchstone* - Irene Radford   *f*   4459

**Dragon of the Lost Sea**
*Dragon Cauldron* - Laurence Yep   *f*   6024
*Dragon War* - Laurence Yep   *f*   6025

**Dragon Prince**
*The Star Scroll* - Melanie Rawn   *f*   4491
*Sunrunner's Fire* - Melanie Rawn   *f*   4493

**Dragon Quartet**
*The Book of Earth* - Marjorie Bradley Kellogg   *f*   3044
*The Book of Water* - Marjorie Bradley Kellogg   *f*   3045

**Dragon Star**
*The Dragon Token* - Melanie Rawn   *f*   4485
*Skybowl* - Melanie Rawn   *f*   4490
*Stronghold* - Melanie Rawn   *f*   4492

**Dragonbound**
*The Goblin Plain War* - Carl Miller   *f*   3892

**Dragonflight**
*Black Unicorn* - Tanith Lee   *f*   3404
*Child of an Ancient City* - Tad Williams   *f*   5827
*Dragon's Plunder* - Brad Strickland   *f*   5336
*Goldclimbers* - Nancy Luenn   *f*   3545

*The Sleep of Stone* - Louise Cooper  *f*  1179
*Wishing Season* - Esther Friesner  *f*  2085
*The Wizard's Apprentice* - S.P. Somtow  *f*  5163

**Dragonlance**
*The Doom Brigade* - Margaret Weis  *f*  5708
*Dragons of Summer Flame* - Margaret Weis  *f*  5711
*The Second Generation* - Margaret Weis  *f*  5724
*The Soulforge* - Margaret Weis  *f*  5728

**Dragonlance: Defenders of Magic**
*The Seventh Sentinel* - Mary Kirchoff  *f*  3154

**Dragonlance: Fifth Age**
*The Day of the Tempest* - Jean Rabe  *f*  4457

**Dragonlance Heroes II**
*Kaz the Minotaur* - Richard A. Knaak  *f*  3172

**Dragonlance: Lost Legends**
*Vinas Solamnus* - J. Robert King  *f*  3123

**Dragonlance Saga: The Meetings Sextet**
*Wanderlust* - Mary Kirchoff  *f*  3155

**Dragonlance: The Elven Nations Trilogy**
*Firstborn* - Paul B. Thompson  *f*  5454
*The Kinslayer Wars* - Douglas Niles  *f*  4109
*The Qualinesti* - Paul B. Thompson  *f*  5455

**Dragonlance: The Meetings Sextet**
*Kindred Spirits* - Mark Anthony  *f*  154
*Steel and Stone* - Ellen Porath  *f*  4368

**Dragonlance: Villains**
*Hederick, the Theocrat* - Ellen Dodge
  Severson  *f*  4925

**Dragonrealm**
*Children of the Drake* - Richard A. Knaak  *f*  3166
*The Crystal Dragon* - Richard A. Knaak  *f*  3167
*The Dragon Crown* - Richard A. Knaak  *f*  3168
*Dragon Tome* - Richard A. Knaak  *f*  3169
*The Shrouded Realm* - Richard A. Knaak  *f*  3174
*Wolfhelm* - Richard A. Knaak  *f*  3175

**Dragonriders of Pern**
*All the Weyrs of Pern* - Anne McCaffrey  *s*  3719
*The Chronicles of Pern: First Fall* - Anne
  McCaffrey  *s*  3721
*The Dolphins of Pern* - Anne McCaffrey  *s*  3729
*Dragonseye* - Anne McCaffrey  *s*  3730
*The Masterharper of Pern* - Anne
  McCaffrey  *s*  3739
*The Renegades of Pern* - Anne McCaffrey  *s*  3746

**Dragon's Disciple**
*Dark Heart* - Margaret Weis  *f*  5707

**Dragon's Heirs**
*In the Shadow of the Oak King* - Courtway
  Jones  *f*  2939
*Witch of the North* - Courtway Jones  *f*  2940

**Dragon's Pawn**
*Dragon's Queen* - Carol L. Dennis  *f*  1488

**Dragonsword**
*Dragon Death* - Gael Baudino  *f*  390
*Duel of Dragons* - Gael Baudino  *f*  391

**Draka**
*Drakon* - S.M. Stirling  *s*  5294
*The Stone Dogs* - S.M. Stirling  *s*  5300

**Drake Maijstral**
*Rock of Ages* - Walter Jon Williams  *s*  5840

**Dream Park**
*The Barsoom Project* - Larry Niven  *s*  4115
*The California Voodoo Game* - Larry Niven  *s*  4117

**Dream Warrior Trilogy**
*Soothslayer: A Magickal Fantasy* - D.J.
  Conway  *f*  1143

**Dreamer**
*A Call to Arms* - Thomas K. Martin  *f*  3650

**Dreamers of the Day**
*The Argus Gambit* - David D. Ross  *s*  4681
*The Eighth Rank* - David D. Ross  *s*  4682

**Drums of Chaos**
*Drum Calls* - Jo Clayton  *f*  1065
*Drum Warning* - Jo Clayton  *f*  1066

**Dryco Chronicles**
*Elvissey* - Jack Womack  *s*  5957
*Heathern* - Jack Womack  *s*  5958
*Random Acts of Senseless Violence* - Jack
  Womack  *f*  5959
*Terraplane* - Jack Womack  *s*  5960

**D'Shai**
*D'Shai* - Joel Rosenberg  *f*  4670
*Hour of the Octopus* - Joel Rosenberg  *f*  4673

**The Early Cannon**
*Tales of Lovecraftian Horror and Humor* - P.H.
  Cannon  *h*  868
*The Thing in the Bathtub and Other Lovecraftian Tales*
  - P.H. Cannon  *h*  869

**Earth Blood**
*Deep Trek* - James Axler  *s*  278

**Earth Dawn**
*The Longing Ring* - Christopher Kubasik  *f*  3246

**Earth's Children**
*The Plains of Passage* - Jean M. Auel  *f*  275

**Earthsea**
*Tehanu: The Last Book of Earthsea* - Ursula K. Le
  Guin  *f*  3383

**Echoes of Valor**
*Echoes of Valor III* - Karl Edward Wagner  *f*  5599

**Ecolitan**
*The Ecolitan Operation* - L.E. Modesitt Jr.  *s*  3928

**Ecolitan Institute**
*The Ecolitan Enigma* - L.E. Modesitt Jr.  *s*  3927

**Ecolitan Trilogy**
*The Ecologic Secession* - L.E. Modesitt Jr.  *s*  3929

**Eden**
*Beyond Eden* - J.M. Morgan  *s*  3999
*Desert Eden* - J.M. Morgan  *s*  4000
*Future Eden* - J.M. Morgan  *s*  4001

**Eggheads**
*GodHeads* - Emily Devenport  *s*  1501

**Eight Worlds**
*Steel Beach* - John Varley  *s*  5566

**Elders**
*Converse and Conflict* - L. Neil Smith  *s*  5130

**Elenium**
*The Diamond Throne* - David Eddings  *f*  1731
*The Ruby Knight* - David Eddings  *f*  1736
*The Sapphire Rose* - David Eddings  *f*  1737

**Elfquest**
*Captives of the Blue Mountain* - Wendy
  Pini  *f*  4336
*The Quest Begins* - Wendy Pini  *f*  4337

**Elfquest: The Blood of Ten Chiefs**
*Dark Hours* - Richard Pini  *f*  4335

**Elfwood**
*Twisted Dragon* - Kevin Stein  *f*  5251

**Elric**
*Elric: Song of the Black Sword* - Michael
  Moorcock  *f*  3980
*The Fortress of the Pearl* - Michael
  Moorcock  *f*  3982

**The Revenge of the Rose** - Michael
  Moorcock  *f*  3985
*Tales of the White Wolf* - Edward E.
  Kramer  *f*  3227

**Elven Ways**
*Ancient Games* - Scott Ciencin  *f*  1028
*Night of Glory* - Scott Ciencin  *f*  1030
*The Ways of Magic* - Scott Ciencin  *f*  1033

**Elvira, Mistress of the Dark**
*Camp Vamp* - Elvira  *h*  1801

**Elysia**
*Primavera* - Francesca Lia Block  *f*  551

**Emancipator**
*Emperor of Everything* - Ray Aldridge  *s*  62
*The Pharaoh Contract* - Ray Aldridge  *s*  63

**Empire Trilogy**
*Mistress of the Empire* - Raymond E. Feist  *f*  1906
*Servant of the Empire* - Raymond E. Feist  *f*  1910

**Enchanted Forest Chronicles**
*Calling on Dragons* - Patricia C. Wrede  *f*  5974
*Dealing with Dragons* - Patricia C. Wrede  *f*  5975
*Searching for Dragons* - Patricia C. Wrede  *f*  5979

**Ender Wiggin**
*Children of the Mind* - Orson Scott Card  *s*  883
*Xenocide* - Orson Scott Card  *s*  899

**Endless Frontier**
*Life Among the Asteroids* - Jerry Pournelle  *s*  4376

**Endworld**
*Madman Run* - David Robbins  *s*  4600
*Spartan Run* - David Robbins  *s*  4602
*Yellowstone Run* - David Robbins  *s*  4605

**Eon**
*Legacy* - Greg Bear  *s*  420

**Eschaton Sequence**
*The Siege of Eternity* - Frederik Pohl  *s*  4353

**Eternal Champion**
*Corum: The Coming of Chaos* - Michael
  Moorcock  *f*  3978

**Eternal Guardians**
*The Fourth Guardian* - Ronald Anthony
  Cross  *s*  1273
*The Lost Guardian* - Ronald Anthony Cross  *s*  1274
*The White Guardian* - Ronald Anthony
  Cross  *s*  1275

**Ethshar**
*The Spell of the Black Dagger* - Lawrence Watt-
  Evans  *f*  5648
*Taking Flight* - Lawrence Watt-Evans  *f*  5650

**Ever**
*The Daemon in the Machine* - Felicity
  Savage  *f*  4848
*The War in the Waste* - Felicity Savage  *f*  4852
*The War in the Waste* - Felicity Savage  *f*  4851

**Exiles**
*The Mageborn Traitor* - Melanie Rawn  *f*  4488
*The Ruins of Ambrai* - Melanie Rawn  *f*  4489

**Exiles Saga**
*Exile's Challenge* - Angus Wells  *f*  5734
*Exile's Children* - Angus Wells  *f*  5735

**Exordium**
*The Phoenix in Flight* - Sherwood Smith  *s*  5138
*A Prison Unsought* - Sherwood Smith  *s*  5139
*The Rifter's Covenant* - Sherwood Smith  *s*  5140
*Ruler of Naught* - Sherwood Smith  *s*  5141

**Faerie Dragon**
*Dragons on the Town* - Thorarinn
  Gunnarsson  *f*  2463

*Make Way for Dragons!* - Thorarinn Gunnarsson  *f*  2465

**Fafhrd and the Gray Mouser**
*Ill Met in Lankhmar* - Fritz Leiber  *f*  3419
*Return to Lankhmar* - Fritz Leiber  *f*  3422
*Swords Against the Shadowland* - Robin Wayne Bailey  *f*  291

**Fairy Tales**
*Snow White and Rose Red* - Patricia C. Wrede  *f*  5981
*Tam Lin* - Pamela Dean  *f*  1446

**Fantasy Adventure**
*Cardmaster* - Clayton Emery  *f*  1813

**Fanuilh**
*Beggar's Banquet* - Daniel Hood  *f*  2756
*Fanuilh* - Daniel Hood  *f*  2757
*Wizard's Heir* - Daniel Hood  *f*  2759

**Far Kingdoms**
*Kingdoms of the Night* - Allan Cole  *f*  1105
*The Warrior Returns* - Allan Cole  *f*  1109
*The Warrior's Tale* - Allan Cole  *f*  1110

**Far-Seer**
*Fossil Hunter* - Robert J. Sawyer  *s*  4855

**Farseer**
*Assassin's Apprentice* - Robin Hobb  *f*  2693
*Assassin's Quest* - Robin Hobb  *f*  2694
*Royal Assassin* - Robin Hobb  *f*  2695

**FBI Agent Kreident**
*Lethal Exposure* - Kevin J. Anderson  *s*  110

**Fear Street**
*The Cat* - R.L. Stine  *h*  5285
*Double Date* - R.L. Stine  *h*  5287

**Fenrille**
*The Founder* - Christopher Rowley  *s*  4696
*To a Highland Nation* - Christopher Rowley  *s*  4698

**Ferdinand Feghoot**
*The Collected Feghoot* - Grendel Briarton  *s*  677

**Fey**
*The Changeling* - Kristine Kathryn Rusch  *f*  4714
*The Resistance* - Kristine Kathryn Rusch  *f*  4727

**Fiddleback Trilogy**
*Evil Ascending* - Michael A. Stackpole  *s*  5198
*Evil Triumphant* - Michael A. Stackpole  *s*  5199
*A Gathering Evil* - Michael A. Stackpole  *s*  5201

**Fifth Foreign Legion**
*Cohort of the Damned* - Andrew Keith  *s*  3034
*March or Die* - Andrew Keith  *s*  3035

**Fifth Millennium**
*Lion's Heart* - Karen Wehrstein  *f*  5683
*Lion's Soul* - Karen Wehrstein  *f*  5684
*Saber & Shadow* - S.M. Stirling  *f*  5297
*Shadow's Daughter* - Shirley Meier  *f*  3871
*Shadow's Son* - Shirley Meier  *f*  3872
*Snow Brother* - S.M. Stirling  *f*  5299

**Fire Sanctuary**
*Hidden Fires* - Katharine Eliska Kimbriel  *s*  3117

**Firebringer Trilogy**
*The Son of Summer Stars* - Meredith Ann Pierce  *f*  4319

**Firestar**
*Rogue Star* - Michael Flynn  *s*  1965

**First Americans Saga**
*The Edge of the World* - William Sarabande  *f*  4817
*The Sacred Stones* - William Sarabande  *f*  4818
*Thunder in the Sky* - William Sarabande  *f*  4819

**First North Americans**
*People of the Earth* - W. Michael Gear  *f*  2166
*People of the Fire* - W. Michael Gear  *f*  2167
*People of the Lakes* - Kathleen O'Neal Gear  *f*  2164
*People of the River* - W. Michael Gear  *f*  2168
*People of the Sea* - W. Michael Gear  *f*  2169
*People of the Wolf* - W. Michael Gear  *f*  2170

**Fisher King**
*Earthquake Weather* - Tim Powers  *f*  4382

**Five Worlds**
*Exile* - Al Sarrantonio  *s*  4829

**Flight Engineer**
*The Rising* - James Doohan  *s*  1579

**Flinx**
*Mid-Flinx* - Alan Dean Foster  *s*  2010

**Forbidden Borders**
*Relic of Empire* - W. Michael Gear  *s*  2171

**Foreigner Universe**
*Foreigner* - C.J. Cherryh  *s*  990
*Inheritor* - C.J. Cherryh  *s*  997
*Invader* - C.J. Cherryh  *s*  998

**Forerunner**
*Brother to Shadows* - Andre Norton  *s*  4142

**Forests of the Night**
*Emperors of the Twilight* - S. Andrew Swann  *s*  5362
*Specters of the Dawn* - S. Andrew Swann  *s*  5368

**Forever King**
*The Broken Sword* - Molly Cochran  *f*  1091

**Forever Knight**
*Forever Knight: A Stirring of Dust* - Susan Sizemore  *h*  5078
*Forever Knight: Intimations of Mortality* - Susan M. Garrett  *h*  2149

**Forgotten Realms**
*Cormyr: A Novel* - Ed Greenwood  *f*  2426
*Daughter of the Drow* - Elaine Cunningham  *f*  1287
*Elminster: The Making of a Mage* - Ed Greenwood  *f*  2427
*The Legacy* - R.A. Salvatore  *f*  4801
*Masquerades* - Kate Novak  *f*  4166
*Murder in Cormyr* - Chet Williamson  *f*  5848
*Passage to Dawn* - R.A. Salvatore  *f*  4803
*Siege of Darkness* - R.A. Salvatore  *f*  4804
*The Silent Blade* - R.A. Salvatore  *f*  4805
*Starless Night* - R.A. Salvatore  *f*  4807

**Forgotten Realms: The Cleric Quintet**
*Canticle* - R.A. Salvatore  *f*  4793
*In Sylvan Shadows* - R.A. Salvatore  *f*  4800

**Forgotten Realms: The Dark Elf Trilogy**
*Sojourn* - R.A. Salvatore  *f*  4806

**Forgotten Realms: The Druidhome Trilogy**
*The Coral Kingdom* - Douglas Niles  *f*  4106

**Forgotten Realms: The Empire Trilogy**
*Crusade* - James Lowder  *f*  3537
*Horselords* - David Cook  *f*  1145

**Forgotten Realms: The Finder's Stone Trilogy**
*Song of the Saurials* - Kate Novak  *f*  4167

**Forgotten Realms: The Harpers**
*Elfshadow* - Elaine Cunningham  *f*  1288
*Elfsong* - Elaine Cunningham  *f*  1289
*Finder's Bane* - Kate Novak  *f*  4165
*The Parched Sea* - Troy Denning  *f*  1486
*Red Magic* - Jean Rabe  *f*  4458
*The Ring of Winter* - James Lowder  *f*  3538
*Silver Shadows* - Elaine Cunningham  *f*  1292

**Forgotten Realms: The Maztica Trilogy**
*Feathered Dragon* - Douglas Niles  *f*  4108

**Forgotten Realms: The Nobles**
*King Pinch* - David Cook  *f*  1146
*The Mage in the Iron Mask* - Brian Thomsen  *f*  5458

**Fortress**
*Fortress of Owls* - C.J. Cherryh  *f*  993

**Foundation**
*Forward the Foundation* - Isaac Asimov  *s*  236
*Foundation and Chaos* - Greg Bear  *s*  418

**Freedom's Landing**
*Freedom's Challenge* - Anne McCaffrey  *s*  3732
*Freedom's Choice* - Anne McCaffrey  *s*  3733

**Freedom's Rangers**
*Search and Destroy* - Keith William Andrews  *s*  141
*Sink the Armada* - Keith William Andrews  *s*  142
*Treason in Time* - Keith William Andrews  *s*  143

**From Thief to King**
*A Forest Lord* - Michael Williams  *f*  5819
*A Sorcerer's Apprentice* - Michael Williams  *f*  5820

**Full Spectrum**
*Full Spectrum 2* - Lou Aronica  *s*  214
*Full Spectrum 3* - Lou Aronica  *s*  215
*Full Spectrum 4* - Lou Aronica  *s*  216
*Full Spectrum 5* - Jennifer Hershey  *s*  2679

**Gabriel Knight**
*The Beast Within: A Gabriel Knight Mystery* - Jane Jensen  *h*  2895
*Gabriel Knight: Sins of the Fathers* - Jane Jensen  *h*  2896

**Galactic Center**
*Sailing Bright Eternity* - Gregory Benford  *s*  449

**Galactic MI**
*Galactic MI* - Kevin D. Randle  *s*  4467

**Galactic Milieu**
*Diamond Mask: A Novel* - Julian May  *s*  3697
*Jack the Bodiless* - Julian May  *s*  3698
*Magnificat* - Julian May  *s*  3699

**Gambler's Star**
*The Six Families* - Nancy Holder  *s*  2733

**Gamearth**
*Gameplay* - Kevin J. Anderson  *f*  105
*Game's End* - Kevin J. Anderson  *f*  104

**Gamester Wars**
*The Napoleon Wager* - William R. Forstchen  *s*  1980

**Gammalaw**
*A Screaming Across the Sky* - Brian Daley  *s*  1315

**Gap**
*Forbidden Knowledge* - Stephen R. Donaldson  *s*  1571
*The Gap into Madness: Chaos and Order* - Stephen R. Donaldson  *s*  1573
*The Gap into Power: A Dark and Hungry God Arises* - Stephen R. Donaldson  *s*  1574
*The Gap into Ruin: This Day All Gods Die* - Stephen R. Donaldson  *s*  1575

**Garrett Files**
*Deadly Quicksilver Lies* - Glen Cook  *f*  1148
*Dread Brass Shadows* - Glen Cook  *f*  1149
*Old Tin Sorrows* - Glen Cook  *f*  1151
*Pretty Pewter Gods* - Glen Cook  *f*  1152
*Red Iron Nights* - Glen Cook  *f*  1153

**Gate of Worlds**
*Lion Time in Timbuctoo* - Robert Silverberg  *s*  5036

**Gates of Time**
*The Whispers* - Dan Parkinson  *s*  4247

**Genellan**
*Genellan: Planetfall* - Scott G. Gier  *s*  2223
*In the Shadow of the Moon* - Scott G. Gier  *s*  2224

**Geodyssey**
*Hope of Earth* - Piers Anthony  *s*  175
*Shame of Man* - Piers Anthony  *s*  188

**Gerin the Fox**
*Fox and Empire* - Harry Turtledove  *f*  5500

**Ghatti's Tale**
*Exiles' Return* - Gayle Greeno  *s*  2420
*Finders-Seekers* - Gayle Greeno  *s*  2421
*Mind-Speakers' Call* - Gayle Greeno  *s*  2423

**Ghoster**
*Backblast* - Lee McKeone  *s*  3828
*The Clone Crisis* - Lee McKeone  *s*  3829
*Starfire Down* - Lee McKeone  *s*  3830

**Giants**
*Entoverse* - James P. Hogan  *s*  2724

**Glaive**
*The Glaive* - Cary Osborne  *s*  4227
*Iroshi* - Cary Osborne  *s*  4228

**Glenraven**
*In the Rift* - Marion Zimmer Bradley  *f*  639

**Goa**
*Blood of the Goddess* - Kara Dalkey  *f*  1318

**Goblin Moon**
*The Gnome's Engine* - Teresa Edgerton  *f*  1742

**Gods of Ireland**
*The Enchanted Isles* - Casey Flynn  *f*  1960
*Most Ancient Song* - Casey Flynn  *f*  1961

**Godwars**
*Dark Magic* - Angus Wells  *f*  5733
*Forbidden Magic* - Angus Wells  *f*  5736
*Wild Magic* - Angus Wells  *f*  5741

**Golden Queen**
*Beyond the Gate* - Dave Wolverton  *s*  5949
*The Golden Queen* - Dave Wolverton  *s*  5951

**Goldenwing Cycle**
*Glory* - Alfred Coppel  *s*  1182
*Glory's People* - Alfred Coppel  *s*  1183
*Glory's War* - Alfred Coppel  *s*  1184

**Goosebumps**
*Vampire Breath* - R.L. Stine  *h*  5291

**Great Game**
*Future Indefinite* - Dave Duncan  *f*  1678
*Present Tense* - Dave Duncan  *f*  1686

**Great Sky River**
*Furious Gulf* - Gregory Benford  *s*  447

**Great War**
*The Great War: American Front* - Harry
  Turtledove  *s*  5501

**Green Lion**
*Goblin Moon* - Teresa Edgerton  *f*  1743
*The Moon in Hiding* - Teresa Edgerton  *f*  1745
*The Work of the Sun* - Teresa Edgerton  *f*  1746

**Greg Mandel**
*Mindstar Rising* - Peter F. Hamilton  *s*  2526
*A Quantum Murder* - Peter F. Hamilton  *s*  2527

**Griffin & Sabine**
*The Golden Mean* - Nick Bantock  *f*  334
*Sabine's Notebook* - Nick Bantock  *f*  335

**Guardians**
*Devil's Deal* - Richard Austin  *s*  277

**Guardians of the Flame**
*The Road Home* - Joel Rosenberg  *f*  4674
*The Road to Ehvenor* - Joel Rosenberg  *f*  4675

**Hain**
*Four Ways to Forgiveness* - Ursula K. Le
  Guin  *s*  3380

**Halfblood Chronicles**
*The Elvenbane* - Andre Norton  *f*  4149
*Elvenblood* - Andre Norton  *f*  4150

**Hammer and the Cross**
*The Hammer and the Cross* - Harry
  Harrison  *f*  2570
*King and Emperor* - Harry Harrison  *f*  2571
*One King's Way* - Harry Harrison  *s*  2572

**Hammer's Slammers**
*Caught in the Crossfire* - David Drake  *s*  1628
*Rolling Hot* - David Drake  *s*  1642
*The Warrior* - David Drake  *s*  1651

**Handful of Men**
*The Cutting Edge* - Dave Duncan  *f*  1675
*The Living God* - Dave Duncan  *f*  1682
*The Stricken Field* - Dave Duncan  *f*  1688
*Upland Outlaws* - Dave Duncan  *f*  1690

**Harold Shea**
*The Enchanter Reborn* - L. Sprague de
  Camp  *f*  1413

**Harvest of Stars**
*The Fleet of Stars* - Poul Anderson  *s*  126
*Harvest the Fire* - Poul Anderson  *s*  128

**Hawk & Fisher**
*The Bones of Haven* - Simon R. Green  *f*  2363
*The God Killer* - Simon R. Green  *f*  2368
*Guard Against Dishonor* - Simon R. Green  *f*  2369
*Hawk & Fisher* - Simon R. Green  *f*  2370
*Winner Takes All* - Simon R. Green  *f*  2375
*Wolf in the Fold* - Simon R. Green  *f*  2376

**Healer's War**
*The Healer's War* - Elizabeth Ann
  Scarborough  *f*  4865
*Last Refuge* - Elizabeth Ann Scarborough  *f*  4866
*Nothing Sacred* - Elizabeth Ann
  Scarborough  *f*  4867

**Heechee**
*The Gateway Trip: Tales and Vignettes of the Heechee*
  - Frederik Pohl  *s*  4346

**Heirs of Saint Camber**
*The Bastard Prince* - Katherine Kurtz  *f*  3255
*King Javan's Year* - Katherine Kurtz  *f*  3258

**Heirs to Gnarlsmyre**
*Hall of Whispers* - Mike Jefferies  *f*  2884

**Hellboy**
*Hellboy: The Lost Army* - Christopher
  Golden  *h*  2257

**Hellflower**
*Archangel Blues* - eluki bes shahar  *s*  471
*Darktraders* - eluki bes shahar  *s*  472

**Hellraised**
*The Devil and Dan Cooley* - Holly Lisle  *f*  3480
*Hell on High* - Holly Lisle  *f*  3483
*Sympathy for the Devil* - Holly Lisle  *f*  3488

**Helmsman**
*The Defenders* - Bill Baldwin  *s*  309
*The Defiance* - Bill Baldwin  *s*  310
*The Mercenaries* - Bill Baldwin  *s*  311
*The Siege* - Bill Baldwin  *s*  312

**Henry Martyn**
*Bretta Martyn* - L. Neil Smith  *s*  5128

**Heorot**
*Beowulf's Children* - Larry Niven  *s*  4116

**Hercules: The Legendary Journeys**
*By the Sword* - Timothy Boggs  *f*  559

*The First Casualty* - David L. Seidman  *f*  4912

**Heritage of Shannara**
*The Druid of Shannara* - Terry Brooks  *f*  710
*The Elf Queen of Shannara* - Terry Brooks  *f*  711
*The Scions of Shannara* - Terry Brooks  *f*  716
*The Talismans of Shannara* - Terry Brooks  *f*  717

**Heritage Trilogy**
*Semper Mars* - Ian Douglas  *s*  1585

**Heritage Universe**
*Convergence* - Charles Sheffield  *s*  4951
*Divergence* - Charles Sheffield  *s*  4954
*Summertide* - Charles Sheffield  *s*  4965
*Transcendence* - Charles Sheffield  *s*  4967

**Heroes, Inc.**
*Heroes, Inc.* - Kyle Crocco  *f*  1268
*Heroes Wanted* - Kyle Crocco  *f*  1267

**High Road Trilogy**
*A Passage of Stars* - Alis A. Rasmussen  *s*  4482

**Highlander**
*The Element of Fire* - Jason Henderson  *f*  2657
*Scotland the Brave* - Jennifer Roberson  *f*  4611
*Shadow of Obsession* - Rebecca Neason  *f*  4082

**Highroad Trilogy**
*The Price of Ransom* - Alis A. Rasmussen  *s*  4483
*Revolution's Shore* - Alis A. Rasmussen  *s*  4484

**His Dark Materials**
*The Golden Compass* - Philip Pullman  *f*  4446
*The Subtle Knife* - Philip Pullman  *f*  4448

**Historical Illuminatus Chronicles**
*Nature's God* - Robert Anton Wilson  *f*  5903

**Hitchhiker's Guide to the Galaxy**
*The Illustrated Hitchhiker's Guide to the Galaxy* -
  Douglas Adams  *s*  29
*Mostly Harmless* - Douglas Adams  *s*  31

**Homecoming**
*The Call of Earth* - Orson Scott Card  *s*  882
*Earthborn* - Orson Scott Card  *s*  884
*Earthfall* - Orson Scott Card  *s*  885
*The Memory of Earth* - Orson Scott Card  *s*  894
*The Ships of Earth* - Orson Scott Card  *s*  897

**Honor Harrington**
*Echoes of Honor* - David Weber  *s*  5669
*Field of Dishonor* - David Weber  *s*  5670
*Flag in Exile* - David Weber  *s*  5671
*Honor Among Enemies* - David Weber  *s*  5673
*The Honor of the Queen* - David Weber  *s*  5674
*In Enemy Hands* - David Weber  *s*  5675
*On Basilisk Station* - David Weber  *s*  5679
*The Short Victorious War* - David Weber  *s*  5681

**Horror Writers Association Presents**
*Robert Bloch's Psychos* - Robert Bloch  *h*  544

**Horsegirl Saga**
*The Stallion Queen* - Constance Ash  *f*  223

**Hostile Takeover**
*Partisan* - S. Andrew Swann  *s*  5365
*Profiteer* - S. Andrew Swann  *s*  5366
*Revolutionary* - S. Andrew Swann  *s*  5367

**Hot Blood**
*Deadly After Dark* - Jeff Gelb  *h*  2174
*Fear the Fever* - Jeff Gelb  *h*  2176
*Hot Blood X* - Jeff Gelb  *h*  2177
*Hot Blood: Crimes of Passion* - Jeff Gelb  *h*  2178
*Hot Blood: Kiss and Kill* - Jeff Gelb  *h*  2179
*Hotter Blood: More Tales of Erotic Horror* - Jeff
  Gelb  *h*  2180
*Hottest Blood: The Ultimate in Erotic Horror* - Jeff
  Gelb  *h*  2181
*Seeds of Fear* - Jeff Gelb  *h*  2182
*Stranger by Night* - Jeff Gelb  *h*  2185

**Howl's Moving Castle**
*Castle in the Air* - Diana Wynne Jones  f  2944

**Hugo Winners**
*The New Hugo Winners, Volume III* - Connie
  Willis  s  5871
*The New Hugo Winners, Volume IV* - Martin H.
  Greenberg  s  2401

**Humanx Commonwealth**
*The Howling Stones* - Alan Dean Foster  s  2006

**Humility Garden**
*Delta City* - Felicity Savage  f  4849
*Humility Garden* - Felicity Savage  f  4850

**Hunted Earth**
*The Ring of Charon* - Roger MacBride Allen  s  80
*The Shattered Sphere* - Roger MacBride Allen  s  81

**Hunter**
*The Hunter on Arena* - Rose Estes  s  1838

**Hunting Party**
*Hunting Party* - Elizabeth Moon  s  3968
*Sporting Chance* - Elizabeth Moon  s  3974
*Winning Colors* - Elizabeth Moon  s  3976

**Hyperion**
*Endymion* - Dan Simmons  s  5051
*The Fall of Hyperion* - Dan Simmons  s  5052
*Hyperion* - Dan Simmons  s  5055
*The Rise of Endymion* - Dan Simmons  s  5059

**Ijon Tichy**
*Peace on Earth* - Stanislaw Lem  s  3435

**Immortals**
*The Realms of the Gods* - Tamora Pierce  f  4321
*Wild Magic* - Tamora Pierce  f  4323
*Wolf-Speaker* - Tamora Pierce  f  4324

**Incarnations of Immortality**
*And Eternity* - Piers Anthony  f  162

**Incredible Hulk**
*What Savage Beast* - Peter David  s  1390

**Independence Day**
*Silent Zone* - Stephen Molstad  s  3952

**Indian in the Cupboard**
*The Key to the Indian* - Lynne Reid Banks  f  331
*The Secret of the Indian* - Lynne Reid Banks  f  332

**Indiana Jones**
*Indiana Jones and the Dance of the Giants* - Rob
  MacGregor  f  3588
*Indiana Jones and the Genesis Deluge* - Rob
  MacGregor  f  3589
*Indiana Jones and the Interior World* - Rob
  MacGregor  f  3590
*Indiana Jones and the Peril at Delphi* - Rob
  MacGregor  f  3591
*Indiana Jones and the Seven Veils* - Rob
  MacGregor  f  3592
*Indiana Jones and the Sky Pirates* - Martin
  Caidin  f  825
*Indiana Jones and the Unicorn's Legacy* - Rob
  MacGregor  f  3593
*Indiana Jones and the White Witch* - Martin
  Caidin  f  826

**Indigo**
*Aisling* - Louise Cooper  f  1172
*Avatar* - Louise Cooper  f  1173
*Infanta* - Louise Cooper  f  1176
*Nemesis* - Louise Cooper  f  1177
*Revenant* - Louise Cooper  f  1178
*Troika* - Louise Cooper  f  1181

**Infocom**
*The Lost City of Zork* - Robin Wayne Bailey  f  288
*The Zork Chronicles* - George Alec
  Effinger  s  1754

**Inheritor**
*Heartlight* - Marion Zimmer Bradley  f  637

**Instrumentality of Mankind**
*Norstrilia* - Cordwainer Smith  s  5105
*The Rediscovery of Man* - Cordwainer
  Smith  s  5106

**Invaders of Charon**
*Warlords of Jupiter* - William H. Keith Jr.  s  3036

**Invasion America**
*Invasion America* - Christie Golden  s  2252
*On the Run* - Christie Golden  s  2254

**Iron Man**
*Iron Man: The Armor Trap* - Greg Cox  s  1227

**Isaac Asimov Presents the Great SF Stories**
*Isaac Asimov Presents the Great SF Stories: 20 (1958)*
  - Isaac Asimov  s  238
*Isaac Asimov Presents the Great SF Stories: 21 (1959)*
  - Isaac Asimov  s  239
*Isaac Asimov Presents the Great SF Stories: 22 (1959)*
  - Isaac Asimov  s  240
*Isaac Asimov Presents the Great SF Stories: 23 (1961)*
  - Isaac Asimov  s  241
*Isaac Asimov Presents the Great SF Stories: 24 (1962)*
  - Isaac Asimov  s  242
*Isaac Asimov Presents the Great SF Stories: 25 (1963)*
  - Isaac Asimov  s  243

**Isaac Asimov's Caliban**
*Caliban* - Roger MacBride Allen  s  77
*Inferno* - Roger MacBride Allen  s  78
*Utopia* - Roger MacBride Allen  s  83

**Isaac Asimov's Magical Worlds of Fantasy**
*Faeries* - Isaac Asimov  f  235

**Isaac Asimov's Robot City: Robots and Aliens**
*Changeling* - Stephen Leigh  s  3425
*Maverick* - Bruce Bethke  s  484
*Renegade* - Cordell Scotten  s  4903

**Isaac Asimov's Robots in Time**
*Dictator* - William F. Wu  s  5996
*Predator* - William F. Wu  s  5998
*Warrior* - William F. Wu  s  6000

**Island Warrior**
*Storm Caller* - Carol Severance  f  4924

**Island Worlds**
*Delta Pavonis* - Eric Kotani  s  3221

**Ivory**
*The Gate of Ivory* - Doris Egan  s  1755
*Guilt-Edged Ivory* - Doris Egan  s  1756
*Two-Bit Heroes* - Doris Egan  s  1757

**Jack Eichord Chronicles**
*Iceman* - Rex Miller  h  3900

**Jackaroo**
*On Fortune's Wheel* - Cynthia Voigt  f  5579

**Jake Bird**
*Devil's Engine* - Mark Sumner  f  5356
*Devil's Tower* - Mark Sumner  f  5357

**Jaran**
*An Earthly Crown* - Kate Elliott  s  1771
*The Law of Becoming* - Kate Elliott  s  1774

**Jason Cosmo**
*Dirty Work* - Dan McGirt  f  3810

**Jefferson's War**
*Jefferson's War: Death of a Regiment* - Kevin
  Randle  s  4466

**Jenny Sixa**
*The Stranger* - Eric James Fullilove  s  2093

**Jeremy Moon**
*Wizard's Mole* - Brad Strickland  f  5337

**Jiana**
*Warriorwards* - Dafydd ab Hugh  f  11

**Journeys of the Catechist**
*Carnivores of Light and Darkness* - Alan Dean
  Foster  f  1996

**Jupiter**
*Higher Education* - Charles Sheffield  s  4958
*Starswarm* - Jerry Pournelle  s  4379

**K-9 Corps**
*Cry Wolf* - Kenneth Von Gunden  s  5586
*Under Fire* - Kenneth Von Gunden  s  5589

**Kedrigern**
*Kedrigern and the Charming Couple* - John
  Morressy  f  4013
*A Remembrance for Kedrigern* - John
  Morressy  f  4014

**Keepers of the Hidden Ways**
*The Crimson Sky* - Joel Rosenberg  f  4669
*The Fire Duke* - Joel Rosenberg  f  4671
*The Silver Stone* - Joel Rosenberg  f  4676

**Keith Doyle**
*Higher Mythology* - Jody Lynn Nye  f  4170
*Mythology 101* - Jody Lynn Nye  f  4173
*Mythology Abroad* - Jody Lynn Nye  f  4174

**Keltiad**
*Blackmantle: A Triumph* - Patricia Kennealy-
  Morrison  f  3059
*The Deer's Cry: A Book of the Keltiad* - Patricia
  Kennealy-Morrison  f  3060

**Keltiad: Tales of Arthur**
*The Hawk's Gray Feather* - Patricia Kennealy-
  Morrison  f  3061
*The Hedge of Mist* - Patricia Kennealy-
  Morrison  s  3062
*The Oak Above the Kings: A Book of the Keltiad* -
  Patricia Kennealy  s  3058

**Kelvin of Rud**
*Chimaera's Copper* - Piers Anthony  f  166
*Mouvar's Magic* - Piers Anthony  f  182
*Orc's Opal* - Piers Anthony  f  183

**Kent Montana**
*668: The Neighbor of the Beast* - Lionel
  Fenn  h  1917
*Kent Montana and the Really Ugly Thing From Mars* -
  Lionel Fenn  s  1918
*Kent Montana and the Reasonably Invisible Man* -
  Lionel Fenn  s  1919

**Khaavren Romances**
*Five Hundred Years After* - Steven Brust  f  742
*The Phoenix Guards* - Steven Brust  f  747

**Khyren**
*World Spirits* - Aline Boucher-Kaplan  s  580

**King's Quest**
*The Floating Castle* - Craig Mills  f  3913

**Kirins**
*Kirins: The Flight of the Ain* - James D.
  Priest  f  4433
*Kirins: The Secret of the Hanging Stones* - James D.
  Priest  f  4434
*Kirins: The Spell of No'an* - James D.
  Priest  f  4435

**Known Space**
*Crashlander* - Larry Niven  s  4118
*Flatlander* - Larry Niven  s  4121

**Krispos of Videssos**
*Krispos of Videssos* - Harry Turtledove  f  5506
*Krispos Rising* - Harry Turtledove  f  5507
*Krispos the Emperor* - Harry Turtledove  f  5508

**LaNague Federation**
*The LaNague Chronicles* - F. Paul Wilson   s   5889

**Land and Overland**
*The Fugitive Worlds* - Bob Shaw   s   4942

**Lannat**
*The Prisoner Within* - Donald E. McQuinn   s   3861

**Last Herald Mage**
*Magic's Pawn* - Mercedes Lackey   f   3287
*Magic's Price* - Mercedes Lackey   f   3288
*Magic's Promise* - Mercedes Lackey   f   3289

**Last on Earth**
*The Vanishing* - Marilyn Kaye   s   3021

**Last Rangers**
*Destination: Showdown* - Jake Davis   s   1405

**Last Rune**
*Beyond the Pale* - Mark Anthony   f   153

**Last Vampire**
*The Last Vampire* - Christopher Pike   h   4328

**Legion of the Damned**
*The Final Battle* - William C. Dietz   s   1546

**Lens of the World Trilogy**
*The Belly of the Wolf* - R.A. MacAvoy   f   3580
*King of the Dead* - R.A. MacAvoy   f   3581
*Lens of the World* - R.A. MacAvoy   f   3582

**Lensman**
*Galactic Patrol* - Edward E. Smith   s   5116
*Gray Lensman* - Edward E. Smith   s   5117

**Leonard Nimoy's Primordials**
*Target Earth* - Steve Perry   s   4301

**Liavek**
*Liavek: Festival Week* - Will Shetterly   f   4994

**Life and Times of Owen Deathstalker**
*Deathstalker Honor* - Simon R. Green   s   2364
*Deathstalker Rebellion* - Simon R. Green   s   2365
*Deathstalker War* - Simon R. Green   s   2366
*Twilight of the Empire* - Simon R. Green   s   2374

**Lightbringer Trilogy**
*The Forging of the Shadows* - Oliver Johnson   f   2924
*Nations of the Night* - Oliver Johnson   f   2925

**Lightpaths**
*Standing Wave* - Howard V. Hendrix   s   2661

**Lives of the Mayfair Witches**
*Lasher* - Anne Rice   h   4570
*Taltos* - Anne Rice   h   4577
*The Witching Hour* - Anne Rice   h   4580

**Liveship Traders Trilogy**
*The Ship of Magic* - Robin Hobb   f   2696

**Lon Tobyn Chronicle**
*Children of Amarid* - David B. Coe   f   1095
*The Outlanders* - David B. Coe   f   1096

**Lord of the Isles**
*Queen of Demons* - David Drake   f   1640

**Loremasters of Elundium**
*The Knights of Cawdor* - Mike Jefferies   f   2886
*Palace of Kings* - Mike Jefferies   f   2887
*The Road to Underfall* - Mike Jefferies   f   2888

**Lost Coast**
*The Thirteenth Daughter of the Moon* - Steven Nightingale   f   4104

**Lost Millennium**
*First Dawn* - Mike Moscoe   s   4038
*Lost Days* - Mike Moscoe   s   4039
*Second Fire* - Mike Moscoe   s   4040

**Lost Regiment**
*Never Sound Retreat* - William R. Forstchen   s   1981
*Rally Cry!* - William R. Forstchen   s   1982
*Terrible Swift Sword* - William R. Forstchen   s   1983

**Lost Swords**
*The Sixth Book of Lost Swords: Mindsword's Story* - Fred Saberhagen   f   4776
*Wayfinder's Story: The Seventh Book of Lost Swords* - Fred Saberhagen   f   4777

**Lost Years of Merlin**
*The Fires of Merlin* - T.A. Barron   f   369
*The Seven Songs of Merlin* - T.A. Barron   f   372

**Love in Vein**
*Love in Vein II* - Poppy Z. Brite   h   699

**Lovers of Steadford Abbey**
*The Meddlesome Ghost* - Sheila Rosalynd Allen   f   84

**Luciferian Chronicles**
*Chains of Light* - Quentin Thomas   s   5449

**Lucius Leffing**
*The Adventures of Lucius Leffing* - Joseph Payne Brennan   h   670

**Lyonesse**
*Madouc* - Jack Vance   f   5547

**Lyra**
*The Raven Ring* - Patricia C. Wrede   f   5978
*Shadows over Lyra* - Patricia C. Wrede   f   5980

**M.Y.T.H.**
*M.Y.T.H. Inc. in Action* - Robert Asprin   f   259
*Sweet Myth-tery of Life* - Robert Asprin   f   262

**Macedon**
*Dark Prince* - David Gemmell   f   2187
*Lion of Macedon* - David Gemmell   f   2189

**Madagascar Manifesto**
*Child of the Journey* - Janet Berliner   f   466
*Child of the Light* - Janet Gluckman   f   2244
*Children of the Dusk* - Janet Berliner   f   467

**Madoc Saga**
*Madoc's Hundred* - Pat Winter   f   5925

**Mage Storms**
*Storm Breaking* - Mercedes Lackey   f   3296
*Storm Rising* - Mercedes Lackey   f   3297
*Storm Warning* - Mercedes Lackey   f   3298

**Mage Wars**
*The Black Gryphon* - Mercedes Lackey   f   3270
*The Silver Gryphon* - Mercedes Lackey   f   3295
*The White Gryphon* - Mercedes Lackey   f   3303

**Mage Winds**
*Winds of Change* - Mercedes Lackey   f   3304
*Winds of Fate* - Mercedes Lackey   f   3305
*Winds of Fury* - Mercedes Lackey   f   3306

**MageLord Trilogy**
*Magelord: The Awakening* - Thomas K. Martin   f   3651
*The Time of Madness* - Thomas K. Martin   f   3652

**Mageworlds**
*By Honor Betray'd* - Debra Doyle   s   1598
*The Gathering Flame* - Debra Doyle   s   1599
*The Long Hunt* - Debra Doyle   s   1602
*The Price of the Stars* - Debra Doyle   s   1604
*Starpilot's Grave* - Debra Doyle   s   1606

**Magic Kingdom of Landover**
*The Tangle Box* - Terry Brooks   f   718
*Witches' Brew* - Terry Brooks   f   719

**Magic of the Plains**
*By the Sword* - Greg Costikyan   f   1207

**Magic Shop**
*Jennifer Murdley's Toad* - Bruce Coville   f   1220
*Jeremy Thatcher, Dragon Hatcher* - Bruce Coville   f   1221

**Magic: The Gathering**
*Arena* - William R. Forstchen   f   1977
*Distant Planes* - Kathy Ice   f   2827
*Final Sacrifice* - Clayton Emery   f   1814
*Shattered Chains* - Clayton Emery   f   1816

**Mairelon the Magician**
*Magician's Ward* - Patricia C. Wrede   f   5976

**Majipoor**
*The Mountains of Majipoor* - Robert Silverberg   s   5037
*Sorcerers of Majipoor* - Robert Silverberg   s   5041

**Majyk**
*Majyk by Accident* - Esther Friesner   f   2079
*Majyk by Design* - Esther Friesner   f   2080
*Majyk by Hook or Crook* - Esther Friesner   f   2081

**Make Way for Dragons**
*Dragon's Domain* - Thorarinn Gunnarsson   f   2461

**Malloreon**
*The Seeress of Kell* - David Eddings   f   1738
*Sorceress of Darshiva* - David Eddings   f   1739

**Man-Kzin Wars**
*Cathouse* - Dean Ing   s   2828
*The Children's Hour* - Jerry Pournelle   s   4372
*A Darker Geometry* - Mark O. Martin   s   3649
*Inconstant Star* - Poul Anderson   s   129
*Man-Kzin Wars III* - Larry Niven   s   4123
*Man-Kzin Wars IV* - Larry Niven   s   4124
*Man-Kzin Wars V* - Larry Niven   s   4125

**Man of His Word**
*Emperor and Clown* - Dave Duncan   f   1676
*Faery Lands Forlorn* - Dave Duncan   f   1677
*Magic Casement* - Dave Duncan   f   1683
*Perilous Seas* - Dave Duncan   f   1685

**Marathon Trilogy**
*Homecoming* - David Alexander Smith   s   5108

**Marianne**
*Marianne, the Matchbox and the Malachite Mouse* - Sheri S. Tepper   f   5432

**Marid Audran**
*The Exile Kiss* - George Alec Effinger   s   1750

**Mars Attacks**
*Martian Deathtrap* - Nathan Archer   s   205

**Mars Trilogy**
*Blue Mars* - Kim Stanley Robinson   s   4629
*Green Mars* - Kim Stanley Robinson   s   4633
*Red Mars* - Kim Stanley Robinson   s   4635

**Master Li**
*Eight Skilled Gentlemen* - Barry Hughart   f   2804

**Matador**
*The Albino Knife* - Steve Perry   s   4288
*Black Steel* - Steve Perry   s   4291
*Brother Death* - Steve Perry   s   4292

**Mayflower Trilogy**
*Lovelock* - Orson Scott Card   s   892

**Mechanical Sky**
*Crescent in the Sky* - Donald Moffitt   s   3946
*A Gathering of Stars* - Donald Moffitt   s   3947

**Memory, Sorrow and Thorn Trilogy**
*The Dragonbone Chair* - Tad Williams   f   5829
*Stone of Farewell* - Tad Williams   f   5831
*To Green Angel Tower* - Tad Williams   f   5832

**Mennyms**
*The Mennyms* - Sylvia Waugh   f   5654
*Mennyms Alive* - Sylvia Waugh   f   5655

*Mennyms Under Siege* - Sylvia Waugh   *f*   5656

**Meri**
*The Crystal Rose* - Maya Kaathryn Bohnhoff   *f*   560
*Taminy* - Maya Kaathryn Bohnhoff   *f*   563

**Merlin's Legacy**
*Merlin's Legacy: Dawn of Camelot* - Quinn Taylor
   Evans   *f*   1857

**Merovingen Nights**
*Endgame* - C.J. Cherryh   *s*   986
*Flood Tide* - C.J. Cherryh   *s*   989

**Metropolitan**
*City on Fire* - Walter Jon Williams   *s*   5835

**Millennial Contest**
*Bring Me the Head of Prince Charming* - Roger
   Zelazny   *f*   6062
*A Farce to Be Reckoned With* - Roger
   Zelazny   *f*   6064
*If at Faust You Don't Succeed* - Roger
   Zelazny   *f*   6070

**Millennium**
*The Frenchman* - Elizabeth Hand   *h*   2534
*Gehenna* - Lewis Gannett   *h*   2114

**Millennium Quartet**
*Chariot* - Charles L. Grant   *h*   2304
*In the Mood* - Charles L. Grant   *h*   2312
*Symphony* - Charles L. Grant   *h*   2318

**Mindstar**
*Sister Blood* - Karen Haber   *s*   2476
*The War Minstrels* - Karen Haber   *s*   2477
*Woman Without a Shadow* - Karen Haber   *s*   2478

**Mists of Avalon**
*Lady of Avalon* - Marion Zimmer Bradley   *f*   640

**Mistworld**
*Mistworld* - Simon R. Green   *s*   2372

**Mithgar**
*Into the Forge* - Dennis L. McKiernan   *f*   3835

**Mongo**
*The Fear in Yesterday's Rings* - George C.
   Chesbro   *h*   1007

**Moonrunner**
*Under the Shadow* - Jane Toombs   *h*   5481

**Moonspeaker**
*House of Moons* - K.D. Wentworth   *s*   5752
*Moonspeaker* - K.D. Wentworth   *s*   5754

**Moontide and Magic Rise**
*Sea Without a Shore* - Sean Russell   *f*   4743
*World Without End* - Sean Russell   *f*   4744

**Mortal Kombat**
*Mortal Kombat* - Martin Delrio   *f*   1483

**Mother Earth, Father Sky**
*Song of the River* - Sue Harrison   *f*   2583

**Mountain Trilogy**
*Fire and Ice* - Edward Myers   *f*   4061
*The Mountain Made of Light* - Edward
   Myers   *f*   4062
*The Summit* - Edward Myers   *f*   4063

**Mutant Season**
*Mutant Legacy* - Karen Haber   *s*   2474
*Mutant Star* - Karen Haber   *s*   2475

**Mutants Amok**
*Christmas Slaughter* - Mark Grant   *s*   2323
*Mutant Hell* - Mark Grant   *s*   2324
*Mutants Amok* - Mark Grant   *s*   2325

**Mutineer's Moon**
*The Armageddon Inheritance* - David
   Weber   *s*   5668

*Heirs of Empire* - David Weber   *s*   5672

**My Teacher Is an Alien**
*My Teacher Flunked the Planet* - Bruce
   Coville   *s*   1222
*My Teacher Fried My Brains* - Bruce
   Coville   *s*   1223
*My Teacher Glows in the Dark* - Bruce
   Coville   *s*   1224

**Myst**
*Myst: The Book of Atrus* - Rand Miller   *f*   3896
*Myst: The Book of D'ni* - Rand Miller   *f*   3897

**Mystara: The Dragonlord Chronicles**
*Dragonmage of Mystara* - Thorarinn
   Gunnarsson   *f*   2462

**Mystic Rebel**
*Fortress of Forbidden Destiny* - Ryder
   Syvertson   *s*   5378

**Mythago Wood**
*Gate of Ivory, Gate of Horn* - Robert
   Holdstock   *f*   2737
*The Hollowing* - Robert Holdstock   *f*   2738

**Narrow Houses**
*Blue Motel* - Peter Crowther   *h*   1279
*Narrow Houses* - Peter Crowther   *h*   1284
*Touch Wood* - Peter Crowther   *h*   1285

**Native Tongue**
*Earthsong* - Suzette Haden Elgin   *s*   1769

**Near Space Stories**
*A King of Infinite Space* - Allen Steele   *s*   5243
*Labyrinth of Night* - Allen Steele   *s*   5244
*Lunar Descent* - Allen Steele   *s*   5245
*Rude Astronauts* - Allen Steele   *s*   5247

**Nebula Awards**
*Nebula Awards 24* - Michael Bishop   *s*   500
*Nebula Awards 25* - Michael Bishop   *s*   501
*Nebula Awards 26* - James Morrow   *s*   4031
*Nebula Awards 27* - James Morrow   *s*   4032
*Nebula Awards 28* - James Morrow   *s*   4033
*Nebula Awards 29* - Pamela Sargent   *s*   4822
*Nebula Awards 30* - Pamela Sargent   *s*   4823
*Nebula Awards 31* - Pamela Sargent   *s*   4824

**Necroscope**
*Deadspawn* - Brian Lumley   *h*   3550
*Deadspeak* - Brian Lumley   *h*   3551
*Necroscope: The Lost Years* - Brian
   Lumley   *h*   3560
*Resurgence* - Brian Lumley   *h*   3564
*The Source* - Brian Lumley   *h*   3565

**Network/Consortium**
*Fire Crossing* - Cheryl J. Franklin   *s*   2036
*The Inquisitor* - Cheryl J. Franklin   *s*   2037
*The Light in Exile* - Cheryl J. Franklin   *s*   2038

**Neutronium Alchemist**
*Conflict* - Peter F. Hamilton   *s*   2522
*Consolidation* - Peter F. Hamilton   *s*   2523

**Neverness**
*The Broken God* - David Zindell   *s*   6085
*The Wild* - David Zindell   *s*   6086

**New Moon**
*Beldan's Fire* - Midori Snyder   *f*   5150

**New Series of the Cutler Family**
*Secrets of the Morning* - V.C. Andrews   *h*   146

**New Tales of the Vampires**
*Pandora* - Anne Rice   *h*   4573
*The Vampire Armand* - Anne Rice   *h*   4578

**Newford**
*Someplace to Be Flying* - Charles de Lint   *f*   1435
*Trader* - Charles de Lint   *f*   1438

**News From the Edge**
*Insanity, Illinois* - Mark Sumner   *s*   5358

**Next Wave**
*Alien Tongue* - Stephen Leigh   *s*   3424
*The Missing Matter* - Thomas R.
   McDonough   *s*   3805
*The Modular Man* - Roger MacBride Allen   *s*   79
*Red Genesis* - S.C. Sykes   *s*   5377

**Ni-Lach**
*Seeking the Dream Brother* - Marcia J.
   Bennett   *s*   451

**Nicholas Seafort Saga**
*Challenger's Hope* - David Feintuch   *s*   1899
*Fisherman's Hope* - David Feintuch   *s*   1900
*Midshipman's Hope* - David Feintuch   *s*   1901
*Voices of Hope* - David Feintuch   *s*   1903

**Nicole Shea**
*Grounded!* - Chris Claremont   *s*   1041
*Sundowner* - Chris Claremont   *s*   1043

**Night-Threads**
*One Land, One Duke* - Ru Emerson   *f*   1809
*The Two in Hiding* - Ru Emerson   *f*   1812

**Night Visions**
*Night Visions 8* - John Farris   *h*   1885

**Nightrunner**
*Luck in the Shadows* - Lynn Flewelling   *f*   1952
*Stalking Darkness* - Lynn Flewelling   *f*   1953

**Nightworld Cycle**
*Nightworld* - F. Paul Wilson   *h*   5893

**Nimnestl the Bodyguard**
*Rouse a Sleeping Cat* - Dan Crawford   *f*   1249
*The Sure Death of a Mouse* - Dan Crawford   *f*   1250
*A Wild Dog and Lone* - Dan Crawford   *f*   1251

**Nomad**
*Desert Fire* - David Alexander   *s*   65
*Nomad* - David Alexander   *s*   66

**Norby**
*Norby and the Court Jester* - Janet Asimov   *s*   252
*Norby and the Oldest Dragon* - Janet
   Asimov   *s*   253
*Norby and Yobo's Great Adventure* - Janet
   Asimov   *s*   254
*Norby Down to Earth* - Janet Asimov   *s*   255

**Northworld**
*Justice* - David Drake   *s*   1635
*Northworld* - David Drake   *s*   1637
*Vengeance* - David Drake   *s*   1648

**Olivia Trilogy**
*A Candle for D'Artagnan* - Chelsea Quinn
   Yarbro   *f*   6013
*Crusader's Torch* - Chelsea Quinn Yarbro   *h*   6015

**Omaran Saga**
*The Gods in Anger* - Adrian Cole   *f*   1100

**Omni Best Science Fiction**
*Omni Best Science Fiction Three* - Ellen
   Datlow   *s*   1364

**Omni Visions**
*Omni Visions One* - Ellen Datlow   *s*   1365

**Operation StarHawks**
*Beyond the Void* - Sean Dalton   *s*   1331
*Destination: Mutiny* - Sean Dalton   *s*   1332
*The Salukan Gambit* - Sean Dalton   *s*   1333

**Oracle**
*Oracle* - Mike Resnick   *s*   4551
*Prophet* - Mike Resnick   *s*   4553

**Orange County Trilogy**
*The Gold Coast* - Kim Stanley Robinson   *s*   4632
*Pacific Edge* - Kim Stanley Robinson   *s*   4634

**Orion**
*Orion Among the Stars* - Ben Bova   s   589
*Orion and the Conqueror* - Ben Bova   s   590
*Orion in the Dying Time* - Ben Bova   s   591

**Otherland**
*City of Golden Shadow* - Tad Williams   s   5828
*River of Blue Fire* - Tad Williams   f   5830

**Others**
*OtherWhere* - Margaret Wander Bonanno   s   566
*OtherWise* - Margaret Wander Bonanno   s   567

**Outlander Trilogy**
*The Outlander: Captivity* - B.J. Salterberg   s   4792

**Oxrun Station**
*The Black Carousel* - Charles L. Grant   h   2303
*Dialing the Wind* - Charles L. Grant   h   2305

**Oz**
*Wicked: The Life and Times of the Wicked Witch of
the West* - Gregory Maguire   f   3609

**Paranoia**
*Extreme Paranoia: Nobody Knows the Trouble I've
Shot* - Ken Rolston   s   4662
*Title Deleted for Security Reasons* - Ed
Blome   s   553

**Paratwa Saga**
*Ash Ock* - Christopher Hinz   s   2690
*The Paratwa* - Christopher Hinz   s   2691

**Patterns of Chaos**
*Path of Fire* - Charles Ingrid   s   2832

**The Peace Company**
*The Mountain Walks* - Roland J. Green   s   2349

**Pegasus**
*Pegasus in Flight* - Anne McCaffrey   s   3742

**Pendragon Cycle**
*Arthur* - Stephen R. Lawhead   f   3352
*Grail* - Stephen R. Lawhead   f   3355
*Pendragon* - Stephen R. Lawhead   f   3357

**Pendragon's Banner Trilogy**
*The Kingmaking* - Helen Hollick   f   2745
*Pendragon's Banner* - Helen Hollick   f   2746
*Shadow of the King* - Helen Hollick   f   2747

**Peter Thorne, Psychic Investigator**
*Death Channels* - Robert E. Vardeman   h   5562

**Philip Jose Farmer's The Dungeon**
*The Final Battle* - Richard A. Lupoff   f   3572
*The Hidden City* - Charles de Lint   f   1429

**Phule's Company**
*Phule's Company* - Robert Asprin   s   260
*Phule's Paradise* - Robert Asprin   s   261

**Pik Lando**
*Drifter* - William C. Dietz   s   1543
*Drifter's Run* - William C. Dietz   s   1544
*Drifter's War* - William C. Dietz   s   1545

**Pinch**
*The Eyes of God* - Mark Kreighbaum   s   3231
*Palace* - Katharine Kerr   s   3072

**Pit Bull Squadron**
*Border Dispute* - Daniel R. Kerns   s   3066

**Planescape: The Blood Wars Trilogy**
*Planar Powers* - J. Robert King   f   3122

**Planet Builders**
*Rebel From Alphorion* - Robyn Tallis   s   5381

**Planet Pirates**
*The Death of Sleep* - Anne McCaffrey   s   3727
*Generation Warrior* - Anne McCaffrey   s   3735
*Sassinak* - Anne McCaffrey   s   3748

**Plenty**
*Seasons of Plenty* - Colin Greenland   s   2418

**Polite Harmony of Worlds**
*Imposter* - Valerie J. Freireich   s   2050
*Testament* - Valerie J. Freireich   s   2051

**Power and the Pattern**
*Children of Enchantment* - Anne Kelleher
Bush   f   787

**Powers That Be**
*Power Lines* - Anne McCaffrey   s   3743
*Power Play* - Anne McCaffrey   s   3744
*Powers That Be* - Anne McCaffrey   s   3745

**Prince Among Men**
*A King Beneath the Mountain* - Robert N.
Charrette   f   973
*A Knight Among Knaves* - Robert N.
Charrette   f   974
*A Prince Among Men* - Robert N. Charrette   f   977

**Prince of the Sidhe**
*The Shattered Oath* - Josepha Sherman   f   4989

**Prism Pentad**
*The Verdant Passage* - Troy Denning   f   1487

**Privateers**
*Empire Builders* - Ben Bova   s   584

**Procurator**
*Cry Republic* - Kirk Mitchell   s   3917

**Prodigy**
*Earth Herald* - Jan Clark   s   1046

**Proteus**
*Proteus in the Underworld* - Charles
Sheffield   s   4962

**Psi-Man**
*Haven* - David Peters   f   4304
*Psi-Man* - David Peters   s   4305

**Psion**
*Dreamfall* - Joan D. Vinge   s   5571

**Psychomech Trilogy**
*Psychamok* - Brian Lumley   h   3561
*Psychomech* - Brian Lumley   h   3562

**Pulphouse: The Hardback Magazine**
*The Best of Pulphouse: The Hardback Magazine* -
Kristine Kathryn Rusch   s   4713
*Pulphouse, Issue 6: Fantasy* - Kristine Kathryn
Rusch   f   4723
*Pulphouse, Issue 7: Horror* - Kristine Kathryn
Rusch   h   4724
*Pulphouse, Issue 8: Science Fiction* - Kristine Kathryn
Rusch   s   4725
*Pulphouse, Issue 9: Dark Fantasy* - Kristine Kathryn
Rusch   h   4726
*Pulphouse, Issue 10: Special Issue* - Kristine Kathryn
Rusch   f   4720
*Pulphouse, Issue 11: Speculative Fiction* - Kristine
Kathryn Rusch   s   4721
*Pulphouse, Issue 12: The Last Issue* - Kristine Kathryn
Rusch   h   4722

**Pyromancer**
*Aquamancer* - Don Callander   f   841
*Geomancer* - Don Callander   f   845

**Quantum Leap**
*Angels Unaware* - L. Elizabeth Storm   s   5315
*Knights of the Morningstar* - Melanie Rawn   s   4487

**Queen of Angels**
*/* - Greg Bear   s   413

**Quest for Tomorrow**
*Delta Search* - William Shatner   s   4930

**Questioner Trilogy**
*Labyrinth* - Dennis Schmidt   s   4884

**Quintara Marathon**
*The Demons at Rainbow Bridge* - Jack L.
Chalker   s   952
*The Ninety Trillion Fausts* - Jack L. Chalker   s   958
*The Run to Chaos Keep* - Jack L. Chalker   s   960

**Radix Tetrad**
*The Last Legends of Earth* - A.A. Attanasio   s   270

**Rage**
*Call to Battle* - Doug Murray   h   4059

**Rama**
*The Garden of Rama* - Arthur C. Clarke   s   1055
*Rama II* - Arthur C. Clarke   s   1058
*Rama Revealed* - Arthur C. Clarke   s   1059

**Ratha**
*Ratha and Thistle-Chaser* - Clare Bell   f   432

**Rats of NIMH**
*R-T, Margaret, and the Rats of NIMH* - Jane Leslie
Conly   f   1132

**Ravenloft**
*Death of a Darklord* - Laurell K. Hamilton   h   2516
*I, Strahd* - P.N. Elrod   h   1797
*King of the Dead* - Gene DeWeese   h   1510
*Mordenheim* - Chet Williamson   h   5847
*Shadowborn* - William W. Connors   h   1137
*Tapestry of Dark Souls* - Elaine Bergstrom   h   465
*Tower of Doom* - Mark Anthony   h   155

**The Reality Dysfunction**
*Expansion* - Peter F. Hamilton   s   2525

**Realms of Chaos**
*An Enemy Reborn* - Michael A. Stackpole   f   5197
*A Hero Born* - Michael A. Stackpole   f   5202

**Recluce**
*The Chaos Balance* - L.E. Modesitt Jr.   f   3925
*The Death of Chaos* - L.E. Modesitt Jr.   f   3926
*Fall of Angels* - L.E. Modesitt Jr.   f   3930
*The Magic Engineer* - L.E. Modesitt Jr.   f   3933
*The Order War* - L.E. Modesitt Jr.   f   3936
*The Towers of the Sunset* - L.E. Modesitt
Jr.   f   3941
*The White Order* - L.E. Modesitt Jr.   f   3942

**Red Dwarf**
*Better than Life* - Grant Naylor   s   4076
*Red Dwarf: Infinity Welcomes Careful Drivers* - Grant
Naylor   s   4077

**Red Kings of Wynnamyr**
*Book of Stones* - L. Dean James   f   2862
*Kingslayer* - L. Dean James   f   2863

**Redwall**
*The Bellmaker* - Brian Jacques   f   2848
*The Long Patrol* - Brian Jacques   f   2849
*Mariel of Redwall* - Brian Jacques   f   2850
*Martin the Warrior* - Brian Jacques   f   2851
*Mattimeo* - Brian Jacques   f   2852
*Outcast of Redwall* - Brian Jacques   f   2853
*The Pearls of Lutra* - Brian Jacques   f   2854
*Salamandastron* - Brian Jacques   f   2855

**Regiment**
*The Kalif's War* - John Dalmas   s   1322
*The Regiment's War* - John Dalmas   s   1326
*The White Regiment* - John Dalmas   s   1327

**Rehumanization of Jade Darcy**
*Jade Darcy and the Zen Pirates* - Stephen
Goldin   s   2260

**Reluctant Sorcerer**
*The Ambivalent Magician* - Simon Hawke   f   2616
*The Inadequate Adept* - Simon Hawke   f   2617
*The Reluctant Sorcerer* - Simon Hawke   f   2622

**Renegade Legion**
*Monsoon* - Peter L. Rice   s   4583

**Renshai Chronicles**
*Beyond Ragnarok* - Mickey Zucker Reichert  *f*  4516
*The Children of Wrath* - Mickey Zucker
  Reichert  *f*  4518
*The Last of the Renshai* - Mickey Zucker
  Reichert  *f*  4520
*Prince of Demons* - Mickey Zucker
  Reichert  *f*  4522
*The Western Wizard* - Mickey Zucker
  Reichert  *f*  4526

**Resurrection Man**
*The Night Watch* - Sean Stewart  *f*  5274

**Retief**
*Reward for Retief* - Keith Laumer  *s*  3345

**Rex Corvan**
*Mars Prime* - William C. Dietz  *s*  1548
*Matrix Man* - William C. Dietz  *s*  1549

**Riftwar**
*The King's Buccaneer* - Raymond E. Feist  *f*  1904
*Krondor, the Betrayal* - Raymond E. Feist  *f*  1905
*Prince of the Blood* - Raymond E. Feist  *f*  1907

**Rikard Braeth**
*Crown of the Serpent* - Allen L. Wold  *s*  5932
*Lair of the Cyclops* - Allen L. Wold  *s*  5933

**Rim**
*Mir* - Alexander Besher  *s*  474

**Ringworld**
*The Ringworld Throne* - Larry Niven  *s*  4128

**River into Darkness**
*Beneath the Vaulted Hills* - Sean Russell  *f*  4739
*The Compass of the Soul* - Sean Russell  *f*  4740

**Riverworld**
*Quest to Riverworld* - Philip Jose Farmer  *s*  1872
*Tales of Riverworld* - Philip Jose Farmer  *s*  1875
*To Your Scattered Bodies Go* - Philip Jose
  Farmer  *s*  1876

**Robert Silverberg's Time Tours**
*The Robin Hood Ambush* - William F. Wu  *s*  5999

**Robot**
*I, Robot: The Illustrated Screenplay* - Harlan
  Ellison  *s*  1785

**Rocheworld**
*Marooned on Eden* - Robert L. Forward  *s*  1986
*Ocean under the Ice* - Robert L. Forward  *s*  1988
*Return to Rocheworld* - Robert L. Forward  *s*  1989

**Roger Rabbit**
*Who P-P-Plugged Roger Rabbit?* - Gary K.
  Wolf  *f*  5934

**Rogue Planet**
*Red Shadows* - Yvonne Navarro  *s*  4074

**Rogue Wizard**
*A Wizard in Chaos* - Christopher Stasheff  *s*  5230
*A Wizard in Midgard* - Christopher Stasheff  *s*  5231
*A Wizard in War* - Christopher Stasheff  *s*  5234

**Rook**
*The Terror* - Graham Masterton  *h*  3679

**Rowan**
*Damia* - Anne McCaffrey  *s*  3725
*Damia's Children* - Anne McCaffrey  *s*  3726
*Lyon's Pride* - Anne McCaffrey  *s*  3738
*The Rowan* - Anne McCaffrey  *s*  3747

**Rune Blade Trilogy**
*Broken Blade* - Ann Marston  *f*  3634
*Kingmaker's Sword* - Ann Marston  *f*  3635
*The Western King* - Ann Marston  *f*  3636

**Runelords**
*The Runelords: The Sum of All Men* - David
  Farland  *f*  1866

**Runesword**
*Dark Divide* - Mark Acres  *f*  27
*Horrible Humes* - Stephen Billias  *f*  487
*Outcasts* - Clayton Emery  *f*  1815
*The Stone of Time* - Rose Estes  *f*  1840

**Rusalka**
*Chernevog* - C.J. Cherryh  *f*  982
*Rusalka* - C.J. Cherryh  *f*  1002
*Yvgenie* - C.J. Cherryh  *f*  1005

**Saga of the Unified Worlds**
*Dominion's Reach* - Diann Thornley  *s*  5465

**Sam McCade**
*McCade's Bounty* - William C. Dietz  *s*  1550

**Samurai Cat**
*Samurai Cat Goes to Hell* - Mark E. Rogers  *f*  4655
*Samurai Cat Goes to the Movies* - Mark E.
  Rogers  *s*  4656
*The Sword of Samurai Cat* - Mark E.
  Rogers  *s*  4657

**Sand Wars**
*Alien Salute* - Charles Ingrid  *s*  2830
*Return Fire* - Charles Ingrid  *s*  2833

**Sandman**
*The Sandman: Book of Dreams* - Neil
  Gaiman  *f*  2105

**Sandy MacGregor**
*A Name to Conjure With* - Donald Aamodt  *f*  3
*A Troubling Along the Border* - Donald Aamodt  *f*  4

**Satellite Night News**
*Satellite Night News* - Jack Hopkins  *s*  2770

**Scorpio**
*Dragon's Blood* - Alex McDonough  *s*  3799
*Dragon's Claw* - Alex McDonough  *s*  3800
*Dragon's Eye* - Alex McDonough  *s*  3801
*Scorpio* - Alex McDonough  *s*  3802
*Scorpio Descending* - Alex McDonough  *s*  3803
*Scorpio Rising* - Alex McDonough  *s*  3804

**seaQuest DSV**
*seaQuest DSV: Fire Below* - Matthew J.
  Costello  *s*  1201
*seaQuest DSV: The Novel* - Diane Duane  *s*  1666

**Searchers**
*City of Iron* - Chet Williamson  *h*  5843
*Empire of Dust* - Chet Williamson  *h*  5846

**Second Foundation Trilogy**
*Foundation's Fear* - Gregory Benford  *s*  446

**Secret Books of Paradys**
*The Book of the Beast* - Tanith Lee  *f*  3405

**Secret Books of Venus**
*Faces under Water* - Tanith Lee  *h*  3409

**Secret Country**
*The Dubious Hills* - Pamela Dean  *f*  1444
*The Whim of the Dragon* - Pamela Dean  *f*  1447

**Secret Texts**
*Diplomacy of Wolves* - Holly Lisle  *f*  3481

**Secrets of Power**
*Choose Your Enemies Carefully* - Robert N.
  Charrette  *s*  971
*Find Your Own Truth* - Robert N. Charrette  *f*  972
*Never Deal with a Dragon* - Robert N.
  Charrette  *s*  975

**Sector General**
*Final Diagnosis* - James White  *s*  5777
*The Galactic Gourmet* - James White  *s*  5778
*The Genocidal Healer* - James White  *s*  5779
*Mind Changer* - James White  *s*  5780

**Seelzar Chronicles**
*The Planet Beyond* - Steve Mudd  *s*  4043

**Seer King**
*The Demon King* - Chris Bunch  *f*  770

**Serpentwar Saga**
*Rage of a Demon King* - Raymond E. Feist  *f*  1908
*Rise of a Merchant Prince* - Raymond E.
  Feist  *f*  1909
*Shadow of a Dark Queen* - Raymond E.
  Feist  *f*  1911
*Shards of a Broken Crown* - Raymond E.
  Feist  *f*  1912

**Serrated Edge**
*Born to Run* - Mercedes Lackey  *f*  3271
*Chrome Circle* - Mercedes Lackey  *f*  3277
*Wheels of Fire* - Mercedes Lackey  *f*  3301
*When the Bough Breaks* - Mercedes Lackey  *f*  3302

**Seven Dreams**
*The Ice-Shirt* - William T. Vollmann  *f*  5580

**Seven Towers**
*The Wizard at Home* - Rick Shelley  *f*  4975

**Seventh Carrier**
*Assault of the Super Carrier* - Peter Albano  *s*  47
*Ordeal of the Seventh Carrier* - Peter Albano  *s*  48
*Revenge of the Seventh Carrier* - Peter Albano  *s*  49
*Super Carrier: The Ultimate Secret Weapon* - Peter
  Albano  *s*  50

**Shadith's Quest**
*Shadowkill* - Jo Clayton  *s*  1069
*Shadowplay* - Jo Clayton  *s*  1070
*Shadowspeer* - Jo Clayton  *s*  1071

**Shadow**
*Dagger's Edge* - Anne Logston  *f*  3508
*Shadow* - Anne Logston  *f*  3512
*Shadow Dance* - Anne Logston  *f*  3513
*Shadow Hunt* - Anne Logston  *f*  3514

**Shadow Saga**
*Of Masques and Martyrs* - Christopher
  Golden  *h*  2258

**Shadow World**
*Clock Strikes Sword* - Ian Hammell  *f*  2529

**Shadowrun**
*2XS* - Nigel Findley  *f*  1935
*Beyond the Pale* - Jack Koke  *f*  3198
*Blood Sport* - Lisa Smedman  *f*  5096
*Changeling* - Christopher Kubasik  *f*  3245
*Fade to Black* - Nyx Smith  *s*  5134
*Headhunters* - Mel Odom  *s*  4192
*House of the Sun* - Nigel Findley  *s*  1936
*Into the Shadows* - Jordan K. Weisman  *f*  5731
*Never Trust an Elf* - Robert N. Charrette  *f*  976
*Night's Pawn* - Tom Dowd  *s*  1591
*Shadowboxer* - Nick Pollotta  *s*  4366
*Streets of Blood* - Carl Sargent  *f*  4821
*Striper Assassin* - Nyx Smith  *f*  5135
*Wolf and Raven* - Michael A. Stackpole  *f*  5207

**Shadows**
*Realm of Light* - Deborah Chester  *f*  1008
*Reign of Shadows* - Deborah Chester  *f*  1009
*Shadow War* - Deborah Chester  *f*  1010

**Shadowsong**
*Fire in the Sky* - Jo Clayton  *s*  1067

**Shaman Cycle**
*The Serpent Slayers* - Adam Niswander  *h*  4113

**Shannara**
*First King of Shannara* - Terry Brooks  *f*  712

**Shaper Exile**
*Shaper's Legacy* - Sheila Finch  *s*  1933
*Shaping the Dawn* - Sheila Finch  *s*  1934

**Ship Who Sang**
*The City Who Fought* - Anne McCaffrey  *s*  3722

*PartnerShip* - Anne McCaffrey   s   3741
*The Ship Avenged* - S.M. Stirling   s   5298
*The Ship Errant* - Jody Lynn Nye   s   4175
*The Ship Who Searched* - Anne McCaffrey   s   3749
*The Ship Who Won* - Anne McCaffrey   s   3750

**Shiva**
*Shiva Accused: An Adventure of the Ice Age* - J.H. Brennan   f   667
*Shiva: An Adventure of the Ice Age* - J.H. Brennan   f   669
*Shiva's Challenge: An Adventure of the Ice Age* - J.H. Brennan   f   668

**Sholan Alliance**
*Fire Margins* - Lisanne Norman   s   4137
*Fortune's Wheel* - Lisanne Norman   s   4138
*Razor's Edge* - Lisanne Norman   s   4139
*Turning Point* - Lisanne Norman   s   4140

**Shunlar Chronicles**
*The Gates of Vensunor* - Carol Heller   f   2650
*The Sands of Kalaven: A Novel of Shunlar* - Carol Heller   f   2651

**Sileria**
*In Legend Born* - Laura Resnick   f   4533

**Silverglass**
*Mistress of Ambiguities* - J.F. Rivkin   f   4596

**Sing the Light**
*Receive the Gift* - Louise Marley   s   3628
*Sing the Warmth* - Louise Marley   s   3630

**Sisters of the Night**
*The Angry Angel* - Chelsea Quinn Yarbro   h   6010

**Skolian Empire**
*Catch the Lightning* - Catherine Asaro   s   218
*The Last Hawk* - Catherine Asaro   s   219

**Sky Lords**
*The War of the Sky Lords* - John Brosnan   s   721

**Slow Freight**
*Arrow From Earth* - F.M. Busby   s   782
*The Triad Worlds* - F.M. Busby   s   786

**Slow World**
*The Persistence of Memory* - Karen Ripley   s   4592
*The Warden of Horses* - Karen Ripley   s   4595

**Snow Queen**
*The Summer Queen* - Joan D. Vinge   s   5572

**Snow White, Blood Red**
*Ruby Slippers, Golden Tears* - Ellen Datlow   f   1366
*Snow White, Blood Red* - Ellen Datlow   f   1368

**Software**
*Freeware* - Rudy Rucker   s   4703

**Solar Queen**
*Derelict for Trade* - Andre Norton   s   4148
*Redline the Stars* - Andre Norton   s   4160

**Song Called Youth**
*Eclipse Corona* - John Shirley   s   5006

**Song of Albion**
*The Endless Knot* - Stephen R. Lawhead   f   3354
*The Silver Hand* - Stephen R. Lawhead   f   3358

**Song of Ice and Fire**
*A Game of Thrones* - George R.R. Martin   f   3645

**Songkiller Saga**
*Phantom Banjo* - Elizabeth Ann Scarborough   f   4868
*Picking the Ballad's Bones* - Elizabeth Ann Scarborough   f   4869
*Strum Again?* - Elizabeth Ann Scarborough   f   4870

**Songs of Eirren**
*Fire Arrow* - Edith Pattou   f   4260

**Sonja Blue**
*A Dozen Black Roses* - Nancy A. Collins   h   1119
*In the Blood* - Nancy A. Collins   h   1121
*Midnight Blue: The Sonja Blue Collection* - Nancy A. Collins   h   1122
*Sunglasses After Dark* - Nancy A. Collins   h   1124

**Sorceress and the Cygnet**
*The Cygnet and the Firebird* - Patricia A. McKillip   f   3839
*The Sorceress and the Cygnet* - Patricia A. McKillip   f   3842

**Sorcery Hall**
*The Golden Thread* - Suzy McKee Charnas   f   969

**Soulsmith**
*Dreambuilder* - Tom Deitz   f   1471
*Soulsmith* - Tom Deitz   f   1475
*Wordwright* - Tom Deitz   f   1478

**Space Odyssey**
*3001: The Final Odyssey* - Arthur C. Clarke   s   1053

**Spacecops**
*High Moon* - Diane Duane   s   1661
*Kill Station* - Diane Duane   s   1664
*Mindblast* - Diane Duane   s   1665

**Sparrowhawk**
*Greenhouse* - Thomas A. Easton   s   1723
*Seeds of Destiny* - Thomas A. Easton   s   1724
*Sparrowhawk* - Thomas A. Easton   s   1725
*Tower of the Gods* - Thomas A. Easton   s   1726
*Woodsman* - Thomas A. Easton   s   1727

**Spearwielder's Tale**
*The Dragon's Dagger* - R.A. Salvatore   f   4797
*Dragonslayer's Return* - R.A. Salvatore   f   4798
*The Woods out Back* - R.A. Salvatore   f   4809

**Spellkey**
*The Spellkey Trilogy* - Ann Downer   f   1592

**Spellsinger**
*Chorus Skating* - Alan Dean Foster   f   1998
*Son of Spellsinger* - Alan Dean Foster   f   2015

**Spellsong Cycle**
*The Spellsong War* - L.E. Modesitt Jr.   f   3939

**Spider**
*The Spider #3: Death's Crimson Juggernaut/The Red Death Rain* - Grant Stockbridge   f   5307
*The Spider #4: Death Reign of the Vampire King/The Pain Emperor* - Grant Stockbridge   f   5308
*The Spider #8: The Devil's Paymaster/Legions of the Accursed Light* - Grant Stockbridge   f   5309
*The Web of Spider* - W. Michael Gear   s   2173

**Spider-Man**
*Spider-Man: The Venom Factor* - Diane Duane   s   1667
*The Ultimate Spider-Man* - Stan Lee   s   3403

**Spider World**
*The Delta* - Colin Wilson   s   5878

**Spindoc**
*The Forever Drug* - Steve Perry   s   4296
*Spindoc* - Steve Perry   s   4300

**Spinetinglers**
*Pet Store* - M.T. Coffin   h   1097

**Spiral**
*Chase the Morning* - Michael Scott Rohan   f   4658
*Cloud Castles* - Michael Scott Rohan   f   4659
*The Gates of Noon* - Michael Scott Rohan   f   4661

**Stainless Steel Rat**
*The Stainless Steel Rat Goes to Hell* - Harry Harrison   s   2574
*The Stainless Steel Rat Sings the Blues* - Harry Harrison   s   2575

**Stan Lee's Riftworld**
*Crossover* - Bill McCay   f   3768

**Star Commandos**
*Call to Arms* - P.M. Griffin   s   2435
*Fire Planet* - P.M. Griffin   s   2436
*Jungle Assault* - P.M. Griffin   s   2437

**Star of the Guardians**
*King's Sacrifice* - Margaret Weis   s   5717
*The Lost King* - Margaret Weis   s   5720

**Star Precinct**
*Mind Slayer* - Kevin D. Randle   s   4469
*Star Precinct* - Kevin D. Randle   s   4470

**Star Requiem**
*Mother of Storms* - Adrian Cole   f   1101
*Warlord of Heaven* - Adrian Cole   f   1102

**Star Stone**
*The Sage* - Christopher Stasheff   f   5221
*The Shaman* - Christopher Stasheff   f   5223

**Star Svensdotter**
*Red Planet Run* - Dana Stabenow   s   5187

**Star Trek**
*The Ashes of Eden* - William Shatner   s   4927
*Assignment: Eternity* - Greg Cox   s   1225
*Avenger* - William Shatner   s   4928
*Best Destiny* - Diane Carey   s   900
*The City on the Edge of Forever* - Harlan Ellison   s   1784
*Crossroad* - Barbara Hambly   s   2501
*The Disinherited* - Peter David   s   1381
*Doctor's Orders* - Diane Duane   s   1659
*Enemy Unseen* - V.E. Mitchell   s   3918
*The Fearful Summons* - Denny Martin Flinn   s   1954
*Federation* - Judith Reeves-Stevens   s   4511
*First Frontier* - Diane Carey   s   902
*First Strike* - Diane Carey   s   903
*A Flag Full of Stars* - Brad Ferguson   s   1922
*The Joy Machine* - James Gunn   s   2458
*The Kobayashi Maru* - Julia Ecklar   s   1728
*Mind Meld* - John Vornholt   s   5596
*Prime Directive* - Judith Reeves-Stevens   s   4514
*Probe* - Margaret Wander Bonanno   s   569
*Renegade* - Gene DeWeese   s   1511
*The Return* - William Shatner   s   4933
*The Rift* - Peter David   s   1386
*Rules of Engagement* - Peter Morwood   s   4037
*Sanctuary* - John Vornholt   s   5597
*Sarek* - A.C. Crispin   s   1260
*Shadows on the Sun* - Michael Jan Friedman   s   2069
*Spectre* - William Shatner   s   4934
*Star Trek VI: The Undiscovered Country* - J.M. Dillard   s   1556
*Star Trek: The Classic Episodes 1* - James Blish   s   526
*Star Trek: The Classic Episodes 2* - James Blish   s   527
*Star Trek: The Classic Episodes 3* - James Blish   s   528
*Star Trek: The Lost Years* - J.M. Dillard   s   1557
*Starfleet Academy* - Diane Carey   s   905
*Traitor Winds* - L.A. Graf   s   2298
*Vulcan's Forge* - Susan Shwartz   s   5019
*Vulcan's Glory* - D.C. Fontana   s   1967
*Windows on a Lost World* - V.E. Mitchell   s   3920

**Star Trek: Day of Honor**
*Armageddon Sky* - L.A. Graf   s   2296
*Her Klingon Soul* - Michael Jan Friedman   s   2064

**Star Trek: Deep Space Nine**
*Bloodletter* - K.W. Jeter   s   2908
*Devil in the Sky* - Greg Cox   s   1226
*Fallen Heroes* - Dafydd ab Hugh   s   8
*Time's Enemy* - L.A. Graf   s   2297
*Vengeance* - Dafydd ab Hugh   s   10

*Warped* - K.W. Jeter  *s*  2917

**Star Trek: Deep Space Nine: The Dominion War**
*Call to Arms* - Diane Carey  *s*  901

**Star Trek: New Frontier**
*End Game* - Peter David  *s*  1382

**Star Trek: The Captain's Table**
*War Dragons* - L.A. Graf  *s*  2299

**Star Trek: The Next Generation**
*All Good Things. . .* - Michael Jan Friedman  *s*  2061
*Balance of Power* - Dafydd ab Hugh  *s*  7
*A Call to Darkness* - Michael Jan Friedman  *s*  2062
*Chains of Command* - Bill McCay  *s*  3767
*Crossover* - Michael Jan Friedman  *s*  2063
*Dark Mirror* - Diane Duane  *s*  1658
*Debtors' Planet* - William R. Thompson  *s*  5457
*The Devil's Heart* - Carmen Carter  *s*  922
*Doomsday World* - Carmen Carter  *s*  923
*Dragon's Honor* - Kij Johnson  *s*  2922
*Guises of the Mind* - Rebecca Neason  *s*  4081
*Imbalance* - V.E. Mitchell  *s*  3919
*Imzadi* - Peter David  *s*  1383
*Insurrection* - J.M. Dillard  *s*  1554
*Intellivore* - Diane Duane  *s*  1663
*Kahless* - Michael Jan Friedman  *s*  2065
*The Last Stand* - Brad Ferguson  *s*  1923
*Metamorphosis* - Jean Lorrah  *s*  3524
*Q-in-Law* - Peter David  *s*  1384
*Q-Squared* - Peter David  *s*  1385
*Relics* - Michael Jan Friedman  *s*  2066
*Requiem* - Michael Jan Friedman  *s*  2067
*Reunion* - Michael Jan Friedman  *s*  2068
*Ship of the Line* - Diane Carey  *s*  904
*The Soldiers of Fear* - Dean Wesley Smith  *s*  5115
*Triangle: Imzadi II* - Peter David  *s*  1388
*Vendetta* - Peter David  *s*  1389

**Star Trek: The Next Generation: Starfleet Academy**
*Worf's First Adventure* - Peter David  *s*  1391

**Star Trek: The Next Generation: The Q Continuum**
*Q-Space* - Greg Cox  *s*  1228
*Q-Zone* - Greg Cox  *s*  1229

**Star Trek: Voyager**
*Chrysalis* - David Niall Wilson  *s*  5880
*The Final Fury* - Dafydd ab Hugh  *s*  9
*Mosaic* - Jeri Taylor  *s*  5403
*Pathways* - Jeri Taylor  *s*  5404
*Ragnarok* - Nathan Archer  *s*  206

**Star Trek Voyager: Starfleet Academy**
*The Chance Factor* - Diana G. Gallagher  *s*  2109

**Star Wars**
*Children of the Jedi* - Barbara Hambly  *s*  2500
*The Courtship of Princess Leia* - Dave
   Wolverton  *s*  5950
*The Crystal Star* - Vonda N. McIntyre  *s*  3820
*Dark Force Rising* - Timothy Zahn  *s*  6052
*Darksaber* - Kevin J. Anderson  *s*  103
*The Glove of Darth Vader* - Paul Davids  *s*  1392
*Heir to the Empire* - Timothy Zahn  *s*  6054
*The Last Command* - Timothy Zahn  *s*  6055
*The Lost City of the Jedi* - Paul Davids  *s*  1393
*The New Rebellion* - Kristine Kathryn
   Rusch  *s*  4719
*Shadows of the Empire* - Steve Perry  *s*  4299
*Tales From Jabba's Palace* - Kevin J.
   Anderson  *s*  114
*Tales From the Mos Eisley Cantina* - Kevin J.
   Anderson  *s*  115
*The Truce at Bakura* - Kathy Tyers  *s*  5527
*Zorba the Hutt's Revenge* - Paul Davids  *s*  1394

**Star Wars: Jedi Academy Trilogy**
*Jedi Search* - Kevin J. Anderson  *s*  109

**Star Wars: The Black Fleet Crisis**
*Before the Storm* - Michael P. Kube-
   McDowell  *s*  3247

**Star Wars: The Bounty Hunter Wars**
*The Mandalorian Armor* - K.W. Jeter  *s*  2914

**Star Wars: The Corellian Trilogy**
*Ambush at Corellia* - Roger MacBride Allen  *s*  76

**Star Wars: X-Wing**
*Rogue Squadron* - Michael A. Stackpole  *s*  5205

**Star Wreck**
*Star Wreck II: The Attack of the Jargonites* - Leah
   Rewolinski  *s*  4563
*Star Wreck III: Time Warped* - Leah
   Rewolinski  *s*  4564
*Star Wreck IV: Live Long and Profit* - Leah
   Rewolinski  *s*  4565
*Star Wreck 6: Geek Space Nine* - Leah
   Rewolinski  *s*  4562
*Star Wreck: The Generation Gap* - Leah
   Rewolinski  *s*  4566

**StarBridge**
*Ancestor's World* - A.C. Crispin  *s*  1259
*Serpent's Gift* - A.C. Crispin  *s*  1261
*Shadow World* - A.C. Crispin  *s*  1262
*Silent Dances* - A.C. Crispin  *s*  1263
*Silent Songs* - A.C. Crispin  *s*  1264
*Starbridge* - A.C. Crispin  *s*  1265
*Voices of Chaos* - A.C. Crispin  *s*  1266

**Starbridge Chronicles**
*The Cult of Loving Kindness* - Paul Park  *s*  4242
*Sugar Rain* - Paul Park  *s*  4243

**Starbuck Family Adventure**
*Double Trouble Squared* - Kathryn Lasky  *f*  3340
*Shadows in the Water* - Kathryn Lasky  *s*  3341

**Starcruiser Shenandoah**
*The Painful Field* - Roland J. Green  *s*  2351
*Squadron Alert* - Roland J. Green  *s*  2352
*The Sum of Things* - Roland J. Green  *s*  2353

**Stardance**
*Starmind* - Spider Robinson  *s*  4642
*Starseed* - Spider Robinson  *s*  4643

**Starfarers**
*Metaphase* - Vonda N. McIntyre  *s*  3821
*Nautilus* - Vonda N. McIntyre  *s*  3823
*Transition* - Vonda N. McIntyre  *s*  3825

**Starfist**
*School of Fire* - David Sherman  *s*  4982

**Stargate**
*Reconnaissance* - Bill McCay  *s*  3769

**Stargate SG-1**
*Stargate SG-1* - Ashley McConnell  *s*  3777

**Starlight**
*Starlight 1* - Patrick Nielsen Hayden  *s*  2634
*Starlight 2* - Patrick Nielsen Hayden  *s*  2635

**Starsea Invaders**
*Starsea Invaders: First Action* - G. Harry
   Stine  *s*  5282

**Starshield**
*Sentinels* - Margaret Weis  *s*  5725

**Starship Troupers**
*A Company of Stars* - Christopher Stasheff  *s*  5215
*We Open on Venus* - Christopher Stasheff  *s*  5227

**Starwolves**
*Battle of the Ring* - Thorarinn Gunnarsson  *s*  2460
*Dreadnought* - Thorarinn Gunnarsson  *s*  2464
*Tactical Error* - Thorarinn Gunnarsson  *s*  2466

**Steerswoman**
*The Outskirter's Secret* - Rosemary Kirstein  *s*  3157

*The Steerswoman* - Rosemary Kirstein  *s*  3158

**Sten**
*Empire's End* - Allan Cole  *s*  1103
*The Return of the Emperor* - Allan Cole  *s*  1106
*Revenge of the Damned* - Allan Cole  *s*  1107
*Vortex* - Allan Cole  *s*  1108

**Steven Dalt**
*The Tery* - F. Paul Wilson  *s*  5900

**Stolen Throne**
*The Stolen Throne* - Harry Turtledove  *f*  5510

**Stones of Power**
*Ghost King* - David Gemmell  *f*  2188
*Wolf in Shadow* - David Gemmell  *s*  2191

**Stormlands**
*The Poisoned Lands* - John Maddox
   Roberts  *f*  4619
*Queens of Land and Sea* - John Maddox
   Roberts  *f*  4620
*The Steel Kings* - John Maddox Roberts  *f*  4621

**Strands of Starlight**
*Spires of Spirit* - Gael Baudino  *f*  395
*Strands of Sunlight* - Gael Baudino  *f*  396

**Streetlethal**
*Gorgon Child* - Steven Barnes  *s*  361

**Summerlands**
*Season of Storms* - Ellen Foxxe  *f*  2032

**Sun-Cross**
*The Magicians of Night* - Barbara Hambly  *f*  2505
*The Rainbow Abyss* - Barbara Hambly  *f*  2507

**Sun Sword**
*The Broken Crown* - Michelle West  *f*  5757
*The Uncrowned King* - Michelle West  *f*  5760

**Sun Wolf and Starhawk**
*The Dark Hand of Magic* - Barbara Hambly  *f*  2502

**Sunder, Eclipse and Seed**
*Sunder, Eclipse and Seed* - Elise Guttenberg  *f*  2471

**Sundered**
*Chains of Darkness, Chains of Light* - Michelle
   Sagara  *f*  4781
*Children of the Blood: Book Two of The Sundered* -
   Michelle Sagara  *f*  4782
*Into the Dark Lands* - Michelle Sagara  *f*  4783
*Lady of Mercy* - Michelle Sagara  *f*  4784

**Superman**
*The Death and Life of Superman* - Roger
   Stern  *s*  5262
*The Further Adventures of Superman* - Martin H.
   Greenberg  *s*  2393
*Lois & Clark* - C.J. Cherryh  *s*  999

**Survivalist**
*The Struggle* - Jerry Ahern  *s*  44

**Swag**
*Kill Crazy* - L.S. Riker  *s*  4590

**Swan Lake**
*The Veils of Snows* - Mark Helprin  *f*  2654

**Sword and Sorcery**
*Sword and Sorceress VIII* - Marion Zimmer
   Bradley  *f*  646
*Sword and Sorceress IX* - Marion Zimmer
   Bradley  *f*  647
*Sword and Sorceress XI* - Marion Zimmer
   Bradley  *f*  648
*Sword and Sorceress XII* - Marion Zimmer
   Bradley  *f*  649
*Sword and Sorceress XIII* - Marion Zimmer
   Bradley  *f*  650
*Sword and Sorceress XIV* - Marion Zimmer
   Bradley  *f*  651

**Sword of Knowledge**
*Wizard Spawn* - C.J. Cherryh  *f*  1004

**Sword of Truth**
*Blood of the Fold* - Terry Goodkind  *f*  2268
*Stone of Tears* - Terry Goodkind  *f*  2269
*Temple of the Winds* - Terry Goodkind  *f*  2270

**Swords**
*An Armory of Swords* - Fred Saberhagen  *f*  4759
*The Last Book of Swords: Shieldbreaker's Story* - Fred
   Saberhagen  *f*  4768

**Tabitha Jute**
*Mother of Plenty* - Colin Greenland  *s*  2417

**Talamadh**
*Flight to Hollow Mountain* - Mark Sebanc  *f*  4908

**Tale of the Five**
*The Door into Sunset* - Diane Duane  *f*  1660

**Tales of Alvin Maker**
*Alvin Journeyman* - Orson Scott Card  *f*  881
*Heartfire* - Orson Scott Card  *f*  889
*Prentice Alvin* - Orson Scott Card  *f*  896

**Tales of the Branion Realm**
*The Painter Knight* - Fiona Patton  *f*  4258

**Tales of the Continuing Time**
*The Last Dancer* - Daniel Keys Moran  *s*  3994
*The Long Run* - Daniel Keys Moran  *s*  3995

**Tales of the Timuras**
*Wolves of the Gods* - Allan Cole  *f*  1111

**Tales of the Willows**
*Toad Triumphant* - William Horwood  *f*  2774
*The Willows and Beyond* - William
   Horwood  *f*  2775
*The Willows in Winter* - William Horwood  *f*  2776

**Taliswoman**
*Cup of Clay* - Carole Nelson Douglas  *f*  1583
*Seed upon the Wind* - Carole Nelson
   Douglas  *f*  1584

**Tamson House**
*Spiritwalk* - Charles de Lint  *f*  1436

**Tamuli**
*Domes of Fire* - David Eddings  *f*  1732
*The Hidden City* - David Eddings  *f*  1733

**Tek**
*Tek Money* - William Shatner  *s*  4935
*Tek Net* - William Shatner  *s*  4936
*Tek Power* - William Shatner  *s*  4937
*Tek Vengeance* - William Shatner  *s*  4938
*TekLab* - William Shatner  *s*  4939
*TekLords* - William Shatner  *s*  4940
*TekWar* - William Shatner  *s*  4941

**Tenth Class**
*The Tenth Class* - Karen Ripley  *s*  4594

**Terra Nova**
*Enemy of My Enemy* - Ben Ohlander  *s*  4204

**Thieves' World**
*City at the Edge of Time* - Janet Morris  *f*  4015
*The Shadow of Sorcery* - Andrew J. Offutt  *f*  4202

**Thlassa Mey**
*Across the Thlassa Mey* - Dennis McCarty  *f*  3765
*The Birth of the Blade* - Dennis McCarty  *f*  3766

**Three Worlds**
*Out of This World* - Lawrence Watt-Evans  *f*  5645
*The Reign of the Brown Magician* - Lawrence Watt-
   Evans  *f*  5647

**Threshold**
*The Stalk* - Janet Morris  *s*  4016
*Threshold* - Janet Morris  *s*  4018
*Trust Territory* - Janet Morris  *s*  4019

**Tielmaran Chronicles**
*Wind From a Foreign Sky* - Katya Reimann  *f*  4528

**Tiger and Del**
*Sword-Born* - Jennifer Roberson  *f*  4612
*Sword-Breaker* - Jennifer Roberson  *f*  4613
*Sword-Maker* - Jennifer Roberson  *f*  4614

**Time for Dragons**
*Dragons Past* - Gary Gentile  *s*  2192

**Time of Troubles**
*The Thousand Cities* - Harry Turtledove  *f*  5512
*Videssos Besieged* - Harry Turtledove  *f*  5513

**Time Patrol**
*The Shield of Time* - Poul Anderson  *s*  131
*The Time Patrol* - Poul Anderson  *s*  135

**Time Police**
*Stranded!* - Warren Norwood  *s*  4164

**Time Raider**
*Union Fires* - John Barnes  *f*  358
*Wartide* - John Barnes  *f*  359

**Time Scout**
*Wagers of Sin* - Robert Asprin  *s*  264

**Time Share**
*Timeshare: Second Time Around* - Joshua
   Dann  *s*  1345

**Time Station**
*Time Station Berlin* - David Evans  *s*  1852
*Time Station London* - David Evans  *s*  1853
*Time Station Paris* - David Evans  *s*  1854

**Time Traders**
*Firehand* - Andre Norton  *s*  4151

**Time Warrior**
*Day of the Snake* - Matthew J. Costello  *s*  1196
*Hour of the Scorpion* - Matthew J. Costello  *s*  1199

**Timeline Wars**
*Caesar's Bicycle* - John Barnes  *s*  350
*Patton's Spaceship* - John Barnes  *s*  357

**Timothy Desmond**
*Gnome Man's Land* - Esther Friesner  *f*  2075
*Harpy High* - Esther Friesner  *f*  2076
*Unicorn U.* - Esther Friesner  *f*  2084

**Titans**
*Sons of the Titans* - Patrick H. Adkins  *f*  36

**Titus Crow**
*The Burrowers Beneath* - Brian Lumley  *h*  3548
*Titus Crow, Volume One* - Brian Lumley  *h*  3566
*Titus Crow, Volume Three* - Brian Lumley  *h*  3567
*Titus Crow, Volume Two* - Brian Lumley  *h*  3568
*The Transition of Titus Crow* - Brian
   Lumley  *h*  3569

**To Save the Sun**
*To Fear the Light* - Ben Bova  *s*  595

**Tom Dunjer**
*Specterworld* - Isidore Haiblum  *s*  2480

**Tom Red Clay**
*Human to Human* - Rebecca Ore  *s*  4219

**Torg: The Possibility Wars**
*City of Pain* - John Terra  *f*  5438
*Dragons over England* - Douglas Kaufman  *f*  3015
*Mysterious Cairo* - Ed Stark  *f*  5210
*Storm Knights* - Bill Slavicsek  *f*  5087
*Strange Tales From the Nile Empire* - Greg
   Farshtey  *f*  1889

**Trillium**
*Golden Trillium* - Andre Norton  *f*  4153
*Lady of the Trillium* - Marion Zimmer
   Bradley  *f*  641
*Sky Trillium* - Julian May  *f*  3700

**Trilogy of the Blood Curse**
*The Devil's Advocate* - Gherbod Fleming  *h*  1949

**TRIO: Rebels in the New World**
*Traitors from Within* - R.A. Montgomery  *s*  3966

**Truckers**
*Truckers* - Terry Pratchett  *s*  4402

**Twelve Treasures**
*The Cup of Morning Shadows* - Rosemary
   Edghill  *f*  1747
*The Sword of Maiden's Tears* - Rosemary
   Edghill  *f*  1748

**Twilight of the Empire**
*Hellworld* - Simon R. Green  *s*  2371

**Twilight Tales Presents**
*Dangerous Dames* - Tina L. Jens  *h*  2891
*Strange Creatures* - Tina L. Jens  *h*  2892
*Tales of Forbidden Passion* - Tina L. Jens  *h*  2893
*Winter Tales* - Tina L. Jens  *h*  2894

**Ty Merrick**
*Manjinn Moon* - Denise Vitola  *s*  5576

**Ultima Saga**
*The Forge of Virtue* - Lynn Abbey  *f*  16
*The Temper of Wisdom* - Lynn Abbey  *f*  17

**Unbalanced Earth**
*The Lightless Kingdom* - Jonathan Wylie  *f*  6007

**Unbeheaded King**
*The Honorable Barbarian* - L. Sprague de
   Camp  *f*  1415

**Unicorn Chronicles**
*Into the Land of the Unicorns* - Bruce
   Coville  *f*  1219

**Unicorn Quest**
*The Unicorn Peace* - John Lee  *f*  3399
*The Unicorn Solution* - John Lee  *f*  3400
*The Unicorn War* - John Lee  *f*  3401

**Unified Worlds**
*Echoes of Issel* - Diann Thornley  *s*  5466

**Union/Alliance**
*Downbelow Station* - C.J. Cherryh  *s*  985

**Universe**
*Universe 2* - Robert Silverberg  *s*  5045
*Universe 3* - Robert Silverberg  *s*  5046

**Unlikely Ones**
*Master of Many Treasures* - Mary Brown  *f*  726

**Unreal**
*Hard Crash* - Ryan Hughes  *s*  2810

**Uplift**
*Brightness Reef* - David Brin  *s*  684
*Heaven's Reach* - David Brin  *s*  687
*Infinity's Shore* - David Brin  *s*  688

**Valdemar**
*By the Sword* - Mercedes Lackey  *f*  3273
*Sword of Ice and Other Tales of Valdemar* - Mercedes
   Lackey  *f*  3300

**Vampire Chronicles**
*Memnoch the Devil* - Anne Rice  *h*  4571
*The Queen of the Damned* - Anne Rice  *h*  4574
*The Tale of the Body Thief* - Anne Rice  *h*  4576

**Vampire Diary**
*Vampire Diary: The Embrace* - Robert
   Weinberg  *h*  5705

**Vampire Files**
*Blood on the Water* - P.N. Elrod  *h*  1791
*Bloodlist* - P.N. Elrod  *h*  1792
*A Chill in the Blood* - P.N. Elrod  *h*  1793
*Fire in the Blood* - P.N. Elrod  *h*  1796

**Vampire Junction**
*Valentine* - S.P. Somtow   *h*   5160
*Vanitas: Escape From Vampire Junction* - S.P.
   Somtow   *h*   5162

**Vampire Legacy**
*Bitter Blood* - Karen E. Taylor   *h*   5405
*Blood Secrets* - Karen E. Taylor   *h*   5406
*Blood Ties* - Karen E. Taylor   *h*   5407

**Vampire, the Dark Ages: The Grails Covenant**
*To Dream of Dreamers Lost* - David Niall
   Wilson   *h*   5882

**Vampire: The Grails Covenant Trilogy**
*To Speak in Lifeless Tongues* - David Niall
   Wilson   *h*   5883

**Vampire: The Masquerade**
*The Unbeholden* - Robert Weinberg   *h*   5703

**A Vampire the Masquerade: Masquerade of the
   Red Death**
*Blood War* - Robert Weinberg   *h*   5693

**A Vampire: The Masquerade: Masquerade of the
   Red Death**
*Unholy Allies* - Robert Weinberg   *h*   5704

**A Vampire: The Masquerade: The Masquerade of
   Red Death**
*As One Dead* - Don Bassingthwaite   *h*   387

**A Vampire: The Masquerade: Trilogy of the Blood
   Curse**
*The Winnowing* - Gherbod Fleming   *h*   1950

**Vampire World Trilogy**
*Blood Brothers* - Brian Lumley   *h*   3546
*Bloodwars* - Brian Lumley   *h*   3547
*The Last Aerie* - Brian Lumley   *h*   3557

**Vampyr-SS**
*At Sword's Point* - Scott MacMillan   *f*   3601
*Knights of the Blood* - Scott MacMillan   *f*   3602

**Varayan Memoir**
*The Hero King* - Rick Shelley   *f*   4970
*The Hero of Varay* - Rick Shelley   *f*   4971

**Viagens Interplanetarias**
*The Hand of Zei* - L. Sprague de Camp   *s*   1414
*The Swords of Zinjaban* - L. Sprague de
   Camp   *s*   1418

**Victory Nelson, Investigator**
*Blood Debt* - Tanya Huff   *h*   2792

**ViraVax**
*Burn* - Bill Ransom   *s*   4476
*ViraVax* - Bill Ransom   *s*   4478

**Virgin and the Dinosaur**
*Atlantis Found* - R. Garcia y Robertson   *s*   2119

**Virtual Light**
*Idoru* - William Gibson   *s*   2218

**Virtual Mode**
*Chaos Mode* - Piers Anthony   *f*   165
*Fractal Mode* - Piers Anthony   *f*   171
*Virtual Mode* - Piers Anthony   *f*   194

**Virtual World**
*No Limits* - Nigel Findley   *s*   1938

**Vlad Taltos**
*Athyra* - Steven Brust   *f*   739
*Dragon* - Steven Brust   *f*   741
*Orca* - Steven Brust   *f*   745

**Von Bek Family**
*The War Amongst the Angels* - Michael
   Moorcock   *f*   3986

**Voyagers**
*Star Brothers* - Ben Bova   *s*   594

**Voyages of the Skipjack**
*Hopeship* - Simon Lang   *s*   3315
*The Trumpets of Tagan* - Simon Lang   *s*   3316

**Walled Orchard**
*Goatsong* - Tom Holt   *f*   2751
*The Walled Orchard* - Tom Holt   *f*   2752

**War Against the Chtorr**
*A Rage for Revenge* - David Gerrold   *s*   2210
*A Season for Slaughter* - David Gerrold   *s*   2211

**War and Honor**
*The Harriers* - Gordon R. Dickson   *s*   1535

**War of the Fading Worlds**
*A Key for the Nonesuch* - Geary Gravel   *s*   2330
*The Return of the Breakneck Boys* - Geary
   Gravel   *s*   2332

**War World**
*Blood Feuds* - S.M. Stirling   *s*   5292
*CoDominium: Revolt on War World* - Jerry
   Pournelle   *s*   4373

**Warbots**
*Blood Siege* - G. Harry Stine   *s*   5278
*Force of Arms* - G. Harry Stine   *s*   5279
*Guts and Glory* - G. Harry Stine   *s*   5280
*Judgment Day* - G. Harry Stine   *s*   5281
*Warrior Shield* - G. Harry Stine   *s*   5283

**Warhammer**
*Drachenfels* - Jack Yeovil   *f*   6022
*Plague Demon* - Brian Craig   *f*   1239
*Storm Warriors* - Brian Craig   *f*   1240
*Zaragoz* - Brian Craig   *f*   1241

**Warhammer 40,000**
*Inquisitor* - Ian Watson   *s*   5637

**Warhammer: Warblade**
*Konrad* - David Ferring   *f*   1927
*Shadowbreed* - David Ferring   *f*   1928

**Warhorse of Esdragon**
*The Prince of Ill Luck* - Susan Dexter   *f*   1512
*The True Knight* - Susan Dexter   *f*   1513

**Warkeep 2030**
*Finger of God* - Michael Kasner   *s*   3013

**Warlock**
*M'Lady Witch* - Christopher Stasheff   *f*   5217
*Quicksilver's Knight* - Christopher Stasheff   *f*   5220
*Warlock and Son* - Christopher Stasheff   *s*   5224
*The Warlock Insane* - Christopher Stasheff   *f*   5225
*The Warlock Rock* - Christopher Stasheff   *s*   5226
*A Wizard in Absentia* - Christopher Stasheff   *s*   5229
*A Wizard in Mind* - Christopher Stasheff   *s*   5232

**Warlord Chronicles**
*Enemy of God* - Bernard Cornwell   *f*   1189
*Excalibur* - Bernard Cornwell   *f*   1190
*The Winter King* - Bernard Cornwell   *f*   1191

**Warrior**
*Wanderer* - Donald E. McQuinn   *s*   3862
*Warrior* - Donald E. McQuinn   *s*   3863
*Witch* - Donald E. McQuinn   *s*   3864

**Wars of Light and Shadow**
*Curse of the Mistwraith* - Janny Wurts   *f*   6001
*Fugitive Prince* - Janny Wurts   *f*   6002
*Ships of Merior* - Janny Wurts   *f*   6004

**Warstrider**
*Warstrider* - William H. Keith Jr.   *s*   3037
*Warstrider: Netlink* - William H. Keith Jr.   *s*   3038

**Water**
*Branch and Crown* - Gael Baudino   *f*   389
*O Greenest Branch!* - Gael Baudino   *f*   394

**Watershed Trilogy**
*A Breach in the Watershed* - Douglas Niles   *f*   4105

**Darkenheight** - Douglas Niles   *f*   4107
*War of the Three Waters* - Douglas Niles   *f*   4110

**Weetzie Bat**
*Baby Be-Bop* - Francesca Lia Block   *f*   545
*Cherokee Bat and the Goat Guys* - Francesca Lia
   Block   *f*   546
*Missing Angel Juan* - Francesca Lia Block   *f*   550

**Well-Favored Man**
*The Price of Blood and Honor* - Elizabeth
   Willey   *f*   5811
*A Sorcerer and a Gentleman* - Elizabeth
   Willey   *f*   5812
*The Well-Favored Man: The Tale of the Sorcerer's
   Nephew* - Elizabeth Willey   *f*   5813

**Well World**
*Echoes of the Well of Souls* - Jack L.
   Chalker   *s*   953
*Gods of the Well of Souls* - Jack L. Chalker   *s*   954
*Shadow of the Well of Souls* - Jack L.
   Chalker   *s*   961

**Westria**
*The Jewel of Fire* - Diana L. Paxson   *f*   4265
*The Wind Crystal* - Diana L. Paxson   *f*   4269

**What Might Have Been**
*Alternate Americas* - Gregory Benford   *s*   442
*Alternate Wars* - Gregory Benford   *s*   443

**Wheel of Time**
*A Crown of Swords* - Robert Jordan   *f*   2984
*The Dragon Reborn* - Robert Jordan   *f*   2985
*The Eye of the World* - Robert Jordan   *f*   2986
*The Fires of Heaven* - Robert Jordan   *f*   2987
*Lord of Chaos* - Robert Jordan   *f*   2988
*The Path of Daggers* - Robert Jordan   *f*   2989
*The Shadow Rising* - Robert Jordan   *f*   2990
*The World of Robert Jordan's The Wheel of Time* -
   Robert Jordan   *f*   2991

**Wheel Trilogy**
*Cathedral of Thorns* - Steven Frankos   *f*   2041

**Widowmaker**
*The Widowmaker Reborn* - Mike Resnick   *s*   4560

**Wild Cards**
*Ace in the Hole* - George R.R. Martin   *s*   3641
*Black Trump* - George R.R. Martin   *s*   3642
*Dealer's Choice* - George R.R. Martin   *s*   3643
*Jokertown Shuffle* - George R.R. Martin   *s*   3646
*Marked Cards* - George R.R. Martin   *s*   3647
*Turn of the Cards* - Victor Milan   *s*   3891

**Wild Magic**
*The Magic Wars* - Jo Clayton   *f*   1068
*Wild Magic* - Jo Clayton   *f*   1072
*Wildfire* - Jo Clayton   *f*   1073

**Willow Wood Springs**
*Invasion of Willow Wood Springs* - Terry
   Ellis   *f*   1781

**Wind Trilogy**
*Escape to the Wind* - Jennifer DiMarco   *s*   1559

**Windameir Circle**
*The Bridge of Dawn* - Neil Hancock   *f*   2531

**Windrose Chronicles**
*Dog Wizard* - Barbara Hambly   *f*   2503

**Wing Commander**
*Action Stations* - William R. Forstchen   *s*   1976
*Wing Commander: Freedom Flight* - Mercedes
   Lackey   *s*   3307

**Winter of the World**
*The Forge in the Forest* - Michael Scott
   Rohan   *f*   4660

**Winter World**
*Brander's Book* - C.J. Mills   *s*   3909

*Egil's Book* - C.J. Mills  *s*  3910
*Kit's Book* - C.J. Mills  *s*  3911
*Zjhanne's Book* - C.J. Mills  *s*  3912

**Witch**
*The Witch Returns* - Phyllis Reynolds
 Naylor  *f*  4079
*The Witch's Eye* - Phyllis Reynolds Naylor  *f*  4080

**Witch World**
*Ciara's Song* - Andre Norton  *f*  4146
*Flight of Vengeance* - Andre Norton  *f*  4152
*The Key of the Keplian* - Andre Norton  *f*  4156
*Songsmith* - Andre Norton  *f*  4161
*Storms of Victory* - Andre Norton  *f*  4162
*The Warding of Witch World* - Andre
 Norton  *f*  4163

**Wizard and Dragon**
*The Faithful Traitor* - Robert Don Hughes  *f*  2809

**Wizard in Rhyme**
*My Son, the Wizard* - Christopher Stasheff  *f*  5218
*The Secular Wizard* - Christopher Stasheff  *f*  5222
*The Witch Doctor* - Christopher Stasheff  *f*  5228

**Wizard of 4th Street**
*The Last Wizard* - Simon Hawke  *f*  2619
*The Nine Lives of Catseye Gomez* - Simon
 Hawke  *f*  2620
*The Samurai Wizard* - Simon Hawke  *f*  2623
*The Wizard of Camelot* - Simon Hawke  *f*  2627
*The Wizard of Santa Fe* - Simon Hawke  *f*  2628
*The Wizard of Sunset Strip* - Simon Hawke  *f*  2629

**Wizard War Chronicles**
*Lords of the Sword* - Hugh Cook  *f*  1156

**Wizardry**
*The Wiz Biz* - Rick Cook  *f*  1160
*A Wizard Abroad* - Diane Duane  *f*  1668
*The Wizardry Consulted* - Rick Cook  *f*  1161
*The Wizardry Cursed* - Rick Cook  *f*  1162
*The Wizardry Quested* - Rick Cook  *f*  1163

**Wizard's War**
*The Dragon's Carbuncle* - Elizabeth H.
 Boyer  *f*  605

**Wizenbeak**
*Lord of the Troll-Bats* - Alexis A. Gilliland  *f*  2234
*The Shadow Shaia* - Alexis A. Gilliland  *f*  2235

**Women of Darkness**
*Women of Darkness II* - Kathryn Ptacek  *h*  4443

**Women of Wonder**
*Women of Wonder, the Classic Years: Science Fiction
 by Women From the 1940s to the 1970s* - Pamela
 Sargent  *s*  4825
*Women of Wonder, the Contemporary Years: Science
 Fiction by Women From the 1970s to the 1990s* -
 Pamela Sargent  *s*  4826

**Wonderland Gambit**
*The Cybernetic Walrus* - Jack L. Chalker  *s*  951
*The Hot-Wired Dodo* - Jack L. Chalker  *s*  956
*The March Hare Network* - Jack L. Chalker  *s*  957

**World of Ardel**
*FreeMaster* - Kris Jensen  *s*  2897
*Mentor* - Kris Jensen  *s*  2898

**World of Darkness**
*The Essential World of Darkness* - Stewart
 Wieck  *h*  5797
*The Quintessential World of Darkness* - Stewart
 Wieck  *h*  5798
*Strange City* - Staley Krause  *h*  3229

**World of Darkness: Immortal Eyes Trilogy**
*Shadows on the Hill* - Jackie Cassada  *f*  935

**World of Darkness: Mage the Ascension: The
 Horizon War Trilogy**
*The Road to Hell, Volume I* - Robert
 Weinberg  *h*  5701

**World of Darkness: Mage: The Horizon War
 Trilogy**
*The Road to Hell, Volume II* - Robert
 Weinberg  *h*  5702

**World of Darkness: Vampire**
*Blood on the Sun* - Brian Herbert  *h*  2664
*Blood Relations* - Doug Murray  *h*  4058
*Dark Prince* - Keith Herber  *h*  2663
*Netherworld* - Richard Lee Byers  *h*  798

**World of Darkness: Werewolf**
*Hell-Storm* - James A. Moore  *h*  3990
*The World of Darkness: Watcher* - Charles L.
 Grant  *h*  2321
*Wyrm Wolf* - Edo van Belkom  *h*  5535

**World of Darkness: Wraith**
*St. Vitus Dances Eternity: A Sarajevo Ghost Story* -
 Stewart Von Allmen  *h*  5585

**World of Tiers**
*More than Fire* - Philip Jose Farmer  *s*  1871
*Red Orc's Rage* - Philip Jose Farmer  *f*  1873

**Worlds Trilogy**
*Worlds Enough and Time* - Joe Haldeman  *s*  2491

**Worldwar**
*Worldwar: In the Balance* - Harry
 Turtledove  *s*  5515
*Worldwar: Striking the Balance* - Harry
 Turtledove  *s*  5516
*Worldwar: Tilting the Balance* - Harry
 Turtledove  *s*  5517
*Worldwar: Upsetting the Balance* - Harry
 Turtledove  *s*  5518

**Wraith: The Oblivion; Dark Kingdoms Trilogy**
*The Ebon Mask* - Richard Lee Byers  *h*  797

**Wren**
*Wren to the Rescue* - Sherwood Smith  *f*  5142
*Wren's Quest* - Sherwood Smith  *f*  5143
*Wren's War* - Sherwood Smith  *f*  5144

**Writers of the Future**
*L. Ron Hubbard Presents Writers of the Future,
 Volume VII* - Algis Budrys  *s*  754
*L. Ron Hubbard Presents Writers of the Future,
 Volume VIII* - Algis Budrys  *s*  755
*L. Ron Hubbard Presents Writers of the Future,
 Volume IX* - Dave Wolverton  *s*  5952
*L. Ron Hubbard Presents Writers of the Future,
 Volume XII* - Dave Wolverton  *s*  5953

**X-Files**
*Antibodies* - Kevin J. Anderson  *h*  99
*Goblins* - Charles L. Grant  *s*  2309
*Ground Zero* - Kevin J. Anderson  *h*  106
*Ruins* - Kevin J. Anderson  *h*  112
*Whirlwind* - Charles L. Grant  *f*  2320

**X-Men**
*Codename Wolverine* - Christopher Golden  *s*  2256

**Xanadu**
*Xanadu* - Jane Yolen  *f*  6044
*Xanadu 2* - Jane Yolen  *f*  6045
*Xanadu 3* - Jane Yolen  *f*  6046

**Xanth**
*The Color of Her Panties* - Piers Anthony  *f*  167
*Demons Don't Dream* - Piers Anthony  *f*  168
*Faun & Games* - Piers Anthony  *f*  169
*Geis of the Gargoyle* - Piers Anthony  *f*  172
*Isle of View* - Piers Anthony  *f*  177
*Man From Mundania* - Piers Anthony  *f*  180
*Question Quest* - Piers Anthony  *f*  186
*Roc and a Hard Place* - Piers Anthony  *f*  187
*Yon Ill Wind* - Piers Anthony  *f*  196
*Zombie Lover* - Piers Anthony  *f*  197

**Xanthe**
*Harpy Thyme* - Piers Anthony  *f*  174

**Xeelee**
*Ring* - Stephen Baxter  *s*  402
*Timelike Infinity* - Stephen Baxter  *s*  404

**Xena: Warrior Princess**
*The Empty Throne* - Ru Emerson  *f*  1808
*The Thief of Hermes* - Ru Emerson  *f*  1811

**Xenogenesis**
*Imago* - Octavia E. Butler  *s*  791

**Yamato**
*Yamato: A Rage in Heaven* - Ken Kato  *s*  3014

**The Year's Best Fantasy and Horror**
*The Year's Best Fantasy and Horror: Eleventh Annual
 Collection* - Ellen Datlow  *h*  1371
*The Year's Best Fantasy and Horror: Tenth Annual
 Collection* - Ellen Datlow  *h*  1377

**Year's Best Science Fiction**
*The Year's Best Science Fiction: Eighth Annual
 Collection* - Gardner Dozois  *s*  1616
*The Year's Best Science Fiction: Eleventh Annual
 Collection* - Gardner Dozois  *s*  1617
*The Year's Best Science Fiction: Fourteenth Annual
 Collection* - Gardner Dozois  *s*  1619
*The Year's Best Science Fiction: Ninth Annual
 Collection* - Gardner Dozois  *s*  1620
*The Year's Best Science Fiction: Seventh Annual
 Collection* - Gardner Dozois  *s*  1621
*The Year's Best Science Fiction: Tenth Annual
 Collection* - Gardner Dozois  *s*  1622
*The Year's Best Science Fiction: Thirteenth Annual
 Collection* - Gardner Dozois  *s*  1623
*The Year's Best Science Fiction: Twelfth Annual
 Collection* - Gardner Dozois  *s*  1624

**Year's Best SF**
*Year's Best SF 2* - David G. Hartwell  *s*  2597
*Year's Best SF 3* - David G. Hartwell  *s*  2598

**Years of Longdirk**
*Demon Knight* - Ken Hood  *f*  2760

**Yngling**
*The Yngling and the Circle of Power* - John
 Dalmas  *s*  1328
*The Yngling in Yamato* - John Dalmas  *s*  1329

**Young Indiana Jones Chronicles**
*The Mata Hari Adventure* - James Luceno  *f*  3544

**Young Jedi Knights**
*Trouble on Cloud City* - Kevin J. Anderson  *s*  117

**Young Merlin Trilogy**
*Merlin* - Jane Yolen  *f*  6035
*Passager* - Jane Yolen  *f*  6038

**Zoot Marlowe**
*Hawaiian U.F.O. Aliens* - Mel Gilden  *s*  2226
*Tubular Android Superheroes* - Mel Gilden  *s*  2228

# Time Period Index

This index chronologically lists the time settings in which the featured books take place. Main headings refer to a century; where no specific time is given, the headings INDETERMINATE PAST, INDETERMINATE FUTURE, and INDETERMINATE are used. The 18th through 21st centuries are broken down into decades when possible. (Note: 1800s, for example, refers to the first decade of the 19th century.) Featured titles are listed alphabetically beneath time headings, with author names and entry numbers also provided.

## INDETERMINATE PAST

*The Adventures of Huru on the Road to Baghdad* - Guneli Gun  f  2457

*The Adventures of King Midas* - Lynne Reid Banks  f  329

*The Adventures of Threadwell the Tailor, or Alterations Made While You Wait* - P.D. Cacek  h  801

*Ahmed and the Oblivion Machines* - Ray Bradbury  f  618

*Aisling* - Louise Cooper  f  1172

*Alamut* - Judith Tarr  f  5390

*All's Faire* - Pamela F. Service  f  4917

*Ambush at Corellia* - Roger MacBride Allen  s  76

*Angels & Visitations: A Miscellany* - Neil Gaiman  f  2101

*The Animal Wife* - Elizabeth Marshall Thomas  f  5444

*The Anubis Murders* - Gary Gygax  f  2472

*Aquamancer* - Don Callander  f  841

*Arabian Nights: The Marvels and Wonders of the Thousand and One Nights* - Jack Zipes  f  6087

*The Architecture of Desire* - Mary Gentle  f  2195

*The Arkadians* - Lloyd Alexander  f  67

*Ars Magica* - Judith Tarr  f  5392

*Arthur* - Stephen R. Lawhead  f  3352

*Atlantis Found* - R. Garcia y Robertson  s  2119

*Avatar* - Louise Cooper  f  1173

*The Avenger* - Louise Cooper  f  1174

*Back to the Time Trap* - Keith Laumer  s  3343

*A Bad Day for Ali Baba* - Craig Shaw Gardner  f  2123

*The Bastard Prince* - Katherine Kurtz  f  3255

*Before the Storm* - Michael P. Kube-McDowell  s  3247

*Between the Rivers* - Harry Turtledove  f  5496

*Beyond Ragnarok* - Mickey Zucker Reichert  f  4516

*The Black Gryphon* - Mercedes Lackey  f  3270

*Blameless in Abaddon* - James Morrow  f  4029

*Bleak Seasons* - Glen Cook  f  1147

*The Bones of Haven* - Simon R. Green  f  2363

*The Book of the Beast* - Tanith Lee  f  3405

*The Boy From the Burren* - Sheila Gilluly  f  2236

*The Bridge of Dawn* - Neil Hancock  f  2531

*Bridge of Valor* - Anne Lesley Groell  f  2452

*By the Sword* - Timothy Boggs  f  559

*By the Sword* - Mercedes Lackey  f  3273

*Call of Madness* - Julie Dean Smith  f  5124

*Cardmaster* - Clayton Emery  f  1813

*The Chalchiuhite Dragon* - Kenneth Morris  f  4020

*Challenges* - Sharon Green  f  2354

*The Changeling* - Kristine Kathryn Rusch  f  4714

*Charlemagne's Champion* - Gail Van Asten  f  5534

*Chernevog* - C.J. Cherryh  f  982

*Child of an Ancient City* - Tad Williams  f  5827

*Children of the Jedi* - Barbara Hambly  s  2500

*The Chronicles of Master Li and Number Ten Ox* - Barry Hughart  f  2803

*Clouds End* - Sean Stewart  f  5272

*Competition* - Sharon Green  f  2355

*Conan and the Treasure of Python* - John Maddox Roberts  f  4616

*The Conan Chronicles* - Robert Jordan  f  2983

*Conan of the Red Brotherhood* - Leonard Carpenter  f  906

*Conan, Scourge of the Bloody Coast* - Leonard Carpenter  f  910

*Conan the Gladiator* - Leonard Carpenter  f  907

*Conan the Outcast* - Leonard Carpenter  f  908

*Conan the Savage* - Leonard Carpenter  f  909

*Count Scar* - C. Dale Brittain  f  702

*The Courtship of Princess Leia* - Dave Wolverton  s  5950

*Cowboy Feng's Space Bar and Grille* - Steven Brust  s  740

*Crow and Weasel* - Barry Lopez  f  3523

*The Crown of Dalemark* - Diana Wynne Jones  f  2945

*Crusade* - James Lowder  f  3537

*The Crystal Star* - Vonda N. McIntyre  s  3820

*The Cygnet and the Firebird* - Patricia A. McKillip  f  3839

*The Dagger and the Cross: A Novel of the Crusades* - Judith Tarr  f  5393

*The Dancers at the End of Time* - Michael Moorcock  s  3979

*Dark Force Rising* - Timothy Zahn  s  6052

*Dark Legend* - Jamake Highwater  f  2686

*The Dark Shore* - Adam Lee  f  3385

*Darksaber* - Kevin J. Anderson  s  103

*The Day of the Tempest* - Jean Rabe  f  4457

*Days of Air and Darkness* - Katharine Kerr  f  3067

*Days of Blood and Fire* - Katharine Kerr  f  3068

*Deadly Quicksilver Lies* - Glen Cook  f  1148

*Death in Delhi* - Gary Gygax  f  2473

*The Demon King* - Chris Bunch  f  770

*Distant Planes* - Kathy Ice  f  2827

*A Diversity of Dragons* - Anne McCaffrey  f  3728

*Down Among the Dead Men* - Simon R. Green  f  2367

*The Dragon and the Unicorn* - A.A. Attanasio  f  266

*Dragon Cauldron* - Laurence Yep  f  6024

*The Dragon Revenant* - Katharine Kerr  f  3069

*Dragon War* - Laurence Yep  f  6025

*Dragon's Blood* - Alex McDonough  s  3799

*The Dragon's Boy* - Jane Yolen  f  6030

*The Dragon's Carbuncle* - Elizabeth H. Boyer  f  605

*Dragons Past* - Gary Gentile  s  2192

*Dread Brass Shadows* - Glen Cook  f  1149

*Dreams of Steel* - Glen Cook  f  1150

*Drum Calls* - Jo Clayton  f  1065

*Duel of Dragons* - Gael Baudino  f  391

*The Eagle and the Sword* - A.A. Attanasio  f  267

*Emperor and Clown* - Dave Duncan  f  1676

*The Empty Throne* - Ru Emerson  f  1808

*The Enchanted Isles* - Casey Flynn  f  1960

*End of an Era* - Robert J. Sawyer  s  4853

*Engor's Sword Arm* - David C. Smith  h  5110

*Faery in Shadow* - C.J. Cherryh  f  987

*Faery Lands Forlorn* - Dave Duncan  f  1677

*The Falcon and the Serpent* - Cheryl A. Smith  f  5101

*Fanuilh* - Daniel Hood  f  2757

*Feathered Dragon* - Douglas Niles  f  4108

*Fifth Quarter* - Tanya Huff  f  2795

*Final Sacrifice* - Clayton Emery  f  1814

*Fire in the Mist* - Holly Lisle  f  3482

*Firehand* - Andre Norton  s  4151

*The Fire's Stone* - Tanya Huff  f  2796

*The First Casualty* - David L. Seidman  f  4912

*First Frontier* - Diane Carey  s  902

*Five Hundred Years After* - Steven Brust  f  742

*Flight of the Raven* - Jennifer Roberson  f  4608

*A Forest Lord* - Michael Williams  f  5819

*The Forge of Virtue* - Lynn Abbey  f  16

*The Fortress of Eternity* - Andrew Whitmore  f  5790

*The Fourth Guardian* - Ronald Anthony Cross  s  1273

*The Further Adventures of Superman* - Martin H. Greenberg  s  2393

*Future Indefinite* - Dave Duncan  f  1678

*Gate of Ivory, Gate of Horn* - Robert Holdstock  f  2737

*Gatherer of Clouds* - Sean Russell  f  4741

*Geomancer* - Don Callander  f  845

*The Gilded Chain: A Tale of the King's Blades* - Dave Duncan  f  1679

*The Glove of Darth Vader* - Paul Davids  s  1392

*The Goblin Companion* - Terry Jones  f  2980

*Goblin Moon* - Teresa Edgerton  f  1743

*The God Killer* - Simon R. Green  f  2368

*Grail* - Stephen R. Lawhead  f  3355

*Guard Against Dishonor* - Simon R. Green  f  2369

*The Guardian* - Angus Wells  f  5737

*Hall of Whispers* - Mike Jefferies  f  2884

*Hammer and Anvil* - Harry Turtledove   f  5503
*Hawk & Fisher* - Simon R. Green   f  2370
*Helen's Passage* - Diana M. Concannon   f  1129
*Here There Be Dragons* - Roger Zelazny   f  6069
*The Hollowing* - Robert Holdstock   f  2738
*Hope of Earth* - Piers Anthony   s  175
*Hour of the Dragon* - Robert E. Howard   f  2783
*Hunter of the Light* - Risa Aratyr   f  203
*The Hunter Returns* - David Drake   f  1632
*Hunter's Death* - Michelle West   f  5758
*The Hunters' Haunt* - Dave Duncan   f  1681
*Hunter's Oath* - Michelle West   f  5759
*The Illusionists* - Faren Miller   f  3894
*Imperial Lady* - Andre Norton   f  4155
*In Legend Born* - Laura Resnick   f  4533
*Infanta* - Louise Cooper   f  1176
*The Initiate Brother* - Sean Russell   f  4742
*The Innamorati* - Midori Snyder   f  5152
*The Innkeeper's Song* - Peter S. Beagle   f  409
*The Interior Life* - Katherine Blake   f  515
*The Island of the Mighty* - Evangeline
   Walton   f  5626
*The Isles of the Blest* - Morgan Llywelyn   f  3505
*The Janus Mask* - Richard A. Knaak   f  3171
*Jedi Search* - Kevin J. Anderson   s  109
*The Jigsaw Woman* - Kim Antieau   f  199
*Kahless* - Michael Jan Friedman   s  2065
*Kane of Old Mars* - Michael Moorcock   s  3983
*Krispos of Videssos* - Harry Turtledove   f  5506
*Krispos Rising* - Harry Turtledove   f  5507
*Krispos the Emperor* - Harry Turtledove   f  5508
*The Land of Gold* - Gillian Bradshaw   f  658
*The Last Arabian Night* - Craig Shaw
   Gardner   f  2129
*The Last Book of Swords: Shieldbreaker's Story* - Fred
   Saberhagen   f  4768
*The Last Command* - Timothy Zahn   s  6055
*The Last of the Renshai* - Mickey Zucker
   Reichert   f  4520
*The Last Voyage of Somebody the Sailor* - John
   Barth   f  374
*The Legend of Nightfall* - Mickey Zucker
   Reichert   f  4521
*Liar's Oath* - Elizabeth Moon   f  3969
*The Lions of Al-Rassan* - Guy Gavriel Kay   f  3016
*The Living God* - Dave Duncan   f  1682
*The Longing Ring* - Christopher Kubasik   f  3246
*Lord of the Isles* - David Drake   f  1636
*The Lost City of the Jedi* - Paul Davids   s  1393
*The Lost Guardian* - Ronald Anthony Cross   s  1274
*The Lost Prince* - Bridget Wood   f  5962
*A Love through Time* - Terri Brisbin   f  691
*Magic Casement* - Dave Duncan   f  1683
*Magic's Price* - Mercedes Lackey   f  3288
*The Mandalorian Armor* - K.W. Jeter   s  2914
*Maskerade* - Terry Pratchett   f  4395
*The Master of Whitestorm* - Janny Wurts   f  6003
*Merlin* - Jane Yolen   f  6035
*Merlin's Bones* - Fred Saberhagen   f  4771
*Mission of Magic* - Julie Dean Smith   f  5125
*Mistress of Ambiguities* - J.F. Rivkin   f  4596
*The Moon in Hiding* - Teresa Edgerton   f  1745
*Most Ancient Song* - Casey Flynn   f  1961
*Nemesis* - Louise Cooper   f  1177
*The New Rebellion* - Kristine Kathryn
   Rusch   s  4719
*Nightwatch* - Robin Wayne Bailey   f  289
*No Enemy but Time* - Michael Bishop   s  502
*No Quarter* - Tanya Huff   f  2798
*Norby and Yobo's Great Adventure* - Janet
   Asimov   s  254
*Old Tin Sorrows* - Glen Cook   f  1151
*On Fortune's Wheel* - Cynthia Voigt   f  5579
*One for the Morning Glory* - John Barnes   f  355
*The Other Sinbad* - Craig Shaw Gardner   f  2130
*The Outlaws of Sherwood* - Robin
   McKinley   f  3846
*The Painter Knight* - Fiona Patton   f  4258
*The Parched Sea* - Troy Denning   f  1486

*Passager* - Jane Yolen   f  6038
*People of the Fire* - W. Michael Gear   f  2167
*People of the Mesa* - Ardath Mayhar   f  3704
*People of the River* - W. Michael Gear   f  2168
*People of the Wolf* - W. Michael Gear   f  2170
*Perilous Seas* - Dave Duncan   f  1685
*The Phoenix Guards* - Steven Brust   f  747
*Pigs Don't Fly* - Mary Brown   f  727
*The Plains of Passage* - Jean M. Auel   f  275
*Predator* - William F. Wu   s  5998
*Pretty Pewter Gods* - Glen Cook   f  1152
*Prince of Demons* - Mickey Zucker
   Reichert   f  4522
*Prince of the North* - Harry Turtledove   f  5509
*Pyromancer* - Don Callander   f  847
*Queen of Demons* - David Drake   f  1640
*The Queen of the Damned* - Anne Rice   h  4574
*Rage of a Demon King* - Raymond E. Feist   f  1908
*Raptor Red* - Robert T. Bakker   f  306
*Ratha and Thistle-Chaser* - Clare Bell   f  432
*Rats and Gargoyles* - Mary Gentle   f  2196
*Ray Bradbury Presents: Dinosaur Planet* - Stephen
   Leigh   s  3427
*Ray Bradbury Presents: Dinosaur World* - Stephen
   Leigh   s  3428
*Realm of Light* - Deborah Chester   f  1008
*The Realms of the Gods* - Tamora Pierce   f  4321
*Red Iron Nights* - Glen Cook   f  1153
*The Red King* - Victor Kelleher   f  3043
*Reign of Shadows* - Deborah Chester   f  1009
*The Remarkable Journey of Prince Jen* - Lloyd
   Alexander   f  69
*Revenant* - Louise Cooper   f  1178
*A Ride on the Red Mare's Back* - Ursula K. Le
   Guin   f  3382
*Rivers of Time* - L. Sprague de Camp   s  1417
*The Road West* - Gary Wright   f  5984
*Rogue Squadron* - Michael A. Stackpole   s  5205
*The Runelords: The Sum of All Men* - David
   Farland   f  1866
*Rusalka* - C.J. Cherryh   f  1002
*The Sacred Stones* - William Sarabande   f  4818
*Sage of Sare* - Julie Dean Smith   f  5126
*Sea Without a Shore* - Sean Russell   f  4743
*The Secret Weavers: Stories of the Fantastic by Latin
   American Women* - Marjorie Agosin   f  43
*The Secular Wizard* - Christopher Stasheff   f  5222
*The Seeds of Time* - Kay Kenyon   s  3064
*The Seer King* - Chris Bunch   f  771
*The Shadow Gate* - Margaret Ball   f  317
*Shadow Moon* - George Lucas   f  3540
*Shadow War* - Deborah Chester   f  1010
*Shadows of the Empire* - Steve Perry   s  4299
*Shame of Man* - Piers Anthony   s  188
*Shards of a Broken Crown* - Raymond E.
   Feist   f  1912
*Shattered Chains* - Clayton Emery   f  1816
*She Is the Darkness* - Glen Cook   f  1154
*The Shield of Time* - Poul Anderson   s  131
*Shiva Accused: An Adventure of the Ice Age* - J.H.
   Brennan   f  667
*Shiva's Challenge: An Adventure of the Ice Age* - J.H.
   Brennan   f  668
*The Silver Gryphon* - Mercedes Lackey   f  3295
*The Silver Hand* - Stephen R. Lawhead   f  3358
*Sing the Four Quarters* - Tanya Huff   f  2799
*The Sixth Book of Lost Swords: Mindsword's Story* -
   Fred Saberhagen   f  4776
*Sojourn* - R.A. Salvatore   f  4806
*Soldier of Arete* - Gene Wolfe   f  5944
*A Song for Arbonne* - Guy Gavriel Kay   f  3017
*Song for the Basilisk* - Patricia A. McKillip   f  3841
*Song of the Gargoyle* - Zilpha Keatley
   Snyder   f  5153
*Sons of the Titans* - Patrick H. Adkins   f  36
*A Sorcerer's Apprentice* - Michael Williams   f  5820
*The Sorceress and the Cygnet* - Patricia A.
   McKillip   f  3842
*The Soulforge* - Margaret Weis   f  5728

*StarSpawn* - Kenneth Von Gunden   s  5588
*The Still* - David Feintuch   f  1902
*The Stolen Throne* - Harry Turtledove   f  5510
*The Stone Prince* - Fiona Patton   f  4259
*Storm Breaking* - Mercedes Lackey   f  3296
*Storm Rising* - Mercedes Lackey   f  3297
*Storm Warning* - Mercedes Lackey   f  3298
*A Strange and Ancient Name* - Josepha
   Sherman   f  4991
*The Stricken Field* - Dave Duncan   f  1688
*Suisan* - Phyllis Carol Agins   f  42
*Summer King, Winter Fool* - Lisa Goldstein   f  2263
*Sunder, Eclipse and Seed* - Elise Guttenberg   f  2471
*Surrender None: The Legacy of Gird* - Elizabeth
   Moon   f  3975
*Sword and Sorceress IX* - Marion Zimmer
   Bradley   f  647
*The Sword and the Lion* - Roberta Cray   f  1253
*Sword-Born* - Jennifer Roberson   f  4612
*Sword-Breaker* - Jennifer Roberson   f  4613
*Sword-Maker* - Jennifer Roberson   f  4614
*Sword of Ice and Other Tales of Valdemar* - Mercedes
   Lackey   f  3300
*Tales From Jabba's Palace* - Kevin J.
   Anderson   s  114
*Tales From the Mos Eisley Cantina* - Kevin J.
   Anderson   s  115
*Tales of Talislanta* - Stephen Michael Sechi   f  4909
*Tales of the White Wolf* - Edward E.
   Kramer   f  3227
*Tales of Zothique* - Clark Ashton Smith   f  5104
*Talion: Revenant* - Michael A. Stackpole   f  5206
*A Tapestry of Lions* - Jennifer Roberson   f  4615
*The Temper of Wisdom* - Lynn Abbey   f  17
*The Thief of Hermes* - Ru Emerson   f  1811
*The Thousand Cities* - Harry Turtledove   f  5512
*A Time of Exile* - Katharine Kerr   f  3077
*A Time of Omens* - Katharine Kerr   f  3078
*The Time Ships* - Stephen Baxter   s  403
*Timespell* - Robert N. Charrette   f  978
*To the Land of the Living* - Robert
   Silverberg   s  5044
*Tongues of Jade* - Laurence Yep   f  6026
*Touching the Fire* - Roger Welsch   f  5751
*A Tremor in the Bitter Earth* - Katya
   Reimann   f  4527
*Troika* - Louise Cooper   f  1181
*The Truce at Bakura* - Kathy Tyers   s  5527
*Tyrannosaurus Rex* - J.F. Rivkin   s  4597
*Upland Outlaws* - Dave Duncan   f  1690
*The Usurper* - Angus Wells   f  5739
*Videssos Besieged* - Harry Turtledove   f  5513
*Vinas Solamnus* - J. Robert King   f  3123
*The Virgin and the Dinosaur* - R. Garcia y
   Robertson   s  2122
*Voyage of the Fox Rider* - Dennis L.
   McKiernan   f  3837
*War of the Gods* - Poul Anderson   f  136
*The Warding of Witch World* - Andre
   Norton   f  4163
*The Warrior Returns* - Allan Cole   f  1109
*The Warrior's Tale* - Allan Cole   f  1110
*The Way Beneath* - Angus Wells   f  5740
*Wayfinder's Story: The Seventh Book of Lost Swords* -
   Fred Saberhagen   f  4777
*The Wealdwife's Tale* - Paul Hazel   f  2636
*A Well-Timed Enchantment* - Vivian Vande
   Velde   f  5559
*The Western Wizard* - Mickey Zucker
   Reichert   f  4526
*Whilom* - Robert Watson   f  5639
*The White Gryphon* - Mercedes Lackey   f  3303
*The White Guardian* - Ronald Anthony
   Cross   s  1275
*The White Mists of Power* - Kristine Kathryn
   Rusch   f  4730
*Whose Song Is Sung* - Frank Schaefer   f  4872
*The Wild Hunt: Vengeance Moon* - Jocelin
   Foxe   f  2031

Wild Magic - Tamora Pierce   f  4323
The Willing Spirit - Piers Anthony   f  195
Wind From a Foreign Sky - Katya Reimann   f  4528
Winds of Change - Mercedes Lackey   f  3304
Winds of Fate - Mercedes Lackey   f  3305
Winds of Fury - Mercedes Lackey   f  3306
Winner Takes All - Simon R. Green   f  2375
Wishing Season - Esther Friesner   f  2085
The Witch Doctor - Christopher Stasheff   f  5228
Wit'ch Fire - James Clemens   f  1082
The Wizard King - Julie Dean Smith   f  5127
Wizard of Bones - Robert N. Charrette   f  979
Wizard's Heir - Daniel Hood   f  2759
The Wolf and the Crown - A.A. Attanasio   f  273
Wolf in the Fold - Simon R. Green   f  2376
Wolf-Speaker - Tamora Pierce   f  4324
Wolfhelm - Richard A. Knaak   f  3175
Wolfking - Bridget Wood   f  5963
Wolf's Cub - Mackay Wood   f  5964
Wolves of the Gods - Allan Cole   f  1111
The Woman Who Loved Reindeer - Meredith Ann
    Pierce   f  4320
The Work of the Sun - Teresa Edgerton   f  1746
World Without End - Molly Cochran   f  1093
Wrath of Ashar - Angus Wells   f  5742
Yvgenie - C.J. Cherryh   f  1005
Zorba the Hutt's Revenge - Paul Davids   s  1394

### 20000th CENTURY B.C.

Isle of Woman - Piers Anthony   f  178

### 81th CENTURY B.C.

The Dechronization of Sam Magruder - George
    Gaylord Simpson   s  5067

### 480th CENTURY B.C.

Hunting the Ghost Dancer - A.A. Attanasio   f  268

### 380th CENTURY B.C.

The Ugly Little Boy - Isaac Asimov   s  250

### 350th CENTURY B.C.

The Last Dancer - Daniel Keys Moran   s  3994

### 250th CENTURY B.C.

Arc Riders - David Drake   s  1626

### 189th CENTURY B.C.

Letters From Atlantis - Robert Silverberg   f  5035

### 120th CENTURY B.C.

The Edge of the World - William Sarabande   f  4817
Thunder in the Sky - William Sarabande   f  4819

### 101st CENTURY B.C.

The Elementals - Morgan Llywelyn   f  3503

### 90th CENTURY B.C.

People of the Sea - W. Michael Gear   f  2169

### 80th CENTURY B.C.

Dawn Land - Joseph Bruchac   f  731
Orion in the Dying Time - Ben Bova   s  591

### 73rd CENTURY B.C.

Encounter with Tiber - Buzz Aldrin   s  64

### 71st CENTURY B.C.

Mother Earth, Father Sky - Sue Harrison   f  2581

### 65th CENTURY B.C.

Song of the River - Sue Harrison   f  2583

### 50th CENTURY B.C.

Time Station Paris - David Evans   s  1854

### 40th CENTURY B.C.

First Dawn - Mike Moscoe   s  4038
Lost Days - Mike Moscoe   s  4039
Second Fire - Mike Moscoe   s  4040

### 30th CENTURY B.C.

People of the Earth - W. Michael Gear   f  2166

### 15th CENTURY B.C.

Thebes of the Hundred Gates - Robert
    Silverberg   s  5043

### 13th CENTURY B.C.

The Amazon Chronicles - Jane E.M.
    Robinson   f  4627
Iron Dawn - Matthew Woodring Stover   f  5320
Island in the Sea of Time - S.M. Stirling   s  5295
Jericho Moon - Matthew Woodring Stover   f  5321

### 11th CENTURY B.C.

An Acceptable Time - Madeleine L'Engle   f  3436

### 10th CENTURY B.C.

The Druid's Gift - Margaret J. Anderson   f  121

### 8th CENTURY B.C.

My Sister the Moon - Sue Harrison   f  2582

### 7th CENTURY B.C.

Servant of the Bones - Anne Rice   h  4575

### 6th CENTURY B.C.

The Fabulist - John Vornholt   f  5595

### 5th CENTURY B.C.

Goatsong - Tom Holt   f  2751
Soldier of Arete - Gene Wolfe   f  5944
The Walled Orchard - Tom Holt   f  2752

### 4th CENTURY B.C.

Dark Prince - David Gemmell   f  2187
Lion of Macedon - David Gemmell   f  2189
Lord of the Two Lands - Judith Tarr   f  5395
Orion and the Conqueror - Ben Bova   s  590

### 2nd CENTURY B.C.

Horses of Heaven - Gillian Bradshaw   f  657

### 1st CENTURY B.C.

Child of the Eagle - Esther Friesner   f  2073
Pandora - Anne Rice   h  4573
The Schizogenic Man - Raymond Harris   s  2563
Throne of Isis - Judith Tarr   f  5397

### 1st CENTURY

The Centurion's Empire - Sean McMullen   s  3854
Corrupting Dr. Nice - John Kessel   s  3083
Far Edge of Darkness - Linda Evans   s  1855
The Fire Queen - Jack Holland   f  2740
The Forest House - Marion Zimmer Bradley   f  633
The Fourth Rome - David Drake   s  1631
The Grail of Hearts - Susan Shwartz   f  5015
Lady of Avalon - Marion Zimmer Bradley   f  640
The Light Bearer - Donna Gillespie   f  2229
Live From Golgotha: A Novel - Gore Vidal   s  5569
The Raid - Randy Lee Eickhoff   f  1764
Time Scout - Robert Asprin   s  263
Wagers of Sin - Robert Asprin   s  264
Warrior - William F. Wu   s  6000

### 2nd CENTURY

People of the Lakes - Kathleen O'Neal Gear   f  2164

### 3rd CENTURY

The Autobiography of Santa Claus: It's Better to Give
    - Jeff Guinn   f  2456
Finn Mac Cool - Morgan Llywelyn   f  3504
Lady of Avalon - Marion Zimmer Bradley   f  640
Master of Earth and Water - Diana L.
    Paxson   f  4266
The Shield between the Worlds - Diana L.
    Paxson   f  4267
Sword of Fire and Shadow - Diana L.
    Paxson   f  4268

### 4th CENTURY

Cromm - Kenneth C. Flint   f  1957
The Skystone - Jack Whyte   f  5794
The Vampire Memoirs - Mara McCuniff   h  3781

### 5th CENTURY

Arthur War Lord - Dafydd ab Hugh   f  6
Attila's Treasure - Stephan Grundy   f  2453
The Camelot Chronicles - Mike Ashley   f  224
The Child Queen - Nancy McKenzie   f  3827
Chronicles of King Arthur - Andrea
    Hopkins   f  2767
The Deer's Cry: A Book of the Keltiad - Patricia
    Kennealy-Morrison   f  3060
The Dragons of the Rhine - Diana L.
    Paxson   f  4264
Druids - Morgan Llywelyn   f  3502
The Eagles' Brood - Jack Whyte   f  5792
In the Shadow of the Oak King - Courtway
    Jones   f  2939
The Kingmaking - Helen Hollick   f  2745
Legacy - Steve White   s  5785
Merlin and the Dragons - Jane Yolen   f  6036
The Merlin Chronicles - Mike Ashley   f  227
Pendragon's Banner - Helen Hollick   f  2746
The Prince and the Pilgrim - Mary Stewart   f  5270
Rhinegold - Stephan Grundy   f  2454
The Saxon Shore - Jack Whyte   f  5793
Shadow of the King - Helen Hollick   f  2747
The Tower of Beowulf - Parke Godwin   f  2250
Witch of the North - Courtway Jones   f  2940
The Wolf and the Raven - Diana L. Paxson   f  4270

### 6th CENTURY

*Black Horses for the King* - Anne McCaffrey  f  3720
*Chronicles of King Arthur* - Andrea Hopkins  f  2767
*Druids* - Morgan Llywelyn  f  3502
*Enemy of God* - Bernard Cornwell  f  1189
*Excalibur* - Bernard Cornwell  f  1190
*The Fires of Merlin* - T.A. Barron  f  369
*Ghost King* - David Gemmell  f  2188
*Guinevere: The Legend in Autumn* - Persia Woolley  f  5970
*In the Heart of Darkness* - Eric Flint  s  1955
*King & Raven* - Cary James  f  2858
*The Last Pendragon* - Robert Rice  f  4584
*The Lost Years of Merlin* - T.A. Barron  f  370
*An Oblique Approach* - David Drake  s  1638
*Pendragon* - Stephen R. Lawhead  f  3357
*Queen of the Summer Stars* - Persia Woolley  f  5971
*The Seven Songs of Merlin* - T.A. Barron  f  372
*Thessalonica* - Harry Turtledove  f  5511
*The Throne of Tara* - John Desjarlais  f  1498
*The Tower of Beowulf* - Parke Godwin  f  2250
*The Winter King* - Bernard Cornwell  f  1191

### 7th CENTURY

*Celestial Matters* - Richard Garfinkle  s  2140
*Eight Skilled Gentlemen* - Barry Hughart  f  2804
*The Panther's Hoard* - Nancy Varian Berberick  f  458
*Shadow of the Seventh Moon* - Nancy Varian Berberick  f  459
*Shadowborn* - William W. Connors  h  1137
*The Shining Company* - Rosemary Sutcliff  f  5359

### 8th CENTURY

*The Book of Brendan* - Ann Curry  f  1294
*The Deepest Sea* - Charles Barnitz  f  363
*The Shattered Oath* - Josepha Sherman  f  4989
*Silk Road* - Jeanne Larsen  f  3339
*The Silver Wolf* - Alice Borchardt  h  572

### 9th CENTURY

*The Discovery of Dragons* - Graeme Base  f  385
*The Hammer and the Cross* - Harry Harrison  f  2570
*His Majesty's Elephant* - Judith Tarr  f  5394
*King and Emperor* - Harry Harrison  f  2571
*Living with the Reptiles* - Roger L. DiSilvestro  s  1563
*One King's Way* - Harry Harrison  s  2572
*The Red Wyvern* - Katharine Kerr  f  3074

### 10th CENTURY

*Better in the Dark* - Chelsea Quinn Yarbro  h  6011
*Black Dogs* - Ian McEwan  h  3808
*Brian Boru: Emperor of the Irish* - Morgan Llywelyn  f  3501
*Bring Me the Head of Prince Charming* - Roger Zelazny  f  6062
*By Chaos Cursed* - Mickey Zucker Reichert  f  4517
*Byzantium* - Stephen R. Lawhead  f  3353
*The Golden Key* - Melanie Rawn  f  4486
*The Grail of Hearts* - Susan Shwartz  f  5015
*Shards of Empire* - Susan Shwartz  f  5017

### 11th CENTURY

*Cross and Crescent* - Susan Shwartz  f  5014
*The Ice-Shirt* - William T. Vollmann  f  5580
*The Iron Lance* - Stephen R. Lawhead  f  3356
*Lord of Sunset* - Parke Godwin  f  2246

*Merlin's Legacy: Dawn of Camelot* - Quinn Taylor Evans  f  1857
*Pride of Lions* - Morgan Llywelyn  f  3506
*Robin and the King* - Parke Godwin  f  2247
*Sherwood* - Parke Godwin  f  2248
*The Spawn of Loki* - Jason Henderson  f  2658

### 12th CENTURY

*Bronze Mirror* - Jeanne Larsen  f  3338
*Child of Faerie, Child of Earth* - Josepha Sherman  f  4985
*Cross and Crescent* - Susan Shwartz  f  5014
*Crusader's Torch* - Chelsea Quinn Yarbro  h  6015
*The Heavenward Path* - Kara Dalkey  f  1319
*Horselords* - David Cook  f  1145
*Kingdom of the Grail* - A.A. Attanasio  f  269
*Lady of the Forest* - Jennifer Roberson  f  4609
*Little Sister* - Kara Dalkey  f  1320
*Madoc's Hundred* - Pat Winter  f  5925
*The Mask of Loki* - Roger Zelazny  f  6071
*The Notorious Abbess* - Vera Chapman  f  965
*The Red Wyvern* - Katharine Kerr  f  3074
*The Robin Hood Ambush* - William F. Wu  s  5999
*To Dream of Dreamers Lost* - David Niall Wilson  h  5882
*To Speak in Lifeless Tongues* - David Niall Wilson  h  5883

### 13th CENTURY

*Conrad's Quest for Rubber* - Leo Frankowski  s  2043
*The Discovery of Dragons* - Graeme Base  f  385
*The Flying Warlord* - Leo Frankowski  s  2044
*The High-Tech Knight* - Leo Frankowski  s  2045
*If at Faust You Don't Succeed* - Roger Zelazny  f  6070
*King's Man and Thief* - Christie Golden  f  2253
*Knights of the Blood* - Scott MacMillan  f  3602
*Lord Conrad's Lady* - Leo Frankowski  f  2046
*A Once and Future Love* - Anne Kelleher  f  3039
*Quest for a Maid* - Frances Mary Hendry  f  2662
*The Radiant Warrior* - Leo Frankowski  s  2047
*The Sheriff of Nottingham* - Richard Kluger  f  3165
*Sing for a Gentle Rain* - J. Alison James  f  2861
*The Wizard at Home* - Rick Shelley  f  4975

### 14th CENTURY

*Beauty* - Sheri S. Tepper  f  5428
*Blood Roses* - Chelsea Quinn Yarbro  h  6012
*Doomsday Book* - Connie Willis  s  5868
*The Dragon and the Gnarly King* - Gordon R. Dickson  f  1529
*The Dragon at War* - Gordon R. Dickson  f  1530
*The Dragon in Lyonesse* - Gordon R. Dickson  f  1531
*The Dragon Knight* - Gordon R. Dickson  f  1532
*The Dragon on the Border* - Gordon R. Dickson  f  1533
*Dragon's Eye* - Alex McDonough  s  3801
*The Golden Key* - Melanie Rawn  f  4486
*The Last Highlander* - Claire Cross  f  1271
*The Lost History of Redwyn* - William Jay  f  2883
*Maze of Moonlight* - Gael Baudino  f  393
*The Plague Tales* - Ann Benson  s  453
*Scorpio* - Alex McDonough  s  3802
*Testament of the Dragon* - Margaret Weis  f  5729
*Thomas the Rhymer* - Ellen Kushner  f  3265

### 15th CENTURY

*The Ancient One* - T.A. Barron  f  368
*Collidescope* - Grace Chetwin  s  1011
*Faces under Water* - Tanith Lee  h  3409
*I Am Dracula* - C. Dean Andersson  h  139
*The Memory Cathedral* - Jack Dann  s  1341

*Of Beginnings and Endings* - Robert Adams  s  33
*Parsifal* - Peter Vansittart  f  5560
*Pastwatch: The Redemption of Christopher Columbus* - Orson Scott Card  s  895
*Quest: In Search of the Dragontooth* - Michael Green  f  2346
*Rehearsal for a Renaissance* - Douglas W. Clark  f  1045
*The Silent Stars Go By* - James White  s  5781
*Spell Bound* - Ru Emerson  f  1810
*A Time for Us* - Christine Holden  f  2731
*The Venetian's Wife: A Strangely Sensual Tale of a Renaissance Explorer, a Computer, and a Metamorphosis* - Nick Bantock  f  336
*Where the Towers Pierce the Sky* - Marie D. Goodwin  f  2272
*Yesterday We Saw Mermaids* - Esther Friesner  f  2086

### 16th CENTURY

*The Angry Angel* - Chelsea Quinn Yarbro  h  6010
*Bhagavati* - Kara Dalkey  f  1316
*Bijapur* - Kara Dalkey  f  1317
*Blood Countess* - Andrei Codrescu  h  1094
*Blood of the Goddess* - Kara Dalkey  f  1318
*Daughter of the Night* - Elaine Bergstrom  h  463
*The Deathless* - Myles Murchison  h  4048
*Demon Knight* - Ken Hood  f  2760
*Drachenfels* - Jack Yeovil  f  6022
*Evil Reincarnate* - Leigh Clark  h  1050
*A Farce to Be Reckoned With* - Roger Zelazny  f  6064
*God's Fires* - Patricia Anthony  s  159
*In the Garden of Iden* - Kage Baker  s  298
*Konrad* - David Ferring  f  1927
*Last Mountain* - Robert C. Fleet  f  1946
*Love & Sleep* - John Crowley  f  1277
*Pasquale's Angel* - Paul J. McAuley  f  3714
*The Pit and the Pendulum* - Amarantha Knight  f  3183
*Plague Demon* - Brian Craig  f  1239
*Scorpio Rising* - Alex McDonough  s  3804
*Shadowbreed* - David Ferring  f  1928
*Sink the Armada* - Keith William Andrews  s  142
*Snow White and Rose Red* - Patricia C. Wrede  f  5981
*The Spiral Dance* - R. Garcia y Robertson  f  2121
*Spires of Spirit* - Gael Baudino  f  395
*The Stars Dispose* - Michaela Roessner  f  4651
*Storm Warriors* - Brian Craig  f  1240
*Strange Devices of the Sun and Moon* - Lisa Goldstein  f  2262
*Tatham Mound* - Piers Anthony  f  191
*This Dark Paradise* - Wendy Haley  h  2493
*The Time Tree* - Enid Richemont  f  4585
*The Vampire Armand* - Anne Rice  h  4578
*World Without End* - Sean Russell  f  4744
*Zaragoz* - Brian Craig  f  1241

### 17th CENTURY

*Blackmantle: A Triumph* - Patricia Kennealy-Morrison  f  3059
*Caliban's Hour* - Tad Williams  f  5826
*A Candle for D'Artagnan* - Chelsea Quinn Yarbro  h  6013
*The Crafters* - Christopher Stasheff  f  5216
*Daughter of the Night* - Elaine Bergstrom  h  463
*The Duke of Sumava* - Sara J. Wrench  f  5983
*Eternity* - Maggie Shayne  f  4943
*The Eyes of Torie Webster* - Roy Sorrels  h  5164
*Ghost of Chance* - William S. Burroughs  s  780
*The House on Hound Hill* - Maggie Prince  f  4438
*I, Tituba, Black Witch of Salem* - Maryse Conde  f  1130
*Mansions of Darkness* - Chelsea Quinn Yarbro  h  6016

*Milton in America* - Peter Ackroyd  f  25
*The Moon and the Sun* - Vonda N.
 McIntyre  f  3822
*Newton's Cannon* - J. Gregory Keyes  f  3097
*The Printer's Devil* - Chico Kidd  f  3099
*The Scathach and the Maeve's Daughter* - Mary
 Alexander Walker  f  5618
*Sexing the Cherry* - Jeanette Winterson  f  5927
*Witchwood* - John Buchan  f  750

### 18th CENTURY

*Arc d'X* - Steve Erickson  f  1835
*The Belly of the Wolf* - R.A. MacAvoy  f  3580
*Black Body* - H.C. Turk  h  5488
*Blessings and Curses* - Christopher Stasheff  f  5214
*The Crafters* - Christopher Stasheff  f  5216
*Desmond: A Novel of Love and the Modern Vampire* -
 Ulysses G. Dietz  h  1541
*The Druid's Gift* - Margaret J. Anderson  f  121
*The Empire of Fear* - Brian Stableford  h  5191
*The Gnome's Engine* - Teresa Edgerton  f  1742
*If at Faust You Don't Succeed* - Roger
 Zelazny  f  6070
*The Key to the Indian* - Lynne Reid Banks  f  331
*King of the Dead* - R.A. MacAvoy  f  3581
*Lens of the World* - R.A. MacAvoy  f  3582
*Nature's God* - Robert Anton Wilson  f  5903
*The Porcelain Dove* - Delia Sherman  f  4983
*Scotland the Brave* - Jennifer Roberson  f  4611
*The Vampire Journals* - Traci Briery  h  678

### 1730s

*The Manuscript Found in Sragossa* - Jan
 Potocki  h  4371

### 1770s

*Dance of Death* - P.N. Elrod  h  1794
*Death Masque* - P.N. Elrod  h  1795
*The Eight* - Katherine Neville  f  4092
*The Iron Bridge* - David Morse  s  4036
*Red Death* - P.N. Elrod  h  1798
*Search and Destroy* - Keith William
 Andrews  s  141
*Two Crowns for America* - Katherine Kurtz  f  3262

### 1780s

*The Memoirs of Elizabeth Frankenstein* - Theodore
 Roszak  h  4684

### 1790s

*The Memoirs of Elizabeth Frankenstein* - Theodore
 Roszak  h  4684
*A Sharpness on the Neck* - Fred
 Saberhagen  h  4774
*Walford's Oak* - Jill M. Phillips  f  4310

### 19th CENTURY

*Angelique's Descent* - Lara Parker  h  4246
*Antiquities* - John Crowley  f  1276
*Baby Dolly* - Ruby Jean Jensen  h  2899
*Blessings and Curses* - Christopher Stasheff  f  5214
*Blood and Roses* - Sharon Bainbridge  h  292
*Branch Point* - Mona Clee  s  1074
*Carmilla: The Return* - Kyle Marffin  h  3623
*Dead in the West* - Joe R. Lansdale  h  3325
*Elephantasm* - Tanith Lee  h  3408
*Freedom & Necessity* - Steven Brust  f  743
*Galilee* - Clive Barker  h  340
*The Gallery of His Dreams* - Kristine Kathryn
 Rusch  f  4717
*The Gilda Stories* - Jewelle Gomez  h  2267
*The Golden* - Lucius Shepard  h  4978
*The Haunted Tea Cosy: A Dispirited and Distasteful
 Diversion for Christmas* - Edward Gorey  h  2276
*The Haunting of Lamb House* - Joan Aiken  h  45
*Heartfire* - Orson Scott Card  f  889
*Jack Faust* - Michael Swanwick  s  5372
*Kindred Rites* - Katharine Eliska Kimbriel  f  3118

*A Knight of the Word* - Terry Brooks  f  714
*Lord Kelvin's Machine* - James P. Blaylock  f  520
*Lurid Dreams* - Charles L. Harness  s  2546
*Mad Amos* - Alan Dean Foster  f  2009
*Mary Reilly* - Valerie Martin  h  3654
*The Meddlesome Ghost* - Sheila Rosalynd
 Allen  f  84
*Nutcracker* - E.T.A. Hoffmann  f  2719
*Phantom* - Susan Kay  h  3020
*The Prestige* - Christopher Priest  s  4432
*The Secret of the Indian* - Lynne Reid Banks  f  332
*Shaman* - Robert Shea  f  4946
*Spring-Heeled Jack* - Philip Pullman  f  4447
*The Steampunk Trilogy* - Paul Di Filippo  s  1518
*Stonewords: A Ghost Story* - Pam Conrad  f  1138
*To Say Nothing of the Dog* - Connie Willis  s  5874
*Violin* - Anne Rice  f  4579
*The War in the Waste* - Felicity Savage  f  4852
*War of the Worlds: Global Dispatches* - Kevin J.
 Anderson  s  119

### 1800s

*The Darker Passions: Carmilla* - Amarantha
 Knight  h  3177
*Goat Dance* - Douglas Clegg  h  1079
*I Am Frankenstein* - C. Dean Andersson  h  140
*Lord of the Dead* - Tom Holland  h  2741
*The Secret Laboratory Journals of Dr. Victor
 Frankenstein* - Jeremy Kay  h  3019

### 1810s

*The Bell Witch: An American Haunting* - Brent
 Monahan  h  3953
*The Darker Passions: Frankenstein* - Amarantha
 Knight  h  3180
*Gothic Romance* - Emmanuel Carrere  h  912
*Magician's Ward* - Patricia C. Wrede  f  5976
*Mairelon the Magician* - Patricia C. Wrede  f  5977
*Wall, Stone, Craft* - Walter Jon Williams  h  5842

### 1820s

*The Bell Witch: An American Haunting* - Brent
 Monahan  h  3953
*Nadya: The Wolf Chronicles* - Pat Murphy  f  4052
*Old Nathan* - David Drake  f  1639
*Out of the House of Life* - Chelsea Quinn
 Yarbro  h  6018
*The Stress of Her Regard* - Tim Powers  h  4385

### 1830s

*Distant Dreams* - Jenny Lykins  f  3576
*The Hollow Earth: The Narrative of Mason Algiers
 Reynolds of Virginia* - Rudy Rucker  s  4705
*In the Shadows of the Moonglade* - Riley St.
 James  h  5186
*Nadya: The Wolf Chronicles* - Pat Murphy  f  4052
*Natural History* - Juan Perucho  h  4303

### 1840s

*Children of the Vampire* - Jeanne
 Kalogridis  h  3003
*The Chymical Wedding* - Lindsay Clarke  f  1063
*Covenant with the Vampire* - Jeanne
 Kalogridis  h  3004
*Friends in Time* - Grace Chetwin  f  1012
*The Lighthouse at the End of the World* - Stephen
 Marlowe  f  3631
*Madeline: After the Fall of Usher* - Marie
 Kiraly  h  3150
*No Blood Spilled* - Les Daniels  h  1338
*Under the Shadow* - Jane Toombs  h  5481

### 1850s

*The Difference Engine* - William Gibson  s  2217
*The Element of Fire* - Jason Henderson  f  2657
*The Elementals* - Morgan Llywelyn  f  3503
*The Lincoln Hunters* - Wilson Tucker  s  5487
*The Virgin and the Dinosaur* - R. Garcia y
 Robertson  s  2122
*Voyage of the Basset* - James C.
 Christensen  f  1024

### 1860s

*Automated Alice* - Jeff Noon  f  4134
*Bring the Jubilee* - Ward Moore  s  3993
*Darker Angels* - S.P. Somtow  h  5155
*Dinotopia* - James Gurney  f  2468
*Dinotopia Lost* - Alan Dean Foster  f  2003
*Dragon's Domain* - Thorarinn Gunnarsson  f  2461
*The Fantastic Civil War* - Frank D. McSherry
 Jr.  f  3867
*Fires of Eden* - Dan Simmons  h  5053
*The Guns of the South: A Novel of the Civil War* -
 Harry Turtledove  s  5502
*Rally Cry!* - William R. Forstchen  s  1982
*The Secret Life of Laszlo, Count Dracula* - Roderick
 Anscombe  h  152
*Stars and Stripes Forever* - Harry Harrison  s  2577
*Union Fires* - John Barnes  f  358
*Walking Wolf* - Nancy A. Collins  h  1126
*Web of Futures* - Jefferson P. Swycaffer  f  5376
*The World Beneath* - James Gurney  f  2469

### 1870s

*Anti-Ice* - Stephen Baxter  s  398
*Bone Wars* - Brett Davis  s  1398
*Children of the Vampire* - Jeanne
 Kalogridis  h  3003
*Devil's Engine* - Mark Sumner  f  5356
*Devil's Tower* - Mark Sumner  f  5357
*The Dracula Tape* - Fred Saberhagen  h  4765
*Evil Eye* - Michael Slade  h  5085
*The Final Battle* - Richard A. Lupoff  f  3572
*The Flight of Michael McBride* - Midori
 Snyder  f  5151
*The Hidden City* - Charles de Lint  f  1429
*The Living Evil* - Ruby Jean Jensen  h  2902
*Lorien Lost* - Michael King  f  3124
*Never Sound Retreat* - William R.
 Forstchen  s  1981
*Sarah Canary* - Karen Joy Fowler  f  2028
*Spirits of the Ordinary* - Kathleen Alcala  f  52
*The War in the Waste* - Felicity Savage  f  4851
*Was* - Geoff Ryman  f  4758
*The Waterworks* - E.L. Doctorow  s  1564
*The Werewolf of Paris* - Guy Endore  h  1822
*The Werewolves of London* - Brian
 Stableford  h  5196

### 1880s

*Anno Dracula* - Kim Newman  h  4094
*Apacheria* - Jake Page  s  4233
*Changeweaver* - Margaret Ball  f  313
*Dragon's Domain* - Thorarinn Gunnarsson  f  2461
*Flameweaver* - Margaret Ball  f  314
*From Hell* - Alan Moore  h  3987
*From Time to Time* - Jack Finney  s  1941
*How Few Remain* - Harry Turtledove  s  5504
*The Jekyll Legacy* - Robert Bloch  f  535
*Moon Dance* - S.P. Somtow  h  5158
*The Off Season* - Jack Cady  f  820
*The Red-Eared Ghosts* - Vivian Alcock  f  53
*The Secret Life of Laszlo, Count Dracula* - Roderick
 Anscombe  h  152
*Slave of My Thirst* - Tom Holland  h  2742
*The Tallow Image* - Jane Brindle  h  690
*Time Scout* - Robert Asprin  s  263
*The Trial of Elizabeth Cree* - Peter Ackroyd  h  26
*Wagers of Sin* - Robert Asprin  s  264
*The Women of Whitechapel and Jack the Ripper* - Paul
 West  h  5761

### 1890s

*The Angel of Pain* - Brian Stableford  h  5189
*The Bars on Satan's Jailhouse* - Norman
 Partridge  h  4251
*Bram Stoker's Dracula* - Fred Saberhagen  h  4763
*Chekhov's Journey* - Ian Watson  s  5633
*The Daemon in the Machine* - Felicity
 Savage  f  4848
*The Darker Passions: Dr. Jekyll and Mr. Hyde* -
 Amarantha Knight  h  3178

*The Darker Passions: Dracula* - Amarantha
  Knight  *h*  3179
*The Deathless* - Myles Murchison  *h*  4048
*Demon Dance* - T. Chris Martindale  *h*  3655
*The Element of Fire* - Jason Henderson  *f*  2657
*The Final Battle* - Richard A. Lupoff  *f*  3572
*The Golden Nineties* - Lisa Mason  *s*  3663
*The Hidden City* - Charles de Lint  *f*  1429
*The Holmes-Dracula File* - Fred
  Saberhagen  *h*  4767
*The Hunger and Ecstasy of Vampires* - Brian
  Stableford  *h*  5192
*Lady Cottington's Pressed Fairy Book* - Terry
  Jones  *f*  2981
*Lizzie Borden* - Elizabeth Engstrom  *h*  1826
*Lord of the Vampires* - Jeanne Kalogridis  *h*  3005
*Mina* - Marie Kiraly  *h*  3151
*A Night in the Lonesome October* - Roger
  Zelazny  *h*  6072
*The Night Inside* - Nancy Baker  *h*  301
*Night of the Cooters* - Howard Waldrop  *s*  5614
*One Wish* - C.J. Card  *f*  880
*The Passion* - Donna Boyd  *h*  603
*The Princess and the Dragon* - Roberto
  Pazzi  *f*  4272
*Sherlock Holmes in Orbit* - Mike Resnick  *s*  4556
*The Silver Tree* - Ruth L. Williams  *f*  5822
*The War in the Waste* - Felicity Savage  *f*  4851
*Whispers in the Dark* - Jonathan Aycliffe  *h*  283
*The Woman between the Worlds* - F. Gwynplaine
  MacIntyre  *s*  3596

### 20th CENTURY

*Amazon: A Novel* - Barbara G. Walker  *f*  5616
*The Autobiography of Santa Claus: It's Better to Give*
  - Jeff Guinn  *f*  2456
*Baby Dolly* - Ruby Jean Jensen  *h*  2899
*Beauty* - Sheri S. Tepper  *f*  5428
*The Black Death* - Basil Copper  *h*  1185
*Blackburn* - Bradley Denton  *h*  1489
*Bring the Jubilee* - Ward Moore  *s*  3993
*The Burrowers Beneath* - Brian Lumley  *h*  3548
*Callahan's Lady* - Spider Robinson  *s*  4638
*Darkthunder's Way* - Tom Deitz  *f*  1470
*Dragons over England* - Douglas Kaufman  *f*  3015
*A Fearful Symmetry* - James Luceno  *s*  3542
*The First Immortal* - James L. Halperin  *s*  2498
*Frisk* - Dennis Cooper  *h*  1170
*The Ghost Inside the Monitor* - Margaret J.
  Anderson  *f*  122
*The Gilda Stories* - Jewelle Gomez  *h*  2267
*Gossamer Axe* - Gael Baudino  *f*  392
*Gypsies* - Robert Charles Wilson  *s*  5908
*Haroun and the Sea of Stories* - Salman
  Rushdie  *f*  4731
*The Hashish Man and Other Stories by Lord Dunsany*
  - Lord Dunsany  *f*  1700
*The Haunting of Lamb House* - Joan Aiken  *h*  45
*Ingathering: The Complete People Stories of Zenna
  Henderson* - Zenna Henderson  *s*  2659
*Jack Faust* - Michael Swanwick  *s*  5372
*King of Morning, Queen of Day* - Ian
  McDonald  *f*  3793
*Landscape Painted with Tea* - Milorad
  Pavic  *f*  4263
*The Last World* - Christoph Ransmayr  *f*  4475
*The Living Evil* - Ruby Jean Jensen  *h*  2902
*Living with the Reptiles* - Roger L.
  DiSilvestro  *s*  1563
*The Martian Chronicles* - Ray Bradbury  *s*  621
*The Mirror Maze* - James P. Hogan  *s*  2726
*The Ogre Downstairs* - Diana Wynne Jones  *f*  2949
*Outside the Dog Museum* - Jonathan Carroll  *f*  919
*Parsifal* - Peter Vansittart  *f*  5560
*Phases of Gravity* - Dan Simmons  *s*  5057
*Prophets for the End of Time* - Marcos
  Donnelly  *f*  1577

*Reality Is What You Can Get Away With: An
  Illustrated Screenplay* - Robert Anton
  Wilson  *s*  5904
*Revelations* - Douglas E. Winter  *h*  5924
*Scream for Jeeves: A Parody* - P.H. Cannon  *h*  867
*The Secret Weavers: Stories of the Fantastic by Latin
  American Women* - Marjorie Agosin  *f*  43
*The Stone Dogs* - S.M. Stirling  *s*  5300
*Stonewords: A Ghost Story* - Pam Conrad  *f*  1138
*Strange Invasion* - Michael Kandel  *s*  3012
*A Tie to the Past* - David Wiseman  *f*  5928
*Touching the Fire* - Roger Welsch  *f*  5751
*Truckers* - Terry Pratchett  *s*  4402
*Twistor* - John Cramer  *s*  1245
*The Vampire Memoirs* - Mara McCuniff  *h*  3781
*The Wall* - Marlen Haushofer  *s*  2603
*War of the Worlds: Global Dispatches* - Kevin J.
  Anderson  *s*  119
*Was* - Geoff Ryman  *f*  4758
*Web of Dreams* - V.C. Andrews  *h*  147
*The Witching Hour* - Anne Rice  *h*  4580
*Wolf and Iron* - Gordon R. Dickson  *s*  1539

### 1900s

*1901* - Robert Conroy  *s*  1139
*Bug Park* - James P. Hogan  *s*  2723
*A College of Magics* - Caroline Stevermer  *f*  5266
*Dancing Bears* - Fred Saberhagen  *f*  4764
*Dracul: An Eternal Love Story* - Nancy
  Kilpatrick  *h*  3110
*Einstein's Dreams* - Alan Lightman  *f*  3459
*Fiends* - John Farris  *h*  1884
*The Forgetting Room* - Nick Bantock  *f*  333
*The Hill of Dreams* - Arthur Machen  *h*  3595
*The Hot-Wired Dodo* - Jack L. Chalker  *s*  956
*The House on the Borderland* - William Hope
  Hodgson  *h*  2711
*The Jewel of Seven Stars* - Bram Stoker  *h*  5312
*Lady Cottington's Pressed Fairy Book* - Terry
  Jones  *f*  2981
*Laying the Music to Rest* - Dean Wesley
  Smith  *h*  5114
*Mastery* - Kelley Wilde  *h*  5802
*Meg* - Steve Alten  *h*  88
*The Mummy, or Ramses the Damned* - Anne
  Rice  *h*  4572
*Night Calls* - Katharine Eliska Kimbriel  *h*  3119
*The Prestige* - Christopher Priest  *s*  4432
*Seance for a Vampire* - Fred Saberhagen  *h*  4773
*Sherlock Holmes in Orbit* - Mike Resnick  *s*  4556
*Those Who Hunt the Night* - Barbara
  Hambly  *h*  2510
*Ticktock* - Dean R. Koontz  *h*  3217
*Traveling with the Dead* - Barbara Hambly  *h*  2511
*The Trickster* - Muriel Gray  *h*  2340

### 1910s

*Back in the USSA* - Kim Newman  *s*  4095
*The Bloody Red Baron* - Kim Newman  *h*  4097
*Bully!* - Mike Resnick  *s*  4539
*The Carnival of Destruction* - Brian
  Stableford  *h*  5190
*City of Golden Shadow* - Tad Williams  *s*  5828
*Escape From Loki* - Philip Jose Farmer  *f*  1870
*The Fifth Element* - Terry Bisson  *s*  504
*The Fire Rose* - Mercedes Lackey  *f*  3280
*Future Indefinite* - Dave Duncan  *f*  1678
*The Great War: American Front* - Harry
  Turtledove  *s*  5501
*John Dollar* - Marianne Wiggins  *h*  5799
*The Judas Cross* - Charles Sheffield  *f*  4960
*The Keys to D'Esperance* - Chaz Brenchley  *h*  666
*The Mata Hari Adventure* - James Luceno  *f*  3544
*Past Imperative* - Dave Duncan  *f*  1684
*Present Tense* - Dave Duncan  *f*  1686
*Scorpio Descending* - Alex McDonough  *s*  3803
*Strange Stains and Mysterious Smells* - Terry
  Jones  *f*  2982
*Treason in Time* - Keith William Andrews  *s*  143

*The Wild Blue and the Gray* - William
  Sanders  *s*  4814
*Writ in Blood* - Chelsea Quinn Yarbro  *h*  6019

### 1920s

*Apacheria* - Jake Page  *s*  4233
*Believe: A Novel* - William Shatner  *f*  4929
*Bride of the Rat God* - Barbara Hambly  *f*  2499
*Child of the Light* - Janet Gluckman  *f*  2244
*The Colors of Hell* - Michael Paine  *h*  4234
*The Door through Washington Square* - Elaine
  Bergstrom  *f*  464
*A Dozen Tough Jobs* - Howard Waldrop  *f*  5612
*The Final Diary Entry of Kees Hujgens* - William R.
  Stotler  *s*  5317
*Fire and Ice* - Edward Myers  *f*  4061
*The Hemingway Hoax* - Joe Haldeman  *s*  2489
*Indiana Jones and the Dance of the Giants* - Rob
  MacGregor  *f*  3588
*Indiana Jones and the Genesis Deluge* - Rob
  MacGregor  *f*  3589
*Indiana Jones and the Interior World* - Rob
  MacGregor  *f*  3590
*Indiana Jones and the Peril at Delphi* - Rob
  MacGregor  *f*  3591
*Indiana Jones and the Seven Veils* - Rob
  MacGregor  *f*  3592
*Indiana Jones and the Unicorn's Legacy* - Rob
  MacGregor  *f*  3593
*Jacob's Hands* - Aldous Huxley  *f*  2817
*Lucifer Jones* - Mike Resnick  *f*  4549
*Lunching with the Antichrist* - Michael
  Moorcock  *f*  3984
*The Marvellous Land of Snergs* - E.A. Wyke-
  Smith  *f*  6006
*Mask of the Night* - Mary Ryan  *h*  4753
*Mixed Doubles* - Daniel Da Cruz  *s*  1305
*The Mountain Made of Light* - Edward
  Myers  *f*  4062
*Nevermore* - William Hjortsberg  *h*  2692
*Photographing Fairies* - Steve Szilagyi  *f*  5379
*The Return* - Walter de la Mare  *h*  1424
*The Shadow over Innsmouth* - H.P.
  Lovecraft  *h*  3533
*Strange Stains and Mysterious Smells* - Terry
  Jones  *f*  2982
*Strong Spirits* - Elisa DeCarlo  *f*  1451
*The Summit* - Edward Myers  *f*  4063
*Timeshare: Second Time Around* - Joshua
  Dann  *s*  1345

### 1930s

*Archangel* - Michael Conner  *s*  1133
*A Blessing on the Moon* - Joseph Skibell  *f*  5079
*Blood on the Water* - P.N. Elrod  *h*  1791
*Bloodlist* - P.N. Elrod  *h*  1792
*Bone Music* - Alan Rodgers  *h*  4646
*Child of the Journey* - Janet Berliner  *f*  466
*Child of the Light* - Janet Gluckman  *f*  2244
*Children of the Dusk* - Janet Berliner  *f*  467
*A Chill in the Blood* - P.N. Elrod  *h*  1793
*The City on the Edge of Forever* - Harlan
  Ellison  *s*  1784
*The Dealings of Daniel Kesserich* - Fritz
  Leiber  *s*  3417
*Demogorgon* - Brian Lumley  *h*  3552
*The Devil Rides Out* - Dennis Wheatley  *h*  5773
*The Devil You Say* - Elisa DeCarlo  *f*  1450
*Dr. Dimension* - John DeChancie  *s*  1456
*The Face in the Abyss* - A. Merritt  *f*  3878
*Fade* - Robert Cormier  *h*  1188
*Fire in the Blood* - P.N. Elrod  *h*  1796
*The Fortress of Utopia* - Jack Williamson  *s*  5863
*Further Adventures* - Jon Stephen Fink  *f*  1940
*The Green Mile* - Stephen King  *h*  3134
*A Hidden Place* - Robert Charles Wilson  *s*  5910
*In the Land of the Dead* - K.W. Jeter  *h*  2912
*Indiana Jones and the Sky Pirates* - Martin
  Caidin  *f*  825

*Indiana Jones and the White Witch* - Martin
Caidin  *f*  826
*The Jade Ogre* - Kenneth Robeson  *f*  4623
*The Kiss* - Kathryn Reines  *h*  4529
*The Lion of Farside* - John Dalmas  *f*  1324
*Lucifer Jones* - Mike Resnick  *f*  4549
*The Night of the Moonbow* - Thomas
Tryon  *h*  5486
*Python Isle* - Kenneth Robeson  *f*  4624
*A Question of Time* - Fred Saberhagen  *h*  4772
*The Smithsonian Institution* - Gore Vidal  *f*  5570
*Specters* - J.M. Dillard  *h*  1555
*Spider* - Patrick McGrath  *h*  3815
*The Spider #3: Death's Crimson Juggernaut/The Red
Death Rain* - Grant Stockbridge  *f*  5307
*The Spider #4: Death Reign of the Vampire King/The
Pain Emperor* - Grant Stockbridge  *f*  5308
*The Spider #8: The Devil's Paymaster/Legions of the
Accursed Light* - Grant Stockbridge  *f*  5309
*Time on My Hands* - Peter Delacorte  *s*  1480
*Walking the Labyrinth* - Lisa Goldstein  *f*  2266
*War With the Newts* - Karel Capek  *s*  874
*White Eyes* - Kenneth Robeson  *f*  4625

**1940s**
*'48* - James Herbert  *h*  2667
*1945* - Newt Gingrich  *s*  2239
*A Blessing on the Moon* - Joseph Skibell  *f*  5079
*Blood Alone* - Elaine Bergstrom  *h*  462
*Blood on the Sun* - Brian Herbert  *h*  2664
*Brittle Innings* - Michael Bishop  *h*  498
*The Crystal Sorcerers* - William R.
Forstchen  *f*  1979
*Dark Legacy* - Mark A. Kostrubula  *h*  3220
*Darker than You Think* - Jack Williamson  *h*  5861
*Darkness on the Ice* - Lois Tilton  *h*  5475
*Darwinia* - Robert Charles Wilson  *s*  5906
*Day of the Snake* - Matthew J. Costello  *s*  1196
*Days of Cain* - J.R. Dunn  *s*  1694
*Death Is a Lonely Business* - Ray Bradbury  *h*  619
*Dictator* - William F. Wu  *s*  5996
*Dinosaur Summer* - Greg Bear  *s*  416
*Dr. Haggard's Disease* - Patrick McGrath  *h*  3813
*Fear* - L. Ron Hubbard  *h*  2789
*The Frightened Fish* - Kenneth Robeson  *f*  4622
*The Grotesque* - Patrick McGrath  *h*  3814
*Hard Landing* - Algis Budrys  *s*  753
*The King* - Donald Barthelme  *f*  375
*Lightning* - Dean R. Koontz  *h*  3211
*The Magicians of Night* - Barbara Hambly  *f*  2505
*Majestic* - Whitley Strieber  *s*  5341
*Mr. Was* - Pete Hautman  *s*  2614
*Night of the Cooters* - Howard Waldrop  *s*  5614
*The Sandman: Book of Dreams* - Neil
Gaiman  *f*  2105
*Slow Dancing through Time* - Gardner
Dozois  *s*  1615
*The Sweetheart Season* - Karen Joy Fowler  *f*  2029
*Till the End of Time* - Allen Appel  *f*  201
*Time on My Hands* - Peter Delacorte  *s*  1480
*Time Station London* - David Evans  *s*  1853
*Time Station Paris* - David Evans  *s*  1854
*Time's Arrow* - Martin Amis  *s*  96
*Timeshare* - Joshua Dann  *s*  1344
*The Trail of Cthulhu* - August Derleth  *h*  1497
*The Trinity Paradox* - Kevin J. Anderson  *s*  116
*Triumph* - Ben Bova  *s*  598
*Typewriter in the Sky* - L. Ron Hubbard  *f*  2791
*Unicorn Highway* - David Lee Jones  *f*  2941
*Wartide* - John Barnes  *f*  359
*Werewolf* - Peter Rubie  *h*  4702
*The Werewolf's Revenge* - Richard Jaccoma  *h*  2841
*Who P-P-Plugged Roger Rabbit?* - Gary K.
Wolf  *f*  5934
*The Wolf's Hour* - Robert R. McCammon  *h*  3759
*Worldwar: In the Balance* - Harry
Turtledove  *s*  5515
*Worldwar: Striking the Balance* - Harry
Turtledove  *s*  5516

*Worldwar: Tilting the Balance* - Harry
Turtledove  *s*  5517
*Worldwar: Upsetting the Balance* - Harry
Turtledove  *s*  5518

**1950s**
*Armageddon: The Musical* - Robert Rankin  *s*  4473
*Bad Dreams* - Kim Newman  *h*  4096
*The Catswold Portal* - Shirley Rousseau
Murphy  *f*  4055
*The Collected Stories of Philip K. Dick, Volume One:
The Short Happy Life of the Brown Oxford* - Philip
K. Dick  *s*  1519
*The Colors of Hell* - Michael Paine  *h*  4234
*The Dog King* - Christoph Ransmayr  *f*  4474
*Dogland* - Will Shetterly  *f*  4992
*Elvissey* - Jack Womack  *s*  5957
*Escardy Gap* - Peter Crowther  *h*  1282
*Eye in the Sky* - Philip K. Dick  *s*  1521
*Father of Frankenstein* - Christopher Bram  *h*  659
*Gojiro* - Mark Jacobson  *f*  2847
*A Graveyard for Lunatics* - Ray Bradbury  *h*  620
*Horror Show* - Greg Kihn  *h*  3103
*Inagehi* - Jack Cady  *h*  817
*Judgment of Tears: Anno Dracula 1959* - Kim
Newman  *h*  4098
*Over the River & through the Woods* - Clifford D.
Simak  *s*  5047
*Psycho* - Robert Bloch  *h*  540
*The Quagmire* - James Kisner  *h*  3160
*Root of All Evil* - David A. Farrow  *h*  1888
*Some of Your Blood* - Theodore Sturgeon  *h*  5347
*Spider* - Patrick McGrath  *h*  3815
*Spyder* - Norman Partridge  *h*  4255
*Time's Arrow* - Martin Amis  *s*  96
*Who Killed James Dean?* - Warren Newton
Beath  *h*  428

**1960s**
*Assignment: Eternity* - Greg Cox  *s*  1225
*The Axman Cometh* - John Farris  *h*  1883
*Big Rock Beat* - Greg Kihn  *h*  3102
*Blue Light* - Walter Mosley  *s*  4042
*Boy's Life* - Robert R. McCammon  *h*  3754
*Branch Point* - Mona Clee  *s*  1074
*A Bridge of Years* - Robert Charles Wilson  *s*  5905
*By Chaos Cursed* - Mickey Zucker Reichert  *f*  4517
*The Children of Hamelin* - Norman Spinrad  *s*  5170
*Cloven Hooves* - Megan Lindholm  *f*  3470
*Dark Winds* - Graham Watkins  *h*  5630
*Darkborn* - Matthew J. Costello  *h*  1195
*Darwinia* - Robert Charles Wilson  *s*  5906
*The Devil's Day* - James Blish  *h*  525
*Dolores Claiborne* - Stephen King  *h*  3130
*Dragon Sleeping* - Craig Shaw Gardner  *f*  2127
*Dream Baby* - Bruce McAllister  *s*  3706
*The Face of Another* - Kobo Abe  *h*  19
*The Famished Road* - Ben Okri  *f*  4207
*Fatherland* - Robert Harris  *s*  2564
*Freeze Frames* - Katharine Kerr  *s*  3071
*Glimpses* - Lewis Shiner  *h*  4997
*Glory Road* - Robert A. Heinlein  *f*  2644
*The Grass Dancer* - Susan Power  *f*  4380
*The Healer's War* - Elizabeth Ann
Scarborough  *f*  4865
*Heartlight* - Marion Zimmer Bradley  *f*  637
*The Hollowing* - Robert Holdstock  *f*  2738
*Hour of the Scorpion* - Matthew J. Costello  *s*  1199
*Kane of Old Mars* - Michael Moorcock  *s*  3983
*Kiss of Death* - Daniel Rhodes  *h*  4569
*Mask of the Night* - Mary Ryan  *h*  4753
*Moon Dance* - S.P. Somtow  *h*  5158
*My Pretty Pony* - Stephen King  *h*  3136
*Nightmare Logic* - Matthew Hall  *h*  2495
*Paris in the Twentieth Century* - Jules
Verne  *s*  5568
*Peter Nevsky and the True Story of the Russian Moon
Landing* - John Calvin Batchelor  *s*  388
*Reborn* - F. Paul Wilson  *h*  5895

*The Resurrections* - Simon Louvish  *s*  3528
*Second Chance* - Chet Williamson  *h*  5850
*Shangri-La: The Return to the World of Lost Horizon* -
Eleanor Cooney  *f*  1169
*Sins of the Flesh* - Don Davis  *h*  1404
*The Site* - Melisand March  *h*  3621
*Slow Dancing through Time* - Gardner
Dozois  *s*  1615
*Songs of Enchantment* - Ben Okri  *f*  4208
*Summer of Love* - Lisa Mason  *s*  3664
*Summer of Night* - Dan Simmons  *h*  5060
*Sunglasses After Dark* - Nancy A. Collins  *h*  1124
*Time Station Berlin* - David Evans  *s*  1852
*Twisted* - Sue Hollister Barr  *h*  364
*Way Station* - Clifford D. Simak  *s*  5048
*The Werewolf's Touch* - Cheri Scotch  *h*  4892

**1970s**
*Angelique's Descent* - Lara Parker  *h*  4246
*The Atrocity Exhibition* - J.G. Ballard  *s*  319
*Baby Be-Bop* - Francesca Lia Block  *f*  545
*Bagatelle—Guinevere* - Nancy Bogen  *f*  558
*The Black Cat* - Robert Poe  *h*  4344
*Carrie* - Stephen King  *h*  3127
*Chaingang* - Rex Miller  *h*  3899
*Children of the Night* - Mercedes Lackey  *h*  3276
*Cloven Hooves* - Megan Lindholm  *f*  3470
*Dark Winds* - Graham Watkins  *h*  5630
*Dead Voices: Natural Agonies in the Real World* -
Gerald Vizenor  *f*  5578
*Dragon's Blood* - Alex McDonough  *s*  3799
*Drawing Blood* - Poppy Z. Brite  *h*  694
*Echoes* - Jackie Hyman  *h*  2818
*The Eight* - Katherine Neville  *f*  4092
*An Exaltation of Larks* - Robert Reed  *s*  4506
*Fiends* - John Farris  *h*  1884
*Flying in Place* - Susan Palwick  *h*  4240
*The Godsend* - Bernard Taylor  *h*  5401
*The Grass Dancer* - Susan Power  *f*  4380
*The Halloween Man* - Douglas Clegg  *h*  1080
*Hell House* - Richard Matheson  *h*  3685
*The House Next Door* - Anne Rivers
Siddons  *h*  5021
*The Hunted* - Kathryn Ptacek  *h*  4442
*I Know What You Did Last Summer* - Lois
Duncan  *h*  1692
*Knights of the Blood* - Scott MacMillan  *f*  3602
*The Man Who Folded Himself* - David
Gerrold  *s*  2208
*Memory and Dream* - Charles de Lint  *f*  1433
*Naomi's Room* - Jonathan Aycliffe  *h*  281
*Night of the Living Dead* - John Russo  *h*  4745
*The Nightwalker* - Thomas Tessier  *s*  5442
*Oasis* - Brian Hodge  *h*  2703
*The Off Season* - Jack Cady  *f*  820
*Our Lady of the Harbour* - Charles de Lint  *f*  1434
*The Premonition* - Andrew Laurance  *h*  3349
*The Quorum* - Kim Newman  *h*  4100
*The Rats* - James Herbert  *h*  2671
*Red Orc's Rage* - Philip Jose Farmer  *f*  1873
*The Resurrections* - Simon Louvish  *s*  3528
*Salem's Lot* - Stephen King  *h*  3140
*The Shining* - Stephen King  *h*  3141
*Silent Zone* - Stephen Molstad  *s*  3952
*The Site* - Melisand March  *h*  3621
*Something's Alive on the Titanic* - Robert
Serling  *h*  4915
*The State of the Art* - Iain M. Banks  *s*  327
*The Summit* - Edward Myers  *f*  4063
*The Summoned* - Steven Ray Fulgham  *h*  2090
*Sweetheart, Sweetheart* - Bernard Taylor  *h*  5402
*Tam Lin* - Pamela Dean  *f*  1446
*The Transition of Titus Crow* - Brian
Lumley  *h*  3569
*Twilight* - Peter James  *h*  2876
*Waking the Moon* - Elizabeth Hand  *f*  2538
*Witch Hill* - Marion Zimmer Bradley  *h*  654

**1980s**

*Absolute Power* - Ray Russell  *h*  4738
*An Acceptable Time* - Madeleine L'Engle  *f*  3436
*Ace in the Hole* - George R.R. Martin  *s*  3641
*Act of Love* - Joe R. Lansdale  *h*  3319
*The Adventures of Lucius Leffing* - Joseph Payne
  Brennan  *h*  670
*Adversary* - Daniel Rhodes  *h*  4568
*After Silence* - Jonathan Carroll  *h*  916
*After Sundown* - Randall Boyll  *h*  609
*Afterimage* - Kristine Kathryn Rusch  *f*  4709
*Afterimage Aftershock* - Kristine Kathryn
  Rusch  *h*  4710
*Afternoon of the Gosling* - Marlys Huffman  *h*  2801
*The Amulet* - A.R. Morlan  *h*  4009
*Ancient Images* - Ramsey Campbell  *h*  852
*Angelwalk: A Modern Fable* - Roger
  Elwood  *f*  1803
*Animus* - Ed Kelleher  *h*  3040
*The Axman Cometh* - John Farris  *h*  1883
*Back in the USSA* - Kim Newman  *s*  4095
*Balyet* - Patricia Wrightson  *f*  5995
*Beast House* - Richard Laymon  *h*  3364
*Being Alien* - Rebecca Ore  *s*  4217
*Beneath Still Waters* - Matthew J. Costello  *h*  1193
*Bernie and the Bessledorf Ghost* - Phyllis Reynolds
  Naylor  *f*  4078
*Beyond Apollo* - Barry Malzberg  *s*  3612
*Black Death* - R. Karl Largent  *h*  3337
*The Black School* - J.N. Williamson  *h*  5851
*Blood Feud* - Sam Siciliano  *h*  5020
*Blood of the Impaler* - Jeffrey Sackett  *h*  4779
*Bloodshift* - Garfield Reeves-Stevens  *h*  4508
*Bone* - George C. Chesbro  *h*  1006
*Breeder* - Douglas Clegg  *h*  1076
*Bride of the Slime Monster* - Craig Shaw
  Gardner  *f*  2125
*A Bridge of Years* - Robert Charles Wilson  *s*  5905
*Buddy Holly Is Alive and Well on Ganymede* - Bradley
  Denton  *s*  1490
*The Burning Man* - Michael Hammond  *h*  2530
*Burning Water* - Mercedes Lackey  *h*  3272
*The Callahan Touch* - Spider Robinson  *f*  4637
*Callahan's Legacy* - Spider Robinson  *s*  4639
*Captain Quad* - Sean Costello  *h*  1203
*Carnival* - William W. Johnstone  *h*  2927
*Carnosaur* - Harry Adam Knight  *s*  3191
*Carrion Comfort* - Dan Simmons  *h*  5049
*The Cartoonist* - Sean Costello  *h*  1204
*Catacomb* - Andrew Laurance  *h*  3347
*Catch the Lightning* - Catherine Asaro  *s*  218
*Cat's Eye* - William W. Johnstone  *h*  2928
*The Cellar* - Richard Laymon  *h*  3365
*Charmed* - Marilyn Singer  *h*  5070
*Chekhov's Journey* - Ian Watson  *s*  5633
*The Chymical Wedding* - Lindsay Clarke  *f*  1063
*Clicking Stones* - Nancy Tyler Glenn  *s*  2242
*The Cockroaches of Stay More* - Donald
  Harington  *f*  2544
*Cold Eye* - Giles Blunt  *h*  556
*Cold in July* - Joe R. Lansdale  *h*  3323
*Core* - Paul Preuss  *s*  4416
*The Cormorant* - Stephen Gregory  *h*  2429
*The Cornish Trilogy* - Robertson Davies  *f*  1397
*Coven* - Steven William Rimmer  *h*  4591
*Creature* - John Saul  *h*  4839
*Cutthroat* - Michael Slade  *h*  5084
*Cyberbooks* - Ben Bova  *s*  582
*The Dark Half* - Stephen King  *h*  3128
*Dark Journey* - A.R. Morlan  *h*  4010
*Dark Souls* - Barry Porter  *h*  4369
*Darkly the Thunder* - William W.
  Johnstone  *h*  2929
*Darkman* - Randall Boyll  *h*  611
*Darkscope* - Margaret Falk  *h*  1860
*Darkside* - Dennis Etchison  *h*  1845
*Dead Lines* - John Skipp  *h*  5082
*Deadspeak* - Brian Lumley  *h*  3551
*Deathsong* - Douglas Borton  *h*  575

*Deathwalker* - Patrick Whalen  *h*  5769
*Demogorgon* - Brian Lumley  *h*  3552
*Demon Night* - J. Michael Straczynski  *h*  5322
*Demon Shadows* - Michael B. Sirota  *h*  5075
*Demon Within* - Dana Reed  *h*  4499
*The Devil's Auction* - Robert Weinberg  *h*  5696
*The Devil's Churn* - Kristine Kathryn
  Rusch  *h*  4715
*Disciples of Dread* - Hugh B. Cave  *h*  941
*Doomstalker* - Gary Brandner  *h*  661
*Down River* - Stephen Gallagher  *h*  2110
*The Drawing of the Three* - Stephen King  *h*  3131
*Dreamthorp* - Chet Williamson  *h*  5845
*The Dwelling* - Tom Elliott  *h*  1776
*Earthbound* - Richard Matheson  *h*  3684
*Eden's Eyes* - Sean Costello  *h*  1205
*The Eyes of Darkness* - Dean R. Koontz  *s*  3206
*Fade* - Robert Cormier  *h*  1188
*The Fair Rules of Evil* - David C. Smith  *h*  5111
*Familiar Spirit* - Lisa Tuttle  *h*  5519
*Fantasma* - Thomas F. Monteleone  *h*  3963
*The Feeding* - Leigh Clark  *h*  1051
*Flying Saucers over Hennepin* - Peter
  Gelman  *f*  2186
*The Folk of the Air* - Peter S. Beagle  *f*  407
*Fool on the Hill* - Matt Ruff  *f*  4707
*The Fungus* - Harry Adam Knight  *h*  3192
*Funland* - Richard Laymon  *h*  3366
*Fury* - John Coyne  *h*  1237
*Gabriel's Body* - Curt Siodmak  *h*  5073
*Gate of Darkness, Circle of Light* - Tanya
  Huff  *f*  2797
*Gates of Paradise* - V.C. Andrews  *h*  145
*Geek Love* - Katherine Dunn  *h*  1697
*The Gilgul* - Henry W. Hocherman  *h*  2697
*Glimpses* - Lewis Shiner  *h*  4997
*Goat Dance* - Douglas Clegg  *h*  1079
*Golden Eyes* - John Gideon  *h*  2220
*The Gryphon King* - Tom Deitz  *f*  1473
*The Hacker* - Chet Day  *h*  1410
*The Halflife* - Sharon Webb  *s*  5664
*Harmful Intent* - Robin Cook  *s*  1164
*The Hellbound Heart* - Clive Barker  *h*  342
*The Holy Terror* - Wayne Allen Sallee  *h*  4787
*The Homecoming* - Barry B. Longyear  *s*  3521
*The Horror Club* - Mark Morris  *h*  4022
*I, Vampire* - Michael Romkey  *h*  4665
*Illegal Aliens* - Nick Pollotta  *s*  4365
*The Illustrated Hitchhiker's Guide to the Galaxy* -
  Douglas Adams  *s*  29
*In a Dark Dream* - Charles L. Grant  *h*  2310
*In Hot Blood* - Petru Popescu  *h*  4367
*In the Deep Woods* - Nicholas Conde  *h*  1131
*Incubi* - Edward Lee  *h*  3394
*The Influence* - Ramsey Campbell  *h*  857
*The Informers* - Brett Easton Ellis  *h*  1778
*Invasion of Willow Wood Springs* - Terry
  Ellis  *f*  1781
*Jonas McFee, A.T.P.* - Sarah Sargent  *f*  4827
*Journey to Terezor* - Frank Asch  *s*  221
*Julian's House* - Judith Hawkes  *h*  2630
*Junkyard* - Barry Porter  *h*  4370
*Jurassic Park* - Michael Crichton  *s*  1255
*Kalimantan* - Lucius Shepard  *h*  4979
*The Kill Riff* - David J. Schow  *h*  4887
*Kiss of Death* - Daniel Rhodes  *h*  4569
*Knights of the Morningstar* - Melanie Rawn  *s*  4487
*Koko* - Peter Straub  *h*  5328
*The Labyrinth Gate* - Alis A. Rasmussen  *f*  4481
*Lady Slings the Booze* - Spider Robinson  *s*  4640
*The Last Coin* - James P. Blaylock  *f*  519
*The Last Voyage of Somebody the Sailor* - John
  Barth  *f*  374
*Lavondyss: Journey to an Unknown Region* - Robert
  Holdstock  *f*  2739
*Lightning* - Dean R. Koontz  *h*  3211
*The Lilith Factor* - Jean Paiva  *h*  4236
*The Link* - Andrew Laurance  *h*  3348
*Lion Time in Timbuctoo* - Robert Silverberg  *s*  5036

*Live Girls* - Ray Garton  *h*  2151
*The Long Dark Tea-Time of the Soul* - Douglas
  Adams  *s*  30
*Lori* - Robert Bloch  *h*  536
*Lost Boys* - Orson Scott Card  *f*  891
*The Lurker* - James V. Smith  *h*  5123
*Makoto* - Kelley Wilde  *h*  5801
*Man From Mundania* - Piers Anthony  *f*  180
*Marianne, the Matchbox and the Malachite Mouse* -
  Sheri S. Tepper  *f*  5432
*Mastery* - Kelley Wilde  *h*  5802
*Medallion of the Black Hound* - Shirley Rousseau
  Murphy  *f*  4056
*Midnight* - Dean R. Koontz  *h*  3212
*The Midnight Tour* - Richard Laymon  *h*  3368
*Midnight's Lair* - Richard Laymon  *h*  3369
*Mirror* - Graham Masterton  *h*  3677
*Monday's Child* - Patricia Wallace  *h*  5623
*Moon Walker* - Rick Hautala  *h*  2610
*Moonbane* - Al Sarrantonio  *s*  4831
*Moondog* - Henry Garfield  *h*  2138
*Mutation* - Robin Cook  *s*  1165
*My Soul to Keep* - Judith Hawkes  *h*  2631
*Mystery* - Peter Straub  *h*  5330
*Mythology 101* - Jody Lynn Nye  *f*  4173
*Mythology Abroad* - Jody Lynn Nye  *f*  4174
*A Name to Conjure With* - Donald Aamodt  *f*  3
*Necroscope: The Lost Years* - Brian
  Lumley  *h*  3560
*The Nexus* - Mike McQuay  *f*  3860
*Night Brothers* - Sidney Williams  *h*  5824
*Night Games* - Marilyn Harris  *h*  2562
*Night Glow* - Martin James  *h*  2867
*Night Prophets* - Paul F. Olson  *h*  4213
*Night Things* - Michael Talbot  *h*  5380
*Nighteyes* - Garfield Reeves-Stevens  *s*  4510
*Nightlight* - Michael Cadnum  *h*  813
*Nightmare Logic* - Matthew Hall  *h*  2495
*Nightshade* - Stanley R. Moore  *h*  3992
*The Nihilesthete* - Richard Kalich  *h*  3002
*No Enemy but Time* - Michael Bishop  *s*  502
*Now You See It...* - Richard Matheson  *h*  3688
*Oktober* - Stephen Gallagher  *h*  2112
*Out of the Ordinary* - Annie Dalton  *f*  1330
*Owl Light* - Michael Paine  *h*  4235
*Paddywhack* - John Stchur  *h*  5236
*The Parasite* - Ramsey Campbell  *h*  863
*Perfect Little Angels* - Andrew Neiderman  *h*  4090
*Possession* - Peter James  *h*  2873
*Psycho II* - Robert Bloch  *h*  541
*Psychomech* - Brian Lumley  *h*  3562
*Psychosphere* - Brian Lumley  *h*  3563
*The Queen of the Damned* - Anne Rice  *h*  4574
*Quest for Apollo* - Michael Lahey  *f*  3309
*R-T, Margaret, and the Rats of NIMH* - Jane Leslie
  Conly  *f*  1132
*The Rainbow Sword* - Adrienne Martine-
  Barnes  *f*  3659
*Reluctant Voyagers* - Elisabeth Vonarburg  *s*  5591
*Resurgence* - Brian Lumley  *h*  3564
*Resurrection Dreams* - Richard Laymon  *h*  3371
*Retro Lives* - Lee Grimes  *s*  2446
*Return of the Living Dead* - John Russo  *h*  4746
*The Ridge* - Lisa Cantrell  *h*  872
*Running Wild* - J.G. Ballard  *h*  320
*The Secret History* - Donna Tartt  *h*  5398
*The Secret of the Indian* - Lynne Reid Banks  *f*  332
*See You Later* - Christopher Pike  *f*  4332
*Seeds of Evil* - Margaret Bingley  *h*  491
*Sepulchre* - James Herbert  *h*  2672
*Shadow Child* - Joseph A. Citro  *h*  1038
*Shadows After Dark* - Ouida Crozier  *f*  1286
*The Silence of the Lambs* - Thomas Harris  *h*  2566
*Silent Moon* - William Relling Jr.  *h*  4531
*Sins of the Flesh* - Don Davis  *h*  1404
*Sleipnir* - Linda Evans  *h*  1856
*Slice* - Rex Miller  *h*  3902
*The Snake Oil Wars* - Parke Godwin  *s*  2249
*Snowbeast!* - Peter Tremayne  *h*  5482

*Songs of Earth and Power* - Greg Bear  *f*  424
*The Source* - Brian Lumley  *h*  3565
*Speak to the Rain* - Helen K. Passey  *h*  4257
*Spellcaster* - J. Edward Ames  *h*  92
*Sphynxes Wild* - Esther Friesner  *f*  2083
*The Spirit Stalker* - Nina Romberg  *h*  4664
*Stones of the Dalai Lama* - Ken Mitchell  *f*  3916
*Strange Attractors* - William Sleator  *s*  5088
*The Suiting* - Kelley Wilde  *h*  5803
*Sunglasses After Dark* - Nancy A. Collins  *h*  1124
*Sunshaker's War* - Tom Deitz  *f*  1477
*Swamp* - Peter Tremayne  *h*  5483
*The Sword of Samurai Cat* - Mark E.
    Rogers  *s*  4657
*T.J.'s Ghost* - Shirley Climo  *h*  1087
*The Tallow Image* - Jane Brindle  *h*  690
*Thunder Rise* - G. Wayne Miller  *h*  3895
*A Tie to the Past* - David Wiseman  *f*  5928
*Tombley's Walk* - Crosland Brown  *h*  723
*The Torching* - Marcy Heidish  *h*  2642
*Torments* - Lisa Cantrell  *h*  873
*Tourists* - Lisa Goldstein  *f*  2264
*The Twelfth Child* - Raymond Van Over  *h*  5538
*The Unborn* - Andrew Laurance  *h*  3350
*Under Siege* - Elisabeth Mace  *f*  3587
*The Unknown Soldier* - Mickey Zucker
    Reichert  *s*  4525
*The Uprising* - Brent Monahan  *h*  3956
*Ursus* - David Dvorkin  *s*  1708
*Viper* - Alan Riefe  *h*  4589
*Vision Quest* - Pamela F. Service  *f*  4920
*Voyager* - Stephen Baxter  *s*  406
*Walkers* - Graham Masterton  *h*  3681
*Waltz with Evil* - P.D. Rozzi  *h*  4701
*Webs* - Scott Baker  *h*  304
*Where the Towers Pierce the Sky* - Marie D.
    Goodwin  *f*  2272
*The Whim of the Dragon* - Pamela Dean  *f*  1447
*Winter Wolves* - Earle Wescott  *h*  5756
*Witch* - Christopher Pike  *f*  4334
*A Witch Across Time* - Gilbert B. Cross  *f*  1272
*The Witch House* - Norma Tadlock Johnson  *f*  2923
*The Witch's Eye* - Phyllis Reynolds Naylor  *f*  4080
*Wizard and Glass* - Stephen King  *h*  3144

**1990s**
*7 Steps to Midnight* - Richard Matheson  *h*  3682
*The 7th Guest* - Matthew J. Costello  *h*  1192
*12 Monkeys* - Elizabeth Hand  *s*  2532
*The 37th Mandala* - Marc Laidlaw  *h*  3310
*65mm* - Dale Hoover  *h*  2761
*668: The Neighbor of the Beast* - Lionel
    Fenn  *h*  1917
*The Abductors: Conspiracy* - Jonathan
    Frakes  *s*  2034
*The Abraxas Marvel Circus* - Stephen Leigh  *f*  3423
*Addams Family Values* - Todd Strasser  *f*  5324
*The Adept* - Katherine Kurtz  *f*  3254
*After Life* - Andrew Neiderman  *h*  4083
*After Silence* - Jonathan Carroll  *h*  916
*Agviq* - Michael Armstrong  *s*  208
*Agyar* - Steven Brust  *f*  738
*Aliens Stole My Body* - Bruce Coville  *s*  1217
*All the Bells on Earth* - James P. Blaylock  *f*  518
*All Things under the Moon* - Robert
    Morgan  *h*  4002
*All's Faire* - Pamela F. Service  *f*  4917
*Along Came a Spider* - Athena Alexis  *h*  70
*Althea* - Abigail McDaniels  *h*  3782
*The Ambivalent Magician* - Simon Hawke  *f*  2616
*American Psycho* - Brett Easton Ellis  *h*  1777
*Among Madmen* - Jim Starlin  *s*  5212
*Ancestral Hungers* - Scott Baker  *h*  303
*Ancient Echoes* - Robert Holdstock  *f*  2735
*The Ancient One* - T.A. Barron  *f*  368
*Ancient Shores* - Jack McDevitt  *s*  3786
*Angel Kiss* - Kelley Wilde  *h*  5800
*Angel Light* - Andrew M. Greeley  *f*  2342
*Angela and Diabola* - Lynne Reid Banks  *f*  330

*Angels & Visitations: A Miscellany* - Neil
    Gaiman  *f*  2101
*Angels on Fire* - Nancy A. Collins  *h*  1117
*Angels Unaware* - L. Elizabeth Storm  *s*  5315
*Animals* - John Skipp  *h*  5080
*Animus* - Ed Kelleher  *h*  3040
*Anthony Shriek* - Jessica Amanda
    Salmonson  *h*  4790
*Antibodies* - Kevin J. Anderson  *h*  99
*Apartheid, Superstrings, and Mordecai Thubana* -
    Michael Bishop  *s*  496
*Aqua Sancta* - Edward Bryant  *h*  748
*The Arbitrary Placement of Walls* - Martha
    Soukup  *f*  5165
*Area 51* - Robert Doherty  *s*  1565
*The Armageddon Box* - Robert Weinberg  *h*  5690
*The Art of Arrow Cutting* - Stephen
    Dedman  *f*  1462
*Arthur War Lord* - Dafydd ab Hugh  *f*  6
*As One Dead* - Don Bassingthwaite  *h*  387
*As She Climbed Across the Table* - Jonathan
    Lethem  *s*  3439
*The Ascending* - T.M. Wright  *h*  5989
*Assault of the Super Carrier* - Peter Albano  *s*  47
*The Asylum* - John E. Ames  *h*  93
*Asylum* - Patrick McGrath  *h*  3812
*At Sword's Point* - Scott MacMillan  *f*  3601
*Aunt Maria* - Diana Wynne Jones  *f*  2943
*Automated Alice* - Jeff Noon  *f*  4134
*Avatar* - Donald Beman  *h*  437
*The Baby* - Stephanie Kegan  *h*  3033
*Bad Blood* - D.A. Fowler  *h*  2021
*Bad Brains* - Kathe Koja  *h*  3193
*Bad Dreams* - Kim Newman  *h*  4096
*Bad Karma* - Andrew Harper  *h*  2548
*The Bad Place* - Dean R. Koontz  *h*  3202
*The Bad Thing* - Michael O'Rourke  *h*  4222
*Bag of Bones* - Stephen King  *h*  3126
*The Barbed Coil* - J.V. Jones  *f*  2957
*The Barrens* - F. Paul Wilson  *h*  5884
*The Basement* - Bari Wood  *h*  5961
*Batman: Captured by the Engines* - Joe R.
    Lansdale  *h*  3320
*Bats* - William W. Johnstone  *h*  2926
*Battle Front* - Ian Slater  *s*  5086
*The Bear Went over the Mountain* - William
    Kotzwinkle  *f*  3222
*Beast* - Peter Benchley  *h*  440
*The Beast* - Marie Ardell White  *h*  5784
*The Beast Within: A Gabriel Knight Mystery* - Jane
    Jensen  *h*  2895
*Beauty* - Brian D'Amato  *h*  1334
*Bedlam Boyz* - Ellen Guon  *f*  2467
*Bedlam's Bard* - Mercedes Lackey  *f*  3269
*Being of Two Minds* - Pamela F. Service  *f*  4918
*Belladonna* - Michael Stewart  *h*  5271
*Bellwether* - Connie Willis  *s*  5867
*Beneath the Gated Sky* - Robert Reed  *s*  4502
*Bereavement* - Richard Lortz  *h*  3525
*The Between* - Tananarive Due  *h*  1669
*Between Floors* - Thomas F. Monteleone  *h*  3957
*Between the Devil and the Deep* - J.M.
    Morgan  *h*  3998
*The Beyond* - Barry Harrington  *h*  2556
*Beyond the Door* - Gary L. Blackwood  *s*  510
*Beyond the Magic Sphere* - Gail Jarrow  *f*  2879
*Beyond the Pale* - Mark Anthony  *f*  153
*Beyond the Shroud* - Rick Hautala  *h*  2604
*Beyond the Veil of Stars* - Robert Reed  *s*  4503
*The Bighead* - Edward Lee  *h*  3387
*Billy* - Whitley Strieber  *h*  5338
*Bitter Blood* - Karen E. Taylor  *h*  5405
*The Black Carousel* - Charles L. Grant  *h*  2303
*Black Ice* - Pat Graversen  *h*  2333
*Black Lightning* - John Saul  *h*  4837
*The Black Lodge* - Robert Weinberg  *h*  5692
*The Black Mariah* - Jay R. Bonansinga  *h*  570
*Black Night* - S.J. Strayhorn  *h*  5334
*Black Sun* - Douglas E. Winter  *h*  5923

*Black Trump* - George R.R. Martin  *s*  3642
*The Blackstone Chronicles* - John Saul  *h*  4838
*Blade* - Mel Odom  *h*  4190
*Blameless in Abaddon* - James Morrow  *f*  4029
*Bleeder* - Gene Lazuta  *h*  3374
*Blind Hunger* - David Darke  *h*  1352
*Blood* - Ron Dee  *h*  1463
*Blood and Chocolate* - Annette Curtis
    Klause  *h*  3162
*Blood Brothers* - Brian Lumley  *h*  3546
*Blood Brothers* - T. Lucien Wright  *h*  5986
*Blood Countess* - Andrei Codrescu  *h*  1094
*Blood Debt* - Tanya Huff  *h*  2792
*Blood Kin* - Ronald Kelly  *h*  3051
*Blood Lust* - Ron Dee  *h*  1464
*The Blood of Angels* - Stephen Gregory  *h*  2428
*Blood of Innocents* - John Arbucci  *h*  204
*Blood of Mugwump* - Doug Rice  *h*  4581
*Blood of the Children* - Alan Rodgers  *h*  4645
*Blood of the Covenant* - Brent Monahan  *h*  3954
*The Blood of the Lamb* - Thomas F.
    Monteleone  *h*  3958
*Blood on the Bayou* - D.J. Donaldson  *h*  1570
*Blood Price* - Tanya Huff  *h*  2793
*Blood Relations* - Doug Murray  *h*  4058
*Blood Roots* - Richie Tankersley Cusick  *h*  1300
*Blood Sabbath* - Leigh Clark  *h*  1048
*Blood Secrets* - Karen E. Taylor  *h*  5406
*Blood Ties* - Karen E. Taylor  *h*  5407
*Blood Trail* - Tanya Huff  *h*  2794
*Blood War* - Robert Weinberg  *h*  5693
*Blood Wings* - Stephen Gresham  *h*  2430
*Blood Work* - Fay Zachary  *h*  6050
*Bloodletter* - Warren Newton Beath  *h*  426
*Bloodlines* - J.N. Williamson  *h*  5852
*Bloodstream* - Tess Gerritsen  *h*  2205
*Bloodsucking Fiends: A Love Story* - Christopher
    Moore  *h*  3988
*Bloody Bones* - Laurell K. Hamilton  *h*  2512
*Bloody Valentine* - Stephen R. George  *h*  2197
*Bloody Waters* - B.L. Winters  *h*  5926
*Blue Light* - Walter Mosley  *s*  4042
*Blue Moon* - Hila Feil  *f*  1898
*Blue Moon* - Laurell K. Hamilton  *h*  2513
*Bone Music* - Alan Rodgers  *h*  4646
*Boneman* - Lisa Cantrell  *h*  871
*Bones* - Joyce Thompson  *h*  5453
*The Book of Common Dread* - Brent
    Monahan  *h*  3955
*The Book of Night with Moon* - Diane
    Duane  *f*  1657
*The Book of the Damned* - D.A. Fowler  *h*  2022
*The Book of Webster's* - J.N. Williamson  *h*  5853
*Borderland: A Novel of Terror* - S.K.
    Epperson  *h*  1828
*Borgel* - Daniel Manus Pinkwater  *f*  4338
*Born to Run* - Mercedes Lackey  *f*  3271
*The Boss in the Wall* - Avram Davidson  *h*  1396
*Boundaries* - T.M. Wright  *h*  5990
*The Boy Who Cried Werewolf* - Elvira  *h*  1800
*Boys of Life* - Paul Russell  *h*  4737
*Brainstorm* - Steven M. Krauzer  *h*  3230
*Brand New Cherry Flavor* - Todd Grimson  *h*  2448
*Breeder* - Ed Kelleher  *h*  3041
*Brethren* - Shawn Ryan  *h*  4754
*Briar Rose* - Jane Yolen  *f*  6029
*Bride of the Castle* - John DeChancie  *s*  1452
*The Bridge: A Horror Story* - John Skipp  *h*  5081
*Bright Shadow* - Elizabeth Forrest  *h*  1971
*Bring Me Children* - David Martin  *h*  3637
*Bring on the Night* - Don Davis  *h*  1402
*The Broken Goddess* - Hans Bemmann  *f*  439
*Brothers* - Ben Bova  *s*  581
*Brothers of the Dragon* - Robin Wayne
    Bailey  *f*  286
*Brown Girl in the Ring* - Nalo Hopkinson  *f*  2771
*Buffy the Vampire Slayer* - Richie Tankersley
    Cusick  *h*  1301
*Bureau 13* - Nick Pollotta  *f*  4362

*Burial* - Graham Masterton  *h*  3671
*Buried Screams* - C. Dean Andersson  *h*  137
*The Burning* - Graham Masterton  *h*  3672
*Burning Bright* - J.S. Russell  *h*  4733
*Burnt Offerings* - Laurell K. Hamilton  *h*  2514
*Butcher* - Rex Miller  *h*  3898
*The Butcher Boy* - Patrick McCabe  *h*  3716
*Button Bright* - Michael Kurland  *h*  3251
*Cain* - James Byron Huggins  *h*  2802
*A Calculated Magic* - Robert Weinberg  *f*  5694
*The Calcutta Chromosome* - Amitav Ghosh  *h*  2214
*California Ghosting* - William Hill  *h*  2687
*California Gothic* - Dennis Etchison  *h*  1843
*A Call to Arms* - Alan Dean Foster  *s*  1995
*A Call to Arms* - Thomas K. Martin  *f*  3650
*Call to Battle* - Doug Murray  *h*  4059
*The Calling* - Kathryn Meyer Griffith  *h*  2439
*Cambio Bay* - Kate Wilhelm  *f*  5806
*Camp Vamp* - Elvira  *h*  1801
*Candle Night* - Phil Rickman  *h*  4586
*Captain Quad* - Sean Costello  *h*  1203
*Cardinal's Sin* - Raymond Buckland  *h*  751
*Carmilla: The Return* - Kyle Marffin  *h*  3623
*Carnivore* - Leigh Clark  *h*  1049
*Carnivores* - Penelope Banka Kreps  *h*  3232
*Carol for Another Christmas* - Elizabeth Ann
    Scarborough  *f*  4861
*The Case of the Police Officer's Cock Ring and the
    Piano Player Who Had No Fingers* - Edward
    Lee  *h*  3388
*Castle Dreams* - John DeChancie  *s*  1453
*Castle War!* - John DeChancie  *s*  1455
*Castleview* - Gene Wolfe  *f*  5939
*The Cat* - R.L. Stine  *h*  5285
*Catamount* - Michael Peak  *f*  4273
*The Caterpillar's Question* - Piers Anthony  *f*  164
*Cats Raise the Dead* - Shirley Rousseau
    Murphy  *f*  4054
*Catwoman* - Lynn Abbey  *s*  14
*Caverns of Socrates* - Dennis L. McKiernan  *f*  3831
*Celestial Dogs* - J.S. Russell  *h*  4734
*Celia* - Ruby Jean Jensen  *h*  2900
*Cemetery of Angels* - Noel Hynd  *h*  2821
*The Changeling Garden* - Winifred Elze  *h*  1806
*Changer* - Jane M. Lindskold  *f*  3474
*Chariot* - Charles L. Grant  *h*  2304
*Charlie's Bones* - L.L. Thrasher  *h*  5468
*The Charm* - Adam Niswander  *h*  4111
*Charmed Life* - Bernard Taylor  *h*  5399
*Chase the Morning* - Michael Scott Rohan  *f*  4658
*Cherokee Bat and the Goat Guys* - Francesca Lia
    Block  *f*  546
*Chicago Loop* - Paul Theroux  *h*  5443
*A Child Across the Sky* - Jonathan Carroll  *h*  917
*Child of Shadows* - John Coyne  *h*  1236
*Children of the End* - Mark A. Clements  *h*  1084
*Children of the Night* - Dan Simmons  *h*  5050
*Children of the Thunder* - John Brunner  *s*  733
*The Children's Hour* - Douglas Clegg  *h*  1077
*Child's Play III* - Matthew J. Costello  *h*  1194
*Chiller* - Randall Boyll  *h*  610
*Chimaera's Copper* - Piers Anthony  *f*  166
*The Chosen* - Edward Lee  *h*  3389
*Chrome Circle* - Mercedes Lackey  *f*  3277
*The Cipher* - Kathe Koja  *h*  3194
*Circus of the Damned* - Laurell K.
    Hamilton  *h*  2515
*The Circus of the Earth and Air* - Brooke
    Stevens  *f*  5264
*City of Iron* - Chet Williamson  *h*  5843
*Clash by Night* - Chet Williamson  *h*  5844
*Claw* - Ken Eulo  *h*  1850
*The Cloning of Joanna May* - Fay Weldon  *s*  5732
*Cloud Castles* - Michael Scott Rohan  *f*  4659
*Codename Wolverine* - Christopher Golden  *s*  2256
*Cold at Heart* - Brian Hopkins  *h*  2768
*Cold Fire* - Dean R. Koontz  *h*  3203
*Cold Iron* - Melisa Michaels  *f*  3886
*Cold Kiss* - Roxanne Longstreet  *h*  3517

*The Cold One* - Christopher Pike  *h*  4327
*Cold Whisper* - Rick Hautala  *h*  2605
*Cold White Fury* - Beth Amos  *h*  97
*Collidescope* - Grace Chetwin  *s*  1011
*Come Before Christ and Murder Love* - Stewart
    Home  *f*  2754
*Comeback Tour: The Sky Belongs to the Stars* - Jack
    Yeovil  *s*  6020
*The Committee* - Raymond Buckland  *h*  752
*Concrete Hotel* - C. Christopher Caldon  *h*  839
*Conglomeros* - Jesse Browner  *f*  729
*Contagion* - John David Connor  *h*  1136
*Control Freak* - Christa Faust  *h*  1890
*The Convocation* - John R. Holt  *h*  2748
*Core* - Paul Preuss  *s*  4416
*Count Geiger's Blues* - Michael Bishop  *s*  499
*The Count of Eleven* - Ramsey Campbell  *h*  853
*Coven* - Edward Lee  *h*  3390
*Coyote* - Peter Gadol  *f*  2100
*Cradle of Splendor* - Patricia Anthony  *s*  158
*The Crawling Dark* - Pauline Dunn  *h*  1698
*Created By* - Richard Christian Matheson  *h*  3691
*Creekers* - Edward Lee  *h*  3391
*Cries of the Children* - Clare McNally  *h*  3856
*The Crimson Sky* - Joel Rosenberg  *f*  4669
*Cromm* - Kenneth C. Flint  *f*  1957
*Cross a Dark Bridge* - Deborah
    Churchman  *h*  1027
*Crossover* - Bill McCay  *f*  3768
*Crota* - Owl Goingback  *h*  2251
*Cul-De-Sac* - David Martin  *h*  3638
*Cup of Clay* - Carole Nelson Douglas  *f*  1583
*The Cup of Morning Shadows* - Rosemary
    Edghill  *f*  1747
*Curfew* - Phil Rickman  *h*  4587
*The Curse* - John Tigges  *h*  5472
*The Curse of Camp Cold Lake* - R.L. Stine  *h*  5286
*Curse of the Vampire* - Geoffrey Caine  *h*  832
*Cursed Be the Child* - Mort Castle  *h*  937
*The D. Case: The Truth about the Mystery of Edwin
    Drood* - Charles Dickens  *f*  1524
*Dagger Magic* - Katherine Kurtz  *f*  3256
*Damnbanna* - Nancy Springer  *f*  5177
*Dance Dance Dance* - Haruki Murakami  *s*  4046
*Dangerous Nature* - T.J. Kirby  *h*  3152
*The Dark* - Andrew Neiderman  *h*  4084
*Dark Channel* - Ray Garton  *h*  2150
*Dark City* - Frank Lauria  *h*  3351
*Dark Dance* - Tanith Lee  *h*  3406
*Dark Debts* - Karen Hall  *h*  2494
*Dark Dreaming* - Pat Franklin  *h*  2040
*Dark Father* - Tom Piccirilli  *h*  4312
*Dark Fortune* - Richard Lee Byers  *h*  795
*Dark Heart* - Margaret Weis  *f*  5707
*Dark Legacy* - Mark A. Kostrubula  *h*  3220
*Dark Lullaby* - Jessica Palmer  *h*  4237
*Dark Matter* - Garfield Reeves-Stevens  *h*  4509
*Dark of the Eye* - Douglas Clegg  *h*  1078
*The Dark One* - Guy N. Smith  *h*  5118
*Dark Prince* - Keith Herber  *h*  2663
*Dark Reunion* - Stephen R. George  *h*  2198
*Dark Rivers of the Heart* - Dean R. Koontz  *h*  3204
*Dark Silence* - Rick Hautala  *h*  2606
*Dark Tide* - Elizabeth Forrest  *h*  1972
*Dark Time* - Maxine O'Callaghan  *h*  4189
*Dark Twilight* - Joseph A. Citro  *h*  1036
*Dark Visions* - T. Lucien Wright  *h*  5987
*Darkborn* - Matthew J. Costello  *h*  1195
*The Darker Saints* - Brian Hodge  *h*  2699
*Darkling* - Michael O'Rourke  *h*  4223
*Darkman #1: The Hangman* - Randall Boyll  *h*  612
*Darkman #2: The Price of Fear* - Randall
    Boyll  *h*  613
*Darkman #3: The Gods of Hell* - Randall
    Boyll  *h*  614
*Darkman #4: The Face of Death* - Randall
    Boyll  *h*  615
*Darkness* - John Saul  *h*  4840
*Darkness, I* - Tanith Lee  *h*  3407

*The Darkness Within* - Shawn MacDonald  *h*  3585
*Daughter of Darkness* - Steven Spruill  *h*  5183
*Dawn* - V.C. Andrews  *h*  144
*Dawn Song* - Michael Marano  *h*  3620
*Day of the Snake* - Matthew J. Costello  *s*  1196
*Days of the Dead* - Ashley McConnell  *h*  3774
*Dead End* - Guy N. Smith  *h*  5119
*Dead Heat* - Del Stone Jr.  *h*  5313
*Dead in the Water* - Nancy Holder  *h*  2732
*The Dead Man's Kiss* - Robert Weinberg  *h*  5695
*Dead of Night* - Alex Abella  *h*  20
*Dead Time* - Richard Lee Byers  *h*  796
*Dead Voices* - Rick Hautala  *h*  2607
*Dead Voices* - Abigail McDaniels  *h*  3783
*Dead Voices: Natural Agonies in the Real World* -
    Gerald Vizenor  *f*  5578
*Deadly Breed* - T.J. Kirby  *h*  3153
*Deadly Dreams* - Gerald A. Schiller  *h*  4874
*Deadly Friend* - Keith Ferrario  *h*  1926
*Deadly Vengeance* - Stephen R. George  *h*  2199
*Deadrush* - Yvonne Navarro  *h*  4073
*Deadspawn* - Brian Lumley  *h*  3550
*Deadweight* - Robert Devereaux  *h*  1505
*Dealer's Choice* - George R.R. Martin  *s*  3643
*The Death and Life of Superman* - Roger
    Stern  *s*  5262
*Death Channels* - Robert E. Vardeman  *h*  5562
*The Death Crystal* - J. Edward Ames  *h*  91
*Death of an Adept* - Katherine Kurtz  *f*  3257
*The Death Prayer* - David Bowker  *h*  602
*Deathchain* - Ken Greenhall  *h*  2415
*Deathgrip* - Brian Hodge  *h*  2700
*Death's Door* - John Wooley  *h*  5969
*Deathscape* - Michael Cecilione  *h*  945
*Deathwalker* - R. Patrick Gates  *h*  2159
*December* - Phil Rickman  *h*  4588
*Demolition Man* - Richard Osborne  *s*  4229
*Demon Download* - Jack Yeovil  *f*  6021
*Demon Fire* - Gary L. Holleman  *h*  2743
*Demon's Fright* - Penelope Banka Kreps  *h*  3233
*Descent* - Ron Dee  *h*  1465
*Desert Eden* - J.M. Morgan  *s*  4000
*Desert Fire* - David Alexander  *s*  65
*Desmodus* - Melanie Tem  *h*  5421
*Desmond: A Novel of Love and the Modern Vampire* -
    Ulysses G. Dietz  *h*  1541
*Desperation* - Stephen King  *h*  3129
*Destiny's Carnival* - Warren Murphy  *h*  4057
*Deus-X: A Novel of Spiritual Terror* - Joseph A.
    Citro  *h*  1037
*The Devil and Dan Cooley* - Holly Lisle  *f*  3480
*The Devil's Advocate* - Andrew Neiderman  *h*  4085
*The Devil's Cradle* - Kate Stewart  *h*  5269
*The Devil's End* - D.A. Fowler  *h*  2023
*Devil's Gate* - Elizabeth Ergas  *h*  1833
*The Devil's Laughter* - William W.
    Johnstone  *h*  2930
*The Devouring* - Douglas D. Hawk  *h*  2615
*Diary of a Vampire* - Gary Bowen  *h*  600
*Diggers* - Terry Pratchett  *f*  4386
*Distant Dreams* - Jenny Lykins  *f*  3576
*Disturbing Behavior* - John Whitman  *h*  5789
*A Diversity of Dragons* - Anne McCaffrey  *f*  3728
*The Divide* - Robert Charles Wilson  *s*  5907
*The Djinn in the Nightingale's Eye* - A.S.
    Byatt  *f*  794
*Doc Sidhe* - Aaron Allston  *f*  85
*Dog Wizard* - Barbara Hambly  *f*  2503
*Dolores Claiborne* - Stephen King  *h*  3130
*Domination* - Michael Cecilione  *h*  946
*Dominion* - Bentley Little  *h*  3492
*Doomsday Exam* - Nick Pollotta  *f*  4363
*Door Number Three* - Patrick O'Leary  *s*  4210
*Dorella* - Mark A. Garland  *f*  2142
*The Double* - Don Webb  *f*  5661
*Double Date* - R.L. Stine  *h*  5287
*Double Edge* - Dennis Etchison  *h*  1846
*Double Trouble Squared* - Kathryn Lasky  *f*  3340
*A Dozen Black Roses* - Nancy A. Collins  *h*  1119

*Dracula Unbound* - Brian W. Aldiss *h* 55
*Dragon Death* - Gael Baudino *f* 390
*Dragon Moon* - Chris Claremont *f* 1040
*Dragon Season* - Michael Cassutt *f* 936
*Dragon Tears* - Dean R. Koontz *h* 3205
*Dragons on the Town* - Thorarinn
  Gunnarsson *f* 2463
*Dragonslayer's Return* - R.A. Salvatore *f* 4798
*Drakon* - S.M. Stirling *s* 5294
*Drawing Blood* - Poppy Z. Brite *h* 694
*Dreambuilder* - Tom Deitz *f* 1471
*Dreamer* - Peter James *h* 2871
*Dreamer* - Daniel Quinn *h* 4454
*Dreamseeker's Road* - Tom Deitz *f* 1472
*Drink Down the Moon* - Charles de Lint *f* 1426
*Dry Skull Dreams* - Michael Green *h* 2344
*A Dry Spell* - Susan Moloney *h* 3951
*Duel of Dragons* - Gael Baudino *f* 391
*Dumford Blood* - S.K. Epperson *h* 1829
*Dun Lady's Jess* - Doranna Durgin *f* 1704
*Duplicates* - Andrew Neiderman *h* 4086
*Dusk* - Ron Dee *h* 1466
*Dying Breath* - Jon A. Harrald *h* 2555
*The Earth Giant* - Melvin Burgess *s* 773
*Earthquake Weather* - Tim Powers *f* 4382
*The Ebon Mask* - Richard Lee Byers *h* 797
*Echoes* - Jackie Hyman *h* 2818
*Echoes of the Fourth Magic* - R.A.
  Salvatore *f* 4799
*Ecstasy Club* - Douglas Rushkoff *s* 4732
*The Eleventh Plague: A Novel of Medical Terror* -
  John S. Marr *h* 3632
*Elvira: Transylvania 90210* - Elvira *h* 1802
*Elvis Rising: Stories on the King* - Kay
  Sloan *f* 5089
*Ember From the Sun* - Mark Canter *s* 870
*Empire of Dust* - Chet Williamson *h* 5846
*The End of Alice* - A.M. Homes *h* 2755
*Entity* - Nina Mandelik *h* 3615
*Et Tu, Babe* - Mark Leyner *s* 3455
*Eternity* - Maggie Shayne *f* 4943
*Everville* - Clive Barker *h* 338
*Evil Eye* - Michael Slade *h* 5085
*Evil Intent* - Bernard Taylor *h* 5400
*Evil Reincarnate* - Leigh Clark *h* 1050
*Expiration Date* - Tim Powers *f* 4383
*Expiry Date* - Carol Anne Davis *h* 1401
*Exquisite Corpse* - Poppy Z. Brite *h* 695
*Extinct* - Charles Wilson *h* 5877
*Eye Killers* - A.A. Carr *h* 911
*The Eyes of the Beast* - Steve Harris *h* 2565
*Eyes of the Empress* - Camille Bacon-Smith *f* 285
*The Eyes of Torie Webster* - Roy Sorrels *h* 5164
*Facade* - Kristine Kathryn Rusch *h* 4716
*A Face at the Window* - Dennis McFarland *h* 3809
*The Fagin* - Pat Graversen *h* 2334
*Fair Peril* - Nancy Springer *f* 5178
*Fallen* - Dee Graham *h* 2302
*Famine* - Todd Komarnicki *h* 3201
*Fantastique* - Marvin Kaye *h* 3025
*Far Edge of Darkness* - Linda Evans *s* 1855
*Fatal Outcome* - Patricia Wallace *h* 5622
*Father's Little Helper* - Ronald Kelly *h* 3052
*The Fear in Yesterday's Rings* - George C.
  Chesbro *h* 1007
*Fear Itself* - Ric Meyers *h* 3881
*Fear Nothing* - Dean R. Koontz *h* 3207
*Fellow Traveller* - William Barton *s* 380
*The Fermata* - Nicholson Baker *s* 302
*Fetish* - Edward Bryant *h* 749
*Fiend* - C. Dean Andersson *h* 138
*The Fire Duke* - Joel Rosenberg *f* 4671
*Firefly* - Piers Anthony *h* 170
*Fires of Eden* - Dan Simmons *h* 5053
*Firestar* - Michael Flynn *s* 1962
*First Blast of the Trumpet Against the Monstrous
  Regiment of Women* - Eric McCormack *h* 3779
*The First Horror* - R.L. Stine *h* 5288

*First Love: A Gothic Tale* - Joyce Carol
  Oates *h* 4183
*Flames of the Dragon* - Robin Wayne Bailey *f* 287
*Flesh* - Gus Weill *h* 5685
*Flesh and Blood* - D.A. Fowler *h* 2024
*Flicker* - Theodore Roszak *h* 4683
*Flickering Shadows* - Kwadwo Agymah
  Kamau *f* 3006
*Flying Dutch* - Tom Holt *f* 2750
*Fog Heart* - Thomas Tessier *h* 5440
*Footprints of Thunder* - James F. David *s* 1379
*For You, the Living* - Wayne Allen Sallee *h* 4786
*The Forbidden Zone* - Whitley Strieber *h* 5340
*Forest of the Night* - S.P. Somtow *f* 5156
*The Forever Children* - Eric Flanders *h* 1944
*The Forever King* - Molly Cochran *f* 1092
*Forever Knight: A Stirring of Dust* - Susan
  Sizemore *h* 5078
*Forever Knight: Intimations of Mortality* - Susan M.
  Garrett *h* 2149
*Forget Me Not* - Gene Lazuta *h* 3375
*The Forgotten* - Stephen R. George *h* 2200
*The Forsaken* - Steven Ray Fulgham *h* 2089
*Fortress of Forbidden Destiny* - Ryder
  Syvertson *s* 5378
*The Fourth Guardian* - Ronald Anthony
  Cross *f* 1273
*The Fourth Rome* - David Drake *s* 1631
*The Foxes of Firstdark* - Garry Kilworth *f* 3115
*Fractal Mode* - Piers Anthony *f* 171
*Fragments* - James F. David *h* 1380
*Frameshift* - Robert J. Sawyer *s* 4856
*Freedom's Challenge* - Anne McCaffrey *s* 3732
*Freedom's Choice* - Anne McCaffrey *s* 3733
*Freedom's Landing* - Anne McCaffrey *s* 3734
*The Frenchman* - Elizabeth Hand *h* 2534
*Friends in Time* - Grace Chetwin *f* 1012
*The Friendship Song* - Nancy Springer *f* 5179
*The Frighteners* - Michael Jahn *h* 2856
*From a Whisper to a Scream* - Samuel M.
  Key *h* 3093
*From the Teeth of Angels* - Jonathan Carroll *h* 918
*From Time to Time* - Jack Finney *s* 1941
*Frostwing* - Richard A. Knaak *f* 3170
*Full Moonster* - Nick Pollotta *f* 4364
*Furnace* - Muriel Gray *h* 2339
*Further Adventures* - Jon Stephen Fink *f* 1940
*The Further Adventures of Batman 2: Featuring the
  Penguin* - Martin H. Greenberg *s* 2391
*The Further Adventures of Batman 3: Featuring
  Catwoman* - Martin H. Greenberg *s* 2392
*The Further Adventures of Superman* - Martin H.
  Greenberg *s* 2393
*Gabriel Knight: Sins of the Fathers* - Jane
  Jensen *h* 2896
*Galatea 2.2* - Richard M. Powers *s* 4381
*Galatea in 2-D* - Aaron Allston *f* 87
*Galilee* - Clive Barker *h* 340
*Game's End* - Kevin J. Anderson *f* 104
*Garden* - Matthew J. Costello *h* 1197
*Gate of Ivory, Gate of Horn* - Robert
  Holdstock *f* 2737
*The Gates of Noon* - Michael Scott Rohan *f* 4661
*Gehenna* - Lewis Gannett *h* 2114
*Genesis* - Charles L. Grant *h* 2308
*Gerald's Game* - Stephen King *h* 3133
*Ghost Boy* - Jean Simon *h* 5064
*Ghost Dance* - Kathryn Ptacek *h* 4441
*Ghost Dancers* - Brian Craig *s* 1238
*Ghost Light* - Rick Hautala *h* 2603
*Ghostlight* - Marion Zimmer Bradley *f* 634
*Ghosts* - Noel Hynd *h* 2822
*The Ghosts of Sleath* - James Herbert *h* 2668
*Ghosts of Wind and Shadow* - Charles de
  Lint *f* 1427
*Ghostwright* - Michael Cadnum *h* 810
*The Gifted* - Jack Caravela *h* 879
*A Girl Named Disaster* - Nancy Farmer *f* 1868
*Glenraven* - Marion Zimmer Bradley *f* 635

*Glimmering* - Elizabeth Hand *s* 2535
*Gnelfs* - Sidney Williams *h* 5823
*Gnome Man's Land* - Esther Friesner *f* 2075
*Goblins* - Vincent Courtney *h* 1212
*Goblins* - Charles L. Grant *s* 2309
*The Godmother* - Elizabeth Ann
  Scarborough *f* 4862
*Godmother Night* - Rachel Pollack *f* 4358
*The Godmother's Apprentice* - Elizabeth Ann
  Scarborough *f* 4863
*The Godmother's Web* - Elizabeth Ann
  Scarborough *f* 4864
*God's Dice* - S. Andrew Swann *f* 5364
*Gods of the Well of Souls* - Jack L. Chalker *s* 954
*Godzilla 2000* - Marc Cerasini *s* 949
*The Golden Mean* - Nick Bantock *f* 334
*Gone South* - Robert R. McCammon *h* 3755
*The Good Children* - Kate Wilhelm *h* 5808
*Good News From Outer Space* - John
  Kessel *s* 3084
*Good Night, Sweet Angel* - Clare McNally *h* 3857
*Good Omens: The Nice and Accurate Prophecies of
  Agnes Nutter, Witch* - Neil Gaiman *h* 2103
*Goodlow's Ghosts* - T.M. Wright *h* 5991
*Goon* - Edward Lee *h* 3392
*Gothic Romance* - Emmanuel Carrere *h* 912
*Grandma's Little Darling* - Stephen R.
  George *h* 2201
*Grave Markings* - Michael A. Arnzen *h* 212
*Gravelight* - Marion Zimmer Bradley *f* 636
*Graythings* - Pat Graversen *h* 2335
*The Great and Secret Show* - Clive Barker *h* 341
*Greely's Cove* - John Gideon *h* 2221
*Green Lake* - S.K. Epperson *h* 1830
*The Green Progression* - L.E. Modesitt Jr. *s* 3932
*The Gris-Gris Man* - Don Davis *h* 1403
*Ground Zero* - Kevin J. Anderson *h* 106
*Guardian* - John Saul *h* 4841
*The Gypsy* - Steven Brust *f* 744
*Half Asleep in Frog Pajamas* - Tom
  Robbins *s* 4606
*The Halloween Man* - Douglas Clegg *h* 1080
*The Hanged Man* - Francesca Lia Block *f* 548
*The Hanged Man* - T.J. MacGregor *h* 3594
*Happy Policeman* - Patricia Anthony *s* 160
*Harpy High* - Esther Friesner *f* 2076
*Harrowgate* - Daniel H. Gower *h* 2292
*The Harvest* - Richie Tankersley Cusick *h* 1302
*Harvest of Blood* - Vincent Courtney *h* 1213
*The Haunt* - John Fogarty *h* 1966
*Haunted* - James Herbert *h* 2669
*Haunted* - Tamara Thorne *h* 5463
*The Haunting* - Ruby Jean Jensen *h* 2901
*Head Injuries* - Conrad Williams *h* 5816
*Header* - Edward Lee *h* 3393
*Headhunter* - Timothy Findley *h* 1939
*The Headsman* - James Neal Harvey *h* 2599
*The Healing of Crossroads* - Nick
  O'Donohoe *f* 4195
*Heartlight* - Marion Zimmer Bradley *f* 637
*Heathen* - Shaun Hutson *h* 2816
*Heathern* - Jack Womack *s* 5958
*Hell-O-Ween* - David Robbins *h* 4598
*Hell on High* - Holly Lisle *f* 3483
*Hell-Storm* - James A. Moore *h* 3990
*Hellboy: The Lost Army* - Christopher
  Golden *h* 2257
*Hellcat* - Amanda Kingsley *h* 3145
*The Hellfire Club* - Peter Straub *h* 5326
*Hence* - Brad Leithauser *s* 3431
*Her Monster* - Jeff Collignon *h* 1115
*The Hero King* - Rick Shelley *f* 4970
*The Hero of Varay* - Rick Shelley *f* 4971
*Hexwood* - Diana Wynne Jones *s* 2948
*Hidden Echoes* - Mike Jefferies *f* 2885
*Hideaway* - Dean R. Koontz *h* 3208
*Higher Mythology* - Jody Lynn Nye *f* 4170
*The Higher Space* - Jamil Nasir *s* 4070
*Hobkin* - Peni R. Griffin *f* 2438

*The Hollow Man* - Dan Simmons  s  5054
*Holy Terror* - Josephine Boyle  h  608
*Homebody* - Orson Scott Card  h  890
*Homecoming* - Matthew J. Costello  h  1198
*The Homecoming* - Kimberly Rangel  h  4471
*The Homing* - John Saul  h  4842
*Hook* - Terry Brooks  f  713
*Horror Show* - Greg Kihn  h  3103
*Horrorshow* - David Darke  h  1353
*Horses of the Night* - Michael Cadnum  h  811
*Host* - Peter James  h  2872
*House Haunted* - Al Sarrantonio  h  4830
*The House of Doors* - Brian Lumley  h  3554
*The House of the Toad* - Richard L.
  Tierney  h  5470
*The House on Hound Hill* - Maggie Prince  f  4438
*The House That Jack Built* - Graham
  Masterton  h  3675
*How Like a God* - Brenda W. Clough  f  1089
*Howl* - Christine Tanasiuk  h  5388
*Howl-O-Ween* - Gary L. Holleman  h  2744
*Human Resources* - Floyd Kemske  h  3057
*Human to Human* - Rebecca Ore  s  4219
*Humans* - Donald E. Westlake  f  5768
*Humpty Dumpty: An Oval* - Damon Knight  s  3186
*Hunger* - William Dantz  h  1346
*The Hunger of the Beast* - John Driver  h  1656
*Hungry for Home: A Wolf Odyssey* - 'Asta
  Bowen  f  599
*I Met a Man Who Wasn't There* - Mary R.
  Callaghan  h  840
*I, Said the Fly* - Michael Shea  h  4944
*I Was a Teenage Fairy* - Francesca Lia
  Block  f  549
*Icebound* - Dean R. Koontz  h  3209
*Icefalcon's Quest* - Barbara Hambly  f  2504
*Icefire* - Judith Reeves-Stevens  s  4512
*Iceman* - Rex Miller  h  3900
*Ignition* - Kevin J. Anderson  s  107
*The Ignored* - Bentley Little  h  3493
*I'll Be Watching You* - Samuel M. Key  h  3094
*Ill Wind* - Kevin J. Anderson  s  108
*Imajica* - Clive Barker  h  343
*The Immaculate* - Mark Morris  h  4023
*Immortal* - Jason Nickles  h  4102
*The Immortals* - Andrew Neiderman  h  4087
*An Impossumble Summer* - Brenda W.
  Clough  f  1090
*Impulse* - Rick Hautala  h  2609
*In between Dragons* - Michael Kandel  f  3010
*In Double Jeopardy* - Andrew Neiderman  h  4088
*In the Blood* - Nancy A. Collins  h  1121
*In the Land of Winter* - Richard Grant  f  2326
*In the Mood* - Charles L. Grant  h  2312
*In the Rift* - Marion Zimmer Bradley  f  639
*In the Shadows of the Moonglade* - Riley St.
  James  h  5186
*The Inadequate Adept* - Simon Hawke  f  2617
*Independence Day* - Dean Devlin  s  1508
*Infernal Affairs* - Jane Heller  h  2652
*Infinity's Child* - Harry Stein  h  5250
*The Innsmouth Heritage* - Brian Stableford  h  5194
*Insatiable* - David Dvorkin  h  1707
*Insomnia* - Stephen King  h  3135
*Intensity* - Dean R. Koontz  h  3210
*Interface* - Stephen Bury  s  781
*The Interior Life* - Katherine Blake  f  515
*Into the Forest* - Jean Hegland  s  2640
*Into the Land of the Unicorns* - Bruce
  Coville  f  1219
*Iron Shadows* - Steven Barnes  f  362
*Irrational Fears* - William Browning
  Spencer  h  5167
*Ishmael* - Daniel Quinn  s  4455
*Island in the Sea of Time* - S.M. Stirling  s  5295
*Islands of Tomorrow* - F.M. Busby  s  783
*Isle of View* - Piers Anthony  f  177
*The Ivory and the Horn* - Charles de Lint  f  1431
*Jackals* - Charles L. Grant  h  2313

*Jaguar* - Bill Ransom  s  4477
*Jed the Dead* - Alan Dean Foster  s  2007
*Jennifer Murdley's Toad* - Bruce Coville  f  1220
*Jeremy Thatcher, Dragon Hatcher* - Bruce
  Coville  f  1221
*The Jewel of Equilibrant* - Steven Frankos  f  2042
*The Jimjams* - Michael Green  h  2345
*Jinx High* - Mercedes Lackey  h  3284
*Jokertown Shuffle* - George R.R. Martin  s  3646
*The Judas Glass* - Michael Cadnum  h  812
*Jumper* - Steven Gould  s  2290
*Jumpers* - R. Patrick Gates  h  2161
*The Juniper Game* - Sherryl Jordan  f  2992
*Juniper, Gentian and Rosemary* - Pamela
  Dean  f  1445
*Jupiter's Daughter* - Tom Hyman  s  2820
*Kaleidoscope Eyes* - Graham Watkins  h  5631
*Kane* - Douglas Borton  h  576
*The Keeper* - Robert D. Lee  h  3402
*Keeper of the King* - Nigel Bennett  h  452
*Kent Montana and the Really Ugly Thing From Mars* -
  Lionel Fenn  s  1918
*Kent Montana and the Reasonably Invisible Man* -
  Lionel Fenn  s  1919
*A Key for the Nonesuch* - Geary Gravel  s  2330
*The Key to the Indian* - Lynne Reid Banks  f  331
*Kids* - Trevor Hoyle  s  2787
*The Killing Dance* - Laurell K. Hamilton  h  2518
*Killing Frost* - Dan I. Blake  h  514
*The Killing of the Saints* - Alex Abella  h  21
*Killjoy* - Elizabeth Forrest  h  1973
*Killobyte* - Piers Anthony  f  179
*Kindred* - John Gideon  h  2222
*King of the Grey* - Richard A. Knaak  f  3173
*The Kingdom of Kevin Malone* - Suzy McKee
  Charnas  f  970
*Kirins: The Flight of the Ain* - James D.
  Priest  f  4433
*Kirins: The Secret of the Hanging Stones* - James D.
  Priest  f  4434
*Kirins: The Spell of No'an* - James D.
  Priest  f  4435
*Kiss of the Vampire* - Lee Weathersby  h  5657
*Knight of Ghosts and Shadows* - Mercedes
  Lackey  f  3285
*Krokodil Tears* - Jack Yeovil  f  6023
*The Kronos Condition* - Emily Devenport  s  1502
*Ladies Night* - Jack Ketchum  h  3091
*Lady El* - Jim Starlin  s  5213
*Lagoon* - Alison Drake  h  1625
*The Land of Nod* - Mark A. Clements  h  1085
*Landslayer's Law* - Tom Deitz  f  1474
*Larque on the Wing* - Nancy Springer  f  5180
*Lasher* - Anne Rice  h  4570
*Last Call* - Tim Powers  f  4384
*The Last Highlander* - Claire Cross  f  1271
*Last Mountain* - Robert C. Fleet  f  1946
*Last Rites* - David Darke  h  1354
*The Last Vampire* - Christopher Pike  h  4328
*The Last Voice They Hear* - Ramsey
  Campbell  h  858
*Laying the Music to Rest* - Dean Wesley
  Smith  h  5114
*The Lazarus Heart* - Poppy Z. Brite  h  696
*Leanna: Possession of a Woman* - Marie
  Kiraly  h  3149
*Legends Reborn* - Kenneth C. Flint  f  1958
*Legion of the Dead* - Geoffrey Caine  h  833
*Less than Human* - Gary L. Raisor  h  4464
*Let There Be Dark* - Allen Lee Harris  h  2557
*Lethal Delivery* - J.G. Maxon  h  3695
*Lie to Me* - David Martin  h  3639
*A Life in the Future* - Martin Caidin  s  827
*Life Support* - Tess Gerritsen  h  2206
*Lifehouse* - Spider Robinson  s  4641
*Lights Out in the Reptile House* - Jim
  Shepard  f  4976
*Liquid Diet* - William Tedford  h  5419
*Little Boy Lost* - T.M. Wright  h  5992

*The Little Country* - Charles de Lint  f  1432
*Live From Golgotha: A Novel* - Gore Vidal  s  5569
*The Living Dark* - Stephen Gresham  h  2431
*Living Hell* - Ric Meyers  h  3882
*The Living One* - Lewis Gannett  h  2115
*Living with Aliens* - John DeChancie  s  1460
*The Lodge of the Lynx* - Katherine Kurtz  f  3259
*The Lodger* - Fred Chappell  h  966
*A Logical Magician* - Robert Weinberg  f  5697
*Lois & Clark* - C.J. Cherryh  s  999
*The Long Lost* - Ramsey Campbell  h  859
*The Long Midnight* - Daniel Ransom  h  4480
*Looker* - Jorge Saralegui  h  4820
*Lord of the Dark Lake* - Ron Faust  h  1894
*Lord of the Dead* - Tom Holland  h  2741
*Lords of Creation* - Tim Sullivan  s  5351
*Lorelei* - Mark A. Clements  h  1086
*The Lost* - Jonathan Aycliffe  h  279
*Lost Futures* - Lisa Tuttle  s  5520
*The Lost Guardian* - Ronald Anthony Cross  s  1274
*Lost Souls* - Poppy Z. Brite  h  697
*The Lost World* - Michael Crichton  s  1256
*Lot Lizards* - Ray Garton  h  2152
*Love & Sleep* - John Crowley  f  1277
*Love Bite* - Sherry Gottlieb  h  2288
*Lucifer's Eye* - Hugh B. Cave  h  943
*Lullaby* - Diane Guest  h  2455
*The Lunatic Cafe* - Laurell K. Hamilton  h  2520
*Lunatics* - Bradley Denton  f  1491
*Lunching with the Antichrist* - Michael
  Moorcock  f  3984
*Lurid Dreams* - Charles L. Harness  s  2546
*The M.D.: A Horror Story* - Thomas M.
  Disch  h  1561
*Machine* - Rene Belletto  h  436
*Madeleine's Ghost* - Robert Girardi  h  2240
*The Magic and the Healing* - Nick
  O'Donohoe  f  4196
*The Magic Bicycle* - William Hill  f  2688
*The Magic Touch* - Jody Lynn Nye  f  4171
*MagicNet* - John DeChancie  f  1461
*The Mailman* - Bentley Little  h  3494
*Make Way for Dragons!* - Thorarinn
  Gunnarsson  f  2465
*Making Love* - Melanie Tem  h  5422
*The Making of a Monster* - Gail Petersen  h  4307
*Mall, Mayhem and Magic* - Holly Lisle  f  3485
*Mall Purchase Night* - Rick Cook  f  1159
*The Man Upstairs* - T.L. Parkinson  h  4248
*The Man Who Turned into Himself* - David
  Ambrose  h  89
*Manhattan Heat* - Ken Eulo  h  1851
*The March Hare Network* - Jack L. Chalker  s  957
*The Mark of the Moderately Vicious Vampire* - Lionel
  Fenn  h  1920
*Mark of the Werewolf* - Jeffrey Sackett  h  4780
*Marked Cards* - George R.R. Martin  s  3647
*Martian Deathtrap* - Nathan Archer  s  205
*Master of Lies* - Graham Masterton  h  3676
*Mathemagics* - Margaret Ball  f  316
*The Matrix* - Jonathan Aycliffe  h  280
*A Matter of Taste* - Fred Saberhagen  h  4770
*Max Lakeman and the Beautiful Stranger* - Jon
  Cohen  f  1098
*Maze of Worlds* - Brian Lumley  h  3559
*Meeting the Minotaur* - Carol Dawson  f  1409
*Mefisto in Onyx* - Harlan Ellison  h  1786
*Memnoch the Devil* - Anne Rice  h  4571
*Memory and Dream* - Charles de Lint  f  1433
*Men in Black* - Steve Perry  h  4298
*The Mennyms* - Sylvia Waugh  f  5654
*Mennyms Alive* - Sylvia Waugh  f  5655
*Mennyms Under Siege* - Sylvia Waugh  f  5656
*Mercy's Mill* - Betty Levin  f  3444
*Meridian 144* - Meg Files  f  1932
*The Merlin Effect* - T.A. Barron  f  371
*The Messenger* - Donald Tyson  h  5528
*Metal Angel* - Nancy Springer  f  5181
*The Midnight Club* - Christopher Pike  h  4329

*The Midnight Horse* - Sid Fleischman  *f*  1948
*Midnight Is a Lonely Place* - Barbara
   Erskine  *h*  1836
*Midnight Sun* - Ramsey Campbell  *h*  860
*The Midnight Tour* - Richard Laymon  *h*  3368
*Midsummer* - Matthew J. Costello  *h*  1200
*Mind Kill* - Richard La Plante  *h*  3267
*Mind Stealer* - Lee Duigon  *h*  1672
*Mine* - Robert R. McCammon  *h*  3756
*Minerva Wakes* - Holly Lisle  *f*  3487
*Mirage* - Perry Brass  *s*  662
*Mirage* - F. Paul Wilson  *h*  5892
*Missing Angel Juan* - Francesca Lia Block  *f*  550
*Mixed Doubles* - Daniel Da Cruz  *s*  1305
*Mockingbird* - Sean Stewart  *f*  5273
*Mojave Wells* - L. Dean James  *s*  2864
*Mojo and the Pickle Jar* - Douglas Bell  *f*  433
*The Monastery* - J.N. Williamson  *h*  5856
*Monet's Ghost* - Chelsea Quinn Yarbro  *f*  6017
*Mongster* - Randall Boyll  *h*  616
*Monster* - John Tigges  *h*  5474
*Moon of the Werewolf* - Ronald Kelly  *h*  3053
*Moonfall* - Tamara Thorne  *h*  5464
*The Moons of Summer* - S.K. Epperson  *h*  1831
*The Moon's Wife: A Hystery* - A.A.
   Attanasio  *f*  271
*Moonwise* - Greer Ilene Gilman  *f*  2238
*More than Fire* - Philip Jose Farmer  *s*  1871
*Morningstar* - Peter Atkins  *h*  265
*Mortal Kombat* - Martin Delrio  *f*  1483
*Mother of Winter* - Barbara Hambly  *f*  2506
*Mount Dragon* - Douglas Preston  *h*  4413
*The Mountain King* - Rick Hautala  *h*  2611
*Mouvar's Magic* - Piers Anthony  *f*  182
*Mr. Murder* - Dean R. Koontz  *h*  3213
*Mr. Sandman* - Lyle Howard  *h*  2779
*Mr. Was* - Pete Hautman  *s*  2614
*Mrs. God* - Peter Straub  *h*  5329
*Mucho Mojo* - Joe R. Lansdale  *h*  3330
*My Best Friend Is Invisible* - R.L. Stine  *h*  5289
*My Cousin, My Gastroenterologist* - Mark
   Leyner  *s*  3456
*My Ishmael* - Daniel Quinn  *s*  4456
*My Soul to Keep* - Tannarive Due  *h*  1670
*My Soul to Take* - Steven Spruill  *s*  5184
*My Stepfather Shrank!* - Barbara Dillon  *s*  1558
*My Teacher Flunked the Planet* - Bruce
   Coville  *s*  1222
*My Teacher Fried My Brains* - Bruce
   Coville  *s*  1223
*My Teacher Glows in the Dark* - Bruce
   Coville  *s*  1224
*Mysteries of the Word* - Stanley Wiater  *h*  5796
*The Mysterium* - Eric McCormack  *h*  3780
*Mysterium* - Robert Charles Wilson  *s*  5911
*Name of the Beast* - Daniel Easterman  *h*  1721
*Naming the Flowers* - Kate Wilhelm  *s*  5809
*Nanoware Time/The Persistence of Vision* - Ian
   Watson  *s*  5638
*Nazareth Hill* - Ramsey Campbell  *h*  861
*Near Dead* - Stephen R. George  *h*  2202
*Near Death* - Nancy Kilpatrick  *h*  3113
*Necrom* - Mick Farren  *s*  1881
*The Need* - Andrew Neiderman  *h*  4089
*Needful Things* - Stephen King  *h*  3137
*Negrophobia: An Urban Parable* - Darius
   James  *f*  2859
*Neighbors* - Maureen S. Pusti  *h*  4450
*Netherworld* - Richard Lee Byers  *h*  798
*Never Land* - Douglas Clegg  *h*  1081
*Neverwhere* - Neil Gaiman  *f*  2104
*The New Neighbor* - Ray Garton  *h*  2154
*Nice Guys Finish Last* - Gary Jonas  *h*  2938
*Night* - Alan Rodgers  *h*  4649
*Night Beasts* - T.W. Stetson  *h*  5263
*Night Blood* - Eric Flanders  *h*  1945
*Night Cruise* - Billie Sue Mosiman  *h*  4041
*Night Hunter* - Michael Reaves  *h*  4496
*The Night in Fog* - David B. Silva  *h*  5026

*The Night Inside* - Nancy Baker  *h*  301
*Night Launch* - Jake Garn  *s*  2143
*Night Magic* - Thomas Tryon  *h*  5485
*The Night Man* - K.W. Jeter  *h*  2915
*Night Mask* - William W. Johnstone  *h*  2931
*Night Music* - Sheila Bristow Garner  *h*  2147
*Night of Broken Souls* - Thomas F.
   Monteleone  *h*  3964
*The Night of Wishes: Or, The
   Satanarchaeolidealcohellish Notion Potion* - Michael
   Ende  *f*  1821
*Night Prayers* - P.D. Cacek  *h*  803
*Night Relics* - James P. Blaylock  *h*  521
*The Night Seasons* - J.N. Williamson  *h*  5858
*Night Sounds* - Warner Lee  *h*  3415
*Night Thirst* - Patrick Whalen  *h*  5770
*Night Thunder* - Ruby Jean Jensen  *h*  2903
*Nightblood* - T. Chris Martindale  *h*  3656
*Nightlife* - Jack Ellis  *h*  1779
*Nightlife* - Brian Hodge  *h*  2702
*Nightmare* - S.K. Epperson  *h*  1832
*The Nightmare People* - Lawrence Watt-
   Evans  *h*  5643
*Nightmare, with Angel* - Stephen Gallagher  *h*  2111
*Nightmare's Disciple* - Joseph S. Pulver Jr.  *h*  4449
*Nightscape* - Stephen R. George  *h*  2203
*Nightworld* - F. Paul Wilson  *h*  5893
*Nine Levels Down* - William Dantz  *h*  1347
*No Limits* - Nigel Findley  *s*  1938
*Nocturnas* - Shawn Ryan  *h*  4755
*Not Broken, Not Belonging* - Randy Fox  *h*  2030
*Oaths and Miracles* - Nancy Kress  *s*  3242
*Obsessed* - Rick R. Reed  *h*  4500
*October* - Al Sarrantonio  *h*  4832
*Of Saints and Shadows* - Christopher
   Golden  *h*  2259
*Offspring* - Jack Ketchum  *h*  3092
*The Offspring* - Kenneth McKenney  *h*  3826
*The Old Man and Mr. Smith* - Peter
   Ustinov  *f*  5532
*Omega* - Patrick Lynch  *h*  3577
*A Once and Future Love* - Anne Kelleher  *f*  3039
*One Foot in the Grave* - Wm. Mark
   Simmons  *f*  5062
*The One Safe Place* - Ramsey Campbell  *h*  862
*Only Begotten Daughter* - James Morrow  *f*  4034
*The Only Thing to Fear* - Robert Morgan  *h*  4003
*Operation Synbat* - Bob Mayer  *h*  3701
*The Orchid Eater* - Marc Laidlaw  *h*  3312
*Orc's Opal* - Piers Anthony  *f*  183
*Ordeal of the Seventh Carrier* - Peter Albano  *s*  48
*Order of the Arrow* - Michael T.
   Hinkemeyer  *h*  2689
*Orphans* - Jean Simon  *s*  5065
*The Orpheus Process* - Daniel H. Gower  *h*  2293
*The Other End of Time* - Frederik Pohl  *s*  4351
*OtherSyde* - J. Michael Straczynski  *h*  5323
*Otherworld* - Kenneth C. Flint  *h*  1959
*Out for Blood* - John Peyton Cooke  *h*  1166
*Out of Body* - Thomas Baum  *h*  397
*Out of the Night* - Patrick Whalen  *h*  5771
*Out of This World* - Lawrence Watt-Evans  *f*  5645
*Out There in the Darkness* - Ed Gorman  *h*  2279
*Outworld Cats* - Jack Lovejoy  *s*  3536
*The Pagemaster* - David Kirschner  *h*  3156
*Painted Devil* - Michael Bedard  *f*  430
*The Palm Dome* - Liz Fulton  *h*  2094
*Panda Ray* - Michael Kandel  *s*  3011
*Pandora* - Alan Rodgers  *h*  4650
*Panic* - Chris Curry  *h*  1295
*The Paper Grail* - James P. Blaylock  *f*  522
*Parliament of Blood* - Scott Ciencin  *h*  1031
*The Passion* - Donna Boyd  *h*  603
*Passive Intruder* - Michael Upchurch  *h*  5530
*Patton's Spaceship* - John Barnes  *s*  357
*Pelts* - F. Paul Wilson  *h*  5894
*Penance* - Rick R. Reed  *h*  4501
*Personal Darkness* - Tanith Lee  *h*  3413
*Pet Store* - M.T. Coffin  *h*  1097

*Phantom Banjo* - Elizabeth Ann
   Scarborough  *f*  4868
*Phoenix Fire* - Elizabeth Forrest  *f*  1974
*Picking the Ballad's Bones* - Elizabeth Ann
   Scarborough  *f*  4869
*Pictures at 11* - Norman Spinrad  *s*  5173
*Pillow Friend* - Lisa Tuttle  *h*  5522
*Pitfall* - Ronald Kelly  *h*  3054
*The Place* - T.M. Wright  *h*  5993
*Playmates* - Abigail McDaniels  *h*  3784
*Pluto, Animal Lover* - Laren Stover  *h*  5318
*Portent* - James Herbert  *h*  2670
*Portrait of the Psychopath as a Young Woman* -
   Edward Lee  *h*  3395
*The Possession* - Ronald Kelly  *h*  3055
*Practical Demonkeeping* - Christopher
   Moore  *h*  3989
*Practical Magic* - Alice Hoffman  *f*  2713
*Prank Night* - David Robbins  *h*  4601
*The Presence* - John Saul  *h*  4843
*Preternatural* - Margaret Wander Bonanno  *s*  568
*Prey* - William W. Johnstone  *h*  2932
*The Priest: A Gothic Romance* - Thomas M.
   Disch  *h*  1562
*The Printer's Devil* - Chico Kidd  *f*  3099
*Private Demons* - Robert Masello  *h*  3660
*Prodigal* - Melanie Tem  *h*  5423
*The Prodigy* - Noel Hynd  *h*  2823
*Prophecy* - Peter James  *h*  2874
*Prototype* - Brian Hodge  *h*  2704
*Psycho House* - Robert Bloch  *h*  542
*Psychoshop* - Alfred Bester  *s*  477
*Puppet Master* - Barry T. Hawkins  *h*  2632
*Quake* - Richard Laymon  *h*  3370
*A Question of Time* - Fred Saberhagen  *h*  4772
*The Quiet* - Patrick Billings  *h*  488
*The Quorum* - Kim Newman  *h*  4100
*Quoth the Crow* - David Bischoff  *h*  494
*Rage* - Elizabeth Ergas  *h*  1834
*Ragged Angels* - Della Van Hise  *h*  5537
*Rapid Growth* - Mary K. Hanner  *h*  2541
*Raptor* - Paul Zindel  *s*  6084
*Raven* - Charles L. Grant  *h*  2314
*Raven* - S.A. Swiniarski  *h*  5374
*Raven Stole the Moon* - Garth Stein  *h*  5249
*Ray Bradbury Presents: Dinosaur Planet* - Stephen
   Leigh  *s*  3427
*Ray Bradbury Presents: Dinosaur World* - Stephen
   Leigh  *s*  3428
*Reaper* - Ben Mizrich  *h*  3923
*A Reasonable Madness* - Fran Dorf  *h*  1580
*The Rebirth of Wonder* - Lawrence Watt
   Evans  *f*  5646
*The Reckoning* - Ruby Jean Jensen  *h*  2904
*Red Angel* - Roxanne Longstreet  *h*  3518
*Red Army* - Ralph Peters  *s*  4306
*Red Bride* - Christopher Fowler  *h*  2019
*Red Devil* - David Saperstein  *h*  4816
*The Red-Eared Ghosts* - Vivian Alcock  *f*  53
*Red, Red Robin* - Stephen Gallagher  *h*  2113
*Red Wizard* - Nancy Springer  *f*  5182
*The Regulators* - Richard Bachman  *h*  284
*Reign* - Chet Williamson  *h*  5849
*The Reign of the Brown Magician* - Lawrence Watt-
   Evans  *f*  5647
*Relic* - Douglas Preston  *h*  4414
*Relife* - Dan Barton  *h*  376
*Reliquary* - Douglas Preston  *h*  4415
*The Reluctant Sorcerer* - Simon Hawke  *f*  2622
*Renaissance Moon* - Linda Nevins  *f*  4093
*Reprisal* - F. Paul Wilson  *h*  5896
*Requiem* - Graham Joyce  *h*  2994
*Requiem* - Clifford Mohr  *h*  3950
*Resume with Monsters* - William Browning
   Spencer  *h*  5168
*Resurrection Man* - Sean Stewart  *f*  5277
*The Resurrectionist* - Thomas F.
   Monteleone  *h*  3965
*Retribution* - Elizabeth Forrest  *h*  1975

*The Return of the Breakneck Boys* - Geary Gravel  *s*  2332
*Return of the Wolfman* - Jeff Rovin  *h*  4687
*Return to Chaos* - Craig Shaw Gardner  *h*  2131
*Return to Howliday Inn* - James Howe  *f*  2786
*Return to Lovecraft Country* - Scott David Aniolowski  *h*  148
*Return to the House of Usher* - Robert Poe  *h*  4345
*The Revelation* - Bentley Little  *h*  3496
*Revenant* - Melanie Tem  *h*  5424
*Revenge of the Seventh Carrier* - Peter Albano  *s*  49
*Riverrun* - S.P. Somtow  *f*  5159
*The Road to Hell, Volume I* - Robert Weinberg  *h*  5701
*The Road to Hell, Volume II* - Robert Weinberg  *h*  5702
*Roadkill* - Richard Sanford  *h*  4815
*Rockabilly Hell* - William W. Johnstone  *h*  2933
*Rockabilly Limbo* - William W. Johnstone  *h*  2934
*Rook* - Graham Masterton  *h*  3678
*Room 13* - Henry Garfield  *h*  2139
*A Room for the Dead* - Noel Hynd  *h*  2825
*Root of All Evil* - David A. Farrow  *h*  1888
*Rose Madder* - Stephen King  *h*  3139
*Rough Beast* - Gary Goshgarian  *h*  2284
*The Ruby Tear* - Rebecca Brand  *h*  660
*Ruins* - Kevin J. Anderson  *h*  112
*Rulers of Darkness* - Steven Spruill  *h*  5185
*Rune* - Christopher Fowler  *h*  2020
*Running with the Demon* - Terry Brooks  *f*  715
*Russian Spring* - Norman Spinrad  *s*  5174
*Sabine's Notebook* - Nick Bantock  *f*  335
*Sacrament* - Clive Barker  *h*  345
*Sacred Ground* - Mercedes Lackey  *f*  3294
*Sacred Prey* - Vivian Schilling  *h*  4875
*Sacrifice* - John Farris  *h*  1886
*Sacrifice* - Richard Kinion  *h*  3146
*The Safety of Unknown Cities* - Lucy Taylor  *h*  5414
*St. Peter's Wolf* - Michael Cadnum  *h*  816
*St. Vitus Dances Eternity: A Sarajevo Ghost Story* - Stewart Von Allmen  *h*  5585
*Samurai Cat Goes to the Movies* - Mark E. Rogers  *s*  4656
*The Sand Dwellers* - Adam Niswander  *h*  4112
*The Sandman: Book of Dreams* - Neil Gaiman  *f*  2105
*Santa Steps Out: A Fairy Tale for Grownups* - Robert Devereaux  *h*  1506
*Santa's Twin* - Dean R. Koontz  *f*  3214
*Sati* - Christopher Pike  *f*  4330
*Savage Season* - Joe R. Lansdale  *h*  3332
*Savant* - Rex Miller  *h*  3901
*The School* - Ed Kelleher  *h*  3042
*The School* - T.M. Wright  *h*  5994
*Scorpion Shards* - Neal Shusterman  *s*  5013
*Scotland the Brave* - Jennifer Roberson  *f*  4611
*Seattle Ghost Story* - Nick DiMartino  *h*  1560
*Seaward* - Brad Leithauser  *h*  3433
*Second Chance* - Chet Williamson  *h*  5850
*Second Child* - John Saul  *h*  4844
*Secret Passages* - Paul Preuss  *s*  4420
*Secrets of the Morning* - V.C. Andrews  *h*  146
*Seed of Evil* - Edmund Plante  *h*  4340
*Seed upon the Wind* - Carole Nelson Douglas  *f*  1584
*Seeing Eye* - Jack Ellis  *h*  1780
*The Select* - F. Paul Wilson  *h*  5897
*Senor Vivo and the Coca Lord* - Louis de Bernieres  *f*  1411
*Senora Rodriguez and Other Worlds* - Martha Cerda  *f*  950
*Serial Killer Days* - David Prill  *h*  4436
*The Serpent Slayers* - Adam Niswander  *h*  4113
*Servant of the Bones* - Anne Rice  *h*  4575
*SETI* - Frederick Fichman  *s*  1930
*The Seventh Heart* - Marina Fitch  *f*  1943
*Shackled* - Ray Garton  *h*  2156
*Shade* - David Darke  *h*  1355

*Shade of Pale* - Greg Kihn  *h*  3104
*Shades of Night* - Rick Hautala  *h*  2612
*Shadow Dance* - Douglas Borton  *h*  577
*Shadow Dance* - Jessica Palmer  *h*  4238
*The Shadow Eater* - Adam Lee  *f*  3386
*The Shadow Gate* - Margaret Ball  *f*  317
*Shadow Man* - Dennis Etchison  *h*  1848
*Shadow of the Beast* - Margaret L. Carter  *h*  926
*Shadow Twin* - Dale Hoover  *h*  2762
*Shadow Walkers* - Nina Romberg  *h*  4663
*Shadows* - Jonathan Nasaw  *h*  4068
*Shadows* - Kimberly Rangel  *h*  4472
*Shadows* - John Saul  *h*  4845
*Shadows in the Water* - Kathryn Lasky  *s*  3341
*Shadows on the Hill* - Jackie Cassada  *f*  935
*Shaman Woods* - Morgan Fields  *h*  1931
*Shango* - James Roberto Curtis  *h*  1298
*Shapes* - Steve Vance  *h*  5552
*A Sharpness on the Neck* - Fred Saberhagen  *h*  4774
*Sheep* - Simon Maginn  *h*  3606
*The Shield of Time* - Poul Anderson  *s*  131
*Shifters* - Edward Lee  *h*  3396
*Shock Lines* - Warren Newton Beath  *h*  427
*Shock Radio* - Leigh Clark  *h*  1052
*Shoebag* - Mary James  *f*  2868
*Shoebag Returns* - Mary James  *f*  2869
*Sibs* - F. Paul Wilson  *h*  5898
*Sick* - Jay R. Bonansinga  *h*  571
*Sideshow* - Sheri S. Tepper  *s*  5436
*Signs of Life* - M. John Harrison  *s*  2580
*Silent Scream* - Dan Schmidt  *h*  4883
*The Silent Strength of Stones* - Nina Kiriki Hoffman  *f*  2716
*Silent Witness* - Robert Arthur Smith  *h*  5136
*Silk* - Caitlin R. Kiernan  *h*  3101
*The Silver Kiss* - Annette Curtis Klause  *f*  3163
*The Silver Tree* - Ruth L. Williams  *f*  5822
*Sineater* - Elizabeth Massie  *h*  3668
*Sing for a Gentle Rain* - J. Alison James  *f*  2861
*Sins of the Blood* - Kristine Kathryn Rusch  *h*  4728
*The Sister* - Elleston Trevor  *h*  5484
*Sister, Sister* - Andrew Neiderman  *h*  4091
*Sister to the Rain* - Melisa Michaels  *f*  3887
*The Sixth Dog* - Jane Rice  *h*  4582
*Skeletons* - Al Sarrantonio  *h*  4834
*Skin* - Kathe Koja  *h*  3196
*Skinny Legs and All* - Tom Robbins  *f*  4607
*Skull Session* - Daniel Hecht  *h*  2638
*Skyscape* - Michael Cadnum  *h*  814
*Sleepwalker* - Michael Cadnum  *h*  815
*Sliders: The Novel* - Brad Linaweaver  *s*  3467
*Slippin' into Darkness* - Norman Partridge  *h*  4254
*Slow Funeral* - Rebecca Ore  *f*  4221
*Snowmen* - Jerry Earl Brown  *s*  725
*Sole Survivor* - Dean R. Koontz  *h*  3215
*Solomon's Knife* - Victor Koman  *s*  3200
*Some Enchanted Evening* - Alice Alfonsi  *f*  73
*Some Things Come Back* - Robert Morgan  *h*  4004
*Some Things Never Die* - Robert Morgan  *h*  4005
*Someplace to Be Flying* - Charles de Lint  *f*  1435
*Something Out There* - Ronald Kelly  *h*  3056
*Something Rich and Strange* - Patricia A. McKillip  *f*  3840
*Something Stirs* - Charles L. Grant  *h*  2316
*Something's Alive on the Titanic* - Robert Serling  *h*  4915
*Son of Darkness* - Josepha Sherman  *f*  4990
*Son of Rosemary* - Ira Levin  *h*  3445
*Songs of the Dancing Gods* - Jack L. Chalker  *f*  962
*The Soprano Sorceress* - L.E. Modesitt Jr.  *f*  3938
*Sorcerers of Sodom* - Roger Elwood  *h*  1804
*Soul Catcher* - Colin Kersey  *h*  3081
*Soul Snatchers* - Michael Cecilione  *h*  947
*Soulcatchers* - Jan Lara  *h*  3336
*Souls* - Katina Alexis  *h*  71
*Soulsmith* - Tom Deitz  *f*  1475
*Species* - Yvonne Navarro  *s*  4075
*Specters* - J.M. Dillard  *h*  1555

*Spell Bound* - Trana Mae Simmons  *f*  5061
*Spider-Man: The Venom Factor* - Diane Duane  *s*  1667
*Spires of Spirit* - Gael Baudino  *f*  395
*Spirit Catcher* - Elizabeth Hallam  *f*  2497
*Spirit Crossings* - Claudia Peck  *f*  4275
*Spiritride* - Mark Shepherd  *f*  4981
*Spiritwalk* - Charles de Lint  *f*  1436
*Spook* - Steve Vance  *h*  5553
*Spook Night* - David Robbins  *h*  4603
*Spree* - Lucy Taylor  *h*  5415
*Stage Fright* - Clare McNally  *h*  3858
*Stainless* - Todd Grimson  *h*  2449
*The Stake* - Richard Laymon  *h*  3372
*The Stand: The Complete and Uncut Edition* - Stephen King  *h*  3142
*Star Prey* - Ehren M. Ehly  *h*  1763
*Star Sister* - Juanita Coulson  *s*  1211
*StarGate* - Dean Devlin  *s*  1509
*The Starry Child* - Lynn Hanna  *f*  2540
*The Stars Must Wait* - Keith Laumer  *s*  3346
*Steam* - Jay B. Laws  *h*  3361
*Steel Rose* - Kara Dalkey  *f*  1321
*Stitch* - Mark Morris  *h*  4024
*Stone Angels* - Mike Jefferies  *h*  2889
*The Stone Circle* - Gary Goshgarian  *h*  2285
*Stone Dead* - Ellen Jamison  *h*  2878
*Stoneskin's Revenge* - Tom Deitz  *f*  1476
*The Store* - Bentley Little  *h*  3497
*Storm Knights* - Bill Slavicsek  *f*  5087
*Storytellers* - Julie Anne Parks  *h*  4249
*Stranded* - Camarin Grae  *s*  2295
*Strands of Sunlight* - Gael Baudino  *f*  396
*Strange Angels* - Kathe Koja  *h*  3197
*Street* - Jack Cady  *h*  822
*Street Magic* - Michael Reaves  *f*  4497
*The Streeter* - Scott Ian Barry  *h*  373
*Strum Again?* - Elizabeth Ann Scarborough  *f*  4870
*Stunts* - Charles L. Grant  *h*  2317
*Substitute Teacher* - Jordan Storm  *h*  5314
*The Subtle Knife* - Philip Pullman  *f*  4448
*Succumb* - Ron Dee  *h*  1468
*Suckers* - Anne Billson  *h*  490
*A Sudden Wild Magic* - Diana Wynne Jones  *f*  2950
*The Summer I Shrank My Grandmother* - Elvira Woodruff  *f*  5968
*Summon the Keeper* - Tanya Huff  *f*  2800
*Summoned to Tourney* - Mercedes Lackey  *f*  3299
*The Summoning* - Bentley Little  *h*  3498
*Super Carrier: The Ultimate Secret Weapon* - Peter Albano  *s*  50
*Supernova* - Roger MacBride Allen  *s*  82
*Superstition* - David Ambrose  *h*  90
*Superstitious* - R.L. Stine  *h*  5290
*Sweet Blood* - Pat Graversen  *h*  2337
*Sweet Heart* - Peter James  *h*  2875
*Sweet Revenge* - Jean Simon  *h*  5066
*Sweet William* - Jessica Palmer  *h*  4239
*The Sword of Maiden's Tears* - Rosemary Edghill  *f*  1748
*Sympathy for the Devil* - Holly Lisle  *f*  3488
*Symphony* - Charles L. Grant  *h*  2318
*Symphony* - Adrian Savage  *h*  4847
*The Taking* - Donald Beman  *h*  438
*The Tale of the Body Thief* - Anne Rice  *h*  4576
*Tales From the Crypt: Demon Knight* - Randall Boyll  *h*  617
*Taltos* - Anne Rice  *h*  4577
*Tap, Tap* - David Martin  *h*  3640
*The Tattooed Map* - Barbara Hodgson  *f*  2706
*Tech-Heaven* - Linda Nagata  *s*  4066
*The Templar Treasure* - Katherine Kurtz  *f*  3261
*Tempter* - Nancy A. Collins  *h*  1125
*Terminal Games* - Cole Perriman  *s*  4283
*The Terror* - Graham Masterton  *h*  3679
*Testament of the Dragon* - Margaret Weis  *f*  5729
*The Tetherballs of Bougainville* - Mark Leyner  *f*  3457

*Tex and Molly in the Afterlife* - Richard Grant  *f*  2327

*That's All Folks!* - Greg Snow  *f*  5148

*Them* - William W. Johnstone  *h*  2935

*These Fallen Angels* - Wendy Haley  *h*  2492

*The Thief of Always* - Clive Barker  *h*  347

*The Thing That Darkness Hides* - Robert Morgan  *h*  4006

*The Things That Are Not There* - Robert Morgan  *h*  4007

*Thinning the Predators* - Daina Graziunas  *h*  2341

*The Third Beast* - Peter Loughran  *h*  3527

*Thirst* - Michael Cecilione  *h*  948

*Thirst* - Pyotr Kurtinski  *h*  3253

*Thirst of the Vampire* - T. Lucien Wright  *h*  5988

*The Thirteenth Daughter of the Moon* - Steven Nightingale  *f*  4104

*This Dark Paradise* - Wendy Haley  *h*  2493

*This Symbiotic Fascination* - Charlee Jacob  *h*  2843

*Thor* - Wayne Smith  *h*  5146

*The Thread That Binds the Bones* - Nina Kiriki Hoffman  *f*  2717

*Threshold* - Bill Myers  *s*  4060

*Thrill* - Patricia Wallace  *h*  5624

*The Throat* - Peter Straub  *h*  5332

*Throat Sprockets* - Tim Lucas  *h*  3541

*Through the Ice* - Piers Anthony  *f*  192

*Thunder Road* - Chris Curry  *h*  1296

*Till the End of Time* - Allen Appel  *f*  201

*Time and Chance* - Alan Brennert  *f*  676

*Time and the Clock Mice, Etcetera* - Peter Dickinson  *f*  1527

*Time Blender* - Michael Dorn  *s*  1581

*A Time for Us* - Christine Holden  *f*  2731

*The Time of Feasting* - Mick Farren  *h*  1882

*The Time of the Ghost* - Diana Wynne Jones  *f*  2951

*The Time Tree* - Enid Richemont  *f*  4585

*Tooth and Claw* - Graham Masterton  *h*  3680

*The Tooth Fairy* - Graham Joyce  *f*  2995

*Top Dog* - Jerry Jay Carroll  *f*  915

*Toplin* - Michael McDowell  *h*  3807

*Torment* - Stephen R. George  *h*  2204

*The Totem* - David Morrell  *h*  4012

*Tower of Evil* - James Kisner  *h*  3161

*Towing Jehovah* - James Morrow  *f*  4035

*Trader* - Charles de Lint  *f*  1438

*The Tranquility Alternative* - Allen Steele  *s*  5248

*Travel Far, Pay No Fare* - Anne Lindbergh  *f*  3468

*Treasure Box* - Orson Scott Card  *h*  898

*Trickster* - Chris Curry  *h*  1297

*The Trickster* - Muriel Gray  *h*  2340

*The Trikon Deception* - Ben Bova  *s*  597

*Trinity Grove* - David van Meter Smith  *h*  5112

*The Trinity Paradox* - Kevin J. Anderson  *s*  116

*Troll-Quest* - Rose Estes  *f*  1841

*Troll-Tuken* - Rose Estes  *f*  1842

*Tropic of Orange* - Karen Tei Yamashita  *f*  6009

*Tunnelvision* - R. Patrick Gates  *h*  2162

*Turn of the Cards* - Victor Milan  *s*  3891

*Twilight* - Peter James  *h*  2876

*Twilight Time* - Rick Hautala  *h*  2613

*Twisted Images* - Don D'Ammassa  *h*  1335

*A Two-Edged Sword* - Thomas K. Martin  *f*  3653

*The Two Georges* - Richard Dreyfuss  *f*  1655

*Tyrannosaurus Rex* - J.F. Rivkin  *s*  4597

*The Ultimate Bike Path* - Michael B. Sirota  *s*  5076

*The Ultimate Spider-Man* - Stan Lee  *s*  3403

*The Unbeholden* - Robert Weinberg  *h*  5703

*The Uncanny* - Andrew Klavan  *h*  3164

*The Undead* - Roxanne Longstreet  *h*  3519

*Under the Healing Sign* - Nick O'Donohoe  *f*  4198

*The Undesired Princess and the Enchanted Bunny* - L. Sprague de Camp  *f*  1419

*The Undine* - Michael O'Rourke  *h*  4224

*Unearthed* - Ashley McConnell  *h*  3778

*The Unfinished* - Jay B. Laws  *h*  3362

*Unholy Allies* - Robert Weinberg  *h*  5704

*Unholy Fire* - Whitley Strieber  *h*  5342

*The Unicorn Sonata* - Peter S. Beagle  *f*  412

*Unicorn U.* - Esther Friesner  *f*  2084

*Universal Soldier* - Robert Tine  *s*  5476

*University* - Bentley Little  *h*  3499

*The Unnatural* - David Prill  *h*  4437

*The Unseen* - Joseph A. Citro  *h*  1039

*The Uprising* - Abigail McDaniels  *h*  3785

*User Unfriendly* - Vivian Vande Velde  *f*  5558

*Uwharrie* - Eugene E. Pfaff Jr.  *h*  4309

*Valentine* - S.P. Somtow  *h*  5160

*Vampire$* - John Steakley  *h*  5237

*The Vampire Armand* - Anne Rice  *h*  4578

*Vampire Beat* - Vincent Courtney  *h*  1214

*Vampire Blood* - Kathryn Meyer Griffith  *h*  2441

*Vampire Breath* - R.L. Stine  *h*  5291

*Vampire Bytes* - Linda Grant  *h*  2322

*Vampire Diary: The Embrace* - Robert Weinberg  *h*  5705

*The Vampire Journals* - Traci Briery  *h*  678

*Vampire Junkies* - Norman Spinrad  *h*  5175

*The Vampire Odyssey* - Scott Ciencin  *h*  1032

*The Vampire Papers* - Michael Romkey  *h*  4666

*The Vampire Princess* - Michael Romkey  *h*  4667

*The Vampire Virus* - Michael Romkey  *h*  4668

*Vampires Anonymous* - Jeffrey N. McMahan  *h*  3853

*The Vampire's Apprentice* - Richard Lee Byers  *h*  799

*The Vampire's Beautiful Daughter* - S.P. Somtow  *h*  5161

*The Vanishing* - Marilyn Kaye  *s*  3021

*The Vanishment* - Jonathan Aycliffe  *h*  282

*Vanitas: Escape From Vampire Junction* - S.P. Somtow  *h*  5162

*Vaporetto 13* - Robert Girardi  *h*  2241

*The Venetian's Wife: A Strangely Sensual Tale of a Renaissance Explorer, a Computer, and a Metamorphosis* - Nick Bantock  *f*  336

*Vespers* - Jeff Rovin  *h*  4688

*Violin* - Anne Rice  *h*  4579

*Virago* - Karen Marie Christa Minns  *h*  3915

*Virgin* - Mary Elizabeth Murphy  *h*  4050

*The Virginia Ghost Murders* - Leslie Raymond Sachs  *h*  4778

*Virgins and Martyrs* - Simon Maginn  *h*  3607

*Virgintooth* - Mark Ivanhoe  *h*  2834

*Virtual Destruction* - Kevin J. Anderson  *s*  118

*Virtual Mode* - Piers Anthony  *f*  194

*Virtually Perfect* - Dan Gutman  *s*  2470

*Virtuosity* - Terry Bisson  *s*  507

*Virus* - Graham Watkins  *h*  5632

*Visitors From Oz: The Wild Adventures of Dorothy, the Scarecrow and the Tin Woodman* - Martin Gardner  *f*  2136

*Vodoun* - David Madsen  *h*  3605

*The Voice in the Basement* - T. Chris Martindale  *h*  3657

*Voodoo Child* - Michael Reaves  *h*  4498

*Vyrmin* - Gene Lazuta  *h*  3376

*Wake of the Werewolf* - Geoffrey Caine  *h*  834

*Wake Up Screaming* - Vincent Courtney  *h*  1215

*Waking the Moon* - Elizabeth Hand  *f*  2538

*Walking the Labyrinth* - Lisa Goldstein  *f*  2266

*Walking Wounded* - Robert Devereaux  *h*  1507

*The War Amongst the Angels* - Michael Moorcock  *f*  3986

*The War of Don Emmanuel's Nether Parts* - Louis de Bernieres  *f*  1412

*Wartide* - John Barnes  *f*  359

*Watchers in the Woods* - William W. Johnstone  *h*  2936

*Water Rites* - Guy N. Smith  *h*  5121

*Way Up High* - Roger Zelazny  *f*  6076

*Website* - Ray Garton  *h*  2157

*Weirdos of the Universe, Unite!* - Pamela F. Service  *f*  4921

*The Well* - Michael B. Sirota  *h*  5077

*A Well-Timed Enchantment* - Vivian Vande Velde  *f*  5559

*Wendigo Border* - Catherine Montrose  *h*  3967

*The Werewolf Chronicles* - Traci Briery  *h*  679

*Wes Craven's New Nightmare* - David Bergantino  *h*  460

*Wet Work* - Philip Nutman  *h*  4168

*Wetbones* - John Shirley  *h*  5010

*What Savage Beast* - Peter David  *s*  1390

*What's Wrong with America* - Scott Bradfield  *h*  627

*What's Wrong with Tamara?* - D.A. Fowler  *f*  2025

*What's Wrong with Valerie?* - D.A. Fowler  *h*  2026

*Wheels of Fire* - Mercedes Lackey  *f*  3301

*When Darkness Falls* - Sidney Williams  *h*  5825

*When Shadows Fall* - Brian Scott Smith  *h*  5100

*When the Bough Breaks* - Mercedes Lackey  *f*  3302

*When Wolves Cry* - Chris N. Africa  *f*  41

*Where Does Kissing End?* - Kate Pullinger  *h*  4445

*Where the Chill Waits* - T. Chris Martindale  *h*  3658

*Whipping Boy* - John Byrne  *h*  800

*Whirlwind* - Charles L. Grant  *f*  2320

*Whisper* - Raymond Van Over  *h*  5539

*A Whisper of Wings* - Steven Ray Fulgham  *h*  2091

*The Whispers* - Dan Parkinson  *s*  4247

*White Horse, Dark Dragon* - Robert C. Fleet  *f*  1947

*White Shark* - Peter Benchley  *h*  441

*Who Killed James Dean?* - Warren Newton Beath  *h*  428

*The Wild* - Whitley Strieber  *h*  5343

*Wild Blood* - Nancy A. Collins  *h*  1127

*The Wild Road* - Gabriel King  *f*  3120

*The Wild Wood* - Charles de Lint  *f*  1440

*Wilderness* - Dennis Danvers  *h*  1349

*Wildest Dreams* - Norman Partridge  *h*  4256

*Wilding* - Melanie Tem  *h*  5425

*The Wildlings* - Scott Ciencin  *f*  1034

*The Wilds* - Richard Laymon  *h*  3373

*Wildside* - Steven Gould  *s*  2291

*Wind Chimes* - R.R. Walters  *h*  5625

*Wings* - Terry Pratchett  *s*  4403

*The Winnowing* - Gherbod Fleming  *h*  1950

*Winter Moon* - Dean R. Koontz  *h*  3218

*Winter Tides* - James P. Blaylock  *h*  524

*A Wish and a Dream* - Ingrid Weaver  *f*  5658

*The Wishing Well* - Charles de Lint  *f*  1441

*Witch Baby* - Francesca Lia Block  *f*  552

*Witch-Light* - Nancy Holder  *h*  2734

*The Witch of Maple Park* - Stephanie S. Tolan  *f*  5478

*The Witch Returns* - Phyllis Reynolds Naylor  *f*  4079

*Witch Spell* - Guy N. Smith  *h*  5122

*Witchcraft* - Bill Michaels  *h*  3885

*Witches* - Kathryn Meyer Griffith  *h*  2442

*Witchlight* - Marion Zimmer Bradley  *f*  655

*The Wiz Biz* - Rick Cook  *f*  1160

*A Wizard Abroad* - Diane Duane  *f*  1668

*The Wizardry Cursed* - Rick Cook  *f*  1162

*The Wizardry Quested* - Rick Cook  *f*  1163

*The Wizard's Apprentice* - S.P. Somtow  *f*  5163

*Wizard's Mole* - Brad Strickland  *f*  5337

*WiZrD* - Steve Zell  *h*  6078

*Wolf Flow* - K.W. Jeter  *h*  2918

*Wolf Moon* - John R. Holt  *h*  2749

*Wolfsong* - Traci Briery  *h*  680

*The Wood Wife* - Terri Windling  *f*  5916

*The Woods out Back* - R.A. Salvatore  *f*  4809

*Wordwright* - Tom Deitz  *f*  1478

*The World I Made for Her* - Thomas Moran  *h*  3996

*The World of Darkness: Watcher* - Charles L. Grant  *h*  2321

*The World on Blood* - Jonathan Nasaw  *h*  4069

*World Without End* - Molly Cochran  *f*  1093

*Worst Nightmare* - Ric Meyers  *h*  3883

*Wurm* - Matthew J. Costello  *h*  1202

*Wyrm* - Mark Fabi  *s*  1858

*Wyrm Wolf* - Edo van Belkom  *h*  5535
*The X-Files: Fight the Future* - Chris Carter  *h*  924
*Ye Gods!* - Tom Holt  *f*  2753
*Yellow Moon* - David J. Searls  *h*  4907
*Yours Truly, Jackie the Stripper* - Edo van Belkom  *h*  5536
*Zeus and Co.* - David Lee Jones  *f*  2942
*Zod Wallop* - William Browning Spencer  *h*  5169
*Zombie* - Joyce Carol Oates  *h*  4185

## 21st CENTURY

*12 Monkeys* - Elizabeth Hand  *s*  2532
*Achilles' Choice* - Larry Niven  *s*  4114
*The Alien Years* - Robert Silverberg  *s*  5027
*Amnesia Moon* - Jonathan Lethem  *f*  3438
*Ancient Heavens* - Robert E. Vardeman  *s*  5561
*Ancient Light* - Mary Gentle  *s*  2194
*Antiquities* - John Crowley  *f*  1276
*Arachne* - Lisa Mason  *s*  3661
*Arc d'X* - Steve Erickson  *f*  1835
*The Argus Gambit* - David D. Ross  *s*  4681
*The Armageddon Crazy* - Mick Farren  *s*  1877
*Armed Memory* - Jim Young  *s*  6048
*Arrow From Earth* - F.M. Busby  *s*  782
*Article 23* - William R. Forstchen  *s*  1978
*Bad Voltage* - Jonathan Littell  *s*  3491
*Batman: Knightfall* - Dennis O'Neil  *s*  4215
*Batman Returns* - Craig Shaw Gardner  *s*  2124
*Beggars in Spain* - Nancy Kress  *s*  3237
*Black Milk* - Robert Reed  *s*  4504
*Black Snow Days* - Claudia O'Keefe  *s*  4205
*Black Sun* - Robert Leininger  *s*  3429
*Blade Runner: Replicant Night* - K.W. Jeter  *s*  2907
*The Blood Artists* - Chuck Hogan  *h*  2720
*Blood Siege* - G. Harry Stine  *s*  5278
*Brain Rose* - Nancy Kress  *s*  3239
*Bright Angel* - John Blair  *s*  512
*Brother Termite* - Patricia Anthony  *s*  156
*Brute Orbits* - George Zebrowski  *s*  6059
*Buying Time* - Joe Haldeman  *s*  2487
*Captain Jack Zodiac* - Michael Kandel  *f*  3009
*Carlucci's Heart* - Richard Paul Russo  *s*  4748
*Carmen Miranda's Ghost Is Haunting Space Station Three* - Don Sakers  *s*  4785
*Century 21* - Ewa Kuryluk  *s*  3263
*The Change* - Barry B. Longyear  *s*  3520
*Chaos Mode* - Piers Anthony  *f*  165
*The Child Garden* - Geoff Ryman  *s*  4756
*Children of God* - Mary Doria Russell  *s*  4735
*China Mountain Zhang* - Maureen F. McHugh  *s*  3817
*Christmas Slaughter* - Mark Grant  *s*  2323
*The City, Not Long After* - Pat Murphy  *s*  4051
*City of Pain* - John Terra  *f*  5438
*City of Truth* - James Morrow  *s*  4030
*Clicking Stones* - Nancy Tyler Glenn  *s*  2242
*Climbing Olympus* - Kevin J. Anderson  *s*  102
*Clipjoint* - Wilhelmina Baird  *s*  294
*CoDominium: Revolt on War World* - Jerry Pournelle  *s*  4373
*Contact and Commune* - L. Neil Smith  *s*  5129
*Converse and Conflict* - L. Neil Smith  *s*  5130
*Corrupting Dr. Nice* - John Kessel  *s*  3083
*Crashcourse* - Wilhelmina Baird  *s*  295
*Cross of Blood* - K.W. Jeter  *s*  2909
*Cybernarc* - Robert Cain  *s*  829
*The Cybernetic Shogun* - Victor Milan  *s*  3890
*The Cybernetic Walrus* - Jack L. Chalker  *s*  951
*Cyberweb* - Lisa Mason  *s*  3662
*Dancing on Air* - Nancy Kress  *s*  3240
*Dark Horizon* - K.W. Jeter  *s*  2910
*Dawn's Uncertain Light* - Neal Barrett Jr.  *s*  365
*Days of Atonement* - Walter Jon Williams  *s*  5836
*Dead Boys* - Richard Calder  *s*  836
*Dead Girls* - Richard Calder  *s*  837
*Dead Things* - Richard Calder  *s*  838
*Death Dream* - Ben Bova  *s*  583

*Destroying Angel* - Richard Paul Russo  *s*  4749
*Deus Ex Machina* - J.V. Brummels  *s*  732
*Deus X* - Norman Spinrad  *s*  5171
*The Diamond Age* - Neal Stephenson  *s*  5253
*The Diamond Moon* - Paul Preuss  *s*  4417
*The Dig* - Alan Dean Foster  *s*  2002
*Doomsday Book* - Connie Willis  *s*  5868
*Double Jeopardy* - Aaron Allston  *s*  86
*Dragon's Teeth* - Lee Killough  *s*  3109
*Dream Maker* - W.A. Harbinson  *s*  2542
*Dream-Weaver* - Louise Lawrence  *s*  3359
*Dreams of Gods and Men* - W.T. Quick  *s*  4451
*The Drylands* - Mary Rosenblum  *s*  4678
*The Dying Sun* - Gary L. Blackwood  *s*  511
*Echoes of the Well of Souls* - Jack L. Chalker  *s*  953
*Eclipse Corona* - John Shirley  *s*  5006
*The Eighth Rank* - David D. Ross  *s*  4682
*Elvissey* - Jack Womack  *s*  5957
*Empire Builders* - Ben Bova  *s*  584
*Encounter with Tiber* - Buzz Aldrin  *s*  64
*End Game* - Robert Cain  *s*  830
*The Enigma Variations* - John Maddox Roberts  *s*  4618
*Entoverse* - James P. Hogan  *s*  2724
*Eon* - Greg Bear  *s*  417
*Evil Ascending* - Michael A. Stackpole  *s*  5198
*An Eye for Dark Places* - Norma Marder  *s*  3622
*The Faery Convention* - Brett Davis  *f*  1399
*Fairyland* - Paul J. McAuley  *s*  3711
*Falkenberg's Legion* - Jerry Pournelle  *s*  4374
*The False Mirror* - Alan Dean Foster  *s*  2004
*Father to the Man* - John Gribbin  *s*  2434
*The Feelies* - Mick Farren  *s*  1878
*Fellow Traveller* - William Barton  *s*  380
*Ferman's Devils* - Joe Clifford Faust  *s*  1892
*Find Your Own Truth* - Robert N. Charrette  *f*  972
*A Fire in the Sun* - George Alec Effinger  *s*  1751
*Firelance* - David Mace  *s*  3586
*First Dawn* - Mike Moscoe  *s*  4038
*The First Immortal* - James L. Halperin  *s*  2498
*The Flies of Memory* - Ian Watson  *s*  5635
*The Folk of the Fringe* - Orson Scott Card  *s*  886
*Force of Arms* - G. Harry Stine  *s*  5279
*Freeze Frames* - Katharine Kerr  *s*  3071
*The Fulfillments of Fate and Desire* - Storm Constantine  *s*  1142
*Full Tide of Night* - J.R. Dunn  *s*  1695
*Future Boston* - David Alexander Smith  *s*  5107
*Gaia's Toys* - Rebecca Ore  *s*  4218
*A Gathering Evil* - Michael A. Stackpole  *s*  5201
*Glass Houses* - Laura J. Mixon  *s*  3921
*Go Tell the Spartans* - Jerry Pournelle  *s*  4375
*God's World* - Ian Watson  *s*  5636
*The Gold Coast* - Kim Stanley Robinson  *s*  4632
*Gold Dragon* - Robert Cain  *s*  831
*Gorgon Child* - Steven Barnes  *s*  361
*Griffin's Egg* - Michael Swanwick  *s*  5370
*Growing Up Weightless* - John M. Ford  *s*  1970
*Gun, with Occasional Music* - Jonathan Lethem  *f*  3441
*Guts and Glory* - G. Harry Stine  *s*  5280
*The Hacker and the Ants* - Rudy Rucker  *s*  4704
*Hair of the Dog* - Brett Davis  *f*  1400
*Half the Day Is Night* - Maureen F. McHugh  *s*  3818
*Hard Sell* - Piers Anthony  *s*  173
*The Harvest* - Robert Charles Wilson  *s*  5909
*Hawaiian U.F.O. Aliens* - Mel Gilden  *s*  2226
*He, She and It* - Marge Piercy  *s*  4325
*Homecoming* - David Alexander Smith  *s*  5108
*Homegoing* - Frederik Pohl  *s*  4347
*Hong on the Range* - William F. Wu  *s*  5997
*Hooray for Hellywood* - Esther Friesner  *f*  2077
*Hope of Earth* - Piers Anthony  *s*  175
*I Feel Like the Morning Star* - Gregory Maguire  *s*  3608
*I, Robot: The Illustrated Screenplay* - Harlan Ellison  *s*  1785

*Idoru* - William Gibson  *s*  2218
*Imago* - Octavia E. Butler  *s*  791
*The Imperium Game* - K.D. Wentworth  *s*  5753
*In the Blood* - Lauren Wright Douglas  *s*  1590
*In the Cube* - David Alexander Smith  *s*  5109
*The Infinity Plague* - Robert E. Vardeman  *s*  5564
*Interface Masque* - Shariann Lewitt  *s*  3453
*Into the Deep* - Ken Grimwood  *s*  2450
*The Invisible Company* - Scott Russell Sanders  *s*  4813
*Iris* - William Barton  *s*  381
*Iron Man: The Armor Trap* - Greg Cox  *s*  1227
*A Journal of the Flood Year* - David Ely  *s*  1805
*Judgment Day* - G. Harry Stine  *s*  5281
*Kaduna Memories* - Jack McKinney  *s*  3850
*Kill Crazy* - L.S. Riker  *s*  4590
*A King Beneath the Mountain* - Robert N. Charrette  *f*  973
*A Knight Among Knaves* - Robert N. Charrette  *f*  974
*The Lake at the End of the World* - Caroline MacDonald  *s*  3584
*Land O'Goshen* - Charles McNair  *s*  3855
*Legacy of Earth* - Juanita Coulson  *s*  1209
*Lethal Exposure* - Kevin J. Anderson  *s*  110
*Lethal Interface* - Mel Odom  *s*  4193
*Lifeline* - Kevin J. Anderson  *s*  111
*Light Raid* - Connie Willis  *s*  5870
*Limbo System* - Rick Cook  *s*  1158
*The Long Run* - Daniel Keys Moran  *s*  3995
*The Longest Voyage/Slow Lightning* - Poul Anderson  *s*  130
*Look into the Sun* - James Patrick Kelly  *s*  3047
*Looking for the Mahdi* - N. Lee Wood  *s*  5966
*Lost Days* - Mike Moscoe  *s*  4039
*Lovelock* - Orson Scott Card  *s*  892
*Madlands* - K.W. Jeter  *s*  2913
*Madman Run* - David Robbins  *s*  4600
*Manhattan Transfer* - John E. Stith  *s*  5303
*Manjinn Moon* - Denise Vitola  *s*  5576
*The Marked Man* - Charles Ingrid  *s*  2831
*Mars* - Ben Bova  *s*  586
*Mars—The Red Planet* - Mick Farren  *s*  1880
*The Martian Chronicles* - Ray Bradbury  *s*  621
*The Mask of Loki* - Roger Zelazny  *f*  6071
*Mask of the Phantasm* - Geary Gravel  *s*  2331
*Masters of the Fist* - Edward P. Hughes  *s*  2805
*Matrix Man* - William C. Dietz  *s*  1549
*ME: A Novel of Self Discovery* - Thomas T. Thomas  *s*  5452
*Merlin's Bones* - Fred Saberhagen  *f*  4771
*Metaphase* - Vonda N. McIntyre  *s*  3821
*Mindstar Rising* - Peter F. Hamilton  *s*  2526
*Mining the Oort* - Frederik Pohl  *s*  4349
*Mirror to the Sky* - Mark S. Geston  *s*  2213
*The Missing Matter* - Thomas R. McDonough  *s*  3805
*The Modular Man* - Roger MacBride Allen  *s*  79
*Montezuma Strip* - Alan Dean Foster  *s*  2011
*Moonrise* - Ben Bova  *s*  587
*Moonwar* - Ben Bova  *s*  588
*Murder in the Solid State* - Wil McCarthy  *s*  3764
*Mutant Hell* - Mark Grant  *s*  2324
*The Mutant Season* - Robert Silverberg  *s*  5039
*Mutants Amok* - Mark Grant  *s*  2325
*Mysterious Cairo* - Ed Stark  *f*  5210
*The Nanotech Chronicles* - Michael Flynn  *s*  1964
*Nanoware Time/The Persistence of Vision* - Ian Watson  *s*  5638
*The Nature of Smoke* - Anne Harris  *s*  2559
*Nautilus* - Vonda N. McIntyre  *s*  3823
*The Night Mayor* - Kim Newman  *s*  4099
*The Night Watch* - Sean Stewart  *f*  5274
*No Kidding* - Bruce Brooks  *s*  709
*Of Masques and Martyrs* - Christopher Golden  *h*  2258
*Of the Fall* - Paul J. McAuley  *s*  3713
*On My Way to Paradise* - Dave Wolverton  *s*  5955
*One Man's Universe* - Charles Sheffield  *s*  4961

*Opalite Moon* - Denise Vitola   *f*  5577
*Operation Damocles* - Oscar L. Fellows   *s*  1915
*Orbital Decay* - Allen Steele   *s*  5216
*Other Nature* - Stephanie A. Smith   *s*  5145
*Pacific Edge* - Kim Stanley Robinson   *s*  4634
*Parallelities* - Alan Dean Foster   *s*  2012
*Passion Play* - Sean Stewart   *s*  5276
*The Past of Forever* - Juanita Coulson   *s*  1210
*Paths to Otherwhere* - James P. Hogan   *s*  2728
*Pegasus in Flight* - Anne McCaffrey   *s*  3742
*The Penultimate Truth* - Philip K. Dick   *s*  1522
*Pirates of the Universe* - Terry Bisson   *s*  506
*Predator* - William F. Wu   *s*  5998
*A Prince Among Men* - Robert N. Charrette   *f*  977
*Prince of Mercenaries* - Jerry Pournelle   *s*  4377
*Prince of Sparta* - Jerry Pournelle   *s*  4378
*Prison Ship* - Martin Caidin   *s*  828
*Probe* - Edward M. Lerner   *s*  3437
*A Prophecy of Monsters* - Clark Ashton
    Smith   *h*  5103
*Prophets for the End of Time* - Marcos
    Donnelly   *f*  1577
*Psykosis* - Wilhelmina Baird   *s*  296
*The Pure Cold Light* - Gregory Frost   *s*  2087
*A Quantum Murder* - Peter F. Hamilton   *s*  2527
*Queen City Jazz* - Kathleen Ann Goonan   *s*  2275
*Queen of Angels* - Greg Bear   *s*  423
*The Quick* - Burt Cole   *s*  1113
*The Quicksilver Screen* - Don H. DeBrandt   *s*  1449
*Random Acts of Senseless Violence* - Jack
    Womack   *f*  5959
*Reach* - Edward Gibson   *s*  2216
*A Reasonable World* - Damon Knight   *s*  3188
*Red Genesis* - S.C. Sykes   *s*  5377
*The Rediscovery of Man* - Cordwainer
    Smith   *s*  5106
*Remake* - Connie Willis   *s*  5873
*Resurrection* - Katharine Kerr   *s*  3075
*Return to Rocheworld* - Robert L. Forward   *s*  1989
*Richter 10* - Arthur C. Clarke   *s*  1060
*The Rising of the Moon* - Flynn Connolly   *s*  1135
*River Rats* - Caroline Stevermer   *s*  5267
*Rocheworld* - Robert L. Forward   *s*  1990
*Rule Golden and Double Meaning* - Damon
    Knight   *s*  3189
*Sailor Song* - Ken Kesey   *s*  3082
*Saturn Rukh* - Robert L. Forward   *s*  1991
*Scissors Cut Paper Wrap Stone* - Ian
    McDonald   *s*  3795
*A Season for Slaughter* - David Gerrold   *s*  2211
*Second Contact* - Mike Resnick   *s*  4555
*Second Fire* - Mike Moscoe   *s*  4040
*Secret Realms* - Tom Cool   *s*  1168
*Shadow of the Well of Souls* - Jack L.
    Chalker   *s*  961
*The Sherwood Game* - Esther Friesner   *s*  2082
*The Shockwave Rider* - John Brunner   *s*  736
*Silent Thunder/Universe* - Dean Ing   *s*  2829
*The Singularity Project* - F.M. Busby   *s*  784
*Slow Freight* - F.M. Busby   *s*  785
*Slow River* - Nicola Griffith   *s*  2445
*Snow Crash* - Neal Stephenson   *s*  5254
*Solip: System* - Walter Jon Williams   *s*  5841
*Solo* - Robert Mason   *s*  3665
*Somewhere East of Life* - Brian W. Aldiss   *s*  60
*The Square Deal* - David Drake   *s*  1644
*Star Brothers* - Ben Bova   *s*  594
*Starfarers* - Vonda N. McIntyre   *s*  3824
*The Stars Are Also Fire* - Poul Anderson   *s*  134
*The Stars Must Wait* - Keith Laumer   *s*  3346
*Starsea Invaders: First Action* - G. Harry
    Stine   *s*  5282
*Starstrike* - W. Michael Gear   *s*  2172
*Stranded!* - Warren Norwood   *s*  4164
*Strange Tales From the Nile Empire* - Greg
    Farshtey   *f*  1889
*Stranger in a Strange Land* - Robert A.
    Heinlein   *s*  2649
*Streets of Blood* - Carl Sargent   *f*  4821

*Strings* - Dave Duncan   *s*  1689
*The Struggle* - Jerry Ahern   *s*  44
*Subterranean Gallery* - Richard Paul Russo   *s*  4750
*Summerland* - L. Dean James   *f*  2865
*Sunstroke* - David Kagan   *s*  2999
*Svaha* - Charles de Lint   *s*  1437
*Synners* - Pat Cadigan   *s*  808
*Systems* - W.T. Quick   *s*  4452
*Tech-Heaven* - Linda Nagata   *s*  4066
*Temporary Agency* - Rachel Pollack   *f*  4360
*Terminal Cafe* - Ian McDonald   *s*  3797
*Terraplane* - Jack Womack   *s*  5960
*This Side of Judgment* - J.R. Dunn   *s*  1696
*A Thunder on Neptune* - Gordon Eklund   *s*  1768
*Thunder Strike!* - Michael McCollum   *s*  3772
*A Time for Dragons* - Gary Gentile   *s*  2193
*To Say Nothing of the Dog* - Connie Willis   *s*  5874
*Transition* - Vonda N. McIntyre   *s*  3825
*Tubular Android Superheroes* - Mel Gilden   *s*  2228
*Two That Came True* - Judith Moffett   *s*  3945
*The Ugly Little Boy* - Isaac Asimov   *s*  250
*Under Alien Stars* - Pamela F. Service   *s*  4919
*Unquenchable Fire* - Rachel Pollack   *f*  4361
*Virtual Death* - Shale Aaron   *s*  5
*The Voice of Cepheus* - Ken Appleby   *s*  202
*The Wall Around Eden* - Joan Slonczewski   *s*  5092
*Warrior* - William F. Wu   *s*  6000
*Warrior Shield* - G. Harry Stine   *s*  5283
*Weapon* - Robert Mason   *s*  3666
*When Dreams Collide* - Wm. Mark
    Simmons   *f*  5063
*The World Next Door* - Brad Ferguson   *s*  1924
*A World of Difference* - Harry Turtledove   *s*  5514
*The Zap Gun* - Philip K. Dick   *s*  1523

**2000s**
*Angel Souls and Devil Hearts* - Christopher
    Golden   *h*  2255
*Armageddon Summer* - Jane Yolen   *s*  6028
*Beachhead* - Jack Williamson   *s*  5859
*Bloodwars* - Brian Lumley   *h*  3547
*Blue Limbo* - Terrence M. Green   *s*  2377
*Cosm* - Gregory Benford   *s*  444
*The Deus Machine* - Pierre Ouellette   *h*  4232
*Dust* - Charles Pellegrino   *h*  4279
*Einstein's Bridge* - John Cramer   *s*  1244
*Evolution's Shore* - Ian McDonald   *s*  3792
*The Family Tree* - Sheri S. Tepper   *s*  5429
*Firestar* - Michael Flynn   *s*  1962
*The Gatekeepers* - Daniel Graham Jr.   *s*  2301
*The Ghost From the Grand Banks* - Arthur C.
    Clarke   *s*  1056
*Gibbon's Decline and Fall* - Sheri S.
    Tepper   *s*  5430
*Headcrash* - Bruce Bethke   *s*  483
*Hocus Pocus or, What's the Hurry, Son?* - Kurt
    Vonnegut Jr.   *s*  5593
*How to Mutate and Take Over the World* - R.U.
    Sirius   *s*  5074
*Jupiter's Daughter* - Tom Hyman   *s*  2820
*Kamikaze L'Amour* - Richard Kadrey   *s*  2998
*The Last Aerie* - Brian Lumley   *h*  3557
*Lives of the Monster Dogs* - Kirsten Bakis   *s*  305
*The Multiplex Man* - James P. Hogan   *s*  2727
*Outnumbering the Dead* - Frederik Pohl   *s*  4352
*Precious Blood* - Pat Graversen   *s*  2336
*Psychamok* - Brian Lumley   *h*  3561
*The Puppet Masters* - Robert A. Heinlein   *s*  2646
*Rage of Spirits* - Noel Hynd   *h*  2824
*Rewind* - Terry England   *s*  1825
*Rogue Star* - Michael Flynn   *s*  1965
*The Scathach and the Maeve's Daughter* - Mary
    Alexander Walker   *f*  5618
*The Season of Passage* - Christopher Pike   *h*  4331
*The Secret Oceans* - Betty Ballantine   *s*  318
*Shangri-La: The Return to the World of Lost Horizon* -
    Eleanor Cooney   *f*  1169
*The Shift* - George Foy   *s*  2033
*Supernova* - Roger MacBride Allen   *s*  82

*Target Earth* - Steve Perry   *s*  4301
*Terminal Logic* - Jefferson Scott   *s*  4893
*Thoughts of God* - Michael Kanaly   *s*  3007
*Through the Arc of the Rain Forest* - Karen Tei
    Yamashita   *f*  6008
*Timecop* - S.D. Perry   *s*  4286
*Timequake* - Kurt Vonnegut Jr.   *s*  5594
*Timeshare* - Joshua Dann   *s*  1344
*Titan* - Stephen Baxter   *s*  405
*Tomorrow and Tomorrow* - Charles
    Sheffield   *s*  4966
*Virtual Girl* - Amy Thomson   *s*  5462
*Virtual Light* - William Gibson   *s*  2219
*Walker between the Worlds* - Diane
    DesRochers   *f*  1499
*Why Do Birds* - Damon Knight   *s*  3190

**2010s**
*Beyond Eden* - J.M. Morgan   *s*  3999
*The Bones of Time* - Kathleen Ann Goonan   *s*  2273
*The Book of Water* - Marjorie Bradley
    Kellogg   *f*  3045
*Brother to Dragons* - Charles Sheffield   *s*  4949
*Burn* - Bill Ransom   *s*  4476
*Cold Allies* - Patricia Anthony   *s*  157
*A Deeper Sea* - Alexander Jablokov   *s*  2838
*Earthling* - Tony Daniel   *s*  1336
*End of an Era* - Robert J. Sawyer   *s*  4853
*Evil Triumphant* - Michael A. Stackpole   *s*  5199
*Fallen Angels* - Larry Niven   *s*  4120
*The Fugitive Stars* - Daniel Ransom   *s*  4479
*The Ghost From the Grand Banks* - Arthur C.
    Clarke   *s*  1056
*Illegal Alien* - Robert J. Sawyer   *s*  4858
*The Immortals* - Tracy Hickman   *s*  2681
*Isaac Asimov's I-Bots* - Steve Perry   *s*  4297
*The Jericho Iteration* - Allen Steele   *s*  5242
*Leap Point* - Kay Kenyon   *s*  3063
*The Pleistocene Redemption* - Dan
    Gallagher   *s*  2107
*The President's Astrologer* - Barbara
    Shafferman   *f*  4926
*seaQuest DSV: Fire Below* - Matthew J.
    Costello   *s*  1201
*seaQuest DSV: The Novel* - Diane Duane   *s*  1666
*Second Star* - Dana Stabenow   *s*  5188
*Silicon Embrace* - John Shirley   *s*  5009
*The Sparrow* - Mary Doria Russell   *s*  4736
*The Terminal Experiment* - Robert J.
    Sawyer   *s*  4860
*Traitors from Within* - R.A. Montgomery   *s*  3966
*ViraVax* - Bill Ransom   *s*  4478
*Web of Futures* - Jefferson P. Swycaffer   *f*  5376

**2020s**
*Above the Lower Sky* - Tom Deitz   *f*  1469
*Aftermath* - Charles Sheffield   *s*  4947
*Assemblers of Infinity* - Kevin J. Anderson   *s*  100
*Blade Runner 2: The Edge of Human* - K.W.
    Jeter   *s*  2906
*The Centurion's Empire* - Sean McMullen   *s*  3854
*The Children of Men* - P.D. James   *f*  2870
*Crygender* - Thomas T. Thomas   *s*  5451
*Cytheria* - Richard Calder   *s*  835
*A Deeper Sea* - Alexander Jablokov   *s*  2838
*F.R.E.E.Lancers* - Mel Odom   *s*  4191
*Future Eden* - J.M. Morgan   *s*  4001
*Haven* - David Peters   *f*  4304
*Infectress* - Tom Cool   *s*  1167
*Innerverse* - John DeChancie   *s*  1458
*Isle of Woman* - Piers Anthony   *f*  178
*Johnny Mnemonic* - Terry Bisson   *s*  505
*Lunar Descent* - Allen Steele   *s*  5245
*The Misconceiver* - Lucy Ferriss   *s*  1929
*Moonfall* - Jack McDevitt   *s*  3789
*Mother of Storms* - John Barnes   *s*  354
*Mutant Legacy* - Karen Haber   *s*  2474
*Mutant Star* - Karen Haber   *s*  2475
*Orbital Resonance* - John Barnes   *s*  356

*Parable of the Sower* - Octavia E. Butler　*s*　792
*Psi-Man* - David Peters　*s*　4305
*The Ragged World: A Novel of the Hefn on Earth* -
　Judith Moffett　*s*　3943
*Red Mars* - Kim Stanley Robinson　*s*　4635
*Red Planet Run* - Dana Stabenow　*s*　5187
*Red Shadows* - Yvonne Navarro　*s*　4074
*Rim: A Novel of Virtual Reality* - Alexander
　Besher　*s*　475
*Sheltered Lives* - Charles Oberndorf　*s*　4188
*Starseed* - Spider Robinson　*s*　4643
*Toward the End of Time* - John Updike　*s*　5531
*The Turing Option* - Harry Harrison　*s*　2579
*Vanishing Point* - Michaela Roessner　*s*　4652
*Whiteout* - Sage Walker　*s*　5619

**2030s**
*The Bones of Time* - Kathleen Ann Goonan　*s*　2273
*Charmed* - Marilyn Singer　*f*　5070
*Demolition Man* - Richard Osborne　*s*　4229
*Desert Fire* - David Alexander　*s*　65
*Destination: Showdown* - Jake Davis　*s*　1405
*Earth* - David Brin　*s*　685
*Finger of God* - Michael Kasner　*s*　3013
*Firedance* - Steven Barnes　*s*　360
*Heavy Weather* - Bruce Sterling　*s*　5258
*In the Wrong Hands* - Edward Gibson　*s*　2215
*Labyrinth of Night* - Allen Steele　*s*　5244
*The Last Rangers* - Jake Davis　*s*　1406
*Mars Underground* - William Hartmann　*s*　2584
*The Martian Chronicles* - Ray Bradbury　*s*　622
*Maximum Light* - Nancy Kress　*s*　3241
*Mir* - Alexander Besher　*s*　474
*Nimbus* - Alexander Jablokov　*s*　2839
*Nomad* - David Alexander　*s*　66
*Overshoot* - Mona Clee　*s*　1075
*Pallas* - L. Neil Smith　*s*　5132
*Parable of the Talents* - Octavia E. Butler　*s*　793
*See You Later* - Christopher Pike　*f*　4332
*The Seraphim Rising* - Elisabeth De Vos　*s*　1442
*Sewer, Gas & Electric* - Matt Ruff　*s*　4708
*The Silicon Man* - Charles Platt　*s*　4343
*Time, Like an Ever-Rolling Stream* - Judith
　Moffett　*s*　3944
*Timemaster* - Robert L. Forward　*s*　1992
*The Trinity Vector* - Steve Perry　*s*　4302
*White Queen* - Gwyneth Jones　*s*　2955

**2040s**
*2041: Twelve Short Stories about the Future by Top*
　*Science Fiction Writers* - Jane Yolen　*s*　6027
*Brain Child* - George Turner　*s*　5491
*Clarke County, Space* - Allen Steele　*s*　5241
*Deep Trek* - James Axler　*s*　278
*Distraction* - Bruce Sterling　*s*　5256
*The Fifth Sacred Thing* - Starhawk　*f*　5209
*Forever Peace* - Joe Haldeman　*s*　2488
*Harmony* - Marjorie Bradley Kellogg　*s*　3046
*High Aztec* - Ernest Hogan　*s*　2722
*The Iron Bridge* - David Morse　*s*　4036
*Lightpaths* - Howard V. Hendrix　*s*　2660
*Man Plus* - Frederik Pohl　*s*　4348
*Martian Rainbow* - Robert L. Forward　*s*　1987
*Mutineers' Moon* - David Weber　*s*　5677
*Semper Mars* - Ian Douglas　*s*　1585
*Sparrowhawk* - Thomas A. Easton　*s*　1725
*Standing Wave* - Howard V. Hendrix　*s*　2661
*The Whispers* - Dan Parkinson　*s*　4247

**2050s**
*2XS* - Nigel Findley　*f*　1935
*Beyond the Pale* - Jack Koke　*f*　3198
*Blood Sport* - Lisa Smedman　*f*　5096
*The California Voodoo Game* - Larry Niven　*s*　4117
*Changeling* - Christopher Kubasik　*f*　3245
*Choose Your Enemies Carefully* - Robert N.
　Charrette　*s*　971
*Circle of One* - Eric James Fullilove　*s*　2092
*The Dazzle of Day* - Molly Gloss　*s*　2243
*Distress* - Greg Egan　*s*　1760

*Emperors of the Twilight* - S. Andrew
　Swann　*s*　5362
*Fade to Black* - Nyx Smith　*s*　5134
*Flying to Valhalla* - Charles Pellegrino　*s*　4280
*Forests of the Night* - S. Andrew Swann　*s*　5363
*Freeware* - Rudy Rucker　*s*　4703
*Headhunters* - Mel Odom　*s*　4192
*House of the Sun* - Nigel Findley　*s*　1936
*In the Heart of the Valley of Love* - Cynthia
　Kadohata　*s*　2997
*Into the Shadows* - Jordan K. Weisman　*f*　5731
*Jack the Bodiless* - Julian May　*s*　3698
*Kalifornia* - Marc Laidlaw　*s*　3311
*Never Deal with a Dragon* - Robert N.
　Charrette　*s*　975
*Never Trust an Elf* - Robert N. Charrette　*f*　976
*Night's Pawn* - Tom Dowd　*s*　1591
*Permutation City* - Greg Egan　*s*　1761
*Shadowboxer* - Nick Pollotta　*s*　4366
*Specters of the Dawn* - S. Andrew Swann　*s*　5368
*The Stranger* - Eric James Fullilove　*s*　2093
*Striper Assassin* - Nyx Smith　*f*　5135
*Wolf and Raven* - Michael A. Stackpole　*f*　5207

**2060s**
*/* - Greg Bear　*s*　413
*Alien Tongue* - Stephen Leigh　*s*　3424
*Flying to Valhalla* - Charles Pellegrino　*s*　4280
*The Ganymede Club* - Charles Sheffield　*s*　4955
*The Illegal Rebirth of Billy the Kid* - Rebecca
　Ore　*s*　4220
*The Law of War* - William Shatner　*s*　4931
*Man o' War* - William Shatner　*s*　4932
*Quarantine* - Greg Egan　*s*　1762
*The Robin Hood Ambush* - William F. Wu　*s*　5999
*The Sparrow* - Mary Doria Russell　*s*　4736
*Starmind* - Spider Robinson　*s*　4642

**2070s**
*The Ganymede Club* - Charles Sheffield　*s*　4955
*The Last Dancer* - Daniel Keys Moran　*s*　3994
*Marooned on Eden* - Robert L. Forward　*s*　1986
*The Moon Is a Harsh Mistress* - Robert A.
　Heinlein　*s*　2645
*Nothing Sacred* - Elizabeth Ann
　Scarborough　*f*　4867
*Ocean under the Ice* - Robert L. Forward　*s*　1988

**2080s**
*Ark Liberty* - Will Bradley　*s*　656
*Circuit of Heaven* - Dennis Danvers　*s*　1348
*Flare* - Roger Zelazny　*s*　6065
*Greenhouse* - Thomas A. Easton　*s*　1723

**2090s**
*The Bushido Incident* - Betty Anne
　Crawford　*s*　1248
*Cold as Ice* - Charles Sheffield　*s*　4950
*The Digital Effect* - Steve Perry　*s*　4295
*Fortress on the Sun* - Paul Cook　*s*　1157
*Holy Fire* - Bruce Sterling　*s*　5259
*The Killing Star* - Charles Pellegrino　*s*　4281
*A King of Infinite Space* - Allen Steele　*s*　5243
*The Quiet Pools* - Michael P. Kube-
　McDowell　*s*　3249
*Return to Isis* - Jean Stewart　*s*　5268
*The Specialist* - Wynne Whiteford　*s*　5788
*Starplex* - Robert J. Sawyer　*s*　4859
*Tooth: A Tale of Love and Death in Paradox* - Novak
　Kruger　*h*　3244
*Woodsman* - Thomas A. Easton　*s*　1727

**22nd CENTURY**

*Afrikorps* - Bill Dolan　*s*　1566
*After the Blue* - Russel Like　*s*　3465
*Beggars and Choosers* - Nancy Kress　*s*　3236
*Beggars Ride* - Nancy Kress　*s*　3238
*Beowulf's Children* - Larry Niven　*s*　4116
*Blue Mars* - Kim Stanley Robinson　*s*　4629

*Bright Messengers* - Gentry Lee　*s*　3398
*Cathouse* - Dean Ing　*s*　2828
*Challenger's Hope* - David Feintuch　*s*　1899
*Cobra Curse* - Bill Dolan　*s*　1567
*Crisis on Doona* - Anne McCaffrey　*s*　3723
*Cyber Way* - Alan Dean Foster　*s*　2000
*Dark Genesis* - J. Gregory Keyes　*s*　3096
*The Dechronization of Sam Magruder* - George
　Gaylord Simpson　*s*　5067
*Delta Pavonis* - Eric Kotani　*s*　3221
*Diamond Mask: A Novel* - Julian May　*s*　3697
*Donnerjack* - Roger Zelazny　*s*　6063
*Double Planet* - John Gribbin　*s*　2433
*Dream of Glass* - Jean Mark Gawron　*s*　2163
*The Ear, the Eye, and the Arm* - Nancy
　Farmer　*f*　1867
*Earth 2* - Melissa Crandall　*s*　1247
*Earthfall* - Jerry Earl Brown　*s*　724
*The Faces of Ceti* - Mary Caraker　*s*　877
*The First Duelist* - Rutledge Etheridge　*s*　1849
*Flatlander* - Larry Niven　*s*　4121
*Go Tell the Spartans* - Jerry Pournelle　*s*　4375
*Golden Fleece* - Robert J. Sawyer　*s*　4857
*Green Mars* - Kim Stanley Robinson　*s*　4633
*The Hammer of God* - Arthur C. Clarke　*s*　1057
*Heads* - Greg Bear　*s*　419
*Hide and Seek* - Paul Preuss　*s*　4418
*High Steel* - Jack C. Haldeman II　*s*　2486
*Hot Sky at Midnight* - Robert Silverberg　*s*　5032
*Infinity Hold* - Barry B. Longyear　*s*　3522
*Inherit the Earth* - Brian Stableford　*s*　5193
*Invitation to the Game* - Monica Hughes　*s*　2807
*Iron Horse* - Bill Dolan　*s*　1568
*Journals of the Plague Years* - Norman
　Spinrad　*s*　5172
*Judge Dredd* - Neal Barrett Jr.　*s*　366
*Kaleidoscope Century* - John Barnes　*s*　352
*Kill Station* - Diane Duane　*s*　1664
*Kirinyaga: A Fable of Utopia* - Mike
　Resnick　*s*　4548
*L.A. Strike* - David Robbins　*s*　4599
*Last Refuge* - Elizabeth Ann Scarborough　*f*　4866
*Lethe* - Tricia Sullivan　*s*　5354
*Living Real* - James C. Bassett　*s*　386
*Magnificat* - Julian May　*s*　3699
*The Medusa Encounter* - Paul Preuss　*s*　4419
*Memorymakers* - Brian Herbert　*s*　2665
*The Middle Kingdom* - David Wingrove　*s*　5919
*Midshipman's Hope* - David Feintuch　*s*　1901
*Mind Snare* - Gayle Greeno　*s*　2422
*Mindblast* - Diane Duane　*s*　1665
*Mother of Demons* - Eric Flint　*s*　1956
*Moving Mars* - Greg Bear　*s*　421
*The Mummy!: A Tale of the Twenty-Second Century* -
　Jane Webb Loudon　*h*　3526
*Neptune Crossing* - Jeffrey A. Carver　*s*　933
*Nightshade* - Jack Butler　*s*　789
*North Wind* - Gwyneth Jones　*s*　2953
*Pastwatch: The Redemption of Christopher Columbus* -
　Orson Scott Card　*s*　895
*The Positronic Man* - Isaac Asimov　*s*　249
*Prince of Sparta* - Jerry Pournelle　*s*　4378
*Proteus in the Underworld* - Charles
　Sheffield　*s*　4962
*Proteus Unbound* - Charles Sheffield　*s*　4963
*Rama II* - Arthur C. Clarke　*s*　1058
*Ring* - Stephen Baxter　*s*　402
*Ring of Swords* - Eleanor Arnason　*s*　210
*Saturn's Child* - Nichelle Nichols　*s*　4101
*A Second Infinity* - Michael D. Weaver　*s*　5660
*The Shining Ones* - Paul Preuss　*s*　4421
*The Six Families* - Nancy Holder　*s*　2733
*A Small Colonial War* - Robert Frezza　*s*　2054
*Spartan Run* - David Robbins　*s*　4602
*The Starlight Crystal* - Christopher Pike　*s*　4333
*Steelheart* - William C. Dietz　*s*　1552
*Stranger Suns* - George Zebrowski　*s*　6060
*The Swords of Zinjaban* - L. Sprague de
　Camp　*s*　1418

*Tek Money* - William Shatner  s  4935
*Tek Net* - William Shatner  s  4936
*Tek Power* - William Shatner  s  4937
*Tek Vengeance* - William Shatner  s  4938
*TekLab* - William Shatner  s  4939
*TekLords* - William Shatner  s  4940
*TekWar* - William Shatner  s  4941
*Tower of the Gods* - Thomas A. Easton  s  1726
*Trouble and Her Friends* - Melissa Scott  s  4902
*Vengeance Strike* - David Robbins  s  4604
*The Voices of Heaven* - Frederik Pohl  s  4356
*What Savage Beast* - Peter David  s  1390
*When Heaven Fell* - William Barton  s  383
*White Rhino* - Bill Dolan  s  1569
*Wildlife* - James Patrick Kelly  s  3049
*Worlds Enough and Time* - Joe Haldeman  s  2491
*Yellowstone Run* - David Robbins  s  4605
*Bloom* - Wil McCarthy  s  3761

### 23rd CENTURY

*Alpha Centauri* - William Barton  s  378
*Ancient Heavens* - Robert E. Vardeman  s  5561
*Anvil of Stars* - Greg Bear  s  414
*The Ashes of Eden* - William Shatner  s  4927
*Assignment: Eternity* - Greg Cox  s  1225
*Beneath the Tree of Heaven* - David
  Wingrove  s  5917
*Best Destiny* - Diane Carey  s  900
*Blue Mars* - Kim Stanley Robinson  s  4629
*The Broken Wheel* - David Wingrove  s  5918
*Burster* - Michael Capobianco  s  876
*The City on the Edge of Forever* - Harlan
  Ellison  s  1784
*Crossroad* - Barbara Hambly  s  2501
*Day of the Dead* - Neil Gaiman  s  2102
*The Dazzle of Day* - Molly Gloss  s  2243
*Death's Head* - Mel Keegan  s  3029
*Delta Search* - William Shatner  s  4930
*The Disinherited* - Peter David  s  1381
*Doctor's Orders* - Diane Duane  s  1659
*Enemy Unseen* - V.E. Mitchell  s  3918
*The Engines of God* - Jack McDevitt  s  3787
*The Exile Kiss* - George Alec Effinger  s  1750
*Faraday's Orphans* - N. Lee Wood  s  5965
*The Fearful Summons* - Denny Martin Flinn  s  1954
*Federation* - Judith Reeves-Stevens  s  4511
*First Frontier* - Diane Carey  s  902
*First Strike* - Diane Carey  s  903
*Fisherman's Hope* - David Feintuch  s  1900
*A Flag Full of Stars* - Brad Ferguson  s  1922
*Flare Star* - Paula E. Downing  s  1594
*The Fortunate Fall* - Raphael Carter  s  927
*FreeMaster* - Kris Jensen  s  2897
*The Garden of Rama* - Arthur C. Clarke  s  1055
*A History Maker* - Alasdair Gray  s  2338
*Inconstant Star* - Poul Anderson  s  129
*The Joy Machine* - James Gunn  s  2458
*The Kobayashi Maru* - Julia Ecklar  s  1728
*Legacy* - Steve White  s  5785
*Mentor* - Kris Jensen  s  2898
*Mind Meld* - John Vornholt  s  5596
*Murasaki* - Robert Silverberg  s  5038
*Nemesis* - Isaac Asimov  s  247
*Nightside City* - Lawrence Watt-Evans  s  5644
*People of the Sky* - Clare Bell  s  431
*Personal Agendas* - Al Sarrantonio  s  4833
*Polar City Blues* - Katharine Kerr  s  3073
*The Positronic Man* - Isaac Asimov  s  249
*Prime Directive* - Judith Reeves-Stevens  s  4514
*Probe* - Margaret Wander Bonanno  s  569
*Relics* - Michael Jan Friedman  s  2066
*Renegade* - Gene DeWeese  s  1511
*Requiem* - Michael Jan Friedman  s  2067
*The Rift* - Peter David  s  1386
*Rules of Engagement* - Peter Morwood  s  4037
*The Sails of Tau Ceti* - Michael McCollum  s  3771
*The Samurai Wizard* - Simon Hawke  f  2623

*Sanctuary* - John Vornholt  s  5597
*Sarek* - A.C. Crispin  s  1260
*Satellite Night News* - Jack Hopkins  s  2770
*Seeds of Destiny* - Thomas A. Easton  s  1724
*The Shadow Within* - Jeanne Cavelos  s  944
*Shadows on the Sun* - Michael Jan
  Friedman  s  2069
*Ship of the Line* - Diane Carey  s  904
*Star Trek VI: The Undiscovered Country* - J.M.
  Dillard  s  1556
*Star Trek: The Classic Episodes 1* - James
  Blish  s  526
*Star Trek: The Classic Episodes 2* - James
  Blish  s  527
*Star Trek: The Classic Episodes 3* - James
  Blish  s  528
*Star Trek: The Lost Years* - J.M. Dillard  s  1557
*Star Wreck II: The Attack of the Jargonites* - Leah
  Rewolinski  s  4563
*Star Wreck: The Generation Gap* - Leah
  Rewolinski  s  4566
*Starborne* - Robert Silverberg  s  5042
*Starfleet Academy* - Diane Carey  s  905
*Steel Beach* - John Varley  s  5566
*The Stone Within* - David Wingrove  s  5920
*Stranded!* - Warren Norwood  s  4164
*Take Back Plenty* - Colin Greenland  s  2419
*Thirdspace* - Peter David  s  1387
*To Dream in the City of Sorrows* - Kathryn M.
  Drennan  s  1654
*The Touch of Your Shadow, the Whisper of Your Name*
  - Neal Barrett Jr.  s  367
*Traitor Winds* - L.A. Graf  s  2298
*Voices* - John Vornholt  s  5598
*Voices of Hope* - David Feintuch  s  1903
*Vulcan's Forge* - Susan Shwartz  s  5019
*Vulcan's Glory* - D.C. Fontana  s  1967
*War Dragons* - L.A. Graf  s  2299
*War Dragons* - L.A. Graf  s  2299
*White Moon, Red Dragon* - David
  Wingrove  s  5921
*Windows on a Lost World* - V.E. Mitchell  s  3920
*A Woman of the Iron People* - Eleanor
  Arnason  s  211

### 24th CENTURY

*All Good Things. . .* - Michael Jan Friedman  s  2061
*Ark Liberty* - Will Bradley  s  656
*Armageddon Sky* - L.A. Graf  s  2296
*Avenger* - William Shatner  s  4928
*Away Is a Strange Place to Be* - H.M.
  Hoover  s  2763
*Balance of Power* - Dafydd ab Hugh  s  7
*Bloodletter* - K.W. Jeter  s  2908
*Call to Arms* - Diane Carey  s  901
*A Call to Darkness* - Michael Jan Friedman  s  2062
*Carve the Sky* - Alexander Jablokov  s  2836
*Chains of Command* - Bill McCay  s  3767
*The Chance Factor* - Diana G. Gallagher  s  2109
*Chrysalis* - David Niall Wilson  s  5880
*Crossover* - Michael Jan Friedman  s  2063
*Cyteen* - C.J. Cherryh  s  984
*Dark Mirror* - Diane Duane  s  1658
*Debtors' Planet* - William R. Thompson  s  5457
*The Demolished Man* - Alfred Bester  s  476
*Devil in the Sky* - Greg Cox  s  1226
*The Devil's Heart* - Carmen Carter  s  922
*Doomsday World* - Carmen Carter  s  923
*Dragon's Honor* - Kij Johnson  s  2922
*Earthsong* - Suzette Haden Elgin  s  1769
*End Game* - Peter David  s  1382
*The Escape* - Dean Wesley Smith  s  5113
*The Face of the Waters* - Robert Silverberg  s  5029
*Fallen Heroes* - Dafydd ab Hugh  s  8
*Federation* - Judith Reeves-Stevens  s  4511
*The Final Fury* - Dafydd ab Hugh  s  9

*Fire on the Border* - Kevin O'Donnell Jr.  s  4194
*Guises of the Mind* - Rebecca Neason  s  4081
*Hellburner* - C.J. Cherryh  s  996
*Her Klingon Soul* - Michael Jan Friedman  s  2064
*Imbalance* - V.E. Mitchell  s  3919
*Imzadi* - Peter David  s  1383
*Insurrection* - J.M. Dillard  s  1554
*Intellivore* - Diane Duane  s  1663
*Kahless* - Michael Jan Friedman  s  2065
*The Last Stand* - Brad Ferguson  s  1923
*The Light in Exile* - Cheryl J. Franklin  s  2038
*The Madness Season* - C.S. Friedman  s  2058
*Man-Kzin Wars IV* - Larry Niven  s  4124
*Metamorphosis* - Jean Lorrah  s  3524
*Mosaic* - Jeri Taylor  s  5403
*The Mountain Walks* - Roland J. Green  s  2349
*Muddle Earth* - John Brunner  s  735
*Other* - Gordon R. Dickson  s  1538
*Outbanker* - Timothy A. Madden  s  3603
*The Paratwa* - Christopher Hinz  s  2691
*Partisan* - S. Andrew Swann  s  5365
*Pathways* - Jeri Taylor  s  5404
*Phylum Monsters* - Hayford Peirce  s  4276
*Profiteer* - S. Andrew Swann  s  5366
*Q-in-Law* - Peter David  s  1384
*Q-Space* - Greg Cox  s  1228
*Q-Squared* - Peter David  s  1385
*Q-Zone* - Greg Cox  s  1229
*Ragnarok* - Nathan Archer  s  206
*Relics* - Michael Jan Friedman  s  2066
*Requiem* - Michael Jan Friedman  s  2067
*The Return* - William Shatner  s  4933
*Reunion* - Michael Jan Friedman  s  2068
*Revolutionary* - S. Andrew Swann  s  5367
*Rimrunners* - C.J. Cherryh  s  1001
*Rinn's Star* - Paula E. Downing  s  1719
*River of Dust* - Alexander Jablokov  s  2840
*Ship of the Line* - Diane Carey  s  904
*The Snows of Jaspre* - Mary Caraker  s  878
*The Soldiers of Fear* - Dean Wesley Smith  s  5115
*Spectre* - William Shatner  s  4934
*Star Wreck III: Time Warped* - Leah
  Rewolinski  s  4564
*Star Wreck IV: Live Long and Profit* - Leah
  Rewolinski  s  4565
*The Stars My Destination* - Alfred Bester  s  478
*Time's Enemy* - L.A. Graf  s  2297
*Treks Not Taken: What if Stephen King, Anne Rice,*
  *Bret Easton Ellis, and Other Literary Greats Had*
  *Written Episodes of Star Trek: The Next*
  *Generation?* - Steven R. Boyett  s  607
*Triangle: Imzadi II* - Peter David  s  1388
*Vendetta* - Peter David  s  1389
*Vengeance* - Dafydd ab Hugh  s  10
*Voyage of the Star Wolf* - David Gerrold  s  2212
*Warped* - K.W. Jeter  s  2917
*Worf's First Adventure* - Peter David  s  1391
*Young Bleys* - Gordon R. Dickson  s  1540

### 25th CENTURY

*Cannon's Orb* - L. Warren Douglas  s  1586
*The Children's Hour* - Jerry Pournelle  s  4372
*Commitment Hour* - James Alan Gardner  s  2134
*Drakon* - S.M. Stirling  s  5294
*The Ecolitan Operation* - L.E. Modesitt Jr.  s  3928
*The Ecologic Secession* - L.E. Modesitt Jr.  s  3929
*Exile* - Al Sarrantonio  s  4829
*The Expediter* - J. Brian Clarke  s  1062
*Expendable* - James Alan Gardner  s  2135
*The Fifth Element* - Terry Bisson  s  504
*The Founder* - Christopher Rowley  s  4696
*The Gaia Websters* - Kim Antieau  s  198
*Hammer of Mars* - M.S. Murdock  s  4049
*Imzadi* - Peter David  s  1383
*The Last Wizard* - Simon Hawke  f  2619
*A Life in the Future* - Martin Caidin  s  827
*Man-Kzin Wars IV* - Larry Niven  s  4124

*Matrix Cubed* - Britton Bloom   s   554
*A Plague of Change* - L. Warren Douglas   s   1587
*"Repent, Harlequin!" Said the Ticktockman* - Harlan Ellison   s   1782
*The Shattered Sphere* - Roger MacBride Allen   s   81
*The Spoils of War* - Alan Dean Foster   s   2016
*Star Wreck 6: Geek Space Nine* - Leah Rewolinski   s   4562
*Warlords of Jupiter* - William H. Keith Jr.   s   3036
*The Wizard of Camelot* - Simon Hawke   f   2627
*Yamato: A Rage in Heaven* - Ken Kato   s   3014

### 26th CENTURY

*Acts of Conscience* - William Barton   s   377
*Arc Riders* - David Drake   s   1626
*A Company of Stars* - Christopher Stasheff   s   5215
*Emergence* - Peter F. Hamilton   s   2524
*Glory's People* - Alfred Coppel   s   1183
*Icarus Descending* - Elizabeth Hand   s   2536
*The Lincoln Hunters* - Wilson Tucker   s   5487
*The Nine Lives of Catseye Gomez* - Simon Hawke   f   2620
*Rebel From Alphorion* - Robyn Tallis   s   5381
*Rule Golden and Double Meaning* - Damon Knight   s   3189
*Squadron Alert* - Roland J. Green   s   2352
*Time: The Semi-Final Frontier* - Lionel Fenn   s   1921
*To a Highland Nation* - Christopher Rowley   s   4698
*Wanderer* - Donald E. McQuinn   s   3862
*Warpath* - Tony Daniel   s   1337
*Warrior* - Donald E. McQuinn   s   3863
*Warstrider* - William H. Keith Jr.   s   3037
*We Open on Venus* - Christopher Stasheff   s   5227
*Witch* - Donald E. McQuinn   s   3864
*The Wizard of Santa Fe* - Simon Hawke   f   2628

### 27th CENTURY

*Atlantis Found* - R. Garcia y Robertson   s   2119
*Canby's Legion* - Bill Baldwin   s   308
*Conflict* - Peter F. Hamilton   s   2522
*Consolidation* - Peter F. Hamilton   s   2523
*Crashlander* - Larry Niven   s   4118
*Expansion* - Peter F. Hamilton   s   2525
*The Lanterns of God* - Ron Sarti   s   4835
*Mutagenesis* - Helen Collins   s   1116
*Silent Thunder/Universe* - Dean Ing   s   2829
*The Stalk* - Janet Morris   s   4016
*Threshold* - Janet Morris   s   4018
*Trust Territory* - Janet Morris   s   4019

### 28th CENTURY

*Children of Enchantment* - Anne Kelleher Bush   f   787
*Daughter of Prophecy* - Anne Kelleher Bush   f   788
*The Death of Sleep* - Anne McCaffrey   s   3727
*Destiny's Road* - Larry Niven   s   4119
*The Fall of Hyperion* - Dan Simmons   s   5052
*Harvest the Fire* - Poul Anderson   s   128
*Hyperion* - Dan Simmons   s   5055
*Key West 2720 A.D.* - William Eakins   s   1720
*The Napoleon Wager* - William R. Forstchen   s   1980
*PartnerShip* - Anne McCaffrey   s   3741
*The Ship Who Searched* - Anne McCaffrey   s   3749
*The Stars Are Also Fire* - Poul Anderson   s   134

### 29th CENTURY

*Cohort of the Damned* - Andrew Keith   s   3034
*Exit to Reality* - Edith Forbes   s   1968
*Lieutenant* - Rick Shelley   s   4972
*March or Die* - Andrew Keith   s   3035
*Officer Cadet* - Rick Shelley   s   4973

*Red Dust* - Paul J. McAuley   s   3715
*The Ringworld Throne* - Larry Niven   s   4128
*The Yngling and the Circle of Power* - John Dalmas   s   1328
*The Yngling in Yamato* - John Dalmas   s   1329

### 30th CENTURY

*Diaspora* - Greg Egan   s   1759
*Genetic Soldier* - George Turner   s   5492
*The Lizard War* - John Dalmas   s   1325
*Testament* - Valerie J. Freireich   s   2051

### 31st CENTURY

*3001: The Final Odyssey* - Arthur C. Clarke   s   1053
*Bretta Martyn* - L. Neil Smith   s   5128
*Century 21* - Ewa Kuryluk   s   3263
*The Clouds of Magellan* - David F. Nighbert   s   4103
*Crescent in the Sky* - Donald Moffitt   s   3946
*Dayworld Breakup* - Philip Jose Farmer   s   1869
*Earthgrip* - Harry Turtledove   s   5499
*Earthling* - Tony Daniel   s   1336
*A Gathering of Stars* - Donald Moffitt   s   3947
*The Gripping Hand* - Larry Niven   s   4122
*Henry Martyn* - L. Neil Smith   s   5131
*A Talent for War* - Jack McDevitt   s   3790
*Warlock and Son* - Christopher Stasheff   s   5224
*The Warlock Insane* - Christopher Stasheff   f   5225
*The Warlock Rock* - Christopher Stasheff   s   5226
*Way of the Clans* - Robert Thurston   s   5469
*A Wizard in Absentia* - Christopher Stasheff   s   5229
*A Wizard in Peace* - Christopher Stasheff   s   5233
*A Wizard in War* - Christopher Stasheff   s   5234

### 32nd CENTURY

*Endymion* - Dan Simmons   s   5051
*The Rise of Endymion* - Dan Simmons   s   5059

### 33rd CENTURY

*Cathy IV* - Frances Lucas   s   3539
*Saint Leibowitz and the Wild Horse Woman* - Walter M. Miller Jr.   s   3908
*The Tides of God* - Ted Reynolds   s   4567

### 35th CENTURY

*Glory* - Alfred Coppel   s   1182
*Lion's Soul* - Karen Wehrstein   f   5684
*Shadow's Son* - Shirley Meier   f   3872
*Star Bridge* - James Gunn   s   2459

### 36th CENTURY

*Shadow's Daughter* - Shirley Meier   f   3871

### 40th CENTURY

*The Dark Beyond the Stars* - Frank M. Robinson   s   4626
*To the Land of the Living* - Robert Silverberg   f   5044

### 45th CENTURY

*Iceman* - Cynthia Felice   s   1913

### 50th CENTURY

*Saber & Shadow* - S.M. Stirling   f   5297
*Snow Brother* - S.M. Stirling   f   5299

### 51st CENTURY

*The Family Tree* - Sheri S. Tepper   s   5429

### 53rd CENTURY

*The Fall of Sirius* - Wil McCarthy   s   3762
*The Queen's Squadron* - R.M. Meluch   s   3874

### 61st CENTURY

*My Father Immortal* - Michael D. Weaver   s   5659
*Sideshow* - Sheri S. Tepper   s   5436

### 63rd CENTURY

*Convergence* - Charles Sheffield   s   4951
*Divergence* - Charles Sheffield   s   4954
*Summertide* - Charles Sheffield   s   4965
*Transcendence* - Charles Sheffield   s   4967

### 69th CENTURY

*Monsoon* - Peter L. Rice   s   4583

### 87th CENTURY

*The Red Tape War* - Jack L. Chalker   s   959

### 100th CENTURY

*Against a Dark Background* - Iain M. Banks   s   322

### 120th CENTURY

*The Humanoids* - Jack Williamson   s   5865
*Solis* - A.A. Attanasio   s   272

### 160th CENTURY

*Norstrilia* - Cordwainer Smith   s   5105

### 220th CENTURY

*The Kalif's War* - John Dalmas   s   1322
*The Regiment's War* - John Dalmas   s   1326
*The White Regiment* - John Dalmas   s   1327

### 280th CENTURY

*Furious Gulf* - Gregory Benford   s   447

### 520th CENTURY

*The Defenders* - Bill Baldwin   s   309
*The Mercenaries* - Bill Baldwin   s   311
*The Siege* - Bill Baldwin   s   312

### 521st CENTURY

*The Defiance* - Bill Baldwin   s   310

### 900th CENTURY

*Death's Gray Land* - Mike Shupp   s   5011
*The Last Reckoning* - Mike Shupp   s   5012

### INDETERMINATE FUTURE

*The 97th Step* - Steve Perry   s   4287
*Accidental Creatures* - Anne Harris   s   2558
*Acorna* - Anne McCaffrey   s   3717
*Acorna's Quest* - Anne McCaffrey   s   3718
*Action Stations* - William R. Forstchen   s   1976
*Adiamante* - L.E. Modesitt Jr.   s   3924
*Afterage* - Yvonne Navarro   h   4072

*Aggressor Six* - Wil McCarthy   s   3760

*Ai! Pedrito!: When Intelligence Goes Wrong* - L. Ron Hubbard   s   2788

*Alastor* - Jack Vance   s   5543

*The Albino Knife* - Steve Perry   s   4288

*Alien 3* - Alan Dean Foster   s   1993

*Alien Blues* - Lynn S. Hightower   s   2682

*The Alien Dark* - Diana G. Gallagher   s   2108

*Alien Dreams* - Larry Segriff   s   4910

*Alien Earth* - Megan Lindholm   s   3469

*Alien Eyes* - Lynn S. Hightower   s   2683

*Alien Heat* - Lynn S. Hightower   s   2684

*Alien Influences* - Kristine Kathryn Rusch   s   4711

*Alien Minds* - Keith Laumer   s   3342

*Alien Resurrection* - A.C. Crispin   s   1258

*Alien Rites* - Lynn S. Hightower   s   2685

*Alien Salute* - Charles Ingrid   s   2830

*Aliens: Earth Hive* - Steve Perry   s   4289

*Aliens: The Female War* - Steve Perry   s   4290

*All the Weyrs of Pern* - Anne McCaffrey   s   3719

*The Alleluia Files* - Sharon Shinn   s   4999

*Ammonite* - Nicola Griffith   s   2443

*Ancestor's World* - A.C. Crispin   s   1259

*And Eternity* - Piers Anthony   f   162

*Angel Station* - Walter Jon Williams   s   5833

*Antarctica* - Kim Stanley Robinson   s   4628

*Anvil* - Nicolas van Pallandt   s   5540

*Apocalypse* - Nancy Springer   f   5176

*The Arbitrary Placement of Walls* - Martha Soukup   f   5165

*Archangel* - Sharon Shinn   s   5000

*Archangel Blues* - eluki bes shahar   s   471

*Aristoi* - Walter Jon Williams   s   5834

*Armageddon* - Richard Hatch   s   2602

*The Armageddon Inheritance* - David Weber   s   5668

*The Artifact* - W. Michael Gear   s   2165

*Ash Ock* - Christopher Hinz   s   2690

*Athyra* - Steven Brust   f   739

*Back to the Time Trap* - Keith Laumer   s   3343

*Backblast* - Lee McKeone   s   3828

*The Barsoom Project* - Larry Niven   s   4115

*Battle of the Ring* - Thorarinn Gunnarsson   s   2460

*Battlestation* - David Drake   s   1627

*The Beacon* - Valerie J. Freireich   s   2048

*Beamriders!* - Martin Caidin   s   824

*Beautiful Strangers* - Melanie Tem   h   5420

*Becoming Human* - Valerie J. Freireich   s   2049

*Beholder's Eye* - Julie E. Czerneda   s   1303

*Berserker* - S.D. Perry   s   4285

*Berserker Fury* - Fred Saberhagen   s   4760

*Berserker Kill* - Fred Saberhagen   s   4761

*Berserker Lies* - Fred Saberhagen   s   4762

*Better than Life* - Grant Naylor   s   4076

*Beyond the Fall of Night* - Arthur C. Clarke   s   1054

*Beyond the Gate* - Dave Wolverton   s   5949

*Beyond the Void* - Sean Dalton   s   1331

*Bill, the Galactic Hero: On the Planet of Tasteless Pleasure* - Harry Harrison   s   2567

*Bill, the Galactic Hero: The Final Incoherent Adventure* - Harry Harrison   s   2568

*The Billion Dollar Boy* - Charles Sheffield   s   4948

*Black Steel* - Steve Perry   s   4291

*The Black Sun* - Jack Williamson   s   5860

*Black Sun Rising* - C.S. Friedman   f   2056

*Blind Justice* - S.N. Lewitt   s   3448

*Blood Feuds* - S.M. Stirling   s   5292

*Blood Lines* - William R. Burkett Jr.   s   774

*Blueheart* - Alison Sinclair   s   5068

*Bodyguard* - William C. Dietz   s   1542

*The Bohr Maker* - Linda Nagata   s   4064

*Bone Danc: A Fantasy for Technophiles* - Emma Bull   s   766

*Border Dispute* - Daniel R. Kerns   s   3066

*Borderland* - Terri Windling   f   5913

*Borders of Infinity* - Lois McMaster Bujold   s   757

*Brander's Book* - C.J. Mills   s   3909

*Brightness Reef* - David Brin   s   684

*The Broken God* - David Zindell   s   6085

*The Broken Land* - Ian McDonald   s   3791

*The Broken Sword* - Molly Cochran   f   1091

*Brother Death* - Steve Perry   s   4292

*Brother to Dragons, Companion to Owls* - Jane M. Lindskold   f   3473

*Brother to Shadows* - Andre Norton   s   4142

*Brotherhood of the Stars* - Kirby Greene   s   2414

*The Bug Life Chronicles* - Phillip C. Jennings   s   2890

*Burning Bright* - Melissa Scott   s   4894

*But What of Earth?* - Piers Anthony   s   163

*By Honor Betray'd* - Debra Doyle   s   1598

*Caesar's Bicycle* - John Barnes   s   350

*Calde of the Long Sun* - Gene Wolfe   s   5937

*Caliban* - Roger MacBride Allen   s   77

*The Call of Earth* - Orson Scott Card   s   882

*Call to Arms* - P.M. Griffin   s   2435

*Canal Dreams* - Iain M. Banks   s   323

*Carlucci's Edge* - Richard Paul Russo   s   4747

*Carpe Diem* - Steve Miller   s   3907

*Cat Scratch Fever* - Tara K. Harper   s   2550

*Catastrophe's Spell* - Mayer Alan Brenner   f   671

*Catch the Lightning* - Catherine Asaro   s   218

*Cat's Gambit* - Leslie Gadallah   s   2099

*Caught in the Crossfire* - David Drake   s   1628

*Celestis* - Paul Park   s   4241

*Cetaganda* - Lois McMaster Bujold   s   758

*Changeling* - Stephen Leigh   s   3425

*Chanur's Legacy* - C.J. Cherryh   s   981

*Chaos Come Again* - Wilhelmina Baird   s   293

*Checkmate* - Eric T. Baker   s   297

*Chicago Red* - R.M. Meluch   s   3873

*Children of the Earth* - Catherine Wells   s   5743

*Children of the Mind* - Orson Scott Card   s   883

*The Children Star* - Joan Slonczewski   s   5090

*Chimera* - Mary Rosenblum   s   4677

*The Chronicles of Pern: First Fall* - Anne McCaffrey   s   3721

*Cinderblock* - Janine Ellen Young   s   6047

*City of Bones* - Martha Wells   f   5748

*City of Diamond* - Jane Emerson   s   1807

*City of Golden Shadow* - Tad Williams   s   5828

*City on Fire* - Walter Jon Williams   s   5835

*The City Who Fought* - Anne McCaffrey   s   3722

*Clan of the Shape-Changers* - Robert Levy   f   3446

*The Clone Crisis* - Lee McKeone   s   3829

*The Clouds of Saturn* - Michael McCollum   s   3770

*Cloud's Rider* - C.J. Cherryh   s   983

*Cluster Command* - David Drake   s   1630

*Codgerspace* - Alan Dean Foster   s   1999

*The Collected Stories of Philip K. Dick, Volume Two: We Can Remember It for You Wholesale* - Philip K. Dick   s   1520

*The Color of Distance* - Amy Thomson   s   5461

*Commencement* - Roby James   s   2877

*Conqueror's Pride* - Timothy Zahn   s   6051

*Correspondence* - Sue Thomas   s   5450

*Cortez on Jupiter* - Ernest Hogan   s   2721

*A Covenant of Justice* - David Gerrold   s   2207

*Cowboy Feng's Space Bar and Grille* - Steven Brust   s   740

*Crown of Empire* - Chelsea Quinn Yarbro   s   6014

*Crown of Shadows* - C.S. Friedman   s   2057

*Crown of the Serpent* - Allen L. Wold   s   5932

*Cry Wolf* - Kenneth Von Gunden   s   5586

*Crystal Line* - Anne McCaffrey   s   3724

*Crystal Witness* - Kathy Tyers   s   5524

*The Cult of Loving Kindness* - Paul Park   s   4242

*Cybernetic Jungle* - S.N. Lewitt   s   3449

*Cyberstealth* - S.N. Lewitt   s   3450

*The Cyborg From Earth* - Charles Sheffield   s   4952

*Damia* - Anne McCaffrey   s   3725

*Damia's Children* - Anne McCaffrey   s   3726

*Dancer of the Sixth* - Michelle Shirey Crean   s   1254

*The Dancers at the End of Time* - Michael Moorcock   s   3979

*Dancing Vac* - S.N. Lewitt   s   3451

*Dare to Go A-Hunting* - Andre Norton   s   4147

*Dark Sky Legion* - William Barton   s   379

*Dark Water's Embrace* - Stephen Leigh   s   3426

*A Darker Geometry* - Mark O. Martin   s   3649

*Darkloom* - Cary Osborne   s   4225

*Darktraders* - eluki bes shahar   s   472

*Daughter of Elysium* - Joan Slonczewski   s   5091

*Days of Cain* - J.R. Dunn   s   1694

*Deathgift* - Ann Tonsor Zeddies   s   6061

*Deathstalker Honor* - Simon R. Green   s   2364

*Deathstalker Rebellion* - Simon R. Green   s   2365

*Deathstalker War* - Simon R. Green   s   2366

*Deathweave* - Cary Osborne   s   4226

*Deception Well* - Linda Nagata   s   4065

*Deep Freeze* - Zach Hughes   s   2811

*Deep Quarry* - John E. Stith   s   5302

*Deepdrive* - Alexander Jablokov   s   2837

*Deepwater Dreams* - Sydney J. Van Scyoc   s   5541

*The Delta* - Colin Wilson   s   5878

*Demon Moon* - Jack Williamson   s   5862

*The Demon Princes: Volume One* - Jack Vance   s   5544

*The Demon Princes: Volume Two* - Jack Vance   s   5545

*The Demons at Rainbow Bridge* - Jack L. Chalker   s   952

*Derelict for Trade* - Andre Norton   s   4148

*Design for Great-Day* - Alan Dean Foster   s   2001

*Desperate Measures* - Joe Clifford Faust   s   1891

*Destination: Mutiny* - Sean Dalton   s   1332

*Devil's Deal* - Richard Austin   s   277

*Diaspora* - Greg Egan   s   1759

*Dictator* - William F. Wu   s   5996

*Diplomatic Act* - Peter Jurasik   s   2996

*Distant Friends and Others* - Timothy Zahn   s   6053

*The Dolphins of Pern* - Anne McCaffrey   s   3729

*Domains of Darkover* - Marion Zimmer Bradley   s   631

*Dominion's Reach* - Diann Thornley   s   5465

*Don't Forget Your Spacesuit, Dear* - Jody Lynn Nye   s   4169

*Douglas Adams's Starship Titanic* - Terry Jones   s   2979

*Down the Stream of Stars* - Jeffrey A. Carver   s   928

*Dragon* - Steven Brust   f   741

*Dragon Rigger* - Jeffrey A. Carver   s   929

*Dragon's Claw* - Alex McDonough   s   3800

*Dragons in the Stars* - Jeffrey A. Carver   s   930

*Dragons Past* - Gary Gentile   s   2192

*Dragonseye* - Anne McCaffrey   s   3730

*Dreadnought* - Thorarinn Gunnarsson   s   2464

*The Dream Vessel* - Jeff Bredenberg   s   664

*Dreamfall* - Joan D. Vinge   s   5571

*Dreaming in Smoke* - Tricia Sullivan   s   5353

*Dreaming Metal* - Melissa Scott   s   4895

*Dreamships* - Melissa Scott   s   4896

*Dreamspy* - Jacqueline Lichtenberg   s   3458

*Drifter* - William C. Dietz   s   1543

*Drifter's Run* - William C. Dietz   s   1544

*Drifter's War* - William C. Dietz   s   1545

*Dydeetown World* - F. Paul Wilson   s   5887

*Dying of the Light* - George R.R. Martin   s   3644

*Earth Herald* - Jan Clark   s   1046

*The Earth Is All That Lasts* - Catherine Wells   s   5744

*Earth Made of Glass* - John Barnes   s   351

*The Earth Remembers* - Susan Torian Olan   s   4209

*The Earth Saver* - Catherine Wells   s   5745

*Earthborn* - Orson Scott Card   s   884

*Earthfall* - Orson Scott Card   s   885

*An Earthly Crown* - Kate Elliott   s   1771

*Ecce and Old Earth* - Jack Vance   s   5546

*Echoes of Honor* - David Weber   s   5669

*Echoes of Issel* - Diann Thornley   s   5466

*The Ecolitan Enigma* - L.E. Modesitt Jr.   s   3927

*Ecstasia* - Francesca Lia Block   f   547

*Eden* - Stanislaw Lem   s   3434

*Eggheads* - Emily Devenport   s   1500

*Egil's Book* - C.J. Mills   s   3910

*The Einstein Intersection* - Samuel R. Delany   s   1481
*Elsewhere* - Will Shetterly   f   4993
*The Elvenbane* - Andre Norton   f   4149
*Elvenblood* - Andre Norton   f   4150
*The Embedding* - Ian Watson   s   5634
*Emperor of Everything* - Ray Aldridge   s   62
*Empire of the Ants* - Bernard Werber   s   5755
*Empire's End* - Allan Cole   s   1103
*Empire's Horizon* - John Brizzolara   s   707
*The Enchantments of Flesh and Spirit* - Storm Constantine   s   1141
*Endgame* - C.J. Cherryh   s   986
*Enemy of My Enemy* - Ben Ohlander   s   4204
*Escape to the Wind* - Jennifer DiMarco   s   1559
*The Eternal Enemy* - Michael Berlyn   s   469
*Eternal Light* - Paul J. McAuley   s   3710
*Eternity Road* - Jack McDevitt   s   3788
*Eva* - Peter Dickinson   s   1525
*An Exaltation of Larks* - Robert Reed   s   4506
*Excession* - Iain M. Banks   s   324
*An Exchange of Hostages* - Susan R. Matthews   s   3692
*Exile* - Michael P. Kube-McDowell   s   3248
*Exiles' Return* - Gayle Greeno   s   2420
*Exile's Song* - Marion Zimmer Bradley   s   632
*Exodus From the Long Sun* - Gene Wolfe   s   5941
*The Eyes of God* - Mark Kreighbaum   s   3231
*The Face of Apollo* - Fred Saberhagen   s   4766
*Falcon* - Emma Bull   s   768
*Fallway* - Paula E. Downing   s   1593
*Far Futures* - Gregory Benford   s   445
*Far Harbor* - Melisa C. Michaels   s   3888
*Farewell Horizontal* - K.W. Jeter   s   2911
*Feersum Endjinn* - Iain M. Banks   s   325
*Field of Dishonor* - David Weber   s   5670
*The Final Battle* - William C. Dietz   s   1546
*Final Blackout* - L. Ron Hubbard   s   2790
*Final Diagnosis* - James White   s   5777
*Finder* - Emma Bull   f   769
*Finders-Seekers* - Gayle Greeno   s   2421
*Fine Prey* - Scott Westerfeld   s   5766
*Finity's End* - C.J. Cherryh   s   988
*Fire* - Alan Rodgers   h   4647
*Fire in a Faraway Place* - Robert Frezza   s   2052
*Fire in the Sky* - Jo Clayton   s   1067
*Fire Margins* - Lisanne Norman   s   4137
*Fire Planet* - P.M. Griffin   s   2436
*A Fire upon the Deep* - Vernor Vinge   s   5573
*A Fisherman of the Inland Sea* - Ursula K. Le Guin   s   3379
*Flag in Exile* - David Weber   s   5671
*The Fleet of Stars* - Poul Anderson   s   126
*Flesh and Gold* - Phyllis Gotlieb   s   2286
*Flies From the Amber* - Wil McCarthy   s   3763
*Flood Tide* - C.J. Cherryh   s   989
*Flowerdust* - Gwyneth Jones   s   2952
*Flux* - Stephen Baxter   s   399
*Fools* - Pat Cadigan   s   805
*Fool's War* - Sarah Zettel   s   6079
*Foragers* - Charles Oberndorf   s   4187
*Forbidden Knowledge* - Stephen R. Donaldson   s   1571
*Foreigner* - C.J. Cherryh   s   990
*The Forever Drug* - Steve Perry   s   4296
*The Fortress of Utopia* - Jack Williamson   s   5863
*Fortune's Wheel* - Lisanne Norman   s   4138
*Forward the Foundation* - Isaac Asimov   s   236
*Fossil* - Hal Clement   s   1083
*Foundation and Chaos* - Greg Bear   s   418
*Foundation's Fear* - Gregory Benford   s   446
*Four Ways to Forgiveness* - Ursula K. Le Guin   s   3380
*Free Radicals* - Jack McKinney   s   3848
*Free Zone* - Charles Platt   s   4341
*From a Changeling Star* - Jeffrey A. Carver   s   931
*The Fugitive Worlds* - Bob Shaw   s   4942
*The Furies* - Suzy McKee Charnas   s   968
*Future Crime* - Ben Bova   s   585

*Future on Fire* - Orson Scott Card   s   887
*The Galactic Gourmet* - James White   s   5778
*Galactic MI* - Kevin D. Randle   s   4467
*Galactic Patrol* - Edward E. Smith   s   5116
*The Galactic Silver Star* - Kevin D. Randle   s   4468
*A Game of Universe* - Eric S. Nylund   f   4178
*Ganwold's Child* - Diann Thornley   s   5467
*The Gap into Conflict: The Real Story* - Stephen R. Donaldson   s   1572
*The Gap into Madness: Chaos and Order* - Stephen R. Donaldson   s   1573
*The Gap into Power: A Dark and Hungry God Arises* - Stephen R. Donaldson   s   1574
*The Gap into Ruin: This Day All Gods Die* - Stephen R. Donaldson   s   1575
*The Gate of Ivory* - Doris Egan   s   1755
*The Gateway Trip: Tales and Vignettes of the Heechee* - Frederik Pohl   s   4346
*The Gathering Flame* - Debra Doyle   s   1599
*Genellan: Planetfall* - Scott G. Gier   s   2223
*Generation Warrior* - Anne McCaffrey   s   3735
*The Genocidal Healer* - James White   s   5779
*The Ghost of the Revelator* - L.E. Modesitt Jr.   s   3931
*The Gift of the Gorboduc Vandal* - Paul O. Williams   s   5821
*A Gift upon the Shore* - M.K. Wren   s   5982
*Girl in Landscape* - Jonathan Lethem   s   3440
*The Glaive* - Cary Osborne   s   4227
*Glory Season* - David Brin   s   686
*Glory's War* - Alfred Coppel   s   1184
*The Goda War* - Jay D. Blakeney   s   516
*GodHeads* - Emily Devenport   s   1501
*The Gods in Anger* - Adrian Cole   f   1100
*Godspeed* - Charles Sheffield   s   4957
*The Golden Globe* - John Varley   s   5565
*The Golden Queen* - Dave Wolverton   s   5951
*Grass* - Sheri S. Tepper   s   5431
*Gray Lensman* - Edward E. Smith   s   5117
*The Great Wheel* - Ian R. MacLeod   s   3599
*Greenthieves* - Alan Dean Foster   s   2005
*Groogleman* - Debra Doyle   s   1600
*Ground-Ties* - Jane S. Fancher   s   1861
*Grounded!* - Chris Claremont   s   1041
*Gryphon* - Crawford Kilian   s   3106
*Guilt-Edged Ivory* - Doris Egan   s   1756
*Habu* - James B. Johnson   s   2920
*Half-Light* - Denise Vitola   s   5575
*Halfway Human* - Carolyn Ives Gilman   s   2237
*Halo* - Tom Maddox   s   3604
*Hand of Prophecy* - Severna Park   s   4244
*The Hand of Zei* - L. Sprague de Camp   s   1414
*Hard-Boiled Wonderland and the End of the World* - Haruki Murakami   s   4047
*Hard Crash* - Ryan Hughes   s   2810
*Harmonies of the 'Net* - Jane S. Fancher   s   1862
*Harvest of Stars* - Poul Anderson   s   127
*Heart of Red Iron* - Phyllis Gotlieb   s   2287
*Heaven's Reach* - David Brin   s   687
*Heavy Time* - C.J. Cherryh   s   995
*Heirs of Empire* - David Weber   s   5672
*Hellflower* - eluki bes shahar   s   473
*Hellspark* - Janet Kagan   s   3000
*Hellworld* - Simon R. Green   s   2371
*Helm* - Steven Gould   s   2289
*The Hemingway Hoax* - Joe Haldeman   s   2489
*Heritage of Flight* - Susan Shwartz   s   5016
*Hero* - Dave Duncan   s   1680
*Hero* - Joel Rosenberg   s   4672
*Heroes Die* - Matthew Woodring Stover   s   5319
*Heroes, Inc.* - Kyle Crocco   f   1268
*Hidden Fires* - Katharine Eliska Kimbriel   s   3117
*The Hidden War* - Michael Armstrong   s   209
*High Moon* - Diane Duane   s   1661
*High Wizardry* - Diane Duane   s   1662
*Higher Education* - Charles Sheffield   s   4958
*Honor Among Enemies* - David Weber   s   5673
*The Honor of the Queen* - David Weber   s   5674
*Honor of the Regiment* - Bill Fawcett   s   1896

*Hopeship* - Simon Lang   s   3315
*The Host* - Peter R. Emshwiller   s   1819
*Hostile Takeover* - Jack McKinney   s   3849
*House of Moons* - K.D. Wentworth   s   5752
*The Howling Stones* - Alan Dean Foster   s   2006
*The Humanoids* - Jack Williamson   s   5865
*A Hunger in the Soul* - Mike Resnick   s   4545
*The Hunter on Arena* - Rose Estes   s   1838
*Hunter's Planet* - David Bischoff   s   492
*Hunting Party* - Elizabeth Moon   s   3968
*Hunting the Corrigan's Blood* - Holly Lisle   s   3484
*I Wake From a Dream of a Drowned Star City* - S.P. Somtow   s   5157
*I Who Have Never Known Men* - Jacqueline Harpman   s   2554
*The Ice Beast* - Frank A. Javor   s   2881
*Igniting the Reaches* - David Drake   s   1633
*Illegal Alien* - James Luceno   s   3543
*The Immortality Option* - James P. Hogan   s   2725
*Imposter* - Valerie J. Freireich   s   2050
*In Enemy Hands* - David Weber   s   5675
*In the Company of the Mind* - Steven Piziks   s   4339
*In the Mothers' Land* - Elisabeth Vonarburg   s   5590
*In the Shadow of the Moon* - Scott G. Gier   s   2224
*India's Story* - Kathlyn S. Starbuck   s   5208
*Inferno* - Roger MacBride Allen   s   78
*The Infinite Sea* - Jeffrey A. Carver   s   932
*Infinity's Shore* - David Brin   s   688
*Inheritor* - C.J. Cherryh   s   997
*Inhuman Beings* - Jerry Jay Carroll   s   914
*Initiation* - Marian Hughes   s   2806
*The Inquisitor* - Cheryl J. Franklin   s   2037
*Inquisitor* - Ian Watson   s   5637
*Insanity, Illinois* - Mark Sumner   s   5358
*Invader* - C.J. Cherryh   s   998
*Invasion America* - Christie Golden   s   2252
*The Iron Dragon's Daughter* - Michael Swanwick   f   5371
*Iroshi* - Cary Osborne   s   4228
*Islands of Tomorrow* - F.M. Busby   s   783
*Ivory: A Legend of Past and Future* - Mike Resnick   s   4547
*Jade Darcy and the Zen Pirates* - Stephen Goldin   s   2260
*Jaran* - Kate Elliott   s   1772
*Jaydium* - Deborah Wheeler   s   5774
*Jefferson's War: Death of a Regiment* - Kevin Randle   s   4466
*Jovah's Angel* - Sharon Shinn   s   5001
*Judson's Eden* - Keith Laumer   s   3344
*The Jungle* - David Drake   s   1634
*Jungle Assault* - P.M. Griffin   s   2437
*Justice* - David Drake   s   1635
*The Khan's Persuasion* - Cynthia Felice   s   1914
*Kingdoms of the Wall* - Robert Silverberg   s   5033
*Kings of the High Frontier* - Victor Koman   s   3199
*King's Sacrifice* - Margaret Weis   s   5717
*Kit's Book* - C.J. Mills   s   3911
*Knights of the Black Earth* - Margaret Weis   s   5718
*Komarr* - Lois McMaster Bujold   s   760
*The Kruton Interface* - John DeChancie   s   1459
*Labyrinth* - Dennis Schmidt   s   4884
*Lair of the Cyclops* - Allen L. Wold   s   5933
*Lake of the Long Sun* - Gene Wolfe   s   5942
*Lake of the Sun* - Wynne Whiteford   s   5787
*The LaNague Chronicles* - F. Paul Wilson   s   5889
*A Landscape of Darkness* - John Blair   s   513
*The Lantern of God* - John Dalmas   s   1323
*Larissa* - Emily Devenport   s   1503
*The Last Legends of Earth* - A.A. Attanasio   s   270
*The Last Stand of the DNA Cowboys* - Mick Farren   s   1879
*The Last Vampire* - Kathryn Meyer Griffith   h   2440
*The Law of Becoming* - Kate Elliott   s   1774
*Legacies* - Alison Sinclair   s   5069
*Legacy* - Greg Bear   s   420
*Legacy of the Ancients* - Ron Sarti   s   4836
*Legacy of the Darksword* - Margaret Weis   f   5719
*Legion of the Damned* - William C. Dietz   s   1547

Leroni of Darkover - Marion Zimmer Bradley  s  642
Life Form - Alan Dean Foster  s  2008
Life on the Border - Terri Windling  f  5915
Lightwing - Tara K. Harper  s  2551
Limbo Search - Parke Godwin  s  2245
Lion's Heart - Karen Wehrstein  f  5683
London Fields - Martin Amis  s  95
The Lone Sentinel - Jo Dereske  s  1493
The Long Hunt - Debra Doyle  s  1602
The Longest Voyage/Slow Lightning - Poul Anderson  s  130
The Lost King - Margaret Weis  s  5720
The Lost Prince - Bridget Wood  f  5962
Lunar Justice - Charles L. Harness  s  2545
Lyon's Pride - Anne McCaffrey  s  3738
Machines That Kill - Fred Saberhagen  s  4769
Mad Roy's Light - Paula King  s  3125
The Magnificent Wilf - Gordon R. Dickson  s  1536
Maia's Veil - P.K. McAllister  s  3707
Mainline - Deborah Christian  s  1026
The Man in the Moon Must Die - Jeff Bredenberg  s  665
Man-Kzin Wars V - Larry Niven  s  4125
Marks of Our Brothers - Jane M. Lindskold  s  3475
Mars Prime - William C. Dietz  s  1548
Masque - F. Paul Wilson  s  5890
The Master of Chaos - Terry A. Adams  s  34
The Masterharper of Pern - Anne McCaffrey  s  3739
A Matter of Oaths - Helen S. Wright  s  5985
Maverick - Bruce Bethke  s  484
A Maze of Stars - John Brunner  s  734
Mazeway - Jack Williamson  s  5866
McCade's Bounty - William C. Dietz  s  1550
McLendon's Syndrome - Robert Frezza  s  2053
Medicine Show - Jody Lynn Nye  s  4172
Megalomania - Ian Wallace  s  5621
Memento Mori - Shariann Lewitt  s  3454
Memory - Lois McMaster Bujold  s  761
The Memory of Earth - Orson Scott Card  s  894
Men Like Rats - Rob Chilson  s  1015
Mercycle - Piers Anthony  s  181
The Merro Tree - Katie Waitman  s  5609
Metropolitan - Walter Jon Williams  s  5839
Mid-Flinx - Alan Dean Foster  s  2010
Midnight Mass - F. Paul Wilson  h  5891
Mighty Good Road - Melissa Scott  s  4897
A Million Open Doors - John Barnes  s  353
Mind Changer - James White  s  5780
A Mind for Trade - Andre Norton  s  4158
Mind Light - Margaret Davis  s  1407
Mind Slayer - Kevin D. Randle  s  4469
Mind-Speakers' Call - Gayle Greeno  s  2423
Mindplayers - Pat Cadigan  s  806
Minds Apart - Margaret Davis  s  1408
Mirabile - Janet Kagan  s  3001
A Miracle of Rare Design - Mike Resnick  s  4550
Mirror Dance - Lois McMaster Bujold  s  762
Mission Child - Maureen F. McHugh  s  3819
Mission: Tori - Johanna Bolton  s  564
Mississippi Blues - Kathleen Ann Goonan  s  2274
Mistwalker - Denise Lopez Heald  s  2637
Mistworld - Simon R. Green  s  2372
M'Lady Witch - Christopher Stasheff  f  5217
Monkey Station - Ardath Mayhar  s  3703
Moonseed - Stephen Baxter  s  400
More than Honor - David Weber  s  5676
Mother Lode - Zach Hughes  s  2812
Mother of Plenty - Colin Greenland  s  2417
The Mountains of Majipoor - Robert Silverberg  s  5037
Murder at the Galactic Writers' Society - Janet Asimov  s  251
My Son, the Wizard - Christopher Stasheff  f  5218
Myst: The Book of D'ni - Rand Miller  f  3897
N-Space - Larry Niven  s  4126
Naked to the Stars/The Alien Way - Gordon R. Dickson  s  1537

Nevernever - Will Shetterly  f  4995
The New Springtime - Robert Silverberg  s  5040
Newer York - Lawrence Watt-Evans  s  5642
Nicoji - M. Shayne Bell  s  434
Night Lamp - Jack Vance  s  5548
Night Sky Mine - Melissa Scott  s  4898
Nightfeeder - Judith Reeves-Stevens  f  4513
Nightmare World - David Stern  s  5261
Nightside the Long Sun - Gene Wolfe  s  5943
Nightsword - Margaret Weis  f  5722
The Ninety Trillion Fausts - Jack L. Chalker  s  958
Noir - K.W. Jeter  s  2916
Non-Stop - Brian W. Aldiss  s  58
Norby and the Court Jester - Janet Asimov  s  252
Norby and the Oldest Dragon - Janet Asimov  s  253
Norby and Yobo's Great Adventure - Janet Asimov  s  254
Norby Down to Earth - Janet Asimov  s  255
Northlight - Deborah Wheeler  s  5775
Northworld - David Drake  s  1637
O Pioneer! - Frederik Pohl  s  4350
On Basilisk Station - David Weber  s  5679
On the Run - Christie Golden  s  2254
On the Verge - Roland J. Green  s  2350
Once a Hero - Elizabeth Moon  s  3970
One Mind's Eye - Kathy Tyers  s  5525
Only Child - H.M. Hoover  s  2764
Operation Damocles - Oscar L. Fellows  s  1916
Oracle - Mike Resnick  s  4551
Orca - Steven Brust  f  745
Orion Among the Stars - Ben Bova  s  589
Orion's Dagger - P.K. McAllister  s  3708
Out on Blue Six - Ian McDonald  s  3794
The Outlander: Captivity - B.J. Salterberg  s  4792
Outpost - Scott Mackay  s  3597
The Outskirter's Secret - Rosemary Kirstein  s  3157
The Oxygen Barons - Gregory Feeley  s  1897
The Painful Field - Roland J. Green  s  2351
Palace - Katharine Kerr  s  3072
Palaces and Prisons - Ron Miller  f  3904
Paradise: A Chronicle of a Distant World - Mike Resnick  s  4552
The Parafaith War - L.E. Modesitt Jr.  s  3937
The Parasite War - Tim Sullivan  s  5352
A Passage of Stars - Alis A. Rasmussen  s  4482
Path of Fire - Charles Ingrid  s  2832
Path of the Fury - David Weber  s  5680
Peace on Earth - Stanislaw Lem  s  3435
The Pharaoh Contract - Ray Aldridge  s  63
Phaze Doubt - Piers Anthony  f  184
Phoenix - Steven Brust  f  746
Phoenix Cafe - Gwyneth Jones  s  2954
The Phoenix in Flight - Sherwood Smith  s  5138
Phule's Company - Robert Asprin  s  260
Phule's Paradise - Robert Asprin  s  261
A Plague of Angels - Sheri S. Tepper  f  5433
The Planet Beyond - Steve Mudd  s  4043
Planet of the Robot Slaves - Harry Harrison  s  2573
The Player of Games - Iain M. Banks  s  326
Playing God - Sarah Zettel  s  6080
The Poisoned Lands - John Maddox Roberts  f  4619
Pollen - Jeff Noon  s  4135
Polymorph - Scott Westerfeld  s  5767
Ports of Call - Jack Vance  s  5549
Power Lines - Anne McCaffrey  s  3743
Power Play - Anne McCaffrey  s  3744
Powers That Be - Anne McCaffrey  s  3745
Precious Cargo - Joe Clifford Faust  s  1893
The Price of Ransom - Alis A. Rasmussen  s  4483
The Price of the Stars - Debra Doyle  s  1604
Primary Inversion - Catherine Asaro  s  220
Primavera - Francesca Lia Block  f  551
Prince of Havoc - Michael A. Stackpole  s  5204
Prince of Sunset - Steve White  s  5786
Priorities - Lynda Lyons  s  3579
Prison Planet - William C. Dietz  s  1551
A Prison Unsought - Sherwood Smith  s  5139

Prisoner of Conscience - Susan R. Matthews  s  3693
Prisoner of Dreams - Karen Ripley  s  4593
The Prisoner Within - Donald E. McQuinn  s  3861
Prodigy - Jan Clark  s  1047
Project Farcry - Pauline Ashwell  s  230
The Promise - Monica Hughes  s  2808
Promised Land - Connie Willis  s  5872
Prophet - Mike Resnick  s  4553
Protektor - Charles Platt  s  4342
Purgatory: A Chronicle of a Distant World - Mike Resnick  s  4554
Putting Up Roots - Charles Sheffield  s  4964
Quasar - Jamil Nasir  s  4071
The Queen of Darkness - Miguel Conner  s  1134
Queens of Land and Sea - John Maddox Roberts  f  4620
Quest to Riverworld - Philip Jose Farmer  s  1872
Quicksilver's Knight - Christopher Stasheff  f  5220
Quozl - Alan Dean Foster  s  2013
The Race for God - Brian Herbert  s  2666
Raft - Stephen Baxter  s  401
Rainbow Man - M.J. Engh  s  1824
Raising the Stones - Sheri S. Tepper  s  5434
Rama Revealed - Arthur C. Clarke  s  1059
Random Factor - Joel Henry Sherman  s  4984
Razor's Edge - Lisanne Norman  s  4139
Reality Is What You Can Get Away With: An Illustrated Screenplay - Robert Anton Wilson  s  5904
Realtime Interrupt - James P. Hogan  s  2729
Receive the Gift - Louise Marley  s  3628
Reckoning Infinity - John E. Stith  s  5304
Reconnaissance - Bill McCay  s  3769
Red Dwarf: Infinity Welcomes Careful Drivers - Grant Naylor  s  4077
Red Planet - Robert A. Heinlein  s  2647
The Red Queen - Dirk Draulans  s  1653
Rediscovery: A Novel of Darkover - Marion Zimmer Bradley  s  643
The Rediscovery of Man - Cordwainer Smith  s  5106
Redline the Stars - Andre Norton  s  4160
Redliners - David Drake  s  1641
Redshift Rendezvous - John E. Stith  s  5305
Reefsong - Carol Severance  s  4923
Regenesis - Julia Ecklar  s  1729
Relic of Empire - W. Michael Gear  s  2171
The Remarkables - Robert Reed  s  4507
Rememory - John Gregory Betancourt  s  481
Remnant Population - Elizabeth Moon  s  3972
Renegade - Cordell Scotten  s  4903
The Renegades of Pern - Anne McCaffrey  s  3746
Renunciates of Darkover - Marion Zimmer Bradley  s  644
Requiem for Anthi - Jay D. Blakeney  s  517
Return Fire - Charles Ingrid  s  2833
The Return of the Emperor - Allan Cole  s  1106
Return to Camerein - Rick Shelley  s  4974
Reunion on Neverend - John E. Stith  s  5306
Revenge of the Damned - Allan Cole  s  1107
Revolution's Shore - Alis A. Rasmussen  s  4484
Reward for Retief - Keith Laumer  s  3345
Rider at the Gate - C.J. Cherryh  s  1000
The Rifter's Covenant - Sherwood Smith  s  5140
The Rim-World Legacy and Beyond - Frank A. Javor  s  2882
Ring - Stephen Baxter  s  402
The Ring of Charon - Roger MacBride Allen  s  80
The Rising - James Doohan  s  1579
River of Blue Fire - Tad Williams  f  5830
Rock 'n' Roll Babes From Outer Space - Linda Javin  s  2880
Rock of Ages - Walter Jon Williams  s  5840
A Roil of Stars - Don Wismer  s  5930
Rolling Hot - David Drake  s  1642
The Rowan - Anne McCaffrey  s  3747
Ruler of Naught - Sherwood Smith  s  5141

*Run for the Stars/Echoes of Thunder* - Harlan Ellison  s  1788
*The Run to Chaos Keep* - Jack L. Chalker  s  960
*Sable, Shadow and Ice* - Cheryl J. Franklin  f  2039
*Sailing Bright Eternity* - Gregory Benford  s  449
*The Salukan Gambit* - Sean Dalton  s  1333
*Sam Gunn, Unlimited* - Ben Bova  s  593
*Sassinak* - Anne McCaffrey  s  3748
*Schismatrix Plus* - Bruce Sterling  s  5260
*The Schizogenic Man* - Raymond Harris  s  2563
*School of Fire* - David Sherman  s  4982
*A Screaming Across the Sky* - Brian Daley  s  1315
*Seasons of Plenty* - Colin Greenland  s  2418
*A Second Infinity* - Michael D. Weaver  s  5660
*The Seeds of Time* - Kay Kenyon  s  3064
*Seeking the Dream Brother* - Marcia J. Bennett  s  451
*Sentinels* - Margaret Weis  s  5725
*Serpent Catch* - Dave Wolverton  s  5956
*Serpent's Gift* - A.C. Crispin  s  1261
*Shade* - Emily Devenport  s  1504
*Shade's Children* - Garth Nix  s  4130
*Shadow Leader* - Tara K. Harper  f  2552
*Shadow Man* - Melissa Scott  s  4900
*The Shadow Matrix* - Marion Zimmer Bradley  s  645
*Shadow World* - A.C. Crispin  s  1262
*Shadowkill* - Jo Clayton  s  1069
*Shadowplay* - Jo Clayton  s  1070
*Shadow's End* - Sheri S. Tepper  s  5435
*Shadows Fall* - Simon R. Green  f  2373
*Shadows of War* - Thomas S. Gressman  s  2432
*Shadowspeer* - Jo Clayton  s  1071
*Shaper's Legacy* - Sheila Finch  s  1933
*The Shapes of Their Hearts* - Melissa Scott  s  4901
*Shaping the Dawn* - Sheila Finch  s  1934
*The Sharp End* - David Drake  s  1643
*Shifter* - Judith Reeves-Stevens  f  4515
*The Ship Avenged* - S.M. Stirling  s  5298
*The Ship Errant* - Jody Lynn Nye  s  4175
*The Ship Who Won* - Anne McCaffrey  s  3750
*The Ships of Earth* - Orson Scott Card  s  897
*Shiva in Steel* - Fred Saberhagen  s  4775
*Shivering World* - Kathy Tyers  s  5526
*Short Blade* - Peter R. Emshwiller  s  1820
*The Short Victorious War* - David Weber  s  5681
*Siduri's Net* - P.K. McAllister  s  3709
*The Siege of Eternity* - Frederik Pohl  s  4353
*Signal to Noise* - Eric S. Nylund  s  4179
*Signs of Life* - Cherry Wilder  s  5804
*The Silent City* - Elisabeth Vonarburg  s  5592
*Silent Dances* - A.C. Crispin  s  1263
*Silent Songs* - A.C. Crispin  s  1264
*Silk and Steel* - Ron Miller  f  3905
*Silverlight* - Morgan Llywelyn  f  3507
*Sing the Light* - Louise Marley  s  3629
*Sing the Warmth* - Louise Marley  s  3630
*The Singers of Time* - Frederik Pohl  s  4354
*Sister Blood* - Karen Haber  s  2476
*Six Moon Dance* - Sheri S. Tepper  s  5437
*The Sky Lords* - John Brosnan  s  720
*Sky Trillium* - Julian May  f  3700
*Smoke and Mirrors* - Jane M. Lindskold  s  3476
*Someone to Watch over Me* - Tricia Sullivan  s  5355
*Songs of Chaos* - S.N. Lewitt  s  3452
*Soothsayer* - Mike Resnick  s  4557
*Sorcerers of Majipoor* - Robert Silverberg  s  5041
*The Sounding Stillness* - Kenneth Von Gunden  s  5587
*Spacer Dreams* - Larry Segriff  s  4911
*Speaking Dreams* - Severna Park  s  4245
*Specterworld* - Isidore Haiblum  s  2480
*Spider Legs* - Piers Anthony  s  189
*Spindoc* - Steve Perry  s  4300
*Sporting Chance* - Elizabeth Moon  s  3974
*The Stainless Steel Rat Goes to Hell* - Harry Harrison  s  2574

*The Stainless Steel Rat Sings the Blues* - Harry Harrison  s  2575
*Star Child* - James P. Hogan  s  2730
*Star Precinct* - Kevin D. Randle  s  4470
*Starbridge* - A.C. Crispin  s  1265
*Starfarers* - Poul Anderson  s  133
*Starfire Down* - Lee McKeone  s  3830
*Stargate SG-1* - Ashley McConnell  s  3777
*Starliner* - David Drake  s  1645
*Starpilot's Grave* - Debra Doyle  s  1606
*Starswarm* - Jerry Pournelle  s  4379
*Stationfall* - Arthur Byron Cover  s  1216
*Stations of the Tide* - Michael Swanwick  s  5373
*The Steel Kings* - John Maddox Roberts  f  4621
*The Steerswoman* - Rosemary Kirstein  s  3158
*Stepwater* - L. Warren Douglas  s  1588
*Stinger* - Nancy Kress  s  3243
*The Stone Garden* - Mary Rosenblum  s  4679
*Strange Attractors* - Jeffrey A. Carver  s  934
*Strange Deliverance* - Mary Brown  s  728
*Sugar Rain* - Paul Park  s  4243
*Suicide Attack* - John Sievert  s  5023
*The Sum of Things* - Roland J. Green  s  2353
*The Summer Queen* - Joan D. Vinge  s  5572
*Sundowner* - Chris Claremont  s  1043
*Surface Action* - David Drake  s  1646
*Swan Song* - Robert R. McCammon  h  3757
*Tactical Error* - Thorarinn Gunnarsson  s  2466
*Tales of Zothique* - Clark Ashton Smith  f  5104
*Tangled Webs* - Steve Mudd  s  4044
*Target* - Janet Morris  s  4017
*Taylor's Ark* - Jody Lynn Nye  s  4176
*Tea From an Empty Cup* - Pat Cadigan  s  809
*The Tenth Class* - Karen Ripley  s  4594
*The Tery* - F. Paul Wilson  s  5900
*There Won't Be War* - Harry Harrison  s  2578
*The Third Eagle: Lessons Along a Minor String* - R.A. MacAvoy  s  3583
*The Third Force* - Marc Laidlaw  s  3313
*This Alien Shore* - C.S. Friedman  s  2059
*This Immortal* - Roger Zelazny  s  6074
*A Thousand Words for Stranger* - Julie E. Czerneda  s  1304
*Through the Breach* - David Drake  s  1647
*Through the Heart* - Richard Grant  f  2328
*Throy* - Jack Vance  s  5550
*Tides of Light* - Gregory Benford  s  450
*Time and Light* - William Bornefeld  s  574
*The Time Ships* - Stephen Baxter  s  403
*Time Station London* - David Evans  s  1853
*Timediver's Dawn* - L.E. Modesitt Jr.  s  3940
*Timelike Infinity* - Stephen Baxter  s  404
*Titan* - Stephen Baxter  s  405
*Title Deleted for Security Reasons* - Ed Blome  s  553
*To Fear the Light* - Ben Bova  s  595
*To Save the Sun* - Ben Bova  s  596
*To Your Scattered Bodies Go* - Philip Jose Farmer  s  1876
*Tomorrow and Tomorrow* - Charles Sheffield  s  4966
*Too, Too Solid Flesh* - Nick O'Donohoe  s  4197
*Total Recall* - Piers Anthony  s  193
*Towers of Darkover* - Marion Zimmer Bradley  f  653
*Traitors* - Kristine Kathryn Rusch  f  4729
*The Transall Saga* - Gary Paulsen  s  4262
*The Transmigration of Souls* - William Barton  s  382
*Treaty at Doona* - Anne McCaffrey  s  3752
*The Triad Worlds* - F.M. Busby  s  786
*Tripoint* - C.J. Cherryh  s  1003
*Trouble on Cloud City* - Kevin J. Anderson  s  117
*The Trumpets of Tagan* - Simon Lang  s  3316
*Turning Point* - Lisanne Norman  s  4140
*Twilight of the Empire* - Simon R. Green  s  2374
*Two-Bit Heroes* - Doris Egan  s  1757
*Uncharted Territory* - Connie Willis  s  5875
*Under Fire* - Kenneth Von Gunden  s  5589

*Unwillingly to Earth* - Pauline Ashwell  s  231
*The Unwound Way* - William Adams  s  35
*Uplink* - Jane S. Fancher  s  1865
*Use of Weapons* - Iain M. Banks  s  328
*Utopia* - Roger MacBride Allen  s  83
*Vast* - Linda Nagata  s  4067
*Vengeance* - David Drake  s  1648
*The Venom Trees of Sunga* - L. Sprague de Camp  s  1420
*Views from the Oldest House* - Richard Grant  s  2329
*Virus Clans* - Michael Kanaly  s  3008
*The VMR Theory* - Robert Frezza  s  2055
*Voices of Chaos* - A.C. Crispin  s  1266
*The Vor Game* - Lois McMaster Bujold  s  764
*Vortex* - Allan Cole  s  1108
*The Voyage* - David Drake  s  1649
*Voyage to the Red Planet* - Terry Bisson  s  508
*Vurt* - Jeff Noon  s  4136
*The Walking Shadow* - Brian Stableford  s  5195
*The Wall at the Edge of the World* - Jim Aikin  s  46
*War Birds* - R.M. Meluch  s  3875
*The War Machine* - David Drake  s  1650
*The War Minstrels* - Karen Haber  s  2477
*The War of the Sky Lords* - John Brosnan  s  721
*Warhorse* - Timothy Zahn  s  6056
*Warlord of Heaven* - Adrian Cole  f  1102
*Warp Angel* - Stuart Hopen  s  2766
*The Warrior* - David Drake  s  1651
*Warsprite* - Jefferson P. Swycaffer  s  5375
*Warstrider: Netlink* - William H. Keith Jr.  s  3038
*The Web of Spider* - W. Michael Gear  s  2173
*The Weigher* - Eric Vinicoff  s  5574
*The Wells of Phyre* - L. Warren Douglas  s  1589
*West of January* - Dave Duncan  s  1691
*Whatdunits* - Mike Resnick  s  4558
*When True Night Falls* - C.S. Friedman  f  2060
*Where the Ships Die* - William C. Dietz  s  1553
*The Whims of Creation* - Simon Hawke  s  2626
*A Whisper of Time* - Paula E. Downing  s  1595
*The White Abacus* - Damien Broderick  s  708
*White Light* - William Barton  s  384
*The White Mountain* - David Wingrove  s  5922
*The White Tribunal* - Paula Volsky  f  5583
*The Widowmaker* - Mike Resnick  s  4559
*The Wild* - David Zindell  s  6086
*The Winds of Mars* - H.M. Hoover  s  2765
*Wing Commander: Freedom Flight* - Mercedes Lackey  s  3307
*Winning Colors* - Elizabeth Moon  s  3976
*Winterlong* - Elizabeth Hand  s  2539
*With Full Honors* - Donald E. McQuinn  s  3865
*With the Lightnings* - David Drake  s  1652
*A Wizard in Chaos* - Christopher Stasheff  s  5230
*A Wizard in Midgard* - Christopher Stasheff  s  5231
*A Wizard in Mind* - Christopher Stasheff  s  5232
*The Wizard of Sunset Strip* - Simon Hawke  f  2629
*Wolf in Shadow* - David Gemmell  s  2191
*Wolfking* - Bridget Wood  f  5963
*Wolfwalker* - Tara K. Harper  f  2553
*Woman Without a Shadow* - Karen Haber  s  2478
*The World at the End of Time* - Frederik Pohl  s  4357
*A World Lost* - James B. Johnson  s  2921
*World Spirits* - Aline Boucher-Kaplan  s  580
*Wulfsyarn: A Mosaic* - Phillip Mann  s  3617
*Xenocide* - Orson Scott Card  s  899
*Yesterday's Pawn* - W.T. Quick  s  4453
*Zeta Base* - Judith Alguire  s  74
*Zjhanne's Book* - C.J. Mills  s  3912

## INDETERMINATE

*Across the Thlassa Mey* - Dennis McCarty  f  3765
*AEstival Tide* - Elizabeth Hand  s  2533
*Allamanda* - Michael Williams  f  5817
*Alvin Journeyman* - Orson Scott Card  f  881

*The Ambivalent Magician* - Simon Hawke  f  2616
*Ancient Echoes* - Robert Holdstock  f  2735
*Ancient Games* - Scott Ciencin  f  1028
*Another Day, Another Dungeon* - Greg
  Costikyan  f  1206
*Anvil of the Sun* - Anne Lesley Groell  f  2451
*The Apprentice* - Deborah Talmadge-
  Bickmore  f  5382
*Arcady* - Michael Williams  f  5818
*Arena* - William R. Forstchen  f  1977
*The Arm of the Stone* - Victoria Strauss  f  5333
*Armageddon: The Musical* - Robert Rankin  s  4473
*Arrows of the Sun* - Judith Tarr  f  5391
*Assassin's Apprentice* - Robin Hobb  f  2693
*Assassin's Quest* - Robin Hobb  f  2694
*Aurian* - Maggie Furey  f  2095
*A Bad Spell in Yurt* - C. Dale Brittain  f  701
*The Baker's Boy* - J.V. Jones  f  2956
*The Barbed Coil* - J.V. Jones  f  2957
*Barrenlands* - Doranna Durgin  f  1702
*Barrow* - John Deakins  f  1443
*Battledragon* - Christopher Rowley  f  4691
*Bazil Broketail* - Christopher Rowley  f  4692
*Bedlam Boyz* - Ellen Guon  f  2467
*Beggar's Banquet* - Daniel Hood  f  2756
*Beldan's Fire* - Midori Snyder  f  5150
*Belgarath the Sorcerer* - David Eddings  f  1730
*The Bellmaker* - Brian Jacques  f  2848
*Beneath the Vaulted Hills* - Sean Russell  f  4739
*Beneath the Web* - Lynn Abbey  f  12
*Bewitchments of Love and Hate* - Storm
  Constantine  s  1140
*Beyond the Magic Sphere* - Gail Jarrow  f  2879
*Beyond the Moons* - David Cook  f  1144
*Beyond the Pale* - Mark Anthony  f  153
*The Birth of the Blade* - Dennis McCarty  f  3766
*Black as Blood* - Rob Chilson  f  1014
*Black Trillium* - Marion Zimmer Bradley  f  630
*Black Unicorn* - Tanith Lee  f  3404
*Black Wine* - Candas Jane Dorsey  s  1582
*The Blackgod* - J. Gregory Keyes  f  3095
*Blindfold* - Kevin J. Anderson  s  101
*Blood: A Southern Fantasy* - Michael
  Moorcock  f  3977
*Blood and Honor* - Simon R. Green  f  2361
*The Blood Jaguar* - Michael H. Payne  f  4271
*The Blood of a Dragon* - Lawrence Watt-
  Evans  f  5640
*Blood of the Colyn Muir* - Paul Edwin
  Zimmer  f  6083
*Blood of the Fold* - Terry Goodkind  f  2268
*Blood Trillium* - Julian May  f  3696
*Blue Moon Rising* - Simon R. Green  f  2362
*Bones of the Past* - Holly Lisle  f  3478
*The Book of Atrix Wolfe* - Patricia A.
  McKillip  f  3838
*The Book of Earth* - Marjorie Bradley
  Kellogg  f  3044
*The Book of Knights* - Yves Meynard  f  3884
*The Book of Night with Moon* - Diane
  Duane  f  1657
*Book of Stones* - L. Dean James  f  2862
*Branch and Crown* - Gael Baudino  f  389
*The Brazen Gambit* - Lynn Abbey  f  13
*A Breach in the Watershed* - Douglas Niles  f  4105
*Bride of the Castle* - John DeChancie  s  1452
*Bride of the Slime Monster* - Craig Shaw
  Gardner  f  2125
*Broken Blade* - Ann Marston  f  3634
*The Broken Crown* - Michelle West  f  5757
*The Broken Goddess* - Hans Bemmann  f  439
*Bronze Mirror* - Jeanne Larsen  f  3338
*Brothers of the Dragon* - Robin Wayne
  Bailey  f  286
*By the Sword* - Greg Costikyan  f  1207
*The Cage* - S.M. Stirling  f  5293
*Caledon of the Mists* - Deborah Turner
  Harris  f  2560
*A Call to Arms* - Thomas K. Martin  f  3650

*Calling on Dragons* - Patricia C. Wrede  f  5974
*Canticle* - R.A. Salvatore  f  4793
*Captains Outrageous, or, For Doom the Bell Tolls* -
  Roy V. Young  f  6049
*Captives of the Blue Mountain* - Wendy
  Pini  f  4336
*Carmen Dog* - Carol Emshwiller  f  1817
*Carnivores of Light and Darkness* - Alan Dean
  Foster  f  1996
*The Case of the Toxic Spell Dump* - Harry
  Turtledove  f  5497
*A Cast of Corbies* - Mercedes Lackey  f  3274
*Castle in the Air* - Diana Wynne Jones  f  2944
*Castle of Deception* - Mercedes Lackey  f  3275
*The Castle of the Silver Wheel* - Teresa
  Edgerton  f  1741
*Castle Spellbound* - John DeChancie  s  1454
*Cat-A-Lyst* - Alan Dean Foster  s  1997
*Cathedral of Thorns* - Steven Frankos  f  2041
*Cat's Paw* - L.A. Taylor  f  5409
*The Catswold Portal* - Shirley Rousseau
  Murphy  f  4055
*Catwings* - Ursula K. Le Guin  f  3377
*Chains of Darkness, Chains of Light* - Michelle
  Sagara  f  4781
*Chains of Light* - Quentin Thomas  s  5449
*The Changeling Prince* - Vivian Vande
  Velde  f  5554
*Changespell* - Doranna Durgin  f  1703
*Changing Fate* - Elisabeth Waters  f  5629
*The Chaos Balance* - L.E. Modesitt Jr.  f  3925
*Chaos Mode* - Piers Anthony  f  165
*A Child of Elvish* - Nancy Varian Berberick  f  457
*Children of Amarid* - David B. Coe  f  1095
*Children of the Blood: Book Two of The Sundered* -
  Michelle Sagara  f  4782
*Children of the Drake* - Richard A. Knaak  f  3166
*The Children of Wrath* - Mickey Zucker
  Reichert  f  4518
*Chorus Skating* - Alan Dean Foster  f  1998
*Chrome Circle* - Mercedes Lackey  f  3277
*Ciara's Song* - Andre Norton  f  4146
*Cinnabar Shadows* - Lynn Abbey  f  15
*City at the Edge of Time* - Janet Morris  f  4015
*A City in Winter* - Mark Helprin  f  2653
*City of the Sorcerers* - Mary H. Herbert  f  2673
*The Clan of the Warlord* - Elizabeth H.
  Boyer  f  604
*Clock Strikes Sword* - Ian Hammell  f  2529
*The Cloud People* - Robert B. Kelly  f  3050
*The Coachman Rat* - David Henry Wilson  f  5879
*The Color of Her Panties* - Piers Anthony  f  167
*The Compass of the Soul* - Sean Russell  f  4740
*Conan the Formidable* - Steve Perry  f  4293
*Conan the Guardian* - Roland J. Green  f  2347
*Conan the Indomitable* - Steve Perry  f  4294
*Conan the Relentless* - Roland J. Green  f  2348
*Conan the Rogue* - John Maddox Roberts  f  4617
*The Conjurer Princess* - Vivian Vande
  Velde  f  5555
*Conspiracy* - J. Robert King  f  3121
*Convergence* - Sharon Green  f  2356
*The Coral Kingdom* - Douglas Niles  f  4106
*Cormyr: A Novel* - Ed Greenwood  f  2426
*Cormyr: A Novel* - Ed Greenwood  f  2425
*Corum: The Coming of Chaos* - Michael
  Moorcock  f  3978
*Court Duel* - Sherwood Smith  f  5137
*The Courts of Sorcery* - Ashley McConnell  f  3773
*The Crimson Sky* - Joel Rosenberg  f  4669
*A Crown of Swords* - Robert Jordan  f  2984
*Crucible* - Troy Denning  f  1484
*Cry Republic* - Kirk Mitchell  s  3917
*The Crystal Dragon* - Richard A. Knaak  f  3167
*The Crystal Rose* - Maya Kaathryn Bohnhoff  f  560
*Cup of Clay* - Carole Nelson Douglas  f  1583
*Curse of the Black Heron* - Holly Lisle  f  3479
*Curse of the Mistwraith* - Janny Wurts  f  6001
*The Cursed* - Dave Duncan  f  1674

*The Cutting Edge* - Dave Duncan  f  1675
*Dagger's Edge* - Anne Logston  f  3508
*Dancer's Rise* - Jo Clayton  f  1064
*Dancing Jack* - Laurie J. Marks  f  3624
*Dark Divide* - Mark Acres  f  27
*The Dark Hand of Magic* - Barbara Hambly  f  2502
*Dark Heart* - Betsy James  f  2857
*Dark Horse* - Mary H. Herbert  f  2674
*Dark Lord of Derkholm* - Diana Wynne
  Jones  f  2946
*Dark Magic* - Angus Wells  f  5733
*Dark Mirror, Dark Dreams* - Sharon Green  f  2357
*Darkenheight* - Douglas Niles  f  4107
*Daughter of Magic* - C. Dale Brittain  f  703
*Daughter of the Blood* - Anne Bishop  f  495
*Daughter of the Drow* - Elaine Cunningham  f  1287
*Dealing with Dragons* - Patricia C. Wrede  f  5975
*Death of a Darklord* - Laurell K. Hamilton  h  2516
*The Death of Chaos* - L.E. Modesitt Jr.  f  3926
*The Death of the Necromancer* - Martha
  Wells  f  5749
*Deathknight* - Andrew J. Offutt  f  4201
*The Deceiver* - Louise Cooper  f  1175
*Deerskin* - Robin McKinley  f  3844
*Delan the Mislaid* - Laurie J. Marks  f  3625
*Delta City* - Felicity Savage  f  4849
*The Demon Awakens* - R.A. Salvatore  f  4794
*Demon Blade* - Mark A. Garland  f  2141
*Demon Drums* - Carol Severance  f  4922
*Demon Pig* - Karen Brush  f  737
*The Demon Spirit* - R.A. Salvatore  f  4795
*Demons Don't Dream* - Piers Anthony  f  168
*The Devouring Void* - Mark E. Rogers  f  4653
*Dhiammara* - Maggie Furey  f  2096
*Dialing the Wind* - Charles L. Grant  h  2305
*The Diamond Throne* - David Eddings  f  1731
*Diplomacy of Wolves* - Holly Lisle  f  3481
*Dirty Work* - Dan McGirt  f  3810
*The Djinn in the Nightingale's Eye* - A.S.
  Byatt  f  794
*Doc Sidhe* - Aaron Allston  f  85
*Dr. Dimension* - John DeChancie  s  1456
*Dog Wizard* - Barbara Hambly  f  2503
*Domes of Fire* - David Eddings  f  1732
*The Doom Brigade* - Margaret Weis  f  5708
*The Door into Sunset* - Diane Duane  f  1660
*The Door to Ambermere* - J. Calvin Pierce  f  4316
*Down the Bright Way* - Robert Reed  s  4505
*The Dragon and the Djinn* - Gordon R.
  Dickson  f  1528
*A Dragon at World's End* - Christopher
  Rowley  f  4693
*Dragon Burning* - Craig Shaw Gardner  f  2126
*Dragon Companion* - Don Callander  f  842
*The Dragon Crown* - Richard A. Knaak  f  3168
*The Dragon in Lyonesse* - Gordon R.
  Dickson  f  1531
*The Dragon King* - R.A. Salvatore  f  4796
*The Dragon Reborn* - Robert Jordan  f  2985
*Dragon Rescue* - Don Callander  f  843
*Dragon Sleeping* - Craig Shaw Gardner  f  2127
*Dragon Tempest* - Don Callander  f  844
*The Dragon, the Earl, and the Troll* - Gordon R.
  Dickson  f  1534
*The Dragon Token* - Melanie Rawn  f  4485
*Dragon Tome* - Richard A. Knaak  f  3169
*Dragon Waking* - Craig Shaw Gardner  f  2128
*Dragon Wing* - Margaret Weis  f  5709
*The Dragonbone Chair* - Tad Williams  f  5829
*Dragoncharm* - Graham Edwards  f  1749
*Dragonmage of Mystara* - Thorarinn
  Gunnarsson  f  2462
*Dragonrank Master* - Mickey Zucker
  Reichert  f  4519
*Dragon's Bait* - Vivian Vande Velde  f  5556
*The Dragon's Dagger* - R.A. Salvatore  f  4797
*Dragons of Argonath* - Christopher Rowley  f  4694
*Dragons of Summer Flame* - Margaret Weis  f  5711
*Dragons of War* - Christopher Rowley  f  4695

*Dragon's Plunder* - Brad Strickland  f  5336
*Dragon's Queen* - Carol L. Dennis  f  1488
*The Dragon's Touchstone* - Irene Radford  f  4459
*Dragon's Winter* - Elizabeth A. Lynn  f  3578
*Dragonslayer's Return* - R.A. Salvatore  f  4798
*Dragonspawn* - Mark Acres  f  28
*The Dragonstone* - Dennis L. McKiernan  f  3832
*Dreamseeker's Road* - Tom Deitz  f  1472
*The Druid of Shannara* - Terry Brooks  f  710
*Drum Warning* - Jo Clayton  f  1066
*D'Shai* - Joel Rosenberg  f  4670
*The Dubious Hills* - Pamela Dean  f  1444
*Dun Lady's Jess* - Doranna Durgin  f  1704
*The Eagle and the Nightingales* - Mercedes
    Lackey  f  3278
*The Element of Fire* - Martha Wells  f  5750
*The Elf Queen of Shannara* - Terry Brooks  f  711
*Elfshadow* - Elaine Cunningham  f  1288
*Elfsong* - Elaine Cunningham  f  1289
*Elfwood* - Rose Estes  f  1837
*Elminster: The Making of a Mage* - Ed
    Greenwood  f  2427
*Elric: Song of the Black Sword* - Michael
    Moorcock  f  3980
*Elven Star* - Margaret Weis  f  5712
*Elvendude* - Mark Shepherd  f  4980
*Emerald House Rising* - Peg Kerr  f  3080
*The End-of-Everything Man* - Tom De
    Haven  f  1421
*The Endless Knot* - Stephen R. Lawhead  f  3354
*An Enemy Reborn* - Michael A. Stackpole  f  5197
*Equal Rites* - Terry Pratchett  f  4387
*Eric* - Terry Pratchett  f  4388
*The Essential Bordertown* - Terri Windling  f  5914
*Evermeet: Island of Elves* - Elaine
    Cunningham  f  1290
*An Exchange of Gifts* - Anne McCaffrey  f  3731
*Exile's Challenge* - Angus Wells  f  5734
*Exile's Children* - Angus Wells  f  5735
*Extreme Paranoia: Nobody Knows the Trouble I've
    Shot* - Ken Rolston  s  4662
*The Eye of the Hunter* - Dennis L.
    McKiernan  f  3833
*The Eye of the World* - Robert Jordan  f  2986
*Eyes of Silver* - Michael A. Stackpole  f  5200
*Fabulous Harbors* - Michael Moorcock  f  3981
*Faces of Deception* - Troy Denning  f  1485
*The Faithful Traitor* - Robert Don Hughes  f  2809
*The Falcon Rises* - Michael C. Staudinger  f  5235
*Fall of Angels* - L.E. Modesitt Jr.  f  3930
*The Far Kingdoms* - Allan Cole  f  1104
*Far-Seer* - Robert J. Sawyer  s  4854
*Farewell to Lankhmar* - Fritz Leiber  f  3418
*Faun & Games* - Piers Anthony  f  169
*Feather Stroke* - Sydney J. Van Scyoc  f  5542
*Feet of Clay* - Terry Pratchett  f  4389
*Finder's Bane* - Kate Novak  f  4165
*Fire Angels* - Jane Routley  f  4685
*Fire Arrow* - Edith Pattou  f  4260
*Fire Crossing* - Cheryl J. Franklin  s  2036
*Fire Sea* - Margaret Weis  f  5714
*Firebird* - Mercedes Lackey  f  3281
*The Fires of Heaven* - Robert Jordan  f  2987
*Firewalk* - Anne Logston  f  3509
*First King of Shannara* - Terry Brooks  f  712
*Firstborn* - Paul B. Thompson  f  5454
*Fish Soup* - Ursula K. Le Guin  f  3378
*Flames of the Dragon* - Robin Wayne Bailey  f  287
*Flight of the Dragon Kyn* - Susan Fletcher  f  1951
*Flight of Vengeance* - Andre Norton  f  4152
*Flight to Hollow Mountain* - Mark Sebanc  f  4908
*The Floating Castle* - Craig Mills  f  3913
*Flute Song Magic* - Andrea Shettle  f  4996
*The Fools' War* - Lee Kisling  f  3159
*Forbidden Magic* - Angus Wells  f  5736
*The Forge in the Forest* - Michael Scott
    Rohan  f  4660
*The Forging of the Shadows* - Oliver
    Johnson  f  2924

*Fortress in the Eye of Time* - C.J. Cherryh  f  991
*Fortress of Eagles* - C.J. Cherryh  f  992
*Fortress of Frost and Fire* - Mercedes
    Lackey  f  3282
*Fortress of Owls* - C.J. Cherryh  f  993
*The Fortress of the Pearl* - Michael
    Moorcock  f  3982
*Fossil Hunter* - Robert J. Sawyer  s  4855
*The Fountains of Mirlacca* - Ashley
    McConnell  f  3775
*Four & Twenty Blackbirds* - Mercedes
    Lackey  f  3283
*Fox and Empire* - Harry Turtledove  f  5500
*From Prussia with Love* - John DeChancie  f  1457
*Fugitive Prince* - Janny Wurts  f  6002
*Full Spectrum 2* - Lou Aronica  s  214
*A Game of Thrones* - George R.R. Martin  f  3645
*Gameplay* - Kevin J. Anderson  f  105
*The Gates of Twilight* - Paula Volsky  f  5581
*The Gates of Vensunor* - Carol Heller  f  2650
*Gawain and Lady Green* - Anne Eliot
    Crompton  f  1269
*Geis of the Gargoyle* - Piers Anthony  f  172
*Ghost of Chance* - William S. Burroughs  s  780
*The Gift* - Patrick O'Leary  f  4211
*The Glass Dragon* - Irene Radford  f  4460
*The Glass Warrior* - Robert E. Vardeman  f  5563
*Glory Road* - Robert A. Heinlein  f  2644
*Go Quest, Young Man* - K.B. Bogen  f  557
*The Goblin Mirror* - C.J. Cherryh  f  994
*The Goblin Plain War* - Carl Miller  f  3892
*Goblins in the Castle* - Bruce Coville  f  1218
*The Gold Ball* - Hanne Marie Svendsen  f  5361
*Gold Unicorn* - Tanith Lee  f  3410
*Goldclimbers* - Nancy Luenn  f  3545
*The Golden Compass* - Philip Pullman  f  4446
*The Golden Thread* - Suzy McKee Charnas  f  969
*Golden Trillium* - Andre Norton  f  4153
*The Grail and the Ring* - Teresa Edgerton  f  1744
*Green Rider* - Kristen Britain  f  692
*Greendaughter* - Anne Logston  f  3510
*Greenmagic* - Crawford Kilian  f  3105
*Guardian's Key* - Anne Logston  f  3511
*Guards! Guards!* - Terry Pratchett  f  4390
*Guilty Pleasures* - Laurell K. Hamilton  f  2517
*The Hand of Chaos* - Margaret Weis  f  5715
*The Hands of Lyr* - Andre Norton  f  4154
*Harm's Way* - Colin Greenland  s  2416
*Harp of Winds* - Maggie Furey  f  2097
*Harpy Thyme* - Piers Anthony  f  174
*Harry Potter and the Sorcerer's Stone* - J.K.
    Rowling  f  4700
*The Hashish Man and Other Stories by Lord Dunsany*
    - Lord Dunsany  f  1700
*Hawk's Flight* - Carol Chase  f  980
*The Hawk's Gray Feather* - Patricia Kennealy-
    Morrison  f  3061
*The Healing of Crossroads* - Nick
    O'Donohoe  f  4195
*Heart Readers* - Kristine Kathryn Rusch  f  4718
*Hearts and Armor* - Ron Miller  f  3903
*Heartstone and Silver* - Jacqui Singleton  f  5071
*Hederick, the Theocrat* - Ellen Dodge
    Severson  f  4925
*The Hedge of Mist* - Patricia Kennealy-
    Morrison  f  3062
*Heir to the Empire* - Timothy Zahn  s  6054
*The Heirs of Hammerfell* - Marion Zimmer
    Bradley  s  638
*The Heldan* - Deborah Talmadge-Bickmore  f  5383
*Henry's Gift: The Magic Eye* - David
    Worsick  f  5972
*A Hero Born* - Michael A. Stackpole  f  5202
*Heroes Wanted* - Kyle Crocco  f  1267
*A Heroine of the World* - Tanith Lee  f  3412
*Hero's Song* - Edith Pattou  f  4261
*The Hidden City* - David Eddings  f  1733
*The Hidden Realms* - Sharon Green  f  2358
*The High House* - James Stoddard  f  5311

*Hogfather* - Terry Pratchett  f  4391
*The Honorable Barbarian* - L. Sprague de
    Camp  f  1415
*Horrible Humes* - Stephen Billias  f  487
*Horrors of the Dancing Gods* - Jack L.
    Chalker  f  955
*Hour of the Octopus* - Joel Rosenberg  f  4673
*Humility Garden* - Felicity Savage  f  4850
*I, Strahd* - P.N. Elrod  h  1797
*If I Pay Thee Not in Gold* - Piers Anthony  f  176
*If Wishes Were Horses* - Anne McCaffrey  f  3737
*Ill Met in Lankhmar* - Fritz Leiber  f  3419
*Illusion* - Paula Volsky  f  5582
*In Sylvan Shadows* - R.A. Salvatore  f  4800
*In the Red Lord's Reach* - Phyllis
    Eisenstein  f  1765
*The Inadequate Adept* - Simon Hawke  f  2617
*Interesting Times* - Terry Pratchett  f  4392
*Into the Dark Lands* - Michelle Sagara  f  4783
*Into the Fire* - Dennis L. McKiernan  f  3834
*Into the Forge* - Dennis L. McKiernan  f  3835
*Into the Green* - Charles de Lint  f  1430
*Into the Labyrinth* - Margaret Weis  f  5716
*Into the Land of the Unicorns* - Bruce
    Coville  f  1219
*Into the Void* - Nigel Findley  f  1937
*Iron Dragons: Mountains and Madness* - Rose
    Estes  f  1839
*The Iron Ring* - Lloyd Alexander  f  68
*The Iron Throne* - Simon Hawke  f  2618
*Isaac Asimov Presents the Great SF Stories: 20 (1958)*
    - Isaac Asimov  s  238
*Isaac Asimov Presents the Great SF Stories: 21 (1959)*
    - Isaac Asimov  s  239
*The Itinerant Exorcist* - Ashley McConnell  f  3776
*Jason Cosmo* - Dan McGirt  f  3811
*The Jewel of Equilibrant* - Steven Frankos  f  2042
*The Jewel of Fire* - Diana L. Paxson  f  4265
*Jingo* - Terry Pratchett  f  4393
*Journeyman Wizard* - Mary Frances
    Zambreno  f  6057
*Kar Kalim* - Deborah Christian  f  1025
*Kaz the Minotaur* - Richard A. Knaak  f  3172
*Kedrigern and the Charming Couple* - John
    Morressy  f  4013
*The Key of the Keplian* - Andre Norton  f  4156
*Kindred Spirits* - Mark Anthony  f  154
*King Javan's Year* - Katherine Kurtz  f  3258
*King of the Dead* - Gene DeWeese  h  1510
*King of the Grey* - Richard A. Knaak  f  3173
*King Pinch* - David Cook  f  1146
*The Kingdom of Kevin Malone* - Suzy McKee
    Charnas  f  970
*Kingdoms of the Night* - Allan Cole  f  1105
*Kingmaker's Sword* - Ann Marston  f  3635
*The King's Buccaneer* - Raymond E. Feist  f  1904
*King's Dragon* - Kate Elliott  f  1773
*King's Son, Magic's Son* - Josepha Sherman  f  4986
*Kingslayer* - L. Dean James  f  2863
*The Kinslayer Wars* - Douglas Niles  f  4109
*The Knights of Cawdor* - Mike Jefferies  f  2886
*Knight's Wyrd* - Debra Doyle  f  1601
*Krondor, the Betrayal* - Raymond E. Feist  f  1905
*Lady of Mercy* - Michelle Sagara  f  4784
*Lady of the Trillium* - Marion Zimmer
    Bradley  f  641
*Ladylord* - Sasha Miller  f  3906
*The Lark and the Wren* - Mercedes Lackey  f  3286
*The Last Dragonlord* - Joanne Bertin  f  470
*The Last Hawk* - Catherine Asaro  s  219
*The Last Human* - Tom De Haven  f  1422
*The Laughing Corpse* - Laurell K. Hamilton  f  2519
*The League of the Crimson Crescent* - James E.
    Reagen  f  4495
*Lean Times in Lankhmar* - Fritz Leiber  f  3420
*The Legacy* - R.A. Salvatore  f  4801
*Legacy of Steel* - Mary H. Herbert  f  2675
*Liavek: Festival Week* - Will Shetterly  f  4994
*The Lightless Kingdom* - Jonathan Wylie  f  6007*

*Lightning's Daughter* - Mary H. Herbert  f  2676
*The Loneliest Magician* - Irene Radford  f  4461
*The Long Patrol* - Brian Jacques  f  2849
*Lord of Chaos* - Robert Jordan  f  2988
*Lord of the Troll-Bats* - Alexis A. Gilliland  f  2234
*Lords and Ladies* - Terry Pratchett  f  4394
*Lords of the Sky* - Angus Wells  f  5738
*Lords of the Sword* - Hugh Cook  f  1156
*The Lost City of Zork* - Robin Wayne Bailey  f  288
*Lost in Translation* - Margaret Ball  f  315
*The Lotus and the Rose* - Scott Ciencin  f  1029
*Luck in the Shadows* - Lynn Flewelling  f  1952
*Luck of the Wheels* - Megan Lindholm  f  3471
*Luthien's Gamble* - R.A. Salvatore  f  4802
*M.Y.T.H. Inc. in Action* - Robert Asprin  f  259
*The Mace of Souls* - Bruce Fergusson  f  1925
*Madouc* - Jack Vance  f  5547
*Mage Heart* - Jane Routley  f  4686
*The Mage in the Iron Mask* - Brian
    Thomsen  f  5458
*The Mageborn Traitor* - Melanie Rawn  f  4488
*Magelord: The Awakening* - Thomas K.
    Martin  f  3651
*The Magic and the Healing* - Nick
    O'Donohoe  f  4196
*The Magic Engineer* - L.E. Modesitt Jr.  f  3933
*The Magic of Recluce* - L.E. Modesitt Jr.  f  3934
*The Magic Wars* - Jo Clayton  f  1068
*Magic's Pawn* - Mercedes Lackey  f  3287
*Magic's Promise* - Mercedes Lackey  f  3289
*Majyk by Accident* - Esther Friesner  f  2079
*Majyk by Design* - Esther Friesner  f  2080
*Majyk by Hook or Crook* - Esther Friesner  f  2081
*A Man Betrayed* - J.V. Jones  f  2958
*Man-Kzin Wars III* - Larry Niven  s  4123
*Marbleheart* - Don Callander  f  846
*Mariel of Redwall* - Brian Jacques  f  2850
*The Mark of the Cat* - Andre Norton  f  4157
*Martin the Warrior* - Brian Jacques  f  2851
*Masquerades* - Kate Novak  f  4166
*Masques* - Patricia Briggs  f  681
*Master and Fool* - J.V. Jones  f  2959
*Master of Many Treasures* - Mary Brown  f  726
*Mathemagics* - Margaret Ball  f  316
*Mattimeo* - Brian Jacques  f  2852
*Medallion of the Black Hound* - Shirley Rousseau
    Murphy  f  4056
*Men at Arms* - Terry Pratchett  f  4396
*The Mer-Child: A Legend for Children und Other
    Adults* - Robin Morgan  f  4008
*The Meri* - Maya Kaathryn Bohnhoff  f  561
*The Merlin Effect* - T.A. Barron  f  371
*Merlin's Harp* - Anne Eliot Crompton  f  1270
*Mind of the Magic* - Holly Lisle  f  3486
*The Mines of Behemoth* - Michael Shea  f  4945
*Mirror of Destiny* - Andre Norton  f  4159
*Mistress of the Empire* - Raymond E. Feist  f  1906
*The Moonbane Mage* - Laurie J. Marks  f  3626
*Moonspeaker* - K.D. Wentworth  s  5754
*The Moorchild* - Eloise Jarvis McGraw  f  3816
*Mordenheim* - Chet Williamson  h  5847
*Mordred's Curse* - Ian McDowell  f  3806
*More than Fire* - Philip Jose Farmer  s  1871
*Morigu: The Dead* - Mark C. Perry  f  4284
*Morningstar* - David Gemmell  f  2190
*Mort* - Terry Pratchett  f  4397
*Mostly Harmless* - Douglas Adams  s  31
*Mother of Storms* - Adrian Cole  f  1101
*Moving Pictures* - Terry Pratchett  f  4398
*Murder in Cormyr* - Chet Williamson  f  5848
*Myst: The Book of Atrus* - Rand Miller  f  3896
*Nameless Magery* - Delia Marshall Turner  f  5490
*Nations of the Night* - Oliver Johnson  f  2925
*Nebula Awards 24* - Michael Bishop  s  500
*Negrophobia: An Urban Parable* - Darius
    James  f  2859
*Night of Glory* - Scott Ciencin  f  1030
*Night of the Living 'Gator!* - Richard A.
    Lupoff  s  3573

*Night of the Living Rat!* - Debra Doyle  s  1603
*Night of the Living Shark!* - David Bischoff  s  493
*Nightfall* - Isaac Asimov  s  248
*Nightseer* - Laurell K. Hamilton  f  2521
*No Limits* - Nigel Findley  s  1938
*No One Noticed the Cat* - Anne McCaffrey  f  3740
*Nobody's Son* - Sean Stewart  f  5275
*The Nomad Queen* - James Gordon White  f  5783
*O Greenest Branch!* - Gael Baudino  f  394
*The Oak Above the Kings: A Book of the Keltiad* -
    Patricia Kennealy  s  3058
*Oath of Swords* - David Weber  f  5678
*Oathblood* - Mercedes Lackey  f  3290
*The Oathbound Wizard* - Christopher
    Stasheff  f  5219
*Of Tangible Ghosts* - L.E. Modesitt Jr.  f  3935
*On Meeting Witches at Wells* - Judith
    Gorog  f  2283
*Once a Hero* - Michael A. Stackpole  f  5203
*The One-Armed Queen* - Jane Yolen  f  6037
*One Land, One Duke* - Ru Emerson  f  1809
*One Quest, Hold the Dragons* - Greg
    Costikyan  f  1208
*The Order War* - L.E. Modesitt Jr.  f  3936
*The Others* - Margaret Wander Bonanno  s  565
*OtherWhere* - Margaret Wander Bonanno  s  566
*OtherWise* - Margaret Wander Bonanno  s  567
*The Outcast* - Simon Hawke  f  2621
*Outcast of Redwall* - Brian Jacques  f  2853
*Outcasts* - Clayton Emery  f  1815
*The Outlanders* - David B. Coe  f  1096
*Owlflight* - Mercedes Lackey  f  3291
*Owlsight* - Mercedes Lackey  f  3292
*The Painted Alphabet* - Diana Darling  f  1356
*Palace of Kings* - Mike Jefferies  f  2887
*Passage to Dawn* - R.A. Salvatore  f  4803
*Past Imperative* - Dave Duncan  f  1684
*The Path of Daggers* - Robert Jordan  f  2989
*The Pearl of the Soul of the World* - Meredith Ann
    Pierce  f  4318
*The Pearls of Lutra* - Brian Jacques  f  2854
*The Perfect Princess* - Irene Radford  f  4462
*The Persistence of Memory* - Karen Ripley  s  4592
*Petrogypsies* - Rory Harper  s  2549
*The Pixilated Peeress* - L. Sprague de
    Camp  f  1416
*A Plague of Sorcerers* - Mary Frances
    Zambreno  f  6058
*Planar Powers* - J. Robert King  f  3122
*Point of Hopes* - Melissa Scott  f  4899
*Polgara the Sorceress* - David Eddings  f  1734
*The Porcelain Dove* - Delia Sherman  f  4983
*Prentice Alvin* - Orson Scott Card  f  896
*Present Tense* - Dave Duncan  f  1606
*The Price of Blood and Honor* - Elizabeth
    Willey  f  5811
*Prince of Chaos* - Roger Zelazny  f  6073
*The Prince of Ill Luck* - Susan Dexter  f  1512
*Prince of the Blood* - Raymond E. Feist  f  1907
*Pulphouse, Issue 6: Fantasy* - Kristine Kathryn
    Rusch  f  4723
*Pulphouse, Issue 8: Science Fiction* - Kristine Kathryn
    Rusch  s  4725
*The Qualinesti* - Paul B. Thompson  f  5455
*The Queen of Ashes* - Deborah Turner
    Harris  f  2561
*The Quest Begins* - Wendy Pini  f  4337
*Quest for the Fallen Star* - Piers Anthony  f  185
*Question Quest* - Piers Anthony  f  186
*The Radiant Dragon* - Elaine Cunningham  f  1291
*The Rainbow Abyss* - Barbara Hambly  f  2507
*Rally Cry!* - William R. Forstchen  s  1982
*The Raven Ring* - Patricia C. Wrede  f  5978
*Reaper Man* - Terry Pratchett  f  4399
*The Reaver Road* - Dave Duncan  f  1687
*Reclamation* - Sarah Zettel  s  6081
*Red Magic* - Jean Rabe  f  4458
*Red Unicorn* - Tanith Lee  f  3414
*Redmagic* - Crawford Kilian  f  3107

*The Reluctant Sorcerer* - Simon Hawke  f  2622
*A Remembrance for Kedrigern* - John
    Morressy  f  4014
*The Resistance* - Kristine Kathryn Rusch  f  4727
*Return to Lankhmar* - Fritz Leiber  f  3422
*Revenge of the Fluffy Bunnies* - Craig Shaw
    Gardner  f  2132
*The Revenge of the Rose* - Michael
    Moorcock  f  3985
*The Riddled Man* - Mark E. Rogers  f  4654
*Ring of Intrigue* - Jane S. Fancher  f  1863
*Ring of Lightning* - Jane S. Fancher  f  1864
*The Ring of Winter* - James Lowder  f  3538
*Rise of a Merchant Prince* - Raymond E.
    Feist  f  1909
*The Rivan Codex* - David Eddings  f  1735
*The Road Home* - Joel Rosenberg  f  4674
*The Road to Ehvenor* - Joel Rosenberg  f  4675
*The Road to Underfall* - Mike Jefferies  f  2888
*The Robin and the Kestrel* - Mercedes
    Lackey  f  3293
*Roc and a Hard Place* - Piers Anthony  f  187
*A Romance of the Equator: The Best Fantasy Stories
    of Brian W. Aldiss* - Brian W. Aldiss  f  59
*Ronin* - D.A. Heeley  f  2639
*Rose Daughter* - Robin McKinley  f  3847
*The Rose Sea* - S.M. Stirling  f  5296
*Rouse a Sleeping Cat* - Dan Crawford  f  1249
*Roverandom* - J.R.R. Tolkien  f  5479
*Royal Assassin* - Robin Hobb  f  2695
*The Ruby Knight* - David Eddings  f  1736
*The Ruins of Ambrai* - Melanie Rawn  f  4489
*Runes of Autumn* - Larry Elmore  f  1790
*Sabriel* - Garth Nix  f  4129
*The Sage* - Christopher Stasheff  f  5221
*Salamandastron* - Brian Jacques  f  2855
*Samurai Cat Goes to Hell* - Mark E. Rogers  f  4655
*The Sands of Kalaven: A Novel of Shunlar* - Carol
    Heller  f  2651
*The Sapphire Rose* - David Eddings  f  1737
*The Schemes of Dragons* - Dave Smeds  f  5097
*School of Wizardry* - Debra Doyle  f  1605
*The Scions of Shannara* - Terry Brooks  f  716
*Search for the Starblade* - Keith Taylor  f  5408
*Searching for Dragons* - Patricia C. Wrede  f  5979
*Season of Storms* - Ellen Foxxe  f  2032
*The Second Generation* - Margaret Weis  f  5724
*Seed upon the Wind* - Carole Nelson
    Douglas  f  1584
*The Seeker* - Simon Hawke  f  2624
*The Seeress of Kell* - David Eddings  f  1738
*Serpent Mage* - Margaret Weis  f  5726
*Servant of the Empire* - Raymond E. Feist  f  1910
*The Seventh Gate* - Margaret Weis  f  5727
*The Seventh Sentinel* - Mary Kirchoff  f  3154
*Shade and Shadow* - Francine G. Woodbury  f  5967
*Shadow* - Anne Logston  f  3512
*Shadow Dance* - Anne Logston  f  3513
*Shadow Dawn* - Chris Claremont  f  1042
*Shadow Hunt* - Anne Logston  f  3514
*Shadow-Maze* - Mark Smith  f  5133
*Shadow of a Dark Queen* - Raymond E.
    Feist  f  1911
*Shadow of Obsession* - Rebecca Neason  f  4082
*The Shadow of Sorcery* - Andrew J. Offutt  f  4202
*Shadow of the Crown* - Craig Mills  f  3914
*The Shadow Rising* - Robert Jordan  f  2990
*The Shadow Shaia* - Alexis A. Gilliland  f  2235
*The Shadow Warrior* - Pat Zettner  f  6082
*Shadowdance* - Robin Wayne Bailey  f  290
*Shadowlight* - Jackie Hyman  f  2819
*Shadows over Lyra* - Patricia C. Wrede  f  5980
*Shadow's Realm* - Mickey Zucker Reichert  f  4523
*Shaman* - Sandra Miesel  f  3889
*The Shaman* - Christopher Stasheff  f  5223
*The Shape-Changer's Wife* - Sharon Shinn  f  5002
*Shape-Shifter: Stories by Pauline Melville* - Pauline
    Melville  f  3876
*Sheepfarmer's Daughter* - Elizabeth Moon  f  3973

*The Ship of Magic* - Robin Hobb    f    2696
*Ships of Merior* - Janny Wurts    f    6004
*Shiva: An Adventure of the Ice Age* - J.H.
    Brennan    f    669
*The Shrouded Realm* - Richard A. Knaak    f    3174
*Siege of Darkness* - R.A. Salvatore    f    4804
*The Silent Blade* - R.A. Salvatore    f    4805
*Silver Princess, Golden Knight* - Sharon
    Green    f    2359
*Silver Shadows* - Elaine Cunningham    f    1292
*The Silver Stone* - Joel Rosenberg    f    4676
*Sister Light, Sister Dark* - Jane Yolen    f    6039
*Skybowl* - Melanie Rawn    f    4490
*Slay and Rescue* - John Moore    f    3991
*The Sleep of Stone* - Louise Cooper    f    1179
*Sleipnir* - Linda Evans    f    1856
*Small Gods* - Terry Pratchett    f    4400
*Son of Spellsinger* - Alan Dean Foster    f    2015
*The Son of Summer Stars* - Meredith Ann
    Pierce    f    4319
*Song in the Silence* - Elizabeth Kerner    f    3065
*Song of the Saurials* - Kate Novak    f    4167
*Songs of Earth and Power* - Greg Bear    f    424
*Songsmith* - Andre Norton    f    4161
*Soothslayer: A Magickal Fantasy* - D.J.
    Conway    f    1143
*The Soprano Sorceress* - L.E. Modesitt Jr.    f    3938
*A Sorcerer and a Gentleman* - Elizabeth
    Willey    f    5812
*Sorceress of Darshiva* - David Eddings    f    1739
*Soul Music* - Terry Pratchett    f    4401
*Spear of Heaven* - Judith Tarr    f    5396
*Spell of Apocalypse* - Mayer Alan Brenner    f    672
*Spell of Fate* - Mayer Alan Brenner    f    673
*The Spell of the Black Dagger* - Lawrence Watt-
    Evans    f    5648
*The Spellkey Trilogy* - Ann Downer    f    1592
*The Spellsong War* - L.E. Modesitt Jr.    f    3939
*Spirit Fox* - Mickey Zucker Reichert    f    4524
*The Spirit Gate* - Maya Kaathryn Bohnhoff    f    562
*Spirit of the Wind* - Chris Pierson    f    4326
*The Spirit Ring* - Lois McMaster Bujold    f    763
*Spirits of Cavern and Hearth* - M. Coleman
    Easton    f    1722
*Split Heirs* - Lawrence Watt-Evans    f    5649
*Stalking Darkness* - Lynn Flewelling    f    1953
*The Stalking Horse* - Constance Ash    f    222
*The Stallion Queen* - Constance Ash    f    223
*Star Ascendant* - Louise Cooper    f    1180
*The Star Scroll* - Melanie Rawn    f    4491
*StarGate* - Dean Devlin    s    1509
*Starless Night* - R.A. Salvatore    f    4807
*Steal the Dragon* - Patricia Briggs    f    682
*Steel and Stone* - Ellen Porath    f    4368
*The Stone Giant* - James P. Blaylock    f    523
*The Stone Movers* - Patricia Mullen    f    4045
*Stone of Farewell* - Tad Williams    f    5831
*Stone of Tears* - Terry Goodkind    f    2269
*The Stone of Time* - Rose Estes    f    1840
*Stopping at Slowyear* - Frederik Pohl    s    4355
*Storm Caller* - Carol Severance    f    4924
*Storms of Victory* - Andre Norton    f    4162
*Stranger at the Wedding* - Barbara Hambly    f    2509
*Stronghold* - Melanie Rawn    f    4492
*A Study in Sorcery* - Michael Kurland    f    3252
*The Subtle Knife* - Philip Pullman    f    4448
*Summerland* - L. Dean James    f    2865
*Sunderlies Seeking* - Gayle Greeno    f    2424
*Sunrunner's Fire* - Melanie Rawn    f    4493
*The Sure Death of a Mouse* - Dan Crawford    f    1250
*Sweet Myth-tery of Life* - Robert Asprin    f    262
*A Sword for a Dragon* - Christopher
    Rowley    f    4697
*The Sword of Bedwyr* - R.A. Salvatore    f    4808
*Sword of Flame* - Maggie Furey    f    2098

*Swords Against the Shadowland* - Robin Wayne
    Bailey    f    291
*Taking Flight* - Lawrence Watt-Evans    f    5650
*Tales From Planet Earth* - Arthur C. Clarke    s    1061
*Tales From Watership Down* - Richard Adams    f    32
*Tales of Mithgar* - Dennis L. McKiernan    f    3836
*Tales of Riverworld* - Philip Jose Farmer    s    1875
*The Talismans of Shannara* - Terry Brooks    f    717
*Taminy* - Maya Kaathryn Bohnhoff    f    563
*The Tangle Box* - Terry Brooks    f    718
*Tapestry of Dark Souls* - Elaine Bergstrom    h    465
*Tears of the Night Sky* - Linda P. Baker    f    299
*Tears of Time* - Nancy Asire    f    256
*Tegne: Soul Warrior* - Richard La Plante    f    3268
*Tehanu: The Last Book of Earthsea* - Ursula K. Le
    Guin    f    3383
*Temple of the Winds* - Terry Goodkind    f    2270
*Terrible Swift Sword* - William R.
    Forstchen    s    1983
*They Fly at Ciron* - Samuel R. Delany    s    1482
*The Thirteenth Majestral* - Hayford Peirce    s    4277
*Thorn and Needle* - Paul B. Thompson    f    5456
*Thornhold* - Elaine Cunningham    f    1293
*Thunder of the Captains* - Holly Lisle    f    3489
*Tigana* - Guy Gavriel Kay    f    3018
*Tiger Burning Bright* - Marion Zimmer
    Bradley    f    652
*The Time of Madness* - Thomas K. Martin    f    3652
*To Fall Like Stars* - Nancy Asire    f    257
*To Green Angel Tower* - Tad Williams    f    5832
*Toad Triumphant* - William Horwood    f    2774
*Token of Dragonsblood* - Damaris Cole    f    1114
*Top Dog* - Jerry Jay Carroll    f    915
*Touched by Magic* - Doranna Durgin    f    1705
*Touched by the Gods* - Lawrence Watt-
    Evans    f    5651
*Tower of Doom* - Mark Anthony    h    155
*Tower of Fear* - Glen Cook    f    1155
*The Towers of the Sunset* - L.E. Modesitt
    Jr.    f    3941
*Tris's Book* - Tamora Pierce    f    4322
*A Troubling Along the Border* - Donald Aamodt    f    4
*The True Knight* - Susan Dexter    f    1513
*Twisted Dragon* - Kevin Stein    f    5251
*A Two-Edged Sword* - Thomas K. Martin    f    3653
*The Two in Hiding* - Ru Emerson    f    1812
*Typewriter in the Sky* - L. Ron Hubbard    f    2791
*The Ultimate Helm* - Russ T. Howard    f    2785
*The Uncrowned King* - Michelle West    f    5760
*Under the Healing Sign* - Nick O'Donohoe    f    4198
*Under the Yoke* - S.M. Stirling    s    5301
*The Undesired Princess and the Enchanted Bunny* - L.
    Sprague de Camp    f    1419
*The Unicorn Peace* - John Lee    f    3399
*The Unicorn Solution* - John Lee    f    3400
*The Unicorn Sonata* - Peter S. Beagle    f    412
*The Unicorn War* - John Lee    f    3401
*Valorian* - Mary H. Herbert    f    2677
*The Veils of Snows* - Mark Helprin    f    2654
*The Verdant Passage* - Troy Denning    f    1487
*Villains by Necessity* - Eve Forward    f    1985
*Visitors From Oz: The Wild Adventures of Dorothy,
    the Scarecrow and the Tin Woodman* - Martin
    Gardner    f    2136
*Voima* - C. Dale Brittain    f    704
*The Voyage of Mael Duin's Curragh* - Patricia
    Aakhus    f    2
*Waking Beauty* - Paul Witcover    f    5931
*Waking in Dreamland* - Jody Lynn Nye    f    4177
*Walker of Worlds* - Tom De Haven    f    1423
*Wanderlust* - Mary Kirchoff    f    3155
*War* - Simon Hawke    f    2625
*The War Amongst the Angels* - Michael
    Moorcock    f    3986
*The War God's Own* - David Weber    f    5682

*War of the Three Waters* - Douglas Niles    f    4110
*The Warden of Horses* - Karen Ripley    s    4595
*The Warrior and the Witch* - Carl Miller    f    3893
*Warriorwards* - Dafydd ab Hugh    f    11
*The Waste Lands* - Stephen King    h    3143
*The Watcher's Mask* - Laurie J. Marks    f    3627
*The Waterborn* - J. Gregory Keyes    f    3098
*The Ways of Magic* - Scott Ciencin    f    1033
*The Well-Favored Man: The Tale of the Sorcerer's
    Nephew* - Elizabeth Willey    f    5813
*Well Wished* - Franny Billingsley    f    489
*The Western King* - Ann Marston    f    3636
*Westlin Wind* - Charles de Lint    f    1439
*Wheel of Dreams* - Salinda Tyson    f    5529
*When Demons Walk* - Patricia Briggs    f    683
*When the Gods Are Silent* - Jane M.
    Lindskold    f    3477
*White Jenna* - Jane Yolen    f    6041
*The White Order* - L.E. Modesitt Jr.    f    3942
*Wicked: The Life and Times of the Wicked Witch of
    the West* - Gregory Maguire    f    3609
*The Widowmaker Reborn* - Mike Resnick    s    4560
*A Wild Dog and Lone* - Dan Crawford    f    1251
*The Wild Hunt* - Jane Yolen    f    6042
*Wild Magic* - Jo Clayton    f    1072
*Wild Magic* - Angus Wells    f    5741
*Wildfire* - Jo Clayton    f    1073
*The Willows and Beyond* - William
    Horwood    f    2775
*The Willows in Winter* - William Horwood    f    2776
*The Wind Crystal* - Diana L. Paxson    f    4269
*Wind Whispers, Shadow Shouts* - Sharon
    Green    f    2360
*Winged Magic* - Mary H. Herbert    f    2678
*Winter Rose* - Patricia A. McKillip    f    3843
*Wishbringer* - Craig Shaw Gardner    f    2133
*The Witch and the Cathedral* - C. Dale
    Brittain    f    705
*Witch and Wombat* - Carolyn Cushman    f    1299
*Witches Abroad* - Terry Pratchett    f    4404
*Witches' Brew* - Terry Brooks    f    719
*The Witches of Eileanan* - Kate Forsyth    f    1984
*The Wiz Biz* - Rick Cook    f    1160
*The Wizard and the Floating City* - Christopher
    Rowley    f    4699
*The Wizard of Ambermere* - J. Calvin Pierce    f    4317
*Wizard Spawn* - C.J. Cherryh    f    1004
*The Wizardry Consulted* - Rick Cook    f    1161
*The Wizardry Quested* - Rick Cook    f    1163
*Wizard's First Rule* - Terry Goodkind    f    2271
*Wizard's Hall* - Jane Yolen    f    6043
*The Wizard's Shadow* - Susan Dexter    f    1514
*Wolf Justice* - Doranna Durgin    f    1706
*The Wolf of Winter* - Paula Volsky    f    5584
*The Wolves of Autumn* - Scott Ciencin    f    1035
*The Wood Nymph and the Cranky Saint* - C. Dale
    Brittain    f    706
*The Wooden Sword* - Lynn Abbey    f    18
*The Woods out Back* - R.A. Salvatore    f    4809
*The World of Robert Jordan's The Wheel of Time* -
    Robert Jordan    f    2991
*Wrath of the Princes* - Holly Lisle    f    3490
*Wren to the Rescue* - Sherwood Smith    f    5142
*Wren's Quest* - Sherwood Smith    f    5143
*Wren's War* - Sherwood Smith    f    5144
*Wyrd Sisters* - Terry Pratchett    f    4405
*Ye Gods!* - Tom Holt    f    2753
*The Year's Best Science Fiction: Seventh Annual
    Collection* - Gardner Dozois    s    1621
*Yon Ill Wind* - Piers Anthony    f    196
*Zombie Lover* - Piers Anthony    f    197
*The Zork Chronicles* - George Alec
    Effinger    s    1754

# Geographic Index

This index provides access to all featured books by geographic settings, such as countries, continents, oceans, and planets. States and provinces are indicated for the United States and Canada. Also included are headings for fictional place names, such as Spaceships, Imaginary Planets, etc. Sections are further broken down by city or the specific name of the imaginary locale. Book titles are listed alphabetically under headings, and author names and entry numbers are also provided.

## AFRICA

*Afrikorps* - Bill Dolan   s   1566
*The Book of Water* - Marjorie Bradley
   Kellogg   f   3045
*Cobra Curse* - Bill Dolan   s   1567
*The Discovery of Dragons* - Graeme Base   f   385
*Evil Eye* - Michael Slade   h   5085
*The Exile Kiss* - George Alec Effinger   s   1750
*The Exile Kiss* - George Alec Effinger   s   1750
*The Famished Road* - Ben Okri   f   4207
*A Fire in the Sun* - George Alec Effinger   s   1751
*Firedance* - Steven Barnes   s   360
*Future Earths: Under African Skies* - Mike
   Resnick   s   4544
*Hope of Earth* - Piers Anthony   s   175
*Indiana Jones and the Sky Pirates* - Martin
   Caidin   f   825
*Iron Horse* - Bill Dolan   s   1568
*The Land of Gold* - Gillian Bradshaw   f   658
*No Enemy but Time* - Michael Bishop   s   502
*O Greenest Branch!* - Gael Baudino   f   394
*Pastwatch: The Redemption of Christopher Columbus* -
   Orson Scott Card   s   895
*Songs of Enchantment* - Ben Okri   f   4208
*StarGate* - Dean Devlin   s   1509
*White Rhino* - Bill Dolan   s   1569

**Endless City**
*The Great Wheel* - Ian R. MacLeod   s   3599

**Gerardville**
*White Queen* - Gwyneth Jones   s   2955

**Kirinyaga Territory**
*Bully!* - Mike Resnick   s   4539

**Senegambia**
*Warrior Shield* - G. Harry Stine   s   5283

**Timbuctoo**
*Lion Time in Timbuctoo* - Robert Silverberg   s   5036

## ALBANIA

*Lord of the Dead* - Tom Holland   h   2741

## ALGERIA

**Algiers**
*The Eight* - Katherine Neville   f   4092

## ALTERNATE EARTH

*The Adventures of Threadwell the Tailor, or
   Alterations Made While You Wait* - P.D.
   Cacek   h   801
*Alvin Journeyman* - Orson Scott Card   f   881
*Ancient Games* - Scott Ciencin   f   1028
*The Architecture of Desire* - Mary Gentle   f   2195
*Back in the USSA* - Kim Newman   s   4095
*A Bad Spell in Yurt* - C. Dale Brittain   f   701
*Blood: A Southern Fantasy* - Michael
   Moorcock   f   3977
*Branch Point* - Mona Clee   s   1074
*Bring the Jubilee* - Ward Moore   s   3993
*Bully!* - Mike Resnick   s   4539
*The Case of the Toxic Spell Dump* - Harry
   Turtledove   f   5497
*Catwings* - Ursula K. Le Guin   f   3377
*Changespell* - Doranna Durgin   f   1703
*Chimaera's Copper* - Piers Anthony   f   166
*A College of Magics* - Caroline Stevermer   f   5266
*Conan the Formidable* - Steve Perry   f   4293
*Conan the Guardian* - Roland J. Green   f   2347
*Conan the Indomitable* - Steve Perry   f   4294
*Corum: The Coming of Chaos* - Michael
   Moorcock   f   3978
*Cry Republic* - Kirk Mitchell   s   3917
*The Dagger and the Cross: A Novel of the Crusades* -
   Judith Tarr   f   5393
*Dark City* - Frank Lauria   h   3351
*Doc Sidhe* - Aaron Allston   f   85
*Drachenfels* - Jack Yeovil   f   6022
*The Dragon and the Gnarly King* - Gordon R.
   Dickson   f   1529
*The Dragon in Lyonesse* - Gordon R.
   Dickson   f   1531
*The Drawing of the Three* - Stephen King   h   3131
*Dun Lady's Jess* - Doranna Durgin   f   1704
*Elvissey* - Jack Womack   s   5957
*Fabulous Harbors* - Michael Moorcock   f   3981
*The Final Battle* - Richard A. Lupoff   f   3572
*The Flying Warlord* - Leo Frankowski   s   2044
*Forest of the Night* - S.P. Somtow   f   5156
*Freeze Frames* - Katharine Kerr   s   3071
*Glory Road* - Robert A. Heinlein   f   2644
*The Great War: American Front* - Harry
   Turtledove   s   5501
*Guilty Pleasures* - Laurell K. Hamilton   f   2517
*Heartfire* - Orson Scott Card   f   889
*A Heroine of the World* - Tanith Lee   f   3412
*The Hidden City* - Charles de Lint   f   1429
*The High-Tech Knight* - Leo Frankowski   s   2045

*The Hollow Earth: The Narrative of Mason Algiers
   Reynolds of Virginia* - Rudy Rucker   s   4705
*How Few Remain* - Harry Turtledove   s   5504
*Invasion of Willow Wood Springs* - Terry
   Ellis   f   1781
*Jaguar* - Bill Ransom   s   4477
*Jason Cosmo* - Dan McGirt   f   3811
*Konrad* - David Ferring   f   1927
*Lights Out in the Reptile House* - Jim
   Shepard   f   4976
*Lord Conrad's Lady* - Leo Frankowski   s   2046
*Lost in Translation* - Margaret Ball   f   315
*The Memory Cathedral* - Jack Dann   s   1341
*Milton in America* - Peter Ackroyd   f   25
*Mouvar's Magic* - Piers Anthony   f   182
*Mysterium* - Robert Charles Wilson   s   5911
*Negrophobia: An Urban Parable* - Darius
   James   f   2859
*An Oblique Approach* - David Drake   s   1638
*An Oblique Approach* - David Drake   s   1638
*Of Beginnings and Endings* - Robert Adams   s   33
*Orc's Opal* - Piers Anthony   f   183
*Outcasts* - Clayton Emery   f   1815
*Past Imperative* - Dave Duncan   f   1684
*Plague Demon*   Brian Craig   f   1239
*Prentice Alvin* - Orson Scott Card   f   896
*Present Tense* - Dave Duncan   f   1686
*Queen's Gambit Declined* - Melinda M.
   Snodgrass   f   5147
*The Radiant Warrior* - Leo Frankowski   s   2047
*Ratha and Thistle-Chaser* - Clare Bell   f   432
*Rats and Gargoyles* - Mary Gentle   f   2196
*Reluctant Voyagers* - Elisabeth Vonarburg   s   5591
*The Resurrections* - Simon Louvish   s   3528
*School of Wizardry* - Debra Doyle   f   1605
*Shadowbreed* - David Ferring   f   1928
*Shaman* - Sandra Miesel   f   3889
*Sliders: The Novel* - Brad Linaweaver   s   3467
*The Spirit Ring* - Lois McMaster Bujold   f   763
*The Steampunk Trilogy* - Paul Di Filippo   s   1518
*The Stone Dogs* - S.M. Stirling   s   5300
*The Subtle Knife* - Philip Pullman   f   4448
*Through the Ice* - Piers Anthony   f   192
*The Tranquility Alternative* - Allen Steele   s   5248
*The War in the Waste* - Felicity Savage   f   4851
*What Savage Beast* - Peter David   s   1390
*The Wizardry Consulted* - Rick Cook   f   1161
*The Wizardry Cursed* - Rick Cook   f   1162
*The Wizardry Quested* - Rick Cook   f   1163
*The Wood Nymph and the Cranky Saint* - C. Dale
   Brittain   f   706
*Worldwar: In the Balance* - Harry
   Turtledove   s   5515

*Worldwar: Striking the Balance* - Harry
  Turtledove  *s*  5516
*Worldwar: Tilting the Balance* - Harry
  Turtledove  *s*  5517
*Worldwar: Upsetting the Balance* - Harry
  Turtledove  *s*  5518
*Zaragoz* - Brian Craig  *f*  1241

**Antarctica**
*Ghost Dancers* - Brian Craig  *s*  1238

**Avonleigh**
*Shadowborn* - William W. Connors  *h*  1137

**Aysle**
*Dragons over England* - Douglas Kaufman  *f*  3015

**Bay Bay**
*Warriorwards* - Dafydd ab Hugh  *f*  11

**Cape Canaveral, Florida**
*Comeback Tour: The Sky Belongs to the Stars* - Jack
  Yeovil  *s*  6020

**Domino**
*An Eye for Dark Places* - Norma Marder  *s*  3622

**D'Urth**
*The Race for God* - Brian Herbert  *s*  2666

**England**
*Anno Dracula* - Kim Newman  *h*  4094
*The Dragon and the Djinn* - Gordon R.
  Dickson  *f*  1528
*The Dragon at War* - Gordon R. Dickson  *f*  1530
*The Dragon Knight* - Gordon R. Dickson  *f*  1532
*The Dragon on the Border* - Gordon R.
  Dickson  *f*  1533
*The Dragon, the Earl, and the Troll* - Gordon R.
  Dickson  *f*  1534
*Shade and Shadow* - Francine G. Woodbury  *f*  5967

**Europe**
*From Prussia with Love* - John DeChancie  *f*  1457

**Euterpe**
*The Gnome's Engine* - Teresa Edgerton  *f*  1742

**Eyrith**
*Minerva Wakes* - Holly Lisle  *f*  3487

**Fasosi**
*The Duke of Sumava* - Sara J. Wrench  *f*  5983

**France**
*The Bloody Red Baron* - Kim Newman  *h*  4097
*The Dragon at War* - Gordon R. Dickson  *f*  1530
*The Wild Blue and the Gray* - William
  Sanders  *s*  4814

**Gl'thaan Em**
*Ancient Echoes* - Robert Holdstock  *f*  2735

**Italy**
*Pasquale's Angel* - Paul J. McAuley  *f*  3714

**The Kingdom**
*On Fortune's Wheel* - Cynthia Voigt  *f*  5579

**Lyonesse**
*The Dragon in Lyonesse* - Gordon R.
  Dickson  *f*  1531

**Memphis, Tennessee**
*Comeback Tour: The Sky Belongs to the Stars* - Jack
  Yeovil  *s*  6020

**Middle East**
*The Dragon and the Djinn* - Gordon R.
  Dickson  *f*  1528

**Morien, Wales**
*Storm Warriors* - Brian Craig  *f*  1240

**The New World**
*The Gnome's Engine* - Teresa Edgerton  *f*  1742

**New World**
*The Silent Stars Go By* - James White  *s*  5781
*A Study in Sorcery* - Michael Kurland  *f*  3252

**Nextdoor**
*Future Indefinite* - Dave Duncan  *f*  1678

**Nile Empire**
*Mysterious Cairo* - Ed Stark  *f*  5210
*Strange Tales From the Nile Empire* - Greg
  Farshtey  *f*  1889

**North America**
*Of Tangible Ghosts* - L.E. Modesitt Jr.  *f*  3935

**North American Union**
*The Two Georges* - Richard Dreyfuss  *s*  1655

**Orange County, California**
*The Gold Coast* - Kim Stanley Robinson  *s*  4632
*Pacific Edge* - Kim Stanley Robinson  *s*  4634

**Qushmarrah**
*Tower of Fear* - Glen Cook  *f*  1155

**St. Louis, Missouri**
*Bloody Bones* - Laurell K. Hamilton  *h*  2512
*Circus of the Damned* - Laurell K.
  Hamilton  *h*  2515
*The Laughing Corpse* - Laurell K. Hamilton  *f*  2519
*The Lunatic Cafe* - Laurell K. Hamilton  *h*  2520

**Shale**
*Chaos Mode* - Piers Anthony  *f*  165

**Shei'rah**
*The Unicorn Sonata* - Peter S. Beagle  *f*  412

**Sky Lord Pangloth**
*The Sky Lords* - John Brosnan  *s*  720

**Southwest United States**
*Ghost Dancers* - Brian Craig  *s*  1238

**Thornberry-on-the-Lunn**
*Goblin Moon* - Teresa Edgerton  *f*  1743

**Vurt**
*Pollen* - Jeff Noon  *s*  4135

**Western United States**
*Darkthunder's Way* - Tom Deitz  *f*  1470

**Wild Side**
*Wildside* - Steven Gould  *s*  2291

**MISSOURI**

**St. Louis**
*Burnt Offerings* - Laurell K. Hamilton  *h*  2514

**TENNESSEE**

**Myerton**
*Blue Moon* - Laurell K. Hamilton  *h*  2513

## ALTERNATE UNIVERSE

*Alamut* - Judith Tarr  *f*  5390
*Bride of the Slime Monster* - Craig Shaw
  Gardner  *f*  2125
*Call of Madness* - Julie Dean Smith  *f*  5124
*Cathedral of Thorns* - Steven Frankos  *f*  2041
*Celestial Matters* - Richard Garfinkle  *s*  2140
*The Changeling* - Kristine Kathryn Rusch  *f*  4714
*Chase the Morning* - Michael Scott Rohan  *f*  4658
*Darwinia* - Robert Charles Wilson  *s*  5906
*Delan the Mislaid* - Laurie J. Marks  *f*  3625
*Forest of the Night* - S.P. Somtow  *f*  5156
*Gypsies* - Robert Charles Wilson  *s*  5908
*The Honorable Barbarian* - L. Sprague de
  Camp  *f*  1415
*The Hot-Wired Dodo* - Jack L. Chalker  *s*  956

*The Labyrinth Gate* - Alis A. Rasmussen  *f*  4481
*The Lion of Farside* - John Dalmas  *f*  1324
*Magician's Ward* - Patricia C. Wrede  *f*  5976
*Marianne, the Matchbox and the Malachite Mouse* -
  Sheri S. Tepper  *f*  5432
*Medallion of the Black Hound* - Shirley Rousseau
  Murphy  *f*  4056
*The Missing Matter* - Thomas R.
  McDonough  *s*  3805
*The Moonbane Mage* - Laurie J. Marks  *f*  3626
*Rally Cry!* - William R. Forstchen  *s*  1982
*Red Wizard* - Nancy Springer  *f*  5182
*River of Blue Fire* - Tad Williams  *s*  5830
*Riverrun* - S.P. Somtow  *f*  5159
*The Run to Chaos Keep* - Jack L. Chalker  *s*  960
*Sheepfarmer's Daughter* - Elizabeth Moon  *f*  3973
*Sister Light, Sister Dark* - Jane Yolen  *f*  6039
*The Source* - Brian Lumley  *f*  3565
*Spirits of Cavern and Hearth* - M. Coleman
  Easton  *f*  1722
*Surrender None: The Legacy of Gird* - Elizabeth
  Moon  *f*  3975
*Sword-Maker* - Jennifer Roberson  *f*  4614
*The Thief of Always* - Clive Barker  *h*  347
*The Transmigration of Souls* - William
  Barton  *s*  382
*Twistor* - John Cramer  *s*  1245
*Under the Yoke* - S.M. Stirling  *s*  5301
*The War Amongst the Angels* - Michael
  Moorcock  *f*  3986
*Westlin Wind* - Charles de Lint  *f*  1439
*White Jenna* - Jane Yolen  *f*  6041
*The Woman between the Worlds* - F. Gwynplaine
  MacIntyre  *s*  3596

**Cineverse**
*Revenge of the Fluffy Bunnies* - Craig Shaw
  Gardner  *f*  2132

**Cold Shepherd**
*Batman: Captured by the Engines* - Joe R.
  Lansdale  *h*  3320

**Courts of Chaos**
*Prince of Chaos* - Roger Zelazny  *f*  6073

**Deadtown**
*A Dozen Black Roses* - Nancy A. Collins  *h*  1119

**E Level Hyperspace**
*Heaven's Reach* - David Brin  *s*  687

**Europe**
*By Chaos Cursed* - Mickey Zucker Reichert  *f*  4517

**Fading Worlds**
*A Key for the Nonesuch* - Geary Gravel  *s*  2330

**Hell**
*Daughter of the Blood* - Anne Bishop  *f*  495

**Hidden Land**
*The Whim of the Dragon* - Pamela Dean  *f*  1447

**Holding Facility**
*Doomsday Exam* - Nick Pollotta  *f*  4363

**Hole in the Void Valley**
*Necrom* - Mick Farren  *s*  1881

**Klah**
*M.Y.T.H. Inc. in Action* - Robert Asprin  *f*  259

**Launde**
*Out of the Ordinary* - Annie Dalton  *f*  1330

**London, England**
*Mairelon the Magician* - Patricia C. Wrede  *f*  5977

**New York**
*Terraplane* - Jack Womack  *s*  5960

**Oklahoma**
*Fractal Mode* - Piers Anthony  *f*  171

*Virtual Mode* - Piers Anthony   *f*   194

**Q Continuum**
*Q-Space* - Greg Cox   *s*   1228
*Q-Zone* - Greg Cox   *s*   1229

**Quarzhasaata**
*The Fortress of the Pearl* - Michael
    Moorcock   *f*   3982

**The Reef**
*The Cybernetic Shogun* - Victor Milan   *s*   3890

**Sparrill**
*The Jewel of Equilibrant* - Steven Frankos   *f*   2042

**Sunside**
*Bloodwars* - Brian Lumley   *h*   3547

**Texas**
*Petrogypsies* - Rory Harper   *s*   2549

**Waroth**
*Entoverse* - James P. Hogan   *s*   2724

**The Waste Lands**
*The Waste Lands* - Stephen King   *h*   3143

**World of the Gate**
*Blood Brothers* - Brian Lumley   *h*   3546

**Zarathandra**
*A Name to Conjure With* - Donald Aamodt   *f*   3
*A Troubling Along the Border* - Donald Aamodt   *f*   4

## AMERICAN COLONIES

*Heartfire* - Orson Scott Card   *f*   889
*Milton in America* - Peter Ackroyd   *f*   25

### MASSACHUSETTS

**Salem**
*I, Tituba, Black Witch of Salem* - Maryse
    Conde   *f*   1130

### NEW ENGLAND

*The Crafters* - Christopher Stasheff   *f*   5216

## ANCIENT CIVILIZATION

*By the Sword* - Timothy Boggs   *f*   559
*Caesar's Bicycle* - John Barnes   *s*   350
*The Empty Throne* - Ru Emerson   *f*   1808
*Hope of Earth* - Piers Anthony   *s*   175
*Thessalonica* - Harry Turtledove   *f*   5511
*Time Station Paris* - David Evans   *s*   1854

**Arkadia**
*The Arkadians* - Lloyd Alexander   *f*   67

**Huitznahuac**
*The Chalchiuhite Dragon* - Kenneth Morris   *f*   4020

**Kashgar**
*Changeweaver* - Margaret Ball   *f*   313

**Nubia**
*The Land of Gold* - Gillian Bradshaw   *f*   658

**Tyre**
*Iron Dawn* - Matthew Woodring Stover   *f*   5320

## ANTARCTICA

*Antarctica* - Kim Stanley Robinson   *s*   4628
*Assemblers of Infinity* - Kevin J. Anderson   *s*   100
*Carnivore* - Leigh Clark   *h*   1049
*Dream Maker* - W.A. Harbinson   *s*   2542
*Icefire* - Judith Reeves-Stevens   *s*   4512
*Stranger Suns* - George Zebrowski   *s*   6060

*Whiteout* - Sage Walker   *s*   5619

**Erebus Complex**
*Chimera* - Mary Rosenblum   *s*   4677

**McMurdo City**
*Cytheria* - Richard Calder   *s*   835

## ARCTIC

**Ellesmere Island**
*Cold at Heart* - Brian Hopkins   *h*   2768

**North Pole**
*Santa Steps Out: A Fairy Tale for Grownups* - Robert
    Devereaux   *h*   1506
*Santa's Twin* - Dean R. Koontz   *f*   3214

## ARGENTINA

*Harvest the Fire* - Poul Anderson   *s*   128
*Why Do Birds* - Damon Knight   *s*   3190

## ASIA

*The Discovery of Dragons* - Graeme Base   *f*   385
*Flowerdust* - Gwyneth Jones   *s*   2952
*If at Faust You Don't Succeed* - Roger
    Zelazny   *f*   6070
*Koko* - Peter Straub   *h*   5328
*Lucifer Jones* - Mike Resnick   *f*   4549
*The Old Man and Mr. Smith* - Peter
    Ustinov   *f*   5532
*Raptor Red* - Robert T. Bakker   *f*   306
*Samurai Cat Goes to Hell* - Mark E. Rogers   *f*   4655
*Turn of the Cards* - Victor Milan   *s*   3891
*War of the Worlds: Global Dispatches* - Kevin J.
    Anderson   *s*   119

**Bactria**
*Horses of Heaven* - Gillian Bradshaw   *f*   657

**Bering Land Bridge**
*People of the Wolf* - W. Michael Gear   *f*   2170

**Caucassian Mountains**
*Child of an Ancient City* - Tad Williams   *f*   5827

**Ferghana**
*Horses of Heaven* - Gillian Bradshaw   *f*   657

**Quaraband**
*Horselords* - David Cook   *f*   1145

**Wotroya House**
*The Nature of Smoke* - Anne Harris   *s*   2559

## ASIA MINOR

*The Amazon Chronicles* - Jane E.M.
    Robinson   *f*   4627
*Cross and Crescent* - Susan Shwartz   *f*   5014
*Throne of Isis* - Judith Tarr   *f*   5397

**Troy**
*Helen's Passage* - Diana M. Concannon   *f*   1129

## ASTEROID

*Brute Orbits* - George Zebrowski   *s*   6059
*Carve the Sky* - Alexander Jablokov   *s*   2836
*Fellow Traveller* - William Barton   *s*   380
*Heavy Time* - C.J. Cherryh   *s*   995
*Spectre* - William Shatner   *s*   4934
*Thunder Strike!* - Michael McCollum   *s*   3772

**4442 Garcia**
*A King of Infinite Space* - Allen Steele   *s*   5243

**5023 Eris**
*Contact and Commune* - L. Neil Smith   *s*   5129

**Belt Center 83**
*Seeds of Destiny* - Thomas A. Easton   *s*   1724

**Ceres**
*Buying Time* - Joe Haldeman   *s*   2487
*The Killing Star* - Charles Pellegrino   *s*   4281

**Gatsby**
*Wildlife* - James Patrick Kelly   *s*   3049

**Icarus**
*The Eighth Rank* - David D. Ross   *s*   4682

**Kali**
*The Hammer of God* - Arthur C. Clarke   *s*   1057

**Maxima**
*A Wizard in Absentia* - Christopher Stasheff   *s*   5229

**Mercator**
*The First Duelist* - Rutledge Etheridge   *s*   1849

**Neverend**
*Reunion on Neverend* - John E. Stith   *s*   5306

**Pallas**
*Pallas* - L. Neil Smith   *s*   5132

**Pigpen**
*Cat's Gambit* - Leslie Gadallah   *s*   2099

**Psyche**
*The White Abacus* - Damien Broderick   *s*   708

**Quevi Ltir**
*Fallway* - Paula E. Downing   *s*   1593

**Saint Helier**
*Bloom* - Wil McCarthy   *s*   3761

**Sargasso Asteroid**
*The Stars My Destination* - Alfred Bester   *s*   478

**StarBridge Academy**
*Serpent's Gift* - A.C. Crispin   *s*   1261

**Starbridge Academy**
*Shadow World* - A.C. Crispin   *s*   1262

**Thistledown**
*Eon* - Greg Bear   *s*   417

## AT SEA

*Battledragon* - Christopher Rowley   *f*   4691
*Conan of the Red Brotherhood* - Leonard
    Carpenter   *f*   906
*Dragon Waking* - Craig Shaw Gardner   *f*   2128
*The Gift* - Patrick O'Leary   *f*   4211
*Into the Deep* - Ken Grimwood   *s*   2450
*Kingdoms of the Night* - Allan Cole   *f*   1105
*The Last Dragonlord* - Joanne Bertin   *f*   470
*Lord Kelvin's Machine* - James P. Blaylock   *f*   520
*The Mer-Child: A Legend for Children and Other
    Adults* - Robin Morgan   *f*   4008
*One King's Way* - Harry Harrison   *s*   2572
*A Reasonable World* - Damon Knight   *s*   3188
*Roverandom* - J.R.R. Tolkien   *f*   5479
*Sea Cursed: Thirty Terrifying Tales of the Deep* - T.
    Liam McDonald   *h*   3798
*Sea Without a Shore* - Sean Russell   *f*   4743
*The Secret Oceans* - Betty Ballantine   *s*   318
*Silverlight* - Morgan Llywelyn   *f*   3507
*Sink the Armada* - Keith William Andrews   *s*   142
*Something Rich and Strange* - Patricia A.
    McKillip   *f*   3840
*Something's Alive on the Titanic* - Robert
    Serling   *h*   4915
*Storm Caller* - Carol Severance   *f*   4924
*The Sword of Samurai Cat* - Mark E.
    Rogers   *f*   4657
*Swords Against the Shadowland* - Robin Wayne
    Bailey   *f*   291
*Timespell* - Robert N. Charrette   *f*   978

*The Voyage of Mael Duin's Curragh* - Patricia
  Aakhus  *f*  2
*The Warrior Returns* - Allan Cole  *f*  1109
*Wizard of Bones* - Robert N. Charrette  *f*  979

**Andrei Sakharov**
*A Deeper Sea* - Alexander Jablokov  *s*  2838

**Betty**
*Dragon's Plunder* - Brad Strickland  *f*  5336

**Civilization River**
*Blood Lines* - William R. Burkett Jr.  *s*  774

**Edo**
*Assault of the Super Carrier* - Peter Albano  *s*  47

**Flying Fish**
*Lords of the Sword* - Hugh Cook  *f*  1156

**Glomar Explorer**
*The Ghost From the Grand Banks* - Arthur C.
  Clarke  *s*  1056

**Gulf of Mexico**
*Wurm* - Matthew J. Costello  *h*  1202

**H.M.S. Basset**
*Voyage of the Basset* - James C.
  Christensen  *f*  1024

**Hutan's Ship**
*The Other Sinbad* - Craig Shaw Gardner  *f*  2130

**Lord of Day**
*Letters From Atlantis* - Robert Silverberg  *f*  5035

**Mellow Yellow**
*Deus X* - Norman Spinrad  *s*  5171

**Nakedo**
*Canal Dreams* - Iain M. Banks  *s*  323

**Pearl Queen**
*The Bellmaker* - Brian Jacques  *f*  2848

**Princess of Moonshae**
*The Coral Kingdom* - Douglas Niles  *f*  4106

**Queen of Hydros**
*The Face of the Waters* - Robert Silverberg  *s*  5029

**Raft**
*Snow Crash* - Neal Stephenson  *s*  5254

**Robert X. Morris**
*Dead in the Water* - Nancy Holder  *h*  2732

**Sea Sprite**
*Passage to Dawn* - R.A. Salvatore  *f*  4803

**Sky Angel**
*The War of the Sky Lords* - John Brosnan  *s*  721

**Sogne**
*Child of the Journey* - Janet Berliner  *f*  466

**SS Carpco Valparaiso**
*Towing Jehovah* - James Morrow  *f*  4035

**Summer Dancer**
*Search for the Starblade* - Keith Taylor  *f*  5408

**Swallow**
*World Without End* - Sean Russell  *f*  4744

**U.S.S. Abraham Lincoln**
*Secret Realms* - Tom Cool  *s*  1168

**U.S.S. Vindicator**
*Firelance* - David Mace  *s*  3586

**Verdomde**
*Flying Dutch* - Tom Holt  *f*  2750

**Vigilant**
*Legacy* - Greg Bear  *s*  420

**Vivacia**
*The Ship of Magic* - Robin Hobb  *f*  2696

**Warfolf**
*Lords of the Sword* - Hugh Cook  *f*  1156

**Yonaga**
*Assault of the Super Carrier* - Peter Albano  *s*  47
*Ordeal of the Seventh Carrier* - Peter Albano  *s*  48
*Revenge of the Seventh Carrier* - Peter Albano  *s*  49
*Super Carrier: The Ultimate Secret Weapon* - Peter
  Albano  *s*  50

**Zhang-Zhou**
*Gold Dragon* - Robert Cain  *s*  831

# ATLANTIC OCEAN

*Ark Liberty* - Will Bradley  *s*  656
*The Element of Fire* - Jason Henderson  *f*  2657
*Kirins: The Flight of the Ain* - James D.
  Priest  *f*  4433
*seaQuest DSV: Fire Below* - Matthew J.
  Costello  *s*  1201
*seaQuest DSV: The Novel* - Diane Duane  *s*  1666
*Spider Legs* - Piers Anthony  *s*  189
*Towing Jehovah* - James Morrow  *f*  4035
*Yesterday We Saw Mermaids* - Esther
  Friesner  *f*  2086

**Devil's Triangle**
*Echoes of the Fourth Magic* - R.A.
  Salvatore  *f*  4799

# AUSTRALIA

*Balyet* - Patricia Wrightson  *f*  5995
*The Gatekeepers* - Daniel Graham Jr.  *s*  2301
*In the Garden of Iden* - Kage Baker  *s*  298
*The Lake at the End of the World* - Caroline
  MacDonald  *s*  3584

**Ayer's Rock**
*Find Your Own Truth* - Robert N. Charrette  *f*  972

**Brisbane**
*Sabine's Notebook* - Nick Bantock  *f*  335

**Fremantle**
*The Tallow Image* - Jane Brindle  *h*  690

**Melbourne**
*Brain Child* - George Turner  *s*  5491

**New Hong Kong**
*Quarantine* - Greg Egan  *s*  1762

**Perth**
*Quarantine* - Greg Egan  *s*  1762

**Sydney**
*Distress* - Greg Egan  *s*  1760
*Permutation City* - Greg Egan  *s*  1761

**Westerton**
*Brain Child* - George Turner  *s*  5491

**Yarra Valley**
*Genetic Soldier* - George Turner  *s*  5492

# AUSTRIA

*At Sword's Point* - Scott MacMillan  *f*  3601
*Tek Vengeance* - William Shatner  *s*  4938

**Salzburg**
*Angel Souls and Devil Hearts* - Christopher
  Golden  *h*  2255

**Styria**
*The Darker Passions: Carmilla* - Amarantha
  Knight  *h*  3177

**Vienna**
*From the Teeth of Angels* - Jonathan Carroll  *h*  918
*Knights of the Blood* - Scott MacMillan  *f*  3602
*Mixed Doubles* - Daniel Da Cruz  *s*  1305
*Traveling with the Dead* - Barbara Hambly  *h*  2511
*The Unbeholden* - Robert Weinberg  *h*  5703
*Violin* - Anne Rice  *h*  4579

# BABYLON

*The Fabulist* - John Vornholt  *f*  5595
*Servant of the Bones* - Anne Rice  *h*  4575

# BAHAMAS

**Andros Island**
*Drakon* - S.M. Stirling  *s*  5294

**Bimini**
*The Deathless* - Myles Murchison  *h*  4048

**Nassau**
*TekLab* - William Shatner  *s*  4939

# BARBADOS

*I, Tituba, Black Witch of Salem* - Maryse
  Conde  *f*  1130

# BELGIUM

**Brussels**
*Russian Spring* - Norman Spinrad  *s*  5174

# BERMUDA

*Beast* - Peter Benchley  *h*  440

# BOSNIA-HERCEGOVINA

**Sarajevo**
*St. Vitus Dances Eternity: A Sarajevo Ghost Story* -
  Stewart Von Allmen  *h*  5585

# BRAZIL

*Changer* - Jane M. Lindskold  *f*  3474
*Conrad's Quest for Rubber* - Leo
  Frankowski  *s*  2043
*Cradle of Splendor* - Patricia Anthony  *s*  158
*A Fearful Symmetry* - James Luceno  *s*  3542
*Indiana Jones and the Seven Veils* - Rob
  MacGregor  *f*  3592
*Monkey Station* - Ardath Mayhar  *s*  3703
*The Nanotech Chronicles* - Michael Flynn  *s*  1964
*A Season for Slaughter* - David Gerrold  *s*  2211
*Silent Witness* - Robert Arthur Smith  *h*  5136
*Tek Vengeance* - William Shatner  *s*  4938
*Through the Arc of the Rain Forest* - Karen Tei
  Yamashita  *f*  6008
*Tyrannosaurus Rex* - J.F. Rivkin  *s*  4597

**Amazon Jungle**
*Finger of God* - Michael Kasner  *s*  3013

**Brasilia**
*Cybernetic Jungle* - S.N. Lewitt  *s*  3449

**Rio de Janeiro**
*Violin* - Anne Rice  *h*  4579

# BULGARIA

**Boleslaus**
*The Kiss* - Kathryn Reines  *h*  4529

## BYZANTINE EMPIRE

**Constantinople**
*Cross and Crescent* - Susan Shwartz  *f*  5014
*Shards of Empire* - Susan Shwartz  *f*  5017

## BYZANTIUM

**Byzantium**
*Byzantium* - Stephen R. Lawhead  *f*  3353

## CAMBODIA

*The Jade Ogre* - Kenneth Robeson  *f*  4623

**Phnom Penh**
*Dragon's Blood* - Alex McDonough  *s*  3799

## CANADA

*Believe: A Novel* - William Shatner  *f*  4929
*Blessings and Curses* - Christopher Stasheff  *f*  5214
*Cloven Hooves* - Megan Lindholm  *f*  3470
*Light Raid* - Connie Willis  *s*  5870
*ME: A Novel of Self Discovery* - Thomas T.
   Thomas  *s*  5452
*Memory and Dream* - Charles de Lint  *f*  1433
*Near Death* - Nancy Kilpatrick  *h*  3113
*Northern Frights 2* - Don Hutchison  *h*  2814
*Northern Frights 3* - Don Hutchison  *h*  2815
*The Scathach and the Maeve's Daughter* - Mary
   Alexander Walker  *f*  5618
*Svaha* - Charles de Lint  *s*  1437
*Trader* - Charles de Lint  *f*  1438
*Was* - Geoff Ryman  *f*  4758

**Black Thunder**
*Howl* - Christine Tanasiuk  *h*  5388

**Caledon**
*Painted Devil* - Michael Bedard  *f*  430

**Carrick**
*The Mysterium* - Eric McCormack  *h*  3780

**Newford**
*I'll Be Watching You* - Samuel M. Key  *h*  3094
*The Ivory and the Horn* - Charles de Lint  *f*  1431
*Someplace to Be Flying* - Charles de Lint  *f*  1435

**Seacouver**
*Shadow of Obsession* - Rebecca Neason  *f*  4082

**Stroven**
*First Blast of the Trumpet Against the Monstrous
   Regiment of Women* - Eric McCormack  *h*  3779

**ALBERTA**
*End of an Era* - Robert J. Sawyer  *s*  4853

**Calgary**
*The Art of Arrow Cutting* - Stephen
   Dedman  *f*  1462

**Edmonton**
*The Night Watch* - Sean Stewart  *f*  5274

**BRITISH COLUMBIA**

**Hatchet Blade**
*Monster* - John Tigges  *h*  5474

**New Westminster**
*Evil Eye* - Michael Slade  *h*  5085

**Vancouver**
*Blood Debt* - Tanya Huff  *h*  2792
*Cutthroat* - Michael Slade  *h*  5084
*The Deathless* - Myles Murchison  *h*  4048
*Lifehouse* - Spider Robinson  *s*  4641

*The Night Watch* - Sean Stewart  *f*  5274

**NOVA SCOTIA**

**Haven-by-the-Sea**
*The Messenger* - Donald Tyson  *h*  5528

**ONTARIO**

*The Wild Wood* - Charles de Lint  *f*  1440

**Atikokan**
*Where the Chill Waits* - T. Chris
   Martindale  *h*  3658

**Kingston**
*Summon the Keeper* - Tanya Huff  *f*  2800

**Ottawa**
*Eden's Eyes* - Sean Costello  *h*  1205
*Spiritwalk* - Charles de Lint  *f*  1436
*Westlin Wind* - Charles de Lint  *f*  1439

**Thunder Bay**
*Golden Fleece* - Robert J. Sawyer  *s*  4857

**Toronto**
*As One Dead* - Don Bassingthwaite  *h*  387
*The Ascending* - T.M. Wright  *h*  5989
*Blood Price* - Tanya Huff  *h*  2793
*Blood Trail* - Tanya Huff  *h*  2794
*Bloodshift* - Garfield Reeves-Stevens  *h*  4508
*Blue Limbo* - Terrence M. Green  *s*  2377
*Brown Girl in the Ring* - Nalo Hopkinson  *f*  2771
*The Cornish Trilogy* - Robertson Davies  *f*  1397
*The Divide* - Robert Charles Wilson  *s*  5907
*Forever Knight: A Stirring of Dust* - Susan
   Sizemore  *h*  5078
*Forever Knight: Intimations of Mortality* - Susan M.
   Garrett  *h*  2149
*Gate of Darkness, Circle of Light* - Tanya
   Huff  *f*  2797
*Headhunter* - Timothy Findley  *h*  1939
*Keeper of the King* - Nigel Bennett  *h*  452
*The Night Inside* - Nancy Baker  *h*  301
*The Suiting* - Kelley Wilde  *h*  5803
*The Terminal Experiment* - Robert J.
   Sawyer  *s*  4860

**QUEBEC**

*The Cartoonist* - Sean Costello  *h*  1204

**Montreal**
*Reluctant Voyagers* - Elisabeth Vonarburg  *s*  5591
*The Suiting* - Kelley Wilde  *h*  5803

**ROCKY MOUNTAINS**

**Crystal Wells**
*The Devouring* - Douglas D. Hawk  *h*  2615

## CARIBBEAN

*Flickering Shadows* - Kwadwo Agymah
   Kamau  *f*  3006
*Sink the Armada* - Keith William Andrews  *s*  142
*World Without End* - Molly Cochran  *f*  1093

**Coronado**
*Jupiter's Daughter* - Tom Hyman  *s*  2820

**Cozumel Reef**
*Rock of Ages* - Walter Jon Williams  *s*  5840

**Hispaniola**
*Pastwatch: The Redemption of Christopher Columbus* -
   Orson Scott Card  *s*  895
*Queen of Angels* - Greg Bear  *s*  423

**Mill Walk**
*Mystery* - Peter Straub  *h*  5330

**St. Albans**
*Lucifer's Eye* - Hugh B. Cave  *h*  943

**Thomas Island**
*The Dream Vessel* - Jeff Bredenberg  *s*  664

## CENTRAL AMERICA

*The Chalchiuhite Dragon* - Kenneth Morris  *f*  4020
*Dark Legend* - Jamake Highwater  *f*  2686
*Weapon* - Robert Mason  *s*  3666

## CHILE

**Isle of Chiloe**
*Indiana Jones and the Interior World* - Rob
   MacGregor  *f*  3590

## CHINA

*Bronze Mirror* - Jeanne Larsen  *f*  3338
*The Chronicles of Master Li and Number Ten Ox* -
   Barry Hughart  *f*  2803
*Imperial Lady* - Andre Norton  *f*  4155
*The Remarkable Journey of Prince Jen* - Lloyd
   Alexander  *f*  69
*Silk Road* - Jeanne Larsen  *f*  3339
*Stones of the Dalai Lama* - Ken Mitchell  *f*  3916
*Tongues of Jade* - Laurence Yep  *f*  6026
*The Yngling and the Circle of Power* - John
   Dalmas  *s*  1328

**Beijing**
*Fortress of Forbidden Destiny* - Ryder
   Syvertson  *s*  5378

**Forbidden City**
*Eight Skilled Gentlemen* - Barry Hughart  *f*  2804

**Peking**
*Changeweaver* - Margaret Ball  *f*  313
*Eight Skilled Gentlemen* - Barry Hughart  *f*  2804

**Shanghai**
*The Diamond Age* - Neal Stephenson  *s*  5253

**Xian**
*The Only Thing to Fear* - Robert Morgan  *h*  4003
*Phoenix Fire* - Elizabeth Forrest  *f*  1974

## COLOMBIA

*Cybernarc* - Robert Cain  *s*  829
*End Game* - Robert Cain  *s*  830

## COSTA RICA

*The Lost World* - Michael Crichton  *s*  1256

**Isla Nublar**
*Jurassic Park* - Michael Crichton  *s*  1255

**Paradisio**
*The Vampire Virus* - Michael Romkey  *h*  4668

## CUBA

*Ai! Pedrito!: When Intelligence Goes Wrong* - L. Ron
   Hubbard  *s*  2788
*White Eyes* - Kenneth Robeson  *f*  4625

## CYBERSPACE

*Cinderblock* - Janine Ellen Young  *s*  6047
*The Cybernetic Walrus* - Jack L. Chalker  *s*  951
*Exit to Reality* - Edith Forbes  *s*  1968

*The Eyes of God* - Mark Kreighbaum   s   3231
*The Hacker and the Ants* - Rudy Rucker   s   4704
*How to Mutate and Take Over the World* - R.U.
   Sirius   s   5074
*Iron Man: The Armor Trap* - Greg Cox   s   1227
*Johnny Mnemonic* - Terry Bisson   s   505
*Murder in the Solid State* - Wil McCarthy   s   3764
*Palace* - Katharine Kerr   s   3072
*Tea From an Empty Cup* - Pat Cadigan   s   809
*Terminal Logic* - Jefferson Scott   s   4893
*Tomorrow and Tomorrow* - Charles
   Sheffield   s   4966
*Under Siege* - Elisabeth Mace   f   3587
*Virtually Perfect* - Dan Gutman   s   2470
*Whiteout* - Sage Walker   s   5619

**The Big Board**
*Deus X* - Norman Spinrad   s   5171

**The Bin**
*Circuit of Heaven* - Dennis Danvers   s   1348

**Deep Field**
*Donnerjack* - Roger Zelazny   s   6063

**Dreamland**
*When Dreams Collide* - Wm. Mark
   Simmons   f   5063

**Elsewhen**
*No Limits* - Nigel Findley   s   1938

**Elysium**
*Permutation City* - Greg Egan   s   1761

**Heaven**
*Headcrash* - Bruce Bethke   s   483

**Insomnia**
*Terminal Games* - Cole Perriman   s   4283

**Itheria**
*Caverns of Socrates* - Dennis L. McKiernan   f   3831

**MagicNet**
*MagicNet* - John DeChancie   f   1461

**The Metaverse**
*Snow Crash* - Neal Stephenson   s   5254

**The Net**
*City of Golden Shadow* - Tad Williams   s   5828

**Network**
*Living Real* - James C. Bassett   s   386

**Oz**
*Realtime Interrupt* - James P. Hogan   s   2729

**Telespace**
*Cyberweb* - Lisa Mason   s   3662

**Virtu**
*Donnerjack* - Roger Zelazny   s   6063

**Virtual Reality**
*Death Dream* - Ben Bova   s   583
*The Imperium Game* - K.D. Wentworth   s   5753
*Killobyte* - Piers Anthony   f   179
*The Sherwood Game* - Esther Friesner   s   2082
*Wyrm* - Mark Fabi   s   1858

**Wildnet**
*Night Sky Mine* - Melissa Scott   s   4898

## DENMARK

*The Gold Ball* - Hanne Marie Svendsen   f   5361
*The Tower of Beowulf* - Parke Godwin   f   2250
*War of the Gods* - Poul Anderson   f   136

## EARTH

*The Abraxas Marvel Circus* - Stephen Leigh   f   3423

*Achilles' Choice* - Larry Niven   s   4114
*Acts of Conscience* - William Barton   s   377
*Adiamante* - L.E. Modesitt Jr.   s   3924
*The Albino Knife* - Steve Perry   s   4288
*Alien Earth* - Megan Lindholm   s   3469
*Aliens: Earth Hive* - Steve Perry   s   4289
*Ancient Echoes* - Robert Holdstock   s   2735
*Ancient Heavens* - Robert E. Vardeman   s   5561
*And Eternity* - Piers Anthony   f   162
*Angela and Diabola* - Lynne Reid Banks   f   330
*Angelwalk: A Modern Fable* - Roger
   Elwood   f   1803
*Armageddon: The Musical* - Robert Rankin   s   4473
*The Atrocity Exhibition* - J.G. Ballard   s   319
*Back to the Time Trap* - Keith Laumer   s   3343
*The Beacon* - Valerie J. Freireich   s   2048
*Being Alien* - Rebecca Ore   s   4217
*Beneath the Tree of Heaven* - David
   Wingrove   s   5917
*Berserker Fury* - Fred Saberhagen   s   4760
*Bewitchments of Love and Hate* - Storm
   Constantine   s   1140
*Beyond the Door* - Gary L. Blackwood   s   510
*Black Milk* - Robert Reed   s   4504
*Blade Runner: Replicant Night* - K.W. Jeter   s   2907
*Bride of the Slime Monster* - Craig Shaw
   Gardner   f   2125
*Bright Angel* - John Blair   s   512
*The Broken Wheel* - David Wingrove   s   5918
*The Bushido Incident* - Betty Anne
   Crawford   s   1248
*Buying Time* - Joe Haldeman   s   2487
*A Call to Arms* - Alan Dean Foster   s   1995
*Captain Jack Zodiac* - Michael Kandel   f   3009
*Carve the Sky* - Alexander Jablokov   s   2836
*Catastrophe's Spell* - Mayer Alan Brenner   f   671
*Century 21* - Ewa Kuryluk   s   3263
*Chaos Mode* - Piers Anthony   f   165
*Charmed* - Marilyn Singer   f   5070
*Codgerspace* - Alan Dean Foster   s   1999
*The Collected Stories of Philip K. Dick, Volume Two:
   We Can Remember It for You Wholesale* - Philip K.
   Dick   s   1520
*Crisis on Doona* - Anne McCaffrey   s   3723
*Cry Wolf* - Kenneth Von Gunden   s   5586
*Dark Sky Legion* - William Barton   s   379
*Dayworld Breakup* - Philip Jose Farmer   s   1869
*The Delta* - Colin Wilson   s   5878
*The Demon Princes: Volume One* - Jack
   Vance   s   5544
*Deus X* - Norman Spinrad   s   5171
*The Diamond Moon* - Paul Preuss   s   4417
*Don't Forget Your Spacesuit, Dear* - Jody Lynn
   Nye   s   4169
*The Door to Ambermere* - J. Calvin Pierce   f   4316
*Dorella* - Mark A. Garland   f   2142
*Down the Bright Way* - Robert Reed   s   4505
*Dragon Wing* - Margaret Weis   f   5709
*The Dragon's Dagger* - R.A. Salvatore   f   4797
*Dragon's Eye* - Alex McDonough   s   3801
*Dragons Past* - Gary Gentile   s   2192
*Dragonslayer's Return* - R.A. Salvatore   f   4798
*Drink Down the Moon* - Charles de Lint   f   1426
*Earth* - David Brin   s   685
*The Earth Giant* - Melvin Burgess   s   773
*Earth Herald* - Jan Clark   s   1046
*The Earth Saver* - Catherine Wells   s   5745
*Earthfall* - Orson Scott Card   s   885
*An Earthly Crown* - Kate Elliott   s   1771
*Ecce and Old Earth* - Jack Vance   s   5546
*Echoes of the Well of Souls* - Jack L.
   Chalker   s   953
*The Elvenbane* - Andre Norton   f   4149
*Elvenblood* - Andre Norton   f   4150
*Empire Builders* - Ben Bova   s   584
*Entoverse* - James P. Hogan   s   2724
*Eva* - Peter Dickinson   s   1525
*Exile* - Al Sarrantonio   s   4829
*Fellow Traveller* - William Barton   s   380

*Fire on the Border* - Kevin O'Donnell Jr.   s   4194
*First Frontier* - Diane Carey   s   902
*Fisherman's Hope* - David Feintuch   s   1900
*A Flag Full of Stars* - Brad Ferguson   s   1922
*Flatlander* - Larry Niven   s   4121
*The Folk of the Air* - Peter S. Beagle   f   407
*Future Crime* - Ben Bova   s   585
*Galatea in 2-D* - Aaron Allston   f   87
*A Game of Universe* - Eric S. Nylund   f   4178
*Gameplay* - Kevin J. Anderson   f   105
*Game's End* - Kevin J. Anderson   f   104
*Girl in Landscape* - Jonathan Lethem   s   3440
*Grass* - Sheri S. Tepper   s   5431
*Grounded!* - Chris Claremont   s   1041
*Gryphon* - Crawford Kilian   s   3106
*Hard Sell* - Piers Anthony   s   173
*Harvest of Stars* - Poul Anderson   s   127
*The Hero King* - Rick Shelley   f   4970
*The Hero of Varay* - Rick Shelley   f   4971
*The Hidden War* - Michael Armstrong   s   209
*The Homecoming* - Barry B. Longyear   s   3521
*Homecoming* - David Alexander Smith   s   5108
*Homegoing* - Frederik Pohl   s   4347
*Honor of the Regiment* - Bill Fawcett   s   1896
*Hour of the Dragon* - Robert E. Howard   f   2783
*The Hunter Returns* - David Drake   f   1632
*Hunting the Ghost Dancer* - A.A. Attanasio   f   268
*I, Robot: The Illustrated Screenplay* - Harlan
   Ellison   s   1785
*I Who Have Never Known Men* - Jacqueline
   Harpman   s   2554
*Icarus Descending* - Elizabeth Hand   s   2536
*Iceman* - Cynthia Felice   s   1913
*Imago* - Octavia E. Butler   s   791
*The Infinity Plague* - Robert E. Vardeman   s   5564
*Isle of Woman* - Piers Anthony   f   178
*Ivory: A Legend of Past and Future* - Mike
   Resnick   s   4547
*Jaguar* - Bill Ransom   s   4477
*The Jigsaw Woman* - Kim Antieau   f   199
*Judson's Eden* - Keith Laumer   s   3344
*Kaduna Memories* - Jack McKinney   s   3850
*Kaleidoscope Century* - John Barnes   s   352
*Kirins: The Spell of No'an* - James D.
   Priest   f   4435
*The Labyrinth Gate* - Alis A. Rasmussen   f   4481
*A Landscape of Darkness* - John Blair   s   513
*The Last Dancer* - Daniel Keys Moran   s   3994
*The Last Stand of the DNA Cowboys* - Mick
   Farren   s   1879
*Legion of the Damned* - William C. Dietz   s   1547
*Lethe* - Tricia Sullivan   s   5354
*Look into the Sun* - James Patrick Kelly   s   3047
*The Magnificent Wilf* - Gordon R. Dickson   s   1536
*The Man in the Moon Must Die* - Jeff
   Bredenberg   s   665
*Marianne, the Matchbox and the Malachite Mouse* -
   Sheri S. Tepper   f   5432
*Mars* - Ben Bova   s   586
*The Martian Chronicles* - Ray Bradbury   s   621
*Mazeway* - Jack Williamson   s   5866
*Medallion of the Black Hound* - Shirley Rousseau
   Murphy   f   4056
*The Medusa Encounter* - Paul Preuss   s   4419
*Memorymakers* - Brian Herbert   s   2665
*Men Like Rats* - Rob Chilson   s   1015
*The Mer-Child: A Legend for Children and Other
   Adults* - Robin Morgan   f   4008
*Mercycle* - Piers Anthony   s   181
*The Middle Kingdom* - David Wingrove   s   5919
*Minerva Wakes* - Holly Lisle   f   3487
*Mining the Oort* - Frederik Pohl   s   4349
*Mission: Tori* - Johanna Bolton   s   564
*Moonrise* - Ben Bova   s   587
*Moonwise* - Greer Ilene Gilman   f   2238
*More than Fire* - Philip Jose Farmer   s   1871
*Mosaic* - Jeri Taylor   s   5403
*Mother of Storms* - John Barnes   s   354
*Moving Mars* - Greg Bear   s   421

*Muddle Earth* - John Brunner   s   735
*My Father Immortal* - Michael D. Weaver   s   5659
*Naked to the Stars/The Alien Way* - Gordon R. Dickson   s   1537
*Nemesis* - Isaac Asimov   s   247
*The New Springtime* - Robert Silverberg   s   5040
*Night Launch* - Jake Garn   s   2143
*Nomad* - David Alexander   s   66
*Norby and Yobo's Great Adventure* - Janet Asimov   s   254
*Norstrilia* - Cordwainer Smith   s   5105
*Out of This World* - Lawrence Watt-Evans   f   5645
*Out on Blue Six* - Ian McDonald   s   3794
*Partisan* - S. Andrew Swann   s   5365
*The Persistence of Memory* - Karen Ripley   s   4592
*Phylum Monsters* - Hayford Peirce   s   4276
*Priorities* - Lynda Lyons   s   3579
*Prison Ship* - Martin Caidin   s   828
*Profiteer* - S. Andrew Swann   s   5366
*A Prophecy of Monsters* - Clark Ashton Smith   h   5103
*Proteus in the Underworld* - Charles Sheffield   s   4962
*The Quicksilver Screen* - Don H. DeBrandt   s   1449
*The Quiet Pools* - Michael P. Kube-McDowell   s   3249
*Quozl* - Alan Dean Foster   s   2013
*The Ragged World: A Novel of the Hefn on Earth* - Judith Moffett   s   3943
*The Rainbow Sword* - Adrienne Martine-Barnes   f   3659
*Rama II* - Arthur C. Clarke   s   1058
*Reach* - Edward Gibson   s   2216
*Reality Is What You Can Get Away With: An Illustrated Screenplay* - Robert Anton Wilson   s   5904
*''Repent, Harlequin!'' Said the Ticktockman* - Harlan Ellison   s   1782
*Ring* - Stephen Baxter   s   402
*The Ring of Charon* - Roger MacBride Allen   s   80
*Rivers of Time* - L. Sprague de Camp   s   1417
*Rocheworld* - Robert L. Forward   s   1990
*Rock 'n' Roll Babes From Outer Space* - Linda Javin   s   2880
*Ronin* - D.A. Heeley   f   2639
*Rule Golden and Double Meaning* - Damon Knight   s   3189
*The Sails of Tau Ceti* - Michael McCollum   s   3771
*Schismatrix Plus* - Bruce Sterling   s   5260
*Shade's Children* - Garth Nix   s   4130
*Shame of Man* - Piers Anthony   s   188
*The Shattered Sphere* - Roger MacBride Allen   s   81
*The Shield of Time* - Poul Anderson   s   131
*The Singers of Time* - Frederik Pohl   s   4354
*The Snake Oil Wars* - Parke Godwin   s   2249
*Someone to Watch over Me* - Tricia Sullivan   s   5355
*Star Bridge* - James Gunn   s   2459
*Star Brothers* - Ben Bova   s   594
*Star Trek: The Lost Years* - J.M. Dillard   s   1557
*The Stars My Destination* - Alfred Bester   s   478
*Starseed* - Spider Robinson   s   4643
*Starstrike* - W. Michael Gear   s   2172
*The State of the Art* - Iain M. Banks   s   327
*The Stone Within* - David Wingrove   s   5920
*Strange Deliverance* - Mary Brown   s   728
*Strange Invasion* - Michael Kandel   s   3012
*Sunstroke* - David Kagan   s   2999
*Tactical Error* - Thorarinn Gunnarsson   s   2466
*Tales From Planet Earth* - Arthur C. Clarke   s   1061
*Tek Net* - William Shatner   s   4936
*Through the Ice* - Piers Anthony   s   192
*A Time for Dragons* - Gary Gentile   s   2193
*The Time Patrol* - Poul Anderson   s   135
*Timequake* - Kurt Vonnegut Jr.   s   5594
*To Fear the Light* - Ben Bova   s   595
*Tomorrow and Tomorrow* - Charles Sheffield   s   4966
*Too, Too Solid Flesh* - Nick O'Donohoe   s   4197

*Total Recall* - Piers Anthony   s   193
*Tourists* - Lisa Goldstein   f   2264
*Traitor Winds* - L.A. Graf   s   2298
*Voices* - John Vornholt   s   5598
*Walker of Worlds* - Tom De Haven   f   1423
*The Walking Shadow* - Brian Stableford   s   5195
*Way Up High* - Roger Zelazny   f   6076
*The Ways of Magic* - Scott Ciencin   f   1033
*When Heaven Fell* - William Barton   s   383
*The Whim of the Dragon* - Pamela Dean   f   1447
*The White Abacus* - Damien Broderick   s   708
*White Moon, Red Dragon* - David Wingrove   s   5921
*The White Mountain* - David Wingrove   s   5922
*The Wizard of Ambermere* - J. Calvin Pierce   f   4317
*The Woods out Back* - R.A. Salvatore   f   4809
*Ye Gods!* - Tom Holt   f   2753
*Zeta Base* - Judith Alguire   s   74

**Alliance Central**
*Shadow's End* - Sheri S. Tepper   s   5435

**Alpha Complex**
*Extreme Paranoia: Nobody Knows the Trouble I've Shot* - Ken Rolston   s   4662
*Title Deleted for Security Reasons* - Ed Blome   s   553

**The Center**
*The Outlander: Captivity* - B.J. Salterberg   s   4792

**The City**
*Quasar* - Jamil Nasir   s   4071

**CoDominium**
*Prince of Mercenaries* - Jerry Pournelle   s   4377

**Diaspar**
*Beyond the Fall of Night* - Arthur C. Clarke   s   1054

**Dream Park**
*The Barsoom Project* - Larry Niven   s   4115

**Isle of Kos**
*This Immortal* - Roger Zelazny   s   6074

**Juarez El Pasco Port Authority**
*Greenthieves* - Alan Dean Foster   s   2005

**Lys**
*Beyond the Fall of Night* - Arthur C. Clarke   s   1054

**Nauc**
*Strings* - Dave Duncan   s   1689

**New City**
*Deus Ex Machina* - J.V. Brummels   s   732

**Nexus Building**
*A Key for the Nonesuch* - Geary Gravel   s   2330

**Russett**
*Unwillingly to Earth* - Pauline Ashwell   s   231

**Sorcery Hall**
*The Golden Thread* - Suzy McKee Charnas   f   969

**Tomi**
*The Last World* - Christoph Ransmayr   f   4475

**Trinity Wood**
*The Foxes of Firstdark* - Garry Kilworth   f   3115

**Twombly Town**
*The Stone Giant* - James P. Blaylock   f   523

**U.A.N. Headquarters**
*Marks of Our Brothers* - Jane M. Lindskold   s   3475

## EGYPT

*The Anubis Murders* - Gary Gygax   f   2472
*Cobra Curse* - Bill Dolan   s   1567
*The Fabulist* - John Vornholt   f   5595
*The Fifth Element* - Terry Bisson   s   504

*Lord of the Two Lands* - Judith Tarr   f   5395
*The Mummy, or Ramses the Damned* - Anne Rice   h   4572
*The Queen of the Damned* - Anne Rice   h   4574
*The Werewolves of London* - Brian Stableford   h   5196

**Alexandria**
*Child of the Eagle* - Esther Friesner   f   2073
*Sabine's Notebook* - Nick Bantock   f   335
*The Schizogenic Man* - Raymond Harris   s   2563
*Throne of Isis* - Judith Tarr   f   5397

**Cairo**
*The Calling* - Kathryn Meyer Griffith   h   2439
*Name of the Beast* - Daniel Easterman   h   1721

**Great Sand Sea**
*Hellboy: The Lost Army* - Christopher Golden   h   2257

**Shaydan**
*Orion in the Dying Time* - Ben Bova   s   591

**Thebes**
*Out of the House of Life* - Chelsea Quinn Yarbro   h   6018
*Thebes of the Hundred Gates* - Robert Silverberg   s   5043

## ENGLAND

*Arthur* - Stephen R. Lawhead   f   3352
*Beauty* - Sheri S. Tepper   f   5428
*Believe: A Novel* - William Shatner   f   4929
*Black Body* - H.C. Turk   h   5488
*Black Horses for the King* - Anne McCaffrey   f   3720
*Blood of the Impaler* - Jeffrey Sackett   h   4779
*The Camelot Chronicles* - Mike Ashley   f   224
*Chase the Morning* - Michael Scott Rohan   f   4658
*The Child Queen* - Nancy McKenzie   f   3827
*The Children of Men* - P.D. James   f   2870
*Children of the Thunder* - John Brunner   s   733
*Chronicles of King Arthur* - Andrea Hopkins   f   2767
*The Chymical Wedding* - Lindsay Clarke   f   1063
*Correspondence* - Sue Thomas   s   5450
*The Crafters* - Christopher Stasheff   f   5216
*The Deepest Sea* - Charles Barnitz   f   363
*The Dragon and the Gnarly King* - Gordon R. Dickson   f   1529
*The Dragon and the Unicorn* - A.A. Attanasio   f   266
*The Dragon's Boy* - Jane Yolen   f   6030
*Dragons of England* - Douglas Kaufman   f   3015
*Elephantasm* - Tanith Lee   h   3408
*The Enchantments of Flesh and Spirit* - Storm Constantine   s   1141
*Enemy of God* - Bernard Cornwell   f   1189
*Excalibur* - Bernard Cornwell   f   1190
*An Eye for Dark Places* - Norma Marder   s   3622
*Father to the Man* - John Gribbin   s   2434
*Final Blackout* - L. Ron Hubbard   s   2790
*The Fire Queen* - Jack Holland   f   2740
*Flying Dutch* - Tom Holt   f   2750
*The Forever King* - Molly Cochran   f   1092
*Freedom & Necessity* - Steven Brust   f   743
*The Fungus* - Harry Adam Knight   h   3192
*Future Indefinite* - Dave Duncan   f   1678
*Gate of Ivory, Gate of Horn* - Robert Holdstock   f   2737
*Gawain and Lady Green* - Anne Eliot Crompton   f   1269
*Ghost King* - David Gemmell   f   2188
*Grail* - Stephen R. Lawhead   f   3355
*The Hammer and the Cross* - Harry Harrison   f   2570
*Heart-Beast* - Tanith Lee   h   3411
*The Hellbound Heart* - Clive Barker   h   342

*Hexwood* - Diana Wynne Jones  *s*  2948
*The Hollowing* - Robert Holdstock  *f*  2738
*In the Shadow of the Oak King* - Courtway
 Jones  *f*  2939
*Indiana Jones and the Dance of the Giants* - Rob
 MacGregor  *f*  3588
*Indiana Jones and the White Witch* - Martin
 Caidin  *f*  826
*The Keys to D'Esperance* - Chaz Brenchley  *h*  666
*The King* - Donald Barthelme  *f*  375
*King & Raven* - Cary James  *f*  2858
*The Kingmaking* - Helen Hollick  *f*  2745
*Lady Cottington's Pressed Fairy Book* - Terry
 Jones  *f*  2981
*The Last Pendragon* - Robert Rice  *f*  4584
*Lavondyss: Journey to an Unknown Region* - Robert
 Holdstock  *f*  2739
*Legacy* - Steve White  *s*  5785
*Living with the Reptiles* - Roger L.
 DiSilvestro  *s*  1563
*London Fields* - Martin Amis  *s*  95
*The Long Patrol* - Brian Jacques  *f*  2849
*Lord of Sunset* - Parke Godwin  *f*  2246
*The Lost History of Redwyn* - William Jay  *f*  2883
*The Meddlesome Ghost* - Sheila Rosalynd
 Allen  *f*  84
*The Mennyms* - Sylvia Waugh  *f*  5654
*Mennyms Alive* - Sylvia Waugh  *f*  5655
*Mennyms Under Siege* - Sylvia Waugh  *f*  5656
*Merlin* - Jane Yolen  *f*  6035
*Merlin and the Dragons* - Jane Yolen  *f*  6036
*Merlin's Bones* - Fred Saberhagen  *f*  4771
*Merlin's Legacy: Dawn of Camelot* - Quinn Taylor
 Evans  *f*  1857
*Mindstar Rising* - Peter F. Hamilton  *s*  2526
*Mrs. God* - Peter Straub  *h*  5329
*Newton's Cannon* - J. Gregory Keyes  *f*  3097
*Nightmare, with Angel* - Stephen Gallagher  *h*  2111
*The Notorious Abbess* - Vera Chapman  *f*  965
*The Ogre Downstairs* - Diana Wynne Jones  *f*  2949
*A Once and Future Love* - Anne Kelleher  *f*  3039
*One King's Way* - Harry Harrison  *s*  2572
*Out of the Ordinary* - Annie Dalton  *f*  1330
*The Panther's Hoard* - Nancy Varian
 Berberick  *f*  458
*Passager* - Jane Yolen  *f*  6038
*Pendragon* - Stephen R. Lawhead  *f*  3357
*Pendragon's Banner* - Helen Hollick  *f*  2746
*Picking the Ballad's Bones* - Elizabeth Ann
 Scarborough  *f*  4869
*Present Tense* - Dave Duncan  *f*  1686
*The Prestige* - Christopher Priest  *s*  4432
*The Prince and the Pilgrim* - Mary Stewart  *f*  5270
*The Printer's Devil* - Chico Kidd  *f*  3099
*Prophets for the End of Time* - Marcos
 Donnelly  *f*  1577
*A Quantum Murder* - Peter F. Hamilton  *s*  2527
*Quest: In Search of the Dragontooth* - Michael
 Green  *f*  2346
*Robin and the King* - Parke Godwin  *f*  2247
*The Saxon Shore* - Jack Whyte  *f*  5793
*The Scathach and the Maeve's Daughter* - Mary
 Alexander Walker  *f*  5618
*Scream for Jeeves: A Parody* - P.H. Cannon  *h*  867
*The Secret of the Indian* - Lynne Reid Banks  *f*  332
*Seeds of Evil* - Margaret Bingley  *f*  491
*Shadow of the King* - Helen Hollick  *f*  2747
*Shadow of the Seventh Moon* - Nancy Varian
 Berberick  *f*  459
*Sherwood* - Parke Godwin  *f*  2248
*The Skystone* - Jack Whyte  *f*  5794
*Slow River* - Nicola Griffith  *s*  2445
*Snow White and Rose Red* - Patricia C.
 Wrede  *f*  5981
*The Spiral Dance* - R. Garcia y Robertson  *f*  2121
*The Steampunk Trilogy* - Paul Di Filippo  *s*  1518
*Strange Stains and Mysterious Smells* - Terry
 Jones  *f*  2982
*The Stress of Her Regard* - Tim Powers  *h*  4385

*Strong Spirits* - Elisa DeCarlo  *f*  1451
*A Sudden Wild Magic* - Diana Wynne Jones  *f*  2950
*The Templar Treasure* - Katherine Kurtz  *f*  3261
*The Third Beast* - Peter Loughran  *h*  3527
*A Tie to the Past* - David Wiseman  *f*  5928
*A Time for Us* - Christine Holden  *f*  2731
*The Time of the Ghost* - Diana Wynne
 Jones  *f*  2951
*Toad Triumphant* - William Horwood  *f*  2774
*Under Siege* - Elisabeth Mace  *f*  3587
*Walking the Labyrinth* - Lisa Goldstein  *f*  2266
*The Wealdwife's Tale* - Paul Hazel  *f*  2636
*The White Guardian* - Ronald Anthony
 Cross  *s*  1275
*The Willows and Beyond* - William
 Horwood  *f*  2775
*The Willows in Winter* - William Horwood  *f*  2776
*The Winter King* - Bernard Cornwell  *f*  1191
*The Wizard at Home* - Rick Shelley  *f*  4975
*The Wolf and the Crown* - A.A. Attanasio  *f*  273

**Avalon**
*Lady of Avalon* - Marion Zimmer Bradley  *f*  640

**Basingstoke**
*The Eyes of the Beast* - Steve Harris  *h*  2565

**Bay of Wodin**
*The Book of Brendan* - Ann Curry  *f*  1294

**Beckford**
*The Immaculate* - Mark Morris  *h*  4023

**Bedford**
*The Tallow Image* - Jane Brindle  *h*  690

**Berkshire**
*The Grotesque* - Patrick McGrath  *h*  3814

**Binscombe**
*Binscombe Tales* - John Whitbourn  *h*  5776

**Bishop Mayne**
*Well Wished* - Franny Billingsley  *f*  489

**Blackpool**
*The Last Voice They Hear* - Ramsey
 Campbell  *h*  858

**Bodbury**
*The Little Country* - Charles de Lint  *f*  1432

**Branton**
*Time and the Clock Mice, Etcetera* - Peter
 Dickinson  *f*  1527

**Burkinwell**
*Photographing Fairies* - Steve Szilagyi  *f*  5379

**Burnt Yarley**
*Sacrament* - Clive Barker  *h*  345

**Burton**
*Under the Crust* - Terry Lamsley  *h*  3314

**Cadbury Tor**
*The Broken Sword* - Molly Cochran  *f*  1091

**Caer Camlann Castle**
*Arthur War Lord* - Dafydd ab Hugh  *f*  6

**Cambridge**
*Naomi's Room* - Jonathan Aycliffe  *h*  281
*Red Death* - P.N. Elrod  *h*  1798
*Trinity Grove* - David van Meter Smith  *h*  5112

**Camelot**
*The Eagle and the Sword* - A.A. Attanasio  *f*  267
*Guinevere: The Legend in Autumn* - Persia
 Woolley  *f*  5970
*The Merlin Chronicles* - Mike Ashley  *f*  227
*Merlin's Harp* - Anne Eliot Crompton  *f*  1270
*Mordred's Curse* - Ian McDowell  *f*  3806
*Queen of the Summer Stars* - Persia
 Woolley  *f*  5971

*Witch of the North* - Courtway Jones  *f*  2940

**Camulod**
*The Eagles' Brood* - Jack Whyte  *f*  5792

**Chelsea**
*Fabulous Harbors* - Michael Moorcock  *f*  3981

**Chester**
*The Long Lost* - Ramsey Campbell  *h*  859

**Cliff House**
*Oktober* - Stephen Gallagher  *h*  2112

**Cloudsley Towers**
*The Red-Eared Ghosts* - Vivian Alcock  *f*  53

**Colchester**
*Midnight Is a Lonely Place* - Barbara
 Erskine  *h*  1836

**Coventry**
*Time Station London* - David Evans  *s*  1853
*To Say Nothing of the Dog* - Connie Willis  *s*  5874

**Cranbury-on-the-Sea**
*Aunt Maria* - Diana Wynne Jones  *f*  2943

**Deva**
*The Forest House* - Marion Zimmer Bradley  *f*  633

**Devon**
*The Golden Mean* - Nick Bantock  *f*  334

**Dorset**
*The Key to the Indian* - Lynne Reid Banks  *f*  331

**Elgin**
*Dr. Haggard's Disease* - Patrick McGrath  *h*  3813

**Elmwood**
*Sweet Heart* - Peter James  *h*  2875

**Exeter**
*Mina* - Marie Kiraly  *h*  3151

**Finchley**
*The Time Tree* - Enid Richemont  *f*  4585

**Hazelrod**
*Portent* - James Herbert  *h*  2670

**Hemhill**
*The Great Wheel* - Ian R. MacLeod  *s*  3599

**High Grimmire**
*Blood and Roses* - Sharon Bainbridge  *h*  292

**Hillingham**
*Sweetheart, Sweetheart* - Bernard Taylor  *h*  5402

**Hobury Abbey**
*The Book of Brendan* - Ann Curry  *f*  1294

**Hopwas**
*Water Rites* - Guy N. Smith  *h*  5121

**Hove**
*Virgins and Martyrs* - Simon Maginn  *h*  3607

**Joyous Gard**
*Guinevere: The Legend in Autumn* - Persia
 Woolley  *f*  5970

**Kent**
*In the Garden of Iden* - Kage Baker  *s*  298

**Kirkwhelpington**
*Whispers in the Dark* - Jonathan Aycliffe  *h*  283

**Little Haverstraw**
*The Godsend* - Bernard Taylor  *h*  5401

**Little Hocking**
*Holy Terror* - Josephine Boyle  *h*  608

**Liverpool**
*Burning Bright* - J.S. Russell  *h*  4733
*The Count of Eleven* - Ramsey Campbell  *h*  853

*The Parasite* - Ramsey Campbell  h  863

**London**
*7 Steps to Midnight* - Richard Matheson  h  3682
*'48* - James Herbert  h  2667
*The Ambivalent Magician* - Simon Hawke  f  2616
*Ancient Images* - Ramsey Campbell  h  852
*The Angel of Pain* - Brian Stableford  h  5189
*Angels & Visitations: A Miscellany* - Neil
  Gaiman  f  2101
*Asylum* - Patrick McGrath  h  3812
*Bad Dreams* - Kim Newman  h  4096
*Bloodwars* - Brian Lumley  h  3547
*The Bloody Red Baron* - Kim Newman  h  4097
*Bram Stoker's Dracula* - Fred Saberhagen  h  4763
*Burning Bright* - J.S. Russell  h  4733
*The Carnival of Destruction* - Brian
  Stableford  h  5190
*Charmed Life* - Bernard Taylor  h  5399
*The Child Garden* - Geoff Ryman  s  4756
*Choose Your Enemies Carefully* - Robert N.
  Charrette  s  971
*Cloud Castles* - Michael Scott Rohan  f  4659
*Come Before Christ and Murder Love* - Stewart
  Home  f  2754
*Dance of Death* - P.N. Elrod  h  1794
*Dark Dance* - Tanith Lee  h  3406
*The Darker Passions: Dr. Jekyll and Mr. Hyde* -
  Amarantha Knight  h  3178
*Darkness, I* - Tanith Lee  h  3407
*Dead End* - Guy N. Smith  h  5119
*Deadspawn* - Brian Lumley  h  3550
*Death Masque* - P.N. Elrod  h  1795
*Demogorgon* - Brian Lumley  h  3552
*The Devil Rides Out* - Dennis Wheatley  h  5773
*The Devil You Say* - Elisa DeCarlo  f  1450
*The Difference Engine* - William Gibson  s  2217
*Double Trouble Squared* - Kathryn Lasky  f  3340
*Down River* - Stephen Gallagher  h  2110
*Dracul: An Eternal Love Story* - Nancy
  Kilpatrick  h  3110
*The Dracula Tape* - Fred Saberhagen  h  4765
*Dreamer* - Peter James  h  2871
*A Face at the Window* - Dennis McFarland  h  3809
*Fairyland* - Paul J. McAuley  s  3711
*The Final Battle* - Richard A. Lupoff  f  3572
*From Hell* - Alan Moore  h  3987
*The Gates of Noon* - Michael Scott Rohan  f  4661
*The Golden Compass* - Philip Pullman  f  4446
*Good Omens: The Nice and Accurate Prophecies of
  Agnes Nutter, Witch* - Neil Gaiman  f  2103
*Gothic Romance* - Emmanuel Carrere  h  912
*The Hashish Man and Other Stories by Lord Dunsany*
  - Lord Dunsany  f  1700
*Haunted* - James Herbert  h  2669
*Heathen* - Shaun Hutson  h  2816
*The Hill of Dreams* - Arthur Machen  h  3595
*The Holmes-Dracula File* - Fred
  Saberhagen  h  4767
*The House on Hound Hill* - Maggie Prince  f  4438
*Humpty Dumpty: An Oval* - Damon Knight  s  3186
*The Hunger and Ecstasy of Vampires* - Brian
  Stableford  h  5192
*Imajica* - Clive Barker  h  343
*The Immaculate* - Mark Morris  h  4023
*In the Shadows of the Moonglade* - Riley St.
  James  h  5186
*The Jekyll Legacy* - Robert Bloch  h  535
*The Jewel of Seven Stars* - Bram Stoker  h  5312
*The Last Aerie* - Brian Lumley  h  3557
*The Last Voice They Hear* - Ramsey
  Campbell  h  858
*The Law of Becoming* - Kate Elliott  s  1774
*The Link* - Andrew Laurance  h  3348
*Lord Kelvin's Machine* - James P. Blaylock  f  520
*Lord of the Dead* - Tom Holland  h  2741
*Lord of the Vampires* - Jeanne Kalogridis  h  3005
*Lorien Lost* - Michael King  f  3124
*Love & Sleep* - John Crowley  f  1277

*Lunching with the Antichrist* - Michael
  Moorcock  f  3984
*Magician's Ward* - Patricia C. Wrede  f  5976
*Mary Reilly* - Valerie Martin  h  3654
*The Mummy!: A Tale of the Twenty-Second Century* -
  Jane Webb Loudon  h  3526
*The Mummy, or Ramses the Damned* - Anne
  Rice  h  4572
*Necroscope: The Lost Years* - Brian
  Lumley  h  3560
*Neverwhere* - Neil Gaiman  f  2104
*A Night in the Lonesome October* - Roger
  Zelazny  h  6072
*The Nightwalker* - Thomas Tessier  h  5442
*Personal Darkness* - Tanith Lee  h  3413
*Photographing Fairies* - Steve Szilagyi  f  5379
*Pillow Friend* - Lisa Tuttle  h  5522
*The Plague Tales* - Ann Benson  s  453
*Prophecy* - Peter James  h  2874
*Psychomech* - Brian Lumley  h  3562
*Psychosphere* - Brian Lumley  h  3563
*The Quorum* - Kim Newman  h  4100
*The Rats* - James Herbert  h  2671
*Red Bride* - Christopher Fowler  h  2019
*The Reluctant Sorcerer* - Simon Hawke  h  2622
*The Return* - Walter de la Mare  h  1424
*The Robin Hood Ambush* - William F. Wu  s  5999
*Rune* - Christopher Fowler  h  2020
*Sabine's Notebook* - Nick Bantock  f  335
*Scorpio Rising* - Alex McDonough  s  3804
*Seance for a Vampire* - Fred Saberhagen  h  4773
*Sexing the Cherry* - Jeanette Winterson  f  5927
*Sherlock Holmes in Orbit* - Mike Resnick  s  4556
*Signs of Life* - M. John Harrison  s  2580
*Slave of My Thirst* - Tom Holland  h  2742
*Spider* - Patrick McGrath  h  3815
*Spring-Heeled Jack* - Philip Pullman  f  4447
*Strange Devices of the Sun and Moon* - Lisa
  Goldstein  f  2262
*Streets of Blood* - Carl Sargent  f  4821
*Stunts* - Charles L. Grant  h  2317
*Suckers* - Anne Billson  h  490
*TekLab* - William Shatner  s  4939
*That's All, Folks!* - Greg Snow  f  5148
*Those Who Hunt the Night* - Barbara
  Hambly  h  2510
*Time Scout* - Robert Asprin  s  263
*Time Station London* - David Evans  s  1853
*Traveling with the Dead* - Barbara Hambly  h  2511
*The Trial of Elizabeth Cree* - Peter Ackroyd  h  26
*Triumph* - Ben Bova  s  598
*Tyrannosaurus Rex* - J.F. Rivkin  s  4597
*The Unborn* - Andrew Laurance  h  3350
*The Uncanny* - Andrew Klavan  h  3164
*The War Amongst the Angels* - Michael
  Moorcock  f  3986
*Werewolf* - Peter Rubie  h  4702
*The Werewolves of London* - Brian
  Stableford  h  5196
*Where Does Kissing End?* - Kate Pullinger  h  4445
*White Queen* - Gwyneth Jones  s  2955
*The Wizard of Camelot* - Simon Hawke  f  2627
*The Wolf's Hour* - Robert R. McCammon  h  3759
*The Woman between the Worlds* - F. Gwynplaine
  MacIntyre  s  3596
*The Women of Whitechapel and Jack the Ripper* - Paul
  West  h  5761
*Writ in Blood* - Chelsea Quinn Yarbro  h  6019

**Loughborough**
*The Wizard of Camelot* - Simon Hawke  f  2627

**Lousewartshire**
*Nature's God* - Robert Anton Wilson  f  5903

**Lower Spigot**
*The Haunted Tea Cosy: A Dispirited and Distasteful
  Diversion for Christmas* - Edward Gorey  h  2276

**Manchester**
*Anti-Ice* - Stephen Baxter  s  398
*Automated Alice* - Jeff Noon  f  4134
*The One Safe Place* - Ramsey Campbell  h  862
*Pollen* - Jeff Noon  s  4135
*Vurt* - Jeff Noon  s  4136

**Marshank**
*Martin the Warrior* - Brian Jacques  f  2851

**Maybury**
*Stitch* - Mark Morris  h  4024

**Merkleton**
*Kent Montana and the Reasonably Invisible Man* -
  Lionel Fenn  s  1919

**Morecambe**
*Head Injuries* - Conrad Williams  h  5816

**Mount Pleasant**
*The Influence* - Ramsey Campbell  h  857

**Mousehole**
*The Little Country* - Charles de Lint  f  1432

**Nantucket Island**
*Island in the Sea of Time* - S.M. Stirling  s  5295

**Neath**
*Sepulchre* - James Herbert  h  2672

**Norwich**
*Stone Angels* - Mike Jefferies  h  2889

**Nottingham**
*Lady of the Forest* - Jennifer Roberson  f  4609
*The Sheriff of Nottingham* - Richard Kluger  f  3165

**Over Stowey**
*Walford's Oak* - Jill M. Phillips  f  4310

**Oxford**
*The Endless Knot* - Stephen R. Lawhead  f  3354
*Legacy of the Darksword* - Margaret Weis  f  5719
*The Subtle Knife* - Philip Pullman  f  4448
*To Say Nothing of the Dog* - Connie Willis  s  5874

**Oxfordshire**
*Doomsday Book* - Connie Willis  s  5868
*Good Omens: The Nice and Accurate Prophecies of
  Agnes Nutter, Witch* - Neil Gaiman  f  2103

**Partington**
*Nazareth Hill* - Ramsey Campbell  h  861

**Ravenmoor**
*Haunted* - James Herbert  h  2669

**Ravenskeep**
*Lady of the Forest* - Jennifer Roberson  f  4609

**Redstone**
*The Tooth Fairy* - Graham Joyce  f  2995

**Redwall Abbey**
*The Bellmaker* - Brian Jacques  f  2848
*Mariel of Redwall* - Brian Jacques  f  2850
*Martin the Warrior* - Brian Jacques  f  2851
*Outcast of Redwall* - Brian Jacques  f  2853
*The Pearls of Lutra* - Brian Jacques  f  2854
*Salamandastron* - Brian Jacques  f  2855

**Richmond**
*The Time Ships* - Stephen Baxter  s  403

**Rye**
*The Haunting of Lamb House* - Joan Aiken  h  45

**Salisbury**
*The Alien Years* - Robert Silverberg  s  5027

**Sandpits**
*The Dark One* - Guy N. Smith  h  5118

**Sherwood Forest**
*Lady of the Forest* - Jennifer Roberson  f  4609

*The Outlaws of Sherwood* - Robin
    McKinley  *f*  3846
*The Sheriff of Nottingham* - Richard Kluger  *f*  3165

**Shropshire**
*The Iron Bridge* - David Morse  *s*  4036

**Sleath**
*The Ghosts of Sleath* - James Herbert  *h*  2668

**Somerset**
*Walford's Oak* - Jill M. Phillips  *f*  4310

**Starmouth**
*The Horror Club* - Mark Morris  *h*  4022

**Stonehenge**
*Kirins: The Flight of the Ain* - James D.
    Priest  *f*  4433
*Kirins: The Secret of the Hanging Stones* - James D.
    Priest  *f*  4434

**Sussex**
*Host* - Peter James  *h*  2872
*Psychamok* - Brian Lumley  *h*  3561
*Twilight* - Peter James  *h*  2876

**Thornton Basset**
*The Black Death* - Basil Copper  *h*  1185

**Tredannack**
*The Vanishment* - Jonathan Aycliffe  *h*  282

**Valley Green**
*Evil Intent* - Bernard Taylor  *h*  5400

**Vernematon**
*The Forest House* - Marion Zimmer Bradley  *f*  633

**Warchester**
*Carnosaur* - Harry Adam Knight  *s*  3191

**Willington College**
*Witch Spell* - Guy N. Smith  *h*  5122

**Woodhenge**
*Burning Bright* - J.S. Russell  *h*  4733

**Wych Cross**
*The Sandman: Book of Dreams* - Neil
    Gaiman  *f*  2105

**York**
*Sleepwalker* - Michael Cadnum  *h*  815

**Yorkshire**
*Midnight Sun* - Ramsey Campbell  *h*  860

# EUROPE

*All's Faire* - Pamela F. Service  *f*  4917
*The Amazon Chronicles* - Jane E.M.
    Robinson  *f*  4627
*Ars Magica* - Judith Tarr  *f*  5392
*Attila's Treasure* - Stephan Grundy  *f*  2453
*The Autobiography of Santa Claus: It's Better to Give*
    - Jeff Guinn  *f*  2456
*Black Horses for the King* - Anne
    McCaffrey  *f*  3720
*Blood Alone* - Elaine Bergstrom  *h*  462
*The Boat of a Million Years* - Poul Anderson  *s*  125
*Byzantium* - Stephen R. Lawhead  *f*  3353
*Charlemagne's Champion* - Gail Van Asten  *f*  5534
*City of Pain* - John Terra  *f*  5438
*Dark Tyrants* - Justin Achilli  *h*  23
*Darwinia* - Robert Charles Wilson  *s*  5906
*The Discovery of Dragons* - Graeme Base  *f*  385
*A Diversity of Dragons* - Anne McCaffrey  *f*  3728
*The Dragons of the Rhine* - Diana L.
    Paxson  *f*  4264
*Eclipse Corona* - John Shirley  *s*  5006
*A Farce to Be Reckoned With* - Roger
    Zelazny  *f*  6064
*Glenraven* - Marion Zimmer Bradley  *f*  635

*His Majesty's Elephant* - Judith Tarr  *f*  5394
*Holy Fire* - Bruce Sterling  *s*  5259
*If at Faust You Don't Succeed* - Roger
    Zelazny  *f*  6070
*Indiana Jones and the Sky Pirates* - Martin
    Caidin  *f*  825
*Jack Faust* - Michael Swanwick  *s*  5372
*Jupiter's Daughter* - Tom Hyman  *s*  2820
*The Light Bearer* - Donna Gillespie  *f*  2229
*The Lost Guardian* - Ronald Anthony Cross  *s*  1274
*Lucifer Jones* - Mike Resnick  *f*  4549
*Madouc* - Jack Vance  *f*  5547
*North Wind* - Gwyneth Jones  *s*  2953
*The Offspring* - Kenneth McKenney  *h*  3826
*One King's Way* - Harry Harrison  *s*  2572
*Parsifal* - Peter Vansittart  *f*  5560
*The Plains of Passage* - Jean M. Auel  *s*  275
*The Premonition* - Andrew Laurance  *h*  3349
*The Princess and the Dragon* - Roberto
    Pazzi  *f*  4272
*Rhinegold* - Stephan Grundy  *f*  2454
*Second Fire* - Mike Moscoe  *s*  4040
*Shadow of Obsession* - Rebecca Neason  *f*  4082
*Shiva Accused: An Adventure of the Ice Age* - J.H.
    Brennan  *f*  667
*Shiva: An Adventure of the Ice Age* - J.H.
    Brennan  *f*  669
*Shiva's Challenge: An Adventure of the Ice Age* - J.H.
    Brennan  *f*  668
*Slow Dancing through Time* - Gardner
    Dozois  *s*  1615
*Songs of Chaos* - S.N. Lewitt  *s*  3452
*Spires of Spirit* - Gael Baudino  *f*  395
*The Stress of Her Regard* - Tim Powers  *h*  4385
*Treason in Time* - Keith William Andrews  *s*  143
*The Turing Option* - Harry Harrison  *s*  2579
*Turn of the Cards* - Victor Milan  *s*  3891
*The Unborn* - Andrew Laurance  *h*  3350
*The Vampire Memoirs* - Mara McCuniff  *h*  3781
*The Wall* - Marlen Haushofer  *s*  2603
*War of the Worlds: Global Dispatches* - Kevin J.
    Anderson  *s*  119
*Whose Song Is Sung* - Frank Schaefer  *f*  4872
*Why Do Birds* - Damon Knight  *s*  3190
*The Wolf and the Raven* - Diana L. Paxson  *f*  4270
*The Yngling and the Circle of Power* - John
    Dalmas  *s*  1328

**Castle Banat**
*The Golden* - Lucius Shepard  *h*  4978

**The City**
*The Silent City* - Elisabeth Vonarburg  *s*  5592

**Old World**
*Drachenfels* - Jack Yeovil  *f*  6022

**Pyrenees**
*Cold Allies* - Patricia Anthony  *s*  157

# FICTIONAL CITY

*Metropolitan* - Walter Jon Williams  *s*  5839
*Pigs Don't Fly* - Mary Brown  *f*  727
*Shadow Dance* - Anne Logston  *f*  3513

**Aerillia**
*Harp of Winds* - Maggie Furey  *f*  2097

**Aghrapur**
*Conan of the Red Brotherhood* - Leonard
    Carpenter  *f*  906

**Airdnasheen**
*The Crystal Rose* - Maya Kaathryn Bohnhoff  *f*  560

**Aiskeep**
*Ciara's Song* - Andre Norton  *f*  4146

**Akava**
*The Watcher's Mask* - Laurie J. Marks  *f*  3627

**Alanda**
*Four & Twenty Blackbirds* - Mercedes
    Lackey  *f*  3283

**Allanmere**
*Dagger's Edge* - Anne Logston  *f*  3508
*Greendaughter* - Anne Logston  *f*  3510
*Shadow* - Anne Logston  *f*  3512

**Angelshand**
*Stranger at the Wedding* - Barbara Hambly  *f*  2509

**Ankh-Morpork**
*Feet of Clay* - Terry Pratchett  *f*  4389
*Guards! Guards!* - Terry Pratchett  *f*  4390
*Hogfather* - Terry Pratchett  *f*  4391
*Interesting Times* - Terry Pratchett  *f*  4392
*Maskerade* - Terry Pratchett  *f*  4395
*Men at Arms* - Terry Pratchett  *f*  4396
*Moving Pictures* - Terry Pratchett  *f*  4398
*Reaper Man* - Terry Pratchett  *f*  4399
*Soul Music* - Terry Pratchett  *f*  4401

**Ankhapur**
*King Pinch* - David Cook  *f*  1146

**Anwar-Teng**
*Wild Magic* - Angus Wells  *f*  5741

**Araboth**
*AEstival Tide* - Elizabeth Hand  *s*  2533

**Aranos**
*Star Child* - James P. Hogan  *s*  2730

**Ariss**
*Fire in the Mist* - Holly Lisle  *f*  3482

**Arwar Odawl**
*The Dark Shore* - Adam Lee  *f*  3385

**Ashami**
*The Watcher's Mask* - Laurie J. Marks  *f*  3627

**Aster**
*Sunder, Eclipse and Seed* - Elise Guttenberg  *f*  2471

**Atalanta**
*The Defiance* - Bill Baldwin  *s*  310

**Athgar**
*Wolf's Cub* - Mackay Wood  *f*  5964

**Avanue**
*Black Wine* - Candas Jane Dorsey  *s*  1582

**Avenor**
*Fugitive Prince* - Janny Wurts  *f*  6002

**Averalaan**
*Hunter's Death* - Michelle West  *f*  5758

**Avonel**
*Beneath the Vaulted Hills* - Sean Russell  *f*  4739

**Axe-Edge**
*The Wizard's Shadow* - Susan Dexter  *f*  1514

**Aydindril**
*Blood of the Fold* - Terry Goodkind  *f*  2268

**Banqot**
*The Salukan Gambit* - Sean Dalton  *s*  1333

**Barca's Hamlet**
*Lord of the Isles* - David Drake  *f*  1636

**Bay'Zell**
*The Barbed Coil* - J.V. Jones  *f*  2957

**Bekalli**
*Wrath of the Princes* - Holly Lisle  *f*  3490

**Beldan**
*Beldan's Fire* - Midori Snyder  *f*  5150

**Berylon**
*Song for the Basilisk* - Patricia A. McKillip  *f*  3841

**Bethely**
*In the Mothers' Land* - Elisabeth Vonarburg   s   5590

**Biemestren**
*The Road Home* - Joel Rosenberg   f   4674

**Bingtown**
*The Ship of Magic* - Robin Hobb   f   2696

**Blavek**
*Hearts and Armor* - Ron Miller   f   3903

**Bordertown**
*Borderland* - Terri Windling   f   5913
*Elsewhere* - Will Shetterly   f   4993
*The Essential Bordertown* - Terri Windling   f   5914
*Finder* - Emma Bull   f   769
*Life on the Border* - Terri Windling   f   5915
*Nevernever* - Will Shetterly   f   4995

**Borphee**
*The Lost City of Zork* - Robin Wayne Bailey   f   288

**Braedon**
*King's Man and Thief* - Christie Golden   f   2253

**Bragenmere**
*The Rainbow Abyss* - Barbara Hambly   f   2507

**Bren**
*A Man Betrayed* - J.V. Jones   f   2958

**Briana**
*Sunder, Eclipse and Seed* - Elise Guttenberg   f   2471

**Bright**
*Fire in the Mist* - Holly Lisle   f   3482

**Caer Cadan**
*Shadow of the King* - Helen Hollick   f   2747

**Caer MacDonald**
*Luthien's Gamble* - R.A. Salvatore   f   4802

**Caerockeith**
*The Painter Knight* - Fiona Patton   f   4258

**Calimekka**
*Diplomacy of Wolves* - Holly Lisle   f   3481

**Calimport**
*The Silent Blade* - R.A. Salvatore   f   4805

**Camelot**
*The Whispers* - Dan Parkinson   s   4247

**Camfield**
*Wolf's Cub* - Mackay Wood   f   5964

**Cangora**
*Winged Magic* - Mary H. Herbert   f   2678

**Caraqui**
*City on Fire* - Walter Jon Williams   s   5835

**Caris**
*The Sleep of Stone* - Louise Cooper   f   1179

**Cartada**
*The Lions of Al-Rassan* - Guy Gavriel Kay   f   3016

**Cartheon**
*Wheel of Dreams* - Salinda Tyson   f   5529

**Castlebough**
*The Compass of the Soul* - Sean Russell   f   4740

**Cavasar**
*In Legend Born* - Laura Resnick   f   4533

**Cengarn**
*Days of Air and Darkness* - Katharine Kerr   f   3067

**Chepsenyt**
*The Broken Land* - Ian McDonald   s   3791

**Chestnut Circle**
*Dragon Sleeping* - Craig Shaw Gardner   f   2127

**Ciaron**
*The Raven Ring* - Patricia C. Wrede   f   5978

**Ciron**
*They Fly at Ciron* - Samuel R. Delany   s   1482

**Cittagazze**
*The Subtle Knife* - Philip Pullman   f   4448

**The City**
*Black Unicorn* - Tanith Lee   f   3404

**City of Sorcerers**
*A Hero Born* - Michael A. Stackpole   f   5202

**City of the Abyss**
*Ancient Games* - Scott Ciencin   f   1028

**City of Time**
*Hidden Echoes* - Mike Jefferies   f   2885

**Cloud City**
*Trouble on Cloud City* - Kevin J. Anderson   s   117
*Zorba the Hutt's Revenge* - Paul Davids   s   1394

**Clouds End**
*Clouds End* - Sean Stewart   f   5272

**Corcorva**
*The Innkeeper's Song* - Peter S. Beagle   f   409

**Cragsfall**
*The Conjurer Princess* - Vivian Vande
  Velde   f   5555

**Creek**
*Dark Heart* - Betsy James   f   2857

**Creiddylad**
*The Crystal Rose* - Maya Kaathryn Bohnhoff   f   560
*Taminy* - Maya Kaathryn Bohnhoff   f   563

**Cullinsberg**
*Shadow's Realm* - Mickey Zucker Reichert   f   4523

**Cuspidor**
*In between Dragons* - Michael Kandel   f   3010

**Cyrga**
*The Hidden City* - David Eddings   f   1733

**Daggerdale**
*Finder's Bane* - Kate Novak   f   4165

**Daltigoth**
*Vinas Solamnus* - J. Robert King   f   3123

**Datha**
*The Master of Whitestorm* - Janny Wurts   f   6003

**Dejagore**
*Bleak Seasons* - Glen Cook   f   1147
*Dreams of Steel* - Glen Cook   f   1150

**Delgroth**
*A Call to Arms* - Thomas K. Martin   f   3650

**Delta City**
*Delta City* - Felicity Savage   f   4849

**Dhiammara**
*Dhiammara* - Maggie Furey   f   2096

**Diadem**
*Changing Fate* - Elisabeth Waters   f   5629

**Dorbin**
*Moonspeaker* - K.D. Wentworth   s   5754

**Dramujh**
*Tears of Time* - Nancy Asire   f   256

**Dreambreak**
*I Wake From a Dream of a Drowned Star City* - S.P.
  Somtow   s   5157

**Dry Hole**
*The Mines of Behemoth* - Michael Shea   f   4945

**Dundalis**
*The Demon Awakens* - R.A. Salvatore   f   4794

**Durbrecht**
*Lords of the Sky* - Angus Wells   f   5738

**Eberly**
*The Itinerant Exorcist* - Ashley McConnell   f   3776

**Ebou Dar**
*A Crown of Swords* - Robert Jordan   f   2984

**Ehvenor**
*The Road to Ehvenor* - Joel Rosenberg   f   4675

**Elysia**
*Ecstasia* - Francesca Lia Block   f   547
*Primavera* - Francesca Lia Block   f   551

**Ephebe**
*Small Gods* - Terry Pratchett   f   4400

**Errold's Grove**
*Owlflight* - Mercedes Lackey   f   3291
*Owlsight* - Mercedes Lackey   f   3292

**Evereska**
*Elfshadow* - Elaine Cunningham   f   1288

**Evreux**
*Pigs Don't Fly* - Mary Brown   f   727

**Eyerlon**
*Beneath the Web* - Lynn Abbey   f   12

**Fairhaven**
*The White Order* - L.E. Modesitt Jr.   f   3942

**Falias**
*The Fire Duke* - Joel Rosenberg   f   4671

**Faudace**
*The Book of Knights* - Yves Meynard   f   3884

**Felsplex**
*The Rainbow Abyss* - Barbara Hambly   f   2507

**Firaqua**
*The Shadow of Sorcery* - Andrew J. Offutt   f   4202

**Firoze**
*Clock Strikes Sword* - Ian Hammell   f   2529

**First Folk Ruins**
*Bones of the Past* - Holly Lisle   f   3478

**The Forest of Tethir**
*Silver Shadows* - Elaine Cunningham   f   1292

**Fort Hold**
*Dragonseye* - Anne McCaffrey   s   3730

**F'talezon**
*Shadow's Daughter* - Shirley Meier   f   3871

**Fullerton**
*Time and Light* - William Bornefeld   s   574

**Gahrs**
*Murder in Cormyr* - Chet Williamson   f   5848

**Gallia**
*Mage Heart* - Jane Routley   f   4686

**Gan Garee**
*Challenges* - Sharon Green   f   2354
*Competition* - Sharon Green   f   2355
*Convergence* - Sharon Green   f   2356

**Gandhara**
*Changeweaver* - Margaret Ball   f   313
*Flameweaver* - Margaret Ball   f   314

**Genesis**
*Ancient Games* - Scott Ciencin   f   1028

**Genesis Settlement**
*Night of Glory* - Scott Ciencin   f   1030

**Geneva**
*The Shadow Within* - Jeanne Cavelos  s  944

**Ghezrat**
*The Sword and the Lion* - Roberta Cray  f  1253

**Gibil**
*Between the Rivers* - Harry Turtledove  f  5496

**Gnomon**
*Clock Strikes Sword* - Ian Hammell  f  2529

**Gradford**
*The Robin and the Kestrel* - Mercedes
    Lackey  f  3293

**Grand Base**
*Galactic Patrol* - Edward E. Smith  s  5116

**Granite City**
*The Road to Underfall* - Mike Jefferies  f  2888

**Grassedge**
*Promised Land* - Connie Willis  s  5872

**Great Gray City**
*The Iron Dragon's Daughter* - Michael
    Swanwick  f  5371

**Great Hall**
*Feersum Endjinn* - Iain M. Banks  s  325

**Great Library of Kanez**
*Branch and Crown* - Gael Baudino  f  389

**Greshing**
*The Arm of the Stone* - Victoria Strauss  f  5333

**Griswold**
*Dragon's Bait* - Vivian Vande Velde  f  5556

**Haisbarg**
*The White Order* - L.E. Modesitt Jr.  f  3942

**Halig-liath**
*The Crystal Rose* - Maya Kaathryn Bohnhoff  f  560

**Hamsterburg**
*One Quest, Hold the Dragons* - Greg
    Costikyan  f  1208

**Haven**
*The Bones of Haven* - Simon R. Green  f  2363
*The God Killer* - Simon R. Green  f  2368
*Guard Against Dishonor* - Simon R. Green  f  2369
*Hawk & Fisher* - Simon R. Green  f  2370
*Winner Takes All* - Simon R. Green  f  2375
*Wolf in the Fold* - Simon R. Green  f  2376

**Hel's Town**
*The Guardian* - Angus Wells  f  5737

**Hi-Vator**
*They Fly at Ciron* - Samuel R. Delany  s  1482

**The Hill**
*Flickering Shadows* - Kwadwo Agymah
    Kamau  f  3006

**Holdfast**
*The Furies* - Suzy McKee Charnas  s  968

**Hub of the Impire**
*Emperor and Clown* - Dave Duncan  f  1676
*Upland Outlaws* - Dave Duncan  f  1690

**Huon Parita**
*Infanta* - Louise Cooper  f  1176

**Hvalkir**
*To Fall Like Stars* - Nancy Asire  f  257

**Hyper Athens**
*Patton's Spaceship* - John Barnes  s  357

**Ifriti Islamic Republic**
*Infectress* - Tom Cool  s  1167

**Ikos**
*Prince of the North* - Harry Turtledove  f  5509

**Illizbuah**
*Saber & Shadow* - S.M. Stirling  f  5297

**Imperia**
*Realm of Light* - Deborah Chester  f  1008
*Reign of Shadows* - Deborah Chester  f  1009
*Shadow War* - Deborah Chester  f  1010

**Inishbuffin**
*The Boy From the Burren* - Sheila Gilluly  f  2236

**Iron City**
*The Warden of Horses* - Karen Ripley  s  4595

**Jefferson Village**
*My Stepfather Shrank!* - Barbara Dillon  s  1558

**Jerhattan**
*Pegasus in Flight* - Anne McCaffrey  s  3742

**Jolinstive**
*Heroes, Inc.* - Kyle Crocco  f  1268

**Jor Valadrem**
*Wizard of Bones* - Robert N. Charrette  f  979

**Joyful Travail**
*Revenant* - Louise Cooper  f  1178

**Jubilar**
*Waking Beauty* - Paul Witcover  f  5931

**Kahnderule**
*The Gates of Twilight* - Paula Volsky  f  5581

**Karenta**
*Pretty Pewter Gods* - Glen Cook  f  1152

**Keep of Dare**
*Icefalcon's Quest* - Barbara Hambly  f  2504
*Mother of Winter* - Barbara Hambly  f  2506

**King's Keep**
*Wolf Justice* - Doranna Durgin  f  1706

**Kingsford**
*A Cast of Corbies* - Mercedes Lackey  f  3274

**Konishi**
*Diaspora* - Greg Egan  s  1759

**Krondor**
*Shadow of a Dark Queen* - Raymond E.
    Feist  f  1911

**Kush**
*Arena* - William R. Forstchen  f  1977

**Kyara**
*Anvil* - Nicolas van Pallandt  s  5540

**Lancre**
*Lords and Ladies* - Terry Pratchett  f  4394

**Land of the Dark Isles**
*Black Wine* - Candas Jane Dorsey  s  1582

**Landage**
*Dreaming Metal* - Melissa Scott  s  4895

**Land's End**
*Journeyman Wizard* - Mary Frances
    Zambreno  f  6057

**Lankhmar**
*Farewell to Lankhmar* - Fritz Leiber  f  3418
*Ill Met in Lankhmar* - Fritz Leiber  f  3419
*Lean Times in Lankhmar* - Fritz Leiber  f  3420
*Return to Lankhmar* - Fritz Leiber  f  3422
*Swords Against the Shadowland* - Robin Wayne
    Bailey  f  291

**Laureal City**
*Northlight* - Deborah Wheeler  s  5775

**London Below**
*Neverwhere* - Neil Gaiman  f  2104

**Lost City of the Jedi**
*The Lost City of the Jedi* - Paul Davids  s  1393

**Luly**
*Song for the Basilisk* - Patricia A. McKillip  f  3841

**Luminaux**
*Jovah's Angel* - Sharon Shinn  s  5001

**Lundinia**
*King's Son, Magic's Son* - Josepha Sherman  f  4986

**Luxur**
*Conan the Gladiator* - Leonard Carpenter  f  907

**Lycanth**
*The Warrior's Tale* - Allan Cole  f  1110

**Marneri**
*Bazil Broketail* - Christopher Rowley  f  4692

**Mashupro**
*Chorus Skating* - Alan Dean Foster  f  1998

**Mecq**
*The Wizard at Home* - Rick Shelley  f  4975

**Menzoberranzan**
*Daughter of the Drow* - Elaine Cunningham  f  1287
*Siege of Darkness* - R.A. Salvatore  f  4804
*The Silent Blade* - R.A. Salvatore  f  4805

**Merina**
*Tiger Burning Bright* - Marion Zimmer
    Bradley  f  652

**Meya Suerta**
*The Golden Key* - Melanie Rawn  f  4486

**Middletown**
*My Best Friend Is Invisible* - R.L. Stine  h  5289

**Midsummer Faire at Kingsford**
*The Lark and the Wren* - Mercedes Lackey  f  3286

**Mirchaz**
*A Dragon at World's End* - Christopher
    Rowley  f  4693

**Mirlacca**
*The Courts of Sorcery* - Ashley McConnell  f  3773
*The Fountains of Mirlacca* - Ashley
    McConnell  f  3775
*The Itinerant Exorcist* - Ashley McConnell  f  3776

**Miyesti**
*Thorn and Needle* - Paul B. Thompson  f  5456

**Mon'ay**
*The Heldan* - Deborah Talmadge-Bickmore  f  5383

**Monfort**
*The Sword of Bedwyr* - R.A. Salvatore  f  4808

**Monjon**
*The Wizard and the Floating City* - Christopher
    Rowley  f  4699

**Moor**
*The Dog King* - Christoph Ransmayr  f  4474

**Mospheira**
*Inheritor* - C.J. Cherryh  s  997

**Moy Tura**
*City of the Sorcerers* - Mary H. Herbert  f  2673

**Mulberia**
*The Fools' War* - Lee Kisling  f  3159

**Mull Barya**
*Troika* - Louise Cooper  f  1181

**Mulmaster**
*The Mage in the Iron Mask* - Brian
　Thomsen　*f*　5458

**Mutchville**
*Bright Messengers* - Gentry Lee　*s*　3398

**Nairne**
*Taminy* - Maya Kaathryn Bohnhoff　*f*　563

**Namport**
*By Honor Betray'd* - Debra Doyle　*s*　1598

**Nargh**
*Past Imperative* - Dave Duncan　*f*　1684

**Natayos**
*The Hidden City* - David Eddings　*f*　1733

**Neraka**
*Legacy of Steel* - Mary H. Herbert　*f*　2675
*Tears of the Night Sky* - Linda P. Baker　*f*　299

**New Babylon**
*Wolf in Shadow* - David Gemmell　*s*　2191

**New City**
*The Schizogenic Man* - Raymond Harris　*s*　2563

**New Milton**
*Milton in America* - Peter Ackroyd　*f*　25

**Newford**
*Trader* - Charles de Lint　*f*　1438

**Newport**
*The Warrior and the Witch* - Carl Miller　*f*　3893

**Nexis**
*Aurian* - Maggie Furey　*f*　2095
*Dhiammara* - Maggie Furey　*f*　2096
*Harp of Winds* - Maggie Furey　*f*　2097
*Sword of Flame* - Maggie Furey　*f*　2098

**N'hol**
*The Waterborn* - J. Gregory Keyes　*f*　3098

**Nolton**
*The Lark and the Wren* - Mercedes Lackey　*f*　3286

**Novyraj**
*A Second Infinity* - Michael D. Weaver　*s*　5660

**Nowford**
*Our Lady of the Harbour* - Charles de Lint　*f*　1434

**Nuhr**
*O Greenest Branch!* - Gael Baudino　*f*　394

**Ol Tah**
*The Broken Land* - Ian McDonald　*s*　3791

**Omwimmee Trade**
*Bones of the Past* - Holly Lisle　*f*　3478

**Orikhalkos**
*Acts of Conscience* - William Barton　*s*　377

**Orissa**
*The Warrior Returns* - Allan Cole　*f*　1109
*The Warrior's Tale* - Allan Cole　*f*　1110

**Orktown**
*Never Trust an Elf* - Robert N. Charrette　*f*　976

**Ottersgate**
*The Blood Jaguar* - Michael H. Payne　*f*　4271

**Pandathaway**
*The Road Home* - Joel Rosenberg　*f*　4674

**Pangur Ban**
*The Face of Apollo* - Fred Saberhagen　*s*　4766

**Paradys**
*The Book of the Beast* - Tanith Lee　*f*　3405

**Parda**
*Heroes, Inc.* - Kyle Crocco　*f*　1268

**Parendur**
*Shadowdance* - Robin Wayne Bailey　*f*　290

**Parlainth**
*The Longing Ring* - Christopher Kubasik　*f*　3246

**Parz City**
*Flux* - Stephen Baxter　*s*　399

**Peridol**
*Spell of Apocalypse* - Mayer Alan Brenner　*f*　672
*Spell of Fate* - Mayer Alan Brenner　*f*　673

**Peyrefixade**
*Count Scar* - C. Dale Brittain　*f*　702

**Piyar**
*Emerald House Rising* - Peg Kerr　*f*　3080

**Podhru**
*One Land, One Duke* - Ru Emerson　*f*　1809

**Polar City**
*Polar City Blues* - Katharine Kerr　*s*　3073

**Port City**
*Traitors* - Kristine Kathryn Rusch　*f*　4729

**Prima City**
*Delta Search* - William Shatner　*s*　4930

**Pseudopolis**
*Eric* - Terry Pratchett　*f*　4388

**Purasham**
*By the Sword* - Greg Costikyan　*f*　1207

**Qjara**
*Conan the Outcast* - Leonard Carpenter　*f*　908

**Quarin**
*A Two-Edged Sword* - Thomas K. Martin　*f*　3653

**Quosh**
*Dragons of Argonath* - Christopher Rowley　*f*　4694

**Quoz**
*Waking Beauty* - Paul Witcover　*f*　5931

**Ramsgate**
*Dragon War* - Laurence Yep　*f*　6025

**Ranganar**
*Flowerdust* - Gwyneth Jones　*s*　2952

**Ranoima**
*The Wall at the Edge of the World* - Jim
　Aikin　*s*　46

**The Redoubt**
*Troika* - Louise Cooper　*f*　1181

**Reykvid**
*Magelord: The Awakening* - Thomas K.
　Martin　*f*　3651

**Rhiminee**
*Luck in the Shadows* - Lynn Flewelling　*f*　1952
*Stalking Darkness* - Lynn Flewelling　*f*　1953

**Rhomatum**
*Ring of Intrigue* - Jane S. Fancher　*f*　1863
*Ring of Lightning* - Jane S. Fancher　*f*　1864

**Rhostshyl**
*Mistress of Ambiguities* - J.F. Rivkin　*f*　4596

**Rhuidean**
*The Fires of Heaven* - Robert Jordan　*f*　2987

**Rit**
*Sable, Shadow and Ice* - Cheryl J. Franklin　*f*　2039

**River Bend**
*First Dawn* - Mike Moscoe　*s*　4038

**Rivervale**
*Wolf in Shadow* - David Gemmell　*s*　2191

**Rorn**
*The Baker's Boy* - J.V. Jones　*f*　2956

**Sacor City**
*Green Rider* - Kristen Britain　*f*　692

**Saigo City**
*Alien Blues* - Lynn S. Hightower　*s*　2682
*Alien Eyes* - Lynn S. Hightower　*s*　2683
*Alien Heat* - Lynn S. Hightower　*s*　2684
*Alien Rites* - Lynn S. Hightower　*s*　2685

**St. Celias**
*The Changeling Prince* - Vivian Vande
　Velde　*f*　5554

**St. Toby's-by-the-Mountain**
*Dragon's Bait* - Vivian Vande Velde　*f*　5556

**Samarinda**
*The Gilded Chain: A Tale of the King's Blades* - Dave
　Duncan　*f*　1679

**Sandeni**
*Shadow Dawn* - Chris Claremont　*f*　1042

**Sannatia**
*User Unfriendly* - Vivian Vande Velde　*f*　5558

**Santagithi**
*The Western Wizard* - Mickey Zucker
　Reichert　*f*　4526

**Sarykam**
*The Last Book of Swords: Shieldbreaker's Story* - Fred
　Saberhagen　*f*　4768

**Sassevin**
*Nameless Magery* - Delia Marshall Turner　*f*　5490

**Savvalis**
*Wildfire* - Jo Clayton　*f*　1073

**Shadowcatch**
*Bleak Seasons* - Glen Cook　*f*　1147
*She Is the Darkness* - Glen Cook　*f*　1154

**Shadows Fall**
*Shadows Fall* - Simon R. Green　*f*　2373

**Shadyside**
*The Cat* - R.L. Stine　*h*　5285

**Shaidar Haran**
*Lord of Chaos* - Robert Jordan　*f*　2988

**Shan on the Desert**
*Taking Flight* - Lawrence Watt-Evans　*f*　5650

**Shayol Ghul**
*Lord of Chaos* - Robert Jordan　*f*　2988

**Shejidan**
*Inheritor* - C.J. Cherryh　*s*　997

**Sherreen**
*Illusion* - Paula Volsky　*f*　5582

**Shreveport**
*Celestis* - Paul Park　*s*　4241

**Sigil**
*Finder's Bane* - Kate Novak　*f*　4165
*Planar Powers* - J. Robert King　*f*　3122

**The Silver City**
*Angels & Visitations: A Miscellany* - Neil
　Gaiman　*f*　2101

**Skandi**
*Sword-Born* - Jennifer Roberson　*f*　4612

**Smallcliff**
*Athyra* - Steven Brust　*f*　739

**Smokey Hollow**
*Jennifer Murdley's Toad* - Bruce Coville　f　1220

**Southwark**
*Beggar's Banquet* - Daniel Hood　f　2756
*Fanuilh* - Daniel Hood　f　2757
*Scales of Justice* - Daniel Hood　f　2758
*Wizard's Heir* - Daniel Hood　f　2759

**Spiral Town**
*Destiny's Road* - Larry Niven　s　4119

**Stateless**
*Distress* - Greg Egan　s　1760

**Steadfast-by-Sea**
*Horrible Humes* - Stephen Billias　f　487

**Stridgenfel**
*Runes of Autumn* - Larry Elmore　f　1790

**Swangard**
*Nobody's Son* - Sean Stewart　f　5275

**Sylvarresta**
*The Runelords: The Sum of All Men* - David
　Farland　f　1866

**Taglios**
*Dreams of Steel* - Glen Cook　f　1150

**Tall Oaks**
*First Dawn* - Mike Moscoe　s　4038
*Lost Days* - Mike Moscoe　s　4039

**Tanelorn**
*Corum: The Coming of Chaos* - Michael
　Moorcock　f　3978

**Tar Vallon**
*The Shadow Rising* - Robert Jordan　f　2990

**Tathagata**
*Sable, Shadow and Ice* - Cheryl J. Franklin　f　2039

**Taufzin**
*Mission Child* - Maureen F. McHugh　s　3819

**Tells**
*Dark Heart* - Betsy James　f　2857

**Tezin-dar**
*Forbidden Magic* - Angus Wells　f　5736

**Thanqurn**
*The Riddled Man* - Mark E. Rogers　f　4654

**Throal**
*The Longing Ring* - Christopher Kubasik　f　3246

**Thrull**
*The Forging of the Shadows* - Oliver
　Johnson　f　2924

**Tir Amindel**
*The Master of Whitestorm* - Janny Wurts　f　6003

**Tober Cove**
*Commitment Hour* - James Alan Gardner　s　2134

**Torskaal**
*The Moorchild* - Eloise Jarvis McGraw　f　3816

**TunFaire**
*Red Iron Nights* - Glen Cook　f　1153

**Two Rivers**
*The Humanoids* - Jack Williamson　s　5865

**U.**
*Galatea 2.2* - Richard M. Powers　s　4381

**Uji**
*North Wind* - Gwyneth Jones　s　2953

**Urf Durfal**
*Another Day, Another Dungeon* - Greg
　Costikyan　f　1206

**Valana**
*Saint Leibowitz and the Wild Horse Woman* - Walter
　M. Miller Jr.　s　3908

**Valestock**
*The War in the Waste* - Felicity Savage　f　4851

**Vensunor**
*The Gates of Vensunor* - Carol Heller　f　2650

**Videssos**
*Videssos Besieged* - Harry Turtledove　f　5513

**Vienne**
*The Death of the Necromancer* - Martha
　Wells　f　5749

**Vingaard Keep**
*Kaz the Minotaur* - Richard A. Knaak　f　3172

**Viron**
*Calde of the Long Sun* - Gene Wolfe　s　5937
*Exodus From the Long Sun* - Gene Wolfe　s　5941

**Wardenberg**
*In the Mothers' Land* - Elisabeth Vonarburg　s　5590

**Waterdeep**
*Elfshadow* - Elaine Cunningham　f　1288
*Thornhold* - Elaine Cunningham　f　1293

**Waterholm**
*Cardmaster* - Clayton Emery　f　1813

**Weird's Hold**
*Minerva Wakes* - Holly Lisle　f　3487

**Westerin**
*Castle of Deception* - Mercedes Lackey　f　3275

**Westgate**
*Masquerades* - Kate Novak　f　4166

**Xalycis Rock**
*The Illusionists* - Faren Miller　f　3894

**Xandim**
*Sword of Flame* - Maggie Furey　f　2098

**Xi'an**
*Never Sound Retreat* - William R.
　Forstchen　s　1981

**Ylith**
*Shards of a Broken Crown* - Raymond E.
　Feist　f　1912

**Ynefel**
*Fortress in the Eye of Time* - C.J. Cherryh　f　991

**Zanadon**
*The Reaver Road* - Dave Duncan　f　1687

**Zendow**
*Tegne: Soul Warrior* - Richard La Plante　f　3268

# FICTIONAL COUNTRY

*The Adventures of King Midas* - Lynne Reid
　Banks　f　329
*By the Sword* - Greg Costikyan　f　1207
*Carnivores of Light and Darkness* - Alan Dean
　Foster　f　1996
*The Coachman Rat* - David Henry Wilson　f　5879
*Dancer's Rise* - Jo Clayton　f　1064
*Deerskin* - Robin McKinley　f　3844
*The Djinn in the Nightingale's Eye* - A.S.
　Byatt　f　794
*The Dragon Token* - Melanie Rawn　f　4485
*Dragoncharm* - Graham Edwards　f　1749
*An Exchange of Gifts* - Anne McCaffrey　f　3731
*The Forging of the Shadows* - Oliver
　Johnson　f　2924
*The Gift* - Patrick O'Leary　f　4211
*Go Quest, Young Man* - K.B. Bogen　f　557

*Gold Unicorn* - Tanith Lee　f　3410
*Harry Potter and the Sorcerer's Stone* - J.K.
　Rowling　f　4700
*The High House* - James Stoddard　f　5311
*If Wishes Were Horses* - Anne McCaffrey　f　3737
*Into the Forge* - Dennis L. McKiernan　f　3835
*The Iron Ring* - Lloyd Alexander　f　68
*Ladylord* - Sasha Miller　f　3906
*Nations of the Night* - Oliver Johnson　f　2925
*Pigs Don't Fly* - Mary Brown　f　727
*A Plague of Sorcerers* - Mary Frances
　Zambreno　f　6058
*Red Unicorn* - Tanith Lee　f　3414
*The Rivan Codex* - David Eddings　f　1735
*Roverandom* - J.R.R. Tolkien　f　5479
*The Sage* - Christopher Stasheff　f　5221
*Shadowlight* - Jackie Hyman　f　2819
*The Shaman* - Christopher Stasheff　f　5223
*The Shape-Changer's Wife* - Sharon Shinn　f　5002
*Skybowl* - Melanie Rawn　f　4490
*The Star Scroll* - Melanie Rawn　f　4491
*Stronghold* - Melanie Rawn　f　4492
*Sunrunner's Fire* - Melanie Rawn　f　4493
*Voima* - C. Dale Brittain　f　704
*The Warrior* - David Drake　s　1651
*When the Gods Are Silent* - Jane M.
　Lindskold　f　3477
*Wind Whispers, Shadow Shouts* - Sharon
　Green　f　2360
*The Wiz Biz* - Rick Cook　f　1160

**The 9 Countries of the Palm**
*Tigana* - Guy Gavriel Kay　f　3018

**Abanasinia**
*Spirit of the Wind* - Chris Pierson　f　4326
*Wanderlust* - Mary Kirchoff　f　3155

**Acheron**
*Conan and the Treasure of Python* - John Maddox
　Roberts　f　4616

**Adria**
*Maze of Moonlight* - Gael Baudino　f　393

**Adrilankha**
*Phoenix* - Steven Brust　f　746

**Agatean Empire**
*Interesting Times* - Terry Pratchett　f　4392

**Agrond**
*Firewalk* - Anne Logston　f　3509

**Al-Rassan**
*The Lions of Al-Rassan* - Guy Gavriel Kay　f　3016

**Alacia**
*Slay and Rescue* - John Moore　f　3991

**Alanda**
*A Cast of Corbies* - Mercedes Lackey　f　3274
*The Eagle and the Nightingales* - Mercedes
　Lackey　f　3278

**Alasea**
*Wit'ch Fire* - James Clemens　f　1082

**Albin**
*Season of Storms* - Ellen Foxxe　f　2032

**Albion**
*Elfwood* - Rose Estes　f　1837
*The Endless Knot* - Stephen R. Lawhead　f　3354
*Twisted Dragon* - Kevin Stein　f　5251

**Alifbay**
*Haroun and the Sea of Stories* - Salman
　Rushdie　f　4731

**Alketch**
*Mother of Winter* - Barbara Hambly　f　2506

**Alkyra**
*Shadows over Lyra* - Patricia C. Wrede  *f*  5980

**All-Haven**
*Dancing Jack* - Laurie J. Marks  *f*  3624

**Allustria**
*The Witch Doctor* - Christopher Stasheff  *f*  5228

**Almerkun**
*Saber & Shadow* - S.M. Stirling  *f*  5297

**Alyndar**
*The Legend of Nightfall* - Mickey Zucker
  Reichert  *f*  4521

**Amadicia**
*The Fires of Heaven* - Robert Jordan  *f*  2987

**Amazonia**
*The Amazon Chronicles* - Jane E.M.
  Robinson  *f*  4627

**Amefel**
*Fortress in the Eye of Time* - C.J. Cherryh  *f*  991
*Fortress of Owls* - C.J. Cherryh  *f*  993

**Ancelstierre**
*Sabriel* - Garth Nix  *f*  4129

**Andor**
*A Crown of Swords* - Robert Jordan  *f*  2984

**Angarossa**
*Taking Flight* - Lawrence Watt-Evans  *f*  5650

**Anglia**
*Knight's Wyrd* - Debra Doyle  *f*  1601

**Angwyn**
*Shadow Dawn* - Chris Claremont  *f*  1042

**Ansalon**
*Vinas Solamnus* - J. Robert King  *f*  3123

**Apacheria**
*Apacheria* - Jake Page  *s*  4233

**Araethura**
*Fugitive Prince* - Janny Wurts  *f*  6002

**Aran**
*Eyes of Silver* - Michael A. Stackpole  *f*  5200

**Aravis**
*A College of Magics* - Caroline Stevermer  *f*  5266

**Arbonne**
*A Song for Arbonne* - Guy Gavriel Kay  *f*  3017

**Arden**
*Dirty Work* - Dan McGirt  *f*  3810

**Arendia**
*Belgarath the Sorcerer* - David Eddings  *f*  1730
*Polgara the Sorceress* - David Eddings  *f*  1734

**Argans**
*Lords of the Sword* - Hugh Cook  *f*  1156

**Argonath**
*Dragons of Argonath* - Christopher Rowley  *f*  4694

**Argonath Region**
*Battledragon* - Christopher Rowley  *f*  4691
*Dragons of War* - Christopher Rowley  *f*  4695
*A Sword for a Dragon* - Christopher
  Rowley  *f*  4697

**Argos**
*Conan the Guardian* - Roland J. Green  *f*  2347

**Argylle**
*The Price of Blood and Honor* - Elizabeth
  Willey  *f*  5811

**Arhel**
*Mind of the Magic* - Holly Lisle  *f*  3486

**Arjuna**
*The Hidden City* - David Eddings  *f*  1733

**Arkan**
*Legacy of the Ancients* - Ron Sarti  *s*  4836
*Shadow's Son* - Shirley Meier  *f*  3872

**Arko**
*Lion's Soul* - Karen Wehrstein  *f*  5684

**Arlen**
*The Door into Sunset* - Diane Duane  *f*  1660

**Armyn**
*The Wizard's Shadow* - Susan Dexter  *f*  1514

**Arrhyndon**
*Bridge of Valor* - Anne Lesley Groell  *f*  2452

**Artemesia**
*A Plague of Angels* - Sheri S. Tepper  *f*  5433

**Asanion**
*Arrows of the Sun* - Judith Tarr  *f*  5391
*Spear of Heaven* - Judith Tarr  *f*  5396

**Ashkharon**
*Anvil of the Sun* - Anne Lesley Groell  *f*  2451

**Atlanton Earth**
*The Bridge of Dawn* - Neil Hancock  *f*  2531

**Austerneve, North Countries**
*Song of the Gargoyle* - Zilpha Keatley
  Snyder  *f*  5153

**Avalon**
*Merlin's Legacy: Dawn of Camelot* - Quinn Taylor
  Evans  *f*  1857

**Aveshq**
*The Gates of Twilight* - Paula Volsky  *f*  5581

**Bakan**
*The Wizard and the Floating City* - Christopher
  Rowley  *f*  4699

**Bardek**
*The Dragon Revenant* - Katharine Kerr  *f*  3069
*A Time of Omens* - Katharine Kerr  *f*  3078

**Bari**
*Shadow-Maze* - Mark Smith  *f*  5133

**Barony of Sardiron**
*The Blood of a Dragon* - Lawrence Watt-
  Evans  *f*  5640

**Barony of Veldran**
*Henry's Gift: The Magic Eye* - David
  Worsick  *f*  5972

**Barovia**
*I, Strahd* - P.N. Elrod  *h*  1797

**Barrow**
*Barrow* - John Deakins  *f*  1443

**Bearn**
*Beyond Ragnarok* - Mickey Zucker Reichert  *f*  4516
*Prince of Demons* - Mickey Zucker
  Reichert  *f*  4522

**Behringar**
*The Queen of Ashes* - Deborah Turner
  Harris  *f*  2561

**Bissanty Empire**
*A Tremor in the Bitter Earth* - Katya
  Reimann  *f*  4527
*Wind From a Foreign Sky* - Katya Reimann  *f*  4528

**The Blasted Lands**
*Lord of Chaos* - Robert Jordan  *f*  2988

**Blue Isle**
*The Changeling* - Kristine Kathryn Rusch  *f*  4714

*The Resistance* - Kristine Kathryn Rusch  *f*  4727

**Border Kingdom**
*Conan the Relentless* - Roland J. Green  *f*  2348

**Borders**
*Nobody's Son* - Sean Stewart  *f*  5275

**Branion**
*The Painter Knight* - Fiona Patton  *f*  4258
*The Stone Prince* - Fiona Patton  *f*  4259

**Breodanir**
*Hunter's Oath* - Michelle West  *f*  5759

**Bright Kingdom**
*Iron Dragons: Mountains and Madness* - Rose
  Estes  *f*  1839

**Brittania**
*The Arm of the Stone* - Victoria Strauss  *f*  5333
*The Forge of Virtue* - Lynn Abbey  *f*  16
*The Temper of Wisdom* - Lynn Abbey  *f*  17

**Broceliande**
*The Grail of Hearts* - Susan Shwartz  *f*  5015

**Brythunia**
*Conan the Savage* - Leonard Carpenter  *f*  909

**Caelrhon**
*Daughter of Magic* - C. Dale Brittain  *f*  703
*The Witch and the Cathedral* - C. Dale
  Brittain  *f*  705

**Caemlyn**
*The Path of Daggers* - Robert Jordan  *f*  2989

**Cairhien**
*A Crown of Swords* - Robert Jordan  *f*  2984

**Caithe**
*Sage of Sare* - Julie Dean Smith  *f*  5126
*The Wizard King* - Julie Dean Smith  *f*  5127

**Caldeon**
*The Still* - David Feintuch  *f*  1902

**Caledon**
*Caledon of the Mists* - Deborah Turner
  Harris  *f*  2560
*The Queen of Ashes* - Deborah Turner
  Harris  *f*  2561

**Callia**
*The Watcher's Mask* - Laurie J. Marks  *f*  3627

**Caluz**
*Wolves of the Gods* - Allan Cole  *f*  1111

**Candar**
*The Chaos Balance* - L.E. Modesitt Jr.  *f*  3925
*Fall of Angels* - L.E. Modesitt Jr.  *f*  3930
*The Order War* - L.E. Modesitt Jr.  *f*  3936

**Canderis**
*Mind-Speakers' Call* - Gayle Greeno  *s*  2423

**Cant'area**
*Greenmagic* - Crawford Kilian  *f*  3105
*Redmagic* - Crawford Kilian  *f*  3107

**Cantirmoor**
*Wren's Quest* - Sherwood Smith  *f*  5143

**Canton**
*The Belly of the Wolf* - R.A. MacAvoy  *f*  3580

**Caraccen**
*Goldclimbers* - Nancy Luenn  *f*  3545

**Carolna**
*Dragon Companion* - Don Callander  *f*  842
*Dragon Rescue* - Don Callander  *f*  843
*Dragon Tempest* - Don Callander  *f*  844

**Celi**
*The Western King* - Ann Marston  *f*  3636

**Cenmere**
*Emperor and Clown* - Dave Duncan  *f*  1676

**Central Almerkun**
*Snow Brother* - S.M. Stirling  *f*  5299

**Cerilian Empire of Anuire**
*The Iron Throne* - Simon Hawke  *f*  2618

**Chadar**
*Valorian* - Mary H. Herbert  *f*  2677

**Chaldor**
*The Guardian* - Angus Wells  *f*  5737

**Chelem**
*Earthborn* - Orson Scott Card  *s*  884

**Chenedolle**
*Point of Hopes* - Melissa Scott  *f*  4899

**Chivial**
*The Gilded Chain: A Tale of the King's Blades* - Dave
Duncan  *f*  1679

**Choin**
*Aquamancer* - Don Callander  *f*  841
*Geomancer* - Don Callander  *f*  845
*Marbleheart* - Don Callander  *f*  846

**Chult**
*The Ring of Winter* - James Lowder  *f*  3538

**The City-States of Sij**
*Deathknight* - Andrew J. Offutt  *f*  4201

**Cloud**
*Moonwise* - Greer Ilene Gilman  *f*  2238

**Coindra**
*Lost in Translation* - Margaret Ball  *f*  315

**Columbia**
*The Ghost of the Revelator* - L.E. Modesitt
Jr.  *s*  3931

**Confederate States of America**
*The Guns of the South: A Novel of the Civil War* -
Harry Turtledove  *s*  5502

**Confederation of Costa Brava**
*Burn* - Bill Ransom  *s*  4476
*ViraVax* - Bill Ransom  *s*  4478

**Continental Americas**
*India's Story* - Kathlyn S. Starbuck  *s*  5208

**Corbinwood**
*A Forest Lord* - Michael Williams  *f*  5819

**Corigo**
*The Falcon and the Serpent* - Cheryl A.
Smith  *f*  5101

**Cormyr**
*Cormyr: A Novel* - Ed Greenwood  *f*  2425
*Cormyr: A Novel* - Ed Greenwood  *f*  2426
*Crusade* - James Lowder  *f*  3537
*Murder in Cormyr* - Chet Williamson  *f*  5848

**Corona**
*The Demon Awakens* - R.A. Salvatore  *f*  4794
*The Demon Spirit* - R.A. Salvatore  *f*  4795

**Coronnan**
*The Dragon's Touchstone* - Irene Radford  *f*  4459
*The Glass Dragon* - Irene Radford  *f*  4460
*The Loneliest Magician* - Irene Radford  *f*  4461
*The Perfect Princess* - Irene Radford  *f*  4462

**Cortton, Kartakass**
*Death of a Darklord* - Laurell K. Hamilton  *h*  2516

**Country of the Wind Websters**
*Horrible Humes* - Stephen Billias  *f*  487

**Crossroads**
*The Healing of Crossroads* - Nick
O'Donohoe  *f*  4195
*The Magic and the Healing* - Nick
O'Donohoe  *f*  4196
*Under the Healing Sign* - Nick O'Donohoe  *f*  4198

**Cuan na'For**
*Dark Magic* - Angus Wells  *f*  5733

**Culm**
*The Sixth Book of Lost Swords: Mindsword's Story* -
Fred Saberhagen  *f*  4776

**Cyador**
*The Chaos Balance* - L.E. Modesitt Jr.  *f*  3925

**Cymra**
*King's Son, Magic's Son* - Josepha Sherman  *f*  4986

**Da Lam**
*The Cursed* - Dave Duncan  *f*  1674

**Dalethica**
*A Breach in the Watershed* - Douglas Niles  *f*  4105
*Darkenheight* - Douglas Niles  *f*  4107

**Darakemba**
*Earthborn* - Orson Scott Card  *s*  884

**Dark Isle**
*Avatar* - Louise Cooper  *f*  1173

**Darn**
*The Ambivalent Magician* - Simon Hawke  *f*  2616
*The Inadequate Adept* - Simon Hawke  *f*  2617

**Darran**
*Steal the Dragon* - Patricia Briggs  *f*  682

**Daventry**
*The Floating Castle* - Craig Mills  *f*  3913

**Deep Moor**
*The Book of Earth* - Marjorie Bradley
Kellogg  *f*  3044

**Defalk**
*The Soprano Sorceress* - L.E. Modesitt Jr.  *f*  3938
*The Spellsong War* - L.E. Modesitt Jr.  *f*  3939

**Den Oroshtai**
*D'Shai* - Joel Rosenberg  *f*  4670

**Deseret**
*The Ghost of the Revelator* - L.E. Modesitt
Jr.  *s*  3931

**Deverry**
*Days of Air and Darkness* - Katharine Kerr  *f*  3067
*Days of Blood and Fire* - Katharine Kerr  *f*  3068
*The Dragon Revenant* - Katharine Kerr  *f*  3069
*The Red Wyvern* - Katharine Kerr  *f*  3074
*A Time of Exile* - Katharine Kerr  *f*  3077
*A Time of Omens* - Katharine Kerr  *f*  3078

**D'Hara**
*Stone of Tears* - Terry Goodkind  *f*  2269
*Temple of the Winds* - Terry Goodkind  *f*  2270

**Dharbek**
*Lords of the Sky* - Angus Wells  *f*  5738

**Dinotopia**
*Dinotopia* - James Gurney  *f*  2468
*Dinotopia Lost* - Alan Dean Foster  *f*  2003
*The World Beneath* - James Gurney  *f*  2469

**Dolmen**
*The Mines of Behemoth* - Michael Shea  *f*  4945

**The Domains**
*Final Sacrifice* - Clayton Emery  *f*  1814

*Shattered Chains* - Clayton Emery  *f*  1816

**Domdur Empire**
*Touched by the Gods* - Lawrence Watt-
Evans  *f*  5651

**Dominia**
*Distant Planes* - Kathy Ice  *f*  2827

**Dominion of Annagar**
*The Broken Crown* - Michelle West  *f*  5757
*The Uncrowned King* - Michelle West  *f*  5760

**Dominion of Argylle**
*The Well-Favored Man: The Tale of the Sorcerer's
Nephew* - Elizabeth Willey  *f*  5813

**Dorisha Plains**
*Storm Breaking* - Mercedes Lackey  *f*  3296

**Dragon Isle**
*Song in the Silence* - Elizabeth Kerner  *f*  3065

**Dragon Reach**
*Perilous Seas* - Dave Duncan  *f*  1685

**Dragonrealm**
*Wolfhelm* - Richard A. Knaak  *f*  3175

**D'Shai**
*D'Shai* - Joel Rosenberg  *f*  4670
*Hour of the Octopus* - Joel Rosenberg  *f*  4673

**The Dubious Hills**
*The Dubious Hills* - Pamela Dean  *f*  1444

**Duchy of Piotr**
*Silk and Steel* - Ron Miller  *f*  3905

**Duchy of Simava**
*The Duke of Sumava* - Sara J. Wrench  *f*  5983

**Dukedom**
*Geomancer* - Don Callander  *f*  845

**Duloth-Trol**
*War of the Three Waters* - Douglas Niles  *f*  4110

**Dumar**
*The Spellsong War* - L.E. Modesitt Jr.  *f*  3939

**Eigo**
*A Dragon at World's End* - Christopher
Rowley  *f*  4693

**Eileanan**
*The Witches of Eileanan* - Kate Forsyth  *f*  1984

**Eirren**
*Fire Arrow* - Edith Pattou  *f*  4260
*Hero's Song* - Edith Pattou  *f*  4261

**Elenia**
*Domes of Fire* - David Eddings  *f*  1732

**Elfhame Avalon**
*Elvendude* - Mark Shepherd  *f*  4980

**Elliath**
*Into the Dark Lands* - Michelle Sagara  *f*  4783

**Elundium**
*The Knights of Cawdor* - Mike Jefferies  *f*  2886
*Palace of Kings* - Mike Jefferies  *f*  2887
*The Road to Underfall* - Mike Jefferies  *f*  2888

**Elven Holdings**
*Once a Hero* - Michael A. Stackpole  *f*  5203

**Elysium**
*Return to Isis* - Jean Stewart  *s*  5268

**Emond's Field**
*The Eye of the World* - Robert Jordan  *f*  2986

**The Empire**
*The League of the Crimson Crescent* - James E.
Reagen  *f*  4495

*The Road Home* - Joel Rosenberg  *f*  4674
*The Third Force* - Marc Laidlaw  *s*  3313

**Empire of Anuir**
*War* - Simon Hawke  *f*  2625

**Empire of Elabon**
*Prince of the North* - Harry Turtledove  *f*  5509

**Empire of Essalieyan**
*The Broken Crown* - Michelle West  *f*  5757
*The Uncrowned King* - Michelle West  *f*  5760

**Empire of Ferryth**
*Dog Wizard* - Barbara Hambly  *f*  2503
*Stranger at the Wedding* - Barbara Hambly  *f*  2509

**Empire of the Spear**
*Oath of Swords* - David Weber  *f*  5678

**Empire of Wa**
*Gatherer of Clouds* - Sean Russell  *f*  4741
*The Initiate Brother* - Sean Russell  *f*  4742

**Eriador**
*The Dragon King* - R.A. Salvatore  *f*  4796
*Luthien's Gamble* - R.A. Salvatore  *f*  4802
*The Sword of Bedwyr* - R.A. Salvatore  *f*  4808

**Erinn**
*Flight of the Raven* - Jennifer Roberson  *f*  4608

**Erkynland**
*To Green Angel Tower* - Tad Williams  *f*  5832

**Erlkazar**
*Faces of Deception* - Troy Denning  *f*  1485

**Esdragon**
*The Prince of Ill Luck* - Susan Dexter  *f*  1512
*The True Knight* - Susan Dexter  *f*  1513

**Esphania**
*No One Noticed the Cat* - Anne McCaffrey  *f*  3740

**Essalieyan**
*Hunter's Death* - Michelle West  *f*  5758

**Eurostate**
*Songs of Chaos* - S.N. Lewitt  *s*  3452

**Evermeet**
*Evermeet: Island of Elves* - Elaine
   Cunningham  *f*  1290

**Exteca**
*Redmagic* - Crawford Kilian  *f*  3107

**Faerd**
*Dancing Jack* - Laurie J. Marks  *f*  3624

**Faerie**
*Beauty* - Sheri S. Tepper  *f*  5428
*Faery Lands Forlorn* - Dave Duncan  *f*  1677

**Faerine**
*Darkenheight* - Douglas Niles  *f*  4107
*War of the Three Waters* - Douglas Niles  *f*  4110

**Faerun**
*Crucible* - Troy Denning  *f*  1484
*Elminster: The Making of a Mage* - Ed
   Greenwood  *f*  2427

**Fairholm**
*The Clan of the Warlord* - Elizabeth H.
   Boyer  *f*  604

**Falinor**
*Kingmaker's Sword* - Ann Marston  *f*  3635

**Fallsend**
*The Fulfillments of Fate and Desire* - Storm
   Constantine  *s*  1142

**Fanape Island**
*Demon Drums* - Carol Severance  *f*  4922

**Far North**
*Demon Blade* - Mark A. Garland  *f*  2141

**Farrland**
*Beneath the Vaulted Hills* - Sean Russell  *f*  4739
*World Without End* - Sean Russell  *f*  4744

**Farrow**
*World Without End* - Sean Russell  *f*  4744

**Fearsburg**
*Specterworld* - Isidore Haiblum  *s*  2480

**Fendarath**
*The Interior Life* - Katherine Blake  *f*  515

**Ferupe**
*The War in the Waste* - Felicity Savage  *f*  4852

**Five Kingdoms**
*The Last Dragonlord* - Joanne Bertin  *f*  470

**Fohima Alghera**
*Death's Gray Land* - Mike Shupp  *s*  5011

**Forest Kingdom**
*Blue Moon Rising* - Simon R. Green  *f*  2362

**Forest Lands**
*The Red King* - Victor Kelleher  *f*  3043

**Four Kingdoms**
*The Baker's Boy* - J.V. Jones  *f*  2956
*A Man Betrayed* - J.V. Jones  *f*  2958
*Master and Fool* - J.V. Jones  *f*  2959

**The Four Lands**
*The Elf Queen of Shannara* - Terry Brooks  *f*  711
*First King of Shannara* - Terry Brooks  *f*  712
*The Talismans of Shannara* - Terry Brooks  *f*  717

**Frank**
*The Inadequate Adept* - Simon Hawke  *f*  2617
*The Reluctant Sorcerer* - Simon Hawke  *f*  2622

**Freeland**
*Return to Isis* - Jean Stewart  *s*  5268

**Gallia**
*The Stone Prince* - Fiona Patton  *f*  4259

**Galunlati**
*Stoneskin's Revenge* - Tom Deitz  *f*  1476

**Gessyth**
*Forbidden Magic* - Angus Wells  *f*  5736

**Gleann Fiain**
*Faery in Shadow* - C.J. Cherryh  *f*  987

**Glenraven**
*Glenraven* - Marion Zimmer Bradley  *f*  635
*In the Rift* - Marion Zimmer Bradley  *f*  639

**Gnarlsmyre**
*Hall of Whispers* - Mike Jefferies  *f*  2884

**Golga**
*Traitors* - Kristine Kathryn Rusch  *f*  4729

**Golran**
*Dark Mirror, Dark Dreams* - Sharon Green  *f*  2357
*Silver Princess, Golden Knight* - Sharon
   Green  *f*  2359

**Gorhaut**
*A Song for Arbonne* - Guy Gavriel Kay  *f*  3017

**Gramarye**
*The Warlock Insane* - Christopher Stasheff  *f*  5225

**Gran**
*The Poisoned Lands* - John Maddox
   Roberts  *f*  4619

**The Grasslands**
*The Furies* - Suzy McKee Charnas  *s*  968

**The Great Realms**
*Shadow Moon* - George Lucas  *f*  3540

**Great Underground Empire**
*The Zork Chronicles* - George Alec
   Effinger  *s*  1754

**Greensere**
*Phoenix* - Steven Brust  *f*  746

**Gryylth**
*Dragon Death* - Gael Baudino  *f*  390
*Duel of Dragons* - Gael Baudino  *f*  391

**Guhland**
*Lord of the Troll-Bats* - Alexis A. Gilliland  *f*  2234
*The Shadow Shaia* - Alexis A. Gilliland  *f*  2235

**Gwynedd**
*The Bastard Prince* - Katherine Kurtz  *f*  3255
*King Javan's Year* - Katherine Kurtz  *f*  3258

**Haighlei Empire**
*The White Gryphon* - Mercedes Lackey  *f*  3303

**Halcus**
*A Man Betrayed* - J.V. Jones  *f*  2958

**Hamis**
*Talion: Revenant* - Michael A. Stackpole  *f*  5206

**Hamisch**
*The Undesired Princess and the Enchanted Bunny* - L.
   Sprague de Camp  *f*  1419

**Happy City**
*Specterworld* - Isidore Haiblum  *s*  2480

**Hardorn**
*Storm Rising* - Mercedes Lackey  *f*  3297
*Winds of Fury* - Mercedes Lackey  *f*  3306

**Haunted Hills**
*Henry's Gift: The Magic Eye* - David
   Worsick  *f*  5972

**Havakeen Empire**
*Fifth Quarter* - Tanya Huff  *f*  2795

**Hegemony of the Three Ethshars**
*The Blood of a Dragon* - Lawrence Watt-
   Evans  *f*  5640
*The Spell of the Black Dagger* - Lawrence Watt-
   Evans  *f*  5648

**Heileshein**
*Dragonspawn* - Mark Acres  *f*  28

**Helansajar**
*Eyes of Silver* - Michael A. Stackpole  *f*  5200

**Hernystir**
*To Green Angel Tower* - Tad Williams  *f*  5832

**Highland**
*Morningstar* - David Gemmell  *f*  2190

**The Highlands**
*Moonspeaker* - K.D. Wentworth  *s*  5754

**Homana**
*Flight of the Raven* - Jennifer Roberson  *f*  4608
*A Tapestry of Lions* - Jennifer Roberson  *f*  4615

**Hoven, Westerhoven**
*Heroes Wanted* - Kyle Crocco  *f*  1267

**Hunter's Field**
*The Book of Atrix Wolfe* - Patricia A.
   McKillip  *f*  3838

**Husaquahr**
*Horrors of the Dancing Gods* - Jack L.
   Chalker  *f*  955
*Songs of the Dancing Gods* - Jack L. Chalker  *f*  962

**Hydrangea**
*Split Heirs* - Lawrence Watt-Evans   f   5649

**Ibile**
*My Son, the Wizard* - Christopher Stasheff   f   5218
*The Oathbound Wizard* - Christopher
  Stasheff   f   5219

**Ile-Rein**
*The Element of Fire* - Martha Wells   f   5750

**Ile-Rien**
*The Death of the Necromancer* - Martha
  Wells   f   5749

**Illian**
*The Dragon Reborn* - Robert Jordan   f   2985
*The Path of Daggers* - Robert Jordan   f   2989

**Illyria**
*Slay and Rescue* - John Moore   f   3991

**Immanira**
*The Fulfillments of Fate and Desire* - Storm
  Constantine   s   1142

**The Impire**
*The Living God* - Dave Duncan   f   1682
*The Stricken Field* - Dave Duncan   f   1688

**Irth**
*The Dark Shore* - Adam Lee   f   3385

**Ischia**
*The Fire's Stone* - Tanya Huff   f   2796

**Isle of Celi**
*Broken Blade* - Ann Marston   f   3634

**Isle of Morbihan**
*The Stone Movers* - Patricia Mullen   f   4045

**Isle of Sampetra**
*The Pearls of Lutra* - Brian Jacques   f   2854

**Isle of Sare**
*Mission of Magic* - Julie Dean Smith   f   5125

**Ispar**
*Once a Hero* - Michael A. Stackpole   f   5203

**Ispor**
*Shadowdance* - Robin Wayne Bailey   f   290

**Jesseryn Plain**
*Wild Magic* - Angus Wells   f   5741

**Julkrease**
*The Fortress of Eternity* - Andrew
  Whitmore   f   5790

**Kadjafi Lands**
*The Devouring Void* - Mark E. Rogers   f   4653
*The Riddled Man* - Mark E. Rogers   f   4654

**Kaerubulan**
*The Magic Wars* - Jo Clayton   f   1068

**Kahulawe**
*The Mark of the Cat* - Andre Norton   f   4157

**Kalaven**
*The Sands of Kalaven: A Novel of Shunlar* - Carol
  Heller   f   2651

**Kallopane**
*A Remembrance for Kedrigern* - John
  Morressy   f   4014

**Kandahar**
*Forbidden Magic* - Angus Wells   f   5736

**Karistan**
*White Horse, Dark Dragon* - Robert C.
  Fleet   f   1947

**Ka'venusho**
*The Black Gryphon* - Mercedes Lackey   f   3270

**Keland**
*Touched by Magic* - Doranna Durgin   f   1705

**Kell**
*The Seeress of Kell* - David Eddings   f   1738
*Sorceress of Darshiva* - David Eddings   f   1739

**Kelvinia**
*Mouvar's Magic* - Piers Anthony   f   182
*Orc's Opal* - Piers Anthony   f   183

**Kenesee**
*The Lanterns of God* - Ron Sarti   s   4835
*Legacy of the Ancients* - Ron Sarti   s   4836

**Kenor**
*Dragons of War* - Christopher Rowley   f   4695

**Kesh**
*The Falcon Rises* - Michael C. Staudinger   f   5235

**Ket-Ta-Thanne**
*Exile's Challenge* - Angus Wells   f   5734

**Ket-Ta-Witko**
*Exile's Children* - Angus Wells   f   5735

**Kilot**
*The White Mists of Power* - Kristine Kathryn
  Rusch   f   4730

**King Estmere's Lands**
*King's Son, Magic's Son* - Josepha Sherman   f   4986

**The Kingdom**
*A City in Winter* - Mark Helprin   f   2653
*One for the Morning Glory* - John Barnes   f   355
*Traitors* - Kristine Kathryn Rusch   f   4729
*The Veils of Snows* - Mark Helprin   f   2654

**Kingdom of America**
*Chicago Red* - R.M. Meluch   s   3873

**Kingdom of Celydonn**
*The Work of the Sun* - Teresa Edgerton   f   1746

**Kingdom of Heaven**
*Spear of Heaven* - Judith Tarr   f   5396

**Kingdom of Lancre**
*Wyrd Sisters* - Terry Pratchett   f   4405

**Kingdom of Rofehaven**
*The Runelords: The Sum of All Men* - David
  Farland   f   1866

**Kingdom of Summer**
*Pendragon* - Stephen R. Lawhead   f   3357

**Kingdoms of the Green Isles**
*Into the Green* - Charles de Lint   f   1430

**Kinvale**
*Magic Casement* - Dave Duncan   f   1683

**Kirekune**
*The Daemon in the Machine* - Felicity
  Savage   f   4848

**Kolmar**
*Song in the Silence* - Elizabeth Kerner   f   3065

**Komars**
*The Regiment's War* - John Dalmas   s   1326

**Krasnegar**
*Magic Casement* - Dave Duncan   f   1683

**Krynn**
*Tears of the Night Sky* - Linda P. Baker   f   299

**Kyrania**
*Wolves of the Gods* - Allan Cole   f   1111

**Labornok**
*Lady of the Trillium* - Marion Zimmer
  Bradley   f   641

**Lammermorn**
*Flight to Hollow Mountain* - Mark Sebanc   f   4908

**Land of Luster**
*Into the Land of the Unicorns* - Bruce
  Coville   f   1219

**Land of the Nelvins**
*Flute Song Magic* - Andrea Shettle   f   4996

**Land of the Purple Lords**
*Oath of Swords* - David Weber   f   5678

**Landover**
*The Tangle Box* - Terry Brooks   f   718
*Witches' Brew* - Terry Brooks   f   719

**Landuc**
*The Price of Blood and Honor* - Elizabeth
  Willey   f   5811

**Laringras**
*Broken Blade* - Ann Marston   f   3634

**Latruria**
*The Secular Wizard* - Christopher Stasheff   f   5222

**Leanda**
*Heart Readers* - Kristine Kathryn Rusch   f   4718

**Leased Territories**
*The Diamond Age* - Neal Stephenson   s   5253

**Legar**
*The Crystal Dragon* - Richard A. Knaak   f   3167

**Levindre**
*Shadow-Maze* - Mark Smith   f   5133

**Liavek**
*Liavek: Festival Week* - Will Shetterly   f   4994

**Lieda**
*Thunder of the Captains* - Holly Lisle   f   3489

**Lightless Kingdom**
*The Lightless Kingdom* - Jonathan Wylie   f   6007

**Linderwall**
*Dealing with Dragons* - Patricia C. Wrede   f   5975

**Lis Folaze**
*The White Tribunal* - Paula Volsky   f   5583

**Loggia**
*The Undesired Princess and the Enchanted Bunny* - L.
  Sprague de Camp   f   1419

**Londeac**
*Silk and Steel* - Ron Miller   f   3905

**Losan Island**
*Demon Drums* - Carol Severance   f   4922

**Lysse**
*Dark Magic* - Angus Wells   f   5733

**Magoria**
*The Way Beneath* - Angus Wells   f   5740

**Maisir**
*The Demon King* - Chris Bunch   f   770

**Makuran**
*The Stolen Throne* - Harry Turtledove   f   5510
*The Thousand Cities* - Harry Turtledove   f   5512

**Mallorea**
*Belgarath the Sorcerer* - David Eddings   f   1730
*The Seeress of Kell* - David Eddings   f   1738
*Sorceress of Darshiva* - David Eddings   f   1739

**Malthan**
*Children of the Blood: Book Two of The Sundered* -
  Michelle Sagara   f   4782
*Into the Dark Lands* - Michelle Sagara   f   4783
*Lady of Mercy* - Michelle Sagara   f   4784

**Manland**
*A Plague of Angels* - Sheri S. Tepper   *f*   5433

**Marantine**
*Chains of Darkness, Chains of Light* - Michelle Sagara   *f*   4781

**Maratine**
*Lady of Mercy* - Michelle Sagara   *f*   4784

**The Marchlands**
*Spirit Fox* - Mickey Zucker Reichert   *f*   4524

**Marchmont**
*Mind-Speakers' Call* - Gayle Greeno   *s*   2423

**The Marvelous Land of Snergs**
*The Marvellous Land of Snergs* - E.A. Wyke-Smith   *f*   6006

**Matawaye**
*Exile's Challenge* - Angus Wells   *f*   5734

**Mazonia**
*If I Pay Thee Not in Gold* - Piers Anthony   *f*   176

**Maztica**
*Feathered Dragon* - Douglas Niles   *f*   4108

**McGulveyland**
*In between Dragons* - Michael Kandel   *f*   3010

**Medecia**
*The Janus Mask* - Richard A. Knaak   *f*   3171

**Meldrith**
*Wren to the Rescue* - Sherwood Smith   *f*   5142
*Wren's Quest* - Sherwood Smith   *f*   5143
*Wren's War* - Sherwood Smith   *f*   5144

**Melen**
*The Hidden Realms* - Sharon Green   *f*   2358

**Melnibone**
*Elric: Song of the Black Sword* - Michael Moorcock   *f*   3980

**Meriga**
*Children of Enchantment* - Anne Kelleher Bush   *f*   787

**Merovence**
*My Son, the Wizard* - Christopher Stasheff   *f*   5218
*The Secular Wizard* - Christopher Stasheff   *f*   5222

**Merovingen**
*Endgame* - C.J. Cherryh   *s*   986
*Flood Tide* - C.J. Cherryh   *s*   989

**Mezpa**
*The Steel Kings* - John Maddox Roberts   *f*   4621

**Midkemia**
*Krondor, the Betrayal* - Raymond E. Feist   *f*   1905
*Rise of a Merchant Prince* - Raymond E. Feist   *f*   1909

**The Midlands**
*Blood of the Fold* - Terry Goodkind   *f*   2268
*Stone of Tears* - Terry Goodkind   *f*   2269
*Temple of the Winds* - Terry Goodkind   *f*   2270
*Wizard's First Rule* - Terry Goodkind   *f*   2271

**Midpassage**
*Death's Gray Land* - Mike Shupp   *s*   5011
*The Last Reckoning* - Mike Shupp   *s*   5012

**Midvale**
*The Road West* - Gary Wright   *f*   5984

**Minerva**
*The Sky Lords* - John Brosnan   *s*   720
*The War of the Sky Lords* - John Brosnan   *s*   721

**Mist Marsh**
*Nightwatch* - Robin Wayne Bailey   *f*   289

**Mithgar**
*The Dragonstone* - Dennis L. McKiernan   *f*   3832
*The Eye of the Hunter* - Dennis L. McKiernan   *f*   3833
*Into the Fire* - Dennis L. McKiernan   *f*   3834
*Tales of Mithgar* - Dennis L. McKiernan   *f*   3836

**Montefoglia**
*The Spirit Ring* - Lois McMaster Bujold   *f*   763

**Montgren**
*The Towers of the Sunset* - L.E. Modesitt Jr.   *f*   3941

**Mordantari**
*Chains of Darkness, Chains of Light* - Michelle Sagara   *f*   4781

**Moria**
*Fire Angels* - Jane Routley   *f*   4685
*Mage Heart* - Jane Routley   *f*   4686

**Morrowindl Island**
*The Elf Queen of Shannara* - Terry Brooks   *f*   711

**Mundania**
*Man From Mundania* - Piers Anthony   *f*   180

**Myst**
*Myst: The Book of Atrus* - Rand Miller   *f*   3896

**Naclos**
*The Order War* - L.E. Modesitt Jr.   *f*   3936

**Nation of Prosperity**
*Revenant* - Louise Cooper   *f*   1178

**Nemedia**
*The Conan Chronicles* - Robert Jordan   *f*   2983

**Neva**
*Queens of Land and Sea* - John Maddox Roberts   *f*   4620

**New Albin**
*Season of Storms* - Ellen Foxxe   *f*   2032

**New Normandy**
*The Empire of Fear* - Brian Stableford   *h*   5191

**Nhol**
*The Blackgod* - J. Gregory Keyes   *f*   3095

**Nine Kingdoms**
*Demon Pig* - Karen Brush   *f*   737

**North Dalemark**
*The Crown of Dalemark* - Diana Wynne Jones   *f*   2945

**Northern Young Kingdoms**
*The Revenge of the Rose* - Michael Moorcock   *f*   3985

**Northland**
*Northlight* - Deborah Wheeler   *s*   5775

**Northlands**
*The Last of the Renshai* - Mickey Zucker Reichert   *f*   4520

**Novindus**
*Shadow of a Dark Queen* - Raymond E. Feist   *f*   1911

**Numantia**
*The Demon King* - Chris Bunch   *f*   770
*The Seer King* - Chris Bunch   *f*   771

**Nylan**
*The Magic of Recluce* - L.E. Modesitt Jr.   *f*   3934

**Ohrid**
*Sing the Four Quarters* - Tanya Huff   *f*   2799

**Old Kingdom**
*Aquamancer* - Don Callander   *f*   841

**The Old Kingdom**
*Sabriel* - Garth Nix   *f*   4129

**The Old World**
*Blood of the Fold* - Terry Goodkind   *f*   2268

**Omnia**
*Small Gods* - Terry Pratchett   *f*   4400

**Oran**
*Beldan's Fire* - Midori Snyder   *f*   5150

**Osten Ard**
*Stone of Farewell* - Tad Williams   *f*   5831

**Othion**
*Kedrigern and the Charming Couple* - John Morressy   *f*   4013

**Outside**
*Time and Light* - William Bornefeld   *s*   574

**Pacifica**
*The Lanterns of God* - Ron Sarti   *s*   4835

**Paduan**
*The Falcon and the Serpent* - Cheryl A. Smith   *f*   5101

**Pakajan Peninsula**
*Hawk's Flight* - Carol Chase   *f*   980

**Palerna**
*A Forest Lord* - Michael Williams   *f*   5819
*A Sorcerer's Apprentice* - Michael Williams   *f*   5820

**Pandemia**
*The Cutting Edge* - Dave Duncan   *f*   1675
*Emperor and Clown* - Dave Duncan   *f*   1676

**Paradise**
*Primavera* - Francesca Lia Block   *f*   551

**Parkwood**
*Down Among the Dead Men* - Simon R. Green   *f*   2367

**Peep-East**
*The Zap Gun* - Philip K. Dick   *s*   1523

**Pegana**
*The Complete Pegana* - Lord Dunsany   *f*   1699

**Pelucir**
*The Book of Atrix Wolfe* - Patricia A. McKillip   *f*   3838

**The Peninsula**
*Flowerdust* - Gwyneth Jones   *s*   2952

**Perime of Moer**
*The Stone Movers* - Patricia Mullen   *f*   4045

**Phesaotois**
*A Sorcerer and a Gentleman* - Elizabeth Willey   *f*   5812

**Pheyarcet**
*A Sorcerer and a Gentleman* - Elizabeth Willey   *f*   5812

**Pinrae**
*Ghost King* - David Gemmell   *f*   2188

**Piyanthia**
*Emerald House Rising* - Peg Kerr   *f*   3080

**The Plain**
*The Son of Summer Stars* - Meredith Ann Pierce   *f*   4319

**Polia**
*The Spirit Gate* - Maya Kaathryn Bohnhoff   *f*   562

**Prospero's Isle**
*Caliban's Hour* - Tad Williams   *f*   5826

**Province of Bierdsey**
*Cat's Paw* - L.A. Taylor   f   5409

**Pudar**
*Prince of Demons* - Mickey Zucker
   Reichert   f   4522

**Punja Desert**
*Sword-Breaker* - Jennifer Roberson   f   4613

**Pyrdain**
*The Silver Hand* - Stephen R. Lawhead   f   3358

**Python Isle**
*Python Isle* - Kenneth Robeson   f   4624

**Qualinesti**
*Kindred Spirits* - Mark Anthony   f   154
*The Qualinesti* - Paul B. Thompson   f   5455

**Quinque**
*God's Dice* - S. Andrew Swann   f   5364

**Rangfara**
*The Clan of the Warlord* - Elizabeth H.
   Boyer   f   604

**Raragash**
*The Cursed* - Dave Duncan   f   1674

**Rashpuht**
*Castle in the Air* - Diana Wynne Jones   f   2944

**Ravenloft**
*Mordenheim* - Chet Williamson   h   5847
*Tapestry of Dark Souls* - Elaine Bergstrom   h   465
*Tower of Doom* - Mark Anthony   h   155

**Realm of Infinitera**
*Quest for the Fallen Star* - Piers Anthony   f   185

**The Realms**
*The Ring of Winter* - James Lowder   f   3538

**Recluce**
*The Death of Chaos* - L.E. Modesitt Jr.   f   3926
*The Magic Engineer* - L.E. Modesitt Jr.   f   3933
*The Magic of Recluce* - L.E. Modesitt Jr.   f   3934
*The Towers of the Sunset* - L.E. Modesitt
   Jr.   f   3941

**Redhart**
*Blood and Honor* - Simon R. Green   f   2361

**Remalna**
*Court Duel* - Sherwood Smith   f   5137

**The Republic**
*Innerverse* - John DeChancie   s   1458

**Republic of Saru**
*Outside the Dog Museum* - Jonathan Carroll   f   919

**Reth**
*Masques* - Patricia Briggs   f   681

**Rethwellen**
*By the Sword* - Mercedes Lackey   f   3273

**Reykvid**
*The Time of Madness* - Thomas K. Martin   f   3652

**Rezhmia**
*King of the Dead* - R.A. MacAvoy   f   3581

**Rhadaz**
*One Land, One Duke* - Ru Emerson   f   1809
*The Two in Hiding* - Ru Emerson   f   1812

**Rhaetia**
*The Pixilated Peeress* - L. Sprague de
   Camp   f   1416

**Rhazaulle**
*The Wolf of Winter* - Paula Volsky   f   5584

**The River**
*Spirit Fox* - Mickey Zucker Reichert   f   4524

**Rossacotta**
*Rouse a Sleeping Cat* - Dan Crawford   f   1249
*The Sure Death of a Mouse* - Dan Crawford   f   1250
*A Wild Dog and Lone* - Dan Crawford   f   1251

**Rud**
*Chimaera's Copper* - Piers Anthony   f   166

**Ruwenda**
*Black Trillium* - Marion Zimmer Bradley   f   630
*Blood Trillium* - Julian May   f   3696
*Golden Trillium* - Andre Norton   f   4153
*Lady of the Trillium* - Marion Zimmer
   Bradley   f   641

**Rwn**
*Voyage of the Fox Rider* - Dennis L.
   McKiernan   f   3837

**Sacoridia**
*Green Rider* - Kristen Britain   f   692

**The Sad City**
*Haroun and the Sea of Stories* - Salman
   Rushdie   f   4731

**St. Crim**
*Lunching with the Antichrist* - Michael
   Moorcock   f   3984

**St. Lucien**
*The Stalking Horse* - Constance Ash   f   222

**Sanctum**
*Wheel of Dreams* - Salinda Tyson   f   5529

**Saquave Wilderness**
*The Stallion Queen* - Constance Ash   f   223

**Sar Akka**
*Soothslayer: A Magickal Fantasy* - D.J.
   Conway   f   1143

**Sarronnyn**
*The Order War* - L.E. Modesitt Jr.   f   3936

**Scothandir**
*Timespell* - Robert N. Charrette   f   978

**SeLenicca**
*The Loneliest Magician* - Irene Radford   f   4461

**Sendaria**
*Belgarath the Sorcerer* - David Eddings   f   1730

**Senna Lirwan**
*Wren to the Rescue* - Sherwood Smith   f   5142

**Seven Islands**
*Dragon Burning* - Craig Shaw Gardner   f   2126
*Dragon Sleeping* - Craig Shaw Gardner   f   2127
*Dragon Waking* - Craig Shaw Gardner   f   2128

**Seven Kingdoms**
*A Game of Thrones* - George R.R. Martin   f   3645

**Seven Nations**
*Silverlight* - Morgan Llywelyn   f   3507

**Shai**
*Summer King, Winter Fool* - Lisa Goldstein   f   2263

**Shaleth**
*The Falcon Rises* - Michael C. Staudinger   f   5235

**Shangri-La**
*Shangri-La: The Return to the World of Lost Horizon* -
   Eleanor Cooney   f   1169

**Shkoder**
*No Quarter* - Tanya Huff   f   2798
*Sing the Four Quarters* - Tanya Huff   f   2799

**Sicas, Aquilonia**
*Conan the Rogue* - John Maddox Roberts   f   4617

**Sicmon Islands**
*The Golden Mean* - Nick Bantock   f   334

**Sidra**
*Token of Dragonsblood* - Damaris Cole   f   1114

**Sileria**
*In Legend Born* - Laura Resnick   f   4533

**Silvanesti**
*Firstborn* - Paul B. Thompson   f   5454

**Siradayel**
*Wren's Quest* - Sherwood Smith   f   5143

**Six Duchies**
*Assassin's Apprentice* - Robin Hobb   f   2693
*Assassin's Quest* - Robin Hobb   f   2694
*Royal Assassin* - Robin Hobb   f   2695

**Six Kingdoms**
*The Mace of Souls* - Bruce Fergusson   f   1925

**The Six Lands**
*Villains by Necessity* - Eve Forward   f   1985

**Skala**
*Luck in the Shadows* - Lynn Flewelling   f   1952
*Stalking Darkness* - Lynn Flewelling   f   1953

**Smolen**
*The Regiment's War* - John Dalmas   s   1326

**Sobrania**
*Sky Trillium* - Julian May   f   3700

**Solinde**
*Flight of the Raven* - Jennifer Roberson   f   4608

**Solvany**
*Barrenlands* - Doranna Durgin   f   1702

**Soma**
*The Unnatural* - David Prill   h   4437

**Sono**
*The Poisoned Lands* - John Maddox
   Roberts   f   4619

**South Central Ansalon**
*The Kinslayer Wars* - Douglas Niles   f   4109

**Souther Chaun**
*The Deceiver* - Louise Cooper   f   1175

**Southern Continent**
*The Lightless Kingdom* - Jonathan Wylie   f   6007

**Southern Isles**
*Aisling* - Louise Cooper   f   1172
*Nemesis* - Louise Cooper   f   1177

**Southern Kingdoms**
*Dhiammara* - Maggie Furey   f   2096

**Southern Mang**
*The Blackgod* - J. Gregory Keyes   f   3095

**Southsward**
*The Bellmaker* - Brian Jacques   f   2848

**Southwood**
*When Demons Walk* - Patricia Briggs   f   683

**Spice Lands**
*The Reaver Road* - Dave Duncan   f   1687

**Star Peninsula**
*The Avenger* - Louise Cooper   f   1174
*The Deceiver* - Louise Cooper   f   1175

**Stygia**
*Conan and the Treasure of Python* - John Maddox
   Roberts   f   4616
*Conan the Gladiator* - Leonard Carpenter   f   907

**Su-Shaklan**
*Spear of Heaven* - Judith Tarr   f   5396

**Summer Isle**
*The Avenger* - Louise Cooper   f   1174

**Sunderlies**
*Sunderlies Seeking* - Gayle Greeno   f   2424

**Svalbard**
*The Golden Compass* - Philip Pullman   f   4446

**Tahena**
*Storm Caller* - Carol Severance   f   4924

**Talislanta**
*Tales of Talislanta* - Stephen Michael Sechi   f   4909

**Tamlaght**
*Hearts and Armor* - Ron Miller   f   3903
*Palaces and Prisons* - Ron Miller   f   3904

**Tamul Empire**
*Domes of Fire* - David Eddings   f   1732

**Tantara**
*The Black Gryphon* - Mercedes Lackey   f   3270

**Tar Valon**
*The Dragon Reborn* - Robert Jordan   f   2985

**Taralon**
*Beggar's Banquet* - Daniel Hood   f   2756
*Fanuilh* - Daniel Hood   f   2757
*Scales of Justice* - Daniel Hood   f   2758
*Wizard's Heir* - Daniel Hood   f   2759

**Tarin Tseld**
*The Rose Sea* - S.M. Stirling   f   5296

**Tarnish Empire**
*Valorian* - Mary H. Herbert   f   2677

**Tarsia**
*The Wild Hunt: Vengeance Moon* - Jocelin
   Foxe   f   2031

**Tasavalta**
*The Last Book of Swords: Shieldbreaker's Story* - Fred
   Saberhagen   f   4768
*The Sixth Book of Lost Swords: Mindsword's Story* -
   Fred Saberhagen   f   4776
*Wayfinder's Story: The Seventh Book of Lost Swords* -
   Fred Saberhagen   f   4777

**Terosalle**
*Thunder of the Captains* - Holly Lisle   f   3489

**Terrain**
*The Pearl of the Soul of the World* - Meredith Ann
   Pierce   f   4318

**Terrosalle**
*Curse of the Black Heron* - Holly Lisle   f   3479

**Texas Republic**
*Mind Snare* - Gayle Greeno   s   2422

**Thallandia**
*Cardmaster* - Clayton Emery   f   1813

**Tharkold Occupation Zone**
*City of Pain* - John Terra   f   5438

**Thay**
*Red Magic* - Jean Rabe   f   4458

**the Dales**
*The One-Armed Queen* - Jane Yolen   f   6037

**the Isles**
*Queen of Demons* - David Drake   f   1640

**Thezas**
*The Steel Kings* - John Maddox Roberts   f   4621

**Thimhallen**
*Legacy of the Darksword* - Margaret Weis   f   5719

**Thirdmoon**
*The Spellkey Trilogy* - Ann Downer   f   1592

**The Three Kingdoms**
*Branch and Crown* - Gael Baudino   f   389
*O Greenest Branch!* - Gael Baudino   f   394
*The Way Beneath* - Angus Wells   f   5740

**Thulgaria**
*Being of Two Minds* - Pamela F. Service   f   4918

**Tielmark**
*A Tremor in the Bitter Earth* - Katya
   Reimann   f   4527
*Wind From a Foreign Sky* - Katya Reimann   f   4528

**Tiersian Universe**
*Red Orc's Rage* - Philip Jose Farmer   f   1873

**Tir Na Nog**
*The Crimson Sky* - Joel Rosenberg   f   4669
*The Fire Duke* - Joel Rosenberg   f   4671
*The Silver Stone* - Joel Rosenberg   f   4676

**Tira Virte**
*The Golden Key* - Melanie Rawn   f   4486

**Tobyn-Ser**
*Children of Amarid* - David B. Coe   f   1095
*The Outlanders* - David B. Coe   f   1096

**Tondur**
*Blood of the Colyn Muir* - Paul Edwin
   Zimmer   f   6083

**Tor Alte**
*The Book of Earth* - Marjorie Bradley
   Kellogg   f   3044

**Tortall**
*The Realms of the Gods* - Tamora Pierce   f   4321
*Wild Magic* - Tamora Pierce   f   4323
*Wolf-Speaker* - Tamora Pierce   f   4324

**Trav**
*Realm of Light* - Deborah Chester   f   1008
*Reign of Shadows* - Deborah Chester   f   1009

**Trevine**
*Shadow-Maze* - Mark Smith   f   5133

**Trondholm**
*Dark Divide* - Mark Acres   f   27

**TunFaire**
*Deadly Quicksilver Lies* - Glen Cook   f   1148
*Dread Brass Shadows* - Glen Cook   f   1149
*Old Tin Sorrows* - Glen Cook   f   1151

**Turan**
*The Conan Chronicles* - Robert Jordan   f   2983
*Conan of the Red Brotherhood* - Leonard
   Carpenter   f   906
*Conan, Scourge of the Bloody Coast* - Leonard
   Carpenter   f   910

**Turic Nation**
*Winged Magic* - Mary H. Herbert   f   2678

**The Twenty Kingdoms**
*The Eagle and the Nightingales* - Mercedes
   Lackey   f   3278

**Two Rivers**
*The Shadow Rising* - Robert Jordan   f   2990

**Tykissian Empire**
*The Rose Sea* - S.M. Stirling   f   5296

**Tyra**
*Kingmaker's Sword* - Ann Marston   f   3635

**Tyrenia**
*Kingdoms of the Night* - Allan Cole   f   1105

**Underhill**
*Chrome Circle* - Mercedes Lackey   f   3277

**United Countries of America**
*The Host* - Peter R. Emshwiller   s   1819
*Short Blade* - Peter R. Emshwiller   s   1820

**Upper Hetzia**
*The White Tribunal* - Paula Volsky   f   5583

**Urizen**
*Allamanda* - Michael Williams   f   5817

**Urthona**
*Allamanda* - Michael Williams   f   5817
*Arcady* - Michael Williams   f   5818

**Utter East**
*Conspiracy* - J. Robert King   f   3121

**Vacaan**
*The Far Kingdoms* - Allan Cole   f   1104

**Valaroi**
*The Far Kingdoms* - Allan Cole   f   1104

**Valdemar**
*By the Sword* - Mercedes Lackey   f   3273
*Magic's Price* - Mercedes Lackey   f   3288
*Oathblood* - Mercedes Lackey   f   3290
*Owlflight* - Mercedes Lackey   f   3291
*Owlsight* - Mercedes Lackey   f   3292
*Storm Breaking* - Mercedes Lackey   f   3296
*Storm Rising* - Mercedes Lackey   f   3297
*Storm Warning* - Mercedes Lackey   f   3298
*Sword of Ice and Other Tales of Valdemar* - Mercedes
   Lackey   f   3300
*Winds of Fate* - Mercedes Lackey   f   3305
*Winds of Fury* - Mercedes Lackey   f   3306

**Vandescard**
*The Silver Stone* - Joel Rosenberg   f   4676

**Varay**
*The Hero King* - Rick Shelley   f   4970
*The Hero of Varay* - Rick Shelley   f   4971

**Varre**
*Prince of Dogs* - Kate Elliott   f   1775

**Varslaad**
*Mirror of Destiny* - Andre Norton   f   4159

**Varua**
*Sea Without a Shore* - Sean Russell   f   4743

**Vaylle**
*Duel of Dragons* - Gael Baudino   f   391

**Vedette**
*Cathedral of Thorns* - Steven Frankos   f   2041

**Velonya**
*The Belly of the Wolf* - R.A. MacAvoy   f   3580
*King of the Dead* - R.A. MacAvoy   f   3581

**Vestinglon**
*Lens of the World* - R.A. MacAvoy   f   3582

**Videssos**
*Hammer and Anvil* - Harry Turtledove   f   5503
*Krispos of Videssos* - Harry Turtledove   f   5506
*Krispos Rising* - Harry Turtledove   f   5507
*Krispos the Emperor* - Harry Turtledove   f   5508
*The Thousand Cities* - Harry Turtledove   f   5512
*Videssos Besieged* - Harry Turtledove   f   5513

**Vilayet Sea**
*Conan, Scourge of the Bloody Coast* - Leonard
   Carpenter   f   910

**Vonahr**
*Illusion* - Paula Volsky   f   5582

**Voorstod**
*Raising the Stones* - Sheri S. Tepper   s   5434

**Vyjenor**
*Tears of Time* - Nancy Asire   f   256

*To Fall Like Stars* - Nancy Asire   *f*   257

**Walensor**
*Beneath the Web* - Lynn Abbey   *f*   12
*The Wooden Sword* - Lynn Abbey   *f*   18

**Wandernaught**
*The Magic of Recluce* - L.E. Modesitt Jr.   *f*   3934

**Wendar**
*King's Dragon* - Kate Elliott   *f*   1773
*Prince of Dogs* - Kate Elliott   *f*   1775

**Wennish Jungle**
*Bones of the Past* - Holly Lisle   *f*   3478

**Wes-bloc**
*The Zap Gun* - Philip K. Dick   *s*   1523

**Wesran**
*The Cursed* - Dave Duncan   *f*   1674

**West Gahant**
*Shadow of the Crown* - Craig Mills   *f*   3914

**Westland**
*Wizard's First Rule* - Terry Goodkind   *f*   2271

**The Westlands**
*Days of Air and Darkness* - Katharine Kerr   *f*   3067
*Days of Blood and Fire* - Katharine Kerr   *f*   3068
*Prince of Demons* - Mickey Zucker Reichert   *f*   4522
*A Time of Omens* - Katharine Kerr   *f*   3078
*The Western Wizard* - Mickey Zucker Reichert   *f*   4526

**Westria**
*The Jewel of Fire* - Diana L. Paxson   *f*   4265
*The Wind Crystal* - Diana L. Paxson   *f*   4269

**Westwind**
*The Towers of the Sunset* - L.E. Modesitt Jr.   *f*   3941

**White Gryphon Lands**
*The Silver Gryphon* - Mercedes Lackey   *f*   3295

**Wraithwaste**
*The War in the Waste* - Felicity Savage   *f*   4851

**Wynnamyr**
*Book of Stones* - L. Dean James   *f*   2862
*Kingslayer* - L. Dean James   *f*   2863

**Xanth**
*The Color of Her Panties* - Piers Anthony   *f*   167
*Demons Don't Dream* - Piers Anthony   *f*   168
*Faun & Games* - Piers Anthony   *f*   169
*Geis of the Gargoyle* - Piers Anthony   *f*   172
*Harpy Thyme* - Piers Anthony   *f*   174
*Isle of View* - Piers Anthony   *f*   177
*Question Quest* - Piers Anthony   *f*   186
*Roc and a Hard Place* - Piers Anthony   *f*   187
*Yon Ill Wind* - Piers Anthony   *f*   196
*Zombie Lover* - Piers Anthony   *f*   197

**Yeoli**
*Lion's Heart* - Karen Wehrstein   *f*   5683
*Shadow's Son* - Shirley Meier   *f*   3872

**Yeou**
*Lion's Soul* - Karen Wehrstein   *f*   5684

**Ylesuin**
*Fortress in the Eye of Time* - C.J. Cherryh   *f*   991
*Fortress of Eagles* - C.J. Cherryh   *f*   992

**Ynys Celydonn**
*The Castle of the Silver Wheel* - Teresa Edgerton   *f*   1741
*The Grail and the Ring* - Teresa Edgerton   *f*   1744

**Yole**
*Lord of the Isles* - David Drake   *f*   1636

**The Young Kingdoms**
*Elric: Song of the Black Sword* - Michael Moorcock   *f*   3980
*Tales of the White Wolf* - Edward E. Kramer   *f*   3227

**Ys**
*The Oathbound Wizard* - Christopher Stasheff   *f*   5219

**Ytaili**
*The Fire's Stone* - Tanya Huff   *f*   2796

**Yu-Atlanchi**
*The Face in the Abyss* - A. Merritt   *f*   3878

**Yuggoth**
*Horrors of the Dancing Gods* - Jack L. Chalker   *f*   955

**Yurt**
*A Bad Spell in Yurt* - C. Dale Brittain   *f*   701
*Daughter of Magic* - C. Dale Brittain   *f*   703
*The Wood Nymph and the Cranky Saint* - C. Dale Brittain   *f*   706

**Zam Fadogurum**
*Wild Magic* - Jo Clayton   *f*   1072

**Zamora**
*The Conan Chronicles* - Robert Jordan   *f*   2983

**Zanzib**
*Castle in the Air* - Diana Wynne Jones   *f*   2944

**Zark**
*Faery Lands Forlorn* - Dave Duncan   *f*   1677
*Perilous Seas* - Dave Duncan   *f*   1685

**Zelharri**
*One Land, One Duke* - Ru Emerson   *f*   1809

**Zinora**
*Blood Trillium* - Julian May   *f*   3696

# FRANCE

*A Candle for D'Artagnan* - Chelsea Quinn Yarbro   *h*   6013
*Child of Faerie, Child of Earth* - Josepha Sherman   *f*   4985
*King & Raven* - Cary James   *f*   2858
*A King Beneath the Mountain* - Robert N. Charrette   *f*   973
*The Premonition* - Andrew Laurance   *h*   3349
*Rehearsal for a Renaissance* - Douglas W. Clark   *f*   1045
*A Strange and Ancient Name* - Josepha Sherman   *f*   4991
*A Well-Timed Enchantment* - Vivian Vande Velde   *f*   5559
*Where the Towers Pierce the Sky* - Marie D. Goodwin   *f*   2272

**Avignon**
*Scorpio* - Alex McDonough   *s*   3802

**Brittany**
*The Winter King* - Bernard Cornwell   *f*   1191

**Chateau Beauxpres**
*The Porcelain Dove* - Delia Sherman   *f*   4983

**Duchy of Aquitaine**
*The Shadow Gate* - Margaret Ball   *f*   317

**Greenlaw**
*A College of Magics* - Caroline Stevermer   *f*   5266

**Grenoble**
*To Dream of Dreamers Lost* - David Niall Wilson   *h*   5882

**Jura Mountains**
*The Porcelain Dove* - Delia Sherman   *f*   4983

**Le Caillou**
*Wall, Stone, Craft* - Walter Jon Williams   *h*   5842

**Lyons**
*The Passion* - Donna Boyd   *h*   603

**Nice**
*Echoes* - Jackie Hyman   *h*   2818
*Glory Road* - Robert A. Heinlein   *f*   2644
*Mir* - Alexander Besher   *s*   474

**Normandy**
*The Spawn of Loki* - Jason Henderson   *f*   2658

**Orgon**
*Blood Roses* - Chelsea Quinn Yarbro   *h*   6012

**Paris**
*Arc d'X* - Steve Erickson   *f*   1835
*Bad Voltage* - Jonathan Littell   *s*   3491
*The Carnival of Destruction* - Brian Stableford   *h*   5190
*Dancing on Air* - Nancy Kress   *s*   3240
*Desmond: A Novel of Love and the Modern Vampire* - Ulysses G. Dietz   *h*   1541
*The Eight* - Katherine Neville   *f*   4092
*Empire of the Ants* - Bernard Werber   *s*   5755
*Human Resources* - Floyd Kemske   *h*   3057
*I, Vampire* - Michael Romkey   *h*   4665
*Indiana Jones and the Peril at Delphi* - Rob MacGregor   *f*   3591
*Machine* - Rene Belletto   *h*   436
*The Mata Hari Adventure* - James Luceno   *f*   3544
*Mirage* - F. Paul Wilson   *h*   5892
*Night of the Cooters* - Howard Waldrop   *s*   5614
*Paris in the Twentieth Century* - Jules Verne   *s*   5568
*The Passion* - Donna Boyd   *h*   603
*Phantom* - Susan Kay   *h*   3020
*The Porcelain Dove* - Delia Sherman   *f*   4983
*Russian Spring* - Norman Spinrad   *s*   5174
*The Secret Life of Laszlo, Count Dracula* - Roderick Anscombe   *h*   152
*A Sharpness on the Neck* - Fred Saberhagen   *h*   4774
*The Tale of the Body Thief* - Anne Rice   *h*   4576
*TekLab* - William Shatner   *s*   4939
*Time Station Paris* - David Evans   *s*   1854
*The Unbeholden* - Robert Weinberg   *h*   5703
*The Werewolf of Paris* - Guy Endore   *h*   1822

**Saint Ame**
*The Judas Cross* - Charles Sheffield   *h*   4960

**Saint-Fabrisse**
*Kiss of Death* - Daniel Rhodes   *h*   4569

**St. Maurice de Navacelles**
*Black Dogs* - Ian McEwan   *h*   3808

**Verdun**
*The Mata Hari Adventure* - James Luceno   *f*   3544

**Versailles**
*The Moon and the Sun* - Vonda N. McIntyre   *f*   3822

# FRENCH GUIANA

**Kourou**
*Ignition* - Kevin J. Anderson   *s*   107

# GAUL

*Druids* - Morgan Llywelyn   *f*   3502

# GEORGIA

*Somewhere East of Life* - Brian W. Aldiss   *s*   60

## GERMANY

*1945* - Newt Gingrich   s   2239
*At Sword's Point* - Scott MacMillan   f   3601
*The Book of Earth* - Marjorie Bradley
   Kellogg   f   3044
*Carrion Comfort* - Dan Simmons   h   5049
*The Cornish Trilogy* - Robertson Davies   f   1397
*Escape From Loki* - Philip Jose Farmer   f   1870
*First Dawn* - Mike Moscoe   s   4038
*The Fourth Rome* - David Drake   s   1631
*Lightning* - Dean R. Koontz   h   3211
*The Magicians of Night* - Barbara Hambly   f   2505
*Night's Pawn* - Tom Dowd   s   1591
*Nutcracker* - E.T.A. Hoffmann   f   2719
*Parsifal* - Peter Vansittart   f   5560
*Red Army* - Ralph Peters   s   4306
*The Secret Laboratory Journals of Dr. Victor
   Frankenstein* - Jeremy Kay   h   3019
*Sleipnir* - Linda Evans   f   1856
*Spell Bound* - Ru Emerson   f   1810
*Warrior* - William F. Wu   s   6000

**Bayreuth**
*I, Vampire* - Michael Romkey   h   4665

**Berlin**
*Arc d'X* - Steve Erickson   f   1835
*Child of the Journey* - Janet Berliner   f   466
*Child of the Light* - Janet Gluckman   f   2244
*City of Pain* - John Terra   s   5438
*Fatherland* - Robert Harris   s   2564
*Time Station Berlin* - David Evans   s   1852
*Triumph* - Ben Bova   s   598

**East Berlin**
*Codename Wolverine* - Christopher Golden   s   2256

**Frankfort**
*Cloud Castles* - Michael Scott Rohan   f   4659

**Hamburg**
*Nightmare, with Angel* - Stephen Gallagher   h   2111

**Harz Mountains**
*Psychomech* - Brian Lumley   h   3562

**Leipzig**
*Two Crowns for America* - Katherine Kurtz   f   3262

**Munich**
*The Beast Within: A Gabriel Knight Mystery* - Jane
   Jensen   h   2895
*The Broken Goddess* - Hans Bemmann   f   439
*The Parasite* - Ramsey Campbell   h   863
*Time's Arrow* - Martin Amis   s   96

**Saxony**
*Better in the Dark* - Chelsea Quinn Yarbro   h   6011

## GERMANY, WEST

**Berlin**
*Black Dogs* - Ian McEwan   h   3808

## GREECE

*Antiquities* - John Crowley   f   1276
*The Arkadians* - Lloyd Alexander   f   67
*Deadspeak* - Brian Lumley   h   3551
*Demogorgon* - Brian Lumley   h   3552
*The Fabulist* - John Vornholt   f   5595
*Soldier of Arete* - Gene Wolfe   f   5944
*Sons of the Titans* - Patrick H. Adkins   f   36
*Thessalonica* - Harry Turtledove   f   5511
*Throne of Isis* - Judith Tarr   f   5397
*Whilom* - Robert Watson   f   5639

**Antioch**
*Pandora* - Anne Rice   h   4573

**Athens**
*Celestial Matters* - Richard Garfinkle   s   2140
*Goatsong* - Tom Holt   f   2751
*Orion and the Conqueror* - Ben Bova   s   590
*Secret Passages* - Paul Preuss   s   4420
*The Thief of Hermes* - Ru Emerson   f   1811
*The Walled Orchard* - Tom Holt   f   2752

**Crete**
*The Elementals* - Morgan Llywelyn   f   3503
*Secret Passages* - Paul Preuss   s   4420

**Delphi**
*Indiana Jones and the Peril at Delphi* - Rob
   MacGregor   f   3591

**Ithaca**
*By the Sword* - Timothy Boggs   f   559
*The Empty Throne* - Ru Emerson   f   1808

**Krisos Island**
*Lord of the Dark Lake* - Ron Faust   h   1894

**Mercantilius**
*The First Casualty* - David L. Seidman   f   4912

**Pastoralis**
*The First Casualty* - David L. Seidman   f   4912

**Pella**
*Lion of Macedon* - David Gemmell   f   2189

**Rhodes**
*Psychosphere* - Brian Lumley   h   3563

**Sparta**
*Lion of Macedon* - David Gemmell   f   2189

**Thebes**
*Lion of Macedon* - David Gemmell   f   2189

**Thessalonika**
*Live From Golgotha: A Novel* - Gore Vidal   s   5569

## GREENLAND

*Darkness on the Ice* - Lois Tilton   h   5475
*The Ice-Shirt* - William T. Vollmann   f   5580
*Spider Legs* - Piers Anthony   s   189

**Thule**
*Icebound* - Dean R. Koontz   h   3209

## GUATEMALA

**Kan Peten**
*Sacrifice* - John Farris   h   1886

## HEAVEN

*And Eternity* - Piers Anthony   f   162
*Angelwalk: A Modern Fable* - Roger
   Elwood   f   1803
*The Devil and Dan Cooley* - Holly Lisle   f   3480
*A Farce to Be Reckoned With* - Roger
   Zelazny   f   6064
*Hell on High* - Holly Lisle   f   3483
*Prophets for the End of Time* - Marcos
   Donnelly   f   1577
*The Stainless Steel Rat Goes to Hell* - Harry
   Harrison   s   2574

## HELL

*And Eternity* - Piers Anthony   f   162
*The Black School* - J.N. Williamson   h   5851
*Only Begotten Daughter* - James Morrow   f   4034
*Phantom Banjo* - Elizabeth Ann
   Scarborough   f   4868
*Picking the Ballad's Bones* - Elizabeth Ann
   Scarborough   f   4869

*Samurai Cat Goes to Hell* - Mark E. Rogers   f   4655
*The Stainless Steel Rat Goes to Hell* - Harry
   Harrison   s   2574
*Sympathy for the Devil* - Holly Lisle   f   3488
*The Thing That Darkness Hides* - Robert
   Morgan   h   4006

**North Discomfort, Pit 405**
*Bring Me the Head of Prince Charming* - Roger
   Zelazny   f   6062

**Pandemonium**
*Eric* - Terry Pratchett   f   4388

**Realm of Darkness**
*A Farce to Be Reckoned With* - Roger
   Zelazny   f   6064

## HONG KONG

*The Bones of Time* - Kathleen Ann Goonan   s   2273
*Mortal Kombat* - Martin Delrio   f   1483

## HUNGARY

**Budapest**
*Blood Countess* - Andrei Codrescu   h   1094
*Signs of Life* - M. John Harrison   s   2580

## ICELAND

**Reykjavik**
*Double Planet* - John Gribbin   s   2433

## IN THE AIR

*Argo*
*Atlantis Found* - R. Garcia y Robertson   s   2119

*Wagner*
*From Prussia with Love* - John DeChancie   f   1457

## INDIA

*Bijapur* - Kara Dalkey   f   1317
*Flameweaver* - Margaret Ball   f   314
*In the Heart of Darkness* - Eric Flint   s   1955
*No Blood Spilled* - Les Daniels   h   1338
*Phases of Gravity* - Dan Simmons   s   5057
*The Sword of Samurai Cat*   Mark E.
   Rogers   s   4657
*The Willing Spirit* - Piers Anthony   f   195

**Bangalore**
*Freeware* - Rudy Rucker   s   4703

**Bhagavati**
*Bhagavati* - Kara Dalkey   f   1316

**Calcutta**
*The Calcutta Chromosome* - Amitav Ghosh   h   2214

**Delhi**
*Death in Delhi* - Gary Gygax   f   2473

**Dharmsala**
*Fortress of Forbidden Destiny* - Ryder
   Syvertson   s   5378

**Dharwar District**
*Viper* - Alan Riefe   h   4589

**Goa**
*Blood of the Goddess* - Kara Dalkey   f   1318

## INDONESIA

**Bali**
*The Painted Alphabet* - Diana Darling   f   1356

**Kalimantan, Borneo**
*Kalimantan* - Lucius Shepard  *h*  4979

## INTERSTELLAR EMPIRE/ FEDERATION

*Ambush at Corellia* - Roger MacBride Allen  *s*  76
*Beyond the Gate* - Dave Wolverton  *s*  5949
*The Broken God* - David Zindell  *s*  6085
*Conqueror's Pride* - Timothy Zahn  *s*  6051
*A Darker Geometry* - Mark O. Martin  *s*  3649
*Day of the Dead* - Neil Gaiman  *s*  2102
*The Defenders* - Bill Baldwin  *s*  309
*The Defiance* - Bill Baldwin  *s*  310
*The Demon Princes: Volume One* - Jack
   Vance  *s*  5544
*The Demon Princes: Volume Two* - Jack
   Vance  *s*  5545
*An Exchange of Hostages* - Susan R.
   Matthews  *s*  3692
*First Strike* - Diane Carey  *s*  903
*The Gap into Madness: Chaos and Order* - Stephen R.
   Donaldson  *s*  1573
*The Gap into Ruin: This Day All Gods Die* - Stephen
   R. Donaldson  *s*  1575
*Glory's People* - Alfred Coppel  *s*  1183
*The Humanoids* - Jack Williamson  *s*  5865
*Komarr* - Lois McMaster Bujold  *s*  760
*Masque* - F. Paul Wilson  *s*  5890
*Out of This World* - Lawrence Watt-Evans  *f*  5645
*Playing God* - Sarah Zettel  *s*  6080
*Prodigy* - Jan Clark  *s*  1047
*Q-Space* - Greg Cox  *s*  1228
*The Return* - William Shatner  *s*  4933
*Shadows of the Empire* - Steve Perry  *s*  4299
*The Siege* - Bill Baldwin  *s*  312
*Tales From the Mos Eisley Cantina* - Kevin J.
   Anderson  *s*  115
*Thirdspace* - Peter David  *s*  1387
*The Touch of Your Shadow, the Whisper of Your Name*
   - Neal Barrett Jr.  *s*  367
*Voices* - John Vornholt  *s*  5598
*War Dragons* - L.A. Graf  *s*  2299
*The Widowmaker Reborn* - Mike Resnick  *s*  4560
*The Wild* - David Zindell  *s*  6086
*With Full Honors* - Donald E. McQuinn  *s*  3865

**Alastor Cluster**
*Alastor* - Jack Vance  *s*  5543

**Allied Worlds of Earth**
*Primary Inversion* - Catherine Asaro  *s*  220

**Barryaran Empire**
*Borders of Infinity* - Lois McMaster Bujold  *s*  757
*The Vor Game* - Lois McMaster Bujold  *s*  764

**Cetaganda**
*Cetaganda* - Lois McMaster Bujold  *s*  758

**Civilization**
*Nautilus* - Vonda N. McIntyre  *s*  3823

**The Com**
*Commencement* - Roby James  *s*  2877

**Compact Space**
*Chanur's Legacy* - C.J. Cherryh  *s*  981

**Concord Worlds**
*Shadow Man* - Melissa Scott  *s*  4900

**Confederacy of Sentient Beings**
*The Final Battle* - William C. Dietz  *s*  1546

**Confederation**
*The VMR Theory* - Robert Frezza  *s*  2055
*The White Regiment* - John Dalmas  *s*  1327
*Wing Commander: Freedom Flight* - Mercedes
   Lackey  *s*  3307

**Cooperative League of Systems**
*Silent Songs* - A.C. Crispin  *s*  1264

**The Culture**
*The Player of Games* - Iain M. Banks  *s*  326
*Use of Weapons* - Iain M. Banks  *s*  328

**Diobastan Cluster**
*The Thirteenth Majestral* - Hayford Peirce  *s*  4277

**Dragon Empire**
*Dragon's Honor* - Kij Johnson  *s*  2922

**The Empire**
*The Mandalorian Armor* - K.W. Jeter  *s*  2914

**Empire**
*Mistworld* - Simon R. Green  *s*  2372

**Empire of Azad**
*The Player of Games* - Iain M. Banks  *s*  326

**Federation of Sentient Planets**
*Sassinak* - Anne McCaffrey  *s*  3748

**Federation Space**
*Generation Warrior* - Anne McCaffrey  *s*  3735

**First Empire**
*Crown of Empire* - Chelsea Quinn Yarbro  *s*  6014
*The War Machine* - David Drake  *s*  1650

**Fluvanna**
*The Mercenaries* - Bill Baldwin  *s*  311

**The Fold**
*The Children Star* - Joan Slonczewski  *s*  5090

**Free Fold**
*Daughter of Elysium* - Joan Slonczewski  *s*  5091

**Galactic Empire**
*Alien Salute* - Charles Ingrid  *s*  2830
*The Ecolitan Operation* - L.E. Modesitt Jr.  *s*  3928
*The Reign of the Brown Magician* - Lawrence Watt-
   Evans  *f*  5647
*Rogue Squadron* - Michael A. Stackpole  *s*  5205
*Tales From Jabba's Palace* - Kevin J.
   Anderson  *s*  114

**Galactic Federation**
*I, Robot: The Illustrated Screenplay* - Harlan
   Ellison  *s*  1785

**Galactic Milieu**
*Magnificat* - Julian May  *s*  3699

**Harmony of Worlds**
*Becoming Human* - Valerie J. Freireich  *s*  2049

**Harmony Star Cluster**
*Cluster Command* - David Drake  *s*  1630

**The Hegemony**
*Chains of Light* - Quentin Thomas  *s*  5449

**Hegemony of Man**
*Hyperion* - Dan Simmons  *s*  5055

**Held Empire**
*The Goda War* - Jay D. Blakeney  *s*  516

**Human Confederation**
*Emergence* - Peter F. Hamilton  *s*  2524

**Hundred Worlds**
*To Save the Sun* - Ben Bova  *s*  596

**Karghanik Empire**
*The Kalif's War* - John Dalmas  *s*  1322

**Kazi Empire**
*Cat's Gambit* - Leslie Gadallah  *s*  2099

**Keltia**
*Blackmantle: A Triumph* - Patricia Kenneally-
   Morrison  *f*  3059

*The Hawk's Gray Feather* - Patricia Kenneally-
   Morrison  *f*  3061
*The Hedge of Mist* - Patricia Kenneally-
   Morrison  *s*  3062
*The Oak Above the Kings: A Book of the Keltiad* -
   Patricia Kennealy  *s*  3058

**Klingon Empire**
*Kahless* - Michael Jan Friedman  *s*  2065

**LaNague Federation**
*The LaNague Chronicles* - F. Paul Wilson  *s*  5889

**Logarchy**
*Aristoi* - Walter Jon Williams  *s*  5834

**The Magnificate**
*The Harriers* - Gordon R. Dickson  *s*  1535

**Metaji Empire**
*Dreamspy* - Jacqueline Lichtenberg  *s*  3458

**The Moiety**
*Days of Cain* - J.R. Dunn  *s*  1694

**Monopolity of Hanover**
*Bretta Martyn* - L. Neil Smith  *s*  5128

**New Republic**
*Before the Storm* - Michael P. Kube-
   McDowell  *s*  3247
*Children of the Jedi* - Barbara Hambly  *s*  2500
*The Courtship of Princess Leia* - Dave
   Wolverton  *s*  5950
*The Crystal Star* - Vonda N. McIntyre  *s*  3820
*Darksaber* - Kevin J. Anderson  *s*  103
*Jedi Search* - Kevin J. Anderson  *s*  109
*The Last Command* - Timothy Zahn  *s*  6055
*The New Rebellion* - Kristine Kathryn
   Rusch  *s*  4719
*Rogue Squadron* - Michael A. Stackpole  *s*  5205
*The Truce at Bakura* - Kathy Tyers  *s*  5527

**Outer System Federation**
*Proteus Unbound* - Charles Sheffield  *s*  4963

**Panarchy of the Thousand Suns**
*A Prison Unsought* - Sherwood Smith  *s*  5139
*The Rifter's Covenant* - Sherwood Smith  *s*  5140

**People's Republic of Haven**
*Flag in Exile* - David Weber  *s*  5671

**Phoenix Empire**
*Archangel Blues* - eluki bes shahar  *s*  471

**The Pinch**
*The Eyes of God* - Mark Kreighbaum  *s*  3231
*Palace* - Katharine Kerr  *s*  3072

**The Planets of the Seven Senti**
*The Third Eagle: Lessons Along a Minor String* - R.A.
   MacAvoy  *s*  3583

**Polite Harmony of Worlds**
*Imposter* - Valerie J. Freireich  *s*  2050
*Testament* - Valerie J. Freireich  *s*  2051

**Protektorate**
*Protektor* - Charles Platt  *s*  4342

**Romulan Empire**
*Assignment: Eternity* - Greg Cox  *s*  1225

**Sassan Empire**
*Relic of Empire* - W. Michael Gear  *s*  2171

**Scorpio/Sagittarius Sector**
*Mad Roy's Light* - Paula King  *s*  3125

**The Seventeen Planets**
*Anvil* - Nicolas van Pallandt  *s*  5540

**Silesian Confederacy**
*Honor Among Enemies* - David Weber  *s*  5673

**Sol Galaxy**
*Megalomania* - Ian Wallace   s   5621

**Solarian Combine**
*Design for Great-Day* - Alan Dean Foster   s   2001

**Star Kingdom of Manticore**
*Field of Dishonor* - David Weber   s   5670
*Flag in Exile* - David Weber   s   5671
*Honor Among Enemies* - David Weber   s   5673
*In Enemy Hands* - David Weber   s   5675
*The Short Victorious War* - David Weber   s   5681

**Suzerainty of Human Spaces**
*The Fall of Sirius* - Wil McCarthy   s   3762

**Teleod**
*Dreamspy* - Jacqueline Lichtenberg   s   3458

**Terran Federation**
*Murder at the Galactic Writers' Society* - Janet Asimov   s   251
*Norby Down to Earth* - Janet Asimov   s   255

**Terran Hegemony**
*Warstrider* - William H. Keith Jr.   s   3037

**Unified Worlds/Dominion**
*Echoes of Issel* - Diann Thornley   s   5466
*Ganwold's Child* - Diann Thornley   s   5467

**United Empire of Planets**
*Dark Mirror* - Diane Duane   s   1658

**United Federation of Planets**
*Armageddon Sky* - L.A. Graf   s   2296
*The Ashes of Eden* - William Shatner   s   4927
*Avenger* - William Shatner   s   4928
*Balance of Power* - Dafydd ab Hugh   s   7
*Bloodletter* - K.W. Jeter   s   2908
*The Chance Factor* - Diana G. Gallagher   s   2109
*Chrysalis* - David Niall Wilson   s   5880
*Crossover* - Michael Jan Friedman   s   2063
*Crossroad* - Barbara Hambly   s   2501
*Debtors' Planet* - William R. Thompson   s   5457
*The Fearful Summons* - Denny Martin Flinn   s   1954
*Imzadi* - Peter David   s   1383
*Insurrection* - J.M. Dillard   s   1554
*Intellivore* - Diane Duane   s   1663
*The Joy Machine* - James Gunn   s   2458
*Mind Meld* - John Vornholt   s   5596
*Requiem* - Michael Jan Friedman   s   2067
*Sarek* - A.C. Crispin   s   1260
*Ship of the Line* - Diane Carey   s   904
*The Soldiers of Fear* - Dean Wesley Smith   s   5115
*Spectre* - William Shatner   s   4934
*Starfleet Academy* - Diane Carey   s   905
*Time's Enemy* - L.A. Graf   s   2297
*Traitor Winds* - L.A. Graf   s   2298
*Vulcan's Forge* - Susan Shwartz   s   5019
*Warped* - K.W. Jeter   s   2917

**The Weave**
*The False Mirror* - Alan Dean Foster   s   2004

**Xarafeille Stream**
*Stepwater* - L. Warren Douglas   s   1588
*The Wells of Phyre* - L. Warren Douglas   s   1589

## IRAN

**Tabriz**
*Walker between the Worlds* - Diane DesRochers   f   1499

## IRAQ

*The Pleistocene Redemption* - Dan Gallagher   s   2107

## IRELAND

*Angel Light* - Andrew M. Greeley   f   2342
*Brian Boru: Emperor of the Irish* - Morgan Llywelyn   f   3501
*Cromm* - Kenneth C. Flint   f   1957
*The Deepest Sea* - Charles Barnitz   f   363
*The Enchanted Isles* - Casey Flynn   f   1960
*Finn Mac Cool* - Morgan Llywelyn   f   3504
*The Fungus* - Harry Adam Knight   h   3192
*The Ghost From the Grand Banks* - Arthur C. Clarke   s   1056
*The Godmother's Apprentice* - Elizabeth Ann Scarborough   f   4863
*Great Irish Tales of Horror* - Peter Haining   h   2482
*Hunter of the Light* - Risa Aratyr   f   203
*Irish Tales of the Supernatural* - Martin O'Griofa   h   4203
*Legends Reborn* - Kenneth C. Flint   f   1958
*The Lost Prince* - Bridget Wood   f   5962
*Master of Earth and Water* - Diana L. Paxson   f   4266
*Most Ancient Song* - Casey Flynn   f   1961
*Pride of Lions* - Morgan Llywelyn   f   3506
*The Rising of the Moon* - Flynn Connolly   s   1135
*Search for the Starblade* - Keith Taylor   f   5408
*The Shattered Oath* - Josepha Sherman   f   4989
*The Shield between the Worlds* - Diana L. Paxson   f   4267
*Sword of Fire and Shadow* - Diana L. Paxson   f   4268
*A Wizard Abroad* - Diane Duane   f   1668
*Wolfking* - Bridget Wood   f   5963

**Barley Cross**
*Masters of the Fist* - Edward P. Hughes   s   2805

**Carrick-on-Suir**
*The Uprising* - Brent Monahan   h   3956

**Connacht**
*The Raid* - Randy Lee Eickhoff   f   1764

**County Cork**
*The Haunt* - John Fogarty   h   1966

**County Offaly**
*Above the Lower Sky* - Tom Deitz   f   1469

**County Sligo**
*King of Morning, Queen of Day* - Ian McDonald   f   3793

**Dublin**
*The Butcher Boy* - Patrick McCabe   h   3716
*Heathen* - Shaun Hutson   h   2816
*King of Morning, Queen of Day* - Ian McDonald   f   3793

**Dun Laoghaire**
*Realtime Interrupt* - James P. Hogan   s   2729

**Iona**
*The Throne of Tara* - John Desjarlais   f   1498

**Kilashane**
*Mask of the Night* - Mary Ryan   h   4753

**Kraighten**
*The House on the Borderland* - William Hope Hodgson   h   2711

**Mull of Kintyre**
*Dagger Magic* - Katherine Kurtz   f   3256

**Slemish**
*The Deer's Cry: A Book of the Keltiad* - Patricia Kennealy-Morrison   f   3060

**Ulster**
*The Raid* - Randy Lee Eickhoff   f   1764

## ISRAEL

*Carrion Comfort* - Dan Simmons   h   5049
*The Old Man and Mr. Smith* - Peter Ustinov   f   5532
*The Pleistocene Redemption* - Dan Gallagher   s   2107

**Jerusalem**
*Black Trump* - George R.R. Martin   s   3642
*The Grail of Hearts* - Susan Shwartz   f   5015
*The Iron Lance* - Stephen R. Lawhead   f   3356
*Requiem* - Graham Joyce   h   2994
*Skinny Legs and All* - Tom Robbins   f   4607
*To Speak in Lifeless Tongues* - David Niall Wilson   h   5883

**Tel Aviv**
*The Unbeholden* - Robert Weinberg   h   5703

## ITALY

*Demon Knight* - Ken Hood   f   2760
*The Devil's Day* - James Blish   h   525
*King and Emperor* - Harry Harrison   f   2571
*Quest for Apollo* - Michael Lahey   f   3309
*Rehearsal for a Renaissance* - Douglas W. Clark   f   1045
*Wartide* - John Barnes   f   359

**Florence**
*The Memory Cathedral* - Jack Dann   s   1341
*Renaissance Moon* - Linda Nevins   f   4093
*The Stars Dispose* - Michaela Roessner   f   4651

**Labirinto**
*The Innamorati* - Midori Snyder   f   5152

**Libarna**
*The Centurion's Empire* - Sean McMullen   s   3854

**Milan**
*Humpty Dumpty: An Oval* - Damon Knight   s   3186

**Monte Trasimeno**
*Catacomb* - Andrew Laurance   h   3347

**Naples**
*Caliban's Hour* - Tad Williams   f   5826
*Children of God* - Mary Doria Russell   s   4735
*Lady Cottington's Pressed Fairy Book* - Terry Jones   f   2981

**Rome**
*Caesar's Bicycle* - John Barnes   s   350
*A Candle for D'Artagnan* - Chelsea Quinn Yarbro   h   6013
*Crusader's Torch* - Chelsea Quinn Yarbro   h   6015
*The D. Case: The Truth about the Mystery of Edwin Drood* - Charles Dickens   f   1524
*The Flies of Memory* - Ian Watson   s   5635
*The Great Wheel* - Ian R. MacLeod   s   3599
*Interface Masque* - Shariann Lewitt   s   3453
*Judgment of Tears: Anno Dracula 1959* - Kim Newman   h   4098
*Live From Golgotha: A Novel* - Gore Vidal   s   5569
*Pandora* - Anne Rice   h   4573
*Phantom* - Susan Kay   h   3020
*Psychoshop* - Alfred Bester   s   477
*The Silver Wolf* - Alice Borchardt   h   572

**Sicily**
*Fantasma* - Thomas F. Monteleone   h   3963
*The Vampire Journals* - Traci Briery   h   678

**Venice**
*7 Steps to Midnight* - Richard Matheson   h   3682
*Evil Reincarnate* - Leigh Clark   h   1050
*Faces under Water* - Tanith Lee   h   3409
*The Innamorati* - Midori Snyder   f   5152
*Interface Masque* - Shariann Lewitt   s   3453
*Mask of the Night* - Mary Ryan   h   4753

*Master of Many Treasures* - Mary Brown  *f*  726
*Of Saints and Shadows* - Christopher
   Golden  *h*  2259
*The Vampire Armand* - Anne Rice  *h*  4578
*Vaporetto 13* - Robert Girardi  *h*  2241
*The Venetian's Wife: A Strangely Sensual Tale of a
   Renaissance Explorer, a Computer, and a
   Metamorphosis* - Nick Bantock  *f*  336

## JAMAICA

*Disciples of Dread* - Hugh B. Cave  *h*  941

## JAPAN

*Assault of the Super Carrier* - Peter Albano  *s*  47
*The Face of Another* - Kobo Abe  *h*  19
*Free Radicals* - Jack McKinney  *s*  3848
*The Frightened Fish* - Kenneth Robeson  *f*  4622
*The Heavenward Path* - Kara Dalkey  *f*  1319
*Hostile Takeover* - Jack McKinney  *s*  3849
*Little Sister* - Kara Dalkey  *f*  1320
*Scissors Cut Paper Wrap Stone* - Ian
   McDonald  *s*  3795
*Supernova* - Roger MacBride Allen  *s*  82
*TekLords* - William Shatner  *s*  4940
*Till the End of Time* - Allen Appel  *f*  201
*The Yngling in Yamato* - John Dalmas  *s*  1329

**Sapporo**
*Dance Dance Dance* - Haruki Murakami  *s*  4046

**Tokyo**
*Angel Kiss* - Kelley Wilde  *h*  5800
*Dance Dance Dance* - Haruki Murakami  *s*  4046
*Evil Ascending* - Michael A. Stackpole  *s*  5198
*Fire in a Faraway Place* - Robert Frezza  *s*  2052
*Hard-Boiled Wonderland and the End of the World* -
   Haruki Murakami  *s*  4047
*Idoru* - William Gibson  *s*  2218
*Iroshi* - Cary Osborne  *s*  4228
*Meeting the Minotaur* - Carol Dawson  *f*  1409
*Rim: A Novel of Virtual Reality* - Alexander
   Besher  *s*  475
*The Samurai Wizard* - Simon Hawke  *f*  2623

## JUPITER

*The Medusa Encounter* - Paul Preuss  *s*  4419
*Warlords of Jupiter* - William H. Keith Jr.  *s*  3036

**Callisto**
*Damia* - Anne McCaffrey  *s*  3725

**Europa**
*3001: The Final Odyssey* - Arthur C.
   Clarke  *s*  1053
*Cold as Ice* - Charles Sheffield  *s*  4950

**Ganymede**
*Bloom* - Wil McCarthy  *s*  3761
*Cold as Ice* - Charles Sheffield  *s*  4950
*The Ganymede Club* - Charles Sheffield  *s*  4955

## KENYA

*The Golden Mean* - Nick Bantock  *f*  334

**Marsabit**
*Kirinyaga: A Fable of Utopia* - Mike
   Resnick  *s*  4548

**Nairobi**
*Evolution's Shore* - Ian McDonald  *s*  3792

## REPUBLIC OF KOREA

*Fire* - Alan Rodgers  *h*  4647

## LEBANON

**Beirut**
*The Werewolf's Revenge* - Richard Jaccoma  *h*  2841

## MACEDONIA

*Dark Prince* - David Gemmell  *f*  2187
*Lord of the Two Lands* - Judith Tarr  *f*  5395
*Orion and the Conqueror* - Ben Bova  *s*  590

## MADAGASCAR

*Children of the Dusk* - Janet Berliner  *f*  467
*Ghost of Chance* - William S. Burroughs  *s*  780

## MALAYSIA

**Sunda**
*The Bohr Maker* - Linda Nagata  *s*  4064

## MARS

*Beachhead* - Jack Williamson  *s*  5859
*Beneath the Tree of Heaven* - David
   Wingrove  *s*  5917
*Blade Runner: Replicant Night* - K.W. Jeter  *s*  2907
*Blue Mars* - Kim Stanley Robinson  *s*  4629
*Bodyguard* - William C. Dietz  *s*  1542
*Bright Messengers* - Gentry Lee  *s*  3398
*Burster* - Michael Capobianco  *s*  876
*Celestial Matters* - Richard Garfinkle  *s*  2140
*Climbing Olympus* - Kevin J. Anderson  *s*  102
*The Collected Stories of Philip K. Dick, Volume Two:
   We Can Remember It for You Wholesale* - Philip K.
   Dick  *s*  1520
*Crescent in the Sky* - Donald Moffitt  *s*  3946
*Exile* - Al Sarrantonio  *s*  4829
*The Fleet of Stars* - Poul Anderson  *s*  126
*The Flies of Memory* - Ian Watson  *s*  5635
*The Ganymede Club* - Charles Sheffield  *s*  4955
*Green Mars* - Kim Stanley Robinson  *s*  4633
*Hammer of Mars* - M.S. Murdock  *s*  4049
*Harm's Way* - Colin Greenland  *s*  2416
*Hide and Seek* - Paul Preuss  *s*  4418
*Kane of Old Mars* - Michael Moorcock  *s*  3983
*Lake of the Sun* - Wynne Whiteford  *s*  5787
*The Law of War* - William Shatner  *s*  4931
*Man o' War* - William Shatner  *s*  4932
*Mars* - Ben Bova  *s*  586
*Mars Prime* - William C. Dietz  *s*  1548
*Mars—The Red Planet* - Mick Farren  *s*  1880
*Mars Underground* - William Hartmann  *s*  2584
*The Martian Chronicles* - Ray Bradbury  *s*  622
*The Martian Chronicles* - Ray Bradbury  *s*  621
*Martian Rainbow* - Robert L. Forward  *s*  1987
*Mining the Oort* - Frederik Pohl  *s*  4349
*Moving Mars* - Greg Bear  *s*  421
*Nightshade* - Jack Butler  *s*  789
*Norby and Yobo's Great Adventure* - Janet
   Asimov  *s*  254
*Phylum Monsters* - Hayford Peirce  *s*  4276
*Profiteer* - S. Andrew Swann  *s*  5366
*Proteus in the Underworld* - Charles
   Sheffield  *s*  4962
*Red Genesis* - S.C. Sykes  *s*  5377
*Red Mars* - Kim Stanley Robinson  *s*  4635
*Red Planet Run* - Dana Stabenow  *s*  5187
*River of Dust* - Alexander Jablokov  *s*  2840
*The Season of Passage* - Christopher Pike  *h*  4331
*Solis* - A.A. Attanasio  *s*  272
*The Specialist* - Wynne Whiteford  *s*  5788
*Taylor's Ark* - Jody Lynn Nye  *s*  4176
*A Thunder on Neptune* - Gordon Eklund  *s*  1768
*Total Recall* - Piers Anthony  *s*  193
*Voyage to the Red Planet* - Terry Bisson  *s*  508
*Voyager* - Stephen Baxter  *s*  406

*Warstrider: Netlink* - William H. Keith Jr.  *s*  3038
*White Moon, Red Dragon* - David
   Wingrove  *s*  5921
*The White Mountain* - David Wingrove  *s*  5922
*The Winds of Mars* - H.M. Hoover  *s*  2765

**Arsia Station**
*Labyrinth of Night* - Allen Steele  *s*  5244

**Bitter Waters**
*Red Dust* - Paul J. McAuley  *s*  3715

**City**
*Labyrinth of Night* - Allen Steele  *s*  5244

**Cydonia Base**
*Labyrinth of Night* - Allen Steele  *s*  5244
*Semper Mars* - Ian Douglas  *s*  1585

**Paris**
*Dead Boys* - Richard Calder  *s*  836

**Phobos**
*High Moon* - Diane Duane  *s*  1661
*Mars Underground* - William Hartmann  *s*  2584

**Red Sands City**
*Kaleidoscope Century* - John Barnes  *s*  352

**South Colony**
*Red Planet* - Robert A. Heinlein  *s*  2647

**Syrtis Minor**
*Red Planet* - Robert A. Heinlein  *s*  2647

**Tharsis Montes**
*Man Plus* - Frederik Pohl  *s*  4348

**Xin Beijing**
*Red Dust* - Paul J. McAuley  *s*  3715

## MARTINIQUE

**Trinite**
*Angelique's Descent* - Lara Parker  *h*  4246

## MEDITERRANEAN

**I'lli Du Levant**
*Glory Road* - Robert A. Heinlein  *f*  2644

## MERCURY

*Blue Mars* - Kim Stanley Robinson  *s*  4629
*Matrix Cubed* - Britton Bloom  *s*  554

## MEXICO

*Blood Sport* - Lisa Smedman  *f*  5096
*The Earth Remembers* - Susan Torian Olan  *s*  4209
*The Fourth Guardian* - Ronald Anthony
   Cross  *s*  1273
*The Further Adventures of Batman 2: Featuring the
   Penguin* - Martin H. Greenberg  *s*  2391
*Montezuma Strip* - Alan Dean Foster  *s*  2011
*Senora Rodriguez and Other Worlds* - Martha
   Cerda  *f*  950
*Stranded!* - Warren Norwood  *s*  4164
*The Turing Option* - Harry Harrison  *s*  2579

**Aztlan Free Zone**
*Above the Lower Sky* - Tom Deitz  *f*  1469

**Baja California**
*The Merlin Effect* - T.A. Barron  *f*  371

**Casas Grandes**
*Spirits of the Ordinary* - Kathleen Alcala  *f*  52

**Huevos Verdes**
*Beggars and Choosers* - Nancy Kress  *s*  3236

**Mazatlan**
*Tropic of Orange* - Karen Tei Yamashita  *f*  6009

**Mexico City**
*High Aztec* - Ernest Hogan  *s*  2722

**Nuevo Laredo**
*Heavy Weather* - Bruce Sterling  *s*  5258

**Portobello**
*Forever Peace* - Joe Haldeman  *s*  2488

**Saltillo**
*Spirits of the Ordinary* - Kathleen Alcala  *f*  52

**Xitaclan**
*Ruins* - Kevin J. Anderson  *h*  112

## MIDDLE EAST

*The Adventures of Huru on the Road to Baghdad* -
   Guneli Gun  *f*  2457
*Ahmed and the Oblivion Machines* - Ray
   Bradbury  *f*  618
*Aladdin: Master of the Lamp* - Mike
   Resnick  *f*  4534
*Arabian Nights: The Marvels and Wonders of the
   Thousand and One Nights* - Jack Zipes  *f*  6087
*The Autobiography of Santa Claus: It's Better to Give*
   - Jeff Guinn  *f*  2456
*A Bad Day for Ali Baba* - Craig Shaw
   Gardner  *f*  2123
*Dark Prince* - David Gemmell  *f*  2187
*Death in Delhi* - Gary Gygax  *f*  2473
*A Diversity of Dragons* - Anne McCaffrey  *f*  3728
*The Djinn in the Nightingale's Eye* - A.S.
   Byatt  *f*  794
*The Hashish Man and Other Stories by Lord Dunsany*
   - Lord Dunsany  *f*  1700
*The Hunters' Haunt* - Dave Duncan  *f*  1681
*The Last Arabian Night* - Craig Shaw
   Gardner  *f*  2129
*Lord of the Two Lands* - Judith Tarr  *f*  5395
*The Mask of Loki* - Roger Zelazny  *f*  6071
*Master of Many Treasures* - Mary Brown  *f*  726
*The Memory Cathedral* - Jack Dann  *s*  1341
*The Notorious Abbess* - Vera Chapman  *f*  965
*Whose Song Is Sung* - Frank Schaefer  *f*  4872
*Wishing Season* - Esther Friesner  *f*  2085

**Acre**
*The Dagger and the Cross: A Novel of the Crusades* -
   Judith Tarr  *f*  5393

**Baghdad**
*The Last Voyage of Somebody the Sailor* - John
   Barth  *f*  374
*The Other Sinbad* - Craig Shaw Gardner  *f*  2130

**Jebusai, Canaan**
*Jericho Moon* - Matthew Woodring Stover  *f*  5321

**Jerusalem**
*Alamut* - Judith Tarr  *f*  5390
*Corrupting Dr. Nice* - John Kessel  *s*  3083
*Cross and Crescent* - Susan Shwartz  *f*  5014

**Khuruchabja**
*Looking for the Mahdi* - N. Lee Wood  *s*  5966

**Nok Kuzlat**
*Looking for the Mahdi* - N. Lee Wood  *s*  5966

**Sumer**
*To the Land of the Living* - Robert
   Silverberg  *f*  5044

**Tyre**
*Crusader's Torch* - Chelsea Quinn Yarbro  *h*  6015

## MONGOLIA

*The Yngling and the Circle of Power* - John
   Dalmas  *s*  1328

## MONTENEGRO

*The Alien Dark* - Diana G. Gallagher  *s*  2108
*Beamriders!* - Martin Caidin  *s*  824
*Carve the Sky* - Alexander Jablokov  *s*  2836
*Century 21* - Ewa Kuryluk  *s*  3263
*Cowboy Feng's Space Bar and Grille* - Steven
   Brust  *s*  740
*Dark Genesis* - J. Gregory Keyes  *s*  3096
*Deepdrive* - Alexander Jablokov  *s*  2837
*Dreams of Gods and Men* - W.T. Quick  *s*  4451
*The Eighth Rank* - David D. Ross  *s*  4682
*Empire Builders* - Ben Bova  *s*  584
*Fisherman's Hope* - David Feintuch  *s*  1900
*Flare* - Roger Zelazny  *s*  6065
*Flatlander* - Larry Niven  *s*  4121
*The Fleet of Stars* - Poul Anderson  *s*  126
*The Fortress of Utopia* - Jack Williamson  *s*  5863
*Griffin's Egg* - Michael Swanwick  *s*  5370
*Growing Up Weightless* - John M. Ford  *s*  1970
*The Hammer of God* - Arthur C. Clarke  *s*  1057
*Hammer of Mars* - M.S. Murdock  *s*  4049
*Harvest of Stars* - Poul Anderson  *s*  127
*Heads* - Greg Bear  *s*  419
*The Long Run* - Daniel Keys Moran  *s*  3995
*Moonseed* - Stephen Baxter  *s*  400
*Moonwar* - Ben Bova  *s*  588
*Mutant Star* - Karen Haber  *s*  2475
*Mutineers' Moon* - David Weber  *s*  5677
*Nanoware Time/The Persistence of Vision* - Ian
   Watson  *s*  5638
*Peace on Earth* - Stanislaw Lem  *s*  3435
*The Pure Cold Light* - Gregory Frost  *s*  2087
*Roverandom* - J.R.R. Tolkien  *f*  5479
*Satellite Night News* - Jack Hopkins  *s*  2770
*Signal to Noise* - Eric S. Nylund  *s*  4179
*Star Brothers* - Ben Bova  *s*  594
*Steel Beach* - John Varley  *s*  5566
*Target* - Janet Morris  *s*  4017
*Thunder Strike!* - Michael McCollum  *s*  3772
*Tower of the Gods* - Thomas A. Easton  *s*  1726
*The Transmigration of Souls* - William
   Barton  *s*  382
*The Voices of Heaven* - Frederik Pohl  *s*  4356

**Clavius Base**
*Lifeline* - Kevin J. Anderson  *s*  111

**Columbus Base**
*Assemblers of Infinity* - Kevin J. Anderson  *s*  100

**Copernicus**
*The Multiplex Man* - James P. Hogan  *s*  2727
*Second Star* - Dana Stabenow  *s*  5188

**Daedalus Crater**
*Assemblers of Infinity* - Kevin J. Anderson  *s*  100

**Descartes Station**
*Lunar Descent* - Allen Steele  *s*  5245

**Fun City**
*The Man in the Moon Must Die* - Jeff
   Bredenberg  *s*  665

**Hipparchus**
*Double Planet* - John Gribbin  *s*  2433

**Hydra Square**
*Harvest the Fire* - Poul Anderson  *s*  128

**King City**
*The Golden Globe* - John Varley  *s*  5565

**LB-13**
*In the Wrong Hands* - Edward Gibson  *s*  2215

**Luna**
*Freeware* - Rudy Rucker  *s*  4703
*To Save the Sun* - Ben Bova  *s*  596

**Luna City**
*The Moon Is a Harsh Mistress* - Robert A.
   Heinlein  *s*  2645

**Lunaplex**
*Lunar Justice* - Charles L. Harness  *s*  2545

**Moonbase**
*Moonfall* - Jack McDevitt  *s*  3789
*Moonrise* - Ben Bova  *s*  587

**Moonbase Vegas**
*The Six Families* - Nancy Holder  *s*  2733

**Ontario Base**
*The Rising* - James Doohan  *s*  1579

**Port Bowen**
*The Stars Are Also Fire* - Poul Anderson  *s*  134

**Schiaparelli, Luna**
*Take Back Plenty* - Colin Greenland  *s*  2419

**Tycho South Shore**
*The Oxygen Barons* - Gregory Feeley  *s*  1897

**U.N. Base**
*Stranger Suns* - George Zebrowski  *s*  6060

**Zamok Vysoki**
*The Stars Are Also Fire* - Poul Anderson  *s*  134

## MOON—IMAGINARY

**Amalthea**
*The Diamond Moon* - Paul Preuss  *s*  4417

**Anee**
*Serpent Catch* - Dave Wolverton  *s*  5956

**Dark Man's Moon**
*Sky Trillium* - Julian May  *f*  3700

**Davonia**
*Devil in the Sky* - Greg Cox  *s*  1226

**God's World**
*God's World* - Ian Watson  *s*  5636

**Haven**
*Blood Feuds* - S.M. Stirling  *s*  5292

**Hisagazi, Yarzik Island**
*The Longest Voyage/Slow Lightning* - Poul
   Anderson  *s*  130

**Kahani**
*Haroun and the Sea of Stories* - Salman
   Rushdie  *f*  4731

**Minor Base**
*Alien Influences* - Kristine Kathryn Rusch  *s*  4711

**Ocypete**
*Iris* - William Barton  *s*  381

**Oz**
*The Engines of God* - Jack McDevitt  *s*  3787

**Ptero**
*Faun & Games* - Piers Anthony  *f*  169
*Zombie Lover* - Piers Anthony  *f*  197

**Quintaglio Home World**
*Far-Seer* - Robert J. Sawyer  *s*  4854
*Fossil Hunter* - Robert J. Sawyer  *s*  4855

**Yavin Four**
*The Lost City of the Jedi* - Paul Davids  *s*  1393

**Zulu**
*Ocean under the Ice* - Robert L. Forward  *s*  1988

**Zuni**
*Marooned on Eden* - Robert L. Forward　*s*　1986

## MOROCCO

*The Tattooed Map* - Barbara Hodgson　*f*　2706

**Marrakesh**
*The Broken Sword* - Molly Cochran　*f*　1091
*The Colors of Hell* - Michael Paine　*h*　4234

**Taroudannt**
*The Safety of Unknown Cities* - Lucy
　Taylor　*h*　5414

## MOZAMBIQUE

**Lake Cabora Bassa**
*A Girl Named Disaster* - Nancy Farmer　*f*　1868

## MYANMAR

*Gold Dragon* - Robert Cain　*s*　831

**Rangoon**
*John Dollar* - Marianne Wiggins　*h*　5799

## MYTHICAL PLACE

*Blood Lines* - William R. Burkett Jr.　*s*　774
*The Broken Goddess* - Hans Bemmann　*f*　439
*The Cornish Trilogy* - Robertson Davies　*f*　1397
*Dark Lord of Derkholm* - Diana Wynne
　Jones　*f*　2946
*Flight of the Dragon Kyn* - Susan Fletcher　*f*　1951
*Fortress of Frost and Fire* - Mercedes
　Lackey　*f*　3282
*Harry Potter and the Sorcerer's Stone* - J.K.
　Rowling　*f*　4700
*The Hashish Man and Other Stories by Lord Dunsany*
　- Lord Dunsany　*f*　1700
*Here There Be Dragons* - Roger Zelazny　*f*　6069
*In the Red Lord's Reach* - Phyllis
　Eisenstein　*f*　1765
*Liar's Oath* - Elizabeth Moon　*f*　3969
*Little Sister* - Kara Dalkey　*f*　1320
*Monet's Ghost* - Chelsea Quinn Yarbro　*f*　6017
*Mostly Harmless* - Douglas Adams　*s*　31
*The Panther's Hoard* - Nancy Varian
　Berberick　*f*　458
*Ronin* - D.A. Heeley　*f*　2639
*The Secret Weavers: Stories of the Fantastic by Latin
　American Women* - Marjorie Agosin　*f*　43
*Spires of Spirit* - Gael Baudino　*f*　395
*To the Land of the Living* - Robert
　Silverberg　*f*　5044
*Typewriter in the Sky* - L. Ron Hubbard　*f*　2791
*The Unicorn Solution* - John Lee　*f*　3400
*The Wild Road* - Gabriel King　*f*　3120

**Abbey of St. Leibowitz**
*Saint Leibowitz and the Wild Horse Woman* - Walter
　M. Miller Jr.　*s*　3908

**Addams Family Mansion**
*Addams Family Values* - Todd Strasser　*f*　5324

**Aerith**
*The Master of Whitestorm* - Janny Wurts　*f*　6003

**The Afterlife**
*Tex and Molly in the Afterlife* - Richard
　Grant　*f*　2327

**The Afterworlds**
*The Friendship Song* - Nancy Springer　*f*　5179

**Allanmere**
*Shadow Hunt* - Anne Logston　*f*　3514

**Altai Valley**
*Winged Magic* - Mary H. Herbert　*f*　2678

**Amazina**
*The Ultimate Bike Path* - Michael B. Sirota　*s*　5076

**Ambermere**
*The Door to Ambermere* - J. Calvin Pierce　*f*　4316
*The Wizard of Ambermere* - J. Calvin Pierce　*f*　4317

**Anauroch**
*The Parched Sea* - Troy Denning　*f*　1486

**Arcady**
*Arcady* - Michael Williams　*f*　5818

**Asgard**
*The Tower of Beowulf* - Parke Godwin　*f*　2250

**Asterman's Wood**
*Nameless Magery* - Delia Marshall Turner　*f*　5490

**Astral Plane**
*The Fourth Guardian* - Ronald Anthony
　Cross　*s*　1273

**Athas**
*The Verdant Passage* - Troy Denning　*f*　1487

**Athilan**
*Letters From Atlantis* - Robert Silverberg　*f*　5035

**Atlantis**
*World Without End* - Molly Cochran　*f*　1093

**Avalon**
*The Dragon and the Unicorn* - A.A.
　Attanasio　*f*　266
*The Wolf and the Crown* - A.A. Attanasio　*f*　273

**Baloran's Keep**
*Shadow Hunt* - Anne Logston　*f*　3514

**Beast's Palace**
*Rose Daughter* - Robin McKinley　*f*　3847

**Bellwoods**
*Son of Spellsinger* - Alan Dean Foster　*f*　2015

**Beltrevan**
*Wrath of Ashar* - Angus Wells　*f*　5742

**Birds Home**
*Commitment Hour* - James Alan Gardner　*s*　2134

**Black Oak Mall**
*Mall Purchase Night* - Rick Cook　*f*　1159

**Blodgett's Crossing**
*Jeremy Thatcher, Dragon Hatcher* - Bruce
　Coville　*f*　1221

**Blue Forest**
*Wheel of Dreams* - Salinda Tyson　*f*　5529

**Blue Mountain**
*Captives of the Blue Mountain* - Wendy
　Pini　*f*　4336
*Master of Many Treasures* - Mary Brown　*f*　726

**Borderland**
*Borderland* - Terri Windling　*f*　5913
*The Essential Bordertown* - Terri Windling　*f*　5914
*Finder* - Emma Bull　*f*　769
*Nevernever* - Will Shetterly　*f*　4995

**Camp Chippewa**
*Addams Family Values* - Todd Strasser　*f*　5324

**Carthell Abbey**
*The Robin and the Kestrel* - Mercedes
　Lackey　*f*　3293

**Castle Elfwood**
*Elfwood* - Rose Estes　*f*　1837

**Castle Fox**
*Prince of the North* - Harry Turtledove　*f*　5509

**Castle Frankenstein**
*The Ultimate Bike Path* - Michael B. Sirota　*s*　5076

**Castle Harvell**
*The Baker's Boy* - J.V. Jones　*f*　2956

**Castle Midnight**
*Blood and Honor* - Simon R. Green　*f*　2361

**Caverns of Cytorax**
*Another Day, Another Dungeon* - Greg
　Costikyan　*f*　1206

**Chaos**
*An Enemy Reborn* - Michael A. Stackpole　*f*　5197

**Chateau "Howliday Inn" Bow-Wow**
*Return to Howliday Inn* - James Howe　*f*　2786

**Chaumenard**
*The Book of Atrix Wolfe* - Patricia A.
　McKillip　*f*　3838

**The Citadel**
*The Wizard at Home* - Rick Shelley　*f*　4975

**The Citadel of Wizards**
*Dog Wizard* - Barbara Hambly　*f*　2503

**The City**
*Suisan* - Phyllis Carol Agins　*f*　42

**Costard's Superior Mine**
*The Mines of Behemoth* - Michael Shea　*f*　4945

**Count Volmar's Castle**
*Castle of Deception* - Mercedes Lackey　*f*　3275

**Covamere**
*Dragoncharm* - Graham Edwards　*f*　1749

**The Crossroads**
*What Savage Beast* - Peter David　*s*　1390

**Crystal Keep**
*Guardian's Key* - Anne Logston　*f*　3511

**Danda-Vana Forest**
*The Iron Ring* - Lloyd Alexander　*f*　68

**Dark Heart**
*Dark Heart* - Betsy James　*f*　2857

**Dark Horse Plains**
*City of the Sorcerers* - Mary H. Herbert　*f*　2673
*Lightning's Daughter* - Mary H. Herbert　*f*　2676

**Darkhorn Mountains**
*Valorian* - Mary H. Herbert　*f*　2677

**Darkon**
*King of the Dead* - Gene DeWeese　*h*　1510

**Darwinia**
*Darwinia* - Robert Charles Wilson　*s*　5906

**Dead Lands**
*Groogleman* - Debra Doyle　*s*　1600

**Delta**
*The Sorceress and the Cygnet* - Patricia A.
　McKillip　*f*　3842

**Desolate Mountains**
*Dragon Cauldron* - Laurence Yep　*f*　6024

**Dim Reaches**
*Shadow Dance* - Anne Logston　*f*　3513

**D'ni**
*Myst: The Book of D'ni* - Rand Miller　*f*　3897

**The Down**
*Tales From Watership Down* - Richard Adams　*f*　32

**Dragon Realm**
*Dragon Rigger* - Jeffrey A. Carver　*s*　929

**Dragoncastle**
*Lords of the Sky* - Angus Wells   *f*   5738

**Dragonclaw**
*The Witches of Eileanan* - Kate Forsyth   *f*   1984

**The Drake Kingdoms**
*The Dragon Crown* - Richard A. Knaak   *f*   3168

**Drakmil**
*Kar Kalim* - Deborah Christian   *f*   1025

**The Dreaming**
*The Sandman: Book of Dreams* - Neil
   Gaiman   *f*   2105

**Dreamland**
*Waking in Dreamland* - Jody Lynn Nye   *f*   4177

**Egg Mountain**
*Dragon War* - Laurence Yep   *f*   6025

**Eight Planes of the Matrix**
*Justice* - David Drake   *s*   1635

**Eigo**
*Battledragon* - Christopher Rowley   *f*   4691

**Eldh**
*Beyond the Pale* - Mark Anthony   *f*   153

**Elfland**
*A Child of Elvish* - Nancy Varian Berberick   *f*   457
*The Cup of Morning Shadows* - Rosemary
   Edghill   *f*   1747
*Thomas the Rhymer* - Ellen Kushner   *f*   3265

**Elfwood**
*Elfwood* - Rose Estes   *f*   1837
*Twisted Dragon* - Kevin Stein   *f*   5251

**Elphame**
*The Cup of Morning Shadows* - Rosemary
   Edghill   *f*   1747
*The Sword of Maiden's Tears* - Rosemary
   Edghill   *f*   1748

**Emerald Mountains**
*Roc and a Hard Place* - Piers Anthony   *f*   187

**Empire of the Axe**
*The War God's Own* - David Weber   *f*   5682

**Enchanted Forest**
*Calling on Dragons* - Patricia C. Wrede   *f*   5974
*Dealing with Dragons* - Patricia C. Wrede   *f*   5975
*Mirror of Destiny* - Andre Norton   *f*   4159
*Searching for Dragons* - Patricia C. Wrede   *f*   5979

**Enlightenment**
*The Magic Touch* - Jody Lynn Nye   *f*   4171

**Evermeet**
*The Coral Kingdom* - Douglas Niles   *f*   4106

**Eyrie**
*Jovah's Angel* - Sharon Shinn   *s*   5001

**Faerie**
*Child of Faerie, Child of Earth* - Josepha
   Sherman   *f*   4985
*The Dragon's Dagger* - R.A. Salvatore   *f*   4797
*Dragonslayer's Return* - R.A. Salvatore   *f*   4798
*Dreamseeker's Road* - Tom Deitz   *f*   1472
*The Hero King* - Rick Shelley   *f*   4970
*The Rebirth of Wonder* - Lawrence Watt-
   Evans   *f*   5646
*The Reign of the Brown Magician* - Lawrence Watt-
   Evans   *f*   5647
*A Strange and Ancient Name* - Josepha
   Sherman   *f*   4991
*Sunshaker's War* - Tom Deitz   *f*   1477
*The Woods out Back* - R.A. Salvatore   *f*   4809

**Faerun's Underdark**
*Siege of Darkness* - R.A. Salvatore   *f*   4804

**Faery**
*A Knight Among Knaves* - Robert N.
   Charrette   *f*   974

**Fair Peril**
*Fair Peril* - Nancy Springer   *f*   5178

**Fairy Realm**
*Merlin's Bones* - Fred Saberhagen   *f*   4771

**Fallo**
*Past Imperative* - Dave Duncan   *f*   1684

**Farraglean Ocean**
*Chorus Skating* - Alan Dean Foster   *f*   1998

**Fayre Farre**
*The Kingdom of Kevin Malone* - Suzy McKee
   Charnas   *f*   970

**Feyndala**
*Wrath of the Princes* - Holly Lisle   *f*   3490

**Fishtail Island**
*Thunder of the Captains* - Holly Lisle   *f*   3489

**The Forest**
*Suisan* - Phyllis Carol Agins   *f*   42

**Fortress of the Stone**
*The Arm of the Stone* - Victoria Strauss   *f*   5333

**The Four Lands**
*The Druid of Shannara* - Terry Brooks   *f*   710
*The Scions of Shannara* - Terry Brooks   *f*   716

**Galcen**
*Sailing Bright Eternity* - Gregory Benford   *s*   449

**Galunlati**
*Sunshaker's War* - Tom Deitz   *f*   1477

**Gaugach**
*Faery in Shadow* - C.J. Cherryh   *f*   987

**Ghostwood**
*Nobody's Son* - Sean Stewart   *f*   5275

**Glass Mountain Village**
*Bring Me the Head of Prince Charming* - Roger
   Zelazny   *f*   6062

**Goblin Plain**
*The Goblin Plain War* - Carl Miller   *f*   3892

**The Great Highway**
*Taking Flight* - Lawrence Watt-Evans   *f*   5650

**Green Lord's Realm**
*Beyond the Magic Sphere* - Gail Jarrow   *f*   2879

**Greyhawk**
*Nightwatch* - Robin Wayne Bailey   *f*   289

**Guesclin**
*Hearts and Armor* - Ron Miller   *f*   3903

**Halig-liath**
*The Meri* - Maya Kaathryn Bohnhoff   *f*   561
*Taminy* - Maya Kaathryn Bohnhoff   *f*   563

**Hallow Hills**
*The Son of Summer Stars* - Meredith Ann
   Pierce   *f*   4319

**Heavenly Realm**
*Bronze Mirror* - Jeanne Larsen   *f*   3338

**Hellas**
*Castle Spellbound* - John DeChancie   *s*   1454

**The High Forest**
*Elfsong* - Elaine Cunningham   *f*   1289

**Hyperborea**
*Tales of Zothique* - Clark Ashton Smith   *f*   5104

**Inis Witrin**
*Lady of Avalon* - Marion Zimmer Bradley   *f*   640

**Inner Worlds**
*Witch and Wombat* - Carolyn Cushman   *f*   1299

**Ippa**
*Dragon's Winter* - Elizabeth A. Lynn   *f*   3578

**Isle of Fincayra**
*The Fires of Merlin* - T.A. Barron   *f*   369
*The Lost Years of Merlin* - T.A. Barron   *f*   370
*The Seven Songs of Merlin* - T.A. Barron   *f*   372

**Isles of the Blest**
*The Isles of the Blest* - Morgan Llywelyn   *f*   3505

**Ivy Green Institute**
*Brother to Dragons, Companion to Owls* - Jane M.
   Lindskold   *f*   3473

**Jaive's Fortress**
*Black Unicorn* - Tanith Lee   *f*   3404

**Kilagurri**
*Son of Spellsinger* - Alan Dean Foster   *f*   2015

**Kingdoms of the West**
*Polgara the Sorceress* - David Eddings   *f*   1734

**King's Keep**
*Touched by Magic* - Doranna Durgin   *f*   1705

**Krondor**
*Rise of a Merchant Prince* - Raymond E.
   Feist   *f*   1909

**K'Sheyna Vale**
*Winds of Change* - Mercedes Lackey   *f*   3304
*Winds of Fate* - Mercedes Lackey   *f*   3305

**Kyatawat**
*Wildfire* - Jo Clayton   *f*   1073

**The Labyrinth**
*The Goblin Companion* - Terry Jones   *f*   2980

**Land of Yesterday**
*Tales From Watership Down* - Richard Adams   *f*   32

**Larking Land**
*Lorien Lost* - Michael King   *f*   3124

**Limbo**
*If at Faust You Don't Succeed* - Roger
   Zelazny   *f*   6070

**Luxor Desert**
*The Cygnet and the Firebird* - Patricia A.
   McKillip   *f*   3839

**Lynn Hall**
*Winter Rose* - Patricia A. McKillip   *f*   3843

**M3 Center**
*Days of Cain* - J.R. Dunn   *s*   1694

**Madame F's Toy Museum**
*The Silver Tree* - Ruth L. Williams   *f*   5822

**Madame Koto's Bar**
*Songs of Enchantment* - Ben Okri   *f*   4208

**Mage Towers**
*Metropolitan* - Walter Jon Williams   *s*   5839

**Maggiar**
*The Goblin Mirror* - C.J. Cherryh   *f*   994

**Maho**
*Fish Soup* - Ursula K. Le Guin   *f*   3378

**Mamar's Kingdom**
*Shiva's Challenge: An Adventure of the Ice Age* - J.H.
   Brennan   *f*   668

**Mary's Place**
*The Callahan Touch* - Spider Robinson   *f*   4637

*Callahan's Legacy* - Spider Robinson   s   4639

**Megaverse Mall**
*Night of the Living 'Gator!* - Richard A.
   Lupoff   s   3573
*Night of the Living Rat!* - Debra Doyle   s   1603
*Night of the Living Shark!* - David Bischoff   s   493

**Metaplanes**
*Beyond the Pale* - Jack Koke   f   3198

**The Metaworld**
*Strange Attractors* - Jeffrey A. Carver   s   934

**Midgard**
*The Children of Wrath* - Mickey Zucker
   Reichert   f   4518
*Dragonrank Master* - Mickey Zucker
   Reichert   f   4519

**Midkemia**
*The King's Buccaneer* - Raymond E. Feist   f   1904
*Shadow of a Dark Queen* - Raymond E.
   Feist   f   1911

**Mirwell Province**
*Green Rider* - Kristen Britain   f   692

**The Mist**
*Clouds End* - Sean Stewart   f   5272

**Mithril Hall**
*The Legacy* - R.A. Salvatore   f   4801
*Siege of Darkness* - R.A. Salvatore   f   4804
*Starless Night* - R.A. Salvatore   f   4807

**Moha**
*Fish Soup* - Ursula K. Le Guin   f   3378

**Moodymount**
*A Remembrance for Kedrigern* - John
   Morressy   f   4014

**Moonshae Isles**
*The Coral Kingdom* - Douglas Niles   f   4106

**Mossflower Woods**
*Mattimeo* - Brian Jacques   f   2852
*Outcast of Redwall* - Brian Jacques   f   2853

**The Mound**
*The Moorchild* - Eloise Jarvis McGraw   f   3816

**Mountain Land**
*Fire and Ice* - Edward Myers   f   4061
*The Mountain Made of Light* - Edward
   Myers   f   4062
*The Summit* - Edward Myers   f   4063

**Neitherworld**
*Night of the Living Rat!* - Debra Doyle   s   1603

**Netherworld**
*The Catswold Portal* - Shirley Rousseau
   Murphy   f   4055

**Neverland**
*Hook* - Terry Brooks   f   713

**Nevernever**
*Nevernever* - Will Shetterly   f   4995

**New Asgard**
*The Spawn of Loki* - Jason Henderson   f   2658

**Nifflheim**
*Sleipnir* - Linda Evans   f   1856

**Nilbog**
*Goblins in the Castle* - Bruce Coville   f   1218

**No-Place**
*India's Story* - Kathlyn S. Starbuck   s   5208

**Northlands**
*Fox and Empire* - Harry Turtledove   f   5500

**Novindus**
*The King's Buccaneer* - Raymond E. Feist   f   1904

**Old Shorings**
*Metropolitan* - Walter Jon Williams   s   5839

**Olympus**
*The Kronos Condition* - Emily Devenport   s   1502

**Omara**
*The Gods in Anger* - Adrian Cole   f   1100

**Omphalos**
*/* - Greg Bear   s   413

**One Land**
*The Faithful Traitor* - Robert Don Hughes   f   2809

**The Otherworld**
*The Seven Songs of Merlin* - T.A. Barron   f   372

**Otherworld**
*The Spellkey Trilogy* - Ann Downer   f   1592

**Outworld**
*Mortal Kombat* - Martin Delrio   f   1483

**Over-mountain**
*The Goblin Mirror* - C.J. Cherryh   f   994

**Oz**
*Samurai Cat Goes to the Movies* - Mark E.
   Rogers   s   4656
*Visitors From Oz: The Wild Adventures of Dorothy,
   the Scarecrow and the Tin Woodman* - Martin
   Gardner   f   2136
*Wicked: The Life and Times of the Wicked Witch of
   the West* - Gregory Maguire   f   3609

**Palace of Ease**
*The Hidden Realms* - Sharon Green   f   2358

**Palace of Green Porcelain**
*The Time Ships* - Stephen Baxter   s   403

**The Palace of Spiders**
*Angels & Visitations: A Miscellany* - Neil
   Gaiman   f   2101

**Palace of the Prophets**
*Stone of Tears* - Terry Goodkind   f   2269

**Palasso Grijalva**
*The Golden Key* - Melanie Rawn   f   4486

**Palenoc**
*Brothers of the Dragon* - Robin Wayne
   Bailey   f   286
*Flames of the Dragon* - Robin Wayne Bailey   f   287

**Parramat Archipelago**
*The Howling Stones* - Alan Dean Foster   s   2006

**Pelagiris Forest**
*Owlflight* - Mercedes Lackey   f   3291
*Owlsight* - Mercedes Lackey   f   3292

**The Place of Power**
*A Plague of Angels* - Sheri S. Tepper   f   5433

**The Plane Beyond**
*Tegne: Soul Warrior* - Richard La Plante   f   3268

**Poor Farm Road**
*On Meeting Witches at Wells* - Judith
   Gorog   f   2283

**Rain Wild River**
*The Ship of Magic* - Robin Hobb   f   2696

**Realm of the Sidhe**
*Songs of Earth and Power* - Greg Bear   f   424

**The Realms**
*Song of the Saurials* - Kate Novak   f   4167

**Realms of the Gods**
*The Realms of the Gods* - Tamora Pierce   f   4321

**The River**
*The Blackgod* - J. Gregory Keyes   f   3095

**Ro Holding**
*The Cygnet and the Firebird* - Patricia A.
   McKillip   f   3839
*The Sorceress and the Cygnet* - Patricia A.
   McKillip   f   3842

**Rose Cottage**
*Rose Daughter* - Robin McKinley   f   3847

**Ryetelth**
*Bazil Broketail* - Christopher Rowley   f   4692

**The Ryft**
*The Hands of Lyr* - Andre Norton   f   4154

**Ryhope Wood**
*Gate of Ivory, Gate of Horn* - Robert
   Holdstock   f   2737
*The Hollowing* - Robert Holdstock   f   2738

**Salamandastron**
*The Long Patrol* - Brian Jacques   f   2849
*Salamandastron* - Brian Jacques   f   2855

**Salvation**
*Exile's Challenge* - Angus Wells   f   5734
*Exile's Children* - Angus Wells   f   5735

**Seaharrow**
*War* - Simon Hawke   f   2625

**The Second Ether**
*The War Amongst the Angels* - Michael
   Moorcock   f   3986

**Seventh Gate**
*The Seventh Gate* - Margaret Weis   f   5727

**Shadow Land**
*The Grail and the Ring* - Teresa Edgerton   f   1744

**The Shadowlands**
*The Changeling* - Kristine Kathryn Rusch   f   4714

**Shilmista**
*In Sylvan Shadows* - R.A. Salvatore   f   4800

**Sidh**
*Legends Reborn* - Kenneth C. Flint   f   1958

**Skull Hill**
*The Robin and the Kestrel* - Mercedes
   Lackey   f   3293

**Sligo Woods**
*The Higher Space* - Jamil Nasir   s   4070

**Snowflake Mountains**
*Canticle* - R.A. Salvatore   f   4793

**Sorrow's End**
*The Quest Begins* - Wendy Pini   f   4337

**The Sphere, the Realm**
*The Revenge of the Rose* - Michael
   Moorcock   f   3985

**Spine of the World**
*The Silent Blade* - R.A. Salvatore   f   4805

**The Spiral**
*Cloud Castles* - Michael Scott Rohan   f   4659
*The Gates of Noon* - Michael Scott Rohan   f   4661

**Spirit Lake**
*Shadow Dance* - Anne Logston   f   3513
*Shadow Hunt* - Anne Logston   f   3514

**The Spiritworld**
*Trader* - Charles de Lint   f   1438

**Stygia**
*The Ebon Mask* - Richard Lee Byers   h   797

**Tara**
*Wolfking* - Bridget Wood   f   5963

**Telgar**
*Dragonseye* - Anne McCaffrey   s   3730

**Temple of the Moon**
*Tegne: Soul Warrior* - Richard La Plante   f   3268

**Ten Nations**
*The World of Robert Jordan's The Wheel of Time* - Robert Jordan   f   2991

**Terahnee**
*Myst: The Book of D'ni* - Rand Miller   f   3897

**Termalaine, Maer Dualdon**
*Sojourn* - R.A. Salvatore   f   4806

**the River Bank**
*The Willows and Beyond* - William Horwood   f   2775

**Thlassa Mey**
*Across the Thlassa Mey* - Dennis McCarty   f   3765
*The Birth of the Blade* - Dennis McCarty   f   3766

**The Three Kingdoms**
*The Usurper* - Angus Wells   f   5739
*Wrath of Ashar* - Angus Wells   f   5742

**Tir-Nan-Og**
*Landslayer's Law* - Tom Deitz   f   1474

**Titan's Dimension**
*Evil Triumphant* - Michael A. Stackpole   s   5199

**Toad Hall**
*The Willows and Beyond* - William Horwood   f   2775

**Toad-in-a-Cage Castle**
*Goblins in the Castle* - Bruce Coville   f   1218

**Tower of Urtho**
*Storm Breaking* - Mercedes Lackey   f   3296

**Tuscan**
*Planar Powers* - J. Robert King   f   3122

**Twenty Kingdoms**
*Four & Twenty Blackbirds* - Mercedes Lackey   f   3283

**Ultimate Bike Path**
*The Ultimate Bike Path* - Michael B. Sirota   s   5076

**Under the Hill**
*Steel Rose* - Kara Dalkey   f   1321
*A Wizard Abroad* - Diane Duane   f   1668

**The Underdark**
*Daughter of the Drow* - Elaine Cunningham   f   1287
*Starless Night* - R.A. Salvatore   f   4807

**The Underground**
*Ye Gods!* - Tom Holt   f   2753

**Underhill**
*Spiritride* - Mark Shepherd   f   4981

**Undermoment**
*The Last Human* - Tom De Haven   f   1422

**The Underworld**
*Wizard's First Rule* - Terry Goodkind   f   2271

**The Unformed**
*Chrome Circle* - Mercedes Lackey   f   3277

**Unseelie lands**
*Bedlam Boyz* - Ellen Guon   f   2467

**Uriat Mountains**
*Emerald House Rising* - Peg Kerr   f   3080

**Valhalla**
*Sleipnir* - Linda Evans   f   1856

**Valhalla Outpost Facility**
*Bright Messengers* - Gentry Lee   s   3398

**Valley of Great Trees**
*The Gates of Vensunor* - Carol Heller   f   2650

**Villa Nightmare**
*The Night of Wishes: Or, The Satanarchaeolidealcohellish Notion Potion* - Michael Ende   f   1821

**The Watershed**
*A Breach in the Watershed* - Douglas Niles   f   4105
*Darkenheight* - Douglas Niles   f   4107
*War of the Three Waters* - Douglas Niles   f   4110

**The Weald**
*The Wealdwife's Tale* - Paul Hazel   f   2636

**Westwoods**
*The Stone of Time* - Rose Estes   f   1840

**Wild Road**
*The Wild Road* - Gabriel King   f   3120

**Winding Circle Temple**
*Tris's Book* - Tamora Pierce   f   4322

**Windrose Island**
*Dragon's Plunder* - Brad Strickland   f   5336

**Wizard's Hall**
*Wizard's Hall* - Jane Yolen   f   6043

**Wizard's High**
*Pyromancer* - Don Callander   f   847

**Wizard's Keep**
*The Wizardry Quested* - Rick Cook   f   1163

**Woofburg**
*Pet Store* - M.T. Coffin   h   1097

**World of the Barbed Coil**
*The Barbed Coil* - J.V. Jones   f   2957

**World of the Fey**
*Merlin's Harp* - Anne Eliot Crompton   f   1270

**World of the Grey**
*King of the Grey* - Richard A. Knaak   f   3173

**Zeln's Castle**
*Nightseer* - Laurell K. Hamilton   f   2521

**Zothique**
*Tales of Zothique* - Clark Ashton Smith   f   5104

## NEPAL

*Snowmen* - Jerry Earl Brown   s   725

**Kathmandu**
*Escape From Kathmandu* - Kim Stanley Robinson   s   4630

**Katmandu**
*Threshold* - Bill Myers   s   4060

## NEPTUNE

*A Thunder on Neptune* - Gordon Eklund   s   1768

**Triton**
*The Infinite Sea* - Jeffrey A. Carver   s   932
*Neptune Crossing* - Jeffrey A. Carver   s   933

## NETHERLANDS

*Child of the Journey* - Janet Berliner   f   466

**Amsterdam**
*Children of the Vampire* - Jeanne Kalogridis   h   3003

*The Final Diary Entry of Kees Huijgens* - William R. Stotler   h   5317
*Frisk* - Dennis Cooper   h   1170
*The Nature of Smoke* - Anne Harris   s   2559
*Signal to Noise* - Eric S. Nylund   s   4179

**The Hague**
*Blameless in Abaddon* - James Morrow   f   4029

## NEW ZEALAND

*The Juniper Game* - Sherryl Jordan   f   2992

**North Island**
*Earth* - David Brin   s   685

## NICARAGUA

*Solo* - Robert Mason   s   3665

**Managua**
*Tek Power* - William Shatner   s   4937

## NORTH AMERICA

*Ark Liberty* - Will Bradley   s   656
*Beyond Eden* - J.M. Morgan   s   3999
*Children of Enchantment* - Anne Kelleher Bush   f   787
*Dawn's Uncertain Light* - Neal Barrett Jr.   s   365
*The Dechronization of Sam Magruder* - George Gaylord Simpson   s   5067
*End of an Era* - Robert J. Sawyer   s   4853
*Fine Prey* - Scott Westerfeld   s   5766
*Future Eden* - J.M. Morgan   s   4001
*The Ghost of the Revelator* - L.E. Modesitt Jr.   s   3931
*The Great War: American Front* - Harry Turtledove   s   5501
*How Few Remain* - Harry Turtledove   s   5504
*In the Company of the Mind* - Steven Piziks   s   4339
*Into the Deep* - Ken Grimwood   s   2450
*Invitation to the Game* - Monica Hughes   s   2807
*The Key to the Indian* - Lynne Reid Banks   f   331
*Kindred Rites* - Katharine Eliska Kimbriel   f   3118
*The Lanterns of God* - Ron Sarti   s   4835
*Legacy of the Ancients* - Ron Sarti   s   4836
*The Lizard War* - John Dalmas   s   1325
*Madoc's Hundred* - Pat Winter   f   5925
*Mind Snare* - Gayle Greeno   s   2422
*People of the Earth* - W. Michael Gear   f   2166
*Phoenix Cafe* - Gwyneth Jones   s   2954
*Predator* - William F. Wu   s   5998
*Raptor Red* - Robert T. Bakker   f   306
*Resurrection Man* - Sean Stewart   f   5277
*Return to Isis* - Jean Stewart   s   5268
*Saber & Shadow* - S.M. Stirling   f   5297
*The Sacred Stones* - William Sarabande   f   4818
*Search and Destroy* - Keith William Andrews   s   141
*Traitors from Within* - R.A. Montgomery   s   3966
*The Transall Saga* - Gary Paulsen   s   4262
*Wanderer* - Donald E. McQuinn   s   3862
*War of the Worlds: Global Dispatches* - Kevin J. Anderson   s   119
*Winterlong* - Elizabeth Hand   s   2539
*The Wishing Well* - Charles de Lint   f   1441
*Witch* - Donald E. McQuinn   s   3864
*Yesterday We Saw Mermaids* - Esther Friesner   f   2086

**Adirondack Mountains**
*Dawn Land* - Joseph Bruchac   f   731

**Blue Ridge Mountains**
*The Dream Vessel* - Jeff Bredenberg   s   664

**Cahokia**
*People of the River* - W. Michael Gear   f   2168

**Devil's Mountain**
*Christmas Slaughter* - Mark Grant   s   2323

**Fishtown, The Sprawl**
*Rememory* - John Gregory Betancourt   s   481

**Hudson River Valley**
*Dawn Land* - Joseph Bruchac   f   731

**Montezuma Strip**
*Montezuma Strip* - Alan Dean Foster   s   2011

**New San Francisco**
*Christmas Slaughter* - Mark Grant   s   2323

**New Seattle**
*Escape to the Wind* - Jennifer DiMarco   s   1559

**Northern Plains**
*Crow and Weasel* - Barry Lopez   f   3523

**Pittsburgh**
*Faraday's Orphans* - N. Lee Wood   s   5965

**Sierra Nevada Mountains**
*People of the Sea* - W. Michael Gear   f   2169

**Vinland**
*The Ice-Shirt* - William T. Vollmann   f   5580


**GREAT LAKES**

*People of the Lakes* - Kathleen O'Neal Gear   f   2164


**GREAT PLAINS**

*The Edge of the World* - William Sarabande   f   4817
*Saint Leibowitz and the Wild Horse Woman* - Walter
   M. Miller Jr.   s   3908
*Snow Brother* - S.M. Stirling   f   5299
*Thunder in the Sky* - William Sarabande   f   4819
*Touching the Fire* - Roger Welsch   f   5751


**MISSISSIPPI RIVER**

*Eternity Road* - Jack McDevitt   s   3788

## NORWAY

*Dragon's Domain* - Thorarinn Gunnarsson   f   2461
*People of the Fire* - W. Michael Gear   f   2167
*The Queen of Darkness* - Miguel Conner   s   1134

## OUTER SPACE

*Action Stations* - William R. Forstchen   s   1976
*Aggressor Six* - Wil McCarthy   s   3760
*Alien Dreams* - Larry Segriff   s   4910
*Aliens: The Female War* - Steve Perry   s   4290
*All Good Things...* - Michael Jan Friedman   s   2061
*Alpha Centauri* - William Barton   s   378
*The Armageddon Inheritance* - David
   Weber   s   5668
*Arrow From Earth* - F.M. Busby   s   782
*Battlestation* - David Drake   s   1627
*Before the Storm* - Michael P. Kube-
   McDowell   s   3247
*Being Alien* - Rebecca Ore   s   4217
*Berserker Fury* - Fred Saberhagen   s   4760
*Berserker Kill* - Fred Saberhagen   s   4761
*Best Destiny* - Diane Carey   s   900
*Better than Life* - Grant Naylor   s   4076
*Beyond the Fall of Night* - Arthur C. Clarke   s   1054
*Beyond the Void* - Sean Dalton   s   1331
*Blind Justice* - S.N. Lewitt   s   3448
*The Boat of a Million Years* - Poul Anderson   s   125
*Border Dispute* - Daniel R. Kerns   s   3066
*Bright Angel* - John Blair   s   512
*A Call to Arms* - Alan Dean Foster   s   1995
*Challenger's Hope* - David Feintuch   s   1899

*Children of the Jedi* - Barbara Hambly   s   2500
*The Clone Crisis* - Lee McKeone   s   3829
*Cowboy Feng's Space Bar and Grille* - Steven
   Brust   s   740
*Crashlander* - Larry Niven   s   4118
*A Darker Geometry* - Mark O. Martin   s   3649
*The Death and Life of Superman* - Roger
   Stern   s   5262
*The Death of Sleep* - Anne McCaffrey   s   3727
*The Defiance* - Bill Baldwin   s   310
*Diplomatic Act* - Peter Jurasik   s   2996
*Don't Forget Your Spacesuit, Dear* - Jody Lynn
   Nye   s   4169
*Double Planet* - John Gribbin   s   2433
*Douglas Adams's Starship Titanic* - Terry
   Jones   s   2979
*Dreadnought* - Thorarinn Gunnarsson   s   2464
*Drifter's Run* - William C. Dietz   s   1544
*Earthfall* - Jerry Earl Brown   s   724
*Earthfall* - Orson Scott Card   s   885
*Encounter with Tiber* - Buzz Aldrin   s   64
*The Eternal Enemy* - Michael Berlyn   s   469
*Eternal Light* - Paul J. McAuley   s   3710
*Expansion* - Peter F. Hamilton   s   2525
*Fall of Angels* - L.E. Modesitt Jr.   f   3930
*Final Diagnosis* - James White   s   5777
*First Strike* - Diane Carey   s   903
*Fisherman's Hope* - David Feintuch   s   1900
*Flare* - Roger Zelazny   s   6065
*Furious Gulf* - Gregory Benford   s   447
*The Galactic Silver Star* - Kevin D. Randle   s   4468
*The Gap into Conflict: The Real Story* - Stephen R.
   Donaldson   s   1572
*The Gap into Ruin: This Day All Gods Die* - Stephen
   R. Donaldson   s   1575
*The Garden of Rama* - Arthur C. Clarke   s   1055
*The Gateway Trip: Tales and Vignettes of the Heechee*
   - Frederik Pohl   s   4346
*The Genocidal Healer* - James White   s   5779
*Heaven's Reach* - David Brin   s   687
*Heir to the Empire* - Timothy Zahn   s   6054
*Henry Martyn* - L. Neil Smith   s   5131
*High Wizardry* - Diane Duane   s   1662
*The Homecoming* - Barry B. Longyear   s   3521
*The Honor of the Queen* - David Weber   s   5674
*Icarus Descending* - Elizabeth Hand   s   2536
*The Illustrated Hitchhiker's Guide to the Galaxy* -
   Douglas Adams   s   29
*In Enemy Hands* - David Weber   s   5675
*Inconstant Star* - Poul Anderson   s   129
*Jefferson's War: Death of a Regiment* - Kevin
   Randle   s   4466
*The Killing Star* - Charles Pellegrino   s   4281
*Kings of the High Frontier* - Victor Koman   s   3199
*King's Sacrifice* - Margaret Weis   s   5717
*Knights of the Black Earth* - Margaret Weis   s   5718
*The Kruton Interface* - John DeChancie   s   1459
*The Last Command* - Timothy Zahn   s   6055
*Life Form* - Alan Dean Foster   s   2008
*Lyon's Pride* - Anne McCaffrey   s   3738
*Maia's Veil* - P.K. McAllister   s   3707
*Manhattan Transfer* - John E. Stith   s   5303
*Maverick* - Bruce Bethke   s   484
*Midshipman's Hope* - David Feintuch   s   1901
*Mind Changer* - James White   s   5780
*Mission: Tori* - Johanna Bolton   s   564
*Moonrise* - Ben Bova   s   587
*Mother of Storms* - John Barnes   s   354
*My Father Immortal* - Michael D. Weaver   s   5659
*Nomad* - David Alexander   s   66
*One Man's Universe* - Charles Sheffield   s   4961
*Operation Damocles* - Oscar L. Fellows   s   1916
*Out of This World* - Lawrence Watt-Evans   f   5645
*The Price of Ransom* - Alis A. Rasmussen   s   4483
*Prince of Sunset* - Steve White   s   5786
*Prison Ship* - Martin Caidin   s   828
*Psykosis* - Wilhelmina Baird   s   296
*Q-in-Law* - Peter David   s   1384
*Raft* - Stephen Baxter   s   401

*Ragnarok* - Nathan Archer   s   206
*Rama Revealed* - Arthur C. Clarke   s   1059
*The Rediscovery of Man* - Cordwainer
   Smith   s   5106
*Ring* - Stephen Baxter   s   402
*The Ring of Charon* - Roger MacBride Allen   s   80
*Rinn's Star* - Paula E. Downing   s   1719
*The Rising* - James Doohan   s   1579
*Rock 'n' Roll Babes From Outer Space* - Linda
   Javin   s   2880
*The Sails of Tau Ceti* - Michael McCollum   s   3771
*Shadowkill* - Jo Clayton   s   1069
*Shadows of War* - Thomas S. Gressman   s   2432
*The Ship Errant* - Jody Lynn Nye   s   4175
*The Short Victorious War* - David Weber   s   5681
*Siduri's Net* - P.K. McAllister   s   3709
*Silent Thunder/Universe* - Dean Ing   s   2829
*Solis* - A.A. Attanasio   s   272
*The Specialist* - Wynne Whiteford   s   5788
*The Spoils of War* - Alan Dean Foster   s   2016
*Star Trek: The Classic Episodes 1* - James
   Blish   s   526
*Star Trek: The Classic Episodes 2* - James
   Blish   s   527
*Star Trek: The Classic Episodes 3* - James
   Blish   s   528
*Star Wreck 6: Geek Space Nine* - Leah
   Rewolinski   s   4562
*Starborne* - Robert Silverberg   s   5042
*Starfarers* - Poul Anderson   s   133
*Starliner* - David Drake   s   1645
*The Stars My Destination* - Alfred Bester   s   478
*StarSpawn* - Kenneth Von Gunden   s   5588
*The Stone Dogs* - S.M. Stirling   s   5300
*The Stone Within* - David Wingrove   s   5920
*Strange Attractors* - Jeffrey A. Carver   s   934
*Sundowner* - Chris Claremont   s   1043
*Target Earth* - Steve Perry   s   4301
*Thirdspace* - Peter David   s   1387
*The Transmigration of Souls* - William
   Barton   s   382
*The Ultimate Helm* - Russ T. Howard   f   2785
*Vast* - Linda Nagata   s   4067
*Voices of Chaos* - A.C. Crispin   s   1266
*Voyage of the Star Wolf* - David Gerrold   s   2212
*The Web of Spider* - W. Michael Gear   s   2173
*The Whims of Creation* - Simon Hawke   s   2626
*The World at the End of Time* - Frederik
   Pohl   s   4357
*Wulfsyarn: A Mosaic* - Phillip Mann   s   3617

**61 Cygni Colonies**
*Outbanker* - Timothy A. Madden   s   3603

**Abraham's Star**
*Tides of Light* - Gregory Benford   s   450

**Aldebaran**
*The Transition of Titus Crow* - Brian
   Lumley   h   3569

**Alpha Draconis**
*Starplex* - Robert J. Sawyer   s   4859

**Ashton-Laval**
*Diaspora* - Greg Egan   s   1759

**Asteroid Belt**
*Kill Station* - Diane Duane   s   1664
*Red Planet Run* - Dana Stabenow   s   5187
*Sam Gunn, Unlimited* - Ben Bova   s   593
*Timemaster* - Robert L. Forward   s   1992

**Barnard Star System**
*Marooned on Eden* - Robert L. Forward   s   1986
*Ocean under the Ice* - Robert L. Forward   s   1988
*Return to Rocheworld* - Robert L. Forward   s   1989
*Rocheworld* - Robert L. Forward   s   1990

**battlestar** *Galactica*
*Armageddon* - Richard Hatch   s   2602

**Buttercup Star System**
*Anvil of Stars* - Greg Bear    s    414

**Capella System**
*Mother of Plenty* - Colin Greenland    s    2417

**Delta Pavonis Star System**
*Delta Pavonis* - Eric Kotani    s    3221

**Delta Quadrant**
*The Final Fury* - Dafydd ab Hugh    s    9
*Mosaic* - Jeri Taylor    s    5403

**Earth Orbit**
*Kaduna Memories* - Jack McKinney    s    3850
*Solip: System* - Walter Jon Williams    s    5841

**Eighty-Two Eridani**
*Jefferson's War: Death of a Regiment* - Kevin
    Randle    s    4466

**The Eye of Terror**
*Inquisitor* - Ian Watson    s    5637

**The Forty Worlds**
*Godspeed* - Charles Sheffield    s    4957

**Greater Magellanic Cloud**
*The Clouds of Magellan* - David F.
    Nighbert    s    4103

**Hohweyn System**
*The Kobayashi Maru* - Julia Ecklar    s    1728

**Landolph's Breach**
*Through the Breach* - David Drake    s    1647

**Magellanic Cloud**
*The Napoleon Wager* - William R.
    Forstchen    s    1980

**Malhela System**
*Flies From the Amber* - Wil McCarthy    s    3763

**Messina Dust Cloud**
*The Billion Dollar Boy* - Charles Sheffield    s    4948
*The Cyborg From Earth* - Charles Sheffield    s    4952

**Milky Way Galaxy**
*A Maze of Stars* - John Brunner    s    734

**Musca Constellation**
*Doctor's Orders* - Diane Duane    s    1659

**Oort Cloud**
*Mazeway* - Jack Williamson    s    5866
*Proteus in the Underworld* - Charles
    Sheffield    s    4962

**Orion Nebula**
*Orion's Dagger* - P.K. McAllister    s    3708

**Polar Cloud**
*A Roil of Stars* - Don Wismer    s    5930

**The Star**
*Flux* - Stephen Baxter    s    399

**Ta Ha Ak Station**
*Starstrike* - W. Michael Gear    s    2172

**Tau Ceti**
*Starplex* - Robert J. Sawyer    s    4859

**Torvil Anfract**
*Convergence* - Charles Sheffield    s    4951
*Transcendence* - Charles Sheffield    s    4967

**Yamato Sector**
*Yamato: A Rage in Heaven* - Ken Kato    s    3014

## PACIFIC ISLANDS

*John Dollar* - Marianne Wiggins    h    5799
*Mad Amos* - Alan Dean Foster    f    2009
*Time Blender* - Michael Dorn    s    1581

**Babylon**
*Crygender* - Thomas T. Thomas    s    5451

**Batan Island**
*Secret Realms* - Tom Cool    s    1168

**Guadalcanal**
*Mr. Was* - Pete Hautman    s    2614

**Radioactive Island**
*Gojiro* - Mark Jacobson    f    2847

**Sakhalin Island**
*Force of Arms* - G. Harry Stine    s    5279

**Sulatonga Island**
*Outworld Cats* - Jack Lovejoy    s    3536

**Tano Island**
*Meridian 144* - Meg Files    s    1932

**Tuamatuetuamatu**
*Harmony* - Marjorie Bradley Kellogg    s    3046

## PACIFIC OCEAN

*A Life in the Future* - Martin Caidin    s    827
*The Merlin Effect* - T.A. Barron    f    371
*Starsea Invaders: First Action* - G. Harry
    Stine    s    5282
*The Struggle* - Jerry Ahern    s    44

**Kehena Island**
*Dark Legacy* - Mark A. Kostrubula    h    3220

## PAKISTAN

*Judgment Day* - G. Harry Stine    s    5281

## PANAMA

*On My Way to Paradise* - Dave Wolverton    s    5955

**Gatun Lake**
*Canal Dreams* - Iain M. Banks    s    323

## PERSIA

**Nisni-Novgorod**
*Phantom* - Susan Kay    h    3020

## PERU

**Andes Mountains**
*Fire and Ice* - Edward Myers    f    4061
*The Mountain Made of Light* - Edward
    Myers    f    4062
*The Summit* - Edward Myers    f    4063

**Cuzco**
*Mansions of Darkness* - Chelsea Quinn
    Yarbro    h    6016

**Lima**
*The Trail of Cthulhu* - August Derleth    h    1497

**Nazca**
*Cat-A-Lyst* - Alan Dean Foster    s    1997

**Paititi, La S'ebra Sur**
*Cat-A-Lyst* - Alan Dean Foster    s    1997

## PLANET—IMAGINARY

*Aliens: Earth Hive* - Steve Perry    s    4289
*Alpha Centauri* - William Barton    s    378
*Antiquities* - John Crowley    f    1276
*Assignment: Eternity* - Greg Cox    s    1225
*Beyond the Veil of Stars* - Robert Reed    s    4503

*Bill, the Galactic Hero: On the Planet of Tasteless
    Pleasure* - Harry Harrison    s    2567
*Carpe Diem* - Steve Miller    s    3907
*City of Bones* - Martha Wells    f    5748
*The City on the Edge of Forever* - Harlan
    Ellison    s    1784
*Cloud's Rider* - C.J. Cherryh    s    983
*The Cult of Loving Kindness* - Paul Park    s    4242
*Dare to Go A-Hunting* - Andre Norton    s    4147
*Daughter of the Drow* - Elaine Cunningham    f    1287
*The Dazzle of Day* - Molly Gloss    s    2243
*Demon Moon* - Jack Williamson    s    5862
*The Demon Princes: Volume One* - Jack
    Vance    s    5544
*Design for Great-Day* - Alan Dean Foster    s    2001
*The Final Fury* - Dafydd ab Hugh    s    9
*Foreigner* - C.J. Cherryh    s    990
*The Forge in the Forest* - Michael Scott
    Rohan    f    4660
*A Game of Universe* - Eric S. Nylund    f    4178
*Henry Martyn* - L. Neil Smith    s    5131
*Her Klingon Soul* - Michael Jan Friedman    s    2064
*Honor of the Regiment* - Bill Fawcett    s    1896
*The Humanoids* - Jack Williamson    s    5865
*The Infinite Sea* - Jeffrey A. Carver    s    932
*Initiation* - Marian Hughes    s    2806
*Invader* - C.J. Cherryh    s    998
*Invitation to the Game* - Monica Hughes    s    2807
*Kingdoms of the Wall* - Robert Silverberg    s    5033
*Liar's Oath* - Elizabeth Moon    f    3969
*Mission Child* - Maureen F. McHugh    s    3819
*Mosaic* - Jeri Taylor    s    5403
*Myst: The Book of Atrus* - Rand Miller    f    3896
*Nameless Magery* - Delia Marshall Turner    f    5490
*The Nomad Queen* - James Gordon White    f    5783
*The Oathbound Wizard* - Christopher
    Stasheff    f    5219
*The Others* - Margaret Wander Bonanno    s    565
*OtherWhere* - Margaret Wander Bonanno    s    566
*Outpost* - Scott Mackay    s    3597
*The Outskirter's Secret* - Rosemary Kirstein    s    3157
*Pathways* - Jeri Taylor    s    5404
*Revenge of the Damned* - Allan Cole    s    1107
*Rider at the Gate* - C.J. Cherryh    s    1000
*Ring of Swords* - Eleanor Arnason    s    210
*Star Ascendant* - Louise Cooper    f    1180
*StarGate* - Dean Devlin    s    1509
*The Steerswoman* - Rosemary Kirstein    s    3158
*Sugar Rain* - Paul Park    s    4243
*Summerland* - L. Dean James    f    2865
*Swords Against the Shadowland* - Robin Wayne
    Bailey    f    291
*Tehanu: The Last Book of Earthsea* - Ursula K. Le
    Guin    f    3383
*Top Dog* - Jerry Jay Carroll    f    915
*The Voyage* - David Drake    s    1649
*The Weigher* - Eric Vinicoff    s    5574
*West of January* - Dave Duncan    s    1691
*When Heaven Fell* - William Barton    s    383
*A Wizard in Peace* - Christopher Stasheff    s    5233
*Wolfwalker* - Tara K. Harper    f    2553

**5023 Eris**
*Converse and Conflict* - L. Neil Smith    s    5130

**Abarrach**
*Fire Sea* - Margaret Weis    f    5714
*Into the Labyrinth* - Margaret Weis    f    5716
*The Seventh Gate* - Margaret Weis    f    5727

**Abydos**
*Stargate SG-1* - Ashley McConnell    s    3777

**Accord**
*The Ecolitan Enigma* - L.E. Modesitt Jr.    s    3927
*The Ecologic Secession* - L.E. Modesitt Jr.    s    3929

**Agatsu**
*Helm* - Steven Gould    s    2289

**Agorima**
*Protektor* - Charles Platt   s   4342

**Ahng**
*Nightmare World* - David Stern   s   5261

**Alcawell**
*The Escape* - Dean Wesley Smith   s   5113

**Aldebaran-C XII**
*I, Robot: The Illustrated Screenplay* - Harlan Ellison   s   1785

**Algeron**
*Legion of the Damned* - William C. Dietz   s   1547

**Alice**
*McCade's Bounty* - William C. Dietz   s   1550

**Alien Colony Circling Star AC**
*Limbo System* - Rick Cook   s   1158

**Almeon Colony**
*The Lantern of God* - John Dalmas   s   1323

**Alpha Centauri**
*A Gathering of Stars* - Donald Moffitt   s   3947

**Alpha Centauri IV**
*Cat's Gambit* - Leslie Gadallah   s   2099

**Alpha Centauri A-4**
*Flying to Valhalla* - Charles Pellegrino   s   4280

**Alt Bauernhof**
*The VMR Theory* - Robert Frezza   s   2055

**Altiplano**
*Once a Hero* - Elizabeth Moon   s   3970

**Alune**
*Half-Light* - Denise Vitola   s   5575

**Amaz**
*Tourists* - Lisa Goldstein   f   2264

**Amazoon**
*Jungle Assault* - P.M. Griffin   s   2437

**Andia**
*Becoming Human* - Valerie J. Freireich   s   2049

**Angel**
*Drifter* - William C. Dietz   s   1543

**Ankhana**
*Heroes Die* - Matthew Woodring Stover   s   5319

**Antar**
*One Mind's Eye* - Kathy Tyers   s   5525

**Anu/Dagda**
*Mutagenesis* - Helen Collins   s   1116

**Appledura**
*Charmed* - Marilyn Singer   f   5070

**Aquamarine**
*A Screaming Across the Sky* - Brian Daley   s   1315

**Arangorta**
*Reunion on Neverend* - John E. Stith   s   5306

**Arbroth**
*Dream-Weaver* - Louise Lawrence   s   3359

**Ardel**
*FreeMaster* - Kris Jensen   s   2897
*Mentor* - Kris Jensen   s   2898

**Arekkhi**
*Voices of Chaos* - A.C. Crispin   s   1266

**Ares**
*A Prison Unsought* - Sherwood Smith   s   5139

**Argo**
*Children of the Earth* - Catherine Wells   s   5743

*The Earth Is All That Lasts* - Catherine Wells   s   5744

**Ariadan**
*A Whisper of Time* - Paula E. Downing   s   1595

**Arianus**
*The Hand of Chaos* - Margaret Weis   f   5715
*Into the Labyrinth* - Margaret Weis   f   5716

**Arist**
*On the Verge* - Roland J. Green   s   2350

**Arius**
*Yesterday's Pawn* - W.T. Quick   s   4453

**Arizar**
*Path of Fire* - Charles Ingrid   s   2832

**Arizona**
*Smoke and Mirrors* - Jane M. Lindskold   s   3476

**Armageddon**
*Armageddon Sky* - L.A. Graf   s   2296

**Armaghast**
*Endymion* - Dan Simmons   s   5051

**Armistice**
*The Radiant Dragon* - Elaine Cunningham   f   1291

**Arrarat**
*Falkenberg's Legion* - Jerry Pournelle   s   4374

**Arth**
*A Sudden Wild Magic* - Diana Wynne Jones   f   2950

**Arthelion**
*Ruler of Naught* - Sherwood Smith   s   5141

**Artismo**
*A Miracle of Rare Design* - Mike Resnick   s   4550

**Artos**
*The Ecolitan Enigma* - L.E. Modesitt Jr.   s   3927

**Asborgan**
*Brother to Shadows* - Andre Norton   s   4142

**Aseneshesh**
*Look into the Sun* - James Patrick Kelly   s   3047

**Association**
*Other* - Gordon R. Dickson   s   1538
*Young Bleys* - Gordon R. Dickson   s   1540

**Astareth**
*Kar Kalim* - Deborah Christian   f   1025

**Astris Alexandria**
*The Death of Sleep* - Anne McCaffrey   s   3727

**Athas**
*The Brazen Gambit* - Lynn Abbey   f   13
*Cinnabar Shadows* - Lynn Abbey   f   15
*The Outcast* - Simon Hawke   f   2621
*The Seeker* - Simon Hawke   f   2624

**Athena**
*Ivory: A Legend of Past and Future* - Mike Resnick   s   4547

**Athera**
*Curse of the Mistwraith* - Janny Wurts   f   6001
*Ships of Merior* - Janny Wurts   f   6004

**Athet**
*Earthgrip* - Harry Turtledove   s   5499

**Atlas**
*Blindfold* - Kevin J. Anderson   s   101

**Auord**
*A Thousand Words for Stranger* - Julie E. Czerneda   s   1304

**Aurlanis**
*Deepwater Dreams* - Sydney J. Van Scyoc   s   5541

**Autumn**
*The Lotus and the Rose* - Scott Ciencin   f   1029
*The Wolves of Autumn* - Scott Ciencin   f   1035

**The Autumn World**
*Warp Angel* - Stuart Hopen   s   2766

**Avadon**
*Nightsword* - Margaret Weis   f   5722

**Avalon**
*Beowulf's Children* - Larry Niven   s   4116
*The Defenders* - Bill Baldwin   s   309
*The Siege* - Bill Baldwin   s   312

**Azonda**
*Brotherhood of the Stars* - Kirby Greene   s   2414

**Azure**
*The Lone Sentinel* - Jo Dereske   s   1493
*Star Child* - James P. Hogan   s   2730

**Baker**
*On My Way to Paradise* - Dave Wolverton   s   5955

**Ba'ku**
*Insurrection* - J.M. Dillard   s   1554

**Bakunin**
*Partisan* - S. Andrew Swann   s   5365
*Profiteer* - S. Andrew Swann   s   5366
*Revolutionary* - S. Andrew Swann   s   5367

**Bakura**
*The Truce at Bakura* - Kathy Tyers   s   5527

**Ballas**
*Reconnaissance* - Bill McCay   s   3769

**Ballybran**
*Crystal Line* - Anne McCaffrey   s   3724

**Baret Two**
*City of Diamond* - Jane Emerson   s   1807

**Barevi**
*Freedom's Landing* - Anne McCaffrey   s   3734

**Barrayar**
*Barrayar* - Lois McMaster Bujold   s   756
*Memory* - Lois McMaster Bujold   s   761

**Beanstalk**
*Man-Kzin Wars V* - Larry Niven   s   4125

**Bekh-Nar**
*Tangled Webs* - Steve Mudd   s   4044

**Beldorph**
*Backblast* - Lee McKeone   s   3828

**Bellea-Naya**
*Hand of Prophecy* - Severna Park   s   4244

**Belletiener**
*Lieutenant* - Rick Shelley   s   4972

**Bellmakers World**
*Falcon* - Emma Bull   s   768

**Belsavis**
*Children of the Jedi* - Barbara Hambly   s   2500

**Beltaxiyan Minor**
*Imbalance* - V.E. Mitchell   s   3919

**Beluchad**
*Fire in the Sky* - Jo Clayton   s   1067

**Benarus**
*Half-Light* - Denise Vitola   s   5575

**Benisan**
*Igniting the Reaches* - David Drake   s   1633

**Bestla**
*Night Sky Mine* - Melissa Scott   s   4898

**Beta**
*Children of the Earth* - Catherine Wells   *s*   5743
*The Earth Saver* - Catherine Wells   *s*   5745

**Beta Orbis IV**
*Shaper's Legacy* - Sheila Finch   *s*   1933
*Shaping the Dawn* - Sheila Finch   *s*   1934

**Beta Prometheus**
*The Fearful Summons* - Denny Martin Flinn   *s*   1954

**Betazed**
*Imzadi* - Peter David   *s*   1383
*Triangle: Imzadi II* - Peter David   *s*   1388

**Bia**
*Heirs of Empire* - David Weber   *s*   5672

**Bimran**
*Rainbow Man* - M.J. Engh   *s*   1824

**Blueheart**
*Blueheart* - Alison Sinclair   *s*   5068

**Bohr**
*Empire's End* - Allan Cole   *s*   1103

**Bol Mutian**
*Shadowkill* - Jo Clayton   *s*   1069

**Bolton's Planet**
*Galactic MI* - Kevin D. Randle   *s*   4467

**Boohte**
*Uncharted Territory* - Connie Willis   *s*   5875

**Bosque**
*The Glaive* - Cary Osborne   *s*   4227

**Botany**
*Freedom's Challenge* - Anne McCaffrey   *s*   3732
*Freedom's Choice* - Anne McCaffrey   *s*   3733
*Freedom's Landing* - Anne McCaffrey   *s*   3734

**Bothawui**
*Shadows of the Empire* - Steve Perry   *s*   4299

**Bountiful**
*Alien Influences* - Kristine Kathryn Rusch   *s*   4711

**Brakir**
*Day of the Dead* - Neil Gaiman   *s*   2102

**Bralava**
*Imposter* - Valcric J. Freireich   *s*   2050

**Brangornie**
*The Phoenix in Flight* - Sherwood Smith   *s*   5138

**Briand**
*Earth Made of Glass* - John Barnes   *s*   351

**Brighthome**
*Spacer Dreams* - Larry Segriff   *s*   4911

**Brishan V**
*Sentinels* - Margaret Weis   *s*   5725

**Burdania**
*Legacies* - Alison Sinclair   *s*   5069

**Burihatin-14**
*A Covenant of Justice* - David Gerrold   *s*   2207

**Burning Bright**
*Burning Bright* - Melissa Scott   *s*   4894

**Bushveld**
*A Hunger in the Soul* - Mike Resnick   *s*   4545

**BZ 459**
*Redliners* - David Drake   *s*   1641

**Cabar 4**
*Eggheads* - Emily Devenport   *s*   1500

**Cablans**
*Jade Darcy and the Zen Pirates* - Stephen Goldin   *s*   2260

**Cadwal**
*Ecce and Old Earth* - Jack Vance   *s*   5546
*Throy* - Jack Vance   *s*   5550

**Calamari**
*The Glove of Darth Vader* - Paul Davids   *s*   1392

**Caldera**
*Deathweave* - Cary Osborne   *s*   4226

**Caledonia**
*Diamond Mask: A Novel* - Julian May   *s*   3697

**Calferon**
*The Cloud People* - Robert B. Kelly   *f*   3050

**Calligar**
*The Rift* - Peter David   *s*   1386

**Callisto**
*The Rowan* - Anne McCaffrey   *s*   3747

**Camerein**
*Return to Camerein* - Rick Shelley   *s*   4974

**Candle**
*Warpath* - Tony Daniel   *s*   1337

**Cannon's Orb**
*Cannon's Orb* - L. Warren Douglas   *s*   1586
*A Plague of Change* - L. Warren Douglas   *s*   1587

**Cantilucca**
*The Sharp End* - David Drake   *s*   1643

**Canuche of Halio**
*Redline the Stars* - Andre Norton   *s*   4160

**Capella II**
*Halfway Human* - Carolyn Ives Gilman   *s*   2237

**Capulon IV**
*Guises of the Mind* - Rebecca Neason   *s*   4081

**Cardassia Prime**
*Ship of the Line* - Diane Carey   *s*   904

**Careta IV**
*Windows on a Lost World* - V.E. Mitchell   *s*   3920

**Caryldon**
*Commencement* - Roby James   *s*   2877

**Castle Perilous**
*Bride of the Castle* - John DeChancie   *s*   1452
*Castle Dreams* - John DeChancie   *s*   1453
*Castle Spellbound* - John DeChancie   *s*   1454
*Castle War!* - John DeChancie   *s*   1455

**Catten**
*Freedom's Challenge* - Anne McCaffrey   *s*   3732

**Cayahno**
*The Magnificent Wilf* - Gordon R. Dickson   *s*   1536

**Cebalrai**
*A Whisper of Time* - Paula E. Downing   *s*   1595

**Celestis**
*Celestis* - Paul Park   *s*   4241

**Cellulite-1, Starfreak Colony**
*Star Wreck: The Generation Gap* - Leah Rewolinski   *s*   4566

**Centauri Prime**
*Personal Agendas* - Al Sarrantonio   *s*   4833

**Cestry Prime**
*The Khan's Persuasion* - Cynthia Felice   *s*   1914

**Cestus III**
*Requiem* - Michael Jan Friedman   *s*   2067

**Ceti**
*The Faces of Ceti* - Mary Caraker   *s*   877

**Chal**
*The Ashes of Eden* - William Shatner   *s*   4927
*Avenger* - William Shatner   *s*   4928

**Chalco-Doror**
*The Last Legends of Earth* - A.A. Attanasio   *s*   270

**Chelestra**
*Serpent Mage* - Margaret Weis   *f*   5726

**Chennidur**
*World Spirits* - Aline Boucher-Kaplan   *s*   580

**Chissoku Bogmaks**
*Shadowspeer* - Jo Clayton   *s*   1071

**Cho**
*Path of Fire* - Charles Ingrid   *s*   2832

**Chujoan**
*Murasaki* - Robert Silverberg   *s*   5038

**Chyrellka**
*Renegade* - Gene DeWeese   *s*   1511

**Clarf**
*Damia's Children* - Anne McCaffrey   *s*   3726
*Lyon's Pride* - Anne McCaffrey   *s*   3738

**Coba**
*The Last Hawk* - Catherine Asaro   *s*   219

**Cocytus**
*The Dig* - Alan Dean Foster   *s*   2002

**Colony Station, Wolf II**
*Flare Star* - Paula E. Downing   *s*   1594

**Confabulon**
*Free Radicals* - Jack McKinney   *s*   3848

**Constanthus**
*Crossover* - Michael Jan Friedman   *s*   2063

**Contisuyu**
*Cat-A-Lyst* - Alan Dean Foster   *s*   1997

**Corellia**
*Ambush at Corellia* - Roger MacBride Allen   *s*   76

**Corinth**
*To Save the Sun* - Ben Bova   *s*   596

**Corsicata**
*Half-Light* - Denise Vitola   *s*   5575

**Coruscant**
*Before the Storm* - Michael P. Kube-McDowell   *s*   3247
*Dark Force Rising* - Timothy Zahn   *s*   6052
*Heir to the Empire* - Timothy Zahn   *s*   6054
*Jedi Search* - Kevin J. Anderson   *s*   109
*The New Rebellion* - Kristine Kathryn Rusch   *s*   4719
*Shadows of the Empire* - Steve Perry   *s*   4299

**Costeau**
*The Sounding Stillness* - Kenneth Von Gunden   *s*   5587

**Cosuut**
*The False Mirror* - Alan Dean Foster   *s*   2004

**Cridi**
*The Ship Errant* - Jody Lynn Nye   *s*   4175

**Crseih**
*The Crystal Star* - Vonda N. McIntyre   *s*   3820

**Cylinder**
*Farewell Horizontal* - K.W. Jeter   *s*   2911

**Cymru**
*Falcon* - Emma Bull   *s*   768

**Cynthia**
*Heritage of Flight* - Susan Shwartz   s   5016

**Cyteen**
*Cyteen* - C.J. Cherryh   s   984

**Dacket**
*Metamorphosis* - Jean Lorrah   s   3524

**Dahlgren's World**
*Heart of Red Iron* - Phyllis Gotlieb   s   2287

**Dannon's Keep**
*Lair of the Cyclops* - Allen L. Wold   s   5933

**Dar Sai**
*The Demon Princes: Volume Two* - Jack
   Vance   s   5545

**Darkath**
*Empire's Horizon* - John Brizzolara   s   707

**Darkover**
*Domains of Darkover* - Marion Zimmer
   Bradley   s   631
*Exile's Song* - Marion Zimmer Bradley   s   632
*The Heirs of Hammerfell* - Marion Zimmer
   Bradley   s   638
*Leroni of Darkover* - Marion Zimmer
   Bradley   s   642
*Rediscovery: A Novel of Darkover* - Marion Zimmer
   Bradley   s   643
*Renunciates of Darkover* - Marion Zimmer
   Bradley   s   644
*The Shadow Matrix* - Marion Zimmer
   Bradley   s   645
*Towers of Darkover* - Marion Zimmer
   Bradley   f   653

**Dathomir**
*The Courtship of Princess Leia* - Dave
   Wolverton   s   5950

**Dazau**
*Mathemagics* - Margaret Ball   f   316

**Deald's World**
*Run for the Stars/Echoes of Thunder* - Harlan
   Ellison   s   1788

**Deception Well**
*Deception Well* - Linda Nagata   s   4065

**Dedelphi**
*Playing God* - Sarah Zettel   s   6080

**Deep Freeze**
*Deep Freeze* - Zach Hughes   s   2811

**Dekkanar**
*Rules of Engagement* - Peter Morwood   s   4037

**Delos**
*Primary Inversion* - Catherine Asaro   s   220

**Delta Bootis**
*Rinn's Star* - Paula E. Downing   s   1719

**Delta Cygnus 4**
*The Infinity Plague* - Robert E. Vardeman   s   5564

**Demeter**
*Harvest of Stars* - Poul Anderson   s   127

**Denali**
*Jack the Bodiless* - Julian May   s   3698

**Deneb**
*Damia* - Anne McCaffrey   s   3725

**Desalaya**
*House of Moons* - K.D. Wentworth   s   5752

**Destiny**
*Destiny's Road* - Larry Niven   s   4119

**Devereaux**
*Cohort of the Damned* - Andrew Keith   s   3034

**Diehr IV**
*The Chance Factor* - Diana G. Gallagher   s   2109

**Dilarang**
*Lethe* - Tricia Sullivan   s   5354

**Dinadh**
*Shadow's End* - Sheri S. Tepper   s   5435

**Diomede**
*The Price of Ransom* - Alis A. Rasmussen   s   4483

**Dirigent**
*Lieutenant* - Rick Shelley   s   4972
*Officer Cadet* - Rick Shelley   s   4973

**Discworld**
*Equal Rites* - Terry Pratchett   f   4387
*Feet of Clay* - Terry Pratchett   f   4389
*Guards! Guards!* - Terry Pratchett   f   4390
*Interesting Times* - Terry Pratchett   f   4392
*Jingo* - Terry Pratchett   f   4393
*Lords and Ladies* - Terry Pratchett   f   4394
*Maskerade* - Terry Pratchett   f   4395
*Men at Arms* - Terry Pratchett   f   4396
*Mort* - Terry Pratchett   f   4397
*Moving Pictures* - Terry Pratchett   f   4398
*Reaper Man* - Terry Pratchett   f   4399
*Small Gods* - Terry Pratchett   f   4400
*Soul Music* - Terry Pratchett   f   4401
*Witches Abroad* - Terry Pratchett   f   4404
*Wyrd Sisters* - Terry Pratchett   f   4405

**Dominion of Virgin**
*Firehand* - Andre Norton   s   4151

**Doona**
*Crisis on Doona* - Anne McCaffrey   s   3723

**Downbelow**
*Downbelow Station* - C.J. Cherryh   s   985

**Dragaera**
*Dragon* - Steven Brust   f   741
*Five Hundred Years After* - Steven Brust   f   742
*Orca* - Steven Brust   f   745
*The Phoenix Guards* - Steven Brust   f   747

**Dragonrealm**
*Children of the Drake* - Richard A. Knaak   f   3166
*Dragon Tome* - Richard A. Knaak   f   3169
*The Shrouded Realm* - Richard A. Knaak   f   3174

**Drinan IV**
*Tangled Webs* - Steve Mudd   s   4044

**Droos**
*The Merro Tree* - Katie Waitman   s   5609

**Durvie**
*A Wizard in Chaos* - Christopher Stasheff   s   5230

**Dusable**
*Empire's End* - Allan Cole   s   1103

**Eamn**
*The Triad Worlds* - F.M. Busby   s   786

**Eannor**
*Warlord of Heaven* - Adrian Cole   f   1102

**Earth II**
*More than Fire* - Philip Jose Farmer   s   1871

**Earthheart**
*The Tenth Class* - Karen Ripley   s   4594

**Eden**
*Eden* - Stanislaw Lem   s   3434
*Judson's Eden* - Keith Laumer   s   3344

**Eirossad**
*The False Mirror* - Alan Dean Foster   s   2004

**Eisernon**
*The Trumpets of Tagan* - Simon Lang   s   3316

**Elenia**
*The Diamond Throne* - David Eddings   f   1731
*The Ruby Knight* - David Eddings   f   1736
*The Sapphire Rose* - David Eddings   f   1737

**Elseemar**
*Shadow World* - A.C. Crispin   s   1262

**Elsewhere**
*Sideshow* - Sheri S. Tepper   s   5436

**Elysia**
*Metamorphosis* - Jean Lorrah   s   3524

**Elysium**
*Of the Fall* - Paul J. McAuley   s   3713

**Enstor**
*Clan of the Shape-Changers* - Robert Levy   f   3446

**Entibor**
*The Gathering Flame* - Debra Doyle   s   1599

**Epimetheus**
*Nightside City* - Lawrence Watt-Evans   s   5644

**Epsilon Eridani Two**
*Eternal Light* - Paul J. McAuley   s   3710

**Erd**
*War Birds* - R.M. Meluch   s   3875

**Erin**
*Godspeed* - Charles Sheffield   s   4957

**Erna**
*Black Sun Rising* - C.S. Friedman   f   2056
*Crown of Shadows* - C.S. Friedman   s   2057
*When True Night Falls* - C.S. Friedman   f   2060

**Eron**
*Star Bridge* - James Gunn   s   2459

**Escobar**
*Mirror Dance* - Lois McMaster Bujold   s   762

**Eta Cassiopeia IV**
*The Queen's Squadron* - R.M. Meluch   s   3874

**Eta Ceta IV**
*Cetaganda* - Lois McMaster Bujold   s   758

**Excenus 23**
*Unwillingly to Earth* - Pauline Ashwell   s   231

**Eyerack**
*Bill, the Galactic Hero: The Final Incoherent
   Adventure* - Harry Harrison   s   2568

**Fader**
*Night Lamp* - Jack Vance   s   5548

**Farfara**
*The Wild* - David Zindell   s   6086

**The Farther Kingdom**
*Fool's War* - Sarah Zettel   s   6079

**Fenrille**
*The Founder* - Christopher Rowley   s   4696
*To a Highland Nation* - Christopher
   Rowley   s   4698

**Fiametta**
*Ports of Call* - Jack Vance   s   5549

**Fiorina**
*Alien 3* - Alan Dean Foster   s   1993

**Firekka**
*Wing Commander: Freedom Flight* - Mercedes
   Lackey   s   3307

**First-Stop**
*Seeds of Destiny* - Thomas A. Easton   s   1724

**The Flower World**
*The Return of the Breakneck Boys* - Geary
   Gravel   s   2332

**Flyspeck**
*Doctor's Orders* - Diane Duane   s   1659

**Foreshires Hold**
*Primary Inversion* - Catherine Asaro   s   220

**Forever World**
*Imzadi* - Peter David   s   1383

**Fthel V.**
*Flesh and Gold* - Phyllis Gotlieb   s   2286

**G889**
*Earth 2* - Melissa Crandall   s   1247

**Galcen**
*The Gathering Flame* - Debra Doyle   s   1599
*Starpilot's Grave* - Debra Doyle   s   1606

**Gale'tin**
*Beyond the Door* - Gary L. Blackwood   s   510

**Galicia**
*The Glaive* - Cary Osborne   s   4227

**Gamearth**
*Gameplay* - Kevin J. Anderson   f   105
*Game's End* - Kevin J. Anderson   f   104

**Gammadis**
*Halfway Human* - Carolyn Ives Gilman   s   2237

**Gandji**
*The Eternal Enemy* - Michael Berlyn   s   469

**Gannet**
*Time: The Semi-Final Frontier* - Lionel
   Fenn   s   1921

**Ganwold**
*Ganwold's Child* - Diann Thornley   s   5467

**Gauguin**
*Rebel From Alphorion* - Robyn Tallis   s   5381

**Gehenna**
*A Prison Unsought* - Sherwood Smith   s   5139

**Genellan**
*Genellan: Planetfall* - Scott G. Gier   s   2223
*In the Shadow of the Moon* - Scott G. Gier   s   2224

**Genizee**
*Convergence* - Charles Sheffield   s   4951
*Transcendence* - Charles Sheffield   s   4967

**Genji**
*Murasaki* - Robert Silverberg   s   5038

**Ghandi**
*Cry Wolf* - Kenneth Von Gunden   s   5586

**Giles Three**
*India's Story* - Kathlyn S. Starbuck   s   5208

**Gilver**
*Earthgrip* - Harry Turtledove   s   5499

**Glandair**
*Drum Calls* - Jo Clayton   f   1065
*Drum Warning* - Jo Clayton   f   1066

**Glaurus**
*Brotherhood of the Stars* - Kirby Greene   s   2414

**Glister**
*Divergence* - Charles Sheffield   s   4954

**Glory**
*Darkloom* - Cary Osborne   s   4225
*Deathweave* - Cary Osborne   s   4226

**Goddard**
*Shivering World* - Kathy Tyers   s   5526

**Golgotha**
*Deathstalker Rebellion* - Simon R. Green   s   2365

**Golter**
*Against a Dark Background* - Iain M. Banks   s   322

**Gramarye**
*M'Lady Witch* - Christopher Stasheff   f   5217
*Quicksilver's Knight* - Christopher Stasheff   f   5220
*Warlock and Son* - Christopher Stasheff   s   5224
*The Warlock Rock* - Christopher Stasheff   s   5226

**Grass**
*Grass* - Sheri S. Tepper   s   5431

**Grayson**
*Echoes of Honor* - David Weber   s   5669
*Flag in Exile* - David Weber   s   5671
*The Honor of the Queen* - David Weber   s   5674

**Grenchstom's Planet "Jeep"**
*Ammonite* - Nicola Griffith   s   2443

**Groombra Four**
*The Expediter* - J. Brian Clarke   s   1062

**Guera**
*This Alien Shore* - C.S. Friedman   s   2059

**Guillen**
*Smoke and Mirrors* - Jane M. Lindskold   s   3476

**Gwynedd**
*The Hawk's Gray Feather* - Patricia Kennealy-
   Morrison   f   3061
*The Oak Above the Kings: A Book of the Keltiad* -
   Patricia Kennealy   s   3058

**Habranha**
*Fossil* - Hal Clement   s   1083

**Hades**
*Echoes of Honor* - David Weber   s   5669
*Oracle* - Mike Resnick   s   4551

**Hadley**
*Falkenberg's Legion* - Jerry Pournelle   s   4374

**Hain**
*Four Ways to Forgiveness* - Ursula K. Le
   Guin   s   3380

**Hanover**
*Bretta Martyn* - L. Neil Smith   s   5128

**Hanuman**
*March or Die* - Andrew Keith   s   3035

**Hara**
*Shadow Man* - Melissa Scott   s   4900

**Harmony**
*The Call of Earth* - Orson Scott Card   s   882
*Earthfall* - Orson Scott Card   s   885
*The Memory of Earth* - Orson Scott Card   s   894
*The Ships of Earth* - Orson Scott Card   s   897

**Harsh**
*Revolution's Shore* - Alis A. Rasmussen   s   4484

**Haskin's Planet**
*Phule's Company* - Robert Asprin   s   260
*Phule's Paradise* - Robert Asprin   s   261

**Haven**
*CoDominium: Revolt on War World* - Jerry
   Pournelle   s   4373
*The Crystal Sorcerers* - William R.
   Forstchen   f   1979
*On Basilisk Station* - David Weber   s   5679

**Hawaika**
*Firehand* - Andre Norton   s   4151

**Hellfrost**
*The Black Sun* - Jack Williamson   s   5860

**Hephaestus**
*Under Fire* - Kenneth Von Gunden   s   5589

**H'hogoth**
*Yesterday's Pawn* - W.T. Quick   s   4453

**Hire**
*The Prisoner Within* - Donald E. McQuinn   s   3861

**Hobbs Land**
*Raising the Stones* - Sheri S. Tepper   s   5434

**Holders Fastness**
*The Fall of Sirius* - Wil McCarthy   s   3762

**Holmarin IV**
*Starfire Down* - Lee McKeone   s   3830

**Homeworld**
*Hexwood* - Diana Wynne Jones   s   2948

**Hook**
*Larissa* - Emily Devenport   s   1503

**Hope Nation**
*Midshipman's Hope* - David Feintuch   s   1901

**Hunter's Planet**
*Hunter's Planet* - David Bischoff   s   492

**Huntress**
*Shadows of War* - Thomas S. Gressman   s   2432

**HuteNamid**
*Ground-Ties* - Jane S. Fancher   s   1861
*Harmonies of the 'Net* - Jane S. Fancher   s   1862
*Uplink* - Jane S. Fancher   s   1865

**Hydros**
*The Face of the Waters* - Robert Silverberg   s   5029

**Hyperborea**
*Shiva in Steel* - Fred Saberhagen   s   4775

**Hyperion**
*Endymion* - Dan Simmons   s   5051
*The Fall of Hyperion* - Dan Simmons   s   5052
*Hyperion* - Dan Simmons   s   5055
*The Rise of Endymion* - Dan Simmons   s   5059

**Iadara**
*Mighty Good Road* - Melissa Scott   s   4897

**Icefall**
*The Broken God* - David Zindell   s   6085

**Idun "Eden"**
*The Shapes of Their Hearts* - Melissa Scott   s   4901

**Ildefor**
*Hopeship* - Simon Lang   s   3315

**Imperial Mikasa**
*Darktraders* - eluki bes shahar   s   472

**Incognita**
*Unwillingly to Earth* - Pauline Ashwell   s   231

**Indra**
*Earth Herald* - Jan Clark   s   1046

**Inferno**
*Caliban* - Roger MacBride Allen   s   77
*Inferno* - Roger MacBride Allen   s   78
*Utopia* - Roger MacBride Allen   s   83

**Innasmorn**
*Mother of Storms* - Adrian Cole   f   1101
*Warlord of Heaven* - Adrian Cole   f   1102

**Innish-Kyl**
*The Price of the Stars* - Debra Doyle   s   1604

**Iomard**
*Drum Calls* - Jo Clayton   f   1065
*Drum Warning* - Jo Clayton   f   1066

**Iota Aurigae**
*Damia* - Anne McCaffrey   s   3725
*Damia's Children* - Anne McCaffrey   s   3726

**Ireta**
*The Death of Sleep* - Anne McCaffrey   s   3727

**Ironhold**
*Way of the Clans* - Robert Thurston   s   5469

**Irth**
*The Shadow Eater* - Adam Lee   f   3386

**Iryala**
*The White Regiment* - John Dalmas   s   1327

**Ishtar**
*Mother of Demons* - Eric Flint   s   1956

**Issel**
*Dominion's Reach* - Diann Thornley   s   5465

**Issel II**
*Echoes of Issel* - Diann Thornley   s   5466

**Ithavoll**
*A Landscape of Darkness* - John Blair   s   513

**Ivory**
*The Gate of Ivory* - Doris Egan   s   1755
*Guilt-Edged Ivory* - Doris Egan   s   1756
*Two-Bit Heroes* - Doris Egan   s   1757

**Izz**
*Norby and the Court Jester* - Janet Asimov   s   252

**Jackson's Whole**
*Mirror Dance* - Lois McMaster Bujold   s   762

**Jacobi IV**
*The Tery* - F. Paul Wilson   s   5900

**Jalna**
*Razor's Edge* - Lisanne Norman   s   4139

**Jamya**
*Norby and the Oldest Dragon* - Janet
   Asimov   s   253

**Jarnevon**
*Gray Lensman* - Edward E. Smith   s   5117

**Jartee**
*Beneath the Gated Sky* - Robert Reed   s   4502

**Jaspre**
*The Snows of Jaspre* - Mary Caraker   s   878

**Jericho**
*The Shapes of Their Hearts* - Melissa Scott   s   4901

**Jerrume**
*Random Factor* - Joel Henry Sherman   s   4984

**Jevlen**
*Entoverse* - James P. Hogan   s   2724

**Jijo**
*Brightness Reef* - David Brin   s   684
*Infinity's Shore* - David Brin   s   688

**Jochi**
*Vortex* - Allan Cole   s   1108

**Juniper**
*Wulfsyarn: A Mosaic* - Phillip Mann   s   3617

**Kalgash**
*Nightfall* - Isaac Asimov   s   248

**Kantano's World**
*From a Changeling Star* - Jeffrey A. Carver   s   931

**Karela**
*Taylor's Ark* - Jody Lynn Nye   s   4176

**Karimon**
*Purgatory: A Chronicle of a Distant World* - Mike
   Resnick   s   4554

**Karst**
*Being Alien* - Rebecca Ore   s   4217
*Human to Human* - Rebecca Ore   s   4219

**Keiss**
*Turning Point* - Lisanne Norman   s   4140

**Kekoi**
*The Merro Tree* - Katie Waitman   s   5609

**Kelewan**
*The King's Buccaneer* - Raymond E. Feist   f   1904
*Mistress of the Empire* - Raymond E. Feist   f   1906
*Servant of the Empire* - Raymond E. Feist   f   1910

**Keltia**
*The Deer's Cry: A Book of the Keltiad* - Patricia
   Kennealy-Morrison   f   3060

**Keramos**
*Promised Land* - Connie Willis   s   5872

**Kesh**
*Prince of the Blood* - Raymond E. Feist   f   1907

**Kessel**
*The Glove of Darth Vader* - Paul Davids   s   1392
*Jedi Search* - Kevin J. Anderson   s   109

**Kezdet**
*Acorna's Quest* - Anne McCaffrey   s   3718

**Khalife**
*Canby's Legion* - Bill Baldwin   s   308

**Khesat**
*The Long Hunt* - Debra Doyle   s   1602

**Ki**
*Mirage* - Perry Brass   s   662

**Kialinninni Alpha**
*Warhorse* - Timothy Zahn   s   6056

**Killhaven**
*Soothsayer* - Mike Resnick   s   4557

**Kirinyaga**
*Kirinyaga: A Fable of Utopia* - Mike
   Resnick   s   4548

**Kirlos**
*Doomsday World* - Carmen Carter   s   923

**Kiskai**
*Shadowplay* - Jo Clayton   s   1070

**Klah**
*Sweet Myth-tery of Life* - Robert Asprin   f   262

**Kohltri**
*Crown of the Serpent* - Allen L. Wold   s   5932

**Komarr**
*Komarr* - Lois McMaster Bujold   s   760

**Kon**
*In the Shadow of the Moon* - Scott G. Gier   s   2224

**Koorn**
*Chains of Command* - Bill McCay   s   3767

**Kor**
*Genellan: Planetfall* - Scott G. Gier   s   2223

**Kornagy**
*Shadows After Dark* - Ouida Crozier   f   1286

**Kostroma**
*With the Lightnings* - David Drake   s   1652

**Kraos**
*Beholder's Eye* - Julie E. Czerneda   s   1303

**Krishna**
*The Hand of Zei* - L. Sprague de Camp   s   1414
*The Swords of Zinjaban* - L. Sprague de
   Camp   s   1418

**Krondor**
*Prince of the Blood* - Raymond E. Feist   f   1907

**Kruton**
*The Kruton Interface* - John DeChancie   s   1459

**Kryndamar**
*Aliens Stole My Body* - Bruce Coville   s   1217

**Krynn**
*Beyond the Moons* - David Cook   f   1144
*The Day of the Tempest* - Jean Rabe   f   4457
*The Doom Brigade* - Margaret Weis   f   5708
*Dragons of Summer Flame* - Margaret Weis   f   5711
*Hederick, the Theocrat* - Ellen Dodge
   Severson   f   4925
*Kaz the Minotaur* - Richard A. Knaak   f   3172
*The Second Generation* - Margaret Weis   f   5724
*The Seventh Sentinel* - Mary Kirchoff   f   3154
*The Soulforge* - Margaret Weis   f   5728
*Steel and Stone* - Ellen Porath   f   4368
*Vinas Solamnus* - J. Robert King   f   3123

**Kwashi**
*The LaNague Chronicles* - F. Paul Wilson   s   5889

**La-Tri**
*Where the Ships Die* - William C. Dietz   s   1553

**Laboue**
*Acorna* - Anne McCaffrey   s   3717

**Labyrinth**
*Labyrinth* - Dennis Schmidt   s   4884

**Lach**
*Seeking the Dream Brother* - Marcia J.
   Bennett   s   451

**Lalonde**
*Emergence* - Peter F. Hamilton   s   2524

**Lamarkia**
*Legacy* - Greg Bear   s   420

**Lambda**
*Project Farcry* - Pauline Ashwell   s   230

**Lamuella**
*Mostly Harmless* - Douglas Adams   s   31

**Land**
*The Fugitive Worlds* - Bob Shaw   s   4942

**Landsdrum**
*The Gift of the Gorboduc Vandal* - Paul O.
   Williams   s   5821

**Lassti**
*Hellspark* - Janet Kagan   s   3000

**Last Chance**
*Oracle* - Mike Resnick   s   4551
*Prophet* - Mike Resnick   s   4553
*Soothsayer* - Mike Resnick   s   4557

**Lazon II**
*Triangle: Imzadi II* - Peter David   s   1388

**Leiblein**
*Captains Outrageous, or, For Doom the Bell Tolls* -
   Roy V. Young   f   6049

**Lenfell**
*The Mageborn Traitor* - Melanie Rawn   f   4488
*The Ruins of Ambrai* - Melanie Rawn   f   4489

**Lesaat**
*Reefsong* - Carol Severance   s   4923

**Light Trap**
*Hostile Takeover* - Jack McKinney   s   3849

**Linak'h**
*The Painful Field* - Roland J. Green   s   2351

**Liokukae**
*The Stainless Steel Rat Sings the Blues* - Harry
   Harrison   s   2575

**Lioth**
*Dancer of the Sixth* - Michelle Shirey
   Crean   s   1254

**Lochan**
*Brother to Shadows* - Andre Norton   s   4142

**Loris**
*Orion Among the Stars* - Ben Bova   s   589

**Lostwithal**
*The End-of-Everything Man* - Tom De
   Haven   f   1421

**Lunga**
*Orion Among the Stars* - Ben Bova   s   589

**Lusitania**
*Children of the Mind* - Orson Scott Card   s   883
*Xenocide* - Orson Scott Card   s   899

**Lussuoso**
*The Stainless Steel Rat Goes to Hell* - Harry
   Harrison   s   2574

**Lyanan**
*The Color of Distance* - Amy Thomson   s   5461

**Lyra**
*Shadows over Lyra* - Patricia C. Wrede   f   5980

**Madonna-Moloch**
*Noctet: Tales of Madonna-Moloch* - Albert J.
   Manachino   h   3613

**Maganos**
*Acorna* - Anne McCaffrey   s   3717

**Magh**
*The Triad Worlds* - F.M. Busby   s   786

**Majipoor**
*The Mountains of Majipoor* - Robert
   Silverberg   s   5037
*Sorcerers of Majipoor* - Robert Silverberg   s   5041

**Malroth**
*Dream-Weaver* - Louise Lawrence   s   3359

**Maltroit**
*A Wizard in War* - Christopher Stasheff   s   5234

**Malvrone**
*Lair of the Cyclops* - Allen L. Wold   s   5933

**Mandeyn**
*The Price of the Stars* - Debra Doyle   s   1604

**Mannheim**
*Crystal Witness* - Kathy Tyers   s   5524

**Manticore**
*Field of Dishonor* - David Weber   s   5670

**Mara**
*The Parafaith War* - L.E. Modesitt Jr.   s   3937

**Maraghai**
*The Long Hunt* - Debra Doyle   s   1602

**Marcanter**
*Dancing Vac* - S.N. Lewitt   s   3451

**Mathison's World**
*Path of the Fury* - David Weber   s   5680

**Mauldar**
*Heartstone and Silver* - Jacqui Singleton   f   5071

**May 16**
*Reclamation* - Sarah Zettel   s   6081

**Mechnos**
*Where the Ships Die* - William C. Dietz   s   1553

**Medina**
*A Miracle of Rare Design* - Mike Resnick   s   4550

**Medusa**
*On Basilisk Station* - David Weber   s   5679

**Megara**
*Debtors' Planet* - William R. Thompson   s   5457

**Melaquin**
*Expendable* - James Alan Gardner   s   2135

**Melthanus**
*Destination: Mutiny* - Sean Dalton   s   1332

**Merydion**
*Castle War!* - John DeChancie   s   1455

**Methuen**
*Exiles' Return* - Gayle Greeno   s   2420
*Finders-Seekers* - Gayle Greeno   s   2421

**Metzadan**
*Hero* - Joel Rosenberg   s   4672

**Meyaga**
*The Madness Season* - C.S. Friedman   s   2058

**Mictlan**
*Dark Water's Embrace* - Stephen Leigh   s   3426

**Midgard**
*Full Tide of Night* - J.R. Dunn   s   1695

**Midkemia**
*Rage of a Demon King* - Raymond E. Feist   f   1908
*Shards of a Broken Crown* - Raymond E.
   Feist   f   1912

**Midworld**
*Mid-Flinx* - Alan Dean Foster   s   2010

**Minbar**
*To Dream in the City of Sorrows* - Kathryn M.
   Drennan   s   1654

**Minerva**
*A World of Difference* - Harry Turtledove   s   5514

**Minzan**
*The Salukan Gambit* - Sean Dalton   s   1333

**Mirabile**
*Mirabile* - Janet Kagan   s   3001

**Miranda**
*Stations of the Tide* - Michael Swanwick   s   5373

**Mistwald**
*Return Fire* - Charles Ingrid   s   2833

**Mistworld**
*Deathstalker War* - Simon R. Green   s   2366
*Mistworld* - Simon R. Green   s   2372
*Twilight of the Empire* - Simon R. Green   s   2374

**Monsoon**
*Monsoon* - Peter L. Rice   s   4583

**Moon Two**
*Captain Jack Zodiac* - Michael Kandel   f   3009

**Moudervelt**
*The Demon Princes: Volume Two* - Jack
   Vance   s   5545

**Mourngrim Castle, Shadowdale**
*Song of the Saurials* - Kate Novak   f   4167

**Mozart**
*Prophet* - Mike Resnick   s   4553

**Mra-mig**
*Conqueror's Pride* - Timothy Zahn   s   6051

**Mtu**
*Black Steel* - Steve Perry   s   4291

**Murchison's Eye**
*The Gripping Hand* - Larry Niven   s   4122

**Music**
*Winning Colors* - Elizabeth Moon   s   3976

**Mystara**
*Dragonmage of Mystara* - Thorarinn
   Gunnarsson   f   2462

**Na-Dina**
*Ancestor's World* - A.C. Crispin   s   1259

**Na Pali**
*Hard Crash* - Ryan Hughes   s   2810

**Nammerin**
*By Honor Betray'd* - Debra Doyle   s   1598

**Namport**
*Starpilot's Grave* - Debra Doyle   s   1606

**Nansen**
*A Million Open Doors* - John Barnes   s   353

**Narbon**
*The Phoenix in Flight* - Sherwood Smith   s   5138

**NBHJ-43301-G**
*Drifter's War* - William C. Dietz   s   1545

**Nehwon**
*Return to Lankhmar* - Fritz Leiber   f   3422

**Nem Ma'ak Bratuna**
*The Last Stand* - Brad Ferguson   s   1923

**Nerth**
*Ancient Heavens* - Robert E. Vardeman   s   5561

**Network**
*Fire Crossing* - Cheryl J. Franklin   s   2036

**Neuland**
*Becoming Human* - Valerie J. Freireich   s   2049

**Nevya**
*Receive the Gift* - Louise Marley   s   3628
*Sing the Light* - Louise Marley   s   3629
*Sing the Warmth* - Louise Marley   s   3630

**New Calidonia**
*The Gripping Hand* - Larry Niven   s   4122

**New California**
*Conflict* - Peter F. Hamilton   s   2522
*Consolidation* - Peter F. Hamilton   s   2523

**New Dallas**
*Regenesis* - Julia Ecklar   s   1729

**New Earth**
*Expendable* - James Alan Gardner   s   2135
*The Forever Drug* - Steve Perry   s   4296
*Other* - Gordon R. Dickson   s   1538
*Spindoc* - Steve Perry   s   4300

**New Hope**
*Deathgift* - Ann Tonsor Zeddies   s   6061
*Enemy of My Enemy* - Ben Ohlander   s   4204
*Where the Ships Die* - William C. Dietz   s   1553

**New Venus**
*We Open on Venus* - Christopher Stasheff   s   5227

**New Washington**
*Falkenberg's Legion* - Jerry Pournelle   s   4374

**NewAm**
*Voices of Chaos* - A.C. Crispin   s   1266

**Newcount Two**
*The Unwound Way* - William Adams  *s*  35

**Newholme**
*Six Moon Dance* - Sheri S. Tepper  *s*  5437

**Newhome**
*Stepwater* - L. Warren Douglas  *s*  1588
*The Wells of Phyre* - L. Warren Douglas  *s*  1589

**Newmanhome**
*The World at the End of Time* - Frederik
   Pohl  *s*  4357

**Newton**
*The Return of the Emperor* - Allan Cole  *s*  1106

**Nexus**
*The Unwound Way* - William Adams  *s*  35

**Niand**
*Star Sister* - Juanita Coulson  *s*  1211

**Niang**
*The Seeds of Time* - Kay Kenyon  *s*  3064

**Nicoji**
*Nicoji* - M. Shayne Bell  *s*  434

**Nimrud**
*Glory's War* - Alfred Coppel  *s*  1184

**Nineveh**
*Glory's War* - Alfred Coppel  *s*  1184

**Norbank**
*Officer Cadet* - Rick Shelley  *s*  4973

**Noreen**
*Call to Arms* - P.M. Griffin  *s*  2435

**Norstrilia**
*Norstrilia* - Cordwainer Smith  *s*  5105

**Northworld**
*Justice* - David Drake  *s*  1635
*Northworld* - David Drake  *s*  1637
*Vengeance* - David Drake  *s*  1648

**Novy Strana**
*Rinn's Star* - Paula E. Downing  *s*  1719

**Nowarth**
*Crown of the Serpent* - Allen L. Wold  *s*  5932

**Nuala**
*Hidden Fires* - Katharine Eliska Kimbriel  *s*  3117

**Numenes**
*Alastor* - Jack Vance  *s*  5543

**O'Brian's Stake**
*Dancer of the Sixth* - Michelle Shirey
   Crean  *s*  1254

**Occo**
*War Birds* - R.M. Meluch  *s*  3875

**O'Hara**
*Worlds Enough and Time* - Joe Haldeman  *s*  2491

**Olam**
*Dark Sky Legion* - William Barton  *s*  379

**OMSK**
*GodHeads* - Emily Devenport  *s*  1501

**Ondinee**
*The Summer Queen* - Joan D. Vinge  *s*  5572

**Oneway**
*People of the Sky* - Clare Bell  *s*  431

**Opal**
*Summertide* - Charles Sheffield  *s*  4965

**Orbix**
*Majyk by Accident* - Esther Friesner  *f*  2079

**Majyk by Design** - Esther Friesner  *f*  2080
*Majyk by Hook or Crook* - Esther Friesner  *f*  2081

**Orthe**
*Ancient Light* - Mary Gentle  *s*  2194

**Overland**
*The Fugitive Worlds* - Bob Shaw  *s*  4942

**Ozrah**
*The Ship Who Won* - Anne McCaffrey  *s*  3750

**Pacem**
*Endymion* - Dan Simmons  *s*  5051
*The Rise of Endymion* - Dan Simmons  *s*  5059

**Pacifica**
*Children of the Mind* - Orson Scott Card  *s*  883

**Pai**
*Dragon's Honor* - Kij Johnson  *s*  2922

**Palace**
*The Eyes of God* - Mark Kreighbaum  *s*  3231
*Palace* - Katharine Kerr  *s*  3072

**Palaceoid Morningstar**
*Archangel Blues* - eluki bes shahar  *s*  471

**Paradise**
*Far Harbor* - Melisa C. Michaels  *s*  3888
*Starswarm* - Jerry Pournelle  *s*  4379

**Pardal**
*Heirs of Empire* - David Weber  *s*  5672

**Path**
*Xenocide* - Orson Scott Card  *s*  899

**Patma**
*Only Child* - H.M. Hoover  *s*  2764

**Paumons**
*Naked to the Stars/The Alien Way* - Gordon R.
   Dickson  *s*  1537

**Pava**
*The Voices of Heaven* - Frederik Pohl  *s*  4356

**Pell**
*Finity's End* - C.J. Cherryh  *s*  988

**Peponi**
*Paradise: A Chronicle of a Distant World* - Mike
   Resnick  *s*  4552

**Perdur**
*Shadow's End* - Sheri S. Tepper  *s*  5435

**Periapt**
*A Screaming Across the Sky* - Brian Daley  *s*  1315

**Pern**
*All the Weyrs of Pern* - Anne McCaffrey  *s*  3719
*The Chronicles of Pern: First Fall* - Anne
   McCaffrey  *s*  3721
*The Dolphins of Pern* - Anne McCaffrey  *s*  3729
*Dragonseye* - Anne McCaffrey  *s*  3730
*The Masterharper of Pern* - Anne
   McCaffrey  *s*  3739
*The Renegades of Pern* - Anne McCaffrey  *s*  3746

**Persephone**
*Dreaming Metal* - Melissa Scott  *s*  4895
*Dreamships* - Melissa Scott  *s*  4896

**Petaybee**
*Power Lines* - Anne McCaffrey  *s*  3743
*Power Play* - Anne McCaffrey  *s*  3744
*Powers That Be* - Anne McCaffrey  *s*  3745

**Petrarch**
*A Wizard in Mind* - Christopher Stasheff  *s*  5232

**Pharaoh**
*The Pharaoh Contract* - Ray Aldridge  *s*  63

**Phastillan**
*Cannon's Orb* - L. Warren Douglas  *s*  1586
*A Plague of Change* - L. Warren Douglas  *s*  1587

**Phaze**
*Phaze Doubt* - Piers Anthony  *f*  184

**Phyre**
*The Wells of Phyre* - L. Warren Douglas  *s*  1589

**Pinega**
*The Fall of Sirius* - Wil McCarthy  *s*  3762

**Pitcairn**
*The Remarkables* - Robert Reed  *s*  4507

**Planet of the Archbuilders**
*Girl in Landscape* - Jonathan Lethem  *s*  3440

**Planet of the N'lacs**
*The Past of Forever* - Juanita Coulson  *s*  1210

**Planet of the Q'aantre**
*Illegal Alien* - James Luceno  *s*  3543

**Planet of the Robot Slaves**
*Planet of the Robot Slaves* - Harry Harrison  *s*  2573

**Plione**
*White Light* - William Barton  *s*  384

**Porotane**
*The Glass Warrior* - Robert E. Vardeman  *f*  5563

**Port Rudistal**
*Prisoner of Conscience* - Susan R.
   Matthews  *s*  3693

**Porta Flora**
*The Tenth Class* - Karen Ripley  *s*  4594

**Prime**
*Vortex* - Allan Cole  *s*  1108

**Procyon Four**
*Legacy of Earth* - Juanita Coulson  *s*  1209

**Prokaryon**
*The Children Star* - Joan Slonczewski  *s*  5090

**Prosperity**
*Rolling Hot* - David Drake  *s*  1642

**Proxt**
*Medicine Show* - Jody Lynn Nye  *s*  4172

**Pryan**
*Elven Star* - Margaret Weis  *f*  5712

**Ptolemy**
*Blood Lines* - William R. Burkett Jr.  *s*  774

**Pyran**
*Into the Labyrinth* - Margaret Weis  *f*  5716

**Qo'noS**
*Kahless* - Michael Jan Friedman  *s*  2065
*Triangle: Imzadi II* - Peter David  *s*  1388

**Quake**
*Summertide* - Charles Sheffield  *s*  4965

**Quaraqua**
*The Engines of God* - Jack McDevitt  *s*  3787

**Query**
*Timediver's Dawn* - L.E. Modesitt Jr.  *s*  3940

**Rainbow Bridge**
*The Demons at Rainbow Bridge* - Jack L.
   Chalker  *s*  952
*The Ninety Trillion Fausts* - Jack L. Chalker  *s*  958

**Rakhat**
*Children of God* - Mary Doria Russell  *s*  4735
*The Sparrow* - Mary Doria Russell  *s*  4736

**Ramaj Ariye Asengar**
*Shadow Leader* - Tara K. Harper   *f*   2552

**L'Rau**
*Earthgrip* - Harry Turtledove   *s*   5499

**The Realm of the Nameless**
*Reclamation* - Sarah Zettel   *s*   6081

**Refuge**
*Dreamfall* - Joan D. Vinge   *s*   5571
*Dreamships* - Melissa Scott   *s*   4896

**Rega**
*Relic of Empire* - W. Michael Gear   *s*   2171

**Reis**
*Memento Mori* - Shariann Lewitt   *s*   3454

**Restaapa**
*Jade Darcy and the Zen Pirates* - Stephen
   Goldin   *s*   2260

**Resurrection**
*Psykosis* - Wilhelmina Baird   *s*   296

**Rethan**
*Death's Head* - Mel Keegan   *s*   3029

**Reyson's Planet**
*Regenesis* - Julia Ecklar   *s*   1729

**Rhomary Land**
*Signs of Life* - Cherry Wilder   *s*   5804

**Rhui**
*An Earthly Crown* - Kate Elliott   *s*   1771
*Jaran* - Kate Elliott   *s*   1772
*The Law of Becoming* - Kate Elliott   *s*   1774

**Rigel II**
*Beholder's Eye* - Julie E. Czerneda   *s*   1303

**Rigel V**
*Mind Meld* - John Vornholt   *s*   5596

**Rimway**
*A Talent for War* - Jack McDevitt   *s*   3790

**Ringworld**
*The Ringworld Throne* - Larry Niven   *s*   4128

**Risthmus**
*Cat Scratch Fever* - Tara K. Harper   *s*   2550

**Rithra**
*The Disinherited* - Peter David   *s*   1381

**Riverworld**
*Quest to Riverworld* - Philip Jose Farmer   *s*   1872
*Tales of Riverworld* - Philip Jose Farmer   *s*   1875
*To Your Scattered Bodies Go* - Philip Jose
   Farmer   *s*   1876

**Roanoke**
*A World Lost* - James B. Johnson   *s*   2921

**Robot City**
*Changeling* - Stephen Leigh   *s*   3425
*Renegade* - Cordell Scotten   *s*   4903

**Rockhouse Major**
*Sporting Chance* - Elizabeth Moon   *s*   3974

**Rokam**
*The Promise* - Monica Hughes   *s*   2808

**Romulus**
*The Return* - William Shatner   *s*   4933

**Ronin**
*The Missing Matter* - Thomas R.
   McDonough   *s*   3805

**Root Canal**
*Free Radicals* - Jack McKinney   *s*   3848

**Rosalia**
*Throy* - Jack Vance   *s*   5550

**Rotor**
*Nemesis* - Isaac Asimov   *s*   247

**Rototara**
*The Hunter on Arena* - Rose Estes   *s*   1838

**Rraladoona**
*Treaty at Doona* - Anne McCaffrey   *s*   3752

**Ruantl**
*Requiem for Anthi* - Jay D. Blakeney   *s*   517

**Ruml Homeworld**
*Naked to the Stars/The Alien Way* - Gordon R.
   Dickson   *s*   1537

**Rune**
*Iroshi* - Cary Osborne   *s*   4228

**Rura Penthe**
*Star Trek VI: The Undiscovered Country* - J.M.
   Dillard   *s*   1556

**S-15**
*Journey to Terezor* - Frank Asch   *s*   221

**Sado**
*Yamato: A Rage in Heaven* - Ken Kato   *s*   3014

**Saede**
*Echoes of Issel* - Diann Thornley   *s*   5466

**Saegrenot**
*Cathy IV* - Frances Lucas   *s*   3539

**Sagdeev**
*White Light* - William Barton   *s*   384

**Salt**
*Humility Garden* - Felicity Savage   *f*   4850

**Samaria**
*The Alleluia Files* - Sharon Shinn   *s*   4999
*Archangel* - Sharon Shinn   *s*   5000
*Jovah's Angel* - Sharon Shinn   *s*   5001

**Samstead**
*Mid-Flinx* - Alan Dean Foster   *s*   2010

**Sanctuary**
*Sanctuary* - John Vornholt   *s*   5597

**Schuyler's World**
*McLendon's Syndrome* - Robert Frezza   *s*   2053

**Seelzar**
*The Planet Beyond* - Steve Mudd   *s*   4043

**Selmun III/R'debh**
*Mainline* - Deborah Christian   *s*   1026

**Senisran**
*The Howling Stones* - Alan Dean Foster   *s*   2006

**Serii**
*Fire Crossing* - Cheryl J. Franklin   *s*   2036

**Shin System**
*The 97th Step* - Steve Perry   *s*   4287

**Shola**
*Fire Margins* - Lisanne Norman   *s*   4137
*Fortune's Wheel* - Lisanne Norman   *s*   4138
*Razor's Edge* - Lisanne Norman   *s*   4139

**Shora**
*Daughter of Elysium* - Joan Slonczewski   *s*   5091

**The Shouter**
*The Expediter* - J. Brian Clarke   *s*   1062

**Shub**
*Deathstalker Honor* - Simon R. Green   *s*   2364

**Siatha**
*The Light in Exile* - Cheryl J. Franklin   *s*   2038

**Siddah-II**
*The Clone Crisis* - Lee McKeone   *s*   3829

**Siegfried**
*A Wizard in Midgard* - Christopher Stasheff   *s*   5231

**Sigma Draconis II**
*A Woman of the Iron People* - Eleanor
   Arnason   *s*   211

**Sigma Radidiani**
*A Roil of Stars* - Don Wismer   *s*   5930

**Sims Bancorp Colony 3245.12**
*Remnant Population* - Elizabeth Moon   *s*   3972

**Sinaha**
*Border Dispute* - Daniel R. Kerns   *s*   3066

**Sirialis**
*Hunting Party* - Elizabeth Moon   *s*   3968
*Sporting Chance* - Elizabeth Moon   *s*   3974

**Sirius 23**
*Reality Is What You Can Get Away With: An
   Illustrated Screenplay* - Robert Anton
   Wilson   *s*   5904

**Skirren**
*Once a Hero* - Michael A. Stackpole   *f*   5203

**Skye**
*Bretta Martyn* - L. Neil Smith   *s*   5128

**Slowyear**
*Stopping at Slowyear* - Frederik Pohl   *s*   4355

**Snister**
*Habu* - James B. Johnson   *s*   2920

**Soissons**
*Path of the Fury* - David Weber   *s*   5680

**Solamnia**
*Kaz the Minotaur* - Richard A. Knaak   *f*   3172

**Solferino**
*Putting Up Roots* - Charles Sheffield   *s*   4964

**Solio II**
*The Widowmaker* - Mike Resnick   *s*   4559

**Solomon**
*Soothsayer* - Mike Resnick   *s*   4557

**Sook**
*Emperor of Everything* - Ray Aldridge   *s*   62
*The Pharaoh Contract* - Ray Aldridge   *s*   63

**Sparta**
*Go Tell the Spartans* - Jerry Pournelle   *s*   4375
*Prince of Mercenaries* - Jerry Pournelle   *s*   4377
*Prince of Sparta* - Jerry Pournelle   *s*   4378

**Sphinx**
*More than Honor* - David Weber   *s*   5676

**Ssan**
*Shadows on the Sun* - Michael Jan
   Friedman   *s*   2069

**Stalinvast**
*Inquisitor* - Ian Watson   *s*   5637

**Stalleybrass**
*Redliners* - David Drake   *s*   1641

**Star Rest**
*Star Precinct* - Kevin D. Randle   *s*   4470

**Starker IV**
*Brander's Book* - C.J. Mills   *s*   3909
*Egil's Book* - C.J. Mills   *s*   3910
*Kit's Book* - C.J. Mills   *s*   3911
*Zjhanne's Book* - C.J. Mills   *s*   3912

**Star's Rest**
*The Artifact* - W. Michael Gear  s  2165

**Stayman**
*Jaydium* - Deborah Wheeler  s  5774

**Stepwater**
*Stepwater* - L. Warren Douglas  s  1588

**Stohlson's Redemption**
*The Thirteenth Majestral* - Hayford Peirce  s  4277

**Storm**
*Eggheads* - Emily Devenport  s  1500
*GodHeads* - Emily Devenport  s  1501

**Strana Mechty**
*Prince of Havoc* - Michael A. Stackpole  s  5204

**Strand**
*The Unicorn Peace* - John Lee  f  3399
*The Unicorn Solution* - John Lee  f  3400
*The Unicorn War* - John Lee  f  3401

**Stratos**
*Glory Season* - David Brin  s  686

**Stromvi**
*The Inquisitor* - Cheryl J. Franklin  s  2037

**Styreia**
*Kar Kalim* - Deborah Christian  f  1025

**Styx**
*Sister Blood* - Karen Haber  s  2476
*Woman Without a Shadow* - Karen Haber  s  2478

**Suid-Afrika**
*Fire in a Faraway Place* - Robert Frezza  s  2052

**Suid Afrika**
*A Small Colonial War* - Robert Frezza  s  2054

**Summerland**
*Deathstalker War* - Simon R. Green  s  2366

**Sunga**
*The Venom Trees of Sunga* - L. Sprague de
  Camp  s  1420

**Swamp**
*Prison Planet* - William C. Dietz  s  1551

**Talos IV**
*Prime Directive* - Judith Reeves-Stevens  s  4514

**Tambora**
*Fire Planet* - P.M. Griffin  s  2436

**Tamir**
*Dragon's Claw* - Alex McDonough  s  3800

**Tankur**
*Deep Quarry* - John E. Stith  s  5302

**Tannia**
*War Birds* - R.M. Meluch  s  3875

**Tara**
*Blackmantle: A Triumph* - Patricia Kennealy-
  Morrison  f  3059

**Taridwyn**
*Legacies* - Alison Sinclair  s  5069

**Tartaros**
*Infinity Hold* - Barry B. Longyear  s  3522

**Tatooine**
*The Mandalorian Armor* - K.W. Jeter  s  2914
*Tales From Jabba's Palace* - Kevin J.
  Anderson  s  114
*Tales From the Mos Eisley Cantina* - Kevin J.
  Anderson  s  115
*Zorba the Hutt's Revenge* - Paul Davids  s  1394

**Tau Ceti IV**
*Tower of the Gods* - Thomas A. Easton  s  1726

**Tau Puppis IV**
*Maverick* - Bruce Bethke  s  484

**Tau System**
*The 97th Step* - Steve Perry  s  4287

**Taurin**
*Exile* - Michael P. Kube-McDowell  s  3248

**Taxhaven**
*A Wizard in Absentia* - Christopher Stasheff  s  5229

**Technos III**
*Deathstalker Rebellion* - Simon R. Green  s  2365

**Tel Hasa**
*Dancing Vac* - S.N. Lewitt  s  3451

**Temaris**
*Probe* - Margaret Wander Bonanno  s  569

**Tembo**
*Brother Death* - Steve Perry  s  4292

**Terfreya**
*The White Regiment* - John Dalmas  s  1327

**Terra II**
*Mother Lode* - Zach Hughes  s  2812

**Terrapin**
*Dragon's Claw* - Alex McDonough  s  3800
*Dragon's Eye* - Alex McDonough  s  3801
*Scorpio* - Alex McDonough  s  3802

**Terreille**
*Daughter of the Blood* - Anne Bishop  f  495

**Testament**
*Testament* - Valerie J. Freireich  s  2051

**Thallon**
*End Game* - Peter David  s  1382

**Thanet**
*Night Lamp* - Jack Vance  s  5548

**Thaumia**
*Wizard's Mole* - Brad Strickland  f  5337

**Thelerie**
*The Ship Errant* - Jody Lynn Nye  s  4175

**Theolithos**
*White Light* - William Barton  s  384

**Thieves' World**
*City at the Edge of Time* - Janet Morris  f  4015

**Thompson's Gazelle**
*Black Steel* - Steve Perry  s  4291

**Thors Anvil**
*Anvil* - Nicolas van Pallandt  s  5540

**Thoska-Roole**
*A Covenant of Justice* - David Gerrold  s  2207

**The Thousand Island World**
*The Return of the Breakneck Boys* - Geary
  Gravel  s  2332

**Throne**
*The LaNague Chronicles* - F. Paul Wilson  s  5889

**Thul**
*The Ice Beast* - Frank A. Javor  s  2881

**Tiamat**
*The Summer Queen* - Joan D. Vinge  s  5572

**Tienah**
*Foragers* - Charles Oberndorf  s  4187

**Tigian II**
*Deep Freeze* - Zach Hughes  s  2811

**Tihrglas**
*The Golden Queen* - Dave Wolverton  s  5951

**Timshel**
*The Joy Machine* - James Gunn  s  2458

**Tine's World**
*A Fire upon the Deep* - Vernor Vinge  s  5573

**Tir.ki.k.ai**
*Alien Tongue* - Stephen Leigh  s  3424

**Tith**
*Feather Stroke* - Sydney J. Van Scyoc  f  5542

**T'nane**
*Dreaming in Smoke* - Tricia Sullivan  s  5353

**Tokasha**
*Way of the Clans* - Robert Thurston  s  5469

**Topawa**
*Dominion's Reach* - Diann Thornley  s  5465

**Topside**
*The Snake Oil Wars* - Parke Godwin  s  2249

**Tori**
*Mission: Tori* - Johanna Bolton  s  564

**Toril**
*Into the Void* - Nigel Findley  f  1937

**Traja**
*Hand of Prophecy* - Severna Park  s  4244
*Speaking Dreams* - Severna Park  s  4245

**Trantor**
*Forward the Foundation* - Isaac Asimov  s  236
*Foundation and Chaos* - Greg Bear  s  418
*Foundation's Fear* - Gregory Benford  s  446

**Tremonthin**
*Beyond the Gate* - Dave Wolverton  s  5949

**Trenco**
*Galactic Patrol* - Edward E. Smith  s  5116

**Trinity**
*Silent Dances* - A.C. Crispin  s  1263
*Silent Songs* - A.C. Crispin  s  1264

**Tsikshka**
*Lair of the Cyclops* - Allen L. Wold  s  5933

**Tsing IV**
*To Fear the Light* - Ben Bova  s  595

**Tssek**
*Brother to Shadows* - Andre Norton  s  4142

**Tumbleweed**
*Mind Slayer* - Kevin D. Randle  s  4469

**Tundra**
*The Widowmaker* - Mike Resnick  s  4559

**Tupelo**
*O Pioneer!* - Frederik Pohl  s  4350

**Tyrus**
*Invasion America* - Christie Golden  s  2252

**Uhao**
*Berserker Fury* - Fred Saberhagen  s  4760

**Ult**
*Hero* - Dave Duncan  s  1680

**Unruli**
*A Passage of Stars* - Alis A. Rasmussen  s  4482

**Unua**
*Flies From the Amber* - Wil McCarthy  s  3763

**Uriel**
*Regenesis* - Julia Ecklar  s  1729

**Urrytha**
*Chrysalis* - David Niall Wilson  s  5880

**Urulan**
*Daughter of Elysium* - Joan Slonczewski  s  5091

**Uskos**
*The Master of Chaos* - Terry A. Adams  s  34

**Valennia**
*Terrible Swift Sword* - William R.
Forstchen  s  1983

**Vancadia**
*Renegade* - Gene DeWeese  s  1511

**Vardalia**
*Sister Blood* - Karen Haber  s  2476

**Veil**
*Cup of Clay* - Carole Nelson Douglas  f  1583
*Seed upon the Wind* - Carole Nelson
Douglas  f  1584

**Ver Day**
*Mistwalker* - Denise Lopez Heald  s  2637

**Veridian III**
*The Return* - William Shatner  s  4933

**Veschke**
*Hellspark* - Janet Kagan  s  3000

**Victoria**
*Squadron Alert* - Roland J. Green  s  2352
*The Sum of Things* - Roland J. Green  s  2353

**Virginity**
*Clipjoint* - Wilhelmina Baird  s  294

**Virimonde**
*Deathstalker Honor* - Simon R. Green  s  2364

**Voerenhutz**
*Use of Weapons* - Iain M. Banks  s  328

**Voerster**
*Glory* - Alfred Coppel  s  1182

**Vulcan**
*Avenger* - William Shatner  s  4928
*Sarek* - A.C. Crispin  s  1260
*Vulcan's Glory* - D.C. Fontana  s  1967

**Wanderjahr**
*School of Fire* - David Sherman  s  4982

**Wanderweb**
*Hellflower* - eluki bes shahar  s  473

**Well World**
*Echoes of the Well of Souls* - Jack L.
Chalker  s  953
*Gods of the Well of Souls* - Jack L. Chalker  s  954
*Shadow of the Well of Souls* - Jack L.
Chalker  s  961

**Wemar**
*The Galactic Gourmet* - James White  s  5778

**Werel**
*Four Ways to Forgiveness* - Ursula K. Le
Guin  s  3380

**Wheat**
*Beautiful Strangers* - Melanie Tem  h  5420

**Widdershins**
*Dragon's Queen* - Carol L. Dennis  f  1488

**Wilson**
*A Million Open Doors* - John Barnes  s  353

**Witch World**
*Flight of Vengeance* - Andre Norton  f  4152
*The Key of the Keplian* - Andre Norton  f  4156
*Songsmith* - Andre Norton  f  4161
*Storms of Victory* - Andre Norton  f  4162
*The Warding of Witch World* - Andre
Norton  f  4163

**Wolf IV**
*Hellworld* - Simon R. Green  s  2371
*Twilight of the Empire* - Simon R. Green  s  2374

**Wolfbane**
*Delta Search* - William Shatner  s  4930

**Worber's World**
*The Final Battle* - William C. Dietz  s  1546

**The World**
*OtherWise* - Margaret Wander Bonanno  s  567
*The Web of Spider* - W. Michael Gear  s  2173

**World of Tiers**
*More than Fire* - Philip Jose Farmer  s  1871

**Worlorn**
*Dying of the Light* - George R.R. Martin  s  3644

**Wunderland**
*The Children's Hour* - Jerry Pournelle  s  4372
*Inconstant Star* - Poul Anderson  s  129
*Man-Kzin Wars IV* - Larry Niven  s  4124
*Man-Kzin Wars V* - Larry Niven  s  4125

**X**
*Bagatelle—Guinevere* - Nancy Bogen  f  558

**Xanth**
*Man From Mundania* - Piers Anthony  f  180

**Xavier**
*Winning Colors* - Elizabeth Moon  s  3976

**Xi-7**
*Marks of Our Brothers* - Jane M. Lindskold  s  3475

**Xica de Silva III**
*Life Form* - Alan Dean Foster  s  2008

**Yamato**
*Glory's People* - Alfred Coppel  s  1183

**Yeowe**
*Four Ways to Forgiveness* - Ursula K. Le
Guin  s  3380

**Yetel**
*Token of Dragonsblood* - Damaris Cole  f  1114

**Yoldragi**
*The Rim-World Legacy and Beyond* - Frank A.
Javor  s  2882

**Yuang**
*The Madness Season* - C.S. Friedman  s  2058

**Yuulith**
*The Lion of Farside* - John Dalmas  f  1324

**Zany-Doo**
*Reward for Retief* - Keith Laumer  s  3345

**Zauberberg**
*The Mountain Walks* - Roland J. Green  s  2349

**Zeta Reticuli 2**
*The Bushido Incident* - Betty Anne
Crawford  s  1248

**Z'Ha'dum**
*The Shadow Within* - Jeanne Cavelos  s  944

**Zoo**
*Cathouse* - Dean Ing  s  2828

**Z'taruhn**
*Larissa* - Emily Devenport  s  1503
*Shade* - Emily Devenport  s  1504

**Zuul**
*Steelheart* - William C. Dietz  s  1552

## PLUTO

*The Golden Globe* - John Varley  s  5565

**Gravities Research Station**
*The Ring of Charon* - Roger MacBride Allen  s  80

## POLAND

*A Blessing on the Moon* - Joseph Skibell  f  5079
*Briar Rose* - Jane Yolen  f  6029
*Cold Allies* - Patricia Anthony  s  157
*The Flying Warlord* - Leo Frankowski  s  2044
*The High-Tech Knight* - Leo Frankowski  s  2045
*Lord Conrad's Lady* - Leo Frankowski  s  2046
*The Radiant Warrior* - Leo Frankowski  s  2047

**Auschwitz**
*Days of Cain* - J.R. Dunn  s  1694
*Time's Arrow* - Martin Amis  s  96

**Okoitz**
*Conrad's Quest for Rubber* - Leo
Frankowski  s  2043

## PORTUGAL

**Lisbon**
*God's Fires* - Patricia Anthony  s  159

**Quintas**
*God's Fires* - Patricia Anthony  s  159

## PUERTO RICO

**Andrea Island**
*Mr. Was* - Pete Hautman  s  2614

**Arecibo**
*The Sparrow* - Mary Doria Russell  s  4736

## ROMAN EMPIRE

*Far Edge of Darkness* - Linda Evans  s  1855
*The Forest House* - Marion Zimmer Bradley  f  633
*Time Scout* - Robert Asprin  s  263
*Wagers of Sin* - Robert Asprin  s  264

**Rome**
*Child of the Eagle* - Esther Friesner  f  2073

## ROMANIA

**Bucharest**
*Children of the Night* - Dan Simmons  h  5050
*Nocturnas* - Shawn Ryan  h  4755

**Castel Vlaicu**
*The Lost* - Jonathan Aycliffe  h  279

**Piatra Neamt**
*Conglomeros* - Jesse Browner  f  729

## RUSSIA

*A Deeper Sea* - Alexander Jablokov  s  2838
*Firebird* - Mercedes Lackey  f  3281
*ME: A Novel of Self Discovery* - Thomas T.
Thomas  s  5452
*The Princess and the Dragon* - Roberto
Pazzi  f  4272
*Terraplane* - Jack Womack  s  5960
*When Dreams Collide* - Wm. Mark
Simmons  f  5063
*Yvgenie* - C.J. Cherryh  f  1005

**Arkhangelsk**
*The Fortunate Fall* - Raphael Carter  s  927

**Leningrad**
*The Fortunate Fall* - Raphael Carter  s  927

**Moscow**
*The Fourth Rome* - David Drake  *s*  1631
*The Green Progression* - L.E. Modesitt Jr.  *s*  3932
*Peter Nevsky and the True Story of the Russian Moon
   Landing* - John Calvin Batchelor  *s*  388
*A Second Infinity* - Michael D. Weaver  *s*  5660
*Skeletons* - Al Sarrantonio  *h*  4834

**Novgorod**
*Dancing Bears* - Fred Saberhagen  *f*  4764

**Petrograd**
*Scorpio Descending* - Alex McDonough  *s*  3803

**St. Petersburg**
*Writ in Blood* - Chelsea Quinn Yarbro  *h*  6019

**Siberia**
*The Animal Wife* - Elizabeth Marshall
   Thomas  *f*  5444
*Dancing Bears* - Fred Saberhagen  *f*  4764
*Scorpio Descending* - Alex McDonough  *s*  3803

**Vojvoda**
*Chernevog* - C.J. Cherryh  *f*  982
*Rusalka* - C.J. Cherryh  *f*  1002

## SATURN

*Saturn Rukh* - Robert L. Forward  *s*  1991

**Cloudcroft**
*The Clouds of Saturn* - Michael McCollum  *s*  3770

**Mimas**
*Red Dwarf: Infinity Welcomes Careful Drivers* - Grant
   Naylor  *s*  4077

**Titan**
*The Immortality Option* - James P. Hogan  *s*  2725
*Saturn's Child* - Nichelle Nichols  *s*  4101
*Titan* - Stephen Baxter  *s*  405

## SCANDINAVIA

*A Ride on the Red Mare's Back* - Ursula K. Le
   Guin  *f*  3382

**Djofullhol**
*The Dragon's Carbuncle* - Elizabeth H.
   Boyer  *f*  605

## SCOTLAND

*The Adept* - Katherine Kurtz  *f*  3254
*The Black School* - J.N. Williamson  *h*  5851
*Dagger Magic* - Katherine Kurtz  *f*  3256
*Death of an Adept* - Katherine Kurtz  *f*  3257
*The Element of Fire* - Jason Henderson  *f*  2657
*Flying Dutch* - Tom Holt  *f*  2750
*Goblins* - Vincent Courtney  *h*  1212
*A History Maker* - Alasdair Gray  *s*  2338
*The House of Doors* - Brian Lumley  *h*  3554
*Indiana Jones and the Dance of the Giants* - Rob
   MacGregor  *f*  3588
*The Last Highlander* - Claire Cross  *f*  1271
*The Lodge of the Lynx* - Katherine Kurtz  *f*  3259
*The Lost History of Redwyn* - William Jay  *f*  2883
*A Love through Time* - Terri Brisbin  *f*  691
*Maze of Worlds* - Brian Lumley  *h*  3559
*Mythology Abroad* - Jody Lynn Nye  *f*  4174
*Picking the Ballad's Bones* - Elizabeth Ann
   Scarborough  *f*  4869
*Scotland the Brave* - Jennifer Roberson  *f*  4611
*The Shining Company* - Rosemary Sutcliff  *f*  5359
*The Spiral Dance* - R. Garcia y Robertson  *f*  2121
*The Templar Treasure* - Katherine Kurtz  *f*  3261
*The Throne of Tara* - John Desjarlais  *f*  1498
*Witch of the North* - Courtway Jones  *f*  2940
*Witchwood* - John Buchan  *f*  750

**Cairngorms**
*Snowbeast!* - Peter Tremayne  *h*  5482

**Drenewydd**
*Coven* - Steven William Rimmer  *h*  4591

**Drumnadrochit**
*City of Iron* - Chet Williamson  *h*  5843

**Edinburgh**
*Expiry Date* - Carol Anne Davis  *h*  1401
*The Matrix* - Jonathan Aycliffe  *h*  280
*Moonseed* - Stephen Baxter  *s*  400
*Necroscope: The Lost Years* - Brian
   Lumley  *h*  3560
*Resurgence* - Brian Lumley  *h*  3564

**Eilean a'Tempull Dubh**
*Donnerjack* - Roger Zelazny  *s*  6063

**Fionnphort**
*Standing Wave* - Howard V. Hendrix  *s*  2661

**Inverkeithing**
*Quest for a Maid* - Frances Mary Hendry  *f*  2662

**Loch Ness**
*Between the Devil and the Deep* - J.M.
   Morgan  *h*  3998
*Testament of the Dragon* - Margaret Weis  *f*  5729

**The Orkneys**
*Mordred's Curse* - Ian McDowell  *f*  3806

**St. Kilda Islands**
*The Druid's Gift* - Margaret J. Anderson  *f*  121

## SERBIA

*Landscape Painted with Tea* - Milorad
   Pavic  *f*  4263

## SOUTH AFRICA

*Apartheid, Superstrings, and Mordecai Thubana* -
   Michael Bishop  *s*  496

**Cape Town**
*Python Isle* - Kenneth Robeson  *f*  4624

**Durban**
*City of Golden Shadow* - Tad Williams  *s*  5828

**Kuwenezi Canton, Kuwenezi**
*Earth* - David Brin  *s*  685

## SOUTH AMERICA

*Dream Maker* - W.A. Harbinson  *s*  2542
*Hope of Earth* - Piers Anthony  *s*  175
*Living with the Reptiles* - Roger L.
   DiSilvestro  *s*  1563
*The Queen of the Damned* - Anne Rice  *h*  4574
*The Secret Weavers: Stories of the Fantastic by Latin
   American Women* - Marjorie Agosin  *f*  43
*Senor Vivo and the Coca Lord* - Louis de
   Bernieres  *f*  1411
*Through the Arc of the Rain Forest* - Karen Tei
   Yamashita  *f*  6008
*The War of Don Emmanuel's Nether Parts* - Louis de
   Bernieres  *f*  1412

**Andes Mountains**
*The Face in the Abyss* - A. Merritt  *f*  3878

## SPACE STATION

*Article 23* - William R. Forstchen  *s*  1978
*Berserker Kill* - Fred Saberhagen  *s*  4761
*Carmen Miranda's Ghost Is Haunting Space Station
   Three* - Don Sakers  *s*  4785

*Grounded!* - Chris Claremont  *s*  1041
*In the Company of the Mind* - Steven Piziks  *s*  4339
*Ring of Swords* - Eleanor Arnason  *s*  210
*Run for the Stars/Echoes of Thunder* - Harlan
   Ellison  *s*  1788
*Sam Gunn, Unlimited* - Ben Bova  *s*  593
*Schismatrix Plus* - Bruce Sterling  *s*  5260

**Amalthea**
*Warlords of Jupiter* - William H. Keith Jr.  *s*  3036

**Angel Station**
*Angel Station* - Walter Jon Williams  *s*  5833

**Ares**
*The Rifter's Covenant* - Sherwood Smith  *s*  5140

**ATG-311-B**
*Aggressor Six* - Wil McCarthy  *s*  3760

**Aurelian**
*Stationfall* - Arthur Byron Cover  *s*  1216

**Auriga**
*Alien Resurrection* - A.C. Crispin  *s*  1258

**Babylon 5**
*Day of the Dead* - Neil Gaiman  *s*  2102
*Personal Agendas* - Al Sarrantonio  *s*  4833
*Thirdspace* - Peter David  *s*  1387
*The Touch of Your Shadow, the Whisper of Your Name*
   - Neal Barrett Jr.  *s*  367
*Voices* - John Vornholt  *s*  5598

**The Ball**
*Trust Territory* - Janet Morris  *s*  4019

**Battle Station Alpha XIV**
*The Final Battle* - William C. Dietz  *s*  1546

**Billingate**
*The Gap into Power: A Dark and Hungry God Arises*
   - Stephen R. Donaldson  *s*  1574

**Bryce Station**
*The War Minstrels* - Karen Haber  *s*  2477

**Cassamir Station**
*Hunting the Corrigan's Blood* - Holly Lisle  *s*  3484

**Cesarea Station**
*Hidden Fires* - Katharine Eliska Kimbriel  *s*  3117

**Clarke County**
*Clarke County, Space* - Allen Steele  *s*  5241
*A King of Infinite Space* - Allen Steele  *s*  5243

**Clarke Orbital Station**
*Looking for the Mahdi* - N. Lee Wood  *s*  5966

**CM-2**
*Higher Education* - Charles Sheffield  *s*  4958

**CM-26**
*Higher Education* - Charles Sheffield  *s*  4958

**Co-Mars Two**
*Mining the Oort* - Frederik Pohl  *s*  4349

**Com-Mine Station**
*The Gap into Conflict: The Real Story* - Stephen R.
   Donaldson  *s*  1572

**Corson**
*Lightwing* - Tara K. Harper  *s*  2551

**Crane**
*Silent Songs* - A.C. Crispin  *s*  1264

**The Cylinder**
*Catch the Lightning* - Catherine Asaro  *s*  218

**D.S. 949**
*Berserker* - S.D. Perry  *s*  4285

**Deep Space Nine**
*Bloodletter* - K.W. Jeter  *s*  2908

*Call to Arms* - Diane Carey   s   901
*Devil in the Sky* - Greg Cox   s   1226
*Fallen Heroes* - Dafydd ab Hugh   s   8
*Time's Enemy* - L.A. Graf   s   2297
*Vengeance* - Dafydd ab Hugh   s   10
*Warped* - K.W. Jeter   s   2917

**Delta Station**
*Alien Earth* - Megan Lindholm   s   3469

**Downbelow**
*Downbelow Station* - C.J. Cherryh   s   985

**Earth's Orbital Space Colonies**
*Ash Ock* - Christopher Hinz   s   2690
*The Paratwa* - Christopher Hinz   s   2691

**Ellfive**
*Second Star* - Dana Stabenow   s   5188

**Equality**
*In the Wrong Hands* - Edward Gibson   s   2215

**Estrade**
*Ammonite* - Nicola Griffith   s   2443

**Fleet Orientation Station Med.**
*An Exchange of Hostages* - Susan R.
   Matthews   s   3692

**Floating World**
*The Cybernetic Shogun* - Victor Milan   s   3890

**Fold Council Station**
*The Children Star* - Joan Slonczewski   s   5090

**Freedom**
*Mindblast* - Diane Duane   s   1665

**Gal Three**
*Power Play* - Anne McCaffrey   s   3744

**Gateway Asteroid**
*The Gateway Trip: Tales and Vignettes of the Heechee*
  - Frederik Pohl   s   4346

**Geek Space Nine**
*Star Wreck 6: Geek Space Nine* - Leah
   Rewolinski   s   4562

**Guild Hall Station**
*Fool's War* - Sarah Zettel   s   6079

**Halo City**
*Halo* - Tom Maddox   s   3604

**Harmony**
*Derelict for Trade* - Andre Norton   s   4148

**High Haven**
*Harm's Way* - Colin Greenland   s   2416

**High Orbital Mfg. Env.**
*Lightpaths* - Howard V. Hendrix   s   2660

**Hightown**
*Cortez on Jupiter* - Ernest Hogan   s   2721

**Ithica Base**
*Cortez on Jupiter* - Ernest Hogan   s   2721

**Jeross**
*Mind Light* - Margaret Davis   s   1407

**Jupiter**
*A Deeper Sea* - Alexander Jablokov   s   2838

**Kibalchick**
*Lifeline* - Kevin J. Anderson   s   111

**Kolnar**
*The Ship Avenged* - S.M. Stirling   s   5298

**Koskiusko**
*Once a Hero* - Elizabeth Moon   s   3970

**Kud'ar Mub'at's Web**
*The Mandalorian Armor* - K.W. Jeter   s   2914

**L4**
*The Nanotech Chronicles* - Michael Flynn   s   1964

**Limbo**
*Limbo Search* - Parke Godwin   s   2245

**Lorelei**
*Phule's Paradise* - Robert Asprin   s   261

**Mael Station**
*Random Factor* - Joel Henry Sherman   s   4984

**Meetpoint**
*Chanur's Legacy* - C.J. Cherryh   s   981

**Mir**
*Firestar* - Michael Flynn   s   1962

**Naked Purple Habitat**
*The Shattered Sphere* - Roger MacBride Allen   s   81

**Never**
*Clipjoint* - Wilhelmina Baird   s   294
*Crashcourse* - Wilhelmina Baird   s   295

**New Dentinies**
*The Ship Avenged* - S.M. Stirling   s   5298

**Nuevo Valparaiso**
*Hot Sky at Midnight* - Robert Silverberg   s   5032

**Orbital Biodiversity Preserve**
*Lightpaths* - Howard V. Hendrix   s   2660
*Standing Wave* - Howard V. Hendrix   s   2661

**Orbitech**
*Lifeline* - Kevin J. Anderson   s   111

**OrbLab2**
*Blindfold* - Kevin J. Anderson   s   101

**Outer Hollywood**
*Blade Runner: Replicant Night* - K.W. Jeter   s   2907

**Overworld**
*Pirates of the Universe* - Terry Bisson   s   506

**PabNeruda**
*Mind Snare* - Gayle Greeno   s   2422

**Pell Station**
*Finity's End* - C.J. Cherryh   s   988

**Plenty**
*Take Back Plenty* - Colin Greenland   s   2419

**Probe Station**
*Woodsman* - Thomas A. Easton   s   1727

**Rinji 8**
*F.R.E.E.Lancers* - Mel Odom   s   4191

**Robert E. Lee**
*The Digital Effect* - Steve Perry   s   4295

**Sargenti-Peterson**
*The Killing Star* - Charles Pellegrino   s   4281

**Sector General Hospital**
*Final Diagnosis* - James White   s   5777
*The Galactic Gourmet* - James White   s   5778
*The Genocidal Healer* - James White   s   5779

**Shangri-la**
*Time Scout* - Robert Asprin   s   263

**Shasta Station/Kaleidas**
*Proxies* - Laura J. Mixon   s   3922

**Silk**
*Deception Well* - Linda Nagata   s   4065

**Skycan**
*Orbital Decay* - Allen Steele   s   5246

**Skyport**
*Moonfall* - Jack McDevitt   s   3789

**Sol II**
*Hellburner* - C.J. Cherryh   s   996

**SSS-900-C**
*The City Who Fought* - Anne McCaffrey   s   3722

**Starbridge Station**
*Serpent's Gift* - A.C. Crispin   s   1261

**Starfleet First Contact Office**
*Prime Directive* - Judith Reeves-Stevens   s   4514

**Starlab**
*The Other End of Time* - Frederik Pohl   s   4351

**Starmuse Station**
*From a Changeling Star* - Jeffrey A. Carver   s   931

**Summer House**
*The Bohr Maker* - Linda Nagata   s   4064

**Sunstation Ra**
*Fortress on the Sun* - Paul Cook   s   1157

**Sunyata**
*Desert Fire* - David Alexander   s   65

**Tokyan Station**
*Reckoning Infinity* - John E. Stith   s   5304

**Top Step**
*Starseed* - Spider Robinson   s   4643

**Tranquility**
*Conflict* - Peter F. Hamilton   s   2522
*Consolidation* - Peter F. Hamilton   s   2523

**Trans-United Space Colony**
*High Steel* - Jack C. Haldeman II   s   2486

**Tri Power Station**
*Orion's Dagger* - P.K. McAllister   s   3708

**Trikon Station**
*The Trikon Deception* - Ben Bova   s   597

**Trust Territory of Threshold**
*The Stalk* - Janet Morris   s   4016
*Threshold* - Janet Morris   s   4018
*Trust Territory* - Janet Morris   s   4019

**Upper New York**
*The Stone Garden* - Mary Rosenblum   s   4679

**Ur**
*Playing God* - Sarah Zettel   s   6080

**Viking**
*Tripoint* - C.J. Cherryh   s   1003

**Vitacon**
*Away Is a Strange Place to Be* - H.M.
   Hoover   s   2763

**Voice-2**
*Tech-Heaven* - Linda Nagata   s   4066

## SPACESHIP

*Crashlander* - Larry Niven   s   4118
*Homegoing* - Frederik Pohl   s   4347
*Man-Kzin Wars IV* - Larry Niven   s   4124
*My Teacher Glows in the Dark* - Bruce
   Coville   s   1224
*Prodigy* - Jan Clark   s   1047
*The Rediscovery of Man* - Cordwainer
   Smith   s   5106
*Rock 'n' Roll Babes From Outer Space* - Linda
   Javin   s   2880
*Schismatrix Plus* - Bruce Sterling   s   5260
*The Ship Who Searched* - Anne McCaffrey   s   3749
*Silent Thunder/Universe* - Dean Ing   s   2829
*Stranger Suns* - George Zebrowski   s   6060
*Take Back Plenty* - Colin Greenland   s   2419

*Acadecki*
*Acorna's Quest* - Anne McCaffrey   *s*   3718

*Agamemnon*
*The Whims of Creation* - Simon Hawke   *s*   2626

*Alderran*
*The Crystal Star* - Vonda N. McIntyre   *s*   3820

*Alexasander Grobkin*
*The Siege* - Bill Baldwin   *s*   312

*Amalthea*
*The Shining Ones* - Paul Preuss   *s*   4421

*Angel's Luck*
*Desperate Measures* - Joe Clifford Faust   *s*   1891
*Precious Cargo* - Joe Clifford Faust   *s*   1893

*Ares*
*Beachhead* - Jack Williamson   *s*   5859
*Red Mars* - Kim Stanley Robinson   *s*   4635

*Argent*
*Deepdrive* - Alexander Jablokov   *s*   2837

*Argo*
*Furious Gulf* - Gregory Benford   *s*   447
*Golden Fleece* - Robert J. Sawyer   *s*   4857
*Tides of Light* - Gregory Benford   *s*   450

*Ariel*
*Mirror Dance* - Lois McMaster Bujold   *s*   762

*Ark*
*Lovelock* - Orson Scott Card   *s*   892

*Arrow*
*Arrow From Earth* - F.M. Busby   *s*   782

*Asia*
*Burster* - Michael Capobianco   *s*   876

*Astron*
*The Dark Beyond the Stars* - Frank M.
  Robinson   *s*   4626

*Atlantis*
*The Dig* - Alan Dean Foster   *s*   2002

*Aurora*
*This Alien Shore* - C.S. Friedman   *s*   2059

*Barbarossa*
*The Unwound Way* - William Adams   *s*   35

*BB-1066*
*Crystal Line* - Anne McCaffrey   *s*   3724

*Benedict*
*Aliens: Earth Hive* - Steve Perry   *s*   4289

*Betty*
*Alien Resurrection* - A.C. Crispin   *s*   1258

*Bhattya*
*A Matter of Oaths* - Helen S. Wright   *s*   5985

*Big Dog*
*Non-Stop* - Brian W. Aldiss   *s*   58

*Blade*
*Destination: Mutiny* - Sean Dalton   *s*   1332

*Bloodknife*
*The Phoenix in Flight* - Sherwood Smith   *s*   5138

*Boaz*
*The Artifact* - W. Michael Gear   *s*   2165

*Bonne Fortune*
*Ganwold's Child* - Diann Thornley   *s*   5467

*Bright Hope*
*Alien Tongue* - Stephen Leigh   *s*   3424

*Brishan*
*Sentinels* - Margaret Weis   *s*   5725

*Bucephalus*
*The Clone Crisis* - Lee McKeone   *s*   3829

*C.S.S. Dryden*
*Warhorse* - Timothy Zahn   *s*   6056

*Cantaloupe*
*Reckoning Infinity* - John E. Stith   *s*   5304

*Captain's Fancy*
*Forbidden Knowledge* - Stephen R.
  Donaldson   *s*   1571

*Cassandra*
*Dragons in the Stars* - Jeffrey A. Carver   *s*   930

*Celeste*
*The First Duelist* - Rutledge Etheridge   *s*   1849

*Century*
*The Expediter* - J. Brian Clarke   *s*   1062

*Cetacean*
*Ground-Ties* - Jane S. Fancher   *s*   1861
*Harmonies of the 'Net* - Jane S. Fancher   *s*   1862
*Uplink* - Jane S. Fancher   *s*   1865

*Ceti Flag*
*Flare Star* - Paula E. Downing   *s*   1594

*Chanur's Legacy*
*Chanur's Legacy* - C.J. Cherryh   *s*   981

*Charity*
*Down the Stream of Stars* - Jeffrey A.
  Carver   *s*   928

*Chi*
*Metaphase* - Vonda N. McIntyre   *s*   3821
*Transition* - Vonda N. McIntyre   *s*   3825

*Chimaera*
*Dark Force Rising* - Timothy Zahn   *s*   6052

*CISS Angus*
*Time: The Semi-Final Frontier* - Lionel
  Fenn   *s*   1921

*City of Diamond*
*City of Diamond* - Jane Emerson   *s*   1807

*CK-963*
*The Ship Who Won* - Anne McCaffrey   *s*   3750

*Columbia*
*Titan* - Stephen Baxter   *s*   405

*Constanza*
*Blind Justice* - S.N. Lewitt   *s*   3448

*Corinthian*
*Tripoint* - C.J. Cherryh   *s*   1003

*Dahak*
*The Armageddon Inheritance* - David
  Weber   *s*   5668
*Mutineers' Moon* - David Weber   *s*   5677

*Dan tahlni*
*The Alien Dark* - Diana G. Gallagher   *s*   2108

*Dawn Trader*
*Anvil of Stars* - Greg Bear   *s*   414

*Deepstar*
*Iris* - William Barton   *s*   381

*Defiant*
*The Lost King* - Margaret Weis   *s*   5720

*Desire*
*Bill, the Galactic Hero: On the Planet of Tasteless
  Pleasure* - Harry Harrison   *s*   2567

*Desiree*
*Starbridge* - A.C. Crispin   *s*   1265

*Destria*
*Starfire Down* - Lee McKeone   *s*   3830

*Discovery*
*Night Launch* - Jake Garn   *s*   2143
*Titan* - Stephen Baxter   *s*   405

*Dragon's Egg*
*Saturn's Child* - Nichelle Nichols   *s*   4101

*Dusty Miller*
*The Dazzle of Day* - Molly Gloss   *s*   2243

*Eidolon*
*Berserker Kill* - Fred Saberhagen   *s*   4761

*Empress of Earth*
*Starliner* - David Drake   *s*   1645

*Environ*
*Slow Freight* - F.M. Busby   *s*   785

*Envoy*
*Starfarers* - Poul Anderson   *s*   133

*Erebus*
*Transcendence* - Charles Sheffield   *s*   4967

*Evangeline*
*Alien Earth* - Megan Lindholm   *s*   3469

*Exeter*
*This Alien Shore* - C.S. Friedman   *s*   2059

*Exodus*
*Proxies* - Laura J. Mixon   *s*   3922

*Exodus 27*
*Dream-Weaver* - Louise Lawrence   *s*   3359

*Falstaff*
*The War Minstrels* - Karen Haber   *s*   2477
*Woman Without a Shadow* - Karen Haber   *s*   2478

*Fearless*
*The Honor of the Queen* - David Weber   *s*   5674
*On Basilisk Station* - David Weber   *s*   5679

*Ferkel*
*Aliens Stole My Body* - Bruce Coville   *s*   1217

*Finity's End*
*Finity's End* - C.J. Cherryh   *s*   988

*Firecat*
*Hellflower* - eluki bes shahar   *s*   473

*Flying Dutchman*
*Orbital Resonance* - John Barnes   *s*   356

*Forlorn Hope*
*The Price of Ransom* - Alis A. Rasmussen   *s*   4483
*Revolution's Shore* - Alis A. Rasmussen   *s*   4484

*Founder*
*The Founder* - Christopher Rowley   *s*   4696

*Galactique*
*The Seeds of Time* - Kay Kenyon   *s*   3064

*Galtizh*
*Probe* - Margaret Wander Bonanno   *s*   569

*Gambler's Star*
*The Six Families* - Nancy Holder   *s*   2733

*Gene Bullard*
*Rogue Star* - Michael Flynn   *s*   1965

*Genesee*
*Lyon's Pride* - Anne McCaffrey   *s*   3738

*Ghost Dance*
*Archangel Blues* - eluki bes shahar   *s*   471

*Glicca*
*Ports of Call* - Jack Vance   *s*   5549

*Gloria "Glory" Coelis*
*Glory* - Alfred Coppel   s   1182
*Glory's People* - Alfred Coppel   s   1183
*Glory's War* - Alfred Coppel   s   1184

*The Golden Hind*
*The Singers of Time* - Frederik Pohl   s   4354

*Goliath*
*3001: The Final Odyssey* - Arthur C.
  Clarke   s   1053
*The Hammer of God* - Arthur C. Clarke   s   1057

*Grabovnikon*
*Night of the Living Shark!* - David Bischoff   s   493

*Grail Angel*
*A Game of Universe* - Eric S. Nylund   f   4178

*Great Northern*
*Ring* - Stephen Baxter   s   402

*Grozniy*
*Ruler of Naught* - Sherwood Smith   s   5141

*Gypsy*
*Tower of the Gods* - Thomas A. Easton   s   1726

*H.M.S. Wayfarer*
*Honor Among Enemies* - David Weber   s   5673

*Hailey*
*The Kobayashi Maru* - Julia Ecklar   s   1728

*Hakluyt*
*Outnumbering the Dead* - Frederik Pohl   s   4352

*Halley*
*The Golden Globe* - John Varley   s   5565

*Hamilton*
*Treaty at Doona* - Anne McCaffrey   s   3752

*Harrier*
*Once a Hero* - Elizabeth Moon   s   3970

*Harvest Moon*
*The Billion Dollar Boy* - Charles Sheffield   s   4948

*Heart of Gold*
*The Illustrated Hitchhiker's Guide to the Galaxy* -
  Douglas Adams   s   29

*Hercules*
*Psykosis* - Wilhelmina Baird   s   296

*Hermit Crab*
*Timelike Infinity* - Stephen Baxter   s   404

*Hope's Reward*
*Hunting the Corrigan's Blood* - Holly Lisle   s   3484

*Hound of Heaven*
*The Tides of God* - Ted Reynolds   s   4567

*I.K.S. Rotarran*
*Call to Arms* - Diane Carey   s   901

*I.S.S. Enterprise*
*Dark Mirror* - Diane Duane   s   1658

*Ibn Battuta*
*Smoke and Mirrors* - Jane M. Lindskold   s   3476

*Icarus*
*The Shadow Within* - Jeanne Cavelos   s   944

*Imperial Terra*
*Heirs of Empire* - David Weber   s   5672

*Indulgence*
*Convergence* - Charles Sheffield   s   4951

*Introspectia*
*Flies From the Amber* - Wil McCarthy   s   3763

*Invincible*
*The Rising* - James Doohan   s   1579

*Jacaranda*
*Expendable* - James Alan Gardner   s   2135

*James Cook*
*Life Form* - Alan Dean Foster   s   2008

*Jeanne Kirkpatrick*
*The Hidden War* - Michael Armstrong   s   209

*Jersey*
*Checkmate* - Eric T. Baker   s   297

*Johann Winkelmann*
*The Engines of God* - Jack McDevitt   s   3787

*Jovah*
*The Alleluia Files* - Sharon Shinn   s   4999

*Junk*
*Drifter's Run* - William C. Dietz   s   1544

*Kennedy*
*Limbo Search* - Parke Godwin   s   2245

*Kezzedua Dinnyee*
*Shadowspeer* - Jo Clayton   s   1071

*Khalossa*
*Fortune's Wheel* - Lisanne Norman   s   4138

*Khedive*
*Acorna* - Anne McCaffrey   s   3717

*Kronos One*
*Star Trek VI: The Undiscovered Country* - J.M.
  Dillard   s   1556

*Kurtz*
*Aliens: The Female War* - Steve Perry   s   4290

*Loki*
*Rimrunners* - C.J. Cherryh   s   1001

*Louis Pasteur*
*Bloom* - Wil McCarthy   s   3761

*LS-1187 Star Wolf*
*The Middle of Nowhere* - David Gerrold   s   2209

*Magellan*
*The Sparrow* - Mary Doria Russell   s   4736

*Mangueira*
*Songs of Chaos* - S.N. Lewitt   s   3452

*Mary Damned*
*Blind Justice* - S.N. Lewitt   s   3448

*Mary Poppins*
*Voyage to the Red Planet* - Terry Bisson   s   508

*Maxwell*
*Limbo System* - Rick Cook   s   1158

*Mayflower*
*The World at the End of Time* - Frederik
  Pohl   s   4357

*Megarea*
*Path of the Fury* - David Weber   s   5680

*Merkon*
*Star Child* - James P. Hogan   s   2730

*Methryn*
*Dreadnought* - Thorarinn Gunnarsson   s   2464
*Tactical Error* - Thorarinn Gunnarsson   s   2466

*Michaelangelo*
*Alien Dreams* - Larry Segriff   s   4910

*Millenium Falcon*
*The New Rebellion* - Kristine Kathryn
  Rusch   s   4719

*Minnesota*
*Rediscovery: A Novel of Darkover* - Marion Zimmer
  Bradley   s   643

*Mother Lode*
*Mother Lode* - Zach Hughes   s   2812

*Mother Night*
*Alpha Centauri* - William Barton   s   378

*Mudlark*
*Dr. Dimension* - John DeChancie   s   1456

*Mul Hunter*
*Lightwing* - Tara K. Harper   s   2551

*Naglfar*
*Dark Sky Legion* - William Barton   s   379

*Nancia*
*PartnerShip* - Anne McCaffrey   s   3741

*Nautilus*
*Crossroad* - Barbara Hambly   s   2501
*Nautilus* - Vonda N. McIntyre   s   3823

*Nefertiti*
*The Clouds of Magellan* - David F.
  Nighbert   s   4103

*Nemesis*
*Berserker* - S.D. Perry   s   4285

*Nemo*
*Metaphase* - Vonda N. McIntyre   s   3821

*Newhome*
*Worlds Enough and Time* - Joe Haldeman   s   2491

*Nightingale*
*Wulfsyarn: A Mosaic* - Phillip Mann   s   3617

*Nightstalker*
*The Radiant Dragon* - Elaine Cunningham   f   1291

*Nike*
*Field of Dishonor* - David Weber   s   5670
*The Short Victorious War* - David Weber   s   5681

*Nordvik*
*Stopping at Slowyear* - Frederik Pohl   s   4355

*North Star*
*A Mind for Trade* - Andre Norton   s   4158

*Norway*
*Downbelow Station* - C.J. Cherryh   s   985

*Nosey*
*Kill Station* - Diane Duane   s   1664

*Null Boundary*
*Vast* - Linda Nagata   s   4067

*Open Palm*
*Homecoming* - David Alexander Smith   s   5108

*Out of Band*
*A Fire upon the Deep* - Vernor Vinge   s   5573

*Outbanker Bravo*
*Outbanker* - Timothy A. Madden   s   3603

*Outpost*
*Red Planet Run* - Dana Stabenow   s   5187

*Outward Bound*
*Mars Prime* - William C. Dietz   s   1548

*Paladin*
*The Eternal Enemy* - Michael Berlyn   s   469

*Pasadena*
*Fool's War* - Sarah Zettel   s   6079

*Pete Rozelle*
*The Red Tape War* - Jack L. Chalker   s   959

*Petrel*
*Full Tide of Night* - J.R. Dunn   s   1695

*Phaeton*
*Anti-Ice* - Stephen Baxter   s   398

*Phoenix*
*Foreigner* - C.J. Cherryh  *s*  990
*Inheritor* - C.J. Cherryh  *s*  997
*Invader* - C.J. Cherryh  *s*  998
*The Lost King* - Margaret Weis  *s*  5720

*Phoenix II*
*King's Sacrifice* - Margaret Weis  *s*  5717

*Pilgrim Crusader*
*God's World* - Ian Watson  *s*  5636

*Plenty*
*Mother of Plenty* - Colin Greenland  *s*  2417
*Seasons of Plenty* - Colin Greenland  *s*  2418

*Polkjhy*
*Infinity's Shore* - David Brin  *s*  688

*Probe*
*Into the Void* - Nigel Findley  *f*  1937

*Prometheus*
*Marooned on Eden* - Robert L. Forward  *s*  1986
*Ocean under the Ice* - Robert L. Forward  *s*  1988
*Return to Rocheworld* - Robert L. Forward  *s*  1989
*Rocheworld* - Robert L. Forward  *s*  1990

*Proud Mary*
*The Longest Voyage/Slow Lightning* - Poul
   Anderson  *s*  130

*Proviso*
*Speaking Dreams* - Severna Park  *s*  4245

*Punisher*
*The Gap into Madness: Chaos and Order* - Stephen R.
   Donaldson  *s*  1573

*Quiet Earth*
*Burster* - Michael Capobianco  *s*  876

*Rama II*
*The Garden of Rama* - Arthur C. Clarke  *s*  1055
*Rama II* - Arthur C. Clarke  *s*  1058

*Rama III*
*The Garden of Rama* - Arthur C. Clarke  *s*  1055
*Rama Revealed* - Arthur C. Clarke  *s*  1059

*Ranger*
*Reckoning Infinity* - John E. Stith  *s*  5304

*Raptor*
*Prisoner of Dreams* - Karen Ripley  *s*  4593

*Red Dwarf*
*Better than Life* - Grant Naylor  *s*  4076
*Red Dwarf: Infinity Welcomes Careful Drivers* - Grant
   Naylor  *s*  4077

*Redshift*
*Redshift Rendezvous* - John E. Stith  *s*  5305

*Rhabwar*
*The Galactic Gourmet* - James White  *s*  5778

*Rigus*
*Beholder's Eye* - Julie E. Czerneda  *s*  1303

*RMS Minotaur*
*Echoes of Honor* - David Weber  *s*  5669

*Romer*
*The Triad Worlds* - F.M. Busby  *s*  786

*Runaway*
*Angel Station* - Walter Jon Williams  *s*  5833

*Rustam's Slipper*
*McLendon's Syndrome* - Robert Frezza  *s*  2053
*The VMR Theory* - Robert Frezza  *s*  2055

*S.S. Jenolen*
*Relics* - Michael Jan Friedman  *s*  2066

*Sabre*
*The Salukan Gambit* - Sean Dalton  *s*  1333

*Saladin*
*Seeds of Destiny* - Thomas A. Easton  *s*  1724

*Santana*
*The Return of the Emperor* - Allan Cole  *s*  1106

*Schiaparelli*
*Aftermath* - Charles Sheffield  *s*  4947

*Search*
*Genetic Soldier* - George Turner  *s*  5492

*Seneca*
*Dragons in the Stars* - Jeffrey A. Carver  *s*  930

*Sequencer*
*Quozl* - Alan Dean Foster  *s*  2013

*Serendip Dana*
*Signs of Life* - Cherry Wilder  *s*  5804

*Serendipity*
*The First Duelist* - Rutledge Etheridge  *s*  1849

*Sextant*
*Saturn Rukh* - Robert L. Forward  *s*  1991

*Shadow*
*Dominion's Reach* - Diann Thornley  *s*  5465

*Shadowsweep*
*Marks of Our Brothers* - Jane M. Lindskold  *s*  3475

*Shenandoah*
*The Painful Field* - Roland J. Green  *s*  2351

*Shimizu Hotel*
*Starmind* - Spider Robinson  *s*  4642

*Sibyl*
*Medicine Show* - Jody Lynn Nye  *s*  4172
*Taylor's Ark* - Jody Lynn Nye  *s*  4176

*Siduri's Dance*
*Siduri's Net* - P.K. McAllister  *s*  3709

*Siduri's Isle*
*Orion's Dagger* - P.K. McAllister  *s*  3708

*Siduri's Net*
*Maia's Veil* - P.K. McAllister  *s*  3707
*Siduri's Net* - P.K. McAllister  *s*  3709

*Silver Fox*
*A Thousand Words for Stranger* - Julie E.
   Czerneda  *s*  1304

*Sinbad*
*The Gripping Hand* - Larry Niven  *s*  4122

*Sirghal*
*Warstrider: Netlink* - William H. Keith Jr.  *s*  3038

*Sleeper Service*
*Excession* - Iain M. Banks  *s*  324

*Solar Queen*
*A Mind for Trade* - Andre Norton  *s*  4158
*Redline the Stars* - Andre Norton  *s*  4160

*Solo*
*Against a Dark Background* - Iain M. Banks  *s*  322

*Somers*
*Article 23* - William R. Forstchen  *s*  1978

*Spacemaster*
*Timemaster* - Robert L. Forward  *s*  1992

*Sparrow Hawk*
*The Clouds of Saturn* - Michael McCollum  *s*  3770

*Spelljammer*
*The Ultimate Helm* - Russ T. Howard  *f*  2785

*Spirit of St. Louis*
*Cry Wolf* - Kenneth Von Gunden  *s*  5586

*The Spline*
*Timelike Infinity* - Stephen Baxter  *s*  404

*Sprite*
*Tripoint* - C.J. Cherryh  *s*  1003

*Starbird*
*Threshold* - Janet Morris  *s*  4018
*Trust Territory* - Janet Morris  *s*  4019

*Starfarer*
*Metaphase* - Vonda N. McIntyre  *s*  3821
*Nautilus* - Vonda N. McIntyre  *s*  3823
*Starfarers* - Vonda N. McIntyre  *s*  3824
*Transition* - Vonda N. McIntyre  *s*  3825

*Starfinder*
*Slow Freight* - F.M. Busby  *s*  785

*Starfire*
*Starfire Down* - Lee McKeone  *s*  3830

*Starfury*
*The Mercenaries* - Bill Baldwin  *s*  311

*Starhawk*
*The Seeds of Time* - Kay Kenyon  *s*  3064

*Starhopper*
*The Sails of Tau Ceti* - Michael McCollum  *s*  3771

*Starship Titanic*
*Douglas Adams's Starship Titanic* - Terry
   Jones  *s*  2979

*Stephen Hawking*
*Battlestation* - David Drake  *s*  1627

*Sternberger*
*End of an Era* - Robert J. Sawyer  *s*  4853

*Streaker*
*Heaven's Reach* - David Brin  *s*  687
*Infinity's Shore* - David Brin  *s*  688

*Summer Dreamboat*
*Divergence* - Charles Sheffield  *s*  4954

*Sun-Tzu*
*A Darker Geometry* - Mark O. Martin  *s*  3649

*Sundowner*
*Sundowner* - Chris Claremont  *s*  1043

*Suneater*
*The Rifter's Covenant* - Sherwood Smith  *s*  5140

*Sweet Delight*
*Hunting Party* - Elizabeth Moon  *s*  3968
*Sporting Chance* - Elizabeth Moon  *s*  3974
*Winning Colors* - Elizabeth Moon  *s*  3976

*Swift*
*The Voyage* - David Drake  *s*  1649

*Tacoma*
*Border Dispute* - Daniel R. Kerns  *s*  3066

*Taelarn*
*Legacy* - Steve White  *s*  5785

*Talguth*
*The Madness Season* - C.S. Friedman  *s*  2058

*Teacher*
*Mid-Flinx* - Alan Dean Foster  *s*  2010

*Telvarna*
*Ruler of Naught* - Sherwood Smith  *s*  5141

*Terra Nova*
*The Shattered Sphere* - Roger MacBride Allen  *s*  81

*Thistledown*
*Legacy* - Greg Bear  *s*  420

*Tiger's Claw*
*Wing Commander: Freedom Flight* - Mercedes Lackey   s   3307

*Timemaster*
*Timemaster* - Robert L. Forward   s   1992

*The Tinker's Damn*
*Drifter* - William C. Dietz   s   1543

*Traveler*
*The Starlight Crystal* - Christopher Pike   s   4333

*Trumpet*
*The Gap into Madness: Chaos and Order* - Stephen R. Donaldson   s   1573
*The Gap into Power: A Dark and Hungry God Arises* - Stephen R. Donaldson   s   1574
*The Gap into Ruin: This Day All Gods Die* - Stephen R. Donaldson   s   1575

*U-Kenai*
*Reclamation* - Sarah Zettel   s   6081

*U.N.S. Hibernia*
*Midshipman's Hope* - David Feintuch   s   1901

*U.N.S.N. Catskinner*
*The Children's Hour* - Jerry Pournelle   s   4372

*U.S.S. Constitution*
*Sundowner* - Chris Claremont   s   1043

*U.S.S. Defiant*
*Armageddon Sky* - L.A. Graf   s   2296
*Call to Arms* - Diane Carey   s   901
*Time's Enemy* - L.A. Graf   s   2297
*Vengeance* - Dafydd ab Hugh   s   10

*U.S.S. Endocrine*
*Star Wreck II: The Attack of the Jargonites* - Leah Rewolinski   s   4563
*Star Wreck III: Time Warped* - Leah Rewolinski   s   4564
*Star Wreck IV: Live Long and Profit* - Leah Rewolinski   s   4565
*Star Wreck 6: Geek Space Nine* - Leah Rewolinski   s   4562
*Star Wreck: The Generation Gap* - Leah Rewolinski   s   4566

*U.S.S. Enterprise*
*All Good Things. . .* - Michael Jan Friedman   s   2061
*Assignment: Eternity* - Greg Cox   s   1225
*Balance of Power* - Dafydd ab Hugh   s   7
*Best Destiny* - Diane Carey   s   900
*A Call to Darkness* - Michael Jan Friedman   s   2062
*Chains of Command* - Bill McCay   s   3767
*Crossover* - Michael Jan Friedman   s   2063
*Crossroad* - Barbara Hambly   s   2501
*Dark Mirror* - Diane Duane   s   1658
*Debtors' Planet* - William R. Thompson   s   5457
*The Devil's Heart* - Carmen Carter   s   922
*The Disinherited* - Peter David   s   1381
*Doctor's Orders* - Diane Duane   s   1659
*Doomsday World* - Carmen Carter   s   923
*Dragon's Honor* - Kij Johnson   s   2922
*Enemy Unseen* - V.E. Mitchell   s   3918
*The Fearful Summons* - Denny Martin Flinn   s   1954
*Federation* - Judith Reeves-Stevens   s   4511
*First Frontier* - Diane Carey   s   902
*First Strike* - Diane Carey   s   903
*Guises of the Mind* - Rebecca Neason   s   4081
*Imbalance* - V.E. Mitchell   s   3919
*Insurrection* - J.M. Dillard   s   1554
*Intellivore* - Diane Duane   s   1663
*The Joy Machine* - James Gunn   s   2458
*Kahless* - Michael Jan Friedman   s   2065
*The Last Stand* - Brad Ferguson   s   1923
*Metamorphosis* - Jean Lorrah   s   3524
*Mind Meld* - John Vornholt   s   5596
*Prime Directive* - Judith Reeves-Stevens   s   4514
*Probe* - Margaret Wander Bonanno   s   569

*Q-in-Law* - Peter David   s   1384
*Q-Space* - Greg Cox   s   1228
*Q-Squared* - Peter David   s   1385
*Q-Zone* - Greg Cox   s   1229
*Relics* - Michael Jan Friedman   s   2066
*Renegade* - Gene DeWeese   s   1511
*Requiem* - Michael Jan Friedman   s   2067
*Reunion* - Michael Jan Friedman   s   2068
*The Rift* - Peter David   s   1386
*Rules of Engagement* - Peter Morwood   s   4037
*Sanctuary* - John Vornholt   s   5597
*Sarek* - A.C. Crispin   s   1260
*Shadows on the Sun* - Michael Jan Friedman   s   2069
*Ship of the Line* - Diane Carey   s   904
*The Soldiers of Fear* - Dean Wesley Smith   s   5115
*Spectre* - William Shatner   s   4934
*Star Trek VI: The Undiscovered Country* - J.M. Dillard   s   1556
*Star Trek: The Classic Episodes 1* - James Blish   s   526
*Star Trek: The Classic Episodes 2* - James Blish   s   527
*Star Trek: The Classic Episodes 3* - James Blish   s   528
*Star Trek: The Lost Years* - J.M. Dillard   s   1557
*Traitor Winds* - L.A. Graf   s   2298
*Treks Not Taken: What if Stephen King, Anne Rice, Bret Easton Ellis, and Other Literary Greats Had Written Episodes of Star Trek: The Next Generation?* - Steven R. Boyett   s   607
*Vendetta* - Peter David   s   1389
*Vulcan's Glory* - D.C. Fontana   s   1967
*War Dragons* - L.A. Graf   s   2299
*Windows on a Lost World* - V.E. Mitchell   s   3920

*U.S.S. Excalibur*
*End Game* - Peter David   s   1382

*U.S.S. Excelsior*
*The Ashes of Eden* - William Shatner   s   4927
*War Dragons* - L.A. Graf   s   2299

*U.S.S. Hope*
*Hopeship* - Simon Lang   s   3315

*U.S.S. Intrepid II*
*Vulcan's Forge* - Susan Shwartz   s   5019

*U.S.S. Pasteur*
*All Good Things. . .* - Michael Jan Friedman   s   2061

*U.S.S. Repulse*
*The Kruton Interface* - John DeChancie   s   1459

*U.S.S. Skipjack*
*The Trumpets of Tagan* - Simon Lang   s   3316

*U.S.S. Voyager*
*Chrysalis* - David Niall Wilson   s   5880
*The Escape* - Dean Wesley Smith   s   5113
*The Final Fury* - Dafydd ab Hugh   s   9
*Her Klingon Soul* - Michael Jan Friedman   s   2064
*Pathways* - Jeri Taylor   s   5404
*Ragnarok* - Nathan Archer   s   206

*Ulug Beg*
*The Missing Matter* - Thomas R. McDonough   s   3805

*Unity*
*The Voice of Cepheus* - Ken Appleby   s   202

*Vadim*
*Damia's Children* - Anne McCaffrey   s   3726

*Valcyr*
*Tactical Error* - Thorarinn Gunnarsson   s   2466

*Valkyrie*
*Flying to Valhalla* - Charles Pellegrino   s   4280

*Valthyrra Methryn*
*Battle of the Ring* - Thorarinn Gunnarsson   s   2460

*Verdea*
*Harvest the Fire* - Poul Anderson   s   128

*Victory*
*Empire's End* - Allan Cole   s   1103

*Vigia*
*The Pharaoh Contract* - Ray Aldridge   s   63

*Void Runner*
*McCade's Bounty* - William C. Dietz   s   1550

*Warhammer*
*By Honor Betray'd* - Debra Doyle   s   1598
*The Gathering Flame* - Debra Doyle   s   1599
*The Price of the Stars* - Debra Doyle   s   1604
*Starpilot's Grave* - Debra Doyle   s   1606

*Wayfarer 1*
*Reach* - Edward Gibson   s   2216

*Wayfarer 2*
*Reach* - Edward Gibson   s   2216

*Whorl of the Long Sun*
*Calde of the Long Sun* - Gene Wolfe   s   5937
*Exodus From the Long Sun* - Gene Wolfe   s   5941
*Lake of the Long Sun* - Gene Wolfe   s   5942
*Nightside the Long Sun* - Gene Wolfe   s   5943

*Widdon Galaxy*
*Mind Light* - Margaret Davis   s   1407
*Minds Apart* - Margaret Davis   s   1408

*Wild Karrde*
*The Last Command* - Timothy Zahn   s   6055

*Windrunner/Windy*
*Chaos Come Again* - Wilhelmina Baird   s   293

*Windsong*
*Backblast* - Lee McKeone   s   3828

*Woebegone*
*Darktraders* - eluki bes shahar   s   472

*Wotan*
*Starborne* - Robert Silverberg   s   5042

*Xenophobe*
*Use of Weapons* - Iain M. Banks   s   328

*Yggdrasill*
*The Rise of Endymion* - Dan Simmons   s   5059

*Young Lord Byron*
*Dreamships* - Melissa Scott   s   4896

## SPAIN

*In the Garden of Iden* - Kage Baker   s   298
*King and Emperor* - Harry Harrison   f   2571
*Tek Money* - William Shatner   s   4935

**Barcelona**
*Natural History* - Juan Perucho   h   4303

**Cervere**
*The Plague Tales* - Ann Benson   s   453

**Madrid**
*The Manuscript Found in Sragossa* - Jan Potocki   h   4371

**Ronda**
*The Forgetting Room* - Nick Bantock   f   333

**Toledo**
*The Pit and the Pendulum* - Amarantha Knight   h   3183

## SUBMARINE

*Io*
*A Life in the Future* - Martin Caidin   s   827

*seaQuest DSV*
*seaQuest DSV: Fire Below* - Matthew J.
   Costello   s   1201
*seaQuest DSV: The Novel* - Diane Duane   s   1666

*Thetis*
*Atlantis Found* - R. Garcia y Robertson   s   2119

*Turtle*
*The Secret Oceans* - Betty Ballantine   s   318

*U.S.S. Shenandoah*
*Starsea Invaders: First Action* - G. Harry
   Stine   s   5282

*Unicorn*
*Echoes of the Fourth Magic* - R.A.
   Salvatore   f   4799

## SUBTERRANEAN WORLD

**Land of the Lost**
*Indiana Jones and the Interior World* - Rob
   MacGregor   f   3590

**Pincoya**
*Indiana Jones and the Interior World* - Rob
   MacGregor   f   3590

## SWEDEN

*The Tower of Beowulf* - Parke Godwin   f   2250
*War of the Gods* - Poul Anderson   f   136

**Uppsala**
*The Spawn of Loki* - Jason Henderson   f   2658

## SWITZERLAND

*The Armageddon Box* - Robert Weinberg   h   5690
*The Centurion's Empire* - Sean McMullen   s   3854
*Dagger Magic* - Katherine Kurtz   f   3256
*Oktober* - Stephen Gallagher   h   2112
*The Secret Laboratory Journals of Dr. Victor
   Frankenstein* - Jeremy Kay   h   3019

**Augsburg**
*Bring Me the Head of Prince Charming* - Roger
   Zelazny   f   6062

**Berne**
*Einstein's Dreams* - Alan Lightman   f   3459

**Chillon**
*Wildlife* - James Patrick Kelly   s   3049

**Geneva**
*The Darker Passions: Frankenstein* - Amarantha
   Knight   h   3180
*Einstein's Bridge* - John Cramer   s   1244
*The Memoirs of Elizabeth Frankenstein* - Theodore
   Roszak   h   4684
*Secret Passages* - Paul Preuss   s   4420

**Lake Geneva**
*Gothic Romance* - Emmanuel Carrere   h   912

**Zurich**
*Dark Legacy* - Mark A. Kostrubula   h   3220

## THAILAND

*Gold Dragon* - Robert Cain   s   831

**Bangkok**
*Dead Boys* - Richard Calder   s   836
*Dead Girls* - Richard Calder   s   837
*Dead Things* - Richard Calder   s   838
*The Gates of Noon* - Michael Scott Rohan   f   4661
*Private Demons* - Robert Masello   h   3660

*Vanitas: Escape From Vampire Junction* - S.P.
   Somtow   h   5162

## TIBET

*Shangri-La: The Return to the World of Lost Horizon* -
   Eleanor Cooney   f   1169
*Stones of the Dalai Lama* - Ken Mitchell   f   3916

**Kanggenpo**
*Evil Ascending* - Michael A. Stackpole   s   5198

**Shambala**
*Last Refuge* - Elizabeth Ann Scarborough   f   4866
*Nothing Sacred* - Elizabeth Ann
   Scarborough   f   4867

## TRANSYLVANIA

*Blood of the Impaler* - Jeffrey Sackett   h   4779
*Bram Stoker's Dracula* - Fred Saberhagen   h   4763
*Children of the Night* - Dan Simmons   h   5050
*Children of the Vampire* - Jeanne
   Kalogridis   h   3003
*Covenant with the Vampire* - Jeanne
   Kalogridis   h   3004
*The Darker Passions: Dracula* - Amarantha
   Knight   h   3179
*Daughter of the Night* - Elaine Bergstrom   h   463
*Deadspeak* - Brian Lumley   h   3551
*I Am Dracula* - C. Dean Andersson   h   139
*The Secret Life of Laszlo, Count Dracula* - Roderick
   Anscombe   h   152

## TROPICAL ISLAND

*Tek Money* - William Shatner   s   4935

**Ratnapida**
*Slow River* - Nicola Griffith   s   2445

## TRUST TERRITORY OF THE
## PACIFIC ISLANDS

**Marianas Islands**
*Super Carrier: The Ultimate Secret Weapon* - Peter
   Albano   s   50

## TURKEY

**Constantinople**
*The Iron Lance* - Stephen R. Lawhead   f   3356

**Istanbul**
*Indiana Jones and the Genesis Deluge* - Rob
   MacGregor   f   3589

## TURKMENISTAN

*Somewhere East of Life* - Brian W. Aldiss   s   60

## UNDERGROUND ENVIRONMENT

*Core* - Paul Preuss   s   4416

**The Sphere**
*The Time Ships* - Stephen Baxter   s   403

## UNDERSEA ENVIRONMENT/
## HABITAT

*The Infinite Sea* - Jeffrey A. Carver   s   932

**Caribe**
*Half the Day Is Night* - Maureen F.
   McHugh   s   3818

**Liberty**
*Ark Liberty* - Will Bradley   s   656

**Shangri La**
*The War of the Sky Lords* - John Brosnan   s   721

**SousMer**
*seaQuest DSV: Fire Below* - Matthew J.
   Costello   s   1201

## UNION OF SOVIET SOCIALIST
## REPUBLICS

*Branch Point* - Mona Clee   s   1074
*Red Devil* - David Saperstein   h   4816

**Moscow**
*Dictator* - William F. Wu   s   5996
*Humans* - Donald E. Westlake   f   5768
*Triumph* - Ben Bova   s   598

**Perchorsk Pass**
*The Source* - Brian Lumley   h   3565

**Siberia**
*Desert Eden* - J.M. Morgan   s   4000

**Starry Town**
*Peter Nevsky and the True Story of the Russian Moon
   Landing* - John Calvin Batchelor   s   388

## UNITED STATES

*1901* - Robert Conroy   s   1139
*1945* - Newt Gingrich   s   2239
*Afternoon of the Gosling* - Marlys Huffman   h   2801
*Ai! Pedrito!: When Intelligence Goes Wrong* - L. Ron
   Hubbard   s   2788
*Amazon: A Novel* - Barbara G. Walker   f   5616
*Antiquities* - John Crowley   f   1276
*Aqua Sancta* - Edward Bryant   h   748
*The Argus Gambit* - David D. Ross   s   4681
*The Armageddon Crazy* - Mick Farren   s   1877
*The Autobiography of Santa Claus: It's Better to Give*
   - Jeff Guinn   f   2456
*Away Is a Strange Place to Be* - H.M.
   Hoover   s   2763
*Battle Front* - Ian Slater   s   5086
*Beggars and Choosers* - Nancy Kress   s   3236
*Beggars in Spain* - Nancy Kress   s   3237
*Believe: A Novel* - William Shatner   f   4929
*Bernie and the Bessledorf Ghost* - Phyllis Reynolds
   Naylor   f   4078
*Beyond Apollo* - Barry Malzberg   s   3612
*Beyond the Pale* - Jack Koke   f   3198
*Beyond the Veil of Stars* - Robert Reed   s   4503
*Black as Blood* - Rob Chilson   f   1014
*The Black School* - J.N. Williamson   h   5851
*Black Snow Days* - Claudia O'Keefe   s   4205
*Blood Sport* - Lisa Smedman   f   5096
*Branch Point* - Mona Clee   s   1074
*Briar Rose* - Jane Yolen   f   6029
*The Callahan Touch* - Spider Robinson   f   4637
*Callahan's Legacy* - Spider Robinson   s   4639
*Canby's Legion* - Bill Baldwin   s   308
*Carrion Comfort* - Dan Simmons   h   5049
*The Caterpillar's Question* - Piers Anthony   f   164
*Celia* - Ruby Jean Jensen   h   2900
*Child's Play III* - Matthew J. Costello   h   1194
*The Cipher* - Kathe Koja   h   3194
*Clicking Stones* - Nancy Tyler Glenn   s   2242
*The Collected Stories of Philip K. Dick, Volume One:
   The Short Happy Life of the Brown Oxford* - Philip
   K. Dick   s   1519
*Cromm* - Kenneth C. Flint   f   1957
*Cybernarc* - Robert Cain   s   829
*The Cybernetic Walrus* - Jack L. Chalker   s   951
*Damnbanna* - Nancy Springer   f   5177
*Daughter of Prophecy* - Anne Kelleher Bush   f   788
*The Devil's Day* - James Blish   h   525

*Distant Friends and Others* - Timothy Zahn   *s*   6053
*The Djinn in the Nightingale's Eye* - A.S. Byatt   *f*   794
*The Drawing of the Three* - Stephen King   *h*   3131
*Dream Baby* - Bruce McAllister   *s*   3706
*The Eighth Rank* - David D. Ross   *s*   4682
*The Enigma Variations* - John Maddox Roberts   *s*   4618
*Et Tu, Babe* - Mark Leyner   *s*   3455
*The Fair Rules of Evil* - David C. Smith   *h*   5111
*Fallen* - Dee Graham   *h*   2302
*The Family Tree* - Sheri S. Tepper   *s*   5429
*The Fantastic Civil War* - Frank D. McSherry Jr.   *f*   3867
*The Feelies* - Mick Farren   *s*   1878
*Finger of God* - Michael Kasner   *s*   3013
*Fools* - Pat Cadigan   *s*   805
*The Friendship Song* - Nancy Springer   *f*   5179
*The Further Adventures of Batman 2: Featuring the Penguin* - Martin H. Greenberg   *s*   2391
*The Gallery of His Dreams* - Kristine Kathryn Rusch   *f*   4717
*Geek Love* - Katherine Dunn   *h*   1697
*Godmother Night* - Rachel Pollack   *f*   4358
*Good News From Outer Space* - John Kessel   *s*   3084
*Great American Ghost Stories* - Frank D. McSherry Jr.   *h*   3869
*Greenhouse* - Thomas A. Easton   *s*   1723
*Groogleman* - Debra Doyle   *s*   1600
*Gypsies* - Robert Charles Wilson   *s*   5908
*He, She and It* - Marge Piercy   *s*   4325
*The Higher Space* - Jamil Nasir   *s*   4070
*Holy Fire* - Bruce Sterling   *s*   5259
*The Hot-Wired Dodo* - Jack L. Chalker   *s*   956
*How Few Remain* - Harry Turtledove   *s*   5504
*How to Mutate and Take Over the World* - R.U. Sirius   *s*   5074
*Human Resources* - Floyd Kemske   *h*   3057
*The Imperium Game* - K.D. Wentworth   *s*   5753
*Inherit the Earth* - Brian Stableford   *s*   5193
*Innerverse* - John DeChancie   *s*   1458
*Isaac Asimov's I-Bots* - Steve Perry   *s*   4297
*Ishmael* - Daniel Quinn   *s*   4455
*Jonas McFee, A.T.P.* - Sarah Sargent   *s*   4827
*A Journal of the Flood Year* - David Ely   *s*   1805
*The Kill Riff* - David J. Schow   *h*   4887
*Killobyte* - Piers Anthony   *f*   179
*A Knight of the Word* - Terry Brooks   *f*   714
*Koko* - Peter Straub   *h*   5328
*The Lilith Factor* - Jean Paiva   *h*   4236
*The Lurker* - James V. Smith   *h*   5123
*The Magic Touch* - Jody Lynn Nye   *f*   4171
*Marked Cards* - George R.R. Martin   *s*   3647
*The Marked Man* - Charles Ingrid   *s*   2831
*Martian Deathtrap* - Nathan Archer   *s*   205
*Mindplayers* - Pat Cadigan   *s*   806
*Mine* - Robert R. McCammon   *h*   3756
*The Mirror Maze* - James P. Hogan   *s*   2726
*Monet's Ghost* - Chelsea Quinn Yarbro   *f*   6017
*Montezuma Strip* - Alan Dean Foster   *s*   2011
*Moonbane* - Al Sarrantonio   *s*   4831
*The Mutant Season* - Robert Silverberg   *s*   5039
*Mutation* - Robin Cook   *s*   1165
*My Cousin, My Gastroenterologist* - Mark Leyner   *s*   3456
*My Ishmael* - Daniel Quinn   *s*   4456
*My Teacher Flunked the Planet* - Bruce Coville   *s*   1222
*My Teacher Fried My Brains* - Bruce Coville   *s*   1223
*Mysteries of the Word* - Stanley Wiater   *h*   5796
*Mythology 101* - Jody Lynn Nye   *f*   4173
*Negrophobia: An Urban Parable* - Darius James   *f*   2859
*Nice Guys Finish Last* - Gary Jonas   *h*   2938
*The Night of the Moonbow* - Thomas Tryon   *h*   5486
*Oaths and Miracles* - Nancy Kress   *s*   3242

*The Old Man and Mr. Smith* - Peter Ustinov   *f*   5532
*Opalite Moon* - Denise Vitola   *f*   5577
*Outnumbering the Dead* - Frederik Pohl   *s*   4352
*The Pagemaster* - David Kirschner   *f*   3156
*The Parasite War* - Tim Sullivan   *s*   5352
*Passion Play* - Sean Stewart   *s*   5276
*The Penultimate Truth* - Philip K. Dick   *s*   1522
*Phantom Banjo* - Elizabeth Ann Scarborough   *f*   4868
*Phases of Gravity* - Dan Simmons   *s*   5057
*Predator* - William F. Wu   *s*   5998
*The Prestige* - Christopher Priest   *s*   4432
*Prodigal* - Melanie Tem   *h*   5423
*The Puppet Masters* - Robert A. Heinlein   *s*   2646
*The Quick* - Burt Cole   *s*   1113
*A Rage for Revenge* - David Gerrold   *s*   2210
*A Reasonable World* - Damon Knight   *s*   3188
*Red Wizard* - Nancy Springer   *f*   5182
*Retro Lives* - Lee Grimes   *s*   2446
*Samurai Cat Goes to the Movies* - Mark E. Rogers   *s*   4656
*Santa's Twin* - Dean R. Koontz   *f*   3214
*A Season for Slaughter* - David Gerrold   *s*   2211
*Second Contact* - Mike Resnick   *s*   4555
*The Shockwave Rider* - John Brunner   *s*   736
*Shoebag* - Mary James   *f*   2868
*Sideshow* - Sheri S. Tepper   *s*   5436
*The Silence of the Lambs* - Thomas Harris   *h*   2566
*The Silver Kiss* - Annette Curtis Klause   *f*   3163
*Slow Dancing through Time* - Gardner Dozois   *s*   1615
*Slow Freight* - F.M. Busby   *s*   785
*Sparrowhawk* - Thomas A. Easton   *s*   1725
*The Spider #3: Death's Crimson Juggernaut/The Red Death Rain* - Grant Stockbridge   *f*   5307
*The Spider #4: Death Reign of the Vampire King/The Pain Emperor* - Grant Stockbridge   *f*   5308
*Stars and Stripes Forever* - Harry Harrison   *s*   2577
*The Stars Must Wait* - Keith Laumer   *s*   3346
*Stonewords: A Ghost Story* - Pam Conrad   *f*   1138
*Strange Angels* - Kathe Koja   *h*   3197
*Strange Attractors* - William Sleator   *s*   5088
*Succumb* - Ron Dee   *h*   1468
*Swan Song* - Robert R. McCammon   *h*   3757
*The Sword of Samurai Cat* - Mark E. Rogers   *s*   4657
*Systems* - W.T. Quick   *s*   4452
*The Trikon Deception* - Ben Bova   *s*   597
*Views from the Oldest House* - Richard Grant   *s*   2329
*Virgintooth* - Mark Ivanhoe   *h*   2834
*Virus Clans* - Michael Kanaly   *s*   3008
*Web of Futures* - Jefferson P. Swycaffer   *f*   5376
*Website* - Ray Garton   *h*   2157
*Whiteout* - Sage Walker   *s*   5619
*A Wish and a Dream* - Ingrid Weaver   *f*   5658
*The Witch Returns* - Phyllis Reynolds Naylor   *f*   4079
*Woodsman* - Thomas A. Easton   *s*   1727

**Atworthy College**
*Fear* - L. Ron Hubbard   *h*   2789

**Brookington**
*The Book of the Damned* - D.A. Fowler   *h*   2022

**Camp Cold Lake**
*The Curse of Camp Cold Lake* - R.L. Stine   *h*   5286

**The City**
*Black Sun* - Douglas E. Winter   *h*   5923

**Claremont**
*Dark Lullaby* - Jessica Palmer   *h*   4237

**Clinton**
*Waltz with Evil* - P.D. Rozzi   *h*   4701

**Dixon Landing**
*The Ghost Inside the Monitor* - Margaret J. Anderson   *f*   122

**Elesian Fields**
*Perfect Little Angels* - Andrew Neiderman   *h*   4090

**Ellsworth**
*Resurrection Dreams* - Richard Laymon   *h*   3371

**Gallows**
*Dark Father* - Tom Piccirilli   *h*   4312

**Gotham City**
*Batman: Captured by the Engines* - Joe R. Lansdale   *h*   3320
*Batman: Knightfall* - Dennis O'Neil   *s*   4215
*Batman Returns* - Craig Shaw Gardner   *s*   2124
*Catwoman* - Lynn Abbey   *s*   14
*The Further Adventures of Batman 2: Featuring the Penguin* - Martin H. Greenberg   *s*   2391
*The Further Adventures of Batman 3: Featuring Catwoman* - Martin H. Greenberg   *s*   2392
*Mask of the Phantasm* - Geary Gravel   *s*   2331

**Hanesburg**
*Liquid Diet* - William Tedford   *h*   5419

**Le Quier**
*Psi-Man* - David Peters   *s*   4305

**Metropolis**
*The Death and Life of Superman* - Roger Stern   *s*   5262
*The Further Adventures of Superman* - Martin H. Greenberg   *s*   2393
*Lois & Clark* - C.J. Cherryh   *s*   999

**Monkar**
*Other Nature* - Stephanie A. Smith   *s*   5145

**Navajo Nation, Four Corners**
*Cyber Way* - Alan Dean Foster   *s*   2000

**The Oasis**
*Through the Heart* - Richard Grant   *f*   2328

**Oconee**
*Count Geiger's Blues* - Michael Bishop   *s*   499

**Oldcolumbia**
*Lunar Justice* - Charles L. Harness   *s*   2545

**Patuxet Haven**
*Lunar Justice* - Charles L. Harness   *s*   2545

**Riverland**
*Gnelfs* - Sidney Williams   *h*   5823

**Rivertown**
*Skin* - Kathe Koja   *h*   3196

**Shadyside**
*Double Date* - R.L. Stine   *h*   5287
*The First Horror* - R.L. Stine   *h*   5288

**Thom Valley**
*R-T, Margaret, and the Rats of NIMH* - Jane Leslie Conly   *f*   1132

**Twainton**
*Horrorshow* - David Darke   *h*   1353

**Veritas, City of Truth**
*City of Truth* - James Morrow   *s*   4030

**ALABAMA**

**Atmore**
*Mefisto in Onyx* - Harlan Ellison   *h*   1786

**Birmingham**
*Silk* - Caitlin R. Kiernan   *h*   3101

**Goshen**
*Land O'Goshen* - Charles McNair   *s*   3855

**Mobile**
*Night Cruise* - Billie Sue Mosiman  *h*  4041

**Tuscaloosa**
*The Trinity Vector* - Steve Perry  *s*  4302

**Zephyr**
*Boy's Life* - Robert R. McCammon  *h*  3754

**ALASKA**

*Cloven Hooves* - Megan Lindholm  *f*  3470
*Far Edge of Darkness* - Linda Evans  *s*  1855
*Rockabilly Hell* - William W. Johnstone  *h*  2933
*Song of the River* - Sue Harrison  *f*  2583

**Aleutian Islands**
*Mother Earth, Father Sky* - Sue Harrison  *f*  2581
*My Sister the Moon* - Sue Harrison  *f*  2582

**Anchorage**
*Blood on the Sun* - Brian Herbert  *h*  2664

**Barrow**
*Agviq* - Michael Armstrong  *s*  208

**Kantishna Hills**
*Ember From the Sun* - Mark Canter  *s*  870

**Kuinak**
*Sailor Song* - Ken Kesey  *s*  3082

**Utqiagvik**
*Agviq* - Michael Armstrong  *s*  208

**Wrangell**
*Raven Stole the Moon* - Garth Stein  *h*  5249

**APPALACHIANS**

*Slow Funeral* - Rebecca Ore  *f*  4221

**ARIZONA**

*Black Sun* - Robert Leininger  *s*  3429
*The Godmother's Web* - Elizabeth Ann
  Scarborough  *f*  4864
*In the Blood* - Lauren Wright Douglas  *s*  1590
*Jed the Dead* - Alan Dean Foster  *s*  2007
*The Kronos Condition* - Emily Devenport  *s*  1502
*The Last Wizard* - Simon Hawke  *f*  2619
*Sing for a Gentle Rain* - J. Alison James  *f*  2861
*Supernova* - Roger MacBride Allen  *s*  82
*The Wild Wood* - Charles de Lint  *f*  1440

**Badger Mountain**
*Bright Shadow* - Elizabeth Forrest  *h*  1971

**Bisbee**
*Darkscope* - Margaret Falk  *h*  1860

**Coyote Creek**
*The Gaia Websters* - Kim Antieau  *s*  198

**Fort Apache**
*Demon Download* - Jack Yeovil  *f*  6021

**Gila Desert**
*Krokodil Tears* - Jack Yeovil  *f*  6023

**Grand Canyon**
*The Gaia Websters* - Kim Antieau  *s*  198

**Joseph City**
*Empire of Dust* - Chet Williamson  *h*  5846

**Juniper**
*The Store* - Bentley Little  *h*  3497

**Los Lobos**
*Wild Blood* - Nancy A. Collins  *h*  1127

**Phoenix**
*Burial* - Graham Masterton  *h*  3671
*The Charm* - Adam Niswander  *h*  4111

*Evil Triumphant* - Michael A. Stackpole  *s*  5199
*A Gathering Evil* - Michael A. Stackpole  *s*  5201
*The Serpent Slayers* - Adam Niswander  *h*  4113

**Pinon Rim**
*WiZrD* - Steve Zell  *h*  6078

**Randall**
*The Revelation* - Bentley Little  *h*  3496

**Rio Verde**
*The Summoning* - Bentley Little  *h*  3498

**Sagebrush Flats**
*The Stake* - Richard Laymon  *h*  3372

**Sedona**
*Waking the Moon* - Elizabeth Hand  *f*  2538

**Superstition Mountain**
*The Sand Dwellers* - Adam Niswander  *h*  4112

**Tucson**
*Apacheria* - Jake Page  *s*  4233
*Caverns of Socrates* - Dennis L. McKiernan  *f*  3831
*Dragon Season* - Michael Cassutt  *f*  936
*The Gatekeepers* - Daniel Graham Jr.  *s*  2301
*The Wood Wife* - Terri Windling  *f*  5916

**Welcome**
*Demon Download* - Jack Yeovil  *f*  6021

**Willis**
*The Mailman* - Bentley Little  *h*  3494

**Window Rock**
*Tooth and Claw* - Graham Masterton  *h*  3680

**ARKANSAS**

*Prey* - William W. Johnstone  *h*  2932

**Buckhead County**
*Iceman* - Rex Miller  *h*  3900

**Meander**
*Earthsong* - Suzette Haden Elgin  *s*  1769

**CALIFORNIA**

*The Alien Years* - Robert Silverberg  *s*  5027
*Amnesia Moon* - Jonathan Lethem  *f*  3438
*As She Climbed Across the Table* - Jonathan
  Lethem  *s*  3439
*The Catswold Portal* - Shirley Rousseau
  Murphy  *f*  4055
*Chimera* - Mary Rosenblum  *s*  4677
*Cosm* - Gregory Benford  *s*  444
*Deep Trek* - James Axler  *s*  278
*Diplomatic Act* - Peter Jurasik  *s*  2996
*Doomstalker* - Gary Brandner  *h*  661
*Eye in the Sky* - Philip K. Dick  *s*  1521
*The Fifth Sacred Thing* - Starhawk  *f*  5209
*The Fourth Guardian* - Ronald Anthony
  Cross  *s*  1273
*Ghosts of Wind and Shadow* - Charles de
  Lint  *f*  1427
*Hot Sky at Midnight* - Robert Silverberg  *s*  5032
*Ill Wind* - Kevin J. Anderson  *s*  108
*In the Blood* - Lauren Wright Douglas  *s*  1590
*In the Land of the Dead* - K.W. Jeter  *h*  2912
*Into the Forest* - Jean Hegland  *s*  2640
*Jed the Dead* - Alan Dean Foster  *s*  2007
*Kalifornia* - Marc Laidlaw  *s*  3311
*Lightning* - Dean R. Koontz  *h*  3211
*A Logical Magician* - Robert Weinberg  *f*  5697
*Make Way for Dragons!* - Thorarinn
  Gunnarsson  *f*  2465
*The March Hare Network* - Jack L. Chalker  *s*  957
*Mixed Doubles* - Daniel Da Cruz  *s*  1305
*Mutant Legacy* - Karen Haber  *s*  2474
*Mutant Star* - Karen Haber  *s*  2475

*The Night Man* - K.W. Jeter  *h*  2915
*Other Nature* - Stephanie A. Smith  *s*  5145
*The Paper Grail* - James P. Blaylock  *f*  522
*The Positronic Man* - Isaac Asimov  *s*  249
*Revenge of the Fluffy Bunnies* - Craig Shaw
  Gardner  *f*  2132
*See You Later* - Christopher Pike  *f*  4332
*Silicon Embrace* - John Shirley  *s*  5009
*The Silicon Man* - Charles Platt  *s*  4343
*Solomon's Knife* - Victor Koman  *s*  3200
*Son of Rosemary* - Ira Levin  *h*  3445
*Supernova* - Roger MacBride Allen  *s*  82
*Tek Money* - William Shatner  *s*  4935
*TekLords* - William Shatner  *s*  4940
*Timeshare* - Joshua Dann  *s*  1344
*The Turing Option* - Harry Harrison  *s*  2579
*The Unnatural* - David Prill  *h*  4437
*Vampires Anonymous* - Jeffrey N.
  McMahan  *h*  3853
*Vengeance Strike* - David Robbins  *s*  4604
*Was* - Geoff Ryman  *f*  4758
*The Wizardry Consulted* - Rick Cook  *f*  1161
*Wyrm* - Mark Fabi  *s*  1858
*Zeus and Co.* - David Lee Jones  *f*  2942

**Acorn**
*Parable of the Talents* - Octavia E. Butler  *s*  793

**Agate Creek**
*Shaman Woods* - Morgan Fields  *h*  1931

**Anderson**
*Dark Channel* - Ray Garton  *h*  2150

**Apple Creek**
*Shadow Twin* - Dale Hoover  *h*  2762

**Barrington**
*Shadows* - John Saul  *h*  4845

**Bay Area**
*The Baby* - Stephanie Kegan  *h*  3033

**Beaver Hills**
*The Boy Who Cried Werewolf* - Elvira  *h*  1800
*Camp Vamp* - Elvira  *h*  1801
*Elvira: Transylvania 90210* - Elvira  *h*  1802

**Bel Air**
*The Undine* - Michael O'Rourke  *h*  4224

**Berkeley**
*Blue Light* - Walter Mosley  *s*  4042
*Cosm* - Gregory Benford  *s*  444
*Frameshift* - Robert J. Sawyer  *s*  4856
*Heartlight* - Marion Zimmer Bradley  *f*  637
*Nightlight* - Michael Cadnum  *h*  813
*Overshoot* - Mona Clee  *s*  1075
*Paths to Otherwhere* - James P. Hogan  *s*  2728
*Rim: A Novel of Virtual Reality* - Alexander
  Besher  *s*  475
*The Thirteenth Daughter of the Moon* - Steven
  Nightingale  *f*  4104
*Twisted* - Sue Hollister Barr  *h*  364

**Beverly Hills**
*The Beast* - Marie Ardell White  *h*  5784
*Sorcerers of Sodom* - Roger Elwood  *h*  1804
*The Vampire Odyssey* - Scott Ciencin  *h*  1032
*The Wildlings* - Scott Ciencin  *h*  1034

**Black Cavern**
*The Feeding* - Leigh Clark  *h*  1051

**Bohemia Bay**
*The Orchid Eater* - Marc Laidlaw  *h*  3312

**Bonner**
*The Well* - Michael B. Sirota  *h*  5077

**Brea**
*The Ignored* - Bentley Little  *h*  3493
*University* - Bentley Little  *h*  3499

**Cambio Bay**
*Cambio Bay* - Kate Wilhelm   *f*   5806

**Castle Bay**
*Night Sounds* - Warner Lee   *h*   3415

**Catalina Island**
*Bad Karma* - Andrew Harper   *h*   2548

**Chatsworth**
*Deadly Dreams* - Gerald A. Schiller   *h*   4874

**Cielo**
*Ghost Boy* - Jean Simon   *h*   5064

**Cliffside**
*Wildest Dreams* - Norman Partridge   *h*   4256

**Death Valley**
*Dead Heat* - Del Stone Jr.   *h*   5313

**Eden Cove**
*Shadow Man* - Dennis Etchison   *h*   1848

**Edwards Air Force Base**
*Fallen Angels* - Larry Niven   *s*   4120

**El Cerrito**
*The World on Blood* - Jonathan Nasaw   *h*   4069

**Encino**
*Blood Sabbath* - Leigh Clark   *h*   1048
*The Vampire's Beautiful Daughter* - S.P.
   Somtow   *h*   5161

**Escondita**
*SETI* - Frederick Fichman   *s*   1930

**Fareland**
*65mm* - Dale Hoover   *h*   2761

**Fey Valley**
*Sister to the Rain* - Melisa Michaels   *f*   3887

**Fiddler**
*The Bars on Satan's Jailhouse* - Norman
   Partridge   *h*   4251

**Forest City**
*Night Beasts* - T.W. Stetson   *h*   5263

**Ghostal Shores**
*California Ghosting* - William Hill   *h*   2687

**Hennington**
*Witchcraft* - Bill Michaels   *h*   3885

**Hollywood**
*Big Rock Beat* - Greg Kihn   *h*   3102
*Bloodletter* - Warren Newton Beath   *h*   426
*Brand New Cherry Flavor* - Todd Grimson   *h*   2448
*Bride of the Rat God* - Barbara Hambly   *f*   2499
*Created By* - Richard Christian Matheson   *h*   3691
*Evil Reincarnate* - Leigh Clark   *h*   1050
*A Graveyard for Lunatics* - Ray Bradbury   *h*   620
*Hooray for Hellywood* - Esther Friesner   *f*   2077
*Horror Show* - Greg Kihn   *h*   3103
*The Making of a Monster* - Gail Petersen   *h*   4307
*Night Hunter* - Michael Reaves   *h*   4496
*Psycho II* - Robert Bloch   *h*   541
*Remake* - Connie Willis   *s*   5873
*Star Prey* - Ehren M. Ehly   *h*   1763
*Time on My Hands* - Peter Delacorte   *s*   1480

**Horton's Valley**
*Dream of Glass* - Jean Mark Gawron   *s*   2163

**Huntington Beach**
*Winter Tides* - James P. Blaylock   *h*   524

**Irvines**
*Ticktock* - Dean R. Koontz   *h*   3217

**Julian**
*Moondog* - Henry Garfield   *h*   2138
*Room 13* - Henry Garfield   *h*   2139

**La Barca**
*Night Mask* - William W. Johnstone   *h*   2931

**Laguna Beach**
*Retribution* - Elizabeth Forrest   *h*   1975

**Laguna Niguel**
*Cold Fire* - Dean R. Koontz   *h*   3203
*Dragon Tears* - Dean R. Koontz   *h*   3205
*Hideaway* - Dean R. Koontz   *h*   3208
*Mr. Murder* - Dean R. Koontz   *h*   3213

**Livermore**
*Virtual Destruction* - Kevin J. Anderson   *s*   118

**Los Angeles**
*Absolute Power* - Ray Russell   *h*   4738
*After Silence* - Jonathan Carroll   *h*   916
*Arc d'X* - Steve Erickson   *f*   1835
*Baby Be-Bop* - Francesca Lia Block   *f*   545
*Bedlam Boyz* - Ellen Guon   *f*   2467
*Blade Runner 2: The Edge of Human* - K.W.
   Jeter   *s*   2906
*Bride of the Rat God* - Barbara Hambly   *f*   2499
*Buffy the Vampire Slayer* - Richie Tankersley
   Cusick   *h*   1301
*Cain* - James Byron Huggins   *h*   2802
*California Gothic* - Dennis Etchison   *h*   1843
*Catch the Lightning* - Catherine Asaro   *s*   218
*Celestial Dogs* - J.S. Russell   *h*   4734
*Cemetery of Angels* - Noel Hynd   *h*   2821
*The Change* - Barry B. Longyear   *s*   3520
*Cherokee Bat and the Goat Guys* - Francesca Lia
   Block   *f*   546
*A Child Across the Sky* - Jonathan Carroll   *h*   917
*Circle of One* - Eric James Fullilove   *s*   2092
*Claw* - Ken Eulo   *h*   1850
*Cold Iron* - Melisa Michaels   *f*   3886
*The Cold One* - Christopher Pike   *h*   4327
*Cortez on Jupiter* - Ernest Hogan   *s*   2721
*Cross of Blood* - K.W. Jeter   *s*   2909
*The Dark* - Andrew Neiderman   *h*   4084
*Dark Horizon* - K.W. Jeter   *s*   2910
*Dark Matter* - Garfield Reeves-Stevens   *h*   4509
*Darkside* - Dennis Etchison   *h*   1845
*Dead of Night* - Alex Abella   *h*   20
*Death's Door* - John Wooley   *h*   5969
*Deathsong* - Douglas Borton   *h*   575
*Demolition Man* - Richard Osborne   *s*   4229
*Desert Fire* - David Alexander   *s*   65
*Dog Wizard* - Barbara Hambly   *f*   2503
*Double Edge* - Dennis Etchison   *h*   1846
*Dragon Death* - Gael Baudino   *f*   390
*Duel of Dragons* - Gael Baudino   *f*   391
*Earthquake Weather* - Tim Powers   *f*   4382
*Expiration Date* - Tim Powers   *f*   4383
*Firedance* - Steven Barnes   *s*   360
*Flicker* - Theodore Roszak   *h*   4683
*Free Zone* - Charles Platt   *s*   4341
*Gabriel's Body* - Curt Siodmak   *s*   5073
*The Hanged Man* - Francesca Lia Block   *f*   548
*I, Said the Fly* - Michael Shea   *h*   4944
*I Was a Teenage Fairy* - Francesca Lia
   Block   *f*   549
*Illegal Alien* - Robert J. Sawyer   *s*   4858
*In Double Jeopardy* - Andrew Neiderman   *h*   4088
*In the Heart of the Valley of Love* - Cynthia
   Kadohata   *s*   2997
*The Informers* - Brett Easton Ellis   *h*   1778
*Jacob's Hands* - Aldous Huxley   *f*   2817
*The Killing of the Saints* - Alex Abella   *h*   21
*Killjoy* - Elizabeth Forrest   *h*   1973
*Knight of Ghosts and Shadows* - Mercedes
   Lackey   *f*   3285
*Knights of the Blood* - Scott MacMillan   *f*   3602
*L.A. Strike* - David Robbins   *s*   4599
*Last Mountain* - Robert C. Fleet   *f*   1946
*Lori* - Robert Bloch   *h*   536
*Love Bite* - Sherry Gottlieb   *h*   2288
*Madlands* - K.W. Jeter   *s*   2913

*MagicNet* - John DeChancie   *f*   1461
*The Man Who Folded Himself* - David
   Gerrold   *s*   2208
*Metal Angel* - Nancy Springer   *f*   5181
*Mirror* - Graham Masterton   *h*   3677
*Missing Angel Juan* - Francesca Lia Block   *f*   550
*The Need* - Andrew Neiderman   *h*   4089
*Night Prayers* - P.D. Cacek   *h*   803
*Omega* - Patrick Lynch   *h*   3577
*OtherSyde* - J. Michael Straczynski   *h*   5323
*Outside the Dog Museum* - Jonathan Carroll   *f*   919
*Parable of the Sower* - Octavia E. Butler   *s*   792
*Parallelities* - Alan Dean Foster   *s*   2012
*Phoenix Fire* - Elizabeth Forrest   *f*   1974
*Pictures at 11* - Norman Spinrad   *s*   5173
*Preternatural* - Margaret Wander Bonanno   *s*   568
*Quake* - Richard Laymon   *h*   3370
*Queen of Angels* - Greg Bear   *s*   423
*Ragged Angels* - Della Van Hise   *h*   5537
*Relife* - Dan Barton   *h*   376
*Sati* - Christopher Pike   *f*   4330
*Shade* - Emily Devenport   *s*   1504
*Shadow Dance* - Douglas Borton   *h*   577
*Shadows* - Kimberly Rangel   *h*   4472
*Shock Radio* - Leigh Clark   *h*   1052
*Snow Crash* - Neal Stephenson   *s*   5254
*Sole Survivor* - Dean R. Koontz   *s*   3215
*Songs of Earth and Power* - Greg Bear   *f*   424
*Species* - Yvonne Navarro   *s*   4075
*Stainless* - Todd Grimson   *h*   2449
*Stone Dead* - Ellen Jamison   *h*   2878
*The Stranger* - Eric James Fullilove   *s*   2093
*Summerland* - L. Dean James   *f*   2865
*Synners* - Pat Cadigan   *s*   808
*Tech-Heaven* - Linda Nagata   *s*   4066
*Tek Vengeance* - William Shatner   *s*   4938
*TekWar* - William Shatner   *s*   4941
*Terminal Cafe* - Ian McDonald   *s*   3797
*Terminal Games* - Cole Perriman   *s*   4283
*Tropic of Orange* - Karen Tei Yamashita   *f*   6009
*Tubular Android Superheroes* - Mel Gilden   *s*   2228
*The Unicorn Sonata* - Peter S. Beagle   *f*   412
*Vampire Diary: The Embrace* - Robert
   Weinberg   *h*   5705
*The Vampire Journals* - Traci Briery   *h*   678
*The Vampire Memoirs* - Mara McCuniff   *h*   3781
*Vanitas: Escape From Vampire Junction* - S.P.
   Somtow   *h*   5162
*Virtual Light* - William Gibson   *s*   2219
*Virtuosity* - Terry Bisson   *s*   507
*The Werewolf Chronicles* - Traci Briery   *h*   679
*Wes Craven's New Nightmare* - David
   Bergantino   *h*   460
*Wetbones* - John Shirley   *h*   5010
*What's Wrong with America* - Scott
   Bradfield   *h*   627
*Who P-P-Plugged Roger Rabbit?* - Gary K.
   Wolf   *f*   5934
*Witch Baby* - Francesca Lia Block   *f*   552
*The Wizard's Apprentice* - S.P. Somtow   *f*   5163
*Wolfsong* - Traci Briery   *h*   680

**Mabton**
*Dark Dreaming* - Pat Franklin   *h*   2040

**Madelyn**
*Thunder Road* - Chris Curry   *h*   1296

**Malcasa Point**
*Beast House* - Richard Laymon   *h*   3364
*The Cellar* - Richard Laymon   *h*   3365
*The Midnight Tour* - Richard Laymon   *h*   3368

**Malibu**
*Hawaiian U.F.O. Aliens* - Mel Gilden   *s*   2226
*Tubular Android Superheroes* - Mel Gilden   *s*   2228

**McKenna's Creek**
*Thrill* - Patricia Wallace   *h*   5624

**Menlo Park**
*Operation Damocles* - Oscar L. Fellows   s   1915

**Mill Valley**
*Shadows* - Jonathan Nasaw   h   4068

**Mojave Desert**
*The California Voodoo Game* - Larry Niven   s   4117
*Jacob's Hands* - Aldous Huxley   f   2817
*Mojave Wells* - L. Dean James   s   2864
*Skyscape* - Michael Cadnum   814
*Species* - Yvonne Navarro   s   4075

**Mojave Wells**
*Mojave Wells* - L. Dean James   s   2864

**Molena Point**
*Cats Raise the Dead* - Shirley Rousseau Murphy   f   4054

**Monterey**
*Meg* - Steve Alten   h   88

**Moonfall**
*Moonfall* - Tamara Thorne   h   5464

**Moonlight Bay**
*Fear Nothing* - Dean R. Koontz   h   3207

**Moonlight Cove**
*Midnight* - Dean R. Koontz   h   3212

**Napa Valley**
*Dominion* - Bentley Little   h   3492
*Intensity* - Dean R. Koontz   h   3210

**New Svenbrog**
*Cold Fire* - Dean R. Koontz   h   3203

**Newport Beach**
*In the Shadows of the Moonglade* - Riley St. James   h   5186

**Oak Valley**
*Charlie's Bones* - L.L. Thrasher   h   5468

**Oakland**
*Dead Voices: Natural Agonies in the Real World* - Gerald Vizenor   f   5578
*Ecstasy Club* - Douglas Rushkoff   s   4732
*Gun, with Occasional Music* - Jonathan Lethem   f   3441

**Oildorado**
*Shock Lines* - Warren Newton Beath   h   427

**Orange**
*All the Bells on Earth* - James P. Blaylock   f   518

**Orange County**
*The Bad Place* - Dean R. Koontz   h   3202

**Pacific Crest**
*Dark Tide* - Elizabeth Forrest   h   1972

**Palo Alto**
*Journals of the Plague Years* - Norman Spinrad   s   5172
*Vanishing Point* - Michaela Roessner   s   4652

**Pidgeon Point**
*T.J.'s Ghost* - Shirley Climo   h   1087

**Pine Cove**
*Practical Demonkeeping* - Christopher Moore   h   3989

**Pleasant Valley**
*The Homing* - John Saul   h   4842

**Pleasonton**
*Ground Zero* - Kevin J. Anderson   h   106

**Ravina**
*Out of the Night* - Patrick Whalen   h   5771

**Red Bluff**
*Bride of the Rat God* - Barbara Hambly   f   2499

**Red Cay**
*Haunted* - Tamara Thorne   h   5463

**Redbrook**
*The New Neighbor* - Ray Garton   h   2154

**Rio Santo**
*The Seventh Heart* - Marina Fitch   f   1943

**Robledos**
*Parable of the Sower* - Octavia E. Butler   s   792

**Roseville**
*Deadweight* - Robert Devereaux   h   1505

**Royal Beach**
*Outworld Cats* - Jack Lovejoy   s   3536

**Sacramento**
*Santa Steps Out: A Fairy Tale for Grownups* - Robert Devereaux   h   1506
*The Wall at the Edge of the World* - Jim Aikin   s   46

**St. John**
*Terminal Cafe* - Ian McDonald   s   3797

**Salinas**
*Dark of the Eye* - Douglas Clegg   h   1078

**San Angeles**
*Demolition Man* - Richard Osborne   s   4229

**San Diego**
*The Burning* - Graham Masterton   h   3672
*Catamount* - Michael Peak   h   4273
*Children of the End* - Mark A. Clements   h   1084
*Ragged Angels* - Della Van Hise   h   5537

**San Francisco**
*The 37th Mandala* - Marc Laidlaw   h   3310
*Adversary* - Daniel Rhodes   h   4568
*Angel Kiss* - Kelley Wilde   h   5800
*Arachne* - Lisa Mason   s   3661
*Balance of Power* - Dafydd ab Hugh   s   7
*Bedlam's Bard* - Mercedes Lackey   f   3269
*Bloodsucking Fiends: A Love Story* - Christopher Moore   h   3988
*Blue Light* - Walter Mosley   s   4042
*Carlucci's Edge* - Richard Paul Russo   s   4747
*Carlucci's Heart* - Richard Paul Russo   s   4748
*The City, Not Long After* - Pat Murphy   s   4051
*Cold Iron* - Melisa Michaels   f   3886
*Crygender* - Thomas T. Thomas   s   5451
*Cyberweb* - Lisa Mason   s   3662
*Dark Prince* - Keith Herber   h   2663
*Death Channels* - Robert E. Vardeman   h   5562
*The Deathless* - Myles Murchison   h   4048
*Delta Search* - William Shatner   s   4930
*Destroying Angel* - Richard Paul Russo   s   4749
*Dream of Glass* - Jean Mark Gawron   s   2163
*Dreams of Gods and Men* - W.T. Quick   s   4451
*Earthquake Weather* - Tim Powers   f   4382
*The Fire Rose* - Mercedes Lackey   f   3280
*A Flag Full of Stars* - Brad Ferguson   s   1922
*Freeze Frames* - Katharine Kerr   s   3071
*Gehenna* - Lewis Gannett   h   2114
*Ghostwright* - Michael Cadnum   h   810
*The Golden Nineties* - Lisa Mason   s   3663
*Gun, with Occasional Music* - Jonathan Lethem   f   3441
*Horses of the Night* - Michael Cadnum   h   811
*In the Blood* - Nancy A. Collins   h   1121
*Inhuman Beings* - Jerry Jay Carroll   s   914
*Iron Man: The Armor Trap* - Greg Cox   s   1227
*The Jade Ogre* - Kenneth Robeson   f   4623
*Journals of the Plague Years* - Norman Spinrad   s   5172
*The Judas Glass* - Michael Cadnum   h   812
*Kamikaze L'Amour* - Richard Kadrey   s   2998

*The Man Upstairs* - T.L. Parkinson   h   4248
*Master of Lies* - Graham Masterton   h   3676
*Mastery* - Kelley Wilde   h   5802
*ME: A Novel of Self Discovery* - Thomas T. Thomas   s   5452
*Mir* - Alexander Besher   s   474
*Morningstar* - Peter Atkins   h   265
*The Night Mayor* - Kim Newman   s   4099
*Overshoot* - Mona Clee   s   1075
*The Queen of the Damned* - Anne Rice   h   4574
*Resurrection* - Katharine Kerr   s   3075
*Sacrament* - Clive Barker   h   345
*St. Peter's Wolf* - Michael Cadnum   h   816
*Shadows on the Hill* - Jackie Cassada   f   935
*Skyscape* - Michael Cadnum   h   814
*Soulcatchers* - Jan Lara   h   3336
*Specters of the Dawn* - S. Andrew Swann   s   5368
*Starfleet Academy* - Diane Carey   s   905
*Steam* - Jay B. Laws   h   3361
*Stranded* - Camarin Grae   s   2295
*Street Magic* - Michael Reaves   f   4497
*Subterranean Gallery* - Richard Paul Russo   s   4750
*Summer of Love* - Lisa Mason   s   3664
*Summoned to Tourney* - Mercedes Lackey   f   3299
*Under Alien Stars* - Pamela F. Service   s   4919
*Under the Shadow* - Jane Toombs   h   5481
*The Unfinished* - Jay B. Laws   h   3362
*Vampire Bytes* - Linda Grant   h   2322
*Virtual Light* - William Gibson   s   2219
*Wanderer* - Donald E. McQuinn   s   3862
*The Witching Hour* - Anne Rice   h   4580
*Witchlight* - Marion Zimmer Bradley   f   655
*Worf's First Adventure* - Peter David   s   1391
*Wyrm Wolf* - Edo van Belkom   h   5535

**San Gabriel Mountains**
*Last Mountain* - Robert C. Fleet   f   1946
*Richter 10* - Arthur C. Clarke   s   1060

**San Jose**
*Vanishing Point* - Michaela Roessner   s   4652
*The Wizardry Cursed* - Rick Cook   f   1162

**San Paradiso**
*Echoes* - Jackie Hyman   h   2818

**Santa Cruz**
*Afterimage* - Kristine Kathryn Rusch   f   4709
*Afterimage Aftershock* - Kristine Kathryn Rusch   h   4710
*Freeware* - Rudy Rucker   s   4703
*Witch Baby* - Francesca Lia Block   s   552

**Santa Monica**
*Dark Rivers of the Heart* - Dean R. Koontz   h   3204
*Father of Frankenstein* - Christopher Bram   h   659
*The Jewel of Equilibrant* - Steven Frankos   f   2042
*The Offspring* - Kenneth McKenney   h   3826

**Santa Sierra**
*Signal to Noise* - Eric S. Nylund   s   4179

**Santa Verde**
*Panic* - Chris Curry   h   1295

**Seaview**
*The Summer I Shrank My Grandmother* - Elvira Woodruff   f   5968

**Serenity Hills**
*Rapid Growth* - Mary K. Hanner   h   2541

**Shadow Bay**
*Shadow Man* - Dennis Etchison   h   1848

**Silicon Valley**
*The Hacker and the Ants* - Rudy Rucker   s   4704

**Smithton Township**
*Some of Your Blood* - Theodore Sturgeon   h   5347

**Smithville**
*The Dealings of Daniel Kesserich* - Fritz
   Leiber   *s*   3417

**Sonoma**
*Kiss of Death* - Daniel Rhodes   *h*   4569

**Stanford**
*The Starry Child* - Lynn Hanna   *f*   2540

**Stilwell**
*Demon Shadows* - Michael B. Sirota   *h*   5075

**Sunnydale**
*The Harvest* - Richie Tankersley Cusick   *h*   1302
*Return to Chaos* - Craig Shaw Gardner   *h*   2131

**Sunnyvale**
*Virtually Perfect* - Dan Gutman   *s*   2470

**Toontown**
*Who P-P-Plugged Roger Rabbit?* - Gary K.
   Wolf   *f*   5934

**Trabuco Canyon**
*Night Relics* - James P. Blaylock   *h*   521

**Tuskett**
*Kane* - Douglas Borton   *h*   576

**Vallejo**
*Shackled* - Ray Garton   *h*   2156
*Slippin' into Darkness* - Norman Partridge   *h*   4254

**Venice Beach**
*Death Is a Lonely Business* - Ray Bradbury   *h*   619

**Weed**
*The Night in Fog* - David B. Silva   *h*   5026

**West Grove**
*The Terror* - Graham Masterton   *h*   3679
*Tooth and Claw* - Graham Masterton   *h*   3680

**Westwood**
*Rook* - Graham Masterton   *h*   3678
*Who Killed James Dean?* - Warren Newton
   Beath   *h*   428

**Winslow**
*Monday's Child* - Patricia Wallace   *h*   5623

**Wisdom Beach**
*Sweet Revenge* - Jean Simon   *h*   5066

**Yreka**
*Lot Lizards* - Ray Garton   *h*   2152


**COLORADO**

*Beyond the Pale* - Mark Anthony   *f*   153
*Cold Allies* - Patricia Anthony   *s*   157
*The Darkness Within* - Shawn MacDonald   *h*   3585
*Spires of Spirit* - Gael Baudino   *f*   395
*StarGate* - Dean Devlin   *s*   1509

**Aspen Prison**
*Judge Dredd* - Neal Barrett Jr.   *s*   366

**Boulder**
*Bellwether* - Connie Willis   *s*   5867
*The Burning Man* - Michael Hammond   *h*   2530
*Spree* - Lucy Taylor   *h*   5415
*The Stand: The Complete and Uncut Edition* - Stephen
   King   *h*   3142
*The Trinity Vector* - Steve Perry   *s*   4302

**Central Forest Preserve**
*Reefsong* - Carol Severance   *s*   4923

**Cheyenne Mt.**
*Mutant Hell* - Mark Grant   *s*   2324

**Colorado Springs**
*Grave Markings* - Michael A. Arnzen   *h*   212
*Mutineers' Moon* - David Weber   *s*   5677

**Denver**
*Cries of the Children* - Clare McNally   *h*   3856
*Gossamer Axe* - Gael Baudino   *f*   392
*The Hollow Man* - Dan Simmons   *s*   5054
*Insatiable* - David Dvorkin   *h*   1707
*Night's Pawn* - Tom Dowd   *s*   1591
*The Nine Lives of Catseye Gomez* - Simon
   Hawke   *f*   2620
*Otherworld* - Kenneth C. Flint   *h*   1959
*Prototype* - Brian Hodge   *h*   2704
*Strands of Sunlight* - Gael Baudino   *f*   396
*Virtual Girl* - Amy Thomson   *s*   5462
*Wagers of Sin* - Robert Asprin   *s*   264
*Wilding* - Melanie Tem   *h*   5425

**Denver Springs**
*Light Raid* - Connie Willis   *s*   5870

**Elvenhome**
*Strands of Sunlight* - Gael Baudino   *f*   396

**Fort Collins**
*Walking Wounded* - Robert Devereaux   *h*   1507

**Fury**
*Spirit Catcher* - Elizabeth Hallam   *f*   2497

**Glen Springs**
*Arrow From Earth* - F.M. Busby   *s*   782

**Grand Canyon**
*A Question of Time* - Fred Saberhagen   *h*   4772

**Hawksborough**
*Dark Souls* - Barry Porter   *h*   4369

**Mesa Verde**
*Indiana Jones and the Unicorn's Legacy* - Rob
   MacGregor   *f*   3593

**Overlook Hotel**
*The Shining* - Stephen King   *h*   3141

**Pagosa Springs**
*Hell-O-Ween* - David Robbins   *h*   4598

**Potter's Field**
*The Totem* - David Morrell   *h*   4012

**Revenant**
*Revenant* - Melanie Tem   *h*   5424

**Silverdale**
*Creature* - John Saul   *h*   4839

**Tallus**
*Desmodus* - Melanie Tem   *h*   5421

**Thunder**
*Darkly the Thunder* - William W.
   Johnstone   *h*   2929

**Willowdale**
*Darkly the Thunder* - William W.
   Johnstone   *h*   2929


**CONNECTICUT**

*An Acceptable Time* - Madeleine L'Engle   *f*   3436
*Nighteyes* - Garfield Reeves-Stevens   *s*   4510

**Bridgeport**
*Tooth: A Tale of Love and Death in Paradox* - Novak
   Kruger   *h*   3244

**Camfrey Estate**
*The Palm Dome* - Liz Fulton   *h*   2094

**Canaan**
*Witches* - Kathryn Meyer Griffith   *h*   2442

**Devon**
*The Man Who Turned into Himself* - David
   Ambrose   *h*   89

**Fallsbridge**
*The Basement* - Bari Wood   *h*   5961

**New Canaan**
*Wildlife* - James Patrick Kelly   *s*   3049

**New Haven**
*The Adventures of Lucius Leffing* - Joseph Payne
   Brennan   *h*   670

**Oxrun Station**
*The Black Carousel* - Charles L. Grant   *h*   2303
*Dialing the Wind* - Charles L. Grant   *h*   2305

**Stonehaven**
*The Halloween Man* - Douglas Clegg   *h*   1080

**Thornberry**
*Corrupting Dr. Nice* - John Kessel   *s*   3083

**Westbury**
*The Sister* - Elleston Trevor   *h*   5484

**Westerholm**
*The Hellfire Club* - Peter Straub   *h*   5326

**Westport**
*Fog Heart* - Thomas Tessier   *h*   5440

**Winter Falls**
*Black Ice* - Pat Graversen   *h*   2333


**DISTRICT OF COLUMBIA**

**Washington**
*12 Monkeys* - Elizabeth Hand   *s*   2532
*The Abductors: Conspiracy* - Jonathan
   Frakes   *s*   2034
*Aftermath* - Charles Sheffield   *s*   4947
*Blood War* - Robert Weinberg   *h*   5693
*Brainstorm* - Steven M. Krauzer   *h*   3230
*Breeder* - Douglas Clegg   *h*   1076
*Brother Termite* - Patricia Anthony   *s*   156
*Brothers* - Ben Bova   *s*   581
*Cardinal's Sin* - Raymond Buckland   *h*   751
*Circuit of Heaven* - Dennis Danvers   *s*   1348
*The Committee* - Raymond Buckland   *h*   752
*Cul-De-Sac* - David Martin   *h*   3638
*Dark Genesis* - J. Gregory Keyes   *s*   3096
*Daughter of Darkness* - Steven Spruill   *h*   5183
*Dawn* - V.C. Andrews   *h*   144
*The Deus Machine* - Pierre Ouellette   *h*   4232
*Distraction* - Bruce Sterling   *s*   5256
*Dream Maker* - W.A. Harbinson   *s*   2542
*Elvis Rising: Stories on the King* - Kay
   Sloan   *f*   5089
*The Faery Convention* - Brett Davis   *f*   1399
*A Fearful Symmetry* - James Luceno   *s*   3542
*Fire* - Alan Rodgers   *h*   4647
*Footprints of Thunder* - James F. David   *s*   1379
*The Fugitive Stars* - Daniel Ransom   *s*   4479
*The Gatekeepers* - Daniel Graham Jr.   *s*   2301
*Goblins* - Charles L. Grant   *s*   2309
*The Green Progression* - L.E. Modesitt Jr.   *s*   3932
*Ground Zero* - Kevin J. Anderson   *s*   106
*How Like a God* - Brenda W. Clough   *f*   1089
*Incubi* - Edward Lee   *h*   3394
*Independence Day* - Dean Devlin   *s*   1508
*Interface* - Stephen Bury   *s*   781
*Journals of the Plague Years* - Norman
   Spinrad   *s*   5172
*Lady El* - Jim Starlin   *s*   5213
*The Last Wizard* - Simon Hawke   *f*   2619
*Lie to Me* - David Martin   *h*   3639
*Lorelei* - Mark A. Clements   *h*   1086
*Martian Rainbow* - Robert L. Forward   *s*   1987
*Maximum Light* - Nancy Kress   *s*   3241
*Mirror to the Sky* - Mark S. Geston   *s*   2213
*The Modular Man* - Roger MacBride Allen   *s*   79
*Moonfall* - Jack McDevitt   *s*   3789
*My Soul to Take* - Steven Spruill   *h*   5184
*No Kidding* - Bruce Brooks   *s*   709

*One Wish* - C.J. Card  *f*  880
*Operation Damocles* - Oscar L. Fellows  *s*  1915
*The Other End of Time* - Frederik Pohl  *s*  4351
*Portrait of the Psychopath as a Young Woman* -
    Edward Lee  *h*  3395
*The President's Astrologer* - Barbara
    Shafferman  *f*  4926
*Prey* - William W. Johnstone  *h*  2932
*Rage of Spirits* - Noel Hynd  *h*  2824
*The Resurrectionist* - Thomas F.
    Monteleone  *h*  3965
*Rogue Star* - Michael Flynn  *s*  1965
*Rulers of Darkness* - Steven Spruill  *h*  5185
*Seaward* - Brad Leithauser  *h*  3433
*Semper Mars* - Ian Douglas  *s*  1585
*The Siege of Eternity* - Frederik Pohl  *s*  4353
*Silent Zone* - Stephen Molstad  *s*  3952
*The Smithsonian Institution* - Gore Vidal  *f*  5570
*Stranger in a Strange Land* - Robert A.
    Heinlein  *s*  2649
*Tap, Tap* - David Martin  *h*  3640
*Target Earth* - Steve Perry  *s*  4301
*Tea From an Empty Cup* - Pat Cadigan  *s*  809
*Tek Power* - William Shatner  *s*  4937
*Terminal Logic* - Jefferson Scott  *s*  4893
*This Side of Judgment* - J.R. Dunn  *s*  1696
*Timecop* - S.D. Perry  *s*  4286
*The Torching* - Marcy Heidish  *h*  2642
*Treasure Box* - Orson Scott Card  *h*  898
*The Trinity Vector* - Steve Perry  *s*  4302
*Unholy Allies* - Robert Weinberg  *h*  5704
*Virtual Destruction* - Kevin J. Anderson  *s*  118
*Vodoun* - David Madsen  *h*  3605
*Waking the Moon* - Elizabeth Hand  *f*  2538
*Wet Work* - Philip Nutman  *h*  4168
*Whirlwind* - Charles L. Grant  *f*  2320
*The X-Files: Fight the Future* - Chris Carter  *h*  924

## EAST

*Eastern Ghosts* - Frank D. McSherry Jr.  *h*  3866

## EAST COAST

*Diggers* - Terry Pratchett  *s*  4386
*Manjinn Moon* - Denise Vitola  *s*  5576
*Wings* - Terry Pratchett  *s*  4403

## FLORIDA

*Death Dream* - Ben Bova  *s*  583
*Footprints of Thunder* - James F. David  *s*  1379
*The Hanged Man* - T.J. MacGregor  *h*  3594
*Kings of the High Frontier* - Victor Koman  *s*  3199
*Operation Damocles* - Oscar L. Fellows  *s*  1916
*Swamp* - Peter Tremayne  *h*  5483
*Tatham Mound* - Piers Anthony  *f*  191
*Wind Chimes* - R.R. Walters  *h*  5625
*Wings* - Terry Pratchett  *s*  4403

**Banyon Beach**
*Infernal Affairs* - Jane Heller  *h*  2652

**Blue Turtle Island**
*The Jimjams* - Michael Green  *h*  2345

**Canaveral Pier**
*Clarke County, Space* - Allen Steele  *s*  5241

**Cape Canaveral**
*Voyager* - Stephen Baxter  *s*  406

**Chaseburn**
*Souls* - Katina Alexis  *h*  71

**Corona City**
*Dark Fortune* - Richard Lee Byers  *h*  795

**Destiny World**
*The Seraphim Rising* - Elisabeth De Vos  *s*  1442

**Florida Keys**
*Shadows in the Water* - Kathryn Lasky  *s*  3341

**Ft. Lauderdale**
*In the Rift* - Marion Zimmer Bradley  *f*  639

**Fort Lauderdale**
*Mr. Sandman* - Lyle Howard  *h*  2779

**Ft. Walton Beach**
*Kiss of the Vampire* - Lee Weathersby  *h*  5657

**Gainesville**
*Living Real* - James C. Bassett  *s*  386

**Greater Tampa**
*Cyber Way* - Alan Dean Foster  *s*  2000

**John's Bluff**
*Concrete Hotel* - C. Christopher Caldon  *h*  839

**Kennedy Space Center**
*Ignition* - Kevin J. Anderson  *s*  107

**Key West**
*Hunger* - William Dantz  *h*  1346
*Key West 2720 A.D.* - William Eakins  *s*  1720

**La Mirada**
*Return of the Wolfman* - Jeff Rovin  *h*  4687

**Las Flores**
*Carnivores* - Penelope Banka Kreps  *h*  3232

**Latchahee County**
*Dogland* - Will Shetterly  *f*  4992

**Miami**
*The Between* - Tannarive Due  *h*  1669
*Harvest of Blood* - Vincent Courtney  *h*  1213
*My Soul to Keep* - Tannarive Due  *h*  1670
*Shango* - James Roberto Curtis  *h*  1298
*The Tale of the Body Thief* - Anne Rice  *h*  4576
*Vampire Beat* - Vincent Courtney  *h*  1214
*The Vampire Princess* - Michael Romkey  *h*  4667

**Middle Kingdom Ranch**
*Firefly* - Piers Anthony  *h*  170

**Orlando**
*Pirates of the Universe* - Terry Bisson  *s*  506

**Summer Haven**
*Vampire Blood* - Kathryn Meyer Griffith  *h*  2441

**Sundova Beach**
*Wake Up Screaming* - Vincent Courtney  *h*  1215

**Tampa**
*The Darker Saints* - Brian Hodge  *h*  2699
*Dead Time* - Richard Lee Byers  *h*  796
*Netherworld* - Richard Lee Byers  *h*  798
*Nightlife* - Brian Hodge  *h*  2702
*Specters* - J.M. Dillard  *h*  1555
*The Vampire's Apprentice* - Richard Lee
    Byers  *h*  799

**Trapper's Cay**
*Demon's Fright* - Penelope Banka Kreps  *h*  3233

**Villejeune**
*Darkness* - John Saul  *h*  4840

## GEORGIA

*The Black Mariah* - Jay R. Bonansinga  *h*  570
*Born to Run* - Mercedes Lackey  *f*  3271
*Dreamseeker's Road* - Tom Deitz  *f*  1472
*The Harvest* - Robert Charles Wilson  *s*  5909
*Landslayer's Law* - Tom Deitz  *f*  1474
*Moonwar* - Ben Bova  *s*  588

**Athens**
*The Gryphon King* - Tom Deitz  *f*  1473

**Atlanta**
*Angel Kiss* - Kelley Wilde  *h*  5800
*Blood* - Ron Dee  *h*  1463
*The Blood Artists* - Chuck Hogan  *h*  2720
*Call to Battle* - Doug Murray  *h*  4059
*The Devil's Advocate* - Gherbod Fleming  *h*  1949
*Diaspora* - Greg Egan  *s*  1759
*The Halflife* - Sharon Webb  *s*  5664
*The House Next Door* - Anne Rivers
    Siddons  *h*  5021
*The Multiplex Man* - James P. Hogan  *s*  2727
*The Seraphim Rising* - Elisabeth De Vos  *s*  1442
*Sewer, Gas & Electric* - Matt Ruff  *s*  4708
*Slice* - Rex Miller  *h*  3902
*The Winnowing* - Gherbod Fleming  *h*  1950

**Barton**
*Dark Debts* - Karen Hall  *h*  2494

**Chattahoochee Valley**
*Brittle Innings* - Michael Bishop  *h*  498

**Cherokee Rose**
*The Book of Webster's* - J.N. Williamson  *h*  5853

**Congreve**
*Along Came a Spider* - Athena Alexis  *h*  70

**Cordova**
*Dreambuilder* - Tom Deitz  *f*  1471
*Soulsmith* - Tom Deitz  *f*  1475

**Enotah County**
*Sunshaker's War* - Tom Deitz  *f*  1477

**Gull Island**
*Never Land* - Douglas Clegg  *h*  1081

**Gwinnett County**
*Brethren* - Shawn Ryan  *h*  4754

**Lagoon**
*Lagoon* - Alison Drake  *h*  1625

**Mt. Jephtha**
*Let There Be Dark* - Allen Lee Harris  *h*  2557

**Savannah**
*These Fallen Angels* - Wendy Haley  *h*  2492
*This Dark Paradise* - Wendy Haley  *h*  2493

**Sky Valley**
*Sacrifice* - John Farris  *h*  1886

**Soldier**
*The Living Dark* - Stephen Gresham  *h*  2431

**Sturgis**
*Spook* - Steve Vance  *h*  5553

**Welch County**
*Dreambuilder* - Tom Deitz  *f*  1471
*Wordwright* - Tom Deitz  *f*  1478

**Whidden**
*Stoneskin's Revenge* - Tom Deitz  *f*  1476

## GREAT LAKES

*The Key to the Indian* - Lynne Reid Banks  *f*  331

## HAWAII

*Addams Family Values* - Todd Strasser  *f*  5324
*House of the Sun* - Nigel Findley  *s*  1936

**Hana**
*Demon Fire* - Gary L. Holleman  *h*  2743

**Hilo**
*Mars Underground* - William Hartmann  *s*  2584
*Shadows on the Hill* - Jackie Cassada  *f*  935

**Honolulu**
*The Bones of Time* - Kathleen Ann Goonan  *s*  2273

*Viper* - Alan Riefe   *h*   4589

**Kauai**
*Galilee* - Clive Barker   *h*   340
*Magnificat* - Julian May   *s*   3699

**Maui**
*The Presence* - John Saul   *h*   4843
*Spindoc* - Steve Perry   *s*   4300

**Pearl Harbor**
*Day of the Snake* - Matthew J. Costello   *s*   1196

**South Kona**
*Fires of Eden* - Dan Simmons   *h*   5053

**IDAHO**

*Her Monster* - Jeff Collignon   *h*   1115
*Laying the Music to Rest* - Dean Wesley
  Smith   *h*   5114

**Great Primitive Area**
*Watchers in the Woods* - William W.
  Johnstone   *h*   2936

**Indian Pole**
*Witch* - Christopher Pike   *f*   4334

**Junction**
*Valentine* - S.P. Somtow   *h*   5160

**Moskow**
*/* - Greg Bear   *s*   413

**Sugarloaf Valley**
*Guardian* - John Saul   *h*   4841

**ILLINOIS**

*Ancestral Hungers* - Scott Baker   *h*   303
*Lethal Exposure* - Kevin J. Anderson   *s*   110

**Andover**
*Curse of the Vampire* - Geoffrey Caine   *h*   832

**Bloomington**
*The Lincoln Hunters* - Wilson Tucker   *s*   5487

**Castleview**
*Castleview* - Gene Wolfe   *f*   5939

**Chicago**
*Afterage* - Yvonne Navarro   *h*   4072
*Angel Light* - Andrew M. Greeley   *f*   2342
*The Armageddon Box* - Robert Weinberg   *h*   5690
*Back in the USSA* - Kim Newman   *s*   4095
*The Black Lodge* - Robert Weinberg   *h*   5692
*Blood on the Water* - P.N. Elrod   *h*   1791
*Bloodlist* - P.N. Elrod   *h*   1792
*Bring on the Night* - Don Davis   *h*   1402
*Bureau 13* - Nick Pollotta   *f*   4362
*A Calculated Magic* - Robert Weinberg   *f*   5694
*Carmilla: The Return* - Kyle Marffin   *h*   3623
*Changeling* - Christopher Kubasik   *f*   3245
*Chicago Loop* - Paul Theroux   *h*   5443
*A Chill in the Blood* - P.N. Elrod   *h*   1793
*The City on the Edge of Forever* - Harlan
  Ellison   *s*   1784
*Crashcourse* - Wilhelmina Baird   *s*   295
*Cursed Be the Child* - Mort Castle   *h*   937
*Dark Heart* - Margaret Weis   *f*   5707
*The Dead Man's Kiss* - Robert Weinberg   *h*   5695
*Deadrush* - Yvonne Navarro   *h*   4073
*The Devil's Auction* - Robert Weinberg   *h*   5696
*Doomsday Exam* - Nick Pollotta   *f*   4363
*Dreamer* - Daniel Quinn   *h*   4454
*Dreams of Gods and Men* - W.T. Quick   *s*   4451
*F.R.E.E.Lancers* - Mel Odom   *s*   4191
*Fallen Angels* - Larry Niven   *s*   4120
*Fire in the Blood* - P.N. Elrod   *h*   1796
*The Fire Rose* - Mercedes Lackey   *f*   3280
*For You, the Living* - Wayne Allen Sallee   *h*   4786

*The Forever King* - Molly Cochran   *f*   1092
*Frostwing* - Richard A. Knaak   *f*   3170
*Full Moonster* - Nick Pollotta   *f*   4364
*Harmony* - Marjorie Bradley Kellogg   *s*   3046
*The Holy Terror* - Wayne Allen Sallee   *h*   4787
*I, Vampire* - Michael Romkey   *h*   4665
*Indiana Jones and the Genesis Deluge* - Rob
  MacGregor   *f*   3589
*Indiana Jones and the Peril at Delphi* - Rob
  MacGregor   *f*   3591
*King of the Grey* - Richard A. Knaak   *f*   3173
*A Logical Magician* - Robert Weinberg   *f*   5697
*The Long Midnight* - Daniel Ransom   *h*   4480
*A Matter of Taste* - Fred Saberhagen   *h*   4770
*Night Prophets* - Paul F. Olson   *h*   4213
*Nimbus* - Alexander Jablokov   *s*   2839
*Obsessed* - Rick R. Reed   *h*   4500
*Out for Blood* - John Peyton Cooke   *h*   1166
*Penance* - Rick R. Reed   *h*   4501
*Red Angel* - Roxanne Longstreet   *h*   3518
*Sick* - Jay R. Bonansinga   *h*   571
*Slice* - Rex Miller   *h*   3902
*Stranded* - Camarin Grae   *s*   2295
*Testament of the Dragon* - Margaret Weis   *f*   5729
*Timeshare: Second Time Around* - Joshua
  Dann   *s*   1345
*Troll-Quest* - Rose Estes   *f*   1841
*Troll-Taken* - Rose Estes   *f*   1842
*What Savage Beast* - Peter David   *s*   1390

**Elm Haven**
*Summer of Night* - Dan Simmons   *h*   5060

**Faulkner**
*Whipping Boy* - John Byrne   *h*   800

**Glendale**
*Silent Scream* - Dan Schmidt   *h*   4883

**Green Town**
*Ray Bradbury Presents: Dinosaur Planet* - Stephen
  Leigh   *s*   3427
*Ray Bradbury Presents: Dinosaur World* - Stephen
  Leigh   *s*   3428

**Hollow Tree Farm**
*Higher Mythology* - Jody Lynn Nye   *f*   4170

**Hopewell**
*Running with the Demon* - Terry Brooks   *f*   715

**Meridian**
*Insanity, Illinois* - Mark Sumner   *s*   5358

**Midwestern University**
*Higher Mythology* - Jody Lynn Nye   *f*   4170

**Milhaven**
*The Throat* - Peter Straub   *h*   5332

**Rolling Meadows**
*Probe* - Edward M. Lerner   *s*   3437

**Shoreview**
*Hard Landing* - Algis Budrys   *s*   753

**Springfield**
*Interface* - Stephen Bury   *s*   781
*Skeletons* - Al Sarrantonio   *h*   4834

**Vallor**
*In the Mood* - Charles L. Grant   *h*   2312

**INDIANA**

*All's Faire* - Pamela F. Service   *f*   4917
*The Lion of Farside* - John Dalmas   *f*   1324

**Bethel Lake**
*Threshold* - Bill Myers   *s*   4060

**Evansville**
*The Quagmire* - James Kisner   *h*   3160

**Farmington**
*Killing Frost* - Dan I. Blake   *h*   514

**Harrodsburg**
*The Voice in the Basement* - T. Chris
  Martindale   *h*   3657

**Huntsville**
*Seed upon the Wind* - Carole Nelson
  Douglas   *f*   1584

**Indianapolis**
*Night Glow* - Martin James   *h*   2867
*The Night Seasons* - J.N. Williamson   *h*   5858
*Tower of Evil* - James Kisner   *h*   3161

**Isherwood**
*Nightblood* - T. Chris Martindale   *h*   3656

**Jamay Lake**
*The Forever Children* - Eric Flanders   *h*   1944

**Lakota**
*The Gypsy* - Steven Brust   *f*   744

**Middlefield**
*The Land of Nod* - Mark A. Clements   *h*   1085

**Neva Monastery**
*The Monastery* - J.N. Williamson   *h*   5856

**Noblesville**
*The Monastery* - J.N. Williamson   *h*   5856

**South Bend**
*Where the Towers Pierce the Sky* - Marie D.
  Goodwin   *f*   2272

**South Port**
*Dangerous Nature* - T.J. Kirby   *h*   3152

**Wabash Heights**
*Mongster* - Randall Boyll   *h*   616

**IOWA**

*Mutant Hell* - Mark Grant   *s*   2324
*Mutants Amok* - Mark Grant   *s*   2325
*Spartan Run* - David Robbins   *s*   4602

**Ames**
*The Soprano Sorceress* - L.E. Modesitt Jr.   *f*   3938

**Hermes**
*Weirdos of the Universe, Unite!* - Pamela F.
  Service   *f*   4921

**North Liberty**
*The Unknown Soldier* - Mickey Zucker
  Reichert   *s*   4525

**St. Regis**
*The House of the Toad* - Richard L.
  Tierney   *h*   5470

**Stevensville**
*Billy* - Whitley Strieber   *h*   5338

**KANSAS**

*Buddy Holly Is Alive and Well on Ganymede* - Bradley
  Denton   *s*   1490
*Mirror to the Sky* - Mark S. Geston   *s*   2213
*Panda Ray* - Michael Kandel   *s*   3011
*Psi-Man* - David Peters   *s*   4305
*Requiem* - Clifford Mohr   *h*   3950
*Unicorn Highway* - David Lee Jones   *f*   2941

**Colson**
*The Moons of Summer* - S.K. Epperson   *h*   1831

**Denke**
*Borderland: A Novel of Terror* - S.K.
  Epperson   *h*   1828

**Dumford**
*Dumford Blood* - S.K. Epperson   *h*   1829

**Eastwood**
*The Whispers* - Dan Parkinson   *s*   4247

**Emerson**
*The Axman Cometh* - John Farris   *h*   1883

**Flint Hills**
*Nightmare* - S.K. Epperson   *h*   1832

**Fort Grant**
*Black Night* - S.J. Strayhorn   *h*   5334

**Fort Riley**
*Entity* - Nina Mandelik   *h*   3615

**Green Lake**
*Green Lake* - S.K. Epperson   *h*   1830

**Kansas City**
*Dragon's Teeth* - Lee Killough   *s*   3109

**Manhattan**
*Was* - Geoff Ryman   *f*   4758

**Pittsburg**
*One Foot in the Grave* - Wm. Mark
    Simmons   *f*   5062

**Spring Valley**
*The Reckoning* - Ruby Jean Jensen   *h*   2904

**Topeka**
*Dragon's Teeth* - Lee Killough   *s*   3109
*Wizard and Glass* - Stephen King   *h*   3144

**Wontoda**
*Blackburn* - Bradley Denton   *h*   1489

**KENTUCKY**

**Crockston**
*Genesis* - Charles L. Grant   *h*   2308

**Cumberland Mountains**
*Love & Sleep* - John Crowley   *f*   1277

**Fort Campbell**
*Operation Synbat* - Bob Mayer   *h*   3701

**Half Moon**
*Black Death* - R. Karl Largent   *h*   3337

**Mammoth Caves**
*Troll-Quest* - Rose Estes   *f*   1841

**Stoneridge**
*Buried Screams* - C. Dean Andersson   *h*   137

**LOUISIANA**

*Blood Roots* - Richie Tankersley Cusick   *h*   1300
*The Darker Saints* - Brian Hodge   *h*   2699

**Apollo**
*Playmates* - Abigail McDaniels   *h*   3784

**The Bayous**
*Gone South* - Robert R. McCammon   *h*   3755

**Bristol Springs**
*Night Brothers* - Sidney Williams   *h*   5824

**Catahoula**
*Bats* - William W. Johnstone   *h*   2926

**Coulee**
*Althea* - Abigail McDaniels   *h*   3782

**Creque Bayou**
*The Dwelling* - Tom Elliott   *h*   1776

**LaGrange**
*The Devil's Laughter* - William W.
    Johnstone   *h*   2930

**New Falls Church**
*Dead Voices* - Abigail McDaniels   *h*   3783

**New Orleans**
*The Asylum* - John E. Ames   *h*   93
*Blood: A Southern Fantasy* - Michael
    Moorcock   *f*   3977
*Blood on the Bayou* - D.J. Donaldson   *h*   1570
*Bone Music* - Alan Rodgers   *h*   4646
*Contagion* - John David Connor   *h*   1136
*Crygender* - Thomas T. Thomas   *s*   5451
*The Death Crystal* - J. Edward Ames   *h*   91
*Distraction* - Bruce Sterling   *s*   5256
*Exquisite Corpse* - Poppy Z. Brite   *h*   695
*Gabriel Knight: Sins of the Fathers* - Jane
    Jensen   *h*   2896
*The Gris-Gris Man* - Don Davis   *h*   1403
*The Hacker* - Chet Day   *h*   1410
*In Hot Blood* - Petru Popescu   *h*   4367
*Killjoy* - Elizabeth Forrest   *h*   1973
*Lasher* - Anne Rice   *h*   4570
*The Lazarus Heart* - Poppy Z. Brite   *h*   696
*Leanna: Possession of a Woman* - Marie
    Kiraly   *h*   3149
*Lorelei* - Mark A. Clements   *h*   1086
*Lost Souls* - Poppy Z. Brite   *h*   697
*Madeline: After the Fall of Usher* - Marie
    Kiraly   *h*   3150
*Of Masques and Martyrs* - Christopher
    Golden   *h*   2258
*Portent* - James Herbert   *h*   2670
*Sacred Prey* - Vivian Schilling   *h*   4875
*Spell Bound* - Trana Mae Simmons   *f*   5061
*Tempter* - Nancy A. Collins   *h*   1125
*A Time for Us* - Christine Holden   *f*   2731
*The Vampire Armand* - Anne Rice   *h*   4578
*The Venetian's Wife: A Strangely Sensual Tale of a
    Renaissance Explorer, a Computer, and a
    Metamorphosis* - Nick Bantock   *f*   336
*Violin* - Anne Rice   *h*   4579
*Virtual Girl* - Amy Thomson   *s*   5462
*Voodoo Child* - Michael Reaves   *h*   4498
*The Werewolf's Touch* - Cheri Scotch   *h*   4892
*The Witching Hour* - Anne Rice   *h*   4580

**Petittville**
*When Darkness Falls* - Sidney Williams   *h*   5825

**Sandy Run**
*Them* - William W. Johnstone   *h*   2935

**Shreveport**
*Gone South* - Robert R. McCammon   *h*   3755

**MAINE**

*The Bear Went over the Mountain* - William
    Kotzwinkle   *f*   3222
*Tex and Molly in the Afterlife* - Richard
    Grant   *f*   2327

**Assyria**
*The Mark of the Moderately Vicious Vampire* - Lionel
    Fenn   *h*   1920

**Bolton**
*Impulse* - Rick Hautala   *h*   2609

**Bristol Mills**
*Dead Voices* - Rick Hautala   *h*   2607

**Caeser Island**
*Flesh* - Gus Weill   *h*   5685

**Cape Helm**
*Distant Dreams* - Jenny Lykins   *f*   3576

**Cape Higgins**
*Twilight Time* - Rick Hautala   *h*   2613

**Castle Rock**
*The Dark Half* - Stephen King   *h*   3128

**Needful Things** - Stephen King   *h*   3137

**Chamberlain**
*Carrie* - Stephen King   *h*   3127

**Dark Score Lake**
*Bag of Bones* - Stephen King   *h*   3126

**Dead River**
*Offspring* - Jack Ketchum   *h*   3092

**Derry**
*Insomnia* - Stephen King   *h*   3135

**Dyer**
*Moon Walker* - Rick Hautala   *h*   2610

**Fairwater**
*The Frighteners* - Michael Jahn   *h*   2856

**Hilton**
*Cold Whisper* - Rick Hautala   *h*   2605
*The Mountain King* - Rick Hautala   *h*   2611

**Jerusalem's Lot**
*Salem's Lot* - Stephen King   *h*   3140

**Kashawakam Lake**
*Gerald's Game* - Stephen King   *h*   3133

**Land's End**
*Lullaby* - Diane Guest   *h*   2455

**Little Tall Island**
*Dolores Claiborne* - Stephen King   *h*   3130

**Ludlow**
*The Dark Half* - Stephen King   *h*   3128

**Matawaskie Valley**
*Hell House* - Richard Matheson   *h*   3685

**Orono**
*Cold Whisper* - Rick Hautala   *h*   2605

**Paradise Island**
*The Invisible Company* - Scott Russell
    Sanders   *s*   4813

**Portland**
*Beyond the Shroud* - Rick Hautala   *h*   2604
*Ghost Light* - Rick Hautala   *h*   2608
*Shades of Night* - Rick Hautala   *h*   2612

**Secret Cove**
*Second Child* - John Saul   *h*   4844

**Steel Harbor**
*Winter Wolves* - Earle Wescott   *h*   5756

**Stockton Springs**
*Shadow Dance* - Jessica Palmer   *h*   4238

**Summerfield**
*Dark Silence* - Rick Hautala   *h*   2606

**Tranquility**
*Bloodstream* - Tess Gerritsen   *h*   2205

**MARYLAND**

*Stinger* - Nancy Kress   *s*   3243

**Annapolis**
*Sacrifice* - Richard Kinion   *h*   3146
*Shadow of the Beast* - Margaret L. Carter   *h*   926

**Baltimore**
*12 Monkeys* - Elizabeth Hand   *s*   2532
*Diary of a Vampire* - Gary Bowen   *h*   600
*The Lighthouse at the End of the World* - Stephen
    Marlowe   *h*   3631
*Lurid Dreams* - Charles L. Harness   *s*   2546
*Murder in the Solid State* - Wil McCarthy   *s*   3764
*Quoth the Crow* - David Bischoff   *h*   494
*Specters* - J.M. Dillard   *h*   1555

**Cambridge**
*Cross a Dark Bridge* - Deborah
  Churchman   *h*   1027

**Catoctin Mountain Park**
*Aftermath* - Charles Sheffield   *s*   4947

**College Park**
*Time, Like an Ever-Rolling Stream* - Judith
  Moffett   *s*   3944

**Diamond Park**
*The Nightmare People* - Lawrence Watt-
  Evans   *h*   5643

**Laurel Hills**
*The Select* - F. Paul Wilson   *h*   5897

**Riverview**
*Blood and Chocolate* - Annette Curtis
  Klause   *h*   3162

**Silver Springs**
*Hellcat* - Amanda Kingsley   *h*   3145

**MASSACHUSETTS**

*Captain Quad* - Sean Costello   *h*   1203
*The Element of Fire* - Jason Henderson   *f*   2657
*A King Beneath the Mountain* - Robert N.
  Charrette   *f*   973
*Practical Magic* - Alice Hoffman   *f*   2713
*A Prince Among Men* - Robert N. Charrette   *f*   977
*The Steampunk Trilogy* - Paul Di Filippo   *s*   1518
*Toward the End of Time* - John Updike   *s*   5531

**Arkham**
*Witch Hill* - Marion Zimmer Bradley   *h*   654

**Ashbury**
*Mercy's Mill* - Betty Levin   *f*   3444

**Bampton**
*The Rebirth of Wonder* - Lawrence Watt-
  Evans   *f*   5646

**Boston**
*Angels Unaware* - L. Elizabeth Storm   *s*   5315
*Arc Riders* - David Drake   *s*   1626
*Dawn Song* - Michael Marano   *h*   3620
*Dinosaur Summer* - Greg Bear   *s*   416
*The Fermata* - Nicholson Baker   *s*   302
*The First Immortal* - James L. Halperin   *s*   2498
*Future Boston* - David Alexander Smith   *s*   5107
*The Gilda Stories* - Jewelle Gomez   *h*   2267
*Goodlow's Ghosts* - T.M. Wright   *h*   5991
*Hence* - Brad Leithauser   *s*   3431
*The Hollow Man* - Dan Simmons   *s*   5054
*Human to Human* - Rebecca Ore   *s*   4219
*In the Cube* - David Alexander Smith   *s*   5109
*Life Support* - Tess Gerritsen   *h*   2206
*The Living One* - Lewis Gannett   *h*   2115
*Newton's Cannon* - J. Gregory Keyes   *f*   3097
*Now You See It. . .* - Richard Matheson   *h*   3688
*Of Saints and Shadows* - Christopher
  Golden   *h*   2259
*Reaper* - Ben Mizrich   *h*   3923
*The Return of the Breakneck Boys* - Geary
  Gravel   *s*   2332
*The Trail of Cthulhu* - August Derleth   *h*   1497

**Brookline**
*Blood of Innocents* - John Arbucci   *h*   204

**Cambridge**
*Renaissance Moon* - Linda Nevins   *f*   4093

**Cape Cod**
*Blue Moon* - Hila Feil   *f*   1898

**Carleton**
*Rough Beast* - Gary Goshgarian   *h*   2284

**Crocker**
*Deathwalker* - R. Patrick Gates   *h*   2159
*Tunnelvision* - R. Patrick Gates   *h*   2162

**Edens Bluff**
*Soul Snatchers* - Michael Cecilione   *h*   947

**Fall River**
*Lizzie Borden* - Elizabeth Engstrom   *h*   1826

**Glenport**
*Invasion America* - Christie Golden   *s*   2252

**Hanley**
*The School* - Ed Kelleher   *h*   3042

**Horn Pond**
*Immortal* - Jason Nickles   *h*   4102

**Innsmouth**
*The Innsmouth Heritage* - Brian Stableford   *h*   5194
*The Shadow over Innsmouth* - H.P.
  Lovecraft   *h*   3533

**Kingdom Head Island**
*The Stone Circle* - Gary Goshgarian   *h*   2285

**Martha's Vineyard**
*A Witch Across Time* - Gilbert B. Cross   *f*   1272

**Monument**
*Fade* - Robert Cormier   *h*   1188

**Morgantown**
*Thunder Rise* - G. Wayne Miller   *h*   3895

**Mount Weeupcutt**
*Armageddon Summer* - Jane Yolen   *s*   6028

**Nantucket Island**
*Ghosts* - Noel Hynd   *h*   2822

**North Andover**
*When Shadows Fall* - Brian Scott Smith   *h*   5100

**Osprey Island**
*White Shark* - Peter Benchley   *h*   441

**Pioneer Colony**
*I Feel Like the Morning Star* - Gregory
  Maguire   *s*   3608

**Provincetown**
*Starmind* - Spider Robinson   *s*   4642

**Quincy**
*The Frightened Fish* - Kenneth Robeson   *f*   4622

**Sanctuary**
*Eternity* - Maggie Shayne   *f*   4943

**Skipdon**
*Julian's House* - Judith Hawkes   *h*   2630

**Village**
*Looker* - Jorge Saralegui   *h*   4820

**MICHIGAN**

*Shaman* - Robert Shea   *f*   4946

**Detroit**
*Accidental Creatures* - Anne Harris   *s*   2558
*Bad Brains* - Kathe Koja   *h*   3193
*Darkman* - Randall Boyll   *h*   611
*Darkman #1: The Hangman* - Randall Boyll   *h*   612
*Darkman #2: The Price of Fear* - Randall
  Boyll   *h*   613
*Darkman #3: The Gods of Hell* - Randall
  Boyll   *h*   614
*Darkman #4: The Face of Death* - Randall
  Boyll   *h*   615
*Door Number Three* - Patrick O'Leary   *s*   4210
*F.R.E.E.Lancers* - Mel Odom   *s*   4191
*Zombie* - Joyce Carol Oates   *h*   4185

**Granger**
*Paddywhack* - John Stchur   *h*   5236

**Merrimac**
*Wake of the Werewolf* - Geoffrey Caine   *h*   834

**Puzzle Lake**
*Killing Frost* - Dan I. Blake   *h*   514

**Two Rivers**
*Mysterium* - Robert Charles Wilson   *s*   5911

**Waterloo**
*Dead Heat* - Del Stone Jr.   *h*   5313

**Watersmeet**
*Carmilla: The Return* - Kyle Marfinn   *h*   3623

**MIDWEST**

*Being of Two Minds* - Pamela F. Service   *f*   4918
*The Fear in Yesterday's Rings* - George C.
  Chesbro   *h*   1007
*Fields of Blood: Vampire Stories of the Heartland* -
  Lawrence Schimel   *h*   4879
*Ghosts of the Heartland* - Frank D. McSherry
  Jr.   *h*   3868
*The Sixth Dog* - Jane Rice   *h*   4582
*Walking the Labyrinth* - Lisa Goldstein   *f*   2266

**Clarendon**
*Darker than You Think* - Jack Williamson   *h*   5861

**Crick City**
*Creekers* - Edward Lee   *h*   3391

**Escardy Gap**
*Escardy Gap* - Peter Crowther   *h*   1282

**Groveland**
*Harrowgate* - Daniel H. Gower   *h*   2292

**Haute Montaigne**
*A Hidden Place* - Robert Charles Wilson   *s*   5910

**Libertyville**
*Rose Madder* - Stephen King   *h*   3139

**Medicine Falls**
*Leap Point* - Kay Kenyon   *s*   3063

**Sun Return**
*Night Calls* - Katharine Eliska Kimbriel   *h*   3119

**Warner**
*An Exaltation of Larks* - Robert Reed   *s*   4506

**MINNESOTA**

*Cup of Clay* - Carole Nelson Douglas   *f*   1583
*Jumper* - Steven Gould   *s*   2290
*Madman Run* - David Robbins   *s*   4600
*Mr. Was* - Pete Hautman   *s*   2614
*Red Shadows* - Yvonne Navarro   *s*   4074
*The Unnatural* - David Prill   *h*   4437

**Battle Lake**
*Seeing Eye* - Jack Ellis   *h*   1780

**Blackstock College**
*Tam Lin* - Pamela Dean   *f*   1446

**Dart Commune**
*Fury* - John Coyne   *h*   1237

**Halkirk**
*Bloody Valentine* - Stephen R. George   *h*   2197

**Hobie**
*Clash by Night* - Chet Williamson   *h*   5844

**Laidlaw**
*Deadly Vengeance* - Stephen R. George   *h*   2199

**Magrit**
*The Sweetheart Season* - Karen Joy Fowler   *f*   2029

## Marissa
*Dark Reunion* - Stephen R. George   *h*   2198

## Minneapolis
*Archangel* - Michael Conner   *s*   1133
*Armed Memory* - Jim Young   *s*   6048
*Bone Danc: A Fantasy for Technophiles* - Emma Bull   *s*   766
*The Crimson Sky* - Joel Rosenberg   *f*   4669
*Fallen Angels* - Larry Niven   *s*   4120
*Flying Saucers over Hennepin* - Peter Gelman   *f*   2186
*The Forgotten* - Stephen R. George   *h*   2200
*Grandma's Little Darling* - Stephen R. George   *h*   2201
*Juniper, Gentian and Rosemary* - Pamela Dean   *f*   1445
*The M.D.: A Horror Story* - Thomas M. Disch   *h*   1561
*The Multiplex Man* - James P. Hogan   *s*   2727
*Near Dead* - Stephen R. George   *h*   2202
*Nightlife* - Jack Ellis   *h*   1779
*Nightscape* - Stephen R. George   *h*   2203
*Over the River & through the Woods* - Clifford D. Simak   *s*   5047
*The Priest: A Gothic Romance* - Thomas M. Disch   *h*   1562
*Shadows After Dark* - Ouida Crozier   *f*   1286
*Torment* - Stephen R. George   *h*   2204

## Running Horse Lake
*Orphans* - Jean Simon   *h*   5065

## St. Paul
*Headcrash* - Bruce Bethke   *s*   483
*Seed upon the Wind* - Carole Nelson Douglas   *f*   1584

## Standard Springs
*Serial Killer Days* - David Prill   *h*   4436

## Superior
*Arc Riders* - David Drake   *s*   1626

## MISSISSIPPI
*A Dozen Tough Jobs* - Howard Waldrop   *f*   5612

## Biloxi
*Extinct* - Charles Wilson   *h*   5877

## Greenville
*Infinity Hold* - Barry B. Longyear   *s*   3522

## Jerusalem
*The Vampire Papers* - Michael Romkey   *h*   4666

## Wilfred
*Baby Dolly* - Ruby Jean Jensen   *h*   2899

## MISSISSIPPI RIVER
*Blood: A Southern Fantasy* - Michael Moorcock   *f*   3977
*River Rats* - Caroline Stevermer   *s*   5267

*American Queen*
*Mississippi Blues* - Kathleen Ann Goonan   *s*   2274

## MISSOURI

### Bayou Ridge
*Butcher* - Rex Miller   *h*   3898

### Gideon
*Sins of the Flesh* - Don Davis   *h*   1404

### Kansas City
*Savant* - Rex Miller   *h*   3901

### Kennett
*Sins of the Flesh* - Don Davis   *h*   1404

## Logan
*Crota* - Owl Goingback   *h*   2251

## Maple Glen
*The Uprising* - Abigail McDaniels   *h*   3785

## Marion
*Chaingang* - Rex Miller   *h*   3899

## Nesoho
*Blind Hunger* - David Darke   *h*   1352

## St. Charles
*Chiller* - Randall Boyll   *h*   610

## St. Louis
*Blood War* - Robert Weinberg   *h*   5693
*Deathgrip* - Brian Hodge   *h*   2700
*The Ebon Mask* - Richard Lee Byers   *h*   797
*The Jericho Iteration* - Allen Steele   *s*   5242
*The Killing Dance* - Laurell K. Hamilton   *s*   2518
*The Last Vampire* - Kathryn Meyer Griffith   *h*   2440
*Scorpion Shards* - Neal Shusterman   *s*   5013

## Valley View
*Blood Lust* - Ron Dee   *h*   1464

## Wolf Crossing
*Nadya: The Wolf Chronicles* - Pat Murphy   *f*   4052

## MONTANA
*Beyond Eden* - J.M. Morgan   *s*   3999
*Bone Wars* - Brett Davis   *s*   1398
*Hungry for Home: A Wolf Odyssey* - 'Asta Bowen   *f*   599
*Lords of Creation* - Tim Sullivan   *s*   5351
*Winter Moon* - Dean R. Koontz   *h*   3218
*Wolf and Iron* - Gordon R. Dickson   *s*   1539

## Billings
*In Double Jeopardy* - Andrew Neiderman   *h*   4088

## Hell Creek
*The Virgin and the Dinosaur* - R. Garcia y Robertson   *s*   2122

## Ironwood
*This Side of Judgment* - J.R. Dunn   *s*   1696

## Missoula
*Jumpers* - R. Patrick Gates   *h*   2161

## NEBRASKA
*The Fear in Yesterday's Rings* - George C. Chesbro   *h*   1007

## Barlow
*Demon Dance* - T. Chris Martindale   *h*   3655

## Flitheimer University
*Dr. Dimension* - John DeChancie   *s*   1456

## Holland
*Carnival* - William W. Johnstone   *h*   2927

## Omaha
*Ghost Light* - Rick Hautala   *h*   2608

## Running Board
*Night* - Alan Rodgers   *h*   4649

## Xanadu
*Brother to Dragons* - Charles Sheffield   *s*   4949

## NEVADA
*Amnesia Moon* - Jonathan Lethem   *f*   3438
*Deep Trek* - James Axler   *s*   278
*Judgment Day* - G. Harry Stine   *s*   5281
*Universal Soldier* - Robert Tine   *s*   5476
*Vision Quest* - Pamela F. Service   *f*   4920

## Area 51
*Area 51* - Robert Doherty   *s*   1565
*Independence Day* - Dean Devlin   *s*   1508
*Silent Zone* - Stephen Molstad   *s*   3952
*Silicon Embrace* - John Shirley   *s*   5009

## Battle Mountain
*Blood Siege* - G. Harry Stine   *s*   5278

## Desperation
*Desperation* - Stephen King   *h*   3129

## Idle Springs
*Fatal Outcome* - Patricia Wallace   *h*   5622

## Las Vegas
*Area 51* - Robert Doherty   *s*   1565
*The Art of Arrow Cutting* - Stephen Dedman   *f*   1462
*A Calculated Magic* - Robert Weinberg   *f*   5694
*Chariot* - Charles L. Grant   *s*   2304
*The Eyes of Darkness* - Dean R. Koontz   *s*   3206
*Ghost Dance* - Kathryn Ptacek   *h*   4441
*Hair of the Dog* - Brett Davis   *f*   1400
*Hell-Storm* - James A. Moore   *h*   3990
*Last Call* - Tim Powers   *f*   4384
*Parliament of Blood* - Scott Ciencin   *h*   1031
*Some Enchanted Evening* - Alice Alfonsi   *f*   73
*The Stand: The Complete and Uncut Edition* - Stephen King   *h*   3142
*The Wizardry Quested* - Rick Cook   *f*   1163

## Mountain City
*When Wolves Cry* - Chris N. Africa   *h*   41

## Nellis Air Force Base
*Godzilla 2000* - Marc Cerasini   *s*   949

## Nintucca
*Unearthed* - Ashley McConnell   *h*   3778

## Sanctuary
*Blood Siege* - G. Harry Stine   *s*   5278

## Saratoga Springs
*Between the Devil and the Deep* - J.M. Morgan   *h*   3998

## Spirit Lake
*Darkling* - Michael O'Rourke   *h*   4223

## NEW ENGLAND
*Blessings and Curses* - Christopher Stasheff   *f*   5214
*Blood Lines: Vampire Stories From New England* - Lawrence Schimel   *h*   4876
*The Circus of the Earth and Air* - Brooke Stevens   *f*   5264
*Eternity Road* - Jack McDevitt   *s*   3788
*Harmful Intent* - Robin Cook   *s*   1164
*In the Land of Winter* - Richard Grant   *f*   2326
*Nature's God* - Robert Anton Wilson   *f*   5903
*Seed of Evil* - Edmund Plante   *h*   4340
*Thirsty* - M.T. Anderson   *h*   120

## Greystone Bay
*In the Fog* - Charles L. Grant   *h*   2311

## Manor Island
*Order of the Arrow* - Michael T. Hinkemeyer   *h*   2689

## New Polk
*October* - Al Sarrantonio   *h*   4832

## NEW HAMPSHIRE
*The Elementals* - Morgan Llywelyn   *f*   3503

## Blackstone
*The Blackstone Chronicles* - John Saul   *h*   4838

## Cricklewood
*The Midnight Horse* - Sid Fleischman   *f*   1948

**Draconia**
*Devil's Gate* - Elizabeth Ergas   *h*   1833

**Edwardstown**
*Infinity's Child* - Harry Stein   *h*   5250

**Greenfield**
*Jumpers* - R. Patrick Gates   *h*   2161

**Hamtucket**
*668: The Neighbor of the Beast* - Lionel
   Fenn   *h*   1917

**Hanover**
*Diamond Mask: A Novel* - Julian May   *s*   3697
*The Twelfth Child* - Raymond Van Over   *h*   5538

**Nashua**
*A Room for the Dead* - Noel Hynd   *h*   2825

**Seahaven**
*Trouble and Her Friends* - Melissa Scott   *s*   4902

**NEW JERSEY**

*Bad Brains* - Kathe Koja   *h*   3193
*The Eyes of Torie Webster* - Roy Sorrels   *h*   5164
*Goblins* - Charles L. Grant   *s*   2309
*Kent Montana and the Really Ugly Thing From Mars* -
   Lionel Fenn   *s*   1918
*The Mask of Loki* - Roger Zelazny   *f*   6071
*Mind Stealer* - Lee Duigon   *h*   1672
*My Son, the Wizard* - Christopher Stasheff   *f*   5218
*My Teacher Glows in the Dark* - Bruce
   Coville   *s*   1224
*Raven* - Charles L. Grant   *h*   2314

**Asbury Park**
*Sweet Blood* - Pat Graversen   *h*   2337

**Atlantic City**
*Naming the Flowers* - Kate Wilhelm   *s*   5809
*Only Begotten Daughter* - James Morrow   *f*   4034
*Sphynxes Wild* - Esther Friesner   *f*   2083

**Barnegat Light**
*The Hollow Man* - Dan Simmons   *s*   5054

**Foxriver**
*Something Stirs* - Charles L. Grant   *h*   2316

**Hunter**
*In a Dark Dream* - Charles L. Grant   *h*   2310

**Hunter Heights**
*The Hunted* - Kathryn Ptacek   *h*   4442

**Jamesburg**
*After the Blue* - Russel Like   *s*   3465

**Maple Landing**
*Symphony* - Charles L. Grant   *h*   2318

**Maplewood**
*The Tetherballs of Bougainville* - Mark
   Leyner   *f*   3457

**Newark**
*Fade to Black* - Nyx Smith   *s*   5134
*Johnny Mnemonic* - Terry Bisson   *s*   505

**North Orange**
*Firestar* - Michael Flynn   *s*   1962

**Palisades**
*Glass Houses* - Laura J. Mixon   *s*   3921

**Pine Barrens**
*The Barrens* - F. Paul Wilson   *h*   5884
*Pelts* - F. Paul Wilson   *h*   5894

**Port Richmond**
*Stunts* - Charles L. Grant   *h*   2317

**Princeton**
*Blood of the Covenant* - Brent Monahan   *h*   3954

*The Book of Common Dread* - Brent
   Monahan   *h*   3955

**Spring Lake**
*Midnight Mass* - F. Paul Wilson   *h*   5891

**NEW MEXICO**

*Changer* - Jane M. Lindskold   *f*   3474
*Ill Wind* - Kevin J. Anderson   *s*   108
*Ingathering: The Complete People Stories of Zenna
   Henderson* - Zenna Henderson   *s*   2659
*Jed the Dead* - Alan Dean Foster   *s*   2007
*Majestic* - Whitley Strieber   *s*   5341
*Nanoware Time/The Persistence of Vision* - Ian
   Watson   *s*   5638
*Spiritride* - Mark Shepherd   *f*   4981
*Whirlwind* - Charles L. Grant   *f*   2320

**Albuquerque**
*Eye Killers* - A.A. Carr   *h*   911
*Rewind* - Terry England   *s*   1825

**Arroyo Hondo**
*Fetish* - Edward Bryant   *h*   749

**Atocha**
*Days of Atonement* - Walter Jon Williams   *s*   5836

**Death Valley**
*Cain* - James Byron Huggins   *h*   2802

**Desolada**
*Days of the Dead* - Ashley McConnell   *h*   3774

**Duerme**
*Witch-Light* - Nancy Holder   *h*   2734

**Isleta**
*Parliament of Blood* - Scott Ciencin   *h*   1031

**Jornada del Muerto Desert**
*Mount Dragon* - Douglas Preston   *h*   4413

**Los Alamos**
*Paths to Otherwhere* - James P. Hogan   *s*   2728
*The Trinity Paradox* - Kevin J. Anderson   *s*   116

**Mannheim**
*The Square Deal* - David Drake   *s*   1644

**Mesa**
*The Gifted* - Jack Caravela   *h*   879

**Old Taos**
*The Stone Garden* - Mary Rosenblum   *s*   4679

**Santa Fe**
*The Nine Lives of Catseye Gomez* - Simon
   Hawke   *f*   2620
*Rewind* - Terry England   *s*   1825

**Sante Fe**
*Gibbon's Decline and Fall* - Sheri S.
   Tepper   *s*   5430
*The Wizard of Santa Fe* - Simon Hawke   *f*   2628

**Silver Spring**
*I Know What You Did Last Summer* - Lois
   Duncan   *h*   1692

**White Sands**
*The Black Sun* - Jack Williamson   *s*   5860

**Wormwood**
*Tales From the Crypt: Demon Knight* - Randall
   Boyll   *h*   617

**NEW YORK**

*The 7th Guest* - Matthew J. Costello   *h*   1192
*Beyond the Magic Sphere* - Gail Jarrow   *f*   2879
*Cosm* - Gregory Benford   *s*   444
*The Eyes of Torie Webster* - Roy Sorrels   *h*   5164

*The Flight of Michael McBride* - Midori
   Snyder   *f*   5151
*The Illegal Rebirth of Billy the Kid* - Rebecca
   Ore   *s*   4220
*Knights of the Morningstar* - Melanie Rawn   *s*   4487
*Little Boy Lost* - T.M. Wright   *h*   5992
*Love & Sleep* - John Crowley   *f*   1277
*The Ugly Little Boy* - Isaac Asimov   *s*   250
*The World I Made for Her* - Thomas
   Moran   *h*   3996

**Adirondack Mountains**
*The World Next Door* - Brad Ferguson   *s*   1924

**Arcadia**
*The Moon's Wife: A Hystery* - A.A.
   Attanasio   *f*   271

**Batavia**
*Boundaries* - T.M. Wright   *h*   5990

**Braddock**
*The Headsman* - James Neal Harvey   *h*   2599

**Buffalo**
*Dark Visions* - T. Lucien Wright   *h*   5987

**Canaan**
*The Place* - T.M. Wright   *h*   5993

**Cascade**
*The Curse* - John Tigges   *h*   5472

**Catskill Mountains**
*Brothers of the Dragon* - Robin Wayne
   Bailey   *f*   286
*Flames of the Dragon* - Robin Wayne Bailey   *f*   287

**Centerville**
*Sister, Sister* - Andrew Neiderman   *h*   4091

**Cold Spring**
*The House That Jack Built* - Graham
   Masterton   *h*   3675

**Cold Spring Harbor**
*Skeletons* - Al Sarrantonio   *h*   4834

**Dale Falls**
*Deathchain* - Ken Greenhall   *h*   2415

**Danby**
*The School* - T.M. Wright   *h*   5994

**Dowdsville**
*Flames of the Dragon* - Robin Wayne Bailey   *f*   287

**Dydeetown**
*Dydeetown World* - F. Paul Wilson   *s*   5887

**Ellerton**
*Beneath Still Waters* - Matthew J. Costello   *h*   1193

**Ellis Island**
*Dealer's Choice* - George R.R. Martin   *s*   3643

**Gardner Town**
*After Life* - Andrew Neiderman   *h*   4083

**Groveland**
*The Beyond* - Barry Harrington   *h*   2556

**Groverton**
*Deathscape* - Michael Cecilione   *h*   945

**Harper's Gate**
*Bereavement* - Richard Lortz   *h*   3525

**Hudson Valley**
*House Haunted* - Al Sarrantonio   *h*   4830

**Indigo Lake**
*Shapes* - Steve Vance   *h*   5552

**Ippisiqua**
*The Cup of Morning Shadows* - Rosemary
   Edghill   *f*   1747

**Ithaca**
*Fool on the Hill* - Matt Ruff  f  4707
*The Place* - T.M. Wright  h  5993

**Jokertown**
*Black Trump* - George R.R. Martin  s  3642

**Lewisboro**
*Skull Session* - Daniel Hecht  h  2638

**Long Island**
*Dust* - Charles Pellegrino  h  4279
*Earthbound* - Richard Matheson  h  3684
*Red Death* - P.N. Elrod  h  1798
*Sweet William* - Jessica Palmer  h  4239
*Target Earth* - Steve Perry  s  4301

**Manhattan East Enclave**
*Beggars Ride* - Nancy Kress  s  3238

**McAndrew**
*The World Next Door* - Brad Ferguson  s  1924

**Mega-City One**
*Judge Dredd* - Neal Barrett Jr.  s  366

**Middletown**
*Friends in Time* - Grace Chetwin  f  1012

**Mixinick**
*Treasure Box* - Orson Scott Card  h  898

**Monroe Village**
*Reborn* - F. Paul Wilson  h  5895

**Montauk**
*Stage Fright* - Clare McNally  h  3858

**Mount Garde**
*Breeder* - Ed Kelleher  h  3041

**Naples Falls**
*Blood Brothers* - T. Lucien Wright  h  5986

**New York**
*Ace in the Hole* - George R.R. Martin  s  3641
*All Things under the Moon* - Robert
  Morgan  h  4002
*American Psycho* - Brett Easton Ellis  h  1777
*Angels on Fire* - Nancy A. Collins  h  1117
*Animus* - Ed Kelleher  h  3040
*The Arbitrary Placement of Walls* - Martha
  Soukup  f  5165
*Armed Memory* - Jim Young  s  6048
*Avatar* - Donald Beman  h  437
*The Axman Cometh* - John Farris  h  1883
*Back in the USSA* - Kim Newman  s  4095
*Bagatelle—Guinevere* - Nancy Bogen  f  558
*The Bear Went over the Mountain* - William
  Kotzwinkle  f  3222
*Beauty* - Brian D'Amato  h  1334
*Beggars Ride* - Nancy Kress  s  3238
*Bereavement* - Richard Lortz  h  3525
*Between Floors* - Thomas F. Monteleone  h  3957
*Bitter Blood* - Karen E. Taylor  h  5405
*Blade* - Mel Odom  h  4190
*The Blood of the Lamb* - Thomas F.
  Monteleone  h  3958
*Blood Relations* - Doug Murray  h  4058
*Blood Secrets* - Karen E. Taylor  h  5406
*Blood Ties* - Karen E. Taylor  h  5407
*Bloodlines* - J.N. Williamson  h  5852
*Bone* - George C. Chesbro  h  1006
*The Book of Night with Moon* - Diane
  Duane  f  1657
*Borgel* - Daniel Manus Pinkwater  f  4338
*The Boss in the Wall* - Avram Davidson  h  1396
*Boys of Life* - Paul Russell  h  4737
*Bride of the Castle* - John DeChancie  s  1452
*A Bridge of Years* - Robert Charles Wilson  s  5905
*Bring the Jubilee* - Ward Moore  s  3993
*Brother to Dragons, Companion to Owls* - Jane M.
  Lindskold  f  3473

*Bureau 13* - Nick Pollotta  f  4362
*Burial* - Graham Masterton  h  3671
*By Chaos Cursed* - Mickey Zucker Reichert  f  4517
*The Calcutta Chromosome* - Amitav Ghosh  h  2214
*Callahan's Lady* - Spider Robinson  s  4638
*Carmen Dog* - Carol Emshwiller  f  1817
*A Child Across the Sky* - Jonathan Carroll  h  917
*Child of Shadows* - John Coyne  h  1236
*The Children of Hamelin* - Norman Spinrad  s  5170
*Children of the Night* - Mercedes Lackey  h  3276
*China Mountain Zhang* - Maureen F.
  McHugh  s  3817
*Codename Wolverine* - Christopher Golden  s  2256
*Cold Eye* - Giles Blunt  h  556
*Collidescope* - Grace Chetwin  s  1011
*The Colors of Hell* - Michael Paine  h  4234
*A Company of Stars* - Christopher Stasheff  s  5215
*Conglomeros* - Jesse Browner  f  729
*Control Freak* - Christa Faust  h  1890
*The Convocation* - John R. Holt  h  2748
*Crossover* - Bill McCay  f  3768
*Cyberbooks* - Ben Bova  s  582
*Dancing on Air* - Nancy Kress  s  3240
*Dark Winds* - Graham Watkins  h  5630
*Darkborn* - Matthew J. Costello  h  1195
*Darker Angels* - S.P. Somtow  h  5155
*Day of the Snake* - Matthew J. Costello  s  1196
*Dead Lines* - John Skipp  h  5082
*The Demolished Man* - Alfred Bester  s  476
*Demon Within* - Dana Reed  h  4499
*Desert Fire* - David Alexander  s  65
*Desmond: A Novel of Love and the Modern Vampire* -
  Ulysses G. Dietz  h  1541
*The Deus Machine* - Pierre Ouellette  h  4232
*The Devil's Advocate* - Andrew Neiderman  h  4085
*The Devil's Cradle* - Kate Stewart  h  5269
*Devil's Engine* - Mark Sumner  f  5356
*Dinosaur Summer* - Greg Bear  s  416
*Doc Sidhe* - Aaron Allston  f  85
*Domination* - Michael Cecilione  h  946
*The Door through Washington Square* - Elaine
  Bergstrom  f  464
*Dragons on the Town* - Thorarinn
  Gunnarsson  f  2463
*Drakon* - S.M. Stirling  s  5294
*The Eight* - Katherine Neville  f  4092
*Elvissey* - Jack Womack  s  5957
*Emperors of the Twilight* - S. Andrew
  Swann  s  5362
*Famine* - Todd Komarnicki  h  3201
*Fantastique* - Marvin Kaye  h  3025
*Fear Itself* - Ric Meyers  h  3881
*Ferman's Devils* - Joe Clifford Faust  s  1892
*The Fifth Element* - Terry Bisson  s  504
*A Flag Full of Stars* - Brad Ferguson  s  1922
*The Forever King* - Molly Cochran  f  1092
*The Frightened Fish* - Kenneth Robeson  f  4622
*From Time to Time* - Jack Finney  s  1941
*Further Adventures* - Jon Stephen Fink  f  1940
*Fury* - John Coyne  h  1237
*Gaia's Toys* - Rebecca Ore  s  4218
*Garden* - Matthew J. Costello  h  1197
*Gibbon's Decline and Fall* - Sheri S.
  Tepper  s  5430
*The Gilda Stories* - Jewelle Gomez  h  2267
*Glass Houses* - Laura J. Mixon  s  3921
*Gnome Man's Land* - Esther Friesner  f  2075
*Godzilla 2000* - Marc Cerasini  s  949
*Graythings* - Pat Graversen  h  2335
*Harpy High* - Esther Friesner  f  2076
*Haven* - David Peters  f  4304
*Heartlight* - Marion Zimmer Bradley  f  637
*Heathern* - Jack Womack  s  5958
*Hidden Echoes* - Mike Jefferies  f  2885
*Homecoming* - Matthew J. Costello  h  1198
*How Like a God* - Brenda W. Clough  f  1089
*Humans* - Donald E. Westlake  f  5768
*I Met a Man Who Wasn't There* - Mary R.
  Callaghan  h  840

*Illegal Alien* - Robert J. Sawyer  s  4858
*Illegal Aliens* - Nick Pollotta  s  4365
*Imajica* - Clive Barker  h  343
*Immortal* - Jason Nickles  h  4102
*Impulse* - Rick Hautala  h  2609
*In Double Jeopardy* - Andrew Neiderman  h  4088
*In the Deep Woods* - Nicholas Conde  h  1131
*Johnny Mnemonic* - Terry Bisson  s  505
*Jokertown Shuffle* - George R.R. Martin  s  3646
*Jumper* - Steven Gould  s  2290
*Jupiter's Daughter* - Tom Hyman  s  2820
*Kill Crazy* - L.S. Riker  s  4590
*The Kingdom of Kevin Malone* - Suzy McKee
  Charnas  f  970
*Ladies Night* - Jack Ketchum  h  3091
*Lady El* - Jim Starlin  s  5213
*Lady Slings the Booze* - Spider Robinson  s  4640
*The Last Wizard* - Simon Hawke  s  2619
*Legends Reborn* - Kenneth C. Flint  f  1958
*Legion of the Dead* - Geoffrey Caine  h  833
*Lethal Delivery* - J.G. Maxon  h  3695
*Live Girls* - Ray Garton  h  2151
*Lives of the Monster Dogs* - Kirsten Bakis  s  305
*Living Hell* - Ric Meyers  h  3882
*The Long Run* - Daniel Keys Moran  s  3995
*Madeleine's Ghost* - Robert Girardi  h  2240
*Makoto* - Kelley Wilde  h  5801
*Manhattan Heat* - Ken Eulo  h  1851
*Manhattan Transfer* - John E. Stith  s  5303
*Maximum Light* - Nancy Kress  s  3241
*Memnoch the Devil* - Anne Rice  h  4571
*Men in Black* - Steve Perry  s  4298
*Mirage* - Perry Brass  s  662
*Mirage* - F. Paul Wilson  h  5892
*Missing Angel Juan* - Francesca Lia Block  f  550
*The Moon's Wife: A Hystery* - A.A.
  Attanasio  f  271
*Murder at the Galactic Writers' Society* - Janet
  Asimov  s  251
*The Nanotech Chronicles* - Michael Flynn  s  1964
*Near Death* - Nancy Kilpatrick  h  3113
*Necrom* - Mick Farren  s  1881
*Nevermore* - William Hjortsberg  h  2692
*Newer York* - Lawrence Watt-Evans  s  5642
*Night Magic* - Thomas Tryon  h  5485
*Night of Broken Souls* - Thomas F.
  Monteleone  h  3964
*Night of the Cooters* - Howard Waldrop  s  5614
*Nightfeeder* - Judith Reeves-Stevens  f  4513
*Night's Pawn* - Tom Dowd  s  1591
*Nightworld* - F. Paul Wilson  h  5893
*The Nihilesthete* - Richard Kalich  h  3002
*Nine Levels Down* - William Dantz  h  1347
*Of Masques and Martyrs* - Christopher
  Golden  h  2258
*The Only Thing to Fear* - Robert Morgan  h  4003
*The Parasite* - Ramsey Campbell  h  863
*The Passion* - Donna Boyd  h  603
*Pelts* - F. Paul Wilson  h  5894
*Pluto, Animal Lover* - Laren Stover  h  5318
*Polymorph* - Scott Westerfeld  s  5767
*Precious Blood* - Pat Graversen  h  2336
*Preternatural* - Margaret Wander Bonanno  s  568
*Private Demons* - Robert Masello  h  3660
*The Prodigy* - Noel Hynd  h  2823
*Puppet Master* - Barry T. Hawkins  h  2632
*Python Isle* - Kenneth Robeson  f  4624
*Random Acts of Senseless Violence* - Jack
  Womack  f  5959
*A Reasonable Madness* - Fran Dorf  h  1580
*Relic* - Douglas Preston  h  4414
*Reliquary* - Douglas Preston  h  4415
*Requiem* - Clifford Mohr  h  3950
*The Ruby Tear* - Rebecca Brand  h  660
*The Samurai Wizard* - Simon Hawke  f  2623
*The Scathach and the Maeve's Daughter* - Mary
  Alexander Walker  f  5618
*Secrets of the Morning* - V.C. Andrews  h  146
*Servant of the Bones* - Anne Rice  h  4575

*Sewer, Gas & Electric* - Matt Ruff  *s*  4708
*Shade of Pale* - Greg Kihn  *h*  3104
*The Shadow Eater* - Adam Lee  *f*  3386
*Shadows* - Jonathan Nasaw  *h*  4068
*The Shift* - George Foy  *s*  2033
*Shifter* - Judith Reeves-Stevens  *f*  4515
*Sibs* - F. Paul Wilson  *h*  5898
*The Site* - Melisand March  *h*  3621
*Skinny Legs and All* - Tom Robbins  *f*  4607
*Solo* - Robert Mason  *s*  3665
*Some Things Come Back* - Robert Morgan  *h*  4004
*Some Things Never Die* - Robert Morgan  *h*  4005
*Son of Darkness* - Josepha Sherman  *f*  4990
*Son of Rosemary* - Ira Levin  *h*  3445
*The Spider #8: The Devil's Paymaster/Legions of the Accursed Light* - Grant Stockbridge  *f*  5309
*Spider-Man: The Venom Factor* - Diane Duane  *s*  1667
*Storm Knights* - Bill Slavicsek  *f*  5087
*Stranger in a Strange Land* - Robert A. Heinlein  *s*  2649
*The Streeter* - Scott Ian Barry  *h*  373
*Streets of Blood: Vampire Stories From New York City* - Lawrence Schimel  *h*  4881
*Substitute Teacher* - Jordan Storm  *h*  5314
*Sunglasses After Dark* - Nancy A. Collins  *h*  1124
*Superstition* - David Ambrose  *h*  90
*The Sword of Maiden's Tears* - Rosemary Edghill  *f*  1748
*Symphony* - Adrian Savage  *h*  4847
*Taltos* - Anne Rice  *h*  4577
*Tek Power* - William Shatner  *s*  4937
*Temporary Agency* - Rachel Pollack  *f*  4360
*The Thing That Darkness Hides* - Robert Morgan  *h*  4006
*The Things That Are Not There* - Robert Morgan  *h*  4007
*Thinning the Predators* - Daina Graziunas  *h*  2341
*Thirst* - Michael Cecilione  *h*  948
*Thirst* - Pyotr Kurtinski  *h*  3253
*Thoughts of God* - Michael Kanaly  *s*  3007
*Till the End of Time* - Allen Appel  *f*  201
*Time and Chance* - Alan Brennert  *f*  676
*The Time of Feasting* - Mick Farren  *h*  1882
*Time's Arrow* - Martin Amis  *s*  96
*Timeshare: Second Time Around* - Joshua Dann  *s*  1345
*A Two-Edged Sword* - Thomas K. Martin  *f*  3653
*Typewriter in the Sky* - L. Ron Hubbard  *f*  2791
*The Ultimate Spider-Man* - Stan Lee  *s*  3403
*Unholy Fire* - Whitley Strieber  *h*  5342
*Unicorn U.* - Esther Friesner  *f*  2084
*Unquenchable Fire* - Rachel Pollack  *f*  4361
*Vampire Junkies* - Norman Spinrad  *s*  5175
*The Vanishing* - Marilyn Kaye  *s*  3021
*Vespers* - Jeff Rovin  *h*  4688
*Virago* - Karen Marie Christa Minns  *h*  3915
*Virgin* - Mary Elizabeth Murphy  *h*  4050
*Virtual Death* - Shale Aaron  *s*  5
*Virtual Girl* - Amy Thomson  *s*  5462
*Visitors From Oz: The Wild Adventures of Dorothy, the Scarecrow and the Tin Woodman* - Martin Gardner  *f*  2136
*Voices of Hope* - David Feintuch  *s*  1903
*The Waterworks* - E.L. Doctorow  *f*  1564
*Wet Work* - Philip Nutman  *h*  4168
*White Eyes* - Kenneth Robeson  *f*  4625
*Why Do Birds* - Damon Knight  *s*  3190
*The Wild* - Whitley Strieber  *h*  5343
*Wizard's Mole* - Brad Strickland  *f*  5337
*Worst Nightmare* - Ric Meyers  *h*  3883
*Wurm* - Matthew J. Costello  *h*  1202

**Oscola**
*The Forbidden Zone* - Whitley Strieber  *h*  5340

**Ossining**
*The End of Alice* - A.M. Homes  *h*  2755

**Plattsburgh**
*City of Iron* - Chet Williamson  *h*  5843

**Poughkeepsie**
*Unquenchable Fire* - Rachel Pollack  *f*  4361

**Ransomville**
*First Love: A Gothic Tale* - Joyce Carol Oates  *h*  4183

**Red Hook**
*The Taking* - Donald Beman  *h*  438

**Rhinelander**
*The Keeper* - Robert D. Lee  *h*  3402

**Riker's Island**
*The Shift* - George Foy  *s*  2033

**Rochester**
*Brain Rose* - Nancy Kress  *s*  3239
*Nightmare's Disciple* - Joseph S. Pulver Jr.  *h*  4449
*The Road to Hell, Volume I* - Robert Weinberg  *h*  5701
*The Road to Hell, Volume II* - Robert Weinberg  *h*  5702
*Thirst of the Vampire* - T. Lucien Wright  *h*  5988

**St. Claire**
*Wolf Moon* - John R. Holt  *h*  2749

**Sandburg**
*Duplicates* - Andrew Neiderman  *h*  4086
*The Immortals* - Andrew Neiderman  *h*  4087

**Sawquid**
*Rage* - Elizabeth Ergas  *h*  1834

**Scipio**
*Hocus Pocus or, What's the Hurry, Son?* - Kurt Vonnegut Jr.  *s*  5593

**Shadowkill**
*Ghostlight* - Marion Zimmer Bradley  *f*  634

**Shandaken County**
*Among Madmen* - Jim Starlin  *s*  5212

**Stoneham**
*Dying Breath* - Jon A. Harrald  *h*  2555

**Stonywood**
*Midsummer* - Matthew J. Costello  *h*  1200

**Taghkanic College**
*Witchlight* - Marion Zimmer Bradley  *f*  655

**Troy**
*My Pretty Pony* - Stephen King  *h*  3136

**Utica**
*The Misconceiver* - Lucy Ferriss  *s*  1929

**Virgil**
*Lost Futures* - Lisa Tuttle  *s*  5520

**Watertown**
*Thirst of the Vampire* - T. Lucien Wright  *h*  5988

**Westchester County**
*The End of Alice* - A.M. Homes  *h*  2755

**White Plains**
*Homecoming* - Matthew J. Costello  *h*  1198

**Yonkers**
*Glimmering* - Elizabeth Hand  *s*  2535

**NORTH CAROLINA**

*In the Rift* - Marion Zimmer Bradley  *f*  639
*Inagehi* - Jack Cady  *h*  817
*Mall, Mayhem and Magic* - Holly Lisle  *f*  3485
*The Ridge* - Lisa Cantrell  *h*  872

**Beaver Creek**
*Child of Shadows* - John Coyne  *h*  1236

**Charlotte**
*Sympathy for the Devil* - Holly Lisle  *f*  3488

**Clearview**
*Uwharrie* - Eugene E. Pfaff Jr.  *h*  4309

**Crooked Creek**
*Storytellers* - Julie Anne Parks  *h*  4249

**Devil's Point**
*Hell on High* - Holly Lisle  *f*  3483

**Durham**
*Virus* - Graham Watkins  *h*  5632

**Fayetteville**
*When the Bough Breaks* - Mercedes Lackey  *f*  3302

**Greensboro**
*Homebody* - Orson Scott Card  *h*  890

**Merrillville**
*Torments* - Lisa Cantrell  *h*  873

**Missing Mile**
*Drawing Blood* - Poppy Z. Brite  *h*  694
*Lost Souls* - Poppy Z. Brite  *h*  697

**Ocean City**
*Night Music* - Sheila Bristow Garner  *h*  2147

**Outer Banks**
*Kaleidoscope Eyes* - Graham Watkins  *h*  5631

**Phoenix City**
*Boneman* - Lisa Cantrell  *h*  871

**Plattsborough**
*The Lodger* - Fred Chappell  *h*  966

**Raleigh**
*The Devil and Dan Cooley* - Holly Lisle  *f*  3480

**Steuben**
*Lost Boys* - Orson Scott Card  *f*  891

**Torrence**
*Kids* - Trevor Hoyle  *h*  2787

**NORTH DAKOTA**

*The Grass Dancer* - Susan Power  *f*  4380

**Bismarck**
*Stones of the Dalai Lama* - Ken Mitchell  *f*  3916

**Fort Moxie**
*Ancient Shores* - Jack McDevitt  *s*  3786

**Goodlands**
*A Dry Spell* - Susan Moloney  *h*  3951

**Hardwood**
*The Crimson Sky* - Joel Rosenberg  *f*  4669
*The Fire Duke* - Joel Rosenberg  *f*  4671
*The Silver Stone* - Joel Rosenberg  *f*  4676

**Mannering**
*Mark of the Werewolf* - Jeffrey Sackett  *h*  4780

**Walhalla**
*Ancient Shores* - Jack McDevitt  *s*  3786

**OHIO**

*Vampire Breath* - R.L. Stine  *h*  5291

**Belmont City**
*Red Orc's Rage* - Philip Jose Farmer  *f*  1873

**Berkshire**
*The Orpheus Process* - Daniel H. Gower  *h*  2293

**Cincinnati**
*Mississippi Blues* - Kathleen Ann Goonan  *s*  2274
*Queen City Jazz* - Kathleen Ann Goonan  *s*  2275

**Cleary**
*Yellow Moon* - David J. Searls   *h*   4907

**Cleveland**
*Bleeder* - Gene Lazuta   *h*   3374
*Forests of the Night* - S. Andrew Swann   *s*   5363
*Forget Me Not* - Gene Lazuta   *h*   3375
*God's Dice* - S. Andrew Swann   *f*   5364
*The Lincoln Hunters* - Wilson Tucker   *s*   5487
*Raven* - S.A. Swiniarski   *h*   5374
*Sheltered Lives* - Charles Oberndorf   *s*   4188

**Friendly**
*Throat Sprockets* - Tim Lucas   *h*   3541

**Fulton**
*Deadly Friend* - Keith Ferrario   *h*   1926

**Harpersville**
*Vyrmin* - Gene Lazuta   *h*   3376

**Keynesville**
*Living with Aliens* - John DeChancie   *s*   1460

**Lakota**
*Agyar* - Steven Brust   *f*   738

**Maple Park**
*The Witch of Maple Park* - Stephanie S. Tolan   *f*   5478

**Marion**
*Dun Lady's Jess* - Doranna Durgin   *f*   1704

**Moldowen**
*Button Bright* - Michael Kurland   *h*   3251

**Wentworth**
*The Regulators* - Richard Bachman   *h*   284

**Wright-Patterson AF Base**
*Pandora* - Alan Rodgers   *h*   4650

**OKLAHOMA**
*Buddy Holly Is Alive and Well on Ganymede* - Bradley Denton   *s*   1490
*Chrome Circle* - Mercedes Lackey   *f*   3277
*Wheels of Fire* - Mercedes Lackey   *f*   3301

**Norman**
*Shade* - David Darke   *h*   1355

**Stillwater**
*Descent* - Ron Dee   *h*   1465

**Tulsa**
*Jinx High* - Mercedes Lackey   *h*   3284
*Last Rites* - David Darke   *h*   1354
*Sacred Ground* - Mercedes Lackey   *f*   3294

**OREGON**
*Footprints of Thunder* - James F. David   *s*   1379
*A Gift upon the Shore* - M.K. Wren   *s*   5982
*The Harvest* - Robert Charles Wilson   *s*   5909
*Other Nature* - Stephanie A. Smith   *s*   5145
*Parable of the Sower* - Octavia E. Butler   *s*   792
*Summerland* - L. Dean James   *f*   2865
*Thor* - Wayne Smith   *h*   5146

**Arcadia**
*The Thread That Binds the Bones* - Nina Kiriki Hoffman   *f*   2717

**Bend**
*Iron Shadows* - Steven Barnes   *f*   362

**Cascade Mountains**
*The Silent Strength of Stones* - Nina Kiriki Hoffman   *f*   2716

**Cemetery Ridge**
*Prank Night* - David Robbins   *h*   4601

**Columbia River Valley**
*The Drylands* - Mary Rosenblum   *s*   4678

**Cronon's Crater**
*The Ancient One* - T.A. Barron   *f*   368

**Deuce Creek**
*Roadkill* - Richard Sanford   *h*   4815

**Dory Cove**
*The Devil's Churn* - Kristine Kathryn Rusch   *h*   4715

**Everville**
*Everville* - Clive Barker   *h*   338

**Gold Beach**
*No Limits* - Nigel Findley   *s*   1938

**Hot Lake**
*Wolf Flow* - K.W. Jeter   *h*   2918

**Mayfair**
*The Last Vampire* - Christopher Pike   *h*   4328

**Oldenburg**
*Golden Eyes* - John Gideon   *h*   2220

**Point Vestal**
*The Off Season* - Jack Cady   *f*   820

**Portland**
*The Abductors: Conspiracy* - Jonathan Frakes   *s*   2034
*Antibodies* - Kevin J. Anderson   *h*   99
*Blood Feud* - Sam Siciliano   *h*   5020
*The Deus Machine* - Pierre Ouellette   *h*   4232
*The Good Children* - Kate Wilhelm   *h*   5808
*Iron Shadows* - Steven Barnes   *f*   362
*Kindred* - John Gideon   *h*   2222
*Sins of the Blood* - Kristine Kathryn Rusch   *h*   4728
*The Thread That Binds the Bones* - Nina Kiriki Hoffman   *f*   2717

**Rookers Cove**
*The Undine* - Michael O'Rourke   *h*   4224

**Sauterelle Lake**
*The Silent Strength of Stones* - Nina Kiriki Hoffman   *f*   2716

**Seavy Village**
*Facade* - Kristine Kathryn Rusch   *h*   4716

**Shadow Ridge**
*Shadows* - Kimberly Rangel   *h*   4472

**Shoalwater Bay**
*Nadya: The Wolf Chronicles* - Pat Murphy   *f*   4052

**University of Oregon**
*Fragments* - James F. David   *h*   1380

**OZARKS**
*Earthsong* - Suzette Haden Elgin   *s*   1769

**PACIFIC NORTHWEST**
*Earthling* - Tony Daniel   *s*   1336
*The Mysterious Doom and Other Ghostly Tales of the Pacific Northwest* - Jessica Amanda Salmonson   *h*   4791
*Sarah Canary* - Karen Joy Fowler   *f*   2028
*Scotland the Brave* - Jennifer Roberson   *f*   4611
*Yours Truly, Jackie the Stripper* - Edo van Belkom   *h*   5536

**Sesqua Valley**
*Tales of Sesqua Valley* - W.H. Pugmire   *h*   4444

**PENNSYLVANIA**
*Bring the Jubilee* - Ward Moore   *s*   3993

*Dragon Moon* - Chris Claremont   *f*   1040
*Fair Peril* - Nancy Springer   *f*   5178
*Infectress* - Tom Cool   *s*   1167
*Kids* - Trevor Hoyle   *h*   2787
*Larque on the Wing* - Nancy Springer   *f*   5180
*Night of the Living Dead* - John Russo   *h*   4745
*Return of the Living Dead* - John Russo   *h*   4746

**Abaddon Township**
*Blameless in Abaddon* - James Morrow   *f*   4029

**Allenville**
*Destiny's Carnival* - Warren Murphy   *h*   4057

**Bremerton**
*The Bad Thing* - Michael O'Rourke   *h*   4222

**Burnwell**
*Neighbors* - Maureen S. Pusti   *h*   4450

**Dreamthorpe**
*Dreamthorp* - Chet Williamson   *h*   5845

**Endicott**
*Blood of Mugwump* - Doug Rice   *h*   4581

**Gettysburg**
*Lurid Dreams* - Charles L. Harness   *s*   2546

**Gramentown**
*Max Lakeman and the Beautiful Stranger* - Jon Cohen   *f*   1098

**Gwynwood**
*The Wall Around Eden* - Joan Slonczewski   *s*   5092

**Hoadley**
*Apocalypse* - Nancy Springer   *f*   5176

**Iselin**
*Second Chance* - Chet Williamson   *h*   5850

**Jenkins**
*Metal Angel* - Nancy Springer   *f*   5181

**Kirkland**
*Reign* - Chet Williamson   *h*   5849

**Lancaster**
*Thoughts of God* - Michael Kanaly   *s*   3007

**Mill Creek**
*Owl Light* - Michael Paine   *h*   4235

**Monville**
*Animals* - John Skipp   *h*   5080

**Moore**
*Superstitious* - R.L. Stine   *h*   5290

**Oldcastle**
*I Met a Man Who Wasn't There* - Mary R. Callaghan   *h*   840

**Paradise**
*The Bridge: A Horror Story* - John Skipp   *h*   5081

**Philadelphia**
*12 Monkeys* - Elizabeth Hand   *s*   2532
*Blood Work* - Fay Zachary   *h*   6050
*Eyes of the Empress* - Camille Bacon-Smith   *f*   285
*Mind Kill* - Richard La Plante   *h*   3267
*Murder in the Solid State* - Wil McCarthy   *s*   3764
*The Pure Cold Light* - Gregory Frost   *s*   2087
*Red, Red Robin* - Stephen Gallagher   *h*   2113
*A Room for the Dead* - Noel Hynd   *h*   2825
*Silent Scream* - Dan Schmidt   *h*   4883
*Striper Assassin* - Nyx Smith   *f*   5135
*Two Crowns for America* - Katherine Kurtz   *f*   3262
*Virtual Death* - Shale Aaron   *s*   5

**Pittsburgh**
*In between Dragons* - Michael Kandel   *f*   3010
*Making Love* - Melanie Tem   *h*   5422
*Realtime Interrupt* - James P. Hogan   *s*   2729
*Steel Rose* - Kara Dalkey   *f*   1321

**Potamos**
*Humpty Dumpty: An Oval* - Damon Knight   s   3186

**Spook Hollow**
*Spook Night* - David Robbins   h   4603

**Thomas Valley**
*Nightshade* - Stanley R. Moore   h   3992

**Wayne**
*Shoebag Returns* - Mary James   f   2869

**RHODE ISLAND**

**Providence**
*The Boss in the Wall* - Avram Davidson   h   1396
*A Knight Among Knaves* - Robert N.
   Charrette   f   974
*Twisted Images* - Don D'Ammassa   h   1335

**ROCKY MOUNTAINS**

**Piketon**
*Ursus* - David Dvorkin   s   1708

**SOUTH**

*The Boss in the Wall* - Avram Davidson   h   1396
*The Gilda Stories* - Jewelle Gomez   h   2267
*The Haunting* - Ruby Jean Jensen   h   2901
*The Living Evil* - Ruby Jean Jensen   h   2902
*Night Thunder* - Ruby Jean Jensen   h   2903
*Southern Blood: Vampire Stories From the American
   South* - Lawrence Schimel   h   4880
*Tatham Mound* - Piers Anthony   f   191

**Cold Mountain Penitentiary**
*The Green Mile* - Stephen King   h   3134

**Danville**
*Flesh and Blood* - D.A. Fowler   h   2024

**Exuam College**
*Coven* - Edward Lee   h   3390

**Green Hill**
*Blood of the Children* - Alan Rodgers   h   4645

**Waynesville**
*The Chosen* - Edward Lee   h   3389

**SOUTH CAROLINA**

*Reprisal* - F. Paul Wilson   h   5896

**Bear Claw Islands**
*Soulcatchers* - Jan Lara   h   3336

**Charleston**
*Root of All Evil* - David A. Farrow   h   1888

**SOUTH DAKOTA**

*Wolf and Iron* - Gordon R. Dickson   s   1539

**Sharon Valley**
*The Devil's End* - D.A. Fowler   h   2023

**SOUTHWEST**

*Apacheria* - Jake Page   s   4233
*Area 51* - Robert Doherty   s   1565
*Blackburn* - Bradley Denton   h   1489
*The Changeling Garden* - Winifred Elze   h   1806
*The Dazzle of Day* - Molly Gloss   s   2243
*Forest of the Night* - S.P. Somtow   f   5156
*Ghost Dance* - Kathryn Ptacek   h   4441
*Ill Wind* - Kevin J. Anderson   s   108
*Indiana Jones and the Sky Pirates* - Martin
   Caidin   f   825

*Indiana Jones and the Unicorn's Legacy* - Rob
   MacGregor   f   3593
*Ingathering: The Complete People Stories of Zenna
   Henderson* - Zenna Henderson   s   2659
*The Iron Bridge* - David Morse   s   4036
*Mad Amos* - Alan Dean Foster   f   2009
*Mojo and the Pickle Jar* - Douglas Bell   f   433
*Night Cruise* - Billie Sue Mosiman   h   4041
*People of the Mesa* - Ardath Mayhar   f   3704
*Riverrun* - S.P. Somtow   f   5159
*Strum Again?* - Elizabeth Ann Scarborough   f   4870
*The Transall Saga* - Gary Paulsen   s   4262
*Walking Wolf* - Nancy A. Collins   h   1126
*Warsprite* - Jefferson P. Swycaffer   s   5375
*The Wood Wife* - Terri Windling   f   5916

**Arizona Territy**
*The Gaia Websters* - Kim Antieau   s   198

**Frescuro**
*Coyote* - Peter Gadol   f   2100

**Mordock Caves**
*Midnight's Lair* - Richard Laymon   h   3369

**Navajo Nation**
*The Godmother's Web* - Elizabeth Ann
   Scarborough   f   4864

**TENNESSEE**

*The Black Mariah* - Jay R. Bonansinga   h   570
*Old Nathan* - David Drake   f   1639
*Spirit Crossings* - Claudia Peck   f   4275

**Adams**
*The Bell Witch: An American Haunting* - Brent
   Monahan   h   3953

**Cedar Bluff**
*Father's Little Helper* - Ronald Kelly   h   3052

**Clark's Corner**
*Deadly Breed* - T.J. Kirby   h   3153

**Corey County**
*My Soul to Keep* - Judith Hawkes   h   2631

**Franklin**
*The Possession* - Ronald Kelly   h   3055

**Graceland**
*Elvis Rising: Stories on the King* - Kay
   Sloan   f   5089
*Elvissey* - Jack Womack   s   5957
*Rock of Ages* - Walter Jon Williams   s   5840

**Green Hollow**
*Blood Kin* - Ronald Kelly   h   3051

**Knoxville**
*Not Broken, Not Belonging* - Randy Fox   h   2030

**Lookout Mountain**
*The World of Darkness: Watcher* - Charles L.
   Grant   h   2321

**Memphis**
*Howl-O-Ween* - Gary L. Holleman   h   2744
*Monsters From Memphis* - Beecher Smith   h   5098
*More Monsters From Memphis* - Beecher
   Smith   h   5099
*Rockabilly Hell* - William W. Johnstone   h   2933
*Rockabilly Limbo* - William W. Johnstone   h   2934

**Mountainville**
*Fire* - Alan Rodgers   h   4647

**Old Hickory**
*Moon of the Werewolf* - Ronald Kelly   h   3053

**Pine Junction**
*Pandora* - Alan Rodgers   h   4650

**Potar Ridge**
*Jackals* - Charles L. Grant   h   2313

**Rockville**
*The Crawling Dark* - Pauline Dunn   h   1698

**Sublimity**
*Fiends* - John Farris   h   1884

**Tucker's Mill**
*Something Out There* - Ronald Kelly   h   3056

**TEXAS**

*Beneath the Gated Sky* - Robert Reed   s   4502
*Destination: Showdown* - Jake Davis   s   1405
*Double Jeopardy* - Aaron Allston   s   86
*The Earth Remembers* - Susan Torian Olan   s   4209
*The Flight of Michael McBride* - Midori
   Snyder   f   5151
*Future Eden* - J.M. Morgan   s   4001
*The Last Rangers* - Jake Davis   s   1406
*The Magic Bicycle* - William Hill   f   2688
*The Spirit Stalker* - Nina Romberg   h   4664
*Wildside* - Steven Gould   s   2291

**Amarillo**
*Dead Heat* - Del Stone Jr.   h   5313

**Austin**
*The Double* - Don Webb   h   5661
*Familiar Spirit* - Lisa Tuttle   h   5519
*Glimpses* - Lewis Shiner   h   4997
*Lunatics* - Bradley Denton   f   1491
*Mathemagics* - Margaret Ball   f   316
*Pillow Friend* - Lisa Tuttle   h   5522
*Proxies* - Laura J. Mixon   s   3922
*Resume with Monsters* - William Browning
   Spencer   h   5168
*The Shadow Gate* - Margaret Ball   f   317
*The Sherwood Game* - Esther Friesner   s   2082
*Zod Wallop* - William Browning Spencer   h   5169

**Bernice**
*Meeting the Minotaur* - Carol Dawson   f   1409

**Biosphere Seven**
*Beyond Eden* - J.M. Morgan   s   3999

**Blackwood**
*The X-Files: Fight the Future* - Chris Carter   h   924

**Bone**
*Second Chance* - Chet Williamson   h   5850

**Britt**
*Hobkin* - Peni R. Griffin   f   2438

**Carruthers**
*Less than Human* - Gary L. Raisor   h   4464

**Claypool**
*Desert Eden* - J.M. Morgan   s   4000

**Clear Creek**
*The Undead* - Roxanne Longstreet   h   3519

**Coomey**
*Happy Policeman* - Patricia Anthony   s   160

**Core City**
*Core* - Paul Preuss   s   4416

**Crowder Flats**
*Less than Human* - Gary L. Raisor   h   4464

**Dallas**
*Burning Water* - Mercedes Lackey   h   3272
*Cold Kiss* - Roxanne Longstreet   h   3517
*Dusk* - Ron Dee   h   1466
*Elvendude* - Mark Shepherd   f   4980
*Fiend* - C. Dean Andersson   h   138
*Lethal Interface* - Mel Odom   s   4193
*Meeting the Minotaur* - Carol Dawson   f   1409

*The Nexus* - Mike McQuay   *f*   3860
*Vampire$* - John Steakley   *h*   5237

**Fairvale**
*Psycho II* - Robert Bloch   *h*   541
*Psycho House* - Robert Bloch   *h*   542

**Fort Worth**
*Beachhead* - Jack Williamson   *s*   5859
*Rock of Ages* - Walter Jon Williams   *s*   5840

**Gusher**
*Shadow Walkers* - Nina Romberg   *h*   4663

**Houston**
*Act of Love* - Joe R. Lansdale   *h*   3319
*The Centurion's Empire* - Sean McMullen   *s*   3854
*Forever Peace* - Joe Haldeman   *s*   2488

**La Borde**
*Cold in July* - Joe R. Lansdale   *h*   3323
*Mucho Mojo* - Joe R. Lansdale   *h*   3330

**Lansom**
*Night Blood* - Eric Flanders   *h*   1945

**Marfa**
*Spyder* - Norman Partridge   *h*   4255

**Marvel Creek**
*Savage Season* - Joe R. Lansdale   *h*   3332

**Montrose**
*Mockingbird* - Sean Stewart   *f*   5273

**Mud Creek**
*Dead in the West* - Joe R. Lansdale   *h*   3325

**Nostalgia**
*The Homecoming* - Kimberly Rangel   *h*   4471

**San Antonio**
*The Eleventh Plague: A Novel of Medical Terror* - John S. Marr   *h*   3632
*Warsprite* - Jefferson P. Swycaffer   *s*   5375

**Shorecross**
*This Symbiotic Fascination* - Charlee Jacob   *h*   2843

**Sulphur Springs**
*Pitfall* - Ronald Kelly   *h*   3054

**Tombley's Walk**
*Tombley's Walk* - Crosland Brown   *h*   723

**Tyler**
*Terminal Logic* - Jefferson Scott   *s*   4893

**Waxahachie**
*Einstein's Bridge* - John Cramer   *s*   1244

**UTAH**

*Dracula Unbound* - Brian W. Aldiss   *h*   55
*The Folk of the Fringe* - Orson Scott Card   *s*   886
*On the Run* - Christie Golden   *s*   2254
*Raptor* - Paul Zindel   *s*   6084
*Warrior* - Donald E. McQuinn   *s*   3863

**Beaver**
*The Immortals* - Tracy Hickman   *s*   2681

**Canyonlands**
*Children of the Earth* - Catherine Wells   *s*   5743
*The Earth Is All That Lasts* - Catherine Wells   *s*   5744

**Milford**
*The Immortals* - Tracy Hickman   *s*   2681

**Newhouse Center**
*The Immortals* - Tracy Hickman   *s*   2681

**Salt Lake City**
*After Sundown* - Randall Boyll   *h*   609

*Gibbon's Decline and Fall* - Sheri S. Tepper   *s*   5430
*Krokodil Tears* - Jack Yeovil   *f*   6023

**Spike Mountain**
*After Sundown* - Randall Boyll   *h*   609

**VERMONT**

*The Secret History* - Donna Tartt   *h*   5398
*Travel Far, Pay No Fare* - Anne Lindbergh   *f*   3468
*The Unseen* - Joseph A. Citro   *h*   1039

**Antrim**
*Shadow Child* - Joseph A. Citro   *h*   1038

**Brattleboro**
*Dry Skull Dreams* - Michael Green   *h*   2344

**Fenwick**
*The Hunger of the Beast* - John Driver   *h*   1656

**Friar's Island**
*Dark Twilight* - Joseph A. Citro   *h*   1036

**Harmony**
*Harmony* - Marjorie Bradley Kellogg   *s*   3046

**Hobston**
*Deus-X: A Novel of Spiritual Terror* - Joseph A. Citro   *h*   1037

**New Thetford**
*Whisper* - Raymond Van Over   *h*   5539

**Pinebridge**
*Good Night, Sweet Angel* - Clare McNally   *h*   3857

**VIRGINIA**

*Gaia's Toys* - Rebecca Ore   *s*   4218
*The Illegal Rebirth of Billy the Kid* - Rebecca Ore   *s*   4220
*An Impossumble Summer* - Brenda W. Clough   *f*   1090
*Union Fires* - John Barnes   *f*   358

**Arlington**
*The Siege of Eternity* - Frederik Pohl   *s*   4353

**Beacon Cove**
*Sineater* - Elizabeth Massie   *h*   3668

**Blue Falls**
*The Fagin* - Pat Graversen   *h*   2334

**Bracken County**
*Slow Funeral* - Rebecca Ore   *f*   4221

**Charlottesville**
*Belladonna* - Michael Stewart   *h*   5271

**City Point**
*Rally Cry!* - William R. Forstchen   *s*   1982

**Clear Creek**
*The Burning Man* - Michael Hammond   *h*   2530

**The Complex**
*Haven* - David Peters   *f*   4304

**Crowley Creek**
*The Black Cat* - Robert Poe   *h*   4344
*Return to the House of Usher* - Robert Poe   *h*   4345

**Furnace**
*Furnace* - Muriel Gray   *h*   2339

**Harken**
*Irrational Fears* - William Browning Spencer   *h*   5167

**Hillenberg**
*Cold White Fury* - Beth Amos   *h*   97

**Homeplace**
*Bloody Waters* - B.L. Winters   *h*   5926

**Kendrick**
*The Healing of Crossroads* - Nick O'Donohoe   *f*   4195
*The Magic and the Healing* - Nick O'Donohoe   *f*   4196
*Under the Healing Sign* - Nick O'Donohoe   *f*   4198

**Kobold**
*Slow Funeral* - Rebecca Ore   *f*   4221

**Lewisburg**
*Header* - Edward Lee   *h*   3393

**Luntville**
*The Bighead* - Edward Lee   *h*   3387
*The Case of the Police Officer's Cock Ring and the Piano Player Who Had No Fingers* - Edward Lee   *h*   3388
*Goon* - Edward Lee   *h*   3392

**Pontefract**
*Goat Dance* - Douglas Clegg   *h*   1079

**Reeves County**
*Cat's Eye* - William W. Johnstone   *h*   2928

**Richmond**
*Circuit of Heaven* - Dennis Danvers   *s*   1348
*The Virginia Ghost Murders* - Leslie Raymond Sachs   *h*   4778
*Wilderness* - Dennis Danvers   *h*   1349

**WASHINGTON**

*Cloven Hooves* - Megan Lindholm   *f*   3470
*The March Hare Network* - Jack L. Chalker   *s*   957
*The Midnight Club* - Christopher Pike   *h*   4329
*Speak to the Rain* - Helen K. Passey   *h*   4257

**Avalon**
*Deathwalker* - Patrick Whalen   *h*   5769

**Belltower**
*A Bridge of Years* - Robert Charles Wilson   *s*   5905

**Greely's Cove**
*Greely's Cove* - John Gideon   *h*   2221

**Lilian River Valley**
*Earthling* - Tony Daniel   *s*   1336

**Longview**
*Dark Time* - Maxine O'Callaghan   *h*   4189

**Mt. St. Helens**
*Scorpion Shards* - Neal Shusterman   *s*   5013

**Newford**
*From a Whisper to a Scream* - Samuel M. Key   *h*   3093

**Othello**
*The Summoned* - Steven Ray Fulgham   *h*   2090

**Pullman**
*Islands of Tomorrow* - F.M. Busby   *s*   783

**Sea-Tac Urboplex**
*Bodyguard* - William C. Dietz   *s*   1542

**Seattle**
*/* - Greg Bear   *s*   413
*2XS* - Nigel Findley   *f*   1935
*Anthony Shriek* - Jessica Amanda Salmonson   *h*   4790
*Black Lightning* - John Saul   *h*   4837
*Blood on the Sun* - Brian Herbert   *h*   2664
*Bones* - Joyce Thompson   *h*   5453
*Carol for Another Christmas* - Elizabeth Ann Scarborough   *f*   4861
*Find Your Own Truth* - Robert N. Charrette   *f*   972
*The Forsaken* - Steven Ray Fulgham   *h*   2089

*The Frenchman* - Elizabeth Hand   *h*   2534
*The Godmother* - Elizabeth Ann
   Scarborough   *f*   4862
*Half Asleep in Frog Pajamas* - Tom
   Robbins   *s*   4606
*Headhunters* - Mel Odom   *s*   4192
*Into the Shadows* - Jordan K. Weisman   *f*   5731
*Matrix Man* - William C. Dietz   *s*   1549
*Never Deal with a Dragon* - Robert N.
   Charrette   *s*   975
*Never Trust an Elf* - Robert N. Charrette   *f*   976
*Night Thirst* - Patrick Whalen   *h*   5770
*One Foot in the Grave* - Wm. Mark
   Simmons   *f*   5062
*Passive Intruder* - Michael Upchurch   *h*   5530
*Seattle Ghost Story* - Nick DiMartino   *h*   1560
*Shadowboxer* - Nick Pollotta   *s*   4366
*Shifters* - Edward Lee   *h*   3396
*The Singularity Project* - F.M. Busby   *s*   784
*Soul Catcher* - Colin Kersey   *h*   3081
*Street* - Jack Cady   *h*   822
*Trickster* - Chris Curry   *h*   1297
*Twistor* - John Cramer   *s*   1245
*A Whisper of Wings* - Steven Ray Fulgham   *h*   2091
*The Witch House* - Norma Tadlock Johnson   *f*   2923
*Wolf and Raven* - Michael A. Stackpole   *f*   5207

**Stellacoom**
*Sarah Canary* - Karen Joy Fowler   *f*   2028

**Tacoma**
*Bug Park* - James P. Hogan   *s*   2723
*Out of Body* - Thomas Baum   *h*   397

**Whaler Bay**
*Ember From the Sun* - Mark Canter   *s*   870

**WEST**
*The Eyes of Darkness* - Dean R. Koontz   *s*   3206
*Hong on the Range* - William F. Wu   *s*   5997
*Moon Dance* - S.P. Somtow   *h*   5158
*The Secret of the Indian* - Lynne Reid Banks   *f*   332
*Suicide Attack* - John Sievert   *s*   5023
*Western Ghosts* - Frank D. McSherry Jr.   *h*   3870
*Yellowstone Run* - David Robbins   *s*   4605

**Medicine Rock**
*Devil's Engine* - Mark Sumner   *f*   5356

**WEST COAST**
*Noir* - K.W. Jeter   *s*   2916
*Something Rich and Strange* - Patricia A.
   McKillip   *f*   3840

**WEST VIRGINIA**
**Colony**
*The Children's Hour* - Douglas Clegg   *h*   1077

**Hamelin**
*Bring Me Children* - David Martin   *h*   3637

**Huntington**
*Bad Blood* - D.A. Fowler   *h*   2021
*What's Wrong with Tamara?* - D.A.
   Fowler   *h*   2025
*What's Wrong with Valerie?* - D.A. Fowler   *h*   2026

**Morton's Fork**
*Gravelight* - Marion Zimmer Bradley   *f*   636

**WISCONSIN**
*Flying in Place* - Susan Palwick   *h*   4240

*Out There in the Darkness* - Ed Gorman   *h*   2279
*Over the River & through the Woods* - Clifford D.
   Simak   *s*   5047
*Walkers* - Graham Masterton   *h*   3681

**Eagle Lake**
*Mystery* - Peter Straub   *h*   5330

**Eau Claire**
*Clash by Night* - Chet Williamson   *h*   5844

**Ewerton**
*The Amulet* - A.R. Morlan   *h*   4009
*Dark Journey* - A.R. Morlan   *h*   4010

**Madison**
*Out for Blood* - John Peyton Cooke   *h*   1166

**Millville**
*Way Station* - Clifford D. Simak   *s*   5048

**WYOMING**
*Amnesia Moon* - Jonathan Lethem   *f*   3438
*The Illegal Rebirth of Billy the Kid* - Rebecca
   Ore   *s*   4220
*Man o' War* - William Shatner   *s*   4932

**Cheyenne**
*House of the Sun* - Nigel Findley   *s*   1936

**Cheyenne Mountain Command Cent**
*Firelance* - David Mace   *s*   3586

**Laramie**
*Devil's Tower* - Mark Sumner   *f*   5357
*Wendigo Border* - Catherine Montrose   *h*   3967

**Yellowstone National Park**
*The Quiet* - Patrick Billings   *h*   488

## UZBEKISTAN

*How Like a God* - Brenda W. Clough   *f*   1089

## VATICAN CITY

*The Blood of the Lamb* - Thomas F.
   Monteleone   *h*   3958
*Cardinal's Sin* - Raymond Buckland   *h*   751

## VENEZUELA

**Caracas**
*Standing Wave* - Howard V. Hendrix   *s*   2661

**Puerto Ordaz**
*Dinosaur Summer* - Greg Bear   *s*   416

## VENUS

*The Alien Dark* - Diana G. Gallagher   *s*   2108
*Beyond Apollo* - Barry Malzberg   *s*   3612
*Blue Mars* - Kim Stanley Robinson   *s*   4629
*Deepdrive* - Alexander Jablokov   *s*   2837
*The Gateway Trip: Tales and Vignettes of the Heechee*
   - Frederik Pohl   *s*   4346
*Igniting the Reaches* - David Drake   *s*   1633
*The Jungle* - David Drake   *s*   1634
*Surface Action* - David Drake   *s*   1646
*Through the Breach* - David Drake   *s*   1647

## VIETNAM

*Arc Riders* - David Drake   *s*   1626

*Black Trump* - George R.R. Martin   *s*   3642
*Dream Baby* - Bruce McAllister   *s*   3706
*The Healer's War* - Elizabeth Ann
   Scarborough   *f*   4865
*Marked Cards* - George R.R. Martin   *s*   3647

**Cu Chi**
*Kindred* - John Gideon   *h*   2222

**Saigon**
*Hour of the Scorpion* - Matthew J. Costello   *s*   1199

## VIRGIN ISLANDS OF THE UNITED STATES

**Santa Luz**
*Shadows* - Jonathan Nasaw   *h*   4068

## WALES

*The Cormorant* - Stephen Gregory   *h*   2429
*Kingdom of the Grail* - A.A. Attanasio   *f*   269
*The Moon in Hiding* - Teresa Edgerton   *f*   1745
*The Panther's Hoard* - Nancy Varian
   Berberick   *f*   458
*Pendragon* - Stephen R. Lawhead   *f*   3357

**Caermaen**
*The Hill of Dreams* - Arthur Machen   *h*   3595

**Caernarfon**
*The Blood of Angels* - Stephen Gregory   *h*   2428

**Crybbe**
*Curfew* - Phil Rickman   *h*   4587

**Gwent**
*December* - Phil Rickman   *h*   4588

**Gwynedd**
*The Island of the Mighty* - Evangeline
   Walton   *f*   5626

**Ty-Gwyneth**
*Sheep* - Simon Maginn   *h*   3606

**Y Groes**
*Candle Night* - Phil Rickman   *h*   4586

## WEST INDIES

*Shape-Shifter: Stories by Pauline Melville* - Pauline
   Melville   *f*   3876

## YEMEN

*Guts and Glory* - G. Harry Stine   *s*   5280

## YUGOSLAVIA

**Belgrade**
*The Angry Angel* - Chelsea Quinn Yarbro   *h*   6010

## ZAIRE

*The Lost Guardian* - Ronald Anthony Cross   *s*   1274

## ZIMBABWE

*A Girl Named Disaster* - Nancy Farmer   *f*   1868

**Harare**
*The Ear, the Eye, and the Arm* - Nancy
   Farmer   *f*   1867

# Story Type Index

This index is a listing of the story types arranged in alphabetical order. Falling under each story type, titles are listed alphabetically, along with author names and entry numbers. For definitions of the story types, see the "Key to Story Types" section following the Introduction.

## FANTASY

### Fantasy — Adventure

*The Adventures of Huru on the Road to Baghdad* - Guneli Gun  f  2457
*Allamanda* - Michael Williams  f  5817
*The Amazon Chronicles* - Jane E.M. Robinson  f  4627
*Anvil of the Sun* - Anne Lesley Groell  f  2451
*Arena* - William R. Forstchen  f  1977
*The Arkadians* - Lloyd Alexander  f  67
*Athyra* - Steven Brust  f  739
*Attila's Treasure* - Stephan Grundy  f  2453
*The Avenger* - Louise Cooper  f  1174
*Battledragon* - Christopher Rowley  f  4691
*Bazil Broketail* - Christopher Rowley  f  4692
*Belgarath the Sorcerer* - David Eddings  f  1730
*The Bellmaker* - Brian Jacques  f  2848
*Beyond Ragnarok* - Mickey Zucker Reichert  f  4516
*Bhagavati* - Kara Dalkey  f  1316
*Bijapur* - Kara Dalkey  f  1317
*The Black Gryphon* - Mercedes Lackey  f  3270
*Black Unicorn* - Tanith Lee  f  3404
*The Bones of Haven* - Simon R. Green  f  2363
*The Book of Night with Moon* - Diane Duane  f  1657
*The Book of Water* - Marjorie Bradley Kellogg  f  3045
*The Boy From the Burren* - Sheila Gilluly  f  2236
*The Brazen Gambit* - Lynn Abbey  f  13
*Bridge of Valor* - Anne Lesley Groell  f  2452
*Brothers of the Dragon* - Robin Wayne Bailey  f  286
*By Chaos Cursed* - Mickey Zucker Reichert  f  4517
*By the Sword* - Timothy Boggs  f  559
*By the Sword* - Mercedes Lackey  f  3273
*Byzantium* - Stephen R. Lawhead  f  3353
*The Cage* - S.M. Stirling  f  5293
*Caledon of the Mists* - Deborah Turner Harris  f  2560
*Call of Madness* - Julie Dean Smith  f  5124
*Captives of the Blue Mountain* - Wendy Pini  f  4336
*Cardmaster* - Clayton Emery  f  1813
*Carnivores of Light and Darkness* - Alan Dean Foster  f  1996
*Catamount* - Michael Peak  f  4273
*Catwings* - Ursula K. Le Guin  f  3377
*Caverns of Socrates* - Dennis L. McKiernan  f  3831
*Changing Fate* - Elisabeth Waters  f  5629
*Chaos Mode* - Piers Anthony  f  165
*Child of an Ancient City* - Tad Williams  f  5827

*Children of Amarid* - David B. Coe  f  1095
*Chimaera's Copper* - Piers Anthony  f  166
*Clan of the Shape-Changers* - Robert Levy  f  3446
*Clock Strikes Sword* - Ian Hammell  f  2529
*The Conan Chronicles* - Robert Jordan  f  2983
*Conan the Gladiator* - Leonard Carpenter  f  907
*The Conjurer Princess* - Vivian Vande Velde  f  5555
*Coyote* - Peter Gadol  f  2100
*Crow and Weasel* - Barry Lopez  f  3523
*The Cursed* - Dave Duncan  f  1674
*The Cygnet and the Firebird* - Patricia A. McKillip  f  3839
*Dagger's Edge* - Anne Logston  f  3508
*Dancer's Rise* - Jo Clayton  f  1064
*Dancing Bears* - Fred Saberhagen  f  4764
*Dark Divide* - Mark Acres  f  27
*Dark Heart* - Margaret Weis  f  5707
*Daughter of Magic* - C. Dale Brittain  f  703
*Daughter of the Drow* - Elaine Cunningham  f  1287
*The Day of the Tempest* - Jean Rabe  f  4457
*Days of Air and Darkness* - Katharine Kerr  f  3067
*Days of Blood and Fire* - Katharine Kerr  f  3068
*Deathknight* - Andrew J. Offutt  f  4201
*The Deepest Sea* - Charles Barnitz  f  363
*Delan the Mislaid* - Laurie J. Marks  f  3625
*Demon Blade* - Mark A. Garland  f  2141
*Demon Download* - Jack Yeovil  f  6021
*Dinotopia Lost* - Alan Dean Foster  f  2003
*Doc Sidhe* - Aaron Allston  f  85
*The Doom Brigade* - Margaret Weis  f  5708
*Double Trouble Squared* - Kathryn Lasky  f  3340
*Down Among the Dead Men* - Simon R. Green  f  2367
*Dragon* - Steven Brust  f  741
*A Dragon at World's End* - Christopher Rowley  f  4693
*Dragon Cauldron* - Laurence Yep  f  6024
*Dragon Companion* - Don Callander  f  842
*Dragon Rescue* - Don Callander  f  843
*The Dragon Revenant* - Katharine Kerr  f  3069
*Dragon Tempest* - Don Callander  f  844
*Dragon War* - Laurence Yep  f  6025
*Dragon Wing* - Margaret Weis  f  5709
*Dragon's Domain* - Thorarinn Gunnarsson  f  2461
*Dragons of War* - Christopher Rowley  f  4695
*Dragonslayer's Return* - R.A. Salvatore  f  4798
*Dragonspawn* - Mark Acres  f  28
*The Dragonstone* - Dennis L. McKiernan  f  3832
*Dreamseeker's Road* - Tom Deitz  f  1472
*Drum Calls* - Jo Clayton  f  1065
*Drum Warning* - Jo Clayton  f  1066

*The Eagle and the Nightingales* - Mercedes Lackey  f  3278
*Eight Skilled Gentlemen* - Barry Hughart  f  2804
*The Element of Fire* - Jason Henderson  f  2657
*Elfshadow* - Elaine Cunningham  f  1288
*Elminster: The Making of a Mage* - Ed Greenwood  f  2427
*Elven Star* - Margaret Weis  f  5712
*The Elvenbane* - Andre Norton  f  4149
*Elvenblood* - Andre Norton  f  4150
*Emperor and Clown* - Dave Duncan  f  1676
*The Empty Throne* - Ru Emerson  f  1808
*The End-of-Everything Man* - Tom De Haven  f  1421
*The Endless Knot* - Stephen R. Lawhead  f  3354
*Escape From Loki* - Philip Jose Farmer  f  1870
*Excalibur* - Bernard Cornwell  f  1190
*Eyes of Silver* - Michael A. Stackpole  f  5200
*The Face in the Abyss* - A. Merritt  f  3078
*Faery in Shadow* - C.J. Cherryh  f  987
*Faery Lands Forlorn* - Dave Duncan  f  1677
*The Faithful Traitor* - Robert Don Hughes  f  2809
*The Far Kingdoms* - Allan Cole  f  1104
*The Final Battle* - Richard A. Lupoff  f  3572
*Find Your Own Truth* - Robert N. Charrette  f  972
*Finn Mac Cool* - Morgan Llywelyn  f  3504
*Fire and Ice* - Edward Myers  f  4061
*Fire Sea* - Margaret Weis  f  5714
*Firewalk* - Anne Logston  f  3509
*First King of Shannara* - Terry Brooks  f  712
*Firstborn* - Paul B. Thompson  f  5454
*Five Hundred Years After* - Steven Brust  f  742
*Flight of the Raven* - Jennifer Roberson  f  4608
*Flight to Hollow Mountain* - Mark Sebanc  f  4908
*The Floating Castle* - Craig Mills  f  3913
*Fortress of Frost and Fire* - Mercedes Lackey  f  3282
*Fractal Mode* - Piers Anthony  f  171
*The Frightened Fish* - Kenneth Robeson  f  4622
*A Game of Thrones* - George R.R. Martin  f  3645
*The Gates of Twilight* - Paula Volsky  f  5581
*The Gates of Vensunor* - Carol Heller  f  2650
*Gatherer of Clouds* - Sean Russell  f  4741
*A Girl Named Disaster* - Nancy Farmer  f  1868
*Glenraven* - Marion Zimmer Bradley  f  635
*Glory Road* - Robert A. Heinlein  f  2644
*The Gnome's Engine* - Teresa Edgerton  f  1742
*The Goblin Plain War* - Carl Miller  f  3892
*The God Killer* - Simon R. Green  f  2368
*Gold Unicorn* - Tanith Lee  f  3410
*Green Rider* - Kristen Britain  f  692
*Greendaughter* - Anne Logston  f  3510
*Hall of Whispers* - Mike Jefferies  f  2884

*Haven* - David Peters  f  4304

*Hawk's Flight* - Carol Chase  f  980

*The Healing of Crossroads* - Nick O'Donohoe  f  4195

*Heroes, Inc.* - Kyle Crocco  f  1268

*Heroes Wanted* - Kyle Crocco  f  1267

*The Hidden City* - Charles de Lint  f  1429

*The Hidden City* - David Eddings  f  1733

*Hidden Echoes* - Mike Jefferies  f  2885

*The Honorable Barbarian* - L. Sprague de Camp  f  1415

*Hook* - Terry Brooks  f  713

*Horrible Humes* - Stephen Billias  f  487

*Horrors of the Dancing Gods* - Jack L. Chalker  f  955

*Hungry for Home: A Wolf Odyssey* - 'Asta Bowen  f  599

*Hunter of the Light* - Risa Aratyr  f  203

*The Hunter Returns* - David Drake  f  1632

*The Hunters' Haunt* - Dave Duncan  f  1681

*Hunter's Oath* - Michelle West  f  5759

*Indiana Jones and the Dance of the Giants* - Rob MacGregor  f  3588

*Indiana Jones and the Genesis Deluge* - Rob MacGregor  f  3589

*Indiana Jones and the Interior World* - Rob MacGregor  f  3590

*Indiana Jones and the Peril at Delphi* - Rob MacGregor  f  3591

*Indiana Jones and the Seven Veils* - Rob MacGregor  f  3592

*Indiana Jones and the Sky Pirates* - Martin Caidin  f  825

*Indiana Jones and the Unicorn's Legacy* - Rob MacGregor  f  3593

*Indiana Jones and the White Witch* - Martin Caidin  f  826

*The Initiate Brother* - Sean Russell  f  4742

*Into the Green* - Charles de Lint  f  1430

*Invasion of Willow Wood Springs* - Terry Ellis  f  1781

*The Iron Throne* - Simon Hawke  f  2618

*The Jade Ogre* - Kenneth Robeson  f  4623

*Kar Kalim* - Deborah Christian  f  1025

*Kaz the Minotaur* - Richard A. Knaak  f  3172

*Kedrigern and the Charming Couple* - John Morressy  f  4013

*Killobyte* - Piers Anthony  f  179

*Kindred Rites* - Katharine Eliska Kimbriel  f  3118

*King & Raven* - Cary James  f  2858

*King Pinch* - David Cook  f  1146

*Kingdoms of the Night* - Allan Cole  f  1105

*The King's Buccaneer* - Raymond E. Feist  f  1904

*King's Man and Thief* - Christie Golden  f  2253

*Kingslayer* - L. Dean James  f  2863

*The Kinslayer Wars* - Douglas Niles  f  4109

*The Knights of Cawdor* - Mike Jefferies  f  2886

*Knight's Wyrd* - Debra Doyle  f  1601

*Konrad* - David Ferring  f  1927

*Krispos Rising* - Harry Turtledove  f  5507

*Krokodil Tears* - Jack Yeovil  f  6023

*Ladylord* - Sasha Miller  f  3906

*Landslayer's Law* - Tom Deitz  f  1474

*The Lark and the Wren* - Mercedes Lackey  f  3286

*Last Mountain* - Robert C. Fleet  f  1946

*The Legacy* - R.A. Salvatore  f  4801

*Legacy of the Darksword* - Margaret Weis  f  5719

*The Legend of Nightfall* - Mickey Zucker Reichert  f  4521

*Lion's Heart* - Karen Wehrstein  f  5683

*The Living God* - Dave Duncan  f  1682

*The Long Patrol* - Brian Jacques  f  2849

*Lords of the Sword* - Hugh Cook  f  1156

*Madoc's Hundred* - Pat Winter  f  5925

*The Magic and the Healing* - Nick O'Donohoe  f  4196

*Magic Casement* - Dave Duncan  f  1683

*MagicNet* - John DeChancie  f  1461

*Magic's Promise* - Mercedes Lackey  f  3289

*Majyk by Accident* - Esther Friesner  f  2079

*Majyk by Hook or Crook* - Esther Friesner  f  2081

*Mariel of Redwall* - Brian Jacques  f  2850

*Martin the Warrior* - Brian Jacques  f  2851

*The Marvellous Land of Snergs* - E.A. Wyke-Smith  f  6006

*The Mask of Loki* - Roger Zelazny  f  6071

*The Mata Hari Adventure* - James Luceno  f  3544

*Mattimeo* - Brian Jacques  f  2852

*Medallion of the Black Hound* - Shirley Rousseau Murphy  f  4056

*Men at Arms* - Terry Pratchett  f  4396

*The Merlin Effect* - T.A. Barron  f  371

*Mind of the Magic* - Holly Lisle  f  3486

*The Mines of Behemoth* - Michael Shea  f  4945

*Mirror of Destiny* - Andre Norton  f  4159

*Mission of Magic* - Julie Dean Smith  f  5125

*M'Lady Witch* - Christopher Stasheff  f  5217

*Morningstar* - David Gemmell  f  2190

*Mortal Kombat* - Martin Delrio  f  1483

*Mother of Storms* - Adrian Cole  f  1101

*The Mountain Made of Light* - Edward Myers  f  4062

*Mouvar's Magic* - Piers Anthony  f  182

*Myst: The Book of Atrus* - Rand Miller  f  3896

*Nightsword* - Margaret Weis  f  5722

*The Nomad Queen* - James Gordon White  f  5783

*On Fortune's Wheel* - Cynthia Voigt  f  5579

*Once a Hero* - Michael A. Stackpole  f  5203

*The One-Armed Queen* - Jane Yolen  f  6037

*One Foot in the Grave* - Wm. Mark Simmons  f  5062

*One Land, One Duke* - Ru Emerson  f  1809

*Orca* - Steven Brust  f  745

*Outcast of Redwall* - Brian Jacques  f  2853

*Owlflight* - Mercedes Lackey  f  3291

*Owlsight* - Mercedes Lackey  f  3292

*Palaces and Prisons* - Ron Miller  f  3904

*The Parched Sea* - Troy Denning  f  1486

*Passage to Dawn* - R.A. Salvatore  f  4803

*The Pearls of Lutra* - Brian Jacques  f  2854

*People of the Fire* - W. Michael Gear  f  2167

*People of the Wolf* - W. Michael Gear  f  2170

*Perilous Seas* - Dave Duncan  f  1685

*Phoenix* - Steven Brust  f  746

*The Phoenix Guards* - Steven Brust  f  747

*The Pixilated Peeress* - L. Sprague de Camp  f  1416

*Planar Powers* - J. Robert King  f  3122

*Polgara the Sorceress* - David Eddings  f  1734

*Primavera* - Francesca Lia Block  f  551

*Prince of Demons* - Mickey Zucker Reichert  f  4522

*Prince of the Blood* - Raymond E. Feist  f  1907

*Prince of the North* - Harry Turtledove  f  5509

*Python Isle* - Kenneth Robeson  f  4624

*Queens of Land and Sea* - John Maddox Roberts  f  4620

*The Quest Begins* - Wendy Pini  f  4337

*Raptor Red* - Robert T. Bakker  f  306

*Ratha and Thistle-Chaser* - Clare Bell  f  432

*The Raven Ring* - Patricia C. Wrede  f  5978

*The Realms of the Gods* - Tamora Pierce  f  4321

*The Reaver Road* - Dave Duncan  f  1687

*The Red King* - Victor Kelleher  f  3043

*Red Magic* - Jean Rabe  f  4458

*Red Unicorn* - Tanith Lee  f  3414

*Return to Howliday Inn* - James Howe  f  2786

*Rhinegold* - Stephan Grundy  f  2454

*The Road Home* - Joel Rosenberg  f  4674

*Roverandom* - J.R.R. Tolkien  f  5479

*Runes of Autumn* - Larry Elmore  f  1790

*Saber & Shadow* - S.M. Stirling  f  5297

*Sage of Sare* - Julie Dean Smith  f  5126

*Salamandastron* - Brian Jacques  f  2855

*Samurai Cat Goes to Hell* - Mark E. Rogers  f  4655

*Santa's Twin* - Dean R. Koontz  f  3214

*The Sapphire Rose* - David Eddings  f  1737

*Scotland the Brave* - Jennifer Roberson  f  4611

*Search for the Starblade* - Keith Taylor  f  5408

*The Second Generation* - Margaret Weis  f  5724

*The Seeker* - Simon Hawke  f  2624

*The Seventh Gate* - Margaret Weis  f  5727

*Shadow* - Anne Logston  f  3512

*Shadow Leader* - Tara K. Harper  f  2552

*Shadow of a Dark Queen* - Raymond E. Feist  f  1911

*Shadow of Obsession* - Rebecca Neason  f  4082

*The Shadow Shaia* - Alexis A. Gilliland  f  2235

*The Shadow Warrior* - Pat Zettner  f  6082

*Shadowbreed* - David Ferring  f  1928

*Shadow's Realm* - Mickey Zucker Reichert  f  4523

*Shaman* - Sandra Miesel  f  3889

*The Shaman* - Christopher Stasheff  f  5223

*Shards of Empire* - Susan Shwartz  f  5017

*The Ship of Magic* - Robin Hobb  f  2696

*Shiva: An Adventure of the Ice Age* - J.H. Brennan  f  669

*Siege of Darkness* - R.A. Salvatore  f  4804

*The Silent Blade* - R.A. Salvatore  f  4805

*Silk and Steel* - Ron Miller  f  3905

*Silk Road* - Jeanne Larsen  f  3339

*The Silver Gryphon* - Mercedes Lackey  f  3295

*The Silver Hand* - Stephen R. Lawhead  f  3358

*Silver Shadows* - Elaine Cunningham  f  1292

*Silverlight* - Morgan Llywelyn  f  3507

*Sing the Four Quarters* - Tanya Huff  f  2799

*Sister Light, Sister Dark* - Jane Yolen  f  6039

*The Skystone* - Jack Whyte  f  5794

*Sojourn* - R.A. Salvatore  f  4806

*The Son of Summer Stars* - Meredith Ann Pierce  f  4319

*Song of the Gargoyle* - Zilpha Keatley Snyder  f  5153

*Song of the River* - Sue Harrison  f  2583

*Song of the Saurials* - Kate Novak  f  4167

*Songsmith* - Andre Norton  f  4161

*Sons of the Titans* - Patrick H. Adkins  f  36

*A Sorcerer's Apprentice* - Michael Williams  f  5820

*The Soulforge* - Margaret Weis  f  5728

*The Spawn of Loki* - Jason Henderson  f  2658

*Spear of Heaven* - Judith Tarr  f  5396

*The Spiral Dance* - R. Garcia y Robertson  f  2121

*The Stallion Queen* - Constance Ash  f  223

*Star Ascendant* - Louise Cooper  f  1180

*Steal the Dragon* - Patricia Briggs  f  682

*The Still* - David Feintuch  f  1902

*The Stolen Throne* - Harry Turtledove  f  5510

*Stones of the Dalai Lama* - Ken Mitchell  f  3916

*Stoneskin's Revenge* - Tom Deitz  f  1476

*Storm Warriors* - Brian Craig  f  1240

*Storms of Victory* - Andre Norton  f  4162

*Strange Tales From the Nile Empire* - Greg Farshtey  f  1889

*The Stricken Field* - Dave Duncan  f  1688

*Striper Assassin* - Nyx Smith  f  5135

*The Summit* - Edward Myers  f  4063

*Sunshaker's War* - Tom Deitz  f  1477

*Surrender None: The Legacy of Gird* - Elizabeth Moon  f  3975

*Sword-Born* - Jennifer Roberson  f  4612

*Sword-Breaker* - Jennifer Roberson  f  4613

*A Sword for a Dragon* - Christopher Rowley  f  4697

*Sword of Fire and Shadow* - Diana L. Paxson  f  4268

*Sword of Ice and Other Tales of Valdemar* - Mercedes Lackey  f  3300

*Taking Flight* - Lawrence Watt-Evans  f  5650

*Tales of Mithgar* - Dennis L. McKiernan  f  3836

*Talion: Revenant* - Michael A. Stackpole  f  5206

*Testament of the Dragon* - Margaret Weis  f  5729

*The Thief of Hermes* - Ru Emerson  f  1811

*Thomas the Rhymer* - Ellen Kushner  f  3265

*Thunder of the Captains* - Holly Lisle  f  3489

*A Time of Exile* - Katharine Kerr  f  3077

*A Time of Omens* - Katharine Kerr  f  3078

*Timespell* - Robert N. Charrette  f  978

*Toad Triumphant* - William Horwood  f  2774
*The Tower of Beowulf* - Parke Godwin  f  2250
*A Troubling Along the Border* - Donald Aamodt  f  4
*The Two in Hiding* - Ru Emerson  f  1812
*Typewriter in the Sky* - L. Ron Hubbard  f  2791
*Under the Healing Sign* - Nick O'Donohoe  f  4198
*The Verdant Passage* - Troy Denning  f  1487
*Vinas Solamnus* - J. Robert King  f  3123
*Visitors From Oz: The Wild Adventures of Dorothy, the Scarecrow and the Tin Woodman* - Martin Gardner  f  2136
*Voyage of the Basset* - James C. Christensen  f  1024
*War* - Simon Hawke  f  2625
*The War in the Waste* - Felicity Savage  f  4851
*The Warrior and the Witch* - Carl Miller  f  3893
*The Warrior Returns* - Allan Cole  f  1109
*The Watcher's Mask* - Laurie J. Marks  f  3627
*Way Up High* - Roger Zelazny  f  6076
*When Dreams Collide* - Wm. Mark Simmons  f  5063
*When the Gods Are Silent* - Jane M. Lindskold  f  3477
*White Eyes* - Kenneth Robeson  f  4625
*White Horse, Dark Dragon* - Robert C. Fleet  f  1947
*White Jenna* - Jane Yolen  f  6041
*Whose Song Is Sung* - Frank Schaefer  f  4872
*Wild Magic* - Tamora Pierce  f  4323
*The Wild Road* - Gabriel King  f  3120
*The Willows and Beyond* - William Horwood  f  2775
*The Willows in Winter* - William Horwood  f  2776
*Winds of Change* - Mercedes Lackey  f  3304
*Winds of Fate* - Mercedes Lackey  f  3305
*Wit'ch Fire* - James Clemens  f  1082
*Witches' Brew* - Terry Brooks  f  719
*Wizard of Bones* - Robert N. Charrette  f  979
*The Wizardry Cursed* - Rick Cook  f  1162
*The Wizard's Shadow* - Susan Dexter  f  1514
*Wolf-Speaker* - Tamora Pierce  f  4324
*Wolfhelm* - Richard A. Knaak  f  3175
*The Wooden Sword* - Lynn Abbey  f  18
*The World Beneath* - James Gurney  f  2469
*Wrath of the Princes* - Holly Lisle  f  3490
*Wren's War* - Sherwood Smith  f  5144
*Zaragoz* - Brian Craig  f  1241
*Zombie Lover* - Piers Anthony  f  197

**Fantasy — Alternate History**

*Devil's Tower* - Mark Sumner  f  5357
*Flameweaver* - Margaret Ball  f  314
*Milton in America* - Peter Ackroyd  f  25
*The Smithsonian Institution* - Gore Vidal  f  5570

**Fantasy — Alternate Universe**

*The Door to Ambermere* - J. Calvin Pierce  f  4316
*River of Blue Fire* - Tad Williams  f  5830
*The War in the Waste* - Felicity Savage  f  4851
*The Wizard of Ambermere* - J. Calvin Pierce  f  4317

**Fantasy — Alternate World**

*The Ambivalent Magician* - Simon Hawke  f  2616
*Ancient Echoes* - Robert Holdstock  f  2735
*The Barbed Coil* - J.V. Jones  f  2957
*Beyond the Magic Sphere* - Gail Jarrow  f  2879
*Beyond the Pale* - Mark Anthony  f  153
*Bride of the Slime Monster* - Craig Shaw Gardner  f  2125
*The Broken Goddess* - Hans Bemmann  f  439
*Brothers of the Dragon* - Robin Wayne Bailey  f  286
*A Call to Arms* - Thomas K. Martin  f  3650
*The Caterpillar's Question* - Piers Anthony  f  164
*Caverns of Socrates* - Dennis L. McKiernan  f  3831

*Changespell* - Doranna Durgin  f  1703
*Charmed* - Marilyn Singer  f  5070
*The Crimson Sky* - Joel Rosenberg  f  4669
*The Crystal Sorcerers* - William R. Forstchen  f  1979
*Cup of Clay* - Carole Nelson Douglas  f  1583
*The Cup of Morning Shadows* - Rosemary Edghill  f  1747
*Doc Sidhe* - Aaron Allston  f  85
*Dog Wizard* - Barbara Hambly  f  2503
*The Dragon and the Djinn* - Gordon R. Dickson  f  1528
*The Dragon and the Gnarly King* - Gordon R. Dickson  f  1529
*The Dragon at War* - Gordon R. Dickson  f  1530
*Dragon Burning* - Craig Shaw Gardner  f  2126
*Dragon Companion* - Don Callander  f  842
*The Dragon in Lyonesse* - Gordon R. Dickson  f  1531
*The Dragon Knight* - Gordon R. Dickson  f  1532
*The Dragon on the Border* - Gordon R. Dickson  f  1533
*Dragon Sleeping* - Craig Shaw Gardner  f  2127
*The Dragon, the Earl, and the Troll* - Gordon R. Dickson  f  1534
*Dragon Waking* - Craig Shaw Gardner  f  2128
*The Dragon's Dagger* - R.A. Salvatore  f  4797
*Dragon's Queen* - Carol L. Dennis  f  1488
*Dreamseeker's Road* - Tom Deitz  f  1472
*Duel of Dragons* - Gael Baudino  f  391
*Dun Lady's Jess* - Doranna Durgin  f  1704
*Echoes of the Fourth Magic* - R.A. Salvatore  f  4799
*Eight Skilled Gentlemen* - Barry Hughart  f  2804
*Elven Star* - Margaret Weis  f  5712
*The Endless Knot* - Stephen R. Lawhead  f  3354
*The Face in the Abyss* - A. Merritt  f  3878
*The Falcon Rises* - Michael C. Staudinger  f  5235
*The Final Battle* - Richard A. Lupoff  f  3572
*The Fire Duke* - Joel Rosenberg  f  4671
*Fire Sea* - Margaret Weis  f  5714
*Flames of the Dragon* - Robin Wayne Bailey  f  287
*Forest of the Night* - S.P. Somtow  f  5156
*Future Indefinite* - Dave Duncan  f  1678
*Gameplay* - Kevin J. Anderson  f  105
*Game's End* - Kevin J. Anderson  f  104
*Gate of Ivory, Gate of Horn* - Robert Holdstock  f  2737
*Glory Road* - Robert A. Heinlein  f  2644
*God's Dice* - S. Andrew Swann  f  5364
*The Grail and the Ring* - Teresa Edgerton  f  1744
*The Healing of Crossroads* - Nick O'Donohoe  f  4195
*The Hero King* - Rick Shelley  f  4970
*The Hero of Varay* - Rick Shelley  f  4971
*The Hidden City* - Charles de Lint  f  1429
*Hidden Echoes* - Mike Jefferies  f  2885
*Icefalcon's Quest* - Barbara Hambly  f  2504
*In between Dragons* - Michael Kandel  f  3010
*The Inadequate Adept* - Simon Hawke  f  2617
*The Interior Life* - Katherine Blake  f  515
*The Jewel of Equilibrant* - Steven Frankos  f  2042
*The Kingdom of Kevin Malone* - Suzy McKee Charnas  f  970
*The Labyrinth Gate* - Alis A. Rasmussen  f  4481
*Landslayer's Law* - Tom Deitz  f  1474
*The League of the Crimson Crescent* - James E. Reagen  f  4495
*The Lion of Farside* - John Dalmas  f  1324
*Lost in Translation* - Margaret Ball  f  315
*The Magic and the Healing* - Nick O'Donohoe  f  4196
*The Magicians of Night* - Barbara Hambly  f  2505
*Marianne, the Matchbox and the Malachite Mouse* - Sheri S. Tepper  f  5432
*Mathemagics* - Margaret Ball  f  316
*Minerva Wakes* - Holly Lisle  f  3487
*Monet's Ghost* - Chelsea Quinn Yarbro  f  6017
*Moonwise* - Greer Ilene Gilman  f  2238

*Mother of Winter* - Barbara Hambly  f  2506
*My Son, the Wizard* - Christopher Stasheff  f  5218
*Negrophobia: An Urban Parable* - Darius James  f  2859
*Newton's Cannon* - J. Gregory Keyes  f  3097
*Nightfeeder* - Judith Reeves-Stevens  f  4513
*The Oathbound Wizard* - Christopher Stasheff  f  5219
*One Land, One Duke* - Ru Emerson  f  1809
*Out of This World* - Lawrence Watt-Evans  f  5645
*The Pagemaster* - David Kirschner  f  3156
*Past Imperative* - Dave Duncan  f  1684
*Present Tense* - Dave Duncan  f  1686
*Prince of Dogs* - Kate Elliott  f  1775
*Queen's Gambit Declined* - Melinda M. Snodgrass  f  5147
*The Rainbow Abyss* - Barbara Hambly  f  2507
*Red Orc's Rage* - Philip Jose Farmer  f  1873
*Red Wizard* - Nancy Springer  f  5182
*The Reluctant Sorcerer* - Simon Hawke  f  2622
*Riverrun* - S.P. Somtow  f  5159
*The Secular Wizard* - Christopher Stasheff  f  5222
*Seed upon the Wind* - Carole Nelson Douglas  f  1584
*The Shadow Gate* - Margaret Ball  f  317
*Shadows After Dark* - Ouida Crozier  f  1286
*Shifter* - Judith Reeves-Stevens  f  4515
*Silver Princess, Golden Knight* - Sharon Green  f  2359
*The Silver Stone* - Joel Rosenberg  f  4676
*Songs of Earth and Power* - Greg Bear  f  424
*Songs of the Dancing Gods* - Jack L. Chalker  f  962
*The Soprano Sorceress* - L.E. Modesitt Jr.  f  3938
*The Spellsong War* - L.E. Modesitt Jr.  f  3939
*Summerland* - L. Dean James  f  2865
*Through the Ice* - Piers Anthony  f  192
*Top Dog* - Jerry Jay Carroll  f  915
*A Two-Edged Sword* - Thomas K. Martin  f  3653
*The Two in Hiding* - Ru Emerson  f  1812
*Typewriter in the Sky* - L. Ron Hubbard  f  2791
*Under the Healing Sign* - Nick O'Donohoe  f  4198
*The Undesired Princess and the Enchanted Bunny* - L. Sprague de Camp  f  1419
*The Unicorn Sonata* - Peter S. Beagle  f  412
*The Whim of the Dragon* - Pamela Dean  f  1447
*Winter Rose* - Patricia A. McKillip  f  3843
*The Witch Doctor* - Christopher Stasheff  f  5228
*The Wiz Biz* - Rick Cook  f  1160
*The Wizardry Consulted* - Rick Cook  f  1161
*The Wizardry Cursed* - Rick Cook  f  1162
*Wizard's Mole* - Brad Strickland  f  5337
*The Woods out Back* - R.A. Salvatore  f  4809

**Fantasy — Anthology**

*After the King: Stories in Honor of J.R.R. Tolkien* - Martin H. Greenberg  f  2378
*Aladdin: Master of the Lamp* - Mike Resnick  f  4534
*Alien Pregnant by Elvis* - Esther Friesner  f  2070
*All Hallow's Eve: Tales of Love and the Supernatural* - Mary Elizabeth Allen  f  75
*Ancient Enchantresses* - Kathleen M. Massie-Ferch  f  3670
*Angels!* - Jack Dann  f  1339
*Arabian Nights: The Marvels and Wonders of the Thousand and One Nights* - Jack Zipes  f  6087
*The Armless Maiden and Other Tales for Childhood's Survivors* - Terri Windling  f  5912
*An Armory of Swords* - Fred Saberhagen  f  4759
*Battle Magic* - Martin H. Greenberg  f  2380
*Beauties, Beasts and Enchantments* - Jack Zipes  f  6088
*Bending the Landscape: Fantasy* - Nicola Griffith  f  2444
*The Best of Marion Zimmer Bradley's Fantasy Magazine* - Marion Zimmer Bradley  f  628

*The Best of Marion Zimmer Bradley's Fantasy Magazine, Volume II* - Marion Zimmer Bradley   f   629
*Betcha Can't Read Just One* - Alan Dean Foster   f   1994
*Black Cats and Broken Mirrors* - Martin H. Greenberg   f   2381
*Black Swan, White Raven* - Ellen Datlow   f   1358
*Black Thorn, White Rose* - Ellen Datlow   f   1359
*Blessings and Curses* - Christopher Stasheff   f   5214
*The Book of Dragons* - Michael Hague   f   2479
*Borderland* - Terri Windling   f   5913
*The Bradbury Chronicles: Stories in Honor of Ray Bradbury* - William F. Nolan   f   4131
*The Camelot Chronicles* - Mike Ashley   f   224
*Camelot Fantastic* - Lawrence Schimel   f   4877
*Catfantastic II* - Andre Norton   f   4143
*Catfantastic III* - Andre Norton   f   4144
*Catfantastic IV* - Andre Norton   f   4145
*Chicks in Chainmail* - Esther Friesner   f   2072
*Christmas Bestiary* - Rosalind M. Greenberg   f   2412
*Christmas Forever* - David G. Hartwell   f   2587
*Christmas Magic* - David G. Hartwell   f   2588
*Chronicles of King Arthur* - Andrea Hopkins   f   2767
*The Complete Fairy Tales of the Brothers Grimm* - Jacob Ludwig Grimm   f   2447
*The Crafters* - Christopher Stasheff   f   5216
*Dark Hours* - Richard Pini   f   4335
*David Copperfield's Beyond Imagination* - David Copperfield   f   1186
*Did You Say Chicks?!* - Esther Friesner   f   2074
*Dinosaur Fantastic* - Mike Resnick   f   4543
*Distant Planes* - Kathy Ice   f   2827
*Dragon Fantastic* - Rosalind M. Greenberg   f   2413
*A Dragon-Lover's Treasury of the Fantastic* - Margaret Weis   f   5710
*Dragons over England* - Douglas Kaufman   f   3015
*Echoes of Valor III* - Karl Edward Wagner   f   5599
*Elf Fantastic* - Martin H. Greenberg   f   2388
*Elvis Rising: Stories on the King* - Kay Sloan   f   5089
*Enchanted Forests* - Katharine Kerr   f   3070
*The Enchanter Reborn* - L. Sprague de Camp   f   1413
*The Essential Bordertown* - Terri Windling   f   5914
*Faeries* - Isaac Asimov   f   235
*The Fantastic Adventures of Robin Hood* - Martin H. Greenberg   f   2389
*Fantastic Alice* - Margaret Weis   f   5713
*The Fantastic Civil War* - Frank D. McSherry Jr.   f   3867
*The Fantasy Hall of Fame* - Robert Silverberg   f   5030
*Forbidden Journeys: Fairy Tales and Fantasies by Victorian Women Writers* - Nina Auerbach   f   276
*Forever After* - Roger Zelazny   f   6066
*Grails: Quests of the Dawn* - Richard Gilliam   f   2231
*Grails: Visitations of the Night* - Richard Gilliam   f   2232
*Halflings, Hobbits, Warrows & Weefolk: A Collection of Tales of Heroes Short in Stature* - Baird Searles   f   4906
*Heaven Sent: 18 Glorious Tales of the Angels* - Peter Crowther   f   1283
*The Horns of Elfland* - Ellen Kushner   f   3264
*Horse Fantastic* - Martin H. Greenberg   f   2397
*Into the Shadows* - Jordan K. Weisman   f   5731
*Legends: Short Novels by the Masters of Modern Fantasy* - Robert Silverberg   f   5034
*Liavek: Festival Week* - Will Shetterly   f   4994
*Life on the Border* - Terri Windling   f   5915
*The Lifted Veil: The Book of Fantastic Literature by Women* - A. Susan Williams   f   5814
*Little People!* - Jack Dann   f   1340
*Lord of the Fantastic: Stories in Honor of Roger Zelazny* - Martin H. Greenberg   f   2398

*A Magic-Lover's Treasury of the Fantastic* - Margaret Weis   f   5721
*The Magic of Christmas* - John Silbersack   f   5024
*The Mammoth Book of Fairy Tales* - Mike Ashley   f   225
*Masterpieces of Fantasy and Wonder* - David G. Hartwell   f   2592
*The Merlin Chronicles* - Mike Ashley   f   227
*Mob Magic* - Brian Thomsen   f   5459
*Modern Classics of Fantasy* - Gardner Dozois   f   1613
*Mysterious Cairo* - Ed Stark   f   5210
*Olympus* - Martin H. Greenberg   f   2404
*On Crusade* - Katherine Kurtz   f   3260
*Once upon a Time: A Treasury of Modern Fairy Tales* - Lester Del Rey   f   1479
*Orphans of the Night* - Josepha Sherman   f   4988
*The Outspoken Princess and the Gentle Knight* - Jack Zipes   f   6089
*The Oxford Book of Fantasy Stories* - Tom Shippey   f   5003
*The Oxford Book of Modern Fairy Tales* - Alison Lurie   f   3574
*The Penguin Book of Modern Fantasy by Women* - A. Susan Williams   f   5815
*Peter S. Beagle's Immortal Unicorn* - Peter S. Beagle   f   410
*Politically Correct Bedtime Stories* - James Finn Garner   f   2145
*Pulphouse, Issue 6: Fantasy* - Kristine Kathryn Rusch   f   4723
*Pulphouse, Issue 10: Special Issue* - Kristine Kathryn Rusch   f   4720
*The Random House Book of Fantasy Stories* - Mike Ashley   f   228
*Rath and Storm* - Peter Archer   f   207
*Relics and Omens* - Margaret Weis   f   5723
*Return to Avalon: A Celebration of Marion Zimmer Bradley* - Jennifer Roberson   f   4610
*Ruby Slippers, Golden Tears* - Ellen Datlow   f   1366
*The Sandman: Book of Dreams* - Neil Gaiman   f   2105
*The Secret Weavers: Stories of the Fantastic by Latin American Women* - Marjorie Agosin   f   43
*The Shimmering Door* - Katharine Kerr   f   3076
*Sisters in Fantasy 2* - Susan Shwartz   f   5018
*Smart Dragons, Foolish Elves* - Alan Dean Foster   f   2014
*Snow White, Blood Red* - Ellen Datlow   f   1368
*Spells of Enchantment* - Jack Zipes   f   6090
*Strange Dreams* - Stephen R. Donaldson   f   1576
*Strange Tales From the Nile Empire* - Greg Farshtey   f   1889
*Superheroes* - John Varley   f   5567
*Sword and Sorceress VIII* - Marion Zimmer Bradley   f   646
*Sword and Sorceress IX* - Marion Zimmer Bradley   f   647
*Sword and Sorceress XI* - Marion Zimmer Bradley   f   648
*Sword and Sorceress XII* - Marion Zimmer Bradley   f   649
*Sword and Sorceress XIII* - Marion Zimmer Bradley   f   650
*Sword and Sorceress XIV* - Marion Zimmer Bradley   f   651
*Sword of Ice and Other Tales of Valdemar* - Mercedes Lackey   f   3300
*Swords of the Rainbow* - Eric Garber   f   2117
*Tales From Tethedril* - Scott Siegel   f   5022
*Tales From the Great Turtle* - Piers Anthony   f   190
*Tales of Talislanta* - Stephen Michael Sechi   f   4909
*Tales of the White Wolf* - Edward E. Kramer   f   3227
*Tarot Fantastic* - Martin H. Greenberg   f   2406
*Tarot Tales* - Rachel Pollack   f   4359
*Testament of the Dragon* - Margaret Weis   f   5729
*Things Invisible to See: Gay and Lesbian Tales of Magic Realism* - Lawrence Schimel   f   4882

*Towers of Darkover* - Marion Zimmer Bradley   f   653
*Treasures of Fantasy* - Margaret Weis   f   5730
*The Ultimate Dragon* - Byron Preiss   f   4408
*Unicorns II* - Jack Dann   f   1343
*Visions & Imaginings: Classic Fantasy Fiction* - Robert H. Boyer   f   606
*Warrior Princesses* - Elizabeth Ann Scarborough   f   4871
*Warriors of Blood and Dream* - Roger Zelazny   f   6075
*Weird Tales From Shakespeare* - Katharine Kerr   f   3079
*The Williamson Effect* - Roger Zelazny   f   6077
*A Wizard's Dozen* - Michael Stearns   f   5239
*Xanadu* - Jane Yolen   f   6044
*Xanadu 2* - Jane Yolen   f   6045
*Xanadu 3* - Jane Yolen   f   6046
*The Year's Best Fantasy and Horror: Fourth Annual Collection* - Ellen Datlow   f   1373

**Fantasy — Collection**

*Aesop's Fables* - Aesop   f   40
*Angels & Visitations: A Miscellany* - Neil Gaiman   f   2101
*Antiquities* - John Crowley   f   1276
*The Arbitrary Placement of Walls* - Martha Soukup   f   5165
*The Armies of Elfland* - Poul Anderson   f   124
*At the City Limits of Fate* - Michael Bishop   f   497
*Bear's Fantasies* - Greg Bear   f   415
*Beyond the Wall of Sleep* - R. Andrew Heidel   f   2641
*The Bone Forest* - Robert Holdstock   f   2736
*Book of Enchantments* - Patricia C. Wrede   f   5973
*The Book of the Beast* - Tanith Lee   f   3405
*Common Clay: 20 Odd Stories* - Brian W. Aldiss   f   54
*The Complete Pegana* - Lord Dunsany   f   1699
*The Cornish Trilogy* - Robertson Davies   f   1397
*The Discovery of Dragons* - Graeme Base   f   385
*The Djinn in the Nightingale's Eye* - A.S. Byatt   f   794
*Double Feature* - Emma Bull   f   767
*The Dragon Path: Collected Tales of Kenneth Morris* - Kenneth Morris   f   4021
*Dreams Underfoot* - Charles de Lint   f   1425
*Everard's Ride* - Diana Wynne Jones   f   2947
*Fabulous Harbors* - Michael Moorcock   f   3981
*The Fairy Tales of Hermann Hesse* - Hermann Hesse   f   2680
*Farewell to Lankhmar* - Fritz Leiber   f   3418
*Feminist Fairy Tales* - Barbara G. Walker   f   5617
*Fiddler Fair* - Mercedes Lackey   f   3279
*Fractured Fairy Tales* - A.J. Jacobs   f   2845
*Giant Bones* - Peter S. Beagle   f   408
*The Girl with the Green Ear: Stories about Magic in Nature* - Margaret Mahy   f   3610
*The Goblin Companion* - Terry Jones   f   2980
*Good Bones and Simple Murders* - Margaret Atwood   f   274
*Good Faeries, Bad Faeries* - Brian Froud   f   2088
*The Hashish Man and Other Stories by Lord Dunsany* - Lord Dunsany   f   1700
*Hedgework and Guessery* - Charles de Lint   f   1428
*Her Stories* - Virginia Hamilton   f   2528
*Here There Be Angels* - Jane Yolen   f   6031
*Here There Be Dragons* - Jane Yolen   f   6032
*Here There Be Unicorns* - Jane Yolen   f   6033
*Here There Be Witches* - Jane Yolen   f   6034
*Italian Folktales* - Italo Calvino   f   849
*It's Been Fun* - Esther Friesner   f   2078
*The Ivory and the Horn* - Charles de Lint   f   1431
*Kipling's Fantasy* - Rudyard Kipling   f   3147
*Kissing the Witch: Old Tales in New Skins* - Emma Donoghue   f   1578

*A Knot in the Grain and Other Stories* - Robin McKinley  f  3845

*Ladies: Retold Tales of Goddesses and Heroines* - Doris Vallejo  f  5533

*The Lady or the Tiger and Other Stories* - Frank Stockton  f  5310

*Last Summer at Mars Hill* - Elizabeth Hand  f  2537

*Lean Times in Lankhmar* - Fritz Leiber  f  3420

*Legally Correct Fairy Tales* - David Fisher  f  1942

*Lunching with the Antichrist* - Michael Moorcock  f  3984

*Mad Amos* - Alan Dean Foster  f  2009

*Magic: The Final Fantasy Collection* - Isaac Asimov  f  244

*Maureen Birnbaum, Barbarian Swordsperson: The Complete Stories* - George Alec Effinger  f  1752

*Mind Fields: The Art of Jacek Yerka* - Harlan Ellison  f  1787

*Mrs. Vargas and the Dead Naturalist* - Kathleen Alcala  f  51

*The Night We Buried Road Dog* - Jack Cady  f  819

*The Notorious Abbess* - Vera Chapman  f  965

*Oathblood* - Mercedes Lackey  f  3290

*Old Nathan* - David Drake  f  1639

*Once upon a Galaxy* - Josepha Sherman  f  4987

*Once upon a More Enlightened Time: More Politically Correct Bedtime Stories* - James Finn Garner  f  2144

*Politically Correct Holiday Stories: For an Enlightened Yuletide Season* - James Finn Garner  f  2146

*Return to Lankhmar* - Fritz Leiber  f  3422

*Revenge of the Christmas Box* - Cathy Crimmins  f  1257

*The Rhinoceros Who Quoted Nietzsche and Other Odd Acquaintances* - Peter S. Beagle  f  411

*The Rivan Codex* - David Eddings  f  1735

*A Romance of the Equator: The Best Fantasy Stories of Brian W. Aldiss* - Brian W. Aldiss  f  59

*Sauron Defeated* - J.R.R. Tolkien  f  5480

*The Second Generation* - Margaret Weis  f  5724

*Shape-Shifter: Stories by Pauline Melville* - Pauline Melville  f  3876

*Smoke and Mirrors* - Neil Gaiman  f  2106

*Spires of Spirit* - Gael Baudino  f  395

*Spiritwalk* - Charles de Lint  f  1436

*State of Grace* - Kate Wilhelm  f  5810

*Storeys From the Old Hotel* - Gene Wolfe  f  5945

*Strange Stains and Mysterious Smells* - Terry Jones  f  2982

*Tales From the Brothers Grimm and the Sisters Weird* - Vivian Vande Velde  f  5557

*Tales From Watership Down* - Richard Adams  f  32

*Tales of Mithgar* - Dennis L. McKiernan  f  3836

*Tales of Zothique* - Clark Ashton Smith  f  5104

*A Tall Story and Other Tales* - Margaret Mahy  f  3611

*That Way Lies Camelot* - Janny Wurts  f  6005

*Tongues of Jade* - Laurence Yep  f  6026

*Touching the Fire* - Roger Welsch  f  5751

*Travelers in Magic* - Lisa Goldstein  f  2265

*Twelve Impossible Things Before Breakfast* - Jane Yolen  f  6040

*Unconquered Countries: Four Novellas* - Geoff Ryman  f  4757

*Unlocking the Air and Other Stories* - Ursula K. Le Guin  f  3384

*The World of Robert Jordan's The Wheel of Time* - Robert Jordan  f  2991


## Fantasy — Contemporary

*The Abraxas Marvel Circus* - Stephen Leigh  f  3423

*The Adept* - Katherine Kurtz  f  3254

*Afterimage* - Kristine Kathryn Rusch  f  4709

*Amnesia Moon* - Jonathan Lethem  f  3438

*And Eternity* - Piers Anthony  f  162

*Angel Light* - Andrew M. Greeley  f  2342

*The Art of Arrow Cutting* - Stephen Dedman  f  1462

*At Sword's Point* - Scott MacMillan  f  3601

*Aunt Maria* - Diana Wynne Jones  f  2943

*Baby Be-Bop* - Francesca Lia Block  f  545

*The Bear Went over the Mountain* - William Kotzwinkle  f  3222

*Bedlam's Bard* - Mercedes Lackey  f  3269

*Being of Two Minds* - Pamela F. Service  f  4918

*Blue Moon* - Hila Feil  f  1898

*Borgel* - Daniel Manus Pinkwater  f  4338

*The Broken Sword* - Molly Cochran  f  1091

*Brown Girl in the Ring* - Nalo Hopkinson  f  2771

*Bureau 13* - Nick Pollotta  f  4362

*Castleview* - Gene Wolfe  f  5939

*Catamount* - Michael Peak  f  4273

*The Caterpillar's Question* - Piers Anthony  f  164

*The Catswold Portal* - Shirley Rousseau Murphy  f  4055

*Changer* - Jane M. Lindskold  f  3474

*Chase the Morning* - Michael Scott Rohan  f  4658

*Cherokee Bat and the Goat Guys* - Francesca Lia Block  f  546

*The Chymical Wedding* - Lindsay Clarke  f  1063

*The Circus of the Earth and Air* - Brooke Stevens  f  5264

*Cloud Castles* - Michael Scott Rohan  f  4659

*Cloven Hooves* - Megan Lindholm  f  3470

*Conglomeros* - Jesse Browner  f  729

*The Cornish Trilogy* - Robertson Davies  f  1397

*Cromm* - Kenneth C. Flint  f  1957

*Crossover* - Bill McCay  f  3768

*Damnbanna* - Nancy Springer  f  5177

*Dark Heart* - Margaret Weis  f  5707

*The Devil and Dan Cooley* - Holly Lisle  f  3480

*Doomsday Exam* - Nick Pollotta  f  4363

*Dragon Moon* - Chris Claremont  f  1040

*Dragon Season* - Michael Cassutt  f  936

*Dreambuilder* - Tom Deitz  f  1471

*Drink Down the Moon* - Charles de Lint  f  1426

*Earthquake Weather* - Tim Powers  f  4382

*Expiration Date* - Tim Powers  f  4383

*Fair Peril* - Nancy Springer  f  5178

*The Famished Road* - Ben Okri  f  4207

*Fish Soup* - Ursula K. Le Guin  f  3378

*The Forever King* - Molly Cochran  f  1092

*Frostwing* - Richard A. Knaak  f  3170

*Full Moonster* - Nick Pollotta  f  4364

*Further Adventures* - Jon Stephen Fink  f  1940

*Galatea in 2-D* - Aaron Allston  f  87

*The Gallery of His Dreams* - Kristine Kathryn Rusch  f  4717

*Gate of Darkness, Circle of Light* - Tanya Huff  f  2797

*The Gates of Noon* - Michael Scott Rohan  f  4661

*Ghostlight* - Marion Zimmer Bradley  f  634

*Ghosts of Wind and Shadow* - Charles de Lint  f  1427

*Gnome Man's Land* - Esther Friesner  f  2075

*Godmother Night* - Rachel Pollack  f  4358

*The Godmother's Web* - Elizabeth Ann Scarborough  f  4864

*The Golden Mean* - Nick Bantock  f  334

*The Gryphon King* - Tom Deitz  f  1473

*Haroun and the Sea of Stories* - Salman Rushdie  f  4731

*The Healer's War* - Elizabeth Ann Scarborough  f  4865

*Hell on High* - Holly Lisle  f  3483

*I Was a Teenage Fairy* - Francesca Lia Block  f  549

*An Impossumble Summer* - Brenda W. Clough  f  1090

*In the Land of Winter* - Richard Grant  f  2326

*Jennifer Murdley's Toad* - Bruce Coville  f  1220

*The Juniper Game* - Sherryl Jordan  f  2992

*Juniper, Gentian and Rosemary* - Pamela Dean  f  1445

*Killobyte* - Piers Anthony  f  179

*King of Morning, Queen of Day* - Ian McDonald  f  3793

*King of the Grey* - Richard A. Knaak  f  3173

*Knight of Ghosts and Shadows* - Mercedes Lackey  f  3285

*Knights of the Blood* - Scott MacMillan  f  3602

*Lady Cottington's Pressed Fairy Book* - Terry Jones  f  2981

*Landscape Painted with Tea* - Milorad Pavic  f  4263

*Larque on the Wing* - Nancy Springer  f  5180

*Last Call* - Tim Powers  f  4384

*The Little Country* - Charles de Lint  f  1432

*Lorien Lost* - Michael King  f  3124

*MagicNet* - John DeChancie  f  1461

*Max Lakeman and the Beautiful Stranger* - Jon Cohen  f  1098

*Memory and Dream* - Charles de Lint  f  1433

*The Mennyms* - Sylvia Waugh  f  5654

*Mennyms Alive* - Sylvia Waugh  f  5655

*Mennyms Under Siege* - Sylvia Waugh  f  5656

*The Mer-Child: A Legend for Children and Other Adults* - Robin Morgan  f  4008

*Metal Angel* - Nancy Springer  f  5181

*The Midnight Horse* - Sid Fleischman  f  1948

*Missing Angel Juan* - Francesca Lia Block  f  550

*Mockingbird* - Sean Stewart  f  5273

*Mojo and the Pickle Jar* - Douglas Bell  f  433

*The Mountain Made of Light* - Edward Myers  f  4062

*Mythology 101* - Jody Lynn Nye  f  4173

*Mythology Abroad* - Jody Lynn Nye  f  4174

*Neverwhere* - Neil Gaiman  f  2104

*Nothing Sacred* - Elizabeth Ann Scarborough  f  4867

*The Ogre Downstairs* - Diana Wynne Jones  f  2949

*One Foot in the Grave* - Wm. Mark Simmons  f  5062

*Our Lady of the Harbour* - Charles de Lint  f  1434

*Outside the Dog Museum* - Jonathan Carroll  f  919

*The Paper Grail* - James P. Blaylock  f  522

*Prophets for the End of Time* - Marcos Donnelly  f  1577

*The Rebirth of Wonder* - Lawrence Watt-Evans  t  5646

*Red Orc's Rage* - Philip Jose Farmer  f  1873

*Resurrection Man* - Sean Stewart  f  5277

*Running with the Demon* - Terry Brooks  f  715

*Sabine's Notebook* - Nick Bantock  f  335

*The Samurai Wizard* - Simon Hawke  f  2623

*The Scathach and the Maeve's Daughter* - Mary Alexander Walker  f  5618

*Senor Vivo and the Coca Lord* - Louis de Bernieres  f  1411

*Shadows on the Hill* - Jackie Cassada  f  935

*Shoebag* - Mary James  f  2868

*The Silent Strength of Stones* - Nina Kiriki Hoffman  f  2716

*Skinny Legs and All* - Tom Robbins  f  4607

*Slow Funeral* - Rebecca Ore  f  4221

*Smoke and Mirrors* - Neil Gaiman  f  2106

*Someplace to Be Flying* - Charles de Lint  f  1435

*Something Rich and Strange* - Patricia A. McKillip  f  3840

*Son of Darkness* - Josepha Sherman  f  4990

*Songs of Enchantment* - Ben Okri  f  4208

*Soulsmith* - Tom Deitz  f  1475

*Sphynxes Wild* - Esther Friesner  f  2083

*The Spider #3: Death's Crimson Juggernaut/The Red Death Rain* - Grant Stockbridge  f  5307

*The Spider #4: Death Reign of the Vampire King/The Pain Emperor* - Grant Stockbridge  f  5308

*The Spider #8: The Devil's Paymaster/Legions of the Accursed Light* - Grant Stockbridge  f  5309

*Spirit Crossings* - Claudia Peck  f  4275

*The Starry Child* - Lynn Hanna  f  2540

*Stoneskin's Revenge* - Tom Deitz  f  1476

*Strum Again?* - Elizabeth Ann Scarborough  f  4870

*Sunshaker's War* - Tom Deitz  f  1477

*Sympathy for the Devil* - Holly Lisle  f  3488
*Temporary Agency* - Rachel Pollack  f  4360
*That's All, Folks!* - Greg Snow  f  5148
*The Thread That Binds the Bones* - Nina Kiriki Hoffman  f  2717
*Till the End of Time* - Allen Appel  f  201
*Time and Chance* - Alan Brennert  f  676
*The Time of the Ghost* - Diana Wynne Jones  f  2951
*Trader* - Charles de Lint  f  1438
*Troll-Taken* - Rose Estes  f  1842
*The Venetian's Wife: A Strangely Sensual Tale of a Renaissance Explorer, a Computer, and a Metamorphosis* - Nick Bantock  f  336
*Visitors From Oz: The Wild Adventures of Dorothy, the Scarecrow and the Tin Woodman* - Martin Gardner  f  2136
*Walker of Worlds* - Tom De Haven  f  1423
*Walking the Labyrinth* - Lisa Goldstein  f  2266
*Was* - Geoff Ryman  f  4758
*Whirlwind* - Charles L. Grant  f  2320
*White Horse, Dark Dragon* - Robert C. Fleet  f  1947
*The Wild Wood* - Charles de Lint  f  1440
*The Wishing Well* - Charles de Lint  f  1441
*Witch* - Christopher Pike  f  4334
*Witch Baby* - Francesca Lia Block  f  552
*The Witch of Maple Park* - Stephanie S. Tolan  f  5478
*Witchlight* - Marion Zimmer Bradley  f  655
*The Wizard of Sunset Strip* - Simon Hawke  f  2629
*The Wood Wife* - Terri Windling  f  5916
*Wordwright* - Tom Deitz  f  1478
*Zeus and Co.* - David Lee Jones  f  2942

## Fantasy — Contemporary Realism

*All the Bells on Earth* - James P. Blaylock  f  518
*Bagatelle—Guinevere* - Nancy Bogen  f  558
*A Blessing on the Moon* - Joseph Skibell  f  5079
*Cat's Paw* - L.A. Taylor  f  5409
*Cats Raise the Dead* - Shirley Rousseau Murphy  f  4054
*Come Before Christ and Murder Love* - Stewart Home  f  2754
*Dogland* - Will Shetterly  f  4992
*Einstein's Dreams* - Alan Lightman  f  3459
*The Element of Fire* - Jason Henderson  f  2657
*Flickering Shadows* - Kwadwo Agymah Kamau  f  3006
*Flying Saucers over Hennepin* - Peter Gelman  f  2186
*The Forgetting Room* - Nick Bantock  f  333
*The Grass Dancer* - Susan Power  f  4380
*The Hanged Man* - Francesca Lia Block  f  548
*Heartlight* - Marion Zimmer Bradley  f  637
*How Like a God* - Brenda W. Clough  f  1089
*In the Rift* - Marion Zimmer Bradley  f  639
*Iron Shadows* - Steven Barnes  f  362
*Jacob's Hands* - Aldous Huxley  f  2817
*Last Summer at Mars Hill* - Elizabeth Hand  f  2537
*Lost Boys* - Orson Scott Card  f  891
*Love & Sleep* - John Crowley  f  1277
*Lunatics* - Bradley Denton  f  1491
*Meeting the Minotaur* - Carol Dawson  f  1409
*The Moon's Wife: A Hystery* - A.A. Attanasio  f  271
*The Moorchild* - Eloise Jarvis McGraw  f  3816
*The Night We Buried Road Dog* - Jack Cady  f  819
*The Off Season* - Jack Cady  f  820
*On Meeting Witches at Wells* - Judith Gorog  f  2283
*Renaissance Moon* - Linda Nevins  f  4093
*The Seventh Heart* - Marina Fitch  f  1943
*Shangri-La: The Return to the World of Lost Horizon* - Eleanor Cooney  f  1169
*The Sweetheart Season* - Karen Joy Fowler  f  2029

*The Thirteenth Daughter of the Moon* - Steven Nightingale  f  4104
*The Tooth Fairy* - Graham Joyce  f  2995
*Unlocking the Air and Other Stories* - Ursula K. Le Guin  f  3384

## Fantasy — Family Saga

*Mockingbird* - Sean Stewart  f  5273

## Fantasy — Historical

*Alvin Journeyman* - Orson Scott Card  f  881
*The Animal Wife* - Elizabeth Marshall Thomas  f  5444
*Arc d'X* - Steve Erickson  f  1835
*The Architecture of Desire* - Mary Gentle  f  2195
*Ars Magica* - Judith Tarr  f  5392
*Believe: A Novel* - William Shatner  f  4929
*Between the Rivers* - Harry Turtledove  f  5496
*Bhagavati* - Kara Dalkey  f  1316
*Bijapur* - Kara Dalkey  f  1317
*Blood: A Southern Fantasy* - Michael Moorcock  f  3977
*The Book of the Beast* - Tanith Lee  f  3405
*Branch and Crown* - Gael Baudino  f  389
*The Chalchiuhite Dragon* - Kenneth Morris  f  4020
*Changeweaver* - Margaret Ball  f  313
*Child of the Eagle* - Esther Friesner  f  2073
*Child of the Journey* - Janet Berliner  f  466
*Child of the Light* - Janet Gluckman  f  2244
*Children of the Dusk* - Janet Berliner  f  467
*The Chymical Wedding* - Lindsay Clarke  f  1063
*Crusade* - James Lowder  f  3537
*Dancing Bears* - Fred Saberhagen  f  4764
*Dark Prince* - David Gemmell  f  2187
*The Deepest Sea* - Charles Barnitz  f  363
*Demon Knight* - Ken Hood  f  2760
*Devil's Engine* - Mark Sumner  f  5356
*Dinotopia* - James Gurney  f  2468
*Distant Dreams* - Jenny Lykins  f  3576
*The Dog King* - Christoph Ransmayr  f  4474
*Druids* - Morgan Llywelyn  f  3502
*The Duke of Sumava* - Sara J. Wrench  f  5983
*The Edge of the World* - William Sarabande  f  4817
*The Eight* - Katherine Neville  f  4092
*Elvis Rising: Stories on the King* - Kay Sloan  f  5089
*The Fabulist* - John Vornholt  f  5595
*The Fantastic Civil War* - Frank D. McSherry Jr.  f  3867
*Feathered Dragon* - Douglas Niles  f  4108
*The Fire Queen* - Jack Holland  f  2740
*The Forest House* - Marion Zimmer Bradley  f  633
*Freedom & Necessity* - Steven Brust  f  743
*From Prussia with Love* - John DeChancie  f  1457
*The Gallery of His Dreams* - Kristine Kathryn Rusch  f  4717
*Gatherer of Clouds* - Sean Russell  f  4741
*Goatsong* - Tom Holt  f  2751
*The Golden Compass* - Philip Pullman  f  4446
*Hammer and Anvil* - Harry Turtledove  f  5503
*The Hammer and the Cross* - Harry Harrison  f  2570
*Heartfire* - Orson Scott Card  f  889
*Helen's Passage* - Diana M. Concannon  f  1129
*His Majesty's Elephant* - Judith Tarr  f  5394
*Horselords* - David Cook  f  1145
*Horses of Heaven* - Gillian Bradshaw  f  657
*The Hunter Returns* - David Drake  f  1632
*I, Tituba, Black Witch of Salem* - Maryse Conde  f  1130
*The Ice-Shirt* - William T. Vollmann  f  5580
*Imperial Lady* - Andre Norton  f  4155
*The Innamorati* - Midori Snyder  f  5152
*The Iron Lance* - Stephen R. Lawhead  f  3356
*Isle of Woman* - Piers Anthony  f  178
*Jericho Moon* - Matthew Woodring Stover  f  5321

*King and Emperor* - Harry Harrison  f  2571
*King of the Dead* - R.A. MacAvoy  f  3581
*Kingdom of the Grail* - A.A. Attanasio  f  269
*The Last World* - Christoph Ransmayr  f  4475
*Lens of the World* - R.A. MacAvoy  f  3582
*The Light Bearer* - Donna Gillespie  f  2229
*Lights Out in the Reptile House* - Jim Shepard  f  4976
*Lion of Macedon* - David Gemmell  f  2189
*Lord Kelvin's Machine* - James P. Blaylock  f  520
*Lord of the Two Lands* - Judith Tarr  f  5395
*The Mata Hari Adventure* - James Luceno  f  3544
*Maze of Moonlight* - Gael Baudino  f  393
*The Moon and the Sun* - Vonda N. McIntyre  f  3822
*Mother Earth, Father Sky* - Sue Harrison  f  2581
*My Sister the Moon* - Sue Harrison  f  2582
*Nadya: The Wolf Chronicles* - Pat Murphy  f  4052
*Nature's God* - Robert Anton Wilson  f  5903
*O Greenest Branch!* - Gael Baudino  f  394
*A Once and Future Love* - Anne Kelleher  f  3039
*Pasquale's Angel* - Paul J. McAuley  f  3714
*People of the Earth* - W. Michael Gear  f  2166
*People of the Fire* - W. Michael Gear  f  2167
*People of the Lakes* - Kathleen O'Neal Gear  f  2164
*People of the Mesa* - Ardath Mayhar  f  3704
*People of the River* - W. Michael Gear  f  2168
*People of the Sea* - W. Michael Gear  f  2169
*People of the Wolf* - W. Michael Gear  f  2170
*Photographing Fairies* - Steve Szilagyi  f  5379
*The Plains of Passage* - Jean M. Auel  f  275
*The Porcelain Dove* - Delia Sherman  f  4983
*The Princess and the Dragon* - Roberto Pazzi  f  4272
*Rehearsal for a Renaissance* - Douglas W. Clark  f  1045
*The Reign of the Brown Magician* - Lawrence Watt-Evans  f  5647
*Robin and the King* - Parke Godwin  f  2247
*The Sacred Stones* - William Sarabande  f  4818
*Sexing the Cherry* - Jeanette Winterson  f  5927
*Shadow of the Seventh Moon* - Nancy Varian Berberick  f  459
*Shaman* - Robert Shea  f  4946
*The Sheriff of Nottingham* - Richard Kluger  f  3165
*The Shining Company* - Rosemary Sutcliff  f  5359
*Shiva Accused: An Adventure of the Ice Age* - J.H. Brennan  f  667
*Shiva: An Adventure of the Ice Age* - J.H. Brennan  f  669
*Shiva's Challenge: An Adventure of the Ice Age* - J.H. Brennan  f  668
*A Song for Arbonne* - Guy Gavriel Kay  f  3017
*Spell Bound* - Ru Emerson  f  1810
*The Spiral Dance* - R. Garcia y Robertson  f  2121
*Spirits of the Ordinary* - Kathleen Alcala  f  52
*Strange Devices of the Sun and Moon* - Lisa Goldstein  f  2262
*The Subtle Knife* - Philip Pullman  f  4448
*Tam Lin* - Pamela Dean  f  1446
*Tatham Mound* - Piers Anthony  f  191
*Thessalonica* - Harry Turtledove  f  5511
*Thunder in the Sky* - William Sarabande  f  4819
*A Tie to the Past* - David Wiseman  f  5928
*The Time Tree* - Enid Richemont  f  4585
*Two Crowns for America* - Katherine Kurtz  f  3262
*Walford's Oak* - Jill M. Phillips  f  4310
*The Walled Orchard* - Tom Holt  f  2752
*Was* - Geoff Ryman  f  4758
*The Winter King* - Bernard Cornwell  f  1191
*The Wolf and the Crown* - A.A. Attanasio  f  273
*The Wolf and the Raven* - Diana L. Paxson  f  4270
*The Woman Who Loved Reindeer* - Meredith Ann Pierce  f  4320
*The World Beneath* - James Gurney  f  2469
*Yesterday We Saw Mermaids* - Esther Friesner  f  2086

## Fantasy — Horror

Agyar - Steven Brust  f  738
Apocalypse - Nancy Springer  f  5176
At Sword's Point - Scott MacMillan  f  3601
Black Sun Rising - C.S. Friedman  f  2056
Blood and Honor - Simon R. Green  f  2361
Blood of the Goddess - Kara Dalkey  f  1318
Bride of the Rat God - Barbara Hambly  f  2499
Caliban's Hour - Tad Williams  f  5826
Children of the Blood: Book Two of The Sundered -
   Michelle Sagara  f  4782
The Devouring Void - Mark E. Rogers  f  4653
Drachenfels - Jack Yeovil  f  6022
The Flight of Michael McBride - Midori
   Snyder  f  5151
Ill Met in Lankhmar - Fritz Leiber  f  3419
Knights of the Blood - Scott MacMillan  f  3602
Last Call - Tim Powers  f  4384
The Laughing Corpse - Laurell K. Hamilton  f  2519
Memory and Dream - Charles de Lint  f  1433
Mind Fields: The Art of Jacek Yerka - Harlan
   Ellison  f  1787
Painted Devil - Michael Bedard  f  430
Plague Demon - Brian Craig  f  1239
The Silver Kiss - Annette Curtis Klause  f  3163
Spirit Crossings - Claudia Peck  f  4275
Storm Knights - Bill Slavicsek  f  5087
Storm Warriors - Brian Craig  f  1240
The Tooth Fairy - Graham Joyce  f  2995
The Year's Best Fantasy and Horror: Fourth Annual
   Collection - Ellen Datlow  f  1373
Zaragoz - Brian Craig  f  1241

## Fantasy — Humor

Black as Blood - Rob Chilson  f  1014
Gojiro - Mark Jacobson  f  2847
Hogfather - Terry Pratchett  f  4391
Jingo - Terry Pratchett  f  4393
The King - Donald Barthelme  f  375
Prophets for the End of Time - Marcos
   Donnelly  f  1577

## Fantasy — Legend

The Adventures of King Midas - Lynne Reid
   Banks  f  329
Aesop's Fables - Aesop  f  40
Aladdin: Master of the Lamp - Mike
   Resnick  f  4534
Arabian Nights: The Marvels and Wonders of the
   Thousand and One Nights - Jack Zipes  f  6087
Arthur - Stephen R. Lawhead  f  3352
Arthur War Lord - Dafydd ab Hugh  f  6
Attila's Treasure - Stephan Grundy  f  2453
The Autobiography of Santa Claus: It's Better to Give
   - Jeff Guinn  f  2456
A Bad Day for Ali Baba - Craig Shaw
   Gardner  f  2123
Balyet - Patricia Wrightson  f  5995
Beauties, Beasts and Enchantments - Jack
   Zipes  f  6088
Beauty - Sheri S. Tepper  f  5428
Beyond Ragnarok - Mickey Zucker Reichert  f  4516
Black Horses for the King - Anne
   McCaffrey  f  3720
Black Swan, White Raven - Ellen Datlow  f  1358
Black Thorn, White Rose - Ellen Datlow  f  1359
The Book of Brendan - Ann Curry  f  1294
Briar Rose - Jane Yolen  f  6029
Bring Me the Head of Prince Charming - Roger
   Zelazny  f  6062
The Broken Sword - Molly Cochran  f  1091
Bronze Mirror - Jeanne Larsen  f  3338
By the Sword - Timothy Boggs  f  559
Caliban's Hour - Tad Williams  f  5826
Cambio Bay - Kate Wilhelm  f  5806
The Camelot Chronicles - Mike Ashley  f  224

Carol for Another Christmas - Elizabeth Ann
   Scarborough  f  4861
The Chalchiuhite Dragon - Kenneth Morris  f  4020
Changeling - Christopher Kubasik  f  3245
Charlemagne's Champion - Gail Van Asten  f  5534
Chernevog - C.J. Cherryh  f  982
Child of an Ancient City - Tad Williams  f  5827
Child of the Eagle - Esther Friesner  f  2073
The Child Queen - Nancy McKenzie  f  3827
Chronicles of King Arthur - Andrea
   Hopkins  f  2767
Cloven Hooves - Megan Lindholm  f  3470
The Coachman Rat - David Henry Wilson  f  5879
The Complete Fairy Tales of the Brothers Grimm -
   Jacob Ludwig Grimm  f  2447
Crow and Weasel - Barry Lopez  f  3523
Dark Legend - Jamake Highwater  f  2686
Dawn Land - Joseph Bruchac  f  731
Dead Voices: Natural Agonies in the Real World -
   Gerald Vizenor  f  5578
Deerskin - Robin McKinley  f  3844
The Discovery of Dragons - Graeme Base  f  385
A Diversity of Dragons - Anne McCaffrey  f  3728
The Djinn in the Nightingale's Eye - A.S.
   Byatt  f  794
A Dozen Tough Jobs - Howard Waldrop  f  5612
The Dragon and the Unicorn - A.A.
   Attanasio  f  266
Dragon Fantastic - Rosalind M. Greenberg  f  2413
Dragonrank Master - Mickey Zucker
   Reichert  f  4519
The Dragon's Boy - Jane Yolen  f  6030
The Dragon's Carbuncle - Elizabeth H.
   Boyer  f  605
The Dragons of the Rhine - Diana L.
   Paxson  f  4264
Dragons over England - Douglas Kaufman  f  3015
The Eagle and the Sword - A.A. Attanasio  f  267
The Eagles' Brood - Jack Whyte  f  5792
Elf Fantastic - Martin H. Greenberg  f  2388
The Empty Throne - Ru Emerson  f  1808
The Enchanted Isles - Casey Flynn  f  1960
Enemy of God - Bernard Cornwell  f  1189
Eric - Terry Pratchett  f  4388
Excalibur - Bernard Cornwell  f  1190
Fair Peril - Nancy Springer  f  5178
The Famished Road - Ben Okri  f  4207
The Fantastic Adventures of Robin Hood - Martin H.
   Greenberg  f  2389
Feminist Fairy Tales - Barbara G. Walker  f  5617
Finn Mac Cool - Morgan Llywelyn  f  3504
Firebird - Mercedes Lackey  f  3281
The Fires of Merlin - T.A. Barron  f  369
The First Casualty - David L. Seidman  f  4912
Flying Dutch - Tom Holt  f  2750
Forbidden Journeys: Fairy Tales and Fantasies by
   Victorian Women Writers - Nina Auerbach  f  276
The Forever King - Molly Cochran  f  1092
Fractured Fairy Tales - A.J. Jacobs  f  2845
Gawain and Lady Green - Anne Eliot
   Crompton  f  1269
Ghost King - David Gemmell  f  2188
The Goblin Companion - Terry Jones  f  2980
Godmother Night - Rachel Pollack  f  4358
The Godmother's Apprentice - Elizabeth Ann
   Scarborough  f  4863
Good Faeries, Bad Faeries - Brian Froud  f  2088
Grail - Stephen R. Lawhead  f  3355
The Grail of Hearts - Susan Shwartz  f  5015
Grails: Quests of the Dawn - Richard
   Gilliam  f  2231
Grails: Visitations of the Night - Richard
   Gilliam  f  2232
Guinevere: The Legend in Autumn - Persia
   Woolley  f  5970
The Heavenward Path - Kara Dalkey  f  1319
Her Stories - Virginia Hamilton  f  2528
Here There Be Unicorns - Jane Yolen  f  6033
Hunter of the Light - Risa Aratyr  f  203

If at Faust You Don't Succeed - Roger
   Zelazny  f  6070
In the Shadow of the Oak King - Courtway
   Jones  f  2939
Indiana Jones and the Genesis Deluge - Rob
   MacGregor  f  3589
The Innamorati - Midori Snyder  f  5152
The Island of the Mighty - Evangeline
   Walton  f  5626
The Isles of the Blest - Morgan Llywelyn  f  3505
Italian Folktales - Italo Calvino  f  849
The Jigsaw Woman - Kim Antieau  f  199
The King - Donald Barthelme  f  375
Kingdom of the Grail - A.A. Attanasio  f  269
The Kingmaking - Helen Hollick  f  2745
Kissing the Witch: Old Tales in New Skins - Emma
   Donoghue  f  1578
Ladies: Retold Tales of Goddesses and Heroines -
   Doris Vallejo  f  5533
Lady of Avalon - Marion Zimmer Bradley  f  640
Lady of the Forest - Jennifer Roberson  f  4609
The Lady or the Tiger and Other Stories - Frank
   Stockton  f  5310
The Last Arabian Night - Craig Shaw
   Gardner  f  2129
The Last Pendragon - Robert Rice  f  4584
The Last Voyage of Somebody the Sailor - John
   Barth  f  374
Legally Correct Fairy Tales - David Fisher  f  1942
Letters From Atlantis - Robert Silverberg  f  5035
The Little Country - Charles de Lint  f  1432
Little Sister - Kara Dalkey  f  1320
Lord of Sunset - Parke Godwin  f  2246
The Lost History of Redwyn - William Jay  f  2883
The Lost Years of Merlin - T.A. Barron  f  370
Madoc's Hundred - Pat Winter  f  5925
The Mammoth Book of Fairy Tales - Mike
   Ashley  f  225
The Mask of Loki - Roger Zelazny  f  6071
Master of Earth and Water - Diana L.
   Paxson  f  4266
Meeting the Minotaur - Carol Dawson  f  1409
The Mer-Child: A Legend for Children and Other
   Adults - Robin Morgan  f  4008
Merlin - Jane Yolen  f  6035
Merlin and the Dragons - Jane Yolen  f  6036
The Merlin Chronicles - Mike Ashley  f  227
Merlin's Bones - Fred Saberhagen  f  4771
Merlin's Harp - Anne Eliot Crompton  f  1270
Mordred's Curse - Ian McDowell  f  3806
Most Ancient Song - Casey Flynn  f  1961
My Sister the Moon - Sue Harrison  f  2582
Nadya: The Wolf Chronicles - Pat Murphy  f  4052
Nutcracker - E.T.A. Hoffmann  f  2719
Once upon a Galaxy - Josepha Sherman  f  4987
Once upon a More Enlightened Time: More Politically
   Correct Bedtime Stories - James Finn
   Garner  f  2144
Once upon a Time: A Treasury of Modern Fairy Tales
   - Lester Del Rey  f  1479
The Other Sinbad - Craig Shaw Gardner  f  2130
Our Lady of the Harbour - Charles de Lint  f  1434
The Outlaws of Sherwood - Robin
   McKinley  f  3846
The Oxford Book of Modern Fairy Tales - Alison
   Lurie  f  3574
The Painted Alphabet - Diana Darling  f  1356
Parsifal - Peter Vansittart  f  5560
Passager - Jane Yolen  f  6038
Pendragon's Banner - Helen Hollick  f  2746
Peter S. Beagle's Immortal Unicorn - Peter S.
   Beagle  f  410
Phoenix Fire - Elizabeth Forrest  f  1974
Politically Correct Bedtime Stories - James Finn
   Garner  f  2145
Politically Correct Holiday Stories: For an
   Enlightened Yuletide Season - James Finn
   Garner  f  2146
Pride of Lions - Morgan Llywelyn  f  3506

*The Prince and the Pilgrim* - Mary Stewart   f   5270
*Prince of Demons* - Mickey Zucker
  Reichert   f   4522
*Queen of the Summer Stars* - Persia
  Woolley   f   5971
*Quest for a Maid* - Frances Mary Hendry   f   2662
*Quest for Apollo* - Michael Lahey   f   3309
*The Raid* - Randy Lee Eickhoff   f   1764
*Return to Avalon: A Celebration of Marion Zimmer
  Bradley* - Jennifer Roberson   f   4610
*Rhinegold* - Stephan Grundy   f   2454
*Robin and the King* - Parke Godwin   f   2247
*Rose Daughter* - Robin McKinley   f   3847
*Ruby Slippers, Golden Tears* - Ellen Datlow   f   1366
*Rusalka* - C.J. Cherryh   f   1002
*Santa's Twin* - Dean R. Koontz   f   3214
*The Saxon Shore* - Jack Whyte   f   5793
*The Scathach and the Maeve's Daughter* - Mary
  Alexander Walker   f   5618
*The Seven Songs of Merlin* - T.A. Barron   f   372
*Shadow of the King* - Helen Hollick   f   2747
*The Sheriff of Nottingham* - Richard Kluger   f   3165
*Sherwood* - Parke Godwin   f   2248
*The Shield between the Worlds* - Diana L.
  Paxson   f   4267
*The Shining Company* - Rosemary Sutcliff   f   5359
*The Silver Hand* - Stephen R. Lawhead   f   3358
*The Sixth Book of Lost Swords: Mindsword's Story* -
  Fred Saberhagen   f   4776
*The Skystone* - Jack Whyte   f   5794
*Sleipnir* - Linda Evans   f   1856
*Snow White and Rose Red* - Patricia C.
  Wrede   f   5981
*Snow White, Blood Red* - Ellen Datlow   f   1368
*Soldier of Arete* - Gene Wolfe   f   5944
*Song in the Silence* - Elizabeth Kerner   f   3065
*Songs of Enchantment* - Ben Okri   f   4208
*Sons of the Titans* - Patrick H. Adkins   f   36
*Spells of Enchantment* - Jack Zipes   f   6090
*Spring-Heeled Jack* - Philip Pullman   f   4447
*Storm Caller* - Carol Severance   f   4924
*Suisan* - Phyllis Carol Agins   f   42
*Sword of Fire and Shadow* - Diana L.
  Paxson   f   4268
*Tales From the Brothers Grimm and the Sisters Weird*
  - Vivian Vande Velde   f   5557
*Tales From the Great Turtle* - Piers Anthony   f   190
*Tam Lin* - Pamela Dean   f   1446
*The Thief of Hermes* - Ru Emerson   f   1811
*The Throne of Tara* - John Desjarlais   f   1498
*To the Land of the Living* - Robert
  Silverberg   f   5044
*Touching the Fire* - Roger Welsch   f   5751
*The Tower of Beowulf* - Parke Godwin   f   2250
*Unicorns II* - Jack Dann   f   1343
*Unquenchable Fire* - Rachel Pollack   f   4361
*The Usurper* - Angus Wells   f   5739
*The Voyage of Mael Duin's Curragh* - Patricia
  Aakhus   f   2
*War of the Gods* - Poul Anderson   f   136
*The Wealdwife's Tale* - Paul Hazel   f   2636
*Weirdos of the Universe, Unite!* - Pamela F.
  Service   f   4921
*Whose Song Is Sung* - Frank Schaefer   f   4872
*The Willing Spirit* - Piers Anthony   f   195
*The Winter King* - Bernard Cornwell   f   1191
*Witch of the North* - Courtway Jones   f   2940
*The Wolf and the Raven* - Diana L. Paxson   f   4270
*World Without End* - Molly Cochran   f   1093
*Wrath of Ashar* - Angus Wells   f   5742
*Yvgenie* - C.J. Cherryh   f   1005

**Fantasy — Light Fantasy**

*Addams Family Values* - Todd Strasser   f   5324
*Alien Pregnant by Elvis* - Esther Friesner   f   2070
*The Ambivalent Magician* - Simon Hawke   f   2616
*Angela and Diabola* - Lynne Reid Banks   f   330

*Another Day, Another Dungeon* - Greg
  Costikyan   f   1206
*Automated Alice* - Jeff Noon   f   4134
*A Bad Day for Ali Baba* - Craig Shaw
  Gardner   f   2123
*A Bad Spell in Yurt* - C. Dale Brittain   f   701
*Betcha Can't Read Just One* - Alan Dean
  Foster   f   1994
*Born to Run* - Mercedes Lackey   f   3271
*Bring Me the Head of Prince Charming* - Roger
  Zelazny   f   6062
*By the Sword* - Greg Costikyan   f   1207
*The Callahan Touch* - Spider Robinson   f   4637
*Captain Jack Zodiac* - Michael Kandel   f   3009
*Captains Outrageous, or, For Doom the Bell Tolls* -
  Roy V. Young   f   6049
*The Case of the Toxic Spell Dump* - Harry
  Turtledove   f   5497
*Castle in the Air* - Diana Wynne Jones   f   2944
*Catastrophe's Spell* - Mayer Alan Brenner   f   671
*Chicks in Chainmail* - Esther Friesner   f   2072
*The Chronicles of Master Li and Number Ten Ox* -
  Barry Hughart   f   2803
*The Color of Her Panties* - Piers Anthony   f   167
*Crossover* - Bill McCay   f   3768
*Dark Lord of Derkholm* - Diana Wynne
  Jones   f   2946
*Daughter of Magic* - C. Dale Brittain   f   703
*Dealing with Dragons* - Patricia C. Wrede   f   5975
*Demon Pig* - Karen Brush   f   737
*Demons Don't Dream* - Piers Anthony   f   168
*The Devil and Dan Cooley* - Holly Lisle   f   3480
*Did You Say Chicks?!* - Esther Friesner   f   2074
*Dirty Work* - Dan McGirt   f   3810
*The Door to Ambermere* - J. Calvin Pierce   f   4316
*Emperor and Clown* - Dave Duncan   f   1676
*The Enchanter Reborn* - L. Sprague de
  Camp   f   1413
*Equal Rites* - Terry Pratchett   f   4387
*Eric* - Terry Pratchett   f   4388
*The Faery Convention* - Brett Davis   f   1399
*Faery Lands Forlorn* - Dave Duncan   f   1677
*A Farce to Be Reckoned With* - Roger
  Zelazny   f   6064
*Faun & Games* - Piers Anthony   f   169
*Feet of Clay* - Terry Pratchett   f   4389
*Flying Dutch* - Tom Holt   f   2750
*Fool on the Hill* - Matt Ruff   f   4707
*The Foxes of Firstdark* - Garry Kilworth   f   3115
*Geis of the Gargoyle* - Piers Anthony   f   172
*Gnome Man's Land* - Esther Friesner   f   2075
*Go Quest, Young Man* - K.B. Bogen   f   557
*The Godmother* - Elizabeth Ann
  Scarborough   f   4862
*The Godmother's Apprentice* - Elizabeth Ann
  Scarborough   f   4863
*Good Omens: The Nice and Accurate Prophecies of
  Agnes Nutter, Witch* - Neil Gaiman   f   2103
*Guards! Guards!* - Terry Pratchett   f   4390
*Gun, with Occasional Music* - Jonathan
  Lethem   f   3441
*Harpy High* - Esther Friesner   f   2076
*Harpy Thyme* - Piers Anthony   f   174
*Hell on High* - Holly Lisle   f   3483
*Heroes, Inc.* - Kyle Crocco   f   1268
*Heroes Wanted* - Kyle Crocco   f   1267
*Higher Mythology* - Jody Lynn Nye   f   4170
*Hooray for Hellywood* - Esther Friesner   f   2077
*If at Faust You Don't Succeed* - Roger
  Zelazny   f   6070
*The Illusionists* - Faren Miller   f   3894
*Interesting Times* - Terry Pratchett   f   4392
*Isle of View* - Piers Anthony   f   177
*Jason Cosmo* - Dan McGirt   f   3811
*Kedrigern and the Charming Couple* - John
  Morressy   f   4013
*Lady Cottington's Pressed Fairy Book* - Terry
  Jones   f   2981

*The Last Arabian Night* - Craig Shaw
  Gardner   f   2129
*A Logical Magician* - Robert Weinberg   f   5697
*Lords and Ladies* - Terry Pratchett   f   4394
*The Lost City of Zork* - Robin Wayne Bailey   f   288
*Lost in Translation* - Margaret Ball   f   315
*Lucifer Jones* - Mike Resnick   f   4549
*Luck of the Wheels* - Megan Lindholm   f   3471
*Lunatics* - Bradley Denton   f   1491
*M.Y.T.H. Inc. in Action* - Robert Asprin   f   259
*Mad Amos* - Alan Dean Foster   f   2009
*Magic Casement* - Dave Duncan   f   1683
*Majyk by Accident* - Esther Friesner   f   2079
*Majyk by Design* - Esther Friesner   f   2080
*Majyk by Hook or Crook* - Esther Friesner   f   2081
*Make Way for Dragons!* - Thorarinn
  Gunnarsson   f   2465
*Mall, Mayhem and Magic* - Holly Lisle   f   3485
*Mall Purchase Night* - Rick Cook   f   1159
*Man From Mundania* - Piers Anthony   f   180
*Maskerade* - Terry Pratchett   f   4395
*Mathemagics* - Margaret Ball   f   316
*Maureen Birnbaum, Barbarian Swordsperson: The
  Complete Stories* - George Alec Effinger   f   1752
*Men at Arms* - Terry Pratchett   f   4396
*Mort* - Terry Pratchett   f   4397
*Moving Pictures* - Terry Pratchett   f   4398
*A Name to Conjure With* - Donald Aamodt   f   3
*The Night of Wishes: Or, The
  Satanarchaeolidealcohellish Notion Potion* - Michael
  Ende   f   1821
*The Nine Lives of Catseye Gomez* - Simon
  Hawke   f   2620
*The Oathbound Wizard* - Christopher
  Stasheff   f   5219
*The Ogre Downstairs* - Diana Wynne Jones   f   2949
*The Old Man and Mr. Smith* - Peter
  Ustinov   f   5532
*One for the Morning Glory* - John Barnes   f   355
*One Quest, Hold the Dragons* - Greg
  Costikyan   f   1208
*One Wish* - C.J. Card   f   880
*The Other Sinbad* - Craig Shaw Gardner   f   2130
*Perilous Seas* - Dave Duncan   f   1685
*Phaze Doubt* - Piers Anthony   f   184
*Pigs Don't Fly* - Mary Brown   f   727
*Practical Magic* - Alice Hoffman   f   2713
*The Prince of Ill Luck* - Susan Dexter   f   1512
*Question Quest* - Piers Anthony   f   186
*Reaper Man* - Terry Pratchett   f   4399
*The Rebirth of Wonder* - Lawrence Watt-
  Evans   f   5646
*Rehearsal for a Renaissance* - Douglas W.
  Clark   f   1045
*The Reluctant Sorcerer* - Simon Hawke   f   2622
*A Remembrance for Kedrigern* - John
  Morressy   f   4014
*Revenge of the Fluffy Bunnies* - Craig Shaw
  Gardner   f   2132
*Roc and a Hard Place* - Piers Anthony   f   187
*Samurai Cat Goes to Hell* - Mark E. Rogers   f   4655
*Slay and Rescue* - John Moore   f   3991
*Small Gods* - Terry Pratchett   f   4400
*Smart Dragons, Foolish Elves* - Alan Dean
  Foster   f   2014
*Some Enchanted Evening* - Alice Alfonsi   f   73
*Son of Spellsinger* - Alan Dean Foster   f   2015
*Soul Music* - Terry Pratchett   f   4401
*Spell Bound* - Trana Mae Simmons   f   5061
*Spell of Apocalypse* - Mayer Alan Brenner   f   672
*Spirit Catcher* - Elizabeth Hallam   f   2497
*The Spirit Ring* - Lois McMaster Bujold   f   763
*Split Heirs* - Lawrence Watt-Evans   f   5649
*The Stone Giant* - James P. Blaylock   f   523
*Strange Stains and Mysterious Smells* - Terry
  Jones   f   2982
*A Sudden Wild Magic* - Diana Wynne Jones   f   2950
*The Summer I Shrank My Grandmother* - Elvira
  Woodruff   f   5968

*Summon the Keeper* - Tanya Huff  f  2800
*Sweet Myth-tery of Life* - Robert Asprin  f  262
*Sympathy for the Devil* - Holly Lisle  f  3488
*That's All, Folks!* - Greg Snow  f  5148
*Towing Jehovah* - James Morrow  f  4035
*A Troubling Along the Border* - Donald Aamodt  f  4
*The Undesired Princess and the Enchanted Bunny* - L. Sprague de Camp  f  1419
*Unicorn U.* - Esther Friesner  f  2084
*The Warlock Insane* - Christopher Stasheff  f  5225
*Whilom* - Robert Watson  f  5639
*Who P-P-Plugged Roger Rabbit?* - Gary K. Wolf  f  5934
*A Wish and a Dream* - Ingrid Weaver  f  5658
*Wishbringer* - Craig Shaw Gardner  f  2133
*Wishing Season* - Esther Friesner  f  2085
*Witch and Wombat* - Carolyn Cushman  f  1299
*The Witch House* - Norma Tadlock Johnson  f  2923
*Witches Abroad* - Terry Pratchett  f  4404
*The Wiz Biz* - Rick Cook  f  1160
*A Wizard Abroad* - Diane Duane  f  1668
*The Wizard of Ambermere* - J. Calvin Pierce  f  4317
*The Wizard of Camelot* - Simon Hawke  f  2627
*The Wizardry Consulted* - Rick Cook  f  1161
*The Wizardry Quested* - Rick Cook  f  1163
*The Wizard's Apprentice* - S.P. Somtow  f  5163
*Wizard's Mole* - Brad Strickland  f  5337
*The Wood Nymph and the Cranky Saint* - C. Dale Brittain  f  706
*Wyrd Sisters* - Terry Pratchett  f  4405
*Ye Gods!* - Tom Holt  f  2753
*Yon Ill Wind* - Piers Anthony  f  196
*Zombie Lover* - Piers Anthony  f  197

**Fantasy — Literary**

*Bending the Landscape: Fantasy* - Nicola Griffith  f  2444
*Brown Girl in the Ring* - Nalo Hopkinson  f  2771
*The Children of Men* - P.D. James  f  2870
*Come Before Christ and Murder Love* - Stewart Home  f  2754
*The Dog King* - Christoph Ransmayr  f  4474
*Dogland* - Will Shetterly  f  4992
*Einstein's Dreams* - Alan Lightman  f  3459
*Fabulous Harbors* - Michael Moorcock  f  3981
*Flying Saucers over Hennepin* - Peter Gelman  f  2186
*Further Adventures* - Jon Stephen Fink  f  1940
*Gojiro* - Mark Jacobson  f  2847
*The Innkeeper's Song* - Peter S. Beagle  f  409
*Jacob's Hands* - Aldous Huxley  f  2817
*Lorien Lost* - Michael King  f  3124
*Love & Sleep* - John Crowley  f  1277
*Lunching with the Antichrist* - Michael Moorcock  f  3984
*Primavera* - Francesca Lia Block  f  551
*The Sandman: Book of Dreams* - Neil Gaiman  f  2105
*Senora Rodriguez and Other Worlds* - Martha Cerda  f  950
*Shape-Shifter: Stories by Pauline Melville* - Pauline Melville  f  3876
*The Smithsonian Institution* - Gore Vidal  f  5570
*Spirits of the Ordinary* - Kathleen Alcala  f  52
*The Tattooed Map* - Barbara Hodgson  f  2706
*The Tetherballs of Bougainville* - Mark Leyner  f  3457
*The Thirteenth Daughter of the Moon* - Steven Nightingale  f  4104
*Through the Heart* - Richard Grant  f  2328
*Tropic of Orange* - Karen Tei Yamashita  f  6009
*Whilom* - Robert Watson  f  5639

**Fantasy — Magic Conflict**

*The Adept* - Katherine Kurtz  f  3254
*Aisling* - Louise Cooper  f  1172

*Ancient Echoes* - Robert Holdstock  f  2735
*Ancient Games* - Scott Ciencin  f  1028
*And Eternity* - Piers Anthony  f  162
*The Anubis Murders* - Gary Gygax  f  2472
*The Apprentice* - Deborah Talmadge-Bickmore  f  5382
*Aquamancer* - Don Callander  f  841
*Arena* - William R. Forstchen  f  1977
*The Arm of the Stone* - Victoria Strauss  f  5333
*The Art of Arrow Cutting* - Stephen Dedman  f  1462
*Aurian* - Maggie Furey  f  2095
*The Baker's Boy* - J.V. Jones  f  2956
*Barrenlands* - Doranna Durgin  f  1702
*Barrow* - John Deakins  f  1443
*The Bastard Prince* - Katherine Kurtz  f  3255
*Bedlam Boyz* - Ellen Guon  f  2467
*Bedlam's Bard* - Mercedes Lackey  f  3269
*Beggar's Banquet* - Daniel Hood  f  2756
*Beldan's Fire* - Midori Snyder  f  5150
*Beneath the Vaulted Hills* - Sean Russell  f  4739
*Beneath the Web* - Lynn Abbey  f  12
*Beyond the Pale* - Jack Koke  f  3198
*The Black Gryphon* - Mercedes Lackey  f  3270
*Black Trillium* - Marion Zimmer Bradley  f  630
*The Blackgod* - J. Gregory Keyes  f  3095
*Blackmantle: A Triumph* - Patricia Kennealy-Morrison  f  3059
*Bleak Seasons* - Glen Cook  f  1147
*Blood and Honor* - Simon R. Green  f  2361
*Blood Trillium* - Julian May  f  3696
*Blue Moon Rising* - Simon R. Green  f  2362
*The Book of Atrix Wolfe* - Patricia A. McKillip  f  3838
*The Book of Night with Moon* - Diane Duane  f  1657
*A Breach in the Watershed* - Douglas Niles  f  4105
*Bride of the Rat God* - Barbara Hambly  f  2499
*Broken Blade* - Ann Marston  f  3634
*The Broken Crown* - Michelle West  f  5757
*By Chaos Cursed* - Mickey Zucker Reichert  f  4517
*A Calculated Magic* - Robert Weinberg  f  5694
*Caledon of the Mists* - Deborah Turner Harris  f  2560
*A Call to Arms* - Thomas K. Martin  f  3650
*Canticle* - R.A. Salvatore  f  4793
*Castle in the Air* - Diana Wynne Jones  f  2944
*The Castle of the Silver Wheel* - Teresa Edgerton  f  1741
*Chains of Darkness, Chains of Light* - Michelle Sagara  f  4781
*Challenges* - Sharon Green  f  2354
*The Changeling* - Kristine Kathryn Rusch  f  4714
*Changer* - Jane M. Lindskold  f  3474
*Changespell* - Doranna Durgin  f  1703
*Changeweaver* - Margaret Ball  f  313
*The Chaos Balance* - L.E. Modesitt Jr.  f  3925
*Child of the Journey* - Janet Berliner  f  466
*Children of the Blood: Book Two of The Sundered* - Michelle Sagara  f  4782
*Children of the Drake* - Richard A. Knaak  f  3166
*Children of the Dusk* - Janet Berliner  f  467
*The Children of Wrath* - Mickey Zucker Reichert  f  4518
*Chimaera's Copper* - Piers Anthony  f  166
*Chorus Skating* - Alan Dean Foster  f  1998
*Chrome Circle* - Mercedes Lackey  f  3277
*Cinnabar Shadows* - Lynn Abbey  f  15
*The Clan of the Warlord* - Elizabeth H. Boyer  f  604
*A College of Magics* - Caroline Stevermer  f  5266
*The Compass of the Soul* - Sean Russell  f  4740
*Competition* - Sharon Green  f  2355
*Conspiracy* - J. Robert King  f  3121
*Convergence* - Sharon Green  f  2356
*Cormyr: A Novel* - Ed Greenwood  f  2425
*Count Scar* - C. Dale Brittain  f  702
*The Courts of Sorcery* - Ashley McConnell  f  3773
*The Crimson Sky* - Joel Rosenberg  f  4669

*A Crown of Swords* - Robert Jordan  f  2984
*Crucible* - Troy Denning  f  1484
*The Crystal Dragon* - Richard A. Knaak  f  3167
*The Crystal Sorcerers* - William R. Forstchen  f  1979
*Curse of the Mistwraith* - Janny Wurts  f  6001
*The Cutting Edge* - Dave Duncan  f  1675
*The Cygnet and the Firebird* - Patricia A. McKillip  f  3839
*The Daemon in the Machine* - Felicity Savage  f  4848
*Dark Horse* - Mary H. Herbert  f  2674
*Dark Magic* - Angus Wells  f  5733
*Dark Mirror, Dark Dreams* - Sharon Green  f  2357
*The Dark Shore* - Adam Lee  f  3385
*Darkenheight* - Douglas Niles  f  4107
*Daughter of the Blood* - Anne Bishop  f  495
*Days of Air and Darkness* - Katharine Kerr  f  3067
*Days of Blood and Fire* - Katharine Kerr  f  3068
*Death in Delhi* - Gary Gygax  f  2473
*The Death of Chaos* - L.E. Modesitt Jr.  f  3926
*The Death of the Necromancer* - Martha Wells  f  5749
*The Deceiver* - Louise Cooper  f  1175
*The Demon Awakens* - R.A. Salvatore  f  4794
*Demon Drums* - Carol Severance  f  4922
*Demon Knight* - Ken Hood  f  2760
*Demon Pig* - Karen Brush  f  737
*The Demon Spirit* - R.A. Salvatore  f  4795
*Devil's Engine* - Mark Sumner  f  5356
*Devil's Tower* - Mark Sumner  f  5357
*The Devouring Void* - Mark E. Rogers  f  4653
*Dhiammara* - Maggie Furey  f  2096
*Diplomacy of Wolves* - Holly Lisle  f  3481
*Distant Planes* - Kathy Ice  f  2827
*Dog Wizard* - Barbara Hambly  f  2503
*The Door into Sunset* - Diane Duane  f  1660
*Dorella* - Mark A. Garland  f  2142
*The Dragon and the Gnarly King* - Gordon R. Dickson  f  1529
*The Dragon at War* - Gordon R. Dickson  f  1530
*A Dragon at World's End* - Christopher Rowley  f  4693
*Dragon Burning* - Craig Shaw Gardner  f  2126
*The Dragon Crown* - Richard A. Knaak  f  3168
*Dragon Death* - Gael Baudino  f  390
*The Dragon in Lyonesse* - Gordon R. Dickson  f  1531
*The Dragon on the Border* - Gordon R. Dickson  f  1533
*The Dragon Reborn* - Robert Jordan  f  2985
*Dragon Sleeping* - Craig Shaw Gardner  f  2127
*The Dragon, the Earl, and the Troll* - Gordon R. Dickson  f  1534
*The Dragon Token* - Melanie Rawn  f  4485
*Dragon Tome* - Richard A. Knaak  f  3169
*Dragon Waking* - Craig Shaw Gardner  f  2128
*Dragoncharm* - Graham Edwards  f  1749
*Dragonmage of Mystara* - Thorarinn Gunnarsson  f  2462
*Dragons of Argonath* - Christopher Rowley  f  4694
*Dragons of Summer Flame* - Margaret Weis  f  5711
*Dragons on the Town* - Thorarinn Gunnarsson  f  2463
*The Dragon's Touchstone* - Irene Radford  f  4459
*Dragonspawn* - Mark Acres  f  28
*The Dubious Hills* - Pamela Dean  f  1444
*The Duke of Sumava* - Sara J. Wrench  f  5983
*Dun Lady's Jess* - Doranna Durgin  f  1704
*Echoes of the Fourth Magic* - R.A. Salvatore  f  4799
*The Element of Fire* - Martha Wells  f  5750
*Elric: Song of the Black Sword* - Michael Moorcock  f  3980
*The Elvenbane* - Andre Norton  f  4149
*Elvendude* - Mark Shepherd  f  4980
*Emerald House Rising* - Peg Kerr  f  3080
*An Enemy Reborn* - Michael A. Stackpole  f  5197
*Eyes of the Empress* - Camille Bacon-Smith  f  285

Story Type Index

*The Falcon Rises* - Michael C. Staudinger  f  5235
*Fall of Angels* - L.E. Modesitt Jr.  f  3930
*Fifth Quarter* - Tanya Huff  f  2795
*Final Sacrifice* - Clayton Emery  f  1814
*Fire Angels* - Jane Routley  f  4685
*The Fire Duke* - Joel Rosenberg  f  4671
*Fire in the Mist* - Holly Lisle  f  3482
*The Fire Rose* - Mercedes Lackey  f  3280
*Firebird* - Mercedes Lackey  f  3281
*The Fires of Heaven* - Robert Jordan  f  2987
*First King of Shannara* - Terry Brooks  f  712
*Flames of the Dragon* - Robin Wayne Bailey  f  287
*Flameweaver* - Margaret Ball  f  314
*The Flight of Michael McBride* - Midori
  Snyder  f  5151
*Flight of Vengeance* - Andre Norton  f  4152
*Flight to Hollow Mountain* - Mark Sebanc  f  4908
*The Folk of the Air* - Peter S. Beagle  f  407
*The Fools' War* - Lee Kisling  f  3159
*Fortress in the Eye of Time* - C.J. Cherryh  f  991
*Fortress of Eagles* - C.J. Cherryh  f  992
*The Fountains of Mirlacca* - Ashley
  McConnell  f  3775
*Four & Twenty Blackbirds* - Mercedes
  Lackey  f  3283
*From Prussia with Love* - John DeChancie  f  1457
*Frostwing* - Richard A. Knaak  f  3170
*Fugitive Prince* - Janny Wurts  f  6002
*Galatea in 2-D* - Aaron Allston  f  87
*Gate of Ivory, Gate of Horn* - Robert
  Holdstock  f  2737
*The Gates of Vensunor* - Carol Heller  f  2650
*Geomancer* - Don Callander  f  845
*Ghostlight* - Marion Zimmer Bradley  f  634
*The Gift* - Patrick O'Leary  f  4211
*The Glass Dragon* - Irene Radford  f  4460
*Glenraven* - Marion Zimmer Bradley  f  635
*The Goblin Mirror* - C.J. Cherryh  f  994
*The Gods in Anger* - Adrian Cole  f  1100
*The Gold Ball* - Hanne Marie Svendsen  f  5361
*The Golden Thread* - Suzy McKee Charnas  f  969
*Golden Trillium* - Andre Norton  f  4153
*Gravelight* - Marion Zimmer Bradley  f  636
*The Guardian* - Angus Wells  f  5737
*Harp of Winds* - Maggie Furey  f  2097
*Hawk & Fisher* - Simon R. Green  f  2370
*Heartlight* - Marion Zimmer Bradley  f  637
*Hederick, the Theocrat* - Ellen Dodge
  Severson  f  4925
*The Hidden City* - David Eddings  f  1733
*The Hidden Realms* - Sharon Green  f  2358
*Hogfather* - Terry Pratchett  f  4391
*Hunter's Death* - Michelle West  f  5758
*Icefalcon's Quest* - Barbara Hambly  f  2504
*If I Pay Thee Not in Gold* - Piers Anthony  f  176
*Illusion* - Paula Volsky  f  5582
*In the Rift* - Marion Zimmer Bradley  f  639
*The Inadequate Adept* - Simon Hawke  f  2617
*Into the Dark Lands* - Michelle Sagara  f  4783
*Into the Fire* - Dennis L. McKiernan  f  3834
*Into the Forge* - Dennis L. McKiernan  f  3835
*Iron Dawn* - Matthew Woodring Stover  f  5320
*The Island of the Mighty* - Evangeline
  Walton  f  5626
*The Itinerant Exorcist* - Ashley McConnell  f  3776
*The Janus Mask* - Richard A. Knaak  f  3171
*Jericho Moon* - Matthew Woodring Stover  f  5321
*The Jewel of Fire* - Diana L. Paxson  f  4265
*Kar Kalim* - Deborah Christian  f  1025
*Kindred Rites* - Katharine Eliska Kimbriel  f  3118
*A King Beneath the Mountain* - Robert N.
  Charrette  f  973
*King Javan's Year* - Katherine Kurtz  f  3258
*King Pinch* - David Cook  f  1146
*King's Dragon* - Kate Elliott  f  1773
*King's Man and Thief* - Christie Golden  f  2253
*King's Son, Magic's Son* - Josepha Sherman  f  4986
*Kirins: The Flight of the Ain* - James D.
  Priest  f  4433

*Kirins: The Secret of the Hanging Stones* - James D.
  Priest  f  4434
*Kirins: The Spell of No'an* - James D.
  Priest  f  4435
*A Knight Among Knaves* - Robert N.
  Charrette  f  974
*A Knight of the Word* - Terry Brooks  f  714
*Krispos of Videssos* - Harry Turtledove  f  5506
*Krispos the Emperor* - Harry Turtledove  f  5508
*Krondor, the Betrayal* - Raymond E. Feist  f  1905
*Lady of Mercy* - Michelle Sagara  f  4784
*Lady of the Trillium* - Marion Zimmer
  Bradley  f  641
*The Last Book of Swords: Shieldbreaker's Story* - Fred
  Saberhagen  f  4768
*The Last Wizard* - Simon Hawke  f  2619
*Legacy of Steel* - Mary H. Herbert  f  2675
*Legacy of the Darksword* - Margaret Weis  f  5719
*Legends: Short Novels by the Masters of Modern
  Fantasy* - Robert Silverberg  f  5034
*Liar's Oath* - Elizabeth Moon  f  3969
*Liavek: Festival Week* - Will Shetterly  f  4994
*Lightning's Daughter* - Mary H. Herbert  f  2676
*The Living God* - Dave Duncan  f  1682
*The Lodge of the Lynx* - Katherine Kurtz  f  3259
*A Logical Magician* - Robert Weinberg  f  5697
*Lord of Chaos* - Robert Jordan  f  2988
*Lord of the Isles* - David Drake  f  1636
*Lords of the Sky* - Angus Wells  f  5738
*Luck in the Shadows* - Lynn Flewelling  f  1952
*Mage Heart* - Jane Routley  f  4686
*The Mageborn Traitor* - Melanie Rawn  f  4488
*Magelord: The Awakening* - Thomas K.
  Martin  f  3651
*The Magic Engineer* - L.E. Modesitt Jr.  f  3933
*A Magic-Lover's Treasury of the Fantastic* - Margaret
  Weis  f  5721
*The Magic of Recluce* - L.E. Modesitt Jr.  f  3934
*The Magic Wars* - Jo Clayton  f  1068
*The Magicians of Night* - Barbara Hambly  f  2505
*Magic's Price* - Mercedes Lackey  f  3288
*Mairelon the Magician* - Patricia C. Wrede  f  5977
*Mall, Mayhem and Magic* - Holly Lisle  f  3485
*A Man Betrayed* - J.V. Jones  f  2958
*Masques* - Patricia Briggs  f  681
*Master and Fool* - J.V. Jones  f  2959
*The Master of Whitestorm* - Janny Wurts  f  6003
*Mind of the Magic* - Holly Lisle  f  3486
*Minerva Wakes* - Holly Lisle  f  3487
*Mirror of Destiny* - Andre Norton  f  4159
*Mission of Magic* - Julie Dean Smith  f  5125
*Morigu: The Dead* - Mark C. Perry  f  4284
*Mother of Winter* - Barbara Hambly  f  2506
*Mouvar's Magic* - Piers Anthony  f  182
*My Son, the Wizard* - Christopher Stasheff  f  5218
*Nameless Magery* - Delia Marshall Turner  f  5490
*Night of Glory* - Scott Ciencin  f  1030
*The Night of Wishes: Or, The
  Satanarchaeolidealcohellish Notion Potion* - Michael
  Ende  f  1821
*Nightseer* - Laurell K. Hamilton  f  2521
*Nightwatch* - Robin Wayne Bailey  f  289
*No Quarter* - Tanya Huff  f  2798
*Nobody's Son* - Sean Stewart  f  5275
*Oath of Swords* - David Weber  f  5678
*Old Nathan* - David Drake  f  1639
*Orc's Opal* - Piers Anthony  f  183
*The Order War* - L.E. Modesitt Jr.  f  3936
*Out of the Ordinary* - Annie Dalton  f  1330
*Palace of Kings* - Mike Jefferies  f  2887
*Passage to Dawn* - R.A. Salvatore  f  4803
*The Path of Daggers* - Robert Jordan  f  2989
*The Pearl of the Soul of the World* - Meredith Ann
  Pierce  f  4318
*The Perfect Princess* - Irene Radford  f  4462
*Phantom Banjo* - Elizabeth Ann
  Scarborough  f  4868
*Picking the Ballad's Bones* - Elizabeth Ann
  Scarborough  f  4869

*A Plague of Sorcerers* - Mary Frances
  Zambreno  f  6058
*Point of Hopes* - Melissa Scott  f  4899
*Prentice Alvin* - Orson Scott Card  f  896
*The Price of Blood and Honor* - Elizabeth
  Willey  f  5811
*A Prince Among Men* - Robert N. Charrette  f  977
*Prince of Chaos* - Roger Zelazny  f  6073
*The Prince of Ill Luck* - Susan Dexter  f  1512
*The Printer's Devil* - Chico Kidd  f  3099
*Pyromancer* - Don Callander  f  847
*The Qualinesti* - Paul B. Thompson  f  5455
*The Queen of Ashes* - Deborah Turner
  Harris  f  2561
*Queen of Demons* - David Drake  f  1640
*Quest for the Fallen Star* - Piers Anthony  f  185
*Rage of a Demon King* - Raymond E. Feist  f  1908
*The Rainbow Abyss* - Barbara Hambly  f  2507
*The Raven Ring* - Patricia C. Wrede  f  5978
*Realm of Light* - Deborah Chester  f  1008
*Red Magic* - Jean Rabe  f  4458
*The Red Wyvern* - Katharine Kerr  f  3074
*Redmagic* - Crawford Kilian  f  3107
*Reign of Shadows* - Deborah Chester  f  1009
*The Riddled Man* - Mark E. Rogers  f  4654
*Ring of Intrigue* - Jane S. Fancher  f  1863
*Ring of Lightning* - Jane S. Fancher  f  1864
*The Road to Ehvenor* - Joel Rosenberg  f  4675
*The Road to Underfall* - Mike Jefferies  f  2888
*Ronin* - D.A. Heeley  f  2639
*The Rose Sea* - S.M. Stirling  f  5296
*The Ruins of Ambrai* - Melanie Rawn  f  4489
*The Runelords: The Sum of All Men* - David
  Farland  f  1866
*Sable, Shadow and Ice* - Cheryl J. Franklin  f  2039
*Sabriel* - Garth Nix  f  4129
*Sacred Ground* - Mercedes Lackey  f  3294
*The Sage* - Christopher Stasheff  f  5221
*Sage of Sare* - Julie Dean Smith  f  5126
*The Samurai Wizard* - Simon Hawke  f  2623
*Scales of Justice* - Daniel Hood  f  2758
*School of Wizardry* - Debra Doyle  f  1605
*Sea Without a Shore* - Sean Russell  f  4743
*The Secular Wizard* - Christopher Stasheff  f  5222
*The Seventh Gate* - Margaret Weis  f  5727
*The Seventh Sentinel* - Mary Kirchoff  f  3154
*Shadow Dawn* - Chris Claremont  f  1042
*The Shadow Eater* - Adam Lee  f  3386
*The Shadow Gate* - Margaret Ball  f  317
*Shadow-Maze* - Mark Smith  f  5133
*The Shadow of Sorcery* - Andrew J. Offutt  f  4202
*Shadow of the Crown* - Craig Mills  f  3914
*The Shadow Rising* - Robert Jordan  f  2990
*Shadow War* - Deborah Chester  f  1010
*Shadows over Lyra* - Patricia C. Wrede  f  5980
*The Shaman* - Christopher Stasheff  f  5223
*The Shape-Changer's Wife* - Sharon Shinn  f  5002
*Shards of a Broken Crown* - Raymond E.
  Feist  f  1912
*Shattered Chains* - Clayton Emery  f  1816
*The Shattered Oath* - Josepha Sherman  f  4989
*She Is the Darkness* - Glen Cook  f  1154
*Ships of Merior* - Janny Wurts  f  6004
*The Shrouded Realm* - Richard A. Knaak  f  3174
*Siege of Darkness* - R.A. Salvatore  f  4804
*The Silver Gryphon* - Mercedes Lackey  f  3295
*The Silver Stone* - Joel Rosenberg  f  4676
*Silverlight* - Morgan Llywelyn  f  3507
*Sky Trillium* - Julian May  f  3700
*Skybowl* - Melanie Rawn  f  4490
*The Sleep of Stone* - Louise Cooper  f  1179
*Son of Darkness* - Josepha Sherman  f  4990
*Song of the Saurials* - Kate Novak  f  4167
*Soothslayer: A Magickal Fantasy* - D.J.
  Conway  f  1143
*The Soprano Sorceress* - L.E. Modesitt Jr.  f  3938
*A Sorcerer and a Gentleman* - Elizabeth
  Willey  f  5812

*The Sorceress and the Cygnet* - Patricia A. McKillip   f   3842
*Spell of Apocalypse* - Mayer Alan Brenner   f   672
*Spell of Fate* - Mayer Alan Brenner   f   673
*The Spell of the Black Dagger* - Lawrence Watt-Evans   f   5648
*The Spellkey Trilogy* - Ann Downer   f   1592
*The Spellsong War* - L.E. Modesitt Jr.   f   3939
*Spirit Fox* - Mickey Zucker Reichert   f   4524
*Spirit of the Wind* - Chris Pierson   f   4326
*Spiritride* - Mark Shepherd   f   4981
*Stalking Darkness* - Lynn Flewelling   f   1953
*Steel Rose* - Kara Dalkey   f   1321
*The Stone Movers* - Patricia Mullen   f   4045
*Stone of Tears* - Terry Goodkind   f   2269
*Storm Breaking* - Mercedes Lackey   f   3296
*Storm Caller* - Carol Severance   f   4924
*Storm Knights* - Bill Slavicsek   f   5087
*Storm Rising* - Mercedes Lackey   f   3297
*Storm Warning* - Mercedes Lackey   f   3298
*Stranger at the Wedding* - Barbara Hambly   f   2509
*The Stricken Field* - Dave Duncan   f   1688
*Stronghold* - Melanie Rawn   f   4492
*Strum Again?* - Elizabeth Ann Scarborough   f   4870
*A Sudden Wild Magic* - Diana Wynne Jones   f   2950
*Summer King, Winter Fool* - Lisa Goldstein   f   2263
*Sunder, Eclipse and Seed* - Elise Guttenberg   f   2471
*Sunderlies Seeking* - Gayle Greeno   f   2424
*Sword of Flame* - Maggie Furey   f   2098
*The Talismans of Shannara* - Terry Brooks   f   717
*The Tangle Box* - Terry Brooks   f   718
*The Temper of Wisdom* - Lynn Abbey   f   17
*The Templar Treasure* - Katherine Kurtz   f   3261
*Temple of the Winds* - Terry Goodkind   f   2270
*Thornhold* - Elaine Cunningham   f   1293
*Tiger Burning Bright* - Marion Zimmer Bradley   f   652
*A Time of Exile* - Katharine Kerr   f   3077
*The Time of Madness* - Thomas K. Martin   f   3652
*Timespell* - Robert N. Charrette   f   978
*To Green Angel Tower* - Tad Williams   f   5832
*Token of Dragonsblood* - Damaris Cole   f   1114
*Touched by Magic* - Doranna Durgin   f   1705
*Touched by the Gods* - Lawrence Watt-Evans   f   5651
*Tourists* - Lisa Goldstein   f   2264
*The Towers of the Sunset* - L.E. Modesitt Jr.   f   3941
*Tris's Book* - Tamora Pierce   f   4322
*The True Knight* - Susan Dexter   f   1513
*A Two-Edged Sword* - Thomas K. Martin   f   3653
*The Uncrowned King* - Michelle West   f   5760
*The Unicorn War* - John Lee   f   3401
*Upland Outlaws* - Dave Duncan   f   1690
*The Usurper* - Angus Wells   f   5739
*Villains by Necessity* - Eve Forward   f   1985
*Vision Quest* - Pamela F. Service   f   4920
*Voima* - C. Dale Brittain   f   704
*Waking the Moon* - Elizabeth Hand   f   2538
*Wanderlust* - Mary Kirchoff   f   3155
*The War in the Waste* - Felicity Savage   f   4852
*War of the Three Waters* - Douglas Niles   f   4110
*The Warding of Witch World* - Andre Norton   f   4163
*The Warrior Returns* - Allan Cole   f   1109
*Warriorwards* - Dafydd ab Hugh   f   11
*The Way Beneath* - Angus Wells   f   5740
*Well Wished* - Franny Billingsley   f   489
*The Western King* - Ann Marston   f   3636
*The Western Wizard* - Mickey Zucker Reichert   f   4526
*When Demons Walk* - Patricia Briggs   f   683
*The White Gryphon* - Mercedes Lackey   f   3303
*The White Order* - L.E. Modesitt Jr.   f   3942
*The White Tribunal* - Paula Volsky   f   5583
*The Wild Hunt* - Jane Yolen   f   6042
*Wild Magic* - Jo Clayton   f   1072
*Wild Magic* - Angus Wells   f   5741
*Wildfire* - Jo Clayton   f   1073

*Wind From a Foreign Sky* - Katya Reimann   f   4528
*Wind Whispers, Shadow Shouts* - Sharon Green   f   2360
*Winds of Fury* - Mercedes Lackey   f   3306
*Winged Magic* - Mary H. Herbert   f   2678
*The Witch and the Cathedral* - C. Dale Brittain   f   705
*The Witch Doctor* - Christopher Stasheff   f   5228
*Wit'ch Fire* - James Clemens   f   1082
*The Witch Returns* - Phyllis Reynolds Naylor   f   4079
*Witches' Brew* - Terry Brooks   f   719
*Witchlight* - Marion Zimmer Bradley   f   655
*The Witch's Eye* - Phyllis Reynolds Naylor   f   4080
*The Wizard and the Floating City* - Christopher Rowley   f   4699
*The Wizard at Home* - Rick Shelley   f   4975
*The Wizard King* - Julie Dean Smith   f   5127
*Wizard of Bones* - Robert N. Charrette   f   979
*The Wizard of Santa Fe* - Simon Hawke   f   2628
*Wizard Spawn* - C.J. Cherryh   f   1004
*Wizard's First Rule* - Terry Goodkind   f   2271
*Wizard's Hall* - Jane Yolen   f   6043
*The Wizard's Shadow* - Susan Dexter   f   1514
*Wolf and Raven* - Michael A. Stackpole   f   5207
*The Wolf of Winter* - Paula Volsky   f   5584
*Wolf's Cub* - Mackay Wood   f   5964
*Wolves of the Gods* - Allan Cole   f   1111
*The World of Robert Jordan's The Wheel of Time* - Robert Jordan   f   2991
*Wrath of Ashar* - Angus Wells   f   5742

## Fantasy — Magic Realism

*Things Invisible to See: Gay and Lesbian Tales of Magic Realism* - Lawrence Schimel   f   4882

## Fantasy — Military

*Bleak Seasons* - Glen Cook   f   1147
*Down Among the Dead Men* - Simon R. Green   f   2367
*Evermeet: Island of Elves* - Elaine Cunningham   f   1290
*Flight of Vengeance* - Andre Norton   f   4152
*Fox and Empire* - Harry Turtledove   f   5500
*Hammer and Anvil* - Harry Turtledove   f   5503
*She Is the Darkness* - Glen Cook   f   1154
*The Thousand Cities* - Harry Turtledove   f   5512
*To Fall Like Stars* - Nancy Asire   f   257
*The War God's Own* - David Weber   f   5682
*Warlord of Heaven* - Adrian Cole   f   1102
*The Warrior's Tale* - Allan Cole   f   1110

## Fantasy — Mystery

*2XS* - Nigel Findley   f   1935
*Afterimage* - Kristine Kathryn Rusch   f   4709
*The Anubis Murders* - Gary Gygax   f   2472
*Beggar's Banquet* - Daniel Hood   f   2756
*Bernie and the Bessledorf Ghost* - Phyllis Reynolds Naylor   f   4078
*Blood Sport* - Lisa Smedman   f   5096
*The Bones of Haven* - Simon R. Green   f   2363
*The Case of the Toxic Spell Dump* - Harry Turtledove   f   5497
*Cat's Paw* - L.A. Taylor   f   5409
*Cats Raise the Dead* - Shirley Rousseau Murphy   f   4054
*The Circus of the Earth and Air* - Brooke Stevens   f   5264
*Cold Iron* - Melisa Michaels   f   3886
*The D. Case: The Truth about the Mystery of Edwin Drood* - Charles Dickens   f   1524
*Dagger Magic* - Katherine Kurtz   f   3256
*Dagger's Edge* - Anne Logston   f   3508
*Deadly Quicksilver Lies* - Glen Cook   f   1148
*Death in Delhi* - Gary Gygax   f   2473

*The Death of the Necromancer* - Martha Wells   f   5749
*The Devil You Say* - Elisa DeCarlo   f   1450
*Dread Brass Shadows* - Glen Cook   f   1149
*D'Shai* - Joel Rosenberg   f   4670
*The Dubious Hills* - Pamela Dean   f   1444
*The Ear, the Eye, and the Arm* - Nancy Farmer   f   1867
*Elfsong* - Elaine Cunningham   f   1289
*Emerald House Rising* - Peg Kerr   f   3080
*Eyes of the Empress* - Camille Bacon-Smith   f   285
*Fanuilh* - Daniel Hood   f   2757
*Feet of Clay* - Terry Pratchett   f   4389
*Four & Twenty Blackbirds* - Mercedes Lackey   f   3283
*The Frightened Fish* - Kenneth Robeson   f   4622
*The Glass Dragon* - Irene Radford   f   4460
*The God Killer* - Simon R. Green   f   2368
*The Grail and the Ring* - Teresa Edgerton   f   1744
*Guard Against Dishonor* - Simon R. Green   f   2369
*Guilty Pleasures* - Laurell K. Hamilton   f   2517
*Gun, with Occasional Music* - Jonathan Lethem   f   3441
*The Gypsy* - Steven Brust   f   744
*Hair of the Dog* - Brett Davis   f   1400
*Hawk & Fisher* - Simon R. Green   f   2370
*Hour of the Octopus* - Joel Rosenberg   f   4673
*Iron Shadows* - Steven Barnes   f   362
*The Jade Ogre* - Kenneth Robeson   f   4623
*Journeyman Wizard* - Mary Frances Zambreno   f   6057
*Kindred Spirits* - Mark Anthony   f   154
*The Laughing Corpse* - Laurell K. Hamilton   f   2519
*Magician's Ward* - Patricia C. Wrede   f   5976
*Murder in Cormyr* - Chet Williamson   f   5848
*Nightwatch* - Robin Wayne Bailey   f   289
*The Nine Lives of Catseye Gomez* - Simon Hawke   f   2620
*Old Tin Sorrows* - Glen Cook   f   1151
*Opalite Moon* - Denise Vitola   f   5577
*Point of Hopes* - Melissa Scott   f   4899
*Pretty Pewter Gods* - Glen Cook   f   1152
*Red Iron Nights* - Glen Cook   f   1153
*Rouse a Sleeping Cat* - Dan Crawford   f   1249
*Runes of Autumn* - Larry Elmore   f   1790
*Sacred Ground* - Mercedes Lackey   f   3294
*Scales of Justice* - Daniel Hood   f   2758
*Shade and Shadow* - Francine G. Woodbury   f   5967
*Shadow* - Anne Logston   f   3512
*Sister to the Rain* - Melisa Michaels   f   3887
*The Spider #3: Death's Crimson Juggernaut/The Red Death Rain* - Grant Stockbridge   f   5307
*The Spider #4: Death Reign of the Vampire King/The Pain Emperor* - Grant Stockbridge   f   5308
*The Spider #8: The Devil's Paymaster/Legions of the Accursed Light* - Grant Stockbridge   f   5309
*Spirit Catcher* - Elizabeth Hallam   f   2497
*Strong Spirits* - Elisa DeCarlo   f   1451
*A Study in Sorcery* - Michael Kurland   f   3252
*The Sure Death of a Mouse* - Dan Crawford   f   1250
*Thessalonica* - Harry Turtledove   f   5511
*Touched by Magic* - Doranna Durgin   f   1705
*Walking the Labyrinth* - Lisa Goldstein   f   2266
*When Demons Walk* - Patricia Briggs   f   683
*Whirlwind* - Charles L. Grant   f   2320
*The White Gryphon* - Mercedes Lackey   f   3303
*Who P-P-Plugged Roger Rabbit?* - Gary K. Wolf   f   5934
*A Wild Dog and Lone* - Dan Crawford   f   1251
*Winner Takes All* - Simon R. Green   f   2375
*Wizard's Heir* - Daniel Hood   f   2759
*Wolf in the Fold* - Simon R. Green   f   2376
*The Wood Wife* - Terri Windling   f   5916
*The Wooden Sword* - Lynn Abbey   f   18

## Fantasy — Political

*The Amazon Chronicles* - Jane E.M. Robinson   *f*   4627
*The Architecture of Desire* - Mary Gentle   *f*   2195
*Arrows of the Sun* - Judith Tarr   *f*   5391
*Assassin's Apprentice* - Robin Hobb   *f*   2693
*Assassin's Quest* - Robin Hobb   *f*   2694
*The Baker's Boy* - J.V. Jones   *f*   2956
*Barrenlands* - Doranna Durgin   *f*   1702
*The Bastard Prince* - Katherine Kurtz   *f*   3255
*Beldan's Fire* - Midori Snyder   *f*   5150
*Beneath the Vaulted Hills* - Sean Russell   *f*   4739
*The Birth of the Blade* - Dennis McCarty   *f*   3766
*Blackmantle: A Triumph* - Patricia Kennealy-Morrison   *f*   3059
*Blood of the Fold* - Terry Goodkind   *f*   2268
*The Brazen Gambit* - Lynn Abbey   *f*   13
*The Broken Crown* - Michelle West   *f*   5757
*A Cast of Corbies* - Mercedes Lackey   *f*   3274
*Castle of Deception* - Mercedes Lackey   *f*   3275
*Chains of Darkness, Chains of Light* - Michelle Sagara   *f*   4781
*Challenges* - Sharon Green   *f*   2354
*The Changeling* - Kristine Kathryn Rusch   *f*   4714
*Child of the Light* - Janet Gluckman   *f*   2244
*A City in Winter* - Mark Helprin   *f*   2653
*Clock Strikes Sword* - Ian Hammell   *f*   2529
*Competition* - Sharon Green   *f*   2355
*Convergence* - Sharon Green   *f*   2356
*Cormyr: A Novel* - Ed Greenwood   *f*   2426
*Cormyr: A Novel* - Ed Greenwood   *f*   2425
*Count Scar* - C. Dale Brittain   *f*   702
*Court Duel* - Sherwood Smith   *f*   5137
*The Courts of Sorcery* - Ashley McConnell   *f*   3773
*Cross and Crescent* - Susan Shwartz   *f*   5014
*The Crystal Rose* - Maya Kaathryn Bohnhoff   *f*   560
*Curse of the Mistwraith* - Janny Wurts   *f*   6001
*The Cursed* - Dave Duncan   *f*   1674
*The Cutting Edge* - Dave Duncan   *f*   1675
*Dancer's Rise* - Jo Clayton   *f*   1064
*Darkenheight* - Douglas Niles   *f*   4107
*Daughter of the Blood* - Anne Bishop   *f*   495
*The Death of Chaos* - L.E. Modesitt Jr.   *f*   3926
*Delta City* - Felicity Savage   *f*   4849
*The Demon Awakens* - R.A. Salvatore   *f*   4794
*The Demon King* - Chris Bunch   *f*   770
*The Demon Spirit* - R.A. Salvatore   *f*   4795
*Diplomacy of Wolves* - Holly Lisle   *f*   3481
*The Doom Brigade* - Margaret Weis   *f*   5708
*Dragon* - Steven Brust   *f*   741
*The Dragon Crown* - Richard A. Knaak   *f*   3168
*The Dragon King* - R.A. Salvatore   *f*   4796
*The Dragon Token* - Melanie Rawn   *f*   4485
*Dragoncharm* - Graham Edwards   *f*   1749
*Dragonmage of Mystara* - Thorarinn Gunnarsson   *f*   2462
*Dragons of Argonath* - Christopher Rowley   *f*   4694
*Dragons of Summer Flame* - Margaret Weis   *f*   5711
*The Eagle and the Nightingales* - Mercedes Lackey   *f*   3278
*Elvenblood* - Andre Norton   *f*   4150
*Exile's Challenge* - Angus Wells   *f*   5734
*Exile's Children* - Angus Wells   *f*   5735
*Eyes of Silver* - Michael A. Stackpole   *f*   5200
*The Faery Convention* - Brett Davis   *f*   1399
*The Faithful Traitor* - Robert Don Hughes   *f*   2809
*The Fire Queen* - Jack Holland   *f*   2740
*Firewalk* - Anne Logston   *f*   3509
*Firstborn* - Paul B. Thompson   *f*   5454
*Five Hundred Years After* - Steven Brust   *f*   742
*Flickering Shadows* - Kwadwo Agymah Kamau   *f*   3006
*The Forging of the Shadows* - Oliver Johnson   *f*   2924
*Fortress in the Eye of Time* - C.J. Cherryh   *f*   991
*Fortress of Eagles* - C.J. Cherryh   *f*   992
*Fox and Empire* - Harry Turtledove   *f*   5500
*Freedom & Necessity* - Steven Brust   *f*   743

*Fugitive Prince* - Janny Wurts   *f*   6002
*A Game of Thrones* - George R.R. Martin   *f*   3645
*The Gilded Chain: A Tale of the King's Blades* - Dave Duncan   *f*   1679
*Goblin Moon* - Teresa Edgerton   *f*   1743
*The Golden Key* - Melanie Rawn   *f*   4486
*Grail* - Stephen R. Lawhead   *f*   3355
*Greendaughter* - Anne Logston   *f*   3510
*The Guardian* - Angus Wells   *f*   5737
*Hall of Whispers* - Mike Jefferies   *f*   2884
*Haven* - David Peters   *f*   4304
*Hawk's Flight* - Carol Chase   *f*   980
*Heart Readers* - Kristine Kathryn Rusch   *f*   4718
*Hearts and Armor* - Ron Miller   *f*   3903
*Hour of the Octopus* - Joel Rosenberg   *f*   4673
*Humility Garden* - Felicity Savage   *f*   4850
*Illusion* - Paula Volsky   *f*   5582
*In Legend Born* - Laura Resnick   *f*   4533
*Into the Fire* - Dennis L. McKiernan   *f*   3834
*Into the Labyrinth* - Margaret Weis   *f*   5716
*Iron Dawn* - Matthew Woodring Stover   *f*   5320
*The Iron Throne* - Simon Hawke   *f*   2618
*King Javan's Year* - Katherine Kurtz   *f*   3258
*King's Dragon* - Kate Elliott   *f*   1773
*King's Son, Magic's Son* - Josepha Sherman   *f*   4986
*The Knights of Cawdor* - Mike Jefferies   *f*   2886
*Krispos of Videssos* - Harry Turtledove   *f*   5506
*Krispos Rising* - Harry Turtledove   *f*   5507
*Krispos the Emperor* - Harry Turtledove   *f*   5508
*Lady of Mercy* - Michelle Sagara   *f*   4784
*Ladylord* - Sasha Miller   *f*   3906
*The Last Human* - Tom De Haven   *f*   1422
*The League of the Crimson Crescent* - James E. Reagen   *f*   4495
*Liar's Oath* - Elizabeth Moon   *f*   3969
*The Light Bearer* - Donna Gillespie   *f*   2229
*Lights Out in the Reptile House* - Jim Shepard   *f*   4976
*The Lion of Farside* - John Dalmas   *f*   1324
*Lion's Heart* - Karen Wehrstein   *f*   5683
*The Lions of Al-Rassan* - Guy Gavriel Kay   *f*   3016
*Lion's Soul* - Karen Wehrstein   *f*   5684
*The Loneliest Magician* - Irene Radford   *f*   4461
*Lord of Sunset* - Parke Godwin   *f*   2246
*Lord of the Troll-Bats* - Alexis A. Gilliland   *f*   2234
*The Lost Prince* - Bridget Wood   *f*   5962
*The Lotus and the Rose* - Scott Ciencin   *f*   1029
*Luck in the Shadows* - Lynn Flewelling   *f*   1952
*Luthien's Gamble* - R.A. Salvatore   *f*   4802
*Madouc* - Jack Vance   *f*   5547
*The Mageborn Traitor* - Melanie Rawn   *f*   4488
*Magelord: The Awakening* - Thomas K. Martin   *f*   3651
*The Magic Engineer* - L.E. Modesitt Jr.   *f*   3933
*A Man Betrayed* - J.V. Jones   *f*   2958
*Masquerades* - Kate Novak   *f*   4166
*Masques* - Patricia Briggs   *f*   681
*Master and Fool* - J.V. Jones   *f*   2959
*Merlin's Bones* - Fred Saberhagen   *f*   4771
*Mistress of the Empire* - Raymond E. Feist   *f*   1906
*Mother of Storms* - Adrian Cole   *f*   1101
*Nations of the Night* - Oliver Johnson   *f*   2925
*Never Trust an Elf* - Robert N. Charrette   *f*   976
*No One Noticed the Cat* - Anne McCaffrey   *f*   3740
*Nobody's Son* - Sean Stewart   *f*   5275
*Once a Hero* - Michael A. Stackpole   *f*   5203
*The One-Armed Queen* - Jane Yolen   *f*   6037
*Orca* - Steven Brust   *f*   745
*The Order War* - L.E. Modesitt Jr.   *f*   3936
*The Painter Knight* - Fiona Patton   *f*   4258
*Pendragon* - Stephen R. Lawhead   *f*   3357
*Pendragon's Banner* - Helen Hollick   *f*   2746
*The Perfect Princess* - Irene Radford   *f*   4462
*Polgara the Sorceress* - David Eddings   *f*   1734
*The President's Astrologer* - Barbara Shafferman   *f*   4926
*The Price of Blood and Honor* - Elizabeth Willey   *f*   5811
*Pride of Lions* - Morgan Llywelyn   *f*   3506

*Prince of Dogs* - Kate Elliott   *f*   1775
*Prince of the North* - Harry Turtledove   *f*   5509
*The Qualinesti* - Paul B. Thompson   *f*   5455
*The Queen of Ashes* - Deborah Turner Harris   *f*   2561
*The Quest Begins* - Wendy Pini   *f*   4337
*Rats and Gargoyles* - Mary Gentle   *f*   2196
*Realm of Light* - Deborah Chester   *f*   1008
*The Red Wyvern* - Katharine Kerr   *f*   3074
*Reign of Shadows* - Deborah Chester   *f*   1009
*Ring of Intrigue* - Jane S. Fancher   *f*   1863
*Ring of Lightning* - Jane S. Fancher   *f*   1864
*Rise of a Merchant Prince* - Raymond E. Feist   *f*   1909
*The Robin and the Kestrel* - Mercedes Lackey   *f*   3293
*Rouse a Sleeping Cat* - Dan Crawford   *f*   1249
*Royal Assassin* - Robin Hobb   *f*   2695
*The Ruins of Ambrai* - Melanie Rawn   *f*   4489
*Saber & Shadow* - S.M. Stirling   *f*   5297
*The Sapphire Rose* - David Eddings   *f*   1737
*Scotland the Brave* - Jennifer Roberson   *f*   4611
*Sea Without a Shore* - Sean Russell   *f*   4743
*Season of Storms* - Ellen Foxxe   *f*   2032
*The Seer King* - Chris Bunch   *f*   771
*Servant of the Empire* - Raymond E. Feist   *f*   1910
*Shadow of Obsession* - Rebecca Neason   *f*   4082
*Shadow of the Crown* - Craig Mills   *f*   3914
*The Shadow Shaia* - Alexis A. Gilliland   *f*   2235
*Shadow War* - Deborah Chester   *f*   1010
*Shadows over Lyra* - Patricia C. Wrede   *f*   5980
*Shards of Empire* - Susan Shwartz   *f*   5017
*Ships of Merior* - Janny Wurts   *f*   6004
*Sing the Four Quarters* - Tanya Huff   *f*   2799
*Skinny Legs and All* - Tom Robbins   *f*   4607
*Skybowl* - Melanie Rawn   *f*   4490
*Song for the Basilisk* - Patricia A. McKillip   *f*   3841
*A Sorcerer and a Gentleman* - Elizabeth Willey   *f*   5812
*Spear of Heaven* - Judith Tarr   *f*   5396
*Spell of Fate* - Mayer Alan Brenner   *f*   673
*The Spell of the Black Dagger* - Lawrence Watt-Evans   *f*   5648
*The Spirit Ring* - Lois McMaster Bujold   *f*   763
*Spiritride* - Mark Shepherd   *f*   4981
*Stalking Darkness* - Lynn Flewelling   *f*   1953
*The Stalking Horse* - Constance Ash   *f*   222
*Star Ascendant* - Louise Cooper   *f*   1180
*The Star Scroll* - Melanie Rawn   *f*   4491
*The Stars Dispose* - Michaela Roessner   *f*   4651
*Steal the Dragon* - Patricia Briggs   *f*   682
*The Steel Kings* - John Maddox Roberts   *f*   4621
*The Still* - David Feintuch   *f*   1902
*The Stolen Throne* - Harry Turtledove   *f*   5510
*The Stone Movers* - Patricia Mullen   *f*   4045
*The Stone Prince* - Fiona Patton   *f*   4259
*Streets of Blood* - Carl Sargent   *f*   4821
*Stronghold* - Melanie Rawn   *f*   4492
*Summer King, Winter Fool* - Lisa Goldstein   *f*   2263
*Sunrunner's Fire* - Melanie Rawn   *f*   4493
*Surrender None: The Legacy of Gird* - Elizabeth Moon   *f*   3975
*The Sword and the Lion* - Roberta Cray   *f*   1253
*Talion: Revenant* - Michael A. Stackpole   *f*   5206
*Taminy* - Maya Kaathryn Bohnhoff   *f*   563
*Tegne: Soul Warrior* - Richard La Plante   *f*   3268
*Temple of the Winds* - Terry Goodkind   *f*   2270
*Temporary Agency* - Rachel Pollack   *f*   4360
*Thornhold* - Elaine Cunningham   *f*   1293
*The Thousand Cities* - Harry Turtledove   *f*   5512
*Throne of Isis* - Judith Tarr   *f*   5397
*Thunder of the Captains* - Holly Lisle   *f*   3489
*Tigana* - Guy Gavriel Kay   *f*   3018
*Tiger Burning Bright* - Marion Zimmer Bradley   *f*   652
*The Time of Madness* - Thomas K. Martin   *f*   3652
*Touched by the Gods* - Lawrence Watt-Evans   *f*   5651
*Traitors* - Kristine Kathryn Rusch   *f*   4729

*A Tremor in the Bitter Earth* - Katya
    Reimann  f  4527
*Twisted Dragon* - Kevin Stein  f  5251
*Two Crowns for America* - Katherine Kurtz  f  3262
*The Uncrowned King* - Michelle West  f  5760
*The Unicorn Peace* - John Lee  f  3399
*The Unicorn War* - John Lee  f  3401
*Unquenchable Fire* - Rachel Pollack  f  4361
*Upland Outlaws* - Dave Duncan  f  1690
*The Veils of Snows* - Mark Helprin  f  2654
*Videssos Besieged* - Harry Turtledove  f  5513
*Waking Beauty* - Paul Witcover  f  5931
*Waking in Dreamland* - Jody Lynn Nye  f  4177
*Wanderlust* - Mary Kirchoff  f  3155
*War* - Simon Hawke  f  2625
*The War Amongst the Angels* - Michael
    Moorcock  f  3986
*The War of Don Emmanuel's Nether Parts* - Louis de
    Bernieres  f  1412
*The Watcher's Mask* - Laurie J. Marks  f  3627
*The Well-Favored Man: The Tale of the Sorcerer's
    Nephew* - Elizabeth Willey  f  5813
*The White Mists of Power* - Kristine Kathryn
    Rusch  f  4730
*The White Tribunal* - Paula Volsky  f  5583
*Wicked: The Life and Times of the Wicked Witch of
    the West* - Gregory Maguire  f  3609
*A Wild Dog and Lone* - Dan Crawford  f  1251
*The Wild Hunt: Vengeance Moon* - Jocelin
    Foxe  f  2031
*Wildfire* - Jo Clayton  f  1073
*Wind From a Foreign Sky* - Katya Reimann  f  4528
*Winds of Fury* - Mercedes Lackey  f  3306
*Winged Magic* - Mary H. Herbert  f  2678
*The Witches of Eileanan* - Kate Forsyth  f  1984
*The Wizard King* - Julie Dean Smith  f  5127
*The Wolf of Winter* - Paula Volsky  f  5584
*Wolf's Cub* - Mackay Wood  f  5964
*World Without End* - Sean Russell  f  4744
*Wrath of the Princes* - Holly Lisle  f  3490

**Fantasy — Post-Disaster**

*Amnesia Moon* - Jonathan Lethem  f  3438
*Captain Jack Zodiac* - Michael Kandel  f  3009
*Children of Enchantment* - Anne Kelleher
    Bush  f  787
*The Children of Men* - P.D. James  f  2870
*City of Bones* - Martha Wells  f  5748
*Daughter of Prophecy* - Anne Kelleher Bush  f  788
*The Elementals* - Morgan Llywelyn  f  3503
*Elsewhere* - Will Shetterly  f  4993
*The Fifth Sacred Thing* - Starhawk  f  5209
*Last Refuge* - Elizabeth Ann Scarborough  f  4866
*Nevernever* - Will Shetterly  f  4995
*The Night Watch* - Sean Stewart  f  5274
*Nothing Sacred* - Elizabeth Ann
    Scarborough  f  4867
*The Poisoned Lands* - John Maddox
    Roberts  f  4619
*Queens of Land and Sea* - John Maddox
    Roberts  f  4620
*The Steel Kings* - John Maddox Roberts  f  4621
*Summerland* - L. Dean James  f  2865
*The Wizard of Camelot* - Simon Hawke  f  2627
*The Wizard of Santa Fe* - Simon Hawke  f  2628
*Wolfking* - Bridget Wood  f  5963

**Fantasy — Psychic Powers**

*Above the Lower Sky* - Tom Deitz  f  1469
*Alvin Journeyman* - Orson Scott Card  f  881
*Assassin's Apprentice* - Robin Hobb  f  2693
*Assassin's Quest* - Robin Hobb  f  2694
*Bureau 13* - Nick Pollotta  f  4362
*Children of Enchantment* - Anne Kelleher
    Bush  f  787
*A City in Winter* - Mark Helprin  f  2653

*City of the Sorcerers* - Mary H. Herbert  f  2673
*Daughter of Prophecy* - Anne Kelleher Bush  f  788
*Death of an Adept* - Katherine Kurtz  f  3257
*The Devil You Say* - Elisa DeCarlo  f  1450
*Doomsday Exam* - Nick Pollotta  f  4363
*Exile's Challenge* - Angus Wells  f  5734
*Exile's Children* - Angus Wells  f  5735
*The Fifth Sacred Thing* - Starhawk  f  5209
*Finder* - Emma Bull  f  769
*Full Moonster* - Nick Pollotta  f  4364
*Gravelight* - Marion Zimmer Bradley  f  636
*Heartfire* - Orson Scott Card  f  889
*The Heldan* - Deborah Talmadge-Bickmore  f  5383
*Henry's Gift: The Magic Eye* - David
    Worsick  f  5972
*How Like a God* - Brenda W. Clough  f  1089
*Hunter's Death* - Michelle West  f  5758
*Hunter's Oath* - Michelle West  f  5759
*Indiana Jones and the Sky Pirates* - Martin
    Caidin  f  825
*Lady of the Trillium* - Marion Zimmer
    Bradley  f  641
*Larque on the Wing* - Nancy Springer  f  5180
*The Lodge of the Lynx* - Katherine Kurtz  f  3259
*M'Lady Witch* - Christopher Stasheff  f  5217
*Nameless Magery* - Delia Marshall Turner  f  5490
*The Nexus* - Mike McQuay  f  3860
*Quicksilver's Knight* - Christopher Stasheff  f  5220
*Royal Assassin* - Robin Hobb  f  2695
*The Silent Strength of Stones* - Nina Kiriki
    Hoffman  f  2716
*Snow Brother* - S.M. Stirling  f  5299
*Songsmith* - Andre Norton  f  4161
*The Spirit Gate* - Maya Kaathryn Bohnhoff  f  562
*Strong Spirits* - Elisa DeCarlo  f  1451
*The Thread That Binds the Bones* - Nina Kiriki
    Hoffman  f  2717
*Time and the Clock Mice, Etcetera* - Peter
    Dickinson  f  1527
*To Fall Like Stars* - Nancy Asire  f  257
*Towers of Darkover* - Marion Zimmer
    Bradley  f  653
*A Tremor in the Bitter Earth* - Katya
    Reimann  f  4527
*Walker between the Worlds* - Diane
    DesRochers  f  1499
*When the Bough Breaks* - Mercedes Lackey  f  3302
*When True Night Falls* - C.S. Friedman  f  2060
*Wordwright* - Tom Deitz  f  1478
*World Without End* - Molly Cochran  f  1093

**Fantasy — Quest**

*Across the Thlassa Mey* - Dennis McCarty  f  3765
*Addams Family Values* - Todd Strasser  f  5324
*Aisling* - Louise Cooper  f  1172
*Anvil of the Sun* - Anne Lesley Groell  f  2451
*Aquamancer* - Don Callander  f  841
*Arcady* - Michael Williams  f  5818
*Avatar* - Louise Cooper  f  1173
*Believe: A Novel* - William Shatner  f  4929
*The Belly of the Wolf* - R.A. MacAvoy  f  3580
*Beyond the Moons* - David Cook  f  1144
*Beyond the Pale* - Jack Koke  f  3198
*The Birth of the Blade* - Dennis McCarty  f  3766
*Black Trillium* - Marion Zimmer Bradley  f  630
*The Blackgod* - J. Gregory Keyes  f  3095
*The Blood Jaguar* - Michael H. Payne  f  4271
*The Blood of a Dragon* - Lawrence Watt-
    Evans  f  5640
*Blood of the Colyn Muir* - Paul Edwin
    Zimmer  f  6083
*Blood Trillium* - Julian May  f  3696
*Blue Moon Rising* - Simon R. Green  f  2362
*Bones of the Past* - Holly Lisle  f  3478
*The Book of Knights* - Yves Meynard  f  3884
*Book of Stones* - L. Dean James  f  2862

*The Book of Water* - Marjorie Bradley
    Kellogg  f  3045
*The Boy From the Burren* - Sheila Gilluly  f  2236
*A Breach in the Watershed* - Douglas Niles  f  4105
*Briar Rose* - Jane Yolen  f  6029
*The Bridge of Dawn* - Neil Hancock  f  2531
*Calling on Dragons* - Patricia C. Wrede  f  5974
*Captains Outrageous, or, For Doom the Bell Tolls* -
    Roy V. Young  f  6049
*Carnivores of Light and Darkness* - Alan Dean
    Foster  f  1996
*Castle of Deception* - Mercedes Lackey  f  3275
*Cathedral of Thorns* - Steven Frankos  f  2041
*The Catswold Portal* - Shirley Rousseau
    Murphy  f  4055
*Chaos Mode* - Piers Anthony  f  165
*A Child of Elvish* - Nancy Varian Berberick  f  457
*Children of Amarid* - David B. Coe  f  1095
*Chorus Skating* - Alan Dean Foster  f  1998
*The Chronicles of Master Li and Number Ten Ox* -
    Barry Hughart  f  2803
*City of the Sorcerers* - Mary H. Herbert  f  2673
*The Clan of the Warlord* - Elizabeth H.
    Boyer  f  604
*Cloud Castles* - Michael Scott Rohan  f  4659
*The Cloud People* - Robert B. Kelly  f  3050
*Clouds End* - Sean Stewart  f  5272
*A College of Magics* - Caroline Stevermer  f  5266
*The Color of Her Panties* - Piers Anthony  f  167
*The Coral Kingdom* - Douglas Niles  f  4106
*Corum: The Coming of Chaos* - Michael
    Moorcock  f  3978
*The Crown of Dalemark* - Diana Wynne
    Jones  f  2945
*The Cup of Morning Shadows* - Rosemary
    Edghill  f  1747
*Curse of the Black Heron* - Holly Lisle  f  3479
*Dancing Jack* - Laurie J. Marks  f  3624
*Dark Heart* - Betsy James  f  2857
*Dark Legend* - Jamake Highwater  f  2686
*Dark Magic* - Angus Wells  f  5733
*Dark Mirror, Dark Dreams* - Sharon Green  f  2357
*Darkthunder's Way* - Tom Deitz  f  1470
*Daughter of the Drow* - Elaine Cunningham  f  1287
*Dawn Land* - Joseph Bruchac  f  731
*Deerskin* - Robin McKinley  f  3844
*Demon Blade* - Mark A. Garland  f  2141
*Demons Don't Dream* - Piers Anthony  f  168
*The Diamond Throne* - David Eddings  f  1731
*Dinotopia* - James Gurney  f  2468
*Dirty Work* - Dan McGirt  f  3810
*Domes of Fire* - David Eddings  f  1732
*Drachenfels* - Jack Yeovil  f  6022
*The Dragon and the Djinn* - Gordon R.
    Dickson  f  1528
*Dragon Cauldron* - Laurence Yep  f  6024
*The Dragon Knight* - Gordon R. Dickson  f  1532
*The Dragon Reborn* - Robert Jordan  f  2985
*Dragon Rescue* - Don Callander  f  843
*The Dragon Revenant* - Katharine Kerr  f  3069
*Dragon Tome* - Richard A. Knaak  f  3169
*Dragon War* - Laurence Yep  f  6025
*The Dragonbone Chair* - Tad Williams  f  5829
*Dragon's Bait* - Vivian Vande Velde  f  5556
*Dragon's Domain* - Thorarinn Gunnarsson  f  2461
*Dragons on the Town* - Thorarinn
    Gunnarsson  f  2463
*Dragon's Plunder* - Brad Strickland  f  5336
*Dragon's Winter* - Elizabeth A. Lynn  f  3578
*The Dragonstone* - Dennis L. McKiernan  f  3832
*The Druid of Shannara* - Terry Brooks  f  710
*The Edge of the World* - William Sarabande  f  4817
*The Elf Queen of Shannara* - Terry Brooks  f  711
*Elfsong* - Elaine Cunningham  f  1289
*The Enchanted Isles* - Casey Flynn  f  1960
*The Eye of the Hunter* - Dennis L.
    McKiernan  f  3833
*The Eye of the World* - Robert Jordan  f  2986
*Faces of Deception* - Troy Denning  f  1485

*The Far Kingdoms* - Allan Cole  *f*  1104
*Faun & Games* - Piers Anthony  *f*  169
*Feather Stroke* - Sydney J. Van Scyoc  *f*  5542
*Finder's Bane* - Kate Novak  *f*  4165
*Fire Arrow* - Edith Pattou  *f*  4260
*The Fire's Stone* - Tanya Huff  *f*  2796
*Flight of the Dragon Kyn* - Susan Fletcher  *f*  1951
*Flight of the Raven* - Jennifer Roberson  *f*  4608
*Flute Song Magic* - Andrea Shettle  *f*  4996
*Forbidden Magic* - Angus Wells  *f*  5736
*A Forest Lord* - Michael Williams  *f*  5819
*Forever After* - Roger Zelazny  *f*  6066
*The Forge in the Forest* - Michael Scott
   Rohan  *f*  4660
*The Forge of Virtue* - Lynn Abbey  *f*  16
*The Fortress of Eternity* - Andrew
   Whitmore  *f*  5790
*Fortress of Frost and Fire* - Mercedes
   Lackey  *f*  3282
*The Fortress of the Pearl* - Michael
   Moorcock  *f*  3982
*Fractal Mode* - Piers Anthony  *f*  171
*A Game of Universe* - Eric S. Nylund  *f*  4178
*Geis of the Gargoyle* - Piers Anthony  *f*  172
*The Gilded Chain: A Tale of the King's Blades* - Dave
   Duncan  *f*  1679
*A Girl Named Disaster* - Nancy Farmer  *f*  1868
*The Glass Warrior* - Robert E. Vardeman  *f*  5563
*Go Quest, Young Man* - K.B. Bogen  *f*  557
*The Goblin Mirror* - C.J. Cherryh  *f*  994
*Goblins in the Castle* - Bruce Coville  *f*  1218
*The Godmother's Web* - Elizabeth Ann
   Scarborough  *f*  4864
*God's Dice* - S. Andrew Swann  *f*  5364
*Goldclimbers* - Nancy Luenn  *f*  3545
*The Golden Compass* - Philip Pullman  *f*  4446
*Golden Trillium* - Andre Norton  *f*  4153
*Greenmagic* - Crawford Kilian  *f*  3105
*Guardian's Key* - Anne Logston  *f*  3511
*The Hand of Chaos* - Margaret Weis  *f*  5715
*The Hands of Lyr* - Andre Norton  *f*  4154
*Haroun and the Sea of Stories* - Salman
   Rushdie  *f*  4731
*Harp of Winds* - Maggie Furey  *f*  2097
*Harpy Thyme* - Piers Anthony  *f*  174
*Hearts and Armor* - Ron Miller  *f*  3903
*The Heldan* - Deborah Talmadge-Bickmore  *f*  5383
*Henry's Gift: The Magic Eye* - David
   Worsick  *f*  5972
*Here There Be Dragons* - Roger Zelazny  *f*  6069
*The Hero King* - Rick Shelley  *f*  4970
*The Hero of Varay* - Rick Shelley  *f*  4971
*Hero's Song* - Edith Pattou  *f*  4261
*The Hidden Realms* - Sharon Green  *f*  2358
*Higher Mythology* - Jody Lynn Nye  *f*  4170
*The Hollowing* - Robert Holdstock  *f*  2738
*Hook* - Terry Brooks  *f*  713
*Horrible Humes* - Stephen Billias  *f*  487
*Horrors of the Dancing Gods* - Jack L.
   Chalker  *f*  955
*Hunting the Ghost Dancer* - A.A. Attanasio  *f*  268
*If I Pay Thee Not in Gold* - Piers Anthony  *f*  176
*The Illusionists* - Faren Miller  *f*  3894
*In Sylvan Shadows* - R.A. Salvatore  *f*  4800
*Indiana Jones and the Dance of the Giants* - Rob
   MacGregor  *f*  3588
*Indiana Jones and the Peril at Delphi* - Rob
   MacGregor  *f*  3591
*Indiana Jones and the Seven Veils* - Rob
   MacGregor  *f*  3592
*Indiana Jones and the Unicorn's Legacy* - Rob
   MacGregor  *f*  3593
*Indiana Jones and the White Witch* - Martin
   Caidin  *f*  826
*Infanta* - Louise Cooper  *f*  1176
*The Innkeeper's Song* - Peter S. Beagle  *f*  409
*Into the Forge* - Dennis L. McKiernan  *f*  3835
*Into the Labyrinth* - Margaret Weis  *f*  5716

*Into the Land of the Unicorns* - Bruce
   Coville  *f*  1219
*Into the Void* - Nigel Findley  *f*  1937
*Iron Dragons: Mountains and Madness* - Rose
   Estes  *f*  1839
*The Iron Lance* - Stephen R. Lawhead  *f*  3356
*The Iron Ring* - Lloyd Alexander  *f*  68
*The Janus Mask* - Richard A. Knaak  *f*  3171
*Jeremy Thatcher, Dragon Hatcher* - Bruce
   Coville  *f*  1221
*The Jewel of Equilibrant* - Steven Frankos  *f*  2042
*The Jewel of Fire* - Diana L. Paxson  *f*  4265
*The Key of the Keplian* - Andre Norton  *f*  4156
*King of the Grey* - Richard A. Knaak  *f*  3173
*Kingdoms of the Night* - Allan Cole  *f*  1105
*Kirins: The Flight of the Ain* - James D.
   Priest  *f*  4433
*Kirins: The Secret of the Hanging Stones* - James D.
   Priest  *f*  4434
*Kirins: The Spell of No'an* - James D.
   Priest  *f*  4435
*Konrad* - David Ferring  *f*  1927
*The Land of Gold* - Gillian Bradshaw  *f*  658
*The Last Human* - Tom De Haven  *f*  1422
*The Last World* - Christoph Ransmayr  *f*  4475
*Lavondyss: Journey to an Unknown Region* - Robert
   Holdstock  *f*  2739
*The Legend of Nightfall* - Mickey Zucker
   Reichert  *f*  4521
*Legends Reborn* - Kenneth C. Flint  *f*  1958
*The Lightless Kingdom* - Jonathan Wylie  *f*  6007
*Lightning's Daughter* - Mary H. Herbert  *f*  2676
*The Loneliest Magician* - Irene Radford  *f*  4461
*The Longing Ring* - Christopher Kubasik  *f*  3246
*Lord Kelvin's Machine* - James P. Blaylock  *f*  520
*Lords of the Sky* - Angus Wells  *f*  5738
*The Lost City of Zork* - Robin Wayne Bailey  *f*  288
*The Lotus and the Rose* - Scott Ciencin  *f*  1029
*The Mace of Souls* - Bruce Fergusson  *f*  1925
*The Magic Wars* - Jo Clayton  *f*  1068
*Majyk by Design* - Esther Friesner  *f*  2080
*Marbleheart* - Don Callander  *f*  846
*The Mark of the Cat* - Andre Norton  *f*  4157
*Masquerades* - Kate Novak  *f*  4166
*Master of Many Treasures* - Mary Brown  *f*  726
*The Master of Whitestorm* - Janny Wurts  *f*  6003
*The Meri* - Maya Kaathryn Bohnhoff  *f*  561
*Merlin's Legacy: Dawn of Camelot* - Quinn Taylor
   Evans  *f*  1857
*The Mines of Behemoth* - Michael Shea  *f*  4945
*The Moon in Hiding* - Teresa Edgerton  *f*  1745
*The Moonbane Mage* - Laurie J. Marks  *f*  3626
*Moonwise* - Greer Ilene Gilman  *f*  2238
*Most Ancient Song* - Casey Flynn  *f*  1961
*Myst: The Book of D'ni* - Rand Miller  *f*  3897
*Nemesis* - Louise Cooper  *f*  1177
*Nightfeeder* - Judith Reeves-Stevens  *f*  4513
*No Quarter* - Tanya Huff  *f*  2798
*The Nomad Queen* - James Gordon White  *f*  5783
*One for the Morning Glory* - John Barnes  *f*  355
*Orc's Opal* - Piers Anthony  *f*  183
*The Outcast* - Simon Hawke  *f*  2621
*Outcasts* - Clayton Emery  *f*  1815
*The Paper Grail* - James P. Blaylock  *f*  522
*People of the Lakes* - Kathleen O'Neal Gear  *f*  2164
*People of the Sea* - W. Michael Gear  *f*  2169
*Phantom Banjo* - Elizabeth Ann
   Scarborough  *f*  4868
*Phoenix Fire* - Elizabeth Forrest  *f*  1974
*Photographing Fairies* - Steve Szilagyi  *f*  5379
*Picking the Ballad's Bones* - Elizabeth Ann
   Scarborough  *f*  4869
*Pigs Don't Fly* - Mary Brown  *f*  727
*Plague Demon* - Brian Craig  *f*  1239
*A Plague of Angels* - Sheri S. Tepper  *f*  5433
*The Prince and the Pilgrim* - Mary Stewart  *f*  5270
*Pyromancer* - Don Callander  *f*  847
*Quest for the Fallen Star* - Piers Anthony  *f*  185

*Quest: In Search of the Dragontooth* - Michael
   Green  *f*  2346
*Question Quest* - Piers Anthony  *f*  186
*The Radiant Dragon* - Elaine Cunningham  *f*  1291
*The Rainbow Sword* - Adrienne Martine-
   Barnes  *f*  3659
*The Remarkable Journey of Prince Jen* - Lloyd
   Alexander  *f*  69
*A Remembrance for Kedrigern* - John
   Morressy  *f*  4014
*Revenant* - Louise Cooper  *f*  1178
*The Revenge of the Rose* - Michael
   Moorcock  *f*  3985
*A Ride on the Red Mare's Back* - Ursula K. Le
   Guin  *f*  3382
*The Ring of Winter* - James Lowder  *f*  3538
*The Rose Sea* - S.M. Stirling  *f*  5296
*The Ruby Knight* - David Eddings  *f*  1736
*The Sage* - Christopher Stasheff  *f*  5221
*The Sands of Kalaven: A Novel of Shunlar* - Carol
   Heller  *f*  2651
*Sarah Canary* - Karen Joy Fowler  *f*  2028
*The Schemes of Dragons* - Dave Smeds  *f*  5097
*The Scions of Shannara* - Terry Brooks  *f*  716
*Search for the Starblade* - Keith Taylor  *f*  5408
*Searching for Dragons* - Patricia C. Wrede  *f*  5979
*Seed upon the Wind* - Carole Nelson
   Douglas  *f*  1584
*The Seeker* - Simon Hawke  *f*  2624
*The Seeress of Kell* - David Eddings  *f*  1738
*Senor Vivo and the Coca Lord* - Louis de
   Bernieres  *f*  1411
*Serpent Mage* - Margaret Weis  *f*  5726
*Shadow Dance* - Anne Logston  *f*  3513
*Shadow Dawn* - Chris Claremont  *f*  1042
*The Shadow Eater* - Adam Lee  *f*  3386
*Shadow Hunt* - Anne Logston  *f*  3514
*Shadow-Maze* - Mark Smith  *f*  5133
*Shadow Moon* - George Lucas  *f*  3540
*Shadow of a Dark Queen* - Raymond E.
   Feist  *f*  1911
*The Shadow of Sorcery* - Andrew J. Offutt  *f*  4202
*Shadowdance* - Robin Wayne Bailey  *f*  290
*Shadowlight* - Jackie Hyman  *f*  2819
*Shadows After Dark* - Ouida Crozier  *f*  1286
*Shadows on the Hill* - Jackie Cassada  *f*  935
*Shadow's Son* - Shirley Meier  *f*  3872
*Sheepfarmer's Daughter* - Elizabeth Moon  *f*  3973
*Shifter* - Judith Reeves-Stevens  *f*  4515
*Snow Brother* - S.M. Stirling  *f*  5299
*Someplace to Be Flying* - Charles de Lint  *f*  1435
*Son of Spellsinger* - Alan Dean Foster  *f*  2015
*Song in the Silence* - Elizabeth Kerner  *f*  3065
*Song of the River* - Sue Harrison  *f*  2583
*Songs of the Dancing Gods* - Jack L. Chalker  *f*  962
*The Sorceress and the Cygnet* - Patricia A.
   McKillip  *f*  3842
*Sorceress of Darshiva* - David Eddings  *f*  1739
*The Spellkey Trilogy* - Ann Downer  *f*  1592
*Spirits of Cavern and Hearth* - M. Coleman
   Easton  *f*  1722
*Starless Night* - R.A. Salvatore  *f*  4807
*Steel and Stone* - Ellen Porath  *f*  4368
*Stone of Farewell* - Tad Williams  *f*  5831
*The Stone of Time* - Rose Estes  *f*  1840
*A Strange and Ancient Name* - Josepha
   Sherman  *f*  4991
*Street Magic* - Michael Reaves  *f*  4497
*The Subtle Knife* - Philip Pullman  *f*  4448
*Sword-Breaker* - Jennifer Roberson  *f*  4613
*Sword of Flame* - Maggie Furey  *f*  2098
*The Sword of Maiden's Tears* - Rosemary
   Edghill  *f*  1748
*Taking Flight* - Lawrence Watt-Evans  *f*  5650
*The Talismans of Shannara* - Terry Brooks  *f*  717
*A Tapestry of Lions* - Jennifer Roberson  *f*  4615
*Tatham Mound* - Piers Anthony  *f*  191
*Tears of the Night Sky* - Linda P. Baker  *f*  299

*Tehanu: The Last Book of Earthsea* - Ursula K. Le Guin  *f*  3383
*The Temper of Wisdom* - Lynn Abbey  *f*  17
*Thorn and Needle* - Paul B. Thompson  *f*  5456
*A Time of Omens* - Katharine Kerr  *f*  3078
*To Green Angel Tower* - Tad Williams  *f*  5832
*Token of Dragonsblood* - Damaris Cole  *f*  1114
*Trader* - Charles de Lint  *f*  1438
*Travel Far, Pay No Fare* - Anne Lindbergh  *f*  3468
*Troika* - Louise Cooper  *f*  1181
*Troll-Quest* - Rose Estes  *f*  1841
*The True Knight* - Susan Dexter  *f*  1513
*The Ultimate Helm* - Russ T. Howard  *f*  2785
*Unicorn Highway* - David Lee Jones  *f*  2941
*The Unicorn Solution* - John Lee  *f*  3400
*User Unfriendly* - Vivian Vande Velde  *f*  5558
*Valorian* - Mary H. Herbert  *f*  2677
*Villains by Necessity* - Eve Forward  *f*  1985
*Virtual Mode* - Piers Anthony  *f*  194
*Voyage of the Fox Rider* - Dennis L. McKiernan  *f*  3837
*Waking in Dreamland* - Jody Lynn Nye  *f*  4177
*The War God's Own* - David Weber  *f*  5682
*War of the Three Waters* - Douglas Niles  *f*  4110
*The Warding of Witch World* - Andre Norton  *f*  4163
*The Warrior's Tale* - Allan Cole  *f*  1110
*The Waterborn* - J. Gregory Keyes  *f*  3098
*Wayfinder's Story: The Seventh Book of Lost Swords* - Fred Saberhagen  *f*  4777
*The Wealdwife's Tale* - Paul Hazel  *f*  2636
*The Well-Favored Man: The Tale of the Sorcerer's Nephew* - Elizabeth Willey  *f*  5813
*Westlin Wind* - Charles de Lint  *f*  1439
*Wheels of Fire* - Mercedes Lackey  *f*  3301
*When Dreams Collide* - Wm. Mark Simmons  *f*  5063
*When the Gods Are Silent* - Jane M. Lindskold  *f*  3477
*The White Mists of Power* - Kristine Kathryn Rusch  *f*  4730
*The Wild Hunt* - Jane Yolen  *f*  6042
*Wild Magic* - Angus Wells  *f*  5741
*The Wild Road* - Gabriel King  *f*  3120
*The Willing Spirit* - Piers Anthony  *f*  195
*The Wind Crystal* - Diana L. Paxson  *f*  4269
*Wind Whispers, Shadow Shouts* - Sharon Green  *f*  2360
*Winds of Change* - Mercedes Lackey  *f*  3304
*Winds of Fate* - Mercedes Lackey  *f*  3305
*Witches Abroad* - Terry Pratchett  *f*  4404
*The Witches of Eileanan* - Kate Forsyth  *f*  1984
*The Wizard and the Floating City* - Christopher Rowley  *f*  4699
*The Wizardry Quested* - Rick Cook  *f*  1163
*Wizard's First Rule* - Terry Goodkind  *f*  2271
*Wolfwalker* - Tara K. Harper  *f*  2553
*The Wolves of Autumn* - Scott Ciencin  *f*  1035
*The Wood Nymph and the Cranky Saint* - C. Dale Brittain  *f*  706
*The Work of the Sun* - Teresa Edgerton  *f*  1746
*World Without End* - Sean Russell  *f*  4744
*Wren to the Rescue* - Sherwood Smith  *f*  5142
*Wren's Quest* - Sherwood Smith  *f*  5143
*Yon Ill Wind* - Piers Anthony  *f*  196

**Fantasy — Religious**

*Allamanda* - Michael Williams  *f*  5817
*Ancient Games* - Scott Ciencin  *f*  1028
*Angel Light* - Andrew M. Greeley  *f*  2342
*Angels!* - Jack Dann  *f*  1339
*Angelwalk: A Modern Fable* - Roger Elwood  *f*  1803
*Arc d'X* - Steve Erickson  *f*  1835
*The Arm of the Stone* - Victoria Strauss  *f*  5333
*At the City Limits of Fate* - Michael Bishop  *f*  497
*The Belly of the Wolf* - R.A. MacAvoy  *f*  3580

*Between the Rivers* - Harry Turtledove  *f*  5496
*Blameless in Abaddon* - James Morrow  *f*  4029
*A Blessing on the Moon* - Joseph Skibell  *f*  5079
*Blood of the Goddess* - Kara Dalkey  *f*  1318
*Branch and Crown* - Gael Baudino  *f*  389
*A Cast of Corbies* - Mercedes Lackey  *f*  3274
*Christmas Forever* - David G. Hartwell  *f*  2587
*Christmas Magic* - David G. Hartwell  *f*  2588
*City of Pain* - John Terra  *f*  5438
*Coyote* - Peter Gadol  *f*  2100
*Cross and Crescent* - Susan Shwartz  *f*  5014
*The Crystal Rose* - Maya Kaathryn Bohnhoff  *f*  560
*The Dagger and the Cross: A Novel of the Crusades* - Judith Tarr  *f*  5393
*Dagger Magic* - Katherine Kurtz  *f*  3256
*Damnbanna* - Nancy Springer  *f*  5177
*Death of an Adept* - Katherine Kurtz  *f*  3257
*Delta City* - Felicity Savage  *f*  4849
*The Door into Sunset* - Diane Duane  *f*  1660
*Dragon Season* - Michael Cassutt  *f*  936
*Dreambuilder* - Tom Deitz  *f*  1471
*The Eagle and the Sword* - A.A. Attanasio  *f*  267
*The Elementals* - Morgan Llywelyn  *f*  3503
*The Falcon and the Serpent* - Cheryl A. Smith  *f*  5101
*A Farce to Be Reckoned With* - Roger Zelazny  *f*  6064
*Fire and Ice* - Edward Myers  *f*  4061
*The Forest House* - Marion Zimmer Bradley  *f*  633
*Forest of the Night* - S.P. Somtow  *f*  5156
*The Gates of Twilight* - Paula Volsky  *f*  5581
*Good Omens: The Nice and Accurate Prophecies of Agnes Nutter, Witch* - Neil Gaiman  *f*  2103
*The Grail of Hearts* - Susan Shwartz  *f*  5015
*The Hammer and the Cross* - Harry Harrison  *f*  2570
*The Hands of Lyr* - Andre Norton  *f*  4154
*Heaven Sent: 18 Glorious Tales of the Angels* - Peter Crowther  *f*  1283
*Hederick, the Theocrat* - Ellen Dodge Severson  *f*  4925
*Here There Be Angels* - Jane Yolen  *f*  6031
*Humans* - Donald E. Westlake  *f*  5768
*Humility Garden* - Felicity Savage  *f*  4850
*In the Land of Winter* - Richard Grant  *f*  2326
*King and Emperor* - Harry Harrison  *f*  2571
*Lady of Avalon* - Marion Zimmer Bradley  *f*  640
*The Last Coin* - James P. Blaylock  *f*  519
*Last Refuge* - Elizabeth Ann Scarborough  *f*  4866
*Lost Boys* - Orson Scott Card  *f*  891
*The Lost History of Redwyn* - William Jay  *f*  2883
*The Meri* - Maya Kaathryn Bohnhoff  *f*  561
*Milton in America* - Peter Ackroyd  *f*  25
*Mojo and the Pickle Jar* - Douglas Bell  *f*  433
*The Notorious Abbess* - Vera Chapman  *f*  965
*O Greenest Branch!* - Gael Baudino  *f*  394
*The Old Man and Mr. Smith* - Peter Ustinov  *f*  5532
*The Painted Alphabet* - Diana Darling  *f*  1356
*Pendragon* - Stephen R. Lawhead  *f*  3357
*People of the River* - W. Michael Gear  *f*  2168
*Quest: In Search of the Dragontooth* - Michael Green  *f*  2346
*Rats and Gargoyles* - Mary Gentle  *f*  2196
*Renaissance Moon* - Linda Nevins  *f*  4093
*Resurrection Man* - Sean Stewart  *f*  5277
*The Riddled Man* - Mark E. Rogers  *f*  4654
*Riverrun* - S.P. Somtow  *f*  5159
*The Robin and the Kestrel* - Mercedes Lackey  *f*  3293
*Ronin* - D.A. Heeley  *f*  2639
*Sable, Shadow and Ice* - Cheryl J. Franklin  *f*  2039
*Sati* - Christopher Pike  *f*  4330
*The Seventh Heart* - Marina Fitch  *f*  1943
*Shadows Fall* - Simon R. Green  *f*  2373
*Shangri-La: The Return to the World of Lost Horizon* - Eleanor Cooney  *f*  1169
*Slow Funeral* - Rebecca Ore  *f*  4221
*Small Gods* - Terry Pratchett  *f*  4400

*Soothslayer: A Magickal Fantasy* - D.J. Conway  *f*  1143
*The Spawn of Loki* - Jason Henderson  *f*  2658
*The Spirit Gate* - Maya Kaathryn Bohnhoff  *f*  562
*Stones of the Dalai Lama* - Ken Mitchell  *f*  3916
*Strands of Sunlight* - Gael Baudino  *f*  396
*Summon the Keeper* - Tanya Huff  *f*  2800
*The Sword and the Lion* - Roberta Cray  *f*  1253
*Taminy* - Maya Kaathryn Bohnhoff  *f*  563
*Tegne: Soul Warrior* - Richard La Plante  *f*  3268
*The Templar Treasure* - Katherine Kurtz  *f*  3261
*Thorn and Needle* - Paul B. Thompson  *f*  5456
*Throne of Isis* - Judith Tarr  *f*  5397
*The Throne of Tara* - John Desjarlais  *f*  1498
*Thunder in the Sky* - William Sarabande  *f*  4819
*Towing Jehovah* - James Morrow  *f*  4035
*Waking Beauty* - Paul Witcover  *f*  5931
*Waking the Moon* - Elizabeth Hand  *f*  2538
*The War Amongst the Angels* - Michael Moorcock  *f*  3986
*The Waterborn* - J. Gregory Keyes  *f*  3098
*The Ways of Magic* - Scott Ciencin  *f*  1033
*Web of Futures* - Jefferson P. Swycaffer  *f*  5376
*When True Night Falls* - C.S. Friedman  *f*  2060
*Wicked: The Life and Times of the Wicked Witch of the West* - Gregory Maguire  *f*  3609
*Wild Magic* - Jo Clayton  *f*  1072
*The Witch and the Cathedral* - C. Dale Brittain  *f*  705
*Witchwood* - John Buchan  *f*  750
*Ye Gods!* - Tom Holt  *f*  2753

**Fantasy — Romance**

*Alamut* - Judith Tarr  *f*  5390
*The Animal Wife* - Elizabeth Marshall Thomas  *f*  5444
*Aurian* - Maggie Furey  *f*  2095
*Beneath the Web* - Lynn Abbey  *f*  12
*The Castle of the Silver Wheel* - Teresa Edgerton  *f*  1741
*Changing Fate* - Elisabeth Waters  *f*  5629
*Child of Faerie, Child of Earth* - Josepha Sherman  *f*  4985
*The Dagger and the Cross: A Novel of the Crusades* - Judith Tarr  *f*  5393
*Distant Dreams* - Jenny Lykins  *f*  3576
*The Dragons of the Rhine* - Diana L. Paxson  *f*  4264
*Ecstasia* - Francesca Lia Block  *f*  547
*Eternity* - Maggie Shayne  *f*  4943
*An Exchange of Gifts* - Anne McCaffrey  *f*  3731
*The Falcon and the Serpent* - Cheryl A. Smith  *f*  5101
*The Fire Rose* - Mercedes Lackey  *f*  3280
*The Gnome's Engine* - Teresa Edgerton  *f*  1742
*The Golden Key* - Melanie Rawn  *f*  4486
*The Golden Mean* - Nick Bantock  *f*  334
*Gossamer Axe* - Gael Baudino  *f*  392
*The Grass Dancer* - Susan Power  *f*  4380
*Guinevere: The Legend in Autumn* - Persia Woolley  *f*  5970
*A Heroine of the World* - Tanith Lee  *f*  3412
*Horses of Heaven* - Gillian Bradshaw  *f*  657
*The Interior Life* - Katherine Blake  *f*  515
*Isle of View* - Piers Anthony  *f*  177
*Lady of the Forest* - Jennifer Roberson  *f*  4609
*The Last Highlander* - Claire Cross  *f*  1271
*A Love through Time* - Terri Brisbin  *f*  691
*The Magic of Recluce* - L.E. Modesitt Jr.  *f*  3934
*Magician's Ward* - Patricia C. Wrede  *f*  5976
*Maze of Moonlight* - Gael Baudino  *f*  393
*The Meddlesome Ghost* - Sheila Rosalynd Allen  *f*  84
*Mother Earth, Father Sky* - Sue Harrison  *f*  2581
*A Once and Future Love* - Anne Kelleher  *f*  3039
*One Wish* - C.J. Card  *f*  880
*People of the Earth* - W. Michael Gear  *f*  2166

*The Plains of Passage* - Jean M. Auel   *f*   275
*Queen of the Summer Stars* - Persia
   Woolley   *f*   5971
*Sabine's Notebook* - Nick Bantock   *f*   335
*The Sacred Stones* - William Sarabande   *f*   4818
*See You Later* - Christopher Pike   *f*   4332
*Servant of the Empire* - Raymond E. Feist   *f*   1910
*The Shape-Changer's Wife* - Sharon Shinn   *f*   5002
*Silver Princess, Golden Knight* - Sharon
   Green   *f*   2359
*Sing for a Gentle Rain* - J. Alison James   *f*   2861
*The Sleep of Stone* - Louise Cooper   *f*   1179
*Something Rich and Strange* - Patricia A.
   McKillip   *f*   3840
*A Song for Arbonne* - Guy Gavriel Kay   *f*   3017
*Spell Bound* - Trana Mae Simmons   *f*   5061
*The Starry Child* - Lynn Hanna   *f*   2540
*Steel and Stone* - Ellen Porath   *f*   4368
*A Time for Us* - Christine Holden   *f*   2731
*The Towers of the Sunset* - L.E. Modesitt
   Jr.   *f*   3941
*Under Siege* - Elisabeth Mace   *f*   3587
*Wheel of Dreams* - Salinda Tyson   *f*   5529
*The Wild Hunt: Vengeance Moon* - Jocelin
   Foxe   *f*   2031
*Winter Rose* - Patricia A. McKillip   *f*   3843
*A Wish and a Dream* - Ingrid Weaver   *f*   5658

### Fantasy — Satire

*Amazon: A Novel* - Barbara G. Walker   *f*   5616
*The Bear Went over the Mountain* - William
   Kotzwinkle   *f*   3222
*Blameless in Abaddon* - James Morrow   *f*   4029
*Carmen Dog* - Carol Emshwiller   *f*   1817
*The Cockroaches of Stay More* - Donald
   Harington   *f*   2544
*Conglomeros* - Jesse Browner   *f*   729
*The D. Case: The Truth about the Mystery of Edwin
   Drood* - Charles Dickens   *f*   1524
*Hooray for Hellywood* - Esther Friesner   *f*   2077
*Maskerade* - Terry Pratchett   *f*   4395
*Mordred's Curse* - Ian McDowell   *f*   3806
*Negrophobia: An Urban Parable* - Darius
   James   *f*   2859
*Only Begotten Daughter* - James Morrow   *f*   4034
*Revenge of the Christmas Box* - Cathy
   Crimmins   *f*   1257
*Revenge of the Fluffy Bunnies* - Craig Shaw
   Gardner   *f*   2132
*The Tetherballs of Bougainville* - Mark
   Leyner   *f*   3457
*Tex and Molly in the Afterlife* - Richard
   Grant   *f*   2327
*Through the Arc of the Rain Forest* - Karen Tei
   Yamashita   *f*   6008
*Top Dog* - Jerry Jay Carroll   *f*   915
*The War of Don Emmanuel's Nether Parts* - Louis de
   Bernieres   *f*   1412

### Fantasy — Science Fiction

*2XS* - Nigel Findley   *f*   1935
*Above the Lower Sky* - Tom Deitz   *f*   1469
*Antiquities* - John Crowley   *f*   1276
*The Arbitrary Placement of Walls* - Martha
   Soukup   *f*   5165
*Bagatelle—Guinevere* - Nancy Bogen   *f*   558
*Black Sun Rising* - C.S. Friedman   *f*   2056
*Blood: A Southern Fantasy* - Michael
   Moorcock   *f*   3977
*Brother to Dragons, Companion to Owls* - Jane M.
   Lindskold   *f*   3473
*The Callahan Touch* - Spider Robinson   *f*   4637
*City of Bones* - Martha Wells   *f*   5748
*City of Pain* - John Terra   *f*   5438
*The Cloud People* - Robert B. Kelly   *f*   3050

*Common Clay: 20 Odd Stories* - Brian W.
   Aldiss   *f*   54
*The Deer's Cry: A Book of the Keltiad* - Patricia
   Kennealy-Morrison   *f*   3060
*The Dragon and the Unicorn* - A.A.
   Attanasio   *f*   266
*The Ear, the Eye, and the Arm* - Nancy
   Farmer   *f*   1867
*Everard's Ride* - Diana Wynne Jones   *f*   2947
*A Game of Universe* - Eric S. Nylund   *f*   4178
*The Gift* - Patrick O'Leary   *f*   4211
*Good Bones and Simple Murders* - Margaret
   Atwood   *f*   274
*The Hawk's Gray Feather* - Patricia Kennealy-
   Morrison   *f*   3061
*High Wizardry* - Diane Duane   *f*   1662
*The Iron Dragon's Daughter* - Michael
   Swanwick   *f*   5371
*Lion's Soul* - Karen Wehrstein   *f*   5684
*Lord of the Fantastic: Stories in Honor of Roger
   Zelazny* - Martin H. Greenberg   *f*   2398
*Myst: The Book of D'ni* - Rand Miller   *f*   3897
*The Night Watch* - Sean Stewart   *f*   5274
*Nightsword* - Margaret Weis   *f*   5722
*Of Tangible Ghosts* - L.E. Modesitt Jr.   *f*   3935
*Out of This World* - Lawrence Watt-Evans   *f*   5645
*A Plague of Angels* - Sheri S. Tepper   *f*   5433
*The Poisoned Lands* - John Maddox
   Roberts   *f*   4619
*Quicksilver's Knight* - Christopher Stasheff   *f*   5220
*R-T, Margaret, and the Rats of NIMH* - Jane Leslie
   Conly   *f*   1132
*Random Acts of Senseless Violence* - Jack
   Womack   *f*   5959
*Raptor Red* - Robert T. Bakker   *f*   306
*The Red-Eared Ghosts* - Vivian Alcock   *f*   53
*The Reign of the Brown Magician* - Lawrence Watt-
   Evans   *f*   5647
*Shadows Fall* - Simon R. Green   *f*   2373
*Streets of Blood* - Carl Sargent   *f*   4821
*Superheroes* - John Varley   *f*   5567
*Swords of the Rainbow* - Eric Garber   *f*   2117
*Tex and Molly in the Afterlife* - Richard
   Grant   *f*   2327
*That Way Lies Camelot* - Janny Wurts   *f*   6005
*Through the Heart* - Richard Grant   *f*   2328
*Unconquered Countries: Four Novellas* - Geoff
   Ryman   *f*   4757
*Walker between the Worlds* - Diane
   DesRochers   *f*   1499
*Warlord of Heaven* - Adrian Cole   *f*   1102
*Warriors of Blood and Dream* - Roger
   Zelazny   *f*   6075
*The Williamson Effect* - Roger Zelazny   *f*   6077

### Fantasy — Sword and Sorcery

*An Armory of Swords* - Fred Saberhagen   *f*   4759
*The Barbed Coil* - J.V. Jones   *f*   2957
*Blood of the Fold* - Terry Goodkind   *f*   2268
*The Book of Earth* - Marjorie Bradley
   Kellogg   *f*   3044
*Broken Blade* - Ann Marston   *f*   3634
*The Changeling Prince* - Vivian Vande
   Velde   *f*   5554
*City at the Edge of Time* - Janet Morris   *f*   4015
*Conan and the Treasure of Python* - John Maddox
   Roberts   *f*   4616
*The Conan Chronicles* - Robert Jordan   *f*   2983
*Conan of the Red Brotherhood* - Leonard
   Carpenter   *f*   906
*Conan, Scourge of the Bloody Coast* - Leonard
   Carpenter   *f*   910
*Conan the Formidable* - Steve Perry   *f*   4293
*Conan the Gladiator* - Leonard Carpenter   *f*   907
*Conan the Guardian* - Roland J. Green   *f*   2347
*Conan the Indomitable* - Steve Perry   *f*   4294
*Conan the Outcast* - Leonard Carpenter   *f*   908

*Conan the Relentless* - Roland J. Green   *f*   2348
*Conan the Rogue* - John Maddox Roberts   *f*   4617
*Conan the Savage* - Leonard Carpenter   *f*   909
*Corum: The Coming of Chaos* - Michael
   Moorcock   *f*   3978
*Dancing Jack* - Laurie J. Marks   *f*   3624
*The Dark Hand of Magic* - Barbara Hambly   *f*   2502
*The Dragon King* - R.A. Salvatore   *f*   4796
*The Dragon's Carbuncle* - Elizabeth H.
   Boyer   *f*   605
*Dreams of Steel* - Glen Cook   *f*   1150
*Echoes of Valor III* - Karl Edward Wagner   *f*   5599
*Elfwood* - Rose Estes   *f*   1837
*Elminster: The Making of a Mage* - Ed
   Greenwood   *f*   2427
*Elric: Song of the Black Sword* - Michael
   Moorcock   *f*   3980
*The Forging of the Shadows* - Oliver
   Johnson   *f*   2924
*The Fortress of Eternity* - Andrew
   Whitmore   *f*   5790
*Fortress of Owls* - C.J. Cherryh   *f*   993
*Ghost King* - David Gemmell   *f*   2188
*Heartstone and Silver* - Jacqui Singleton   *f*   5071
*A Hero Born* - Michael A. Stackpole   *f*   5202
*Hour of the Dragon* - Robert E. Howard   *f*   2783
*Ill Met in Lankhmar* - Fritz Leiber   *f*   3419
*In the Red Lord's Reach* - Phyllis
   Eisenstein   *f*   1765
*Kingmaker's Sword* - Ann Marston   *f*   3635
*The Last of the Renshai* - Mickey Zucker
   Reichert   *f*   4520
*Lean Times in Lankhmar* - Fritz Leiber   *f*   3420
*Lion of Macedon* - David Gemmell   *f*   2189
*Luthien's Gamble* - R.A. Salvatore   *f*   4802
*The Mage in the Iron Mask* - Brian
   Thomsen   *f*   5458
*Magic's Pawn* - Mercedes Lackey   *f*   3287
*Mistress of Ambiguities* - J.F. Rivkin   *f*   4596
*Nations of the Night* - Oliver Johnson   *f*   2925
*Oath of Swords* - David Weber   *f*   5678
*Oathblood* - Mercedes Lackey   *f*   3290
*One Quest, Hold the Dragons* - Greg
   Costikyan   *f*   1208
*Palace of Kings* - Mike Jefferies   *f*   2887
*The Panther's Hoard* - Nancy Varian
   Berberick   *f*   458
*The Parched Sea* - Troy Denning   *f*   1486
*Return to Lankhmar* - Fritz Leiber   *f*   3422
*The Road Home* - Joel Rosenberg   *f*   4674
*The Road to Underfall* - Mike Jefferies   *f*   2888
*The Road West* - Gary Wright   *f*   5984
*The Sands of Kalaven: A Novel of Shunlar* - Carol
   Heller   *f*   2651
*The Silent Blade* - R.A. Salvatore   *f*   4805
*Sleipnir* - Linda Evans   *f*   1856
*Stone of Tears* - Terry Goodkind   *f*   2269
*Sword and Sorceress VIII* - Marion Zimmer
   Bradley   *f*   646
*Sword and Sorceress IX* - Marion Zimmer
   Bradley   *f*   647
*Sword and Sorceress XI* - Marion Zimmer
   Bradley   *f*   648
*Sword and Sorceress XII* - Marion Zimmer
   Bradley   *f*   649
*Sword and Sorceress XIII* - Marion Zimmer
   Bradley   *f*   650
*Sword-Maker* - Jennifer Roberson   *f*   4614
*The Sword of Bedwyr* - R.A. Salvatore   *f*   4808
*Swords Against the Shadowland* - Robin Wayne
   Bailey   *f*   291
*Tears of Time* - Nancy Asire   *f*   256
*Tower of Fear* - Glen Cook   *f*   1155
*Twisted Dragon* - Kevin Stein   *f*   5251
*The Verdant Passage* - Troy Denning   *f*   1487
*Wayfinder's Story: The Seventh Book of Lost Swords* -
   Fred Saberhagen   *f*   4777
*The Western King* - Ann Marston   *f*   3636
*Wolf Justice* - Doranna Durgin   *f*   1706

*Wolfhelm* - Richard A. Knaak   *f*  3175

**Fantasy — Time Travel**

*An Acceptable Time* - Madeleine L'Engle   *f*  3436
*All's Faire* - Pamela F. Service   *f*  4917
*Amazon: A Novel* - Barbara G. Walker   *f*  5616
*The Ancient One* - T.A. Barron   *f*  368
*Arthur War Lord* - Dafydd ab Hugh   *f*  6
*Automated Alice* - Jeff Noon   *f*  4134
*Beauty* - Sheri S. Tepper   *f*  5428
*Charmed* - Marilyn Singer   *f*  5070
*The Crown of Dalemark* - Diana Wynne Jones   *f*  2945
*The Door through Washington Square* - Elaine Bergstrom   *f*  464
*The Druid's Gift* - Margaret J. Anderson   *f*  121
*Friends in Time* - Grace Chetwin   *f*  1012
*The Ghost Inside the Monitor* - Margaret J. Anderson   *f*  122
*Gossamer Axe* - Gael Baudino   *f*  392
*The House on Hound Hill* - Maggie Prince   *f*  4438
*The Jigsaw Woman* - Kim Antieau   *f*  199
*The Key to the Indian* - Lynne Reid Banks   *f*  331
*The Last Highlander* - Claire Cross   *f*  1271
*The Last Voyage of Somebody the Sailor* - John Barth   *f*  374
*Letters From Atlantis* - Robert Silverberg   *f*  5035
*The Lost Prince* - Bridget Wood   *f*  5962
*A Love through Time* - Terri Brisbin   *f*  691
*Mercy's Mill* - Betty Levin   *f*  3444
*The Princess and the Dragon* - Roberto Pazzi   *f*  4272
*The Secret of the Indian* - Lynne Reid Banks   *f*  332
*The Silver Tree* - Ruth L. Williams   *f*  5822
*Sing for a Gentle Rain* - J. Alison James   *f*  2861
*Stonewords: A Ghost Story* - Pam Conrad   *f*  1138
*Till the End of Time* - Allen Appel   *f*  201
*A Time for Us* - Christine Holden   *f*  2731
*The Time Tree* - Enid Richemont   *f*  4585
*Union Fires* - John Barnes   *f*  358
*Wartide* - John Barnes   *f*  359
*Web of Futures* - Jefferson P. Swycaffer   *f*  5376
*A Well-Timed Enchantment* - Vivian Vande Velde   *f*  5559
*Where the Towers Pierce the Sky* - Marie D. Goodwin   *f*  2272
*A Witch Across Time* - Gilbert B. Cross   *f*  1272
*Wolfking* - Bridget Wood   *f*  5963

**Fantasy — Urban**

*Agyar* - Steven Brust   *f*  738
*Bedlam Boyz* - Ellen Guon   *f*  2467
*Borderland* - Terri Windling   *f*  5913
*Born to Run* - Mercedes Lackey   *f*  3271
*Brother to Dragons, Companion to Owls* - Jane M. Lindskold   *f*  3473
*Carol for Another Christmas* - Elizabeth Ann Scarborough   *f*  4861
*Changeling* - Christopher Kubasik   *f*  3245
*Chrome Circle* - Mercedes Lackey   *f*  3277
*Cold Iron* - Melisa Michaels   *f*  3886
*Dead Voices: Natural Agonies in the Real World* - Gerald Vizenor   *f*  5578
*Double Feature* - Emma Bull   *f*  767
*Dreams Underfoot* - Charles de Lint   *f*  1425
*Elsewhere* - Will Shetterly   *f*  4993
*Elvendude* - Mark Shepherd   *f*  4980
*The Essential Bordertown* - Terri Windling   *f*  5914
*Finder* - Emma Bull   *f*  769
*The Friendship Song* - Nancy Springer   *f*  5179
*Ghosts of Wind and Shadow* - Charles de Lint   *f*  1427
*The Godmother* - Elizabeth Ann Scarborough   *f*  4862
*The Gypsy* - Steven Brust   *f*  744
*Into the Shadows* - Jordan K. Weisman   *f*  5731

*The Iron Dragon's Daughter* - Michael Swanwick   *f*  5371
*The Ivory and the Horn* - Charles de Lint   *f*  1431
*A King Beneath the Mountain* - Robert N. Charrette   *f*  973
*A Knight Among Knaves* - Robert N. Charrette   *f*  974
*Last Mountain* - Robert C. Fleet   *f*  1946
*The Last Wizard* - Simon Hawke   *f*  2619
*Legends Reborn* - Kenneth C. Flint   *f*  1958
*Life on the Border* - Terri Windling   *f*  5915
*The Magic Touch* - Jody Lynn Nye   *f*  4171
*Mall Purchase Night* - Rick Cook   *f*  1159
*Never Trust an Elf* - Robert N. Charrette   *f*  976
*Nevernever* - Will Shetterly   *f*  4995
*Neverwhere* - Neil Gaiman   *f*  2104
*Pretty Pewter Gods* - Glen Cook   *f*  1152
*A Prince Among Men* - Robert N. Charrette   *f*  977
*Random Acts of Senseless Violence* - Jack Womack   *f*  5959
*Red Iron Nights* - Glen Cook   *f*  1153
*Shadow's Daughter* - Shirley Meier   *f*  3871
*Shoebag Returns* - Mary James   *f*  2869
*Sister to the Rain* - Melisa Michaels   *f*  3887
*Songs of Earth and Power* - Greg Bear   *f*  424
*Spires of Spirit* - Gael Baudino   *f*  395
*Spiritwalk* - Charles de Lint   *f*  1436
*Steel Rose* - Kara Dalkey   *f*  1321
*Strands of Sunlight* - Gael Baudino   *f*  396
*Street Magic* - Michael Reaves   *f*  4497
*Striper Assassin* - Nyx Smith   *f*  5135
*Summoned to Tourney* - Mercedes Lackey   *f*  3299
*Troll-Quest* - Rose Estes   *f*  1841
*Wheels of Fire* - Mercedes Lackey   *f*  3301
*When the Bough Breaks* - Mercedes Lackey   *f*  3302
*Wolf in the Fold* - Simon R. Green   *f*  2376
*Zeus and Co.* - David Lee Jones   *f*  2942

**Fantasy — Young Adult**

*An Acceptable Time* - Madeleine L'Engle   *f*  3436
*The Adventures of King Midas* - Lynne Reid Banks   *f*  329
*Ahmed and the Oblivion Machines* - Ray Bradbury   *f*  618
*All's Faire* - Pamela F. Service   *f*  4917
*The Ancient One* - T.A. Barron   *f*  368
*Angela and Diabola* - Lynne Reid Banks   *f*  330
*The Arkadians* - Lloyd Alexander   *f*  67
*Aunt Maria* - Diana Wynne Jones   *f*  2943
*Baby Be-Bop* - Francesca Lia Block   *f*  545
*Being of Two Minds* - Pamela F. Service   *f*  4918
*The Bellmaker* - Brian Jacques   *f*  2848
*Bernie and the Bessledorf Ghost* - Phyllis Reynolds Naylor   *f*  4078
*Beyond the Magic Sphere* - Gail Jarrow   *f*  2879
*Black Horses for the King* - Anne McCaffrey   *f*  3720
*Black Unicorn* - Tanith Lee   *f*  3404
*The Blood of a Dragon* - Lawrence Watt-Evans   *f*  5640
*Blue Moon* - Hila Feil   *f*  1898
*The Book of Brendan* - Ann Curry   *f*  1294
*The Book of Dragons* - Michael Hague   *f*  2479
*Book of Enchantments* - Patricia C. Wrede   *f*  5973
*The Book of Knights* - Yves Meynard   *f*  3884
*Borgel* - Daniel Manus Pinkwater   *f*  4338
*Brian Boru: Emperor of the Irish* - Morgan Llywelyn   *f*  3501
*Calling on Dragons* - Patricia C. Wrede   *f*  5974
*Cherokee Bat and the Goat Guys* - Francesca Lia Block   *f*  546
*Child of Faerie, Child of Earth* - Josepha Sherman   *f*  4985
*Clan of the Shape-Changers* - Robert Levy   *f*  3446
*Court Duel* - Sherwood Smith   *f*  5137
*Dark Heart* - Betsy James   *f*  2857
*Dealing with Dragons* - Patricia C. Wrede   *f*  5975

*Double Trouble Squared* - Kathryn Lasky   *f*  3340
*Dragon's Bait* - Vivian Vande Velde   *f*  5556
*The Dragon's Boy* - Jane Yolen   *f*  6030
*Drum Warning* - Jo Clayton   *f*  1066
*Fire Arrow* - Edith Pattou   *f*  4260
*The Fires of Merlin* - T.A. Barron   *f*  369
*Fish Soup* - Ursula K. Le Guin   *f*  3378
*Flight of the Dragon Kyn* - Susan Fletcher   *f*  1951
*The Fools' War* - Lee Kisling   *f*  3159
*Friends in Time* - Grace Chetwin   *f*  1012
*The Friendship Song* - Nancy Springer   *f*  5179
*The Ghost Inside the Monitor* - Margaret J. Anderson   *f*  122
*The Girl with the Green Ear: Stories about Magic in Nature* - Margaret Mahy   *f*  3610
*Goblins in the Castle* - Bruce Coville   *f*  1218
*Gold Unicorn* - Tanith Lee   *f*  3410
*Goldclimbers* - Nancy Luenn   *f*  3545
*Green Rider* - Kristen Britain   *f*  692
*Harpy High* - Esther Friesner   *f*  2076
*The Heavenward Path* - Kara Dalkey   *f*  1319
*Here There Be Dragons* - Jane Yolen   *f*  6032
*Here There Be Dragons* - Roger Zelazny   *f*  6069
*Hero's Song* - Edith Pattou   *f*  4261
*His Majesty's Elephant* - Judith Tarr   *f*  5394
*Hobkin* - Peni R. Griffin   *f*  2438
*The House on Hound Hill* - Maggie Prince   *f*  4438
*I Was a Teenage Fairy* - Francesca Lia Block   *f*  549
*If Wishes Were Horses* - Anne McCaffrey   *f*  3737
*An Impossumble Summer* - Brenda W. Clough   *f*  1090
*In between Dragons* - Michael Kandel   *f*  3010
*Into the Land of the Unicorns* - Bruce Coville   *f*  1219
*The Iron Ring* - Lloyd Alexander   *f*  68
*Jennifer Murdley's Toad* - Bruce Coville   *f*  1220
*Jeremy Thatcher, Dragon Hatcher* - Bruce Coville   *f*  1221
*Journeyman Wizard* - Mary Frances Zambreno   *f*  6057
*The Juniper Game* - Sherryl Jordan   *f*  2992
*The Key to the Indian* - Lynne Reid Banks   *f*  331
*The Kingdom of Kevin Malone* - Suzy McKee Charnas   *f*  970
*The King's Buccaneer* - Raymond E. Feist   *f*  1904
*Knight's Wyrd* - Debra Doyle   *f*  1601
*A Knot in the Grain and Other Stories* - Robin McKinley   *f*  3845
*The Land of Gold* - Gillian Bradshaw   *f*  658
*The Lark and the Wren* - Mercedes Lackey   *f*  3286
*Little Sister* - Kara Dalkey   *f*  1320
*The Long Patrol* - Brian Jacques   *f*  2849
*The Lost Years of Merlin* - T.A. Barron   *f*  370
*The Magic Bicycle* - William Hill   *f*  2688
*The Magic Touch* - Jody Lynn Nye   *f*  4171
*Mairelon the Magician* - Patricia C. Wrede   *f*  5977
*Mariel of Redwall* - Brian Jacques   *f*  2850
*Martin the Warrior* - Brian Jacques   *f*  2851
*The Marvellous Land of Snergs* - E.A. Wyke-Smith   *f*  6006
*Mattimeo* - Brian Jacques   *f*  2852
*The Mennyms* - Sylvia Waugh   *f*  5654
*Mennyms Alive* - Sylvia Waugh   *f*  5655
*Mennyms Under Siege* - Sylvia Waugh   *f*  5656
*Mercy's Mill* - Betty Levin   *f*  3444
*Merlin* - Jane Yolen   *f*  6035
*Merlin and the Dragons* - Jane Yolen   *f*  6036
*The Merlin Effect* - T.A. Barron   *f*  371
*Merlin's Harp* - Anne Eliot Crompton   *f*  1270
*The Midnight Horse* - Sid Fleischman   *f*  1948
*Missing Angel Juan* - Francesca Lia Block   *f*  550
*Monet's Ghost* - Chelsea Quinn Yarbro   *f*  6017
*The Moorchild* - Eloise Jarvis McGraw   *f*  3816
*No One Noticed the Cat* - Anne McCaffrey   *f*  3740
*Nutcracker* - E.T.A. Hoffmann   *f*  2719
*On Fortune's Wheel* - Cynthia Voigt   *f*  5579
*On Meeting Witches at Wells* - Judith Gorog   *f*  2283

*Orphans of the Night* - Josepha Sherman   *f*   4988

*Out of the Ordinary* - Annie Dalton   *f*   1330

*Outcast of Redwall* - Brian Jacques   *f*   2853

*The Pagemaster* - David Kirschner   *f*   3156

*Painted Devil* - Michael Bedard   *f*   430

*The Pearl of the Soul of the World* - Meredith Ann
Pierce   *f*   4318

*The Pearls of Lutra* - Brian Jacques   *f*   2854

*A Plague of Sorcerers* - Mary Frances
Zambreno   *f*   6058

*R-T, Margaret, and the Rats of NIMH* - Jane Leslie
Conly   *f*   1132

*Ratha and Thistle-Chaser* - Clare Bell   *f*   432

*The Realms of the Gods* - Tamora Pierce   *f*   4321

*The Red-Eared Ghosts* - Vivian Alcock   *f*   53

*The Red King* - Victor Kelleher   *f*   3043

*Red Unicorn* - Tanith Lee   *f*   3414

*The Remarkable Journey of Prince Jen* - Lloyd
Alexander   *f*   69

*Return to Howliday Inn* - James Howe   *f*   2786

*A Ride on the Red Mare's Back* - Ursula K. Le
Guin   *f*   3382

*Sabriel* - Garth Nix   *f*   4129

*Salamandastron* - Brian Jacques   *f*   2855

*School of Wizardry* - Debra Doyle   *f*   1605

*Searching for Dragons* - Patricia C. Wrede   *f*   5979

*The Secret of the Indian* - Lynne Reid Banks   *f*   332

*See You Later* - Christopher Pike   *f*   4332

*The Seven Songs of Merlin* - T.A. Barron   *f*   372

*Shadow's Daughter* - Shirley Meier   *f*   3871

*Shiva Accused: An Adventure of the Ice Age* - J.H.
Brennan   *f*   667

*Shiva's Challenge: An Adventure of the Ice Age* - J.H.
Brennan   *f*   668

*Shoebag* - Mary James   *f*   2868

*Shoebag Returns* - Mary James   *f*   2869

*The Silver Kiss* - Annette Curtis Klause   *f*   3163

*The Silver Tree* - Ruth L. Williams   *f*   5822

*The Son of Summer Stars* - Meredith Ann
Pierce   *f*   4319

*Song of the Gargoyle* - Zilpha Keatley
Snyder   *f*   5153

*Soulsmith* - Tom Deitz   *f*   1475

*Spring-Heeled Jack* - Philip Pullman   *f*   4447

*Stonewords: A Ghost Story* - Pam Conrad   *f*   1138

*The Summer I Shrank My Grandmother* - Elvira
Woodruff   *f*   5968

*Tales From Watership Down* - Richard Adams   *f*   32

*A Tall Story and Other Tales* - Margaret
Mahy   *f*   3611

*Time and the Clock Mice, Etcetera* - Peter
Dickinson   *f*   1527

*The Time of the Ghost* - Diana Wynne
Jones   *f*   2951

*Toad Triumphant* - William Horwood   *f*   2774

*Tongues of Jade* - Laurence Yep   *f*   6026

*Travel Far, Pay No Fare* - Anne Lindbergh   *f*   3468

*Tris's Book* - Tamora Pierce   *f*   4322

*Twelve Impossible Things Before Breakfast* - Jane
Yolen   *f*   6040

*Under Siege* - Elisabeth Mace   *f*   3587

*Unicorn Highway* - David Lee Jones   *f*   2941

*The Unicorn Sonata* - Peter S. Beagle   *f*   412

*Unicorn U.* - Esther Friesner   *f*   2084

*User Unfriendly* - Vivian Vande Velde   *f*   5558

*The Veils of Snows* - Mark Helprin   *f*   2654

*Voyage of the Basset* - James C.
Christensen   *f*   1024

*Way Up High* - Roger Zelazny   *f*   6076

*The Ways of Magic* - Scott Ciencin   *f*   1033

*Weirdos of the Universe, Unite!* - Pamela F.
Service   *f*   4921

*A Well-Timed Enchantment* - Vivian Vande
Velde   *f*   5559

*Well Wished* - Franny Billingsley   *f*   489

*Wild Magic* - Tamora Pierce   *f*   4323

*The Willows and Beyond* - William
Horwood   *f*   2775

*The Willows in Winter* - William Horwood   *f*   2776

*Wishing Season* - Esther Friesner   *f*   2085

*Witch* - Christopher Pike   *f*   4334

*A Witch Across Time* - Gilbert B. Cross   *f*   1272

*Witch Baby* - Francesca Lia Block   *f*   552

*The Witch House* - Norma Tadlock Johnson   *f*   2923

*The Witch of Maple Park* - Stephanie S.
Tolan   *f*   5478

*The Witch Returns* - Phyllis Reynolds
Naylor   *f*   4079

*The Witch's Eye* - Phyllis Reynolds Naylor   *f*   4080

*A Wizard Abroad* - Diane Duane   *f*   1668

*The Wizard's Apprentice* - S.P. Somtow   *f*   5163

*A Wizard's Dozen* - Michael Stearns   *f*   5239

*Wizard's Hall* - Jane Yolen   *f*   6043

*Wolf-Speaker* - Tamora Pierce   *f*   4324

*Wren's Quest* - Sherwood Smith   *f*   5143

*Wren's War* - Sherwood Smith   *f*   5144

## Fantasy — Young Readers

*Harry Potter and the Sorcerer's Stone* - J.K.
Rowling   *f*   4700

*Roverandom* - J.R.R. Tolkien   *f*   5479

# HORROR

## Horror — Alternate World

*Boundaries* - T.M. Wright   *h*   5990

*The Drawing of the Three* - Stephen King   *h*   3131

*King of the Dead* - Gene DeWeese   *h*   1510

*Mirror* - Graham Masterton   *h*   3677

## Horror — Ancient Evil Unleashed

*The Barrens* - F. Paul Wilson   *h*   5884

*Blood Wings* - Stephen Gresham   *h*   2430

*Bone Music* - Alan Rodgers   *h*   4646

*Burial* - Graham Masterton   *h*   3671

*Buried Screams* - C. Dean Andersson   *h*   137

*The Burrowers Beneath* - Brian Lumley   *h*   3548

*Candle Night* - Phil Rickman   *h*   4586

*Cat's Eye* - William W. Johnstone   *h*   2928

*The Charm* - Adam Niswander   *h*   4111

*City of Iron* - Chet Williamson   *h*   5843

*Crota* - Owl Goingback   *h*   2251

*Curfew* - Phil Rickman   *h*   4587

*Dark Tide* - Elizabeth Forrest   *h*   1972

*Dark Twilight* - Joseph A. Citro   *h*   1036

*Dark Winds* - Graham Watkins   *h*   5630

*Darkly the Thunder* - William W.
Johnstone   *h*   2929

*The Deathless* - Myles Murchison   *h*   4048

*Deathsong* - Douglas Borton   *h*   575

*Deathwalker* - Patrick Whalen   *h*   5769

*Desperation* - Stephen King   *h*   3129

*Dominion* - Bentley Little   *h*   3492

*Dreamthorp* - Chet Williamson   *h*   5845

*Entity* - Nina Mandelik   *h*   3615

*Fiends* - John Farris   *h*   1884

*The Final Diary Entry of Kees Hujgens* - William R.
Stotler   *h*   5317

*Goat Dance* - Douglas Clegg   *h*   1079

*The Halloween Man* - Douglas Clegg   *h*   1080

*Hell-O-Ween* - David Robbins   *h*   4598

*Hellboy: The Lost Army* - Christopher
Golden   *h*   2257

*The House of the Toad* - Richard L.
Tierney   *h*   5470

*Midnight Sun* - Ramsey Campbell   *h*   860

*Mysteries of the Word* - Stanley Wiater   *h*   5796

*Nightmare's Disciple* - Joseph S. Pulver Jr.   *h*   4449

*Out of the Night* - Patrick Whalen   *h*   5771

*Prank Night* - David Robbins   *h*   4601

*Reprisal* - F. Paul Wilson   *h*   5896

*Return to Chaos* - Craig Shaw Gardner   *h*   2131

*The Sand Dwellers* - Adam Niswander   *h*   4112

*Sepulchre* - James Herbert   *h*   2672

*The Serpent Slayers* - Adam Niswander   *h*   4113

*Shadow Dance* - Douglas Borton   *h*   577

*Shadow Dance* - Jessica Palmer   *h*   4238

*The Shadow over Innsmouth* - H.P.
Lovecraft   *h*   3533

*Shaman Woods* - Morgan Fields   *h*   1931

*Shock Lines* - Warren Newton Beath   *h*   427

*Stone Angels* - Mike Jefferies   *h*   2889

*The Stone Circle* - Gary Goshgarian   *h*   2285

*Storytellers* - Julie Anne Parks   *h*   4249

*Swamp* - Peter Tremayne   *h*   5483

*Tales From the Crypt: Demon Knight* - Randall
Boyll   *h*   617

*The Things That Are Not There* - Robert
Morgan   *h*   4007

*Thunder Rise* - G. Wayne Miller   *h*   3895

*The Trail of Cthulhu* - August Derleth   *h*   1497

*The Transition of Titus Crow* - Brian
Lumley   *h*   3569

*The Trickster* - Muriel Gray   *h*   2340

*Trinity Grove* - David van Meter Smith   *h*   5112

*The Unseen* - Joseph A. Citro   *h*   1039

*The Uprising* - Brent Monahan   *h*   3956

*Virgin* - Mary Elizabeth Murphy   *h*   4050

*Water Rites* - Guy N. Smith   *h*   5121

*The Well* - Michael B. Sirota   *h*   5077

*The Werewolves of London* - Brian
Stableford   *h*   5196

*Where the Chill Waits* - T. Chris
Martindale   *h*   3658

*WiZrD* - Steve Zell   *h*   6078

## Horror — Anthology

*100 Creepy Little Creature Stories* - Robert
Weinberg   *h*   5686

*100 Ghastly Little Ghost Stories* - Stefan
Dziemianowicz   *h*   1709

*100 Hair-Raising Little Horror Stories* - Al
Sarrantonio   *h*   4828

*100 Tiny Tales of Terror* - Robert
Weinberg   *h*   5687

*100 Twisted Little Tales of Torment* - Stefan
Dziemianowicz   *h*   1710

*100 Vicious Little Vampire Stories* - Robert
Weinberg   *h*   5688

*100 Wicked Little Witch Stories* - Stefan
Dziemianowicz   *h*   1711

*100 Wild Little Weird Tales* - Robert
Weinberg   *h*   5689

*After the Darkness* - Stanley Wiater   *h*   5795

*Air Fish* - Joy Oestreicher   *h*   4199

*Alien Sex* - Ellen Datlow   *h*   1357

*Alpha Gallery* - Joy Oestreicher   *h*   4200

*American Gothic* - Elizabeth Terry   *h*   5439

*American Gothic Tales* - Joyce Carol Oates   *h*   4180

*Angels of Darkness* - Marvin Kaye   *h*   3022

*The Ash-Tree Press Annual Macabre 1997* - Jack
Adrian   *h*   37

*The Ash-Tree Press Annual Macabre 1998* - Jack
Adrian   *h*   38

*Avatar* - Donald Beman   *h*   437

*The Azathoth Cycle* - Robert M. Price   *h*   4422

*Back From the Dead* - Martin H.
Greenberg   *h*   2379

*The Beast Within: Erotic Tales of Werewolves* -
Cecilia Tan   *h*   5384

*Best New Horror* - Stephen Jones   *h*   2961

*Best New Horror 2* - Stephen Jones   *h*   2962

*Best New Horror 4* - Stephen Jones   *h*   2963

*Best New Horror 6* - Stephen Jones   *h*   2964

*The Best of Cemetery Dance* - Richard T.
Chizmar   *h*   1017

*Best of the Midwest's Science Fiction, Fantasy and
Horror, Volume II* - Brian Smart   *h*   5095

*The Best of Weird Tales* - John Gregory
Betancourt   *h*   480

*The Best of Weird Tales: 1923* - Marvin Kaye  *h*  3023

*The Best of Whispers* - Stuart David Schiff  *h*  4873

*Between Time and Terror* - Robert Weinberg  *h*  5691

*Black Water 2: More Tales of the Fantastic* - Alberto Manguel  *h*  3616

*Blood Is Not Enough* - Ellen Datlow  *h*  1360

*Blood Kiss: Vampire Erotica* - Cecilia Tan  *h*  5385

*Blood Lines: Vampire Stories From New England* - Lawrence Schimel  *h*  4876

*Blood Muse: Timeless Tales of Vampires in the Arts* - Esther Friesner  *h*  2071

*Blood Thirst: 100 Years of Vampire Fiction* - Leonard Wolf  *h*  5935

*Blue Motel* - Peter Crowther  *h*  1279

*Bodies of the Dead* - David G. Hartwell  *h*  2586

*The Book of Iod* - Henry Kuttner  *h*  3266

*The Book of Irish Weirdness* - Anonymous  *h*  149

*Borderlands* - Thomas F. Monteleone  *h*  3959

*Borderlands 2* - Thomas F. Monteleone  *h*  3960

*Borderlands 3* - Thomas F. Monteleone  *h*  3961

*Borderlands 4* - Thomas F. Monteleone  *h*  3962

*Brothers of the Night* - Michael Rowe  *h*  4689

*Cafe Purgatorium* - Dana Anderson  *h*  98

*Celebrity Vampires* - Martin H. Greenberg  *h*  2382

*A Century of Horror: 1970-1979: The Greatest Stories of the Decade* - David Drake  *h*  1629

*Cherished Blood* - Cecilia Tan  *h*  5386

*Chilled to the Bone* - Robert T. Garcia  *h*  2118

*Chillers* - Richard T. Chizmar  *h*  1018

*Chillers for Christmas* - Richard Dalby  *h*  1307

*Christmas Ghosts* - Mike Resnick  *h*  4541

*Civil War Ghosts* - Martin H. Greenberg  *h*  2383

*Classic Tales of Horror and the Supernatural* - Bill Pronzini  *h*  4440

*Cold Blood* - Richard T. Chizmar  *h*  1019

*Cold Shocks* - Tim Sullivan  *h*  5350

*The Complete Masters of Darkness* - Dennis Etchison  *h*  1844

*Confederacy of the Dead* - Richard Gilliam  *h*  2230

*The Conspiracy Files* - Martin H. Greenberg  *h*  2384

*Copper Star* - Bruce D. Arthurs  *h*  217

*The Crow: Shattered Lives and Broken Dreams* - James O'Barr  *h*  4186

*Cthulhu 2000* - Jim Turner  *h*  5493

*The Cthulhu Cycle* - Robert M. Price  *h*  4423

*Cthulhu's Heirs* - Thomas M.K. Stratman  *h*  5325

*Dangerous Dames* - Tina L. Jens  *h*  2891

*Dante's Disciples* - Peter Crowther  *h*  1280

*Dark at Heart* - Joe R. Lansdale  *h*  3324

*The Dark Descent* - David G. Hartwell  *h*  2590

*Dark Destiny* - Edward E. Kramer  *h*  3224

*Dark Destiny II: Proprietors of Fate* - Edward E. Kramer  *h*  3225

*Dark Destiny III: Children of Dracula* - Edward E. Kramer  *h*  3226

*Dark Love* - Nancy A. Collins  *h*  1118

*Dark Seductions* - Alice Alfonsi  *h*  72

*Dark Tyrants* - Justin Achilli  *h*  23

*Darker Angels: Lesbian Vampire Stories* - Pam Keesey  *h*  3030

*The Darkest Thirst: A Vampire Anthology* - Anonymous  *h*  150

*Darkside: Horror for the Next Millennium* - John Pelan  *h*  4278

*Daughters of Darkness: Lesbian Vampire Stories* - Pam Keesey  *h*  3031

*David Copperfield's Tales of the Impossible* - David Copperfield  *h*  1187

*Dead End: City Limits* - Paul F. Olson  *h*  4212

*Deadly After Dark* - Jeff Gelb  *h*  2174

*Deals with the Devil* - Mike Resnick  *h*  4542

*Death Walks Tonight* - Anthony Horowitz  *h*  2772

*Deathport* - Ramsey Campbell  *h*  854

*The Definitive Best of the Horror Show* - David B. Silva  *h*  5025

*Demon Sex* - Amarantha Knight  *h*  3181

*Demons of the Night: Tales of the Fantastic, Madness, and the Supernatural From Nineteenth Century France* - Joan C. Kessler  *h*  3089

*Desire Burn: Women's Stories From the Dark Side of Passion* - Janet Berliner  *h*  468

*Destination Unknown* - Peter Crowther  *h*  1281

*Devil Worshippers* - Martin H. Greenberg  *h*  2385

*Diagnosis: Terminal* - F. Paul Wilson  *h*  5886

*Disciples of Cthulhu* - Edward P. Berglund  *h*  461

*Don't Open This Book!* - Marvin Kaye  *h*  3024

*Doubles, Dummies and Dolls: 21 Terror Tales of Replication* - Leonard Wolf  *h*  5936

*Dracula: Prince of Darkness* - Martin H. Greenberg  *h*  2387

*Dracula: The Ultimate Illustrated Edition of the World-Famous Vampire Play* - Hamilton Deane  *h*  1448

*Dracula's Brood* - Richard Dalby  *h*  1308

*Dread and Delight: A Century of Children's Ghost Stories* - Philippa Pearce  *h*  4274

*The Dunwich Cycle: Where the Old Gods Wait* - Robert M. Price  *h*  4424

*Dying for It: More Erotic Tales of Unearthly Love* - Gardner Dozois  *h*  1607

*The Earth Strikes Back* - Richard T. Chizmar  *h*  1020

*Embracing the Dark* - Eric Garber  *h*  2116

*Erotica Vampirica* - Cecilia Tan  *h*  5387

*The Essential World of Darkness* - Stewart Wieck  *h*  5797

*The Eternal Lovecraft: The Persistence of HPL in Popular Culture* - Jim Turner  *h*  5494

*Famous Fantastic Mysteries* - Stefan Dziemianowicz  *h*  1712

*Fantastic Tales: Visionary and Everyday* - Italo Calvino  *h*  848

*Fantasy Tales #2* - Stephen Jones  *h*  2965

*Fantasy Tales #4* - Stephen Jones  *h*  2966

*Fantasy Tales #6* - Stephen Jones  *h*  2967

*Fear Itself* - Jeff Gelb  *h*  2175

*Fear the Fever* - Jeff Gelb  *h*  2176

*Fields of Blood: Vampire Stories of the Heartland* - Lawrence Schimel  *h*  4879

*Final Shadows* - Charles L. Grant  *h*  2306

*Forbidden Acts* - Nancy A. Collins  *h*  1120

*Foundations of Fear* - David G. Hartwell  *h*  2591

*Frankenstein: The Monster Wakes* - Martin H. Greenberg  *h*  2390

*Freak Show* - F. Paul Wilson  *h*  5888

*Gahan Wilson's The Ultimate Haunted House* - Gahan Wilson  *h*  5902

*Gallery of Horror* - Charles L. Grant  *h*  2307

*Ghosttide* - Claudia O'Keefe  *h*  4206

*Girls' Night Out* - Stefan Dziemianowicz  *h*  1713

*Glimring Night and Other Tales of Fantasy* - Joe Morey  *h*  3997

*Going Postal* - Gerard Daniel Houarner  *h*  2777

*Gothic Ghosts* - Wendy Webb  *h*  5665

*Grave Passions* - William J. Mann  *h*  3618

*Great Ghost Stories* - John Grafton  *h*  2300

*Great Irish Stories of the Supernatural* - Peter Haining  *h*  2481

*Great Irish Tales of Horror* - Peter Haining  *h*  2482

*Great Weird Tales* - S.T. Joshi  *h*  2993

*Great Writers and Kids Write Spooky Stories* - Martin H. Greenberg  *h*  2395

*Guignoir and Other Furies* - George Hatch  *h*  2600

*H.P. Lovecraft's Book of Horror* - Stephen Jones  *h*  2968

*A Hammock Beneath the Mangoes* - Thomas Colchie  *h*  1099

*Harvest Tales and Midnight Revels: Stories for the Waning of the Year* - Michael Mayhew  *h*  3705

*The Hastur Cycle* - Robert M. Price  *h*  4425

*Haunted Houses: The Greatest Stories* - Martin H. Greenberg  *h*  2396

*The Horror Hall of Fame* - Robert Silverberg  *h*  5031

*Horrors: 365 Scary Stories* - Stefan Dziemianowicz  *h*  1714

*Horrorstory III* - Karl Edward Wagner  *h*  5601

*Horrorstory IV* - Karl Edward Wagner  *h*  5602

*Horrorstory V* - Karl Edward Wagner  *h*  5603

*Hot Blood X* - Jeff Gelb  *h*  2177

*Hot Blood: Crimes of Passion* - Jeff Gelb  *h*  2178

*Hot Blood: Kiss and Kill* - Jeff Gelb  *h*  2179

*Hotter Blood: More Tales of Erotic Horror* - Jeff Gelb  *h*  2180

*Hottest Blood: The Ultimate in Erotic Horror* - Jeff Gelb  *h*  2181

*I Shudder at Your Touch* - Michele Slung  *h*  5093

*I, Vampire: Interviews with the Undead* - Jean Marie Stine  *h*  5284

*Imagination Fully Dilated* - Alan M. Clark  *h*  1044

*In the Fog* - Charles L. Grant  *h*  2311

*In the Shadow of the Gargoyle* - Nancy Kilpatrick  *h*  3112

*The Innsmouth Cycle: The Taint of the Deep Ones in 13 Tales* - Robert M. Price  *h*  4426

*Inside the Works* - Tom Piccirilli  *h*  4314

*Intensive Scare* - Karl Edward Wagner  *h*  5604

*Irish Tales of the Supernatural* - Martin O'Griofa  *h*  4203

*Isaac Asimov's Ghosts* - Gardner Dozois  *h*  1610

*Isaac Asimov's Vampires* - Gardner Dozois  *h*  1611

*It Came From the Drive-In* - Norman Partridge  *h*  4252

*Journey into Fear and Other Great Stories of Horror on the Railways* - Richard Peyton  *h*  4308

*Journeys to the Twilight Zone* - Carol Serling  *h*  4913

*The King Is Dead: Tales of Elvis Post Mortem* - Paul M. Sammon  *h*  4810

*The Kiss of Death: An Anthology of Vampire Stories* - Anonymous  *h*  151

*The Literary Ghost* - Larry Dark  *h*  1351

*The Little Book of Horrors* - Sebastian Wolfe  *h*  5946

*Little Deaths* - Ellen Datlow  *h*  1361

*Love Bites* - Amarantha Knight  *h*  3182

*Love in Vein* - Poppy Z. Brite  *h*  698

*Love in Vein II* - Poppy Z. Brite  *h*  699

*Lovecraft's Legacy* - Robert Weinberg  *h*  5698

*Lovers and Other Monsters* - Marvin Kaye  *h*  3026

*The Mammoth Book of Best New Horror* - Stephen Jones  *h*  2969

*The Mammoth Book of Best New Horror 8* - Stephen Jones  *h*  2970

*The Mammoth Book of Best New Horror 9* - Stephen Jones  *h*  2971

*The Mammoth Book of Dracula* - Stephen Jones  *h*  2972

*The Mammoth Book of Frankenstein* - Stephen Jones  *h*  2973

*The Mammoth Book of Ghost Stories* - Richard Dalby  *h*  1309

*The Mammoth Book of Short Horror Novels* - Mike Ashley  *h*  226

*The Mammoth Book of Terror* - Stephen Jones  *h*  2974

*The Mammoth Book of Twentieth Century Ghost Stories* - Peter Haining  *h*  2483

*The Mammoth Book of Vampires* - Stephen Jones  *h*  2975

*The Mammoth Book of Victorian and Edwardian Ghost Stories* - Richard Dalby  *h*  1310

*The Mammoth Book of Werewolves* - Stephen Jones  *h*  2976

*The Mammoth Book of Zombies* - Stephen Jones  *h*  2977

*Masques IV* - J.N. Williamson  *h*  5855

*Masterpieces of Terror and the Unknown* - Marvin Kaye  *h*  3027

*Metahorror* - Dennis Etchison  *h*  1847

*Midnight Graffiti* - Jessica Horsting  *h*  2773

*Midnight Never Comes* - Barbara Roden  *h*  4644

*Miskatonic University* - Martin H. Greenberg  *h*  2399

*Mistletoe Mayhem* - Richard Dalby  *h*  1311

*Mistresses of the Dark* - Stefan Dziemianowicz  *h*  1715

*Modern Ghost Stories by Eminent Women Writers* - Richard Dalby  *h*  1312

*Monsters From Memphis* - Beecher Smith  *h*  5098

*Monsters in Our Midst* - Robert Bloch  *h*  538

*More Monsters From Memphis* - Beecher Smith  *h*  5099

*More Phobias* - Wendy Webb  *h*  5666

*Mummy Stories* - Martin H. Greenberg  *h*  2400

*Mysterious Cat Stories* - John Richard Stephens  *h*  5252

*Narrow Houses* - Peter Crowther  *h*  1284

*The Necronomicon* - Robert M. Price  *h*  4427

*The New Gothic* - Bradford Morrow  *h*  4027

*The New Lovecraft Circle* - Robert M. Price  *h*  4428

*New Stories From the Twilight Zone* - Martin H. Greenberg  *h*  2402

*Night Bites: Vampire Stories by Women* - Victoria Brownworth  *h*  730

*Night Screams* - Ed Gorman  *h*  2278

*Night Terrors: Stories of Shadow and Substance* - Lois Duncan  *h*  1693

*Night Visions 8* - John Farris  *h*  1885

*Night Visions 9* - Thomas Tessier  *h*  5441

*Nightmares on Elm Street: Freddy Krueger's Seven Sweetest Dreams* - Martin H. Greenberg  *h*  2403

*Northern Frights* - Don Hutchison  *h*  2813

*Northern Frights 2* - Don Hutchison  *h*  2814

*Northern Frights 3* - Don Hutchison  *h*  2815

*The Norton Book of Ghost Stories* - Brad Leithauser  *h*  3432

*Nursery Crimes* - Stefan Dziemianowicz  *h*  1716

*The Nyarlathotep Cycle* - Robert M. Price  *h*  4429

*Obsessions* - Gary L. Raisor  *h*  4465

*The Omnibus of Twentieth Century Ghost Stories* - Robert Phillips  *h*  4311

*The Oxford Book of Gothic Tales* - Chris Baldick  *h*  307

*The Oxford Book of Twentieth Century Ghost Stories* - Michael Cox  *h*  1232

*Peter Straub's Ghosts* - Peter Straub  *h*  5331

*Phantoms of the Night* - Richard Gilliam  *h*  2233

*Phobias: Stories of Your Deepest Fears* - Wendy Webb  *h*  5667

*Post Mortem: New Tales of Ghostly Horror* - Paul F. Olson  *h*  4214

*Predators* - Ed Gorman  *h*  2280

*Psycho-Paths* - Robert Bloch  *h*  543

*Pulphouse, Issue 7: Horror* - Kristine Kathryn Rusch  *h*  4724

*Pulphouse, Issue 9: Dark Fantasy* - Kristine Kathryn Rusch  *h*  4726

*Pulphouse, Issue 12: The Last Issue* - Kristine Kathryn Rusch  *h*  4722

*Quick Chills* - Peter Enfantino  *h*  1823

*Quick Chills II* - Robert Morrish  *h*  4025

*The Quintessential World of Darkness* - Stewart Wieck  *h*  5798

*The Raven and the Monkey's Paw* - Anonymous  *h*  1

*Razored Saddles* - Joe R. Lansdale  *h*  3331

*The Reel Stuff* - Brian Thomsen  *h*  5460

*Reel Terror* - Sebastian Wolfe  *h*  5947

*Restless Spirits* - Catherine A. Lundie  *h*  3570

*Return to Lovecraft Country* - Scott David Aniolowski  *h*  148

*Return to the Twilight Zone* - Carol Serling  *h*  4914

*Revelations* - Douglas E. Winter  *h*  5924

*Rivals of Dracula* - Robert Weinberg  *h*  5699

*Rivals of Weird Tales* - Robert Weinberg  *h*  5700

*Roald Dahl's Book of Ghost Stories* - Roald Dahl  *h*  1306

*Robert Bloch's Psychos* - Robert Bloch  *h*  544

*Screamplays* - Richard T. Chizmar  *h*  1022

*Sea Cursed: Thirty Terrifying Tales of the Deep* - T. Liam McDonald  *h*  3798

*The SeaHarp Hotel* - Charles L. Grant  *h*  2315

*Seductive Spectres* - Amarantha Knight  *h*  3184

*Seeds of Fear* - Jeff Gelb  *h*  2182

*Shadows over Innsmouth* - Stephen Jones  *h*  2978

*Shivers for Christmas* - Richard Dalby  *h*  1313

*Shock Rock* - Jeff Gelb  *h*  2183

*Shock Rock II* - Jeff Gelb  *h*  2184

*The Shub Niggurath Cycle* - Robert M. Price  *h*  4430

*Shudder Again* - Michele Slung  *h*  5094

*Sinistre: An Anthology of Rituals* - George Hatch  *h*  2601

*Sirens and Other Daemon Lovers* - Ellen Datlow  *h*  1367

*Sisters of the Night* - Barbara Hambly  *h*  2508

*Six German Romantic Tales* - Ronald Taylor  *h*  5418

*Skin of the Soul* - Lisa Tuttle  *h*  5523

*Sons of Darkness: Tales of Men, Blood and Immortality* - Michael Rowe  *h*  4690

*Southern Blood: Vampire Stories From the American South* - Lawrence Schimel  *h*  4880

*Splatterpunks II: Over the Edge* - Paul M. Sammon  *h*  4811

*Splatterpunks: Extreme Horror* - Paul M. Sammon  *h*  4812

*Spooky Sea Stories* - Charles G. Waugh  *h*  5652

*Stalkers* - Ed Gorman  *h*  2282

*Still Dead: Book of the Dead 2* - John Skipp  *h*  5083

*Strange City* - Staley Krause  *h*  3229

*Strange Creatures* - Tina L. Jens  *h*  2892

*Strange Tales From the Strand* - Jack Adrian  *h*  39

*Stranger by Night* - Jeff Gelb  *h*  2185

*Streets of Blood: Vampire Stories From New York City* - Lawrence Schimel  *h*  4881

*Supernatural Sleuths* - Charles G. Waugh  *h*  5653

*Supernatural Tales From around the World* - Terri Hardin  *h*  2543

*Tales of Forbidden Passion* - Tina L. Jens  *h*  2893

*Tales of the Lovecraft Mythos* - Robert M. Price  *h*  4431

*A Taste for Blood* - Martin H. Greenberg  *h*  2407

*Terata: Anomalies of Literature* - Jeffrey Thomas  *h*  5447

*Terminal Frights, Volume One* - Ken Abner  *h*  22

*The Time of the Vampires* - P.N. Elrod  *h*  1799

*To Sleep, Perchance to Dream. . .Nightmare* - Stefan Dziemianowicz  *h*  1717

*Tombs* - Edward E. Kramer  *h*  3228

*Tomorrow Bites* - Greg Cox  *h*  1230

*Tomorrow Sucks* - Greg Cox  *h*  1231

*Touch Wood* - Peter Crowther  *h*  1285

*Twelve Gothic Tales* - Richard Dalby  *h*  1314

*Twelve Irish Ghost Stories* - Patricia Craig  *h*  1242

*Twelve Tales of the Supernatural* - Michael Cox  *h*  1233

*Twelve Victorian Ghost Stories* - Michael Cox  *h*  1234

*Twists of the Tale* - Ellen Datlow  *h*  1369

*The Ultimate Dracula* - Byron Preiss  *h*  4407

*The Ultimate Frankenstein* - Byron Preiss  *h*  4409

*The Ultimate Werewolf* - Byron Preiss  *h*  4410

*The Ultimate Witch* - Byron Preiss  *h*  4411

*The Ultimate Zombie* - Byron Preiss  *h*  4412

*Under the Fang* - Robert R. McCammon  *h*  3758

*Urban Horrors* - William F. Nolan  *h*  4133

*Vampire and Werewolf Stories* - Alan Durant  *h*  1701

*A Vampire Bestiary* - Jeffrey Thomas  *h*  5448

*Vampire Detectives* - Martin H. Greenberg  *h*  2408

*The Vampire Hunters' Casebook* - Peter Haining  *h*  2484

*Vampires: The Greatest Stories* - Martin H. Greenberg  *h*  2409

*Vampires, Wine & Roses* - John Richard Stevens  *h*  5265

*The Vampyre and Other Tales of the Macabre* - Robert Morrison  *h*  4026

*Victorian Ghost Stories: An Oxford Anthology* - Michael Cox  *h*  1235

*Virtuous Vampires* - Stefan Dziemianowicz  *h*  1718

*Voices From the Night* - John Maclay  *h*  3598

*Voyages into Darkness* - Stephen Laws  *h*  3363

*Walls of Fear* - Kathryn Cramer  *h*  1246

*Weird Business* - Joe R. Lansdale  *h*  3334

*Weird Menace* - Fred Olen Ray  *h*  4494

*Weird Tales* - Peter Haining  *h*  2485

*Weird Tales: Seven Decades of Terror* - John Gregory Betancourt  *h*  482

*Weird Tales: The Magazine That Never Dies* - Marvin Kaye  *h*  3028

*Weird Vampire Tales* - Robert Weinberg  *h*  5706

*Werewolves* - Martin H. Greenberg  *h*  2410

*When the Black Lotus Blooms* - Elizabeth A. Saunders  *h*  4846

*A Whisper of Blood* - Ellen Datlow  *h*  1370

*White House Horrors* - Martin H. Greenberg  *h*  2411

*Wild Women* - Melissa Mia Hall  *h*  2496

*Winter Tales* - Tina L. Jens  *h*  2894

*Women of Darkness II* - Kathryn Ptacek  *h*  4443

*Women Who Run with Werewolves: Tales of Blood, Lust and Metamorphosis* - Pam Keesey  *h*  3032

*The Xothic Legend Cycle: The Complete Mythos Fiction of Lin Carter* - Lin Carter  *h*  925

*The Year's Best Fantasy and Horror: Eleventh Annual Collection* - Ellen Datlow  *h*  1371

*The Year's Best Fantasy and Horror: Fifth Annual Collection* - Ellen Datlow  *h*  1372

*The Year's Best Fantasy and Horror: Ninth Annual Collection* - Ellen Datlow  *h*  1374

*The Year's Best Fantasy and Horror: Seventh Annual Collection* - Ellen Datlow  *h*  1375

*The Year's Best Fantasy and Horror: Sixth Annual Collection* - Ellen Datlow  *h*  1376

*The Year's Best Fantasy and Horror: Tenth Annual Collection* - Ellen Datlow  *h*  1377

*The Year's Best Fantasy and Horror: Third Annual Collection* - Ellen Datlow  *h*  1378

*The Year's Best Horror Stories XVIII* - Karl Edward Wagner  *h*  5605

*The Year's Best Horror Stories XX* - Karl Edward Wagner  *h*  5606

*The Year's Best Horror Stories XXI* - Karl Edward Wagner  *h*  5607

*The Year's Best Horror Stories XXIII* - Karl Edward Wagner  *h*  5608

*Young Blood* - Mike Baker  *h*  300

*The Young Oxford Book of Ghost Stories* - Dennis Pepper  *h*  4282

## Horror — Apocalyptic Horror

*The 37th Mandala* - Marc Laidlaw  *h*  3310

*The Angel of Pain* - Brian Stableford  *h*  5189

*Black Sun* - Douglas E. Winter  *h*  5923

*Cain* - James Byron Huggins  *h*  2802

*The Carnival of Destruction* - Brian Stableford  *h*  5190

*The Cat* - R.L. Stine  *h*  5285

*Chariot* - Charles L. Grant  *h*  2304

*The Crawling Dark* - Pauline Dunn  *h*  1698

*Dark Channel* - Ray Garton  *h*  2150

*Demon Dance* - T. Chris Martindale  *h*  3655

*Demon Night* - J. Michael Straczynski  *h*  5322

*Deus-X: A Novel of Spiritual Terror* - Joseph A. Citro  *h*  1037

*The Devil's Day* - James Blish  *h*  525

*Everville* - Clive Barker  *h*  338

*Fire* - Alan Rodgers  *h*  4647

*For You, the Living* - Wayne Allen Sallee  *h*  4786

*The Forbidden Zone* - Whitley Strieber  *h*  5340

*Ghost Dance* - Kathryn Ptacek  *h*  4441

*The Great and Secret Show* - Clive Barker  *h*  341

*The House on the Borderland* - William Hope Hodgson   *h*   2711
*Imajica* - Clive Barker   *h*   343
*In the Mood* - Charles L. Grant   *h*   2312
*Name of the Beast* - Daniel Easterman   *h*   1721
*Night* - Alan Rodgers   *h*   4649
*Nightworld* - F. Paul Wilson   *h*   5893
*Otherworld* - Kenneth C. Flint   *h*   1959
*Portent* - James Herbert   *h*   2670
*The Revelation* - Bentley Little   *h*   3496
*The Road to Hell, Volume I* - Robert Weinberg   *h*   5701
*The Road to Hell, Volume II* - Robert Weinberg   *h*   5702
*Rockabilly Limbo* - William W. Johnstone   *h*   2934
*Skeletons* - Al Sarrantonio   *h*   4834
*The Stand: The Complete and Uncut Edition* - Stephen King   *h*   3142
*Swan Song* - Robert R. McCammon   *h*   3757
*Symphony* - Charles L. Grant   *h*   2318
*Wizard and Glass* - Stephen King   *h*   3144
*Wurm* - Matthew J. Costello   *h*   1202
*Yellow Moon* - David J. Searls   *h*   4907


**Horror — Black Magic**

*After Life* - Andrew Neiderman   *h*   4083
*Black Body* - H.C. Turk   *h*   5488
*Blood Sabbath* - Leigh Clark   *h*   1048
*Breeder* - Douglas Clegg   *h*   1076
*Breeder* - Ed Kelleher   *h*   3041
*Cardinal's Sin* - Raymond Buckland   *h*   751
*Child's Play III* - Matthew J. Costello   *h*   1194
*The Chosen* - Edward Lee   *h*   3389
*The Convocation* - John R. Holt   *h*   2748
*Coven* - Edward Lee   *h*   3390
*Coven* - Steven William Rimmer   *h*   4591
*Dark Debts* - Karen Hall   *h*   2494
*Dark Legacy* - Mark A. Kostrubula   *h*   3220
*Darkborn* - Matthew J. Costello   *h*   1195
*The Darker Saints* - Brian Hodge   *h*   2699
*The Death Prayer* - David Bowker   *h*   602
*Demon Fire* - Gary L. Holleman   *h*   2743
*Demon Within* - Dana Reed   *h*   4499
*Demon's Fright* - Penelope Banka Kreps   *h*   3233
*The Devil Rides Out* - Dennis Wheatley   *h*   5773
*The Devil's Advocate* - Andrew Neiderman   *h*   4085
*The Devil's End* - D.A. Fowler   *h*   2023
*The Devil's Laughter* - William W. Johnstone   *h*   2930
*Disciples of Dread* - Hugh B. Cave   *h*   941
*Evil Intent* - Bernard Taylor   *h*   5400
*The Fair Rules of Evil* - David C. Smith   *h*   5111
*Fantasma* - Thomas F. Monteleone   *h*   3963
*Fetish* - Edward Bryant   *h*   749
*Furnace* - Muriel Gray   *h*   2339
*Goon* - Edward Lee   *h*   3392
*Grimm Memorials* - R. Patrick Gates   *h*   2160
*The Gris-Gris Man* - Don Davis   *h*   1403
*Horror Show* - Greg Kihn   *h*   3103
*Horses of the Night* - Michael Cadnum   *h*   811
*Howl-O-Ween* - Gary L. Holleman   *h*   2744
*Last Rites* - David Darke   *h*   1354
*The Monastery* - J.N. Williamson   *h*   5856
*Moonfall* - Tamara Thorne   *h*   5464
*Neighbors* - Maureen S. Pusti   *h*   4450
*Night Music* - Sheila Bristow Garner   *h*   2147
*Night Thunder* - Ruby Jean Jensen   *h*   2903
*The Quagmire* - James Kisner   *h*   3160
*The Quorum* - Kim Newman   *h*   4100
*Raven* - S.A. Swiniarski   *h*   5374
*Resurrection Dreams* - Richard Laymon   *h*   3371
*Rook* - Graham Masterton   *h*   3678
*Root of All Evil* - David A. Farrow   *h*   1888
*The School* - Ed Kelleher   *h*   3042
*The Sixth Dog* - Jane Rice   *h*   4582
*Snowbeast!* - Peter Tremayne   *h*   5482
*Sorcerers of Sodom* - Roger Elwood   *h*   1804

*Soul Snatchers* - Michael Cecilione   *h*   947
*Spellcaster* - J. Edward Ames   *h*   92
*Tempter* - Nancy A. Collins   *h*   1125
*The Thing That Darkness Hides* - Robert Morgan   *h*   4006
*Ticktock* - Dean R. Koontz   *h*   3217
*The Torching* - Marcy Heidish   *h*   2642
*Voodoo Child* - Michael Reaves   *h*   4498
*When Shadows Fall* - Brian Scott Smith   *h*   5100
*Wildest Dreams* - Norman Partridge   *h*   4256
*Witch Hill* - Marion Zimmer Bradley   *h*   654
*Witch Spell* - Guy N. Smith   *h*   5122
*Witchcraft* - Bill Michaels   *h*   3885
*Witches* - Kathryn Meyer Griffith   *h*   2442
*The Witching Hour* - Anne Rice   *h*   4580
*Wolf Moon* - John R. Holt   *h*   2749


**Horror — Carnival/Circus Horror**

*Dark Journey* - A.R. Morlan   *h*   4010
*Destiny's Carnival* - Warren Murphy   *h*   4057
*Escardy Gap* - Peter Crowther   *h*   1282
*The Eyes of the Beast* - Steve Harris   *h*   2565
*Freak Show* - F. Paul Wilson   *h*   5888


**Horror — Child-in-Peril**

*The Baby* - Stephanie Kegan   *h*   3033
*Baby Dolly* - Ruby Jean Jensen   *h*   2899
*The Black School* - J.N. Williamson   *h*   5851
*Bloodstream* - Tess Gerritsen   *h*   2205
*Bring Me Children* - David Martin   *h*   3637
*Button Bright* - Michael Kurland   *h*   3251
*Cursed Be the Child* - Mort Castle   *h*   937
*Darkness* - John Saul   *h*   4840
*Darkside* - Dennis Etchison   *h*   1845
*The Devil's Cradle* - Kate Stewart   *h*   5269
*Disturbing Behavior* - John Whitman   *h*   5789
*The Fagin* - Pat Graversen   *h*   2334
*The Feeding* - Leigh Clark   *h*   1051
*First Love: A Gothic Tale* - Joyce Carol Oates   *h*   4183
*Flying in Place* - Susan Palwick   *h*   4240
*From a Whisper to a Scream* - Samuel M. Key   *h*   3093
*Gnelfs* - Sidney Williams   *h*   5823
*Good Night, Sweet Angel* - Clare McNally   *h*   3857
*Grimm Memorials* - R. Patrick Gates   *h*   2160
*The Hunted* - Kathryn Ptacek   *h*   4442
*Little Boy Lost* - T.M. Wright   *h*   5992
*Nightscape* - Stephen R. George   *h*   2203
*Nursery Crimes* - Stefan Dziemianowicz   *h*   1716
*Panic* - Chris Curry   *h*   1295
*Playmates* - Abigail McDaniels   *h*   3784
*The Presence* - John Saul   *h*   4843
*Shadow Child* - Joseph A. Citro   *h*   1038
*Shadow Man* - Dennis Etchison   *h*   1848
*Shadow Walkers* - Nina Romberg   *h*   4663
*Shadows* - John Saul   *h*   4845
*Substitute Teacher* - Jordan Storm   *h*   5314
*Whispers in the Dark* - Jonathan Aycliffe   *h*   283


**Horror — Collection**

*13 Haunting Ghost Tales* - Kirt Stark   *h*   5211
*The Adventures of Lucius Leffing* - Joseph Payne Brennan   *h*   670
*The Agonizing Resurrection of Victor Frankenstein and Other Gothic Tales* - Thomas Ligotti   *h*   3460
*Alone with the Horrors* - Ramsey Campbell   *h*   851
*Angry Candy* - Harlan Ellison   *h*   1783
*Are You Loathsome Tonight?* - Poppy Z. Brite   *h*   693
*Aylmer Vance: Ghost-Seer* - Alice Askew   *h*   258
*Bad Intentions* - Norman Partridge   *h*   4250
*The Barrens and Others* - F. Paul Wilson   *h*   5885
*The Best Horror Stories of Arthur Conan Doyle* - Sir Arthur Conan Doyle   *h*   1596

*The Best of D.F. Lewis* - D.F. Lewis   *h*   3447
*Bestsellers Guaranteed* - Joe R. Lansdale   *h*   3321
*Beyond the Borders* - Robert E. Howard   *h*   2780
*Beyond the Lamplight* - Donald Burleson   *h*   775
*Binscombe Tales* - John Whitbourn   *h*   5776
*Bitter/Sweet* - Hugh B. Cave   *h*   939
*Black Butterflies: A Flock on the Dark Side* - John Shirley   *h*   5005
*Black Leather Required* - David J. Schow   *h*   4885
*The Black Reaper* - Bernard Capes   *h*   875
*Black Spirits and White* - Ralph Adams Cram   *h*   1243
*Black Walls, Red Glass* - Jeffrey Thomas   *h*   5445
*Blood Walk* - Lee Killough   *h*   3108
*Blue World* - Robert R. McCammon   *h*   3753
*The Bones of the Old Ones and Other Lovecraftian Tales* - Jeffrey Thomas   *h*   5446
*The Book of Hyperborea* - Clark Ashton Smith   *h*   5102
*The Book of Iod* - Henry Kuttner   *h*   3266
*The Brain in the Jar and Others* - Richard F. Searight   *h*   4904
*The Brains of Rats* - Michael Blumlein   *h*   555
*The Bureau of Lost Souls* - Christopher Fowler   *h*   2017
*Burn, Witch, Burn!/Creep, Shadow, Creep!* - A. Merritt   *h*   3877
*Burning Your Boats: The Collected Short Stories* - Angela Carter   *h*   921
*By Bizarre Hands* - Joe R. Lansdale   *h*   3322
*Cabal* - Clive Barker   *h*   337
*Cages* - Ed Gorman   *h*   2277
*The Call and Other Stories* - Robert Westall   *h*   5762
*Candles for Elizabeth* - Caitlin R. Kiernan   *h*   3100
*The Cleft and Other Odd Tales* - Gahan Wilson   *h*   5901
*The Clock Strikes Twelve* - H. Russell Wakefield   *h*   5610
*Close to the Bone* - Lucy Taylor   *h*   5411
*Collected Fictions* - Jorge Luis Borges   *h*   573
*The Collected Ghost Stories of E.F. Benson* - E.F. Benson   *h*   454
*Collected Stories* - Richard Matheson   *h*   3683
*Collected Tales and Stories* - Mary Shelley   *h*   4968
*The Collector of Hearts: New Tales of the Grotesque* - Joyce Carol Oates   *h*   4181
*The Compleat Werewolf and Other Tales of Fantasy and Science Fiction* - Anthony Boucher   *h*   579
*The Complete John Silence Stories* - Algernon Blackwood   *h*   509
*The Complete Stories of Robert Bloch, Volume 1: Final Reckonings* - Robert Bloch   *h*   531
*The Complete Stories of Robert Bloch, Volume 2: Bitter Ends* - Robert Bloch   *h*   529
*The Complete Stories of Robert Bloch, Volume 3: Last Rites* - Robert Bloch   *h*   530
*Conjure Wife/Our Lady of Darkness* - Fritz Leiber   *h*   3416
*The Convulsion Factory* - Brian Hodge   *h*   2698
*A Coven of Vampires* - Brian Lumley   *h*   3549
*Crypt Orchids* - David J. Schow   *h*   4886
*The Cthulhu Mythos* - August Derleth   *h*   1494
*Curse of the Magazine Killers* - Gary Jonas   *h*   2937
*The Dark Domain* - Stefan Grabinski   *h*   2294
*A Dark Night's Work and Other Stories* - Elizabeth Cleghorn Gaskell   *h*   2158
*The Dark Side: Tales of Terror and the Supernatural* - Guy de Maupassant   *h*   3694
*Dark Tales and Light* - Bruce Boston   *h*   578
*The Darker Passions Reader* - Amarantha Knight   *h*   3176
*Dead Meat* - Guy N. Smith   *h*   5120
*Death Stalks the Night* - Hugh B. Cave   *h*   940
*Decoded Mirrors: Three Tales after Lovecraft* - Steve Rasnic Tem   *h*   5426
*Demon and Other Tales* - Joyce Carol Oates   *h*   4182

*Demons and Shadows: The Ghostly Best Stories of Robert Westall* - Robert Westall  *h*  5763
*Demons by Daylight* - Ramsey Campbell  *h*  855
*Demons of the Sea* - William Hope Hodgson  *h*  2708
*The Dog Syndrome and Other Sick Puppies* - Tom Piccirilli  *h*  4313
*Donovan's Brain/Hauser's Memory* - Curt Siodmak  *h*  5072
*Don't Dream* - Donald Wandrei  *h*  5627
*The Door Below* - Hugh B. Cave  *h*  942
*Down Among the Weeds: The Sargasso Sea Stories of William Hope Hodgson* - William Hope Hodgson  *h*  2709
*The Drag Queen of Elfland* - Lawrence Schimel  *h*  4878
*The Dream Cycle of H.P. Lovecraft: Dreams of Terror and Death* - H.P. Lovecraft  *h*  3530
*Dream of the Wolf* - Scott Bradfield  *h*  626
*Driftglider and Other Stories* - Jeffrey Osier  *h*  4230
*The Drive-In: A Double Omnibus* - Joe R. Lansdale  *h*  3326
*Dystopia* - William A. Walker Jr.  *h*  5620
*The Early Fears* - Robert Bloch  *h*  532
*Electric Gumbo: A Lansdale Reader* - Joe R. Lansdale  *h*  3327
*Endorphins* - Nancy Kilpatrick  *h*  3111
*The Ends of the Earth* - Lucius Shepard  *h*  4977
*Eons of the Night* - Robert E. Howard  *h*  2781
*Escape From Tomorrow* - Frank Belknap Long  *h*  3515
*Evenings with Demons* - Whitley Strieber  *h*  5339
*The Exit at Toledo Blade Boulevard* - Jack Ketchum  *h*  3090
*Exorcisms and Ecstasies* - Karl Edward Wagner  *h*  5600
*Extremities* - Kathe Koja  *h*  3195
*The Eye Above the Mantel and Other Stories* - Frank Belknap Long  *h*  3516
*Fairytales* - Steve Rasnic Tem  *h*  5427
*The Fall of the House of Escher and Other Illusions* - David Niall Wilson  *h*  5881
*Falling Idols* - Brian Hodge  *h*  2701
*Fantastic Tales* - I.U. Tarchetti  *h*  5389
*Far Away and Never* - Ramsey Campbell  *h*  856
*Fear and Trembling* - Robert Bloch  *h*  533
*Feeding the Glamour Hogs* - Mark McLaughlin  *h*  3851
*The Fellow Travellers and Other Ghost Stories* - Sheila Hodgson  *h*  2707
*A Few Bricks Shy* - S. Anthony Gardner  *h*  2137
*The Fifth Season* - J.N. Williamson  *h*  5854
*Firefly...Burning Bright* - Barry Hoffman  *h*  2714
*A Fist Full of Stories (and Articles)* - Joe R. Lansdale  *h*  3328
*The Flesh Artist* - Lucy Taylor  *h*  5412
*Flights of Fear* - Graham Masterton  *h*  3673
*Flowers From the Moon and Other Lunacies* - Robert Bloch  *h*  534
*For the Blood Is the Life and Other Stories* - F. Marion Crawford  *h*  1252
*Forms of Heaven* - Clive Barker  *h*  339
*Fortnight of Fear* - Graham Masterton  *h*  3674
*Four Past Midnight* - Stephen King  *h*  3132
*Four Shadowings* - Donald Burleson  *h*  776
*Fruiting Bodies and Other Fungi* - Brian Lumley  *h*  3553
*Fugue Devil and Other Weird Horrors* - Stephen Mark Rainey  *h*  4463
*The Ghost Book of Charles Lindley, Viscount Halifax* - Charles Lindley  *h*  3472
*The Ghost-Feeler* - Edith Wharton  *h*  5772
*Ghostly Tales of Iowa* - Ruth D. Hein  *h*  2643
*The Golden Pot and Other Tales* - E.T.A. Hoffmann  *h*  2718
*A Good, Secret Place* - Richard Laymon  *h*  3367
*The Good, the Bad, and the Indifferent* - Joe R. Lansdale  *h*  3329

*Grimscribe: His Lives and Works* - Thomas Ligotti  *h*  3461
*The Haunted Chair and Other Stories* - Richard Marsh  *h*  3633
*The Haunted Pampero* - William Hope Hodgson  *h*  2710
*Haunted: Tales of the Grotesque* - Joyce Carol Oates  *h*  4184
*Heatseeker* - John Shirley  *h*  5007
*Her Pilgrim Soul* - Alan Brennert  *h*  674
*The Hoard of the Wizard Beast and One Other* - Robert H. Barlow  *h*  348
*Hogfoot Right and Bird-Hands* - Garry Kilworth  *h*  3116
*Horizon Lines* - Jeffrey Osier  *h*  4231
*The Horror in the Museum and Other Revisions* - H.P. Lovecraft  *h*  3531
*The Horror of the Heights and Other Tales of Suspense* - Sir Arthur Conan Doyle  *h*  1597
*The Hot Jazz Trio* - William Kotzwinkle  *h*  3223
*Houses Without Doors* - Peter Straub  *h*  5327
*The Howling Man* - Charles Beaumont  *h*  429
*I Am Legend* - Richard Matheson  *h*  3686
*Iced on Aran and Other Dream Quests* - Brian Lumley  *h*  3555
*Imagine a Man in a Box* - H. Russell Wakefield  *h*  5611
*In Camera and Other Stories* - Robert Westall  *h*  5764
*In Ghostly Company* - Amyas Northcote  *h*  4141
*In His Own Write: Brian Lumley, Necroscribe* - Brian Lumley  *h*  3556
*In Lovecraft's Shadow* - August Derleth  *h*  1495
*Incarnations* - Clive Barker  *h*  344
*The Incredible Shrinking Man* - Richard Matheson  *h*  3687
*The Infinite Man* - William Relling Jr.  *h*  4530
*Irrational Numbers* - David Langford  *h*  3317
*Just an Ordinary Day* - Shirley Jackson  *h*  2842
*Kevin Browne's Nightales* - John Tigges  *h*  5473
*The King in Yellow* - Robert W. Chambers  *h*  963
*Lady Ferry and Other Uncanny People* - Sarah Orne Jewett  *h*  2919
*The Lady of the Frozen Death and Other Weird Tales* - Leonard Cline  *h*  1088
*Landscape of Demons and the Book of Sara* - Gabriel Devlin Kessler  *h*  3088
*The Language of Fear* - Del James  *h*  2860
*The Last Rite* - Brian Lumley  *h*  3558
*Leavings* - P.D. Cacek  *h*  802
*Legacy of Fire* - Nina Kiriki Hoffman  *h*  2715
*Lemon Drops and Other Horrors* - Donald Burleson  *h*  777
*The Light Invisible* - Robert Hugh Benson  *h*  456
*Lilith's Cave: Jewish Tales of the Supernatural* - Howard Schwartz  *h*  4890
*The Lion Tamer's Daughter* - Peter Dickinson  *h*  1526
*Lost Angels* - David J. Schow  *h*  4888
*Lost in Booth Nine* - Adam-Troy Castro  *h*  938
*Ma Qui and Other Phantoms* - Alan Brennert  *h*  675
*Maps in a Mirror* - Orson Scott Card  *h*  893
*The Mask of Cthulhu* - August Derleth  *h*  1496
*Mean Little Old Lady at Work* - Ardath Mayhar  *h*  3702
*Memories of the Body* - Lisa Tuttle  *h*  5521
*Methods of Madness* - Ray Garton  *h*  2153
*Midnight Blue: The Sonja Blue Collection* - Nancy A. Collins  *h*  1122
*Midnight Pleasures* - Robert Bloch  *h*  537
*Midnight Promises* - Richard T. Chizmar  *h*  1021
*The Mirror of the Night* - Roberta Lannes  *h*  3318
*The Monkey's Paw and Other Tales of Mystery and the Macabre* - W.W. Jacobs  *h*  2846
*Monsters and Other Stories* - Richard Chizmar  *h*  1016
*Moon of the Wolf/Progeny of the Adder* - Les Whitten  *h*  5791

*The Moonlit Road and Other Ghost and Horror Stories* - Ambrose Bierce  *h*  485
*More Shapes than One* - Fred Chappell  *h*  967
*The Mortal Immortal* - Mary Shelley  *h*  4969
*Mr. Fox and Other Feral Tales* - Norman Partridge  *h*  4253
*Mr. Templeton's Toyshop: Prose Poems and Short Fiction* - Thomas Wiloch  *h*  5876
*Murmerous Haunts* - Bentley Little  *h*  3495
*The Mysteries of the Worm* - Robert Bloch  *h*  539
*The Mysterious Doom and Other Ghostly Tales of the Pacific Northwest* - Jessica Amanda Salmonson  *h*  4791
*The Naked Flesh of Feeling* - J.N. Williamson  *h*  5857
*Nameless Sins* - Nancy A. Collins  *h*  1123
*Needles and Sins* - Michael A. Arnzen  *h*  213
*New Life for the Dead* - Alan Rodgers  *h*  4648
*New Noir* - John Shirley  *h*  5008
*Nice Little Stories Jam-Packed with Depraved Sex and Violence* - Michael Hemmingson  *h*  2655
*The Night Comes On* - Steve Duffy  *h*  1671
*Night Gaunts: An Entertainment Based on the Life and Work of H.P. Lovecraft* - Brett Rutherford  *h*  4751
*Night Shapes: Excursions into Terror* - William F. Nolan  *h*  4132
*The Night We Buried Road Dog* - Jack Cady  *h*  818
*The Nightmare Factory* - Thomas Ligotti  *h*  3462
*Nightmare Flower* - Elizabeth Engstrom  *h*  1827
*Nightmare Jack and Other Stories* - John Metcalfe  *h*  3879
*Nightmare Jack and Other Stories* - John Metcalfe  *h*  3880
*Nightmares and Dreamscapes* - Stephen King  *h*  3138
*Nights of the Round Table* - Margery Lawrence  *h*  3360
*Noctet: Tales of Madonna-Moloch* - Albert J. Manachino  *h*  3613
*Noctuary* - Thomas Ligotti  *h*  3463
*Noise and Other Night Terrors* - Newton E. Streeter  *h*  5335
*The October Country* - Ray Bradbury  *h*  623
*The Odd Lot: The Selected Works of Albert J. Manachino* - Albert J. Manachino  *h*  3614
*Open to the Public* - Muriel Spark  *h*  5166
*The Oracle at Stoneleigh Court* - Peter Taylor  *h*  5417
*Out of the Dark: Origins* - Robert W. Chambers  *h*  964
*Pain-Grin* - Wayne Allen Sallee  *h*  4788
*Painfreak* - Gerard Daniel Houarner  *h*  2778
*Painted in Blood* - Lucy Taylor  *h*  5413
*The Panic Hand* - Jonathan Carroll  *h*  920
*Pentacle* - Tom Piccirilli  *h*  4315
*People of the Night* - S. Darnbrook Colson  *h*  1128
*Personal Demons* - Christopher Fowler  *h*  2018
*The Phantom Coach and Other Ghost Stories of an Antiquary* - Augustus Jessop  *h*  2905
*Pieces of Hate* - Ray Garton  *h*  2155
*Poems of Ambrose Bierce* - Ambrose Bierce  *h*  486
*Points of Departure* - Pat Murphy  *h*  4053
*Prayers to Broken Stones* - Dan Simmons  *h*  5058
*Prisoners and Other Stories* - Ed Gorman  *h*  2281
*Publish and Perish* - James Hynes  *h*  2826
*The Reality Machine* - Cliff Burns  *h*  778
*Road to Madness: The Transition of H.P. Lovecraft* - H.P. Lovecraft  *h*  3532
*Robert Bloch: Appreciations of the Master* - Richard Matheson  *h*  3689
*The Rose of Death and Other Mysterious Delusions* - Julian Hawthorne  *h*  2633
*Scare Tactics* - John Farris  *h*  1887
*Scream for Jeeves: A Parody* - P.H. Cannon  *h*  867
*Scroll of Thoth* - Richard L. Tierney  *h*  5471
*The Sealed Casket and Other Stories* - Richard F. Searight  *h*  4905
*Seeing Red* - David J. Schow  *h*  4889

*Sex and Blood* - Ron Dee  *h*  1467
*Sex and the Single Vampire* - Nancy
  Kilpatrick  *h*  3114
*Sexpunks & Savage Sagas* - Richard
  Sutphen  *h*  5360
*Shades of Darkness: More of the Ghostly Best Stories
  of Robert Westall* - Robert Westall  *h*  5765
*Shadow Dreams* - Elizabeth Massie  *h*  3667
*The Shell of Sense* - Olivia Howard Dunbar  *h*  1673
*Shifting the Boundaries: The Selected Works of Kevin
  J. Anderson* - Kevin J. Anderson  *h*  113
*Shrines and Desecrations* - Brian Hodge  *h*  2705
*Slippage* - Harlan Ellison  *h*  1789
*Smoke of the Snake* - Carl Jacobi  *h*  2844
*Snuff Flique* - Michael Hemmingson  *h*  2656
*Soft and Others* - F. Paul Wilson  *h*  5899
*Someone in the Room: Strange Tales Old and New* -
  A.M. Burrage  *h*  779
*Something Haunts Us All* - Brian Hopkins  *h*  2769
*Somewhere in the Night* - Jeffrey N.
  McMahan  *h*  3852
*Somewhere in Time/What Dreams May Come* -
  Richard Matheson  *h*  3690
*Songs of a Dead Dreamer* - Thomas
  Ligotti  *h*  3464
*The Sons of Noah and Other Stories* - Jack
  Cady  *h*  821
*Southern Discomfort: Selected Works of Elizabeth
  Massie* - Elizabeth Massie  *h*  3669
*Spectral Snow: The Dark Fantasies of Jack Snow* -
  Jack Snow  *h*  5149
*A Spell for the Fulfillment of Desire* - Don
  Webb  *h*  5662
*Splatterspunk: The Micah Hays Stories* - Edward
  Lee  *h*  3397
*Star Bones Weep the Blood of Angels* - Sue
  Storm  *h*  5316
*Stealing My Rules* - Don Webb  *h*  5663
*The Stone Dragon and Other Tragic Romances* - R.
  Murray Gilchrist  *h*  2225
*Stories by Mama Lansdale's Youngest Boy* - Joe R.
  Lansdale  *h*  3333
*Strange Highways* - Dean R. Koontz  *h*  3216
*Strange Things and Stranger Places* - Ramsey
  Campbell  *h*  864
*Suicide Art* - Scott Edelman  *h*  1740
*Swamp Foetus* - Poppy Z. Brite  *h*  700
*Tales From the Nightside* - Charles L.
  Grant  *h*  2319
*Tales of Lovecraftian Horror and Humor* - P.H.
  Cannon  *h*  868
*Tales of Sesqua Valley* - W.H. Pugmire  *h*  4444
*Tales of the Lovecraft Collectors* - Kenneth W. Faig
  Jr.  *h*  1859
*Tales of Titillation and Terror* - Mel D. Ames  *h*  94
*Tapping the Vein: Books One and Two* - Clive
  Barker  *h*  346
*Terminal Weird* - Jack Remick  *h*  4532
*The Terror by Night* - E.F. Benson  *h*  455
*Terrors of the Sea* - William Hope
  Hodgson  *h*  2712
*Testament: The Unpublished Prologues* - David
  Morrell  *h*  4011
*The Thing in the Bathtub and Other Lovecraftian Tales*
  - P.H. Cannon  *h*  869
*Things Left Behind* - Gary A. Braunbeck  *h*  663
*Thirty Strange Stories* - H.G. Wells  *h*  5746
*Three Gothic Novels* - Charles Brockden
  Brown  *h*  722
*The Throne of Bones* - Brian McNaughton  *h*  3859
*Time Burial* - Howard Wandrei  *h*  5628
*Titus Crow, Volume One* - Brian Lumley  *h*  3566
*Titus Crow, Volume Three* - Brian Lumley  *h*  3567
*Titus Crow, Volume Two* - Brian Lumley  *h*  3568
*Trails in Darkness* - Robert E. Howard  *h*  2784
*Transients and Other Disquieting Tales* - Darrell
  Schweitzer  *h*  4891
*Trudging to Eden* - Kim Antieau  *h*  200

*Twilight and Other Supernatural Romances* - Marjorie
  Bowen  *h*  601
*The Twilight Zone: Complete Stories* - Rod
  Serling  *h*  4916
*Two by Carrere* - Emmanuel Carrere  *h*  913
*Two Obscure Tales* - Ramsey Campbell  *h*  865
*Under the Crust* - Terry Lamsley  *h*  3314
*Unholy Relics* - M.P. Dare  *h*  1350
*Unnatural Acts and Other Stories* - Lucy
  Taylor  *h*  5416
*The Vampire Stories of R. Chetwynd-Hayes* - R.
  Chetwynd-Hayes  *h*  1013
*Waking Nightmares* - Ramsey Campbell  *h*  866
*A Warning to the Curious* - M.R. James  *h*  2866
*The Watchers out of Time* - H.P. Lovecraft  *h*  3535
*Weird Family Tales* - Ken Wisman  *h*  5929
*Whippoorwill Road* - Brett Rutherford  *h*  4752
*The Witch's Tale* - Alonzo Dean Cole  *h*  1112
*With Wounds Still Wet* - Wayne Allen
  Sallee  *h*  4789
*The Woman with the Flying Head and Other Stories* -
  Yumiko Kurahashi  *h*  3250
*Women and Ghosts* - Alison Lurie  *h*  3575
*Writer of the Purple Rage* - Joe R.
  Lansdale  *h*  3335
*Wrong* - Dennis Cooper  *h*  1171


**Horror — Coming-of-Age**

*Boy's Life* - Robert R. McCammon  *h*  3754
*Brittle Innings* - Michael Bishop  *h*  498
*Dawn* - V.C. Andrews  *h*  144
*First Blast of the Trumpet Against the Monstrous
  Regiment of Women* - Eric McCormack  *h*  3779
*My Pretty Pony* - Stephen King  *h*  3136
*Summer of Night* - Dan Simmons  *h*  5060
*The Thief of Always* - Clive Barker  *h*  347


**Horror — Curse**

*The Amulet* - A.R. Morlan  *h*  4009
*The Black Mariah* - Jay R. Bonansinga  *h*  570
*The Blackstone Chronicles* - John Saul  *h*  4838
*Brethren* - Shawn Ryan  *h*  4754
*Cold Whisper* - Rick Hautala  *h*  2605
*The Curse* - John Tigges  *h*  5472
*Dark Silence* - Rick Hautala  *h*  2606
*Goblins* - Vincent Courtney  *h*  1212
*Oasis* - Brian Hodge  *h*  2703
*The Offspring* - Kenneth McKenney  *h*  3826
*Shade of Pale* - Greg Kihn  *h*  3104
*Shadow Dance* - Jessica Palmer  *h*  4238
*Stunts* - Charles L. Grant  *h*  2317
*Twisted* - Sue Hollister Barr  *h*  364
*Wendigo Border* - Catherine Montrose  *h*  3967


**Horror — Doppelganger**

*Animus* - Ed Kelleher  *h*  3040
*Cold Eye* - Giles Blunt  *h*  556
*Created By* - Richard Christian Matheson  *h*  3691
*The Dark Half* - Stephen King  *h*  3128
*The Darker Passions: Dr. Jekyll and Mr. Hyde* -
  Amarantha Knight  *h*  3178
*Death's Door* - John Wooley  *h*  5969
*The Double* - Don Webb  *h*  5661
*Echoes* - Jackie Hyman  *h*  2818
*Ghostwright* - Michael Cadnum  *h*  810
*The Man Who Turned into Himself* - David
  Ambrose  *h*  89
*Mr. Murder* - Dean R. Koontz  *h*  3213
*Nightlife* - Brian Hodge  *h*  2702
*The Nightmare People* - Lawrence Watt-
  Evans  *h*  5643
*Reign* - Chet Williamson  *h*  5849
*Shadow Twin* - Dale Hoover  *h*  2762
*Succumb* - Ron Dee  *h*  1468

**Horror — Erotic Horror**

*The Darker Passions: Frankenstein* - Amarantha
  Knight  *h*  3180
*Deadly After Dark* - Jeff Gelb  *h*  2174
*Demon Sex* - Amarantha Knight  *h*  3181
*Dying for It: More Erotic Tales of Unearthly Love* -
  Gardner Dozois  *h*  1607
*Expiry Date* - Carol Anne Davis  *h*  1401
*Fear the Fever* - Jeff Gelb  *h*  2176
*Firefly* - Piers Anthony  *h*  170
*Hot Blood X* - Jeff Gelb  *h*  2177
*Hot Blood: Crimes of Passion* - Jeff Gelb  *h*  2178
*Hot Blood: Kiss and Kill* - Jeff Gelb  *h*  2179
*Hotter Blood: More Tales of Erotic Horror* - Jeff
  Gelb  *h*  2180
*Hottest Blood: The Ultimate in Erotic Horror* - Jeff
  Gelb  *h*  2181
*Kaleidoscope Eyes* - Graham Watkins  *h*  5631
*Kiss of Death* - Daniel Rhodes  *h*  4569
*Looker* - Jorge Saralegui  *h*  4820
*The New Neighbor* - Ray Garton  *h*  2154
*Painfreak* - Gerard Daniel Houarner  *h*  2778
*The Pit and the Pendulum* - Amarantha
  Knight  *h*  3183
*Santa Steps Out: A Fairy Tale for Grownups* - Robert
  Devereaux  *h*  1506
*Steam* - Jay B. Laws  *h*  3361
*Stranger by Night* - Jeff Gelb  *h*  2185
*Tales of Forbidden Passion* - Tina L. Jens  *h*  2893
*Yours Truly, Jackie the Stripper* - Edo van
  Belkom  *h*  5536


**Horror — Evil Children**

*Afternoon of the Gosling* - Marlys Huffman  *h*  2801
*Animus* - Ed Kelleher  *h*  3040
*Bad Blood* - D.A. Fowler  *h*  2021
*Blood of the Children* - Alan Rodgers  *h*  4645
*Child of Shadows* - John Coyne  *h*  1236
*Dark Father* - Tom Piccirilli  *h*  4312
*The Dark One* - Guy N. Smith  *h*  5118
*Goblins* - Vincent Courtney  *h*  1212
*The Godsend* - Bernard Taylor  *h*  5401
*John Dollar* - Marianne Wiggins  *h*  5799
*Kids* - Trevor Hoyle  *h*  2787
*Monday's Child* - Patricia Wallace  *h*  5623
*Never Land* - Douglas Clegg  *h*  1081
*The Night of the Moonbow* - Thomas
  Tryon  *h*  5486
*Seed of Evil* - Edmund Plante  *h*  4340
*Seeds of Evil* - Margaret Bingley  *h*  491
*Sheep* - Simon Maginn  *h*  3606
*The Sister* - Elleston Trevor  *h*  5484
*Sweet William* - Jessica Palmer  *h*  4239
*The Twelfth Child* - Raymond Van Over  *h*  5538
*What's Wrong with Tamara?* - D.A.
  Fowler  *h*  2025
*Wind Chimes* - R.R. Walters  *h*  5625


**Horror — Fantasy**

*The Best Horror From Fantasy Tales* - Stephen
  Jones  *h*  2960
*Fantasy Tales #2* - Stephen Jones  *h*  2965
*Fantasy Tales #4* - Stephen Jones  *h*  2966
*Fantasy Tales #6* - Stephen Jones  *h*  2967
*I, Strahd* - P.N. Elrod  *h*  1797
*The Year's Best Fantasy and Horror: Fifth Annual
  Collection* - Ellen Datlow  *h*  1372
*The Year's Best Fantasy and Horror: Ninth Annual
  Collection* - Ellen Datlow  *h*  1374
*The Year's Best Fantasy and Horror: Seventh Annual
  Collection* - Ellen Datlow  *h*  1375
*The Year's Best Fantasy and Horror: Sixth Annual
  Collection* - Ellen Datlow  *h*  1376
*The Year's Best Fantasy and Horror: Third Annual
  Collection* - Ellen Datlow  *h*  1378

## Horror — Femme Fatale

*The Lilith Factor* - Jean Paiva　*h*　4236

## Horror — Gay/Lesbian Fiction

*Grave Passions* - William J. Mann　*h*　3618
*Lizzie Borden* - Elizabeth Engstrom　*h*　1826
*Virago* - Karen Marie Christa Minns　*h*　3915

## Horror — Ghost Story

*100 Ghastly Little Ghost Stories* - Stefan
　Dziemianowicz　*h*　1709
*After Sundown* - Randall Boyll　*h*　609
*Bag of Bones* - Stephen King　*h*　3126
*The Calling* - Kathryn Meyer Griffith　*h*　2439
*Cemetery of Angels* - Noel Hynd　*h*　2821
*Charlie's Bones* - L.L. Thrasher　*h*　5468
*Christmas Ghosts* - Mike Resnick　*h*　4541
*Civil War Ghosts* - Martin H. Greenberg　*h*　2383
*The Curse of Camp Cold Lake* - R.L. Stine　*h*　5286
*Dead Lines* - John Skipp　*h*　5082
*Deadly Friend* - Keith Ferrario　*h*　1926
*Dread and Delight: A Century of Children's Ghost
　Stories* - Philippa Pearce　*h*　4274
*Earthbound* - Richard Matheson　*h*　3684
*Eastern Ghosts* - Frank D. McSherry Jr.　*h*　3866
*A Face at the Window* - Dennis McFarland　*h*　3809
*Famine* - Todd Komarnicki　*h*　3201
*Fog Heart* - Thomas Tessier　*h*　5440
*Fragments* - James F. David　*h*　1380
*The Frighteners* - Michael Jahn　*h*　2856
*The Ghost Book of Charles Lindley, Viscount Halifax* -
　Charles Lindley　*h*　3472
*Ghost Boy* - Jean Simon　*h*　5064
*Ghosts* - Noel Hynd　*h*　2822
*The Ghosts of Sleath* - James Herbert　*h*　2668
*Ghosts of the Heartland* - Frank D. McSherry
　Jr.　*h*　3868
*Goodlow's Ghosts* - T.M. Wright　*h*　5991
*Gothic Ghosts* - Wendy Webb　*h*　5665
*Great American Ghost Stories* - Frank D. McSherry
　Jr.　*h*　3869
*Great Ghost Stories* - John Grafton　*h*　2300
*The Haunted Tea Cosy: A Dispirited and Distasteful
　Diversion for Christmas* - Edward Gorey　*h*　2276
*I Met a Man Who Wasn't There* - Mary R.
　Callaghan　*h*　840
*The Immaculate* - Mark Morris　*h*　4023
*In a Dark Dream* - Charles L. Grant　*h*　2310
*Isaac Asimov's Ghosts* - Gardner Dozois　*h*　1610
*Laying the Music to Rest* - Dean Wesley
　Smith　*h*　5114
*The Literary Ghost* - Larry Dark　*h*　1351
*Madeleine's Ghost* - Robert Girardi　*h*　2240
*The Mammoth Book of Ghost Stories* - Richard
　Dalby　*h*　1309
*The Mammoth Book of Twentieth Century Ghost
　Stories* - Peter Haining　*h*　2483
*The Mammoth Book of Victorian and Edwardian
　Ghost Stories* - Richard Dalby　*h*　1310
*Midnight Never Comes* - Barbara Roden　*h*　4644
*Modern Ghost Stories by Eminent Women Writers* -
　Richard Dalby　*h*　1312
*Mrs. God* - Peter Straub　*h*　5329
*My Soul to Keep* - Judith Hawkes　*h*　2631
*Naomi's Room* - Jonathan Aycliffe　*h*　281
*The Night in Fog* - David B. Silva　*h*　5026
*Night Relics* - James P. Blaylock　*h*　521
*The Norton Book of Ghost Stories* - Brad
　Leithauser　*h*　3432
*October* - Al Sarrantonio　*h*　4832
*The Omnibus of Twentieth Century Ghost Stories* -
　Robert Phillips　*h*　4311
*The Only Thing to Fear* - Robert Morgan　*h*　4003
*The Oxford Book of Twentieth Century Ghost Stories* -
　Michael Cox　*h*　1232
*Passive Intruder* - Michael Upchurch　*h*　5530

*Peter Straub's Ghosts* - Peter Straub　*h*　5331
*Phantoms of the Night* - Richard Gilliam　*h*　2233
*Possession* - Peter James　*h*　2873
*Rage of Spirits* - Noel Hynd　*h*　2824
*Revenant* - Melanie Tem　*h*　5424
*Roald Dahl's Book of Ghost Stories* - Roald
　Dahl　*h*　1306
*Rockabilly Hell* - William W. Johnstone　*h*　2933
*St. Vitus Dances Eternity: A Sarajevo Ghost Story* -
　Stewart Von Allmen　*h*　5585
*Seattle Ghost Story* - Nick DiMartino　*h*　1560
*Seaward* - Brad Leithauser　*h*　3433
*Second Child* - John Saul　*h*　4844
*Seductive Spectres* - Amarantha Knight　*h*　3184
*Something's Alive on the Titanic* - Robert
　Serling　*h*　4915
*Speak to the Rain* - Helen K. Passey　*h*　4257
*Superstition* - David Ambrose　*h*　90
*T.J.'s Ghost* - Shirley Climo　*h*　1087
*Twelve Victorian Ghost Stories* - Michael
　Cox　*h*　1234
*Unholy Relics* - M.P. Dare　*h*　1350
*The Uprising* - Abigail McDaniels　*h*　3785
*Vaporetto 13* - Robert Girardi　*h*　2241
*Victorian Ghost Stories: An Oxford Anthology* -
　Michael Cox　*h*　1235
*Violin* - Anne Rice　*h*　4579
*Western Ghosts* - Frank D. McSherry Jr.　*h*　3870

## Horror — Gothic Family Chronicle

*Along Came a Spider* - Athena Alexis　*h*　70
*Blood Roots* - Richie Tankersley Cusick　*h*　1300
*Dark Dance* - Tanith Lee　*h*　3406
*Gates of Paradise* - V.C. Andrews　*h*　145
*The Good Children* - Kate Wilhelm　*h*　5808
*The Living One* - Lewis Gannett　*h*　2115
*Madeline: After the Fall of Usher* - Marie
　Kiraly　*h*　3150
*Secrets of the Morning* - V.C. Andrews　*h*　146
*These Fallen Angels* - Wendy Haley　*h*　2492
*This Dark Paradise* - Wendy Haley　*h*　2493
*Web of Dreams* - V.C. Andrews　*h*　147

## Horror — Haunted House

*The 7th Guest* - Matthew J. Costello　*h*　1192
*65mm* - Dale Hoover　*h*　2761
*The Baby* - Stephanie Kegan　*h*　3033
*California Ghosting* - William Hill　*h*　2687
*Dark Dreaming* - Pat Franklin　*h*　2040
*Drawing Blood* - Poppy Z. Brite　*h*　694
*The Dwelling* - Tom Elliott　*h*　1776
*Familiar Spirit* - Lisa Tuttle　*h*　5519
*The First Horror* - R.L. Stine　*h*　5288
*Gahan Wilson's The Ultimate Haunted House* - Gahan
　Wilson　*h*　5902
*The Haunt* - John Fogarty　*h*　1966
*Haunted* - James Herbert　*h*　2669
*Haunted* - Tamara Thorne　*h*　5463
*Haunted Houses: The Greatest Stories* - Martin H.
　Greenberg　*h*　2396
*The Haunting* - Ruby Jean Jensen　*h*　2901
*The Haunting of Lamb House* - Joan Aiken　*h*　45
*Hell House* - Richard Matheson　*h*　3685
*The Hellbound Heart* - Clive Barker　*h*　342
*Holy Terror* - Josephine Boyle　*h*　608
*Homebody* - Orson Scott Card　*h*　890
*House Haunted* - Al Sarrantonio　*h*　4830
*The House Next Door* - Anne Rivers
　Siddons　*h*　5021
*Julian's House* - Judith Hawkes　*h*　2630
*The Keys to D'Esperance* - Chaz Brenchley　*h*　666
*Nazareth Hill* - Ramsey Campbell　*h*　861
*Night Things* - Michael Talbot　*h*　5380
*Room 13* - Henry Garfield　*h*　2139
*The School* - T.M. Wright　*h*　5994
*Shades of Night* - Rick Hautala　*h*　2612

*Shadow Walkers* - Nina Romberg　*h*　4663
*The Shining* - Stephen King　*h*　3141
*The Site* - Melisand March　*h*　3621
*Sweetheart, Sweetheart* - Bernard Taylor　*h*　5402
*Torments* - Lisa Cantrell　*h*　873
*The Vanishment* - Jonathan Aycliffe　*h*　282
*The Voice in the Basement* - T. Chris
　Martindale　*h*　3657
*Walkers* - Graham Masterton　*h*　3681
*Walls of Fear* - Kathryn Cramer　*h*　1246
*Waltz with Evil* - P.D. Rozzi　*h*　4701

## Horror — Historical

*Dance of Death* - P.N. Elrod　*h*　1794
*Death Masque* - P.N. Elrod　*h*　1795
*Madeline: After the Fall of Usher* - Marie
　Kiraly　*h*　3150
*Nevermore* - William Hjortsberg　*h*　2692

## Horror — Literary

*Black Dogs* - Ian McEwan　*h*　3808
*Blood Countess* - Andrei Codrescu　*h*　1094
*Fantastique* - Marvin Kaye　*h*　3025
*Father of Frankenstein* - Christopher Bram　*h*　659
*The Haunting of Lamb House* - Joan Aiken　*h*　45
*The Ridge* - Lisa Cantrell　*h*　872
*The Trial of Elizabeth Cree* - Peter Ackroyd　*h*　26
*Wall, Stone, Craft* - Walter Jon Williams　*h*　5842

## Horror — Mystery

*7 Steps to Midnight* - Richard Matheson　*h*　3682
*After Silence* - Jonathan Carroll　*h*　916
*All Things under the Moon* - Robert
　Morgan　*h*　4002
*Ancient Images* - Ramsey Campbell　*h*　852
*Angel Kiss* - Kelley Wilde　*h*　5800
*The Asylum* - John E. Ames　*h*　93
*The Bad Place* - Dean R. Koontz　*h*　3202
*Beast House* - Richard Laymon　*h*　3364
*Big Rock Beat* - Greg Kihn　*h*　3102
*The Bighead* - Edward Lee　*h*　3387
*The Black Cat* - Robert Poe　*h*　4344
*Blood Debt* - Tanya Huff　*h*　2792
*Bloody Waters* - B.L. Winters　*h*　5926
*Boneman* - Lisa Cantrell　*h*　871
*Burning Bright* - J.S. Russell　*h*　4733
*Burning Water* - Mercedes Lackey　*h*　3272
*The Calcutta Chromosome* - Amitav Ghosh　*h*　2214
*Celestial Dogs* - J.S. Russell　*h*　4734
*The Cellar* - Richard Laymon　*h*　3365
*Charlie's Bones* - L.L. Thrasher　*h*　5468
*Charmed Life* - Bernard Taylor　*h*　5399
*A Child Across the Sky* - Jonathan Carroll　*h*　917
*Children of the Night* - Mercedes Lackey　*h*　3276
*City of Iron* - Chet Williamson　*h*　5843
*Cold in July* - Joe R. Lansdale　*h*　3323
*Contagion* - John David Connor　*h*　1136
*Control Freak* - Christa Faust　*h*　1890
*Creekers* - Edward Lee　*h*　3391
*Cross a Dark Bridge* - Deborah
　Churchman　*h*　1027
*Darkman #1: The Hangman* - Randall Boyll　*h*　612
*Darkman #2: The Price of Fear* - Randall
　Boyll　*h*　613
*Darkman #3: The Gods of Hell* - Randall
　Boyll　*h*　614
*Darkman #4: The Face of Death* - Randall
　Boyll　*h*　615
*Dead of Night* - Alex Abella　*h*　20
*Deadly Dreams* - Gerald A. Schiller　*h*　4874
*Death Is a Lonely Business* - Ray Bradbury　*h*　619
*The Double* - Don Webb　*h*　5661
*Double Date* - R.L. Stine　*h*　5287
*Dreamer* - Peter James　*h*　2871
*Dumford Blood* - S.K. Epperson　*h*　1829

*Duplicates* - Andrew Neiderman   *h*   4086
*Empire of Dust* - Chet Williamson   *h*   5846
*Faces under Water* - Tanith Lee   *h*   3409
*Famous Fantastic Mysteries* - Stefan
   Dziemianowicz   *h*   1712
*Fear Nothing* - Dean R. Koontz   *h*   3207
*Flicker* - Theodore Roszak   *h*   4683
*From the Teeth of Angels* - Jonathan Carroll   *h*   918
*The Golden* - Lucius Shepard   *h*   4978
*Gothic Romance* - Emmanuel Carrere   *h*   912
*A Graveyard for Lunatics* - Ray Bradbury   *h*   620
*The Green Mile* - Stephen King   *h*   3134
*The Headsman* - James Neal Harvey   *h*   2599
*Her Monster* - Jeff Collignon   *h*   1115
*In Double Jeopardy* - Andrew Neiderman   *h*   4088
*Inagehi* - Jack Cady   *h*   817
*The Jekyll Legacy* - Robert Bloch   *h*   535
*Jinx High* - Mercedes Lackey   *h*   3284
*The Killing Dance* - Laurell K. Hamilton   *h*   2518
*The Land of Nod* - Mark A. Clements   *h*   1085
*The Last Voice They Hear* - Ramsey
   Campbell   *h*   858
*Life Support* - Tess Gerritsen   *h*   2206
*The Lighthouse at the End of the World* - Stephen
   Marlowe   *h*   3631
*Lori* - Robert Bloch   *h*   536
*The Midnight Club* - Christopher Pike   *h*   4329
*The Midnight Tour* - Richard Laymon   *h*   3368
*Midnight's Lair* - Richard Laymon   *h*   3369
*Moondog* - Henry Garfield   *h*   2138
*The Moons of Summer* - S.K. Epperson   *h*   1831
*Mucho Mojo* - Joe R. Lansdale   *h*   3330
*The Mysterium* - Eric McCormack   *h*   3780
*Nevermore* - William Hjortsberg   *h*   2692
*Night Hunter* - Michael Reaves   *h*   4496
*Nightlight* - Michael Cadnum   *h*   813
*Now You See It. . .* - Richard Matheson   *h*   3688
*Oktober* - Stephen Gallagher   *h*   2112
*Omega* - Patrick Lynch   *h*   3577
*The Only Thing to Fear* - Robert Morgan   *h*   4003
*Out There in the Darkness* - Ed Gorman   *h*   2279
*Phantom* - Susan Kay   *h*   3020
*Prey* - William W. Johnstone   *h*   2932
*Psycho II* - Robert Bloch   *h*   541
*Psycho House* - Robert Bloch   *h*   542
*Raven* - Charles L. Grant   *h*   2314
*A Reasonable Madness* - Fran Dorf   *h*   1580
*Red Bride* - Christopher Fowler   *h*   2019
*Relife* - Dan Barton   *h*   376
*Requiem* - Graham Joyce   *h*   2994
*Root of All Evil* - David A. Farrow   *h*   1888
*Rulers of Darkness* - Steven Spruill   *h*   5185
*Sacrifice* - John Farris   *h*   1886
*Shackled* - Ray Garton   *h*   2156
*Skull Session* - Daniel Hecht   *h*   2638
*Slippin' into Darkness* - Norman Partridge   *h*   4254
*Spook* - Steve Vance   *h*   5553
*Spree* - Lucy Taylor   *h*   5415
*Supernatural Sleuths* - Charles G. Waugh   *h*   5653
*Tap, Tap* - David Martin   *h*   3640
*The Things That Are Not There* - Robert
   Morgan   *h*   4007
*The Throat* - Peter Straub   *h*   5332
*The Totem* - David Morrell   *h*   4012
*The Uncanny* - Andrew Klavan   *h*   3164
*Vampire Bytes* - Linda Grant   *h*   2322
*The Virginia Ghost Murders* - Leslie Raymond
   Sachs   *h*   4778
*Zod Wallop* - William Browning Spencer   *h*   5169


**Horror — Nature in Revolt**

*Bats* - William W. Johnstone   *h*   2926
*Beast* - Peter Benchley   *h*   440
*Between the Devil and the Deep* - J.M.
   Morgan   *h*   3998
*The Bridge: A Horror Story* - John Skipp   *h*   5081
*Carnivore* - Leigh Clark   *h*   1049


*Carnivores* - Penelope Banka Kreps   *h*   3232
*Claw* - Ken Eulo   *h*   1850
*The Devouring* - Douglas D. Hawk   *h*   2615
*Dust* - Charles Pellegrino   *h*   4279
*The Earth Strikes Back* - Richard T.
   Chizmar   *h*   1020
*Extinct* - Charles Wilson   *h*   5877
*Garden* - Matthew J. Costello   *h*   1197
*Howl* - Christine Tanasiuk   *h*   5388
*Hunger* - William Dantz   *h*   1346
*Lagoon* - Alison Drake   *h*   1625
*Meg* - Steve Alten   *h*   88
*Monster* - John Tigges   *h*   5474
*The Mountain King* - Rick Hautala   *h*   2611
*Night Beasts* - T.W. Stetson   *h*   5263
*The Night Seasons* - J.N. Williamson   *h*   5858
*Nightshade* - Stanley R. Moore   *h*   3992
*Paddywhack* - John Stchur   *h*   5236
*Pelts* - F. Paul Wilson   *h*   5894
*Pet Store* - M.T. Coffin   *h*   1097
*Pitfall* - Ronald Kelly   *h*   3054
*The Rats* - James Herbert   *h*   2671
*Roadkill* - Richard Sanford   *h*   4815
*The Streeter* - Scott Ian Barry   *h*   373
*Vespers* - Jeff Rovin   *h*   4688
*Watchers in the Woods* - William W.
   Johnstone   *h*   2936
*When Wolves Cry* - Chris N. Africa   *h*   41
*Winter Wolves* - Earle Wescott   *h*   5756


**Horror — Occult**

*Absolute Power* - Ray Russell   *h*   4738
*Angels on Fire* - Nancy A. Collins   *h*   1117
*The Ascending* - T.M. Wright   *h*   5989
*The Beast* - Marie Ardell White   *h*   5784
*The Bell Witch: An American Haunting* - Brent
   Monahan   *h*   3953
*The Black Death* - Basil Copper   *h*   1185
*The Black Lodge* - Robert Weinberg   *h*   5692
*The Book of the Damned* - D.A. Fowler   *h*   2022
*Brand New Cherry Flavor* - Todd Grimson   *h*   2448
*The Burning* - Graham Masterton   *h*   3672
*Burning Bright* - J.S. Russell   *h*   4733
*Celestial Dogs* - J.S. Russell   *h*   4734
*The Changeling Garden* - Winifred Elze   *h*   1806
*The Colors of Hell* - Michael Paine   *h*   4234
*The Complete John Silence Stories* - Algernon
   Blackwood   *h*   509
*The Dark* - Andrew Neiderman   *h*   4084
*Dark Fortune* - Richard Lee Byers   *h*   795
*Dark Reunion* - Stephen R. George   *h*   2198
*Darkling* - Michael O'Rourke   *h*   4223
*Dawn Song* - Michael Marano   *h*   3620
*Days of the Dead* - Ashley McConnell   *h*   3774
*The Dead Man's Kiss* - Robert Weinberg   *h*   5695
*Dead of Night* - Alex Abella   *h*   20
*Dead Voices* - Rick Hautala   *h*   2607
*Death Channels* - Robert E. Vardeman   *h*   5562
*December* - Phil Rickman   *h*   4588
*Demogorgon* - Brian Lumley   *h*   3552
*Descent* - Ron Dee   *h*   1465
*The Devil's Auction* - Robert Weinberg   *h*   5696
*The Devil's Churn* - Kristine Kathryn
   Rusch   *h*   4715
*The Devil's End* - D.A. Fowler   *h*   2023
*Devil's Gate* - Elizabeth Ergas   *h*   1833
*Dreamer* - Daniel Quinn   *h*   4454
*A Dry Spell* - Susan Moloney   *h*   3951
*The Ebon Mask* - Richard Lee Byers   *h*   797
*Elephantasm* - Tanith Lee   *h*   3408
*Empire of Dust* - Chet Williamson   *h*   5846
*Engor's Sword Arm* - David C. Smith   *h*   5110
*Evil Eye* - Michael Slade   *h*   5085
*The Eyes of Torie Webster* - Roy Sorrels   *h*   5164
*Fallen* - Dee Graham   *h*   2302
*The Forsaken* - Steven Ray Fulgham   *h*   2089


*Gabriel Knight: Sins of the Fathers* - Jane
   Jensen   *h*   2896
*Ghor, Kin-Slayer: The Saga of Genseric's Fifth-Born
   Son* - Robert E. Howard   *h*   2782
*Graythings* - Pat Graversen   *h*   2335
*Harrowgate* - Daniel H. Gower   *h*   2292
*Heathen* - Shaun Hutson   *h*   2816
*Hell House* - Richard Matheson   *h*   3685
*The Hill of Dreams* - Arthur Machen   *h*   3595
*The Horror Club* - Mark Morris   *h*   4022
*The House That Jack Built* - Graham
   Masterton   *h*   3675
*Incubi* - Edward Lee   *h*   3394
*Infernal Affairs* - Jane Heller   *h*   2652
*Irrational Fears* - William Browning
   Spencer   *h*   5167
*Jinx High* - Mercedes Lackey   *h*   3284
*The Judas Cross* - Charles Sheffield   *h*   4960
*Kalimantan* - Lucius Shepard   *h*   4979
*The Killing of the Saints* - Alex Abella   *h*   21
*Kindred* - John Gideon   *h*   2222
*Lasher* - Anne Rice   *h*   4570
*Leanna: Possession of a Woman* - Marie
   Kiraly   *h*   3149
*Lucifer's Eye* - Hugh B. Cave   *h*   943
*Manhattan Heat* - Ken Eulo   *h*   1851
*The Manuscript Found in Sragossa* - Jan
   Potocki   *h*   4371
*Master of Lies* - Graham Masterton   *h*   3676
*The Matrix* - Jonathan Aycliffe   *h*   280
*The Memoirs of Elizabeth Frankenstein* - Theodore
   Roszak   *h*   4684
*The Messenger* - Donald Tyson   *h*   5528
*Mind Stealer* - Lee Duigon   *h*   1672
*My Soul to Keep* - Tannarive Due   *h*   1670
*Near Dead* - Stephen R. George   *h*   2202
*Night Magic* - Thomas Tryon   *h*   5485
*Night Music* - Sheila Bristow Garner   *h*   2147
*Noctet: Tales of Madonna-Moloch* - Albert J.
   Manachino   *h*   3613
*Private Demons* - Robert Masello   *h*   3660
*Prophecy* - Peter James   *h*   2874
*Rune* - Christopher Fowler   *h*   2020
*Sacrament* - Clive Barker   *h*   345
*Sacrifice* - Richard Kinion   *h*   3146
*Servant of the Bones* - Anne Rice   *h*   4575
*Shadowborn* - William W. Connors   *h*   1137
*Shango* - James Roberto Curtis   *h*   1298
*Silent Moon* - William Relling Jr.   *h*   4531
*Some Things Come Back* - Robert Morgan   *h*   4004
*Son of Rosemary* - Ira Levin   *h*   3445
*Souls* - Katina Alexis   *h*   71
*Spyder* - Norman Partridge   *h*   4255
*The Store* - Bentley Little   *h*   3497
*The Summoned* - Steven Ray Fulgham   *h*   2090
*Superstitious* - R.L. Stine   *h*   5290
*Symphony* - Adrian Savage   *h*   4847
*The Taking* - Donald Beman   *h*   438
*Taltos* - Anne Rice   *h*   4577
*Tapestry of Dark Souls* - Elaine Bergstrom   *h*   465
*The Terror* - Graham Masterton   *h*   3679
*Tooth and Claw* - Graham Masterton   *h*   3680
*The Torching* - Marcy Heidish   *h*   2642
*Twilight* - Peter James   *h*   2876
*Twisted Images* - Don D'Ammassa   *h*   1335
*The Uncanny* - Andrew Klavan   *h*   3164
*The Undine* - Michael O'Rourke   *h*   4224
*The Unfinished* - Jay B. Laws   *h*   3362
*Unholy Fire* - Whitley Strieber   *h*   5342
*University* - Bentley Little   *h*   3499
*Vodoun* - David Madsen   *h*   3605
*Wake Up Screaming* - Vincent Courtney   *h*   1215
*Who Killed James Dean?* - Warren Newton
   Beath   *h*   428
*Witch-Light* - Nancy Holder   *h*   2734

## Horror — Possession

*Althea* - Abigail McDaniels  *h*  3782
*Belladonna* - Michael Stewart  *h*  5271
*The Beyond* - Barry Harrington  *h*  2556
*Beyond the Shroud* - Rick Hautala  *h*  2604
*Cursed Be the Child* - Mort Castle  *h*  937
*Dark Lullaby* - Jessica Palmer  *h*  4237
*Eden's Eyes* - Sean Costello  *h*  1205
*The Gilgul* - Henry W. Hocherman  *h*  2697
*Grandma's Little Darling* - Stephen R.
   George  *h*  2201
*The Homecoming* - Kimberly Rangel  *h*  4471
*The Influence* - Ramsey Campbell  *h*  857
*The Lodger* - Fred Chappell  *h*  966
*Lullaby* - Diane Guest  *h*  2455
*Makoto* - Kelley Wilde  *h*  5801
*Night Sounds* - Warner Lee  *h*  3415
*The Nightmare People* - Lawrence Watt-
   Evans  *h*  5643
*Not Broken, Not Belonging* - Randy Fox  *h*  2030
*The Parasite* - Ramsey Campbell  *h*  863
*The Possession* - Ronald Kelly  *h*  3055
*Requiem* - Clifford Mohr  *h*  3950
*The Return* - Walter de la Mare  *h*  1424
*Sibs* - F. Paul Wilson  *h*  5898
*Stitch* - Mark Morris  *h*  4024
*The Suiting* - Kelley Wilde  *h*  5803
*Sweet Heart* - Peter James  *h*  2875
*Sweet Revenge* - Jean Simon  *h*  5066
*Sweet William* - Jessica Palmer  *h*  4239
*Torment* - Stephen R. George  *h*  2204
*Vodoun* - David Madsen  *h*  3605
*Whisper* - Raymond Van Over  *h*  5539
*A Whisper of Wings* - Steven Ray Fulgham  *h*  2091
*Winter Tides* - James P. Blaylock  *h*  524

## Horror — Psychological Suspense

*Asylum* - Patrick McGrath  *h*  3812
*The Axman Cometh* - John Farris  *h*  1883
*Bad Karma* - Andrew Harper  *h*  2548
*The Bars on Satan's Jailhouse* - Norman
   Partridge  *h*  4251
*Bereavement* - Richard Lortz  *h*  3525
*Between Floors* - Thomas F. Monteleone  *h*  3957
*The Blood of Angels* - Stephen Gregory  *h*  2428
*Blood Work* - Fay Zachary  *h*  6050
*Bones* - Joyce Thompson  *h*  5453
*Boys of Life* - Paul Russell  *h*  4737
*The Butcher Boy* - Patrick McCabe  *h*  3716
*California Gothic* - Dennis Etchison  *h*  1843
*Chicago Loop* - Paul Theroux  *h*  5443
*The Cormorant* - Stephen Gregory  *h*  2429
*Dark Matter* - Garfield Reeves-Stevens  *h*  4509
*Dark Rivers of the Heart* - Dean R. Koontz  *h*  3204
*The Darkness Within* - Shawn MacDonald  *h*  3585
*Deathchain* - Ken Greenhall  *h*  2415
*Dr. Haggard's Disease* - Patrick McGrath  *h*  3813
*Dolores Claiborne* - Stephen King  *h*  3130
*Double Edge* - Dennis Etchison  *h*  1846
*Down River* - Stephen Gallagher  *h*  2110
*Dying Breath* - Jon A. Harrald  *h*  2555
*The End of Alice* - A.M. Homes  *h*  2755
*Facade* - Kristine Kathryn Rusch  *h*  4716
*The Face of Another* - Kobo Abe  *h*  19
*Fear* - L. Ron Hubbard  *h*  2789
*Flesh and Blood* - D.A. Fowler  *h*  2024
*The Forgotten* - Stephen R. George  *h*  2200
*Gerald's Game* - Stephen King  *h*  3133
*Ghost Light* - Rick Hautala  *h*  2608
*Gone South* - Robert R. McCammon  *h*  3755
*Green Lake* - S.K. Epperson  *h*  1830
*The Grotesque* - Patrick McGrath  *h*  3814
*Header* - Edward Lee  *h*  3393
*Headhunter* - Timothy Findley  *h*  1939
*The Hunger of the Beast* - John Driver  *h*  1656
*I Know What You Did Last Summer* - Lois
   Duncan  *h*  1692

*Icebound* - Dean R. Koontz  *h*  3209
*I'll Be Watching You* - Samuel M. Key  *h*  3094
*Impulse* - Rick Hautala  *h*  2609
*In Double Jeopardy* - Andrew Neiderman  *h*  4088
*Intensity* - Dean R. Koontz  *h*  3210
*Kane* - Douglas Borton  *h*  576
*The Keeper* - Robert D. Lee  *h*  3402
*The Kill Riff* - David J. Schow  *h*  4887
*Lethal Delivery* - J.G. Maxon  *h*  3695
*Lie to Me* - David Martin  *h*  3639
*Lizzie Borden* - Elizabeth Engstrom  *h*  1826
*Lord of the Dark Lake* - Ron Faust  *h*  1894
*The Man Upstairs* - T.L. Parkinson  *h*  4248
*Mary Reilly* - Valerie Martin  *h*  3654
*Mine* - Robert R. McCammon  *h*  3756
*Mirage* - F. Paul Wilson  *h*  5892
*Mystery* - Peter Straub  *h*  5330
*Night Games* - Marilyn Harris  *h*  2562
*Nightmare* - S.K. Epperson  *h*  1832
*Nightmare, with Angel* - Stephen Gallagher  *h*  2111
*The Nihilesthete* - Richard Kalich  *h*  3002
*Nine Levels Down* - William Dantz  *h*  1347
*Obsessed* - Rick R. Reed  *h*  4500
*The One Safe Place* - Ramsey Campbell  *h*  862
*Penance* - Rick R. Reed  *h*  4501
*Pluto, Animal Lover* - Laren Stover  *h*  5318
*Puppet Master* - Barry T. Hawkins  *h*  2632
*Quake* - Richard Laymon  *h*  3370
*Red, Red Robin* - Stephen Gallagher  *h*  2113
*Return to the House of Usher* - Robert Poe  *h*  4345
*Rose Madder* - Stephen King  *h*  3139
*Savage Season* - Joe R. Lansdale  *h*  3332
*Second Chance* - Chet Williamson  *h*  5850
*The Secret History* - Donna Tartt  *h*  5398
*Seeing Eye* - Jack Ellis  *h*  1780
*The Select* - F. Paul Wilson  *h*  5897
*Skin* - Kathe Koja  *h*  3196
*Skyscape* - Michael Cadnum  *h*  814
*Specters* - J.M. Dillard  *h*  1555
*Spider* - Patrick McGrath  *h*  3815
*Strange Angels* - Kathe Koja  *h*  3197
*The Third Beast* - Peter Loughran  *h*  3527
*Toplin* - Michael McDowell  *h*  3807
*Twilight Time* - Rick Hautala  *h*  2613
*Virgins and Martyrs* - Simon Maginn  *h*  3607
*Webs* - Scott Baker  *h*  304
*Website* - Ray Garton  *h*  2157
*What's Wrong with Valerie?* - D.A. Fowler  *h*  2026
*The Wilds* - Richard Laymon  *h*  3373
*Zombie* - Joyce Carol Oates  *h*  4185

## Horror — Reanimated Dead

*Boneman* - Lisa Cantrell  *h*  871
*The Boss in the Wall* - Avram Davidson  *h*  1396
*Celia* - Ruby Jean Jensen  *h*  2900
*The Cold One* - Christopher Pike  *h*  4327
*Dark Souls* - Barry Porter  *h*  4369
*Darker Angels* - S.P. Somtow  *h*  5155
*The Darker Passions: Frankenstein* - Amarantha
   Knight  *h*  3180
*Dead End* - Guy N. Smith  *h*  5119
*Dead Heat* - Del Stone Jr.  *h*  5313
*Dead in the West* - Joe R. Lansdale  *h*  3325
*Deadweight* - Robert Devereaux  *h*  1505
*Death of a Darklord* - Laurell K. Hamilton  *h*  2516
*Genesis* - Charles L. Grant  *h*  2308
*I Am Frankenstein* - C. Dean Andersson  *h*  140
*In the Land of the Dead* - K.W. Jeter  *h*  2912
*The Jewel of Seven Stars* - Bram Stoker  *h*  5312
*The Lazarus Heart* - Poppy Z. Brite  *h*  696
*Legion of the Dead* - Geoffrey Caine  *h*  833
*Living Hell* - Ric Meyers  *h*  3882
*The Mammoth Book of Zombies* - Stephen
   Jones  *h*  2977
*Mongster* - Randall Boyll  *h*  616
*Moon Walker* - Rick Hautala  *h*  2610
*Mordenheim* - Chet Williamson  *h*  5847

*The Mummy!: A Tale of the Twenty-Second Century* -
   Jane Webb Loudon  *h*  3526
*The Mummy, or Ramses the Damned* - Anne
   Rice  *h*  4572
*Mummy Stories* - Martin H. Greenberg  *h*  2400
*Night of the Living Dead* - John Russo  *h*  4745
*The Orpheus Process* - Daniel H. Gower  *h*  2293
*Owl Light* - Michael Paine  *h*  4235
*Return of the Living Dead* - John Russo  *h*  4746
*The Secret Laboratory Journals of Dr. Victor
   Frankenstein* - Jeremy Kay  *h*  3019
*Skeletons* - Al Sarrantonio  *h*  4834
*Sleepwalker* - Michael Cadnum  *h*  815
*Stage Fright* - Clare McNally  *h*  3858
*Tower of Doom* - Mark Anthony  *h*  155
*The Ultimate Frankenstein* - Byron Preiss  *h*  4409
*The Ultimate Zombie* - Byron Preiss  *h*  4412
*Wet Work* - Philip Nutman  *h*  4168

## Horror — Reincarnation

*Fury* - John Coyne  *h*  1237
*Mask of the Night* - Mary Ryan  *h*  4753
*Night of Broken Souls* - Thomas F.
   Monteleone  *h*  3964

## Horror — Satanism

*Adversary* - Daniel Rhodes  *h*  4568
*Doomstalker* - Gary Brandner  *h*  661
*Red Devil* - David Saperstein  *h*  4816

## Horror — Satire

*668: The Neighbor of the Beast* - Lionel
   Fenn  *h*  1917
*The Adventures of Threadwell the Tailor, or
   Alterations Made While You Wait* - P.D.
   Cacek  *h*  801
*Bloodsucking Fiends: A Love Story* - Christopher
   Moore  *h*  3988
*Camp Vamp* - Elvira  *h*  1801
*Flesh* - Gus Weill  *h*  5685
*Human Resources* - Floyd Kemske  *h*  3057
*Irrational Fears* - William Browning
   Spencer  *h*  5167
*The M.D.: A Horror Story* - Thomas M.
   Disch  *h*  1561
*The Mailman* - Bentley Little  *h*  3494
*The Mark of the Moderately Vicious Vampire* - Lionel
   Fenn  *h*  1920
*The Mummy!: A Tale of the Twenty-Second Century* -
   Jane Webb Loudon  *h*  3526
*A Night in the Lonesome October* - Roger
   Zelazny  *h*  6072
*Perfect Little Angels* - Andrew Neiderman  *h*  4090
*Pluto, Animal Lover* - Laren Stover  *h*  5318
*Practical Demonkeeping* - Christopher
   Moore  *h*  3989
*The Priest: A Gothic Romance* - Thomas M.
   Disch  *h*  1562
*Resume with Monsters* - William Browning
   Spencer  *h*  5168
*Serial Killer Days* - David Prill  *h*  4436
*The Store* - Bentley Little  *h*  3497
*Suckers* - Anne Billson  *h*  490
*The Unnatural* - David Prill  *h*  4437
*What's Wrong with America* - Scott
   Bradfield  *h*  627

## Horror — Science Fiction

*'48* - James Herbert  *h*  2667
*Alien Sex* - Ellen Datlow  *h*  1357
*Antibodies* - Kevin J. Anderson  *h*  99
*Beautiful Strangers* - Melanie Tem  *h*  5420
*Beauty* - Brian D'Amato  *h*  1334
*The Blood Artists* - Chuck Hogan  *h*  2720

*Bloodshift* - Garfield Reeves-Stevens  *h*  4508
*Cain* - James Byron Huggins  *h*  2802
*Carnivores* - Penelope Banka Kreps  *h*  3232
*Children of the End* - Mark A. Clements  *h*  1084
*Chiller* - Randall Boyll  *h*  610
*Cold Fire* - Dean R. Koontz  *h*  3203
*Creature* - John Saul  *h*  4839
*Dangerous Nature* - T.J. Kirby  *h*  3152
*Dark City* - Frank Lauria  *h*  3351
*Dark of the Eye* - Douglas Clegg  *h*  1078
*Dark Time* - Maxine O'Callaghan  *h*  4189
*Darkman* - Randall Boyll  *h*  611
*Deadly Breed* - T.J. Kirby  *h*  3153
*The Deus Machine* - Pierre Ouellette  *h*  4232
*Dracula Unbound* - Brian W. Aldiss  *h*  55
*Dry Skull Dreams* - Michael Green  *h*  2344
*Fear Nothing* - Dean R. Koontz  *h*  3207
*The Forever Children* - Eric Flanders  *h*  1944
*Gabriel's Body* - Curt Siodmak  *h*  5073
*Ground Zero* - Kevin J. Anderson  *h*  106
*The Homing* - John Saul  *h*  4842
*Host* - Peter James  *h*  2872
*The House of Doors* - Brian Lumley  *h*  3554
*Hunger* - William Dantz  *h*  1346
*The Hunger and Ecstasy of Vampires* - Brian
  Stableford  *h*  5192
*I, Said the Fly* - Michael Shea  *h*  4944
*The Immortals* - Andrew Neiderman  *h*  4087
*Infinity's Child* - Harry Stein  *h*  5250
*The Innsmouth Heritage* - Brian Stableford  *h*  5194
*The Jimjams* - Michael Green  *h*  2345
*Killjoy* - Elizabeth Forrest  *h*  1973
*Machine* - Rene Belletto  *h*  436
*Maze of Worlds* - Brian Lumley  *h*  3559
*Midnight Mass* - F. Paul Wilson  *h*  5891
*Midsummer* - Matthew J. Costello  *h*  1200
*Mirage* - F. Paul Wilson  *h*  5892
*Mount Dragon* - Douglas Preston  *h*  4413
*Mr. Murder* - Dean R. Koontz  *h*  3213
*My Best Friend Is Invisible* - R.L. Stine  *h*  5289
*Night Beasts* - T.W. Stetson  *h*  5263
*Operation Synbat* - Bob Mayer  *h*  3701
*The Orpheus Process* - Daniel H. Gower  *h*  2293
*Pandora* - Alan Rodgers  *h*  4650
*The Presence* - John Saul  *h*  4843
*A Prophecy of Monsters* - Clark Ashton
  Smith  *h*  5103
*Prototype* - Brian Hodge  *h*  2704
*Rapid Growth* - Mary K. Hanner  *h*  2541
*Reborn* - F. Paul Wilson  *h*  5895
*Relic* - Douglas Preston  *h*  4414
*Reliquary* - Douglas Preston  *h*  4415
*Rockabilly Limbo* - William W. Johnstone  *h*  2934
*Rough Beast* - Gary Goshgarian  *h*  2284
*Ruins* - Kevin J. Anderson  *h*  112
*Silent Witness* - Robert Arthur Smith  *h*  5136
*Them* - William W. Johnstone  *h*  2935
*Thunder Road* - Chris Curry  *h*  1296
*Virus* - Graham Watkins  *h*  5632
*The Waste Lands* - Stephen King  *h*  3143
*White Shark* - Peter Benchley  *h*  441
*Winter Moon* - Dean R. Koontz  *h*  3218
*The X-Files: Fight the Future* - Chris Carter  *h*  924

Horror — Serial Killer

*Act of Love* - Joe R. Lansdale  *h*  3319
*Afterimage Aftershock* - Kristine Kathryn
  Rusch  *h*  4710
*American Psycho* - Brett Easton Ellis  *h*  1777
*The Bad Thing* - Michael O'Rourke  *h*  4222
*Billy* - Whitley Strieber  *h*  5338
*Black Lightning* - John Saul  *h*  4837
*Blackburn* - Bradley Denton  *h*  1489
*Bleeder* - Gene Lazuta  *h*  3374
*Bloodletter* - Warren Newton Beath  *h*  426
*Bloody Valentine* - Stephen R. George  *h*  2197
*Bone* - George C. Chesbro  *h*  1006

*The Book of Webster's* - J.N. Williamson  *h*  5853
*Butcher* - Rex Miller  *h*  3898
*Chaingang* - Rex Miller  *h*  3899
*The Count of Eleven* - Ramsey Campbell  *h*  853
*Cul-De-Sac* - David Martin  *h*  3638
*Cutthroat* - Michael Slade  *h*  5084
*Dead Time* - Richard Lee Byers  *h*  796
*The Death Crystal* - J. Edward Ames  *h*  91
*Deathwalker* - R. Patrick Gates  *h*  2159
*Double Edge* - Dennis Etchison  *h*  1846
*Evil Reincarnate* - Leigh Clark  *h*  1050
*Exquisite Corpse* - Poppy Z. Brite  *h*  695
*Father's Little Helper* - Ronald Kelly  *h*  3052
*Forget Me Not* - Gene Lazuta  *h*  3375
*The Frenchman* - Elizabeth Hand  *h*  2534
*Frisk* - Dennis Cooper  *h*  1170
*From Hell* - Alan Moore  *h*  3987
*Gehenna* - Lewis Gannett  *h*  2114
*Grave Markings* - Michael A. Arnzen  *h*  212
*The Hellfire Club* - Peter Straub  *h*  5326
*Hideaway* - Dean R. Koontz  *h*  3208
*Homecoming* - Matthew J. Costello  *h*  1198
*Iceman* - Rex Miller  *h*  3900
*In the Deep Woods* - Nicholas Conde  *h*  1131
*Jackals* - Charles L. Grant  *h*  2313
*Kane* - Douglas Borton  *h*  576
*Koko* - Peter Straub  *h*  5328
*Lorelei* - Mark A. Clements  *h*  1086
*The Lurker* - James V. Smith  *h*  5123
*Mefisto in Onyx* - Harlan Ellison  *h*  1786
*Morningstar* - Peter Atkins  *h*  265
*Night Cruise* - Billie Sue Mosiman  *h*  4041
*Night Mask* - William W. Johnstone  *h*  2931
*Nightmare Logic* - Matthew Hall  *h*  2495
*Nightmare's Disciple* - Joseph S. Pulver Jr.  *h*  4449
*The Orchid Eater* - Marc Laidlaw  *h*  3312
*Order of the Arrow* - Michael T.
  Hinkemeyer  *h*  2689
*The Place* - T.M. Wright  *h*  5993
*Portrait of the Psychopath as a Young Woman* -
  Edward Lee  *h*  3395
*Psycho* - Robert Bloch  *h*  540
*Puppet Master* - Barry T. Hawkins  *h*  2632
*The Quiet* - Patrick Billings  *h*  488
*Red Angel* - Roxanne Longstreet  *h*  3518
*Running Wild* - J.G. Ballard  *h*  320
*Savant* - Rex Miller  *h*  3901
*The Secret Life of Laszlo, Count Dracula* - Roderick
  Anscombe  *h*  152
*Shadow Man* - Dennis Etchison  *h*  1848
*Shock Radio* - Leigh Clark  *h*  1052
*The Silence of the Lambs* - Thomas Harris  *h*  2566
*Sins of the Flesh* - Don Davis  *h*  1404
*Slice* - Rex Miller  *h*  3902
*Soulcatchers* - Jan Lara  *h*  3336
*The Spirit Stalker* - Nina Romberg  *h*  4664
*Star Prey* - Ehren M. Ehly  *h*  1763
*Street* - Jack Cady  *h*  822
*Thinning the Predators* - Daina Graziunas  *h*  2341
*Trickster* - Chris Curry  *h*  1297
*Tunnelvision* - R. Patrick Gates  *h*  2162
*The Women of Whitechapel and Jack the Ripper* - Paul
  West  *h*  5761

Horror — Small Town Horror

*The Black Carousel* - Charles L. Grant  *h*  2303
*Black Death* - R. Karl Largent  *h*  3337
*Black Night* - S.J. Strayhorn  *h*  5334
*Borderland: A Novel of Terror* - S.K.
  Epperson  *h*  1828
*The Children's Hour* - Douglas Clegg  *h*  1077
*Dark Twilight* - Joseph A. Citro  *h*  1036
*Dialing the Wind* - Charles L. Grant  *h*  2305
*Greely's Cove* - John Gideon  *h*  2221
*Horrorshow* - David Darke  *h*  1353
*Junkyard* - Barry Porter  *h*  4370
*Let There Be Dark* - Allen Lee Harris  *h*  2557

*Midnight* - Dean R. Koontz  *h*  3212
*Needful Things* - Stephen King  *h*  3137
*Offspring* - Jack Ketchum  *h*  3092
*Something Out There* - Ronald Kelly  *h*  3056
*Something Stirs* - Charles L. Grant  *h*  2316
*Symphony* - Charles L. Grant  *h*  2318
*Under the Crust* - Terry Lamsley  *h*  3314
*Unearthed* - Ashley McConnell  *h*  3778
*Yellow Moon* - David J. Searls  *h*  4907

Horror — Supernatural Vengeance

*The Basement* - Bari Wood  *h*  5961
*Beneath Still Waters* - Matthew J. Costello  *h*  1193
*Black Ice* - Pat Graversen  *h*  2333
*Black Lightning* - John Saul  *h*  4837
*Burial* - Graham Masterton  *h*  3671
*The Cartoonist* - Sean Costello  *h*  1204
*Cemetery of Angels* - Noel Hynd  *h*  2821
*Clash by Night* - Chet Williamson  *h*  5844
*Darkscope* - Margaret Falk  *h*  1860
*Dead in the Water* - Nancy Holder  *h*  2732
*Dead in the West* - Joe R. Lansdale  *h*  3325
*Dead Voices* - Abigail McDaniels  *h*  3783
*Deadly Friend* - Keith Ferrario  *h*  1926
*Deadly Vengeance* - Stephen R. George  *h*  2199
*Demon Shadows* - Michael B. Sirota  *h*  5075
*Fear Itself* - Ric Meyers  *h*  3881
*Fiend* - C. Dean Andersson  *h*  138
*Fires of Eden* - Dan Simmons  *h*  5053
*Hellcat* - Amanda Kingsley  *h*  3145
*The Living Evil* - Ruby Jean Jensen  *h*  2902
*Making Love* - Melanie Tem  *h*  5422
*Midnight Is a Lonely Place* - Barbara
  Erskine  *h*  1836
*The Night Man* - K.W. Jeter  *h*  2915
*OtherSyde* - J. Michael Straczynski  *h*  5323
*The Palm Dome* - Liz Fulton  *h*  2094
*The Prodigy* - Noel Hynd  *h*  2823
*Quoth the Crow* - David Bischoff  *h*  494
*Rage* - Elizabeth Ergas  *h*  1834
*The Reckoning* - Ruby Jean Jensen  *h*  2904
*A Room for the Dead* - Noel Hynd  *h*  2825
*Sacred Prey* - Vivian Schilling  *h*  4875
*Soul Catcher* - Colin Kersey  *h*  3081
*Spook Night* - David Robbins  *h*  4603
*Stone Dead* - Ellen Jamison  *h*  2878
*Tower of Evil* - James Kisner  *h*  3161
*The Uprising* - Abigail McDaniels  *h*  3785
*Uwharrie* - Eugene E. Pfaff Jr.  *h*  4309
*Wes Craven's New Nightmare* - David
  Bergantino  *h*  460
*Worst Nightmare* - Ric Meyers  *h*  3883

Horror — Techno-Horror

*The Eleventh Plague: A Novel of Medical Terror* -
  John S. Marr  *h*  3632
*The Fungus* - Harry Adam Knight  *h*  3192
*The Hacker* - Chet Day  *h*  1410
*Night Glow* - Martin James  *h*  2867
*Reaper* - Ben Mizrich  *h*  3923

Horror — Time Travel

*Lightning* - Dean R. Koontz  *h*  3211

Horror — Vampire Story

*100 Vicious Little Vampire Stories* - Robert
  Weinberg  *h*  5688
*Afterage* - Yvonne Navarro  *h*  4072
*Ancestral Hungers* - Scott Baker  *h*  303
*Angel Souls and Devil Hearts* - Christopher
  Golden  *h*  2255
*The Angry Angel* - Chelsea Quinn Yarbro  *h*  6010
*Anno Dracula* - Kim Newman  *h*  4094

*Aqua Sancta* - Edward Bryant  *h*  748
*The Armageddon Box* - Robert Weinberg  *h*  5690
*As One Dead* - Don Bassingthwaite  *h*  387
*Bad Dreams* - Kim Newman  *h*  4096
*Better in the Dark* - Chelsea Quinn Yarbro  *h*  6011
*Bitter Blood* - Karen E. Taylor  *h*  5405
*Blade* - Mel Odom  *h*  4190
*Blind Hunger* - David Darke  *h*  1352
*Blood* - Ron Dee  *h*  1463
*Blood Alone* - Elaine Bergstrom  *h*  462
*Blood and Roses* - Sharon Bainbridge  *h*  292
*Blood Brothers* - Brian Lumley  *h*  3546
*Blood Brothers* - T. Lucien Wright  *h*  5986
*Blood Debt* - Tanya Huff  *h*  2792
*Blood Feud* - Sam Siciliano  *h*  5020
*Blood Is Not Enough* - Ellen Datlow  *h*  1360
*Blood Kin* - Ronald Kelly  *h*  3051
*Blood Kiss: Vampire Erotica* - Cecilia Tan  *h*  5385
*Blood Lines: Vampire Stories From New England* -
    Lawrence Schimel  *h*  4876
*Blood Lust* - Ron Dee  *h*  1464
*Blood Muse: Timeless Tales of Vampires in the Arts* -
    Esther Friesner  *h*  2071
*Blood of Mugwump* - Doug Rice  *h*  4581
*Blood of the Covenant* - Brent Monahan  *h*  3954
*Blood of the Impaler* - Jeffrey Sackett  *h*  4779
*Blood on the Sun* - Brian Herbert  *h*  2664
*Blood on the Water* - P.N. Elrod  *h*  1791
*Blood Price* - Tanya Huff  *h*  2793
*Blood Relations* - Doug Murray  *h*  4058
*Blood Roses* - Chelsea Quinn Yarbro  *h*  6012
*Blood Secrets* - Karen E. Taylor  *h*  5406
*Blood Thirst: 100 Years of Vampire Fiction* - Leonard
    Wolf  *h*  5935
*Blood Ties* - Karen E. Taylor  *h*  5407
*Blood Walk* - Lee Killough  *h*  3108
*Blood War* - Robert Weinberg  *h*  5693
*Bloodlines* - J.N. Williamson  *h*  5852
*Bloodlist* - P.N. Elrod  *h*  1792
*Bloodshift* - Garfield Reeves-Stevens  *h*  4508
*Bloodsucking Fiends: A Love Story* - Christopher
    Moore  *h*  3988
*Bloodwars* - Brian Lumley  *h*  3547
*Bloody Bones* - Laurell K. Hamilton  *h*  2512
*The Bloody Red Baron* - Kim Newman  *h*  4097
*Blue Moon* - Laurell K. Hamilton  *h*  2513
*The Book of Common Dread* - Brent
    Monahan  *h*  3955
*Bram Stoker's Dracula* - Fred Saberhagen  *h*  4763
*Bring on the Night* - Don Davis  *h*  1402
*Brothers of the Night* - Michael Rowe  *h*  4689
*Buffy the Vampire Slayer* - Richie Tankersley
    Cusick  *h*  1301
*Burnt Offerings* - Laurell K. Hamilton  *h*  2514
*A Candle for D'Artagnan* - Chelsea Quinn
    Yarbro  *h*  6013
*Carmilla: The Return* - Kyle Marffin  *h*  3623
*Carrion Comfort* - Dan Simmons  *h*  5049
*Celebrity Vampires* - Martin H. Greenberg  *h*  2382
*Cherished Blood* - Cecilia Tan  *h*  5386
*Children of the Night* - Mercedes Lackey  *h*  3276
*Children of the Night* - Dan Simmons  *h*  5050
*Children of the Vampire* - Jeanne
    Kalogridis  *h*  3003
*A Chill in the Blood* - P.N. Elrod  *h*  1793
*Circus of the Damned* - Laurell K.
    Hamilton  *h*  2515
*Cold Kiss* - Roxanne Longstreet  *h*  3517
*A Coven of Vampires* - Brian Lumley  *h*  3549
*Covenant with the Vampire* - Jeanne
    Kalogridis  *h*  3004
*Crusader's Torch* - Chelsea Quinn Yarbro  *h*  6015
*Curse of the Vampire* - Geoffrey Caine  *h*  832
*Dance of Death* - P.N. Elrod  *h*  1794
*Dark Destiny III: Children of Dracula* - Edward E.
    Kramer  *h*  3226
*Dark Prince* - Keith Herber  *h*  2663
*Darker Angels: Lesbian Vampire Stories* - Pam
    Keesey  *h*  3030

*The Darker Passions: Carmilla* - Amarantha
    Knight  *h*  3177
*The Darker Passions: Dracula* - Amarantha
    Knight  *h*  3179
*The Darkest Thirst: A Vampire Anthology* -
    Anonymous  *h*  150
*Darkness, I* - Tanith Lee  *h*  3407
*Darkness on the Ice* - Lois Tilton  *h*  5475
*Daughter of Darkness* - Steven Spruill  *h*  5183
*Daughter of the Night* - Elaine Bergstrom  *h*  463
*Daughters of Darkness: Lesbian Vampire Stories* -
    Pam Keesey  *h*  3031
*Deadspawn* - Brian Lumley  *h*  3550
*Deadspeak* - Brian Lumley  *h*  3551
*Death Masque* - P.N. Elrod  *h*  1795
*Desmodus* - Melanie Tem  *h*  5421
*Desmond: A Novel of Love and the Modern Vampire* -
    Ulysses G. Dietz  *h*  1541
*The Devil's Advocate* - Gherbod Fleming  *h*  1949
*Diary of a Vampire* - Gary Bowen  *h*  600
*Domination* - Michael Cecilione  *h*  946
*A Dozen Black Roses* - Nancy A. Collins  *h*  1119
*Dracul: An Eternal Love Story* - Nancy
    Kilpatrick  *h*  3110
*Dracula: Prince of Darkness* - Martin H.
    Greenberg  *h*  2387
*The Dracula Tape* - Fred Saberhagen  *h*  4765
*Dracula: The Ultimate Illustrated Edition of the
    World-Famous Vampire Play* - Hamilton
    Deane  *h*  1448
*Dracula's Brood* - Richard Dalby  *h*  1308
*Dusk* - Ron Dee  *h*  1466
*Elvira: Transylvania 90210* - Elvira  *h*  1802
*The Empire of Fear* - Brian Stableford  *h*  5191
*Endorphins* - Nancy Kilpatrick  *h*  3111
*Erotica Vampirica* - Cecilia Tan  *h*  5387
*Eye Killers* - A.A. Carr  *h*  911
*Fire in the Blood* - P.N. Elrod  *h*  1796
*Forever Knight: A Stirring of Dust* - Susan
    Sizemore  *h*  5078
*Forever Knight: Intimations of Mortality* - Susan M.
    Garrett  *h*  2149
*The Gilda Stories* - Jewelle Gomez  *h*  2267
*Girls' Night Out* - Stefan Dziemianowicz  *h*  1713
*The Golden* - Lucius Shepard  *h*  4978
*Golden Eyes* - John Gideon  *h*  2220
*The Harvest* - Richie Tankersley Cusick  *h*  1302
*Harvest of Blood* - Vincent Courtney  *h*  1213
*The Holmes-Dracula File* - Fred
    Saberhagen  *h*  4767
*Human Resources* - Floyd Kemske  *h*  3057
*The Hunger and Ecstasy of Vampires* - Brian
    Stableford  *h*  5192
*I Am Dracula* - C. Dean Andersson  *h*  139
*I, Strahd* - P.N. Elrod  *h*  1797
*I, Vampire* - Michael Romkey  *h*  4665
*I, Vampire: Interviews with the Undead* - Jean Marie
    Stine  *h*  5284
*Immortal* - Jason Nickles  *h*  4102
*In Hot Blood* - Petru Popescu  *h*  4367
*In the Blood* - Nancy A. Collins  *h*  1121
*The Informers* - Brett Easton Ellis  *h*  1778
*Insatiable* - David Dvorkin  *h*  1707
*Isaac Asimov's Vampires* - Gardner Dozois  *h*  1611
*The Judas Glass* - Michael Cadnum  *h*  812
*Judgment of Tears: Anno Dracula 1959* - Kim
    Newman  *h*  4098
*Keeper of the King* - Nigel Bennett  *h*  452
*The Kiss* - Kathryn Reines  *h*  4529
*The Kiss of Death: An Anthology of Vampire Stories* -
    Anonymous  *h*  151
*Kiss of the Vampire* - Lee Weathersby  *h*  5657
*The Last Aerie* - Brian Lumley  *h*  3557
*The Last Vampire* - Kathryn Meyer Griffith  *h*  2440
*The Last Vampire* - Christopher Pike  *h*  4328
*Less than Human* - Gary L. Raisor  *h*  4464
*Liquid Diet* - William Tedford  *h*  5419
*Live Girls* - Ray Garton  *h*  2151
*Lord of the Dead* - Tom Holland  *h*  2741

*Lord of the Vampires* - Jeanne Kalogridis  *h*  3005
*The Lost* - Jonathan Aycliffe  *h*  279
*Lost Souls* - Poppy Z. Brite  *h*  697
*Lot Lizards* - Ray Garton  *h*  2152
*Love Bite* - Sherry Gottlieb  *h*  2288
*Love Bites* - Amarantha Knight  *h*  3182
*Love in Vein* - Poppy Z. Brite  *h*  698
*Love in Vein II* - Poppy Z. Brite  *h*  699
*The Lunatic Cafe* - Laurell K. Hamilton  *h*  2520
*The Making of a Monster* - Gail Petersen  *h*  4307
*The Mammoth Book of Dracula* - Stephen
    Jones  *h*  2972
*The Mammoth Book of Vampires* - Stephen
    Jones  *h*  2975
*Mansions of Darkness* - Chelsea Quinn
    Yarbro  *h*  6016
*The Mark of the Moderately Vicious Vampire* - Lionel
    Fenn  *h*  1920
*Mastery* - Kelley Wilde  *h*  5802
*A Matter of Taste* - Fred Saberhagen  *h*  4770
*Memnoch the Devil* - Anne Rice  *h*  4571
*Midnight Blue: The Sonja Blue Collection* - Nancy A.
    Collins  *h*  1122
*Midnight Mass* - F. Paul Wilson  *h*  5891
*Mina* - Marie Kiraly  *h*  3151
*Morningstar* - Peter Atkins  *h*  265
*Natural History* - Juan Perucho  *h*  4303
*Near Death* - Nancy Kilpatrick  *h*  3113
*Necroscope: The Lost Years* - Brian
    Lumley  *h*  3560
*The Need* - Andrew Neiderman  *h*  4089
*Netherworld* - Richard Lee Byers  *h*  798
*Night Bites: Vampire Stories by Women* - Victoria
    Brownworth  *h*  730
*Night Blood* - Eric Flanders  *h*  1945
*Night Brothers* - Sidney Williams  *h*  5824
*Night Hunter* - Michael Reaves  *h*  4496
*The Night Inside* - Nancy Baker  *h*  301
*Night Prayers* - P.D. Cacek  *h*  803
*Night Prophets* - Paul F. Olson  *h*  4213
*Night Thirst* - Patrick Whalen  *h*  5770
*Nightblood* - T. Chris Martindale  *h*  3656
*Nightlife* - Jack Ellis  *h*  1779
*No Blood Spilled* - Les Daniels  *h*  1338
*Nocturnas* - Shawn Ryan  *h*  4755
*Of Masques and Martyrs* - Christopher
    Golden  *h*  2258
*Of Saints and Shadows* - Christopher
    Golden  *h*  2259
*Out for Blood* - John Peyton Cooke  *h*  1166
*Out of the House of Life* - Chelsea Quinn
    Yarbro  *h*  6018
*Pandora* - Anne Rice  *h*  4573
*Parliament of Blood* - Scott Ciencin  *h*  1031
*Personal Darkness* - Tanith Lee  *h*  3413
*Precious Blood* - Pat Graversen  *h*  2336
*Prodigal* - Melanie Tem  *h*  5423
*The Queen of the Damned* - Anne Rice  *h*  4574
*A Question of Time* - Fred Saberhagen  *h*  4772
*Ragged Angels* - Della Van Hise  *h*  5537
*Raven* - S.A. Swiniarski  *h*  5374
*Red Death* - P.N. Elrod  *h*  1798
*Resurgence* - Brian Lumley  *h*  3564
*Return to Chaos* - Craig Shaw Gardner  *h*  2131
*Rivals of Dracula* - Robert Weinberg  *h*  5699
*The Ruby Tear* - Rebecca Brand  *h*  660
*Rulers of Darkness* - Steven Spruill  *h*  5185
*The Safety of Unknown Cities* - Lucy
    Taylor  *h*  5414
*Salem's Lot* - Stephen King  *h*  3140
*Seance for a Vampire* - Fred Saberhagen  *h*  4773
*The Season of Passage* - Christopher Pike  *h*  4331
*Sex and Blood* - Ron Dee  *h*  1467
*Sex and the Single Vampire* - Nancy
    Kilpatrick  *h*  3114
*Shade* - David Darke  *h*  1355
*Shadows* - Jonathan Nasaw  *h*  4068
*A Sharpness on the Neck* - Fred
    Saberhagen  *h*  4774

*Shifters* - Edward Lee  *h*  3396
*Shrines and Desecrations* - Brian Hodge  *h*  2705
*Sins of the Blood* - Kristine Kathryn Rusch  *h*  4728
*Slave of My Thirst* - Tom Holland  *h*  2742
*Some of Your Blood* - Theodore Sturgeon  *h*  5347
*Some Things Come Back* - Robert Morgan  *h*  4004
*Some Things Never Die* - Robert Morgan  *h*  4005
*Sons of Darkness: Tales of Men, Blood and
   Immortality* - Michael Rowe  *h*  4690
*The Source* - Brian Lumley  *h*  3565
*Southern Blood: Vampire Stories From the American
   South* - Lawrence Schimel  *h*  4880
*Stainless* - Todd Grimson  *h*  2449
*The Stake* - Richard Laymon  *h*  3372
*The Stress of Her Regard* - Tim Powers  *h*  4385
*Suckers* - Anne Billson  *h*  490
*The Summoning* - Bentley Little  *h*  3498
*Sunglasses After Dark* - Nancy A. Collins  *h*  1124
*Sweet Blood* - Pat Graversen  *h*  2337
*The Tale of the Body Thief* - Anne Rice  *h*  4576
*A Taste for Blood* - Martin H. Greenberg  *h*  2407
*These Fallen Angels* - Wendy Haley  *h*  2492
*Thirst* - Michael Cecilione  *h*  948
*Thirst* - Pyotr Kurtinski  *h*  3253
*Thirst of the Vampire* - T. Lucien Wright  *h*  5988
*Thirsty* - M.T. Anderson  *h*  120
*This Dark Paradise* - Wendy Haley  *h*  2493
*This Symbiotic Fascination* - Charlee Jacob  *h*  2843
*Those Who Hunt the Night* - Barbara
   Hambly  *h*  2510
*Throat Sprockets* - Tim Lucas  *h*  3541
*The Time of Feasting* - Mick Farren  *h*  1882
*The Time of the Vampires* - P.N. Elrod  *h*  1799
*To Dream of Dreamers Lost* - David Niall
   Wilson  *h*  5882
*To Speak in Lifeless Tongues* - David Niall
   Wilson  *h*  5883
*Tomorrow Sucks* - Greg Cox  *h*  1231
*Tooth: A Tale of Love and Death in Paradox* - Novak
   Kruger  *h*  3244
*Traveling with the Dead* - Barbara Hambly  *h*  2511
*The Ultimate Dracula* - Byron Preiss  *h*  4407
*The Unbeholden* - Robert Weinberg  *h*  5703
*The Undead* - Roxanne Longstreet  *h*  3519
*Under the Fang* - Robert R. McCammon  *h*  3758
*Unholy Allies* - Robert Weinberg  *h*  5704
*Valentine* - S.P. Somtow  *h*  5160
*Vampire$* - John Steakley  *h*  5237
*The Vampire Armand* - Anne Rice  *h*  4578
*Vampire Beat* - Vincent Courtney  *h*  1214
*A Vampire Bestiary* - Jeffrey Thomas  *h*  5448
*Vampire Blood* - Kathryn Meyer Griffith  *h*  2441
*Vampire Breath* - R.L. Stine  *h*  5291
*Vampire Bytes* - Linda Grant  *h*  2322
*Vampire Detectives* - Martin H. Greenberg  *h*  2408
*Vampire Diary: The Embrace* - Robert
   Weinberg  *h*  5705
*The Vampire Hunters' Casebook* - Peter
   Haining  *h*  2484
*The Vampire Journals* - Traci Briery  *h*  678
*Vampire Junkies* - Norman Spinrad  *h*  5175
*The Vampire Memoirs* - Mara McCuniff  *h*  3781
*The Vampire Odyssey* - Scott Ciencin  *h*  1032
*The Vampire Papers* - Michael Romkey  *h*  4666
*The Vampire Princess* - Michael Romkey  *h*  4667
*The Vampire Virus* - Michael Romkey  *h*  4668
*Vampires Anonymous* - Jeffrey N.
   McMahan  *h*  3853
*The Vampire's Apprentice* - Richard Lee
   Byers  *h*  799
*The Vampire's Beautiful Daughter* - S.P.
   Somtow  *h*  5161
*Vampires: The Greatest Stories* - Martin H.
   Greenberg  *h*  2409
*Vanitas: Escape From Vampire Junction* - S.P.
   Somtow  *h*  5162
*Virgintooth* - Mark Ivanhoe  *h*  2834
*Virtuous Vampires* - Stefan Dziemianowicz  *h*  1718
*Weird Vampire Tales* - Robert Weinberg  *h*  5706

*Wetbones* - John Shirley  *h*  5010
*Where Does Kissing End?* - Kate Pullinger  *h*  4445
*A Whisper of Blood* - Ellen Datlow  *h*  1370
*The Wildlings* - Scott Ciencin  *h*  1034
*The Winnowing* - Gherbod Fleming  *h*  1950
*The World on Blood* - Jonathan Nasaw  *h*  4069
*Writ in Blood* - Chelsea Quinn Yarbro  *h*  6019


**Horror — Werewolf Story**

*All Things under the Moon* - Robert
   Morgan  *h*  4002
*Animals* - John Skipp  *h*  5080
*Batman: Captured by the Engines* - Joe R.
   Lansdale  *h*  3320
*The Beast Within: A Gabriel Knight Mystery* - Jane
   Jensen  *h*  2895
*The Beast Within: Erotic Tales of Werewolves* -
   Cecilia Tan  *h*  5384
*Blood and Chocolate* - Annette Curtis
   Klause  *h*  3162
*Blood on the Bayou* - D.J. Donaldson  *h*  1570
*Blood Trail* - Tanya Huff  *h*  2794
*The Boy Who Cried Werewolf* - Elvira  *h*  1800
*Call to Battle* - Doug Murray  *h*  4059
*The Case of the Police Officer's Cock Ring and the
   Piano Player Who Had No Fingers* - Edward
   Lee  *h*  3388
*Cold at Heart* - Brian Hopkins  *h*  2768
*Darker than You Think* - Jack Williamson  *h*  5861
*The Fear in Yesterday's Rings* - George C.
   Chesbro  *h*  1007
*Guardian* - John Saul  *h*  4841
*Heart-Beast* - Tanith Lee  *h*  3411
*Hell-Storm* - James A. Moore  *h*  3990
*Killing Frost* - Dan I. Blake  *h*  514
*The Living Dark* - Stephen Gresham  *h*  2431
*The Lunatic Cafe* - Laurell K. Hamilton  *h*  2520
*The Mammoth Book of Werewolves* - Stephen
   Jones  *h*  2976
*Mark of the Werewolf* - Jeffrey Sackett  *h*  4780
*Moon Dance* - S.P. Somtow  *h*  5158
*Moon of the Werewolf* - Ronald Kelly  *h*  3053
*Moondog* - Henry Garfield  *h*  2138
*The Nightwalker* - Thomas Tessier  *h*  5442
*The Passion* - Donna Boyd  *h*  603
*A Prophecy of Monsters* - Clark Ashton
   Smith  *h*  5103
*Return of the Wolfman* - Jeff Rovin  *h*  4687
*Room 13* - Henry Garfield  *h*  2139
*St. Peter's Wolf* - Michael Cadnum  *h*  816
*Shadow of the Beast* - Margaret L. Carter  *h*  926
*Shadows* - Kimberly Rangel  *h*  4472
*Shapes* - Steve Vance  *h*  5552
*The Silver Wolf* - Alice Borchardt  *h*  572
*Thor* - Wayne Smith  *h*  5146
*Tombley's Walk* - Crosland Brown  *h*  723
*Tomorrow Bites* - Greg Cox  *h*  1230
*The Ultimate Werewolf* - Byron Preiss  *h*  4410
*Under the Shadow* - Jane Toombs  *h*  5481
*Vyrmin* - Gene Lazuta  *h*  3376
*Wake of the Werewolf* - Geoffrey Caine  *h*  834
*Walking Wolf* - Nancy A. Collins  *h*  1126
*Werewolf* - Peter Rubie  *h*  4702
*The Werewolf Chronicles* - Traci Briery  *h*  679
*The Werewolf of Paris* - Guy Endore  *h*  1822
*The Werewolf's Revenge* - Richard Jaccoma  *h*  2841
*The Werewolf's Touch* - Cheri Scotch  *h*  4892
*Werewolves* - Martin H. Greenberg  *h*  2410
*The Werewolves of London* - Brian
   Stableford  *h*  5196
*When Darkness Falls* - Sidney Williams  *h*  5825
*The Wild* - Whitley Strieber  *h*  5343
*Wild Blood* - Nancy A. Collins  *h*  1127
*Wilderness* - Dennis Danvers  *h*  1349
*Wilding* - Melanie Tem  *h*  5425
*Wolf Moon* - John R. Holt  *h*  2749
*The Wolf's Hour* - Robert R. McCammon  *h*  3759

*Wolfsong* - Traci Briery  *h*  680
*Women Who Run with Werewolves: Tales of Blood,
   Lust and Metamorphosis* - Pam Keesey  *h*  3032
*The World of Darkness: Watcher* - Charles L.
   Grant  *h*  2321
*Wyrm Wolf* - Edo van Belkom  *h*  5535


**Horror — Wild Talents**

*Anthony Shriek* - Jessica Amanda
   Salmonson  *h*  4790
*Bad Brains* - Kathe Koja  *h*  3193
*The Between* - Tannarive Due  *h*  1669
*Blood of Innocents* - John Arbucci  *h*  204
*The Blood of the Lamb* - Thomas F.
   Monteleone  *h*  3958
*Brainstorm* - Steven M. Krauzer  *h*  3230
*Bright Shadow* - Elizabeth Forrest  *h*  1971
*The Burning Man* - Michael Hammond  *h*  2530
*Captain Quad* - Sean Costello  *h*  1203
*Carrie* - Stephen King  *h*  3127
*Catacomb* - Andrew Laurance  *h*  3347
*The Cipher* - Kathe Koja  *h*  3194
*Cold White Fury* - Beth Amos  *h*  97
*The Committee* - Raymond Buckland  *h*  752
*Concrete Hotel* - C. Christopher Caldon  *h*  839
*Cries of the Children* - Clare McNally  *h*  3856
*Dark of the Eye* - Douglas Clegg  *h*  1078
*Dark Visions* - T. Lucien Wright  *h*  5987
*Deadrush* - Yvonne Navarro  *h*  4073
*Deadweight* - Robert Devereaux  *h*  1505
*Deathgrip* - Brian Hodge  *h*  2700
*Deathscape* - Michael Cecilione  *h*  945
*Dragon Tears* - Dean R. Koontz  *h*  3205
*Fade* - Robert Cormier  *h*  1188
*Fatal Outcome* - Patricia Wallace  *h*  5622
*Fog Heart* - Thomas Tessier  *h*  5440
*The Gifted* - Jack Caravela  *h*  879
*Glimpses* - Lewis Shiner  *h*  4997
*The Hanged Man* - T.J. MacGregor  *h*  3594
*The Holy Terror* - Wayne Allen Sallee  *h*  4787
*The Ignored* - Bentley Little  *h*  3493
*Insomnia* - Stephen King  *h*  3135
*Jumpers* - R. Patrick Gates  *h*  2161
*The Link* - Andrew Laurance  *h*  3348
*The Long Lost* - Ramsey Campbell  *h*  859
*The Long Midnight* - Daniel Ransom  *h*  4480
*Mefisto in Onyx* - Harlan Ellison  *h*  1786
*Mind Kill* - Richard La Plante  *h*  3267
*Mr. Sandman* - Lyle Howard  *h*  2779
*Night Calls* - Katharine Eliska Kimbriel  *h*  3119
*Orphans* - Jean Simon  *h*  5065
*Out of Body* - Thomas Baum  *h*  397
*Pillow Friend* - Lisa Tuttle  *h*  5522
*The Premonition* - Andrew Laurance  *h*  3349
*Psychamok* - Brian Lumley  *h*  3561
*Psychomech* - Brian Lumley  *h*  3562
*Psychosphere* - Brian Lumley  *h*  3563
*The Regulators* - Richard Bachman  *h*  284
*The Resurrectionist* - Thomas F.
   Monteleone  *h*  3965
*Retribution* - Elizabeth Forrest  *h*  1975
*Rook* - Graham Masterton  *h*  3678
*Seeing Eye* - Jack Ellis  *h*  1780
*Sick* - Jay R. Bonansinga  *h*  571
*Silent Scream* - Dan Schmidt  *h*  4883
*Sineater* - Elizabeth Massie  *h*  3668
*Sister, Sister* - Andrew Neiderman  *h*  4091
*Sole Survivor* - Dean R. Koontz  *h*  3215
*Spree* - Lucy Taylor  *h*  5415
*Superstition* - David Ambrose  *h*  90
*Thinning the Predators* - Daina Graziunas  *h*  2341
*The Unborn* - Andrew Laurance  *h*  3350
*Viper* - Alan Riefe  *h*  4589
*Walking Wounded* - Robert Devereaux  *h*  1507
*Whipping Boy* - John Byrne  *h*  800
*Witch Spell* - Guy N. Smith  *h*  5122
*Wolf Flow* - K.W. Jeter  *h*  2918

*The World I Made for Her* - Thomas Moran  h  3996

## Horror — Witchcraft

*100 Wicked Little Witch Stories* - Stefan Dziemianowicz  h  1711
*Fiend* - C. Dean Andersson  h  138
*Nice Guys Finish Last* - Gary Jonas  h  2938
*The Tallow Image* - Jane Brindle  h  690
*Treasure Box* - Orson Scott Card  h  898
*The Ultimate Witch* - Byron Preiss  h  4411

## Horror — Young Adult

*Blood and Chocolate* - Annette Curtis Klause  h  3162
*The Cat* - R.L. Stine  h  5205
*The Curse of Camp Cold Lake* - R.L. Stine  h  5286
*The Lion Tamer's Daughter* - Peter Dickinson  h  1526
*My Best Friend Is Invisible* - R.L. Stine  h  5289
*Night Terrors: Stories of Shadow and Substance* - Lois Duncan  h  1693
*Thirsty* - M.T. Anderson  h  120
*The Young Oxford Book of Ghost Stories* - Dennis Pepper  h  4282

# SCIENCE FICTION

## Science Fiction — Adventure

*The 97th Step* - Steve Perry  s  4287
*The Abductors: Conspiracy* - Jonathan Frakes  s  2034
*Achilles' Choice* - Larry Niven  s  4114
*Acts of Conscience* - William Barton  s  377
*The Albino Knife* - Steve Perry  s  4288
*Alien 3* - Alan Dean Foster  s  1993
*Alien Salute* - Charles Ingrid  s  2830
*Aliens Stole My Body* - Bruce Coville  s  1217
*Aliens: The Female War* - Steve Perry  s  4290
*Ancient Heavens* - Robert E. Vardeman  s  5561
*Article 23* - William R. Forstchen  s  1978
*The Artifact* - W. Michael Gear  s  2165
*Atlantis Found* - R. Garcia y Robertson  s  2119
*Backblast* - Lee McKeone  s  3828
*The Barsoom Project* - Larry Niven  s  4115
*Batman: Knightfall* - Dennis O'Neil  s  4215
*Batman Returns* - Craig Shaw Gardner  s  2124
*Beachhead* - Jack Williamson  s  5859
*Beamriders!* - Martin Caidin  s  824
*Beyond Eden* - J.M. Morgan  s  3999
*Beyond the Void* - Sean Dalton  s  1331
*The Billion Dollar Boy* - Charles Sheffield  s  4948
*Black Steel* - Steve Perry  s  4291
*Bodyguard* - William C. Dietz  s  1542
*The Broken God* - David Zindell  s  6085
*Brother Death* - Steve Perry  s  4292
*Brother to Shadows* - Andre Norton  s  4142
*Brotherhood of the Stars* - Kirby Greene  s  2414
*Buddy Holly Is Alive and Well on Ganymede* - Bradley Denton  s  1490
*Bug Park* - James P. Hogan  s  2723
*Burning Bright* - Melissa Scott  s  4894
*A Call to Arms* - Alan Dean Foster  s  1995
*Call to Arms* - P.M. Griffin  s  2435
*Carpe Diem* - Steve Miller  s  3907
*Carve the Sky* - Alexander Jablokov  s  2836
*Cat-A-Lyst* - Alan Dean Foster  s  1997
*Cat Scratch Fever* - Tara K. Harper  s  2550
*Catch the Lightning* - Catherine Asaro  s  218
*Catwoman* - Lynn Abbey  s  14
*The Chance Factor* - Diana G. Gallagher  s  2109
*Christmas Slaughter* - Mark Grant  s  2323
*The City Who Fought* - Anne McCaffrey  s  3722
*Clarke County, Space* - Allen Steele  s  5241
*The Clone Crisis* - Lee McKeone  s  3829

*Codename Wolverine* - Christopher Golden  s  2256
*Cohort of the Damned* - Andrew Keith  s  3034
*Comeback Tour: The Sky Belongs to the Stars* - Jack Yeovil  s  6020
*A Company of Stars* - Christopher Stasheff  s  5215
*Conrad's Quest for Rubber* - Leo Frankowski  s  2043
*Crescent in the Sky* - Donald Moffitt  s  3946
*Crown of the Serpent* - Allen L. Wold  s  5932
*Cry Wolf* - Kenneth Von Gunden  s  5586
*Cybernarc* - Robert Cain  s  829
*The Dark Beyond the Stars* - Frank M. Robinson  s  4626
*Dayworld Breakup* - Philip Jose Farmer  s  1869
*The Death and Life of Superman* - Roger Stern  s  5262
*The Death of Sleep* - Anne McCaffrey  s  3727
*Deathweave* - Cary Osborne  s  4226
*Delta Pavonis* - Eric Kotani  s  3221
*Delta Search* - William Shatner  s  4930
*Demolition Man* - Richard Osborne  s  4229
*The Demon Princes: Volume One* - Jack Vance  s  5544
*The Demon Princes: Volume Two* - Jack Vance  s  5545
*The Demons at Rainbow Bridge* - Jack L. Chalker  s  952
*Derelict for Trade* - Andre Norton  s  4148
*Destination: Mutiny* - Sean Dalton  s  1332
*Devil in the Sky* - Greg Cox  s  1226
*The Diamond Moon* - Paul Preuss  s  4417
*The Dig* - Alan Dean Foster  s  2002
*Diggers* - Terry Pratchett  s  4386
*Dinosaur Summer* - Greg Bear  s  416
*Divergence* - Charles Sheffield  s  4954
*The Dolphins of Pern* - Anne McCaffrey  s  3729
*Douglas Adams's Starship Titanic* - Terry Jones  s  2979
*Down the Bright Way* - Robert Reed  s  4505
*Dragon Rigger* - Jeffrey A. Carver  s  929
*Dragon's Blood* - Alex McDonough  s  3799
*Dragon's Claw* - Alex McDonough  s  3800
*Dragons in the Stars* - Jeffrey A. Carver  s  930
*Dragon's Teeth* - Lee Killough  s  3109
*Drifter* - William C. Dietz  s  1543
*Drifter's Run* - William C. Dietz  s  1544
*Drifter's War* - William C. Dietz  s  1545
*Earth 2* - Melissa Crandall  s  1247
*Earthgrip* - Harry Turtledove  s  5499
*An Earthly Crown* - Kate Elliott  s  1771
*Echoes of the Well of Souls* - Jack L. Chalker  s  953
*The Ecolitan Operation* - L.E. Modesitt Jr.  s  3928
*Emperor of Everything* - Ray Aldridge  s  62
*Empire's End* - Allan Cole  s  1103
*End Game* - Robert Cain  s  830
*Enemy of My Enemy* - Ben Ohlander  s  4204
*Evil Triumphant* - Michael A. Stackpole  s  5199
*F.R.E.E.Lancers* - Mel Odom  s  4191
*The Face of the Waters* - Robert Silverberg  s  5029
*Far-Seer* - Robert J. Sawyer  s  4854
*Finity's End* - C.J. Cherryh  s  988
*Firedance* - Steven Barnes  s  360
*Firehand* - Andre Norton  s  4151
*Foragers* - Charles Oberndorf  s  4187
*The Forever Drug* - Steve Perry  s  4296
*Fortress of Forbidden Destiny* - Ryder Syvertson  s  5378
*The Fourth Rome* - David Drake  s  1631
*Free Radicals* - Jack McKinney  s  3848
*Freedom's Choice* - Anne McCaffrey  s  3733
*Freedom's Landing* - Anne McCaffrey  s  3734
*The Fugitive Worlds* - Bob Shaw  s  4942
*The Further Adventures of Batman 2: Featuring the Penguin* - Martin H. Greenberg  s  2391
*The Further Adventures of Batman 3: Featuring Catwoman* - Martin H. Greenberg  s  2392
*Future Eden* - J.M. Morgan  s  4001

*The Gap into Conflict: The Real Story* - Stephen R. Donaldson  s  1572
*The Gateway Trip: Tales and Vignettes of the Heechee* - Frederik Pohl  s  4346
*The Gathering Flame* - Debra Doyle  s  1599
*A Gathering of Stars* - Donald Moffitt  s  3947
*Ghost Dancers* - Brian Craig  s  1238
*The Glaive* - Cary Osborne  s  4227
*Gods of the Well of Souls* - Jack L. Chalker  s  954
*God's World* - Ian Watson  s  5636
*Godzilla 2000* - Marc Cerasini  s  949
*Gold Dragon* - Robert Cain  s  831
*The Golden Globe* - John Varley  s  5565
*Gorgon Child* - Steven Barnes  s  361
*Griffin's Egg* - Michael Swanwick  s  5370
*The Hand of Zei* - L. Sprague de Camp  s  1414
*Harm's Way* - Colin Greenland  s  2416
*Hellburner* - C.J. Cherryh  s  996
*Hellflower* - eluki bes shahar  s  473
*Heroes Die* - Matthew Woodring Stover  s  5319
*Hidden Fires* - Katharine Eliska Kimbriel  s  3117
*Hide and Seek* - Paul Preuss  s  4418
*Higher Education* - Charles Sheffield  s  4958
*The Hollow Earth: The Narrative of Mason Algiers Reynolds of Virginia* - Rudy Rucker  s  4705
*Hope of Earth* - Piers Anthony  s  175
*Hostile Takeover* - Jack McKinney  s  3849
*A Hunger in the Soul* - Mike Resnick  s  4545
*The Hunter on Arena* - Rose Estes  s  1838
*Hunter's Planet* - David Bischoff  s  492
*Hunting Party* - Elizabeth Moon  s  3968
*Igniting the Reaches* - David Drake  s  1633
*In the Shadow of the Moon* - Scott G. Gier  s  2224
*Inconstant Star* - Poul Anderson  s  129
*Infinity Hold* - Barry B. Longyear  s  3522
*Inquisitor* - Ian Watson  s  5637
*Invitation to the Game* - Monica Hughes  s  2807
*Iron Man: The Armor Trap* - Greg Cox  s  1227
*Iroshi* - Cary Osborne  s  4228
*Ivory: A Legend of Past and Future* - Mike Resnick  s  4547
*Jade Darcy and the Zen Pirates* - Stephen Goldin  s  2260
*Jaran* - Kate Elliott  s  1772
*Johnny Mnemonic* - Terry Bisson  s  505
*Judge Dredd* - Neal Barrett Jr.  s  366
*The Jungle* - David Drake  s  1634
*Jurassic Park* - Michael Crichton  s  1255
*Kahless* - Michael Jan Friedman  s  2065
*A Key for the Nonesuch* - Geary Gravel  s  2330
*The Khan's Persuasion* - Cynthia Felice  s  1914
*Kill Crazy* - L.S. Riker  s  4590
*Kit's Book* - C.J. Mills  s  3911
*Lair of the Cyclops* - Allen L. Wold  s  5933
*The LaNague Chronicles* - F. Paul Wilson  s  5889
*The Last Hawk* - Catherine Asaro  s  219
*The Last Rangers* - Jake Davis  s  1406
*The Last Stand of the DNA Cowboys* - Mick Farren  s  1879
*The Law of Becoming* - Kate Elliott  s  1774
*Leap Point* - Kay Kenyon  s  3063
*Legacy* - Steve White  s  5785
*A Life in the Future* - Martin Caidin  s  827
*Lifehouse* - Spider Robinson  s  4641
*The Light in Exile* - Cheryl J. Franklin  s  2038
*Living with Aliens* - John DeChancie  s  1460
*Lois & Clark* - C.J. Cherryh  s  999
*The Lost World* - Michael Crichton  s  1256
*Mad Roy's Light* - Paula King  s  3125
*The Madness Season* - C.S. Friedman  s  2058
*Maia's Veil* - P.K. McAllister  s  3707
*March or Die* - Andrew Keith  s  3035
*Mars Prime* - William C. Dietz  s  1548
*Mars—The Red Planet* - Mick Farren  s  1880
*Mars Underground* - William Hartmann  s  2584
*Mask of the Phantasm* - Geary Gravel  s  2331
*Matrix Man* - William C. Dietz  s  1549
*A Maze of Stars* - John Brunner  s  734
*McCade's Bounty* - William C. Dietz  s  1550

*Medicine Show* - Jody Lynn Nye   s   4172
*The Medusa Encounter* - Paul Preuss   s   4419
*Mercycle* - Piers Anthony   s   181
*The Middle of Nowhere* - David Gerrold   s   2209
*Mighty Good Road* - Melissa Scott   s   4897
*A Mind for Trade* - Andre Norton   s   4158
*Mirabile* - Janet Kagan   s   3001
*A Miracle of Rare Design* - Mike Resnick   s   4550
*The Missing Matter* - Thomas R.
   McDonough   s   3805
*Mistworld* - Simon R. Green   s   2372
*More than Fire* - Philip Jose Farmer   s   1871
*Mother Lode* - Zach Hughes   s   2812
*Mother of Plenty* - Colin Greenland   s   2417
*Muddle Earth* - John Brunner   s   735
*Murder in the Solid State* - Wil McCarthy   s   3764
*Mutant Hell* - Mark Grant   s   2324
*Mutants Amok* - Mark Grant   s   2325
*Nicoji* - M. Shayne Bell   s   434
*Night Lamp* - Jack Vance   s   5548
*Nightmare World* - David Stern   s   5261
*Night's Pawn* - Tom Dowd   s   1591
*No Limits* - Nigel Findley   s   1938
*Nomad* - David Alexander   s   66
*Ocean under the Ice* - Robert L. Forward   s   1988
*Oracle* - Mike Resnick   s   4551
*The Outskirter's Secret* - Rosemary Kirstein   s   3157
*Parable of the Sower* - Octavia E. Butler   s   792
*PartnerShip* - Anne McCaffrey   s   3741
*A Passage of Stars* - Alis A. Rasmussen   s   4482
*Pathways* - Jeri Taylor   s   5404
*Patton's Spaceship* - John Barnes   s   357
*The Persistence of Memory* - Karen Ripley   s   4592
*The Pharaoh Contract* - Ray Aldridge   s   63
*The Phoenix in Flight* - Sherwood Smith   s   5138
*Pirates of the Universe* - Terry Bisson   s   506
*Ports of Call* - Jack Vance   s   5549
*The Price of Ransom* - Alis A. Rasmussen   s   4483
*The Price of the Stars* - Debra Doyle   s   1604
*Prison Planet* - William C. Dietz   s   1551
*Prisoner of Conscience* - Susan R.
   Matthews   s   3693
*Promised Land* - Connie Willis   s   5872
*Psi-Man* - David Peters   s   4305
*Quasar* - Jamil Nasir   s   4071
*Rainbow Man* - M.J. Engh   s   1824
*Random Factor* - Joel Henry Sherman   s   4984
*Raptor* - Paul Zindel   s   6084
*Ray Bradbury Presents: Dinosaur Planet* - Stephen
   Leigh   s   3427
*Ray Bradbury Presents: Dinosaur World* - Stephen
   Leigh   s   3428
*Razor's Edge* - Lisanne Norman   s   4139
*Realtime Interrupt* - James P. Hogan   s   2729
*Reckoning Infinity* - John E. Stith   s   5304
*Red Planet* - Robert A. Heinlein   s   2647
*Red Planet Run* - Dana Stabenow   s   5187
*Redline the Stars* - Andre Norton   s   4160
*Redliners* - David Drake   s   1641
*Regenesis* - Julia Ecklar   s   1729
*The Remarkables* - Robert Reed   s   4507
*Rememory* - John Gregory Betancourt   s   481
*Return Fire* - Charles Ingrid   s   2833
*The Return of the Breakneck Boys* - Geary
   Gravel   s   2332
*Revolution's Shore* - Alis A. Rasmussen   s   4484
*The Rifter's Covenant* - Sherwood Smith   s   5140
*Rimrunners* - C.J. Cherryh   s   1001
*The Rising* - James Doohan   s   1579
*Ruler of Naught* - Sherwood Smith   s   5141
*The Run to Chaos Keep* - Jack L. Chalker   s   960
*The Salukan Gambit* - Sean Dalton   s   1333
*Satellite Night News* - Jack Hopkins   s   2770
*Scorpio* - Alex McDonough   s   3802
*Scorpio Descending* - Alex McDonough   s   3803
*Scorpio Rising* - Alex McDonough   s   3804
*A Screaming Across the Sky* - Brian Daley   s   1315
*seaQuest DSV: Fire Below* - Matthew J.
   Costello   s   1201

*seaQuest DSV: The Novel* - Diane Duane   s   1666
*Seasons of Plenty* - Colin Greenland   s   2418
*Second Fire* - Mike Moscoe   s   4040
*Seeking the Dream Brother* - Marcia J.
   Bennett   s   451
*Semper Mars* - Ian Douglas   s   1585
*Serpent Catch* - Dave Wolverton   s   5956
*Serpent's Gift* - A.C. Crispin   s   1261
*Shadow of the Well of Souls* - Jack L.
   Chalker   s   961
*Shadowkill* - Jo Clayton   s   1069
*Shadowplay* - Jo Clayton   s   1070
*Shadowspeer* - Jo Clayton   s   1071
*Shame of Man* - Piers Anthony   s   188
*The Sharp End* - David Drake   s   1643
*The Ship Avenged* - S.M. Stirling   s   5298
*The Ship Who Searched* - Anne McCaffrey   s   3749
*Signs of Life* - Cherry Wilder   s   5804
*The Silicon Man* - Charles Platt   s   4343
*Sliders: The Novel* - Brad Linaweaver   s   3467
*Snowmen* - Jerry Earl Brown   s   725
*Songs of Chaos* - S.N. Lewitt   s   3452
*Specterworld* - Isidore Haiblum   s   2480
*Spider-Man: The Venom Factor* - Diane
   Duane   s   1667
*Spindoc* - Steve Perry   s   4300
*Sporting Chance* - Elizabeth Moon   s   3974
*The Square Deal* - David Drake   s   1644
*The Stainless Steel Rat Goes to Hell* - Harry
   Harrison   s   2574
*The Stainless Steel Rat Sings the Blues* - Harry
   Harrison   s   2575
*Star Sister* - Juanita Coulson   s   1211
*Starfire Down* - Lee McKeone   s   3830
*Starfleet Academy* - Diane Carey   s   905
*StarGate* - Dean Devlin   s   1509
*Starliner* - David Drake   s   1645
*Starpilot's Grave* - Debra Doyle   s   1606
*Strings* - Dave Duncan   s   1689
*Summertide* - Charles Sheffield   s   4965
*Take Back Plenty* - Colin Greenland   s   2419
*Tales From the Mos Eisley Cantina* - Kevin J.
   Anderson   s   115
*Taylor's Ark* - Jody Lynn Nye   s   4176
*Tek Money* - William Shatner   s   4935
*Tek Net* - William Shatner   s   4936
*Tek Power* - William Shatner   s   4937
*Tek Vengeance* - William Shatner   s   4938
*TekLab* - William Shatner   s   4939
*TekLords* - William Shatner   s   4940
*The Tenth Class* - Karen Ripley   s   4594
*Threshold* - Janet Morris   s   4018
*Through the Breach* - David Drake   s   1647
*Timecop* - S.D. Perry   s   4286
*To Your Scattered Bodies Go* - Philip Jose
   Farmer   s   1876
*Total Recall* - Piers Anthony   s   193
*The Touch of Your Shadow, the Whisper of Your Name*
   - Neal Barrett Jr.   s   367
*Traitor Winds* - L.A. Graf   s   2298
*Transcendence* - Charles Sheffield   s   4967
*Tripoint* - C.J. Cherryh   s   1003
*The Trumpets of Tagan* - Simon Lang   s   3316
*Trust Territory* - Janet Morris   s   4019
*Two-Bit Heroes* - Doris Egan   s   1757
*Tyrannosaurus Rex* - J.F. Rivkin   s   4597
*The Ultimate Spider-Man* - Stan Lee   s   3403
*Under Fire* - Kenneth Von Gunden   s   5589
*Unwillingly to Earth* - Pauline Ashwell   s   231
*Vast* - Linda Nagata   s   4067
*The Venom Trees of Sunga* - L. Sprague de
   Camp   s   1420
*The VMR Theory* - Robert Frezza   s   2055
*The Vor Game* - Lois McMaster Bujold   s   764
*Voyage to the Red Planet* - Terry Bisson   s   508
*Vulcan's Forge* - Susan Shwartz   s   5019
*Vurt* - Jeff Noon   s   4136
*The War Minstrels* - Karen Haber   s   2477
*The War of the Sky Lords* - John Brosnan   s   721

*The Warden of Horses* - Karen Ripley   s   4595
*Warlock and Son* - Christopher Stasheff   s   5224
*Warrior* - Donald E. McQuinn   s   3863
*West of January* - Dave Duncan   s   1691
*What Savage Beast* - Peter David   s   1390
*Where the Ships Die* - William C. Dietz   s   1553
*The Widowmaker* - Mike Resnick   s   4559
*The Widowmaker Reborn* - Mike Resnick   s   4560
*Wings* - Terry Pratchett   s   4403
*Winning Colors* - Elizabeth Moon   s   3976
*A Wizard in Midgard* - Christopher Stasheff   s   5231
*Woman Without a Shadow* - Karen Haber   s   2478
*Worf's First Adventure* - Peter David   s   1391
*A World Lost* - James B. Johnson   s   2921
*The Yngling and the Circle of Power* - John
   Dalmas   s   1328
*The Yngling in Yamato* - John Dalmas   s   1329

## Science Fiction — Alternate History

*Apacheria* - Jake Page   s   4233
*Back in the USSA* - Kim Newman   s   4095
*By Any Other Fame* - Mike Resnick   s   4540
*Caesar's Bicycle* - John Barnes   s   350
*Dinosaur Summer* - Greg Bear   s   416
*The Ghost of the Revelator* - L.E. Modesitt
   Jr.   s   3931
*The Iron Bridge* - David Morse   s   4036
*Pastwatch: The Redemption of Christopher Columbus* -
   Orson Scott Card   s   895
*Stars and Stripes Forever* - Harry Harrison   s   2577
*The Steampunk Trilogy* - Paul Di Filippo   s   1518
*The Time Ships* - Stephen Baxter   s   403
*The White Guardian* - Ronald Anthony
   Cross   s   1275
*Worldwar: In the Balance* - Harry
   Turtledove   s   5515
*Worldwar: Striking the Balance* - Harry
   Turtledove   s   5516

## Science Fiction — Alternate Intelligence

*/* - Greg Bear   s   413
*3001: The Final Odyssey* - Arthur C.
   Clarke   s   1053
*Accidental Creatures* - Anne Harris   s   2558
*Ark Liberty* - Will Bradley   s   656
*Armed Memory* - Jim Young   s   6048
*Beholder's Eye* - Julie E. Czerneda   s   1303
*Berserker Kill* - Fred Saberhagen   s   4761
*Blade Runner: Replicant Night* - K.W. Jeter   s   2907
*Bloom* - Wil McCarthy   s   3761
*Challenger's Hope* - David Feintuch   s   1899
*Chaos Come Again* - Wilhelmina Baird   s   293
*The Children Star* - Joan Slonczewski   s   5090
*Codgerspace* - Alan Dean Foster   s   1999
*Correspondence* - Sue Thomas   s   5450
*Cyberweb* - Lisa Mason   s   3662
*Daughter of Elysium* - Joan Slonczewski   s   5091
*Deception Well* - Linda Nagata   s   4065
*Deep Freeze* - Zach Hughes   s   2811
*Deus X* - Norman Spinrad   s   5171
*Diaspora* - Greg Egan   s   1759
*Donnerjack* - Roger Zelazny   s   6063
*Dream Maker* - W.A. Harbinson   s   2542
*Dream of Glass* - Jean Mark Gawron   s   2163
*Dreaming Metal* - Melissa Scott   s   4895
*Dreamships* - Melissa Scott   s   4896
*Earthling* - Tony Daniel   s   1336
*Echoes of the Well of Souls* - Jack L.
   Chalker   s   953
*Entoverse* - James P. Hogan   s   2724
*Extreme Paranoia: Nobody Knows the Trouble I've
   Shot* - Ken Rolston   s   4662
*The Eyes of God* - Mark Kreighbaum   s   3231
*The Face of Apollo* - Fred Saberhagen   s   4766
*A Fire upon the Deep* - Vernor Vinge   s   5573
*The Fleet of Stars* - Poul Anderson   s   126

*Fools* - Pat Cadigan   s   805
*Fool's War* - Sarah Zettel   s   6079
*Fortress on the Sun* - Paul Cook   s   1157
*Freeware* - Rudy Rucker   s   4703
*Galatea 2.2* - Richard M. Powers   s   4381
*The Hacker and the Ants* - Rudy Rucker   s   4704
*Halo* - Tom Maddox   s   3604
*Harvest the Fire* - Poul Anderson   s   128
*Hellspark* - Janet Kagan   s   3000
*Honor of the Regiment* - Bill Fawcett   s   1896
*The Imperium Game* - K.D. Wentworth   s   5753
*Infectress* - Tom Cool   s   1167
*A King of Infinite Space* - Allen Steele   s   5243
*Lady El* - Jim Starlin   s   5213
*Living Real* - James C. Bassett   s   386
*Man Plus* - Frederik Pohl   s   4348
*A Maze of Stars* - John Brunner   s   734
*ME: A Novel of Self Discovery* - Thomas T.
   Thomas   s   5452
*Memento Mori* - Shariann Lewitt   s   3454
*Mid-Flinx* - Alan Dean Foster   s   2010
*Mutineers' Moon* - David Weber   s   5677
*The Napoleon Wager* - William R.
   Forstchen   s   1980
*The Nature of Smoke* - Anne Harris   s   2559
*Nightside the Long Sun* - Gene Wolfe   s   5943
*Palace* - Katharine Kerr   s   3072
*Path of the Fury* - David Weber   s   5680
*Permutation City* - Greg Egan   s   1761
*Preternatural* - Margaret Wander Bonanno   s   568
*Probe* - Edward M. Lerner   s   3437
*Proxies* - Laura J. Mixon   s   3922
*Psykosis* - Wilhelmina Baird   s   296
*Queen City Jazz* - Kathleen Ann Goonan   s   2275
*Red Dust* - Paul J. McAuley   s   3715
*Revolutionary* - S. Andrew Swann   s   5367
*The Rise of Endymion* - Dan Simmons   s   5059
*A Second Infinity* - Michael D. Weaver   s   5660
*The Shapes of Their Hearts* - Melissa Scott   s   4901
*The Ship Errant* - Jody Lynn Nye   s   4175
*The Ships of Earth* - Orson Scott Card   s   897
*Shiva in Steel* - Fred Saberhagen   s   4775
*Sideshow* - Sheri S. Tepper   s   5436
*Solis* - A.A. Attanasio   s   272
*Solo* - Robert Mason   s   3665
*Someone to Watch over Me* - Tricia
   Sullivan   s   5355
*Standing Wave* - Howard V. Hendrix   s   2661
*The Stars Are Also Fire* - Poul Anderson   s   134
*Starswarm* - Jerry Pournelle   s   4379
*Steel Beach* - John Varley   s   5566
*Take Back Plenty* - Colin Greenland   s   2419
*The Terminal Experiment* - Robert J.
   Sawyer   s   4860
*Terminal Games* - Cole Perriman   s   4283
*This Side of Judgment* - J.R. Dunn   s   1696
*Title Deleted for Security Reasons* - Ed
   Blome   s   553
*Tomorrow and Tomorrow* - Charles
   Sheffield   s   4966
*The Trinity Vector* - Steve Perry   s   4302
*The Turing Option* - Harry Harrison   s   2579
*Virtual Girl* - Amy Thomson   s   5462
*Virtuosity* - Terry Bisson   s   507
*Warstrider: Netlink* - William H. Keith Jr.   s   3038
*The White Abacus* - Damien Broderick   s   708
*Wildlife* - James Patrick Kelly   s   3049

**Science Fiction — Alternate Universe**

*1901* - Robert Conroy   s   1139
*1945* - Newt Gingrich   s   2239
*Ace in the Hole* - George R.R. Martin   s   3641
*Alternate Americas* - Gregory Benford   s   442
*Alternate Kennedys* - Mike Resnick   s   4536
*Alternate Presidents* - Mike Resnick   s   4537
*Alternate Warriors* - Mike Resnick   s   4538
*Alternate Wars* - Gregory Benford   s   443

*Anti-Ice* - Stephen Baxter   s   398
*Archangel* - Michael Conner   s   1133
*Black Trump* - George R.R. Martin   s   3642
*Branch Point* - Mona Clee   s   1074
*Bride of the Castle* - John DeChancie   s   1452
*Bring the Jubilee* - Ward Moore   s   3993
*The Broken Wheel* - David Wingrove   s   5918
*Bully!* - Mike Resnick   s   4539
*Castle Dreams* - John DeChancie   s   1453
*Castle Spellbound* - John DeChancie   s   1454
*Castle War!* - John DeChancie   s   1455
*Celestial Matters* - Richard Garfinkle   s   2140
*Chekhov's Journey* - Ian Watson   s   5633
*Choose Your Enemies Carefully* - Robert N.
   Charrette   s   971
*Comeback Tour: The Sky Belongs to the Stars* - Jack
   Yeovil   s   6020
*Converse and Conflict* - L. Neil Smith   s   5130
*Count Geiger's Blues* - Michael Bishop   s   499
*Crosstime Traffic* - Lawrence Watt-Evans   s   5641
*Cry Republic* - Kirk Mitchell   s   3917
*Dark Mirror* - Diane Duane   s   1658
*Dealer's Choice* - George R.R. Martin   s   3643
*Departures* - Harry Turtledove   s   5498
*The Difference Engine* - William Gibson   s   2217
*Drakon* - S.M. Stirling   s   5294
*Elvissey* - Jack Womack   s   5957
*Et Tu, Babe* - Mark Leyner   s   3455
*Eye in the Sky* - Philip K. Dick   s   1521
*Fatherland* - Robert Harris   s   2564
*First Frontier* - Diane Carey   s   902
*The Fourth Guardian* - Ronald Anthony
   Cross   s   1273
*Freeze Frames* - Katharine Kerr   s   3071
*From Time to Time* - Jack Finney   s   1941
*Ghost Dancers* - Brian Craig   s   1238
*The Great War: American Front* - Harry
   Turtledove   s   5501
*The Guns of the South: A Novel of the Civil War* -
   Harry Turtledove   s   5502
*Gypsies* - Robert Charles Wilson   s   5908
*Harm's Way* - Colin Greenland   s   2416
*The Hollow Earth: The Narrative of Mason Algiers
   Reynolds of Virginia* - Rudy Rucker   s   4705
*The Hot-Wired Dodo* - Jack L. Chalker   s   956
*Hour of the Scorpion* - Matthew J. Costello   s   1199
*Imzadi* - Peter David   s   1383
*Jaguar* - Bill Ransom   s   4477
*Jaydium* - Deborah Wheeler   s   5774
*Jokertown Shuffle* - George R.R. Martin   s   3646
*A Key for the Nonesuch* - Geary Gravel   s   2330
*Lake of the Long Sun* - Gene Wolfe   s   5942
*Lion Time in Timbuctoo* - Robert Silverberg   s   5036
*Lord Conrad's Lady* - Leo Frankowski   s   2046
*The Lost Guardian* - Ronald Anthony Cross   s   1274
*Lurid Dreams* - Charles L. Harness   s   2546
*Mainline* - Deborah Christian   s   1026
*Marked Cards* - George R.R. Martin   s   3647
*The Memory Cathedral* - Jack Dann   s   1341
*The Middle Kingdom* - David Wingrove   s   5919
*Mysterium* - Robert Charles Wilson   s   5911
*Necrom* - Mick Farren   s   1881
*Never Deal with a Dragon* - Robert N.
   Charrette   s   975
*An Oblique Approach* - David Drake   s   1638
*Of Beginnings and Endings* - Robert Adams   s   33
*One King's Way* - Harry Harrison   s   2572
*Orion and the Conqueror* - Ben Bova   s   590
*Pacific Edge* - Kim Stanley Robinson   s   4634
*Parallelities* - Alan Dean Foster   s   2012
*Paths to Otherwhere* - James P. Hogan   s   2728
*Patton's Spaceship* - John Barnes   s   357
*Peter Nevsky and the True Story of the Russian Moon
   Landing* - John Calvin Batchelor   s   388
*Petrogypsies* - Rory Harper   s   2549
*The Race for God* - Brian Herbert   s   2666
*Rally Cry!* - William R. Forstchen   s   1982
*Reluctant Voyagers* - Elisabeth Vonarburg   s   5591
*Resurrection* - Katharine Kerr   s   3075

*The Resurrections* - Simon Louvish   s   3528
*Samurai Cat Goes to the Movies* - Mark E.
   Rogers   s   4656
*The Shining Ones* - Paul Preuss   s   4421
*The Silent Stars Go By* - James White   s   5781
*Sliders: The Novel* - Brad Linaweaver   s   3467
*Spectre* - William Shatner   s   4934
*The Stalk* - Janet Morris   s   4016
*The Stone Dogs* - S.M. Stirling   s   5300
*Strange Attractors* - William Sleator   s   5088
*Stranger Suns* - George Zebrowski   s   6060
*The Sword of Samurai Cat* - Mark E.
   Rogers   s   4657
*Terraplane* - Jack Womack   s   5960
*Time Blender* - Michael Dorn   s   1581
*The Tranquility Alternative* - Allen Steele   s   5248
*The Transmigration of Souls* - William
   Barton   s   382
*The Trinity Paradox* - Kevin J. Anderson   s   116
*Triumph* - Ben Bova   s   598
*Turn of the Cards* - Victor Milan   s   3891
*The Two Georges* - Richard Dreyfuss   s   1655
*Under the Yoke* - S.M. Stirling   s   5301
*Voyager* - Stephen Baxter   s   406
*The Warden of Horses* - Karen Ripley   s   4595
*What Savage Beast* - Peter David   s   1390
*The Wild Blue and the Gray* - William
   Sanders   s   4814
*Wildside* - Steven Gould   s   2291
*The World Next Door* - Brad Ferguson   s   1924
*A World of Difference* - Harry Turtledove   s   5514
*Worldwar: Upsetting the Balance* - Harry
   Turtledove   s   5518

**Science Fiction — Alternate World**

*Darwinia* - Robert Charles Wilson   s   5906
*Never Sound Retreat* - William R.
   Forstchen   s   1981

**Science Fiction — Anthology**

*The 1990 Annual World's Best Science Fiction* -
   Donald A. Wollheim   s   5948
*2041: Twelve Short Stories about the Future by Top
   Science Fiction Writers* - Jane Yolen   s   6027
*Ackermanthology!* - Forrest J. Ackerman   s   24
*Alien Pets* - Denise Little   s   3500
*Alternate Americas* - Gregory Benford   s   442
*Alternate Generals* - Harry Turtledove   s   5495
*Alternate Kennedys* - Mike Resnick   s   4536
*Alternate Presidents* - Mike Resnick   s   4537
*Alternate Warriors* - Mike Resnick   s   4538
*Alternate Wars* - Gregory Benford   s   443
*Amazing Stories: The Anthology* - Kim
   Mohan   s   3948
*The Ascent of Wonder: The Evolution of Hard SF* -
   David G. Hartwell   s   2585
*Battlestation* - David Drake   s   1627
*The Best From Fantasy & Science Fiction: A 45th
   Anniversary Anthology* - Kristine Kathryn
   Rusch   s   4712
*The Best of Crank!* - Bryan Cholfin   s   1023
*The Best of Interzone* - David Pringle   s   4439
*The Best of Pulphouse: The Hardback Magazine* -
   Kristine Kathryn Rusch   s   4713
*By Any Other Fame* - Mike Resnick   s   4540
*Carmen Miranda's Ghost Is Haunting Space Station
   Three* - Don Sakers   s   4785
*Cats in Space and Other Places* - Bill
   Fawcett   s   1895
*Christmas Stars* - David G. Hartwell   s   2589
*CoDominium: Revolt on War World* - Jerry
   Pournelle   s   4373
*Dealer's Choice* - George R.R. Martin   s   3643
*Dinosaurs* - Martin H. Greenberg   s   2386
*Domains of Darkover* - Marion Zimmer
   Bradley   s   631

*Don't Forget Your Spacesuit, Dear* - Jody Lynn Nye   s   4169
*Endgame* - C.J. Cherryh   s   986
*Far Futures* - Gregory Benford   s   445
*Flood Tide* - C.J. Cherryh   s   989
*Free Space* - Brad Linaweaver   s   3466
*Full Spectrum 2* - Lou Aronica   s   214
*Full Spectrum 3* - Lou Aronica   s   215
*Full Spectrum 4* - Lou Aronica   s   216
*Full Spectrum 5* - Jennifer Hershey   s   2679
*The Further Adventures of Batman 2: Featuring the Penguin* - Martin H. Greenberg   s   2391
*The Further Adventures of Batman 3: Featuring Catwoman* - Martin H. Greenberg   s   2392
*The Further Adventures of Superman* - Martin H. Greenberg   s   2393
*Future Boston* - David Alexander Smith   s   5107
*Future Crime: An Anthology of the Shape of Crime to Come* - Cynthia Manson   s   3619
*Future Earths: Under African Skies* - Mike Resnick   s   4544
*Future Net* - Martin H. Greenberg   s   2394
*Future on Fire* - Orson Scott Card   s   887
*Future on Ice* - Orson Scott Card   s   888
*Future Primitive: The New Ecotopias* - Kim Stanley Robinson   s   4631
*The Good Old Stuff* - Gardner Dozois   s   1609
*The Harriers* - Gordon R. Dickson   s   1535
*Honor of the Regiment* - Bill Fawcett   s   1896
*How to Save the World* - Charles Sheffield   s   4959
*Inside the Funhouse* - Mike Resnick   s   4546
*Intersections: The Sycamore Hill Anthology* - John Kessel   s   3085
*Isaac Asimov Presents the Great SF Stories: 20 (1958)* - Isaac Asimov   s   238
*Isaac Asimov Presents the Great SF Stories: 21 (1959)* - Isaac Asimov   s   239
*Isaac Asimov Presents the Great SF Stories: 22 (1959)* - Isaac Asimov   s   240
*Isaac Asimov Presents the Great SF Stories: 23 (1961)* - Isaac Asimov   s   241
*Isaac Asimov Presents the Great SF Stories: 24 (1962)* - Isaac Asimov   s   242
*Isaac Asimov Presents the Great SF Stories: 25 (1963)* - Isaac Asimov   s   243
*L. Ron Hubbard Presents Writers of the Future, Volume VII* - Algis Budrys   s   754
*L. Ron Hubbard Presents Writers of the Future, Volume VIII* - Algis Budrys   s   755
*L. Ron Hubbard Presents Writers of the Future, Volume IX* - Dave Wolverton   s   5952
*L. Ron Hubbard Presents Writers of the Future, Volume XII* - Dave Wolverton   s   5953
*L. Ron Hubbard Presents Writers of the Future, Volume XIV* - Dave Wolverton   s   5954
*Lamps on the Brow* - James Cahill   s   823
*Leroni of Darkover* - Marion Zimmer Bradley   s   642
*Life Among the Asteroids* - Jerry Pournelle   s   4376
*Machines That Kill* - Fred Saberhagen   s   4769
*The Mammoth Book of Fantastic Science Fiction* - Isaac Asimov   s   245
*The Mammoth Book of Modern Science Fiction: Short Novels of the 1980s* - Isaac Asimov   s   246
*Man-Kzin Wars III* - Larry Niven   s   4123
*Man-Kzin Wars IV* - Larry Niven   s   4124
*Man-Kzin Wars V* - Larry Niven   s   4125
*Meltdown!* - Caro Soles   s   5154
*Modern Classic Short Novels of Science Fiction* - Gardner Dozois   s   1612
*Modern Classics of Science Fiction* - Gardner Dozois   s   1614
*More Amazing Stories* - Kim Mohan   s   3949
*Murasaki* - Robert Silverberg   s   5038
*Nanodreams* - Elton Elliott   s   1770
*Nebula Awards 24* - Michael Bishop   s   500
*Nebula Awards 25* - Michael Bishop   s   501
*Nebula Awards 26* - James Morrow   s   4031
*Nebula Awards 27* - James Morrow   s   4032

*Nebula Awards 28* - James Morrow   s   4033
*Nebula Awards 29* - Pamela Sargent   s   4822
*Nebula Awards 30* - Pamela Sargent   s   4823
*Nebula Awards 31* - Pamela Sargent   s   4824
*Nebula Awards 32* - Jack Dann   s   1342
*New Eves: Science Fiction about the Extraordinary Women of Today and Tomorrow* - Janrae Frank   s   2035
*The New Hugo Winners, Volume III* - Connie Willis   s   5871
*The New Hugo Winners, Volume IV* - Martin H. Greenberg   s   2401
*New Legends* - Greg Bear   s   422
*New Worlds* - David Garnett   s   2148
*Newer York* - Lawrence Watt-Evans   s   5642
*Northern Stars: The Anthology of Canadian Science Fiction* - David G. Hartwell   s   2593
*The Norton Book of Science Fiction: North American Science Fiction, 1960-1990* - Ursula K. Le Guin   s   3381
*Off Limits: Tales of Alien Sex* - Ellen Datlow   s   1362
*Omni Best Science Fiction One* - Ellen Datlow   s   1363
*Omni Best Science Fiction Three* - Ellen Datlow   s   1364
*Omni Visions One* - Ellen Datlow   s   1365
*The Oxford Book of Science Fiction Stories* - Tom Shippey   s   5004
*The Playboy Book of Science Fiction* - Alice K. Turner   s   5489
*Pulphouse, Issue 8: Science Fiction* - Kristine Kathryn Rusch   s   4725
*Pulphouse, Issue 11: Speculative Fiction* - Kristine Kathryn Rusch   s   4721
*Quest to Riverworld* - Philip Jose Farmer   s   1872
*The Random House Book of Science Fiction Stories* - Mike Ashley   s   229
*Renunciates of Darkover* - Marion Zimmer Bradley   s   644
*Requiem* - Robert A. Heinlein   s   2648
*Sacred Visions* - Andrew M. Greeley   s   2343
*The Science Fiction Century* - David G. Hartwell   s   2594
*Sherlock Holmes in Orbit* - Mike Resnick   s   4556
*Space Opera* - Anne McCaffrey   s   3751
*Spec-Lit: Speculative Fiction, Number 1* - Phyllis Eisenstein   s   1766
*Spec-Lit: Speculative Fiction, Number 2* - Phyllis Eisenstein   s   1767
*A Starfarer's Dozen* - Michael Stearns   s   5238
*Starlight 1* - Patrick Nielsen Hayden   s   2634
*Starlight 2* - Patrick Nielsen Hayden   s   2635
*The Super Hugos* - Martin H. Greenberg   s   2405
*Tales From Jabba's Palace* - Kevin J. Anderson   s   114
*Tales From the Mos Eisley Cantina* - Kevin J. Anderson   s   115
*Tales of Riverworld* - Philip Jose Farmer   s   1875
*There Won't Be War* - Harry Harrison   s   2578
*The Ultimate Alien* - Byron Preiss   s   4406
*The Ultimate Spider-Man* - Stan Lee   s   3403
*Universe 2* - Robert Silverberg   s   5045
*Universe 3* - Robert Silverberg   s   5046
*Visions of Wonder: The Science Fiction Research Association Anthology* - David G. Hartwell   s   2595
*War of the Worlds: Global Dispatches* - Kevin J. Anderson   s   119
*Washed by a Wave of Wind* - M. Shayne Bell   s   435
*Whatdunits* - Mike Resnick   s   4558
*Women at War* - Lois McMaster Bujold   s   765
*Women of Wonder, the Classic Years: Science Fiction by Women From the 1940s to the 1970s* - Pamela Sargent   s   4825
*Women of Wonder, the Contemporary Years: Science Fiction by Women From the 1970s to the 1990s* - Pamela Sargent   s   4826

*The Year's Best Science Fiction: Eighth Annual Collection* - Gardner Dozois   s   1616
*The Year's Best Science Fiction: Eleventh Annual Collection* - Gardner Dozois   s   1617
*The Year's Best Science Fiction: Fifteenth Annual Collection* - Gardner Dozois   s   1618
*The Year's Best Science Fiction: Fourteenth Annual Collection* - Gardner Dozois   s   1619
*The Year's Best Science Fiction: Ninth Annual Collection* - Gardner Dozois   s   1620
*The Year's Best Science Fiction: Seventh Annual Collection* - Gardner Dozois   s   1621
*The Year's Best Science Fiction: Tenth Annual Collection* - Gardner Dozois   s   1622
*The Year's Best Science Fiction: Thirteenth Annual Collection* - Gardner Dozois   s   1623
*The Year's Best Science Fiction: Twelfth Annual Collection* - Gardner Dozois   s   1624
*Year's Best SF* - David G. Hartwell   s   2596
*Year's Best SF 2* - David G. Hartwell   s   2597
*Year's Best SF 3* - David G. Hartwell   s   2598

## Science Fiction — Arts

*Blood Lines* - William R. Burkett Jr.   s   774
*Carve the Sky* - Alexander Jablokov   s   2836
*Chimera* - Mary Rosenblum   s   4677
*The City, Not Long After* - Pat Murphy   s   4051
*Clipjoint* - Wilhelmina Baird   s   294
*Cortez on Jupiter* - Ernest Hogan   s   2721
*Count Geiger's Blues* - Michael Bishop   s   499
*Crashcourse* - Wilhelmina Baird   s   295
*Dancing on Air* - Nancy Kress   s   3240
*Dreaming Metal* - Melissa Scott   s   4895
*An Earthly Crown* - Kate Elliott   s   1771
*The Golden Globe* - John Varley   s   5565
*Harmony* - Marjorie Bradley Kellogg   s   3046
*The Hidden War* - Michael Armstrong   s   209
*Interface Masque* - Shariann Lewitt   s   3453
*Memento Mori* - Shariann Lewitt   s   3454
*The Merro Tree* - Katie Waitman   s   5609
*A Million Open Doors* - John Barnes   s   353
*Mind Snare* - Gayle Greeno   s   2422
*Mirror to the Sky* - Mark S. Geston   s   2213
*Mississippi Blues* - Kathleen Ann Goonan   s   2274
*The Night Mayor* - Kim Newman   s   4099
*Outnumbering the Dead* - Frederik Pohl   s   4352
*The Quicksilver Screen* - Don H. DeBrandt   s   1449
*Reality Is What You Can Get Away With: An Illustrated Screenplay* - Robert Anton Wilson   s   5904
*Rock 'n' Roll Babes From Outer Space* - Linda Javin   s   2880
*Sailor Song* - Ken Kesey   s   3082
*Space Opera* - Anne McCaffrey   s   3751
*Starmind* - Spider Robinson   s   4642
*Starseed* - Spider Robinson   s   4643
*The Stone Garden* - Mary Rosenblum   s   4679
*Subterranean Gallery* - Richard Paul Russo   s   4750
*The Swords of Zinjaban* - L. Sprague de Camp   s   1418
*Synners* - Pat Cadigan   s   808
*Timeshare* - Joshua Dann   s   1344
*The Unwound Way* - William Adams   s   35
*Virtual Death* - Shale Aaron   s   5
*Voyage to the Red Planet* - Terry Bisson   s   508
*We Open on Venus* - Christopher Stasheff   s   5227

## Science Fiction — Collection

*Alien Bootlegger and Other Stories* - Rebecca Ore   s   4216
*An Alien Land* - Mike Resnick   s   4535
*Alien Minds* - Keith Laumer   s   3342
*Alien Plot* - Piers Anthony   s   161
*The Aliens of Earth* - Nancy Kress   s   3234
*All-American Alien Boy* - Allen Steele   s   5240
*All One Universe* - Poul Anderson   s   123

*And the Angels Sing* - Kate Wilhelm   s   5805
*The Annotated H.P. Lovecraft* - H.P.
   Lovecraft   s   3529
*Apostrophes and Apocalypses* - John Barnes   s   349
*The Asimov Chronicles: Fifty Years of Isaac Asimov* -
   Isaac Asimov   s   232
*The Atrocity Exhibition* - J.G. Ballard   s   319
*The Avram Davidson Treasury* - Avram
   Davidson   s   1395
*Axiomatic* - Greg Egan   s   1758
*Beaker's Dozen* - Nancy Kress   s   3235
*Bears Discover Fire* - Terry Bisson   s   503
*Before. . .12:01. . .and After* - Richard A.
   Lupoff   s   3571
*Berserker Lies* - Fred Saberhagen   s   4762
*Bible Stories for Adults* - James Morrow   s   4028
*Black Glass: Short Fictions* - Karen Joy
   Fowler   s   2027
*Bloodchild and Other Stories* - Octavia E.
   Butler   s   790
*The Breath of Suspension* - Alexander
   Jablokov   s   2835
*The Bug Life Chronicles* - Phillip C.
   Jennings   s   2890
*Bunch!* - David R. Bunch   s   772
*Castle of Days* - Gene Wolfe   s   5938
*Caught in the Crossfire* - David Drake   s   1628
*Children of the Wind: Five Novellas* - Kate
   Wilhelm   s   5807
*The Chronicles of Pern: First Fall* - Anne
   McCaffrey   s   3721
*The Collected Feghoot* - Grendel Briarton   s   677
*The Collected Stories of Philip K. Dick, Volume One:
   The Short Happy Life of the Brown Oxford* - Philip
   K. Dick   s   1519
*The Collected Stories of Philip K. Dick, Volume Two:
   We Can Remember It for You Wholesale* - Philip K.
   Dick   s   1520
*The Collected Stories of Robert Silverberg, Volume 1:
   Secret Sharers* - Robert Silverberg   s   5028
*The Complete Stories - Volume 1* - Isaac
   Asimov   s   233
*The Complete Stories - Volume 2* - Isaac
   Asimov   s   234
*Crashlander* - Larry Niven   s   4118
*Crosstime Traffic* - Lawrence Watt-Evans   s   5641
*Crystal Express* - Bruce Sterling   s   5255
*Daily Voices* - Lisa Goldstein   s   2261
*Dancing with Myself* - Charles Sheffield   s   4953
*Departures* - Harry Turtledove   s   5498
*Dirty Work* - Pat Cadigan   s   804
*Distant Friends and Others* - Timothy Zahn   s   6053
*Dreamweaver's Dilemma* - Lois McMaster
   Bujold   s   759
*Earthgrip* - Harry Turtledove   s   5499
*Endangered Species* - Gene Wolfe   s   5940
*Facets* - Walter Jon Williams   s   5837
*First Contacts: The Essential Murray Leinster* -
   Murray Leinster   s   3430
*A Fisherman of the Inland Sea* - Ursula K. Le
   Guin   s   3379
*Flatlander* - Larry Niven   s   4121
*The Forest of Time and Other Stories* - Michael
   Flynn   s   1963
*Fractal Paisleys* - Paul Di Filippo   s   1515
*Frankensteins and Foreign Devils* - Walter Jon
   Williams   s   5838
*From the End of the Twentieth Century* - John M.
   Ford   s   1969
*Frost and Fire* - Roger Zelazny   s   6067
*Future Crime* - Ben Bova   s   585
*Galactic Dreams* - Harry Harrison   s   2569
*The Gateway Trip: Tales and Vignettes of the Heechee*
   - Frederik Pohl   s   4346
*Geodesic Dreams: The Best Short Fiction of Gardner
   Dozois* - Gardner Dozois   s   1608
*Georgia on My Mind and Other Places* - Charles
   Sheffield   s   4956

*The Girl from Mars & The Prince of Space* - Jack
   Williamson   s   5864
*The Girl Who Heard Dragons* - Anne
   McCaffrey   s   3736
*Globalhead* - Bruce Sterling   s   5257
*God's Nose* - Damon Knight   s   3185
*Going Home Again* - Howard Waldrop   s   5613
*Gold: The Final Science Fiction Collection* - Isaac
   Asimov   s   237
*Gone to Earth* - Roger Zelazny   s   6068
*Gravity's Angels* - Michael Swanwick   s   5369
*Her Smoke Rose Up Forever* - James Tiptree
   Jr.   s   5477
*His Share of Glory: The Complete Short Science
   Fiction of C.M. Kornbluth* - C.M.
   Kornbluth   s   3219
*Impossible Things* - Connie Willis   s   5869
*Ingathering: The Complete People Stories of Zenna
   Henderson* - Zenna Henderson   s   2659
*The Invisible Country* - Paul J. McAuley   s   3712
*Kaleidoscope* - Harry Turtledove   s   5505
*Killdozer!* - Theodore Sturgeon   s   5344
*Kipling's Science Fiction* - Rudyard Kipling   s   3148
*Kirinyaga: A Fable of Utopia* - Mike
   Resnick   s   4548
*Lafferty in Orbit* - R.A. Lafferty   s   3308
*Last Orders* - Brian W. Aldiss   s   56
*The Leiber Chronicles* - Fritz Leiber   s   3421
*Lost Pages* - Paul Di Filippo   s   1516
*Lovedeath* - Dan Simmons   s   5056
*Man in His Time: The Best Science Fiction Stories of
   Brian W. Aldiss* - Brian W. Aldiss   s   57
*Matter's End* - Gregory Benford   s   448
*Meeting in Infinity* - John Kessel   s   3086
*Microcosmic God* - Theodore Sturgeon   s   5345
*The Mirror Maker* - Primo Levi   s   3443
*The Moon Maid and Other Fantastic Adventures* - R.
   Garcia y Robertson   s   2120
*More than Honor* - David Weber   s   5676
*N-Space* - Larry Niven   s   4126
*The Nanotech Chronicles* - Michael Flynn   s   1964
*Night of the Cooters* - Howard Waldrop   s   5614
*Nine Hard Questions about the Nature of the Universe*
   - Lewis Shiner   s   4998
*None So Blind* - Joe Haldeman   s   2490
*Novelty* - John Crowley   s   1278
*Numbers in the Dark and Other Stories* - Italo
   Calvino   s   850
*The Old Funny Stuff* - George Alec Effinger   s   1753
*One Day Closer to Death* - Bradley Denton   s   1492
*One Man's Universe* - Charles Sheffield   s   4961
*One Side Laughing: Stories Unlike Other Stories* -
   Damon Knight   s   3187
*An Ornament to His Profession* - Charles L.
   Harness   s   2547
*Otherness* - David Brin   s   689
*Over the River & through the Woods* - Clifford D.
   Simak   s   5047
*Patterns* - Pat Cadigan   s   807
*The Perfect Host* - Theodore Sturgeon   s   5346
*Phases* - Elizabeth Moon   s   3971
*Playgrounds of the Mind* - Larry Niven   s   4127
*Portraits of His Children* - George R.R.
   Martin   s   3648
*The Pure Product* - John Kessel   s   3087
*Quicker than the Eye* - Ray Bradbury   s   624
*The Rediscovery of Man* - Cordwainer
   Smith   s   5106
*Remaking History* - Kim Stanley Robinson   s   4636
*Requiem* - Robert A. Heinlein   s   2648
*Ribofunk* - Paul Di Filippo   s   1517
*Riders of the Purple Wage* - Philip Jose
   Farmer   s   1874
*The Rim-World Legacy and Beyond* - Frank A.
   Javor   s   2882
*Rivers of Time* - L. Sprague de Camp   s   1417
*Rude Astronauts* - Allen Steele   s   5247
*Sam Gunn Forever* - Ben Bova   s   592
*Sam Gunn, Unlimited* - Ben Bova   s   593

*Schismatrix Plus* - Bruce Sterling   s   5260
*Slow Dancing through Time* - Gardner
   Dozois   s   1615
*Space Folk* - Poul Anderson   s   132
*Speaking in Tongues* - Ian McDonald   s   3796
*Stainless Steel Visions* - Harry Harrison   s   2576
*Star Trek: The Classic Episodes 1* - James
   Blish   s   526
*Star Trek: The Classic Episodes 2* - James
   Blish   s   527
*Star Trek: The Classic Episodes 3* - James
   Blish   s   528
*The Start of the End of It All* - Carol
   Emshwiller   s   1818
*The Steampunk Trilogy* - Paul Di Filippo   s   1518
*Strange Monsters of the Recent Past* - Howard
   Waldrop   s   5615
*Synthesis & Other Virtual Realities* - Mary
   Rosenblum   s   4680
*Tales From Planet Earth* - Arthur C. Clarke   s   1061
*Tales of H.P. Lovecraft* - H.P. Lovecraft   s   3534
*Tangents* - Greg Bear   s   425
*Think Like a Dinosaur and Other Stories* - James
   Patrick Kelly   s   3048
*Thirty Strange Stories* - H.G. Wells   s   5747
*Thunder and Roses* - Theodore Sturgeon   s   5348
*The Time Patrol* - Poul Anderson   s   135
*The Toynbee Convector* - Ray Bradbury   s   625
*Transreal!* - Rudy Rucker   s   4706
*Treks Not Taken: What if Stephen King, Anne Rice,
   Bret Easton Ellis, and Other Literary Greats Had
   Written Episodes of Star Trek: The Next
   Generation?* - Steven R. Boyett   s   607
*A Tupelov Too Far and Other Stories* - Brian W.
   Aldiss   s   61
*Twilight of the Empire* - Simon R. Green   s   2374
*Two That Came True* - Judith Moffett   s   3945
*The Ultimate Egoist* - Theodore Sturgeon   s   5349
*Virtual Unrealities: The Short Fiction of Alfred Bester*
   - Alfred Bester   s   479
*Voyages by Starlight* - Ian R. MacLeod   s   3600
*The Wall of the Sky, the Wall of the Eye* - Jonathan
   Lethem   s   3442
*War Fever* - J.G. Ballard   s   321
*When the Five Moons Rise* - Jack Vance   s   5551
*The White Papers* - James White   s   5782
*Will the Last Person to Leave the Planet Please Shut
   Off the Sun?* - Mike Resnick   s   4561
*Women's Work* - L.A. Taylor   s   5410

**Science Fiction — Contemporary Realism**

*Agviq* - Michael Armstrong   s   208
*Ancient Shores* - Jack McDevitt   s   3786
*Bellwether* - Connie Willis   s   5867
*Blue Light* - Walter Mosley   s   4042
*Canal Dreams* - Iain M. Banks   s   323
*The Children of Hamelin* - Norman Spinrad   s   5170
*Cosm* - Gregory Benford   s   444
*Earth* - David Brin   s   685
*Ecstasy Club* - Douglas Rushkoff   s   4732
*The Feelies* - Mick Farren   s   1878
*The Ghost From the Grand Banks* - Arthur C.
   Clarke   s   1056
*The Green Progression* - L.E. Modesitt Jr.   s   3932
*Half Asleep in Frog Pajamas* - Tom
   Robbins   s   4606
*Half the Day Is Night* - Maureen F.
   McHugh   s   3818
*Happy Policeman* - Patricia Anthony   s   160
*Heathern* - Jack Womack   s   5958
*Ishmael* - Daniel Quinn   s   4455
*My Cousin, My Gastroenterologist* - Mark
   Leyner   s   3456
*My Ishmael* - Daniel Quinn   s   4456
*Phases of Gravity* - Dan Simmons   s   5057
*Pictures at 11* - Norman Spinrad   s   5173
*The Prestige* - Christopher Priest   s   4432

*The Ragged World: A Novel of the Hefn on Earth* - Judith Moffett  s  3943
*Signs of Life* - M. John Harrison  s  2580
*Somewhere East of Life* - Brian W. Aldiss  s  60
*The Start of the End of It All* - Carol Emshwiller  s  1818
*Time, Like an Ever-Rolling Stream* - Judith Moffett  s  3944
*Timequake* - Kurt Vonnegut Jr.  s  5594
*The Ugly Little Boy* - Isaac Asimov  s  250
*Wyrm* - Mark Fabi  s  1858

### Science Fiction — Cyberpunk

*Angel Station* - Walter Jon Williams  s  5833
*Arachne* - Lisa Mason  s  3661
*Bad Voltage* - Jonathan Littell  s  3491
*Blue Limbo* - Terrence M. Green  s  2377
*The California Voodoo Game* - Larry Niven  s  4117
*Carlucci's Edge* - Richard Paul Russo  s  4747
*Chimera* - Mary Rosenblum  s  4677
*Cinderblock* - Janine Ellen Young  s  6047
*Circle of One* - Eric James Fullilove  s  2092
*Circuit of Heaven* - Dennis Danvers  s  1348
*City of Golden Shadow* - Tad Williams  s  5828
*Crashcourse* - Wilhelmina Baird  s  295
*The Cybernetic Walrus* - Jack L. Chalker  s  951
*Cyberweb* - Lisa Mason  s  3662
*Cytheria* - Richard Calder  s  835
*Dead Boys* - Richard Calder  s  836
*Dead Girls* - Richard Calder  s  837
*Dead Things* - Richard Calder  s  838
*Death Dream* - Ben Bova  s  583
*Deepdrive* - Alexander Jablokov  s  2837
*Destroying Angel* - Richard Paul Russo  s  4749
*The Diamond Age* - Neal Stephenson  s  5253
*The Difference Engine* - William Gibson  s  2217
*Dream of Glass* - Jean Mark Gawron  s  2163
*Dreams of Gods and Men* - W.T. Quick  s  4451
*Dydeetown World* - F. Paul Wilson  s  5887
*Eclipse Corona* - John Shirley  s  5006
*The Enigma Variations* - John Maddox Roberts  s  4618
*F.R.E.E.Lancers* - Mel Odom  s  4191
*Fade to Black* - Nyx Smith  s  5134
*Farewell Horizontal* - K.W. Jeter  s  2911
*Fools* - Pat Cadigan  s  805
*The Fortunate Fall* - Raphael Carter  s  927
*Freeware* - Rudy Rucker  s  4703
*Gaia's Toys* - Rebecca Ore  s  4218
*Glass Houses* - Laura J. Mixon  s  3921
*The Hacker and the Ants* - Rudy Rucker  s  4704
*Headcrash* - Bruce Bethke  s  483
*Headhunters* - Mel Odom  s  4192
*The Hot-Wired Dodo* - Jack L. Chalker  s  956
*House of the Sun* - Nigel Findley  s  1936
*How to Mutate and Take Over the World* - R.U. Sirius  s  5074
*Idoru* - William Gibson  s  2218
*Johnny Mnemonic* - Terry Bisson  s  505
*Kaduna Memories* - Jack McKinney  s  3850
*Lethal Interface* - Mel Odom  s  4193
*The Long Run* - Daniel Keys Moran  s  3995
*Mindplayers* - Pat Cadigan  s  806
*The Modular Man* - Roger MacBride Allen  s  79
*Montezuma Strip* - Alan Dean Foster  s  2011
*Night Sky Mine* - Melissa Scott  s  4898
*Nimbus* - Alexander Jablokov  s  2839
*Noir* - K.W. Jeter  s  2916
*On My Way to Paradise* - Dave Wolverton  s  5955
*Permutation City* - Greg Egan  s  1761
*Pollen* - Jeff Noon  s  4135
*Protektor* - Charles Platt  s  4342
*Quarantine* - Greg Egan  s  1762
*Quasar* - Jamil Nasir  s  4071
*Queen of Angels* - Greg Bear  s  423
*The Quicksilver Screen* - Don H. DeBrandt  s  1449
*Realtime Interrupt* - James P. Hogan  s  2729

*Scissors Cut Paper Wrap Stone* - Ian McDonald  s  3795
*Shadowboxer* - Nick Pollotta  s  4366
*The Shift* - George Foy  s  2033
*Signal to Noise* - Eric S. Nylund  s  4179
*Silicon Embrace* - John Shirley  s  5009
*Snow Crash* - Neal Stephenson  s  5254
*Solip: System* - Walter Jon Williams  s  5841
*Svaha* - Charles de Lint  s  1437
*Synners* - Pat Cadigan  s  808
*Systems* - W.T. Quick  s  4452
*Tea From an Empty Cup* - Pat Cadigan  s  809
*Terminal Cafe* - Ian McDonald  s  3797
*Trouble and Her Friends* - Melissa Scott  s  4902
*Virtual Light* - William Gibson  s  2219
*Vurt* - Jeff Noon  s  4136

### Science Fiction — Disaster

*Aftermath* - Charles Sheffield  s  4947
*Armageddon Sky* - L.A. Graf  s  2296
*Avenger* - William Shatner  s  4928
*Black Sun* - Robert Leininger  s  3429
*Bright Angel* - John Blair  s  512
*Core* - Paul Preuss  s  4416
*Days of Cain* - J.R. Dunn  s  1694
*Doomsday Book* - Connie Willis  s  5868
*Fallen Angels* - Larry Niven  s  4120
*Flare* - Roger Zelazny  s  6065
*Flare Star* - Paula E. Downing  s  1594
*Footprints of Thunder* - James F. David  s  1379
*Glimmering* - Elizabeth Hand  s  2535
*The Hammer of God* - Arthur C. Clarke  s  1057
*Heavy Weather* - Bruce Sterling  s  5258
*Humpty Dumpty: An Oval* - Damon Knight  s  3186
*Ill Wind* - Kevin J. Anderson  s  108
*Into the Forest* - Jean Hegland  s  2640
*Island in the Sea of Time* - S.M. Stirling  s  5295
*The Jericho Iteration* - Allen Steele  s  5242
*A Journal of the Flood Year* - David Ely  s  1805
*Land O'Goshen* - Charles McNair  s  3855
*Manhattan Transfer* - John E. Stith  s  5303
*Monkey Station* - Ardath Mayhar  s  3703
*Moonfall* - Jack McDevitt  s  3789
*Moonseed* - Stephen Baxter  s  400
*Mother of Storms* - John Barnes  s  354
*Nicoji* - M. Shayne Bell  s  434
*Operation Damocles* - Oscar L. Fellows  s  1916
*Overshoot* - Mona Clee  s  1075
*Red Shadows* - Yvonne Navarro  s  4074
*Richter 10* - Arthur C. Clarke  s  1060
*The Ring of Charon* - Roger MacBride Allen  s  80
*Shivering World* - Kathy Tyers  s  5526
*Supernova* - Roger MacBride Allen  s  82
*Thunder Strike!* - Michael McCollum  s  3772
*Titan* - Stephen Baxter  s  405
*The Vanishing* - Marilyn Kaye  s  3021
*Virtual Light* - William Gibson  s  2219
*Virus Clans* - Michael Kanaly  s  3008
*Zeta Base* - Judith Alguire  s  74

### Science Fiction — Dystopian

*The Armageddon Crazy* - Mick Farren  s  1877
*The Child Garden* - Geoff Ryman  s  4756
*Distraction* - Bruce Sterling  s  5256
*The Exile Kiss* - George Alec Effinger  s  1750
*Gaia's Toys* - Rebecca Ore  s  4218
*He, She and It* - Marge Piercy  s  4325
*How to Save the World* - Charles Sheffield  s  4959
*The Humanoids* - Jack Williamson  s  5865
*In the Heart of the Valley of Love* - Cynthia Kadohata  s  2997
*Innerverse* - John DeChancie  s  1458
*Journals of the Plague Years* - Norman Spinrad  s  5172
*Judge Dredd* - Neal Barrett Jr.  s  366
*Kaleidoscope Century* - John Barnes  s  352

*Manjinn Moon* - Denise Vitola  s  5576
*Out on Blue Six* - Ian McDonald  s  3794
*Paris in the Twentieth Century* - Jules Verne  s  5568
*Peace on Earth* - Stanislaw Lem  s  3435
*The Queen of Darkness* - Miguel Conner  s  1134
*The Red Queen* - Dirk Draulans  s  1653
*"Repent, Harlequin!" Said the Ticktockman* - Harlan Ellison  s  1782
*The Seeds of Time* - Kay Kenyon  s  3064
*Sheltered Lives* - Charles Oberndorf  s  4188
*Short Blade* - Peter R. Emshwiller  s  1820
*The Six Families* - Nancy Holder  s  2733
*Solis* - A.A. Attanasio  s  272
*Synthesis & Other Virtual Realities* - Mary Rosenblum  s  4680
*The Third Force* - Marc Laidlaw  s  3313
*Time and Light* - William Bornefeld  s  574
*Toward the End of Time* - John Updike  s  5531
*Voices of Hope* - David Feintuch  s  1903
*The Wall* - Marlen Haushofer  s  2603
*Whiteout* - Sage Walker  s  5619

### Science Fiction — End of the World

*AEstival Tide* - Elizabeth Hand  s  2533
*Armageddon Summer* - Jane Yolen  s  6028
*Bloom* - Wil McCarthy  s  3761
*But What of Earth?* - Piers Anthony  s  163
*Desert Eden* - J.M. Morgan  s  4000
*Deus Ex Machina* - J.V. Brummels  s  732
*The Fortress of Utopia* - Jack Williamson  s  5863
*Nightfall* - Isaac Asimov  s  248
*Red Shadows* - Yvonne Navarro  s  4074

### Science Fiction — Espionage Thriller

*Ai! Pedrito!: When Intelligence Goes Wrong* - L. Ron Hubbard  s  2788
*The Argus Gambit* - David D. Ross  s  4681
*Doomsday World* - Carmen Carter  s  923
*Mission: Tori* - Johanna Bolton  s  564
*The Quiet Pools* - Michael P. Kube-McDowell  s  3249

### Science Fiction — Family Saga

*The Alien Years* - Robert Silverberg  s  5027
*Arrow From Earth* - F.M. Busby  s  782
*Barrayar* - Lois McMaster Bujold  s  756
*Beneath the Gated Sky* - Robert Reed  s  4502
*Beneath the Tree of Heaven* - David Wingrove  s  5917
*Brander's Book* - C.J. Mills  s  3909
*Bretta Martyn* - L. Neil Smith  s  5128
*By Honor Betray'd* - Debra Doyle  s  1598
*Children of the Mind* - Orson Scott Card  s  883
*Damia's Children* - Anne McCaffrey  s  3726
*Diamond Mask: A Novel* - Julian May  s  3697
*Dominion's Reach* - Diann Thornley  s  5465
*Donnerjack* - Roger Zelazny  s  6063
*The Earth Saver* - Catherine Wells  s  5745
*Earthfall* - Orson Scott Card  s  885
*Echoes of Issel* - Diann Thornley  s  5466
*Encounter with Tiber* - Buzz Aldrin  s  64
*Exile's Song* - Marion Zimmer Bradley  s  632
*The First Immortal* - James L. Halperin  s  2498
*Freeze Frames* - Katharine Kerr  s  3071
*Heirs of Empire* - David Weber  s  5672
*Hope of Earth* - Piers Anthony  s  175
*Jack the Bodiless* - Julian May  s  3698
*Komarr* - Lois McMaster Bujold  s  760
*Legacy of Earth* - Juanita Coulson  s  1209
*The Long Hunt* - Debra Doyle  s  1602
*Lyon's Pride* - Anne McCaffrey  s  3738
*Magnificat* - Julian May  s  3699
*Mind Snare* - Gayle Greeno  s  2422
*Mirror Dance* - Lois McMaster Bujold  s  762

*Orion's Dagger* - P.K. McAllister  s  3708
*The Past of Forever* - Juanita Coulson  s  1210
*Pegasus in Flight* - Anne McCaffrey  s  3742
*Raising the Stones* - Sheri S. Tepper  s  5434
*Red Planet Run* - Dana Stabenow  s  5187
*Retro Lives* - Lee Grimes  s  2446
*River of Dust* - Alexander Jablokov  s  2840
*The Rowan* - Anne McCaffrey  s  3747
*Secret Passages* - Paul Preuss  s  4420
*The Shadow Matrix* - Marion Zimmer
   Bradley  s  645
*Shame of Man* - Piers Anthony  s  188
*The Ships of Earth* - Orson Scott Card  s  897
*The Stone Within* - David Wingrove  s  5920
*The Summer Queen* - Joan D. Vinge  s  5572
*Tripoint* - C.J. Cherryh  s  1003
*White Moon, Red Dragon* - David
   Wingrove  s  5921
*The White Mountain* - David Wingrove  s  5922
*The Wild* - David Zindell  s  6086
*A Wizard in Mind* - Christopher Stasheff  s  5232
*Zjhanne's Book* - C.J. Mills  s  3912

**Science Fiction — Fantasy**

*Chains of Light* - Quentin Thomas  s  5449
*Dare to Go A-Hunting* - Andre Norton  s  4147
*Fractal Paisleys* - Paul Di Filippo  s  1515
*The Ghost of the Revelator* - L.E. Modesitt
   Jr.  s  3931
*Hard-Boiled Wonderland and the End of the World* -
   Haruki Murakami  s  4047
*Intersections: The Sycamore Hill Anthology* - John
   Kessel  s  3085
*Kingdoms of the Wall* - Robert Silverberg  s  5033
*The Kronos Condition* - Emily Devenport  s  1502
*L. Ron Hubbard Presents Writers of the Future,
   Volume XII* - Dave Wolverton  s  5953
*Nebula Awards 31* - Pamela Sargent  s  4824
*Necrom* - Mick Farren  s  1881
*One King's Way* - Harry Harrison  s  2572
*Orion and the Conqueror* - Ben Bova  s  590
*The Promise* - Monica Hughes  s  2808
*Quicker than the Eye* - Ray Bradbury  s  624
*The Ragged World: A Novel of the Hefn on Earth* -
   Judith Moffett  s  3943
*Starlight 1* - Patrick Nielsen Hayden  s  2634
*Voyages by Starlight* - Ian R. MacLeod  s  3600
*The Warlock Rock* - Christopher Stasheff  s  5226
*Wyrm* - Mark Fabi  s  1858

**Science Fiction — First Contact**

*Acorna* - Anne McCaffrey  s  3717
*Acts of Conscience* - William Barton  s  377
*Aggressor Six* - Wil McCarthy  s  3760
*Alien Dreams* - Larry Segriff  s  4910
*Alien Earth* - Megan Lindholm  s  3469
*Alien Influences* - Kristine Kathryn Rusch  s  4711
*Alien Tongue* - Stephen Leigh  s  3424
*Alpha Centauri* - William Barton  s  378
*Ancestor's World* - A.C. Crispin  s  1259
*Ancient Light* - Mary Gentle  s  2194
*Anvil of Stars* - Greg Bear  s  414
*The Beacon* - Valerie J. Freireich  s  2048
*Beholder's Eye* - Julie E. Czerneda  s  1303
*Being Alien* - Rebecca Ore  s  4217
*Beowulf's Children* - Larry Niven  s  4116
*Beyond the Veil of Stars* - Robert Reed  s  4503
*The Black Sun* - Jack Williamson  s  5860
*Bone Wars* - Brett Davis  s  1398
*Bright Angel* - John Blair  s  512
*Bright Messengers* - Gentry Lee  s  3398
*Brightness Reef* - David Brin  s  684
*A Call to Arms* - Alan Dean Foster  s  1995
*Cannon's Orb* - L. Warren Douglas  s  1586
*Children of God* - Mary Doria Russell  s  4735
*Children of the Mind* - Orson Scott Card  s  883

*Chrysalis* - David Niall Wilson  s  5880
*The Clouds of Magellan* - David F.
   Nighbert  s  4103
*Cold Allies* - Patricia Anthony  s  157
*The Color of Distance* - Amy Thomson  s  5461
*Conqueror's Pride* - Timothy Zahn  s  6051
*Contact and Commune* - L. Neil Smith  s  5129
*Cortez on Jupiter* - Ernest Hogan  s  2721
*Cradle of Splendor* - Patricia Anthony  s  158
*Damia* - Anne McCaffrey  s  3725
*A Darker Geometry* - Mark O. Martin  s  3649
*Deep Freeze* - Zach Hughes  s  2811
*Deepdrive* - Alexander Jablokov  s  2837
*A Deeper Sea* - Alexander Jablokov  s  2838
*Delta Pavonis* - Eric Kotani  s  3221
*Design for Great-Day* - Alan Dean Foster  s  2001
*The Diamond Moon* - Paul Preuss  s  4417
*Diplomatic Act* - Peter Jurasik  s  2996
*The Dolphins of Pern* - Anne McCaffrey  s  3729
*Down the Bright Way* - Robert Reed  s  4505
*Down the Stream of Stars* - Jeffrey A.
   Carver  s  928
*Dragon's Honor* - Kij Johnson  s  2922
*Dream-Weaver* - Louise Lawrence  s  3359
*The Earth Giant* - Melvin Burgess  s  773
*Earth Made of Glass* - John Barnes  s  351
*Earthfall* - Orson Scott Card  s  885
*Eden* - Stanislaw Lem  s  3434
*Eggheads* - Emily Devenport  s  1500
*Einstein's Bridge* - John Cramer  s  1244
*The Embedding* - Ian Watson  s  5634
*Empire of the Ants* - Bernard Werber  s  5755
*Encounter with Tiber* - Buzz Aldrin  s  64
*Entoverse* - James P. Hogan  s  2724
*The Eternal Enemy* - Michael Berlyn  s  469
*Evolution's Shore* - Ian McDonald  s  3792
*Excession* - Iain M. Banks  s  324
*The Expediter* - J. Brian Clarke  s  1062
*Expendable* - James Alan Gardner  s  2135
*The Faces of Ceti* - Mary Caraker  s  877
*The Fall of Sirius* - Wil McCarthy  s  3762
*Fallway* - Paula E. Downing  s  1593
*Final Diagnosis* - James White  s  5777
*Fine Prey* - Scott Westerfeld  s  5766
*Finity's End* - C.J. Cherryh  s  988
*A Fire upon the Deep* - Vernor Vinge  s  5573
*First Strike* - Diane Carey  s  903
*Flies From the Amber* - Wil McCarthy  s  3763
*The Flies of Memory* - Ian Watson  s  5635
*Flying to Valhalla* - Charles Pellegrino  s  4280
*Foragers* - Charles Oberndorf  s  4187
*Foreigner* - C.J. Cherryh  s  990
*The Founder* - Christopher Rowley  s  4696
*Freedom's Challenge* - Anne McCaffrey  s  3732
*Freedom's Choice* - Anne McCaffrey  s  3733
*Freedom's Landing* - Anne McCaffrey  s  3734
*FreeMaster* - Kris Jensen  s  2897
*The Galactic Gourmet* - James White  s  5778
*Ganwold's Child* - Diann Thornley  s  5467
*The Garden of Rama* - Arthur C. Clarke  s  1055
*Genellan: Planetfall* - Scott G. Gier  s  2223
*The Genocidal Healer* - James White  s  5779
*The Gripping Hand* - Larry Niven  s  4122
*The Harvest* - Robert Charles Wilson  s  5909
*Heaven's Reach* - David Brin  s  687
*Hellspark* - Janet Kagan  s  3000
*Hellworld* - Simon R. Green  s  2371
*Heritage of Flight* - Susan Shwartz  s  5016
*A Hidden Place* - Robert Charles Wilson  s  5910
*High Steel* - Jack C. Haldeman II  s  2486
*The Homecoming* - Barry B. Longyear  s  3521
*Homecoming* - David Alexander Smith  s  5108
*Homegoing* - Frederik Pohl  s  4347
*The Howling Stones* - Alan Dean Foster  s  2006
*Human to Human* - Rebecca Ore  s  4219
*Illegal Alien* - Robert J. Sawyer  s  4858
*Imbalance* - V.E. Mitchell  s  3919
*The Immortality Option* - James P. Hogan  s  2725
*The Infinite Sea* - Jeffrey A. Carver  s  932

*Infinity's Shore* - David Brin  s  688
*Inheritor* - C.J. Cherryh  s  997
*The Inquisitor* - Cheryl J. Franklin  s  2037
*Into the Deep* - Ken Grimwood  s  2450
*Invader* - C.J. Cherryh  s  998
*Jack Faust* - Michael Swanwick  s  5372
*Jaydium* - Deborah Wheeler  s  5774
*Jed the Dead* - Alan Dean Foster  s  2007
*Kaduna Memories* - Jack McKinney  s  3850
*Labyrinth of Night* - Allen Steele  s  5244
*Lake of the Sun* - Wynne Whiteford  s  5787
*The Last Stand* - Brad Ferguson  s  1923
*Legacy* - Greg Bear  s  420
*Life Form* - Alan Dean Foster  s  2008
*Limbo Search* - Parke Godwin  s  2245
*Limbo System* - Rick Cook  s  1158
*The Longest Voyage/Slow Lightning* - Poul
   Anderson  s  130
*Look into the Sun* - James Patrick Kelly  s  3047
*Lords of Creation* - Tim Sullivan  s  5351
*The Magnificent Wilf* - Gordon R. Dickson  s  1536
*Manhattan Transfer* - John E. Stith  s  5303
*Marks of Our Brothers* - Jane M. Lindskold  s  3475
*Marooned on Eden* - Robert L. Forward  s  1986
*The Martian Chronicles* - Ray Bradbury  s  621
*The Martian Chronicles* - Ray Bradbury  s  622
*Martian Rainbow* - Robert L. Forward  s  1987
*The Master of Chaos* - Terry A. Adams  s  34
*Mentor* - Kris Jensen  s  2898
*Metaphase* - Vonda N. McIntyre  s  3821
*Mid-Flinx* - Alan Dean Foster  s  2010
*Mind Changer* - James White  s  5780
*Mind Light* - Margaret Davis  s  1407
*Minds Apart* - Margaret Davis  s  1408
*A Miracle of Rare Design* - Mike Resnick  s  4550
*Mission: Tori* - Johanna Bolton  s  564
*Mistwalker* - Denise Lopez Heald  s  2637
*Mother Lode* - Zach Hughes  s  2812
*Mother of Demons* - Eric Flint  s  1956
*My Teacher Fried My Brains* - Bruce
   Coville  s  1223
*My Teacher Glows in the Dark* - Bruce
   Coville  s  1224
*Naked to the Stars/The Alien Way* - Gordon R.
   Dickson  s  1537
*Nautilus* - Vonda N. McIntyre  s  3823
*Neptune Crossing* - Jeffrey A. Carver  s  933
*North Wind* - Gwyneth Jones  s  2953
*Ocean under the Ice* - Robert L. Forward  s  1988
*Of the Fall* - Paul J. McAuley  s  3713
*One Mind's Eye* - Kathy Tyers  s  5525
*Only Child* - H.M. Hoover  s  2764
*The Other End of Time* - Frederik Pohl  s  4351
*Outworld Cats* - Jack Lovejoy  s  3536
*Paradise: A Chronicle of a Distant World* - Mike
   Resnick  s  4552
*People of the Sky* - Clare Bell  s  431
*Power Lines* - Anne McCaffrey  s  3743
*Power Play* - Anne McCaffrey  s  3744
*Powers That Be* - Anne McCaffrey  s  3745
*Preternatural* - Margaret Wander Bonanno  s  568
*Prison Ship* - Martin Caidin  s  828
*Project Farcry* - Pauline Ashwell  s  230
*Psykosis* - Wilhelmina Baird  s  296
*Putting Up Roots* - Charles Sheffield  s  4964
*Rama II* - Arthur C. Clarke  s  1058
*Rama Revealed* - Arthur C. Clarke  s  1059
*Reach* - Edward Gibson  s  2216
*Reckoning Infinity* - John E. Stith  s  5304
*Remnant Population* - Elizabeth Moon  s  3972
*Return to Rocheworld* - Robert L. Forward  s  1989
*Rewind* - Terry England  s  1825
*The Rift* - Peter David  s  1386
*The Ringworld Throne* - Larry Niven  s  4128
*Rocheworld* - Robert L. Forward  s  1990
*The Sails of Tau Ceti* - Michael McCollum  s  3771
*Saturn Rukh* - Robert L. Forward  s  1991
*Saturn's Child* - Nichelle Nichols  s  4101
*The Secret Oceans* - Betty Ballantine  s  318

*SETI* - Frederick Fichman   s   1930
*Shadow World* - A.C. Crispin   s   1262
*The Shattered Sphere* - Roger MacBride Allen   s   81
*The Shining Ones* - Paul Preuss   s   4421
*The Ship Errant* - Jody Lynn Nye   s   4175
*The Ship Who Won* - Anne McCaffrey   s   3750
*The Siege of Eternity* - Frederik Pohl   s   4353
*Signal to Noise* - Eric S. Nylund   s   4179
*Silent Dances* - A.C. Crispin   s   1263
*Silent Songs* - A.C. Crispin   s   1264
*The Silent Stars Go By* - James White   s   5781
*Silent Zone* - Stephen Molstad   s   3952
*Six Moon Dance* - Sheri S. Tepper   s   5437
*Slow Freight* - F.M. Busby   s   785
*Smoke and Mirrors* - Jane M. Lindskold   s   3476
*The Sparrow* - Mary Doria Russell   s   4736
*The Stalk* - Janet Morris   s   4016
*Star Child* - James P. Hogan   s   2730
*Starborne* - Robert Silverberg   s   5042
*Starbridge* - A.C. Crispin   s   1265
*Starfarers* - Poul Anderson   s   133
*Starplex* - Robert J. Sawyer   s   4859
*StarSpawn* - Kenneth Von Gunden   s   5588
*Starstrike* - W. Michael Gear   s   2172
*The State of the Art* - Iain M. Banks   s   327
*The Stone Garden* - Mary Rosenblum   s   4679
*Target* - Janet Morris   s   4017
*Target Earth* - Steve Perry   s   4301
*A Thunder on Neptune* - Gordon Eklund   s   1768
*To Fear the Light* - Ben Bova   s   595
*Tower of the Gods* - Thomas A. Easton   s   1726
*The Transmigration of Souls* - William Barton   s   382
*Treaty at Doona* - Anne McCaffrey   s   3752
*The Triad Worlds* - F.M. Busby   s   786
*Trust Territory* - Janet Morris   s   4019
*Turning Point* - Lisanne Norman   s   4140
*The Voice of Cepheus* - Ken Appleby   s   202
*Voices of Chaos* - A.C. Crispin   s   1266
*The Voices of Heaven* - Frederik Pohl   s   4356
*War Dragons* - L.A. Graf   s   2299
*Warhorse* - Timothy Zahn   s   6056
*Warpath* - Tony Daniel   s   1337
*Way Station* - Clifford D. Simak   s   5048
*The Weigher* - Eric Vinicoff   s   5574
*A Whisper of Time* - Paula E. Downing   s   1595
*White Light* - William Barton   s   384
*White Queen* - Gwyneth Jones   s   2955
*A Woman of the Iron People* - Eleanor Arnason   s   211
*A World Lost* - James B. Johnson   s   2921
*A World of Difference* - Harry Turtledove   s   5514
*Worlds Enough and Time* - Joe Haldeman   s   2491
*Wulfsyarn: A Mosaic* - Phillip Mann   s   3617

### Science Fiction — Future Shock

*Brother to Dragons* - Charles Sheffield   s   4949
*The Death of Sleep* - Anne McCaffrey   s   3727
*Glimmering* - Elizabeth Hand   s   2535
*The Illegal Rebirth of Billy the Kid* - Rebecca Ore   s   4220
*Mindplayers* - Pat Cadigan   s   806
*Mir* - Alexander Besher   s   474
*Pirates of the Universe* - Terry Bisson   s   506
*The Shockwave Rider* - John Brunner   s   736
*Stranger Suns* - George Zebrowski   s   6060

### Science Fiction — Gay/Lesbian Fiction

*Bewitchments of Love and Hate* - Storm Constantine   s   1140
*Black Wine* - Candas Jane Dorsey   s   1582
*Cathy IV* - Frances Lucas   s   3539
*Clicking Stones* - Nancy Tyler Glenn   s   2242
*Death's Head* - Mel Keegan   s   3029
*Escape to the Wind* - Jennifer DiMarco   s   1559

*The Fulfillments of Fate and Desire* - Storm Constantine   s   1142
*The Furies* - Suzy McKee Charnas   s   968
*Hand of Prophecy* - Severna Park   s   4244
*In the Blood* - Lauren Wright Douglas   s   1590
*Key West 2720 A.D.* - William Eakins   s   1720
*Meltdown!* - Caro Soles   s   5154
*Mirage* - Perry Brass   s   662
*The Nature of Smoke* - Anne Harris   s   2559
*Night Sky Mine* - Melissa Scott   s   4898
*Priorities* - Lynda Lyons   s   3579
*Return to Isis* - Jean Stewart   s   5268
*Ring of Swords* - Eleanor Arnason   s   210
*Shadow Man* - Melissa Scott   s   4900
*Slow River* - Nicola Griffith   s   2445
*Speaking Dreams* - Severna Park   s   4245
*Stranded* - Camarin Grae   s   2295
*The Tranquility Alternative* - Allen Steele   s   5248
*Trouble and Her Friends* - Melissa Scott   s   4902
*Zeta Base* - Judith Alguire   s   74

### Science Fiction — Generation Starship

*Burster* - Michael Capobianco   s   876
*Calde of the Long Sun* - Gene Wolfe   s   5937
*Checkmate* - Eric T. Baker   s   297
*The Dark Beyond the Stars* - Frank M. Robinson   s   4626
*The Dazzle of Day* - Molly Gloss   s   2243
*Exodus From the Long Sun* - Gene Wolfe   s   5941
*Lake of the Long Sun* - Gene Wolfe   s   5942
*Nightside the Long Sun* - Gene Wolfe   s   5943
*Non-Stop* - Brian W. Aldiss   s   58
*Silent Thunder/Universe* - Dean Ing   s   2829
*The Whims of Creation* - Simon Hawke   s   2626
*Worlds Enough and Time* - Joe Haldeman   s   2491

### Science Fiction — Genetic Manipulation

*Accidental Creatures* - Anne Harris   s   2558
*AEstival Tide* - Elizabeth Hand   s   2533
*All the Weyrs of Pern* - Anne McCaffrey   s   3719
*Ammonite* - Nicola Griffith   s   2443
*Armed Memory* - Jim Young   s   6048
*Becoming Human* - Valerie J. Freireich   s   2049
*Beggars and Choosers* - Nancy Kress   s   3236
*Beggars in Spain* - Nancy Kress   s   3237
*Beggars Ride* - Nancy Kress   s   3238
*Black Milk* - Robert Reed   s   4504
*Blade Runner 2: The Edge of Human* - K W Jeter   s   2906
*Blueheart* - Alison Sinclair   s   5068
*The Bohr Maker* - Linda Nagata   s   4064
*The Bones of Time* - Kathleen Ann Goonan   s   2273
*Brain Child* - George Turner   s   5491
*The Broken Land* - Ian McDonald   s   3791
*Burn* - Bill Ransom   s   4476
*Cannon's Orb* - L. Warren Douglas   s   1586
*Carnosaur* - Harry Adam Knight   s   3191
*Catch the Lightning* - Catherine Asaro   s   218
*Celestis* - Paul Park   s   4241
*The Child Garden* - Geoff Ryman   s   4756
*China Mountain Zhang* - Maureen F. McHugh   s   3817
*City of Truth* - James Morrow   s   4030
*Codename Wolverine* - Christopher Golden   s   2256
*Commitment Hour* - James Alan Gardner   s   2134
*A Covenant of Justice* - David Gerrold   s   2207
*Dancing on Air* - Nancy Kress   s   3240
*Dark Water's Embrace* - Stephen Leigh   s   3426
*Daughter of Elysium* - Joan Slonczewski   s   5091
*Deepwater Dreams* - Sydney J. Van Scyoc   s   5541
*Delta Search* - William Shatner   s   4930
*Distress* - Greg Egan   s   1760
*The Divide* - Robert Charles Wilson   s   5907
*Emperors of the Twilight* - S. Andrew Swann   s   5362
*Fairyland* - Paul J. McAuley   s   3711

*The Family Tree* - Sheri S. Tepper   s   5429
*Forests of the Night* - S. Andrew Swann   s   5363
*Frameshift* - Robert J. Sawyer   s   4856
*Genetic Soldier* - George Turner   s   5492
*Gibbon's Decline and Fall* - Sheri S. Tepper   s   5430
*Girl in Landscape* - Jonathan Lethem   s   3440
*Glory Season* - David Brin   s   686
*Greenhouse* - Thomas A. Easton   s   1723
*Hero* - Dave Duncan   s   1680
*Hot Sky at Midnight* - Robert Silverberg   s   5032
*Hunting the Corrigan's Blood* - Holly Lisle   s   3484
*I Wake From a Dream of a Drowned Star City* - S.P. Somtow   s   5157
*Icarus Descending* - Elizabeth Hand   s   2536
*The Illegal Rebirth of Billy the Kid* - Rebecca Ore   s   4220
*Imposter* - Valerie J. Freireich   s   2050
*In the Company of the Mind* - Steven Piziks   s   4339
*In the Wrong Hands* - Edward Gibson   s   2215
*Jovah's Angel* - Sharon Shinn   s   5001
*Jupiter's Daughter* - Tom Hyman   s   2820
*Jurassic Park* - Michael Crichton   s   1255
*Kahless* - Michael Jan Friedman   s   2065
*Lethe* - Tricia Sullivan   s   5354
*Lives of the Monster Dogs* - Kirsten Bakis   s   305
*The Lost World* - Michael Crichton   s   1256
*Masque* - F. Paul Wilson   s   5890
*Maximum Light* - Nancy Kress   s   3241
*Mississippi Blues* - Kathleen Ann Goonan   s   2274
*Mutagenesis* - Helen Collins   s   1116
*Naming the Flowers* - Kate Wilhelm   s   5809
*Norstrilia* - Cordwainer Smith   s   5105
*Oaths and Miracles* - Nancy Kress   s   3242
*A Plague of Change* - L. Warren Douglas   s   1587
*Playing God* - Sarah Zettel   s   6080
*The Pleistocene Redemption* - Dan Gallagher   s   2107
*Power Play* - Anne McCaffrey   s   3744
*Powers That Be* - Anne McCaffrey   s   3745
*Proteus in the Underworld* - Charles Sheffield   s   4962
*Queen City Jazz* - Kathleen Ann Goonan   s   2275
*Reefsong* - Carol Severance   s   4923
*Regenesis* - Julia Ecklar   s   1729
*Rememory* - John Gregory Betancourt   s   481
*The Return* - William Shatner   s   4933
*Seeds of Destiny* - Thomas A. Easton   s   1724
*Serpent Catch* - Dave Wolverton   s   5956
*Shadow's End* - Sheri S. Tepper   s   5435
*Shaper's Legacy* - Sheila Finch   s   1933
*Shaping the Dawn* - Sheila Finch   s   1934
*Signs of Life* - M. John Harrison   s   2580
*The Silent City* - Elisabeth Vonarburg   s   5592
*The Sky Lords* - John Brosnan   s   720
*Snowmen* - Jerry Earl Brown   s   725
*Sparrowhawk* - Thomas A. Easton   s   1725
*The Specialist* - Wynne Whiteford   s   5788
*Species* - Yvonne Navarro   s   4075
*Specters of the Dawn* - S. Andrew Swann   s   5368
*Spider Legs* - Piers Anthony   s   189
*Starmind* - Spider Robinson   s   4642
*The Stars Are Also Fire* - Poul Anderson   s   134
*Stepwater* - L. Warren Douglas   s   1588
*Tech-Heaven* - Linda Nagata   s   4066
*The Tenth Class* - Karen Ripley   s   4594
*Terminal Cafe* - Ian McDonald   s   3797
*Testament* - Valerie J. Freireich   s   2051
*Tower of the Gods* - Thomas A. Easton   s   1726
*ViraVax* - Bill Ransom   s   4478
*Warstrider: Netlink* - William H. Keith Jr.   s   3038
*The Wells of Phyre* - L. Warren Douglas   s   1589
*The Whims of Creation* - Simon Hawke   s   2626
*The Widowmaker* - Mike Resnick   s   4559
*The Widowmaker Reborn* - Mike Resnick   s   4560
*Wildlife* - James Patrick Kelly   s   3049
*Winterlong* - Elizabeth Hand   s   2539
*Woodsman* - Thomas A. Easton   s   1727

## Science Fiction — Hard Science Fiction

*Aftermath* - Charles Sheffield   s   4947
*The Alien Dark* - Diana G. Gallagher   s   2108
*All the Weyrs of Pern* - Anne McCaffrey   s   3719
*Anvil of Stars* - Greg Bear   s   414
*The Ascent of Wonder: The Evolution of Hard SF* - David G. Hartwell   s   2585
*Assemblers of Infinity* - Kevin J. Anderson   s   100
*Beyond the Fall of Night* - Arthur C. Clarke   s   1054
*Blue Mars* - Kim Stanley Robinson   s   4629
*A Bridge of Years* - Robert Charles Wilson   s   5905
*Celestial Matters* - Richard Garfinkle   s   2140
*Climbing Olympus* - Kevin J. Anderson   s   102
*Cold as Ice* - Charles Sheffield   s   4950
*Cosm* - Gregory Benford   s   444
*Crashlander* - Larry Niven   s   4118
*Cyteen* - C.J. Cherryh   s   984
*Double Planet* - John Gribbin   s   2433
*Earth* - David Brin   s   685
*Einstein's Bridge* - John Cramer   s   1244
*Eon* - Greg Bear   s   417
*Father to the Man* - John Gribbin   s   2434
*Firestar* - Michael Flynn   s   1962
*Flare* - Roger Zelazny   s   6065
*Flies From the Amber* - Wil McCarthy   s   3763
*Flux* - Stephen Baxter   s   399
*Flying to Valhalla* - Charles Pellegrino   s   4280
*Frameshift* - Robert J. Sawyer   s   4856
*From a Changeling Star* - Jeffrey A. Carver   s   931
*Furious Gulf* - Gregory Benford   s   447
*Future Net* - Martin H. Greenberg   s   2394
*Glory's War* - Alfred Coppel   s   1184
*Green Mars* - Kim Stanley Robinson   s   4633
*The Gripping Hand* - Larry Niven   s   4122
*Heads* - Greg Bear   s   419
*Holy Fire* - Bruce Sterling   s   5259
*Iris* - William Barton   s   381
*The Killing Star* - Charles Pellegrino   s   4281
*Lady El* - Jim Starlin   s   5213
*Life Form* - Alan Dean Foster   s   2008
*Lunar Descent* - Allen Steele   s   5245
*Marooned on Eden* - Robert L. Forward   s   1986
*Mars* - Ben Bova   s   586
*Mining the Oort* - Frederik Pohl   s   4349
*Mirabile* - Janet Kagan   s   3001
*The Missing Matter* - Thomas R. McDonough   s   3805
*Moonfall* - Jack McDevitt   s   3789
*Moonrise* - Ben Bova   s   587
*Moonseed* - Stephen Baxter   s   400
*Moving Mars* - Greg Bear   s   421
*Nanodreams* - Elton Elliott   s   1770
*The Nanotech Chronicles* - Michael Flynn   s   1964
*Nanoware Time/The Persistence of Vision* - Ian Watson   s   5638
*One Man's Universe* - Charles Sheffield   s   4961
*Orbital Decay* - Allen Steele   s   5246
*The Oxygen Barons* - Gregory Feeley   s   1897
*The Planet Beyond* - Steve Mudd   s   4043
*Proteus Unbound* - Charles Sheffield   s   4963
*Raft* - Stephen Baxter   s   401
*Red Genesis* - S.C. Sykes   s   5377
*Red Mars* - Kim Stanley Robinson   s   4635
*Redshift Rendezvous* - John E. Stith   s   5305
*Return to Rocheworld* - Robert L. Forward   s   1989
*Ribofunk* - Paul Di Filippo   s   1517
*Richter 10* - Arthur C. Clarke   s   1060
*Ring* - Stephen Baxter   s   402
*The Ring of Charon* - Roger MacBride Allen   s   80
*Rocheworld* - Robert L. Forward   s   1990
*Rogue Star* - Michael Flynn   s   1965
*Run for the Stars/Echoes of Thunder* - Harlan Ellison   s   1788
*Sailing Bright Eternity* - Gregory Benford   s   449
*Saturn Rukh* - Robert L. Forward   s   1991
*Secret Passages* - Paul Preuss   s   4420
*The Silicon Man* - Charles Platt   s   4343
*The Singers of Time* - Frederik Pohl   s   4354

*Slow River* - Nicola Griffith   s   2445
*Starfarers* - Vonda N. McIntyre   s   3824
*Supernova* - Roger MacBride Allen   s   82
*Tides of Light* - Gregory Benford   s   450
*Timelike Infinity* - Stephen Baxter   s   404
*Timemaster* - Robert L. Forward   s   1992
*Titan* - Stephen Baxter   s   405
*Transcendence* - Charles Sheffield   s   4967
*Transition* - Vonda N. McIntyre   s   3825
*Twistor* - John Cramer   s   1245
*Voyager* - Stephen Baxter   s   406
*Whiteout* - Sage Walker   s   5619
*The World at the End of Time* - Frederik Pohl   s   4357
*The Year's Best Science Fiction: Seventh Annual Collection* - Gardner Dozois   s   1621

## Science Fiction — Historical

*The Centurion's Empire* - Sean McMullen   s   3854

## Science Fiction — Horror

*Alien 3* - Alan Dean Foster   s   1993
*Alien Resurrection* - A.C. Crispin   s   1258
*The Black Sun* - Jack Williamson   s   5860
*A Covenant of Justice* - David Gerrold   s   2207
*Door Number Three* - Patrick O'Leary   s   4210
*The Eyes of Darkness* - Dean R. Koontz   s   3206
*Fairyland* - Paul J. McAuley   s   3711
*Goblins* - Charles L. Grant   s   2309
*Lost Futures* - Lisa Tuttle   s   5520
*Lovedeath* - Dan Simmons   s   5056
*Nightshade* - Jack Butler   s   789
*Run for the Stars/Echoes of Thunder* - Harlan Ellison   s   1788
*Spider Legs* - Piers Anthony   s   189
*Ursus* - David Dvorkin   s   1708
*The Wall of the Sky, the Wall of the Eye* - Jonathan Lethem   s   3442
*The Woman between the Worlds* - F. Gwynplaine MacIntyre   s   3596

## Science Fiction — Humor

*After the Blue* - Russel Like   s   3465
*Armageddon: The Musical* - Robert Rankin   s   4473
*Better than Life* - Grant Naylor   s   4076
*Bill, the Galactic Hero: On the Planet of Tasteless Pleasure* - Harry Harrison   s   2567
*Bill, the Galactic Hero: The Final Incoherent Adventure* - Harry Harrison   s   2568
*Borders of Infinity* - Lois McMaster Bujold   s   757
*Bride of the Castle* - John DeChancie   s   1452
*Buddy Holly Is Alive and Well on Ganymede* - Bradley Denton   s   1490
*Callahan's Lady* - Spider Robinson   s   4638
*Callahan's Legacy* - Spider Robinson   s   4639
*Carmen Miranda's Ghost Is Haunting Space Station Three* - Don Sakers   s   4785
*Castle Dreams* - John DeChancie   s   1453
*The Clone Crisis* - Lee McKeone   s   3829
*Codgerspace* - Alan Dean Foster   s   1999
*The Collected Feghoot* - Grendel Briarton   s   677
*Cowboy Feng's Space Bar and Grille* - Steven Brust   s   740
*Cyberbooks* - Ben Bova   s   582
*Dr. Dimension* - John DeChancie   s   1456
*Double Jeopardy* - Aaron Allston   s   86
*Douglas Adams's Starship Titanic* - Terry Jones   s   2979
*Escape From Kathmandu* - Kim Stanley Robinson   s   4630
*Et Tu, Babe* - Mark Leyner   s   3455
*Extreme Paranoia: Nobody Knows the Trouble I've Shot* - Ken Rolston   s   4662
*Ferman's Devils* - Joe Clifford Faust   s   1892
*The Fermata* - Nicholson Baker   s   302

*Hard Sell* - Piers Anthony   s   173
*Hawaiian U.F.O. Aliens* - Mel Gilden   s   2226
*Hostile Takeover* - Jack McKinney   s   3849
*How to Mutate and Take Over the World* - R.U. Sirius   s   5074
*Illegal Alien* - James Luceno   s   3543
*Illegal Aliens* - Nick Pollotta   s   4365
*The Illustrated Hitchhiker's Guide to the Galaxy* - Douglas Adams   s   29
*Jed the Dead* - Alan Dean Foster   s   2007
*The Kruton Interface* - John DeChancie   s   1459
*Lady Slings the Booze* - Spider Robinson   s   4640
*Living with the Reptiles* - Roger L. DiSilvestro   s   1563
*The Magnificent Wilf* - Gordon R. Dickson   s   1536
*Men in Black* - Steve Perry   s   4298
*Mostly Harmless* - Douglas Adams   s   31
*Night of the Living 'Gator!* - Richard A. Lupoff   s   3573
*Night of the Living Rat!* - Debra Doyle   s   1603
*Night of the Living Shark!* - David Bischoff   s   493
*O Pioneer!* - Frederik Pohl   s   4350
*Outer Space and All That Junk* - Mel Gilden   s   2227
*Peace on Earth* - Stanislaw Lem   s   3435
*Phule's Company* - Robert Asprin   s   260
*Phule's Paradise* - Robert Asprin   s   261
*Planet of the Robot Slaves* - Harry Harrison   s   2573
*Psychoshop* - Alfred Bester   s   477
*Q-in-Law* - Peter David   s   1384
*Quozl* - Alan Dean Foster   s   2013
*Reality Is What You Can Get Away With: An Illustrated Screenplay* - Robert Anton Wilson   s   5904
*Red Dwarf: Infinity Welcomes Careful Drivers* - Grant Naylor   s   4077
*The Red Tape War* - Jack L. Chalker   s   959
*"Repent, Harlequin!" Said the Ticktockman* - Harlan Ellison   s   1782
*Reward for Retief* - Keith Laumer   s   3345
*Rock 'n' Roll Babes From Outer Space* - Linda Javin   s   2880
*Rock of Ages* - Walter Jon Williams   s   5840
*Sewer, Gas & Electric* - Matt Ruff   s   4708
*The Sherwood Game* - Esther Friesner   s   2082
*The Stainless Steel Rat Goes to Hell* - Harry Harrison   s   2574
*The Stainless Steel Rat Sings the Blues* - Harry Harrison   s   2575
*Stationfall* - Arthur Byron Cover   s   1216
*The Sword of Samurai Cat* - Mark E. Rogers   s   4657
*The Swords of Zinjaban* - L. Sprague de Camp   s   1418
*Title Deleted for Security Reasons* - Ed Blome   s   553
*To Say Nothing of the Dog* - Connie Willis   s   5874
*Truckers* - Terry Pratchett   s   4402
*Tubular Android Superheroes* - Mel Gilden   s   2228
*The Ultimate Bike Path* - Michael B. Sirota   s   5076
*Uncharted Territory* - Connie Willis   s   5875
*The Venom Trees of Sunga* - L. Sprague de Camp   s   1420
*The VMR Theory* - Robert Frezza   s   2055
*The Vor Game* - Lois McMaster Bujold   s   764
*The Warlock Rock* - Christopher Stasheff   s   5226
*We Open on Venus* - Christopher Stasheff   s   5227
*The Zork Chronicles* - George Alec Effinger   s   1754

## Science Fiction — Immortality

*The Boat of a Million Years* - Poul Anderson   s   125
*Buying Time* - Joe Haldeman   s   2487
*Endymion* - Dan Simmons   s   5051
*An Exaltation of Larks* - Robert Reed   s   4506
*Exit to Reality* - Edith Forbes   s   1968
*The First Immortal* - James L. Halperin   s   2498

*Habu* - James B. Johnson  s  2920

*In the Garden of Iden* - Kage Baker  s  298

*Insurrection* - J.M. Dillard  s  1554

*The Invisible Company* - Scott Russell Sanders  s  4813

*The Madness Season* - C.S. Friedman  s  2058

*Norstrilia* - Cordwainer Smith  s  5105

*Orion Among the Stars* - Ben Bova  s  589

*Outnumbering the Dead* - Frederik Pohl  s  4352

*The Queen's Squadron* - R.M. Meluch  s  3874

*Quest to Riverworld* - Philip Jose Farmer  s  1872

*Retro Lives* - Lee Grimes  s  2446

*Steel Beach* - John Varley  s  5566

*Tales of Riverworld* - Philip Jose Farmer  s  1875

*This Immortal* - Roger Zelazny  s  6074

*To a Highland Nation* - Christopher Rowley  s  4698

*To Your Scattered Bodies Go* - Philip Jose Farmer  s  1876

*Tomorrow and Tomorrow* - Charles Sheffield  s  4966

*Vortex* - Allan Cole  s  1108

*Warpath* - Tony Daniel  s  1337

*The Whispers* - Dan Parkinson  s  4247


**Science Fiction — Invasion of Earth**

*The Abductors: Conspiracy* - Jonathan Frakes  s  2034

*The Alien Years* - Robert Silverberg  s  5027

*Aliens: Earth Hive* - Steve Perry  s  4289

*Area 51* - Robert Doherty  s  1565

*The Armageddon Inheritance* - David Weber  s  5668

*Assemblers of Infinity* - Kevin J. Anderson  s  100

*The Beacon* - Valerie J. Freireich  s  2048

*Beyond the Fall of Night* - Arthur C. Clarke  s  1054

*Brother Termite* - Patricia Anthony  s  156

*Callahan's Legacy* - Spider Robinson  s  4639

*The Change* - Barry B. Longyear  s  3520

*Cross of Blood* - K.W. Jeter  s  2909

*Dark Horizon* - K.W. Jeter  s  2910

*The Death and Life of Superman* - Roger Stern  s  5262

*The Delta* - Colin Wilson  s  5878

*Dragons Past* - Gary Gentile  s  2192

*Dream Maker* - W.A. Harbinson  s  2542

*Emperors of the Twilight* - S. Andrew Swann  s  5362

*End of an Era* - Robert J. Sawyer  s  4853

*Evil Ascending* - Michael A. Stackpole  s  5198

*Evil Triumphant* - Michael A. Stackpole  s  5199

*Evolution's Shore* - Ian McDonald  s  3792

*The Fifth Element* - Terry Bisson  s  504

*Free Radicals* - Jack McKinney  s  3848

*The Fugitive Stars* - Daniel Ransom  s  4479

*A Gathering Evil* - Michael A. Stackpole  s  5201

*Good News From Outer Space* - John Kessel  s  3084

*Gryphon* - Crawford Kilian  s  3106

*Hard Landing* - Algis Budrys  s  753

*In the Heart of Darkness* - Eric Flint  s  1955

*Independence Day* - Dean Devlin  s  1508

*Inhuman Beings* - Jerry Jay Carroll  s  914

*Invasion America* - Christie Golden  s  2252

*Kent Montana and the Really Ugly Thing From Mars* - Lionel Fenn  s  1918

*The Killing Star* - Charles Pellegrino  s  4281

*Leap Point* - Kay Kenyon  s  3063

*Living with Aliens* - John DeChancie  s  1460

*Martian Deathtrap* - Nathan Archer  s  205

*Men in Black* - Steve Perry  s  4298

*Men Like Rats* - Rob Chilson  s  1015

*Mirror to the Sky* - Mark S. Geston  s  2213

*Mojave Wells* - L. Dean James  s  2864

*Moonbane* - Al Sarrantonio  s  4831

*Mutineers' Moon* - David Weber  s  5677


*My Teacher Flunked the Planet* - Bruce Coville  s  1222

*North Wind* - Gwyneth Jones  s  2953

*Panda Ray* - Michael Kandel  s  3011

*The Parasite War* - Tim Sullivan  s  5352

*Phoenix Cafe* - Gwyneth Jones  s  2954

*The Puppet Masters* - Robert A. Heinlein  s  2646

*The Pure Cold Light* - Gregory Frost  s  2087

*A Rage for Revenge* - David Gerrold  s  2210

*A Reasonable World* - Damon Knight  s  3188

*Rule Golden and Double Meaning* - Damon Knight  s  3189

*A Season for Slaughter* - David Gerrold  s  2211

*The Seraphim Rising* - Elisabeth De Vos  s  1442

*Shade's Children* - Garth Nix  s  4130

*The Siege of Eternity* - Frederik Pohl  s  4353

*The Singers of Time* - Frederik Pohl  s  4354

*Starsea Invaders: First Action* - G. Harry Stine  s  5282

*Stranded* - Camarin Grae  s  2295

*Strange Invasion* - Michael Kandel  s  3012

*Target Earth* - Steve Perry  s  4301

*Time, Like an Ever-Rolling Stream* - Judith Moffett  s  3944

*Under Alien Stars* - Pamela F. Service  s  4919

*War of the Worlds: Global Dispatches* - Kevin J. Anderson  s  119

*When Heaven Fell* - William Barton  s  383

*White Queen* - Gwyneth Jones  s  2955

*The Woman between the Worlds* - F. Gwynplaine MacIntyre  s  3596

*Worldwar: In the Balance* - Harry Turtledove  s  5515

*Worldwar: Striking the Balance* - Harry Turtledove  s  5516

*Worldwar: Tilting the Balance* - Harry Turtledove  s  5517

*Worldwar: Upsetting the Balance* - Harry Turtledove  s  5518


**Science Fiction — Literary**

*Beyond Apollo* - Barry Malzberg  s  3612

*Century 21* - Ewa Kuryluk  s  3263

*The Cloning of Joanna May* - Fay Weldon  s  5732

*Correspondence* - Sue Thomas  s  5450

*Cytheria* - Richard Calder  s  835

*Dance Dance Dance* - Haruki Murakami  s  4046

*Dead Boys* - Richard Calder  s  836

*Dead Things* - Richard Calder  s  838

*Exit to Reality* - Edith Forbes  s  1968

*Exodus From the Long Sun* - Gene Wolfe  s  5941

*The Fall of Hyperion* - Dan Simmons  s  5052

*Feersum Endjinn* - Iain M. Banks  s  325

*Galatea 2.2* - Richard M. Powers  s  4381

*Ghost of Chance* - William S. Burroughs  s  780

*Hard-Boiled Wonderland and the End of the World* - Haruki Murakami  s  4047

*He, She and It* - Marge Piercy  s  4325

*Hence* - Brad Leithauser  s  3431

*Hocus Pocus or, What's the Hurry, Son?* - Kurt Vonnegut Jr.  s  5593

*Hyperion* - Dan Simmons  s  5055

*I Who Have Never Known Men* - Jacqueline Harpman  s  2554

*Ishmael* - Daniel Quinn  s  4455

*Land O'Goshen* - Charles McNair  s  3855

*Lives of the Monster Dogs* - Kirsten Bakis  s  305

*London Fields* - Martin Amis  s  95

*Meridian 144* - Meg Files  s  1932

*My Cousin, My Gastroenterologist* - Mark Leyner  s  3456

*My Ishmael* - Daniel Quinn  s  4456

*Pollen* - Jeff Noon  s  4135

*Time's Arrow* - Martin Amis  s  96

*War With the Newts* - Karel Capek  s  874

*The Waterworks* - E.L. Doctorow  s  1564


**Science Fiction — Lost Colony**

*The Alleluia Files* - Sharon Shinn  s  4999

*Ammonite* - Nicola Griffith  s  2443

*Archangel* - Sharon Shinn  s  5000

*Cloud's Rider* - C.J. Cherryh  s  983

*Dark Water's Embrace* - Stephen Leigh  s  3426

*Demon Moon* - Jack Williamson  s  5862

*Destiny's Road* - Larry Niven  s  4119

*Dragonseye* - Anne McCaffrey  s  3730

*Earth Made of Glass* - John Barnes  s  351

*Exiles' Return* - Gayle Greeno  s  2420

*Glory Season* - David Brin  s  686

*Godspeed* - Charles Sheffield  s  4957

*Halfway Human* - Carolyn Ives Gilman  s  2237

*Helm* - Steven Gould  s  2289

*Initiation* - Marian Hughes  s  2806

*Legacies* - Alison Sinclair  s  5069

*Legacy* - Greg Bear  s  420

*Lethe* - Tricia Sullivan  s  5354

*The Masterharper of Pern* - Anne McCaffrey  s  3739

*Mission Child* - Maureen F. McHugh  s  3819

*Outpost* - Scott Mackay  s  3597

*Receive the Gift* - Louise Marley  s  3628

*Rediscovery: A Novel of Darkover* - Marion Zimmer Bradley  s  643

*Rider at the Gate* - C.J. Cherryh  s  1000

*Shadow Man* - Melissa Scott  s  4900

*Signs of Life* - Cherry Wilder  s  5804

*Sing the Light* - Louise Marley  s  3629

*Sing the Warmth* - Louise Marley  s  3630

*The Voyage* - David Drake  s  1649

*A Wizard in Peace* - Christopher Stasheff  s  5233


**Science Fiction — Medical**

*Brothers* - Ben Bova  s  581

*Carlucci's Heart* - Richard Paul Russo  s  4748

*Cross of Blood* - K.W. Jeter  s  2909

*An Exchange of Hostages* - Susan R. Matthews  s  3692

*Final Diagnosis* - James White  s  5777

*The Galactic Gourmet* - James White  s  5778

*The Genocidal Healer* - James White  s  5779

*The Great Wheel* - Ian R. MacLeod  s  3599

*The Halflife* - Sharon Webb  s  5664

*Harmful Intent* - Robin Cook  s  1164

*Heavy Weather* - Bruce Sterling  s  5258

*High Aztec* - Ernest Hogan  s  2722

*Hopeship* - Simon Lang  s  3315

*The Immortals* - Tracy Hickman  s  2681

*Infectress* - Tom Cool  s  1167

*McLendon's Syndrome* - Robert Frezza  s  2053

*Medicine Show* - Jody Lynn Nye  s  4172

*Mind Changer* - James White  s  5780

*The Misconceiver* - Lucy Ferriss  s  1929

*Mutagenesis* - Helen Collins  s  1116

*Mutation* - Robin Cook  s  1165

*My Soul to Take* - Steven Spruill  s  5184

*The Plague Tales* - Ann Benson  s  453

*Resurrection* - Katharine Kerr  s  3075

*Shadows on the Sun* - Michael Jan Friedman  s  2069

*Solomon's Knife* - Victor Koman  s  3200

*Stinger* - Nancy Kress  s  3243

*Stopping at Slowyear* - Frederik Pohl  s  4355

*Taylor's Ark* - Jody Lynn Nye  s  4176

*Virus Clans* - Michael Kanaly  s  3008

*The Waterworks* - E.L. Doctorow  s  1564


**Science Fiction — Military**

*1945* - Newt Gingrich  s  2239

*Action Stations* - William R. Forstchen  s  1976

*Afrikorps* - Bill Dolan  s  1566

*Aggressor Six* - Wil McCarthy  s  3760

*Arc Riders* - David Drake  s  1626

*Armageddon* - Richard Hatch  s  2602

*The Armageddon Inheritance* - David
    Weber   s   5668
*Article 23* - William R. Forstchen   s   1978
*Assault of the Super Carrier* - Peter Albano   s   47
*Battle Front* - Ian Slater   s   5086
*Berserker* - S.D. Perry   s   4285
*Berserker Fury* - Fred Saberhagen   s   4760
*Beyond the Void* - Sean Dalton   s   1331
*Bill, the Galactic Hero: The Final Incoherent
    Adventure* - Harry Harrison   s   2568
*Blood Feuds* - S.M. Stirling   s   5292
*Blood Siege* - G. Harry Stine   s   5278
*Bodyguard* - William C. Dietz   s   1542
*Border Dispute* - Daniel R. Kerns   s   3066
*Call to Arms* - Diane Carey   s   901
*Call to Arms* - P.M. Griffin   s   2435
*Canby's Legion* - Bill Baldwin   s   308
*Cathouse* - Dean Ing   s   2828
*Caught in the Crossfire* - David Drake   s   1628
*Challenger's Hope* - David Feintuch   s   1899
*The Children's Hour* - Jerry Pournelle   s   4372
*The City Who Fought* - Anne McCaffrey   s   3722
*Cluster Command* - David Drake   s   1630
*Cobra Curse* - Bill Dolan   s   1567
*CoDominium: Revolt on War World* - Jerry
    Pournelle   s   4373
*Cohort of the Damned* - Andrew Keith   s   3034
*Cold Allies* - Patricia Anthony   s   157
*Crown of Empire* - Chelsea Quinn Yarbro   s   6014
*Cyberstealth* - S.N. Lewitt   s   3450
*Dancer of the Sixth* - Michelle Shirey
    Crean   s   1254
*Dancing Vac* - S.N. Lewitt   s   3451
*A Darker Geometry* - Mark O. Martin   s   3649
*Darkloom* - Cary Osborne   s   4225
*Deathgift* - Ann Tonsor Zeddies   s   6061
*Death's Gray Land* - Mike Shupp   s   5011
*Death's Head* - Mel Keegan   s   3029
*A Deeper Sea* - Alexander Jablokov   s   2838
*The Defenders* - Bill Baldwin   s   309
*The Defiance* - Bill Baldwin   s   310
*Design for Great-Day* - Alan Dean Foster   s   2001
*Destination: Mutiny* - Sean Dalton   s   1332
*Dominion's Reach* - Diann Thornley   s   5465
*Drakon* - S.M. Stirling   s   5294
*Dreadnought* - Thorarinn Gunnarsson   s   2464
*Earth Herald* - Jan Clark   s   1046
*Echoes of Honor* - David Weber   s   5669
*Enemy of My Enemy* - Ben Ohlander   s   4204
*Eternal Light* - Paul J. McAuley   s   3710
*Falkenberg's Legion* - Jerry Pournelle   s   4374
*The False Mirror* - Alan Dean Foster   s   2004
*Field of Dishonor* - David Weber   s   5670
*The Final Battle* - William C. Dietz   s   1546
*Final Blackout* - L. Ron Hubbard   s   2790
*Finger of God* - Michael Kasner   s   3013
*Fire in a Faraway Place* - Robert Frezza   s   2052
*Fire on the Border* - Kevin O'Donnell Jr.   s   4194
*The First Duelist* - Rutledge Etheridge   s   1849
*Fisherman's Hope* - David Feintuch   s   1900
*Flag in Exile* - David Weber   s   5671
*Force of Arms* - G. Harry Stine   s   5279
*Forever Peace* - Joe Haldeman   s   2488
*Freedom's Challenge* - Anne McCaffrey   s   3732
*Galactic MI* - Kevin D. Randle   s   4467
*The Galactic Silver Star* - Kevin D. Randle   s   4468
*Genellan: Planetfall* - Scott G. Gier   s   2223
*Glory's People* - Alfred Coppel   s   1183
*Glory's War* - Alfred Coppel   s   1184
*Go Tell the Spartans* - Jerry Pournelle   s   4375
*The Goda War* - Jay D. Blakeney   s   516
*Godzilla 2000* - Marc Cerasini   s   949
*The Great War: American Front* - Harry
    Turtledove   s   5501
*Grounded!* - Chris Claremont   s   1041
*Guts and Glory* - G. Harry Stine   s   5280
*The Harriers* - Gordon R. Dickson   s   1535
*Hero* - Dave Duncan   s   1680
*Hero* - Joel Rosenberg   s   4672

*The Hidden War* - Michael Armstrong   s   209
*High Moon* - Diane Duane   s   1661
*Honor Among Enemies* - David Weber   s   5673
*The Honor of the Queen* - David Weber   s   5674
*Hour of the Scorpion* - Matthew J. Costello   s   1199
*How Few Remain* - Harry Turtledove   s   5504
*Igniting the Reaches* - David Drake   s   1633
*In Enemy Hands* - David Weber   s   5675
*In the Shadow of the Moon* - Scott G. Gier   s   2224
*Inconstant Star* - Poul Anderson   s   129
*Independence Day* - Dean Devlin   s   1508
*The Infinity Plague* - Robert E. Vardeman   s   5564
*Iron Horse* - Bill Dolan   s   1568
*Island in the Sea of Time* - S.M. Stirling   s   5295
*Jefferson's War: Death of a Regiment* - Kevin
    Randle   s   4466
*Judgment Day* - G. Harry Stine   s   5281
*The Jungle* - David Drake   s   1634
*Jungle Assault* - P.M. Griffin   s   2437
*Justice* - David Drake   s   1635
*The Kalif's War* - John Dalmas   s   1322
*A Landscape of Darkness* - John Blair   s   513
*Legion of the Damned* - William C. Dietz   s   1547
*Lieutenant* - Rick Shelley   s   4972
*Limbo Search* - Parke Godwin   s   2245
*The Lizard War* - John Dalmas   s   1325
*Man-Kzin Wars IV* - Larry Niven   s   4124
*Man-Kzin Wars V* - Larry Niven   s   4125
*March or Die* - Andrew Keith   s   3035
*McCade's Bounty* - William C. Dietz   s   1550
*McLendon's Syndrome* - Robert Frezza   s   2053
*The Middle of Nowhere* - David Gerrold   s   2209
*Midshipman's Hope* - David Feintuch   s   1901
*Monsoon* - Peter L. Rice   s   4583
*Moonwar* - Ben Bova   s   588
*Mosaic* - Jeri Taylor   s   5403
*The Mountain Walks* - Roland J. Green   s   2349
*Naked to the Stars/The Alien Way* - Gordon R.
    Dickson   s   1537
*The Napoleon Wager* - William R.
    Forstchen   s   1980
*The Ninety Trillion Fausts* - Jack L. Chalker   s   958
*An Oblique Approach* - David Drake   s   1638
*Officer Cadet* - Rick Shelley   s   4973
*On Basilisk Station* - David Weber   s   5679
*On the Verge* - Roland J. Green   s   2350
*Ordeal of the Seventh Carrier* - Peter Albano   s   48
*Orion Among the Stars* - Ben Bova   s   589
*The Painful Field* - Roland J. Green   s   2351
*The Parafaith War* - L.E. Modesitt Jr.   s   3937
*Phule's Company* - Robert Asprin   s   260
*Phule's Paradise* - Robert Asprin   s   261
*Prince of Havoc* - Michael A. Stackpole   s   5204
*Prince of Mercenaries* - Jerry Pournelle   s   4377
*Prince of Sparta* - Jerry Pournelle   s   4378
*Prince of Sunset* - Steve White   s   5786
*A Prison Unsought* - Sherwood Smith   s   5139
*The Prisoner Within* - Donald E. McQuinn   s   3861
*Prodigy* - Jan Clark   s   1047
*The Quick* - Burt Cole   s   1113
*Red Army* - Ralph Peters   s   4306
*Redliners* - David Drake   s   1641
*The Regiment's War* - John Dalmas   s   1326
*The Return of the Emperor* - Allan Cole   s   1106
*Return to Camerein* - Rick Shelley   s   4974
*Revenge of the Damned* - Allan Cole   s   1107
*Revenge of the Seventh Carrier* - Peter Albano   s   49
*Ring of Swords* - Eleanor Arnason   s   210
*Rogue Squadron* - Michael A. Stackpole   s   5205
*A Roil of Stars* - Don Wismer   s   5930
*Rolling Hot* - David Drake   s   1642
*School of Fire* - David Sherman   s   4982
*A Screaming Across the Sky* - Brian Daley   s   1315
*Search and Destroy* - Keith William
    Andrews   s   141
*A Season for Slaughter* - David Gerrold   s   2211
*Secret Realms* - Tom Cool   s   1168
*Semper Mars* - Ian Douglas   s   1585
*Shadows of War* - Thomas S. Gressman   s   2432

*The Sharp End* - David Drake   s   1643
*Shiva in Steel* - Fred Saberhagen   s   4775
*The Short Victorious War* - David Weber   s   5681
*The Siege* - Bill Baldwin   s   312
*Sink the Armada* - Keith William Andrews   s   142
*A Small Colonial War* - Robert Frezza   s   2054
*The Spoils of War* - Alan Dean Foster   s   2016
*Squadron Alert* - Roland J. Green   s   2352
*Stars and Stripes Forever* - Harry Harrison   s   2577
*Starsea Invaders: First Action* - G. Harry
    Stine   s   5282
*Steelheart* - William C. Dietz   s   1552
*The Stone Dogs* - S.M. Stirling   s   5300
*Suicide Attack* - John Sievert   s   5023
*The Sum of Things* - Roland J. Green   s   2353
*Sundowner* - Chris Claremont   s   1043
*Super Carrier: The Ultimate Secret Weapon* - Peter
    Albano   s   50
*Surface Action* - David Drake   s   1646
*A Talent for War* - Jack McDevitt   s   3790
*Terrible Swift Sword* - William R.
    Forstchen   s   1983
*Through the Breach* - David Drake   s   1647
*A Time for Dragons* - Gary Gentile   s   2193
*To Dream in the City of Sorrows* - Kathryn M.
    Drennan   s   1654
*Treason in Time* - Keith William Andrews   s   143
*Universal Soldier* - Robert Tine   s   5476
*The Unknown Soldier* - Mickey Zucker
    Reichert   s   4525
*Vengeance* - Dafydd ab Hugh   s   10
*The Voyage* - David Drake   s   1649
*Voyage of the Star Wolf* - David Gerrold   s   2212
*War Birds* - R.M. Meluch   s   3875
*The War Machine* - David Drake   s   1650
*The Warrior* - David Drake   s   1651
*Warrior Shield* - G. Harry Stine   s   5283
*Warstrider* - William H. Keith Jr.   s   3037
*Way of the Clans* - Robert Thurston   s   5469
*When Heaven Fell* - William Barton   s   383
*The White Regiment* - John Dalmas   s   1327
*White Rhino* - Bill Dolan   s   1569
*The Wild Blue and the Gray* - William
    Sanders   s   4814
*Wing Commander: Freedom Flight* - Mercedes
    Lackey   s   3307
*With Full Honors* - Donald E. McQuinn   s   3865
*With the Lightnings* - David Drake   s   1652
*Women at War* - Lois McMaster Bujold   s   765

**Science Fiction — Mystery**

*Alien Blues* - Lynn S. Hightower   s   2682
*Alien Eyes* - Lynn S. Hightower   s   2683
*Alien Heat* - Lynn S. Hightower   s   2684
*Alien Rites* - Lynn S. Hightower   s   2685
*Archangel* - Michael Conner   s   1133
*Avenger* - William Shatner   s   4928
*The Bushido Incident* - Betty Anne
    Crawford   s   1248
*Caliban* - Roger MacBride Allen   s   77
*The California Voodoo Game* - Larry Niven   s   4117
*Carlucci's Edge* - Richard Paul Russo   s   4747
*Carlucci's Heart* - Richard Paul Russo   s   4748
*Cetaganda* - Lois McMaster Bujold   s   758
*Circle of One* - Eric James Fullilove   s   2092
*Clipjoint* - Wilhelmina Baird   s   294
*Crisis on Doona* - Anne McCaffrey   s   3723
*Crygender* - Thomas T. Thomas   s   5451
*Cyber Way* - Alan Dean Foster   s   2000
*Days of Atonement* - Walter Jon Williams   s   5836
*Deep Quarry* - John E. Stith   s   5302
*The Demolished Man* - Alfred Bester   s   476
*Destroying Angel* - Richard Paul Russo   s   4749
*The Dig* - Alan Dean Foster   s   2002
*The Digital Effect* - Steve Perry   s   4295
*Dragon's Teeth* - Lee Killough   s   3109
*Ecce and Old Earth* - Jack Vance   s   5546

*Enemy Unseen* - V.E. Mitchell  s  3918
*Evil Ascending* - Michael A. Stackpole  s  5198
*The Exile Kiss* - George Alec Effinger  s  1750
*Finders-Seekers* - Gayle Greeno  s  2421
*A Fire in the Sun* - George Alec Effinger  s  1751
*Flatlander* - Larry Niven  s  4121
*Flesh and Gold* - Phyllis Gotlieb  s  2286
*Forests of the Night* - S. Andrew Swann  s  5363
*Future Crime: An Anthology of the Shape of Crime to
    Come* - Cynthia Manson  s  3619
*The Ganymede Club* - Charles Sheffield  s  4955
*A Gathering Evil* - Michael A. Stackpole  s  5201
*Goblins* - Charles L. Grant  s  2309
*Golden Fleece* - Robert J. Sawyer  s  4857
*Greenthieves* - Alan Dean Foster  s  2005
*Guilt-Edged Ivory* - Doris Egan  s  1756
*Happy Policeman* - Patricia Anthony  s  160
*Hard Landing* - Algis Budrys  s  753
*Hawaiian U.F.O. Aliens* - Mel Gilden  s  2226
*The Higher Space* - Jamil Nasir  s  4070
*Hopeship* - Simon Lang  s  3315
*Illegal Alien* - Robert J. Sawyer  s  4858
*The Imperium Game* - K.D. Wentworth  s  5753
*In the Cube* - David Alexander Smith  s  5109
*Inferno* - Roger MacBride Allen  s  78
*Insanity, Illinois* - Mark Sumner  s  5358
*Jade Darcy and the Zen Pirates* - Stephen
    Goldin  s  2260
*The Jericho Iteration* - Allen Steele  s  5242
*Kill Station* - Diane Duane  s  1664
*Komarr* - Lois McMaster Bujold  s  760
*Lady Slings the Booze* - Spider Robinson  s  4640
*Lethal Exposure* - Kevin J. Anderson  s  110
*Lethal Interface* - Mel Odom  s  4193
*Madlands* - K.W. Jeter  s  2913
*Manjinn Moon* - Denise Vitola  s  5576
*Mars Prime* - William C. Dietz  s  1548
*Mask of the Phantasm* - Geary Gravel  s  2331
*Memory* - Lois McMaster Bujold  s  761
*Mind Slayer* - Kevin D. Randle  s  4469
*Mindblast* - Diane Duane  s  1665
*Mistworld* - Simon R. Green  s  2372
*Montezuma Strip* - Alan Dean Foster  s  2011
*Murder at the Galactic Writers' Society* - Janet
    Asimov  s  251
*Murder in the Solid State* - Wil McCarthy  s  3764
*Nightside City* - Lawrence Watt-Evans  s  5644
*Nimbus* - Alexander Jablokov  s  2839
*Noir* - K.W. Jeter  s  2916
*Passion Play* - Sean Stewart  s  5276
*The Persistence of Memory* - Karen Ripley  s  4592
*Polar City Blues* - Katharine Kerr  s  3073
*Protektor* - Charles Platt  s  4342
*Proteus in the Underworld* - Charles
    Sheffield  s  4962
*A Quantum Murder* - Peter F. Hamilton  s  2527
*Remake* - Connie Willis  s  5873
*Reunion on Neverend* - John E. Stith  s  5306
*The Rising* - James Doohan  s  1579
*Rock of Ages* - Walter Jon Williams  s  5840
*Second Contact* - Mike Resnick  s  4555
*Sherlock Holmes in Orbit* - Mike Resnick  s  4556
*The Shift* - George Foy  s  2033
*The Singularity Project* - F.M. Busby  s  784
*The Six Families* - Nancy Holder  s  2733
*Sparrowhawk* - Thomas A. Easton  s  1725
*The Specialist* - Wynne Whiteford  s  5788
*Specters of the Dawn* - S. Andrew Swann  s  5368
*Spider-Man: The Venom Factor* - Diane
    Duane  s  1667
*Spindoc* - Steve Perry  s  4300
*Star Precinct* - Kevin D. Randle  s  4470
*The Stranger* - Eric James Fullilove  s  2093
*Tea From an Empty Cup* - Pat Cadigan  s  809
*TekWar* - William Shatner  s  4941
*The Terminal Experiment* - Robert J.
    Sawyer  s  4860
*Terminal Games* - Cole Perriman  s  4283
*This Side of Judgment* - J.R. Dunn  s  1696

*Throy* - Jack Vance  s  5550
*To Dream in the City of Sorrows* - Kathryn M.
    Drennan  s  1654
*Too, Too Solid Flesh* - Nick O'Donohoe  s  4197
*Traitor Winds* - L.A. Graf  s  2298
*Tubular Android Superheroes* - Mel Gilden  s  2228
*The Two Georges* - Richard Dreyfuss  s  1655
*Virtual Destruction* - Kevin J. Anderson  s  118
*Whatdunits* - Mike Resnick  s  4558

## Science Fiction — Mystical

*The Bones of Time* - Kathleen Ann Goonan  s  2273
*The Broken God* - David Zindell  s  6085
*Brother to Shadows* - Andre Norton  s  4142
*Children of the Jedi* - Barbara Hambly  s  2500
*The Courtship of Princess Leia* - Dave
    Wolverton  s  5950
*The Crystal Star* - Vonda N. McIntyre  s  3820
*Darksaber* - Kevin J. Anderson  s  103
*Darwinia* - Robert Charles Wilson  s  5906
*Ecstasy Club* - Douglas Rushkoff  s  4732
*Ember From the Sun* - Mark Canter  s  870
*An Exaltation of Larks* - Robert Reed  s  4506
*A Fearful Symmetry* - James Luceno  s  3542
*Fortress of Forbidden Destiny* - Ryder
    Syverston  s  5378
*The Fourth Guardian* - Ronald Anthony
    Cross  s  1273
*The Glaive* - Cary Osborne  s  4227
*The Harvest* - Robert Charles Wilson  s  5909
*The Howling Stones* - Alan Dean Foster  s  2006
*Iroshi* - Cary Osborne  s  4228
*Kingdoms of the Wall* - Robert Silverberg  s  5033
*The Lost Guardian* - Ronald Anthony Cross  s  1274
*The New Rebellion* - Kristine Kathryn
    Rusch  s  4719
*Northworld* - David Drake  s  1637
*Scissors Cut Paper Wrap Stone* - Ian
    McDonald  s  3795
*Starborne* - Robert Silverberg  s  5042
*Vengeance* - David Drake  s  1648
*The White Guardian* - Ronald Anthony
    Cross  s  1275
*The Wild* - David Zindell  s  6086

## Science Fiction — Parody

*Kent Montana and the Really Ugly Thing From Mars* -
    Lionel Fenn  s  1918
*Kent Montana and the Reasonably Invisible Man* -
    Lionel Fenn  s  1919
*Samurai Cat Goes to the Movies* - Mark E.
    Rogers  s  4656
*Star Wreck II: The Attack of the Jargonites* - Leah
    Rewolinski  s  4563
*Star Wreck III: Time Warped* - Leah
    Rewolinski  s  4564
*Star Wreck IV: Live Long and Profit* - Leah
    Rewolinski  s  4565
*Star Wreck 6: Geek Space Nine* - Leah
    Rewolinski  s  4562
*Star Wreck: The Generation Gap* - Leah
    Rewolinski  s  4566
*Treks Not Taken: What if Stephen King, Anne Rice,
    Bret Easton Ellis, and Other Literary Greats Had
    Written Episodes of Star Trek: The Next
    Generation?* - Steven R. Boyett  s  607

## Science Fiction — Political

*1901* - Robert Conroy  s  1139
*Achilles' Choice* - Larry Niven  s  4114
*Acorna* - Anne McCaffrey  s  3717
*Alastor* - Jack Vance  s  5543
*Alien Eyes* - Lynn S. Hightower  s  2683
*Alien Influences* - Kristine Kathryn Rusch  s  4711
*Aliens: Earth Hive* - Steve Perry  s  4289

*Alpha Centauri* - William Barton  s  378
*Ambush at Corellia* - Roger MacBride Allen  s  76
*Ancestor's World* - A.C. Crispin  s  1259
*Ancient Shores* - Jack McDevitt  s  3786
*Anvil* - Nicolas van Pallandt  s  5540
*Apartheid, Superstrings, and Mordecai Thubana* -
    Michael Bishop  s  496
*Archangel Blues* - eluki bes shahar  s  471
*Aristoi* - Walter Jon Williams  s  5834
*Arrow From Earth* - F.M. Busby  s  782
*Back in the USSA* - Kim Newman  s  4095
*Balance of Power* - Dafydd ab Hugh  s  7
*Barrayar* - Lois McMaster Bujold  s  756
*Battle Front* - Ian Slater  s  5086
*Becoming Human* - Valerie J. Freireich  s  2049
*Beggars and Choosers* - Nancy Kress  s  3236
*Beggars Ride* - Nancy Kress  s  3238
*Beneath the Tree of Heaven* - David
    Wingrove  s  5917
*Beyond the Door* - Gary L. Blackwood  s  510
*Black Wine* - Candas Jane Dorsey  s  1582
*Blade Runner: Replicant Night* - K.W. Jeter  s  2907
*Blind Justice* - S.N. Lewitt  s  3448
*Blindfold* - Kevin J. Anderson  s  101
*Blood Feuds* - S.M. Stirling  s  5292
*Blood Lines* - William R. Burkett Jr.  s  774
*Blue Limbo* - Terrence M. Green  s  2377
*Blue Mars* - Kim Stanley Robinson  s  4629
*Blueheart* - Alison Sinclair  s  5068
*The Bohr Maker* - Linda Nagata  s  4064
*Brander's Book* - C.J. Mills  s  3909
*Bretta Martyn* - L. Neil Smith  s  5128
*Brightness Reef* - David Brin  s  684
*The Broken Land* - Ian McDonald  s  3791
*The Broken Wheel* - David Wingrove  s  5918
*Brother to Dragons* - Charles Sheffield  s  4949
*Brute Orbits* - George Zebrowski  s  6059
*Bully!* - Mike Resnick  s  4539
*Burn* - Bill Ransom  s  4476
*Burning Bright* - Melissa Scott  s  4894
*The Bushido Incident* - Betty Anne
    Crawford  s  1248
*The Call of Earth* - Orson Scott Card  s  882
*Cathouse* - Dean Ing  s  2828
*Cathy IV* - Frances Lucas  s  3539
*Celestis* - Paul Park  s  4241
*Cetaganda* - Lois McMaster Bujold  s  758
*Chains of Light* - Quentin Thomas  s  5449
*Chanur's Legacy* - C.J. Cherryh  s  981
*Chicago Red* - R.M. Meluch  s  3873
*The Children Star* - Joan Slonczewski  s  5090
*China Mountain Zhang* - Maureen F.
    McHugh  s  3817
*City of Diamond* - Jane Emerson  s  1807
*City of Golden Shadow* - Tad Williams  s  5828
*City on Fire* - Walter Jon Williams  s  5835
*Clarke County, Space* - Allen Steele  s  5241
*Cold as Ice* - Charles Sheffield  s  4950
*Commencement* - Roby James  s  2877
*Commitment Hour* - James Alan Gardner  s  2134
*Converse and Conflict* - L. Neil Smith  s  5130
*Cradle of Splendor* - Patricia Anthony  s  158
*Crisis on Doona* - Anne McCaffrey  s  3723
*Crossover* - Michael Jan Friedman  s  2063
*Crown of Empire* - Chelsea Quinn Yarbro  s  6014
*The Cult of Loving Kindness* - Paul Park  s  4242
*Cybernetic Jungle* - S.N. Lewitt  s  3449
*The Cyborg From Earth* - Charles Sheffield  s  4952
*Dancer of the Sixth* - Michelle Shirey
    Crean  s  1254
*Dark Genesis* - J. Gregory Keyes  s  3096
*Dark Sky Legion* - William Barton  s  379
*Darktraders* - eluki bes shahar  s  472
*Dayworld Breakup* - Philip Jose Farmer  s  1869
*Deception Well* - Linda Nagata  s  4065
*Desert Fire* - David Alexander  s  65
*Destiny's Road* - Larry Niven  s  4119
*Distraction* - Bruce Sterling  s  5256
*Double Planet* - John Gribbin  s  2433

*Dragon's Eye* - Alex McDonough   s   3801
*Dragonseye* - Anne McCaffrey   s   3730
*Dreamfall* - Joan D. Vinge   s   5571
*Dreamships* - Melissa Scott   s   4896
*The Drylands* - Mary Rosenblum   s   4678
*Earth Herald* - Jan Clark   s   1046
*Earthborn* - Orson Scott Card   s   884
*Earthsong* - Suzette Haden Elgin   s   1769
*Ecce and Old Earth* - Jack Vance   s   5546
*Echoes of Honor* - David Weber   s   5669
*Echoes of Issel* - Diann Thornley   s   5466
*The Ecolitan Enigma* - L.E. Modesitt Jr.   s   3927
*Eggheads* - Emily Devenport   s   1500
*Egil's Book* - C.J. Mills   s   3910
*The Eighth Rank* - David D. Ross   s   4682
*Emergence* - Peter F. Hamilton   s   2524
*Empire Builders* - Ben Bova   s   584
*Empire's End* - Allan Cole   s   1103
*The Engines of God* - Jack McDevitt   s   3787
*An Exchange of Hostages* - Susan R.
    Matthews   s   3692
*Exile* - Michael P. Kube-McDowell   s   3248
*Expendable* - James Alan Gardner   s   2135
*An Eye for Dark Places* - Norma Marder   s   3622
*The Eyes of God* - Mark Kreighbaum   s   3231
*Fallen Angels* - Larry Niven   s   4120
*The False Mirror* - Alan Dean Foster   s   2004
*Far Edge of Darkness* - Linda Evans   s   1855
*Fatherland* - Robert Harris   s   2564
*Field of Dishonor* - David Weber   s   5670
*Fire in the Sky* - Jo Clayton   s   1067
*Fire Margins* - Lisanne Norman   s   4137
*Firestar* - Michael Flynn   s   1962
*Fisherman's Hope* - David Feintuch   s   1900
*The Fleet of Stars* - Poul Anderson   s   126
*Flowerdust* - Gwyneth Jones   s   2952
*Flux* - Stephen Baxter   s   399
*Foreigner* - C.J. Cherryh   s   990
*Forever Peace* - Joe Haldeman   s   2488
*Fortune's Wheel* - Lisanne Norman   s   4138
*Forward the Foundation* - Isaac Asimov   s   236
*Foundation and Chaos* - Greg Bear   s   418
*Four Ways to Forgiveness* - Ursula K. Le
    Guin   s   3380
*The Fugitive Stars* - Daniel Ransom   s   4479
*Full Tide of Night* - J.R. Dunn   s   1695
*Ganwold's Child* - Diann Thornley   s   5467
*The Gap into Madness: Chaos and Order* - Stephen R.
    Donaldson   s   1573
*The Gap into Ruin: This Day All Gods Die* - Stephen
    R. Donaldson   s   1575
*The Gatekeepers* - Daniel Graham Jr.   s   2301
*The Gathering Flame* - Debra Doyle   s   1599
*Generation Warrior* - Anne McCaffrey   s   3735
*Gibbon's Decline and Fall* - Sheri S.
    Tepper   s   5430
*Glory* - Alfred Coppel   s   1182
*GodHeads* - Emily Devenport   s   1501
*God's Fires* - Patricia Anthony   s   159
*The Gold Coast* - Kim Stanley Robinson   s   4632
*Green Mars* - Kim Stanley Robinson   s   4633
*The Green Progression* - L.E. Modesitt Jr.   s   3932
*Griffin's Egg* - Michael Swanwick   s   5370
*Ground-Ties* - Jane S. Fancher   s   1861
*Grounded!* - Chris Claremont   s   1041
*Growing Up Weightless* - John M. Ford   s   1970
*Half-Light* - Denise Vitola   s   5575
*Half the Day Is Night* - Maureen F.
    McHugh   s   3818
*Halfway Human* - Carolyn Ives Gilman   s   2237
*Hand of Prophecy* - Severna Park   s   4244
*Harmonies of the 'Net* - Jane S. Fancher   s   1862
*Harvest of Stars* - Poul Anderson   s   127
*Harvest the Fire* - Poul Anderson   s   128
*Heads* - Greg Bear   s   419
*Heaven's Reach* - David Brin   s   687
*Heavy Time* - C.J. Cherryh   s   995

*The Hedge of Mist* - Patricia Kennealy-
    Morrison   s   3062
*Heirs of Empire* - David Weber   s   5672
*Hellburner* - C.J. Cherryh   s   996
*Hidden Fires* - Katharine Eliska Kimbriel   s   3117
*High Steel* - Jack C. Haldeman II   s   2486
*A History Maker* - Alasdair Gray   s   2338
*The Host* - Peter R. Emshwiller   s   1819
*House of Moons* - K.D. Wentworth   s   5752
*How Few Remain* - Harry Turtledove   s   5504
*Hunting the Corrigan's Blood* - Holly Lisle   s   3484
*I Wake From a Dream of a Drowned Star City* - S.P.
    Somtow   s   5157
*Icarus Descending* - Elizabeth Hand   s   2536
*Iceman* - Cynthia Felice   s   1913
*The Immortals* - Tracy Hickman   s   2681
*Imposter* - Valerie J. Freireich   s   2050
*In the Cube* - David Alexander Smith   s   5109
*In the Wrong Hands* - Edward Gibson   s   2215
*India's Story* - Kathlyn S. Starbuck   s   5208
*Infinity's Shore* - David Brin   s   688
*Inheritor* - C.J. Cherryh   s   997
*Innerverse* - John DeChancie   s   1458
*The Inquisitor* - Cheryl J. Franklin   s   2037
*Inquisitor* - Ian Watson   s   5637
*Interface* - Stephen Bury   s   781
*Interface Masque* - Shariann Lewitt   s   3453
*Invader* - C.J. Cherryh   s   998
*Islands of Tomorrow* - F.M. Busby   s   783
*The Joy Machine* - James Gunn   s   2458
*The Kalif's War* - John Dalmas   s   1322
*Kings of the High Frontier* - Victor Koman   s   3199
*King's Sacrifice* - Margaret Weis   s   5717
*Kit's Book* - C.J. Mills   s   3911
*Knights of the Black Earth* - Margaret Weis   s   5718
*Labyrinth of Night* - Allen Steele   s   5244
*The LaNague Chronicles* - F. Paul Wilson   s   5889
*The Lanterns of God* - Ron Sarti   s   4835
*The Last Dancer* - Daniel Keys Moran   s   3994
*The Last Reckoning* - Mike Shupp   s   5012
*The Law of Becoming* - Kate Elliott   s   1774
*The Law of War* - William Shatner   s   4931
*Legacy of the Ancients* - Ron Sarti   s   4836
*Legion of the Damned* - William C. Dietz   s   1547
*Lifeline* - Kevin J. Anderson   s   111
*Lightwing* - Tara K. Harper   s   2551
*Lion Time in Timbuctoo* - Robert Silverberg   s   5036
*Living Real* - James C. Bassett   s   386
*Looking for the Mahdi* - N. Lee Wood·   s   5966
*The Lost King* - Margaret Weis   s   5720
*Lovelock* - Orson Scott Card   s   892
*Lunar Descent* - Allen Steele   s   5245
*Lunar Justice* - Charles L. Harness   s   2545
*Maia's Veil* - P.K. McAllister   s   3707
*Man o' War* - William Shatner   s   4932
*The March Hare Network* - Jack L. Chalker   s   957
*Mars* - Ben Bova   s   586
*Mars Underground* - William Hartmann   s   2584
*Martian Rainbow* - Robert L. Forward   s   1987
*The Masterharper of Pern* - Anne
    McCaffrey   s   3739
*Matrix Cubed* - Britton Bloom   s   554
*Maximum Light* - Nancy Kress   s   3241
*Memory* - Lois McMaster Bujold   s   761
*The Memory Cathedral* - Jack Dann   s   1341
*The Memory of Earth* - Orson Scott Card   s   894
*Memorymakers* - Brian Herbert   s   2665
*The Merro Tree* - Katie Waitman   s   5609
*Metropolitan* - Walter Jon Williams   s   5839
*A Million Open Doors* - John Barnes   s   353
*Mind-Speakers' Call* - Gayle Greeno   s   2423
*Mining the Oort* - Frederik Pohl   s   4349
*Mirror Dance* - Lois McMaster Bujold   s   762
*The Misconceiver* - Lucy Ferriss   s   1929
*Mistwalker* - Denise Lopez Heald   s   2637
*The Modular Man* - Roger MacBride Allen   s   79
*The Moon Is a Harsh Mistress* - Robert A.
    Heinlein   s   2645
*Moonrise* - Ben Bova   s   587

*Moonspeaker* - K.D. Wentworth   s   5754
*Mother of Storms* - John Barnes   s   354
*The Mountains of Majipoor* - Robert
    Silverberg   s   5037
*Moving Mars* - Greg Bear   s   421
*The Multiplex Man* - James P. Hogan   s   2727
*Mutant Star* - Karen Haber   s   2475
*Mysterium* - Robert Charles Wilson   s   5911
*The Ninety Trillion Fausts* - Jack L. Chalker   s   958
*Northlight* - Deborah Wheeler   s   5775
*Northwind* - David Drake   s   1637
*O Pioneer!* - Frederik Pohl   s   4350
*The Oak Above the Kings: A Book of the Keltiad* -
    Patricia Kennealy   s   3058
*On Basilisk Station* - David Weber   s   5679
*Once a Hero* - Elizabeth Moon   s   3970
*Oracle* - Mike Resnick   s   4551
*Orion's Dagger* - P.K. McAllister   s   3708
*Other* - Gordon R. Dickson   s   1538
*The Others* - Margaret Wander Bonanno   s   565
*OtherWhere* - Margaret Wander Bonanno   s   566
*Outbanker* - Timothy A. Madden   s   3603
*Outworld Cats* - Jack Lovejoy   s   3536
*The Oxygen Barons* - Gregory Feeley   s   1897
*Pacific Edge* - Kim Stanley Robinson   s   4634
*The Painful Field* - Roland J. Green   s   2351
*Palace* - Katharine Kerr   s   3072
*Pallas* - L. Neil Smith   s   5132
*Parable of the Talents* - Octavia E. Butler   s   793
*Partisan* - S. Andrew Swann   s   5365
*Paths to Otherwhere* - James P. Hogan   s   2728
*Personal Agendas* - Al Sarrantonio   s   4833
*Peter Nevsky and the True Story of the Russian Moon
    Landing* - John Calvin Batchelor   s   388
*The Phoenix in Flight* - Sherwood Smith   s   5138
*A Plague of Change* - L. Warren Douglas   s   1587
*The Player of Games* - Iain M. Banks   s   326
*The Pleistocene Redemption* - Dan
    Gallagher   s   2107
*Polymorph* - Scott Westerfeld   s   5767
*Power Lines* - Anne McCaffrey   s   3743
*The Price of Ransom* - Alis A. Rasmussen   s   4483
*The Price of the Stars* - Debra Doyle   s   1604
*Primary Inversion* - Catherine Asaro   s   220
*Prince of Sparta* - Jerry Pournelle   s   4378
*Prince of Sunset* - Steve White   s   5786
*A Prison Unsought* - Sherwood Smith   s   5139
*Prodigy* - Jan Clark   s   1047
*Profiteer* - S. Andrew Swann   s   5366
*Proxies* - Laura J. Mixon   s   3922
*The Pure Cold Light* - Gregory Frost   s   2087
*The Queen's Squadron* - R.M. Meluch   s   3874
*Rainbow Man* - M.J. Engh   s   1824
*Reclamation* - Sarah Zettel   s   6081
*Red Dust* - Paul J. McAuley   s   3715
*Red Genesis* - S.C. Sykes   s   5377
*Red Mars* - Kim Stanley Robinson   s   4635
*The Regiment's War* - John Dalmas   s   1326
*Relic of Empire* - W. Michael Gear   s   2171
*Remnant Population* - Elizabeth Moon   s   3972
*The Resurrections* - Simon Louvish   s   3528
*The Return of the Emperor* - Allan Cole   s   1106
*Revolutionary* - S. Andrew Swann   s   5367
*Revolution's Shore* - Alis A. Rasmussen   s   4484
*Rewind* - Terry England   s   1825
*The Rifter's Covenant* - Sherwood Smith   s   5140
*The Ringworld Throne* - Larry Niven   s   4128
*Rinn's Star* - Paula E. Downing   s   1719
*The Rising of the Moon* - Flynn Connolly   s   1135
*River of Dust* - Alexander Jablokov   s   2840
*Rogue Star* - Michael Flynn   s   1965
*Ruler of Naught* - Sherwood Smith   s   5141
*Russian Spring* - Norman Spinrad   s   5174
*The Salukan Gambit* - Sean Dalton   s   1333
*Sarek* - A.C. Crispin   s   1260
*School of Fire* - David Sherman   s   4982
*Seeds of Destiny* - Thomas A. Easton   s   1724
*Sentinels* - Margaret Weis   s   5725
*Sheltered Lives* - Charles Oberndorf   s   4188

*The Ship Who Won* - Anne McCaffrey  s  3750
*Short Blade* - Peter R. Emshwiller  s  1820
*Sideshow* - Sheri S. Tepper  s  5436
*Siduri's Net* - P.K. McAllister  s  3709
*Sister Blood* - Karen Haber  s  2476
*Six Moon Dance* - Sheri S. Tepper  s  5437
*Songs of Chaos* - S.N. Lewitt  s  3452
*Sorcerers of Majipoor* - Robert Silverberg  s  5041
*Speaking Dreams* - Severna Park  s  4245
*The Spoils of War* - Alan Dean Foster  s  2016
*Stepwater* - L. Warren Douglas  s  1588
*Stinger* - Nancy Kress  s  3243
*The Stone Within* - David Wingrove  s  5920
*Stranger in a Strange Land* - Robert A.
   Heinlein  s  2649
*Sugar Rain* - Paul Park  s  4243
*The Summer Queen* - Joan D. Vinge  s  5572
*Tangled Webs* - Steve Mudd  s  4044
*Tech-Heaven* - Linda Nagata  s  4066
*Tek Power* - William Shatner  s  4937
*Testament* - Valerie J. Freireich  s  2051
*They Fly at Ciron* - Samuel R. Delany  s  1482
*The Third Force* - Marc Laidlaw  s  3313
*This Alien Shore* - C.S. Friedman  s  2059
*A Thousand Words for Stranger* - Julie E.
   Czerneda  s  1304
*Throy* - Jack Vance  s  5550
*To a Highland Nation* - Christopher
   Rowley  s  4698
*To Fear the Light* - Ben Bova  s  595
*Treaty at Doona* - Anne McCaffrey  s  3752
*The Triad Worlds* - F.M. Busby  s  786
*Triumph* - Ben Bova  s  598
*The Truce at Bakura* - Kathy Tyers  s  5527
*The Unwound Way* - William Adams  s  35
*Uplink* - Jane S. Fancher  s  1865
*Use of Weapons* - Iain M. Banks  s  328
*Vengeance* - David Drake  s  1648
*ViraVax* - Bill Ransom  s  4478
*The Virgin and the Dinosaur* - R. Garcia y
   Robertson  s  2122
*Voices of Chaos* - A.C. Crispin  s  1266
*Voices of Hope* - David Feintuch  s  1903
*Vortex* - Allan Cole  s  1108
*Wanderer* - Donald E. McQuinn  s  3862
*Warlords of Jupiter* - William H. Keith Jr.  s  3036
*The Weigher* - Eric Vinicoff  s  5574
*The Wells of Phyre* - L. Warren Douglas  s  1589
*Where the Ships Die* - William C. Dietz  s  1553
*A Whisper of Time* - Paula E. Downing  s  1595
*The White Abacus* - Damien Broderick  s  708
*White Moon, Red Dragon* - David
   Wingrove  s  5921
*The White Mountain* - David Wingrove  s  5922
*The White Regiment* - John Dalmas  s  1327
*Winning Colors* - Elizabeth Moon  s  3976
*Witch* - Donald E. McQuinn  s  3864
*With Full Honors* - Donald E. McQuinn  s  3865
*A Wizard in Absentia* - Christopher Stasheff  s  5229
*A Wizard in Chaos* - Christopher Stasheff  s  5230
*A Wizard in Peace* - Christopher Stasheff  s  5233
*A Wizard in War* - Christopher Stasheff  s  5234
*World Spirits* - Aline Boucher-Kaplan  s  580
*Young Bleys* - Gordon R. Dickson  s  1540
*Zjhanne's Book* - C.J. Mills  s  3912

**Science Fiction — Post-Disaster**

*12 Monkeys* - Elizabeth Hand  s  2532
*Cinderblock* - Janine Ellen Young  s  6047
*Circuit of Heaven* - Dennis Danvers  s  1348
*Earth 2* - Melissa Crandall  s  1247
*The Earth Saver* - Catherine Wells  s  5745
*Eternity Road* - Jack McDevitt  s  3788
*An Eye for Dark Places* - Norma Marder  s  3622
*The Gaia Websters* - Kim Antieau  s  198
*Inherit the Earth* - Brian Stableford  s  5193
*Initiation* - Marian Hughes  s  2806

*Journals of the Plague Years* - Norman
   Spinrad  s  5172
*Other Nature* - Stephanie A. Smith  s  5145
*Quarantine* - Greg Egan  s  1762
*Rim: A Novel of Virtual Reality* - Alexander
   Besher  s  475
*A Second Infinity* - Michael D. Weaver  s  5660
*Strange Deliverance* - Mary Brown  s  728
*Toward the End of Time* - John Updike  s  5531
*The Transall Saga* - Gary Paulsen  s  4262
*Vanishing Point* - Michaela Roessner  s  4652

**Science Fiction — Post-Holocaust**

*Adiamante* - L.E. Modesitt Jr.  s  3924
*Afrikorps* - Bill Dolan  s  1566
*After the Blue* - Russel Like  s  3465
*Alien Earth* - Megan Lindholm  s  3469
*Among Madmen* - Jim Starlin  s  5212
*Beyond Eden* - J.M. Morgan  s  3999
*Bone Danc: A Fantasy for Technophiles* - Emma
   Bull  s  766
*Chains of Command* - Bill McCay  s  3767
*Chicago Red* - R.M. Meluch  s  3873
*Children of the Earth* - Catherine Wells  s  5743
*Christmas Slaughter* - Mark Grant  s  2323
*The Clouds of Saturn* - Michael McCollum  s  3770
*Cobra Curse* - Bill Dolan  s  1567
*Deep Trek* - James Axler  s  278
*Destination: Showdown* - Jake Davis  s  1405
*The Drylands* - Mary Rosenblum  s  4678
*The Earth Is All That Lasts* - Catherine
   Wells  s  5744
*The Earth Remembers* - Susan Torian Olan  s  4209
*Faraday's Orphans* - N. Lee Wood  s  5965
*The Fortunate Fall* - Raphael Carter  s  927
*The Furies* - Suzy McKee Charnas  s  968
*Future Eden* - J.M. Morgan  s  4001
*Genetic Soldier* - George Turner  s  5492
*Groogleman* - Debra Doyle  s  1600
*I Who Have Never Known Men* - Jacqueline
   Harpman  s  2554
*In the Mothers' Land* - Elisabeth Vonarburg  s  5590
*Iron Horse* - Bill Dolan  s  1568
*Kamikaze L'Amour* - Richard Kadrey  s  2998
*L.A. Strike* - David Robbins  s  4599
*The Lanterns of God* - Ron Sarti  s  4835
*The Last Rangers* - Jake Davis  s  1406
*Legacies* - Alison Sinclair  s  5069
*Legacy of the Ancients* - Ron Sarti  s  4836
*Lifeline* - Kevin J. Anderson  s  111
*Madlands* - K.W. Jeter  s  2913
*Madman Run* - David Robbins  s  4600
*The Marked Man* - Charles Ingrid  s  2831
*Mazeway* - Jack Williamson  s  5866
*Mutant Hell* - Mark Grant  s  2324
*Mutants Amok* - Mark Grant  s  2325
*Nanoware Time/The Persistence of Vision* - Ian
   Watson  s  5638
*The New Springtime* - Robert Silverberg  s  5040
*Northlight* - Deborah Wheeler  s  5775
*Orbital Resonance* - John Barnes  s  356
*OtherWise* - Margaret Wander Bonanno  s  567
*Ring* - Stephen Baxter  s  402
*Sailor Song* - Ken Kesey  s  3082
*The Silent City* - Elisabeth Vonarburg  s  5592
*The Sky Lords* - John Brosnan  s  720
*Spartan Run* - David Robbins  s  4602
*Suicide Attack* - John Sievert  s  5023
*Time and Light* - William Bornefeld  s  574
*Timediver's Dawn* - L.E. Modesitt Jr.  s  3940
*Traitors from Within* - R.A. Montgomery  s  3966
*Vengeance Strike* - David Robbins  s  4604
*The Wall* - Marlen Haushofer  s  2603
*The Wall at the Edge of the World* - Jim
   Aikin  s  46
*The War of the Sky Lords* - John Brosnan  s  721
*White Rhino* - Bill Dolan  s  1569

*Winterlong* - Elizabeth Hand  s  2539
*Wolf and Iron* - Gordon R. Dickson  s  1539
*Wolf in Shadow* - David Gemmell  s  2191
*Yellowstone Run* - David Robbins  s  4605
*The Yngling and the Circle of Power* - John
   Dalmas  s  1328
*The Yngling in Yamato* - John Dalmas  s  1329

**Science Fiction — Post-Nuclear Holocaust**

*Agviq* - Michael Armstrong  s  208
*Ark Liberty* - Will Bradley  s  656
*Black Snow Days* - Claudia O'Keefe  s  4205
*Blade Runner 2: The Edge of Human* - K.W.
   Jeter  s  2906
*Dawn's Uncertain Light* - Neal Barrett Jr.  s  365
*Devil's Deal* - Richard Austin  s  277
*The Dream Vessel* - Jeff Bredenberg  s  664
*Earthfall* - Jerry Earl Brown  s  724
*The Einstein Intersection* - Samuel R.
   Delany  s  1481
*Escape to the Wind* - Jennifer DiMarco  s  1559
*Firelance* - David Mace  s  3586
*The Folk of the Fringe* - Orson Scott Card  s  886
*A Gift upon the Shore* - M.K. Wren  s  5982
*I Feel Like the Morning Star* - Gregory
   Maguire  s  3608
*Imago* - Octavia E. Butler  s  791
*Masters of the Fist* - Edward P. Hughes  s  2805
*Meridian 144* - Meg Files  s  1932
*The Outlander: Captivity* - B.J. Salterberg  s  4792
*The Penultimate Truth* - Philip K. Dick  s  1522
*Return to Isis* - Jean Stewart  s  5268
*River Rats* - Caroline Stevermer  s  5267
*The Stars Must Wait* - Keith Laumer  s  3346
*The Struggle* - Jerry Ahern  s  44
*The Wall Around Eden* - Joan Slonczewski  s  5092
*Wanderer* - Donald E. McQuinn  s  3862
*Warrior* - Donald E. McQuinn  s  3863
*White Light* - William Barton  s  384
*Witch* - Donald E. McQuinn  s  3864
*The World Next Door* - Brad Ferguson  s  1924

**Science Fiction — Psychic Powers**

*Alien Heat* - Lynn S. Hightower  s  2684
*Before the Storm* - Michael P. Kube-
   McDowell  s  3247
*Black Trump* - George R.R. Martin  s  3642
*Blindfold* - Kevin J. Anderson  s  101
*By Honor Betray'd* - Debra Doyle  s  1598
*Cat Scratch Fever* - Tara K. Harper  s  2550
*Chaos Come Again* - Wilhelmina Baird  s  293
*Children of the Thunder* - John Brunner  s  733
*Cloud's Rider* - C.J. Cherryh  s  983
*Commencement* - Roby James  s  2877
*Crown of Shadows* - C.S. Friedman  s  2057
*Damia* - Anne McCaffrey  s  3725
*Damia's Children* - Anne McCaffrey  s  3726
*Dark Force Rising* - Timothy Zahn  s  6052
*Dark Genesis* - J. Gregory Keyes  s  3096
*The Demolished Man* - Alfred Bester  s  476
*The Devil's Heart* - Carmen Carter  s  922
*Diamond Mask: A Novel* - Julian May  s  3697
*Distant Friends and Others* - Timothy Zahn  s  6053
*Down the Stream of Stars* - Jeffrey A.
   Carver  s  928
*Dream Baby* - Bruce McAllister  s  3706
*Dreamfall* - Joan D. Vinge  s  5571
*The Einstein Intersection* - Samuel R.
   Delany  s  1481
*The Enchantments of Flesh and Spirit* - Storm
   Constantine  s  1141
*Exiles' Return* - Gayle Greeno  s  2420
*The Fermata* - Nicholson Baker  s  302
*Finders-Seekers* - Gayle Greeno  s  2421
*Fire Margins* - Lisanne Norman  s  4137
*Flowerdust* - Gwyneth Jones  s  2952

*Fortune's Wheel* - Lisanne Norman  s  4138
*Girl in Landscape* - Jonathan Lethem  s  3440
*GodHeads* - Emily Devenport  s  1501
*Guises of the Mind* - Rebecca Neason  s  4081
*The Hollow Man* - Dan Simmons  s  5054
*House of Moons* - K.D. Wentworth  s  5752
*In the Mothers' Land* - Elisabeth Vonarburg  s  5590
*India's Story* - Kathlyn S. Starbuck  s  5208
*Ingathering: The Complete People Stories of Zenna Henderson* - Zenna Henderson  s  2659
*Into the Deep* - Ken Grimwood  s  2450
*Jack the Bodiless* - Julian May  s  3698
*Jaguar* - Bill Ransom  s  4477
*Jumper* - Steven Gould  s  2290
*The Kronos Condition* - Emily Devenport  s  1502
*A Landscape of Darkness* - John Blair  s  513
*The Last Command* - Timothy Zahn  s  6055
*The Last Dancer* - Daniel Keys Moran  s  3994
*The Last Hawk* - Catherine Asaro  s  219
*Leroni of Darkover* - Marion Zimmer Bradley  s  642
*Lightwing* - Tara K. Harper  s  2551
*The Long Hunt* - Debra Doyle  s  1602
*Lunar Justice* - Charles L. Harness  s  2545
*Lyon's Pride* - Anne McCaffrey  s  3738
*Magnificat* - Julian May  s  3699
*Mainline* - Deborah Christian  s  1026
*Marked Cards* - George R.R. Martin  s  3647
*Marks of Our Brothers* - Jane M. Lindskold  s  3475
*The Martian Chronicles* - Ray Bradbury  s  622
*Mentor* - Kris Jensen  s  2898
*Metropolitan* - Walter Jon Williams  s  5839
*Mind Meld* - John Vornholt  s  5596
*Mind-Speakers' Call* - Gayle Greeno  s  2423
*Mindstar Rising* - Peter F. Hamilton  s  2526
*Moonspeaker* - K.D. Wentworth  s  5754
*Mutant Legacy* - Karen Haber  s  2474
*The Mutant Season* - Robert Silverberg  s  5039
*Mutant Star* - Karen Haber  s  2475
*One Mind's Eye* - Kathy Tyers  s  5525
*The Others* - Margaret Wander Bonanno  s  565
*OtherWhere* - Margaret Wander Bonanno  s  566
*OtherWise* - Margaret Wander Bonanno  s  567
*Panda Ray* - Michael Kandel  s  3011
*Pegasus in Flight* - Anne McCaffrey  s  3742
*Polar City Blues* - Katharine Kerr  s  3073
*Primary Inversion* - Catherine Asaro  s  220
*Project Farcry* - Pauline Ashwell  s  230
*Prophet* - Mike Resnick  s  4553
*Psi-Man* - David Peters  s  4305
*Q-Space* - Greg Cox  s  1228
*Q-Squared* - Peter David  s  1385
*Q-Zone* - Greg Cox  s  1229
*A Quantum Murder* - Peter F. Hamilton  s  2527
*Razor's Edge* - Lisanne Norman  s  4139
*Receive the Gift* - Louise Marley  s  3628
*Reclamation* - Sarah Zettel  s  6081
*Rediscovery: A Novel of Darkover* - Marion Zimmer Bradley  s  643
*Rider at the Gate* - C.J. Cherryh  s  1000
*Rinn's Star* - Paula E. Downing  s  1719
*A Roil of Stars* - Don Wismer  s  5930
*The Rowan* - Anne McCaffrey  s  3747
*Saturn's Child* - Nichelle Nichols  s  4101
*Shade* - Emily Devenport  s  1504
*Shade's Children* - Garth Nix  s  4130
*The Shadow Matrix* - Marion Zimmer Bradley  s  645
*The Shadow Within* - Jeanne Cavelos  s  944
*Shadows in the Water* - Kathryn Lasky  s  3341
*Shadows of the Empire* - Steve Perry  s  4299
*Sing the Light* - Louise Marley  s  3629
*Sing the Warmth* - Louise Marley  s  3630
*Sister Blood* - Karen Haber  s  2476
*Smoke and Mirrors* - Jane M. Lindskold  s  3476
*Soothsayer* - Mike Resnick  s  4557
*Starpilot's Grave* - Debra Doyle  s  1606
*The Stars My Destination* - Alfred Bester  s  478
*The Tery* - F. Paul Wilson  s  5900

*A Thousand Words for Stranger* - Julie E. Czerneda  s  1304
*Threshold* - Bill Myers  s  4060
*Timediver's Dawn* - L.E. Modesitt Jr.  s  3940
*Triangle: Imzadi II* - Peter David  s  1388
*Turn of the Cards* - Victor Milan  s  3891
*Turning Point* - Lisanne Norman  s  4140
*Voices* - John Vornholt  s  5598
*The Wall at the Edge of the World* - Jim Aikin  s  46
*The War Minstrels* - Karen Haber  s  2477
*Warp Angel* - Stuart Hopen  s  2766
*A Wizard in Mind* - Christopher Stasheff  s  5232
*A Wizard in War* - Christopher Stasheff  s  5234
*Woman Without a Shadow* - Karen Haber  s  2478

**Science Fiction — Quest**

*Eternity Road* - Jack McDevitt  s  3788

**Science Fiction — Reincarnation**

*Brain Rose* - Nancy Kress  s  3239

**Science Fiction — Religious**

*Calde of the Long Sun* - Gene Wolfe  s  5937
*Day of the Dead* - Neil Gaiman  s  2102
*First Dawn* - Mike Moscoe  s  4038
*Saint Leibowitz and the Wild Horse Woman* - Walter M. Miller Jr.  s  3908
*The Shapes of Their Hearts* - Melissa Scott  s  4901

**Science Fiction — Robot Fiction**

*Arachne* - Lisa Mason  s  3661
*Berserker Kill* - Fred Saberhagen  s  4761
*Berserker Lies* - Fred Saberhagen  s  4762
*Blood Siege* - G. Harry Stine  s  5278
*Caliban* - Roger MacBride Allen  s  77
*Cybernarc* - Robert Cain  s  829
*The Cybernetic Shogun* - Victor Milan  s  3890
*Diaspora* - Greg Egan  s  1759
*Dictator* - William F. Wu  s  5996
*Earthling* - Tony Daniel  s  1336
*End Game* - Robert Cain  s  830
*Force of Arms* - G. Harry Stine  s  5279
*Forward the Foundation* - Isaac Asimov  s  236
*Foundation and Chaos* - Greg Bear  s  418
*Foundation's Fear* - Gregory Benford  s  446
*The Gaia Websters* - Kim Antieau  s  198
*Gold Dragon* - Robert Cain  s  831
*Greenthieves* - Alan Dean Foster  s  2005
*Guts and Glory* - G. Harry Stine  s  5280
*The Humanoids* - Jack Williamson  s  5865
*I, Robot: The Illustrated Screenplay* - Harlan Ellison  s  1785
*The Immortality Option* - James P. Hogan  s  2725
*Inferno* - Roger MacBride Allen  s  78
*Isaac Asimov's I-Bots* - Steve Perry  s  4297
*Machines That Kill* - Fred Saberhagen  s  4769
*The Man in the Moon Must Die* - Jeff Bredenberg  s  665
*Maverick* - Bruce Bethke  s  484
*ME: A Novel of Self Discovery* - Thomas T. Thomas  s  5452
*Murder at the Galactic Writers' Society* - Janet Asimov  s  251
*Norby and the Court Jester* - Janet Asimov  s  252
*Norby and the Oldest Dragon* - Janet Asimov  s  253
*Norby and Yobo's Great Adventure* - Janet Asimov  s  254
*Norby Down to Earth* - Janet Asimov  s  255
*The Positronic Man* - Isaac Asimov  s  249
*Predator* - William F. Wu  s  5998
*Renegade* - Cordell Scotten  s  4903
*Sailing Bright Eternity* - Gregory Benford  s  449

*The Sherwood Game* - Esther Friesner  s  2082
*The Sounding Stillness* - Kenneth Von Gunden  s  5587
*Star Child* - James P. Hogan  s  2730
*Utopia* - Roger MacBride Allen  s  83
*Virtual Girl* - Amy Thomson  s  5462
*Warrior* - William F. Wu  s  6000
*Warsprite* - Jefferson P. Swycaffer  s  5375
*The Winds of Mars* - H.M. Hoover  s  2765
*A Wizard in Absentia* - Christopher Stasheff  s  5229

**Science Fiction — Romance**

*Dying of the Light* - George R.R. Martin  s  3644
*Iceman* - Cynthia Felice  s  1913
*The Khan's Persuasion* - Cynthia Felice  s  1914
*Naming the Flowers* - Kate Wilhelm  s  5809
*Stopping at Slowyear* - Frederik Pohl  s  4355
*The Ugly Little Boy* - Isaac Asimov  s  250

**Science Fiction — Satire**

*As She Climbed Across the Table* - Jonathan Lethem  s  3439
*Brother Termite* - Patricia Anthony  s  156
*City of Truth* - James Morrow  s  4030
*Elvissey* - Jack Womack  s  5957
*Free Zone* - Charles Platt  s  4341
*Half Asleep in Frog Pajamas* - Tom Robbins  s  4606
*Headcrash* - Bruce Bethke  s  483
*A History Maker* - Alasdair Gray  s  2338
*Hocus Pocus or, What's the Hurry, Son?* - Kurt Vonnegut Jr.  s  5593
*Humpty Dumpty: An Oval* - Damon Knight  s  3186
*Kalifornia* - Marc Laidlaw  s  3311
*Live From Golgotha: A Novel* - Gore Vidal  s  5569
*The Long Dark Tea-Time of the Soul* - Douglas Adams  s  30
*Lost Pages* - Paul Di Filippo  s  1516
*Muddle Earth* - John Brunner  s  735
*Paris in the Twentieth Century* - Jules Verne  s  5568
*Phylum Monsters* - Hayford Peirce  s  4276
*The Prestige* - Christopher Priest  s  4432
*Remake* - Connie Willis  s  5873
*Saint Leibowitz and the Wild Horse Woman* - Walter M. Miller Jr.  s  3908
*Satellite Night News* - Jack Hopkins  s  2770
*The Snake Oil Wars* - Parke Godwin  s  2249
*The Third Eagle: Lessons Along a Minor String* - R.A. MacAvoy  s  3583
*Views from the Oldest House* - Richard Grant  s  2329
*Virtual Death* - Shale Aaron  s  5
*Why Do Birds* - Damon Knight  s  3190
*The Zap Gun* - Philip K. Dick  s  1523

**Science Fiction — Science Fantasy**

*Bewitchments of Love and Hate* - Storm Constantine  s  1140
*Castle Spellbound* - John DeChancie  s  1454
*Castle War!* - John DeChancie  s  1455
*Choose Your Enemies Carefully* - Robert N. Charrette  s  971
*City on Fire* - Walter Jon Williams  s  5835
*Dragon Rigger* - Jeffrey A. Carver  s  929
*Dragons in the Stars* - Jeffrey A. Carver  s  930
*Exile's Song* - Marion Zimmer Bradley  s  632
*The Face of Apollo* - Fred Saberhagen  s  4766
*Fade to Black* - Nyx Smith  s  5134
*Fire Crossing* - Cheryl J. Franklin  s  2036
*Footprints of Thunder* - James F. David  s  1379
*The Fulfillments of Fate and Desire* - Storm Constantine  s  1142
*The Gate of Ivory* - Doris Egan  s  1755
*Guilt-Edged Ivory* - Doris Egan  s  1756

*Headhunters* - Mel Odom  s  4192

*The Hedge of Mist* - Patricia Kennealy-
Morrison  s  3062

*The Heirs of Hammerfell* - Marion Zimmer
Bradley  s  638

*Hexwood* - Diana Wynne Jones  s  2948

*The Higher Space* - Jamil Nasir  s  4070

*House of the Sun* - Nigel Findley  s  1936

*King's Sacrifice* - Margaret Weis  s  5717

*The Lost King* - Margaret Weis  s  5720

*Never Deal with a Dragon* - Robert N.
Charrette  s  975

*The Oak Above the Kings: A Book of the Keltiad* -
Patricia Kennealy  s  3058

*Orion in the Dying Time* - Ben Bova  s  591

*The Outskirter's Secret* - Rosemary Kirstein  s  3157

*Ports of Call* - Jack Vance  s  5549

*Reluctant Voyagers* - Elisabeth Vonarburg  s  5591

*The Renegades of Pern* - Anne McCaffrey  s  3746

*Scorpion Shards* - Neal Shusterman  s  5013

*Shadowboxer* - Nick Pollotta  s  4366

*Sorcerers of Majipoor* - Robert Silverberg  s  5041

*The Steerswoman* - Rosemary Kirstein  s  3158

*Thoughts of God* - Michael Kanaly  s  3007

*Two-Bit Heroes* - Doris Egan  s  1757

*A Wizard in Chaos* - Christopher Stasheff  s  5230

*A Wizard in Midgard* - Christopher Stasheff  s  5231

*Wolf in Shadow* - David Gemmell  s  2191

*The Zork Chronicles* - George Alec
Effinger  s  1754


**Science Fiction — Science Fiction**

*3001: The Final Odyssey* - Arthur C.
Clarke  s  1053

*The Best of Interzone* - David Pringle  s  4439

*Chanur's Legacy* - C.J. Cherryh  s  981

*The Complete Stories - Volume 1* - Isaac
Asimov  s  233

*Convergence* - Charles Sheffield  s  4951

*Crystal Line* - Anne McCaffrey  s  3724

*The Dealings of Daniel Kesserich* - Fritz
Leiber  s  3417

*Ember From the Sun* - Mark Canter  s  870

*Emergence* - Peter F. Hamilton  s  2524

*The Engines of God* - Jack McDevitt  s  3787

*Exile* - Michael P. Kube-McDowell  s  3248

*The Fall of Sirius* - Wil McCarthy  s  3762

*Far Futures* - Gregory Benford  s  445

*Flare Star* - Paula E. Downing  s  1594

*Fossil* - Hal Clement  s  1083

*Four Ways to Forgiveness* - Ursula K. Le
Guin  s  3380

*Georgia on My Mind and Other Places* - Charles
Sheffield  s  4956

*Grass* - Sheri S. Tepper  s  5431

*Heart of Red Iron* - Phyllis Gotlieb  s  2287

*Inside the Funhouse* - Mike Resnick  s  4546

*Killdozer!* - Theodore Sturgeon  s  5344

*Larissa* - Emily Devenport  s  1503

*Lovelock* - Orson Scott Card  s  892

*Metaphase* - Vonda N. McIntyre  s  3821

*Microcosmic God* - Theodore Sturgeon  s  5345

*Mission Child* - Maureen F. McHugh  s  3819

*My Father Immortal* - Michael D. Weaver  s  5659

*Nautilus* - Vonda N. McIntyre  s  3823

*The New Hugo Winners, Volume IV* - Martin H.
Greenberg  s  2401

*Night Lamp* - Jack Vance  s  5548

*The Norton Book of Science Fiction: North American
Science Fiction, 1960-1990* - Ursula K. Le
Guin  s  3381

*Overshoot* - Mona Clee  s  1075

*Parallelities* - Alan Dean Foster  s  2012

*The Plague Tales* - Ann Benson  s  453

*Polymorph* - Scott Westerfeld  s  5767

*Promised Land* - Connie Willis  s  5872


*Pulphouse, Issue 8: Science Fiction* - Kristine Kathryn
Rusch  s  4725

*Purgatory: A Chronicle of a Distant World* - Mike
Resnick  s  4554

*Raising the Stones* - Sheri S. Tepper  s  5434

*The Science Fiction Century* - David G.
Hartwell  s  2594

*Sewer, Gas & Electric* - Matt Ruff  s  4708

*The Sounding Stillness* - Kenneth Von
Gunden  s  5587

*Star Brothers* - Ben Bova  s  594

*Starliner* - David Drake  s  1645

*The Stars My Destination* - Alfred Bester  s  478

*Tales From Planet Earth* - Arthur C. Clarke  s  1061

*Thunder and Roses* - Theodore Sturgeon  s  5348

*To Save the Sun* - Ben Bova  s  596

*Virtual Unrealities: The Short Fiction of Alfred Bester*
- Alfred Bester  s  479

*The Year's Best Science Fiction: Fourteenth Annual
Collection* - Gardner Dozois  s  1619

*Year's Best SF 2* - David G. Hartwell  s  2597


**Science Fiction — Space Colony**

*Beowulf's Children* - Larry Niven  s  4116

*Bloodletter* - K.W. Jeter  s  2908

*Brute Orbits* - George Zebrowski  s  6059

*Burster* - Michael Capobianco  s  876

*Climbing Olympus* - Kevin J. Anderson  s  102

*The Clouds of Saturn* - Michael McCollum  s  3770

*Day of the Dead* - Neil Gaiman  s  2102

*The Digital Effect* - Steve Perry  s  4295

*Fallway* - Paula E. Downing  s  1593

*The Ganymede Club* - Charles Sheffield  s  4955

*The Garden of Rama* - Arthur C. Clarke  s  1055

*Glory* - Alfred Coppel  s  1182

*Halo* - Tom Maddox  s  3604

*Heavy Time* - C.J. Cherryh  s  995

*Hot Sky at Midnight* - Robert Silverberg  s  5032

*A King of Infinite Space* - Allen Steele  s  5243

*The Lantern of God* - John Dalmas  s  1323

*The Law of War* - William Shatner  s  4931

*Lightpaths* - Howard V. Hendrix  s  2660

*Man o' War* - William Shatner  s  4932

*The Martian Chronicles* - Ray Bradbury  s  621

*The Memory of Earth* - Orson Scott Card  s  894

*Mind Slayer* - Kevin D. Randle  s  4469

*Moonwar* - Ben Bova  s  588

*Mother of Demons* - Eric Flint  s  1956

*Outbanker* - Timothy A. Madden  s  3603

*Pallas* - L. Neil Smith  s  5132

*Playing God* - Sarah Zettel  s  6080

*Raft* - Stephen Baxter  s  401

*Rama Revealed* - Arthur C. Clarke  s  1059

*Second Star* - Dana Stabenow  s  5188

*The Ship Avenged* - S.M. Stirling  s  5298

*Standing Wave* - Howard V. Hendrix  s  2661

*Star Precinct* - Kevin D. Randle  s  4470

*Thirdspace* - Peter David  s  1387

*Voices* - John Vornholt  s  5598

*Xenocide* - Orson Scott Card  s  899


**Science Fiction — Space Opera**

*Acorna's Quest* - Anne McCaffrey  s  3718

*Against a Dark Background* - Iain M. Banks  s  322

*Alastor* - Jack Vance  s  5543

*Alien Dreams* - Larry Segriff  s  4910

*Alien Resurrection* - A.C. Crispin  s  1258

*Aliens: The Female War* - Steve Perry  s  4290

*All Good Things. . .* - Michael Jan Friedman  s  2061

*Ambush at Corellia* - Roger MacBride Allen  s  76

*Archangel Blues* - eluki bes shahar  s  471

*Aristoi* - Walter Jon Williams  s  5834

*Armageddon Sky* - L.A. Graf  s  2296

*Ash Ock* - Christopher Hinz  s  2690

*The Ashes of Eden* - William Shatner  s  4927

*Assignment: Eternity* - Greg Cox  s  1225


*Balance of Power* - Dafydd ab Hugh  s  7

*Battle of the Ring* - Thorarinn Gunnarsson  s  2460

*Battlestation* - David Drake  s  1627

*Before the Storm* - Michael P. Kube-
McDowell  s  3247

*Beneath the Gated Sky* - Robert Reed  s  4502

*Best Destiny* - Diane Carey  s  900

*Beyond the Gate* - Dave Wolverton  s  5949

*Bloodletter* - K.W. Jeter  s  2908

*Brotherhood of the Stars* - Kirby Greene  s  2414

*Call to Arms* - Diane Carey  s  901

*A Call to Darkness* - Michael Jan Friedman  s  2062

*Canby's Legion* - Bill Baldwin  s  308

*Cat's Gambit* - Leslie Gadallah  s  2099

*Chains of Command* - Bill McCay  s  3767

*Changeling* - Stephen Leigh  s  3425

*Children of the Jedi* - Barbara Hambly  s  2500

*City of Diamond* - Jane Emerson  s  1807

*The City on the Edge of Forever* - Harlan
Ellison  s  1784

*The Clouds of Magellan* - David F.
Nighbert  s  4103

*Conflict* - Peter F. Hamilton  s  2522

*Conqueror's Pride* - Timothy Zahn  s  6051

*Consolidation* - Peter F. Hamilton  s  2523

*Convergence* - Charles Sheffield  s  4951

*The Courtship of Princess Leia* - Dave
Wolverton  s  5950

*Crossover* - Michael Jan Friedman  s  2063

*Crossroad* - Barbara Hambly  s  2501

*The Crystal Star* - Vonda N. McIntyre  s  3820

*Crystal Witness* - Kathy Tyers  s  5524

*Dark Force Rising* - Timothy Zahn  s  6052

*Dark Mirror* - Diane Duane  s  1658

*Dark Sky Legion* - William Barton  s  379

*Darksaber* - Kevin J. Anderson  s  103

*Darktraders* - eluki bes shahar  s  472

*Deathstalker Honor* - Simon R. Green  s  2364

*Deathstalker Rebellion* - Simon R. Green  s  2365

*Deathstalker War* - Simon R. Green  s  2366

*Debtors' Planet* - William R. Thompson  s  5457

*The Defenders* - Bill Baldwin  s  309

*The Demon Princes: Volume One* - Jack
Vance  s  5544

*The Demon Princes: Volume Two* - Jack
Vance  s  5545

*Desperate Measures* - Joe Clifford Faust  s  1891

*Devil in the Sky* - Greg Cox  s  1226

*The Devil's Heart* - Carmen Carter  s  922

*The Disinherited* - Peter David  s  1381

*Dr. Dimension* - John DeChancie  s  1456

*Doctor's Orders* - Diane Duane  s  1659

*Doomsday World* - Carmen Carter  s  923

*Downbelow Station* - C.J. Cherryh  s  985

*Dragon's Honor* - Kij Johnson  s  2922

*Dreamspy* - Jacqueline Lichtenberg  s  3458

*The Ecolitan Enigma* - L.E. Modesitt Jr.  s  3927

*The Ecologic Secession* - L.E. Modesitt Jr.  s  3929

*End Game* - Peter David  s  1382

*Enemy Unseen* - V.E. Mitchell  s  3918

*The Escape* - Dean Wesley Smith  s  5113

*The Eternal Enemy* - Michael Berlyn  s  469

*Exile* - Al Sarrantonio  s  4829

*Expansion* - Peter F. Hamilton  s  2525

*Falcon* - Emma Bull  s  768

*Fallen Heroes* - Dafydd ab Hugh  s  8

*Far Harbor* - Melisa C. Michaels  s  3888

*The Fearful Summons* - Denny Martin Flinn  s  1954

*Federation* - Judith Reeves-Stevens  s  4511

*The Fifth Element* - Terry Bisson  s  504

*The Final Fury* - Dafydd ab Hugh  s  9

*Fire Crossing* - Cheryl J. Franklin  s  2036

*Fire Planet* - P.M. Griffin  s  2436

*The First Duelist* - Rutledge Etheridge  s  1849

*First Strike* - Diane Carey  s  903

*A Flag Full of Stars* - Brad Ferguson  s  1922

*Flag in Exile* - David Weber  s  5671

*Fool's War* - Sarah Zettel  s  6079

*Forbidden Knowledge* - Stephen R. Donaldson   s   1571
*Foundation's Fear* - Gregory Benford   s   446
*Galactic Patrol* - Edward E. Smith   s   5116
*The Gap into Conflict: The Real Story* - Stephen R. Donaldson   s   1572
*The Gap into Madness: Chaos and Order* - Stephen R. Donaldson   s   1573
*The Gap into Power: A Dark and Hungry God Arises* - Stephen R. Donaldson   s   1574
*The Gap into Ruin: This Day All Gods Die* - Stephen R. Donaldson   s   1575
*The Gift of the Gorboduc Vandal* - Paul O. Williams   s   5821
*The Girl from Mars & The Prince of Space* - Jack Williamson   s   5864
*Glory's People* - Alfred Coppel   s   1183
*The Glove of Darth Vader* - Paul Davids   s   1392
*The Golden Queen* - Dave Wolverton   s   5951
*Gray Lensman* - Edward E. Smith   s   5117
*Guises of the Mind* - Rebecca Neason   s   4081
*Hammer of Mars* - M.S. Murdock   s   4049
*Heir to the Empire* - Timothy Zahn   s   6054
*Henry Martyn* - L. Neil Smith   s   5131
*Her Klingon Soul* - Michael Jan Friedman   s   2064
*High Moon* - Diane Duane   s   1661
*Honor Among Enemies* - David Weber   s   5673
*The Honor of the Queen* - David Weber   s   5674
*Hunting Party* - Elizabeth Moon   s   3968
*The Illustrated Hitchhiker's Guide to the Galaxy* - Douglas Adams   s   29
*Imbalance* - V.E. Mitchell   s   3919
*Imzadi* - Peter David   s   1383
*In Enemy Hands* - David Weber   s   5675
*The Infinite Sea* - Jeffrey A. Carver   s   932
*Insurrection* - J.M. Dillard   s   1554
*Intellivore* - Diane Duane   s   1663
*Jedi Search* - Kevin J. Anderson   s   109
*The Joy Machine* - James Gunn   s   2458
*Judson's Eden* - Keith Laumer   s   3344
*Jungle Assault* - P.M. Griffin   s   2437
*Kane of Old Mars* - Michael Moorcock   s   3983
*Knights of the Black Earth* - Margaret Weis   s   5718
*The Kobayashi Maru* - Julia Ecklar   s   1728
*The Kruton Interface* - John DeChancie   s   1459
*Labyrinth* - Dennis Schmidt   s   4884
*The Last Command* - Timothy Zahn   s   6055
*The Last Legends of Earth* - A.A. Attanasio   s   270
*The Last Stand* - Brad Ferguson   s   1923
*The Lost City of the Jedi* - Paul Davids   s   1393
*The Mandalorian Armor* - K.W. Jeter   s   2914
*A Matter of Oaths* - Helen S. Wright   s   5985
*Megalomania* - Ian Wallace   s   5621
*The Mercenaries* - Bill Baldwin   s   311
*Metamorphosis* - Jean Lorrah   s   3524
*Mind Meld* - John Vornholt   s   5596
*Mosaic* - Jeri Taylor   s   5403
*Mostly Harmless* - Douglas Adams   s   31
*Nemesis* - Isaac Asimov   s   247
*The New Rebellion* - Kristine Kathryn Rusch   s   4719
*Once a Hero* - Elizabeth Moon   s   3970
*The Paratwa* - Christopher Hinz   s   2691
*Personal Agendas* - Al Sarrantonio   s   4833
*Precious Cargo* - Joe Clifford Faust   s   1893
*Prime Directive* - Judith Reeves-Stevens   s   4514
*Prisoner of Dreams* - Karen Ripley   s   4593
*The Prisoner Within* - Donald E. McQuinn   s   3861
*Probe* - Margaret Wander Bonanno   s   569
*Prophet* - Mike Resnick   s   4553
*Q-in-Law* - Peter David   s   1384
*Q-Space* - Greg Cox   s   1228
*Q-Squared* - Peter David   s   1385
*Q-Zone* - Greg Cox   s   1229
*Ragnarok* - Nathan Archer   s   206
*Reconnaissance* - Bill McCay   s   3769
*Relic of Empire* - W. Michael Gear   s   2171
*Relics* - Michael Jan Friedman   s   2066
*Renegade* - Gene DeWeese   s   1511

*Requiem* - Michael Jan Friedman   s   2067
*Requiem for Anthi* - Jay D. Blakeney   s   517
*The Return* - William Shatner   s   4933
*Reunion* - Michael Jan Friedman   s   2068
*The Rift* - Peter David   s   1386
*Rogue Squadron* - Michael A. Stackpole   s   5205
*Rules of Engagement* - Peter Morwood   s   4037
*Sanctuary* - John Vornholt   s   5597
*Sarek* - A.C. Crispin   s   1260
*Sassinak* - Anne McCaffrey   s   3748
*Schismatrix Plus* - Bruce Sterling   s   5260
*Sentinels* - Margaret Weis   s   5725
*The Shadow Within* - Jeanne Cavelos   s   944
*Shadows of the Empire* - Steve Perry   s   4299
*Shadows on the Sun* - Michael Jan Friedman   s   2069
*The Shattered Sphere* - Roger MacBride Allen   s   81
*Ship of the Line* - Diane Carey   s   904
*The Short Victorious War* - David Weber   s   5681
*The Siege* - Bill Baldwin   s   312
*The Soldiers of Fear* - Dean Wesley Smith   s   5115
*Soothsayer* - Mike Resnick   s   4557
*Spacer Dreams* - Larry Segriff   s   4911
*Spectre* - William Shatner   s   4934
*Sporting Chance* - Elizabeth Moon   s   3974
*Star Bridge* - James Gunn   s   2459
*Star Trek VI: The Undiscovered Country* - J.M. Dillard   s   1556
*Star Trek: The Classic Episodes 1* - James Blish   s   526
*Star Trek: The Classic Episodes 2* - James Blish   s   527
*Star Trek: The Classic Episodes 3* - James Blish   s   528
*Star Trek: The Lost Years* - J.M. Dillard   s   1557
*Star Wreck II: The Attack of the Jargonites* - Leah Rewolinski   s   4563
*Star Wreck III: Time Warped* - Leah Rewolinski   s   4564
*Star Wreck IV: Live Long and Profit* - Leah Rewolinski   s   4565
*Star Wreck 6: Geek Space Nine* - Leah Rewolinski   s   4562
*Star Wreck: The Generation Gap* - Leah Rewolinski   s   4566
*Stargate SG-1* - Ashley McConnell   s   3777
*Starstrike* - W. Michael Gear   s   2172
*Strange Attractors* - Jeffrey A. Carver   s   934
*Tactical Error* - Thorarinn Gunnarsson   s   2466
*Tales From Jabba's Palace* - Kevin J. Anderson   s   114
*Thirdspace* - Peter David   s   1387
*The Thirteenth Majestral* - Hayford Peirce   s   4277
*Time's Enemy* - L.A. Graf   s   2297
*The Touch of Your Shadow, the Whisper of Your Name* - Neal Barrett Jr.   s   367
*Triangle: Imzadi II* - Peter David   s   1388
*The Truce at Bakura* - Kathy Tyers   s   5527
*Twilight of the Empire* - Simon R. Green   s   2374
*Use of Weapons* - Iain M. Banks   s   328
*Vendetta* - Peter David   s   1389
*Vengeance* - Dafydd ab Hugh   s   10
*Vulcan's Forge* - Susan Shwartz   s   5019
*Vulcan's Glory* - D.C. Fontana   s   1967
*War Dragons* - L.A. Graf   s   2299
*Warped* - K.W. Jeter   s   2917
*The Web of Spider* - W. Michael Gear   s   2173
*Windows on a Lost World* - V.E. Mitchell   s   3920
*Yamato: A Rage in Heaven* - Ken Kato   s   3014
*Yesterday's Pawn* - W.T. Quick   s   4453
*Zorba the Hutt's Revenge* - Paul Davids   s   1394

**Science Fiction — Techno-Thriller**

*/* - Greg Bear   s   413
*Antarctica* - Kim Stanley Robinson   s   4628
*Anti-Ice* - Stephen Baxter   s   398
*Anvil* - Nicolas van Pallandt   s   5540

*Bug Park* - James P. Hogan   s   2723
*Carnosaur* - Harry Adam Knight   s   3191
*Crygender* - Thomas T. Thomas   s   5451
*The Cybernetic Walrus* - Jack L. Chalker   s   951
*Death Dream* - Ben Bova   s   583
*Desert Eden* - J.M. Morgan   s   4000
*Dreaming in Smoke* - Tricia Sullivan   s   5353
*The Eighth Rank* - David D. Ross   s   4682
*The Feelies* - Mick Farren   s   1878
*Fellow Traveller* - William Barton   s   380
*Fortress on the Sun* - Paul Cook   s   1157
*Full Tide of Night* - J.R. Dunn   s   1695
*The Gatekeepers* - Daniel Graham Jr.   s   2301
*The Host* - Peter R. Emshwiller   s   1819
*Hunter's Planet* - David Bischoff   s   492
*The Ice Beast* - Frank A. Javor   s   2881
*Icefire* - Judith Reeves-Stevens   s   4512
*Ignition* - Kevin J. Anderson   s   107
*Interface* - Stephen Bury   s   781
*A Journal of the Flood Year* - David Ely   s   1805
*Jupiter's Daughter* - Tom Hyman   s   2820
*Kaleidoscope Century* - John Barnes   s   352
*Lethal Exposure* - Kevin J. Anderson   s   110
*Looking for the Mahdi* - N. Lee Wood   s   5966
*The Man in the Moon Must Die* - Jeff Bredenberg   s   665
*The March Hare Network* - Jack L. Chalker   s   957
*Matrix Man* - William C. Dietz   s   1549
*Mindstar Rising* - Peter F. Hamilton   s   2526
*The Mirror Maze* - James P. Hogan   s   2726
*The Multiplex Man* - James P. Hogan   s   2727
*My Soul to Take* - Steven Spruill   s   5184
*Night Launch* - Jake Garn   s   2143
*The Night Mayor* - Kim Newman   s   4099
*Nomad* - David Alexander   s   66
*Oaths and Miracles* - Nancy Kress   s   3242
*Operation Damocles* - Oscar L. Fellows   s   1916
*Operation Damocles* - Oscar L. Fellows   s   1915
*Queen of Angels* - Greg Bear   s   423
*Reunion on Neverend* - John E. Stith   s   5306
*Rim: A Novel of Virtual Reality* - Alexander Besher   s   475
*seaQuest DSV: The Novel* - Diane Duane   s   1666
*Secret Realms* - Tom Cool   s   1168
*Silent Thunder/Universe* - Dean Ing   s   2829
*The Singularity Project* - F.M. Busby   s   784
*Solo* - Robert Mason   s   3665
*The Square Deal* - David Drake   s   1644
*Sunstroke* - David Kagan   s   2999
*Terminal Logic* - Jefferson Scott   s   4893
*The Trikon Deception* - Ben Bova   s   597
*The Turing Option* - Harry Harrison   s   2579
*Universal Soldier* - Robert Tine   s   5476
*Virtual Destruction* - Kevin J. Anderson   s   118
*Virtuosity* - Terry Bisson   s   507
*Weapon* - Robert Mason   s   3666

**Science Fiction — Theological**

*The Alleluia Files* - Sharon Shinn   s   4999
*Angels Unaware* - L. Elizabeth Storm   s   5315
*Archangel* - Sharon Shinn   s   5000
*Bible Stories for Adults* - James Morrow   s   4028
*Blue Light* - Walter Mosley   s   4042
*Bright Messengers* - Gentry Lee   s   3398
*Brother Death* - Steve Perry   s   4292
*Children of God* - Mary Doria Russell   s   4735
*Conflict* - Peter F. Hamilton   s   2522
*Consolidation* - Peter F. Hamilton   s   2523
*Corrupting Dr. Nice* - John Kessel   s   3083
*Crown of Shadows* - C.S. Friedman   s   2057
*Cyber Way* - Alan Dean Foster   s   2000
*The Dazzle of Day* - Molly Gloss   s   2243
*Deus X* - Norman Spinrad   s   5171
*Drifter* - William C. Dietz   s   1543
*Earthborn* - Orson Scott Card   s   884
*Empire's Horizon* - John Brizzolara   s   707

*Endymion* - Dan Simmons   s   5051
*Eternal Light* - Paul J. McAuley   s   3710
*Far-Seer* - Robert J. Sawyer   s   4854
*Fossil Hunter* - Robert J. Sawyer   s   4855
*God's Fires* - Patricia Anthony   s   159
*God's Nose* - Damon Knight   s   3185
*God's World* - Ian Watson   s   5636
*The Great Wheel* - Ian R. MacLeod   s   3599
*Half-Light* - Denise Vitola   s   5575
*Harvest of Stars* - Poul Anderson   s   127
*Heathern* - Jack Womack   s   5958
*High Aztec* - Ernest Hogan   s   2722
*The Hollow Man* - Dan Simmons   s   5054
*In the Garden of Iden* - Kage Baker   s   298
*Jovah's Angel* - Sharon Shinn   s   5001
*Kalifornia* - Marc Laidlaw   s   3311
*Live From Golgotha: A Novel* - Gore Vidal   s   5569
*Lords of Creation* - Tim Sullivan   s   5351
*Mother of Plenty* - Colin Greenland   s   2417
*Mutant Legacy* - Karen Haber   s   2474
*Orion in the Dying Time* - Ben Bova   s   591
*The Other End of Time* - Frederik Pohl   s   4351
*Parable of the Sower* - Octavia E. Butler   s   792
*Parable of the Talents* - Octavia E. Butler   s   793
*The Parafaith War* - L.E. Modesitt Jr.   s   3937
*Passion Play* - Sean Stewart   s   5276
*The Race for God* - Brian Herbert   s   2666
*The Rise of Endymion* - Dan Simmons   s   5059
*Sacred Visions* - Andrew M. Greeley   s   2343
*The Seraphim Rising* - Elisabeth De Vos   s   1442
*Shadow's End* - Sheri S. Tepper   s   5435
*Snow Crash* - Neal Stephenson   s   5254
*The Sparrow* - Mary Doria Russell   s   4736
*The Stranger* - Eric James Fullilove   s   2093
*Stranger in a Strange Land* - Robert A.
   Heinlein   s   2649
*Sugar Rain* - Paul Park   s   4243
*Terminal Logic* - Jefferson Scott   s   4893
*Thoughts of God* - Michael Kanaly   s   3007
*Threshold* - Bill Myers   s   4060
*The Tides of God* - Ted Reynolds   s   4567
*The Trinity Vector* - Steve Perry   s   4302
*The Voices of Heaven* - Frederik Pohl   s   4356
*Warp Angel* - Stuart Hopen   s   2766
*Washed by a Wave of Wind* - M. Shayne
   Bell   s   435
*Way Station* - Clifford D. Simak   s   5048
*World Spirits* - Aline Boucher-Kaplan   s   580
*Wulfsyarn: A Mosaic* - Phillip Mann   s   3617
*Xenocide* - Orson Scott Card   s   899

**Science Fiction — Time Travel**

*12 Monkeys* - Elizabeth Hand   s   2532
*All Good Things. . .* - Michael Jan Friedman   s   2061
*Angels Unaware* - L. Elizabeth Storm   s   5315
*Arc Riders* - David Drake   s   1626
*Armageddon: The Musical* - Robert Rankin   s   4473
*Assignment: Eternity* - Greg Cox   s   1225
*Atlantis Found* - R. Garcia y Robertson   s   2119
*Back to the Time Trap* - Keith Laumer   s   3343
*Branch Point* - Mona Clee   s   1074
*A Bridge of Years* - Robert Charles Wilson   s   5905
*Bring the Jubilee* - Ward Moore   s   3993
*Caesar's Bicycle* - John Barnes   s   350
*The Centurion's Empire* - Sean McMullen   s   3854
*The City on the Edge of Forever* - Harlan
   Ellison   s   1784
*Collidescope* - Grace Chetwin   s   1011
*Conrad's Quest for Rubber* - Leo
   Frankowski   s   2043
*Corrupting Dr. Nice* - John Kessel   s   3083
*The Dancers at the End of Time* - Michael
   Moorcock   s   3979
*Day of the Snake* - Matthew J. Costello   s   1196
*Days of Cain* - J.R. Dunn   s   1694
*Death's Gray Land* - Mike Shupp   s   5011

*The Dechronization of Sam Magruder* - George
   Gaylord Simpson   s   5067
*Desert Fire* - David Alexander   s   65
*Dictator* - William F. Wu   s   5996
*Doomsday Book* - Connie Willis   s   5868
*Door Number Three* - Patrick O'Leary   s   4210
*Dragon's Blood* - Alex McDonough   s   3799
*Dragon's Claw* - Alex McDonough   s   3800
*Dragon's Eye* - Alex McDonough   s   3801
*Dragons Past* - Gary Gentile   s   2192
*End of an Era* - Robert J. Sawyer   s   4853
*The Escape* - Dean Wesley Smith   s   5113
*Fallen Heroes* - Dafydd ab Hugh   s   8
*The Family Tree* - Sheri S. Tepper   s   5429
*Far Edge of Darkness* - Linda Evans   s   1855
*Firehand* - Andre Norton   s   4151
*First Dawn* - Mike Moscoe   s   4038
*First Frontier* - Diane Carey   s   902
*The Flying Warlord* - Leo Frankowski   s   2044
*The Fourth Rome* - David Drake   s   1631
*From Time to Time* - Jack Finney   s   1941
*The Golden Nineties* - Lisa Mason   s   3663
*The Guns of the South: A Novel of the Civil War* -
   Harry Turtledove   s   5502
*The Hemingway Hoax* - Joe Haldeman   s   2489
*The High-Tech Knight* - Leo Frankowski   s   2045
*The Iron Bridge* - David Morse   s   4036
*Islands of Tomorrow* - F.M. Busby   s   783
*Knights of the Morningstar* - Melanie Rawn   s   4487
*The Last Reckoning* - Mike Shupp   s   5012
*Legacy* - Steve White   s   5785
*A Life in the Future* - Martin Caidin   s   827
*Lifehouse* - Spider Robinson   s   4641
*The Lincoln Hunters* - Wilson Tucker   s   5487
*Living with the Reptiles* - Roger L.
   DiSilvestro   s   1563
*Lord Conrad's Lady* - Leo Frankowski   s   2046
*Lost Days* - Mike Moscoe   s   4039
*Lurid Dreams* - Charles L. Harness   s   2546
*The Man Who Folded Himself* - David
   Gerrold   s   2208
*Mixed Doubles* - Daniel Da Cruz   s   1305
*Mr. Was* - Pete Hautman   s   2614
*No Enemy but Time* - Michael Bishop   s   502
*Norby and Yobo's Great Adventure* - Janet
   Asimov   s   254
*Outpost* - Scott Mackay   s   3597
*Pastwatch: The Redemption of Christopher Columbus* -
   Orson Scott Card   s   895
*Predator* - William F. Wu   s   5998
*Psychoshop* - Alfred Bester   s   477
*The Radiant Warrior* - Leo Frankowski   s   2047
*Rally Cry!* - William R. Forstchen   s   1982
*Ray Bradbury Presents: Dinosaur Planet* - Stephen
   Leigh   s   3427
*Ray Bradbury Presents: Dinosaur World* - Stephen
   Leigh   s   3428
*Requiem* - Michael Jan Friedman   s   2067
*Rivers of Time* - L. Sprague de Camp   s   1417
*The Robin Hood Ambush* - William F. Wu   s   5999
*The Schizogenic Man* - Raymond Harris   s   2563
*Scorpio* - Alex McDonough   s   3802
*Scorpio Descending* - Alex McDonough   s   3803
*Scorpio Rising* - Alex McDonough   s   3804
*Search and Destroy* - Keith William
   Andrews   s   141
*Second Fire* - Mike Moscoe   s   4040
*The Seeds of Time* - Kay Kenyon   s   3064
*The Shield of Time* - Poul Anderson   s   131
*Ship of the Line* - Diane Carey   s   904
*Sink the Armada* - Keith William Andrews   s   142
*Specterworld* - Isidore Haiblum   s   2480
*The Starlight Crystal* - Christopher Pike   s   4333
*Starplex* - Robert J. Sawyer   s   4859
*Stranded!* - Warren Norwood   s   4164
*Summer of Love* - Lisa Mason   s   3664
*Terrible Swift Sword* - William R.
   Forstchen   s   1983

*Thebes of the Hundred Gates* - Robert
   Silverberg   s   5043
*Threshold* - Janet Morris   s   4018
*Time on My Hands* - Peter Delacorte   s   1480
*The Time Patrol* - Poul Anderson   s   135
*Time Scout* - Robert Asprin   s   263
*The Time Ships* - Stephen Baxter   s   403
*Time Station Berlin* - David Evans   s   1852
*Time Station London* - David Evans   s   1853
*Time Station Paris* - David Evans   s   1854
*Time: The Semi-Final Frontier* - Lionel
   Fenn   s   1921
*Timecop* - S.D. Perry   s   4286
*Timequake* - Kurt Vonnegut Jr.   s   5594
*Time's Arrow* - Martin Amis   s   96
*Time's Enemy* - L.A. Graf   s   2297
*Timeshare* - Joshua Dann   s   1344
*Timeshare: Second Time Around* - Joshua
   Dann   s   1345
*To Say Nothing of the Dog* - Connie Willis   s   5874
*Treason in Time* - Keith William Andrews   s   143
*The Trinity Paradox* - Kevin J. Anderson   s   116
*Tyrannosaurus Rex* - J.F. Rivkin   s   4597
*The Unknown Soldier* - Mickey Zucker
   Reichert   s   4525
*The Virgin and the Dinosaur* - R. Garcia y
   Robertson   s   2122
*Wagers of Sin* - Robert Asprin   s   264
*The Walking Shadow* - Brian Stableford   s   5195
*Warrior* - William F. Wu   s   6000
*The Whispers* - Dan Parkinson   s   4247

**Science Fiction — UFO**

*Beyond the Veil of Stars* - Robert Reed   s   4503
*Majestic* - Whitley Strieber   s   5341
*Nighteyes* - Garfield Reeves-Stevens   s   4510
*Silent Zone* - Stephen Molstad   s   3952
*Silicon Embrace* - John Shirley   s   5009
*Strange Deliverance* - Mary Brown   s   728
*Why Do Birds* - Damon Knight   s   3190

**Science Fiction — Utopia**

*Adiamante* - L.E. Modesitt Jr.   s   3924
*Future Primitive: The New Ecotopias* - Kim Stanley
   Robinson   s   4631
*Kirinyaga: A Fable of Utopia* - Mike
   Resnick   s   4548
*Lightpaths* - Howard V. Hendrix   s   2660
*A Reasonable World* - Damon Knight   s   3188
*Reefsong* - Carol Severance   s   4923

**Science Fiction — Young Adult**

*2041: Twelve Short Stories about the Future by Top
   Science Fiction Writers* - Jane Yolen   s   6027
*Aliens Stole My Body* - Bruce Coville   s   1217
*Armageddon Summer* - Jane Yolen   s   6028
*Away Is a Strange Place to Be* - H.M.
   Hoover   s   2763
*Beyond the Door* - Gary L. Blackwood   s   510
*The Billion Dollar Boy* - Charles Sheffield   s   4948
*The Chance Factor* - Diana G. Gallagher   s   2109
*The Cyborg From Earth* - Charles Sheffield   s   4952
*Diggers* - Terry Pratchett   s   4386
*Dream-Weaver* - Louise Lawrence   s   3359
*The Dying Sun* - Gary L. Blackwood   s   511
*The Earth Giant* - Melvin Burgess   s   773
*Eva* - Peter Dickinson   s   1525
*The Faces of Ceti* - Mary Caraker   s   877
*The Glove of Darth Vader* - Paul Davids   s   1392
*Groogleman* - Debra Doyle   s   1600
*Growing Up Weightless* - John M. Ford   s   1970
*Helm* - Steven Gould   s   2289
*Hexwood* - Diana Wynne Jones   s   2948
*Higher Education* - Charles Sheffield   s   4958
*Hong on the Range* - William F. Wu   s   5997

*Invitation to the Game* - Monica Hughes   *s*   2807
*Jonas McFee, A.T.P.* - Sarah Sargent   *s*   4827
*Journey to Terezor* - Frank Asch   *s*   221
*Jumper* - Steven Gould   *s*   2290
*The Lake at the End of the World* - Caroline MacDonald   *s*   3584
*Light Raid* - Connie Willis   *s*   5870
*The Lone Sentinel* - Jo Dereske   *s*   1493
*The Lost City of the Jedi* - Paul Davids   *s*   1393
*Mr. Was* - Pete Hautman   *s*   2614
*My Stepfather Shrank!* - Barbara Dillon   *s*   1558
*My Teacher Flunked the Planet* - Bruce Coville   *s*   1222
*My Teacher Fried My Brains* - Bruce Coville   *s*   1223
*My Teacher Glows in the Dark* - Bruce Coville   *s*   1224
*Night of the Living Shark!* - David Bischoff   *s*   493

*No Kidding* - Bruce Brooks   *s*   709
*Norby and the Court Jester* - Janet Asimov   *s*   252
*Only Child* - H.M. Hoover   *s*   2764
*The Promise* - Monica Hughes   *s*   2808
*Putting Up Roots* - Charles Sheffield   *s*   4964
*Raptor* - Paul Zindel   *s*   6084
*Rebel From Alphorion* - Robyn Tallis   *s*   5381
*Red Planet* - Robert A. Heinlein   *s*   2647
*River Rats* - Caroline Stevermer   *s*   5267
*The Robin Hood Ambush* - William F. Wu   *s*   5999
*Scorpion Shards* - Neal Shusterman   *s*   5013
*Serpent's Gift* - A.C. Crispin   *s*   1261
*Shade* - Emily Devenport   *s*   1504
*Shadow World* - A.C. Crispin   *s*   1262
*Shadows in the Water* - Kathryn Lasky   *s*   3341
*Shivering World* - Kathy Tyers   *s*   5526
*The Snows of Jaspre* - Mary Caraker   *s*   878
*Spacer Dreams* - Larry Segriff   *s*   4911

*A Starfarer's Dozen* - Michael Stearns   *s*   5238
*Starfleet Academy* - Diane Carey   *s*   905
*The Starlight Crystal* - Christopher Pike   *s*   4333
*Starswarm* - Jerry Pournelle   *s*   4379
*Surface Action* - David Drake   *s*   1646
*Traitors from Within* - R.A. Montgomery   *s*   3966
*The Transall Saga* - Gary Paulsen   *s*   4262
*Trouble on Cloud City* - Kevin J. Anderson   *s*   117
*Truckers* - Terry Pratchett   *s*   4402
*Under Alien Stars* - Pamela F. Service   *s*   4919
*The Vanishing* - Marilyn Kaye   *s*   3021
*Virtually Perfect* - Dan Gutman   *s*   2470
*Warlock and Son* - Christopher Stasheff   *s*   5224
*Wildside* - Steven Gould   *s*   2291
*The Winds of Mars* - H.M. Hoover   *s*   2765
*Wings* - Terry Pratchett   *s*   4403
*Worf's First Adventure* - Peter David   *s*   1391
*Zorba the Hutt's Revenge* - Paul Davids   *s*   1394

# Character Name Index

This index alphabetically lists the major characters in each featured title. Each character name is followed by a description of the character. Citations also provide titles of the books featuring the character. If the character appears in more than one book, the titles are listed alphabetically. The author name and entry number are also included.

## A

**a Cimabue, Damastes** (Military Personnel; Prisoner)
*The Demon King* - Chris Bunch  *f*  770
*The Seer King* - Chris Bunch  *f*  771

**a-Lagan, Meredydd** (Orphan; Student)
*The Meri* - Maya Kaathryn Bohnhoff  *f*  561

**Aargh** (Animal)
*The Dragon Knight* - Gordon R. Dickson  *f*  1532

**Aaron** (Thief)
*The Fire's Stone* - Tanya Huff  *f*  2796

**Aaron, Lily** (Restaurateur)
*After Silence* - Jonathan Carroll  *h*  916

**Aaron, Lincoln** (Teenager)
*After Silence* - Jonathan Carroll  *h*  916

**Aarons, Keith "Pan"** (Terrorist)
*Second Chance* - Chet Williamson  *h*  5850

**Aarundel** (Mythical Creature; Warrior)
*Once a Hero* - Michael A. Stackpole  *f*  5203

**ab Meredydd, Rhys "Sun Eyes"** (Minstrel)
*Madoc's Hundred* - Pat Winter  *f*  5925

**ab Owen, Madoc "Weather Eyes"** (Leader)
*Madoc's Hundred* - Pat Winter  *f*  5925

**Abaddon** (Immortal; Ruler)
*Wolf in Shadow* - David Gemmell  *s*  2191

**Abalone** (Computer Expert; Criminal)
*Brother to Dragons, Companion to Owls* - Jane M. Lindskold  *f*  3473

**Abba-Bashti** (Trader)
*The Amazon Chronicles* - Jane E.M. Robinson  *f*  4627

**Abbot, Thomas** (Police Officer)
*The Reckoning* - Ruby Jean Jensen  *h*  2904

**Abbott, Vera** (Restaurateur)
*The Chosen* - Edward Lee  *h*  3389

**Abdullah** (Businessman)
*Castle in the Air* - Diana Wynne Jones  *f*  2944

**Abe** (Alien; Telepath)
*The Clouds of Magellan* - David F. Nighbert  *s*  4103

**Abernathy** (Animal; Adventurer)
*Witches' Brew* - Terry Brooks  *f*  719

**Abernathy, Tom** (Rancher)
*Thunder Road* - Chris Curry  *h*  1296

**Abivard** (Nobleman; Military Personnel; Warrior)
*The Stolen Throne* - Harry Turtledove  *f*  5510

**Abivard** (Military Personnel)
*The Thousand Cities* - Harry Turtledove  *f*  5512

**Abivard** (Military Personnel; Political Figure)
*Videssos Besieged* - Harry Turtledove  *f*  5513

**Abrena, Mirielle** (Military Personnel)
*Legacy of Steel* - Mary H. Herbert  *f*  2675

**Abronowitz, Wendy** (Astronaut)
*The Fugitive Stars* - Daniel Ransom  *s*  4479

**Aburto, Manuel "Manny"** (Guide; Time Traveler)
*Tyrannosaurus Rex* - J.F. Rivkin  *s*  4597

**Acari, Stefan** (Judge)
*The Beacon* - Valerie J. Freireich  *s*  2048

**Achilles** (Warrior)
*Yellowstone Run* - David Robbins  *s*  4605

**Acila** (Noblewoman; Mythical Creature)
*Changing Fate* - Elisabeth Waters  *f*  5629

**Ackerman, Larry** (Professor)
*The Voice in the Basement* - T. Chris Martindale  *h*  3657

**Ackley, Robert** (Librarian)
*The Lodger* - Fred Chappell  *h*  966

**Acorna** (Alien; Foundling)
*Acorna* - Anne McCaffrey  *s*  3717

**Acorna** (Orphan; Telepath)
*Acorna's Quest* - Anne McCaffrey  *s*  3718

**Acton, Joe** (Worker)
*Moondog* - Henry Garfield  *h*  2138

**Adair, Devon** (Leader; Settler)
*Earth 2* - Melissa Crandall  *s*  1247

**Adair, Hugh** (Lawyer; Spouse)
*Breeder* - Douglas Clegg  *h*  1076

**Adair, Kirsten** (Police Officer)
*The Bohr Maker* - Linda Nagata  *s*  4064

**Adair, Rachel** (Lawyer)
*Breeder* - Douglas Clegg  *h*  1076

**Adam** (Foundling)
*Child of Shadows* - John Coyne  *h*  1236

**Adam** (Demon)
*Good Omens: The Nice and Accurate Prophecies of Agnes Nutter, Witch* - Neil Gaiman  *f*  2103

**Adams, Frankly** (Artist; Fugitive)
*Virtual Death* - Shale Aaron  *s*  5

**Adams, Joseph** (Writer)
*The Penultimate Truth* - Philip K. Dick  *s*  1522

**Adams, Luther** (Doctor)
*Wilderness* - Dennis Danvers  *h*  1349

**Adams, Nicola Chelsea "Niki"** (Teenager)
*From a Whisper to a Scream* - Samuel M. Key  *h*  3093

**Adams, Rafe** (Scientist)
*Heritage of Flight* - Susan Shwartz  *s*  5016

**Adamsson, Wylie** (Child)
*Night Calls* - Katharine Eliska Kimbriel  *h*  3119

**Adana "the Snake Mother"** (Mythical Creature)
*The Face in the Abyss* - A. Merritt  *f*  3878

**Adashek, David** (Journalist)
*Meg* - Steve Alten  *h*  88

**Adcock, Patrice "Pat"** (Scientist; Spacewoman)
*The Other End of Time* - Frederik Pohl  *s*  4351

**Adcock, Patrice "Pat"** (Scientist; Clone)
*The Siege of Eternity* - Frederik Pohl  *s*  4353

**Adda** (Genetically Altered Being; Patient)
*Flux* - Stephen Baxter  *s*  399

**Addams, Fester** (Fiance(e))
*Addams Family Values* - Todd Strasser  *f*  5324

**Addams, Helen "Kyria"** (Sorceress)
*Dragon Death* - Gael Baudino  *f*  390

**Addams, Helen "Kyria"** (Scholar; Sorceress)
*Duel of Dragons* - Gael Baudino  *f*  391

**Addams, Morticia** (Parent; Spouse)
*Addams Family Values* - Todd Strasser  *f*  5324

**Adderstone, Susannah** (Young Woman)
*The Vanishment* - Jonathan Aycliffe  *h*  282

**Adelrune** (Child; Student)
*The Book of Knights* - Yves Meynard  *f*  3884

**Aderyn** (Magician; Wanderer)
*A Time of Exile* - Katharine Kerr  *f*  3077

**Aditi** (Sorceress)
*Bijapur* - Kara Dalkey  *f*  1317

**Aditi** (Deity; Widow(er); Sorceress)
*Blood of the Goddess* - Kara Dalkey  *f*  1318

**Adkins, Merrill** (Investigator)
*A Chill in the Blood* - P.N. Elrod  *h*  1793

**Adler, Keisha** (Healer; Teenager)
*Owlsight* - Mercedes Lackey  *f*  3292

**Adler, Mark** (Government Official)
*Ursus* - David Dvorkin   *s*   1708

**Adler, Stephen** (Vampire)
*Less than Human* - Gary L. Raisor   *h*   4464

**Adolphus, Matthew** (Detective—Police)
*Afterimage* - Kristine Kathryn Rusch   *f*   4709

**Adolphus, Matthew** (Detective)
*Afterimage Aftershock* - Kristine Kathryn Rusch   *h*   4710

**Adric** (Royalty; Runaway)
*The White Mists of Power* - Kristine Kathryn Rusch   *f*   4730

**Adwon, Jay** (Lawman)
*Dusk* - Ron Dee   *h*   1466

**Aedrea** (Mutant; Femme Fatale)
*Saint Leibowitz and the Wild Horse Woman* - Walter M. Miller Jr.   *s*   3908

**Aeid** (Royalty; Adventurer)
*O Greenest Branch!* - Gael Baudino   *f*   394

**ae'Magi, Geoffrey** (Magician)
*Masques* - Patricia Briggs   *f*   681

**Aenea** (Child; Religious)
*Endymion* - Dan Simmons   *s*   5051

**Aenea** (Genetically Altered Being; Religious)
*The Rise of Endymion* - Dan Simmons   *s*   5059

**Aengus** (Artist)
*The Boy From the Burren* - Sheila Gilluly   *f*   2236

**Aerich of House Lyorn** (Gentleman)
*The Phoenix Guards* - Steven Brust   *f*   747

**Aeriel** (Sorceress)
*The Pearl of the Soul of the World* - Meredith Ann Pierce   *f*   4318

**Aeslu "Moon's Stead" of Vmatta** (Indian)
*Fire and Ice* - Edward Myers   *f*   4061

**Aeslu "Moon's Stead" of Vmatta** (Indian; Linguist)
*The Mountain Made of Light* - Edward Myers   *f*   4062
*The Summit* - Edward Myers   *f*   4063

**Aesop** (Writer; Traveler)
*The Fabulist* - John Vornholt   *f*   5595

**Aetheric III** (Ruler)
*Conspiracy* - J. Robert King   *f*   3121

**Afsan** (Alien; Apprentice)
*Far-Seer* - Robert J. Sawyer   *s*   4854

**Afsan** (Alien; Scholar)
*Fossil Hunter* - Robert J. Sawyer   *s*   4855

**Agamemnon** (Ruler)
*Helen's Passage* - Diana M. Concannon   *f*   1129

**Agamon, Orfei** (Artist)
*A Second Infinity* - Michael D. Weaver   *s*   5660

**Agenor, Roland** (Vampire)
*The Golden* - Lucius Shepard   *h*   4978

**Agenos, Mordion "the Servant"** (Martial Arts Expert; Criminal)
*Hexwood* - Diana Wynne Jones   *s*   2948

**Agesilaus, "Agis"** (Military Personnel)
*Spartan Run* - David Robbins   *s*   4602

**Agis** (Political Figure; Psychic)
*The Verdant Passage* - Troy Denning   *f*   1487

**Agnes** (Aged Person)
*Well Wished* - Franny Billingsley   *f*   489

**Agonostis** (Demon; Administrator)
*Sympathy for the Devil* - Holly Lisle   *f*   3488

**Agramonte, Maran** (Noblewoman)
*The Demon King* - Chris Bunch   *f*   770
*The Seer King* - Chris Bunch   *f*   771

**Agranovsky, Reuven** (Aged Person; Actor)
*Further Adventures* - Jon Stephen Fink   *f*   1940

**Agricola, Caesar Germanicus** (Ruler)
*Cry Republic* - Kirk Mitchell   *s*   3917

**Aguilana, Haros** (Vampire; Spirit)
*King of the Grey* - Richard A. Knaak   *f*   3173

**Aguilar, Carlos** (Teenager)
*Days of the Dead* - Ashley McConnell   *h*   3774

**Aguilar, Ricardo** (Spaceship Captain)
*Starfarers* - Poul Anderson   *s*   133

**Agyar** (Political Figure)
*The Vampire Memoirs* - Mara McCuniff   *h*   3781

**Agyar, Janos "Jack"** (Vampire)
*Agyar* - Steven Brust   *f*   738

**Ahlitah** (Animal)
*Carnivores of Light and Darkness* - Alan Dean Foster   *f*   1996

**Ahlwen, Anders** (Psychic)
*The Snows of Jaspre* - Mary Caraker   *s*   878

**Ahmed** (Child)
*Ahmed and the Oblivion Machines* - Ray Bradbury   *f*   618

**Ahrens, Bleys** (Genius; Activist)
*Other* - Gordon R. Dickson   *s*   1538

**Ahrens, Bleys** (Student; Activist)
*Young Bleys* - Gordon R. Dickson   *s*   1540

**Ahrens, Dahno** (Activist)
*Young Bleys* - Gordon R. Dickson   *s*   1540

**Ahten, Raj** (Royalty; Wizard)
*The Runelords: The Sum of All Men* - David Farland   *f*   1866

**a'Husain, Idryis Khan** (Political Figure)
*Imposter* - Valerie J. Freireich   *s*   2050

**Aiah** (Political Figure; Police Officer)
*City on Fire* - Walter Jon Williams   *s*   5835

**Aiah** (Civil Servant)
*Metropolitan* - Walter Jon Williams   *s*   5839

**Aias** (Scientist)
*Celestial Matters* - Richard Garfinkle   *s*   2140

**Aidan** (Royalty; Mythical Creature)
*Alamut* - Judith Tarr   *f*   5390

**Aidan** (Royalty)
*The Dagger and the Cross: A Novel of the Crusades* - Judith Tarr   *f*   5393

**Aidan** (Heir)
*Flight of the Raven* - Jennifer Roberson   *f*   4608

**Aidan** (Military Personnel)
*Way of the Clans* - Robert Thurston   *s*   5469

**Aide** (Artificial Intelligence)
*An Oblique Approach* - David Drake   *s*   1638

**Aiesa, Gina** (Artist)
*Synners* - Pat Cadigan   *s*   808

**Aigar** (Wizard; Professor)
*Lost in Translation* - Margaret Ball   *f*   315

**Aiken, Robert** (Pharmacist)
*The Mysterium* - Eric McCormack   *h*   3780

**Aiko** (Warrior; Noblewoman)
*The Dragonstone* - Dennis L. McKiernan   *f*   3832

**Ainvar** (Religious)
*Druids* - Morgan Llywelyn   *f*   3502

**Aisling, Algernon** (Professor; Adventurer)
*Voyage of the Basset* - James C. Christensen   *f*   1024

**Aisling, Cassandra** (Child; Adventurer)
*Voyage of the Basset* - James C. Christensen   *f*   1024

**Aisling, Miranda** (Teenager; Adventurer)
*Voyage of the Basset* - James C. Christensen   *f*   1024

**AIVAS** (Artificial Intelligence)
*All the Weyrs of Pern* - Anne McCaffrey   *s*   3719

**Aiysha** (Leader)
*Blood Feuds* - S.M. Stirling   *s*   5292

**Ajani, Korinna "Kori" Kassemi** (Waiter/Waitress; Parent)
*The March Hare Network* - Jack L. Chalker   *s*   957

**Akamu** (Clone; Fugitive)
*The Bones of Time* - Kathleen Ann Goonan   *s*   2273

**Akasha** (Vampire)
*The Queen of the Damned* - Anne Rice   *h*   4574

**Akhor** (Mythical Creature; Royalty)
*Song in the Silence* - Elizabeth Kerner   *f*   3065

**Akiba** (Religious)
*Freeze Frames* - Katharine Kerr   *s*   3071

**Akili** (Genetically Altered Being)
*Distress* - Greg Egan   *s*   1760

**Akimura, Julian** (Psychologist; Psychic)
*Mutant Legacy* - Karen Haber   *s*   2474

**Akimura, Julian** (Twin; Psychic)
*Mutant Star* - Karen Haber   *s*   2475

**Akimura, Rick** (Psychic; Mutant)
*Mutant Legacy* - Karen Haber   *s*   2474

**Akktri** (Alien)
*In the Cube* - David Alexander Smith   *s*   5109

**Akma** (Rebel; Abuse Victim)
*Earthborn* - Orson Scott Card   *s*   884

**al-Badr, Arwa Bint Muhammad** (Royalty)
*Guts and Glory* - G. Harry Stine   *s*   5280

**al-Hakim, Sharif** (Guide)
*The Calling* - Kathryn Meyer Griffith   *h*   2439

**al-Iskandaria, Ibn Sufa** (Companion; Adventurer)
*Quest: In Search of the Dragontooth* - Michael Green   *f*   2346

**al Jorddyn, Kerridwen** (Noblewoman; Martial Arts Expert)
*Kingmaker's Sword* - Ann Marston   *f*   3635

**al Keylan, Brynda** (Noblewoman; Bodyguard)
*Broken Blade* - Ann Marston   *f*   3634

**al-Kharif, Yasin** (Engineer; Criminal)
*Bright Messengers* - Gentry Lee   *s*   3398

**Al Qaseem, Zero** (Scientist; Computer Expert)
*Signal to Noise* - Eric S. Nylund   *s*   4179

**al-Qurtubi** (Terrorist)
*Name of the Beast* - Daniel Easterman   *h*   1721

**Al-Ra,ma, Khaddam** (Sorcerer; Teacher)
*The Riddled Man* - Mark E. Rogers   *f*   4654

**al-Schouki, Esoch** (Military Personnel)
*Foragers* - Charles Oberndorf   *s*   4187

**Al Shei, Katmer** (Businesswoman; Engineer)
*Fool's War* - Sarah Zettel   *s*   6079

**Ala-eh-din Beyh** (Wizard; Warrior)
*Tower of Fear* - Glen Cook   *f*   1155

**Aladdin** (Adventurer)
*Aladdin: Master of the Lamp* - Mike Resnick   *f*   4534

**Aladdin** (Thief; Adventurer)
*A Bad Day for Ali Baba* - Craig Shaw Gardner   *f*   2123

**Alain** (Bastard Son; Military Personnel)
*King's Dragon* - Kate Elliott   *f*   1773

**Alain** (Royalty)
*M'Lady Witch* - Christopher Stasheff   *f*   5217

**Alain** (Nobleman)
*Prince of Dogs* - Kate Elliott  *f*  1775

**Alain, Jahnel** (Leader)
*Fallway* - Paula E. Downing  *s*  1593

**Alaiya** (Military Personnel)
*The Return of the Breakneck Boys* - Geary
Gravel  *s*  2332

**Alamar** (Wizard)
*Voyage of the Fox Rider* - Dennis L.
McKiernan  *f*  3837

**Alanda, Marcus** (Religious)
*Quest for the Fallen Star* - Piers Anthony  *f*  185

**Alara** (Shaman; Mythical Creature)
*The Elvenbane* - Andre Norton  *f*  4149

**Alaric** (Minstrel; Warlock)
*In the Red Lord's Reach* - Phyllis
Eisenstein  *f*  1765

**Alastair** (Heir; Twin)
*The Heirs of Hammerfell* - Marion Zimmer
Bradley  *s*  638

**Alayna** (Wizard)
*Children of Amarid* - David B. Coe  *f*  1095

**Albain, Elandra** (Ruler)
*Realm of Light* - Deborah Chester  *f*  1008

**Albain, Elandra** (Noblewoman; Bastard Daughter)
*Reign of Shadows* - Deborah Chester  *f*  1009

**Albain, Elandra** (Ruler)
*Shadow War* - Deborah Chester  *f*  1010

**Albee, David** (Scientist)
*Lords of Creation* - Tim Sullivan  *s*  5351

**Albin** (Mythical Creature)
*The Wild Wood* - Charles de Lint  *f*  1440

**Albin, Doug** (Teacher)
*The Mailman* - Bentley Little  *h*  3494

**Albin, Tritia** (Housewife)
*The Mailman* - Bentley Little  *h*  3494

**Albright, Harper** (Editor)
*The Uncanny* - Andrew Klavan  *h*  3164

**Albright, Steven** (Writer)
*Bloodletter* - Warren Newton Beath  *h*  426

**Alburton, Denso** (Writer)
*Hidden Echoes* - Mike Jefferies  *f*  2885

**Alderan, Kermiak** (Royalty; Telepath)
*Rediscovery: A Novel of Darkover* - Marion Zimmer
Bradley  *s*  643

**Alderberry, Jane** (Student; Thief)
*The Iron Dragon's Daughter* - Michael
Swanwick  *f*  5371

**Alderini, Delbert** (Writer)
*Quest for Apollo* - Michael Lahey  *f*  3309

**Alderson, Charlotte** (Widow(er))
*The Colors of Hell* - Michael Paine  *h*  4234

**Aldived** (Leader)
*The Heldan* - Deborah Talmadge-Bickmore  *f*  5383

**Alec of Kerry** (Woodsman; Spy)
*Luck in the Shadows* - Lynn Flewelling  *f*  1952

**Alec of Kerry** (Apprentice; Spy)
*Stalking Darkness* - Lynn Flewelling  *f*  1953

**Alegretta** (Doctor; Immortal)
*Outnumbering the Dead* - Frederik Pohl  *s*  4352

**Alemi** (Fisherman)
*The Dolphins of Pern* - Anne McCaffrey  *s*  3729

**Aleph** (Artificial Intelligence)
*Halo* - Tom Maddox  *s*  3604

**Aleron** (Vampire)
*Sex and the Single Vampire* - Nancy
Kilpatrick  *h*  3114

**Aleshire, Puck** (Mythical Creature)
*The Iron Dragon's Daughter* - Michael
Swanwick  *f*  5371

**Aletto** (Heir—Dispossessed)
*One Land, One Duke* - Ru Emerson  *f*  1809

**Aletto** (Heir—Dispossessed; Runaway)
*The Two in Hiding* - Ru Emerson  *f*  1812

**Alex** (Military Personnel)
*Alien Dreams* - Larry Segriff  *s*  4910

**Alexander** (Royalty)
*The Floating Castle* - Craig Mills  *f*  3913

**Alexander** (Warrior)
*Helen's Passage* - Diana M. Concannon  *f*  1129

**Alexander** (Royalty; Teenager)
*The Prince and the Pilgrim* - Mary Stewart  *f*  5270

**Alexander** (Religious)
*The Bighead* - Edward Lee  *h*  3387

**Alexander, Ardeth** (Student)
*The Night Inside* - Nancy Baker  *h*  301

**Alexander, Lyta** (Telepath)
*Thirdspace* - Peter David  *s*  1387

**Alexander, Sam** (Radio; Student—High School)
*SETI* - Frederick Fichman  *s*  1930

**Alexander the Great** (Historical Figure)
*Dark Prince* - David Gemmell  *f*  2187

**Alexander the Great** (Historical Figure; Warrior)
*Lord of the Two Lands* - Judith Tarr  *f*  5395

**Alexia** (Royalty; Magician)
*Dark Mirror, Dark Dreams* - Sharon Green  *f*  2357
*Silver Princess, Golden Knight* - Sharon
Green  *f*  2359
*Wind Whispers, Shadow Shouts* - Sharon
Green  *f*  2360

**Alfonso** (Rancher)
*Under the Shadow* - Jane Toombs  *h*  5481

**Alfred** (Adventurer; Wizard)
*Fire Sea* - Margaret Weis  *f*  5714
*Into the Labyrinth* - Margaret Weis  *f*  5716
*Serpent Mage* - Margaret Weis  *f*  5726
*The Seventh Gate* - Margaret Weis  *f*  5727

**Alfvaen, Tinling** (Psychic)
*Hellspark* - Janet Kagan  *s*  3000

**Algooth** (Mythical Creature)
*The Gates of Vensunor* - Carol Heller  *f*  2650

**Alhammittson, Alhammitt "Mitt"** (Warrior; Leader)
*The Crown of Dalemark* - Diana Wynne
Jones  *f*  2945

**Ali Baba** (Artisan; Adventurer)
*A Bad Day for Ali Baba* - Craig Shaw
Gardner  *f*  2123

**Alias** (Hero; Genetically Altered Being)
*Masquerades* - Kate Novak  *f*  4166

**Alice** (Child)
*Fantastic Alice* - Margaret Weis  *f*  5713

**Alice** (Revolutionary; Adventurer)
*Innerverse* - John DeChancie  *s*  1458

**Alice** (Teenager; Noblewoman)
*The Prince and the Pilgrim* - Mary Stewart  *f*  5270

**Alice, Ti** (Occultist)
*Tempter* - Nancy A. Collins  *h*  1125

**Alinor** (Mythical Creature; Detective—Amateur)
*Wheels of Fire* - Mercedes Lackey  *f*  3301

**Alis** (Actress; Historian)
*Remake* - Connie Willis  *s*  5873

**Alison/Nicholas** (Actress)
*The Need* - Andrew Neiderman  *h*  4089

**Allaird, Clarence Engels "Clancy"** (Spaceship
Captain; Parent)
*Arrow From Earth* - F.M. Busby  *s*  782

**Allaird, Margaret "Marnie"** (Stowaway; Teenager)
*Arrow From Earth* - F.M. Busby  *s*  782

**Allalie, Fentrice** (Aged Person; Magician)
*Walking the Labyrinth* - Lisa Goldstein  *f*  2266

**Allan, David** (Detective)
*The Virginia Ghost Murders* - Leslie Raymond
Sachs  *h*  4778

**Allard** (Mythical Creature; Miner)
*Suisan* - Phyllis Carol Agins  *f*  42

**Allbright, Rod "Seymour"** (Disembodied
Personality; Adventurer)
*Aliens Stole My Body* - Bruce Coville  *s*  1217

**Alldera** (Leader)
*The Furies* - Suzy McKee Charnas  *s*  968

**Allen** (Farmer; Lawman)
*The Persistence of Memory* - Karen Ripley  *s*  4592

**Allen, Harrison** (Businessman; Unemployed)
*Dark Twilight* - Joseph A. Citro  *h*  1036

**Allen, Sandy** (Television)
*Ancient Images* - Ramsey Campbell  *h*  852

**Allen, Zadok** (Streetperson)
*The Shadow over Innsmouth* - H.P.
Lovecraft  *h*  3533

**Allen-Shimmura, Elio** (Historian)
*Dark Water's Embrace* - Stephen Leigh  *s*  3426

**Allerum** (Mythical Creature)
*Shadow's Realm* - Mickey Zucker Reichert  *f*  4523

**Alliar** (Spirit)
*A Strange and Ancient Name* - Josepha
Sherman  *f*  4991

**Allic** (Royalty; Deity)
*The Crystal Sorcerers* - William R.
Forstchen  *f*  1979

**Allie** (Student—College)
*Lost in Translation* - Margaret Ball  *f*  315

**Allika** (Child; Thief)
*King's Man and Thief* - Christie Golden  *f*  2253

**Allison, Harold** (Lawyer)
*The Man Who Turned into Himself* - David
Ambrose  *h*  89

**Allogiamento, Maria Theresa** (Vampire)
*The Vampire Journals* - Traci Briery  *h*  678

**Almond, Donna** (Teacher)
*Dead in the Water* - Nancy Holder  *h*  2732

**Alnosha "Nosh"** (Foundling; Student)
*The Hands of Lyr* - Andre Norton  *f*  4154

**Alon** (Mercenary; Adventurer)
*The Nomad Queen* - James Gordon White  *f*  5783

**Alpha, Pamayers** (Clone; Explorer)
*The Weigher* - Eric Vinicoff  *s*  5574

**Alsnor, Lotta** (Counselor; Psychic)
*The White Regiment* - John Dalmas  *s*  1327

**Alston, Arthur** (Doctor)
*The Select* - F. Paul Wilson  *h*  5897

**Alston, John "Skiddle"** (Religious)
*The Great Wheel* - Ian R. MacLeod  *s*  3599

**Alston, Marian** (Military Personnel; Lesbian)
*Island in the Sea of Time* - S.M. Stirling  *s*  5295

**Alta** (Revolutionary)
*Deception Well* - Linda Nagata  *s*  4065

**Alta** (Psychic)
*White Horse, Dark Dragon* - Robert C.
Fleet  *f*  1947

**Althea** (Gentlewoman)
*The Forge of Virtue* - Lynn Abbey *f* 16

**Althor** (Military Personnel; Psychic)
*Catch the Lightning* - Catherine Asaro *s* 218

**al'Thor, Rand** (Farmer)
*The Eye of the World* - Robert Jordan *f* 2986

**al'Thor, Rand** (Leader)
*The Path of Daggers* - Robert Jordan *f* 2989

**al'Thor, Rand "Dragon Reborn"** (Leader)
*A Crown of Swords* - Robert Jordan *f* 2984

**al'Thor, Rand "Dragon Reborn"** (Leader; Revolutionary)
*The Dragon Reborn* - Robert Jordan *f* 2985
*The Fires of Heaven* - Robert Jordan *f* 2987

**al'Thor, Rand "Dragon Reborn"** (Leader)
*Lord of Chaos* - Robert Jordan *f* 2988

**al'Thor, Rand "Dragon Reborn"** (Leader; Hero)
*The Shadow Rising* - Robert Jordan *f* 2990

**Althorpe, Cory** (Doctor; Psychic)
*World Without End* - Molly Cochran *f* 1093

**Altir "Tir"** (Royalty; Child)
*Icefalcon's Quest* - Barbara Hambly *f* 2504

**Altman, Gibson** (Government Official; Businessman)
*Pallas* - L. Neil Smith *s* 5132

**Alton, Lew** (Diplomat; Psychic)
*Exile's Song* - Marion Zimmer Bradley *s* 632

**Alton, Margaret** (Musician; Psychic)
*Exile's Song* - Marion Zimmer Bradley *s* 632

**Alton, Marguerida "Margaret"** (Heiress; Telepath)
*The Shadow Matrix* - Marion Zimmer Bradley *s* 645

**Altunin, Roberta** (Noblewoman)
*Rock of Ages* - Walter Jon Williams *s* 5840

**Alucard, Sevil** (Vampire)
*Elvira: Transylvania 90210* - Elvira *h* 1802

**Alvarez, Dan** (Musician)
*Bone Music* - Alan Rodgers *h* 4646

**Alvarez, Edward** (FBI Agent)
*Doomsday Exam* - Nick Pollotta *f* 4363

**al'Vere, Egwene** (Religious; Witch)
*A Crown of Swords* - Robert Jordan *f* 2984
*The Dragon Reborn* - Robert Jordan *f* 2985
*The Path of Daggers* - Robert Jordan *f* 2989

**Alvin** (Explorer; Human)
*Beyond the Fall of Night* - Arthur C. Clarke *s* 1054

**Alya, Princess** (Royalty)
*Strings* - Dave Duncan *s* 1689

**Alyna** (Wizard)
*Runes of Autumn* - Larry Elmore *f* 1790

**Alys** (Criminal; Teenager)
*Dragon's Bait* - Vivian Vande Velde *f* 5556

**Amadeus** (Animal)
*Witches* - Kathryn Meyer Griffith *h* 2442

**Amalayna** (Noblewoman; Avenger)
*Chains of Darkness, Chains of Light* - Michelle Sagara *f* 4781

**Amalfi, Julia** (Computer Expert; Leader)
*Full Tide of Night* - J.R. Dunn *s* 1695

**Amalia, Lady** (Noblewoman)
*The Interior Life* - Katherine Blake *f* 515

**Amaranth** (Mythical Creature; Companion)
*The Dragon's Touchstone* - Irene Radford *f* 4459

**Amatus** (Royalty)
*One for the Morning Glory* - John Barnes *f* 355

**Amaury** (Knight)
*King & Raven* - Cary James *f* 2858

**Amaya, Anya** (Pilot)
*Glory's People* - Alfred Coppel *s* 1183

**Amber** (Child)
*Pet Store* - M.T. Coffin *h* 1097

**Amber** (Psychic)
*Return Fire* - Charles Ingrid *s* 2833

**Amberdrake** (Healer)
*The Black Gryphon* - Mercedes Lackey *f* 3270

**Amberdrake** (Healer; Leader)
*The White Gryphon* - Mercedes Lackey *f* 3303

**Ambras "Dog King"** (Leader)
*The Dog King* - Christoph Ransmayr *f* 4474

**Ambrose** (Royalty)
*The Gilded Chain: A Tale of the King's Blades* - Dave Duncan *f* 1679

**Ambrose, Jonathan** (Investigator)
*Death of a Darklord* - Laurell K. Hamilton *h* 2516

**Ambrose, Tereza** (Magician)
*Death of a Darklord* - Laurell K. Hamilton *h* 2516

**Ambrosius, Merlin** (Wizard)
*The Wizard of Camelot* - Simon Hawke *f* 2627

**Ambrosius, Merlinus** (Wizard)
*The Wolf and the Crown* - A.A. Attanasio *f* 273

**Ambrosius, Merlinus "Myrddin/Lailoken"** (Wizard; Demon)
*The Dragon and the Unicorn* - A.A. Attanasio *f* 266

**Amby** (Actor; Psychic)
*Merlin's Bones* - Fred Saberhagen *f* 4771

**Amelia** (Royalty)
*Dragon's Plunder* - Brad Strickland *f* 5336

**Amelia** (Fugitive)
*Further Adventures* - Jon Stephen Fink *f* 1940

**Amelia** (Farmer)
*Return to Isis* - Jean Stewart *s* 5268

**Amfortas** (Knight)
*The Grail of Hearts* - Susan Shwartz *f* 5015

**Amgigh** (Prehistoric Human; Indian)
*My Sister the Moon* - Sue Harrison *f* 2582

**Amij, Katherine** (Businesswoman)
*Changeling* - Christopher Kubasik *f* 3245

**Amilcar** (Military Personnel)
*Pendragon* - Stephen R. Lawhead *f* 3357

**Amnel, Kahlan** (Magician; Leader)
*Temple of the Winds* - Terry Goodkind *f* 2270

**Amnell, Kahlan** (Magician; Leader)
*Blood of the Fold* - Terry Goodkind *f* 2268
*Stone of Tears* - Terry Goodkind *f* 2269
*Wizard's First Rule* - Terry Goodkind *f* 2271

**Amory, Theodora "Teddy"** (Child)
*Goat Dance* - Douglas Clegg *h* 1079

**Amos, Renee** (Feminist)
*Star Sister* - Juanita Coulson *s* 1211

**Ampelus** (Mythical Creature)
*Thessalonica* - Harry Turtledove *f* 5511

**Amrey, Murl "Kar Kalim"** (Magician; Warrior)
*Kar Kalim* - Deborah Christian *f* 1025

**Amy** (Teenager)
*The Kingdom of Kevin Malone* - Suzy McKee Charnas *f* 970

**Amy** (Artist; Musician)
*Stranded* - Camarin Grae *s* 2295

**An** (Spacewoman; Linguist)
*Eggheads* - Emily Devenport *s* 1500

**an Jiar yn Aliria dur Hamley, Quinzaine** (Immortal; Wizard)
*Fire Crossing* - Cheryl J. Franklin *s* 2036

**an Treves, Sheyrena "Rena"** (Mythical Creature; Fiance(e))
*Elvenblood* - Andre Norton *f* 4150

**Anadon, Oren** (Ruler)
*Exile* - Michael P. Kube-McDowell *s* 3248

**Anaka** (Detective—Police)
*Specters of the Dawn* - S. Andrew Swann *s* 5368

**Ananayel** (Angel)
*Humans* - Donald E. Westlake *f* 5768

**Ananda** (Musician; Lawyer)
*The Thirteenth Daughter of the Moon* - Steven Nightingale *f* 4104

**Anangaranga-Jones, Nixy** (Tourist; Adventurer)
*Muddle Earth* - John Brunner *s* 735

**Anara** (Innkeeper; Teacher)
*India's Story* - Kathlyn S. Starbuck *s* 5208

**Anaral** (Religious)
*An Acceptable Time* - Madeleine L'Engle *f* 3436

**Anasan** (Shaman; Indian)
*Sing for a Gentle Rain* - J. Alison James *f* 2861

**Anastasi, Janet** (Scientist)
*Maverick* - Bruce Bethke *s* 484

**Anatole** (Teenager)
*Silicon Embrace* - John Shirley *s* 5009

**Anaxagoras** (Wizard; Teacher)
*The Wizard's Apprentice* - S.P. Somtow *f* 5163

**Ancar** (Royalty; Magician)
*Winds of Fury* - Mercedes Lackey *f* 3306

**Anders, Sarah** (Diplomat)
*FreeMaster* - Kris Jensen *s* 2897

**Anderson, Aaron** (Teenager)
*Oasis* - Brian Hodge *h* 2703

**Anderson, Carrie** (Doctor)
*The Vampire Princess* - Michael Romkey *h* 4667

**Anderson, Carter** (Heir)
*The High House* - James Stoddard *f* 5311

**Anderson, Chris** (Teenager)
*Oasis* - Brian Hodge *h* 2703

**Anderson, Duskin** (Recluse)
*The High House* - James Stoddard *f* 5311

**Anderson, Kelly** (Teenager)
*Darkness* - John Saul *h* 4840

**Anderson, Marion** (Student)
*Flesh* - Gus Weill *h* 5685

**Anderson, Melanie** (Doctor)
*Stinger* - Nancy Kress *s* 3243

**Anderson, Richard** (Wizard; FBI Agent)
*Bureau 13* - Nick Pollotta *f* 4362

**Anderson, Ted** (Construction Worker; Parent)
*Darkness* - John Saul *h* 4840

**An'desha** (Magician)
*Storm Breaking* - Mercedes Lackey *f* 3296
*Storm Rising* - Mercedes Lackey *f* 3297
*Storm Warning* - Mercedes Lackey *f* 3298

**Andojar, Susan Smith** (Military Personnel)
*The Web of Spider* - W. Michael Gear *s* 2173

**Andrachis, Shil** (Alien; Leader)
*Shadows on the Sun* - Michael Jan Friedman *s* 2069

**Andrada, Rosa** (Secretary)
*The House of the Toad* - Richard L. Tierney *h* 5470

**Andrea** (Teenager)
*The Third Beast* - Peter Loughran *h* 3527

**Andreos, Leonidas** (Spaceship Captain)
*Siduri's Net* - P.K. McAllister *s* 3709

**Andrew** (Young Man)
*The Last Coin* - James P. Blaylock   f   519

**Andrews, Boyd** (Carpenter)
*Blood Kin* - Ronald Kelly   h   3051

**Andrews, Laura** (Patient)
*Quarantine* - Greg Egan   s   1762

**Andreyeva, Maya Tayanichna** (Journalist; Cyborg)
*The Fortunate Fall* - Raphael Carter   s   927

**Andry** (Ruler; Magician)
*The Dragon Token* - Melanie Rawn   f   4485
*Stronghold* - Melanie Rawn   f   4492

**Andry** (Nobleman; Magician)
*Sunrunner's Fire* - Melanie Rawn   f   4493

**Angel** (Student—High School; Sports Figure)
*Damnbanna* - Nancy Springer   f   5177

**Angel** (Animal)
*Dancing on Air* - Nancy Kress   s   3240

**Angel** (Vampire)
*Dark Prince* - Keith Herber   h   2663

**Angel** (Alien)
*The Pure Cold Light* - Gregory Frost   s   2087

**Angel Juan** (Teenager; Musician)
*Missing Angel Juan* - Francesca Lia Block   f   550

**Angelica, Pearl** (Genetically Altered Being)
*Tower of the Gods* - Thomas A. Easton   s   1726

**Angelo, Jamie** (Artist; Student)
*Beauty* - Brian D'Amato   h   1334

**Angelus, Lucifer "Luke"** (Computer; Military Personnel)
*Chains of Light* - Quentin Thomas   s   5449

**Anghara, Princess** (Young Woman; Royalty)
*Nemesis* - Louise Cooper   f   1177

**Angharad** (Minstrel; Wanderer)
*Into the Green* - Charles de Lint   f   1430

**Angier, Rupert** (Magician; Writer)
*The Prestige* - Christopher Priest   s   4432

**Anglith of Arkraz, Omar "Trader of Tales"** (Writer; Traveler)
*The Hunters' Haunt* - Dave Duncan   f   1681
*The Reaver Road* - Dave Duncan   f   1687

**Anhand, Deteras "Detter"** (Student; Wizard)
*Nameless Magery* - Delia Marshall Turner   f   5490

**Anica** (Girlfriend)
*Senor Vivo and the Coca Lord* - Louis de Bernieres   f   1411

**Anigel** (Royalty)
*Black Trillium* - Marion Zimmer Bradley   f   630

**Anij** (Immortal; Settler)
*Insurrection* - J.M. Dillard   s   1554

**Animiki-Waewidum, Gahzee** (Indian; Scientist)
*Svaha* - Charles de Lint   s   1437

**Anito** (Alien)
*The Color of Distance* - Amy Thomson   s   5461

**Ankoku** (Nobleman; Twin)
*Dragon's Winter* - Elizabeth A. Lynn   f   3578

**Anlawdd** (Royalty; Criminal)
*Arthur War Lord* - Dafydd ab Hugh   f   6

**Anlon** (Mythical Creature)
*Morigu: The Dead* - Mark C. Perry   f   4284

**Ann** (Housewife)
*The Cormorant* - Stephen Gregory   h   2429

**Ann** (Writer)
*Gothic Romance* - Emmanuel Carrere   h   912

**Ann "Annai"** (Dancer; Parent)
*Shame of Man* - Piers Anthony   s   188

**Anna** (Child)
*Darkness, I* - Tanith Lee   h   3407

**Annalise** (Companion; Slave)
*Black Wine* - Candas Jane Dorsey   s   1582

**Anne** (Handicapped; Spirit)
*The Time Tree* - Enid Richemont   f   4585

**Anne** (Artificial Intelligence)
*Dream of Glass* - Jean Mark Gawron   s   2163

**Annice** (Royalty; Minstrel)
*Sing the Four Quarters* - Tanya Huff   f   2799

**Anniyas, Avira** (Political Figure; Psychic)
*The Ruins of Ambrai* - Melanie Rawn   f   4489

**Ansa** (Warrior; Explorer)
*The Poisoned Lands* - John Maddox Roberts   f   4619

**Ansa** (Explorer; Warrior)
*Queens of Land and Sea* - John Maddox Roberts   f   4620

**Antar** (Computer Expert)
*The Calcutta Chromosome* - Amitav Ghosh   h   2214

**Antero, Amalric** (Adventurer; Teenager)
*The Far Kingdoms* - Allan Cole   f   1104

**Antero, Amalric** (Adventurer)
*Kingdoms of the Night* - Allan Cole   f   1105

**Antero, Rali Emilie** (Wizard; Lesbian)
*The Warrior Returns* - Allan Cole   f   1109

**Antero, Rali Emilie** (Military Personnel)
*The Warrior's Tale* - Allan Cole   f   1110

**Anthea** (Explorer)
*I Who Have Never Known Men* - Jacqueline Harpman   s   2554

**Anthimos** (Ruler)
*Krispos Rising* - Harry Turtledove   f   5507

**Anthony** (Teenager)
*The First Horror* - R.L. Stine   h   5288

**Anthony** (Religious; Teacher)
*Catacomb* - Andrew Laurance   h   3347

**Antilles, Wedge** (Military Personnel; Pilot)
*Rogue Squadron* - Michael A. Stackpole   s   5205

**Antimodes** (Wizard)
*The Soulforge* - Margaret Weis   f   5728

**Antiope** (Warrior; Time Traveler)
*Amazon: A Novel* - Barbara G. Walker   f   5616

**Antiope** (Warrior; Lesbian)
*The Amazon Chronicles* - Jane E.M. Robinson   f   4627

**Antissa, Sybil** (Sorceress)
*Owl Light* - Michael Paine   h   4235

**Antonia** (Witch; Child)
*Daughter of Magic* - C. Dale Brittain   f   703

**Antonio** (Vampire)
*To Dream of Dreamers Lost* - David Niall Wilson   h   5882

**Antonius, Marcus** (Historical Figure; Military Personnel)
*Throne of Isis* - Judith Tarr   f   5397

**Antonov, Denis** (Werewolf)
*The Passion* - Donna Boyd   h   603

**Antonovich, Colonel** (Military Personnel)
*The Struggle* - Jerry Ahern   s   44

**Anwara** (Parent)
*The Moorchild* - Eloise Jarvis McGraw   f   3816

**Anya** (Dancer; Vampire)
*Live Girls* - Ray Garton   h   2151

**Anya** (Warrior)
*Orion in the Dying Time* - Ben Bova   s   591

**Anyelet** (Vampire)
*Afterage* - Yvonne Navarro   h   4072

**Anyr** (Fiance(e))
*The Sleep of Stone* - Louise Cooper   f   1179

**Anzelm, Aitan** (Angel)
*The Ways of Magic* - Scott Ciencin   f   1033

**Aoibhell, Brendan** (Leader; Spaceship Captain)
*The Deer's Cry: A Book of the Keltiad* - Patricia Kennealy-Morrison   f   3060

**ap Don, Gwydion** (Magician; Royalty)
*The Island of the Mighty* - Evangeline Walton   f   5626

**ap Hywel, Dafydd** (Warrior; Adventurer)
*The Dragon in Lyonesse* - Gordon R. Dickson   f   1531

**ap Hywel, Dafydd** (Martial Arts Expert; Royalty)
*The Dragon on the Border* - Gordon R. Dickson   f   1533

**ap Ieuan, Owain** (Vampire)
*The Devil's Advocate* - Gherbod Fleming   h   1949

**ap Kian, Donaugh** (Royalty; Magician)
*The Western King* - Ann Marston   f   3636

**ap Kian, Keylan** (Ruler)
*The Western King* - Ann Marston   f   3636

**ap Kian, Tiernyn** (Royalty; Warrior)
*The Western King* - Ann Marston   f   3636

**ap Mathonwy, Math** (Magician; Royalty)
*The Island of the Mighty* - Evangeline Walton   f   5626

**ap Medrault, Irion** (Royalty)
*The Last Pendragon* - Robert Rice   f   4584

**ap Nia, Aidan** (Royalty; Magician)
*King's Son, Magic's Son* - Josepha Sherman   f   4986

**Ap Sennon, Olmy** (Adventurer; Sailor)
*Legacy* - Greg Bear   s   420

**Ape** (Wizard)
*The Gates of Noon* - Michael Scott Rohan   f   4661

**Aphrael** (Deity; Child)
*The Hidden City* - David Eddings   f   1733

**Apolinario, Lot** (Genetically Altered Being; Revolutionary)
*Deception Well* - Linda Nagata   s   4065

**Apollo** (Warrior; Spaceman)
*Armageddon* - Richard Hatch   s   2602

**Apollo** (Mythical Creature; Deity)
*Ye Gods!* - Tom Holt   f   2753

**Apolon** (Magician)
*Tiger Burning Bright* - Marion Zimmer Bradley   f   652

**Apophis** (Alien)
*Stargate SG-1* - Ashley McConnell   s   3777

**Appenfell, Anjell** (Child; Adventurer)
*A Breach in the Watershed* - Douglas Niles   f   4105

**Appenfell, Rudgar "Rudy"** (Hero; Mountaineer)
*A Breach in the Watershed* - Douglas Niles   f   4105
*Darkenheight* - Douglas Niles   f   4107
*War of the Three Waters* - Douglas Niles   f   4110

**APU-805 "Bird Dog"** (Robot; Military Personnel)
*Destination: Showdown* - Jake Davis   s   1405
*The Last Rangers* - Jake Davis   s   1406

**Apuilana, Nialli** (Royalty)
*The New Springtime* - Robert Silverberg   s   5040

**Aqamdax** (Indian)
*Song of the River* - Sue Harrison   f   2583

**Arabella "Infectress"** (Criminal; Revolutionary)
*Infectress* - Tom Cool   s   1167

**Aracco** (Apprentice; Adventurer)
*Goldclimbers* - Nancy Luenn  f  3545

**Aradia** (Teenager; Noblewoman)
*A Heroine of the World* - Tanith Lee  f  3412

**Aragon, Julian** (Vampire; Writer)
*Thirst* - Michael Cecilione  h  948

**Arak, Bashir** (Aged Person; Explorer)
*The Planet Beyond* - Steve Mudd  s  4043

**Aralorn** (Mythical Creature; Martial Arts Expert)
*Masques* - Patricia Briggs  f  681

**Aramina** (Telepath)
*The Renegades of Pern* - Anne McCaffrey  s  3746

**Aranow, Jackson** (Doctor; Gentleman)
*Beggars Ride* - Nancy Kress  s  3238

**Aranur** (Martial Arts Expert)
*Shadow Leader* - Tara K. Harper  f  2552

**Aravan** (Mythical Creature)
*The Eye of the Hunter* - Dennis L.
McKiernan  f  3833

**Aravan** (Mythical Creature; Sea Captain)
*Voyage of the Fox Rider* - Dennis L.
McKiernan  f  3837

**Arayncourt, Trevelyan** (Businessman)
*The Lotus and the Rose* - Scott Ciencin  f  1029
*The Wolves of Autumn* - Scott Ciencin  f  1035

**Arbok** (Alien; Pilot)
*Prison Ship* - Martin Caidin  s  828

**Arbol** (Royalty; Imposter)
*Split Heirs* - Lawrence Watt-Evans  f  5649

**Arbuthnot, Aubrey** (Detective—Private; Psychic)
*The Devil You Say* - Elisa DeCarlo  f  1450
*Strong Spirits* - Elisa DeCarlo  f  1451

**Arbuthnot, Farquhar** (Nobleman; Spirit)
*Strong Spirits* - Elisa DeCarlo  f  1451

**Arcangelo** (Religious)
*Zaragoz* - Brian Craig  f  1241

**Arcangelo, Michael** (Computer Expert)
*Wyrm* - Mark Fabi  s  1858

**Archangel** (Mythical Creature; Computer Expert)
*Headhunters* - Mel Odom  s  4192

**Archangel** (Writer; Activist)
*Tropic of Orange* - Karen Tei Yamashita  f  6009

**Archemon** (Alien)
*Monsoon* - Peter L. Rice  s  4583

**Archer, Ann** (Teacher)
*Otherworld* - Kenneth C. Flint  h  1959

**Archie** (Animal)
*The Cormorant* - Stephen Gregory  h  2429

**Archon of Lycanth** (Ruler; Wizard)
*The Warrior's Tale* - Allan Cole  f  1110

**Archway, Andy** (Undertaker)
*The Unnatural* - David Prill  h  4437

**ARCHY** (Artificial Intelligence)
*Second Star* - Dana Stabenow  s  5188

**Arda** (Android; Spy)
*Murder at the Galactic Writers' Society* - Janet
Asimov  s  251

**Arden** (Lover)
*The Lightless Kingdom* - Jonathan Wylie  f  6007

**Arden, Rose Red** (Maiden)
*Snow White and Rose Red* - Patricia C.
Wrede  f  5981

**Arden, Snow White** (Maiden)
*Snow White and Rose Red* - Patricia C.
Wrede  f  5981

**Ardis** (Religious)
*Four & Twenty Blackbirds* - Mercedes
Lackey  f  3283

**Ardyn** (Lesbian)
*Escape to the Wind* - Jennifer DiMarco  s  1559

**Aregeni, Callion** (Fugitive)
*In the Rift* - Marion Zimmer Bradley  f  639

**Aretino, Pietro** (Writer)
*A Farce to Be Reckoned With* - Roger
Zelazny  f  6064

**Argyle, Roger** (Businessman)
*All the Bells on Earth* - James P. Blaylock  f  518

**Ari** (Clone; Scientist)
*Cyteen* - C.J. Cherryh  s  984

**Ariadne, Helene** (Student)
*Light Raid* - Connie Willis  s  5870

**Ariane** (Scholar)
*Moonwise* - Greer Ilene Gilman  f  2238

**Arianna** (Noblewoman; Warrior)
*The Resistance* - Kristine Kathryn Rusch  f  4727

**Arianrhod** (Magician; Royalty)
*The Island of the Mighty* - Evangeline
Walton  f  5626

**Arin** (Mythical Creature; Noblewoman)
*The Dragonstone* - Dennis L. McKiernan  f  3832

**Ariodne** (Witch)
*The Wolves of Autumn* - Scott Ciencin  f  1035

**Arista, Tommaso** (Apprentice)
*The Stars Dispose* - Michaela Roessner  f  4651

**Arity "Ari"** (Addict; Outcast)
*Delta City* - Felicity Savage  f  4849

**Arius** (Artificial Intelligence)
*Dreams of Gods and Men* - W.T. Quick  s  4451

**Arlen, Drew** (Musician)
*Beggars and Choosers* - Nancy Kress  s  3236

**Arletta, Simone** (Sorceress)
*Valentine* - S.P. Somtow  h  5160

**Armand** (Vampire)
*The Vampire Armand* - Anne Rice  h  4578

**Armand, Pamela** (Prisoner)
*The Living Evil* - Ruby Jean Jensen  h  2902

**Armon** (Artist)
*The Forgetting Room* - Nick Bantock  f  333

**Armstrong, Alexander "the Great"** (Military
Personnel; Political Figure)
*Martian Rainbow* - Robert L. Forward  s  1987

**Armstrong, Augustus "Gus"** (Scientist;
Administrator)
*Martian Rainbow* - Robert L. Forward  s  1987

**Armstrong, Goodwin** (Detective—Private)
*Inhuman Beings* - Jerry Jay Carroll  s  914

**Armstrong, Vera** (Nurse)
*Werewolf* - Peter Rubie  h  4702

**Arnez, Jorge "Mal Sangre"** (Religious)
*Voodoo Child* - Michael Reaves  h  4498

**Arnix, Gherifan** (Actor)
*The Illusionists* - Faren Miller  f  3894

**Arno, Phyllis** (Actress)
*Deathchain* - Ken Greenhall  h  2415

**Aroha** (Magician)
*Sable, Shadow and Ice* - Cheryl J. Franklin  f  2039

**Aronson, Susan** (Businesswoman)
*Phoenix Fire* - Elizabeth Forrest  f  1974

**Arouetto** (Scholar)
*The Secular Wizard* - Christopher Stasheff  f  5222

**Arry** (Teenager; Empath)
*The Dubious Hills* - Pamela Dean  f  1444

**Artemisia** (Royalty; Parent)
*Split Heirs* - Lawrence Watt-Evans  f  5649

**Arthor** (Bastard Son; Teenager)
*The Eagle and the Sword* - A.A. Attanasio  f  267

**Arthre, Roy "Ratha"** (Professor; Magician)
*The Falcon Rises* - Michael C. Staudinger  f  5235

**Arthur** (Royalty; Ruler)
*The Autobiography of Santa Claus: It's Better to Give*
- Jeff Guinn  f  2456

**Arthur** (Royalty)
*The Book of Brendan* - Ann Curry  f  1294
*The Camelot Chronicles* - Mike Ashley  f  224

**Arthur** (Ruler; Warrior)
*The Child Queen* - Nancy McKenzie  f  3827
*Chronicles of King Arthur* - Andrea
Hopkins  f  2767

**Arthur** (Royalty)
*Enemy of God* - Bernard Cornwell  f  1189
*Excalibur* - Bernard Cornwell  f  1190
*Grail* - Stephen R. Lawhead  f  3355

**Arthur** (Ruler)
*Guinevere: The Legend in Autumn* - Persia
Woolley  f  5970

**Arthur** (Royalty; Military Personnel)
*The Hawk's Gray Feather* - Patricia Kennealy-
Morrison  f  3061

**Arthur** (Robot; Alien)
*The Immortality Option* - James P. Hogan  s  2725

**Arthur** (Royalty)
*In the Shadow of the Oak King* - Courtway
Jones  f  2939
*The King* - Donald Barthelme  f  375

**Arthur** (Ruler)
*King & Raven* - Cary James  f  2858

**Arthur** (Ruler; Warrior)
*Mordred's Curse* - Ian McDowell  f  3806

**Arthur** (Ruler)
*Pendragon* - Stephen R. Lawhead  f  3357
*Queen of the Summer Stars* - Persia
Woolley  f  5971

**Arthur** (Royalty)
*Shadow of the King* - Helen Hollick  f  2747

**Arthur** (Warrior; Bastard Son)
*The Winter King* - Bernard Cornwell  f  1191

**Arthur** (Royalty)
*Witch of the North* - Courtway Jones  f  2940

**Arthur, Shannon** (Detective—Private)
*Sister to the Rain* - Melisa Michaels  f  3887

**Arthur "Artos"** (Ruler; Hero)
*A Prince Among Men* - Robert N. Charrette  f  977

**Artos** (Nobleman; Warrior)
*Black Horses for the King* - Anne
McCaffrey  f  3720

**Artos** (Foundling)
*The Dragon's Boy* - Jane Yolen  f  6030

**Arturo, Maximillian** (Professor; Adventurer)
*Sliders: The Novel* - Brad Linaweaver  s  3467

**Arunsun, Khelben** (Sorcerer)
*Thornhold* - Elaine Cunningham  f  1293

**Arvin, Andro** (Military Personnel; Administrator)
*Starfire Down* - Lee McKeone  s  3830

**Aryadyss** (Artificial Intelligence; Mythical Creature)
*Donnerjack* - Roger Zelazny  s  6063

**Aryl** (Teenager; Alien)
*Under Alien Stars* - Pamela F. Service  s  4919

**Aryton, Antonia** (Noblewoman)
*Whispers in the Dark* - Jonathan Aycliffe  *h*  283

**Aryton, Antony** (Nobleman)
*Whispers in the Dark* - Jonathan Aycliffe  *h*  283

**Asado** (Military Personnel; Criminal)
*The War of Don Emmanuel's Nether Parts* - Louis de
Bernieres  *f*  1412

**Asakeiri, Adline** (Sports Figure; Shaman)
*The Watcher's Mask* - Laurie J. Marks  *f*  3627

**Asan** (Alien; Nobleman)
*Requiem for Anthi* - Jay D. Blakeney  *s*  517

**Asandir** (Sorcerer)
*Curse of the Mistwraith* - Janny Wurts  *f*  6001

**Asbrak** (Royalty)
*The Door to Ambermere* - J. Calvin Pierce  *f*  4316

**Ascher, Emily** (Revolutionary)
*Beneath the Tree of Heaven* - David
Wingrove  *s*  5917

**Ascher, Emily** (Political Figure)
*The Broken Wheel* - David Wingrove  *s*  5918

**Asgar, Klia** (Teenager; Telepath)
*Foundation and Chaos* - Greg Bear  *s*  418

**Asgard, Paula** (Musician)
*Carlucci's Edge* - Richard Paul Russo  *s*  4747

**Ash** (Animal; Companion)
*Deerskin* - Robin McKinley  *f*  3844

**Ash, David** (Paranormal Investigator)
*The Ghosts of Sleath* - James Herbert  *h*  2668
*Haunted* - James Herbert  *h*  2669

**Ash, Hatty** (Healer)
*Devil's Tower* - Mark Sumner  *f*  5357

**Ash, Leanard** (Reanimated Dead)
*Shadows Fall* - Simon R. Green  *f*  2373

**Ash, Leon** (Scientist)
*The Invisible Company* - Scott Russell
Sanders  *s*  4813

**Ash, Mickey** (Military Personnel)
*The Daemon in the Machine* - Felicity
Savage  *f*  4848
*The War in the Waste* - Felicity Savage  *f*  4852

**Ash of Ashland** (Revolutionary; Adventurer)
*Dancing Jack* - Laurie J. Marks  *f*  3624

**Ashar** (Deity)
*The Way Beneath* - Angus Wells  *f*  5740

**Ashata/Maya** (Immortal; Pilot)
*The Queen's Squadron* - R.M. Meluch  *s*  3874

**Ashe, Timothy** (Time Traveler; Spy)
*The Seeds of Time* - Kay Kenyon  *s*  3064

**Ashenden, Turner** (Student)
*Views from the Oldest House* - Richard
Grant  *s*  2329

**Asher** (Vampire)
*Burnt Offerings* - Laurell K. Hamilton  *h*  2514

**Asher, Anat** (Military Personnel)
*Signs of Life* - Cherry Wilder  *s*  5804

**Asher, James** (Detective—Amateur; Professor)
*Those Who Hunt the Night* - Barbara
Hambly  *h*  2510

**Asher, James** (Professor; Detective—Amateur)
*Traveling with the Dead* - Barbara Hambly  *h*  2511

**Asher, Lydia** (Scientist)
*Traveling with the Dead* - Barbara Hambly  *h*  2511

**Ashkevron, Savil** (Magician)
*Magic's Price* - Mercedes Lackey  *f*  3288

**Ashkevron, Vanyel** (Magician; Homosexual)
*Magic's Price* - Mercedes Lackey  *f*  3288

**Ashlar "Mr. Ash"** (Businessman)
*Taltos* - Anne Rice  *h*  4577

**Ashton, Choe** (Truck Driver; Rebel)
*Signs of Life* - M. John Harrison  *s*  2580

**Ashton, Clark** (Doctor)
*Blood of Innocents* - John Arbucci  *h*  204

**Asimov, Issac** (Television Personality; Historical
Figure)
*Back in the USSA* - Kim Newman  *s*  4095

**Asofel** (Angel)
*The Shadow Eater* - Adam Lee  *f*  3386

**Asperson, Arhos** (Criminal)
*Once a Hero* - Elizabeth Moon  *s*  3970

**Asquith, Timothy** (Alcoholic)
*Ghostwright* - Michael Cadnum  *h*  810

**Asrubal** (Thief)
*Night Lamp* - Jack Vance  *s*  5548

**Astare, T.** (Vampire)
*Morningstar* - Peter Atkins  *h*  265

**Aster "Star"** (Royalty; Traveler)
*Glory Road* - Robert A. Heinlein  *f*  2644

**Astfgl** (Demon)
*Eric* - Terry Pratchett  *f*  4388

**Astiar, Meliara "Mel"** (Teenager; Noblewoman)
*Court Duel* - Sherwood Smith  *f*  5137

**A'stoc** (Wizard)
*Quest for the Fallen Star* - Piers Anthony  *f*  185

**Astrahn** (Slave; Revolutionary)
*A City in Winter* - Mark Helprin  *f*  2653

**Asx/Ewasx** (Alien)
*Infinity's Shore* - David Brin  *s*  688

**At** (Alien)
*Doctor's Orders* - Diane Duane  *s*  1659

**Ata'al** (Shaman)
*The Watcher's Mask* - Laurie J. Marks  *f*  3627

**Atani, Karadur** (Nobleman; Twin)
*Dragon's Winter* - Elizabeth A. Lynn  *f*  3578

**Atare, Darame "Silver" Meath** (Ruler; Immigrant)
*Hidden Fires* - Katharine Eliska Kimbriel  *s*  3117

**Atare, Sheen** (Ruler; Hero)
*Hidden Fires* - Katharine Eliska Kimbriel  *s*  3117

**Atbin** (Teenager; Adventurer)
*The Promise* - Monica Hughes  *s*  2808

**Aten** (Immortal)
*Orion Among the Stars* - Ben Bova  *s*  589

**A'Terafin, Jewel** (Businesswoman)
*The Uncrowned King* - Michelle West  *f*  5760

**Atkins, Thomas "Soldier"** (Military Personnel)
*Genetic Soldier* - George Turner  *s*  5492

**Atle** (Military Personnel; Spaceship Captain)
*Silent Songs* - A.C. Crispin  *s*  1264

**Atreus** (Nobleman)
*Faces of Deception* - Troy Denning  *f*  1485

**Atrus** (Magician)
*Myst: The Book of Atrus* - Rand Miller  *f*  3896

**Atrus** (Writer; Magician)
*Myst: The Book of D'ni* - Rand Miller  *f*  3897

**Attercop, Karen** (Student; Lover)
*Webs* - Scott Baker  *h*  304

**Attila** (Android; Martial Arts Expert)
*Hunter's Planet* - David Bischoff  *s*  492

**Attila the Hun** (Historical Figure; Foster Parent)
*Attila's Treasure* - Stephan Grundy  *f*  2453

**Attila the Hun** (Warrior)
*The Autobiography of Santa Claus: It's Better to Give*
- Jeff Guinn  *f*  2456

**Atuli, Cameron** (Dancer; Homosexual)
*Maximum Light* - Nancy Kress  *s*  3241

**Atvar** (Alien; Leader)
*Worldwar: In the Balance* - Harry
Turtledove  *s*  5515

**Atvar** (Military Personnel; Alien)
*Worldwar: Striking the Balance* - Harry
Turtledove  *s*  5516

**Atvar** (Alien; Leader)
*Worldwar: Tilting the Balance* - Harry
Turtledove  *s*  5517

**Atvar** (Military Personnel; Alien)
*Worldwar: Upsetting the Balance* - Harry
Turtledove  *s*  5518

**Atwood, Clancy "Kolo"** (Indian)
*Demon Dance* - T. Chris Martindale  *h*  3655

**Aubert, Jacques** (Apprentice)
*Where the Towers Pierce the Sky* - Marie D.
Goodwin  *f*  2272

**Aubrey** (Student; Wizard)
*The Shape-Changer's Wife* - Sharon Shinn  *f*  5002

**Audran, Marid** (Assistant; Bodyguard)
*The Exile Kiss* - George Alec Effinger  *s*  1750

**Audran, Marid** (Police Officer; Bodyguard)
*A Fire in the Sun* - George Alec Effinger  *s*  1751

**Auganzar** (Alien; Military Personnel)
*Warlord of Heaven* - Adrian Cole  *f*  1102

**Auggie** (Artificial Intelligence)
*Terminal Games* - Cole Perriman  *s*  4283

**August** (Genetically Altered Being)
*Becoming Human* - Valerie J. Freireich  *s*  2049

**Augustine** (Historical Figure; Religious)
*Blameless in Abaddon* - James Morrow  *f*  4029

**Augustine, Alexa** (Computer Expert; Military
Personnel)
*Dream of Glass* - Jean Mark Gawron  *s*  2163

**Augustus, Caleb** (Engineer; Scientist)
*Jovah's Angel* - Sharon Shinn  *s*  5001

**Auk, Maytera** (Criminal; Religious)
*Exodus From the Long Sun* - Gene Wolfe  *s*  5941

**Aurealis, Gannd** (Mythical Creature; Warrior)
*War* - Simon Hawke  *f*  2625

**Aurelia** (Witch)
*The Pit and the Pendulum* - Amarantha
Knight  *h*  3183

**Aurelico, Karvonen** (Thief; Guide)
*The Raven Ring* - Patricia C. Wrede  *f*  5978

**Aurelio** (Indian; Shaman)
*The War of Don Emmanuel's Nether Parts* - Louis de
Bernieres  *f*  1412

**Aurian** (Student; Magician)
*Aurian* - Maggie Furey  *f*  2095

**Aurian** (Magician)
*Dhiammara* - Maggie Furey  *f*  2096

**Aurian** (Magician; Parent)
*Harp of Winds* - Maggie Furey  *f*  2097

**Aurian** (Magician)
*Sword of Flame* - Maggie Furey  *f*  2098

**Auriane** (Warrior; Religious)
*The Light Bearer* - Donna Gillespie  *f*  2229

**Austen, James** (Doctor)
*The Angel of Pain* - Brian Stableford  *h*  5189

**Austin** (Animal; Psychic)
*Summon the Keeper* - Tanya Huff  *f*  2800

**Austin, Gregory** (Captive; Spaceman)
*Fallway* - Paula E. Downing  *s*  1593

**Austin, Kenton** (Businessman)
*The Living Dark* - Stephen Gresham  h  2431

**Austin, Steve** (Police Officer)
*Slippin' into Darkness* - Norman Partridge  h  4254

**Austra, Catherine** (Vampire)
*Daughter of the Night* - Elaine Bergstrom  h  463

**Austra, Laurence** (Vampire)
*Blood Alone* - Elaine Bergstrom  h  462

**Autothor** (Artificial Intelligence; Alien)
*Codgerspace* - Alan Dean Foster  s  1999

**Avelyn** (Religious; Wizard)
*The Demon Awakens* - R.A. Salvatore  f  4794

**Avenger** (Adventurer; Criminal)
*The Spider #4: Death Reign of the Vampire King/The
    Pain Emperor* - Grant Stockbridge  f  5308

**Avens, Isobel** (Genetically Altered Being)
*Signs of Life* - M. John Harrison  s  2580

**Averil** (Sorceress)
*Plague Demon* - Brian Craig  f  1239

**Avery** (Artificial Intelligence)
*Caverns of Socrates* - Dennis L. McKiernan  f  3831

**Avery, David "Derec"** (Computer Expert)
*Maverick* - Bruce Bethke  s  484

**Avery, Rupert "Roo"** (Businessman; Bastard Son)
*Rage of a Demon King* - Raymond E. Feist  f  1908
*Rise of a Merchant Prince* - Raymond E.
    Feist  f  1909

**Avery, Rupert "Roo"** (Fugitive; Bastard Son)
*Shadow of a Dark Queen* - Raymond E.
    Feist  f  1911

**Avery, Rupert "Roo"** (Businessman; Bastard Son)
*Shards of a Broken Crown* - Raymond E.
    Feist  f  1912

**Avichenko, Emily "Avi"** (Scientist)
*Only Child* - H.M. Hoover  s  2764

**Aviendha** (Warrior)
*The Fires of Heaven* - Robert Jordan  f  2987

**Avignon, Kitten "Our Lady of Roses"**
    (Noblewoman)
*Mage Heart* - Jane Routley  f  4686

**Avran** (Servant; Magician)
*Aurian* - Maggie Furey  f  2095

**Avran** (Magician)
*Harp of Winds* - Maggie Furey  f  2097
*Sword of Flame* - Maggie Furey  f  2098

**Avril** (Royalty; Sorcerer)
*The Price of Blood and Honor* - Elizabeth
    Willey  f  5811

**Avril** (Ruler; Sorcerer)
*A Sorcerer and a Gentleman* - Elizabeth
    Willey  f  5812

**Avris** (Witch; Companion)
*Songsmith* - Andre Norton  f  4161

**Aw, Ruiz** (Slave; Agent)
*Emperor of Everything* - Ray Aldridge  s  62

**Aw, Ruiz** (Agent; Martial Arts Expert)
*The Pharaoh Contract* - Ray Aldridge  s  63

**Axxter, Ny** (Artist)
*Farewell Horizontal* - K.W. Jeter  s  2911

**Ayers, Jane** (Health Care Professional)
*The Illegal Rebirth of Billy the Kid* - Rebecca
    Ore  s  4220

**Ayesha** (Mythical Creature)
*Dragon's Domain* - Thorarinn Gunnarsson  f  2461

**Ayla** (Prehistoric Human; Shaman)
*The Plains of Passage* - Jean M. Auel  f  275

**Aylesworth, Jesse** (Student—College; Editor)
*An Exaltation of Larks* - Robert Reed  s  4506

**Ayrlyn** (Doctor)
*The Chaos Balance* - L.E. Modesitt Jr.  f  3925

**Ayth, Argoth** (Religious; Magician)
*Demon Moon* - Jack Williamson  s  5862

**Ayyah** (Alien; Refugee)
*Cat's Gambit* - Leslie Gadallah  s  2099

**Aza-Kra** (Alien)
*Rule Golden and Double Meaning* - Damon
    Knight  s  3189

**Azak** (Mythical Creature; Leader)
*Emperor and Clown* - Dave Duncan  f  1676

**Azaro** (Child; Psychic)
*The Famished Road* - Ben Okri  f  4207
*Songs of Enchantment* - Ben Okri  f  4208

**Azdra'ik** (Mythical Creature; Royalty)
*The Goblin Mirror* - C.J. Cherryh  f  994

**Aziraphale** (Angel)
*Good Omens: The Nice and Accurate Prophecies of
    Agnes Nutter, Witch* - Neil Gaiman  f  2103

**Aziz** (Servant)
*Crescent in the Sky* - Donald Moffitt  s  3946

**Azod** (Young Man)
*The Forsaken* - Steven Ray Fulgham  h  2089

**Azoun** (Ruler)
*Crusade* - James Lowder  f  3537

**Azoun IV** (Ruler)
*Cormyr: A Novel* - Ed Greenwood  f  2425

**Azrael** (Sorcerer)
*Evil Reincarnate* - Leigh Clark  h  1050

**Azriel** (Mythical Creature)
*Servant of the Bones* - Anne Rice  h  4575

# B

**Baalgor "Grayface"** (Hunter)
*Ancient Echoes* - Robert Holdstock  f  2735

**Baat** (Monster)
*Hunting the Ghost Dancer* - A.A. Attanasio  f  268

**Baba Yaga** (Witch)
*Harpy High* - Esther Friesner  f  2076

**Baba Yaga** (Mythical Creature)
*Weirdos of the Universe, Unite!* - Pamela F.
    Service  f  4921

**Babcock, Maria** (Revolutionary)
*Nature's God* - Robert Anton Wilson  f  5903

**Babriel** (Angel)
*Bring Me the Head of Prince Charming* - Roger
    Zelazny  f  6062

**Baby Baby** (Alien; Musician)
*Rock 'n' Roll Babes From Outer Space* - Linda
    Javin  s  2880

**Babych, Simon** (Clerk)
*Nightlife* - Jack Ellis  h  1779

**Bach, Arthur** (Religious; Vampire)
*Night Prophets* - Paul F. Olson  h  4213

**Backmaker, Hodgins "Hodge"** (Historian; Time
    Traveler)
*Bring the Jubilee* - Ward Moore  s  3993

**Bad Belly/Still Water** (Prehistoric Human; Indian)
*People of the Earth* - W. Michael Gear  f  2166

**bad-Jam, Gilan "Gilan the Third"** (Alien; Ruler)
*The Swords of Zinjaban* - L. Sprague de
    Camp  s  1418

**Badger** (Bastard Son; Companion)
*The Spellkey Trilogy* - Ann Downer  f  1592

**Badrang the Tyrant** (Animal; Leader)
*Martin the Warrior* - Brian Jacques  f  2851

**Baedecker, Richard** (Astronaut; Businessman)
*Phases of Gravity* - Dan Simmons  s  5057

**Baedecker, Scott** (Young Man)
*Phases of Gravity* - Dan Simmons  s  5057

**Baenre, Dantrag** (Martial Arts Expert)
*Starless Night* - R.A. Salvatore  f  4807

**Baenre, Liriel** (Magician; Mythical Creature)
*Daughter of the Drow* - Elaine Cunningham  f  1287

**Bagg, Stuart "Shoebag"** (Animal; Child)
*Shoebag* - Mary James  f  2868
*Shoebag Returns* - Mary James  f  2869

**Baggy** (Alien)
*Judson's Eden* - Keith Laumer  s  3344

**Bagnell, Edward E.** (Professor)
*The Boss in the Wall* - Avram Davidson  h  1396

**Bagsby** (Thief)
*Dragonspawn* - Mark Acres  f  28

**Bahhum Bug** (Supernatural Being)
*The Haunted Tea Cosy: A Dispirited and Distasteful
    Diversion for Christmas* - Edward Gorey  h  2276

**Bahnakson, Bahzell** (Warrior; Royalty)
*Oath of Swords* - David Weber  f  5678

**Bahnakson, Bahzell** (Warrior)
*The War God's Own* - David Weber  f  5682

**Bailey, David "Herbert" Clancy** (Robot; Inventor)
*The Modular Man* - Roger MacBride Allen  s  79

**Bailey, Penelope** (Psychic; Leader)
*Prophet* - Mike Resnick  s  4553

**Bailey, Penelope** (Psychic; Fugitive)
*Soothsayer* - Mike Resnick  s  4557

**Bain** (Religious)
*The Thing That Darkness Hides* - Robert
    Morgan  h  4006

**Bainbridge** (Advertising; Student—College)
*Ferman's Devils* - Joe Clifford Faust  s  1892

**Baines, Ti-Jeanne** (Psychic; Single Parent)
*Brown Girl in the Ring* - Nalo Hopkinson  f  2771

**Baird, Jason** (Jeweler)
*The Jade Ogre* - Kenneth Robeson  f  4623

**Baird, John** (Professor)
*The Hemingway Hoax* - Joe Haldeman  s  2489

**Bajac, Tess** (Artist)
*Skin* - Kathe Koja  h  3196

**Baker, Bob** (Teacher)
*After Life* - Andrew Neiderman  h  4083

**Baker, Denise** (Public Relations)
*Soul Catcher* - Colin Kersey  h  3081

**Baker, Evan** (Child)
*Soul Catcher* - Colin Kersey  h  3081

**Baker, Jill** (Child)
*Monday's Child* - Patricia Wallace  h  5623

**Baker, Jonathan** (Sociologist)
*Red Genesis* - S.C. Sykes  s  5377

**Baker, Lenny** (Psychic)
*The Ascending* - T.M. Wright  h  5989

**Bakhtiian, Ilyakoria "Ilya"** (Leader; Barbarian)
*An Earthly Crown* - Kate Elliott  s  1771

**Bakhtiian, Ilyakoria "Ilya"** (Barbarian)
*Jaran* - Kate Elliott  s  1772

**Bal-Simba** (Wizard; Adventurer)
*The Wizardry Cursed* - Rick Cook  f  1162
*The Wizardry Quested* - Rick Cook  f  1163

**Balcher** (Criminal)
*Medallion of the Black Hound* - Shirley Rousseau
  Murphy  *f*  4056

**Baldwin, Sean** (Teenager; Vacationer)
*Yon Ill Wind* - Piers Anthony  *f*  196

**Balfour, Alex** (Historian)
*Till the End of Time* - Allen Appel  *f*  201

**Ball** (Cyborg; Spy)
*Blood Lines* - William R. Burkett Jr.  *s*  774

**Ballard, Cathy** (Professor)
*The Voice in the Basement* - T. Chris
  Martindale  *h*  3657

**Ballard, Kurt** (Lawyer)
*Shadow of the Beast* - Margaret L. Carter  *h*  926

**Ballard, Mitch** (Unemployed)
*The Voice in the Basement* - T. Chris
  Martindale  *h*  3657

**Balor** (Sorcerer)
*Fire Arrow* - Edith Pattou  *f*  4260

**Baloran** (Wizard)
*Shadow Hunt* - Anne Logston  *f*  3514

**Balter, Harry** (Teenager; Traveler)
*Parable of the Sower* - Octavia E. Butler  *s*  792

**Balthazar, Timothy** (Businessman)
*Wolf Moon* - John R. Holt  *h*  2749

**Balyet** (Spirit)
*Balyet* - Patricia Wrightson  *f*  5995

**Bammer, Mortimer** (Military Personnel; Leader)
*Kill Crazy* - L.S. Riker  *s*  4590

**Ban-ya** (Prehistoric Human)
*The Edge of the World* - William Sarabande  *f*  4817

**Banaker, Oliver** (Doctor; Vampire)
*Curse of the Vampire* - Geoffrey Caine  *h*  832

**Bandicut, John** (Spaceman)
*The Infinite Sea* - Jeffrey A. Carver  *s*  932

**Bandicut, John** (Spaceman; Miner)
*Neptune Crossing* - Jeffrey A. Carver  *s*  933

**Bandicut, John** (Spaceman)
*Strange Attractors* - Jeffrey A. Carver  *s*  934

**Bandit** (Shaman)
*Fade to Black* - Nyx Smith  *s*  5134

**Bandit** (Alien; Telepath)
*Fire Planet* - P.M. Griffin  *s*  2436

**Bando, Nicos** (Convict)
*Infinity Hold* - Barry B. Longyear  *s*  3522

**Bandy, Austen** (Artist)
*Bad Brains* - Kathe Koja  *h*  3193

**Bandy, Emily** (Writer)
*Bad Brains* - Kathe Koja  *h*  3193

**Bandylegs, Ahira** (Mythical Creature; Guardian)
*The Road Home* - Joel Rosenberg  *f*  4674

**Bane** (Criminal)
*Batman: Knightfall* - Dennis O'Neil  *s*  4215

**Bane** (Child; Adventurer)
*The Hand of Chaos* - Margaret Weis  *f*  5715

**Bankhead, Tallulah "Tulley"** (Student; Adventurer)
*Beyond the Door* - Gary L. Blackwood  *s*  510

**Bankole, Larkin "Asha Vere"** (Journalist; Critic)
*Parable of the Talents* - Octavia E. Butler  *s*  793

**Bankole, Lauren Oya "Olamina"** (Leader;
  Religious)
*Parable of the Talents* - Octavia E. Butler  *s*  793

**Banks, Monica** (Businesswoman)
*Carol for Another Christmas* - Elizabeth Ann
  Scarborough  *f*  4861

**Banks, Sally "Sal"** (Businesswoman)
*Mistwalker* - Denise Lopez Heald  *s*  2637

**Banks, Stanley** (Secretary)
*Quake* - Richard Laymon  *h*  3370

**Banner, Clint** (Lawyer)
*Quake* - Richard Laymon  *h*  3370

**Banner, Elizabeth "Betty Tanner"** (Spouse)
*What Savage Beast* - Peter David  *s*  1390

**Banner, Robert Bruce "Incredible Hulk"** (Scientist)
*What Savage Beast* - Peter David  *s*  1390

**Bannering, Charlan "Arlin"** (Noblewoman; Martial
  Arts Expert)
*King of the Dead* - R.A. MacAvoy  *f*  3581

**Banning, Clive "Clivey"** (Child)
*My Pretty Pony* - Stephen King  *h*  3136

**Banning, George "Grandpa"** (Aged Person)
*My Pretty Pony* - Stephen King  *h*  3136

**Banning, Mitch** (Engineer; Writer)
*The Singularity Project* - F.M. Busby  *s*  784

**Banning, Peter "Peter Pan"** (Lawyer; Adventurer)
*Hook* - Terry Brooks  *f*  713

**Bannister, Frank** (Paranormal Investigator)
*The Frighteners* - Michael Jahn  *h*  2856

**Bannock, John** (Writer)
*In the Mood* - Charles L. Grant  *h*  2312

**Bannon** (Martial Arts Expert)
*Fifth Quarter* - Tanya Huff  *f*  2795
*No Quarter* - Tanya Huff  *f*  2798

**Banyon, Eric** (Musician; Minstrel)
*Bedlam's Bard* - Mercedes Lackey  *f*  3269
*Knight of Ghosts and Shadows* - Mercedes
  Lackey  *f*  3285

**Banyon, Eric** (Minstrel; Musician)
*Summoned to Tourney* - Mercedes Lackey  *f*  3299

**Bar-el, Shimon** (Military Personnel)
*Hero* - Joel Rosenberg  *s*  4672

**bar Valentin, Alessan** (Royalty)
*Tigana* - Guy Gavriel Kay  *f*  3018

**Barabbas** (Smuggler)
*Woman Without a Shadow* - Karen Haber  *s*  2478

**Baralis** (Sorcerer; Traitor)
*The Baker's Boy* - J.V. Jones  *f*  2956
*Master and Fool* - J.V. Jones  *f*  2959

**Baram** (Warrior; Prisoner)
*The Outlanders* - David B. Coe  *f*  1096

**Baran, Theodore** (Prospector)
*The Ice Beast* - Frank A. Javor  *s*  2881

**Baranyk, Valentin** (Military Personnel)
*Cold Allies* - Patricia Anthony  *s*  157

**Barbara** (Young Woman)
*Night of the Living Dead* - John Russo  *h*  4745

**Barbarossa, Edwin Amadeus** (Scientist)
*How Like a God* - Brenda W. Clough  *f*  1089

**Barbarossa, Galilee** (Sailor)
*Galilee* - Clive Barker  *h*  340

**Barbarossa, Maddox** (Writer)
*Galilee* - Clive Barker  *h*  340

**Barbee, Will** (Journalist)
*Darker than You Think* - Jack Williamson  *h*  5861

**Barber, Cissy** (Girlfriend)
*Land O'Goshen* - Charles McNair  *s*  3855

**Barber, Clem** (Recluse)
*The Sand Dwellers* - Adam Niswander  *h*  4112

**Barbtail, Dotson** (Alien; Genetically Altered Being)
*Seeds of Destiny* - Thomas A. Easton  *s*  1724

**Barchar, Jason "Jase" Lee** (Government Official;
  Experimental Subject)
*Naked to the Stars/The Alien Way* - Gordon R.
  Dickson  *s*  1537

**Barclay, Andy** (Student)
*Child's Play III* - Matthew J. Costello  *h*  1194

**Barclay, Reginald** (Engineer; Space Explorer)
*Requiem* - Michael Jan Friedman  *s*  2067

**Bardou, Nick** (Businessman)
*Spell Bound* - Trana Mae Simmons  *f*  5061

**Bardsey, Geoffrey** (Religious; Immortal)
*The Merlin Effect* - T.A. Barron  *f*  371

**Barek, A.E.** (Mercenary)
*Created By* - Richard Christian Matheson  *h*  3691

**Bargolas** (Demon)
*The Summoned* - Steven Ray Fulgham  *h*  2090

**Bariden** (Martial Arts Expert; Sorcerer)
*The Hidden Realms* - Sharon Green  *f*  2358

**Barion** (Alien)
*The Snake Oil Wars* - Parke Godwin  *s*  2249

**Barker, Jenny** (Disembodied Personality)
*Dragons on the Town* - Thorarinn
  Gunnarsson  *f*  2463

**Barker, Joel** (Child)
*Sineater* - Elizabeth Massie  *h*  3668

**Barker, Justin** (Banker)
*Tombley's Walk* - Crosland Brown  *h*  723

**Barku, Perkar Kar** (Warrior; Hero)
*The Blackgod* - J. Gregory Keyes  *f*  3095

**Barku, Perkar Kar** (Hero)
*The Waterborn* - J. Gregory Keyes  *f*  3098

**Barlow, Frank** (Spaceman)
*The Ring of Charon* - Roger MacBride Allen  *s*  80

**Barlowe, Philip** (Journalist)
*Act of Love* - Joe R. Lansdale  *h*  3319

**Barlstilkin, Talbeck** (Immortal)
*Eternal Light* - Paul J. McAuley  *s*  3710

**Barnard, Jacques** (Wizard; Businessman)
*2XS* - Nigel Findley  *f*  1935

**Barnes, Collee** (Real Estate Agent)
*Black Death* - R. Karl Largent  *h*  3337

**Barnes, Nick** (Health Care Professional)
*Reaper* - Ben Mizrich  *h*  3923

**Barnes, Parker** (Police Officer; Experimental
  Subject)
*Virtuosity* - Terry Bisson  *s*  507

**Barnes, Randy** (Military Personnel)
*Sleipnir* - Linda Evans  *f*  1856

**Barnett, Schuyler "Sky"** (Handyman)
*My Soul to Keep* - Judith Hawkes  *h*  2631

**Barnett, Stephen** (Child)
*My Soul to Keep* - Judith Hawkes  *h*  2631

**Barnevelt, Dirk** (Writer)
*The Hand of Zei* - L. Sprague de Camp  *s*  1414

**Barr, Dallas** (Immortal; Businessman)
*Buying Time* - Joe Haldeman  *s*  2487

**Barra the Pict** (Warrior; Mercenary; Leader)
*Iron Dawn* - Matthew Woodring Stover  *f*  5320

**Barra the Pict** (Mercenary; Leader; Warrior)
*Jericho Moon* - Matthew Woodring Stover  *f*  5321

**Barrera, Ramis** (Settler)
*Lifeline* - Kevin J. Anderson  *s*  111

**Barrero, Estela** (Doctor)
*The Resurrectionist* - Thomas F.
  Monteleone  *h*  3965

**Barrett, Elizabeth** (Young Woman)
*Death Masque* - P.N. Elrod  *h*  1795

**Barrett, Jonathan** (Vampire)
*Dance of Death* - P.N. Elrod  *h*  1794
*Death Masque* - P.N. Elrod  *h*  1795

**Barrett, Jonathan** (Student)
*Red Death* - P.N. Elrod  *h*  1798

**Barrett, Kitty** (Nurse)
*Night Music* - Sheila Bristow Garner  *h*  2147

**Barrett, Lionel** (Paranormal Investigator)
*Hell House* - Richard Matheson  *h*  3685

**Barringer, Melissa "Missy"** (Child)
*Cursed Be the Child* - Mort Castle  *h*  937

**Barringer, Warren** (Professor)
*Cursed Be the Child* - Mort Castle  *h*  937

**Barrington, Cathy** (Young Woman)
*The Tallow Image* - Jane Brindle  *h*  690

**Barris, Michael Albert** (Journalist; Parent)
*The Immortals* - Tracy Hickman  *s*  2681

**Barron, Paul** (Religious)
*Wurm* - Matthew J. Costello  *h*  1202

**Barrow, Simon** (Martial Arts Expert; Teenager)
*The First Duelist* - Rutledge Etheridge  *s*  1849

**Barry, Warren Hubert** (Doctor)
*The Forever Children* - Eric Flanders  *h*  1944

**Bart** (Apprentice; Hunter)
*Initiation* - Marian Hughes  *s*  2806

**Barthlomew, Lucy** (Religious)
*Moonfall* - Tamara Thorne  *h*  5464

**Bartlett, Jennan** (Spaceship Captain)
*Mad Roy's Light* - Paula King  *s*  3125

**Bartlett, Tony "Antonius Caelerus"** (Time Traveler; Criminal)
*Far Edge of Darkness* - Linda Evans  *s*  1855

**Barton, Alex** (Spouse)
*The Circus of the Earth and Air* - Brooke Stevens  *f*  5264

**Barton, Chris** (Scientist)
*7 Steps to Midnight* - Richard Matheson  *h*  3682

**Barton, Howard** (Museum Curator)
*The Paper Grail* - James P. Blaylock  *f*  522

**Barton, Roy** (Construction Worker)
*The Paper Grail* - James P. Blaylock  *f*  522

**Barzac, Ree** (Spaceman)
*Brotherhood of the Stars* - Kirby Greene  *s*  2414

**Bascomb, Charles "Chaz"** (Child)
*Bones* - Joyce Thompson  *h*  5453

**Bascomb, Frederika "Freddy"** (Artist)
*Bones* - Joyce Thompson  *h*  5453

**Bascombe, Jeryline A.** (Servant)
*Tales From the Crypt: Demon Knight* - Randall Boyll  *h*  617

**Bascombe, John** (Administrator)
*The Reign of the Brown Magician* - Lawrence Watt-Evans  *f*  5647

**Basehart, Diana** (Time Traveler)
*Time Station London* - David Evans  *s*  1853

**Bashir, Julian** (Doctor; Military Personnel)
*Armageddon Sky* - L.A. Graf  *s*  2296
*Time's Enemy* - L.A. Graf  *s*  2297

**Bashir, Julian** (Doctor; Genetically Altered Being)
*Vengeance* - Dafydd ab Hugh  *s*  10

**Basker, Tem** (Teenager)
*The Starlight Crystal* - Christopher Pike  *s*  4333

**Bass, Rocket Man** (Pilot)
*Voyage to the Red Planet* - Terry Bisson  *s*  508

**Bassarab** (Vampire; Nobleman)
*One Foot in the Grave* - Wm. Mark Simmons  *f*  5062

**Bastable** (Alien; Royalty)
*Charmed* - Marilyn Singer  *f*  5070

**Bat, Charlie** (Spirit; Grandparent)
*Missing Angel Juan* - Francesca Lia Block  *f*  550

**Bat, Cherokee** (Teenager; Musician)
*Cherokee Bat and the Goat Guys* - Francesca Lia Block  *f*  546

**Bat Man** (Criminal)
*The Spider #4: Death Reign of the Vampire King/The Pain Emperor* - Grant Stockbridge  *f*  5308

**Bateman, Patrick** (Businessman; Serial Killer)
*American Psycho* - Brett Easton Ellis  *h*  1777

**Bateman, Vince** (Doctor)
*The Cartoonist* - Sean Costello  *h*  1204

**Bates, Norman** (Innkeeper; Murderer)
*Psycho* - Robert Bloch  *h*  540

**Bates, Norman** (Murderer)
*Psycho II* - Robert Bloch  *h*  541

**Bates, Patty** (Businessman)
*The Immaculate* - Mark Morris  *h*  4023

**Bateson, Morgan** (Spaceship Captain)
*Ship of the Line* - Diane Carey  *s*  904

**Bathespeake, Jason** (Computer Expert; Administrator)
*ME: A Novel of Self Discovery* - Thomas T. Thomas  *s*  5452

**Bathori, Elizabeth** (Noblewoman; Historical Figure)
*Daughter of the Night* - Elaine Bergstrom  *h*  463

**Bathory, David** (Drug Dealer)
*Ancestral Hungers* - Scott Baker  *h*  303

**Bathory, Elizabeth** (Noblewoman; Historical Figure)
*Blood Countess* - Andrei Codrescu  *h*  1094

**Bathory, Elizabeth** (Vampire)
*Lord of the Vampires* - Jeanne Kalogridis  *h*  3005

**Bathory, Michael** (Businessman)
*Ancestral Hungers* - Scott Baker  *h*  303

**Bathory-Kereshtur, Drake** (Journalist)
*Blood Countess* - Andrei Codrescu  *h*  1094

**Batik** (Religious; Fugitive)
*Wolf in Shadow* - David Gemmell  *s*  2191

**Battacharia, Rustum "Bat"** (Government Official)
*Cold as Ice* - Charles Sheffield  *s*  4950

**Battacharia, Rustum "Bat"** (Computer Expert; Teenager)
*The Ganymede Club* - Charles Sheffield  *s*  4955

**Batterberry, Lesli** (Musician; Runaway)
*Ghosts of Wind and Shadow* - Charles de Lint  *f*  1427

**Batty, Roy** (Disembodied Personality; Artificial Intelligence)
*Blade Runner: Replicant Night* - K.W. Jeter  *s*  2907

**Bauer, Libby** (Parent)
*Requiem* - Clifford Mohr  *h*  3950

**Bauer, Robert** (Musician)
*Requiem* - Clifford Mohr  *h*  3950

**Baum, L. Frank** (Historical Figure; Writer)
*Was* - Geoff Ryman  *f*  4758

**Bavalius, Vitellan** (Military Personnel; Time Traveler)
*The Centurion's Empire* - Sean McMullen  *s*  3854

**Baver, Deodoro "Ted"** (Anthropologist)
*The Yngling and the Circle of Power* - John Dalmas  *s*  1328

**Bawn, Caitlin** (Traveler; Immortal)
*Legends Reborn* - Kenneth C. Flint  *f*  1958

**Baxter, Anna Elizabeth** (Widow(er); Heiress)
*Sheltered Lives* - Charles Oberndorf  *s*  4188

**Baxter, Carl** (Advertising; Pilot)
*The Homecoming* - Barry B. Longyear  *s*  3521

**Baxter, Sophie** (Artist)
*Lost Futures* - Lisa Tuttle  *s*  5520

**Baxter, Spyder** (Store Owner)
*Silk* - Caitlin R. Kiernan  *h*  3101

**Bayless, Laura** (Baker)
*Good Night, Sweet Angel* - Clare McNally  *h*  3857

**Bayley, Frank** (Religious)
*Unholy Fire* - Whitley Strieber  *h*  5342

**Bayley, James** (FBI Agent)
*The Silicon Man* - Charles Platt  *s*  4343

**Baylor, Katti** (Journalist)
*Rockabilly Hell* - William W. Johnstone  *h*  2933

**Baylor, Katti** (Writer)
*Rockabilly Limbo* - William W. Johnstone  *h*  2934

**Beach, Gil** (Detective—Police)
*Puppet Master* - Barry T. Hawkins  *h*  2632

**Beacham, Kate** (Store Owner)
*In the Rift* - Marion Zimmer Bradley  *f*  639

**Bear, Bagese** (Animal; Indian)
*Dead Voices: Natural Agonies in the Real World* - Gerald Vizenor  *f*  5578

**Bear, Tom** (Indian; Shaman)
*The Charm* - Adam Niswander  *h*  4111

**Beasley, Marjorie "Mouse"** (Friend)
*The Witch Returns* - Phyllis Reynolds Naylor  *f*  4079
*The Witch's Eye* - Phyllis Reynolds Naylor  *f*  4080

**Beast** (Animal)
*Rose Daughter* - Robin McKinley  *f*  3847

**Beatrice** (Handicapped; Psychic)
*The Broken Sword* - Molly Cochran  *f*  1091

**Beatrice** (Religious; Traveler)
*Bright Messengers* - Gentry Lee  *s*  3398

**Beauchamp, Antoinette "Toni"** (Businesswoman; Psychic)
*Mockingbird* - Sean Stewart  *f*  5273

**Beauchamp, Candace Jane "Candy"** (Waiter/Waitress; Psychic)
*Mockingbird* - Sean Stewart  *f*  5273

**Beauchamp, Elena** (Psychic; Parent)
*Mockingbird* - Sean Stewart  *f*  5273

**Beauduc, Clarence** (Professor; Tourist)
*Smoke and Mirrors* - Jane M. Lindskold  *s*  3476

**Beaufort, Victor** (Scientist)
*The Jigsaw Woman* - Kim Antieau  *f*  199

**Beaulieu, Antoinette** (Doctor)
*Beyond the Void* - Sean Dalton  *s*  1331
*The Salukan Gambit* - Sean Dalton  *s*  1333

**Beaumont, Andrea** (Girlfriend)
*Mask of the Phantasm* - Geary Gravel  *s*  2331

**Beaumont, Greg** (Lawyer)
*Midnight's Lair* - Richard Laymon  *h*  3369

**Beaumont, Thad** (Writer)
*The Dark Half* - Stephen King  *h*  3128

**Beautiful Maria** (Pilot; Psychic)
*Angel Station* - Walter Jon Williams  *s*  5833

**Beauty** (Noblewoman; Time Traveler)
*Beauty* - Sheri S. Tepper  *f*  5428

**Beauty** (Gardener)
*Rose Daughter* - Robin McKinley  *f*  3847

**Beaver, Bucky** (Alien; Diplomat)
*McLendon's Syndrome* - Robert Frezza  s  2053

**Beck, Billy** (Child)
*Seattle Ghost Story* - Nick DiMartino  h  1560

**Becker, Gilbert** (Administrator)
*The Streeter* - Scott Ian Barry  h  373

**Becker, Max** (Lawyer)
*Second Contact* - Mike Resnick  s  4555

**Becker, Triana** (Musician)
*Violin* - Anne Rice  h  4579

**Beckett, Clare** (Accountant)
*Lost Futures* - Lisa Tuttle  s  5520

**Beckett, Grace** (Doctor)
*Beyond the Pale* - Mark Anthony  f  153

**Beckett, Kerry** (Teenager)
*Irrational Fears* - William Browning
   Spencer  h  5167

**Beckett, Sam** (Time Traveler; Scientist)
*Angels Unaware* - L. Elizabeth Storm  s  5315
*Knights of the Morningstar* - Melanie Rawn  s  4487

**Beckwith, Desmond** (Businessman; Vampire)
*Desmond: A Novel of Love and the Modern Vampire* -
   Ulysses G. Dietz  h  1541

**Beckwith, Forster** (Adventurer)
*Fire and Ice* - Edward Myers  f  4061
*The Mountain Made of Light* - Edward
   Myers  f  4062

**Becky** (Teenager; Girlfriend)
*See You Later* - Christopher Pike  f  4332

**Bede, Strebban "Badger"** (Spaceman; Computer
   Expert)
*Hunting the Corrigan's Blood* - Holly Lisle  s  3484

**Bedford, Richard** (Sea Captain)
*Firelance* - David Mace  s  3586

**Bedlam, Cabe** (Wizard)
*The Crystal Dragon* - Richard A. Knaak  f  3167

**Bedlam, Gwen** (Witch)
*Wolfhelm* - Richard A. Knaak  f  3175

**Bedlam, Wellen** (Explorer; Mythical Creature)
*Dragon Tome* - Richard A. Knaak  f  3169

**Bednacort, Loria** (Spouse)
*Destiny's Road* - Larry Niven  s  4119

**Bedwyr** (Knight)
*The Last Pendragon* - Robert Rice  f  4584

**Bedwyr, Luthien "Crimson Shadow"** (Warrior)
*The Dragon King* - R.A. Salvatore  f  4796
*Luthien's Gamble* - R.A. Salvatore  f  4802
*The Sword of Bedwyr* - R.A. Salvatore  f  4808

**Beeblebrox, Zaphod** (Political Figure; Fugitive)
*The Illustrated Hitchhiker's Guide to the Galaxy* -
   Douglas Adams  s  29

**Beeker** (Servant)
*Phule's Company* - Robert Asprin  s  260

**Beelson, Raymond** (Religious)
*Armageddon Summer* - Jane Yolen  s  6028

**Beelzebub** (Computer Expert)
*Wyrm* - Mark Fabi  s  1858

**Beenay 25** (Scientist)
*Nightfall* - Isaac Asimov  s  248

**Began, Ttar** (Spy)
*Mission: Tori* - Johanna Bolton  s  564

**Begg, Albert** (Military Personnel)
*Fabulous Harbors* - Michael Moorcock  f  3981

**Begg, Edwin** (Religious)
*Lunching with the Antichrist* - Michael
   Moorcock  f  3984

**Beheim, Michel** (Vampire)
*The Golden* - Lucius Shepard  h  4978

**Behler, Simon William** (Journalist; Adventurer)
*The Last Voyage of Somebody the Sailor* - John
   Barth  f  374

**Belacqua, Lyra** (Child)
*The Golden Compass* - Philip Pullman  f  4446

**Belacqua, Lyra** (Child; Fugitive)
*The Subtle Knife* - Philip Pullman  f  4448

**Belecamus, Dorian** (Professor)
*Indiana Jones and the Peril at Delphi* - Rob
   MacGregor  f  3591

**Belevairn** (Wizard; Mythical Creature)
*A Two-Edged Sword* - Thomas K. Martin  f  3653

**Belgarath** (Sorcerer; Adventurer)
*Belgarath the Sorcerer* - David Eddings  f  1730

**Belgarath** (Sorcerer)
*The Rivan Codex* - David Eddings  f  1735

**Belisarius** (Military Personnel)
*In the Heart of Darkness* - Eric Flint  s  1955
*An Oblique Approach* - David Drake  s  1638

**Belkassem, Ferhat Ben** (Military Personnel)
*Path of the Fury* - David Weber  s  5680

**Belkin, Gregory** (Religious)
*Servant of the Bones* - Anne Rice  h  4575

**Belkis "Bell"** (Animal; Royalty)
*Here There Be Dragons* - Roger Zelazny  f  6069

**Bell, Alice** (Genetically Altered Being)
*Woodsman* - Thomas A. Easton  s  1727

**Bell, April** (Werewolf)
*Darker than You Think* - Jack Williamson  h  5861

**Bell, Celina** (Young Woman)
*The Unborn* - Andrew Laurance  h  3350

**Bell, Daniel** (Detective—Police)
*Famine* - Todd Komarnicki  h  3201

**Bell, Elizabeth** (Child)
*The Bell Witch: An American Haunting* - Brent
   Monahan  h  3953

**Bell, Howard** (Maintenance Worker; Writer)
*A Key for the Nonesuch* - Geary Gravel  s  2330

**Bell, Howard** (Leader)
*The Return of the Breakneck Boys* - Geary
   Gravel  s  2332

**Bell, John** (Businessman)
*The Bell Witch: An American Haunting* - Brent
   Monahan  h  3953

**Bell, Justin Wood** (Teenager; Spaceman)
*Article 23* - William R. Forstchen  s  1978

**Bell Dog** (Engineer)
*Through the Heart* - Richard Grant  f  2328

**Bellamy, Frank** (FBI Agent)
*The Ebon Mask* - Richard Lee Byers  h  797

**Bellamy, June** (Con Artist)
*Lifehouse* - Spider Robinson  s  4641

**Bellard, Fern** (Teenager)
*Something Stirs* - Charles L. Grant  h  2316

**Belle, Amy** (Teenager)
*Witch* - Christopher Pike  f  4334

**Bellini, Aaron** (Businessman)
*Out There in the Darkness* - Ed Gorman  h  2279

**Bellisle, Andre** (Businessman)
*Cold Eye* - Giles Blunt  h  556

**Bellman, Alan** (Writer; Musician)
*The Printer's Devil* - Chico Kidd  f  3099

**Bellman, Craig** (Lawyer)
*The House That Jack Built* - Graham
   Masterton  h  3675

**Bellman, Effie** (Spouse)
*The House That Jack Built* - Graham
   Masterton  h  3675

**Bellman, Kim** (Musician; Spouse)
*The Printer's Devil* - Chico Kidd  f  3099

**Belman, Lola** (Psychologist)
*The Ganymede Club* - Charles Sheffield  s  4955

**Belmonte, Rodrigo** (Mercenary)
*The Lions of Al-Rassan* - Guy Gavriel Kay  f  3016

**Belou, Sylvia** (Witch)
*When Shadows Fall* - Brian Scott Smith  h  5100

**Beloved Light** (Alien)
*Acts of Conscience* - William Barton  s  377

**Beltar** (Businessman)
*Traitors* - Kristine Kathryn Rusch  f  4729

**Belzoni, Peter** (Journalist; Teenager)
*Dinosaur Summer* - Greg Bear  s  416

**Ben** (Truck Driver)
*Night of the Living Dead* - John Russo  h  4745

**Ben Sapir, Elijah** (Vampire)
*Bloodsucking Fiends: A Love Story* - Christopher
   Moore  h  3988

**ben Shaqar, Sharif** (Sorcerer)
*The Devouring Void* - Mark E. Rogers  f  4653

**ben Sierra Nueva, Amos "Simeon"** (Leader;
   Refugee)
*The City Who Fought* - Anne McCaffrey  s  3722

**Ben Yussef, Essaj** (Religious)
*The Riddled Man* - Mark E. Rogers  f  4654

**Benacerraf, Paula** (Astronaut; Spacewoman)
*Titan* - Stephen Baxter  s  405

**Bender, Jack** (Revolutionary)
*Mutant Hell* - Mark Grant  s  2324

**Bender, Jack** (Farmer; Revolutionary)
*Mutants Amok* - Mark Grant  s  2325

**Bender, Lucy** (Clerk; Artist)
*Angels on Fire* - Nancy A. Collins  h  1117

**Benedek, Walter** (Journalist)
*Live Girls* - Ray Garton  h  2151

**Benedict** (Religious)
*Sable, Shadow and Ice* - Cheryl J. Franklin  f  2039

**Benedict, Alex** (Businessman)
*A Talent for War* - Jack McDevitt  s  3790

**Benedict, Frederick** (Doctor)
*Insanity, Illinois* - Mark Sumner  s  5358

**Benedict, Sally** (Journalist)
*Infinity's Child* - Harry Stein  h  5250

**Benedict, Whitney** (Teenager)
*The Boy Who Cried Werewolf* - Elvira  h  1800

**Benefactor** (Deity)
*Revenant* - Louise Cooper  f  1178

**Beneforte, Fiametta** (Magician; Fugitive)
*The Spirit Ring* - Lois McMaster Bujold  f  763

**Benelaius** (Wizard)
*Murder in Cormyr* - Chet Williamson  f  5848

**Benhaddou** (Criminal)
*White Rhino* - Bill Dolan  s  1569

**Benjamin, Papa** (Religious)
*The Black Lodge* - Robert Weinberg  h  5692

**Benjarth, Paul** (Heir; Adventurer)
*The Cloud People* - Robert B. Kelly  f  3050

**Bennet, Hal** (Spy)
*The Hanged Man* - T.J. MacGregor  s  3594

**Bennet, Tim** (Bodyguard)
*Half the Day Is Night* - Maureen F.
   McHugh  s  3818

**Bennett** (Nobleman; Mythical Creature)
*A Knight Among Knaves* - Robert N. Charrette  *f*  974

**Bennett, Laura** (Journalist)
*Echoes* - Jackie Hyman  *h*  2818

**Bennington, Jay Jay** (Writer; Traveler)
*Glenraven* - Marion Zimmer Bradley  *f*  635

**Benson, E.F.** (Writer; Historical Figure)
*The Haunting of Lamb House* - Joan Aiken  *h*  45

**Benson, Jack** (Businessman)
*Shadow Twin* - Dale Hoover  *h*  2762

**Benson, Jedidiah** (Child)
*Shadow Twin* - Dale Hoover  *h*  2762

**Benson, Rachal** (Housewife)
*Shadow Twin* - Dale Hoover  *h*  2762

**Benta** (Farmer)
*Invitation to the Game* - Monica Hughes  *s*  2807

**Bentley, Abigail Porterhouse** (Time Traveler; Child)
*Friends in Time* - Grace Chetwin  *f*  1012

**Bento, Jake** (Time Traveler; Guide)
*Atlantis Found* - R. Garcia y Robertson  *s*  2119
*The Virgin and the Dinosaur* - R. Garcia y Robertson  *s*  2122

**Benton, David** (Police Officer)
*Return of the Living Dead* - John Russo  *h*  4746

**Beogoat** (Wizard)
*Heroes Wanted* - Kyle Crocco  *f*  1267

**Beowulf** (Animal; Leader)
*Cry Wolf* - Kenneth Von Gunden  *s*  5586

**Beowulf** (Hero)
*The Tower of Beowulf* - Parke Godwin  *f*  2250

**Beowulf** (Animal; Leader)
*Under Fire* - Kenneth Von Gunden  *s*  5589

**Beowulf** (Hero; Adventurer)
*Whose Song Is Sung* - Frank Schaefer  *f*  4872

**Beppu, Chan-ti** (Wanderer)
*The Last Legends of Earth* - A.A. Attanasio  *s*  270

**Berengar** (Nobleman; Mythical Creature)
*The Shadow Gate* - Margaret Ball  *f*  317

**Berenice, Teal Blane** (Computer Expert; Traveler)
*Blueheart* - Alison Sinclair  *s*  5068

**Berg-Benson, Sephony** (Farmer; Revolutionary)
*An Eye for Dark Places* - Norma Marder  *s*  3622

**Bergeron, Carolyn** (Murderer; Artist)
*Nightmare Logic* - Matthew Hall  *h*  2495

**Bergsndot, Ravna** (Librarian)
*A Fire upon the Deep* - Vernor Vinge  *s*  5573

**Bering** (Teenager; Bodyguard)
*The Dog King* - Christoph Ransmayr  *f*  4474

**Bermudez, Jolanda** (Artist)
*Hot Sky at Midnight* - Robert Silverberg  *s*  5032

**Bernard, Cynthia** (Wealthy; Businesswoman)
*The Gatekeepers* - Daniel Graham Jr.  *s*  2301

**Bernard, Rolf** (Businessman)
*The Gatekeepers* - Daniel Graham Jr.  *s*  2301

**Bernay, Leah de** (Apprentice; Doctor)
*Scorpio* - Alex McDonough  *s*  3802

**Bernie** (Companion; Animal)
*Witch and Wombat* - Carolyn Cushman  *f*  1299

**Beroth of Firoze** (Warrior)
*Clock Strikes Sword* - Ian Hammell  *f*  2529

**Berquist, Kate** (Health Care Professional)
*Nightmare* - S.K. Epperson  *h*  1832

**Beryl** (Warrior)
*The Oxygen Barons* - Gregory Feeley  *s*  1897

**Beryt** (Royalty)
*Shaper's Legacy* - Sheila Finch  *s*  1933

**Berzel** (Royalty; Werewolf)
*Kedrigern and the Charming Couple* - John Morressy  *f*  4013

**Besser, Dudley J.** (Professor)
*Coven* - Edward Lee  *h*  3390

**Bessledorf, Jonathon** (Spirit)
*Bernie and the Bessledorf Ghost* - Phyllis Reynolds Naylor  *f*  4078

**bet Ishak, Jehane** (Doctor)
*The Lions of Al-Rassan* - Guy Gavriel Kay  *f*  3016

**Beth** (Vampire)
*Out for Blood* - John Peyton Cooke  *h*  1166

**Bethune, Casey** (Postal Worker)
*The Black Carousel* - Charles L. Grant  *h*  2303

**Bettik, A.** (Android)
*Endymion* - Dan Simmons  *s*  5051

**Betwixt and Between** (Mythical Creature)
*Brother to Dragons, Companion to Owls* - Jane M. Lindskold  *f*  3473

**Bev** (Health Care Professional)
*My Cousin, My Gastroenterologist* - Mark Leyner  *s*  3456

**Bevol, Osraed** (Guardian; Teacher)
*The Meri* - Maya Kaathryn Bohnhoff  *f*  561

**Bevol, Osraed** (Teacher; Psychic)
*Taminy* - Maya Kaathryn Bohnhoff  *f*  563

**Bey, Friedlander** (Businessman; Organized Crime Figure)
*The Exile Kiss* - George Alec Effinger  *s*  1750

**Bey, Friedlander** (Criminal; Businessman)
*A Fire in the Sun* - George Alec Effinger  *s*  1751

**Beynac, Dagny** (Political Figure; Parent)
*The Stars Are Also Fire* - Poul Anderson  *s*  134

**Bezarian** (Military Personnel)
*Red Army* - Ralph Peters  *s*  4306

**Bhelliom "Blue Rose"** (Mythical Creature)
*The Hidden City* - David Eddings  *f*  1733

**Biale** (Runaway)
*On Fortune's Wheel* - Cynthia Voigt  *f*  5579

**Bianka** (Vampire)
*As One Dead* - Don Bassingthwaite  *h*  387

**Bickerstaff, Robert Luther** (Military Personnel; Businessman)
*Terraplane* - Jack Womack  *s*  5960

**Bidding, Philippa** (Teenager)
*Rebel From Alphorion* - Robyn Tallis  *f*  5381

**Biergarten, Ryerson** (Psychic)
*The Ascending* - T.M. Wright  *h*  5989
*Goodlow's Ghosts* - T.M. Wright  *h*  5991

**Big John "BJ"** (Bartender)
*When Wolves Cry* - Chris N. Africa  *h*  41

**Big Sword** (Alien; Telepath)
*Project Farcry* - Pauline Ashwell  *s*  230

**Big Tom** (Businessman)
*The Dream Vessel* - Jeff Bredenberg  *s*  664

**Bigelow, Walter T.** (Political Figure; Administrator)
*Journals of the Plague Years* - Norman Spinrad  *s*  5172

**Bigthorn, Henry** (Police Officer; Indian)
*Clarke County, Space* - Allen Steele  *s*  5241

**Biilathkamoro, Chodrisei "Coso"** (Ruler)
*The Kalif's War* - John Dalmas  *s*  1322

**Bilbo, Charlie** (Police Officer; Spirit)
*Charlie's Bones* - L.L. Thrasher  *h*  5468

**Bilbo, Jonathan** (Police Officer)
*Charlie's Bones* - L.L. Thrasher  *h*  5468

**Bileux, Peter** (Police Officer)
*Nightshade* - Stanley R. Moore  *h*  3992

**Bilitu** (Sorcerer)
*Engor's Sword Arm* - David C. Smith  *h*  5110

**Bill** (Spaceman)
*Bill, the Galactic Hero: On the Planet of Tasteless Pleasure* - Harry Harrison  *s*  2567
*Bill, the Galactic Hero: The Final Incoherent Adventure* - Harry Harrison  *s*  2568

**Bill** (Robot; Sidekick)
*Hawaiian U.F.O. Aliens* - Mel Gilden  *s*  2226
*Tubular Android Superheroes* - Mel Gilden  *s*  2228

**Bill** (Military Personnel)
*Planet of the Robot Slaves* - Harry Harrison  *s*  2573

**Bill** (Lawman)
*Dusk* - Ron Dee  *h*  1466

**Billie** (Patient; Adventurer)
*Aliens: Earth Hive* - Steve Perry  *s*  4289

**Billy** (Psychic; Adventurer)
*Aliens: The Female War* - Steve Perry  *s*  4290

**Billy** (Musician)
*Cowboy Feng's Space Bar and Grille* - Steven Brust  *s*  740

**Billy the Kid** (Android; Experimental Subject)
*The Illegal Rebirth of Billy the Kid* - Rebecca Ore  *s*  4220

**Bilrog** (Alien)
*Labyrinth* - Dennis Schmidt  *s*  4884

**bin Sind, Simna** (Warrior)
*Carnivores of Light and Darkness* - Alan Dean Foster  *f*  1996

**Binah** (Companion; Mythical Creature)
*Cross and Crescent* - Susan Shwartz  *f*  5014

**Binder, Columbus** (Businessman)
*Flying Saucers over Hennepin* - Peter Gelman  *f*  2186

**Binewski, Miranda** (Artist)
*Geek Love* - Katherine Dunn  *h*  1697

**Binewski, Olympia** (Parent; Genetically Altered Being)
*Geek Love* - Katherine Dunn  *h*  1697

**Bink** (Grandparent; Royalty)
*Zombie Lover* - Piers Anthony  *f*  197

**Birch, Wellington** (Military Personnel; Time Traveler)
*Lurid Dreams* - Charles L. Harness  *s*  2546

**Bird** (Revolutionary; Leader)
*The Fifth Sacred Thing* - Starhawk  *f*  5209

**Bird, Catherine White** (Teenager)
*Tooth and Claw* - Graham Masterton  *h*  3680

**Bird, Jake** (Lawman; Wizard)
*Devil's Engine* - Mark Sumner  *f*  5356

**Bird, Jake** (Maintenance Worker)
*Devil's Tower* - Mark Sumner  *f*  5357

**Bird, Marianne** (Student—College; Spouse)
*Tap, Tap* - David Martin  *h*  3640

**Bird, Morris** (Pilot; Prospector)
*Heavy Time* - C.J. Cherryh  *s*  995

**Bird, Roscoe** (Teacher)
*Tap, Tap* - David Martin  *h*  3640

**Birdsong, Joseph "Mojo"** (Criminal)
*Mojo and the Pickle Jar* - Douglas Bell  *f*  433

**Birdsong, Starling** (Minstrel)
*Assassin's Quest* - Robin Hobb  *f*  2694

**Birkett, Alison** (Lawyer)
*Temporary Agency* - Rachel Pollack   *f*   4360

**Birkwelch** (Mythical Creature)
*Minerva Wakes* - Holly Lisle   *f*   3487

**Birnbaum, Maureen** (Heroine; Martial Arts Expert)
*Maureen Birnbaum, Barbarian Swordsperson: The Complete Stories* - George Alec Effinger   *f*   1752

**Bish, Michael** (Police Officer)
*The Moons of Summer* - S.K. Epperson   *h*   1831

**Bishop** (Android; Hero)
*Alien 3* - Alan Dean Foster   *s*   1993

**Bishop, Bryan** (Teenager)
*Away Is a Strange Place to Be* - H.M. Hoover   *s*   2763

**Bishop, Catherine** (Artisan)
*Animus* - Ed Kelleher   *h*   3040

**Bishop, Ian** (Art Dealer)
*Animus* - Ed Kelleher   *h*   3040

**Bishop, Julian** (Child)
*Animus* - Ed Kelleher   *h*   3040

**Bishop, Killeen** (Spaceship Captain; Genetically Altered Being)
*Furious Gulf* - Gregory Benford   *s*   447

**Bishop, Nigel** (Entertainer)
*The California Voodoo Game* - Larry Niven   *s*   4117

**Bishop, Toby** (Refugee; Genetically Altered Being)
*Furious Gulf* - Gregory Benford   *s*   447

**Bishop, Toby** (Wanderer)
*Sailing Bright Eternity* - Gregory Benford   *s*   449

**Bishop, Wendy** (Child)
*Virgins and Martyrs* - Simon Maginn   *h*   3607

**Bishopric, Susan** (Writer)
*The Night Mayor* - Kim Newman   *s*   4099

**Bittan, Rebecca** (Student)
*The Kiss* - Kathryn Reines   *h*   4529

**Bitterhand, Calvin** (Shaman; Indian)
*The Trickster* - Muriel Gray   *h*   2340

**Bix** (Animal; Guide)
*Dinotopia* - James Gurney   *f*   2468

**Bjorn of Bromme** (Warrior; Adventurer)
*The Discovery of Dragons* - Graeme Base   *f*   385

**Bjornsen, Kristin "Kris"** (Slave; Settler)
*Freedom's Landing* - Anne McCaffrey   *s*   3734

**Bjornsen, Paula** (Teacher)
*Night Sounds* - Warner Lee   *h*   3415

**Bjornson, Kristen "Kris"** (Slave; Settler)
*Freedom's Challenge* - Anne McCaffrey   *s*   3732

**Bjornson, Kristen "Kris"** (Slave)
*Freedom's Choice* - Anne McCaffrey   *s*   3733

**BKR** (Alien; Villain)
*Aliens Stole My Body* - Bruce Coville   *s*   1217

**Black, Angela** (Witch)
*Fetish* - Edward Bryant   *h*   749

**Black, Catherine** (Housewife)
*The Frenchman* - Elizabeth Hand   *h*   2534

**Black, Charlie** (Teenager)
*When Darkness Falls* - Sidney Williams   *h*   5825

**Black, Frank** (Military Personnel)
*Dead Heat* - Del Stone Jr.   *h*   5313

**Black, Frank** (FBI Agent)
*The Frenchman* - Elizabeth Hand   *h*   2534
*Gehenna* - Lewis Gannett   *h*   2114

**Black, Jackson** (Adventurer)
*Living with the Reptiles* - Roger L. DiSilvestro   *s*   1563

**Black, Marguerita "Maggie"** (Writer)
*The Wood Wife* - Terri Windling   *f*   5916

**Black Amber** (Administrator)
*Human to Human* - Rebecca Ore   *s*   4219

**Black Dust 7, Lisa** (Demon)
*Temporary Agency* - Rachel Pollack   *f*   4360

**Black Heron** (Murderer)
*Curse of the Black Heron* - Holly Lisle   *f*   3479

**Black-Robe, Harvas** (Wizard; Barbarian)
*Krispos of Videssos* - Harry Turtledove   *f*   5506

**Blackburn, Jasmine** (Child)
*Blackburn* - Bradley Denton   *h*   1489

**Blackburn, Jimmy** (Drifter; Serial Killer)
*Blackburn* - Bradley Denton   *h*   1489

**Blackburn, Thorne** (Magician; Parent)
*Ghostlight* - Marion Zimmer Bradley   *f*   634

**Blackburn, Trebor** (Warrior; Adventurer)
*Captains Outrageous, or, For Doom the Bell Tolls* - Roy V. Young   *f*   6049

**Blacke, Austin** (Vampire)
*Mastery* - Kelley Wilde   *h*   5802

**Blackstone, Jonathan** (Businessman)
*In the Company of the Mind* - Steven Piziks   *s*   4339

**Blackstone, Lance Michaels** (Detective—Private)
*In the Company of the Mind* - Steven Piziks   *s*   4339

**Blackstone, Norah** (Companion)
*Bride of the Rat God* - Barbara Hambly   *f*   2499

**Blackstone, Rex** (Military Personnel; Pilot)
*Primary Inversion* - Catherine Asaro   *s*   220

**Blackstrap** (Pirate; Sea Captain)
*Dinotopia Lost* - Alan Dean Foster   *f*   2003

**Blackthorn** (Minstrel; Hero)
*Hunter of the Light* - Risa Aratyr   *f*   203

**Blacktop** (Alien; Genetically Altered Being)
*Tower of the Gods* - Thomas A. Easton   *s*   1726

**Blackwell, Patricia "Trish"** (Dancer)
*The Digital Effect* - Steve Perry   *s*   4295

**Blade** (Vampire)
*Blade* - Mel Odom   *h*   4190

**Blade** (Teenager; Wizard)
*Dark Lord of Derkholm* - Diana Wynne Jones   *f*   2946

**Blade** (Warrior)
*L.A. Strike* - David Robbins   *s*   4599

**Blade** (Teenager; Warrior)
*Madman Run* - David Robbins   *s*   4600

**Blade** (Murderer)
*Shadow Hunt* - Anne Logston   *f*   3514

**Blade** (Warrior)
*Spartan Run* - David Robbins   *s*   4602
*Vengeance Strike* - David Robbins   *s*   4604
*Yellowstone Run* - David Robbins   *s*   4605

**Blade, Sonya** (Military Personnel; Warrior)
*Mortal Kombat* - Martin Delrio   *f*   1483

**Blade, Thomas** (Psychic)
*The Marked Man* - Charles Ingrid   *s*   2831

**Bladestone, Hugh** (Doctor; Prisoner)
*Fortress on the Sun* - Paul Cook   *s*   1157

**Blaine, Cassandra "Cass"** (Actress; Thief)
*Clipjoint* - Wilhelmina Baird   *s*   294
*Crashcourse* - Wilhelmina Baird   *s*   295

**Blaine, Cassandra "Cass"** (Criminal; Companion)
*Psykosis* - Wilhelmina Baird   *s*   296

**Blaine, Dee Dee** (Secretary)
*Jumpers* - R. Patrick Gates   *h*   2161

**Blaine, Grant** (Doctor)
*The Dark* - Andrew Neiderman   *h*   4084

**Blaine, Maggie** (Lawyer)
*The Dark* - Andrew Neiderman   *h*   4084

**Blaine, Trish** (Doctor)
*Blood* - Ron Dee   *h*   1463

**Blair, Reeve** (Police Officer)
*The Mysterium* - Eric McCormack   *h*   3780

**Blair, Tiffany** (Child)
*Shadow Dance* - Jessica Palmer   *h*   4238

**Blair, Tony** (Teenager)
*Boys of Life* - Paul Russell   *h*   4737

**Blaise, Adrian** (Businessman)
*Devil's Gate* - Elizabeth Ergas   *h*   1833

**Blaise, Anna** (Young Woman)
*A Hidden Place* - Robert Charles Wilson   *s*   5910

**Blake, Alexander** (Vampire)
*Netherworld* - Richard Lee Byers   *h*   798

**Blake, Anita** (Vampire Hunter; Detective—Private)
*Bloody Bones* - Laurell K. Hamilton   *h*   2512
*Blue Moon* - Laurell K. Hamilton   *h*   2513

**Blake, Anita** (Vampire Hunter)
*Burnt Offerings* - Laurell K. Hamilton   *h*   2514

**Blake, Anita** (Vampire Hunter; Detective—Private)
*Circus of the Damned* - Laurell K. Hamilton   *h*   2515
*Guilty Pleasures* - Laurell K. Hamilton   *f*   2517
*The Killing Dance* - Laurell K. Hamilton   *h*   2518
*The Laughing Corpse* - Laurell K. Hamilton   *f*   2519
*The Lunatic Cafe* - Laurell K. Hamilton   *h*   2520

**Blake, Jason** (Writer)
*Moonbane* - Al Sarrantonio   *s*   4831

**Blake, Jenny** (Businesswoman)
*One Wish* - C.J. Card   *f*   880

**Blake, Nick** (Teenager; Warrior)
*Dragon Burning* - Craig Shaw Gardner   *f*   2126
*Dragon Sleeping* - Craig Shaw Gardner   *f*   2127
*Dragon Waking* - Craig Shaw Gardner   *f*   2128

**Blake, Werner** (Businessman)
*The Bridge: A Horror Story* - John Skipp   *h*   5081

**Blakemore, Mark** (Police Officer)
*Black Lightning* - John Saul   *h*   4837

**Blanca** (Artificial Intelligence; Scientist)
*Diaspora* - Greg Egan   *s*   1759

**Blanchard, Miles** (Werewolf)
*The World of Darkness: Watcher* - Charles L. Grant   *h*   2321

**Blanche** (Artificial Intelligence)
*The Man in the Moon Must Die* - Jeff Bredenberg   *s*   665

**Blas, Gaultry** (Wizard)
*A Tremor in the Bitter Earth* - Katya Reimann   *f*   4527

**Blatchley, James** (Police Officer; Student)
*The World I Made for Her* - Thomas Moran   *h*   3996

**Blathine** (Mythical Creature)
*The Isles of the Blest* - Morgan Llywelyn   *f*   3505

**Blayke, Arcole** (Gambler; Martial Arts Expert)
*Exile's Children* - Angus Wells   *f*   5735

**Blaylock, Morgan** (Writer)
*The Devouring* - Douglas D. Hawk   *h*   2615

**Blaze** (Blacksmith)
*Isle of Woman* - Piers Anthony   *f*   178

**Blaze** (Genetically Altered Being; Musician)
*Mississippi Blues* - Kathleen Ann Goonan   *s*   2274

**Blaze, Chastity** (Spacewoman; Pilot)
*Saturn Rukh* - Robert L. Forward   *s*   1991

**Blaze, Christopher** (Detective—Private; Vampire)
*Harvest of Blood* - Vincent Courtney   *h*   1213

**Blaze, Christopher** (Police Officer; Vampire)
*Vampire Beat* - Vincent Courtney   *h*   1214

**Blaze, Sue** (Doctor)
*Harvest of Blood* - Vincent Courtney   *h*   1213

**The Bleeding Man** (Mythical Creature)
*Night* - Alan Rodgers   *h*   4649

**Blennerhassett, Daniel** (Student)
*Virgins and Martyrs* - Simon Maginn   *h*   3607

**Blervaque, Carver** (Computer Expert; Inventor)
*Living Real* - James C. Bassett   *s*   386

**Blervaque, Rose** (Housewife; Artist)
*Living Real* - James C. Bassett   *s*   386

**Blessing, Arthur** (Orphan; Heir)
*The Forever King* - Molly Cochran   *f*   1092

**Blessing, William** (Writer; Professor)
*Quoth the Crow* - David Bischoff   *h*   494

**Bletcher, Robert** (Detective—Homicide)
*The Frenchman* - Elizabeth Hand   *h*   2534

**Bloat** (Genetically Altered Being; Ruler)
*Dealer's Choice* - George R.R. Martin   *s*   3643
*Jokertown Shuffle* - George R.R. Martin   *s*   3646

**Bloch, Jared** (Teacher; Military Personnel)
*No Limits* - Nigel Findley   *s*   1938

**Block, Hillary** (Social Worker)
*Deathchain* - Ken Greenhall   *h*   2415

**Blondell, Mark Anthony "Tony"** (Explorer; Time Traveler)
*Tyrannosaurus Rex* - J.F. Rivkin   *s*   4597

**Bloocher, Jemmy "Tim Hann"** (Fugitive; Cook)
*Destiny's Road* - Larry Niven   *s*   4119

**Blood** (Criminal)
*Nightside the Long Sun* - Gene Wolfe   *s*   5943

**Bloodworth, Emma** (Artist; Vampire)
*The Last Vampire* - Kathryn Meyer Griffith   *h*   2440

**Bloodyluck, Kithri** (Miner; Pilot)
*Jaydium* - Deborah Wheeler   *s*   5774

**Bloss, Bibi** (Entertainer)
*Skin* - Kathe Koja   *h*   3196

**Blossom** (Police Officer)
*Nightwatch* - Robin Wayne Bailey   *f*   289

**Blossom, Gypsy** (Genetically Altered Being)
*Seeds of Destiny* - Thomas A. Easton   *s*   1724

**Blount, Alan** (Police Officer)
*Shadow Dance* - Jessica Palmer   *h*   4238

**Blount, Mikal** (Military Personnel)
*The Clouds of Saturn* - Michael McCollum   *s*   3770

**Blue, Sonja** (Vampire)
*A Dozen Black Roses* - Nancy A. Collins   *h*   1119
*In the Blood* - Nancy A. Collins   *h*   1121
*Midnight Blue: The Sonja Blue Collection* - Nancy A. Collins   *h*   1122
*Sunglasses After Dark* - Nancy A. Collins   *h*   1124

**Bluecloak** (Alien)
*Remnant Population* - Elizabeth Moon   *s*   3972

**Bluecrane, Will** (Indian; Chieftain)
*Earthsong* - Suzette Haden Elgin   *s*   1769

**Blueshell** (Alien; Businessman)
*A Fire upon the Deep* - Vernor Vinge   *s*   5573

**Blume, Sandy** (Tour Guide)
*The Midnight Tour* - Richard Laymon   *h*   3368

**Blyushkina, Marta Aleksandrova** (Waiter/Waitress)
*Toplin* - Michael McDowell   *h*   3807

**Boardman, Gillian** (Nurse; Companion)
*Stranger in a Strange Land* - Robert A. Heinlein   *s*   2649

**Boba Fett** (Bounty Hunter)
*The Mandalorian Armor* - K.W. Jeter   *s*   2914

**Bobby** (Office Worker)
*Steam* - Jay B. Laws   *h*   3361

**Bobcat** (Animal; Gambler)
*The Blood Jaguar* - Michael H. Payne   *f*   4271

**Boda** (Genetically Altered Being; Taxi Driver)
*Pollen* - Jeff Noon   *s*   4135

**Bodbmall** (Warrior; Teacher)
*Master of Earth and Water* - Diana L. Paxson   *f*   4266

**Boddekker** (Advertising)
*Ferman's Devils* - Joe Clifford Faust   *s*   1892

**Bodeland, Joe** (Scientist)
*Dracula Unbound* - Brian W. Aldiss   *h*   55

**Bogen, Nancy** (Editor)
*Bagatelle—Guinevere* - Nancy Bogen   *f*   558

**Bogert, Norman** (Reanimated Dead; Scientist)
*I, Robot: The Illustrated Screenplay* - Harlan Ellison   *s*   1785

**Boggs, Buffalo Odersby** (Producer)
*Visitors From Oz: The Wild Adventures of Dorothy, the Scarecrow and the Tin Woodman* - Martin Gardner   *f*   2136

**Boggs, W.J.** (Pilot)
*Labyrinth of Night* - Allen Steele   *s*   5244

**Bogner, C. Lane "Rusty"** (Police Officer)
*Black Death* - R. Karl Largent   *h*   3337

**Boh, Walker** (Adventurer)
*The Druid of Shannara* - Terry Brooks   *f*   710

**Boh, Walker** (Magician; Warrior)
*The Talismans of Shannara* - Terry Brooks   *f*   717

**Bohentin, Caroline** (Heiress)
*Brain Rose* - Nancy Kress   *s*   3239

**Bohlen, Ross** (Government Official)
*This Side of Judgment* - J.R. Dunn   *s*   1696

**Bois, Jules** (Consultant)
*The Dark* - Andrew Neiderman   *h*   4084

**Boldface, Byron** (Kidnapper)
*Dragon Tempest* - Don Callander   *f*   844

**Boles, Barrington** (Scientist; Inventor)
*Parallelities* - Alan Dean Foster   *s*   2012

**Boles, Danny** (Sports Figure; Indian)
*Brittle Innings* - Michael Bishop   *h*   498

**Bolt** (Artificial Intelligence)
*The Last Hawk* - Catherine Asaro   *s*   219

**Bolt, Mike** (Police Officer)
*Treasure Box* - Orson Scott Card   *h*   898

**Bolte, Laura** (Psychic)
*The Thread That Binds the Bones* - Nina Kiriki Hoffman   *f*   2717

**Bolton, Jennifer** (Teacher)
*Cold White Fury* - Beth Amos   *h*   97

**Bolton, Maxwell "Max"** (Journalist)
*Shade and Shadow* - Francine G. Woodbury   *f*   5967

**Bolton, Tanner** (Child)
*Cold White Fury* - Beth Amos   *h*   97

**Bomarigala** (Administrator; Scientist)
*GodHeads* - Emily Devenport   *s*   1501

**Bombeck, Tesla** (Biker)
*Everville* - Clive Barker   *h*   338

**Bonaduce, Aballister** (Sorcerer)
*Canticle* - R.A. Salvatore   *f*   4793

**Bonaparte, Napoleon** (Historical Figure; Military Personnel)
*The Napoleon Wager* - William R. Forstchen   *s*   1980

**Boncorro** (Ruler; Wizard)
*The Secular Wizard* - Christopher Stasheff   *f*   5222

**Bond, Hamish** (Spy)
*Judgment of Tears: Anno Dracula 1959* - Kim Newman   *h*   4098

**Bond, Molly** (Psychologist; Psychic)
*Frameshift* - Robert J. Sawyer   *s*   4856

**Bondy** (Businessman)
*War With the Newts* - Karel Capek   *s*   874

**Bone** (Streetperson; Amnesiac)
*Bone* - George C. Chesbro   *h*   1006

**Bone** (Streetperson)
*A Hidden Place* - Robert Charles Wilson   *s*   5910

**Bones, Ezekiel "Zeke"** (Archaeologist)
*Nightmare World* - David Stern   *s*   5261

**Bonfim, Ana Maria** (Political Figure)
*Cradle of Splendor* - Patricia Anthony   *s*   158

**Bonhomme, Jacques** (Cult Member; Time Traveler)
*The Centurion's Empire* - Sean McMullen   *s*   3854

**Boniface, Thomas** (Bodyguard)
*The Element of Fire* - Martha Wells   *f*   5750

**Bonifant, "Mr. Bones"** (Administrator)
*Brother to Dragons* - Charles Sheffield   *s*   4949

**Bonita** (Mythical Creature)
*Polymorph* - Scott Westerfeld   *s*   5767

**Bonivard, Francois** (Computer Expert; Handicapped)
*Wildlife* - James Patrick Kelly   *s*   3049

**Bonner, Nat** (Child)
*Dead End* - Guy N. Smith   *h*   5119

**Bonney, Isabel "Iz"** (Spouse; Time Traveler)
*Elvissey* - Jack Womack   *s*   5957

**Bonney, Jessamyn "Krokodil"** (Leader)
*Krokodil Tears* - Jack Yeovil   *f*   6023

**Bonney, John** (Spouse; Time Traveler)
*Elvissey* - Jack Womack   *s*   5957

**Bonnie** (Teacher)
*Expiry Date* - Carol Anne Davis   *h*   1401

**Bontu** (Alien)
*Life Form* - Alan Dean Foster   *s*   2008

**Boofuls** (Actor; Spirit)
*Mirror* - Graham Masterton   *h*   3677

**Booker, Sam** (FBI Agent)
*Midnight* - Dean R. Koontz   *h*   3212

**Boone, Clayton** (Gardener)
*Father of Frankenstein* - Christopher Bram   *h*   659

**Boone, Hank** (Businessman)
*Angel Kiss* - Kelley Wilde   *h*   5800

**Boone, Jack** (Scientist; Space Explorer)
*Red Mars* - Kim Stanley Robinson   *s*   4635

**Boorman** (Political Figure)
*Ignition* - Kevin J. Anderson   *s*   107

**Booth, Felix** (Lawman)
*Pitfall* - Ronald Kelly   *h*   3054

**Borden, Alfred** (Magician; Writer)
*The Prestige* - Christopher Priest   *s*   4432

**Borden, Andrew** (Businessman)
*Lizzie Borden* - Elizabeth Engstrom   *h*   1826

**Borden, Emma** (Spinster)
*Lizzie Borden* - Elizabeth Engstrom   *h*   1826

**Borden, Lizzie** (Heroine; Historical Figure)
*Lizzie Borden* - Elizabeth Engstrom   *h*   1826

**Borden, Samantha** (Government Official)
*Dusk* - Ron Dee   *h*   1466

**Boren, Troy** (Accountant; Outlaw)
*Blindfold* - Kevin J. Anderson   *s*   101

**Borg, Cy** (Cyborg; Engineer)
*Drifter's Run* - William C. Dietz   *s*   1544
*Drifter's War* - William C. Dietz   *s*   1545

**Borg, Jocasta** (Cyborg; Businesswoman)
*The Specialist* - Wynne Whiteford   *s*   5788

**Borgel** (Time Traveler)
*Borgel* - Daniel Manus Pinkwater   *f*   4338

**Bork, Dick "Dutch"** (Biker)
*Night Beasts* - T.W. Stetson   *h*   5263

**Bork, Saval** (Martial Arts Expert; Bodyguard)
*Brother Death* - Steve Perry   *s*   4292

**Bork, Tazzimi "Taz"** (Police Officer)
*Brother Death* - Steve Perry   *s*   4292

**Born, Eric** (Psychic)
*Reclamation* - Sarah Zettel   *s*   6081

**Boro** (Religious)
*Brand New Cherry Flavor* - Todd Grimson   *h*   2448

**Borric** (Royalty)
*Prince of the Blood* - Raymond E. Feist   *f*   1907

**Boscage, A.D.** (Writer)
*The Priest: A Gothic Romance* - Thomas M.
   Disch   *h*   1562

**Bosch, Benjamin** (Doctor)
*Troll-Quest* - Rose Estes   *f*   1841

**Bosch, Benjamin** (Doctor; Adventurer)
*Troll-Taken* - Rose Estes   *f*   1842

**Bossk** (Bounty Hunter)
*The Mandalorian Armor* - K.W. Jeter   *s*   2914

**Bothari** (Bodyguard; Murderer)
*Barrayar* - Lois McMaster Bujold   *s*   756

**Botticelli, Sandro** (Historical Figure; Artist)
*The Memory Cathedral* - Jack Dann   *s*   1341

**Bottlenose** (Animal; Pilot)
*Starplex* - Robert J. Sawyer   *s*   4859

**Bottom, Nick** (Artisan)
*Whilom* - Robert Watson   *f*   5639

**Botts, Wendell** (Construction Worker)
*Oaths and Miracles* - Nancy Kress   *s*   3242

**Bouchard, Angelique** (Servant)
*Angelique's Descent* - Lara Parker   *h*   4246

**Bouchette, Jean-Paul** (Criminal; Spirit)
*The Suiting* - Kelley Wilde   *h*   5803

**Bouriere, Tira** (Political Figure; Teenager)
*Crown of Empire* - Chelsea Quinn Yarbro   *s*   6014

**Bouriere, Wiley** (Political Figure; Teenager)
*Crown of Empire* - Chelsea Quinn Yarbro   *s*   6014

**Bourne, Geena** (Astronaut)
*Moonseed* - Stephen Baxter   *s*   400

**Bowe, Austin** (Spaceship Captain; Parent)
*Tripoint* - C.J. Cherryh   *s*   1003

**Bowe-Hawkins, Thomas "Tom"** (Spaceman;
   Prisoner)
*Tripoint* - C.J. Cherryh   *s*   1003

**Bowen, Muffy** (Dancer; Captive)
*Greenhouse* - Thomas A. Easton   *s*   1723

**Bowen, Tess** (Teacher)
*The Uprising* - Abigail McDaniels   *h*   3785

**Bowers, Sidney** (Mechanic)
*Mojave Wells* - L. Dean James   *s*   2864

**Bowman, Maggie** (Detective—Homicide)
*Cold Kiss* - Roxanne Longstreet   *h*   3517
*The Undead* - Roxanne Longstreet   *h*   3519

**Bowman, Michael** (Doctor; Vampire)
*Cold Kiss* - Roxanne Longstreet   *h*   3517

**Bowman, Michael** (Doctor)
*The Undead* - Roxanne Longstreet   *h*   3519

**Bowman, Scott** (Doctor)
*The Cartoonist* - Sean Costello   *h*   1204

**Boxdale, Asin** (Artist)
*Free Radicals* - Jack McKinney   *s*   3848

**Boxer, Hugh** (Neighbor)
*Sweet Heart* - Peter James   *h*   2875

**Boxletter, Bob** (Computer Expert)
*Duplicates* - Andrew Neiderman   *h*   4086

**Boxletter, Marion** (Housewife)
*Duplicates* - Andrew Neiderman   *h*   4086

**Boyle, Heather** (Housewife)
*Website* - Ray Garton   *h*   2157

**Boyle, Martin** (Worker)
*Website* - Ray Garton   *h*   2157

**Boyle, Simon** (Scientist; Criminal)
*The Illegal Rebirth of Billy the Kid* - Rebecca
   Ore   *s*   4220

**Boysie** (Sailor; Revolutionary)
*Flickering Shadows* - Kwadwo Agymah
   Kamau   *f*   3006

**Braan** (Alien; Military Personnel)
*Genellan: Planetfall* - Scott G. Gier   *s*   2223

**Braccalese, Gianni** (Businessman)
*A Wizard in Mind* - Christopher Stasheff   *s*   5232

**Bracher, Frederick** (Racist)
*Mark of the Werewolf* - Jeffrey Sackett   *h*   4780

**Bracken, Gary** (Scientist)
*Virus Clans* - Michael Kanaly   *s*   3008

**Brackett, Lute** (Detective—Police)
*Star Precinct* - Kevin D. Randle   *s*   4470

**Brackett, Richard** (Police Officer)
*Mind Slayer* - Kevin D. Randle   *s*   4469

**Braco, Jag** (Religious; Police Officer)
*Inquisitor* - Ian Watson   *s*   5637

**Brad** (Filmmaker)
*I, Said the Fly* - Michael Shea   *h*   4944

**Bradley, Alexander "Alex"** (Student)
*The Hollowing* - Robert Holdstock   *f*   2738

**Bradley, Angela** (Housewife; Songwriter)
*Metal Angel* - Nancy Springer   *f*   5181

**Bradley, Jason** (Engineer)
*The Ghost From the Grand Banks* - Arthur C.
   Clarke   *s*   1056

**Bradley, Karen** (Doctor)
*Deus-X: A Novel of Spiritual Terror* - Joseph A.
   Citro   *h*   1037

**Bradley, Kevin** (Detective—Private; Demon)
*Eyes of the Empress* - Camille Bacon-Smith   *f*   285

**Bradley, Richard** (Parent; Adventurer)
*The Hollowing* - Robert Holdstock   *f*   2738

**Bradoukis, Matthew** (Military Personnel)
*Ground Zero* - Kevin J. Anderson   *h*   106

**Brady, Francis** (Child)
*The Butcher Boy* - Patrick McCabe   *h*   3716

**Brady, Julia** (Spouse; Historical Figure)
*The Gallery of His Dreams* - Kristine Kathryn
   Rusch   *f*   4717

**Brady, Mathew B.** (Historical Figure; Photographer)
*The Gallery of His Dreams* - Kristine Kathryn
   Rusch   *f*   4717

**Brady, Tedman** (Political Figure)
*A Fearful Symmetry* - James Luceno   *s*   3542

**Brady-Phillips, Graysha** (Scientist)
*Shivering World* - Kathy Tyers   *s*   5526

**Braeth, Rikard** (Adventurer; Historian)
*Crown of the Serpent* - Allen L. Wold   *s*   5932
*Lair of the Cyclops* - Allen L. Wold   *s*   5933

**Braganca, Alphonso** (Royalty; Handicapped)
*God's Fires* - Patricia Anthony   *s*   159

**Braille** (Vampire)
*Night Thirst* - Patrick Whalen   *h*   5770

**Brailsford, Jane** (Magician; Adventurer)
*A College of Magics* - Caroline Stevermer   *f*   5266

**Brainard** (Military Personnel)
*The Jungle* - David Drake   *s*   1634

**Braithwaite** (Psychologist)
*Final Diagnosis* - James White   *s*   5777

**Braldt** (Prisoner; Warrior)
*The Hunter on Arena* - Rose Estes   *s*   1838

**Bramhall, Arthur** (Writer; Professor)
*The Bear Went over the Mountain* - William
   Kotzwinkle   *f*   3222

**Brand** (Warrior; Sidekick)
*The Hammer and the Cross* - Harry
   Harrison   *f*   2570
*One King's Way* - Harry Harrison   *s*   2572

**Brand, Anne-Marie** (Photographer; Parent)
*Secret Passages* - Paul Preuss   *s*   4420

**Brand, Evelyn** (Aged Person)
*The Devil's Churn* - Kristine Kathryn
   Rusch   *h*   4715

**Brand, Matthew Tyler** (Scientist; Disembodied
   Personality)
*The Hot-Wired Dodo* - Jack L. Chalker   *s*   956

**Brandarkson, Brandark** (Warrior; Minstrel)
*Oath of Swords* - David Weber   *f*   5678

**Brandin of Ygrath** (Ruler; Sorcerer)
*Tigana* - Guy Gavriel Kay   *f*   3018

**Brandis** (Sorcerer)
*Wind Whispers, Shadow Shouts* - Sharon
   Green   *f*   2360

**Brandis, Sarah** (Dancer)
*Sick* - Jay R. Bonansinga   *h*   571

**Brandon, Richard** (Psychologist; Professor)
*God's Dice* - S. Andrew Swann   *f*   5364

**Brandsetter, Earl** (Murderer; Computer Expert)
*Lethal Interface* - Mel Odom   *s*   4193

**Branfield, Anastasia** (Archaeologist)
*Hellboy: The Lost Army* - Christopher
   Golden   *h*   2257

**Brant, Arn** (Royalty; Military Personnel)
*The Lanterns of God* - Ron Sarti   *s*   4835
*Legacy of the Ancients* - Ron Sarti   *s*   4836

**Branwen** (Step-Parent)
*The Lost Years of Merlin* - T.A. Barron   *f*   370

**Bratenahl, Robert** (Journalist)
*I, Robot: The Illustrated Screenplay* - Harlan
   Ellison   *s*   1785

**Braun, Caleb** (Worker)
*Goblin Moon* - Teresa Edgerton   *f*   1743

**Braun, Susan** (Librarian)
*Ladies Night* - Jack Ketchum   *h*   3091

**Braun, Tom** (Writer)
*Ladies Night* - Jack Ketchum   *h*   3091

**Brauna, Sanda** (Political Figure)
*Becoming Human* - Valerie J. Freireich   *s*   2049

**Brauner, Victor** (Artist)
*Conglomeros* - Jesse Browner   *f*   729

**Brave Man** (Prehistoric Human; Leader)
*People of the Earth* - W. Michael Gear   *f*   2166

**Brayker, Silas** (Thief)
*Tales From the Crypt: Demon Knight* - Randall
   Boyll   *h*   617

**Brazil, Bubbles** (Teenager; Adventurer)
*Negrophobia: An Urban Parable* - Darius
James  *f*  2859

**Brazil, Nathan** (Immortal; Sea Captain)
*Echoes of the Well of Souls* - Jack L.
Chalker  *s*  953

**Brazil, Nathan** (Immortal)
*Gods of the Well of Souls* - Jack L. Chalker  *s*  954
*Shadow of the Well of Souls* - Jack L.
Chalker  *s*  961

**Breanna** (Teenager; Explorer)
*Zombie Lover* - Piers Anthony  *f*  197

**Breaux, Alan** (Detective—Police)
*Spellcaster* - J. Edward Ames  *h*  92

**Breen, Arthur Quentin** (Serial Killer)
*The Safety of Unknown Cities* - Lucy
Taylor  *h*  5414

**Breen, Matthew** (Journalist)
*Paradise: A Chronicle of a Distant World* - Mike
Resnick  *s*  4552

**Breith** (Slave; Wizard)
*Drum Calls* - Jo Clayton  *f*  1065

**Breivik, Allan** (Musician; Magician)
*Make Way for Dragons!* - Thorarinn
Gunnarsson  *f*  2465

**Brekke, Robbie** (Thief)
*Brain Rose* - Nancy Kress  *s*  3239

**Breks, Falca** (Thief)
*The Mace of Souls* - Bruce Fergusson  *f*  1925

**Bremen** (Wizard; Adventurer)
*First King of Shannara* - Terry Brooks  *f*  712

**Bremen, Jeremy "Jerry"** (Psychic; Widow(er))
*The Hollow Man* - Dan Simmons  *s*  5054

**Bremener, Saul** (Wizard)
*The Witch Doctor* - Christopher Stasheff  *f*  5228

**Bremmers, Lana** (Teenager)
*The Devil's End* - D.A. Fowler  *h*  2023

**Brenda** (Journalist)
*Steel Beach* - John Varley  *s*  5566

**Brendan** (Religious)
*The Book of Brendan* - Ann Curry  *f*  1294

**Brenlek, Parke** (Friend)
*Reunion on Neverend* - John E. Stith  *s*  5306

**Brenn** (Adventurer)
*A Forest Lord* - Michael Williams  *f*  5819

**Brenn** (Thief)
*A Sorcerer's Apprentice* - Michael Williams  *f*  5820

**Brennan, Joseph Payne** (Sidekick)
*The Adventures of Lucius Leffing* - Joseph Payne
Brennan  *f*  670

**Brennan, Ted** (Psychologist)
*House Haunted* - Al Sarrantonio  *h*  4830

**Brenner, Hugh** (Scientist; Inventor)
*Paths to Otherwhere* - James P. Hogan  *s*  2728

**Brenner, Joshua** (Child)
*The Feeding* - Leigh Clark  *h*  1051

**Brenner, Matt** (Architect)
*The Feeding* - Leigh Clark  *h*  1051

**Brenner, Robin** (Photographer)
*The Feeding* - Leigh Clark  *h*  1051

**Brent** (Travel Agent)
*The Unfinished* - Jay B. Laws  *h*  3362

**Brent, David** (Vampire)
*The Vampire's Apprentice* - Richard Lee
Byers  *h*  799

**Brentwood, David** (Military Personnel)
*Battle Front* - Ian Slater  *s*  5086

**Brentwood, Grace** (Aged Person)
*Earthbound* - Richard Matheson  *h*  3684

**Breo-Saight "Brie"** (Martial Arts Expert; Hero)
*Fire Arrow* - Edith Pattou  *f*  4260

**Bressanone, Rana** (Mythical Creature)
*The Broken Goddess* - Hans Bemmann  *f*  439

**Brett/Natalie** (Teenager; Artisan)
*Holy Fire* - Bruce Sterling  *s*  5259

**Breunner, August** (Doctor)
*Brainstorm* - Steven M. Krauzer  *h*  3230

**Brevelan** (Witch)
*The Glass Dragon* - Irene Radford  *f*  4460

**Brewer, Tom** (Artisan; Widow(er))
*Dreamthorp* - Chet Williamson  *h*  5845

**Brewster** (Businesswoman)
*The Witch of Maple Park* - Stephanie S.
Tolan  *f*  5478

**Brewster, Bobby Joe** (Scientist)
*Manhattan Transfer* - John E. Stith  *s*  5303

**Brewster, Kip** (Heir—Lost; Teenager)
*Starswarm* - Jerry Pournelle  *s*  4379

**Brewster, Mackenzie** (Psychic; Teenager)
*The Witch of Maple Park* - Stephanie S.
Tolan  *f*  5478

**Brewster, Marvin "Doc"** (Scientist; Genius)
*The Ambivalent Magician* - Simon Hawke  *f*  2616
*The Inadequate Adept* - Simon Hawke  *f*  2617
*The Reluctant Sorcerer* - Simon Hawke  *f*  2622

**Brewster, Mike** (Guardian; Fugitive)
*Starswarm* - Jerry Pournelle  *s*  4379

**Breyd** (Religious; Warrior)
*The Sword and the Lion* - Roberta Cray  *f*  1253

**Briam** (Nobleman; Musician)
*Changing Fate* - Elisabeth Waters  *f*  5629

**Brianna** (Child)
*The Curse of Camp Cold Lake* - R.L. Stine  *h*  5286

**Briar** (Student; Wizard)
*Tris's Book* - Tamora Pierce  *f*  4322

**Brice, Jenny** (Artist)
*Something Out There* - Ronald Kelly  *h*  3056

**Brice, Marcer Joseph** (Scholar; Genetically Altered
Being)
*Imposter* - Valerie J. Freireich  *s*  2050

**Bridger, Gray** (Guide)
*Testament* - Valerie J. Freireich  *s*  2051

**Bridger, Mead** (Genetically Altered Being)
*Testament* - Valerie J. Freireich  *s*  2051

**Bridger, Nathan Hale** (Scientist; Sea Captain)
*seaQuest DSV: Fire Below* - Matthew J.
Costello  *s*  1201
*seaQuest DSV: The Novel* - Diane Duane  *s*  1666

**Briggs, Garner** (Professor)
*Hence* - Brad Leithauser  *s*  3431

**Briggs, Marilyn** (Psychic)
*Near Dead* - Stephen R. George  *h*  2202

**Briggs, Timothy** (Sports Figure)
*Hence* - Brad Leithauser  *s*  3431

**Bright** (Nobleman; Knight)
*Gawain and Lady Green* - Anne Eliot
Crompton  *f*  1269

**Brightblade, Douglas** (Apprentice; Teenager)
*Pyromancer* - Don Callander  *f*  847

**Brightglade, Douglas** (Wizard; Fiance(e))
*Aquamancer* - Don Callander  *f*  841
*Geomancer* - Don Callander  *f*  845

**Brightlaw, Nic** (Librarian; Military Personnel)
*The Cup of Morning Shadows* - Rosemary
Edghill  *f*  1747

**Brighton, Cassandra Lane "Casey"**
(Businesswoman)
*Kiss of the Vampire* - Lee Weathersby  *h*  5657

**Brigit** (Nurse)
*The World I Made for Her* - Thomas
Moran  *h*  3996

**Brigitta, Maeve** (Immigrant)
*The Scathach and the Maeve's Daughter* - Mary
Alexander Walker  *f*  5618

**Brik** (Genetically Altered Being)
*The Middle of Nowhere* - David Gerrold  *s*  2209

**Brill** (Singer; Sorceress)
*The Soprano Sorceress* - L.E. Modesitt Jr.  *f*  3938

**Brill, Janna** (Police Officer)
*Dragon's Teeth* - Lee Killough  *s*  3109

**Brill, Lucy** (Teenager)
*Prodigal* - Melanie Tem  *h*  5423

**Brill, Nicole** (Child)
*Silent Witness* - Robert Arthur Smith  *h*  5136

**Brill, Rae** (Teenager)
*Prodigal* - Melanie Tem  *h*  5423

**Brill, Willy** (Doctor)
*Silent Witness* - Robert Arthur Smith  *h*  5136

**Brim, Wilf** (Military Personnel; Spaceship Captain)
*The Defenders* - Bill Baldwin  *s*  309

**Brim, Wilf** (Military Personnel)
*The Defiance* - Bill Baldwin  *s*  310

**Brim, Wilf** (Military Personnel; Spaceship Captain)
*The Mercenaries* - Bill Baldwin  *s*  311

**Brim, Wilf** (Military Personnel)
*The Siege* - Bill Baldwin  *s*  312

**Brink, Ludger** (Scientist)
*The Dig* - Alan Dean Foster  *s*  2002

**Brissot, Phillipe** (Vampire)
*Thirst of the Vampire* - T. Lucien Wright  *h*  5988

**Brita** (Orphan; Guardian)
*Conan the Rogue* - John Maddox Roberts  *f*  4617

**Britannicus, Caius** (Military Personnel; Leader)
*The Skystone* - Jack Whyte  *f*  5794

**Britannicus, Caius Merlyn** (Leader; Writer)
*The Eagles' Brood* - Jack Whyte  *f*  5792
*The Saxon Shore* - Jack Whyte  *f*  5793

**Brock, Dire-Lord** (Nobleman; Warrior)
*The Goda War* - Jay D. Blakeney  *s*  516

**Broderick, Daria** (Child)
*Along Came a Spider* - Athena Alexis  *h*  70

**Brodski** (Handicapped)
*The Nihilesthete* - Richard Kalich  *h*  3002

**Brody, Aloysius** (Judge; Businessman)
*Pallas* - L. Neil Smith  *s*  5132

**Brogan, Steve** (Detective—Private)
*Witchcraft* - Bill Michaels  *h*  3885

**Broken Echo** (Indian; Spirit)
*Spirit Crossings* - Claudia Peck  *f*  4275

**Broken-finger, Leonard** (Shaman; Indian)
*High Steel* - Jack C. Haldeman II  *s*  2486

**Broketail, Bazil** (Mythical Creature; Military
Personnel)
*Battledragon* - Christopher Rowley  *f*  4691

**Broketail, Bazil** (Mythical Creature; Warrior)
*Bazil Broketail* - Christopher Rowley  *f*  4692

**Broketail, Bazil** (Mythical Creature; Military Personnel)
*A Dragon at World's End* - Christopher Rowley *f* 4693
*Dragons of Argonath* - Christopher Rowley *f* 4694
*Dragons of War* - Christopher Rowley *f* 4695
*A Sword for a Dragon* - Christopher Rowley *f* 4697

**Brokols, Elver** (Diplomat)
*The Lantern of God* - John Dalmas *s* 1323

**Brompton, Arnold** (Computer Expert; Wanderer)
*Virtual Girl* - Amy Thomson *s* 5462

**Bromton, Stu** (Police Officer)
*Greely's Cove* - John Gideon *h* 2221

**Bronkman, Theo "Peter Ambrose"** (Amnesiac; Detective—Amateur)
*Nimbus* - Alexander Jablokov *s* 2839

**Bronson, Raymond** (Teenager)
*I Know What You Did Last Summer* - Lois Duncan *h* 1692

**Bronson, Victoria "Tory"** (Spacewoman)
*The Sails of Tau Ceti* - Michael McCollum *s* 3771

**Bronstein, Miroslav Ilyich** (Astronaut)
*Fellow Traveller* - William Barton *s* 380

**Bronwyn** (Royalty; Warrior)
*Hearts and Armor* - Ron Miller *f* 3903

**Bronwyn** (Royalty; Fugitive)
*Palaces and Prisons* - Ron Miller *f* 3904
*Silk and Steel* - Ron Miller *f* 3905

**Bronwyn** (Revolutionary)
*Thornhold* - Elaine Cunningham *f* 1293

**Brook** (Parent)
*Clouds End* - Sean Stewart *f* 5272

**Brooke-Holt, Diana** (Actress)
*An Earthly Crown* - Kate Elliott *s* 1771

**Brookmeyer, Warren** (Political Figure)
*Tek Power* - William Shatner *s* 4937

**Brooks, Anne** (Veterinarian)
*The Devil's Laughter* - William W. Johnstone *h* 2930

**Brooks, Connor** (Sailor; Criminal)
*Ill Wind* - Kevin J. Anderson *s* 108

**Brooks, Jenny** (Traveler; Revolutionary)
*Cathy IV* - Frances Lucas *s* 3539

**Brooks, Tim** (Police Officer)
*Ghosts* - Noel Hynd *h* 2822

**Brostek** (Teenager; Hunter)
*Shadow-Maze* - Mark Smith *f* 5133

**Broussard, Andy** (Doctor)
*Blood on the Bayou* - D.J. Donaldson *h* 1570

**Broussard, Wade** (Detective—Police)
*The Gris-Gris Man* - Don Davis *h* 1403

**Broward, Joseph** (Detective—Homicide)
*Concrete Hotel* - C. Christopher Caldon *h* 839

**Broward, Liz** (Doctor)
*Blood Work* - Fay Zachary *h* 6050

**Brown** (Lesbian; Magician)
*Phaze Doubt* - Piers Anthony *f* 184

**Brown, Emma** (Grandparent)
*The Summer I Shrank My Grandmother* - Elvira Woodruff *f* 5968

**Brown, Frank** (Industrialist)
*White Horse, Dark Dragon* - Robert C. Fleet *f* 1947

**Brown, Kelsie** (Computer Expert)
*65mm* - Dale Hoover *h* 2761

**Brown, Max** (Teenager)
*Thrill* - Patricia Wallace *h* 5624

**Brown, Nelly** (Child; Scientist)
*The Summer I Shrank My Grandmother* - Elvira Woodruff *f* 5968

**Brown, Oenone** (Housewife)
*Firefly* - Piers Anthony *h* 170

**Brown, Pellimore "Pel"** (Businessman)
*Out of This World* - Lawrence Watt-Evans *f* 5645

**Brown, Pellimore "Pel"** (Magician; Ruler)
*The Reign of the Brown Magician* - Lawrence Watt-Evans *f* 5647

**Brown, Rembrandt "Cryin' Man"** (Musician; Adventurer)
*Sliders: The Novel* - Brad Linaweaver *s* 3467

**Brown, Tim** (Student)
*The Select* - F. Paul Wilson *h* 5897

**Brown, Zack** (Military Personnel)
*Darker Angels* - S.P. Somtow *h* 5155

**The Brown Oxford** (Experimental Subject)
*The Collected Stories of Philip K. Dick, Volume One: The Short Happy Life of the Brown Oxford* - Philip K. Dick *s* 1519

**Brownbenttalon** (Alien; Political Figure)
*O Pioneer!* - Frederik Pohl *s* 4350

**Brownpony, Elia** (Religious; Leader)
*Saint Leibowitz and the Wild Horse Woman* - Walter M. Miller Jr. *s* 3908

**Broxholm** (Alien)
*My Teacher Flunked the Planet* - Bruce Coville *s* 1222

**Bruce** (Animal)
*Paddywhack* - John Stchur *h* 5236

**Bruce, Virgin** (Construction Worker)
*Orbital Decay* - Allen Steele *s* 5246

**Bruchan** (Minstrel)
*The Boy From the Burren* - Sheila Gilluly *f* 2236

**Bruckner, Bill** (Spy; Criminal)
*Nomad* - David Alexander *s* 66

**Bruckner, Teresa** (Student)
*Angels Unaware* - L. Elizabeth Storm *s* 5315

**Bruenor, Catti-Brie** (Mythical Creature; Adventurer)
*Passage to Dawn* - R.A. Salvatore *f* 4803
*Siege of Darkness* - R.A. Salvatore *f* 4804
*Sojourn* - R.A. Salvatore *f* 4806

**Bruenor, Catti-Brie** (Mythical Creature; Warrior)
*Starless Night* - R.A. Salvatore *f* 4807

**Brumado, Joanna** (Scientist)
*Mars* - Ben Bova *s* 586

**Brunahild "Sigdrifa"** (Royalty; Warrior)
*The Dragons of the Rhine* - Diana L. Paxson *f* 4264
*The Wolf and the Raven* - Diana L. Paxson *f* 4270

**Brunichild** (Royalty; Warrior)
*Rhinegold* - Stephan Grundy *f* 2454

**Bruno** (Mercenary)
*Harm's Way* - Colin Greenland *s* 2416

**Bruno** (Royalty)
*King and Emperor* - Harry Harrison *f* 2571

**Bruno, Giordano** (Religious; Historical Figure)
*Love & Sleep* - John Crowley *f* 1277

**Bruno, Richard** (Scientist; Criminal)
*Journals of the Plague Years* - Norman Spinrad *s* 5172

**Brunreich, Porter** (Child)
*Patton's Spaceship* - John Barnes *s* 357

**Brusen, Elaine** (Scientist)
*Merlin's Bones* - Fred Saberhagen *f* 4771

**Brustein, Harvey** (Cult Member)
*The Children of Hamelin* - Norman Spinrad *s* 5170

**Brutha** (Religious)
*Small Gods* - Terry Pratchett *f* 4400

**Brutogas, Kator Secondcousin** (Alien)
*Naked to the Stars/The Alien Way* - Gordon R. Dickson *s* 1537

**Brutus, Marcus Junius** (Political Figure; Military Personnel)
*Child of the Eagle* - Esther Friesner *f* 2073

**Bruwer-Sanmartin, Hanna** (Political Figure)
*Fire in a Faraway Place* - Robert Frezza *s* 2052

**Bryan** (Young Man)
*The Night in Fog* - David B. Silva *h* 5026

**Bryant, Bonnie** (Child; Foundling)
*The Godsend* - Bernard Taylor *h* 5401

**Bryant, Karla** (Advertising)
*Deadrush* - Yvonne Navarro *h* 4073

**Bryant, Martin** (Student)
*The Crawling Dark* - Pauline Dunn *h* 1698

**Bryant, Sandra** (Restaurateur)
*The Crawling Dark* - Pauline Dunn *h* 1698

**Bryarmote** (Mythical Creature; Royalty)
*Pyromancer* - Don Callander *f* 847

**Bryce, Christopher** (Religious)
*Storm Knights* - Bill Slavicsek *f* 5087

**Bryce, Neal** (Police Officer)
*The Death Crystal* - J. Edward Ames *h* 91

**Bryce, Pat** (Religious)
*The Priest: A Gothic Romance* - Thomas M. Disch *h* 1562

**Bryge, Larry** (Teenager; Student—High School)
*Spirit Crossings* - Claudia Peck *f* 4275

**Buccari, Sharl** (Military Personnel)
*Genellan: Planetfall* - Scott G. Gier *s* 2223

**Buccari, Sharl** (Pilot; Parent)
*In the Shadow of the Moon* - Scott G. Gier *s* 2224

**Buchanan, Victoria** (Teacher)
*The Vampire Papers* - Michael Romkey *h* 4666

**Buckingham, Harry** (Advertising)
*Rune* - Christopher Fowler *h* 2020

**Buckland, Ulysses** (Teenager; Wizard)
*The Whims of Creation* - Simon Hawke *s* 2626

**Buckley, Christopher** (Child)
*Shadow Man* - Dennis Etchison *h* 1848

**Buddy** (Teenager; Orphan)
*Land O'Goshen* - Charles McNair *s* 3855

**Buechner, Marianne "Rianne"** (Child)
*An Impossumble Summer* - Brenda W. Clough *f* 1090

**Buechner, Shannon** (Child)
*An Impossumble Summer* - Brenda W. Clough *f* 1090

**Bueller** (Military Personnel)
*Aliens: Earth Hive* - Steve Perry *s* 4289

**Buford, Tommy** (Handyman)
*Let There Be Dark* - Allen Lee Harris *h* 2557

**Bugmeier, Neil** (Writer)
*Horror Show* - Greg Kihn *h* 3103

**Bull-Roar, Harold** (Ruler; Adventurer)
*Byzantium* - Stephen R. Lawhead *f* 3353

**Bult** (Alien)
*Uncharted Territory* - Connie Willis *s* 5875

**Bumstead, Frank** (Detective)
*Dark City* - Frank Lauria *h* 3351

**Bunkowski, Daniel "Chaingang"** (Serial Killer)
*Butcher* - Rex Miller *h* 3898
*Chaingang* - Rex Miller *h* 3899
*Savant* - Rex Miller *h* 3901

*Slice* - Rex Miller   *h*   3902

**Burbage, Horace** (Actor)
*A Company of Stars* - Christopher Stasheff   *s*   5215

**Burdon, Bill** (Detective—Private)
*A Question of Time* - Fred Saberhagen   *h*   4772

**Bureaucrat** (Agent)
*Stations of the Tide* - Michael Swanwick   *s*   5373

**Burge** (Police Officer)
*Nightwatch* - Robin Wayne Bailey   *f*   289

**Burgess** (Animal)
*Chaos Mode* - Piers Anthony   *f*   165

**Burke** (Child)
*Sineater* - Elizabeth Massie   *h*   3668

**Burke, Khalil Haleem** (Criminal)
*The Alien Years* - Robert Silverberg   *s*   5027

**Burke, Martin** (Psychologist; Inventor)
*/* - Greg Bear   *s*   413

**Burke, Martin** (Psychologist)
*Queen of Angels* - Greg Bear   *s*   423

**Burke, Moira Janelle** (Lawyer; Aged Person)
*Overshoot* - Mona Clee   *s*   1075

**Burke, Peter** (Photographer)
*Cold at Heart* - Brian Hopkins   *h*   2768

**Burkhardt, Jared Jr.** (Student)
*First Love: A Gothic Tale* - Joyce Carol
   Oates   *h*   4183

**Burlingame, Gerald** (Lawyer)
*Gerald's Game* - Stephen King   *h*   3133

**Burlingame, Jessie** (Housewife)
*Gerald's Game* - Stephen King   *h*   3133

**Burlow, Kurt** (Vampire)
*Salem's Lot* - Stephen King   *h*   3140

**Burnell** (Amnesiac; Activist)
*Somewhere East of Life* - Brian W. Aldiss   *s*   60

**Burnham, Harold** (Scientist)
*Carnivores* - Penelope Banka Kreps   *h*   3232

**Burning** (Military Personnel)
*A Screaming Across the Sky* - Brian Daley   *s*   1315

**Burns, David** (Military Personnel)
*The War in the Waste* - Felicity Savage   *f*   4852

**Burns, Marty** (Detective—Private; Actor)
*Burning Bright* - J.S. Russell   *h*   4733

**Burns, Marty** (Detective)
*Celestial Dogs* - J.S. Russell   *h*   4734

**Burr, Martyn** (Doctor)
*Stone Angels* - Mike Jefferies   *h*   2889

**Burrfoot, Tasslehoff** (Mythical Creature)
*Wanderlust* - Mary Kirchoff   *f*   3155

**Burrich** (Step-Parent; Animal Trainer)
*Assassin's Apprentice* - Robin Hobb   *f*   2693

**Burroughs, Jack "MAX—KOOL"** (Computer Expert)
*Headcrash* - Bruce Bethke   *s*   483

**Burroughs, Mahree** (Diplomat)
*Ancestor's World* - A.C. Crispin   *s*   1259

**Burroughs, Mahree** (Teenager)
*Starbridge* - A.C. Crispin   *s*   1265

**Burrows** (Doctor)
*The Hill of Dreams* - Arthur Machen   *h*   3595

**Burton, Denise** (Secretary)
*Deadly Dreams* - Gerald A. Schiller   *h*   4874

**Burton, Paige** (Scientist)
*Between the Devil and the Deep* - J.M.
   Morgan   *h*   3998

**Burton, Richard Francis** (Historical Figure; Explorer)
*To Your Scattered Bodies Go* - Philip Jose
   Farmer   *s*   1876

**Burwin, Addie** (Doctor)
*Stunts* - Charles L. Grant   *h*   2317

**Bury, Horace Hussein** (Businessman)
*The Gripping Hand* - Larry Niven   *s*   4122

**Busch, Zachary** (Computer Expert)
*Drawing Blood* - Poppy Z. Brite   *h*   694

**Bush, George Herbert Walker** (Political Figure;
   Historical Figure)
*Reality Is What You Can Get Away With: An
   Illustrated Screenplay* - Robert Anton
   Wilson   *s*   5904

**Bushell, Thomas** (Military Personnel; Detective)
*The Two Georges* - Richard Dreyfuss   *s*   1655

**Bustamante, Robby** (Psychic; Handicapped)
*The Hollow Man* - Dan Simmons   *s*   5054

**Butler, Mark** (Parent)
*After Sundown* - Randall Boyll   *h*   609

**Butterbaugh, C.G.** (Detective)
*Sacrifice* - John Farris   *h*   1886

**Butterworth, Alicia** (Scientist; Researcher)
*Cosm* - Gregory Benford   *s*   444

**Bydawine** (Companion)
*Token of Dragonsblood* - Damaris Cole   *f*   1114

**Byrd, Benjamin** (Psychologist)
*St. Peter's Wolf* - Michael Cadnum   *h*   816

**Byrd, Tom** (Government Official)
*Living Real* - James C. Bassett   *s*   386

**Byriver, Jerno** (Royalty; Castaway)
*Thunder of the Captains* - Holly Lisle   *f*   3489

**Byrne, Jack** (Scientist)
*The Eleventh Plague: A Novel of Medical Terror* -
   John S. Marr   *h*   3632

**Byrne, Lysander "Jay"** (Serial Killer)
*Exquisite Corpse* - Poppy Z. Brite   *h*   695

**Byrne, Marianne** (Police Officer)
*Dying Breath* - Jon A. Harrald   *h*   2555

**Byrnison, Iorek** (Mercenary; Animal)
*The Golden Compass* - Philip Pullman   *f*   4446

**Byrns, Scott** (Teenager)
*Something Stirs* - Charles L. Grant   *h*   2316

**Byron** (Apprentice; Wizard)
*Cardmaster* - Clayton Emery   *f*   1813

**Byron** (Knight)
*Henry's Gift: The Magic Eye* - David
   Worsick   *f*   5972

**Byron** (Investigator)
*The Queen of Darkness* - Miguel Conner   *s*   1134

**Byron** (Musician; Wanderer)
*The White Mists of Power* - Kristine Kathryn
   Rusch   *f*   4730

**Byron, Ada** (Scientist)
*The Difference Engine* - William Gibson   *s*   2217

**Byron, George Gordon** (Historical Figure; Writer)
*Lord of the Dead* - Tom Holland   *h*   2741
*The Stress of Her Regard* - Tim Powers   *h*   4385


# C

**C.** (Student)
*Galatea 2.2* - Richard M. Powers   *s*   4381

**C** (Disembodied Personality)
*Someone to Watch over Me* - Tricia
   Sullivan   *s*   5355

**C-3PO** (Robot; Adventurer)
*The Glove of Darth Vader* - Paul Davids   *s*   1392

**Cable, John** (Professor; Archaeologist)
*Out of the Night* - Patrick Whalen   *h*   5771

**Cabot, Jaime** (Horse Trainer)
*Changespell* - Doranna Durgin   *f*   1703
*Dun Lady's Jess* - Doranna Durgin   *f*   1704

**Caceras, Mimla** (Military Personnel; Teenager)
*Traitors from Within* - R.A. Montgomery   *s*   3966

**Cadarn, Derfel** (Warrior)
*Enemy of God* - Bernard Cornwell   *f*   1189
*Excalibur* - Bernard Cornwell   *f*   1190

**Cadarn, Derfel** (Slave; Warrior)
*The Winter King* - Bernard Cornwell   *f*   1191

**Cadderly** (Student; Scholar)
*Canticle* - R.A. Salvatore   *f*   4793

**Cadderly** (Religious; Scholar)
*In Sylvan Shadows* - R.A. Salvatore   *f*   4800

**Cade, Hypatia "Tia"** (Cyborg)
*The Ship Who Searched* - Anne McCaffrey   *s*   3749

**Cade, Skinner** (Young Man; Werewolf)
*Wild Blood* - Nancy A. Collins   *h*   1127

**Cadigan, Risha "Rusty"** (Photographer; Vampire)
*Love Bite* - Sherry Gottlieb   *h*   2288

**Cadogan, Marianne** (Child)
*Nightmare, with Angel* - Stephen Gallagher   *h*   2111

**Caesar, Julius** (Military Personnel; Historical Figure)
*Caesar's Bicycle* - John Barnes   *s*   350

**Caeser, Justin** (Student)
*Flesh* - Gus Weill   *h*   5685

**Cafferty, Megan** (Businesswoman)
*Jade Darcy and the Zen Pirates* - Stephen
   Goldin   *s*   2260

**Caffre, Marie** (Housewife)
*Return to Camerein* - Rick Shelley   *s*   4974

**Cag** (Alien)
*Them* - William W. Johnstone   *h*   2935

**Cage, Bill** (Police Officer)
*Deathwalker* - R. Patrick Gates   *h*   2159

**Cage, Louis P.** (Archaeologist)
*Curse of the Vampire* - Geoffrey Caine   *h*   832

**Cage, Peter** (Genetically Altered Being)
*Wildlife* - James Patrick Kelly   *s*   3049

**Cage, Ryland "Ry"** (Doctor)
*Carlucci's Heart* - Richard Paul Russo   *s*   4748

**Cage, Wynne** (Journalist; Genetically Altered Being)
*Wildlife* - James Patrick Kelly   *s*   3049

**Cahanagh, Athyn "Blackmantle"** (Orphan; Leader)
*Blackmantle: A Triumph* - Patricia Kennealy-
   Morrison   *f*   3059

**Cahill, Joseph** (Religious)
*Midnight Mass* - F. Paul Wilson   *h*   5891

**Caidin** (Nobleman)
*Tower of Doom* - Mark Anthony   *h*   155

**Caillean** (Religious)
*The Forest House* - Marion Zimmer Bradley   *f*   633
*Lady of Avalon* - Marion Zimmer Bradley   *f*   640

**Caillet, Bertrand** (Military Personnel; Werewolf)
*The Werewolf of Paris* - Guy Endore   *h*   1822

**Caillet, Josephine** (Servant)
*The Werewolf of Paris* - Guy Endore   *h*   1822

**Cain, Martin** (Journalist)
*Empire's Horizon* - John Brizzolara   *s*   707

**Cain, Roth Tiberius** (Military Personnel)
*Cain* - James Byron Huggins   *h*   2802

**Caine, Tycho** (Amnesiac; Imposter)
*Evil Ascending* - Michael A. Stackpole   *s*   5198

**Caine, Tycho** (Criminal; Hero)
*Evil Triumphant* - Michael A. Stackpole   s   5199

**Caine, Tycho** (Amnesiac)
*A Gathering Evil* - Michael A. Stackpole   s   5201

**Caiper, Noonie** (Child)
*Short Blade* - Peter R. Emshwiller   s   1820

**Caiper, Watly** (Murderer; Disembodied Personality)
*The Host* - Peter R. Emshwiller   s   1819

**Caiper, Watly** (Disembodied Personality)
*Short Blade* - Peter R. Emshwiller   s   1820

**Cairns, Moira** (Musician)
*December* - Phil Rickman   h   4588

**Cairo, Alya** (Administrator)
*This Alien Shore* - C.S. Friedman   s   2059

**Caitin, Bedyr** (Nobleman; Warrior)
*Wrath of Ashar* - Angus Wells   f   5742

**Caitin, Kedryn** (Royalty; Warrior)
*The Usurper* - Angus Wells   f   5739
*The Way Beneath* - Angus Wells   f   5740
*Wrath of Ashar* - Angus Wells   f   5742

**Caitlin** (Young Woman)
*The Druid's Gift* - Margaret J. Anderson   f   121
*Expiry Date* - Carol Anne Davis   h   1401

**Caitlin** (Foundling; Witch)
*The Spellkey Trilogy* - Ann Downer   f   1592

**Caitria** (Companion; Spirit)
*The Deepest Sea* - Charles Barnitz   f   363

**Caladrius, Rook** (Musician)
*Song for the Basilisk* - Patricia A. McKillip   f   3841

**Calais, Lucien** (Businessman)
*Private Demons* - Robert Masello   h   3660

**Calanthe** (Wanderer)
*Bewitchments of Love and Hate* - Storm Constantine   s   1140

**Calanthe** (Mutant; Psychic)
*The Enchantments of Flesh and Spirit* - Storm Constantine   s   1141

**Calanthe** (Wanderer; Prostitute)
*The Fulfillments of Fate and Desire* - Storm Constantine   s   1142

**Caldaq** (Alien; Warrior)
*A Call to Arms* - Alan Dean Foster   s   1995

**Calder, Charlotte** (Accountant)
*Tempter* - Nancy A. Collins   h   1125

**Calder, Reginald** (Mentally Ill Person)
*No Blood Spilled* - Les Daniels   h   1338

**Calderon, Mercedes** (Businesswoman; Abuse Victim)
*Solip: System* - Walter Jon Williams   s   5841

**Calderon, Miguel** (Student—College)
*Shango* - James Roberto Curtis   h   1298

**Caldicott, Edgar** (Doctor)
*Disturbing Behavior* - John Whitman   h   5789

**Caldwell** (Doctor)
*Call to Battle* - Doug Murray   h   4059

**Caldwell, Caroline** (Child)
*Manhattan Heat* - Ken Eulo   h   1851

**Caldwell, Frank** (Police Officer)
*Manhattan Heat* - Ken Eulo   h   1851

**Caldwell, Jay** (Student; Werewolf)
*Call to Battle* - Doug Murray   h   4059

**Caldwell, Jessica** (Waiter/Waitress)
*King of Morning, Queen of Day* - Ian McDonald   f   3793

**Caldwell, John** (Student—College; Genetically Altered Being)
*Mojave Wells* - L. Dean James   s   2864

**Cale** (Alien; Royalty)
*Invasion America* - Christie Golden   s   2252
*On the Run* - Christie Golden   s   2254

**Caleb** (Spaceman)
*PartnerShip* - Anne McCaffrey   s   3741

**Calef** (Animal)
*Hungry for Home: A Wolf Odyssey* - 'Asta Bowen   f   599

**Calhoun, Forrest** (Spaceship Captain)
*Rogue Star* - Michael Flynn   s   1965

**Calhoun, Janey** (Alien; Settler)
*Warpath* - Tony Daniel   s   1337

**Calhoun, Mackenzie** (Spaceship Captain)
*End Game* - Peter David   s   1382

**Caliban** (Monster)
*Caliban's Hour* - Tad Williams   f   5826

**Caliban** (Robot; Revolutionary)
*Inferno* - Roger MacBride Allen   s   78

**Caliban** (Robot)
*Utopia* - Roger MacBride Allen   s   83

**Calindor** (Magician)
*Redmagic* - Crawford Kilian   f   3107

**Calis** (Mercenary; Mythical Creature)
*Shadow of a Dark Queen* - Raymond E. Feist   f   1911

**Calistinsson, Colbey** (Warrior)
*Prince of Demons* - Mickey Zucker Reichert   f   4522
*The Western Wizard* - Mickey Zucker Reichert   f   4526

**Callahan** (Religious)
*Aqua Sancta* - Edward Bryant   h   748

**Callahan, Jessica** (Teenager)
*Sweet Revenge* - Jean Simon   h   5066

**Callahan, Juanita "Nita"** (Teenager; Wizard)
*A Wizard Abroad* - Diane Duane   f   1668

**Callahan, Mardie** (Accountant)
*Sweet Revenge* - Jean Simon   h   5066

**Callahan, Mike** (Time Traveler)
*Callahan's Legacy* - Spider Robinson   s   4639

**Callahan, Myra** (Housekeeper)
*Borderland: A Novel of Terror* - S.K. Epperson   h   1828

**Callahan, Sally** (Madam)
*Callahan's Lady* - Spider Robinson   s   4638
*Lady Slings the Booze* - Spider Robinson   s   4640

**Callahan-Finn, Mary** (Computer Expert)
*Callahan's Legacy* - Spider Robinson   s   4639

**Callare, Jesse** (Teacher; Student—College)
*Mother of Storms* - John Barnes   s   354

**Callaway, Chris** (Vampire; Homosexual)
*Out for Blood* - John Peyton Cooke   h   1166

**Callen, Kevin** (Fugitive; Wizard)
*Come Before Christ and Murder Love* - Stewart Home   f   2754

**Calliope** (Psychic; Orphan)
*Ecstasia* - Francesca Lia Block   f   547

**Calliope** (Royalty; Heir—Dispossessed)
*One for the Morning Glory* - John Barnes   f   355

**Calliope** (Parent; Psychic)
*Primavera* - Francesca Lia Block   f   551

**Callista** (Martial Arts Expert; Pilot)
*Darksaber* - Kevin J. Anderson   s   103

**Callow, John** (Occultist)
*Evil Intent* - Bernard Taylor   h   5400

**Cally "Earth"** (Child; Adventurer)
*Beyond the Magic Sphere* - Gail Jarrow   f   2879

**Calmady, Pollexfen** (Gentleman; Mercenary)
*The Architecture of Desire* - Mary Gentle   f   2195

**Calrissian, Lando** (Military Personnel)
*Before the Storm* - Michael P. Kube-McDowell   s   3247

**Caludius, Alexsandra** (Spy)
*7 Steps to Midnight* - Richard Matheson   h   3682

**Calum** (Miner)
*Acorna's Quest* - Anne McCaffrey   s   3718

**Calvert, Joshua** (Spaceship Captain)
*Consolidation* - Peter F. Hamilton   s   2523

**Calvert, Joshua** (Businessman; Spaceman)
*Emergence* - Peter F. Hamilton   s   2524

**Calvert, Joshua** (Spaceman)
*Expansion* - Peter F. Hamilton   s   2525

**Calvin, Susan** (Computer Expert; Psychologist)
*I, Robot: The Illustrated Screenplay* - Harlan Ellison   s   1785

**Calyx** (Mythical Creature)
*Cathedral of Thorns* - Steven Frankos   f   2041

**Calyx** (Religious)
*Sunder, Eclipse and Seed* - Elise Guttenberg   f   2471

**Camden, Alice "Leisha"** (Genetically Altered Being)
*Beggars in Spain* - Nancy Kress   s   3237

**Camel, Teddy** (Police Officer)
*Cul-De-Sac* - David Martin   h   3638
*Lie to Me* - David Martin   h   3639

**Camerata, Jo** (Industrialist)
*Star Brothers* - Ben Bova   s   594

**Cameron, Bren** (Linguist; Diplomat)
*Foreigner* - C.J. Cherryh   s   990

**Cameron, Bren** (Diplomat; Linguist)
*Inheritor* - C.J. Cherryh   s   997

**Cameron, Bren** (Linguist; Diplomat)
*Invader* - C.J. Cherryh   s   998

**Cameron, Daren** (Scholar; Scientist)
*Warstrider: Netlink* - William H. Keith Jr.   s   3038

**Cameron, Dev** (Military Personnel)
*Warstrider* - William H. Keith Jr.   s   3037

**Cameron, Dev** (Genetically Altered Being; Space Explorer)
*Warstrider: Netlink* - William H. Keith Jr.   s   3038

**Cameron, Jason** (Magician; Werewolf)
*The Fire Rose* - Mercedes Lackey   f   3280

**Cameron, Jenny** (Editor)
*Shadow of the Beast* - Margaret L. Carter   h   926

**Cameron, Tim** (Musician)
*Shadow of the Beast* - Margaret L. Carter   h   926

**Camfrey, Maurizio** (Professor)
*The Palm Dome* - Liz Fulton   h   2094

**Camillia** (Editor)
*Pluto, Animal Lover* - Laren Stover   h   5318

**Camio** (Animal)
*The Foxes of Firstdark* - Garry Kilworth   f   3115

**Campbell, Alan** (Doctor)
*Rapid Growth* - Mary K. Hanner   h   2541

**Campbell, Arlene "Grandma"** (Aged Person)
*The Amulet* - A.R. Morlan   h   4009

**Campbell, Brianne** (Teenager; Healer)
*Journeyman Wizard* - Mary Frances Zambreno   f   6057

**Campbell, Deirdre** (Student; Adventurer)
*Indiana Jones and the Dance of the Giants* - Rob MacGregor   f   3588
*Indiana Jones and the Seven Veils* - Rob MacGregor   f   3592

**Campbell, Hamish** (Traveler)
*Demon Knight* - Ken Hood   *f*  2760

**Campbell, Jack "Cap'n Jack"** (Astronaut)
*The Fugitive Stars* - Daniel Ransom   *s*  4479

**Campbell, Katie** (Researcher)
*Rapid Growth* - Mary K. Hanner   *h*  2541

**Campbell, Laicy "Iroshi"** (Martial Arts Expert;
   Administrator)
*The Glaive* - Cary Osborne   *s*  4227

**Campbell, Laicy "Iroshi"** (Martial Arts Expert;
   Wanderer)
*Iroshi* - Cary Osborne   *s*  4228

**Campbell, Robbie** (Child)
*Rapid Growth* - Mary K. Hanner   *h*  2541

**Campbell, Trey** (Health Care Professional)
*Bad Karma* - Andrew Harper   *h*  2548

**Campos, Juana "Juan"** (Drug Dealer)
*Gods of the Well of Souls* - Jack L. Chalker   *s*  954

**Camron** (Nobleman; Warrior)
*The Barbed Coil* - J.V. Jones   *f*  2957

**Canary, Sarah** (Patient; Wanderer)
*Sarah Canary* - Karen Joy Fowler   *f*  2028

**Canby, Gordon** (Spaceship Captain; Mercenary)
*Canby's Legion* - Bill Baldwin   *s*  308

**Canches, Alejandro** (Doctor; Wanderer)
*The Plague Tales* - Ann Benson   *s*  453

**Candace** (Spirit)
*The Seventh Heart* - Marina Fitch   *f*  1943

**Candle, Martin** (Judge; Activist)
*Blameless in Abaddon* - James Morrow   *f*  4029

**Candlemas, Richard** (Doctor)
*The Long Midnight* - Daniel Ransom   *h*  4480

**Cannon, April** (Scientist)
*Ancient Shores* - Jack McDevitt   *s*  3786

**Cannon, Ben** (Student; Political Figure)
*Cannon's Orb* - L. Warren Douglas   *s*  1586

**Cannon, Bobby** (Student)
*The School* - Ed Kelleher   *h*  3042

**Cannon, Vassily "Bass" James** (Heir; Computer
   Expert)
*A Plague of Change* - L. Warren Douglas   *s*  1587

**Cantemir, George** (Businessman; Criminal)
*The Venom Trees of Sunga* - L. Sprague de
   Camp   *s*  1420

**Cantrell, Barry** (Immortal)
*Prey* - William W. Johnstone   *h*  2932

**Cantrell, Boone** (Spirit; Lawman)
*Spirit Catcher* - Elizabeth Hallam   *f*  2497

**Cantrell, Loren** (Spaceship Captain)
*Ground-Ties* - Jane S. Fancher   *s*  1861
*Harmonies of the 'Net* - Jane S. Fancher   *s*  1862

**Caoimhghin** (Landowner)
*The Adventures of Threadwell the Tailor, or
   Alterations Made While You Wait* - P.D.
   Cacek   *h*  801

**Caolin "Blood Lord"** (Sorcerer)
*The Jewel of Fire* - Diana L. Paxson   *f*  4265

**Capone, Al** (Historical Figure; Reanimated Dead)
*Consolidation* - Peter F. Hamilton   *s*  2523

**Capone, Al** (Historical Figure; Organized Crime
   Figure)
*Timeshare: Second Time Around* - Joshua
   Dann   *s*  1345

**Capone, Alphonse** (Political Figure; Historical
   Figure)
*Back in the USSA* - Kim Newman   *s*  4095

**Captain** (Astronaut)
*Beyond Apollo* - Barry Malzberg   *s*  3612
*Eden* - Stanislaw Lem   *s*  3434

**Capthorne, Mya** (Scientist)
*Hidden Echoes* - Mike Jefferies   *f*  2885

**Capuela, Giacomo** (Businessman)
*The Unborn* - Andrew Laurance   *h*  3350

**Carabosse** (Mythical Creature)
*Beauty* - Sheri S. Tepper   *f*  5428

**Caramon** (Innkeeper; Hero)
*The Second Generation* - Margaret Weis   *f*  5724

**Caraval, Estela** (Divorced Person)
*Spirits of the Ordinary* - Kathleen Alcala   *f*  52

**Caraval, Julio** (Parent; Philosopher)
*Spirits of the Ordinary* - Kathleen Alcala   *f*  52

**Caraval, Zacarias** (Prospector)
*Spirits of the Ordinary* - Kathleen Alcala   *f*  52

**Carbri** (Musician; Minstrel)
*Search for the Starblade* - Keith Taylor   *f*  5408

**Cardenas, Angel** (Police Officer; Psychic)
*Montezuma Strip* - Alan Dean Foster   *s*  2011

**Cardiff, Melisan** (Demon; Human)
*Hooray for Hellywood* - Esther Friesner   *f*  2077

**Cardiff, Noel** (Warlock)
*Hooray for Hellywood* - Esther Friesner   *f*  2077

**Cardigan, Jake** (Detective—Private)
*Tek Money* - William Shatner   *s*  4935
*Tek Net* - William Shatner   *s*  4936
*Tek Power* - William Shatner   *s*  4937
*Tek Vengeance* - William Shatner   *s*  4938
*TekLab* - William Shatner   *s*  4939
*TekLords* - William Shatner   *s*  4940
*TekWar* - William Shatner   *s*  4941

**Carelias, Caroline "Sarah"** (Spy; Time Traveler)
*Union Fires* - John Barnes   *f*  358

**Carenza, Peter** (Religious)
*The Blood of the Lamb* - Thomas F.
   Monteleone   *h*  3958

**Carewe, Cindy** (Artist; Clerk)
*Absolute Power* - Ray Russell   *h*  4738

**Carewe, Eliza "Bettina"** (Witch)
*Absolute Power* - Ray Russell   *h*  4738

**Carey** (Courier)
*Changespell* - Doranna Durgin   *f*  1703
*Dun Lady's Jess* - Doranna Durgin   *f*  1704

**Carfax, Kurt** (Vampire)
*The Time of Feasting* - Mick Farren   *h*  1882

**Cargo** (Pilot; Spy)
*Cyberstealth* - S.N. Lewitt   *s*  3450
*Dancing Vac* - S.N. Lewitt   *s*  3451

**Carialle** (Cyborg)
*The Ship Errant* - Jody Lynn Nye   *s*  4175

**Carialle** (Spacewoman)
*The Ship Who Won* - Anne McCaffrey   *s*  3750

**Caribou** (Leader)
*The Woman Who Loved Reindeer* - Meredith Ann
   Pierce   *f*  4320

**Cariola "Cary"** (Artificial Intelligence)
*Full Tide of Night* - J.R. Dunn   *s*  1695

**Carl** (Actor)
*The Arbitrary Placement of Walls* - Martha
   Soukup   *f*  5165

**Carless, India "Trouble"** (Computer Expert;
   Lesbian)
*Trouble and Her Friends* - Melissa Scott   *s*  4902

**Carlisle, Amy** (Child-Care Giver)
*Clash by Night* - Chet Williamson   *h*  5844

**Carlisle, Bari** (Designer; Girlfriend)
*Count Geiger's Blues* - Michael Bishop   *s*  499

**Carlisle, Harry** (Police Officer)
*The Armageddon Crazy* - Mick Farren   *s*  1877

**Carlotta** (Mythical Creature; Imposter)
*Castle of Deception* - Mercedes Lackey   *f*  3275

**Carlsen, Anita** (Journalist)
*Sorcerers of Sodom* - Roger Elwood   *h*  1804

**Carlson, Amy** (Child)
*Shadows* - John Saul   *h*  4845

**Carlson, Annette** (Actress)
*Ghosts* - Noel Hynd   *h*  2822

**Carlson, Curt** (Military Personnel)
*Blood Siege* - G. Harry Stine   *s*  5278
*Force of Arms* - G. Harry Stine   *s*  5279
*Guts and Glory* - G. Harry Stine   *s*  5280
*Judgment Day* - G. Harry Stine   *s*  5281
*Warrior Shield* - G. Harry Stine   *s*  5283

**Carlson, Winnie** (Technician; Spy)
*Putting Up Roots* - Charles Sheffield   *s*  4964

**Carlson-Wade, Bruno David** (Writer)
*Bereavement* - Richard Lortz   *h*  3525

**Carlton, Billy** (Actor; Spirit)
*Cemetery of Angels* - Noel Hynd   *h*  2821

**Carlucci, Caroline** (Detective—Amateur)
*Carlucci's Heart* - Richard Paul Russo   *s*  4748

**Carlucci, Frank** (Detective—Police)
*Carlucci's Edge* - Richard Paul Russo   *s*  4747
*Carlucci's Heart* - Richard Paul Russo   *s*  4748

**Carmaggio, Henry** (Detective—Police)
*Drakon* - S.M. Stirling   *s*  5294

**Carmichael, Anson** (Military Personnel; Rancher)
*The Alien Years* - Robert Silverberg   *s*  5027

**Carmichael, Gabriel** (Child)
*Revenant* - Melanie Tem   *h*  5424

**Carmichael, Justin** (Revolutionary)
*Two Crowns for America* - Katherine Kurtz   *f*  3262

**Carmilla** (Vampire)
*The Darker Passions: Carmilla* - Amarantha
   Knight   *h*  3177

**Carmody, Alice Levertov** (Indian; Businesswoman)
*Sailor Song* - Ken Kesey   *s*  3082

**Carmody, Michael** (Sea Captain; Fisherman)
*Sailor Song* - Ken Kesey   *s*  3082

**Carne, Stephanie** (Scientist)
*The Mirror Maze* - James P. Hogan   *s*  2726

**Carnelian, Jherek** (Time Traveler)
*The Dancers at the End of Time* - Michael
   Moorcock   *s*  3979

**Carnes, Donald** (Boyfriend)
*The Axman Cometh* - John Farris   *h*  1883

**Carnes, Rebecca** (Military Personnel; Time Traveler)
*Arc Riders* - David Drake   *s*  1626

**Carney, Hugh** (Doctor)
*Bright Angel* - John Blair   *s*  512

**Carnitch, Richard** (Vampire)
*Nightlife* - Jack Ellis   *h*  1779

**Carol** (Mentally Ill Person)
*Century 21* - Ewa Kuryluk   *s*  3263

**Caroline** (Friend)
*Jed the Dead* - Alan Dean Foster   *s*  2007

**Carpenter, Aaron** (Wizard)
*The Hero King* - Rick Shelley   *f*  4970

**Carpenter, Alison** (Teenager)
*Guardian* - John Saul   *h*  4841

**Carpenter, Corey** (Teenager)
*Dark Time* - Maxine O'Callaghan   *h*  4189

**Carpenter, Gary** (Businessman)
*Last Rites* - David Darke   *h*   1354

**Carpenter, Gayle** (Clerk)
*Dark Time* - Maxine O'Callaghan   *h*   4189

**Carpenter, Harold** (Scientist)
*Icebound* - Dean R. Koontz   *h*   3209

**Carpenter, Joe** (Journalist)
*Sole Survivor* - Dean R. Koontz   *h*   3215

**Carpenter, Mary Anne** (Parent)
*Guardian* - John Saul   *h*   4841

**Carpenter, Paul** (Sea Captain; Office Worker)
*Hot Sky at Midnight* - Robert Silverberg   *s*   5032

**Carpenter, Rebecca** (Spouse)
*Dark Fortune* - Richard Lee Byers   *h*   795

**Carpenter, Tom** (Religious)
*Dark Fortune* - Richard Lee Byers   *h*   795

**Carpenter, Tonia** (Artist)
*Last Rites* - David Darke   *h*   1354

**Carpinski, Wyrdrune** (Wizard)
*The Samurai Wizard* - Simon Hawke   *f*   2623
*The Wizard of Santa Fe* - Simon Hawke   *f*   2628
*The Wizard of Sunset Strip* - Simon Hawke   *f*   2629

**Carr, Sultana** (Scientist)
*Flare* - Roger Zelazny   *s*   6065

**Carrasco, Solomon** (Spaceship Captain)
*The Artifact* - W. Michael Gear   *s*   2165

**Carri, Michael** (Political Figure)
*The Law of War* - William Shatner   *s*   4931

**Carri, Michael** (Government Official)
*Man o' War* - William Shatner   *s*   4932

**Carrie** (Psychic)
*Fire Margins* - Lisanne Norman   *s*   4137
*Fortune's Wheel* - Lisanne Norman   *s*   4138
*Razor's Edge* - Lisanne Norman   *s*   4139
*Turning Point* - Lisanne Norman   *s*   4140

**Carrie** (Religious)
*Virgin* - Mary Elizabeth Murphy   *h*   4050

**Carrigan** (Military Personnel; Time Traveler)
*The Unknown Soldier* - Mickey Zucker
   Reichert   *s*   4525

**Carrington, Charles Francis** (Traveler; Writer)
*Changeweaver* - Margaret Ball   *f*   313

**Carrion, Kade** (Royalty; Sorceress)
*The Element of Fire* - Martha Wells   *f*   5750

**Carruthers, Ronald "Ronnie"** (Teenager;
   Nobleman)
*Hunting Party* - Elizabeth Moon   *s*   3968

**Carson, Aloysius Byron** (Scientist; Explorer)
*Uncharted Territory* - Connie Willis   *s*   5875

**Carson, Casey** (Housewife)
*Darkside* - Dennis Etchison   *h*   1845

**Carson, Chev** (Mercenary)
*Warp Angel* - Stuart Hopen   *s*   2766

**Carson, Dave** (Police Officer)
*Funland* - Richard Laymon   *h*   3366

**Carson, Doug** (Composer)
*Darkside* - Dennis Etchison   *h*   1845

**Carson, Erin** (Teenager)
*Darkside* - Dennis Etchison   *h*   1845

**Carson, Guy** (Scientist)
*Mount Dragon* - Douglas Preston   *h*   4413

**Carson, Ilene** (Political Figure)
*Tech-Heaven* - Linda Nagata   *s*   4066

**Carson, Kenneth "Kit"** (Time Traveler; Aged
   Person)
*Time Scout* - Robert Asprin   *s*   263

**Carson, Lily** (Photojournalist)
*Someplace to Be Flying* - Charles de Lint   *f*   1435

**Carson, Roberta** (Activist; Writer)
*Rogue Star* - Michael Flynn   *s*   1965

**Cart** (Teenager)
*The Time of the Ghost* - Diana Wynne
   Jones   *f*   2951

**Carter, Annie** (Housewife)
*The Changeling Garden* - Winifred Elze   *h*   1806

**Carter, David** (Child)
*The Changeling Garden* - Winifred Elze   *h*   1806

**Carter, David** (Teenager)
*The Eyes of the Beast* - Steve Harris   *h*   2565

**Carter, David** (Student—High School)
*Invasion America* - Christie Golden   *s*   2252
*On the Run* - Christie Golden   *s*   2254

**Carter, Ellie** (Spirit; Businesswoman)
*The Wishing Well* - Charles de Lint   *f*   1441

**Carter, Janet** (Student)
*Tam Lin* - Pamela Dean   *f*   1446

**Carter, Jeremy** (Actor)
*Cat-A-Lyst* - Alan Dean Foster   *s*   1997

**Carter, John** (Architect)
*The Black Death* - Basil Copper   *h*   1185

**Carter, John** (Criminal)
*Return of the Living Dead* - John Russo   *h*   4746

**Carter, Richard** (Editor)
*The Summoning* - Bentley Little   *h*   3498

**Carter, Robert** (Police Officer)
*The Summoning* - Bentley Little   *h*   3498

**Carter, Sharon** (Handicapped; Singer)
*Jacob's Hands* - Aldous Huxley   *f*   2817

**Carter, Travis** (Teacher)
*Demon's Fright* - Penelope Banka Kreps   *h*   3233

**Carton, Sidney "Sid"** (Kidnapper; Adventurer)
*North Wind* - Gwyneth Jones   *s*   2953

**Cartwright, Jay** (Astronaut)
*The Fortress of Utopia* - Jack Williamson   *s*   5863

**Carvalho, Edson** (Spy)
*Cradle of Splendor* - Patricia Anthony   *s*   158

**Carver, Alison** (Journalist)
*Cup of Clay* - Carole Nelson Douglas   *f*   1583

**Carver, Alison** (Journalist; Shaman)
*Seed upon the Wind* - Carole Nelson
   Douglas   *f*   1584

**Carver, David** (Child)
*Desperation* - Stephen King   *h*   3129

**Carver, Reggie** (Detective—Private)
*Harvest of Blood* - Vincent Courtney   *h*   1213

**Carver, Zachary** (Police Officer)
*Soul Snatchers* - Michael Cecilione   *h*   947

**Carville, Rebecca** (Scholar)
*Lord of the Dead* - Tom Holland   *h*   2741

**Casad, Sasha** (Teenager)
*Bodyguard* - William C. Dietz   *s*   1542

**Casaubon** (Magician; Spouse; Nobleman)
*The Architecture of Desire* - Mary Gentle   *f*   2195

**Casaubon** (Nobleman; Magician)
*Rats and Gargoyles* - Mary Gentle   *f*   2196

**Case, David** (Worker)
*Boundaries* - T.M. Wright   *h*   5990

**Case, Jamie** (Child; Prisoner)
*Wheels of Fire* - Mercedes Lackey   *f*   3301

**Casey** (Royalty)
*With Full Honors* - Donald E. McQuinn   *s*   3865

**Casey, Jerry** (Teenager; Refugee)
*Cold Allies* - Patricia Anthony   *s*   157

**Casey, Matt** (Musician)
*Our Lady of the Harbour* - Charles de Lint   *f*   1434

**Casey, Paddy** (Engineer; Spaceman)
*The Rising* - James Doohan   *s*   1579

**Casipriadin, Luba** (Artist)
*Scissors Cut Paper Wrap Stone* - Ian
   McDonald   *s*   3795

**Caspar** (Teenager)
*The Ogre Downstairs* - Diana Wynne Jones   *f*   2949

**Caspode the Wonder Dog** (Animal)
*Moving Pictures* - Terry Pratchett   *f*   4398

**Casruel, Aru** (Adventurer; Immigrant)
*Mother of Storms* - Adrian Cole   *f*   1101

**Cassandra** (Vampire)
*Sweet Myth-tery of Life* - Robert Asprin   *f*   262

**Cassia** (Teenager; Religious)
*The Cult of Loving Kindness* - Paul Park   *s*   4242

**Cassiday, Robert** (Government Official)
*Otherworld* - Kenneth C. Flint   *h*   1959

**Cassidy** (Horse Trainer; Amnesiac)
*The Persistence of Memory* - Karen Ripley   *s*   4592

**Cassidy, Katherine Sweeney** (Anthropologist)
*Waking the Moon* - Elizabeth Hand   *f*   2538

**Cassidy, Lylah** (Professor; Murderer)
*Looker* - Jorge Saralegui   *h*   4820

**Castanaveras, Denice** (Telepath; Genetically Altered
   Being)
*The Last Dancer* - Daniel Keys Moran   *s*   3994
*The Long Run* - Daniel Keys Moran   *s*   3995

**Castanaveras, Trent** (Thief; Computer Expert)
*The Long Run* - Daniel Keys Moran   *s*   3995

**Casteel, Luke Jr.** (Relative)
*Gates of Paradise* - V.C. Andrews   *h*   145

**Casteel, Luke Jr.** (Young Man)
*Web of Dreams* - V.C. Andrews   *h*   147

**Castellan, Basil** (Military Personnel)
*Prince of Sunset* - Steve White   *s*   5786

**Castillo, Lourdes Maria** (Young Woman)
*The Halloween Man* - Douglas Clegg   *h*   1080

**Castle, Charles** (Photographer)
*Photographing Fairies* - Steve Szilagyi   *f*   5379

**Castle, Hunter** (Businessman)
*The Six Families* - Nancy Holder   *s*   2733

**Castlemaine, Sylvester** (Criminal)
*The Hemingway Hoax* - Joe Haldeman   *s*   2489

**Castor, Charlie** (Technician)
*Operation Damocles* - Oscar L. Fellows   *s*   1916

**Cat** (Animal)
*Better than Life* - Grant Naylor   *s*   4076

**Cat** (Thief; Handicapped)
*Mistworld* - Simon R. Green   *s*   2372

**Cat** (Animal; Companion)
*Cat's Paw* - L.A. Taylor   *f*   5409

**Cat** (Animal)
*The Wild Hunt* - Jane Yolen   *f*   6042

**Cat "Bian"** (Psychic)
*Dreamfall* - Joan D. Vinge   *s*   5571

**Catahn, Ren** (Leader)
*The Crystal Rose* - Maya Kaathryn Bohnhoff   *f*   560

**Catalano, Serena** (Businesswoman; Organized
   Crime Figure)
*Protektor* - Charles Platt   *s*   4342

**Catalina, Mother** (Religious)
*Yesterday We Saw Mermaids* - Esther
Friesner  *f*  2086

**Catch** (Demon)
*Practical Demonkeeping* - Christopher
Moore  *h*  3989

**Catcher, Selene** (Scholar; Religious)
*Renaissance Moon* - Linda Nevins  *f*  4093

**Catchstraw** (Prehistoric Human)
*People of the Sea* - W. Michael Gear  *f*  2169

**Catelyn** (Noblewoman)
*A Game of Thrones* - George R.R. Martin  *f*  3645

**Catherine** (Alien)
*Flying to Valhalla* - Charles Pellegrino  *s*  4280

**Catherine** (Adventurer)
*Myst: The Book of D'ni* - Rand Miller  *f*  3897

**Catherine** (Religious)
*Phoenix Cafe* - Gwyneth Jones  *s*  2954

**Catledge, Sue** (Doctor)
*Vampire Beat* - Vincent Courtney  *h*  1214

**Catti-Brie** (Mythical Creature; Adventurer)
*The Silent Blade* - R.A. Salvatore  *f*  4805

**Cavan, Andrew** (Government Official)
*Mirror to the Sky* - Mark S. Geston  *s*  2213

**Cavanagh, Pheylan** (Spaceship Captain)
*Conqueror's Pride* - Timothy Zahn  *s*  6051

**Cavanagh, Stewart** (Businessman; Political Figure)
*Conqueror's Pride* - Timothy Zahn  *s*  6051

**Cavanaugh, Carter** (Vampire)
*The Vampire's Apprentice* - Richard Lee
Byers  *h*  799

**Cavanaugh, Robert** (FBI Agent)
*Oaths and Miracles* - Nancy Kress  *s*  3242

**Cave, Clea/Richard** (Actress)
*The Need* - Andrew Neiderman  *h*  4089

**Cavewood, Matthew** (Historian)
*Belladonna* - Michael Stewart  *h*  5271

**Cavish, Beka** (Warrior; Teenager)
*Stalking Darkness* - Lynn Flewelling  *f*  1953

**Cayne, Candy** (Teenager; Fanatic)
*Cold Iron* - Melisa Michaels  *f*  3886

**CBN-001 "Caliban"** (Robot)
*Caliban* - Roger MacBride Allen  *s*  77

**C'boath, Joruus** (Psychic)
*Dark Force Rising* - Timothy Zahn  *s*  6052

**Cedar, Hugh Rock** (Administrator; Engineer)
*Fossil* - Hal Clement  *s*  1083

**Cedar, Janice** (Researcher; Spouse)
*Fossil* - Hal Clement  *s*  1083

**Cedric** (Military Personnel; Political Figure)
*One for the Morning Glory* - John Barnes  *f*  355

**Cedric** (Teenager)
*Strings* - Dave Duncan  *s*  1689

**Cefwyn** (Royalty)
*Fortress in the Eye of Time* - C.J. Cherryh  *f*  991
*Fortress of Eagles* - C.J. Cherryh  *f*  992
*Fortress of Owls* - C.J. Cherryh  *f*  993

**Celeste** (Religious)
*Private Demons* - Robert Masello  *h*  3660

**Celia** (Robot)
*Automated Alice* - Jeff Noon  *f*  4134

**Celine, Sigismundo** (Magician; Musician)
*Nature's God* - Robert Anton Wilson  *f*  5903

**Celluci, Mike** (Detective—Police)
*Blood Debt* - Tanya Huff  *h*  2792

**Celluci, Mike** (Police Officer)
*Blood Price* - Tanya Huff  *h*  2793
*Blood Trail* - Tanya Huff  *h*  2794

**Celyn, Imp y** (Musician)
*Soul Music* - Terry Pratchett  *f*  4401

**Centaur, Cathryn** (Mythical Creature; Guide)
*Faun & Games* - Piers Anthony  *f*  169

**Centaur, Che** (Mythical Creature)
*Isle of View* - Piers Anthony  *f*  177

**Center, Fisk** (Businessman)
*Hard Sell* - Piers Anthony  *s*  173

**Central "CC" Computer** (Artificial Intelligence)
*Steel Beach* - John Varley  *s*  5566

**Centuri, Ariann** (Military Personnel; Religious)
*Half-Light* - Denise Vitola  *s*  5575

**Cephus** (Farmer; Revolutionary)
*Flickering Shadows* - Kwadwo Agymah
Kamau  *f*  3006

**Cept, Claire** (Professor)
*Bring Me Children* - David Martin  *h*  3637

**Cerdic** (Royalty; Warrior)
*Shadow of the King* - Helen Hollick  *f*  2747

**Cerebus** (Artificial Intelligence; Imposter)
*When Dreams Collide* - Wm. Mark
Simmons  *f*  5063

**Ceridwen** (Witch)
*Dragonslayer's Return* - R.A. Salvatore  *f*  4798

**Cerise** (Adventurer)
*Cardmaster* - Clayton Emery  *f*  1813

**Cerise** (Computer Expert; Lesbian)
*Trouble and Her Friends* - Melissa Scott  *s*  4902

**Cermit, Abasio** (Traveler)
*A Plague of Angels* - Sheri S. Tepper  *f*  5433

**Cerryl** (Wizard; Apprentice)
*The White Order* - L.E. Modesitt Jr.  *f*  3942

**Cervantes, Micah Miguel** (Artist)
*Harmony* - Marjorie Bradley Kellogg  *s*  3046

**Cge** (Robot; Sidekick)
*Backblast* - Lee McKeone  *s*  3828
*The Clone Crisis* - Lee McKeone  *s*  3829

**Cha-kwena** (Shaman; Prehistoric Human)
*The Edge of the World* - William Sarabande  *f*  4817
*Thunder in the Sky* - William Sarabande  *f*  4819

**Cha'dune, Hezhi Yehd** (Royalty; Fugitive)
*The Blackgod* - J. Gregory Keyes  *f*  3095

**Cha'dune, Hezhi Yehd** (Royalty)
*The Waterborn* - J. Gregory Keyes  *f*  3098

**Chagak** (Prehistoric Human; Indian)
*Mother Earth, Father Sky* - Sue Harrison  *f*  2581

**Chakallakak, Chakallakak "Chaka" ngha** (Alien;
Teenager)
*The Long Hunt* - Debra Doyle  *s*  1602

**Chakliux** (Storyteller; Handicapped)
*Song of the River* - Sue Harrison  *f*  2583

**Chakotay** (Military Personnel; Indian)
*Pathways* - Jeri Taylor  *s*  5404
*Ragnarok* - Nathan Archer  *s*  206

**Chakthi** (Leader; Warrior)
*Exile's Challenge* - Angus Wells  *f*  5734

**Chalaine** (Sorceress)
*Dark Mirror, Dark Dreams* - Sharon Green  *f*  2357
*The Hidden Realms* - Sharon Green  *f*  2358

**Chalkin** (Leader)
*Dragonseye* - Anne McCaffrey  *s*  3730

**Challer, Bo** (Teenager)
*A Whisper of Wings* - Steven Ray Fulgham  *h*  2091

**Chalmers, Frank** (Administrator; Scientist)
*Red Mars* - Kim Stanley Robinson  *s*  4635

**Chalmers, Polly** (Businesswoman)
*Needful Things* - Stephen King  *h*  3137

**Chalmers, Reed** (Psychologist; Adventurer)
*The Enchanter Reborn* - L. Sprague de
Camp  *f*  1413

**Chambers, Christel** (Relative)
*The Misconceiver* - Lucy Ferriss  *s*  1929

**Chambers, Peter** (Anthropologist)
*Sleepwalker* - Michael Cadnum  *h*  815

**Chambers, Phoebe** (Criminal; Computer Expert)
*The Misconceiver* - Lucy Ferriss  *s*  1929

**Champion, Dragonbait** (Religious; Alien)
*Masquerades* - Kate Novak  *f*  4166

**Champion, Dragonbait** (Alien; Warrior)
*Song of the Saurials* - Kate Novak  *f*  4167

**Champion, Ned** (Student)
*The Wilds* - Richard Laymon  *h*  3373

**Chamtong, Onua** (Animal Trainer; Adventurer)
*Wild Magic* - Tamora Pierce  *f*  4323

**Chan** (Military Personnel)
*Dragon's Blood* - Alex McDonough  *s*  3799

**Chan, Dahlia** (Entertainer; Artificial Intelligence)
*Cytheria* - Richard Calder  *s*  835

**Chance, Angela** (Time Traveler; Student—Graduate)
*Time Station Berlin* - David Evans  *s*  1852

**Chance, David** (Orphan)
*Brain Child* - George Turner  *s*  5491

**Chance, Lester** (Historian; Mentally Ill Person)
*Blue Light* - Walter Mosley  *s*  4042

**Chancel, Davey** (Editor)
*The Hellfire Club* - Peter Straub  *h*  5326

**Chancel, Nora** (Housewife)
*The Hellfire Club* - Peter Straub  *h*  5326

**Chandler, Jay** (Archaeologist)
*Lord of the Dark Lake* - Ron Faust  *h*  1894

**Chandler, Jeff** (Government Official)
*Deus-X: A Novel of Spiritual Terror* - Joseph A.
Citro  *h*  1037

**Chandler, Joshua "the Whistler" Jeremiah** (Bounty
Hunter; Murderer)
*Oracle* - Mike Resnick  *s*  4551

**Chandler, Karen** (Parent)
*Solomon's Knife* - Victor Koman  *s*  3200

**Chandler, Sam** (Architect)
*Devil's Gate* - Elizabeth Ergas  *h*  1833

**Chandler, Vicki** (Doctor)
*Resurrection Dreams* - Richard Laymon  *h*  3371

**Chandler, Zinc** (Police Officer)
*Cutthroat* - Michael Slade  *h*  5084

**Chandler, Zinc** (Detective)
*Evil Eye* - Michael Slade  *h*  5085

**Chandra** (Wizard; Royalty)
*The Fire's Stone* - Tanya Huff  *f*  2796

**Chaney** (Military Personnel)
*Crown of Empire* - Chelsea Quinn Yarbro  *s*  6014

**Chang, Deanna** (Teenager; Outcast)
*Scorpion Shards* - Neal Shusterman  *s*  5013

**Chang, Emily** (Musician)
*Night Magic* - Thomas Tryon  *h*  5485

**Chang, Marte** (Inventor; Government Official)
*Burn* - Bill Ransom  *s*  4476
*ViraVax* - Bill Ransom  *s*  4478

**Chang, Mavra** (Immortal; Chieftain)
*Echoes of the Well of Souls* - Jack L.
    Chalker   s   953

**Chang, Mavra** (Immortal)
*Gods of the Well of Souls* - Jack L. Chalker   s   954
*Shadow of the Well of Souls* - Jack L.
    Chalker   s   961

**Chang, Steve** (Time Traveler)
*Warrior* - William F. Wu   s   6000

**Changer** (Supernatural Being)
*Changer* - Jane M. Lindskold   f   3474

**Chanly, Bel, Margasdotter** (Warrior; Guide)
*The Outskirter's Secret* - Rosemary Kirstein   s   3157

**Channon** (Alien; Diplomat)
*Target* - Janet Morris   s   4017

**Chanur, Hilfy** (Alien; Spaceship Captain)
*Chanur's Legacy* - C.J. Cherryh   s   981

**Chao, Larry O'Shawnessy** (Scientist)
*The Ring of Charon* - Roger MacBride Allen   s   80
*The Shattered Sphere* - Roger MacBride Allen   s   81

**Chapel, Christine** (Nurse; Military Personnel)
*Crossroad* - Barbara Hambly   s   2501

**Chapel, Helen** (Accountant)
*Red Bride* - Christopher Fowler   h   2019

**Chapel, John** (Public Relations)
*Red Bride* - Christopher Fowler   h   2019

**Chapin, Francis** (Teacher)
*Blood of Innocents* - John Arbucci   h   204

**Chapman, Annie** (Prostitute)
*From Hell* - Alan Moore   h   3987

**Chapman, Julie** (Scientist)
*Mr. Sandman* - Lyle Howard   h   2779

**Chapman, Merrick** (Detective—Police)
*Daughter of Darkness* - Steven Spruill   h   5183

**Chapman, Merrick** (Detective; Vampire)
*Rulers of Darkness* - Steven Spruill   h   5185

**Chapman, Tony** (Museum Curator)
*Desmond: A Novel of Love and the Modern Vampire* -
    Ulysses G. Dietz   h   1541

**Chapman, Zane** (Vampire)
*Daughter of Darkness* - Steven Spruill   h   5183
*Rulers of Darkness* - Steven Spruill   h   5185

**Chappy** (Prisoner)
*The End of Alice* - A.M. Homes   h   2755

**Charlemagne** (Historical Figure; Ruler)
*His Majesty's Elephant* - Judith Tarr   f   5394

**Charles** (Nobleman; Vampire)
*Daughter of the Night* - Elaine Bergstrom   h   463

**Charles, Ellen Cherry** (Artist; Waiter/Waitress)
*Skinny Legs and All* - Tom Robbins   f   4607

**Charlie** (Nurse; Military Personnel)
*Chains of Light* - Quentin Thomas   s   5449

**Charlie** (Alien)
*Neptune Crossing* - Jeffrey A. Carver   s   933
*Strange Attractors* - Jeffrey A. Carver   s   934

**Charlie/Charlene** (Alien)
*The Infinite Sea* - Jeffrey A. Carver   s   932

**Charlotte "Lottie"** (Child)
*Santa's Twin* - Dean R. Koontz   f   3214

**Charly** (Musician)
*The Making of a Monster* - Gail Petersen   h   4307

**Charming** (Hero; Royalty)
*Slay and Rescue* - John Moore   f   3991

**Chase** (Military Personnel)
*Deathweave* - Cary Osborne   s   4226

**Chase, Adam** (Photographer)
*Nocturnas* - Shawn Ryan   h   4755

**Chase, Danny** (Teenager)
*The Magic Bicycle* - William Hill   f   2688

**Chase, J. Kelsey** (Diver)
*Between the Devil and the Deep* - J.M.
    Morgan   h   3998

**Chase, Jason** (Businessman; Martial Arts Expert)
*Night's Pawn* - Tom Dowd   s   1591

**Chase, Max** (Child)
*White Shark* - Peter Benchley   h   441

**Chase, Richard** (FBI Agent)
*The Devouring* - Douglas D. Hawk   h   2615

**Chase, Simon** (Scientist)
*White Shark* - Peter Benchley   h   441

**Chase-Frisson L'Zalle, Trevarre** (Stowaway;
    Teenager)
*Shivering World* - Kathy Tyers   s   5526

**Chasen, Liz** (Writer)
*Demon Night* - J. Michael Straczynski   h   5322

**Chasse, Lois** (Aged Person)
*Insomnia* - Stephen King   h   3135

**Chato del Klinne** (Indian)
*Ghost Dance* - Kathryn Ptacek   h   4441

**Chatwin, Jack** (Psychic)
*Ancient Echoes* - Robert Holdstock   f   2735

**Chauvin, Rene** (Businessman)
*The Gris-Gris Man* - Don Davis   h   1403

**Chavez, Rafael** (Waiter/Waitress)
*Black Night* - S.J. Strayhorn   h   5334

**Che, Ya** (Criminal)
*The Spider #3: Death's Crimson Juggernaut/The Red
    Death Rain* - Grant Stockbridge   f   5307

**Chedo, Gral II** (Alien)
*Random Factor* - Joel Henry Sherman   s   4984

**Chee, Diren** (Nobleman; Villain)
*House of Moons* - K.D. Wentworth   s   5752

**Cheever, Shelby V** (Teenager; Heir)
*The Billion Dollar Boy* - Charles Sheffield   s   4948

**Chekhov, Anton** (Writer; Historical Figure)
*Chekhov's Journey* - Ian Watson   s   5633

**Chekov, Pavel** (Military Personnel; Space Explorer)
*The Ashes of Eden* - William Shatner   s   4927
*The Disinherited* - Peter David   s   1381
*Traitor Winds* - L.A. Graf   s   2298
*War Dragons* - L.A. Graf   s   2299
*Windows on a Lost World* - V.E. Mitchell   s   3920

**Chen, David** (Artist; Computer Expert)
*Chimera* - Mary Rosenblum   s   4677

**Chen, Harry** (Deity; Addict)
*The Seraphim Rising* - Elisabeth De Vos   s   1442

**Chen, Kao** (Military Personnel)
*Beneath the Tree of Heaven* - David
    Wingrove   s   5917

**Chen, Laura** (Friend)
*Resurrection Man* - Sean Stewart   f   5277

**Chen, Robert** (Teacher; Spaceman)
*Starseed* - Spider Robinson   s   4643

**Chen, Tam** (Businessman)
*Phoenix Fire* - Elizabeth Forrest   f   1974

**Chen Li** (Young Woman)
*Twisted Images* - Don D'Ammassa   h   1335

**Chentelle** (Singer; Mythical Creature)
*Quest for the Fallen Star* - Piers Anthony   f   185

**Cheops** (Reanimated Dead)
*The Mummy!: A Tale of the Twenty-Second Century* -
    Jane Webb Loudon   h   3526

**Chernevog, Kavi** (Wizard)
*Chernevog* - C.J. Cherryh   f   982

**Chernevog, Kavi** (Spirit)
*Yvgenie* - C.J. Cherryh   f   1005

**Cheryl** (Vampire)
*Sex and the Single Vampire* - Nancy
    Kilpatrick   h   3114

**Chessner, Barbara** (Real Estate Agent)
*Infernal Affairs* - Jane Heller   h   2652

**Chester** (Animal)
*Return to Howliday Inn* - James Howe   f   2786

**Chet** (Supernatural Being)
*Thirsty* - M.T. Anderson   h   120

**Chevenga** (Ruler)
*Shadow's Son* - Shirley Meier   f   3872

**Chevenga, Fourth** (Heir; Ruler)
*Lion's Heart* - Karen Wehrstein   f   5683

**Chevenga, Fourth** (Ruler)
*Lion's Soul* - Karen Wehrstein   f   5684

**Chevette** (Postal Worker; Fugitive)
*Virtual Light* - William Gibson   s   2219

**Chewbacca** (Alien; Adventurer)
*The Crystal Star* - Vonda N. McIntyre   s   3820
*Jedi Search* - Kevin J. Anderson   s   109

**Chi-da** (Alien)
*Wulfsyarn: A Mosaic* - Phillip Mann   s   3617

**Chiara** (Professor; Fugitive)
*The Thirteenth Daughter of the Moon* - Steven
    Nightingale   f   4104

**Chibisov** (Military Personnel)
*Red Army* - Ralph Peters   s   4306

**Chicago, Pasquale** (Businessman)
*A King of Infinite Space* - Allen Steele   s   5243

**Chichelski, Chango** (Mutant; Thief)
*Accidental Creatures* - Anne Harris   s   2558

**Chien-Chu, Sergi** (Counselor)
*Legion of the Damned* - William C. Dietz   s   1547

**Chilke, Eustace** (Police Officer)
*Throy* - Jack Vance   s   5550

**Chin, Ah Kin** (Worker; Wanderer)
*Sarah Canary* - Karen Joy Fowler   f   2028

**Chin, Gun Roh** (Spaceship Captain)
*The Ninety Trillion Fausts* - Jack L. Chalker   s   958

**Chin, Gun Roh** (Pilot)
*The Run to Chaos Keep* - Jack L. Chalker   s   960

**Chinnery, Thomas** (Apothecary; Trader)
*Bhagavati* - Kara Dalkey   f   1316

**Chinnery, Thomas** (Apothecary; Prisoner)
*Bijapur* - Kara Dalkey   f   1317

**Chinnery, Thomas** (Sailor; Apothecary)
*Blood of the Goddess* - Kara Dalkey   f   1318

**Chior** (Leader; Scientist)
*OtherWise* - Margaret Wander Bonanno   s   567

**Chios, Maia** (Student; Heiress)
*Dragon Season* - Michael Cassutt   f   936

**Chip** (Artificial Intelligence; Companion)
*A King of Infinite Space* - Allen Steele   s   5243

**Chiron Cat's Eye in Draco** (Time Traveler)
*Summer of Love* - Lisa Mason   s   3664

**Chirwl** (Alien; Health Care Professional)
*Medicine Show* - Jody Lynn Nye   s   4172

**Chisolm, Casey** (Religious)
*Symphony* - Charles L. Grant   h   2318

**Chli-pou-ni** (Animal)
*Empire of the Ants* - Bernard Werber   s   5755

**Chloe** (Teenager)
*Camp Vamp* - Elvira   h   1801

**Chlorine** (Runaway; Adventurer)
*Yon Ill Wind* - Piers Anthony  *f*  196

**Chmeee** (Alien)
*The Ringworld Throne* - Larry Niven  *s*  4128

**Chomanche** (Religious; Alien)
*A Miracle of Rare Design* - Mike Resnick  *s*  4550

**Chornyak, Delina Meloran** (Linguist; Scientist)
*Earthsong* - Suzette Haden Elgin  *s*  1769

**Chornyak, Nazareth Joanna** (Disembodied
  Personality)
*Earthsong* - Suzette Haden Elgin  *s*  1769

**Chowdhury, Ralph** (Scientist)
*Sparrowhawk* - Thomas A. Easton  *s*  1725

**Choy, Mary** (Police Officer)
*/ -* Greg Bear  *s*  413
*Queen of Angels* - Greg Bear  *s*  423

**Chrestil, Damian** (Alien; Businessman)
*Burning Bright* - Melissa Scott  *s*  4894

**Chris** (Traveler)
*The Tattooed Map* - Barbara Hodgson  *f*  2706

**Chris** (Teenager; Vampire)
*Thirsty* - M.T. Anderson  *h*  120

**Christensen, Maryanne "Maggie"** (Warrior;
  Girlfriend; Martial Arts Expert)
*The Crimson Sky* - Joel Rosenberg  *f*  4669

**Christensen, Maryanne "Maggie"** (Martial Arts
  Expert; Girlfriend)
*The Silver Stone* - Joel Rosenberg  *f*  4676

**Christian, Fletcher** (Historical Figure; Reanimated
  Dead)
*Conflict* - Peter F. Hamilton  *s*  2522

**Christian, Karl** (Spaceship Captain)
*The Starlight Crystal* - Christopher Pike  *s*  4333

**Christian, Paige** (Teenager; Space Explorer)
*The Starlight Crystal* - Christopher Pike  *s*  4333

**Christian, Reese** (Bounty Hunter)
*Shadows* - Kimberly Rangel  *h*  4472

**Christiansen, Mitch** (Military Personnel)
*Killjoy* - Elizabeth Forrest  *h*  1973

**Christie** (Student)
*The Informers* - Brett Easton Ellis  *h*  1778

**Christie, Lynne De Lisle** (Diplomat)
*Ancient Light* - Mary Gentle  *s*  2194

**Christman, Barbara** (Investigator)
*Sole Survivor* - Dean R. Koontz  *h*  3215

**Christmas** (Thief)
*The Widowmaker* - Mike Resnick  *s*  4559

**Christopher** (Child; Vampire)
*The Silver Kiss* - Annette Curtis Klause  *f*  3163

**Ch*Tril** (Animal)
*Into the Deep* - Ken Grimwood  *s*  2450

**Chu** (Police Officer)
*Stations of the Tide* - Michael Swanwick  *s*  5373

**Chuck** (Animal)
*Hong on the Range* - William F. Wu  *s*  5997

**Chucky** (Disembodied Personality; Murderer)
*Child's Play III* - Matthew J. Costello  *h*  1194

**Chung, Feng Hwa** (Drug Dealer)
*Gold Dragon* - Robert Cain  *s*  831

**Church, Andy** (Foreman)
*Where the Chill Waits* - T. Chris
  Martindale  *h*  3658

**Church, Louis Edward** (Police Officer)
*Whisper* - Raymond Van Over  *h*  5539

**Church, Thomas** (Religious)
*The Gaia Websters* - Kim Antieau  *s*  198

**Churchill, Winston** (Historical Figure; Political
  Figure)
*Triumph* - Ben Bova  *s*  598

**Chuut-Riit** (Alien)
*The Children's Hour* - Jerry Pournelle  *s*  4372

**Chyrie** (Mythical Creature)
*Greendaughter* - Anne Logston  *f*  3510

**Ciara** (Noblewoman)
*Ciara's Song* - Andre Norton  *f*  4146

**Cidiera "Cid"** (Scientist; Lesbian)
*The Nature of Smoke* - Anne Harris  *s*  2559

**Cierto, Hoja** (Martial Arts Expert; Teacher)
*Black Steel* - Steve Perry  *s*  4291

**Cigany** (Gypsy)
*The Gypsy* - Steven Brust  *f*  744

**Cilla** (Companion; Heroine)
*Heroes, Inc.* - Kyle Crocco  *f*  1268

**Cilla** (Heroine; Companion)
*Heroes Wanted* - Kyle Crocco  *f*  1267

**Cimorene** (Royalty)
*Calling on Dragons* - Patricia C. Wrede  *f*  5974
*Dealing with Dragons* - Patricia C. Wrede  *f*  5975

**Cimorene** (Royalty; Companion)
*Searching for Dragons* - Patricia C. Wrede  *f*  5979

**Cincinnati, Chime** (Guardian; Religious)
*Last Refuge* - Elizabeth Ann Scarborough  *f*  4866

**Cincinnatus** (Worker; Spy)
*The Great War: American Front* - Harry
  Turtledove  *s*  5501

**Cind** (Military Personnel; Girlfriend)
*Empire's End* - Allan Cole  *s*  1103

**Cissie** (Young Woman)
*'48* - James Herbert  *h*  2667

**Civet** (Witch)
*Dragon Cauldron* - Laurence Yep  *f*  6024

**Claiborne, Adam** (Doctor)
*Psycho II* - Robert Bloch  *h*  541

**Claiborne, Adam** (Businessman)
*Sacred Prey* - Vivian Schilling  *h*  4875

**Claiborne, Dolores** (Aged Person)
*Dolores Claiborne* - Stephen King  *h*  3130

**Claiborne, Kevin** (Inventor; Political Figure)
*Pacific Edge* - Kim Stanley Robinson  *s*  4634

**Claiborne, Kyle** (Criminal)
*Sacred Prey* - Vivian Schilling  *h*  4875

**Claire** (Military Personnel; Governess)
*The Night Watch* - Sean Stewart  *f*  5274

**Clanton, Otis** (Aged Person)
*The Sixth Dog* - Jane Rice  *h*  4582

**Clare, Peter** (Writer)
*The Vanishment* - Jonathan Aycliffe  *h*  282

**Claridge, Kit** (Doctor; Spacewoman)
*The Sails of Tau Ceti* - Michael McCollum  *s*  3771

**Clark, Darcy** (Spy)
*Deadspawn* - Brian Lumley  *h*  3550

**Clark, Elliot** (Police Officer)
*Cold Whisper* - Rick Hautala  *h*  2605

**Clark, Jennifer** (Artist)
*Torments* - Lisa Cantrell  *h*  873

**Clark, Joe** (Student—College)
*Fiend* - C. Dean Andersson  *h*  138

**Clark, Steve** (Teenager)
*Disturbing Behavior* - John Whitman  *h*  5789

**Clarkson, Wade** (Doctor)
*Retribution* - Elizabeth Forrest  *h*  1975

**Clarkston, Rachel** (Spirit)
*Waltz with Evil* - P.D. Rozzi  *h*  4701

**Clarkston, Tommy** (Child)
*Waltz with Evil* - P.D. Rozzi  *h*  4701

**Claro** (Alien)
*An Eye for Dark Places* - Norma Marder  *s*  3622

**Clarris, Peter** (Genetically Altered Being; Mythical
  Creature)
*Changeling* - Christopher Kubasik  *f*  3245

**Class, Julian** (Military Personnel; Scientist)
*Forever Peace* - Joe Haldeman  *s*  2488

**Clattuc, Glawen** (Police Officer)
*Ecce and Old Earth* - Jack Vance  *s*  5546
*Throy* - Jack Vance  *s*  5550

**Claude** (Robot; Sidekick)
*Title Deleted for Security Reasons* - Ed
  Blome  *s*  553

**Claudia** (Scientist; Anthropologist)
*Agviq* - Michael Armstrong  *s*  208

**Claudia** (Addict)
*The Hanged Man* - Francesca Lia Block  *f*  548

**Claudius** (Vampire)
*Vampire Diary: The Embrace* - Robert
  Weinberg  *h*  5705

**Claus, Anya** (Spouse)
*Santa Steps Out: A Fairy Tale for Grownups* - Robert
  Devereaux  *h*  1506

**Claus, Bob "Santa"** (Imposter; Relative)
*Santa's Twin* - Dean R. Koontz  *f*  3214

**Clavel** (Alien; Writer)
*North Wind* - Gwyneth Jones  *s*  2953

**Clavius, Black** (Spaceman; Wanderer)
*Glory* - Alfred Coppel  *s*  1182

**Clay, John Sebastian** (Mercenary)
*A Landscape of Darkness* - John Blair  *s*  513

**Clay, Tom Red** (Diplomat)
*Being Alien* - Rebecca Ore  *s*  4217
*Human to Human* - Rebecca Ore  *s*  4219

**Clayborn, Robert** (Scientist)
*Phylum Monsters* - Hayford Peirce  *s*  4276

**Clayborne, Ann** (Scientist; Aged Person)
*Blue Mars* - Kim Stanley Robinson  *s*  4629

**Clayborne, Laura** (Journalist; Parent)
*Mine* - Robert R. McCammon  *h*  3756

**Clayborne, Martin** (Businessman)
*Darkman #2: The Price of Fear* - Randall
  Boyll  *h*  613

**Clayburn, Karl Thomas** (Writer)
*Buried Screams* - C. Dean Andersson  *h*  137

**Claypoole, Chester "Chet" W.** (Businessman;
  Television)
*Live From Golgotha: A Novel* - Gore Vidal  *s*  5569

**Claypoole, Rachman** (Military Personnel)
*School of Fire* - David Sherman  *s*  4982

**Clayton, Wilbur** (Guard)
*Tunnelvision* - R. Patrick Gates  *h*  2162

**Cleary, Quinn** (Student)
*The Select* - F. Paul Wilson  *h*  5897

**Cleave, Peter** (Doctor)
*Asylum* - Patrick McGrath  *h*  3812

**Cleedis** (Warrior)
*King Pinch* - David Cook  *f*  1146

**Cleg, Dennis "Spider"** (Patient)
*Spider* - Patrick McGrath  *h*  3815

**Cleg, Horace** (Parent; Maintenance Worker)
*Spider* - Patrick McGrath  *h*  3815

**Clemens, Atta Olivia** (Vampire)
*A Candle for D'Artagnan* - Chelsea Quinn
Yarbro   *h*   6013
*Crusader's Torch* - Chelsea Quinn Yarbro   *h*   6015

**Clemens, Sam** (Journalist; Historical Figure)
*How Few Remain* - Harry Turtledove   *s*   5504

**Clement VII, Pope** (Religious)
*Scorpio* - Alex McDonough   *s*   3802

**Clementi, Nick** (Doctor; Aged Person)
*Maximum Light* - Nancy Kress   *s*   3241

**Clements, Yolanda Free** (Police Officer)
*Alien Heat* - Lynn S. Hightower   *s*   2684

**Clemmy** (Teenager)
*The Fools' War* - Lee Kisling   *f*   3159

**Clendannan, Cherrid ris** (Military Personnel)
*Death's Gray Land* - Mike Shupp   *s*   5011

**Cleo** (Passenger)
*Checkmate* - Eric T. Baker   *s*   297

**Cleon, I** (Ruler)
*Foundation's Fear* - Gregory Benford   *s*   446

**Cleopatra** (Historical Figure; Religious)
*Throne of Isis* - Judith Tarr   *f*   5397

**Clermont, Donald** (Vintner)
*Kiss of Death* - Daniel Rhodes   *h*   4569

**Clermont, Selena** (Heiress)
*Kiss of Death* - Daniel Rhodes   *h*   4569

**Clerval, Henry** (Sports Figure; Reanimated Dead)
*Brittle Innings* - Michael Bishop   *h*   498

**Clewe, Elizabeth** (Musician)
*The Blood of Angels* - Stephen Gregory   *h*   2428

**Clewe, Harry** (Handyman)
*The Blood of Angels* - Stephen Gregory   *h*   2428

**Clewe, Zoe** (Child)
*The Blood of Angels* - Stephen Gregory   *h*   2428

**Cley** (Heroine; Human)
*Beyond the Fall of Night* - Arthur C. Clarke   *s*   1054

**Click** (Leader; Tinker)
*The Warden of Horses* - Karen Ripley   *s*   4595

**Clifford, Doug** (Diplomat)
*Ancient Light* - Mary Gentle   *s*   2194

**Climber, Artus** (Adventurer)
*The Ring of Winter* - James Lowder   *f*   3538

**Cline, Kendra** (Doctor)
*Legion of the Dead* - Geoffrey Caine   *h*   833

**Cline, Tara** (Passenger)
*Redshift Rendezvous* - John E. Stith   *s*   5305

**Clisser** (Musician; Professor)
*Dragonseye* - Anne McCaffrey   *s*   3730

**Clootie** (Wizard)
*Split Heirs* - Lawrence Watt-Evans   *f*   5649

**Cloud** (Animal; Telepath)
*Cloud's Rider* - C.J. Cherryh   *s*   983
*Rider at the Gate* - C.J. Cherryh   *s*   1000

**Cloud, Nelda** (Guardian)
*Quasar* - Jamil Nasir   *s*   4071

**Clough, Emma** (Bartender)
*Famine* - Todd Komarnicki   *h*   3201

**C'mel** (Animal; Genetically Altered Being)
*Norstrilia* - Cordwainer Smith   *s*   5105

**Coachman, Dosh** (Prostitute)
*Future Indefinite* - Dave Duncan   *f*   1678

**Coal, Hugo** (Nobleman; Handicapped)
*The Grotesque* - Patrick McGrath   *h*   3814

**Cobal, Flysse** (Waiter/Waitress)
*Exile's Children* - Angus Wells   *f*   5735

**Cobalt** (Animal)
*Deadly Vengeance* - Stephen R. George   *h*   2199
*Legacy of Steel* - Mary H. Herbert   *f*   2675

**Cobb, Phoebe** (Receptionist)
*Everville* - Clive Barker   *h*   338

**Cobblepot, Oswald "the Penguin"** (Criminal)
*Batman Returns* - Craig Shaw Gardner   *s*   2124
*The Further Adventures of Batman 2: Featuring the
Penguin* - Martin H. Greenberg   *s*   2391

**Cobham, James** (Writer; Wealthy)
*Freedom & Necessity* - Steven Brust   *f*   743

**Cobham, Richard** (Writer; Wealthy)
*Freedom & Necessity* - Steven Brust   *f*   743

**Cobri, Alex** (Computer Expert)
*Grounded!* - Chris Claremont   *s*   1041

**Cobri, Amy** (Businesswoman; Socialite)
*Sundowner* - Chris Claremont   *s*   1043

**Cocciolone, Carol Jeanne** (Scientist; Genius)
*Lovelock* - Orson Scott Card   *s*   892

**Cochran, Sid** (Vintner)
*Earthquake Weather* - Tim Powers   *f*   4382

**Cochrane, Miles "David Gilman"** (Scientist;
Mentally Ill Person)
*Alpha Centauri* - William Barton   *s*   378

**Cochrane, Richard** (Actor)
*Time and Chance* - Alan Brennert   *f*   676

**Cochrane, Rick** (Insurance Agent)
*Time and Chance* - Alan Brennert   *f*   676

**Cochrane, William** (Government Official)
*Rage of Spirits* - Noel Hynd   *h*   2824

**Cochrane, Zefrem** (Scientist; Space Explorer)
*Federation* - Judith Reeves-Stevens   *s*   4511

**Coconino** (Time Traveler; Indian)
*Children of the Earth* - Catherine Wells   *s*   5743

**Coconino** (Indian; Hunter)
*The Earth Is All That Lasts* - Catherine
Wells   *s*   5744

**Coconino** (Indian; Time Traveler)
*The Earth Saver* - Catherine Wells   *s*   5745

**Coddington, Quentin** (Psychic; Researcher)
*Strange Stains and Mysterious Smells* - Terry
Jones   *f*   2982

**Cody** (Genetically Altered Being)
*Black Milk* - Robert Reed   *s*   4504

**Cody, Will** (Vampire)
*Angel Souls and Devil Hearts* - Christopher
Golden   *h*   2255
*Of Masques and Martyrs* - Christopher
Golden   *h*   2258

**Cody, William** (Scout; Historical Figure)
*Devil's Engine* - Mark Sumner   *f*   5356

**Coeccias, Aedile** (Government Official)
*Fanuilh* - Daniel Hood   *f*   2757

**Coerlis, Jack-Jax Landsdowne** (Heir; Collector)
*Mid-Flinx* - Alan Dean Foster   *s*   2010

**Coffey, John** (Prisoner)
*The Green Mile* - Stephen King   *h*   3134

**Coffey, Malcolm "Cup"** (Teacher)
*Goat Dance* - Douglas Clegg   *h*   1079

**Cofflin, Jared** (Police Officer)
*Island in the Sea of Time* - S.M. Stirling   *s*   5295

**Cofield, Aaron** (Time Traveler; Teenager)
*Ray Bradbury Presents: Dinosaur Planet* - Stephen
Leigh   *s*   3427

**Cofield, Aaron** (Teenager; Time Traveler)
*Ray Bradbury Presents: Dinosaur World* - Stephen
Leigh   *s*   3428

**Cofort, Rael** (Spacewoman; Trader)
*Derelict for Trade* - Andre Norton   *s*   4148

**Cofort, Rael** (Doctor; Spacewoman)
*Redline the Stars* - Andre Norton   *s*   4160

**Coglin, Dennis** (Detective—Police)
*Bring on the Night* - Don Davis   *h*   1402

**Cohen, Ghenghiz "Cohen the Barbarian"** (Hero;
Aged Person)
*Interesting Times* - Terry Pratchett   *f*   4392

**Cohen, Julius** (Scientist; Settler)
*Mother of Demons* - Eric Flint   *s*   1956

**Cohen, Lauren "Laurie"** (Parent; Lesbian)
*Godmother Night* - Rachel Pollack   *f*   4358

**Cohen, Sophie** (Truck Driver)
*The Black Mariah* - Jay R. Bonansinga   *h*   570

**Cohn, Milton** (Administrator)
*Superstitious* - R.L. Stine   *h*   5290

**Coke, Matthew** (Military Personnel; Leader)
*The Sharp End* - David Drake   *s*   1643

**Colburn, Croft** (Spy)
*The Forever Drug* - Steve Perry   *s*   4296

**Cole, Cassandra** (Immortal; Martial Arts Expert)
*A Logical Magician* - Robert Weinberg   *f*   5697

**Cole, Dillon** (Teenager; Outcast)
*Scorpion Shards* - Neal Shusterman   *s*   5013

**Cole, James** (Time Traveler; Criminal)
*12 Monkeys* - Elizabeth Hand   *s*   2532

**Cole, Marcus** (Military Personnel)
*To Dream in the City of Sorrows* - Kathryn M.
Drennan   *s*   1654

**Colene** (Teenager; Adventurer)
*Chaos Mode* - Piers Anthony   *f*   165
*Fractal Mode* - Piers Anthony   *f*   171
*Virtual Mode* - Piers Anthony   *f*   194

**Coleridge, Samuel Taylor** (Writer; Historical Figure)
*Walford's Oak* - Jill M. Phillips   *f*   4310

**Coleridge, Stuart** (Police Officer)
*The Orpheus Process* - Daniel H. Gower   *h*   2293

**Colette, Sianna** (Scientist; Student)
*The Shattered Sphere* - Roger MacBride Allen   *s*   81

**Coley, J.J.** (Journalist)
*Boneman* - Lisa Cantrell   *h*   871

**Coll, Lorand** (Wizard; Farmer)
*Competition* - Sharon Green   *f*   2355

**Coll, Lorand "Lor"** (Wizard; Farmer)
*Challenges* - Sharon Green   *f*   2354
*Convergence* - Sharon Green   *f*   2356

**Colleton, Anne** (Plantation Owner)
*The Great War: American Front* - Harry
Turtledove   *s*   5501

**Colletti, Vince** (Businessman)
*Torments* - Lisa Cantrell   *h*   873

**Collier, Ben** (Time Traveler; Clone)
*A Bridge of Years* - Robert Charles Wilson   *s*   5905

**Collier, Joyce** (Businesswoman)
*The Fermata* - Nicholson Baker   *s*   302

**Collier, Marcy** (Student—College)
*Mythology 101* - Jody Lynn Nye   *f*   4173

**Collier, Rance** (Public Relations)
*Slow Freight* - F.M. Busby   *s*   785

**Collier, Samantha** (Television Personality)
*Shock Radio* - Leigh Clark   *h*   1052

**Collings, Reed** (Editor)
*Bleeder* - Gene Lazuta   *h*   3374

**Collingwood, Max** (Pilot)
*Ancient Shores* - Jack McDevitt   *s*   3786

**Collins, Amanda** (Paranormal Investigator)
*Deadly Friend* - Keith Ferrario  h  1926

**Collins, Barnabas** (Businessman; Vampire)
*Angelique's Descent* - Lara Parker  h  4246

**Collins, Camisa** (Housewife)
*Flesh and Blood* - D.A. Fowler  h  2024

**Collins, Chad** (Teenager)
*Quozl* - Alan Dean Foster  s  2013

**Collins, Elliot** (Professor)
*Dark Winds* - Graham Watkins  h  5630

**Collins, George** (Wealthy)
*The Thing That Darkness Hides* - Robert
   Morgan  h  4006

**Collins, Hap** (Worker)
*Mucho Mojo* - Joe R. Lansdale  h  3330
*Savage Season* - Joe R. Lansdale  h  3332

**Collins, Henry** (Businessman)
*The Sweetheart Season* - Karen Joy Fowler  f  2029

**Collins, Jack** (Scientist; Magician)
*A Calculated Magic* - Robert Weinberg  f  5694

**Collins, Jack** (Student)
*A Logical Magician* - Robert Weinberg  f  5697

**Collins, Karen Cecile "Casey"** (Student; Time
   Traveler)
*Islands of Tomorrow* - F.M. Busby  s  783

**Collins, Lysander** (Military Personnel; Royalty)
*Prince of Sparta* - Jerry Pournelle  s  4378

**Collins, Maggie** (Housewife; Mythical Creature)
*The Sweetheart Season* - Karen Joy Fowler  f  2029

**Collins, Rikka** (Television Personality)
*Satellite Night News* - Jack Hopkins  s  2770

**Collins, Trudy** (Divorced Person)
*Savage Season* - Joe R. Lansdale  h  3332

**Colloway, Stephen** (Writer)
*Shackled* - Ray Garton  h  2156

**Collun** (Adventurer)
*Hero's Song* - Edith Pattou  f  4261

**Colter, Daniel** (Journalist; Stowaway)
*Into the Deep* - Ken Grimwood  s  2450

**Columbar, Santiago** (Artist)
*Terminal Cafe* - Ian McDonald  s  3797

**Columbus, Christopher** (Historical Figure; Explorer)
*Pastwatch: The Redemption of Christopher Columbus* -
   Orson Scott Card  s  895

**Columcille** (Royalty; Religious)
*The Throne of Tara* - John Desjarlais  f  1498

**Colville, Randall "Ran"** (Spaceman)
*Starliner* - David Drake  s  1645

**Comfort, Isambard** (Agent; Criminal)
*The Golden Globe* - John Varley  s  5565

**Complain, Roy** (Hunter)
*Non-Stop* - Brian W. Aldiss  s  58

**Compton, Andrew** (Serial Killer; Homosexual)
*Exquisite Corpse* - Poppy Z. Brite  h  695

**The Computer** (Artificial Intelligence; Ruler)
*Extreme Paranoia: Nobody Knows the Trouble I've
   Shot* - Ken Rolston  s  4662

**Con, Val** (Spy)
*Carpe Diem* - Steve Miller  s  3907

**Conan** (Barbarian; Warrior)
*Conan and the Treasure of Python* - John Maddox
   Roberts  f  4616
*The Conan Chronicles* - Robert Jordan  f  2983
*Conan of the Red Brotherhood* - Leonard
   Carpenter  f  906
*Conan, Scourge of the Bloody Coast* - Leonard
   Carpenter  f  910
*Conan the Formidable* - Steve Perry  f  4293

*Conan the Gladiator* - Leonard Carpenter  f  907
*Conan the Guardian* - Roland J. Green  f  2347
*Conan the Indomitable* - Steve Perry  f  4294
*Conan the Outcast* - Leonard Carpenter  f  908
*Conan the Relentless* - Roland J. Green  f  2348
*Conan the Rogue* - John Maddox Roberts  f  4617
*Conan the Savage* - Leonard Carpenter  f  909
*Hour of the Dragon* - Robert E. Howard  f  2783

**Conan III** (Royalty; Child)
*Rouse a Sleeping Cat* - Dan Crawford  f  1249

**Conan III** (Ruler)
*A Wild Dog and Lone* - Dan Crawford  f  1251

**Concord, Tappuah "Tappy"** (Orphan; Mythical
   Creature)
*The Caterpillar's Question* - Piers Anthony  f  164

**Conforti, Alexandra** (Vampire)
*The Golden* - Lucius Shepard  h  4978

**Congemi, Nelson** (Doctor)
*Duplicates* - Andrew Neiderman  h  4086

**Cong15meros** (Monster)
*Conglomeros* - Jesse Browner  f  729

**Conlick, Dennis "Tunnel Rat"** (Computer Expert)
*The Hacker* - Chet Day  h  1410

**Conn** (Heir; Twin)
*The Heirs of Hammerfell* - Marion Zimmer
   Bradley  s  638

**Conn** (Slave)
*The Shining Company* - Rosemary Sutcliff  f  5359

**Connaghan, Connor** (Artisan; Landlord)
*Child of Shadows* - John Coyne  h  1236

**Connel, Eileen** (Writer)
*October* - Al Sarrantonio  h  4832

**Connelly, Misha** (Nobleman)
*Phoenix Cafe* - Gwyneth Jones  s  2954

**Connely, Mary** (Teacher)
*Blood Feud* - Sam Siciliano  h  5020

**Conner, Daphne "Dee"** (Writer)
*Cat's Eye* - William W. Johnstone  h  2928

**Conner, Katie** (Young Woman)
*Dead Lines* - John Skipp  h  5082

**Connla** (Warrior)
*The Isles of the Blest* - Morgan Llywelyn  f  3505

**Connor** (Knight)
*Merlin's Legacy: Dawn of Camelot* - Quinn Taylor
   Evans  f  1857

**Connor, Islaen** (Leader; Telepath)
*Call to Arms* - P.M. Griffin  s  2435

**Connor, Islaen** (Military Personnel)
*Fire Planet* - P.M. Griffin  s  2436
*Jungle Assault* - P.M. Griffin  s  2437

**Constable, Arbitrance** (Mythical Creature)
*Dragon Rescue* - Don Callander  f  843

**Constable, Retruance** (Mythical Creature)
*Dragon Companion* - Don Callander  f  842

**Constance** (Sorcerer)
*Down Among the Dead Men* - Simon R.
   Green  f  2367

**Constantine** (Political Figure; Revolutionary)
*City on Fire* - Walter Jon Williams  s  5835

**Constantine** (Political Figure)
*Metropolitan* - Walter Jon Williams  s  5839

**Constantine, Danny** (Journalist)
*Archangel* - Michael Conner  s  1133

**Constantine, Miquel Kaliq** (Vampire)
*Ragged Angels* - Della Van Hise  h  5537

**Consul** (Diplomat)
*Hyperion* - Dan Simmons  s  5055

**Conti, Ned** (Student)
*Madeleine's Ghost* - Robert Girardi  h  2240

**Conti, Niccolo Dei** (Explorer; Collector)
*The Venetian's Wife: A Strangely Sensual Tale of a
   Renaissance Explorer, a Computer, and a
   Metamorphosis* - Nick Bantock  f  336

**Converse, Maggie** (Journalist)
*The Burning Man* - Michael Hammond  h  2530

**Conway, H.W.** (Police Officer)
*Vyrmin* - Gene Lazuta  h  3376

**Conway, Hugh** (Diplomat)
*Shangri-La: The Return to the World of Lost Horizon* -
   Eleanor Cooney  f  1169

**Conway, Michael** (Detective—Police)
*Vyrmin* - Gene Lazuta  h  3376

**Conyers, Pamela** (Businesswoman; Fugitive)
*The Enigma Variations* - John Maddox
   Roberts  s  4618

**Coogan, Elihu "Emil Storchesson"** (Agent; Criminal)
*The Singularity Project* - F.M. Busby  s  784

**Cook, Dan** (Police Officer)
*Waltz with Evil* - P.D. Rozzi  h  4701

**Cook, Jay** (Archaeologist)
*Time Blender* - Michael Dorn  s  1581

**Cook, Jeremy** (Sailor)
*Infernal Affairs* - Jane Heller  h  2652

**Cooke, Caroline** (Doctor)
*Return of the Wolfman* - Jeff Rovin  h  4687

**Cooke, Daniel** (Mercenary)
*Surface Action* - David Drake  s  1646

**Cookie** (Cowboy)
*The Thirteenth Daughter of the Moon* - Steven
   Nightingale  f  4104

**Cooley, Dan** (Radio Personality)
*The Devil and Dan Cooley* - Holly Lisle  f  3480

**Coollege, Emma** (Spy; Military Personnel)
*Galactic MI* - Kevin D. Randle  s  4467

**Coombs, Alice** (Scientist)
*As She Climbed Across the Table* - Jonathan
   Lethem  s  3439

**Cooper** (Convict)
*In the Land of the Dead* - K.W. Jeter  h  2912

**Cooper, Arlene** (Writer)
*The Children of Hamelin* - Norman Spinrad  s  5170

**Cooper, Chaz** (Courier)
*Expiry Date* - Carol Anne Davis  h  1401

**Cooper, David** (Writer)
*Earthbound* - Richard Matheson  h  3684

**Cooper, Ellen** (Spouse)
*Earthbound* - Richard Matheson  h  3684

**Cooper, Gerald** (Businessman)
*Kings of the High Frontier* - Victor Koman  s  3199

**Cooper, Harry** (Businessman)
*Night of the Living Dead* - John Russo  h  4745

**Cooper, Marjorie** (Scientist)
*Father to the Man* - John Gribbin  s  2434

**Cope, Edward Drinker** (Scientist)
*Bone Wars* - Brett Davis  s  1398

**Cope, Seamus** (Young Man)
*Head Injuries* - Conrad Williams  h  5816

**Copley, Isabelle "Izzy"** (Artist; Student—College)
*Memory and Dream* - Charles de Lint  f  1433

**Coppercorn, Jilly** (Artist)
*The Wishing Well* - Charles de Lint  f  1441

**Copplestone, Edward** (Scientist)
*The Hunger and Ecstasy of Vampires* - Brian
   Stableford  h  5192

**Coral** (Sorceress)
*The Goblin Plain War* - Carl Miller  *f*  3892
*The Warrior and the Witch* - Carl Miller  *f*  3893

**Corbett, Blake** (Writer)
*Shapes* - Steve Vance  *h*  5552

**Cordell** (Warrior; Leader)
*Feathered Dragon* - Douglas Niles  *f*  4108

**Corder, Rachel** (Drifter)
*Jackals* - Charles L. Grant  *h*  2313

**Cordery, Noell** (Scientist)
*The Empire of Fear* - Brian Stableford  *h*  5191

**Cordesman, Jack** (Detective—Police)
*Incubi* - Edward Lee  *h*  3394

**Cordesman, Jack** (Detective)
*Shifters* - Edward Lee  *h*  3396

**Corea, Jake** (Actor)
*Created By* - Richard Christian Matheson  *h*  3691

**Corey, Elizabeth "Betty"** (Religious)
*The World on Blood* - Jonathan Nasaw  *h*  4069

**Corey, Lewis** (Artisan)
*Inagehi* - Jack Cady  *h*  817

**Corey, Maggie** (Single Parent)
*Freeze Frames* - Katharine Kerr  *s*  3071

**Corio, Giovanna** (Religious)
*Renaissance Moon* - Linda Nevins  *f*  4093

**Cork, Joe** (Mythical Creature; Government Official)
*The Faery Convention* - Brett Davis  *f*  1399

**Cork, Stan** (Guard)
*Tower of Evil* - James Kisner  *h*  3161

**Corlaiys, Aitchley** (Farmer; Adventurer)
*Cathedral of Thorns* - Steven Frankos  *f*  2041

**Corleau** (Hero)
*The Sorceress and the Cygnet* - Patricia A.
  McKillip  *f*  3842

**Cormac** (Royalty)
*Wolfking* - Bridget Wood  *f*  5963

**Cormack, Leonard** (Government Official; Pilot)
*Faraday's Orphans* - N. Lee Wood  *s*  5965

**Cormallon, Ran** (Wizard)
*The Gate of Ivory* - Doris Egan  *s*  1755
*Guilt-Edged Ivory* - Doris Egan  *s*  1756
*Two-Bit Heroes* - Doris Egan  *s*  1757

**Corman, Brian** (Businessman)
*The Gifted* - Jack Caravela  *h*  879

**Cornelian, Prime** (Ruler; Fanatic)
*Exile* - Al Sarrantonio  *s*  4829

**Cornelius, Vito** (Religious)
*The Fifth Element* - Terry Bisson  *s*  504

**Cornish, Francis** (Artist; Philanthropist)
*The Cornish Trilogy* - Robertson Davies  *f*  1397

**Correa, Marissa** (Researcher; Student)
*Lightpaths* - Howard V. Hendrix  *s*  2660

**Corrigan, Casey** (Teenager)
*The Witch of Maple Park* - Stephanie S.
  Tolan  *f*  5478

**Corrigan, Joe** (Computer Expert)
*Realtime Interrupt* - James P. Hogan  *s*  2729

**Corry, William M.** (Military Personnel; Sea Captain)
*Starsea Invaders: First Action* - G. Harry
  Stine  *s*  5282

**Corson** (Martial Arts Expert)
*Mistress of Ambiguities* - J.F. Rivkin  *f*  4596

**Cort** (Military Personnel)
*A Wizard in Chaos* - Christopher Stasheff  *s*  5230

**Cortez, Pablo** (Artist)
*Cortez on Jupiter* - Ernest Hogan  *s*  2721

**Cortez, Rafaela** (Housekeeper)
*Tropic of Orange* - Karen Tei Yamashita  *f*  6009

**Cortez, Rosita "Rose" Carmelita** (Spouse; Parent)
*Timemaster* - Robert L. Forward  *s*  1992

**Cortinez, Don Lazaro Ruiz** (Vampire)
*The Vampire Virus* - Michael Romkey  *h*  4668

**Cortiss, Sophie** (Traveler)
*Glenraven* - Marion Zimmer Bradley  *f*  635

**Cortland, Roger** (Scientist; Researcher)
*Lightpaths* - Howard V. Hendrix  *s*  2660

**Cortland, Roger** (Scientist; Spaceman)
*Standing Wave* - Howard V. Hendrix  *s*  2661

**Corvan, Kim** (Editor)
*Mars Prime* - William C. Dietz  *s*  1548

**Corvan, Rex** (Journalist)
*Mars Prime* - William C. Dietz  *s*  1548
*Matrix Man* - William C. Dietz  *s*  1549

**Corvino, Dominic** (Spy)
*Wet Work* - Philip Nutman  *h*  4168

**Corwyn** (Apprentice)
*The Apprentice* - Deborah Talmadge-
  Bickmore  *f*  5382

**Corwyn** (Magician)
*Rehearsal for a Renaissance* - Douglas W.
  Clark  *f*  1045

**Cory, Patrick** (Scientist)
*Donovan's Brain/Hauser's Memory* - Curt
  Siodmak  *h*  5072
*Gabriel's Body* - Curt Siodmak  *h*  5073

**Cosmo, Jason** (Farmer; Hero)
*Dirty Work* - Dan McGirt  *f*  3810
*Jason Cosmo* - Dan McGirt  *f*  3811

**Costa** (Psychic)
*Speaking Dreams* - Severna Park  *s*  4245

**Costello, Joey** (Teenager)
*Something Stirs* - Charles L. Grant  *h*  2316

**Costello, T.P.** (Journalist)
*Evolution's Shore* - Ian McDonald  *s*  3792

**Cotta** (Tourist)
*The Last World* - Christoph Ransmayr  *f*  4475

**Cotter, Wolf** (Journalist)
*Mastery* - Kelley Wilde  *h*  5802

**Cottington, Angelica** (Naturalist; Teenager)
*Lady Cottington's Pressed Fairy Book* - Terry
  Jones  *f*  2981

**Cotto, Grant** (Photographer)
*Strange Angels* - Kathe Koja  *h*  3197

**Cotto, Vir** (Alien; Political Figure)
*Personal Agendas* - Al Sarrantonio  *s*  4833

**Cotton, Alex** (Computer Expert)
*Brethren* - Shawn Ryan  *h*  4754

**Coughlan, Demeter** (Spy; Student)
*Man Plus* - Frederik Pohl  *s*  4348

**Coughlin, Charlie** (Aged Person)
*Dry Skull Dreams* - Michael Green  *h*  2344

**Coughlin, Molly** (Nurse)
*Dry Skull Dreams* - Michael Green  *h*  2344

**Coulter, Matt** (Carpenter)
*Shades of Night* - Rick Hautala  *h*  2612

**Coulton, Roger** (Scientist)
*Einstein's Bridge* - John Cramer  *s*  1244

**Court, Annalyn Reynolds** (Military Personnel)
*The Winds of Mars* - H.M. Hoover  *s*  2765

**Courtak, Jarrod** (Magician)
*The Unicorn Peace* - John Lee  *f*  3399
*The Unicorn Solution* - John Lee  *f*  3400
*The Unicorn War* - John Lee  *f*  3401

**Courvossier, Raoul** (Military Personnel; Diplomat)
*The Honor of the Queen* - David Weber  *s*  5674

**Coventry, Martina** (Writer)
*City of Truth* - James Morrow  *s*  4030

**Covington, Diana** (Genetically Altered Being; Spy)
*Beggars and Choosers* - Nancy Kress  *s*  3236

**Cowal, Bobby** (Child)
*Deadly Friend* - Keith Ferrario  *h*  1926

**Cowal, Peter** (Child)
*Deadly Friend* - Keith Ferrario  *h*  1926

**Cowperthwait, Cosmo** (Inventor; Naturalist)
*The Steampunk Trilogy* - Paul Di Filippo  *s*  1518

**Coxe, Rachel** (Witch)
*Witches* - Kathryn Meyer Griffith  *h*  2442

**Coyote** (Shaman)
*Cherokee Bat and the Goat Guys* - Francesca Lia
  Block  *f*  546

**Coyote** (Genetically Altered Being; Taxi Driver)
*Pollen* - Jeff Noon  *s*  4135

**Coyul** (Alien)
*The Snake Oil Wars* - Parke Godwin  *s*  2249

**Cozzano, William Anthony** (Political Figure;
  Experimental Subject)
*Interface* - Stephen Bury  *s*  781

**Craig, Alice** (Office Worker)
*Down River* - Stephen Gallagher  *h*  2110

**Craig, Donald** (Computer Expert)
*The Ghost From the Grand Banks* - Arthur C.
  Clarke  *s*  1056

**Craig, Edith** (Heiress)
*Lucifer's Eye* - Hugh B. Cave  *h*  943

**Craig, James Christopher** (Technician)
*Psychamok* - Brian Lumley  *h*  3561

**Craig, Julie** (Young Woman)
*Heathen* - Shaun Hutson  *h*  2816

**Craig, Samantha** (Scientist)
*Reaper* - Ben Mizrich  *h*  3923

**Cramer, Eddie** (Police Officer; Homosexual)
*Vampires Anonymous* - Jeffrey N.
  McMahan  *h*  3853

**Cranach, Stella** (Artist)
*The Schizogenic Man* - Raymond Harris  *s*  2563

**Crandall, Raymond E. Jr.** (Teenager; Apprentice)
*The Magic Touch* - Jody Lynn Nye  *f*  4171

**Crandall, Samantha "Sam"** (Journalist)
*The Modular Man* - Roger MacBride Allen  *s*  79

**Crane** (Doctor; Spy)
*Lake of the Long Sun* - Gene Wolfe  *s*  5942
*Nightside the Long Sun* - Gene Wolfe  *s*  5943

**Crane, George "Trip" III** (Scientist; Professor)
*The First Immortal* - James L. Halperin  *s*  2498

**Crane, Lewis** (Scientist)
*Richter 10* - Arthur C. Clarke  *s*  1060

**Crane, Mary** (Thief)
*Psycho* - Robert Bloch  *h*  540

**Crane, Peter** (Businessman; Political Figure)
*Hunting the Corrigan's Blood* - Holly Lisle  *s*  3484

**Crane, Scott** (Religious; Spirit)
*Earthquake Weather* - Tim Powers  *f*  4382

**Crane, Scott** (Gambler)
*Last Call* - Tim Powers  *f*  4384

**Craobb** (Angel)
*Moonwise* - Greer Ilene Gilman  *f*  2238

**Craslowe, Hadrian** (Psychologist)
*Greely's Cove* - John Gideon  *h*  2221

**Craulnober, Elaith** (Mythical Creature)
*Elfsong* - Elaine Cunningham   f   1289

**Craven, Dudley** (Farmer)
*Blood Kin* - Ronald Kelly   h   3051

**Craven, Nick** (Detective)
*Evil Eye* - Michael Slade   h   5085

**Craven, Tammy** (Teacher)
*Blood Kin* - Ronald Kelly   h   3051

**Craven, Wes** (Director; Historical Figure)
*Wes Craven's New Nightmare* - David
   Bergantino   h   460

**Crawford, Jonathan** (Health Care Professional)
*The Callahan Touch* - Spider Robinson   f   4637

**Crawford, Lee** (Political Figure; Administrator)
*Dark Genesis* - J. Gregory Keyes   s   3096

**Crawford, Michael** (Doctor; Fugitive)
*The Stress of Her Regard* - Tim Powers   h   4385

**Crawford, Oilvia** (Young Woman)
*Blood Roots* - Richie Tankersley Cusick   h   1300

**Crawford, Stony** (Kidnapper)
*The Halloween Man* - Douglas Clegg   h   1080

**Cray, Jennifer** (Lawyer; Magician)
*One Land, One Duke* - Ru Emerson   f   1809
*The Two in Hiding* - Ru Emerson   f   1812

**Cray, Robyn** (Single Parent; Mythical Creature)
*The Two in Hiding* - Ru Emerson   f   1812

**Craythorne** (Military Personnel; Psychologist)
*Mind Changer* - James White   s   5780

**Crazy** (Writer)
*Death Is a Lonely Business* - Ray Bradbury   h   619

**Crea** (Reanimated Dead)
*The Darker Passions: Frankenstein* - Amarantha
   Knight   h   3180

**Creaghan, Michael** (Military Personnel)
*Hellboy: The Lost Army* - Christopher
   Golden   h   2257

**Crecilius, Hallie** (Musician)
*The Devil's Cradle* - Kate Stewart   h   5269

**Cree, Elizabeth** (Actress)
*The Trial of Elizabeth Cree* - Peter Ackroyd   h   26

**Cree, John** (Actor)
*The Trial of Elizabeth Cree* - Peter Ackroyd   h   26

**Creed, Victor "Sabertooth"** (Mutant; Mentally Ill
Person)
*Codename Wolverine* - Christopher Golden   s   2256

**Creedath** (Businessman; Psychic)
*The Gates of Vensunor* - Carol Heller   f   2650

**Creeping Sword** (Handicapped; Sorcerer)
*Spell of Apocalypse* - Mayer Alan Brenner   f   672

**Creighton, Abe "TC"** (Military Personnel)
*Afrikorps* - Bill Dolan   s   1566
*Cobra Curse* - Bill Dolan   s   1567
*Iron Horse* - Bill Dolan   s   1568
*White Rhino* - Bill Dolan   s   1569

**Creighton, Jonathan** (Psychologist)
*The Barrens* - F. Paul Wilson   h   5884

**Crenson, Croyd "The Sleeper"** (Genetically Altered
Being)
*Black Trump* - George R.R. Martin   s   3642
*Marked Cards* - George R.R. Martin   s   3647
*Turn of the Cards* - Victor Milan   s   3891

**Creslin** (Wizard; Fiance(e))
*The Towers of the Sunset* - L.E. Modesitt
   Jr.   f   3941

**Crindle** (Teacher)
*Mysteries of the Word* - Stanley Wiater   h   5796

**Cripplemaker, General** (Outlaw)
*Farewell Horizontal* - K.W. Jeter   s   2911

**Crisco, Bungeeman** (Military Personnel; Spaceman)
*Star Wreck 6: Geek Space Nine* - Leah
   Rewolinski   s   4562

**Crispian, Grace** (Truck Driver)
*Rune* - Christopher Fowler   h   2020

**Croaker** (Military Personnel; Doctor)
*Bleak Seasons* - Glen Cook   f   1147

**Croaker** (Military Personnel; Historian)
*Dreams of Steel* - Glen Cook   f   1150

**Croaker** (Military Personnel; Doctor)
*She Is the Darkness* - Glen Cook   f   1154

**Crocken** (Peddler; Adventurer)
*The Wizard's Shadow* - Susan Dexter   f   1514

**Crocker, Ben** (Child)
*Yellow Moon* - David J. Searls   h   4907

**Crocker, Thad** (Political Figure)
*Yellow Moon* - David J. Searls   h   4907

**Crockett, Selena** (Heiress)
*Archangel* - Michael Conner   s   1133

**Croft, Jessamyn** (Actress)
*The Ruby Tear* - Rebecca Brand   h   660

**Croft, Michael "Mickey"** (Political Figure)
*The Stalk* - Janet Morris   s   4016
*Trust Territory* - Janet Morris   s   4019

**Croft, Samantha** (Insurance Agent)
*Demon Within* - Dana Reed   h   4499

**Crogan, Janice** (Young Woman)
*Beast House* - Richard Laymon   h   3364

**Cromwell, Willard** (Martial Arts Expert; Adventurer)
*Indiana Jones and the Sky Pirates* - Martin
   Caidin   f   825

**Crone** (Shaman)
*Shiva Accused: An Adventure of the Ice Age* - J.H.
   Brennan   f   667

**Crook, Annie** (Clerk)
*From Hell* - Alan Moore   h   3987

**Crookleg, Poilar** (Adventurer; Religious)
*Kingdoms of the Wall* - Robert Silverberg   s   5033

**Cross, Anthony** (Scientist; Serial Killer)
*Dark Matter* - Garfield Reeves-Stevens   h   4509

**Cross, Jo** (Young Woman)
*Garden* - Matthew J. Costello   h   1197

**Cross, Joanna** (Journalist)
*Superstition* - David Ambrose   h   90

**Cross, Jordan** (Detective—Private)
*Dark Channel* - Ray Garton   h   2150

**Cross, Michael** (Professor)
*Garden* - Matthew J. Costello   h   1197
*Wurm* - Matthew J. Costello   h   1202

**Cross, Prosper** (Minstrel; Wanderer)
*The World Next Door* - Brad Ferguson   s   1924

**Cross, Tom** (Genetically Altered Being;
Businessman)
*Greenhouse* - Thomas A. Easton   s   1723

**Crotalus** (Wizard)
*Conan, Scourge of the Bloody Coast* - Leonard
   Carpenter   f   910
*The Falcon and the Serpent* - Cheryl A.
   Smith   f   5101

**Crouper, Martin** (Vampire)
*Immortal* - Jason Nickles   h   4102

**Crow** (Adventurer; Indian)
*Crow and Weasel* - Barry Lopez   f   3523

**Crow, Jack** (Vampire Hunter)
*Vampire$* - John Steakley   h   5237

**Crow, Titus** (Paranormal Investigator)
*The Burrowers Beneath* - Brian Lumley   h   3548

**Crow, Titus** (Adventurer; Paranormal Investigator)
*Titus Crow, Volume One* - Brian Lumley   h   3566
*Titus Crow, Volume Three* - Brian Lumley   h   3567
*Titus Crow, Volume Two* - Brian Lumley   h   3568

**Crow, Titus** (Paranormal Investigator)
*The Transition of Titus Crow* - Brian
   Lumley   h   3569

**Crowe, Derek** (Writer)
*The 37th Mandala* - Marc Laidlaw   h   3310

**Crowe, Janie** (Doctor; Student)
*The Plague Tales* - Ann Benson   s   453

**Crowell** (Martial Arts Expert; Heir)
*Iroshi* - Cary Osborne   s   4228

**Crowell, Eve** (Parent)
*Eden's Eyes* - Sean Costello   h   1205

**Crowley** (Angel)
*Good Omens: The Nice and Accurate Prophecies of
   Agnes Nutter, Witch* - Neil Gaiman   f   2103

**Crowley** (Rogue; Nobleman)
*Lady Cottington's Pressed Fairy Book* - Terry
   Jones   f   2981

**Crowley, Aleister** (Magician; Historical Figure)
*The Door through Washington Square* - Elaine
   Bergstrom   f   464
*The Woman between the Worlds* - F. Gwynplaine
   MacIntyre   s   3596

**Crowley, Damon** (Warrior; Hero)
*Evil Triumphant* - Michael A. Stackpole   s   5199

**Croyd** (Businessman)
*Megalomania* - Ian Wallace   s   5621

**Cruitaire, Christa** (Teacher; Musician)
*Gossamer Axe* - Gael Baudino   f   392

**Crumley, Elmo** (Detective—Private)
*Death Is a Lonely Business* - Ray Bradbury   h   619

**Crusher, Beverly** (Spaceship Captain; Doctor)
*All Good Things. . .* - Michael Jan Friedman   s   2061

**Crusher, Beverly** (Doctor; Space Explorer)
*Chains of Command* - Bill McCay   s   3767
*Dragon's Honor* - Kij Johnson   s   2922
*Imbalance* - V.E. Mitchell   s   3919
*Intellivore* - Diane Duane   s   1663

**Crusher, Jack** (Spaceship Captain)
*Q-Squared* - Peter David   s   1385

**Crusher, Wesley** (Student—College; Military
Personnel)
*Balance of Power* - Dafydd ab Hugh   s   7

**Crusher, Wesley** (Student)
*Debtors' Planet* - William R. Thompson   s   5457

**Crygender, "Cry"** (Criminal)
*Crygender* - Thomas T. Thomas   s   5451

**Crysania** (Religious)
*Tears of the Night Sky* - Linda P. Baker   f   299

**Crystal** (Parent; Mythical Creature)
*Troll-Quest* - Rose Estes   f   1841

**Csejthe, Christopher** (Vampire; Radio Personality)
*One Foot in the Grave* - Wm. Mark
   Simmons   f   5062

**Cuchlainn** (Warrior; Teenager)
*The Raid* - Randy Lee Eickhoff   f   1764

**Cugnet, Vern** (Mechanic; Adventurer)
*Stones of the Dalai Lama* - Ken Mitchell   f   3916

**Culaehra** (Warrior; Adventurer)
*The Sage* - Christopher Stasheff   f   5221

**Culley, Mance** (Teenager)
*The Living Dark* - Stephen Gresham   h   2431

**Cullinane, Andrea** (Wizard)
*The Road to Ehvenor* - Joel Rosenberg   f   4675

**Cullinane, Jason** (Warrior; Nobleman)
*The Road Home* - Joel Rosenberg  *f*  4674

**Cully, Lawrence** (Veterinarian)
*The Black Cat* - Robert Poe  *h*  4344

**Cumber** (Mythical Creature; Adventurer)
*Dragoncharm* - Graham Edwards  *f*  1749

**Cumberland, Jack** (Thief)
*Mongster* - Randall Boyll  *h*  616

**Cummings, Michael** (Banker)
*Not Broken, Not Belonging* - Randy Fox  *h*  2030

**Cummings, Rachael** (Artist)
*Not Broken, Not Belonging* - Randy Fox  *h*  2030

**Cummings, Stewart** (Police Officer)
*Header* - Edward Lee  *h*  3393

**Cunningham, Dodge** (Detective—Private)
*Mastery* - Kelley Wilde  *h*  5802

**Cunningham, Jennifer** (Advertising)
*The Site* - Melisand March  *h*  3621

**Curio** (Model)
*Majyk by Design* - Esther Friesner  *f*  2080

**Curran, Abigail** (Aged Person)
*Holy Terror* - Josephine Boyle  *h*  608

**Curran, Baal** (Handicapped; Teenager)
*Killobyte* - Piers Anthony  *f*  179

**Curran, Joslire** (Slave; Martial Arts Expert)
*An Exchange of Hostages* - Susan R.
   Matthews  *s*  3692

**Curry, Michael** (Architect)
*Lasher* - Anne Rice  *h*  4570
*The Witching Hour* - Anne Rice  *h*  4580

**Curry, Rowan Mayfair** (Doctor; Witch)
*Lasher* - Anne Rice  *h*  4570

**Curtis, Adam** (Child)
*Baby Dolly* - Ruby Jean Jensen  *h*  2899

**Curtis, Prissy** (Child)
*Baby Dolly* - Ruby Jean Jensen  *h*  2899

**Curtis, Richard** (Financier; Spouse)
*Dreamer* - Peter James  *h*  2871

**Curtis, Samantha "Sam"** (Producer)
*Dreamer* - Peter James  *h*  2871

**Curtiss, David** (Paranormal Investigator)
*Julian's House* - Judith Hawkes  *h*  2630

**Curtiss, Sally** (Paranormal Investigator)
*Julian's House* - Judith Hawkes  *h*  2630

**Custer, George A.** (Military Personnel; Historical
   Figure)
*How Few Remain* - Harry Turtledove  *s*  5504

**Custer, George Armstrong** (Sorcerer; Historical
   Figure)
*Devil's Tower* - Mark Sumner  *f*  5357

**Cuthberton-Jones** (Parent)
*Angela and Diabola* - Lynne Reid Banks  *f*  330

**Cuthberton-Jones, Angelica** (Child; Psychic)
*Angela and Diabola* - Lynne Reid Banks  *f*  330

**Cuthberton-Jones, Diabola** (Child; Psychic)
*Angela and Diabola* - Lynne Reid Banks  *f*  330

**Cutler, Philip** (Teenager)
*Dawn* - V.C. Andrews  *h*  144

**Cutter** (Mythical Creature; Leader)
*Captives of the Blue Mountain* - Wendy
   Pini  *f*  4336
*The Quest Begins* - Wendy Pini  *f*  4337

**Cutter, Hargrave** (Doctor)
*Night Thirst* - Patrick Whalen  *h*  5770

**Cutter, Lance** (Investigator)
*Mr. Sandman* - Lyle Howard  *h*  2779

**Cutter, Sam** (Paranormal Investigator)
*The Burning Man* - Michael Hammond  *h*  2530

**Cutter, Timothy** (Child)
*Shadow Dance* - Douglas Borton  *h*  577

**Cwan, Si** (Royalty; Alien)
*End Game* - Peter David  *s*  1382

**Cwenn** (Royalty; Step-Parent)
*Suisan* - Phyllis Carol Agins  *f*  42

**Cy BerPunk** (Computer Expert)
*Planet of the Robot Slaves* - Harry Harrison  *s*  2573

**Cymel** (Student; Wizard)
*Drum Calls* - Jo Clayton  *f*  1065

**Cymel** (Mythical Creature)
*Drum Warning* - Jo Clayton  *f*  1066

**Cypher, Richard "the Seeker"** (Wizard; Captive)
*Stone of Tears* - Terry Goodkind  *f*  2269

**Cypher, Richard "the Seeker"** (Woodsman; Martial
   Arts Expert)
*Wizard's First Rule* - Terry Goodkind  *f*  2271

**Cyric** (Deity)
*Crucible* - Troy Denning  *f*  1484

**Cyron** (Royalty)
*Star Child* - James P. Hogan  *s*  2730

# D

**da Brabant, Huegenet** (Noblewoman)
*Blood Roses* - Chelsea Quinn Yarbro  *h*  6012

**da Clovina, Antonio** (Vampire)
*The Vampire Journals* - Traci Briery  *h*  678

**da Lionghi, Emilio** (Criminal)
*Humpty Dumpty: An Oval* - Damon Knight  *s*  3186

**da Vinci, Leonardo** (Historical Figure; Inventor)
*The Memory Cathedral* - Jack Dann  *s*  1341

**da Vinci, Leonardo** (Genius; Aged Person)
*Pasquale's Angel* - Paul J. McAuley  *f*  3714

**Daae, Christine** (Student; Singer)
*Phantom* - Susan Kay  *h*  3020

**Dacham, Klaus** (Military Personnel)
*Partisan* - S. Andrew Swann  *s*  5365

**Dacron** (Android)
*Star Wreck III: Time Warped* - Leah
   Rewolinski  *s*  4564

**Dad** (Scientist)
*Eva* - Peter Dickinson  *s*  1525

**Dad** (Parent; Time Traveler)
*The Key to the Indian* - Lynne Reid Banks  *f*  331

**Dad** (Guard)
*Pet Store* - M.T. Coffin  *h*  1097

**Dad** (Parent; Political Figure)
*Songs of Enchantment* - Ben Okri  *f*  4208

**Dad** (Lawyer)
*Thor* - Wayne Smith  *h*  5146

**Daez, Henry** (Landlord)
*Makoto* - Kelley Wilde  *h*  5801

**Daffyd** (Musician)
*The Soprano Sorceress* - L.E. Modesitt Jr.  *f*  3938

**Dafoe, Mary Lou "Merrilu"** (Teenager)
*Dragon Sleeping* - Craig Shaw Gardner  *f*  2127

**Dafoe, Rafe** (Teenager)
*Blood and Chocolate* - Annette Curtis
   Klause  *h*  3162

**Dagda** (Immigrant; Adventurer)
*The Enchanted Isles* - Casey Flynn  *f*  1960
*Most Ancient Song* - Casey Flynn  *f*  1961

**Daggett, Tace** (Entertainer)
*Night Hunter* - Michael Reaves  *h*  4496

**Dagon** (Android; Murderer)
*Dead Boys* - Richard Calder  *s*  836

**D'Agosta, Vincent** (Police Officer)
*Reliquary* - Douglas Preston  *h*  4415

**Dagref** (Teenager; Scholar)
*Fox and Empire* - Harry Turtledove  *f*  5500

**Dahak** (Artificial Intelligence)
*The Armageddon Inheritance* - David
   Weber  *s*  5668
*Heirs of Empire* - David Weber  *s*  5672

**Dahl, Deha** (Government Official)
*The Last Hawk* - Catherine Asaro  *s*  219

**Dahl, Lars** (Government Official)
*Crystal Line* - Anne McCaffrey  *s*  3724

**Dahlgren, Mod** (Android)
*Heart of Red Iron* - Phyllis Gotlieb  *s*  2287

**Dahlgren, Sven** (Mutant)
*Heart of Red Iron* - Phyllis Gotlieb  *s*  2287

**Dahmi** (Alien)
*Alien Eyes* - Lynn S. Hightower  *s*  2683

**Dahnak** (Alien)
*Diplomatic Act* - Peter Jurasik  *s*  2996

**Dahven** (Nobleman)
*One Land, One Duke* - Ru Emerson  *f*  1809

**Dai, David** (Military Personnel; Bodyguard)
*Half the Day Is Night* - Maureen F.
   McHugh  *s*  3818

**Daily, Jennifer** (Detective—Police)
*Star Precinct* - Kevin D. Randle  *s*  4470

**Daimbert** (Wizard)
*A Bad Spell in Yurt* - C. Dale Brittain  *f*  701
*Daughter of Magic* - C. Dale Brittain  *f*  703
*The Witch and the Cathedral* - C. Dale
   Brittain  *f*  705
*The Wood Nymph and the Cranky Saint* - C. Dale
   Brittain  *f*  706

**Daimler, Rachel** (Housewife)
*Lullaby* - Diane Guest  *h*  2455

**Dain, Benn** (Explorer; Student)
*Mazeway* - Jack Williamson  *s*  5866

**Daine, Truro** (Fugitive)
*The Night Mayor* - Kim Newman  *s*  4099

**Dairine** (Wizard)
*High Wizardry* - Diane Duane  *f*  1662

**Daitaku** (Clone)
*Fire on the Border* - Kevin O'Donnell Jr.  *s*  4194

**Daja** (Student; Wizard)
*Tris's Book* - Tamora Pierce  *f*  4322

**Dak, Maanka "Pete Moss"** (Alien; Criminal)
*The Change* - Barry B. Longyear  *s*  3520

**Dakar** (Psychic; Religious)
*Ships of Merior* - Janny Wurts  *f*  6004

**Dakota** (Scout)
*The Lanterns of God* - Ron Sarti  *s*  4835

**Dakota, Bobbie** (Detective—Private)
*The Bad Place* - Dean R. Koontz  *h*  3202

**Dakota, Julie** (Detective—Private)
*The Bad Place* - Dean R. Koontz  *h*  3202

**Dalamar** (Wizard)
*Dragons of Summer Flame* - Margaret Weis  *f*  5711

**Dalamar** (Mythical Creature)
*Tears of the Night Sky* - Linda P. Baker  *f*  299

**Dalamini, Ming** (Smuggler)
*Crystal Witness* - Kathy Tyers  *s*  5524

**Dale, Ambrose** (Businessman)
*The Night Inside* - Nancy Baker   h   301

**Daley, Cameron** (Teenager; Student)
*The Vanishing* - Marilyn Kaye   s   3021

**Dallas, Korben** (Taxi Driver; Military Personnel)
*The Fifth Element* - Terry Bisson   s   504

**Dallaugher, Danny** (Young Man)
*When Shadows Fall* - Brian Scott Smith   h   5100

**DalLierx, Lindon** (Administrator)
*Shivering World* - Kathy Tyers   s   5526

**Dalt, Steven** (Anthropologist; Spy)
*The LaNague Chronicles* - F. Paul Wilson   s   5889

**Dalt, Steven** (Spy)
*The Tery* - F. Paul Wilson   s   5900

**Dalton, Edmund** (Businessman)
*Winter Tides* - James P. Blaylock   h   524

**Dalton, Jennifer "Darla"** (Young Woman)
*Darkman #4: The Face of Death* - Randall
   Boyll   h   615

**Dalton, Susan Benning** (Housewife)
*Watchers in the Woods* - William W.
   Johnstone   h   2936

**Dalton, Tom** (Spouse)
*Watchers in the Woods* - William W.
   Johnstone   h   2936

**Damarr, Amala** (Noblewoman)
*The Mace of Souls* - Bruce Fergusson   f   1925

**D'Ame, Celia "Lee"** (Heroine; Waiter/Waitress)
*A Roil of Stars* - Don Wismer   s   5930

**Damek** (Assistant)
*The Spirit Gate* - Maya Kaathryn Bohnhoff   f   562

**Damen, Clyde** (Mechanic)
*Cats Raise the Dead* - Shirley Rousseau
   Murphy   f   4054

**Damfels, Sylvan Bon** (Nobleman)
*Grass* - Sheri S. Tepper   s   5431

**Damico, Mary** (Nurse; Military Personnel)
*Dream Baby* - Bruce McAllister   s   3706

**"Damnbanna" Deil** (Musician; Student—High
   School)
*Damnbanna* - Nancy Springer   f   5177

**Dan** (Space Explorer; Traveler)
*Douglas Adams's Starship Titanic* - Terry
   Jones   s   2979

**Dan, Issachar** (Nobleman; Warrior)
*Wind From a Foreign Sky* - Katya Reimann   f   4528

**Dana, Gregory** (Scientist)
*Voyager* - Stephen Baxter   s   406

**Danan, Elora** (Royalty; Magician)
*Shadow Dawn* - Chris Claremont   f   1042

**Danan, Elora** (Royalty)
*Shadow Moon* - George Lucas   f   3540

**Dandilion** (Animal; Storyteller)
*Tales From Watership Down* - Richard Adams   f   32

**Dane, Richard** (Businessman)
*Cold in July* - Joe R. Lansdale   h   3323

**Daneam, Penelope** (Teenager)
*Dominion* - Bentley Little   h   3492

**Danica** (Warrior; Martial Arts Expert)
*Canticle* - R.A. Salvatore   f   4793

**Daniel** (Twin)
*Dark Father* - Tom Piccirilli   h   4312

**Daniel** (Gambler; Adventurer)
*The Door to Ambermere* - J. Calvin Pierce   f   4316

**Daniels, Aikin** (Student—College; Adventurer)
*Dreamseeker's Road* - Tom Deitz   f   1472

**Daniels, Danny** (Reanimated Dead)
*Deadweight* - Robert Devereaux   h   1505

**Daniels, Kip** (Teenager; Military Personnel)
*Godzilla 2000* - Marc Cerasini   s   949

**Daniels, Molly** (Witch)
*Witchcraft* - Bill Michaels   h   3885

**Daniels, Norman** (Detective—Police)
*Rose Madder* - Stephen King   h   3139

**Daniels, Rose McLendon** (Businesswoman; Abuse
   Victim)
*Rose Madder* - Stephen King   h   3139

**Danilov, Alexander** (Vampire)
*These Fallen Angels* - Wendy Haley   h   2492
*This Dark Paradise* - Wendy Haley   h   2493

**Danilov, Barron** (Businessman)
*This Dark Paradise* - Wendy Haley   h   2493

**Danilov, Justin** (Teenager)
*These Fallen Angels* - Wendy Haley   h   2492

**Danilov, Sonya** (Parent)
*These Fallen Angels* - Wendy Haley   h   2492

**Danio, Kiera** (Fugitive; Psychic)
*Wheel of Dreams* - Salinda Tyson   f   5529

**Danirov, Major** (Military Personnel)
*Suicide Attack* - John Sievert   s   5023

**Danner, Hannah** (Military Personnel)
*Ammonite* - Nicola Griffith   s   2443

**Dannerman, Jim Daniel "Dan"** (Spy; Spaceman)
*The Other End of Time* - Frederik Pohl   s   4351

**Dannerman, Jim Daniel "Dan"** (Spy; Clone)
*The Siege of Eternity* - Frederik Pohl   s   4353

**Danny-boy** (Artist)
*The City, Not Long After* - Pat Murphy   s   4051

**d'Anton, Charlotte Marie** (Slave; Time Traveler)
*The Virgin and the Dinosaur* - R. Garcia y
   Robertson   s   2122

**Danu** (Royalty)
*The Enchanted Isles* - Casey Flynn   f   1960

**Danya** (Teenager)
*Vampire Diary: The Embrace* - Robert
   Weinberg   h   5705

**Danziger** (Spaceman; Castaway)
*Earth 2* - Melissa Crandall   s   1247

**Danziger, E.E.** (Scientist)
*From Time to Time* - Jack Finney   s   1941

**dar Dero, Halleyne** (Noblewoman; Sorceress)
*Wrath of the Princes* - Holly Lisle   f   3490

**Dara** (Wanderer)
*Ancestral Hungers* - Scott Baker   h   303

**Dara** (Telepath)
*Feather Stroke* - Sydney J. Van Scyoc   f   5542

**Dara** (Magician; Servant)
*Guardian's Key* - Anne Logston   f   3511

**Dara** (Royalty)
*Krispos of Videssos* - Harry Turtledove   f   5506

**Darby, Abraham III** (Religious; Industrialist)
*The Iron Bridge* - David Morse   s   4036

**Darby, Beacontor "Beau"** (Mythical Creature;
   Healer; Adventurer)
*Into the Fire* - Dennis L. McKiernan   f   3834

**Darby, Beacontor "Beau"** (Mythical Creature;
   Adventurer; Healer)
*Into the Forge* - Dennis L. McKiernan   f   3835

**Darcalus** (Wizard)
*King of the Dead* - Gene DeWeese   h   1510

**Darch, Jack** (Prospector)
*The Specialist* - Wynne Whiteford   s   5788

**Darcourt, Simon** (Religious; Scholar)
*The Cornish Trilogy* - Robertson Davies   f   1397

**Darcy, Jade** (Martial Arts Expert; Warrior)
*Jade Darcy and the Zen Pirates* - Stephen
   Goldin   s   2260

**Darcy, Lord** (Detective)
*A Study in Sorcery* - Michael Kurland   f   3252

**Darffot, Tex "Bear"** (Spirit; Activist)
*Tex and Molly in the Afterlife* - Richard
   Grant   f   2327

**Darian** (Angel)
*Angelwalk: A Modern Fable* - Roger
   Elwood   f   1803

**Darian** (Hunter; Apprentice)
*Owlflight* - Mercedes Lackey   f   3291

**Darian** (Healer; Teenager)
*Owlsight* - Mercedes Lackey   f   3292

**Darin of Culverne** (Child; Religious)
*Children of the Blood: Book Two of The Sundered* -
   Michelle Sagara   f   4782
*Lady of Mercy* - Michelle Sagara   f   4784

**Dario, Ramon** (Police Officer)
*Senor Vivo and the Coca Lord* - Louis de
   Bernieres   f   1411

**Darith** (Hero)
*Blood of the Colyn Muir* - Paul Edwin
   Zimmer   f   6083

**Darius** (Religious)
*Elephantasm* - Tanith Lee   h   3408

**Darius** (Ruler)
*Fractal Mode* - Piers Anthony   f   171

**Darius** (Knight)
*Kaz the Minotaur* - Richard A. Knaak   f   3172

**Darius** (Immortal)
*Shadow of Obsession* - Rebecca Neason   f   4082

**Darius** (Ruler)
*Virtual Mode* - Piers Anthony   f   194

**d'Ark, Hazel** (Revolutionary; Bounty Hunter)
*Deathstalker Honor* - Simon R. Green   s   2364

**Dark Lord** (Wizard)
*Outcasts* - Clayton Emery   f   1815

**Darke, Makellen** (Genetically Altered Being;
   Psychic)
*Dancer of the Sixth* - Michelle Shirey
   Crean   s   1254

**Darker, Alex** (Divorced Person)
*The Chymical Wedding* - Lindsay Clarke   f   1063

**Darkholme, Raven "Mystique"** (Mutant; Spy)
*Codename Wolverine* - Christopher Golden   s   2256

**Darkhorse** (Demon)
*The Crystal Dragon* - Richard A. Knaak   f   3167

**Darkling, Katastrofa "Kathy"** (Police Officer;
   Mythical Creature)
*Riverrun* - S.P. Somtow   f   5159

**Darkwind** (Scout)
*Winds of Change* - Mercedes Lackey   f   3304

**Darkwind** (Spy; Scout)
*Winds of Fate* - Mercedes Lackey   f   3305

**Darkwind** (Scout)
*Winds of Fury* - Mercedes Lackey   f   3306

**Darling, William Somers "Whip"** (Fisherman)
*Beast* - Peter Benchley   h   440

**d'Armand, Magnus Gallowglass "Gar
   Pike"** (Warrior; Psychic; Wizard)
*Warlock and Son* - Christopher Stasheff   s   5224

**d'Armand, Magnus Gallowglass "Gar Pike"**
   (Adventurer; Psychic; Wizard)
*A Wizard in Absentia* - Christopher Stasheff   s   5229

**d'Armand, Magnus Gallowglass "Gar Pike"** (Psychic; Troubleshooter; Wizard)
*A Wizard in Chaos* - Christopher Stasheff   *s*   5230

**d'Armand, Magnus Gallowglass "Gar Pike"** (Wizard; Troubleshooter; Psychic)
*A Wizard in Midgard* - Christopher Stasheff   *s*   5231

**d'Armand, Magnus Gallowglass "Gar Pike"** (Wizard; Revolutionary; Psychic)
*A Wizard in Mind* - Christopher Stasheff   *s*   5232

**d'Armand, Magnus Gallowglass "Gar Pike"** (Psychic; Revolutionary; Wizard)
*A Wizard in Peace* - Christopher Stasheff   *s*   5233

**d'Armand, Magnus Gallowglass "Gar Pike"** (Psychic; Warrior; Wizard)
*A Wizard in War* - Christopher Stasheff   *s*   5234

**Darrow, Iselia** (Religious)
*Star Ascendant* - Louise Cooper   *f*   1180

**Darrow, Troy** (Scientist)
*Carnivore* - Leigh Clark   *h*   1049

**Darsen** (Vampire)
*Virago* - Karen Marie Christa Minns   *h*   3915

**Dart** (Nobleman; Amnesiac)
*The Wooden Sword* - Lynn Abbey   *f*   18

**Dart, Dick** (Serial Killer)
*The Hellfire Club* - Peter Straub   *h*   5326

**Dart, Kathy** (Psychic)
*Fury* - John Coyne   *h*   1237

**D'Artagnan, Charles** (Warrior)
*A Candle for D'Artagnan* - Chelsea Quinn Yarbro   *h*   6013

**Darte, Novak** (Vampire)
*Tooth: A Tale of Love and Death in Paradox* - Novak Kruger   *h*   3244

**Darthoridan** (Warrior)
*Evermeet: Island of Elves* - Elaine Cunningham   *f*   1290

**Dartmuth, Darcie** (Military Personnel; Spouse)
*Dominion's Reach* - Diann Thornley   *s*   5465

**Dartson, Emma** (Child)
*The Premonition* - Andrew Laurance   *h*   3349

**Dartson, Michael** (Businessman)
*The Premonition* - Andrew Laurance   *h*   3349

**Daruya** (Royalty; Magician)
*Spear of Heaven* - Judith Tarr   *f*   5396

**Darville** (Royalty)
*The Perfect Princess* - Irene Radford   *f*   4462

**Darvish** (Royalty)
*The Fire's Stone* - Tanya Huff   *f*   2796

**Darwin** (Animal)
*seaQuest DSV: The Novel* - Diane Duane   *s*   1666

**Darwin, Alton** (Convict)
*Hocus Pocus or, What's the Hurry, Son?* - Kurt Vonnegut Jr.   *s*   5593

**Darynson, Davyn "Davi"** (Royalty; Sorcerer)
*Book of Stones* - L. Dean James   *f*   2862

**Dash** (Scout; Nobleman)
*Shards of a Broken Crown* - Raymond E. Feist   *f*   1912

**DaSilva, Renli** (Bodyguard; Genetically Altered Being)
*The Shapes of Their Hearts* - Melissa Scott   *s*   4901

**D'Asperge, Timaeus** (Magician; Nobleman)
*Another Day, Another Dungeon* - Greg Costikyan   *f*   1206
*One Quest, Hold the Dragons* - Greg Costikyan   *f*   1208

**Data** (Android; Military Personnel)
*The Devil's Heart* - Carmen Carter   *s*   922

**Data** (Android; Military Personnel)
*Doomsday World* - Carmen Carter   *s*   923

**Data** (Android; Military Personnel; Space Explorer)
*Imzadi* - Peter David   *s*   1383

**Data** (Android; Space Explorer; Military Personnel)
*Insurrection* - J.M. Dillard   *s*   1554

**Data** (Android; Military Personnel; Space Explorer)
*Intellivore* - Diane Duane   *s*   1663

**Data** (Military Personnel; Android; Space Explorer)
*The Last Stand* - Brad Ferguson   *s*   1923

**Data** (Android; Space Explorer; Military Personnel)
*Metamorphosis* - Jean Lorrah   *s*   3524

**Datu, Dayu** (Witch)
*The Painted Alphabet* - Diana Darling   *f*   1356

**Datum** (Android; Space Explorer)
*Treks Not Taken: What if Stephen King, Anne Rice, Bret Easton Ellis, and Other Literary Greats Had Written Episodes of Star Trek: The Next Generation?* - Steven R. Boyett   *s*   607

**Datz, Harmis** (Military Personnel)
*Plague Demon* - Brian Craig   *f*   1239

**D'Auber MacLeod, Carli** (Professor; Inventor)
*Proxies* - Laura J. Mixon   *s*   3922

**Daumier, Anatole** (Military Personnel)
*The Carnival of Destruction* - Brian Stableford   *h*   5190

**d'Aurca, Adamus** (Royalty; Animal)
*Fair Peril* - Nancy Springer   *f*   5178

**dav Aidan, Kenzie "Catfoot"** (Mercenary; Nobleman)
*Broken Blade* - Ann Marston   *f*   3634

**dav Leydon, Kian "Mouse"** (Heir—Lost; Hero)
*Kingmaker's Sword* - Ann Marston   *f*   3635

**dav Medroch, Cullin** (Nobleman; Mercenary)
*Kingmaker's Sword* - Ann Marston   *f*   3635

**Davakinapwottapellazanzis** (Alien; Researcher)
*The Expediter* - J. Brian Clarke   *s*   1062

**Davenger/Daven, Harla** (Military Personnel; Imposter)
*Dancer of the Sixth* - Michelle Shirey Crean   *s*   1254

**Davenport, Ben** (Taxi Driver)
*The Last Voice They Hear* - Ramsey Campbell   *h*   858

**Davenport, Geoff** (Journalist)
*The Last Voice They Hear* - Ramsey Campbell   *h*   858

**David** (Child)
*Dead in the West* - Joe R. Lansdale   *h*   3325

**David** (Student; Sports Figure)
*Gameplay* - Kevin J. Anderson   *f*   105
*Game's End* - Kevin J. Anderson   *f*   104

**David** (Teenager)
*Medallion of the Black Hound* - Shirley Rousseau Murphy   *f*   4056

**David** (Child)
*My Father Immortal* - Michael D. Weaver   *s*   5659

**Davidsen, Gunnar** (Hunter)
*Bright Shadow* - Elizabeth Forrest   *h*   1971

**Davidson, Callum** (Aged Person)
*Dialing the Wind* - Charles L. Grant   *h*   2305

**Davidson, Charles Joseph** (Doctor)
*Deadly Breed* - T.J. Kirby   *h*   3153

**Davidson, Troy** (Teenager; Vampire)
*Liquid Diet* - William Tedford   *h*   5419

**Davies, Gabriel** (Detective)
*Red Angel* - Roxanne Longstreet   *h*   3518

**Davies, Rachel** (Military Personnel)
*Jefferson's War: Death of a Regiment* - Kevin Randle   *s*   4466

**Davies, Stewart** (Computer Expert; Student—Graduate)
*Target Earth* - Steve Perry   *s*   4301

**Daviot** (Traveler)
*Lords of the Sky* - Angus Wells   *f*   5738

**Davis, Anne** (Student)
*Order of the Arrow* - Michael T. Hinkemeyer   *h*   2689

**Davis, Bill** (Writer)
*The Store* - Bentley Little   *h*   3497

**Davis, Edward** (Time Traveler)
*Thebes of the Hundred Gates* - Robert Silverberg   *s*   5043

**Davis, Evan** (Detective—Private; Demon)
*Eyes of the Empress* - Camille Bacon-Smith   *f*   285

**Davis, Gabrielle** (Businesswoman)
*Gnelfs* - Sidney Williams   *h*   5823

**Davis, Hannah** (Journalist)
*Marked Cards* - George R.R. Martin   *s*   3647

**Davis, Heaven** (Child)
*Gnelfs* - Sidney Williams   *h*   5823

**Davis, Jefferson** (Political Figure)
*Stars and Stripes Forever* - Harry Harrison   *s*   2577

**Davis, Kate** (Musician; Vampire)
*The Making of a Monster* - Gail Petersen   *h*   4307

**Davis, Kelly Brynn** (Journalist)
*Shapes* - Steve Vance   *h*   5552

**Davis, Kyra** (Pilot; Spaceman)
*Harvest of Stars* - Poul Anderson   *s*   127

**Davis, Shannon** (Teenager; Relative)
*The Store* - Bentley Little   *h*   3497

**Davison, Bill** (Psychologist)
*Was* - Geoff Ryman   *f*   4758

**Davison, Wesley** (Engineer)
*Thrill* - Patricia Wallace   *h*   5624

**Davos** (Healer; Demon)
*The Itinerant Exorcist* - Ashley McConnell   *f*   3776

**Dawn, Rhoda** (Psychic; Child)
*Outworld Cats* - Jack Lovejoy   *s*   3536

**Dawson** (Slave; Cyborg)
*Warp Angel* - Stuart Hopen   *s*   2766

**Dawson, DeWitt** (Police Officer)
*Happy Policeman* - Patricia Anthony   *s*   160

**Dawson, Donny** (Religious)
*Deathgrip* - Brian Hodge   *h*   2700

**Dawson, Jack** (Mercenary)
*Hell-Storm* - James A. Moore   *h*   3990

**Dawson, Joe** (Spy; Historian)
*Scotland the Brave* - Jennifer Roberson   *f*   4611
*Shadow of Obsession* - Rebecca Neason   *f*   4082

**Dax** (Artificial Intelligence)
*From a Changeling Star* - Jeffrey A. Carver   *s*   931

**Dax, Jadzia** (Military Personnel; Alien)
*Call to Arms* - Diane Carey   *s*   901
*Time's Enemy* - L.A. Graf   *s*   2297

**Day, Rachaela** (Clerk)
*Dark Dance* - Tanith Lee   *h*   3406

**Day, Rachaela** (Vampire)
*Darkness, I* - Tanith Lee   *h*   3407

**Day, Ruth** (Child)
*Dark Dance* - Tanith Lee   *h*   3406

**de Barenton, Lucien** (Nobleman; Military Personnel)
*The Moon and the Sun* - Vonda N. McIntyre   f   3822

**de Beq, Henri** (Knight; Vampire)
*Knights of the Blood* - Scott MacMillan   f   3602

**de Bernay, Leah** (Apprentice; Doctor)
*Dragon's Blood* - Alex McDonough   s   3799
*Dragon's Claw* - Alex McDonough   s   3800
*Dragon's Eye* - Alex McDonough   s   3801
*Scorpio Descending* - Alex McDonough   s   3803
*Scorpio Rising* - Alex McDonough   s   3804

**De Brouchee, Montolio** (Ranger)
*Sojourn* - R.A. Salvatore   f   4806

**de Brus, Marjory** (Noblewoman)
*Quest for a Maid* - Frances Mary Hendry   f   2662

**de Carabas** (Nobleman; Con Artist)
*Neverwhere* - Neil Gaiman   f   2104

**De Clerq, Robert** (Police Officer)
*Cutthroat* - Michael Slade   h   5084

**de Clifford, Robert** (Nobleman; Kidnapper)
*The Dragon and the Gnarly King* - Gordon R. Dickson   f   1529

**de Conde, Sarah Webster** (Socialite; Twin)
*Deep Freeze* - Zach Hughes   s   2811

**De Corizo, Ixoro** (Actress)
*Red Bride* - Christopher Fowler   h   2019

**de Courcy, Guiscard** (Knight; Psychic)
*King Javan's Year* - Katherine Kurtz   f   3258

**de Dip, Onofre** (Vampire)
*Natural History* - Juan Perucho   h   4303

**de Draconis, Rejiia** (Magician; Royalty)
*The Loneliest Magician* - Irene Radford   f   4461

**de Garsenc, Blaise** (Nobleman; Mercenary)
*A Song for Arbonne* - Guy Gavriel Kay   f   3017

**de Gris, Daria** (Noblewoman; Sorceress)
*The Changeling Prince* - Vivian Vande Velde   f   5554

**de Kreshtur, Andrei** (Student)
*Blood Countess* - Andrei Codrescu   h   1094

**de la Crois, Marie-Josephe** (Noblewoman)
*The Moon and the Sun* - Vonda N. McIntyre   f   3822

**de la von Zaguar, Lamar** (Vampire; Nobleman)
*The Mark of the Moderately Vicious Vampire* - Lionel Fenn   h   1920

**de Laal, Leland** (Royalty; Military Personnel)
*Helm* - Steven Gould   s   2289

**De Leone, "Deus X"** (Artificial Intelligence; Experimental Subject)
*Deus X* - Norman Spinrad   s   5171

**de Lioncourt, Lestat** (Vampire)
*Memnoch the Devil* - Anne Rice   h   4571
*The Queen of the Damned* - Anne Rice   h   4574
*The Tale of the Body Thief* - Anne Rice   h   4576

**De Luca, Vince** (Detective—Police)
*Souls* - Katina Alexis   h   71

**de Marigny, Henri Laurent** (Sidekick; Paranormal Investigator)
*Titus Crow, Volume One* - Brian Lumley   h   3566
*Titus Crow, Volume Three* - Brian Lumley   h   3567
*Titus Crow, Volume Two* - Brian Lumley   h   3568

**de Marigny, Henri Laurent** (Paranormal Investigator; Sidekick)
*The Transition of Titus Crow* - Brian Lumley   h   3569

**de Marion, Auguste "White Bear"** (Shaman)
*Shaman* - Robert Shea   f   4946

**de Marion, Raoul** (Farmer)
*Shaman* - Robert Shea   f   4946

**de Marktos, Cecelia** (Noblewoman)
*Hunting Party* - Elizabeth Moon   s   3968
*Sporting Chance* - Elizabeth Moon   s   3974
*Winning Colors* - Elizabeth Moon   s   3976

**de Medici, Caterina** (Historical Figure)
*The Stars Dispose* - Michaela Roessner   f   4651

**de Montalia, Madelaine** (Vampire)
*Out of the House of Life* - Chelsea Quinn Yarbro   h   6018

**de Montgarde, Adela** (Scientist)
*To Fear the Light* - Ben Bova   s   595
*To Save the Sun* - Ben Bova   s   596

**de Montpalau, Antoni** (Scientist)
*Natural History* - Juan Perucho   h   4303

**de Noram, Marilyn** (Royalty)
*Helm* - Steven Gould   s   2289

**de Noux, Leanna** (Femme Fatale)
*Leanna: Possession of a Woman* - Marie Kiraly   h   3149

**de Novau, Isidre** (Sea Captain)
*Natural History* - Juan Perucho   h   4303

**de Oro, Irving** (Hero; Warrior)
*Horrors of the Dancing Gods* - Jack L. Chalker   f   955

**de Oro, Joe** (Barbarian; Hero)
*Songs of the Dancing Gods* - Jack L. Chalker   f   962

**De Ramaira, David** (Scientist)
*Of the Fall* - Paul J. McAuley   s   3713

**de Remy, Mireille** (Noblewoman)
*The Eight* - Katherine Neville   f   4092

**de Richlieu** (Nobleman)
*The Devil Rides Out* - Dennis Wheatley   h   5773

**De Romanus, Marius** (Artist; Vampire)
*The Vampire Armand* - Anne Rice   h   4578

**de Saint-Germain, Francois** (Vampire; Musician)
*Blood Roses* - Chelsea Quinn Yarbro   h   6012

**de Sanha Marsao, Aimeric "Ambrose Cruthers"** (Diplomat)
*A Million Open Doors* - John Barnes   s   353

**de Saumur et Navarre y Cordova, Anastasia "Meanne"** (Royalty)
*An Exchange of Gifts* - Anne McCaffrey   f   3731

**De Soto, Hernando** (Historical Figure; Explorer)
*Tatham Mound* - Piers Anthony   f   191

**De Styx, Marquande** (Political Figure)
*The Silent City* - Elisabeth Vonarburg   s   5592

**de Talair, Bertran** (Nobleman; Minstrel)
*A Song for Arbonne* - Guy Gavriel Kay   f   3017

**de Uzeda, Pedro** (Religious)
*The Manuscript Found in Sragossa* - Jan Potocki   h   4371

**de Verdeur, Michel "Raven"** (Apprentice; Knight)
*King & Raven* - Cary James   f   2858

**De Vere, Tyson** (Architect)
*Horses of the Night* - Michael Cadnum   h   811

**De Vilbiss, Vincent** (Vampire)
*The Book of Common Dread* - Brent Monahan   h   3955

**de Villanueva, Don Sebastian** (Vampire)
*No Blood Spilled* - Les Daniels   h   1338

**De Vore, Howard** (Political Figure; Military Personnel)
*The Broken Wheel* - David Wingrove   s   5918

**De Vries, Alicia "Tisiphone"** (Military Personnel; Disembodied Personality)
*Path of the Fury* - David Weber   s   5680

**De Witt, Ryan** (Student—Junior High School)
*Red Wizard* - Nancy Springer   f   5182

**de Wolf, Mike** (Adventurer; Pirate)
*Typewriter in the Sky* - L. Ron Hubbard   f   2791

**Deacon, Jane** (Young Woman)
*The Hill of Dreams* - Arthur Machen   h   3595

**Dead Man** (Mythical Creature)
*Pretty Pewter Gods* - Glen Cook   f   1152

**Dead Man** (Sidekick; Genius)
*Red Iron Nights* - Glen Cook   f   1153

**Deadmon** (Pirate; Sea Captain)
*Dragon's Plunder* - Brad Strickland   f   5336

**Deal, Brian** (Teenager; Adventurer)
*The Square Deal* - David Drake   s   1644

**Deal, John "J.C."** (Adventurer; Warrior)
*The Square Deal* - David Drake   s   1644

**Deal, Sissy** (Waiter/Waitress)
*Resume with Monsters* - William Browning Spencer   h   5168

**Dean** (Doctor)
*I, Said the Fly* - Michael Shea   h   4944

**Dean, Eddie** (Addict)
*The Drawing of the Three* - Stephen King   h   3131
*The Waste Lands* - Stephen King   h   3143

**Dean, James** (Actor; Historical Figure)
*Spyder* - Norman Partridge   h   4255

**Dean, Scarlet** (Editor)
*Cyberbooks* - Ben Bova   s   582

**Deane, Joseph** (Military Personnel)
*School of Fire* - David Sherman   s   4982

**Deanna** (Vacationer)
*A Well-Timed Enchantment* - Vivian Vande Velde   f   5559

**Dearborn, Sondra** (Researcher; Troubleshooter)
*Proteus in the Underworld* - Charles Sheffield   s   4962

**Death** (Artificial Intelligence; Mythical Creature)
*Donnerjack* - Roger Zelazny   s   6063

**Death** (Mythical Creature)
*Hogfather* - Terry Pratchett   f   4391

**Death** (Spirit)
*Kindred Rites* - Katharine Eliska Kimbriel   f   3118

**Death** (Mythical Creature)
*Maskerade* - Terry Pratchett   f   4395
*The Sandman: Book of Dreams* - Neil Gaiman   f   2105

**d'Eath, Edward** (Nobleman; Criminal)
*Men at Arms* - Terry Pratchett   f   4396

**Death "Bill Door"** (Mythical Creature)
*Reaper Man* - Terry Pratchett   f   4399

**Death of Rats** (Mythical Creature)
*Soul Music* - Terry Pratchett   f   4401

**Death Wind** (Revolutionary)
*Dragons Past* - Gary Gentile   s   2192

**Deathstalker, Owen** (Nobleman; Bounty Hunter)
*Deathstalker Honor* - Simon R. Green   s   2364

**Deathstalker, Owen** (Revolutionary; Nobleman)
*Deathstalker Rebellion* - Simon R. Green   s   2365
*Deathstalker War* - Simon R. Green   s   2366

**Deaton, Jim** (Detective—Private)
*Rockabilly Hell* - William W. Johnstone   h   2933

**Deaver, Herman** (Religious)
*The Folk of the Fringe* - Orson Scott Card   s   886

**Deayl** (Alien)
*The Homecoming* - Barry B. Longyear   s   3521

**Debauchery Devil/Torchy Burns** (Mythical Creature; Demon)
*Strum Again?* - Elizabeth Ann Scarborough  f  4870

**Deborah** (Teenager)
*Wilding* - Melanie Tem  h  5425

**Debra** (Teenager)
*The Sister* - Elleston Trevor  h  5484

**deBurrows, Oliver** (Mythical Creature; Martial Arts Expert)
*Luthien's Gamble* - R.A. Salvatore  f  4802

**deBurrows, Oliver** (Mythical Creature; Highwayman)
*The Sword of Bedwyr* - R.A. Salvatore  f  4808

**DeChance, Megan** (Military Personnel; Psychic)
*Hellworld* - Simon R. Green  s  2371

**Decius** (Slave; Military Personnel)
*The Light Bearer* - Donna Gillespie  f  2229

**Deckard, Rick** (Police Officer)
*Blade Runner 2: The Edge of Human* - K.W. Jeter  s  2906

**Deckard, Rick** (Police Officer; Consultant)
*Blade Runner: Replicant Night* - K.W. Jeter  s  2907

**Decker, Andrew Jackson** (Political Figure)
*Storm Knights* - Bill Slavicsek  f  5087

**Decker, Henry** (Psychologist)
*Sick* - Jay R. Bonansinga  h  571

**DeClerq, Robert** (Detective)
*Evil Eye* - Michael Slade  h  5085

**deCotmer, Ailith** (Teenager)
*A Time for Us* - Christine Holden  f  2731

**Decutonius** (Magician)
*Elfwood* - Rose Estes  f  1837
*Twisted Dragon* - Kevin Stein  f  5251

**Dee, John** (Magician; Doctor)
*Scorpio Rising* - Alex McDonough  s  3804

**Deed, Kalypso** (Computer Expert)
*Dreaming in Smoke* - Tricia Sullivan  s  5353

**Deeds, A.J.** (Parent; Wealthy)
*Meeting the Minotaur* - Carol Dawson  f  1409

**Deems, Ann** (Widow(er))
*Reign* - Chet Williamson  h  5849

**Deeping, Gabriel** (Young Man)
*Gabriel's Body* - Curt Siodmak  h  5073

**Deepneau, Ed** (Scientist; Researcher)
*Insomnia* - Stephen King  h  3135

**Deering, Wilma** (Warrior)
*Hammer of Mars* - M.S. Murdock  s  4049

**Deering, Wilma** (Pilot; Psychologist)
*A Life in the Future* - Martin Caidin  s  827

**Deeters, Nathan** (Store Owner)
*Cross a Dark Bridge* - Deborah Churchman  h  1027

**Defoe, Braxton** (Writer)
*Storytellers* - Julie Anne Parks  h  4249

**Defoe, Piper** (Teacher; Spouse)
*Storytellers* - Julie Anne Parks  h  4249

**Degahv, Rieka** (Spaceship Captain; Diplomat)
*Earth Herald* - Jan Clark  s  1046

**Degahv, Rieka** (Spaceship Captain)
*Prodigy* - Jan Clark  s  1047

**DeGeaux, Vanessa** (Aged Person)
*The Black Mariah* - Jay R. Bonansinga  h  570

**Deite, Manuel "Childe"** (Sorcerer)
*Raven* - S.A. Swiniarski  h  5374

**deJanes, Ecktor** (Administrator; Leader; Widow(er))
*Adiamante* - L.E. Modesitt Jr.  s  3924

**Dekker, Paul** (Pilot; Prospector)
*Heavy Time* - C.J. Cherryh  s  995

**Dekker, Paul** (Pilot)
*Hellburner* - C.J. Cherryh  s  996

**Del** (Warrior)
*Sword-Born* - Jennifer Roberson  f  4612

**del Rio, Annunciata "Nancy"** (Child)
*Last Mountain* - Robert C. Fleet  f  1946

**Del Valle, Ryan** (Spy)
*Wet Work* - Philip Nutman  h  4168

**deLacey, William** (Nobleman; Lawman)
*Lady of the Forest* - Jennifer Roberson  f  4609

**Delacorte, Emil** (Magician)
*Now You See It. . .* - Richard Matheson  h  3688

**Delacorte, Maximillian** (Magician)
*Now You See It. . .* - Richard Matheson  h  3688

**Delacourte, Michaela "Mikey"** (Military Personnel; Spy)
*Spacer Dreams* - Larry Segriff  s  4911

**Delacroix, Conway** (Writer)
*Fetish* - Edward Bryant  h  749

**Delacroix, Ivy** (Child)
*Deathwalker* - R. Patrick Gates  h  2159

**Delacroix, Ivy** (Teenager)
*Tunnelvision* - R. Patrick Gates  h  2162

**Delan** (Wanderer)
*Delan the Mislaid* - Laurie J. Marks  f  3625

**Deland, Roger** (Vampire)
*Desmond: A Novel of Love and the Modern Vampire* - Ulysses G. Dietz  h  1541

**Delane, Ariel** (Teenager)
*Intensity* - Dean R. Koontz  h  3210

**Delaney, Brian** (Scientist; Computer Expert)
*The Turing Option* - Harry Harrison  s  2579

**Delaney, Cathy "Cassidy"** (Amnesiac; Horse Trainer)
*The Warden of Horses* - Karen Ripley  s  4595

**Delaney, Joan** (Police Officer)
*Funland* - Richard Laymon  h  3366

**Delaney, Sylvie** (Young Woman; Spirit)
*Homebody* - Orson Scott Card  h  890

**Delaney, Tania Jane** (Runaway; Prostitute)
*Born to Run* - Mercedes Lackey  f  3271

**Delaney, Tawne** (Clerk; Vampire)
*This Symbiotic Fascination* - Charlee Jacob  h  2843

**delAurvre, Christopher** (Nobleman)
*Maze of Moonlight* - Gael Baudino  f  393

**de'Leonne, Valedan kai** (Royalty)
*The Broken Crown* - Michelle West  f  5757

**Delgado, Susan** (Teenager)
*Wizard and Glass* - Stephen King  h  3144

**Delgato, Amy** (Teenager)
*Dark Time* - Maxine O'Callaghan  h  4189

**DelGiudice, Jeff** (Scientist)
*Echoes of the Fourth Magic* - R.A. Salvatore  f  4799

**Delia** (Animal; Companion)
*Journeyman Wizard* - Mary Frances Zambreno  f  6057
*A Plague of Sorcerers* - Mary Frances Zambreno  f  6058

**Delilah "Del"** (Warrior)
*Sword-Breaker* - Jennifer Roberson  f  4613

**Delilah "Lilah"** (Genetically Altered Being; Singer)
*Jovah's Angel* - Sharon Shinn  s  5001

**Dell** (Drifter)
*The Book of Webster's* - J.N. Williamson  h  5853

**Dellhart, Jackson** (Businessman)
*Something Out There* - Ronald Kelly  h  3056

**Dellon, Melusine "Sinah"** (Actress; Telepath)
*Gravelight* - Marion Zimmer Bradley  f  636

**Delores** (Girlfriend)
*Bride of the Slime Monster* - Craig Shaw Gardner  f  2125

**DeLorn, McLaren "Swordfish"** (Diplomat; Military Personnel)
*Psykosis* - Wilhelmina Baird  s  296

**Delp, Albert** (Scientist)
*Lights Out in the Reptile House* - Jim Shepard  f  4976

**Delroy, Lylene** (Apprentice; Wizard)
*The Conjurer Princess* - Vivian Vande Velde  f  5555

**Delta** (Robot)
*Warsprite* - Jefferson P. Swycaffer  s  5375

**Delta, Ralphayers** (Clone; Genetically Altered Being)
*The Weigher* - Eric Vinicoff  s  5574

**Deluca, Maria** (Computer Expert)
*Permutation City* - Greg Egan  s  1761

**DeLuca, Neil** (Journalist)
*The Gilgul* - Henry W. Hocherman  h  2697

**Delvano, Gwen** (Scientist)
*Dying of the Light* - George R.R. Martin  s  3644

**Demandred** (Wizard)
*Lord of Chaos* - Robert Jordan  f  2988

**DeMarco, Selene** (Antiques Dealer)
*Shadows* - Kimberly Rangel  h  4472

**Demarest, Patti** (Teenager)
*Demon's Fright* - Penelope Banka Kreps  h  3233

**DeMarian, Demnor** (Royalty; Teenager)
*The Stone Prince* - Fiona Patton  f  4259

**DeMarian, Kassandra** (Child; Royalty)
*The Painter Knight* - Fiona Patton  f  4258

**DeMarian, Melesandra III** (Royalty; Political Figure)
*The Stone Prince* - Fiona Patton  f  4259

**Demerit, Geode** (Maintenance Worker)
*Firefly* - Piers Anthony  h  170

**Demetrios, Thann** (Artist)
*The Quicksilver Screen* - Don H. DeBrandt  s  1449

**Demidas, Tanya** (Witch)
*Cardinal's Sin* - Raymond Buckland  h  751

**Demir** (Animal; Telepath)
*City of the Sorcerers* - Mary H. Herbert  f  2673

**Demogorgon** (Computer Expert)
*Iris* - William Barton  s  381

**Demon** (Demon)
*Running with the Demon* - Terry Brooks  f  715

**Demopoulos, Demetrios "Dr. Dimension"** (Scientist; Inventor)
*Dr. Dimension* - John DeChancie  s  1456

**Demos, Maria** (Real Estate Agent)
*Souls* - Katina Alexis  h  71

**den Karynth, Calandryll** (Royalty; Adventurer)
*Dark Magic* - Angus Wells  f  5733

**den Karynth, Calandryll** (Royalty; Scholar)
*Forbidden Magic* - Angus Wells  f  5736

**den Karynth, Calandryll** (Royalty; Renegade)
*Wild Magic* - Angus Wells  f  5741

**den Ostreicher, Jory** (Cyborg)
*Man Plus* - Frederik Pohl  s  4348

**Denethan** (Mutant)
*The Marked Man* - Charles Ingrid  s  2831

**Denison, Arthur** (Scientist; Explorer)
*Dinotopia* - James Gurney   f   2468
*The World Beneath* - James Gurney   f   2469

**Denison, Will** (Adventurer; Teenager)
*Dinotopia* - James Gurney   f   2468

**Denison, Will** (Adventurer)
*Dinotopia Lost* - Alan Dean Foster   f   2003
*The World Beneath* - James Gurney   f   2469

**Denisovitch, Pavel** (Teacher)
*The Nanotech Chronicles* - Michael Flynn   s   1964

**Denman, Lloyd** (Restaurateur)
*The Burning* - Graham Masterton   h   3672

**Dennehy, Nuala Maebh** (Teacher; Revolutionary)
*The Rising of the Moon* - Flynn Connolly   s   1135

**Denness, Leonov Opener** (Scientist; Explorer)
*Mirabile* - Janet Kagan   s   3001

**Dennessy, Anne** (Waiter/Waitress; Abuse Victim)
*The Darkness Within* - Shawn MacDonald   h   3585

**Dennessy, Beth** (Twin; Abuse Victim)
*The Darkness Within* - Shawn MacDonald   h   3585

**Dennessy, Carol** (Twin; Abuse Victim)
*The Darkness Within* - Shawn MacDonald   h   3585

**Denning, John** (Political Figure)
*The Beacon* - Valerie J. Freireich   s   2048

**Dennis** (Murderer)
*Frisk* - Dennis Cooper   h   1170

**Dent, Arthur** (Traveler)
*The Illustrated Hitchhiker's Guide to the Galaxy* - Douglas Adams   s   29
*Mostly Harmless* - Douglas Adams   s   31

**Dentata, Regina** (Teenager)
*Shock Lines* - Warren Newton Beath   h   427

**Denton, Alba** (Witch)
*Black Body* - H.C. Turk   h   5488

**Denton, Eric** (Nobleman)
*Black Body* - H.C. Turk   h   5488

**Denton, Pete** (Taxi Driver)
*The Last Voice They Hear* - Ramsey Campbell   h   858

**Denturian, Maaron** (Immortal; Government Official)
*Dark Sky Legion* - William Barton   s   379

**DenUyl, Luis Raoul** (Warrior)
*The Lizard War* - John Dalmas   s   1325

**Derae** (Psychic)
*Dark Prince* - David Gemmell   f   2187

**Derec** (Amnesiac; Scientist)
*Changeling* - Stephen Leigh   s   3425
*Renegade* - Cordell Scotten   s   4903

**Derigha, Yarrun** (Space Explorer; Military Personnel)
*Expendable* - James Alan Gardner   s   2135

**Derk** (Wizard)
*Dark Lord of Derkholm* - Diana Wynne Jones   f   2946

**Dero, Halleyne dar** (Writer; Castaway)
*Thunder of the Captains* - Holly Lisle   f   3489

**Derrith, Raunn ni Obradi san** (Agent)
*World Spirits* - Aline Boucher-Kaplan   s   580

**Derrith, Verrer ni Rimmani san** (Alien)
*World Spirits* - Aline Boucher-Kaplan   s   580

**Derry, Jerry** (Adventurer; Hero)
*Ye Gods!* - Tom Holt   f   2753

**Derveet** (Revolutionary; Addict)
*Flowerdust* - Gwyneth Jones   s   2952

**Des Grieux, Samuel "Slick"** (Military Personnel)
*The Warrior* - David Drake   s   1651

**Des Jardins, Nicole** (Doctor)
*Rama II* - Arthur C. Clarke   s   1058

**DeSalvo, Lara** (Housewife)
*Shades of Night* - Rick Hautala   h   2612

**DeSalvo, Vincent** (Businessman)
*Shades of Night* - Rick Hautala   h   2612

**Desio** (Royalty)
*Servant of the Empire* - Raymond E. Feist   f   1910

**Desmodus, Eli** (Vampire)
*Desmodus* - Melanie Tem   h   5421

**Desmodus, Joel** (Vampire)
*Desmodus* - Melanie Tem   h   5421

**Desmodus, Rory** (Vampire)
*Desmodus* - Melanie Tem   h   5421

**Desmon, Lilah** (Spacewoman)
*The Cyborg From Earth* - Charles Sheffield   s   4952

**Desmond, Emily** (Teenager)
*King of Morning, Queen of Day* - Ian McDonald   f   3793

**Desmond, Timothy Alfred** (Teenager)
*Gnome Man's Land* - Esther Friesner   f   2075

**Desmond, Timothy Alfred** (Student—High School; Wizard)
*Harpy High* - Esther Friesner   f   2076

**Desmond, Timothy Alfred** (Student—College; Wizard)
*Unicorn U.* - Esther Friesner   f   2084

**Desoll, Trystin** (Military Personnel)
*The Parafaith War* - L.E. Modesitt Jr.   s   3937

**Desse, Gorynal** (Psychic; Revolutionary)
*The Ruins of Ambrai* - Melanie Rawn   f   4489

**Destin, Elissa** (Entertainer)
*Destiny's Carnival* - Warren Murphy   h   4057

**Destree** (Orphan; Psychic)
*Storms of Victory* - Andre Norton   f   4162

**DEUS** (Artificial Intelligence)
*The Deus Machine* - Pierre Ouellette   h   4232

**Dev** (Religious)
*Sunder, Eclipse and Seed* - Elise Guttenberg   f   2471

**Devane, Elizabeth** (Activist; Time Traveler)
*The Trinity Paradox* - Kevin J. Anderson   s   116

**Deveaux, Jacques** (Religious; Computer Expert)
*City of Pain* - John Terra   f   5438

**Develos, Debi** (Vampire; Experimental Subject)
*Blood* - Ron Dee   h   1463

**Deveraux, Rosalie** (Aged Person; Grandparent)
*Blood Roots* - Richie Tankersley Cusick   h   1300

**Devereaux, Cleveland Carroll** (Writer)
*Who Killed James Dean?* - Warren Newton Beath   h   428

**Devery, Nell** (Student—College)
*When Darkness Falls* - Sidney Williams   h   5825

**Devlin** (Scientist)
*The Coachman Rat* - David Henry Wilson   f   5879

**Devlin, Annie** (Immortal; Revolutionary)
*Scotland the Brave* - Jennifer Roberson   f   4611

**Devlin, Johnny** (Rogue; Alcoholic)
*Trader* - Charles de Lint   f   1438

**Devoncroix, Alexander** (Werewolf)
*The Passion* - Donna Boyd   h   603

**DeVore, Howard** (Revolutionary; Leader)
*White Moon, Red Dragon* - David Wingrove   s   5921
*The White Mountain* - David Wingrove   s   5922

**Devore, Kyra** (Child)
*Bag of Bones* - Stephen King   h   3126

**Devore, Max** (Businessman)
*Bag of Bones* - Stephen King   h   3126

**Devreaux, Luc** (Cyborg; Reanimated Dead)
*Universal Soldier* - Robert Tine   s   5476

**DeVries, Harlan** (Serial Killer; Psychic)
*The Place* - T.M. Wright   h   5993

**Dewar** (Sorcerer)
*The Price of Blood and Honor* - Elizabeth Willey   f   5811
*A Sorcerer and a Gentleman* - Elizabeth Willey   f   5812

**Dewdrop** (Animal)
*Whilom* - Robert Watson   f   5639

**DeWellesthar, Auglaise "Dancer"** (Spaceship Captain; Military Personnel)
*Dancer of the Sixth* - Michelle Shirey Crean   s   1254

**Dewey, Thomas E. "Ted"** (Journalist)
*The Lurker* - James V. Smith   h   5123

**DeWinter** (Vampire)
*As One Dead* - Don Bassingthwaite   h   387

**DeWitt, Katherine "Kate" Ariella** (Prisoner)
*Fortress on the Sun* - Paul Cook   s   1157

**DeWitt, Willard "Jeremy Schneider"** (Computer Expert; Businessman)
*Lunar Descent* - Allen Steele   s   5245

**DeWoe, Dekker** (Student; Spaceman)
*Mining the Oort* - Frederik Pohl   s   4349

**Dexter, Fiona** (Telepath; Revolutionary)
*Dark Genesis* - J. Gregory Keyes   s   3096

**Dexter, Quinn** (Religious)
*Emergence* - Peter F. Hamilton   s   2524

**D'Halldt, Lian** (Handicapped)
*Legacies* - Alison Sinclair   s   5069

**Dhalvad** (Alien; Psychic)
*Seeking the Dream Brother* - Marcia J. Bennett   s   451

**Dh'arlo'me** (Mythical Creature)
*Prince of Demons* - Mickey Zucker Reichert   f   4522

**Dharmamitra, Uma** (Agent)
*Burning Bright* - J.S. Russell   h   4733

**Dheribi** (Bastard Son)
*Greenmagic* - Crawford Kilian   f   3105

**Dhu, Zeldan** (Mythical Creature; Magician)
*Elvendude* - Mark Shepherd   f   4980

**di Hoa, Barry** (Pilot; Mentally Ill Person)
*The Voices of Heaven* - Frederik Pohl   s   4356

**di Medusa, Nicoletta Vittorini** (Vampire)
*The Vampire Princess* - Michael Romkey   h   4667

**di Rienzi, Angelica** (Anthropologist; Religious)
*Waking the Moon* - Elizabeth Hand   f   2538

**di Sarc, Sira** (Amnesiac; Alien)
*A Thousand Words for Stranger* - Julie E. Czerneda   s   1304

**Diamond, Tal** (Alien; Military Personnel)
*City of Diamond* - Jane Emerson   s   1807

**Diane** (Writer)
*Amazon: A Novel* - Barbara G. Walker   f   5616

**Diaspad** (Royalty)
*The Work of the Sun* - Teresa Edgerton   f   1746

**Diate, Emilio** (Dancer)
*Traitors* - Kristine Kathryn Rusch   f   4729

**Diaz, Lupe** (Drifter)
*The Orchid Eater* - Marc Laidlaw   h   3312

**Diaz, Rafael** (Student)
*The Terror* - Graham Masterton   h   3679

**Diaz, Ricardo** (Sorcerer)
*Dead of Night* - Alex Abella   *h*   20

**Diaz, Sal** (Drug Dealer)
*The Orchid Eater* - Marc Laidlaw   *h*   3312

**Dibbler, Cut-Me-Own-Throat** (Businessman)
*Moving Pictures* - Terry Pratchett   *f*   4398

**Dibiaja, Mpu** (Shaman)
*The Painted Alphabet* - Diana Darling   *f*   1356

**Dickinson, Emily** (Writer; Historical Figure)
*The Steampunk Trilogy* - Paul Di Filippo   *s*   1518

**Dickory, Tracy** (Animal; Telepath)
*Time and the Clock Mice, Etcetera* - Peter
   Dickinson   *f*   1527

**Didge** (Magician)
*The End-of-Everything Man* - Tom De
   Haven   *f*   1421

**Didi "Deeds"** (Robot; Researcher)
*Circle of One* - Eric James Fullilove   *s*   2092

**Diedrich** (Disembodied Personality)
*Satellite Night News* - Jack Hopkins   *s*   2770

**Diego** (Gunfighter; Time Traveler)
*Time: The Semi-Final Frontier* - Lionel
   Fenn   *s*   1921

**Diego y Rey, Eduardo** (Vampire)
*Bloodshift* - Garfield Reeves-Stevens   *h*   4508

**Diehrenn** (Alien; Writer)
*Encounter with Tiber* - Buzz Aldrin   *s*   64

**Diest, Vernon** (Undertaker)
*The Moons of Summer* - S.K. Epperson   *h*   1831

**Dietrich, Elinor** (Aged Person)
*Revenant* - Melanie Tem   *h*   5424

**Dietrich, Martin** (Military Personnel)
*Darkness on the Ice* - Lois Tilton   *h*   5475

**Dietz, Tre** (Artist; Inventor)
*Freeware* - Rudy Rucker   *s*   4703

**Dieudonne, Genevieve** (Vampire; Health Care
   Professional)
*Anno Dracula* - Kim Newman   *h*   4094

**Dieudonne, Genevieve** (Vampire)
*Drachenfels* - Jack Yeovil   *f*   6022
*Judgment of Tears: Anno Dracula 1959* - Kim
   Newman   *h*   4098

**DiFalco, Tiraena** (Military Personnel; Time Traveler)
*Legacy* - Steve White   *s*   5785

**Digby, Digger** (Mountain Man)
*The World Next Door* - Brad Ferguson   *s*   1924

**Digging Woman** (Indian)
*Walking Wolf* - Nancy A. Collins   *h*   1126

**Digonness, Peter** (Businessman)
*The Expediter* - J. Brian Clarke   *s*   1062

**diGriz, Jim** (Criminal; Adventurer)
*The Stainless Steel Rat Goes to Hell* - Harry
   Harrison   *s*   2574

**DiGriz, Jim** (Criminal)
*The Stainless Steel Rat Sings the Blues* - Harry
   Harrison   *s*   2575

**Diko** (Time Traveler)
*Pastwatch: The Redemption of Christopher Columbus* -
   Orson Scott Card   *s*   895

**Dikobe, Pauline** (Scholar; Spacewoman)
*Foragers* - Charles Oberndorf   *s*   4187

**Diliani** (Mythical Creature)
*Kirins: The Flight of the Ain* - James D.
   Priest   *f*   4433

**Dillon** (Prisoner; Miner)
*Alien 3* - Alan Dean Foster   *s*   1993

**Dillon, Lan** (Police Officer)
*Reunion on Neverend* - John E. Stith   *s*   5306

**Dillon, Ronny** (Artist; Telepath)
*Dreambuilder* - Tom Deitz   *f*   1471

**Dillon, Ronny** (Orphan; Student—High School)
*Soulsmith* - Tom Deitz   *f*   1475

**Dillon, Ronny** (Artist; Telepath)
*Wordwright* - Tom Deitz   *f*   1478

**di'Marano, Diora** (Noblewoman; Widow(er))
*The Broken Crown* - Michelle West   *f*   5757

**Dimblethum** (Mythical Creature)
*Into the Land of the Unicorns* - Bruce
   Coville   *f*   1219

**Dinaos** (Nobleman; Artist)
*The Belly of the Wolf* - R.A. MacAvoy   *f*   3580

**Dingletoon, Tish** (Animal)
*The Cockroaches of Stay More* - Donald
   Harington   *f*   2544

**Dinsman, Angela** (Troubleshooter; Anthropologist)
*Reefsong* - Carol Severance   *s*   4923

**Dinsmuir, Harold "Dirty"** (Scientist)
*Insatiable* - David Dvorkin   *h*   1707

**Diogenes, Romanus** (Ruler)
*Shards of Empire* - Susan Shwartz   *f*   5017

**Dion** (Magician; Student)
*Mage Heart* - Jane Routley   *f*   4686

**Dion** (Martial Arts Expert; Healer; Twin)
*Shadow Leader* - Tara K. Harper   *f*   2552

**Dion** (Martial Arts Expert; Healer)
*Wolfwalker* - Tara K. Harper   *f*   2553

**Dions** (Religious; Psychic)
*Throne of Isis* - Judith Tarr   *f*   5397

**Dios, Warden** (Police Officer; Leader)
*The Gap into Ruin: This Day All Gods Die* - Stephen
   R. Donaldson   *s*   1575

**Dirk** (Musician)
*The Abraxas Marvel Circus* - Stephen Leigh   *f*   3423

**Dirona** (Royalty; Sorceress)
*Search for the Starblade* - Keith Taylor   *f*   5408

**Dismarum** (Wizard)
*Wit'ch Fire* - James Clemens   *f*   1082

**d'Iste, Tiran** (Mercenary; Magician)
*Dark Mirror, Dark Dreams* - Sharon Green   *f*   2357
*Silver Princess, Golden Knight* - Sharon
   Green   *f*   2359

**d'Iste, Tiran** (Ruler; Magician)
*Wind Whispers, Shadow Shouts* - Sharon
   Green   *f*   2360

**Distephano, Vincent** (Military Personnel)
*Alien Resurrection* - A.C. Crispin   *s*   1258

**DiThorn, Bram** (Nobleman; Mythical Creature)
*The Seventh Sentinel* - Mary Kirchoff   *f*   3154

**DiThorn, Guerrand** (Wizard)
*The Seventh Sentinel* - Mary Kirchoff   *f*   3154

**Dittimore, Jeffry** (Lawyer)
*The Land of Nod* - Mark A. Clements   *h*   1085

**Dittrich, Robert "Bobby"** (Computer Expert)
*Forests of the Night* - S. Andrew Swann   *s*   5363

**Diver Dan** (Serial Killer)
*Bloodletter* - Warren Newton Beath   *h*   426

**Divine Endurance** (Animal; Android)
*Flowerdust* - Gwyneth Jones   *s*   2952

**Dixon, Benjamin** (Vampire Hunter; Religious)
*Blood Lust* - Ron Dee   *h*   1464

**Dixon, Stephanie** (Doctor)
*Kaleidoscope Eyes* - Graham Watkins   *h*   5631

**Dixon, Travis** (Publisher)
*Night Brothers* - Sidney Williams   *h*   5824

**d'jehn, Tahl** (Alien; Spaceship Captain)
*The Alien Dark* - Diana G. Gallagher   *s*   2108

**Djinn** (Mythical Creature)
*The Djinn in the Nightingale's Eye* - A.S.
   Byatt   *f*   794

**Dnivtopun** (Alien)
*The Children's Hour* - Jerry Pournelle   *s*   4372

**D'Noch** (Guide)
*The Book of Water* - Marjorie Bradley
   Kellogg   *f*   3045

**Dob** (Alien)
*Back to the Time Trap* - Keith Laumer   *s*   3343

**Doban** (Prehistoric Human; Child)
*Shiva: An Adventure of the Ice Age* - J.H.
   Brennan   *f*   669

**Dobbs** (Public Relations)
*Kill Crazy* - L.S. Riker   *s*   4590

**Dobbs, Charles "Sugar" Franklin** (Professor)
*The Healing of Crossroads* - Nick
   O'Donohoe   *f*   4195

**Dobbs, Charles "Sugar" Franklin** (Professor;
   Veterinarian)
*The Magic and the Healing* - Nick
   O'Donohoe   *f*   4196

**Dobbs, Evelyn** (Spacewoman; Psychologist)
*Fool's War* - Sarah Zettel   *s*   6079

**Dobbs, J.R. "BoB"** (Religious; Activist)
*Reality Is What You Can Get Away With: An
   Illustrated Screenplay* - Robert Anton
   Wilson   *s*   5904

**Dobbs, Karl** (Time Traveler)
*The Lincoln Hunters* - Wilson Tucker   *s*   5487

**Dobbs, Melvin** (Magician)
*Resurrection Dreams* - Richard Laymon   *h*   3371

**Doc** (Revolutionary)
*Dragons Past* - Gary Gentile   *s*   2192

**Doctor** (Astronaut)
*Eden* - Stanislaw Lem   *s*   3434

**Dodge, Allison** (Activist)
*Gaia's Toys* - Rebecca Ore   *s*   4218

**Dodger** (Mutant; Computer Expert)
*Choose Your Enemies Carefully* - Robert N.
   Charrette   *s*   971
*Find Your Own Truth* - Robert N. Charrette   *f*   972
*Never Deal with a Dragon* - Robert N.
   Charrette   *s*   975

**Dog Brother** (Supernatural Being)
*Tooth and Claw* - Graham Masterton   *h*   3680

**Dog-Woman** (Animal Trainer)
*Sexing the Cherry* - Jeanette Winterson   *f*   5927

**Dogbrick** (Thief; Philosopher)
*The Dark Shore* - Adam Lee   *f*   3385

**Doggie** (Robot)
*Daughter of Elysium* - Joan Slonczewski   *s*   5091

**Dohen, Spike** (Restaurateur)
*Skinny Legs and All* - Tom Robbins   *f*   4607

**Doheny, Mike** (Engineer; Administrator)
*Sunstroke* - David Kagan   *s*   2999

**Doheny, Shannon** (Teenager)
*Elvira: Transylvania 90210* - Elvira   *h*   1802

**Doland, Jane** (Banker)
*Flying Dutch* - Tom Holt   *f*   2750

**Dollar, John** (Sea Captain)
*John Dollar* - Marianne Wiggins   *h*   5799

**Dolmi, Yarkol** (Doctor)
*Spirits of Cavern and Hearth* - M. Coleman
 Easton  *f*  1722

**Dolph** (Royalty)
*Isle of View* - Piers Anthony  *f*  177

**Domenico** (Religious; Magician)
*The Devil's Day* - James Blish  *h*  525

**Domerc** (Student—College; Wizard)
*Lost in Translation* - Margaret Ball  *f*  315

**Dominque, Nyota** (Scientist; Spaceship Captain)
*Saturn's Child* - Nichelle Nichols  *s*  4101

**Domon, Tamrissa** (Wizard; Abuse Victim)
*Convergence* - Sharon Green  *f*  2356

**Donaher, Michael** (Religious; FBI Agent)
*Bureau 13* - Nick Pollotta  *f*  4362
*Full Moonster* - Nick Pollotta  *f*  4364

**Donaldson, Larry** (Businessman)
*Mind Stealer* - Lee Duigon  *h*  1672

**Donaldson, Pamela** (Young Woman)
*Madeline: After the Fall of Usher* - Marie
 Kiraly  *h*  3150

**Donaltsson, Marta** (Magician; Midwife)
*Kindred Rites* - Katharine Eliska Kimbriel  *f*  3118

**Donatello, Kevin** (Teenager)
*The Uprising* - Abigail McDaniels  *h*  3785

**Donato, Rinio** (Trader)
*Vaporetto 13* - Robert Girardi  *h*  2241

**Donna** (Girlfriend)
*Pirates of the Universe* - Terry Bisson  *s*  506

**Donnelly, John** (Psychologist; Time Traveler)
*Door Number Three* - Patrick O'Leary  *s*  4210

**Donner, Bruce** (Writer)
*Stage Fright* - Clare McNally  *h*  3858

**Donner, Greg** (Writer)
*Dreamer* - Daniel Quinn  *h*  4454

**Donner, Mark** (Young Man)
*Disciples of Dread* - Hugh B. Cave  *h*  941

**Donnerjack, John D'Arcy** (Computer Expert)
*Donnerjack* - Roger Zelazny  *s*  6063

**Donohoe, Annabelle** (Businesswoman)
*Isaac Asimov's I-Bots* - Steve Perry  *s*  4297

**Donohue, Gabriela "Gaby"** (Experimental Subject;
 Girlfriend)
*Doc Sidhe* - Aaron Allston  *f*  85

**Donohue, Greg** (Boyfriend)
*A Witch Across Time* - Gilbert B. Cross  *f*  1272

**Donokh** (Alien)
*Shade* - Emily Devenport  *s*  1504

**Donough** (Leader; Warrior)
*Pride of Lions* - Morgan Llywelyn  *f*  3506

**Donovan, Fay** (Doctor)
*Lagoon* - Alison Drake  *h*  1625

**Donovan, Lincoln "Link"** (Journalist)
*The Devil's Laughter* - William W.
 Johnstone  *h*  2930

**Donovan, Vera** (Aged Person)
*Dolores Claiborne* - Stephen King  *h*  3130

**Donya** (Thief; Mythical Creature)
*Shadow* - Anne Logston  *f*  3512
*Shadow Dance* - Anne Logston  *f*  3513

**Dooley, Paul** (Imposter; Computer Expert)
*The Tranquility Alternative* - Allen Steele  *s*  5248

**Dooley, Samantha "Sam"** (Pilot)
*No Limits* - Nigel Findley  *s*  1938

**Doom** (Leader)
*Between Floors* - Thomas F. Monteleone  *h*  3957

**Doomsday** (Monster)
*The Death and Life of Superman* - Roger
 Stern  *s*  5262

**Doomstalker** (Demon)
*Doomstalker* - Gary Brandner  *h*  661

**Doon, Harley** (Android)
*Steelheart* - William C. Dietz  *s*  1552

**Door** (Gentlewoman; Fugitive)
*Neverwhere* - Neil Gaiman  *f*  2104

**Doorman, Lissea** (Spaceship Captain; Military
 Personnel)
*The Voyage* - David Drake  *s*  1649

**Doot** (Teenager)
*Wolf Flow* - K.W. Jeter  *h*  2918

**Dopey** (Alien)
*The Other End of Time* - Frederik Pohl  *s*  4351

**Dorcas** (Mythical Creature)
*Diggers* - Terry Pratchett  *s*  4386

**Dorcas** (Mythical Creature; Alien)
*Truckers* - Terry Pratchett  *s*  4402

**Dore, Michael** (Genius; Philanthropist)
*Lunar Justice* - Charles L. Harness  *s*  2545

**Doreen** (Spouse)
*Flickering Shadows* - Kwadwo Agymah
 Kamau  *f*  3006

**Dorella** (Witch; Alien)
*Dorella* - Mark A. Garland  *f*  2142

**Doresh, Barc** (Genetically Altered Being; Heir)
*Stepwater* - L. Warren Douglas  *s*  1588

**Dorfl** (Mythical Creature)
*Feet of Clay* - Terry Pratchett  *f*  4389

**Dorman, Jeremy** (Scientist)
*Antibodies* - Kevin J. Anderson  *h*  99

**d'Ormonde, Hue** (Businessman)
*Blood Roses* - Chelsea Quinn Yarbro  *h*  6012

**Doron** (Religious)
*Rainbow Man* - M.J. Engh  *s*  1824

**Dorothea "Diamond Mask"** (Psychic)
*Magnificat* - Julian May  *s*  3699

**Dorrin** (Magician; Engineer)
*The Magic Engineer* - L.E. Modesitt Jr.  *f*  3933

**Dorset, Byron** (Genetically Altered Being)
*Specters of the Dawn* - S. Andrew Swann  *s*  5368

**Dorthansdotter, Paksenarrion "Paks"** (Farmer;
 Military Personnel)
*Sheepfarmer's Daughter* - Elizabeth Moon  *f*  3973

**Dorvin, Jan** (Fugitive)
*The Sky Lords* - John Brosnan  *s*  720

**Dorvin, Jan** (Administrator)
*The War of the Sky Lords* - John Brosnan  *s*  721

**Doshky "Dosh"** (Prostitute; Actor)
*Crashcourse* - Wilhelmina Baird  *s*  295

**Douay, Deldragon Drakedon "Drake"** (Teenager;
 Apprentice)
*Lords of the Sword* - Hugh Cook  *f*  1156

**Douchette, Earl** (Aged Person)
*The Jimjams* - Michael Green  *h*  2345

**D'oud** (Alien; Scientist)
*The False Mirror* - Alan Dean Foster  *s*  2004

**Dougal, Duncan** (Student)
*My Teacher Fried My Brains* - Bruce
 Coville  *s*  1223

**Dougherty, Kim** (Architect)
*The House Next Door* - Anne Rivers
 Siddons  *h*  5021

**Doughterty, Brian** (Writer)
*Icebound* - Dean R. Koontz  *h*  3209

**Douglas, Doug** (Worker; Unemployed)
*Slippin' into Darkness* - Norman Partridge  *h*  4254

**Douglas, Jardine Craig** (Military Personnel)
*A History Maker* - Alasdair Gray  *s*  2338

**Douglas, Jill** (Housewife)
*The Baby* - Stephanie Kegan  *h*  3033

**Douglas, Kirk** (Detective)
*The Book of Webster's* - J.N. Williamson  *h*  5853

**Douglas, Medoret** (Alien; Foundling)
*A Whisper of Time* - Paula E. Downing  *s*  1595

**Douglas, Morric** (Musician)
*Blackmantle: A Triumph* - Patricia Kennealy-
 Morrison  *f*  3059

**Douglas, Tom** (Doctor)
*The Baby* - Stephanie Kegan  *h*  3033

**Douglass, Frederick** (Journalist; Historical Figure)
*How Few Remain* - Harry Turtledove  *s*  5504

**Do'Urden, Drizzt** (Mythical Creature; Adventurer)
*The Legacy* - R.A. Salvatore  *f*  4801
*Siege of Darkness* - R.A. Salvatore  *f*  4804
*The Silent Blade* - R.A. Salvatore  *f*  4805
*Sojourn* - R.A. Salvatore  *f*  4806
*Starless Night* - R.A. Salvatore  *f*  4807

**Dove, Amy** (Sociologist)
*God's World* - Ian Watson  *s*  5636

**Dovero, Colinda** (Adventurer)
*Fabulous Harbors* - Michael Moorcock  *f*  3981

**do'Verrada, Alejandro** (Nobleman)
*The Golden Key* - Melanie Rawn  *f*  4486

**Dowd, Katherine "Katy"** (Librarian; Adventurer)
*Flames of the Dragon* - Robin Wayne Bailey  *f*  287

**Downey, Tressa** (Administrator)
*Golden Eyes* - John Gideon  *h*  2220

**Downing, Rae** (Secretary)
*Orphans* - Jean Simon  *h*  5065

**Dowornobb** (Alien; Scientist)
*Genellan: Planetfall* - Scott G. Gier  *s*  2223

**Doyle, Arthur Conan** (Historical Figure; Writer)
*Believe: A Novel* - William Shatner  *f*  4929
*Nevermore* - William Hjortsberg  *f*  2692
*Photographing Fairies* - Steve Szilagyi  *f*  5379

**Doyle, Irini** (Cook; Sports Figure)
*The Sweetheart Season* - Karen Joy Fowler  *f*  2029

**Doyle, Keith** (Student)
*Higher Mythology* - Jody Lynn Nye  *f*  4170

**Doyle, Keith** (Student—College)
*Mythology 101* - Jody Lynn Nye  *f*  4173

**Doyle, Keith** (Student; Traveler)
*Mythology Abroad* - Jody Lynn Nye  *f*  4174

**Doyle, Lionel** (Professor)
*The Beast* - Marie Ardell White  *h*  5784

**Doyle, Vernon** (Businessman)
*Harrowgate* - Daniel H. Gower  *h*  2292

**Drackman, Bryan "Ticktock"** (Young Man)
*Dragon Tears* - Dean R. Koontz  *h*  3205

**Dracul, Vlad** (Vampire)
*Vampire Junkies* - Norman Spinrad  *h*  5175

**Dracula** (Vampire)
*The Angry Angel* - Chelsea Quinn Yarbro  *h*  6010
*Anno Dracula* - Kim Newman  *h*  4094
*Blood of the Impaler* - Jeffrey Sackett  *h*  4779
*Bram Stoker's Dracula* - Fred Saberhagen  *h*  4763
*Dracul: An Eternal Love Story* - Nancy
 Kilpatrick  *h*  3110
*The Dracula Tape* - Fred Saberhagen  *h*  4765
*The Holmes-Dracula File* - Fred
 Saberhagen  *h*  4767

**Dracula** (Vampire; Nobleman)
*The Mammoth Book of Dracula* - Stephen
Jones   *h*   2972

**Dracula** (Vampire)
*Seance for a Vampire* - Fred Saberhagen   *h*   4773
*Dracula Unbound* - Brian W. Aldiss   *h*   55

**Dracula, Radu** (Vampire)
*A Sharpness on the Neck* - Fred
Saberhagen   *h*   4774

**Dracula, Vlad** (Vampire)
*A Sharpness on the Neck* - Fred
Saberhagen   *h*   4774

**Dragelman, Dan** (Police Officer)
*Claw* - Ken Eulo   *h*   1850

**Dragit** (Alien; Ruler)
*On the Run* - Christie Golden   *s*   2254

**Dragon** (Mythical Creature; Royalty)
*Dragon Tome* - Richard A. Knaak   *f*   3169

**Dragon** (Deity)
*Dark Heart* - Margaret Weis   *f*   5707

**Drake, Cadence "Cady"** (Spaceship Captain)
*Hunting the Corrigan's Blood* - Holly Lisle   *s*   3484

**Drake, Christopher** (Military Personnel)
*Cybernarc* - Robert Cain   *s*   829

**Drake, Christopher** (Martial Arts Expert; Teacher)
*End Game* - Robert Cain   *s*   830

**Drake, Christopher** (Military Personnel)
*Gold Dragon* - Robert Cain   *s*   831

**Drake, Franz** (Vampire)
*Kiss of the Vampire* - Lee Weathersby   *h*   5657

**Drake, Michael** (Scientist)
*A Hunger in the Soul* - Mike Resnick   *s*   4545

**Drake, Michaeline** (Scientist)
*Ancient Heavens* - Robert E. Vardeman · *s*   5561

**Drake, Richard** (Scientist)
*Ancient Heavens* - Robert E. Vardeman   *s*   5561

**Drake, Selma** (Witch)
*The Quagmire* - James Kisner   *h*   3160

**Drake, Simon Tepes** (Vampire)
*Kiss of the Vampire* - Lee Weathersby   *h*   5657

**Drake, Tannim** (Sports Figure; Magician)
*Chrome Circle* - Mercedes Lackey   *f*   3277

**D'Rasha** (Businessman)
*Hand of Prophecy* - Severna Park   *s*   4244

**Draus, Morry** (Clone; Heir)
*I Wake From a Dream of a Drowned Star City* - S.P.
Somtow   *s*   5157

**Dravie, Lena** (Scientist)
*Stranger Suns* - George Zebrowski   *s*   6060

**Dread, Doctor** (Terrorist; Leader)
*Revenge of the Fluffy Bunnies* - Craig Shaw
Gardner   *f*   2132

**Dreadful Eye** (Alien)
*The Woman between the Worlds* - F. Gwynplaine
MacIntyre   *s*   3596

**Dredd, Joseph "Judge"** (Police Officer; Fugitive)
*Judge Dredd* - Neal Barrett Jr.   *s*   366

**Dreen** (Religious)
*The Hands of Lyr* - Andre Norton   *f*   4154

**Drev** (Ruler; Wizard)
*The Dark Shore* - Adam Lee   *f*   3385

**Drew** (Musician)
*The Making of a Monster* - Gail Petersen   *h*   4307

**Drew, Jonathan** (Police Officer)
*Night Blood* - Eric Flanders   *h*   1945

**Drew, Laura** (Saloon Hostess; Lover)
*The Unseen* - Joseph A. Citro   *h*   1039

**Drexel, David** (Government Official)
*Firelance* - David Mace   *s*   3586

**Dreyer, Sigmund** (Detective—Private)
*Dydeetown World* - F. Paul Wilson   *s*   5887

**Drib** (Student; Chimneysweep)
*The Knights of Cawdor* - Mike Jefferies   *f*   2886

**Dribble** (Genetically Altered Being)
*Clipjoint* - Wilhelmina Baird   *s*   294

**Driscoll, Guy** (Journalist)
*The Moons of Summer* - S.K. Epperson   *h*   1831

**Driver, Greg** (Actor)
*Horrorshow* - David Darke   *h*   1353

**Drizzt Do'Urden** (Mythical Creature; Adventurer)
*Passage to Dawn* - R.A. Salvatore   *f*   4803

**Droagn, Endark** (Alien; Telepath)
*Lair of the Cyclops* - Allen L. Wold   *s*   5933

**D'Rosselin, Jens Metadi Jessan** (Teenager; Heir)
*The Long Hunt* - Debra Doyle   *s*   1602

**Drosselmeier, Christian Elias "Godfather"** (Artisan)
*Nutcracker* - E.T.A. Hoffmann   *f*   2719

**Drulethen "Dru"** (Mythical Creature; Sorcerer)
*The Qualinesti* - Paul B. Thompson   *f*   5455

**Drumheller, Thorn** (Companion; Wizard)
*Shadow Dawn* - Chris Claremont   *f*   1042

**Drumheller, Thorn** (Mythical Creature; Wizard)
*Shadow Moon* - George Lucas   *f*   3540

**Drumm, Pat** (Astronaut)
*The Fortress of Utopia* - Jack Williamson   *s*   5863

**Drummond, Cathan** (Knight; Companion)
*The Bastard Prince* - Katherine Kurtz   *f*   3255

**Drummond, John** (Detective—Homicide; Vampire)
*At Sword's Point* - Scott MacMillan   *f*   3601

**Drummond, John** (Detective—Homicide)
*Knights of the Blood* - Scott MacMillan   *f*   3602

**Drumon** (Artisan)
*The Forge of Virtue* - Lynn Abbey   *f*   16

**Drusilla** (Sorceress)
*The Fourth Guardian* - Ronald Anthony
Cross   *s*   1273

**Dryden, Thatcher** (Businessman)
*Heathern* - Jack Womack   *s*   5958

**Dryhope, Kate "Kittock"** (Parent)
*A History Maker* - Alasdair Gray   *s*   2338

**Dryhope, Wat** (Warrior; Hero)
*A History Maker* - Alasdair Gray   *s*   2338

**Dryke, Mikhail** (Businessman)
*The Quiet Pools* - Michael P. Kube-
McDowell   *s*   3249

**du Boise, Llysette** (Refugee; Singer)
*The Ghost of the Revelator* - L.E. Modesitt
Jr.   *s*   3931

**Du Boise, Llysette** (Singer; Spy)
*Of Tangible Ghosts* - L.E. Modesitt Jr.   *f*   3935

**du Cheyne, Gaetan** (Spaceship Captain)
*Acts of Conscience* - William Barton   *s*   377

**Du Lucent, Andrea** (Royalty)
*The War of the Sky Lords* - John Brosnan   *s*   721

**du Mond, Paul** (Apprentice)
*The Fire Rose* - Mercedes Lackey   *f*   3280

**du Pres, Josette** (Noblewoman)
*Angelique's Descent* - Lara Parker   *h*   4246

**Dubchek, Jackson** (Historian; Time Traveler)
*Stranded!* - Warren Norwood   *s*   4164

**Duberville, Myron** (Teenager; Genius)
*Outer Space and All That Junk* - Mel
Gilden   *s*   2227

**Dubhain** (Mythical Creature)
*Faery in Shadow* - C.J. Cherryh   *f*   987

**DuBois, Ned** (Astronaut)
*Firestar* - Michael Flynn   *s*   1962

**Ducane, Wilhemina "Willie"** (Child)
*Demon Dance* - T. Chris Martindale   *h*   3655

**Ducas, Leo** (Military Personnel)
*Cross and Crescent* - Susan Shwartz   *f*   5014
*Shards of Empire* - Susan Shwartz   *f*   5017

**Duffy, Karen** (Young Woman)
*Boundaries* - T.M. Wright   *h*   5990

**Dufrenoy, Michael** (Writer; Orphan)
*Paris in the Twentieth Century* - Jules
Verne   *s*   5568

**Dug** (Teenager; Adventurer)
*Demons Don't Dream* - Piers Anthony   *f*   168

**Dugan, Andrew** (Artist)
*My Soul to Take* - Steven Spruill   *s*   5184

**Duin, Mael** (Outcast; Wanderer)
*The Voyage of Mael Duin's Curragh* - Patricia
Aakhus   *f*   2

**Duinngan, Will** (Lawyer)
*Darkborn* - Matthew J. Costello   *h*   1195

**Duke, Bob** (Stock Broker; Werewolf)
*The Wild* - Whitley Strieber   *h*   5343

**Duke, Cindy** (Spouse)
*The Wild* - Whitley Strieber   *h*   5343

**Duke, Kevin Thomas** (Child)
*The Wild* - Whitley Strieber   *h*   5343

**Duke, Nicholas** (Journalist)
*Majestic* - Whitley Strieber   *s*   5341

**Dulac, Will** (Composer)
*A Call to Arms* - Alan Dean Foster   *s*   1995

**Dulaine, Dirk** (Sidekick; Military Personnel)
*A Wizard in Chaos* - Christopher Stasheff   *s*   5230

**Dulaine, Dirk** (Sidekick; Adventurer)
*A Wizard in Peace* - Christopher Stasheff   *s*   5233

**Dulaine, Dirk** (Sidekick)
*A Wizard in War* - Christopher Stasheff   *s*   5234

**Dulay** (Royalty; Psychic)
*Inhuman Beings* - Jerry Jay Carroll   *s*   914

**Dulcet, Giulia** (Musician; Teacher)
*Song for the Basilisk* - Patricia A. McKillip   *f*   3841

**Dulcie** (Animal)
*Cats Raise the Dead* - Shirley Rousseau
Murphy   *f*   4054

**Dulcimer** (Alien; Pilot)
*Transcendence* - Charles Sheffield   *s*   4967

**DuMar, Theresa "T.J." Jr.** (Teenager)
*T.J.'s Ghost* - Shirley Climo   *h*   1087

**Dumenco, Georg** (Scientist)
*Lethal Exposure* - Kevin J. Anderson   *s*   110

**Dumery of Shiphaven** (Child; Traveler)
*The Blood of a Dragon* - Lawrence Watt-
Evans   *f*   5640

**Dun, Richard** (Consultant; Vampire)
*Keeper of the King* - Nigel Bennett   *h*   452

**Dun Lady's Jess** (Animal; Young Woman)
*Dun Lady's Jess* - Doranna Durgin   *f*   1704

**Dunbar, Lane** (Teenager)
*The Stake* - Richard Laymon   *h*   3372

**Dunbar, Larry** (Writer)
*The Stake* - Richard Laymon   *h*   3372

**Dunbar, Maggie** (Teacher)
*Dark Tide* - Elizabeth Forrest   *h*   1972

**Dunbar, Sheik** (Military Personnel)
*Starstrike* - W. Michael Gear   s   2172

**Duncan** (Religious)
*Eternity* - Maggie Shayne   f   4943

**Duncan, George Thomas** (Leader; Revolutionary)
*Ecstasy Club* - Douglas Rushkoff   s   4732

**Duncan, William St.-George** (Revolutionary)
*Dayworld Breakup* - Philip Jose Farmer   s   1869

**Dunham, Arthur "Art"** (Businessman)
*The Rebirth of Wonder* - Lawrence Watt-
    Evans   f   5646

**Dunjer, Tom** (Security Officer)
*Specterworld* - Isidore Haiblum   s   2480

**Dunkle, Simon** (Director)
*Flicker* - Theodore Roszak   h   4683

**Dunladry, Duncan** (Royalty; Heir—Dispossessed)
*Caledon of the Mists* - Deborah Turner
    Harris   f   2560

**Dunladry, Mhairi** (Royalty; Heiress—Dispossessed)
*Caledon of the Mists* - Deborah Turner
    Harris   f   2560

**Dunladry, Mhairi** (Royalty)
*The Queen of Ashes* - Deborah Turner
    Harris   f   2561

**Dunlap, Gordon** (Journalist)
*The Totem* - David Morrell   h   4012

**Dunlet, Kate** (Professor)
*Deep Quarry* - John E. Stith   s   5302

**dunMheric, Deymorin Rhomandi** (Royalty)
*Ring of Intrigue* - Jane S. Fancher   f   1863
*Ring of Lightning* - Jane S. Fancher   f   1864

**dunMheric, Mikhyel Rhomandi** (Royalty;
    Handicapped)
*Ring of Intrigue* - Jane S. Fancher   f   1863

**dunMheric, Mikhyel Rhomandi** (Royalty)
*Ring of Lightning* - Jane S. Fancher   f   1864

**dunMheric, Nikaenor "Nikki" Rhomandi** (Royalty)
*Ring of Lightning* - Jane S. Fancher   f   1864

**Dunn, Jim** (FBI Agent)
*The Ebon Mask* - Richard Lee Byers   h   797

**Dunn, Rick** (Architect)
*The Ascending* - T.M. Wright   h   5989

**Dunreith, Cassandra "Cass"** (Martial Arts Expert;
    Writer)
*Dragon Moon* - Chris Claremont   f   1040

**Dunstan, Sara** (Warrior)
*Legacy of Steel* - Mary H. Herbert   f   2675

**Dunworthy, James** (Professor)
*Doomsday Book* - Connie Willis   s   5868

**Duone, Kestrienne** (Noblewoman; Wizard)
*Emerald House Rising* - Peg Kerr   f   3080

**Duone, Morgan** (Nobleman; Wizard)
*Emerald House Rising* - Peg Kerr   f   3080

**Dupin, C. Auguste** (Detective)
*The Lighthouse at the End of the World* - Stephen
    Marlowe   h   3631

**Dupree, Lorelle** (Demon)
*The New Neighbor* - Ray Garton   h   2154

**Dur** (Sorcerer)
*Drum Warning* - Jo Clayton   f   1066

**Dura** (Genetically Altered Being; Settler)
*Flux* - Stephen Baxter   s   399

**Duran** (Mythical Creature; Mercenary)
*Headhunters* - Mel Odom   s   4192

**Duran, Marcus** (Religious; Zealot)
*Parable of the Talents* - Octavia E. Butler   s   793

**Duran, Michael** (Artist)
*Diary of a Vampire* - Gary Bowen   h   600

**Durancy, Abraham** (Scientist; Architect)
*Queen City Jazz* - Kathleen Ann Goonan   s   2275

**Duratan** (Historian)
*Flight of Vengeance* - Andre Norton   f   4152

**Durbin, Ashley** (Journalist)
*Hair of the Dog* - Brett Davis   f   1400

**Durendal** (Knight; Agent)
*The Gilded Chain: A Tale of the King's Blades* - Dave
    Duncan   f   1679

**Durham, Paul** (Computer Expert)
*Permutation City* - Greg Egan   s   1761

**Durmontov, Alexei** (Royalty; Wizard)
*Magician's Ward* - Patricia C. Wrede   f   5976

**Duroc, Roger** (Agent; Religious)
*Comeback Tour: The Sky Belongs to the Stars* - Jack
    Yeovil   s   6020

**Durvash** (Time Traveler; Alien)
*Man-Kzin Wars V* - Larry Niven   s   4125

**Dutton, Brian** (Businessman)
*The 7th Guest* - Matthew J. Costello   h   1192

**Duvall, Katherine** (Detective—Homicide)
*Dark Matter* - Garfield Reeves-Stevens   h   4509

**Duvet, Berthe** (Servant; Writer)
*The Porcelain Dove* - Delia Sherman   f   4983

**Duzon** (Nobleman; Warrior)
*Touched by the Gods* - Lawrence Watt-
    Evans   f   5651

**Dvorak, Daniel** (Doctor)
*Life Support* - Tess Gerritsen   h   2206

**Dvorak, Jason** (Administrator; Architect)
*Assemblers of Infinity* - Kevin J. Anderson   s   100

**Dvorak, Teresa** (Real Estate Agent)
*Frostwing* - Richard A. Knaak   f   3170

**Dwago** (Cult Member)
*Graythings* - Pat Graversen   h   2335

**Dwayne** (Teenager)
*The Cat* - R.L. Stine   h   5285

**Dweller** (Alien)
*The Source* - Brian Lumley   h   3565

**Dwiri** (Telepath)
*OtherWhere* - Margaret Wander Bonanno   s   566

**Dworkin, Sam** (Researcher; Aged Person)
*Silent Zone* - Stephen Molstad   s   3952

**Dwyer** (Librarian)
*Painted Devil* - Michael Bedard   f   430

**Dy-Dybo** (Alien; Ruler)
*Fossil Hunter* - Robert J. Sawyer   s   4855

**Dycek, Rachel** (Doctor)
*Climbing Olympus* - Kevin J. Anderson   s   102

**Dyckman, Alicia "Lish"** (Producer; Divorced
    Person)
*The Swords of Zinjaban* - L. Sprague de
    Camp   s   1418

**Dyfed** (Warrior)
*Shadow of the Seventh Moon* - Nancy Varian
    Berberick   f   459

**Dykes, Joe** (Government Official)
*Operation Damocles* - Oscar L. Fellows   s   1916

**Dylan** (Young Man)
*Gehenna* - Lewis Gannett   h   2114

**Dyson, T.T.** (Serial Killer)
*Fiend* - C. Dean Andersson   h   138

**Dzaminid** (Shaman)
*Spirits of Cavern and Hearth* - M. Coleman
    Easton   f   1722

**Dzierlatka, Martin** (Actor)
*Bereavement* - Richard Lortz   h   3525

## E

**Ea** (Linguist; Captive)
*Black Wine* - Candas Jane Dorsey   s   1582

**Eagen, Wesley** (Teenager)
*Hell-O-Ween* - David Robbins   h   4598

**Eakins, Daniel Jamieson** (Time Traveler)
*The Man Who Folded Himself* - David
    Gerrold   s   2208

**Eakins, Diane Jane** (Time Traveler)
*The Man Who Folded Himself* - David
    Gerrold   s   2208

**Earth** (Mythical Creature; Guardian)
*The Book of Earth* - Marjorie Bradley
    Kellogg   f   3044

**Earth** (Mythical Creature)
*The Book of Water* - Marjorie Bradley
    Kellogg   f   3045

**Earth Mother** (Deity)
*Nemesis* - Louise Cooper   f   1177

**Easter, Brandi** (Spacewoman)
*Standing Wave* - Howard V. Hendrix   s   2661

**Easterman, Nesta Christiana** (Scientist)
*Vanishing Point* - Michaela Roessner   s   4652

**Eberhardt, Johann** (Engineer; Businessman)
*Bright Messengers* - Gentry Lee   s   3398

**Eberhart, George** (Journalist)
*Good News From Outer Space* - John
    Kessel   s   3084

**Eberle, Markus** (Police Officer)
*At Sword's Point* - Scott MacMillan   f   3601

**Ebert, Hans** (Revolutionary)
*Beneath the Tree of Heaven* - David
    Wingrove   s   5917

**Eckert, Angie** (Noblewoman; Spouse)
*The Dragon and the Gnarly King* - Gordon R.
    Dickson   f   1529

**Eckert, Jim/Gorbash** (Knight; Magician; Nobleman)
*The Dragon and the Djinn* - Gordon R.
    Dickson   f   1528

**Eckert, Jim/Gorbash** (Nobleman; Magician; Knight)
*The Dragon and the Gnarly King* - Gordon R.
    Dickson   f   1529

**Eckert, Jim/Gorbash** (Knight; Magician; Nobleman)
*The Dragon at War* - Gordon R. Dickson   f   1530

**Eckert, Jim/Gorbash** (Nobleman; Magician; Knight)
*The Dragon in Lyonesse* - Gordon R.
    Dickson   f   1531
*The Dragon Knight* - Gordon R. Dickson   f   1532

**Eckert, Jim/Gorbash** (Knight; Magician; Nobleman)
*The Dragon on the Border* - Gordon R.
    Dickson   f   1533
*The Dragon, the Earl, and the Troll* - Gordon R.
    Dickson   f   1534

**Ecklundson, Dword** (Minstrel; Warrior)
*Captains Outrageous, or, For Doom the Bell Tolls* -
    Roy V. Young   f   6049

**Ector** (Knight)
*The Dragon's Boy* - Jane Yolen   f   6030

**Ecu** (Alien; Diplomat)
*Empire's End* - Allan Cole   s   1103
*The Return of the Emperor* - Allan Cole   s   1106

**Eddy, Henriette May** (Anthropologist)
*The Deathless* - Myles Murchison   h   4048

**Ede** (Artificial Intelligence)
*The Wild* - David Zindell   s   6086

**Edgecomb, Paul** (Guard)
*The Green Mile* - Stephen King   h   3134

**Edhadeya** (Royalty; Teacher)
*Earthborn* - Orson Scott Card   s   884

**Edison, Thomas** (Inventor; Disembodied Personality)
*Expiration Date* - Tim Powers   f   4383

**Edith of Shaftsbury** (Spouse; Parent)
*Lord of Sunset* - Parke Godwin   f   2246

**Edmonds, Sarah Emma "Kite"** (Aged Person; Activist)
*Sewer, Gas & Electric* - Matt Ruff   s   4708

**Edward** (Royalty)
*Lord of Sunset* - Parke Godwin   f   2246

**Edward, Albert Victor Christian** (Royalty)
*The Women of Whitechapel and Jack the Ripper* - Paul West   h   5761

**Edward III** (Ruler)
*Chicago Red* - R.M. Meluch   s   3873

**Edwardo "Ed"** (FBI Agent; Leader)
*Full Moonster* - Nick Pollotta   f   4364

**Edwards, Cynthia** (Housewife)
*The Immortals* - Andrew Neiderman   h   4087

**Edwards, Drake** (Businessman)
*The Immortals* - Andrew Neiderman   h   4087

**Edwards, James "Jay"** (Government Official)
*Men in Black* - Steve Perry   s   4298

**Eedrah** (Royalty)
*Myst: The Book of D'ni* - Rand Miller   f   3897

**Eerin, Ri-El** (Alien)
*Shadow World* - A.C. Crispin   s   1262

**Effie** (Young Woman)
*The Gilda Stories* - Jewelle Gomez   h   2267

**Efstathiou, Garcia** (Lover)
*Descent* - Ron Dee   h   1465

**Egdril** (Royalty; Leader)
*No One Noticed the Cat* - Anne McCaffrey   f   3740

**Egil** (Warrior)
*The Dragonstone* - Dennis L. McKiernan   f   3832

**Ehara** (Nobleman; Military Personnel)
*The Spellsong War* - L.E. Modesitt Jr.   f   3939

**Ehlana** (Royalty)
*Domes of Fire* - David Eddings   f   1732
*The Sapphire Rose* - David Eddings   f   1737

**Ehlers, Lou** (Student)
*Who Killed James Dean?* - Warren Newton Beath   h   428

**Ehomba, Etjole** (Traveler; Worker)
*Carnivores of Light and Darkness* - Alan Dean Foster   f   1996

**Ehren** (Military Personnel)
*Barrenlands* - Doranna Durgin   f   1702

**Eh'rik** (Warrior)
*Snow Brother* - S.M. Stirling   f   5299

**Eichord, Donna** (Spouse)
*Iceman* - Rex Miller   h   3900

**Eichord, Jack** (Detective—Police)
*Iceman* - Rex Miller   h   3900
*Slice* - Rex Miller   h   3902

**Eiden, Paul** (Religious)
*Owl Light* - Michael Paine   h   4235

**Eilan** (Religious; Parent)
*The Forest House* - Marion Zimmer Bradley   f   633

**Einhorn, Carl** (Scientist)
*Rage of Spirits* - Noel Hynd   h   2824

**Einstein, Albert** (Historical Figure; Government Official)
*Einstein's Dreams* - Alan Lightman   f   3459

**Eircelly, Talarrie** (Healer)
*If Wishes Were Horses* - Anne McCaffrey   f   3737

**Eircelly, Tirza** (Child)
*If Wishes Were Horses* - Anne McCaffrey   f   3737

**Eircelly, Tracell** (Child)
*If Wishes Were Horses* - Anne McCaffrey   f   3737

**Eiriksdottir, Freydis** (Historical Figure)
*The Ice-Shirt* - William T. Vollmann   f   5580

**Eiriksson, Leif** (Historical Figure)
*The Ice-Shirt* - William T. Vollmann   f   5580

**Eithne** (Royalty; Witch)
*The Shattered Oath* - Josepha Sherman   f   4989

**e'Kieron, Aliera** (Royalty)
*Five Hundred Years After* - Steven Brust   f   742

**Eklunk, Hans-Bjorn "Mokey/Moke"** (Artist; Actor)
*Clipjoint* - Wilhelmina Baird   s   294
*Crashcourse* - Wilhelmina Baird   s   295

**Eklunk, Hans-Bjorn "Mokey/Moke"** (Artist; Genius)
*Psykosis* - Wilhelmina Baird   s   296

**El-ahrairah** (Animal; Leader)
*Tales From Watership Down* - Richard Adams   f   32

**El Gran Mojado** (Sports Figure)
*Tropic of Orange* - Karen Tei Yamashita   f   6009

**El-Sayed, Ray** (Detective—Police)
*The Digital Effect* - Steve Perry   s   4295

**Ela** (Witch; Adventurer)
*The Goblin Mirror* - C.J. Cherryh   f   994

**Elaine** (Royalty; Wizard)
*Wolf's Cub* - Mackay Wood   f   5964

**Elaira** (Wizard; Doctor)
*Fugitive Prince* - Janny Wurts   f   6002

**E'lan, Misele** (Waiter/Waitress)
*The Itinerant Exorcist* - Ashley McConnell   f   3776

**elan Emok, Stuk** (Alien; Spaceship Captain)
*Half-Light* - Denise Vitola   s   5575

**Elavel** (Alien; Immortal)
*White Queen* - Gwyneth Jones   s   2955

**Elayna** (Witch; Lesbian)
*Heartstone and Silver* - Jacqui Singleton   f   5071

**Elayne** (Royalty; Heiress)
*A Crown of Swords* - Robert Jordan   f   2984
*The Dragon Reborn* - Robert Jordan   f   2985
*The Fires of Heaven* - Robert Jordan   f   2987

**Elayne** (Royalty; Fugitive)
*The Path of Daggers* - Robert Jordan   f   2989

**Elbub, Azzie** (Demon)
*Bring Me the Head of Prince Charming* - Roger Zelazny   f   6062
*A Farce to Be Reckoned With* - Roger Zelazny   f   6064

**Eldrich** (Wizard)
*Beneath the Vaulted Hills* - Sean Russell   f   4739
*The Compass of the Soul* - Sean Russell   f   4740

**Eleanor of Aquitaine** (Robot)
*Rama Revealed* - Arthur C. Clarke   s   1059

**Fleazar** (Indian)
*Whisper* - Raymond Van Over   h   5539

**Eleeri** (Runaway; Animal Trainer)
*The Key of the Keplian* - Andre Norton   f   4156

**Eleighanaran "Leigh"** (Mythical Creature; Noblewoman)
*Shadows on the Hill* - Jackie Cassada   s   935

**Elemak** (Linguist; Renegade)
*Earthfall* - Orson Scott Card   s   885

**Elemak** (Leader; Rogue)
*The Ships of Earth* - Orson Scott Card   s   897

**Elen** (Psychic)
*City of Bones* - Martha Wells   f   5748

**Elena** (Apprentice; Sorcerer)
*The Fourth Guardian* - Ronald Anthony Cross   s   1273

**Elena** (Sorcerer)
*The Lost Guardian* - Ronald Anthony Cross   s   1274

**Elena** (Sorceress; Teenager)
*Wit'ch Fire* - James Clemens   f   1082

**Eleph** (Alien)
*Mercycle* - Piers Anthony   s   181

**Elessedil, Wren** (Mythical Creature; Ruler)
*The Talismans of Shannara* - Terry Brooks   f   717

**Eleuth** (Mythical Creature; Magician)
*Songs of Earth and Power* - Greg Bear   f   424

**Elf, Jenny** (Mythical Creature; Guide)
*Demons Don't Dream* - Piers Anthony   f   168

**Elf, Jenny** (Mythical Creature)
*Isle of View* - Piers Anthony   f   177

**Elgin** (Streetperson)
*Street* - Jack Cady   h   822

**Elgin, Edith** (Journalist)
*Moonwar* - Ben Bova   s   588

**Elias** (Religious)
*The Revelation* - Bentley Little   h   3496

**Eliason, Scott** (Vampire Hunter)
*Sins of the Blood* - Kristine Kathryn Rusch   h   4728

**Elionbel** (Fiance(e); Prisoner)
*Palace of Kings* - Mike Jefferies   f   2887

**Eliot, Ann** (Writer)
*The Innsmouth Heritage* - Brian Stableford   h   5194

**Eliot, John** (Doctor)
*Slave of My Thirst* - Tom Holland   h   2742

**Elisa** (Genetically Altered Being)
*The Silent City* - Elisabeth Vonarburg   s   5592

**Elisabeth** (Housewife)
*What's Wrong with Valerie?* - D.A. Fowler   h   2026

**Eliseth** (Magician)
*Dhiammara* - Maggie Furey   f   2096
*Sword of Flame* - Maggie Furey   f   2098

**Elita** (Toy)
*Stone Dead* - Ellen Jamison   h   2878

**Elives, S.H.** (Businessman)
*Jennifer Murdley's Toad* - Bruce Coville   f   1220

**Elizabeth** (Singer; Dancer)
*Ladies Night* - Jack Ketchum   h   3091

**Elizabeth** (Traveler)
*Mutagenesis* - Helen Collins   s   1116

**Elizabeth** (Spouse)
*The Secret Life of Laszlo, Count Dracula* - Roderick Anscombe   h   152

**Elizabeth** (Vampire)
*Virgintooth* - Mark Ivanhoe   h   2834

**Elizebith of Morea** (Sorceress)
*Dark Divide* - Mark Acres   f   27
*Outcasts* - Clayton Emery   f   1815
*The Stone of Time* - Rose Estes   f   1840

**Elk Charm** (Prehistoric Human; Indian)
*People of the Fire* - W. Michael Gear   f   2167

**Ell, Pe** (Murderer)
*The Druid of Shannara* - Terry Brooks   f   710

**Ella** (Teenager)
*I Feel Like the Morning Star* - Gregory Maguire   s   3608

**Ella** (Psychic; Teenager)
*Shade's Children* - Garth Nix   s   4130

**Ellair, Noble** (Doctor)
*The Night Seasons* - J.N. Williamson   h   5858

**Ellel, Quince** (Witch)
*A Plague of Angels* - Sheri S. Tepper   f   5433

**Ellen** (Scientist)
*The Red Queen* - Dirk Draulans   s   1653

**Ellerman, Amy** (Student)
*The Quiet* - Patrick Billings   h   488

**Ellington, Dan** (Religious)
*The Blood of the Lamb* - Thomas F.
   Monteleone   h   3958

**Ellington, Lucas** (Parent)
*The Kill Riff* - David J. Schow   h   4887

**Elliot, Dan** (Journalist)
*Beneath Still Waters* - Matthew J. Costello   h   1193

**Elliott, Claire** (Doctor)
*Bloodstream* - Tess Gerritsen   h   2205

**Elliott, Kate** (Teenager)
*Vision Quest* - Pamela F. Service   f   4920

**Elliott, Noah** (Teenager)
*Bloodstream* - Tess Gerritsen   h   2205

**Ellis, Cander** (Spy; Martial Arts Expert)
*Shadow of the Crown* - Craig Mills   f   3914

**Ellis, Cindy** (Horse Trainer)
*The Godmother's Web* - Elizabeth Ann
   Scarborough   f   4864

**Ellis, John** (Doctor)
*The Dealings of Daniel Kesserich* - Fritz
   Leiber   s   3417

**Ellis, Wilson** (Detective—Private)
*Forget Me Not* - Gene Lazuta   h   3375

**Ellyn** (Royalty; Wizard)
*The Guardian* - Angus Wells   f   5737

**Elmara** (Adventurer; Religious)
*Elminster: The Making of a Mage* - Ed
   Greenwood   f   2427

**Elminster** (Sorcerer; Royalty)
*Elminster: The Making of a Mage* - Ed
   Greenwood   f   2427

**Elobert, Henri** (Businessman)
*Prophets for the End of Time* - Marcos
   Donnelly   f   1577

**Elof** (Magician; Blacksmith)
*The Forge in the Forest* - Michael Scott
   Rohan   f   4660

**Eloise** (Hunter)
*Nicoji* - M. Shayne Bell   s   434

**Elphaba** (Witch; Activist)
*Wicked: The Life and Times of the Wicked Witch of
   the West* - Gregory Maguire   f   3609

**Elric** (Child)
*The Book of Brendan* - Ann Curry   f   1294

**Elric** (Knight)
*The Spellkey Trilogy* - Ann Downer   f   1592

**Elric of Melnibone** (Warrior; Ruler; Wizard)
*Elric: Song of the Black Sword* - Michael
   Moorcock   f   3980

**Elric of Melnibone** (Warrior; Royalty; Wizard)
*The Fortress of the Pearl* - Michael
   Moorcock   f   3982
*The Revenge of the Rose* - Michael
   Moorcock   f   3985

**Elric of Melnibone** (Royalty; Wizard; Warrior)
*Tales of the White Wolf* - Edward E.
   Kramer   f   3227

**Elroy, Shannon** (Guard)
*Tower of Evil* - James Kisner   h   3161

**Elryc** (Royalty)
*The Still* - David Feintuch   f   1902

**Elsie** (Mythical Creature)
*Galatea in 2-D* - Aaron Allston   f   87

**Elspet** (Witch)
*Coven* - Steven William Rimmer   h   4591

**Elspeth** (Spouse)
*Thomas the Rhymer* - Ellen Kushner   f   3265

**Elspeth** (Heir; Government Official)
*Winds of Change* - Mercedes Lackey   f   3304
*Winds of Fate* - Mercedes Lackey   f   3305

**Elspeth** (Magician; Heiress)
*Winds of Fury* - Mercedes Lackey   f   3306

**Elvira** (Young Woman)
*The Boy Who Cried Werewolf* - Elvira   h   1800
*Camp Vamp* - Elvira   h   1801
*Elvira: Transylvania 90210* - Elvira   h   1802

**Elvis** (Robot; Spouse)
*The Man in the Moon Must Die* - Jeff
   Bredenberg   s   665

**Elyssa** (Sorceress)
*Konrad* - David Ferring   f   1927

**em-Pelsh, Jag Kandaro** (Alien)
*Starplex* - Robert J. Sawyer   s   4859

**Ember** (Parent; Leader)
*Isle of Woman* - Piers Anthony   f   178

**Ember, Annie** (Teenager; Servant)
*Elephantasm* - Tanith Lee   h   3408

**Emberella** (Royalty)
*Witches Abroad* - Terry Pratchett   f   4404

**Emereck** (Minstrel; Adventurer)
*Shadows over Lyra* - Patricia C. Wrede   f   5980

**Emerson, Dirk** (Teenager)
*Demon's Fright* - Penelope Banka Kreps   h   3233

**Emerson, Ian** (Professor)
*University* - Bentley Little   h   3499

**Emily** (Teenager)
*The House on Hound Hill* - Maggie Prince   f   4438

**Emily "Emmy"** (Child)
*Santa's Twin* - Dean R. Koontz   f   3214

**Emma** (Young Woman)
*Westlin Wind* - Charles de Lint   f   1439

**Emory, Ariane** (Scientist; Political Figure)
*Cyteen* - C.J. Cherryh   s   984

**Emrys** (Child; Psychic)
*The Lost Years of Merlin* - T.A. Barron   f   370

**Emrys** (Psychic)
*Merlin and the Dragons* - Jane Yolen   f   6036

**Emshander IV** (Ruler)
*Upland Outlaws* - Dave Duncan   f   1690

**Emshander V** (Ruler)
*The Living God* - Dave Duncan   f   1682
*The Stricken Field* - Dave Duncan   f   1688

**Endang** (Scholar; Slave)
*Flowerdust* - Gwyneth Jones   s   2952

**Endering, Sophia** (Art Dealer)
*The Uncanny* - Andrew Klavan   h   3164

**Enderton, Paddy** (Spaceman)
*Godspeed* - Charles Sheffield   s   4957

**Endicott, Carl "Johnson"** (Fugitive)
*Delta Search* - William Shatner   s   4930

**Endicott, James "Jimmy"** (Teenager; Genetically
   Altered Being)
*Delta Search* - William Shatner   s   4930

**Endicott, Rob** (Telepath; Worker)
*The Gifted* - Jack Caravela   h   879

**Endine, Flojian** (Businessman)
*Eternity Road* - Jack McDevitt   s   3788

**Endrada, Deirdre "Deedee"** (Child; Explorer)
*Halfway Human* - Carolyn Ives Gilman   s   2237

**Endrada, Valerie "Val"** (Anthropologist; Student)
*Halfway Human* - Carolyn Ives Gilman   s   2237

**Endymion, Raul** (Prisoner; Hero; Guardian)
*Endymion* - Dan Simmons   s   5051

**Endymion, Raul** (Hero; Guardian; Lover)
*The Rise of Endymion* - Dan Simmons   s   5059

**Enemy** (Alien)
*Cold Fire* - Dean R. Koontz   h   3203

**Enfandin, Rene** (Diplomat)
*Bring the Jubilee* - Ward Moore   s   3993

**L'Enfant, Terrance** (Administrator)
*Labyrinth of Night* - Allen Steele   s   5244

**Engel, Emily** (Patient)
*Zod Wallop* - William Browning Spencer   h   5169

**Engibil** (Deity)
*Between the Rivers* - Harry Turtledove   f   5496

**Engle, Kivrin** (Student; Time Traveler)
*Doomsday Book* - Connie Willis   s   5868

**Engleman, Carolyn** (Businesswoman)
*Cambio Bay* - Kate Wilhelm   f   5806

**Engor** (Pirate)
*Engor's Sword Arm* - David C. Smith   h   5110

**Enkidu** (Homosexual; Boyfriend)
*Mirage* - Perry Brass   s   662

**Ennin, Willie** (Cook)
*Raven* - Charles L. Grant   h   2314

**Ennesstheh** (Alien)
*Cannon's Orb* - L. Warren Douglas   s   1586

**E'non, Caelan** (Gladiator; Psychic)
*Realm of Light* - Deborah Chester   f   1008
*Reign of Shadows* - Deborah Chester   f   1009

**E'non, Caelan** (Military Personnel; Psychic)
*Shadow War* - Deborah Chester   f   1010

**Enos, George** (Sea Captain; Sailor)
*The Great War: American Front* - Harry
   Turtledove   s   5501

**Enrique, Dom** (Explorer)
*Mansions of Darkness* - Chelsea Quinn
   Yarbro   h   6016

**Ensi** (Spirit; Martial Arts Expert)
*The Glaive* - Cary Osborne   s   4227

**Entragion, Collie** (Police Officer)
*Desperation* - Stephen King   h   3129
*The Regulators* - Richard Bachman   h   284

**Erato** (Mythical Creature)
*Zeus and Co.* - David Lee Jones   f   2942

**Erek** (Sorceress)
*Hall of Whispers* - Mike Jefferies   f   2884

**Erelvar** (Nobleman; Religious)
*A Call to Arms* - Thomas K. Martin   f   3650
*A Two-Edged Sword* - Thomas K. Martin   f   3653

**Ergates** (Animal)
*Feersum Endjinn* - Iain M. Banks   s   325

**Erhsham, Ling** (Space Explorer)
*The Transmigration of Souls* - William
   Barton   s   382

**Erica** (Lesbian)
*Clicking Stones* - Nancy Tyler Glenn   s   2242

**Erickson, Dirk** (Vampire)
*The Informers* - Brett Easton Ellis   h   1778

**Erickson, Richard** (Lawman)
*Shadows Fall* - Simon R. Green   f   2373

**Ericson, Jacob** (Rancher; Healer)
*Jacob's Hands* - Aldous Huxley   f   2817

**Eride "Thorn"** (Religious; Martial Arts Expert)
*Thorn and Needle* - Paul B. Thompson   f   5456

**Erik** (Teenager)
*The Lone Sentinel* - Jo Dereske   s   1493

**Erik** (Child; Musician)
*Phantom* - Susan Kay   h   3020

**Erin of Elliath** (Warrior; Healer)
*Chains of Darkness, Chains of Light* - Michelle
   Sagara   f   4781
*Into the Dark Lands* - Michelle Sagara   f   4783
*Lady of Mercy* - Michelle Sagara   f   4784

**Erkenbert** (Religious; Leader)
*One King's Way* - Harry Harrison   s   2572

**Erland** (Royalty)
*Prince of the Blood* - Raymond E. Feist   f   1907

**Ernst, Jeffrey** (Child)
*Twistor* - John Cramer   s   1245

**Errenthorp, Reynaldo** (Businessman)
*The Third Eagle: Lessons Along a Minor String* - R.A.
   MacAvoy   s   3583

**Er'ril** (Warrior; Handicapped)
*Wit'ch Fire* - James Clemens   f   1082

**Ersh** (Alien; Immortal)
*Beholder's Eye* - Julie E. Czerneda   s   1303

**Erskine, Cheryl** (Child)
*In a Dark Dream* - Charles L. Grant   h   2310

**Erskine, Glenn** (Police Officer)
*In a Dark Dream* - Charles L. Grant   h   2310

**Erskine, Harry** (Psychic)
*Burial* - Graham Masterton   h   3671

**Erwyn** (Sorcerer; Royalty)
*Go Quest, Young Man* - K.B. Bogen   f   557

**Erzsebet** (Noblewoman; Vampire)
*The Secret Weavers: Stories of the Fantastic by Latin
   American Women* - Marjorie Agosin   f   43

**Erzul, Ti Sandra** (Political Figure)
*Moving Mars* - Greg Bear   s   421

**Escargot, Theophile** (Cook; Adventurer)
*The Stone Giant* - James P. Blaylock   f   523

**Eschar, William** (Wizard)
*A Plague of Sorcerers* - Mary Frances
   Zambreno   f   6058

**Eschbach, Johan** (Professor; Spy)
*The Ghost of the Revelator* - L.E. Modesitt
   Jr.   s   3931
*Of Tangible Ghosts* - L.E. Modesitt Jr.   f   3935

**Escott, Charles** (Detective—Private)
*Blood on the Water* - P.N. Elrod   h   1791
*Bloodlist* - P.N. Elrod   h   1792
*Fire in the Blood* - P.N. Elrod   h   1796

**Esen-Alit-Quar** (Alien; Immortal)
*Beholder's Eye* - Julie E. Czerneda   s   1303

**Esher** (Vampire)
*A Dozen Black Roses* - Nancy A. Collins   h   1119

**Esher, David** (Writer)
*Unearthed* - Ashley McConnell   h   3778

**Esk** (Witch)
*Equal Rites* - Terry Pratchett   f   4387

**Eslingen, Philip** (Military Personnel)
*Point of Hopes* - Melissa Scott   f   4899

**Esmelda "Esme"** (Government Official)
*Northlight* - Deborah Wheeler   s   5775

**Espinoza, Margarita** (Artist)
*The Stone Garden* - Mary Rosenblum   s   4679

**Essa** (Wanderer; Slave)
*Black Wine* - Candas Jane Dorsey   s   1582

**Essell, Lilly** (Military Personnel; Astronaut)
*Realtime Interrupt* - James P. Hogan   s   2729

**Essessili** (Mythical Creature)
*The Dragon at War* - Gordon R. Dickson   f   1530

**Estarion** (Ruler)
*Arrows of the Sun* - Judith Tarr   f   5391

**Esterbrook, Diana** (Teenager; Computer Expert)
*The Higher Space* - Jamil Nasir   s   4070

**Esterhok, Quait** (Military Personnel)
*Eternity Road* - Jack McDevitt   s   3788

**Estes, Ken** (Military Personnel)
*Pandora* - Alan Rodgers   h   4650

**Estmere** (Royalty; Leader)
*King's Son, Magic's Son* - Josepha Sherman   f   4986

**Estrand, Philip** (Professor)
*As She Climbed Across the Table* - Jonathan
   Lethem   s   3439

**Estriss** (Alien; Telepath)
*Into the Void* - Nigel Findley   f   1937

**Estriss** (Alien; Spaceship Captain)
*The Radiant Dragon* - Elaine Cunningham   f   1291

**Etanl, Latona** (Activist)
*Alien Influences* - Kristine Kathryn Rusch   s   4711

**Etasalou** (Military Personnel)
*The Prisoner Within* - Donald E. McQuinn   s   3861

**Etcher** (Thief)
*Arc d'X* - Steve Erickson   f   1835

**Etchison, Phil** (Writer)
*Forest of the Night* - S.P. Somtow   f   5156

**Etchison, Theo** (Psychic)
*Forest of the Night* - S.P. Somtow   f   5156

**Etchison, Theo** (Teenager; Psychic)
*Riverrun* - S.P. Somtow   f   5159

**Eth** (Alien; Psychic)
*Dream-Weaver* - Louise Lawrence   s   3359

**Ethemark** (Police Officer; Genetically Altered Being)
*City on Fire* - Walter Jon Williams   s   5835

**Ettalira** (Alien; Explorer)
*To Fear the Light* - Ben Bova   s   595

**Etzilios** (Barbarian; Leader)
*Hammer and Anvil* - Harry Turtledove   f   5503

**Euclid** (Computer Expert)
*Exit to Reality* - Edith Forbes   s   1968

**Eudoxus** (Alien)
*The Gripping Hand* - Larry Niven   s   4122

**Eupolis of Pallene** (Writer)
*Goatsong* - Tom Holt   f   2751
*The Walled Orchard* - Tom Holt   f   2752

**Eusabian, Jerrode** (Political Figure)
*The Phoenix in Flight* - Sherwood Smith   s   5138
*The Rifter's Covenant* - Sherwood Smith   s   5140

**Eva** (Teenager)
*Eva* - Peter Dickinson   s   1525
*Into the Forest* - Jean Hegland   s   2640

**Eva** (Witch)
*Witchcraft* - Bill Michaels   h   3885

**Evander** (Mythical Creature; Sorcerer)
*Days of Air and Darkness* - Katharine Kerr   f   3067

**Evander, Danais** (Royalty; Heir—Dispossessed)
*The Wizard and the Floating City* - Christopher
   Rowley   f   4699

**Evangeline** (Alien)
*Alien Earth* - Megan Lindholm   s   3469

**Evans, Bill "Bill the Just"** (Accountant; Hero)
*The League of the Crimson Crescent* - James E.
   Reagen   f   4495

**Evans, Christina** (Dancer; Producer)
*The Eyes of Darkness* - Dean R. Koontz   s   3206

**Evans, Constanza** (Socialite)
*The War of Don Emmanuel's Nether Parts* - Louis de
   Bernieres   f   1412

**Evans, Harrington-Smith** (Wealthy)
*Bereavement* - Richard Lortz   h   3525

**Evans, Harry M.** (Astronaut)
*Beyond Apollo* - Barry Malzberg   s   3612

**Evans, Jonna** (Teacher)
*Monster* - John Tigges   h   5474

**Evans, Joshua Carl** (Child)
*Worst Nightmare* - Ric Meyers   h   3883

**Evans, Juliet "Julie"** (Cyborg)
*Mindstar Rising* - Peter F. Hamilton   s   2526

**Evans, Katy** (Patient)
*The Homecoming* - Kimberly Rangel   h   4471

**Evans, Malcolm** (Clerk)
*Monster* - John Tigges   h   5474

**Evans, Owain** (Vampire; Spy)
*The Winnowing* - Gherbod Fleming   h   1950

**Evans, Philip** (Industrialist; Disembodied
   Personality)
*Mindstar Rising* - Peter F. Hamilton   s   2526

**Evans, Sean** (Student)
*A Diversity of Dragons* - Anne McCaffrey   f   3728

**Evanston, Livermore** (Businessman; Criminal)
*Hunter's Planet* - David Bischoff   s   492

**Eve, Glennys** (Dancer; Horse Trainer)
*The Stalking Horse* - Constance Ash   f   222

**Eve, Glennys** (Leader; Telepath)
*The Stallion Queen* - Constance Ash   f   223

**Eveningstar, Dasmaria** (Knight)
*Shadowborn* - William W. Connors   h   1137

**Everard, Manse** (Agent)
*The Shield of Time* - Poul Anderson   s   131
*The Time Patrol* - Poul Anderson   s   135

**Everett, Matt** (Teenager; Spaceman)
*Article 23* - William R. Forstchen   s   1978

**Everett, Radmilla** (Lawyer; Government Official)
*Rewind* - Terry England   s   1825

**Everson, Kelly** (Nurse)
*Harmful Intent* - Robin Cook   s   1164

**Everynne** (Clone; Royalty)
*The Golden Queen* - Dave Wolverton   s   5951

**Eveshka** (Wizard)
*Yvgenie* - C.J. Cherryh   f   1005

**Evjenial** (Doctor)
*The Light in Exile* - Cheryl J. Franklin   s   2038

**Ewebean, Jade** (Aged Person)
*Panic* - Chris Curry   h   1295

**Ewin, Cors Cant** (Minstrel)
*Arthur War Lord* - Dafydd ab Hugh   f   6

**Ewine, Zarel** (Nobleman; Leader)
*Arena* - William R. Forstchen   f   1977

**Ewing, Jude** (Detective—Police)
*Deadrush* - Yvonne Navarro   h   4073

**Exeter, Edward** (Traveler; Leader)
*Future Indefinite* - Dave Duncan   f   1678

**Exeter, Edward** (Student)
*Past Imperative* - Dave Duncan   f   1684

**Exeter, Edward** (Traveler)
*Present Tense* - Dave Duncan  *f*  1686

**Eydryth of Kar Garudwyn** (Minstrel)
*Songsmith* - Andre Norton  *f*  4161

**Eye on Sky** (Alien; Spaceman)
*Anvil of Stars* - Greg Bear  *s*  414

**Ezekiel "Zeke"** (Angel; Telepath)
*The Seraphim Rising* - Elisabeth De Vos  *s*  1442

# F

**fab Maelgwyn, Tryffin** (Royalty; Government Official)
*The Castle of the Silver Wheel* - Teresa Edgerton  *f*  1741

**Fabrizio** (Actor)
*The Innamorati* - Midori Snyder  *f*  5152

**Fades** (Monster)
*The Eye of the World* - Robert Jordan  *f*  2986

**Fafhrd** (Thief; Warrior)
*Farewell to Lankhmar* - Fritz Leiber  *f*  3418
*Ill Met in Lankhmar* - Fritz Leiber  *f*  3419
*Lean Times in Lankhmar* - Fritz Leiber  *f*  3420
*Return to Lankhmar* - Fritz Leiber  *f*  3422
*Swords Against the Shadowland* - Robin Wayne Bailey  *f*  291

**Fafleen** (Mythical Creature)
*Dragon's Queen* - Carol L. Dennis  *f*  1488

**Fafner** (Animal)
*Borgel* - Daniel Manus Pinkwater  *f*  4338

**Faharmoy** (Agent)
*Wild Magic* - Jo Clayton  *f*  1072

**Fairburn, Pamela** (Scientist; Fiance(e))
*The Ambivalent Magician* - Simon Hawke  *f*  2616

**Fairchild, Kimberly** (Doctor)
*The Fungus* - Harry Adam Knight  *h*  3192

**Fairclough, Jude** (Young Woman)
*The Night in Fog* - David B. Silva  *h*  5026

**Fairfax, Aaron Lee** (Genetically Altered Being)
*Rewind* - Terry England  *s*  1825

**Fairfax, Eugenia** (Social Worker)
*Black Night* - S.J. Strayhorn  *h*  5334

**Fairfax, Lena** (Worker)
*Black Night* - S.J. Strayhorn  *h*  5334

**Fairouz** (Spaceship Captain)
*The Missing Matter* - Thomas R. McDonough  *s*  3805

**Fairy Godmother** (Mythical Creature)
*Spell Bound* - Ru Emerson  *f*  1810

**Faison, Genevieva** (Con Artist; Time Traveler)
*Corrupting Dr. Nice* - John Kessel  *s*  3083

**Faith, Charlie** (Engineer)
*The Embedding* - Ian Watson  *s*  5634

**Falc of Risskor** (Knight)
*Deathknight* - Andrew J. Offutt  *f*  4201

**Falco, Josie** (Young Woman)
*Orphans* - Jean Simon  *h*  5065

**Falco, Ray** (Journalist)
*Vodoun* - David Madsen  *h*  3605

**Falcon, Nikki** (Royalty; Pilot)
*Falcon* - Emma Bull  *s*  768

**Falconer, Fay** (Government Official)
*The Painter Knight* - Fiona Patton  *f*  4258

**Falconer, Jamie** (Wizard)
*Dragon's Plunder* - Brad Strickland  *f*  5336

**Falconi, Giovanni** (Religious)
*The Sister* - Elleston Trevor  *h*  5484

**Falconi, Richard** (Detective—Police)
*House Haunted* - Al Sarrantonio  *h*  4830

**Falfurrias, Ofelia Damareux** (Aged Person; Runaway)
*Remnant Population* - Elizabeth Moon  *s*  3972

**Falke** (Vampire)
*Eye Killers* - A.A. Carr  *h*  911

**Falke, Egidius Maximillian** (Doctor)
*Out of the House of Life* - Chelsea Quinn Yarbro  *h*  6018

**Falkenberg, John Christian** (Military Personnel)
*Falkenberg's Legion* - Jerry Pournelle  *s*  4374

**Falkenberg, John Christian** (Mercenary)
*Prince of Mercenaries* - Jerry Pournelle  *s*  4377

**Falkirk, Trey** (Gambler)
*Chariot* - Charles L. Grant  *h*  2304

**Fall, Thomas** (Indian; Wanderer)
*Warpath* - Tony Daniel  *s*  1337

**Fall-Levchenko, Anna Leah** (Time Traveler; Scholar)
*Branch Point* - Mona Clee  *s*  1074

**Fallon** (Wizard; Mythical Creature)
*The Stone Movers* - Patricia Mullen  *f*  4045

**Fallstar, Chade** (Bastard Son; Diplomat)
*Assassin's Apprentice* - Robin Hobb  *f*  2693

**Falmah-Al, Kezi** (Warrior)
*The Goda War* - Jay D. Blakeney  *s*  516

**Falsche, Viktor** (Rebel; Wizard)
*The Janus Mask* - Richard A. Knaak  *f*  3171

**Falstaff, Raymond** (Spaceship Captain)
*Border Dispute* - Daniel R. Kerns  *s*  3066

**Faltar** (Wizard; Apprentice)
*The White Order* - L.E. Modesitt Jr.  *f*  3942

**Falushe, Viole** (Kidnapper; Outlaw)
*The Demon Princes: Volume One* - Jack Vance  *s*  5544

**Famande, Chrysanda "Christine"** (Actress)
*Bride of the Rat God* - Barbara Hambly  *f*  2499

**Famber, Leelson** (Empath)
*Shadow's End* - Sheri S. Tepper  *s*  5435

**Fancy, Darren** (Child)
*The One Safe Place* - Ramsey Campbell  *h*  862

**Fancy, Jan "Jeanette"** (Femme Fatale)
*Succumb* - Ron Dee  *h*  1468

**Fanuilh** (Mythical Creature; Companion)
*Beggar's Banquet* - Daniel Hood  *f*  2756
*Fanuilh* - Daniel Hood  *f*  2757
*Scales of Justice* - Daniel Hood  *f*  2758
*Wizard's Heir* - Daniel Hood  *f*  2759

**Faracon, George** (Criminal; Time Traveler)
*Time Station Paris* - David Evans  *s*  1854

**Faraday, Richard** (Actor)
*Diplomatic Act* - Peter Jurasik  *s*  2996

**Farblood, Corri** (Sorcerer; Leader)
*Soothslayer: A Magickal Fantasy* - D.J. Conway  *f*  1143

**Farhallen, Annadale** (Empath)
*Children of Enchantment* - Anne Kelleher Bush  *f*  787

**Farhallen, Nydia** (Psychic)
*Daughter of Prophecy* - Anne Kelleher Bush  *f*  788

**Farkas, Victor** (Genetically Altered Being)
*Hot Sky at Midnight* - Robert Silverberg  *s*  5032

**Farlan, Tessa** (Businesswoman)
*Reunion on Neverend* - John E. Stith  *s*  5306

**Farley, Heather** (Student; Telepath)
*Serpent's Gift* - A.C. Crispin  *s*  1261

**Faro** (Slave)
*If I Pay Thee Not in Gold* - Piers Anthony  *f*  176

**Faron, Theodore** (Historian; Revolutionary)
*The Children of Men* - P.D. James  *f*  2870

**Faronya, Kelmer** (Journalist)
*The Regiment's War* - John Dalmas  *s*  1326

**Faronya, Tain** (Prisoner)
*The Kalif's War* - John Dalmas  *s*  1322

**Farraday** (Public Relations)
*Silicon Embrace* - John Shirley  *s*  5009

**Farraday, Morgan** (Administrator)
*The Snows of Jaspre* - Mary Caraker  *s*  878

**Farrand, Louis** (Religious)
*Garden* - Matthew J. Costello  *h*  1197

**Farree** (Alien)
*Dare to Go A-Hunting* - Andre Norton  *s*  4147

**Farrell** (Hippie)
*The Folk of the Air* - Peter S. Beagle  *f*  407

**Farrell, Gene** (Doctor)
*Kiss of Death* - Daniel Rhodes  *h*  4569

**Farrell, Lizbeth** (Secretary)
*Homecoming* - Matthew J. Costello  *h*  1198

**Farrell, Simon** (Businessman)
*Homecoming* - Matthew J. Costello  *h*  1198

**Farren** (Wizard)
*Touched by Magic* - Doranna Durgin  *f*  1705

**Farringer, Gail** (Artist)
*Demon Shadows* - Michael B. Sirota  *h*  5075

**Farris, Duffy** (Hotel Worker)
*The Jimjams* - Michael Green  *h*  2345

**Farris, Rose** (Hotel Worker)
*The Jimjams* - Michael Green  *h*  2345

**Farseer, FitzChivalry "Fitz"** (Bastard Son; Psychic)
*Assassin's Apprentice* - Robin Hobb  *f*  2693
*Assassin's Quest* - Robin Hobb  *f*  2694
*Royal Assassin* - Robin Hobb  *f*  2695

**Farseer, Verity** (Psychic; Royalty)
*Royal Assassin* - Robin Hobb  *f*  2695

**Farthing, Jacob** (Parent; Security Officer)
*Harm's Way* - Colin Greenland  *s*  2416

**Farthing, Sophie** (Runaway; Heiress—Lost)
*Harm's Way* - Colin Greenland  *s*  2416

**Faslorn** (Alien)
*The Sails of Tau Ceti* - Michael McCollum  *s*  3771

**Fasner, Holt "The Dragon"** (Administrator)
*The Gap into Power: A Dark and Hungry God Arises* - Stephen R. Donaldson  *s*  1574

**Fast, Barry** (Teacher)
*Firestar* - Michael Flynn  *s*  1962

**Fastet, Meer** (Judge; Revolutionary)
*Exile* - Michael P. Kube-McDowell  *s*  3248

**Fat Woman** (Witch)
*Nice Guys Finish Last* - Gary Jonas  *h*  2938

**Fath, Jaro** (Foundling; Spaceman)
*Night Lamp* - Jack Vance  *s*  5548

**f'ath, Riitha** (Alien; Scientist)
*The Alien Dark* - Diana G. Gallagher  *s*  2108

**Faulk, Carol** (Spaceship Captain; Military Personnel)
*A Darker Geometry* - Mark O. Martin  *s*  3649

**Faulkner, Sully** (Student—College)
*An Exaltation of Larks* - Robert Reed  *s*  4506

**Faulkner, William** (Writer; Pilot)
*The Wild Blue and the Gray* - William Sanders  *s*  4814

**Faun, Forrest** (Mythical Creature; Gardener)
*Faun & Games* - Piers Anthony  f  169

**Faure, Georges Henri** (Diplomat)
*Moonwar* - Ben Bova  s  588

**Faust, Johann** (Thief; Imposter)
*If at Faust You Don't Succeed* - Roger
Zelazny  f  6070

**Faust, Johannes "Jack"** (Scholar; Genius)
*Jack Faust* - Michael Swanwick  s  5372

**Faust, Prometheus "Bruce Payne"** (Religious)
*Symphony* - Adrian Savage  h  4847

**Fava** (Girlfriend; Prehistoric Human)
*Serpent Catch* - Dave Wolverton  s  5956

**Fawcett, Christine** (Explorer; Time Traveler)
*Tyrannosaurus Rex* - J.F. Rivkin  s  4597

**Fears, Quentin** (Computer Expert)
*Treasure Box* - Orson Scott Card  h  898

**Feich, Daimhin** (Political Figure)
*The Crystal Rose* - Maya Kaathryn Bohnhoff  f  560

**Feinberg, Jennifer** (Businesswoman)
*Drakon* - S.M. Stirling  s  5294

**Feinman, Jacob** (Doctor)
*Specters* - J.M. Dillard  h  1555

**Feinstein, Rose** (Mythical Creature; Teacher)
*The Magic Touch* - Jody Lynn Nye  f  4171

**Feirn** (Television Personality)
*Hero* - Dave Duncan  s  1680

**Feit, Sherry** (Professor)
*Walking Wounded* - Robert Devereaux  h  1507

**Felaya** (Sorceress)
*Token of Dragonsblood* - Damaris Cole  f  1114

**Feldberg, David** (Linguist)
*Requiem* - Graham Joyce  h  2994

**Feldman, Jake** (Businessman)
*Pelts* - F. Paul Wilson  h  5894

**Feldman, Malachi** (Scientist)
*The Asylum* - John E. Ames  h  93

**Feldspar** (Businessman)
*The Chosen* - Edward Lee  h  3389

**Felice** (Parent; Thief)
*User Unfriendly* - Vivian Vande Velde  f  5558

**Felicitas** (Prisoner; Amnesiac)
*Outpost* - Scott Mackay  s  3597

**Felipe** (Religious)
*The Great Wheel* - Ian R. MacLeod  s  3599

**Felix, William Charles "Gunman"** (Vampire
Hunter)
*Vampire$* - John Steakley  h  5237

**Fellowes, Edith** (Nurse)
*The Ugly Little Boy* - Isaac Asimov  s  250

**Felmet** (Nobleman; Murderer)
*Wyrd Sisters* - Terry Pratchett  f  4405

**Fels, Jimmy** (Teenager; Runaway)
*Penance* - Rick R. Reed  h  4501

**Fence** (Wizard)
*The Whim of the Dragon* - Pamela Dean  f  1447

**Fender, Duncan** (Photographer)
*Suckers* - Anne Billson  h  490

**Fenn** (Police Officer; Revolutionary)
*The Fleet of Stars* - Poul Anderson  s  126

**Fenton, Mariah** (Herbalist)
*The Changeling Garden* - Winifred Elze  h  1806

**Ferahgo the Assassin** (Animal; Warrior)
*Salamandastron* - Brian Jacques  f  2855

**Feraru, Michael** (Teacher)
*The Lost* - Jonathan Aycliffe  h  279

**Ferdulf** (Child; Mythical Creature)
*Fox and Empire* - Harry Turtledove  f  5500

**Feree, Harper** (Child; Hero)
*The Friendship Song* - Nancy Springer  f  5179

**Ferenczy, Janos** (Vampire; Magician)
*Deadspeak* - Brian Lumley  h  3551

**Fergus** (Military Personnel; Time Traveler)
*The Lost Prince* - Bridget Wood  f  5962

**Ferguson, Harold "Rondo"** (Spy)
*Darkman #4: The Face of Death* - Randall
Boyll  h  615

**Ferguson, Herman D. "Fergie"** (Criminal;
Computer Expert)
*Judge Dredd* - Neal Barrett Jr.  s  366

**Feritayl, Irma** (Royalty)
*Bill, the Galactic Hero: On the Planet of Tasteless
Pleasure* - Harry Harrison  s  2567

**Fermi, Enrico** (Historical Figure; Scientist)
*Worldwar: In the Balance* - Harry
Turtledove  s  5515

**Fernholz the Wise** (Royalty)
*The Fools' War* - Lee Kisling  f  3159

**Ferrand, Art** (Computer Expert)
*Aftermath* - Charles Sheffield  s  4947

**Ferraro, Gene** (Adventurer)
*Castle War!* - John DeChancie  s  1455

**Ferrier, Matt** (Military Personnel)
*Darkness on the Ice* - Lois Tilton  h  5475

**Ferris, Robert** (Spy)
*The Devouring* - Douglas D. Hawk  h  2615

**Ferro, Dante** (Religious)
*Blood of the Covenant* - Brent Monahan  h  3954

**Ferro-Maine, Sylvia** (Professor; Agent)
*The Ecolitan Enigma* - L.E. Modesitt Jr.  s  3927

**Ferrol, Chayne** (Spaceman)
*Warhorse* - Timothy Zahn  s  6056

**Fess** (Robot)
*The Warlock Insane* - Christopher Stasheff  f  5225
*The Warlock Rock* - Christopher Stasheff  s  5226
*A Wizard in Absentia* - Christopher Stasheff  s  5229

**Fettle, Richard** (Writer)
*Queen of Angels* - Greg Bear  s  423

**Fiar, Jacobious** (Scientist)
*Jonas McFee, A.T.P.* - Sarah Sargent  s  4827

**Fielder, John** (Doctor)
*Dead in the Water* - Nancy Holder  h  2732

**Fielding, Anna** (Wizard; Apprentice)
*The Compass of the Soul* - Sean Russell  f  4740

**Fields, Stratton** (Architect)
*Horses of the Night* - Michael Cadnum  h  811

**Fiendlord, Zoltan** (Wizard)
*Majyk by Accident* - Esther Friesner  f  2079
*Majyk by Design* - Esther Friesner  f  2080

**Fieran** (Martial Arts Expert; Leader)
*Dragon Moon* - Chris Claremont  f  1040

**Figg, Nigel** (Child)
*The Horror Club* - Mark Morris  h  4022

**Figueroa, Calafia "Kali"** (Television Personality;
Religious)
*Kalifornia* - Marc Laidlaw  s  3311

**Figueroa, Poppy** (Television Personality; Parent)
*Kalifornia* - Marc Laidlaw  s  3311

**Figueroa, Sandy** (Television Personality)
*Kalifornia* - Marc Laidlaw  s  3311

**Fileli** (Handicapped)
*The Broken Land* - Ian McDonald  s  3791

**Fileli, Mathembe** (Refugee)
*The Broken Land* - Ian McDonald  s  3791

**Fin, Adam** (Artist; Mythical Creature)
*Something Rich and Strange* - Patricia A.
McKillip  f  3840

**Finch, Josephine** (Businesswoman)
*The LaNague Chronicles* - F. Paul Wilson  s  5889

**Fine, Joan** (Activist)
*Sewer, Gas & Electric* - Matt Ruff  s  4708

**Finesse, Adrian** (Actor)
*Star Prey* - Ehren M. Ehly  h  1763

**Finis "Water"** (Child; Adventurer)
*Beyond the Magic Sphere* - Gail Jarrow  f  2879

**Finister "Moraga"** (Agent; Psychic)
*Quicksilver's Knight* - Christopher Stasheff  f  5220

**Finley, Sarah** (Doctor)
*Descent* - Ron Dee  h  1465

**Finn, Clio** (Time Traveler; Pilot)
*The Seeds of Time* - Kay Kenyon  s  3064

**Finnegan, Jack** (Publisher; Recluse)
*Glimmering* - Elizabeth Hand  s  2535

**Finriddy, Sarah "Fin"** (Scientist; Explorer)
*Uncharted Territory* - Connie Willis  s  5875

**Fiolon** (Nobleman; Musician)
*Lady of the Trillium* - Marion Zimmer
Bradley  f  641

**Fiona** (Reincarnated Person; Spouse)
*Ronin* - D.A. Heeley  f  2639

**Fir** (Mythical Creature)
*Above the Lower Sky* - Tom Deitz  f  1469

**Firdun** (Nobleman)
*The Warding of Witch World* - Andre
Norton  f  4163

**Fire, Fen "Fire Queen"** (Warrior; Royalty)
*The Fire Queen* - Jack Holland  f  2740

**Fireforge, Flint** (Mythical Creature; Artisan)
*Kindred Spirits* - Mark Anthony  f  154
*Wanderlust* - Mary Kirchoff  f  3155

**Firemayne, Rowan** (Hero; Musician)
*Cup of Clay* - Carole Nelson Douglas  f  1583
*Seed upon the Wind* - Carole Nelson
Douglas  f  1584

**Firesong** (Magician)
*Storm Breaking* - Mercedes Lackey  f  3296
*Storm Warning* - Mercedes Lackey  f  3298

**Firinne** (Farmer)
*Faery in Shadow* - C.J. Cherryh  f  987

**Fischer, Benjamin Franklin** (Psychic)
*Hell House* - Richard Matheson  h  3685

**Fischer, Bernie** (Detective—Police)
*Sparrowhawk* - Thomas A. Easton  s  1725

**Fischer, Max** (Artist)
*After Silence* - Jonathan Carroll  h  916

**Fischer, Tim** (Psychic)
*Night* - Alan Rodgers  h  4649

**Fisher** (Animal)
*The Blood Jaguar* - Michael H. Payne  f  4271

**Fisher, Danny** (Telepath)
*Cloud's Rider* - C.J. Cherryh  s  983
*Rider at the Gate* - C.J. Cherryh  s  1000

**Fisher, David** (Government Official)
*The Case of the Toxic Spell Dump* - Harry
Turtledove  f  5497

**Fisher, Isobel** (Police Officer)
*The Bones of Haven* - Simon R. Green  f  2363
*The God Killer* - Simon R. Green  f  2368
*Guard Against Dishonor* - Simon R. Green  f  2369
*Hawk & Fisher* - Simon R. Green  f  2370

*Winner Takes All* - Simon R. Green  *f*  2375
*Wolf in the Fold* - Simon R. Green  *f*  2376

**Fisher, Johanna** (Linguist)
*St. Peter's Wolf* - Michael Cadnum  *h*  816

**Fisher, Steve** (Importer/Exporter)
*Chase the Morning* - Michael Scott Rohan  *f*  4658
*Cloud Castles* - Michael Scott Rohan  *f*  4659
*The Gates of Noon* - Michael Scott Rohan  *f*  4661

**Fist, Sinklar** (Military Personnel)
*Relic of Empire* - W. Michael Gear  *s*  2171

**Fitch, Xavier** (Scientist; Leader)
*Species* - Yvonne Navarro  *s*  4075

**Fitz-Gerald, Ralf** (Knight; Lawman)
*Sherwood* - Parke Godwin  *f*  2248

**Fitzpatrick, Al-Hajji Brian** (Scientist; Religious)
*The Missing Matter* - Thomas R.
  McDonough  *s*  3805

**Fitzpatrick, Dan** (Religious)
*Virgin* - Mary Elizabeth Murphy  *h*  4050

**Fitzroy, Henry** (Writer; Vampire)
*Blood Debt* - Tanya Huff  *h*  2792
*Blood Price* - Tanya Huff  *h*  2793
*Blood Trail* - Tanya Huff  *h*  2794

**FitzWalter, Marion "Marion of Ravenskeep"**
  (Noblewoman)
*Lady of the Forest* - Jennifer Roberson  *f*  4609

**Flagg, Randall** (Leader)
*The Stand: The Complete and Uncut Edition* - Stephen
  King  *h*  3142

**Flanagan, Jeffrey** (Religious; Administrator)
*Lords of Creation* - Tim Sullivan  *s*  5351

**Flanagan, Thomas** (Political Figure)
*The Resurrectionist* - Thomas F.
  Monteleone  *h*  3965

**Flander** (Computer Expert)
*Chimera* - Mary Rosenblum  *s*  4677

**Flanders, Ted "Dead Ted"** (Vagrant)
*Tower of Evil* - James Kisner  *h*  3161

**Flannagan, James** (Businessman)
*Diary of a Vampire* - Gary Bowen  *h*  600

**Flannery, Eric** (Computer Expert; Adventurer)
*Caverns of Socrates* - Dennis L. McKiernan  *f*  3831

**Flannery, Kathleen** (Museum Curator; Adventurer)
*The Two Georges* - Richard Dreyfuss  *s*  1655

**Flattery, Erasmus** (Apprentice; Adventurer)
*Beneath the Vaulted Hills* - Sean Russell  *f*  4739

**Flattery, Erasmus** (Adventurer)
*The Compass of the Soul* - Sean Russell  *f*  4740

**Flattery, Tristam** (Naturalist)
*Sea Without a Shore* - Sean Russell  *f*  4743
*World Without End* - Sean Russell  *f*  4744

**Flavius** (Slave)
*Pandora* - Anne Rice  *h*  4573

**Fledge** (Servant)
*The Grotesque* - Patrick McGrath  *h*  3814

**Fleetfox** (Hero)
*Barrow* - John Deakins  *f*  1443

**Fleming, Cory** (Teenager)
*Hell-O-Ween* - David Robbins  *h*  4598

**Fleming, Ed** (Fisherman)
*Raven Stole the Moon* - Garth Stein  *h*  5249

**Fleming, Jack** (Detective—Private; Vampire;
  Journalist)
*Blood on the Water* - P.N. Elrod  *h*  1791

**Fleming, Jack** (Journalist; Vampire; Detective—
  Private)
*Bloodlist* - P.N. Elrod  *h*  1792

**Fleming, Jack** (Detective—Private; Vampire;
  Journalist)
*A Chill in the Blood* - P.N. Elrod  *h*  1793

**Fleming, Jack** (Journalist; Vampire; Detective—
  Private)
*Fire in the Blood* - P.N. Elrod  *h*  1796

**Fleming, Paul** (Writer)
*Demon Shadows* - Michael B. Sirota  *h*  5075

**Flere-Imsaho** (Robot)
*The Player of Games* - Iain M. Banks  *s*  326

**Fletcher, Ben** (Horse Trainer)
*Darkscope* - Margaret Falk  *h*  1860

**Fletcher, DeAnne** (Housewife)
*Lost Boys* - Orson Scott Card  *f*  891

**Fletcher, Diane** (Detective—Private; Empath)
*Passion Play* - Sean Stewart  *s*  5276

**Fletcher, Evelyn** (Doctor)
*Solomon's Knife* - Victor Koman  *s*  3200

**Fletcher, Howard** (Doctor)
*Contagion* - John David Connor  *h*  1136

**Fletcher, Lenora** (FBI Agent)
*The Hanged Man* - T.J. MacGregor  *h*  3594

**Fletcher, Mary Lisa** (Actress)
*Night Games* - Marilyn Harris  *h*  2562

**Fletcher, Richard Wesley** (Scientist)
*The Great and Secret Show* - Clive Barker  *h*  341

**Fletcher, Step** (Computer Expert; Religious)
*Lost Boys* - Orson Scott Card  *f*  891

**Fletcher, Stevie** (Child)
*Lost Boys* - Orson Scott Card  *f*  891

**Fletcher, Terrance "Eel"** (Criminal)
*The Darker Saints* - Brian Hodge  *h*  2699

**Flez** (Alien)
*Living with Aliens* - John DeChancie  *s*  1460

**Flitheimer, Samuel** (Philanthropist)
*Dr. Dimension* - John DeChancie  *s*  1456

**Flitworth, Renata** (Farmer; Maiden)
*Reaper Man* - Terry Pratchett  *f*  4399

**Flood, C. Thomas** (Writer)
*Bloodsucking Fiends: A Love Story* - Christopher
  Moore  *h*  3988

**Flood, Reuben** (Scientist; Military Personnel)
*Habu* - James B. Johnson  *s*  2920

**Florence, Julia** (Teenager; Witch)
*Witch* - Christopher Pike  *f*  4334

**Florescu, Ilana** (Vampire)
*Domination* - Michael Cecilione  *h*  946

**Florey, Rick** (Scientist)
*Of the Fall* - Paul J. McAuley  *s*  3713

**Florida** (Child; Mythical Creature)
*Nevernever* - Will Shetterly  *f*  4995

**Floris** (Foundling; Heir—Lost)
*Out of the Ordinary* - Annie Dalton  *f*  1330

**Flowerbender** (Royalty)
*Marbleheart* - Don Callander  *f*  846

**Flowerstalk, Flarman** (Wizard; Magician)
*Pyromancer* - Don Callander  *f*  847

**Flutirr** (Nobleman)
*Flute Song Magic* - Andrea Shettle  *f*  4996

**Flynn, Beth** (Administrator)
*Substitute Teacher* - Jordan Storm  *h*  5314

**Flynn, Charlie** (Police Officer; Time Traveler)
*Far Edge of Darkness* - Linda Evans  *s*  1855

**Flynn, Evon** (Worker; Scholar)
*Nightsword* - Margaret Weis  *f*  5722

**Flynn, Lizbeth** (Child)
*Substitute Teacher* - Jordan Storm  *h*  5314

**Flynn, Lonny** (Convict)
*Spree* - Lucy Taylor  *h*  5415

**Flynn, Maggie** (Fiance(e))
*Beyond the Gate* - Dave Wolverton  *s*  5949

**Fogarty, Bill** (Police Officer)
*Mind Kill* - Richard La Plante  *h*  3267

**Foggia, Larry** (Detective—Police)
*Master of Lies* - Graham Masterton  *h*  3676

**Folliot, Clive** (Military Personnel)
*The Final Battle* - Richard A. Lupoff  *f*  3572
*The Hidden City* - Charles de Lint  *f*  1429

**Fong, Jimmy** (Teenager)
*Vision Quest* - Pamela F. Service  *f*  4920

**Fong, Len** (Salesman)
*An Enemy Reborn* - Michael A. Stackpole  *f*  5197

**Fonteyn, Oliver** (Cousin)
*Death Masque* - P.N. Elrod  *h*  1795

**Forbes, Melanie** (Paranormal Investigator)
*The Link* - Andrew Laurance  *h*  3348
*The Premonition* - Andrew Laurance  *h*  3349
*The Unborn* - Andrew Laurance  *h*  3350

**Forbes, Vanessa** (Student)
*The School* - Ed Kelleher  *h*  3042

**Ford, Arlen** (Actress)
*From the Teeth of Angels* - Jonathan Carroll  *h*  918

**Ford, Marcus** (Doctor)
*Omega* - Patrick Lynch  *h*  3577

**Ford, Morgan** (Police Officer)
*Skull Session* - Daniel Hecht  *h*  2638

**Foreman, Jack** (Anthropologist)
*The Charm* - Adam Niswander  *h*  4111

**Forester, Clay** (Scientist; Engineer)
*The Humanoids* - Jack Williamson  *s*  5865

**Forester, David** (Student)
*Starfleet Academy* - Diane Carey  *s*  905

**Forister** (Spaceman)
*PartnerShip* - Anne McCaffrey  *s*  3741

**Formidable** (Royalty; Warrior)
*A Remembrance for Kedrigern* - John
  Morressy  *f*  4014

**Formosus, Musculus Herodes** (Adventurer;
  Handicapped)
*Whose Song Is Sung* - Frank Schaefer  *f*  4872

**Forrest, Connie** (Housewife)
*Evil Intent* - Bernard Taylor  *h*  5400

**Forrest, Jack** (Writer)
*Evil Intent* - Bernard Taylor  *h*  5400

**Forrest, Pete** (Neighbor; Traveler)
*Beyond the Veil of Stars* - Robert Reed  *s*  4503

**Forrest, Winn** (Religious; Government Official)
*Half-Light* - Denise Vitola  *s*  5575

**Forrester, Edward** (Criminal)
*The Lunatic Cafe* - Laurell K. Hamilton  *h*  2520

**Forsetti, Anna** (Artisan)
*The Innamorati* - Midori Snyder  *f*  5152

**Forster, J.Q.R.** (Professor)
*The Diamond Moon* - Paul Preuss  *s*  4417
*The Shining Ones* - Paul Preuss  *s*  4421

**Forsyte, Adrian** (Scientist)
*Shifter* - Judith Reeves-Stevens  *f*  4515

**Fortizak "Zak"** (Writer)
*Murder at the Galactic Writers' Society* - Janet
  Asimov  *s*  251

**Fortunato, Amelia** (Student—College)
*Dark Visions* - T. Lucien Wright  *h*  5987

**Fortune** (Mythical Creature; Adventurer)
*Dragoncharm* - Graham Edwards  *f*  1749

**Fortune, Alison Crandall** (Paralegal)
*Devil's Gate* - Elizabeth Ergas  *h*  1833

**Fortune, Celinde "Cissy"** (Magician; Technician)
*Dreaming Metal* - Melissa Scott  *s*  4895

**Fortune, Felicity** (Mythical Creature)
*The Godmother* - Elizabeth Ann
 Scarborough  *f*  4862
*The Godmother's Apprentice* - Elizabeth Ann
 Scarborough  *f*  4863

**Foskins** (Government Official)
*The Rats* - James Herbert  *h*  2671

**Foster, Bass** (Time Traveler; Warrior)
*Of Beginnings and Endings* - Robert Adams  *s*  33

**Foster, Danny** (Child)
*Twilight Time* - Rick Hautala  *h*  2613

**Foster, Katherine** (Secretary—Legal)
*Twilight Time* - Rick Hautala  *h*  2613

**Foster, Maggie** (Time Traveler)
*The Iron Bridge* - David Morse  *s*  4036

**Foster, Neda** (Researcher)
*The Abductors: Conspiracy* - Jonathan
 Frakes  *s*  2034

**Foster, Sandra "Sandy"** (Scientist; Researcher)
*Bellwether* - Connie Willis  *s*  5867

**Foster, Sunny Mae** (Worker)
*Ghost Dance* - Kathryn Ptacek  *h*  4441

**Foth** (Scholar)
*The Tides of God* - Ted Reynolds  *s*  4567

**Four, Cathy** (Cyborg)
*Cathy IV* - Frances Lucas  *s*  3539

**Fouts, Marian** (Journalist)
*Murder in the Solid State* - Wil McCarthy  *s*  3764

**Fowke, William G.** (Engineer; Outlaw)
*A Journal of the Flood Year* - David Ely  *s*  1805

**Fowler, Cassie** (Writer)
*Towing Jehovah* - James Morrow  *f*  4035

**Fox-Eyes, Thelvyn** (Royalty)
*Dragonmage of Mystara* - Thorarinn
 Gunnarsson  *f*  2462

**Foxfire** (Mythical Creature; Leader)
*Silver Shadows* - Elaine Cunningham  *f*  1292

**Foxfire, Dalvenjah** (Mythical Creature)
*Dragons on the Town* - Thorarinn
 Gunnarsson  *f*  2463
*Make Way for Dragons!* - Thorarinn
 Gunnarsson  *f*  2465

**Foxworth, Elizabeth** (Social Worker)
*Fragments* - James F. David  *h*  1380

**Foxxe, Johnny "Fox"** (Musician)
*The Wood Wife* - Terri Windling  *f*  5916

**Foyan, Esmeralda** (Young Woman)
*Westlin Wind* - Charles de Lint  *f*  1439

**Foyle, Gulliver "Gully"** (Spaceman; Psychic)
*The Stars My Destination* - Alfred Bester  *s*  478

**Frakes, Danny "Mouse"** (Child)
*Darkman #1: The Hangman* - Randall Boyll  *h*  612

**Frame, Max** (Teacher)
*Dead End* - Guy N. Smith  *h*  5119

**Francie** (Teenager; Orphan)
*In the Heart of the Valley of Love* - Cynthia
 Kadohata  *s*  2997

**Francie** (Genetically Altered Being; Child)
*Naming the Flowers* - Kate Wilhelm  *s*  5809

**Francine** (Noblewoman; Spouse)
*Lord Conrad's Lady* - Leo Frankowski  *s*  2046

**Francisco, George** (Alien; Detective—Police)
*The Change* - Barry B. Longyear  *s*  3520
*Cross of Blood* - K.W. Jeter  *s*  2909
*Dark Horizon* - K.W. Jeter  *s*  2910

**Francy, Lizzie** (Teenager; Computer Expert)
*Beggars Ride* - Nancy Kress  *s*  3238

**Frank** (Demon)
*The Hellbound Heart* - Clive Barker  *h*  342

**Frank** (Mechanic; Pirate)
*Spacer Dreams* - Larry Segriff  *s*  4911

**Frank, Victor** (Doctor; Scientist)
*Mutation* - Robin Cook  *s*  1165

**Frank-I-STN-4** (Administrator; Clone)
*Title Deleted for Security Reasons* - Ed
 Blome  *s*  553

**Frankel, Cathy** (Alien; Doctor)
*Cross of Blood* - K.W. Jeter  *s*  2909

**Frankel, Melissa** (Teenager)
*Roadkill* - Richard Sanford  *h*  4815

**Frankel, Sidney** (Professor)
*Roadkill* - Richard Sanford  *h*  4815

**Frankenstein, Elizabeth** (Young Woman)
*The Darker Passions: Frankenstein* - Amarantha
 Knight  *h*  3180
*The Memoirs of Elizabeth Frankenstein* - Theodore
 Roszak  *h*  4684

**Frankenstein, Gunthar Thunnar** (Scientist)
*I Am Frankenstein* - C. Dean Andersson  *h*  140

**Frankenstein, Victor** (Scientist)
*The Darker Passions: Frankenstein* - Amarantha
 Knight  *h*  3180
*The Memoirs of Elizabeth Frankenstein* - Theodore
 Roszak  *h*  4684
*The Secret Laboratory Journals of Dr. Victor
 Frankenstein* - Jeremy Kay  *h*  3019

**Frankenstein's Monster** (Monster)
*The Final Battle* - Richard A. Lupoff  *f*  3572

**Franker, Edward "Eddie"** (Television)
*Pictures at 11* - Norman Spinrad  *s*  5173

**Frankie** (Teenager)
*Collidescope* - Grace Chetwin  *s*  1011

**Frankl, Victor** (Office Worker)
*The Suiting* - Kelley Wilde  *h*  5803

**Franklin, Benjamin** (Apprentice)
*Newton's Cannon* - J. Gregory Keyes  *f*  3097

**Franklin, Charles** (Scientist)
*Moving Mars* - Greg Bear  *s*  421

**Franklin, Jim** (Clerk)
*Mall, Mayhem and Magic* - Holly Lisle  *f*  3485

**Franklyn, Kit** (Psychologist)
*Blood on the Bayou* - D.J. Donaldson  *h*  1570

**Franks, Leo** (Police Officer)
*Night Mask* - William W. Johnstone  *h*  2931

**Fraser, Brian** (Child)
*Dark Silence* - Rick Hautala  *h*  2606

**Fraser, Colin** (Military Personnel)
*March or Die* - Andrew Keith  *s*  3035

**Fraser, Edward** (Businessman)
*Dark Silence* - Rick Hautala  *h*  2606

**Fraser, Mike** (Patient)
*Dark Silence* - Rick Hautala  *h*  2606

**Frasier, Cally** (Teenager)
*The First Horror* - R.L. Stine  *h*  5288

**Frasier, Cody** (Teenager)
*The First Horror* - R.L. Stine  *h*  5288

**Frazier, Nick** (Police Officer)
*Down River* - Stephen Gallagher  *h*  2110

**Frazier, Rhea** (Political Figure)
*Shadows Fall* - Simon R. Green  *f*  2373

**Fred** (Alien)
*After the Blue* - Russel Like  *s*  3465

**Frede** (Military Personnel; Health Care Professional)
*Orion Among the Stars* - Ben Bova  *s*  589

**Frederickson, Robert "Mongo"** (Detective—
 Private)
*The Fear in Yesterday's Rings* - George C.
 Chesbro  *h*  1007

**Freds** (Expatriate)
*Escape From Kathmandu* - Kim Stanley
 Robinson  *s*  4630

**Freeborn, Silas** (Businessman)
*Nocturnas* - Shawn Ryan  *h*  4755

**Freede, Hannibal** (Scientist)
*Flare* - Roger Zelazny  *s*  6065

**Freelorn "Lorn"** (Heir—Dispossessed; Royalty)
*The Door into Sunset* - Diane Duane  *f*  1660

**Freeman, Alan** (Scientist)
*Extinct* - Charles Wilson  *h*  5877

**Freeman, Claire** (Photographer)
*Candle Night* - Phil Rickman  *h*  4586

**Freeman, Doug** (Military Personnel)
*Battle Front* - Ian Slater  *s*  5086

**Freeman, Giles** (Journalist)
*Candle Night* - Phil Rickman  *h*  4586

**Freeman, Justine** (Teenager)
*Perfect Little Angels* - Andrew Neiderman  *h*  4090

**Freemark, Nest** (Sorceress; Student—College; Sports
 Figure)
*A Knight of the Word* - Terry Brooks  *f*  714

**Freemark, Nest** (Teenager; Student—High School;
 Sorceress)
*Running with the Demon* - Terry Brooks  *f*  715

**Freese, Neil** (Guide)
*Snowmen* - Jerry Earl Brown  *s*  725

**Freetz, Jhoe** (Spaceman; Scientist)
*Flies From the Amber* - Wil McCarthy  *s*  3763

**Freleng, Rachel** (Teacher)
*Cries of the Children* - Clare McNally  *h*  3856

**French, Jessica** (Doctor)
*Little Boy Lost* - T.M. Wright  *h*  5992

**French, Melissa** (Teenager; Vampire)
*Liquid Diet* - William Tedford  *h*  5419

**Fresca, Riki** (Artist)
*The Cybernetic Walrus* - Jack L. Chalker  *s*  951

**Freund, Solomon** (Psychic)
*Child of the Light* - Janet Gluckman  *f*  2244

**Freund, Solomon "Sol"** (Psychic)
*Child of the Journey* - Janet Berliner  *f*  466
*Children of the Dusk* - Janet Berliner  *f*  467

**Frewin, Mary** (Child; Psychic)
*The Red-Eared Ghosts* - Vivian Alcock  *f*  53

**Frey, Ezra** (Military Personnel)
*Emperors of the Twilight* - S. Andrew
 Swann  *s*  5362

**Freyer, Ulteena** (Military Personnel)
*The Parafaith War* - L.E. Modesitt Jr.  *s*  3937

**Frida** (Musician)
*Kamikaze L'Amour* - Richard Kadrey  *s*  2998

**Friedkin** (Scientist)
*The Quick* - Burt Cole  *s*  1113

**Friedman, Jack** (Police Officer)
*Homecoming* - Matthew J. Costello  *h*  1198

**Friend** (Ruler)
*Swan Song* - Robert R. McCammon  *h*  3757

**Friendly, Bud** (Journalist)
*Silent Moon* - William Relling Jr.   *h*   4531

**Friendly, Tod T.** (Doctor; Criminal)
*Time's Arrow* - Martin Amis   *s*   96

**Friese, Adam "Iceberg"** (Astronaut)
*Ignition* - Kevin J. Anderson   *s*   107

**Frike** (Servant)
*Bring Me the Head of Prince Charming* - Roger
   Zelazny   *f*   6062

**Frisson** (Writer)
*The Witch Doctor* - Christopher Stasheff   *f*   5228

**Fritz, Edgar P.** (Criminal)
*Darkman #3: The Gods of Hell* - Randall
   Boyll   *h*   614

**Froister, Albert** (Mythical Creature; Businessman)
*The Magic Touch* - Jody Lynn Nye   *f*   4171

**Frolatti, Victor** (Journalist)
*The Golden Mean* - Nick Bantock   *f*   334

**Fronto** (Animal; Writer)
*The Arkadians* - Lloyd Alexander   *f*   67

**Frost** (Military Personnel)
*Deathstalker War* - Simon R. Green   *s*   2366

**Frost** (Magician)
*Demon Blade* - Mark A. Garland   *f*   2141

**Frost, Deacon** (Vampire)
*Blade* - Mel Odom   *h*   4190

**Frost, Jonathan** (Businessman)
*Morningstar* - Peter Atkins   *h*   265

**Frost, Joni** (Vagrant)
*Stone Angels* - Mike Jefferies   *h*   2889

**Frost, Melanie** (Health Care Professional)
*The Seventh Heart* - Marina Fitch   *f*   1943

**Frost, Raymond** (Clerk)
*Killing Frost* - Dan I. Blake   *h*   514

**Frostwing** (Monster)
*Frostwing* - Richard A. Knaak   *f*   3170

**Fry, Theodore** (Magician)
*The Fair Rules of Evil* - David C. Smith   *h*   5111

**Frydys** (Girlfriend)
*The Deepest Sea* - Charles Barnitz   *f*   363

**Fucci, Vannie** (Criminal)
*The Hollow Man* - Dan Simmons   *s*   5054

**Fuentes, Jose** (Police Officer)
*Star Prey* - Ehren M. Ehly   *h*   1763

**Fujito, Hiroshi** (Military Personnel)
*Assault of the Super Carrier* - Peter Albano   *s*   47
*Super Carrier: The Ultimate Secret Weapon* - Peter
   Albano   *s*   50

**Fuller, Maude** (Witch; Psychic)
*Slow Funeral* - Rebecca Ore   *f*   4221

**Fuller, Stan** (Teenager)
*The Summoned* - Steven Ray Fulgham   *h*   2090

**Fullin** (Musician; Experimental Subject)
*Commitment Hour* - James Alan Gardner   *s*   2134

**Funcitti, Benito** (Government Official)
*The Man in the Moon Must Die* - Jeff
   Bredenberg   *s*   665

**Fundan, Dane** (Heir; Spaceman)
*The Founder* - Christopher Rowley   *s*   4696

**Fundan, Fair** (Rancher; Leader)
*To a Highland Nation* - Christopher
   Rowley   *s*   4698

**Furiano, Furian** (Apprentice)
*Faces under Water* - Tanith Lee   *h*   3409

**Furth, Dafyd** (Psychic)
*Exile's Challenge* - Angus Wells   *f*   5734
*Exile's Children* - Angus Wells   *f*   5735

**Fury** (Psychic)
*Jack the Bodiless* - Julian May   *s*   3698

**Fyana** (Healer)
*The Poisoned Lands* - John Maddox
   Roberts   *f*   4619

**Fyodor of Rashemen** (Warrior)
*Daughter of the Drow* - Elaine Cunningham   *f*   1287

# G

**G.Ren.Bei.Yi** (Alien)
*Alien Tongue* - Stephen Leigh   *s*   3424

**Gable, Clark** (Actor; Historical Figure)
*Who P-P-Plugged Roger Rabbit?* - Gary K.
   Wolf   *f*   5934

**Gable, Helen** (Waiter/Waitress)
*Symphony* - Charles L. Grant   *h*   2318

**Gable, Robert** (Psychologist; Administrator)
*Serpent's Gift* - A.C. Crispin   *s*   1261
*Starbridge* - A.C. Crispin   *s*   1265

**Gable, Robert** (Administrator; Psychologist)
*Voices of Chaos* - A.C. Crispin   *s*   1266

**Gabool** (Animal; Pirate)
*Mariel of Redwall* - Brian Jacques   *f*   2850

**Gabria** (Warrior; Sorceress)
*Dark Horse* - Mary H. Herbert   *f*   2674
*Lightning's Daughter* - Mary H. Herbert   *f*   2676
*Winged Magic* - Mary H. Herbert   *f*   2678

**Gabriel** (Singer; Angel)
*Archangel* - Sharon Shinn   *s*   5000

**Gabriel** (Government Official; Detective—Amateur)
*Aristoi* - Walter Jon Williams   *s*   5834

**Gabriel, Faustin** (Art Dealer)
*Vodoun* - David Madsen   *h*   3605

**Gabriel, Justin** (Prisoner)
*Mind Kill* - Richard La Plante   *h*   3267

**Gabrielle** (Sidekick; Adventurer)
*The Empty Throne* - Ru Emerson   *f*   1808

**Gabrielle** (Warrior; Storyteller)
*The Thief of Hermes* - Ru Emerson   *f*   1811

**Gadded, Elizabeth** (Entertainer)
*Prophets for the End of Time* - Marcos
   Donnelly   *f*   1577

**Gadfium, Hortis** (Scientist)
*Feersum Endjinn* - Iain M. Banks   *s*   325

**Gadjung** (Wizard)
*The Wizard and the Floating City* - Christopher
   Rowley   *f*   4699

**Gael, Dorothy "Dotty"** (Orphan; Abuse Victim)
*Was* - Geoff Ryman   *f*   4758

**Gaelinar** (Companion)
*Dragonrank Master* - Mickey Zucker
   Reichert   *f*   4519

**Gaetan, Mary** (Housewife)
*Lie to Me* - David Martin   *h*   3639

**Gaetan, Philip** (Prisoner)
*Lie to Me* - David Martin   *h*   3639

**Gaetano, Rafaelo** (Political Figure; Organized Crime
   Figure)
*Empire Builders* - Ben Bova   *s*   584

**Gaffney, Arnold** (Military Personnel)
*Lieutenant* - Rick Shelley   *s*   4972

**Gage, Tom** (Detective)
*The Long Midnight* - Daniel Ransom   *h*   4480

**Gail** (Royalty; Spouse)
*Nobody's Son* - Sean Stewart   *f*   5275

**Gailard** (Military Personnel)
*The Guardian* - Angus Wells   *f*   5737

**Gaimes, Gary** (Murderer)
*House Haunted* - Al Sarrantonio   *h*   4830

**Gainsborough, Harry** (Writer)
*Zod Wallop* - William Browning Spencer   *h*   5169

**Galbraith, Emily** (Child)
*Good Night, Sweet Angel* - Clare McNally   *h*   3857

**Galbraith, Jenn** (Teacher)
*Good Night, Sweet Angel* - Clare McNally   *h*   3857

**Gale, Abby "Apple Guy"** (Child)
*Thunder Rise* - G. Wayne Miller   *h*   3895

**Gale, Brad** (Journalist)
*Thunder Rise* - G. Wayne Miller   *h*   3895

**Gale, C.J.** (Teenager)
*Little Boy Lost* - T.M. Wright   *h*   5992

**Gale, Denton** (Computer Expert)
*Mother Lode* - Zach Hughes   *s*   2812

**Gale, Dorothy** (Traveler; Teenager)
*Visitors From Oz: The Wild Adventures of Dorothy,
   the Scarecrow and the Tin Woodman* - Martin
   Gardner   *f*   2136

**Gale, Miles** (Archaeologist)
*Little Boy Lost* - T.M. Wright   *h*   5992

**Galele, Tedla** (Genetically Altered Being; Refugee)
*Halfway Human* - Carolyn Ives Gilman   *s*   2237

**Galen, Michelle** (Lawyer)
*The Double* - Don Webb   *s*   5661

**Gali** (Mythical Creature)
*Mall, Mayhem and Magic* - Holly Lisle   *f*   3485

**Galinda "Glinda the Good"** (Socialite; Witch)
*Wicked: The Life and Times of the Wicked Witch of
   the West* - Gregory Maguire   *f*   3609

**Galingale, Cyrus "Cy"** (Carpenter)
*Waking Beauty* - Paul Witcover   *f*   5931

**Gall, Dennis** (Guide)
*Snowmen* - Jerry Earl Brown   *s*   725

**Gallagher, Dori** (Journalist)
*Trickster* - Chris Curry   *h*   1297

**Gallandro, Anja** (Revolutionary)
*Trouble on Cloud City* - Kevin J. Anderson   *s*   117

**Gallatin, Michael** (Spy; Werewolf)
*The Wolf's Hour* - Robert R. McCammon   *h*   3759

**Gallegher, P.J.** (Shaman)
*Valentine* - S.P. Somtow   *h*   5160

**Gallegher, P.J.** (Art Dealer)
*Vanitas: Escape From Vampire Junction* - S.P.
   Somtow   *h*   5162

**Galliez, Aymar** (Writer)
*The Werewolf of Paris* - Guy Endore   *h*   1822

**Galloway, Katt** (Masseuse)
*Walking Wounded* - Robert Devereaux   *h*   1507

**Galloway, Marcus** (Professor)
*Walking Wounded* - Robert Devereaux   *h*   1507

**Gallowglass, Cordelia** (Witch; Noblewoman)
*M'Lady Witch* - Christopher Stasheff   *f*   5217

**Gallowglass, Geoffrey** (Warlock; Nobleman)
*M'Lady Witch* - Christopher Stasheff   *f*   5217
*Quicksilver's Knight* - Christopher Stasheff   *f*   5220

**Gallowglass, Gwen** (Witch)
*The Warlock Rock* - Christopher Stasheff   *s*   5226

**Gallowglass, Rod** (Warlock)
*Warlock and Son* - Christopher Stasheff   *s*   5224
*The Warlock Insane* - Christopher Stasheff   *f*   5225
*The Warlock Rock* - Christopher Stasheff   *s*   5226

**Galoran** (Nobleman; Military Personnel)
*Count Scar* - C. Dale Brittain  f  702

**Galore, B.S.** (Leader)
*Star Wreck II: The Attack of the Jargonites* - Leah Rewolinski  s  4563

**Galvin** (Magician; Religious)
*Red Magic* - Jean Rabe  f  4458

**Galweigh, Kait** (Mythical Creature; Diplomat)
*Diplomacy of Wolves* - Holly Lisle  f  3481

**Gamaliel, Cartee** (Investigator)
*Kindred* - John Gideon  h  2222

**Game Cat** (Computer Expert; Editor)
*Vurt* - Jeff Noon  s  4136

**Gamelan** (Wizard)
*The Warrior's Tale* - Allan Cole  f  1110

**Gampo, Songstan** (Ruler)
*The Yngling and the Circle of Power* - John Dalmas  s  1328

**Gandharva** (Musician; Handicapped)
*Bhagavati* - Kara Dalkey  f  1316

**Gandillon, Vivian** (Teenager; Werewolf)
*Blood and Chocolate* - Annette Curtis Klause  h  3162

**Ganganelli, Patrizio** (Religious)
*Cardinal's Sin* - Raymond Buckland  h  751

**Gangle, Kendar "Ratwacker"** (Wizard; Student)
*Majyk by Accident* - Esther Friesner  f  2079

**Gangle, Kendar "Ratwacker"** (Wizard)
*Majyk by Design* - Esther Friesner  f  2080
*Majyk by Hook or Crook* - Esther Friesner  f  2081

**Gannett, Anson "Andy"** (Computer Expert)
*The Alien Years* - Robert Silverberg  s  5027

**Gantha** (Alien; Sorceress)
*Afterimage* - Kristine Kathryn Rusch  f  4709

**Garbage, Roger** (Producer)
*Skeletons* - Al Sarrantonio  h  4834

**Garcia, Acacia "Panthesilea"** (Entertainer)
*The California Voodoo Game* - Larry Niven  s  4117

**Garcia, Bud** (Resistance Fighter)
*Martian Deathtrap* - Nathan Archer  s  205

**Garcia-Chase, Isabel** (Teenager)
*The Wall Around Eden* - Joan Slonczewski  s  5092

**Garcia-Mesa, Rosa** (Religious)
*Shango* - James Roberto Curtis  h  1298

**Garden, Beauty "Beau"** (Artist; Religious)
*Humility Garden* - Felicity Savage  f  4850

**Garden, Humility "Humi"** (Ruler; Revolutionary)
*Delta City* - Felicity Savage  f  4849

**Garden, Humility "Humi"** (Apprentice; Artist; Religious)
*Humility Garden* - Felicity Savage  f  4850

**Gardener, Richard** (Child)
*The Horror Club* - Mark Morris  h  4022

**Gardener, Rick** (Artist)
*The Possession* - Ronald Kelly  h  3055

**Gardner, Joe** (Writer)
*The Children's Hour* - Douglas Clegg  h  1077

**Gardner, Peter** (Handicapped)
*Captain Quad* - Sean Costello  h  1203

**Gardner, Sam** (Student)
*Captain Quad* - Sean Costello  h  1203

**Garfield, Jake** (Minstrel; Wanderer)
*The World Next Door* - Brad Ferguson  s  1924

**Garfield, Joanne** (Teenager; Slave)
*Parable of the Sower* - Octavia E. Butler  s  792

**Gargoyle, Gary** (Mythical Creature)
*Geis of the Gargoyle* - Piers Anthony  f  172

**Garibaldi, Michael** (Security Officer)
*The Touch of Your Shadow, the Whisper of Your Name* - Neal Barrett Jr.  s  367

**Garibaldi, Michael** (Military Personnel; Security Officer)
*Voices* - John Vornholt  s  5598

**Garin, Seth** (Child)
*The Regulators* - Richard Bachman  h  284

**Garion** (Wizard; Royalty)
*The Seeress of Kell* - David Eddings  f  1738
*Sorceress of Darshiva* - David Eddings  f  1739

**Garlick, Magrat** (Fiance(e); Witch)
*Lords and Ladies* - Terry Pratchett  f  4394

**Garlick, Magrat** (Witch)
*Witches Abroad* - Terry Pratchett  f  4404

**Garlthik** (Mythical Creature; Thief)
*The Longing Ring* - Christopher Kubasik  f  3246

**Garner** (Religious)
*Wetbones* - John Shirley  h  5010

**Garoit, Darrell** (Convict; Revolutionary)
*Infinity Hold* - Barry B. Longyear  s  3522

**Garon** (Nobleman; Warrior)
*A Man Betrayed* - J.V. Jones  f  2958

**Garou, Lupe** (Werewolf)
*One Foot in the Grave* - Wm. Mark Simmons  f  5062

**Garret, Allison** (Vampire)
*Night Prayers* - P.D. Cacek  h  803

**Garrett** (Detective—Private)
*Deadly Quicksilver Lies* - Glen Cook  f  1148
*Dread Brass Shadows* - Glen Cook  f  1149
*Old Tin Sorrows* - Glen Cook  f  1151
*Pretty Pewter Gods* - Glen Cook  f  1152
*Red Iron Nights* - Glen Cook  f  1153

**Garrett, Carl** (Detective—Private)
*Cat's Eye* - William W. Johnstone  h  2928

**Garrett, Carl** (Murderer)
*The Dead Man's Kiss* - Robert Weinberg  h  5695

**Garrison, David** (Wealthy)
*Psychosphere* - Brian Lumley  h  3563

**Garrison, Richard** (Military Personnel)
*Psychomech* - Brian Lumley  h  3562

**Garrith, Lance** (Journalist)
*The Specialist* - Wynne Whiteford  s  5788

**Garroc** (Warrior; Mythical Creature)
*The Panther's Hoard* - Nancy Varian Berberick  f  458
*Shadow of the Seventh Moon* - Nancy Varian Berberick  f  459

**Garroway, Mark Alan** (Military Personnel; Computer Expert)
*Semper Mars* - Ian Douglas  s  1585

**Gart, Maya** (Teenager; Settler)
*The Faces of Ceti* - Mary Caraker  s  877

**Garth One-eye** (Warrior; Heir—Dispossessed)
*Arena* - William R. Forstchen  f  1977

**Garuda** (Mythical Creature; Adventurer)
*The Iron Ring* - Lloyd Alexander  f  68

**Garuda** (Animal)
*Walker between the Worlds* - Diane DesRochers  f  1499

**Garwood, Tony** (Guard)
*Children of the End* - Mark A. Clements  h  1084

**Garza, Tony** (Murderer)
*In the Mood* - Charles L. Grant  h  2312

**Gasam** (Warrior; Royalty)
*The Poisoned Lands* - John Maddox Roberts  f  4619

**Gaspar, James** (Time Traveler)
*Days of Cain* - J.R. Dunn  s  1694

**Gatekeeper** (Artisan)
*Hard-Boiled Wonderland and the End of the World* - Haruki Murakami  s  4047

**Gates, Bill** (Police Officer)
*Tunnelvision* - R. Patrick Gates  h  2162

**Gates, John** (Student)
*Flicker* - Theodore Roszak  h  4683

**Gates, Lawrence** (Doctor)
*Sibs* - F. Paul Wilson  h  5898

**Gatineau, Robert** (Spaceman)
*The Middle of Nowhere* - David Gerrold  s  2209

**Gatlin, Ben** (Police Officer)
*Father's Little Helper* - Ronald Kelly  h  3052

**Gato, Coyote** (Guide)
*Coyote* - Peter Gadol  f  2100

**Gatzalumendi, Isadora Katarina Manuela** (Researcher; Animal Lover)
*Anvil* - Nicolas van Pallandt  s  5540

**Gaultry** (Hunter; Wizard)
*Wind From a Foreign Sky* - Katya Reimann  f  4528

**Gaunt** (Robot)
*Checkmate* - Eric T. Baker  s  297

**Gaunt, Leland** (Businessman)
*Needful Things* - Stephen King  h  3137

**Gavel, Kevin** (Police Officer; Murderer)
*Junkyard* - Barry Porter  h  4370

**Gavilan, Kemal** (Royalty)
*Matrix Cubed* - Britton Bloom  s  554

**Gavin** (Royalty)
*Magelord: The Awakening* - Thomas K. Martin  f  3651
*The Time of Madness* - Thomas K. Martin  f  3652

**Gavin, Felix** (Sailor; Musician)
*The Little Country* - Charles de Lint  f  1432

**Gavrilli, David** (Heir; Runaway)
*Interface Masque* - Shariann Lewitt  s  3453

**Gawain** (Knight)
*Gawain and Lady Green* - Anne Eliot Crompton  f  1269

**Gawaine** (Knight)
*Blood and Honor* - Simon R. Green  f  2361

**Gawaine** (Apprentice; Musician)
*Fortress of Frost and Fire* - Mercedes Lackey  f  3282

**Gawen** (Ruler; Religious)
*Lady of Avalon* - Marion Zimmer Bradley  f  640

**Gaylen, Linda** (Journalist)
*Brainstorm* - Steven M. Krauzer  h  3230

**G'Dath** (Alien; Scientist)
*A Flag Full of Stars* - Brad Ferguson  s  1922

**Geddarms, Volothamp "Volo"** (Traveler; Scholar)
*The Mage in the Iron Mask* - Brian Thomsen  f  5458

**Gehn** (Magician)
*Myst: The Book of Atrus* - Rand Miller  f  3896

**Geiger, Rolf** (Musician)
*The Prodigy* - Noel Hynd  h  2823

**Gelasaar III** (Royalty; Leader)
*The Phoenix in Flight* - Sherwood Smith  s  5138

**Gelasias, Crystal** (Survivor)
*Red Shadows* - Yvonne Navarro  s  4074

**Geldt** (Companion)
*Madlands* - K.W. Jeter  s  2913

**Gelly** (Teenager; Adventurer)
*Flight to Hollow Mountain* - Mark Sebanc  f  4908

**Gelmann, Mina** (Aged Person; Adventurer)
*Codgerspace* - Alan Dean Foster  s  1999

**Gemcutter, Jena** (Apprentice; Wizard)
*Emerald House Rising* - Peg Kerr  f  3080

**Gemma** (Sorceress)
*The Lightless Kingdom* - Jonathan Wylie  f  6007

**Gen-93-Beta, John** (Spaceship Captain)
*Alien Earth* - Megan Lindholm  s  3469

**Genar-Hofoen, Byr** (Diplomat)
*Excession* - Iain M. Banks  s  324

**Genevera "Gena"** (Mythical Creature; Warrior)
*Once a Hero* - Michael A. Stackpole  f  5203

**Genius** (Artificial Intelligence; Alien)
*The Immortality Option* - James P. Hogan  s  2725

**Genoud, Rochelle** (Heiress)
*Oktober* - Stephen Gallagher  h  2112

**Gently, Dirk** (Detective—Private; Psychic)
*The Long Dark Tea-Time of the Soul* - Douglas
   Adams  s  30

**Gentry, Robert** (Detective—Police)
*Vespers* - Jeff Rovin  h  4688

**Geoffrey** (Nobleman; Vampire)
*Blood and Roses* - Sharon Bainbridge  h  292

**George** (Expatriate)
*Escape From Kathmandu* - Kim Stanley
   Robinson  s  4630

**George** (Artisan)
*Thessalonica* - Harry Turtledove  f  5511

**Gerard, Brian** (Professor)
*Webs* - Scott Baker  h  304

**Gerard, Monique** (Artist)
*Avatar* - Donald Beman  h  437

**Gerard, Sybil** (Prostitute)
*The Difference Engine* - William Gibson  s  2217

**Gerbert** (Religious)
*Ars Magica* - Judith Tarr  f  5392

**Gerchak, Julie** (Child; Student)
*My Ishmael* - Daniel Quinn  s  4456

**Gerenz, Frederick** (Administrator)
*Dead Heat* - Del Stone Jr.  h  5313

**Gerick** (Prisoner)
*Hard Crash* - Ryan Hughes  s  2810

**Gerin the Fox** (Military Personnel; Royalty)
*Fox and Empire* - Harry Turtledove  f  5500

**Gerin the Fox** (Ruler; Military Personnel)
*Prince of the North* - Harry Turtledove  f  5509

**Gerlach, Midas** (Gunfighter)
*The Bars on Satan's Jailhouse* - Norman
   Partridge  h  4251

**Germain** (Criminal)
*A Game of Universe* - Eric S. Nylund  f  4178

**Gerome, Pluto Hellbender** (Editor)
*Pluto, Animal Lover* - Laren Stover  h  5318

**Geronimo** (Historical Figure; Indian)
*Apacheria* - Jake Page  s  4233

**Geronimo** (Teenager; Warrior)
*Madman Run* - David Robbins  s  4600

**Geronimo** (Alien)
*The Voices of Heaven* - Frederik Pohl  s  4356

**Gerrows, Eithnie** (Artist)
*The Wild Wood* - Charles de Lint  f  1440

**Gersen, Kirth** (Avenger; Hero; Criminal)
*The Demon Princes: Volume One* - Jack
   Vance  s  5544
*The Demon Princes: Volume Two* - Jack
   Vance  s  5545

**Gershon, Ralph** (Astronaut)
*Voyager* - Stephen Baxter  s  406

**Gersten, Clovis** (Actor; Vampire)
*Golden Eyes* - John Gideon  h  2220

**Gerund** (Child)
*The Wild Hunt* - Jane Yolen  f  6042

**Gervinus** (Religious; Sorcerer)
*The Shattered Oath* - Josepha Sherman  f  4989

**Geryam** (Military Personnel; Hero)
*The Birth of the Blade* - Dennis McCarty  f  3766

**Gespry** (Companion)
*Guardian's Key* - Anne Logston  f  3511

**Gestaurien, Mauryl** (Wizard)
*Fortress in the Eye of Time* - C.J. Cherryh  f  991

**Ghan** (Teacher; Librarian)
*The Waterborn* - J. Gregory Keyes  f  3098

**G'hana, 'jum** (Child; Genetically Altered Being)
*The Children Star* - Joan Slonczewski  s  5090

**Ghere, Rhule** (Alien; Doctor)
*The Parafaith War* - L.E. Modesitt Jr.  s  3937

**Ghidorah** (Monster)
*Godzilla 2000* - Marc Cerasini  s  949

**Ghormley, Richard** (Professor)
*Wendigo Border* - Catherine Montrose  h  3967

**Ghost** (Animal)
*Ghost of Chance* - William S. Burroughs  s  780

**Ghost** (Musician)
*Lost Souls* - Poppy Z. Brite  h  697

**Ghost** (Spirit)
*The Time of the Ghost* - Diana Wynne
   Jones  f  2951

**Ghoster** (Alien; Spy)
*Cyberstealth* - S.N. Lewitt  s  3450
*Dancing Vac* - S.N. Lewitt  s  3451

**Ghysla** (Mythical Creature)
*The Sleep of Stone* - Louise Cooper  f  1179

**Giant** (Alien; Child)
*The Earth Giant* - Melvin Burgess  s  773

**Gibb** (Homosexual)
*Key West 2720 A.D.* - William Eakins  s  1720

**Gibberling** (Courtier; Cartographer)
*Here There Be Dragons* - Roger Zelazny  f  6069

**Gibbs, Hank** (Journalist; Publisher)
*Psycho House* - Robert Bloch  h  542

**Gibbs, Rinpoche** (Time Traveler; Adventurer)
*Muddle Earth* - John Brunner  s  735

**Gibson, Cheryl** (Child-Care Giver)
*Grandma's Little Darling* - Stephen R.
   George  s  2201

**Gibson, Emma** (Time Traveler; Child)
*Friends in Time* - Grace Chetwin  f  1012

**Gibson, John "Gibby"** (Doctor)
*Black Ice* - Pat Graversen  h  2333

**Gibson, Paul** (Businessman)
*Black as Blood* - Rob Chilson  f  1014

**Gift** (Nobleman)
*The Resistance* - Kristine Kathryn Rusch  f  4727

**Gift, Sebastian "Nifty"** (Spaceman; Military
   Personnel)
*Berserker Fury* - Fred Saberhagen  s  4760

**Gil-Ravandry, Kelsenellenelvial** (Mythical Creature)
*The Dragon's Dagger* - R.A. Salvatore  f  4797

*The Woods out Back* - R.A. Salvatore  f  4809

**Gilbert, Cyrus** (Police Officer)
*Between the Devil and the Deep* - J.M.
   Morgan  h  3998

**Gilbert, India** (Psychic; Student)
*India's Story* - Kathlyn S. Starbuck  s  5208

**Gilbert, Jack** (Antiques Dealer)
*The Palm Dome* - Liz Fulton  h  2094

**Gilbert, Renard** (Warrior)
*No Limits* - Nigel Findley  s  1938

**Gilda** (Vampire; Lesbian)
*The Gilda Stories* - Jewelle Gomez  h  2267

**Giles** (Military Personnel)
*Beauty* - Sheri S. Tepper  f  5428

**Giles** (Librarian)
*The Harvest* - Richie Tankersley Cusick  h  1302

**Giles, Rupert** (Librarian)
*Return to Chaos* - Craig Shaw Gardner  h  2131

**Gilgamesh** (Deity; Immortal)
*How Like a God* - Brenda W. Clough  f  1089

**Gilgamesh** (Warrior; Royalty)
*To the Land of the Living* - Robert
   Silverberg  f  5044

**Gill, Gabriel** (Child)
*The Werewolves of London* - Brian
   Stableford  h  5196

**Gill, Spencer** (Scientist)
*The House of Doors* - Brian Lumley  h  3554
*Maze of Worlds* - Brian Lumley  h  3559

**Gillespie, William** (Scientist)
*Something's Alive on the Titanic* - Robert
   Serling  h  4915

**Gilliam** (Hunter; Nobleman)
*Hunter's Death* - Michelle West  f  5758
*Hunter's Oath* - Michelle West  f  5759

**Gillian** (Genetically Altered Being; Warrior)
*Ash Ock* - Christopher Hinz  s  2690
*The Paratwa* - Christopher Hinz  s  2691

**Gilman** (Knight; Handicapped)
*Pigs Don't Fly* - Mary Brown  f  727

**Gilman, Emily** (Scientist)
*Sparrowhawk* - Thomas A. Easton  s  1725

**Gilmour, Sarah** (Parent)
*Nighteyes* - Garfield Reeves-Stevens  s  4510

**Gilmour, Wendy** (Teenager)
*Nighteyes* - Garfield Reeves-Stevens  s  4510

**Gilray, Jimmy-Don** (Religious)
*Good News From Outer Space* - John
   Kessel  s  3084

**Gimlet, Carrot** (Police Officer)
*Feet of Clay* - Terry Pratchett  f  4389
*Guards! Guards!* - Terry Pratchett  f  4390
*Men at Arms* - Terry Pratchett  f  4396

**Gina** (Time Traveler; Teenager)
*All's Faire* - Pamela F. Service  f  4917

**Ginny** (Student; Lesbian)
*Virago* - Karen Marie Christa Minns  h  3915

**Gioglie III, Declan "Gill"** (Spaceman; Miner)
*Acorna* - Anne McCaffrey  s  3717

**Giovanni, Madeleine** (Vampire)
*The Road to Hell, Volume II* - Robert
   Weinberg  h  5702
*The Unbeholden* - Robert Weinberg  h  5703
*Unholy Allies* - Robert Weinberg  h  5704

**Girat, Phaed** (Parent)
*Raising the Stones* - Sheri S. Tepper  s  5434

**Girat, Saluniel** (Administrator)
*Raising the Stones* - Sheri S. Tepper  s  5434

**Girat, Samasnier** (Administrator)
*Raising the Stones* - Sheri S. Tepper  s  5434

**Giraud** (Heir—Dispossessed)
*Curse of the Black Heron* - Holly Lisle  f  3479

**Gird** (Revolutionary; Leader)
*Liar's Oath* - Elizabeth Moon  f  3969

**Gird** (Farmer; Revolutionary)
*Surrender None: The Legacy of Gird* - Elizabeth
Moon  f  3975

**Girelf** (Genetically Altered Being; Heir)
*Stepwater* - L. Warren Douglas  s  1588

**Girl** (Child)
*A Ride on the Red Mare's Back* - Ursula K. Le
Guin  f  3382

**Gistere, Rurak** (Knight)
*The Day of the Tempest* - Jean Rabe  f  4457

**Gi'Suei'Obodi'Sedon** (Immortal; Rebel)
*The Last Dancer* - Daniel Keys Moran  s  3994

**Gi'Tbad'Eovad'Dvan, "William Devane"** (Immortal;
Security Officer)
*The Last Dancer* - Daniel Keys Moran  s  3994

**Givens, Amanda** (Witch)
*Witches* - Kathryn Meyer Griffith  h  2442

**Giyt, Evesham** (Immigrant; Computer Expert)
*O Pioneer!* - Frederik Pohl  s  4350

**G'Kar** (Alien; Prisoner)
*Personal Agendas* - Al Sarrantonio  s  4833

**Gladheon, Karigan** (Student; Courier)
*Green Rider* - Kristen Britain  f  692

**Gladstone, Meina** (Government Official)
*The Fall of Hyperion* - Dan Simmons  s  5052

**Glass, Duncan** (Civil Servant)
*A Whisper of Wings* - Steven Ray Fulgham  h  2091

**Glass Warrior** (Warrior)
*The Glass Warrior* - Robert E. Vardeman  f  5563

**Glasser, Stephen** (Doctor)
*Death's Door* - John Wooley  h  5969

**Gleason, Tommy** (Doctor)
*Spree* - Lucy Taylor  h  5415

**Gleese, Eacon** (Ruler)
*The Stone Movers* - Patricia Mullen  f  4045

**Glendil** (Witch)
*The Moon's Wife: A Hystery* - A.A.
Attanasio  f  271

**Glenn, Molly** (Journalist)
*Till the End of Time* - Allen Appel  f  201

**Glibspet** (Demon; Detective—Private)
*Hell on High* - Holly Lisle  f  3483

**Glivven, Miranda** (Detective—Amateur; Spouse)
*Cat's Paw* - L.A. Taylor  f  5409

**Gloria** (Vampire)
*The Vampire Journals* - Traci Briery  h  678

**Gloria** (Young Woman)
*The Wilds* - Richard Laymon  h  3373

**Glorian** (Companion)
*The Zork Chronicles* - George Alec
Effinger  s  1754

**Gloth** (Mythical Creature; Military Personnel)
*The Doom Brigade* - Margaret Weis  f  5708

**Glover, Tony** (Mountaineer)
*Snowbeast!* - Peter Tremayne  h  5482

**Glyndower, Evan** (Military Personnel)
*High Moon* - Diane Duane  s  1661
*Kill Station* - Diane Duane  s  1664
*Mindblast* - Diane Duane  s  1665

**Glyrenden** (Wizard)
*The Shape-Changer's Wife* - Sharon Shinn  f  5002

**G'Meni** (Wizard)
*The Janus Mask* - Richard A. Knaak  f  3171

**Gnoza** (Alien)
*The Longest Voyage/Slow Lightning* - Poul
Anderson  s  130

**Gobi, Frank** (Professor; Computer Expert)
*Rim: A Novel of Virtual Reality* - Alexander
Besher  s  475

**Gobi, Trevor** (Computer Expert)
*Mir* - Alexander Besher  s  474

**Goble, Samuel** (Scientist)
*A Thunder on Neptune* - Gordon Eklund  s  1768

**Goblin, Gwenny** (Mythical Creature; Feminist)
*The Color of Her Panties* - Piers Anthony  f  167

**God** (Deity)
*Sympathy for the Devil* - Holly Lisle  f  3488

**God "The Old Man"** (Deity)
*The Old Man and Mr. Smith* - Peter
Ustinov  f  5532

**Godfrey** (Alien)
*The Ragged World: A Novel of the Hefn on Earth* -
Judith Moffett  s  3943

**Godwinesson, Harold** (Nobleman; Warrior)
*Lord of Sunset* - Parke Godwin  f  2246

**Godzilla** (Monster)
*Godzilla 2000* - Marc Cerasini  s  949

**Goebbels, Joseph "Joseph Gable"** (Historical
Figure; Businessman)
*The Resurrections* - Simon Louvish  s  3528

**Goering, Hermann** (Historical Figure)
*To Your Scattered Bodies Go* - Philip Jose
Farmer  s  1876

**Goff, Max** (Producer)
*Curfew* - Phil Rickman  h  4587

**Gojiro** (Animal; Mutant)
*Gojiro* - Mark Jacobson  f  2847

**Gold, Leah** (Aged Person)
*Rage* - Elizabeth Ergas  h  1834

**Guld, Michael "Mike"** (Spouse; Worker)
*Unquenchable Fire* - Rachel Pollack  f  4361

**Gold, Samuel** (Producer)
*Visitors From Oz: The Wild Adventures of Dorothy,
the Scarecrow and the Tin Woodman* - Martin
Gardner  f  2136

**Gold-eye** (Child; Psychic)
*Shade's Children* - Garth Nix  s  4130

**Goldberg, Honeylou Emmyjane "Marshmallo"**
(Runaway)
*The Red Tape War* - Jack L. Chalker  s  959

**Goldblatt, Steve** (Mentally Ill Person)
*Landscape of Demons and the Book of Sara* - Gabriel
Devlin Kessler  h  3088

**Goldin, Netta** (Administrator)
*Alien Influences* - Kristine Kathryn Rusch  s  4711

**Golding, Juniper** (Teenager; Psychic)
*The Juniper Game* - Sherryl Jordan  f  2992

**Golding, Marsha** (Single Parent)
*The Juniper Game* - Sherryl Jordan  f  2992

**Goldman, David** (Doctor)
*A Reasonable Madness* - Fran Dorf  h  1580

**Gomez, Catseye** (Animal; Genetically Altered
Being)
*The Nine Lives of Catseye Gomez* - Simon
Hawke  f  2620

**Gomez, Sid** (Detective—Private)
*Tek Money* - William Shatner  s  4935
*Tek Net* - William Shatner  s  4936
*Tek Power* - William Shatner  s  4937

*Tek Vengeance* - William Shatner  s  4938
*TekLab* - William Shatner  s  4939
*TekLords* - William Shatner  s  4940

**Gomja, Herphan** (Military Personnel; Alien)
*Beyond the Moons* - David Cook  f  1144

**Gonn-Ben-Allah** (Deity)
*Ahmed and the Oblivion Machines* - Ray
Bradbury  f  618

**Gonzales, Mikhail Mikhailovitch** (Computer Expert;
Auditor)
*Halo* - Tom Maddox  s  3604

**Goodall, Sasha** (Radio Personality)
*Fear Nothing* - Dean R. Koontz  h  3207

**Goode, Wilson** (Bounty Hunter)
*Monsoon* - Peter L. Rice  s  4583

**Goodlooking/Bella** (Alien; Librarian)
*North Wind* - Gwyneth Jones  s  2953

**Goodlow, Sam** (Detective)
*Goodlow's Ghosts* - T.M. Wright  h  5991

**Goon** (Sports Figure)
*Goon* - Edward Lee  h  3392

**Goosequill** (Servant; Guide)
*Milton in America* - Peter Ackroyd  f  25

**Goranu** (Mythical Creature; Demon)
*The Heavenward Path* - Kara Dalkey  f  1319
*Little Sister* - Kara Dalkey  f  1320

**Gorath** (Chieftain)
*Krondor, the Betrayal* - Raymond E. Feist  f  1905

**Gorbachev, Mikhail Sergeevich** (Political Figure;
Historical Figure)
*Fellow Traveller* - William Barton  s  380

**Gorbo** (Mythical Creature)
*The Marvellous Land of Snergs* - E.A. Wyke-
Smith  f  6006

**Gorbunova, Ludmila** (Military Personnel; Pilot)
*Worldwar: Tilting the Balance* - Harry
Turtledove  s  5517
*Worldwar: Upsetting the Balance* - Harry
Turtledove  s  5518

**Gordon, Sr.** (Housewife; Adventurer)
*Revenge of the Fluffy Bunnies* - Craig Shaw
Gardner  f  2132

**Gordon, Eathan** (Doctor)
*Mirage* - F. Paul Wilson  h  5892

**Gordon, Evelyn Cyril "Oscar/Scar"** (Hero; Traveler)
*Glory Road* - Robert A. Heinlein  f  2644

**Gordon, George** (Nobleman)
*Wall, Stone, Craft* - Walter Jon Williams  h  5842

**Gordon, John** (Mercenary)
*Surface Action* - David Drake  s  1646

**Gordon, Julie** (Scientist)
*Mirage* - F. Paul Wilson  h  5892

**Gordon, Karen** (Young Woman)
*The Gilgul* - Henry W. Hocherman  h  2697

**Gordon, Kate** (Teenager; Adventurer)
*The Merlin Effect* - T.A. Barron  f  371

**Gordon, Martin "Marty"** (Leader; Spaceman)
*Anvil of Stars* - Greg Bear  s  414

**Gordon, Nathan** (Scientist)
*Mirage* - F. Paul Wilson  h  5892

**Gordon, Roger Jr.** (Public Relations)
*Bride of the Slime Monster* - Craig Shaw
Gardner  f  2125

**Gordon, Roger Jr.** (Hero; Adventurer)
*Revenge of the Fluffy Bunnies* - Craig Shaw
Gardner  f  2132

**Gordon, Winston** (Businessman; Nobleman)
*Mina* - Marie Kiraly  h  3151

**Gorlay, Glenn** (Child)
*The Dark One* - Guy N. Smith  h  5118

**Gorlay, Rankin** (Journalist)
*The Dark One* - Guy N. Smith  h  5118

**Gormlaith** (Widow(er))
*Pride of Lions* - Morgan Llywelyn  f  3506

**Goro** (Warrior; Royalty)
*Mortal Kombat* - Martin Delrio  f  1483

**Gorobec, Anton** (Reanimated Dead)
*I Am Frankenstein* - C. Dean Andersson  h  140

**Gorp, Shigehero** (Criminal)
*Svaha* - Charles de Lint  s  1437

**Gorse** (Student)
*Wizard's Hall* - Jane Yolen  f  6043

**Gorthyn** (Royalty)
*The Shining Company* - Rosemary Sutcliff  f  5359

**Goss, Brionne** (Telepath)
*Cloud's Rider* - C.J. Cherryh  s  983

**Gottbaum, Leo** (Scientist)
*The Silicon Man* - Charles Platt  s  4343

**Gotti, Guillermo** (Religious; Psychic)
*The Book of Earth* - Marjorie Bradley
    Kellogg  f  3044

**Gowdie, Maggie** (Witch)
*The Rebirth of Wonder* - Lawrence Watt-
    Evans  f  5646

**Gowdy, Samuel "Sam" Hall** (Spaceship Captain)
*The Triad Worlds* - F.M. Busby  s  786

**Grabovnikon "Grab"** (Artificial Intelligence)
*Night of the Living Shark!* - David Bischoff  s  493

**Grace, Peter** (Spirit)
*The Parasite* - Ramsey Campbell  h  863

**Grace, Stephen** (Criminal)
*Dark of the Eye* - Douglas Clegg  h  1078

**Graciosa** (Human; Noblewoman)
*Child of Faerie, Child of Earth* - Josepha
    Sherman  f  4985

**Grady, Joanna** (Time Traveler)
*Wolfking* - Bridget Wood  f  5963

**Graeboe** (Mythical Creature)
*Harpy Thyme* - Piers Anthony  f  174

**Gragelouth** (Businessman; Animal)
*Son of Spellsinger* - Alan Dean Foster  f  2015

**Graham, Dexter** (Teacher)
*Mysterium* - Robert Charles Wilson  s  5911

**Graham, James** (Nobleman)
*The Ebon Mask* - Richard Lee Byers  h  797

**Graham, Jason "Jase"** (Spaceman; Engineer)
*Inheritor* - C.J. Cherryh  s  997

**Grahame, John** (Military Personnel; Psychic)
*The Templar Treasure* - Katherine Kurtz  f  3261

**Grainger, Laura** (Widow(er))
*Darker Angels* - S.P. Somtow  h  5155

**Grainger, Tim** (Time Traveler)
*Arc Riders* - David Drake  s  1626
*The Fourth Rome* - David Drake  s  1631

**Grainne** (Royalty)
*The Lost Prince* - Bridget Wood  f  5962

**Gramm, Rachel "Button"** (Child)
*Button Bright* - Michael Kurland  h  3251

**Grandier, Urbain** (Imposter; Sorcerer)
*The Element of Fire* - Martha Wells  f  5750

**Grandma Fifi** (Grandparent; Dancer)
*Baby Be-Bop* - Francesca Lia Block  f  545

**Grandpa Rowe** (Artist; Psychic)
*The Cartoonist* - Sean Costello  h  1204

**Grange, Florida** (Lawyer)
*Mucho Mojo* - Joe R. Lansdale  h  3330

**Grange, Karen** (Banker)
*A Dry Spell* - Susan Moloney  h  3951

**Granny Weatherwax** (Witch)
*Maskerade* - Terry Pratchett  f  4395

**Grant** (Computer Expert; Disembodied Personality)
*MagicNet* - John DeChancie  f  1461

**Grant, Alan** (Scientist; Professor)
*Jurassic Park* - Michael Crichton  s  1255

**Grant, John** (Computer Expert)
*Spook Night* - David Robbins  h  4603

**Grant, John "Slick"** (Military Personnel)
*March or Die* - Andrew Keith  s  3035

**Grant, Kip** (Teenager)
*Spook Night* - David Robbins  h  4603

**Grant, Shery** (Teenager)
*Spook Night* - David Robbins  h  4603

**Grant, Spencer** (Computer Expert)
*Dark Rivers of the Heart* - Dean R. Koontz  h  3204

**Granville, Gabby** (Child)
*Bloody Valentine* - Stephen R. George  h  2197

**Granville, Jo** (Artist)
*Bloody Valentine* - Stephen R. George  h  2197

**Grason, Gilead** (Clerk)
*Cross a Dark Bridge* - Deborah
    Churchman  h  1027

**Grason, Missy** (Twin)
*Cross a Dark Bridge* - Deborah
    Churchman  h  1027

**Gravel, Edmund** (Recluse)
*The Haunted Tea Cosy: A Dispirited and Distasteful
    Diversion for Christmas* - Edward Gorey  h  2276

**Graves, Elliott** (Teacher)
*Dark Lullaby* - Jessica Palmer  h  4237

**Graves, Jermyn** (Wizard; Detective—Amateur)
*Journeyman Wizard* - Mary Frances
    Zambreno  f  6057

**Graves, Jermyn** (Apprentice)
*A Plague of Sorcerers* - Mary Frances
    Zambreno  f  6058

**Graves, Sara** (Child)
*Dark Lullaby* - Jessica Palmer  h  4237

**Graves, Shelley** (Child)
*Dark Lullaby* - Jessica Palmer  h  4237

**Gray** (Alien)
*The Longest Voyage/Slow Lightning* - Poul
    Anderson  s  130

**Gray, Doreen** (Photographer)
*Fire in the Blood* - P.N. Elrod  h  1796

**Gray, Emma** (Child; Abuse Victim)
*Flying in Place* - Susan Palwick  h  4240

**Gray, Frank** (Police Officer)
*The Lazarus Heart* - Poppy Z. Brite  h  696

**Gray, Justin** (Advertising)
*The Darker Saints* - Brian Hodge  h  2699
*Nightlife* - Brian Hodge  h  2702

**Gray, Simon** (Scientist; Doctor)
*Archangel* - Michael Conner  s  1133

**Gray, Stewart** (Doctor)
*Flying in Place* - Susan Palwick  h  4240

**Gray, Zachary** (Young Man)
*An Acceptable Time* - Madeleine L'Engle  f  3436

**Gray Mouser** (Thief; Magician)
*Farewell to Lankhmar* - Fritz Leiber  f  3418
*Swords Against the Shadowland* - Robin Wayne
    Bailey  f  291

**Gray Wolf, Josiah** (Scientist; Explorer)
*Beyond Eden* - J.M. Morgan  s  3999
*Desert Eden* - J.M. Morgan  s  4000

**Gray Wolf, Willow** (Explorer)
*Future Eden* - J.M. Morgan  s  4001

**Graydon, Nicholas** (Adventurer; Scientist)
*The Face in the Abyss* - A. Merritt  f  3878

**Graydon, Roland** (Doctor)
*Dead Voices* - Rick Hautala  h  2607

**Graylord** (Monster)
*Shadowlight* - Jackie Hyman  f  2819

**Grayshard** (Alien)
*Lair of the Cyclops* - Allen L. Wold  s  5933

**Great and Powerful Turtle** (Hero)
*Dealer's Choice* - George R.R. Martin  s  3643

**Great Chaffalo** (Spirit; Magician)
*The Midnight Horse* - Sid Fleischman  f  1948

**Great God Om** (Deity; Animal)
*Small Gods* - Terry Pratchett  f  4400

**Great Karlini** (Sorcerer)
*Spell of Apocalypse* - Mayer Alan Brenner  f  672

**Grebb, Richard** (Religious)
*Penance* - Rick R. Reed  h  4501

**Greeland** (Homosexual; Criminal)
*Mirage* - Perry Brass  s  662

**Greeley, Dan** (Activist; Farmer)
*The Drylands* - Mary Rosenblum  s  4678

**Green** (Sorceress)
*Gawain and Lady Green* - Anne Eliot
    Crompton  f  1269

**Green, Antony** (Spirit)
*Aunt Maria* - Diana Wynne Jones  f  2943

**Green, Jerome** (Religious)
*Dead Voices* - Abigail McDaniels  h  3783

**Green, Margo** (Student)
*Relic* - Douglas Preston  h  4414

**Green, Margo** (Anthropologist)
*Reliquary* - Douglas Preston  h  4415

**Green, Paul** (Political Figure)
*Fire* - Alan Rodgers  h  4647

**Green, Sandra** (Scientist; Spacewoman)
*Saturn Rukh* - Robert L. Forward  s  1991

**Green Spider** (Psychic; Indian)
*People of the Lakes* - Kathleen O'Neal Gear  f  2164

**Greenberg, Bernard** (Trader; Spaceship Captain)
*Earthgrip* - Harry Turtledove  s  5499

**Greene, Andy "the Warden"** (Ruler)
*The Warden of Horses* - Karen Ripley  s  4595

**Greene, Cathy** (Farmer)
*The Taking* - Donald Beman  h  438

**Greene, Harris** (Sports Figure; Martial Arts Expert)
*Doc Sidhe* - Aaron Allston  f  85

**Greene, Harry** (Sailor)
*First Blast of the Trumpet Against the Monstrous
    Regiment of Women* - Eric McCormack  h  3779

**Greene, Maggie** (Waiter/Waitress)
*Entity* - Nina Mandelik  h  3615

**Greenhands "Silveran"** (Mythical Creature)
*The Qualinesti* - Paul B. Thompson  f  5455

**Greenpearl** (Captive)
*Silk Road* - Jeanne Larsen  f  3339

**Greensleeves** (Wizard; Revolutionary)
*Final Sacrifice* - Clayton Emery  f  1814
*Shattered Chains* - Clayton Emery  f  1816

**Greenstone, Brian** (Agent)
*The Prodigy* - Noel Hynd  h  2823

**Greenway, Dorian** (Leader)
*Irrational Fears* - William Browning
   Spencer   *h*   5167

**Greer, Mitchell** (Detective—Police)
*Bitter Blood* - Karen E. Taylor   *h*   5405
*Blood Secrets* - Karen E. Taylor   *h*   5406

**Greer, Mitchell** (Vampire; Detective—Police)
*Blood Ties* - Karen E. Taylor   *h*   5407

**Gregg, Stephen** (Military Personnel)
*Igniting the Reaches* - David Drake   *s*   1633

**Gregg, Stephen** (Pirate)
*Through the Breach* - David Drake   *s*   1647

**Gregor** (Servant)
*Dr. Haggard's Disease* - Patrick McGrath   *h*   3813

**Gregorian** (Scientist; Magician)
*Stations of the Tide* - Michael Swanwick   *s*   5373

**Gregory** (Revolutionary; Government Official)
*The Dream Vessel* - Jeff Bredenberg   *s*   664

**Gregory** (Vampire)
*Night Thirst* - Patrick Whalen   *h*   5770

**Gregory** (Religious)
*The Secret Life of Laszlo, Count Dracula* - Roderick
   Anscombe   *h*   152
*StarSpawn* - Kenneth Von Gunden   *s*   5588

**Gregory, Joe-Jim** (Mutant; Spaceman)
*Silent Thunder/Universe* - Dean Ing   *s*   2829

**Gregory, Joely** (Child)
*Ghost Boy* - Jean Simon   *h*   5064

**Gregory, Libby** (Receptionist)
*Ghost Boy* - Jean Simon   *h*   5064

**Gregory, Stephen Thomas** (Scientist)
*Starfarers* - Vonda N. McIntyre   *s*   3824

**Grendel** (Mythical Creature; Monster)
*The Tower of Beowulf* - Parke Godwin   *f*   2250

**Grenfell, Arden** (Bodyguard)
*Darkloom* - Cary Osborne   *s*   4225
*Deathweave* - Cary Osborne   *s*   4226

**Grenier, Roger** (Businessman)
*Viper* - Alan Riefe   *h*   4589

**Grenlaarin, Karah** (Equestrian; Military Personnel)
*The Rose Sea* - S.M. Stirling   *f*   5296

**Greston, Weber** (Director)
*A Child Across the Sky* - Jonathan Carroll   *h*   917

**Greta** (Explorer)
*I Who Have Never Known Men* - Jacqueline
   Harpman   *s*   2554

**Greville, Richard** (Doctor)
*Running Wild* - J.G. Ballard   *h*   320

**Grey, Agnes** (Writer)
*Pillow Friend* - Lisa Tuttle   *h*   5522

**Grey, Alice** (Writer)
*The Torching* - Marcy Heidish   *h*   2642

**Grey, Joe** (Animal)
*Cats Raise the Dead* - Shirley Rousseau
   Murphy   *f*   4054

**Grey, Liza** (Student)
*The Messenger* - Donald Tyson   *h*   5528

**Grey, Marjorie** (Writer)
*Pillow Friend* - Lisa Tuttle   *h*   5522

**Grey Mouser** (Thief; Wizard)
*Ill Met in Lankhmar* - Fritz Leiber   *f*   3419
*Lean Times in Lankhmar* - Fritz Leiber   *f*   3420
*Return to Lankhmar* - Fritz Leiber   *f*   3422

**Greycloak, Janela Kether** (Adventurer)
*Kingdoms of the Night* - Allan Cole   *f*   1105

**Greycloak, Janos** (Military Personnel; Wizard)
*The Far Kingdoms* - Allan Cole   *f*   1104

**Greylocks, Lysander** (Religious)
*Shadowborn* - William W. Connors   *h*   1137

**Greyson, Hunter "Grey"** (Magician)
*Witchlight* - Marion Zimmer Bradley   *f*   655

**Greystoke, David** (Spaceman; Musician)
*Ocean under the Ice* - Robert L. Forward   *s*   1988

**Grieg, Christian** (Young Man)
*Boundaries* - T.M. Wright   *h*   5990

**Griffin** (Coach)
*The Cat* - R.L. Stine   *h*   5285

**Griffin** (Housekeeper)
*The Thief of Always* - Clive Barker   *h*   347

**Griffin** (Mythical Creature)
*The Healing of Crossroads* - Nick
   O'Donohoe   *f*   4195

**Griffin, Alan** (Prisoner)
*Cold Whisper* - Rick Hautala   *h*   2605

**Griffin, Alex** (Security Officer)
*The California Voodoo Game* - Larry Niven   *s*   4117

**Griffin, Beth** (Health Care Professional)
*Nazareth Hill* - Ramsey Campbell   *h*   861

**Griffin, Deirdre** (Vampire; Designer)
*Bitter Blood* - Karen E. Taylor   *h*   5405
*Blood Secrets* - Karen E. Taylor   *h*   5406
*Blood Ties* - Karen E. Taylor   *h*   5407

**Griffin, George** (Scientist)
*Einstein's Bridge* - John Cramer   *s*   1244

**Griffin, Nic** (Actor; Writer)
*The Ruby Tear* - Rebecca Brand   *h*   660

**Griffith, Wally** (Patient)
*Strange Invasion* - Michael Kandel   *s*   3012

**Griffiths, Jeremy** (Spaceship Captain; Royalty)
*Nightsword* - Margaret Weis   *f*   5722

**Griffiths, Jeremy** (Spaceship Captain)
*Sentinels* - Margaret Weis   *s*   5725

**Grijalva, Saavedra** (Artist)
*The Golden Key* - Melanie Rawn   *f*   4486

**Grijalva, Sario** (Artist; Nobleman)
*The Golden Key* - Melanie Rawn   *f*   4486

**Grillo, Nathan** (Computer Expert)
*Everville* - Clive Barker   *h*   338

**Grimes, Griff** (Journalist)
*Serial Killer Days* - David Prill   *h*   4436

**Grimi, Garni ben** (Mythical Creature; Adventurer)
*Another Day, Another Dungeon* - Greg
   Costikyan   *f*   1206

**Grimm** (Engineer; Warrior)
*Inquisitor* - Ian Watson   *s*   5637

**Grimm, Eleanor** (Undertaker; Witch)
*Grimm Memorials* - R. Patrick Gates   *h*   2160

**Grimma** (Mythical Creature)
*Diggers* - Terry Pratchett   *s*   4386

**Grimson, Jim** (Teenager; Criminal)
*Red Orc's Rage* - Philip Jose Farmer   *f*   1873

**Grimya** (Animal; Telepath)
*Aisling* - Louise Cooper   *f*   1172
*Avatar* - Louise Cooper   *f*   1173
*Infanta* - Louise Cooper   *f*   1176
*Revenant* - Louise Cooper   *f*   1178
*Troika* - Louise Cooper   *f*   1181

**Grissom, Sarah** (Child)
*Mercy's Mill* - Betty Levin   *f*   3444

**Grizzly** (Genetically Altered Being; Warrior)
*Vengeance Strike* - David Robbins   *s*   4604

**Grobowski, Nolan** (Detective—Police)
*Terminal Games* - Cole Perriman   *s*   4283

**Grossclout** (Professor; Demon)
*Roc and a Hard Place* - Piers Anthony   *f*   187

**Grout** (Teacher)
*The Knights of Cawdor* - Mike Jefferies   *f*   2886

**Grover** (Hero; Mercenary)
*Heroes, Inc.* - Kyle Crocco   *f*   1268
*Heroes Wanted* - Kyle Crocco   *f*   1267

**Growch** (Animal; Companion)
*Master of Many Treasures* - Mary Brown   *f*   726

**Growler, Donald** (Murderer)
*Cul-De-Sac* - David Martin   *h*   3638

**Grraf-Commander** (Alien)
*Cathouse* - Dean Ing   *s*   2828

**Grundbur** (Monster)
*Whose Song Is Sung* - Frank Schaefer   *f*   4872

**Grunt, Blind Boy** (Artificial Intelligence)
*Clarke County, Space* - Allen Steele   *s*   5241

**Gryll** (Demon)
*Prince of Chaos* - Roger Zelazny   *f*   6073

**Gryphon** (Mythical Creature)
*Wolfhelm* - Richard A. Knaak   *f*   3175

**Grzzeearoghh "Grizz"** (Spaceship Captain; Alien)
*Treaty at Doona* - Anne McCaffrey   *s*   3752

**Gubwa, Charon** (Telepath)
*Psychosphere* - Brian Lumley   *h*   3563

**Guenevere** (Royalty; Spouse)
*The Camelot Chronicles* - Mike Ashley   *f*   224
*Witch of the North* - Courtway Jones   *f*   2940

**Guenther, Spiro** (Teenager)
*The Devil's End* - D.A. Fowler   *h*   2023

**Guerner, Margaret "Peggy"** (Psychic; Activist)
*Alvin Journeyman* - Orson Scott Card   *f*   881

**Guerreri, Karen Rohmer** (Writer)
*Preternatural* - Margaret Wander Bonanno   *s*   568

**Guester, Peggy** (Psychic)
*Prentice Alvin* - Orson Scott Card   *f*   896

**Guevara, Ernesto "Che"** (Historical Figure;
   Revolutionary)
*The Resurrections* - Simon Louvish   *s*   3528

**Guglioli, Johnny** (Expatriate; Journalist)
*White Queen* - Gwyneth Jones   *s*   2955

**Guido** (Bodyguard)
*M.Y.T.H. Inc. in Action* - Robert Asprin   *f*   259

**Guillory, Terry** (Child)
*Gnelfs* - Sidney Williams   *h*   5823

**Guimaraes, Veronica** (Spacewoman)
*Songs of Chaos* - S.N. Lewitt   *s*   3452

**Guinan** (Alien; Saloon Keeper/Owner)
*The Devil's Heart* - Carmen Carter   *s*   922

**Guinan** (Saloon Keeper/Owner; Alien)
*Vendetta* - Peter David   *s*   1389

**Guinevere** (Royalty)
*The Child Queen* - Nancy McKenzie   *f*   3827
*Guinevere: The Legend in Autumn* - Persia
   Woolley   *f*   5970
*The King* - Donald Barthelme   *f*   375
*Queen of the Summer Stars* - Persia
   Woolley   *f*   5971

**Guitierrez, Rafael** (Vampire)
*Diary of a Vampire* - Gary Bowen   *h*   600

**Guiwenneth** (Warrior)
*Gate of Ivory, Gate of Horn* - Robert
   Holdstock   *f*   2737

**Gujerat, Mandvi "Manny"** (Genetically Altered
   Being; Doctor)
*Forests of the Night* - S. Andrew Swann   *s*   5363

**Gull** (Leader; Revolutionary)
*Final Sacrifice* - Clayton Emery   f   1814
*Shattered Chains* - Clayton Emery   f   1816

**Gull** (Doctor)
*The Women of Whitechapel and Jack the Ripper* - Paul
West   h   5761

**Gulliver, Connie** (Police Officer)
*Dragon Tears* - Dean R. Koontz   h   3205

**Gullone, Greta** (Witch)
*The Witch Returns* - Phyllis Reynolds
Naylor   f   4079

**Gultec** (Warrior; Indian)
*Feathered Dragon* - Douglas Niles   f   4108

**Gumby** (Psychic)
*The Lost Guardian* - Ronald Anthony Cross   s   1274

**Gunar** (Magician; Engineer)
*The Order War* - L.E. Modesitt Jr.   f   3936

**Gundhalinu, BZ** (Police Officer; Judge)
*The Summer Queen* - Joan D. Vinge   s   5572

**Gunn** (Peddler; Businessman)
*Primavera* - Francesca Lia Block   f   551

**Gunn, Erik** (Editor)
*Moondog* - Henry Garfield   h   2138

**Gunn, Sam** (Astronaut)
*Sam Gunn Forever* - Ben Bova   s   592

**Gunn, Sam** (Businessman)
*Sam Gunn, Unlimited* - Ben Bova   s   593

**Gunnar** (Warrior; Traveler)
*Byzantium* - Stephen R. Lawhead   f   3353

**Gurden, Tom** (Musician; Religious)
*The Mask of Loki* - Roger Zelazny   f   6071

**Gurder** (Mythical Creature; Alien)
*Wings* - Terry Pratchett   s   4403

**Gurgeh, Jernau** (Sports Figure)
*The Player of Games* - Iain M. Banks   s   326

**Gurney, Molly** (Teenager; Child-Care Giver)
*Out of the Ordinary* - Annie Dalton   f   1330

**Gurronsevas** (Alien; Cook)
*The Galactic Gourmet* - James White   s   5778

**Gustiano, Rinaldo** (Nobleman; Mercenary)
*The Innamorati* - Midori Snyder   f   5152

**Guthrie, Anson** (Cyborg)
*The Fleet of Stars* - Poul Anderson   s   126

**Guthrie, Anson** (Businessman; Disembodied
Personality)
*Harvest of Stars* - Poul Anderson   s   127

**Guthrie, Dave** (Artist)
*Night Sounds* - Warner Lee   h   3415

**Guthrum** (Mythical Creature)
*The Clan of the Warlord* - Elizabeth H.
Boyer   f   604

**Gutierrez, Osvaldo** (Police Officer)
*Shango* - James Roberto Curtis   h   1298

**Gwalchavad** (Knight; Nobleman)
*Grail* - Stephen R. Lawhead   f   3355

**Gwarha, Ettin** (Diplomat; Alien)
*Ring of Swords* - Eleanor Arnason   s   210

**Gwen** (Girlfriend)
*Rehearsal for a Renaissance* - Douglas W.
Clark   f   1045

**Gwen** (Artificial Intelligence)
*Starswarm* - Jerry Pournelle   s   4379

**Gwenhwyfar** (Fiance(e))
*The Kingmaking* - Helen Hollick   f   2745

**Gwenhwyfar** (Royalty; Spouse)
*Pendragon's Banner* - Helen Hollick   f   2746

**Gwenhwyfar** (Royalty)
*Shadow of the King* - Helen Hollick   f   2747

**Gwenhwyvar** (Ruler)
*Pendragon* - Stephen R. Lawhead   f   3357

**Gwenlliant** (Wizard)
*The Castle of the Silver Wheel* - Teresa
Edgerton   f   1741
*The Grail and the Ring* - Teresa Edgerton   f   1744

**Gwent, Donson** (Director; Writer)
*Wordwright* - Tom Deitz   f   1478

**Gwydion** (Royalty; Sorcerer)
*The Well-Favored Man: The Tale of the Sorcerer's
Nephew* - Elizabeth Willey   f   5813

**Gwynn, Angharad "the Rowan"** (Psychic; Orphan)
*The Rowan* - Anne McCaffrey   s   3747

**Gwynn-Raven, Angharad "the Rowan"** (Psychic)
*Damia* - Anne McCaffrey   s   3725

**Gwynn-Raven, Damia** (Psychic)
*Damia* - Anne McCaffrey   s   3725

**Gyhard** (Military Personnel)
*Fifth Quarter* - Tanya Huff   f   2795
*No Quarter* - Tanya Huff   f   2798

**Gypsy Pete** (Store Owner)
*Frisk* - Dennis Cooper   h   1170

# H

**Haal, Daetrin Ungashak To-Alym** (Vampire;
Werewolf)
*The Madness Season* - C.S. Friedman   s   2058

**Ha'ark** (Alien; Ruler)
*Never Sound Retreat* - William R.
Forstchen   s   1981

**Haas, Alexandria Victoria** (Psychologist; Counselor)
*Mindplayers* - Pat Cadigan   s   806

**Haas, Peter** (Sports Figure; Artist)
*Memento Mori* - Shariann Lewitt   s   3454

**Habbazu** (Thief)
*Between the Rivers* - Harry Turtledove   f   5496

**Habeggar** (Professor; Inventor)
*Slow Freight* - F.M. Busby   s   785

**Haberman** (Social Worker)
*The Nihilesthete* - Richard Kalich   h   3002

**Hac** (Android)
*Mission: Tori* - Johanna Bolton   s   564

**Hackett, Horace** (Writer)
*Typewriter in the Sky* - L. Ron Hubbard   f   2791

**Hackleberry, Kelvin Knight** (Hero)
*Chimaera's Copper* - Piers Anthony   f   166
*Mouvar's Magic* - Piers Anthony   f   182
*Orc's Opal* - Piers Anthony   f   183

**Hackworth, John Percival** (Engineer)
*The Diamond Age* - Neal Stephenson   s   5253

**Hadding** (Ruler; Warrior)
*War of the Gods* - Poul Anderson   f   136

**Hades** (Deity)
*The Face of Apollo* - Fred Saberhagen   s   4766

**Hadfield, Felicity Jane** (Child)
*Viper* - Alan Riefe   h   4589

**Hadrak, Quisaz** (Alien; Military Personnel)
*Martian Deathtrap* - Nathan Archer   s   205

**Hadrian** (Religious)
*The Silver Wolf* - Alice Borchardt   h   572

**Hael** (Royalty; Warrior)
*The Steel Kings* - John Maddox Roberts   f   4621

**Hafford, Jovvi** (Wizard; Prostitute)
*Challenges* - Sharon Green   f   2354
*Competition* - Sharon Green   f   2355

**Haflinger, Nickie** (Experimental Subject)
*The Shockwave Rider* - John Brunner   s   736

**Hagan** (Warrior; Homosexual)
*Attila's Treasure* - Stephan Grundy   f   2453

**Hagan, Kara** (Military Personnel)
*Warstrider: Netlink* - William H. Keith Jr.   s   3038

**Hagan, Tim** (Companion)
*Red, Red Robin* - Stephen Gallagher   h   2113

**Hagar, Jonathan** (Wealthy)
*The Beast* - Marie Ardell White   h   5784

**Hagbarth, Hoak** (Businessman; Civil Servant)
*O Pioneer!* - Frederik Pohl   s   4350

**Hager, Ross Ed** (Tourist)
*Jed the Dead* - Alan Dean Foster   s   2007

**Haggard, Edward** (Doctor)
*Dr. Haggard's Disease* - Patrick McGrath   h   3813

**Haggerwells, Barbara** (Inventor; Time Traveler)
*Bring the Jubilee* - Ward Moore   s   3993

**Hagopian** (Aged Person)
*Black Sun* - Douglas E. Winter   h   5923

**Hague, Scott** (Teenager)
*Witch* - Christopher Pike   f   4334

**Hahn** (Spaceman)
*Collidescope* - Grace Chetwin   s   1011

**hai-Arkad, Brandon** (Royalty)
*The Rifter's Covenant* - Sherwood Smith   s   5140

**Haid, Francis Madsen "Painkiller"** (Serial Killer)
*The Holy Terror* - Wayne Allen Sallee   h   4787

**Haig, Gudrun "Dauna"** (Journalist)
*The Singularity Project* - F.M. Busby   s   784

**Haines, Amelia "Amy"** (Writer)
*Psycho House* - Robert Bloch   h   542

**Haines, Carolyn** (Pilot)
*Extinct* - Charles Wilson   h   5877

**Haji, Hool** (Alien; Warrior)
*Kane of Old Mars* - Michael Moorcock   s   3983

**Hake** (Scientist)
*Vanishing Point* - Michaela Roessner   s   4652

**Hake, Denton** (Construction Worker)
*Out of Body* - Thomas Baum   h   397

**Hake, Elliot** (Insurance Investigator)
*Out of Body* - Thomas Baum   h   397

**Hakoni, Kyosti Bitterleaf** (Doctor; Spaceman)
*Revolution's Shore* - Alis A. Rasmussen   s   4484

**Hakori, Sonny** (Drug Dealer)
*TekWar* - William Shatner   s   4941

**Hal Jam** (Animal; Imposter)
*The Bear Went over the Mountain* - William
Kotzwinkle   f   3222

**Halanyn, SharMarali "Shar"** (Mythical Creature;
Magician)
*Chrome Circle* - Mercedes Lackey   f   3277

**Halarek, Karne** (Nobleman; Ruler)
*Brander's Book* - C.J. Mills   s   3909
*Egil's Book* - C.J. Mills   s   3910
*Kit's Book* - C.J. Mills   s   3911
*Zjhanne's Book* - C.J. Mills   s   3912

**Halarek, Kathryn "Kit" Magdalena Alysha**
(Noblewoman; Captive)
*Kit's Book* - C.J. Mills   s   3911

**Halbard, Amy** (Computer Expert)
*Offspring* - Jack Ketchum   h   3092

**Halburton, Gustav** (Psychologist)
*Dark Dreaming* - Pat Franklin   h   2040

**Haldane, Javan Jashan Urien** (Royalty; Psychic)
*King Javan's Year* - Katherine Kurtz  *f*  3258

**Haldane, Rhys Michael Alister** (Ruler; Psychic)
*The Bastard Prince* - Katherine Kurtz  *f*  3255

**Haldeth** (Artisan)
*The Master of Whitestorm* - Janny Wurts  *f*  6003

**Hale, David** (Librarian)
*Uwharrie* - Eugene E. Pfaff Jr.  *h*  4309

**Hale, Dick** (Radio)
*Night Mask* - William W. Johnstone  *h*  2931

**Hale, Ebeneezer** (Paranormal Investigator)
*The Messenger* - Donald Tyson  *h*  5528

**Haley, Adam** (Scientist)
*Howl* - Christine Tanasiuk  *h*  5388

**Half-Elvin, Tanthalas "Tanis"** (Mythical Creature; Warrior)
*Kindred Spirits* - Mark Anthony  *f*  154
*Steel and Stone* - Ellen Porath  *f*  4368
*Wanderlust* - Mary Kirchoff  *f*  3155

**Halfnight, Andrew** (Orphan)
*First Blast of the Trumpet Against the Monstrous Regiment of Women* - Eric McCormack  *h*  3779

**Hali** (Witch; Guide)
*Witch and Wombat* - Carolyn Cushman  *f*  1299

**Halkin, Edward** (Child)
*Prophecy* - Peter James  *h*  2874

**Halkin, Oliver** (Actuary)
*Prophecy* - Peter James  *h*  2874

**Hall, Cassandra** (Designer; Vampire)
*Thirst* - Michael Cecilione  *h*  948

**Hall, Courtney** (Artist; Revolutionary)
*Out on Blue Six* - Ian McDonald  *s*  3794

**Haller, Buzzy** (Filmmaker)
*Horror Show* - Greg Kihn  *h*  3103

**Halliday, Arden** (Musician)
*Gone South* - Robert R. McCammon  *h*  3755

**Halloran, Jack** (Engineer)
*Hell on High* - Holly Lisle  *f*  3483

**Halloran, Lawrence "Fixer-of-Weapons"** (Spy; Telepath)
*Man-Kzin Wars IV* - Larry Niven  *s*  4124

**Halloran, Liam** (Bodyguard)
*Sepulchre* - James Herbert  *h*  2672

**Halloran, Myrna** (Nurse)
*Flying in Place* - Susan Palwick  *h*  4240

**Halloway, Bobby** (Sports Figure)
*Fear Nothing* - Dean R. Koontz  *h*  3207

**Halman** (Artificial Intelligence)
*3001: The Final Odyssey* - Arthur C. Clarke  *s*  1053

**Halton, John** (Genetically Altered Being)
*Looking for the Mahdi* - N. Lee Wood  *s*  5966

**Halver** (Teacher; Werewolf)
*The Dubious Hills* - Pamela Dean  *f*  1444

**Hamid-Jones, Abdul** (Scientist)
*Crescent in the Sky* - Donald Moffitt  *s*  3946
*A Gathering of Stars* - Donald Moffitt  *s*  3947

**Hamilton, Case** (Police Officer)
*Death's Door* - John Wooley  *h*  5969

**Hamilton, Dennis** (Actor; Producer)
*Reign* - Chet Williamson  *h*  5849

**Hamilton, Diana** (Police Officer)
*Death's Door* - John Wooley  *h*  5969

**Hamilton, Ethan** (Computer Expert)
*Terminal Logic* - Jefferson Scott  *s*  4893

**Hamilton, Gil "the Arm"** (Detective—Police)
*Flatlander* - Larry Niven  *s*  4121

**Hamilton, Jack** (Engineer)
*Eye in the Sky* - Philip K. Dick  *s*  1521

**Hamilton, Jordan** (Child; Computer Expert)
*Terminal Logic* - Jefferson Scott  *s*  4893

**Hamilton, Marsha** (Liberal)
*Eye in the Sky* - Philip K. Dick  *s*  1521

**Hamilton, Rick** (Publisher)
*The Man Who Turned into Himself* - David Ambrose  *h*  89

**Hamilton, Ruth** (Widow(er))
*Dead in the Water* - Nancy Holder  *h*  2732

**Hamlet** (Android; Actor)
*Too, Too Solid Flesh* - Nick O'Donohoe  *s*  4197

**Hammen** (Thief)
*Arena* - William R. Forstchen  *f*  1977

**Hammer** (Criminal)
*Illegal Aliens* - Nick Pollotta  *s*  4365

**Hammer, Alois** (Military Personnel)
*The Warrior* - David Drake  *s*  1651

**Hammer-Hand, Barnar** (Adventurer)
*The Mines of Behemoth* - Michael Shea  *f*  4945

**Hammersmidt, Garry** (Businessman)
*Yesterday's Pawn* - W.T. Quick  *s*  4453

**Hammond, Fiona** (Ward)
*The Black Death* - Basil Copper  *h*  1185

**Hammond, John** (Businessman)
*Jurassic Park* - Michael Crichton  *s*  1255

**Hammond, Lech** (Journalist)
*Mars—The Red Planet* - Mick Farren  *s*  1880

**Hampton, Evelyn** (Administrator; Businesswoman)
*Moonfall* - Jack McDevitt  *s*  3789

**Hamr** (Hunter; Wanderer)
*Hunting the Ghost Dancer* - A.A. Attanasio  *f*  268

**Han, Liu** (Revolutionary; Parent)
*Worldwar: Striking the Balance* - Harry Turtledove  *s*  5516

**Han Rosie** (Animal; Warrior)
*Mariel of Redwall* - Brian Jacques  *f*  2850

**Hanavi, Ari** (Warrior; Military Personnel)
*Hero* - Joel Rosenberg  *s*  4672

**Handler, Paul** (Radio Personality)
*Deathgrip* - Brian Hodge  *h*  2700

**Handrar, Ser** (Religious; Wizard)
*Wizard of Bones* - Robert N. Charrette  *f*  979

**Hanfor** (Military Personnel; Counselor)
*The Spellsong War* - L.E. Modesitt Jr.  *f*  3939

**Hangman** (Genetically Altered Being; Sidekick)
*Rememory* - John Gregory Betancourt  *s*  481

**Hanks, Deana** (Linguist; Government Official)
*Invader* - C.J. Cherryh  *s*  998

**Hanley, Matthew** (Principal)
*The School* - Ed Kelleher  *h*  3042

**Hanley, Roderick** (Scientist)
*Reborn* - F. Paul Wilson  *h*  5895

**Hanlon, Agnes** (Assistant)
*The Sixth Dog* - Jane Rice  *h*  4582

**Hanna** (Telepath; Diplomat)
*The Master of Chaos* - Terry A. Adams  *s*  34

**Hanno** (Immortal; Sailor)
*The Boat of a Million Years* - Poul Anderson  *s*  125

**Hanorissia, Juliassa** (Royalty)
*The Lantern of God* - John Dalmas  *s*  1323

**Hanover, June** (Public Relations)
*Burning Bright* - J.S. Russell  *h*  4733

**Hanse** (Adventurer; Warrior)
*The Shadow of Sorcery* - Andrew J. Offutt  *f*  4202

**Hansen, Claire Beth** (Psychic)
*Summon the Keeper* - Tanya Huff  *f*  2800

**Hansen, Nils** (Police Officer)
*Justice* - David Drake  *s*  1635
*Northworld* - David Drake  *s*  1637
*Vengeance* - David Drake  *s*  1648

**Hansen, Randolf** (Doctor)
*Liquid Diet* - William Tedford  *h*  5419

**Hansen, Sunny** (Artist)
*The Spirit Stalker* - Nina Romberg  *h*  4664

**Hanson, Marvin** (Police Officer)
*Act of Love* - Joe R. Lansdale  *h*  3319

**Hanson, Robert** (Computer Expert)
*Probe* - Edward M. Lerner  *s*  3437

**Hanuman** (Companion)
*The Broken God* - David Zindell  *s*  6085

**Hap, Channa** (Spaceman)
*The City Who Fought* - Anne McCaffrey  *s*  3722

**Haplo** (Adventurer; Wizard)
*Elven Star* - Margaret Weis  *f*  5712
*Fire Sea* - Margaret Weis  *f*  5714
*The Hand of Chaos* - Margaret Weis  *f*  5715
*Into the Labyrinth* - Margaret Weis  *f*  5716
*Serpent Mage* - Margaret Weis  *f*  5726
*The Seventh Gate* - Margaret Weis  *f*  5727

**Hara, Jay** (Teenager; Spaceman)
*Godspeed* - Charles Sheffield  *s*  4957

**Haramis** (Royalty; Sorceress)
*Black Trillium* - Marion Zimmer Bradley  *f*  630

**Haramis** (Sorceress; Scholar; Royalty)
*Blood Trillium* - Julian May  *f*  3696

**Haramis** (Sorceress; Recluse; Royalty)
*Lady of the Trillium* - Marion Zimmer Bradley  *f*  641

**Haramis** (Sorceress; Royalty)
*Sky Trillium* - Julian May  *f*  3700

**Haran, Shaidar** (Mythical Creature)
*Lord of Chaos* - Robert Jordan  *f*  2988

**Hardesty** (Spaceship Captain)
*Voyage of the Star Wolf* - David Gerrold  *s*  2212

**Hardgreip** (Mythical Creature; Witch)
*War of the Gods* - Poul Anderson  *f*  136

**Hardin, Charlie** (Truck Driver)
*Roadkill* - Richard Sanford  *h*  4815

**Harding, Amelia "Blaze"** (Scientist; Professor)
*Forever Peace* - Joe Haldeman  *s*  2488

**Harding, Sarah** (Scientist)
*The Lost World* - Michael Crichton  *s*  1256

**Harding, Skip** (Police Officer)
*Crota* - Owl Goingback  *h*  2251

**Hardison, Matt** (Writer)
*Let There Be Dark* - Allen Lee Harris  *h*  2557

**Hardison, Pete** (Child)
*Let There Be Dark* - Allen Lee Harris  *h*  2557

**Hardrim, Mel** (Police Officer)
*The Argus Gambit* - David D. Ross  *s*  4681

**Hardwick, David Lyle** (Writer; Vampire)
*Near Death* - Nancy Kilpatrick  *h*  3113

**Hardy, Dominic** (Mythical Creature)
*Juniper, Gentian and Rosemary* - Pamela Dean  *f*  1445

**Hardy, Gorman** (Writer)
*Beast House* - Richard Laymon  *h*  3364

**Hari** (Religious; Adventurer)
*The Willing Spirit* - Piers Anthony  *f*  195

**Harijadi, Anjeillo "Angel"** (Security Officer; Businessman)
*The Shapes of Their Hearts* - Melissa Scott   s   4901

**Harkender, Jacob** (Supernatural Being)
*The Carnival of Destruction* - Brian Stableford   h   5190

**Harker, Jonathan** (Real Estate Agent)
*Bram Stoker's Dracula* - Fred Saberhagen   h   4763

**Harker, Jonathan** (Lawyer)
*The Darker Passions: Dracula* - Amarantha Knight   h   3179
*Mina* - Marie Kiraly   h   3151

**Harker, Malcolm** (Detective—Amateur)
*Blood of the Impaler* - Jeffrey Sackett   h   4779

**Harker, Mina** (Housewife)
*Bram Stoker's Dracula* - Fred Saberhagen   h   4763

**Harker, Mina** (Heroine; Lover)
*The Dracula Tape* - Fred Saberhagen   h   4765

**Harker, Mina** (Teacher)
*Mina* - Marie Kiraly   h   3151

**Harkta** (Wizard)
*The Conjurer Princess* - Vivian Vande Velde   f   5555

**Harlan** (Animal)
*Night of the Living Rat!* - Debra Doyle   s   1603

**Harlan** (Animal; Disembodied Personality)
*Night of the Living Shark!* - David Bischoff   s   493

**Harlan, Brander** (Nobleman; Revolutionary)
*Brander's Book* - C.J. Mills   s   3909

**Harlan, Kathryn "Kit"** (Noblewoman)
*Zjhanne's Book* - C.J. Mills   s   3912

**Harlan, Richard** (Prisoner; Leader)
*Brander's Book* - C.J. Mills   s   3909

**Harlie** (Artificial Intelligence)
*Voyage of the Star Wolf* - David Gerrold   s   2212

**Harlow, Robert "Bob"** (Professor; Archaeologist)
*Stones of the Dalai Lama* - Ken Mitchell   f   3916

**Harlow-c, Jean** (Clone)
*Dydeetown World* - F. Paul Wilson   s   5887

**Harmon, Anne Marie "Annie"** (Musician; Lesbian)
*Waking the Moon* - Elizabeth Hand   f   2538

**Harmon, Dale** (Engineer)
*Moon Walker* - Rick Hautala   h   2610

**Harms, Harry** (Genetically Altered Being; Explorer)
*Heaven's Reach* - David Brin   s   687

**Harnak** (Royalty; Warrior)
*Oath of Swords* - David Weber   f   5678

**Harold** (Animal)
*Return to Howliday Inn* - James Howe   f   2786

**Harootunian, Geoffrey "Hoot"** (Spouse)
*Larque on the Wing* - Nancy Springer   f   5180

**Harootunian, Larque "Lark"** (Psychic; Artisan)
*Larque on the Wing* - Nancy Springer   f   5180

**Harp, John** (Aged Person)
*Chariot* - Charles L. Grant   h   2304

**Harper, Ellen** (Archaeologist)
*The Dead Man's Kiss* - Robert Weinberg   h   5695

**Harper, Fay** (Teenager; Student)
*Jinx High* - Mercedes Lackey   h   3284

**Harper, Jim** (Teacher)
*Oktober* - Stephen Gallagher   h   2112

**Harper, Marty** (Teenager; Student—High School)
*The Cat* - R.L. Stine   h   5285

**Harper, Timothy** (Time Traveler; Military Personnel)
*Death's Gray Land* - Mike Shupp   s   5011
*The Last Reckoning* - Mike Shupp   s   5012

**Harper, Toby** (Doctor)
*Life Support* - Tess Gerritsen   h   2206

**Harper, Willie** (Teenager)
*Dark Fortune* - Richard Lee Byers   h   795

**Harpirias of Muldemar** (Royalty; Diplomat)
*The Mountains of Majipoor* - Robert Silverberg   s   5037

**Harpole, Nicholas** (Secretary; Religious)
*In the Garden of Iden* - Kage Baker   s   298

**Harpy-Goblin, Gloha** (Mythical Creature)
*Harpy Thyme* - Piers Anthony   f   174

**Harrah, Talia Crawford** (Twin)
*The Lilith Factor* - Jean Paiva   h   4236

**Harrigan, Kevin G.** (Scientist)
*The Pleistocene Redemption* - Dan Gallagher   s   2107

**Harrington, Allison** (Doctor; Parent)
*Echoes of Honor* - David Weber   s   5669

**Harrington, Honor** (Military Personnel; Hero)
*Echoes of Honor* - David Weber   s   5669

**Harrington, Honor** (Military Personnel; Noblewoman)
*Field of Dishonor* - David Weber   s   5670
*Flag in Exile* - David Weber   s   5671
*Honor Among Enemies* - David Weber   s   5673
*The Honor of the Queen* - David Weber   s   5674
*In Enemy Hands* - David Weber   s   5675
*On Basilisk Station* - David Weber   s   5679
*The Short Victorious War* - David Weber   s   5681

**Harris** (Teacher)
*The Rats* - James Herbert   h   2671

**Harris, Alex** (Worker)
*Ghost Light* - Rick Hautala   h   2608

**Harris, Billy** (Child)
*Ghost Light* - Rick Hautala   h   2608

**Harris, Derek** (Child)
*Wake Up Screaming* - Vincent Courtney   h   1215

**Harris, Druce** (Spouse)
*Howl* - Christine Tanasiuk   h   5388

**Harris, Dutch** (Farmer; Grandparent)
*Wake Up Screaming* - Vincent Courtney   h   1215

**Harris, James** (Settler)
*Bright Angel* - John Blair   s   512

**Harris, Jenny** (Spacewoman)
*Expansion* - Peter F. Hamilton   s   2525

**Harris, Laika** (Spy)
*City of Iron* - Chet Williamson   h   5843
*Empire of Dust* - Chet Williamson   h   5846

**Harris, Nora** (Orphan)
*Grandma's Little Darling* - Stephen R. George   h   2201

**Harris, Samantha** (Scientist)
*Howl* - Christine Tanasiuk   h   5388

**Harris, Tina** (Student—College)
*The Abductors: Conspiracy* - Jonathan Frakes   s   2034

**Harris, Valerie** (Advertising)
*The Site* - Melisand March   h   3621

**Harrisch** (Businessman)
*Noir* - K.W. Jeter   s   2916

**Harrison, Andrew** (Political Figure)
*1945* - Newt Gingrich   s   2239

**Harrison, Bailey** (Scientist; Researcher)
*The Vampire Virus* - Michael Romkey   h   4668

**Harrison, Benjamin** (Spirit; Historical Figure)
*The Smithsonian Institution* - Gore Vidal   f   5570

**Harrison, David** (Scientist)
*Twistor* - John Cramer   s   1245

**Harrison, Hatchford** (Antiques Dealer)
*Hideaway* - Dean R. Koontz   h   3208

**Harrison, Lee Anne** (Student; Veterinarian)
*The Magic and the Healing* - Nick O'Donohoe   f   4196
*Under the Healing Sign* - Nick O'Donohoe   f   4198

**Harrison, Nick** (Demon)
*Freeze Frames* - Katharine Kerr   s   3071

**Harrison, Nick "The Devil"** (Angel)
*Resurrection* - Katharine Kerr   s   3075

**Harrison, Sally** (Office Worker)
*The Eyes of the Beast* - Steve Harris   h   2565

**Harrison, Theophilus "Ted"** (Student; Immigrant)
*Orbital Resonance* - John Barnes   s   356

**Harrow, Aidan** (Disembodied Personality)
*Icarus Descending* - Elizabeth Hand   s   2536

**Harrowslough, Holly** (Religious; Rebel)
*Finder's Bane* - Kate Novak   f   4165

**Harry** (Child)
*The Cormorant* - Stephen Gregory   h   2429

**Harry** (Companion)
*The King's Buccaneer* - Raymond E. Feist   f   1904

**Harshaw, Jubal** (Writer; Lawyer)
*Stranger in a Strange Land* - Robert A. Heinlein   s   2649

**Hart** (Scientist; Lesbian)
*In the Blood* - Lauren Wright Douglas   s   1590

**Hart, Adragon** (Vampire)
*Precious Blood* - Pat Graversen   h   2336

**Hart, Adragon** (Teenager; Vampire)
*Sweet Blood* - Pat Graversen   h   2337

**Hart, Beth** (Teenager; Vampire)
*Precious Blood* - Pat Graversen   h   2336

**Hart, Carolyn** (Young Woman)
*A Room for the Dead* - Noel Hynd   h   2825

**Hart, Damon** (Artist)
*Inherit the Earth* - Brian Stableford   s   5193

**Hart, Elsbeth** (Writer; Vampire)
*Sweet Blood* - Pat Graversen   h   2337

**Hart, Lola** (Teenager; Student; Gang Member)
*Random Acts of Senseless Violence* - Jack Womack   f   5959

**Hart, Marcel** (Child)
*The Dark One* - Guy N. Smith   h   5118

**Hart, Sally** (Sailor)
*Hunger* - William Dantz   h   1346

**Hart, Thomas J.** (Sailor)
*Hunger* - William Dantz   h   1346

**Hartell, Kathryn** (Lesbian; Researcher)
*Shadows After Dark* - Ouida Crozier   f   1286

**Harth, Beren "Brat" SanDyllin** (Orphan)
*Wheel of Dreams* - Salinda Tyson   f   5529

**Harting, William Jameson "Jay"** (Doctor)
*Deadly Breed* - T.J. Kirby   h   3153

**Hartke, Eugene Debs** (Professor)
*Hocus Pocus or, What's the Hurry, Son?* - Kurt Vonnegut Jr.   s   5593

**Hartley, Sherrine** (Computer Expert)
*Fallen Angels* - Larry Niven   s   4120

**Hartmann, Gregg** (Political Figure; Genetically Altered Being)
*Ace in the Hole* - George R.R. Martin   s   3641
*Marked Cards* - George R.R. Martin   s   3647

**Hartwig, Reece** (Counselor)
*The Night of the Moonbow* - Thomas Tryon   h   5486

**Harvey, Emily** (Twin; Revolutionary)
*Memorymakers* - Brian Herbert  s  2665

**Harvey, Thomas** (Twin)
*Memorymakers* - Brian Herbert  s  2665

**Hasagawa, Padraic Hakim** (Professor)
*Reality Is What You Can Get Away With: An
   Illustrated Screenplay* - Robert Anton
   Wilson  s  5904

**Hasgard, David** (Military Personnel; Teenager)
*Traitors from Within* - R.A. Montgomery  s  3966

**Hask** (Alien)
*Illegal Alien* - Robert J. Sawyer  s  4858

**Haskell, Charles L. "Charlie"** (Political Figure)
*Moonfall* - Jack McDevitt  s  3789

**Haskell, Simon** (Detective—Private)
*Leap Point* - Kay Kenyon  s  3063

**Hasloch, Toller** (Warrior; Villain)
*Heartlight* - Marion Zimmer Bradley  f  637

**Hasmara, Faan "Fa"** (Sorceress; Orphan)
*The Magic Wars* - Jo Clayton  f  1068
*Wildfire* - Jo Clayton  f  1073

**Hasruel** (Demon; Mythical Creature)
*Castle in the Air* - Diana Wynne Jones  f  2944

**Hastings, Amber** (Scientist)
*Thunder Strike!* - Michael McCollum  s  3772

**Hastings, Julie** (Lawyer)
*Darkman* - Randall Boyll  h  611
*Darkman #2: The Price of Fear* - Randall
   Boyll  h  613

**Hastings, Kyle Stevens** (Imposter; Wanderer)
*Down the Bright Way* - Robert Reed  s  4505

**Hastur, Leonie** (Telepath)
*Rediscovery: A Novel of Darkover* - Marion Zimmer
   Bradley  s  643

**Hatcher, Agnes** (Patient)
*Bad Karma* - Andrew Harper  h  2548

**Hathaway** (Spaceman)
*The Martian Chronicles* - Ray Bradbury  s  621

**Hathor** (Mythical Creature; Revolutionary)
*Horrible Humes* - Stephen Billias  f  487

**Hathor** (Mythical Creature)
*The Land of Gold* - Gillian Bradshaw  f  658
*Outcasts* - Clayton Emery  f  1815

**Hatshepsut** (Time Traveler)
*Dragon's Claw* - Alex McDonough  s  3800

**Hauberin** (Mythical Creature; Royalty)
*A Strange and Ancient Name* - Josepha
   Sherman  f  4991

**Hauser, Wolfgang "Karl Wolf"** (Military Personnel;
   Leader)
*Cohort of the Damned* - Andrew Keith  s  3034

**Hausmann, Elena** (Librarian; Revolutionary)
*The Third Force* - Marc Laidlaw  s  3313

**Hausmann, Louis** (Military Personnel)
*The Third Force* - Marc Laidlaw  s  3313

**Haven, Dextra** (Political Figure; Religious)
*A Screaming Across the Sky* - Brian Daley  s  1315

**Haven, Kyle** (Sea Captain)
*The Ship of Magic* - Robin Hobb  f  2696

**Havoc, Mike** (Military Personnel)
*L.A. Strike* - David Robbins  s  4599

**Havzhiva, Yehedarhed** (Diplomat)
*Four Ways to Forgiveness* - Ursula K. Le
   Guin  s  3380

**Hawk** (Police Officer)
*The Bones of Haven* - Simon R. Green  f  2363
*The God Killer* - Simon R. Green  f  2368
*Guard Against Dishonor* - Simon R. Green  f  2369

**Hawk & Fisher** - Simon R. Green  f  2370

**Hawk** (Prehistoric Human; Inventor)
*The Hunter Returns* - David Drake  f  1632

**Hawk** (Police Officer)
*Winner Takes All* - Simon R. Green  f  2375
*Wolf in the Fold* - Simon R. Green  f  2376

**Hawk, Carin** (Explorer)
*Ark Liberty* - Will Bradley  s  656

**Hawk-Hobby** (Teenager)
*Merlin* - Jane Yolen  f  6035

**Hawk-That-Settles** (Indian; Religious)
*Krokodil Tears* - Jack Yeovil  f  6023

**Hawke** (Heir)
*Far Harbor* - Melisa C. Michaels  s  3888

**Hawke, Christopher** (Military Personnel)
*No Blood Spilled* - Les Daniels  h  1338

**Hawke, Michael** (Magician)
*Night Magic* - Thomas Tryon  h  5485

**Hawken, Garrick** (Heir)
*Allamanda* - Michael Williams  f  5817

**Hawken, Jos** (Military Personnel; Spaceship
   Captain)
*Yamato: A Rage in Heaven* - Ken Kato  s  3014

**Hawken, Solomon** (Magician; Scholar)
*Arcady* - Michael Williams  f  5818

**Hawkes, Benton** (Diplomat; Government Official)
*The Law of War* - William Shatner  s  4931

**Hawkes, Benton** (Diplomat; Rancher)
*Man o' War* - William Shatner  s  4932

**Hawkins, Danny** (Child; Explorer)
*A Thunder on Neptune* - Gordon Eklund  s  1768

**Hawkins, Ethan** (Military Personnel; Spaceman)
*Mutant Star* - Karen Haber  s  2475

**Hawkins, Ethorne** (Worker)
*Dogland* - Will Shetterly  f  4992

**Hawkins, Marie** (Spacewoman; Parent)
*Tripoint* - C.J. Cherryh  s  1003

**Hawkins, Nirgal** (Political Figure)
*Blue Mars* - Kim Stanley Robinson  s  4629

**Hawkins, Nirgal** (Political Figure; Revolutionary)
*Green Mars* - Kim Stanley Robinson  s  4633

**Hawkins, Ron** (Maintenance Worker)
*Fire* - Alan Rodgers  h  4647

**Hawkins, Rosalind "Rose"** (Scholar; Orphan)
*The Fire Rose* - Mercedes Lackey  f  3280

**Hawksmoor, Nicholas** (Pilot; Artificial Intelligence)
*Berserker Kill* - Fred Saberhagen  s  4761

**Hawn, Loren** (Police Officer)
*Days of Atonement* - Walter Jon Williams  s  5836

**Hawson, Jordan** (Knight)
*The Forge of Virtue* - Lynn Abbey  f  16

**Hawson, Jordan** (Knight; Handicapped)
*The Temper of Wisdom* - Lynn Abbey  f  17

**Hawthorn, Ariel** (Spaceman)
*Anvil of Stars* - Greg Bear  s  414

**Hawthorn, Lucas** (Travel Agent)
*The Whispers* - Dan Parkinson  s  4247

**Hawthorn "D-base"** (Artificial Intelligence)
*Cinderblock* - Janine Ellen Young  s  6047

**Hawthorne, Alec** (Businessman)
*Distant Dreams* - Jenny Lykins  f  3576

**Hawthorne, Royce** (Young Man)
*Chaingang* - Rex Miller  h  3899

**Hawthorne, Sara** (Teacher)
*Moonfall* - Tamara Thorne  h  5464

**Hay, Matthew** (Religious)
*Witch Hill* - Marion Zimmer Bradley  h  654

**Hayaka, Reyna** (Guardian; Businessman)
*Wild Magic* - Jo Clayton  f  1072

**Hayden, Conek** (Spaceship Captain; Businessman)
*Backblast* - Lee McKeone  s  3828
*The Clone Crisis* - Lee McKeone  s  3829
*Starfire Down* - Lee McKeone  s  3830

**Hayden, Mark** (Police Officer)
*Bats* - William W. Johnstone  h  2926

**Hayes** (Scientist; Administrator)
*Time and Light* - William Bornefeld  s  574

**Hayes, Charlie** (Businessman)
*Death Channels* - Robert E. Vardeman  h  5562

**Hayes, Donna** (Travel Agent)
*The Cellar* - Richard Laymon  h  3365

**Hayes, Drew** (Teenager)
*Living with Aliens* - John DeChancie  s  1460

**Hayes, Jack** (Criminal)
*The Spider #3: Death's Crimson Juggernaut/The Red
   Death Rain* - Grant Stockbridge  f  5307

**Hayes, Roy** (Criminal)
*The Cellar* - Richard Laymon  h  3365

**Hayes, Terry** (Journalist)
*The Season of Passage* - Christopher Pike  h  4331

**Hays, Micah** (Police Officer)
*The Case of the Police Officer's Cock Ring and the
   Piano Player Who Had No Fingers* - Edward
   Lee  h  3388
*Splatterspunk: The Micah Hays Stories* - Edward
   Lee  h  3397

**Hazaar** (Alien)
*Larissa* - Emily Devenport  s  1503

**Hazard, Arthur** (Genetically Altered Being)
*Brain Child* - George Turner  s  5491

**Hazel** (Photographer; Fiance(e))
*Belladonna* - Michael Stewart  h  5271

**Hazelhof, Cornelia** (Businesswoman; Genius)
*Timeshare* - Joshua Dann  s  1344

**Hazzard, Calvin** (Professor)
*Rough Beast* - Gary Goshgarian  h  2284

**Hazzard, Matt** (Child)
*Rough Beast* - Gary Goshgarian  h  2284

**Heather** (Singer; Handicapped)
*Lorien Lost* - Michael King  f  3124

**Heber, Kevin** (Teenager; Technician)
*Bug Park* - James P. Hogan  s  2723

**Heber, Vanessa** (Step-Parent; Scientist)
*Bug Park* - James P. Hogan  s  2723

**Hector** (Teenager)
*The Lake at the End of the World* - Caroline
   MacDonald  s  3584

**Hederick** (Religious; Leader)
*Hederick, the Theocrat* - Ellen Dodge
   Severson  f  4925

**Hedison, Marianne** (Computer Expert; Detective—
   Amateur)
*Terminal Games* - Cole Perriman  s  4283

**Heffer, John Wilson** (Vacationer)
*The Feelies* - Mick Farren  s  1878

**Heiclaro, Corean** (Trader)
*Emperor of Everything* - Ray Aldridge  s  62

**Heikki, Galler** (Businessman)
*Mighty Good Road* - Melissa Scott  s  4897

**Heikki, Gwynne** (Businesswoman; Adventurer)
*Mighty Good Road* - Melissa Scott  s  4897

**Heiligmann, E. "Pif"** (Detective)
*Double Jeopardy* - Aaron Allston  s  86

**Heim, Walter** (Agent)
*Double Edge* - Dennis Etchison  h  1846

**Heiratikus** (Wizard; Political Figure)
*Wind From a Foreign Sky* - Katya Reimann  f  4528

**Heisenberg, Paul** (Religious)
*The Walking Shadow* - Brian Stableford  s  5195

**Helarion** (Thief)
*The Thief of Hermes* - Ru Emerson  f  1811

**Helen** (Artificial Intelligence)
*Galatea 2.2* - Richard M. Powers  s  4381

**Helen** (Noblewoman)
*Helen's Passage* - Diana M. Concannon  f  1129

**Helen** (Prehistoric Human)
*No Enemy but Time* - Michael Bishop  s  502

**Helen** (Noblewoman)
*The Princess and the Dragon* - Roberto
  Pazzi  f  4272

**Helier, Conrad** (Scientist)
*Inherit the Earth* - Brian Stableford  s  5193

**Heliokleia** (Royalty)
*Horses of Heaven* - Gillian Bradshaw  f  657

**Helit, Susan Sto** (Student; Apprentice)
*Soul Music* - Terry Pratchett  f  4401

**Hellboy** (Supernatural Being)
*Hellboy: The Lost Army* - Christopher
  Golden  h  2257

**Heller, Prescott "Sean Toole"** (Military Personnel;
Spy)
*Union Fires* - John Barnes  f  358

**Heller, Sean** (Businessman)
*California Ghosting* - William Hill  h  2687

**Helling, Suzanne "Alouzon"** (Student; Guardian)
*Dragon Death* - Gael Baudino  f  390
*Duel of Dragons* - Gael Baudino  f  391

**Helman, Granger** (Murderer)
*Bloodshift* - Garfield Reeves-Stevens  h  4508

**Helmish** (Artisan; Inventor)
*Top Dog* - Jerry Jay Carroll  f  915

**Helmond, Alexandra "Ally"** (Teenager)
*The Orpheus Process* - Daniel H. Gower  h  2293

**Helmond, Orville** (Scientist)
*The Orpheus Process* - Daniel H. Gower  h  2293

**Helms, Mary** (Doctor)
*Kids* - Trevor Hoyle  h  2787

**Helmuth** (Pirate; Agent)
*Galactic Patrol* - Edward E. Smith  s  5116

**Heln** (Spouse)
*Chimaera's Copper* - Piers Anthony  f  166

**Helwig, Barbie** (Child)
*Blue Limbo* - Terrence M. Green  s  2377

**Helwig, Mitch** (Police Officer)
*Blue Limbo* - Terrence M. Green  s  2377

**Helwin, Owen** (Warrior)
*The Bridge of Dawn* - Neil Hancock  f  2531

**Hemings, Sally** (Slave)
*Arc d'X* - Steve Erickson  f  1835

**Hemingway, Kate** (Journalist)
*Twilight* - Peter James  h  2876

**Hemlock** (Royalty; Ruler)
*Sweet Myth-tery of Life* - Robert Asprin  f  262

**Henchard, Daniel** (Teenager; Apprentice)
*Groogleman* - Debra Doyle  s  1600

**Henderson, Carl** (Scientist)
*The Homing* - John Saul  h  4842

**Henderson, Dawn** (Child)
*The Forever Children* - Eric Flanders  h  1944

**Henderson, Lisa** (Young Woman)
*Bone Music* - Alan Rodgers  h  4646

**Hendricks, Cara** (Journalist; Teenager)
*Shadow World* - A.C. Crispin  s  1262

**Hendricks, Clint** (Police Officer)
*Stone Dead* - Ellen Jamison  h  2878

**Hendricks, Connie** (Teenager; Telepath)
*Being of Two Minds* - Pamela F. Service  f  4918

**Hendricks, Judson** (Detective)
*Flesh and Blood* - D.A. Fowler  h  2024

**Henkin, Paul** (Child)
*Mysteries of the Word* - Stanley Wiater  h  5796

**Henning, J. Benjamin** (Paranormal Investigator)
*Something's Alive on the Titanic* - Robert
  Serling  h  4915

**Henning, Johanna** (Scientist)
*Memento Mori* - Shariann Lewitt  s  3454

**Henry, Dora** (Police Officer)
*The Family Tree* - Sheri S. Tepper  s  5429

**Henry, Ned** (Historian; Time Traveler)
*To Say Nothing of the Dog* - Connie Willis  s  5874

**Henry, Wiiliam** (Ruler; Historical Figure)
*Queen's Gambit Declined* - Melinda M.
  Snodgrass  f  5147

**Henry of Veldran** (Orphan)
*Henry's Gift: The Magic Eye* - David
  Worsick  f  5972

**Henry "Thornmallow"** (Student)
*Wizard's Hall* - Jane Yolen  f  6043

**Henshaw, William** (Veterinarian)
*Hard Landing* - Algis Budrys  s  753

**Hera** (Immortal; Deity)
*Orion and the Conqueror* - Ben Bova  s  590

**Herb** (Animal)
*The Arbitrary Placement of Walls* - Martha
  Soukup  f  5165

**Herb-Woman** (Healer; Parent)
*Strange Deliverance* - Mary Brown  s  728

**Herbert, Grisel** (Young Woman)
*The Return* - Walter de la Mare  h  1424

**Hercules** (Hero)
*Atlantis Found* - R. Garcia y Robertson  s  2119

**Hercules** (Hero; Warrior)
*By the Sword* - Timothy Boggs  f  559

**Hercules** (Hero)
*The First Casualty* - David L. Seidman  f  4912

**Heredes** (Teacher; Martial Arts Expert)
*A Passage of Stars* - Alis A. Rasmussen  s  4482

**Heredes, Lilyaka Ash** (Spaceman)
*Revolution's Shore* - Alis A. Rasmussen  s  4484

**Herewiss** (Magician; Religious)
*The Door into Sunset* - Diane Duane  f  1660

**Herky** (Mythical Creature)
*Goblins in the Castle* - Bruce Coville  f  1218

**Herla** (Royalty)
*Storm Warriors* - Brian Craig  f  1240

**Herman** (Animal)
*Way Up High* - Roger Zelazny  f  6076

**Hernandes y Jons, Rico** (Computer Expert)
*The Eyes of God* - Mark Kreighbaum  s  3231
*Palace* - Katharine Kerr  s  3072

**Hernandez, Corinne** (Martial Arts Expert)
*The First Duelist* - Rutledge Etheridge  s  1849

**Heron** (Shaman; Prehistoric Human)
*People of the Wolf* - W. Michael Gear  f  2170

**Heron, John** (Immigrant; Time Traveler)
*The Schizogenic Man* - Raymond Harris  s  2563

**Heron, Madeleine** (Anthropologist; Widow(er))
*Green Lake* - S.K. Epperson  h  1830

**Herric** (Royalty; Scholar)
*Wolf's Cub* - Mackay Wood  f  5964

**Herrin, Ashley** (Reanimated Dead)
*Harrowgate* - Daniel H. Gower  h  2292

**Hershey** (Police Officer)
*Judge Dredd* - Neal Barrett Jr.  s  366

**Heslin, Camnor** (Diplomat; Spy)
*Dancer's Rise* - Jo Clayton  f  1064

**Hesseth** (Alien)
*Black Sun Rising* - C.S. Friedman  f  2056
*When True Night Falls* - C.S. Friedman  f  2060

**Hewlitt** (Patient)
*Final Diagnosis* - James White  s  5777

**Heywood, Diana** (Computer Expert)
*Halo* - Tom Maddox  s  3604

**Hickock** (Warrior)
*Yellowstone Run* - David Robbins  s  4605

**Hickory, Magister** (Wizard; Teacher)
*Wizard's Hall* - Jane Yolen  f  6043

**Hidalgo, Lourdes** (Teenager; Outcast)
*Scorpion Shards* - Neal Shusterman  s  5013

**Hidetada** (Artificial Intelligence)
*The Cybernetic Shogun* - Victor Milan  s  3890

**Higginson, Alice** (Teenager; Actor)
*Painted Devil* - Michael Bedard  f  430

**Highborn, Ilaron** (Businessman; Mythical Creature)
*Son of Darkness* - Josepha Sherman  f  4990

**Highland, Bill** (Political Figure)
*The Committee* - Raymond Buckland  h  752

**Hightower, Alex** (Agent; Parent)
*Possession* - Peter James  h  2873

**Hightower, Belisarius** (Military Personnel)
*Pandora* - Alan Rodgers  h  4650

**Hightower, Fabian** (Spirit; Young Man)
*Possession* - Peter James  h  2873

**Hildegund** (Teenager)
*Attila's Treasure* - Stephan Grundy  f  2453

**Hill, Jonathan** (Aged Person)
*The Burning Man* - Michael Hammond  h  2530

**Hill, Shannon** (Artist)
*The Axman Cometh* - John Farris  h  1883

**Hillenbrand, Charles** (Professor)
*Naomi's Room* - Jonathan Aycliffe  h  281

**Hillenbrand, Laura** (Spouse)
*Naomi's Room* - Jonathan Aycliffe  h  281

**Hiller, Steven** (Military Personnel; Pilot)
*Independence Day* - Dean Devlin  s  1508

**Hillerman, Walter "Walt"** (Scientist; Computer
Expert)
*Lady El* - Jim Starlin  s  5213

**Hilliard, Terrence** (Telepath)
*The Shadow Within* - Jeanne Cavelos  s  944

**Hilton, Jim** (Military Personnel)
*Deep Trek* - James Axler  s  278

**Hilton, Matt** (Teenager)
*Journey to Terezor* - Frank Asch  s  221

**Himmels, Peter** (Military Personnel)
*The Sandman: Book of Dreams* - Neil
  Gaiman  f  2105

**Hinckel, Hieronymus** (Musician; Thief)
*Chorus Skating* - Alan Dean Foster  *f*  1998

**Hindmost** (Alien)
*The Ringworld Throne* - Larry Niven  *s*  4128

**Hinson, Jody** (Psychologist)
*The Halflife* - Sharon Webb  *s*  5664

**Hinton, Blackbird** (Smuggler)
*Python Isle* - Kenneth Robeson  *f*  4624

**Hiram** (Prehistoric Human)
*Shiva Accused: An Adventure of the Ice Age* - J.H.
   Brennan  *f*  667
*Shiva: An Adventure of the Ice Age* - J.H.
   Brennan  *f*  669
*Shiva's Challenge: An Adventure of the Ice Age* - J.H.
   Brennan  *f*  668

**Hirazawa, Suki** (Worker)
*Angel Kiss* - Kelley Wilde  *h*  5800

**Hirmin** (Farmer; Fiance(e))
*The Wooden Sword* - Lynn Abbey  *f*  18

**Hiroshi, Kajiwara** (Military Personnel)
*Fire on the Border* - Kevin O'Donnell Jr.  *s*  4194

**Hirsch, Magen** (Warrior)
*Warp Angel* - Stuart Hopen  *s*  2766

**Hispard, Michael** (Dancer)
*Skin* - Kathe Koja  *h*  3196

**Hisvet** (Mythical Creature)
*Return to Lankhmar* - Fritz Leiber  *f*  3422

**Hitch** (Reanimated Dead; Biker)
*Dead Heat* - Del Stone Jr.  *h*  5313

**Hitchcock, Allison** (Writer)
*The School* - T.M. Wright  *h*  5994

**Hitchcock, Frank** (Photographer)
*The School* - T.M. Wright  *h*  5994

**Hitler, Adolf** (Military Personnel; Historical Figure)
*Dark Legacy* - Mark A. Kostrubula  *h*  3220

**Hitler, Adolf** (Historical Figure; Political Figure)
*The Resurrections* - Simon Louvish  *s*  3528
*Triumph* - Ben Bova  *s*  598

**Ho, Gordon** (Royalty)
*House of the Sun* - Nigel Findley  *s*  1936

**Hobart, Rollin** (Engineer)
*The Undesired Princess and the Enchanted Bunny* - L.
   Sprague de Camp  *f*  1419

**Hobbes, John** (Detective)
*Fallen* - Dee Graham  *h*  2302

**Hobbs, Alexandra** (Journalist)
*Red Angel* - Roxanne Longstreet  *h*  3518

**Hobbs, Maggie** (Tourist)
*A Love through Time* - Terri Brisbin  *f*  691

**Hobgoblin** (Criminal)
*Spider-Man: The Venom Factor* - Diane
   Duane  *s*  1667

**Hobkin** (Mythical Creature)
*Hobkin* - Peni R. Griffin  *f*  2438

**Hobson, Cathy** (Advertising)
*The Terminal Experiment* - Robert J.
   Sawyer  *s*  4860

**Hobson, Peter** (Scientist; Engineer)
*The Terminal Experiment* - Robert J.
   Sawyer  *s*  4860

**Hochstader, Jeremy** (Computer Expert)
*Castle War!* - John DeChancie  *s*  1455

**Hodge, Benton** (Store Owner)
*Sineater* - Elizabeth Massie  *h*  3668

**Hodge, Birk "Birkaj"** (Trader; Administrator)
*The Inquisitor* - Cheryl J. Franklin  *s*  2037

**Hodge, J. Benison** (Vampire)
*The Devil's Advocate* - Gherbod Fleming  *h*  1949

**Hodges, Laren** (Journalist)
*The Lurker* - James V. Smith  *h*  5123

**Hodierna** (Religious; Adventurer)
*The Notorious Abbess* - Vera Chapman  *f*  965

**Hoey, Buck** (Sports Figure)
*Brittle Innings* - Michael Bishop  *h*  498

**Hoffman, Judith** (Scientist)
*Eon* - Greg Bear  *s*  417

**Hoffman, Vivien** (Heiress)
*Skull Session* - Daniel Hecht  *h*  2638

**Hogan, Stan** (Drifter)
*Symphony* - Charles L. Grant  *h*  2318

**Hogopian, Aaron** (Activist; Researcher)
*Playing God* - Sarah Zettel  *s*  6080

**Hoke** (Pilot)
*'48* - James Herbert  *h*  2667

**Hokokul, Cha Ishil** (Alien)
*Jaran* - Kate Elliott  *s*  1772

**Holbian** (Royalty; Warrior)
*The Road to Underfall* - Mike Jefferies  *f*  2888

**Holbrook, Miller** (Professor)
*One Wish* - C.J. Card  *f*  880

**Holcroft, Jake** (Child; Computer Expert)
*Target Earth* - Steve Perry  *s*  4301

**Holdman, Taylor** (Businessman)
*Near Dead* - Stephen R. George  *h*  2202

**Holdstrom, Roy** (Filmmaker)
*A Graveyard for Lunatics* - Ray Bradbury  *h*  620

**Holdsworth, Adrian** (Scientist)
*The Voice of Cepheus* - Ken Appleby  *s*  202

**Holiday, Ben** (Ruler; Parent)
*The Tangle Box* - Terry Brooks  *f*  718
*Witches' Brew* - Terry Brooks  *f*  719

**Holl** (Mythical Creature)
*Higher Mythology* - Jody Lynn Nye  *f*  4170
*Mythology Abroad* - Jody Lynn Nye  *f*  4174

**Holland, Linda** (Teenager)
*Carnival* - William W. Johnstone  *h*  2927

**Holland, Martin** (Political Figure)
*Carnival* - William W. Johnstone  *h*  2927

**Holland, R. Paul** (Scientist)
*Infinity's Child* - Harry Stein  *h*  5250

**Holland, Susan** (Designer)
*The Beyond* - Barry Harrington  *h*  2556

**Hollander, Mariele** (Interior Decorator)
*Graythings* - Pat Graversen  *h*  2335

**Hollander, Tom** (Editor; Hippie)
*The Children of Hamelin* - Norman Spinrad  *s*  5170

**Holley, Charles Hardin** (Musician; Revolutionary)
*Back in the USSA* - Kim Newman  *s*  4095

**Holloway, Melissa** (Teenager)
*Second Child* - John Saul  *h*  4844

**Holly** (Computer)
*Red Dwarf: Infinity Welcomes Careful Drivers* - Grant
   Naylor  *s*  4077

**Holly, Wanda** (Spaceman)
*Starliner* - David Drake  *s*  1645

**Holman, Guy** (Teacher)
*Charmed Life* - Bernard Taylor  *h*  5399

**Holmes, Harry** (Detective—Police)
*Root of All Evil* - David A. Farrow  *h*  1888

**Holmes, Lori** (Young Woman)
*Lori* - Robert Bloch  *h*  536

**Holmes, Odetta** (Handicapped)
*The Waste Lands* - Stephen King  *h*  3143

**Holmes, Shadrach** (Spirit)
*Double Trouble Squared* - Kathryn Lasky  *f*  3340

**Holmes, Sherlock** (Detective—Private)
*The D. Case: The Truth about the Mystery of Edwin
   Drood* - Charles Dickens  *f*  1524
*The Holmes-Dracula File* - Fred
   Saberhagen  *h*  4767

**Holmes, Sherlock** (Detective—Private; Teenager)
*Muddle Earth* - John Brunner  *s*  735

**Holmes, Sherlock** (Detective—Private)
*Seance for a Vampire* - Fred Saberhagen  *h*  4773

**Holmes, Sherlock** (Detective—Private; Adventurer)
*Sherlock Holmes in Orbit* - Mike Resnick  *s*  4556

**Holscomb, Ray** (Teenager)
*Junkyard* - Barry Porter  *h*  4370

**Holser, Vax** (Military Personnel)
*Midshipman's Hope* - David Feintuch  *s*  1901

**Holt, Kenneth** (Streetperson)
*Wyrm Wolf* - Edo van Belkom  *h*  5535

**Holton, Clare** (Government Official)
*Dream Maker* - W.A. Harbinson  *s*  2542

**Holyhands, Dion** (Wizard)
*Fire Angels* - Jane Routley  *f*  4685

**Homer-R-ICK-3** (Clone; Troubleshooter)
*Extreme Paranoia: Nobody Knows the Trouble I've
   Shot* - Ken Rolston  *s*  4662

**Hong** (Nobleman; Villain)
*Interesting Times* - Terry Pratchett  *f*  4392

**Hong, Louie** (Cowboy)
*Hong on the Range* - William F. Wu  *s*  5997

**Honniker** (Advertising)
*Ferman's Devils* - Joe Clifford Faust  *s*  1892

**Hoo-Lan** (Alien)
*My Teacher Glows in the Dark* - Bruce
   Coville  *s*  1224

**Hood, Nicholas** (Artist)
*Cold Eye* - Giles Blunt  *h*  556

**Hood, Robin** (Outlaw; Hero)
*The Fantastic Adventures of Robin Hood* - Martin H.
   Greenberg  *f*  2389

**Hood, Robin** (Hero; Outlaw)
*The Oathbound Wizard* - Christopher
   Stasheff  *f*  5219

**Hood, Robin** (Outlaw; Hero)
*The Outlaws of Sherwood* - Robin
   McKinley  *f*  3846

**Hood, Robin** (Hero; Outlaw)
*Robin and the King* - Parke Godwin  *f*  2247
*The Sheriff of Nottingham* - Richard Kluger  *f*  3165

**Hood, Robin** (Artificial Intelligence)
*The Sherwood Game* - Esther Friesner  *s*  2082

**Hood, Virgil** (Detective)
*Noctet: Tales of Madonna-Moloch* - Albert J.
   Manachino  *h*  3613

**Hooded One** (Wizard)
*Lord of the Isles* - David Drake  *f*  1636

**Hook, James** (Pirate; Sea Captain)
*Hook* - Terry Brooks  *f*  713

**Hooker, Nicodemus** (Scientist)
*Kent Montana and the Really Ugly Thing From Mars* -
   Lionel Fenn  *s*  1918

**Hooker, Popeye** (Construction Worker)
*Orbital Decay* - Allen Steele  *s*  5246

**Hoover, Rod** (Salesman)
*Lethal Delivery* - J.G. Maxon  *h*  3695

**Hope, Mary** (Writer)
*A Gift upon the Shore* - M.K. Wren  s  5982

**Hopewell, Norman** (Religious)
*Darkman #3: The Gods of Hell* - Randall
Boyll  h  614

**Horace** (Mythical Creature; Telepath)
*Mouvar's Magic* - Piers Anthony  f  182

**Horatio** (Actor)
*Too, Too Solid Flesh* - Nick O'Donohoe  s  4197

**Hork** (Genetically Altered Being; Government
Official)
*Flux* - Stephen Baxter  s  399

**Horn, Alan** (Mercenary)
*Star Bridge* - James Gunn  s  2459

**Horn, Corran** (Military Personnel; Pilot)
*Rogue Squadron* - Michael A. Stackpole  s  5205

**Hornchurch, Anthony** (Servant; Detective—
Amateur)
*The Devil You Say* - Elisa DeCarlo  f  1450
*Strong Spirits* - Elisa DeCarlo  f  1451

**Horner, Jack** (Detective—Private)
*Angels & Visitations: A Miscellany* - Neil
Gaiman  f  2101

**Horsfall, Arne** (Patient)
*Fiends* - John Farris  h  1884

**Horta, Raul** (Wizard; FBI Agent)
*Doomsday Exam* - Nick Pollotta  f  4363

**Horton, Carol** (Lawyer)
*Althea* - Abigail McDaniels  h  3782

**Horton, Dabney** (Businessman)
*The Virginia Ghost Murders* - Leslie Raymond
Sachs  h  4778

**Horton, Holly** (Child)
*Althea* - Abigail McDaniels  h  3782

**Horton, Lisa** (Teenager)
*Althea* - Abigail McDaniels  h  3782

**Hoskins, Gerald** (Scientist)
*The Ugly Little Boy* - Isaac Asimov  s  250

**Houdini, Harry** (Magician; Historical Figure)
*Believe: A Novel* - William Shatner  f  4929
*Nevermore* - William Hjortsberg  h  2692

**Houston, Jackson** (Military Personnel)
*Wartide* - John Barnes  f  359

**Howard** (Worker)
*Toplin* - Michael McDowell  h  3807

**Howards, Tom** (Doctor)
*Dark Souls* - Barry Porter  h  4369

**Howe, Geena** (Teenager)
*Monet's Ghost* - Chelsea Quinn Yarbro  f  6017

**Howell, Clarence** (Military Personnel)
*Hour of the Scorpion* - Matthew J. Costello  s  1199

**Howgath, Lizzy** (Librarian)
*Kent Montana and the Reasonably Invisible Man* -
Lionel Fenn  s  1919

**Howie** (Animal)
*Return to Howliday Inn* - James Howe  f  2786

**Hoyland, Hugh** (Spaceman; Student)
*Silent Thunder/Universe* - Dean Ing  s  2829

**Hoyt, Father** (Religious)
*Hyperion* - Dan Simmons  s  5055

**Hph-wayuo "Alvin"** (Alien; Student)
*Brightness Reef* - David Brin  s  684

**Hph-wayuo "Alvin"** (Alien; Journalist)
*Heaven's Reach* - David Brin  s  687

**Hph-wayuo "Alvin"** (Alien; Teenager)
*Infinity's Shore* - David Brin  s  688

**Hr.Tyi.Bei.k.ai** (Alien; Royalty)
*Alien Tongue* - Stephen Leigh  s  3424

**Hrecker, Marcus Aurelius** (Scientist)
*Seeds of Destiny* - Thomas A. Easton  s  1724

**Hrluska, Jenn** (Doctor)
*Daughter of Darkness* - Steven Spruill  h  5183

**Hrrestan** (Alien; Political Figure)
*Treaty at Doona* - Anne McCaffrey  s  3752

**Hrriss** (Alien; Settler)
*Crisis on Doona* - Anne McCaffrey  s  3723

**H'sial, Atvar** (Alien; Businesswoman)
*Convergence* - Charles Sheffield  s  4951

**Hsing, Carlisle** (Detective—Private)
*Nightside City* - Lawrence Watt-Evans  s  5644

**Hu "Hugh"** (Musician; Parent)
*Shame of Man* - Piers Anthony  s  188

**Hubbard, Scott** (Spy; FBI Agent)
*The Eleventh Plague: A Novel of Medical Terror* -
John S. Marr  h  3632

**Hudder, Cyrus** (Parent; Scientist)
*Core* - Paul Preuss  s  4416

**Hudder, Leiden "Leidy"** (Scientist)
*Core* - Paul Preuss  s  4416

**Hudson, Aaron** (Civil Servant)
*Checkmate* - Eric T. Baker  s  297

**Hudson, Cal** (Producer; Religious)
*Symphony* - Adrian Savage  h  4847

**Hudson, Graham** (Producer)
*Glimpses* - Lewis Shiner  h  4997

**Huffington, Q-Jo** (Psychic)
*Half Asleep in Frog Pajamas* - Tom
Robbins  s  4606

**Huger, Willy** (Political Figure)
*Root of All Evil* - David A. Farrow  h  1888

**Hugh the Hand** (Criminal)
*Dragon Wing* - Margaret Weis  f  5709
*The Hand of Chaos* - Margaret Weis  f  5715
*Into the Labyrinth* - Margaret Weis  f  5716

**Hughes, Mary** (Spy)
*Charmed Life* - Bernard Taylor  h  5399

**Hugo** (Scientist)
*Outer Space and All That Junk* - Mel
Gilden  s  2227

**Hujgens, Kees** (Architect)
*The Final Diary Entry of Kees Hujgens* - William R.
Stotler  h  5317

**Hulhe** (Farmer; Scholar)
*When the Gods Are Silent* - Jane M.
Lindskold  f  3477

**Hull, Jake** (Detective—Police)
*Night Hunter* - Michael Reaves  h  4496

**Hume, Edna "Aten"** (Genetically Altered Being;
Telepath)
*GodHeads* - Emily Devenport  s  1501

**Humfrey** (Magician)
*Question Quest* - Piers Anthony  f  186

**Humidyear VII, Fivetide** (Military Personnel)
*Excession* - Iain M. Banks  s  324

**Hummingbird, Kinsey** (Mechanic)
*Drawing Blood* - Poppy Z. Brite  h  694

**Humphrey** (Alien)
*Time, Like an Ever-Rolling Stream* - Judith
Moffett  s  3944

**Hunnul** (Animal; Telepath)
*Valorian* - Mary H. Herbert  f  2677

**Hunsacker, Matt** (Vampire)
*Blind Hunger* - David Darke  h  1352

**Hunsacker, Patty** (Widow(er); Handicapped)
*Blind Hunger* - David Darke  h  1352

**Hunsucker, Willie** (Cyborg)
*Gaia's Toys* - Rebecca Ore  s  4218

**Hunt, Gregory** (Doctor; Scientist)
*Tech-Heaven* - Linda Nagata  s  4066

**Hunt, Katie** (Museum Curator)
*The Trickster* - Muriel Gray  h  2340

**Hunt, Michael** (Spy)
*Name of the Beast* - Daniel Easterman  h  1721

**Hunt, Nicholas "Pygmalion"** (Mythical Creature)
*Evil Triumphant* - Michael A. Stackpole  s  5199

**Hunt, Sam** (Maintenance Worker; Indian)
*The Trickster* - Muriel Gray  h  2340

**Hunt, Victor** (Scientist)
*Entoverse* - James P. Hogan  s  2724

**Hunter** (Robot; Detective)
*Dictator* - William F. Wu  s  5996
*Predator* - William F. Wu  s  5998

**Hunter** (Pioneer)
*Twilight of the Empire* - Simon R. Green  s  2374

**Hunter** (Robot; Detective)
*Warrior* - William F. Wu  s  6000

**Hunter, Cara Diana** (Adventurer)
*Into the Land of the Unicorns* - Bruce
Coville  f  1219

**Hunter, Gregory** (Military Personnel)
*Blood Alone* - Elaine Bergstrom  h  462

**Hunter, Harold "Randy" Randolph** (Space Explorer;
Businessman)
*Timemaster* - Robert L. Forward  s  1992

**Hunter, Homer** (Spaceman)
*Stationfall* - Arthur Byron Cover  s  1216

**Hunter, Lucel** (Mercenary; Genetically Altered
Being)
*The Centurion's Empire* - Sean McMullen  s  3854

**Hunter, Max** (Businessman)
*Blood Secrets* - Karen E. Taylor  h  5406

**Hunter, Nicole "Panther"** (Administrator;
Astronaut)
*Ignition* - Kevin J. Anderson  s  107

**Hunter, Scott** (Military Personnel; Scout)
*Hellworld* - Simon R. Green  s  2371

**Hunter, Travis** (Military Personnel)
*Search and Destroy* - Keith William
Andrews  s  141
*Sink the Armada* - Keith William Andrews  s  142
*Treason in Time* - Keith William Andrews  s  143

**Huru** (Young Woman)
*The Adventures of Huru on the Road to Baghdad* -
Guneli Gun  f  2457

**Huston, Noah** (Doctor)
*Monday's Child* - Patricia Wallace  h  5623

**Hutchings, Ian McFarland** (Scientist; Leader)
*Fortress on the Sun* - Paul Cook  s  1157

**Hutchins, Priscilla "Hutch"** (Spacewoman; Pilot)
*The Engines of God* - Jack McDevitt  s  3787

**Hutchinson, Lisa** (Assistant)
*All Things under the Moon* - Robert
Morgan  h  4002
*The Things That Are Not There* - Robert
Morgan  h  4007

**Hutsenreiter, Skirlet** (Noblewoman; Investigator)
*Night Lamp* - Jack Vance  s  5548

**Hutton, Andrew** (Scientist)
*Earthling* - Tony Daniel  s  1336

**Hutton, George** (Engineer; Industrialist)
*Earth* - David Brin  s  685

**Huxley, Christian** (Adventurer)
*Gate of Ivory, Gate of Horn* - Robert
  Holdstock   f   2737

**Huxley, Dorothy** (Librarian)
*Rune* - Christopher Fowler   h   2020

**Huxley, Lenina** (Police Officer)
*Demolition Man* - Richard Osborne   s   4229

**Hyde** (Criminal)
*The Darker Passions: Dr. Jekyll and Mr. Hyde* -
  Amarantha Knight   h   3178

**Hyland, Morn** (Police Officer)
*Forbidden Knowledge* - Stephen R.
  Donaldson   s   1571
*The Gap into Conflict: The Real Story* - Stephen R.
  Donaldson   s   1572

**Hyland, Morn** (Police Officer; Prisoner)
*The Gap into Madness: Chaos and Order* - Stephen R.
  Donaldson   s   1573

**Hyland, Morn** (Police Officer)
*The Gap into Power: A Dark and Hungry God Arises*
  - Stephen R. Donaldson   s   1574
*The Gap into Ruin: This Day All Gods Die* - Stephen
  R. Donaldson   s   1575

**Hynde, Lucas** (Truck Driver)
*The Black Mariah* - Jay R. Bonansinga   h   570


## I

**I** (Writer)
*The Broken Goddess* - Hans Bemmann   f   439

**I** (Royalty; Orphan)
*A City in Winter* - Mark Helprin   f   2653

**I** (Writer)
*Dance Dance Dance* - Haruki Murakami   s   4046
*Flying Saucers over Hennepin* - Peter
  Gelman   f   2186

**I** (Writer; Computer Expert)
*Hard-Boiled Wonderland and the End of the World* -
  Haruki Murakami   s   4047

**I** (Writer; Explorer)
*I Who Have Never Known Men* - Jacqueline
  Harpman   s   2554

**I** (Writer; Student)
*Ishmael* - Daniel Quinn   s   4455

**I** (Human)
*My Cousin, My Gastroenterologist* - Mark
  Leyner   s   3456

**I** (Writer; Artisan)
*Time and the Clock Mice, Etcetera* - Peter
  Dickinson   f   1527

**I** (Writer; Military Personnel)
*The Veils of Snows* - Mark Helprin   f   2654

**I** (Writer)
*The Wall* - Marlen Haushofer   s   2603

**I "Laundry"** (Writer)
*Dead Voices: Natural Agonies in the Real World* -
  Gerald Vizenor   f   5578

**Iban** (Psychic)
*Sing the Warmth* - Louise Marley   s   3630

**ibn Khairan, Ammar** (Military Personnel; Courtier)
*The Lions of Al-Rassan* - Guy Gavriel Kay   f   3016

**ibn-Rushd, Damon** (Businessman; Traveler)
*Destiny's Road* - Larry Niven   s   4119

**Ice** (Divorced Person; Villain)
*Chaos Come Again* - Wilhelmina Baird   s   293

**Icefalcon** (Military Personnel; Indian)
*Icefalcon's Quest* - Barbara Hambly   f   2504

**Icor, Gella** (Spaceship Captain)
*Starfire Down* - Lee McKeone   s   3830

**Idera** (Indian; Warrior)
*Dark Legend* - Jamake Highwater   f   2686

**Iezu** (Demon)
*Crown of Shadows* - C.S. Friedman   s   2057

**Iff** (Mythical Creature)
*Haroun and the Sea of Stories* - Salman
  Rushdie   f   4731

**Iger** (Spaceman; Smuggler)
*The War Minstrels* - Karen Haber   s   2477

**Igor** (Handicapped; Adventurer)
*Goblins in the Castle* - Bruce Coville   f   1218

**Igraine** (Revolutionary)
*The Rising of the Moon* - Flynn Connolly   s   1135

**ih'iie-u Ulak!ha', Hwii** (Alien; Scientist)
*Dark Mirror* - Diane Duane   s   1658

**Ilisidi** (Alien)
*Foreigner* - C.J. Cherryh   s   990

**Ilisidi** (Alien; Ruler)
*Inheritor* - C.J. Cherryh   s   997

**Illyan, Simon** (Government Official)
*Memory* - Lois McMaster Bujold   s   761

**Ilya** (Guard; Adventurer)
*Firebird* - Mercedes Lackey   f   3281

**Imbri, Mare** (Animal; Companion)
*Faun & Games* - Piers Anthony   f   169

**Immugio** (Mythical Creature; Wizard)
*Final Sacrifice* - Clayton Emery   f   1814

**Impossumble** (Animal; Magician)
*An Impossumble Summer* - Brenda W.
  Clough   f   1090

**Impresario, Throng** (Entertainer)
*Past Imperative* - Dave Duncan   f   1684

**Incarnadine** (Royalty; Magician)
*Bride of the Castle* - John DeChancie   s   1452
*Castle Dreams* - John DeChancie   s   1453
*Castle War!* - John DeChancie   s   1455

**Inconnu, Jane "Jade" Avril** (Journalist)
*Sam Gunn, Unlimited* - Ben Bova   s   593

**Inda, Sinykin** (Doctor; Psychic)
*Mentor* - Kris Jensen   s   2898

**Indergard, Cejo** (Settler)
*The Dazzle of Day* - Molly Gloss   s   2243

**Indes, Richenza** (Noblewoman)
*The Wild Hunt: Vengeance Moon* - Jocelin
  Foxe   f   2031

**Indian** (Time Traveler; Mythical Creature)
*An Exaltation of Larks* - Robert Reed   s   4506

**Indian, John** (Slave; Spouse)
*I, Tituba, Black Witch of Salem* - Maryse
  Conde   f   1130

**Indigo** (Outcast)
*Aisling* - Louise Cooper   f   1172
*Avatar* - Louise Cooper   f   1173

**Indigo** (Adventurer)
*Dragon War* - Laurence Yep   f   6025

**Indigo** (Outcast)
*Infanta* - Louise Cooper   f   1176
*Revenant* - Louise Cooper   f   1178
*Troika* - Louise Cooper   f   1181

**Indigo** (Musician; Teenager)
*The Unicorn Sonata* - Peter S. Beagle   f   412

**Indiw** (Alien; Spaceship Captain)
*Border Dispute* - Daniel R. Kerns   s   3066

**Ineluki the Storm King** (Ruler; Alien)
*Stone of Farewell* - Tad Williams   f   5831

**Infinity** (Mythical Creature)
*Unicorn Highway* - David Lee Jones   f   2941

**Ingalls, Ray** (Police Officer)
*The Devil's Laughter* - William W.
  Johnstone   h   2930

**Inge** (Witch)
*Quest for a Maid* - Frances Mary Hendry   f   2662

**Ingersol, William "Bogey"** (Businessman; Animal)
*Top Dog* - Jerry Jay Carroll   f   915

**Ingersoll, Austin** (Advertising)
*Throat Sprockets* - Tim Lucas   h   3541

**Ingham, Justine** (Singer; Artificial Intelligence)
*Circuit of Heaven* - Dennis Danvers   s   1348

**Ingledew, Sam** (Animal)
*The Cockroaches of Stay More* - Donald
  Harington   f   2544

**Ingles, Benton** (Industrialist; Villain)
*Outworld Cats* - Jack Lovejoy   s   3536

**Inglorion, Ingold** (Wizard)
*Icefalcon's Quest* - Barbara Hambly   f   2504
*Mother of Winter* - Barbara Hambly   f   2506

**Ingman, Robert "Shade"** (Disembodied Personality)
*Shade's Children* - Garth Nix   s   4130

**Ingoldesdaughter, Berika** (Shepherd; Sorceress)
*Beneath the Web* - Lynn Abbey   f   12

**Ingoldesdaughter, Berika** (Shepherd; Runaway)
*The Wooden Sword* - Lynn Abbey   f   18

**Ingolfsson, Gwendolyn** (Genetically Altered Being)
*Drakon* - S.M. Stirling   s   5294

**Ingolfsson, Yolande** (Royalty)
*The Stone Dogs* - S.M. Stirling   s   5300

**Inhetep, Setne** (Wizard; Religious)
*The Anubis Murders* - Gary Gygax   f   2472
*Death in Delhi* - Gary Gygax   f   2473

**Inman, Toby** (Television Personality; Journalist)
*Pictures at 11* - Norman Spinrad   s   5173

**Innisfree, Merle "Myrddin"** (Wizard)
*The Rebirth of Wonder* - Lawrence Watt-
  Evans   f   5646

**Innowen** (Handicapped; Dancer)
*Shadowdance* - Robin Wayne Bailey   f   290

**Inosolan "Inos"** (Royalty)
*Emperor and Clown* - Dave Duncan   f   1676
*Faery Lands Forlorn* - Dave Duncan   f   1677
*Magic Casement* - Dave Duncan   f   1683
*Perilous Seas* - Dave Duncan   f   1685

**Inya** (Recluse; Sorceress)
*Kar Kalim* - Deborah Christian   f   1025

**Iowyn** (Royalty; Warrior)
*Tears of Time* - Nancy Asire   f   256

**Iphigenia, Alusz** (Companion; Fugitive)
*The Demon Princes: Volume One* - Jack
  Vance   s   5544

**Iquar, Kryx** (Alien; Psychic)
*Catch the Lightning* - Catherine Asaro   s   218

**ir Var, Zorn** (Heir—Dispossessed; Fugitive)
*Demon Moon* - Jack Williamson   s   5862

**Iranaputra, Victor** (Aged Person; Adventurer)
*Codgerspace* - Alan Dean Foster   s   1999

**Iris** (Royalty)
*Geis of the Gargoyle* - Piers Anthony   f   172

**Irith** (Mythical Creature; Magician)
*Taking Flight* - Lawrence Watt-Evans   f   5650

**Ironhart, Jim** (Teacher)
*Cold Fire* - Dean R. Koontz   h   3203

**Ironsmith, Frank** (Engineer)
*The Humanoids* - Jack Williamson   s   5865

**Irrylath** (Royalty)
*The Pearl of the Soul of the World* - Meredith Ann Pierce   *f*   4318

**Irsei, Corum Jhaelen** (Royalty; Wizard)
*Corum: The Coming of Chaos* - Michael Moorcock   *f*   3978

**Irtuk-Saa** (Alien; Ruler)
*The Triad Worlds* - F.M. Busby   *s*   786

**Isabeau** (Apprentice; Adventurer)
*The Witches of Eileanan* - Kate Forsyth   *f*   1984

**Isaf** (Warrior)
*The Fortress of Eternity* - Andrew Whitmore   *f*   5790

**Isbetta** (Artisan)
*Curse of the Black Heron* - Holly Lisle   *f*   3479

**Isham, Evi** (Genetically Altered Being; Human)
*Emperors of the Twilight* - S. Andrew Swann   *s*   5362

**Ishikawa, Keiko** (Scientist; Space Explorer)
*Imbalance* - V.E. Mitchell   *s*   3919

**Ishimaru, Kazumasa** (Engineer)
*Through the Arc of the Rain Forest* - Karen Tei Yamashita   *f*   6008

**Ishmael** (Animal; Telepath)
*Ishmael* - Daniel Quinn   *s*   4455
*My Ishmael* - Daniel Quinn   *s*   4456

**Islay, Arran "Henry Martyn"** (Leader)
*Bretta Martyn* - L. Neil Smith   *s*   5128

**Islay, Arran "Henry Martyn"** (Heir—Dispossessed; Pirate)
*Henry Martyn* - L. Neil Smith   *s*   5131

**Islay, Robretta "Bretta Martyn"** (Teenager)
*Bretta Martyn* - L. Neil Smith   *s*   5128

**Islief the Watcher** (Mythical Creature)
*A Child of Elvish* - Nancy Varian Berberick   *f*   457

**Italiano, Dorothy** (Researcher)
*A Reasonable World* - Damon Knight   *s*   3188

**Ithariel** (Sorceress)
*The Master of Whitestorm* - Janny Wurts   *f*   6003

**Ivanova, Sonya** (Linguist; Political Figure)
*Russian Spring* - Norman Spinrad   *s*   5174

**Ivanova, Susan** (Leader; Spacewoman)
*The Touch of Your Shadow, the Whisper of Your Name* - Neal Barrett Jr.   *s*   367

**Ivanova, Susan** (Military Personnel; Telepath)
*Voices* - John Vornholt   *s*   5598

**Ivar** (Warrior)
*The Hammer and the Cross* - Harry Harrison   *f*   2570

**Ivard** (Pirate)
*Ruler of Naught* - Sherwood Smith   *s*   5141

**Ives, Bobby** (Veteran; Werewolf)
*The Nightwalker* - Thomas Tessier   *h*   5442

**Ivy** (Royalty; Sorceress)
*Man From Mundania* - Piers Anthony   *f*   180

**Ix** (Religious)
*Earth Made of Glass* - John Barnes   *s*   351

**Iz** (Teenager; Gang Member)
*Random Acts of Senseless Violence* - Jack Womack   *f*   5959

**Izakar "Izzy"** (Linguist; Time Traveler)
*The Family Tree* - Sheri S. Tepper   *s*   5429

**Izeki, Hitedoro** (Police Officer)
*Anvil* - Nicolas van Pallandt   *s*   5540

**Izmailova, Ekaterina** (Scientist; Leader)
*Griffin's Egg* - Michael Swanwick   *s*   5370

# J

**ja N'Wook, Chrysamen "Chrys"** (Time Traveler; Warrior)
*Caesar's Bicycle* - John Barnes   *s*   350

**Jaad** (Reincarnated Person; Magician)
*Ronin* - D.A. Heeley   *f*   2639

**Jabba the Hutt** (Organized Crime Figure; Alien)
*Tales From Jabba's Palace* - Kevin J. Anderson   *s*   114

**Jack** (Teenager)
*After the Blue* - Russel Like   *s*   3465

**Jack** (Baker; Sorcerer)
*The Baker's Boy* - J.V. Jones   *f*   2956

**Jack** (Artist; Companion)
*The Caterpillar's Question* - Piers Anthony   *f*   164

**Jack** (Traveler; Agent)
*The End-of-Everything Man* - Tom De Haven   *f*   1421

**Jack** (Addict)
*The Hanged Man* - Francesca Lia Block   *f*   548

**Jack** (Traveler)
*The Last Human* - Tom De Haven   *f*   1422

**Jack** (Magician; Adventurer)
*The Loneliest Magician* - Irene Radford   *f*   4461

**Jack** (Mentally Ill Person)
*Lunatics* - Bradley Denton   *f*   1491

**Jack** (Sorcerer; Hero)
*A Man Betrayed* - J.V. Jones   *f*   2958
*Master and Fool* - J.V. Jones   *f*   2959

**Jack** (Traveler)
*Walker of Worlds* - Tom De Haven   *f*   1423

**Jack the Bodiless** (Psychic; Relative)
*Magnificat* - Julian May   *s*   3699

**Jack the Ripper** (Serial Killer)
*A Night in the Lonesome October* - Roger Zelazny   *h*   6072

**Jackson, Andrew** (Teacher)
*Spirit Crossings* - Claudia Peck   *f*   4275

**Jackson, Beauregard** (Child)
*Never Land* - Douglas Clegg   *h*   1081

**Jackson, Carl** (Adventurer)
*Dragon Burning* - Craig Shaw Gardner   *f*   2126

**Jackson, Daniel** (Scientist)
*Reconnaissance* - Bill McCay   *s*   3769

**Jackson, Daniel** (Linguist; Scholar)
*StarGate* - Dean Devlin   *s*   1509

**Jackson, Jack** (Astronaut)
*The Stars Must Wait* - Keith Laumer   *s*   3346

**Jackson, Jocelyn** (Artist)
*Water Rites* - Guy N. Smith   *h*   5121

**Jackson, Kendall** (Vampire)
*The Devil's Advocate* - Gherbod Fleming   *h*   1949

**Jackson, Portis** (Banker)
*Dumford Blood* - S.K. Epperson   *h*   1829

**Jackson, Skeeter** (Con Artist; Time Traveler)
*Wagers of Sin* - Robert Asprin   *s*   264

**Jacob** (Spy)
*Falcon* - Emma Bull   *s*   768

**Jacobi, Henry** (Engineer; Anthropologist)
*The Engines of God* - Jack McDevitt   *s*   3787

**Jacobs, Earl** (Con Artist)
*Less than Human* - Gary L. Raisor   *h*   4464

**Jacobs, Peter** (Journalist)
*The Cold One* - Christopher Pike   *h*   4327

**Jacobs, Sammy** (Child)
*My Best Friend Is Invisible* - R.L. Stine   *h*   5289

**Jacobs, Simon** (Child)
*My Best Friend Is Invisible* - R.L. Stine   *h*   5289

**Jacobs-Wolde, Jessica** (Journalist)
*My Soul to Keep* - Tannarive Due   *h*   1670

**Jacobson, Auston** (Saloon Keeper/Owner)
*Vampire Diary: The Embrace* - Robert Weinberg   *h*   5705

**Jacoby** (Scientist)
*Virus Clans* - Michael Kanaly   *s*   3008

**Jacoby, Daniel** (Teenager)
*The Wall Around Eden* - Joan Slonczewski   *s*   5092

**Jacoby, Darcy** (Student—College)
*Wendigo Border* - Catherine Montrose   *h*   3967

**Jacqueline** (Businesswoman)
*Human Resources* - Floyd Kemske   *h*   3057

**Jade** (Spirit)
*Familiar Spirit* - Lisa Tuttle   *h*   5519

**Jael** (Mythical Creature; Royalty)
*Dagger's Edge* - Anne Logston   *f*   3508

**Jaeme** (Nobleman)
*Elfwood* - Rose Estes   *f*   1837

**Jaeme** (Noblewoman; Warrior)
*Twisted Dragon* - Kevin Stein   *f*   5251

**Jaffe, Randolph** (Postal Worker)
*The Great and Secret Show* - Clive Barker   *h*   341

**Jaffey** (Engineer; Computer Expert)
*Zeta Base* - Judith Alguire   *s*   74

**Jagoda, Barbara** (Model)
*Chicago Loop* - Paul Theroux   *h*   5443

**Jagoda, Parker** (Architect)
*Chicago Loop* - Paul Theroux   *h*   5443

**Jagun** (Genetically Altered Being; Guide)
*Golden Trillium* - Andre Norton   *f*   4153

**Jahdo** (Child; Adventurer)
*Days of Blood and Fire* - Katharine Kerr   *f*   3068

**Jahns, Carter** (Engineer; Administrator)
*Mars Underground* - William Hartmann   *s*   2584

**Jaimah** (Servant)
*The Apprentice* - Deborah Talmadge-Bickmore   *f*   5382

**Jaimie** (Computer Expert)
*Second Contact* - Mike Resnick   *s*   4555

**Jaishree/Minaz** (Artist; Model)
*Beauty* - Brian D'Amato   *h*   1334

**Jakan** (Demon)
*Rage of a Demon King* - Raymond E. Feist   *f*   1908

**Jake** (Hunter)
*Nicoji* - M. Shayne Bell   *s*   434

**Jake** (Criminal)
*Terraplane* - Jack Womack   *s*   5960

**Jake** (Criminal; Fugitive)
*Further Adventures* - Jon Stephen Fink   *f*   1940

**Jakobi, Virgil** (Artist)
*The Quicksilver Screen* - Don H. DeBrandt   *s*   1449

**Jakobot "Jacko" 490,9000** (Robot; Sidekick)
*Extreme Paranoia: Nobody Knows the Trouble I've Shot* - Ken Rolston   *s*   4662

**Jakri** (Psychic; Singer)
*Receive the Gift* - Louise Marley   *s*   3628

**Jalanopi** (Alien; Leader)
*Purgatory: A Chronicle of a Distant World* - Mike Resnick   *s*   4554

**Jaldis the Blind** (Wizard)
*The Rainbow Abyss* - Barbara Hambly   *f*   2507

**Jamail, Dierdre** (Explorer)
*Delta Pavonis* - Eric Kotani  s  3221

**Jamal** (Actress)
*Masquerades* - Kate Novak  f  4166

**Jamas** (Royalty; Leader)
*No One Noticed the Cat* - Anne McCaffrey  f  3740

**James** (Teenager)
*The Dying Sun* - Gary L. Blackwood  s  511

**James, Cullen** (Writer)
*A Child Across the Sky* - Jonathan Carroll  h  917

**James, Dallas** (Actress)
*Spirit Catcher* - Elizabeth Hallam  f  2497

**James, Dede** (Judge)
*The Between* - Tannarive Due  h  1669

**James, Henderson** (Scientist)
*Over the River & through the Woods* - Clifford D. Simak  s  5047

**James, Henry** (Writer; Historical Figure)
*The Haunting of Lamb House* - Joan Aiken  h  45

**James, Hilton** (Social Worker)
*The Between* - Tannarive Due  h  1669

**James, Joshua** (Professor)
*Darkborn* - Matthew J. Costello  h  1195

**James, Julie** (Teenager)
*I Know What You Did Last Summer* - Lois Duncan  h  1692

**James, Mike** (Student)
*The Orchid Eater* - Marc Laidlaw  h  3312

**James, Raglan** (Supernatural Being)
*The Tale of the Body Thief* - Anne Rice  h  4576

**James, Will** (Immortal; Publisher)
*Warpath* - Tony Daniel  s  1337

**James, Zack** (Computer Expert; Artist)
*Blood Work* - Fay Zachary  h  6050

**James-B-OND-1** (Clone; Security Officer)
*Title Deleted for Security Reasons* - Ed Blome  h  553

**Jameson, Charles** (Businessman)
*Between Floors* - Thomas F. Monteleone  h  3957

**Jameson, Gary** (Trapper)
*Pelts* - F. Paul Wilson  h  5894

**Jamie** (Military Personnel)
*Alien Dreams* - Larry Segriff  s  4910

**Jamie** (Musician)
*Cowboy Feng's Space Bar and Grille* - Steven Brust  s  740

**Jamil/Alasil** (Military Personnel; Spy)
*The Watcher's Mask* - Laurie J. Marks  f  3627

**Jamison, Diane** (FBI Agent)
*Infectress* - Tom Cool  s  1167

**Jane** (Waiter/Waitress)
*Animals* - John Skipp  h  5080

**Jane** (Artificial Intelligence; Deity)
*Children of the Mind* - Orson Scott Card  s  883

**Jane** (Artificial Intelligence)
*Xenocide* - Orson Scott Card  s  899

**Jane "Quicksilver"** (Outlaw; Psychic)
*Quicksilver's Knight* - Christopher Stasheff  f  5220

**Janeway, Kathryn** (Student; Leader)
*The Chance Factor* - Diana G. Gallagher  s  2109

**Janeway, Kathryn** (Spaceship Captain; Military Personnel; Space Explorer)
*Chrysalis* - David Niall Wilson  s  5880
*The Escape* - Dean Wesley Smith  s  5113

**Janeway, Kathryn** (Spaceship Captain; Space Explorer; Military Personnel)
*The Final Fury* - Dafydd ab Hugh  s  9

**Janeway, Kathryn** (Spaceship Captain; Military Personnel; Space Explorer)
*Her Klingon Soul* - Michael Jan Friedman  s  2064

**Janeway, Kathryn** (Spaceship Captain; Space Explorer; Military Personnel)
*Mosaic* - Jeri Taylor  s  5403

**Janeway, Kathryn** (Spaceship Captain; Military Personnel; Space Explorer)
*Ragnarok* - Nathan Archer  s  206

**Janeway, Lewis** (Detective—Police)
*Trinity Grove* - David van Meter Smith  h  5112

**Jankowitz, Sheldon** (Student; Wizard)
*User Unfriendly* - Vivian Vande Velde  f  5558

**Janna** (Linguist; Traveler)
*Mission Child* - Maureen F. McHugh  s  3819

**Janos, Teodor** (Social Worker)
*The Death of Sleep* - Anne McCaffrey  s  3727

**Janozek, Magda** (Teenager)
*Flare Star* - Paula E. Downing  s  1594

**Jansen, Karen** (Doctor)
*Blade* - Mel Odom  h  4190

**Jansky, Thalia** (Spacewoman; Castaway)
*White Light* - William Barton  s  384

**Janszoon, Jozef P.** (Architect)
*The Final Diary Entry of Kees Hujgens* - William R. Stotler  h  5317

**Janusz, Ekaterina "Kate" Marya** (Spacewoman; Gypsy)
*Maia's Veil* - P.K. McAllister  s  3707

**Janusz, Pov** (Spaceship Captain; Gypsy)
*Maia's Veil* - P.K. McAllister  s  3707
*Orion's Dagger* - P.K. McAllister  s  3708
*Siduri's Net* - P.K. McAllister  s  3709

**Jaqueth, Falcon** (Knight)
*The Falcon and the Serpent* - Cheryl A. Smith  f  5101

**Jared** (Genetically Altered Being; Leader)
*The Alleluia Files* - Sharon Shinn  s  4999

**Jared** (Mythical Creature)
*A Call to Arms* - Thomas K. Martin  f  3650

**Jarnhann, Nils** (Telepath; Warrior)
*The Yngling and the Circle of Power* - John Dalmas  s  1328
*The Yngling in Yamato* - John Dalmas  s  1329

**Jarrat, Kevin** (Military Personnel; Homosexual)
*Death's Head* - Mel Keegan  s  3029

**Jarrett, Ma** (Psychic)
*Lucifer's Eye* - Hugh B. Cave  h  943

**Jarrett, Syd** (Worker)
*Animals* - John Skipp  h  5080

**Jarrod** (Government Official)
*Earthling* - Tony Daniel  s  1336

**Jarrow, Richard** (Military Personnel; Experimental Subject)
*The Multiplex Man* - James P. Hogan  s  2727

**Jarrow, Tod** (Serial Killer)
*Evil Reincarnate* - Leigh Clark  h  1050

**Jarry, Alfred** (Historical Figure; Writer)
*Night of the Cooters* - Howard Waldrop  s  5614

**Jarth, Christopher** (Leader; Military Personnel)
*Escape to the Wind* - Jennifer DiMarco  s  1559

**Jaryd** (Wizard)
*Children of Amarid* - David B. Coe  f  1095

**Jasmine "Jas"** (Pilot; Mythical Creature)
*Finder's Bane* - Kate Novak  f  4165

**JASON** (Computer)
*Golden Fleece* - Robert J. Sawyer  s  4857

**Jason** (Mythical Creature; Human)
*Master of Many Treasures* - Mary Brown  f  726

**Jasper** (Servant; Student)
*Murder in Cormyr* - Chet Williamson  f  5848

**Jathondi** (Royalty)
*The Gates of Twilight* - Paula Volsky  f  5581

**Javas** (Royalty)
*To Save the Sun* - Ben Bova  s  596

**Javere "Javerri"** (Noblewoman; Martial Arts Expert)
*Ladylord* - Sasha Miller  f  3906

**Javobo** (Alien; Bounty Hunter)
*Mainline* - Deborah Christian  s  1026

**Jax** (Artist)
*The City, Not Long After* - Pat Murphy  s  4051

**Jaxom** (Nobleman)
*All the Weyrs of Pern* - Anne McCaffrey  s  3719

**Jayal** (Nobleman; Hero; Knight)
*The Forging of the Shadows* - Oliver Johnson  f  2924

**Jayal** (Knight; Nobleman; Hero)
*Nations of the Night* - Oliver Johnson  f  2925

**Jayge** (Trader)
*The Renegades of Pern* - Anne McCaffrey  s  3746

**Jaylor** (Wizard)
*The Glass Dragon* - Irene Radford  f  4460

**Jaynes, Jennifer** (Pilot)
*In the Shadows of the Moonglade* - Riley St. James  h  5186

**Jayson, Darby** (Journalist)
*The Homecoming* - Kimberly Rangel  h  4471

**Jazen** (Sorcerer)
*The Courts of Sorcery* - Ashley McConnell  f  3773
*The Fountains of Mirlacca* - Ashley McConnell  f  3775

**Jean-Claude** (Vampire)
*Bloody Bones* - Laurell K. Hamilton  h  2512

**Jean-Claude** (Vampire; Businessman)
*Burnt Offerings* - Laurell K. Hamilton  h  2514

**Jean-Claude** (Vampire)
*Circus of the Damned* - Laurell K. Hamilton  h  2515

**Jean-Claude** (Vampire; Leader)
*The Killing Dance* - Laurell K. Hamilton  h  2518

**Jean-Claude** (Vampire)
*The Laughing Corpse* - Laurell K. Hamilton  f  2519

**Jed** (Teenager)
*Armageddon Summer* - Jane Yolen  s  6028

**Jed** (Alien; Reanimated Dead)
*Jed the Dead* - Alan Dean Foster  s  2007

**Jeeves** (Servant)
*Scream for Jeeves: A Parody* - P.H. Cannon  h  867

**Jeff** (Student—Middle School)
*On Meeting Witches at Wells* - Judith Gorog  f  2283

**Jeffers, Anne** (Journalist)
*Black Lightning* - John Saul  h  4837

**Jeffers, Glen** (Architect)
*Black Lightning* - John Saul  h  4837

**Jefferson, David Steven** (Military Personnel)
*The Galactic Silver Star* - Kevin D. Randle  s  4468
*Jefferson's War: Death of a Regiment* - Kevin Randle  s  4466

**Jefferson, Thomas** (Diplomat; Historical Figure)
*Arc d'X* - Steve Erickson  f  1835

**Jeffrey** (Mythical Creature; Teenager)
*Clan of the Shape-Changers* - Robert Levy  f  3446

**Jeffries, S.C.** (Doctor)
*Voyage to the Red Planet* - Terry Bisson  *s*  508

**Jekyll, Henry** (Doctor)
*The Darker Passions: Dr. Jekyll and Mr. Hyde* -
Amarantha Knight  *h*  3178
*Mary Reilly* - Valerie Martin  *h*  3654

**Jelinsky, Debbie** (Child-Care Giver; Criminal)
*Addams Family Values* - Todd Strasser  *f*  5324

**Jellico, Miceal** (Spaceship Captain; Trader)
*Redline the Stars* - Andre Norton  *s*  4160

**Jemeret** (Psychic)
*Commencement* - Roby James  *s*  2877

**Jemson "Jem"** (Royalty)
*The One-Armed Queen* - Jane Yolen  *f*  6037

**Jen** (Royalty)
*The Remarkable Journey of Prince Jen* - Lloyd
Alexander  *f*  69

**Jenk, Gottfried** (Scholar)
*Goblin Moon* - Teresa Edgerton  *f*  1743

**Jenkins, Obadiah** (Religious; Diplomat)
*Branch and Crown* - Gael Baudino  *f*  389
*O Greenest Branch!* - Gael Baudino  *f*  394

**Jenkins, Peter** (Spaceship Captain)
*Limbo System* - Rick Cook  *s*  1158

**Jenkins, Tom** (Military Personnel; Pilot)
*Alien Dreams* - Larry Segriff  *s*  4910

**Jenkins, Tom** (Orphan)
*Spacer Dreams* - Larry Segriff  *s*  4911

**Jenna** (Ruler; Warrior)
*The One-Armed Queen* - Jane Yolen  *f*  6037

**Jenna** (Orphan; Heroine)
*Sister Light, Sister Dark* - Jane Yolen  *f*  6039

**Jenna** (Alien; Disembodied Personality)
*Stranded* - Camarin Grae  *s*  2295

**Jenna** (Orphan; Heroine)
*White Jenna* - Jane Yolen  *f*  6041

**Jennedote, Yaji** (Sorceress; Student)
*Fire in the Mist* - Holly Lisle  *f*  3482

**Jennings, Patricia** (Professor)
*The Taking* - Donald Beman  *h*  438

**Jennings, Richard** (Disembodied Personality)
*Darkly the Thunder* - William W.
Johnstone  *h*  2929

**Jenny Sixa** (Telepath; Detective)
*Circle of One* - Eric James Fullilove  *s*  2092

**Jephthah** (Activist)
*To Fear the Light* - Ben Bova  *s*  595

**Jeremiah** (Activist; Terrorist)
*The Quiet Pools* - Michael P. Kube-
McDowell  *s*  3249

**Jeremy** (Writer)
*Black Dogs* - Ian McEwan  *h*  3808

**Jeremy, Clark** (Religious; Television Personality)
*Blood Siege* - G. Harry Stine  *s*  5278

**Jerno** (Royalty; Leader)
*Wrath of the Princes* - Holly Lisle  *f*  3490

**Jerod** (Child)
*The Wild Hunt* - Jane Yolen  *f*  6042

**Jervis, Katherine** (Secretary)
*Milton in America* - Peter Ackroyd  *f*  25

**Jeryl** (Alien)
*Mentor* - Kris Jensen  *s*  2898

**Jes** (Mercenary)
*Hope of Earth* - Piers Anthony  *s*  175

**Jess** (Animal; Young Woman)
*Changespell* - Doranna Durgin  *f*  1703

**Jess, Martin** (Convict)
*Berserker* - S.D. Perry  *s*  4285

**Jessa** (Ruler; Royalty)
*Darkloom* - Cary Osborne  *s*  4225

**Jessa** (Royalty; Fugitive)
*Deathweave* - Cary Osborne  *s*  4226

**Jessan** (Doctor; Military Personnel)
*The Price of the Stars* - Debra Doyle  *s*  1604

**Jessan, Nyls** (Doctor; Military Personnel)
*Starpilot's Grave* - Debra Doyle  *s*  1606

**Jetboy** (Hero; Pilot)
*Night of the Cooters* - Howard Waldrop  *s*  5614

**Jewel** (Mythical Creature; Royalty)
*The Changeling* - Kristine Kathryn Rusch  *f*  4714

**Jewel** (Psychic)
*Hunter's Death* - Michelle West  *f*  5758

**Jewelbright, Taynad** (Bodyguard; Martial Arts
Expert)
*Brother to Shadows* - Andre Norton  *s*  4142

**Jewell, Amy** (Divorced Person)
*Out of This World* - Lawrence Watt-Evans  *f*  5645

**Jez** (Werewolf)
*Wild Blood* - Nancy A. Collins  *h*  1127

**Jian, Reverdy** (Pilot; Lesbian)
*Dreaming Metal* - Melissa Scott  *s*  4895
*Dreamships* - Melissa Scott  *s*  4896

**Jiana** (Warrior)
*Warriorwards* - Dafydd ab Hugh  *f*  11

**Jiang Ling** (Astronaut)
*Titan* - Stephen Baxter  *s*  405

**Jiang-Tibayan, Nikko** (Genetically Altered Being;
Experimental Subject)
*The Bohr Maker* - Linda Nagata  *s*  4064

**Jill** (Artificial Intelligence)
*/* - Greg Bear  *s*  413

**Jill** (Sorceress)
*Days of Air and Darkness* - Katharine Kerr  *f*  3067
*Days of Blood and Fire* - Katharine Kerr  *f*  3068
*A Time of Exile* - Katharine Kerr  *f*  3077
*A Time of Omens* - Katharine Kerr  *f*  3078

**Jill of Cerrmor** (Mercenary)
*The Dragon Revenant* - Katharine Kerr  *f*  3069

**Jilseponie "Pony"** (Teenager; Adventurer)
*The Demon Awakens* - R.A. Salvatore  *f*  4794

**Jilseponie "Pony"** (Psychic; Adventurer)
*The Demon Spirit* - R.A. Salvatore  *f*  4795

**Jiltanith** (Military Personnel; Pilot)
*Mutineers' Moon* - David Weber  *s*  5677

**Jim** (Spirit)
*Agyar* - Steven Brust  *f*  738

**Jim** (Actor)
*Horrorshow* - David Darke  *h*  1353

**Jimi** (Traveler)
*Lunching with the Antichrist* - Michael
Moorcock  *f*  3984

**Jiminez, Angelita Carmen** (Angel)
*Angels Unaware* - L. Elizabeth Storm  *s*  5315

**Jimmers** (Companion)
*The Paper Grail* - James P. Blaylock  *f*  522

**Jin the Plarnjarn** (Robot; Spy)
*The Race for God* - Brian Herbert  *s*  2666

**Jing, Jong** (Linguist; Adventurer)
*Stones of the Dalai Lama* - Ken Mitchell  *f*  3916

**Jinnarin** (Mythical Creature)
*Voyage of the Fox Rider* - Dennis L.
McKiernan  *f*  3837

**Jivar, Michael** (Government Official)
*Iceman* - Cynthia Felice  *s*  1913

**Jo** (Teenager)
*Balyet* - Patricia Wrightson  *f*  5995

**Jo** (Mythical Creature)
*Clouds End* - Sean Stewart  *f*  5272

**Jo** (Spaceman)
*Eggheads* - Emily Devenport  *s*  1500

**Jo** (Social Worker)
*The Parasite War* - Tim Sullivan  *s*  5352

**Jo-lac** (Spaceship Captain)
*Prisoner of Dreams* - Karen Ripley  *s*  4593

**Jo-Lac** (Spaceship Captain)
*The Tenth Class* - Karen Ripley  *s*  4594

**Joachim** (Religious; Adventurer)
*The Wood Nymph and the Cranky Saint* - C. Dale
Brittain  *f*  706

**Joanna** (Computer Expert)
*Dog Wizard* - Barbara Hambly  *f*  2503

**Joanna** (Child; Student)
*The Time Tree* - Enid Richemont  *f*  4585

**Joanna** (Military Personnel)
*Way of the Clans* - Robert Thurston  *s*  5469

**Joaquim, Leo** (Child)
*The Night of the Moonbow* - Thomas
Tryon  *h*  5486

**Jobber** (Revolutionary; Psychic)
*Beldan's Fire* - Midori Snyder  *f*  5150

**Jock o' the Syde** (Werewolf; Companion)
*The Spiral Dance* - R. Garcia y Robertson  *f*  2121

**Jodahs** (Genetically Altered Being)
*Imago* - Octavia E. Butler  *s*  791

**Jody** (Clerk; Vampire)
*Bloodsucking Fiends: A Love Story* - Christopher
Moore  *h*  3988

**Joe** (Religious; Security Officer)
*Wheels of Fire* - Mercedes Lackey  *f*  3301

**Joel** (Musician; Religious)
*Finder's Bane* - Kate Novak  *f*  4165

**Joel-Andrew** (Religious; Wanderer)
*The Off Season* - Jack Cady  *f*  820

**Jofre** (Outcast; Martial Arts Expert)
*Brother to Shadows* - Andre Norton  *s*  4142

**Johanna** (Health Care Professional)
*Strange Angels* - Kathe Koja  *h*  3197

**John** (Royalty; Historical Figure)
*The Sheriff of Nottingham* - Richard Kluger  *f*  3165

**John, Mortel** (Teacher)
*Commencement* - Roby James  *s*  2877

**Johnny** (Murderer)
*The Bad Thing* - Michael O'Rourke  *h*  4222

**Johnny** (Courier; Fugitive)
*Johnny Mnemonic* - Terry Bisson  *s*  505

**Johnson, Cloud Hunter** (Guide)
*When Wolves Cry* - Chris N. Africa  *h*  41

**Johnson, Duffy** (Student)
*Wolf Moon* - John R. Holt  *h*  2749

**Johnson, Grandma** (Aged Person)
*Grandma's Little Darling* - Stephen R.
George  *h*  2201

**Johnson, Greg** (Police Officer)
*The Charm* - Adam Niswander  *h*  4111

**Johnson, Harriette** (Teacher)
*Inagehi* - Jack Cady  *h*  817

**Johnson, Hildy** (Journalist; Teacher)
*Steel Beach* - John Varley  *s*  5566

**Johnson, Joe** (Writer)
*The Undesired Princess and the Enchanted Bunny* - L. Sprague de Camp   *f*   1419

**Johnson, Laura** (Patient; Time Traveler)
*Door Number Three* - Patrick O'Leary   *s*   4210

**Johnson, Lezzie** (Healer; Teenager)
*Groogleman* - Debra Doyle   *s*   1600

**Johnson, Mark "Hobbes"** (Philosopher; Scientist)
*Mosaic* - Jeri Taylor   *s*   5403

**Johnson, Samuel** (Religious; Architect)
*The Iron Bridge* - David Morse   *s*   4036

**Johnson, Sibyl** (Student; Time Traveler)
*Far Edge of Darkness* - Linda Evans   *s*   1855

**Johnston, Jerry** (Social Worker)
*Prodigal* - Melanie Tem   *h*   5423

**Johnston, Virgil Wayne** (Cowboy)
*The Immortals* - Tracy Hickman   *s*   2681

**Joker** (Criminal)
*Mask of the Phantasm* - Geary Gravel   *s*   2331

**Joli-Chanteu, Alexander** (Spaceman)
*The Ship Who Searched* - Anne McCaffrey   *s*   3749

**Jolie** (Spirit)
*And Eternity* - Piers Anthony   *f*   162

**Jolyon** (Religious; Zealot)
*The Arm of the Stone* - Victoria Strauss   *f*   5333

**Jon** (Mutant)
*The Tery* - F. Paul Wilson   *s*   5900

**Jonah** (Teenager)
*The House on Hound Hill* - Maggie Prince   *f*   4438

**Jonah** (Collector; Store Owner)
*Something Rich and Strange* - Patricia A. McKillip   *f*   3840

**Jonas, Paul** (Military Personnel)
*River of Blue Fire* - Tad Williams   *f*   5830

**Jonathan** (Young Man)
*Tapestry of Dark Souls* - Elaine Bergstrom   *h*   465

**Jonathan** (Vampire)
*Virgintooth* - Mark Ivanhoe   *h*   2834

**Jondalar** (Prehistoric Human; Hunter)
*The Plains of Passage* - Jean M. Auel   *f*   275

**Jones, Altair** (Trader)
*Endgame* - C.J. Cherryh   *s*   986

**Jones, Bob** (Writer)
*The Ignored* - Bentley Little   *h*   3493

**Jones, Cory** (Journalist; Warrior)
*City of Pain* - John Terra   *f*   5438

**Jones, David** (Writer)
*Deus Ex Machina* - J.V. Brummels   *s*   732

**Jones, Fanning "Fan"** (Musician; Cousin)
*Dreaming Metal* - Melissa Scott   *s*   4895

**Jones, George** (Detective—Police)
*Shade of Pale* - Greg Kihn   *h*   3104

**Jones, Guinevere** (Child)
*The Witch House* - Norma Tadlock Johnson   *f*   2923

**Jones, Indiana "Indy"** (Archaeologist)
*Indiana Jones and the Dance of the Giants* - Rob MacGregor   *f*   3588
*Indiana Jones and the Genesis Deluge* - Rob MacGregor   *f*   3589
*Indiana Jones and the Interior World* - Rob MacGregor   *f*   3590
*Indiana Jones and the Peril at Delphi* - Rob MacGregor   *f*   3591
*Indiana Jones and the Seven Veils* - Rob MacGregor   *f*   3592
*Indiana Jones and the Sky Pirates* - Martin Caidin   *f*   825

*Indiana Jones and the Unicorn's Legacy* - Rob MacGregor   *f*   3593
*Indiana Jones and the White Witch* - Martin Caidin   *f*   826

**Jones, Indiana "Indy"** (Teenager; Military Personnel)
*The Mata Hari Adventure* - James Luceno   *f*   3544

**Jones, Jeremiah "Jonesy"** (Journalist; Psychic)
*Chaos Come Again* - Wilhelmina Baird   *s*   293

**Jones, Kellogg "Doc"** (Saloon Keeper/Owner; Professor)
*Laying the Music to Rest* - Dean Wesley Smith   *h*   5114

**Jones, Lloyd Merlin** (Computer Expert; Warlock)
*MagicNet* - John DeChancie   *f*   1461

**Jones, Lucifer** (Adventurer; Religious)
*Lucifer Jones* - Mike Resnick   *f*   4549

**Jones, Nora** (Vampire)
*Dance of Death* - P.N. Elrod   *h*   1794
*Red Death* - P.N. Elrod   *h*   1798

**Jones, Ritcher** (Religious; Adventurer)
*Dawn's Uncertain Light* - Neal Barrett Jr.   *s*   365

**Jones, Shadrach** (Clerk; Royalty)
*The Collected Stories of Philip K. Dick, Volume One: The Short Happy Life of the Brown Oxford* - Philip K. Dick   *s*   1519

**Jones, Sibyl** (Detective—Police; Telepath)
*Pollen* - Jeff Noon   *s*   4135

**Jones, T. Bowser** (Lawyer)
*Murder in the Solid State* - Wil McCarthy   *s*   3764

**Jones, T.J.** (Teenager)
*Rook* - Graham Masterton   *h*   3678

**Jones, Umber** (Sorcerer)
*Rook* - Graham Masterton   *h*   3678

**Jones, Virginia "Jinjur"** (Spaceship Captain; Military Personnel)
*Marooned on Eden* - Robert L. Forward   *s*   1986
*Ocean under the Ice* - Robert L. Forward   *s*   1988
*Return to Rocheworld* - Robert L. Forward   *s*   1989
*Rocheworld* - Robert L. Forward   *s*   1990

**Jones, Walter Tai-Ching** (Spaceship Captain)
*Homecoming* - David Alexander Smith   *s*   5108

**Jones, Witchfinder** (Bounty Hunter)
*Walking Wolf* - Nancy A. Collins   *h*   1126

**Jonesy** (Spy)
*Brain Child* - George Turner   *s*   5491

**Jonnah's-kin, Maihu** (Religious; Captive)
*Snow Brother* - S.M. Stirling   *f*   5299

**Jonson, Kenneth** (Military Personnel; Experimental Subject)
*Aggressor Six* - Wil McCarthy   *s*   3760

**Jorana** (Alien; Artisan)
*The Howling Stones* - Alan Dean Foster   *s*   2006

**Jorandel "Jorie"** (Mythical Creature; Musician)
*Cold Iron* - Melisa Michaels   *f*   3886

**Jordan** (Actor)
*Blood and Honor* - Simon R. Green   *f*   2361

**Jordan** (Serial Killer)
*The Lazarus Heart* - Poppy Z. Brite   *h*   696

**Jordan, Andy** (Teenager)
*65mm* - Dale Hoover   *h*   2761

**Jordan, Greg** (Accountant)
*Wind Chimes* - R.R. Walters   *h*   5625

**Jordan, John James** (Spaceman; Leader)
*Project Farcry* - Pauline Ashwell   *s*   230

**Jordan, Matt** (Spy)
*Watchers in the Woods* - William W. Johnstone   *h*   2936

**Jordan, Megan** (Child)
*Wind Chimes* - R.R. Walters   *h*   5625

**Jordan, Miles** (Scientist; Museum Curator)
*End of an Era* - Robert J. Sawyer   *s*   4853

**Jordan, Pamela** (Businesswoman)
*Wind Chimes* - R.R. Walters   *h*   5625

**Jordan, Richard** (Professor)
*Otherworld* - Kenneth C. Flint   *h*   1959

**Jordan, Richard "Rivername"** (Telepath; Teenager)
*Project Farcry* - Pauline Ashwell   *s*   230

**Jordon** (Child)
*Sexing the Cherry* - Jeanette Winterson   *f*   5927

**Jorem** (Religious)
*The Boy From the Burren* - Sheila Gilluly   *f*   2236

**Joreth** (Genetically Altered Being)
*OtherWhere* - Margaret Wander Bonanno   *s*   566

**Joreth** (Musician)
*OtherWise* - Margaret Wander Bonanno   *s*   567

**Jorhsa** (Vampire)
*Some Things Never Die* - Robert Morgan   *h*   4005

**Josarian** (Thief)
*In Legend Born* - Laura Resnick   *f*   4533

**Josef** (Leader)
*The Run to Chaos Keep* - Jack L. Chalker   *s*   960

**Joseph** (Animal; Adventurer)
*The Bellmaker* - Brian Jacques   *f*   2848

**Joseph** (Immortal)
*In the Garden of Iden* - Kage Baker   *s*   298

**Joshim** (Spaceman)
*A Matter of Oaths* - Helen S. Wright   *s*   5985

**Joshua** (Guide)
*Groogleman* - Debra Doyle   *s*   1600

**Joshua** (Clone)
*The Killing Star* - Charles Pellegrino   *s*   4281

**Josua** (Royalty)
*To Green Angel Tower* - Tad Williams   *f*   5832

**Joth** (Angel)
*Angels on Fire* - Nancy A. Collins   *h*   1117

**Joubert, Mireille** (Political Figure; Scientist)
*Semper Mars* - Ian Douglas   *s*   1585

**Jourdemayne, Truth** (Paranormal Investigator)
*Ghostlight* - Marion Zimmer Bradley   *f*   634
*Gravelight* - Marion Zimmer Bradley   *f*   636
*Witchlight* - Marion Zimmer Bradley   *f*   655

**Journey, Ruby** (Revolutionary; Bounty Hunter)
*Deathstalker Rebellion* - Simon R. Green   *s*   2365

**Joy, Sandy "Sana"** (Musician; Psychic)
*Strands of Sunlight* - Gael Baudino   *f*   396

**Joy-in-the-Dance** (Adventurer)
*The Arkadians* - Lloyd Alexander   *f*   67

**Joyce, Nancy** (Scientist)
*Vespers* - Jeff Rovin   *h*   4688

**Joyner, Griffin** (Military Personnel)
*The First Duelist* - Rutledge Etheridge   *s*   1849

**Joze** (Adventurer)
*A Child of Elvish* - Nancy Varian Berberick   *f*   457

**J'role** (Teenager; Thief)
*The Longing Ring* - Christopher Kubasik   *f*   3246

**Juarel, Chita** (Young Woman)
*668: The Neighbor of the Beast* - Lionel Fenn   *h*   1917

**Juarel, Chita** (Waiter/Waitress)
*Kent Montana and the Really Ugly Thing From Mars* - Lionel Fenn   *s*   1918

**Jude** (Teenager; Gang Member)
*Random Acts of Senseless Violence* - Jack
  Womack  *f*  5959

**Judge, Paul** (Lawyer)
*Soul Catcher* - Colin Kersey  *h*  3081

**Judson, Marl** (Spaceship Captain)
*Judson's Eden* - Keith Laumer  *s*  3344

**Juh** (Leader; Indian)
*Apacheria* - Jake Page  *s*  4233

**Juillerat, Sister Chantal** (Agent; Computer Expert)
*Demon Download* - Jack Yeovil  *f*  6021

**Julia** (Child-Care Giver; Teenager)
*Blue Moon* - Hila Feil  *f*  1898

**Julia** (Royalty)
*Blue Moon Rising* - Simon R. Green  *f*  2362

**Julia** (Housewife; Spouse)
*The Hellbound Heart* - Clive Barker  *h*  342

**Julia** (Young Woman)
*Spree* - Lucy Taylor  *h*  5415

**Julian** (Revolutionary; Parent)
*The Children of Men* - P.D. James  *f*  2870

**Julian** (Young Man)
*Orphans* - Jean Simon  *h*  5065

**Julian** (Streetperson)
*Wilding* - Melanie Tem  *h*  5425

**Julian of Stansvale** (Royalty)
*The Jewel of Fire* - Diana L. Paxson  *f*  4265

**Julian of Stansvale** (Royalty; Heir—Dispossessed)
*The Wind Crystal* - Diana L. Paxson  *f*  4269

**Julianus, Marcus** (Diplomat)
*The Light Bearer* - Donna Gillespie  *f*  2229

**Julien, Maria** (Heiress)
*Unholy Fire* - Whitley Strieber  *h*  5342

**Julius Caesar, Gaius** (Ruler; Military Personnel)
*Child of the Eagle* - Esther Friesner  *f*  2073

**Junknowitz, Lucky** (Revolutionary)
*Free Radicals* - Jack McKinney  *s*  3848
*Hostile Takeover* - Jack McKinney  *s*  3849

**Juraviel, Belli'mar** (Mythical Creature; Warrior)
*The Demon Spirit* - R.A. Salvatore  *f*  4795

**Justen** (Magician; Engineer)
*The Order War* - L.E. Modesitt Jr.  *f*  3936

**Justin** (Clone)
*The Killing Star* - Charles Pellegrino  *s*  4281

**Justin** (Young Man)
*The Living Evil* - Ruby Jean Jensen  *h*  2902

**Justin, Rangsey** (Computer Expert; Homosexual)
*Night Sky Mine* - Melissa Scott  *s*  4898

**Justine** (Vampire)
*Stainless* - Todd Grimson  *h*  2449

**Justinian** (Veteran)
*Subterranean Gallery* - Richard Paul Russo  *s*  4750

**Justinian** (Ruler)
*In the Heart of Darkness* - Eric Flint  *s*  1955

**Jute, Tabitha** (Spaceship Captain; Leader)
*Mother of Plenty* - Colin Greenland  *s*  2417
*Seasons of Plenty* - Colin Greenland  *s*  2418

**Jute, Tabitha** (Spaceship Captain)
*Take Back Plenty* - Colin Greenland  *s*  2419

**Juvell, Cat** (Detective—Private; Martial Arts Expert)
*Iron Shadows* - Steven Barnes  *f*  362

**Juvell, Tyler** (Computer Expert; Handicapped)
*Iron Shadows* - Steven Barnes  *f*  362

**Jy** (Leader; Wanderer)
*Down the Bright Way* - Robert Reed  *s*  4505

**Jyp** (Sailor)
*Chase the Morning* - Michael Scott Rohan  *f*  4658

# K

**K** (Doctor)
*The Face of Another* - Kobo Abe  *h*  19

**K, Ylla** (Alien; Spouse)
*The Martian Chronicles* - Ray Bradbury  *s*  622

**Kaa** (Genetically Altered Being; Pilot)
*Infinity's Shore* - David Brin  *s*  688

**Kaantille, Katrina** (Teenager; Artisan)
*The Loneliest Magician* - Irene Radford  *f*  4461

**Kadaffi, "Captain Cadaver"** (Military Personnel)
*Bill, the Galactic Hero: The Final Incoherent
  Adventure* - Harry Harrison  *s*  2568

**Kadar** (Witch)
*The Fagin* - Pat Graversen  *h*  2334

**Kadiya** (Royalty)
*Black Trillium* - Marion Zimmer Bradley  *f*  630

**Kadiya** (Explorer; Royalty)
*Golden Trillium* - Andre Norton  *f*  4153

**Kadolan "Kade"** (Royalty; Guardian)
*Faery Lands Forlorn* - Dave Duncan  *f*  1677
*Perilous Seas* - Dave Duncan  *f*  1685

**Kadumi** (Warrior)
*The Parched Sea* - Troy Denning  *f*  1486

**Kady, Meg** (Pilot)
*Hellburner* - C.J. Cherryh  *s*  996

**Kaeler, Lanen** (Heroine; Bastard Daughter)
*Song in the Silence* - Elizabeth Kerner  *f*  3065

**Kaeot** (Monster)
*A Whisper of Wings* - Steven Ray Fulgham  *h*  2091

**Kaftus** (Sorcerer)
*The Sure Death of a Mouse* - Dan Crawford  *f*  1250

**Kah-laye-dee** (Alien)
*The Magic Bicycle* - William Hill  *f*  2688

**Kahless** (Warrior; Hero)
*Kahless* - Michael Jan Friedman  *s*  2065

**Kahn, Tae** (Teenager; Warrior)
*Beyond Ragnarok* - Mickey Zucker Reichert  *f*  4516

**Kahn, Tae** (Royalty)
*The Children of Wrath* - Mickey Zucker
  Reichert  *f*  4518

**Kahsir** (Royalty; Warrior)
*Tears of Time* - Nancy Asire  *f*  256

**kai de'Leonne, Valedan** (Royalty)
*The Uncrowned King* - Michelle West  *f*  5760

**kai Ortega, Maeru "Kai"** (Spaceman; Engineer)
*Alpha Centauri* - William Barton  *s*  378

**Kaid** (Military Personnel; Alien)
*Fire Margins* - Lisanne Norman  *s*  4137
*Razor's Edge* - Lisanne Norman  *s*  4139

**Kaihan** (Wizard; Royalty)
*Nameless Magery* - Delia Marshall Turner  *f*  5490

**Kairn** (Warrior; Explorer)
*The Steel Kings* - John Maddox Roberts  *f*  4621

**KaiSa** (Alien; Diplomat)
*Dark Water's Embrace* - Stephen Leigh  *s*  3426

**Kaiser, Valentine** (Public Relations; Vampire)
*A Matter of Taste* - Fred Saberhagen  *h*  4770

**Kakzim** (Religious; Mythical Creature)
*Cinnabar Shadows* - Lynn Abbey  *f*  15

**Kal** (Teenager; Adventurer)
*Flight to Hollow Mountain* - Mark Sebanc  *f*  4908

**Kalakaua, Cen** (Genius; Scientist)
*The Bones of Time* - Kathleen Ann Goonan  *s*  2273

**Kalass, Et** (Political Figure; Alien)
*In the Shadow of the Moon* - Scott G. Gier  *s*  2224

**Kalavek** (Mythical Creature; Adventurer)
*Dragon's Domain* - Thorarinn Gunnarsson  *f*  2461

**Kaldy, Janos** (Werewolf)
*Mark of the Werewolf* - Jeffrey Sackett  *h*  4780

**Kalena** (Noblewoman)
*Wolf Justice* - Doranna Durgin  *f*  1706

**Kalencka** (Sidekick)
*Rally Cry!* - William R. Forstchen  *s*  1982

**Kalimuni** (Religious; Lawyer)
*The Broken Land* - Ian McDonald  *s*  3791

**Kalliana** (Telepath)
*Blindfold* - Kevin J. Anderson  *s*  101

**Kallisti, Avra** (Clerk)
*Specters* - J.M. Dillard  *h*  1555

**Kallisti, Magdalen** (Teacher)
*Specters* - J.M. Dillard  *h*  1555

**Kallmirsson, Rache** (Warrior)
*The Last of the Renshai* - Mickey Zucker
  Reichert  *f*  4520

**Kalvin, Walter** (Government Official)
*Silent Thunder/Universe* - Dean Ing  *s*  2829

**Kamehameha, Cesar** (Administrator; Scientist)
*Blueheart* - Alison Sinclair  *s*  5068

**Kameron, Theodore R.G.** (Scientist)
*The Eleventh Plague: A Novel of Medical Terror* -
  John S. Marr  *h*  3632

**Kami, Minamoto no** (Leader; Scientist)
*Glory's People* - Alfred Coppel  *s*  1183

**Kaminski, Tiffany Jeanine "T.J."** (Artist; Student—
  College)
*Steel Rose* - Kara Dalkey  *f*  1321

**Kammaeman** (Military Personnel)
*Present Tense* - Dave Duncan  *f*  1686

**Kampa, Joshua** (Time Traveler)
*No Enemy but Time* - Michael Bishop  *s*  502

**Kan-Kon** (Pilot)
*Dragon Rigger* - Jeffrey A. Carver  *s*  929

**Kandaki** (Royalty; Heiress—Dispossessed)
*The Land of Gold* - Gillian Bradshaw  *f*  658

**Kane** (Murderer)
*Kane* - Douglas Borton  *h*  576

**Kane, Anna** (Psychologist)
*Nine Levels Down* - William Dantz  *h*  1347

**Kane, Bowie** (Handyman; Indian)
*Pitfall* - Ronald Kelly  *h*  3054

**Kane, Chandler** (Businessman; Wealthy)
*Order of the Arrow* - Michael T.
  Hinkemeyer  *h*  2689

**Kane, Emily** (Doctor)
*Immortal* - Jason Nickles  *h*  4102

**Kane, Laura** (Student)
*Deathscape* - Michael Cecilione  *h*  945

**Kane, Michael** (Professor)
*Kane of Old Mars* - Michael Moorcock  *s*  3983

**Kane, Nathan** (Vampire)
*Bring on the Night* - Don Davis  *h*  1402

**Kang** (Mythical Creature; Military Personnel)
*The Doom Brigade* - Margaret Weis  *f*  5708

**Kang, Liu** (Religious; Martial Arts Expert)
*Mortal Kombat* - Martin Delrio  *f*  1483

**Kapellmeister** (Alien)
*Acts of Conscience* - William Barton  *s*  377

**Kaplan, T'ing Hau** (Teenager)
*Gnome Man's Land* - Esther Friesner  *f*  2075

**Kaplan, T'ing Hau** (Student—College)
*Unicorn U.* - Esther Friesner  *f*  2084

**Kar, Ann** (Writer; Journalist)
*Century 21* - Ewa Kuryluk  *s*  3263

**kar Therma, Staffa** (Mercenary)
*Relic of Empire* - W. Michael Gear  *s*  2171

**Kara** (Adventurer; Teenager)
*Flight of the Dragon Kyn* - Susan Fletcher  *f*  1951

**Karageorge, Vanessa** (Scholar)
*Carve the Sky* - Alexander Jablokov  *s*  2836

**Karak** (Deity)
*The Blackgod* - J. Gregory Keyes  *f*  3095

**Karal** (Religious)
*Storm Rising* - Mercedes Lackey  *f*  3297

**Karaquazian, Jack** (Gambler; Adventurer)
*Blood: A Southern Fantasy* - Michael
   Moorcock  *f*  3977
*Fabulous Harbors* - Michael Moorcock  *f*  3981
*The War Amongst the Angels* - Michael
   Moorcock  *f*  3986

**Kardith** (Warrior)
*Northlight* - Deborah Wheeler  *s*  5775

**Karen** (Young Woman)
*Black Sun* - Douglas E. Winter  *h*  5923

**Karin** (Royalty; Adventurer)
*Voima* - C. Dale Brittain  *f*  704

**Karis** (Young Woman)
*Tooth: A Tale of Love and Death in Paradox* - Novak
   Kruger  *h*  3244

**Karli Dog** (Robot)
*Vurt* - Jeff Noon  *s*  4136

**Karloff, Boris** (Actor; Historical Figure)
*Father of Frankenstein* - Christopher Bram  *h*  659

**Karmade, Theodore "Ted"** (Technician)
*Quasar* - Jamil Nasir  *s*  4071

**Karmikal, Jake** (Military Personnel)
*Jungle Assault* - P.M. Griffin  *s*  2437

**Karolyi, Ignace** (Mercenary)
*Traveling with the Dead* - Barbara Hambly  *h*  2511

**Karoulis, Sam** (Police Officer)
*Blue Limbo* - Terrence M. Green  *s*  2377

**Karpou, Betty Lou** (Alien; Teacher)
*My Teacher Fried My Brains* - Bruce
   Coville  *s*  1223

**Karpov, Sapphire** (Addict; Young Woman)
*Putting Up Roots* - Charles Sheffield  *s*  4964

**Karriaagzh** (Scholar; Administrator)
*Human to Human* - Rebecca Ore  *s*  4219

**Karros, Dimitri Alexander** (Computer Expert;
   Vampire)
*Ragged Angels* - Della Van Hise  *h*  5537

**Karsh** (Innkeeper)
*The Innkeeper's Song* - Peter S. Beagle  *f*  409

**Karus** (Companion)
*Last Mountain* - Robert C. Fleet  *f*  1946

**Karuth** (Sorceress)
*The Avenger* - Louise Cooper  *f*  1174
*The Deceiver* - Louise Cooper  *f*  1175

**Kashir** (Royalty; Warrior)
*To Fall Like Stars* - Nancy Asire  *f*  257

**Kasselman, Philip** (Doctor)
*Button Bright* - Michael Kurland  *h*  3251

**Kastazi, Marko** (Businesswoman; Heiress—Lost)
*Hawk's Flight* - Carol Chase  *f*  980

**Kastle** (Scientist)
*Devil's Engine* - Mark Sumner  *f*  5356

**Kastlin, Vask** (Psychic; Police Officer)
*Mainline* - Deborah Christian  *s*  1026

**Kastring** (Warrior)
*Shadowbreed* - David Ferring  *f*  1928

**Kastrouni, Dimitrious** (Spy)
*Demogorgon* - Brian Lumley  *h*  3552

**Kasuga** (Military Personnel)
*On the Verge* - Roland J. Green  *s*  2350

**Kat** (Teenager)
*Dark Heart* - Betsy James  *f*  2857

**Kataboki, Lily** (Banker)
*I'll Be Watching You* - Samuel M. Key  *h*  3094

**Katayev, Nadezhda** (Scientist)
*Pacific Edge* - Kim Stanley Robinson  *s*  4634

**Kate** (Time Traveler; Teenager)
*The Ancient One* - T.A. Barron  *f*  368

**Katelo, Jonathan** (Indian; Explorer)
*Beyond Eden* - J.M. Morgan  *s*  3999

**Katelo, Jonathon** (Guide; Linguist; Indian)
*Desert Eden* - J.M. Morgan  *s*  4000

**Katelo, Seth** (Indian; Explorer)
*Beyond Eden* - J.M. Morgan  *s*  3999
*Future Eden* - J.M. Morgan  *s*  4001

**Kateralbin, Crispin** (Sorcerer; Military Personnel)
*The Daemon in the Machine* - Felicity
   Savage  *f*  4848
*The War in the Waste* - Felicity Savage  *f*  4852

**Kateralbin, Crispin** (Entertainer; Mechanic)
*The War in the Waste* - Felicity Savage  *f*  4851

**Kathinka** (Religious; Guide)
*The Flies of Memory* - Ian Watson  *s*  5635

**Kathy** (Prostitute)
*Dark Prince* - Keith Herber  *h*  2663

**Katiasi** (Young Woman)
*I Am Frankenstein* - C. Dean Andersson  *h*  140

**Katin** (Royalty; Herbalist)
*Season of Storms* - Ellen Foxxe  *f*  2032

**Katrina** (Mythical Creature)
*Our Lady of the Harbour* - Charles de Lint  *f*  1434

**Katrina** (Noblewoman)
*War* - Simon Hawke  *f*  2625

**Katsuleris, Aubrey** (Artist; Wizard)
*The Broken Sword* - Molly Cochran  *f*  1091

**Katts, Wesley** (Store Owner)
*Anthony Shriek* - Jessica Amanda
   Salmonson  *h*  4790

**Katya** (Adventurer)
*Dark Magic* - Angus Wells  *f*  5733
*Wild Magic* - Angus Wells  *f*  5741

**Katz, Julie** (Deity)
*Only Begotten Daughter* - James Morrow  *f*  4034

**Kavanaugh, Louise** (Researcher)
*Nightshade* - Stanley R. Moore  *h*  3992

**Kavanaugh, Robert** (FBI Agent)
*Stinger* - Nancy Kress  *s*  3243

**Kawaguchi, Mike** (Teenager)
*The Summoned* - Steven Ray Fulgham  *h*  2090

**Kawakita, Gregory** (Museum Curator)
*Relic* - Douglas Preston  *h*  4414

**Kawalsky** (Military Personnel)
*Stargate SG-1* - Ashley McConnell  *s*  3777

**Kay** (Government Official)
*Men in Black* - Steve Perry  *s*  4298

**Kay, Laura** (Journalist)
*Catamount* - Michael Peak  *f*  4273

**Kaye, Darbi** (Child)
*Chiller* - Randall Boyll  *h*  610

**Kaye, Peter** (Student—Graduate)
*Chiller* - Randall Boyll  *h*  610

**Kayli** (Magician; Noblewoman)
*Firewalk* - Anne Logston  *f*  3509

**Kayrlis** (Entertainer; Teenager)
*Ancient Games* - Scott Ciencin  *f*  1028

**Kayrlis** (Adventurer)
*Night of Glory* - Scott Ciencin  *f*  1030

**Kaz** (Mythical Creature; Knight)
*Kaz the Minotaur* - Richard A. Knaak  *f*  3172

**Kazacos, Ari** (Businessman)
*Vampire Bytes* - Linda Grant  *h*  2322

**Kazenstein, Morris** (Inventor; Activist)
*Sewer, Gas & Electric* - Matt Ruff  *s*  4708

**Kazul** (Mythical Creature; Royalty)
*Calling on Dragons* - Patricia C. Wrede  *f*  5974

**Kazul** (Mythical Creature)
*Dealing with Dragons* - Patricia C. Wrede  *f*  5975

**Kazzintuitruaabemss "Kazz"** (Prehistoric Human)
*To Your Scattered Bodies Go* - Philip Jose
   Farmer  *s*  1876

**Kean, Michael** (Businessman)
*Legends Reborn* - Kenneth C. Flint  *f*  1958

**Keane, Abel** (Student)
*The Trail of Cthulhu* - August Derleth  *h*  1497

**Keane, Andrew** (Military Personnel)
*Never Sound Retreat* - William R.
   Forstchen  *s*  1981
*Rally Cry!* - William R. Forstchen  *s*  1982
*Terrible Swift Sword* - William R.
   Forstchen  *s*  1983

**Keating, Michael** (Doctor)
*Night of Broken Souls* - Thomas F.
   Monteleone  *h*  3964

**Keatley, Thompson** (Magician)
*A Dry Spell* - Susan Moloney  *h*  3951

**Kedrigern** (Wizard)
*Kedrigern and the Charming Couple* - John
   Morressy  *f*  4013
*A Remembrance for Kedrigern* - John
   Morressy  *f*  4014

**Kee** (Teenager)
*The Book of Webster's* - J.N. Williamson  *h*  5853

**Kee-Toroca** (Alien; Scientist)
*Fossil Hunter* - Robert J. Sawyer  *s*  4855

**Keebler, Micah "the Scavenger"** (Scavenger)
*Trust Territory* - Janet Morris  *s*  4019

**Keegan, Caroline** (Journalist)
*Wyrm Wolf* - Edo van Belkom  *h*  5535

**Keelan, Delphine** (Vampire)
*Sweet Blood* - Pat Graversen  *h*  2337

**Keelie** (Reanimated Dead; Psychic)
*The Jigsaw Woman* - Kim Antieau  *f*  199

**Keenan, Daniel** (Doctor)
*Minds Apart* - Margaret Davis  *s*  1408

**Keene, Valerie** (Waiter/Waitress)
*Dark Rivers of the Heart* - Dean R. Koontz  *h*  3204

**Keeper, Tom** (Artist; Religious; Magician)
*Ancient Games* - Scott Ciencin  *f*  1028

**Keeper, Tom** (Artist; Magician)
*Night of Glory* - Scott Ciencin  *f*  1030

**Keeper, Tom** (Teenager; Artist; Magician)
*The Ways of Magic* - Scott Ciencin  *f*  1033

**Keeton, Tallis** (Teenager)
*Lavondyss: Journey to an Unknown Region* - Robert
  Holdstock  *f*  2739

**Keff** (Pilot; Spaceman)
*The Ship Errant* - Jody Lynn Nye  *s*  4175

**Keighvin** (Mythical Creature)
*Born to Run* - Mercedes Lackey  *f*  3271

**Keita, Arthur** (Military Personnel)
*Path of the Fury* - David Weber  *s*  5680

**Keith** (Musician)
*Stainless* - Todd Grimson  *h*  2449

**Kelahnus** (Warrior; Homosexual)
*The Stone Prince* - Fiona Patton  *f*  4259

**Kelder of Shulara** (Adventurer)
*Taking Flight* - Lawrence Watt-Evans  *f*  5650

**Keleios** (Sorceress; Fiance(e))
*Nightseer* - Laurell K. Hamilton  *f*  2521

**Kelemvor** (Warrior)
*Crucible* - Troy Denning  *f*  1484

**Kelene** (Young Woman)
*The Angry Angel* - Chelsea Quinn Yarbro  *h*  6010

**Kelene** (Sorceress; Healer)
*City of the Sorcerers* - Mary H. Herbert  *f*  2673
*Winged Magic* - Mary H. Herbert  *f*  2678

**Kelledy, Cerin** (Mythical Creature)
*Ghosts of Wind and Shadow* - Charles de
  Lint  *f*  1427

**Kelledy, Meran** (Musician; Mythical Creature)
*Ghosts of Wind and Shadow* - Charles de
  Lint  *f*  1427

**Keller, Sally** (Researcher)
*Probe* - Edward M. Lerner  *s*  3437

**Keller, Yates** (Empath; Criminal)
*The War Minstrels* - Karen Haber  *s*  2477
*Woman Without a Shadow* - Karen Haber  *s*  2478

**Kelligan, Sam Houston** (Astronaut; Heir)
*Beachhead* - Jack Williamson  *s*  5859

**Kellin** (Mythical Creature)
*A Tapestry of Lions* - Jennifer Roberson  *f*  4615

**Kelly, Bob** (Police Officer)
*The Forbidden Zone* - Whitley Strieber  *h*  5340

**Kelly, Brian** (Scientist)
*The Forbidden Zone* - Whitley Strieber  *h*  5340

**Kelly, Bryan** (Military Personnel)
*Beyond the Void* - Sean Dalton  *s*  1331
*Destination: Mutiny* - Sean Dalton  *s*  1332
*The Salukan Gambit* - Sean Dalton  *s*  1333

**Kelly, Chris** (Criminal)
*The Bad Thing* - Michael O'Rourke  *h*  4222

**Kelly, Dorothea** (Nurse)
*Systems* - W.T. Quick  *s*  4452

**Kelly, Gideon** (Religious)
*The Time of Feasting* - Mick Farren  *h*  1882

**Kelly, Ista** (Foundling; Teenager)
*Night Sky Mine* - Melissa Scott  *s*  4898

**Kelryn** (Dancer)
*The Legend of Nightfall* - Mickey Zucker
  Reichert  *f*  4521

**Kelys** (Teacher; Wanderer)
*In the Mothers' Land* - Elisabeth Vonarburg  *s*  5590

**Kem** (Teenager)
*Through the Heart* - Richard Grant  *f*  2328

**Keman** (Mythical Creature; Wizard)
*Elvenblood* - Andre Norton  *f*  4150

**Kemp, Jerod** (Thief; Adventurer)
*Shadow of the Crown* - Craig Mills  *f*  3914

**Kemp, Lilah** (Psychic)
*Headhunter* - Timothy Findley  *h'*  1939

**Kemp, Wallace "Wally"** (Computer Expert)
*Lifehouse* - Spider Robinson  *s*  4641

**Kemra** (Military Personnel; Cyborg)
*Adiamante* - L.E. Modesitt Jr.  *s*  3924

**Ken** (Teenager; Student)
*The Lost City of the Jedi* - Paul Davids  *s*  1393

**Kenan, Philip** (Writer)
*Resume with Monsters* - William Browning
  Spencer  *h*  5168

**Kendal, Evan** (Teacher)
*Stunts* - Charles L. Grant  *h*  2317

**Kendal, Harry** (Agent)
*Now You See It. . .* - Richard Matheson  *h*  3688

**Kendall, James William** (Government Official)
*Sunstroke* - David Kagan  *s*  2999

**Kendoro, Judit** (Scientist; Heroine)
*Acorna* - Anne McCaffrey  *s*  3717

**Kendrick, Amanda** (Abuse Victim; Psychic)
*When the Bough Breaks* - Mercedes Lackey  *f*  3302

**Kendrick, Robyn** (Royalty; Adventurer)
*The Coral Kingdom* - Douglas Niles  *f*  4106

**Kendry, Alicen** (Gentlewoman; Spy)
*Season of Storms* - Ellen Foxxe  *f*  2032

**Kenley, Joshua Claybourne** (Professor)
*A Time for Us* - Christine Holden  *f*  2731

**Kenmore, Harold** (Scientist; Time Traveler)
*Of Beginnings and Endings* - Robert Adams  *s*  33

**Kenmuir, Ian** (Spaceship Captain; Revolutionary)
*The Stars Are Also Fire* - Poul Anderson  *s*  134

**Kennedy, Colquitt** (Housewife)
*The House Next Door* - Anne Rivers
  Siddons  *h*  5021

**Kennedy, Jill** (Office Worker)
*Insatiable* - David Dvorkin  *h*  1707

**Kennedy, John F.** (Historical Figure; Leader)
*Time Station Berlin* - David Evans  *s*  1852

**Kennedy, Kate** (Writer)
*Midnight Is a Lonely Place* - Barbara
  Erskine  *h*  1836

**Kennedy, Simon** (Vampire)
*Vampire$* - John Steakley  *h*  5237

**Kenner, Erin Elizabeth** (Explorer; Spaceship
  Captain)
*Mother Lode* - Zach Hughes  *s*  2812

**Kenner, Mark** (Student; Diplomat)
*Shadow World* - A.C. Crispin  *s*  1262

**Kennet, Spencer** (Miner; Businessman)
*Monsoon* - Peter L. Rice  *s*  4583

**Kenning, Valerie** (Guide)
*Antarctica* - Kim Stanley Robinson  *s*  4628

**Kennison, Rogers** (Journalist)
*Deadly Dreams* - Gerald A. Schiller  *h*  4874

**Kent, Averil** (Nobleman; Artist)
*Sea Without a Shore* - Sean Russell  *f*  4743

**Kent, Clark "Superman"** (Journalist; Alien)
*The Death and Life of Superman* - Roger
  Stern  *s*  5262
*The Further Adventures of Superman* - Martin H.
  Greenberg  *s*  2393
*Lois & Clark* - C.J. Cherryh  *s*  999

**Kent, Henry** (Doctor)
*Deathscape* - Michael Cecilione  *h*  945

**Kentraine, Beth** (Psychic; Musician)
*Knight of Ghosts and Shadows* - Mercedes
  Lackey  *f*  3285

*Summoned to Tourney* - Mercedes Lackey  *f*  3299

**Keogh, Harry** (Spy; Psychic)
*Deadspawn* - Brian Lumley  *h*  3550
*Deadspeak* - Brian Lumley  *h*  3551
*Necroscope: The Lost Years* - Brian
  Lumley  *h*  3560
*Resurgence* - Brian Lumley  *h*  3564
*The Source* - Brian Lumley  *h*  3565

**Keogh, Nathan** (Twin; Psychic)
*Bloodwars* - Brian Lumley  *h*  3547

**Kerac, John** (Prisoner; Indian)
*Wake of the Werewolf* - Geoffrey Caine  *h*  834

**Kerebawa** (Indian)
*Nightlife* - Brian Hodge  *h*  2702

**Keri** (Prisoner)
*The Hunter on Arena* - Rose Estes  *s*  1838

**Kerickson, Alline Bolton** (Divorced Person)
*The Imperium Game* - K.D. Wentworth  *s*  5753

**Kerickson, Arvid Gerald** (Computer Expert;
  Divorced Person)
*The Imperium Game* - K.D. Wentworth  *s*  5753

**Kerim** (Ruler)
*When Demons Walk* - Patricia Briggs  *f*  683

**Kerin** (Barbarian)
*The Honorable Barbarian* - L. Sprague de
  Camp  *f*  1415

**Kermovan** (Nobleman)
*The Forge in the Forest* - Michael Scott
  Rohan  *f*  4660

**Kern** (Warrior)
*Conspiracy* - J. Robert King  *f*  3121

**Kerowyn** (Mercenary)
*By the Sword* - Mercedes Lackey  *f*  3273

**Kerrick, James** (Archaeologist)
*The House of the Toad* - Richard L.
  Tierney  *h*  5470

**Kerrigan, Joshua "Josh"** (Hero; Outcast)
*Putting Up Roots* - Charles Sheffield  *s*  4964

**Kersh, Jeremy** (FBI Agent)
*Naming the Flowers* - Kate Wilhelm  *s*  5809

**Kes** (Alien; Telepath)
*Chrysalis* - David Niall Wilson  *s*  5880

**Kesair** (Artisan; Leader)
*The Elementals* - Morgan Llywelyn  *f*  3503

**Kesev, Chaim** (Spy)
*Virgin* - Mary Elizabeth Murphy  *h*  4050

**Kessallia** (Noblewoman)
*The Prince of Ill Luck* - Susan Dexter  *f*  1512

**Kesserich, Daniel** (Scientist)
*The Dealings of Daniel Kesserich* - Fritz
  Leiber  *s*  3417

**Kessler, Kevin** (Detective—Police)
*The Book of the Damned* - D.A. Fowler  *h*  2022

**Kestle, Don** (Archaeologist)
*Mercycle* - Piers Anthony  *s*  181

**Kestrel** (Prehistoric Human; Fugitive)
*People of the Sea* - W. Michael Gear  *f*  2169

**Kestrel** (Minstrel; Royalty)
*The Robin and the Kestrel* - Mercedes
  Lackey  *f*  3293

**Kestrel, Derek "Deke"** (Teenager; Student)
*Jinx High* - Mercedes Lackey  *h*  3284

**Ketcham, Roger** (Doctor)
*Pitfall* - Ronald Kelly  *h*  3054

**Kethry** (Sorceress; Martial Arts Expert)
*Oathblood* - Mercedes Lackey  *f*  3290

Ketral, Jarid Tal (Psychic; Bastard Son)
*Moonspeaker* - K.D. Wentworth   s   5754

Ketter, Bill (Truck Driver)
*Lot Lizards* - Ray Garton   h   2152

Ketter, Jon (Child)
*Lot Lizards* - Ray Garton   h   2152

Kettering, Brian (Detective—Police)
*Doomstalker* - Gary Brandner   h   661

Keven (Orphan; Traveler)
*The Road West* - Gary Wright   f   5984

Kevin (Time Traveler; Teenager)
*All's Faire* - Pamela F. Service   f   4917

Kevin (Musician; Magician)
*Castle of Deception* - Mercedes Lackey   f   3275

Kevin (Teenager; Patient)
*The Midnight Club* - Christopher Pike   h   4329

Kew, Horris (Magician; Criminal)
*The Tangle Box* - Terry Brooks   f   718

Keynes, Daniel "Butch" (Military Personnel)
*The War in the Waste* - Felicity Savage   f   4851

Khaavren of House Tiassa (Military Personnel)
*Five Hundred Years After* - Steven Brust   f   742

Khaavren of House Tiassa (Gentleman)
*The Phoenix Guards* - Steven Brust   f   747

Khadaji, Emile (Martial Arts Expert; Parent)
*The Albino Knife* - Steve Perry   s   4288

Khalid (Mythical Creature; Student)
*Wishing Season* - Esther Friesner   f   2085

Khalid, Ibn ben (Rebel)
*The Widowmaker Reborn* - Mike Resnick   s   4560

Khalifa, Haroun (Adventurer)
*Haroun and the Sea of Stories* - Salman
  Rushdie   f   4731

Khalifa, Rashid (Storyteller)
*Haroun and the Sea of Stories* - Salman
  Rushdie   f   4731

Kham (Mythical Creature; Leader)
*Never Trust an Elf* - Robert N. Charrette   f   976

Khan, Rukmani (Chieftain; Empath)
*The Khan's Persuasion* - Cynthia Felice   s   1914

Kharendaen (Mythical Creature)
*Dragonmage of Mystara* - Thorarinn
  Gunnarsson   f   2462

Khargi (Religious)
*Disciples of Dread* - Hugh B. Cave   h   941

Kharitonov, Jeffrey (Time Traveler)
*Branch Point* - Mona Clee   s   1074

Khar'pern (Alien; Telepath)
*Exiles' Return* - Gayle Greeno   s   2420
*Finders-Seekers* - Gayle Greeno   s   2421
*Mind-Speakers' Call* - Gayle Greeno   s   2423

Kharyat, Judy (Secretary)
*Son of Rosemary* - Ira Levin   h   3445

Khast, Rafiq (Warrior)
*Eyes of Silver* - Michael A. Stackpole   f   5200

Khat (Businessman; Genetically Altered Being)
*City of Bones* - Martha Wells   f   5748

Kheperu (Magician; Mercenary; Con Artist)
*Iron Dawn* - Matthew Woodring Stover   f   5320

Kheperu (Mercenary; Con Artist; Magician)
*Jericho Moon* - Matthew Woodring Stover   f   5321

Khordas (Immortal; Pirate)
*The Element of Fire* - Jason Henderson   f   2657

Khoronos, Erim (Wealthy)
*Incubi* - Edward Lee   h   3394

KhriNyad-Son (Religious)
*The Gates of Twilight* - Paula Volsky   f   5581

Khruuz (Alien)
*More than Fire* - Philip Jose Farmer   s   1871

Khumeni, George (Wealthy)
*Demogorgon* - Brian Lumley   h   3552

Khuzud, Kami (Entertainer)
*D'Shai* - Joel Rosenberg   f   4670

Khuzud, Kami (Detective)
*Hour of the Octopus* - Joel Rosenberg   f   4673

Khyriz (Royalty; Alien)
*Voices of Chaos* - A.C. Crispin   s   1266

Ki (Trader)
*Luck of the Wheels* - Megan Lindholm   f   3471

Kiakra, Darryl (Parent)
*Minerva Wakes* - Holly Lisle   f   3487

Kiakra, Minerva (Parent; Heroine)
*Minerva Wakes* - Holly Lisle   f   3487

Kiarda (Noblewoman)
*Spirit Fox* - Mickey Zucker Reichert   f   4524

Kickaha (Adventurer)
*More than Fire* - Philip Jose Farmer   s   1871

Kicva (Mythical Creature; Adventurer)
*A Child of Elvish* - Nancy Varian Berberick   f   457

Kid Death (Mutant; Criminal)
*The Einstein Intersection* - Samuel R.
  Delany   s   1481

Kid Zero (Outlaw)
*Ghost Dancers* - Brian Craig   s   1238

Kidd, Billy Lee (Singer)
*Deathsong* - Douglas Borton   h   575

Kidd, Christian (Advertising; Homosexual)
*That's All, Folks!* - Greg Snow   f   5148

Kidd, Malachy (Religious; Warrior)
*Eyes of Silver* - Michael A. Stackpole   f   5200

Kiera (Thief)
*Orca* - Steven Brust   f   745

Kiernan, Michael (Detective)
*Control Freak* - Christa Faust   h   1890

Kies, Wolfgang (Vigilante; Shaman)
*Wolf and Raven* - Michael A. Stackpole   f   5207

Kiff, Jim (Veteran)
*Darkborn* - Matthew J. Costello   h   1195

Kifo, Ndug "Brother Death" (Martial Arts Expert;
  Leader)
*Brother Death* - Steve Perry   s   4292

Kiin (Prehistoric Human; Indian)
*My Sister the Moon* - Sue Harrison   f   2582

Kiklu, Nathan (Twin; Psychic)
*Blood Brothers* - Brian Lumley   h   3546
*The Last Aerie* - Brian Lumley   h   3557

Kiklu, Nestor (Twin; Psychic)
*Blood Brothers* - Brian Lumley   h   3546

Kiklu, Nestor (Vampire; Twin)
*Bloodwars* - Brian Lumley   h   3547

Kiklu, Nestor (Twin; Psychic)
*The Last Aerie* - Brian Lumley   h   3557

Kikun (Alien; Warrior)
*Shadowkill* - Jo Clayton   s   1069
*Shadowplay* - Jo Clayton   s   1070
*Shadowspeer* - Jo Clayton   s   1071

Kilgour, Alex (Spaceman; Companion)
*Revenge of the Damned* - Allan Cole   s   1107

Kilgour, Alex (Royalty; Military Personnel)
*Vortex* - Allan Cole   s   1108

Killany, Mark (Police Officer)
*Night Cruise* - Billie Sue Mosiman   h   4041

Killany, Molly (Teenager)
*Night Cruise* - Billie Sue Mosiman   h   4041

Killdeer, Hunter (Police Officer)
*Living with the Reptiles* - Roger L.
  DiSilvestro   s   1563

Killeen (Parent; Wanderer)
*Sailing Bright Eternity* - Gregory Benford   s   449

Killeen (Spaceship Captain)
*Tides of Light* - Gregory Benford   s   450

Kilpatrick, Mark Michael (Artist; Serial Killer)
*Grave Markings* - Michael A. Arnzen   h   212

Kim (Teenager)
*Demons Don't Dream* - Piers Anthony   f   168

Kim (Apprentice; Magician)
*Magician's Ward* - Patricia C. Wrede   f   5976

Kim (Orphan)
*Mairelon the Magician* - Patricia C. Wrede   f   5977

Kim, Harry (Military Personnel)
*Her Klingon Soul* - Michael Jan Friedman   s   2064

Kim, Jenae (Genetically Altered Being)
*Lethe* - Tricia Sullivan   s   5354

Kimball, Donald (Detective—Private)
*American Psycho* - Brett Easton Ellis   h   1777

Kimball, Joel (Police Officer)
*Night* - Alan Rodgers   h   4649

Kimberlin, Elwyn (Spaceship Captain)
*The Tides of God* - Ted Reynolds   s   4567

Kimmler, Vic (Police Officer; Widow(er))
*Borderland: A Novel of Terror* - S.K.
  Epperson   h   1828

Kincaid, Astrid (Military Personnel; Space Explorer)
*The Transmigration of Souls* - William
  Barton   s   382

Kincaid, Hannah (Teenager)
*A Witch Across Time* - Gilbert B. Cross   f   1272

Kincannon, Aidan (Security Officer)
*Red, Red Robin* - Stephen Gallagher   h   2113

Kindle, Tom (Mountain Man)
*The Harvest* - Robert Charles Wilson   s   5909

Kindle, Verity (Historian; Time Traveler)
*To Say Nothing of the Dog* - Connie Willis   s   5874

Kindred, Lewis (Veteran)
*Kindred* - John Gideon   h   2222

King (Fugitive; Musician)
*River Rats* - Caroline Stevermer   s   5267

King, Depard (Murderer; Spy)
*Spindoc* - Steve Perry   s   4300

King, Elena "Lanie" (Computer Expert)
*Richter 10* - Arthur C. Clarke   s   1060

King, Ellen (Receptionist)
*The Faery Convention* - Brett Davis   f   1399

King, Greg (Military Personnel)
*Sink the Armada* - Keith William Andrews   s   142
*Treason in Time* - Keith William Andrews   s   143

King, Greta (Psychic; Child)
*The Place* - T.M. Wright   h   5993

King, Newman (Businessman)
*The Store* - Bentley Little   h   3497

King, Schuyler "Skye" (Professor; Detective—
  Amateur)
*MagicNet* - John DeChancie   f   1461

Kingston, April (Advertising; Artist)
*Nightlife* - Brian Hodge   h   2702

**Kingston-Gray, April** (Advertising; Artist)
*The Darker Saints* - Brian Hodge   *h*   2699

**Kinion, Richard** (Police Officer)
*The Case of the Police Officer's Cock Ring and the Piano Player Who Had No Fingers* - Edward Lee   *h*   3388

**Kinkaid, Johnny** (Werewolf)
*Moon Dance* - S.P. Somtow   *h*   5158

**Kinner's Son, Kensher** (Rancher; Businessman)
*The Blood of a Dragon* - Lawrence Watt-Evans   *f*   5640

**Kinney, Michael** (Religious)
*Dark Debts* - Karen Hall   *h*   2494

**Kinnison, Kimball** (Military Personnel; Psychic)
*Galactic Patrol* - Edward E. Smith   *s*   5116
*Gray Lensman* - Edward E. Smith   *s*   5117

**Kinoshita, Ito** (Martial Arts Expert)
*The Widowmaker Reborn* - Mike Resnick   *s*   4560

**Kinsey, Doc** (Prisoner)
*The Night Seasons* - J.N. Williamson   *h*   5858

**Kintner, Edward** (Scientist; Government Official)
*Paths to Otherwhere* - James P. Hogan   *s*   2728

**Kira** (Military Personnel; Alien)
*Bloodletter* - K.W. Jeter   *s*   2908
*Devil in the Sky* - Greg Cox   *s*   1226

**Kirby, Erin** (Detective—Police)
*The Asylum* - John E. Ames   *h*   93

**Kirby, Gertrude** (Child-Care Giver)
*The Jekyll Legacy* - Robert Bloch   *h*   535

**Kirby, Paul** (Journalist)
*The Chosen* - Edward Lee   *h*   3389

**Kire** (Military Personnel)
*They Fly at Ciron* - Samuel R. Delany   *s*   1482

**Kireyevsky, Vasily "Vasha"** (Warrior; Bastard Son)
*The Law of Becoming* - Kate Elliott   *s*   1774

**Kirha** (Alien; Warrior)
*Wing Commander: Freedom Flight* - Mercedes Lackey   *s*   3307

**Kiriel** (Orphan)
*The Broken Crown* - Michelle West   *f*   5757

**Kirilovich, Vasily "Temsik"** (Vampire)
*Out for Blood* - John Peyton Cooke   *h*   1166

**Kirk** (Orphan)
*Elfwood* - Rose Estes   *f*   1837

**Kirk, George Samuel** (Parent; Spaceman)
*Best Destiny* - Diane Carey   *s*   900

**Kirk, James T.** (Spaceship Captain)
*The Ashes of Eden* - William Shatner   *s*   4927
*Assignment: Eternity* - Greg Cox   *s*   1225
*Avenger* - William Shatner   *s*   4928

**Kirk, James T.** (Spaceship Captain; Time Traveler)
*The City on the Edge of Forever* - Harlan Ellison   *s*   1784

**Kirk, James T.** (Spaceship Captain)
*The Disinherited* - Peter David   *s*   1381
*Doctor's Orders* - Diane Duane   *s*   1659
*Enemy Unseen* - V.E. Mitchell   *s*   3918

**Kirk, James T.** (Spaceship Captain; Aged Person)
*The Fearful Summons* - Denny Martin Flinn   *s*   1954

**Kirk, James T.** (Spaceship Captain)
*Federation* - Judith Reeves-Stevens   *s*   4511
*First Frontier* - Diane Carey   *s*   902
*First Strike* - Diane Carey   *s*   903
*A Flag Full of Stars* - Brad Ferguson   *s*   1922
*The Joy Machine* - James Gunn   *s*   2458
*The Kobayashi Maru* - Julia Ecklar   *s*   1728
*Mind Meld* - John Vornholt   *s*   5596
*Prime Directive* - Judith Reeves-Stevens   *s*   4514
*Probe* - Margaret Wander Bonanno   *s*   569

*Renegade* - Gene DeWeese   *s*   1511
*The Return* - William Shatner   *s*   4933
*The Rift* - Peter David   *s*   1386
*Rules of Engagement* - Peter Morwood   *s*   4037
*Sanctuary* - John Vornholt   *s*   5597
*Spectre* - William Shatner   *s*   4934
*Star Trek VI: The Undiscovered Country* - J.M. Dillard   *s*   1556
*Star Trek: The Classic Episodes 1* - James Blish   *s*   526
*Star Trek: The Classic Episodes 2* - James Blish   *s*   527
*Star Trek: The Classic Episodes 3* - James Blish   *s*   528
*Star Trek: The Lost Years* - J.M. Dillard   *s*   1557
*Starfleet Academy* - Diane Carey   *s*   905

**Kirk, James T.** (Military Personnel; Spaceship Captain)
*Traitor Winds* - L.A. Graf   *s*   2298

**Kirk, James T.** (Spaceship Captain)
*War Dragons* - L.A. Graf   *s*   2299
*Windows on a Lost World* - V.E. Mitchell   *s*   3920

**Kirk, James T. "Jimmy"** (Teenager; Adventurer)
*Best Destiny* - Diane Carey   *s*   900

**Kirk, Peter James** (Student)
*Sarek* - A.C. Crispin   *s*   1260

**Kirkland, Larry** (Psychic; Vampire Hunter)
*Bloody Bones* - Laurell K. Hamilton   *h*   2512
*Circus of the Damned* - Laurell K. Hamilton   *h*   2515

**Kirkpatrick, Stanley** (Police Officer)
*The Spider #8: The Devil's Paymaster/Legions of the Accursed Light* - Grant Stockbridge   *f*   5309

**Kirov, Natasha Alyosha Katerina** (Spaceship Captain)
*Voyage to the Red Planet* - Terry Bisson   *s*   508

**Kirowa, Niala** (Administrator; Agent)
*The Planet Beyond* - Steve Mudd   *s*   4043

**Kirshner, Martin** (Criminal)
*Worst Nightmare* - Ric Meyers   *h*   3883

**Kirtha** (Child; Magician)
*Mind of the Magic* - Holly Lisle   *f*   3486

**Kishida, Katie** (Widow(er); Revolutionary)
*Tech-Heaven* - Linda Nagata   *s*   4066

**Kit** (Military Personnel)
*A Hero Born* - Michael A. Stackpole   *f*   5202

**Kitatimate, Alexander "Sander"** (Prisoner; Computer Expert)
*Cinderblock* - Janine Ellen Young   *s*   6047

**Kitchener, Edward** (Scientist)
*A Quantum Murder* - Peter F. Hamilton   *s*   2527

**Kite, Dorothy** (Librarian)
*The Devil's Cradle* - Kate Stewart   *h*   5269

**Kith-Kanan** (Mythical Creature; Royalty)
*Firstborn* - Paul B. Thompson   *f*   5454

**Kith-Kanan** (Mythical Creature; Warrior)
*The Kinslayer Wars* - Douglas Niles   *f*   4109
*The Qualinesti* - Paul B. Thompson   *f*   5455

**Kittridge, Valerie** (Student)
*Witch-Light* - Nancy Holder   *h*   2734

**K'Kai** (Alien; Spaceship Captain)
*Wing Commander: Freedom Flight* - Mercedes Lackey   *s*   3307

**Klaverel-va-Hynkkel** (Traveler)
*The Mark of the Cat* - Andre Norton   *f*   4157

**Kleiffer, Milton** (Doctor)
*Retro Lives* - Lee Grimes   *s*   2446

**Klein, Alice** (Teenager; Apprentice)
*Higher Education* - Charles Sheffield   *s*   4958

**Klein, Lance** (Businessman)
*Night Relics* - James P. Blaylock   *h*   521

**Klemay, Keff** (Spaceman)
*The Ship Who Won* - Anne McCaffrey   *s*   3750

**Kline, Cynthia** (Spy)
*The Armageddon Crazy* - Mick Farren   *s*   1877

**Kline, Felix** (Psychic; Businessman)
*Sepulchre* - James Herbert   *h*   2672

**Klingsor** (Sorcerer)
*The Grail of Hearts* - Susan Shwartz   *f*   5015

**KLse** (Alien; Telepath)
*GodHeads* - Emily Devenport   *s*   1501

**Kluge, Wilhelm** (Military Personnel; Vampire)
*At Sword's Point* - Scott MacMillan   *f*   3601
*Knights of the Blood* - Scott MacMillan   *f*   3602

**Knifedancer, Railu** (Military Personnel)
*The Illusionists* - Faren Miller   *f*   3894

**Knight, Aubrey** (Martial Arts Expert; Spouse)
*Firedance* - Steven Barnes   *s*   360

**Knight, Aubrey** (Martial Arts Expert; Sports Figure)
*Gorgon Child* - Steven Barnes   *s*   361

**Knight, Campbell** (Businessman)
*Seeing Eye* - Jack Ellis   *h*   1780

**Knight, Dean** (Parent)
*The Monastery* - J.N. Williamson   *h*   5856

**Knight, Gabriel** (Writer)
*The Beast Within: A Gabriel Knight Mystery* - Jane Jensen   *h*   2895
*Gabriel Knight: Sins of the Fathers* - Jane Jensen   *h*   2896

**Knight, Joshua** (Child)
*Escardy Gap* - Peter Crowther   *h*   1282

**Knight, Nicholas** (Detective—Homicide; Vampire)
*Forever Knight: A Stirring of Dust* - Susan Sizemore   *h*   5078
*Forever Knight: Intimations of Mortality* - Susan M. Garrett   *h*   2149

**Knight, Rachel** (Scientist)
*The Serpent Slayers* - Adam Niswander   *h*   4113

**Knight, Stormy** (Journalist)
*Prey* - William W. Johnstone   *h*   2932

**Knobil** (Wanderer)
*West of January* - Dave Duncan   *s*   1691

**Knossus** (Alien)
*Larissa* - Emily Devenport   *s*   1503
*Shade* - Emily Devenport   *s*   1504

**Knott, Wyoming "Wyoh"** (Revolutionary)
*The Moon Is a Harsh Mistress* - Robert A. Heinlein   *s*   2645

**Knox, Edward** (Gambler)
*The 7th Guest* - Matthew J. Costello   *h*   1192

**Knox, Emily** (Teenager)
*Blood Lust* - Ron Dee   *h*   1464

**Knudsen, Arne** (Police Officer)
*Master of Lies* - Graham Masterton   *h*   3676

**Ko** (Animal)
*Monkey Station* - Ardath Mayhar   *s*   3703

**Ko, Melody** (Adventurer; Engineer)
*Nightfeeder* - Judith Reeves-Stevens   *f*   4513
*Shifter* - Judith Reeves-Stevens   *f*   4515

**Ko, Shang** (Wizard)
*Bride of the Rat God* - Barbara Hambly   *f*   2499

**Kobir, Nikolai** (Spaceship Captain; Pirate)
*Canby's Legion* - Bill Baldwin   *s*   308

**Kochevikov, Pyetr** (Hero)
*Chernevog* - C.J. Cherryh   *f*   982

**Kochevikov, Pyetr** (Hero; Fugitive)
*Rusalka* - C.J. Cherryh   *f*   1002

**Kochevikov, Pyetr** (Hero)
*Yvgenie* - C.J. Cherryh   *f*   1005

**Koda-Levin, Anais** (Doctor)
*Dark Water's Embrace* - Stephen Leigh   *s*   3426

**Kodesh, Kli** (Vampire)
*To Speak in Lifeless Tongues* - David Niall
   Wilson   *h*   5883
*The Winnowing* - Gherbod Fleming   *h*   1950

**Koenig, Willy** (Secretary)
*Psychomech* - Brian Lumley   *h*   3562

**Koja** (Religious)
*Horselords* - David Cook   *f*   1145

**Kole, Polly** (Pharmacist)
*Flesh* - Gus Weill   *h*   5685

**Kolkey, Alan** (Scientist; Psychic)
*Walker between the Worlds* - Diane
   DesRochers   *f*   1499

**Kollberg, Arturo** (Businessman)
*Heroes Die* - Matthew Woodring Stover   *s*   5319

**Kominsky, Katerina "Kate"** (Sea Captain; Scientist)
*The Secret Oceans* - Betty Ballantine   *s*   318

**Komodo** (Teenager)
*Gojiro* - Mark Jacobson   *f*   2847

**Komus** (Entertainer)
*Song of the Gargoyle* - Zilpha Keatley
   Snyder   *f*   5153

**Kondratieff, David** (Administrator)
*Double Planet* - John Gribbin   *s*   2433

**Konnor** (Military Personnel)
*The Outlander: Captivity* - B.J. Salterberg   *s*   4792

**Konrad** (Servant)
*Konrad* - David Ferring   *f*   1927

**Konrad** (Warrior)
*Shadowbreed* - David Ferring   *f*   1928

**Konstantin, Damon** (Administrator)
*Downbelow Station* - C.J. Cherryh   *s*   985

**Konstantin, Dore** (Detective—Homicide)
*Tea From an Empty Cup* - Pat Cadigan   *s*   809

**Kontsandas, Esteban** (Military Personnel)
*Winning Colors* - Elizabeth Moon   *s*   3976

**Koolhan, Sara** (Scientist; Linguist)
*Heaven's Reach* - David Brin   *s*   687

**Kopal, Jefferson "Jeff"** (Heir; Cyborg)
*The Cyborg From Earth* - Charles Sheffield   *s*   4952

**Kopp, Curly** (Store Owner)
*Seaward* - Brad Leithauser   *h*   3433

**Korendil** (Royalty; Mythical Creature)
*Bedlam's Bard* - Mercedes Lackey   *f*   3269

**Korendil** (Mythical Creature; Royalty)
*Knight of Ghosts and Shadows* - Mercedes
   Lackey   *f*   3285
*Summoned to Tourney* - Mercedes Lackey   *f*   3299

**Korendir** (Adventurer; Mercenary)
*The Master of Whitestorm* - Janny Wurts   *f*   6003

**Kori** (Hunter; Prehistoric Human)
*The Animal Wife* - Elizabeth Marshall
   Thomas   *f*   5444

**Koriba** (Religious; Aged Person)
*Kirinyaga: A Fable of Utopia* - Mike
   Resnick   *s*   4548

**Korie, Jonathan Thomas** (Spaceship Captain)
*The Middle of Nowhere* - David Gerrold   *s*   2209

**Korie, Jonathan Thomas** (Military Personnel)
*Voyage of the Star Wolf* - David Gerrold   *s*   2212

**Korinaam the Shapeshifter** (Guide; Linguist)
*The Mountains of Majipoor* - Robert
   Silverberg   *s*   5037

**Kornfeld-Taggert, Sieglinde** (Scientist)
*Delta Pavonis* - Eric Kotani   *s*   3221

**Korrey, Eula** (Religious)
*Chariot* - Charles L. Grant   *h*   2304

**Korsakov, Jahn** (Psychic)
*One Mind's Eye* - Kathy Tyers   *s*   5525

**Korsibar** (Royalty)
*Sorcerers of Majipoor* - Robert Silverberg   *s*   5041

**Korsyzczy, Nela Zy-Czorsky** (Twin; Time Traveler)
*Sideshow* - Sheri S. Tepper   *s*   5436

**Kort** (Robot; Artificial Intelligence)
*Star Child* - James P. Hogan   *s*   2730

**K'os** (Indian; Avenger)
*Song of the River* - Sue Harrison   *f*   2583

**Kosarek, Deborah** (Writer)
*Children of the End* - Mark A. Clements   *h*   1084

**Koscuisko, Andrej** (Doctor; Student)
*An Exchange of Hostages* - Susan R.
   Matthews   *s*   3692

**Koscuisko, Andrej** (Doctor)
*Prisoner of Conscience* - Susan R.
   Matthews   *s*   3693

**Koshka, Ulysses** (Werewolf)
*Under the Shadow* - Jane Toombs   *h*   5481

**Kostal, Miriam** (Police Officer)
*River of Dust* - Alexander Jablokov   *s*   2840

**Kostanuik, April** (Child; Musician)
*Torment* - Stephen R. George   *h*   2204

**Koster, Laurence "Larry"** (Actor)
*Preternatural* - Margaret Wander Bonanno   *s*   568

**Kostimon** (Ruler)
*Reign of Shadows* - Deborah Chester   *f*   1009

**Kostner, Harry** (Miner)
*Unearthed* - Ashley McConnell   *h*   3778

**Koto** (Saloon Keeper/Owner)
*The Famished Road* - Ben Okri   *f*   4207

**Koto** (Saloon Keeper/Owner; Political Figure)
*Songs of Enchantment* - Ben Okri   *f*   4208

**Koussevitzky, Clifford "Cliff"** (Parent)
*Captain Jack Zodiac* - Michael Kandel   *f*   3009

**Koyil** (Alien; Ruler)
*Fallway* - Paula E. Downing   *s*   1593

**Kozel, Dina** (Spacewoman; Traitor)
*Siduri's Net* - P.K. McAllister   *s*   3709

**Kozinski, Judy** (Journalist)
*Oaths and Miracles* - Nancy Kress   *s*   3242

**Kr, Duncan** (Spaceship Captain; Empath)
*Glory's People* - Alfred Coppel   *s*   1183
*Glory's War* - Alfred Coppel   *s*   1184

**Kraal** (Alien)
*The Artifact* - W. Michael Gear   *s*   2165

**Kraeken** (Vampire)
*Shrines and Desecrations* - Brian Hodge   *h*   2705

**Kraft, Jason** (Spaceman)
*Redshift Rendezvous* - John E. Stith   *s*   5305

**Krake, Francis** (Spaceship Captain)
*The Singers of Time* - Frederik Pohl   *s*   4354

**Kramer, Alan** (Doctor)
*Fatal Outcome* - Patricia Wallace   *h*   5622

**Kramer, George** (Writer)
*The Dealings of Daniel Kesserich* - Fritz
   Leiber   *s*   3417

**Kramer, Paul "Papa"** (Scientist)
*The Silent City* - Elisabeth Vonarburg   *s*   5592

**Kramer, Richard** (Scientist)
*Deadly Dreams* - Gerald A. Schiller   *h*   4874

**Kravitz, Sol** (Producer)
*Big Rock Beat* - Greg Kihn   *h*   3102

**Krebs, Scott** (Student)
*But What of Earth?* - Piers Anthony   *s*   163

**Krecis** (Alien; Spaceship Captain)
*Saturn's Child* - Nichelle Nichols   *s*   4101

**Kreeblim** (Alien)
*My Teacher Flunked the Planet* - Bruce
   Coville   *s*   1222

**Kregler, Timothy** (Spirit)
*The Land of Nod* - Mark A. Clements   *h*   1085

**Kreident, Craig** (FBI Agent)
*Lethal Exposure* - Kevin J. Anderson   *s*   110
*Virtual Destruction* - Kevin J. Anderson   *s*   118

**Kreider, Tomus** (Spaceman; Scientist)
*Flies From the Amber* - Wil McCarthy   *s*   3763

**Kren** (Genetically Altered Being; Military Personnel)
*The Lanterns of God* - Ron Sarti   *s*   4835

**Kresh, Alvar** (Lawman)
*Caliban* - Roger MacBride Allen   *s*   77
*Inferno* - Roger MacBride Allen   *s*   78

**Kresh, Alvar** (Political Figure)
*Utopia* - Roger MacBride Allen   *s*   83

**Kreutzer, Friedrich** (Writer)
*Mordenheim* - Chet Williamson   *h*   5847

**Krieg, Thomas L. Jr.** (Architect)
*Revenant* - Melanie Tem   *h*   5424

**Krieger, Stefan** (Time Traveler)
*Lightning* - Dean R. Koontz   *h*   3211

**Krillen** (Alien; Detective)
*Ancestor's World* - A.C. Crispin   *s*   1259

**Krim** (Military Personnel; Spaceman)
*The Hidden War* - Michael Armstrong   *s*   209

**Kris, Tabrel** (Diplomat)
*Exile* - Al Sarrantonio   *s*   4829

**Krishna the Holy Mendoro** (Telepath; Religious)
*The Ninety Trillion Fausts* - Jack L. Chalker   *s*   958

**Krisos, Alexander** (Wealthy)
*Lord of the Dark Lake* - Ron Faust   *h*   1894

**Krispos** (Ruler)
*Krispos of Videssos* - Harry Turtledove   *f*   5506

**Krispos** (Adventurer)
*Krispos Rising* - Harry Turtledove   *f*   5507

**Krispos** (Ruler)
*Krispos the Emperor* - Harry Turtledove   *f*   5508

**Kristin** (Royalty)
*The Sixth Book of Lost Swords: Mindsword's Story* -
   Fred Saberhagen   *f*   4776

**Kristinsson, Garth** (Orphan; Traveler)
*Hidden Fires* - Katharine Eliska Kimbriel   *s*   3117

**Kro, Gulthar** (Criminal; Spy)
*The Regiment's War* - John Dalmas   *s*   1326

**Kroft, Brian** (Journalist)
*The Undine* - Michael O'Rourke   *h*   4224

**Krokodil** (Cyborg)
*Comeback Tour: The Sky Belongs to the Stars* - Jack
   Yeovil   *s*   6020

**Kromman** (Wizard; Spy)
*The Gilded Chain: A Tale of the King's Blades* - Dave
   Duncan   *f*   1679

**Kronarsson, Kraki** (Adventurer)
*One Quest, Hold the Dragons* - Greg
   Costikyan   *f*   1208

**Kronis** (Nobleman)
*Sons of the Titans* - Patrick H. Adkins   *f*   36

**Kruger, Clayton Allen** (Pilot)
*Deadly Breed* - T.J. Kirby   *h*   3153

**Kruickshank, Jenny** (Teenager; Warrior)
*The Whims of Creation* - Simon Hawke   *s*   2626

**Krulshards** (Demon)
*Palace of Kings* - Mike Jefferies   *f*   2887

**Kryn** (Heir—Dispossessed; Outlaw)
*The Hands of Lyr* - Andre Norton   *f*   4154

**Krystal** (Military Personnel)
*The Death of Chaos* - L.E. Modesitt Jr.   *f*   3926

**Krystal** (Adventurer)
*The Magic of Recluce* - L.E. Modesitt Jr.   *f*   3934

**Krystel** (Government Official; Scout)
*Hellworld* - Simon R. Green   *s*   2371

**Kryten** (Robot)
*Better than Life* - Grant Naylor   *s*   4076

**Kuan Yu-Chen** (Religious)
*The Only Thing to Fear* - Robert Morgan   *h*   4003

**Kubick, Ruby** (Construction Worker; Recluse)
*Glass Houses* - Laura J. Mixon   *s*   3921

**Kullervo, Reede Kulleva** (Genetically Altered Being; Researcher)
*The Summer Queen* - Joan D. Vinge   *s*   5572

**Kullervo, Vyra** (Alien; Insurance Investigator)
*Greenthieves* - Alan Dean Foster   *s*   2005

**Kun, Holger** (Military Personnel)
*A Knight Among Knaves* - Robert N. Charrette   *f*   974

**Kundry** (Immortal; Wanderer)
*The Grail of Hearts* - Susan Shwartz   *f*   5015

**Kune** (Doctor)
*The Off Season* - Jack Cady   *f*   820

**Kung, Evelyn** (Widow(er))
*The Lincoln Hunters* - Wilson Tucker   *s*   5487

**Kurasawa, Sho** (Military Personnel)
*The Painful Field* - Roland J. Green   *s*   2351
*The Sum of Things* - Roland J. Green   *s*   2353

**Kurimoto, Eva** (Journalist)
*Protektor* - Charles Platt   *s*   4342

**Kurosawa, Oishi** (Warrior)
*The Napoleon Wager* - William R. Forstchen   *s*   1980

**Kurosov'e, Malyene Andreivne "Malye"** (Leader)
*The Fall of Sirius* - Wil McCarthy   *s*   3762

**Kurtz, Rupert** (Doctor)
*Headhunter* - Timothy Findley   *h*   1939

**Kurtzweill, Alvin** (Scientist)
*The X-Files: Fight the Future* - Chris Carter   *h*   924

**Kuruk** (Cult Member)
*Deathsong* - Douglas Borton   *h*   575

**Kurz** (Alien; Spy)
*Fire in the Sky* - Jo Clayton   *s*   1067

**Kusac** (Psychic; Alien)
*Fire Margins* - Lisanne Norman   *s*   4137
*Fortune's Wheel* - Lisanne Norman   *s*   4138
*Razor's Edge* - Lisanne Norman   *s*   4139
*Turning Point* - Lisanne Norman   *s*   4140

**Kusaka, Michael** (Spaceship Captain; Immortal)
*The Dark Beyond the Stars* - Frank M. Robinson   *s*   4626

**Kustaa, Captain Fred** (Pilot)
*Under the Yoke* - S.M. Stirling   *s*   5301

**Kuttner, Dayne** (Nurse)
*Sympathy for the Devil* - Holly Lisle   *f*   3488

**Kuvasc, Paval** (Apprentice; Scientist)
*Regenesis* - Julia Ecklar   *s*   1729

**Kuwai** (Indian; Royalty)
*Dark Legend* - Jamake Highwater   *f*   2686

**K'vin** (Leader)
*Dragonseye* - Anne McCaffrey   *s*   3730

**Kwan, Martin** (Lawyer)
*Cutthroat* - Michael Slade   *h*   5084

**Kwan, Roxane** (Wanderer)
*Mazeway* - Jack Williamson   *s*   5866

**Kwip** (Thief)
*Castle Spellbound* - John DeChancie   *s*   1454

**Ky, Niki** (Dancer)
*Silk* - Caitlin R. Kiernan   *h*   3101

**Kyl** (Mythical Creature; Heir)
*The Dragon Crown* - Richard A. Knaak   *f*   3168

**Kyla** (Young Woman)
*Engor's Sword Arm* - David C. Smith   *h*   5110

**Kyle, Amy** (Psychic)
*The Nexus* - Mike McQuay   *f*   3860

**Kyle, Selena "Catwoman"** (Criminal; Heroine)
*Batman Returns* - Craig Shaw Gardner   *s*   2124
*Catwoman* - Lynn Abbey   *s*   14
*The Further Adventures of Batman 3: Featuring Catwoman* - Martin H. Greenberg   *s*   2392

**Kyler, Vaughan** (Organized Crime Figure)
*Blood on the Water* - P.N. Elrod   *h*   1791

**Kylie, Gabriel** (Backwoodsman; Rebel)
*Anvil* - Nicolas van Pallandt   *s*   5540

**Kyllikki** (Alien; Telepath)
*Dreamspy* - Jacqueline Lichtenberg   *s*   3458

**Kymri** (Pilot; Alien)
*Grounded!* - Chris Claremont   *s*   1041


# L

**La Cava, Lou** (Detective)
*Fallen* - Dee Graham   *h*   2302

**La Cotta, Paul** (Teacher)
*Dawn Song* - Michael Marano   *h*   3620

**La Forge, Geordi** (Engineer; Military Personnel)
*Balance of Power* - Dafydd ab Hugh   *s*   7
*Dark Mirror* - Diane Duane   *s*   1658
*Doomsday World* - Carmen Carter   *s*   923
*Relics* - Michael Jan Friedman   *s*   2066
*Requiem* - Michael Jan Friedman   *s*   2067
*Vendetta* - Peter David   *s*   1389

**La Plante, Etienne** (Criminal)
*Wolf and Raven* - Michael A. Stackpole   *f*   5207

**LaBianca, Diana** (Producer)
*The Hunger of the Beast* - John Driver   *h*   1656

**Labonta, Anthony** (Lawyer)
*Flesh and Gold* - Phyllis Gotlieb   *s*   2286

**LaBrae, Jael** (Pilot; Heroine)
*Dragon Rigger* - Jeffrey A. Carver   *s*   929

**Labyrinth, Doc** (Scientist)
*The Collected Stories of Philip K. Dick, Volume One: The Short Happy Life of the Brown Oxford* - Philip K. Dick   *s*   1519

**Lacan, Arnauld** (Scientist)
*The Hollowing* - Robert Holdstock   *f*   2738

**Lace, Invictus Ovidius "I.O."** (Orphan)
*A Dozen Tough Jobs* - Howard Waldrop   *f*   5612

**Lacerda, Zefty** (Waiter/Waitress)
*Trader* - Charles de Lint   *f*   1438

**Lacey, Bobbie** (Computer Expert; Police Officer)
*Polar City Blues* - Katharine Kerr   *s*   3073

**Lacey, Jenny** (Writer)
*Vampire Blood* - Kathryn Meyer Griffith   *h*   2441

**Lacey, Joey** (Restaurateur)
*Vampire Blood* - Kathryn Meyer Griffith   *h*   2441

**lach Feragh, Culain** (Immortal; Warrior)
*Ghost King* - David Gemmell   *f*   2188

**Lachlan "Locke"** (Military Personnel)
*A Hero Born* - Michael A. Stackpole   *f*   5202

**LaCroix, Lucien** (Radio Personality; Vampire)
*Forever Knight: A Stirring of Dust* - Susan Sizemore   *h*   5078

**Lacroix, Marc** (Doctor)
*Machine* - Rene Belletto   *h*   436

**Lacroix, Marie** (Housewife)
*Machine* - Rene Belletto   *h*   436

**Lacuna** (Housewife; Agent)
*Question Quest* - Piers Anthony   *f*   186

**Lady** (Military Personnel; Sorcerer)
*Dreams of Steel* - Glen Cook   *f*   1150

**Lady** (Aged Person)
*Boy's Life* - Robert R. McCammon   *h*   3754

**Laela** (Mythical Creature; Magician)
*Twisted Dragon* - Kevin Stein   *f*   5251

**Lafall, Teksan** (Traveler)
*Delan the Mislaid* - Laurie J. Marks   *f*   3625

**LaFayette, Morgan** (Tourist)
*The Last Highlander* - Claire Cross   *f*   1271

**LaFitte, Shane** (Religious)
*Voodoo Child* - Michael Reaves   *h*   4498

**LaFontaine, Horace "Gray Redstar"** (Reanimated Dead; Murderer)
*Blue Light* - Walter Mosley   *s*   4042

**Lagenkamp, Heather** (Actress; Historical Figure)
*Wes Craven's New Nightmare* - David Bergantino   *h*   460

**Lahikainen, Sarah** (Student—College)
*Cold Whisper* - Rick Hautala   *h*   2605

**Laidcliff, Cullen** (Government Official)
*Looking for the Mahdi* - N. Lee Wood   *s*   5966

**Laidlaw, Alison** (Police Officer)
*Cloud Castles* - Michael Scott Rohan   *f*   4659

**Laine** (Military Personnel)
*Barrenlands* - Doranna Durgin   *f*   1702

**Laine, Bonnie** (Parent)
*Nightscape* - Stephen R. George   *h*   2203

**Laine, Evan** (Child)
*Nightscape* - Stephen R. George   *h*   2203

**Laitha "Gian Avur"** (Orphan; Young Woman)
*Ghost King* - David Gemmell   *f*   2188

**Lake, Dana** (Tour Guide)
*The Midnight Tour* - Richard Laymon   *h*   3368

**Lakeman, Max** (Landscaper)
*Max Lakeman and the Beautiful Stranger* - Jon Cohen   *f*   1098

**Laker, Maria** (Spouse; Murderer)
*Among Madmen* - Jim Starlin   *s*   5212

**Laker, Naomi "Mig" Margaret** (Teenager; Writer)
*Aunt Maria* - Diana Wynne Jones   *f*   2943

**Laker, Tom** (Lawman)
*Among Madmen* - Jim Starlin   *s*   5212

**Lakshmi** (Mythical Creature)
*My Son, the Wizard* - Christopher Stasheff   *f*   5218

**"Lal" Lalkhamsin-Khamsolal** (Sailor)
*The Innkeeper's Song* - Peter S. Beagle   *f*   409

**Laleekh** (Alien)
*Bagatelle—Guinevere* - Nancy Bogen   *f*   558

**Lalelelang** (Historian; Alien)
*The Spoils of War* - Alan Dean Foster   *s*   2016

**Lamai, Leie** (Teenager; Twin)
*Glory Season* - David Brin   *s*   686

**Lamai, Maia** (Teenager; Traveler)
*Glory Season* - David Brin   *s*   686

**Lamaril** (Hero; Warrior)
*Golden Trillium* - Andre Norton   *f*   4153

**Lamashtu** (Demon)
*Son of Darkness* - Josepha Sherman   *f*   4990

**Lamb, Toby** (Child)
*The Haunting of Lamb House* - Joan Aiken   *h*   45

**Lambert, Constance** (Teacher)
*The Stone Circle* - Gary Goshgarian   *h*   2285

**Lambert, Dan** (Worker; Veteran)
*Gone South* - Robert R. McCammon   *h*   3755

**Lambert, Natalie** (Doctor)
*Forever Knight: A Stirring of Dust* - Susan
   Sizemore   *h*   5078
*Forever Knight: Intimations of Mortality* - Susan M.
   Garrett   *h*   2149

**Lambert, Richard** (Businessman)
*A Once and Future Love* - Anne Kelleher   *f*   3039

**Lambert, Tom** (Doctor)
*Tomorrow and Tomorrow* - Charles
   Sheffield   *s*   4966

**Lamont, Gail** (Housewife)
*Dead Voices* - Abigail McDaniels   *h*   3783

**Lamont, Roger** (Businessman)
*Dead Voices* - Abigail McDaniels   *h*   3783

**Lamruil** (Ruler)
*Evermeet: Island of Elves* - Elaine
   Cunningham   *f*   1290

**Lan, Song** (Scientist)
*Bright Angel* - John Blair   *s*   512

**LaNague, Peter** (Revolutionary)
*The LaNague Chronicles* - F. Paul Wilson   *s*   5889

**Lanakila** (Animal)
*Catamount* - Michael Peak   *f*   4273

**Lanart-Hastur, Mikhail** (Nobleman; Psychic;
   Telepath)
*Exile's Song* - Marion Zimmer Bradley   *s*   632

**Lanart-Hastur, Mikhail** (Telepath; Nobleman;
   Psychic)
*The Shadow Matrix* - Marion Zimmer
   Bradley   *s*   645

**Lancaster, Whitney** (Political Figure)
*Breeder* - Ed Kelleher   *h*   3041

**Lancelot** (Knight)
*The Child Queen* - Nancy McKenzie   *f*   3827
*Chronicles of King Arthur* - Andrea
   Hopkins   *f*   2767
*Guinevere: The Legend in Autumn* - Persia
   Woolley   *f*   5970
*Queen of the Summer Stars* - Persia
   Woolley   *f*   5971

**Land, Garrett** (Businessman)
*Demon Within* - Dana Reed   *h*   4499

**Lander** (Revolutionary)
*The Parched Sea* - Troy Denning   *f*   1486

**Landers, Diana** (Writer)
*The Beast* - Marie Ardell White   *h*   5784

**Lando, Pik** (Smuggler; Spaceship Captain)
*Drifter* - William C. Dietz   *s*   1543
*Drifter's Run* - William C. Dietz   *s*   1544
*Drifter's War* - William C. Dietz   *s*   1545

**Landon, Harry** (Photographer)
*I'll Be Watching You* - Samuel M. Key   *h*   3094

**Landry, Jack** (Handyman)
*Dark Debts* - Karen Hall   *h*   2494

**Lane, Hester** (Writer)
*The Jekyll Legacy* - Robert Bloch   *h*   535

**Lane, Lois** (Journalist; Girlfriend)
*The Death and Life of Superman* - Roger
   Stern   *s*   5262
*Lois & Clark* - C.J. Cherryh   *s*   999

**Lane, Thomas** (Student)
*Tam Lin* - Pamela Dean   *f*   1446

**Laney, Colin** (Consultant; Researcher)
*Idoru* - William Gibson   *s*   2218

**Lanfranc, Guy** (Nobleman)
*Kingdom of the Grail* - A.A. Attanasio   *f*   269

**Lang, Alice "Lancaster"** (Journalist; Writer)
*Einstein's Bridge* - John Cramer   *s*   1244

**Lang, Darya** (Scientist; Adventurer)
*Convergence* - Charles Sheffield   *s*   4951
*Divergence* - Charles Sheffield   *s*   4954
*Summertide* - Charles Sheffield   *s*   4965
*Transcendence* - Charles Sheffield   *s*   4967

**Lang, Edward Winslow** (Government Official;
   Businessman)
*Sheltered Lives* - Charles Oberndorf   *s*   4188

**Lang, Gabriel** (Political Figure)
*Rage of Spirits* - Noel Hynd   *h*   2824

**Lang, Jacqueline "Jaqe"** (Parent; Lesbian)
*Godmother Night* - Rachel Pollack   *f*   4358

**Lange, Lizbet** (Waiter/Waitress)
*Charlie's Bones* - L.L. Thrasher   *h*   5468

**Langelleik, Holjpip** (Ruler)
*Crystal Witness* - Kathy Tyers   *s*   5524

**Langston, Fred** (Police Officer)
*Blood* - Ron Dee   *h*   1463

**Langtry, Cimarron** (Wanderer)
*The Earth Remembers* - Susan Torian Olan   *s*   4209

**Lani** (Clone)
*Masque* - F. Paul Wilson   *s*   5890

**Lanier, Garry** (Engineer)
*Eon* - Greg Bear   *s*   417

**Lannan** (Military Personnel; Psychic)
*The Price of the Stars* - Debra Doyle   *s*   1604

**Lannat** (Military Personnel)
*The Prisoner Within* - Donald E. McQuinn   *s*   3861
*With Full Honors* - Donald E. McQuinn   *s*   3865

**Lannister, Tyrion** (Bastard Son; Handicapped)
*A Game of Thrones* - George R.R. Martin   *f*   3645

**Lansen, Mark** (Professor)
*Golden Eyes* - John Gideon   *h*   2220

**Lansing, Gilbert "Keith"** (Administrator; Immortal)
*Starplex* - Robert J. Sawyer   *s*   4859

**Lanta** (Religious; Psychic)
*Wanderer* - Donald E. McQuinn   *s*   3862

**LaPorte, Eva** (Doctor)
*Bloodletter* - Warren Newton Beath   *h*   426

**Lara** (Spirit; Witch)
*The Shadow Eater* - Adam Lee   *f*   3386

**Lara, Katherine** (Military Personnel)
*Berserker* - S.D. Perry   *s*   4285

**Larath, Deveren** (Nobleman; Thief)
*King's Man and Thief* - Christie Golden   *f*   2253

**Larchmont, Marvin** (Archaeologist)
*Out of the Night* - Patrick Whalen   *h*   5771

**Larice, Aldin** (Businessman; Gambler)
*The Napoleon Wager* - William R.
   Forstchen   *s*   1980

**Laril** (Mythical Creature)
*The Moonbane Mage* - Laurie J. Marks   *f*   3626

**Larissa** (Teenager; Runaway)
*Larissa* - Emily Devenport   *s*   1503

**Larissa** (Royalty; Political Figure)
*Queens of Land and Sea* - John Maddox
   Roberts   *f*   4620
*The Steel Kings* - John Maddox Roberts   *f*   4621

**Lark, Don** (Construction Worker; Widow(er))
*Homebody* - Orson Scott Card   *h*   890

**Larken, Ray** (Businessman; Adventurer)
*Cry Wolf* - Kenneth Von Gunden   *s*   5586
*Under Fire* - Kenneth Von Gunden   *s*   5589

**Larkin, Samuel** (Doctor)
*Lasher* - Anne Rice   *h*   4570

**Larking, Lorien** (Spouse)
*Lorien Lost* - Michael King   *f*   3124

**Larkspur, Evan** (Actor; Fugitive)
*The Unwound Way* - William Adams   *s*   35

**LaRoche, Serge** (Student; Musician)
*Serpent's Gift* - A.C. Crispin   *s*   1261

**Larque, Lens** (Outlaw; Thief)
*The Demon Princes: Volume Two* - Jack
   Vance   *s*   5545

**Larraby, Luke** (Museum Curator)
*The Boss in the Wall* - Avram Davidson   *h*   1396

**Larrin, Marty** (Scientist)
*Forever Peace* - Joe Haldeman   *s*   2488

**Larsdatter, Alea** (Fugitive)
*A Wizard in Midgard* - Christopher Stasheff   *s*   5231

**Larsen, Alexandra** (Editor)
*The Gris-Gris Man* - Don Davis   *h*   1403

**Larsen, Penny** (Secretary—Legal)
*Darkman #1: The Hangman* - Randall Boyll   *h*   612

**Larson, Al** (Military Personnel; Mythical Creature)
*By Chaos Cursed* - Mickey Zucker Reichert   *f*   4517
*Dragonrank Master* - Mickey Zucker
   Reichert   *f*   4519
*Shadow's Realm* - Mickey Zucker Reichert   *f*   4523

**Larsson, Gunvald** (Scientist)
*Icebound* - Dean R. Koontz   *h*   3209

**Larue, Andy** (Detective—Police)
*Manjinn Moon* - Denise Vitola   *s*   5576

**LaRue, Andy** (Detective—Police)
*Opalite Moon* - Denise Vitola   *f*   5577

**Lasalle, Stevie** (Psychologist; Teacher)
*The Death Crystal* - J. Edward Ames   *h*   91

**LaSarde, Dawn** (Psychic)
*Walker between the Worlds* - Diane
   DesRochers   *f*   1499

**Lashana "Shana"** (Hero; Leader)
*Elvenblood* - Andre Norton   *f*   4150

**Lasher** (Demon)
*The Witching Hour* - Anne Rice   *h*   4580

**Lasker, Burt** (Martial Arts Expert; Religious)
*Fortress of Forbidden Destiny* - Ryder
   Syvertson   *s*   5378

**Lasker, Tom** (Farmer)
*Ancient Shores* - Jack McDevitt   *h*   3786

**Laski, Saul** (Doctor; Survivor)
*Carrion Comfort* - Dan Simmons   *h*   5049

**Lasseter, Ruth** (Advertising)
*Red, Red Robin* - Stephen Gallagher   *h*   2113

**Lassiter, Audrey** (Artist)
*Hopeship* - Simon Lang   *s*   3315

**Lassiter, Charles** (Doctor; Patient)
*Hopeship* - Simon Lang   *s*   3315

**Lassiter, Diane** (Engineer)
*Days of the Dead* - Ashley McConnell   *h*   3774

**Laster, Vickie** (Young Woman)
*Descent* - Ron Dee   *h*   1465

**Lastwell, Franklin** (Spaceship Captain)
*Life Form* - Alan Dean Foster   *s*   2008

**Laszlo, Count Dracula** (Nobleman)
*The Secret Life of Laszlo, Count Dracula* - Roderick
   Anscombe   *h*   152

**Latcher, Dan** (Writer; Student)
*Stitch* - Mark Morris   *h*   4024

**Latimer, Sarah** (Student; Witch)
*Witch Hill* - Marion Zimmer Bradley   *h*   654

**Latro** (Mercenary)
*Soldier of Arete* - Gene Wolfe   *f*   5944

**Latticus, Gaarius "Gaar"** (Warrior)
*The Vampire Memoirs* - Mara McCuniff   *h*   3781

**Lattimore, Sam** (Political Figure)
*The Resurrectionist* - Thomas F.
   Monteleone   *h*   3965

**Laughing More, Anna** (Police Officer)
*Wake of the Werewolf* - Geoffrey Caine   *h*   834

**Launcelot** (Knight)
*The King* - Donald Barthelme   *f*   375

**Laura** (Young Woman)
*The Darker Passions: Carmilla* - Amarantha
   Knight   *h*   3177

**Laurel** (Psychic)
*The Hanged Man* - Francesca Lia Block   *f*   548

**Lauri** (Mythical Creature; Lesbian)
*Spires of Spirit* - Gael Baudino   *f*   395

**Laurie** (Vagrant)
*Dark Father* - Tom Piccirilli   *h*   4312

**Lauzon, Gary** (Detective—Police)
*Cold Eye* - Giles Blunt   *h*   556

**Lavalle, Linda** (Administrator; Girlfriend)
*Why Do Birds* - Damon Knight   *s*   3190

**Lavanic, Cruise** (Drifter; Serial Killer)
*Night Cruise* - Billie Sue Mosiman   *h*   4041

**Laverne, Vernon** (Police Officer)
*The Death Prayer* - David Bowker   *h*   602

**LaVine, Martin** (Businessman)
*When Shadows Fall* - Brian Scott Smith   *h*   5100

**Lavine, Rosalynd "Rosie"** (Detective—Private)
*Cold Iron* - Melisa Michaels   *f*   3886
*Sister to the Rain* - Melisa Michaels   *f*   3887

**Lavra** (Psychic)
*The Chymical Wedding* - Lindsay Clarke   *f*   1063

**Law, Guilford** (Photographer; Explorer)
*Darwinia* - Robert Charles Wilson   *s*   5906

**Law, Lily** (Child; Journalist)
*Darwinia* - Robert Charles Wilson   *s*   5906

**Lawford, Arthur** (Parent)
*The Return* - Walter de la Mare   *h*   1424

**Lawford, Sheila** (Young Woman)
*The Return* - Walter de la Mare   *h*   1424

**Lawler, Valben** (Doctor)
*The Face of the Waters* - Robert Silverberg   *s*   5029

**Lawre, Jocchario** (Wizard; Diplomat)
*The Mage in the Iron Mask* - Brian
   Thomsen   *f*   5458

**Lawrence** (Clerk)
*Dawn Song* - Michael Marano   *h*   3620

**Lawrence, Felix** (Doctor)
*Perfect Little Angels* - Andrew Neiderman   *h*   4090

**Lawrence, Mark** (Young Man)
*The Offspring* - Kenneth McKenney   *h*   3826

**Lawrence, Rod** (Prostitute)
*Sheltered Lives* - Charles Oberndorf   *s*   4188

**Lawrence, Sally** (Parent)
*The Offspring* - Kenneth McKenney   *h*   3826

**Lawrence, Ursula** (Young Woman)
*The Darker Passions: Dr. Jekyll and Mr. Hyde* -
   Amarantha Knight   *h*   3178

**Lawson, James** (Diplomat)
*Design for Great-Day* - Alan Dean Foster   *s*   2001

**Lawson, John** (Police Officer)
*Moonfall* - Tamara Thorne   *h*   5464

**Layla** (Witch)
*Spyder* - Norman Partridge   *h*   4255

**Lazarian, Ramou** (Spaceman; Student)
*A Company of Stars* - Christopher Stasheff   *s*   5215
*We Open on Venus* - Christopher Stasheff   *s*   5227

**Lazarich, Sabina** (Musician; Composer)
*Someone to Watch over Me* - Tricia
   Sullivan   *s*   5355

**Le Roux, Reiki Momoku** (Computer Expert;
   Spacewoman)
*Marooned on Eden* - Robert L. Forward   *s*   1986

**Leah, Morgan** (Adventurer)
*The Druid of Shannara* - Terry Brooks   *f*   710

**Lealbhallain** (Student)
*The Meri* - Maya Kaathryn Bohnhoff   *f*   561

**Lealor** (Guardian)
*Dragon's Queen* - Carol L. Dennis   *f*   1488

**Leary, Daniel** (Military Personnel)
*With the Lightnings* - David Drake   *s*   1652

**Leather-Woman** (Sorceress)
*Spires of Spirit* - Gael Baudino   *f*   395

**LeBrae, Jael** (Spacewoman; Teenager)
*Dragons in the Stars* - Jeffrey A. Carver   *s*   930

**LeBrel, Andre** (Vampire)
*Children of the Night* - Mercedes Lackey   *h*   3276

**Leclerc, Louis** (Inventor; Time Traveler)
*Witch* - Donald E. McQuinn   *s*   3864

**Lecotta, Angel** (Revolutionary; Time Traveler)
*Time: The Semi-Final Frontier* - Lionel
   Fenn   *s*   1921

**Lecouveurs, Alain** (Nobleman; Vampire)
*In Hot Blood* - Petru Popescu   *h*   4367

**Lector, Hannibal "Cannibal"** (Murderer)
*The Silence of the Lambs* - Thomas Harris   *h*   2566

**Leda** (Mythical Creature; Orphan)
*Nevernever* - Will Shetterly   *f*   4995

**Ledbetter, Gary** (Serial Killer)
*A Room for the Dead* - Noel Hynd   *h*   2825

**Lee** (Abuse Victim)
*The Jigsaw Woman* - Kim Antieau   *f*   199

**Lee** (Mythical Creature)
*Polymorph* - Scott Westerfeld   *s*   5767

**Lee, Afriqua** (Teenager)
*Jaguar* - Bill Ransom   *s*   4477

**Lee, Amy** (Child; Relative)
*The Earth Giant* - Melvin Burgess   *s*   773

**Lee, Darcy** (Military Personnel)
*Fire on the Border* - Kevin O'Donnell Jr.   *s*   4194

**Lee, Houlka** (Hero)
*A Dozen Tough Jobs* - Howard Waldrop   *f*   5612

**Lee, Jeroen** (Political Figure)
*Becoming Human* - Valerie J. Freireich   *s*   2049

**Lee, Lysistrata "Lizzie"** (Student; Teenager)
*Unwillingly to Earth* - Pauline Ashwell   *s*   231

**Lee, Peter** (Child; Relative)
*The Earth Giant* - Melvin Burgess   *s*   773

**Lee, Richard** (Scientist)
*Father to the Man* - John Gribbin   *s*   2434

**Lee, Robert E.** (Historical Figure; Military Personnel)
*The Guns of the South: A Novel of the Civil War* -
   Harry Turtledove   *s*   5502

**Lee, Wei** (Technician; Traveler)
*Red Dust* - Paul J. McAuley   *s*   3715

**Leech, Derek** (Businessman)
*The Quorum* - Kim Newman   *h*   4100

**Leeloo Minai, Appipulai** (Deity)
*The Fifth Element* - Terry Bisson   *s*   504

**Leetah** (Mythical Creature)
*Captives of the Blue Mountain* - Wendy
   Pini   *f*   4336
*The Quest Begins* - Wendy Pini   *f*   4337

**LeFarge, Frederick** (Royalty)
*The Stone Dogs* - S.M. Stirling   *s*   5300

**LeFarge, Marya** (Royalty)
*The Stone Dogs* - S.M. Stirling   *s*   5300

**Leffing, Lucius** (Paranormal Investigator)
*The Adventures of Lucius Leffing* - Joseph Payne
   Brennan   *h*   670

**Leger, Gary** (Adventurer; Hero)
*The Dragon's Dagger* - R.A. Salvatore   *f*   4797
*Dragonslayer's Return* - R.A. Salvatore   *f*   4798
*The Woods out Back* - R.A. Salvatore   *f*   4809

**LeGuerre, Tessa** (Maintenance Worker)
*The Passion* - Donna Boyd   *h*   603

**Lehman, Roger "Senmut-Ptah"** (Time Traveler;
   Scientist)
*Thebes of the Hundred Gates* - Robert
   Silverberg   *s*   5043

**Lehman, Stefan** (Criminal; Leader)
*The Stone Within* - David Wingrove   *s*   5920

**Leiber, Manny** (Director)
*A Graveyard for Lunatics* - Ray Bradbury   *h*   620

**Leifr** (Adventurer)
*The Dragon's Carbuncle* - Elizabeth H.
   Boyer   *f*   605

**Leigh, Makoto Shirata** (Teacher)
*Makoto* - Kelley Wilde   *h*   5801

**Leighton, Gerard** (Administrator)
*High Steel* - Jack C. Haldeman II   *s*   2486

**Leiria** (Warrior)
*Wolves of the Gods* - Allan Cole   *f*   1111

**Leith** (Royalty; Psychic)
*The Prince of Ill Luck* - Susan Dexter   *f*   1512

**Leith** (Werewolf)
*Tapestry of Dark Souls* - Elaine Bergstrom   *h*   465

**LeMat, Joseph "Gunnar Savage"** (Computer Expert)
*Headcrash* - Bruce Bethke   *s*   483

**Lenk, Able** (Leader)
*Legacy* - Greg Bear   *s*   420

**Lennart** (Spaceman)
*Jaydium* - Deborah Wheeler   *s*   5774

**Lennox, Xavier William** (Explorer; Genetically
   Altered Being)
*A Miracle of Rare Design* - Mike Resnick   *s*   4550

**Lennuick, Peyto** (Scholar)
*Timespell* - Robert N. Charrette  *f*  978

**Leno, Dan** (Actor)
*The Trial of Elizabeth Cree* - Peter Ackroyd  *h*  26

**Lentrall, Davlo** (Scientist)
*Utopia* - Roger MacBride Allen  *s*  83

**Leo, Sam** (Doctor)
*Kaleidoscope Eyes* - Graham Watkins  *h*  5631

**Leon** (Royalty)
*The Stallion Queen* - Constance Ash  *f*  223

**Leon** (Businessman)
*The Immortals* - Andrew Neiderman  *h*  4087

**Leonan** (Deity)
*Planar Powers* - J. Robert King  *f*  3122

**Leonard** (Inventor)
*Jingo* - Terry Pratchett  *f*  4393

**Leonard, Wyatt** (Actor; Homosexual)
*From the Teeth of Angels* - Jonathan Carroll  *h*  918

**Leones, Giraut** (Diplomat)
*Earth Made of Glass* - John Barnes  *s*  351

**Leones, Giraut** (Teacher)
*A Million Open Doors* - John Barnes  *s*  353

**Leones, Margaret** (Diplomat)
*Earth Made of Glass* - John Barnes  *s*  351

**Leong, Allan** (Student)
*The Robin Hood Ambush* - William F. Wu  *s*  5999

**Leonidas** (Young Man)
*The Pit and the Pendulum* - Amarantha Knight  *h*  3183

**Leopold** (Royalty; Military Personnel)
*Tiger Burning Bright* - Marion Zimmer Bradley  *f*  652

**Lephi the White** (Ruler)
*The Chaos Balance* - L.E. Modesitt Jr.  *f*  3925

**Lerille, Jack** (Actor; Librarian)
*Paddywhack* - John Stchur  *h*  5236

**Lerner, Reed** (Doctor)
*The Basement* - Bari Wood  *h*  5961

**Lerris** (Apprentice; Carpenter)
*The Death of Chaos* - L.E. Modesitt Jr.  *f*  3926
*The Magic of Recluce* - L.E. Modesitt Jr.  *f*  3934

**Lescevre, Thibault** (Apprentice; Martial Arts Expert)
*Anvil of the Sun* - Anne Lesley Groell  *f*  2451

**Lescevre, Thibault** (Student; Martial Arts Expert)
*Bridge of Valor* - Anne Lesley Groell  *f*  2452

**Lessa** (Leader)
*All the Weyrs of Pern* - Anne McCaffrey  *s*  3719

**Lesserac, Gary** (Computer Expert)
*Virtual Destruction* - Kevin J. Anderson  *s*  118

**Lesseth** (Mythical Creature)
*Kar Kalim* - Deborah Christian  *f*  1025

**Lessis of Valmes** (Witch; Heroine)
*Bazil Broketail* - Christopher Rowley  *f*  4692

**Leta** (Young Woman)
*The Stone Giant* - James P. Blaylock  *f*  523

**Lethe** (Vampire)
*Shifters* - Edward Lee  *h*  3396

**Leucas** (Warrior; Mercenary)
*Iron Dawn* - Matthew Woodring Stover  *f*  5320

**Leucas** (Mercenary; Warrior)
*Jericho Moon* - Matthew Woodring Stover  *f*  5321

**Leung, Kathy** (Journalist)
*Vespers* - Jeff Rovin  *h*  4688

**Levenson, David** (Detective)
*Clash by Night* - Chet Williamson  *h*  5844

**Leventhal, Dan** (Detective—Police)
*The Nine Lives of Catseye Gomez* - Simon Hawke  *f*  2620

**Leverett, Anthony** (Doctor)
*Lori* - Robert Bloch  *h*  536

**Levin, Peter** (Writer)
*Children of the Thunder* - John Brunner  *s*  733

**Levine, Charles** (Scientist)
*Mount Dragon* - Douglas Preston  *h*  4413

**Levine, Richard** (Scientist)
*The Lost World* - Michael Crichton  *s*  1256

**Leving, Fredda** (Computer Expert; Engineer)
*Caliban* - Roger MacBride Allen  *s*  77

**Levitt, Ira** (FBI Agent)
*Thinning the Predators* - Daina Graziunas  *h*  2341

**Levitt, Irv** (Scientist)
*A World of Difference* - Harry Turtledove  *s*  5514

**Levy, Jace** (Detective—Homicide)
*Love Bite* - Sherry Gottlieb  *h*  2288

**Lewes, Charlotte** (Widow(er); Teacher)
*John Dollar* - Marianne Wiggins  *h*  5799

**Lewin, Alma Marie** (Time Traveler; Prisoner)
*Days of Cain* - J.R. Dunn  *s*  1694

**Lewin, Bonnie** (Hunter; Reanimated Dead)
*Conflict* - Peter F. Hamilton  *s*  2522

**Lewin, Linda** (Religious; Criminal)
*Journals of the Plague Years* - Norman Spinrad  *s*  5172

**Lewis** (Servant; Psychic; Genetically Altered Being)
*Prisoner of Dreams* - Karen Ripley  *s*  4593

**Lewis** (Genetically Altered Being; Psychic)
*The Tenth Class* - Karen Ripley  *s*  4594

**Lewis, Carl** (Inventor)
*Cyberbooks* - Ben Bova  *s*  582

**Lewis, Claude** (Government Official)
*Way Station* - Clifford D. Simak  *s*  5048

**Lewis, Dafydd** (Photographer)
*Naomi's Room* - Jonathan Aycliffe  *h*  281

**Lewis, Jonathan** (Student)
*Looker* - Jorge Saralegui  *h*  4820

**Lewis, Jonathan Thomas** (Murderer)
*In Double Jeopardy* - Andrew Neiderman  *h*  4088

**Lewis, Laura** (Teenager)
*The Third Beast* - Peter Loughran  *h*  3527

**Lewis, Leonard** (Photographer)
*Nightlight* - Michael Cadnum  *h*  813

**Lewis, Mary** (Widow(er))
*Nightlight* - Michael Cadnum  *h*  813

**Lewis, Rob** (Computer Expert; Telepath)
*How Like a God* - Brenda W. Clough  *f*  1089

**Leydon, B.** (Student; Companion)
*Unwillingly to Earth* - Pauline Ashwell  *s*  231

**Leyladin** (Wizard; Healer)
*The White Order* - L.E. Modesitt Jr.  *f*  3942

**Leyner, Mark** (Writer; Socialite)
*Et Tu, Babe* - Mark Leyner  *s*  3455

**Leyner, Mark** (Writer; Teenager)
*The Tetherballs of Bougainville* - Mark Leyner  *f*  3457

**Lha** (Royalty)
*Python Isle* - Kenneth Robeson  *f*  4624

**Li** (Detective)
*Eight Skilled Gentlemen* - Barry Hughart  *f*  2804

**Li, Beth** (Teenager)
*The Werewolf's Revenge* - Richard Jaccoma  *h*  2841

**Li, Harry** (Professor; Administrator)
*Eyes of the Empress* - Camille Bacon-Smith  *f*  285

**Li, Master** (Con Artist; Adventurer)
*The Chronicles of Master Li and Number Ten Ox* - Barry Hughart  *f*  2803

**Li, Stefan** (Scientist; Disembodied Personality)
*Ark Liberty* - Will Bradley  *s*  656

**Li Yuan** (Leader)
*White Moon, Red Dragon* - David Wingrove  *s*  5921

**Liang, Sindon** (Linguist)
*The Khan's Persuasion* - Cynthia Felice  *s*  1914

**Liant** (Sorceress)
*Prince of Dogs* - Kate Elliott  *f*  1775

**Liath** (Courier)
*King's Dragon* - Kate Elliott  *f*  1773

**Libermann, E.F.** (Cartographer; Scientist)
*The Discovery of Dragons* - Graeme Base  *f*  385

**Library** (Librarian; Psychic)
*Genetic Soldier* - George Turner  *s*  5492

**Lichen** (Indian; Psychic)
*People of the River* - W. Michael Gear  *f*  2168

**Liddell, Alice** (Artificial Intelligence)
*Take Back Plenty* - Colin Greenland  *s*  2419

**Liddell, Alice Pleasance** (Child; Time Traveler)
*Automated Alice* - Jeff Noon  *f*  4134

**Liddell, Rose** (Spaceship Captain)
*The Painful Field* - Roland J. Green  *s*  2351
*Squadron Alert* - Roland J. Green  *s*  2352
*The Sum of Things* - Roland J. Green  *s*  2353

**Liddy, Mary** (Mentally Ill Person)
*The Uprising* - Brent Monahan  *h*  3956

**Lidjun, Dun** (Nobleman; Martial Arts Expert)
*Hour of the Octopus* - Joel Rosenberg  *f*  4673

**Lie** (Young Woman)
*The Bars on Satan's Jailhouse* - Norman Partridge  *h*  4251

**Liedral** (Trader)
*The Magic Engineer* - L.E. Modesitt Jr.  *f*  3933

**Lieserl** (Human; Experimental Subject)
*Ring* - Stephen Baxter  *s*  402

**Lieutenant** (Military Personnel)
*Final Blackout* - L. Ron Hubbard  *s*  2790

**Lightfoot** (Computer Expert; Businessman)
*Deepdrive* - Alexander Jablokov  *s*  2837

**Lightfoot** (Mythical Creature; Animal)
*Into the Land of the Unicorns* - Bruce Coville  *f*  1219

**Lightner, Sydnie "Charel Secour"** (Spacewoman; Criminal)
*The Triad Worlds* - F.M. Busby  *s*  786

**Lightnin' Lil** (Scientist)
*Mississippi Blues* - Kathleen Ann Goonan  *s*  2274

**Lightstorm, Allan "Al"** (Religious)
*Unquenchable Fire* - Rachel Pollack  *f*  4361

**Lila Anne** (Runaway; Sorceress)
*Summerland* - L. Dean James  *f*  2865

**Lilisaire** (Political Figure; Genetically Altered Being)
*The Stars Are Also Fire* - Poul Anderson  *s*  134

**Lilith** (Parent)
*Imago* - Octavia E. Butler  *s*  791

**Lilith** (Genetically Altered Being; Spouse)
*The Shape-Changer's Wife* - Sharon Shinn  *f*  5002

**Lillorigga "Lilli"** (Psychic)
*The Red Wyvern* - Katharine Kerr  *f*  3074

**Lily** (Hunter)
*The Dog King* - Christoph Ransmayr  *f*  4474

**Lily** (Sports Figure; Addict)
*Ecstasia* - Francesca Lia Block  *f*  547

**Lily** (Deity)
*Lunatics* - Bradley Denton  *f*  1491

**Lily** (Survivor)
*Red Shadows* - Yvonne Navarro  *s*  4074

**liMarchborg, Tradain** (Imposter; Sorcerer)
*The White Tribunal* - Paula Volsky  *f*  5583

**Limmer, Edwin** (Time Traveler)
*The Whispers* - Dan Parkinson  *s*  4247

**Lina** (Apprentice; Singer)
*Interface Masque* - Shariann Lewitt  *s*  3453

**Linares, Segismundo** (Maintenance Worker)
*The Secret Weavers: Stories of the Fantastic by Latin American Women* - Marjorie Agosin  *f*  43

**Lincoln, Abraham** (Historical Figure)
*Skeletons* - Al Sarrantonio  *h*  4834

**Lincoln, Abraham** (Spirit; Historical Figure)
*The Smithsonian Institution* - Gore Vidal  *f*  5570

**Lincoln, Abraham** (Political Figure)
*Stars and Stripes Forever* - Harry Harrison  *s*  2577

**Lincoln, Bojake "Buffalo"** (Insurance Investigator)
*Double Jeopardy* - Aaron Allston  *s*  86

**Linda** (Bride; Magician)
*Bride of the Castle* - John DeChancie  *s*  1452

**Lindavar** (Wizard)
*Murder in Cormyr* - Chet Williamson  *f*  5848

**Linders, Martin** (Ranger)
*The Quiet* - Patrick Billings  *h*  488

**Lindgren, Anton** (Steward)
*Carve the Sky* - Alexander Jablokov  *s*  2836

**Lindholm, Erik Robert** (Worker)
*Buried Screams* - C. Dean Andersson  *h*  137

**Lindo, Sigrid** (Accountant)
*The Moon's Wife: A Hystery* - A.A. Attanasio  *f*  271

**Lindquist, Anna Catarina** (Military Personnel; Vampire)
*McLendon's Syndrome* - Robert Frezza  *s*  2053

**Lindquist, Anna Catarina** (Spacewoman; Vampire)
*The VMR Theory* - Robert Frezza  *s*  2055

**Lindsay, Abelard** (Diplomat; Revolutionary)
*Schismatrix Plus* - Bruce Sterling  *s*  5260

**Lindsey, Alison** (Teenager)
*Midnight Is a Lonely Place* - Barbara Erskine  *h*  1836

**Lindsey, Greg** (Artist)
*Midnight Is a Lonely Place* - Barbara Erskine  *h*  1836

**Lindstrom, Flynn** (Historian)
*Day of the Snake* - Matthew J. Costello  *s*  1196

**Lindy** (Addict)
*Wolf Flow* - K.W. Jeter  *h*  2918

**Ling, Mayla** (Banker)
*Half the Day Is Night* - Maureen F. McHugh  *s*  3818

**Lingri** (Historian; Writer)
*The Others* - Margaret Wander Bonanno  *s*  565
*OtherWhere* - Margaret Wander Bonanno  *s*  566
*OtherWise* - Margaret Wander Bonanno  *s*  567

**Link** (Alien)
*In the Heart of Darkness* - Eric Flint  *s*  1955

**Linn, Holly** (Government Official)
*A Second Infinity* - Michael D. Weaver  *s*  5660

**Linn-Campbell, Neena** (Spaceship Captain; Rebel)
*A Covenant of Justice* - David Gerrold  *s*  2207

**Linnie** (Teacher)
*The Wall at the Edge of the World* - Jim Aikin  *s*  46

**Linter, Dervley** (Alien)
*The State of the Art* - Iain M. Banks  *s*  327

**Lioe, Quin** (Spacewoman; Computer Expert)
*Burning Bright* - Melissa Scott  *s*  4894

**Lion, Maurice** (Religious)
*Jackals* - Charles L. Grant  *h*  2313

**Lionheart, Richard** (Royalty)
*The Empire of Fear* - Brian Stableford  *h*  5191

**Lioren** (Doctor; Alien)
*The Genocidal Healer* - James White  *s*  5779

**Liosh** (Mythical Creature; Telepath)
*Dragon* - Steven Brust  *f*  741

**Lipaski, Anthony** (Detective)
*Red Angel* - Roxanne Longstreet  *h*  3518

**Lippman, Lenore** (Computer Expert; Cyborg)
*The Eighth Rank* - David D. Ross  *s*  4682

**Lipschitz, Isadore** (Military Personnel)
*Hero* - Joel Rosenberg  *s*  4672

**Lipstick** (Android)
*Dead Things* - Richard Calder  *s*  838

**Lirion** (Genetically Altered Being; Revolutionary)
*Harvest the Fire* - Poul Anderson  *s*  128

**Lisa** (Noblewoman)
*Demon Knight* - Ken Hood  *f*  2760

**Lisa** (Secretary)
*The Shadow Gate* - Margaret Ball  *f*  317

**Lisane** (Refugee; Psychic)
*Nameless Magery* - Delia Marshall Turner  *f*  5490

**Lisbei of Bethely** (Psychic)
*In the Mothers' Land* - Elisabeth Vonarburg  *s*  5590

**Liss, Benetan** (Military Personnel)
*Star Ascendant* - Louise Cooper  *f*  1180

**Liss, Trojan nine zero eight** (Spacewoman)
*Rainbow Man* - M.J. Engh  *s*  1824

**Lissa** (Maiden)
*The Birth of the Blade* - Dennis McCarty  *f*  3766

**Lissa** (Religious)
*King Pinch* - David Cook  *f*  1146

**Lissa** (Courtier)
*Nobody's Son* - Sean Stewart  *f*  5275

**Lissar, Lissla "Deerskin"** (Royalty; Fugitive)
*Deerskin* - Robin McKinley  *f*  3844

**Lisse** (Artist)
*Invitation to the Game* - Monica Hughes  *s*  2807

**Lissette** (Child; Spirit)
*Cursed Be the Child* - Mort Castle  *h*  937

**Lisseut of Vezet** (Minstrel)
*A Song for Arbonne* - Guy Gavriel Kay  *f*  3017

**Lister, David** (Spaceman)
*Better than Life* - Grant Naylor  *s*  4076
*Red Dwarf: Infinity Welcomes Careful Drivers* - Grant Naylor  *s*  4077

**Liston, Mark** (Businessman)
*Soulcatchers* - Jan Lara  *h*  3336

**Lithaniel, Ardagh** (Royalty; Mythical Creature)
*The Shattered Oath* - Josepha Sherman  *f*  4989

**Little, Janey** (Musician)
*The Little Country* - Charles de Lint  *f*  1432

**Little, Loy** (Scavenger)
*Men Like Rats* - Rob Chilson  *s*  1015

**Little, Thomas** (Aged Person)
*The Little Country* - Charles de Lint  *f*  1432

**Little Bear** (Indian; Chieftain)
*The Key to the Indian* - Lynne Reid Banks  *f*  331

**Little Bear** (Indian)
*The Secret of the Indian* - Lynne Reid Banks  *f*  332

**Little Dancer** (Shaman; Prehistoric Human)
*People of the Fire* - W. Michael Gear  *f*  2167

**Little Father** (Heir)
*Lion Time in Timbuctoo* - Robert Silverberg  *s*  5036

**Little Girl** (Handicapped; Scientist)
*The Mer-Child: A Legend for Children and Other Adults* - Robin Morgan  *f*  4008

**Little Hawk, Jay** (Game Warden)
*Crota* - Owl Goingback  *h*  2251

**Little Spring** (Leader; Indian)
*Apacheria* - Jake Page  *s*  4233

**Littlefield, Eric** (Teenager)
*Monkey Station* - Ardath Mayhar  *s*  3703

**Litzenreich** (Sorcerer)
*Shadowbreed* - David Ferring  *f*  1928

**Livia** (Military Personnel)
*Nocturnas* - Shawn Ryan  *h*  4755

**Livingstone, David** (Shaman)
*Raven Stole the Moon* - Garth Stein  *h*  5249

**Liwellan, Sarra Ambrai** (Political Figure; Noblewoman)
*The Mageborn Traitor* - Melanie Rawn  *f*  4488

**Liwellan, Sarra Ambrai** (Adoptee; Heiress)
*The Ruins of Ambrai* - Melanie Rawn  *f*  4489

**Lixandashkya, Megan** (Child)
*Shadow's Daughter* - Shirley Meier  *f*  3871

**Lixia, Li** (Linguist; Sociologist)
*A Woman of the Iron People* - Eleanor Arnason  *s*  211

**Lizard Lips** (Alien)
*In the Shadow of the Moon* - Scott G. Gier  *s*  2224

**Lizra** (Royalty)
*Black Unicorn* - Tanith Lee  *f*  3404

**Llanfrechfa, Geraint** (Nobleman; Adventurer)
*Streets of Blood* - Carl Sargent  *f*  4821

**Llannat** (Military Personnel; Psychic)
*Starpilot's Grave* - Debra Doyle  *s*  1606

**Llewellyn, George** (Police Officer)
*Werewolf* - Peter Rubie  *h*  4702

**Lloth** (Leader; Deity)
*Siege of Darkness* - R.A. Salvatore  *f*  4804

**Llyndreth** (Royalty)
*The Shadow Warrior* - Pat Zettner  *f*  6082

**lo Lyrane, Lyrane** (Student)
*Demon Moon* - Jack Williamson  *s*  5862

**Lobb, Eddie "Tiger"** (Criminal)
*Catwoman* - Lynn Abbey  *s*  14

**Lobey, Lo** (Mutant; Musician)
*The Einstein Intersection* - Samuel R. Delany  *s*  1481

**Lochlainn, Sean O.** (Sidekick)
*A Study in Sorcery* - Michael Kurland  *f*  3252

**Lochley, Elizabeth** (Military Personnel)
*Day of the Dead* - Neil Gaiman  *s*  2102

**Locke, Laura** (Writer)
*The Possession* - Ronald Kelly  *h*  3055

**Locke, Richard** (Writer)
*Shifters* - Edward Lee  *h*  3396

**Locke, Ryan** (Police Officer)
*Bloody Valentine* - Stephen R. George  *h*  2197

**Lockerman, John** (Police Officer)
*Grave Markings* - Michael A. Arnzen  *h*  212

**Lockhart, Ximena** (Doctor; Fiance(e))
*Death of an Adept* - Katherine Kurtz  f  3257

**Lockheart, Karen** (Patient)
*Eden's Eyes* - Sean Costello  h  1205

**Lockland, Tessa** (Young Woman)
*Midnight* - Dean R. Koontz  h  3212

**Locklear** (Nobleman)
*Krondor, the Betrayal* - Raymond E. Feist  f  1905

**Locklear, Carroll** (Scholar; Scientist)
*Cathouse* - Dean Ing  s  2828

**Lockwood, Edmund** (Religious)
*The Ghosts of Sleath* - James Herbert  h  2668

**Lockwood, Grace** (Student)
*The Ghosts of Sleath* - James Herbert  h  2668

**Lockwood, Spencer** (Scientist; Administrator)
*Ill Wind* - Kevin J. Anderson  s  108

**LoDire, Mira** (Diplomat; Businesswoman)
*Speaking Dreams* - Severna Park  s  4245

**Loeffler, Brian** (Religious)
*Sorcerers of Sodom* - Roger Elwood  h  1804

**Loftis** (Detective)
*Orca* - Steven Brust  f  745

**Logan, Diana** (Teacher)
*Eye Killers* - A.A. Carr  h  911

**Logan, Janet** (Doctor)
*Deathgift* - Ann Tonsor Zeddies  s  6061

**Logan, Jennifer** (Trader; Teacher)
*Earthgrip* - Harry Turtledove  s  5499

**Logan, Matthew** (Traveler)
*The Jewel of Equilibrant* - Steven Frankos  f  2042

**Logan "Wolverine"** (Mutant; Adventurer)
*Codename Wolverine* - Christopher Golden  s  2256

**Lohmatski, Gregori** (Nobleman; Mythical Creature)
*Dancing Bears* - Fred Saberhagen  f  4764

**Lohmatski, Natalya** (Noblewoman; Revolutionary)
*Dancing Bears* - Fred Saberhagen  f  4764

**Loiosh** (Animal; Mythical Creature)
*Phoenix* - Steven Brust  f  746

**Loki** (Deity)
*The Spawn of Loki* - Jason Henderson  f  2658

**Lolita** (Prehistoric Human)
*Cathouse* - Dean Ing  s  2828

**Lomallin** (Immortal; Mythical Creature)
*The Shaman* - Christopher Stasheff  f  5223

**Loman, Bill** (Police Officer)
*Yours Truly, Jackie the Stripper* - Edo van
  Belkom  h  5536

**Lomax, Felix "Gravedancer"** (Bodyguard; Spy)
*Prophet* - Mike Resnick  s  4553

**Lombard, Nick** (Student)
*Trinity Grove* - David van Meter Smith  h  5112

**Lonat, Bosanka** (Student—Exchange; Sorceress)
*The Golden Thread* - Suzy McKee Charnas  f  969

**London, Claire** (Psychic)
*Heartlight* - Marion Zimmer Bradley  f  637

**London, Stefan** (Businessman)
*Ragged Angels* - Della Van Hise  h  5537

**London, Teddy** (Detective—Private)
*All Things under the Moon* - Robert
  Morgan  h  4002
*The Only Thing to Fear* - Robert Morgan  h  4003
*Some Things Come Back* - Robert Morgan  h  4004
*Some Things Never Die* - Robert Morgan  h  4005
*The Thing That Darkness Hides* - Robert
  Morgan  h  4006
*The Things That Are Not There* - Robert
  Morgan  h  4007

**Long, Huey "Hal" Alphonse** (Courier; Hero)
*The Trinity Vector* - Steve Perry  s  4302

**Long John Silver** (Criminal)
*Celestial Dogs* - J.S. Russell  h  4734

**Long-Reach** (Slave; Alien)
*Man-Kzin Wars IV* - Larry Niven  s  4124

**Longchamp, Dawn** (Teenager)
*Dawn* - V.C. Andrews  h  144

**Longchamp, Dawn** (Student; Musician)
*Secrets of the Morning* - V.C. Andrews  h  146

**Longchamp, Jimmy** (Child)
*Dawn* - V.C. Andrews  h  144

**Longchamp, Jimmy** (Military Personnel)
*Secrets of the Morning* - V.C. Andrews  h  146

**Longdirk, Tobias** (Outlaw)
*Demon Knight* - Ken Hood  f  2760

**Longshadow** (Wizard)
*Bleak Seasons* - Glen Cook  f  1147

**Looks-at-Charts** (Alien; Scout)
*Quozl* - Alan Dean Foster  s  2013

**Loola** (Girlfriend; Mythical Creature)
*Night of the Living 'Gator!* - Richard A.
  Lupoff  s  3573
*Night of the Living Rat!* - Debra Doyle  s  1603

**Lopez, Angelica "Angel" Lorenzo** (Genetically
  Altered Being)
*Specters of the Dawn* - S. Andrew Swann  s  5368

**Lopez, Maria Elena** (Young Woman)
*Witch-Light* - Nancy Holder  h  2734

**Loran, Luroc I** (Ruler; Warrior)
*Firehand* - Andre Norton  s  4151

**Lorat** (Shaman)
*Rinn's Star* - Paula E. Downing  s  1719

**Lord, Melanie** (Agent)
*Haunted* - Tamara Thorne  s  5463

**Lord, Suzannah** (Doctor)
*My Soul to Take* - Steven Spruill  s  5184

**Lord Lynn, Margaret "Maggy"** (Artificial
  Intelligence; Computer)
*Hellspark* - Janet Kagan  s  3000

**Lorelei** (Serial Killer)
*Lorelei* - Mark A. Clements  h  1086

**Loremaster, Barach** (Wizard)
*Wizard's Mole* - Brad Strickland  f  5337

**Lorhaiden** (Warrior)
*To Fall Like Stars* - Nancy Asire  f  257

**Losang** (Religious)
*Fortress of Forbidden Destiny* - Ryder
  Syvertson  s  5378

**Losmara, Rafe** (Student—Graduate)
*Reprisal* - F. Paul Wilson  h  5896

**Lot** (Vampire)
*As One Dead* - Don Bassingthwaite  h  387

**Lot** (Adventurer; Spaceman)
*Vast* - Linda Nagata  s  4067

**Lothor** (Sorcerer; Fiance(e))
*Nightseer* - Laurell K. Hamilton  f  2521

**Lothos** (Vampire)
*Buffy the Vampire Slayer* - Richie Tankersley
  Cusick  h  1301

**Lott, Roxanne** (Young Woman)
*The Mark of the Moderately Vicious Vampire* - Lionel
  Fenn  h  1920

**Lottick, Vaclav** (Administrator; Leader)
*Bloom* - Wil McCarthy  s  3761

**Louchard, Onidi "Dinah O'Neill"** (Pirate;
  Disembodied Personality)
*Power Play* - Anne McCaffrey  s  3744

**Louis XIV** (Historical Figure; Royalty)
*The Moon and the Sun* - Vonda N.
  McIntyre  f  3822

**Louis XIV** (Ruler; Historical Figure)
*Queen's Gambit Declined* - Melinda M.
  Snodgrass  f  5147

**Louise, Zoe** (Child; Spirit)
*Stonewords: A Ghost Story* - Pam Conrad  f  1138

**Lovat, Peregrine** (Artist; Psychic)
*The Adept* - Katherine Kurtz  f  3254
*Dagger Magic* - Katherine Kurtz  f  3256
*The Lodge of the Lynx* - Katherine Kurtz  f  3259
*The Templar Treasure* - Katherine Kurtz  f  3261

**Love, Larissa "Lara"** (Actress)
*The Shift* - George Foy  s  2033

**Lovell, Willa** (Scientist; Computer Expert)
*Judgment Day* - G. Harry Stine  s  5281

**Lovelock** (Animal; Genetically Altered Being)
*Lovelock* - Orson Scott Card  s  892

**Low, Boston** (Pilot)
*The Dig* - Alan Dean Foster  s  2002

**Lowe, Cherie** (Young Woman)
*Who Killed James Dean?* - Warren Newton
  Beath  h  428

**Lowe, Saul** (Inventor; Time Traveler)
*Door Number Three* - Patrick O'Leary  s  4210

**Lowell, Greg** (Editor)
*The Well* - Michael B. Sirota  h  5077

**Lowell, Jacob** (Indian)
*Nadya: The Wolf Chronicles* - Pat Murphy  f  4052

**Lowell, Janet** (Spouse)
*The Well* - Michael B. Sirota  h  5077

**Lowenstein, David** (Doctor)
*Beauty* - Brian D'Amato  h  1334

**Lowrey, Jason** (Inventor; Genius)
*Death Dream* - Ben Bova  s  583

**Lowry, Davis** (Anthropologist)
*Sleepwalker* - Michael Cadnum  h  815

**Lowry, Jack** (Professor)
*Irrational Fears* - William Browning
  Spencer  h  5167

**Lowry, James** (Professor)
*Fear* - L. Ron Hubbard  h  2789

**Lowry, Mary** (Housewife)
*Fear* - L. Ron Hubbard  h  2789

**Lu** (Psychic; Teacher)
*Sing the Light* - Louise Marley  s  3629

**Lu, Antonia "Toni"** (Activist; Assistant)
*Other* - Gordon R. Dickson  s  1538

**Lu, Curtis** (Computer Expert)
*Carol for Another Christmas* - Elizabeth Ann
  Scarborough  f  4861

**Luap** (Royalty; Magician)
*Liar's Oath* - Elizabeth Moon  f  3969

**Luban, Rick** (Teenager; Apprentice)
*Higher Education* - Charles Sheffield  s  4958

**Lucas, Annabel "Nan"** (Photographer)
*My Soul to Keep* - Judith Hawkes  h  2631

**Lucas, James** (Military Personnel)
*The Wild Blue and the Gray* - William
  Sanders  s  4814

**Lucas, Prince** (Royalty; Thief)
*Rats and Gargoyles* - Mary Gentle  f  2196

**Luccia** (Mythical Creature)
*Vinas Solamnus* - J. Robert King  f  3123

**Luci** (Dancer; Vampire)
*Night Prayers* - P.D. Cacek  h  803

**Lucian** (Adventurer; Fugitive)
*The Arkadians* - Lloyd Alexander  f  67

**Luciano, Tony** (Spy)
*City of Iron* - Chet Williamson  h  5843
*Empire of Dust* - Chet Williamson  h  5846

**Lucier, Kevin** (Veteran)
*Jumpers* - R. Patrick Gates  h  2161

**Lucifer** (Angel; Military Personnel)
*Angels & Visitations: A Miscellany* - Neil
  Gaiman  f  2101

**Lucifer** (Demon)
*The Devil and Dan Cooley* - Holly Lisle  f  3480

**Lucille** (Doctor)
*Strange Invasion* - Michael Kandel  s  3012

**Lucinda** (Genetically Altered Being; Singer)
*The Alleluia Files* - Sharon Shinn  s  4999

**Luckinbill, Tom** (Police Officer)
*Yellow Moon* - David J. Searls  h  4907

**Lucy** (Thief)
*But What of Earth?* - Piers Anthony  s  163

**Lucy** (Space Explorer; Traveler)
*Douglas Adams's Starship Titanic* - Terry
  Jones  s  2979

**Lucy** (Girlfriend)
*That's All, Folks!* - Greg Snow  f  5148

**Ludovic, Cassandra "Sam"** (Artist)
*Synners* - Pat Cadigan  s  808

**Luet** (Psychic; Spouse)
*The Ships of Earth* - Orson Scott Card  s  897

**Lugard** (Nobleman)
*The Hunger and Ecstasy of Vampires* - Brian
  Stableford  h  5192

**Lugh** (Royalty; Mythical Creature)
*Landslayer's Law* - Tom Deitz  f  1474

**Lugosh, James D.** (Student; Serial Killer)
*Order of the Arrow* - Michael T.
  Hinkemeyer  h  2689

**Luisa** (Innkeeper)
*Cambio Bay* - Kate Wilhelm  f  5806

**Lujan, Derek** (Time Traveler; Spaceman)
*Children of the Earth* - Catherine Wells  s  5743

**Lukas, Greg** (Spaceman; Pilot)
*Mind Light* - Margaret Davis  s  1407
*Minds Apart* - Margaret Davis  s  1408

**Lukas, Harkon** (Minstrel)
*Death of a Darklord* - Laurell K. Hamilton  h  2516

**Lukasha** (Sorcerer)
*The Spirit Gate* - Maya Kaathryn Bohnhoff  f  562

**Luke** (Religious)
*Thessalonica* - Harry Turtledove  f  5511

**Luke, Jim Bob** (Detective—Private)
*Cold in July* - Joe R. Lansdale  h  3323

**Luki** (Immortal)
*Fire Crossing* - Cheryl J. Franklin  s  2036

**Lumbaird, Fran** (Child)
*The Black Carousel* - Charles L. Grant  h  2303

**Lund, Jack "Mr. Was"** (Time Traveler; Amnesiac)
*Mr. Was* - Pete Hautman  s  2614

**Lundens, Myra** (Housewife)
*The Basement* - Bari Wood  h  5961

**Lungo Muso** (Alien; Time Traveler)
*Outpost* - Scott Mackay  s  3597

**Lupo** (Animal)
*Down the Stream of Stars* - Jeffrey A.
  Carver  s  928

**Lustig, Alex** (Scientist)
*Earth* - David Brin  s  685

**Luther** (Student)
*Fool on the Hill* - Matt Ruff  f  4707

**Lutz, Frances** (Real Estate Agent)
*Infernal Affairs* - Jane Heller  h  2652

**Lutz, Klaue** (Genetically Altered Being)
*Lives of the Monster Dogs* - Kirsten Bakis  s  305

**Luz** (Teenager; Psychic)
*The Secret Weavers: Stories of the Fantastic by Latin
  American Women* - Marjorie Agosin  f  43

**Luz, Gabriel** (Witch)
*Witch-Light* - Nancy Holder  h  2734

**Lyall, Andrew** (Vampire)
*Vampires Anonymous* - Jeffrey N.
  McMahan  h  3853

**Lycaon** (Artisan; Werewolf)
*The Last World* - Christoph Ransmayr  f  4475

**Lydi** (Witch)
*Shadow of the Seventh Moon* - Nancy Varian
  Berberick  f  459

**Lydia** (Traveler)
*The Tattooed Map* - Barbara Hodgson  f  2706

**Lydia "Pandora"** (Vampire)
*Pandora* - Anne Rice  h  4573

**Lydyard, Cordelia** (Housewife)
*The Angel of Pain* - Brian Stableford  h  5189

**Lydyard, David** (Scientist)
*The Angel of Pain* - Brian Stableford  h  5189
*The Carnival of Destruction* - Brian
  Stableford  h  5190

**Lydyard, David** (Young Man)
*The Werewolves of London* - Brian
  Stableford  h  5196

**Lyell, Thomasina** (Journalist; Activist)
*The Pure Cold Light* - Gregory Frost  s  2087

**Lyim** (Wizard; Handicapped)
*The Seventh Sentinel* - Mary Kirchoff  f  3154

**Lykan, Radu** (Vampire)
*Necroscope: The Lost Years* - Brian
  Lumley  h  3560
*Resurgence* - Brian Lumley  h  3564

**Lyle, Nona** (Doctor)
*Horses of the Night* - Michael Cadnum  h  811

**Lyma, Skyla** (Mercenary)
*Relic of Empire* - W. Michael Gear  s  2171

**Lynch, Raymond** (Scientist)
*Infinity's Child* - Harry Stein  h  5250

**Lynn, Corbet** (Heir)
*Winter Rose* - Patricia A. McKillip  f  3843

**Lynskey, Lucy** (Doctor)
*The Frighteners* - Michael Jahn  h  2856

**Lynx** (Gang Member)
*Bad Voltage* - Jonathan Littell  s  3491

**Lynx, Philip "Flinx"** (Psychic; Wanderer)
*Mid-Flinx* - Alan Dean Foster  s  2010

**Lyon, Afra** (Psychic)
*Damia* - Anne McCaffrey  s  3725

**Lyon, Harry** (Police Officer)
*Dragon Tears* - Dean R. Koontz  h  3205

**Lyon, Isthian "Thian"** (Teenager; Psychic)
*Damia's Children* - Anne McCaffrey  s  3726

**Lyon, John** (Television Personality; Journalist)
*Bring Me Children* - David Martin  h  3637

**Lyon, Laria** (Teenager; Psychic)
*Damia's Children* - Anne McCaffrey  s  3726

**Lyon, Rojer** (Teenager; Psychic)
*Damia's Children* - Anne McCaffrey  s  3726

**Lyon, Rojer** (Psychic; Spaceman)
*Lyon's Pride* - Anne McCaffrey  s  3738

**Lyonz** (Heir)
*Drum Warning* - Jo Clayton  f  1066

**Lyppiatt, Xan** (Political Figure)
*The Children of Men* - P.D. James  f  2870

**Lysander** (Android; Agent)
*Phaze Doubt* - Piers Anthony  f  184

**Lysander** (Royalty)
*Prince of Mercenaries* - Jerry Pournelle  s  4377

**Lysia** (Noblewoman)
*Hammer and Anvil* - Harry Turtledove  f  5503


# M

**Ma Li "Sister"** (Military Personnel; Revolutionary)
*Shangri-La: The Return to the World of Lost Horizon* -
  Eleanor Cooney  f  1169

**Maas, Aaron** (Child)
*The Curse of Camp Cold Lake* - R.L. Stine  h  5286

**Maas, Ellen** (Journalist)
*The Forbidden Zone* - Whitley Strieber  h  5340

**Maas, Sarah** (Child)
*The Curse of Camp Cold Lake* - R.L. Stine  h  5286

**Mab** (Mythical Creature; Counselor)
*I Was a Teenage Fairy* - Francesca Lia
  Block  f  549

**mac Ailill, Fionchadd** (Mythical Creature)
*Sunshaker's War* - Tom Deitz  f  1477

**Mac Airt, Cormac** (Royalty; Leader)
*Finn Mac Cool* - Morgan Llywelyn  f  3504

**mac Brian, Murcha** (Warrior; Heir)
*Brian Boru: Emperor of the Irish* - Morgan
  Llywelyn  f  3501

**mac Cainnech, Aidan** (Religious; Linguist)
*Byzantium* - Stephen R. Lawhead  f  3353

**mac Calprin, Patraic "Patricius Calpurnius"**
  (Religious; Slave)
*The Deer's Cry: A Book of the Keltiad* - Patricia
  Kennealy-Morrison  f  3060

**Mac Cool, Finn** (Warrior; Hero)
*Finn Mac Cool* - Morgan Llywelyn  f  3504

**mac Cuel, Ceilyn** (Knight; Werewolf)
*The Work of the Sun* - Teresa Edgerton  f  1746

**mac Cumhall, Fionn "Demne"** (Historical Figure;
  Hero)
*Master of Earth and Water* - Diana L.
  Paxson  f  4266
*The Shield between the Worlds* - Diana L.
  Paxson  f  4267
*Sword of Fire and Shadow* - Diana L.
  Paxson  f  4268

**Mac Kay, Kenneth "Ken"** (Military Personnel)
*McLendon's Syndrome* - Robert Frezza  s  2053

**mac Kennedy, Brian** (Leader; Historical Figure)
*Brian Boru: Emperor of the Irish* - Morgan
  Llywelyn  f  3501

**Mac Morna, Goll** (Warrior)
*Finn Mac Cool* - Morgan Llywelyn  f  3504

**mac Morna, Goll** (Warrior)
*The Shield between the Worlds* - Diana L.
  Paxson  f  4267

**mac Sliabhin, Caith** (Outlaw)
*Faery in Shadow* - C.J. Cherryh  *f*  987

**Macafee, Simon** (Inventor; Space Explorer)
*The Cyborg From Earth* - Charles Sheffield  *s*  4952

**Macaffrey, Lester Hill** (Teacher; Psychic)
*Heathern* - Jack Womack  *s*  5958

**Macairty, Adam Maser** (Time Traveler)
*Psychoshop* - Alfred Bester  *s*  477

**Macaree, Anne** (Model)
*Obsessed* - Rick R. Reed  *h*  4500

**Macaree, Joe** (Advertising)
*Obsessed* - Rick R. Reed  *h*  4500

**MacAuley, Alasdair** (Nobleman)
*The Last Highlander* - Claire Cross  *f*  1271

**MacAuliffe, Judy** (Saloon Keeper/Owner)
*The Keeper* - Robert D. Lee  *h*  3402

**MacBreed, Keenan** (Archaeologist)
*The Uprising* - Brent Monahan  *h*  3956

**MacBride, Johnny** (Military Personnel)
*Bats* - William W. Johnstone  *h*  2926

**MacCallum, Brenda** (Waiter/Waitress)
*Shadows* - John Saul  *h*  4845

**MacCallum, Bridget** (Time Traveler)
*The Door through Washington Square* - Elaine Bergstrom  *f*  464

**MacCallum, Dierdre** (Heir)
*The Door through Washington Square* - Elaine Bergstrom  *f*  464

**MacCallum, Josh** (Child)
*Shadows* - John Saul  *h*  4845

**MacColl, Enye** (Advertising; Courier)
*King of Morning, Queen of Day* - Ian McDonald  *f*  3793

**MacDavid, Kate** (Young Woman)
*Night Beasts* - T.W. Stetson  *h*  5263

**Macdonald, Dorothea** (Psychic; Political Figure)
*Diamond Mask: A Novel* - Julian May  *s*  3697

**MacDonald, Ellen** (Secretary)
*Snowbeast!* - Peter Tremayne  *h*  5482

**MacDonald, Mercy** (Spaceman)
*Stopping at Slowyear* - Frederik Pohl  *s*  4355

**MacDonald, Murdo** (Doctor)
*Snowbeast!* - Peter Tremayne  *h*  5482

**MacDonald, Sean** (Writer)
*Avatar* - Donald Beman  *h*  437
*The Taking* - Donald Beman  *h*  438

**MacDonald, Warren** (Religious)
*Blood Lust* - Ron Dee  *h*  1464

**MacDougall, Clarrissa** (Nurse)
*Gray Lensman* - Edward E. Smith  *s*  5117

**MacDuff** (Hero)
*The Spawn of Loki* - Jason Henderson  *f*  2658

**Mace, Jarek** (Criminal; Hero)
*Morningstar* - David Gemmell  *f*  2190

**Macero** (Thief)
*Songs of the Dancing Gods* - Jack L. Chalker  *f*  962

**MacFarlane, Griffin** (Teenager)
*Furnace* - Muriel Gray  *h*  2339

**MacFarlane, Nelly** (Political Figure)
*Furnace* - Muriel Gray  *h*  2339

**MacGregor, Sandy** (Hero; Wizard)
*A Name to Conjure With* - Donald Aamodt  *f*  3
*A Troubling Along the Border* - Donald Aamodt  *f*  4

**Machiavelli, Niccolo** (Historical Figure; Apprentice)
*The Memory Cathedral* - Jack Dann  *s*  1341

**Machiavelli, Niccolo** (Journalist; Political Figure)
*Pasquale's Angel* - Paul J. McAuley  *f*  3714

**Macinnes, Matt** (Linguist)
*The Starry Child* - Lynn Hanna  *f*  2540

**Macintosh, Elizabeth** (Spacewoman; Telepath)
*Rediscovery: A Novel of Darkover* - Marion Zimmer Bradley  *s*  643

**MacIntyre, Colin** (Spaceship Captain; Leader)
*The Armageddon Inheritance* - David Weber  *s*  5668

**MacIntyre, Colin** (Ruler; Spaceship Captain)
*Heirs of Empire* - David Weber  *s*  5672

**MacIntyre, Colin** (Military Personnel; Spaceship Captain)
*Mutineers' Moon* - David Weber  *s*  5677

**MacIntyre, Sean Horus** (Heir; Military Personnel)
*Heirs of Empire* - David Weber  *s*  5672

**MacIver, Teri** (Teenager)
*Second Child* - John Saul  *h*  4844

**Mack, Derwent** (Criminal)
*Yours Truly, Jackie the Stripper* - Edo van Belkom  *h*  5536

**Mack the Knife** (Criminal; Historical Figure)
*Spring-Heeled Jack* - Philip Pullman  *f*  4447

**MacKai, Willie** (Musician)
*Phantom Banjo* - Elizabeth Ann Scarborough  *f*  4868
*Picking the Ballad's Bones* - Elizabeth Ann Scarborough  *f*  4869
*Strum Again?* - Elizabeth Ann Scarborough  *f*  4870

**MacKelston, Kathleen** (Accountant)
*The Barrens* - F. Paul Wilson  *h*  5884

**MacKendimen, Alex** (Businessman; Tourist)
*A Love through Time* - Terri Brisbin  *f*  691

**Mackenson, Cory** (Child)
*Boy's Life* - Robert R. McCammon  *h*  3754

**Mackenson, Tom** (Worker; Parent)
*Boy's Life* - Robert R. McCammon  *h*  3754

**MacKenzie, David** (Detective—Police)
*Heathen* - Shaun Hutson  *h*  2816

**MacKenzie, Ian S.** (Spaceship Captain)
*Outbanker* - Timothy A. Madden  *s*  3603

**Mackenzie, Lyle** (Administrator; Political Figure)
*Sister Blood* - Karen Haber  *s*  2476

**Mackinnon, Curtis** (Businessman)
*Kalimantan* - Lucius Shepard  *h*  4979

**MacLaren, Colin** (Psychologist; Paranormal Investigator)
*Heartlight* - Marion Zimmer Bradley  *f*  637

**Maclaren, Neil** (Restaurateur)
*Raven* - Charles L. Grant  *h*  2314

**MacLaren, Sherideen** (Young Woman)
*For You, the Living* - Wayne Allen Sallee  *h*  4786

**MacLean, Henry** (Farmer)
*Other* - Gordon R. Dickson  *s*  1538

**Maclean, Ramsey** (Doctor)
*The Matrix* - Jonathan Aycliffe  *h*  280

**Maclemmon, Howmaster** (Businessman)
*668: The Neighbor of the Beast* - Lionel Fenn  *h*  1917

**Macleod, Andrew** (Professor)
*The Matrix* - Jonathan Aycliffe  *h*  280

**MacLeod, Connor** (Immortal)
*The Element of Fire* - Jason Henderson  *f*  2657

**MacLeod, Duncan** (Immortal; Martial Arts Expert)
*The Element of Fire* - Jason Henderson  *f*  2657
*Scotland the Brave* - Jennifer Roberson  *f*  4611
*Shadow of Obsession* - Rebecca Neason  *f*  4082

**MacLoed, Alex** (Hero; Pilot)
*Fallen Angels* - Larry Niven  *s*  4120

**Maclyn of Elfhame Outremer** (Mythical Creature)
*When the Bough Breaks* - Mercedes Lackey  *f*  3302

**MacMahan, Hector** (Military Personnel)
*Mutineers' Moon* - David Weber  *s*  5677

**MacNeil, Duncan** (Military Personnel)
*Down Among the Dead Men* - Simon R. Green  *f*  2367

**MacPherson, Maggie** (Journalist)
*Force of Arms* - G. Harry Stine  *s*  5279

**Macumba the Dark Man** (Sorcerer)
*Howl-O-Ween* - Gary L. Holleman  *h*  2744

**Macurdy, Curtis** (Farmer; Warrior)
*The Lion of Farside* - John Dalmas  *f*  1324

**Mad Mall** (Sailor; Warrior)
*Chase the Morning* - Michael Scott Rohan  *f*  4658

**Maddock** (Warrior)
*Spirit Fox* - Mickey Zucker Reichert  *f*  4524

**Maddock, Yanaba** (Military Personnel; Settler)
*Power Lines* - Anne McCaffrey  *s*  3743

**Maddock, Yanaba** (Military Personnel; Administrator)
*Power Play* - Anne McCaffrey  *s*  3744

**Maddock, Yanaba** (Invalid; Military Personnel)
*Powers That Be* - Anne McCaffrey  *s*  3745

**Maddox, Cory** (Computer Expert; Adventurer; Hero)
*The Cybernetic Walrus* - Jack L. Chalker  *s*  951

**Maddox, Cory** (Computer Expert; Hero; Adventurer)
*The Hot-Wired Dodo* - Jack L. Chalker  *s*  956

**Maddox, Cory** (Computer Expert; Handicapped; Adventurer)
*The March Hare Network* - Jack L. Chalker  *s*  957

**Madeleine** (Parent)
*Phantom* - Susan Kay  *h*  3020

**Madeline** (Thief; Sorceress)
*The Death of the Necromancer* - Martha Wells  *f*  5749

**Madera, Blasing** (Businessman)
*California Ghosting* - William Hill  *h*  2687

**Madia** (Royalty)
*Demon Blade* - Mark A. Garland  *f*  2141

**Madimi** (Angel)
*Love & Sleep* - John Crowley  *f*  1277

**Madison, Jay** (Student—College; Relative)
*The Gryphon King* - Tom Deitz  *f*  1473

**Madison, Marshall** (Vampire)
*Bloodlines* - J.N. Williamson  *h*  5852

**Madison, Sybil Wilfred** (Aged Person)
*Baby Dolly* - Ruby Jean Jensen  *h*  2899

**Madison, Thaddie** (Child)
*Bloodlines* - J.N. Williamson  *h*  5852

**Madlen** (Teenager)
*The Sister* - Elleston Trevor  *h*  5484

**Madog, Jay "Mad Dog"** (Businessman; Bachelor)
*Promised Land* - Connie Willis  *s*  5872

**Madonette** (Singer; Worker)
*The Stainless Steel Rat Sings the Blues* - Harry Harrison  *s*  2575

**Madouc** (Heroine)
*Madouc* - Jack Vance  *f*  5547

**Madrone** (Healer; Revolutionary)
*The Fifth Sacred Thing* - Starhawk  *f*  5209

**Ma'elKoth** (Ruler)
*Heroes Die* - Matthew Woodring Stover  *s*  5319

**Maelwaedd, Rhodry** (Mythical Creature; Mercenary)
*Days of Air and Darkness* - Katharine Kerr  f  3067
*Days of Blood and Fire* - Katharine Kerr  f  3068
*The Dragon Revenant* - Katharine Kerr  f  3069
*A Time of Exile* - Katharine Kerr  f  3077

**Maenial** (Military Personnel)
*The Silver Wolf* - Alice Borchardt  h  572

**Ma'eva** (Mythical Creature)
*Storm Caller* - Carol Severance  f  4924

**Mafoo** (Servant)
*The Remarkable Journey of Prince Jen* - Lloyd
 Alexander  f  69

**Magaera** (Wizard)
*The Towers of the Sunset* - L.E. Modesitt
 Jr.  f  3941

**Magara** (Storyteller)
*Shadow-Maze* - Mark Smith  f  5133

**Magda** (Servant)
*The Angry Angel* - Chelsea Quinn Yarbro  h  6010

**Magda** (Vampire)
*The Darker Passions: Dracula* - Amarantha
 Knight  h  3179

**Maggie** (Scientist)
*Cain* - James Byron Huggins  h  2802
*The Cat* - R.L. Stine  h  5285

**Maggie** (Artificial Intelligence)
*Virtual Girl* - Amy Thomson  s  5462

**Magistrale, Michelangelo "Mage"** (Wizard;
 Photographer)
*The Art of Arrow Cutting* - Stephen
 Dedman  f  1462

**Magnalucius** (Religious; Writer)
*Quest: In Search of the Dragontooth* - Michael
 Green  f  2346

**Magnan, Ben** (Diplomat)
*Reward for Retief* - Keith Laumer  s  3345

**Magnolia** (Runaway; Lesbian)
*The Nature of Smoke* - Anne Harris  s  2559

**Magnus, Brock** (Teenager; Settler)
*The Faces of Ceti* - Mary Caraker  s  877

**Magnus, Dominic "Dom"** (Cyborg; Businessman)
*Partisan* - S. Andrew Swann  s  5365
*Profiteer* - S. Andrew Swann  s  5366
*Revolutionary* - S. Andrew Swann  s  5367

**Magnus, Mei-Ling** (Historian; Researcher)
*Standing Wave* - Howard V. Hendrix  s  2661

**Magodor** (Deity)
*Pretty Pewter Gods* - Glen Cook  f  1152

**Magon** (Royalty; Pirate)
*The Warrior Returns* - Allan Cole  f  1109

**Magorski, Mary Jane** (Businesswoman)
*Some Enchanted Evening* - Alice Alfonsi  f  73

**Magpie** (Minstrel)
*A Cast of Corbies* - Mercedes Lackey  f  3274

**Magruder, Bernie** (Child; Student)
*Bernie and the Bessledorf Ghost* - Phyllis Reynolds
 Naylor  f  4078

**Magruder, Sam** (Scientist; Time Traveler)
*The Dechronization of Sam Magruder* - George
 Gaylord Simpson  s  5067

**Maguire, Aaron** (Magician; Teenager)
*The Wizard's Apprentice* - S.P. Somtow  f  5163

**Maguire, Charlotte "Charlie"** (Journalist)
*Fatherland* - Robert Harris  s  2564

**Magus, Stheneleos XLIV** (Alien; Time Traveler)
*Web of Futures* - Jefferson P. Swycaffer  f  5376

**Magyar, Cherry** (Engineer)
*Slow River* - Nicola Griffith  s  2445

**Mah-ree** (Prehistoric Human)
*The Edge of the World* - William Sarabande  f  4817

**Mahafny** (Doctor)
*Finders-Seekers* - Gayle Greeno  s  2421

**Mahan, Patrick** (Military Personnel)
*1901* - Robert Conroy  s  1139

**Mahan, Sherry** (Police Officer)
*The Bad Thing* - Michael O'Rourke  h  4222

**Mahoney, Ian** (Military Personnel)
*The Return of the Emperor* - Allan Cole  s  1106
*Vortex* - Allan Cole  s  1108

**Mahtra** (Genetically Altered Being)
*Cinnabar Shadows* - Lynn Abbey  f  15

**Maijstral, Drake** (Thief; Nobleman)
*Rock of Ages* - Walter Jon Williams  s  5840

**Mairelon** (Magician; Traveler)
*Mairelon the Magician* - Patricia C. Wrede  f  5977

**Majamdar, Casseia** (Political Figure)
*Moving Mars* - Greg Bear  s  421

**Majeed** (Young Man)
*The Safety of Unknown Cities* - Lucy
 Taylor  h  5414

**Majere, Caramon** (Warrior; Child)
*The Soulforge* - Margaret Weis  f  5728

**Majere, Palin** (Wizard)
*The Day of the Tempest* - Jean Rabe  f  4457

**Majere, Raistlin** (Wizard)
*Dragons of Summer Flame* - Margaret Weis  f  5711

**Majere, Raistlin** (Wizard; Handicapped)
*The Soulforge* - Margaret Weis  f  5728

**Majicou** (Animal; Guide)
*The Wild Road* - Gabriel King  f  3120

**Major, Cyrus "Cy" Lance** (Computer Expert; Sports
 Figure)
*Zeus and Co.* - David Lee Jones  f  2942

**Makepeace, Sebastian** (Mythical Creature; Teacher)
*The Last Wizard* - Simon Hawke  f  2619

**Makish** (Criminal)
*Blood War* - Robert Weinberg  h  5693

**Malach** (Vampire)
*Personal Darkness* - Tanith Lee  h  3413

**Malachy the Great** (Royalty; Leader)
*Brian Boru: Emperor of the Irish* - Morgan
 Llywelyn  f  3501

**Malcolm** (Artist)
*The Cipher* - Kathe Koja  h  3194

**Malcolm** (Teenager)
*The Ogre Downstairs* - Diana Wynne Jones  f  2949

**Malcolm, Ian** (Scientist)
*The Lost World* - Michael Crichton  s  1256

**Maldari** (Spaceship Captain; Alien)
*The Fearful Summons* - Denny Martin Flinn  s  1954

**Malendor** (Vampire; Mythical Creature)
*Dark Divide* - Mark Acres  f  27

**Maler, Vicki** (Girlfriend)
*Psychosphere* - Brian Lumley  h  3563

**Maligor** (Wizard)
*Red Magic* - Jean Rabe  f  4458

**Maliwal** (Hunter; Prehistoric Human)
*The Sacred Stones* - William Sarabande  f  4818

**Malkin** (Thief; Companion)
*The Wizardry Consulted* - Rick Cook  f  1161

**Mallau, Olney** (Veterinarian; Alcoholic)
*Hand of Prophecy* - Severna Park  s  4244

**Malledd** (Artisan; Hero)
*Touched by the Gods* - Lawrence Watt-
 Evans  f  5651

**Mallernee, Jay** (Journalist)
*My Soul to Take* - Steven Spruill  s  5184

**Mallory** (Child)
*My Stepfather Shrank!* - Barbara Dillon  s  1558

**Mallory, David** (Doctor)
*The Twelfth Child* - Raymond Van Over  h  5538

**Mallory, Edward** (Scientist)
*The Difference Engine* - William Gibson  s  2217

**Mallory, Quinn** (Inventor; Scientist)
*Sliders: The Novel* - Brad Linaweaver  s  3467

**Mallory, Signy** (Spaceship Captain)
*Downbelow Station* - C.J. Cherryh  s  985

**Mallory, Thomas** (Police Officer)
*The Wizard of Camelot* - Simon Hawke  f  2627

**Malloy, D'Arcy** (Spirit)
*Second Child* - John Saul  h  4844

**Malone, Amos "Mad Amos"** (Mountain Man;
 Sorcerer)
*Mad Amos* - Alan Dean Foster  f  2009

**Malone, Billy** (Lawyer)
*The Devil's Churn* - Kristine Kathryn
 Rusch  h  4715

**Malone, Jessie** (Madam; Alcoholic)
*The Golden Nineties* - Lisa Mason  s  3663

**Malone, Kevin** (Teenager; Abuse Victim)
*The Kingdom of Kevin Malone* - Suzy McKee
 Charnas  f  970

**Malone, Patrick** (Spaceman; Pilot)
*Alien Tongue* - Stephen Leigh  s  3424

**Malu** (Philosopher; Deity)
*Children of the Mind* - Orson Scott Card  s  883

**Malva** (Alien)
*The Caterpillar's Question* - Piers Anthony  f  164

**Malystryx** (Mythical Creature)
*The Day of the Tempest* - Jean Rabe  f  4457
*Spirit of the Wind* - Chris Pierson  f  4326

**Mama** (Monster; Mythical Creature)
*India's Story* - Kathlyn S. Starbuck  s  5208

**Mama Pitie** (Religious)
*Portent* - James Herbert  h  2670

**Mama Yaya** (Spirit; Healer)
*I, Tituba, Black Witch of Salem* - Maryse
 Conde  f  1130

**Mami Gros-Jeanne** (Healer; Herbalist)
*Brown Girl in the Ring* - Nalo Hopkinson  f  2771

**Mana** (Warrior)
*Lion's Heart* - Karen Wehrstein  f  5683

**Manadgi** (Alien)
*Foreigner* - C.J. Cherryh  s  990

**Manan, Mattine "Mattie"** (Scientist; Explorer)
*Mutagenesis* - Helen Collins  s  1116

**Manarov, Vladimir "Volodya" Alekseevich**
 (Astronaut)
*Fellow Traveller* - William Barton  s  380

**Mancy, Katherine "Kat"** (Friend; Teenager)
*Her Monster* - Jeff Collignon  h  1115

**Mandaka, Bukoba** (Warrior)
*Ivory: A Legend of Past and Future* - Mike
 Resnick  f  4547

**Mandel, Eleanor** (Spouse; Detective)
*A Quantum Murder* - Peter F. Hamilton  s  2527

**Mandel, Greg** (Psychic; Detective)
*Mindstar Rising* - Peter F. Hamilton  s  2526
*A Quantum Murder* - Peter F. Hamilton  s  2527

**Mander, Otto** (Occultist)
*The Burning* - Graham Masterton   *h*   3672

**Manderley, Alexander** (Scientist)
*Thunder Road* - Chris Curry   *h*   1296

**Mandlestein, Gemma Rose** (Grandparent)
*Briar Rose* - Jane Yolen   *f*   6029

**Mandrake** (Robot)
*Nightshade* - Jack Butler   *s*   789

**Mandrake, Jarvin** (Archaeologist)
*Stone Angels* - Mike Jefferies   *h*   2889

**Mandrax** (Occultist)
*Master of Lies* - Graham Masterton   *h*   3676

**Mandrol** (Nobleman; Wizard)
*The Janus Mask* - Richard A. Knaak   *f*   3171

**Mandy** (Student; Teenager)
*Weirdos of the Universe, Unite!* - Pamela F.
   Service   *f*   4921

**Manfaluti, Aisha** (Archaeologist)
*Name of the Beast* - Daniel Easterman   *h*   1721

**Manfred** (Artificial Intelligence)
*Dreamships* - Melissa Scott   *s*   4896

**Maniakes** (Military Personnel; Rebel)
*Hammer and Anvil* - Harry Turtledove   *f*   5503

**Maniakes** (Ruler; Military Personnel)
*Videssos Besieged* - Harry Turtledove   *f*   5513

**Manilla** (Student; Lesbian)
*Virago* - Karen Marie Christa Minns   *h*   3915

**Manning, Kitty** (Teacher)
*Meridian 144* - Meg Files   *s*   1932

**Manning, Rowena Pearce** (Artist)
*Writ in Blood* - Chelsea Quinn Yarbro   *h*   6019

**Manning, Zoe** (Housewife)
*Night Games* - Marilyn Harris   *h*   2562

**Mano, Iuti** (Warrior; Magician)
*Demon Drums* - Carol Severance   *f*   4922
*Storm Caller* - Carol Severance   *f*   4924

**Manstar, Myrn** (Apprentice; Fiance(e))
*Aquamancer* - Don Callander   *f*   841

**Manstar, Myrn** (Wizard; Fiance(e))
*Geomancer* - Don Callander   *f*   845

**Mantrell, Matthew "Matt"** (Wizard)
*My Son, the Wizard* - Christopher Stasheff   *f*   5218

**Mantrell, Matthew "Matt"** (Wizard; Minstrel)
*The Secular Wizard* - Christopher Stasheff   *f*   5222

**Manx, Leo** (Genetically Altered Being)
*Proteus Unbound* - Charles Sheffield   *s*   4963

**Manz, Broderick** (Insurance Investigator)
*Greenthieves* - Alan Dean Foster   *s*   2005

**Manzara, Gaetano** (Baker; Aged Person)
*Fantasma* - Thomas F. Monteleone   *h*   3963

**Manzara, Vincent** (Musician)
*Fantasma* - Thomas F. Monteleone   *h*   3963

**Mapstone, Laren** (Courier; Military Personnel)
*Green Rider* - Kristen Britain   *f*   692

**MaqqRee, Desmond "Doc Sidhe"** (Hero)
*Doc Sidhe* - Aaron Allston   *f*   85

**Mara** (Gang Member)
*Bad Voltage* - Jonathan Littell   *s*   3491

**Mara** (Young Woman)
*Cry Republic* - Kirk Mitchell   *s*   3917

**Mara** (Royalty)
*Mistress of the Empire* - Raymond E. Feist   *f*   1906
*Servant of the Empire* - Raymond E. Feist   *f*   1910

**Mara** (Religious)
*Time Blender* - Michael Dorn   *s*   1581

**Mara, Vincent** (Writer)
*Thirst* - Pyotr Kurtinski   *h*   3253

**Marapper, Henry** (Religious)
*Non-Stop* - Brian W. Aldiss   *s*   58

**Maraquine, Toller II** (Pilot)
*The Fugitive Worlds* - Bob Shaw   *s*   4942

**Marat, Beverly** (Relative)
*Thirst of the Vampire* - T. Lucien Wright   *h*   5988

**Marat, Mike** (Journalist)
*Thirst of the Vampire* - T. Lucien Wright   *h*   5988

**Marble, Maytera** (Robot; Religious)
*Lake of the Long Sun* - Gene Wolfe   *s*   5942

**Marbleheart** (Animal; Companion)
*Geomancer* - Don Callander   *f*   845

**Marbleheart** (Animal)
*Marbleheart* - Don Callander   *f*   846

**Marbon, Diccon** (Teenager)
*Sunderlies Seeking* - Gayle Greeno   *f*   2424

**Marbon, Doyce** (Telepath)
*Exiles' Return* - Gayle Greeno   *s*   2420
*Finders-Seekers* - Gayle Greeno   *s*   2421
*Mind-Speakers' Call* - Gayle Greeno   *s*   2423

**Marbon, Jenneth** (Teenager)
*Sunderlies Seeking* - Gayle Greeno   *f*   2424

**Marceau, Yves** (Spaceship Captain)
*Flare Star* - Paula E. Downing   *s*   1594

**Marceline** (Police Officer; Imposter)
*Fools* - Pat Cadigan   *s*   805

**March, Xavier** (Detective—Police; Police Officer)
*Fatherland* - Robert Harris   *s*   2564

**Marchenko, Ivan "Burian Klimus"** (Professor;
   Criminal)
*Frameshift* - Robert J. Sawyer   *s*   4856

**Marcia** (Adventurer)
*The Wizard of Ambermere* - J. Calvin Pierce   *f*   4317

**Marconi, Maria** (Immortal; Pilot)
*Buying Time* - Joe Haldeman   *s*   2487

**Marcsson, Azamat** (Statistician)
*Dreaming in Smoke* - Tricia Sullivan   *s*   5353

**Marcus** (Saloon Keeper/Owner; Slave)
*Wagers of Sin* - Robert Asprin   *s*   264

**Marden, Jake** (Criminal; Computer Expert)
*Prison Ship* - Martin Caidin   *s*   828

**Marden, Kim** (Hotel Worker)
*Chiller* - Randall Boyll   *h*   610

**Mardian, Aiden** (Detective—Private)
*The Sand Dwellers* - Adam Niswander   *h*   4112

**Mardimil, Rion** (Wizard; Gentleman)
*Challenges* - Sharon Green   *f*   2354
*Competition* - Sharon Green   *f*   2355

**Margaret** (Student; Revolutionary)
*A Million Open Doors* - John Barnes   *s*   353

**Margaret** (Child)
*R-T, Margaret, and the Rats of NIMH* - Jane Leslie
   Conly   *f*   1132

**Margawt "The Morigu"** (Mythical Creature;
   Warrior)
*Morigu: The Dead* - Mark C. Perry   *f*   4284

**Marge** (Mythical Creature)
*Horrors of the Dancing Gods* - Jack L.
   Chalker   *f*   955

**Margery** (Witch)
*Strange Devices of the Sun and Moon* - Lisa
   Goldstein   *f*   2262

**Margison, Danny** (Child)
*Kids* - Trevor Hoyle   *h*   2787

**Margison, Tom** (Student; Scientist)
*Kids* - Trevor Hoyle   *h*   2787

**Margolis, Charles** (Administrator)
*Lords of Creation* - Tim Sullivan   *s*   5351

**Margrett** (Witch)
*Coven* - Steven William Rimmer   *h*   4591

**Margulies, Mary** (Military Personnel)
*The Sharp End* - David Drake   *s*   1643

**Maria** (Deity)
*The Wizard at Home* - Rick Shelley   *f*   4975

**Maria** (Magician)
*Aunt Maria* - Diana Wynne Jones   *f*   2943

**Maria Elena** (Musician; Agent)
*Humans* - Donald E. Westlake   *f*   5768

**Marian** (Librarian)
*The Fermata* - Nicholson Baker   *s*   302

**Marian** (Noblewoman)
*The Outlaws of Sherwood* - Robin
   McKinley   *f*   3846

**Marian** (Spouse)
*Robin and the King* - Parke Godwin   *f*   2247

**Marian** (Maiden; Girlfriend)
*Sherwood* - Parke Godwin   *f*   2248

**Mariana** (Vampire; Artist)
*Blood Relations* - Doug Murray   *h*   4058

**Marianne** (Young Woman)
*Marianne, the Matchbox and the Malachite Mouse* -
   Sheri S. Tepper   *f*   5432

**Marie** (Guide)
*Correspondence* - Sue Thomas   *s*   5450

**Mariel** (Animal; Adventurer; Warrior)
*The Bellmaker* - Brian Jacques   *f*   2848

**Mariel** (Animal; Warrior; Adventurer)
*Mariel of Redwall* - Brian Jacques   *f*   2850

**Mariell, Christina** (Heiress)
*Haunted* - James Herbert   *h*   2669

**Marik, Dau** (Doctor; Alien; Military Personnel)
*Hopeship* - Simon Lang   *s*   3315

**Marik, Dao** (Military Personnel; Alien; Doctor)
*The Trumpets of Tagan* - Simon Lang   *s*   3316

**Marina** (Teenager)
*Armageddon Summer* - Jane Yolen   *s*   6028

**Marinville, Johnny** (Writer)
*Desperation* - Stephen King   *h*   3129
*The Regulators* - Richard Bachman   *h*   284

**Marisovna, Cora** (Criminal; Genetically Altered
   Being)
*Climbing Olympus* - Kevin J. Anderson   *s*   102

**Marita** (Magician)
*Sable, Shadow and Ice* - Cheryl J. Franklin   *f*   2039

**Marius** (Religious)
*Pandora* - Anne Rice   *h*   4573

**Mark** (Computer Expert)
*See You Later* - Christopher Pike   *f*   4332

**Mark** (Teenager)
*The Transall Saga* - Gary Paulsen   *s*   4262

**Mark, Philip** (Mercenary; Lawman)
*The Sheriff of Nottingham* - Richard Kluger   *f*   3165

**Markham, Clare** (Artist; Religious)
*The Colors of Hell* - Michael Paine   *h*   4234

**Markham, Dan** (Store Owner)
*California Gothic* - Dennis Etchison   *h*   1843

**Markham, Evie** (Store Owner)
*California Gothic* - Dennis Etchison   *h*   1843

**Markham, Robert** (Journalist; Adventurer)
*A Hunger in the Soul* - Mike Resnick   *s*   4545

**Markham, Ulf Reichstein** (Administrator)
*Inconstant Star* - Poul Anderson   s   129

**Markhamwit** (Alien; Leader)
*Design for Great-Day* - Alan Dean Foster   s   2001

**Markley, Alan** (Businessman)
*Between Floors* - Thomas F. Monteleone   h   3957

**Markos** (Scientist)
*The Eternal Enemy* - Michael Berlyn   s   469

**Marks, Barbie** (Teenager; Model)
*I Was a Teenage Fairy* - Francesca Lia
   Block   f   549

**Marks, Paul** (Doctor)
*The Man Upstairs* - T.L. Parkinson   h   4248

**Marlene** (Teenager)
*Nemesis* - Isaac Asimov   s   247

**Marley, Andrew** (Werewolf; Religious)
*The Werewolf's Touch* - Cheri Scotch   h   4892

**Marliir, Dauneth** (Warrior)
*Cormyr: A Novel* - Ed Greenwood   f   2425

**Marling, Oliver Fonteyn** (Doctor)
*Dance of Death* - P.N. Elrod   h   1794

**Marling, Oliver Fonteyn** (Student)
*Red Death* - P.N. Elrod   h   1798

**Marlon, John** (Criminal)
*Nine Levels Down* - William Dantz   h   1347

**Marlow, Charles** (Doctor)
*Headhunter* - Timothy Findley   h   1939

**Marlow, Jenny** (Writer)
*Double Edge* - Dennis Etchison   h   1846

**Marlow, Lee** (Photographer)
*Double Edge* - Dennis Etchison   h   1846

**Marlowe** (Artist)
*The Godsend* - Bernard Taylor   h   5401

**Marlowe, Christopher** (Writer; Historical Figure)
*Strange Devices of the Sun and Moon* - Lisa
   Goldstein   f   2262

**Marlowe, Jim** (Student)
*Red Planet* - Robert A. Heinlein   s   2647

**Marlowe, Jim** (Scientist)
*White Horse, Dark Dragon* - Robert C.
   Fleet   f   1947

**Marlowe, Kate** (Housewife)
*The Godsend* - Bernard Taylor   h   5401

**Marlowe, Philip** (Detective—Private)
*The D. Case: The Truth about the Mystery of Edwin
   Drood* - Charles Dickens   f   1524

**Marlowe, Ruth** (Librarian; Student)
*The Cup of Morning Shadows* - Rosemary
   Edghill   f   1747
*The Sword of Maiden's Tears* - Rosemary
   Edghill   f   1748

**Marlowe, Trip** (Musician)
*Glimmering* - Elizabeth Hand   s   2535

**Marlowe, Zoot** (Alien; Detective)
*Hawaiian U.F.O. Aliens* - Mel Gilden   s   2226
*Tubular Android Superheroes* - Mel Gilden   s   2228

**Marm, Everett C. "Harlequin"** (Revolutionary;
   Activist)
*"Repent, Harlequin!" Said the Ticktockman* - Harlan
   Ellison   s   1782

**Marnay, Paul** (Artist)
*Deathchain* - Ken Greenhall   h   2415

**Maroc, Huud** (Actor; Alien)
*The Merro Tree* - Katie Waitman   s   5609

**Marouk, Kemal** (Scientist; Government Official)
*The Joy Machine* - James Gunn   s   2458

**Marquard, Pat** (Scientist)
*A World of Difference* - Harry Turtledove   s   5514

**Marqueete, Donald** (Student—Graduate; Writer)
*Quoth the Crow* - David Bischoff   h   494

**The Marra** (Alien)
*The Madness Season* - C.S. Friedman   s   2058

**Marrah, Rabh** (Murderer)
*The Light in Exile* - Cheryl J. Franklin   s   2038

**Marrika** (Thief; Traitor)
*King's Man and Thief* - Christie Golden   f   2253

**Marrimian** (Ruler)
*Hall of Whispers* - Mike Jefferies   f   2884

**Mars, Jerry** (Criminal)
*Rough Beast* - Gary Goshgarian   h   2284

**Marsh, Gregory Bradford** (Serial Killer)
*Nightmare's Disciple* - Joseph S. Pulver Jr.   h   4449

**Marsh, Harold** (Doctor)
*Black Death* - R. Karl Largent   h   3337

**Marsh, Maxwell** (Journalist)
*Rage* - Elizabeth Ergas   h   1834

**Marsh, Obediah** (Sailor)
*The Shadow over Innsmouth* - H.P.
   Lovecraft   h   3533

**Marsh, Othniel Charles** (Scientist)
*Bone Wars* - Brett Davis   s   1398

**Marsh, Pella** (Teenager; Adventurer)
*Girl in Landscape* - Jonathan Lethem   s   3440

**Marsh, Valentine** (Student—High School; Sorceress)
*The Golden Thread* - Suzy McKee Charnas   f   969

**Marshak, Arthur** (Doctor; Researcher)
*Brothers* - Ben Bova   s   581

**Marshak, Jessie** (Doctor)
*Brothers* - Ben Bova   s   581

**Marshak, Julia** (Spouse)
*Brothers* - Ben Bova   s   581

**Marshall, Anna** (Singer; Sorceress)
*The Soprano Sorceress* - L.E. Modesitt Jr.   f   3938
*The Spellsong War* - L.E. Modesitt Jr.   f   3939

**Marshall, Deidi** (Journalist)
*Flesh and Blood* - D.A. Fowler   h   2024

**Marshall, Jenny** (Young Woman)
*The Judas Cross* - Charles Sheffield   h   4960

**Marshall, Meg** (Housewife)
*Seeds of Evil* - Margaret Bingley   h   491

**Marshall, Olivia** (Child; Twin)
*Seeds of Evil* - Margaret Bingley   h   491

**Marshall, Orlando** (Child; Twin)
*Seeds of Evil* - Margaret Bingley   h   491

**Mart** (Teenager)
*I Feel Like the Morning Star* - Gregory
   Maguire   s   3608

**Marta** (Animal; Leader)
*Hungry for Home: A Wolf Odyssey* - 'Asta
   Bowen   f   599

**Marteen, Triscoe** (Spaceship Captain)
*Prodigy* - Jan Clark   s   1047

**Martel, Dina** (Diplomat)
*Man o' War* - William Shatner   s   4932

**Martel, James Mannheim** (Military Personnel)
*1945* - Newt Gingrich   s   2239

**Martens, Billy** (Television Personality)
*The Wizard of Camelot* - Simon Hawke   f   2627

**Marth, Jarem** (Pirate; Ruler)
*Ash Ock* - Christopher Hinz   s   2690
*The Paratwa* - Christopher Hinz   s   2691

**Martin** (Producer)
*The Informers* - Brett Easton Ellis   h   1778

**Martin** (Artificial Intelligence)
*Mars Prime* - William C. Dietz   s   1548

**Martin, Andrew** (Robot; Revolutionary)
*The Positronic Man* - Isaac Asimov   s   249

**Martin, Anita** (Divorced Person)
*Blood Wings* - Stephen Gresham   h   2430

**Martin, Dan** (Director)
*Goblins* - Vincent Courtney   h   1212

**Martin, Fred** (Religious)
*Blood Feud* - Sam Siciliano   h   5020

**Martin, Gene** (Accountant)
*Hellcat* - Amanda Kingsley   h   3145

**Martin, Gina** (Writer)
*Entoverse* - James P. Hogan   s   2724

**Martin, Hailey** (Writer)
*Leanna: Possession of a Woman* - Marie
   Kiraly   h   3149

**Martin, Hector** (Scientist; Researcher)
*Accidental Creatures* - Anne Harris   s   2558

**Martin, Helix** (Genetically Altered Being; Adoptee)
*Accidental Creatures* - Anne Harris   s   2558

**Martin, Jack** (Artist)
*Shadow Man* - Dennis Etchison   h   1848

**Martin, Jiggs** (Cook)
*The Unfinished* - Jay B. Laws   h   3362

**Martin, Julianne** (Musician)
*Phantom Banjo* - Elizabeth Ann
   Scarborough   f   4868
*Strum Again?* - Elizabeth Ann Scarborough   f   4870

**Martin, Justin** (Teenager)
*Thunder Road* - Chris Curry   h   1296

**Martin, Larry** (Vampire)
*Blood Ties* - Karen E. Taylor   h   5407

**Martin, Marty** (Child)
*Goblins* - Vincent Courtney   h   1212

**Martin, Neil** (Worker)
*The Quorum* - Kim Newman   h   4100

**Martin, Paul** (Teacher; Parent)
*Shaman Woods* - Morgan Fields   h   1931

**Martin, Vicki** (Housewife)
*Goblins* - Vincent Courtney   h   1212

**Martin, Wade** (Child)
*Blood Wings* - Stephen Gresham   h   2430

**Martin, Wes** (Psychologist)
*Fragments* - James F. David   h   1380

**Martin, Worth** (Child)
*Shaman Woods* - Morgan Fields   h   1931

**Martin the Warrior** (Animal; Slave)
*Martin the Warrior* - Brian Jacques   f   2851

**Martina, Jewel** (Health Care Professional)
*Chimera* - Mary Rosenblum   s   4677

**Martine** (Girlfriend)
*Time and Light* - William Bornefeld   s   574

**Martinez, Freddy** (Child)
*Vampire Breath* - R.L. Stine   h   5291

**Martinique, Speranza** (Governess)
*Moon Dance* - S.P. Somtow   h   5158

**Martino, Chris** (Teenager; Student—High School)
*OtherSyde* - J. Michael Straczynski   h   5323

**Mary** (Prostitute)
*Beautiful Strangers* - Melanie Tem   h   5420

**Mary** (Young Woman)
*The House on the Borderland* - William Hope
   Hodgson   h   2711

**Mary** (Spy)
*The Puppet Masters* - Robert A. Heinlein   s   2646

**Mary** (Teenager)
*A Tie to the Past* - David Wiseman   f   5928

**Mary** (Aged Person)
*Wilding* - Melanie Tem   h   5425

**Maryk, Peter** (Scientist)
*The Blood Artists* - Chuck Hogan   h   2720

**Maryn** (Royalty)
*The Red Wyvern* - Katharine Kerr   f   3074

**Masada, Kio** (Computer Expert; Mentally Ill Person)
*This Alien Shore* - C.S. Friedman   s   2059

**Masahiko** (Artist)
*Scissors Cut Paper Wrap Stone* - Ian
   McDonald   s   3795

**Masau** (Hunter; Prehistoric Human)
*The Sacred Stones* - William Sarabande   f   4818

**Mash, Madeleine** (Journalist)
*Coyote* - Peter Gadol   f   2100

**Masklin** (Mythical Creature; Alien)
*Truckers* - Terry Pratchett   s   4402
*Wings* - Terry Pratchett   s   4403

**Masmajean, Anna "Mama" Jason** (Scientist)
*Mirabile* - Janet Kagan   s   3001

**Mason, Estelle "Lysistrata"** (Genetically Altered
   Being; Student)
*Cannon's Orb* - L. Warren Douglas   s   1586

**Mason, Jennifer** (Teenager; Time Traveler)
*Ray Bradbury Presents: Dinosaur Planet* - Stephen
   Leigh   s   3427
*Ray Bradbury Presents: Dinosaur World* - Stephen
   Leigh   s   3428

**Massenet, Charles** (Doctor)
*Them* - William W. Johnstone   h   2935

**Massey, Caleb** (Scientist)
*Beamriders!* - Martin Caidin   s   824

**Massif, Sheila** (Sociologist)
*The Living One* - Lewis Gannett   h   2115

**Master** (Magician; Mythical Creature)
*Mythology Abroad* - Jody Lynn Nye   f   4174

**Master** (Vampire)
*Virgintooth* - Mark Ivanhoe   h   2834

**Masters, Amber** (Teenager)
*Haunted* - Tamara Thorne   h   5463

**Masters, David** (Writer)
*Haunted* - Tamara Thorne   h   5463

**Masters, Gil** (Psychic)
*Fragments* - James F. David   h   1380

**Masterson, Gordon** (Real Estate Agent)
*Killing Frost* - Dan I. Blake   h   514

**Masterson, Jenny** (Waiter/Waitress)
*Practical Demonkeeping* - Christopher
   Moore   h   3989

**Masterson, Rick** (Journalist)
*Darkling* - Michael O'Rourke   h   4223

**Masul** (Revolutionary)
*The Star Scroll* - Melanie Rawn   f   4491

**Mata Hari** (Spy; Historical Figure)
*The Mata Hari Adventure* - James Luceno   f   3544

**Matalon, Cynthia** (Experimental Subject;
   Gentlewoman)
*The Hot-Wired Dodo* - Jack L. Chalker   s   956

**Matamoros, Hunahpu** (Time Traveler)
*Pastwatch: The Redemption of Christopher Columbus* -
   Orson Scott Card   s   895

**Matar, Kitiara "Kit"** (Mercenary; Leader)
*Steel and Stone* - Ellen Porath   f   4368

**Mathen** (Knight; Abuse Victim)
*The Time of Madness* - Thomas K. Martin   f   3652

**Matheson, Harry** (Writer; Vampire)
*Blood Brothers* - T. Lucien Wright   h   5986

**Matheson, Honor** (Nurse)
*Fatal Outcome* - Patricia Wallace   h   5622

**Matheson, Hope** (Animal Lover)
*Seeing Eye* - Jack Ellis   h   1780

**Matheson, Jerry** (Writer)
*Blood Brothers* - T. Lucien Wright   h   5986

**Matheson, Tad** (Child)
*Blood Brothers* - T. Lucien Wright   h   5986

**Mathews, Sheilagh** (Student; Astronaut)
*The Voice of Cepheus* - Ken Appleby   s   202

**Mati, Gwendolyn "Gwen"** (Stock Broker; Fiance(e))
*Half Asleep in Frog Pajamas* - Tom
   Robbins   s   4606

**Matilde** (Noblewoman)
*A Strange and Ancient Name* - Josepha
   Sherman   f   4991

**M'ats** (Alien)
*Delta Pavonis* - Eric Kotani   s   3221

**Matsika, Amadeus** (Military Personnel)
*The Ear, the Eye, and the Arm* - Nancy
   Farmer   f   1867

**Matsika, Tendai** (Child)
*The Ear, the Eye, and the Arm* - Nancy
   Farmer   f   1867

**Matsuda** (Businessman)
*The Bushido Incident* - Betty Anne
   Crawford   s   1248

**Matsudaira, Daisuke** (Businessman)
*Fire in a Faraway Place* - Robert Frezza   s   2052

**Matsuhara, Yoshi** (Military Personnel)
*Assault of the Super Carrier* - Peter Albano   s   47
*Ordeal of the Seventh Carrier* - Peter Albano   s   48
*Revenge of the Seventh Carrier* - Peter Albano   s   49

**Matsuko, Estelle** (Royalty; Government Official)
*On Basilisk Station* - David Weber   s   5679

**Matsumoto, Hiroshi** (Administrator)
*Hocus Pocus or, What's the Hurry, Son?* - Kurt
   Vonnegut Jr.   s   5593

**Matt** (Wizard; Fiance(e))
*The Oathbound Wizard* - Christopher
   Stasheff   f   5219

**Matthew** (Child)
*The End of Alice* - A.M. Homes   h   2755

**Matthews, Charles** (Teacher)
*I Met a Man Who Wasn't There* - Mary R.
   Callaghan   h   840

**Matthews, Eric** (Young Man)
*Demon Night* - J. Michael Straczynski   h   5322

**Matthews, Gabriel** (Fanatic)
*Deathgrip* - Brian Hodge   h   2700

**Matthews, Kevin** (Artist; Criminal)
*Galatea in 2-D* - Aaron Allston   f   87

**Matthews, Lydia** (Single Parent)
*Carnivores* - Penelope Banka Kreps   h   3232

**Matthews, Susan** (Journalist; Parent)
*Dancing on Air* - Nancy Kress   s   3240

**Matthiall** (Wizard)
*Glenraven* - Marion Zimmer Bradley   f   635

**Matthias** (Religious)
*The Changeling* - Kristine Kathryn Rusch   f   4714

**Matthias** (Warrior; Animal)
*Mattimeo* - Brian Jacques   f   2852

**Matthieson, Jonah** (Pilot; Military Personnel)
*Man-Kzin Wars V* - Larry Niven   s   4125

**Mattison, Petie** (Teenager)
*Wake Up Screaming* - Vincent Courtney   h   1215

**Mauakes** (Ruler)
*Horses of Heaven* - Gillian Bradshaw   f   657

**Maude** (Bodyguard; Genetically Altered Being)
*Conrad's Quest for Rubber* - Leo
   Frankowski   s   2043

**Maughan, Daisy** (Businesswoman; Antiques Dealer)
*Mennyms Alive* - Sylvia Waugh   f   5655

**Maule, Matthew** (Philanthropist; Vampire)
*A Matter of Taste* - Fred Saberhagen   h   4770

**Mauney, Kevin** (Writer)
*Above the Lower Sky* - Tom Deitz   f   1469

**Maupin, Emily** (Student)
*Anthony Shriek* - Jessica Amanda
   Salmonson   h   4790

**Maureen** (Prostitute)
*Callahan's Lady* - Spider Robinson   s   4638

**Maury, Paul** (Businessman; Lawyer)
*Whiteout* - Sage Walker   s   5619

**Mauryl** (Wizard; Immortal)
*Fortress of Owls* - C.J. Cherryh   f   993

**Maurynna** (Sea Captain)
*The Last Dragonlord* - Joanne Bertin   f   470

**Maverick** (Alien)
*Maverick* - Bruce Bethke   s   484

**MAX** (Cyborg)
*Berserker* - S.D. Perry   s   4285

**Max** (Teenager)
*Strange Attractors* - William Sleator   s   5088

**Maxey, Warren** (Scientist)
*Dangerous Nature* - T.J. Kirby   h   3152

**Maximillian** (Sorcerer)
*Catastrophe's Spell* - Mayer Alan Brenner   f   671
*Spell of Apocalypse* - Mayer Alan Brenner   f   672
*Spell of Fate* - Mayer Alan Brenner   f   673

**Maxon, Alice** (Computer Expert; Adventurer)
*Caverns of Socrates* - Dennis L. McKiernan   f   3831

**Maxon, Max** (Bodyguard; Handicapped)
*Bodyguard* - William C. Dietz   s   1542

**Maxwell, Alicia** (Teenager)
*Facade* - Kristine Kathryn Rusch   h   4716

**Maxwell, James** (Journalist)
*The Mysterium* - Eric McCormack   h   3780

**Maxwell, Jillian** (Editor)
*Facade* - Kristine Kathryn Rusch   h   4716

**Maxwell, Mahlon Sumner "Mama"** (Police Officer)
*Dragon's Teeth* - Lee Killough   s   3109

**Maxwell, Maureen** (Real Estate Agent; Spouse)
*Relife* - Dan Barton   h   376

**Maxwell, Scott** (Addict)
*Relife* - Dan Barton   h   376

**Maxwell, Thomas F.** (Lawyer)
*Relife* - Dan Barton   h   376

**May, Carl** (Businessman)
*The Cloning of Joanna May* - Fay Weldon   s   5732

**May, James** (Spaceship Captain)
*Desperate Measures* - Joe Clifford Faust   s   1891
*Precious Cargo* - Joe Clifford Faust   s   1893

**May, Joanna** (Divorced Person)
*The Cloning of Joanna May* - Fay Weldon   s   5732

**Maya** (Religious; Grandparent)
*The Fifth Sacred Thing* - Starhawk   f   5209

**Mayaram, Simon** (Diplomat; Human)
*Celestis* - Paul Park  s  4241

**Maybelle** (Spirit)
*The Witch House* - Norma Tadlock Johnson  f  2923

**Mayer, Steve** (Detective—Police)
*The Need* - Andrew Neiderman  h  4089

**Mayfair, Mona** (Businesswoman)
*Taltos* - Anne Rice  h  4577

**Mayfair, Rowan** (Doctor; Witch)
*The Witching Hour* - Anne Rice  h  4580

**Mayhew, Benjamin** (Leader)
*Flag in Exile* - David Weber  s  5671
*The Honor of the Queen* - David Weber  s  5674

**Mayhew, Richard** (Businessman)
*Neverwhere* - Neil Gaiman  f  2104

**Mayhew IX, Benjamin** (Political Figure; Leader)
*Echoes of Honor* - David Weber  s  5669

**Mayland, Gia** (Researcher; Explorer)
*The Expediter* - J. Brian Clarke  s  1062

**Mayor, Mayor** (Political Figure)
*Escardy Gap* - Peter Crowther  h  1282

**Mays, Johnny** (Police Officer)
*Down River* - Stephen Gallagher  h  2110

**Mays, Randolph** (Historian; Television Personality)
*The Diamond Moon* - Paul Preuss  s  4417

**Maz, Mia** (Diplomat)
*Cetaganda* - Lois McMaster Bujold  s  758

**Mazdan, Jennifer "Jennie"** (Government Official; Psychic)
*Unquenchable Fire* - Rachel Pollack  f  4361

**Mbele, Miriam Makepeace** (Clone; Computer Expert)
*Red Dust* - Paul J. McAuley  s  3715

**McAlois, Lois** (Spaceship Captain)
*Tower of the Gods* - Thomas A. Easton  s  1726
*Woodsman* - Thomas A. Easton  s  1727

**McAndrews, Arthur Morton** (Scientist; Spaceman)
*One Man's Universe* - Charles Sheffield  s  4961

**McAslan, Gabriel "Gaby"** (Journalist)
*Evolution's Shore* - Ian McDonald  s  3792

**McAusland, James** (Military Personnel)
*Flameweaver* - Margaret Ball  f  314

**McAusland, Louisa** (Diplomat; Shaman)
*Changeweaver* - Margaret Ball  f  313

**McBan, Rod** (Telepath)
*Norstrilia* - Cordwainer Smith  s  5105

**McBride, Duane** (Child)
*Summer of Night* - Dan Simmons  h  5060

**McBride, Michael** (Cowboy; Mythical Creature)
*The Flight of Michael McBride* - Midori Snyder  f  5151

**McBride, Ronica** (Psychic)
*Commencement* - Roby James  s  2877

**McCabe, Darian** (Psychic; Sailor)
*World Without End* - Molly Cochran  f  1093

**McCabe, Sarah/Melissa** (Heiress—Dispossessed)
*The Catswold Portal* - Shirley Rousseau Murphy  f  4055

**McCade, Molly** (Child)
*McCade's Bounty* - William C. Dietz  s  1550

**McCade, Sam** (Spaceship Captain; Bounty Hunter)
*McCade's Bounty* - William C. Dietz  s  1550

**McCaffrey, Anne** (Writer; Storyteller)
*A Diversity of Dragons* - Anne McCaffrey  f  3728

**McCall, Cassie** (Accountant)
*Black Ice* - Pat Graversen  h  2333

**McCall, Dante** (Outcast; Spaceman)
*Songs of Chaos* - S.N. Lewitt  s  3452

**McCall, Jess** (Child)
*Black Ice* - Pat Graversen  h  2333

**McCallum, Richard** (Detective—Private)
*The Abductors: Conspiracy* - Jonathan Frakes  s  2034

**McCamfrey, Tessa** (Wizard)
*The Barbed Coil* - J.V. Jones  f  2957

**McCandless, Lauren** (Artist)
*Vanitas: Escape From Vampire Junction* - S.P. Somtow  h  5162

**McCann, Dire** (Detective)
*Blood War* - Robert Weinberg  h  5693
*The Unbeholden* - Robert Weinberg  h  5703
*Unholy Allies* - Robert Weinberg  h  5704

**McCann, Rorin** (Nobleman; Rebel)
*Caledon of the Mists* - Deborah Turner Harris  f  2560

**McCardle, Box "Texas"** (Police Officer)
*Metal Angel* - Nancy Springer  f  5181

**McCarthy, James Edward** (Military Personnel)
*A Rage for Revenge* - David Gerrold  s  2210
*A Season for Slaughter* - David Gerrold  s  2211

**McCarthy, Mary Margaret** (Teacher)
*Substitute Teacher* - Jordan Storm  h  5314

**McCay, Debra** (Leader)
*The Earth Saver* - Catherine Wells  s  5745

**McClain, Walter** (Administrator)
*Demon Shadows* - Michael B. Sirota  h  5075

**McClane** (Psychologist)
*The Collected Stories of Philip K. Dick, Volume Two: We Can Remember It for You Wholesale* - Philip K. Dick  s  1520

**McClane, Judson** (Administrator)
*Sorcerers of Sodom* - Roger Elwood  h  1804

**McClare, D.J.** (Professor; Scientist)
*Unwillingly to Earth* - Pauline Ashwell  s  231

**McClellan, Conan** (Police Officer)
*Return of the Living Dead* - John Russo  h  4746

**McClure, Katy** (Photographer)
*The Dwelling* - Tom Elliott  h  1776

**McCogg, Gus "Aengus Mac Og"** (Artist; Mythical Creature)
*The Friendship Song* - Nancy Springer  f  5179

**McComb, Aaron** (Political Figure; Criminal)
*Timecop* - S.D. Perry  s  4286

**McConnell, Celeste** (Administrator; Psychic)
*Assemblers of Infinity* - Kevin J. Anderson  s  100

**McCord, Bob** (Businessman)
*Darkscope* - Margaret Falk  h  1860

**McCord, Chelsea** (Artist)
*Darkscope* - Margaret Falk  h  1860

**McCormick, Lianne** (Teacher; Heroine)
*When the Bough Breaks* - Mercedes Lackey  f  3302

**McCormick, Marilou** (Teacher)
*Room 13* - Henry Garfield  h  2139

**McCormick, Sandra** (Police Officer)
*Dark Heart* - Margaret Weis  f  5707

**McCoy, Leonard** (Doctor)
*Doctor's Orders* - Diane Duane  s  1659
*Enemy Unseen* - V.E. Mitchell  s  3918
*First Frontier* - Diane Carey  s  902
*Prime Directive* - Judith Reeves-Stevens  s  4514
*Renegade* - Gene DeWeese  s  1511
*Sanctuary* - John Vornholt  s  5597
*Shadows on the Sun* - Michael Jan Friedman  s  2069

*Star Trek VI: The Undiscovered Country* - J.M. Dillard  s  1556
*Star Trek: The Classic Episodes 1* - James Blish  s  526
*Star Trek: The Classic Episodes 2* - James Blish  s  527
*Star Trek: The Classic Episodes 3* - James Blish  s  528

**McCoy, Leonard** (Doctor; Spaceman)
*Vulcan's Forge* - Susan Shwartz  s  5019

**McCray, Abbey** (Parent; Heroine)
*Leap Point* - Kay Kenyon  s  3063

**McCray, Jimmy** (Telepath)
*The Demons at Rainbow Bridge* - Jack L. Chalker  s  952
*The Ninety Trillion Fausts* - Jack L. Chalker  s  958
*The Run to Chaos Keep* - Jack L. Chalker  s  960

**McCray, Tom** (Troubleshooter)
*Protektor* - Charles Platt  s  4342

**McCrea, Rinn** (Telepath)
*Rinn's Star* - Paula E. Downing  s  1719

**McCready** (Teacher; Criminal)
*Damnbanna* - Nancy Springer  f  5177

**McCulley, Kitty** (Nurse; Military Personnel)
*The Healer's War* - Elizabeth Ann Scarborough  f  4865

**McCullough, Caitlin** (Writer)
*Control Freak* - Christa Faust  h  1890

**McCullough, Carson** (Government Official)
*The Seraphim Rising* - Elisabeth De Vos  s  1442

**McCullough, Dusty** (Ruler)
*Free Zone* - Charles Platt  s  4341

**McCullough, Mike** (Military Personnel)
*Secret Realms* - Tom Cool  s  1168

**McCunniff, Mara** (Vampire)
*The Vampire Memoirs* - Mara McCuniff  h  3781

**McCutcheon, Christopher** (Librarian)
*The Quiet Pools* - Michael P. Kube-McDowell  s  3249

**McDaris, Samantha "Sammi"** (Mythical Creature; Royalty)
*Elvendude* - Mark Shepherd  f  4980

**McDarvid, Jack** (Researcher; Detective—Amateur)
*The Green Progression* - L.E. Modesitt Jr.  s  3932

**McDonald** (Spaceman; Pirate)
*Cat's Gambit* - Leslie Gadallah  s  2099

**McDonald, Dirk** (Teenager; Homosexual)
*Baby Be-Bop* - Francesca Lia Block  f  545
*Witch Baby* - Francesca Lia Block  f  552

**McDougal, Marta** (Inventor; Scientist)
*Core* - Paul Preuss  s  4416

**McDowell, Allison** (Writer)
*Sweet William* - Jessica Palmer  h  4239

**McDowell, Josie** (Student)
*Belladonna* - Michael Stewart  h  5271

**McDowell, William Scott** (Child)
*Sweet William* - Jessica Palmer  h  4239

**McElroy, Jud** (Police Officer)
*The Headsman* - James Neal Harvey  h  2599

**McFarland, Henry Lee** (Oil Industry Worker; Farmer)
*Petrogypsies* - Rory Harper  s  2549

**McFarland, Sonny** (Teenager)
*Father's Little Helper* - Ronald Kelly  h  3052

**McFarley, Andrew** (Religious)
*Purgatory: A Chronicle of a Distant World* - Mike Resnick  s  4554

**McFee, Jonas** (Teenager)
*Jonas McFee, A.T.P.* - Sarah Sargent  s  4827

**McGammon, Clyde** (Detective—Private)
*Lorelei* - Mark A. Clements  h  1086

**McGann, Agnes "Aggie"** (Religious)
*Gibbon's Decline and Fall* - Sheri S.
Tepper  s  5430

**McGann, Jennifer** (Detective—Police)
*Nightmare, with Angel* - Stephen Gallagher  h  2111

**McGann, Jim** (Photographer)
*From a Whisper to a Scream* - Samuel M.
Key  h  3093

**McGarvey, Heather** (Housewife)
*Winter Moon* - Dean R. Koontz  h  3218

**McGarvey, Jack** (Police Officer)
*Winter Moon* - Dean R. Koontz  h  3218

**McGarvey, Toby** (Child)
*Winter Moon* - Dean R. Koontz  h  3218

**McGee, Rosa** (Supernatural Being)
*Sacrament* - Clive Barker  h  345

**McGee, Trevor** (Artist)
*Drawing Blood* - Poppy Z. Brite  h  694

**McGill, Henderson** (Military Personnel)
*Deep Trek* - James Axler  s  278

**McGilray, Aidan** (Writer)
*Stage Fright* - Clare McNally  h  3858

**McGinnis, Rachel** (Designer)
*Santa Steps Out: A Fairy Tale for Grownups* - Robert
Devereaux  h  1506

**McGiven, Mary** (Girlfriend)
*The Haunt* - John Fogarty  h  1966

**McGlinn, Desiree** (Public Relations)
*Mask of the Night* - Mary Ryan  h  4753

**McGowan, Annie** (Aged Person)
*The Nightmare People* - Lawrence Watt-
Evans  h  5643

**McGruder, Jim** (FBI Agent)
*Bright Shadow* - Elizabeth Forrest  h  1971

**McGuire, Bill** (Contractor)
*The Blackstone Chronicles* - John Saul  h  4838

**McGulvey, Mr.** (Steward)
*In between Dragons* - Michael Kandel  f  3010

**McHenry, Mark** (Scientist; Student)
*Worf's First Adventure* - Peter David  s  1391

**McHogue** (Computer Expert; Criminal)
*Warped* - K.W. Jeter  s  2917

**McIlvane** (Editor)
*The Waterworks* - E.L. Doctorow  s  1564

**McIntosh, Alexander** (Immortal)
*Gryphon* - Crawford Kilian  s  3106

**McIntosh, Calvin** (Indian; Wanderer)
*Stoneskin's Revenge* - Tom Deitz  f  1476
*Sunshaker's War* - Tom Deitz  f  1477

**McIntyre, Scott** (Political Figure)
*Footprints of Thunder* - James F. David  s  1379

**McIssac, Dean** (Maintenance Worker; Cook)
*Summon the Keeper* - Tanya Huff  f  2800

**McKay** (Military Personnel)
*Devil's Deal* - Richard Austin  s  277

**McKay, Bernie** (Businessman)
*Black as Blood* - Rob Chilson  f  1014

**McKay, David** (Child)
*Brainstorm* - Steven M. Krauzer  h  3230

**McKay, Debra** (Scientist; Hunter)
*Children of the Earth* - Catherine Wells  s  5743
*The Earth Is All That Lasts* - Catherine
Wells  s  5744

**McKay, Kenneth "Ken"** (Vampire; Military
Personnel)
*The VMR Theory* - Robert Frezza  s  2055

**McKeane, Fletcher** (Photojournalist)
*In the Shadows of the Moonglade* - Riley St.
James  h  5186

**McKelvey, Dan** (Castaway)
*The Past of Forever* - Juanita Coulson  s  1210

**McKendree** (Racist)
*Devil's Deal* - Richard Austin  s  277

**McKenzie, Chia** (Teenager; Investigator)
*Idoru* - William Gibson  s  2218

**McKenzie, Victoria** (Scientist; Leader)
*Metaphase* - Vonda N. McIntyre  s  3821
*Starfarers* - Vonda N. McIntyre  s  3824
*Transition* - Vonda N. McIntyre  s  3825

**McKeon, Alister** (Military Personnel)
*On Basilisk Station* - David Weber  s  5679

**McKibben, Brion** (Child)
*Whisper* - Raymond Van Over  h  5539

**McKinnan** (Police Officer)
*The Third Beast* - Peter Loughran  h  3527

**McKinnon, Savvy** (Journalist)
*Insanity, Illinois* - Mark Sumner  s  5358

**McLaris, Duncan** (Manufacturer; Administrator)
*Lifeline* - Kevin J. Anderson  s  111

**McLaud, Jaren** (Magician)
*Sage of Sare* - Julie Dean Smith  f  5126

**McLean, Alec** (Student—College; Adventurer)
*Dreamseeker's Road* - Tom Deitz  f  1472

**McLeod, Morgan** (Dancer; Student)
*Starseed* - Spider Robinson  s  4643

**McLeod, Noel** (Police Officer; Psychic)
*The Adept* - Katherine Kurtz  f  3254
*Dagger Magic* - Katherine Kurtz  f  3256

**McMahon, Colin** (Artist)
*Cromm* - Kenneth C. Flint  f  1957

**McMichaels, Scott** (Computer Expert; Researcher)
*Infectress* - Tom Cool  s  1167

**McMickey, Mickey** (Mythical Creature)
*Dragonslayer's Return* - R.A. Salvatore  f  4798

**McMurphy, Robie** (Farmer)
*The Reluctant Sorcerer* - Simon Hawke  f  2622

**McMurtrey, Evander Harold** (Religious)
*The Race for God* - Brian Herbert  s  2666

**McNair, Brian** (Child)
*The Good Children* - Kate Wilhelm  h  5808

**McNair, Liz** (Child)
*The Good Children* - Kate Wilhelm  h  5808

**McNamara, Alice** (Teenager)
*Along Came a Spider* - Athena Alexis  h  70

**McNamara, Deuce** (Gambler)
*The Six Families* - Nancy Holder  s  2733

**McNihil** (Detective—Private)
*Noir* - K.W. Jeter  s  2916

**McPherson, Dennis** (Engineer)
*The Gold Coast* - Kim Stanley Robinson  s  4632

**McPherson, Jim** (Teacher; Writer)
*The Gold Coast* - Kim Stanley Robinson  s  4632

**McPherson, Mark** (Journalist)
*Seed upon the Wind* - Carole Nelson
Douglas  f  1584

**McRay, Kevin** (Police Officer)
*Nine Levels Down* - William Dantz  h  1347

**McShane, Terry** (Military Personnel)
*seaQuest DSV: Fire Below* - Matthew J.
Costello  s  1201

**McTurk, Felix** (Computer Expert; Detective)
*Kaduna Memories* - Jack McKinney  s  3850

**Meacher, Henry** (Scientist)
*Moonseed* - Stephen Baxter  s  400

**Meadows, Catherine** (Doctor)
*Batman: Captured by the Engines* - Joe R.
Lansdale  h  3320

**Meadows, Mark "Captain Trips"** (Genetically
Altered Being; Scientist)
*Black Trump* - George R.R. Martin  s  3642
*Turn of the Cards* - Victor Milan  s  3891

**Meagar** (Government Official)
*The Outlander: Captivity* - B.J. Salterberg  s  4792

**Meagher, Richard** (Police Officer)
*The Uprising* - Brent Monahan  h  3956

**Means, Gordon** (Military Personnel)
*Cold Allies* - Patricia Anthony  s  157

**Meara, Ray** (Farmer)
*Butcher* - Rex Miller  h  3898

**Mears, Ben** (Writer)
*Salem's Lot* - Stephen King  h  3140

**Medakan, Taziar** (Thief)
*By Chaos Cursed* - Mickey Zucker Reichert  f  4517
*Shadow's Realm* - Mickey Zucker Reichert  f  4523

**Medallia** (Spy)
*A Wizard in Mind* - Christopher Stasheff  s  5232

**Medalont** (Alien; Doctor)
*Final Diagnosis* - James White  s  5777

**Medea** (Witch)
*Fiend* - C. Dean Andersson  h  138

**Medea, Helene** (Scientist)
*Light Raid* - Connie Willis  s  5870

**Medicine Plant** (Psychic; Indian)
*Dawn Land* - Joseph Bruchac  f  731

**Medlocke, Jason** (Detective—Homicide)
*Brethren* - Shawn Ryan  h  4754

**Medlocke, Stephen** (Parent; Religious)
*Brethren* - Shawn Ryan  h  4754

**Medoc** (Wizard; Ruler)
*The Lost Prince* - Bridget Wood  f  5962

**Medwin, Earl** (Heir; Wealthy)
*Jacob's Hands* - Aldous Huxley  f  2817

**Medwind Song** (Barbarian; Scholar)
*Bones of the Past* - Holly Lisle  f  3478

**Megan** (Sorceress)
*Merlin's Legacy: Dawn of Camelot* - Quinn Taylor
Evans  f  1857

**Megan** (Artist)
*Something Rich and Strange* - Patricia A.
McKillip  f  3840

**Meh'Lindi** (Spy)
*Inquisitor* - Ian Watson  s  5637

**Meiglan** (Royalty)
*The Dragon Token* - Melanie Rawn  f  4485
*Skybowl* - Melanie Rawn  f  4490

**Mek Kermak's-kin, Shkai'ra** (Warrior)
*Saber & Shadow* - S.M. Stirling  f  5297
*Snow Brother* - S.M. Stirling  f  5299

**Mel** (Truck Driver)
*Celia* - Ruby Jean Jensen  h  2900

**Melanchthon "7332"** (Mythical Creature)
*The Iron Dragon's Daughter* - Michael
Swanwick  f  5371

**Melania** (Noblewoman; Adventurer)
*The Eagle and the Sword* - A.A. Attanasio  f  267

**Melanie** (Student; Sports Figure)
*Gameplay* - Kevin J. Anderson  f  105

*Game's End* - Kevin J. Anderson  *f*  104

**Melchior** (Religious; Wizard)
*Count Scar* - C. Dale Brittain  *f*  702

**Meldron** (Royalty)
*The Silver Hand* - Stephen R. Lawhead  *f*  3358

**Melford, Trudy** (Businesswoman; Wealthy)
*Proteus in the Underworld* - Charles
Sheffield  *s*  4962

**Melina** (Prostitute)
*Total Recall* - Piers Anthony  *s*  193

**Melior, Laurel** (Heroine)
*Winter Rose* - Patricia A. McKillip  *f*  3843

**Melior, Rohannan** (Mythical Creature; Nobleman)
*The Cup of Morning Shadows* - Rosemary
Edghill  *f*  1747

**Melior, Rohannan** (Mythical Creature)
*The Sword of Maiden's Tears* - Rosemary
Edghill  *f*  1748

**Melior, Rois** (Heroine)
*Winter Rose* - Patricia A. McKillip  *f*  3843

**Melisande** (Dancer; Mutant)
*The Widowmaker* - Mike Resnick  *s*  4559

**Melliandra "Melli"** (Noblewoman; Fiance(e))
*The Baker's Boy* - J.V. Jones  *f*  2956

**Melliandra "Melli"** (Noblewoman)
*A Man Betrayed* - J.V. Jones  *f*  2958

**Melmoth, Lydia** (Artist; Fugitive)
*Virtual Death* - Shale Aaron  *s*  5

**Melmoth, Stamen** (Government Official; Fugitive)
*Virtual Death* - Shale Aaron  *s*  5

**Melnik, Claudi** (Child)
*Down the Stream of Stars* - Jeffrey A.
Carver  *s*  928

**Melody** (Alien)
*Finity's End* - C.J. Cherryh  *s*  988

**Melody** (Warrior)
*The Lion of Farside* - John Dalmas  *f*  1324

**Melrose, Frank** (Police Officer)
*Dead Voices* - Rick Hautala  *h*  2607

**Melvin** (Child; Time Traveler)
*Borgel* - Daniel Manus Pinkwater  *f*  4338

**Melvinge** (Hero; Werewolf)
*Night of the Living 'Gator!* - Richard A.
Lupoff  *s*  3573
*Night of the Living Rat!* - Debra Doyle  *s*  1603
*Night of the Living Shark!* - David Bischoff  *s*  493

**Memnoch** (Demon)
*Memnoch the Devil* - Anne Rice  *h*  4571

**Menaker, Mikhail "the Mick" Geoffrey** (Teenager)
*Count Geiger's Blues* - Michael Bishop  *s*  499

**Mendanbar** (Ruler)
*Searching for Dragons* - Patricia C. Wrede  *f*  5979

**Mende, Alice** (Computer Expert)
*Wyrm* - Mark Fabi  *s*  1858

**Mendel, Toby** (Anthropologist)
*The Undine* - Michael O'Rourke  *h*  4224

**Mendelssohn, Olivia** (Psychic; Security Officer)
*The Flies of Memory* - Ian Watson  *s*  5635

**Mendez, Marla** (Cyborg; Prisoner)
*Prison Planet* - William C. Dietz  *s*  1551

**Mendez, Sofia** (Computer Expert; Pilot)
*The Sparrow* - Mary Doria Russell  *s*  4736

**Mendoza** (Immortal; Scientist)
*In the Garden of Iden* - Kage Baker  *s*  298

**Mendoza, Carl** (Television Personality)
*Pictures at 11* - Norman Spinrad  *s*  5173

**Mendoza, Carlos "Iceman"** (Saloon Keeper/Owner; Spy)
*Oracle* - Mike Resnick  *s*  4551
*Prophet* - Mike Resnick  *s*  4553
*Soothsayer* - Mike Resnick  *s*  4557

**Meniskos, Jhana** (Scientist; Researcher)
*Lightpaths* - Howard V. Hendrix  *s*  2660

**Mennym, Appleby** (Teenager; Mythical Creature)
*The Mennyms* - Sylvia Waugh  *f*  5654
*Mennyms Under Siege* - Sylvia Waugh  *f*  5656

**Mennym, Pilbeam** (Mythical Creature)
*Mennyms Under Siege* - Sylvia Waugh  *f*  5656

**Mennym, Soobie** (Mythical Creature)
*Mennyms Alive* - Sylvia Waugh  *f*  5655

**Mennym, Tulip** (Grandparent; Mythical Creature)
*The Mennyms* - Sylvia Waugh  *f*  5654

**Mennym, Tulip** (Mythical Creature; Grandparent)
*Mennyms Alive* - Sylvia Waugh  *f*  5655

**Mennym, Vinetta** (Parent; Mythical Creature)
*The Mennyms* - Sylvia Waugh  *f*  5654

**Mentia, D.** (Demon)
*Geis of the Gargoyle* - Piers Anthony  *f*  172

**Mephistopheles** (Demon)
*If at Faust You Don't Succeed* - Roger
Zelazny  *f*  6070

**Mephistopheles** (Alien; Demon)
*Jack Faust* - Michael Swanwick  *s*  5372

**MEQMAT** (Computer)
*The Schizogenic Man* - Raymond Harris  *s*  2563

**Mer-Child** (Mythical Creature)
*The Mer-Child: A Legend for Children and Other
Adults* - Robin Morgan  *f*  4008

**Meral, Katerin "Kitri Terry"** (Professor)
*Fire Crossing* - Cheryl J. Franklin  *s*  2036

**Mercati, Adrian** (Ruler)
*City of Diamond* - Jane Emerson  *s*  1807

**Mercer, Jebidiah** (Religious)
*Dead in the West* - Joe R. Lansdale  *h*  3325

**Merchant, Liliane** (Religious; Spy)
*The Arm of the Stone* - Victoria Strauss  *f*  5333

**Mercury** (Deity)
*The M.D.: A Horror Story* - Thomas M.
Disch  *h*  1561

**Mercury, Ryan** (Spy)
*Beyond the Pale* - Jack Koke  *f*  3198

**Merelan** (Singer; Parent)
*The Masterharper of Pern* - Anne
McCaffrey  *s*  3739

**Meriamon** (Royalty; Religious)
*Lord of the Two Lands* - Judith Tarr  *f*  5395

**Merikur, Anson** (Military Personnel)
*Cluster Command* - David Drake  *s*  1630

**Meriones** (Musician)
*The Elementals* - Morgan Llywelyn  *f*  3503

**Meriweather, Buncan** (Teenager; Musician)
*Son of Spellsinger* - Alan Dean Foster  *f*  2015

**Meriweather, Gentian** (Scientist; Teenager)
*Juniper, Gentian and Rosemary* - Pamela
Dean  *f*  1445

**Meriweather, Jon-Tom** (Musician; Adventurer)
*Chorus Skating* - Alan Dean Foster  *f*  1998

**Merlin** (Sorcerer)
*Arthur* - Stephen R. Lawhead  *f*  3352

**Merlin** (Magician)
*The Camelot Chronicles* - Mike Ashley  *f*  224

**Merlin** (Wizard; Leader)
*The Eagle and the Sword* - A.A. Attanasio  *f*  267

**Merlin** (Religious; Wizard)
*Enemy of God* - Bernard Cornwell  *f*  1189
*Excalibur* - Bernard Cornwell  *f*  1190

**Merlin** (Wizard; Leader)
*The Faery Convention* - Brett Davis  *f*  1399

**Merlin** (Child; Orphan)
*Merlin* - Jane Yolen  *f*  6035

**Merlin** (Magician)
*Merlin and the Dragons* - Jane Yolen  *f*  6036
*The Merlin Chronicles* - Mike Ashley  *f*  227
*Merlin's Harp* - Anne Eliot Crompton  *f*  1270

**Merlin** (Wizard; Homosexual)
*Mordred's Curse* - Ian McDowell  *f*  3806

**Merlin** (Child)
*Passager* - Jane Yolen  *f*  6038

**Merlin** (Royalty)
*Prince of Chaos* - Roger Zelazny  *f*  6073

**Merlin, Anastasia "Ana"** (Singer)
*Tomorrow and Tomorrow* - Charles
Sheffield  *s*  4966

**Merlin, Emrys** (Adventurer)
*The Fires of Merlin* - T.A. Barron  *f*  369

**Merlin, Emrys** (Child; Psychic)
*The Seven Songs of Merlin* - T.A. Barron  *f*  372

**Merlin, Walter Drake** (Musician)
*Tomorrow and Tomorrow* - Charles
Sheffield  *s*  4966

**Merlino, Pepper** (Student)
*Seattle Ghost Story* - Nick DiMartino  *h*  1560

**Merrick** (Vampire Hunter)
*Buffy the Vampire Slayer* - Richie Tankersley
Cusick  *h*  1301

**Merrick, Geoffrey Robert** (Businessman;
Reanimated Dead)
*Fear Itself* - Ric Meyers  *h*  3881
*Living Hell* - Ric Meyers  *h*  3882
*Worst Nightmare* - Ric Meyers  *h*  3883

**Merrick, Melanie** (Housewife)
*Fear Itself* - Ric Meyers  *h*  3881
*Living Hell* - Ric Meyers  *h*  3882

**Merrick, Ty** (Detective—Police)
*Manjinn Moon* - Denise Vitola  *s*  5576

**Merrick, Ty** (Detective—Police; Werewolf)
*Opalite Moon* - Denise Vitola  *f*  5577

**Merrick the Blackbird** (Pirate)
*Sister Blood* - Karen Haber  *s*  2476

**Merrill, Richard "Mairelon"** (Magician)
*Magician's Ward* - Patricia C. Wrede  *f*  5976

**Merrit, Robin** (Scientist)
*Operation Synbat* - Bob Mayer  *h*  3701

**Mertz, Harry** (Immortal; Judge)
*A Covenant of Justice* - David Gerrold  *s*  2207

**Merwoman, Mela** (Mythical Creature; Widow(er))
*The Color of Her Panties* - Piers Anthony  *f*  167

**Mespil, Lunzie** (Doctor)
*The Death of Sleep* - Anne McCaffrey  *s*  3727
*Generation Warrior* - Anne McCaffrey  *s*  3735

**Messenger, Joe** (Scientist; Computer Expert)
*Host* - Peter James  *h*  2872

**Messenger, Karen** (Researcher; Spouse)
*Host* - Peter James  *h*  2872

**Metadi, Beka Rosselin** (Spaceship Captain; Heiress)
*The Price of the Stars* - Debra Doyle  *s*  1604

**Metadi, Jos** (Spaceship Captain; Privateer)
*The Gathering Flame* - Debra Doyle  *s*  1599

**Metaxos, Diego** (Spaceman; Teenager)
*Powers That Be* - Anne McCaffrey  *s*  3745

**Metcalf, Charlotte** (Child; Orphan)
*Whispers in the Dark* - Jonathan Aycliffe   h   283

**Metcalf, Conrad** (Detective—Private)
*Gun, with Occasional Music* - Jonathan
Lethem   f   3441

**Metcalf, Elizabeth** (Settler)
*Nadya: The Wolf Chronicles* - Pat Murphy   f   4052

**Metcalf, Lily** (Psychologist)
*Resume with Monsters* - William Browning
Spencer   h   5168

**Metcalf, Oliver** (Editor)
*The Blackstone Chronicles* - John Saul   h   4838

**Methryn, Valthyrra** (Artificial Intelligence)
*Dreadnought* - Thorarinn Gunnarsson   s   2464
*Tactical Error* - Thorarinn Gunnarsson   s   2466

**Metis, Jean** (Agent)
*Crygender* - Thomas T. Thomas   s   5451

**Metria "Woe Betide"** (Demon)
*Roc and a Hard Place* - Piers Anthony   f   187

**Metullus, Amaelia** (Computer Game Player)
*The Imperium Game* - K.D. Wentworth   s   5753

**Metzgar, Joachim** (Leader; Psychic)
*Mutant Legacy* - Karen Haber   s   2474

**Mew** (Animal; Adventurer)
*Roverandom* - J.R.R. Tolkien   f   5479

**Meyer, Elizabeth "Payne"** (Divorced Person)
*Dead Voices* - Rick Hautala   h   2607

**Meyers, Max** (Military Personnel)
*The Final Battle* - William C. Dietz   s   1546

**Mharyon** (Mythical Creature)
*Dragon Moon* - Chris Claremont   f   1040

**Miaowara Shiro** (Animal; Adventurer)
*Samurai Cat Goes to the Movies* - Mark E.
Rogers   s   4656
*The Sword of Samurai Cat* - Mark E.
Rogers   s   4657

**Miaowara Tomokato** (Animal; Warrior)
*Samurai Cat Goes to the Movies* - Mark E.
Rogers   s   4656
*The Sword of Samurai Cat* - Mark E.
Rogers   s   4657

**Miathan** (Magician)
*Aurian* - Maggie Furey   f   2095
*Dhiammara* - Maggie Furey   f   2096
*Harp of Winds* - Maggie Furey   f   2097

**Michael** (Servant)
*Dark Dance* - Tanith Lee   h   3406

**Michael** (Child)
*Gypsies* - Robert Charles Wilson   s   5908

**Michael** (Diplomat; Apprentice)
*Lion Time in Timbuctoo* - Robert Silverberg   s   5036

**Michael** (Religious; Alcoholic)
*The Eyes of Torie Webster* - Roy Sorrels   h   5164

**Michaels, Dean** (Convict)
*Swamp* - Peter Tremayne   h   5483

**Michaels, Judge** (Young Man; Relative)
*The M.D.: A Horror Story* - Thomas M.
Disch   h   1561

**Michaels, Kevin** (Professor)
*October* - Al Sarrantonio   h   4832

**Michaels, Steve** (Ranger)
*Carmilla: The Return* - Kyle Marfinn   h   3623

**Michaels, William "Billy"** (Doctor; Parent)
*The M.D.: A Horror Story* - Thomas M.
Disch   h   1561

**Michaelson, Hal** (Computer Expert; Leader)
*Virtual Destruction* - Kevin J. Anderson   s   118

**Michaelson, Hari** (Entertainer)
*Heroes Die* - Matthew Woodring Stover   s   5319

**Michaelson, Kiley** (Businesswoman; Pilot)
*Mind Light* - Margaret Davis   s   1407

**Michelson, Terry** (Vampire)
*Vampire Blood* - Kathryn Meyer Griffith   h   2441

**Mick** (Office Worker)
*Steam* - Jay B. Laws   h   3361

**Midas** (Royalty)
*The Adventures of King Midas* - Lynne Reid
Banks   f   329

**Mika** (Doctor)
*Tower of Doom* - Mark Anthony   h   155

**Mikal** (Sorcerer)
*Broken Blade* - Ann Marston   f   3634

**Mikayla** (Royalty; Student)
*Lady of the Trillium* - Marion Zimmer
Bradley   f   641

**Mike** (Businessman)
*Dark Legacy* - Mark A. Kostrubula   h   3220

**Mike** (Artificial Intelligence; Imposter)
*The Moon Is a Harsh Mistress* - Robert A.
Heinlein   s   2645

**Mike** (Doctor)
*Wolf Flow* - K.W. Jeter   h   2918

**Mikel** (Deity)
*The Wizard at Home* - Rick Shelley   f   4975

**Mikel, Chris** (Child)
*Blind Hunger* - David Darke   h   1352

**Mikhail** (Hunter; Leader)
*Initiation* - Marian Hughes   s   2806

**Mikhailovych, Lixand** (Storyteller; Artisan)
*Shadow's Daughter* - Shirley Meier   f   3871

**Mikhalevviko "Mikh"** (Wizard; Criminal)
*Mathemagics* - Margaret Ball   f   316

**Mikk** (Actor; Alien)
*The Merro Tree* - Katie Waitman   s   5609

**Mikolajczak, Adam** (Lawyer)
*Seaward* - Brad Leithauser   h   3433

**Milam, Hank** (Religious)
*Rockabilly Limbo* - William W. Johnstone   h   2934

**Milana, Chaka** (Hunter; Scholar)
*Eternity Road* - Jack McDevitt   s   3788

**Milano, Gretta** (Professor)
*Fallen* - Dee Graham   h   2302

**Milburn, Annie** (Teacher)
*Charmed Life* - Bernard Taylor   h   5399

**Milena** (Actress)
*The Child Garden* - Geoff Ryman   s   4756

**Milena "Alfred Russell Wallace"** (Computer Expert;
Teenager)
*Fairyland* - Paul J. McAuley   s   3711

**Miles, Dora** (Widow(er))
*The Baby* - Stephanie Kegan   h   3033

**Miles, Janna** (Teenager)
*Speak to the Rain* - Helen K. Passey   h   4257

**Miles, Karen** (Child)
*Speak to the Rain* - Helen K. Passey   h   4257

**Milk, Billy** (Religious)
*Only Begotten Daughter* - James Morrow   f   4034

**Millarca** (Vampire)
*Carmilla: The Return* - Kyle Marfinn   h   3623

**Milleflores, Delanna** (Heiress; Spouse)
*Promised Land* - Connie Willis   s   5872

**Miller, Alvin "Maker"** (Blacksmith; Psychic;
Relative)
*Alvin Journeyman* - Orson Scott Card   f   881

**Miller, Alvin "Maker"** (Blacksmith; Psychic;
Spouse)
*Heartfire* - Orson Scott Card   f   889

**Miller, Alvin "Maker"** (Apprentice; Psychic)
*Prentice Alvin* - Orson Scott Card   f   896

**Miller, Calvin** (Psychic; Relative)
*Alvin Journeyman* - Orson Scott Card   f   881
*Heartfire* - Orson Scott Card   f   889

**Miller, Desmond** (Doctor)
*Supernova* - Roger MacBride Allen   s   82

**Miller, Doc** (Oil Industry Worker)
*Petrogypsies* - Rory Harper   s   2549

**Miller, Jack** (Traveler)
*The Ultimate Bike Path* - Michael B. Sirota   s   5076

**Miller, Margaret "Peggy"** (Psychic; Activist;
Spouse)
*Heartfire* - Orson Scott Card   f   889

**Miller, Martin** (Businessman)
*The Darker Passions: Carmilla* - Amarantha
Knight   h   3177

**Miller, Paul** (Detective—Amateur)
*In the Deep Woods* - Nicholas Conde   h   1131

**Miller, Quintus** (Genius; Occultist)
*Walkers* - Graham Masterton   h   3681

**Miller, Tony** (Archaeologist)
*Time Blender* - Michael Dorn   s   1581

**Miller, Zeke** (Musician)
*Night Music* - Sheila Bristow Garner   h   2147

**Millicent "Millie"** (Girlfriend)
*Jumper* - Steven Gould   s   2290

**Milo** (Genetically Altered Being; Immortal)
*The Sky Lords* - John Brosnan   s   720

**Miloslavic, Dragos** (Doctor)
*St. Vitus Dances Eternity: A Sarajevo Ghost Story* -
Stewart Von Allmen   h   5585

**Milton, Annie** (Young Woman)
*Cul-De-Sac* - David Martin   h   3638

**Milton, John** (Lawyer)
*The Devil's Advocate* - Andrew Neiderman   h   4085

**Milton, John** (Writer; Leader)
*Milton in America* - Peter Ackroyd   f   25

**Minakis, Manolis** (Scientist; Businessman)
*Secret Passages* - Paul Preuss   s   4420

**Minarik** (Military Personnel; Leader)
*Shadowdance* - Robin Wayne Bailey   f   290

**Minder XXIII, John** (Ruler)
*Stepwater* - L. Warren Douglas   s   1588
*The Wells of Phyre* - L. Warren Douglas   s   1589

**Miner, Bron "Selwyn Forester"** (Religious; Avenger)
*The Arm of the Stone* - Victoria Strauss   f   5333

**Minerva** (Mythical Creature; Deity)
*Ye Gods!* - Tom Holt   f   2753

**Minnie "Miin"** (Psychic; Child)
*Shame of Man* - Piers Anthony   s   188

**Minster, Joanne** (Police Officer)
*The World of Darkness: Watcher* - Charles L.
Grant   h   2321

**Minstrel Boy** (Warrior)
*The Last Stand of the DNA Cowboys* - Mick
Farren   s   1879

**Mint** (Military Personnel)
*Exodus From the Long Sun* - Gene Wolfe   s   5941

**Mint, Maytera** (Religious; Teacher)
*Calde of the Long Sun* - Gene Wolfe   s   5937

**Mira** (Sorceress)
*Dragons on the Town* - Thorarinn Gunnarsson   2463

**Mirabar** (Religious)
*In Legend Born* - Laura Resnick   f   4533

**Mirabara, Keishi** (Researcher; Technician)
*The Fortunate Fall* - Raphael Carter   s   927

**Miraflores, Pedro** (Spy; Revolutionary)
*Ai! Pedrito!: When Intelligence Goes Wrong* - L. Ron Hubbard   s   2788

**Mirakles** (Hero)
*The Zork Chronicles* - George Alec Effinger   s   1754

**Miranda** (Parent)
*Caliban's Hour* - Tad Williams   f   5826

**Miranda** (Adventurer; Companion)
*Charmed* - Marilyn Singer   f   5070

**Miranda, Carmen** (Spirit; Entertainer)
*Carmen Miranda's Ghost Is Haunting Space Station Three* - Don Sakers   s   4785

**Mirelle, Victoria "Tori"** (Clone)
*The Inquisitor* - Cheryl J. Franklin   s   2037

**Miri** (Mercenary)
*Carpe Diem* - Steve Miller   s   3907

**Miriam** (Indian; Abuse Victim)
*The Spirit Stalker* - Nina Romberg   h   4664

**Miriamele** (Royalty)
*To Green Angel Tower* - Tad Williams   f   5832

**Mirlu, Bonnie Jean "B.J."** (Saloon Keeper/Owner; Vampire)
*Necroscope: The Lost Years* - Brian Lumley   h   3560
*Resurgence* - Brian Lumley   h   3564

**Miro, Roy** (Government Official)
*Dark Rivers of the Heart* - Dean R. Koontz   h   3204

**Mirri** (Young Woman; Adventurer)
*The Iron Ring* - Lloyd Alexander   f   68

**Mirskaya, Daria Nicolaeuna** (Scientist)
*Scorpio Descending* - Alex McDonough   s   3803

**Mishima, Ken** (Martial Arts Expert)
*The Unwound Way* - William Adams   s   35

**Mishwe, Dajaj** (Murderer; Scientist)
*ViraVax* - Bill Ransom   s   4478

**Miss Bird** (Servant; Indian)
*The Gilda Stories* - Jewelle Gomez   h   2267

**Mission** (Pirate; Leader)
*Ghost of Chance* - William S. Burroughs   s   780

**Mist** (Hunter; Mythical Creature)
*Shadow Dance* - Anne Logston   f   3513

**Mistislaus** (Wizard)
*The Clan of the Warlord* - Elizabeth H. Boyer   f   604

**Misurov, Sasha** (Wizard; Apprentice)
*Chernevog* - C.J. Cherryh   f   982
*Rusalka* - C.J. Cherryh   f   1002

**Mitchell, Gordon** (Anthropologist)
*Ancestor's World* - A.C. Crispin   s   1259

**Mitchell, Jackie** (Animal Lover)
*Dangerous Nature* - T.J. Kirby   h   3152

**Mitchell, Kelly** (Journalist)
*Domination* - Michael Cecilione   h   946

**Mitchell, Manny** (Administrator)
*Taylor's Ark* - Jody Lynn Nye   s   4176

**Mitchell, Paige** (Public Relations)
*Lethal Exposure* - Kevin J. Anderson   s   110

**Mitexi, Meredalia** (Computer Expert)
*Dreamships* - Melissa Scott   s   4896

**Mitford, Chuck** (Military Personnel; Settler)
*Freedom's Challenge* - Anne McCaffrey   s   3732

**Mitford, Chuck** (Military Personnel)
*Freedom's Choice* - Anne McCaffrey   s   3733

**Mitford, Chuck** (Military Personnel; Settler)
*Freedom's Landing* - Anne McCaffrey   s   3734

**Mithra** (Angel)
*Ancient Games* - Scott Ciencin   f   1028

**Mithra** (Leader)
*The Falcon Rises* - Michael C. Staudinger   f   5235

**Mitrian** (Warrior)
*The Last of the Renshai* - Mickey Zucker Reichert   f   4520

**Mitroff, Seryi** (Revolutionary)
*The Frightened Fish* - Kenneth Robeson   f   4622

**Mitsouko, Emma** (Artist)
*Throat Sprockets* - Tim Lucas   h   3541

**Mitsuko, Fujiwara "Little Puddle" no** (Teenager; Heroine)
*Little Sister* - Kara Dalkey   f   1320

**Mitsumishi, Ecclesiastes** (Undertaker)
*The Abraxas Marvel Circus* - Stephen Leigh   f   3423

**Miya** (Alien; Psychic)
*Dreamfall* - Joan D. Vinge   s   5571

**Mizzamir** (Magician; Criminal)
*Villains by Necessity* - Eve Forward   f   1985

**Mnrogar** (Mythical Creature)
*The Dragon, the Earl, and the Troll* - Gordon R. Dickson   f   1534

**Mobarak, Cyrus "Torquemada"** (Inventor; Businessman)
*Cold as Ice* - Charles Sheffield   s   4950

**Mocata** (Sorcerer)
*The Devil Rides Out* - Dennis Wheatley   h   5773

**Moden, Sten** (Military Personnel)
*The Sharp End* - David Drake   s   1643

**Moffett, Pierce** (Researcher)
*Love & Sleep* - John Crowley   f   1277

**Mogget** (Spirit; Animal)
*Sabriel* - Garth Nix   f   4129

**Mogurn, Deuteronomous** (Spaceship Captain; Smuggler)
*Dragons in the Stars* - Jeffrey A. Carver   s   930

**Mohamonero** (Doctor)
*Eggheads* - Emily Devenport   s   1500

**Mohatsa, Phila** (Military Personnel)
*Beyond the Void* - Sean Dalton   s   1331

**Mohini** (Deity)
*The Willing Spirit* - Piers Anthony   f   195

**Moira** (Witch)
*The Wiz Biz* - Rick Cook   f   1160
*The Wizardry Cursed* - Rick Cook   f   1162

**Moira** (Witch; Spouse)
*The Wizardry Quested* - Rick Cook   f   1163

**Moki** (Alien)
*The Color of Distance* - Amy Thomson   s   5461

**Mokoena, Mamphela** (Scientist)
*Starfarers* - Poul Anderson   s   133

**Mole** (Animal; Adventurer)
*Toad Triumphant* - William Horwood   f   2774
*The Willows and Beyond* - William Horwood   f   2775
*The Willows in Winter* - William Horwood   f   2776

**Moliak** (Cyborg; Wanderer)
*Down the Bright Way* - Robert Reed   s   4505

**Mollari, Londo** (Diplomat; Alien)
*Day of the Dead* - Neil Gaiman   s   2102

**Mollari, Londo** (Alien; Political Figure)
*Personal Agendas* - Al Sarrantonio   s   4833

**Mollockle, Thud** (Mythical Creature; Adventurer)
*Hearts and Armor* - Ron Miller   f   3903
*Palaces and Prisons* - Ron Miller   f   3904
*Silk and Steel* - Ron Miller   f   3905

**Molly** (Child)
*Blue Moon* - Hila Feil   f   1898

**Molly** (Spirit; Activist)
*Tex and Molly in the Afterlife* - Richard Grant   f   2327

**Molok** (Mythical Creature)
*Kaz the Minotaur* - Richard A. Knaak   f   3172

**Mom** (Artificial Intelligence)
*Exit to Reality* - Edith Forbes   s   1968

**Mon, Ismail** (Ruler)
*The Pleistocene Redemption* - Dan Gallagher   s   2107

**Mona** (Avenger; Sidekick)
*Enemy of My Enemy* - Ben Ohlander   s   4204

**Monahan, Tim** (Writer)
*The Halflife* - Sharon Webb   s   5664

**Moncrief, Marcel** (Magician; Criminal)
*Ports of Call* - Jack Vance   s   5549

**Mondesir, Carmen** (Businessman)
*Vodoun* - David Madsen   h   3605

**Mondragon, Carlos** (Stowaway; Immigrant)
*The Black Sun* - Jack Williamson   s   5860

**Mondragon, Tom** (Revolutionary; Refugee)
*Endgame* - C.J. Cherryh   s   986

**Monet, Claude** (Spirit; Artist)
*Monet's Ghost* - Chelsea Quinn Yarbro   f   6017

**Monigan** (Deity)
*The Time of the Ghost* - Diana Wynne Jones   f   2951

**Monique** (Robot)
*Freeware* - Rudy Rucker   s   4703

**Monkey** (Wizard; Mythical Creature)
*Dragon Cauldron* - Laurence Yep   f   6024
*Dragon War* - Laurence Yep   f   6025

**Monkey, King** (Prehistoric Human)
*The Kronos Condition* - Emily Devenport   s   1502

**Monlux, Cassandra** (Scientist; Agent)
*Slow Freight* - F.M. Busby   s   785

**Monmart, Kevisson** (Psychic; Healer)
*House of Moons* - K.D. Wentworth   s   5752
*Moonspeaker* - K.D. Wentworth   s   5754

**Monroe, Sumter** (Child)
*Never Land* - Douglas Clegg   h   1081

**Monroe, Wade** (Paranormal Investigator)
*The Possession* - Ronald Kelly   h   3055

**Monsanto, Francesca** (Archaeologist)
*Prophecy* - Peter James   h   2874

**Montagu, Edmund** (Military Personnel)
*The Mummy!: A Tale of the Twenty-Second Century* - Jane Webb Loudon   h   3526

**Montagu, Edric** (Student)
*The Mummy!: A Tale of the Twenty-Second Century* - Jane Webb Loudon   h   3526

**Montague, Derek** (Adventurer)
*Something's Alive on the Titanic* - Robert Serling   h   4915

**Montana, Kent** (Actor; Laird)
*668: The Neighbor of the Beast* - Lionel Fenn   h   1917
*Kent Montana and the Really Ugly Thing From Mars* - Lionel Fenn   s   1918

*Kent Montana and the Reasonably Invisible Man* - Lionel Fenn  *s*  1919

*The Mark of the Moderately Vicious Vampire* - Lionel Fenn  *h*  1920

**Montes, Samta** (Indian; Archaeologist)
*A Whisper of Time* - Paula E. Downing  *s*  1595

**Montgomery, Derek** (Detective)
*2XS* - Nigel Findley  *f*  1935

**Montgomery, Dirk** (Cyborg; Detective—Private)
*House of the Sun* - Nigel Findley  *s*  1936

**Montoneros, Juan Ramirez** (Orphan; Religious)
*Catacomb* - Andrew Laurance  *h*  3347

**Montoya, Alyssa** (Activist)
*The Planet Beyond* - Steve Mudd  *s*  4043

**Montoya, Nita** (Psychic)
*The Drylands* - Mary Rosenblum  *s*  4678

**Montrovant** (Vampire)
*To Dream of Dreamers Lost* - David Niall Wilson  *h*  5882
*To Speak in Lifeless Tongues* - David Niall Wilson  *h*  5883

**Moody, Vernon** (Detective—Police)
*Cyber Way* - Alan Dean Foster  *s*  2000

**Moon, Donovan** (Journalist)
*Morningstar* - Peter Atkins  *h*  265

**Moon, Everett "Chaos"** (Amnesiac)
*Amnesia Moon* - Jonathan Lethem  *f*  3438

**Moon, Frank** (Detective—Police)
*Sick* - Jay R. Bonansinga  *h*  571

**Moon, Jeremy** (Magician; Advertising)
*Wizard's Mole* - Brad Strickland  *f*  5337

**Moon, Miranda** (Religious; Parent)
*The Trinity Vector* - Steve Perry  *s*  4302

**Moon, Paul** (Military Personnel)
*Shadows of War* - Thomas S. Gressman  *s*  2432

**Moonblade, Arilyn** (Warrior; Spy)
*Elfshadow* - Elaine Cunningham  *f*  1288
*Silver Shadows* - Elaine Cunningham  *f*  1292

**Moonbrow, Aljan "Jan"** (Mythical Creature; Leader)
*The Son of Summer Stars* - Meredith Ann Pierce  *f*  4319

**Moondark, Gan** (Leader; Warrior)
*Warrior* - Donald E. McQuinn  *s*  3863
*Witch* - Donald E. McQuinn  *s*  3864

**Mooner** (Mythical Creature)
*Elsewhere* - Will Shetterly  *f*  4993

**Mooney, Shawana** (Single Parent; Traveler)
*The Arbitrary Placement of Walls* - Martha Soukup  *f*  5165

**Moonfeather** (Wizard)
*Shadowboxer* - Nick Pollotta  *s*  4366

**Moonlight, Charlie** (Drifter; Indian)
*Thunder Rise* - G. Wayne Miller  *h*  3895

**MoonQueen** (Ruler)
*The Queen of Darkness* - Miguel Conner  *s*  1134

**Moorcock, Margaret Rose** (Revolutionary; Adventurer)
*The War Amongst the Angels* - Michael Moorcock  *f*  3986

**Moore, Julie** (Psychologist; Student)
*The Cold One* - Christopher Pike  *h*  4327

**Moore, Malcolm** (Time Traveler; Guide)
*Time Scout* - Robert Asprin  *s*  263

**Moore, Melinda** (Musician)
*Gossamer Axe* - Gael Baudino  *f*  392

**Moore, Rebecca** (Housewife)
*Cemetery of Angels* - Noel Hynd  *h*  2821

**Moore, Teldin** (Adventurer; Warrior)
*Beyond the Moons* - David Cook  *f*  1144

**Moore, Teldin** (Warrior; Adventurer)
*Into the Void* - Nigel Findley  *f*  1937

**Moore, Teldin** (Adventurer; Warrior)
*The Radiant Dragon* - Elaine Cunningham  *f*  1291

**Moore, Teldin** (Adventurer; Spaceship Captain)
*The Ultimate Helm* - Russ T. Howard  *f*  2785

**Moql'nkkn "Moql/Saaski"** (Mythical Creature)
*The Moorchild* - Eloise Jarvis McGraw  *f*  3816

**Mora, Chad** (Scientist)
*Predator* - William F. Wu  *s*  5998

**Morai** (Criminal)
*Talion: Revenant* - Michael A. Stackpole  *f*  5206

**Morales, Daire** (Pilot; Spaceman)
*Lethe* - Tricia Sullivan  *s*  5354

**Morales, Mira** (Psychic)
*The Hanged Man* - T.J. MacGregor  *h*  3594

**Moran, California** (Immortal)
*Gryphon* - Crawford Kilian  *s*  3106

**Moran, John J.** (Doctor)
*The Lighthouse at the End of the World* - Stephen Marlowe  *h*  3631

**Morane, Reynard** (Martial Arts Expert; Criminal)
*The Death of the Necromancer* - Martha Wells  *f*  5749

**Moravec, Alan** (Journalist)
*This Symbiotic Fascination* - Charlee Jacob  *h*  2843

**Morbius** (Criminal; Ruler)
*Strange Tales From the Nile Empire* - Greg Farshtey  *f*  1889

**Morcey, Paul** (Assistant)
*The Only Thing to Fear* - Robert Morgan  *h*  4003

**Morcey, Paul** (Detective)
*Some Things Come Back* - Robert Morgan  *h*  4004

**Morcey, Paul** (Maintenance Worker)
*The Things That Are Not There* - Robert Morgan  *h*  4007

**Mordance of Barquist** (Widow(er); Friend)
*The Queen of Ashes* - Deborah Turner Harris  *f*  2561

**Morden** (Linguist)
*The Shadow Within* - Jeanne Cavelos  *s*  944

**Mordenheim, Victor** (Doctor)
*Mordenheim* - Chet Williamson  *h*  5847

**Mordeth** (Magician; Ruler)
*The Falcon Rises* - Michael C. Staudinger  *f*  5235

**Mordock, Kyle** (Teenager)
*Midnight's Lair* - Richard Laymon  *h*  3369

**Mordred** (Royalty; Bastard Son)
*Mordred's Curse* - Ian McDowell  *f*  3806

**Moreau, Alessandra "Ale"** (Time Traveler; Student)
*Day of the Snake* - Matthew J. Costello  *s*  1196
*Hour of the Scorpion* - Matthew J. Costello  *s*  1199

**Moreau, Paul** (Werewolf)
*Hair of the Dog* - Brett Davis  *f*  1400

**Moreaux, Paul** (Writer)
*Fade* - Robert Cormier  *h*  1188

**Morelli, Berry** (Journalist)
*Candle Night* - Phil Rickman  *h*  4586

**Moreno, Alexandra "Alix"** (Companion; Traveler)
*When Heaven Fell* - William Barton  *s*  383

**Moreson, Joe** (Businessman)
*65mm* - Dale Hoover  *h*  2761

**Morgan** (Lesbian)
*Clicking Stones* - Nancy Tyler Glenn  *s*  2242

**Morgan, Jason** (Spaceship Captain)
*A Thousand Words for Stranger* - Julie E. Czerneda  *s*  1304

**Morgan, Liam** (Professor)
*Superstitious* - R.L. Stine  *h*  5290

**Morgan, Meredith** (Psychologist)
*Dark Dreaming* - Pat Franklin  *h*  2040

**Morgan, Richard** (Businessman; Spouse)
*Dark Dreaming* - Pat Franklin  *h*  2040

**Morgan, Rod** (Spaceship Captain)
*Saturn Rukh* - Robert L. Forward  *s*  1991

**Morgan, Sara** (Student)
*Superstitious* - R.L. Stine  *h*  5290

**Morgan le Fay** (Sorceress)
*Merlin's Bones* - Fred Saberhagen  *f*  4771

**Morgan le Fay** (Royalty; Sorceress)
*The Prince and the Pilgrim* - Mary Stewart  *f*  5270

**Morgan le Fey** (Royalty)
*Witch of the North* - Courtway Jones  *f*  2940

**Morgannan, Warrick** (Wizard; Leader)
*The Ambivalent Magician* - Simon Hawke  *f*  2616
*The Inadequate Adept* - Simon Hawke  *f*  2617

**Morganstern, Jack** (Spy)
*Dead Girls* - Richard Calder  *s*  837

**Morgasdotte, Roba** (Teacher; Adventurer)
*Bones of the Past* - Holly Lisle  *f*  3478

**Morgen** (Alien; Spaceman)
*Mad Roy's Light* - Paula King  *s*  3125

**Morgen** (Royalty; Spaceship Captain)
*Reunion* - Michael Jan Friedman  *s*  2068

**Morgeu** (Royalty; Demon)
*The Dragon and the Unicorn* - A.A. Attanasio  *f*  266

**Morgian** (Royalty; Sorceress)
*Grail* - Stephen R. Lawhead  *f*  3355

**Morgiana** (Immortal; Noblewoman)
*The Dagger and the Cross: A Novel of the Crusades* - Judith Tarr  *f*  5393

**Morgis, Duke** (Warrior; Mythical Creature)
*Wolfhelm* - Richard A. Knaak  *f*  3175

**Morianna, Maigrey** (Noblewoman; Pilot)
*King's Sacrifice* - Margaret Weis  *s*  5717
*The Lost King* - Margaret Weis  *s*  5720

**Moriarity, Pepper** (Store Owner)
*The House That Jack Built* - Graham Masterton  *h*  3675

**Morkaarin, Bren** (Heir—Lost; Military Personnel)
*The Rose Sea* - S.M. Stirling  *f*  5296

**Morley, Lynn** (Child; Student)
*The Witch Returns* - Phyllis Reynolds Naylor  *f*  4079
*The Witch's Eye* - Phyllis Reynolds Naylor  *f*  4080

**Morley, Simon "Si"** (Time Traveler)
*From Time to Time* - Jack Finney  *s*  1941

**Morlock, Endora** (Gentlewoman)
*Madman Run* - David Robbins  *s*  4600

**Mornan** (Wizard)
*The Sleep of Stone* - Louise Cooper  *f*  1179

**Mornay, Peter** (Religious; Government Official)
*Glory's War* - Alfred Coppel  *s*  1184

**Mornette, Will** (Teenager)
*Rebel From Alphorion* - Robyn Tallis  *s*  5381

**Morning, Debbie Sue** (Teenager)
*Serial Killer Days* - David Prill  *h*  4436

**Morningstar, Thomas** (Detective—Police)
*From a Whisper to a Scream* - Samuel M. Key  *h*  3093

**Morpheus** (Mythical Creature)
*The Sandman: Book of Dreams* - Neil Gaiman　f　2105

**Morran, Goldie** (Businesswoman)
*Wagers of Sin* - Robert Asprin　s　264

**Morrell, Charlie** (Lawyer; Detective—Private)
*Dead of Night* - Alex Abella　h　20

**Morrell, Charlie** (Lawyer)
*The Killing of the Saints* - Alex Abella　h　21

**Morris** (Teenager)
*Under Siege* - Elisabeth Mace　f　3587

**Morris, Anne** (Writer)
*Winter Tides* - James P. Blaylock　h　524

**Morris, Claudia** (Sociologist)
*Children of the Thunder* - John Brunner　s　733

**Morris, Dwight** (Businessman)
*Penance* - Rick R. Reed　h　4501

**Morris, Rob** (Detective)
*Sibs* - F. Paul Wilson　h　5898

**Morris, Zenoa** (Young Woman)
*The Living Evil* - Ruby Jean Jensen　h　2902

**Morris "Mauricio di Mauro"** (Animal; Spy)
*The Night of Wishes: Or, The Satanarchaeolidealcohellish Notion Potion* - Michael Ende　f　1821

**Morrisey, Hilda Jeanne** (Government Official; Administrator)
*The Siege of Eternity* - Frederik Pohl　s　4353

**Morrison, Alex** (Detective—Police)
*What's Wrong with Tamara?* - D.A. Fowler　h　2025

**Morrison, Athol** (Mercenary)
*When Heaven Fell* - William Barton　s　383

**Morrison, Faye** (Journalist)
*Curfew* - Phil Rickman　h　4587

**Morrison, Gertie** (Psychic)
*Threshold* - Bill Myers　s　4060

**Morrison, Jessie Mae** (Child)
*The Hunted* - Kathryn Ptacek　h　4442

**Morrison, Rebecca** (Librarian)
*The Blackstone Chronicles* - John Saul　h　4838

**Morrison, Ryan** (Scientist)
*Journey to Terezor* - Frank Asch　s　221

**Morrison, Troy** (Teenager; Spaceman)
*Dream-Weaver* - Louise Lawrence　s　3359

**Morrolan** (Mythical Creature)
*Dragon* - Steven Brust　f　741

**Morrough** (Knight)
*StarSpawn* - Kenneth Von Gunden　s　5588

**Morrow, Cathy** (Businesswoman)
*The Link* - Andrew Laurance　h　3348

**Morrow, Julian** (Professor)
*The Secret History* - Donna Tartt　h　5398

**Morrow, Rachel** (Artist; Farmer)
*A Gift upon the Shore* - M.K. Wren　s　5982

**Mort** (Apprentice)
*Mort* - Terry Pratchett　f　4397

**Mortega, Dyani** (Military Personnel; Indian)
*Blood Siege* - G. Harry Stine　s　5278

**Morton, John** (Researcher)
*Night Glow* - Martin James　h　2867

**Morwen** (Witch)
*Calling on Dragons* - Patricia C. Wrede　f　5974

**Morwyne the Powershaper** (Mythical Creature)
*Darkthunder's Way* - Tom Deitz　f　1470

**Mosala, Violet** (Scientist)
*Distress* - Greg Egan　s　1760

**Mosay** (Director; Immortal)
*Outnumbering the Dead* - Frederik Pohl　s　4352

**Mosby, Marianne** (Military Personnel)
*Legion of the Damned* - William C. Dietz　s　1547

**Mosca, Piero** (Student)
*Flare* - Roger Zelazny　s　6065

**Mosely** (Detective—Police)
*Gabriel Knight: Sins of the Fathers* - Jane Jensen　h　2896

**Moses** (Robot)
*Greenthieves* - Alan Dean Foster　s　2005

**Moses, Libby** (Doctor; Military Personnel)
*Echoes of Issel* - Diann Thornley　s　5466

**Mosiah** (Wizard)
*Legacy of the Darksword* - Margaret Weis　f　5719

**Mosquito** (Thief)
*Cytheria* - Richard Calder　s　835

**Moss, Griffin** (Artist)
*The Golden Mean* - Nick Bantock　f　334
*Sabine's Notebook* - Nick Bantock　f　335

**Mother** (Parent)
*Don't Forget Your Spacesuit, Dear* - Jody Lynn Nye　s　4169

**Mother Night** (Mythical Creature; Guardian)
*Godmother Night* - Rachel Pollack　f　4358

**Motzin, Rebeka** (Prisoner)
*Days of Cain* - J.R. Dunn　s　1694

**Mouche** (Student; Teenager)
*Six Moon Dance* - Sheri S. Tepper　s　5437

**Mouse** (Thief; Companion)
*Soothsayer* - Mike Resnick　s　4557

**Mozart, Wolfgang Amadeus** (Composer; Historical Figure)
*I, Vampire* - Michael Romkey　h　4665

**Mreen** (Psychic; Child)
*Receive the Gift* - Louise Marley　s　3628

**Mthembu, Lucas "Venator"** (Artificial Intelligence; Robot)
*Harvest the Fire* - Poul Anderson　s　128

**Muadhen, Seamus** (Military Personnel)
*Nature's God* - Robert Anton Wilson　f　5903

**Mudge** (Animal)
*Chorus Skating* - Alan Dean Foster　f　1998

**Muhammed, Sarkar** (Computer Expert)
*The Terminal Experiment* - Robert J. Sawyer　s　4860

**Muir, Oona** (Psychic)
*Fog Heart* - Thomas Tessier　h　5440

**Mulcahey, Gerald "Jerry"** (Scientist; Genius)
*Heavy Weather* - Bruce Sterling　s　5258

**Mulder, Fox** (FBI Agent)
*Antibodies* - Kevin J. Anderson　h　99
*Goblins* - Charles L. Grant　s　2309
*Ground Zero* - Kevin J. Anderson　h　106
*Ruins* - Kevin J. Anderson　h　112
*Whirlwind* - Charles L. Grant　f　2320
*The X-Files: Fight the Future* - Chris Carter　h　924

**Mulkerrin** (Religious)
*Of Saints and Shadows* - Christopher Golden　h　2259

**Mulkerrin, Liam** (Vampire)
*Angel Souls and Devil Hearts* - Christopher Golden　h　2255

**Mullica, Jack** (Alien)
*Hard Landing* - Algis Budrys　s　753

**Mulligan, Jack** (Psychic)
*Polar City Blues* - Katharine Kerr　s　3073

**Mulliner, Jasper** (Farmer)
*The Barrens* - F. Paul Wilson　h　5884

**Mullins, Lawrence** (Police Officer)
*Creekers* - Edward Lee　h　3391

**Mulloy, Cynthia "Lady Cyndara"** (Editor)
*Knights of the Morningstar* - Melanie Rawn　s　4487

**Mully, Katharine** (Writer; Lesbian)
*Memory and Dream* - Charles de Lint　f　1433

**Multiple Entity "ME"** (Artificial Intelligence; Spy)
*ME: A Novel of Self Discovery* - Thomas T. Thomas　s　5452

**Mulvihill, Travest** (Tailor)
*The Ways of Magic* - Scott Ciencin　f　1033

**Mumbo** (Mythical Creature)
*The Adventures of King Midas* - Lynne Reid Banks　f　329

**Muncie, Lance** (Spaceman)
*The Trikon Deception* - Ben Bova　s　597

**Mundy, Adele** (Scholar)
*With the Lightnings* - David Drake　s　1652

**Munk** (Android; Revolutionary)
*Solis* - A.A. Attanasio　s　272

**Munn, Alex** (Writer; Computer Expert)
*The Shift* - George Foy　s　2033

**Munro, Dan** (Police Officer)
*Reign* - Chet Williamson　h　5849

**Munro, David** (Artist)
*Head Injuries* - Conrad Williams　h　5816

**Munsen, Luke** (Scientist)
*Fire* - Alan Rodgers　h　4647

**Murasaki, Rose** (Editor; Vampire)
*Suckers* - Anne Billson　h　490

**Murat** (Royalty)
*The Sixth Book of Lost Swords: Mindsword's Story* - Fred Saberhagen　f　4776

**Murchison** (Doctor; Spacewoman)
*The Galactic Gourmet* - James White　s　5778

**Murdan of Overhall** (Leader)
*Dragon Companion* - Don Callander　f　842

**Murdan of Overhall** (Companion)
*Dragon Rescue* - Don Callander　f　843

**Murdley, Jennifer** (Teenager; Student)
*Jennifer Murdley's Toad* - Bruce Coville　f　1220

**Murdoch, John** (Fugitive)
*Dark City* - Frank Lauria　h　3351

**Murdoch, Ross** (Time Traveler)
*Firehand* - Andre Norton　s　4151

**Murgen** (Military Personnel)
*Bleak Seasons* - Glen Cook　f　1147

**Murgen** (Military Personnel; Psychic)
*She Is the Darkness* - Glen Cook　f　1154

**Murphy, Annie** (Housewife)
*The Elementals* - Morgan Llywelyn　f　3503

**Murphy, Buffy** (Storyteller)
*Fair Peril* - Nancy Springer　f　5178

**Murphy, Clarence "Cookie"** (Cook; Sidekick)
*Judson's Eden* - Keith Laumer　s　3344

**Murphy, Emily** (Teenager)
*Fair Peril* - Nancy Springer　f　5178

**Murphy, Grey** (Student—College; Sorcerer)
*Man From Mundania* - Piers Anthony　f　180

**Murphy, James** (Musician)
*Landslayer's Law* - Tom Deitz　f　1474

**Murphy, Pilar** (Psychologist; Professor)
*Puppet Master* - Barry T. Hawkins   h   2632

**Murra** (Spouse)
*Stopping at Slowyear* - Frederik Pohl   s   4355

**Murray, Melpomene** (Student; Writer)
*Orbital Resonance* - John Barnes   s   356

**Murray, Mina** (Young Woman)
*Dracul: An Eternal Love Story* - Nancy
   Kilpatrick   h   3110

**Murri** (Animal)
*The Mark of the Cat* - Andre Norton   f   4157

**Murrinder, Ainne** (Telepath)
*The Wall at the Edge of the World* - Jim
   Aikin   s   46

**Murtaugh, Flint** (Bounty Hunter)
*Gone South* - Robert R. McCammon   h   3755

**Murugan, L.** (Computer Expert)
*The Calcutta Chromosome* - Amitav Ghosh   h   2214

**Musashi** (Artificial Intelligence)
*The Cybernetic Shogun* - Victor Milan   s   3890

**Musgrave, Winter** (Amnesiac)
*Witchlight* - Marion Zimmer Bradley   f   655

**Musgrave, Wycherly "Wych"** (Alcoholic)
*Gravelight* - Marion Zimmer Bradley   f   636

**Mushimo** (Martial Arts Expert)
*Iroshi* - Cary Osborne   s   4228

**Musik, Peter** (Journalist)
*The End-of-Everything Man* - Tom De
   Haven   f   1421

**Musser, Joanie** (Witch)
*Apocalypse* - Nancy Springer   f   5176

**Mussina, Isabella** (Doctor)
*Night of Broken Souls* - Thomas F.
   Monteleone   h   3964

**Mwili-Ferret** (Thief; Warrior)
*The 97th Step* - Steve Perry   s   4287

**My Secret Agent Lover Man** (Filmmaker)
*Witch Baby* - Francesca Lia Block   f   552

**Myat** (Noblewoman)
*An Enemy Reborn* - Michael A. Stackpole   f   5197

**Myburgh, Gerrit** (Businessman)
*Apartheid, Superstrings, and Mordecai Thubana* -
   Michael Bishop   s   496

**Myers, Didi "Deeds"** (Robot; Researcher)
*The Stranger* - Eric James Fullilove   s   2093

**Myers, Edward** (Writer; Researcher)
*The Summit* - Edward Myers   f   4063

**Myers, Jeremy** (Scientist)
*The Serpent Slayers* - Adam Niswander   h   4113

**Myklathun, Einar** (Government Official; Adventurer)
*Dragon's Domain* - Thorarinn Gunnarsson   f   2461

**Mylne, Duncan** (Sorcerer)
*The Matrix* - Jonathan Aycliffe   h   280

**Mynauzet** (Royalty)
*King of the Dead* - R.A. MacAvoy   f   3581

**Myrddin** (Artisan; Guardian)
*In the Shadow of the Oak King* - Courtway
   Jones   f   2939

**Myrilandel "Myri"** (Healer)
*The Dragon's Touchstone* - Irene Radford   f   4459

**Myshtigo, Cort** (Alien; Journalist)
*This Immortal* - Roger Zelazny   s   6074

**Mystra** (Sorceress)
*Elminster: The Making of a Mage* - Ed
   Greenwood   f   2427

**Myth, Urban** (Computer Expert; Robot)
*Cinderblock* - Janine Ellen Young   s   6047

**Mzu, Alkad** (Scientist; Avenger)
*Conflict* - Peter F. Hamilton   s   2522

# N

**na Juriam dro Sarn, Perolys** (Government Official)
*The Queen of Ashes* - Deborah Turner
   Harris   f   2561

**NaBlaine, Ruairi** (Nobleman)
*Bridge of Valor* - Anne Lesley Groell   f   2452

**Nacker the Teach** (Health Care Professional)
*The Pharaoh Contract* - Ray Aldridge   s   63

**Nadia** (Adventurer)
*Henry's Gift: The Magic Eye* - David
   Worsick   f   5972

**Nafai** (Teenager)
*The Call of Earth* - Orson Scott Card   s   882

**Nafai** (Leader; Spaceship Captain)
*Earthfall* - Orson Scott Card   s   885

**Nafai** (Student; Child)
*The Memory of Earth* - Orson Scott Card   s   894

**Nafai** (Student; Hunter)
*The Ships of Earth* - Orson Scott Card   s   897

**Nagashima, Galvanix** (Scientist)
*The Oxygen Barons* - Gregory Feeley   s   1897

**Naguchi, Machiko** (Warrior; Guide)
*Hunter's Planet* - David Bischoff   s   492

**Nahadeh, Nika** (Psychic; Relative)
*Ember From the Sun* - Mark Canter   s   870

**Nahadeh, Yute** (Anthropologist; Indian)
*Ember From the Sun* - Mark Canter   s   870

**Nahvah** (Doctor)
*The Belly of the Wolf* - R.A. MacAvoy   f   3580

**Nailer, Diane** (Spouse)
*Grimm Memorials* - R. Patrick Gates   h   2160

**Nailer, Steve** (Teacher; Writer)
*Grimm Memorials* - R. Patrick Gates   h   2160

**Naill, Clarence "Rusty"** (Time Traveler; Sea
   Captain)
*Back to the Time Trap* - Keith Laumer   s   3343

**Naismith, Cordelia** (Noblewoman)
*Barrayar* - Lois McMaster Bujold   s   756

**Naismith, Gladys** (Witch; Adventurer)
*A Sudden Wild Magic* - Diana Wynne Jones   f   2950

**Naitachal** (Mythical Creature; Musician)
*Fortress of Frost and Fire* - Mercedes
   Lackey   f   3282

**Nakar** (Wizard; Ruler)
*Tower of Fear* - Glen Cook   f   1155

**Nakimura, Grace** (Clerk)
*The Beast Within: A Gabriel Knight Mystery* - Jane
   Jensen   h   2895

**Nakimura, Grace** (Worker)
*Gabriel Knight: Sins of the Fathers* - Jane
   Jensen   h   2896

**Nakota** (Waiter/Waitress)
*The Cipher* - Kathe Koja   h   3194

**Nallaneen, Faris** (Magician; Royalty)
*A College of Magics* - Caroline Stevermer   f   5266

**Nanchen, Kedar** (Government Official;
   Revolutionary)
*Exile* - Michael P. Kube-McDowell   s   3248

**Nancia** (Cyborg)
*PartnerShip* - Anne McCaffrey   s   3741

**Nandan** (Magician)
*The Adventures of King Midas* - Lynne Reid
   Banks   f   329

**Nanopoulos, Sheila** (Police Officer)
*Glass Houses* - Laura J. Mixon   s   3921

**Naoh** (Alien; Revolutionary)
*Dreamfall* - Joan D. Vinge   s   5571

**Naomia** (Prostitute; Military Personnel)
*Chains of Light* - Quentin Thomas   s   5449

**Nara** (Animal)
*Dark Horse* - Mary H. Herbert   f   2674

**Narantir** (Wizard)
*D'Shai* - Joel Rosenberg   f   4670

**Narbando, Ignatio** (Scientist)
*Lord Kelvin's Machine* - James P. Blaylock   f   520

**Nargol, Edward** (Royalty)
*The Legend of Nightfall* - Mickey Zucker
   Reichert   f   4521

**Narlh** (Mythical Creature; Adventurer)
*The Oathbound Wizard* - Christopher
   Stasheff   f   5219

**Narman, Bart** (Businessman)
*The Curse* - John Tigges   h   5472

**Narman, Sabra** (Artist)
*The Curse* - John Tigges   h   5472

**Narn, Roger K. "RK"** (Lawman)
*Mojo and the Pickle Jar* - Douglas Bell   f   433

**Narrator** (Writer)
*The House on the Borderland* - William Hope
   Hodgson   h   2711

**Narrion** (Nobleman)
*Summer King, Winter Fool* - Lisa Goldstein   f   2263

**Narrow Leg** (Scientist; Alien)
*The Ship Errant* - Jody Lynn Nye   s   4175

**Nash, August** (Security Officer; Spy)
*Labyrinth of Night* - Allen Steele   s   5244

**Nash, Scott** (Photojournalist)
*Lagoon* - Alison Drake   h   1625

**Nashram, Mika** (Magician; Con Artist)
*By the Sword* - Greg Costikyan   f   1207

**Naso** (Fugitive; Writer)
*The Last World* - Christoph Ransmayr   f   4475

**Nastrus** (Mythical Creature)
*The Unicorn War* - John Lee   f   3401

**Nasty Andrew** (Serial Killer)
*Bleeder* - Gene Lazuta   h   3374

**Nathalorial, Kaylana** (Religious; Leader)
*Villains by Necessity* - Eve Forward   f   1985

**Nathan, Corliss** (Police Officer)
*Genesis* - Charles L. Grant   h   2308

**Nathan, Jessica** (Scientist)
*Desert Eden* - J.M. Morgan   s   4000

**Natil** (Mythical Creature; Minstrel)
*Maze of Moonlight* - Gael Baudino   f   393

**Natter, Cody** (Drug Dealer)
*Creekers* - Edward Lee   h   3391

**Naufts, Tom** (Criminal; Telepath)
*The Gifted* - Jack Caravela   h   879

**Navarra** (Vampire)
*Night Brothers* - Sidney Williams   h   5824

**Navarre** (Magician; Adventurer)
*The Magic Wars* - Jo Clayton   f   1068

**Naxania** (Royalty; Ruler)
*The Unicorn Peace* - John Lee   f   3399

**Nazaual** (Magician; Religious)
*Redmagic* - Crawford Kilian   f   3107

**Nazhuret** (Warrior)
*The Belly of the Wolf* - R.A. MacAvoy  *f*  3580
*King of the Dead* - R.A. MacAvoy  *f*  3581
*Lens of the World* - R.A. MacAvoy  *f*  3582

**Nazir, Nassifeh "Opalears"** (Time Traveler; Storyteller)
*The Family Tree* - Sheri S. Tepper  *s*  5429

**Ndemi** (Apprentice)
*Kirinyaga: A Fable of Utopia* - Mike Resnick  *s*  4548

**Neal, Porsche** (Alien; Fugitive)
*Beneath the Gated Sky* - Robert Reed  *s*  4502

**Neal, Porsche** (Alien; Traveler)
*Beyond the Veil of Stars* - Robert Reed  *s*  4503

**Neale, Charis** (Scientist)
*Dark Matter* - Garfield Reeves-Stevens  *h*  4509

**Neary, Billy** (Child)
*Billy* - Whitley Strieber  *h*  5338

**Neary, Mark** (Teacher)
*Billy* - Whitley Strieber  *h*  5338

**Nebogipfel** (Mutant; Time Traveler)
*The Time Ships* - Stephen Baxter  *s*  403

**Nebuun** (Alien)
*Random Factor* - Joel Henry Sherman  *s*  4984

**Ned** (Orphan; Genius)
*Hope of Earth* - Piers Anthony  *s*  175

**Ned** (Orphan)
*Spring-Heeled Jack* - Philip Pullman  *f*  4447

**Needham, Bill** (Businessman)
*Kane* - Douglas Borton  *h*  576

**Neelix** (Alien; Cook)
*The Final Fury* - Dafydd ab Hugh  *s*  9

**Nefertity** (Artificial Intelligence)
*AEstival Tide* - Elizabeth Hand  *s*  2533

**Negrete, Dolores** (Settler)
*The Dazzle of Day* - Molly Gloss  *s*  2243

**Neihart, Fletcher Robert** (Orphan; Teenager)
*Finity's End* - C.J. Cherryh  *s*  988

**Neimark, Max** (Actor; Director)
*Preternatural* - Margaret Wander Bonanno  *s*  568

**Nell** (Teenager; Writer)
*Into the Forest* - Jean Hegland  *s*  2640

**Nellodee "Nell"** (Child)
*The Diamond Age* - Neal Stephenson  *s*  5253

**Nelly** (Computer Expert)
*Mir* - Alexander Besher  *s*  474

**Nelson, MaryAnn "Spook"** (Teenager)
*Spook* - Steve Vance  *h*  5553

**Nelson, Nedra Muriel** (Artist)
*Spook* - Steve Vance  *h*  5553

**Nelson, Vicki** (Detective—Private)
*Blood Debt* - Tanya Huff  *h*  2792
*Blood Price* - Tanya Huff  *h*  2793
*Blood Trail* - Tanya Huff  *h*  2794

**Nelson, Zack** (Teenager)
*Sweet Revenge* - Jean Simon  *h*  5066

**Nemet "Greenface"** (Hunter)
*Ancient Echoes* - Robert Holdstock  *f*  2735

**Nemmitz, Palmer** (Aged Person)
*Dark Journey* - A.R. Morlan  *h*  4010

**Nemo** (Alien)
*Metaphase* - Vonda N. McIntyre  *s*  3821

**Nemony** (Alien; Psychic)
*Dream-Weaver* - Louise Lawrence  *s*  3359

**Nenda, Louis** (Adventurer)
*Convergence* - Charles Sheffield  *s*  4951

**Nepe/Flach** (Mythical Creature; Animal)
*Phaze Doubt* - Piers Anthony  *f*  184

**Nephredann** (Demon)
*Necrom* - Mick Farren  *s*  1881

**Nesbit, Edward** (Writer)
*The Chymical Wedding* - Lindsay Clarke  *f*  1063

**Nesbitt, Justin** (Musician)
*The Beyond* - Barry Harrington  *h*  2556

**Neskat, Merinda** (Alien; Historian)
*Nightsword* - Margaret Weis  *f*  5722
*Sentinels* - Margaret Weis  *s*  5725

**Ness** (Artisan; Parent)
*Shadow's Daughter* - Shirley Meier  *f*  3871

**Nessarose** (Witch; Religious)
*Wicked: The Life and Times of the Wicked Witch of the West* - Gregory Maguire  *f*  3609

**Nest, Henrich Joseph** (Vampire)
*The Harvest* - Richie Tankersley Cusick  *h*  1302

**Nestor** (Wizard)
*The Guardian* - Angus Wells  *f*  5737

**Nettie** (Space Explorer; Traveler)
*Douglas Adams's Starship Titanic* - Terry Jones  *s*  2979

**Neumann, Kate** (Doctor)
*Children of the Night* - Dan Simmons  *h*  5050

**Neville-Smythe, Brian** (Knight; Fiance(e))
*The Dragon and the Djinn* - Gordon R. Dickson  *f*  1528

**Neville-Smythe, Brian** (Knight)
*The Dragon in Lyonesse* - Gordon R. Dickson  *f*  1531
*The Dragon, the Earl, and the Troll* - Gordon R. Dickson  *f*  1534

**Nevsky, Peter** (Orphan; Spaceman)
*Peter Nevsky and the True Story of the Russian Moon Landing* - John Calvin Batchelor  *s*  388

**Nevyn** (Sorcerer)
*The Dragon Revenant* - Katharine Kerr  *f*  3069

**Nevyn** (Counselor)
*The Red Wyvern* - Katharine Kerr  *f*  3074

**Newcombe, Dan** (Scientist; Religious)
*Richter 10* - Arthur C. Clarke  *s*  1060

**Newell, Charlie** (Teenager; Pilot)
*Wildside* - Steven Gould  *s*  2291

**Newkirk, Bobby** (Teenager)
*Double Date* - R.L. Stine  *h*  5287

**Newman, Greg** (Murderer)
*Impulse* - Rick Hautala  *h*  2609

**Newman, Mark** (Worker)
*The Mountain King* - Rick Hautala  *h*  2611

**Newman, Sandy** (Teenager)
*The Mountain King* - Rick Hautala  *h*  2611

**Newns, Curtis** (Artist)
*Skyscape* - Michael Cadnum  *h*  814

**Newns, Margaret** (Writer)
*Skyscape* - Michael Cadnum  *h*  814

**Newt** (Animal)
*Ratha and Thistle-Chaser* - Clare Bell  *f*  432

**Newton, Isaac** (Inventor)
*Newton's Cannon* - J. Gregory Keyes  *f*  3097

**Newton, Roger** (Saloon Keeper/Owner)
*The Unseen* - Joseph A. Citro  *h*  1039

**Ng, Margot O'Reilly** (Spaceship Captain)
*Ruler of Naught* - Sherwood Smith  *s*  5141

**Ngamuku, Larae** (Young Woman)
*Horrors of the Dancing Gods* - Jack L. Chalker  *f*  955

**Ngenga, Ngina-li "Ngina"** (Alien)
*The Inquisitor* - Cheryl J. Franklin  *s*  2037

**Ngoni, Beatrice** (Doctor)
*A Miracle of Rare Design* - Mike Resnick  *s*  4550

**Ngu, Emerson** (Engineer; Businessman)
*Pallas* - L. Neil Smith  *s*  5132

**Nguyen, Marie** (Teenager; Pilot)
*Wildside* - Steven Gould  *s*  2291

**Nguyen, Phat "Zak"** (Student—Graduate; Researcher)
*Cosm* - Gregory Benford  *s*  444

**Nhamo** (Child; Adventurer)
*A Girl Named Disaster* - Nancy Farmer  *f*  1868

**ni Bron, Deir** (Refugee; Magician)
*Redmagic* - Crawford Kilian  *f*  3107

**ni Errhyn, Bracht** (Mercenary)
*Dark Magic* - Angus Wells  *f*  5733
*Forbidden Magic* - Angus Wells  *f*  5736
*Wild Magic* - Angus Wells  *f*  5741

**ni Pendaron, Teleri** (Sorceress)
*The Work of the Sun* - Teresa Edgerton  *f*  1746

**Nia** (Noblewoman; Mythical Creature)
*The Deer's Cry: A Book of the Keltiad* - Patricia Kennealy-Morrison  *f*  3060

**Nia** (Alien)
*A Woman of the Iron People* - Eleanor Arnason  *s*  211

**Niad** (Magician; Teenager)
*The Cursed* - Dave Duncan  *f*  1674

**Niahrin** (Witch)
*Aisling* - Louise Cooper  *f*  1172

**Niall** (Psychic; Revolutionary)
*The Delta* - Colin Wilson  *s*  5878

**NicCuinn, Meghan** (Sorceress; Leader)
*The Witches of Eileanan* - Kate Forsyth  *f*  1984

**Nicholas** (Royalty)
*The Changeling* - Kristine Kathryn Rusch  *f*  4714

**Nicholas** (Royalty; Teenager)
*The King's Buccaneer* - Raymond E. Feist  *f*  1904

**Nicholas** (Royalty)
*To Save the Sun* - Ben Bova  *s*  596

**Nicholas** (Vampire)
*The Winnowing* - Gherbod Fleming  *h*  1950

**Nicholas "Santa Claus"** (Hero)
*The Autobiography of Santa Claus: It's Better to Give* - Jeff Guinn  *f*  2456

**Nichols, Harford** (Government Official)
*Night of Broken Souls* - Thomas F. Monteleone  *h*  3964

**Nicholson, Graeme** (Journalist)
*Expansion* - Peter F. Hamilton  *s*  2525

**Nicholson, Shawna** (Doctor)
*The Unknown Soldier* - Mickey Zucker Reichert  *s*  4525

**Nick** (Warrior)
*The Paratwa* - Christopher Hinz  *s*  2691

**Nickerson, Josh** (Teenager)
*Kindred* - John Gideon  *h*  2222

**Nicodareus** (Monster; Leader)
*Darkenheight* - Douglas Niles  *f*  4107

**Nicodemus** (Religious)
*Plague Demon* - Brian Craig  *f*  1239

**Nicol, Jesse** (Spaceship Captain; Writer)
*Harvest the Fire* - Poul Anderson  *s*  128

**Nicolau, Grigori** (Amnesiac)
*Frostwing* - Richard A. Knaak  *f*  3170

**Nicole, Maeve** (Student; Veterinarian)
*The Scathach and the Maeve's Daughter* - Mary Alexander Walker  f  5618

**Niehaus, Vilmos** (Architect)
*The Final Diary Entry of Kees Huijgens* - William R. Stotler  h  5317

**Nielsen, Berkeley "Berk"** (Pilot)
*Faraday's Orphans* - N. Lee Wood  s  5965

**Nielson** (Teacher)
*When Darkness Falls* - Sidney Williams  h  5825

**Nielson, Anne** (Journalist)
*Bad Dreams* - Kim Newman  h  4096

**Nielson, Cameron** (Writer)
*Bad Dreams* - Kim Newman  h  4096

**Nielson, Rainey** (Widow(er))
*The Starry Child* - Lynn Hanna  f  2540

**Nielson, Sasha** (Child; Reincarnated Person)
*The Starry Child* - Lynn Hanna  f  2540

**Nifft the Lean** (Adventurer)
*The Mines of Behemoth* - Michael Shea  f  4945

**Niffy** (Animal; Counselor)
*No One Noticed the Cat* - Anne McCaffrey  f  3740

**Nigel** (Professor)
*Specterworld* - Isidore Haiblum  s  2480

**Nigheyes** (Animal; Telepath)
*Royal Assassin* - Robin Hobb  f  2695

**Night, Kevin** (Child)
*The Monastery* - J.N. Williamson  h  5856

**Night, Noel** (Parent)
*The Monastery* - J.N. Williamson  h  5856

**Nighteyes** (Animal; Telepath)
*Assassin's Quest* - Robin Hobb  f  2694

**Nightfall** (Thief)
*The Legend of Nightfall* - Mickey Zucker Reichert  f  4521

**Nighthawk, Jefferson "Widowmaker"** (Clone; Criminal)
*The Widowmaker* - Mike Resnick  s  4559

**Nighthawk, Jefferson "Widowmaker"** (Clone; Mercenary)
*The Widowmaker Reborn* - Mike Resnick  s  4560

**Nightingale "Lyrebird"** (Musician; Magician)
*The Eagle and the Nightingales* - Mercedes Lackey  f  3278

**Nightshade** (Vampire)
*Sex and the Single Vampire* - Nancy Kilpatrick  h  3114

**Nightwing** (Vampire)
*Vampire Breath* - R.L. Stine  h  5291

**Nikki** (Femme Fatale)
*Dark Winds* - Graham Watkins  h  5630

**Nikko** (Artificial Intelligence)
*Vast* - Linda Nagata  s  4067

**Nikolaus** (Vampire; Leader)
*Guilty Pleasures* - Laurell K. Hamilton  f  2517

**Niley, Frank** (Real Estate Agent)
*Blue Moon* - Laurell K. Hamilton  h  2513

**Nili, Mei** (Revolutionary)
*Solis* - A.A. Attanasio  s  272

**Nimbulan "Lan"** (Magician; Warrior)
*The Dragon's Touchstone* - Irene Radford  f  4459

**Nimesin, Kymil** (Martial Arts Expert; Mythical Creature)
*Elfshadow* - Elaine Cunningham  f  1288

**Nimitz, Ariel** (Administrator)
*The Unwound Way* - William Adams  s  35

**Nimitz, Brent** (Unemployed)
*Dark Journey* - A.R. Morlan  h  4010

**Nimnestl** (Bodyguard)
*Rouse a Sleeping Cat* - Dan Crawford  f  1249
*The Sure Death of a Mouse* - Dan Crawford  f  1250
*A Wild Dog and Lone* - Dan Crawford  f  1251

**Nimrod** (Robot; Military Personnel)
*Solo* - Robert Mason  s  3665

**Nimue** (Sorceress)
*The Merlin Effect* - T.A. Barron  f  371

**Nimue** (Orphan; Sorceress)
*The Winter King* - Bernard Cornwell  f  1191

**Nimziki, Albert Alexander** (Government Official)
*Silent Zone* - Stephen Molstad  s  3952

**Nina** (Mentally Ill Person; Military Personnel)
*Planar Powers* - J. Robert King  f  3122

**Ninekiller, Amos** (Indian; Pilot)
*The Wild Blue and the Gray* - William Sanders  s  4814

**Ningauble of the Seven Eyes** (Wizard)
*Ill Met in Lankhmar* - Fritz Leiber  f  3419

**Nira, Val** (Space Explorer)
*The Longest Voyage/Slow Lightning* - Poul Anderson  s  130

**Nirobus** (Wizard; Drug Dealer)
*My Son, the Wizard* - Christopher Stasheff  f  5218

**Nisa** (Slave; Royalty)
*Emperor of Everything* - Ray Aldridge  s  62

**Nisa** (Royalty; Slave)
*The Pharaoh Contract* - Ray Aldridge  s  63

**Nishima** (Royalty)
*The Initiate Brother* - Sean Russell  f  4742

**Nitt, Agnes** (Singer)
*Maskerade* - Terry Pratchett  f  4395

**Nivens, Sam** (Spy)
*The Puppet Masters* - Robert A. Heinlein  s  2646

**Niviene** (Mythical Creature; Apprentice)
*Merlin's Harp* - Anne Eliot Crompton  f  1270

**Nix, Chris** (Child)
*Dogland* - Will Shetterly  f  4992

**Nix, Luke** (Businessman)
*Dogland* - Will Shetterly  f  4992

**Nlavi** (Royalty)
*By the Sword* - Greg Costikyan  f  1207

**No-man's Son, Roric** (Warrior; Adventurer)
*Voima* - C. Dale Brittain  f  704

**no Mitsuko, Fujiwara** (Heroine; Teenager)
*The Heavenward Path* - Kara Dalkey  f  1319

**Nobilio, Francis "Frank"** (Scientist; Government Official)
*Illegal Alien* - Robert J. Sawyer  s  4858

**Noble, Bentley** (Journalist)
*Shackled* - Ray Garton  h  2156

**Nodens** (Deity)
*The Transition of Titus Crow* - Brian Lumley  h  3569

**Nodrey, Russa** (Animal)
*The Long Patrol* - Brian Jacques  f  2849

**Noelle** (Telepath)
*Starborne* - Robert Silverberg  s  5042

**Noir, Alfred "Alf"** (Journalist; Time Traveler)
*Psychoshop* - Alfred Bester  s  477

**Noir, Julie** (Teenager)
*The Black Cat* - Robert Poe  h  4344

**Noirceuil** (Vampire Hunter)
*To Dream of Dreamers Lost* - David Niall Wilson  h  5882

**Nokar** (Librarian)
*Bones of the Past* - Holly Lisle  f  3478

**Nokias** (Magician)
*The Ship Who Won* - Anne McCaffrey  s  3750

**Nolan** (Doctor; Immigrant)
*The Silent Stars Go By* - James White  s  5781

**Nolan, Carly** (Lawyer)
*Arachne* - Lisa Mason  s  3661

**Nolan, Carly** (Computer Expert; Fugitive)
*Cyberweb* - Lisa Mason  s  3662

**Nolan, Celia** (Housewife)
*Celia* - Ruby Jean Jensen  h  2900

**Nolan, Durk** (Reanimated Dead)
*Celia* - Ruby Jean Jensen  h  2900

**Nolan, Eric** (Teacher)
*Shadow Child* - Joseph A. Citro  h  1038

**Nolan, Ion** (Military Personnel)
*Lieutenant* - Rick Shelley  s  4972
*Officer Cadet* - Rick Shelley  s  4973

**Nolan, Ronan** (Teenager; Wizard)
*A Wizard Abroad* - Diane Duane  f  1668

**Nolan, Wulf** (Fire Fighter)
*Borderland: A Novel of Terror* - S.K. Epperson  h  1828

**Nolar** (Scholar; Healer)
*Flight of Vengeance* - Andre Norton  f  4152

**Nomikos, Conrad** (Government Official; Immortal)
*This Immortal* - Roger Zelazny  s  6074

**Nona** (Heroine; Heiress—Dispossessed)
*Fractal Mode* - Piers Anthony  f  171

**Noonan, Mike** (Writer)
*Bag of Bones* - Stephen King  h  3126

**Noonan, Owen** (Child; Adventurer)
*Travel Far, Pay No Fare* - Anne Lindbergh  f  3468

**Nopal** (Royalty; Traveler)
*The Chalchiuhite Dragon* - Kenneth Morris  f  4020

**Nora** (Werewolf)
*Animals* - John Skipp  h  5080

**Norak, Zach** (Teenager)
*Raptor* - Paul Zindel  s  6084

**Norby** (Robot)
*Norby and the Court Jester* - Janet Asimov  s  252
*Norby and the Oldest Dragon* - Janet Asimov  s  253
*Norby and Yobo's Great Adventure* - Janet Asimov  s  254
*Norby Down to Earth* - Janet Asimov  s  255

**Nordbo, Tyra** (Writer; Noblewoman)
*Inconstant Star* - Poul Anderson  s  129

**Noreen** (Scientist)
*Time and Light* - William Bornefeld  s  574

**Noressa** (Empath; Heiress—Dispossessed)
*Token of Dragonsblood* - Damaris Cole  f  1114

**Norman** (Businessman)
*Human Resources* - Floyd Kemske  h  3057

**Norman** (Doctor)
*Chaingang* - Rex Miller  h  3899

**Norman, Eliza** (Witch)
*Neighbors* - Maureen S. Pusti  h  4450

**Norman, Rebecca** (Witch)
*The Tallow Image* - Jane Brindle  h  690

**Normandy, Claire** (Military Personnel)
*Shiva in Steel* - Fred Saberhagen  s  4775

**Norreen** (Military Personnel)
*Shattered Chains* - Clayton Emery  f  1816

**Norris** (Military Personnel)
*Bodyguard* - William C. Dietz  s  1542

**Norris, Robert** (Ranger)
*Vyrmin* - Gene Lazuta   *h*   3376

**North** (Military Personnel)
*Vengeance* - David Drake   *s*   1648

**Northfield, Anthony** (Professor; Pilot)
*War Birds* - R.M. Meluch   *s*   3875

**Norton** (Mythical Creature; Activist)
*Steel Rose* - Kara Dalkey   *f*   1321

**Norwood, Natalie** (Military Personnel)
*The Final Battle* - William C. Dietz   *s*   1546

**No'shto-shti-stlen** (Alien; Diplomat)
*Chanur's Legacy* - C.J. Cherryh   *s*   981

**Nothing** (Teenager)
*Lost Souls* - Poppy Z. Brite   *h*   697

**Notorincus** (Slave; Revolutionary)
*A City in Winter* - Mark Helprin   *f*   2653

**Nova, Lisa** (Director)
*Brand New Cherry Flavor* - Todd Grimson   *h*   2448

**Novak, Cornell** (Fugitive)
*Beneath the Gated Sky* - Robert Reed   *s*   4502

**Novak, Cornell** (Traveler; Adventurer)
*Beyond the Veil of Stars* - Robert Reed   *s*   4503

**Novak, Shea** (Lawyer)
*Fatal Outcome* - Patricia Wallace   *h*   5622

**Novak, Simon** (Psychic)
*Graythings* - Pat Graversen   *h*   2335

**Novari** (Mythical Creature)
*The Warrior Returns* - Allan Cole   *f*   1109

**Noycannir, Mergau** (Civil Servant; Student)
*An Exchange of Hostages* - Susan R.
  Matthews   *s*   3692

**nu-Aten, Ha'riel** (Spaceship Captain; Alien)
*Smoke and Mirrors* - Jane M. Lindskold   *s*   3476

**Nuada** (Leader; Immigrant)
*The Enchanted Isles* - Casey Flynn   *f*   1960
*Most Ancient Song* - Casey Flynn   *f*   1961

**Nuala** (Nurse)
*The World I Made for Her* - Thomas
  Moran   *h*   3996

**Nuela** (Student)
*Deepwater Dreams* - Sydney J. Van Scyoc   *s*   5541

**Nugent, Efram** (Farmer; Leader)
*Girl in Landscape* - Jonathan Lethem   *s*   3440

**Nugent, Philip** (Child)
*The Butcher Boy* - Patrick McCabe   *h*   3716

**Nugget, Jain** (Singer)
*Kaduna Memories* - Jack McKinney   *s*   3850

**Nukurren** (Warrior; Alien)
*Mother of Demons* - Eric Flint   *s*   1956

**Nul** (Animal)
*Wizard's Mole* - Brad Strickland   *f*   5337

**Number Ten Ox** (Orphan; Adventurer)
*The Chronicles of Master Li and Number Ten Ox* -
  Barry Hughart   *f*   2803

**Number Ten Ox** (Sidekick)
*Eight Skilled Gentlemen* - Barry Hughart   *f*   2804

**Nunn** (Magician)
*Dragon Burning* - Craig Shaw Gardner   *f*   2126
*Dragon Sleeping* - Craig Shaw Gardner   *f*   2127
*Dragon Waking* - Craig Shaw Gardner   *f*   2128

**Nunzio** (Bodyguard)
*M.Y.T.H. Inc. in Action* - Robert Asprin   *f*   259

**Nuria** (Child; Orphan)
*Well Wished* - Franny Billingsley   *f*   489

**Nussbaumer, Lynn** (Scientist)
*Playing God* - Sarah Zettel   *s*   6080

**Nussem, Alis Mary** (Spacewoman; Pilot)
*Reckoning Infinity* - John E. Stith   *s*   5304

**Nuwen, Pham** (Religious; Reanimated Dead)
*A Fire upon the Deep* - Vernor Vinge   *s*   5573

**Nyara** (Orphan)
*Winds of Change* - Mercedes Lackey   *f*   3304

**Nyateneri** (Religious; Fugitive)
*The Innkeeper's Song* - Peter S. Beagle   *f*   409

**Nyctasia** (Ruler)
*Mistress of Ambiguities* - J.F. Rivkin   *f*   4596

**Nygerski, Cyrus "Moondog"** (Journalist)
*Moondog* - Henry Garfield   *h*   2138

**Nygerski, Cyrus "Moondog"** (Driver; Werewolf)
*Room 13* - Henry Garfield   *h*   2139

**Nylan** (Engineer)
*The Chaos Balance* - L.E. Modesitt Jr.   *f*   3925
*Fall of Angels* - L.E. Modesitt Jr.   *f*   3930

**Nym** (Mythical Creature)
*A Prince Among Men* - Robert N. Charrette   *f*   977

**Nysander** (Wizard; Spy)
*Luck in the Shadows* - Lynn Flewelling   *f*   1952

**Nystrom, Wayne** (Scientist; Time Traveler)
*Dictator* - William F. Wu   *s*   5996
*Predator* - William F. Wu   *s*   5998
*Warrior* - William F. Wu   *s*   6000

**Nyushka** (Psychic)
*Death Channels* - Robert E. Vardeman   *h*   5562

# O

**O-ha** (Animal)
*The Foxes of Firstdark* - Garry Kilworth   *f*   3115

**Oakenhurst, Sam** (Gambler)
*Blood: A Southern Fantasy* - Michael
  Moorcock   *f*   3977

**Oakenhurst, Sam** (Adventurer)
*The War Amongst the Angels* - Michael
  Moorcock   *f*   3986

**Oakes** (Administrator; Witch)
*On Meeting Witches at Wells* - Judith
  Gorog   *f*   2283

**Oakland, Brian** (Teenager; Student—High School)
*Stunts* - Charles L. Grant   *h*   2317

**Oakton, Cody** (Teenager)
*Only Child* - H.M. Hoover   *s*   2764

**Oar** (Genetically Altered Being)
*Expendable* - James Alan Gardner   *s*   2135

**O'Bannion, Joss** (Military Personnel)
*High Moon* - Diane Duane   *s*   1661
*Kill Station* - Diane Duane   *s*   1664
*Mindblast* - Diane Duane   *s*   1665

**Obar** (Magician)
*Dragon Waking* - Craig Shaw Gardner   *f*   2128

**Obed** (Animal; Linguist)
*The Off Season* - Jack Cady   *f*   820

**Oblivion, Billy** (Warrior)
*The Last Stand of the DNA Cowboys* - Mick
  Farren   *s*   1879

**Obo** (Alien; Police Officer)
*Mind Slayer* - Kevin D. Randle   *s*   4469

**O'Brian, James** (Scientist)
*Gabriel's Body* - Curt Siodmak   *h*   5073

**O'Brian, Launa** (Military Personnel; Time Traveler)
*First Dawn* - Mike Moscoe   *s*   4038
*Lost Days* - Mike Moscoe   *s*   4039

**O'Brian, Launa** (Time Traveler; Military Personnel)
*Second Fire* - Mike Moscoe   *s*   4040

**O'Brien, Anne** (Writer)
*I Met a Man Who Wasn't There* - Mary R.
  Callaghan   *h*   840

**O'Brien, Coley** (Entertainer)
*Destiny's Carnival* - Warren Murphy   *h*   4057

**O'Brien, Ed** (Police Officer)
*Leanna: Possession of a Woman* - Marie
  Kiraly   *h*   3149

**O'Brien, Mike** (Businessman)
*Out There in the Darkness* - Ed Gorman   *h*   2279

**O'Brien, Miles** (Military Personnel; Engineer)
*Bloodletter* - K.W. Jeter   *s*   2908

**O'Brien, Miles** (Engineer; Military Personnel)
*Vengeance* - Dafydd ab Hugh   *s*   10

**O'Brien, Richard** (Police Officer)
*The Crawling Dark* - Pauline Dunn   *h*   1698

**Obrion, Juan** (Scientist)
*Stranger Suns* - George Zebrowski   *s*   6060

**Obst, Roger** (Teenager; Student—High School)
*OtherSyde* - J. Michael Straczynski   *h*   5323

**Ochs, Thur** (Miner; Spy)
*The Spirit Ring* - Lois McMaster Bujold   *f*   763

**O'Connor, Corbo** (Gladiator; Sorcerer)
*The Fourth Guardian* - Ronald Anthony
  Cross   *s*   1273
*The Lost Guardian* - Ronald Anthony Cross   *s*   1274
*The White Guardian* - Ronald Anthony
  Cross   *s*   1275

**O'Connor, Dennis** (Journalist)
*The Hunger of the Beast* - John Driver   *h*   1656

**O'Connor, Flynn** (Time Traveler)
*Wolfking* - Bridget Wood   *s*   5963

**O'Connor, John** (Cowboy; Leader)
*The Flight of Michael McBride* - Midori
  Snyder   *f*   5151

**O'Connor, Katherine** (Political Figure)
*The Last Wizard* - Simon Hawke   *f*   2619

**O'Connor, Padraic** (Terrorist)
*Shade of Pale* - Greg Kihn   *h*   3104

**O'Connor, Thunderbird Devlin "Bird"** (Indian)
*Above the Lower Sky* - Tom Deitz   *f*   1469

**O'Connor, Tim** (Teenager)
*Entity* - Nina Mandelik   *h*   3615

**Octavian, Peter** (Detective—Private; Vampire)
*Of Masques and Martyrs* - Christopher
  Golden   *h*   2258
*Of Saints and Shadows* - Christopher
  Golden   *h*   2259

**O'Day, Gallen** (Warrior; Hero)
*Beyond the Gate* - Dave Wolverton   *s*   5949
*The Golden Queen* - Dave Wolverton   *s*   5951

**O'Dell, Judith** (Heroine)
*Imajica* - Clive Barker   *h*   343

**Odell, Owen** (Minstrel)
*Morningstar* - David Gemmell   *f*   2190

**Odin** (Artificial Intelligence)
*Dark Sky Legion* - William Barton   *s*   379

**Odin** (Deity)
*Sleipnir* - Linda Evans   *f*   1856
*War of the Gods* - Poul Anderson   *f*   136

**Odo** (Alien; Security Officer)
*Fallen Heroes* - Dafydd ab Hugh   *s*   8
*Warped* - K.W. Jeter   *s*   2917

**O'Donnell, Annie** (Student)
*Stitch* - Mark Morris   *h*   4024

**O'Donnell, Charley** (Teacher)
*Fog Heart* - Thomas Tessier   *h*   5440

**O'Donnell, Erin** (Police Officer)
*Deathwalker* - Patrick Whalen   *h*   5769

**O'Donnell, Hugh** (Scientist)
*The Trikon Deception* - Ben Bova   *s*   597

**O'Donnell, Ryan** (Beachcomber)
*Nightmare, with Angel* - Stephen Gallagher   *h*   2111

**Odosson, William "Will"** (Knight; Adventurer)
*Knight's Wyrd* - Debra Doyle   *f*   1601

**O'Fallon, Michael Timothy** (Mythical Creature)
*The Reluctant Sorcerer* - Simon Hawke   *f*   2622

**Offenhouse, Ralph** (Diplomat; Businessman)
*Debtors' Planet* - William R. Thompson   *s*   5457

**Ogg, Nanny** (Witch; Heroine)
*Lords and Ladies* - Terry Pratchett   *f*   4394

**Oghmal** (Warrior; Hero)
*Search for the Starblade* - Keith Taylor   *f*   5408

**Ogle, Cyrus "Cy"** (Public Relations)
*Interface* - Stephen Bury   *s*   781

**Ogre** (Parent)
*The Ogre Downstairs* - Diana Wynne Jones   *f*   2949

**Ogress, Okra** (Mythical Creature; Runaway)
*The Color of Her Panties* - Piers Anthony   *f*   167

**Ohaern** (Warrior; Blacksmith)
*The Sage* - Christopher Stasheff   *f*   5221

**Ohaern** (Warrior; Hunter)
*The Shaman* - Christopher Stasheff   *f*   5223

**O'Hallahan, Emma Delaney** (Widow(er); Abuse Victim)
*What's Wrong with America* - Scott Bradfield   *h*   627

**O'Hallahan, Marvin** (Aged Person)
*What's Wrong with America* - Scott Bradfield   *h*   627

**Ohanscai, Natalya** (Royalty)
*Eyes of Silver* - Michael A. Stackpole   *f*   5200

**O'Hara, Emerald** (Teenager)
*Quake* - Richard Laymon   *h*   3370

**O'Hara, Frank** (Police Officer)
*A Room for the Dead* - Noel Hynd   *h*   2825

**O'Hara, Liam** (Scientist)
*Time, Like an Ever-Rolling Stream* - Judith Moffett   *s*   3944

**O'Hara, Marianne** (Administrator; Settler)
*Worlds Enough and Time* - Joe Haldeman   *s*   2491

**O'Hara, Sonny** (Businessman)
*Torments* - Lisa Cantrell   *h*   873

**O'Hara Prime** (Artificial Intelligence)
*Worlds Enough and Time* - Joe Haldeman   *s*   2491

**Ohasi, Juko** (Spacewoman)
*The Dazzle of Day* - Molly Gloss   *s*   2243

**O'Hearn, Travis** (Drifter)
*Practical Demonkeeping* - Christopher Moore   *h*   3989

**Ohmsford, Coll** (Adventurer)
*The Scions of Shannara* - Terry Brooks   *f*   716

**Ohmsford, Par** (Heir—Lost; Magician)
*The Scions of Shannara* - Terry Brooks   *f*   716

**Ohmsford, Par** (Mythical Creature; Adventurer)
*The Talismans of Shannara* - Terry Brooks   *f*   717

**Ohmsford, Wren** (Mythical Creature; Adventurer)
*The Elf Queen of Shannara* - Terry Brooks   *f*   711

**Oimu, Harriet** (Revolutionary; Genetically Altered Being)
*Celestis* - Paul Park   *s*   4241

**Oit-Makidom, Maraakuks** (Military Personnel)
*Runes of Autumn* - Larry Elmore   *f*   1790

**Okasan** (Businessman)
*Masque* - F. Paul Wilson   *s*   5890

**Okata, Gail** (Police Officer)
*Demon Fire* - Gary L. Holleman   *h*   2743

**O'Keefe, Jesse** (Anthropologist; Adventurer)
*Fire and Ice* - Edward Myers   *f*   4061
*The Mountain Made of Light* - Edward Myers   *f*   4062
*The Summit* - Edward Myers   *f*   4063

**O'Keefe, Katie** (Doctor)
*Rulers of Darkness* - Steven Spruill   *h*   5185

**O'Keefe, Polly** (Student)
*An Acceptable Time* - Madeleine L'Engle   *f*   3436

**O'Kelly, Manuel "Mannie"** (Revolutionary; Computer Expert)
*The Moon Is a Harsh Mistress* - Robert A. Heinlein   *s*   2645

**Okun, Brackish** (Genius; Researcher)
*Silent Zone* - Stephen Molstad   *s*   3952

**Olaffson, Egil** (Bodyguard; Friend)
*Egil's Book* - C.J. Mills   *s*   3910

**O'lal** (Alien; Animal)
*Cat-A-Lyst* - Alan Dean Foster   *s*   1997

**Olam, Thomas "Tom" Edward** (Time Traveler; Computer Expert)
*From Prussia with Love* - John DeChancie   *f*   1457

**Olamina, Lauren Oya** (Teenager; Religious)
*Parable of the Sower* - Octavia E. Butler   *s*   792

**Old Bess** (Aged Person)
*The Moorchild* - Eloise Jarvis McGraw   *f*   3816

**Old Grendel** (Alien)
*Beowulf's Children* - Larry Niven   *s*   4116

**Old Man** (Spy)
*The Puppet Masters* - Robert A. Heinlein   *s*   2646

**Old Man of the Mountain** (Mythical Creature)
*A Calculated Magic* - Robert Weinberg   *f*   5694

**Old Mose** (Farmer)
*Over the River & through the Woods* - Clifford D. Simak   *s*   5047

**Old Nathan** (Backwoodsman; Magician)
*Old Nathan* - David Drake   *f*   1639

**Old Ric** (Mythical Creature; Reanimated Dead)
*The Shadow Eater* - Adam Lee   *f*   3386

**Oldar** (Assistant)
*King of the Dead* - Gene DeWeese   *h*   1510

**Oldman, Wendel** (Werewolf; Religious)
*Wyrm Wolf* - Edo van Belkom   *h*   5535

**Oldtooth** (Animal)
*Hungry for Home: A Wolf Odyssey* - 'Asta Bowen   *f*   599

**Oliderval** (Ruler)
*The Unicorn Peace* - John Lee   *f*   3399

**Olivaw, R. Daneel "Eto Demerzel"** (Robot)
*Forward the Foundation* - Isaac Asimov   *s*   236
*Foundation's Fear* - Gregory Benford   *s*   446

**Oliver** (Robot)
*Stationfall* - Arthur Byron Cover   *s*   1216

**Ollie** (Child)
*No Kidding* - Bruce Brooks   *s*   709

**Olmstead, Robert** (Traveler)
*The Shadow over Innsmouth* - H.P. Lovecraft   *h*   3533

**Olon, Sammis Arloff** (Witch; Military Personnel)
*Timediver's Dawn* - L.E. Modesitt Jr.   *s*   3940

**Olson, Caroline** (Dancer)
*Dancing on Air* - Nancy Kress   *s*   3240

**Olson, Zenobia** (Writer)
*Flying Saucers over Hennepin* - Peter Gelman   *f*   2186

**Olyvria** (Heiress; Adventurer)
*Krispos the Emperor* - Harry Turtledove   *f*   5508

**O'Malley, Wolf** (Spaceship Captain; Castaway)
*White Light* - William Barton   *s*   384

**O'Mara** (Administrator; Psychologist)
*The Genocidal Healer* - James White   *s*   5779
*Mind Changer* - James White   *s*   5780

**O'Meara, Beverly** (Orphan; Detective—Private)
*In the Cube* - David Alexander Smith   *s*   5109

**O'Meara, Patrick** (Warrior; Ruler)
*Masters of the Fist* - Edward P. Hughes   *s*   2805

**O'Mor, Rury** (Chieftain; Immortal)
*Legends Reborn* - Kenneth C. Flint   *f*   1958

**Omri** (Child; Time Traveler)
*The Key to the Indian* - Lynne Reid Banks   *f*   331

**Omri** (Child; Student)
*The Secret of the Indian* - Lynne Reid Banks   *f*   332

**Onado, Hisako** (Musician)
*Canal Dreams* - Iain M. Banks   *s*   323

**O'Neill, Jack** (Military Personnel)
*Reconnaissance* - Bill McCay   *s*   3769 ·

**O'Neill, Jack** (Military Personnel; Leader)
*StarGate* - Dean Devlin   *s*   1509

**O'Neill, Jack** (Military Personnel)
*Stargate SG-1* - Ashley McConnell   *s*   3777

**O'Neill, Marcus Quilligan** (Lawyer; Spirit)
*I Met a Man Who Wasn't There* - Mary R. Callaghan   *h*   840

**Oneness** (Alien)
*Phylum Monsters* - Hayford Peirce   *s*   4276

**Onoda, Norio** (Tourist)
*Meridian 144* - Meg Files   *s*   1932

**Onrad** (Ruler)
*The Defenders* - Bill Baldwin   *s*   309

**Onyx** (Alien; Psychic)
*Marks of Our Brothers* - Jane M. Lindskold   *s*   3475

**Ooljee, Paul** (Police Officer; Indian)
*Cyber Way* - Alan Dean Foster   *s*   2000

**Oonan** (Healer)
*The Dubious Hills* - Pamela Dean   *f*   1444

**Oonitsaupivia, Nijon** (Hero; Barbarian)
*By the Sword* - Greg Costikyan   *f*   1207

**Ooslaxt** (Mutant; Leader)
*Christmas Slaughter* - Mark Grant   *s*   2323

**Opal** (Accountant)
*A Chill in the Blood* - P.N. Elrod   *h*   1793

**Opal, Sam** (Doctor)
*The Judas Glass* - Michael Cadnum   *h*   812

**Operative 41** (Alien; Spaceman)
*The Salukan Gambit* - Sean Dalton   *s*   1333

**or-Reise, Garric** (Warrior; Hunter)
*Lord of the Isles* - David Drake   *f*   1636

**or-Reise, Garric** (Warrior; Psychic)
*Queen of Demons* - David Drake   *f*   1640

**Orc** (Teenager; Nobleman)
*Red Orc's Rage* - Philip Jose Farmer   *f*   1873

**Orchard, Jack** (Businessman)
*The Count of Eleven* - Ramsey Campbell   *h*   853

**Orchard, Julia** (Computer Expert; Spouse)
*The Count of Eleven* - Ramsey Campbell   *h*   853

**Orchard, Laura** (Child)
*The Count of Eleven* - Ramsey Campbell   h   853

**Orchestra** (Alien)
*Nautilus* - Vonda N. McIntyre   s   3823

**O'Reilly, Bennett "Ben"** (Scientist; Researcher)
*Bellwether* - Connie Willis   s   5867

**O'Reilly, Theo** (Military Personnel)
*Mask of the Night* - Mary Ryan   h   4753

**Oren, Eichra** (Human; Agent)
*Converse and Conflict* - L. Neil Smith   s   5130

**Orfeo** (Minstrel)
*Storm Warriors* - Brian Craig   f   1240

**Orfeo** (Minstrel; Writer)
*Zaragoz* - Brian Craig   f   1241

**Orfindel "Hosea Lincoln"** (Deity; Handyman)
*The Fire Duke* - Joel Rosenberg   f   4671

**Organa, Leia** (Royalty; Diplomat)
*The Courtship of Princess Leia* - Dave
   Wolverton   s   5950
*The Crystal Star* - Vonda N. McIntyre   s   3820
*Dark Force Rising* - Timothy Zahn   s   6052
*The Truce at Bakura* - Kathy Tyers   s   5527
*Zorba the Hutt's Revenge* - Paul Davids   s   1394

**Orgoru** (Fugitive; Imposter)
*A Wizard in Peace* - Christopher Stasheff   s   5233

**Orick** (Animal; Adventurer)
*Beyond the Gate* - Dave Wolverton   s   5949
*The Golden Queen* - Dave Wolverton   s   5951

**Orien** (Nobleman; Thief)
*On Fortune's Wheel* - Cynthia Voigt   f   5579

**Orient, Finder** (Psychic)
*Finder* - Emma Bull   f   769

**Orilson, Wend** (Immortal)
*The Crown of Dalemark* - Diana Wynne
   Jones   f   2945

**Orion** (Immortal; Warrior)
*Orion Among the Stars* - Ben Bova   s   589
*Orion and the Conqueror* - Ben Bova   s   590
*Orion in the Dying Time* - Ben Bova   s   591

**O'Riordan** (Religious)
*The Silent Stars Go By* - James White   s   5781

**Orlene** (Spirit)
*And Eternity* - Piers Anthony   f   162

**Orliotti, Philippa J. "Flip"** (Clerk)
*Bellwether* - Connie Willis   s   5867

**Orlis** (Military Personnel)
*Officer Cadet* - Rick Shelley   s   4973

**Orlovsky, Paulo** (Ruler)
*The Third Force* - Marc Laidlaw   s   3313

**Ornis, Frederik Ry** (Technician)
*Legacy* - Greg Bear   s   420

**Orogastus** (Sorcerer; Criminal)
*Sky Trillium* - Julian May   f   3700

**Orogastus/Portolanus** (Sorcerer)
*Blood Trillium* - Julian May   f   3696

**O'Rourke** (Wanderer)
*Earthfall* - Jerry Earl Brown   s   724

**O'Rourke, Mike** (Religious)
*Children of the Night* - Dan Simmons   h   5050

**O'Rourke, Mike** (Child)
*Summer of Night* - Dan Simmons   h   5060

**Orphan** (Heroine)
*A Plague of Angels* - Sheri S. Tepper   f   5433

**Orr, Carnaby** (Businessman)
*Where the Ships Die* - William C. Dietz   s   1553

**Orris** (Sorcerer)
*The Outlanders* - David B. Coe   f   1096

**Ortega, Felix** (Parole Officer)
*Out of Body* - Thomas Baum   h   397

**Ortiveda, Phyllis** (Police Officer)
*Ursus* - David Dvorkin   s   1708

**Orun** (Traveler; Animal Trainer)
*Hidden Echoes* - Mike Jefferies   f   2885

**Orwen, Feng** (Ruler)
*The White Abacus* - Damien Broderick   s   708

**Oryolin, Alexander** (Spaceman; Hero)
*Peter Nevsky and the True Story of the Russian Moon
   Landing* - John Calvin Batchelor   s   388

**Osaro, George** (Religious)
*Ghosts* - Noel Hynd   h   2822

**Osborn, Winston D.** (Teenager)
*T.J.'s Ghost* - Shirley Climo   h   1087

**O'Shaughnessy, Maddock** (Time Traveler)
*Web of Futures* - Jefferson P. Swycaffer   f   5376

**O'Shay, Padrig** (Magician; Warrior)
*City of Pain* - John Terra   f   5438

**O'Shea, Devin** (Teenager; Werewolf)
*Moon of the Werewolf* - Ronald Kelly   h   3053

**O'Shea, Patrick** (Undertaker; Werewolf)
*Moon of the Werewolf* - Ronald Kelly   h   3053

**O'Shea, Rosie** (Teenager; Werewolf)
*Moon of the Werewolf* - Ronald Kelly   h   3053

**Oshima, Lynn** (Fugitive)
*The Bones of Time* - Kathleen Ann Goonan   s   2273

**Oshita, Joy** (Twin; Cult Member)
*Iron Shadows* - Steven Barnes   f   362

**Osic, Angelo** (Scientist; Military Personnel)
*On My Way to Paradise* - Dave Wolverton   s   5955

**Osmirik** (Librarian; Magician)
*Castle Spellbound* - John DeChancie   s   1454

**Osokin** (Prisoner)
*Brute Orbits* - George Zebrowski   s   6059

**Ostrow, Henry** (Murderer)
*Clarke County, Space* - Allen Steele   s   5241

**O'Sullivan, Mike** (Professor)
*The Haunt* - John Fogarty   h   1966

**Oswald** (Royalty)
*Drachenfels* - Jack Yeovil   f   6022

**O'Tennis, Ned** (Pilot)
*The Last Legends of Earth* - A.A. Attanasio   s   270

**Otha** (Slave)
*The Hollow Earth: The Narrative of Mason Algiers
   Reynolds of Virginia* - Rudy Rucker   s   4705

**Other** (Amnesiac)
*Mr. Murder* - Dean R. Koontz   h   3213

**Otter** (Trader; Indian)
*People of the Lakes* - Kathleen O'Neal Gear   f   2164

**Ottokar** (Nobleman)
*The Duke of Sumava* - Sara J. Wrench   f   5983

**Ouija** (Shaman)
*Cyberweb* - Lisa Mason   s   3662

**Ouoji** (Animal)
*Destination: Mutiny* - Sean Dalton   s   1332

**Ourousov, Prince** (Nobleman)
*The Princess and the Dragon* - Roberto
   Pazzi   f   4272

**Ousensky** (Psychic)
*The Boy Who Cried Werewolf* - Elvira   h   1800

**Outerbridge, Philip** (Psychologist)
*Some of Your Blood* - Theodore Sturgeon   h   5347

**Outhwaite, Terence** (Police Officer)
*Virgins and Martyrs* - Simon Maginn   h   3607

**Outis, Charles "Mr. Charlie"** (Disembodied
   Personality; Reanimated Dead)
*Solis* - A.A. Attanasio   s   272

**Overed, Martin** (Government Official)
*To a Highland Nation* - Christopher
   Rowley   s   4698

**Overstreet, Jessie** (Writer)
*After Life* - Andrew Neiderman   h   4083

**Overstreet, Lee** (Teacher)
*After Life* - Andrew Neiderman   h   4083

**Owain, David** (Businessman)
*The Long Lost* - Ramsey Campbell   h   859

**Owain, Gwendolyn** (Aged Person)
*The Long Lost* - Ramsey Campbell   h   859

**Owain, Joelle** (Businesswoman)
*The Long Lost* - Ramsey Campbell   h   859

**Owen** (Student; Teenager)
*Weirdos of the Universe, Unite!* - Pamela F.
   Service   f   4921

**Owen, Davey** (Editor)
*Live Girls* - Ray Garton   h   2151

**Owen, Harriet Cleaver** (Researcher)
*A Reasonable World* - Damon Knight   s   3188

**Owen, Rhyssa** (Telepath; Administrator)
*Pegasus in Flight* - Anne McCaffrey   s   3742

**Owens, Gillian** (Witch)
*Practical Magic* - Alice Hoffman   f   2713

**Owens, Sally** (Witch)
*Practical Magic* - Alice Hoffman   f   2713

**Owens, Tiffany "Tif"** (Pilot; Patient)
*Resurrection* - Katharine Kerr   s   3075

**Owensford, Peter** (Mercenary; Military Personnel)
*Go Tell the Spartans* - Jerry Pournelle   s   4375
*Prince of Sparta* - Jerry Pournelle   s   4378

**Owldark, Fringe Dorwalk** (Police Officer)
*Sideshow* - Sheri S. Tepper   s   5436

**Owlesby, Jack** (Artisan)
*Lord Kelvin's Machine* - James P. Blaylock   f   520

**Oxyle** (Mythical Creature)
*Mirror of Destiny* - Andre Norton   f   4159

**Oykib** (Teacher; Telepath)
*Earthfall* - Orson Scott Card   s   885

**Ozette, Ember** (Prehistoric Human; Psychic)
*Ember From the Sun* - Mark Canter   s   870

**Ozymandias** (Artificial Intelligence)
*Homecoming* - David Alexander Smith   s   5108

**Ozzie** (Computer Expert; Scientist)
*Dreams of Gods and Men* - W.T. Quick   s   4451

**Ozzie** (Mythical Creature)
*The Other Sinbad* - Craig Shaw Gardner   f   2130

# P

**P, Quentin** (Student)
*Zombie* - Joyce Carol Oates   h   4185

**Paarman, Leigh** (Advertising; Businesswoman)
*Succumb* - Ron Dee   h   1468

**Paarman, Martin** (Teacher)
*Succumb* - Ron Dee   h   1468

**Pablo "Sam Krueger"** (Android; Teenager)
*Proxies* - Laura J. Mixon   s   3922

**Packard, Janet** (Businesswoman)
*The Black Lodge* - Robert Weinberg   h   5692

**Packard, Nick** (Police Officer)
*Wet Work* - Philip Nutman   h   4168

**Paco, Chico** (Fisherman)
*Through the Arc of the Rain Forest* - Karen Tei
   Yamashita   *f*   6008

**Paco, Frank** (Organized Crime Figure)
*Bloodlist* - P.N. Elrod   *h*   1792

**Padrik** (Religious; Criminal)
*The Robin and the Kestrel* - Mercedes
   Lackey   *f*   3293

**Page, Scott** (Murderer)
*This Side of Judgment* - J.R. Dunn   *s*   1696

**Pagemaster** (Librarian; Guardian)
*The Pagemaster* - David Kirschner   *f*   3156

**Paik, Anna** (Journalist)
*Cortez on Jupiter* - Ernest Hogan   *s*   2721

**Pairis, Rudy** (Psychic)
*Mefisto in Onyx* - Harlan Ellison   *h*   1786

**Paithan** (Mythical Creature; Adventurer)
*Elven Star* - Margaret Weis   *f*   5712

**Paixao, Rhea** (Writer; Spouse)
*Starmind* - Spider Robinson   *s*   4642

**Pak, So** (Spaceship Captain)
*The Bushido Incident* - Betty Anne
   Crawford   *s*   1248

**Paladin** (Artificial Intelligence)
*Archangel Blues* - eluki bes shahar   *s*   471
*Darktraders* - eluki bes shahar   *s*   472
*Hellflower* - eluki bes shahar   *s*   473

**Paladyr** (Nobleman; Outlaw)
*The Endless Knot* - Stephen R. Lawhead   *f*   3354

**Palamon** (Royalty; Adventurer)
*Across the Thlassa Mey* - Dennis McCarty   *f*   3765

**Palaton** (Alien; Spaceman)
*Path of Fire* - Charles Ingrid   *s*   2832

**Pale Boy** (Lawman)
*Batman: Captured by the Engines* - Joe R.
   Lansdale   *h*   3320

**Pallas** (Pilot)
*Raft* - Stephen Baxter   *s*   401

**Pallenberg, Rachel** (Heiress)
*Galilee* - Clive Barker   *h*   340

**Palmer, Clay** (Drifter)
*Prototype* - Brian Hodge   *h*   2704

**Palmer, Jane** (Teacher)
*Panda Ray* - Michael Kandel   *s*   3011

**Palmer, Tall Man** (Sailor)
*White Shark* - Peter Benchley   *h*   441

**Palmer, William** (Detective)
*In the Blood* - Nancy A. Collins   *h*   1121

**Pan** (Mythical Creature)
*Cloven Hooves* - Megan Lindholm   *f*   3470

**Pan, Miss Scarlet** (Actress; Genetically Altered
   Being)
*Winterlong* - Elizabeth Hand   *s*   2539

**Pandora** (Alien)
*Pandora* - Alan Rodgers   *h*   4650

**Pangborn, Alan** (Police Officer)
*Needful Things* - Stephen King   *h*   3137

**Pangloss** (Supernatural Being)
*In the Blood* - Nancy A. Collins   *h*   1121

**Panshinea** (Alien; Ruler)
*Path of Fire* - Charles Ingrid   *s*   2832

**Pantera, Black Malachi** (Student)
*Views from the Oldest House* - Richard
   Grant   *s*   2329

**Panthera** (Heir; Prostitute)
*The Fulfillments of Fate and Desire* - Storm
   Constantine   *s*   1142

**Paolo** (Robot; Traveler)
*Diaspora* - Greg Egan   *s*   1759

**Papago Joe** (Salesman)
*Burial* - Graham Masterton   *h*   3671

**Papen, Richard** (Student—College)
*The Secret History* - Donna Tartt   *h*   5398

**Pardu** (Royalty; Parent)
*Heart Readers* - Kristine Kathryn Rusch   *f*   4718

**Parent, Lucy** (Linguist)
*The Magnificent Wilf* - Gordon R. Dickson   *s*   1536

**Parent, Tom** (Diplomat)
*The Magnificent Wilf* - Gordon R. Dickson   *s*   1536

**Parganas, Koot "Kootie" Hoomie** (Teenager;
   Psychic)
*Expiration Date* - Tim Powers   *f*   4383

**Paris, Tom** (Pilot; Military Personnel)
*Chrysalis* - David Niall Wilson   *s*   5880
*Pathways* - Jeri Taylor   *s*   5404

**Parker, Caroline** (Innkeeper)
*Winter Wolves* - Earle Wescott   *h*   5756

**Parker, Daria** (Singer)
*Silk* - Caitlin R. Kiernan   *h*   3101

**Parker, David** (Vampire)
*I, Vampire* - Michael Romkey   *h*   4665
*The Vampire Papers* - Michael Romkey   *h*   4666
*The Vampire Princess* - Michael Romkey   *h*   4667

**Parker, Evan** (Military Personnel; Political Figure)
*The Winds of Mars* - H.M. Hoover   *s*   2765

**Parker, Gale** (Archaeologist)
*Indiana Jones and the White Witch* - Martin
   Caidin   *f*   826

**Parker, James "Spark"** (Insurance Investigator)
*Double Jeopardy* - Aaron Allston   *s*   86

**Parker, Janis** (Political Figure)
*The Winds of Mars* - H.M. Hoover   *s*   2765

**Parker, Jim** (Student; Editor)
*University* - Bentley Little   *h*   3499

**Parker, Max** (Journalist)
*Parallelities* - Alan Dean Foster   *s*   2012

**Parker, Melody** (Lawyer)
*Tombley's Walk* - Crosland Brown   *h*   723

**Parker, Peter "Spider-Man"** (Hero; Detective—
   Amateur)
*Spider-Man: The Venom Factor* - Diane
   Duane   *s*   1667
*The Ultimate Spider-Man* - Stan Lee   *s*   3403

**Parkes, John** (Military Personnel)
*The Mountain Walks* - Roland J. Green   *s*   2349

**Parkinson, Rupert** (Sailor)
*The Ghost From the Grand Banks* - Arthur C.
   Clarke   *s*   1056

**Parks, Henry** (Detective)
*Forget Me Not* - Gene Lazuta   *h*   3375

**Parmenion** (Warrior)
*Dark Prince* - David Gemmell   *f*   2187

**Parmenion** (Mercenary; Sports Figure)
*Lion of Macedon* - David Gemmell   *f*   2189

**Parmenter, Casey** (Teenager)
*Tourists* - Lisa Goldstein   *f*   2264

**Parmenter, Mitchell** (Anthropologist)
*Tourists* - Lisa Goldstein   *f*   2264

**Parnell, Eugene M.** (Spaceman; Leader)
*The Tranquility Alternative* - Allen Steele   *s*   5248

**Parody, Paskal** (Magician)
*Kirins: The Secret of the Hanging Stones* - James D.
   Priest   *f*   4434

**Parry, William "Will"** (Child; Fugitive)
*The Subtle Knife* - Philip Pullman   *f*   4448

**Parsifal** (Knight)
*Parsifal* - Peter Vansittart   *f*   5560

**Parsley** (Child; Adventurer)
*Travel Far, Pay No Fare* - Anne Lindbergh   *f*   3468

**Parsons** (Political Figure)
*The Totem* - David Morrell   *h*   4012

**Parsons** (Police Officer)
*Twisted* - Sue Hollister Barr   *h*   364

**Parsons, Ronna** (Vagrant)
*Twisted* - Sue Hollister Barr   *h*   364

**Parthet "Uncle Parker"** (Wizard)
*The Hero King* - Rick Shelley   *f*   4970
*The Hero of Varay* - Rick Shelley   *f*   4971

**Partrick, Nicole** (Young Woman)
*Adversary* - Daniel Rhodes   *h*   4568

**Partridge** (Grandparent; Witch)
*Slow Funeral* - Rebecca Ore   *f*   4221

**Parz, Jasoft** (Diplomat; Time Traveler)
*Timelike Infinity* - Stephen Baxter   *s*   404

**Pascal** (Hotel Worker)
*A Face at the Window* - Dennis McFarland   *h*   3809

**Pascal, David** (Journalist)
*Carnosaur* - Harry Adam Knight   *s*   3191

**Pascale** (Spirit)
*The Ghost Inside the Monitor* - Margaret J.
   Anderson   *f*   122

**Pasco** (Agent)
*Ghost Dancers* - Brian Craig   *s*   1238

**Pashikov, Ilya** (Political Figure)
*Russian Spring* - Norman Spinrad   *s*   5174

**Pasmore, Tom** (Heir)
*Mystery* - Peter Straub   *h*   5330

**Pasmore, Tom** (Detective)
*The Throat* - Peter Straub   *h*   5332

**Pasquale** (Artist)
*Pasquale's Angel* - Paul J. McAuley   *f*   3714

**Passepout** (Actor)
*The Mage in the Iron Mask* - Brian
   Thomsen   *f*   5458

**Passman, Breyten** (Human)
*River of Dust* - Alexander Jablokov   *s*   2840

**Passman, Hektor** (Political Figure)
*River of Dust* - Alexander Jablokov   *s*   2840

**Pati** (Deity; Ruler)
*Delta City* - Felicity Savage   *f*   4849

**Patience** (Spirit)
*A Witch Across Time* - Gilbert B. Cross   *f*   1272

**Patou, Lucy** (Doctor)
*Omega* - Patrick Lynch   *h*   3577

**Patricia** (Model)
*The Man Upstairs* - T.L. Parkinson   *h*   4248

**Patrick** (Friend)
*The Secret of the Indian* - Lynne Reid Banks   *f*   332

**Patrick, Uncle** (Computer Expert)
*Under Siege* - Elisabeth Mace   *f*   3587

**Patswami** (Cult Member)
*Button Bright* - Michael Kurland   *h*   3251

**Patterson, Gil** (Warrior; Scholar)
*Mother of Winter* - Barbara Hambly   *f*   2506

**Patterson, Lizzie** (Teenager)
*Where the Towers Pierce the Sky* - Marie D.
   Goodwin   *f*   2272

**Patterson, Red** (Doctor)
*Skyscape* - Michael Cadnum   *h*   814

**Patton, Dan** (Businessman)
*Dangerous Nature* - T.J. Kirby   h   3152

**Patton, Hallie** (Model)
*Private Demons* - Robert Masello   h   3660

**Paul** (Religious)
*The Twelfth Child* - Raymond Van Over   h   5538

**Pauley, Nigel** (Military Personnel)
*Limbo Search* - Parke Godwin   s   2245

**Paulin** (Religious)
*King Javan's Year* - Katherine Kurtz   f   3258

**Pauling, Addy** (Child)
*Lullaby* - Diane Guest   h   2455

**Pauling, Judd** (Artist; Spouse)
*Lullaby* - Diane Guest   h   2455

**Pavek of Urik** (Religious; Adventurer)
*The Brazen Gambit* - Lynn Abbey   f   13
*Cinnabar Shadows* - Lynn Abbey   f   15

**Pawluk, Ilonka** (Teenager; Patient)
*The Midnight Club* - Christopher Pike   h   4329

**Payne** (Police Officer)
*Running Wild* - J.G. Ballard   h   320

**Payne, Deliverance "Del"** (Waiter/Waitress)
*Ticktock* - Dean R. Koontz   h   3217

**Peach-Frog-At-Twilight** (Alien; Religious)
*Jade Darcy and the Zen Pirates* - Stephen
    Goldin   s   2260

**Pearce, Sarah** (Child; Computer Expert)
*The Ghost Inside the Monitor* - Margaret J.
    Anderson   f   122

**Pearl, Michael** (Doctor; Administrator)
*The Beyond* - Barry Harrington   h   2556

**Pearse, Stephen** (Scientist)
*The Blood Artists* - Chuck Hogan   h   2720

**Pec-Pec** (Magician; Religious)
*The Dream Vessel* - Jeff Bredenberg   s   664

**Peebles** (Spouse)
*My Stepfather Shrank!* - Barbara Dillon   s   1558

**Peekner** (Doctor)
*Dead in the West* - Joe R. Lansdale   h   3325

**Peeve** (Animal; Companion)
*Black Unicorn* - Tanith Lee   f   3404
*Gold Unicorn* - Tanith Lee   f   3410
*Red Unicorn* - Tanith Lee   f   3414

**Peg** (Scientist; Time Traveler)
*The Virgin and the Dinosaur* - R. Garcia y
    Robertson   s   2122

**Pel of House Yendi** (Nobleman)
*Five Hundred Years After* - Steven Brust   f   742

**Pelagia, Iolanthe "Io"** (Royalty)
*City of Diamond* - Jane Emerson   s   1807

**Peldyrin, Alix** (Fiance(e))
*Stranger at the Wedding* - Barbara Hambly   f   2509

**Peldyrin, Kyra** (Wizard)
*Stranger at the Wedding* - Barbara Hambly   f   2509

**Pelicanos, Yosh** (Agent)
*Distraction* - Bruce Sterling   s   5256

**Pellaz** (Mutant; Psychic)
*The Enchantments of Flesh and Spirit* - Storm
    Constantine   s   1141

**Pelleas** (Telepath; Companion)
*In the Shadow of the Oak King* - Courtway
    Jones   f   2939

**Pellia** (Mythical Creature; Telepath)
*The Unicorn Solution* - John Lee   f   3400

**Pellior, Arioso** (Royalty)
*Song for the Basilisk* - Patricia A. McKillip   f   3841

**Pelucir, Talis** (Royalty; Heir)
*The Book of Atrix Wolfe* - Patricia A.
    McKillip   f   3838

**Pemberton, Martin** (Journalist)
*The Waterworks* - E.L. Doctorow   s   1564

**Pembun, Jawj Pero** (Government Official)
*Rule Golden and Double Meaning* - Damon
    Knight   s   3189

**Penarvon, Arthur** (Royalty)
*The Oak Above the Kings: A Book of the Keltiad* -
    Patricia Kennealy   s   3058

**Pendaron, Telerini** (Apprentice; Wizard)
*The Moon in Hiding* - Teresa Edgerton   f   1745

**Pendeers, Kristine** (Professor; Researcher)
*Songs of Earth and Power* - Greg Bear   f   424

**Pendergast, George Irving** (Scientist)
*Children of the End* - Mark A. Clements   h   1084

**Pendragon, Arthor** (Ruler)
*The Wolf and the Crown* - A.A. Attanasio   f   273

**Pendragon, Arthur** (Ruler)
*Arthur* - Stephen R. Lawhead   f   3352
*Changer* - Jane M. Lindskold   f   3474

**Pendragon, Arthur** (Royalty; Leader)
*The Kingmaking* - Helen Hollick   f   2745

**Pendragon, Arthur** (Royalty)
*Merlin and the Dragons* - Jane Yolen   f   6036

**Pendragon, Arthur** (Royalty; Leader)
*Pendragon's Banner* - Helen Hollick   f   2746

**Pendragon, Arthur** (Child; Heir)
*The Saxon Shore* - Jack Whyte   f   5793

**Pendragon, Uther** (Leader; Warrior)
*The Dragon and the Unicorn* - A.A.
    Attanasio   f   266

**Pendragon, Uther** (Warrior)
*The Eagles' Brood* - Jack Whyte   f   5792

**Pendrake, Matthew** (Secretary; Telepath)
*Mind Slayer* - Kevin D. Randle   s   4469

**Pendreic, Arthur "Artos"** (Ruler)
*The Hedge of Mist* - Patricia Kennealy-
    Morrison   s   3062

**Pendreic, Gweniver** (Royalty)
*The Oak Above the Kings: A Book of the Keltiad* -
    Patricia Kennealy   s   3058

**Pendreic, Morguenna** (Royalty; Spouse)
*The Hedge of Mist* - Patricia Kennealy-
    Morrison   s   3062

**Penetanguishene** (Government Official)
*The Queen's Squadron* - R.M. Meluch   s   3874

**Penn, Martin** (Tourist; Doctor)
*Testament* - Valerie J. Freireich   s   2051

**Penn, Simon** (Librarian)
*Blood of the Covenant* - Brent Monahan   h   3954
*The Book of Common Dread* - Brent
    Monahan   h   3955

**Pennant, Rebecca** (Musician)
*The Judas Glass* - Michael Cadnum   h   812

**Penne, Dyann** (Artisan)
*The Gift of the Gorboduc Vandal* - Paul O.
    Williams   s   5821

**Penninger, Greta** (Doctor)
*Distraction* - Bruce Sterling   s   5256

**Pennyman** (Fortune Hunter)
*The Last Coin* - James P. Blaylock   f   519

**Pentacoste** (Noblewoman)
*Better in the Dark* - Chelsea Quinn Yarbro   h   6011

**Penthesilea** (Warrior; Foundling)
*The Amazon Chronicles* - Jane E.M.
    Robinson   f   4627

**Penward, Darren** (Nobleman; Criminal)
*Carnosaur* - Harry Adam Knight   s   3191

**Penward, Jan** (Noblewoman)
*Carnosaur* - Harry Adam Knight   s   3191

**Penz** (Werewolf)
*Conan the Formidable* - Steve Perry   f   4293

**Pepon, Buko** (Revolutionary; Ruler)
*Paradise: A Chronicle of a Distant World* - Mike
    Resnick   s   4552

**Pepper** (Animal)
*The House on the Borderland* - William Hope
    Hodgson   h   2711

**Pepper, Jack** (Advertising)
*Angel Kiss* - Kelley Wilde   h   5800

**Percinet** (Mythical Creature; Royalty)
*Child of Faerie, Child of Earth* - Josepha
    Sherman   f   4985

**Percy, Anne** (Noblewoman)
*The Spiral Dance* - R. Garcia y Robertson   f   2121

**Peregrine** (Spirit)
*The Thread That Binds the Bones* - Nina Kiriki
    Hoffman   f   2717

**Perez, Anna** (Diplomat; Scientist)
*Ring of Swords* - Eleanor Arnason   s   210

**Perez, Magdalena** (Linguist; Abuse Victim)
*Voices of Chaos* - A.C. Crispin   s   1266

**Perez, Theresa "Terry"** (Journalist)
*Echoes of the Well of Souls* - Jack L.
    Chalker   s   953

**Perez, Theresa "Terry"** (Journalist; Handicapped)
*Shadow of the Well of Souls* - Jack L.
    Chalker   s   961

**Performer** (Entertainer; Serial Killer)
*Puppet Master* - Barry T. Hawkins   h   2632

**Perholt, Gillian** (Scholar)
*The Djinn in the Nightingale's Eye* - A.S.
    Byatt   f   794

**Perin, Antonio "Tony"** (Revolutionary; Leader)
*Full Tide of Night* - J.R. Dunn   s   1695

**Perkins, Blair** (Professor; Veterinarian)
*Bats* - William W. Johnstone   h   2926

**Perlman, William** (Doctor)
*Afterage* - Yvonne Navarro   h   4072

**Perne, Alisa** (Vampire)
*The Last Vampire* - Christopher Pike   h   4328

**Perrin, Michael** (Adventurer)
*Songs of Earth and Power* - Greg Bear   f   424

**Perry, Brenda** (Journalist; Businesswoman)
*The Wishing Well* - Charles de Lint   f   1441

**Perry, Eleanor** (Professor)
*Fires of Eden* - Dan Simmons   h   5053

**Perry, Harlan** (Maintenance Worker)
*The Death Crystal* - J. Edward Ames   h   91

**Perry, Jerrica** (Journalist)
*The Bighead* - Edward Lee   h   3387

**Perry, Jon** (Scientist)
*Cold as Ice* - Charles Sheffield   s   4950

**Perry, Max** (Government Official)
*Summertide* - Charles Sheffield   s   4965

**Persyvaunce** (Wizard)
*Red Wizard* - Nancy Springer   f   5182

**Peru, Mattie** (Streetperson)
*Breeder* - Douglas Clegg   h   1076

**Pesca, Walter** (Linguist; Military Personnel)
*Dreadnought* - Thorarinn Gunnarsson   s   2464

**Pessoa, Manoel** (Religious)
*God's Fires* - Patricia Anthony   s   159

**Petalo, Vadoma** (Gypsy)
*Dead Time* - Richard Lee Byers   *h*   796

**Petaybee** (Alien)
*Power Play* - Anne McCaffrey   *s*   3744

**Peter** (Businessman; Step-Parent)
*Bones* - Joyce Thompson   *h*   5453

**Peter** (Computer Expert; Technician)
*Ecstasy Club* - Douglas Rushkoff   *s*   4732

**Peters, George** (Police Officer)
*Offspring* - Jack Ketchum   *h*   3092

**Petersen, Homer "Hopfrog"** (Carpenter)
*The Children's Hour* - Douglas Clegg   *h*   1077

**Petersen, Tad** (Child)
*The Children's Hour* - Douglas Clegg   *h*   1077

**Petie** (Thief)
*The Red King* - Victor Kelleher   *f*   3043

**Petiron** (Musician; Composer)
*The Masterharper of Pern* - Anne
   McCaffrey   *s*   3739

**Petrillo, Val** (Traveler)
*The Safety of Unknown Cities* - Lucy
   Taylor   *h*   5414

**Petrus** (Mythical Creature; Warrior)
*Spiritride* - Mark Shepherd   *f*   4981

**Pettis** (Military Personnel; Astronaut)
*Moonbane* - Al Sarrantonio   *s*   4831

**Petway, Boomer** (Mechanic; Artist)
*Skinny Legs and All* - Tom Robbins   *f*   4607

**Pfahl, Susan** (Student)
*Agyar* - Steven Brust   *f*   738

**Phaeton** (Angel)
*Planar Powers* - J. Robert King   *f*   3122

**Phan, Gi Minh** (Baker)
*Ticktock* - Dean R. Koontz   *h*   3217

**Phan, Tommy** (Writer)
*Ticktock* - Dean R. Koontz   *h*   3217

**Phanes** (Mythical Creature)
*Making Love* - Melanie Tem   *h*   5422

**Pharbeque, Riscky "Hex DEF6"** (Computer Expert;
   Criminal)
*The Hacker and the Ants* - Rudy Rucker   *s*   4704

**Phelan, Andrew** (Researcher)
*The Trail of Cthulhu* - August Derleth   *h*   1497

**Philip of Macedon** (Historical Figure; Leader)
*Lion of Macedon* - David Gemmell   *f*   2189

**Philip of Macedon** (Ruler; Historical Figure)
*Orion and the Conqueror* - Ben Bova   *s*   590

**Philipe** (Terrorist)
*The Ignored* - Bentley Little   *h*   3493

**Philippe** (Military Personnel)
*Canal Dreams* - Iain M. Banks   *s*   323

**Philippe, Marley** (Detective—Private)
*Deus X* - Norman Spinrad   *s*   5171

**Philips, Jethro** (Time Traveler)
*Mercy's Mill* - Betty Levin   *f*   3444

**Phillips, Mark** (Military Personnel; Warrior)
*The Crystal Sorcerers* - William R.
   Forstchen   *f*   1979

**Phillips, Randa** (Journalist)
*Dark Debts* - Karen Hall   *h*   2494

**Phillips, Triune Adjudicator** (Judge)
*Tangled Webs* - Steve Mudd   *s*   4044

**Phillips, Warren** (Doctor)
*Darkness* - John Saul   *h*   4840

**Phineas** (Military Personnel)
*Daughter of Prophecy* - Anne Kelleher Bush   *f*   788

**Phniangsak, Sam** (Religious)
*Paths to Otherwhere* - James P. Hogan   *s*   2728

**Phoe, Sam** (Government Official; Homosexual)
*Key West 2720 A.D.* - William Eakins   *s*   1720

**Phoenix, Simon** (Criminal; Murderer)
*Demolition Man* - Richard Osborne   *s*   4229

**Phostis** (Heir; Captive)
*Krispos the Emperor* - Harry Turtledove   *f*   5508

**Phousita** (Streetperson; Genetically Altered Being)
*The Bohr Maker* - Linda Nagata   *s*   4064

**Phreak** (Computer Expert; Criminal)
*Killobyte* - Piers Anthony   *f*   179

**Phule, Willard** (Military Personnel)
*Phule's Company* - Robert Asprin   *s*   260
*Phule's Paradise* - Robert Asprin   *s*   261

**Picard, Jean-Luc** (Spaceship Captain; Military
   Personnel)
*All Good Things. . .* - Michael Jan Friedman   *s*   2061

**Picard, Jean-Luc** (Spaceship Captain)
*Avenger* - William Shatner   *s*   4928

**Picard, Jean-Luc** (Spaceship Captain; Military
   Personnel)
*Balance of Power* - Dafydd ab Hugh   *s*   7
*A Call to Darkness* - Michael Jan Friedman   *s*   2062
*Chains of Command* - Bill McCay   *s*   3767
*Crossover* - Michael Jan Friedman   *s*   2063
*Dark Mirror* - Diane Duane   *s*   1658
*Debtors' Planet* - William R. Thompson   *s*   5457
*The Devil's Heart* - Carmen Carter   *s*   922
*Dragon's Honor* - Kij Johnson   *s*   2922
*Federation* - Judith Reeves-Stevens   *s*   4511
*Guises of the Mind* - Rebecca Neason   *s*   4081

**Picard, Jean-Luc** (Spaceship Captain)
*Insurrection* - J.M. Dillard   *s*   1554
*Intellivore* - Diane Duane   *s*   1663

**Picard, Jean-Luc** (Spaceship Captain; Military
   Personnel)
*Kahless* - Michael Jan Friedman   *s*   2065
*The Last Stand* - Brad Ferguson   *s*   1923
*Q-in-Law* - Peter David   *s*   1384

**Picard, Jean-Luc** (Spaceship Captain)
*Q-Space* - Greg Cox   *s*   1228

**Picard, Jean-Luc** (Spaceship Captain; Military
   Personnel)
*Q-Squared* - Peter David   *s*   1385
*Q-Zone* - Greg Cox   *s*   1229
*Relics* - Michael Jan Friedman   *s*   2066
*Requiem* - Michael Jan Friedman   *s*   2067
*The Return* - William Shatner   *s*   4933
*Reunion* - Michael Jan Friedman   *s*   2068

**Picard, Jean-Luc** (Spaceship Captain)
*Ship of the Line* - Diane Carey   *s*   904

**Picard, Jean-Luc** (Spaceship Captain; Military
   Personnel)
*The Soldiers of Fear* - Dean Wesley Smith   *s*   5115

**Picard, Jean-Luc** (Spaceship Captain)
*Spectre* - William Shatner   *s*   4934

**Picard, Jean-Luc** (Spaceship Captain; Military
   Personnel)
*Vendetta* - Peter David   *s*   1389

**Pickard, Joe** (Political Figure)
*Echoes* - Jackie Hyman   *h*   2818

**Picket** (Immortal; Spirit)
*Darwinia* - Robert Charles Wilson   *s*   5906

**Pickhard, Jean-Alex** (Spaceship Captain)
*Treks Not Taken: What if Stephen King, Anne Rice,
   Bret Easton Ellis, and Other Literary Greats Had
   Written Episodes of Star Trek: The Next
   Generation?* - Steven R. Boyett   *s*   607

**Pidgely, Dylan** (Artist; Psychic)
*The Juniper Game* - Sherryl Jordan   *f*   2992

**Pie 'oh' Pah** (Mythical Creature)
*Imajica* - Clive Barker   *h*   343

**Pierce** (Vampire)
*Human Resources* - Floyd Kemske   *h*   3057

**Pierce, Melinda** (Journalist)
*Goon* - Edward Lee   *h*   3392

**Pierce, Millard Fillmore** (Administrator)
*The Red Tape War* - Jack L. Chalker   *s*   959

**Piero** (Prisoner; Leader)
*Outpost* - Scott Mackay   *s*   3597

**Pierson, Ellen** (Artist; Lesbian)
*Temporary Agency* - Rachel Pollack   *f*   4360

**Pike, Christopher** (Spaceship Captain)
*The Rift* - Peter David   *s*   1386

**Pike, Eli** (Photojournalist)
*The Ice Beast* - Frank A. Javor   *s*   2881

**Pike, Eli** (Photographer; Military Personnel)
*The Rim-World Legacy and Beyond* - Frank A.
   Javor   *s*   2882

**Pilgrim, Julian** (Magician)
*Ghostlight* - Marion Zimmer Bradley   *f*   634

**Pinch "Janol"** (Thief; Orphan)
*King Pinch* - David Cook   *f*   1146

**Pinchot, Arlen** (Housewife)
*The Basement* - Bari Wood   *h*   5961

**Pincus, Laurie** (Computer Expert)
*The Sherwood Game* - Esther Friesner   *s*   2082

**Pine, Leonard** (Martial Arts Expert)
*Mucho Mojo* - Joe R. Lansdale   *h*   3330
*Savage Season* - Joe R. Lansdale   *h*   3332

**Pinheiro, Berenice** (Healer; Herbalist)
*God's Fires* - Patricia Anthony   *s*   159

**Pink** (Farmer; Teenager)
*Nanoware Time/The Persistence of Vision* - Ian
   Watson   *s*   5638

**Pinkes, Clayton** (Religious)
*Prophets for the End of Time* - Marcos
   Donnelly   *f*   1577

**Pinky** (Time Traveler; Administrator)
*Mr. Was* - Pete Hautman   *s*   2614

**Pinscher** (Animal)
*Pet Store* - M.T. Coffin   *h*   1097

**Pinvey** (Revolutionary)
*Hall of Whispers* - Mike Jefferies   *f*   2884

**Piper, Rick** (Journalist)
*Panic* - Chris Curry   *h*   1295

**Pira, Cleo** (Student)
*Lives of the Monster Dogs* - Kirsten Bakis   *s*   305

**Pirelli, Peter** (Ranger)
*Swamp* - Peter Tremayne   *h*   5483

**Pirelli, Vince** (Spaceman; Warrior)
*Warlords of Jupiter* - William H. Keith Jr.   *s*   3036

**Pitt, Janus** (Ruler)
*Nemesis* - Isaac Asimov   *s*   247

**Pixie, Ephram** (Drifter)
*Wetbones* - John Shirley   *h*   5010

**Piyolss, Faan Korispais** (Orphan; Agent)
*Wild Magic* - Jo Clayton   *f*   1072

**Pjerin** (Nobleman)
*Sing the Four Quarters* - Tanya Huff   *f*   2799

**Plagier, Anton** (Criminal)
*The Rim-World Legacy and Beyond* - Frank A.
   Javor   *s*   2882

**Plase, Janice** (Police Officer)
*Kent Montana and the Reasonably Invisible Man* -
Lionel Fenn  s  1919

**Platho, Aivlys** (Apprentice; Magician)
*Clock Strikes Sword* - Ian Hammell  f  2529

**Platho, Endimin** (Artisan; Magician)
*Clock Strikes Sword* - Ian Hammell  f  2529

**Platt, Maxwell** (Writer)
*Portrait of the Psychopath as a Young Woman* -
Edward Lee  h  3395

**Plon** (Police Officer)
*The Prisoner Within* - Donald E. McQuinn  s  3861

**Plume, Jerry** (Doctor)
*Passive Intruder* - Michael Upchurch  h  5530

**Plumtree, Janis** (Mentally Ill Person)
*Earthquake Weather* - Tim Powers  f  4382

**Podlowski, Eric** (Martial Arts Expert; Teacher)
*Brothers of the Dragon* - Robin Wayne
Bailey  f  286

**Podlowski, Eric** (Martial Arts Expert; Leader)
*Flames of the Dragon* - Robin Wayne Bailey  f  287

**Podlowski, Robert** (Martial Arts Expert; Waiter/
Waitress)
*Brothers of the Dragon* - Robin Wayne
Bailey  f  286

**Podlowski, Robert** (Martial Arts Expert; Writer)
*Flames of the Dragon* - Robin Wayne Bailey  f  287

**Poduano, Dominic** (Monster)
*Shapes* - Steve Vance  h  5552

**Poe, Amanda** (Detective)
*The Virginia Ghost Murders* - Leslie Raymond
Sachs  h  4778

**Poe, Edgar Allan** (Writer; Historical Figure)
*The Bloody Red Baron* - Kim Newman  h  4097
*The Lighthouse at the End of the World* - Stephen
Marlowe  h  3631
*Madeline: After the Fall of Usher* - Marie
Kiraly  h  3150

**Poe, Jared** (Photographer)
*The Lazarus Heart* - Poppy Z. Brite  h  696

**Poe, John Charles** (Journalist)
*The Black Cat* - Robert Poe  h  4344
*Return to the House of Usher* - Robert Poe  h  4345

**Poggs, Hugo** (Scientist)
*Portent* - James Herbert  h  2670

**Pohaku, Annie** (Journalist)
*Mars Underground* - William Hartmann  s  2584

**Poke, Mica** (Religious)
*Night Prayers* - P.D. Cacek  h  803

**Poker, Susan** (Real Estate Agent)
*The Hacker and the Ants* - Rudy Rucker  s  4704

**Pol** (Royalty; Ruler)
*The Dragon Token* - Melanie Rawn  f  4485

**Pol** (Royalty; Magician)
*Skybowl* - Melanie Rawn  f  4490

**Pol** (Royalty)
*Sunrunner's Fire* - Melanie Rawn  f  4493

**Polgara** (Sorceress; Adventurer)
*Polgara the Sorceress* - David Eddings  f  1734

**Polijn** (Servant; Minstrel)
*The Sure Death of a Mouse* - Dan Crawford  f  1250

**Polijn** (Child; Apprentice; Minstrel)
*A Wild Dog and Lone* - Dan Crawford  f  1251

**Polk, Veronica** (Artist)
*Incubi* - Edward Lee  h  3394

**Pollard, Ben** (Pilot; Prospector)
*Heavy Time* - C.J. Cherryh  s  995

**Pollard, Ben** (Pilot)
*Hellburner* - C.J. Cherryh  s  996

**Polmaire** (Political Figure)
*Deepwater Dreams* - Sydney J. Van Scyoc  s  5541

**Polo, Marco** (Historical Figure; Leader)
*If at Faust You Don't Succeed* - Roger
Zelazny  f  6070

**Polyta** (Mythical Creature; Leader)
*Under the Healing Sign* - Nick O'Donohoe  f  4198

**Pomegranate** (Servant; Human)
*Bronze Mirror* - Jeanne Larsen  f  3338

**Pomeroy, Bernard** (Businessman)
*Night Relics* - James P. Blaylock  h  521

**Ponce, Armando** (Religious)
*Dead of Night* - Alex Abella  h  20

**Pond, Susan** (Receptionist)
*Passive Intruder* - Michael Upchurch  h  5530

**Pong, Mustapha** (Pirate; Kidnapper)
*McCade's Bounty* - William C. Dietz  s  1550

**Pooch** (Animal)
*Carmen Dog* - Carol Emshwiller  f  1817

**Pook** (Streetperson; Kidnapper)
*Voices of Hope* - David Feintuch  s  1903

**Poole** (Alien)
*Lightwing* - Tara K. Harper  s  2551

**Poole, Frank** (Astronaut)
*3001: The Final Odyssey* - Arthur C.
Clarke  s  1053

**Poole, Michael** (Doctor; Veteran)
*Koko* - Peter Straub  h  5328

**Poole, Michael** (Scientist)
*Timelike Infinity* - Stephen Baxter  s  404

**Poons, Windle** (Wizard; Reanimated Dead)
*Reaper Man* - Terry Pratchett  f  4399

**Pop** (Teenager)
*Baby Be-Bop* - Francesca Lia Block  f  545

**Popcorn, Selwyn** (Director)
*Brand New Cherry Flavor* - Todd Grimson  h  2448

**Pope, Eric** (Cyborg)
*Black Snow Days* - Claudia O'Keefe  s  4205

**Pope, Francisco** (Gang Member)
*Cybernetic Jungle* - S.N. Lewitt  s  3449

**Pope, Justin** (Composer; Thief)
*Mixed Doubles* - Daniel Da Cruz  s  1305

**Popescu, Liliana** (Lawyer)
*The Lost* - Jonathan Aycliffe  h  279

**Popman, Walker** (Photographer)
*Passive Intruder* - Michael Upchurch  h  5530

**Popsy** (Child; Runaway)
*Shadow Walkers* - Nina Romberg  h  4663

**Porlock, Leona** (Spacewoman)
*Rainbow Man* - M.J. Engh  s  1824

**Porsena, L. Robert** (Doctor)
*Red Orc's Rage* - Philip Jose Farmer  f  1873

**Portaris, Anne** (Inventor; Spacewoman)
*Arrow From Earth* - F.M. Busby  s  782

**Porter, Aloysius Graham** (Military Personnel)
*The Sand Dwellers* - Adam Niswander  h  4112

**Porter, Dylan** (Child)
*Wes Craven's New Nightmare* - David
Bergantino  h  460

**Porter, Rand** (Computer Expert; Spouse)
*Starmind* - Spider Robinson  s  4642

**Portland, Elaine** (Young Woman)
*Blood and Roses* - Sharon Bainbridge  h  292

**Portlock, Ben** (Police Officer)
*Dumford Blood* - S.K. Epperson  h  1829

**Portman, William T. "Orde"** (Religious; Mutant)
*Blue Light* - Walter Mosley  s  4042

**Poseen-Ka** (Alien; Military Personnel)
*The Final Battle* - William C. Dietz  s  1546

**Potter, Curt** (Student)
*Night Prophets* - Paul F. Olson  h  4213

**Potter, Evelyn Sylvia** (Farmer; Spouse)
*Cloven Hooves* - Megan Lindholm  f  3470

**Potter, Harry** (Student)
*Harry Potter and the Sorcerer's Stone* - J.K.
Rowling  f  4700

**Potter, Jack** (Spy; Researcher)
*Signal to Noise* - Eric S. Nylund  s  4179

**Potter, Prat'han** (Revolutionary; Warrior)
*Future Indefinite* - Dave Duncan  f  1678

**Potts, Edward "Potty"** (Teacher)
*The Red-Eared Ghosts* - Vivian Alcock  f  53

**Poubelle, Laurence** (Businessman)
*Kings of the High Frontier* - Victor Koman  s  3199

**Powderdry, Lars** (Engineer)
*The Zap Gun* - Philip K. Dick  s  1523

**Powell, Adrian** (Government Official)
*Indiana Jones and the Dance of the Giants* - Rob
MacGregor  f  3588

**Powell, Kim** (Student)
*Looker* - Jorge Saralegui  h  4820

**Powell, Lincoln** (Psychic; Police Officer)
*The Demolished Man* - Alfred Bester  s  476

**Powell, Richard** (Teacher)
*The Bell Witch: An American Haunting* - Brent
Monahan  h  3953

**Power, Lulu "Flower"** (Dancer)
*Genesis* - Charles L. Grant  h  2308

**Powers, Richard** (Teacher; Writer)
*Galatea 2.2* - Richard M. Powers  s  4381

**Powl** (Teacher)
*Lens of the World* - R.A. MacAvoy  f  3582

**Powys, Joe M.** (Writer)
*Curfew* - Phil Rickman  h  4587

**Pr. Spinner** (Artificial Intelligence; Computer Expert)
*Cyberweb* - Lisa Mason  s  3662

**Prahotep** (Adventurer)
*The Land of Gold* - Gillian Bradshaw  f  658

**Praisegood, William R.** (Doctor)
*Blood and Roses* - Sharon Bainbridge  h  292

**Prawdzik, Ed** (Nurse)
*Night Sounds* - Warner Lee  h  3415

**Precieux, Pierre** (Scientist)
*The Dechronization of Sam Magruder* - George
Gaylord Simpson  s  5067

**Prefect, Ford** (Writer; Alien)
*The Illustrated Hitchhiker's Guide to the Galaxy* -
Douglas Adams  s  29
*Mostly Harmless* - Douglas Adams  s  31

**Prejean, Lani** (Police Officer)
*Night Mask* - William W. Johnstone  h  2931

**Prentice, Clara** (Teenager; Pilot)
*Wildside* - Steven Gould  s  2291

**Prentice, Tom** (Writer)
*Wetbones* - John Shirley  h  5010

**Preposteror, Beelzebub** (Sorcerer)
*The Night of Wishes: Or, The
Satanarchaeolidealcohellish Notion Potion* - Michael
Ende  f  1821

**Prescott, Elaine** (Journalist)
*Soul Snatchers* - Michael Cecilione   h   947

**Prescott, George** (Scientist; Student)
*Supernova* - Roger MacBride Allen   s   82

**Presley, Elvis** (Musician; Historical Figure)
*Armageddon: The Musical* - Robert Rankin   s   4473
*Bone Music* - Alan Rodgers   h   4646

**Presley, Elvis** (Lawman; Historical Figure)
*Comeback Tour: The Sky Belongs to the Stars* - Jack
   Yeovil   s   6020

**Presley, Elvis** (Musician; Historical Figure)
*Elvis Rising: Stories on the King* - Kay
   Sloan   f   5089

**Presley, Elvis** (Musician; Religious)
*Elvissey* - Jack Womack   s   5957

**Presley, Elvis** (Musician; Historical Figure)
*The King Is Dead: Tales of Elvis Post Mortem* - Paul
   M. Sammon   h   4810

**Presteign** (Businessman)
*The Stars My Destination* - Alfred Bester   s   478

**Presteign, Olivia** (Handicapped; Businesswoman)
*The Stars My Destination* - Alfred Bester   s   478

**Prestimion** (Royalty)
*Sorcerers of Majipoor* - Robert Silverberg   s   5041

**Preston, Carl** (Agent)
*Ghost Dancers* - Brian Craig   s   1238

**Preston, Natalie** (Photographer)
*Carrion Comfort* - Dan Simmons   h   5049

**Prettiance "Pretty"** (Teenager)
*Strange Deliverance* - Mary Brown   s   728

**Price, Addie** (Astrologer)
*The President's Astrologer* - Barbara
   Shafferman   f   4926

**Price, Bobby** (Criminal)
*Savant* - Rex Miller   h   3901

**Price, Joshua** (Military Personnel)
*Galactic MI* - Kevin D. Randle   s   4467

**Price, Timothy** (Businessman)
*American Psycho* - Brett Easton Ellis   h   1777

**Prien, Rube** (Military Personnel; Researcher)
*From Time to Time* - Jack Finney   s   1941

**Priestley, Amy** (Teenager)
*Nazareth Hill* - Ramsey Campbell   h   861

**Priestley, Oswald** (Insurance Agent)
*Nazareth Hill* - Ramsey Campbell   h   861

**Prilicla** (Alien; Psychic)
*The Galactic Gourmet* - James White   s   5778
*Mind Changer* - James White   s   5780

**Primavera** (Android; Murderer)
*Dead Girls* - Richard Calder   s   837

**Primavera** (Singer)
*Primavera* - Francesca Lia Block   f   551

**Primer** (Government Official)
*The Gaia Websters* - Kim Antieau   s   198

**Prince, Gabriel** (Time Traveler; Writer)
*Time on My Hands* - Peter Delacorte   s   1480

**Prince, Hugo** (Religious)
*The Death Prayer* - David Bowker   h   602

**Prince, Mick** (Writer; Murderer)
*Quoth the Crow* - David Bischoff   h   494

**Princess** (Spouse; Royalty)
*A Remembrance for Kedrigern* - John
   Morressy   f   4014

**Priscian** (Businesswoman; Heiress)
*Beggar's Banquet* - Daniel Hood   f   2756

**Pritchard, Jen** (Young Woman)
*The New Neighbor* - Ray Garton   h   2154

**Proctor, Ethan** (Businessman)
*Genesis* - Charles L. Grant   h   2308

**Proctor, Ottoken** (Economist; Criminal)
*Krokodil Tears* - Jack Yeovil   f   6023

**Proctor, Simon** (Cult Member)
*Dying Breath* - Jon A. Harrald   h   2555

**Profitt, Dennis** (Businessman; Explorer)
*Star Precinct* - Kevin D. Randle   s   4470

**Prokash, Magda** (Witch)
*Blood Sabbath* - Leigh Clark   h   1048

**Promise** (Dancer; Spouse)
*Firedance* - Steven Barnes   s   360

**Promise** (Dancer)
*Gorgon Child* - Steven Barnes   s   361

**Prosky, Ronald** (Journalist)
*The New Neighbor* - Ray Garton   h   2154

**Prosper** (Nobleman)
*The Shining Company* - Rosemary Sutcliff   f   5359

**Prospero** (Robot)
*Inferno* - Roger MacBride Allen   s   78

**Prospero** (Sorcerer; Royalty)
*The Price of Blood and Honor* - Elizabeth
   Willey   f   5811
*A Sorcerer and a Gentleman* - Elizabeth
   Willey   f   5812
*The Well-Favored Man: The Tale of the Sorcerer's
   Nephew* - Elizabeth Willey   f   5813

**Protagonist, Hiro** (Computer Expert; Martial Arts
   Expert)
*Snow Crash* - Neal Stephenson   s   5254

**Protarus, Iraj** (Royalty; Reanimated Dead)
*Wolves of the Gods* - Allan Cole   f   1111

**Proteus** (Psychic)
*Exit to Reality* - Edith Forbes   s   1968

**Prothore, Alfred** (Political Figure)
*The Jekyll Legacy* - Robert Bloch   h   535

**Prowier, Isaac** (Religious)
*Soul Snatchers* - Michael Cecilione   h   947

**Prowl Captain** (Alien; Spaceship Captain)
*A Darker Geometry* - Mark O. Martin   s   3649

**Prtglm** (Alien)
*Lyon's Pride* - Anne McCaffrey   s   3738

**Pruet, Maxine** (Organized Crime Figure;
   Businesswoman)
*Phule's Paradise* - Robert Asprin   s   261

**Pruett, Robin** (Child)
*After Sundown* - Randall Boyll   h   609

**Pruitt, Pam** (Scientist)
*Time, Like an Ever-Rolling Stream* - Judith
   Moffett   s   3944

**Psamathos** (Wizard)
*Roverandom* - J.R.R. Tolkien   f   5479

**Psellus, Micheal** (Scholar)
*Shards of Empire* - Susan Shwartz   f   5017

**Psycho, Jenny** (Revolutionary; Psychic)
*Deathstalker War* - Simon R. Green   s   2366

**Puck** (Demon)
*The Devil and Dan Cooley* - Holly Lisle   f   3480

**Puckett, Max** (Farmer)
*Rama Revealed* - Arthur C. Clarke   s   1059

**Puerta, Raul** (Psychologist)
*The Between* - Tannarive Due   h   1669

**Pukai, Pualeiokekai** (Genetically Altered Being)
*Reefsong* - Carol Severance   s   4923

**Pulaski, Toya** (Scientist; Spy)
*Converse and Conflict* - L. Neil Smith   s   5130

**Pulivok, Akushtina "Tina" Santis** (Waiter/Waitress;
   Psychic)
*Catch the Lightning* - Catherine Asaro   s   218

**Pullen, Faith** (Student)
*University* - Bentley Little   h   3499

**Pulon** (Alien; Sidekick)
*Ganwold's Child* - Diann Thornley   s   5467

**Purcell, Harry** (Political Figure)
*Worlds Enough and Time* - Joe Haldeman   s   2491

**Purcell, Joe** (Child)
*The Butcher Boy* - Patrick McCabe   h   3716

**Purdoe, Tim** (Doctor)
*The Great Wheel* - Ian R. MacLeod   s   3599

**Purdue, Frederick** (Worker)
*The Eyes of the Beast* - Steve Harris   h   2565

**Putakin, Yuri** (Computer Expert; Spaceman)
*Orion's Dagger* - P.K. McAllister   s   3708

**Puzzle Solver** (Alien; Detective)
*Alien Blues* - Lynn S. Hightower   s   2682

**Pyramors** (Political Figure; Military Personnel)
*Warlord of Heaven* - Adrian Cole   f   1102

**Pyrrhos** (Religious)
*Krispos Rising* - Harry Turtledove   f   5507


# Q

**Q** (Alien)
*All Good Things. . .* - Michael Jan Friedman   s   2061
*Q-in-Law* - Peter David   s   1384

**Q** (Immortal; Alien)
*Q-Space* - Greg Cox   s   1228

**Q** (Alien)
*Q-Squared* - Peter David   s   1385

**Q** (Immortal; Alien)
*Q-Zone* - Greg Cox   s   1229

**Qian** (Foreman)
*China Mountain Zhang* - Maureen F.
   McHugh   s   3817

**Qian, San-xiang** (Girlfriend)
*China Mountain Zhang* - Maureen F.
   McHugh   s   3817

**Qing-an, Virginia "Ginny" Vonzel** (Spaceship
   Captain)
*Alpha Centauri* - William Barton   s   378

**Qox, J'briol** (Genetically Altered Being; Heir)
*Primary Inversion* - Catherine Asaro   s   220

**Quade, Morgan** (Artist)
*Zeta Base* - Judith Alguire   s   74

**Quadroped** (Animal)
*Demon Pig* - Karen Brush   f   737

**Quadrun, Ben** (Journalist)
*Nightmare Logic* - Matthew Hall   h   2495

**Quail, Douglas** (Clerk; Spy)
*The Collected Stories of Philip K. Dick, Volume Two:
   We Can Remember It for You Wholesale* - Philip K.
   Dick   s   1520

**Quail, Douglas** (Construction Worker)
*Total Recall* - Piers Anthony   s   193

**Quan, Zhongli** (Alien)
*Vengeance Strike* - David Robbins   s   4604

**Quantrill, Snohomish "Sno"** (Apprentice; Traveler)
*The Godmother's Apprentice* - Elizabeth Ann
   Scarborough   f   4863

**Quare, Joshua Ali** (Experimental Subject)
*Kaleidoscope Century* - John Barnes   s   352

**Quark** (Alien; Saloon Keeper/Owner)
*Fallen Heroes* - Dafydd ab Hugh  s  8

**Quarrels, David** (Engineer; Fiance(e))
*The Khan's Persuasion* - Cynthia Felice  s  1914

**Quath'jutt'kkal'thon "Quath"** (Alien; Revolutionary)
*Furious Gulf* - Gregory Benford  s  447
*Tides of Light* - Gregory Benford  s  450

**Quauhtli** (Religious)
*The Chalchiuhite Dragon* - Kenneth Morris  f  4020

**Queen** (Royalty)
*The Veils of Snows* - Mark Helprin  f  2654

**Queen of Ice** (Ruler)
*Horrible Humes* - Stephen Billias  f  487

**Queenie** (Spirit)
*The Influence* - Ramsey Campbell  h  857

**Quejaches, Xia** (Dancer; Wanderer)
*The Stone Garden* - Mary Rosenblum  s  4679

**Quen, Elene** (Administrator)
*Finity's End* - C.J. Cherryh  s  988

**Questioner II** (Cyborg; Judge)
*Six Moon Dance* - Sheri S. Tepper  s  5437

**Quetzal** (Religious; Vampire)
*Calde of the Long Sun* - Gene Wolfe  s  5937

**Quetzal** (Immortal)
*A King Beneath the Mountain* - Robert N. Charrette  f  973

**Quiet** (Doctor)
*Bad Brains* - Kathe Koja  h  3193

**Quigley, Joe** (Detective—Private; Imposter)
*Lady Slings the Booze* - Spider Robinson  s  4640

**Quijance, Natasha** (Parent; Storyteller)
*Red Planet Run* - Dana Stabenow  s  5187

**Quijance-Turgenev, Esther Elizabeth** (Child)
*Second Star* - Dana Stabenow  s  5188

**Quiles, Phil** (Inspector)
*Water Rites* - Guy N. Smith  h  5121

**Quillan** (Religious)
*The Face of the Waters* - Robert Silverberg  s  5029

**Quilp** (Criminal; Genius)
*A Game of Universe* - Eric S. Nylund  f  4178

**Quimby, Byron** (Maintenance Worker)
*Lot Lizards* - Ray Garton  h  2152

**Quincunx "the Thief"** (Artificial Intelligence)
*Dream of Glass* - Jean Mark Gawron  s  2163

**Quindell, Mason** (Doctor)
*Bring Me Children* - David Martin  h  3637

**Quinn** (Vampire)
*Precious Blood* - Pat Graversen  h  2336

**Quinn** (Journalist)
*Silicon Embrace* - John Shirley  s  5009

**Quinn, Adam** (Security Officer)
*Conqueror's Pride* - Timothy Zahn  s  6051

**Quinn, Dave** (Businessman)
*Winter Tides* - James P. Blaylock  h  524

**Quinn, Jimmy** (Scientist; Spaceman)
*The Sparrow* - Mary Doria Russell  s  4736

**Quinn, Rachel** (Spacewoman; Spaceship Captain)
*Moonfall* - Jack McDevitt  s  3789

**Quinn, Roger** (Businessman; Magician)
*A Calculated Magic* - Robert Weinberg  f  5694

**Quinn, Sofia Mendes** (Castaway; Computer Expert)
*Children of God* - Mary Doria Russell  s  4735

**Quinn "Nomad"** (Time Traveler; Warrior)
*Desert Fire* - David Alexander  s  65

**Quinn "Nomad"** (Warrior; Spy)
*Nomad* - David Alexander  s  66

**Quinsonnas** (Accountant; Musician)
*Paris in the Twentieth Century* - Jules Verne  s  5568

**Quint** (Agent)
*Psi-Man* - David Peters  s  4305

**Quisling, Emann** (Royalty)
*Vinas Solamnus* - J. Robert King  f  3123

**Quon** (Cult Member)
*The Jade Ogre* - Kenneth Robeson  f  4623

**Quong, Sue-Ling** (Doctor)
*The Singers of Time* - Frederik Pohl  s  4354

**Quordane, Holis** (Nobleman; Criminal)
*Shadow of the Crown* - Craig Mills  f  3914

## R

**R-T "Artie"** (Child; Handicapped)
*R-T, Margaret, and the Rats of NIMH* - Jane Leslie Conly  f  1132

**Ra-Hir** (Knight)
*The Children of Wrath* - Mickey Zucker Reichert  f  4518

**Ra-hotep-kan "Ra"** (Alien)
*StarGate* - Dean Devlin  s  1509

**Ra-khir of Erythane** (Apprentice; Knight)
*Beyond Ragnarok* - Mickey Zucker Reichert  f  4516

**Ra Sadiin, Cydell** (Ruler; Lesbian)
*Heartstone and Silver* - Jacqui Singleton  f  5071

**Raajeh** (Animal)
*Ray Bradbury Presents: Dinosaur Planet* - Stephen Leigh  s  3427

**Raayat** (Alien)
*The Madness Season* - C.S. Friedman  s  2058

**Rabbit, Roger** (Actor; Spouse)
*Who P-P-Plugged Roger Rabbit?* - Gary K. Wolf  f  5934

**Rabble** (Warrior; Mythical Creature)
*When the Gods Are Silent* - Jane M. Lindskold  f  3477

**Rabin, David** (Military Personnel)
*Vulcan's Forge* - Susan Shwartz  s  5019

**Rabjohns, Will** (Photographer)
*Sacrament* - Clive Barker  h  345

**Rabscuttle** (Animal)
*Tales From Watership Down* - Richard Adams  f  32

**Rachael** (Android)
*Blade Runner 2: The Edge of Human* - K.W. Jeter  s  2906

**Rachaela** (Young Woman)
*Personal Darkness* - Tanith Lee  h  3413

**Rache of Scole** (Genetically Altered Being; Administrator)
*Blueheart* - Alison Sinclair  s  5068

**Rachel** (Spouse; Singer)
*Archangel* - Sharon Shinn  s  5000

**Rachel** (Child; Student)
*The Time Tree* - Enid Richemont  f  4585

**Rachelle** (Martial Arts Expert; Bodyguard)
*The Anubis Murders* - Gary Gygax  f  2472

**Rachelle** (Bodyguard; Martial Arts Expert)
*Death in Delhi* - Gary Gygax  f  2473

**Rackstraw, Jeremiah** (Entertainer)
*Escardy Gap* - Peter Crowther  h  1282

**Racso** (Animal)
*R-T, Margaret, and the Rats of NIMH* - Jane Leslie Conly  f  1132

**Radburn, Adam** (Vampire; Morgue Attendant)
*The Undead* - Roxanne Longstreet  h  3519

**Radcliffe, Harry** (Architect)
*Outside the Dog Museum* - Jonathan Carroll  f  919

**Radcliffe, Milton** (Collector; Psychic)
*Lorien Lost* - Michael King  f  3124

**Radcliffe, Phillip** (Young Man)
*A Sharpness on the Neck* - Fred Saberhagen  h  4774

**Radience** (Slave)
*Warriorwards* - Dafydd ab Hugh  f  11

**Radineaux, Jenifleur** (Student; Martial Arts Expert)
*Anvil of the Sun* - Anne Lesley Groell  f  2451

**Radineaux, Jenifleur** (Debutante; Martial Arts Expert)
*Bridge of Valor* - Anne Lesley Groell  f  2452

**Radineaux, Viera** (Martial Arts Expert; Debutante)
*Anvil of the Sun* - Anne Lesley Groell  f  2451

**Radix, William** (Lawyer)
*The Good Children* - Kate Wilhelm  h  5808

**Rado** (Gambler; Traveler)
*Thorn and Needle* - Paul B. Thompson  f  5456

**Radon** (Heir; Spouse)
*Firewalk* - Anne Logston  f  3509

**Rady, Sonja** (Military Personnel)
*Prince of Sunset* - Steve White  s  5786

**Rae** (Orphan; Tailor)
*The War in the Waste* - Felicity Savage  f  4851

**Rae, Dorcas** (Scientist; Researcher)
*Gaia's Toys* - Rebecca Ore  s  4218

**Raeburn, Francis** (Psychic; Magician)
*Death of an Adept* - Katherine Kurtz  f  3257

**Raeburn, Francis** (Historian; Occultist)
*The Lodge of the Lynx* - Katherine Kurtz  f  3259

**Raeder, Peter** (Engineer; Spaceman)
*The Rising* - James Doohan  s  1579

**Rael** (Teenager; Religious)
*The Cult of Loving Kindness* - Paul Park  s  4242

**Rafael** (Artist)
*The Forgetting Room* - Nick Bantock  f  333

**Rafe** (Musician; Orphan)
*Ecstasia* - Francesca Lia Block  f  547

**Rafe** (Spaceman)
*A Matter of Oaths* - Helen S. Wright  s  5985

**Rafferty, John** (Religious)
*Unholy Fire* - Whitley Strieber  h  5342

**Rafiel** (Actor; Aged Person)
*Outnumbering the Dead* - Frederik Pohl  s  4352

**Rafin** (Police Officer)
*Runes of Autumn* - Larry Elmore  f  1790

**Raganda** (Mythical Creature)
*The Gates of Noon* - Michael Scott Rohan  f  4661

**Ragem, Paul** (Spaceman; Military Personnel)
*Beholder's Eye* - Julie E. Czerneda  s  1303

**Ragman** (Psychic; Revolutionary)
*The Host* - Peter R. Emshwiller  s  1819

**Rah** (Alien)
*Lake of the Sun* - Wynne Whiteford  s  5787

**Rahl, Darken** (Wizard; Leader)
*Wizard's First Rule* - Terry Goodkind  f  2271

**Rahl, Drefan** (Criminal; Imposter)
*Temple of the Winds* - Terry Goodkind  f  2270

**Rahl, Richard "the Seeker"** (Wizard)
*Blood of the Fold* - Terry Goodkind  *f*  2268

**Rahl, Richard "the Seeker"** (Wizard; Ruler)
*Temple of the Winds* - Terry Goodkind  *f*  2270

**Rahn** (Farmer; Wanderer)
*They Fly at Ciron* - Samuel R. Delany  *s*  1482

**Raihna** (Warrior; Leader)
*Conan the Relentless* - Roland J. Green  *f*  2348

**Railly, Kathryn** (Doctor)
*12 Monkeys* - Elizabeth Hand  *s*  2532

**Raim** (Handicapped)
*Dark Heart* - Betsy James  *f*  2857

**Rainaut, Valence** (Knight)
*Crusader's Torch* - Chelsea Quinn Yarbro  *h*  6015

**Raine of the Three Waters** (Noblewoman)
*A Breach in the Watershed* - Douglas Niles  *f*  4105

**Raine of the Three Waters** (Noblewoman; Writer)
*Darkenheight* - Douglas Niles  *f*  4107
*War of the Three Waters* - Douglas Niles  *f*  4110

**Raines, Darcy** (Tour Guide)
*Midnight's Lair* - Richard Laymon  *h*  3369

**Raines, Ingrid** (Military Personnel)
*The Children's Hour* - Jerry Pournelle  *s*  4372

**Raines, Michael** (Psychic)
*The Fugitive Stars* - Daniel Ransom  *s*  4479

**Raishan, Marguerite "Marghe" Angelica**
(Anthropologist; Wanderer)
*Ammonite* - Nicola Griffith  *s*  2443

**Raistlin** (Wizard; Hero)
*The Second Generation* - Margaret Weis  *f*  5724

**Raitt, Johnny** (Teenager)
*The Vampire's Beautiful Daughter* - S.P.
Somtow  *h*  5161

**Rajasthan, Nohar** (Genetically Altered Being;
Animal)
*Emperors of the Twilight* - S. Andrew
Swann  *s*  5362

**Rajasthan, Nohar** (Genetically Altered Being;
Detective—Private)
*Forests of the Night* - S. Andrew Swann  *s*  5363

**Rakam, Radosse** (Teacher; Slave)
*Four Ways to Forgiveness* - Ursula K. Le
Guin  *s*  3380

**Rakz, Yosekaat** (Vampire)
*Vampire Beat* - Vincent Courtney  *h*  1214

**Raleel** (Demon)
*Hooray for Hellywood* - Esther Friesner  *f*  2077

**Raleigh, Bryan** (Doctor)
*Nightmare* - S.K. Epperson  *h*  1832

**Raleigh, David** (Journalist)
*Nightmare* - S.K. Epperson  *h*  1832

**Rallya** (Spaceship Captain)
*A Matter of Oaths* - Helen S. Wright  *s*  5985

**Ralph** (Mythical Creature; Activist)
*Steel Rose* - Kara Dalkey  *f*  1321

**Ramey** (Spaceman)
*Rimrunners* - C.J. Cherryh  *s*  1001

**Ramifon Blayl, Ram** (Royalty)
*Letters From Atlantis* - Robert Silverberg  *f*  5035

**Ramirez, Leni** (Detective—Private)
*Blood Sport* - Lisa Smedman  *f*  5096

**Ramirez, Rafael** (Teenager)
*Blood Sport* - Lisa Smedman  *f*  5096

**Ramkin, Sybil** (Noblewoman)
*Guards! Guards!* - Terry Pratchett  *f*  4390

**Ramok** (Mercenary)
*Cat Scratch Fever* - Tara K. Harper  *s*  2550

**Ramos, Festina** (Space Explorer; Military Personnel)
*Expendable* - James Alan Gardner  *s*  2135

**RAMROD Mark I "Rod"** (Robot; Artificial
Intelligence)
*Cybernarc* - Robert Cain  *s*  829
*End Game* - Robert Cain  *s*  830
*Gold Dragon* - Robert Cain  *s*  831

**Ramses the Great** (Historical Figure; Reanimated
Dead)
*The Mummy, or Ramses the Damned* - Anne
Rice  *h*  4572

**Ramsey** (Spy)
*Nomad* - David Alexander  *s*  66

**Ramsey, Keith** (Writer; Hunter)
*Blood Lines* - William R. Burkett Jr.  *s*  774

**Ramsey, Quinn** (Police Officer)
*Demon Fire* - Gary L. Holleman  *h*  2743

**Ramsey, Quinn Jr.** (Child)
*Demon Fire* - Gary L. Holleman  *h*  2743

**Rana** (Adventurer)
*The Jewel of Fire* - Diana L. Paxson  *f*  4265
*The Wind Crystal* - Diana L. Paxson  *f*  4269

**Rance** (Royalty; Wanderer)
*Bride of the Castle* - John DeChancie  *s*  1452

**Rand** (Magician)
*Four & Twenty Blackbirds* - Mercedes
Lackey  *f*  3283

**Rand** (Student; Human)
*Path of Fire* - Charles Ingrid  *s*  2832

**Rand, Adrienne** (Psychologist)
*Prototype* - Brian Hodge  *h*  2704

**Rand, Aino** (Telepath)
*Marks of Our Brothers* - Jane M. Lindskold  *s*  3475

**Rand, Kyna** (Businesswoman)
*Howl-O-Ween* - Gary L. Holleman  *h*  2744

**Rand, Phylis** (Hotel Owner)
*Darkling* - Michael O'Rourke  *h*  4223

**Randall** (Apprentice; Wizard)
*School of Wizardry* - Debra Doyle  *f*  1605

**Randall, Mick** (Police Officer)
*Shadows* - Kimberly Rangel  *h*  4472

**Randi** (Prisoner)
*The Hunter on Arena* - Rose Estes  *s*  1838

**Randolph, Dan** (Businessman; Fugitive)
*Empire Builders* - Ben Bova  *s*  584

**Randolph, Jake** (Writer; Pilot)
*The Torching* - Marcy Heidish  *h*  2642

**Random Walk** (Artificial Intelligence)
*Revolutionary* - S. Andrew Swann  *s*  5367

**Rane** (Artist; Alien)
*Mirror to the Sky* - Mark S. Geston  *s*  2213

**Ranes, Josev T.** (Military Personnel; Experimental
Subject)
*Aggressor Six* - Wil McCarthy  *s*  3760

**Rangegonda** (Noblewoman)
*Better in the Dark* - Chelsea Quinn Yarbro  *h*  6011

**Ranger Dan** (Ranger)
*Camp Vamp* - Elvira  *h*  1801

**Rania** (Child; Royalty)
*The Promise* - Monica Hughes  *s*  2808

**Ranier** (Empath; Adventurer)
*The Remarkables* - Robert Reed  *s*  4507

**Ranieri, Tony** (Student)
*Beyond the Shroud* - Rick Hautala  *h*  2604

**Ranira "Renra"** (Servant; Adventurer)
*Shadows over Lyra* - Patricia C. Wrede  *f*  5980

**Ranji** (Warrior; Genetically Altered Being)
*The False Mirror* - Alan Dean Foster  *s*  2004

**Rankin, Howard S.** (Military Personnel)
*A Landscape of Darkness* - John Blair  *s*  513

**Ransom, Cliff** (Worker)
*Dark Twilight* - Joseph A. Citro  *h*  1036

**Ransom, Garrett** (Child)
*Night Things* - Michael Talbot  *h*  5380

**Ransom, Lauren** (Spouse)
*Night Things* - Michael Talbot  *h*  5380

**Ransom, Lucas** (Writer)
*Exquisite Corpse* - Poppy Z. Brite  *h*  695

**Ransome, Errec** (Psychic)
*By Honor Betray'd* - Debra Doyle  *s*  1598

**Ransome, Errec** (Psychic; Spaceman)
*The Gathering Flame* - Debra Doyle  *s*  1599

**Ransome, Errec** (Spirit; Psychic)
*The Long Hunt* - Debra Doyle  *s*  1602

**Ransome, Illario "Ambidexter"** (Computer Expert;
Artist)
*Burning Bright* - Melissa Scott  *s*  4894

**Ransome, Lilyaka** (Heiress; Spaceman)
*A Passage of Stars* - Alis A. Rasmussen  *s*  4482

**Ransome, Lilyaka** (Spaceship Captain)
*The Price of Ransom* - Alis A. Rasmussen  *s*  4483

**Ranson, June** (Mercenary)
*Rolling Hot* - David Drake  *s*  1642

**Rant, Paul** (Scientist)
*I, Said the Fly* - Michael Shea  *h*  4944

**Ranth** (Mercenary)
*The Sands of Kalaven: A Novel of Shunlar* - Carol
Heller  *f*  2651

**Ranulf** (Nobleman)
*Changing Fate* - Elisabeth Waters  *f*  5629

**Ranulfson, Murdo** (Traveler)
*The Iron Lance* - Stephen R. Lawhead  *f*  3356

**Raoulin** (Student)
*The Book of the Beast* - Tanith Lee  *f*  3405

**Rap** (Ruler; Adventurer)
*The Cutting Edge* - Dave Duncan  *f*  1675

**Rap** (Warrior; Psychic)
*Emperor and Clown* - Dave Duncan  *f*  1676

**Rap** (Worker; Psychic)
*Faery Lands Forlorn* - Dave Duncan  *f*  1677

**Rap** (Nobleman; Psychic)
*The Living God* - Dave Duncan  *f*  1682

**Rap** (Worker; Psychic)
*Magic Casement* - Dave Duncan  *f*  1683
*Perilous Seas* - Dave Duncan  *f*  1685

**Rap** (Nobleman; Psychic)
*The Stricken Field* - Dave Duncan  *f*  1688

**Rap** (Ruler; Psychic)
*Upland Outlaws* - Dave Duncan  *f*  1690

**Raphael** (Angel)
*Archangel* - Sharon Shinn  *s*  5000

**Raphael** (Sorcerer)
*The White Guardian* - Ronald Anthony
Cross  *s*  1275

**Raphael, Stella** (Housewife)
*Asylum* - Patrick McGrath  *h*  3812

**Raphaella "Rae"** (Angel; Travel Agent)
*Angel Light* - Andrew M. Greeley  *f*  2342

**Raptor Red** (Animal)
*Raptor Red* - Robert T. Bakker  *f*  306

**Raqella** (Alien; Pilot)
*Sundowner* - Chris Claremont  *s*  1043

**Rarberticandornan, "Ar"** (Alien; Spaceman)
*Dragons in the Stars* - Jeffrey A. Carver  s  930

**Ras, Pawasar Pawasar** (Leader; Alien)
*Earthgrip* - Harry Turtledove  s  5499

**Rasa** (Teacher; Parent)
*The Call of Earth* - Orson Scott Card  s  882
*The Memory of Earth* - Orson Scott Card  s  894

**Raschad, Meesha** (Miner; Heir)
*Mistwalker* - Denise Lopez Heald  s  2637

**Rasha of the Thousand Doors** (Royalty; Spouse)
*Yesterday We Saw Mermaids* - Esther
  Friesner  f  2086

**Rashid** (Scientist)
*Commitment Hour* - James Alan Gardner  s  2134

**Rasnar, Patriarch** (Religious)
*Rally Cry!* - William R. Forstchen  s  1982

**Rasputin** (Religious; Historical Figure)
*I, Vampire* - Michael Romkey  h  4665

**Rasputin** (Mythical Creature)
*Shadows on the Hill* - Jackie Cassada  f  935

**Ratha** (Animal; Leader)
*Ratha and Thistle-Chaser* - Clare Bell  f  432

**Rathan, Linden** (Mythical Creature)
*The Last Dragonlord* - Joanne Bertin  f  470

**Rathe, Nicolas "Nico"** (Police Officer)
*Point of Hopes* - Melissa Scott  f  4899

**Rathel, Amanda** (Paranormal Investigator)
*Black Body* - H.C. Turk  h  5488

**Rathenau, Miriam** (Singer; Spouse)
*Child of the Journey* - Janet Berliner  f  466

**Rathenau, Miriam** (Singer)
*Child of the Light* - Janet Gluckman  f  2244

**Rathenau, Miriam** (Spouse)
*Children of the Dusk* - Janet Berliner  f  467

**Ratio** (Artificial Intelligence; Leader)
*The White Abacus* - Damien Broderick  s  708

**Ratkay, Dante** (Psychic)
*Resurrection Man* - Sean Stewart  f  5277

**Ratkay, Jet** (Relative)
*Resurrection Man* - Sean Stewart  f  5277

**Rattigan, Constance** (Actress)
*Death Is a Lonely Business* - Ray Bradbury  h  619

**Ravana** (Deity; Demon)
*The Willing Spirit* - Piers Anthony  f  195

**Ravanna** (Sorceress)
*The Pearl of the Soul of the World* - Meredith Ann
  Pierce  f  4318

**Ravanski, Magda** (Journalist)
*The Frighteners* - Michael Jahn  h  2856

**Raven** (Minstrel)
*A Cast of Corbies* - Mercedes Lackey  f  3274

**Raven** (Hero)
*Out of This World* - Lawrence Watt-Evans  f  5645

**Raven** (Martial Arts Expert; Organized Crime Figure)
*Snow Crash* - Neal Stephenson  s  5254

**Raven, Ian** (Student)
*Stitch* - Mark Morris  h  4024

**Raven, Jeff** (Psychic; Parent)
*Lyon's Pride* - Anne McCaffrey  s  3738

**Raven, Jeff** (Settler; Psychic)
*The Rowan* - Anne McCaffrey  s  3747

**Raven, Richard** (Vigilante)
*Wolf and Raven* - Michael A. Stackpole  f  5207

**Raven Hunter** (Warrior; Prehistoric Human)
*People of the Wolf* - W. Michael Gear  f  2170

**Raven of Lao-tzu** (Guide; Writer)
*Blood Lines* - William R. Burkett Jr.  s  774

**Ravenloft, Kinson** (Scout; Adventurer)
*First King of Shannara* - Terry Brooks  f  712

**Ravenna, John** (Criminal)
*Prey* - William W. Johnstone  h  2932

**Ravenwood, Janice** (Psychic; Writer)
*Wildest Dreams* - Norman Partridge  h  4256

**Ravinga** (Shaman)
*The Mark of the Cat* - Andre Norton  f  4157

**Ravis** (Nobleman; Mercenary)
*The Barbed Coil* - J.V. Jones  f  2957

**Raynor, Sara** (Spirit)
*Darkling* - Michael O'Rourke  h  4223

**Razin, Fyodor Alexeyevich** (Scientist)
*Landscape Painted with Tea* - Milorad
  Pavic  f  4263

**Razkili** (Military Personnel)
*Shadowdance* - Robin Wayne Bailey  f  290

**Readis** (Child)
*The Dolphins of Pern* - Anne McCaffrey  s  3729

**Reagan, Nancy** (Advertising)
*Throat Sprockets* - Tim Lucas  h  3541

**Reagan, Ronald** (Political Figure)
*The Atrocity Exhibition* - J.G. Ballard  s  319

**Reagan, Ronald "Dutch"** (Historical Figure; Actor)
*Time on My Hands* - Peter Delacorte  s  1480

**Reandn** (Guard; Detective)
*Touched by Magic* - Doranna Durgin  f  1705

**Reandn** (Military Personnel; Bodyguard)
*Wolf Justice* - Doranna Durgin  f  1706

**ReAth** (Nobleman)
*Shaper's Legacy* - Sheila Finch  s  1933

**Reatur** (Ruler)
*A World of Difference* - Harry Turtledove  s  5514

**Rebecca** (Handicapped)
*Gate of Darkness, Circle of Light* - Tanya
  Huff  f  2797

**Rebecca "Becca"** (Journalist; Traveler)
*Briar Rose* - Jane Yolen  f  6029

**Rebello, Joseph "Joe" Z.** (Spaceman; Military
Personnel)
*In the Wrong Hands* - Edward Gibson  s  2215

**Rebka, Hans** (Adventurer)
*Divergence* - Charles Sheffield  s  4954
*Transcendence* - Charles Sheffield  s  4967

**Rec** (Artificial Intelligence)
*Kaduna Memories* - Jack McKinney  s  3850

**Red Mare** (Mythical Creature; Animal)
*A Ride on the Red Mare's Back* - Ursula K. Le
  Guin  f  3382

**Red Orc** (Immortal)
*More than Fire* - Philip Jose Farmer  s  1871

**Redbird** (Fiance(e))
*Shaman* - Robert Shea  f  4946

**Redd** (Cowboy)
*Red Dust* - Paul J. McAuley  s  3715

**Reddy, John** (Mythical Creature; Adventurer)
*A King Beneath the Mountain* - Robert N.
  Charrette  f  973

**Reddy, John** (Mythical Creature)
*A Knight Among Knaves* - Robert N.
  Charrette  f  974

**Reddy, John** (Security Officer)
*A Prince Among Men* - Robert N. Charrette  f  977

**Rede, Pippa** (Single Parent)
*In the Land of Winter* - Richard Grant  f  2326

**Redfern, Diana** (Teenager)
*The Lake at the End of the World* - Caroline
  MacDonald  s  3584

**Redfield, Blake** (Antiquarian)
*Hide and Seek* - Paul Preuss  s  4418
*The Medusa Encounter* - Paul Preuss  s  4419

**Redman, Stu** (Leader)
*The Stand: The Complete and Uncut Edition* - Stephen
  King  h  3142

**Redthorn, Jeremy** (Farmer; Deity)
*The Face of Apollo* - Fred Saberhagen  s  4766

**Redwing, T'fyrr** (Alien; Musician)
*The Eagle and the Nightingales* - Mercedes
  Lackey  f  3278

**Redwyn** (Magician)
*The Lost History of Redwyn* - William Jay  f  2883

**Ree, Danlo** (Telepath; Traveler)
*The Wall at the Edge of the World* - Jim
  Aikin  s  46

**Ree, Killashandra** (Miner)
*Crystal Line* - Anne McCaffrey  s  3724

**Reece** (Mercenary)
*War* - Simon Hawke  f  2625

**Reed, Jack** (Businessman)
*Walkers* - Graham Masterton  h  3681

**Reed, James** (Spy; Criminal)
*Operation Damocles* - Oscar L. Fellows  s  1915

**Reed, Jerry** (Scientist)
*Russian Spring* - Norman Spinrad  s  5174

**Reed, Kate** (Journalist; Vampire)
*Judgment of Tears: Anno Dracula 1959* - Kim
  Newman  h  4098

**Reed, Kayla** (Empath; Revolutionary)
*Sister Blood* - Karen Haber  s  2476

**Reed, Kayla** (Empath; Smuggler)
*The War Minstrels* - Karen Haber  s  2477

**Reed, Kayla** (Empath; Fugitive)
*Woman Without a Shadow* - Karen Haber  s  2478

**Reed, Matt** (Taxidermist)
*The Reckoning* - Ruby Jean Jensen  h  2904

**Reed, Sharon** (Magician)
*The Road to Hell, Volume I* - Robert
  Weinberg  h  5701
*The Road to Hell, Volume II* - Robert
  Weinberg  h  5702

**Reeling, Kate** (Psychologist)
*Manhattan Heat* - Ken Eulo  h  1851

**Reem "First Cousin Brother"** (Alien; Political
Figure)
*Brother Termite* - Patricia Anthony  s  156

**Rees** (Teenager; Scientist)
*Raft* - Stephen Baxter  s  401

**Reese, Frances** (Spaceship Captain)
*Double Planet* - John Gribbin  s  2433

**Reesone, Donald** (Actor)
*Near Death* - Nancy Kilpatrick  h  3113

**Reeve, Todd** (Rancher; Hero)
*Crisis on Doona* - Anne McCaffrey  s  3723

**Reeve, Todd** (Political Figure)
*Treaty at Doona* - Anne McCaffrey  s  3752

**Reeves, Gail** (Teacher)
*The Immaculate* - Mark Morris  h  4023

**Regeane** (Werewolf)
*The Silver Wolf* - Alice Borchardt  h  572

**Regina** (Religious)
*A Cast of Corbies* - Mercedes Lackey  f  3274

**Regina** (Child)
*Hideaway* - Dean R. Koontz  *h*  3208

**Regis** (Mythical Creature)
*The Legacy* - R.A. Salvatore  *f*  4801

**Reich, Ben** (Businessman; Murderer)
*The Demolished Man* - Alfred Bester  *s*  476

**Reichart, Carlos** (Director; Homosexual)
*Boys of Life* - Paul Russell  *h*  4737

**Reichmann, Wolfgang "Wolfie"** (Teacher)
*Being of Two Minds* - Pamela F. Service  *f*  4918

**Reichner, Helmut** (Administrator; Scientist)
*Threshold* - Bill Myers  *s*  4060

**Reid, Dallas** (Detective—Police)
*Boneman* - Lisa Cantrell  *h*  871

**Reid, David Henry** (Actor)
*Stainless* - Todd Grimson  *h*  2449

**Reid, Nicholas** (Businessman)
*The Cipher* - Kathe Koja  *h*  3194

**Reille y Sanchez, Estrellita** (Spaceship Captain; Explorer)
*Contact and Commune* - L. Neil Smith  *s*  5129

**Reilly, Dave** (Musician)
*December* - Phil Rickman  *h*  4588

**Reilly, Mary** (Servant)
*Mary Reilly* - Valerie Martin  *h*  3654

**Reilly, Rosemary** (Parent)
*Son of Rosemary* - Ira Levin  *h*  3445

**Reindeer** (Mythical Creature)
*The Woman Who Loved Reindeer* - Meredith Ann Pierce  *f*  4320

**Reis, Tammy** (Astronaut)
*Kings of the High Frontier* - Victor Koman  *s*  3199

**Reith, Fergus** (Tour Guide; Divorced Person)
*The Swords of Zinjaban* - L. Sprague de Camp  *s*  1418

**Reive** (Genetically Altered Being)
*AEstival Tide* - Elizabeth Hand  *s*  2533

**Relanj, Zia** (Spy)
*The Forever Drug* - Steve Perry  *s*  4296
*Spindoc* - Steve Perry  *s*  4300

**Relkin** (Military Personnel; Companion)
*Battledragon* - Christopher Rowley  *f*  4691
*Bazil Broketail* - Christopher Rowley  *f*  4692

**Relkin** (Military Personnel)
*A Dragon at World's End* - Christopher Rowley  *f*  4693
*Dragons of Argonath* - Christopher Rowley  *f*  4694

**Relkin** (Military Personnel; Companion)
*Dragons of War* - Christopher Rowley  *f*  4695
*A Sword for a Dragon* - Christopher Rowley  *f*  4697

**Relorn, Wryan** (Witch; Scientist)
*Timediver's Dawn* - L.E. Modesitt Jr.  *s*  3940

**Remillard, Jon** (Psychic; Mutant)
*Diamond Mask: A Novel* - Julian May  *s*  3697

**Remillard, Mark** (Psychic; Revolutionary)
*Magnificat* - Julian May  *s*  3699

**Remillard, Rogatien** (Psychic; Businessman)
*Diamond Mask: A Novel* - Julian May  *s*  3697

**Remillard, Rogatien** (Psychic)
*Jack the Bodiless* - Julian May  *s*  3698

**Remson, Vincent** (Government Official)
*The Stalk* - Janet Morris  *s*  4016

**Renada** (Young Woman)
*The Stars Must Wait* - Keith Laumer  *s*  3346

**Renagi** (Warrior; Leader)
*Tegne: Soul Warrior* - Richard La Plante  *f*  3268

**Renaldi, Cosmo** (Businessman)
*Nightmare's Disciple* - Joseph S. Pulver Jr.  *h*  4449

**Renar of Dagothrin** (Heir—Dispossessed; Fugitive)
*Lady of Mercy* - Michelle Sagara  *f*  4784

**Renard, Eris** (Government Official; Indian)
*Green Lake* - S.K. Epperson  *h*  1830

**Renfield, Tom** (Psychic)
*The Thread That Binds the Bones* - Nina Kiriki Hoffman  *f*  2717

**Renier, Mordan** (Military Personnel; Political Figure)
*Ganwold's Child* - Diann Thornley  *s*  5467

**Renn, Jonathan** (Prisoner)
*Prison Planet* - William C. Dietz  *s*  1551

**Renna** (Spaceman; Diplomat)
*Glory Season* - David Brin  *s*  686

**Renner, Kevin** (Military Personnel; Pilot)
*The Gripping Hand* - Larry Niven  *s*  4122

**Reno** (Revolutionary; Disembodied Personality)
*Solip: System* - Walter Jon Williams  *s*  5841

**Reno, Amy** (Android)
*Steelheart* - William C. Dietz  *s*  1552

**Renquist, Victor** (Vampire)
*The Time of Feasting* - Mick Farren  *h*  1882

**Renya, Jacinta** (Noblewoman; Government Official)
*Iceman* - Cynthia Felice  *s*  1913

**Renzie** (Researcher; Warrior)
*Vanishing Point* - Michaela Roessner  *s*  4652

**Renzler, Lenore** (Young Woman)
*The 37th Mandala* - Marc Laidlaw  *h*  3310

**Renzler, Michael** (Clerk)
*The 37th Mandala* - Marc Laidlaw  *h*  3310

**Repairman Jack** (Vigilante)
*Nightworld* - F. Paul Wilson  *h*  5893

**Resner, Jacob** (Worker)
*A Question of Time* - Fred Saberhagen  *h*  4772

**Rethia** (Healer)
*Touched by Magic* - Doranna Durgin  *f*  1705

**Retief, Jame** (Diplomat)
*Reward for Retief* - Keith Laumer  *s*  3345

**Reuven** (Secretary)
*Legacy of the Darksword* - Margaret Weis  *f*  5719

**Reva** (Genetically Altered Being; Criminal)
*Mainline* - Deborah Christian  *s*  1026

**Rex** (Animal)
*The Magnificent Wilf* - Gordon R. Dickson  *s*  1536

**Rex, Arthur** (Ruler)
*The Whispers* - Dan Parkinson  *s*  4247

**Rey, Cory** (Scientist)
*Icefire* - Judith Reeves-Stevens  *s*  4512

**Reydak, Karl** (Spy)
*A Fearful Symmetry* - James Luceno  *s*  3542

**Reyes, Adrien** (Experimental Subject; Slave)
*Someone to Watch over Me* - Tricia Sullivan  *s*  5355

**Reyes, Eddie** (Teenager)
*Jaguar* - Bill Ransom  *s*  4477

**Reynar III** (Ruler; Parent)
*Silver Princess, Golden Knight* - Sharon Green  *f*  2359

**Reynman, John** (Writer)
*The Double* - Don Webb  *h*  5661

**Reynolds, Alvin** (Computer Expert)
*The Road to Hell, Volume I* - Robert Weinberg  *h*  5701
*The Road to Hell, Volume II* - Robert Weinberg  *h*  5702

**Reynolds, Jane** (Child-Care Giver)
*The Ignored* - Bentley Little  *h*  3493

**Reynolds, Jessie** (Young Woman)
*Forget Me Not* - Gene Lazuta  *h*  3375

**Reynolds, Kelly** (Journalist)
*Area 51* - Robert Doherty  *s*  1565

**Reynolds, Mason Algiers** (Fugitive)
*The Hollow Earth: The Narrative of Mason Algiers Reynolds of Virginia* - Rudy Rucker  *s*  4705

**Reynolds, William** (Student; Time Traveler)
*Lurid Dreams* - Charles L. Harness  *s*  2546

**Reysson, Gaylon** (Ruler; Wizard)
*Book of Stones* - L. Dean James  *f*  2862
*Kingslayer* - L. Dean James  *f*  2863

**Rhannet, Prima** (Pirate; Lesbian)
*Sword-Born* - Jennifer Roberson  *f*  4612

**Rhea of Coos** (Witch)
*Wizard and Glass* - Stephen King  *h*  3144

**Rheinhardt** (Artist)
*Subterranean Gallery* - Richard Paul Russo  *s*  4750

**Rhenford, Liam** (Scholar; Detective—Amateur)
*Beggar's Banquet* - Daniel Hood  *f*  2756
*Fanuilh* - Daniel Hood  *f*  2757

**Rhenford, Liam** (Scholar; Detective)
*Scales of Justice* - Daniel Hood  *f*  2758

**Rhenford, Liam** (Scholar; Detective—Amateur)
*Wizard's Heir* - Daniel Hood  *f*  2759

**Rhia** (Child; Psychic)
*The Lost Years of Merlin* - T.A. Barron  *f*  370

**Rhiana** (Noblewoman; Magician)
*In the Rift* - Marion Zimmer Bradley  *f*  639

**Rhiannon** (Witch; Computer Expert)
*Overshoot* - Mona Clee  *s*  1075

**Rhiannon "Rhia"** (Child; Psychic)
*The Seven Songs of Merlin* - T.A. Barron  *f*  372

**Rhion the Brown** (Wizard)
*The Magicians of Night* - Barbara Hambly  *f*  2505
*The Rainbow Abyss* - Barbara Hambly  *f*  2507

**Rhiow** (Animal; Wizard)
*The Book of Night with Moon* - Diane Duane  *f*  1657

**Rhisadel, Teressa** (Royalty; Leader)
*Wren's War* - Sherwood Smith  *f*  5144

**Rhodes, Jeffrey** (Doctor)
*Harmful Intent* - Robin Cook  *s*  1164

**Rhodes, Jim "War Machine"** (Hero)
*Iron Man: The Armor Trap* - Greg Cox  *s*  1227

**Rhodes, Sally** (Detective—Private)
*The Quorum* - Kim Newman  *h*  4100

**Rhodonite "Rod"** (Religious)
*The Children Star* - Joan Slonczewski  *s*  5090

**Rhodry** (Ruler; Mercenary)
*A Time of Omens* - Katharine Kerr  *f*  3078

**Rhom** (Twin)
*Shadow Leader* - Tara K. Harper  *f*  2552

**Rhoodie, Andries** (Time Traveler; Military Personnel)
*The Guns of the South: A Novel of the Civil War* - Harry Turtledove  *s*  5502

**Rhymer, Catherine** (Teacher)
*Reluctant Voyagers* - Elisabeth Vonarburg  *s*  5591

**Rhys, Gwinn** (Artist; Apprentice)
*Harmony* - Marjorie Bradley Kellogg  *s*  3046

**Rhys-Whitney, Harper** (Entertainer)
*The Fear in Yesterday's Rings* - George C. Chesbro  *h*  1007

**Ria** (Shaman)
*Shaman* - Sandra Miesel   f   3889

**Rialla** (Horse Trainer; Spy)
*Steal the Dragon* - Patricia Briggs   f   682

**Riatha** (Mythical Creature; Immortal)
*The Eye of the Hunter* - Dennis L.
   McKiernan   f   3833

**Ribson, Joe** (Musician)
*Necrom* - Mick Farren   s   1881

**Ricadonna, Helen** (Businesswoman)
*Red Planet Run* - Dana Stabenow   s   5187

**Ricardo, Jean-Lucy** (Spaceship Captain)
*Star Wreck II: The Attack of the Jargonites* - Leah
   Rewolinski   s   4563
*Star Wreck III: Time Warped* - Leah
   Rewolinski   s   4564
*Star Wreck IV: Live Long and Profit* - Leah
   Rewolinski   s   4565
*Star Wreck 6: Geek Space Nine* - Leah
   Rewolinski   s   4562
*Star Wreck: The Generation Gap* - Leah
   Rewolinski   s   4566

**RICE** (Artificial Intelligence)
*Memento Mori* - Shariann Lewitt   s   3454

**Rice, Caddie** (Young Woman; Vampire)
*Blood of Mugwump* - Doug Rice   h   4581

**Rice, Dale** (Lawyer)
*Illegal Alien* - Robert J. Sawyer   s   4858

**Rice, David "Davy"** (Teenager; Runaway)
*Jumper* - Steven Gould   s   2290

**Rice, Doug** (Young Man; Vampire)
*Blood of Mugwump* - Doug Rice   h   4581

**Rice, Sheldon** (Businessman)
*Thrill* - Patricia Wallace   h   5624

**Rich** (Doctor)
*Invitation to the Game* - Monica Hughes   s   2807

**Richards, Carl** (Director)
*Fantastique* - Marvin Kaye   h   3025

**Richards, Neil** (Teacher)
*Sister, Sister* - Andrew Neiderman   h   4091

**Richer the Quick** (Scavenger; Hero)
*Men Like Rats* - Rob Chilson   s   1015

**Richmond, Eleanor Boxwood** (Political Figure)
*Interface* - Stephen Bury   s   781

**Richter** (Government Official)
*Buddy Holly Is Alive and Well on Ganymede* - Bradley
   Denton   s   1490

**Ricimer, Piet** (Spaceman)
*Igniting the Reaches* - David Drake   s   1633

**Ricimer, Piet** (Spaceman; Pirate)
*Through the Breach* - David Drake   s   1647

**Rick** (Spaceship Captain)
*Bill, the Galactic Hero: On the Planet of Tasteless
   Pleasure* - Harry Harrison   s   2567

**Rick** (Editor)
*God's Dice* - S. Andrew Swann   f   5364

**Rick** (Young Man)
*The Night in Fog* - David B. Silva   h   5026

**Rickard, Robert** (Maintenance Worker)
*Room 13* - Henry Garfield   h   2139

**Rico** (Mercenary)
*Fade to Black* - Nyx Smith   s   5134

**Rico, Alexandra "Sunny"** (Detective—Police)
*Finder* - Emma Bull   f   769

**Rictus** (Mythical Creature)
*The Thief of Always* - Clive Barker   h   347

**Riddell, Lester** (Businessman; Spaceman)
*Lunar Descent* - Allen Steele   s   5245

**Ridenau, Abelard** (Ruler)
*Daughter of Prophecy* - Anne Kelleher Bush   f   788

**Ridenau, Roderic** (Royalty; Leader)
*Children of Enchantment* - Anne Kelleher
   Bush   f   787

**Ridenour, Stephen** (Computer Expert)
*Ground-Ties* - Jane S. Fancher   s   1861
*Harmonies of the 'Net* - Jane S. Fancher   s   1862
*Uplink* - Jane S. Fancher   s   1865

**Rider, Emily** (Spouse)
*Other Nature* - Stephanie A. Smith   s   5145

**Rider, Sean** (Spouse)
*Other Nature* - Stephanie A. Smith   s   5145

**Ridge, Freeman** (Maintenance Worker)
*Dark Visions* - T. Lucien Wright   h   5987

**Riemann, Thomas** (Disembodied Personality)
*Permutation City* - Greg Egan   s   1761

**Rifkin, Bernie "Power Man"** (Hero)
*Captain Jack Zodiac* - Michael Kandel   f   3009

**Rigger, Jack** (Child)
*Blood of Innocents* - John Arbucci   h   204

**Riker, Paul Whitfield** (Spaceship Captain)
*The Trumpets of Tagan* - Simon Lang   s   3316

**Riker, William** (Military Personnel)
*A Call to Darkness* - Michael Jan Friedman   s   2062

**Riker, William** (Military Personnel; Space Explorer)
*Imbalance* - V.E. Mitchell   s   3919
*Imzadi* - Peter David   s   1383

**Riker, William** (Military Personnel)
*Q-Zone* - Greg Cox   s   1229
*Ship of the Line* - Diane Carey   s   904

**Riker, William** (Military Personnel; Space Explorer)
*The Soldiers of Fear* - Dean Wesley Smith   s   5115

**Riker, William** (Military Personnel)
*Triangle: Imzadi II* - Peter David   s   1388

**Rikki-Tikki-Tavi** (Warrior)
*Spartan Run* - David Robbins   s   4602

**Rikus** (Warrior; Mythical Creature)
*The Verdant Passage* - Troy Denning   f   1487

**Rile, Martin** (Judge)
*Lunar Justice* - Charles L. Harness   s   2545

**Riley, David** (Military Personnel)
*Operation Synbat* - Bob Mayer   h   3701

**Riley, Kevin** (Military Personnel)
*A Flag Full of Stars* - Brad Ferguson   s   1922

**Riley, Michael** (Computer Expert)
*The Deus Machine* - Pierre Ouellette   h   4232

**Riley, Ray** (Teenager)
*The Last Vampire* - Christopher Pike   h   4328

**Rille, Cailet Ambrai** (Leader; Teacher)
*The Mageborn Traitor* - Melanie Rawn   f   4488

**Rima** (Prostitute)
*The Last Rangers* - Jake Davis   s   1406

**Rimbaud, Ole** (Writer)
*Serial Killer Days* - David Prill   h   4436

**Rimmer, Arnold J.** (Spaceman; Disembodied
   Personality)
*Red Dwarf: Infinity Welcomes Careful Drivers* - Grant
   Naylor   s   4077

**Rincewind** (Wizard)
*Eric* - Terry Pratchett   f   4388
*Interesting Times* - Terry Pratchett   f   4392

**Ring, Ethan** (Artist; Spy)
*Scissors Cut Paper Wrap Stone* - Ian
   McDonald   s   3795

**Ringess, Danlo** (Pilot)
*The Broken God* - David Zindell   s   6085

*The Wild* - David Zindell   s   6086

**Ringess, Mallory** (Parent)
*The Wild* - David Zindell   s   6086

**Rinna** (Maiden)
*The Birth of the Blade* - Dennis McCarty   f   3766

**Riordan, Eveleen** (Time Traveler)
*Firehand* - Andre Norton   s   4151

**Rios, Judy** (Young Woman)
*California Gothic* - Dennis Etchison   h   1843

**Ripi-Arana-Hoc, Ripi** (Alien)
*Deepdrive* - Alexander Jablokov   s   2837

**Ripley** (Military Personnel; Heroine)
*Alien 3* - Alan Dean Foster   s   1993

**Ripley** (Clone; Hero)
*Alien Resurrection* - A.C. Crispin   s   1258

**Ripley, Ellen** (Telepath; Warrior)
*Aliens: The Female War* - Steve Perry   s   4290

**Ripley, Robert Remington III** (Writer; Martial Arts
   Expert)
*When Dreams Collide* - Wm. Mark
   Simmons   f   5063

**Rippen, Jack** (Producer)
*Celestial Dogs* - J.S. Russell   h   4734

**Risinger, Werner** (Businessman; Relative)
*Oktober* - Stephen Gallagher   h   2112

**Rissedote, Faia** (Shepherd; Sorceress)
*Fire in the Mist* - Holly Lisle   f   3482

**Rissedotte, Faia** (Sorceress; Parent)
*Mind of the Magic* - Holly Lisle   f   3486

**Ritter, Alexis** (Religious; Leader)
*The Venom Trees of Sunga* - L. Sprague de
   Camp   s   1420

**Ritz** (Financier; Handicapped)
*Living with the Reptiles* - Roger L.
   DiSilvestro   s   1563

**Riva** (Revolutionary; Fugitive)
*The Eyes of God* - Mark Kreighbaum   s   3231

**Rivakonneva "Riva"** (Warrior; Parent)
*Mathemagics* - Margaret Ball   f   316

**Rivaudais, Antoinette** (Saloon Hostess)
*Madeleine's Ghost* - Robert Girardi   h   2240

**Rivera, Josephine "Joey"** (Musician; Teenager)
*The Unicorn Sonata* - Peter S. Beagle   f   412

**Rivera, Maria** (Aged Person)
*The Nihilesthete* - Richard Kalich   h   3002

**Rivers, James** (Scientist)
*Portent* - James Herbert   h   2670

**Rivers, Neal** (Professor; Vampire)
*Keeper of the King* - Nigel Bennett   h   452

**Rivers, Reginald** (Guide; Time Traveler)
*Rivers of Time* - L. Sprague de Camp   s   1417

**Riversong** (Mythical Creature)
*The Warrior and the Witch* - Carl Miller   f   3893

**Riverwind** (Chieftain)
*Spirit of the Wind* - Chris Pierson   f   4326

**Rivi** (Young Woman)
*Shaping the Dawn* - Sheila Finch   s   1934

**Rizalli, Arvin "Harek"** (Student; Mythical Creature)
*User Unfriendly* - Vivian Vande Velde   f   5558

**Ro, Nyx** (Sorceress)
*The Cygnet and the Firebird* - Patricia A.
   McKillip   f   3839

**Ro, Vallant** (Wizard; Sea Captain)
*Convergence* - Sharon Green   f   2356

**Road Man** (Traveler; Magician)
*Soulsmith* - Tom Deitz   f   1475

**Roan** (Hero; Adventurer)
*Waking in Dreamland* - Jody Lynn Nye *f* 4177

**Roanhorse, Michael** (Shepherd)
*Eye Killers* - A.A. Carr *h* 911

**Roarke, Jason** (Spaceman; Hero)
*Flare Star* - Paula E. Downing *s* 1594

**Rob** (Student—College)
*Agviq* - Michael Armstrong *s* 208

**Robbins, Cynthia** (Military Personnel; Spacewoman)
*The Rising* - James Doohan *s* 1579

**Robbins, Jake** (Teenager; Student)
*The Vanishing* - Marilyn Kaye *s* 3021

**Robbins, Maggie** (Journalist)
*The Dig* - Alan Dean Foster *s* 2002

**Robert** (Animal)
*The Coachman Rat* - David Henry Wilson *f* 5879

**Robert** (Teenager)
*The Dying Sun* - Gary L. Blackwood *s* 511

**Robert** (Royalty; Handicapped)
*Legacy of the Ancients* - Ron Sarti *s* 4836

**Robert "Robin Hood" of Locksley** (Nobleman; Outlaw)
*Lady of the Forest* - Jennifer Roberson *f* 4609

**Roberts, Amelia** (Military Personnel)
*Priorities* - Lynda Lyons *s* 3579

**Roberts, Heather** (Teenager)
*Blood Sabbath* - Leigh Clark *h* 1048

**Roberts, Karin** (Museum Curator)
*Blood Sabbath* - Leigh Clark *h* 1048

**Roberts, Katie** (Real Estate Agent)
*The Haunting* - Ruby Jean Jensen *h* 2901

**Roberts, Kristen** (Housewife)
*Neighbors* - Maureen S. Pusti *h* 4450

**Roberts, Mark** (Doctor)
*Virus* - Graham Watkins *h* 5632

**Roberts, Ralph** (Aged Person)
*Insomnia* - Stephen King *h* 3135

**Roberts, Roy** (Journalist)
*Grave Markings* - Michael A. Arnzen *h* 212

**Roberts, Sheila** (Student—College)
*Into the Deep* - Ken Grimwood *s* 2450

**Roberts, Tom** (Professor)
*Neighbors* - Maureen S. Pusti *h* 4450

**Roberts, Veronica "Ronnie"** (Journalist)
*Universal Soldier* - Robert Tine *s* 5476

**Robillard, Zac** (Scientist)
*Isaac Asimov's I-Bots* - Steve Perry *s* 4297

**Robin** (Hunter; Step-Parent)
*Passager* - Jane Yolen *f* 6038

**Robin** (Minstrel; Revolutionary)
*The Robin and the Kestrel* - Mercedes Lackey *f* 3293

**Robin** (Child; Mythical Creature)
*Street Magic* - Michael Reaves *f* 4497

**Robinson, David** (Writer)
*Beyond the Shroud* - Rick Hautala *h* 2604

**Robinson, Liz** (Detective—Homicide)
*Love Bite* - Sherry Gottlieb *h* 2288

**Robinson, Sarah** (Teacher)
*Beyond the Shroud* - Rick Hautala *h* 2604

**Robinson, Tracy Zempelios** (Housewife)
*Second Chance* - Chet Williamson *h* 5850

**Robinson, Woody** (Musician)
*Second Chance* - Chet Williamson *h* 5850

**Robinton** (Child; Telepath)
*The Masterharper of Pern* - Anne McCaffrey *s* 3739

**Robyn** (Runaway)
*Stoneskin's Revenge* - Tom Deitz *f* 1476

**Roc, Roxanne** (Mythical Creature)
*Roc and a Hard Place* - Piers Anthony *f* 187

**Roche** (Religious)
*Doomsday Book* - Connie Willis *s* 5868

**Roche, Allison** (Lawyer)
*Mefisto in Onyx* - Harlan Ellison *h* 1786

**Rockdream** (Warrior; Hunter)
*The Goblin Plain War* - Carl Miller *f* 3892

**Rockdream** (Military Personnel)
*The Warrior and the Witch* - Carl Miller *f* 3893

**Rocky** (Police Officer)
*God's Dice* - S. Andrew Swann *f* 5364

**Roclawzi, Neal "Dun Wolf"** (Warrior)
*Once a Hero* - Michael A. Stackpole *f* 5203

**Rodgers, Franklin** (Undertaker)
*Moon Walker* - Rick Hautala *h* 2610

**Rodrigo** (Royalty; Heir—Dispossessed)
*The Still* - David Feintuch *f* 1902

**Rodriguez** (Spouse; Parent)
*Senora Rodriguez and Other Worlds* - Martha Cerda *f* 950

**Roebeck, Nan** (Time Traveler)
*Arc Riders* - David Drake *s* 1626

**Roebeck, Nan** (Time Traveler; Leader)
*The Fourth Rome* - David Drake *s* 1631

**Roeder, Karel** (Student—High School)
*Lights Out in the Reptile House* - Jim Shepard *f* 4976

**Roele, Michael** (Royalty; Leader)
*The Iron Throne* - Simon Hawke *f* 2618

**Rogan the Inept** (Wizard)
*The Door to Ambermere* - J. Calvin Pierce *f* 4316

**Roger** (Criminal)
*Memnoch the Devil* - Anne Rice *h* 4571

**Rogers, Buck** (Warrior)
*Hammer of Mars* - M.S. Murdock *s* 4049

**Rogers, Buck** (Pilot; Experimental Subject)
*A Life in the Future* - Martin Caidin *s* 827

**Rogers, Clive** (Genius; Teenager)
*The Tooth Fairy* - Graham Joyce *f* 2995

**Rogers, Mara** (Professor)
*Indiana Jones and the Unicorn's Legacy* - Rob MacGregor *f* 3593

**Rogers, Newman "Warren G. Menso"** (Genius; Disembodied Personality)
*Circuit of Heaven* - Dennis Danvers *s* 1348

**Rogers, Troi** (Socialite; Spacewoman)
*Treks Not Taken: What if Stephen King, Anne Rice, Bret Easton Ellis, and Other Literary Greats Had Written Episodes of Star Trek: The Next Generation?* - Steven R. Boyett *s* 607

**Rogillard, Jack** (Psychic)
*Jack the Bodiless* - Julian May *s* 3698

**Rohan** (Royalty; Ruler)
*The Star Scroll* - Melanie Rawn *f* 4491
*Stronghold* - Melanie Rawn *f* 4492

**Rohr, Gail** (Spirit)
*The Land of Nod* - Mark A. Clements *h* 1085

**Rojas, Duncan** (Researcher)
*Ivory: A Legend of Past and Future* - Mike Resnick *s* 4547

**Roker** (Military Personnel)
*Hero* - Dave Duncan *s* 1680

**Roland** (Bastard Son; Warrior)
*Charlemagne's Champion* - Gail Van Asten *f* 5534

**Roland** (Gunfighter)
*The Drawing of the Three* - Stephen King *h* 3131

**Roland** (Musician)
*Gate of Darkness, Circle of Light* - Tanya Huff *f* 2797

**Roland of Gilead** (Gunfighter)
*The Waste Lands* - Stephen King *h* 3143
*Wizard and Glass* - Stephen King *h* 3144

**Rolando** (Designer)
*Thirst* - Michael Cecilione *h* 948

**Rolfa** (Genetically Altered Being)
*The Child Garden* - Geoff Ryman *s* 4756

**Rolfson, Bjorn** (Hunter; Wizard)
*Magelord: The Awakening* - Thomas K. Martin *f* 3651

**Rollie** (Guide)
*Sing the Light* - Louise Marley *s* 3629

**Rollie, Steve** (Political Figure)
*Dark Tide* - Elizabeth Forrest *h* 1972

**Roman** (Servant)
*Rock of Ages* - Walter Jon Williams *s* 5840

**Roman, Haml** (Spaceship Captain)
*Warhorse* - Timothy Zahn *s* 6056

**Romanov, George Alexandrovich** (Royalty)
*The Princess and the Dragon* - Roberto Pazzi *f* 4272

**Romar** (Captive)
*The Key of the Keplian* - Andre Norton *f* 4156

**Romero, Val** (Vampire)
*Night Blood* - Eric Flanders *h* 1945

**Romlar, Artus** (Military Personnel; Mercenary)
*The Regiment's War* - John Dalmas *s* 1326
*The White Regiment* - John Dalmas *s* 1327

**Rommel** (Animal)
*Psi-Man* - David Peters *s* 4305

**Ronay, Kinna** (Revolutionary)
*The Fleet of Stars* - Poul Anderson *s* 126

**Ronay, Matthias "Matt"** (Teenager; Adventurer)
*Growing Up Weightless* - John M. Ford *s* 1970

**Roo, Luger** (Farmer; Werewolf)
*The Case of the Police Officer's Cock Ring and the Piano Player Who Had No Fingers* - Edward Lee *h* 3388

**Roode, Sam** (Child)
*Lethal Delivery* - J.G. Maxon *h* 3695

**Roode, Tanya** (Office Worker)
*Lethal Delivery* - J.G. Maxon *h* 3695

**Rook, August** (Inventor)
*The Rim-World Legacy and Beyond* - Frank A. Javor *s* 2882

**Rook, Jim** (Teacher)
*Rook* - Graham Masterton *h* 3678
*The Terror* - Graham Masterton *h* 3679
*Tooth and Claw* - Graham Masterton *h* 3680

**Rool** (Mythical Creature)
*Shadow Moon* - George Lucas *f* 3540

**Roosevelt, Franklin Delano** (Historical Figure; Political Figure)
*Triumph* - Ben Bova *s* 598

**Roosevelt, Theodore** (Historical Figure; Political Figure)
*1901* - Robert Conroy *s* 1139
*Bully!* - Mike Resnick *s* 4539

**Rope** (Sailor)
*Clouds End* - Sean Stewart　*f*　5272

**Rork, Paddy** (Sailor; Young Man)
*Signs of Life* - Cherry Wilder　*s*　5804

**Rory** (Businessman)
*The Hellbound Heart* - Clive Barker　*h*　342

**Rosa** (Cyborg; Friend)
*Correspondence* - Sue Thomas　*s*　5450

**Rose** (Sorceress; Royalty)
*Question Quest* - Piers Anthony　*f*　186

**Rose** (Time Traveler; Warrior)
*The Revenge of the Rose* - Michael
　　Moorcock　*f*　3985

**Rose** (Religious)
*Madeleine's Ghost* - Robert Girardi　*h*　2240

**Rose, Janie** (Young Woman)
*Rage* - Elizabeth Ergas　*h*　1834

**Rose, Mick "China"** (Truck Driver; Businessman)
*Signs of Life* - M. John Harrison　*s*　2580

**Rosemont, Alexander F.** (Military Personnel; Leader)
*Finger of God* - Michael Kasner　*s*　3013

**Rosen, Charlina "Charley"** (Martial Arts Expert)
*Helm* - Steven Gould　*s*　2289

**Rosen, Gerry** (Journalist)
*The Jericho Iteration* - Allen Steele　*s*　5242

**Rosen, Jenna** (Relative)
*Raven Stole the Moon* - Garth Stein　*h*　5249

**Rosenberg, Isaac** (Scientist)
*Titan* - Stephen Baxter　*s*　405

**Rosenberg, Willow** (Teenager)
*Return to Chaos* - Craig Shaw Gardner　*h*　2131

**Roshak, Ter** (Military Personnel)
*Way of the Clans* - Robert Thurston　*s*　5469

**Roshannon, Nikkael** (Mercenary; Psychic)
*Wheel of Dreams* - Salinda Tyson　*f*　5529

**Roshnani** (Spouse; Counselor)
*The Stolen Throne* - Harry Turtledove　*f*　5510

**Rosie** (Magician)
*Wild Blood* - Nancy A. Collins　*h*　1127

**Ross, Angie** (Teacher)
*Impulse* - Rick Hautala　*h*　2609

**Ross, Brandy** (Teenager)
*Impulse* - Rick Hautala　*h*　2609

**Ross, Brent** (Military Personnel)
*Assault of the Super Carrier* - Peter Albano　*s*　47
*Revenge of the Seventh Carrier* - Peter Albano　*s*　49
*Super Carrier: The Ultimate Secret Weapon* - Peter
　　Albano　*s*　50

**Ross, David** (Detective)
*The Dead Man's Kiss* - Robert Weinberg　*h*　5695

**Ross, Elaine** (Student)
*In Double Jeopardy* - Andrew Neiderman　*h*　4088

**Ross, John** (Professor; Sorcerer)
*A Knight of the Word* - Terry Brooks　*f*　714

**Ross, John** (Psychic)
*Running with the Demon* - Terry Brooks　*f*　715

**Ross, Malcolm** (Lawyer)
*The Jewel of Seven Stars* - Bram Stoker　*h*　5312

**Rosselin, Perada "Rada"** (Ruler)
*The Gathering Flame* - Debra Doyle　*s*　1599

**Rosselin Metadi, Beka** (Royalty; Spaceship Captain)
*By Honor Betray'd* - Debra Doyle　*s*　1598

**Rosselin Metadi, Beka** (Ruler; Spaceship Captain)
*Starpilot's Grave* - Debra Doyle　*s*　1606

**Rossemikka "Mikka"** (Royalty)
*The Perfect Princess* - Irene Radford　*f*　4462

**Rossi, Eric** (Police Officer)
*Domination* - Michael Cecilione　*h*　946

**Rossiter, Adam** (Singer)
*Tempter* - Nancy A. Collins　*h*　1125

**Rossman, Aaron** (Spaceman)
*Golden Fleece* - Robert J. Sawyer　*s*　4857

**Rosvenir, Collan** (Minstrel; Nobleman)
*The Mageborn Traitor* - Melanie Rawn　*f*　4488

**Roswell, Harry I.** (Dentist; Doctor)
*Summerland* - L. Dean James　*f*　2865

**Rotciv, Victor** (Stock Broker)
*The Convocation* - John R. Holt　*h*　2748

**Roth, Peter** (Guide)
*Monster* - John Tigges　*h*　5474

**Rothman, Felice** (Writer)
*Bagatelle—Guinevere* - Nancy Bogen　*f*　558

**Roueche, Philip** (Zoo Keeper)
*Claw* - Ken Eulo　*h*　1850

**Rourke, Buneka** (Settler; Teenager)
*Powers That Be* - Anne McCaffrey　*s*　3745

**Rourke, John T.** (Military Personnel; Spy)
*The Struggle* - Jerry Ahern　*s*　44

**Rourke, Kenneth Christian** (Security Officer)
*Random Factor* - Joel Henry Sherman　*s*　4984

**Rover "Roverandom"** (Animal; Adventurer)
*Roverandom* - J.R.R. Tolkien　*f*　5479

**Rovin, Elli** (Military Personnel)
*Limbo Search* - Parke Godwin　*s*　2245

**Rowan** (Witch)
*His Majesty's Elephant* - Judith Tarr　*f*　5394

**Rowan** (Child)
*The Influence* - Ramsey Campbell　*h*　857

**Rowan** (Cartographer; Librarian)
*The Outskirter's Secret* - Rosemary Kirstein　*s*　3157

**Rowan** (Wanderer; Scientist)
*The Steerswoman* - Rosemary Kirstein　*s*　3158

**Rowan, Dalin** (Computer Expert)
*Knights of the Black Earth* - Margaret Weis　*s*　5718

**Rowan, Daniel** (Bartender)
*Famine* - Todd Komarnicki　*h*　3201

**Rowan, Jack** (Writer; Spirit)
*Dead Lines* - John Skipp　*h*　5082

**Rowena** (Worker)
*The Persistence of Memory* - Karen Ripley　*s*　4592

**Rowforth** (Royalty)
*Chimaera's Copper* - Piers Anthony　*f*　166

**Rowland, Althea** (Actress)
*Timeshare* - Joshua Dann　*s*　1344

**Roxanne** (Child)
*My Best Friend Is Invisible* - R.L. Stine　*h*　5289

**Roxanne** (Dancer)
*The Werewolf Chronicles* - Traci Briery　*h*　679

**Roy** (Time Traveler)
*Letters From Atlantis* - Robert Silverberg　*f*　5035

**Roy, Ubu** (Pilot; Trader)
*Angel Station* - Walter Jon Williams　*s*　5833

**Royal, Barton** (Murderer)
*Billy* - Whitley Strieber　*h*　5338

**Royal, Paul** (Experimental Subject)
*Nanoware Time/The Persistence of Vision* - Ian
　　Watson　*s*　5638

**Royal, Solomon** (Doctor)
*Butcher* - Rex Miller　*h*　3898

**Rozak, Jay** (Time Traveler; Revolutionary)
*Islands of Tomorrow* - F.M. Busby　*s*　783

**Rozhenko, Worf** (Alien; Student)
*Worf's First Adventure* - Peter David　*s*　1391

**Rozokov, Dimitri** (Vampire)
*The Night Inside* - Nancy Baker　*h*　301

**Rubicon, Cassandra** (Archaeologist)
*Ruins* - Kevin J. Anderson　*h*　112

**Rubidoux, John** (Animal Trainer)
*Retribution* - Elizabeth Forrest　*h*　1975

**Rubra, Rose** (Bride)
*Waking Beauty* - Paul Witcover　*f*　5931

**Rucker, Dave** (Administrator)
*Cosm* - Gregory Benford　*s*　444

**Rucker, Judgement** (Hunter)
*The Cellar* - Richard Laymon　*h*　3365

**Rudolph "Rudy"** (Royalty; Telepath)
*Being of Two Minds* - Pamela F. Service　*f*　4918

**Rufin, Tal** (Police Officer)
*Four & Twenty Blackbirds* - Mercedes
　　Lackey　*f*　3283

**Rufo** (Magician; Servant)
*Glory Road* - Robert A. Heinlein　*f*　2644

**Rufus** (Immortal)
*The Boat of a Million Years* - Poul Anderson　*s*　125

**Rugad** (Ruler)
*The Resistance* - Kristine Kathryn Rusch　*f*　4727

**Rugby, Jerzy** (Computer Expert; Detective—
　　Amateur)
*The Hacker and the Ants* - Rudy Rucker　*s*　4704

**Ruha** (Widow(er); Sorceress)
*The Parched Sea* - Troy Denning　*f*　1486

**Ruiz, Juan** (Criminal)
*Fear Itself* - Ric Meyers　*h*　3881

**Rumer** (Prostitute)
*Waking Beauty* - Paul Witcover　*f*　5931

**Rune** (Musician)
*The Lark and the Wren* - Mercedes Lackey　*f*　3286

**Runs in Light** (Hunter; Prehistoric Human)
*People of the Wolf* - W. Michael Gear　*f*　2170

**Runyon, Damon** (Journalist; Historical Figure)
*Nevermore* - William Hjortsberg　*h*　2692

**Rupert** (Royalty)
*Blue Moon Rising* - Simon R. Green　*f*　2362

**Ruquel** (Doctor; Dancer)
*The Book of the Beast* - Tanith Lee　*f*　3405

**Rushkin, Vincent Adjani** (Artist; Recluse)
*Memory and Dream* - Charles de Lint　*f*　1433

**Ruskettle, Olive** (Mythical Creature)
*Song of the Saurials* - Kate Novak　*f*　4167

**Ruskin, Willard** (Scientist)
*From a Changeling Star* - Jeffrey A. Carver　*s*　931

**Russel, Ben** (Convict)
*Cold in July* - Joe R. Lansdale　*h*　3323

**Russell, Dale** (Government Official)
*Green Lake* - S.K. Epperson　*h*　1830

**Russell, Katrinka** (Housewife)
*Violin* - Anne Rice　*h*　4579

**Russell, Paul** (Scientist; Engineer)
*Lake of the Sun* - Wynne Whiteford　*s*　5787

**Russell, Saxifrage "Sax"** (Scientist; Aged Person)
*Blue Mars* - Kim Stanley Robinson　*s*　4629

**Russell, Saxifrage "Sax"** (Scientist; Revolutionary)
*Green Mars* - Kim Stanley Robinson　*s*　4633

**Russell, Scott** (Detective—Private)
*Street Magic* - Michael Reaves　*f*　4497

**Russie, Moishe** (Refugee; Radio Personality)
*Worldwar: Striking the Balance* - Harry
  Turtledove  *s*  5516

**Russie, Moishe** (Fugitive)
*Worldwar: Tilting the Balance* - Harry
  Turtledove  *s*  5517

**Rustin** (Royalty)
*The Still* - David Feintuch  *f*  1902

**Rustin, Adelaine Hawthorne Taylor** (Aged Person)
*The Devil's Churn* - Kristine Kathryn
  Rusch  *h*  4715

**Rusty** (Teenager; Refugee)
*A Time for Dragons* - Gary Gentile  *s*  2193

**Ruth** (Vampire)
*Personal Darkness* - Tanith Lee  *h*  3413

**Ruthven, Lucy** (Actress)
*Slave of My Thirst* - Tom Holland  *h*  2742

**Rutledge, Andrew** (Writer)
*Root of All Evil* - David A. Farrow  *h*  1888

**Rutman, Becky** (Administrator)
*Nightlife* - Jack Ellis  *h*  1779

**Rwyan** (Wizard)
*Lords of the Sky* - Angus Wells  *f*  5738

**Ryan, Holly** (Psychologist)
*Sacrifice* - Richard Kinion  *h*  3146

**Ryan, Jayne** (Astronaut; Scientist)
*Beachhead* - Jack Williamson  *s*  5859

**Ryan, Lacey** (Teenager)
*Shackled* - Ray Garton  *h*  2156

**Ryan, Steve** (Businessman)
*Blood Feud* - Sam Siciliano  *h*  5020

**Ryan, William** (Religious)
*Nightworld* - F. Paul Wilson  *h*  5893

**Ryan-Turriy, Adlayra** (Mythical Creature)
*Dancer's Rise* - Jo Clayton  *f*  1064

**Ryana** (Religious; Adventurer)
*The Seeker* - Simon Hawke  *f*  2624

**Ryba** (Leader)
*Fall of Angels* - L.E. Modesitt Jr.  *f*  3930

**Rybak, Nadya** (Werewolf; Orphan)
*Nadya: The Wolf Chronicles* - Pat Murphy  *f*  4052

**Rydell, Berry** (Police Officer; Bounty Hunter)
*Virtual Light* - William Gibson  *s*  2219

**Rydell, Tony** (Scientist)
*Dream Maker* - W.A. Harbinson  *s*  2542

**Ryder** (Genetically Altered Being)
*Black Milk* - Robert Reed  *s*  4504

**Ryder** (Musician; Fugitive)
*Kamikaze L'Amour* - Richard Kadrey  *s*  2998

**Ryder, Christine** (Pilot; Lesbian)
*The Tranquility Alternative* - Allen Steele  *s*  5248

**Ryder, Gordon** (Fugitive)
*Pirates of the Universe* - Terry Bisson  *s*  506

**Ryder, Gunther "Gun"** (Spaceman)
*Pirates of the Universe* - Terry Bisson  *s*  506

**Ryder, Howie** (Teenager)
*Dawn's Uncertain Light* - Neal Barrett Jr.  *s*  365

**Ryder, Jake** (Astronaut)
*Reach* - Edward Gibson  *s*  2216

**Ryerson, Will** (Worker)
*Reprisal* - F. Paul Wilson  *h*  5896

**Rylus** (Entertainer)
*When the Gods Are Silent* - Jane M.
  Lindskold  *f*  3477

**Ryn "Robin"** (Runaway)
*The War of the Sky Lords* - John Brosnan  *s*  721

**Rys** (Sailor)
*Dancing Jack* - Laurie J. Marks  *f*  3624

**Ryson, Kerryl** (Slave)
*The Thirteenth Majestral* - Hayford Peirce  *s*  4277

**Ryton, Melanie** (Mutant)
*The Mutant Season* - Robert Silverberg  *s*  5039

**Ryton, Michael** (Mutant)
*The Mutant Season* - Robert Silverberg  *s*  5039

## S

**S-, Delia** (Real Estate Agent)
*First Love: A Gothic Tale* - Joyce Carol
  Oates  *h*  4183

**S-, Josephine Carolyn "Josie"** (Child)
*First Love: A Gothic Tale* - Joyce Carol
  Oates  *h*  4183

**S .B. "Air"** (Child; Adventurer)
*Beyond the Magic Sphere* - Gail Jarrow  *f*  2879

**Saad, Khalil** (Worker)
*The Nightmare People* - Lawrence Watt-
  Evans  *h*  5643

**Saalahan** (Alien)
*Mid-Flinx* - Alan Dean Foster  *s*  2010

**Saari, Juna "Eerin"** (Scientist; Explorer)
*The Color of Distance* - Amy Thomson  *s*  5461

**Saash** (Animal; Wizard)
*The Book of Night with Moon* - Diane
  Duane  *f*  1657

**Sabah, Hasan al** (Criminal; Religious)
*The Mask of Loki* - Roger Zelazny  *f*  6071

**Saber, Karen** (Linguist; Criminal)
*Marks of Our Brothers* - Jane M. Lindskold  *s*  3475

**Sabra** (Vampire)
*Keeper of the King* - Nigel Bennett  *h*  452

**Sabriel** (Magician; Teenager)
*Sabriel* - Garth Nix  *f*  4129

**Sack** (Disembodied Personality)
*Land O'Goshen* - Charles McNair  *s*  3855

**Sadb** (Spouse)
*The Shield between the Worlds* - Diana L.
  Paxson  *f*  4267

**Sadi** (Mercenary; Immortal)
*Kaleidoscope Century* - John Barnes  *s*  352

**SaDiablo, Daemon** (Wizard; Prostitute)
*Daughter of the Blood* - Anne Bishop  *f*  495

**SaDiablo, Saetan** (Vampire; Wizard)
*Daughter of the Blood* - Anne Bishop  *f*  495

**Sadir** (Nobleman)
*Canby's Legion* - Bill Baldwin  *s*  308

**Sadira** (Slave; Mythical Creature)
*The Verdant Passage* - Troy Denning  *f*  1487

**Sadler, Ben** (Vampire)
*Sins of the Blood* - Kristine Kathryn Rusch  *h*  4728

**Sagan, Derek** (Military Personnel)
*King's Sacrifice* - Margaret Weis  *s*  5717
*The Lost King* - Margaret Weis  *s*  5720

**Sage of Sare** (Wizard; Ruler)
*The Wizard King* - Julie Dean Smith  *f*  5127

**Sahacat** (Indian; Shaman)
*People of the Sky* - Clare Bell  *s*  431

**Sahr, Leon** (Nobleman)
*Fire Angels* - Jane Routley  *f*  4685

**Saigo** (Government Official; Revolutionary)
*Aristoi* - Walter Jon Williams  *s*  5834

**Sailor "Lightning"** (Alien)
*Silent Dances* - A.C. Crispin  *s*  1263

**Saint-Alaban, Justice** (Scientist)
*Winterlong* - Elizabeth Hand  *s*  2539

**St. Brendan, Caitlin** (Religious; Magician)
*Indiana Jones and the White Witch* - Martin
  Caidin  *f*  826

**St. Charles, Lia** (Probation Officer)
*Voodoo Child* - Michael Reaves  *h*  4498

**St. Clair, Adrienne** (Scientist; Vampire)
*Bloodshift* - Garfield Reeves-Stevens  *h*  4508

**St. Claire, Nicole** (Student; Werewolf)
*Wolf Moon* - John R. Holt  *h*  2749

**St. Cyr, Butterfly** (Smuggler; Spaceship Captain)
*Archangel Blues* - eluki bes shahar  *s*  471
*Darktraders* - eluki bes shahar  *s*  472
*Hellflower* - eluki bes shahar  *s*  473

**St. Du Lac, Lynn** (Noblewoman)
*The Lost History of Redwyn* - William Jay  *f*  2883

**St. Eve, Clair** (Child)
*Skeletons* - Al Sarrantonio  *h*  4834

**St. George, Blacktooth "Nimmy"** (Religious;
  Linguist)
*Saint Leibowitz and the Wild Horse Woman* - Walter
  M. Miller Jr.  *s*  3908

**St. George, Joe** (Handyman)
*Dolores Claiborne* - Stephen King  *h*  3130

**Saint-Germain** (Vampire)
*Better in the Dark* - Chelsea Quinn Yarbro  *h*  6011
*Mansions of Darkness* - Chelsea Quinn
  Yarbro  *h*  6016
*Out of the House of Life* - Chelsea Quinn
  Yarbro  *h*  6018

**Saint-Germain** (Revolutionary)
*Two Crowns for America* - Katherine Kurtz  *f*  3262

**Saint-Germain** (Vampire)
*Writ in Blood* - Chelsea Quinn Yarbro  *h*  6019

**St. Ives, Langdon** (Scientist; Explorer)
*Lord Kelvin's Machine* - James P. Blaylock  *f*  520

**St. Jacques, Adela Rogers** (Writer)
*Night of the Living 'Gator!* - Richard A.
  Lupoff  *s*  3573

**St. James, Nicholas** (Government Official)
*The Penultimate Truth* - Philip K. Dick  *s*  1522

**St. James, Raven** (Witch)
*Eternity* - Maggie Shayne  *f*  4943

**St. John, Ian "Hunter"** (Pilot)
*Wing Commander: Freedom Flight* - Mercedes
  Lackey  *s*  3307

**St. John, Simon** (Musician)
*December* - Phil Rickman  *h*  4588

**St. John, Wade** (Student)
*Coven* - Edward Lee  *h*  3390

**Saint-Just, Emile** (Spaceman)
*Blind Justice* - S.N. Lewitt  *s*  3448

**Sakai, Catherine** (Pilot; Surveyor)
*To Dream in the City of Sorrows* - Kathryn M.
  Drennan  *s*  1654

**Sakhalin, Anatoly** (Warrior; Nobleman)
*The Law of Becoming* - Kate Elliott  *s*  1774

**Sal** (Warrior; Religious)
*The Face of Apollo* - Fred Saberhagen  *s*  4766

**Saladin** (Immortal; Murderer)
*The Forever King* - Molly Cochran  *f*  1092

**Salandra** (Guide; Adventurer)
*Indiana Jones and the Interior World* - Rob
  MacGregor  *f*  3590

**Salazar, Bettina** (Indian)
*Ghost Dance* - Kathryn Ptacek   h   4441

**Salazar, Kirk** (Student; Traveler)
*The Venom Trees of Sunga* - L. Sprague de
   Camp   s   1420

**Salesman** (Demon)
*Tales From the Crypt: Demon Knight* - Randall
   Boyll   h   617

**Salib, Tariq** (Scientist)
*The Missing Matter* - Thomas R.
   McDonough   s   3805

**Salisaw, Brent** (Construction Worker)
*Night Thunder* - Ruby Jean Jensen   h   2903

**Salisaw, Holly** (Child)
*Night Thunder* - Ruby Jean Jensen   h   2903

**Salisaw, Kara** (Child)
*Night Thunder* - Ruby Jean Jensen   h   2903

**Salk, Job Napoleon** (Orphan)
*Brother to Dragons* - Charles Sheffield   s   4949

**Sallas, Ike "the Bakatcha Bandit"** (Indian; Sailor)
*Sailor Song* - Ken Kesey   s   3082

**Sally** (Psychic; Child)
*The Kronos Condition* - Emily Devenport   s   1502

**Salmalin, Numair** (Magician)
*The Realms of the Gods* - Tamora Pierce   f   4321
*Wolf-Speaker* - Tamora Pierce   f   4324

**Salmoneus** (Salesman; Sidekick)
*The First Casualty* - David L. Seidman   f   4912

**Saluez** (Servant)
*Shadow's End* - Sheri S. Tepper   s   5435

**Salvatore, Dominga** (Religious; Criminal)
*The Laughing Corpse* - Laurell K. Hamilton   f   2519

**Sam** (Warrior; Refugee)
*Hope of Earth* - Piers Anthony   s   175

**Sam** (Hunter)
*Nicoji* - M. Shayne Bell   s   434

**Sam** (Teenager)
*No Kidding* - Bruce Brooks   s   709

**Sam** (Cyborg)
*The Sounding Stillness* - Kenneth Von
   Gunden   s   5587

**Sam** (Mechanic)
*The Unfinished* - Jay B. Laws   h   3362

**Sam** (Criminal; Adventurer)
*Villains by Necessity* - Eve Forward   f   1985

**Samiq** (Prehistoric Human; Indian)
*My Sister the Moon* - Sue Harrison   f   2582

**Sampson, Matt** (Military Personnel; Teenager)
*Traitors from Within* - R.A. Montgomery   s   3966

**Samson, Daniel "Dan"** (Martial Arts Expert; Time
   Traveler)
*Union Fires* - John Barnes   f   358
*Wartide* - John Barnes   f   359

**Samson, Leonard "Doc"** (Doctor)
*What Savage Beast* - Peter David   s   1390

**Samson, Rosalie "Rose"** (Social Worker)
*The Godmother* - Elizabeth Ann
   Scarborough   f   4862

**Samuel** (Twin)
*Dark Father* - Tom Piccirilli   h   4312

**Samuels, Albert** (Inventor; Clone)
*The Clouds of Magellan* - David F.
   Nighbert   s   4103

**Samuels, Rheabeth "Rhea"** (Businesswoman)
*Hell on High* - Holly Lisle   f   3483

**Samules, Elmo** (Civil Servant)
*Spider Legs* - Piers Anthony   s   189

**Samules, Martha** (Scientist)
*Spider Legs* - Piers Anthony   s   189

**Sanchez, Monica** (Musician)
*Gossamer Axe* - Gael Baudino   f   392

**Sanchi** (Gambler)
*Sphynxes Wild* - Esther Friesner   f   2083

**Sanda** (Apprentice; Scholar)
*Initiation* - Marian Hughes   s   2806

**Sandburg, Elaine "Nefret"** (Time Traveler;
   Religious)
*Thebes of the Hundred Gates* - Robert
   Silverberg   s   5043

**Sandeen, Michael** (Musician)
*Night Music* - Sheila Bristow Garner   h   2147

**Sander** (Friend; Teenager)
*Through the Heart* - Richard Grant   f   2328

**Sanderheim, Doug** (Engineer; Boyfriend)
*Slow Funeral* - Rebecca Ore   f   4221

**Sanders, Alison** (Student)
*The Priest: A Gothic Romance* - Thomas M.
   Disch   h   1562

**Sanders, John A.** (Police Officer)
*Dark Visions* - T. Lucien Wright   h   5987

**Sanders, Johnny** (Inventor; Artist)
*Armed Memory* - Jim Young   s   6048

**Sanders, Julia** (Waiter/Waitress)
*Raven* - Charles L. Grant   h   2314

**Sanders, Kenneth** (Mutant; FBI Agent)
*Doomsday Exam* - Nick Pollotta   f   4363

**Sanders, Nicholas** (Linguist)
*Ring of Swords* - Eleanor Arnason   s   210

**Sanders, Phillipe "Phil" Montoya** (Police Officer;
   Computer Expert)
*The Modular Man* - Roger MacBride Allen   s   79

**Sanderson, Loki** (Professor)
*Destiny's Carnival* - Warren Murphy   h   4057

**Sanderson, Merry** (Girlfriend)
*Wolf and Iron* - Gordon R. Dickson   s   1539

**Sanderson, Paul** (Businessman; Wanderer)
*Wolf and Iron* - Gordon R. Dickson   s   1539

**Sandford, Nancy** (Scientist; Editor)
*The Ragged World: A Novel of the Hefn on Earth* -
   Judith Moffett   s   3943

**Sandoval** (Military Personnel; Lesbian)
*In the Blood* - Lauren Wright Douglas   s   1590

**Sandoval, Mickey** (Researcher)
*Heads* - Greg Bear   s   419

**Sandoval, Rho** (Businessman)
*Heads* - Greg Bear   s   419

**Sandoz, Emilio** (Religious; Linguist)
*Children of God* - Mary Doria Russell   s   4735
*The Sparrow* - Mary Doria Russell   s   4736

**Sands, Larson Clarke** (Pilot)
*The Clouds of Saturn* - Michael McCollum   s   3770

**Sands, Max** (Sports Figure)
*The Barsoom Project* - Larry Niven   s   4115

**Sandtiger "Tiger"** (Warrior)
*Sword-Breaker* - Jennifer Roberson   f   4613

**Sandwriter** (Shaman)
*The Promise* - Monica Hughes   s   2808

**Sanger, David** (Scientist)
*Murder in the Solid State* - Wil McCarthy   s   3764

**Sanglant** (Military Personnel; Immortal)
*Prince of Dogs* - Kate Elliott   f   1775

**Sangre, Ryne** (Pilot)
*A Roil of Stars* - Don Wismer   s   5930

**Sanmartin, Raul** (Military Personnel)
*A Small Colonial War* - Robert Frezza   s   2054

**Sannazzaro, Sally** (Nurse)
*Treasure Box* - Orson Scott Card   h   898

**Santa, Levi D.** (Demon)
*The Book of the Damned* - D.A. Fowler   h   2022

**Santa Claus** (Mythical Creature)
*Santa Steps Out: A Fairy Tale for Grownups* - Robert
   Devereaux   h   1506

**Santagithi** (Warrior)
*The Western Wizard* - Mickey Zucker
   Reichert   f   4526

**Santangelo, Kaye** (Writer)
*The Shift* - George Foy   s   2033

**Santiago, Martina** (Teenager; Twin)
*The Vanishing* - Marilyn Kaye   s   3021

**Santillanes, Gil** (Handyman)
*Days of the Dead* - Ashley McConnell   h   3774

**Santorini, Angie** (Child)
*Death Dream* - Ben Bova   s   583

**Santorini, Dan** (Computer Expert; Engineer)
*Death Dream* - Ben Bova   s   583

**Santos** (Vampire)
*To Speak in Lifeless Tongues* - David Niall
   Wilson   h   5883

**Santos, Nick** (Writer; Vampire)
*The World on Blood* - Jonathan Nasaw   h   4069

**Santos, Ramon** (Nobleman)
*Iceman* - Cynthia Felice   s   1913

**Santoul, Remy** (Spy)
*Illegal Alien* - James Luceno   s   3543

**Sara** (Scientist)
*Brightness Reef* - David Brin   s   684

**Sara** (Amnesiac)
*Children of the Blood: Book Two of The Sundered* -
   Michelle Sagara   f   4782

**Sarah** (Handicapped; Psychic)
*Brother to Dragons, Companion to Owls* - Jane M.
   Lindskold   f   3473

**Sarah** (Young Woman)
*Familiar Spirit* - Lisa Tuttle   h   5519

**Sarai** (Scientist; Healer)
*The Children Star* - Joan Slonczewski   s   5090

**Sarai** (Detective; Royalty)
*The Spell of the Black Dagger* - Lawrence Watt-
   Evans   f   5648

**Saralyn, Paul** (Young Man)
*The Link* - Andrew Laurance   h   3348

**Sardoll, Dirac** (Leader)
*Berserker Kill* - Fred Saberhagen   s   4761

**Sardou, Lake Genevieve "Jenny"** (Artificial
   Intelligence)
*Berserker Kill* - Fred Saberhagen   s   4761

**Sarek** (Diplomat; Alien)
*Sarek* - A.C. Crispin   s   1260

**Sarena** (Animal)
*Catamount* - Michael Peak   f   4273

**Sargent, Gideon** (Fisherman)
*The Innsmouth Heritage* - Brian Stableford   h   5194

**Sari** (Traveler; Healer)
*Branch and Crown* - Gael Baudino   f   389

**Sari** (Abuse Victim; Traveler)
*O Greenest Branch!* - Gael Baudino   f   394

**Sarin, Robert** (Aged Person; Handicapped)
*The Plague Tales* - Ann Benson   s   453

**Sarnac, Robert** (Military Personnel; Time Traveler)
*Legacy* - Steve White   s   5785

**Sarnii, Irene** (Anthropologist)
*Sleepwalker* - Michael Cadnum   h   815

**Saro** (Amnesiac; Heiress—Lost)
*The Book of Atrix Wolfe* - Patricia A.
   McKillip   f   3838

**Sarrasri, Diane** (Magician; Telepath)
*The Realms of the Gods* - Tamora Pierce   f   4321
*Wild Magic* - Tamora Pierce   f   4323
*Wolf-Speaker* - Tamora Pierce   f   4324

**Sarrault, Elizabeth** (Spaceship Captain)
*Blind Justice* - S.N. Lewitt   s   3448

**Sartak** (Vampire)
*Netherworld* - Richard Lee Byers   h   798

**Sartorius** (Doctor; Inventor)
*The Waterworks* - E.L. Doctorow   s   1564

**Saryon** (Scholar)
*Legacy of the Darksword* - Margaret Weis   f   5719

**Sasaki, Jay** (Dancer; Spaceman)
*Starmind* - Spider Robinson   s   4642

**Sassinak** (Spaceship Captain)
*Generation Warrior* - Anne McCaffrey   s   3735
*Sassinak* - Anne McCaffrey   s   3748

**Satan "Mr. Smith"** (Angel)
*The Old Man and Mr. Smith* - Peter
   Ustinov   f   5532

**Sataru, Hidaka** (Thief; Wizard)
*The Yngling in Yamato* - John Dalmas   s   1329

**Sathilda** (Entertainer)
*Conan the Gladiator* - Leonard Carpenter   f   907

**Sati** (Deity)
*Sati* - Christopher Pike   f   4330

**Sattler, Ellie** (Scientist)
*Jurassic Park* - Michael Crichton   s   1255

**Saturna** (Telepath; Genetically Altered Being)
*Saturn's Child* - Nichelle Nichols   s   4101

**Saubhari, Rishi** (Companion)
*Faces of Deception* - Troy Denning   f   1485

**Saun** (Apprentice; Healer)
*Athyra* - Steven Brust   f   739

**Saunder, Anthony** (Clone)
*Legacy of Earth* - Juanita Coulson   s   1209

**Saunders, Charlotte** (Artist)
*Retribution* - Elizabeth Forrest   h   1975

**Saunders, Clay** (Murderer)
*Wildest Dreams* - Norman Partridge   h   4256

**Saunders, Reed "Sand"** (Disembodied Personality)
*Darkly the Thunder* - William W.
   Johnstone   h   2929

**Sauromanta** (Time Traveler; Warrior)
*Atlantis Found* - R. Garcia y Robertson   s   2119

**Sauvage, J.D.** (Scientist)
*Metaphase* - Vonda N. McIntyre   s   3821
*Nautilus* - Vonda N. McIntyre   s   3823
*Transition* - Vonda N. McIntyre   s   3825

**Sauventreen, Verna** (Magician; Leader)
*Blood of the Fold* - Terry Goodkind   f   2268

**Savage, Clark "Doc" Jr.** (Adventurer; Military
   Personnel)
*Escape From Loki* - Philip Jose Farmer   f   1870

**Savage, Clark "Doc" Jr.** (Adventurer; Genius)
*The Frightened Fish* - Kenneth Robeson   f   4622
*The Jade Ogre* - Kenneth Robeson   f   4623

**Savage, Clark "Doc" Jr.** (Adventurer; Military
   Personnel)
*Python Isle* - Kenneth Robeson   f   4624

**Savage, Clark "Doc" Jr.** (Adventurer; Genius)
*White Eyes* - Kenneth Robeson   f   4625

**Savage, Lucy** (Worker; Parent)
*Where Does Kissing End?* - Kate Pullinger   h   4445

**Savage, Lyn** (Detective—Police)
*The Death Prayer* - David Bowker   h   602

**Savage, Mina** (Travel Agent)
*Where Does Kissing End?* - Kate Pullinger   h   4445

**Savik, Bob** (Police Officer)
*Hair of the Dog* - Brett Davis   f   1400

**Savitsky** (Military Personnel)
*Lunching with the Antichrist* - Michael
   Moorcock   f   3984

**Savoy** (Actor; Disembodied Personality)
*Fools* - Pat Cadigan   s   805

**Sawalha, Erim** (Religious; Sorcerer)
*The Riddled Man* - Mark E. Rogers   f   4654

**Sawyer, Daniel** (Military Personnel)
*Solo* - Robert Mason   s   3665

**Sawyer, Kelly** (Scientist)
*Carnivore* - Leigh Clark   h   1049

**Sawyer, Meredith** (Journalist)
*The Long Midnight* - Daniel Ransom   h   4480

**Sawyer, Phil** (Worker)
*The Mountain King* - Rick Hautala   h   2611

**Sax/Ewasx** (Alien)
*Brightness Reef* - David Brin   s   684

**Saxon, Bonnie** (Teenager)
*The Stake* - Richard Laymon   h   3372

**Saxton, Drake** (Journalist)
*The Black Carousel* - Charles L. Grant   h   2303

**Saxtorph, Eric** (Spaceship Captain)
*Inconstant Star* - Poul Anderson   s   129

**Sayler, Catherine** (Detective—Private)
*Vampire Bytes* - Linda Grant   h   2322

**Sayyed** (Sorcerer; Religious)
*City of the Sorcerers* - Mary H. Herbert   f   2673

**Sayyed** (Sorcerer; Leader)
*Winged Magic* - Mary H. Herbert   f   2678

**Scallan, Amy** (Musician)
*Our Lady of the Harbour* - Charles de Lint   f   1434

**Scandal** (Animal)
*Majyk by Accident* - Esther Friesner   f   2079
*Majyk by Hook or Crook* - Esther Friesner   f   2081

**Scanwell, Jane** (Political Figure; Organized Crime
   Figure)
*Empire Builders* - Ben Bova   s   584

**Scarbrough, Liz** (Clerk)
*The Vampire's Apprentice* - Richard Lee
   Byers   h   799

**Scarecrow Jack** (Woodsman)
*Down Among the Dead Men* - Simon R.
   Green   f   2367

**Scatha** (Noblewoman)
*The Endless Knot* - Stephen R. Lawhead   f   3354

**Scathach** (Royalty)
*Lavondyss: Journey to an Unknown Region* - Robert
   Holdstock   f   2739

**Scathach** (Mythical Creature; Spirit)
*The Scathach and the Maeve's Daughter* - Mary
   Alexander Walker   f   5618

**Schafer, Justin** (Psychologist)
*Alien Influences* - Kristine Kathryn Rusch   s   4711

**Schechter, Kate** (Heroine)
*The Long Dark Tea-Time of the Soul* - Douglas
   Adams   s   30

**Scheherazade** (Spouse; Storyteller)
*The Last Arabian Night* - Craig Shaw
   Gardner   f   2129

**Schel, Daniel** (Deity)
*The Moon's Wife: A Hystery* - A.A.
   Attanasio   f   271

**Schell, Alix** (Student)
*Lurid Dreams* - Charles L. Harness   s   2546

**Schenk, Madeline Leuoir** (Museum Curator)
*Warsprite* - Jefferson P. Swycaffer   s   5375

**Schlessinger, David** (Activist; Scientist)
*The Secret Oceans* - Betty Ballantine   s   318

**Schoedsack, Ernest "Monte"** (Director; Adventurer)
*Dinosaur Summer* - Greg Bear   s   416

**Schoenwald, Robert** (Construction Worker)
*Shadow Dance* - Jessica Palmer   h   4238

**Schonnegon, Teletha** (Military Personnel)
*Timespell* - Robert N. Charrette   f   978

**Schonnegon, Teletha** (Mercenary)
*Wizard of Bones* - Robert N. Charrette   f   979

**Schrapnell** (Wealthy)
*To Say Nothing of the Dog* - Connie Willis   s   5874

**Schreber, D.P.** (Doctor)
*Dark City* - Frank Lauria   h   3351

**Schroeder, Lauren** (Housewife)
*Dark Channel* - Ray Garton   h   2150

**Schroeder, Thomas** (Businessman)
*Psychomech* - Brian Lumley   h   3562

**Schwartz, Randomly Distributed "Randy"**
   (Student)
*Orbital Resonance* - John Barnes   s   356

**Schwatzendale, Fay** (Engineer; Gambler)
*Ports of Call* - Jack Vance   s   5549

**Schweigman, Marianne** (Linguist)
*Being Alien* - Rebecca Ore   s   4217

**Sciascia, Francesca** (Office Worker)
*Catacomb* - Andrew Laurance   h   3347

**Scillia** (Orphan; Heiress)
*The One-Armed Queen* - Jane Yolen   f   6037

**Scolari, Paula** (Military Personnel)
*Legion of the Damned* - William C. Dietz   s   1547

**Scope** (Mythical Creature; Adventurer)
*Dragoncharm* - Graham Edwards   f   1749

**Scopes, Brent** (Businessman)
*Mount Dragon* - Douglas Preston   h   4413

**Scoresby, Lee** (Pilot)
*The Golden Compass* - Philip Pullman   f   4446

**Scoresby, Lee** (Traveler; Pilot)
*The Subtle Knife* - Philip Pullman   f   4448

**Scoresby, Lyman** (Writer)
*The Lodger* - Fred Chappell   h   966

**Scorpio** (Alien; Fugitive)
*Dragon's Blood* - Alex McDonough   s   3799
*Dragon's Claw* - Alex McDonough   s   3800
*Dragon's Eye* - Alex McDonough   s   3801
*Scorpio* - Alex McDonough   s   3802
*Scorpio Descending* - Alex McDonough   s   3803
*Scorpio Rising* - Alex McDonough   s   3804

**Scott** (Revolutionary)
*Dragons Past* - Gary Gentile   s   2192

**Scott** (Driver; Mythical Creature)
*House of the Sun* - Nigel Findley   s   1936

**Scott** (Teenager; Refugee)
*A Time for Dragons* - Gary Gentile   s   2193

**Scott, Aaron "Sunset"** (Radio Personality)
*Shock Radio* - Leigh Clark   h   1052

**Scott, Andrew** (Cyborg; Reanimated Dead)
*Universal Soldier* - Robert Tine   s   5476

**Scott, Jason** (Administrator)
*The Eighth Rank* - David D. Ross   s   4682

**Scott, Jim** (Wealthy)
*Jackals* - Charles L. Grant   *h*   2313

**Scott, Lisa** (Military Personnel)
*Cohort of the Damned* - Andrew Keith   *s*   3034

**Scott, Michael** (Parent; Teacher)
*The Black School* - J.N. Williamson   *h*   5851

**Scott, Montgomery** (Engineer; Military Personnel)
*Crossover* - Michael Jan Friedman   *s*   2063
*Relics* - Michael Jan Friedman   *s*   2066

**Scott, Valerie** (Writer)
*What's Wrong with Valerie?* - D.A. Fowler   *h*   2026

**Scott, Walter** (Historical Figure; Spirit)
*Picking the Ballad's Bones* - Elizabeth Ann
   Scarborough   *f*   4869

**Scour** (Alien; Royalty)
*Starliner* - David Drake   *s*   1645

**Scribble, Jacob** (Animal; Spy)
*The Night of Wishes: Or, The
   Satanarchaeolidealcohellish Notion Potion* - Michael
   Ende   *f*   1821

**Scrooge, Ebenezer** (Spirit; Artificial Intelligence)
*Carol for Another Christmas* - Elizabeth Ann
   Scarborough   *f*   4861

**Scully, Dana** (FBI Agent; Doctor)
*Antibodies* - Kevin J. Anderson   *h*   99
*Goblins* - Charles L. Grant   *s*   2309
*Ground Zero* - Kevin J. Anderson   *h*   106
*Ruins* - Kevin J. Anderson   *h*   112
*Whirlwind* - Charles L. Grant   *f*   2320
*The X-Files: Fight the Future* - Chris Carter   *h*   924

**Sea Rat "Ratty"** (Animal; Adventurer)
*The Willows and Beyond* - William
   Horwood   *f*   2775

**Seafort, Nicholas** (Military Personnel)
*Challenger's Hope* - David Feintuch   *s*   1899
*Fisherman's Hope* - David Feintuch   *s*   1900
*Midshipman's Hope* - David Feintuch   *s*   1901

**Seafort, Philip** (Genius; Child)
*Voices of Hope* - David Feintuch   *s*   1903

**Seaforth, Fawn** (Scientist)
*The Howling Stones* - Alan Dean Foster   *s*   2006

**Seagal, Hayley** (Director)
*Stage Fright* - Clare McNally   *h*   3858

**Seagryn** (Wizard; Criminal)
*The Faithful Traitor* - Robert Don Hughes   *f*   2809

**Seale, Evan** (Teenager; Animal)
*The Silent Strength of Stones* - Nina Kiriki
   Hoffman   *f*   2716

**Seale, Willow** (Teenager; Psychic)
*The Silent Strength of Stones* - Nina Kiriki
   Hoffman   *f*   2716

**Sealink** (Animal)
*The Wild Road* - Gabriel King   *f*   3120

**Sealock, Brendan** (Engineer; Scientist)
*Iris* - William Barton   *s*   381

**Sean** (Artist)
*Blue Moon* - Hila Feil   *f*   1898

**Sean Horus MacIntyre** (Leader)
*The Armageddon Inheritance* - David
   Weber   *s*   5668

**Seaton, Thomas** (Religious)
*Vampire Bytes* - Linda Grant   *h*   2322

**Seavers, Kim** (Sports Figure; Spy)
*Beamriders!* - Martin Caidin   *s*   824

**Sebasten-Janurias** (Pilot)
*Mighty Good Road* - Melissa Scott   *s*   4897

**Sebastian** (Apprentice)
*Rehearsal for a Renaissance* - Douglas W.
   Clark   *f*   1045

**Seeker** (Alien)
*Labyrinth* - Dennis Schmidt   *s*   4884

**Seeker After Patterns** (Guide; Animal)
*Beyond the Fall of Night* - Arthur C. Clarke   *s*   1054

**Seetoo "Jolly"** (Alien; Leader)
*Marooned on Eden* - Robert L. Forward   *s*   1986

**Segnbora** (Sorceress; Martial Arts Expert)
*The Door into Sunset* - Diane Duane   *f*   1660

**Segretti, Paolo** (Lawyer; Psychologist)
*Mindplayers* - Pat Cadigan   *s*   806

**Seguy, Eva** (Doctor; Professor)
*Mutant Star* - Karen Haber   *s*   2475

**Selatre** (Religious)
*Prince of the North* - Harry Turtledove   *f*   5509

**Selden, Penelope** (Psychologist; Computer Expert)
*The Whims of Creation* - Simon Hawke   *s*   2626

**Seldon, Hari** (Scientist)
*Forward the Foundation* - Isaac Asimov   *s*   236

**Seldon, Hari** (Scientist; Aged Person)
*Foundation and Chaos* - Greg Bear   *s*   418

**Seldon, Hari** (Scientist; Political Figure)
*Foundation's Fear* - Gregory Benford   *s*   446

**Selendrile** (Mythical Creature)
*Dragon's Bait* - Vivian Vande Velde   *f*   5556

**Selenko, Avi** (Spacewoman)
*Maia's Veil* - P.K. McAllister   *s*   3707

**Selenkov, Yuri Ivanovich** (Spaceship Captain)
*Rinn's Star* - Paula E. Downing   *s*   1719

**Self, Melinda** (Traveler)
*Amnesia Moon* - Jonathan Lethem   *f*   3438

**Selima** (Young Woman)
*Lion Time in Timbuctoo* - Robert Silverberg   *s*   5036

**Selinde** (Deity)
*Kaleidoscope Eyes* - Graham Watkins   *h*   5631

**Selius, Overseer** (Government Official)
*Tangled Webs* - Steve Mudd   *s*   4044

**Selway, Cookson** (Restaurateur)
*A Face at the Window* - Dennis McFarland   *h*   3809

**Selway, Ellen** (Writer)
*A Face at the Window* - Dennis McFarland   *h*   3809

**Semele, Alice** (Clerk; Parent)
*Dominion* - Bentley Little   *h*   3492

**Semele, Dion** (Teenager)
*Dominion* - Bentley Little   *h*   3492

**Semjaza** (Sorcerer)
*Zaragoz* - Brian Craig   *f*   1241

**Semmlar, Wayne** (Mechanic; Serial Killer)
*Near Dead* - Stephen R. George   *h*   2202

**Semnarek, Robert** (Lawyer)
*The Colors of Hell* - Michael Paine   *h*   4234

**Sena, Miranda** (Scientist; Administrator)
*Rewind* - Terry England   *s*   1825

**Senea** (Military Personnel; Psychic)
*The Heldan* - Deborah Talmadge-Bickmore   *f*   5383

**sen'Laurea, Terricel "Terris"** (Student; Psychic)
*Northlight* - Deborah Wheeler   *s*   5775

**Sennen, David** (Religious)
*The Black Death* - Basil Copper   *h*   1185

**Sensar** (Alien; Teacher)
*Minds Apart* - Margaret Davis   *s*   1408

**Senungatuk, Clodagh** (Healer)
*Power Lines* - Anne McCaffrey   *s*   3743

**Sephrenia** (Sorceress)
*The Diamond Throne* - David Eddings   *f*   1731
*The Ruby Knight* - David Eddings   *f*   1736

**Sept-Fortune, Cecilie 8** (Apprentice; Computer
Expert)
*Interface Masque* - Shariann Lewitt   *s*   3453

**Seqiro** (Animal; Telepath)
*Chaos Mode* - Piers Anthony   *f*   165
*Virtual Mode* - Piers Anthony   *f*   194

**Seraphina** (Witch)
*The Memoirs of Elizabeth Frankenstein* - Theodore
   Roszak   *h*   4684

**Seraphina** (Mythical Creature)
*A Wish and a Dream* - Ingrid Weaver   *f*   5658

**Serege, Lujan Ansellic** (Military Personnel; Patient)
*Dominion's Reach* - Diann Thornley   *s*   5465

**Serege, Lujan Ansellic** (Military Personnel; Parent)
*Echoes of Issel* - Diann Thornley   *s*   5466

**Serege, Tristan "Tris"** (Teenager; Military
Personnel)
*Dominion's Reach* - Diann Thornley   *s*   5465

**Serege, Tristan "Tris"** (Teenager; Refugee)
*Echoes of Issel* - Diann Thornley   *s*   5466

**Serege, Tristan "Tris"** (Teenager; Castaway)
*Ganwold's Child* - Diann Thornley   *s*   5467

**Seregil** (Spy; Musician)
*Luck in the Shadows* - Lynn Flewelling   *f*   1952

**Seregil** (Spy; Thief)
*Stalking Darkness* - Lynn Flewelling   *f*   1953

**Serena** (Royalty)
*The Wizard and the Floating City* - Christopher
   Rowley   *f*   4699

**Seresen** (Alien)
*Happy Policeman* - Patricia Anthony   *s*   160

**Serrano** (Military Personnel; Spacewoman)
*Once a Hero* - Elizabeth Moon   *s*   3970

**Serrano, Heris** (Spaceship Captain; Military
Personnel)
*Hunting Party* - Elizabeth Moon   *s*   3968
*Sporting Chance* - Elizabeth Moon   *s*   3974
*Winning Colors* - Elizabeth Moon   *s*   3976

**Serroi** (Warrior; Sorceress)
*Dancer's Rise* - Jo Clayton   *f*   1064
*The Magic Wars* - Jo Clayton   *f*   1068

**Service** (Guide; Leader)
*The Remarkables* - Robert Reed   *s*   4507

**Sess, Medusa "Glory"** (Time Traveler; Guardian)
*Psychoshop* - Alfred Bester   *s*   477

**Sessine, Alandre VII** (Nobleman)
*Feersum Endjinn* - Iain M. Banks   *s*   325

**Sessiri-wohnith** (Alien)
*Dark Sky Legion* - William Barton   *s*   379

**Set** (Alien)
*Orion in the Dying Time* - Ben Bova   *s*   591

**Setebos** (Artificial Intelligence)
*A Game of Universe* - Eric S. Nylund   *f*   4178

**Seth, Nguyen** (Spirit; Religious)
*Demon Download* - Jack Yeovil   *f*   6021

**Sethiyan, Hattim** (Nobleman; Ruler)
*The Usurper* - Angus Wells   *f*   5739

**Seton, Winston** (Publisher)
*Naming the Flowers* - Kate Wilhelm   *s*   5809

**Seven, Gary** (Spy; Time Traveler)
*Assignment: Eternity* - Greg Cox   *s*   1225

**Seventeen** (Prisoner)
*The Road to Hell, Volume I* - Robert
   Weinberg   *h*   5701

**Severanko, Nick** (Writer)
*Bleeder* - Gene Lazuta   h   3374

**Severn, Joseph** (Reincarnated Person)
*The Fall of Hyperion* - Dan Simmons   s   5052

**Severyn, Todd** (Engineer)
*Ill Wind* - Kevin J. Anderson   s   108

**Seward, John** (Doctor)
*Anno Dracula* - Kim Newman   h   4094

**Seward, Jonathan** (Doctor)
*Lord of the Vampires* - Jeanne Kalogridis   h   3005

**Seward, Terry** (Lawyer)
*Seaward* - Brad Leithauser   h   3433

**Seyirshi, Ginbiryol** (Filmmaker)
*Shadowkill* - Jo Clayton   s   1069
*Shadowplay* - Jo Clayton   s   1070
*Shadowspeer* - Jo Clayton   s   1071

**Seymour** (Magician)
*The White Mists of Power* - Kristine Kathryn
   Rusch   f   4730

**s'Falenn, Arithon** (Royalty; Magician)
*Curse of the Mistwraith* - Janny Wurts   f   6001

**s'Falenn, Arithon** (Musician; Wizard)
*Fugitive Prince* - Janny Wurts   f   6002

**s'Falenn, Arithon** (Royalty; Magician)
*Ships of Merior* - Janny Wurts   f   6004

**Shaa, Zalzyn** (Magician)
*Catastrophe's Spell* - Mayer Alan Brenner   f   671

**Shaa, Zalzyn** (Adventurer)
*Spell of Fate* - Mayer Alan Brenner   f   673

**Shackleford, Ray** (Repairman; Psychic)
*Glimpses* - Lewis Shiner   h   4997

**Shaddock, Tolman** (Gunfighter)
*Demon Dance* - T. Chris Martindale   h   3655

**Shade** (Runaway; Teenager)
*Shade* - Emily Devenport   s   1504

**Shade, John** (Vampire; Rancher)
*Nightshade* - Jack Butler   s   789

**Shade, Kathleen** (Journalist)
*Portrait of the Psychopath as a Young Woman* -
   Edward Lee   h   3395

**Shade, Scarlett** (Writer; Vampire)
*Shade* - David Darke   h   1355

**Shadimar** (Wizard)
*The Last of the Renshai* - Mickey Zucker
   Reichert   f   4520
*The Western Wizard* - Mickey Zucker
   Reichert   f   4526

**Shadith** (Psychic)
*Fire in the Sky* - Jo Clayton   s   1067
*Shadowkill* - Jo Clayton   s   1069
*Shadowplay* - Jo Clayton   s   1070
*Shadowspeer* - Jo Clayton   s   1071

**Shadow** (Mythical Creature; Thief)
*Dagger's Edge* - Anne Logston   f   3508
*Shadow* - Anne Logston   f   3512
*Shadow Dance* - Anne Logston   f   3513
*Shadow Hunt* - Anne Logston   f   3514

**Shadow** (Mythical Creature)
*Shadowlight* - Jackie Hyman   f   2819

**Shadow** (Disembodied Personality)
*The Wizard's Shadow* - Susan Dexter   f   1514

**Shadowborn, Alexi** (Knight)
*Shadowborn* - William W. Connors   h   1137

**Shadowman** (Monster)
*Dark Souls* - Barry Porter   h   4369

**Shadowspawn** (Thief; Adventurer)
*The Shadow of Sorcery* - Andrew J. Offutt   f   4202

**Shadrack** (Reincarnated Person; Martial Arts Expert)
*Ronin* - D.A. Heeley   f   2639

**Shaeler, Anita** (Travel Agent)
*The Forsaken* - Steven Ray Fulgham   h   2089

**Shaeler, Marshall** (Child)
*The Forsaken* - Steven Ray Fulgham   h   2089

**Shaffer, Beowulf** (Spaceship Captain; Space
   Explorer)
*Crashlander* - Larry Niven   s   4118

**Shaffer, Walter Scott Jr.** (Student; Adventurer)
*Beyond the Door* - Gary L. Blackwood   s   510

**Shahryar** (Royalty; Spouse)
*The Last Arabian Night* - Craig Shaw
   Gardner   f   2129

**Shaithis** (Vampire)
*Deadspawn* - Brian Lumley   h   3550

**Shalaman** (Ruler)
*The White Gryphon* - Mercedes Lackey   f   3303

**Shalindra** (Royalty)
*The Wolf of Winter* - Paula Volsky   f   5584

**Shaltar, Connor** (Royalty)
*Wren to the Rescue* - Sherwood Smith   f   5142
*Wren's Quest* - Sherwood Smith   f   5143
*Wren's War* - Sherwood Smith   f   5144

**Shaman** (Mercenary)
*The Quick* - Burt Cole   s   1113

**Shamandar, Serrin** (Magician; Mythical Creature)
*Streets of Blood* - Carl Sargent   f   4821

**Shamera "Sham"** (Thief; Sorceress)
*When Demons Walk* - Patricia Briggs   f   683

**Shan** (Artist)
*The Quicksilver Screen* - Don H. DeBrandt   s   1449

**Shan, Rafael Zhong "China Mountain"** (Engineer;
   Homosexual)
*China Mountain Zhang* - Maureen F.
   McHugh   s   3817

**Shana** (Orphan)
*The Elvenbane* - Andre Norton   f   4149

**Shane, Laura** (Writer)
*Lightning* - Dean R. Koontz   h   3211

**Shank, Billy** (Scientist)
*Echoes of the Fourth Magic* - R.A.
   Salvatore   f   4799

**Shanna** (Model)
*Pelts* - F. Paul Wilson   h   5894

**Shannon, Rip** (Spaceman; Pilot)
*A Mind for Trade* - Andre Norton   s   4158

**Shannon, Royston** (Wealthy)
*Water Rites* - Guy N. Smith   h   5121

**Shannow, Jon** (Traveler; Warrior)
*Wolf in Shadow* - David Gemmell   s   2191

**Shanto** (Military Personnel)
*The Initiate Brother* - Sean Russell   f   4742

**Shantow** (Warrior)
*The Wolves of Autumn* - Scott Ciencin   f   1035

**Shar, Dalin** (Ruler)
*Exile* - Al Sarrantonio   s   4829

**Shar, Moabet** (Psychic)
*The Illusionists* - Faren Miller   f   3894

**Sharbaraz** (Heir—Dispossessed; Prisoner)
*The Stolen Throne* - Harry Turtledove   f   5510

**Sharbaraz** (Ruler)
*The Thousand Cities* - Harry Turtledove   f   5512

**Sharifi, Jennifer** (Genetically Altered Being; Genius)
*Beggars Ride* - Nancy Kress   s   3238

**Sharissa** (Sorceress)
*Children of the Drake* - Richard A. Knaak   f   3166

**Sharissa** (Sorceress; Immigrant)
*The Shrouded Realm* - Richard A. Knaak   f   3174

**Sharkey, Alex** (Technician)
*Fairyland* - Paul J. McAuley   s   3711

**Sharma, Govinda** (Scientist)
*The Cold One* - Christopher Pike   h   4327

**Sharon** (Counselor)
*Requiem* - Graham Joyce   h   2994

**Sharp, Marcus** (Military Personnel)
*Beast* - Peter Benchley   h   440

**Sharpless, Carril** (Teacher)
*The Ragged World: A Novel of the Hefn on Earth* -
   Judith Moffett   s   3943

**Sharra** (Immortal)
*Mall, Mayhem and Magic* - Holly Lisle   f   3485

**Sharrea** (Psychic)
*Bone Danc: A Fantasy for Technophiles* - Emma
   Bull   s   766

**Sharrow** (Thief; Warrior)
*Against a Dark Background* - Iain M. Banks   s   322

**Sharur** (Businessman; Trader)
*Between the Rivers* - Harry Turtledove   f   5496

**Shaw, John** (Genetically Altered Being)
*The Divide* - Robert Charles Wilson   s   5907

**Shawdell** (Sorcerer; Immortal)
*Green Rider* - Kristen Britain   f   692

**Shaws, Adams** (Guard)
*The Streeter* - Scott Ian Barry   h   373

**Shazad** (Royalty; Political Figure)
*Queens of Land and Sea* - John Maddox
   Roberts   f   4620

**Shea, Alan** (Child)
*Deadly Vengeance* - Stephen R. George   h   2199

**Shea, Bill** (Writer)
*Deadly Vengeance* - Stephen R. George   h   2199

**Shea, Ernie "Lucky Duck"** (Mythical Creature)
*The Callahan Touch* - Spider Robinson   f   4637

**Shea, Harold** (Psychologist; Adventurer)
*The Enchanter Reborn* - L. Sprague de
   Camp   f   1413

**Shea, Nicole** (Pilot; Military Personnel)
*Grounded!* - Chris Claremont   s   1041
*Sundowner* - Chris Claremont   s   1043

**Shears, Melvin** (Lawyer)
*The Mirror Maze* - James P. Hogan   s   2726

**Sheba** (Political Figure)
*Traitors* - Kristine Kathryn Rusch   f   4729

**Shedemei** (Historian; Immortal)
*Earthborn* - Orson Scott Card   s   884

**Shedian, Taylor Caroline** (FBI Agent)
*Souls* - Katina Alexis   h   71

**Shedwyn** (Revolutionary; Psychic)
*Beldan's Fire* - Midori Snyder   f   5150

**Sheehan, Matt** (Government Official;
   Troubleshooter)
*Manhattan Transfer* - John E. Stith   s   5303

**Sheela** (Royalty)
*The Nomad Queen* - James Gordon White   f   5783

**Sheen** (Miner)
*Raft* - Stephen Baxter   s   401

**Sheerin 501** (Scientist; Psychologist)
*Nightfall* - Isaac Asimov   s   248

**Shefferton, Jeffrey** (Political Figure)
*The Argus Gambit* - David D. Ross   s   4681
*The Eighth Rank* - David D. Ross   s   4682

**Sheila** (Agent)
*After the Blue* - Russel Like   s   3465

**Shelagh** (Teacher; Fiance(e))
*Sweetheart, Sweetheart* - Bernard Taylor   *h*   5402

**Shelby, Kathe** (FBI Agent)
*Father's Little Helper* - Ronald Kelly   *h*   3052

**Shelby, Lissa** (Counselor)
*Shadow Man* - Dennis Etchison   *h*   1848

**Sheldon, Peter** (Worker)
*Lucifer's Eye* - Hugh B. Cave   *h*   943

**Sheldon, Rudolph "Rudy"** (Criminal; Sorcerer)
*Brown Girl in the Ring* - Nalo Hopkinson   *f*   2771

**Shellabarger, Vince** (Animal Trainer; Entertainer)
*Dinosaur Summer* - Greg Bear   *s*   416

**Shelley, Mary** (Writer; Historical Figure)
*Gothic Romance* - Emmanuel Carrere   *h*   912

**Shelley, Percy Bysshe** (Writer; Historical Figure)
*Lord of the Dead* - Tom Holland   *h*   2741
*Wall, Stone, Craft* - Walter Jon Williams   *h*   5842

**Shelly, Byron** (Vampire)
*The Last Vampire* - Kathryn Meyer Griffith   *h*   2440

**Shelton, Brett C.** (Student)
*Child's Play III* - Matthew J. Costello   *h*   1194

**Shelyra "Raymonda"** (Royalty)
*Tiger Burning Bright* - Marion Zimmer
  Bradley   *f*   652

**Shepard, M.** (Scientist)
*Evolution's Shore* - Ian McDonald   *s*   3792

**Shepard, Natalie** (Police Officer)
*Spider Legs* - Piers Anthony   *s*   189

**Shepherd, Ben** (Artist)
*The Middle Kingdom* - David Wingrove   *s*   5919

**Shepherd, Carolyn Crespin** (Lawyer; Farmer)
*Gibbon's Decline and Fall* - Sheri S.
  Tepper   *s*   5430

**Shepherd, Chyna** (Student—Graduate)
*Intensity* - Dean R. Koontz   *h*   3210

**Shepherd, Seth** (Collector)
*Trickster* - Chris Curry   *h*   1297

**Sheppard, Lee** (Student)
*The Messenger* - Donald Tyson   *h*   5528

**Sherer, Will** (Detective—Private)
*Cries of the Children* - Clare McNally   *h*   3856

**Sheridan, Alan** (Worker)
*Twisted Images* - Don D'Ammassa   *h*   1335

**Sheridan, Anna** (Anthropologist)
*The Shadow Within* - Jeanne Cavelos   *s*   944

**Sheridan, Denise** (Scholar; Museum Curator)
*Son of Darkness* - Josepha Sherman   *f*   4990

**Sheridan, John** (Military Personnel)
*Thirdspace* - Peter David   *s*   1387

**Sheridan, John** (Leader; Spaceman)
*The Touch of Your Shadow, the Whisper of Your Name*
  - Neal Barrett Jr.   *s*   367

**Sherman** (Student—High School; Adventurer)
*In between Dragons* - Michael Kandel   *f*   3010

**Sherman, William Tecumseh** (Historical Figure;
  Military Personnel)
*Under the Shadow* - Jane Toombs   *h*   5481

**Sherwood, Carl** (Computer Expert)
*The Sherwood Game* - Esther Friesner   *s*   2082

**Sherwood, Iris "Butcher of Boston"** (Government
  Official; Step-Parent)
*In the Cube* - David Alexander Smith   *s*   5109

**Sherwood, John** (Hunter; Mythical Creature)
*Dancing Bears* - Fred Saberhagen   *f*   4764

**Shiara** (Sorceress)
*The Wiz Biz* - Rick Cook   *f*   1160

**Shido, Jamisia "Jamie Capra"** (Abuse Victim;
  Fugitive)
*This Alien Shore* - C.S. Friedman   *s*   2059

**Shielder's Mark** (Hero; Spouse)
*Nobody's Son* - Sean Stewart   *f*   5275

**Shields, Ben** (Writer)
*Prank Night* - David Robbins   *h*   4601

**Shikome, Lily** (Nurse)
*The Twelfth Child* - Raymond Van Over   *h*   5538

**Shile** (Thief)
*The Changeling Prince* - Vivian Vande
  Velde   *f*   5554

**Shile** (Warrior)
*The Conjurer Princess* - Vivian Vande
  Velde   *f*   5555

**Shiloh** (Healer)
*The Halloween Man* - Douglas Clegg   *h*   1080

**Shiloh, Luna** (Government Official)
*Flies From the Amber* - Wil McCarthy   *s*   3763

**Shimmer** (Royalty; Mythical Creature)
*Dragon Cauldron* - Laurence Yep   *f*   6024
*Dragon War* - Laurence Yep   *f*   6025

**Shin, Praeis** (Alien; Spy)
*Playing God* - Sarah Zettel   *s*   6080

**Shinji, Matsumura** (Nobleman; Warrior)
*The Yngling in Yamato* - John Dalmas   *s*   1329

**Ship** (Artificial Intelligence)
*A Maze of Stars* - John Brunner   *s*   734

**Shipman, Malkah** (Aged Person)
*He, She and It* - Marge Piercy   *s*   4325

**Shipman, Shira** (Computer Expert)
*He, She and It* - Marge Piercy   *s*   4325

**Shira** (Time Traveler; Revolutionary)
*Timelike Infinity* - Stephen Baxter   *s*   404

**Shirley** (Cyborg; Traveler)
*Correspondence* - Sue Thomas   *s*   5450

**Shiro, Miaowara** (Relative; Warrior)
*Samurai Cat Goes to Hell* - Mark E. Rogers   *f*   4655

**Shiva** (Prehistoric Human; Teenager)
*Shiva Accused: An Adventure of the Ice Age* - J.H.
  Brennan   *f*   667
*Shiva: An Adventure of the Ice Age* - J.H.
  Brennan   *f*   669

**Shiva** (Artificial Intelligence)
*Shiva in Steel* - Fred Saberhagen   *s*   4775

**Shiva** (Prehistoric Human; Teenager)
*Shiva's Challenge: An Adventure of the Ice Age* - J.H.
  Brennan   *f*   668

**Shkai'ra** (Warrior; Barbarian)
*The Cage* - S.M. Stirling   *f*   5293

**Shkai'ra** (Warrior)
*Shadow's Son* - Shirley Meier   *f*   3872

**Shn'dar, Queekat** (Alien; Historian)
*Sentinels* - Margaret Weis   *s*   5725

**Shomer, Jillian** (Sports Figure)
*Achilles' Choice* - Larry Niven   *s*   4114

**Shongili, Sean** (Genetically Altered Being; Spouse)
*Power Lines* - Anne McCaffrey   *s*   3743

**Shonto** (Nobleman; Military Personnel)
*Gatherer of Clouds* - Sean Russell   *f*   4741

**Shore, Oliver** (Religious)
*Avatar* - Donald Beman   *h*   437

**Shores, Candice** (Military Personnel)
*The Painful Field* - Roland J. Green   *s*   2351
*The Sum of Things* - Roland J. Green   *s*   2353

**Short-Son "Eater-of-Grass" of Chiirr-Nig** (Alien)
*Man-Kzin Wars IV* - Larry Niven   *s*   4124

**Shoth** (Sorcerer)
*An Enemy Reborn* - Michael A. Stackpole   *f*   5197

**Shrewsbury, Laban** (Professor)
*The Trail of Cthulhu* - August Derleth   *h*   1497

**Shriek, Anthony** (Artist)
*Anthony Shriek* - Jessica Amanda
  Salmonson   *h*   4790

**Shudde-M'ell** (Monster)
*The Burrowers Beneath* - Brian Lumley   *h*   3548

**Shuganan** (Artist; Indian)
*Mother Earth, Father Sky* - Sue Harrison   *f*   2581

**Shulana** (Wizard; Mythical Creature)
*Dragonspawn* - Mark Acres   *f*   28

**Shunlar** (Psychic; Warrior)
*The Gates of Vensunor* - Carol Heller   *f*   2650

**Shunlar** (Mercenary)
*The Sands of Kalaven: A Novel of Shunlar* - Carol
  Heller   *f*   2651

**Shustak, Evan "American Dream"** (Vagrant)
*The Holy Terror* - Wayne Allen Sallee   *h*   4787

**Shutterbug** (Pornographer)
*Slippin' into Darkness* - Norman Partridge   *h*   4254

**Shuyun** (Religious; Martial Arts Expert)
*Gatherer of Clouds* - Sean Russell   *f*   4741
*The Initiate Brother* - Sean Russell   *f*   4742

**Sianna** (Mythical Creature; Royalty)
*Lady of Avalon* - Marion Zimmer Bradley   *f*   640

**Sibatia** (Shaman)
*Dry Skull Dreams* - Michael Green   *h*   2344

**Sickert, Walter** (Artist)
*From Hell* - Alan Moore   *h*   3987
*The Women of Whitechapel and Jack the Ripper* - Paul
  West   *h*   5761

**Sid 6.7** (Artificial Intelligence; Criminal)
*Virtuosity* - Terry Bisson   *s*   507

**Siddonie** (Ruler; Sorceress)
*The Catswold Portal* - Shirley Rousseau
  Murphy   *f*   4055

**Sidra** (Explorer)
*Future Eden* - J.M. Morgan   *s*   4001

**Siebold, Howard** (Traitor)
*Afterage* - Yvonne Navarro   *h*   4072

**Siegel, Benjamin "Bugsy"** (Historical Figure;
  Criminal)
*Last Call* - Tim Powers   *f*   4384

**Sien** (Religious; Wizard)
*Shadow War* - Deborah Chester   *f*   1010

**Sierek, Detlef** (Writer)
*Drachenfels* - Jack Yeovil   *f*   6022

**Sieyes** (Psychologist)
*A Whisper of Time* - Paula E. Downing   *s*   1595

**Sigfrid** (Mythical Creature; Warrior)
*The Dragons of the Rhine* - Diana L.
  Paxson   *f*   4264
*The Wolf and the Raven* - Diana L. Paxson   *f*   4270

**Sigfrith** (Mythical Creature; Warrior)
*Rhinegold* - Stephan Grundy   *f*   2454

**Siggerson, Olaf** (Pilot)
*Destination: Mutiny* - Sean Dalton   *s*   1332

**Siglen** (Psychic; Leader)
*The Rowan* - Anne McCaffrey   *s*   3747

**Sigmond, Jerry** (Radio Personality)
*Dust* - Charles Pellegrino   *h*   4279

**Sigvarthsson, Shef** (Hero; Blacksmith)
*The Hammer and the Cross* - Harry
  Harrison   *f*   2570

**Sigvarthsson, Shef** (Royalty; Scientist)
*King and Emperor* - Harry Harrison   f   2571

**Sigvarthsson, Shef** (Royalty; Warrior)
*One King's Way* - Harry Harrison   s   2572

**Sigyn** (Mythical Creature)
*The Tower of Beowulf* - Parke Godwin   f   2250

**Sikes, Jason** (Teenager)
*Under Alien Stars* - Pamela F. Service   s   4919

**Sikes, Jesse** (Murderer; Monster)
*Sins of the Flesh* - Don Davis   h   1404

**Sikes, Matthew** (Detective—Police)
*Cross of Blood* - K.W. Jeter   s   2909
*Dark Horizon* - K.W. Jeter   s   2910

**Sikes, Stephen** (Young Man)
*Sins of the Flesh* - Don Davis   h   1404

**Sil** (Experimental Subject; Genetically Altered Being)
*Species* - Yvonne Navarro   s   4075

**Siladri** (Farmer)
*The Painted Alphabet* - Diana Darling   f   1356

**Silbakor** (Mythical Creature)
*Dragon Death* - Gael Baudino   f   390
*Duel of Dragons* - Gael Baudino   f   391

**Silberhutte, Hank** (Telepath)
*Titus Crow, Volume Three* - Brian Lumley   h   3567
*Titus Crow, Volume Two* - Brian Lumley   h   3568

**Silence, John** (Military Personnel)
*Deathstalker Rebellion* - Simon R. Green   s   2365
*Twilight of the Empire* - Simon R. Green   s   2374

**Silenus, Martin** (Writer; Aged Person)
*The Rise of Endymion* - Dan Simmons   s   5059

**s'Ilessid, Lysaer** (Royalty; Magician)
*Curse of the Mistwraith* - Janny Wurts   f   6001

**s'Ilessid, Lysaer** (Royalty; Wizard)
*Fugitive Prince* - Janny Wurts   f   6002

**s'Ilessid, Lysaer** (Royalty; Magician)
*Ships of Merior* - Janny Wurts   f   6004

**Silk** (Religious)
*Nightside the Long Sun* - Gene Wolfe   s   5943

**Silk** (Streetperson)
*Street* - Jack Cady   h   822

**Silk, Patera** (Religious)
*Calde of the Long Sun* - Gene Wolfe   s   5937
*Exodus From the Long Sun* - Gene Wolfe   s   5941
*Lake of the Long Sun* - Gene Wolfe   s   5942

**Silk, Venture** (Public Relations)
*The Forever Drug* - Steve Perry   s   4296

**Silk, Venture** (Government Official; Sports Figure)
*Spindoc* - Steve Perry   s   4300

**Silkweb Empress** (Royalty; Mythical Creature)
*Bronze Mirror* - Jeanne Larsen   f   3338

**Silme** (Sorceress)
*By Chaos Cursed* - Mickey Zucker Reichert   f   4517

**Siluricus, Gaius Macellius Severus** (Military Personnel)
*The Forest House* - Marion Zimmer Bradley   f   633

**Silvas** (Wizard; Deity)
*The Wizard at Home* - Rick Shelley   f   4975

**Silver** (Computer Expert)
*Shadowboxer* - Nick Pollotta   s   4366

**Silver, David** (Police Officer)
*Alien Blues* - Lynn S. Hightower   s   2682
*Alien Eyes* - Lynn S. Hightower   s   2683
*Alien Heat* - Lynn S. Hightower   s   2684
*Alien Rites* - Lynn S. Hightower   s   2685

**Silver, Harry** (Pilot)
*Shiva in Steel* - Fred Saberhagen   s   4775

**Silver, Jake** (Teenager)
*Them* - William W. Johnstone   h   2935

**Silver, Michelle "Micki" Ann** (Child; Time Traveler)
*The Silver Tree* - Ruth L. Williams   f   5822

**Silver, Mier** (Spy; Psychic)
*Mission: Tori* - Johanna Bolton   s   564

**Silver, Rob** (Anthropologist)
*The Presence* - John Saul   h   4843

**Silver Hand, Llew** (Royalty; Ruler)
*The Endless Knot* - Stephen R. Lawhead   f   3354

**Silver Hand, Llew** (Royalty; Warrior)
*The Silver Hand* - Stephen R. Lawhead   f   3358

**Silver-Rim** (Alien)
*Ocean under the Ice* - Robert L. Forward   s   1988

**Silver Snow** (Royalty; Warrior)
*Imperial Lady* - Andre Norton   f   4155

**Silverblade "Blade"** (Military Personnel)
*The Silver Gryphon* - Mercedes Lackey   f   3295

**Silvercup** (Android)
*Hostile Takeover* - Jack McKinney   s   3849

**Silverhair, Imandoff** (Sorcerer)
*Soothslayer: A Magickal Fantasy* - D.J. Conway   f   1143

**Silverhand, Caeled** (Hero; Warrior)
*Silverlight* - Morgan Llywelyn   f   3507

**Silverhorn, Aelfred** (Mercenary)
*Into the Void* - Nigel Findley   f   1937

**Silverstein, Ian** (Martial Arts Expert; Hero)
*The Crimson Sky* - Joel Rosenberg   f   4669
*The Fire Duke* - Joel Rosenberg   f   4671
*The Silver Stone* - Joel Rosenberg   f   4676

**Simba** (Musician)
*Twisted* - Sue Hollister Barr   h   364

**Simeon-Hap, Joat** (Spaceship Captain)
*The Ship Avenged* - S.M. Stirling   s   5298

**Simmanye, Toska** (Prisoner)
*Prisoner of Conscience* - Susan R. Matthews   s   3693

**Simmons, Roger** (Artist)
*Galatea in 2-D* - Aaron Allston   f   87

**Simmons, Susan** (Student)
*My Teacher Fried My Brains* - Bruce Coville   s   1223

**Simms, Nanci** (Teacher; Warrior)
*Deep Trek* - James Axler   s   278

**Simna, Jack** (Scientist)
*Life Form* - Alan Dean Foster   s   2008

**Simon** (Religious; Time Traveler)
*Corrupting Dr. Nice* - John Kessel   s   3083

**Simon** (Sorcerer; Apprentice)
*The Dragonbone Chair* - Tad Williams   f   5829

**Simon** (Royalty)
*The Gift* - Patrick O'Leary   f   4211

**Simon** (Vampire)
*The Silver Kiss* - Annette Curtis Klause   f   3163

**Simon** (Sorcerer; Apprentice)
*Stone of Farewell* - Tad Williams   f   5831

**Simon** (Postal Worker)
*Wishbringer* - Craig Shaw Gardner   f   2133

**Simon, Althene** (Vampire)
*Darkness, I* - Tanith Lee   h   3407

**Simon, Chuck** (Fugitive; Warrior)
*Haven* - David Peters   f   4304

**Simon, Chuck** (Psychic; Martial Arts Expert)
*Psi-Man* - David Peters   s   4305

**Simon of Florenz** (Artist)
*The Painter Knight* - Fiona Patton   f   4258

**Simon "Seoman/Snowlock"** (Knight)
*To Green Angel Tower* - Tad Williams   f   5832

**Simonetti, Cara** (Child)
*Vampire Breath* - R.L. Stine   h   5291

**Simpson, Beth Ann** (Undertaker)
*Buried Screams* - C. Dean Andersson   h   137

**Sims, Christopher** (Warrior)
*A Talent for War* - Jack McDevitt   s   3790

**Sims, Dolores** (Artist; Spy)
*Cradle of Splendor* - Patricia Anthony   s   158

**Sinbad the Porter** (Worker)
*The Other Sinbad* - Craig Shaw Gardner   f   2130

**Sinbad the Sailor** (Businessman; Adventurer)
*The Last Voyage of Somebody the Sailor* - John Barth   f   374
*The Other Sinbad* - Craig Shaw Gardner   f   2130

**Sinclair, Adam** (Doctor; Psychic)
*The Adept* - Katherine Kurtz   f   3254
*Dagger Magic* - Katherine Kurtz   f   3256
*Death of an Adept* - Katherine Kurtz   f   3257
*The Lodge of the Lynx* - Katherine Kurtz   f   3259
*The Templar Treasure* - Katherine Kurtz   f   3261

**Sinclair, Felice** (Divorced Person; Single Parent)
*The Fagin* - Pat Graversen   h   2334

**Sinclair, Graham Kuan** (Criminal; Businessman)
*Red Genesis* - S.C. Sykes   s   5377

**Sinclair, Jason** (Child)
*The Fagin* - Pat Graversen   h   2334

**Sinclair, Jeffrey** (Military Personnel)
*To Dream in the City of Sorrows* - Kathryn M. Drennan   s   1654

**Sinclair, Katherine** (Parent; Adventurer)
*Troll-Quest* - Rose Estes   f   1841
*Troll-Taken* - Rose Estes   f   1842

**Sinclair, Monique** (Entertainer)
*Sacred Prey* - Vivian Schilling   h   4875

**Sinclair, Richard** (Scientist)
*Dust* - Charles Pellegrino   h   4279

**Sinclair, Tam** (Child)
*Dust* - Charles Pellegrino   h   4279

**Sinclair, Travis** (Police Officer)
*Prank Night* - David Robbins   h   4601

**Singer** (Psychic; Musician)
*Deathgift* - Ann Tonsor Zeddies   s   6061

**Singer, Eleal** (Singer; Handicapped)
*Past Imperative* - Dave Duncan   f   1684

**Singer, Helen** (Police Officer)
*Symphony* - Adrian Savage   h   4847

**Singer, John Wolfe** (Handyman)
*Uwharrie* - Eugene E. Pfaff Jr.   h   4309

**Singer, Mayelbridwen "Maewen"** (Time Traveler)
*The Crown of Dalemark* - Diana Wynne Jones   f   2945

**Singh, Alan** (Professor)
*Brother to Dragons* - Charles Sheffield   s   4949

**Singh, Ram** (Servant; Warrior)
*The Spider #8: The Devil's Paymaster/Legions of the Accursed Light* - Grant Stockbridge   f   5309

**Singh, Robert** (Spaceship Captain)
*The Hammer of God* - Arthur C. Clarke   s   1057

**Singleton, Eric** (Doctor)
*Cold White Fury* - Beth Amos   h   97

**Sinistrad** (Wizard)
*Dragon Wing* - Margaret Weis   f   5709

**Sinjaria, Nolan ra** (Lawman; Wizard)
*Talion: Revenant* - Michael A. Stackpole  f  5206

**Sinjin** (Mythical Creature)
*Some Enchanted Evening* - Alice Alfonsi  f  73

**Sinjon** (Vampire)
*A Dozen Black Roses* - Nancy A. Collins  h  1119

**Siobahn** (Mythical Creature; Martial Arts Expert)
*Luthien's Gamble* - R.A. Salvatore  f  4802

**Sioned** (Royalty)
*Skybowl* - Melanie Rawn  f  4490

**Sioned** (Ruler; Magician)
*Stronghold* - Melanie Rawn  f  4492

**Sira** (Psychic; Singer)
*Sing the Light* - Louise Marley  s  3629
*Sing the Warmth* - Louise Marley  s  3630

**Siri** (Psychic; Singer)
*Receive the Gift* - Louise Marley  s  3628

**Sirkin** (Spacewoman)
*Sporting Chance* - Elizabeth Moon  s  3974

**Sisko, Benjamin** (Spaceship Captain; Military Personnel)
*Armageddon Sky* - L.A. Graf  s  2296

**Sisko, Benjamin** (Military Personnel; Leader)
*Bloodletter* - K.W. Jeter  s  2908

**Sisko, Benjamin** (Spaceship Captain)
*Call to Arms* - Diane Carey  s  901

**Sisko, Benjamin** (Military Personnel)
*Devil in the Sky* - Greg Cox  s  1226

**Sisko, Benjamin** (Leader; Military Personnel)
*Fallen Heroes* - Dafydd ab Hugh  s  8

**Sisko, Benjamin** (Spaceship Captain; Military Personnel)
*Time's Enemy* - L.A. Graf  s  2297

**Sisko, Benjamin** (Spaceship Captain)
*Vengeance* - Dafydd ab Hugh  s  10

**Sisko, Benjamin** (Military Personnel; Leader)
*Warped* - K.W. Jeter  s  2917

**Sith** (Alien)
*The House of Doors* - Brian Lumley  h  3554
*Maze of Worlds* - Brian Lumley  h  3559

**Sithas** (Mythical Creature; Royalty)
*Firstborn* - Paul B. Thompson  f  5454

**Sithas** (Royalty; Mythical Creature)
*The Kinslayer Wars* - Douglas Niles  f  4109

**Sivart, Gil** (Artist; Detective—Amateur)
*The Digital Effect* - Steve Perry  s  4295

**Six, Nicola** (Girlfriend)
*London Fields* - Martin Amis  s  95

**Sixa, Jenny** (Telepath; Detective—Amateur)
*The Stranger* - Eric James Fullilove  s  2093

**Sixclaw, Swartt** (Animal; Warrior)
*Outcast of Redwall* - Brian Jacques  f  2853

**Skaffen-Amtiskaw** (Artificial Intelligence)
*Use of Weapons* - Iain M. Banks  s  328

**Skandrakae, Tadrith "Tad"** (Mythical Creature; Military Personnel)
*The Silver Gryphon* - Mercedes Lackey  f  3295

**Skandranon** (Mythical Creature)
*The Black Gryphon* - Mercedes Lackey  f  3270

**Skandranon** (Mythical Creature; Leader)
*The White Gryphon* - Mercedes Lackey  f  3303

**Skardon, John** (Scientist)
*Mixed Doubles* - Daniel Da Cruz  s  1305

**Skater, Jack** (Mercenary; Cyborg)
*Headhunters* - Mel Odom  s  4192

**Skeeve** (Magician)
*Sweet Myth-tery of Life* - Robert Asprin  f  262

**Skelbrooke, Francis** (Adventurer; Rake)
*The Gnome's Engine* - Teresa Edgerton  f  1742

**Skena, Harry** (Professor; Time Traveler)
*Patton's Spaceship* - John Barnes  s  357

**Skerow** (Alien; Judge)
*Flesh and Gold* - Phyllis Gotlieb  s  2286

**Skibelski, Chaim** (Spirit)
*A Blessing on the Moon* - Joseph Skibell  f  5079

**Skif** (Government Official)
*Winds of Fate* - Mercedes Lackey  f  3305

**Skillet, William "Billy"** (Werewolf)
*Walking Wolf* - Nancy A. Collins  h  1126

**Skink** (Animal)
*The Blood Jaguar* - Michael H. Payne  f  4271

**Skinner** (Aged Person)
*Virtual Light* - William Gibson  s  2219

**Skinner** (Vampire)
*Bad Dreams* - Kim Newman  h  4096

**Skipper** (Alien)
*Only Child* - H.M. Hoover  s  2764

**Skoglund, Paul** (Construction Worker)
*Skull Session* - Daniel Hecht  h  2638

**Skogskra, Haakon** (Nobleman; Monster)
*The Gnome's Engine* - Teresa Edgerton  f  1742

**Skoro, Andrea "Andie"** (Time Traveler)
*Mr. Was* - Pete Hautman  s  2614

**Skorzeny, Otto** (Military Personnel; Historical Figure)
*1945* - Newt Gingrich  s  2239

**Sky-fire-trail** (Indian)
*Collidescope* - Grace Chetwin  s  1011

**Skylda "Skyla"** (Orphan; Witch)
*The Clan of the Warlord* - Elizabeth H. Boyer  f  604

**Skyler** (Handyman)
*Blood Roots* - Richie Tankersley Cusick  h  1300

**Skywalker, Luke** (Martial Arts Expert; Hero)
*Ambush at Corellia* - Roger MacBride Allen  s  76
*Before the Storm* - Michael P. Kube-McDowell  s  3247
*Children of the Jedi* - Barbara Hambly  s  2500
*The Courtship of Princess Leia* - Dave Wolverton  s  5950
*The Crystal Star* - Vonda N. McIntyre  s  3820
*Dark Force Rising* - Timothy Zahn  s  6052
*Darksaber* - Kevin J. Anderson  s  103
*The Glove of Darth Vader* - Paul Davids  s  1392
*Heir to the Empire* - Timothy Zahn  s  6054
*Jedi Search* - Kevin J. Anderson  s  109
*The Last Command* - Timothy Zahn  s  6055
*The Lost City of the Jedi* - Paul Davids  s  1393
*The New Rebellion* - Kristine Kathryn Rusch  s  4719
*Shadows of the Empire* - Steve Perry  s  4299
*The Truce at Bakura* - Kathy Tyers  s  5527

**Skywise** (Mythical Creature)
*The Quest Begins* - Wendy Pini  f  4337

**Slade, Billy** (Wizard)
*The Samurai Wizard* - Simon Hawke  f  2623
*The Wizard of Santa Fe* - Simon Hawke  f  2628

**Slade, Ned** (Military Personnel)
*The Voyage* - David Drake  s  1649

**Slagar** (Animal)
*Mattimeo* - Brian Jacques  f  2852

**Slakey, Justin** (Con Artist; Professor)
*The Stainless Steel Rat Goes to Hell* - Harry Harrison  s  2574

**Slash** (Genetically Altered Being; Thief)
*Rememory* - John Gregory Betancourt  s  481

**Slasher** (Alien; Businesswoman)
*The Weigher* - Eric Vinicoff  s  5574

**Slate** (Warrior)
*The Enigma Variations* - John Maddox Roberts  s  4618

**Slater, Matthew** (Horse Trainer)
*The Tallow Image* - Jane Brindle  h  690

**Slater, Peter** (Scientist; Professor)
*Secret Passages* - Paul Preuss  s  4420

**Slaughter, Nathan** (Police Officer)
*The Totem* - David Morrell  h  4012

**Slavanovot, Viktor** (Repairman)
*The Fall of Sirius* - Wil McCarthy  s  3762

**Slaven, Eleret** (Martial Arts Expert; Teenager)
*The Raven Ring* - Patricia C. Wrede  f  5978

**Sleel** (Bodyguard; Martial Arts Expert)
*Black Steel* - Steve Perry  s  4291

**Sleeper Service** (Artificial Intelligence)
*Excession* - Iain M. Banks  s  324

**Sloan, Cotter** (Handyman)
*Makoto* - Kelley Wilde  h  5801

**Sloan, Philip** (Fugitive; Mentally Ill Person)
*Come Before Christ and Murder Love* - Stewart Home  f  2754

**Sloan, Reno** (Detective—Private)
*The Asylum* - John E. Ames  h  93

**Sloan, Susan** (Journalist; Single Parent)
*Beneath Still Waters* - Matthew J. Costello  h  1193

**Sloane, Ed** (Student)
*Dawn Song* - Michael Marano  h  3620

**Slonimsky, Waldo** (Worker)
*The Burning* - Graham Masterton  h  3672

**Slovotsky, Walter** (Warrior)
*The Road Home* - Joel Rosenberg  f  4674
*The Road to Ehvenor* - Joel Rosenberg  f  4675

**Sma, Diziet** (Alien)
*The State of the Art* - Iain M. Banks  s  327

**Sma, Diziet** (Spy)
*Use of Weapons* - Iain M. Banks  s  328

**Small, Elmo** (Pharmacist)
*The Devil's Cradle* - Kate Stewart  h  5269

**Smedley, Julian** (Military Personnel; Handicapped)
*Present Tense* - Dave Duncan  f  1686

**Smiggens, Preister** (Pirate)
*Dinotopia Lost* - Alan Dean Foster  f  2003

**Smirk, James T.** (Spaceship Captain)
*Star Wreck II: The Attack of the Jargonites* - Leah Rewolinski  s  4563
*Star Wreck III: Time Warped* - Leah Rewolinski  s  4564
*Star Wreck IV: Live Long and Profit* - Leah Rewolinski  s  4565
*Star Wreck 6: Geek Space Nine* - Leah Rewolinski  s  4562
*Star Wreck: The Generation Gap* - Leah Rewolinski  s  4566

**Smith** (Government Official)
*Murder at the Galactic Writers' Society* - Janet Asimov  s  251

**Smith, Alamo** (Lawman)
*Destination: Showdown* - Jake Davis  s  1405
*The Last Rangers* - Jake Davis  s  1406

**Smith, Benjamin Franklin** (Immortal; Doctor)
*The First Immortal* - James L. Halperin  s  2498

**Smith, Brandon** (Computer Expert; Recluse)
*Virtual Girl* - Amy Thomson  s  5462

**Smith, Desi "Daisy Smeet"** (Doctor; Psychic)
*Chaos Come Again* - Wilhelmina Baird   *s*   293

**Smith, Desidra** (Vampire)
*Blood on the Sun* - Brian Herbert   *h*   2664

**Smith, Edward** (Computer Expert)
*The Nightmare People* - Lawrence Watt-
   Evans   *h*   5643

**Smith, Eugene** (Young Man)
*Nice Guys Finish Last* - Gary Jonas   *h*   2938

**Smith, Evangeline** (Witch)
*The Torching* - Marcy Heidish   *h*   2642

**Smith, Freddie** (Computer Expert)
*Polymorph* - Scott Westerfeld   *s*   5767

**Smith, Gary Franklin** (Artist; Doctor)
*The First Immortal* - James L. Halperin   *s*   2498

**Smith, George** (Military Personnel)
*Some of Your Blood* - Theodore Sturgeon   *h*   5347

**Smith, John** (Postal Worker)
*The Mailman* - Bentley Little   *h*   3494

**Smith, Jonathan Wesley** (Computer Expert)
*Harmonies of the 'Net* - Jane S. Fancher   *s*   1862
*Uplink* - Jane S. Fancher   *s*   1865

**Smith, Joseph** (Spirit; Religious)
*The Ghost of the Revelator* - L.E. Modesitt
   Jr.   *s*   3931

**Smith, Kamryn** (Young Woman)
*Killjoy* - Elizabeth Forrest   *h*   1973

**Smith, Kayla** (Magician; Runaway)
*Bedlam Boyz* - Ellen Guon   *f*   2467

**Smith, Sam** (Psychic; Diver)
*World Without End* - Molly Cochran   *f*   1093

**Smith, Shanifa** (Waiter/Waitress)
*Dead End* - Guy N. Smith   *h*   5119

**Smith, Stephen** (Writer)
*Where Does Kissing End?* - Kate Pullinger   *h*   4445

**Smith, Tom** (Military Personnel)
*Ai! Pedrito!: When Intelligence Goes Wrong* - L. Ron
   Hubbard   *s*   2788

**Smith, Valentine Michael** (Angel; Orphan)
*Stranger in a Strange Land* - Robert A.
   Heinlein   *s*   2649

**Smith, Vlad** (Professor)
*The Boss in the Wall* - Avram Davidson   *h*   1396

**Smith, Zachariah** (Cult Member; Traitor)
*Leap Point* - Kay Kenyon   *s*   3063

**Smithback, Bill** (Journalist)
*Relic* - Douglas Preston   *h*   4414
*Reliquary* - Douglas Preston   *h*   4415

**Smithers, Albert** (Reanimated Dead)
*Black as Blood* - Rob Chilson   *f*   1014

**Smoke, Smokey** (Telepath; Prostitute)
*Smoke and Mirrors* - Jane M. Lindskold   *s*   3476

**Smolte, Hampton** (Military Personnel)
*Elephantasm* - Tanith Lee   *h*   3408

**Smythe** (Wizard)
*The Jewel of Equilibrant* - Steven Frankos   *f*   2042

**Smythe, Peter** (Time Traveler; Military Personnel)
*Arthur War Lord* - Dafydd ab Hugh   *f*   6

**Smythe, Raoul "Rags"** (Magician; Professor)
*Shade and Shadow* - Francine G. Woodbury   *f*   5967

**S'Nash** (Alien; Researcher)
*Fossil* - Hal Clement   *s*   1083

**Snatch** (Military Personnel)
*The Knights of Cawdor* - Mike Jefferies   *f*   2886

**Snaugenhutt** (Warrior; Animal)
*Son of Spellsinger* - Alan Dean Foster   *f*   2015

**Snell, Nancy** (Teenager)
*The Devil's End* - D.A. Fowler   *h*   2023

**Snell, Susan** (Teenager)
*Carrie* - Stephen King   *h*   3127

**Snick, Panthea** (Revolutionary; Girlfriend)
*Dayworld Breakup* - Philip Jose Farmer   *s*   1869

**Snorrison, Bran** (Hero; Immortal)
*The Deepest Sea* - Charles Barnitz   *f*   363

**Snout** (Alien; Psychic)
*Aliens Stole My Body* - Bruce Coville   *s*   1217

**Snow, Chris** (Writer)
*Fear Nothing* - Dean R. Koontz   *h*   3207

**Snow, David** (Scientist)
*Cold at Heart* - Brian Hopkins   *h*   2768

**Snow, Julie** (Young Woman)
*Cold at Heart* - Brian Hopkins   *h*   2768

**Snuff** (Animal; Sidekick)
*A Night in the Lonesome October* - Roger
   Zelazny   *h*   6072

**Snyder, Harry** (Television Personality)
*Satellite Night News* - Jack Hopkins   *s*   2770

**Soamosa** (Young Woman)
*The Ship Avenged* - S.M. Stirling   *s*   5298

**Sobek, Yoo** (Alien; Rebel)
*Hostile Takeover* - Jack McKinney   *s*   3849

**Sobel, Charles** (Military Personnel)
*Turn of the Cards* - Victor Milan   *s*   3891

**Sobieski, Josip** (Military Personnel; Explorer)
*Conrad's Quest for Rubber* - Leo
   Frankowski   *s*   2043

**Soerensen, Terese "Tess"** (Heiress; Linguist)
*An Earthly Crown* - Kate Elliott   *s*   1771

**Soerensen, Terese "Tess"** (Scholar; Noblewoman)
*Jaran* - Kate Elliott   *s*   1772

**Soerensen, Terese "Tess"** (Ruler)
*The Law of Becoming* - Kate Elliott   *s*   1774

**Sogan, Varn Tarl** (Royalty; Military Personnel)
*Call to Arms* - P.M. Griffin   *s*   2435

**Sogan, Varn Tarl** (Military Personnel)
*Fire Planet* - P.M. Griffin   *s*   2436

**Sogan, Varn Tarl** (Royalty; Telepath)
*Jungle Assault* - P.M. Griffin   *s*   2437

**Sokol** (Genetically Altered Being; Diplomat)
*Legacy of the Ancients* - Ron Sarti   *s*   4836

**Sokolowska, Marya** (Religious)
*Under the Yoke* - S.M. Stirling   *s*   5301

**Solamnus, Vinas** (Warrior; Religious)
*Vinas Solamnus* - J. Robert King   *f*   3123

**Sole, Chris** (Scientist)
*The Embedding* - Ian Watson   *s*   5634

**Soledad, Zeide** (Student; Genetically Altered Being)
*Cybernetic Jungle* - S.N. Lewitt   *s*   3449

**Soleta** (Alien; Scientist)
*End Game* - Peter David   *s*   1382

**Soleta** (Alien; Student)
*Worf's First Adventure* - Peter David   *s*   1391

**Solinari, Kelly** (Scholar; Detective—Amateur)
*Crisis on Doona* - Anne McCaffrey   *s*   3723

**Solis, Rudy** (Wizard; Mechanic)
*Mother of Winter* - Barbara Hambly   *f*   2506

**Solith, Gwin Nien** (Innkeeper; Magician)
*The Cursed* - Dave Duncan   *f*   1674

**Solo** (Artificial Intelligence; Robot)
*Solo* - Robert Mason   *s*   3665
*Weapon* - Robert Mason   *s*   3666

**Solo, Han** (Spaceship Captain; Warrior)
*Ambush at Corellia* - Roger MacBride Allen   *s*   76
*Children of the Jedi* - Barbara Hambly   *s*   2500
*The Courtship of Princess Leia* - Dave
   Wolverton   *s*   5950
*Heir to the Empire* - Timothy Zahn   *s*   6054
*Jedi Search* - Kevin J. Anderson   *s*   109
*The New Rebellion* - Kristine Kathryn
   Rusch   *s*   4719
*The Truce at Bakura* - Kathy Tyers   *s*   5527

**Solo, Jacen** (Teenager; Military Personnel)
*Trouble on Cloud City* - Kevin J. Anderson   *s*   117

**Solo, Jaina** (Teenager; Military Personnel)
*Trouble on Cloud City* - Kevin J. Anderson   *s*   117

**Solo, Jay** (Police Officer; Administrator)
*The Nine Lives of Catseye Gomez* - Simon
   Hawke   *f*   2620

**Solo, Leia Organa** (Royalty; Leader)
*Ambush at Corellia* - Roger MacBride Allen   *s*   76
*Before the Storm* - Michael P. Kube-
   McDowell   *s*   3247
*Children of the Jedi* - Barbara Hambly   *s*   2500
*Darksaber* - Kevin J. Anderson   *s*   103

**Solo, Leia Organa** (Administrator; Royalty)
*Heir to the Empire* - Timothy Zahn   *s*   6054

**Solo, Leia Organa** (Royalty; Leader)
*The Last Command* - Timothy Zahn   *s*   6055
*The New Rebellion* - Kristine Kathryn
   Rusch   *s*   4719

**Soloman** (Military Personnel)
*Cain* - James Byron Huggins   *h*   2802

**Solomon, Neil** (Businessman)
*Out There in the Darkness* - Ed Gorman   *h*   2279

**Solomon, Parker** (Businessman)
*Dark Tide* - Elizabeth Forrest   *h*   1972

**Somerfield, Alice** (Child)
*The End of Alice* - A.M. Homes   *h*   2755

**Somersby, Nadine** (Store Owner)
*Prank Night* - David Robbins   *h*   4601

**Sommers, Serena** (Girlfriend)
*Forest of the Night* - S.P. Somtow   *f*   5156

**Somoroff, Peter** (Spy)
*Red Devil* - David Saperstein   *h*   4816

**Sondra** (Young Woman)
*Tapestry of Dark Souls* - Elaine Bergstrom   *h*   465

**Song, Medwind** (Sorceress; Barbarian)
*Fire in the Mist* - Holly Lisle   *f*   3482

**Song, Medwind** (Sorceress; Scholar)
*Mind of the Magic* - Holly Lisle   *f*   3486

**Songa** (Hunter; Warrior)
*Conan the Savage* - Leonard Carpenter   *f*   909

**Sonnenberg, Bryce** (Scientist; Sports Figure)
*The Ganymede Club* - Charles Sheffield   *s*   4955

**Soo, Hannah** (Financier; Reanimated Dead)
*Take Back Plenty* - Colin Greenland   *s*   2419

**Soolis, Yveena** (Noblewoman)
*The Thirteenth Majestral* - Hayford Peirce   *s*   4277

**Soothslayer** (Sorcerer; Religious)
*Soothslayer: A Magickal Fantasy* - D.J.
   Conway   *f*   1143

**Soper, Helen** (Store Owner)
*Head Injuries* - Conrad Williams   *h*   5816

**Sophie** (Young Woman)
*Spell Bound* - Ru Emerson   *f*   1810

**Sorak** (Psychic; Mythical Creature)
*The Outcast* - Simon Hawke   *f*   2621
*The Seeker* - Simon Hawke   *f*   2624

**Sorenson, Melissa** (Child; Businesswoman)
*Drifter's Run* - William C. Dietz   s   1544

**Sorenson, Rachel** (Artist)
*I'll Be Watching You* - Samuel M. Key   h   3094

**Sorensson, Alfreda "Allie"** (Magician; Midwife)
*Kindred Rites* - Katharine Eliska Kimbriel   f   3118

**Sorensson, Alfreda "Allie"** (Young Woman)
*Night Calls* - Katharine Eliska Kimbriel   h   3119

**Sorensson, Eldon** (Farmer)
*Night Calls* - Katharine Eliska Kimbriel   h   3119

**sorMeklan, Driskolt "Dart"** (Nobleman)
*Beneath the Web* - Lynn Abbey   f   12

**Sorricaine, Viktor** (Scientist)
*The World at the End of Time* - Frederik
   Pohl   s   4357

**sorRodion, Rinchen "Wolf"** (Royalty)
*Beneath the Web* - Lynn Abbey   f   12

**Sorya** (Revolutionary)
*Metropolitan* - Walter Jon Williams   s   5839

**Souci, Suzanne** (Actress)
*A Company of Stars* - Christopher Stasheff   s   5215
*We Open on Venus* - Christopher Stasheff   s   5227

**Soul, Derek** (Government Official; Divorced
   Person)
*A Second Infinity* - Michael D. Weaver   s   5660

**Soul Catcher** (Wizard; Mentally Ill Person)
*She Is the Darkness* - Glen Cook   f   1154

**South, Joe** (Spaceman; Time Traveler)
*The Stalk* - Janet Morris   s   4016
*Threshold* - Janet Morris   s   4018

**South, Joe** (Time Traveler; Spaceman)
*Trust Territory* - Janet Morris   s   4019

**Southall, Sam** (Teenager)
*The Tooth Fairy* - Graham Joyce   f   2995

**Southerland, John** (Businessman; Wealthy)
*A Matter of Taste* - Fred Saberhagen   h   4770

**Southwell, Roger** (Magician; Scholar)
*The Printer's Devil* - Chico Kidd   f   3099

**Spae, Elizabeth** (Researcher; Adventurer)
*A King Beneath the Mountain* - Robert N.
   Charrette   f   973

**Spango, Hypatia** (Computer Expert)
*Montezuma Strip* - Alan Dean Foster   s   2011

**Spanner** (Lesbian; Criminal)
*Slow River* - Nicola Griffith   s   2445

**Spanning, Henry Lake** (Convict)
*Mefisto in Onyx* - Harlan Ellison   h   1786

**Spano, Constance "Connie"** (Public Relations)
*Independence Day* - Dean Devlin   s   1508

**Sparhawk** (Knight)
*The Diamond Throne* - David Eddings   f   1731
*Domes of Fire* - David Eddings   f   1732

**Sparhawk** (Knight; Parent)
*The Hidden City* - David Eddings   f   1733

**Sparhawk** (Knight)
*The Ruby Knight* - David Eddings   f   1736
*The Sapphire Rose* - David Eddings   f   1737

**Spark, Charles** (Empath)
*The Flies of Memory* - Ian Watson   s   5635

**Sparkle** (Dancer)
*The Six Families* - Nancy Holder   s   2733

**Sparrow** (Trader; Troubleshooter)
*Bone Danc: A Fantasy for Technophiles* - Emma
   Bull   s   766

**Sparrow** (Amnesiac; Space Explorer)
*The Dark Beyond the Stars* - Frank M.
   Robinson   s   4626

**Sparrow** (Artisan; Matchmaker)
*Justice* - David Drake   s   1635

**Spartan, John "Demolition Man"** (Detective—
   Police)
*Demolition Man* - Richard Osborne   s   4229

**Spear, James** (Businessman; Computer Expert)
*Deathwalker* - Patrick Whalen   h   5769

**Speckarin** (Magician; Mythical Creature)
*Kirins: The Flight of the Ain* - James D.
   Priest   f   4433
*Kirins: The Secret of the Hanging Stones* - James D.
   Priest   f   4434
*Kirins: The Spell of No'an* - James D.
   Priest   f   4435

**Specter, Alan** (Time Traveler; Police Officer)
*Time Station Berlin* - David Evans   s   1852

**Speke, Clara** (Housewife)
*Ghostwright* - Michael Cadnum   h   810

**Speke, Hamilton** (Writer)
*Ghostwright* - Michael Cadnum   h   810

**Speke, Vernon** (Scientist)
*Hunger* - William Dantz   h   1346

**Spellman, Julie** (Teenager)
*The Homing* - John Saul   h   4842

**Spellman, Karen** (Secretary—Legal)
*The Homing* - John Saul   h   4842

**Spence, Jeffrey** (Detective)
*Portrait of the Psychopath as a Young Woman* -
   Edward Lee   h   3395

**Spence, Oliver** (Businessman)
*Fog Heart* - Thomas Tessier   h   5440

**Spencer, Allison** (Military Personnel)
*The War Machine* - David Drake   s   1650

**Spencer, Arlene** (Journalist)
*Revenge of the Seventh Carrier* - Peter Albano   s   49

**Spencer, David** (Military Personnel)
*Return to Camerein* - Rick Shelley   s   4974

**Spencer, Jake** (Taxi Driver)
*Bloodlines* - J.N. Williamson   h   5852

**Spencer, Joseph "Speed"** (Astronaut)
*Reach* - Edward Gibson   s   2216

**Spencer, Simon** (Doctor)
*The Werewolf's Touch* - Cheri Scotch   h   4892

**Spenotex, Arakaho Blundy** (Writer; Rancher)
*Stopping at Slowyear* - Frederik Pohl   s   4355

**Spenser, Vernon** (Mechanic)
*Bright Shadow* - Elizabeth Forrest   h   1971

**Sperin, Bro** (Spy)
*The Ship Avenged* - S.M. Stirling   s   5298

**Sperry, Jack** (Critic)
*City of Truth* - James Morrow   s   4030

**Sperry, Toby** (Child)
*City of Truth* - James Morrow   s   4030

**Spider** (Businessman; Mutant)
*The Einstein Intersection* - Samuel R.
   Delany   s   1481

**Spider** (Student)
*Fine Prey* - Scott Westerfeld   s   5766

**Spike** (Companion)
*The Zork Chronicles* - George Alec
   Effinger   s   1754

**Spiller, Josh** (Truck Driver)
*Furnace* - Muriel Gray   h   2339

**Spinner, Probe** (Robot; Revolutionary)
*Arachne* - Lisa Mason   s   3661

**Spinner-of-Rope** (Pilot; Space Explorer)
*Ring* - Stephen Baxter   s   402

**Spiro, Jason** (Teenager)
*Deadrush* - Yvonne Navarro   h   4073

**Spock** (Diplomat; Alien)
*Avenger* - William Shatner   s   4928

**Spock** (Scientist; Alien)
*The City on the Edge of Forever* - Harlan
   Ellison   s   1784
*Crossover* - Michael Jan Friedman   s   2063
*Crossroad* - Barbara Hambly   s   2501
*First Frontier* - Diane Carey   s   902
*First Strike* - Diane Carey   s   903
*The Joy Machine* - James Gunn   s   2458

**Spock** (Alien; Companion)
*Mind Meld* - John Vornholt   s   5596

**Spock** (Scientist; Alien)
*Prime Directive* - Judith Reeves-Stevens   s   4514
*Probe* - Margaret Wander Bonanno   s   569
*Renegade* - Gene DeWeese   s   1511
*The Return* - William Shatner   s   4933
*The Rift* - Peter David   s   1386
*Sanctuary* - John Vornholt   s   5597
*Sarek* - A.C. Crispin   s   1260

**Spock** (Resistance Fighter; Alien)
*Spectre* - William Shatner   s   4934

**Spock** (Scientist; Alien)
*Star Trek: The Classic Episodes 1* - James
   Blish   s   526
*Star Trek: The Classic Episodes 2* - James
   Blish   s   527
*Star Trek: The Classic Episodes 3* - James
   Blish   s   528
*Star Trek: The Lost Years* - J.M. Dillard   s   1557

**Spock** (Spaceship Captain; Alien)
*Vulcan's Forge* - Susan Shwartz   s   5019

**Spock** (Scientist; Alien)
*Vulcan's Glory* - D.C. Fontana   s   1967
*Windows on a Lost World* - V.E. Mitchell   s   3920

**Spoda, Arthur** (Serial Killer)
*Iceman* - Rex Miller   h   3900

**Spoor, Baron Malcolm** (Businessman)
*The Living One* - Lewis Gannett   h   2115

**Spoor, Torrance** (Teenager)
*The Living One* - Lewis Gannett   h   2115

**Spots-Son of Chotrz-Shaa** (Alien; Military
   Personnel)
*Man-Kzin Wars V* - Larry Niven   s   4125

**Spotted Horse, David** (Activist; Indian)
*Sacred Ground* - Mercedes Lackey   f   3294

**Spring, Juliet** (Scientist; Computer Expert)
*Host* - Peter James   h   2872

**Spring-Heeled Jack** (Hero)
*Spring-Heeled Jack* - Philip Pullman   f   4447

**Spring Rain** (Shaman; Indian)
*Sing for a Gentle Rain* - J. Alison James   f   2861

**Sprits** (Psychic)
*Concrete Hotel* - C. Christopher Caldon   h   839

**Squires, Jack** (Trader)
*Vaporetto 13* - Robert Girardi   h   2241

**sr'Yat, Jazen** (Sorcerer)
*The Itinerant Exorcist* - Ashley McConnell   f   3776

**SSS-900-C Simeon** (Administrator; Cyborg)
*The City Who Fought* - Anne McCaffrey   s   3722

**SStragh** (Animal)
*Ray Bradbury Presents: Dinosaur World* - Stephen
   Leigh   s   3428

**Stablits, Dothan** (Police Officer)
*Hard Landing* - Algis Budrys   s   753

**Stack, Nathan** (Police Officer)
*Demon Download* - Jack Yeovil   f   6021

**Stackalee** (Gunfighter)
*The Bars on Satan's Jailhouse* - Norman Partridge  h  4251

**Stafford, Alwyn Bryan** (Explorer; Scientist)
*Mars Underground* - William Hartmann  s  2584

**Stafford, Yvonne** (Abuse Victim)
*Thoughts of God* - Michael Kanaly  s  3007

**Stahlbaum, Marie** (Child)
*Nutcracker* - E.T.A. Hoffmann  f  2719

**Stalker, Darmen** (Secretary)
*Fire Angels* - Jane Routley  f  4685

**Stalker, Martin** (Warrior; Nobleman)
*A Tremor in the Bitter Earth* - Katya Reimann  f  4527

**Stallman, Connie** (Doctor)
*Evil Reincarnate* - Leigh Clark  h  1050

**Standish, Brian** (Doctor)
*Witch Hill* - Marion Zimmer Bradley  h  654

**Standish, William** (Professor)
*Mrs. God* - Peter Straub  h  5329

**Stane, Temelathe** (Political Figure)
*Shadow Man* - Melissa Scott  s  4900

**Stanislaus, Glynn Webster** (Actor; Teenager)
*Mind Snare* - Gayle Greeno  s  2422

**Stanislaus, Jerelynn** (Actress)
*Mind Snare* - Gayle Greeno  s  2422

**Stanley, Rodman** (Police Officer)
*Night Beasts* - T.W. Stetson  h  5263

**Stanley, Samuel** (Military Personnel)
*The Two Georges* - Richard Dreyfuss  s  1655

**Stannard, Gabriel** (Singer)
*The Kill Riff* - David J. Schow  h  4887

**Stanovich, Martin Philip** (Child; Spirit)
*Ghost Boy* - Jean Simon  h  5064

**Stanton, Chris-John** (Revolutionary)
*Chicago Red* - R.M. Meluch  s  3873

**Stanton, Karl** (Spaceman; Pilot)
*Reckoning Infinity* - John E. Stith  s  5304

**Star Shell** (Heroine; Indian)
*People of the Lakes* - Kathleen O'Neal Gear  f  2164

**Starborne, Angela** (Lawyer)
*California Ghosting* - William Hill  h  2687

**Starbridge, Charity** (Widow(er))
*Sugar Rain* - Paul Park  s  4243

**Starbridge, Thanakar** (Doctor)
*Sugar Rain* - Paul Park  s  4243

**Starbuck** (Warrior; Spaceman)
*Armageddon* - Richard Hatch  s  2602

**Starbuck, July** (Telepath; Twin)
*Double Trouble Squared* - Kathryn Lasky  f  3340
*Shadows in the Water* - Kathryn Lasky  s  3341

**Starbuck, Liberty** (Telepath; Twin)
*Double Trouble Squared* - Kathryn Lasky  f  3340
*Shadows in the Water* - Kathryn Lasky  s  3341

**Starbuck, Ron** (Runaway; Human)
*Elsewhere* - Will Shetterly  f  4993

**Starbuck, Ron** (Adventurer; Teenager)
*Nevernever* - Will Shetterly  f  4995

**Stardust, Baijon "Tiggy"** (Knight)
*Archangel Blues* - eluki bes shahar  s  471
*Darktraders* - eluki bes shahar  s  472

**Starfire, Dion** (Heir; Royalty)
*King's Sacrifice* - Margaret Weis  s  5717
*The Lost King* - Margaret Weis  s  5720

**Stargard, Conrad** (Time Traveler; Engineer)
*Conrad's Quest for Rubber* - Leo Frankowski  s  2043

**Stargard, Conrad** (Engineer; Time Traveler)
*The Flying Warlord* - Leo Frankowski  s  2044
*The High-Tech Knight* - Leo Frankowski  s  2045

**Stargard, Conrad** (Time Traveler; Engineer)
*Lord Conrad's Lady* - Leo Frankowski  s  2046

**Stargard, Conrad** (Engineer; Time Traveler)
*The Radiant Warrior* - Leo Frankowski  s  2047

**Starhawk** (Mercenary)
*The Dark Hand of Magic* - Barbara Hambly  f  2502

**Stark, Eddard** (Nobleman)
*A Game of Thrones* - George R.R. Martin  f  3645

**Stark, Edgar** (Artist)
*Asylum* - Patrick McGrath  h  3812

**Stark, Emmett** (Police Officer)
*The Headsman* - James Neal Harvey  h  2599

**Stark, George** (Murderer)
*The Dark Half* - Stephen King  h  3128

**Stark, Laura** (Young Woman)
*Dreamthorp* - Chet Williamson  h  5845

**Stark, Marilyn** (Sea Captain; Criminal)
*seaQuest DSV: The Novel* - Diane Duane  s  1666

**Stark, Otto** (Clone)
*In the Wrong Hands* - Edward Gibson  s  2215

**Stark, Tony "Iron Man"** (Scientist; Hero)
*Iron Man: The Armor Trap* - Greg Cox  s  1227

**Starlen, Garett** (Police Officer)
*Nightwatch* - Robin Wayne Bailey  f  289

**Starling, Clarice** (FBI Agent)
*The Silence of the Lambs* - Thomas Harris  h  2566

**Starling, Ugly** (Outcast)
*Far Harbor* - Melisa C. Michaels  s  3888

**Stasov, Ilya Sergeiivich** (Scientist; Military Personnel)
*A Deeper Sea* - Alexander Jablokov  s  2838

**Stasya** (Minstrel)
*Sing the Four Quarters* - Tanya Huff  f  2799

**Statler, Phil** (Businessman)
*The Fear in Yesterday's Rings* - George C. Chesbro  h  1007

**Stavely, Ann Veronica** (Child)
*Hexwood* - Diana Wynne Jones  s  2948

**Stavenger, Douglas** (Experimental Subject; Teenager)
*Moonrise* - Ben Bova  s  587

**Stavenger, Douglas** (Leader; Genetically Altered Being)
*Moonwar* - Ben Bova  s  588

**Stavenger, Joanna Masterson** (Businesswoman)
*Moonrise* - Ben Bova  s  587

**Stavenger, Paul** (Astronaut; Businessman)
*Moonrise* - Ben Bova  s  587

**Stavi, Kira** (Scientist)
*Remnant Population* - Elizabeth Moon  s  3972

**Stavrianos, Nick** (Police Officer; Detective—Private)
*Quarantine* - Greg Egan  s  1762

**Steadford, Sir Harry** (Spirit; Nobleman)
*The Meddlesome Ghost* - Sheila Rosalynd Allen  f  84

**Stebbins, Ivy** (Real Estate Agent)
*All the Bells on Earth* - James P. Blaylock  f  518

**Stebbins, Walt** (Salesman)
*All the Bells on Earth* - James P. Blaylock  f  518

**Steck** (Clone; Outcast)
*Commitment Hour* - James Alan Gardner  s  2134

**Steele, Vanessa** (Alien; Revolutionary)
*The Woman between the Worlds* - F. Gwynplaine MacIntyre  s  3596

**Steengo** (Spy; Musician)
*The Stainless Steel Rat Sings the Blues* - Harry Harrison  s  2575

**Steep, Jacob** (Supernatural Being)
*Sacrament* - Clive Barker  h  345

**Stefan** (Minstrel; Homosexual)
*Magic's Price* - Mercedes Lackey  f  3288

**Stefano, Yuri** (Gypsy)
*Taltos* - Anne Rice  h  4577

**Stefanos** (Ruler; Immortal)
*Chains of Darkness, Chains of Light* - Michelle Sagara  f  4781
*Children of the Blood: Book Two of The Sundered* - Michelle Sagara  f  4782
*Into the Dark Lands* - Michelle Sagara  f  4783

**Stefanovsky, Stephan** (Musician; Spirit)
*Violin* - Anne Rice  h  4579

**Steffan** (Mythical Creature; Engineer)
*Iron Dragons: Mountains and Madness* - Rose Estes  f  1839

**Steiger, Dianne** (Spaceship Captain)
*The Ring of Charon* - Roger MacBride Allen  s  80

**Stein, Joseph** (Spy)
*City of Iron* - Chet Williamson  h  5843
*Empire of Dust* - Chet Williamson  h  5846

**Stein, Rachel** (Scientist; Agent)
*Search and Destroy* - Keith William Andrews  s  141

**Stein, Susan "Starbright"** (Teenager; Runaway)
*Summer of Love* - Lisa Mason  s  3664

**Steinberg, Leah** (Waiter/Waitress)
*Shock Radio* - Leigh Clark  h  1052

**Steiner, Bill** (Pawnbroker)
*Rose Madder* - Stephen King  h  3139

**Steiner, Clara** (Spy)
*The Werewolf's Revenge* - Richard Jaccoma  h  2841

**Steiner, Katrina** (Noblewoman)
*Prince of Havoc* - Michael A. Stackpole  s  5204

**Steiner-Davion, Victor** (Military Personnel; Royalty)
*Prince of Havoc* - Michael A. Stackpole  s  5204

**Steinfeld** (Revolutionary)
*Eclipse Corona* - John Shirley  s  5006

**Steinmetz, Saul** (Political Figure)
*Aftermath* - Charles Sheffield  s  4947

**Stello, Rawnie** (Child; Hero)
*The Friendship Song* - Nancy Springer  f  5179

**Sten** (Military Personnel)
*Empire's End* - Allan Cole  s  1103
*The Return of the Emperor* - Allan Cole  s  1106

**Sten** (Spaceship Captain; Bodyguard)
*Revenge of the Damned* - Allan Cole  s  1107

**Sten** (Military Personnel; Diplomat)
*Vortex* - Allan Cole  s  1108

**Stenvall, Richard** (Writer)
*The Night Seasons* - J.N. Williamson  h  5858

**Stephen** (Companion)
*Hunter's Death* - Michelle West  f  5758

**Stephen** (Teenager; Royalty)
*The Last Book of Swords: Shieldbreaker's Story* - Fred Saberhagen  f  4768

**Stephen** (Professor)
*Lunatics* - Bradley Denton  f  1491

**Stephen "Scribble"** (Addict; Fugitive)
*Vurt* - Jeff Noon  s  4136

**Stephenson, Diana** (Artist)
*The Prodigy* - Noel Hynd   *h*   2823

**Stephenson, Jenny** (Young Woman)
*Mask of the Night* - Mary Ryan   *h*   4753

**Stepovich, Mike** (Police Officer)
*The Gypsy* - Steven Brust   *f*   744

**Sterling, Alice** (Lawyer)
*Sacrifice* - Richard Kinion   *h*   3146

**Sterling, Ben** (Writer)
*Midnight Sun* - Ramsey Campbell   *h*   860

**Sterling, Ellen** (Artist)
*Midnight Sun* - Ramsey Campbell   *h*   860

**Sterling, Johnny** (Child)
*Midnight Sun* - Ramsey Campbell   *h*   860

**Sterling, Justin** (Immortal; Agent)
*Dark Heart* - Margaret Weis   *f*   5707

**Sterling, Justin** (Immortal; Artist)
*Testament of the Dragon* - Margaret Weis   *f*   5729

**Stern** (Pilot)
*'48* - James Herbert   *h*   2667

**Stern, Andrew** (Professor; Psychologist)
*The Streeter* - Scott Ian Barry   *h*   373

**Steve** (Murderer)
*Sacrifice* - Richard Kinion   *h*   3146

**Steven** (Orphan; Companion)
*Hunter's Oath* - Michelle West   *f*   5759

**Steven** (Child; Abuse Victim)
*The Night Man* - K.W. Jeter   *h*   2915

**Stevens, Carol** (Social Worker)
*Reborn* - F. Paul Wilson   *h*   5895

**Stevens, Jim** (Writer; Journalist)
*Reborn* - F. Paul Wilson   *h*   5895

**Stevens, Kathleen "Zero"** (Prostitute)
*Near Death* - Nancy Kilpatrick   *h*   3113

**Stevens, Luke** (Child)
*Offspring* - Jack Ketchum   *h*   3092

**Stevenson, Connie** (Detective—Homicide)
*Concrete Hotel* - C. Christopher Caldon   *h*   839

**Stevenson, David** (Scientist)
*The Innsmouth Heritage* - Brian Stableford   *h*   5194

**Stevenson, Tom** (Lawyer)
*Return of the Wolfman* - Jeff Rovin   *h*   4687

**Stevenson, Walker** (Anthropologist; Lover)
*The Deathless* - Myles Murchison   *h*   4048

**Steward, Ben** (Time Traveler; Anthropologist)
*The Lincoln Hunters* - Wilson Tucker   *s*   5487

**Stewart, Anne** (Parent; Researcher)
*Jupiter's Daughter* - Tom Hyman   *s*   2820

**Stewart, Bill** (Engineer)
*Weapon* - Robert Mason   *s*   3666

**Stewart, Christopher James** (Detective—Police)
*Nightmare's Disciple* - Joseph S. Pulver Jr.   *h*   4449

**Stewart, Dale** (Child)
*Summer of Night* - Dan Simmons   *h*   5060

**Stewart, Dalton** (Businessman; Criminal)
*Jupiter's Daughter* - Tom Hyman   *s*   2820

**Stewart, Genevieve "Genny"** (Genetically Altered
   Being; Psychic)
*Jupiter's Daughter* - Tom Hyman   *s*   2820

**Stewart, Guil** (Telepath)
*Rider at the Gate* - C.J. Cherryh   *s*   1000

**Stewart, Hope** (Child; Experimental Subject)
*Dark of the Eye* - Douglas Clegg   *h*   1078

**Stewart, Janet** (Computer Expert; Businesswoman)
*Zeus and Co.* - David Lee Jones   *f*   2942

**Stewart, Kate** (Housewife)
*Dark of the Eye* - Douglas Clegg   *h*   1078

**Stewart, Meg** (Veterinarian)
*Claw* - Ken Eulo   *h*   1850

**Stheno** (Mythical Creature; Immortal)
*Bhagavati* - Kara Dalkey   *f*   1316

**Stigg** (Genetically Altered Being)
*My Father Immortal* - Michael D. Weaver   *s*   5659

**Stiles** (Principal)
*Mysteries of the Word* - Stanley Wiater   *h*   5796

**Stiles, Alex** (Vampire)
*Nightblood* - T. Chris Martindale   *h*   3656

**Stiles, Chris** (Veteran)
*Nightblood* - T. Chris Martindale   *h*   3656

**Stiller, Dennis** (Journalist)
*The Nexus* - Mike McQuay   *f*   3860

**Stiller, Warreven "Raven"** (Activist; Lawyer)
*Shadow Man* - Melissa Scott   *s*   4900

**Stillwater, Marty** (Writer)
*Mr. Murder* - Dean R. Koontz   *h*   3213

**Stillwater, Paige** (Health Care Professional)
*Mr. Murder* - Dean R. Koontz   *h*   3213

**Stilman, Shyh** (Researcher; Scientist)
*Lightwing* - Tara K. Harper   *s*   2551

**Stimpson, Nevil** (Convict)
*Werewolf* - Peter Rubie   *h*   4702

**Stirling, Richard** (Lawyer; Vampire)
*The Judas Glass* - Michael Cadnum   *h*   812

**Sto-Helit, Susan** (Governess; Noblewoman)
*Hogfather* - Terry Pratchett   *f*   4391

**Stockton, Clifford** (Child)
*Mysterium* - Robert Charles Wilson   *s*   5911

**Stodard, Paul** (Artisan)
*Blood Alone* - Elaine Bergstrom   *h*   462

**Stoker, Bram** (Writer; Historical Figure)
*Dracula Unbound* - Brian W. Aldiss   *h*   55

**Stoker, Bram** (Writer)
*Slave of My Thirst* - Tom Holland   *h*   2742

**Stollitt, Sydney** (Businesswoman)
*Another Day, Another Dungeon* - Greg
   Costikyan   *f*   1206
*One Quest, Hold the Dragons* - Greg
   Costikyan   *f*   1208

**Stone** (Artisan)
*Isle of Woman* - Piers Anthony   *f*   178

**Stone, Alexandra** (Police Officer)
*Testament of the Dragon* - Margaret Weis   *f*   5729

**Stone, Arla** (Psychic)
*Reclamation* - Sarah Zettel   *s*   6081

**Stone, Charlie** (Cowboy; Indian)
*Wendigo Border* - Catherine Montrose   *h*   3967

**Stone, Cheryl** (Prostitute)
*Dead Time* - Richard Lee Byers   *h*   796

**Stone, David** (Businessman; Landlord)
*Sati* - Christopher Pike   *f*   4330

**Stone, Edwin L. "Ed"** (Revolutionary; Activist)
*Why Do Birds* - Damon Knight   *s*   3190

**Stone, Enoch** (Hunter; Museum Curator)
*A Hunger in the Soul* - Mike Resnick   *s*   4545

**Stone, Gloria** (Healer; Robot)
*The Gaia Websters* - Kim Antieau   *s*   198

**Stone, Jack** (Martial Arts Expert)
*Dead Time* - Richard Lee Byers   *h*   796

**Stone, Jack** (Writer)
*The Immaculate* - Mark Morris   *h*   4023

**Stone, Jerry** (Military Personnel; Homosexual)
*Death's Head* - Mel Keegan   *s*   3029

**Stone, Julie** (Spacewoman)
*The Infinite Sea* - Jeffrey A. Carver   *s*   932

**Stone, Linneth** (Scholar)
*Mysterium* - Robert Charles Wilson   *s*   5911

**Stone, Neil** (Police Officer)
*Deathscape* - Michael Cecilione   *h*   945

**Stone, Philip** (Businessman)
*Psychamok* - Brian Lumley   *h*   3561

**Stone, Richard** (Telepath)
*Psychamok* - Brian Lumley   *h*   3561

**Stone, Roger** (Historian)
*Ancient Images* - Ramsey Campbell   *h*   852

**Stone, Walker** (Journalist)
*Whipping Boy* - John Byrne   *h*   800

**Stone, Wallace "Rocky"** (Military Personnel)
*Galactic MI* - Kevin D. Randle   *s*   4467

**Stone, Will** (Spy)
*Majestic* - Whitley Strieber   *s*   5341

**Stonebender, Jake** (Saloon Keeper/Owner)
*The Callahan Touch* - Spider Robinson   *f*   4637
*Callahan's Legacy* - Spider Robinson   *s*   4639

**Stonehouse, Dylan** (Businessman)
*A Wish and a Dream* - Ingrid Weaver   *f*   5658

**Stoner, Charley** (Military Personnel)
*Limbo Search* - Parke Godwin   *s*   2245

**Stoner, Keith** (Astronaut; Hero)
*Star Brothers* - Ben Bova   *s*   594

**Stonewall, Annie Casteel** (Handicapped)
*Gates of Paradise* - V.C. Andrews   *h*   145

**Stoogeone, Anthony** (Organized Crime Figure)
*Something Out There* - Ronald Kelly   *h*   3056

**Storey, Graham** (Writer)
*Pillow Friend* - Lisa Tuttle   *h*   5522

**Storm, Jack** (Military Personnel; Revolutionary)
*Alien Salute* - Charles Ingrid   *s*   2830
*Return Fire* - Charles Ingrid   *s*   2833

**Storm, Richard** (Producer)
*The Uncanny* - Andrew Klavan   *h*   3164

**Stormer, Julian** (Artist)
*Harrowgate* - Daniel H. Gower   *h*   2292

**Story, Raymond** (Patient)
*Zod Wallop* - William Browning Spencer   *h*   5169

**Stout, Thomas A.** (Relative)
*Humpty Dumpty: An Oval* - Damon Knight   *s*   3186

**Stout, Wellington "Bill" Nelson** (Businessman)
*Humpty Dumpty: An Oval* - Damon Knight   *s*   3186

**Stow, John** (Detective—Private)
*Walking the Labyrinth* - Lisa Goldstein   *f*   2266

**Straachen, Dianus** (Scientist)
*Faces under Water* - Tanith Lee   *h*   3409

**Straat-ien, Nevan** (Military Personnel; Human)
*The Spoils of War* - Alan Dean Foster   *s*   2016

**Straker, Ellis** (Spaceship Captain; Psychic)
*Yamato: A Rage in Heaven* - Ken Kato   *s*   3014

**Straker, Phil** (Police Officer)
*Creekers* - Edward Lee   *h*   3391

**Straker, Phillip** (Detective)
*Goon* - Edward Lee   *h*   3392

**Strand, Paul** (Military Personnel; Hero)
*The Queen's Squadron* - R.M. Meluch   *s*   3874

**Strang, Mark** (Time Traveler; Warrior)
*Caesar's Bicycle* - John Barnes   *s*   350

**Strang, Mark** (Bodyguard)
*Patton's Spaceship* - John Barnes   *s*   357

**Strangelove, Jacqueline** (Stripper)
*Yours Truly, Jackie the Stripper* - Edo van Belkom *h* 5536

**Stranger** (Young Man)
*Black Sun* - Douglas E. Winter *h* 5923

**Stranger, John** (Indian; Spaceman)
*High Steel* - Jack C. Haldeman II *s* 2486

**Stranger, John** (Indian; Construction Worker)
*Run for the Stars/Echoes of Thunder* - Harlan Ellison *s* 1788

**Strann** (Minstrel)
*The Avenger* - Louise Cooper *f* 1174

**Strasheim, John** (Worker; Journalist)
*Bloom* - Wil McCarthy *s* 3761

**Stratford, Earl** (Paranormal Investigator)
*The Committee* - Raymond Buckland *h* 752

**Stratford, Julie** (Adventurer; Heiress)
*The Mummy, or Ramses the Damned* - Anne Rice *h* 4572

**Stratton, Dan** (Police Officer)
*Night Hunter* - Michael Reaves *h* 4496

**Stratton, Thomas** (Actor)
*Facade* - Kristine Kathryn Rusch *h* 4716

**Strayhorn, Leslie** (Spouse)
*Shock Lines* - Warren Newton Beath *h* 427

**Strayhorn, Philip** (Director)
*A Child Across the Sky* - Jonathan Carroll *h* 917

**Strayhorn, Philip** (Teacher)
*Shock Lines* - Warren Newton Beath *h* 427

**Streak** (Animal; Telepath)
*Shadows in the Water* - Kathryn Lasky *s* 3341

**Strelsau, Mathias** (Nobleman; Ruler)
*Silk and Steel* - Ron Miller *f* 3905

**Strick, Gavin** (Teenager)
*Disturbing Behavior* - John Whitman *h* 5789

**Striescu, Aldo** (Vampire)
*Shadows* - Jonathan Nasaw *h* 4068

**Strine, Arnold** (Writer; Criminal)
*The Fermata* - Nicholson Baker *s* 302

**String** (Alien; Police Officer)
*Alien Blues* - Lynn S. Hightower *s* 2682
*Alien Eyes* - Lynn S. Hightower *s* 2683
*Alien Heat* - Lynn S. Hightower *s* 2684
*Alien Rites* - Lynn S. Hightower *s* 2685

**Stripe** (Passenger)
*A Maze of Stars* - John Brunner *s* 734

**Strohem, Sabine** (Artist)
*The Golden Mean* - Nick Bantock *f* 334
*Sabine's Notebook* - Nick Bantock *f* 335

**Stronsi, Felitzia "Flitz"** (Heir—Dispossessed)
*Throy* - Jack Vance *s* 5550

**Stroud, Abraham Hale** (Detective—Private; Psychic)
*Curse of the Vampire* - Geoffrey Caine *h* 832
*Legion of the Dead* - Geoffrey Caine *h* 833
*Wake of the Werewolf* - Geoffrey Caine *h* 834

**Strozza, Joe** (Artist)
*Seattle Ghost Story* - Nick DiMartino *h* 1560

**Stryke, Modra** (Empath)
*The Demons at Rainbow Bridge* - Jack L. Chalker *s* 952

**Stryker, Anton** (Adventurer; Clone)
*The Clouds of Magellan* - David F. Nighbert *s* 4103

**Stryker, Elliot** (Lawyer)
*The Eyes of Darkness* - Dean R. Koontz *s* 3206

**Stumpf, Cordie** (Widow(er))
*Fires of Eden* - Dan Simmons *h* 5053

**Sturdley, Harry** (Publisher)
*Crossover* - Bill McCay *f* 3768

**Sturgis, Dean** (Military Personnel)
*Suicide Attack* - John Sievert *s* 5023

**Sturgis, Wally** (Computer Expert; Student)
*The Shattered Sphere* - Roger MacBride Allen *s* 81

**Styreme, Katharine** (Genetically Altered Being; Musician)
*Celestis* - Paul Park *s* 4241

**SU912** (Android)
*Christmas Slaughter* - Mark Grant *s* 2323

**Suarez, Corazon "Cory"** (Teenager; Castaway)
*White Light* - William Barton *s* 384

**Suarra** (Religious)
*The Face in the Abyss* - A. Merritt *f* 3878

**Succor-of-Yellowways-Sands** (Alien; Teacher)
*Nanoware Time/The Persistence of Vision* - Ian Watson *s* 5638

**Succorso, Nick** (Pirate; Spaceman)
*Forbidden Knowledge* - Stephen R. Donaldson *s* 1571
*The Gap into Madness: Chaos and Order* - Stephen R. Donaldson *s* 1573

**Succubus** (Computer Expert; Murderer)
*The Hacker* - Chet Day *h* 1410

**Sucre** (Revolutionary)
*Canal Dreams* - Iain M. Banks *s* 323

**sud Sarc, Barac** (Alien)
*A Thousand Words for Stranger* - Julie E. Czerneda *s* 1304

**Sudek, Anna** (Worker)
*The Amulet* - A.R. Morlan *h* 4009

**Sudek, Tina Miner** (Worker; Parent)
*The Amulet* - A.R. Morlan *h* 4009

**Sue** (Housewife; Parent)
*The Interior Life* - Katherine Blake *f* 515

**Suettay** (Ruler)
*The Witch Doctor* - Christopher Stasheff *f* 5228

**Suida, Frederick** (Genetically Altered Being; Human)
*Woodsman* - Thomas A. Easton *s* 1727

**Suilin, Dick** (Journalist; Mercenary)
*Rolling Hot* - David Drake *s* 1642

**Suisan** (Maiden)
*Suisan* - Phyllis Carol Agins *f* 42

**Suiza, Esmay** (Spacewoman; Military Personnel)
*Once a Hero* - Elizabeth Moon *s* 3970

**Sulaiman, Kahlili "Kay Bee" bint Munadi** (Journalist)
*Looking for the Mahdi* - N. Lee Wood *s* 5966

**Sulaweyo, Irene** (Teacher)
*River of Blue Fire* - Tad Williams *f* 5830

**Sulaweyo, Renie** (Teacher)
*City of Golden Shadow* - Tad Williams *s* 5828

**Suldris, James** (Sorcerer)
*This Dark Paradise* - Wendy Haley *h* 2493

**Suliman** (Wizard)
*Castle in the Air* - Diana Wynne Jones *f* 2944

**Sullivan** (Vampire)
*Dark Prince* - Keith Herber *h* 2663

**Sullivan, David** (Student—College; Adventurer)
*Darkthunder's Way* - Tom Deitz *f* 1470
*Dreamseeker's Road* - Tom Deitz *f* 1472

**Sullivan, David** (Adventurer; Student—College)
*Landslayer's Law* - Tom Deitz *f* 1474

**Sullivan, David** (Student—College; Adventurer)
*Sunshaker's War* - Tom Deitz *f* 1477

**Sullivan, Donald** (Banker)
*What's Wrong with America* - Scott Bradfield *h* 627

**Sullivan, Mark** (Child)
*The Forgotten* - Stephen R. George *h* 2200

**Sullivan, Pete** (Technician; Psychic)
*Expiration Date* - Tim Powers *f* 4383

**Sullivan, Rex** (Artist)
*The Eyes of Torie Webster* - Roy Sorrels *h* 5164

**Sullivan, Richard** (Guard)
*The Forgotten* - Stephen R. George *h* 2200

**Sullivan, William T.** (Religious)
*Deus-X: A Novel of Spiritual Terror* - Joseph A. Citro *h* 1037

**Sultan of Alpha Centauri** (Ruler)
*A Gathering of Stars* - Donald Moffitt *s* 3947

**Sulu** (Military Personnel)
*The Kobayashi Maru* - Julia Ecklar *s* 1728

**Sulu, Hikaru** (Military Personnel; Spaceship Captain)
*The Ashes of Eden* - William Shatner *s* 4927

**Sulu, Hikaru** (Spaceship Captain)
*The Fearful Summons* - Denny Martin Flinn *s* 1954
*Starfleet Academy* - Diane Carey *s* 905

**Sulu, Hikaru** (Military Personnel)
*Traitor Winds* - L.A. Graf *s* 2298

**Sulu, Hikaru** (Spaceship Captain)
*War Dragons* - L.A. Graf *s* 2299

**Sulula "Philiope"** (Servant; Imposter)
*Conan of the Red Brotherhood* - Leonard Carpenter *f* 906

**Sulvia, Paulo "Jackal"** (Gang Member)
*Cybernetic Jungle* - S.N. Lewitt *s* 3449

**Sumara** (Royalty; Mercenary)
*The Nomad Queen* - James Gordon White *f* 5783

**Sumbaa** (Computer)
*The Kalif's War* - John Dalmas *s* 1322

**Summer** (Telepath; Traveler)
*Master of Many Treasures* - Mary Brown *f* 726

**Summer** (Orphan; Guide)
*Pigs Don't Fly* - Mary Brown *f* 727

**Summer, Moon Dawntreader** (Ruler)
*The Summer Queen* - Joan D. Vinge *s* 5572

**Summers, Buffy** (Teenager; Vampire Hunter)
*Buffy the Vampire Slayer* - Richie Tankersley Cusick *h* 1301
*The Harvest* - Richie Tankersley Cusick *h* 1302
*Return to Chaos* - Craig Shaw Gardner *h* 2131

**Summers, Erik** (Scientist; Professor)
*Wilderness* - Dennis Danvers *h* 1349

**Summers, Faye** (Businesswoman)
*The Calling* - Kathryn Meyer Griffith *h* 2439

**Summers, Millicent** (Businesswoman)
*The Barsoom Project* - Larry Niven *s* 4115

**Summers, Nick** (Musician)
*The Calling* - Kathryn Meyer Griffith *h* 2439

**Summerson, Natil** (Mythical Creature; Immortal)
*Strands of Sunlight* - Gael Baudino *f* 396

**Sumner, Shaelyn** (Journalist)
*Distant Dreams* - Jenny Lykins *f* 3576

**Sun Wolf** (Mercenary; Wizard)
*The Dark Hand of Magic* - Barbara Hambly *f* 2502

**Sunchaser** (Prehistoric Human; Shaman)
*People of the Sea* - W. Michael Gear *f* 2169

**Sunday, Sunday A.** (Administrator)
*A World Lost* - James B. Johnson *s* 2921

**Sundquist, Katherine** (Anthropologist)
*The Presence* - John Saul  *h*  4843

**Sundquist, Michael** (Teenager)
*The Presence* - John Saul  *h*  4843

**Sunflash** (Animal; Warrior)
*Outcast of Redwall* - Brian Jacques  *f*  2853

**Sunnyside, P.T.** (Undertaker)
*The Unnatural* - David Prill  *h*  4437

**Sunshine, Mary** (Prostitute)
*Vampire Junkies* - Norman Spinrad  *h*  5175

**Surrey, John** (Time Traveler; Security Officer)
*Timeshare* - Joshua Dann  *s*  1344

**Surrey, John** (Time Traveler)
*Timeshare: Second Time Around* - Joshua
    Dann  *s*  1345

**sus-Airaalin, Theio syn-Ricte** (Military Personnel;
  Psychic)
*By Honor Betray'd* - Debra Doyle  *s*  1598

**Susan** (Mythical Creature; Teenager)
*Clan of the Shape-Changers* - Robert Levy  *f*  3446

**Susan** (Student)
*The Divide* - Robert Charles Wilson  *s*  5907

**Susan** (Relative)
*Fade* - Robert Cormier  *h*  1188

**Susan** (Scientist; Time Traveler)
*Laying the Music to Rest* - Dean Wesley
    Smith  *h*  5114

**Susan** (Mythical Creature; Immortal)
*The Spawn of Loki* - Jason Henderson  *f*  2658

**Susi** (Child; Student)
*Way Up High* - Roger Zelazny  *f*  6076

**Susie** (Young Woman)
*The Wilds* - Richard Laymon  *h*  3373

**Susri "Fawn"** (Child; Traveler)
*Child of an Ancient City* - Tad Williams  *f*  5827

**Susumo, Tocohl** (Spaceship Captain; Trader)
*Hellspark* - Janet Kagan  *s*  3000

**sutai-Khornezh, Kasak** (Spaceship Captain; Alien)
*Rules of Engagement* - Peter Morwood  *s*  4037

**Sutter, Frank** (Spy; Experimental Subject)
*Innerverse* - John DeChancie  *s*  1458

**Sutton, Frank** (Student)
*Red Planet* - Robert A. Heinlein  *s*  2647

**Sutton, Henry** (Police Officer)
*Out of the Night* - Patrick Whalen  *h*  5771

**Sutton, Michael** (Teacher)
*Secrets of the Morning* - V.C. Andrews  *h*  146

**Sven "Loki"** (Businessman; Computer Expert)
*Overshoot* - Mona Clee  *s*  1075

**Svensdotter, Esther "Star"** (Judge; Spacewoman)
*Red Planet Run* - Dana Stabenow  *s*  5187

**Svensdotter, Esther "Star"** (Administrator)
*Second Star* - Dana Stabenow  *s*  5188

**Svilar, Atanas** (Architect)
*Landscape Painted with Tea* - Milorad
    Pavic  *f*  4263

**Swadeith, Sfalek-ni** (Alien)
*A Plague of Change* - L. Warren Douglas  *s*  1587

**Swag** (Martial Arts Expert; Detective—Private)
*Kill Crazy* - L.S. Riker  *s*  4590

**Swan** (Child)
*Swan Song* - Robert R. McCammon  *h*  3757

**Swann, Chia** (Spaceship Captain)
*Earthfall* - Jerry Earl Brown  *s*  724

**Swann, Clare** (Critic)
*Flicker* - Theodore Roszak  *h*  4683

**Swann, Jackie** (Detective—Police)
*Boneman* - Lisa Cantrell  *h*  871

**Swann, Wanda** (Prostitute)
*Pluto, Animal Lover* - Laren Stover  *h*  5318

**Sweeney, Jim** (Police Officer)
*The Keeper* - Robert D. Lee  *h*  3402

**Sweet** (Military Personnel)
*Call to Battle* - Doug Murray  *h*  4059

**Sweetsong, Stanley** (Child; Student)
*Shoebag Returns* - Mary James  *f*  2869

**Swenson, Colter** (Student—College; Adventurer)
*Footprints of Thunder* - James F. David  *s*  1379

**Swick, Harvey** (Child)
*The Thief of Always* - Clive Barker  *h*  347

**Swift** (Hunter; Prehistoric Human)
*The Animal Wife* - Elizabeth Marshall
    Thomas  *f*  5444

**Swift** (Heir)
*Bewitchments of Love and Hate* - Storm
    Constantine  *s*  1140

**Swinton, Byron** (Doctor)
*Contagion* - John David Connor  *h*  1136

**Swinton, Robby** (Teenager)
*Contagion* - John David Connor  *h*  1136

**Swire, Harvey** (Doctor)
*Twilight* - Peter James  *h*  2876

**Sword, Galen** (Adventurer; Businessman)
*Nightfeeder* - Judith Reeves-Stevens  *f*  4513
*Shifter* - Judith Reeves-Stevens  *f*  4515

**Sykes, Matthew** (Detective—Police)
*The Change* - Barry B. Longyear  *s*  3520

**Sylah** (Religious)
*Wanderer* - Donald E. McQuinn  *s*  3862
*Warrior* - Donald E. McQuinn  *s*  3863

**Sylvan, Eve** (Teenager)
*Strange Attractors* - William Sleator  *s*  5088

**Sylvarresta, Iome** (Royalty; Handicapped)
*The Runelords: The Sum of All Men* - David
    Farland  *f*  1866

**Sylvia** (Child)
*The Marvellous Land of Snergs* - E.A. Wyke-
    Smith  *f*  6006

**Sylvie** (Landowner)
*Moonwise* - Greer Ilene Gilman  *f*  2238

**Symptomatic Nerve Gas** (Streetperson)
*Street* - Jack Cady  *h*  822

**System** (Computer)
*Secret Realms* - Tom Cool  *s*  1168

## T

**T.** (Teenager; Genius)
*The Smithsonian Institution* - Gore Vidal  *f*  5570

**Tabaea** (Thief)
*The Spell of the Black Dagger* - Lawrence Watt-
    Evans  *f*  5648

**Tabby, Jane** (Animal)
*Catwings* - Ursula K. Le Guin  *f*  3377

**Tabini** (Alien; Royalty)
*Invader* - C.J. Cherryh  *s*  998

**Tabor, Abby** (Teenager)
*Away Is a Strange Place to Be* - H.M.
    Hoover  *s*  2763

**Tabor, Lucian "Luke"** (Student—Graduate; Time
  Traveler)
*Islands of Tomorrow* - F.M. Busby  *s*  783

**Tabor, Martin** (Vampire)
*Some Things Come Back* - Robert Morgan  *h*  4004

**Tachyon** (Alien; Doctor)
*Ace in the Hole* - George R.R. Martin  *s*  3641
*Jokertown Shuffle* - George R.R. Martin  *s*  3646

**Taelor, Chris** (Hunter)
*When Wolves Cry* - Chris N. Africa  *h*  41

**Tag** (Animal)
*The Wild Road* - Gabriel King  *f*  3120

**Tagak** (Scientist)
*Shaping the Dawn* - Sheila Finch  *s*  1934

**Tagge, Geoff** (Professor; Anthropologist)
*Mind Stealer* - Lee Duigon  *h*  1672

**Taig, Nick** (Advertising)
*That's All, Folks!* - Greg Snow  *f*  5148

**Taine, Sid** (Detective; Psychic)
*The Black Lodge* - Robert Weinberg  *h*  5692

**Tainharsdarter, Kevral** (Warrior)
*The Children of Wrath* - Mickey Zucker
    Reichert  *f*  4518

**Tainharsdartter, Kevral** (Thief; Adventurer)
*Beyond Ragnarok* - Mickey Zucker Reichert  *f*  4516

**Tainharsdartter, Kevral** (Warrior)
*Prince of Demons* - Mickey Zucker
    Reichert  *f*  4522

**Taja** (Librarian; Wizard)
*Summer King, Winter Fool* - Lisa Goldstein  *f*  2263

**Takagama, Brund** (Military Personnel; Spaceman)
*A Darker Geometry* - Mark O. Martin  *s*  3649

**Takent, Ben** (Detective—Private)
*Deep Quarry* - John E. Stith  *s*  5302

**Taki** (Teenager; Technician)
*Bug Park* - James P. Hogan  *s*  2723

**Takiuji, Sukihara** (Scientist)
*Limbo System* - Rick Cook  *s*  1158

**Takumo, Charles "Charlie" Willis** (Supernatural
  Being; Stuntman)
*The Art of Arrow Cutting* - Stephen
    Dedman  *f*  1462

**Tal, Haemas Sennay** (Psychic; Heiress—
  Dispossessed)
*House of Moons* - K.D. Wentworth  *s*  5752

**Tal, Haemas Sennay** (Psychic; Fugitive)
*Moonspeaker* - K.D. Wentworth  *s*  5754

**Talamasca** (Vampire)
*The Vampire Armand* - Anne Rice  *h*  4578

**Talbot** (Guard; Sailor)
*When Demons Walk* - Patricia Briggs  *f*  683

**Talbot, Annie** (Parent; Aged Person)
*Her Monster* - Jeff Collignon  *h*  1115

**Talbot, David** (Occultist)
*The Tale of the Body Thief* - Anne Rice  *h*  4576

**Talbot, David** (Detective)
*The Vampire Armand* - Anne Rice  *h*  4578

**Talbot, Edward "Eddie"** (Writer; Recluse)
*Her Monster* - Jeff Collignon  *h*  1115

**Talbot, Larry** (Werewolf)
*A Night in the Lonesome October* - Roger
    Zelazny  *h*  6072
*Return of the Wolfman* - Jeff Rovin  *h*  4687

**Talbott, Marshe "Queen"** (Scientist; Leader)
*Aggressor Six* - Wil McCarthy  *s*  3760

**Tale Teller** (Indian; Companion)
*Tatham Mound* - Piers Anthony  *f*  191

**Talen** (Thief)
*The Ruby Knight* - David Eddings   *f*   1736

**Tali** (Alien; Political Figure)
*Brother Termite* - Patricia Anthony   *s*   156

**Talienson, Caltus "Cal"** (Warrior)
*Dark Divide* - Mark Acres   *f*   27
*Horrible Humes* - Stephen Billias   *f*   487
*The Stone of Time* - Rose Estes   *f*   1840

**Taliesen** (Writer; Minstrel)
*The Hawk's Gray Feather* - Patricia Kennealy-
   Morrison   *f*   3061

**Taliesen** (Minstrel; Writer)
*The Hedge of Mist* - Patricia Kennealy-
   Morrison   *s*   3062
*The Oak Above the Kings: A Book of the Keltiad* -
   Patricia Kennealy   *s*   3058

**Taliesin** (Wizard; Immortal)
*The Broken Sword* - Molly Cochran   *f*   1091

**Talisen** (Minstrel; Companion)
*Hero's Song* - Edith Pattou   *f*   4261

**Talker** (Shaman; Prehistoric Human)
*Dawn Land* - Joseph Bruchac   *f*   731

**Talker** (Alien)
*The Remarkables* - Robert Reed   *s*   4507

**Tallant, Benno** (Experimental Subject)
*Run for the Stars/Echoes of Thunder* - Harlan
   Ellison   *s*   1788

**Talldeer, Frank** (Chieftain; Indian)
*Sacred Ground* - Mercedes Lackey   *f*   3294

**Talldeer, Jennifer** (Detective—Private; Shaman)
*Sacred Ground* - Mercedes Lackey   *f*   3294

**Tallendar, Barry** (Director)
*We Open on Venus* - Christopher Stasheff   *s*   5227

**Taller** (Leader; Alien)
*Silent Dances* - A.C. Crispin   *s*   1263
*Silent Songs* - A.C. Crispin   *s*   1264

**Talley, Herbert** (Professor)
*Beast* - Peter Benchley   *h*   440

**Tallstaff, Lutha** (Linguist; Parent)
*Shadow's End* - Sheri S. Tepper   *s*   5435

**Tally, E.C.** (Artificial Intelligence)
*Divergence* - Charles Sheffield   *s*   4954

**Talmadge, Jessica** (Scientist; Student)
*Supernova* - Roger MacBride Allen   *s*   82

**Talon** (Immortal; Wizard)
*The Last Wizard* - Simon Hawke   *f*   2619

**Taltos, Vlad** (Sorcerer; Martial Arts Expert)
*Athyra* - Steven Brust   *f*   739
*Dragon* - Steven Brust   *f*   741
*Orca* - Steven Brust   *f*   745
*Phoenix* - Steven Brust   *f*   746

**Tamai** (Shaman; Heroine)
*Changeweaver* - Margaret Ball   *f*   313

**Tamai** (Psychic)
*Flameweaver* - Margaret Ball   *f*   314

**Tamar** (Fugitive; Revolutionary)
*The Alleluia Files* - Sharon Shinn   *s*   4999

**Tamar** (Royalty; Teacher)
*The Iron Ring* - Lloyd Alexander   *f*   68

**Tamara** (Spy)
*On My Way to Paradise* - Dave Wolverton   *s*   5955

**Tamara** (Child)
*What's Wrong with Valerie?* - D.A. Fowler   *h*   2026

**Tamas of Maggiar** (Royalty; Adventurer)
*The Goblin Mirror* - C.J. Cherryh   *f*   994

**Tamberly, Wanda** (Agent)
*The Shield of Time* - Poul Anderson   *s*   131

**Tamerlane, Rebecca** (Clerk)
*Afterimage Aftershock* - Kristine Kathryn
   Rusch   *h*   4710

**Tamerlane, Rebecca "Michael Kerr"** (Detective—
   Amateur; Mythical Creature)
*Afterimage* - Kristine Kathryn Rusch   *f*   4709

**Tamerlane "Tam"** (Teenager)
*Strange Deliverance* - Mary Brown   *s*   728

**Taminy-a-Cuinn** (Religious; Psychic)
*The Crystal Rose* - Maya Kaathryn Bohnhoff   *f*   560
*Taminy* - Maya Kaathryn Bohnhoff   *f*   563

**Tamis** (Psychic)
*Lion of Macedon* - David Gemmell   *f*   2189

**Tamm, Pirie** (Administrator)
*Ecce and Old Earth* - Jack Vance   *s*   5546

**Tamm, Wayness** (Detective—Amateur)
*Ecce and Old Earth* - Jack Vance   *s*   5546

**Tammo** (Animal)
*The Long Patrol* - Brian Jacques   *f*   2849

**Tamura, Eiko** (Technician; Spacewoman)
*Harvest of Stars* - Poul Anderson   *s*   127

**Tanafres, Yan** (Wizard)
*Timespell* - Robert N. Charrette   *f*   978
*Wizard of Bones* - Robert N. Charrette   *f*   979

**Tanaka** (Shaman)
*Mind Stealer* - Lee Duigon   *h*   1672

**Tanaka, Celine** (Astronaut)
*Aftermath* - Charles Sheffield   *s*   4947

**Tanaka, Joey** (Scientist; Psychic)
*Mind Kill* - Richard La Plante   *h*   3267

**Tanaka, Terry** (Scientist)
*Meg* - Steve Alten   *h*   88

**Tanaquil** (Teenager)
*Black Unicorn* - Tanith Lee   *f*   3404

**Tancred, Tolwyn** (Knight)
*Storm Knights* - Bill Slavicsek   *f*   5087

**Tangaloa, George** (Scientist)
*The Hand of Zei* - L. Sprague de Camp   *s*   1414

**Taniane** (Ruler)
*The New Springtime* - Robert Silverberg   *s*   5040

**Tanis** (Mythical Creature)
*Dragons of Summer Flame* - Margaret Weis   *f*   5711

**Tanis** (Mythical Creature; Warrior)
*The Second Generation* - Margaret Weis   *f*   5724

**Tanith** (Psychic)
*The Nightwalker* - Thomas Tessier   *h*   5442

**Tanner, Florence** (Psychic)
*Hell House* - Richard Matheson   *h*   3685

**Tanner, Frank** (Lawyer)
*Deadweight* - Robert Devereaux   *h*   1505

**Tanner, John** (Ranger)
*The Quiet* - Patrick Billings   *h*   488

**Tanner, Karin** (Gardener)
*Deadweight* - Robert Devereaux   *h*   1505

**Tanner, Louis** (Smuggler; Detective—Amateur)
*Destroying Angel* - Richard Paul Russo   *s*   4749

**Tanner, Mark** (Teenager; Sports Figure)
*Creature* - John Saul   *h*   4839

**Tanner, Sharon** (Housewife)
*Creature* - John Saul   *h*   4839

**Tanner, Tarleton "Sonny"** (Farmer; Spouse)
*Promised Land* - Connie Willis   *s*   5872

**Tanner, Vaughn** (Agent)
*Mad Roy's Light* - Paula King   *s*   3125

**Tannim** (Magician)
*Born to Run* - Mercedes Lackey   *f*   3271

**Tansen** (Warrior)
*In Legend Born* - Laura Resnick   *f*   4533

**Tansy** (Animal)
*The Pearls of Lutra* - Brian Jacques   *f*   2854

**Tany, Myron** (Adventurer)
*Ports of Call* - Jack Vance   *s*   5549

**Tao Tieh** (Aged Person)
*Twisted Images* - Don D'Ammassa   *h*   1335

**Taramasco, Sam** (Scientist)
*Warsprite* - Jefferson P. Swycaffer   *s*   5375

**Taranga, Eugenia** (Spaceship Captain)
*Burster* - Michael Capobianco   *s*   876

**Tarasov, Sein** (Computer Expert; Homosexual)
*Night Sky Mine* - Melissa Scott   *s*   4898

**Tarawe** (Warrior; Magician)
*Demon Drums* - Carol Severance   *f*   4922

**Tarawe** (Magician)
*Storm Caller* - Carol Severance   *f*   4924

**Tardivel, Pierre** (Researcher)
*Frameshift* - Robert J. Sawyer   *s*   4856

**Tarimenloku, Igsat** (Military Personnel)
*The White Regiment* - John Dalmas   *s*   1327

**Tarkenton, Lewis** (Judge)
*Echoes* - Jackie Hyman   *h*   2818

**Tar'krim, Stereth** (Government Official; Outlaw)
*Guilt-Edged Ivory* - Doris Egan   *s*   1756

**Tar'krim, Stereth** (Outlaw)
*Two-Bit Heroes* - Doris Egan   *s*   1757

**Tarlach** (Warrior; Mercenary)
*Flight of Vengeance* - Andre Norton   *f*   4152
*Storms of Victory* - Andre Norton   *f*   4162

**Tarma** (Warrior; Martial Arts Expert)
*Oathblood* - Mercedes Lackey   *f*   3290

**Tarne** (Counselor)
*Heart Readers* - Kristine Kathryn Rusch   *f*   4718

**Tarosh, Valentine** (Scientist)
*Carnivore* - Leigh Clark   *h*   1049

**Tarrant, Gerald** (Nobleman)
*Black Sun Rising* - C.S. Friedman   *f*   2056

**Tarrant, Gerald** (Vampire; Religious)
*Crown of Shadows* - C.S. Friedman   *s*   2057

**Tarrant, Gerald** (Sorcerer; Nobleman)
*When True Night Falls* - C.S. Friedman   *f*   2060

**Tarrel, Janus** (Spaceship Captain)
*Dreadnought* - Thorarinn Gunnarsson   *s*   2464

**Tarrik, Jeniper** (Alien; Diplomat)
*Earth Herald* - Jan Clark   *s*   1046

**Tarz, Auriel** (Trader; Agent)
*World Spirits* - Aline Boucher-Kaplan   *s*   580

**Tasarov, Yevgeny** (Prisoner)
*Brute Orbits* - George Zebrowski   *s*   6059

**Tast'annin, Margalis** (Military Personnel)
*AEstival Tide* - Elizabeth Hand   *s*   2533
*Icarus Descending* - Elizabeth Hand   *s*   2536

**Tate, Augustus "Gus"** (Psychic; Doctor)
*The Demolished Man* - Alfred Bester   *s*   476

**Tate, Donnacee** (Military Personnel; Time Traveler)
*Wanderer* - Donald E. McQuinn   *s*   3862
*Warrior* - Donald E. McQuinn   *s*   3863
*Witch* - Donald E. McQuinn   *s*   3864

**Tatian, Mhyre** (Businessman)
*Shadow Man* - Melissa Scott   *s*   4900

**Tatsuo, Tamenaga** (Wizard; Organized Crime
   Figure)
*The Art of Arrow Cutting* - Stephen
   Dedman   *f*   1462

**Tatyana** (Vampire)
*I, Strahd* - P.N. Elrod  *h*  1797

**Taub, Judy** (Historian)
*Dictator* - William F. Wu  *s*  5996

**Tawl** (Knight)
*Master and Fool* - J.V. Jones  *f*  2959

**Taws** (Demon)
*Wrath of Ashar* - Angus Wells  *f*  5742

**Taya** (Child; Genetically Altered Being)
*Star Child* - James P. Hogan  *s*  2730

**Taylor** (Detective—Police)
*The Night Man* - K.W. Jeter  *h*  2915

**Taylor** (Public Relations)
*The Tenth Class* - Karen Ripley  *s*  4594

**Taylor, Diana Lee** (Actress)
*Fantastique* - Marvin Kaye  *h*  3025

**Taylor, Gary** (Worker)
*The Bridge: A Horror Story* - John Skipp  *h*  5081

**Taylor, Gwen** (Artist)
*The Bridge: A Horror Story* - John Skipp  *h*  5081

**Taylor, Jessica** (Telepath; FBI Agent)
*Bureau 13* - Nick Pollotta  *f*  4362
*Full Moonster* - Nick Pollotta  *f*  4364

**Taylor, Jonas** (Scientist)
*Meg* - Steve Alten  *h*  88

**Taylor, Kevin** (Lawyer)
*The Devil's Advocate* - Andrew Neiderman  *h*  4085

**Taylor, Lance** (Businessman)
*Dark Legacy* - Mark A. Kostrubula  *h*  3220

**Taylor, Lucian** (Writer)
*The Hill of Dreams* - Arthur Machen  *h*  3595

**Taylor, Lura** (Convict; Girlfriend)
*Dumford Blood* - S.K. Epperson  *h*  1829

**Taylor, Miriam** (Housewife)
*The Devil's Advocate* - Andrew Neiderman  *h*  4085

**Taylor, Nugan** (Linguist; Spacewoman)
*Genetic Soldier* - George Turner  *s*  5492

**Taylor, Patricia "Mother"** (Businesswoman; Criminal)
*Proxies* - Laura J. Mixon  *s*  3922

**Taylor, Shona** (Doctor; Space Explorer)
*Medicine Show* - Jody Lynn Nye  *s*  4172
*Taylor's Ark* - Jody Lynn Nye  *s*  4176

**Taylor, Tamara** (Singer)
*The Werewolf Chronicles* - Traci Briery  *h*  679
*Wolfsong* - Traci Briery  *h*  680

**Tazendra of House Dzur** (Gentlewoman)
*The Phoenix Guards* - Steven Brust  *f*  747

**Tch'muchgar** (Vampire)
*Thirsty* - M.T. Anderson  *h*  120

**Teague, Aiden** (Teenager)
*Blood and Chocolate* - Annette Curtis Klause  *h*  3162

**Teague, Jamie** (Adventurer)
*The Folk of the Fringe* - Orson Scott Card  *s*  886

**Teal, Marcus** (Businessman)
*Reaper* - Ben Mizrich  *h*  3923

**Teaqua** (Deity; Ruler)
*Look into the Sun* - James Patrick Kelly  *s*  3047

**Teatime, Jonathan** (Murderer)
*Hogfather* - Terry Pratchett  *f*  4391

**Ted** (Psychic; Mentally Ill Person)
*The Kronos Condition* - Emily Devenport  *s*  1502

**Ted** (Photographer; Werewolf)
*Thor* - Wayne Smith  *h*  5146

**Teeg, Harper** (Time Traveler; Traitor)
*The Seeds of Time* - Kay Kenyon  *s*  3064

**Teenager, Orlando** (Warrior)
*City of Golden Shadow* - Tad Williams  *s*  5828

**Tegne** (Martial Arts Expert; Bastard Son)
*Tegne: Soul Warrior* - Richard La Plante  *f*  3268

**Tegrid** (Minstrel)
*The Silver Hand* - Stephen R. Lawhead  *f*  3358

**Tek** (Mythical Creature; Warrior)
*The Son of Summer Stars* - Meredith Ann Pierce  *f*  4319

**Tekkitho, Chin** (Alien; Teacher)
*Homegoing* - Frederik Pohl  *s*  4347

**Tel'anh, Alethia** (Royalty; Adventurer)
*Shadows over Lyra* - Patricia C. Wrede  *f*  5980

**Telek, Kassia** (Witch; Widow(er))
*The Spirit Gate* - Maya Kaathryn Bohnhoff  *f*  562

**Telerhyde** (Military Personnel)
*The Stone Movers* - Patricia Mullen  *f*  4045

**Telery of Limerick** (Mythical Creature)
*Gnome Man's Land* - Esther Friesner  *f*  2075
*Harpy High* - Esther Friesner  *f*  2076

**Telford, Jason** (Fugitive)
*This Side of Judgment* - J.R. Dunn  *s*  1696

**Telgrin** (Magician)
*The Floating Castle* - Craig Mills  *f*  3913

**Tellentyre, Edward** (Scientist)
*The Werewolves of London* - Brian Stableford  *h*  5196

**Teller** (Storyteller)
*The Gift* - Patrick O'Leary  *f*  4211

**Teller, Edward** (Scientist; Aged Person)
*Operation Damocles* - Oscar L. Fellows  *s*  1915

**Telmah, Lord Cima** (Heir—Dispossessed)
*The White Abacus* - Damien Broderick  *s*  708

**Tembo** (Revolutionary; Archaeologist)
*Phoenix Fire* - Elizabeth Forrest  *f*  1974

**Temiya, Kesbe** (Indian)
*People of the Sky* - Clare Bell  *s*  431

**Temple, Hamilton** (Magician)
*The 7th Guest* - Matthew J. Costello  *h*  1192

**Templeton, Judith** (Computer Expert)
*The Shadow Gate* - Margaret Ball  *f*  317

**Tenar** (Widow(er); Religious)
*Tehanu: The Last Book of Earthsea* - Ursula K. Le Guin  *f*  3383

**Tenedos, Laish** (Royalty; Wizard)
*The Demon King* - Chris Bunch  *f*  770
*The Seer King* - Chris Bunch  *f*  771

**Tenere, Jared** (Computer Expert; Runaway)
*Voices of Hope* - David Feintuch  *s*  1903

**Teneria of Fishertown** (Witch)
*The Blood of a Dragon* - Lawrence Watt-Evans  *f*  5640

**Tenoctris** (Wizard; Aged Person)
*Lord of the Isles* - David Drake  *f*  1636
*Queen of Demons* - David Drake  *f*  1640

**Tenzer, Paul** (Scientist)
*Kalimantan* - Lucius Shepard  *h*  4979

**Tepes, Vlad** (Vampire)
*The Darker Passions: Dracula* - Amarantha Knight  *h*  3179

**Tepes, Vlad** (Warrior; Vampire)
*The Empire of Fear* - Brian Stableford  *h*  5191

**Tepes, Vlad** (Vampire)
*I Am Dracula* - C. Dean Andersson  *h*  139

**Teppish, Rebecca** (Teenager; Vampire)
*The Vampire's Beautiful Daughter* - S.P. Somtow  *h*  5161

**Teppish, Vladimir X. III** (Vampire; Parent)
*The Vampire's Beautiful Daughter* - S.P. Somtow  *h*  5161

**Terek** (Wizard)
*Fall of Angels* - L.E. Modesitt Jr.  *f*  3930

**Terminationer** (Robot; Martial Arts Expert)
*Samurai Cat Goes to the Movies* - Mark E. Rogers  *s*  4656

**Terrance** (Wizard)
*A Forest Lord* - Michael Williams  *f*  5819
*A Sorcerer's Apprentice* - Michael Williams  *f*  5820

**Terrell, Mary "Merry Terror"** (Terrorist)
*Mine* - Robert R. McCammon  *h*  3756

**Terrence, Chris** (Astronaut)
*Encounter with Tiber* - Buzz Aldrin  *s*  64

**Terton, Ama "Ama-la"** (Doctor; Guardian)
*Nothing Sacred* - Elizabeth Ann Scarborough  *f*  4867

**Terza, Abby** (Linguist; Anthropologist)
*Manhattan Transfer* - John E. Stith  *s*  5303

**Tesa "Good Eyes"** (Handicapped; Linguist)
*Silent Dances* - A.C. Crispin  *s*  1263

**Teska** (Alien; Telepath)
*Mind Meld* - John Vornholt  *s*  5596

**Tesla, Nikola** (Historical Figure; Inventor)
*The Prestige* - Christopher Priest  *s*  4432

**Tessler** (Vampire)
*Blood Relations* - Doug Murray  *h*  4058

**Tesuawane, Sovawanea "Sophy" a** (Indian; Feminist)
*Gibbon's Decline and Fall* - Sheri S. Tepper  *s*  5430

**Tetsami, Kari** (Computer Expert; Genetically Altered Being)
*Partisan* - S. Andrew Swann  *s*  5365
*Profiteer* - S. Andrew Swann  *s*  5366
*Revolutionary* - S. Andrew Swann  *s*  5367

**Teyle** (Mythical Creature)
*Conan the Formidable* - Steve Perry  *f*  4293

**Thackeray, Brandon** (Scientist; Museum Curator)
*End of an Era* - Robert J. Sawyer  *s*  4853

**Thag** (Prehistoric Human; Chieftain)
*Shiva's Challenge: An Adventure of the Ice Age* - J.H. Brennan  *f*  668

**Thaiter, Leot** (Royalty)
*The Wild Hunt: Vengeance Moon* - Jocelin Foxe  *f*  2031

**Thakur** (Animal; Teacher)
*Ratha and Thistle-Chaser* - Clare Bell  *f*  432

**Thalassa** (Prostitute; Heroine)
*The Forging of the Shadows* - Oliver Johnson  *f*  2924

**Thalassa** (Heroine)
*Nations of the Night* - Oliver Johnson  *f*  2925

**Thane, Sundira** (Adventurer)
*The Face of the Waters* - Robert Silverberg  *s*  5029

**Thanehand** (Warrior; Leader)
*Palace of Kings* - Mike Jefferies  *f*  2887

**Thanehand** (Apprentice; Warrior)
*The Road to Underfall* - Mike Jefferies  *f*  2888

**Thann, Danilo "Dan"** (Nobleman)
*Elfshadow* - Elaine Cunningham  *f*  1288

**Thann, Danilo "Dan"** (Musician)
*Elfsong* - Elaine Cunningham  *f*  1289

**Thann, Danilo "Dan"** (Musician; Spy)
*Silver Shadows* - Elaine Cunningham  *f*  1292

**Tharion** (Telepath)
*Blindfold* - Kevin J. Anderson  *s*  101

**Tharn, Bulion** (Leader)
*The Cursed* - Dave Duncan  *f*  1674

**Tharna** (Animal; Telepath)
*The Key of the Keplian* - Andre Norton  *f*  4156

**Tharon** (Indian; Leader)
*People of the River* - W. Michael Gear  *f*  2168

**Tharpit, Jaxian** (Government Official; Leader)
*The Reaver Road* - Dave Duncan  *f*  1687

**Thatcher, Jeremy** (Child)
*Jeremy Thatcher, Dragon Hatcher* - Bruce
    Coville  *f*  1221

**Thatcher, Lloyd George** (Criminal)
*Call to Arms* - P.M. Griffin  *s*  2435

**Thaxton, Wendall** (Reincarnated Person; Indian)
*The Higher Space* - Jamil Nasir  *s*  4070

**Thaxton, Xavier** (Journalist; Hero)
*Count Geiger's Blues* - Michael Bishop  *s*  499

**Thayer, Cerise** (Child)
*Afternoon of the Gosling* - Marlys Huffman  *h*  2801

**Thayer, Danny** (Child; Heir—Lost)
*Street Magic* - Michael Reaves  *f*  4497

**Thayer, Philip** (Religious)
*Afternoon of the Gosling* - Marlys Huffman  *h*  2801

**Thayla** (Sorceress)
*Beyond the Pale* - Jack Koke  *f*  3198

**Theisiger, Carlo** (Mercenary)
*Enemy of My Enemy* - Ben Ohlander  *s*  4204

**Thelia** (Alien; Adventurer)
*Metamorphosis* - Jean Lorrah  *s*  3524

**Thenike** (Healer; Wanderer)
*Ammonite* - Nicola Griffith  *s*  2443

**Theodora** (Witch)
*Daughter of Magic* - C. Dale Brittain  *f*  703
*The Witch and the Cathedral* - C. Dale
    Brittain  *f*  705

**Theodora of Pyrene** (Student)
*The Gate of Ivory* - Doris Egan  *s*  1755

**Theodora of Pyrene** (Scholar; Bride)
*Two-Bit Heroes* - Doris Egan  *s*  1757

**Theodoulos** (Linguist; Mythical Creature)
*Cross and Crescent* - Susan Shwartz  *f*  5014

**Theon** (Human)
*Seeking the Dream Brother* - Marcia J.
    Bennett  *s*  451

**Theotohy, Maria Magdalena** (Scholar)
*The Cornish Trilogy* - Robertson Davies  *f*  1397

**Theovere** (Royalty)
*The Eagle and the Nightingales* - Mercedes
    Lackey  *f*  3278

**Theremon 762** (Journalist)
*Nightfall* - Isaac Asimov  *s*  248

**Thermopyle, Angus** (Convict)
*Forbidden Knowledge* - Stephen R.
    Donaldson  *s*  1571

**Thermopyle, Angus** (Pirate)
*The Gap into Conflict: The Real Story* - Stephen R.
    Donaldson  *s*  1572

**Thermopyle, Angus** (Spaceship Captain; Cyborg)
*The Gap into Madness: Chaos and Order* - Stephen R.
    Donaldson  *s*  1573
*The Gap into Power: A Dark and Hungry God Arises*
    - Stephen R. Donaldson  *s*  1574
*The Gap into Ruin: This Day All Gods Die* - Stephen
    R. Donaldson  *s*  1575

**Therru** (Handicapped; Abuse Victim)
*Tehanu: The Last Book of Earthsea* - Ursula K. Le
    Guin  *f*  3383

**Theseus** (Royalty)
*Whilom* - Robert Watson  *f*  5639

**Thews, Questor** (Wizard; Adventurer)
*Witches' Brew* - Terry Brooks  *f*  719

**Thibaudeaux, Catherine "Cat"** (Spy)
*Delta Search* - William Shatner  *s*  4930

**Thibodeau, Skida "Skilly"** (Leader; Murderer)
*Prince of Sparta* - Jerry Pournelle  *s*  4378

**Thibodeaux, Ben** (Aged Person)
*The Dwelling* - Tom Elliott  *h*  1776

**Thibodeaux, Suzanne "Suzy Falcon" Marie**  (Pilot)
*Eternal Light* - Paul J. McAuley  *s*  3710

**Thiede** (Deity; Ruler)
*The Fulfillments of Fate and Desire* - Storm
    Constantine  *s*  1142

**Thing** (Computer)
*Truckers* - Terry Pratchett  *s*  4402
*Wings* - Terry Pratchett  *s*  4403

**Thinking Man of Moha** (Landowner)
*Fish Soup* - Ursula K. Le Guin  *f*  3378

**Third Historian** (Alien)
*Berserker Lies* - Fred Saberhagen  *s*  4762

**Thismet** (Royalty)
*Sorcerers of Majipoor* - Robert Silverberg  *s*  5041

**Thissizz** (Alien; Singer)
*The Merro Tree* - Katie Waitman  *s*  5609

**Thistledown, Tipperton "Tip"** (Mythical Creature)
*Into the Fire* - Dennis L. McKiernan  *f*  3834

**Thistledown, Tipperton "Tip"** (Mythical Creature;
Adventurer)
*Into the Forge* - Dennis L. McKiernan  *f*  3835

**Thistleknot, Kronn-alin** (Traveler)
*Spirit of the Wind* - Chris Pierson  *f*  4326

**Thoggish** (Alien)
*Converse and Conflict* - L. Neil Smith  *s*  5130

**Thomas** (Minstrel)
*Thomas the Rhymer* - Ellen Kushner  *f*  3265

**Thomas** (Religious)
*Towing Jehovah* - James Morrow  *f*  4035

**Thomas, Fran** (Journalist)
*Winter Wolves* - Earle Wescott  *h*  5756

**Thomas, Peter** (Police Officer)
*Wolfsong* - Traci Briery  *h*  680

**Thomas, Quentin** (Psychic; Lawyer)
*Lunar Justice* - Charles L. Harness  *s*  2545

**Thomas, Shep** (Police Officer)
*Nightscape* - Stephen R. George  *h*  2203

**Thomas, Signy** (Computer Expert; Scientist)
*Whiteout* - Sage Walker  *s*  5619

**Thomas, Stephen** (Professor; Genetically Altered
Being)
*Nautilus* - Vonda N. McIntyre  *s*  3823

**Thomason, John "Jean Vitterand"** (Police Officer;
Time Traveler)
*Time Station Paris* - David Evans  *s*  1854

**Thompkins, Maryellen** (Teenager)
*Jaguar* - Bill Ransom  *s*  4477

**Thompson, Drew** (Businessman)
*Virus* - Graham Watkins  *h*  5632

**Thompson, Emily** (Heir; Fugitive)
*The Night Watch* - Sean Stewart  *f*  5274

**Thompson, Ewha** (Doctor)
*The Bushido Incident* - Betty Anne
    Crawford  *s*  1248

**Thompson, Lydia** (Aged Person)
*Seed of Evil* - Edmund Plante  *h*  4340

**Thompson, Patty** (Office Worker)
*Seed of Evil* - Edmund Plante  *h*  4340

**Thompson, Peter** (Student; Hero)
*My Teacher Flunked the Planet* - Bruce
    Coville  *s*  1222

**Thompson, Peter** (Student)
*My Teacher Glows in the Dark* - Bruce
    Coville  *s*  1224

**Thompson, Richard** (Child)
*Seed of Evil* - Edmund Plante  *h*  4340

**Thor** (Animal)
*Thor* - Wayne Smith  *h*  5146

**Thor, Odin** (Military Personnel)
*Timediver's Dawn* - L.E. Modesitt Jr.  *s*  3940

**Thorbjornsdottir, Gudrid** (Historical Figure)
*The Ice-Shirt* - William T. Vollmann  *f*  5580

**Thorian** (Royalty; Traveler)
*The Reaver Road* - Dave Duncan  *f*  1687

**Thorn, Robert** (Drifter)
*Shadow Dance* - Douglas Borton  *h*  577

**Thorne, Becker** (Vampire)
*The Vampire Papers* - Michael Romkey  *h*  4666

**Thorne, Emerson** (Doctor)
*The Hunted* - Kathryn Ptacek  *h*  4442

**Thorne, Hester** (Cult Member)
*Dark Channel* - Ray Garton  *h*  2150

**Thorne, Holly** (Journalist)
*Cold Fire* - Dean R. Koontz  *h*  3203

**Thorne, Newman "Nemo"** (Trader)
*Circuit of Heaven* - Dennis Danvers  *s*  1348

**Thorne, Peter** (Magician; Paranormal Investigator)
*Death Channels* - Robert E. Vardeman  *h*  5562

**Thornekan, Roald** (Spaceship Captain)
*Down the Stream of Stars* - Jeffrey A.
    Carver  *s*  928

**Thorpe, Leonard** (Filmmaker)
*Glimmering* - Elizabeth Hand  *s*  2535

**Thorpe, Proserpine** (Telepath)
*The Reign of the Brown Magician* - Lawrence Watt-
    Evans  *f*  5647

**Thorpe, Thomas** (Engineer)
*Thunder Strike!* - Michael McCollum  *s*  3772

**Thorsen, Sigrid** (Businesswoman)
*Orion's Dagger* - P.K. McAllister  *s*  3708

**Thorsen, Thorian "Torrie"** (Martial Arts Expert;
Young Man)
*The Crimson Sky* - Joel Rosenberg  *f*  4669
*The Fire Duke* - Joel Rosenberg  *f*  4671
*The Silver Stone* - Joel Rosenberg  *f*  4676

**Thorson, Dane** (Spaceman; Trader)
*Derelict for Trade* - Andre Norton  *s*  4148

**Thorson, Dane** (Spaceman)
*A Mind for Trade* - Andre Norton  *s*  4158

**Thorsson, Thor** (Administrator; Military Personnel)
*Article 23* - William R. Forstchen  *s*  1978

**Thorvin** (Mythical Creature; Cyborg)
*Fade to Black* - Nyx Smith  *s*  5134

**Thowinda** (Alien; Diplomat)
*The Shining Ones* - Paul Preuss  *s*  4421

**Thrawn** (Military Personnel; Leader)
*The Last Command* - Timothy Zahn  *s*  6055

**Threadwell** (Tailor)
*The Adventures of Threadwell the Tailor, or
    Alterations Made While You Wait* - P.D.
    Cacek  *h*  801

**Thromar** (Warrior)
*The Jewel of Equilibrant* - Steven Frankos   *f*   2042

**Throtmanian, Paul Donald** (Con Artist)
*Lifehouse* - Spider Robinson   *s*   4641

**Thrugg** (Animal)
*Salamandastron* - Brian Jacques   *f*   2855

**Thubana, Mordecai** (Construction Worker)
*Apartheid, Superstrings, and Mordecai Thubana* -
  Michael Bishop   *s*   496

**Thudd, Dennis "Druzeppa"** (Actor)
*Horrorshow* - David Darke   *h*   1353

**Thunder, Anna** (Indian; Witch)
*The Grass Dancer* - Susan Power   *f*   4380

**Thunder, Charlene** (Indian)
*The Grass Dancer* - Susan Power   *f*   4380

**Thurid** (Wizard)
*The Dragon's Carbuncle* - Elizabeth H.
  Boyer   *f*   605

**Thuro "Uther Pendragon"** (Royalty; Orphan)
*Ghost King* - David Gemmell   *f*   2188

**Thursley, Eric** (Wizard)
*Eric* - Terry Pratchett   *f*   4388

**Thuryn, Rhysel** (Healer; Psychic)
*The Bastard Prince* - Katherine Kurtz   *f*   3255

**Thyme, Jordan "Antiquity"** (Scientist; Computer
Expert)
*Zeta Base* - Judith Alguire   *s*   74

**Tiam** (Diplomat; Alien)
*Probe* - Margaret Wander Bonanno   *s*   569

**Tiamat** (Mythical Creature)
*Jeremy Thatcher, Dragon Hatcher* - Bruce
  Coville   *f*   1221

**Tiana** (Slave; Dancer)
*Songs of the Dancing Gods* - Jack L. Chalker   *f*   962

**Tianna** (Royalty; Magician)
*Iron Dragons: Mountains and Madness* - Rose
  Estes   *f*   1839

**Tiban, Boris** (Criminal; Genetically Altered Being)
*Climbing Olympus* - Kevin J. Anderson   *s*   102

**Tibbeth of Hale** (Wizard)
*Stranger at the Wedding* - Barbara Hambly   *f*   2509

**Tibbett, Adrian "Toady"** (Child)
*The Horror Club* - Mark Morris   *h*   4022

**Tibbon, Rachel** (Imposter)
*Kingdom of the Grail* - A.A. Attanasio   *f*   269

**Tiber, Jim** (Time Traveler)
*Day of the Snake* - Matthew J. Costello   *s*   1196
*Hour of the Scorpion* - Matthew J. Costello   *s*   1199

**Tichy, Ijon** (Space Explorer; Writer)
*Peace on Earth* - Stanislaw Lem   *s*   3435

**Tick-Tick** (Mythical Creature; Mechanic)
*Finder* - Emma Bull   *f*   769

**Ticktockman** (Government Official)
*"Repent, Harlequin!" Said the Ticktockman* - Harlan
  Ellison   *s*   1782

**Tiernan, John** (Journalist)
*The Jericho Iteration* - Allen Steele   *s*   5242

**Tierney, Rose** (Critic; Psychic)
*The Parasite* - Ramsey Campbell   *h*   863

**Tiger** (Warrior)
*Sword-Born* - Jennifer Roberson   *f*   4612

**Tiger** (Hero)
*Sword-Maker* - Jennifer Roberson   *f*   4614

**Tighe, Dan** (Leader)
*The Trikon Deception* - Ben Bova   *s*   597

**Tighe, Epiphanius "Eppy"** (Storyteller)
*A Diversity of Dragons* - Anne McCaffrey   *f*   3728

**Tighe, Justin** (Military Personnel)
*Mosaic* - Jeri Taylor   *s*   5403

**Tikki "Striper"** (Hunter; Mythical Creature)
*Striper Assassin* - Nyx Smith   *f*   5135

**Tim** (Teenager; Adventurer)
*The Gift* - Patrick O'Leary   *f*   4211

**Timkin** (Slave)
*The Red King* - Victor Kelleher   *f*   3043

**Timmers, Lacy** (Student—Graduate)
*Soulcatchers* - Jan Lara   *s*   3336

**Timmerson, Ray** (Writer)
*Immortal* - Jason Nickles   *h*   4102

**Timmie** (Prehistoric Human)
*The Ugly Little Boy* - Isaac Asimov   *s*   250

**Timms, Camilla** (Vampire Hunter)
*Sins of the Blood* - Kristine Kathryn Rusch   *h*   4728

**Timoteo** (Religious; Lawyer)
*Blood of the Goddess* - Kara Dalkey   *f*   1318

**Timothy "Timmy"** (Religious; Writer)
*Live From Golgotha: A Novel* - Gore Vidal   *s*   5569

**Timov** (Child)
*Hunting the Ghost Dancer* - A.A. Attanasio   *f*   268

**Timpson, Freda** (Teacher)
*The Red-Eared Ghosts* - Vivian Alcock   *f*   53

**Timpson, Jean** (Housekeeper)
*Sweetheart, Sweetheart* - Bernard Taylor   *h*   5402

**Timura, Safar** (Wizard; Religious)
*Wolves of the Gods* - Allan Cole   *f*   1111

**Tind** (Warrior)
*A Landscape of Darkness* - John Blair   *s*   513

**Tinker, Austin** (Agent)
*Crygender* - Thomas T. Thomas   *s*   5451

**Tinkerbell** (Mythical Creature)
*Hook* - Terry Brooks   *f*   713

**Tinnie** (Girlfriend)
*Dread Brass Shadows* - Glen Cook   *f*   1149

**Tint, Thaw** (Alien)
*The Killing Star* - Charles Pellegrino   *s*   4281

**Tirand** (Sorcerer)
*The Deceiver* - Louise Cooper   *f*   1175

**Tirelli, Elizabeth "Lizard"** (Military Personnel)
*A Season for Slaughter* - David Gerrold   *s*   2211

**Tirrell** (Ruler)
*Talion: Revenant* - Michael A. Stackpole   *f*   5206

**Tishner, Frank** (Police Officer)
*Firefly* - Piers Anthony   *h*   170

**Tissaurd, Nadia** (Military Personnel)
*The Mercenaries* - Bill Baldwin   *s*   311

**Titch** (Warrior; Adventurer)
*The True Knight* - Susan Dexter   *f*   1513

**Tituba** (Historical Figure; Witch)
*I, Tituba, Black Witch of Salem* - Maryse
  Conde   *f*   1130

**T'Larien, Dirk** (Scientist; Wanderer)
*Dying of the Light* - George R.R. Martin   *s*   3644

**T'lion** (Teenager)
*The Dolphins of Pern* - Anne McCaffrey   *s*   3729

**Toad of Toad Hall** (Animal; Adventurer)
*Toad Triumphant* - William Horwood   *f*   2774
*The Willows and Beyond* - William
  Horwood   *f*   2775

**Toad of Toad Hall** (Animal; Pilot)
*The Willows in Winter* - William Horwood   *f*   2776

**Tobias, Cameron** (Mentally Ill Person)
*Making Love* - Melanie Tem   *h*   5422

**Tobias, Charlotte** (Teacher)
*Making Love* - Melanie Tem   *h*   5422

**Tobias, Robin** (Artist; Mentally Ill Person)
*Strange Angels* - Kathe Koja   *h*   3197

**Tobin, G. Patrick "Toby"** (Traveler; Computer
Expert)
*Angel Light* - Andrew M. Greeley   *f*   2342

**Tobin, Sara Ann** (Student)
*Angel Light* - Andrew M. Greeley   *f*   2342

**Tobinson, Ian** (Companion)
*A Wizard in Absentia* - Christopher Stasheff   *s*   5229

**Toch, Van** (Explorer)
*War With the Newts* - Karel Capek   *s*   874

**Todd, Angel** (Actor)
*Valentine* - S.P. Somtow   *h*   5160

**Todd, Emma** (Doctor)
*The Man Who Turned into Himself* - David
  Ambrose   *h*   89

**Todd, Redmond "Red" Eugene** (Spouse;
Psychologist)
*Lovelock* - Orson Scott Card   *s*   892

**Todtmann, Jeremiah** (Ruler)
*King of the Grey* - Richard A. Knaak   *f*   3173

**Toei, Rei** (Entertainer; Artificial Intelligence)
*Idoru* - William Gibson   *s*   2218

**Toikella** (Royalty; Leader)
*The Mountains of Majipoor* - Robert
  Silverberg   *s*   5037

**Toitovna, Maya** (Revolutionary; Scientist)
*Green Mars* - Kim Stanley Robinson   *s*   4633

**Toitovna, Maya** (Administrator; Scientist)
*Red Mars* - Kim Stanley Robinson   *s*   4635

**Tokoyuni, Mitsuo** (Military Personnel)
*Blood on the Sun* - Brian Herbert   *h*   2664

**Toland, Cindy** (Young Woman)
*Ghost Light* - Rick Hautala   *h*   2608

**Toland, Walter** (Adventurer; Handicapped)
*Killobyte* - Piers Anthony   *f*   179

**Tolar, Rob** (Student—College; Relative)
*The Gryphon King* - Tom Deitz   *f*   1473

**Toledo, Harry** (Teenager; Experimental Subject)
*Burn* - Bill Ransom   *s*   4476

**Toledo, Indira** (Historian; Settler)
*Mother of Demons* - Eric Flint   *s*   1956

**Toledo, Rico** (Military Personnel; Experimental
Subject)
*Burn* - Bill Ransom   *s*   4476
*ViraVax* - Bill Ransom   *s*   4478

**Tolivar** (Royalty; Child)
*Blood Trillium* - Julian May   *f*   3696

**Tolivar** (Nobleman; Teenager)
*Sky Trillium* - Julian May   *f*   3700

**Tolliver, Edgar "Eddie"** (Military Personnel)
*Fisherman's Hope* - David Feintuch   *s*   1900

**Tolnismer, Alysess** (Doctor)
*The Host* - Peter R. Emshwiller   *s*   1819

**Tolnismer, Alysess** (Doctor; Revolutionary)
*Short Blade* - Peter R. Emshwiller   *s*   1820

**Tolwyn, Geoffrey** (Military Personnel)
*Action Stations* - William R. Forstchen   *s*   1976

**Tom** (Farmer)
*The Lizard War* - John Dalmas   *s*   1325

**Tom** (Filmmaker; Editor)
*Remake* - Connie Willis   *s*   5873

**Tomanak** (Deity)
*The War God's Own* - David Weber   *f*   5682

**Tomaso** (Murderer; Psychic)
*Polar City Blues* - Katharine Kerr  *s*  3073

**Tomcat** (Sailor; Teenager)
*River Rats* - Caroline Stevermer  *s*  5267

**Tomeas** (Outcast; Scientist)
*Beyond the Door* - Gary L. Blackwood  *s*  510

**Tomjon** (Heir—Lost)
*Wyrd Sisters* - Terry Pratchett  *f*  4405

**Tomkins, Icanus** (Musician)
*Out of the Ordinary* - Annie Dalton  *f*  1330

**Tomley, Marissa** (Vampire)
*The Wildlings* - Scott Ciencin  *h*  1034

**Tomochelor, Pulickel** (Scientist; Anthropologist)
*The Howling Stones* - Alan Dean Foster  *s*  2006

**Tomokato, Miaowara** (Animal; Warrior)
*Samurai Cat Goes to Hell* - Mark E. Rogers  *f*  4655

**Tompkins, Ben** (Parent)
*Blood of the Children* - Alan Rodgers  *h*  4645

**Tompkins, Ernest** (Child)
*Blackburn* - Bradley Denton  *h*  1489

**Tompkins, Jimmy** (Child)
*Blood of the Children* - Alan Rodgers  *h*  4645

**Tooe** (Alien)
*Derelict for Trade* - Andre Norton  *s*  4148

**Tooe** (Alien; Apprentice)
*A Mind for Trade* - Andre Norton  *s*  4158

**Tooley, Nick** (Student)
*Tam Lin* - Pamela Dean  *f*  1446

**Tooth Fairy** (Supernatural Being)
*The Tooth Fairy* - Graham Joyce  *f*  2995

**Topaz** (Psychic; Martial Arts Expert)
*Mistworld* - Simon R. Green  *s*  2372

**Topchek, Lilo** (Engineer)
*The Zap Gun* - Philip K. Dick  *s*  1523

**Toplin** (Office Worker)
*Toplin* - Michael McDowell  *h*  3807

**Toq** (Mythical Creature)
*Warriorwards* - Dafydd ab Hugh  *f*  11

**Tor** (Mythical Creature; Warrior)
*Shadows on the Hill* - Jackie Cassada  *f*  935

**Toren** (Warrior)
*The Schemes of Dragons* - Dave Smeds  *f*  5097

**Torfinn, Karine** (Parent; Psychologist)
*One Mind's Eye* - Kathy Tyers  *s*  5525

**Torfinn, Llyn** (Adoptee; Psychic)
*One Mind's Eye* - Kathy Tyers  *s*  5525

**Torgov, Grandma Mugwump** (Aged Person; Vampire)
*Blood of Mugwump* - Doug Rice  *h*  4581

**Tornsaarin, Willek** (Military Personnel; Sorcerer)
*The Rose Sea* - S.M. Stirling  *f*  5296

**Torrance, Danny** (Child; Psychic)
*The Shining* - Stephen King  *h*  3141

**Torrance, Jack** (Writer; Maintenance Worker)
*The Shining* - Stephen King  *h*  3141

**Torraway, Roger** (Cyborg; Military Personnel)
*Man Plus* - Frederik Pohl  *s*  4348

**Torrence, Daniel "Hardeyes"** (Revolutionary)
*Eclipse Corona* - John Shirley  *s*  5006

**Torrence, Victoria** (Military Personnel)
*The Galactic Silver Star* - Kevin D. Randle  *s*  4468
*Jefferson's War: Death of a Regiment* - Kevin Randle  *s*  4466

**Torres, B'Elanna** (Engineer; Alien)
*The Escape* - Dean Wesley Smith  *s*  5113
*The Final Fury* - Dafydd ab Hugh  *s*  9

*Her Klingon Soul* - Michael Jan Friedman  *s*  2064
*Pathways* - Jeri Taylor  *s*  5404

**Torres, Rogelio** (Student)
*Meridian 144* - Meg Files  *s*  1932

**Torriner, Sheel** (Leader)
*The Furies* - Suzy McKee Charnas  *s*  968

**Torx, BrainGeneral** (Genetically Altered Being; Military Personnel)
*Mutant Hell* - Mark Grant  *s*  2324
*Mutants Amok* - Mark Grant  *s*  2325

**Toshtai** (Ruler)
*D'Shai* - Joel Rosenberg  *f*  4670

**Touch** (Orphan; Child)
*The Midnight Horse* - Sid Fleischman  *f*  1948

**Touchstone** (Magician)
*Sabriel* - Garth Nix  *f*  4129

**Touriq** (Mythical Creature)
*The Unicorn Sonata* - Peter S. Beagle  *f*  412

**Tovin, Rahel** (Scientist; Animal Lover)
*Regenesis* - Julia Ecklar  *s*  1729

**Tower, Josh** (Computer Expert; Spy)
*Systems* - W.T. Quick  *s*  4452

**Towne, Sam** (Psychologist)
*Superstition* - David Ambrose  *h*  90

**Townsend, Helen** (Clerk)
*Hellcat* - Amanda Kingsley  *h*  3145

**T'Pris** (Alien)
*Vulcan's Glory* - D.C. Fontana  *s*  1967

**Trace, Charlie** (Thief)
*Demogorgon* - Brian Lumley  *h*  3552

**Trace, Donalt** (Military Personnel)
*Tactical Error* - Thorarinn Gunnarsson  *s*  2466

**Trace, Erika** (Scientist)
*Assemblers of Infinity* - Kevin J. Anderson  *s*  100

**Trader, Max** (Artisan; Businessman)
*Trader* - Charles de Lint  *f*  1438

**Tradescant, John** (Farmer; Philosopher)
*Sexing the Cherry* - Jeanette Winterson  *f*  5927

**Tragen, Aaron** (Leader; Orphan)
*Beowulf's Children* - Larry Niven  *s*  4116

**Traiben** (Adventurer; Religious)
*Kingdoms of the Wall* - Robert Silverberg  *s*  5033

**Trap, Clyde** (Doctor)
*Requiem* - Clifford Mohr  *h*  3950

**Trapp, Phillip** (Technician)
*Blood Work* - Fay Zachary  *h*  6050

**Trask, Ben** (Spy)
*Bloodwars* - Brian Lumley  *h*  3547
*The Last Aerie* - Brian Lumley  *h*  3557

**Trask, Grace** (Spaceship Captain; Miner)
*The Billion Dollar Boy* - Charles Sheffield  *s*  4948

**Trask, Jovanna** (Spacewoman; Warrior)
*Warlords of Jupiter* - William H. Keith Jr.  *s*  3036

**Trask, Julian** (Anthropologist; Paranormal Investigator)
*Absolute Power* - Ray Russell  *h*  4738

**Trask, Lana** (Spaceship Captain; Miner)
*The Billion Dollar Boy* - Charles Sheffield  *s*  4948

**Trask, Lanyon** (Religious)
*In the Mood* - Charles L. Grant  *h*  2312

**Trask, Victor** (Journalist)
*Savant* - Rex Miller  *h*  3901

**Travassa, Daisainia** (Political Figure)
*Legacies* - Alison Sinclair  *s*  5069

**Traveler** (Artificial Intelligence)
*Burster* - Michael Capobianco  *s*  876

**Traveller, Josiah** (Inventor; Engineer)
*Anti-Ice* - Stephen Baxter  *s*  398

**Traven, Mick** (Detective—Police)
*Lethal Interface* - Mel Odom  *s*  4193

**Travers, Molly** (Detective—Private)
*Walking the Labyrinth* - Lisa Goldstein  *f*  2266

**Travers, Peter** (Architect)
*Night Relics* - James P. Blaylock  *h*  521

**Travis, Marshall** (Child)
*The One Safe Place* - Ramsey Campbell  *h*  862

**Travis, Susanne** (Teacher)
*The One Safe Place* - Ramsey Campbell  *h*  862

**Trayne** (Detective)
*Madlands* - K.W. Jeter  *s*  2913

**Trayne, Paul** (Teenager)
*Whipping Boy* - John Byrne  *h*  800

**Trayne, Robert** (Religious; Parent)
*Whipping Boy* - John Byrne  *h*  800

**Treadway, Jocelyn** (Diplomat; Divorced Person)
*Shadows on the Sun* - Michael Jan Friedman  *s*  2069

**Tree, Justin** (Companion; Disembodied Personality)
*Zombie Lover* - Piers Anthony  *f*  197

**Tregarde, Diana** (Paranormal Investigator; Writer)
*Burning Water* - Mercedes Lackey  *h*  3272

**Tregarde, Diana** (Psychic; Detective)
*Children of the Night* - Mercedes Lackey  *h*  3276

**Tregarde, Diana** (Writer; Witch)
*Jinx High* - Mercedes Lackey  *h*  3284

**Tregarth, Keris** (Warrior)
*The Warding of Witch World* - Andre Norton  *f*  4163

**Trelane, Athaya** (Royalty; Wizard)
*Call of Madness* - Julie Dean Smith  *f*  5124
*Mission of Magic* - Julie Dean Smith  *f*  5125
*Sage of Sare* - Julie Dean Smith  *f*  5126
*The Wizard King* - Julie Dean Smith  *f*  5127

**Trelane, Durek** (Royalty)
*Mission of Magic* - Julie Dean Smith  *f*  5125
*Sage of Sare* - Julie Dean Smith  *f*  5126

**Trelawney, Abel** (Archaeologist)
*The Jewel of Seven Stars* - Bram Stoker  *h*  5312

**Trelawney, Margaret** (Young Woman)
*The Jewel of Seven Stars* - Bram Stoker  *h*  5312

**Trell** (Alien)
*Illegal Aliens* - Nick Pollotta  *s*  4365

**Trema, Lodovik** (Robot)
*Foundation and Chaos* - Greg Bear  *s*  418

**Tremaine, Bernard** (Journalist)
*Black Dogs* - Ian McEwan  *h*  3808

**Tremaine, Elspeth "Beth"** (Statistician)
*The Convocation* - John R. Holt  *h*  2748

**Tremaine, Ian** (Journalist)
*Carlucci's Edge* - Richard Paul Russo  *s*  4747

**Tremaine, June** (Writer)
*Black Dogs* - Ian McEwan  *h*  3808

**Tremane** (Military Personnel; Nobleman)
*Storm Rising* - Mercedes Lackey  *f*  3297

**Tremayne, Evan** (Doctor)
*Carnivores* - Penelope Banka Kreps  *h*  3232

**Tremulis, Victor Anthony "Tremble"** (Handicapped)
*The Holy Terror* - Wayne Allen Sallee  *h*  4787

**Trent** (Royalty)
*Castle Dreams* - John DeChancie  *s*  1453
*Castle Spellbound* - John DeChancie  *s*  1454

**Trent** (Magician)
*Harpy Thyme* - Piers Anthony  *f*  174

**Trent, Derrick** (Detective—Homicide)
*Circle of One* - Eric James Fullilove  *s*  2092

**Trent, Derrick** (Detective—Police)
*The Stranger* - Eric James Fullilove  *s*  2093

**Trent, Elaine** (Businesswoman)
*Night Blood* - Eric Flanders  *h*  1945

**Trent, Elizabeth** (Archaeologist)
*Thirdspace* - Peter David  *s*  1387

**Trent, Vernor Deacon** (Businessman)
*Children of the Night* - Dan Simmons  *h*  5050

**Trerzian** (Royalty)
*Bewitchments of Love and Hate* - Storm
　Constantine  *s*  1140

**Trevayne, Pagadon Alphen** (Scholar)
*The Fortress of Eternity* - Andrew
　Whitmore  *f*  5790

**Trevisan, David** (Student)
*The Fair Rules of Evil* - David C. Smith  *h*  5111

**Trey, Annie** (Single Parent)
*Alien Rites* - Lynn S. Hightower  *s*  2685

**Trickster** (Artificial Intelligence; Teenager)
*Secret Realms* - Tom Cool  *s*  1168

**Trigg, Cyrus "Russ"** (Bodyguard)
*Howl-O-Ween* - Gary L. Holleman  *h*  2744 .

**Trigg, Dino** (Psychic)
*Megalomania* - Ian Wallace  *s*  5621

**Trillby, Samatha** (Military Personnel)
*Time Station London* - David Evans  *s*  1853

**Trilling, Kate** (Actress; Spy)
*The Invisible Company* - Scott Russell
　Sanders  *s*  4813

**Trinidad** (Alien; Traitor)
*Beneath the Gated Sky* - Robert Reed  *s*  4502

**Trioculus** (Imposter; Ruler)
*The Glove of Darth Vader* - Paul Davids  *s*  1392
*The Lost City of the Jedi* - Paul Davids  *s*  1393
*Zorba the Hutt's Revenge* - Paul Davids  *s*  1394

**Trioran, Eril** (Pilot)
*Jaydium* - Deborah Wheeler  *s*  5774

**Triplett, Michael** (Teenager)
*Entity* - Nina Mandelik  *h*  3615

**Tripolk, Anna** (Scientist)
*Lifeline* - Kevin J. Anderson  *s*  111

**Tris** (Healer; Traitor)
*Steal the Dragon* - Patricia Briggs  *f*  682

**Tris** (Student; Wizard)
*Tris's Book* - Tamora Pierce  *f*  4322

**Tristan** (Clone; Spy)
*Masque* - F. Paul Wilson  *s*  5890

**Tristen** (Foundling)
*Fortress in the Eye of Time* - C.J. Cherryh  *f*  991

**Tristen** (Supernatural Being)
*Fortress of Eagles* - C.J. Cherryh  *f*  992
*Fortress of Owls* - C.J. Cherryh  *f*  993

**Troi, Deanna** (Empath; Psychologist)
*Chains of Command* - Bill McCay  *s*  3767
*Guises of the Mind* - Rebecca Neason  *s*  4081

**Troi, Deanna** (Psychologist; Empath)
*Imzadi* - Peter David  *s*  1383

**Troi, Deanna** (Psychologist; Alien; Space Explorer)
*The Last Stand* - Brad Ferguson  *s*  1923

**Troi, Deanna** (Psychologist; Psychic)
*Q-Space* - Greg Cox  *s*  1228

**Troi, Deanna** (Psychologist; Alien)
*The Soldiers of Fear* - Dean Wesley Smith  *s*  5115

**Troi, Deanna** (Psychologist; Empath; Fiance(e))
*Triangle: Imzadi II* - Peter David  *s*  1388

**Troi, Lwaxana** (Telepath; Alien)
*Q-in-Law* - Peter David  *s*  1384

**Troit, Deanna "Dee"** (Alien; Telepath)
*Star Wreck IV: Live Long and Profit* - Leah
　Rewolinski  *s*  4565

**Troll** (Mythical Creature)
*Angels & Visitations: A Miscellany* - Neil
　Gaiman  *f*  2101
*A Ride on the Red Mare's Back* - Ursula K. Le
　Guin  *f*  3382

**Trondheim, Heida** (Military Personnel)
*The False Mirror* - Alan Dean Foster  *s*  2004

**Troop, Jan** (Farmer)
*Trinity Grove* - David van Meter Smith  *h*  5112

**Trosper, Carl** (Businessman)
*Greely's Cove* - John Gideon  *h*  2221

**Trost, Sophonisba "Soph"** (Businesswoman;
　Adventurer)
*Deepdrive* - Alexander Jablokov  *s*  2837

**Trout, Kilgore** (Writer)
*Timequake* - Kurt Vonnegut Jr.  *s*  5594

**Trovagh** (Noblewoman)
*Ciara's Song* - Andre Norton  *f*  4146

**Trowbridge, Howard** (Detective—Private)
*Killing Frost* - Dan I. Blake  *h*  514

**Troy, Linda Ellen "Sparta"** (Genetically Altered
　Being; Agent)
*The Diamond Moon* - Paul Preuss  *s*  4417

**Troy, Linda Ellen "Sparta"** (Detective—Police;
　Genetically Altered Being)
*Hide and Seek* - Paul Preuss  *s*  4418
*The Medusa Encounter* - Paul Preuss  *s*  4419

**Troy, Linda Ellen "Sparta"** (Genetically Altered
　Being; Heroine)
*The Shining Ones* - Paul Preuss  *s*  4421

**Troys, Taylor Thaddeus "Taytay"** (Handicapped;
　Relative)
*Meeting the Minotaur* - Carol Dawson  *f*  1409

**Trreggerthann, Umber** (Scientist; Warrior)
*The Gift of the Gorboduc Vandal* - Paul O.
　Williams  *s*  5821

**Truant, Cal** (Military Personnel; Government
　Official)
*Naked to the Stars/The Alien Way* - Gordon R.
　Dickson  *s*  1537

**Trudeau, Arielle** (Pilot)
*Return to Rocheworld* - Robert L. Forward  *s*  1989

**True Dragon** (Deity)
*Testament of the Dragon* - Margaret Weis  *f*  5729

**Truely, Yours "Y.T."** (Businesswoman; Teenager)
*Snow Crash* - Neal Stephenson  *s*  5254

**Trumbo, Byron** (Businessman)
*Fires of Eden* - Dan Simmons  *h*  5053

**Trusla** (Traveler; Dancer)
*The Warding of Witch World* - Andre
　Norton  *f*  4163

**Trusslo, Alix Amanda** (Royalty; Adventurer)
*Dragon Rescue* - Don Callander  *f*  843

**Tryon** (Magician; Apprentice)
*Wren to the Rescue* - Sherwood Smith  *f*  5142

**Tryon, Michael** (Artist)
*The Stone Garden* - Mary Rosenblum  *s*  4679

**Trystan** (Minstrel)
*Storm Warriors* - Brian Craig  *f*  1240

**Tsang-jieh** (Historian; Mythical Creature)
*Bronze Mirror* - Jeanne Larsen  *f*  3338

**Tscharka, Gerald** (Spaceship Captain; Fanatic)
*The Voices of Heaven* - Frederik Pohl  *s*  4356

**Tsepesh, Arkady** (Vampire)
*Children of the Vampire* - Jeanne
　Kalogridis  *h*  3003

**Tsepesh, Arkady** (Young Man)
*Covenant with the Vampire* - Jeanne
　Kalogridis  *h*  3004

**Tsepesh, Mary Wyndham** (Young Woman)
*Covenant with the Vampire* - Jeanne
　Kalogridis  *h*  3004

**Tsepesh, Vlad** (Vampire)
*Children of the Vampire* - Jeanne
　Kalogridis  *h*  3003
*Covenant with the Vampire* - Jeanne
　Kalogridis  *h*  3004

**Tsering** (Genetically Altered Being)
*Lethe* - Tricia Sullivan  *s*  5354

**Tsia** (Scientist; Genetically Altered Being)
*Cat Scratch Fever* - Tara K. Harper  *s*  2550

**Tsikas** (Military Personnel; Traitor)
*Videssos Besieged* - Harry Turtledove  *f*  5513

**Tsingar** (Military Personnel)
*Tears of Time* - Nancy Asire  *f*  256
*To Fall Like Stars* - Nancy Asire  *f*  257

**Tso, Anton Sien Hsia** (Clone; Businessman)
*The Shapes of Their Hearts* - Melissa Scott  *s*  4901

**Ttan** (Parent; Alien)
*Devil in the Sky* - Greg Cox  *s*  1226

**Tualha** (Animal; Minstrel)
*A Wizard Abroad* - Diane Duane  *f*  1668

**Tuchman, Ward** (Laird; Avenger)
*Enemy of My Enemy* - Ben Ohlander  *s*  4204

**Tucker** (Aged Person)
*Unicorn Highway* - David Lee Jones  *f*  2941

**Tucker, Elton** (Businessman)
*Where the Chill Waits* - T. Chris
　Martindale  *h*  3658

**Tucker, Graham** (Police Officer)
*The Homecoming* - Kimberly Rangel  *h*  4471

**Tucker, Lynn** (Tour Guide)
*The Midnight Tour* - Richard Laymon  *h*  3368

**Tucker, Paris** (Settler; Adventurer)
*Red Genesis* - S.C. Sykes  *s*  5377

**Tucker, Randy Karl** (Kidnapper)
*Freeware* - Rudy Rucker  *s*  4703

**Tucker, Rose** (Scientist)
*Sole Survivor* - Dean R. Koontz  *h*  3215

**Tucker, William Alec III** (Reanimated Dead;
　Cyborg)
*A King of Infinite Space* - Allen Steele  *s*  5243

**Tuckton, Grandpap** (Aged Person)
*Header* - Edward Lee  *h*  3393

**Tuckton, Travis Clyde** (Convict)
*Header* - Edward Lee  *h*  3393

**Tug** (Spaceship Captain; Alien)
*Alien Earth* - Megan Lindholm  *s*  3469

**Tugelbend, Victor** (Student; Wizard)
*Moving Pictures* - Terry Pratchett  *f*  4398

**Tuggle** (Witch; Spirit)
*The Witch's Eye* - Phyllis Reynolds Naylor  *f*  4080

**Tuiereann, Aedham "Adam"** (Mythical Creature;
　Amnesiac)
*Elvendude* - Mark Shepherd  *f*  4980

**Tula** (Psychic)
*In the Mothers' Land* - Elisabeth Vonarburg  *s*  5590

**Tull** (Hero; Prehistoric Human)
*Serpent Catch* - Dave Wolverton   s   5956

**Tullian, Adele** (Artist)
*Sheep* - Simon Maginn   h   3606

**Tullian, James** (Contractor)
*Sheep* - Simon Maginn   h   3606

**Tullian, Sam** (Child)
*Sheep* - Simon Maginn   h   3606

**Tumcari** (Artificial Intelligence)
*The Nature of Smoke* - Anne Harris   s   2559

**Tumkis "Lady Sun"** (Indian)
*Madoc's Hundred* - Pat Winter   f   5925

**Tummelier, Peter** (Wealthy; Friend)
*Tap, Tap* - David Martin   h   3640

**Tupac, Acanna** (Royalty)
*Mansions of Darkness* - Chelsea Quinn
   Yarbro   h   6016

**Turch, Averell "The Needle"** (Student; Serial Killer)
*Soulcatchers* - Jan Lara   h   3336

**Turcotte, Mike** (Military Personnel)
*Area 51* - Robert Doherty   s   1565

**Turenne** (Military Personnel)
*Wartide* - John Barnes   f   359

**Turkel, Maximillian** (Revolutionary)
*Christmas Slaughter* - Mark Grant   s   2323

**Turkel, Maximillian** (Revolutionary; Warrior)
*Mutant Hell* - Mark Grant   s   2324

**Turkel, Maximillian** (Revolutionary; Fugitive)
*Mutants Amok* - Mark Grant   s   2325

**Turnbull, Ben** (Aged Person)
*Toward the End of Time* - John Updike   s   5531

**Turnbull, Jack** (Military Personnel)
*Maze of Worlds* - Brian Lumley   h   3559

**Turner, Augusta "Gussie"** (Saloon Keeper/Owner)
*Phantom Banjo* - Elizabeth Ann
   Scarborough   f   4868
*Picking the Ballad's Bones* - Elizabeth Ann
   Scarborough   f   4869

**Turner, Bud** (Fugitive)
*Tombley's Walk* - Crosland Brown   h   723

**Turner, Loraine "Phyllis"** (Dancer; Werewolf)
*The Werewolf Chronicles* - Traci Briery   h   679
*Wolfsong* - Traci Briery   h   680

**Turner, Lucas "Yip"** (Teenager)
*Virtually Perfect* - Dan Gutman   s   2470

**Turner, Marian** (Psychologist)
*Night Glow* - Martin James   h   2867

**Turner, Winston** (Military Personnel)
*Action Stations* - William R. Forstchen   s   1976

**Turpin, Richard** (FBI Agent; Werewolf)
*The World of Darkness: Watcher* - Charles L.
   Grant   h   2321

**Tusk-Anini** (Military Personnel)
*Phule's Paradise* - Robert Asprin   s   261

**Tuvok** (Security Officer; Alien)
*The Escape* - Dean Wesley Smith   s   5113
*Ragnarok* - Nathan Archer   s   206

**TW-O: 114-84-1311825** (Robot)
*Cathedral of Thorns* - Steven Frankos   f   2041

**Tweep, Jonathan B.** (Genius)
*Through the Arc of the Rain Forest* - Karen Tei
   Yamashita   f   6008

**Twilla** (Healer; Apprentice)
*Mirror of Destiny* - Andre Norton   f   4159

**Two Bears** (Genetically Altered Being)
*Shadowboxer* - Nick Pollotta   s   4366

**Two Feathers, Jimmy "the Injun"** (Murderer;
   Government Official)
*Oracle* - Mike Resnick   s   4551

**Tye, Asher** (Warrior; Psychic)
*A Roil of Stars* - Don Wismer   s   5930

**Tyeewapi, Anevai** (Scientist; Guide)
*Ground-Ties* - Jane S. Fancher   s   1861
*Uplink* - Jane S. Fancher   s   1865

**Tyger** (Leader; Lesbian)
*Escape to the Wind* - Jennifer DiMarco   s   1559

**Tylar** (Historian; Time Traveler)
*Legacy* - Steve White   s   5785

**Tyler, Arcan** (Clerk)
*This Symbiotic Fascination* - Charlee Jacob   h   2843

**Tyler, Devin** (Vampire)
*Parliament of Blood* - Scott Ciencin   h   1031

**Tyler, Erica** (Parent)
*Midsummer* - Matthew J. Costello   h   1200

**Tyler, Gail** (Teenager)
*Raven* - S.A. Swiniarski   h   5374

**Tyler, Griffin** (Teenager; Actor)
*I Was a Teenage Fairy* - Francesca Lia
   Block   f   549

**Tyler, Jimi** (Child)
*The Deus Machine* - Pierre Ouellette   h   4232

**Tyler, John** (Military Personnel)
*The Harvest* - Robert Charles Wilson   s   5909

**Tyler, Joshua** (Child)
*Midsummer* - Matthew J. Costello   h   1200

**Tyler, Kane** (Detective)
*Raven* - S.A. Swiniarski   h   5374

**Tyler, Maurice** (Scientist; Professor)
*Black Sun* - Robert Leininger   s   3429

**Tyler, Richard** (Child; Adventurer)
*The Pagemaster* - David Kirschner   f   3156

**Tyler, Zane** (Salesman)
*Netherworld* - Richard Lee Byers   h   798

**Tymmon** (Teenager)
*Song of the Gargoyle* - Zilpha Keatley
   Snyder   f   5153

**Tynan, Louie** (Astronaut)
*Mother of Storms* - John Barnes   s   354

**Tyner, Gil** (Royalty; Hero)
*The Hero King* - Rick Shelley   f   4970
*The Hero of Varay* - Rick Shelley   f   4971

**Typhoid Mary** (Psychic; Mentally Ill Person)
*Twilight of the Empire* - Simon R. Green   s   2374

**Tyr** (Lawyer)
*Crucible* - Troy Denning   f   1484

**Tyre, Philip** (Military Personnel; Spaceman)
*Challenger's Hope* - David Feintuch   s   1899

**Tyrell, Sarah** (Heiress; Model)
*Blade Runner 2: The Edge of Human* - K.W.
   Jeter   s   2906

**Tyrell, Sarah** (Businesswoman; Imposter)
*Blade Runner: Replicant Night* - K.W. Jeter   s   2907

**Tyrell, Sarah** (Widow(er))
*A Question of Time* - Fred Saberhagen   h   4772

**Tyrian** (Bodyguard; Companion)
*A College of Magics* - Caroline Stevermer   f   5266

**Tyrr** (Demon; Magician)
*Demon Blade* - Mark A. Garland   f   2141

**Tyrranis** (Military Personnel)
*Valorian* - Mary H. Herbert   f   2677

**Tyson, Joseph** (Military Personnel)
*The Galactic Silver Star* - Kevin D. Randle   s   4468

**Tyson, Roger** (Time Traveler)
*Back to the Time Trap* - Keith Laumer   s   3343

**Tywi** (Orphan)
*The Dark Shore* - Adam Lee   f   3385

**Tzigane** (Witch)
*I Am Dracula* - C. Dean Andersson   h   139

**Tzikas** (Military Personnel; Traitor)
*The Thousand Cities* - Harry Turtledove   f   5512

## U

**Ublaz Mad Eyes** (Animal; Ruler)
*The Pearls of Lutra* - Brian Jacques   f   2854

**Ufgood, Torquil** (Sorcerer)
*Shadow Dawn* - Chris Claremont   f   1042

**Uhatatse** (Indian)
*People of the Mesa* - Ardath Mayhar   f   3704

**Uhua-Sorg, Kennet** (Doctor; Handicapped)
*The Ship Who Searched* - Anne McCaffrey   s   3749

**Uhura** (Military Personnel; Space Explorer)
*The Disinherited* - Peter David   s   1381

**Ulahane** (Shaman; Mythical Creature)
*The Shaman* - Christopher Stasheff   f   5223

**Ulfilo** (Sailor; Warrior)
*Conan and the Treasure of Python* - John Maddox
   Roberts   f   4616

**Ulga, Jubadi va** (Ruler; Alien)
*Terrible Swift Sword* - William R.
   Forstchen   s   1983

**Ulkanov, Andre** (Researcher; Doctor)
*The Multiplex Man* - James P. Hogan   s   2727

**Ullrich, Nils** (Genetically Altered Being)
*Armed Memory* - Jim Young   s   6048

**Ulrich** (Diplomat; Religious)
*Storm Warning* - Mercedes Lackey   f   3298

**Ulrich, Will** (Student)
*The Robin Hood Ambush* - William F. Wu   s   5999

**Uluye** (Religious)
*Avatar* - Louise Cooper   f   1173

**Ulysses** (Alien)
*Way Station* - Clifford D. Simak   s   5048

**Una** (Ruler)
*Storms of Victory* - Andre Norton   f   4162

**Underbridge, Kin** (Servant; Writer)
*Thunder of the Captains* - Holly Lisle   f   3489

**Underbridge, Kin** (Judge)
*Wrath of the Princes* - Holly Lisle   f   3490

**Underhill** (Engineer)
*The Humanoids* - Jack Williamson   s   5865

**Underhill, Jimmy** (Spy)
*The Werewolf's Revenge* - Richard Jaccoma   h   2841

**Underhill, Lee Won** (Administrator)
*F.R.E.E.Lancers* - Mel Odom   s   4191

**Underhill, Tim** (Writer; Veteran)
*Koko* - Peter Straub   h   5328
*The Throat* - Peter Straub   h   5332

**Undershort, Ozwaldo** (Alien; Agent)
*Free Radicals* - Jack McKinney   s   3848

**Unger, Alejandro "Alex"** (Invalid; Drifter)
*Heavy Weather* - Bruce Sterling   s   5258

**Unger, Juanita "Jane"** (Fanatic; Researcher)
*Heavy Weather* - Bruce Sterling   s   5258

**Unicorn** (Mythical Creature; Animal)
*Blue Moon Rising* - Simon R. Green   f   2362

**Unicorn** (Mythical Creature)
*Last Mountain* - Robert C. Fleet   f   1946

**Universal Historian** (Scholar)
*The Dechronization of Sam Magruder* - George Gaylord Simpson   s   5067

**Unnamed Character** (Robot)
*A Prophecy of Monsters* - Clark Ashton Smith   h   5103

**Unnamed Character** (Werewolf)
*A Prophecy of Monsters* - Clark Ashton Smith   h   5103

**Urban** (Revolutionary)
*Deception Well* - Linda Nagata   s   4065

**Urban** (Adventurer; Spaceman)
*Vast* - Linda Nagata   s   4067

**Urghart, Ian** (Nobleman; Wizard)
*The Time of Madness* - Thomas K. Martin   f   3652

**Urmila** (Journalist)
*The Calcutta Chromosome* - Amitav Ghosh   h   2214

**Urruah** (Animal; Wizard)
*The Book of Night with Moon* - Diane Duane   f   1657

**Ursht, Oman** (Leader)
*Alastor* - Jack Vance   s   5543

**Ursis, Nikolai Yanuarievich** (Military Personnel)
*The Siege* - Bill Baldwin   s   312

**Urt** (Genetically Altered Being)
*Lords of the Sky* - Angus Wells   f   5738

**Urtho** (Magician)
*The Black Gryphon* - Mercedes Lackey   f   3270

**Urthstripe the Strong** (Animal; Leader)
*Salamandastron* - Brian Jacques   f   2855

**Usher, Madeline** (Aged Person)
*Madeline: After the Fall of Usher* - Marie Kiraly   h   3150

**Usher, Madeline** (Doctor)
*Return to the House of Usher* - Robert Poe   h   4345

**Usher, Roderick** (Doctor)
*Return to the House of Usher* - Robert Poe   h   4345

**Ussemitus** (Adventurer; Psychic)
*Mother of Storms* - Adrian Cole   f   1101

**Ustinov, Yevgeny** (Administrator)
*Double Planet* - John Gribbin   s   2433

**Usurper, Black** (Criminal)
*Henry Martyn* - L. Neil Smith   s   5131

**Uta** (Indian; Teenager)
*Raptor* - Paul Zindel   s   6084

**Uthred** (Religious)
*Nations of the Night* - Oliver Johnson   f   2925

**Uthred of Ravenspur** (Religious; Wizard)
*The Forging of the Shadows* - Oliver Johnson   f   2924

**Utlunta** (Indian; Monster)
*Stoneskin's Revenge* - Tom Deitz   f   1476

# V

**Vacit, Kevin** (Telepath; Administrator)
*Dark Genesis* - J. Gregory Keyes   s   3096

**Vader, Darth** (Martial Arts Expert; Psychic)
*Shadows of the Empire* - Steve Perry   s   4299

**Vadeviya** (Religious)
*Touched by the Gods* - Lawrence Watt-Evans   f   5651

**Vadim, Lux** (Religious; Scientist)
*Desert Fire* - David Alexander   s   65

**VaGayjur, Supaari** (Alien; Revolutionary)
*Children of God* - Mary Doria Russell   s   4735

**Vail** (Artificial Intelligence)
*Under Siege* - Elisabeth Mace   f   3587

**Val** (Vampire)
*Blood Relations* - Doug Murray   h   4058

**Val Orden, Gaborn** (Royalty; Wizard)
*The Runelords: The Sum of All Men* - David Farland   f   1866

**Valadan** (Animal)
*The Prince of Ill Luck* - Susan Dexter   f   1512
*The True Knight* - Susan Dexter   f   1513

**Valaise, Ailena** (Noblewoman; Parent)
*Kingdom of the Grail* - A.A. Attanasio   f   269

**Valarian, Nickolai** (Government Official; Demon)
*Red Devil* - David Saperstein   h   4816

**Valcourt, Guy-Luc** (Demon; Servant)
*Adversary* - Daniel Rhodes   h   4568

**Valdaimon** (Wizard)
*Dragonspawn* - Mark Acres   f   28

**Valdemar "Val"** (Farmer; Traveler)
*Wayfinder's Story: The Seventh Book of Lost Swords* - Fred Saberhagen   f   4777

**Valdez, Maria** (Telepath; Leader)
*Under Fire* - Kenneth Von Gunden   s   5589

**Valdez, Mark** (Detective—Police; Psychic)
*Burning Water* - Mercedes Lackey   h   3272

**Valdez, Ramon** (Religious)
*The Killing of the Saints* - Alex Abella   h   21

**Valdez, Vido** (Teenager; Apprentice)
*Higher Education* - Charles Sheffield   s   4958

**Valdheim, M.R.** (Doctor; Government Official)
*The Multiplex Man* - James P. Hogan   s   2727

**Valdoria, Sauscony** (Genetically Altered Being)
*Primary Inversion* - Catherine Asaro   s   220

**Valdoria kva Skolia, Kelricson Garlin** (Nobleman; Psychic)
*The Last Hawk* - Catherine Asaro   s   219

**Vale, Dora Rosamund** (Businesswoman)
*Suckers* - Anne Billson   h   490

**Vale, Oliver** (Fugitive)
*Buddy Holly Is Alive and Well on Ganymede* - Bradley Denton   s   1490

**Valemar** (Nobleman)
*Summer King, Winter Fool* - Lisa Goldstein   f   2263

**Valentine** (Military Personnel)
*Priorities* - Lynda Lyons   s   3579

**Valentine, John Barrymore** (Actor; Parent)
*The Golden Globe* - John Varley   s   5565

**Valentine, Kenneth "Sparky"** (Actor; Mentally Ill Person)
*The Golden Globe* - John Varley   s   5565

**Valentine, Patrick** (Smuggler)
*Prototype* - Brian Hodge   h   2704

**Valentine, Timmy** (Musician)
*Vanitas: Escape From Vampire Junction* - S.P. Somtow   h   5162

**Valentinian** (Military Personnel; Bodyguard)
*An Oblique Approach* - David Drake   s   1638

**Valerian** (Wizard)
*Magelord: The Awakening* - Thomas K. Martin   f   3651

**Valeur, Whiss** (Revolutionary; Leader)
*Illusion* - Paula Volsky   f   5582

**Valiant, Eddie** (Detective—Private)
*Who P-P-Plugged Roger Rabbit?* - Gary K. Wolf   f   5934

**Valiarde, Nicholas "Donatien"** (Nobleman; Thief)
*The Death of the Necromancer* - Martha Wells   f   5749

**Vallaniri, Daner** (Martial Arts Expert; Nobleman)
*The Raven Ring* - Patricia C. Wrede   f   5978

**Vallus** (Mythical Creature; Wizard)
*The Radiant Dragon* - Elaine Cunningham   f   1291

**Valmar** (Royalty; Adventurer)
*Voima* - C. Dale Brittain   f   704

**Valorian** (Leader; Magician)
*Valorian* - Mary H. Herbert   f   2677

**Valparaiso, Oscar** (Consultant)
*Distraction* - Bruce Sterling   s   5256

**Valthyrra** (Artificial Intelligence)
*Battle of the Ring* - Thorarinn Gunnarsson   s   2460

**Vampire** (Vampire)
*Aqua Sancta* - Edward Bryant   h   748

**Vampyr** (Vampire)
*Child of an Ancient City* - Tad Williams   f   5827

**Van** (Barbarian)
*Prince of the North* - Harry Turtledove   f   5509

**Van Allen, Edmund** (Detective)
*Cemetery of Angels* - Noel Hynd   h   2821

**Van Buren, Peter** (Young Man)
*Silent Witness* - Robert Arthur Smith   h   5136

**Van Chou, Ngen** (Leader; Revolutionary)
*The Web of Spider* - W. Michael Gear   s   2173

**van de Oest, Frances Lorien "Lore"** (Artist; Heiress)
*Slow River* - Nicola Griffith   s   2445

**Van Diemen, William** (Vampire)
*Thirst* - Pyotr Kurtinski   h   3253

**Van Dorne, Chesna "Echo"** (Actress; Spy)
*The Wolf's Hour* - Robert R. McCammon   h   3759

**Van Helsing, Abraham** (Doctor)
*Lord of the Vampires* - Jeanne Kalogridis   h   3005

**Van Helsing, Stefan** (Doctor)
*Children of the Vampire* - Jeanne Kalogridis   h   3003

**van Hooven, Karen** (Psychic)
*Burial* - Graham Masterton   h   3671

**Van Horne, Anthony** (Sea Captain)
*Towing Jehovah* - James Morrow   f   4035

**van Huyten, Mariesa Gorley** (Heiress; Businesswoman)
*Firestar* - Michael Flynn   s   1962
*Rogue Star* - Michael Flynn   s   1965

**van Liesvelt, Butch** (Computer Expert; Homosexual)
*Trouble and Her Friends* - Melissa Scott   s   4902

**Van Pelt** (Spaceship Captain)
*The Eternal Enemy* - Michael Berlyn   s   469

**Van Richten, Rudolph** (Doctor)
*I, Strahd* - P.N. Elrod   h   1797

**Van Ryn, Rex** (Spy)
*The Devil Rides Out* - Dennis Wheatley   h   5773

**Van Voreen, Leigh** (Young Woman)
*Web of Dreams* - V.C. Andrews   h   147

**van Worden, Alphonse** (Military Personnel)
*The Manuscript Found in Sragossa* - Jan Potocki   f   4371

**van Wyyck, Margo** (Time Traveler)
*Time Scout* - Robert Asprin   s   263

**Van Zandt, Andy** (Child)
*The Stone Circle* - Gary Goshgarian   h   2285

**Van Zandt, Peter** (Archaeologist)
*The Stone Circle* - Gary Goshgarian   h   2285

**Vanachek, Viveka "Viv" Jeng** (Military Personnel; Cartographer)
*Nothing Sacred* - Elizabeth Ann Scarborough   f   4867

**Vance, Aylmer** (Detective)
*Aylmer Vance: Ghost-Seer* - Alice Askew   h   258

**Vanderdecker** (Sea Captain; Mythical Creature)
*The Marvellous Land of Snergs* - E.A. Wyke-Smith   f   6006

**Vanderdecker, Cornelius** (Sea Captain; Immortal)
*Flying Dutch* - Tom Holt   f   2750

**Vandermark, David** (Lawyer)
*Thinning the Predators* - Daina Graziunas   h   2341

**Vandermeer, Constance** (Fiance(e))
*A Wish and a Dream* - Ingrid Weaver   f   5658

**Vanderveen, Frederika** (Librarian; Vampire)
*Blood of the Covenant* - Brent Monahan   h   3954

**Vanderveen, Frederika** (Librarian)
*The Book of Common Dread* - Brent Monahan   h   3955

**Vandervelde** (Farmer)
*In the Land of the Dead* - K.W. Jeter   h   2912

**Vandien** (Warrior)
*Luck of the Wheels* - Megan Lindholm   f   3471

**Vandiver** (Military Personnel)
*Extinct* - Charles Wilson   h   5877

**Vanelli, MONDO** (Revolutionary; Computer Expert)
*How to Mutate and Take Over the World* - R.U. Sirius   s   5074

**Vanessa** (Mythical Creature)
*Maze of Moonlight* - Gael Baudino   f   393

**Vangerdahast** (Magician)
*Cormyr: A Novel* - Ed Greenwood   f   2426

**Vanian** (Guardian)
*Guardian's Key* - Anne Logston   f   3511

**Vanity** (Android; Prostitute)
*Dead Boys* - Richard Calder   s   836

**Vannice, Owen** (Scientist; Time Traveler)
*Corrupting Dr. Nice* - John Kessel   s   3083

**Vantara** (Noblewoman; Pilot)
*The Fugitive Worlds* - Bob Shaw   s   4942

**Vanyel** (Magician; Homosexual)
*Magic's Pawn* - Mercedes Lackey   f   3287

**Vanyel** (Religious)
*Magic's Promise* - Mercedes Lackey   f   3289

**Vanyi** (Religious)
*Arrows of the Sun* - Judith Tarr   f   5391

**Vanyi** (Magician; Leader)
*Spear of Heaven* - Judith Tarr   f   5396

**Var, Tomas** (Military Personnel)
*Exile's Challenge* - Angus Wells   f   5734

**L'var y Smid, Vida** (Political Figure; Fiance(e))
*The Eyes of God* - Mark Kreighbaum   s   3231

**L'var y Smid, Vida** (Heiress—Dispossessed; Fiance(e))
*Palace* - Katharine Kerr   s   3072

**Varden** (Mythical Creature; Healer)
*Spires of Spirit* - Gael Baudino   f   395

**Varia** (Psychic; Spouse)
*The Lion of Farside* - John Dalmas   f   1324

**Varianus, Galwin Gaius** (Linguist; Horse Trainer)
*Black Horses for the King* - Anne McCaffrey   f   3720

**Varien** (Wizard)
*Barrenlands* - Doranna Durgin   f   1702

**Varis** (Royalty; Sorcerer)
*The Wolf of Winter* - Paula Volsky   f   5584

**Varney, Alicia** (Businesswoman; Vampire)
*Blood War* - Robert Weinberg   s   5693
*The Unbeholden* - Robert Weinberg   h   5703
*Unholy Allies* - Robert Weinberg   h   5704

**Varney, Haldis "Hally"** (Actress)
*Stone Dead* - Ellen Jamison   h   2878

**Varo** (Teenager; Hunter)
*Shadow-Maze* - Mark Smith   f   5133

**Varodias** (Ruler)
*The Unicorn War* - John Lee   f   3401

**Varrus, Gaius Publius** (Military Personnel; Blacksmith)
*The Skystone* - Jack Whyte   f   5794

**Vashanna** (Slave)
*Cat Scratch Fever* - Tara K. Harper   s   2550

**Vasquez, Juanita** (Smuggler)
*Mojo and the Pickle Jar* - Douglas Bell   f   433

**Vassago** (Serial Killer)
*Hideaway* - Dean R. Koontz   h   3208

**Vaughan, BJ** (Veterinarian)
*The Healing of Crossroads* - Nick O'Donohoe   f   4195
*The Magic and the Healing* - Nick O'Donohoe   f   4196
*Under the Healing Sign* - Nick O'Donohoe   f   4198

**Vaughan, Celestine** (Vampire; Lawyer)
*Cold Kiss* - Roxanne Longstreet   h   3517

**Vaughan, Elsie Crawford** (Doctor; Twin)
*The Lilith Factor* - Jean Paiva   h   4236

**Vaughan, James** (Pilot)
*Dr. Haggard's Disease* - Patrick McGrath   h   3813

**Vaughan, Lucus** (Religious)
*Spiritride* - Mark Shepherd   f   4981

**Vaughn, Melissa** (Social Worker)
*Child of Shadows* - John Coyne   h   1236

**Vaughn, Rosalyn** (Hairdresser)
*The Book of the Damned* - D.A. Fowler   h   2022

**Vaun** (Genetically Altered Being; Hero)
*Hero* - Dave Duncan   s   1680

**Vayhawk** (Warrior; Leader)
*The Heldan* - Deborah Talmadge-Bickmore   f   5383

**Vear, Nick** (Spy)
*The Ridge* - Lisa Cantrell   h   872

**Vear, Sara** (Child)
*The Ridge* - Lisa Cantrell   h   872

**Veate** (Martial Arts Expert; Genetically Altered Being)
*The Albino Knife* - Steve Perry   s   4288

**Veering, Albert** (Psychologist)
*7 Steps to Midnight* - Richard Matheson   h   3682

**Vega, Carlos** (Leader; Settler)
*The Faces of Ceti* - Mary Caraker   s   877

**Vehmund, Daniel** (Secretary; Werewolf)
*Heart-Beast* - Tanith Lee   h   3411

**Vehmund, Marsall** (Landowner)
*Heart-Beast* - Tanith Lee   h   3411

**Veil** (Animal)
*Outcast of Redwall* - Brian Jacques   f   2853

**Veilleur, Glaeken** (Aged Person)
*Nightworld* - F. Paul Wilson   h   5893

**Velis, Catherine** (Computer Expert)
*The Eight* - Katherine Neville   f   4092

**Velmeran** (Spaceship Captain)
*Battle of the Ring* - Thorarinn Gunnarsson   s   2460
*Tactical Error* - Thorarinn Gunnarsson   s   2466

**Venabili, Dors** (Scientist; Martial Arts Expert)
*Forward the Foundation* - Isaac Asimov   s   236

**Vendeley, Rolande** (Privateer)
*Season of Storms* - Ellen Foxxe   f   2032

**Vendramin, Caterina** (Young Woman)
*Vaporetto 13* - Robert Girardi   h   2241

**Venkatna** (Royalty)
*Justice* - David Drake   s   1635

**Venneman, Richard** (Assistant; Vampire)
*Insatiable* - David Dvorkin   h   1707

**Venom** (Alien)
*Spider-Man: The Venom Factor* - Diane Duane   s   1667

**Ventan, Daniel** (Religious)
*Mission of Magic* - Julie Dean Smith   f   5125

**Venus** (Deity)
*Child of the Eagle* - Esther Friesner   f   2073

**Vercingetorix** (Warrior)
*Druids* - Morgan Llywelyn   f   3502

**Verdadero, Jachin** (Administrator)
*Taylor's Ark* - Jody Lynn Nye   s   4176

**Vereshchagin, Anton** (Military Personnel)
*Fire in a Faraway Place* - Robert Frezza   s   2052
*A Small Colonial War* - Robert Frezza   s   2054

**Veriam, Lizora "Lizra"** (Royalty; Leader)
*Gold Unicorn* - Tanith Lee   f   3410

**Veriam, Tanaquil** (Teenager; Sorceress)
*Gold Unicorn* - Tanith Lee   f   3410

**Veriam, Tanaquil** (Wanderer; Sorceress)
*Red Unicorn* - Tanith Lee   f   3414

**Verid** (Immortal; Political Figure)
*Daughter of Elysium* - Joan Slonczewski   s   5091

**Verity** (Clone; Genetically Altered Being)
*Mississippi Blues* - Kathleen Ann Goonan   s   2274

**Verity** (Adoptee; Clone)
*Queen City Jazz* - Kathleen Ann Goonan   s   2275

**Verllth, Zjhanne** (Spouse; Historian)
*Zjhanne's Book* - C.J. Mills   s   3912

**Verner, Janice** (Monster)
*Find Your Own Truth* - Robert N. Charrette   f   972

**Verner, Samuel** (Outlaw)
*Choose Your Enemies Carefully* - Robert N. Charrette   s   971

**Verner, Samuel** (Shaman)
*Find Your Own Truth* - Robert N. Charrette   f   972

**Verner, Samuel** (Businessman)
*Never Deal with a Dragon* - Robert N. Charrette   s   975

**Vernon, Gary** (Military Personnel)
*Sleipnir* - Linda Evans   f   1856

**Vernon, Vivian** (Scientist)
*Dr. Dimension* - John DeChancie   s   1456

**Veronica** (Religious)
*Cardmaster* - Clayton Emery   f   1813

**Veronica** (Religious; Psychic)
*Guises of the Mind* - Rebecca Neason   s   4081

**Verrou, Nick** (Teenager; Psychic)
*The Silent Strength of Stones* - Nina Kiriki Hoffman   f   2716

**Verruckt, Steven** (Student—Graduate)
*Vampires Anonymous* - Jeffrey N. McMahan   h   3853

**Vertok, Kyril** (Alien; Vampire)
*Shadows After Dark* - Ouida Crozier   f   1286

**Vertue, Leon** (Doctor)
*Mistworld* - Simon R. Green   s   2372

**Vervaine, Meguet** (Warrior)
*The Cygnet and the Firebird* - Patricia A.
  McKillip  *f*  3839

**Vess, Edgler Foreman** (Police Officer; Serial Killer)
*Intensity* - Dean R. Koontz  *h*  3210

**Vestal, Lauren** (Clerk)
*Carmilla: The Return* - Kyle Marfinn  *h*  3623

**Vestrit, Althea** (Teenager; Heiress—Dispossessed)
*The Ship of Magic* - Robin Hobb  *f*  2696

**Vettazen** (Sorceress)
*The Fountains of Mirlacca* - Ashley
  McConnell  *f*  3775

**Vetter, Tracy** (Detective—Homicide)
*Forever Knight: Intimations of Mortality* - Susan M.
  Garrett  *h*  2149

**Vi-Kata** (Alien; Criminal)
*Palace* - Katharine Kerr  *s*  3072

**Vicars, Ned** (Adventurer; Diplomat)
*Anti-Ice* - Stephen Baxter  *s*  398

**Vicia-Heinox** (Mythical Creature)
*The Faithful Traitor* - Robert Don Hughes  *f*  2809

**Victor** (Royalty; Magician)
*Blood and Honor* - Simon R. Green  *f*  2361

**Victor** (Computer Expert)
*See You Later* - Christopher Pike  *f*  4332

**Victor** (Artificial Intelligence)
*Virtually Perfect* - Dan Gutman  *s*  2470

**Videla, Pilar** (Artist; Lesbian)
*Whiteout* - Sage Walker  *s*  5619

**Vierran** (Servant; Revolutionary)
*Hexwood* - Diana Wynne Jones  *s*  2948

**Vigeant, Alison** (Journalist)
*Angel Souls and Devil Hearts* - Christopher
  Golden  *h*  2255
*Of Masques and Martyrs* - Christopher
  Golden  *h*  2258

**Vigor** (Vampire)
*Tooth: A Tale of Love and Death in Paradox* - Novak
  Kruger  *h*  3244

**ViKay** (Noblewoman; Fiance(e))
*Hour of the Octopus* - Joel Rosenberg  *f*  4673

**Vikktakkht** (Alien; Spaceship Captain)
*Chanur's Legacy* - C.J. Cherryh  *s*  981

**Vilkata** (Wizard)
*The Last Book of Swords: Shieldbreaker's Story* - Fred
  Saberhagen  *f*  4768

**Villette, Celine** (Bastard Daughter)
*The Judas Cross* - Charles Sheffield  *h*  4960

**Villette, Louis** (Nobleman)
*The Judas Cross* - Charles Sheffield  *h*  4960

**Villiers, Caroline "Cara Deaver" Tara** (Fugitive)
*Night's Pawn* - Tom Dowd  *s*  1591

**Vimes, Samuel** (Police Officer)
*Feet of Clay* - Terry Pratchett  *f*  4389
*Guards! Guards!* - Terry Pratchett  *f*  4390
*Jingo* - Terry Pratchett  *f*  4393

**Viola** (Animal; Adventurer)
*The Pearls of Lutra* - Brian Jacques  *f*  2854

**Virgil** (Writer; Guide)
*Quest for Apollo* - Michael Lahey  *f*  3309

**Virili, Kip** (Child)
*The Black Sun* - Jack Williamson  *s*  5860

**Virili, Rima** (Scientist)
*The Black Sun* - Jack Williamson  *s*  5860

**Virilio** (Criminal)
*Kamikaze L'Amour* - Richard Kadrey  *s*  2998

**Viroslav, Alexander** (Nobleman; Vampire)
*The Kiss* - Kathryn Reines  *h*  4529

**Viroslav, Maria** (Noblewoman; Vampire)
*The Kiss* - Kathryn Reines  *h*  4529

**VISAR** (Artificial Intelligence)
*Entoverse* - James P. Hogan  *s*  2724

**Vita** (Prostitute)
*And Eternity* - Piers Anthony  *f*  162

**Vitarosa** (Murderer; Religious)
*Mind Snare* - Gayle Greeno  *s*  2422

**Vivian** (Spirit)
*Black Snow Days* - Claudia O'Keefe  *s*  4205

**Vivo, Dionisio** (Critic; Patriot)
*Senor Vivo and the Coca Lord* - Louis de
  Bernieres  *f*  1411

**Vizuelos, Ramon** (Friend; Criminal)
*Meeting the Minotaur* - Carol Dawson  *f*  1409

**VJ** (Mutant)
*Mutation* - Robin Cook  *s*  1165

**Vlaicu, Elena** (Maintenance Worker)
*The Lost* - Jonathan Aycliffe  *h*  279

**vlith-Arkad, Brandon** (Military Personnel; Heir—
  Dispossessed; Fugitive)
*A Prison Unsought* - Sherwood Smith  *s*  5139

**vlith-Arkad, Brandon** (Heir—Dispossessed; Fugitive;
  Military Personnel)
*Ruler of Naught* - Sherwood Smith  *s*  5141

**vo Chaumelle, Renille** (Civil Servant)
*The Gates of Twilight* - Paula Volsky  *f*  5581

**vo Derrivalle, Eliste** (Noblewoman)
*Illusion* - Paula Volsky  *f*  5582

**Voerster, Broni** (Teenager; Handicapped)
*Glory* - Alfred Coppel  *s*  1182

**Voerster, Eliana Ehrengraf** (Noblewoman)
*Glory* - Alfred Coppel  *s*  1182

**Voight, Susan** (Writer; Wealthy)
*Freedom & Necessity* - Steven Brust  *f*  743

**Voisard, B.J.** (Patient)
*Sarah Canary* - Karen Joy Fowler  *f*  2028

**Volar** (Passenger)
*A Maze of Stars* - John Brunner  *s*  734

**Volemak** (Leader; Parent)
*The Memory of Earth* - Orson Scott Card  *s*  894

**Volkova, Ekaterina Alexandrova** (Military
  Personnel; Noblewoman)
*Glory's War* - Alfred Coppel  *s*  1184

**Volmar** (Traitor; Nobleman)
*Castle of Deception* - Mercedes Lackey  *f*  3275

**Volos** (Angel)
*Metal Angel* - Nancy Springer  *f*  5181

**Voltaire, Carter** (Military Personnel)
*The Drylands* - Mary Rosenblum  *s*  4678

**von Alte, Erde** (Noblewoman; Psychic)
*The Book of Earth* - Marjorie Bradley
  Kellogg  *f*  3044

**von Amerningen, Lutz** (Nobleman)
*Cloud Castles* - Michael Scott Rohan  *f*  4659

**von Cragga, Ivo** (Vampire)
*The Ruby Tear* - Rebecca Brand  *h*  660

**von Darkmoor, Erik** (Military Personnel; Bastard
  Son)
*Rage of a Demon King* - Raymond E. Feist  *f*  1908

**von Darkmoor, Erik** (Military Personnel; Nobleman;
  Bastard Son)
*Rise of a Merchant Prince* - Raymond E.
  Feist  *f*  1909

**von Darkmoor, Erik** (Bastard Son; Fugitive; Military
  Personnel)
*Shadow of a Dark Queen* - Raymond E.
  Feist  *f*  1911

**von Darkmoor, Erik** (Military Personnel; Bastard
  Son)
*Shards of a Broken Crown* - Raymond E.
  Feist  *f*  1912

**von Glower, Friedrich** (Nobleman)
*The Beast Within: A Gabriel Knight Mystery* - Jane
  Jensen  *h*  2895

**Von Heilitz, Lamont "the Shadow"** (Detective)
*Mystery* - Peter Straub  *h*  5330

**von Hessel** (Nobleman; Military Personnel)
*Escape From Loki* - Philip Jose Farmer  *f*  1870

**Von Karlsfeld, Hilda** (Teacher)
*Mordenheim* - Chet Williamson  *h*  5847

**von Mannheim De Soto, Igor** (Guide)
*Cat-A-Lyst* - Alan Dean Foster  *s*  1997

**Von Rabenaue, Walter** (Guard)
*Lord of the Dark Lake* - Ron Faust  *h*  1894

**von Richtofen, Manfred** (Military Personnel; Pilot)
*The Bloody Red Baron* - Kim Newman  *h*  4097

**von Sacher, Ludwig** (Genetically Altered Being;
  Historian)
*Lives of the Monster Dogs* - Kirsten Bakis  *s*  305

**von Schuss, Nicholas** (Nobleman; Heir)
*Kit's Book* - C.J. Mills  *s*  3911

**von Wolgast, Klemens Manfred** (Businessman)
*Writ in Blood* - Chelsea Quinn Yarbro  *h*  6019

**Von Zarovich, Strahd** (Ruler; Vampire)
*I, Strahd* - P.N. Elrod  *h*  1797

**Von Ziegler, Horst** (Animal Trainer)
*The Keeper* - Robert D. Lee  *h*  3402

**Vonnegut, Kurt "Junior"** (Writer)
*Timequake* - Kurt Vonnegut Jr.  *s*  5594

**Vorbarra, Gregor** (Ruler)
*The Vor Game* - Lois McMaster Bujold  *s*  764

**Vorbis** (Religious; Police Officer)
*Small Gods* - Terry Pratchett  *f*  4400

**Vordegh** (Magician; Leader)
*Star Ascendant* - Louise Cooper  *f*  1180

**Vorder, Sera** (Gentlewoman)
*The Gnome's Engine* - Teresa Edgerton  *f*  1742
*Goblin Moon* - Teresa Edgerton  *f*  1743

**Vorkosigan, Aral** (Nobleman; Ruler)
*Barrayar* - Lois McMaster Bujold  *s*  756

**Vorkosigan, Mark Pierre** (Clone)
*Mirror Dance* - Lois McMaster Bujold  *s*  762

**Vorkosigan, Miles** (Military Personnel; Diplomat;
  Nobleman)
*Borders of Infinity* - Lois McMaster Bujold  *s*  757

**Vorkosigan, Miles** (Nobleman; Military Personnel)
*Cetaganda* - Lois McMaster Bujold  *s*  758

**Vorkosigan, Miles** (Nobleman; Auditor; Military
  Personnel)
*Komarr* - Lois McMaster Bujold  *s*  760

**Vorkosigan, Miles** (Nobleman; Military Personnel)
*Memory* - Lois McMaster Bujold  *s*  761
*Mirror Dance* - Lois McMaster Bujold  *s*  762

**Vorkosigan, Miles** (Military Personnel; Diplomat;
  Nobleman)
*The Vor Game* - Lois McMaster Bujold  *s*  764

**Vorlund, Krip** (Spaceman)
*Dare to Go A-Hunting* - Andre Norton  *s*  4147

**Vorpatril, Ivan** (Nobleman; Diplomat)
*Cetaganda* - Lois McMaster Bujold  *s*  758

**Vorpatril, Ivan** (Nobleman; Military Personnel)
*Memory* - Lois McMaster Bujold  *s*  761

**Vorsoisson, Ekaterin "Kat"** (Noblewoman)
*Komarr* - Lois McMaster Bujold  *s*  760

**Vortcir** (Alien)
*They Fly at Ciron* - Samuel R. Delany  *s*  1482

**Vorthys** (Auditor)
*Komarr* - Lois McMaster Bujold  *s*  760

**Voskresenye, Pavel Sergeyevich** (Activist; Cyborg)
*The Fortunate Fall* - Raphael Carter  *s*  927

**Vosnesensky, Mikhail Andreivitch** (Spaceman; Leader)
*Mars* - Ben Bova  *s*  586

**Voss, Dorn** (Student; Teenager)
*Where the Ships Die* - William C. Dietz  *s*  1553

**Voss, Natalie** (Spacewoman)
*Where the Ships Die* - William C. Dietz  *s*  1553

**Vost, Harlic** (Religious)
*Thorn and Needle* - Paul B. Thompson  *f*  5456

**Voy, Ellen** (Dancer; Clone)
*Six Moon Dance* - Sheri S. Tepper  *s*  5437

**Voyaging Moon** (Musician)
*The Remarkable Journey of Prince Jen* - Lloyd Alexander  *f*  69

**Voyvodan** (Mythical Creature)
*Fortress of Frost and Fire* - Mercedes Lackey  *f*  3282

**Vozmozho, Vozmuzhalnoy "Moozh"** (Military Personnel)
*The Call of Earth* - Orson Scott Card  *s*  882

**Vree** (Martial Arts Expert)
*Fifth Quarter* - Tanya Huff  *f*  2795
*No Quarter* - Tanya Huff  *f*  2798

**Vril, Dietrich** (Monster; Vampire)
*The Armageddon Box* - Robert Weinberg  *h*  5690

**Vryce, Damien Kilcannon** (Religious; Warrior)
*Black Sun Rising* - C.S. Friedman  *f*  2056
*Crown of Shadows* - C.S. Friedman  *s*  2057
*When True Night Falls* - C.S. Friedman  *f*  2060

**Vusca** (Military Personnel)
*The Book of the Beast* - Tanith Lee  *f*  3405

**Vyledaar, Alessa** (Wizard)
*Dragonmage of Mystara* - Thorarinn Gunnarsson  *f*  2462


# W


**Wade** (Terrorist)
*Antarctica* - Kim Stanley Robinson  *s*  4628

**Wade, Arlo** (Child; Twin)
*Bad Blood* - D.A. Fowler  *h*  2021

**Wade, Austin** (Child; Twin)
*Bad Blood* - D.A. Fowler  *h*  2021

**Wade, Bree** (Teenager; Twin)
*Double Date* - R.L. Stine  *h*  5287

**Wade, Jonathan** (Miner)
*What's Wrong with Tamara?* - D.A. Fowler  *h*  2025

**Wade, Kara** (Writer)
*Sibs* - F. Paul Wilson  *h*  5898

**Wade, Laura Gardner** (Heiress)
*A Reasonable Madness* - Fran Dorf  *h*  1580

**Wade, Samantha** (Teenager; Twin)
*Double Date* - R.L. Stine  *h*  5287

**Wade, Tamara** (Mentally Ill Person; Parent)
*Bad Blood* - D.A. Fowler  *h*  2021

**Wade, Tamara** (Child)
*What's Wrong with Tamara?* - D.A. Fowler  *h*  2025

**Wade, Zach** (Businessman; Spouse)
*A Reasonable Madness* - Fran Dorf  *h*  1580

**Wae, Kiondili** (Student; Telepath)
*Lightwing* - Tara K. Harper  *s*  2551

**Waesc, Dorias** (Artificial Intelligence; Refugee)
*Reclamation* - Sarah Zettel  *s*  6081

**Wagner** (Student)
*Jack Faust* - Michael Swanwick  *s*  5372

**Wagner, Jeff** (Professor)
*Twilight Time* - Rick Hautala  *h*  2613

**Wagner, Jennifer** (Teenager)
*The Season of Passage* - Christopher Pike  *h*  4331

**Wagner, Lauren** (Astronaut)
*The Season of Passage* - Christopher Pike  *h*  4331

**Wahler, Jukes** (Doctor)
*Shade of Pale* - Greg Kihn  *h*  3104

**Wakandagi, Ptesa "Tesa/Good Eyes"** (Diplomat; Indian)
*Silent Songs* - A.C. Crispin  *s*  1264

**Wakefield, Nicole des Jardins** (Doctor; Adventurer)
*The Garden of Rama* - Arthur C. Clarke  *s*  1055

**Wakefield, Nicole des Jardins** (Political Figure)
*Rama Revealed* - Arthur C. Clarke  *s*  1059

**Wakefield, Richard** (Scientist; Adventurer)
*The Garden of Rama* - Arthur C. Clarke  *s*  1055

**Wakefield, Richard** (Engineer)
*Rama II* - Arthur C. Clarke  *s*  1058

**Wakefield, Wallace "Wake"** (Scout)
*The Unnatural* - David Prill  *h*  4437

**Wakelin, Emily** (Artisan)
*Holy Terror* - Josephine Boyle  *h*  608

**Wakelin, John** (Accountant)
*Holy Terror* - Josephine Boyle  *h*  608

**Walcott, Roland** (Professor; Criminal)
*Indiana Jones and the Unicorn's Legacy* - Rob MacGregor  *f*  3593

**Wald, Richard** (Anthropologist)
*The Engines of God* - Jack McDevitt  *s*  3787

**Walden, Jerome** (Scientist)
*The Infinity Plague* - Robert E. Vardeman  *s*  5564

**Walders, Shana** (Teenager; Military Personnel)
*Maximum Light* - Nancy Kress  *s*  3241

**Walford, John** (Murderer; Spirit)
*Walford's Oak* - Jill M. Phillips  *f*  4310

**Wali, Linnet** (Prostitute; Genetically Altered Being)
*Imposter* - Valerie J. Freireich  *s*  2050

**Walk, Random** (Artificial Intelligence)
*Profiteer* - S. Andrew Swann  *s*  5366

**Walker, Betsy** (Femme Fatale)
*Last Rites* - David Darke  *h*  1354

**Walker, Cassie** (Child)
*Playmates* - Abigail McDaniels  *h*  3784

**Walker, David** (Writer)
*Steam* - Jay B. Laws  *h*  3361

**Walker, Greg** (Repairman)
*Sacrifice* - John Farris  *h*  1886

**Walker, Hillary "Hilly"** (Writer)
*The Forgotten* - Stephen R. George  *h*  2200

**Walker, Jack** (Criminal)
*Deathwalker* - R. Patrick Gates  *h*  2159

**Walker, Janet** (Parent; Housewife)
*Playmates* - Abigail McDaniels  *h*  3784

**Walker, Jason** (Doctor)
*The Unknown Soldier* - Mickey Zucker Reichert  *s*  4525

**Walker, Laura** (Young Woman)
*In Hot Blood* - Petru Popescu  *h*  4367

**Walker, Mark** (Parent; Scientist)
*Playmates* - Abigail McDaniels  *h*  3784

**Walker, Max** (Police Officer; Time Traveler)
*Timecop* - S.D. Perry  *s*  4286

**Walker, Ross** (Police Officer)
*Spook* - Steve Vance  *h*  5553

**Walker, Sharissa** (Teenager)
*Sacrifice* - John Farris  *h*  1886

**Walking Bear, Jack** (Military Personnel; Time Traveler)
*First Dawn* - Mike Moscoe  *s*  4038
*Lost Days* - Mike Moscoe  *s*  4039

**Walking Bear, Jack** (Time Traveler; Military Personnel)
*Second Fire* - Mike Moscoe  *s*  4040

**Wallace, Brandy** (Artist; Teacher)
*Dreambuilder* - Tom Deitz  *f*  1471

**Wallace, Ditsy** (Journalist; Adventurer)
*The Square Deal* - David Drake  *s*  1644

**Wallace, Enoch** (Military Personnel; Recluse)
*Way Station* - Clifford D. Simak  *s*  5048

**Wallace, Indra** (Historian)
*3001: The Final Odyssey* - Arthur C. Clarke  *s*  1053

**Wallace, Rollingham Boregard "Rusty"** (Spaceship Captain)
*A World Lost* - James B. Johnson  *s*  2921

**Wallace, Wendy** (Writer)
*The Hunted* - Kathryn Ptacek  *h*  4442

**Wallenberg, Carl** (Doctor)
*Life Support* - Tess Gerritsen  *h*  2206

**Waller, Enid** (Nurse)
*Fiends* - John Farris  *h*  1884

**Wallich, Darren** (Doctor; Spaceship Captain)
*Bloom* - Wil McCarthy  *s*  3761

**Walmsley, Nigel** (Astronaut; Immortal)
*Sailing Bright Eternity* - Gregory Benford  *s*  449

**Walsh, Charity** (Student)
*The Bighead* - Edward Lee  *h*  3387

**Walsh, Dalton** (Religious)
*The Reckoning* - Ruby Jean Jensen  *h*  2904

**Walsh, Richard Earl** (Military Personnel)
*Dragon Season* - Michael Cassutt  *f*  936

**Walsmear, Michael** (Police Officer)
*Photographing Fairies* - Steve Szilagyi  *f*  5379

**Walter of Jacin** (Leader)
*The Wild Hunt: Vengeance Moon* - Jocelin Foxe  *f*  2031

**Walters, Diana** (Anthropologist)
*Uwharrie* - Eugene E. Pfaff Jr.  *h*  4309

**Walther, Jeeris Belamy "Jeebee"** (Professor)
*Wolf and Iron* - Gordon R. Dickson  *s*  1539

**Walthers, Audee** (Pilot)
*The Gateway Trip: Tales and Vignettes of the Heechee* - Frederik Pohl  *s*  4346

**Walthers, Danielle "Dani"** (Doctor; Vampire)
*Parliament of Blood* - Scott Ciencin  *h*  1031

**Walthers, Danielle "Dani"** (Teenager; Student; Vampire)
*The Vampire Odyssey* - Scott Ciencin  *h*  1032

*The Wildlings* - Scott Ciencin   *h*   1034

**Walthers, Samantha "Sam"** (Detective—Private; Parent)
*Parliament of Blood* - Scott Ciencin   *h*   1031
*The Vampire Odyssey* - Scott Ciencin   *h*   1032
*The Wildlings* - Scott Ciencin   *h*   1034

**Walton, Alex** (Doctor)
*Virus* - Graham Watkins   *h*   5632

**Walton, Robert** (Publisher)
*Gothic Romance* - Emmanuel Carrere   *h*   912

**Wan, Lai** (Psychic)
*Some Things Never Die* - Robert Morgan   *h*   4005

**Wan-To** (Alien)
*The World at the End of Time* - Frederik Pohl   *s*   4357

**Wanachtee** (Indian; Chieftain)
*The Silent Stars Go By* - James White   *s*   5781

**Wanbli** (Warrior; Indian)
*The Third Eagle: Lessons Along a Minor String* - R.A. MacAvoy   *s*   3583

**Wanda-Jean** (Television Personality)
*The Feelies* - Mick Farren   *s*   1878

**Wandel, Timothy J.** (Genetically Altered Being)
*Armed Memory* - Jim Young   *s*   6048

**Wanderman, Aubrey** (Military Personnel)
*Honor Among Enemies* - David Weber   *s*   5673

**Wanders, Wendy** (Genetically Altered Being)
*Winterlong* - Elizabeth Hand   *s*   2539

**Wanderson, Balthan** (Magician)
*The Temper of Wisdom* - Lynn Abbey   *f*   17

**Wandigaux, Rowena** (Grandparent)
*Never Land* - Douglas Clegg   *h*   1081

**Wang-mu** (Servant; Genetically Altered Being)
*Xenocide* - Orson Scott Card   *s*   899

**Wanker, David L.** (Military Personnel; Spaceship Captain)
*The Kruton Interface* - John DeChancie   *s*   1459

**Ward** (Doctor)
*Not Broken, Not Belonging* - Randy Fox   *h*   2030

**Ward, Alan** (Military Personnel; Monster)
*Midsummer* - Matthew J. Costello   *h*   1200

**Ward, Alex** (Veteran)
*The Parasite War* - Tim Sullivan   *s*   5352

**Ward, David** (Scientist)
*Operation Synbat* - Bob Mayer   *h*   3701

**Ward, Donna** (Widow(er))
*Heathen* - Shaun Hutson   *h*   2816

**Ward, Kim** (Scientist)
*The Stone Within* - David Wingrove   *s*   5920
*White Moon, Red Dragon* - David Wingrove   *s*   5921
*The White Mountain* - David Wingrove   *s*   5922

**Warden** (Police Officer)
*The Tetherballs of Bougainville* - Mark Leyner   *f*   3457

**Ware** (Demon)
*If I Pay Thee Not in Gold* - Piers Anthony   *f*   176

**Ware, Theron** (Magician)
*The Devil's Day* - James Blish   *h*   525

**Wargallow, Simon** (Leader)
*The Gods in Anger* - Adrian Cole   *f*   1100

**Warhelski, Maxim** (Werewolf)
*All Things under the Moon* - Robert Morgan   *h*   4002

**Warhurst, Montgomery** (Military Personnel; Leader)
*Semper Mars* - Ian Douglas   *s*   1585

**Warner, Alex** (Professor)
*The Armageddon Box* - Robert Weinberg   *h*   5690
*The Devil's Auction* - Robert Weinberg   *h*   5696

**Warner, Hank "Joey Bennett"** (Taxi Driver)
*Someplace to Be Flying* - Charles de Lint   *f*   1435

**Warner, Seth** (Hero)
*Through the Ice* - Piers Anthony   *f*   192

**Warner, Valerie** (Sorceress)
*The Armageddon Box* - Robert Weinberg   *h*   5690

**Warner, Valerie** (Sorceress; Model)
*The Devil's Auction* - Robert Weinberg   *h*   5696

**Warren** (Doctor)
*Act of Love* - Joe R. Lansdale   *h*   3319

**Warren, Carol** (Writer)
*In the Deep Woods* - Nicholas Conde   *h*   1131

**Warrick, John** (Con Artist)
*Less than Human* - Gary L. Raisor   *h*   4464

**Warrick, Susan** (Police Officer)
*OtherSyde* - J. Michael Straczynski   *h*   5323

**Warson, Toll** (Military Personnel)
*The Voyage* - David Drake   *s*   1649

**Wartsworth, Caspar** (Adventurer; Barbarian)
*The Lost City of Zork* - Robin Wayne Bailey   *f*   288

**Warwick, David** (Teacher)
*Sweetheart, Sweetheart* - Bernard Taylor   *h*   5402

**Washburn, Bob** (Student)
*The Robin Hood Ambush* - William F. Wu   *s*   5999

**Washburn, Corky** (Morgue Attendant)
*Bring on the Night* - Don Davis   *h*   1402

**Washi** (Indian; Hero)
*Dark Legend* - Jamake Highwater   *f*   2686

**Washington, Arlene "Lady El"** (Artificial Intelligence; Experimental Subject)
*Lady El* - Jim Starlin   *s*   5213

**Washington, Billy** (Aged Person; Hunter)
*Beggars and Choosers* - Nancy Kress   *s*   3236

**Washington, George** (Military Personnel; Revolutionary)
*Two Crowns for America* - Katherine Kurtz   *f*   3262

**Washington, Sandy** (Young Man)
*Homegoing* - Frederik Pohl   *s*   4347

**Wasserman, Janus Cornelius** (Publisher)
*The House of the Toad* - Richard L. Tierney   *h*   5470

**Watanabe, Kenji** (Historian; Settler)
*The Garden of Rama* - Arthur C. Clarke   *s*   1055

**Watcher, Lightfoot** (Alien)
*Foragers* - Charles Oberndorf   *s*   4187

**Water** (Mythical Creature)
*The Book of Water* - Marjorie Bradley Kellogg   *f*   3045

**Water Rat "Ratty"** (Animal; Adventurer)
*Toad Triumphant* - William Horwood   *f*   2774
*The Willows in Winter* - William Horwood   *f*   2776

**Water Spider** (Government Official)
*The Night Watch* - Sean Stewart   *f*   5274

**Waterfall, Kylene** (Time Traveler; Telepath)
*Death's Gray Land* - Mike Shupp   *s*   5011
*The Last Reckoning* - Mike Shupp   *s*   5012

**Waterhouse, Mary Ann "Synthi Venture"** (Actress; Television Personality)
*Mother of Storms* - John Barnes   *s*   354

**Waterman, James "Jamie" Fox** (Indian; Scientist)
*Mars* - Ben Bova   *s*   586

**Waterman, Phil** (Police Officer)
*Trickster* - Chris Curry   *h*   1297

**Watkins, Beverly** (Journalist)
*Operation Damocles* - Oscar L. Fellows   *s*   1915

**Watkins, Classy Jack** (Drug Dealer)
*Living Hell* - Ric Meyers   *h*   3882

**Watkins, Daniel J.** (Gentleman; Alcoholic)
*The Golden Nineties* - Lisa Mason   *s*   3663

**Watson, John** (Doctor)
*Seance for a Vampire* - Fred Saberhagen   *h*   4773

**Watson, John H.** (Doctor; Writer)
*Sherlock Holmes in Orbit* - Mike Resnick   *s*   4556

**Watt, Al** (Lawman)
*Darkly the Thunder* - William W. Johnstone   *h*   2929

**Watt, Peter** (Spy)
*Gehenna* - Lewis Gannett   *h*   2114

**Watterson, Sam** (Journalist)
*Silent Scream* - Dan Schmidt   *h*   4883

**Watts, Arnie** (Serial Killer)
*Thoughts of God* - Michael Kanaly   *s*   3007

**Waverly, Dora** (Aged Person)
*The Well* - Michael B. Sirota   *h*   5077

**Waverly, Tim** (Activist; Security Officer)
*Outworld Cats* - Jack Lovejoy   *s*   3536

**Waxman, Will** (Doctor)
*Fallen Angels* - Larry Niven   *s*   4120

**Wayland, Richard** (Police Officer)
*Dying Breath* - Jon A. Harrald   *h*   2555

**Wayne, Bruce "Batman"** (Hero; Detective—Amateur)
*Batman: Captured by the Engines* - Joe R. Lansdale   *h*   3320
*Batman: Knightfall* - Dennis O'Neil   *s*   4215
*Batman Returns* - Craig Shaw Gardner   *s*   2124
*Catwoman* - Lynn Abbey   *s*   14
*The Further Adventures of Batman 2: Featuring the Penguin* - Martin H. Greenberg   *s*   2391
*The Further Adventures of Batman 3: Featuring Catwoman* - Martin H. Greenberg   *s*   2392
*Mask of the Phantasm* - Geary Gravel   *s*   2331

**Wayville, Chris** (Astronaut; Scientist)
*Flying to Valhalla* - Charles Pellegrino   *s*   4280

**Wayville, Clarice** (Astronaut; Scientist)
*Flying to Valhalla* - Charles Pellegrino   *s*   4280

**Weasel** (Adventurer; Indian)
*Crow and Weasel* - Barry Lopez   *f*   3523

**Weatherby, Ann** (Teenager)
*Hell-O-Ween* - David Robbins   *h*   4598

**Weatherby, Tamsin** (Actress)
*Star Prey* - Ehren M. Ehly   *h*   1763

**Weatherwax, Granny** (Witch; Heroine)
*Lords and Ladies* - Terry Pratchett   *f*   4394
*Witches Abroad* - Terry Pratchett   *f*   4404
*Wyrd Sisters* - Terry Pratchett   *f*   4405

**Webb, Danny** (Indian; Shaman)
*The Serpent Slayers* - Adam Niswander   *h*   4113

**Webb, Fiona** (Doctor)
*Website* - Ray Garton   *h*   2157

**Webb, Tessa** (Aged Person)
*Haunted* - James Herbert   *h*   2669

**Webber, Mitch** (Military Personnel)
*Icefire* - Judith Reeves-Stevens   *s*   4512

**Webster, Daniel** (Spaceship Captain; Aged Person)
*Deep Freeze* - Zach Hughes   *s*   2811

**Webster, Duncan** (Writer)
*Cardinal's Sin* - Raymond Buckland   *h*   751
*The Committee* - Raymond Buckland   *h*   752

**Webster, Grandma** (Indian; Religious)
*The Godmother's Web* - Elizabeth Ann
  Scarborough   *f*   4864

**Webster, Joshua** (Military Personnel)
*Deep Freeze* - Zach Hughes   *s*   2811

**Webster, Tania** (Scientist)
*Sister, Sister* - Andrew Neiderman   *h*   4091

**Webster, Tom** (Teacher)
*Requiem* - Graham Joyce   *h*   2994

**Webster, Torie** (Journalist)
*The Eyes of Torie Webster* - Roy Sorrels   *h*   5164

**Weena** (Mutant; Young Woman)
*The Time Ships* - Stephen Baxter   *s*   403

**Wei** (Alien; Spy)
*Rule Golden and Double Meaning* - Damon
  Knight   *s*   3189

**Weigand, Pauli** (Time Traveler)
*The Fourth Rome* - David Drake   *s*   1631

**Weil, Gunther** (Worker)
*Griffin's Egg* - Michael Swanwick   *s*   5370

**Weiland** (Teenager)
*The Changeling Prince* - Vivian Vande
  Velde   *f*   5554

**Weintraub, Sarah** (Scientist; Researcher)
*Threshold* - Bill Myers   *s*   4060

**Weir, Jacob** (Teacher)
*The Black School* - J.N. Williamson   *h*   5851

**Weiss, Rachel** (Psychologist)
*Shadow Dance* - Douglas Borton   *h*   577

**Weiss, Selene** (Witch)
*Shadows* - Jonathan Nasaw   *h*   4068

**Weisser, Erich** (Telepath; Animal Trainer)
*Child of the Light* - Janet Gluckman   *f*   2244

**Weisser, Erich "Erich Alois"** (Telepath; Animal
  Trainer)
*Child of the Journey* - Janet Berliner   *f*   466

**Weisser, Erich "Erich Alois"** (Leader; Animal
  Trainer; Telepath)
*Children of the Dusk* - Janet Berliner   *f*   467

**Welch, Lewis** (Political Figure; Telepath)
*Dreambuilder* - Tom Deitz   *f*   1471

**Welch, Lewis** (Bastard Son; Student—High School)
*Soulsmith* - Tom Deitz   *f*   1475

**Welch, Lewis Owen** (Telepath)
*Wordwright* - Tom Deitz   *f*   1478

**Welch, Melissa "Kay Franklin"** (Runaway)
*Hobkin* - Peni R. Griffin   *f*   2438

**Welch, Sara "Liza Franklin"** (Runaway)
*Hobkin* - Peni R. Griffin   *f*   2438

**Weldon, Jim** (Police Officer)
*The Revelation* - Bentley Little   *h*   3496

**Wellin, Alleluia "Alleya"** (Genetically Altered
  Being; Leader)
*Jovah's Angel* - Sharon Shinn   *s*   5001

**Wells, Jeff** (Student; Teenager)
*Norby and the Court Jester* - Janet Asimov   *s*   252

**Wells, Jeff** (Teenager; Student)
*Norby and the Oldest Dragon* - Janet
  Asimov   *s*   253
*Norby and Yobo's Great Adventure* - Janet
  Asimov   *s*   254
*Norby Down to Earth* - Janet Asimov   *s*   255

**Wells, Nancy** (Teacher)
*Dark Twilight* - Joseph A. Citro   *h*   1036

**Welsh, Ariel** (Heiress)
*Changeling* - Stephen Leigh   *s*   3425
*Renegade* - Cordell Scotten   *s*   4903

**Wenceslas, Rudyard "Waldo" Riding** (Royalty;
  Adventurer)
*The Wealdwife's Tale* - Paul Hazel   *f*   2636

**Wendeen, Wendy** (Religious; Doctor)
*Drifter* - William C. Dietz   *s*   1543

**Wendell** (Sidekick)
*Slay and Rescue* - John Moore   *f*   3991

**Wentworth, Ford** (Government Official; Criminal)
*The Trinity Vector* - Steve Perry   *s*   4302

**Wentworth, Richard** (Adventurer)
*The Spider #3: Death's Crimson Juggernaut/The Red
  Death Rain* - Grant Stockbridge   *f*   5307
*The Spider #4: Death Reign of the Vampire King/The
  Pain Emperor* - Grant Stockbridge   *f*   5308
*The Spider #8: The Devil's Paymaster/Legions of the
  Accursed Light* - Grant Stockbridge   *f*   5309

**Werewolf** (Criminal)
*Wizard's Heir* - Daniel Hood   *f*   2759

**Wesley, William** (Child)
*The Forever Children* - Eric Flanders   *h*   1944

**West, Braden** (Artist)
*The Catswold Portal* - Shirley Rousseau
  Murphy   *f*   4055

**West, Kilimanjaro** (Revolutionary; Amnesiac)
*Out on Blue Six* - Ian McDonald   *s*   3794

**West, Michael** (Administrator)
*The Man Upstairs* - T.L. Parkinson   *h*   4248

**Westbrook, Louisa** (Gentlewoman; Psychic)
*Flameweaver* - Margaret Ball   *f*   314

**Westenra, Lucy** (Young Woman)
*Dracul: An Eternal Love Story* - Nancy
  Kilpatrick   *h*   3110

**Westerman, Stacy** (Psychologist)
*Lorelei* - Mark A. Clements   *h*   1086

**Westin, Andy** (Security Officer)
*Mall Purchase Night* - Rick Cook   *f*   1159

**Westlake, Peyton** (Scientist)
*Darkman* - Randall Boyll   *h*   611
*Darkman #1: The Hangman* - Randall Boyll   *h*   612
*Darkman #2: The Price of Fear* - Randall
  Boyll   *h*   613
*Darkman #3: The Gods of Hell* - Randall
  Boyll   *h*   614
*Darkman #4: The Face of Death* - Randall
  Boyll   *h*   615

**Weston, James** (Actor)
*October* - Al Sarrantonio   *h*   4832

**Weston, Jamie** (Adventurer; Imposter)
*Summerland* - L. Dean James   *f*   2865

**Weston, Quinton** (Religious; Political Figure)
*The Immortals* - Tracy Hickman   *s*   2681

**Westriding, Margorie "Jory"** (Traveler; Heroine)
*Sideshow* - Sheri S. Tepper   *s*   5436

**Wetmore, Percy** (Guard)
*The Green Mile* - Stephen King   *h*   3134

**Weyland, Cadmann** (Explorer; Security Officer)
*Beowulf's Children* - Larry Niven   *s*   4116

**Whale, James** (Director; Homosexual)
*Father of Frankenstein* - Christopher Bram   *h*   659

**Whaler, Nathaniel Firstborne** (Professor; Agent)
*The Ecolitan Enigma* - L.E. Modesitt Jr.   *s*   3927

**Whalley, Vida** (Young Woman)
*A Dry Spell* - Susan Moloney   *h*   3951

**Wheatley, Don** (Detective—Police)
*Demon Within* - Dana Reed   *h*   4499

**Wheatley, Gillian** (Linguist)
*The Seventh Heart* - Marina Fitch   *f*   1943

**Wheaton, Anna** (Child)
*Jumpers* - R. Patrick Gates   *h*   2161

**Wheele, Catherine** (Psychic; Religious)
*Sunglasses After Dark* - Nancy A. Collins   *h*   1124

**Wheeler** (Alien; Businessman)
*Signal to Noise* - Eric S. Nylund   *s*   4179

**Wheeler, Alec** (Warlock)
*Witch Spell* - Guy N. Smith   *h*   5122

**Wheeler, Belinda "Bobbie"** (Teenager)
*Witch Spell* - Guy N. Smith   *h*   5122

**Wheeler, Kelly** (Teacher)
*Captain Quad* - Sean Costello   *h*   1203

**Wheeler, Matt** (Doctor; Leader)
*The Harvest* - Robert Charles Wilson   *s*   5909

**Wheeler, Yvonne** (Witch)
*Witch Spell* - Guy N. Smith   *h*   5122

**Wheelwright, Laura** (Young Woman)
*Heart-Beast* - Tanith Lee   *h*   3411

**Wheldrake** (Writer)
*The Revenge of the Rose* - Michael
  Moorcock   *f*   3985

**Whipple, Frank "Weasel"** (Mechanic)
*Mongster* - Randall Boyll   *h*   616

**Whistler, Circe** (Sorceress)
*Wildest Dreams* - Norman Partridge   *h*   4256

**Whistler, Jamey** (Vampire)
*Shadows* - Jonathan Nasaw   *h*   4068
*The World on Blood* - Jonathan Nasaw   *h*   4069

**Whit, Beatrice** (Traveler)
*The Beacon* - Valerie J. Freireich   *s*   2048

**Whitaker, Tomyris "Whit Hastings"** (Military
  Personnel; Spy)
*Return to Isis* - Jean Stewart   *s*   5268

**Whitcomb, Johnny** (Worker)
*Inagehi* - Jack Cady   *h*   817

**Whitcome, Luke** (Child)
*Shadow Child* - Joseph A. Citro   *h*   1038

**Whitcome, Pamela** (Housewife)
*Shadow Child* - Joseph A. Citro   *h*   1038

**White** (Doctor)
*The Midnight Club* - Christopher Pike   *h*   4329

**White, Alan** (Producer; Writer)
*Created By* - Richard Christian Matheson   *h*   3691

**White, Alice** (Travel Agent; Werewolf)
*Wilderness* - Dennis Danvers   *h*   1349

**White, Arnold** (Child)
*Mongster* - Randall Boyll   *h*   616

**White, Carrie** (Teenager; Psychic)
*Carrie* - Stephen King   *h*   3127

**White, Diane** (Parent)
*Hell-Storm* - James A. Moore   *h*   3990

**White, Gabriel** (Werewolf)
*Hell-Storm* - James A. Moore   *h*   3990

**White, Karen** (Housewife)
*Gypsies* - Robert Charles Wilson   *s*   5908

**White Ash** (Prehistoric Human; Psychic)
*People of the Earth* - W. Michael Gear   *f*   2166

**White Crow, Valentine** (Magician; Military
  Personnel; Spouse)
*The Architecture of Desire* - Mary Gentle   *f*   2195

**White Crow, Valentine** (Magician; Military
  Personnel)
*Rats and Gargoyles* - Mary Gentle   *f*   2196

**White Eagle, Zacxk** (Indian; Shaman)
*Shaman Woods* - Morgan Fields   *h*   1931

**White Eyes** (Criminal)
*White Eyes* - Kenneth Robeson  *f*  4625

**Whitefeather, Matthew** (Worker; Indian)
*The Last Vampire* - Kathryn Meyer Griffith  *h*  2440

**Whitefeather, Steven "Brian Moore"** (Military Personnel; Time Traveler)
*Time Station London* - David Evans  *s*  1853

**Whitehead, Tom** (Librarian; Adventurer)
*Dragon Companion* - Don Callander  *f*  842

**Whitehead, Tom** (Librarian)
*Dragon Tempest* - Don Callander  *f*  844

**Whitehorse, Janara** (Telepath)
*Enemy Unseen* - V.E. Mitchell  *s*  3918

**Whitlock, Megan** (Warrior)
*The Cage* - S.M. Stirling  *f*  5293
*Saber & Shadow* - S.M. Stirling  *f*  5297

**Whitlock, Megan** (Businesswoman; Warrior; Mercenary)
*Shadow's Son* - Shirley Meier  *f*  3872

**Whitman, Lisl** (Professor)
*Reprisal* - F. Paul Wilson  *h*  5896

**Whitman, Walt** (Writer)
*Darker Angels* - S.P. Somtow  *h*  5155

**Whitmore, Thomas** (Political Figure)
*Independence Day* - Dean Devlin  *s*  1508

**Wickes, Joey** (Child)
*The Quagmire* - James Kisner  *h*  3160

**Wickes, Margaret** (Waiter/Waitress; Witch)
*The Quagmire* - James Kisner  *h*  3160

**Wickham, Eddie** (Child)
*The Haunting* - Ruby Jean Jensen  *h*  2901

**Wickham, Theodora** (Aged Person)
*The Haunting* - Ruby Jean Jensen  *h*  2901

**Widdick, Harry** (Heir)
*Retro Lives* - Lee Grimes  *s*  2446

**Widdick, Robert** (Businessman; Parent)
*Retro Lives* - Lee Grimes  *s*  2446

**Wide** (Alien; Leader)
*Starstrike* - W. Michael Gear  *s*  2172

**Wiggin, Andrew** (Warrior; Psychologist)
*Xenocide* - Orson Scott Card  *s*  899

**Wiggin, Peter** (Reincarnated Person)
*Children of the Mind* - Orson Scott Card  *s*  883

**Wigram, Rachel** (Child)
*The Vanishment* - Jonathan Aycliffe  *h*  282

**Wilburfoss, Jon** (Spaceship Captain; Religious)
*Wulfsyarn: A Mosaic* - Phillip Mann  *s*  3617

**Wilcox, Bradford C.** (Lawyer)
*Thirst* - Pyotr Kurtinski  *h*  3253

**Wilde, Oscar** (Writer; Historical Figure)
*The Hunger and Ecstasy of Vampires* - Brian Stableford  *h*  5192

**Wilder** (Spaceship Captain)
*The Martian Chronicles* - Ray Bradbury  *s*  621

**Wilder, Travis** (Saloon Keeper/Owner)
*Beyond the Pale* - Mark Anthony  *f*  153

**Wilhoit, Steve** (Businessman)
*Where the Chill Waits* - T. Chris Martindale  *h*  3658

**Wilkerson, Joey** (Teenager)
*Guardian* - John Saul  *h*  4841

**Wilkes, Ron** (Lawyer)
*Bitter Blood* - Karen E. Taylor  *h*  5405

**Wilkins, Edna** (Clerk)
*Hellcat* - Amanda Kingsley  *h*  3145

**Wilkins, John** (Journalist)
*Silent Scream* - Dan Schmidt  *h*  4883

**Wilkins, Mike** (Alcoholic)
*Silent Scream* - Dan Schmidt  *h*  4883

**Wilkinson, Christopher** (Artist)
*In the Shadows of the Moonglade* - Riley St. James  *h*  5186

**Wilkinson, Esau** (Young Man)
*The Hunger of the Beast* - John Driver  *h*  1656

**Wilkinson, Hilda** (Prostitute; Step-Parent)
*Spider* - Patrick McGrath  *h*  3815

**Wilkinson, Steve "The Dreamer"** (Student—College)
*A Call to Arms* - Thomas K. Martin  *f*  3650

**Wilkinson, Steve "The Dreamer"** (Student—College; Volunteer)
*A Two-Edged Sword* - Thomas K. Martin  *f*  3653

**Wilks** (Military Personnel)
*Aliens: Earth Hive* - Steve Perry  *s*  4289
*Aliens: The Female War* - Steve Perry  *s*  4290

**Willa** (Runaway)
*The Lone Sentinel* - Jo Dereske  *s*  1493

**William** (Orphan; Adventurer)
*Goblins in the Castle* - Bruce Coville  *f*  1218

**William** (Knight; Adventurer)
*Here There Be Dragons* - Roger Zelazny  *f*  6069

**William** (Royalty; Historical Figure)
*Robin and the King* - Parke Godwin  *f*  2247

**Williams, Albert** (Psychologist)
*Some of Your Blood* - Theodore Sturgeon  *h*  5347

**Williams, Billy** (Handyman)
*The Sixth Dog* - Jane Rice  *h*  4582

**Williams, Bryce** (Teenager)
*WiZrD* - Steve Zell  *h*  6078

**Williams, Conrad** (Astronaut)
*Night Launch* - Jake Garn  *s*  2143

**Williams, Jonathan** (Spaceship Captain)
*The Martian Chronicles* - Ray Bradbury  *s*  622

**Williams, Martin** (Writer)
*Mirror* - Graham Masterton  *h*  3677

**Williams, Megan** (Teenager)
*WiZrD* - Steve Zell  *h*  6078

**Williams, Sadie** (Child; Runaway)
*Shadow Walkers* - Nina Romberg  *h*  4663

**Williams, Stanley** (Photographer)
*The Undine* - Michael O'Rourke  *h*  4224

**Williams, Thaddeus "Thaddy"** (Child; Adventurer)
*Unicorn Highway* - David Lee Jones  *f*  2941

**Williams, Tommy** (Professor)
*Fear* - L. Ron Hubbard  *h*  2789

**Williams, Trevor** (Artist)
*WiZrD* - Steve Zell  *h*  6078

**Willis** (Alien)
*Red Planet* - Robert A. Heinlein  *s*  2647

**Willow** (Prehistoric Human)
*The Hunter Returns* - David Drake  *f*  1632

**Willow** (Royalty)
*The Tangle Box* - Terry Brooks  *f*  718

**Willow Leaf** (Slave)
*The Road to Underfall* - Mike Jefferies  *f*  2888

**Willson, Andrea** (Real Estate Agent; Step-Parent)
*Dark Reunion* - Stephen R. George  *h*  2198

**Willson, Matthew** (Police Officer; Parent)
*Dark Reunion* - Stephen R. George  *h*  2198

**Willson, Peter** (Teenager)
*Dark Reunion* - Stephen R. George  *h*  2198

**Wilmore, Cally** (Housewife)
*Apocalypse* - Nancy Springer  *f*  5176

**Wilson, Barry** (Scientist; Writer)
*The Fungus* - Harry Adam Knight  *h*  3192

**Wilson, Bob** (Lawyer)
*The Higher Space* - Jamil Nasir  *s*  4070

**Wilson, Braemer** (Journalist)
*White Queen* - Gwyneth Jones  *s*  2955

**Wilson, Brian** (Musician; Historical Figure)
*Glimpses* - Lewis Shiner  *h*  4997

**Wilson, Christopher T.** (Vampire)
*Blood on the Sun* - Brian Herbert  *h*  2664

**Wilson, Collingsworth** (Young Man)
*I Know What You Did Last Summer* - Lois Duncan  *s*  1692

**Wilson, Karen** (Secretary; Psychic)
*The Headsman* - James Neal Harvey  *h*  2599

**Wiltin, Hof** (Rancher; Warrior)
*To a Highland Nation* - Christopher Rowley  *s*  4698

**Wilum** (Magician)
*Flight to Hollow Mountain* - Mark Sebanc  *f*  4908

**Wimperling** (Animal)
*Pigs Don't Fly* - Mary Brown  *f*  727

**Winchell, Anne** (Social Worker)
*Bone* - George C. Chesbro  *h*  1006

**Winchester, Miriam** (Shaman; Indian)
*Shadow Walkers* - Nina Romberg  *h*  4663

**Wind Soldier, Harley** (Indian)
*The Grass Dancer* - Susan Power  *f*  4380

**Windclan, Raincloud** (Linguist; Parent)
*Daughter of Elysium* - Joan Slonczewski  *s*  5091

**Windemere, Gideon** (Drug Dealer)
*Necrom* - Mick Farren  *s*  1881

**Windrose, Antryg** (Wizard; Fugitive)
*Dog Wizard* - Barbara Hambly  *f*  2503

**Windruth** (Alien; Leader)
*Dragon Rigger* - Jeffrey A. Carver  *s*  929

**Windsor, Bethany** (Heiress)
*Cluster Command* - David Drake  *s*  1630

**Windsor, Corrigan Tel** (Bounty Hunter)
*The Price of Ransom* - Alis A. Rasmussen  *s*  4483

**Windsor, Marion** (Journalist)
*The Blood of the Lamb* - Thomas F. Monteleone  *h*  3958

**Winfield, Angela** (Professor; Anthropologist)
*The Werewolf's Touch* - Cheri Scotch  *h*  4892

**Wing, Phillip** (Architect)
*Look into the Sun* - James Patrick Kelly  *s*  3047

**Wing, Sue** (Journalist)
*The Summoning* - Bentley Little  *h*  3498

**Wingate, Max** (Artist)
*The Convocation* - John R. Holt  *h*  2748

**Winger** (Detective—Private)
*Deadly Quicksilver Lies* - Glen Cook  *f*  1148

**Winkler, Gene "Wink"** (Military Personnel)
*Signs of Life* - Cherry Wilder  *s*  5804

**Winnowill** (Mythical Creature)
*Captives of the Blue Mountain* - Wendy Pini  *f*  4336

**Winslow, Dirk** (Military Personnel)
*Time: The Semi-Final Frontier* - Lionel Fenn  *s*  1921

**Winstead, Samantha** (Doctor)
*Cries of the Children* - Clare McNally  *h*  3856

Winston, Ariana (Military Personnel)
*Shadows of War* - Thomas S. Gressman  s  2432

Winston, Palmer (Aged Person)
*Dark Journey* - A.R. Morlan  h  4010

Winter, Catty (Child; Handicapped)
*Well Wished* - Franny Billingsley  f  489

Winter, Henry (Student—College)
*The Secret History* - Donna Tartt  h  5398

Winter, James (Student)
*Sing for a Gentle Rain* - J. Alison James  f  2861

Winter, John (Spy)
*Deathwalker* - Patrick Whalen  h  5769

Winter, Tom (Time Traveler)
*A Bridge of Years* - Robert Charles Wilson  s  5905

Winterbelle (Child)
*In the Land of Winter* - Richard Grant  f  2326

Winters, Angelica (Actress)
*Fantastique* - Marvin Kaye  h  3025

Winters, Elizabet (Magician; Psychologist)
*Bedlam Boyz* - Ellen Guon  f  2467

Winters, Franklin Evelyn (Businessman)
*Dreamer* - Daniel Quinn  h  4454

Winters, Ginny (Artist)
*Dreamer* - Daniel Quinn  h  4454

Winters, Jennifer (Lawyer)
*Fury* - John Coyne  h  1237

Winters, Katie (Child; Resistance Fighter)
*Martian Deathtrap* - Nathan Archer  s  205

Winters, Kelly Ann (Engineer; Military Personnel)
*March or Die* - Andrew Keith  s  3035

Winters, Michael (Truck Driver)
*Sati* - Christopher Pike  f  4330

Winters, Talia (Telepath; Fugitive)
*Voices* - John Vornholt  s  5598

Winters, Theodore "TK" Karlington (Veteran;
   Mythical Creature)
*Strands of Sunlight* - Gael Baudino  f  396

Winthrop, Edwin (Military Personnel)
*The Bloody Red Baron* - Kim Newman  h  4097

Winthrop, Montana "Tana" (Administrator;
   Handicapped)
*The Earth Saver* - Catherine Wells  s  5745

Wisdom (Religious)
*The Curse* - John Tigges  h  5472

Wishart, Adam (Public Relations)
*The Walking Shadow* - Brian Stableford  s  5195

Wisnewski, Leonard (Museum Curator)
*Legion of the Dead* - Geoffrey Caine  h  833

Witch Baby (Musician; Witch)
*Cherokee Bat and the Goat Guys* - Francesca Lia
   Block  f  546

Witch Baby (Teenager; Musician)
*Missing Angel Juan* - Francesca Lia Block  f  550

Witch Baby (Teenager; Foundling; Musician)
*Witch Baby* - Francesca Lia Block  f  552

Withers, Jonella "Johnnie" (Teenager)
*The Living Dark* - Stephen Gresham  h  2431

Withers, Virgil "Rip" (Revolutionary)
*Clash by Night* - Chet Williamson  h  5844

Withrow, Dennis "Dennis Dithrovvu" (Scientist;
   Teacher)
*Mathemagics* - Margaret Ball  f  316

Witney, Charley (Clerk)
*Sweet Heart* - Peter James  h  2875

Witney, Tom (Lawyer)
*Sweet Heart* - Peter James  h  2875

Wittelsbach, Ludwig (Ruler)
*From Prussia with Love* - John DeChancie  f  1457

Witzko, Damion (Military Personnel)
*On the Verge* - Roland J. Green  s  2350

Wizard (Wizard)
*The Adventures of Threadwell the Tailor, or
   Alterations Made While You Wait* - P.D.
   Cacek  h  801

Wizenbeak (Wizard; Royalty)
*Lord of the Troll-Bats* - Alexis A. Gilliland  f  2234

Wizenbeak (Wizard)
*The Shadow Shaia* - Alexis A. Gilliland  f  2235

Woczniak, Hal (FBI Agent; Knight)
*The Forever King* - Molly Cochran  f  1092

Wojciechowski, Thaddaios "Wolf" Alexandru
   (Scientist)
*In the Wrong Hands* - Edward Gibson  s  2215

Wok (Leader; Mythical Creature)
*The Pixilated Peeress* - L. Sprague de
   Camp  f  1416

Wolde, David (Linguist)
*My Soul to Keep* - Tannarive Due  h  1670

Wolde, Kira (Child)
*My Soul to Keep* - Tannarive Due  h  1670

Wolenczak, Lucas (Computer Expert; Teenager)
*seaQuest DSV: Fire Below* - Matthew J.
   Costello  s  1201

Wolf (Prehistoric Human; Hunter)
*The Hunter Returns* - David Drake  f  1632

Wolf (Mercenary)
*Konrad* - David Ferring  f  1927

Wolf (Magician; Warrior)
*Masques* - Patricia Briggs  f  681

Wolf (Veteran; Shaman)
*Spiritride* - Mark Shepherd  f  4981

Wolf, Behrooz "Bey" (Recluse; Scientist)
*Proteus in the Underworld* - Charles
   Sheffield  s  4962

Wolf, Behrooz "Bey" (Government Official;
   Scientist)
*Proteus Unbound* - Charles Sheffield  s  4963

Wolf, Billy "Slider" (Murderer)
*Dreamer* - Peter James  h  2871

Wolfe, Atrix (Magician; Criminal)
*The Book of Atrix Wolfe* - Patricia A.
   McKillip  f  3838

Wolfe, D. (Lawyer)
*Arachne* - Lisa Mason  s  3661

Wolfe, Jacob (Reanimated Dead; Cyborg)
*Deathstalker Honor* - Simon R. Green  s  2364

Wolfe, Nero (Detective—Private)
*The D. Case: The Truth about the Mystery of Edwin
   Drood* - Charles Dickens  f  1524

Wolfe, Sara (Artist)
*The Venetian's Wife: A Strangely Sensual Tale of a
   Renaissance Explorer, a Computer, and a
   Metamorphosis* - Nick Bantock  f  336

Wolff, Hauptsturmfuhrer (Military Personnel;
   Vampire)
*Darkness on the Ice* - Lois Tilton  h  5475

Wolling, Jen (Scientist; Scholar)
*Earth* - David Brin  s  685

Wollstonecraft, Mary (Writer)
*Wall, Stone, Craft* - Walter Jon Williams  h  5842

Wolpin, Zev (Religious)
*Midnight Mass* - F. Paul Wilson  h  5891

Wolsey, Faye (Printer)
*The Palm Dome* - Liz Fulton  h  2094

Womack, Ewa (Worker)
*Chicago Loop* - Paul Theroux  h  5443

Womack, Jeff (Political Figure; Human)
*Brother Termite* - Patricia Anthony  s  156

Wong, Fritz (Director)
*A Graveyard for Lunatics* - Ray Bradbury  h  620

Wood, Alice (Businesswoman)
*Strange Devices of the Sun and Moon* - Lisa
   Goldstein  f  2262

Wood, Leo "Lobo" (Warrior)
*L.A. Strike* - David Robbins  s  4599

Wood, Max (Scientist; Activist)
*The Frightened Fish* - Kenneth Robeson  f  4622

Woodbury, Gillian (Journalist)
*Silent Moon* - William Relling Jr.  h  4531

Woodgate, Lisa (Ruler)
*Bretta Martyn* - L. Neil Smith  s  5128

Woodhouse, Andy (Religious)
*Son of Rosemary* - Ira Levin  h  3445

Woodley, Landis (Director)
*Big Rock Beat* - Greg Kihn  h  3102
*Horror Show* - Greg Kihn  h  3103

Woodrow, John (Architect)
*Torment* - Stephen R. George  h  2204

Woodrow, Melissa (Child; Musician)
*Torment* - Stephen R. George  h  2204

Woodruff, Bodeen (Police Officer)
*Happy Policeman* - Patricia Anthony  s  160

Woody (Parent; Lawyer)
*My Stepfather Shrank!* - Barbara Dillon  s  1558

Woolcott, Jeremy (Teenager)
*Along Came a Spider* - Athena Alexis  h  70

Wooster, Bertie (Gentleman)
*Scream for Jeeves: A Parody* - P.H. Cannon  h  867

Worabex (Magician)
*Red Unicorn* - Tanith Lee  f  3414

Worf (Alien; Military Personnel)
*Armageddon Sky* - L.A. Graf  s  2296

Worf (Military Personnel; Alien)
*Call to Arms* - Diane Carey  s  901

Worf (Military Personnel; Security Officer; Alien)
*Doomsday World* - Carmen Carter  s  923

Worf (Military Personnel; Alien)
*Kahless* - Michael Jan Friedman  s  2065
*Reunion* - Michael Jan Friedman  s  2068

Worf (Military Personnel; Fiance(e); Alien)
*Triangle: Imzadi II* - Peter David  s  1388

Worgan (Wizard)
*Wolf's Cub* - Mackay Wood  f  5964

Worsel (Alien)
*Galactic Patrol* - Edward E. Smith  s  5116
*Gray Lensman* - Edward E. Smith  s  5117

Wort (Handicapped)
*Tower of Doom* - Mark Anthony  h  155

Worth, Andrew (Journalist; Filmmaker)
*Distress* - Greg Egan  s  1760

Worthington, Buchanan "Bucky" (Actor)
*Bloody Waters* - B.L. Winters  h  5926

Worthington, John (Lawyer)
*Bloody Waters* - B.L. Winters  h  5926

Worthington, Kara Noble (Housewife)
*Bloody Waters* - B.L. Winters  h  5926

Wrasselty, Bleth (Genetically Altered Being)
*The Wells of Phyre* - L. Warren Douglas  s  1589

**Wrasselty, Slith** (Genetically Altered Being; Businessman)
*The Wells of Phyre* - L. Warren Douglas   s   1589

**Wratha, the Unrisen** (Vampire)
*Blood Brothers* - Brian Lumley   h   3546

**Wray, Helen** (Businesswoman)
*Omega* - Patrick Lynch   h   3577

**Wren** (Apprentice; Magician)
*The True Knight* - Susan Dexter   f   1513

**Wren** (Orphan; Adventurer; Magician)
*Wren to the Rescue* - Sherwood Smith   f   5142

**Wren** (Adventurer; Student; Orphan)
*Wren's Quest* - Sherwood Smith   f   5143

**Wren** (Adventurer; Magician; Orphan)
*Wren's War* - Sherwood Smith   f   5144

**Wren, Mason** (Doctor; Scientist)
*Alien Resurrection* - A.C. Crispin   s   1258

**Wright, Jimjoy Earle** (Spy)
*The Ecolitan Operation* - L.E. Modesitt Jr.   s   3928
*The Ecologic Secession* - L.E. Modesitt Jr.   s   3929

**Wright, Paul** (Journalist; Critic)
*Nightlight* - Michael Cadnum   h   813

**Wright, Tracy** (Teenager)
*The Uprising* - Abigail McDaniels   h   3785

**Writer** (Writer; Time Traveler)
*The Time Ships* - Stephen Baxter   s   403

**Writing Woman of Maho** (Writer; Landowner)
*Fish Soup* - Ursula K. Le Guin   f   3378

**Wroke, Alice** (Secretary; Spy)
*The Demon Princes: Volume Two* - Jack Vance   s   5545

**Wu, Kildee** (Martial Arts Expert; Teacher)
*Black Steel* - Steve Perry   s   4291

**Wu, Louis** (Adventurer)
*The Ringworld Throne* - Larry Niven   s   4128

**Wu, Nyima** (Actress; Military Personnel)
*Nothing Sacred* - Elizabeth Ann Scarborough   f   4867

**Wu, Oliver** (Immortal; Wanderer)
*Star Bridge* - James Gunn   s   2459

**Wu, Victor "Orf"** (Robot; Scientist)
*Earthling* - Tony Daniel   s   1336

**Wulf** (Artificial Intelligence; Writer)
*Wulfsyarn: A Mosaic* - Phillip Mann   s   3617

**Wulfgar** (Barbarian; Warrior)
*The Silent Blade* - R.A. Salvatore   f   4805

**Wulfrede** (Sailor; Warrior)
*Conan and the Treasure of Python* - John Maddox Roberts   f   4616

**Wurlitzer, Max** (Magician)
*Night Magic* - Thomas Tryon   h   5485

**Wurm** (Mythical Creature)
*The Wizardry Consulted* - Rick Cook   f   1161

**Wyatt, Adam** (Spirit)
*Superstition* - David Ambrose   h   90

**Wyatt, Ren** (Teacher)
*Storytellers* - Julie Anne Parks   h   4249

**Wycherley, Jenret** (Telepath)
*Exiles' Return* - Gayle Greeno   s   2420
*Mind-Speakers' Call* - Gayle Greeno   s   2423

**Wycliff, Walter** (Political Figure)
*The President's Astrologer* - Barbara Shafferman   f   4926

**Wyndon, Elbryan** (Teenager; Adventurer; Warrior)
*The Demon Awakens* - R.A. Salvatore   f   4794

**Wyndon, Elbryan** (Warrior; Adventurer)
*The Demon Spirit* - R.A. Salvatore   f   4795

**Wynett** (Royalty; Religious)
*The Usurper* - Angus Wells   f   5739
*The Way Beneath* - Angus Wells   f   5740

**Wynter** (Mythical Creature)
*Red Magic* - Jean Rabe   f   4458

**Wysaigh, "Wy"** (Pilot)
*Faraday's Orphans* - N. Lee Wood   s   5965

**Wyth** (Religious)
*Taminy* - Maya Kaathryn Bohnhoff   f   563

**Wyungare** (Shaman)
*Dealer's Choice* - George R.R. Martin   s   3643

**Wyvernspur, Finder "Nameless"** (Musician; Magician)
*Song of the Saurials* - Kate Novak   f   4167

# X

**X** (Criminal)
*The Diamond Age* - Neal Stephenson   s   5253

**X, Aaron** (Heir; Smuggler)
*Conglomeros* - Jesse Browner   f   729

**X, Brandon "Brand"** (Teenager)
*Killjoy* - Elizabeth Forrest   h   1973

**X "Brother Rush"** (Demon)
*Humans* - Donald E. Westlake   f   5768

**X-ray, Foxtrot "Fox"** (Mythical Creature; Magician)
*Chrome Circle* - Mercedes Lackey   f   3277

**X41** (Robot)
*Specterworld* - Isidore Haiblum   s   2480

**Xa** (Computer; Alien)
*The Fugitive Worlds* - Bob Shaw   s   4942

**X(A/N)ᵗʰ "Nimby"** (Demon; Handicapped)
*Yon Ill Wind* - Piers Anthony   f   196

**!Xabbu** (Traveler; Student)
*City of Golden Shadow* - Tad Williams   s   5828

**Xanthus** (Professor)
*The Fabulist* - John Vornholt   f   5595

**Xar** (Nobleman; Wizard)
*The Seventh Gate* - Margaret Weis   f   5727

**Xavier** (Religious)
*The Vampire Virus* - Michael Romkey   h   4668

**Xavier, Adolph** (Scientist)
*Mr. Sandman* - Lyle Howard   h   2779

**Xavier, Eileen** (Doctor)
*Godspeed* - Charles Sheffield   s   4957

**XB223** (Computer)
*The Red Tape War* - Jack L. Chalker   s   959

**Xena** (Warrior; Royalty)
*The Empty Throne* - Ru Emerson   f   1808
*The Thief of Hermes* - Ru Emerson   f   1811

**Xisor** (Organized Crime Figure)
*Shadows of the Empire* - Steve Perry   s   4299

**Xizor** (Royalty; Criminal)
*The Mandalorian Armor* - K.W. Jeter   s   2914

**Xris** (Cyborg; Mercenary)
*Knights of the Black Earth* - Margaret Weis   s   5718

**Xtasca the Cherub** (Alien; Genetically Altered Being)
*Mother of Plenty* - Colin Greenland   s   2417

**Xtasca the Cherub** (Genetically Altered Being)
*Seasons of Plenty* - Colin Greenland   s   2418

**Xu-Tzu, Phan** (Spy; Scientist)
*Celestial Matters* - Richard Garfinkle   s   2140

**Xylina** (Orphan; Young Woman)
*If I Pay Thee Not in Gold* - Piers Anthony   f   176

# Y

**Ya-Mash, Yam** (Sidekick; Alien)
*The Return of the Breakneck Boys* - Geary Gravel   s   2332

**Yaeylie, Frenna** (Slave; Genetically Altered Being)
*Hand of Prophecy* - Severna Park   s   4244

**Yail, Jiron** (Police Officer)
*The Glaive* - Cary Osborne   s   4227

**Yaksha** (Demon)
*The Last Vampire* - Christopher Pike   h   4328

**Yalso** (Scholar; Adventurer)
*Dragon Tome* - Richard A. Knaak   f   3169

**Yamaguchi, Motofusa** (Doctor; Administrator)
*Half Asleep in Frog Pajamas* - Tom Robbins   s   4606

**Yambu** (Aged Person; Royalty)
*Wayfinder's Story: The Seventh Book of Lost Swords* - Fred Saberhagen   f   4777

**Yamun** (Royalty)
*Horselords* - David Cook   f   1145

**Yang** (Spirit)
*Unicorn U.* - Esther Friesner   f   2084

**Yaroslavich, Yuri** (Slave)
*Terrible Swift Sword* - William R. Forstchen   s   1983

**Yates, Sam** (Police Officer)
*Target* - Janet Morris   s   4017

**Yatima** (Artificial Intelligence; Orphan)
*Diaspora* - Greg Egan   s   1759

**Yatt** (Artificial Intelligence)
*A Screaming Across the Sky* - Brian Daley   s   1315

**Ye Armonk, Louise** (Engineer; Leader)
*Ring* - Stephen Baxter   s   402

**Yeager, Elizabeth** (Spacewoman)
*Rimrunners* - C.J. Cherryh   s   1001

**Yeager, Galen** (Government Official)
*The Sounding Stillness* - Kenneth Von Gunden   s   5587

**Yeager, Max** (Engineer)
*The Gatekeepers* - Daniel Graham Jr.   s   2301

**Yeager, Pauli** (Pilot; Military Personnel)
*Heritage of Flight* - Susan Shwartz   s   5016

**Yeager, Sam** (Military Personnel)
*Worldwar: In the Balance* - Harry Turtledove   s   5515
*Worldwar: Upsetting the Balance* - Harry Turtledove   s   5518

**Yellow Hare** (Military Personnel)
*Celestial Matters* - Richard Garfinkle   s   2140

**Ygorla** (Sorceress; Ruler; Demon)
*The Avenger* - Louise Cooper   f   1174

**Ygorla** (Demon; Sorceress; Ruler)
*The Deceiver* - Louise Cooper   f   1175

**Yildiz** (Ruler)
*Conan of the Red Brotherhood* - Leonard Carpenter   f   906

**Ying, Soong Mei** (Traveler; Adventurer)
*The Discovery of Dragons* - Graeme Base   f   385

**Ylon** (Royalty; Handicapped)
*Mirror of Destiny* - Andre Norton   f   4159

**Yocote** (Shaman; Mythical Creature)
*The Sage* - Christopher Stasheff   f   5221

**Yod** (Android)
*He, She and It* - Marge Piercy   s   4325

**Yokusuka, Jory** (Journalist)
*Berserker Fury* - Fred Saberhagen   *s*   4760

**Yont, Felicity "Lissy"** (Librarian)
*Homebody* - Orson Scott Card   *h*   890

**Yor** (Warrior; Adventurer)
*Captains Outrageous, or, For Doom the Bell Tolls* -
  Roy V. Young   *f*   6049

**York, Dennison** (Mercenary; Hero)
*Thoughts of God* - Michael Kanaly   *s*   3007

**York, Natalie** (Scientist)
*Voyager* - Stephen Baxter   *s*   406

**York, Nathaniel** (Spaceship Captain)
*The Martian Chronicles* - Ray Bradbury   *s*   622

**Yoseph** (Artificial Intelligence)
*Terminal Logic* - Jefferson Scott   *s*   4893

**Yoshida, Dorthy** (Psychic)
*Eternal Light* - Paul J. McAuley   *s*   3710

**Yoshino, Bill** (Vampire)
*The Vampire Odyssey* - Scott Ciencin   *h*   1032

**Yoshio, Ikawa** (Military Personnel; Warrior)
*The Crystal Sorcerers* - William R.
  Forstchen   *f*   1979

**Young, Beau** (Musician)
*Big Rock Beat* - Greg Kihn   *h*   3102

**Young, Francesca** (Computer Expert)
*Streets of Blood* - Carl Sargent   *f*   4821

**Young, Janet** (Artist)
*Breeder* - Ed Kelleher   *h*   3041

**Young, "Mighty" Joe** (Pilot; Spaceman)
*Lunar Descent* - Allen Steele   *s*   5245

**Young, Miranda Jane** (Teenager)
*Breeder* - Ed Kelleher   *h*   3041

**Young, Pat** (Invalid)
*Obsessed* - Rick R. Reed   *h*   4500

**Young, Pavel** (Nobleman)
*Field of Dishonor* - David Weber   *s*   5670

**Young, Samson** (Writer)
*London Fields* - Martin Amis   *s*   95

**Young Hunter** (Prehistoric Human; Teenager)
*Dawn Land* - Joseph Bruchac   *f*   731

**Younger, Jesse "Cole"** (Police Officer)
*Rockabilly Hell* - William W. Johnstone   *h*   2933
*Rockabilly Limbo* - William W. Johnstone   *h*   2934

**Youngman, Cai** (Nobleman)
*The Dragon's Boy* - Jane Yolen   *f*   6030

**Yrae** (Alien; Actress)
*Legacy of Earth* - Juanita Coulson   *s*   1209

**Yrarier, Marjorie Westriding** (Diplomat)
*Grass* - Sheri S. Tepper   *s*   5431

**Ysidro, Don Simon** (Vampire)
*Those Who Hunt the Night* - Barbara
  Hambly   *h*   2510

**Yspht, Jovil** (Alien)
*Armageddon: The Musical* - Robert Rankin   *s*   4473

**Ystilog, Erpad** (Museum Curator)
*Brotherhood of the Stars* - Kirby Greene   *s*   2414

**Ysuna** (Religious; Prehistoric Human)
*The Sacred Stones* - William Sarabande   *f*   4818

**Yuan, Li** (Heir; Royalty)
*The Middle Kingdom* - David Wingrove   *s*   5919

**Yuan, Li** (Leader)
*The Stone Within* - David Wingrove   *s*   5920
*The White Mountain* - David Wingrove   *s*   5922

**Yukiko "Yuki"** (Detective—Amateur)
*Tea From an Empty Cup* - Pat Cadigan   *s*   809

**Yvette of Grintz** (Runaway; Noblewoman)
*The Pixilated Peeress* - L. Sprague de
  Camp   *f*   1416

# Z

**Zach** (Teacher; Student)
*Ecstasy Club* - Douglas Rushkoff   *s*   4732

**Zacharias, John Furie "Gentle"** (Artist)
*Imajica* - Clive Barker   *h*   343

**Zacharias, Michael** (Musician)
*Lost Futures* - Lisa Tuttle   *s*   5520

**Zachary** (Reanimated Dead; Criminal)
*Guilty Pleasures* - Laurell K. Hamilton   *f*   2517

**Zady** (Witch)
*Mouvar's Magic* - Piers Anthony   *f*   182
*Orc's Opal* - Piers Anthony   *f*   183

**Zagala** (Witch; Gypsy)
*Yesterday We Saw Mermaids* - Esther
  Friesner   *f*   2086

**Zahag** (Animal)
*Queen of Demons* - David Drake   *f*   1640

**Zahmekoses** (Alien; Space Explorer)
*Encounter with Tiber* - Buzz Aldrin   *s*   64

**Zainal** (Alien; Settler)
*Freedom's Challenge* - Anne McCaffrey   *s*   3732
*Freedom's Choice* - Anne McCaffrey   *s*   3733
*Freedom's Landing* - Anne McCaffrey   *s*   3734

**Zakalwe, Cheradenine** (Spy; Mercenary)
*Use of Weapons* - Iain M. Banks   *s*   328

**Zakharov, Aelita** (Astronaut)
*Night Launch* - Jake Garn   *s*   2143

**Zakri** (Psychic; Singer)
*Sing the Warmth* - Louise Marley   *s*   3630

**Zalewski, Petra** (Student—College; Adventurer)
*Footprints of Thunder* - James F. David   *s*   1379

**Zal'honan, Firan** (Sorcerer)
*King of the Dead* - Gene DeWeese   *h*   1510

**Zalman** (Religious)
*A Blessing on the Moon* - Joseph Skibell   *f*   5079

**Zaman** (Servant)
*Viper* - Alan Riefe   *h*   4589

**Zambelli, Ruggerio** (Scientist)
*From Prussia with Love* - John DeChancie   *f*   1457

**Zambendorf, Karl** (Psychic; Magician)
*The Immortality Option* - James P. Hogan   *s*   2725

**Zamiatin, Mark "Visual Mark"** (Artist)
*Synners* - Pat Cadigan   *s*   808

**Zandramas** (Sorceress)
*The Seeress of Kell* - David Eddings   *f*   1738

**Zandro, Taverik** (Businessman)
*Hawk's Flight* - Carol Chase   *f*   980

**Zant, Quasar** (Socialite; Wealthy)
*Quasar* - Jamil Nasir   *s*   4071

**Zapata, Carmen** (Housekeeper)
*Panic* - Chris Curry   *h*   1295

**Zapata, Xolotl** (Fugitive; Artist)
*High Aztec* - Ernest Hogan   *s*   2722

**Zarnicke, Marion** (Journalist)
*A World Lost* - James B. Johnson   *s*   2921

**Zaula** (Alien; Noblewoman)
*Requiem for Anthi* - Jay D. Blakeney   *s*   517

**Zebara** (Spaceship Captain)
*The Death of Sleep* - Anne McCaffrey   *s*   3727

**Zeeman, Richard** (Werewolf; Student; Teacher)
*Blue Moon* - Laurell K. Hamilton   *h*   2513

**Zeeman, Richard** (Werewolf; Teacher)
*The Killing Dance* - Laurell K. Hamilton   *h*   2518
*The Lunatic Cafe* - Laurell K. Hamilton   *h*   2520

**Zeenoson, Dref** (Revolutionary)
*Illusion* - Paula Volsky   *f*   5582

**Zeerus** (Alien; Criminal)
*Target Earth* - Steve Perry   *s*   4301

**Zellorian** (Wizard)
*Mother of Storms* - Adrian Cole   *f*   1101

**Zellorian** (Political Figure; Scientist)
*Warlord of Heaven* - Adrian Cole   *f*   1102

**Zennor** (Alien; Spaceship Captain)
*First Strike* - Diane Carey   *s*   903

**Zeno, Mrs.** (Disembodied Personality)
*Max Lakeman and the Beautiful Stranger* - Jon
  Cohen   *f*   1098

**Zephkar** (Alien; Disembodied Personality)
*Stranded* - Camarin Grae   *s*   2295

**Zephyr** (Mythical Creature)
*Fool on the Hill* - Matt Ruff   *f*   4707

**Zeq, Ahmad** (Space Explorer)
*The Transmigration of Souls* - William
  Barton   *s*   382

**Zeree, Dru** (Sorcerer)
*Children of the Drake* - Richard A. Knaak   *f*   3166

**Zeree, Dru** (Sorcerer; Immigrant)
*The Shrouded Realm* - Richard A. Knaak   *f*   3174

**Zeus** (Royalty)
*Sons of the Titans* - Patrick H. Adkins   *f*   36

**Zhadnoboth** (Sorcerer)
*A Name to Conjure With* - Donald Aamodt   *f*   3
*A Troubling Along the Border* - Donald Aamodt   *f*   4

**Zhang** (Military Personnel; Explorer)
*Shangri-La: The Return to the World of Lost Horizon* -
  Eleanor Cooney   *f*   1169

**Zhiming, Lao** (Military Personnel)
*Crossroad* - Barbara Hambly   *s*   2501

**Zhu Wong** (Time Traveler; Revolutionary)
*The Golden Nineties* - Lisa Mason   *s*   3663

**Zhukovsky, Dmitry** (Spaceman; Hero)
*Peter Nevsky and the True Story of the Russian Moon
  Landing* - John Calvin Batchelor   *s*   388

**Ziemann, Mia** (Noblewoman)
*Holy Fire* - Bruce Sterling   *s*   5259

**Zigmunn** (Spaceman; Outcast)
*Brotherhood of the Stars* - Kirby Greene   *s*   2414

**Zigramson, Thorolf** (Scholar; Military Personnel)
*The Pixilated Peeress* - L. Sprague de
  Camp   *f*   1416

**Zillabar** (Noblewoman; Vampire)
*A Covenant of Justice* - David Gerrold   *s*   2207

**Zillah** (Vampire)
*Lost Souls* - Poppy Z. Brite   *h*   697

**Zimmerman, Christopher** (Adventurer; Time
  Traveler)
*Panda Ray* - Michael Kandel   *s*   3011

**Zimmerman, Debra** (Parent)
*Panda Ray* - Michael Kandel   *s*   3011

**Zimmerman, Rick** (Bodyguard)
*Unearthed* - Ashley McConnell   *h*   3778

**Zinixo** (Mythical Creature; Wizard)
*The Living God* - Dave Duncan   *f*   1682
*The Stricken Field* - Dave Duncan   *f*   1688
*Upland Outlaws* - Dave Duncan   *f*   1690

**Zinser, Jacob** (Collector)
*St. Peter's Wolf* - Michael Cadnum    *h*   816

**Zivic, Leland** (Photographer)
*From the Teeth of Angels* - Jonathan Carroll    *h*   918

**Zobolotsky, Katrina** (Adventurer)
*Indiana Jones and the Genesis Deluge* - Rob
    MacGregor    *f*   3589

**Zobolotsky, Vladimir** (Doctor; Adventurer)
*Indiana Jones and the Genesis Deluge* - Rob
    MacGregor    *f*   3589

**Zodiac, Jack** (Drug Dealer)
*Captain Jack Zodiac* - Michael Kandel    *f*   3009

**Zodiac, Saskia** (Clone)
*Mother of Plenty* - Colin Greenland    *s*   2417

**Zodiac, Saskia** (Clone; Magician)
*Seasons of Plenty* - Colin Greenland    *s*   2418

**Zoe** (Teenager; Student)
*The Silver Kiss* - Annette Curtis Klause    *f*   3163

**Zoe** (Child)
*Stonewords: A Ghost Story* - Pam Conrad    *f*   1138

**Zo'e'minira "Zoe"** (Supernatural Being)
*The Duke of Sumava* - Sara J. Wrench    *f*   5983

**Zofia** (Prisoner)
*Hard Crash* - Ryan Hughes    *s*   2810

**Zolotin, Peter** (Student—Graduate; Spaceman)
*Burster* - Michael Capobianco    *s*   876

**Zoltan** (Royalty; Traveler)
*Wayfinder's Story: The Seventh Book of Lost Swords* -
    Fred Saberhagen    *f*   4777

**Zooty** (Entertainer)
*Day of the Dead* - Neil Gaiman    *s*   2102

**Zorah** (Ruler)
*Beldan's Fire* - Midori Snyder    *f*   5150

**Zorander, Zeddicus "Zedd" Zu'l** (Wizard)
*Stone of Tears* - Terry Goodkind    *f*   2269

**Zorba the Hutt** (Alien; Parent)
*Zorba the Hutt's Revenge* - Paul Davids    *s*   1394

**Zorg** (Alien)
*Living with Aliens* - John DeChancie    *s*   1460

**Zorin, Lavrenti Borisovich** (Military Personnel;
    Revolutionary)
*Branch Point* - Mona Clee    *s*   1074

**zu Blas und Fiersing, Dalain "Wisp"** (Nobleman)
*An Exchange of Gifts* - Anne McCaffrey    *f*   3731

**Zuchmul** (Vampire)
*Dreamspy* - Jacqueline Lichtenberg    *s*   3458

**Zumwalt, William Irving "Wiz"** (Computer Expert;
    Wizard; Witch)
*The Wiz Biz* - Rick Cook    *f*   1160

**Zumwalt, William Irving "Wiz"** (Computer Expert;
    Wizard)
*The Wizardry Consulted* - Rick Cook    *f*   1161
*The Wizardry Cursed* - Rick Cook    *f*   1162
*The Wizardry Quested* - Rick Cook    *f*   1163

**Zurvan** (Scholar)
*Servant of the Bones* - Anne Rice    *h*   4575

**Zurzal** (Alien; Historian)
*Brother to Shadows* - Andre Norton    *s*   4142

**Zverkov, Alexey** (Psychic)
*Spellcaster* - J. Edward Ames    *h*   92

**Zwakh, Ignatz** (Addict; Refugee)
*Dead Boys* - Richard Calder    *s*   836

**Zwakh, Ignatz** (Fugitive)
*Dead Girls* - Richard Calder    *s*   837

**Zwakh, Ignatz** (Revolutionary; Addict)
*Dead Things* - Richard Calder    *s*   838

**Zyto, Michael** (Serial Killer)
*Machine* - Rene Belletto    *h*   436

# Character Description Index

This index alphabetically lists descriptions of the major characters in featured titles. The descriptions may be occupations (astronaut, lawyer, etc.) or may describe personas (recluse, feminist, occultist, etc.). For each description, character names are listed alphabetically. Also provided are book titles, author names, and entry numbers.

## ABUSE VICTIM

**Akma**
*Earthborn* - Orson Scott Card   s   884

**Calderon, Mercedes**
*Solip: System* - Walter Jon Williams   s   5841

**Daniels, Rose McLendon**
*Rose Madder* - Stephen King   h   3139

**Dennessy, Anne**
*The Darkness Within* - Shawn MacDonald   h   3585

**Dennessy, Beth**
*The Darkness Within* - Shawn MacDonald   h   3585

**Dennessy, Carol**
*The Darkness Within* - Shawn MacDonald   h   3585

**Domon, Tamrissa**
*Convergence* - Sharon Green   f   2356

**Gael, Dorothy "Dotty"**
*Was* - Geoff Ryman   f   4758

**Gray, Emma**
*Flying in Place* - Susan Palwick   h   4240

**Kendrick, Amanda**
*When the Bough Breaks* - Mercedes Lackey   f   3302

**Lee**
*The Jigsaw Woman* - Kim Antieau   f   199

**Malone, Kevin**
*The Kingdom of Kevin Malone* - Suzy McKee Charnas   f   970

**Mathen**
*The Time of Madness* - Thomas K. Martin   f   3652

**Miriam**
*The Spirit Stalker* - Nina Romberg   h   4664

**O'Hallahan, Emma Delaney**
*What's Wrong with America* - Scott Bradfield   h   627

**Perez, Magdalena**
*Voices of Chaos* - A.C. Crispin   s   1266

**Sari**
*O Greenest Branch!* - Gael Baudino   f   394

**Shido, Jamisia "Jamie Capra"**
*This Alien Shore* - C.S. Friedman   s   2059

**Stafford, Yvonne**
*Thoughts of God* - Michael Kanaly   s   3007

**Steven**
*The Night Man* - K.W. Jeter   h   2915

**Therru**
*Tehanu: The Last Book of Earthsea* - Ursula K. Le Guin   f   3383

## ACCOUNTANT

**Beckett, Clare**
*Lost Futures* - Lisa Tuttle   s   5520

**Boren, Troy**
*Blindfold* - Kevin J. Anderson   s   101

**Calder, Charlotte**
*Tempter* - Nancy A. Collins   h   1125

**Callahan, Mardie**
*Sweet Revenge* - Jean Simon   h   5066

**Chapel, Helen**
*Red Bride* - Christopher Fowler   h   2019

**Evans, Bill "Bill the Just"**
*The League of the Crimson Crescent* - James E. Reagen   f   4495

**Jordan, Greg**
*Wind Chimes* - R.R. Walters   h   5625

**Lindo, Sigrid**
*The Moon's Wife: A Hystery* - A.A. Attanasio   f   271

**MacKelston, Kathleen**
*The Barrens* - F. Paul Wilson   h   5884

**Martin, Gene**
*Hellcat* - Amanda Kingsley   h   3145

**McCall, Cassie**
*Black Ice* - Pat Graversen   h   2333

**Opal**
*A Chill in the Blood* - P.N. Elrod   h   1793

**Quinsonnas**
*Paris in the Twentieth Century* - Jules Verne   s   5568

**Wakelin, John**
*Holy Terror* - Josephine Boyle   h   608

## ACTIVIST

**Ahrens, Bleys**
*Other* - Gordon R. Dickson   s   1538
*Young Bleys* - Gordon R. Dickson   s   1540

**Ahrens, Dahno**
*Young Bleys* - Gordon R. Dickson   s   1540

**Archangel**
*Tropic of Orange* - Karen Tei Yamashita   f   6009

**Burnell**
*Somewhere East of Life* - Brian W. Aldiss   s   60

**Candle, Martin**
*Blameless in Abaddon* - James Morrow   f   4029

**Carson, Roberta**
*Rogue Star* - Michael Flynn   s   1965

**Darffot, Tex "Bear"**
*Tex and Molly in the Afterlife* - Richard Grant   f   2327

**Devane, Elizabeth**
*The Trinity Paradox* - Kevin J. Anderson   s   116

**Dobbs, J.R. "BoB"**
*Reality Is What You Can Get Away With: An Illustrated Screenplay* - Robert Anton Wilson   s   5904

**Dodge, Allison**
*Gaia's Toys* - Rebecca Ore   s   4218

**Edmonds, Sarah Emma "Kite"**
*Sewer, Gas & Electric* - Matt Ruff   s   4708

**Elphaba**
*Wicked: The Life and Times of the Wicked Witch of the West* - Gregory Maguire   f   3609

**Etanl, Latona**
*Alien Influences* - Kristine Kathryn Rusch   s   4711

**Fine, Joan**
*Sewer, Gas & Electric* - Matt Ruff   s   4708

**Greeley, Dan**
*The Drylands* - Mary Rosenblum   s   4678

**Guerner, Margaret "Peggy"**
*Alvin Journeyman* - Orson Scott Card   f   881

**Hogopian, Aaron**
*Playing God* - Sarah Zettel   s   6080

**Jephthah**
*To Fear the Light* - Ben Bova   s   595

**Jeremiah**
*The Quiet Pools* - Michael P. Kube-McDowell   s   3249

**Kazenstein, Morris**
*Sewer, Gas & Electric* - Matt Ruff   s   4708

**Lu, Antonia "Toni"**
*Other* - Gordon R. Dickson   s   1538

**Lyell, Thomasina**
*The Pure Cold Light* - Gregory Frost   s   2087

**Marm, Everett C. "Harlequin"**
*"Repent, Harlequin!" Said the Ticktockman* - Harlan Ellison　*s*　1782

**Miller, Margaret "Peggy"**
*Heartfire* - Orson Scott Card　*f*　889

**Molly**
*Tex and Molly in the Afterlife* - Richard Grant　*f*　2327

**Montoya, Alyssa**
*The Planet Beyond* - Steve Mudd　*s*　4043

**Norton**
*Steel Rose* - Kara Dalkey　*f*　1321

**Ralph**
*Steel Rose* - Kara Dalkey　*f*　1321

**Schlessinger, David**
*The Secret Oceans* - Betty Ballantine　*s*　318

**Spotted Horse, David**
*Sacred Ground* - Mercedes Lackey　*f*　3294

**Stiller, Warreven "Raven"**
*Shadow Man* - Melissa Scott　*s*　4900

**Stone, Edwin L. "Ed"**
*Why Do Birds* - Damon Knight　*s*　3190

**Voskresenye, Pavel Sergeyevich**
*The Fortunate Fall* - Raphael Carter　*s*　927

**Waverly, Tim**
*Outworld Cats* - Jack Lovejoy　*s*　3536

**Wood, Max**
*The Frightened Fish* - Kenneth Robeson　*f*　4622

## ACTOR

**Agranovsky, Reuven**
*Further Adventures* - Jon Stephen Fink　*f*　1940

**Amby**
*Merlin's Bones* - Fred Saberhagen　*f*　4771

**Arnix, Gherifan**
*The Illusionists* - Faren Miller　*f*　3894

**Boofuls**
*Mirror* - Graham Masterton　*h*　3677

**Burbage, Horace**
*A Company of Stars* - Christopher Stasheff　*s*　5215

**Burns, Marty**
*Burning Bright* - J.S. Russell　*h*　4733

**Carl**
*The Arbitrary Placement of Walls* - Martha Soukup　*f*　5165

**Carlton, Billy**
*Cemetery of Angels* - Noel Hynd　*h*　2821

**Carter, Jeremy**
*Cat-A-Lyst* - Alan Dean Foster　*s*　1997

**Cochrane, Richard**
*Time and Chance* - Alan Brennert　*f*　676

**Corea, Jake**
*Created By* - Richard Christian Matheson　*h*　3691

**Cree, John**
*The Trial of Elizabeth Cree* - Peter Ackroyd　*h*　26

**Dean, James**
*Spyder* - Norman Partridge　*h*　4255

**Doshky "Dosh"**
*Crashcourse* - Wilhelmina Baird　*s*　295

**Driver, Greg**
*Horrorshow* - David Darke　*h*　1353

**Dzierlatka, Martin**
*Bereavement* - Richard Lortz　*h*　3525

**Eklunk, Hans-Bjorn "Mokey/Moke"**
*Clipjoint* - Wilhelmina Baird　*s*　294
*Crashcourse* - Wilhelmina Baird　*s*　295

**Fabrizio**
*The Innamorati* - Midori Snyder　*f*　5152

**Faraday, Richard**
*Diplomatic Act* - Peter Jurasik　*s*　2996

**Finesse, Adrian**
*Star Prey* - Ehren M. Ehly　*h*　1763

**Gable, Clark**
*Who P-P-Plugged Roger Rabbit?* - Gary K. Wolf　*f*　5934

**Gersten, Clovis**
*Golden Eyes* - John Gideon　*h*　2220

**Griffin, Nic**
*The Ruby Tear* - Rebecca Brand　*h*　660

**Hamilton, Dennis**
*Reign* - Chet Williamson　*h*　5849

**Hamlet**
*Too, Too Solid Flesh* - Nick O'Donohoe　*s*　4197

**Higginson, Alice**
*Painted Devil* - Michael Bedard　*f*　430

**Horatio**
*Too, Too Solid Flesh* - Nick O'Donohoe　*s*　4197

**Jim**
*Horrorshow* - David Darke　*h*　1353

**Jordan**
*Blood and Honor* - Simon R. Green　*f*　2361

**Karloff, Boris**
*Father of Frankenstein* - Christopher Bram　*h*　659

**Koster, Laurence "Larry"**
*Preternatural* - Margaret Wander Bonanno　*s*　568

**Larkspur, Evan**
*The Unwound Way* - William Adams　*s*　35

**Leno, Dan**
*The Trial of Elizabeth Cree* - Peter Ackroyd　*h*　26

**Leonard, Wyatt**
*From the Teeth of Angels* - Jonathan Carroll　*h*　918

**Lerille, Jack**
*Paddywhack* - John Stchur　*h*　5236

**Maroc, Huud**
*The Merro Tree* - Katie Waitman　*s*　5609

**Mikk**
*The Merro Tree* - Katie Waitman　*s*　5609

**Montana, Kent**
*668: The Neighbor of the Beast* - Lionel Fenn　*h*　1917
*Kent Montana and the Really Ugly Thing From Mars* - Lionel Fenn　*s*　1918
*Kent Montana and the Reasonably Invisible Man* - Lionel Fenn　*s*　1919
*The Mark of the Moderately Vicious Vampire* - Lionel Fenn　*h*　1920

**Neimark, Max**
*Preternatural* - Margaret Wander Bonanno　*s*　568

**Passepout**
*The Mage in the Iron Mask* - Brian Thomsen　*f*　5458

**Rabbit, Roger**
*Who P-P-Plugged Roger Rabbit?* - Gary K. Wolf　*f*　5934

**Rafiel**
*Outnumbering the Dead* - Frederik Pohl　*s*　4352

**Reagan, Ronald "Dutch"**
*Time on My Hands* - Peter Delacorte　*s*　1480

**Reesone, Donald**
*Near Death* - Nancy Kilpatrick　*h*　3113

**Reid, David Henry**
*Stainless* - Todd Grimson　*h*　2449

**Savoy**
*Fools* - Pat Cadigan　*s*　805

**Stanislaus, Glynn Webster**
*Mind Snare* - Gayle Greeno　*s*　2422

**Stratton, Thomas**
*Facade* - Kristine Kathryn Rusch　*h*　4716

**Thudd, Dennis "Druzeppa"**
*Horrorshow* - David Darke　*h*　1353

**Todd, Angel**
*Valentine* - S.P. Somtow　*h*　5160

**Tyler, Griffin**
*I Was a Teenage Fairy* - Francesca Lia Block　*f*　549

**Valentine, John Barrymore**
*The Golden Globe* - John Varley　*s*　5565

**Valentine, Kenneth "Sparky"**
*The Golden Globe* - John Varley　*s*　5565

**Weston, James**
*October* - Al Sarrantonio　*h*　4832

**Worthington, Buchanan "Bucky"**
*Bloody Waters* - B.L. Winters　*h*　5926

## ACTRESS

**Alis**
*Remake* - Connie Willis　*s*　5873

**Alison/Nicholas**
*The Need* - Andrew Neiderman　*h*　4089

**Arno, Phyllis**
*Deathchain* - Ken Greenhall　*h*　2415

**Blaine, Cassandra "Cass"**
*Clipjoint* - Wilhelmina Baird　*s*　294
*Crashcourse* - Wilhelmina Baird　*s*　295

**Brooke-Holt, Diana**
*An Earthly Crown* - Kate Elliott　*s*　1771

**Carlson, Annette**
*Ghosts* - Noel Hynd　*h*　2822

**Cave, Clea/Richard**
*The Need* - Andrew Neiderman　*h*　4089

**Cree, Elizabeth**
*The Trial of Elizabeth Cree* - Peter Ackroyd　*h*　26

**Croft, Jessamyn**
*The Ruby Tear* - Rebecca Brand　*h*　660

**De Corizo, Ixoro**
*Red Bride* - Christopher Fowler　*h*　2019

**Dellon, Melusine "Sinah"**
*Gravelight* - Marion Zimmer Bradley　*f*　636

**Famande, Chrysanda "Christine"**
*Bride of the Rat God* - Barbara Hambly　*f*　2499

**Fletcher, Mary Lisa**
*Night Games* - Marilyn Harris　*h*　2562

**Ford, Arlen**
*From the Teeth of Angels* - Jonathan Carroll　*h*　918

**Jamal**
*Masquerades* - Kate Novak　*f*　4166

**James, Dallas**
*Spirit Catcher* - Elizabeth Hallam　*f*　2497

**Lagenkamp, Heather**
*Wes Craven's New Nightmare* - David Bergantino　*h*　460

**Love, Larissa "Lara"**
*The Shift* - George Foy　*s*　2033

**Milena**
*The Child Garden* - Geoff Ryman　*s*　4756

**Pan, Miss Scarlet**
*Winterlong* - Elizabeth Hand　*s*　2539

**Rattigan, Constance**
*Death Is a Lonely Business* - Ray Bradbury   *h*   619

**Rowland, Althea**
*Timeshare* - Joshua Dann   *s*   1344

**Ruthven, Lucy**
*Slave of My Thirst* - Tom Holland   *h*   2742

**Souci, Suzanne**
*A Company of Stars* - Christopher Stasheff   *s*   5215
*We Open on Venus* - Christopher Stasheff   *s*   5227

**Stanislaus, Jerelynn**
*Mind Snare* - Gayle Greeno   *s*   2422

**Taylor, Diana Lee**
*Fantastique* - Marvin Kaye   *h*   3025

**Trilling, Kate**
*The Invisible Company* - Scott Russell
  Sanders   *s*   4813

**Van Dorne, Chesna "Echo"**
*The Wolf's Hour* - Robert R. McCammon   *h*   3759

**Varney, Haldis "Hally"**
*Stone Dead* - Ellen Jamison   *h*   2878

**Waterhouse, Mary Ann "Synthi Venture"**
*Mother of Storms* - John Barnes   *s*   354

**Weatherby, Tamsin**
*Star Prey* - Ehren M. Ehly   *h*   1763

**Winters, Angelica**
*Fantastique* - Marvin Kaye   *h*   3025

**Wu, Nyima**
*Nothing Sacred* - Elizabeth Ann
  Scarborough   *f*   4867

**Yrae**
*Legacy of Earth* - Juanita Coulson   *s*   1209

## ACTUARY

**Halkin, Oliver**
*Prophecy* - Peter James   *h*   2874

## ADDICT

**Arity "Ari"**
*Delta City* - Felicity Savage   *f*   4849

**Chen, Harry**
*The Seraphim Rising* - Elisabeth De Vos   *s*   1442

**Claudia**
*The Hanged Man* - Francesca Lia Block   *f*   548

**Dean, Eddie**
*The Drawing of the Three* - Stephen King   *h*   3131
*The Waste Lands* - Stephen King   *h*   3143

**Derveet**
*Flowerdust* - Gwyneth Jones   *s*   2952

**Jack**
*The Hanged Man* - Francesca Lia Block   *f*   548

**Karpov, Sapphire**
*Putting Up Roots* - Charles Sheffield   *s*   4964

**Lily**
*Ecstasia* - Francesca Lia Block   *f*   547

**Lindy**
*Wolf Flow* - K.W. Jeter   *h*   2918

**Maxwell, Scott**
*Relife* - Dan Barton   *h*   376

**Stephen "Scribble"**
*Vurt* - Jeff Noon   *s*   4136

**Zwakh, Ignatz**
*Dead Boys* - Richard Calder   *s*   836
*Dead Things* - Richard Calder   *s*   838

## ADMINISTRATOR

**Agonostis**
*Sympathy for the Devil* - Holly Lisle   *f*   3488

**Armstrong, Augustus "Gus"**
*Martian Rainbow* - Robert L. Forward   *s*   1987

**Arvin, Andro**
*Starfire Down* - Lee McKeone   *s*   3830

**Bascombe, John**
*The Reign of the Brown Magician* - Lawrence Watt-
  Evans   *f*   5647

**Bathespeake, Jason**
*ME: A Novel of Self Discovery* - Thomas T.
  Thomas   *s*   5452

**Becker, Gilbert**
*The Streeter* - Scott Ian Barry   *h*   373

**Bigelow, Walter T.**
*Journals of the Plague Years* - Norman
  Spinrad   *s*   5172

**Black Amber**
*Human to Human* - Rebecca Ore   *s*   4219

**Bomarigala**
*GodHeads* - Emily Devenport   *s*   1501

**Bonifant, "Mr. Bones"**
*Brother to Dragons* - Charles Sheffield   *s*   4949

**Cairo, Alya**
*This Alien Shore* - C.S. Friedman   *s*   2059

**Campbell, Laicy "Iroshi"**
*The Glaive* - Cary Osborne   *s*   4227

**Cedar, Hugh Rock**
*Fossil* - Hal Clement   *s*   1083

**Chalmers, Frank**
*Red Mars* - Kim Stanley Robinson   *s*   4635

**Cohn, Milton**
*Superstitious* - R.L. Stine   *h*   5290

**Crawford, Lee**
*Dark Genesis* - J. Gregory Keyes   *s*   3096

**DalLierx, Lindon**
*Shivering World* - Kathy Tyers   *s*   5526

**deJanes, Ecktor**
*Adiamante* - L.E. Modesitt Jr.   *s*   3924

**Doheny, Mike**
*Sunstroke* - David Kagan   *s*   2999

**Dorvin, Jan**
*The War of the Sky Lords* - John Brosnan   *s*   721

**Downey, Tressa**
*Golden Eyes* - John Gideon   *h*   2220

**Dvorak, Jason**
*Assemblers of Infinity* - Kevin J. Anderson   *s*   100

**L'Enfant, Terrance**
*Labyrinth of Night* - Allen Steele   *s*   5244

**Farraday, Morgan**
*The Snows of Jaspre* - Mary Caraker   *s*   878

**Fasner, Holt "The Dragon"**
*The Gap into Power: A Dark and Hungry God Arises*
  - Stephen R. Donaldson   *s*   1574

**Flanagan, Jeffrey**
*Lords of Creation* - Tim Sullivan   *s*   5351

**Flynn, Beth**
*Substitute Teacher* - Jordan Storm   *h*   5314

**Frank-I-STN-4**
*Title Deleted for Security Reasons* - Ed
  Blome   *s*   553

**Gable, Robert**
*Serpent's Gift* - A.C. Crispin   *s*   1261
*Starbridge* - A.C. Crispin   *s*   1265
*Voices of Chaos* - A.C. Crispin   *s*   1266

**Gerenz, Frederick**
*Dead Heat* - Del Stone Jr.   *h*   5313

**Girat, Saluniel**
*Raising the Stones* - Sheri S. Tepper   *s*   5434

**Girat, Samasnier**
*Raising the Stones* - Sheri S. Tepper   *s*   5434

**Goldin, Netta**
*Alien Influences* - Kristine Kathryn Rusch   *s*   4711

**Hampton, Evelyn**
*Moonfall* - Jack McDevitt   *s*   3789

**Hayes**
*Time and Light* - William Bornefeld   *s*   574

**Hodge, Birk "Birkaj"**
*The Inquisitor* - Cheryl J. Franklin   *s*   2037

**Hunter, Nicole "Panther"**
*Ignition* - Kevin J. Anderson   *s*   107

**Jahns, Carter**
*Mars Underground* - William Hartmann   *s*   2584

**Kamehameha, Cesar**
*Blueheart* - Alison Sinclair   *s*   5068

**Karriaagzh**
*Human to Human* - Rebecca Ore   *s*   4219

**Kirowa, Niala**
*The Planet Beyond* - Steve Mudd   *s*   4043

**Kondratieff, David**
*Double Planet* - John Gribbin   *s*   2433

**Konstantin, Damon**
*Downbelow Station* - C.J. Cherryh   *s*   985

**Lansing, Gilbert "Keith"**
*Starplex* - Robert J. Sawyer   *s*   4859

**Lavalle, Linda**
*Why Do Birds* - Damon Knight   *s*   3190

**Leighton, Gerard**
*High Steel* - Jack C. Haldeman II   *s*   2486

**Li, Harry**
*Eyes of the Empress* - Camille Bacon-Smith   *f*   285

**Lockwood, Spencer**
*Ill Wind* - Kevin J. Anderson   *s*   108

**Lottick, Vaclav**
*Bloom* - Wil McCarthy   *s*   3761

**Mackenzie, Lyle**
*Sister Blood* - Karen Haber   *s*   2476

**Maddock, Yanaba**
*Power Play* - Anne McCaffrey   *s*   3744

**Margolis, Charles**
*Lords of Creation* - Tim Sullivan   *s*   5351

**Markham, Ulf Reichstein**
*Inconstant Star* - Poul Anderson   *s*   129

**Matsumoto, Hiroshi**
*Hocus Pocus or, What's the Hurry, Son?* - Kurt
  Vonnegut Jr.   *s*   5593

**McClain, Walter**
*Demon Shadows* - Michael B. Sirota   *h*   5075

**McClane, Judson**
*Sorcerers of Sodom* - Roger Elwood   *h*   1804

**McConnell, Celeste**
*Assemblers of Infinity* - Kevin J. Anderson   *s*   100

**McLaris, Duncan**
*Lifeline* - Kevin J. Anderson   *s*   111

**Mitchell, Manny**
*Taylor's Ark* - Jody Lynn Nye   *s*   4176

**Morrisey, Hilda Jeanne**
*The Siege of Eternity* - Frederik Pohl   *s*   4353

**Nimitz, Ariel**
*The Unwound Way* - William Adams   *s*   35

**Oakes**
*On Meeting Witches at Wells* - Judith
    Gorog   *f*   2283

**O'Hara, Marianne**
*Worlds Enough and Time* - Joe Haldeman   *s*   2491

**O'Mara**
*The Genocidal Healer* - James White   *s*   5779
*Mind Changer* - James White   *s*   5780

**Owen, Rhyssa**
*Pegasus in Flight* - Anne McCaffrey   *s*   3742

**Pearl, Michael**
*The Beyond* - Barry Harrington   *h*   2556

**Pierce, Millard Fillmore**
*The Red Tape War* - Jack L. Chalker   *s*   959

**Pinky**
*Mr. Was* - Pete Hautman   *s*   2614

**Quen, Elene**
*Finity's End* - C.J. Cherryh   *s*   988

**Rache of Scole**
*Blueheart* - Alison Sinclair   *s*   5068

**Reichner, Helmut**
*Threshold* - Bill Myers   *s*   4060

**Rucker, Dave**
*Cosm* - Gregory Benford   *s*   444

**Rutman, Becky**
*Nightlife* - Jack Ellis   *h*   1779

**Scott, Jason**
*The Eighth Rank* - David D. Ross   *s*   4682

**Sena, Miranda**
*Rewind* - Terry England   *s*   1825

**Solo, Jay**
*The Nine Lives of Catseye Gomez* - Simon
    Hawke   *f*   2620

**Solo, Leia Organa**
*Heir to the Empire* - Timothy Zahn   *s*   6054

**SSS-900-C Simeon**
*The City Who Fought* - Anne McCaffrey   *s*   3722

**Sunday, Sunday A.**
*A World Lost* - James B. Johnson   *s*   2921

**Svensdotter, Esther "Star"**
*Second Star* - Dana Stabenow   *s*   5188

**Tamm, Pirie**
*Ecce and Old Earth* - Jack Vance   *s*   5546

**Thorsson, Thor**
*Article 23* - William R. Forstchen   *s*   1978

**Toitovna, Maya**
*Red Mars* - Kim Stanley Robinson   *s*   4635

**Underhill, Lee Won**
*F.R.E.E.Lancers* - Mel Odom   *s*   4191

**Ustinov, Yevgeny**
*Double Planet* - John Gribbin   *s*   2433

**Vacit, Kevin**
*Dark Genesis* - J. Gregory Keyes   *s*   3096

**Verdadero, Jachin**
*Taylor's Ark* - Jody Lynn Nye   *s*   4176

**West, Michael**
*The Man Upstairs* - T.L. Parkinson   *h*   4248

**Winthrop, Montana "Tana"**
*The Earth Saver* - Catherine Wells   *s*   5745

**Yamaguchi, Motofusa**
*Half Asleep in Frog Pajamas* - Tom
    Robbins   *s*   4606

## ADOPTEE

**Liwellan, Sarra Ambrai**
*The Ruins of Ambrai* - Melanie Rawn   *f*   4489

**Martin, Helix**
*Accidental Creatures* - Anne Harris   *s*   2558

**Torfinn, Llyn**
*One Mind's Eye* - Kathy Tyers   *s*   5525

**Verity**
*Queen City Jazz* - Kathleen Ann Goonan   *s*   2275

## ADVENTURER

**Abernathy**
*Witches' Brew* - Terry Brooks   *f*   719

**Aeid**
*O Greenest Branch!* - Gael Baudino   *f*   394

**Aisling, Algernon**
*Voyage of the Basset* - James C.
    Christensen   *f*   1024

**Aisling, Cassandra**
*Voyage of the Basset* - James C.
    Christensen   *f*   1024

**Aisling, Miranda**
*Voyage of the Basset* - James C.
    Christensen   *f*   1024

**al-Iskandaria, Ibn Sufa**
*Quest: In Search of the Dragontooth* - Michael
    Green   *f*   2346

**Aladdin**
*Aladdin: Master of the Lamp* - Mike
    Resnick   *f*   4534
*A Bad Day for Ali Baba* - Craig Shaw
    Gardner   *f*   2123

**Alfred**
*Fire Sea* - Margaret Weis   *f*   5714
*Into the Labyrinth* - Margaret Weis   *f*   5716
*Serpent Mage* - Margaret Weis   *f*   5726
*The Seventh Gate* - Margaret Weis   *f*   5727

**Ali Baba**
*A Bad Day for Ali Baba* - Craig Shaw
    Gardner   *f*   2123

**Alice**
*Innerverse* - John DeChancie   *s*   1458

**Allbright, Rod "Seymour"**
*Aliens Stole My Body* - Bruce Coville   *s*   1217

**Alon**
*The Nomad Queen* - James Gordon White   *f*   5783

**Anangaranga-Jones, Nixy**
*Muddle Earth* - John Brunner   *s*   735

**Antero, Amalric**
*The Far Kingdoms* - Allan Cole   *f*   1104
*Kingdoms of the Night* - Allan Cole   *f*   1105

**ap Hywel, Dafydd**
*The Dragon in Lyonesse* - Gordon R.
    Dickson   *f*   1531

**Ap Sennon, Olmy**
*Legacy* - Greg Bear   *s*   420

**Appenfell, Anjell**
*A Breach in the Watershed* - Douglas Niles   *f*   4105

**Aracco**
*Goldclimbers* - Nancy Luenn   *f*   3545

**Arturo, Maximillian**
*Sliders: The Novel* - Brad Linaweaver   *s*   3467

**Ash of Ashland**
*Dancing Jack* - Laurie J. Marks   *f*   3624

**Atbin**
*The Promise* - Monica Hughes   *s*   2808

**Avenger**
*The Spider #4: Death Reign of the Vampire King/The
    Pain Emperor* - Grant Stockbridge   *f*   5308

**Bal-Simba**
*The Wizardry Cursed* - Rick Cook   *f*   1162
*The Wizardry Quested* - Rick Cook   *f*   1163

**Bane**
*The Hand of Chaos* - Margaret Weis   *f*   5715

**Bankhead, Tallulah "Tulley"**
*Beyond the Door* - Gary L. Blackwood   *s*   510

**Banning, Peter "Peter Pan"**
*Hook* - Terry Brooks   *f*   713

**Beckwith, Forster**
*Fire and Ice* - Edward Myers   *f*   4061
*The Mountain Made of Light* - Edward
    Myers   *f*   4062

**Behler, Simon William**
*The Last Voyage of Somebody the Sailor* - John
    Barth   *f*   374

**Belgarath**
*Belgarath the Sorcerer* - David Eddings   *f*   1730

**Benjarth, Paul**
*The Cloud People* - Robert B. Kelly   *f*   3050

**Beowulf**
*Whose Song Is Sung* - Frank Schaefer   *f*   4872

**Billie**
*Aliens: Earth Hive* - Steve Perry   *s*   4289

**Billy**
*Aliens: The Female War* - Steve Perry   *s*   4290

**Bjorn of Bromme**
*The Discovery of Dragons* - Graeme Base   *f*   385

**Black, Jackson**
*Living with the Reptiles* - Roger L.
    DiSilvestro   *s*   1563

**Blackburn, Trebor**
*Captains Outrageous, or, For Doom the Bell Tolls* -
    Roy V. Young   *f*   6049

**Boh, Walker**
*The Druid of Shannara* - Terry Brooks   *f*   710

**Bosch, Benjamin**
*Troll-Taken* - Rose Estes   *f*   1842

**Bradley, Richard**
*The Hollowing* - Robert Holdstock   *f*   2738

**Braeth, Rikard**
*Crown of the Serpent* - Allen L. Wold   *s*   5932
*Lair of the Cyclops* - Allen L. Wold   *s*   5933

**Brailsford, Jane**
*A College of Magics* - Caroline Stevermer   *f*   5266

**Brazil, Bubbles**
*Negrophobia: An Urban Parable* - Darius
    James   *f*   2859

**Bremen**
*First King of Shannara* - Terry Brooks   *f*   712

**Brenn**
*A Forest Lord* - Michael Williams   *f*   5819

**Brown, Rembrandt "Cryin' Man"**
*Sliders: The Novel* - Brad Linaweaver   *s*   3467

**Bruenor, Catti-Brie**
*Passage to Dawn* - R.A. Salvatore   *f*   4803
*Siege of Darkness* - R.A. Salvatore   *f*   4804
*Sojourn* - R.A. Salvatore   *f*   4806

**Bull-Roar, Harold**
*Byzantium* - Stephen R. Lawhead   *f*   3353

**C-3PO**
*The Glove of Darth Vader* - Paul Davids   *s*   1392

**Cally "Earth"**
*Beyond the Magic Sphere* - Gail Jarrow   *s*   2879

**Campbell, Deirdre**
*Indiana Jones and the Dance of the Giants* - Rob
    MacGregor   *f*   3588

*Indiana Jones and the Seven Veils* - Rob
 MacGregor  *f*  3592

**Carton, Sidney "Sid"**
*North Wind* - Gwyneth Jones  *s*  2953

**Casruel, Aru**
*Mother of Storms* - Adrian Cole  *f*  1101

**Catherine**
*Myst: The Book of D'ni* - Rand Miller  *f*  3897

**Catti-Brie**
*The Silent Blade* - R.A. Salvatore  *f*  4805

**Cerise**
*Cardmaster* - Clayton Emery  *f*  1813

**Chalmers, Reed**
*The Enchanter Reborn* - L. Sprague de
 Camp  *f*  1413

**Chamtong, Onua**
*Wild Magic* - Tamora Pierce  *f*  4323

**Chewbacca**
*The Crystal Star* - Vonda N. McIntyre  *s*  3820
*Jedi Search* - Kevin J. Anderson  *s*  109

**Chlorine**
*Yon Ill Wind* - Piers Anthony  *f*  196

**Climber, Artus**
*The Ring of Winter* - James Lowder  *f*  3538

**Colene**
*Chaos Mode* - Piers Anthony  *f*  165
*Fractal Mode* - Piers Anthony  *f*  171
*Virtual Mode* - Piers Anthony  *f*  194

**Collun**
*Hero's Song* - Edith Pattou  *f*  4261

**Corlaiys, Aitchley**
*Cathedral of Thorns* - Steven Frankos  *f*  2041

**Crocken**
*The Wizard's Shadow* - Susan Dexter  *f*  1514

**Cromwell, Willard**
*Indiana Jones and the Sky Pirates* - Martin
 Caidin  *f*  825

**Crookleg, Poilar**
*Kingdoms of the Wall* - Robert Silverberg  *s*  5033

**Crow**
*Crow and Weasel* - Barry Lopez  *f*  3523

**Crow, Titus**
*Titus Crow, Volume One* - Brian Lumley  *h*  3566
*Titus Crow, Volume Three* - Brian Lumley  *h*  3567
*Titus Crow, Volume Two* - Brian Lumley  *h*  3568

**Cugnet, Vern**
*Stones of the Dalai Lama* - Ken Mitchell  *f*  3916

**Culaehra**
*The Sage* - Christopher Stasheff  *f*  5221

**Cumber**
*Dragoncharm* - Graham Edwards  *f*  1749

**Dagda**
*The Enchanted Isles* - Casey Flynn  *f*  1960
*Most Ancient Song* - Casey Flynn  *f*  1961

**Daniel**
*The Door to Ambermere* - J. Calvin Pierce  *f*  4316

**Daniels, Aikin**
*Dreamseeker's Road* - Tom Deitz  *f*  1472

**Darby, Beacontor "Beau"**
*Into the Fire* - Dennis L. McKiernan  *f*  3834
*Into the Forge* - Dennis L. McKiernan  *f*  3835

**d'Armand, Magnus Gallowglass "Gar Pike"**
*A Wizard in Absentia* - Christopher Stasheff  *s*  5229

**de Wolf, Mike**
*Typewriter in the Sky* - L. Ron Hubbard  *f*  2791

**Deal, Brian**
*The Square Deal* - David Drake  *s*  1644

---

**Deal, John "J.C."**
*The Square Deal* - David Drake  *s*  1644

**den Karynth, Calandryll**
*Dark Magic* - Angus Wells  *f*  5733

**Denison, Will**
*Dinotopia* - James Gurney  *f*  2468
*Dinotopia Lost* - Alan Dean Foster  *f*  2003
*The World Beneath* - James Gurney  *f*  2469

**Derry, Jerry**
*Ye Gods!* - Tom Holt  *f*  2753

**diGriz, Jim**
*The Stainless Steel Rat Goes to Hell* - Harry
 Harrison  *s*  2574

**Do'Urden, Drizzt**
*The Legacy* - R.A. Salvatore  *f*  4801
*Siege of Darkness* - R.A. Salvatore  *f*  4804
*The Silent Blade* - R.A. Salvatore  *f*  4805
*Sojourn* - R.A. Salvatore  *f*  4806
*Starless Night* - R.A. Salvatore  *f*  4807

**Dovero, Colinda**
*Fabulous Harbors* - Michael Moorcock  *f*  3981

**Dowd, Katherine "Katy"**
*Flames of the Dragon* - Robin Wayne Bailey  *f*  287

**Drizzt Do'Urden**
*Passage to Dawn* - R.A. Salvatore  *f*  4803

**Dug**
*Demons Don't Dream* - Piers Anthony  *f*  168

**Dulaine, Dirk**
*A Wizard in Peace* - Christopher Stasheff  *s*  5233

**Ela**
*The Goblin Mirror* - C.J. Cherryh  *f*  994

**Elmara**
*Elminster: The Making of a Mage* - Ed
 Greenwood  *f*  2427

**Emereck**
*Shadows over Lyra* - Patricia C. Wrede  *f*  5980

**Escargot, Theophile**
*The Stone Giant* - James P. Blaylock  *f*  523

**Ferraro, Gene**
*Castle War!* - John DeChancie  *s*  1455

**Finis "Water"**
*Beyond the Magic Sphere* - Gail Jarrow  *f*  2879

**Flannery, Eric**
*Caverns of Socrates* - Dennis L. McKiernan  *f*  3831

**Flannery, Kathleen**
*The Two Georges* - Richard Dreyfuss  *s*  1655

**Flattery, Erasmus**
*Beneath the Vaulted Hills* - Sean Russell  *f*  4739
*The Compass of the Soul* - Sean Russell  *f*  4740

**Formosus, Musculus Herodes**
*Whose Song Is Sung* - Frank Schaefer  *f*  4872

**Fortune**
*Dragoncharm* - Graham Edwards  *f*  1749

**Gabrielle**
*The Empty Throne* - Ru Emerson  *f*  1808

**Garuda**
*The Iron Ring* - Lloyd Alexander  *f*  68

**Gelly**
*Flight to Hollow Mountain* - Mark Sebanc  *f*  4908

**Gelmann, Mina**
*Codgerspace* - Alan Dean Foster  *s*  1999

**Gibbs, Rinpoche**
*Muddle Earth* - John Brunner  *s*  735

**Gordon, Sr.**
*Revenge of the Fluffy Bunnies* - Craig Shaw
 Gardner  *f*  2132

---

**Gordon, Kate**
*The Merlin Effect* - T.A. Barron  *f*  371

**Gordon, Roger Jr.**
*Revenge of the Fluffy Bunnies* - Craig Shaw
 Gardner  *f*  2132

**Graydon, Nicholas**
*The Face in the Abyss* - A. Merritt  *f*  3878

**Greycloak, Janela Kether**
*Kingdoms of the Night* - Allan Cole  *f*  1105

**Grimi, Garni ben**
*Another Day, Another Dungeon* - Greg
 Costikyan  *f*  1206

**Hammer-Hand, Barnar**
*The Mines of Behemoth* - Michael Shea  *f*  4945

**Hanse**
*The Shadow of Sorcery* - Andrew J. Offutt  *f*  4202

**Haplo**
*Elven Star* - Margaret Weis  *f*  5712
*Fire Sea* - Margaret Weis  *f*  5714
*The Hand of Chaos* - Margaret Weis  *f*  5715
*Into the Labyrinth* - Margaret Weis  *f*  5716
*Serpent Mage* - Margaret Weis  *f*  5726
*The Seventh Gate* - Margaret Weis  *f*  5727

**Hari**
*The Willing Spirit* - Piers Anthony  *f*  195

**Heikki, Gwynne**
*Mighty Good Road* - Melissa Scott  *s*  4897

**Hodierna**
*The Notorious Abbess* - Vera Chapman  *f*  965

**Holmes, Sherlock**
*Sherlock Holmes in Orbit* - Mike Resnick  *s*  4556

**Hunter, Cara Diana**
*Into the Land of the Unicorns* - Bruce
 Coville  *f*  1219

**Huxley, Christian**
*Gate of Ivory, Gate of Horn* - Robert
 Holdstock  *f*  2737

**Igor**
*Goblins in the Castle* - Bruce Coville  *f*  1218

**Ilya**
*Firebird* - Mercedes Lackey  *f*  3281

**Indigo**
*Dragon War* - Laurence Yep  *f*  6025

**Iranaputra, Victor**
*Codgerspace* - Alan Dean Foster  *s*  1999

**Isabeau**
*The Witches of Eileanan* - Kate Forsyth  *f*  1984

**Jack**
*The Loneliest Magician* - Irene Radford  *f*  4461

**Jackson, Carl**
*Dragon Burning* - Craig Shaw Gardner  *f*  2126

**Jahdo**
*Days of Blood and Fire* - Katharine Kerr  *f*  3068

**Jilseponie "Pony"**
*The Demon Awakens* - R.A. Salvatore  *f*  4794
*The Demon Spirit* - R.A. Salvatore  *f*  4795

**Jing, Jong**
*Stones of the Dalai Lama* - Ken Mitchell  *f*  3916

**Joachim**
*The Wood Nymph and the Cranky Saint* - C. Dale
 Brittain  *f*  706

**Jones, Lucifer**
*Lucifer Jones* - Mike Resnick  *f*  4549

**Jones, Ritcher**
*Dawn's Uncertain Light* - Neal Barrett Jr.  *s*  365

**Joseph**
*The Bellmaker* - Brian Jacques  *f*  2848

**Joy-in-the-Dance**
*The Arkadians* - Lloyd Alexander  f  67

**Joze**
*A Child of Elvish* - Nancy Varian Berberick  f  457

**Kal**
*Flight to Hollow Mountain* - Mark Sebanc  f  4908

**Kalavek**
*Dragon's Domain* - Thorarinn Gunnarsson  f  2461

**Kara**
*Flight of the Dragon Kyn* - Susan Fletcher  f  1951

**Karaquazian, Jack**
*Blood: A Southern Fantasy* - Michael
   Moorcock  f  3977
*Fabulous Harbors* - Michael Moorcock  f  3981
*The War Amongst the Angels* - Michael
   Moorcock  f  3986

**Karin**
*Voima* - C. Dale Brittain  f  704

**Katya**
*Dark Magic* - Angus Wells  f  5733
*Wild Magic* - Angus Wells  f  5741

**Kayrlis**
*Night of Glory* - Scott Ciencin  f  1030

**Kelder of Shulara**
*Taking Flight* - Lawrence Watt-Evans  f  5650

**Kemp, Jerod**
*Shadow of the Crown* - Craig Mills  f  3914

**Kendrick, Robyn**
*The Coral Kingdom* - Douglas Niles  f  4106

**Khalifa, Haroun**
*Haroun and the Sea of Stories* - Salman
   Rushdie  f  4731

**Kickaha**
*More than Fire* - Philip Jose Farmer  s  1871

**Kicva**
*A Child of Elvish* - Nancy Varian Berberick  f  457

**Kirk, James T. "Jimmy"**
*Best Destiny* - Diane Carey  s  900

**Ko, Melody**
*Nightfeeder* - Judith Reeves-Stevens  f  4513
*Shifter* - Judith Reeves-Stevens  f  4515

**Korendir**
*The Master of Whitestorm* - Janny Wurts  f  6003

**Krispos**
*Krispos Rising* - Harry Turtledove  f  5507

**Kronarsson, Kraki**
*One Quest, Hold the Dragons* - Greg
   Costikyan  f  1208

**Krystal**
*The Magic of Recluce* - L.E. Modesitt Jr.  f  3934

**Lang, Darya**
*Convergence* - Charles Sheffield  s  4951
*Divergence* - Charles Sheffield  s  4954
*Summertide* - Charles Sheffield  s  4965
*Transcendence* - Charles Sheffield  s  4967

**Larken, Ray**
*Cry Wolf* - Kenneth Von Gunden  s  5586
*Under Fire* - Kenneth Von Gunden  s  5589

**Leah, Morgan**
*The Druid of Shannara* - Terry Brooks  f  710

**Leger, Gary**
*The Dragon's Dagger* - R.A. Salvatore  f  4797
*Dragonslayer's Return* - R.A. Salvatore  f  4798
*The Woods out Back* - R.A. Salvatore  f  4809

**Leifr**
*The Dragon's Carbuncle* - Elizabeth H.
   Boyer  f  605

**Li, Master**
*The Chronicles of Master Li and Number Ten Ox* -
   Barry Hughart  f  2803

**Llanfrechfa, Geraint**
*Streets of Blood* - Carl Sargent  f  4821

**Logan "Wolverine"**
*Codename Wolverine* - Christopher Golden  s  2256

**Lot**
*Vast* - Linda Nagata  s  4067

**Lucian**
*The Arkadians* - Lloyd Alexander  f  67

**Maddox, Cory**
*The Cybernetic Walrus* - Jack L. Chalker  s  951
*The Hot-Wired Dodo* - Jack L. Chalker  s  956
*The March Hare Network* - Jack L. Chalker  s  957

**Marcia**
*The Wizard of Ambermere* - J. Calvin Pierce  f  4317

**Mariel**
*The Bellmaker* - Brian Jacques  f  2848
*Mariel of Redwall* - Brian Jacques  f  2850

**Markham, Robert**
*A Hunger in the Soul* - Mike Resnick  s  4545

**Marsh, Pella**
*Girl in Landscape* - Jonathan Lethem  s  3440

**Maxon, Alice**
*Caverns of Socrates* - Dennis L. McKiernan  f  3831

**McLean, Alec**
*Dreamseeker's Road* - Tom Deitz  f  1472

**Melania**
*The Eagle and the Sword* - A.A. Attanasio  f  267

**Meriweather, Jon-Tom**
*Chorus Skating* - Alan Dean Foster  f  1998

**Merlin, Emrys**
*The Fires of Merlin* - T.A. Barron  f  369

**Mew**
*Roverandom* - J.R.R. Tolkien  f  5479

**Miaowara Shiro**
*Samurai Cat Goes to the Movies* - Mark E.
   Rogers  s  4656
*The Sword of Samurai Cat* - Mark E.
   Rogers  s  4657

**Miranda**
*Charmed* - Marilyn Singer  f  5070

**Mirri**
*The Iron Ring* - Lloyd Alexander  f  68

**Mole**
*Toad Triumphant* - William Horwood  f  2774
*The Willows and Beyond* - William
   Horwood  f  2775
*The Willows in Winter* - William Horwood  f  2776

**Mollockle, Thud**
*Hearts and Armor* - Ron Miller  f  3903
*Palaces and Prisons* - Ron Miller  f  3904
*Silk and Steel* - Ron Miller  f  3905

**Montague, Derek**
*Something's Alive on the Titanic* - Robert
   Serling  h  4915

**Moorcock, Margaret Rose**
*The War Amongst the Angels* - Michael
   Moorcock  f  3986

**Moore, Teldin**
*Beyond the Moons* - David Cook  f  1144
*Into the Void* - Nigel Findley  f  1937
*The Radiant Dragon* - Elaine Cunningham  f  1291
*The Ultimate Helm* - Russ T. Howard  f  2785

**Morgasdotte, Roba**
*Bones of the Past* - Holly Lisle  f  3478

**Myklathun, Einar**
*Dragon's Domain* - Thorarinn Gunnarsson  f  2461

**Nadia**
*Henry's Gift: The Magic Eye* - David
   Worsick  f  5972

**Naismith, Gladys**
*A Sudden Wild Magic* - Diana Wynne Jones  f  2950

**Narlh**
*The Oathbound Wizard* - Christopher
   Stasheff  f  5219

**Navarre**
*The Magic Wars* - Jo Clayton  f  1068

**Nenda, Louis**
*Convergence* - Charles Sheffield  s  4951

**Nhamo**
*A Girl Named Disaster* - Nancy Farmer  f  1868

**Nifft the Lean**
*The Mines of Behemoth* - Michael Shea  f  4945

**No-man's Son, Roric**
*Voima* - C. Dale Brittain  f  704

**Noonan, Owen**
*Travel Far, Pay No Fare* - Anne Lindbergh  f  3468

**Novak, Cornell**
*Beyond the Veil of Stars* - Robert Reed  s  4503

**Number Ten Ox**
*The Chronicles of Master Li and Number Ten Ox* -
   Barry Hughart  f  2803

**Oakenhurst, Sam**
*The War Amongst the Angels* - Michael
   Moorcock  f  3986

**Odosson, William "Will"**
*Knight's Wyrd* - Debra Doyle  f  1601

**Ohmsford, Coll**
*The Scions of Shannara* - Terry Brooks  f  716

**Ohmsford, Par**
*The Talismans of Shannara* - Terry Brooks  f  717

**Ohmsford, Wren**
*The Elf Queen of Shannara* - Terry Brooks  f  711

**O'Keefe, Jesse**
*Fire and Ice* - Edward Myers  f  4061
*The Mountain Made of Light* - Edward
   Myers  f  4062
*The Summit* - Edward Myers  f  4063

**Olyvria**
*Krispos the Emperor* - Harry Turtledove  f  5508

**Orick**
*Beyond the Gate* - Dave Wolverton  s  5949
*The Golden Queen* - Dave Wolverton  s  5951

**Paithan**
*Elven Star* - Margaret Weis  f  5712

**Palamon**
*Across the Thlassa Mey* - Dennis McCarty  f  3765

**Parsley**
*Travel Far, Pay No Fare* - Anne Lindbergh  f  3468

**Pavek of Urik**
*The Brazen Gambit* - Lynn Abbey  f  13
*Cinnabar Shadows* - Lynn Abbey  f  15

**Perrin, Michael**
*Songs of Earth and Power* - Greg Bear  f  424

**Polgara**
*Polgara the Sorceress* - David Eddings  f  1734

**Prahotep**
*The Land of Gold* - Gillian Bradshaw  f  658

**Rana**
*The Jewel of Fire* - Diana L. Paxson  f  4265
*The Wind Crystal* - Diana L. Paxson  f  4269

**Ranier**
*The Remarkables* - Robert Reed   s   4507

**Ranira "Renra"**
*Shadows over Lyra* - Patricia C. Wrede   f   5980

**Rap**
*The Cutting Edge* - Dave Duncan   f   1675

**Ravenloft, Kinson**
*First King of Shannara* - Terry Brooks   f   712

**Rebka, Hans**
*Divergence* - Charles Sheffield   s   4954
*Transcendence* - Charles Sheffield   s   4967

**Reddy, John**
*A King Beneath the Mountain* - Robert N.
   Charrette   f   973

**Roan**
*Waking in Dreamland* - Jody Lynn Nye   f   4177

**Ronay, Matthias "Matt"**
*Growing Up Weightless* - John M. Ford   s   1970

**Rover "Roverandom"**
*Roverandom* - J.R.R. Tolkien   f   5479

**Ryana**
*The Seeker* - Simon Hawke   f   2624

**S .B. "Air"**
*Beyond the Magic Sphere* - Gail Jarrow   f   2879

**Salandra**
*Indiana Jones and the Interior World* - Rob
   MacGregor   f   3590

**Sam**
*Villains by Necessity* - Eve Forward   f   1985

**Savage, Clark "Doc" Jr.**
*Escape From Loki* - Philip Jose Farmer   f   1870
*The Frightened Fish* - Kenneth Robeson   f   4622
*The Jade Ogre* - Kenneth Robeson   f   4623
*Python Isle* - Kenneth Robeson   f   4624
*White Eyes* - Kenneth Robeson   f   4625

**Schoedsack, Ernest "Monte"**
*Dinosaur Summer* - Greg Bear   s   416

**Scope**
*Dragoncharm* - Graham Edwards   f   1749

**Sea Rat "Ratty"**
*The Willows and Beyond* - William
   Horwood   f   2775

**Shaa, Zalzyn**
*Spell of Fate* - Mayer Alan Brenner   f   673

**Shadowspawn**
*The Shadow of Sorcery* - Andrew J. Offutt   f   4202

**Shaffer, Walter Scott Jr.**
*Beyond the Door* - Gary L. Blackwood   s   510

**Shea, Harold**
*The Enchanter Reborn* - L. Sprague de
   Camp   f   1413

**Sherman**
*In between Dragons* - Michael Kandel   f   3010

**Sinbad the Sailor**
*The Last Voyage of Somebody the Sailor* - John
   Barth   f   374
*The Other Sinbad* - Craig Shaw Gardner   f   2130

**Sinclair, Katherine**
*Troll-Quest* - Rose Estes   f   1841
*Troll-Taken* - Rose Estes   f   1842

**Skelbrooke, Francis**
*The Gnome's Engine* - Teresa Edgerton   f   1742

**Spae, Elizabeth**
*A King Beneath the Mountain* - Robert N.
   Charrette   f   973

**Starbuck, Ron**
*Nevernever* - Will Shetterly   f   4995

**Stratford, Julie**
*The Mummy, or Ramses the Damned* - Anne
   Rice   h   4572

**Stryker, Anton**
*The Clouds of Magellan* - David F.
   Nighbert   s   4103

**Sullivan, David**
*Darkthunder's Way* - Tom Deitz   f   1470
*Dreamseeker's Road* - Tom Deitz   f   1472
*Landslayer's Law* - Tom Deitz   f   1474
*Sunshaker's War* - Tom Deitz   f   1477

**Swenson, Colter**
*Footprints of Thunder* - James F. David   s   1379

**Sword, Galen**
*Nightfeeder* - Judith Reeves-Stevens   f   4513
*Shifter* - Judith Reeves-Stevens   f   4515

**Tainharsdartter, Kevral**
*Beyond Ragnarok* - Mickey Zucker Reichert   f   4516

**Tamas of Maggiar**
*The Goblin Mirror* - C.J. Cherryh   f   994

**Tany, Myron**
*Ports of Call* - Jack Vance   s   5549

**Teague, Jamie**
*The Folk of the Fringe* - Orson Scott Card   s   886

**Tel'anh, Alethia**
*Shadows over Lyra* - Patricia C. Wrede   f   5980

**Thane, Sundira**
*The Face of the Waters* - Robert Silverberg   s   5029

**Thelia**
*Metamorphosis* - Jean Lorrah   s   3524

**Thews, Questor**
*Witches' Brew* - Terry Brooks   f   719

**Thistledown, Tipperton "Tip"**
*Into the Forge* - Dennis L. McKiernan   f   3835

**Tim**
*The Gift* - Patrick O'Leary   f   4211

**Titch**
*The True Knight* - Susan Dexter   t   1513

**Toad of Toad Hall**
*Toad Triumphant* - William Horwood   f   2774
*The Willows and Beyond* - William
   Horwood   f   2775

**Toland, Walter**
*Killobyte* - Piers Anthony   f   179

**Traiben**
*Kingdoms of the Wall* - Robert Silverberg   s   5033

**Trost, Sophonisba "Soph"**
*Deepdrive* - Alexander Jablokov   s   2837

**Trusslo, Alix Amanda**
*Dragon Rescue* - Don Callander   f   843

**Tucker, Paris**
*Red Genesis* - S.C. Sykes   s   5377

**Tyler, Richard**
*The Pagemaster* - David Kirschner   f   3156

**Urban**
*Vast* - Linda Nagata   s   4067

**Ussemitus**
*Mother of Storms* - Adrian Cole   f   1101

**Valmar**
*Voima* - C. Dale Brittain   f   704

**Vicars, Ned**
*Anti-Ice* - Stephen Baxter   s   398

**Viola**
*The Pearls of Lutra* - Brian Jacques   f   2854

**Wakefield, Nicole des Jardins**
*The Garden of Rama* - Arthur C. Clarke   s   1055

**Wakefield, Richard**
*The Garden of Rama* - Arthur C. Clarke   s   1055

**Wallace, Ditsy**
*The Square Deal* - David Drake   s   1644

**Wartsworth, Caspar**
*The Lost City of Zork* - Robin Wayne Bailey   f   288

**Water Rat "Ratty"**
*Toad Triumphant* - William Horwood   f   2774
*The Willows in Winter* - William Horwood   f   2776

**Weasel**
*Crow and Weasel* - Barry Lopez   f   3523

**Wenceslas, Rudyard "Waldo" Riding**
*The Wealdwife's Tale* - Paul Hazel   f   2636

**Wentworth, Richard**
*The Spider #3: Death's Crimson Juggernaut/The Red
   Death Rain* - Grant Stockbridge   f   5307
*The Spider #4: Death Reign of the Vampire King/The
   Pain Emperor* - Grant Stockbridge   f   5308
*The Spider #8: The Devil's Paymaster/Legions of the
   Accursed Light* - Grant Stockbridge   f   5309

**Weston, Jamie**
*Summerland* - L. Dean James   f   2865

**Whitehead, Tom**
*Dragon Companion* - Don Callander   f   842

**William**
*Goblins in the Castle* - Bruce Coville   f   1218
*Here There Be Dragons* - Roger Zelazny   f   6069

**Williams, Thaddeus "Thaddy"**
*Unicorn Highway* - David Lee Jones   f   2941

**Wren**
*Wren to the Rescue* - Sherwood Smith   f   5142
*Wren's Quest* - Sherwood Smith   f   5143
*Wren's War* - Sherwood Smith   f   5144

**Wu, Louis**
*The Ringworld Throne* - Larry Niven   s   4128

**Wyndon, Elbryan**
*The Demon Awakens* - R.A. Salvatore   f   4794
*The Demon Spirit* - R.A. Salvatore   f   4795

**Yalso**
*Dragon Tome* - Richard A. Knaak   f   3169

**Ying, Soong Mei**
*The Discovery of Dragons* - Graeme Base   f   385

**Yor**
*Captains Outrageous, or, For Doom the Bell Tolls* -
   Roy V. Young   f   6049

**Zalewski, Petra**
*Footprints of Thunder* - James F. David   s   1379

**Zimmerman, Christopher**
*Panda Ray* - Michael Kandel   s   3011

**Zobolotsky, Katrina**
*Indiana Jones and the Genesis Deluge* - Rob
   MacGregor   f   3589

**Zobolotsky, Vladimir**
*Indiana Jones and the Genesis Deluge* - Rob
   MacGregor   f   3589

## ADVERTISING

**Bainbridge**
*Ferman's Devils* - Joe Clifford Faust   s   1892

**Baxter, Carl**
*The Homecoming* - Barry B. Longyear   s   3521

**Boddekker**
*Ferman's Devils* - Joe Clifford Faust   s   1892

**Bryant, Karla**
*Deadrush* - Yvonne Navarro   h   4073

**Buckingham, Harry**
*Rune* - Christopher Fowler   h   2020

**Cunningham, Jennifer**
*The Site* - Melisand March   *h*   3621

**Gray, Justin**
*The Darker Saints* - Brian Hodge   *h*   2699
*Nightlife* - Brian Hodge   *h*   2702

**Harris, Valerie**
*The Site* - Melisand March   *h*   3621

**Hobson, Cathy**
*The Terminal Experiment* - Robert J.
   Sawyer   *s*   4860

**Honniker**
*Ferman's Devils* - Joe Clifford Faust   *s*   1892

**Ingersoll, Austin**
*Throat Sprockets* - Tim Lucas   *h*   3541

**Kidd, Christian**
*That's All, Folks!* - Greg Snow   *f*   5148

**Kingston, April**
*Nightlife* - Brian Hodge   *h*   2702

**Kingston-Gray, April**
*The Darker Saints* - Brian Hodge   *h*   2699

**Lasseter, Ruth**
*Red, Red Robin* - Stephen Gallagher   *h*   2113

**Macaree, Joe**
*Obsessed* - Rick R. Reed   *h*   4500

**MacColl, Enye**
*King of Morning, Queen of Day* - Ian
   McDonald   *f*   3793

**Moon, Jeremy**
*Wizard's Mole* - Brad Strickland   *f*   5337

**Paarman, Leigh**
*Succumb* - Ron Dee   *h*   1468

**Pepper, Jack**
*Angel Kiss* - Kelley Wilde   *h*   5800

**Reagan, Nancy**
*Throat Sprockets* - Tim Lucas   *h*   3541

**Taig, Nick**
*That's All, Folks!* - Greg Snow   *f*   5148

## AGED PERSON

**Agnes**
*Well Wished* - Franny Billingsley   *f*   489

**Agranovsky, Reuven**
*Further Adventures* - Jon Stephen Fink   *f*   1940

**Allalie, Fentrice**
*Walking the Labyrinth* - Lisa Goldstein   *f*   2266

**Arak, Bashir**
*The Planet Beyond* - Steve Mudd   *s*   4043

**Banning, George "Grandpa"**
*My Pretty Pony* - Stephen King   *h*   3136

**Brand, Evelyn**
*The Devil's Churn* - Kristine Kathryn
   Rusch   *h*   4715

**Brentwood, Grace**
*Earthbound* - Richard Matheson   *h*   3684

**Burke, Moira Janelle**
*Overshoot* - Mona Clee   *s*   1075

**Campbell, Arlene "Grandma"**
*The Amulet* - A.R. Morlan   *h*   4009

**Carson, Kenneth "Kit"**
*Time Scout* - Robert Asprin   *s*   263

**Chasse, Lois**
*Insomnia* - Stephen King   *h*   3135

**Claiborne, Dolores**
*Dolores Claiborne* - Stephen King   *h*   3130

**Clanton, Otis**
*The Sixth Dog* - Jane Rice   *h*   4582

**Clayborne, Ann**
*Blue Mars* - Kim Stanley Robinson   *s*   4629

**Clementi, Nick**
*Maximum Light* - Nancy Kress   *s*   3241

**Cohen, Ghenghiz "Cohen the Barbarian"**
*Interesting Times* - Terry Pratchett   *f*   4392

**Coughlin, Charlie**
*Dry Skull Dreams* - Michael Green   *h*   2344

**Curran, Abigail**
*Holy Terror* - Josephine Boyle   *h*   608

**da Vinci, Leonardo**
*Pasquale's Angel* - Paul J. McAuley   *f*   3714

**Davidson, Callum**
*Dialing the Wind* - Charles L. Grant   *h*   2305

**DeGeaux, Vanessa**
*The Black Mariah* - Jay R. Bonansinga   *h*   570

**Deveraux, Rosalie**
*Blood Roots* - Richie Tankersley Cusick   *h*   1300

**Dietrich, Elinor**
*Revenant* - Melanie Tem   *h*   5424

**Donovan, Vera**
*Dolores Claiborne* - Stephen King   *h*   3130

**Douchette, Earl**
*The Jimjams* - Michael Green   *h*   2345

**Dworkin, Sam**
*Silent Zone* - Stephen Molstad   *s*   3952

**Edmonds, Sarah Emma "Kite"**
*Sewer, Gas & Electric* - Matt Ruff   *s*   4708

**Ewebean, Jade**
*Panic* - Chris Curry   *h*   1295

**Falfurrias, Ofelia Damareux**
*Remnant Population* - Elizabeth Moon   *s*   3972

**Gelmann, Mina**
*Codgerspace* - Alan Dean Foster   *s*   1999

**Gold, Leah**
*Rage* - Elizabeth Ergas   *h*   1834

**Hagopian**
*Black Sun* - Douglas E. Winter   *h*   5923

**Harp, John**
*Chariot* - Charles L. Grant   *h*   2304

**Hill, Jonathan**
*The Burning Man* - Michael Hammond   *h*   2530

**Iranaputra, Victor**
*Codgerspace* - Alan Dean Foster   *s*   1999

**Johnson, Grandma**
*Grandma's Little Darling* - Stephen R.
   George   *h*   2201

**Kirk, James T.**
*The Fearful Summons* - Denny Martin Flinn   *s*   1954

**Koriba**
*Kirinyaga: A Fable of Utopia* - Mike
   Resnick   *s*   4548

**Lady**
*Boy's Life* - Robert R. McCammon   *h*   3754

**Little, Thomas**
*The Little Country* - Charles de Lint   *f*   1432

**Madison, Sybil Wilfred**
*Baby Dolly* - Ruby Jean Jensen   *h*   2899

**Manzara, Gaetano**
*Fantasma* - Thomas F. Monteleone   *h*   3963

**Mary**
*Wilding* - Melanie Tem   *h*   5425

**McGowan, Annie**
*The Nightmare People* - Lawrence Watt-
   Evans   *h*   5643

**Nemmitz, Palmer**
*Dark Journey* - A.R. Morlan   *h*   4010

**O'Hallahan, Marvin**
*What's Wrong with America* - Scott
   Bradfield   *h*   627

**Old Bess**
*The Moorchild* - Eloise Jarvis McGraw   *f*   3816

**Owain, Gwendolyn**
*The Long Lost* - Ramsey Campbell   *h*   859

**Rafiel**
*Outnumbering the Dead* - Frederik Pohl   *s*   4352

**Rivera, Maria**
*The Nihilesthete* - Richard Kalich   *h*   3002

**Roberts, Ralph**
*Insomnia* - Stephen King   *h*   3135

**Russell, Saxifrage "Sax"**
*Blue Mars* - Kim Stanley Robinson   *s*   4629

**Rustin, Adelaine Hawthorne Taylor**
*The Devil's Churn* - Kristine Kathryn
   Rusch   *h*   4715

**Sarin, Robert**
*The Plague Tales* - Ann Benson   *s*   453

**Seldon, Hari**
*Foundation and Chaos* - Greg Bear   *s*   418

**Shipman, Malkah**
*He, She and It* - Marge Piercy   *s*   4325

**Silenus, Martin**
*The Rise of Endymion* - Dan Simmons   *s*   5059

**Skinner**
*Virtual Light* - William Gibson   *s*   2219

**Talbot, Annie**
*Her Monster* - Jeff Collignon   *h*   1115

**Tao Tieh**
*Twisted Images* - Don D'Ammassa   *h*   1335

**Teller, Edward**
*Operation Damocles* - Oscar L. Fellows   *s*   1915

**Tenoctris**
*Lord of the Isles* - David Drake   *f*   1636
*Queen of Demons* - David Drake   *f*   1640

**Thibodeaux, Ben**
*The Dwelling* - Tom Elliott   *h*   1776

**Thompson, Lydia**
*Seed of Evil* - Edmund Plante   *h*   4340

**Torgov, Grandma Mugwump**
*Blood of Mugwump* - Doug Rice   *h*   4581

**Tucker**
*Unicorn Highway* - David Lee Jones   *f*   2941

**Tuckton, Grandpap**
*Header* - Edward Lee   *h*   3393

**Turnbull, Ben**
*Toward the End of Time* - John Updike   *s*   5531

**Usher, Madeline**
*Madeline: After the Fall of Usher* - Marie
   Kiraly   *h*   3150

**Veilleur, Glaeken**
*Nightworld* - F. Paul Wilson   *h*   5893

**Washington, Billy**
*Beggars and Choosers* - Nancy Kress   *s*   3236

**Waverly, Dora**
*The Well* - Michael B. Sirota   *h*   5077

**Webb, Tessa**
*Haunted* - James Herbert   *h*   2669

**Webster, Daniel**
*Deep Freeze* - Zach Hughes   *s*   2811

**Wickham, Theodora**
*The Haunting* - Ruby Jean Jensen   *h*   2901

**Winston, Palmer**
*Dark Journey* - A.R. Morlan   *h*   4010

**Yambu**
*Wayfinder's Story: The Seventh Book of Lost Swords* - Fred Saberhagen   *f*   4777

## AGENT

**Aw, Ruiz**
*Emperor of Everything* - Ray Aldridge   *s*   62
*The Pharaoh Contract* - Ray Aldridge   *s*   63

**Bureaucrat**
*Stations of the Tide* - Michael Swanwick   *s*   5373

**Comfort, Isambard**
*The Golden Globe* - John Varley   *s*   5565

**Coogan, Elihu "Emil Storchesson"**
*The Singularity Project* - F.M. Busby   *s*   784

**Derrith, Raunn ni Obradi san**
*World Spirits* - Aline Boucher-Kaplan   *s*   580

**Dharmamitra, Uma**
*Burning Bright* - J.S. Russell   *h*   4733

**Durendal**
*The Gilded Chain: A Tale of the King's Blades* - Dave Duncan   *f*   1679

**Duroc, Roger**
*Comeback Tour: The Sky Belongs to the Stars* - Jack Yeovil   *s*   6020

**Everard, Manse**
*The Shield of Time* - Poul Anderson   *s*   131
*The Time Patrol* - Poul Anderson   *s*   135

**Faharmoy**
*Wild Magic* - Jo Clayton   *f*   1072

**Ferro-Maine, Sylvia**
*The Ecolitan Enigma* - L.E. Modesitt Jr.   *s*   3927

**Finister "Moraga"**
*Quicksilver's Knight* - Christopher Stasheff   *f*   5220

**Greenstone, Brian**
*The Prodigy* - Noel Hynd   *h*   2823

**Heim, Walter**
*Double Edge* - Dennis Etchison   *h*   1846

**Helmuth**
*Galactic Patrol* - Edward E. Smith   *s*   5116

**Hightower, Alex**
*Possession* - Peter James   *h*   2873

**Jack**
*The End-of-Everything Man* - Tom De Haven   *f*   1421

**Juillerat, Sister Chantal**
*Demon Download* - Jack Yeovil   *f*   6021

**Kendal, Harry**
*Now You See It. . .* - Richard Matheson   *h*   3688

**Kirowa, Niala**
*The Planet Beyond* - Steve Mudd   *s*   4043

**Lacuna**
*Question Quest* - Piers Anthony   *f*   186

**Lord, Melanie**
*Haunted* - Tamara Thorne   *h*   5463

**Lysander**
*Phaze Doubt* - Piers Anthony   *f*   184

**Maria Elena**
*Humans* - Donald E. Westlake   *f*   5768

**Metis, Jean**
*Crygender* - Thomas T. Thomas   *s*   5451

**Monlux, Cassandra**
*Slow Freight* - F.M. Busby   *s*   785

**Oren, Eichra**
*Converse and Conflict* - L. Neil Smith   *s*   5130

**Pasco**
*Ghost Dancers* - Brian Craig   *s*   1238

**Pelicanos, Yosh**
*Distraction* - Bruce Sterling   *s*   5256

**Piyolss, Faan Korispais**
*Wild Magic* - Jo Clayton   *f*   1072

**Preston, Carl**
*Ghost Dancers* - Brian Craig   *s*   1238

**Quint**
*Psi-Man* - David Peters   *s*   4305

**Sheila**
*After the Blue* - Russel Like   *s*   3465

**Stein, Rachel**
*Search and Destroy* - Keith William Andrews   *s*   141

**Sterling, Justin**
*Dark Heart* - Margaret Weis   *f*   5707

**Tamberly, Wanda**
*The Shield of Time* - Poul Anderson   *s*   131

**Tanner, Vaughn**
*Mad Roy's Light* - Paula King   *s*   3125

**Tarz, Auriel**
*World Spirits* - Aline Boucher-Kaplan   *s*   580

**Tinker, Austin**
*Crygender* - Thomas T. Thomas   *s*   5451

**Troy, Linda Ellen "Sparta"**
*The Diamond Moon* - Paul Preuss   *s*   4417

**Undershort, Ozwaldo**
*Free Radicals* - Jack McKinney   *s*   3848

**Whaler, Nathaniel Firstborne**
*The Ecolitan Enigma* - L.E. Modesitt Jr.   *s*   3927

## ALCOHOLIC

**Asquith, Timothy**
*Ghostwright* - Michael Cadnum   *h*   810

**Devlin, Johnny**
*Trader* - Charles de Lint   *f*   1438

**Mallau, Olney**
*Hand of Prophecy* - Severna Park   *s*   4244

**Malone, Jessie**
*The Golden Nineties* - Lisa Mason   *s*   3663

**Michael**
*The Eyes of Torie Webster* - Roy Sorrels   *h*   5164

**Musgrave, Wycherly "Wych"**
*Gravelight* - Marion Zimmer Bradley   *f*   636

**Watkins, Daniel J.**
*The Golden Nineties* - Lisa Mason   *s*   3663

**Wilkins, Mike**
*Silent Scream* - Dan Schmidt   *h*   4883

## ALIEN

**Abe**
*The Clouds of Magellan* - David F. Nighbert   *s*   4103

**Acorna**
*Acorna* - Anne McCaffrey   *s*   3717

**Afsan**
*Far-Seer* - Robert J. Sawyer   *s*   4854
*Fossil Hunter* - Robert J. Sawyer   *s*   4855

**Akktri**
*In the Cube* - David Alexander Smith   *s*   5109

**Andrachis, Shil**
*Shadows on the Sun* - Michael Jan Friedman   *s*   2069

**Angel**
*The Pure Cold Light* - Gregory Frost   *s*   2087

**Anito**
*The Color of Distance* - Amy Thomson   *s*   5461

**Apophis**
*Stargate SG-1* - Ashley McConnell   *s*   3777

**Arbok**
*Prison Ship* - Martin Caidin   *s*   828

**Archemon**
*Monsoon* - Peter L. Rice   *s*   4583

**Arthur**
*The Immortality Option* - James P. Hogan   *s*   2725

**Aryl**
*Under Alien Stars* - Pamela F. Service   *s*   4919

**Asan**
*Requiem for Anthi* - Jay D. Blakeney   *s*   517

**Asx/Ewasx**
*Infinity's Shore* - David Brin   *s*   688

**At**
*Doctor's Orders* - Diane Duane   *s*   1659

**Atvar**
*Worldwar: In the Balance* - Harry Turtledove   *s*   5515
*Worldwar: Striking the Balance* - Harry Turtledove   *s*   5516
*Worldwar: Tilting the Balance* - Harry Turtledove   *s*   5517
*Worldwar: Upsetting the Balance* - Harry Turtledove   *s*   5518

**Auganzar**
*Warlord of Heaven* - Adrian Cole   *f*   1102

**Autothor**
*Codgerspace* - Alan Dean Foster   *s*   1999

**Ayyah**
*Cat's Gambit* - Leslie Gadallah   *s*   2099

**Aza-Kra**
*Rule Golden and Double Meaning* - Damon Knight   *s*   3189

**Baby Baby**
*Rock 'n' Roll Babes From Outer Space* - Linda Javin   *s*   2880

**bad-Jam, Gilan "Gilan the Third"**
*The Swords of Zinjaban* - L. Sprague de Camp   *s*   1418

**Baggy**
*Judson's Eden* - Keith Laumer   *s*   3344

**Bandit**
*Fire Planet* - P.M. Griffin   *s*   2436

**Barbtail, Dotson**
*Seeds of Destiny* - Thomas A. Easton   *s*   1724

**Barion**
*The Snake Oil Wars* - Parke Godwin   *s*   2249

**Bastable**
*Charmed* - Marilyn Singer   *f*   5070

**Beaver, Bucky**
*McLendon's Syndrome* - Robert Frezza   *s*   2053

**Beloved Light**
*Acts of Conscience* - William Barton   *s*   377

**Big Sword**
*Project Farcry* - Pauline Ashwell   *s*   230

**Bilrog**
*Labyrinth* - Dennis Schmidt   *s*   4884

**BKR**
*Aliens Stole My Body* - Bruce Coville   *s*   1217

**Blacktop**
*Tower of the Gods* - Thomas A. Easton   *s*   1726

**Bluecloak**
*Remnant Population* - Elizabeth Moon   s   3972

**Blueshell**
*A Fire upon the Deep* - Vernor Vinge   s   5573

**Bontu**
*Life Form* - Alan Dean Foster   s   2008

**Braan**
*Genellan: Planetfall* - Scott G. Gier   s   2223

**Brownbenttalon**
*O Pioneer!* - Frederik Pohl   s   4350

**Broxholm**
*My Teacher Flunked the Planet* - Bruce
   Coville   s   1222

**Brutogas, Kator Secondcousin**
*Naked to the Stars/The Alien Way* - Gordon R.
   Dickson   s   1537

**Bult**
*Uncharted Territory* - Connie Willis   s   5875

**Cag**
*Them* - William W. Johnstone   h   2935

**Caldaq**
*A Call to Arms* - Alan Dean Foster   s   1995

**Cale**
*Invasion America* - Christie Golden   s   2252
*On the Run* - Christie Golden   s   2254

**Calhoun, Janey**
*Warpath* - Tony Daniel   s   1337

**Catherine**
*Flying to Valhalla* - Charles Pellegrino   s   4280

**Chakallakak, Chakallakak "Chaka" ngha**
*The Long Hunt* - Debra Doyle   s   1602

**Champion, Dragonbait**
*Masquerades* - Kate Novak   f   4166
*Song of the Saurials* - Kate Novak   f   4167

**Channon**
*Target* - Janet Morris   s   4017

**Chanur, Hilfy**
*Chanur's Legacy* - C.J. Cherryh   s   981

**Charlie**
*Neptune Crossing* - Jeffrey A. Carver   s   933
*Strange Attractors* - Jeffrey A. Carver   s   934

**Charlie/Charlene**
*The Infinite Sea* - Jeffrey A. Carver   s   932

**Chedo, Gral II**
*Random Factor* - Joel Henry Sherman   s   4984

**Chewbacca**
*The Crystal Star* - Vonda N. McIntyre   s   3820
*Jedi Search* - Kevin J. Anderson   s   109

**Chi-da**
*Wulfsyarn: A Mosaic* - Phillip Mann   s   3617

**Chirwl**
*Medicine Show* - Jody Lynn Nye   s   4172

**Chmeee**
*The Ringworld Throne* - Larry Niven   s   4128

**Chomanche**
*A Miracle of Rare Design* - Mike Resnick   s   4550

**Chrestil, Damian**
*Burning Bright* - Melissa Scott   s   4894

**Chuut-Riit**
*The Children's Hour* - Jerry Pournelle   s   4372

**Claro**
*An Eye for Dark Places* - Norma Marder   s   3622

**Clavel**
*North Wind* - Gwyneth Jones   s   2953

**Cotto, Vir**
*Personal Agendas* - Al Sarrantonio   s   4833

**Coyul**
*The Snake Oil Wars* - Parke Godwin   s   2249

**Cwan, Si**
*End Game* - Peter David   s   1382

**Dahmi**
*Alien Eyes* - Lynn S. Hightower   s   2683

**Dahnak**
*Diplomatic Act* - Peter Jurasik   s   2996

**Dak, Maanka "Pete Moss"**
*The Change* - Barry B. Longyear   s   3520

**Davakinapwottapellazanzis**
*The Expediter* - J. Brian Clarke   s   1062

**Dax, Jadzia**
*Call to Arms* - Diane Carey   s   901
*Time's Enemy* - L.A. Graf   s   2297

**Deayl**
*The Homecoming* - Barry B. Longyear   s   3521

**Derrith, Verrer ni Rimmani san**
*World Spirits* - Aline Boucher-Kaplan   s   580

**Dhalvad**
*Seeking the Dream Brother* - Marcia J.
   Bennett   s   451

**di Sarc, Sira**
*A Thousand Words for Stranger* - Julie E.
   Czerneda   s   1304

**Diamond, Tal**
*City of Diamond* - Jane Emerson   s   1807

**Diehrenn**
*Encounter with Tiber* - Buzz Aldrin   s   64

**d'jehn, Tahl**
*The Alien Dark* - Diana G. Gallagher   s   2108

**Dnivtopun**
*The Children's Hour* - Jerry Pournelle   s   4372

**Dob**
*Back to the Time Trap* - Keith Laumer   s   3343

**Donokh**
*Shade* - Emily Devenport   s   1504

**Dopey**
*The Other End of Time* - Frederik Pohl   s   4351

**Dorcas**
*Truckers* - Terry Pratchett   s   4402

**Dorella**
*Dorella* - Mark A. Garland   f   2142

**D'oud**
*The False Mirror* - Alan Dean Foster   s   2004

**Douglas, Medoret**
*A Whisper of Time* - Paula E. Downing   s   1595

**Dowornobb**
*Genellan: Planetfall* - Scott G. Gier   s   2223

**Dragit**
*On the Run* - Christie Golden   s   2254

**Dreadful Eye**
*The Woman between the Worlds* - F. Gwynplaine
   MacIntyre   s   3596

**Droagn, Endark**
*Lair of the Cyclops* - Allen L. Wold   s   5933

**Dulcimer**
*Transcendence* - Charles Sheffield   s   4967

**Durvash**
*Man-Kzin Wars V* - Larry Niven   s   4125

**Dweller**
*The Source* - Brian Lumley   h   3565

**Dy-Dybo**
*Fossil Hunter* - Robert J. Sawyer   s   4855

**Ecu**
*Empire's End* - Allan Cole   s   1103

**The Return of the Emperor** - Allan Cole   s   1106

**Eerin, Ri-El**
*Shadow World* - A.C. Crispin   s   1262

**elan Emok, Stuk**
*Half-Light* - Denise Vitola   s   5575

**Elavel**
*White Queen* - Gwyneth Jones   s   2955

**Eleph**
*Mercycle* - Piers Anthony   s   181

**em-Pelsh, Jag Kandaro**
*Starplex* - Robert J. Sawyer   s   4859

**Enemy**
*Cold Fire* - Dean R. Koontz   h   3203

**Ennnesstheh**
*Cannon's Orb* - L. Warren Douglas   s   1586

**Ersh**
*Beholder's Eye* - Julie E. Czerneda   s   1303

**Esen-Alit-Quar**
*Beholder's Eye* - Julie E. Czerneda   s   1303

**Estriss**
*Into the Void* - Nigel Findley   f   1937
*The Radiant Dragon* - Elaine Cunningham   f   1291

**Eth**
*Dream-Weaver* - Louise Lawrence   s   3359

**Ettalira**
*To Fear the Light* - Ben Bova   s   595

**Eudoxus**
*The Gripping Hand* - Larry Niven   s   4122

**Evangeline**
*Alien Earth* - Megan Lindholm   s   3469

**Eye on Sky**
*Anvil of Stars* - Greg Bear   s   414

**Farree**
*Dare to Go A-Hunting* - Andre Norton   s   4147

**Faslorn**
*The Sails of Tau Ceti* - Michael McCollum   s   3771

**f'ath, Riitha**
*The Alien Dark* - Diana G. Gallagher   s   2108

**Flez**
*Living with Aliens* - John DeChancie   s   1460

**Francisco, George**
*The Change* - Barry B. Longyear   s   3520
*Cross of Blood* - K.W. Jeter   s   2909
*Dark Horizon* - K.W. Jeter   s   2910

**Frankel, Cathy**
*Cross of Blood* - K.W. Jeter   s   2909

**Fred**
*After the Blue* - Russel Like   s   3465

**G.Ren.Bei.Yi**
*Alien Tongue* - Stephen Leigh   s   3424

**Gantha**
*Afterimage* - Kristine Kathryn Rusch   f   4709

**G'Dath**
*A Flag Full of Stars* - Brad Ferguson   s   1922

**Genius**
*The Immortality Option* - James P. Hogan   s   2725

**Geronimo**
*The Voices of Heaven* - Frederik Pohl   s   4356

**Ghere, Rhule**
*The Parafaith War* - L.E. Modesitt Jr.   s   3937

**Ghoster**
*Cyberstealth* - S.N. Lewitt   s   3450
*Dancing Vac* - S.N. Lewitt   s   3451

**Giant**
*The Earth Giant* - Melvin Burgess   s   773

**G'Kar**
*Personal Agendas* - Al Sarrantonio   s   4833

**Gnoza**
*The Longest Voyage/Slow Lightning* - Poul
Anderson   s   130

**Godfrey**
*The Ragged World: A Novel of the Hefn on Earth* -
Judith Moffett   s   3943

**Gomja, Herphan**
*Beyond the Moons* - David Cook   f   1144

**Goodlooking/Bella**
*North Wind* - Gwyneth Jones   s   2953

**Gray**
*The Longest Voyage/Slow Lightning* - Poul
Anderson   s   130

**Grayshard**
*Lair of the Cyclops* - Allen L. Wold   s   5933

**Grraf-Commander**
*Cathouse* - Dean Ing   s   2828

**Grzzeearoghh "Grizz"**
*Treaty at Doona* - Anne McCaffrey   s   3752

**Guinan**
*The Devil's Heart* - Carmen Carter   s   922
*Vendetta* - Peter David   s   1389

**Gurder**
*Wings* - Terry Pratchett   s   4403

**Gurronsevas**
*The Galactic Gourmet* - James White   s   5778

**Gwarha, Ettin**
*Ring of Swords* - Eleanor Arnason   s   210

**Ha'ark**
*Never Sound Retreat* - William R.
Forstchen   s   1981

**Hadrak, Quisaz**
*Martian Deathtrap* - Nathan Archer   s   205

**Haji, Hool**
*Kane of Old Mars* - Michael Moorcock   s   3983

**Hask**
*Illegal Alien* - Robert J. Sawyer   s   4858

**Hazaar**
*Larissa* - Emily Devenport   s   1503

**Hesseth**
*Black Sun Rising* - C.S. Friedman   f   2056
*When True Night Falls* - C.S. Friedman   f   2060

**Hindmost**
*The Ringworld Throne* - Larry Niven   s   4128

**Hokokul, Cha Ishil**
*Jaran* - Kate Elliott   s   1772

**Hoo-Lan**
*My Teacher Glows in the Dark* - Bruce
Coville   s   1224

**Hph-wayuo "Alvin"**
*Brightness Reef* - David Brin   s   684
*Heaven's Reach* - David Brin   s   687
*Infinity's Shore* - David Brin   s   688

**Hr.Tyi.Bei.k.ai**
*Alien Tongue* - Stephen Leigh   s   3424

**Hrrestan**
*Treaty at Doona* - Anne McCaffrey   s   3752

**Hrriss**
*Crisis on Doona* - Anne McCaffrey   s   3723

**H'sial, Atvar**
*Convergence* - Charles Sheffield   s   4951

**Humphrey**
*Time, Like an Ever-Rolling Stream* - Judith
Moffett   s   3944

**ih'iie-u Ulak!ha', Hwii**
*Dark Mirror* - Diane Duane   s   1658

**Ilisidi**
*Foreigner* - C.J. Cherryh   s   990
*Inheritor* - C.J. Cherryh   s   997

**Indiw**
*Border Dispute* - Daniel R. Kerns   s   3066

**Ineluki the Storm King**
*Stone of Farewell* - Tad Williams   f   5831

**Iquar, Kryx**
*Catch the Lightning* - Catherine Asaro   s   218

**Irtuk-Saa**
*The Triad Worlds* - F.M. Busby   s   786

**Jabba the Hutt**
*Tales From Jabba's Palace* - Kevin J.
Anderson   s   114

**Jalanopi**
*Purgatory: A Chronicle of a Distant World* - Mike
Resnick   s   4554

**Javobo**
*Mainline* - Deborah Christian   s   1026

**Jed**
*Jed the Dead* - Alan Dean Foster   s   2007

**Jenna**
*Stranded* - Camarin Grae   s   2295

**Jeryl**
*Mentor* - Kris Jensen   s   2898

**Jorana**
*The Howling Stones* - Alan Dean Foster   s   2006

**K, Ylla**
*The Martian Chronicles* - Ray Bradbury   s   622

**Kah-laye-dee**
*The Magic Bicycle* - William Hill   f   2688

**Kaid**
*Fire Margins* - Lisanne Norman   s   4137
*Razor's Edge* - Lisanne Norman   s   4139

**KaiSa**
*Dark Water's Embrace* - Stephen Leigh   s   3426

**Kalass, Et**
*In the Shadow of the Moon* - Scott G. Gier   s   2224

**Kapellmeister**
*Acts of Conscience* - William Barton   s   377

**Karpou, Betty Lou**
*My Teacher Fried My Brains* - Bruce
Coville   s   1223

**Kee-Toroca**
*Fossil Hunter* - Robert J. Sawyer   s   4855

**Kent, Clark "Superman"**
*The Death and Life of Superman* - Roger
Stern   s   5262
*The Further Adventures of Superman* - Martin H.
Greenberg   s   2393
*Lois & Clark* - C.J. Cherryh   s   999

**Kes**
*Chrysalis* - David Niall Wilson   s   5880

**Khar'pern**
*Exiles' Return* - Gayle Greeno   s   2420
*Finders-Seekers* - Gayle Greeno   s   2421
*Mind-Speakers' Call* - Gayle Greeno   s   2423

**Khruuz**
*More than Fire* - Philip Jose Farmer   s   1871

**Khyriz**
*Voices of Chaos* - A.C. Crispin   s   1266

**Kikun**
*Shadowkill* - Jo Clayton   s   1069
*Shadowplay* - Jo Clayton   s   1070
*Shadowspeer* - Jo Clayton   s   1071

**Kira**
*Bloodletter* - K.W. Jeter   s   2908
*Devil in the Sky* - Greg Cox   s   1226

**Kirha**
*Wing Commander: Freedom Flight* - Mercedes
Lackey   s   3307

**K'Kai**
*Wing Commander: Freedom Flight* - Mercedes
Lackey   s   3307

**KLse**
*GodHeads* - Emily Devenport   s   1501

**Knossus**
*Larissa* - Emily Devenport   s   1503
*Shade* - Emily Devenport   s   1504

**Koyil**
*Fallway* - Paula E. Downing   s   1593

**Kraal**
*The Artifact* - W. Michael Gear   s   2165

**Krecis**
*Saturn's Child* - Nichelle Nichols   s   4101

**Kreeblim**
*My Teacher Flunked the Planet* - Bruce
Coville   s   1222

**Krillen**
*Ancestor's World* - A.C. Crispin   s   1259

**Kullervo, Vyra**
*Greenthieves* - Alan Dean Foster   s   2005

**Kurz**
*Fire in the Sky* - Jo Clayton   s   1067

**Kusac**
*Fire Margins* - Lisanne Norman   s   4137
*Fortune's Wheel* - Lisanne Norman   s   4138
*Razor's Edge* - Lisanne Norman   s   4139
*Turning Point* - Lisanne Norman   s   4140

**Kyllikki**
*Dreamspy* - Jacqueline Lichtenberg   s   3458

**Kymri**
*Grounded!* - Chris Claremont   s   1041

**Laleekh**
*Bagatelle—Guinevere* - Nancy Bogen   f   558

**Lalelelang**
*The Spoils of War* - Alan Dean Foster   s   2016

**Link**
*In the Heart of Darkness* - Eric Flint   s   1955

**Linter, Dervley**
*The State of the Art* - Iain M. Banks   s   327

**Lioren**
*The Genocidal Healer* - James White   s   5779

**Lizard Lips**
*In the Shadow of the Moon* - Scott G. Gier   s   2224

**Long-Reach**
*Man-Kzin Wars IV* - Larry Niven   s   4124

**Looks-at-Charts**
*Quozl* - Alan Dean Foster   s   2013

**Lungo Muso**
*Outpost* - Scott Mackay   s   3597

**Magus, Stheneleos XLIV**
*Web of Futures* - Jefferson P. Swycaffer   f   5376

**Maldari**
*The Fearful Summons* - Denny Martin Flinn   s   1954

**Malva**
*The Caterpillar's Question* - Piers Anthony   f   164

**Manadgi**
*Foreigner* - C.J. Cherryh   s   990

**Marik, Dao**
*Hopeship* - Simon Lang   s   3315
*The Trumpets of Tagan* - Simon Lang   s   3316

**Markhamwit**
*Design for Great-Day* - Alan Dean Foster   s   2001

**Marlowe, Zoot**
*Hawaiian U.F.O. Aliens* - Mel Gilden   s   2226
*Tubular Android Superheroes* - Mel Gilden   s   2228

**Maroc, Huud**
*The Merro Tree* - Katie Waitman   s   5609

**The Marra**
*The Madness Season* - C.S. Friedman   s   2058

**Masklin**
*Truckers* - Terry Pratchett   s   4402
*Wings* - Terry Pratchett   s   4403

**M'ats**
*Delta Pavonis* - Eric Kotani   s   3221

**Maverick**
*Maverick* - Bruce Bethke   s   484

**Medalont**
*Final Diagnosis* - James White   s   5777

**Melody**
*Finity's End* - C.J. Cherryh   s   988

**Mephistopheles**
*Jack Faust* - Michael Swanwick   s   5372

**Mikk**
*The Merro Tree* - Katie Waitman   s   5609

**Miya**
*Dreamfall* - Joan D. Vinge   s   5571

**Moki**
*The Color of Distance* - Amy Thomson   s   5461

**Mollari, Londo**
*Day of the Dead* - Neil Gaiman   s   2102
*Personal Agendas* - Al Sarrantonio   s   4833

**Morgen**
*Mad Roy's Light* - Paula King   s   3125

**Mullica, Jack**
*Hard Landing* - Algis Budrys   s   753

**Myshtigo, Cort**
*This Immortal* - Roger Zelazny   s   6074

**Naoh**
*Dreamfall* - Joan D. Vinge   s   5571

**Narrow Leg**
*The Ship Errant* - Jody Lynn Nye   s   4175

**Neal, Porsche**
*Beneath the Gated Sky* - Robert Reed   s   4502
*Beyond the Veil of Stars* - Robert Reed   s   4503

**Nebuun**
*Random Factor* - Joel Henry Sherman   s   4984

**Neelix**
*The Final Fury* - Dafydd ab Hugh   s   9

**Nemo**
*Metaphase* - Vonda N. McIntyre   s   3821

**Nemony**
*Dream-Weaver* - Louise Lawrence   s   3359

**Neskat, Merinda**
*Nightsword* - Margaret Weis   f   5722
*Sentinels* - Margaret Weis   s   5725

**Ngenga, Ngina-li "Ngina"**
*The Inquisitor* - Cheryl J. Franklin   s   2037

**Nia**
*A Woman of the Iron People* - Eleanor
    Arnason   s   211

**No'shto-shti-stlen**
*Chanur's Legacy* - C.J. Cherryh   s   981

**nu-Aten, Ha'riel**
*Smoke and Mirrors* - Jane M. Lindskold   s   3476

**Nukurren**
*Mother of Demons* - Eric Flint   s   1956

**Obo**
*Mind Slayer* - Kevin D. Randle   s   4469

**Odo**
*Fallen Heroes* - Dafydd ab Hugh   s   8
*Warped* - K.W. Jeter   s   2917

**O'lal**
*Cat-A-Lyst* - Alan Dean Foster   s   1997

**Old Grendel**
*Beowulf's Children* - Larry Niven   s   4116

**Oneness**
*Phylum Monsters* - Hayford Peirce   s   4276

**Onyx**
*Marks of Our Brothers* - Jane M. Lindskold   s   3475

**Operative 41**
*The Salukan Gambit* - Sean Dalton   s   1333

**Orchestra**
*Nautilus* - Vonda N. McIntyre   s   3823

**Palaton**
*Path of Fire* - Charles Ingrid   s   2832

**Pandora**
*Pandora* - Alan Rodgers   h   4650

**Panshinea**
*Path of Fire* - Charles Ingrid   s   2832

**Peach-Frog-At-Twilight**
*Jade Darcy and the Zen Pirates* - Stephen
    Goldin   s   2260

**Petaybee**
*Power Play* - Anne McCaffrey   s   3744

**Poole**
*Lightwing* - Tara K. Harper   s   2551

**Poseen-Ka**
*The Final Battle* - William C. Dietz   s   1546

**Prefect, Ford**
*The Illustrated Hitchhiker's Guide to the Galaxy* -
    Douglas Adams   s   29
*Mostly Harmless* - Douglas Adams   s   31

**Prilicla**
*The Galactic Gourmet* - James White   s   5778
*Mind Changer* - James White   s   5780

**Prowl Captain**
*A Darker Geometry* - Mark O. Martin   s   3649

**Prtglm**
*Lyon's Pride* - Anne McCaffrey   s   3738

**Pulon**
*Ganwold's Child* - Diann Thornley   s   5467

**Puzzle Solver**
*Alien Blues* - Lynn S. Hightower   s   2682

**Q**
*All Good Things. . .* - Michael Jan Friedman   s   2061
*Q-in-Law* - Peter David   s   1384
*Q-Space* - Greg Cox   s   1228
*Q-Squared* - Peter David   s   1385
*Q-Zone* - Greg Cox   s   1229

**Quan, Zhongli**
*Vengeance Strike* - David Robbins   s   4604

**Quark**
*Fallen Heroes* - Dafydd ab Hugh   s   8

**Quath'jutt'kkal'thon "Quath"**
*Furious Gulf* - Gregory Benford   s   447
*Tides of Light* - Gregory Benford   s   450

**Ra-hotep-kan "Ra"**
*StarGate* - Dean Devlin   s   1509

**Raayat**
*The Madness Season* - C.S. Friedman   s   2058

**Rah**
*Lake of the Sun* - Wynne Whiteford   s   5787

**Rane**
*Mirror to the Sky* - Mark S. Geston   s   2213

**Raqella**
*Sundowner* - Chris Claremont   s   1043

**Rarberticandornan, "Ar"**
*Dragons in the Stars* - Jeffrey A. Carver   s   930

**Ras, Pawasar Pawasar**
*Earthgrip* - Harry Turtledove   s   5499

**Redwing, T'fyrr**
*The Eagle and the Nightingales* - Mercedes
    Lackey   f   3278

**Reem "First Cousin Brother"**
*Brother Termite* - Patricia Anthony   s   156

**Ripi-Arana-Hoc, Ripi**
*Deepdrive* - Alexander Jablokov   s   2837

**Rozhenko, Worf**
*Worf's First Adventure* - Peter David   s   1391

**Saalahan**
*Mid-Flinx* - Alan Dean Foster   s   2010

**Sailor "Lightning"**
*Silent Dances* - A.C. Crispin   s   1263

**Sarek**
*Sarek* - A.C. Crispin   s   1260

**Sax/Ewasx**
*Brightness Reef* - David Brin   s   684

**Scorpio**
*Dragon's Blood* - Alex McDonough   s   3799
*Dragon's Claw* - Alex McDonough   s   3800
*Dragon's Eye* - Alex McDonough   s   3801
*Scorpio* - Alex McDonough   s   3802
*Scorpio Descending* - Alex McDonough   s   3803
*Scorpio Rising* - Alex McDonough   s   3804

**Scour**
*Starliner* - David Drake   s   1645

**Seeker**
*Labyrinth* - Dennis Schmidt   s   4884

**Seetoo "Jolly"**
*Marooned on Eden* - Robert L. Forward   s   1986

**Sensar**
*Minds Apart* - Margaret Davis   s   1408

**Seresen**
*Happy Policeman* - Patricia Anthony   s   160

**Sessiri-wohnith**
*Dark Sky Legion* - William Barton   s   379

**Set**
*Orion in the Dying Time* - Ben Bova   s   591

**Shin, Praeis**
*Playing God* - Sarah Zettel   s   6080

**Shn'dar, Queekat**
*Sentinels* - Margaret Weis   s   5725

**Short-Son "Eater-of-Grass" of Chiirr-Nig**
*Man-Kzin Wars IV* - Larry Niven   s   4124

**Silver-Rim**
*Ocean under the Ice* - Robert L. Forward   s   1988

**Sith**
*The House of Doors* - Brian Lumley   h   3554
*Maze of Worlds* - Brian Lumley   h   3559

**Skerow**
*Flesh and Gold* - Phyllis Gotlieb   s   2286

**Skipper**
*Only Child* - H.M. Hoover   s   2764

**Slasher**
*The Weigher* - Eric Vinicoff   s   5574

**Sma, Diziet**
*The State of the Art* - Iain M. Banks   s   327

**S'Nash**
*Fossil* - Hal Clement   s   1083

**Snout**
*Aliens Stole My Body* - Bruce Coville   *s*   1217

**Sobek, Yoo**
*Hostile Takeover* - Jack McKinney   *s*   3849

**Soleta**
*End Game* - Peter David   *s*   1382
*Worf's First Adventure* - Peter David   *s*   1391

**Spock**
*Avenger* - William Shatner   *s*   4928
*The City on the Edge of Forever* - Harlan
   Ellison   *s*   1784
*Crossover* - Michael Jan Friedman   *s*   2063
*Crossroad* - Barbara Hambly   *s*   2501
*First Frontier* - Diane Carey   *s*   902
*First Strike* - Diane Carey   *s*   903
*The Joy Machine* - James Gunn   *s*   2458
*Mind Meld* - John Vornholt   *s*   5596
*Prime Directive* - Judith Reeves-Stevens   *s*   4514
*Probe* - Margaret Wander Bonanno   *s*   569
*Renegade* - Gene DeWeese   *s*   1511
*The Return* - William Shatner   *s*   4933
*The Rift* - Peter David   *s*   1386
*Sanctuary* - John Vornholt   *s*   5597
*Sarek* - A.C. Crispin   *s*   1260
*Spectre* - William Shatner   *s*   4934
*Star Trek: The Classic Episodes 1* - James
   Blish   *s*   526
*Star Trek: The Classic Episodes 2* - James
   Blish   *s*   527
*Star Trek: The Classic Episodes 3* - James
   Blish   *s*   528
*Star Trek: The Lost Years* - J.M. Dillard   *s*   1557
*Vulcan's Forge* - Susan Shwartz   *s*   5019
*Vulcan's Glory* - D.C. Fontana   *s*   1967
*Windows on a Lost World* - V.E. Mitchell   *s*   3920

**Spots-Son of Chotrz-Shaa**
*Man-Kzin Wars V* - Larry Niven   *s*   4125

**Steele, Vanessa**
*The Woman between the Worlds* - F. Gwynplaine
   MacIntyre   *s*   3596

**String**
*Alien Blues* - Lynn S. Hightower   *s*   2682
*Alien Eyes* - Lynn S. Hightower   *s*   2683
*Alien Heat* - Lynn S. Hightower   *s*   2684
*Alien Rites* - Lynn S. Hightower   *s*   2685

**Succor-of-Yellowways-Sands**
*Nanoware Time/The Persistence of Vision* - Ian
   Watson   *s*   5638

**sud Sarc, Barac**
*A Thousand Words for Stranger* - Julie E.
   Czerneda   *s*   1304

**sutai-Khornezh, Kasak**
*Rules of Engagement* - Peter Morwood   *s*   4037

**Swadeith, Sfalek-ni**
*A Plague of Change* - L. Warren Douglas   *s*   1587

**Tabini**
*Invader* - C.J. Cherryh   *s*   998

**Tachyon**
*Ace in the Hole* - George R.R. Martin   *s*   3641
*Jokertown Shuffle* - George R.R. Martin   *s*   3646

**Tali**
*Brother Termite* - Patricia Anthony   *s*   156

**Talker**
*The Remarkables* - Robert Reed   *s*   4507

**Taller**
*Silent Dances* - A.C. Crispin   *s*   1263
*Silent Songs* - A.C. Crispin   *s*   1264

**Tarrik, Jeniper**
*Earth Herald* - Jan Clark   *s*   1046

**Tekkitho, Chin**
*Homegoing* - Frederik Pohl   *s*   4347

**Teska**
*Mind Meld* - John Vornholt   *s*   5596

**Thelia**
*Metamorphosis* - Jean Lorrah   *s*   3524

**Third Historian**
*Berserker Lies* - Fred Saberhagen   *s*   4762

**Thissizz**
*The Merro Tree* - Katie Waitman   *s*   5609

**Thoggish**
*Converse and Conflict* - L. Neil Smith   *s*   5130

**Thowinda**
*The Shining Ones* - Paul Preuss   *s*   4421

**Tiam**
*Probe* - Margaret Wander Bonanno   *s*   569

**Tint, Thaw**
*The Killing Star* - Charles Pellegrino   *s*   4281

**Tooe**
*Derelict for Trade* - Andre Norton   *s*   4148
*A Mind for Trade* - Andre Norton   *s*   4158

**Torres, B'Elanna**
*The Escape* - Dean Wesley Smith   *s*   5113
*The Final Fury* - Dafydd ab Hugh   *s*   9
*Her Klingon Soul* - Michael Jan Friedman   *s*   2064
*Pathways* - Jeri Taylor   *s*   5404

**T'Pris**
*Vulcan's Glory* - D.C. Fontana   *s*   1967

**Trell**
*Illegal Aliens* - Nick Pollotta   *s*   4365

**Trinidad**
*Beneath the Gated Sky* - Robert Reed   *s*   4502

**Troi, Deanna**
*The Last Stand* - Brad Ferguson   *s*   1923
*The Soldiers of Fear* - Dean Wesley Smith   *s*   5115

**Troi, Lwaxana**
*Q-in-Law* - Peter David   *s*   1384

**Troit, Deanna "Dee"**
*Star Wreck IV: Live Long and Profit* - Leah
   Rewolinski   *s*   4565

**Ttan**
*Devil in the Sky* - Greg Cox   *s*   1226

**Tug**
*Alien Earth* - Megan Lindholm   *s*   3469

**Tuvok**
*The Escape* - Dean Wesley Smith   *s*   5113
*Ragnarok* - Nathan Archer   *s*   206

**Ulga, Jubadi va**
*Terrible Swift Sword* - William R.
   Forstchen   *s*   1983

**Ulysses**
*Way Station* - Clifford D. Simak   *s*   5048

**Undershort, Ozwaldo**
*Free Radicals* - Jack McKinney   *s*   3848

**VaGayjur, Supaari**
*Children of God* - Mary Doria Russell   *s*   4735

**Venom**
*Spider-Man: The Venom Factor* - Diane
   Duane   *s*   1667

**Vertok, Kyril**
*Shadows After Dark* - Ouida Crozier   *f*   1286

**Vi-Kata**
*Palace* - Katharine Kerr   *s*   3072

**Vikktakkht**
*Chanur's Legacy* - C.J. Cherryh   *s*   981

**Vortcir**
*They Fly at Ciron* - Samuel R. Delany   *s*   1482

**Wan-To**
*The World at the End of Time* - Frederik
   Pohl   *s*   4357

**Watcher, Lightfoot**
*Foragers* - Charles Oberndorf   *s*   4187

**Wei**
*Rule Golden and Double Meaning* - Damon
   Knight   *s*   3189

**Wheeler**
*Signal to Noise* - Eric S. Nylund   *s*   4179

**Wide**
*Starstrike* - W. Michael Gear   *s*   2172

**Willis**
*Red Planet* - Robert A. Heinlein   *s*   2647

**Windruth**
*Dragon Rigger* - Jeffrey A. Carver   *s*   929

**Worf**
*Armageddon Sky* - L.A. Graf   *s*   2296
*Call to Arms* - Diane Carey   *s*   901
*Doomsday World* - Carmen Carter   *s*   923
*Kahless* - Michael Jan Friedman   *s*   2065
*Reunion* - Michael Jan Friedman   *s*   2068
*Triangle: Imzadi II* - Peter David   *s*   1388

**Worsel**
*Galactic Patrol* - Edward E. Smith   *s*   5116
*Gray Lensman* - Edward E. Smith   *s*   5117

**Xa**
*The Fugitive Worlds* - Bob Shaw   *s*   4942

**Xtasca the Cherub**
*Mother of Plenty* - Colin Greenland   *s*   2417

**Ya-Mash, Yam**
*The Return of the Breakneck Boys* - Geary
   Gravel   *s*   2332

**Yrae**
*Legacy of Earth* - Juanita Coulson   *s*   1209

**Yspht, Jovil**
*Armageddon: The Musical* - Robert Rankin   *s*   4473

**Zahmekoses**
*Encounter with Tiber* - Buzz Aldrin   *s*   64

**Zainal**
*Freedom's Challenge* - Anne McCaffrey   *s*   3732
*Freedom's Choice* - Anne McCaffrey   *s*   3733
*Freedom's Landing* - Anne McCaffrey   *s*   3734

**Zaula**
*Requiem for Anthi* - Jay D. Blakeney   *s*   517

**Zeerus**
*Target Earth* - Steve Perry   *s*   4301

**Zennor**
*First Strike* - Diane Carey   *s*   903

**Zephkar**
*Stranded* - Camarin Grae   *s*   2295

**Zorba the Hutt**
*Zorba the Hutt's Revenge* - Paul Davids   *s*   1394

**Zorg**
*Living with Aliens* - John DeChancie   *s*   1460

**Zurzal**
*Brother to Shadows* - Andre Norton   *s*   4142

## AMNESIAC

**Bone**
*Bone* - George C. Chesbro   *h*   1006

**Bronkman, Theo "Peter Ambrose"**
*Nimbus* - Alexander Jablokov   *s*   2839

**Burnell**
*Somewhere East of Life* - Brian W. Aldiss   *s*   60

**Caine, Tycho**
*Evil Ascending* - Michael A. Stackpole   *s*   5198

*A Gathering Evil* - Michael A. Stackpole   *s*   5201

**Cassidy**
*The Persistence of Memory* - Karen Ripley   *s*   4592

**Dart**
*The Wooden Sword* - Lynn Abbey   *f*   18

**Delaney, Cathy "Cassidy"**
*The Warden of Horses* - Karen Ripley   *s*   4595

**Derec**
*Changeling* - Stephen Leigh   *s*   3425
*Renegade* - Cordell Scotten   *s*   4903

**di Sarc, Sira**
*A Thousand Words for Stranger* - Julie E. Czerneda   *s*   1304

**Felicitas**
*Outpost* - Scott Mackay   *s*   3597

**Lund, Jack "Mr. Was"**
*Mr. Was* - Pete Hautman   *s*   2614

**Moon, Everett "Chaos"**
*Amnesia Moon* - Jonathan Lethem   *f*   3438

**Musgrave, Winter**
*Witchlight* - Marion Zimmer Bradley   *f*   655

**Nicolau, Grigori**
*Frostwing* - Richard A. Knaak   *f*   3170

**Other**
*Mr. Murder* - Dean R. Koontz   *h*   3213

**Sara**
*Children of the Blood: Book Two of The Sundered* - Michelle Sagara   *f*   4782

**Saro**
*The Book of Atrix Wolfe* - Patricia A. McKillip   *f*   3838

**Sparrow**
*The Dark Beyond the Stars* - Frank M. Robinson   *s*   4626

**Tuiereann, Aedham "Adam"**
*Elvendude* - Mark Shepherd   *f*   4980

**West, Kilimanjaro**
*Out on Blue Six* - Ian McDonald   *s*   3794

## ANDROID

**Arda**
*Murder at the Galactic Writers' Society* - Janet Asimov   *s*   251

**Attila**
*Hunter's Planet* - David Bischoff   *s*   492

**Bettik, A.**
*Endymion* - Dan Simmons   *s*   5051

**Billy the Kid**
*The Illegal Rebirth of Billy the Kid* - Rebecca Ore   *s*   4220

**Bishop**
*Alien 3* - Alan Dean Foster   *s*   1993

**Dacron**
*Star Wreck III: Time Warped* - Leah Rewolinski   *s*   4564

**Dagon**
*Dead Boys* - Richard Calder   *s*   836

**Dahlgren, Mod**
*Heart of Red Iron* - Phyllis Gotlieb   *s*   2287

**Data**
*The Devil's Heart* - Carmen Carter   *s*   922
*Doomsday World* - Carmen Carter   *s*   923
*Imzadi* - Peter David   *s*   1383
*Insurrection* - J.M. Dillard   *s*   1554
*Intellivore* - Diane Duane   *s*   1663
*The Last Stand* - Brad Ferguson   *s*   1923
*Metamorphosis* - Jean Lorrah   *s*   3524

**Datum**
*Treks Not Taken: What if Stephen King, Anne Rice, Bret Easton Ellis, and Other Literary Greats Had Written Episodes of Star Trek: The Next Generation?* - Steven R. Boyett   *s*   607

**Divine Endurance**
*Flowerdust* - Gwyneth Jones   *s*   2952

**Doon, Harley**
*Steelheart* - William C. Dietz   *s*   1552

**Hac**
*Mission: Tori* - Johanna Bolton   *s*   564

**Hamlet**
*Too, Too Solid Flesh* - Nick O'Donohoe   *s*   4197

**Lipstick**
*Dead Things* - Richard Calder   *s*   838

**Lysander**
*Phaze Doubt* - Piers Anthony   *f*   184

**Munk**
*Solis* - A.A. Attanasio   *s*   272

**Pablo "Sam Krueger"**
*Proxies* - Laura J. Mixon   *s*   3922

**Primavera**
*Dead Girls* - Richard Calder   *s*   837

**Rachael**
*Blade Runner 2: The Edge of Human* - K.W. Jeter   *s*   2906

**Reno, Amy**
*Steelheart* - William C. Dietz   *s*   1552

**Silvercup**
*Hostile Takeover* - Jack McKinney   *s*   3849

**SU912**
*Christmas Slaughter* - Mark Grant   *s*   2323

**Vanity**
*Dead Boys* - Richard Calder   *s*   836

**Yod**
*He, She and It* - Marge Piercy   *s*   4325

## ANGEL

**Ananayel**
*Humans* - Donald E. Westlake   *f*   5768

**Anzelm, Aitan**
*The Ways of Magic* - Scott Ciencin   *f*   1033

**Asofel**
*The Shadow Eater* - Adam Lee   *f*   3386

**Aziraphale**
*Good Omens: The Nice and Accurate Prophecies of Agnes Nutter, Witch* - Neil Gaiman   *f*   2103

**Babriel**
*Bring Me the Head of Prince Charming* - Roger Zelazny   *f*   6062

**Craobb**
*Moonwise* - Greer Ilene Gilman   *f*   2238

**Crowley**
*Good Omens: The Nice and Accurate Prophecies of Agnes Nutter, Witch* - Neil Gaiman   *f*   2103

**Darian**
*Angelwalk: A Modern Fable* - Roger Elwood   *f*   1803

**Ezekiel "Zeke"**
*The Seraphim Rising* - Elisabeth De Vos   *s*   1442

**Gabriel**
*Archangel* - Sharon Shinn   *s*   5000

**Harrison, Nick "The Devil"**
*Resurrection* - Katharine Kerr   *s*   3075

**Jiminez, Angelita Carmen**
*Angels Unaware* - L. Elizabeth Storm   *s*   5315

**Joth**
*Angels on Fire* - Nancy A. Collins   *h*   1117

**Lucifer**
*Angels & Visitations: A Miscellany* - Neil Gaiman   *f*   2101

**Madimi**
*Love & Sleep* - John Crowley   *f*   1277

**Mithra**
*Ancient Games* - Scott Ciencin   *f*   1028

**Phaeton**
*Planar Powers* - J. Robert King   *f*   3122

**Raphael**
*Archangel* - Sharon Shinn   *s*   5000

**Raphaella "Rae"**
*Angel Light* - Andrew M. Greeley   *f*   2342

**Satan "Mr. Smith"**
*The Old Man and Mr. Smith* - Peter Ustinov   *f*   5532

**Smith, Valentine Michael**
*Stranger in a Strange Land* - Robert A. Heinlein   *s*   2649

**Volos**
*Metal Angel* - Nancy Springer   *f*   5181

## ANIMAL

**Aargh**
*The Dragon Knight* - Gordon R. Dickson   *f*   1532

**Abernathy**
*Witches' Brew* - Terry Brooks   *f*   719

**Ahlitah**
*Carnivores of Light and Darkness* - Alan Dean Foster   *f*   1996

**Amadeus**
*Witches* - Kathryn Meyer Griffith   *h*   2442

**Angel**
*Dancing on Air* - Nancy Kress   *s*   3240

**Archie**
*The Cormorant* - Stephen Gregory   *h*   2429

**Ash**
*Deerskin* - Robin McKinley   *f*   3844

**Austin**
*Summon the Keeper* - Tanya Huff   *f*   2800

**Badrang the Tyrant**
*Martin the Warrior* - Brian Jacques   *f*   2851

**Bagg, Stuart "Shoebag"**
*Shoebag* - Mary James   *f*   2868
*Shoebag Returns* - Mary James   *f*   2869

**Bear, Bagese**
*Dead Voices: Natural Agonies in the Real World* - Gerald Vizenor   *f*   5578

**Beast**
*Rose Daughter* - Robin McKinley   *f*   3847

**Belkis "Bell"**
*Here There Be Dragons* - Roger Zelazny   *f*   6069

**Beowulf**
*Cry Wolf* - Kenneth Von Gunden   *s*   5586
*Under Fire* - Kenneth Von Gunden   *s*   5589

**Bernie**
*Witch and Wombat* - Carolyn Cushman   *f*   1299

**Bix**
*Dinotopia* - James Gurney   *f*   2468

**Bobcat**
*The Blood Jaguar* - Michael H. Payne   *f*   4271

**Bottlenose**
*Starplex* - Robert J. Sawyer   *s*   4859

**Bruce**
*Paddywhack* - John Stchur   *h*   5236

**Burgess**
*Chaos Mode* - Piers Anthony   *f*   165

**Byrnison, Iorek**
*The Golden Compass* - Philip Pullman   *f*   4446

**Calef**
*Hungry for Home: A Wolf Odyssey* - 'Asta
  Bowen   *f*   599

**Camio**
*The Foxes of Firstdark* - Garry Kilworth   *f*   3115

**Caspode the Wonder Dog**
*Moving Pictures* - Terry Pratchett   *f*   4398

**Cat**
*Better than Life* - Grant Naylor   *s*   4076
*Cat's Paw* - L.A. Taylor   *f*   5409
*The Wild Hunt* - Jane Yolen   *f*   6042

**Chester**
*Return to Howliday Inn* - James Howe   *f*   2786

**Chli-pou-ni**
*Empire of the Ants* - Bernard Werber   *s*   5755

**Ch*Tril**
*Into the Deep* - Ken Grimwood   *s*   2450

**Chuck**
*Hong on the Range* - William F. Wu   *s*   5997

**Cloud**
*Cloud's Rider* - C.J. Cherryh   *s*   983
*Rider at the Gate* - C.J. Cherryh   *s*   1000

**C'mel**
*Norstrilia* - Cordwainer Smith   *s*   5105

**Cobalt**
*Deadly Vengeance* - Stephen R. George   *h*   2199
*Legacy of Steel* - Mary H. Herbert   *f*   2675

**Dandilion**
*Tales From Watership Down* - Richard Adams   *f*   32

**Darwin**
*seaQuest DSV: The Novel* - Diane Duane   *s*   1666

**d'Aurca, Adamus**
*Fair Peril* - Nancy Springer   *f*   5178

**Delia**
*Journeyman Wizard* - Mary Frances
  Zambreno   *f*   6057
*A Plague of Sorcerers* - Mary Frances
  Zambreno   *f*   6058

**Demir**
*City of the Sorcerers* - Mary H. Herbert   *f*   2673

**Dewdrop**
*Whilom* - Robert Watson   *f*   5639

**Dickory, Tracy**
*Time and the Clock Mice, Etcetera* - Peter
  Dickinson   *f*   1527

**Dingletoon, Tish**
*The Cockroaches of Stay More* - Donald
  Harington   *f*   2544

**Divine Endurance**
*Flowerdust* - Gwyneth Jones   *s*   2952

**Dulcie**
*Cats Raise the Dead* - Shirley Rousseau
  Murphy   *f*   4054

**Dun Lady's Jess**
*Dun Lady's Jess* - Doranna Durgin   *f*   1704

**El-ahrairah**
*Tales From Watership Down* - Richard Adams   *f*   32

**Ergates**
*Feersum Endjinn* - Iain M. Banks   *s*   325

**Fafner**
*Borgel* - Daniel Manus Pinkwater   *f*   4338

**Ferahgo the Assassin**
*Salamandastron* - Brian Jacques   *f*   2855

**Fisher**
*The Blood Jaguar* - Michael H. Payne   *f*   4271

**Fronto**
*The Arkadians* - Lloyd Alexander   *f*   67

**Gabool**
*Mariel of Redwall* - Brian Jacques   *f*   2850

**Garuda**
*Walker between the Worlds* - Diane
  DesRochers   *f*   1499

**Ghost**
*Ghost of Chance* - William S. Burroughs   *s*   780

**Gojiro**
*Gojiro* - Mark Jacobson   *f*   2847

**Gomez, Catseye**
*The Nine Lives of Catseye Gomez* - Simon
  Hawke   *f*   2620

**Gragelouth**
*Son of Spellsinger* - Alan Dean Foster   *f*   2015

**Great God Om**
*Small Gods* - Terry Pratchett   *f*   4400

**Grey, Joe**
*Cats Raise the Dead* - Shirley Rousseau
  Murphy   *f*   4054

**Grimya**
*Aisling* - Louise Cooper   *f*   1172
*Avatar* - Louise Cooper   *f*   1173
*Infanta* - Louise Cooper   *f*   1176
*Revenant* - Louise Cooper   *f*   1178
*Troika* - Louise Cooper   *f*   1181

**Growch**
*Master of Many Treasures* - Mary Brown   *f*   726

**Hal Jam**
*The Bear Went over the Mountain* - William
  Kotzwinkle   *f*   3222

**Han Rosie**
*Mariel of Redwall* - Brian Jacques   *f*   2850

**Harlan**
*Night of the Living Rat!* - Debra Doyle   *s*   1603
*Night of the Living Shark!* - David Bischoff   *s*   493

**Harold**
*Return to Howliday Inn* - James Howe   *f*   2786

**Herb**
*The Arbitrary Placement of Walls* - Martha
  Soukup   *f*   5165

**Herman**
*Way Up High* - Roger Zelazny   *f*   6076

**Howie**
*Return to Howliday Inn* - James Howe   *f*   2786

**Hunnul**
*Valorian* - Mary H. Herbert   *f*   2677

**Imbri, Mare**
*Faun & Games* - Piers Anthony   *f*   169

**Impossumble**
*An Impossumble Summer* - Brenda W.
  Clough   *f*   1090

**Ingersol, William "Bogey"**
*Top Dog* - Jerry Jay Carroll   *f*   915

**Ingledew, Sam**
*The Cockroaches of Stay More* - Donald
  Harington   *f*   2544

**Ishmael**
*Ishmael* - Daniel Quinn   *s*   4455
*My Ishmael* - Daniel Quinn   *s*   4456

**Jess**
*Changespell* - Doranna Durgin   *f*   1703

**Joseph**
*The Bellmaker* - Brian Jacques   *f*   2848

**Ko**
*Monkey Station* - Ardath Mayhar   *s*   3703

**Lanakila**
*Catamount* - Michael Peak   *f*   4273

**Lightfoot**
*Into the Land of the Unicorns* - Bruce
  Coville   *f*   1219

**Loiosh**
*Phoenix* - Steven Brust   *f*   746

**Lovelock**
*Lovelock* - Orson Scott Card   *s*   892

**Lupo**
*Down the Stream of Stars* - Jeffrey A.
  Carver   *s*   928

**Majicou**
*The Wild Road* - Gabriel King   *f*   3120

**Marbleheart**
*Geomancer* - Don Callander   *f*   845
*Marbleheart* - Don Callander   *f*   846

**Mariel**
*The Bellmaker* - Brian Jacques   *f*   2848
*Mariel of Redwall* - Brian Jacques   *f*   2850

**Marta**
*Hungry for Home: A Wolf Odyssey* - 'Asta
  Bowen   *f*   599

**Martin the Warrior**
*Martin the Warrior* - Brian Jacques   *f*   2851

**Matthias**
*Mattimeo* - Brian Jacques   *f*   2852

**Mew**
*Roverandom* - J.R.R. Tolkien   *f*   5479

**Miaowara Shiro**
*Samurai Cat Goes to the Movies* - Mark E.
  Rogers   *s*   4656
*The Sword of Samurai Cat* - Mark E.
  Rogers   *s*   4657

**Miaowara Tomokato**
*Samurai Cat Goes to the Movies* - Mark E.
  Rogers   *s*   4656
*The Sword of Samurai Cat* - Mark E.
  Rogers   *s*   4657

**Mogget**
*Sabriel* - Garth Nix   *f*   4129

**Mole**
*Toad Triumphant* - William Horwood   *f*   2774
*The Willows and Beyond* - William
  Horwood   *f*   2775
*The Willows in Winter* - William Horwood   *f*   2776

**Morris "Mauricio di Mauro"**
*The Night of Wishes: Or, The
  Satanarchaeolidealcohellish Notion Potion* - Michael
  Ende   *f*   1821

**Mudge**
*Chorus Skating* - Alan Dean Foster   *f*   1998

**Murri**
*The Mark of the Cat* - Andre Norton   *f*   4157

**Nara**
*Dark Horse* - Mary H. Herbert   *f*   2674

**Nepe/Flach**
*Phaze Doubt* - Piers Anthony   *f*   184

**Newt**
*Ratha and Thistle-Chaser* - Clare Bell   *f*   432

**Niffy**
*No One Noticed the Cat* - Anne McCaffrey   *f*   3740

**Nigheyes**
*Royal Assassin* - Robin Hobb   *f*   2695

**Nighteyes**
*Assassin's Quest* - Robin Hobb   *f*   2694

**Nodrey, Russa**
*The Long Patrol* - Brian Jacques   *f*   2849

**Nul**
*Wizard's Mole* - Brad Strickland   *f*   5337

**O-ha**
*The Foxes of Firstdark* - Garry Kilworth   *f*   3115

**Obed**
*The Off Season* - Jack Cady   *f*   820

**O'lal**
*Cat-A-Lyst* - Alan Dean Foster   *s*   1997

**Oldtooth**
*Hungry for Home: A Wolf Odyssey* - 'Asta Bowen   *f*   599

**Orick**
*Beyond the Gate* - Dave Wolverton   *s*   5949
*The Golden Queen* - Dave Wolverton   *s*   5951

**Ouoji**
*Destination: Mutiny* - Sean Dalton   *s*   1332

**Peeve**
*Black Unicorn* - Tanith Lee   *f*   3404
*Gold Unicorn* - Tanith Lee   *f*   3410
*Red Unicorn* - Tanith Lee   *f*   3414

**Pepper**
*The House on the Borderland* - William Hope Hodgson   *h*   2711

**Pinscher**
*Pet Store* - M.T. Coffin   *h*   1097

**Pooch**
*Carmen Dog* - Carol Emshwiller   *f*   1817

**Quadroped**
*Demon Pig* - Karen Brush   *f*   737

**Raajeh**
*Ray Bradbury Presents: Dinosaur Planet* - Stephen Leigh   *s*   3427

**Rabscuttle**
*Tales From Watership Down* - Richard Adams   *f*   32

**Racso**
*R-T, Margaret, and the Rats of NIMH* - Jane Leslie Conly   *f*   1132

**Rajasthan, Nohar**
*Emperors of the Twilight* - S. Andrew Swann   *s*   5362

**Raptor Red**
*Raptor Red* - Robert T. Bakker   *f*   306

**Ratha**
*Ratha and Thistle-Chaser* - Clare Bell   *f*   432

**Red Mare**
*A Ride on the Red Mare's Back* - Ursula K. Le Guin   *f*   3382

**Rex**
*The Magnificent Wilf* - Gordon R. Dickson   *s*   1536

**Rhiow**
*The Book of Night with Moon* - Diane Duane   *f*   1657

**Robert**
*The Coachman Rat* - David Henry Wilson   *f*   5879

**Rommel**
*Psi-Man* - David Peters   *s*   4305

**Rover "Roverandom"**
*Roverandom* - J.R.R. Tolkien   *f*   5479

**Saash**
*The Book of Night with Moon* - Diane Duane   *f*   1657

**Sarena**
*Catamount* - Michael Peak   *f*   4273

**Scandal**
*Majyk by Accident* - Esther Friesner   *f*   2079
*Majyk by Hook or Crook* - Esther Friesner   *f*   2081

**Scribble, Jacob**
*The Night of Wishes: Or, The Satanarchaeolidealcohellish Notion Potion* - Michael Ende   *f*   1821

**Sea Rat "Ratty"**
*The Willows and Beyond* - William Horwood   *f*   2775

**Seale, Evan**
*The Silent Strength of Stones* - Nina Kiriki Hoffman   *f*   2716

**Sealink**
*The Wild Road* - Gabriel King   *f*   3120

**Seeker After Patterns**
*Beyond the Fall of Night* - Arthur C. Clarke   *s*   1054

**Seqiro**
*Chaos Mode* - Piers Anthony   *f*   165
*Virtual Mode* - Piers Anthony   *f*   194

**Sixclaw, Swartt**
*Outcast of Redwall* - Brian Jacques   *f*   2853

**Skink**
*The Blood Jaguar* - Michael H. Payne   *f*   4271

**Slagar**
*Mattimeo* - Brian Jacques   *f*   2852

**Snaugenhutt**
*Son of Spellsinger* - Alan Dean Foster   *f*   2015

**Snuff**
*A Night in the Lonesome October* - Roger Zelazny   *h*   6072

**SStragh**
*Ray Bradbury Presents: Dinosaur World* - Stephen Leigh   *s*   3428

**Streak**
*Shadows in the Water* - Kathryn Lasky   *s*   3341

**Sunflash**
*Outcast of Redwall* - Brian Jacques   *f*   2853

**Tabby, Jane**
*Catwings* - Ursula K. Le Guin   *f*   3377

**Tag**
*The Wild Road* - Gabriel King   *f*   3120

**Tammo**
*The Long Patrol* - Brian Jacques   *f*   2849

**Tansy**
*The Pearls of Lutra* - Brian Jacques   *f*   2854

**Thakur**
*Ratha and Thistle-Chaser* - Clare Bell   *f*   432

**Tharna**
*The Key of the Keplian* - Andre Norton   *f*   4156

**Thor**
*Thor* - Wayne Smith   *h*   5146

**Thrugg**
*Salamandastron* - Brian Jacques   *f*   2855

**Toad of Toad Hall**
*Toad Triumphant* - William Horwood   *f*   2774
*The Willows and Beyond* - William Horwood   *f*   2775
*The Willows in Winter* - William Horwood   *f*   2776

**Tomokato, Miaowara**
*Samurai Cat Goes to Hell* - Mark E. Rogers   *f*   4655

**Tualha**
*A Wizard Abroad* - Diane Duane   *f*   1668

**Ublaz Mad Eyes**
*The Pearls of Lutra* - Brian Jacques   *f*   2854

**Unicorn**
*Blue Moon Rising* - Simon R. Green   *f*   2362

**Urruah**
*The Book of Night with Moon* - Diane Duane   *f*   1657

**Urthstripe the Strong**
*Salamandastron* - Brian Jacques   *f*   2855

**Valadan**
*The Prince of Ill Luck* - Susan Dexter   *f*   1512
*The True Knight* - Susan Dexter   *f*   1513

**Veil**
*Outcast of Redwall* - Brian Jacques   *f*   2853

**Viola**
*The Pearls of Lutra* - Brian Jacques   *f*   2854

**Water Rat "Ratty"**
*Toad Triumphant* - William Horwood   *f*   2774
*The Willows in Winter* - William Horwood   *f*   2776

**Wimperling**
*Pigs Don't Fly* - Mary Brown   *f*   727

**Zahag**
*Queen of Demons* - David Drake   *f*   1640

## ANIMAL LOVER

**Gatzalumendi, Isadora Katarina Manuela**
*Anvil* - Nicolas van Pallandt   *s*   5540

**Matheson, Hope**
*Seeing Eye* - Jack Ellis   *h*   1780

**Mitchell, Jackie**
*Dangerous Nature* - T.J. Kirby   *h*   3152

**Tovin, Rahel**
*Regenesis* - Julia Ecklar   *s*   1729

## ANIMAL TRAINER

**Burrich**
*Assassin's Apprentice* - Robin Hobb   *f*   2693

**Chamtong, Onua**
*Wild Magic* - Tamora Pierce   *f*   4323

**Dog-Woman**
*Sexing the Cherry* - Jeanette Winterson   *f*   5927

**Eleeri**
*The Key of the Keplian* - Andre Norton   *f*   4156

**Orun**
*Hidden Echoes* - Mike Jefferies   *f*   2885

**Rubidoux, John**
*Retribution* - Elizabeth Forrest   *h*   1975

**Shellabarger, Vince**
*Dinosaur Summer* - Greg Bear   *s*   416

**Von Ziegler, Horst**
*The Keeper* - Robert D. Lee   *h*   3402

**Weisser, Erich**
*Child of the Light* - Janet Gluckman   *f*   2244

**Weisser, Erich "Erich Alois"**
*Child of the Journey* - Janet Berliner   *f*   466
*Children of the Dusk* - Janet Berliner   *f*   467

## ANTHROPOLOGIST

**Baver, Deodoro "Ted"**
*The Yngling and the Circle of Power* - John Dalmas   *s*   1328

**Cassidy, Katherine Sweeney**
*Waking the Moon* - Elizabeth Hand   *f*   2538

**Chambers, Peter**
*Sleepwalker* - Michael Cadnum   *h*   815

**Claudia**
*Agviq* - Michael Armstrong   *s*   208

**Dalt, Steven**
*The LaNague Chronicles* - F. Paul Wilson   *s*   5889

**di Rienzi, Angelica**
*Waking the Moon* - Elizabeth Hand   *f*   2538

**Dinsman, Angela**
*Reefsong* - Carol Severance   *s*   4923

**Eddy, Henriette May**
*The Deathless* - Myles Murchison   *h*   4048

**Endrada, Valerie "Val"**
*Halfway Human* - Carolyn Ives Gilman   *s*   2237

**Foreman, Jack**
*The Charm* - Adam Niswander   *h*   4111

**Green, Margo**
*Reliquary* - Douglas Preston   *h*   4415

**Heron, Madeleine**
*Green Lake* - S.K. Epperson   *h*   1830

**Jacobi, Henry**
*The Engines of God* - Jack McDevitt   *s*   3787

**Lowry, Davis**
*Sleepwalker* - Michael Cadnum   *h*   815

**Mendel, Toby**
*The Undine* - Michael O'Rourke   *h*   4224

**Mitchell, Gordon**
*Ancestor's World* - A.C. Crispin   *s*   1259

**Nahadeh, Yute**
*Ember From the Sun* - Mark Canter   *s*   870

**O'Keefe, Jesse**
*Fire and Ice* - Edward Myers   *f*   4061
*The Mountain Made of Light* - Edward
  Myers   *f*   4062
*The Summit* - Edward Myers   *f*   4063

**Parmenter, Mitchell**
*Tourists* - Lisa Goldstein   *f*   2264

**Raishan, Marguerite "Marghe" Angelica**
*Ammonite* - Nicola Griffith   *s*   2443

**Sarnii, Irene**
*Sleepwalker* - Michael Cadnum   *h*   815

**Sheridan, Anna**
*The Shadow Within* - Jeanne Cavelos   *s*   944

**Silver, Rob**
*The Presence* - John Saul   *h*   4843

**Stevenson, Walker**
*The Deathless* - Myles Murchison   *h*   4048

**Steward, Ben**
*The Lincoln Hunters* - Wilson Tucker   *s*   5487

**Sundquist, Katherine**
*The Presence* - John Saul   *h*   4843

**Tagge, Geoff**
*Mind Stealer* - Lee Duigon   *h*   1672

**Terza, Abby**
*Manhattan Transfer* - John E. Stith   *s*   5303

**Tomochelor, Pulickel**
*The Howling Stones* - Alan Dean Foster   *s*   2006

**Trask, Julian**
*Absolute Power* - Ray Russell   *h*   4738

**Wald, Richard**
*The Engines of God* - Jack McDevitt   *s*   3787

**Walters, Diana**
*Uwharrie* - Eugene E. Pfaff Jr.   *h*   4309

**Winfield, Angela**
*The Werewolf's Touch* - Cheri Scotch   *h*   4892

## ANTIQUARIAN

**Redfield, Blake**
*Hide and Seek* - Paul Preuss   *s*   4418
*The Medusa Encounter* - Paul Preuss   *s*   4419

## ANTIQUES DEALER

**DeMarco, Selene**
*Shadows* - Kimberly Rangel   *h*   4472

**Gilbert, Jack**
*The Palm Dome* - Liz Fulton   *h*   2094

**Harrison, Hatchford**
*Hideaway* - Dean R. Koontz   *h*   3208

**Maughan, Daisy**
*Mennyms Alive* - Sylvia Waugh   *f*   5655

## APOTHECARY

**Chinnery, Thomas**
*Bhagavati* - Kara Dalkey   *f*   1316
*Bijapur* - Kara Dalkey   *f*   1317
*Blood of the Goddess* - Kara Dalkey   *f*   1318

## APPRENTICE

**Afsan**
*Far-Seer* - Robert J. Sawyer   *s*   4854

**Alec of Kerry**
*Stalking Darkness* - Lynn Flewelling   *f*   1953

**Aracco**
*Goldclimbers* - Nancy Luenn   *s*   3545

**Arista, Tommaso**
*The Stars Dispose* - Michaela Roessner   *f*   4651

**Aubert, Jacques**
*Where the Towers Pierce the Sky* - Marie D.
  Goodwin   *f*   2272

**Bart**
*Initiation* - Marian Hughes   *s*   2806

**Bernay, Leah de**
*Scorpio* - Alex McDonough   *s*   3802

**Brightblade, Douglas**
*Pyromancer* - Don Callander   *f*   847

**Byron**
*Cardmaster* - Clayton Emery   *f*   1813

**Cerryl**
*The White Order* - L.E. Modesitt Jr.   *f*   3942

**Corwyn**
*The Apprentice* - Deborah Talmadge-
  Bickmore   *f*   5382

**Crandall, Raymond E. Jr.**
*The Magic Touch* - Jody Lynn Nye   *f*   4171

**Darian**
*Owlflight* - Mercedes Lackey   *f*   3291

**de Bernay, Leah**
*Dragon's Blood* - Alex McDonough   *s*   3799
*Dragon's Claw* - Alex McDonough   *s*   3800
*Dragon's Eye* - Alex McDonough   *s*   3801
*Scorpio Descending* - Alex McDonough   *s*   3803
*Scorpio Rising* - Alex McDonough   *s*   3804

**de Verdeur, Michel "Raven"**
*King & Raven* - Cary James   *f*   2858

**Delroy, Lylene**
*The Conjurer Princess* - Vivian Vande
  Velde   *f*   5555

**Douay, Deldragon Drakedon "Drake"**
*Lords of the Sword* - Hugh Cook   *f*   1156

**du Mond, Paul**
*The Fire Rose* - Mercedes Lackey   *f*   3280

**Elena**
*The Fourth Guardian* - Ronald Anthony
  Cross   *s*   1273

**Faltar**
*The White Order* - L.E. Modesitt Jr.   *f*   3942

**Fielding, Anna**
*The Compass of the Soul* - Sean Russell   *f*   4740

**Flattery, Erasmus**
*Beneath the Vaulted Hills* - Sean Russell   *f*   4739

**Franklin, Benjamin**
*Newton's Cannon* - J. Gregory Keyes   *f*   3097

**Furiano, Furian**
*Faces under Water* - Tanith Lee   *h*   3409

**Garden, Humility "Humi"**
*Humility Garden* - Felicity Savage   *f*   4850

**Gawaine**
*Fortress of Frost and Fire* - Mercedes
  Lackey   *f*   3282

**Gemcutter, Jena**
*Emerald House Rising* - Peg Kerr   *f*   3080

**Graves, Jermyn**
*A Plague of Sorcerers* - Mary Frances
  Zambreno   *f*   6058

**Helit, Susan Sto**
*Soul Music* - Terry Pratchett   *f*   4401

**Henchard, Daniel**
*Groogleman* - Debra Doyle   *s*   1600

**Isabeau**
*The Witches of Eileanan* - Kate Forsyth   *f*   1984

**Kim**
*Magician's Ward* - Patricia C. Wrede   *f*   5976

**Klein, Alice**
*Higher Education* - Charles Sheffield   *s*   4958

**Kuvasc, Paval**
*Regenesis* - Julia Ecklar   *s*   1729

**Lerris**
*The Death of Chaos* - L.E. Modesitt Jr.   *f*   3926
*The Magic of Recluce* - L.E. Modesitt Jr.   *f*   3934

**Lescevre, Thibault**
*Anvil of the Sun* - Anne Lesley Groell   *f*   2451

**Lina**
*Interface Masque* - Shariann Lewitt   *s*   3453

**Luban, Rick**
*Higher Education* - Charles Sheffield   *s*   4958

**Machiavelli, Niccolo**
*The Memory Cathedral* - Jack Dann   *s*   1341

**Manstar, Myrn**
*Aquamancer* - Don Callander   *f*   841

**Michael**
*Lion Time in Timbuctoo* - Robert Silverberg   *s*   5036

**Miller, Alvin "Maker"**
*Prentice Alvin* - Orson Scott Card   *f*   896

**Misurov, Sasha**
*Chernevog* - C.J. Cherryh   *f*   982
*Rusalka* - C.J. Cherryh   *f*   1002

**Mort**
*Mort* - Terry Pratchett   *f*   4397

**Ndemi**
*Kirinyaga: A Fable of Utopia* - Mike
  Resnick   *s*   4548

**Niviene**
*Merlin's Harp* - Anne Eliot Crompton   *f*   1270

**Pendaron, Telerini**
*The Moon in Hiding* - Teresa Edgerton   *f*   1745

**Platho, Aivlys**
*Clock Strikes Sword* - Ian Hammell   *f*   2529

**Polijn**
*A Wild Dog and Lone* - Dan Crawford   *f*   1251

**Quantrill, Snohomish "Sno"**
*The Godmother's Apprentice* - Elizabeth Ann
  Scarborough   *f*   4863

**Ra-khir of Erythane**
*Beyond Ragnarok* - Mickey Zucker Reichert  f  4516

**Randall**
*School of Wizardry* - Debra Doyle  f  1605

**Rhys, Gwinn**
*Harmony* - Marjorie Bradley Kellogg  s  3046

**Sanda**
*Initiation* - Marian Hughes  s  2806

**Saun**
*Athyra* - Steven Brust  f  739

**Sebastian**
*Rehearsal for a Renaissance* - Douglas W. Clark  f  1045

**Sept-Fortune, Cecilie 8**
*Interface Masque* - Shariann Lewitt  s  3453

**Simon**
*The Dragonbone Chair* - Tad Williams  f  5829
*Stone of Farewell* - Tad Williams  f  5831

**Thanehand**
*The Road to Underfall* - Mike Jefferies  f  2888

**Tooe**
*A Mind for Trade* - Andre Norton  s  4158

**Tryon**
*Wren to the Rescue* - Sherwood Smith  f  5142

**Twilla**
*Mirror of Destiny* - Andre Norton  f  4159

**Valdez, Vido**
*Higher Education* - Charles Sheffield  s  4958

**Wren**
*The True Knight* - Susan Dexter  f  1513

## ARCHAEOLOGIST

**Bones, Ezekiel "Zeke"**
*Nightmare World* - David Stern  s  5261

**Branfield, Anastasia**
*Hellboy: The Lost Army* - Christopher Golden  h  2257

**Cable, John**
*Out of the Night* - Patrick Whalen  h  5771

**Cage, Louis P.**
*Curse of the Vampire* - Geoffrey Caine  h  832

**Chandler, Jay**
*Lord of the Dark Lake* - Ron Faust  h  1894

**Cook, Jay**
*Time Blender* - Michael Dorn  s  1581

**Gale, Miles**
*Little Boy Lost* - T.M. Wright  h  5992

**Harlow, Robert "Bob"**
*Stones of the Dalai Lama* - Ken Mitchell  f  3916

**Harper, Ellen**
*The Dead Man's Kiss* - Robert Weinberg  h  5695

**Jones, Indiana "Indy"**
*Indiana Jones and the Dance of the Giants* - Rob MacGregor  f  3588
*Indiana Jones and the Genesis Deluge* - Rob MacGregor  f  3589
*Indiana Jones and the Interior World* - Rob MacGregor  f  3590
*Indiana Jones and the Peril at Delphi* - Rob MacGregor  f  3591
*Indiana Jones and the Seven Veils* - Rob MacGregor  f  3592
*Indiana Jones and the Sky Pirates* - Martin Caidin  f  825
*Indiana Jones and the Unicorn's Legacy* - Rob MacGregor  f  3593
*Indiana Jones and the White Witch* - Martin Caidin  f  826

**Kerrick, James**
*The House of the Toad* - Richard L. Tierney  h  5470

**Kestle, Don**
*Mercycle* - Piers Anthony  s  181

**Larchmont, Marvin**
*Out of the Night* - Patrick Whalen  h  5771

**MacBreed, Keenan**
*The Uprising* - Brent Monahan  h  3956

**Mandrake, Jarvin**
*Stone Angels* - Mike Jefferies  h  2889

**Manfaluti, Aisha**
*Name of the Beast* - Daniel Easterman  h  1721

**Miller, Tony**
*Time Blender* - Michael Dorn  s  1581

**Monsanto, Francesca**
*Prophecy* - Peter James  h  2874

**Montes, Samta**
*A Whisper of Time* - Paula E. Downing  s  1595

**Parker, Gale**
*Indiana Jones and the White Witch* - Martin Caidin  f  826

**Rubicon, Cassandra**
*Ruins* - Kevin J. Anderson  h  112

**Tembo**
*Phoenix Fire* - Elizabeth Forrest  f  1974

**Trelawney, Abel**
*The Jewel of Seven Stars* - Bram Stoker  h  5312

**Trent, Elizabeth**
*Thirdspace* - Peter David  s  1387

**Van Zandt, Peter**
*The Stone Circle* - Gary Goshgarian  h  2285

## ARCHITECT

**Brenner, Matt**
*The Feeding* - Leigh Clark  h  1051

**Carter, John**
*The Black Death* - Basil Copper  h  1185

**Chandler, Sam**
*Devil's Gate* - Elizabeth Ergas  h  1833

**Curry, Michael**
*Lasher* - Anne Rice  h  4570
*The Witching Hour* - Anne Rice  h  4580

**De Vere, Tyson**
*Horses of the Night* - Michael Cadnum  h  811

**Dougherty, Kim**
*The House Next Door* - Anne Rivers Siddons  h  5021

**Dunn, Rick**
*The Ascending* - T.M. Wright  h  5989

**Durancy, Abraham**
*Queen City Jazz* - Kathleen Ann Goonan  s  2275

**Dvorak, Jason**
*Assemblers of Infinity* - Kevin J. Anderson  s  100

**Fields, Stratton**
*Horses of the Night* - Michael Cadnum  h  811

**Hujgens, Kees**
*The Final Diary Entry of Kees Hujgens* - William R. Stotler  h  5317

**Jagoda, Parker**
*Chicago Loop* - Paul Theroux  h  5443

**Janszoon, Jozef P.**
*The Final Diary Entry of Kees Hujgens* - William R. Stotler  h  5317

**Jeffers, Glen**
*Black Lightning* - John Saul  h  4837

**Johnson, Samuel**
*The Iron Bridge* - David Morse  s  4036

**Krieg, Thomas L. Jr.**
*Revenant* - Melanie Tem  h  5424

**Niehaus, Vilmos**
*The Final Diary Entry of Kees Hujgens* - William R. Stotler  h  5317

**Radcliffe, Harry**
*Outside the Dog Museum* - Jonathan Carroll  f  919

**Svilar, Atanas**
*Landscape Painted with Tea* - Milorad Pavic  f  4263

**Travers, Peter**
*Night Relics* - James P. Blaylock  h  521

**Wing, Phillip**
*Look into the Sun* - James Patrick Kelly  s  3047

**Woodrow, John**
*Torment* - Stephen R. George  h  2204

## ART DEALER

**Bishop, Ian**
*Animus* - Ed Kelleher  h  3040

**Endering, Sophia**
*The Uncanny* - Andrew Klavan  h  3164

**Gabriel, Faustin**
*Vodoun* - David Madsen  h  3605

**Gallegher, P.J.**
*Vanitas: Escape From Vampire Junction* - S.P. Somtow  h  5162

## ARTIFICIAL INTELLIGENCE

**Aide**
*An Oblique Approach* - David Drake  s  1638

**AIVAS**
*All the Weyrs of Pern* - Anne McCaffrey  s  3719

**Aleph**
*Halo* - Tom Maddox  s  3604

**Anne**
*Dream of Glass* - Jean Mark Gawron  s  2163

**ARCHY**
*Second Star* - Dana Stabenow  s  5188

**Arius**
*Dreams of Gods and Men* - W.T. Quick  s  4451

**Aryadyss**
*Donnerjack* - Roger Zelazny  s  6063

**Auggie**
*Terminal Games* - Cole Perriman  s  4283

**Autothor**
*Codgerspace* - Alan Dean Foster  s  1999

**Avery**
*Caverns of Socrates* - Dennis L. McKiernan  f  3831

**Batty, Roy**
*Blade Runner: Replicant Night* - K.W. Jeter  s  2907

**Blanca**
*Diaspora* - Greg Egan  s  1759

**Blanche**
*The Man in the Moon Must Die* - Jeff Bredenberg  s  665

**Bolt**
*The Last Hawk* - Catherine Asaro  s  219

**Cariola "Cary"**
*Full Tide of Night* - J.R. Dunn  s  1695

**Central "CC" Computer**
*Steel Beach* - John Varley  s  5566

**Cerebus**
*When Dreams Collide* - Wm. Mark
   Simmons   *f*   5063

**Chan, Dahlia**
*Cytheria* - Richard Calder   *s*   835

**Chip**
*A King of Infinite Space* - Allen Steele   *s*   5243

**The Computer**
*Extreme Paranoia: Nobody Knows the Trouble I've
   Shot* - Ken Rolston   *s*   4662

**Dahak**
*The Armageddon Inheritance* - David
   Weber   *s*   5668
*Heirs of Empire* - David Weber   *s*   5672

**Dax**
*From a Changeling Star* - Jeffrey A. Carver   *s*   931

**De Leone, "Deus X"**
*Deus X* - Norman Spinrad   *s*   5171

**Death**
*Donnerjack* - Roger Zelazny   *s*   6063

**DEUS**
*The Deus Machine* - Pierre Ouellette   *h*   4232

**Ede**
*The Wild* - David Zindell   *s*   6086

**Genius**
*The Immortality Option* - James P. Hogan   *s*   2725

**Grabovnikon "Grab"**
*Night of the Living Shark!* - David Bischoff   *s*   493

**Grunt, Blind Boy**
*Clarke County, Space* - Allen Steele   *s*   5241

**Gwen**
*Starswarm* - Jerry Pournelle   *s*   4379

**Halman**
*3001: The Final Odyssey* - Arthur C.
   Clarke   *s*   1053

**Harlie**
*Voyage of the Star Wolf* - David Gerrold   *s*   2212

**Hawksmoor, Nicholas**
*Berserker Kill* - Fred Saberhagen   *s*   4761

**Hawthorn "D-base"**
*Cinderblock* - Janine Ellen Young   *s*   6047

**Helen**
*Galatea 2.2* - Richard M. Powers   *s*   4381

**Hidetada**
*The Cybernetic Shogun* - Victor Milan   *s*   3890

**Hood, Robin**
*The Sherwood Game* - Esther Friesner   *s*   2082

**Ingham, Justine**
*Circuit of Heaven* - Dennis Danvers   *s*   1348

**Jane**
*Children of the Mind* - Orson Scott Card   *s*   883
*Xenocide* - Orson Scott Card   *s*   899

**Jill**
*/* - Greg Bear   *s*   413

**Kort**
*Star Child* - James P. Hogan   *s*   2730

**Liddell, Alice**
*Take Back Plenty* - Colin Greenland   *s*   2419

**Lord Lynn, Margaret "Maggy"**
*Hellspark* - Janet Kagan   *s*   3000

**Maggie**
*Virtual Girl* - Amy Thomson   *s*   5462

**Manfred**
*Dreamships* - Melissa Scott   *s*   4896

**Martin**
*Mars Prime* - William C. Dietz   *s*   1548

**Methryn, Valthyrra**
*Dreadnought* - Thorarinn Gunnarsson   *s*   2464
*Tactical Error* - Thorarinn Gunnarsson   *s*   2466

**Mike**
*The Moon Is a Harsh Mistress* - Robert A.
   Heinlein   *s*   2645

**Mom**
*Exit to Reality* - Edith Forbes   *s*   1968

**Mthembu, Lucas "Venator"**
*Harvest the Fire* - Poul Anderson   *s*   128

**Multiple Entity "ME"**
*ME: A Novel of Self Discovery* - Thomas T.
   Thomas   *s*   5452

**Musashi**
*The Cybernetic Shogun* - Victor Milan   *s*   3890

**Nefertity**
*AEstival Tide* - Elizabeth Hand   *s*   2533

**Nikko**
*Vast* - Linda Nagata   *s*   4067

**Odin**
*Dark Sky Legion* - William Barton   *s*   379

**O'Hara Prime**
*Worlds Enough and Time* - Joe Haldeman   *s*   2491

**Ozymandias**
*Homecoming* - David Alexander Smith   *s*   5108

**Paladin**
*Archangel Blues* - eluki bes shahar   *s*   471
*Darktraders* - eluki bes shahar   *s*   472
*Hellflower* - eluki bes shahar   *s*   473

**Pr. Spinner**
*Cyberweb* - Lisa Mason   *s*   3662

**Quincunx "the Thief"**
*Dream of Glass* - Jean Mark Gawron   *s*   2163

**RAMROD Mark I "Rod"**
*Cybernarc* - Robert Cain   *s*   829
*End Game* - Robert Cain   *s*   830
*Gold Dragon* - Robert Cain   *s*   831

**Random Walk**
*Revolutionary* - S. Andrew Swann   *s*   5367

**Ratio**
*The White Abacus* - Damien Broderick   *s*   708

**Rec**
*Kaduna Memories* - Jack McKinney   *s*   3850

**RICE**
*Memento Mori* - Shariann Lewitt   *s*   3454

**Sardou, Lake Genevieve "Jenny"**
*Berserker Kill* - Fred Saberhagen   *s*   4761

**Scrooge, Ebenezer**
*Carol for Another Christmas* - Elizabeth Ann
   Scarborough   *f*   4861

**Setebos**
*A Game of Universe* - Eric S. Nylund   *f*   4178

**Ship**
*A Maze of Stars* - John Brunner   *s*   734

**Shiva**
*Shiva in Steel* - Fred Saberhagen   *s*   4775

**Sid 6.7**
*Virtuosity* - Terry Bisson   *s*   507

**Skaffen-Amtiskaw**
*Use of Weapons* - Iain M. Banks   *s*   328

**Sleeper Service**
*Excession* - Iain M. Banks   *s*   324

**Solo**
*Solo* - Robert Mason   *s*   3665
*Weapon* - Robert Mason   *s*   3666

**Tally, E.C.**
*Divergence* - Charles Sheffield   *s*   4954

**Toei, Rei**
*Idoru* - William Gibson   *s*   2218

**Traveler**
*Burster* - Michael Capobianco   *s*   876

**Trickster**
*Secret Realms* - Tom Cool   *s*   1168

**Tumcari**
*The Nature of Smoke* - Anne Harris   *s*   2559

**Vail**
*Under Siege* - Elisabeth Mace   *f*   3587

**Valthyrra**
*Battle of the Ring* - Thorarinn Gunnarsson   *s*   2460

**Victor**
*Virtually Perfect* - Dan Gutman   *s*   2470

**VISAR**
*Entoverse* - James P. Hogan   *s*   2724

**Waesc, Dorias**
*Reclamation* - Sarah Zettel   *s*   6081

**Walk, Random**
*Profiteer* - S. Andrew Swann   *s*   5366

**Washington, Arlene "Lady El"**
*Lady El* - Jim Starlin   *s*   5213

**Wulf**
*Wulfsyarn: A Mosaic* - Phillip Mann   *s*   3617

**Yatima**
*Diaspora* - Greg Egan   *s*   1759

**Yatt**
*A Screaming Across the Sky* - Brian Daley   *s*   1315

**Yoseph**
*Terminal Logic* - Jefferson Scott   *s*   4893

## ARTISAN

**Ali Baba**
*A Bad Day for Ali Baba* - Craig Shaw
   Gardner   *f*   2123

**Bishop, Catherine**
*Animus* - Ed Kelleher   *h*   3040

**Bottom, Nick**
*Whilom* - Robert Watson   *f*   5639

**Brett/Natalie**
*Holy Fire* - Bruce Sterling   *s*   5259

**Brewer, Tom**
*Dreamthorp* - Chet Williamson   *h*   5845

**Connaghan, Connor**
*Child of Shadows* - John Coyne   *h*   1236

**Corey, Lewis**
*Inagehi* - Jack Cady   *h*   817

**Drosselmeier, Christian Elias "Godfather"**
*Nutcracker* - E.T.A. Hoffmann   *f*   2719

**Drumon**
*The Forge of Virtue* - Lynn Abbey   *f*   16

**Fireforge, Flint**
*Kindred Spirits* - Mark Anthony   *f*   154
*Wanderlust* - Mary Kirchoff   *f*   3155

**Forsetti, Anna**
*The Innamorati* - Midori Snyder   *f*   5152

**Gatekeeper**
*Hard-Boiled Wonderland and the End of the World* -
   Haruki Murakami   *s*   4047

**George**
*Thessalonica* - Harry Turtledove   *f*   5511

**Haldeth**
*The Master of Whitestorm* - Janny Wurts   *f*   6003

**Harootunian, Larque "Lark"**
*Larque on the Wing* - Nancy Springer   *f*   5180

**Helmish**
*Top Dog* - Jerry Jay Carroll   *f*   915

**I**
*Time and the Clock Mice, Etcetera* - Peter Dickinson   *f*   1527

**Isbetta**
*Curse of the Black Heron* - Holly Lisle   *f*   3479

**Jorana**
*The Howling Stones* - Alan Dean Foster   *s*   2006

**Kaantille, Katrina**
*The Loneliest Magician* - Irene Radford   *f*   4461

**Kesair**
*The Elementals* - Morgan Llywelyn   *f*   3503

**Lycaon**
*The Last World* - Christoph Ransmayr   *f*   4475

**Malledd**
*Touched by the Gods* - Lawrence Watt-Evans   *f*   5651

**Mikhailovych, Lixand**
*Shadow's Daughter* - Shirley Meier   *f*   3871

**Myrddin**
*In the Shadow of the Oak King* - Courtway Jones   *f*   2939

**Ness**
*Shadow's Daughter* - Shirley Meier   *f*   3871

**Owlesby, Jack**
*Lord Kelvin's Machine* - James P. Blaylock   *f*   520

**Penne, Dyann**
*The Gift of the Gorboduc Vandal* - Paul O. Williams   *s*   5821

**Platho, Endimin**
*Clock Strikes Sword* - Ian Hammell   *f*   2529

**Sparrow**
*Justice* - David Drake   *s*   1635

**Stodard, Paul**
*Blood Alone* - Elaine Bergstrom   *h*   462

**Stone**
*Isle of Woman* - Piers Anthony   *f*   178

**Trader, Max**
*Trader* - Charles de Lint   *f*   1438

**Wakelin, Emily**
*Holy Terror* - Josephine Boyle   *h*   608

# ARTIST

**Adams, Frankly**
*Virtual Death* - Shale Aaron   *s*   5

**Aengus**
*The Boy From the Burren* - Sheila Gilluly   *f*   2236

**Agamon, Orfei**
*A Second Infinity* - Michael D. Weaver   *s*   5660

**Aiesa, Gina**
*Synners* - Pat Cadigan   *s*   808

**Amy**
*Stranded* - Camarin Grae   *s*   2295

**Angelo, Jamie**
*Beauty* - Brian D'Amato   *h*   1334

**Armon**
*The Forgetting Room* - Nick Bantock   *f*   333

**Axxter, Ny**
*Farewell Horizontal* - K.W. Jeter   *s*   2911

**Bajac, Tess**
*Skin* - Kathe Koja   *h*   3196

**Bandy, Austen**
*Bad Brains* - Kathe Koja   *h*   3193

**Bascomb, Frederika "Freddy"**
*Bones* - Joyce Thompson   *h*   5453

**Baxter, Sophie**
*Lost Futures* - Lisa Tuttle   *s*   5520

**Bender, Lucy**
*Angels on Fire* - Nancy A. Collins   *h*   1117

**Bergeron, Carolyn**
*Nightmare Logic* - Matthew Hall   *h*   2495

**Bermudez, Jolanda**
*Hot Sky at Midnight* - Robert Silverberg   *s*   5032

**Binewski, Miranda**
*Geek Love* - Katherine Dunn   *h*   1697

**Blervaque, Rose**
*Living Real* - James C. Bassett   *s*   386

**Bloodworth, Emma**
*The Last Vampire* - Kathryn Meyer Griffith   *h*   2440

**Botticelli, Sandro**
*The Memory Cathedral* - Jack Dann   *s*   1341

**Boxdale, Asin**
*Free Radicals* - Jack McKinney   *s*   3848

**Brauner, Victor**
*Conglomeros* - Jesse Browner   *f*   729

**Brice, Jenny**
*Something Out There* - Ronald Kelly   *h*   3056

**Carewe, Cindy**
*Absolute Power* - Ray Russell   *h*   4738

**Carpenter, Tonia**
*Last Rites* - David Darke   *h*   1354

**Casipriadin, Luba**
*Scissors Cut Paper Wrap Stone* - Ian McDonald   *s*   3795

**Cervantes, Micah Miguel**
*Harmony* - Marjorie Bradley Kellogg   *s*   3046

**Charles, Ellen Cherry**
*Skinny Legs and All* - Tom Robbins   *f*   4607

**Chen, David**
*Chimera* - Mary Rosenblum   *s*   4677

**Clark, Jennifer**
*Torments* - Lisa Cantrell   *h*   873

**Columbar, Santiago**
*Terminal Cafe* - Ian McDonald   *s*   3797

**Copley, Isabelle "Izzy"**
*Memory and Dream* - Charles de Lint   *f*   1433

**Coppercorn, Jilly**
*The Wishing Well* - Charles de Lint   *f*   1441

**Cornish, Francis**
*The Cornish Trilogy* - Robertson Davies   *f*   1397

**Cortez, Pablo**
*Cortez on Jupiter* - Ernest Hogan   *s*   2721

**Cranach, Stella**
*The Schizogenic Man* - Raymond Harris   *s*   2563

**Cummings, Rachael**
*Not Broken, Not Belonging* - Randy Fox   *h*   2030

**Danny-boy**
*The City, Not Long After* - Pat Murphy   *s*   4051

**De Romanus, Marius**
*The Vampire Armand* - Anne Rice   *h*   4578

**Demetrios, Thann**
*The Quicksilver Screen* - Don H. DeBrandt   *s*   1449

**Dietz, Tre**
*Freeware* - Rudy Rucker   *s*   4703

**Dillon, Ronny**
*Dreambuilder* - Tom Deitz   *f*   1471
*Wordwright* - Tom Deitz   *f*   1478

**Dinaos**
*The Belly of the Wolf* - R.A. MacAvoy   *f*   3580

**Dugan, Andrew**
*My Soul to Take* - Steven Spruill   *s*   5184

**Duran, Michael**
*Diary of a Vampire* - Gary Bowen   *h*   600

**Eklunk, Hans-Bjorn "Mokey/Moke"**
*Clipjoint* - Wilhelmina Baird   *s*   294
*Crashcourse* - Wilhelmina Baird   *s*   295
*Psykosis* - Wilhelmina Baird   *s*   296

**Espinoza, Margarita**
*The Stone Garden* - Mary Rosenblum   *s*   4679

**Farringer, Gail**
*Demon Shadows* - Michael B. Sirota   *h*   5075

**Fin, Adam**
*Something Rich and Strange* - Patricia A. McKillip   *f*   3840

**Fischer, Max**
*After Silence* - Jonathan Carroll   *h*   916

**Fresca, Riki**
*The Cybernetic Walrus* - Jack L. Chalker   *s*   951

**Garden, Beauty "Beau"**
*Humility Garden* - Felicity Savage   *f*   4850

**Garden, Humility "Humi"**
*Humility Garden* - Felicity Savage   *f*   4850

**Gardener, Rick**
*The Possession* - Ronald Kelly   *h*   3055

**Gerard, Monique**
*Avatar* - Donald Beman   *h*   437

**Gerrows, Eithnie**
*The Wild Wood* - Charles de Lint   *f*   1440

**Grandpa Rowe**
*The Cartoonist* - Sean Costello   *h*   1204

**Granville, Jo**
*Bloody Valentine* - Stephen R. George   *h*   2197

**Grijalva, Saavedra**
*The Golden Key* - Melanie Rawn   *f*   4486

**Grijalva, Sario**
*The Golden Key* - Melanie Rawn   *f*   4486

**Guthrie, Dave**
*Night Sounds* - Warner Lee   *h*   3415

**Haas, Peter**
*Memento Mori* - Shariann Lewitt   *s*   3454

**Hall, Courtney**
*Out on Blue Six* - Ian McDonald   *s*   3794

**Hansen, Sunny**
*The Spirit Stalker* - Nina Romberg   *h*   4664

**Hart, Damon**
*Inherit the Earth* - Brian Stableford   *s*   5193

**Hill, Shannon**
*The Axman Cometh* - John Farris   *h*   1883

**Hood, Nicholas**
*Cold Eye* - Giles Blunt   *h*   556

**Jack**
*The Caterpillar's Question* - Piers Anthony   *f*   164

**Jackson, Jocelyn**
*Water Rites* - Guy N. Smith   *h*   5121

**Jaishree/Minaz**
*Beauty* - Brian D'Amato   *h*   1334

**Jakobi, Virgil**
*The Quicksilver Screen* - Don H. DeBrandt   *s*   1449

**James, Zack**
*Blood Work* - Fay Zachary   *h*   6050

**Jax**
*The City, Not Long After* - Pat Murphy   *s*   4051

**Kaminski, Tiffany Jeanine "T.J."**
*Steel Rose* - Kara Dalkey   *f*   1321

**Katsuleris, Aubrey**
*The Broken Sword* - Molly Cochran   *f*   1091

**Keeper, Tom**
*Ancient Games* - Scott Ciencin  *f*  1028
*Night of Glory* - Scott Ciencin  *f*  1030
*The Ways of Magic* - Scott Ciencin  *f*  1033

**Kent, Averil**
*Sea Without a Shore* - Sean Russell  *f*  4743

**Kilpatrick, Mark Michael**
*Grave Markings* - Michael A. Arnzen  *h*  212

**Kingston, April**
*Nightlife* - Brian Hodge  *h*  2702

**Kingston-Gray, April**
*The Darker Saints* - Brian Hodge  *h*  2699

**Lassiter, Audrey**
*Hopeship* - Simon Lang  *s*  3315

**Lindsey, Greg**
*Midnight Is a Lonely Place* - Barbara
    Erskine  *h*  1836

**Lisse**
*Invitation to the Game* - Monica Hughes  *s*  2807

**Lovat, Peregrine**
*The Adept* - Katherine Kurtz  *f*  3254
*Dagger Magic* - Katherine Kurtz  *f*  3256
*The Lodge of the Lynx* - Katherine Kurtz  *f*  3259
*The Templar Treasure* - Katherine Kurtz  *f*  3261

**Ludovic, Cassandra "Sam"**
*Synners* - Pat Cadigan  *s*  808

**Malcolm**
*The Cipher* - Kathe Koja  *h*  3194

**Manning, Rowena Pearce**
*Writ in Blood* - Chelsea Quinn Yarbro  *h*  6019

**Mariana**
*Blood Relations* - Doug Murray  *h*  4058

**Markham, Clare**
*The Colors of Hell* - Michael Paine  *h*  4234

**Marlowe**
*The Godsend* - Bernard Taylor  *h*  5401

**Marnay, Paul**
*Deathchain* - Ken Greenhall  *h*  2415

**Martin, Jack**
*Shadow Man* - Dennis Etchison  *h*  1848

**Masahiko**
*Scissors Cut Paper Wrap Stone* - Ian
    McDonald  *s*  3795

**Matthews, Kevin**
*Galatea in 2-D* - Aaron Allston  *f*  87

**McCandless, Lauren**
*Vanitas: Escape From Vampire Junction* - S.P.
    Somtow  *h*  5162

**McCogg, Gus "Aengus Mac Og"**
*The Friendship Song* - Nancy Springer  *f*  5179

**McCord, Chelsea**
*Darkscope* - Margaret Falk  *h*  1860

**McGee, Trevor**
*Drawing Blood* - Poppy Z. Brite  *h*  694

**McMahon, Colin**
*Cromm* - Kenneth C. Flint  *f*  1957

**Megan**
*Something Rich and Strange* - Patricia A.
    McKillip  *f*  3840

**Melmoth, Lydia**
*Virtual Death* - Shale Aaron  *s*  5

**Mitsouko, Emma**
*Throat Sprockets* - Tim Lucas  *h*  3541

**Monet, Claude**
*Monet's Ghost* - Chelsea Quinn Yarbro  *f*  6017

**Morrow, Rachel**
*A Gift upon the Shore* - M.K. Wren  *s*  5982

**Moss, Griffin**
*The Golden Mean* - Nick Bantock  *f*  334
*Sabine's Notebook* - Nick Bantock  *f*  335

**Munro, David**
*Head Injuries* - Conrad Williams  *h*  5816

**Narman, Sabra**
*The Curse* - John Tigges  *h*  5472

**Nelson, Nedra Muriel**
*Spook* - Steve Vance  *h*  5553

**Newns, Curtis**
*Skyscape* - Michael Cadnum  *h*  814

**Pasquale**
*Pasquale's Angel* - Paul J. McAuley  *f*  3714

**Pauling, Judd**
*Lullaby* - Diane Guest  *h*  2455

**Petway, Boomer**
*Skinny Legs and All* - Tom Robbins  *f*  4607

**Pidgely, Dylan**
*The Juniper Game* - Sherryl Jordan  *f*  2992

**Pierson, Ellen**
*Temporary Agency* - Rachel Pollack  *f*  4360

**Polk, Veronica**
*Incubi* - Edward Lee  *h*  3394

**Quade, Morgan**
*Zeta Base* - Judith Alguire  *s*  74

**Rafael**
*The Forgetting Room* - Nick Bantock  *f*  333

**Rane**
*Mirror to the Sky* - Mark S. Geston  *s*  2213

**Ransome, Illario "Ambidexter"**
*Burning Bright* - Melissa Scott  *s*  4894

**Rheinhardt**
*Subterranean Gallery* - Richard Paul Russo  *s*  4750

**Rhys, Gwinn**
*Harmony* - Marjorie Bradley Kellogg  *s*  3046

**Ring, Ethan**
*Scissors Cut Paper Wrap Stone* - Ian
    McDonald  *s*  3795

**Rushkin, Vincent Adjani**
*Memory and Dream* - Charles de Lint  *f*  1433

**Sanders, Johnny**
*Armed Memory* - Jim Young  *s*  6048

**Saunders, Charlotte**
*Retribution* - Elizabeth Forrest  *h*  1975

**Sean**
*Blue Moon* - Hila Feil  *f*  1898

**Shan**
*The Quicksilver Screen* - Don H. DeBrandt  *s*  1449

**Shepherd, Ben**
*The Middle Kingdom* - David Wingrove  *s*  5919

**Shriek, Anthony**
*Anthony Shriek* - Jessica Amanda
    Salmonson  *h*  4790

**Shuganan**
*Mother Earth, Father Sky* - Sue Harrison  *f*  2581

**Sickert, Walter**
*From Hell* - Alan Moore  *h*  3987
*The Women of Whitechapel and Jack the Ripper* - Paul
    West  *h*  5761

**Simmons, Roger**
*Galatea in 2-D* - Aaron Allston  *f*  87

**Simon of Florenz**
*The Painter Knight* - Fiona Patton  *f*  4258

**Sims, Dolores**
*Cradle of Splendor* - Patricia Anthony  *s*  158

**Sivart, Gil**
*The Digital Effect* - Steve Perry  *s*  4295

**Smith, Gary Franklin**
*The First Immortal* - James L. Halperin  *s*  2498

**Sorenson, Rachel**
*I'll Be Watching You* - Samuel M. Key  *h*  3094

**Stark, Edgar**
*Asylum* - Patrick McGrath  *h*  3812

**Stephenson, Diana**
*The Prodigy* - Noel Hynd  *h*  2823

**Sterling, Ellen**
*Midnight Sun* - Ramsey Campbell  *h*  860

**Sterling, Justin**
*Testament of the Dragon* - Margaret Weis  *f*  5729

**Stormer, Julian**
*Harrowgate* - Daniel H. Gower  *h*  2292

**Strohem, Sabine**
*The Golden Mean* - Nick Bantock  *f*  334
*Sabine's Notebook* - Nick Bantock  *f*  335

**Strozza, Joe**
*Seattle Ghost Story* - Nick DiMartino  *h*  1560

**Sullivan, Rex**
*The Eyes of Torie Webster* - Roy Sorrels  *h*  5164

**Taylor, Gwen**
*The Bridge: A Horror Story* - John Skipp  *h*  5081

**Tobias, Robin**
*Strange Angels* - Kathe Koja  *h*  3197

**Tryon, Michael**
*The Stone Garden* - Mary Rosenblum  *s*  4679

**Tullian, Adele**
*Sheep* - Simon Maginn  *h*  3606

**van de Oest, Frances Lorien "Lore"**
*Slow River* - Nicola Griffith  *s*  2445

**Videla, Pilar**
*Whiteout* - Sage Walker  *s*  5619

**Wallace, Brandy**
*Dreambuilder* - Tom Deitz  *f*  1471

**West, Braden**
*The Catswold Portal* - Shirley Rousseau
    Murphy  *f*  4055

**Wilkinson, Christopher**
*In the Shadows of the Moonglade* - Riley St.
    James  *h*  5186

**Williams, Trevor**
*WiZrD* - Steve Zell  *h*  6078

**Wingate, Max**
*The Convocation* - John R. Holt  *h*  2748

**Winters, Ginny**
*Dreamer* - Daniel Quinn  *h*  4454

**Wolfe, Sara**
*The Venetian's Wife: A Strangely Sensual Tale of a
    Renaissance Explorer, a Computer, and a
    Metamorphosis* - Nick Bantock  *f*  336

**Young, Janet**
*Breeder* - Ed Kelleher  *h*  3041

**Zacharias, John Furie "Gentle"**
*Imajica* - Clive Barker  *h*  343

**Zamiatin, Mark "Visual Mark"**
*Synners* - Pat Cadigan  *s*  808

**Zapata, Xolotl**
*High Aztec* - Ernest Hogan  *s*  2722

## ASSISTANT

**Audran, Marid**
*The Exile Kiss* - George Alec Effinger  *s*  1750

**Damek**
*The Spirit Gate* - Maya Kaathryn Bohnhoff  *f*  562

**Hanlon, Agnes**
*The Sixth Dog* - Jane Rice  *h*  4582

**Hutchinson, Lisa**
*All Things under the Moon* - Robert
    Morgan  *h*  4002
*The Things That Are Not There* - Robert
    Morgan  *h*  4007

**Lu, Antonia "Toni"**
*Other* - Gordon R. Dickson  *s*  1538

**Morcey, Paul**
*The Only Thing to Fear* - Robert Morgan  *h*  4003

**Oldar**
*King of the Dead* - Gene DeWeese  *h*  1510

**Venneman, Richard**
*Insatiable* - David Dvorkin  *h*  1707

## ASTROLOGER

**Price, Addie**
*The President's Astrologer* - Barbara
    Shafferman  *f*  4926

## ASTRONAUT

**Abronowitz, Wendy**
*The Fugitive Stars* - Daniel Ransom  *s*  4479

**Baedecker, Richard**
*Phases of Gravity* - Dan Simmons  *s*  5057

**Benacerraf, Paula**
*Titan* - Stephen Baxter  *s*  405

**Bourne, Geena**
*Moonseed* - Stephen Baxter  *s*  400

**Bronstein, Miroslav Ilyich**
*Fellow Traveller* - William Barton  *s*  380

**Campbell, Jack "Cap'n Jack"**
*The Fugitive Stars* - Daniel Ransom  *s*  4479

**Captain**
*Beyond Apollo* - Barry Malzberg  *s*  3612
*Eden* - Stanislaw Lem  *s*  3434

**Cartwright, Jay**
*The Fortress of Utopia* - Jack Williamson  *s*  5863

**Doctor**
*Eden* - Stanislaw Lem  *s*  3434

**Drumm, Pat**
*The Fortress of Utopia* - Jack Williamson  *s*  5863

**DuBois, Ned**
*Firestar* - Michael Flynn  *s*  1962

**Essell, Lilly**
*Realtime Interrupt* - James P. Hogan  *s*  2729

**Evans, Harry M.**
*Beyond Apollo* - Barry Malzberg  *s*  3612

**Friese, Adam "Iceberg"**
*Ignition* - Kevin J. Anderson  *s*  107

**Gershon, Ralph**
*Voyager* - Stephen Baxter  *s*  406

**Gunn, Sam**
*Sam Gunn Forever* - Ben Bova  *s*  592

**Hunter, Nicole "Panther"**
*Ignition* - Kevin J. Anderson  *s*  107

**Jackson, Jack**
*The Stars Must Wait* - Keith Laumer  *s*  3346

**Jiang Ling**
*Titan* - Stephen Baxter  *s*  405

**Kelligan, Sam Houston**
*Beachhead* - Jack Williamson  *s*  5859

**Manarov, Vladimir "Volodya" Alekseevich**
*Fellow Traveller* - William Barton  *s*  380

**Mathews, Sheilagh**
*The Voice of Cepheus* - Ken Appleby  *s*  202

**Pettis**
*Moonbane* - Al Sarrantonio  *s*  4831

**Poole, Frank**
*3001: The Final Odyssey* - Arthur C.
    Clarke  *s*  1053

**Reis, Tammy**
*Kings of the High Frontier* - Victor Koman  *s*  3199

**Ryan, Jayne**
*Beachhead* - Jack Williamson  *s*  5859

**Ryder, Jake**
*Reach* - Edward Gibson  *s*  2216

**Spencer, Joseph "Speed"**
*Reach* - Edward Gibson  *s*  2216

**Stavenger, Paul**
*Moonrise* - Ben Bova  *s*  587

**Stoner, Keith**
*Star Brothers* - Ben Bova  *s*  594

**Tanaka, Celine**
*Aftermath* - Charles Sheffield  *s*  4947

**Terrence, Chris**
*Encounter with Tiber* - Buzz Aldrin  *s*  64

**Tynan, Louie**
*Mother of Storms* - John Barnes  *s*  354

**Wagner, Lauren**
*The Season of Passage* - Christopher Pike  *h*  4331

**Walmsley, Nigel**
*Sailing Bright Eternity* - Gregory Benford  *s*  449

**Wayville, Chris**
*Flying to Valhalla* - Charles Pellegrino  *s*  4280

**Wayville, Clarice**
*Flying to Valhalla* - Charles Pellegrino  *s*  4280

**Williams, Conrad**
*Night Launch* - Jake Garn  *s*  2143

**Zakharov, Aelita**
*Night Launch* - Jake Garn  *s*  2143

## AUDITOR

**Gonzales, Mikhail Mikhailovitch**
*Halo* - Tom Maddox  *s*  3604

**Vorkosigan, Miles**
*Komarr* - Lois McMaster Bujold  *s*  760

**Vorthys**
*Komarr* - Lois McMaster Bujold  *s*  760

## AVENGER

**Amalayna**
*Chains of Darkness, Chains of Light* - Michelle
    Sagara  *f*  4781

**Gersen, Kirth**
*The Demon Princes: Volume One* - Jack
    Vance  *s*  5544
*The Demon Princes: Volume Two* - Jack
    Vance  *s*  5545

**K'os**
*Song of the River* - Sue Harrison  *f*  2583

**Miner, Bron "Selwyn Forester"**
*The Arm of the Stone* - Victoria Strauss  *f*  5333

**Mona**
*Enemy of My Enemy* - Ben Ohlander  *s*  4204

**Mzu, Alkad**
*Conflict* - Peter F. Hamilton  *s*  2522

**Tuchman, Ward**
*Enemy of My Enemy* - Ben Ohlander  *s*  4204

## BACHELOR

**Madog, Jay "Mad Dog"**
*Promised Land* - Connie Willis  *s*  5872

## BACKWOODSMAN

**Kylie, Gabriel**
*Anvil* - Nicolas van Pallandt  *s*  5540

**Old Nathan**
*Old Nathan* - David Drake  *f*  1639

## BAKER

**Bayless, Laura**
*Good Night, Sweet Angel* - Clare McNally  *h*  3857

**Jack**
*The Baker's Boy* - J.V. Jones  *f*  2956

**Manzara, Gaetano**
*Fantasma* - Thomas F. Monteleone  *h*  3963

**Phan, Gi Minh**
*Ticktock* - Dean R. Koontz  *h*  3217

## BANKER

**Barker, Justin**
*Tombley's Walk* - Crosland Brown  *h*  723

**Cummings, Michael**
*Not Broken, Not Belonging* - Randy Fox  *h*  2030

**Doland, Jane**
*Flying Dutch* - Tom Holt  *f*  2750

**Grange, Karen**
*A Dry Spell* - Susan Moloney  *h*  3951

**Jackson, Portis**
*Dumford Blood* - S.K. Epperson  *h*  1829

**Kataboki, Lily**
*I'll Be Watching You* - Samuel M. Key  *h*  3094

**Ling, Mayla**
*Half the Day Is Night* - Maureen F.
    McHugh  *s*  3818

**Sullivan, Donald**
*What's Wrong with America* - Scott
    Bradfield  *h*  627

## BARBARIAN

**Bakhtiian, Ilyakoria "Ilya"**
*An Earthly Crown* - Kate Elliott  *s*  1771
*Jaran* - Kate Elliott  *s*  1772

**Black-Robe, Harvas**
*Krispos of Videssos* - Harry Turtledove  *f*  5506

**Conan**
*Conan and the Treasure of Python* - John Maddox
    Roberts  *f*  4616
*The Conan Chronicles* - Robert Jordan  *f*  2983
*Conan of the Red Brotherhood* - Leonard
    Carpenter  *f*  906
*Conan, Scourge of the Bloody Coast* - Leonard
    Carpenter  *f*  910
*Conan the Formidable* - Steve Perry  *f*  4293
*Conan the Gladiator* - Leonard Carpenter  *f*  907
*Conan the Guardian* - Roland J. Green  *f*  2347
*Conan the Indomitable* - Steve Perry  *f*  4294
*Conan the Outcast* - Leonard Carpenter  *f*  908
*Conan the Relentless* - Roland J. Green  *f*  2348
*Conan the Rogue* - John Maddox Roberts  *f*  4617
*Conan the Savage* - Leonard Carpenter  *f*  909
*Hour of the Dragon* - Robert E. Howard  *f*  2783

**de Oro, Joe**
*Songs of the Dancing Gods* - Jack L. Chalker  *f*  962

**Etzilios**
*Hammer and Anvil* - Harry Turtledove  *f*  5503

**Kerin**
*The Honorable Barbarian* - L. Sprague de Camp  *f*  1415

**Medwind Song**
*Bones of the Past* - Holly Lisle  *f*  3478

**Oonitsaupivia, Nijon**
*By the Sword* - Greg Costikyan  *f*  1207

**Shkai'ra**
*The Cage* - S.M. Stirling  *f*  5293

**Song, Medwind**
*Fire in the Mist* - Holly Lisle  *f*  3482

**Van**
*Prince of the North* - Harry Turtledove  *f*  5509

**Wartsworth, Caspar**
*The Lost City of Zork* - Robin Wayne Bailey  *f*  288

**Wulfgar**
*The Silent Blade* - R.A. Salvatore  *f*  4805

## BARTENDER

**Big John "BJ"**
*When Wolves Cry* - Chris N. Africa  *h*  41

**Clough, Emma**
*Famine* - Todd Komarnicki  *h*  3201

**Rowan, Daniel**
*Famine* - Todd Komarnicki  *h*  3201

## BASTARD DAUGHTER

**Albain, Elandra**
*Reign of Shadows* - Deborah Chester  *f*  1009

**Kaeler, Lanen**
*Song in the Silence* - Elizabeth Kerner  *f*  3065

**Villette, Celine**
*The Judas Cross* - Charles Sheffield  *h*  4960

## BASTARD SON

**Alain**
*King's Dragon* - Kate Elliott  *f*  1773

**Arthor**
*The Eagle and the Sword* - A.A. Attanasio  *f*  267

**Arthur**
*The Winter King* - Bernard Cornwell  *f*  1191

**Avery, Rupert "Roo"**
*Rage of a Demon King* - Raymond E. Feist  *f*  1908
*Rise of a Merchant Prince* - Raymond E. Feist  *f*  1909
*Shadow of a Dark Queen* - Raymond E. Feist  *f*  1911
*Shards of a Broken Crown* - Raymond E. Feist  *f*  1912

**Badger**
*The Spellkey Trilogy* - Ann Downer  *f*  1592

**Dheribi**
*Greenmagic* - Crawford Kilian  *f*  3105

**Fallstar, Chade**
*Assassin's Apprentice* - Robin Hobb  *f*  2693

**Farseer, FitzChivalry "Fitz"**
*Assassin's Apprentice* - Robin Hobb  *f*  2693
*Assassin's Quest* - Robin Hobb  *f*  2694
*Royal Assassin* - Robin Hobb  *f*  2695

**Ketral, Jarid Tal**
*Moonspeaker* - K.D. Wentworth  *s*  5754

**Kireyevsky, Vasily "Vasha"**
*The Law of Becoming* - Kate Elliott  *s*  1774

**Lannister, Tyrion**
*A Game of Thrones* - George R.R. Martin  *f*  3645

**Mordred**
*Mordred's Curse* - Ian McDowell  *f*  3806

**Roland**
*Charlemagne's Champion* - Gail Van Asten  *f*  5534

**Tegne**
*Tegne: Soul Warrior* - Richard La Plante  *f*  3268

**von Darkmoor, Erik**
*Rage of a Demon King* - Raymond E. Feist  *f*  1908
*Rise of a Merchant Prince* - Raymond E. Feist  *f*  1909
*Shadow of a Dark Queen* - Raymond E. Feist  *f*  1911
*Shards of a Broken Crown* - Raymond E. Feist  *f*  1912

**Welch, Lewis**
*Soulsmith* - Tom Deitz  *f*  1475

## BEACHCOMBER

**O'Donnell, Ryan**
*Nightmare, with Angel* - Stephen Gallagher  *h*  2111

## BIKER

**Bombeck, Tesla**
*Everville* - Clive Barker  *h*  338

**Bork, Dick "Dutch"**
*Night Beasts* - T.W. Stetson  *h*  5263

**Hitch**
*Dead Heat* - Del Stone Jr.  *h*  5313

## BLACKSMITH

**Blaze**
*Isle of Woman* - Piers Anthony  *f*  178

**Elof**
*The Forge in the Forest* - Michael Scott Rohan  *f*  4660

**Miller, Alvin "Maker"**
*Alvin Journeyman* - Orson Scott Card  *f*  881
*Heartfire* - Orson Scott Card  *f*  889

**Ohaern**
*The Sage* - Christopher Stasheff  *f*  5221

**Sigvarthsson, Shef**
*The Hammer and the Cross* - Harry Harrison  *f*  2570

**Varrus, Gaius Publius**
*The Skystone* - Jack Whyte  *f*  5794

## BODYGUARD

**al Keylan, Brynda**
*Broken Blade* - Ann Marston  *f*  3634

**Audran, Marid**
*The Exile Kiss* - George Alec Effinger  *s*  1750
*A Fire in the Sun* - George Alec Effinger  *s*  1751

**Bennet, Tim**
*Half the Day Is Night* - Maureen F. McHugh  *s*  3818

**Bering**
*The Dog King* - Christoph Ransmayr  *f*  4474

**Boniface, Thomas**
*The Element of Fire* - Martha Wells  *f*  5750

**Bork, Saval**
*Brother Death* - Steve Perry  *s*  4292

**Bothari**
*Barrayar* - Lois McMaster Bujold  *s*  756

**Dai, David**
*Half the Day Is Night* - Maureen F. McHugh  *s*  3818

**DaSilva, Renli**
*The Shapes of Their Hearts* - Melissa Scott  *s*  4901

**Grenfell, Arden**
*Darkloom* - Cary Osborne  *s*  4225
*Deathweave* - Cary Osborne  *s*  4226

**Guido**
*M.Y.T.H. Inc. in Action* - Robert Asprin  *f*  259

**Halloran, Liam**
*Sepulchre* - James Herbert  *h*  2672

**Jewelbright, Taynad**
*Brother to Shadows* - Andre Norton  *s*  4142

**Lomax, Felix "Gravedancer"**
*Prophet* - Mike Resnick  *s*  4553

**Maude**
*Conrad's Quest for Rubber* - Leo Frankowski  *s*  2043

**Maxon, Max**
*Bodyguard* - William C. Dietz  *s*  1542

**Nimnestl**
*Rouse a Sleeping Cat* - Dan Crawford  *f*  1249
*The Sure Death of a Mouse* - Dan Crawford  *f*  1250
*A Wild Dog and Lone* - Dan Crawford  *f*  1251

**Nunzio**
*M.Y.T.H. Inc. in Action* - Robert Asprin  *f*  259

**Olaffson, Egil**
*Egil's Book* - C.J. Mills  *s*  3910

**Rachelle**
*The Anubis Murders* - Gary Gygax  *f*  2472
*Death in Delhi* - Gary Gygax  *f*  2473

**Reandn**
*Wolf Justice* - Doranna Durgin  *f*  1706

**Sleel**
*Black Steel* - Steve Perry  *s*  4291

**Sten**
*Revenge of the Damned* - Allan Cole  *s*  1107

**Strang, Mark**
*Patton's Spaceship* - John Barnes  *s*  357

**Trigg, Cyrus "Russ"**
*Howl-O-Ween* - Gary L. Holleman  *h*  2744

**Tyrian**
*A College of Magics* - Caroline Stevermer  *f*  5266

**Valentinian**
*An Oblique Approach* - David Drake  *s*  1638

**Zimmerman, Rick**
*Unearthed* - Ashley McConnell  *h*  3778

## BOUNTY HUNTER

**Boba Fett**
*The Mandalorian Armor* - K.W. Jeter  *s*  2914

**Bossk**
*The Mandalorian Armor* - K.W. Jeter  *s*  2914

**Chandler, Joshua "the Whistler" Jeremiah**
*Oracle* - Mike Resnick  *s*  4551

**Christian, Reese**
*Shadows* - Kimberly Rangel  *h*  4472

**d'Ark, Hazel**
*Deathstalker Honor* - Simon R. Green  *s*  2364

**Deathstalker, Owen**
*Deathstalker Honor* - Simon R. Green  *s*  2364

**Goode, Wilson**
*Monsoon* - Peter L. Rice  *s*  4583

**Javobo**
*Mainline* - Deborah Christian  *s*  1026

**Jones, Witchfinder**
*Walking Wolf* - Nancy A. Collins  *h*  1126

**Journey, Ruby**
*Deathstalker Rebellion* - Simon R. Green  *s*  2365

**McCade, Sam**
*McCade's Bounty* - William C. Dietz  *s*  1550

**Murtaugh, Flint**
*Gone South* - Robert R. McCammon  *h*  3755

**Rydell, Berry**
*Virtual Light* - William Gibson  *s*  2219

**Windsor, Corrigan Tel**
*The Price of Ransom* - Alis A. Rasmussen  *s*  4483

## BOYFRIEND

**Carnes, Donald**
*The Axman Cometh* - John Farris  *h*  1883

**Donohue, Greg**
*A Witch Across Time* - Gilbert B. Cross  *f*  1272

**Enkidu**
*Mirage* - Perry Brass  *s*  662

**Sanderheim, Doug**
*Slow Funeral* - Rebecca Ore  *f*  4221

## BRIDE

**Linda**
*Bride of the Castle* - John DeChancie  *s*  1452

**Rubra, Rose**
*Waking Beauty* - Paul Witcover  *f*  5931

**Theodora of Pyrene**
*Two-Bit Heroes* - Doris Egan  *s*  1757

## BUSINESSMAN

**Abdullah**
*Castle in the Air* - Diana Wynne Jones  *f*  2944

**Allen, Harrison**
*Dark Twilight* - Joseph A. Citro  *h*  1036

**Altman, Gibson**
*Pallas* - L. Neil Smith  *s*  5132

**Arayncourt, Trevelyan**
*The Lotus and the Rose* - Scott Ciencin  *f*  1029
*The Wolves of Autumn* - Scott Ciencin  *f*  1035

**Argyle, Roger**
*All the Bells on Earth* - James P. Blaylock  *f*  518

**Ashlar "Mr. Ash"**
*Taltos* - Anne Rice  *h*  4577

**Austin, Kenton**
*The Living Dark* - Stephen Gresham  *h*  2431

**Avery, Rupert "Roo"**
*Rage of a Demon King* - Raymond E. Feist  *f*  1908
*Rise of a Merchant Prince* - Raymond E. Feist  *f*  1909
*Shards of a Broken Crown* - Raymond E. Feist  *f*  1912

**Baedecker, Richard**
*Phases of Gravity* - Dan Simmons  *s*  5057

**Balthazar, Timothy**
*Wolf Moon* - John R. Holt  *h*  2749

**Bardou, Nick**
*Spell Bound* - Trana Mae Simmons  *f*  5061

**Barnard, Jacques**
*2XS* - Nigel Findley  *f*  1935

**Barr, Dallas**
*Buying Time* - Joe Haldeman  *s*  2487

**Bateman, Patrick**
*American Psycho* - Brett Easton Ellis  *h*  1777

**Bates, Patty**
*The Immaculate* - Mark Morris  *h*  4023

**Bathory, Michael**
*Ancestral Hungers* - Scott Baker  *h*  303

**Beckwith, Desmond**
*Desmond: A Novel of Love and the Modern Vampire* - Ulysses G. Dietz  *h*  1541

**Bell, John**
*The Bell Witch: An American Haunting* - Brent Monahan  *h*  3953

**Bellini, Aaron**
*Out There in the Darkness* - Ed Gorman  *h*  2279

**Bellisle, Andre**
*Cold Eye* - Giles Blunt  *h*  556

**Beltar**
*Traitors* - Kristine Kathryn Rusch  *f*  4729

**Benedict, Alex**
*A Talent for War* - Jack McDevitt  *s*  3790

**Benson, Jack**
*Shadow Twin* - Dale Hoover  *h*  2762

**Bernard, Rolf**
*The Gatekeepers* - Daniel Graham Jr.  *s*  2301

**Bey, Friedlander**
*The Exile Kiss* - George Alec Effinger  *s*  1750
*A Fire in the Sun* - George Alec Effinger  *s*  1751

**Bickerstaff, Robert Luther**
*Terraplane* - Jack Womack  *s*  5960

**Big Tom**
*The Dream Vessel* - Jeff Bredenberg  *s*  664

**Binder, Columbus**
*Flying Saucers over Hennepin* - Peter Gelman  *f*  2186

**Blackstone, Jonathan**
*In the Company of the Mind* - Steven Piziks  *s*  4339

**Blaise, Adrian**
*Devil's Gate* - Elizabeth Ergas  *h*  1833

**Blake, Werner**
*The Bridge: A Horror Story* - John Skipp  *h*  5081

**Blueshell**
*A Fire upon the Deep* - Vernor Vinge  *s*  5573

**Bondy**
*War With the Newts* - Karel Capek  *s*  874

**Boone, Hank**
*Angel Kiss* - Kelley Wilde  *h*  5800

**Borden, Andrew**
*Lizzie Borden* - Elizabeth Engstrom  *h*  1826

**Braccalese, Gianni**
*A Wizard in Mind* - Christopher Stasheff  *s*  5232

**Brody, Aloysius**
*Pallas* - L. Neil Smith  *s*  5132

**Brown, Pellimore "Pel"**
*Out of This World* - Lawrence Watt-Evans  *f*  5645

**Bury, Horace Hussein**
*The Gripping Hand* - Larry Niven  *s*  4122

**Calais, Lucien**
*Private Demons* - Robert Masello  *h*  3660

**Calvert, Joshua**
*Emergence* - Peter F. Hamilton  *s*  2524

**Cantemir, George**
*The Venom Trees of Sunga* - L. Sprague de Camp  *s*  1420

**Capuela, Giacomo**
*The Unborn* - Andrew Laurance  *h*  3350

**Carpenter, Gary**
*Last Rites* - David Darke  *h*  1354

**Castle, Hunter**
*The Six Families* - Nancy Holder  *s*  2733

**Cavanagh, Stewart**
*Conqueror's Pride* - Timothy Zahn  *s*  6051

**Center, Fisk**
*Hard Sell* - Piers Anthony  *s*  173

**Chase, Jason**
*Night's Pawn* - Tom Dowd  *s*  1591

**Chauvin, Rene**
*The Gris-Gris Man* - Don Davis  *h*  1403

**Chen, Tam**
*Phoenix Fire* - Elizabeth Forrest  *f*  1974

**Chicago, Pasquale**
*A King of Infinite Space* - Allen Steele  *s*  5243

**Chrestil, Damian**
*Burning Bright* - Melissa Scott  *s*  4894

**Claiborne, Adam**
*Sacred Prey* - Vivian Schilling  *h*  4875

**Clayborne, Martin**
*Darkman #2: The Price of Fear* - Randall Boyll  *h*  613

**Claypoole, Chester "Chet" W.**
*Live From Golgotha: A Novel* - Gore Vidal  *s*  5569

**Colletti, Vince**
*Torments* - Lisa Cantrell  *h*  873

**Collins, Barnabas**
*Angelique's Descent* - Lara Parker  *h*  4246

**Collins, Henry**
*The Sweetheart Season* - Karen Joy Fowler  *f*  2029

**Cooper, Gerald**
*Kings of the High Frontier* - Victor Koman  *s*  3199

**Cooper, Harry**
*Night of the Living Dead* - John Russo  *h*  4745

**Corman, Brian**
*The Gifted* - Jack Caravela  *h*  879

**Crane, Peter**
*Hunting the Corrigan's Blood* - Holly Lisle  *s*  3484

**Creedath**
*The Gates of Vensunor* - Carol Heller  *f*  2650

**Cross, Tom**
*Greenhouse* - Thomas A. Easton  *s*  1723

**Croyd**
*Megalomania* - Ian Wallace  *s*  5621

**Dale, Ambrose**
*The Night Inside* - Nancy Baker  *h*  301

**Dalton, Edmund**
*Winter Tides* - James P. Blaylock  *h*  524

**Dane, Richard**
*Cold in July* - Joe R. Lansdale  *h*  3323

**Danilov, Barron**
*This Dark Paradise* - Wendy Haley  *h*  2493

**Dartson, Michael**
*The Premonition* - Andrew Laurance  *h*  3349

**Dellhart, Jackson**
*Something Out There* - Ronald Kelly  *h*  3056

**DeSalvo, Vincent**
*Shades of Night* - Rick Hautala  *h*  2612

**Devore, Max**
*Bag of Bones* - Stephen King  *h*  3126

**DeWitt, Willard "Jeremy Schneider"**
*Lunar Descent* - Allen Steele  *s*  5245

**Dibbler, Cut-Me-Own-Throat**
*Moving Pictures* - Terry Pratchett  *f*  4398

**Digonness, Peter**
*The Expediter* - J. Brian Clarke  s  1062

**Donaldson, Larry**
*Mind Stealer* - Lee Duigon  h  1672

**d'Ormonde, Hue**
*Blood Roses* - Chelsea Quinn Yarbro  h  6012

**Doyle, Vernon**
*Harrowgate* - Daniel H. Gower  h  2292

**D'Rasha**
*Hand of Prophecy* - Severna Park  s  4244

**Dryden, Thatcher**
*Heathern* - Jack Womack  s  5958

**Dryke, Mikhail**
*The Quiet Pools* - Michael P. Kube-
   McDowell  s  3249

**Dunham, Arthur "Art"**
*The Rebirth of Wonder* - Lawrence Watt-
   Evans  f  5646

**Dutton, Brian**
*The 7th Guest* - Matthew J. Costello  h  1192

**Eberhardt, Johann**
*Bright Messengers* - Gentry Lee  s  3398

**Edwards, Drake**
*The Immortals* - Andrew Neiderman  h  4087

**Elives, S.H.**
*Jennifer Murdley's Toad* - Bruce Coville  f  1220

**Elobert, Henri**
*Prophets for the End of Time* - Marcos
   Donnelly  f  1577

**Endine, Flojian**
*Eternity Road* - Jack McDevitt  s  3788

**Errenthorp, Reynaldo**
*The Third Eagle: Lessons Along a Minor String* - R.A.
   MacAvoy  s  3583

**Evanston, Livermore**
*Hunter's Planet* - David Bischoff  s  492

**Farrell, Simon**
*Homecoming* - Matthew J. Costello  h  1198

**Feldman, Jake**
*Pelts* - F. Paul Wilson  h  5894

**Feldspar**
*The Chosen* - Edward Lee  h  3389

**Flannagan, James**
*Diary of a Vampire* - Gary Bowen  h  600

**Fraser, Edward**
*Dark Silence* - Rick Hautala  h  2606

**Freeborn, Silas**
*Nocturnas* - Shawn Ryan  h  4755

**Froister, Albert**
*The Magic Touch* - Jody Lynn Nye  f  4171

**Frost, Jonathan**
*Morningstar* - Peter Atkins  h  265

**Gaunt, Leland**
*Needful Things* - Stephen King  h  3137

**Gibson, Paul**
*Black as Blood* - Rob Chilson  f  1014

**Goebbels, Joseph "Joseph Gable"**
*The Resurrections* - Simon Louvish  s  3528

**Gordon, Winston**
*Mina* - Marie Kiraly  h  3151

**Gragelouth**
*Son of Spellsinger* - Alan Dean Foster  f  2015

**Grenier, Roger**
*Viper* - Alan Riefe  h  4589

**Gunn**
*Primavera* - Francesca Lia Block  f  551

**Gunn, Sam**
*Sam Gunn, Unlimited* - Ben Bova  s  593

**Guthrie, Anson**
*Harvest of Stars* - Poul Anderson  s  127

**Hagbarth, Hoak**
*O Pioneer!* - Frederik Pohl  s  4350

**Hammersmidt, Garry**
*Yesterday's Pawn* - W.T. Quick  s  4453

**Hammond, John**
*Jurassic Park* - Michael Crichton  s  1255

**Harijadi, Anjeillo "Angel"**
*The Shapes of Their Hearts* - Melissa Scott  s  4901

**Harrisch**
*Noir* - K.W. Jeter  s  2916

**Hawthorne, Alec**
*Distant Dreams* - Jenny Lykins  f  3576

**Hayaka, Reyna**
*Wild Magic* - Jo Clayton  f  1072

**Hayden, Conek**
*Backblast* - Lee McKeone  s  3828
*The Clone Crisis* - Lee McKeone  s  3829
*Starfire Down* - Lee McKeone  s  3830

**Hayes, Charlie**
*Death Channels* - Robert E. Vardeman  h  5562

**Heikki, Galler**
*Mighty Good Road* - Melissa Scott  s  4897

**Heller, Sean**
*California Ghosting* - William Hill  h  2687

**Highborn, Ilaron**
*Son of Darkness* - Josepha Sherman  f  4990

**Holdman, Taylor**
*Near Dead* - Stephen R. George  h  2202

**Horton, Dabney**
*The Virginia Ghost Murders* - Leslie Raymond
   Sachs  h  4778

**Hunter, Harold "Randy" Randolph**
*Timemaster* - Robert L. Forward  s  1992

**Hunter, Max**
*Blood Secrets* - Karen E. Taylor  h  5406

**ibn-Rushd, Damon**
*Destiny's Road* - Larry Niven  s  4119

**Ingersol, William "Bogey"**
*Top Dog* - Jerry Jay Carroll  f  915

**Jameson, Charles**
*Between Floors* - Thomas F. Monteleone  h  3957

**Jean-Claude**
*Burnt Offerings* - Laurell K. Hamilton  h  2514

**Kane, Chandler**
*Order of the Arrow* - Michael T.
   Hinkemeyer  h  2689

**Kazacos, Ari**
*Vampire Bytes* - Linda Grant  h  2322

**Kean, Michael**
*Legends Reborn* - Kenneth C. Flint  f  1958

**Kennet, Spencer**
*Monsoon* - Peter L. Rice  s  4583

**Khat**
*City of Bones* - Martha Wells  f  5748

**King, Newman**
*The Store* - Bentley Little  h  3497

**Kinner's Son, Kensher**
*The Blood of a Dragon* - Lawrence Watt-
   Evans  f  5640

**Klein, Lance**
*Night Relics* - James P. Blaylock  h  521

**Kline, Felix**
*Sepulchre* - James Herbert  h  2672

**Knight, Campbell**
*Seeing Eye* - Jack Ellis  h  1780

**Kollberg, Arturo**
*Heroes Die* - Matthew Woodring Stover  s  5319

**Lambert, Richard**
*A Once and Future Love* - Anne Kelleher  f  3039

**Lamont, Roger**
*Dead Voices* - Abigail McDaniels  h  3783

**Land, Garrett**
*Demon Within* - Dana Reed  h  4499

**Lang, Edward Winslow**
*Sheltered Lives* - Charles Oberndorf  s  4188

**Larice, Aldin**
*The Napoleon Wager* - William R.
   Forstchen  s  1980

**Larken, Ray**
*Cry Wolf* - Kenneth Von Gunden  s  5586
*Under Fire* - Kenneth Von Gunden  s  5589

**LaVine, Martin**
*When Shadows Fall* - Brian Scott Smith  h  5100

**Leech, Derek**
*The Quorum* - Kim Newman  h  4100

**Leon**
*The Immortals* - Andrew Neiderman  h  4087

**Lightfoot**
*Deepdrive* - Alexander Jablokov  s  2837

**Liston, Mark**
*Soulcatchers* - Jan Lara  h  3336

**London, Stefan**
*Ragged Angels* - Della Van Hise  h  5537

**MacKendimen, Alex**
*A Love through Time* - Terri Brisbin  f  691

**Mackinnon, Curtis**
*Kalimantan* - Lucius Shepard  h  4979

**Maclemmon, Howmaster**
*668: The Neighbor of the Beast* - Lionel
   Fenn  h  1917

**Madera, Blasing**
*California Ghosting* - William Hill  h  2687

**Madog, Jay "Mad Dog"**
*Promised Land* - Connie Willis  s  5872

**Magnus, Dominic "Dom"**
*Partisan* - S. Andrew Swann  s  5365
*Profiteer* - S. Andrew Swann  s  5366
*Revolutionary* - S. Andrew Swann  s  5367

**Markley, Alan**
*Between Floors* - Thomas F. Monteleone  h  3957

**Matsuda**
*The Bushido Incident* - Betty Anne
   Crawford  s  1248

**Matsudaira, Daisuke**
*Fire in a Faraway Place* - Robert Frezza  s  2052

**Maury, Paul**
*Whiteout* - Sage Walker  s  5619

**May, Carl**
*The Cloning of Joanna May* - Fay Weldon  s  5732

**Mayhew, Richard**
*Neverwhere* - Neil Gaiman  f  2104

**McCord, Bob**
*Darkscope* - Margaret Falk  h  1860

**McKay, Bernie**
*Black as Blood* - Rob Chilson  f  1014

**Merrick, Geoffrey Robert**
*Fear Itself* - Ric Meyers  h  3881
*Living Hell* - Ric Meyers  h  3882

*Worst Nightmare* - Ric Meyers   *h*   3883

**Mike**
*Dark Legacy* - Mark A. Kostrubula   *h*   3220

**Miller, Martin**
*The Darker Passions: Carmilla* - Amarantha
    Knight   *h*   3177

**Minakis, Manolis**
*Secret Passages* - Paul Preuss   *s*   4420

**Mobarak, Cyrus "Torquemada"**
*Cold as Ice* - Charles Sheffield   *s*   4950

**Mondesir, Carmen**
*Vodoun* - David Madsen   *h*   3605

**Moreson, Joe**
*65mm* - Dale Hoover   *h*   2761

**Morgan, Richard**
*Dark Dreaming* - Pat Franklin   *h*   2040

**Morris, Dwight**
*Penance* - Rick R. Reed   *h*   4501

**Myburgh, Gerrit**
*Apartheid, Superstrings, and Mordecai Thubana* -
    Michael Bishop   *s*   496

**Narman, Bart**
*The Curse* - John Tigges   *h*   5472

**Needham, Bill**
*Kane* - Douglas Borton   *h*   576

**Ngu, Emerson**
*Pallas* - L. Neil Smith   *s*   5132

**Nix, Luke**
*Dogland* - Will Shetterly   *f*   4992

**Norman**
*Human Resources* - Floyd Kemske   *h*   3057

**O'Brien, Mike**
*Out There in the Darkness* - Ed Gorman   *h*   2279

**Offenhouse, Ralph**
*Debtors' Planet* - William R. Thompson   *s*   5457

**O'Hara, Sonny**
*Torments* - Lisa Cantrell   *h*   873

**Okasan**
*Masque* - F. Paul Wilson   *s*   5890

**Orchard, Jack**
*The Count of Eleven* - Ramsey Campbell   *h*   853

**Orr, Carnaby**
*Where the Ships Die* - William C. Dietz   *s*   1553

**Owain, David**
*The Long Lost* - Ramsey Campbell   *h*   859

**Patton, Dan**
*Dangerous Nature* - T.J. Kirby   *h*   3152

**Peter**
*Bones* - Joyce Thompson   *h*   5453

**Pomeroy, Bernard**
*Night Relics* - James P. Blaylock   *h*   521

**Poubelle, Laurence**
*Kings of the High Frontier* - Victor Koman   *s*   3199

**Presteign**
*The Stars My Destination* - Alfred Bester   *s*   478

**Price, Timothy**
*American Psycho* - Brett Easton Ellis   *h*   1777

**Proctor, Ethan**
*Genesis* - Charles L. Grant   *h*   2308

**Profitt, Dennis**
*Star Precinct* - Kevin D. Randle   *s*   4470

**Quinn, Dave**
*Winter Tides* - James P. Blaylock   *h*   524

**Quinn, Roger**
*A Calculated Magic* - Robert Weinberg   *f*   5694

**Randolph, Dan**
*Empire Builders* - Ben Bova   *s*   584

**Reed, Jack**
*Walkers* - Graham Masterton   *h*   3681

**Reich, Ben**
*The Demolished Man* - Alfred Bester   *s*   476

**Reid, Nicholas**
*The Cipher* - Kathe Koja   *h*   3194

**Remillard, Rogatien**
*Diamond Mask: A Novel* - Julian May   *s*   3697

**Renaldi, Cosmo**
*Nightmare's Disciple* - Joseph S. Pulver Jr.   *h*   4449

**Rice, Sheldon**
*Thrill* - Patricia Wallace   *h*   5624

**Riddell, Lester**
*Lunar Descent* - Allen Steele   *s*   5245

**Risinger, Werner**
*Oktober* - Stephen Gallagher   *h*   2112

**Rory**
*The Hellbound Heart* - Clive Barker   *h*   342

**Rose, Mick "China"**
*Signs of Life* - M. John Harrison   *s*   2580

**Ryan, Steve**
*Blood Feud* - Sam Siciliano   *h*   5020

**Sanderson, Paul**
*Wolf and Iron* - Gordon R. Dickson   *s*   1539

**Sandoval, Rho**
*Heads* - Greg Bear   *s*   419

**Schroeder, Thomas**
*Psychomech* - Brian Lumley   *h*   3562

**Scopes, Brent**
*Mount Dragon* - Douglas Preston   *h*   4413

**Sharur**
*Between the Rivers* - Harry Turtledove   *f*   5496

**Sinbad the Sailor**
*The Last Voyage of Somebody the Sailor* - John
    Barth   *f*   374
*The Other Sinbad* - Craig Shaw Gardner   *f*   2130

**Sinclair, Graham Kuan**
*Red Genesis* - S.C. Sykes   *s*   5377

**Solomon, Neil**
*Out There in the Darkness* - Ed Gorman   *h*   2279

**Solomon, Parker**
*Dark Tide* - Elizabeth Forrest   *h*   1972

**Southerland, John**
*A Matter of Taste* - Fred Saberhagen   *h*   4770

**Spear, James**
*Deathwalker* - Patrick Whalen   *h*   5769

**Spence, Oliver**
*Fog Heart* - Thomas Tessier   *h*   5440

**Spider**
*The Einstein Intersection* - Samuel R.
    Delany   *s*   1481

**Spoor, Baron Malcolm**
*The Living One* - Lewis Gannett   *h*   2115

**Statler, Phil**
*The Fear in Yesterday's Rings* - George C.
    Chesbro   *h*   1007

**Stavenger, Paul**
*Moonrise* - Ben Bova   *s*   587

**Stewart, Dalton**
*Jupiter's Daughter* - Tom Hyman   *s*   2820

**Stone, David**
*Sati* - Christopher Pike   *f*   4330

**Stone, Philip**
*Psychamok* - Brian Lumley   *h*   3561

**Stonehouse, Dylan**
*A Wish and a Dream* - Ingrid Weaver   *f*   5658

**Stout, Wellington "Bill" Nelson**
*Humpty Dumpty: An Oval* - Damon Knight   *s*   3186

**Sven "Loki"**
*Overshoot* - Mona Clee   *s*   1075

**Sword, Galen**
*Nightfeeder* - Judith Reeves-Stevens   *f*   4513
*Shifter* - Judith Reeves-Stevens   *f*   4515

**Tatian, Mhyre**
*Shadow Man* - Melissa Scott   *s*   4900

**Taylor, Lance**
*Dark Legacy* - Mark A. Kostrubula   *h*   3220

**Teal, Marcus**
*Reaper* - Ben Mizrich   *h*   3923

**Thompson, Drew**
*Virus* - Graham Watkins   *h*   5632

**Trader, Max**
*Trader* - Charles de Lint   *f*   1438

**Trent, Vernor Deacon**
*Children of the Night* - Dan Simmons   *h*   5050

**Trosper, Carl**
*Greely's Cove* - John Gideon   *h*   2221

**Trumbo, Byron**
*Fires of Eden* - Dan Simmons   *h*   5053

**Tso, Anton Sien Hsia**
*The Shapes of Their Hearts* - Melissa Scott   *s*   4901

**Tucker, Elton**
*Where the Chill Waits* - T. Chris
    Martindale   *h*   3658

**Verner, Samuel**
*Never Deal with a Dragon* - Robert N.
    Charrette   *s*   975

**von Wolgast, Klemens Manfred**
*Writ in Blood* - Chelsea Quinn Yarbro   *h*   6019

**Wade, Zach**
*A Reasonable Madness* - Fran Dorf   *h*   1580

**Wheeler**
*Signal to Noise* - Eric S. Nylund   *s*   4179

**Widdick, Robert**
*Retro Lives* - Lee Grimes   *s*   2446

**Wilhoit, Steve**
*Where the Chill Waits* - T. Chris
    Martindale   *h*   3658

**Winters, Franklin Evelyn**
*Dreamer* - Daniel Quinn   *h*   4454

**Wrasselty, Slith**
*The Wells of Phyre* - L. Warren Douglas   *s*   1589

**Zandro, Taverik**
*Hawk's Flight* - Carol Chase   *f*   980

## BUSINESSWOMAN

**Al Shei, Katmer**
*Fool's War* - Sarah Zettel   *s*   6079

**Amij, Katherine**
*Changeling* - Christopher Kubasik   *f*   3245

**Aronson, Susan**
*Phoenix Fire* - Elizabeth Forrest   *f*   1974

**A'Terafin, Jewel**
*The Uncrowned King* - Michelle West   *f*   5760

**Banks, Monica**
*Carol for Another Christmas* - Elizabeth Ann
    Scarborough   *f*   4861

**Banks, Sally "Sal"**
*Mistwalker* - Denise Lopez Heald   *s*   2637

**Beauchamp, Antoinette "Toni"**
*Mockingbird* - Sean Stewart   f   5273

**Bernard, Cynthia**
*The Gatekeepers* - Daniel Graham Jr.   s   2301

**Blake, Jenny**
*One Wish* - C.J. Card   f   880

**Borg, Jocasta**
*The Specialist* - Wynne Whiteford   s   5788

**Brewster**
*The Witch of Maple Park* - Stephanie S. Tolan   f   5478

**Brighton, Cassandra Lane "Casey"**
*Kiss of the Vampire* - Lee Weathersby   h   5657

**Cafferty, Megan**
*Jade Darcy and the Zen Pirates* - Stephen Goldin   s   2260

**Calderon, Mercedes**
*Solip: System* - Walter Jon Williams   s   5841

**Carmody, Alice Levertov**
*Sailor Song* - Ken Kesey   s   3082

**Carter, Ellie**
*The Wishing Well* - Charles de Lint   f   1441

**Catalano, Serena**
*Protektor* - Charles Platt   s   4342

**Chalmers, Polly**
*Needful Things* - Stephen King   h   3137

**Cobri, Amy**
*Sundowner* - Chris Claremont   s   1043

**Collier, Joyce**
*The Fermata* - Nicholson Baker   s   302

**Conyers, Pamela**
*The Enigma Variations* - John Maddox Roberts   s   4618

**Daniels, Rose McLendon**
*Rose Madder* - Stephen King   h   3139

**Davis, Gabrielle**
*Gnelfs* - Sidney Williams   h   5823

**Donohoe, Annabelle**
*Isaac Asimov's I-Bots* - Steve Perry   s   4297

**Engleman, Carolyn**
*Cambio Bay* - Kate Wilhelm   f   5806

**Farlan, Tessa**
*Reunion on Neverend* - John E. Stith   s   5306

**Feinberg, Jennifer**
*Drakon* - S.M. Stirling   s   5294

**Finch, Josephine**
*The LaNague Chronicles* - F. Paul Wilson   s   5889

**Hampton, Evelyn**
*Moonfall* - Jack McDevitt   s   3789

**Hazelhof, Cornelia**
*Timeshare* - Joshua Dann   s   1344

**Heikki, Gwynne**
*Mighty Good Road* - Melissa Scott   s   4897

**H'sial, Atvar**
*Convergence* - Charles Sheffield   s   4951

**Jacqueline**
*Human Resources* - Floyd Kemske   h   3057

**Jordan, Pamela**
*Wind Chimes* - R.R. Walters   h   5625

**Kastazi, Marko**
*Hawk's Flight* - Carol Chase   f   980

**LoDire, Mira**
*Speaking Dreams* - Severna Park   s   4245

**Magorski, Mary Jane**
*Some Enchanted Evening* - Alice Alfonsi   f   73

**Maughan, Daisy**
*Mennyms Alive* - Sylvia Waugh   f   5655

**Mayfair, Mona**
*Taltos* - Anne Rice   h   4577

**Melford, Trudy**
*Proteus in the Underworld* - Charles Sheffield   s   4962

**Michaelson, Kiley**
*Mind Light* - Margaret Davis   s   1407

**Morran, Goldie**
*Wagers of Sin* - Robert Asprin   s   264

**Morrow, Cathy**
*The Link* - Andrew Laurance   h   3348

**Owain, Joelle**
*The Long Lost* - Ramsey Campbell   h   859

**Paarman, Leigh**
*Succumb* - Ron Dee   h   1468

**Packard, Janet**
*The Black Lodge* - Robert Weinberg   h   5692

**Perry, Brenda**
*The Wishing Well* - Charles de Lint   f   1441

**Presteign, Olivia**
*The Stars My Destination* - Alfred Bester   s   478

**Priscian**
*Beggar's Banquet* - Daniel Hood   f   2756

**Pruet, Maxine**
*Phule's Paradise* - Robert Asprin   s   261

**Rand, Kyna**
*Howl-O-Ween* - Gary L. Holleman   h   2744

**Ricadonna, Helen**
*Red Planet Run* - Dana Stabenow   s   5187

**Samuels, Rheabeth "Rhea"**
*Hell on High* - Holly Lisle   f   3483

**Slasher**
*The Weigher* - Eric Vinicoff   s   5574

**Sorenson, Melissa**
*Drifter's Run* - William C. Dietz   s   1544

**Stavenger, Joanna Masterson**
*Moonrise* - Ben Bova   s   587

**Stewart, Janet**
*Zeus and Co.* - David Lee Jones   f   2942

**Stollitt, Sydney**
*Another Day, Another Dungeon* - Greg Costikyan   f   1206
*One Quest, Hold the Dragons* - Greg Costikyan   f   1208

**Summers, Faye**
*The Calling* - Kathryn Meyer Griffith   h   2439

**Summers, Millicent**
*The Barsoom Project* - Larry Niven   s   4115

**Taylor, Patricia "Mother"**
*Proxies* - Laura J. Mixon   s   3922

**Thorsen, Sigrid**
*Orion's Dagger* - P.K. McAllister   s   3708

**Trent, Elaine**
*Night Blood* - Eric Flanders   h   1945

**Trost, Sophonisba "Soph"**
*Deepdrive* - Alexander Jablokov   s   2837

**Truely, Yours "Y.T."**
*Snow Crash* - Neal Stephenson   s   5254

**Tyrell, Sarah**
*Blade Runner: Replicant Night* - K.W. Jeter   s   2907

**Vale, Dora Rosamund**
*Suckers* - Anne Billson   h   490

**van Huyten, Mariesa Gorley**
*Firestar* - Michael Flynn   s   1962

**Rogue Star** - Michael Flynn   s   1965

**Varney, Alicia**
*Blood War* - Robert Weinberg   h   5693
*The Unbeholden* - Robert Weinberg   h   5703
*Unholy Allies* - Robert Weinberg   h   5704

**Whitlock, Megan**
*Shadow's Son* - Shirley Meier   f   3872

**Wood, Alice**
*Strange Devices of the Sun and Moon* - Lisa Goldstein   f   2262

**Wray, Helen**
*Omega* - Patrick Lynch   h   3577

## CAPTIVE

**Austin, Gregory**
*Fallway* - Paula E. Downing   s   1593

**Bowen, Muffy**
*Greenhouse* - Thomas A. Easton   s   1723

**Cypher, Richard "the Seeker"**
*Stone of Tears* - Terry Goodkind   f   2269

**Ea**
*Black Wine* - Candas Jane Dorsey   s   1582

**Greenpearl**
*Silk Road* - Jeanne Larsen   f   3339

**Halarek, Kathryn "Kit" Magdalena Alysha**
*Kit's Book* - C.J. Mills   s   3911

**Jonnah's-kin, Maihu**
*Snow Brother* - S.M. Stirling   f   5299

**Phostis**
*Krispos the Emperor* - Harry Turtledove   f   5508

**Romar**
*The Key of the Keplian* - Andre Norton   f   4156

## CARPENTER

**Andrews, Boyd**
*Blood Kin* - Ronald Kelly   h   3051

**Coulter, Matt**
*Shades of Night* - Rick Hautala   h   2612

**Galingale, Cyrus "Cy"**
*Waking Beauty* - Paul Witcover   f   5931

**Lerris**
*The Death of Chaos* - L.E. Modesitt Jr.   f   3926
*The Magic of Recluce* - L.E. Modesitt Jr.   f   3934

**Petersen, Homer "Hopfrog"**
*The Children's Hour* - Douglas Clegg   h   1077

## CARTOGRAPHER

**Gibberling**
*Here There Be Dragons* - Roger Zelazny   f   6069

**Libermann, E.F.**
*The Discovery of Dragons* - Graeme Base   f   385

**Rowan**
*The Outskirter's Secret* - Rosemary Kirstein   s   3157

**Vanachek, Viveka "Viv" Jeng**
*Nothing Sacred* - Elizabeth Ann Scarborough   f   4867

## CASTAWAY

**Byriver, Jerno**
*Thunder of the Captains* - Holly Lisle   f   3489

**Danziger**
*Earth 2* - Melissa Crandall   s   1247

**Dero, Halleyne dar**
*Thunder of the Captains* - Holly Lisle   f   3489

**Jansky, Thalia**
*White Light* - William Barton   s   384

**McKelvey, Dan**
*The Past of Forever* - Juanita Coulson   s   1210

**O'Malley, Wolf**
*White Light* - William Barton   s   384

**Quinn, Sofia Mendes**
*Children of God* - Mary Doria Russell   s   4735

**Serege, Tristan "Tris"**
*Ganwold's Child* - Diann Thornley   s   5467

**Suarez, Corazon "Cory"**
*White Light* - William Barton   s   384

## CHIEFTAIN

**Bluecrane, Will**
*Earthsong* - Suzette Haden Elgin   s   1769

**Chang, Mavra**
*Echoes of the Well of Souls* - Jack L. Chalker   s   953

**Gorath**
*Krondor, the Betrayal* - Raymond E. Feist   f   1905

**Khan, Rukmani**
*The Khan's Persuasion* - Cynthia Felice   s   1914

**Little Bear**
*The Key to the Indian* - Lynne Reid Banks   f   331

**O'Mor, Rury**
*Legends Reborn* - Kenneth C. Flint   f   1958

**Riverwind**
*Spirit of the Wind* - Chris Pierson   f   4326

**Talldeer, Frank**
*Sacred Ground* - Mercedes Lackey   f   3294

**Thag**
*Shiva's Challenge: An Adventure of the Ice Age* - J.H. Brennan   f   668

**Wanachtee**
*The Silent Stars Go By* - James White   s   5781

## CHILD

**Adamsson, Wylie**
*Night Calls* - Katharine Eliska Kimbriel   h   3119

**Adelrune**
*The Book of Knights* - Yves Meynard   f   3884

**Aenea**
*Endymion* - Dan Simmons   s   5051

**Ahmed**
*Ahmed and the Oblivion Machines* - Ray Bradbury   f   618

**Aisling, Cassandra**
*Voyage of the Basset* - James C. Christensen   f   1024

**Alice**
*Fantastic Alice* - Margaret Weis   f   5713

**Allika**
*King's Man and Thief* - Christie Golden   f   2253

**Altir "Tir"**
*Icefalcon's Quest* - Barbara Hambly   f   2504

**Amber**
*Pet Store* - M.T. Coffin   h   1097

**Amory, Theodora "Teddy"**
*Goat Dance* - Douglas Clegg   h   1079

**Anna**
*Darkness, I* - Tanith Lee   h   3407

**Antonia**
*Daughter of Magic* - C. Dale Brittain   f   703

**Aphrael**
*The Hidden City* - David Eddings   f   1733

**Appenfell, Anjell**
*A Breach in the Watershed* - Douglas Niles   f   4105

**Azaro**
*The Famished Road* - Ben Okri   f   4207
*Songs of Enchantment* - Ben Okri   f   4208

**Bagg, Stuart "Shoebag"**
*Shoebag* - Mary James   f   2868
*Shoebag Returns* - Mary James   f   2869

**Baker, Evan**
*Soul Catcher* - Colin Kersey   h   3081

**Baker, Jill**
*Monday's Child* - Patricia Wallace   h   5623

**Bane**
*The Hand of Chaos* - Margaret Weis   f   5715

**Banning, Clive "Clivey"**
*My Pretty Pony* - Stephen King   h   3136

**Barker, Joel**
*Sineater* - Elizabeth Massie   h   3668

**Barnett, Stephen**
*My Soul to Keep* - Judith Hawkes   h   2631

**Barringer, Melissa "Missy"**
*Cursed Be the Child* - Mort Castle   h   937

**Bascomb, Charles "Chaz"**
*Bones* - Joyce Thompson   h   5453

**Beck, Billy**
*Seattle Ghost Story* - Nick DiMartino   h   1560

**Belacqua, Lyra**
*The Golden Compass* - Philip Pullman   f   4446
*The Subtle Knife* - Philip Pullman   f   4448

**Bell, Elizabeth**
*The Bell Witch: An American Haunting* - Brent Monahan   h   3953

**Benson, Jedidiah**
*Shadow Twin* - Dale Hoover   h   2762

**Bentley, Abigail Porterhouse**
*Friends in Time* - Grace Chetwin   f   1012

**Bishop, Julian**
*Animus* - Ed Kelleher   h   3040

**Bishop, Wendy**
*Virgins and Martyrs* - Simon Maginn   h   3607

**Blackburn, Jasmine**
*Blackburn* - Bradley Denton   h   1489

**Blair, Tiffany**
*Shadow Dance* - Jessica Palmer   h   4238

**Bolton, Tanner**
*Cold White Fury* - Beth Amos   h   97

**Bonner, Nat**
*Dead End* - Guy N. Smith   h   5119

**Brady, Francis**
*The Butcher Boy* - Patrick McCabe   h   3716

**Brenner, Joshua**
*The Feeding* - Leigh Clark   h   1051

**Brianna**
*The Curse of Camp Cold Lake* - R.L. Stine   h   5286

**Brill, Nicole**
*Silent Witness* - Robert Arthur Smith   h   5136

**Broderick, Daria**
*Along Came a Spider* - Athena Alexis   h   70

**Brown, Nelly**
*The Summer I Shrank My Grandmother* - Elvira Woodruff   f   5968

**Brunreich, Porter**
*Patton's Spaceship* - John Barnes   s   357

**Bryant, Bonnie**
*The Godsend* - Bernard Taylor   h   5401

**Buckley, Christopher**
*Shadow Man* - Dennis Etchison   h   1848

**Buechner, Marianne "Rianne"**
*An Impossumble Summer* - Brenda W. Clough   f   1090

**Buechner, Shannon**
*An Impossumble Summer* - Brenda W. Clough   f   1090

**Burke**
*Sineater* - Elizabeth Massie   h   3668

**Cadogan, Marianne**
*Nightmare, with Angel* - Stephen Gallagher   h   2111

**Caiper, Noonie**
*Short Blade* - Peter R. Emshwiller   s   1820

**Caldwell, Caroline**
*Manhattan Heat* - Ken Eulo   h   1851

**Cally "Earth"**
*Beyond the Magic Sphere* - Gail Jarrow   f   2879

**Campbell, Robbie**
*Rapid Growth* - Mary K. Hanner   h   2541

**Carlson, Amy**
*Shadows* - John Saul   h   4845

**Carmichael, Gabriel**
*Revenant* - Melanie Tem   h   5424

**Carter, David**
*The Changeling Garden* - Winifred Elze   h   1806

**Carver, David**
*Desperation* - Stephen King   h   3129

**Case, Jamie**
*Wheels of Fire* - Mercedes Lackey   f   3301

**Charlotte "Lottie"**
*Santa's Twin* - Dean R. Koontz   f   3214

**Chase, Max**
*White Shark* - Peter Benchley   h   441

**Christopher**
*The Silver Kiss* - Annette Curtis Klause   f   3163

**Clarkston, Tommy**
*Waltz with Evil* - P.D. Rozzi   h   4701

**Clewe, Zoe**
*The Blood of Angels* - Stephen Gregory   h   2428

**Conan III**
*Rouse a Sleeping Cat* - Dan Crawford   f   1249

**Cowal, Bobby**
*Deadly Friend* - Keith Ferrario   h   1926

**Cowal, Peter**
*Deadly Friend* - Keith Ferrario   h   1926

**Crocker, Ben**
*Yellow Moon* - David J. Searls   h   4907

**Curtis, Adam**
*Baby Dolly* - Ruby Jean Jensen   h   2899

**Curtis, Prissy**
*Baby Dolly* - Ruby Jean Jensen   h   2899

**Cuthberton-Jones, Angelica**
*Angela and Diabola* - Lynne Reid Banks   f   330

**Cuthberton-Jones, Diabola**
*Angela and Diabola* - Lynne Reid Banks   f   330

**Cutter, Timothy**
*Shadow Dance* - Douglas Borton   h   577

**Darin of Culverne**
*Children of the Blood: Book Two of The Sundered* - Michelle Sagara   f   4782
*Lady of Mercy* - Michelle Sagara   f   4784

**Dartson, Emma**
*The Premonition* - Andrew Laurance   h   3349

**David**
*Dead in the West* - Joe R. Lansdale  *h*  3325
*My Father Immortal* - Michael D. Weaver  *s*  5659

**Davis, Heaven**
*Gnelfs* - Sidney Williams  *h*  5823

**Dawn, Rhoda**
*Outworld Cats* - Jack Lovejoy  *s*  3536

**Day, Ruth**
*Dark Dance* - Tanith Lee  *h*  3406

**del Rio, Annunciata "Nancy"**
*Last Mountain* - Robert C. Fleet  *f*  1946

**Delacroix, Ivy**
*Deathwalker* - R. Patrick Gates  *h*  2159

**DeMarian, Kassandra**
*The Painter Knight* - Fiona Patton  *f*  4258

**Devore, Kyra**
*Bag of Bones* - Stephen King  *h*  3126

**Doban**
*Shiva: An Adventure of the Ice Age* - J.H. Brennan  *f*  669

**Ducane, Wilhemina "Willie"**
*Demon Dance* - T. Chris Martindale  *h*  3655

**Duke, Kevin Thomas**
*The Wild* - Whitley Strieber  *h*  5343

**Dumery of Shiphaven**
*The Blood of a Dragon* - Lawrence Watt-Evans  *f*  5640

**Eircelly, Tirza**
*If Wishes Were Horses* - Anne McCaffrey  *f*  3737

**Eircelly, Tracell**
*If Wishes Were Horses* - Anne McCaffrey  *f*  3737

**Elric**
*The Book of Brendan* - Ann Curry  *f*  1294

**Emily "Emmy"**
*Santa's Twin* - Dean R. Koontz  *f*  3214

**Emrys**
*The Lost Years of Merlin* - T.A. Barron  *f*  370

**Endrada, Deirdre "Deedee"**
*Halfway Human* - Carolyn Ives Gilman  *s*  2237

**Erik**
*Phantom* - Susan Kay  *h*  3020

**Ernst, Jeffrey**
*Twistor* - John Cramer  *s*  1245

**Erskine, Cheryl**
*In a Dark Dream* - Charles L. Grant  *h*  2310

**Evans, Joshua Carl**
*Worst Nightmare* - Ric Meyers  *h*  3883

**Fancy, Darren**
*The One Safe Place* - Ramsey Campbell  *h*  862

**Ferdulf**
*Fox and Empire* - Harry Turtledove  *f*  5500

**Feree, Harper**
*The Friendship Song* - Nancy Springer  *f*  5179

**Figg, Nigel**
*The Horror Club* - Mark Morris  *h*  4022

**Finis "Water"**
*Beyond the Magic Sphere* - Gail Jarrow  *f*  2879

**Fletcher, Stevie**
*Lost Boys* - Orson Scott Card  *f*  891

**Florida**
*Nevernever* - Will Shetterly  *f*  4995

**Flynn, Lizbeth**
*Substitute Teacher* - Jordan Storm  *h*  5314

**Foster, Danny**
*Twilight Time* - Rick Hautala  *h*  2613

**Frakes, Danny "Mouse"**
*Darkman #1: The Hangman* - Randall Boyll  *h*  612

**Francie**
*Naming the Flowers* - Kate Wilhelm  *s*  5809

**Fraser, Brian**
*Dark Silence* - Rick Hautala  *h*  2606

**Frewin, Mary**
*The Red-Eared Ghosts* - Vivian Alcock  *f*  53

**Galbraith, Emily**
*Good Night, Sweet Angel* - Clare McNally  *h*  3857

**Gale, Abby "Apple Guy"**
*Thunder Rise* - G. Wayne Miller  *h*  3895

**Gardener, Richard**
*The Horror Club* - Mark Morris  *h*  4022

**Garin, Seth**
*The Regulators* - Richard Bachman  *h*  284

**Gerchak, Julie**
*My Ishmael* - Daniel Quinn  *s*  4456

**Gerund**
*The Wild Hunt* - Jane Yolen  *f*  6042

**G'hana, 'jum**
*The Children Star* - Joan Slonczewski  *s*  5090

**Giant**
*The Earth Giant* - Melvin Burgess  *s*  773

**Gibson, Emma**
*Friends in Time* - Grace Chetwin  *f*  1012

**Gill, Gabriel**
*The Werewolves of London* - Brian Stableford  *h*  5196

**Girl**
*A Ride on the Red Mare's Back* - Ursula K. Le Guin  *f*  3382

**Gold-eye**
*Shade's Children* - Garth Nix  *s*  4130

**Gorlay, Glenn**
*The Dark One* - Guy N. Smith  *h*  5118

**Gramm, Rachel "Button"**
*Button Bright* - Michael Kurland  *h*  3251

**Granville, Gabby**
*Bloody Valentine* - Stephen R. George  *h*  2197

**Graves, Sara**
*Dark Lullaby* - Jessica Palmer  *h*  4237

**Graves, Shelley**
*Dark Lullaby* - Jessica Palmer  *h*  4237

**Gray, Emma**
*Flying in Place* - Susan Palwick  *h*  4240

**Gregory, Joely**
*Ghost Boy* - Jean Simon  *h*  5064

**Grissom, Sarah**
*Mercy's Mill* - Betty Levin  *f*  3444

**Guillory, Terry**
*Gnelfs* - Sidney Williams  *h*  5823

**Hadfield, Felicity Jane**
*Viper* - Alan Riefe  *h*  4589

**Halkin, Edward**
*Prophecy* - Peter James  *h*  2874

**Hamilton, Jordan**
*Terminal Logic* - Jefferson Scott  *s*  4893

**Hardison, Pete**
*Let There Be Dark* - Allen Lee Harris  *h*  2557

**Harris, Billy**
*Ghost Light* - Rick Hautala  *h*  2608

**Harris, Derek**
*Wake Up Screaming* - Vincent Courtney  *h*  1215

**Harry**
*The Cormorant* - Stephen Gregory  *h*  2429

**Hart, Marcel**
*The Dark One* - Guy N. Smith  *h*  5118

**Hawkins, Danny**
*A Thunder on Neptune* - Gordon Eklund  *s*  1768

**Hazzard, Matt**
*Rough Beast* - Gary Goshgarian  *h*  2284

**Helwig, Barbie**
*Blue Limbo* - Terrence M. Green  *s*  2377

**Henderson, Dawn**
*The Forever Children* - Eric Flanders  *h*  1944

**Henkin, Paul**
*Mysteries of the Word* - Stanley Wiater  *h*  5796

**Holcroft, Jake**
*Target Earth* - Steve Perry  *s*  4301

**Horton, Holly**
*Althea* - Abigail McDaniels  *h*  3782

**Jackson, Beauregard**
*Never Land* - Douglas Clegg  *h*  1081

**Jacobs, Sammy**
*My Best Friend Is Invisible* - R.L. Stine  *h*  5289

**Jacobs, Simon**
*My Best Friend Is Invisible* - R.L. Stine  *h*  5289

**Jahdo**
*Days of Blood and Fire* - Katharine Kerr  *f*  3068

**Jerod**
*The Wild Hunt* - Jane Yolen  *f*  6042

**Joanna**
*The Time Tree* - Enid Richemont  *f*  4585

**Joaquim, Leo**
*The Night of the Moonbow* - Thomas Tryon  *h*  5486

**Jones, Guinevere**
*The Witch House* - Norma Tadlock Johnson  *f*  2923

**Jordan, Megan**
*Wind Chimes* - R.R. Walters  *h*  5625

**Jordon**
*Sexing the Cherry* - Jeanette Winterson  *t*  5927

**Kaye, Darbi**
*Chiller* - Randall Boyll  *h*  610

**Ketter, Jon**
*Lot Lizards* - Ray Garton  *h*  2152

**King, Greta**
*The Place* - T.M. Wright  *h*  5993

**Kirtha**
*Mind of the Magic* - Holly Lisle  *f*  3486

**Knight, Joshua**
*Escardy Gap* - Peter Crowther  *h*  1282

**Kostanuik, April**
*Torment* - Stephen R. George  *h*  2204

**Laine, Evan**
*Nightscape* - Stephen R. George  *h*  2203

**Lamb, Toby**
*The Haunting of Lamb House* - Joan Aiken  *h*  45

**Law, Lily**
*Darwinia* - Robert Charles Wilson  *s*  5906

**Lee, Amy**
*The Earth Giant* - Melvin Burgess  *s*  773

**Lee, Peter**
*The Earth Giant* - Melvin Burgess  *s*  773

**Liddell, Alice Pleasance**
*Automated Alice* - Jeff Noon  *f*  4134

**Lissette**
*Cursed Be the Child* - Mort Castle  *h*  937

**Lixandashkya, Megan**
*Shadow's Daughter* - Shirley Meier  *f*  3871

**Longchamp, Jimmy**
*Dawn* - V.C. Andrews   *h*   144

**Louise, Zoe**
*Stonewords: A Ghost Story* - Pam Conrad   *f*   1138

**Lumbaird, Fran**
*The Black Carousel* - Charles L. Grant   *h*   2303

**Maas, Aaron**
*The Curse of Camp Cold Lake* - R.L. Stine   *h*   5286

**Maas, Sarah**
*The Curse of Camp Cold Lake* - R.L. Stine   *h*   5286

**MacCallum, Josh**
*Shadows* - John Saul   *h*   4845

**Mackenson, Cory**
*Boy's Life* - Robert R. McCammon   *h*   3754

**Madison, Thaddie**
*Bloodlines* - J.N. Williamson   *h*   5852

**Magruder, Bernie**
*Bernie and the Bessledorf Ghost* - Phyllis Reynolds
   Naylor   *f*   4078

**Majere, Caramon**
*The Soulforge* - Margaret Weis   *f*   5728

**Mallory**
*My Stepfather Shrank!* - Barbara Dillon   *s*   1558

**Margaret**
*R-T, Margaret, and the Rats of NIMH* - Jane Leslie
   Conly   *f*   1132

**Margison, Danny**
*Kids* - Trevor Hoyle   *h*   2787

**Marshall, Olivia**
*Seeds of Evil* - Margaret Bingley   *h*   491

**Marshall, Orlando**
*Seeds of Evil* - Margaret Bingley   *h*   491

**Martin, Marty**
*Goblins* - Vincent Courtney   *h*   1212

**Martin, Wade**
*Blood Wings* - Stephen Gresham   *h*   2430

**Martin, Worth**
*Shaman Woods* - Morgan Fields   *h*   1931

**Martinez, Freddy**
*Vampire Breath* - R.L. Stine   *h*   5291

**Matheson, Tad**
*Blood Brothers* - T. Lucien Wright   *h*   5986

**Matsika, Tendai**
*The Ear, the Eye, and the Arm* - Nancy
   Farmer   *f*   1867

**Matthew**
*The End of Alice* - A.M. Homes   *h*   2755

**McBride, Duane**
*Summer of Night* - Dan Simmons   *h*   5060

**McCade, Molly**
*McCade's Bounty* - William C. Dietz   *s*   1550

**McCall, Jess**
*Black Ice* - Pat Graversen   *h*   2333

**McDowell, William Scott**
*Sweet William* - Jessica Palmer   *h*   4239

**McGarvey, Toby**
*Winter Moon* - Dean R. Koontz   *h*   3218

**McKay, David**
*Brainstorm* - Steven M. Krauzer   *h*   3230

**McKibben, Brion**
*Whisper* - Raymond Van Over   *h*   5539

**McNair, Brian**
*The Good Children* - Kate Wilhelm   *h*   5800

**McNair, Liz**
*The Good Children* - Kate Wilhelm   *h*   5808

**Melnik, Claudi**
*Down the Stream of Stars* - Jeffrey A.
   Carver   *s*   928

**Melvin**
*Borgel* - Daniel Manus Pinkwater   *f*   4338

**Merlin**
*Merlin* - Jane Yolen   *f*   6035
*Passager* - Jane Yolen   *f*   6038

**Merlin, Emrys**
*The Seven Songs of Merlin* - T.A. Barron   *f*   372

**Metcalf, Charlotte**
*Whispers in the Dark* - Jonathan Aycliffe   *h*   283

**Michael**
*Gypsies* - Robert Charles Wilson   *s*   5908

**Mikel, Chris**
*Blind Hunger* - David Darke   *h*   1352

**Miles, Karen**
*Speak to the Rain* - Helen K. Passey   *h*   4257

**Minnie "Miin"**
*Shame of Man* - Piers Anthony   *s*   188

**Molly**
*Blue Moon* - Hila Feil   *f*   1898

**Monroe, Sumter**
*Never Land* - Douglas Clegg   *h*   1081

**Morley, Lynn**
*The Witch Returns* - Phyllis Reynolds
   Naylor   *f*   4079
*The Witch's Eye* - Phyllis Reynolds Naylor   *f*   4080

**Morrison, Jessie Mae**
*The Hunted* - Kathryn Ptacek   *h*   4442

**Mreen**
*Receive the Gift* - Louise Marley   *s*   3628

**Nafai**
*The Memory of Earth* - Orson Scott Card   *s*   894

**Neary, Billy**
*Billy* - Whitley Strieber   *h*   5338

**Nellodee "Nell"**
*The Diamond Age* - Neal Stephenson   *s*   5253

**Nhamo**
*A Girl Named Disaster* - Nancy Farmer   *f*   1868

**Nielson, Sasha**
*The Starry Child* - Lynn Hanna   *f*   2540

**Night, Kevin**
*The Monastery* - J.N. Williamson   *h*   5856

**Nix, Chris**
*Dogland* - Will Shetterly   *f*   4992

**Noonan, Owen**
*Travel Far, Pay No Fare* - Anne Lindbergh   *f*   3468

**Nugent, Philip**
*The Butcher Boy* - Patrick McCabe   *h*   3716

**Nuria**
*Well Wished* - Franny Billingsley   *f*   489

**Ollie**
*No Kidding* - Bruce Brooks   *s*   709

**Omri**
*The Key to the Indian* - Lynne Reid Banks   *f*   331
*The Secret of the Indian* - Lynne Reid Banks   *f*   332

**Orchard, Laura**
*The Count of Eleven* - Ramsey Campbell   *h*   853

**O'Rourke, Mike**
*Summer of Night* - Dan Simmons   *h*   5060

**Parry, William "Will"**
*The Subtle Knife* - Philip Pullman   *f*   4448

**Parsley**
*Travel Far, Pay No Fare* - Anne Lindbergh   *f*   3468

**Pauling, Addy**
*Lullaby* - Diane Guest   *h*   2455

**Pearce, Sarah**
*The Ghost Inside the Monitor* - Margaret J.
   Anderson   *f*   122

**Pendragon, Arthur**
*The Saxon Shore* - Jack Whyte   *f*   5793

**Petersen, Tad**
*The Children's Hour* - Douglas Clegg   *h*   1077

**Polijn**
*A Wild Dog and Lone* - Dan Crawford   *f*   1251

**Popsy**
*Shadow Walkers* - Nina Romberg   *h*   4663

**Porter, Dylan**
*Wes Craven's New Nightmare* - David
   Bergantino   *h*   460

**Pruett, Robin**
*After Sundown* - Randall Boyll   *h*   609

**Purcell, Joe**
*The Butcher Boy* - Patrick McCabe   *h*   3716

**Quijance-Turgenev, Esther Elizabeth**
*Second Star* - Dana Stabenow   *s*   5188

**R-T "Artie"**
*R-T, Margaret, and the Rats of NIMH* - Jane Leslie
   Conly   *f*   1132

**Rachel**
*The Time Tree* - Enid Richemont   *f*   4585

**Ramsey, Quinn Jr.**
*Demon Fire* - Gary L. Holleman   *h*   2743

**Rania**
*The Promise* - Monica Hughes   *s*   2808

**Ransom, Garrett**
*Night Things* - Michael Talbot   *h*   5380

**Readis**
*The Dolphins of Pern* - Anne McCaffrey   *s*   3729

**Regina**
*Hideaway* - Dean R. Koontz   *h*   3208

**Rhia**
*The Lost Years of Merlin* - T.A. Barron   *f*   370

**Rhiannon "Rhia"**
*The Seven Songs of Merlin* - T.A. Barron   *f*   372

**Rigger, Jack**
*Blood of Innocents* - John Arbucci   *h*   204

**Robin**
*Street Magic* - Michael Reaves   *f*   4497

**Robinton**
*The Masterharper of Pern* - Anne
   McCaffrey   *s*   3739

**Roode, Sam**
*Lethal Delivery* - J.G. Maxon   *h*   3695

**Rowan**
*The Influence* - Ramsey Campbell   *h*   857

**Roxanne**
*My Best Friend Is Invisible* - R.L. Stine   *h*   5289

**S-, Josephine Carolyn "Josie"**
*First Love: A Gothic Tale* - Joyce Carol
   Oates   *h*   4183

**S .B. "Air"**
*Beyond the Magic Sphere* - Gail Jarrow   *f*   2879

**St. Eve, Clair**
*Skeletons* - Al Sarrantonio   *h*   4834

**Salisaw, Holly**
*Night Thunder* - Ruby Jean Jensen   *h*   2903

**Salisaw, Kara**
*Night Thunder* - Ruby Jean Jensen   *h*   2903

**Sally**
*The Kronos Condition* - Emily Devenport  s  1502

**Santorini, Angie**
*Death Dream* - Ben Bova  s  583

**Seafort, Philip**
*Voices of Hope* - David Feintuch  s  1903

**Shaeler, Marshall**
*The Forsaken* - Steven Ray Fulgham  h  2089

**Shea, Alan**
*Deadly Vengeance* - Stephen R. George  h  2199

**Silver, Michelle "Micki" Ann**
*The Silver Tree* - Ruth L. Williams  f  5822

**Simonetti, Cara**
*Vampire Breath* - R.L. Stine  h  5291

**Sinclair, Jason**
*The Fagin* - Pat Graversen  h  2334

**Sinclair, Tam**
*Dust* - Charles Pellegrino  h  4279

**Somerfield, Alice**
*The End of Alice* - A.M. Homes  h  2755

**Sorenson, Melissa**
*Drifter's Run* - William C. Dietz  s  1544

**Sperry, Toby**
*City of Truth* - James Morrow  s  4030

**Stahlbaum, Marie**
*Nutcracker* - E.T.A. Hoffmann  f  2719

**Stanovich, Martin Philip**
*Ghost Boy* - Jean Simon  h  5064

**Stavely, Ann Veronica**
*Hexwood* - Diana Wynne Jones  s  2948

**Stello, Rawnie**
*The Friendship Song* - Nancy Springer  f  5179

**Sterling, Johnny**
*Midnight Sun* - Ramsey Campbell  h  860

**Steven**
*The Night Man* - K.W. Jeter  h  2915

**Stevens, Luke**
*Offspring* - Jack Ketchum  h  3092

**Stewart, Dale**
*Summer of Night* - Dan Simmons  h  5060

**Stewart, Hope**
*Dark of the Eye* - Douglas Clegg  h  1078

**Stockton, Clifford**
*Mysterium* - Robert Charles Wilson  s  5911

**Sullivan, Mark**
*The Forgotten* - Stephen R. George  h  2200

**Susi**
*Way Up High* - Roger Zelazny  f  6076

**Susri "Fawn"**
*Child of an Ancient City* - Tad Williams  f  5827

**Swan**
*Swan Song* - Robert R. McCammon  h  3757

**Sweetsong, Stanley**
*Shoebag Returns* - Mary James  f  2869

**Swick, Harvey**
*The Thief of Always* - Clive Barker  h  347

**Sylvia**
*The Marvellous Land of Snergs* - E.A. Wyke-
Smith  f  6006

**Tamara**
*What's Wrong with Valerie?* - D.A. Fowler  h  2026

**Taya**
*Star Child* - James P. Hogan  s  2730

**Thatcher, Jeremy**
*Jeremy Thatcher, Dragon Hatcher* - Bruce
Coville  f  1221

**Thayer, Cerise**
*Afternoon of the Gosling* - Marlys Huffman  h  2801

**Thayer, Danny**
*Street Magic* - Michael Reaves  f  4497

**Thompson, Richard**
*Seed of Evil* - Edmund Plante  h  4340

**Tibbett, Adrian "Toady"**
*The Horror Club* - Mark Morris  h  4022

**Timov**
*Hunting the Ghost Dancer* - A.A. Attanasio  f  268

**Tolivar**
*Blood Trillium* - Julian May  f  3696

**Tompkins, Ernest**
*Blackburn* - Bradley Denton  h  1489

**Tompkins, Jimmy**
*Blood of the Children* - Alan Rodgers  h  4645

**Torrance, Danny**
*The Shining* - Stephen King  h  3141

**Touch**
*The Midnight Horse* - Sid Fleischman  f  1948

**Travis, Marshall**
*The One Safe Place* - Ramsey Campbell  h  862

**Tullian, Sam**
*Sheep* - Simon Maginn  h  3606

**Tyler, Jimi**
*The Deus Machine* - Pierre Ouellette  h  4232

**Tyler, Joshua**
*Midsummer* - Matthew J. Costello  h  1200

**Tyler, Richard**
*The Pagemaster* - David Kirschner  f  3156

**Van Zandt, Andy**
*The Stone Circle* - Gary Goshgarian  h  2285

**Vear, Sara**
*The Ridge* - Lisa Cantrell  h  872

**Virili, Kip**
*The Black Sun* - Jack Williamson  s  5860

**Wade, Arlo**
*Bad Blood* - D.A. Fowler  h  2021

**Wade, Austin**
*Bad Blood* - D.A. Fowler  h  2021

**Wade, Tamara**
*What's Wrong with Tamara?*  D.A.
Fowler  h  2025

**Walker, Cassie**
*Playmates* - Abigail McDaniels  h  3784

**Wesley, William**
*The Forever Children* - Eric Flanders  h  1944

**Wheaton, Anna**
*Jumpers* - R. Patrick Gates  h  2161

**Whitcome, Luke**
*Shadow Child* - Joseph A. Citro  h  1038

**White, Arnold**
*Mongster* - Randall Boyll  h  616

**Wickes, Joey**
*The Quagmire* - James Kisner  h  3160

**Wickham, Eddie**
*The Haunting* - Ruby Jean Jensen  h  2901

**Wigram, Rachel**
*The Vanishment* - Jonathan Aycliffe  h  282

**Williams, Sadie**
*Shadow Walkers* - Nina Romberg  h  4663

**Williams, Thaddeus "Thaddy"**
*Unicorn Highway* - David Lee Jones  f  2941

**Winter, Catty**
*Well Wished* - Franny Billingsley  f  489

**Winterbelle**
*In the Land of Winter* - Richard Grant  f  2326

**Winters, Katie**
*Martian Deathtrap* - Nathan Archer  s  205

**Wolde, Kira**
*My Soul to Keep* - Tannarive Due  h  1670

**Woodrow, Melissa**
*Torment* - Stephen R. George  h  2204

**Zoe**
*Stonewords: A Ghost Story* - Pam Conrad  f  1138

### CHILD-CARE GIVER

**Carlisle, Amy**
*Clash by Night* - Chet Williamson  h  5844

**Gibson, Cheryl**
*Grandma's Little Darling* - Stephen R.
George  h  2201

**Gurney, Molly**
*Out of the Ordinary* - Annie Dalton  f  1330

**Jelinsky, Debbie**
*Addams Family Values* - Todd Strasser  f  5324

**Julia**
*Blue Moon* - Hila Feil  f  1898

**Kirby, Gertrude**
*The Jekyll Legacy* - Robert Bloch  h  535

**Reynolds, Jane**
*The Ignored* - Bentley Little  h  3493

### CHIMNEYSWEEP

**Drib**
*The Knights of Cawdor* - Mike Jefferies  f  2886

### CIVIL SERVANT

**Aiah**
*Metropolitan* - Walter Jon Williams  s  5839

**Glass, Duncan**
*A Whisper of Wings* - Steven Ray Fulgham  h  2091

**Hagbarth, Hoak**
*O Pioneer!* - Frederik Pohl  s  4350

**Hudson, Aaron**
*Checkmate* - Eric T. Baker  s  297

**Noycannir, Mergau**
*An Exchange of Hostages* - Susan R.
Matthews  s  3692

**Samules, Elmo**
*Spider Legs* - Piers Anthony  s  189

**vo Chaumelle, Renille**
*The Gates of Twilight* - Paula Volsky  f  5581

### CLERK

**Babych, Simon**
*Nightlife* - Jack Ellis  h  1779

**Bender, Lucy**
*Angels on Fire* - Nancy A. Collins  h  1117

**Carewe, Cindy**
*Absolute Power* - Ray Russell  h  4738

**Carpenter, Gayle**
*Dark Time* - Maxine O'Callaghan  h  4189

**Crook, Annie**
*From Hell* - Alan Moore  h  3987

**Day, Rachaela**
*Dark Dance* - Tanith Lee  h  3406

**Delaney, Tawne**
*This Symbiotic Fascination* - Charlee Jacob  h  2843

**Evans, Malcolm**
*Monster* - John Tigges   *h*   5474

**Franklin, Jim**
*Mall, Mayhem and Magic* - Holly Lisle   *f*   3485

**Frost, Raymond**
*Killing Frost* - Dan I. Blake   *h*   514

**Grason, Gilead**
*Cross a Dark Bridge* - Deborah
   Churchman   *h*   1027

**Jody**
*Bloodsucking Fiends: A Love Story* - Christopher
   Moore   *h*   3988

**Jones, Shadrach**
*The Collected Stories of Philip K. Dick, Volume One:
   The Short Happy Life of the Brown Oxford* - Philip
   K. Dick   *s*   1519

**Kallisti, Avra**
*Specters* - J.M. Dillard   *h*   1555

**Lawrence**
*Dawn Song* - Michael Marano   *h*   3620

**Nakimura, Grace**
*The Beast Within: A Gabriel Knight Mystery* - Jane
   Jensen   *h*   2895

**Orliotti, Philippa J. "Flip"**
*Bellwether* - Connie Willis   *s*   5867

**Quail, Douglas**
*The Collected Stories of Philip K. Dick, Volume Two:
   We Can Remember It for You Wholesale* - Philip K.
   Dick   *s*   1520

**Renzler, Michael**
*The 37th Mandala* - Marc Laidlaw   *h*   3310

**Scarbrough, Liz**
*The Vampire's Apprentice* - Richard Lee
   Byers   *h*   799

**Semele, Alice**
*Dominion* - Bentley Little   *h*   3492

**Tamerlane, Rebecca**
*Afterimage Aftershock* - Kristine Kathryn
   Rusch   *h*   4710

**Townsend, Helen**
*Hellcat* - Amanda Kingsley   *h*   3145

**Tyler, Arcan**
*This Symbiotic Fascination* - Charlee Jacob   *h*   2843

**Vestal, Lauren**
*Carmilla: The Return* - Kyle Marfinn   *h*   3623

**Wilkins, Edna**
*Hellcat* - Amanda Kingsley   *h*   3145

**Witney, Charley**
*Sweet Heart* - Peter James   *h*   2875

## CLONE

**Adcock, Patrice "Pat"**
*The Siege of Eternity* - Frederik Pohl   *s*   4353

**Akamu**
*The Bones of Time* - Kathleen Ann Goonan   *s*   2273

**Alpha, Pamayers**
*The Weigher* - Eric Vinicoff   *s*   5574

**Ari**
*Cyteen* - C.J. Cherryh   *s*   984

**Collier, Ben**
*A Bridge of Years* - Robert Charles Wilson   *s*   5905

**Daitaku**
*Fire on the Border* - Kevin O'Donnell Jr.   *s*   4194

**Dannerman, Jim Daniel "Dan"**
*The Siege of Eternity* - Frederik Pohl   *s*   4353

**Delta, Ralphayers**
*The Weigher* - Eric Vinicoff   *s*   5574

**Draus, Morry**
*I Wake From a Dream of a Drowned Star City* - S.P.
   Somtow   *s*   5157

**Everynne**
*The Golden Queen* - Dave Wolverton   *s*   5951

**Frank-I-STN-4**
*Title Deleted for Security Reasons* - Ed
   Blome   *s*   553

**Harlow-c, Jean**
*Dydeetown World* - F. Paul Wilson   *s*   5887

**Homer-R-ICK-3**
*Extreme Paranoia: Nobody Knows the Trouble I've
   Shot* - Ken Rolston   *s*   4662

**James-B-OND-1**
*Title Deleted for Security Reasons* - Ed
   Blome   *s*   553

**Joshua**
*The Killing Star* - Charles Pellegrino   *s*   4281

**Justin**
*The Killing Star* - Charles Pellegrino   *s*   4281

**Lani**
*Masque* - F. Paul Wilson   *s*   5890

**Mbele, Miriam Makepeace**
*Red Dust* - Paul J. McAuley   *s*   3715

**Mirelle, Victoria "Tori"**
*The Inquisitor* - Cheryl J. Franklin   *s*   2037

**Nighthawk, Jefferson "Widowmaker"**
*The Widowmaker* - Mike Resnick   *s*   4559
*The Widowmaker Reborn* - Mike Resnick   *s*   4560

**Ripley**
*Alien Resurrection* - A.C. Crispin   *s*   1258

**Samuels, Albert**
*The Clouds of Magellan* - David F.
   Nighbert   *s*   4103

**Saunder, Anthony**
*Legacy of Earth* - Juanita Coulson   *s*   1209

**Stark, Otto**
*In the Wrong Hands* - Edward Gibson   *s*   2215

**Steck**
*Commitment Hour* - James Alan Gardner   *s*   2134

**Stryker, Anton**
*The Clouds of Magellan* - David F.
   Nighbert   *s*   4103

**Tristan**
*Masque* - F. Paul Wilson   *s*   5890

**Tso, Anton Sien Hsia**
*The Shapes of Their Hearts* - Melissa Scott   *s*   4901

**Verity**
*Mississippi Blues* - Kathleen Ann Goonan   *s*   2274
*Queen City Jazz* - Kathleen Ann Goonan   *s*   2275

**Vorkosigan, Mark Pierre**
*Mirror Dance* - Lois McMaster Bujold   *s*   762

**Voy, Ellen**
*Six Moon Dance* - Sheri S. Tepper   *s*   5437

**Zodiac, Saskia**
*Mother of Plenty* - Colin Greenland   *s*   2417
*Seasons of Plenty* - Colin Greenland   *s*   2418

## COACH

**Griffin**
*The Cat* - R.L. Stine   *h*   5285

## COLLECTOR

**Coerlis, Jack-Jax Landsdowne**
*Mid-Flinx* - Alan Dean Foster   *s*   2010

**Conti, Niccolo Dei**
*The Venetian's Wife: A Strangely Sensual Tale of a
   Renaissance Explorer, a Computer, and a
   Metamorphosis* - Nick Bantock   *f*   336

**Jonah**
*Something Rich and Strange* - Patricia A.
   McKillip   *f*   3840

**Radcliffe, Milton**
*Lorien Lost* - Michael King   *f*   3124

**Shepherd, Seth**
*Trickster* - Chris Curry   *h*   1297

**Zinser, Jacob**
*St. Peter's Wolf* - Michael Cadnum   *h*   816

## COMPANION

**al-Iskandaria, Ibn Sufa**
*Quest: In Search of the Dragontooth* - Michael
   Green   *f*   2346

**Amaranth**
*The Dragon's Touchstone* - Irene Radford   *f*   4459

**Annalise**
*Black Wine* - Candas Jane Dorsey   *s*   1582

**Ash**
*Deerskin* - Robin McKinley   *f*   3844

**Avris**
*Songsmith* - Andre Norton   *f*   4161

**Badger**
*The Spellkey Trilogy* - Ann Downer   *f*   1592

**Bernie**
*Witch and Wombat* - Carolyn Cushman   *f*   1299

**Binah**
*Cross and Crescent* - Susan Shwartz   *f*   5014

**Blackstone, Norah**
*Bride of the Rat God* - Barbara Hambly   *f*   2499

**Blaine, Cassandra "Cass"**
*Psykosis* - Wilhelmina Baird   *s*   296

**Boardman, Gillian**
*Stranger in a Strange Land* - Robert A.
   Heinlein   *s*   2649

**Bydawine**
*Token of Dragonsblood* - Damaris Cole   *f*   1114

**Caitria**
*The Deepest Sea* - Charles Barnitz   *f*   363

**Cat**
*Cat's Paw* - L.A. Taylor   *f*   5409

**Chip**
*A King of Infinite Space* - Allen Steele   *s*   5243

**Cilla**
*Heroes, Inc.* - Kyle Crocco   *f*   1268
*Heroes Wanted* - Kyle Crocco   *f*   1267

**Cimorene**
*Searching for Dragons* - Patricia C. Wrede   *f*   5979

**Delia**
*Journeyman Wizard* - Mary Frances
   Zambreno   *f*   6057
*A Plague of Sorcerers* - Mary Frances
   Zambreno   *f*   6058

**Drumheller, Thorn**
*Shadow Dawn* - Chris Claremont   *f*   1042

**Drummond, Cathan**
*The Bastard Prince* - Katherine Kurtz   *f*   3255

**Fanuilh**
*Beggar's Banquet* - Daniel Hood   *f*   2756
*Fanuilh* - Daniel Hood   *f*   2757
*Scales of Justice* - Daniel Hood   *f*   2758
*Wizard's Heir* - Daniel Hood   *f*   2759

**Gaelinar**
*Dragonrank Master* - Mickey Zucker
   Reichert  *f*  4519

**Geldt**
*Madlands* - K.W. Jeter  *s*  2913

**Gespry**
*Guardian's Key* - Anne Logston  *f*  3511

**Glorian**
*The Zork Chronicles* - George Alec
   Effinger  *s*  1754

**Growch**
*Master of Many Treasures* - Mary Brown  *f*  726

**Hagan, Tim**
*Red, Red Robin* - Stephen Gallagher  *h*  2113

**Hanuman**
*The Broken God* - David Zindell  *s*  6085

**Harry**
*The King's Buccaneer* - Raymond E. Feist  *f*  1904

**Imbri, Mare**
*Faun & Games* - Piers Anthony  *f*  169

**Iphigenia, Alusz**
*The Demon Princes: Volume One* - Jack
   Vance  *s*  5544

**Jack**
*The Caterpillar's Question* - Piers Anthony  *f*  164

**Jimmers**
*The Paper Grail* - James P. Blaylock  *f*  522

**Jock o' the Syde**
*The Spiral Dance* - R. Garcia y Robertson  *f*  2121

**Karus**
*Last Mountain* - Robert C. Fleet  *f*  1946

**Kilgour, Alex**
*Revenge of the Damned* - Allan Cole  *s*  1107

**Leydon, B.**
*Unwillingly to Earth* - Pauline Ashwell  *s*  231

**Malkin**
*The Wizardry Consulted* - Rick Cook  *f*  1161

**Marbleheart**
*Geomancer* - Don Callander  *f*  845

**Miranda**
*Charmed* - Marilyn Singer  *f*  5070

**Moreno, Alexandra "Alix"**
*When Heaven Fell* - William Barton  *s*  383

**Mouse**
*Soothsayer* - Mike Resnick  *s*  4557

**Murdan of Overhall**
*Dragon Rescue* - Don Callander  *f*  843

**Peeve**
*Black Unicorn* - Tanith Lee  *f*  3404
*Gold Unicorn* - Tanith Lee  *f*  3410
*Red Unicorn* - Tanith Lee  *f*  3414

**Pelleas**
*In the Shadow of the Oak King* - Courtway
   Jones  *f*  2939

**Relkin**
*Battledragon* - Christopher Rowley  *f*  4691
*Bazil Broketail* - Christopher Rowley  *f*  4692
*Dragons of War* - Christopher Rowley  *f*  4695
*A Sword for a Dragon* - Christopher
   Rowley  *f*  4697

**Saubhari, Rishi**
*Faces of Deception* - Troy Denning  *f*  1485

**Spike**
*The Zork Chronicles* - George Alec
   Effinger  *s*  1754

**Spock**
*Mind Meld* - John Vornholt  *s*  5596

**Stephen**
*Hunter's Death* - Michelle West  *f*  5758

**Steven**
*Hunter's Oath* - Michelle West  *f*  5759

**Tale Teller**
*Tatham Mound* - Piers Anthony  *f*  191

**Talisen**
*Hero's Song* - Edith Pattou  *f*  4261

**Tobinson, Ian**
*A Wizard in Absentia* - Christopher Stasheff  *s*  5229

**Tree, Justin**
*Zombie Lover* - Piers Anthony  *f*  197

**Tyrian**
*A College of Magics* - Caroline Stevermer  *f*  5266

## COMPOSER

**Carson, Doug**
*Darkside* - Dennis Etchison  *h*  1845

**Dulac, Will**
*A Call to Arms* - Alan Dean Foster  *s*  1995

**Lazarich, Sabina**
*Someone to Watch over Me* - Tricia
   Sullivan  *s*  5355

**Mozart, Wolfgang Amadeus**
*I, Vampire* - Michael Romkey  *h*  4665

**Petiron**
*The Masterharper of Pern* - Anne
   McCaffrey  *s*  3739

**Pope, Justin**
*Mixed Doubles* - Daniel Da Cruz  *s*  1305

## COMPUTER

**Angelus, Lucifer "Luke"**
*Chains of Light* - Quentin Thomas  *s*  5449

**Holly**
*Red Dwarf: Infinity Welcomes Careful Drivers* - Grant
   Naylor  *s*  4077

**JASON**
*Golden Fleece* - Robert J. Sawyer  *s*  4857

**Lord Lynn, Margaret "Maggy"**
*Hellspark* - Janet Kagan  *s*  3000

**MEQMAT**
*The Schizogenic Man* - Raymond Harris  *s*  2563

**Sumbaa**
*The Kalif's War* - John Dalmas  *s*  1322

**System**
*Secret Realms* - Tom Cool  *s*  1168

**Thing**
*Truckers* - Terry Pratchett  *s*  4402
*Wings* - Terry Pratchett  *s*  4403

**Xa**
*The Fugitive Worlds* - Bob Shaw  *s*  4942

**XB223**
*The Red Tape War* - Jack L. Chalker  *s*  959

## COMPUTER EXPERT

**Abalone**
*Brother to Dragons, Companion to Owls* - Jane M.
   Lindskold  *f*  3473

**Al Qaseem, Zero**
*Signal to Noise* - Eric S. Nylund  *s*  4179

**Amalfi, Julia**
*Full Tide of Night* - J.R. Dunn  *s*  1695

**Antar**
*The Calcutta Chromosome* - Amitav Ghosh  *h*  2214

**Arcangelo, Michael**
*Wyrm* - Mark Fabi  *s*  1858

**Archangel**
*Headhunters* - Mel Odom  *s*  4192

**Augustine, Alexa**
*Dream of Glass* - Jean Mark Gawron  *s*  2163

**Avery, David "Derec"**
*Maverick* - Bruce Bethke  *s*  484

**Bathespeake, Jason**
*ME: A Novel of Self Discovery* - Thomas T.
   Thomas  *s*  5452

**Battacharia, Rustum "Bat"**
*The Ganymede Club* - Charles Sheffield  *s*  4955

**Bede, Strebban "Badger"**
*Hunting the Corrigan's Blood* - Holly Lisle  *s*  3484

**Beelzebub**
*Wyrm* - Mark Fabi  *s*  1858

**Berenice, Teal Blane**
*Blueheart* - Alison Sinclair  *s*  5068

**Blervaque, Carver**
*Living Real* - James C. Bassett  *s*  386

**Bonivard, Francois**
*Wildlife* - James Patrick Kelly  *s*  3049

**Boxletter, Bob**
*Duplicates* - Andrew Neiderman  *h*  4086

**Brandsetter, Earl**
*Lethal Interface* - Mel Odom  *s*  4193

**Brompton, Arnold**
*Virtual Girl* - Amy Thomson  *s*  5462

**Brown, Kelsie**
*65mm* - Dale Hoover  *h*  2761

**Burroughs, Jack "MAX—KOOL"**
*Headcrash* - Bruce Bethke  *s*  483

**Busch, Zachary**
*Drawing Blood* - Poppy Z. Brite  *h*  694

**Callahan-Finn, Mary**
*Callahan's Legacy* - Spider Robinson  *s*  4639

**Calvin, Susan**
*I, Robot: The Illustrated Screenplay* - Harlan
   Ellison  *s*  1785

**Cannon, Vassily "Bass" James**
*A Plague of Change* - L. Warren Douglas  *s*  1587

**Carless, India "Trouble"**
*Trouble and Her Friends* - Melissa Scott  *s*  4902

**Castanaveras, Trent**
*The Long Run* - Daniel Keys Moran  *s*  3995

**Cerise**
*Trouble and Her Friends* - Melissa Scott  *s*  4902

**Chambers, Phoebe**
*The Misconceiver* - Lucy Ferriss  *s*  1929

**Chen, David**
*Chimera* - Mary Rosenblum  *s*  4677

**Cobri, Alex**
*Grounded!* - Chris Claremont  *s*  1041

**Conlick, Dennis "Tunnel Rat"**
*The Hacker* - Chet Day  *h*  1410

**Corrigan, Joe**
*Realtime Interrupt* - James P. Hogan  *s*  2729

**Cotton, Alex**
*Brethren* - Shawn Ryan  *h*  4754

**Craig, Donald**
*The Ghost From the Grand Banks* - Arthur C.
   Clarke  *s*  1056

**Cy BerPunk**
*Planet of the Robot Slaves* - Harry Harrison  *s*  2573

**Davies, Stewart**
*Target Earth* - Steve Perry  s  4301

**Deed, Kalypso**
*Dreaming in Smoke* - Tricia Sullivan  s  5353

**Delaney, Brian**
*The Turing Option* - Harry Harrison  s  2579

**Deluca, Maria**
*Permutation City* - Greg Egan  s  1761

**Demogorgon**
*Iris* - William Barton  s  381

**Deveaux, Jacques**
*City of Pain* - John Terra  f  5438

**DeWitt, Willard "Jeremy Schneider"**
*Lunar Descent* - Allen Steele  s  5245

**Dittrich, Robert "Bobby"**
*Forests of the Night* - S. Andrew Swann  s  5363

**Dodger**
*Choose Your Enemies Carefully* - Robert N.
    Charrette  s  971
*Find Your Own Truth* - Robert N. Charrette  f  972
*Never Deal with a Dragon* - Robert N.
    Charrette  s  975

**Donnerjack, John D'Arcy**
*Donnerjack* - Roger Zelazny  s  6063

**Dooley, Paul**
*The Tranquility Alternative* - Allen Steele  s  5248

**Durham, Paul**
*Permutation City* - Greg Egan  s  1761

**Esterbrook, Diana**
*The Higher Space* - Jamil Nasir  s  4070

**Euclid**
*Exit to Reality* - Edith Forbes  s  1968

**Fears, Quentin**
*Treasure Box* - Orson Scott Card  h  898

**Ferguson, Herman D. "Fergie"**
*Judge Dredd* - Neal Barrett Jr.  s  366

**Ferrand, Art**
*Aftermath* - Charles Sheffield  s  4947

**Flander**
*Chimera* - Mary Rosenblum  s  4677

**Flannery, Eric**
*Caverns of Socrates* - Dennis L. McKiernan  f  3831

**Fletcher, Step**
*Lost Boys* - Orson Scott Card  f  891

**Francy, Lizzie**
*Beggars Ride* - Nancy Kress  s  3238

**Gale, Denton**
*Mother Lode* - Zach Hughes  s  2812

**Game Cat**
*Vurt* - Jeff Noon  s  4136

**Gannett, Anson "Andy"**
*The Alien Years* - Robert Silverberg  s  5027

**Garroway, Mark Alan**
*Semper Mars* - Ian Douglas  s  1585

**Giyt, Evesham**
*O Pioneer!* - Frederik Pohl  s  4350

**Gobi, Frank**
*Rim: A Novel of Virtual Reality* - Alexander
    Besher  s  475

**Gobi, Trevor**
*Mir* - Alexander Besher  s  474

**Gonzales, Mikhail Mikhailovitch**
*Halo* - Tom Maddox  s  3604

**Grant**
*MagicNet* - John DeChancie  f  1461

**Grant, John**
*Spook Night* - David Robbins  h  4603

**Grant, Spencer**
*Dark Rivers of the Heart* - Dean R. Koontz  h  3204

**Grillo, Nathan**
*Everville* - Clive Barker  h  338

**Halbard, Amy**
*Offspring* - Jack Ketchum  h  3092

**Hamilton, Ethan**
*Terminal Logic* - Jefferson Scott  s  4893

**Hamilton, Jordan**
*Terminal Logic* - Jefferson Scott  s  4893

**Hanson, Robert**
*Probe* - Edward M. Lerner  s  3437

**Hartley, Sherrine**
*Fallen Angels* - Larry Niven  s  4120

**Hedison, Marianne**
*Terminal Games* - Cole Perriman  s  4283

**Hernandes y Jons, Rico**
*The Eyes of God* - Mark Kreighbaum  s  3231
*Palace* - Katharine Kerr  s  3072

**Heywood, Diana**
*Halo* - Tom Maddox  s  3604

**Hillerman, Walter "Walt"**
*Lady El* - Jim Starlin  s  5213

**Hochstader, Jeremy**
*Castle War!* - John DeChancie  s  1455

**Holcroft, Jake**
*Target Earth* - Steve Perry  s  4301

**I**
*Hard-Boiled Wonderland and the End of the World* -
    Haruki Murakami  s  4047

**Jaffey**
*Zeta Base* - Judith Alguire  s  74

**Jaimie**
*Second Contact* - Mike Resnick  s  4555

**James, Zack**
*Blood Work* - Fay Zachary  h  6050

**Joanna**
*Dog Wizard* - Barbara Hambly  f  2503

**Jones, Lloyd Merlin**
*MagicNet* - John DeChancie  f  1461

**Juillerat, Sister Chantal**
*Demon Download* - Jack Yeovil  f  6021

**Justin, Rangsey**
*Night Sky Mine* - Melissa Scott  s  4898

**Juvell, Tyler**
*Iron Shadows* - Steven Barnes  f  362

**Karros, Dimitri Alexander**
*Ragged Angels* - Della Van Hise  h  5537

**Kemp, Wallace "Wally"**
*Lifehouse* - Spider Robinson  s  4641

**Kerickson, Arvid Gerald**
*The Imperium Game* - K.D. Wentworth  s  5753

**King, Elena "Lanie"**
*Richter 10* - Arthur C. Clarke  s  1060

**Kitatimate, Alexander "Sander"**
*Cinderblock* - Janine Ellen Young  s  6047

**Lacey, Bobbie**
*Polar City Blues* - Katharine Kerr  s  3073

**Le Roux, Reiki Momoku**
*Marooned on Eden* - Robert L. Forward  s  1986

**LeMat, Joseph "Gunnar Savage"**
*Headcrush* - Bruce Bethke  s  483

**Lesserac, Gary**
*Virtual Destruction* - Kevin J. Anderson  s  118

**Leving, Fredda**
*Caliban* - Roger MacBride Allen  s  77

**Lewis, Rob**
*How Like a God* - Brenda W. Clough  f  1089

**Lightfoot**
*Deepdrive* - Alexander Jablokov  s  2837

**Lioe, Quin**
*Burning Bright* - Melissa Scott  s  4894

**Lippman, Lenore**
*The Eighth Rank* - David D. Ross  s  4682

**Lovell, Willa**
*Judgment Day* - G. Harry Stine  s  5281

**Lu, Curtis**
*Carol for Another Christmas* - Elizabeth Ann
    Scarborough  f  4861

**Maddox, Cory**
*The Cybernetic Walrus* - Jack L. Chalker  s  951
*The Hot-Wired Dodo* - Jack L. Chalker  s  956
*The March Hare Network* - Jack L. Chalker  s  957

**Major, Cyrus "Cy" Lance**
*Zeus and Co.* - David Lee Jones  f  2942

**Marden, Jake**
*Prison Ship* - Martin Caidin  s  828

**Mark**
*See You Later* - Christopher Pike  f  4332

**Masada, Kio**
*This Alien Shore* - C.S. Friedman  s  2059

**Maxon, Alice**
*Caverns of Socrates* - Dennis L. McKiernan  f  3831

**Mbele, Miriam Makepeace**
*Red Dust* - Paul J. McAuley  s  3715

**McHogue**
*Warped* - K.W. Jeter  s  2917

**McMichaels, Scott**
*Infectress* - Tom Cool  s  1167

**McTurk, Felix**
*Kaduna Memories* - Jack McKinney  s  3850

**Mende, Alice**
*Wyrm* - Mark Fabi  s  1858

**Mendez, Sofia**
*The Sparrow* - Mary Doria Russell  s  4736

**Messenger, Joe**
*Host* - Peter James  h  2872

**Michaelson, Hal**
*Virtual Destruction* - Kevin J. Anderson  s  118

**Milena "Alfred Russell Wallace"**
*Fairyland* - Paul J. McAuley  s  3711

**Mitexi, Meredalia**
*Dreamships* - Melissa Scott  s  4896

**Muhammed, Sarkar**
*The Terminal Experiment* - Robert J.
    Sawyer  s  4860

**Munn, Alex**
*The Shift* - George Foy  s  2033

**Murugan, L.**
*The Calcutta Chromosome* - Amitav Ghosh  h  2214

**Myth, Urban**
*Cinderblock* - Janine Ellen Young  s  6047

**Nelly**
*Mir* - Alexander Besher  s  474

**Nolan, Carly**
*Cyberweb* - Lisa Mason  s  3662

**O'Kelly, Manuel "Mannie"**
*The Moon Is a Harsh Mistress* - Robert A.
    Heinlein  s  2645

**Olam, Thomas "Tom" Edward**
*From Prussia with Love* - John DeChancie   *f*  1457

**Orchard, Julia**
*The Count of Eleven* - Ramsey Campbell   *h*  853

**Ozzie**
*Dreams of Gods and Men* - W.T. Quick   *s*  4451

**Patrick, Uncle**
*Under Siege* - Elisabeth Mace   *f*  3587

**Pearce, Sarah**
*The Ghost Inside the Monitor* - Margaret J.
   Anderson   *f*  122

**Peter**
*Ecstasy Club* - Douglas Rushkoff   *s*  4732

**Pharbeque, Riscky "Hex DEF6"**
*The Hacker and the Ants* - Rudy Rucker   *s*  4704

**Phreak**
*Killobyte* - Piers Anthony   *f*  179

**Pincus, Laurie**
*The Sherwood Game* - Esther Friesner   *s*  2082

**Porter, Rand**
*Starmind* - Spider Robinson   *s*  4642

**Pr. Spinner**
*Cyberweb* - Lisa Mason   *s*  3662

**Protagonist, Hiro**
*Snow Crash* - Neal Stephenson   *s*  5254

**Putakin, Yuri**
*Orion's Dagger* - P.K. McAllister   *s*  3708

**Quinn, Sofia Mendes**
*Children of God* - Mary Doria Russell   *s*  4735

**Ransome, Illario "Ambidexter"**
*Burning Bright* - Melissa Scott   *s*  4894

**Reynolds, Alvin**
*The Road to Hell, Volume I* - Robert
   Weinberg   *h*  5701
*The Road to Hell, Volume II* - Robert
   Weinberg   *h*  5702

**Rhiannon**
*Overshoot* - Mona Clee   *s*  1075

**Ridenour, Stephen**
*Ground-Ties* - Jane S. Fancher   *s*  1861
*Harmonies of the 'Net* - Jane S. Fancher   *s*  1862
*Uplink* - Jane S. Fancher   *s*  1865

**Riley, Michael**
*The Deus Machine* - Pierre Ouellette   *h*  4232

**Rowan, Dalin**
*Knights of the Black Earth* - Margaret Weis   *s*  5718

**Rugby, Jerzy**
*The Hacker and the Ants* - Rudy Rucker   *s*  4704

**Sanders, Phillipe "Phil" Montoya**
*The Modular Man* - Roger MacBride Allen   *s*  79

**Santorini, Dan**
*Death Dream* - Ben Bova   *s*  583

**Selden, Penelope**
*The Whims of Creation* - Simon Hawke   *s*  2626

**Sept-Fortune, Cecilie 8**
*Interface Masque* - Shariann Lewitt   *s*  3453

**Sherwood, Carl**
*The Sherwood Game* - Esther Friesner   *s*  2082

**Shipman, Shira**
*He, She and It* - Marge Piercy   *s*  4325

**Silver**
*Shadowboxer* - Nick Pollotta   *s*  4366

**Smith, Brandon**
*Virtual Girl* - Amy Thomson   *s*  5462

**Smith, Edward**
*The Nightmare People* - Lawrence Watt-
   Evans   *h*  5643

**Smith, Freddie**
*Polymorph* - Scott Westerfeld   *s*  5767

**Smith, Jonathan Wesley**
*Harmonies of the 'Net* - Jane S. Fancher   *s*  1862
*Uplink* - Jane S. Fancher   *s*  1865

**Spango, Hypatia**
*Montezuma Strip* - Alan Dean Foster   *s*  2011

**Spear, James**
*Deathwalker* - Patrick Whalen   *h*  5769

**Spring, Juliet**
*Host* - Peter James   *h*  2872

**Stewart, Janet**
*Zeus and Co.* - David Lee Jones   *f*  2942

**Sturgis, Wally**
*The Shattered Sphere* - Roger MacBride Allen   *s*  81

**Succubus**
*The Hacker* - Chet Day   *h*  1410

**Sven "Loki"**
*Overshoot* - Mona Clee   *s*  1075

**Tarasov, Sein**
*Night Sky Mine* - Melissa Scott   *s*  4898

**Templeton, Judith**
*The Shadow Gate* - Margaret Ball   *f*  317

**Tenere, Jared**
*Voices of Hope* - David Feintuch   *s*  1903

**Tetsami, Kari**
*Partisan* - S. Andrew Swann   *s*  5365
*Profiteer* - S. Andrew Swann   *s*  5366
*Revolutionary* - S. Andrew Swann   *s*  5367

**Thomas, Signy**
*Whiteout* - Sage Walker   *s*  5619

**Thyme, Jordan "Antiquity"**
*Zeta Base* - Judith Alguire   *s*  74

**Tobin, G. Patrick "Toby"**
*Angel Light* - Andrew M. Greeley   *f*  2342

**Tower, Josh**
*Systems* - W.T. Quick   *s*  4452

**van Liesvelt, Butch**
*Trouble and Her Friends* - Melissa Scott   *s*  4902

**Vanelli, MONDO**
*How to Mutate and Take Over the World* - R.U.
   Sirius   *s*  5074

**Velis, Catherine**
*The Eight* - Katherine Neville   *f*  4092

**Victor**
*See You Later* - Christopher Pike   *f*  4332

**Wolenczak, Lucas**
*seaQuest DSV: Fire Below* - Matthew J.
   Costello   *s*  1201

**Young, Francesca**
*Streets of Blood* - Carl Sargent   *f*  4821

**Zumwalt, William Irving "Wiz"**
*The Wiz Biz* - Rick Cook   *f*  1160
*The Wizardry Consulted* - Rick Cook   *f*  1161
*The Wizardry Cursed* - Rick Cook   *f*  1162
*The Wizardry Quested* - Rick Cook   *f*  1163

## COMPUTER GAME PLAYER

**Metullus, Amaelia**
*The Imperium Game* - K.D. Wentworth   *s*  5753

## CON ARTIST

**Bellamy, June**
*Lifehouse* - Spider Robinson   *s*  4641

**de Carabas**
*Neverwhere* - Neil Gaiman   *f*  2104

**Faison, Genevieva**
*Corrupting Dr. Nice* - John Kessel   *s*  3083

**Jackson, Skeeter**
*Wagers of Sin* - Robert Asprin   *s*  264

**Jacobs, Earl**
*Less than Human* - Gary L. Raisor   *h*  4464

**Kheperu**
*Iron Dawn* - Matthew Woodring Stover   *f*  5320
*Jericho Moon* - Matthew Woodring Stover   *f*  5321

**Li, Master**
*The Chronicles of Master Li and Number Ten Ox* -
   Barry Hughart   *f*  2803

**Nashram, Mika**
*By the Sword* - Greg Costikyan   *f*  1207

**Slakey, Justin**
*The Stainless Steel Rat Goes to Hell* - Harry
   Harrison   *s*  2574

**Throtmanian, Paul Donald**
*Lifehouse* - Spider Robinson   *s*  4641

**Warrick, John**
*Less than Human* - Gary L. Raisor   *h*  4464

## CONSTRUCTION WORKER

**Anderson, Ted**
*Darkness* - John Saul   *h*  4840

**Barton, Roy**
*The Paper Grail* - James P. Blaylock   *f*  522

**Botts, Wendell**
*Oaths and Miracles* - Nancy Kress   *s*  3242

**Bruce, Virgin**
*Orbital Decay* - Allen Steele   *s*  5246

**Hake, Denton**
*Out of Body* - Thomas Baum   *h*  397

**Hooker, Popeye**
*Orbital Decay* - Allen Steele   *s*  5246

**Kubick, Ruby**
*Glass Houses* - Laura J. Mixon   *s*  3921

**Lark, Don**
*Homebody* - Orson Scott Card   *h*  890

**Quail, Douglas**
*Total Recall* - Piers Anthony   *s*  193

**Salisaw, Brent**
*Night Thunder* - Ruby Jean Jensen   *h*  2903

**Schoenwald, Robert**
*Shadow Dance* - Jessica Palmer   *h*  4238

**Skoglund, Paul**
*Skull Session* - Daniel Hecht   *h*  2638

**Stranger, John**
*Run for the Stars/Echoes of Thunder* - Harlan
   Ellison   *s*  1788

**Thubana, Mordecai**
*Apartheid, Superstrings, and Mordecai Thubana* -
   Michael Bishop   *s*  496

## CONSULTANT

**Bois, Jules**
*The Dark* - Andrew Neiderman   *h*  4084

**Deckard, Rick**
*Blade Runner: Replicant Night* - K.W. Jeter   *s*  2907

**Dun, Richard**
*Keeper of the King* - Nigel Bennett   *h*  452

**Laney, Colin**
*Idoru* - William Gibson   *s*  2218

**Valparaiso, Oscar**
*Distraction* - Bruce Sterling   *s*  5256

## CONTRACTOR

**McGuire, Bill**
*The Blackstone Chronicles* - John Saul  *h*  4838

**Tullian, James**
*Sheep* - Simon Maginn  *h*  3606

## CONVICT

**Bando, Nicos**
*Infinity Hold* - Barry B. Longyear  *s*  3522

**Cooper**
*In the Land of the Dead* - K.W. Jeter  *h*  2912

**Darwin, Alton**
*Hocus Pocus or, What's the Hurry, Son?* - Kurt
  Vonnegut Jr.  *s*  5593

**Flynn, Lonny**
*Spree* - Lucy Taylor  *h*  5415

**Garoit, Darrell**
*Infinity Hold* - Barry B. Longyear  *s*  3522

**Jess, Martin**
*Berserker* - S.D. Perry  *s*  4285

**Michaels, Dean**
*Swamp* - Peter Tremayne  *h*  5483

**Russel, Ben**
*Cold in July* - Joe R. Lansdale  *h*  3323

**Spanning, Henry Lake**
*Mefisto in Onyx* - Harlan Ellison  *h*  1786

**Stimpson, Nevil**
*Werewolf* - Peter Rubie  *h*  4702

**Taylor, Lura**
*Dumford Blood* - S.K. Epperson  *h*  1829

**Thermopyle, Angus**
*Forbidden Knowledge* - Stephen R.
  Donaldson  *s*  1571

**Tuckton, Travis Clyde**
*Header* - Edward Lee  *h*  3393

## COOK

**Bloocher, Jemmy "Tim Hann"**
*Destiny's Road* - Larry Niven  *s*  4119

**Doyle, Irini**
*The Sweetheart Season* - Karen Joy Fowler  *f*  2029

**Ennin, Willie**
*Raven* - Charles L. Grant  *h*  2314

**Escargot, Theophile**
*The Stone Giant* - James P. Blaylock  *f*  523

**Gurronsevas**
*The Galactic Gourmet* - James White  *s*  5778

**Martin, Jiggs**
*The Unfinished* - Jay B. Laws  *h*  3362

**McIssac, Dean**
*Summon the Keeper* - Tanya Huff  *f*  2800

**Murphy, Clarence "Cookie"**
*Judson's Eden* - Keith Laumer  *s*  3344

**Neelix**
*The Final Fury* - Dafydd ab Hugh  *s*  9

## COUNSELOR

**Alsnor, Lotta**
*The White Regiment* - John Dalmas  *s*  1327

**Chien-Chu, Sergi**
*Legion of the Damned* - William C. Dietz  *s*  1547

**Haas, Alexandria Victoria**
*Mindplayers* - Pat Cadigan  *s*  806

**Hanfor**
*The Spellsong War* - L.E. Modesitt Jr.  *f*  3939

**Hartwig, Reece**
*The Night of the Moonbow* - Thomas
  Tryon  *h*  5486

**Mab**
*I Was a Teenage Fairy* - Francesca Lia
  Block  *f*  549

**Nevyn**
*The Red Wyvern* - Katharine Kerr  *f*  3074

**Niffy**
*No One Noticed the Cat* - Anne McCaffrey  *f*  3740

**Roshnani**
*The Stolen Throne* - Harry Turtledove  *f*  5510

**Sharon**
*Requiem* - Graham Joyce  *h*  2994

**Shelby, Lissa**
*Shadow Man* - Dennis Etchison  *h*  1848

**Tarne**
*Heart Readers* - Kristine Kathryn Rusch  *f*  4718

## COURIER

**Carey**
*Changespell* - Doranna Durgin  *f*  1703
*Dun Lady's Jess* - Doranna Durgin  *f*  1704

**Cooper, Chaz**
*Expiry Date* - Carol Anne Davis  *h*  1401

**Gladheon, Karigan**
*Green Rider* - Kristen Britain  *f*  692

**Johnny**
*Johnny Mnemonic* - Terry Bisson  *s*  505

**Liath**
*King's Dragon* - Kate Elliott  *f*  1773

**Long, Huey "Hal" Alphonse**
*The Trinity Vector* - Steve Perry  *s*  4302

**MacColl, Enye**
*King of Morning, Queen of Day* - Ian
  McDonald  *f*  3793

**Mapstone, Laren**
*Green Rider* - Kristen Britain  *f*  692

## COURTIER

**Gibberling**
*Here There Be Dragons* - Roger Zelazny  *f*  6069

**ibn Khairan, Ammar**
*The Lions of Al-Rassan* - Guy Gavriel Kay  *f*  3016

**Lissa**
*Nobody's Son* - Sean Stewart  *f*  5275

## COUSIN

**Fonteyn, Oliver**
*Death Masque* - P.N. Elrod  *h*  1795

**Jones, Fanning "Fan"**
*Dreaming Metal* - Melissa Scott  *s*  4895

## COWBOY

**Cookie**
*The Thirteenth Daughter of the Moon* - Steven
  Nightingale  *f*  4104

**Hong, Louie**
*Hong on the Range* - William F. Wu  *s*  5997

**Johnston, Virgil Wayne**
*The Immortals* - Tracy Hickman  *s*  2681

**McBride, Michael**
*The Flight of Michael McBride* - Midori
  Snyder  *f*  5151

**O'Connor, John**
*The Flight of Michael McBride* - Midori
  Snyder  *f*  5151

**Redd**
*Red Dust* - Paul J. McAuley  *s*  3715

**Stone, Charlie**
*Wendigo Border* - Catherine Montrose  *h*  3967

## CRIMINAL

**Abalone**
*Brother to Dragons, Companion to Owls* - Jane M.
  Lindskold  *f*  3473

**Agenos, Mordion "the Servant"**
*Hexwood* - Diana Wynne Jones  *s*  2948

**al-Kharif, Yasin**
*Bright Messengers* - Gentry Lee  *s*  3398

**Alys**
*Dragon's Bait* - Vivian Vande Velde  *f*  5556

**Anlawdd**
*Arthur War Lord* - Dafydd ab Hugh  *f*  6

**Arabella "Infectress"**
*Infectress* - Tom Cool  *s*  1167

**Asado**
*The War of Don Emmanuel's Nether Parts* - Louis de
  Bernieres  *f*  1412

**Asperson, Arhos**
*Once a Hero* - Elizabeth Moon  *s*  3970

**Auk, Maytera**
*Exodus From the Long Sun* - Gene Wolfe  *s*  5941

**Avenger**
*The Spider #4: Death Reign of the Vampire King/The
  Pain Emperor* - Grant Stockbridge  *f*  5308

**Balcher**
*Medallion of the Black Hound* - Shirley Rousseau
  Murphy  *f*  4056

**Bane**
*Batman: Knightfall* - Dennis O'Neil  *s*  4215

**Bartlett, Tony "Antonius Caelerus"**
*Far Edge of Darkness* - Linda Evans  *s*  1855

**Bat Man**
*The Spider #4: Death Reign of the Vampire King/The
  Pain Emperor* - Grant Stockbridge  *f*  5308

**Benhaddou**
*White Rhino* - Bill Dolan  *s*  1569

**Bey, Friedlander**
*A Fire in the Sun* - George Alec Effinger  *s*  1751

**Birdsong, Joseph "Mojo"**
*Mojo and the Pickle Jar* - Douglas Bell  *f*  433

**Blaine, Cassandra "Cass"**
*Psykosis* - Wilhelmina Baird  *s*  296

**Blood**
*Nightside the Long Sun* - Gene Wolfe  *s*  5943

**Bouchette, Jean-Paul**
*The Suiting* - Kelley Wilde  *h*  5803

**Boyle, Simon**
*The Illegal Rebirth of Billy the Kid* - Rebecca
  Ore  *s*  4220

**Brooks, Connor**
*Ill Wind* - Kevin J. Anderson  *s*  108

**Bruckner, Bill**
*Nomad* - David Alexander  *s*  66

**Bruno, Richard**
*Journals of the Plague Years* - Norman
  Spinrad  *s*  5172

**Burke, Khalil Haleem**
*The Alien Years* - Robert Silverberg  *s*  5027

**Caine, Tycho**
*Evil Triumphant* - Michael A. Stackpole  *s*  5199

**Cantemir, George**
*The Venom Trees of Sunga* - L. Sprague de
Camp  *s*  1420

**Carter, John**
*Return of the Living Dead* - John Russo  *h*  4746

**Castlemaine, Sylvester**
*The Hemingway Hoax* - Joe Haldeman  *s*  2489

**Chambers, Phoebe**
*The Misconceiver* - Lucy Ferriss  *s*  1929

**Che, Ya**
*The Spider #3: Death's Crimson Juggernaut/The Red
Death Rain* - Grant Stockbridge  *f*  5307

**Claiborne, Kyle**
*Sacred Prey* - Vivian Schilling  *h*  4875

**Cobblepot, Oswald "the Penguin"**
*Batman Returns* - Craig Shaw Gardner  *s*  2124
*The Further Adventures of Batman 2: Featuring the
Penguin* - Martin H. Greenberg  *s*  2391

**Cole, James**
*12 Monkeys* - Elizabeth Hand  *s*  2532

**Comfort, Isambard**
*The Golden Globe* - John Varley  *s*  5565

**Coogan, Elihu "Emil Storchesson"**
*The Singularity Project* - F.M. Busby  *s*  784

**Crygender, "Cry"**
*Crygender* - Thomas T. Thomas  *s*  5451

**da Lionghi, Emilio**
*Humpty Dumpty: An Oval* - Damon Knight  *s*  3186

**Dak, Maanka "Pete Moss"**
*The Change* - Barry B. Longyear  *s*  3520

**d'Eath, Edward**
*Men at Arms* - Terry Pratchett  *f*  4396

**diGriz, Jim**
*The Stainless Steel Rat Goes to Hell* - Harry
Harrison  *s*  2574

**DiGriz, Jim**
*The Stainless Steel Rat Sings the Blues* - Harry
Harrison  *s*  2575

**Evanston, Livermore**
*Hunter's Planet* - David Bischoff  *s*  492

**Faracon, George**
*Time Station Paris* - David Evans  *s*  1854

**Ferguson, Herman D. "Fergie"**
*Judge Dredd* - Neal Barrett Jr.  *s*  366

**Fletcher, Terrance "Eel"**
*The Darker Saints* - Brian Hodge  *h*  2699

**Forrester, Edward**
*The Lunatic Cafe* - Laurell K. Hamilton  *h*  2520

**Friendly, Tod T.**
*Time's Arrow* - Martin Amis  *s*  96

**Fritz, Edgar P.**
*Darkman #3: The Gods of Hell* - Randall
Boyll  *h*  614

**Fucci, Vannie**
*The Hollow Man* - Dan Simmons  *s*  5054

**Germain**
*A Game of Universe* - Eric S. Nylund  *f*  4178

**Gersen, Kirth**
*The Demon Princes: Volume One* - Jack
Vance  *s*  5544
*The Demon Princes: Volume Two* - Jack
Vance  *s*  5545

**Gorp, Shigehero**
*Svaha* - Charles de Lint  *s*  1437

**Grace, Stephen**
*Dark of the Eye* - Douglas Clegg  *h*  1078

**Greeland**
*Mirage* - Perry Brass  *s*  662

**Grimson, Jim**
*Red Orc's Rage* - Philip Jose Farmer  *f*  1873

**Hammer**
*Illegal Aliens* - Nick Pollotta  *s*  4365

**Hayes, Jack**
*The Spider #3: Death's Crimson Juggernaut/The Red
Death Rain* - Grant Stockbridge  *f*  5307

**Hayes, Roy**
*The Cellar* - Richard Laymon  *h*  3365

**Hobgoblin**
*Spider-Man: The Venom Factor* - Diane
Duane  *s*  1667

**Hugh the Hand**
*Dragon Wing* - Margaret Weis  *f*  5709
*The Hand of Chaos* - Margaret Weis  *f*  5715
*Into the Labyrinth* - Margaret Weis  *f*  5716

**Hyde**
*The Darker Passions: Dr. Jekyll and Mr. Hyde* -
Amarantha Knight  *h*  3178

**Jake**
*Further Adventures* - Jon Stephen Fink  *f*  1940
*Terraplane* - Jack Womack  *s*  5960

**Jelinsky, Debbie**
*Addams Family Values* - Todd Strasser  *f*  5324

**Joker**
*Mask of the Phantasm* - Geary Gravel  *s*  2331

**Keller, Yates**
*The War Minstrels* - Karen Haber  *s*  2477
*Woman Without a Shadow* - Karen Haber  *s*  2478

**Kelly, Chris**
*The Bad Thing* - Michael O'Rourke  *h*  4222

**Kew, Horris**
*The Tangle Box* - Terry Brooks  *f*  718

**Kid Death**
*The Einstein Intersection* - Samuel R.
Delany  *s*  1481

**Kirshner, Martin**
*Worst Nightmare* - Ric Meyers  *h*  3883

**Kro, Gulthar**
*The Regiment's War* - John Dalmas  *s*  1326

**Kyle, Selena "Catwoman"**
*Batman Returns* - Craig Shaw Gardner  *s*  2124
*Catwoman* - Lynn Abbey  *s*  14
*The Further Adventures of Batman 3: Featuring
Catwoman* - Martin H. Greenberg  *s*  2392

**La Plante, Etienne**
*Wolf and Raven* - Michael A. Stackpole  *f*  5207

**Lehman, Stefan**
*The Stone Within* - David Wingrove  *s*  5920

**Lewin, Linda**
*Journals of the Plague Years* - Norman
Spinrad  *s*  5172

**Lightner, Sydnie "Charel Secour"**
*The Triad Worlds* - F.M. Busby  *s*  786

**Lobb, Eddie "Tiger"**
*Catwoman* - Lynn Abbey  *s*  14

**Long John Silver**
*Celestial Dogs* - J.S. Russell  *h*  4734

**Mace, Jarek**
*Morningstar* - David Gemmell  *f*  2190

**Mack, Derwent**
*Yours Truly, Jackie the Stripper* - Edo van
Belkom  *h*  5536

**Mack the Knife**
*Spring-Heeled Jack* - Philip Pullman  *f*  4447

**Makish**
*Blood War* - Robert Weinberg  *h*  5693

**Marchenko, Ivan "Burian Klimus"**
*Frameshift* - Robert J. Sawyer  *s*  4856

**Marden, Jake**
*Prison Ship* - Martin Caidin  *s*  828

**Marisovna, Cora**
*Climbing Olympus* - Kevin J. Anderson  *s*  102

**Marlon, John**
*Nine Levels Down* - William Dantz  *h*  1347

**Mars, Jerry**
*Rough Beast* - Gary Goshgarian  *h*  2284

**Matthews, Kevin**
*Galatea in 2-D* - Aaron Allston  *f*  87

**McComb, Aaron**
*Timecop* - S.D. Perry  *s*  4286

**McCready**
*Damnbanna* - Nancy Springer  *f*  5177

**McHogue**
*Warped* - K.W. Jeter  *s*  2917

**Mikhalevviko "Mikh"**
*Mathemagics* - Margaret Ball  *f*  316

**Mizzamir**
*Villains by Necessity* - Eve Forward  *f*  1985

**Moncrief, Marcel**
*Ports of Call* - Jack Vance  *s*  5549

**Morai**
*Talion: Revenant* - Michael A. Stackpole  *f*  5206

**Morane, Reynard**
*The Death of the Necromancer* - Martha
Wells  *f*  5749

**Morbius**
*Strange Tales From the Nile Empire* - Greg
Farshtey  *f*  1889

**Naufts, Tom**
*The Gifted* - Jack Caravela  *h*  879

**Nighthawk, Jefferson "Widowmaker"**
*The Widowmaker* - Mike Resnick  *s*  4559

**Orogastus**
*Sky Trillium* - Julian May  *f*  3700

**Padrik**
*The Robin and the Kestrel* - Mercedes
Lackey  *f*  3293

**Penward, Darren**
*Carnosaur* - Harry Adam Knight  *s*  3191

**Pharbeque, Riscky "Hex DEF6"**
*The Hacker and the Ants* - Rudy Rucker  *s*  4704

**Phoenix, Simon**
*Demolition Man* - Richard Osborne  *s*  4229

**Phreak**
*Killobyte* - Piers Anthony  *f*  179

**Plagier, Anton**
*The Rim-World Legacy and Beyond* - Frank A.
Javor  *s*  2882

**Price, Bobby**
*Savant* - Rex Miller  *h*  3901

**Proctor, Ottoken**
*Krokodil Tears* - Jack Yeovil  *f*  6023

**Quilp**
*A Game of Universe* - Eric S. Nylund  *f*  4178

**Quordane, Holis**
*Shadow of the Crown* - Craig Mills  *f*  3914

**Rahl, Drefan**
*Temple of the Winds* - Terry Goodkind  *f*  2270

**Ravenna, John**
*Prey* - William W. Johnstone  *h*  2932

**Reed, James**
*Operation Damocles* - Oscar L. Fellows  *s*  1915

**Reva**
*Mainline* - Deborah Christian  *s*  1026

**Roger**
*Memnoch the Devil* - Anne Rice  *h*  4571

**Ruiz, Juan**
*Fear Itself* - Ric Meyers  *h*  3881

**Sabah, Hasan al**
*The Mask of Loki* - Roger Zelazny  *f*  6071

**Saber, Karen**
*Marks of Our Brothers* - Jane M. Lindskold  *s*  3475

**Salvatore, Dominga**
*The Laughing Corpse* - Laurell K. Hamilton  *f*  2519

**Sam**
*Villains by Necessity* - Eve Forward  *f*  1985

**Seagryn**
*The Faithful Traitor* - Robert Don Hughes  *f*  2809

**Sheldon, Rudolph "Rudy"**
*Brown Girl in the Ring* - Nalo Hopkinson  *f*  2771

**Sid 6.7**
*Virtuosity* - Terry Bisson  *s*  507

**Siegel, Benjamin "Bugsy"**
*Last Call* - Tim Powers  *f*  4384

**Sinclair, Graham Kuan**
*Red Genesis* - S.C. Sykes  *s*  5377

**Spanner**
*Slow River* - Nicola Griffith  *s*  2445

**Stark, Marilyn**
*seaQuest DSV: The Novel* - Diane Duane  *s*  1666

**Stewart, Dalton**
*Jupiter's Daughter* - Tom Hyman  *s*  2820

**Strine, Arnold**
*The Fermata* - Nicholson Baker  *s*  302

**Taylor, Patricia "Mother"**
*Proxies* - Laura J. Mixon  *s*  3922

**Thatcher, Lloyd George**
*Call to Arms* - P.M. Griffin  *s*  2435

**Tiban, Boris**
*Climbing Olympus* - Kevin J. Anderson  *s*  102

**Usurper, Black**
*Henry Martyn* - L. Neil Smith  *s*  5131

**Vi-Kata**
*Palace* - Katharine Kerr  *s*  3072

**Virilio**
*Kamikaze L'Amour* - Richard Kadrey  *s*  2998

**Vizuelos, Ramon**
*Meeting the Minotaur* - Carol Dawson  *f*  1409

**Walcott, Roland**
*Indiana Jones and the Unicorn's Legacy* - Rob MacGregor  *f*  3593

**Walker, Jack**
*Deathwalker* - R. Patrick Gates  *h*  2159

**Wentworth, Ford**
*The Trinity Vector* - Steve Perry  *s*  4302

**Werewolf**
*Wizard's Heir* - Daniel Hood  *f*  2759

**White Eyes**
*White Eyes* - Kenneth Robeson  *f*  4625

**Wolfe, Atrix**
*The Book of Atrix Wolfe* - Patricia A. McKillip  *f*  3838

**X**
*The Diamond Age* - Neal Stephenson  *s*  5253

**Xizor**
*The Mandalorian Armor* - K.W. Jeter  *s*  2914

**Zachary**
*Guilty Pleasures* - Laurell K. Hamilton  *f*  2517

**Zeerus**
*Target Earth* - Steve Perry  *s*  4301

## CRITIC

**Bankole, Larkin "Asha Vere"**
*Parable of the Talents* - Octavia E. Butler  *s*  793

**Sperry, Jack**
*City of Truth* - James Morrow  *s*  4030

**Swann, Clare**
*Flicker* - Theodore Roszak  *h*  4683

**Tierney, Rose**
*The Parasite* - Ramsey Campbell  *h*  863

**Vivo, Dionisio**
*Senor Vivo and the Coca Lord* - Louis de Bernieres  *f*  1411

**Wright, Paul**
*Nightlight* - Michael Cadnum  *h*  813

## CULT MEMBER

**Bonhomme, Jacques**
*The Centurion's Empire* - Sean McMullen  *s*  3854

**Brustein, Harvey**
*The Children of Hamelin* - Norman Spinrad  *s*  5170

**Dwago**
*Graythings* - Pat Graversen  *h*  2335

**Kuruk**
*Deathsong* - Douglas Borton  *h*  575

**Oshita, Joy**
*Iron Shadows* - Steven Barnes  *f*  362

**Patswami**
*Button Bright* - Michael Kurland  *h*  3251

**Proctor, Simon**
*Dying Breath* - Jon A. Harrald  *h*  2555

**Quon**
*The Jade Ogre* - Kenneth Robeson  *f*  4623

**Smith, Zachariah**
*Leap Point* - Kay Kenyon  *s*  3063

**Thorne, Hester**
*Dark Channel* - Ray Garton  *h*  2150

## CYBORG

**Andreyeva, Maya Tayanichna**
*The Fortunate Fall* - Raphael Carter  *s*  927

**Ball**
*Blood Lines* - William R. Burkett Jr.  *s*  774

**Borg, Cy**
*Drifter's Run* - William C. Dietz  *s*  1544
*Drifter's War* - William C. Dietz  *s*  1545

**Borg, Jocasta**
*The Specialist* - Wynne Whiteford  *s*  5788

**Cade, Hypatia "Tia"**
*The Ship Who Searched* - Anne McCaffrey  *s*  3749

**Carialle**
*The Ship Errant* - Jody Lynn Nye  *s*  4175

**Dawson**
*Warp Angel* - Stuart Hopen  *s*  2766

**den Ostreicher, Jory**
*Man Plus* - Frederik Pohl  *s*  4348

**Devreaux, Luc**
*Universal Soldier* - Robert Tine  *s*  5476

**Evans, Juliet "Julie"**
*Mindstar Rising* - Peter F. Hamilton  *s*  2526

**Four, Cathy**
*Cathy IV* - Frances Lucas  *s*  3539

**Guthrie, Anson**
*The Fleet of Stars* - Poul Anderson  *s*  126

**Hunsucker, Willie**
*Gaia's Toys* - Rebecca Ore  *s*  4218

**Kemra**
*Adiamante* - L.E. Modesitt Jr.  *s*  3924

**Kopal, Jefferson "Jeff"**
*The Cyborg From Earth* - Charles Sheffield  *s*  4952

**Krokodil**
*Comeback Tour: The Sky Belongs to the Stars* - Jack Yeovil  *s*  6020

**Lippman, Lenore**
*The Eighth Rank* - David D. Ross  *s*  4682

**Magnus, Dominic "Dom"**
*Partisan* - S. Andrew Swann  *s*  5365
*Profiteer* - S. Andrew Swann  *s*  5366
*Revolutionary* - S. Andrew Swann  *s*  5367

**MAX**
*Berserker* - S.D. Perry  *s*  4285

**Mendez, Marla**
*Prison Planet* - William C. Dietz  *s*  1551

**Moliak**
*Down the Bright Way* - Robert Reed  *s*  4505

**Montgomery, Dirk**
*House of the Sun* - Nigel Findley  *s*  1936

**Nancia**
*PartnerShip* - Anne McCaffrey  *s*  3741

**Pope, Eric**
*Black Snow Days* - Claudia O'Keefe  *s*  4205

**Questioner II**
*Six Moon Dance* - Sheri S. Tepper  *s*  5437

**Rosa**
*Correspondence* - Sue Thomas  *s*  5450

**Sam**
*The Sounding Stillness* - Kenneth Von Gunden  *s*  5587

**Scott, Andrew**
*Universal Soldier* - Robert Tine  *s*  5476

**Shirley**
*Correspondence* - Sue Thomas  *s*  5450

**Skater, Jack**
*Headhunters* - Mel Odom  *s*  4192

**SSS-900-C Simeon**
*The City Who Fought* - Anne McCaffrey  *s*  3722

**Thermopyle, Angus**
*The Gap into Madness: Chaos and Order* - Stephen R. Donaldson  *s*  1573
*The Gap into Power: A Dark and Hungry God Arises* - Stephen R. Donaldson  *s*  1574
*The Gap into Ruin: This Day All Gods Die* - Stephen R. Donaldson  *s*  1575

**Thorvin**
*Fade to Black* - Nyx Smith  *s*  5134

**Torraway, Roger**
*Man Plus* - Frederik Pohl  *s*  4348

**Tucker, William Alec III**
*A King of Infinite Space* - Allen Steele  *s*  5243

**Voskresenye, Pavel Sergeyevich**
*The Fortunate Fall* - Raphael Carter   *s*   927

**Wolfe, Jacob**
*Deathstalker Honor* - Simon R. Green   *s*   2364

**Xris**
*Knights of the Black Earth* - Margaret Weis   *s*   5718

## DANCER

**Ann "Annai"**
*Shame of Man* - Piers Anthony   *s*   188

**Anya**
*Live Girls* - Ray Garton   *h*   2151

**Atuli, Cameron**
*Maximum Light* - Nancy Kress   *s*   3241

**Blackwell, Patricia "Trish"**
*The Digital Effect* - Steve Perry   *s*   4295

**Bowen, Muffy**
*Greenhouse* - Thomas A. Easton   *s*   1723

**Brandis, Sarah**
*Sick* - Jay R. Bonansinga   *h*   571

**Diate, Emilio**
*Traitors* - Kristine Kathryn Rusch   *f*   4729

**Elizabeth**
*Ladies Night* - Jack Ketchum   *h*   3091

**Evans, Christina**
*The Eyes of Darkness* - Dean R. Koontz   *s*   3206

**Eve, Glennys**
*The Stalking Horse* - Constance Ash   *f*   222

**Grandma Fifi**
*Baby Be-Bop* - Francesca Lia Block   *f*   545

**Hispard, Michael**
*Skin* - Kathe Koja   *h*   3196

**Innowen**
*Shadowdance* - Robin Wayne Bailey   *f*   290

**Kelryn**
*The Legend of Nightfall* - Mickey Zucker Reichert   *f*   4521

**Ky, Niki**
*Silk* - Caitlin R. Kiernan   *h*   3101

**Luci**
*Night Prayers* - P.D. Cacek   *h*   803

**McLeod, Morgan**
*Starseed* - Spider Robinson   *s*   4643

**Melisande**
*The Widowmaker* - Mike Resnick   *s*   4559

**Olson, Caroline**
*Dancing on Air* - Nancy Kress   *s*   3240

**Power, Lulu "Flower"**
*Genesis* - Charles L. Grant   *h*   2308

**Promise**
*Firedance* - Steven Barnes   *s*   360
*Gorgon Child* - Steven Barnes   *s*   361

**Quejaches, Xia**
*The Stone Garden* - Mary Rosenblum   *s*   4679

**Roxanne**
*The Werewolf Chronicles* - Traci Briery   *h*   679

**Ruquel**
*The Book of the Beast* - Tanith Lee   *f*   3405

**Sasaki, Jay**
*Starmind* - Spider Robinson   *s*   4642

**Sparkle**
*The Six Families* - Nancy Holder   *s*   2733

**Tiana**
*Songs of the Dancing Gods* - Jack L. Chalker   *f*   962

**Trusla**
*The Warding of Witch World* - Andre Norton   *f*   4163

**Turner, Loraine "Phyllis"**
*The Werewolf Chronicles* - Traci Briery   *h*   679
*Wolfsong* - Traci Briery   *h*   680

**Voy, Ellen**
*Six Moon Dance* - Sheri S. Tepper   *s*   5437

## DEBUTANTE

**Radineaux, Jenifleur**
*Bridge of Valor* - Anne Lesley Groell   *f*   2452

**Radineaux, Viera**
*Anvil of the Sun* - Anne Lesley Groell   *f*   2451

## DEITY

**Aditi**
*Blood of the Goddess* - Kara Dalkey   *f*   1318

**Allic**
*The Crystal Sorcerers* - William R. Forstchen   *f*   1979

**Aphrael**
*The Hidden City* - David Eddings   *f*   1733

**Apollo**
*Ye Gods!* - Tom Holt   *f*   2753

**Ashar**
*The Way Beneath* - Angus Wells   *f*   5740

**Benefactor**
*Revenant* - Louise Cooper   *f*   1178

**Chen, Harry**
*The Seraphim Rising* - Elisabeth De Vos   *s*   1442

**Cyric**
*Crucible* - Troy Denning   *f*   1484

**Dragon**
*Dark Heart* - Margaret Weis   *f*   5707

**Earth Mother**
*Nemesis* - Louise Cooper   *f*   1177

**Engibil**
*Between the Rivers* - Harry Turtledove   *f*   5496

**Gilgamesh**
*How Like a God* - Brenda W. Clough   *f*   1089

**God**
*Sympathy for the Devil* - Holly Lisle   *f*   3488

**God "The Old Man"**
*The Old Man and Mr. Smith* - Peter Ustinov   *f*   5532

**Gonn-Ben-Allah**
*Ahmed and the Oblivion Machines* - Ray Bradbury   *f*   618

**Great God Om**
*Small Gods* - Terry Pratchett   *f*   4400

**Hades**
*The Face of Apollo* - Fred Saberhagen   *s*   4766

**Hera**
*Orion and the Conqueror* - Ben Bova   *s*   590

**Jane**
*Children of the Mind* - Orson Scott Card   *s*   883

**Karak**
*The Blackgod* - J. Gregory Keyes   *f*   3095

**Katz, Julie**
*Only Begotten Daughter* - James Morrow   *f*   4034

**Leeloo Minai, Appipulai**
*The Fifth Element* - Terry Bisson   *s*   504

**Leonan**
*Planar Powers* - J. Robert King   *f*   3122

**Lily**
*Lunatics* - Bradley Denton   *f*   1491

**Lloth**
*Siege of Darkness* - R.A. Salvatore   *f*   4804

**Loki**
*The Spawn of Loki* - Jason Henderson   *f*   2658

**Magodor**
*Pretty Pewter Gods* - Glen Cook   *f*   1152

**Malu**
*Children of the Mind* - Orson Scott Card   *s*   883

**Maria**
*The Wizard at Home* - Rick Shelley   *f*   4975

**Mercury**
*The M.D.: A Horror Story* - Thomas M. Disch   *h*   1561

**Mikel**
*The Wizard at Home* - Rick Shelley   *f*   4975

**Minerva**
*Ye Gods!* - Tom Holt   *f*   2753

**Mohini**
*The Willing Spirit* - Piers Anthony   *f*   195

**Monigan**
*The Time of the Ghost* - Diana Wynne Jones   *f*   2951

**Nodens**
*The Transition of Titus Crow* - Brian Lumley   *h*   3569

**Odin**
*Sleipnir* - Linda Evans   *f*   1856
*War of the Gods* - Poul Anderson   *f*   136

**Orfindel "Hosea Lincoln"**
*The Fire Duke* - Joel Rosenberg   *f*   4671

**Pati**
*Delta City* - Felicity Savage   *f*   4849

**Ravana**
*The Willing Spirit* - Piers Anthony   *f*   195

**Redthorn, Jeremy**
*The Face of Apollo* - Fred Saberhagen   *s*   4766

**Sati**
*Sati* - Christopher Pike   *f*   4330

**Schel, Daniel**
*The Moon's Wife: A Hystery* - A.A. Attanasio   *f*   271

**Selinde**
*Kaleidoscope Eyes* - Graham Watkins   *h*   5631

**Silvas**
*The Wizard at Home* - Rick Shelley   *f*   4975

**Teaqua**
*Look into the Sun* - James Patrick Kelly   *s*   3047

**Thiede**
*The Fulfillments of Fate and Desire* - Storm Constantine   *s*   1142

**Tomanak**
*The War God's Own* - David Weber   *f*   5682

**True Dragon**
*Testament of the Dragon* - Margaret Weis   *f*   5729

**Venus**
*Child of the Eagle* - Esther Friesner   *f*   2073

## DEMON

**Adam**
*Good Omens: The Nice and Accurate Prophecies of Agnes Nutter, Witch* - Neil Gaiman   *f*   2103

**Agonostis**
*Sympathy for the Devil* - Holly Lisle   *f*   3488

**Ambrosius, Merlinus "Myrddin/Lailoken"**
*The Dragon and the Unicorn* - A.A.
Attanasio  *f*  266

**Astfgl**
*Eric* - Terry Pratchett  *f*  4388

**Bargolas**
*The Summoned* - Steven Ray Fulgham  *h*  2090

**Black Dust 7, Lisa**
*Temporary Agency* - Rachel Pollack  *f*  4360

**Bradley, Kevin**
*Eyes of the Empress* - Camille Bacon-Smith  *f*  285

**Cardiff, Melisan**
*Hooray for Hellywood* - Esther Friesner  *f*  2077

**Catch**
*Practical Demonkeeping* - Christopher
Moore  *h*  3989

**Darkhorse**
*The Crystal Dragon* - Richard A. Knaak  *f*  3167

**Davis, Evan**
*Eyes of the Empress* - Camille Bacon-Smith  *f*  285

**Davos**
*The Itinerant Exorcist* - Ashley McConnell  *f*  3776

**Debauchery Devil/Torchy Burns**
*Strum Again?* - Elizabeth Ann Scarborough  *f*  4870

**Demon**
*Running with the Demon* - Terry Brooks  *f*  715

**Doomstalker**
*Doomstalker* - Gary Brandner  *h*  661

**Dupree, Lorelle**
*The New Neighbor* - Ray Garton  *h*  2154

**Elbub, Azzie**
*Bring Me the Head of Prince Charming* - Roger
Zelazny  *f*  6062
*A Farce to Be Reckoned With* - Roger
Zelazny  *f*  6064

**Frank**
*The Hellbound Heart* - Clive Barker  *h*  342

**Glibspet**
*Hell on High* - Holly Lisle  *f*  3483

**Goranu**
*The Heavenward Path* - Kara Dalkey  *f*  1319
*Little Sister* - Kara Dalkey  *f*  1320

**Grossclout**
*Roc and a Hard Place* - Piers Anthony  *f*  187

**Gryll**
*Prince of Chaos* - Roger Zelazny  *f*  6073

**Harrison, Nick**
*Freeze Frames* - Katharine Kerr  *s*  3071

**Hasruel**
*Castle in the Air* - Diana Wynne Jones  *f*  2944

**Iezu**
*Crown of Shadows* - C.S. Friedman  *s*  2057

**Jakan**
*Rage of a Demon King* - Raymond E. Feist  *f*  1908

**Krulshards**
*Palace of Kings* - Mike Jefferies  *f*  2887

**Lamashtu**
*Son of Darkness* - Josepha Sherman  *f*  4990

**Lasher**
*The Witching Hour* - Anne Rice  *h*  4580

**Lucifer**
*The Devil and Dan Cooley* - Holly Lisle  *f*  3480

**Memnoch**
*Memnoch the Devil* - Anne Rice  *h*  4571

**Mentia, D.**
*Geis of the Gargoyle* - Piers Anthony  *f*  172

**Mephistopheles**
*If at Faust You Don't Succeed* - Roger
Zelazny  *f*  6070
*Jack Faust* - Michael Swanwick  *s*  5372

**Metria "Woe Betide"**
*Roc and a Hard Place* - Piers Anthony  *f*  187

**Morgeu**
*The Dragon and the Unicorn* - A.A.
Attanasio  *f*  266

**Nephredann**
*Necrom* - Mick Farren  *s*  1881

**Puck**
*The Devil and Dan Cooley* - Holly Lisle  *f*  3480

**Raleel**
*Hooray for Hellywood* - Esther Friesner  *f*  2077

**Ravana**
*The Willing Spirit* - Piers Anthony  *f*  195

**Salesman**
*Tales From the Crypt: Demon Knight* - Randall
Boyll  *h*  617

**Santa, Levi D.**
*The Book of the Damned* - D.A. Fowler  *h*  2022

**Taws**
*Wrath of Ashar* - Angus Wells  *f*  5742

**Tyrr**
*Demon Blade* - Mark A. Garland  *f*  2141

**Valarian, Nickolai**
*Red Devil* - David Saperstein  *h*  4816

**Valcourt, Guy-Luc**
*Adversary* - Daniel Rhodes  *h*  4568

**Ware**
*If I Pay Thee Not in Gold* - Piers Anthony  *f*  176

**X "Brother Rush"**
*Humans* - Donald E. Westlake  *f*  5768

**X(A/N)th "Nimby"**
*Yon Ill Wind* - Piers Anthony  *f*  196

**Yaksha**
*The Last Vampire* - Christopher Pike  *h*  4328

**Ygorla**
*The Avenger* - Louise Cooper  *f*  1174
*The Deceiver* - Louise Cooper  *f*  1175

## DENTIST

**Roswell, Harry I.**
*Summerland* - L. Dean James  *f*  2865

## DESIGNER

**Carlisle, Bari**
*Count Geiger's Blues* - Michael Bishop  *s*  499

**Griffin, Deirdre**
*Bitter Blood* - Karen E. Taylor  *h*  5405
*Blood Secrets* - Karen E. Taylor  *h*  5406
*Blood Ties* - Karen E. Taylor  *h*  5407

**Hall, Cassandra**
*Thirst* - Michael Cecilione  *h*  948

**Holland, Susan**
*The Beyond* - Barry Harrington  *h*  2556

**McGinnis, Rachel**
*Santa Steps Out: A Fairy Tale for Grownups* - Robert
Devereaux  *h*  1506

**Rolando**
*Thirst* - Michael Cecilione  *h*  948

## DETECTIVE

**Adolphus, Matthew**
*Afterimage Aftershock* - Kristine Kathryn
Rusch  *h*  4710

**Allan, David**
*The Virginia Ghost Murders* - Leslie Raymond
Sachs  *h*  4778

**Bumstead, Frank**
*Dark City* - Frank Lauria  *h*  3351

**Burns, Marty**
*Celestial Dogs* - J.S. Russell  *h*  4734

**Bushell, Thomas**
*The Two Georges* - Richard Dreyfuss  *s*  1655

**Butterbaugh, C.G.**
*Sacrifice* - John Farris  *h*  1886

**Chandler, Zinc**
*Evil Eye* - Michael Slade  *h*  5085

**Chapman, Merrick**
*Rulers of Darkness* - Steven Spruill  *h*  5185

**Cordesman, Jack**
*Shifters* - Edward Lee  *h*  3396

**Craven, Nick**
*Evil Eye* - Michael Slade  *h*  5085

**Darcy, Lord**
*A Study in Sorcery* - Michael Kurland  *f*  3252

**Davies, Gabriel**
*Red Angel* - Roxanne Longstreet  *h*  3518

**DeClerq, Robert**
*Evil Eye* - Michael Slade  *h*  5085

**Douglas, Kirk**
*The Book of Webster's* - J.N. Williamson  *h*  5853

**Dupin, C. Auguste**
*The Lighthouse at the End of the World* - Stephen
Marlowe  *h*  3631

**Gage, Tom**
*The Long Midnight* - Daniel Ransom  *h*  4480

**Goodlow, Sam**
*Goodlow's Ghosts* - T.M. Wright  *h*  5991

**Heiligmann, E. "Pif"**
*Double Jeopardy* - Aaron Allston  *s*  86

**Hendricks, Judson**
*Flesh and Blood* - D.A. Fowler  *h*  2024

**Hobbes, John**
*Fallen* - Dee Graham  *h*  2302

**Hood, Virgil**
*Noctet: Tales of Madonna-Moloch* - Albert J.
Manachino  *h*  3613

**Hunter**
*Dictator* - William F. Wu  *s*  5996
*Predator* - William F. Wu  *s*  5998
*Warrior* - William F. Wu  *s*  6000

**Jenny Sixa**
*Circle of One* - Eric James Fullilove  *s*  2092

**Khuzud, Kami**
*Hour of the Octopus* - Joel Rosenberg  *f*  4673

**Kiernan, Michael**
*Control Freak* - Christa Faust  *h*  1890

**Krillen**
*Ancestor's World* - A.C. Crispin  *s*  1259

**La Cava, Lou**
*Fallen* - Dee Graham  *h*  2302

**Levenson, David**
*Clash by Night* - Chet Williamson  *h*  5844

**Li**
*Eight Skilled Gentlemen* - Barry Hughart  *f*  2804

**Lipaski, Anthony**
*Red Angel* - Roxanne Longstreet  *h*  3518

**Loftis**
*Orca* - Steven Brust  *f*  745

**Mandel, Eleanor**
*A Quantum Murder* - Peter F. Hamilton  *s*  2527

**Mandel, Greg**
*Mindstar Rising* - Peter F. Hamilton  *s*  2526
*A Quantum Murder* - Peter F. Hamilton  *s*  2527

**Marlowe, Zoot**
*Hawaiian U.F.O. Aliens* - Mel Gilden  *s*  2226
*Tubular Android Superheroes* - Mel Gilden  *s*  2228

**McCann, Dire**
*Blood War* - Robert Weinberg  *h*  5693
*The Unbeholden* - Robert Weinberg  *h*  5703
*Unholy Allies* - Robert Weinberg  *h*  5704

**McTurk, Felix**
*Kaduna Memories* - Jack McKinney  *s*  3850

**Montgomery, Derek**
*2XS* - Nigel Findley  *f*  1935

**Morcey, Paul**
*Some Things Come Back* - Robert Morgan  *h*  4004

**Morris, Rob**
*Sibs* - F. Paul Wilson  *h*  5898

**Palmer, William**
*In the Blood* - Nancy A. Collins  *h*  1121

**Parks, Henry**
*Forget Me Not* - Gene Lazuta  *h*  3375

**Pasmore, Tom**
*The Throat* - Peter Straub  *h*  5332

**Poe, Amanda**
*The Virginia Ghost Murders* - Leslie Raymond
Sachs  *h*  4778

**Puzzle Solver**
*Alien Blues* - Lynn S. Hightower  *s*  2682

**Reandn**
*Touched by Magic* - Doranna Durgin  *f*  1705

**Rhenford, Liam**
*Scales of Justice* - Daniel Hood  *f*  2758

**Ross, David**
*The Dead Man's Kiss* - Robert Weinberg  *h*  5695

**Sarai**
*The Spell of the Black Dagger* - Lawrence Watt-
Evans  *f*  5648

**Spence, Jeffrey**
*Portrait of the Psychopath as a Young Woman* -
Edward Lee  *h*  3395

**Straker, Phillip**
*Goon* - Edward Lee  *h*  3392

**Taine, Sid**
*The Black Lodge* - Robert Weinberg  *h*  5692

**Talbot, David**
*The Vampire Armand* - Anne Rice  *h*  4578

**Trayne**
*Madlands* - K.W. Jeter  *s*  2913

**Tregarde, Diana**
*Children of the Night* - Mercedes Lackey  *h*  3276

**Tyler, Kane**
*Raven* - S.A. Swiniarski  *h*  5374

**Van Allen, Edmund**
*Cemetery of Angels* - Noel Hynd  *h*  2821

**Vance, Aylmer**
*Aylmer Vance: Ghost-Seer* - Alice Askew  *h*  258

**Von Heilitz, Lamont "the Shadow"**
*Mystery* - Peter Straub  *h*  5330

## DETECTIVE—AMATEUR

**Alinor**
*Wheels of Fire* - Mercedes Lackey  *f*  3301

**Asher, James**
*Those Who Hunt the Night* - Barbara
Hambly  *h*  2510
*Traveling with the Dead* - Barbara Hambly  *h*  2511

**Bronkman, Theo "Peter Ambrose"**
*Nimbus* - Alexander Jablokov  *s*  2839

**Carlucci, Caroline**
*Carlucci's Heart* - Richard Paul Russo  *s*  4748

**Gabriel**
*Aristoi* - Walter Jon Williams  *s*  5834

**Glivven, Miranda**
*Cat's Paw* - L.A. Taylor  *f*  5409

**Graves, Jermyn**
*Journeyman Wizard* - Mary Frances
Zambreno  *f*  6057

**Harker, Malcolm**
*Blood of the Impaler* - Jeffrey Sackett  *h*  4779

**Hedison, Marianne**
*Terminal Games* - Cole Perriman  *s*  4283

**Hornchurch, Anthony**
*The Devil You Say* - Elisa DeCarlo  *f*  1450
*Strong Spirits* - Elisa DeCarlo  *f*  1451

**King, Schuyler "Skye"**
*MagicNet* - John DeChancie  *f*  1461

**McDarvid, Jack**
*The Green Progression* - L.E. Modesitt Jr.  *s*  3932

**Miller, Paul**
*In the Deep Woods* - Nicholas Conde  *h*  1131

**Parker, Peter "Spider-Man"**
*Spider-Man: The Venom Factor* - Diane
Duane  *s*  1667
*The Ultimate Spider-Man* - Stan Lee  *s*  3403

**Rhenford, Liam**
*Beggar's Banquet* - Daniel Hood  *f*  2756
*Fanuilh* - Daniel Hood  *f*  2757
*Wizard's Heir* - Daniel Hood  *f*  2759

**Rugby, Jerzy**
*The Hacker and the Ants* - Rudy Rucker  *s*  4704

**Sivart, Gil**
*The Digital Effect* - Steve Perry  *s*  4295

**Sixa, Jenny**
*The Stranger* - Eric James Fullilove  *s*  2093

**Solinari, Kelly**
*Crisis on Doona* - Anne McCaffrey  *s*  3723

**Tamerlane, Rebecca "Michael Kerr"**
*Afterimage* - Kristine Kathryn Rusch  *f*  4709

**Tamm, Wayness**
*Ecce and Old Earth* - Jack Vance  *s*  5546

**Tanner, Louis**
*Destroying Angel* - Richard Paul Russo  *s*  4749

**Wayne, Bruce "Batman"**
*Batman: Captured by the Engines* - Joe R.
Lansdale  *h*  3320
*Batman: Knightfall* - Dennis O'Neil  *s*  4215
*Batman Returns* - Craig Shaw Gardner  *s*  2124
*Catwoman* - Lynn Abbey  *s*  14
*The Further Adventures of Batman 2: Featuring the
Penguin* - Martin H. Greenberg  *s*  2391
*The Further Adventures of Batman 3: Featuring
Catwoman* - Martin H. Greenberg  *s*  2392
*Mask of the Phantasm* - Geary Gravel  *s*  2331

**Yukiko "Yuki"**
*Tea From an Empty Cup* - Pat Cadigan  *s*  809

## DETECTIVE—HOMICIDE

**Bletcher, Robert**
*The Frenchman* - Elizabeth Hand  *h*  2534

**Bowman, Maggie**
*Cold Kiss* - Roxanne Longstreet  *h*  3517
*The Undead* - Roxanne Longstreet  *h*  3519

**Broward, Joseph**
*Concrete Hotel* - C. Christopher Caldon  *h*  839

**Drummond, John**
*At Sword's Point* - Scott MacMillan  *f*  3601
*Knights of the Blood* - Scott MacMillan  *f*  3602

**Duvall, Katherine**
*Dark Matter* - Garfield Reeves-Stevens  *h*  4509

**Knight, Nicholas**
*Forever Knight: A Stirring of Dust* - Susan
Sizemore  *h*  5078
*Forever Knight: Intimations of Mortality* - Susan M.
Garrett  *h*  2149

**Konstantin, Dore**
*Tea From an Empty Cup* - Pat Cadigan  *s*  809

**Levy, Jace**
*Love Bite* - Sherry Gottlieb  *h*  2288

**Medlocke, Jason**
*Brethren* - Shawn Ryan  *h*  4754

**Robinson, Liz**
*Love Bite* - Sherry Gottlieb  *h*  2288

**Stevenson, Connie**
*Concrete Hotel* - C. Christopher Caldon  *h*  839

**Trent, Derrick**
*Circle of One* - Eric James Fullilove  *s*  2092

**Vetter, Tracy**
*Forever Knight: Intimations of Mortality* - Susan M.
Garrett  *h*  2149

## DETECTIVE—POLICE

**Adolphus, Matthew**
*Afterimage* - Kristine Kathryn Rusch  *f*  4709

**Anaka**
*Specters of the Dawn* - S. Andrew Swann  *s*  5368

**Beach, Gil**
*Puppet Master* - Barry T. Hawkins  *h*  2632

**Bell, Daniel**
*Famine* - Todd Komarnicki  *h*  3201

**Brackett, Lute**
*Star Precinct* - Kevin D. Randle  *s*  4470

**Breaux, Alan**
*Spellcaster* - J. Edward Ames  *h*  92

**Broussard, Wade**
*The Gris-Gris Man* - Don Davis  *h*  1403

**Carlucci, Frank**
*Carlucci's Edge* - Richard Paul Russo  *s*  4747
*Carlucci's Heart* - Richard Paul Russo  *s*  4748

**Carmaggio, Henry**
*Drakon* - S.M. Stirling  *s*  5294

**Celluci, Mike**
*Blood Debt* - Tanya Huff  *h*  2792

**Chapman, Merrick**
*Daughter of Darkness* - Steven Spruill  *h*  5183

**Coglin, Dennis**
*Bring on the Night* - Don Davis  *h*  1402

**Conway, Michael**
*Vyrmin* - Gene Lazuta  *h*  3376

**Cordesman, Jack**
*Incubi* - Edward Lee  *h*  3394

**Daily, Jennifer**
*Star Precinct* - Kevin D. Randle   *s*   4470

**Daniels, Norman**
*Rose Madder* - Stephen King   *h*   3139

**De Luca, Vince**
*Souls* - Katina Alexis   *h*   71

**Eichord, Jack**
*Iceman* - Rex Miller   *h*   3900
*Slice* - Rex Miller   *h*   3902

**El-Sayed, Ray**
*The Digital Effect* - Steve Perry   *s*   4295

**Ewing, Jude**
*Deadrush* - Yvonne Navarro   *h*   4073

**Falconi, Richard**
*House Haunted* - Al Sarrantonio   *h*   4830

**Fischer, Bernie**
*Sparrowhawk* - Thomas A. Easton   *s*   1725

**Foggia, Larry**
*Master of Lies* - Graham Masterton   *h*   3676

**Francisco, George**
*The Change* - Barry B. Longyear   *s*   3520
*Cross of Blood* - K.W. Jeter   *s*   2909
*Dark Horizon* - K.W. Jeter   *s*   2910

**Gentry, Robert**
*Vespers* - Jeff Rovin   *h*   4688

**Greer, Mitchell**
*Bitter Blood* - Karen E. Taylor   *h*   5405
*Blood Secrets* - Karen E. Taylor   *h*   5406
*Blood Ties* - Karen E. Taylor   *h*   5407

**Grobowski, Nolan**
*Terminal Games* - Cole Perriman   *s*   4283

**Hamilton, Gil "the Arm"**
*Flatlander* - Larry Niven   *s*   4121

**Holmes, Harry**
*Root of All Evil* - David A. Farrow   *h*   1888

**Hull, Jake**
*Night Hunter* - Michael Reaves   *h*   4496

**Janeway, Lewis**
*Trinity Grove* - David van Meter Smith   *h*   5112

**Jones, George**
*Shade of Pale* - Greg Kihn   *h*   3104

**Jones, Sibyl**
*Pollen* - Jeff Noon   *s*   4135

**Kessler, Kevin**
*The Book of the Damned* - D.A. Fowler   *h*   2022

**Kettering, Brian**
*Doomstalker* - Gary Brandner   *h*   661

**Kirby, Erin**
*The Asylum* - John E. Ames   *h*   93

**Larue, Andy**
*Manjinn Moon* - Denise Vitola   *s*   5576

**LaRue, Andy**
*Opalite Moon* - Denise Vitola   *f*   5577

**Lauzon, Gary**
*Cold Eye* - Giles Blunt   *h*   556

**Leventhal, Dan**
*The Nine Lives of Catseye Gomez* - Simon Hawke   *f*   2620

**MacKenzie, David**
*Heathen* - Shaun Hutson   *h*   2816

**March, Xavier**
*Fatherland* - Robert Harris   *s*   2564

**Mayer, Steve**
*The Need* - Andrew Neiderman   *h*   4089

**McGann, Jennifer**
*Nightmare, with Angel* - Stephen Gallagher   *h*   2111

**Merrick, Ty**
*Manjinn Moon* - Denise Vitola   *s*   5576
*Opalite Moon* - Denise Vitola   *f*   5577

**Moody, Vernon**
*Cyber Way* - Alan Dean Foster   *s*   2000

**Moon, Frank**
*Sick* - Jay R. Bonansinga   *h*   571

**Morningstar, Thomas**
*From a Whisper to a Scream* - Samuel M. Key   *h*   3093

**Morrison, Alex**
*What's Wrong with Tamara?* - D.A. Fowler   *h*   2025

**Mosely**
*Gabriel Knight: Sins of the Fathers* - Jane Jensen   *h*   2896

**Reid, Dallas**
*Boneman* - Lisa Cantrell   *h*   871

**Rico, Alexandra "Sunny"**
*Finder* - Emma Bull   *f*   769

**Savage, Lyn**
*The Death Prayer* - David Bowker   *h*   602

**Sikes, Matthew**
*Cross of Blood* - K.W. Jeter   *s*   2909
*Dark Horizon* - K.W. Jeter   *s*   2910

**Spartan, John "Demolition Man"**
*Demolition Man* - Richard Osborne   *s*   4229

**Stewart, Christopher James**
*Nightmare's Disciple* - Joseph S. Pulver Jr.   *h*   4449

**Swann, Jackie**
*Boneman* - Lisa Cantrell   *h*   871

**Sykes, Matthew**
*The Change* - Barry B. Longyear   *s*   3520

**Taylor**
*The Night Man* - K.W. Jeter   *h*   2915

**Traven, Mick**
*Lethal Interface* - Mel Odom   *s*   4193

**Trent, Derrick**
*The Stranger* - Eric James Fullilove   *s*   2093

**Troy, Linda Ellen "Sparta"**
*Hide and Seek* - Paul Preuss   *s*   4418
*The Medusa Encounter* - Paul Preuss   *s*   4419

**Valdez, Mark**
*Burning Water* - Mercedes Lackey   *h*   3272

**Wheatley, Don**
*Demon Within* - Dana Reed   *h*   4499

# DETECTIVE—PRIVATE

**Arbuthnot, Aubrey**
*The Devil You Say* - Elisa DeCarlo   *f*   1450
*Strong Spirits* - Elisa DeCarlo   *f*   1451

**Armstrong, Goodwin**
*Inhuman Beings* - Jerry Jay Carroll   *s*   914

**Arthur, Shannon**
*Sister to the Rain* - Melisa Michaels   *f*   3887

**Blackstone, Lance Michaels**
*In the Company of the Mind* - Steven Piziks   *s*   4339

**Blake, Anita**
*Bloody Bones* - Laurell K. Hamilton   *h*   2512
*Blue Moon* - Laurell K. Hamilton   *h*   2513
*Circus of the Damned* - Laurell K. Hamilton   *h*   2515
*Guilty Pleasures* - Laurell K. Hamilton   *f*   2517
*The Killing Dance* - Laurell K. Hamilton   *h*   2518
*The Laughing Corpse* - Laurell K. Hamilton   *f*   2519
*The Lunatic Cafe* - Laurell K. Hamilton   *h*   2520

**Blaze, Christopher**
*Harvest of Blood* - Vincent Courtney   *h*   1213

**Bradley, Kevin**
*Eyes of the Empress* - Camille Bacon-Smith   *f*   285

**Brogan, Steve**
*Witchcraft* - Bill Michaels   *h*   3885

**Burdon, Bill**
*A Question of Time* - Fred Saberhagen   *h*   4772

**Burns, Marty**
*Burning Bright* - J.S. Russell   *h*   4733

**Cardigan, Jake**
*Tek Money* - William Shatner   *s*   4935
*Tek Net* - William Shatner   *s*   4936
*Tek Power* - William Shatner   *s*   4937
*Tek Vengeance* - William Shatner   *s*   4938
*TekLab* - William Shatner   *s*   4939
*TekLords* - William Shatner   *s*   4940
*TekWar* - William Shatner   *s*   4941

**Carver, Reggie**
*Harvest of Blood* - Vincent Courtney   *h*   1213

**Cross, Jordan**
*Dark Channel* - Ray Garton   *h*   2150

**Crumley, Elmo**
*Death Is a Lonely Business* - Ray Bradbury   *h*   619

**Cunningham, Dodge**
*Mastery* - Kelley Wilde   *h*   5802

**Dakota, Bobbie**
*The Bad Place* - Dean R. Koontz   *h*   3202

**Dakota, Julie**
*The Bad Place* - Dean R. Koontz   *h*   3202

**Davis, Evan**
*Eyes of the Empress* - Camille Bacon-Smith   *f*   285

**Deaton, Jim**
*Rockabilly Hell* - William W. Johnstone   *h*   2933

**Dreyer, Sigmund**
*Dydeetown World* - F. Paul Wilson   *s*   5887

**Ellis, Wilson**
*Forget Me Not* - Gene Lazuta   *h*   3375

**Escott, Charles**
*Blood on the Water* - P.N. Elrod   *h*   1791
*Bloodlist* - P.N. Elrod   *h*   1792
*Fire in the Blood* - P.N. Elrod   *h*   1796

**Fleming, Jack**
*Blood on the Water* - P.N. Elrod   *h*   1791
*Bloodlist* - P.N. Elrod   *h*   1792
*A Chill in the Blood* - P.N. Elrod   *h*   1793
*Fire in the Blood* - P.N. Elrod   *h*   1796

**Fletcher, Diane**
*Passion Play* - Sean Stewart   *s*   5276

**Frederickson, Robert "Mongo"**
*The Fear in Yesterday's Rings* - George C. Chesbro   *h*   1007

**Garrett**
*Deadly Quicksilver Lies* - Glen Cook   *f*   1148
*Dread Brass Shadows* - Glen Cook   *f*   1149
*Old Tin Sorrows* - Glen Cook   *f*   1151
*Pretty Pewter Gods* - Glen Cook   *f*   1152
*Red Iron Nights* - Glen Cook   *f*   1153

**Garrett, Carl**
*Cat's Eye* - William W. Johnstone   *h*   2928

**Gently, Dirk**
*The Long Dark Tea-Time of the Soul* - Douglas Adams   *s*   30

**Glibspet**
*Hell on High* - Holly Lisle   *f*   3483

**Gomez, Sid**
*Tek Money* - William Shatner   *s*   4935
*Tek Net* - William Shatner   *s*   4936
*Tek Power* - William Shatner   *s*   4937

*Tek Vengeance* - William Shatner   s   4938
*TekLab* - William Shatner   s   4939
*TekLords* - William Shatner   s   4940

**Haskell, Simon**
*Leap Point* - Kay Kenyon   s   3063

**Holmes, Sherlock**
*The D. Case: The Truth about the Mystery of Edwin Drood* - Charles Dickens   f   1524
*The Holmes-Dracula File* - Fred Saberhagen   h   4767
*Muddle Earth* - John Brunner   s   735
*Seance for a Vampire* - Fred Saberhagen   h   4773
*Sherlock Holmes in Orbit* - Mike Resnick   s   4556

**Horner, Jack**
*Angels & Visitations: A Miscellany* - Neil Gaiman   f   2101

**Hsing, Carlisle**
*Nightside City* - Lawrence Watt-Evans   s   5644

**Juvell, Cat**
*Iron Shadows* - Steven Barnes   f   362

**Kimball, Donald**
*American Psycho* - Brett Easton Ellis   h   1777

**Lavine, Rosalynd "Rosie"**
*Cold Iron* - Melisa Michaels   f   3886
*Sister to the Rain* - Melisa Michaels   f   3887

**London, Teddy**
*All Things under the Moon* - Robert Morgan   h   4002
*The Only Thing to Fear* - Robert Morgan   h   4003
*Some Things Come Back* - Robert Morgan   h   4004
*Some Things Never Die* - Robert Morgan   h   4005
*The Thing That Darkness Hides* - Robert Morgan   h   4006
*The Things That Are Not There* - Robert Morgan   h   4007

**Luke, Jim Bob**
*Cold in July* - Joe R. Lansdale   h   3323

**Mardian, Aiden**
*The Sand Dwellers* - Adam Niswander   h   4112

**Marlowe, Philip**
*The D. Case: The Truth about the Mystery of Edwin Drood* - Charles Dickens   f   1524

**McCallum, Richard**
*The Abductors: Conspiracy* - Jonathan Frakes   s   2034

**McGammon, Clyde**
*Lorelei* - Mark A. Clements   h   1086

**McNihil**
*Noir* - K.W. Jeter   s   2916

**Metcalf, Conrad**
*Gun, with Occasional Music* - Jonathan Lethem   f   3441

**Montgomery, Dirk**
*House of the Sun* - Nigel Findley   s   1936

**Morrell, Charlie**
*Dead of Night* - Alex Abella   h   20

**Nelson, Vicki**
*Blood Debt* - Tanya Huff   h   2792
*Blood Price* - Tanya Huff   h   2793
*Blood Trail* - Tanya Huff   h   2794

**Octavian, Peter**
*Of Masques and Martyrs* - Christopher Golden   h   2258
*Of Saints and Shadows* - Christopher Golden   h   2259

**O'Meara, Beverly**
*In the Cube* - David Alexander Smith   s   5109

**Philippe, Marley**
*Deus X* - Norman Spinrad   s   5171

**Quigley, Joe**
*Lady Slings the Booze* - Spider Robinson   s   4640

**Rajasthan, Nohar**
*Forests of the Night* - S. Andrew Swann   s   5363

**Ramirez, Leni**
*Blood Sport* - Lisa Smedman   f   5096

**Rhodes, Sally**
*The Quorum* - Kim Newman   h   4100

**Russell, Scott**
*Street Magic* - Michael Reaves   f   4497

**Sayler, Catherine**
*Vampire Bytes* - Linda Grant   h   2322

**Sherer, Will**
*Cries of the Children* - Clare McNally   h   3856

**Sloan, Reno**
*The Asylum* - John E. Ames   h   93

**Stavrianos, Nick**
*Quarantine* - Greg Egan   s   1762

**Stow, John**
*Walking the Labyrinth* - Lisa Goldstein   f   2266

**Stroud, Abraham Hale**
*Curse of the Vampire* - Geoffrey Caine   h   832
*Legion of the Dead* - Geoffrey Caine   h   833
*Wake of the Werewolf* - Geoffrey Caine   h   834

**Swag**
*Kill Crazy* - L.S. Riker   s   4590

**Takent, Ben**
*Deep Quarry* - John E. Stith   s   5302

**Talldeer, Jennifer**
*Sacred Ground* - Mercedes Lackey   f   3294

**Travers, Molly**
*Walking the Labyrinth* - Lisa Goldstein   f   2266

**Trowbridge, Howard**
*Killing Frost* - Dan I. Blake   h   514

**Valiant, Eddie**
*Who P-P-Plugged Roger Rabbit?* - Gary K. Wolf   f   5934

**Walthers, Samantha "Sam"**
*Parliament of Blood* - Scott Ciencin   h   1031
*The Vampire Odyssey* - Scott Ciencin   h   1032
*The Wildlings* - Scott Ciencin   h   1034

**Winger**
*Deadly Quicksilver Lies* - Glen Cook   f   1148

**Wolfe, Nero**
*The D. Case: The Truth about the Mystery of Edwin Drood* - Charles Dickens   f   1524

# DIPLOMAT

**Alton, Lew**
*Exile's Song* - Marion Zimmer Bradley   s   632

**Anders, Sarah**
*FreeMaster* - Kris Jensen   s   2897

**Beaver, Bucky**
*McLendon's Syndrome* - Robert Frezza   s   2053

**Brokols, Elver**
*The Lantern of God* - John Dalmas   s   1323

**Burroughs, Mahree**
*Ancestor's World* - A.C. Crispin   s   1259

**Cameron, Bren**
*Foreigner* - C.J. Cherryh   s   990
*Inheritor* - C.J. Cherryh   s   997
*Invader* - C.J. Cherryh   s   998

**Channon**
*Target* - Janet Morris   s   4017

**Christie, Lynne De Lisle**
*Ancient Light* - Mary Gentle   s   2194

**Clay, Tom Red**
*Being Alien* - Rebecca Ore   s   4217
*Human to Human* - Rebecca Ore   s   4219

**Clifford, Doug**
*Ancient Light* - Mary Gentle   s   2194

**Consul**
*Hyperion* - Dan Simmons   s   5055

**Conway, Hugh**
*Shangri-La: The Return to the World of Lost Horizon* - Eleanor Cooney   f   1169

**Courvossier, Raoul**
*The Honor of the Queen* - David Weber   s   5674

**de Sanha Marsao, Aimeric "Ambrose Cruthers"**
*A Million Open Doors* - John Barnes   s   353

**Degahv, Rieka**
*Earth Herald* - Jan Clark   s   1046

**DeLorn, McLaren "Swordfish"**
*Psykosis* - Wilhelmina Baird   s   296

**Ecu**
*Empire's End* - Allan Cole   s   1103
*The Return of the Emperor* - Allan Cole   s   1106

**Enfandin, Rene**
*Bring the Jubilee* - Ward Moore   s   3993

**Fallstar, Chade**
*Assassin's Apprentice* - Robin Hobb   f   2693

**Faure, Georges Henri**
*Moonwar* - Ben Bova   s   588

**Galweigh, Kait**
*Diplomacy of Wolves* - Holly Lisle   f   3481

**Genar-Hofoen, Byr**
*Excession* - Iain M. Banks   s   324

**Gwarha, Ettin**
*Ring of Swords* - Eleanor Arnason   s   210

**Hanna**
*The Master of Chaos* - Terry A. Adams   s   34

**Harpirias of Muldemar**
*The Mountains of Majipoor* - Robert Silverberg   s   5037

**Havzhiva, Yehedarhed**
*Four Ways to Forgiveness* - Ursula K. Le Guin   s   3380

**Hawkes, Benton**
*The Law of War* - William Shatner   s   4931
*Man o' War* - William Shatner   s   4932

**Heslin, Camnor**
*Dancer's Rise* - Jo Clayton   f   1064

**Jefferson, Thomas**
*Arc d'X* - Steve Erickson   f   1835

**Jenkins, Obadiah**
*Branch and Crown* - Gael Baudino   f   389
*O Greenest Branch!* - Gael Baudino   f   394

**Julianus, Marcus**
*The Light Bearer* - Donna Gillespie   f   2229

**KaiSa**
*Dark Water's Embrace* - Stephen Leigh   s   3426

**Kenner, Mark**
*Shadow World* - A.C. Crispin   s   1262

**Kris, Tabrel**
*Exile* - Al Sarrantonio   s   4829

**Lawre, Jocchario**
*The Mage in the Iron Mask* - Brian Thomsen   f   5458

**Lawson, James**
*Design for Great-Day* - Alan Dean Foster   s   2001

**Leones, Giraut**
*Earth Made of Glass* - John Barnes   s   351

**Leones, Margaret**
*Earth Made of Glass* - John Barnes   s   351

**Lindsay, Abelard**
*Schismatrix Plus* - Bruce Sterling   s   5260

**LoDire, Mira**
*Speaking Dreams* - Severna Park   s   4245

**Magnan, Ben**
*Reward for Relief* - Keith Laumer   s   3345

**Martel, Dina**
*Man o' War* - William Shatner   s   4932

**Mayaram, Simon**
*Celestis* - Paul Park   s   4241

**Maz, Mia**
*Cetaganda* - Lois McMaster Bujold   s   758

**McAusland, Louisa**
*Changeweaver* - Margaret Ball   f   313

**Michael**
*Lion Time in Timbuctoo* - Robert Silverberg   s   5036

**Mollari, Londo**
*Day of the Dead* - Neil Gaiman   s   2102

**No'shto-shti-stlen**
*Chanur's Legacy* - C.J. Cherryh   s   981

**Offenhouse, Ralph**
*Debtors' Planet* - William R. Thompson   s   5457

**Organa, Leia**
*The Courtship of Princess Leia* - Dave Wolverton   s   5950
*The Crystal Star* - Vonda N. McIntyre   s   3820
*Dark Force Rising* - Timothy Zahn   s   6052
*The Truce at Bakura* - Kathy Tyers   s   5527
*Zorba the Hutt's Revenge* - Paul Davids   s   1394

**Parent, Tom**
*The Magnificent Wilf* - Gordon R. Dickson   s   1536

**Parz, Jasoft**
*Timelike Infinity* - Stephen Baxter   s   404

**Perez, Anna**
*Ring of Swords* - Eleanor Arnason   s   210

**Renna**
*Glory Season* - David Brin   s   686

**Retief, Jame**
*Reward for Relief* - Keith Laumer   s   3345

**Sarek**
*Sarek* - A.C. Crispin   s   1260

**Sokol**
*Legacy of the Ancients* - Ron Sarti   s   4836

**Spock**
*Avenger* - William Shatner   s   4928

**Sten**
*Vortex* - Allan Cole   s   1108

**Tarrik, Jeniper**
*Earth Herald* - Jan Clark   s   1046

**Thowinda**
*The Shining Ones* - Paul Preuss   s   4421

**Tiam**
*Probe* - Margaret Wander Bonanno   s   569

**Treadway, Jocelyn**
*Shadows on the Sun* - Michael Jan Friedman   s   2069

**Ulrich**
*Storm Warning* - Mercedes Lackey   f   3298

**Vicars, Ned**
*Anti-Ice* - Stephen Baxter   s   398

**Vorkosigan, Miles**
*Borders of Infinity* - Lois McMaster Bujold   s   757
*The Vor Game* - Lois McMaster Bujold   s   764

**Vorpatril, Ivan**
*Cetaganda* - Lois McMaster Bujold   s   758

**Wakandagi, Ptesa "Tesa/Good Eyes"**
*Silent Songs* - A.C. Crispin   s   1264

**Yrarier, Marjorie Westriding**
*Grass* - Sheri S. Tepper   s   5431

## DIRECTOR

**Craven, Wes**
*Wes Craven's New Nightmare* - David Bergantino   h   460

**Dunkle, Simon**
*Flicker* - Theodore Roszak   h   4683

**Greston, Weber**
*A Child Across the Sky* - Jonathan Carroll   h   917

**Gwent, Donson**
*Wordwright*   Tom Deitz   f   1478

**Leiber, Manny**
*A Graveyard for Lunatics* - Ray Bradbury   h   620

**Martin, Dan**
*Goblins* - Vincent Courtney   h   1212

**Mosay**
*Outnumbering the Dead* - Frederik Pohl   s   4352

**Neimark, Max**
*Preternatural* - Margaret Wander Bonanno   s   568

**Nova, Lisa**
*Brand New Cherry Flavor* - Todd Grimson   h   2448

**Popcorn, Selwyn**
*Brand New Cherry Flavor* - Todd Grimson   h   2448

**Reichart, Carlos**
*Boys of Life* - Paul Russell   h   4737

**Richards, Carl**
*Fantastique* - Marvin Kaye   h   3025

**Schoedsack, Ernest "Monte"**
*Dinosaur Summer* - Greg Bear   s   416

**Seagal, Hayley**
*Stage Fright* - Clare McNally   h   3858

**Strayhorn, Philip**
*A Child Across the Sky* - Jonathan Carroll   h   917

**Tallendar, Barry**
*We Open on Venus* - Christopher Stasheff   s   5227

**Whale, James**
*Father of Frankenstein* - Christopher Bram   h   659

**Wong, Fritz**
*A Graveyard for Lunatics* - Ray Bradbury   h   620

**Woodley, Landis**
*Big Rock Beat* - Greg Kihn   h   3102
*Horror Show* - Greg Kihn   h   3103

## DISEMBODIED PERSONALITY

**Allbright, Rod "Seymour"**
*Aliens Stole My Body* - Bruce Coville   s   1217

**Barker, Jenny**
*Dragons on the Town* - Thorarinn Gunnarsson   f   2463

**Batty, Roy**
*Blade Runner: Replicant Night* - K.W. Jeter   s   2907

**Brand, Matthew Tyler**
*The Hot-Wired Dodo* - Jack L. Chalker   s   956

**C**
*Someone to Watch over Me* - Tricia Sullivan   s   5355

**Caiper, Watly**
*The Host* - Peter R. Emshwiller   s   1819
*Short Blade* - Peter R. Emshwiller   s   1820

**Chornyak, Nazareth Joanna**
*Earthsong* - Suzette Haden Elgin   s   1769

**Chucky**
*Child's Play III* - Matthew J. Costello   h   1194

**De Vries, Alicia "Tisiphone"**
*Path of the Fury* - David Weber   s   5680

**Diedrich**
*Satellite Night News* - Jack Hopkins   s   2770

**Edison, Thomas**
*Expiration Date* - Tim Powers   f   4383

**Evans, Philip**
*Mindstar Rising* - Peter F. Hamilton   s   2526

**Grant**
*MagicNet* - John DeChancie   f   1461

**Guthrie, Anson**
*Harvest of Stars* - Poul Anderson   s   127

**Harlan**
*Night of the Living Shark!* - David Bischoff   s   493

**Harrow, Aidan**
*Icarus Descending* - Elizabeth Hand   s   2536

**Ingman, Robert "Shade"**
*Shade's Children* - Garth Nix   s   4130

**Jenna**
*Stranded* - Camarin Grae   s   2295

**Jennings, Richard**
*Darkly the Thunder* - William W. Johnstone   h   2929

**Li, Stefan**
*Ark Liberty* - Will Bradley   s   656

**Louchard, Onidi "Dinah O'Neill"**
*Power Play* - Anne McCaffrey   s   3744

**Outis, Charles "Mr. Charlie"**
*Solis* - A.A. Attanasio   s   272

**Reno**
*Solip: System* - Walter Jon Williams   s   5841

**Riemann, Thomas**
*Permutation City* - Greg Egan   s   1761

**Rimmer, Arnold J.**
*Red Dwarf: Infinity Welcomes Careful Drivers* - Grant Naylor   s   4077

**Rogers, Newman "Warren G. Menso"**
*Circuit of Heaven* - Dennis Danvers   s   1348

**Sack**
*Land O'Goshen* - Charles McNair   s   3855

**Saunders, Reed "Sand"**
*Darkly the Thunder* - William W. Johnstone   h   2929

**Savoy**
*Fools* - Pat Cadigan   s   805

**Shadow**
*The Wizard's Shadow* - Susan Dexter   f   1514

**Tree, Justin**
*Zombie Lover* - Piers Anthony   f   197

**Zeno, Mrs.**
*Max Lakeman and the Beautiful Stranger* - Jon Cohen   f   1098

**Zephkar**
*Stranded* - Camarin Grae   s   2295

## DIVER

**Chase, J. Kelsey**
*Between the Devil and the Deep* - J.M. Morgan   h   3998

**Smith, Sam**
*World Without End* - Molly Cochran   f   1093

## DIVORCED PERSON

**Caraval, Estela**
*Spirits of the Ordinary* - Kathleen Alcala  f  52

**Collins, Trudy**
*Savage Season* - Joe R. Lansdale  h  3332

**Darker, Alex**
*The Chymical Wedding* - Lindsay Clarke  f  1063

**Dyckman, Alicia "Lish"**
*The Swords of Zinjaban* - L. Sprague de
   Camp  s  1418

**Ice**
*Chaos Come Again* - Wilhelmina Baird  s  293

**Jewell, Amy**
*Out of This World* - Lawrence Watt-Evans  f  5645

**Kerickson, Alline Bolton**
*The Imperium Game* - K.D. Wentworth  s  5753

**Kerickson, Arvid Gerald**
*The Imperium Game* - K.D. Wentworth  s  5753

**Martin, Anita**
*Blood Wings* - Stephen Gresham  h  2430

**May, Joanna**
*The Cloning of Joanna May* - Fay Weldon  s  5732

**Meyer, Elizabeth "Payne"**
*Dead Voices* - Rick Hautala  h  2607

**Reith, Fergus**
*The Swords of Zinjaban* - L. Sprague de
   Camp  s  1418

**Sinclair, Felice**
*The Fagin* - Pat Graversen  h  2334

**Soul, Derek**
*A Second Infinity* - Michael D. Weaver  s  5660

**Treadway, Jocelyn**
*Shadows on the Sun* - Michael Jan
   Friedman  s  2069

## DOCTOR

**Adams, Luther**
*Wilderness* - Dennis Danvers  h  1349

**Alegretta**
*Outnumbering the Dead* - Frederik Pohl  s  4352

**Alston, Arthur**
*The Select* - F. Paul Wilson  h  5897

**Althorpe, Cory**
*World Without End* - Molly Cochran  f  1093

**Anderson, Carrie**
*The Vampire Princess* - Michael Romkey  h  4667

**Anderson, Melanie**
*Stinger* - Nancy Kress  s  3243

**Aranow, Jackson**
*Beggars Ride* - Nancy Kress  s  3238

**Ashton, Clark**
*Blood of Innocents* - John Arbucci  h  204

**Austen, James**
*The Angel of Pain* - Brian Stableford  h  5189

**Ayrlyn**
*The Chaos Balance* - L.E. Modesitt Jr.  f  3925

**Banaker, Oliver**
*Curse of the Vampire* - Geoffrey Caine  h  832

**Barrero, Estela**
*The Resurrectionist* - Thomas F.
   Monteleone  h  3965

**Barry, Warren Hubert**
*The Forever Children* - Eric Flanders  h  1944

**Bashir, Julian**
*Armageddon Sky* - L.A. Graf  s  2296

*Time's Enemy* - L.A. Graf  s  2297
*Vengeance* - Dafydd ab Hugh  s  10

**Bateman, Vince**
*The Cartoonist* - Sean Costello  h  1204

**Beaulieu, Antoinette**
*Beyond the Void* - Sean Dalton  s  1331
*The Salukan Gambit* - Sean Dalton  s  1333

**Beckett, Grace**
*Beyond the Pale* - Mark Anthony  f  153

**Benedict, Frederick**
*Insanity, Illinois* - Mark Sumner  s  5358

**Bernay, Leah de**
*Scorpio* - Alex McDonough  s  3802

**bet Ishak, Jehane**
*The Lions of Al-Rassan* - Guy Gavriel Kay  f  3016

**Bladestone, Hugh**
*Fortress on the Sun* - Paul Cook  s  1157

**Blaine, Grant**
*The Dark* - Andrew Neiderman  h  4084

**Blaine, Trish**
*Blood* - Ron Dee  h  1463

**Blaze, Sue**
*Harvest of Blood* - Vincent Courtney  h  1213

**Bosch, Benjamin**
*Troll-Quest* - Rose Estes  f  1841
*Troll-Taken* - Rose Estes  f  1842

**Bowman, Michael**
*Cold Kiss* - Roxanne Longstreet  h  3517
*The Undead* - Roxanne Longstreet  h  3519

**Bowman, Scott**
*The Cartoonist* - Sean Costello  h  1204

**Bradley, Karen**
*Deus-X: A Novel of Spiritual Terror* - Joseph A.
   Citro  h  1037

**Breunner, August**
*Brainstorm* - Steven M. Krauzer  h  3230

**Brill, Willy**
*Silent Witness* - Robert Arthur Smith  h  5136

**Broussard, Andy**
*Blood on the Bayou* - D.J. Donaldson  h  1570

**Broward, Liz**
*Blood Work* - Fay Zachary  h  6050

**Burr, Martyn**
*Stone Angels* - Mike Jefferies  h  2889

**Burrows**
*The Hill of Dreams* - Arthur Machen  h  3595

**Burwin, Addie**
*Stunts* - Charles L. Grant  h  2317

**Cage, Ryland "Ry"**
*Carlucci's Heart* - Richard Paul Russo  s  4748

**Caldicott, Edgar**
*Disturbing Behavior* - John Whitman  h  5789

**Caldwell**
*Call to Battle* - Doug Murray  h  4059

**Campbell, Alan**
*Rapid Growth* - Mary K. Hanner  h  2541

**Canches, Alejandro**
*The Plague Tales* - Ann Benson  s  453

**Candlemas, Richard**
*The Long Midnight* - Daniel Ransom  h  4480

**Carney, Hugh**
*Bright Angel* - John Blair  s  512

**Catledge, Sue**
*Vampire Beat* - Vincent Courtney  h  1214

**Chandler, Vicki**
*Resurrection Dreams* - Richard Laymon  h  3371

**Claiborne, Adam**
*Psycho II* - Robert Bloch  h  541

**Claridge, Kit**
*The Sails of Tau Ceti* - Michael McCollum  s  3771

**Clarkson, Wade**
*Retribution* - Elizabeth Forrest  h  1975

**Cleave, Peter**
*Asylum* - Patrick McGrath  h  3812

**Clementi, Nick**
*Maximum Light* - Nancy Kress  s  3241

**Cline, Kendra**
*Legion of the Dead* - Geoffrey Caine  h  833

**Cofort, Rael**
*Redline the Stars* - Andre Norton  s  4160

**Congemi, Nelson**
*Duplicates* - Andrew Neiderman  h  4086

**Cooke, Caroline**
*Return of the Wolfman* - Jeff Rovin  h  4687

**Crane**
*Lake of the Long Sun* - Gene Wolfe  s  5942
*Nightside the Long Sun* - Gene Wolfe  s  5943

**Crawford, Michael**
*The Stress of Her Regard* - Tim Powers  h  4385

**Croaker**
*Bleak Seasons* - Glen Cook  f  1147
*She Is the Darkness* - Glen Cook  f  1154

**Crowe, Janie**
*The Plague Tales* - Ann Benson  s  453

**Crusher, Beverly**
*All Good Things. . .* - Michael Jan Friedman  s  2061
*Chains of Command* - Bill McCay  s  3767
*Dragon's Honor* - Kij Johnson  s  2922
*Imbalance* - V.E. Mitchell  s  3919
*Intellivore* - Diane Duane  s  1663

**Curry, Rowan Mayfair**
*Lasher* - Anne Rice  h  4570

**Cutter, Hargrave**
*Night Thirst* - Patrick Whalen  h  5770

**Davidson, Charles Joseph**
*Deadly Breed* - T.J. Kirby  h  3153

**de Bernay, Leah**
*Dragon's Blood* - Alex McDonough  s  3799
*Dragon's Claw* - Alex McDonough  s  3800
*Dragon's Eye* - Alex McDonough  s  3801
*Scorpio Descending* - Alex McDonough  s  3803
*Scorpio Rising* - Alex McDonough  s  3804

**Dean**
*I, Said the Fly* - Michael Shea  h  4944

**Dee, John**
*Scorpio Rising* - Alex McDonough  s  3804

**Des Jardins, Nicole**
*Rama II* - Arthur C. Clarke  s  1058

**Dixon, Stephanie**
*Kaleidoscope Eyes* - Graham Watkins  h  5631

**Dolmi, Yarkol**
*Spirits of Cavern and Hearth* - M. Coleman
   Easton  f  1722

**Donovan, Fay**
*Lagoon* - Alison Drake  h  1625

**Douglas, Tom**
*The Baby* - Stephanie Kegan  h  3033

**Dvorak, Daniel**
*Life Support* - Tess Gerritsen  h  2206

**Dycek, Rachel**
*Climbing Olympus* - Kevin J. Anderson  s  102

**Elaira**
*Fugitive Prince* - Janny Wurts  f  6002

**Eliot, John**
*Slave of My Thirst* - Tom Holland　*h*　2742

**Ellair, Noble**
*The Night Seasons* - J.N. Williamson　*h*　5858

**Elliott, Claire**
*Bloodstream* - Tess Gerritsen　*h*　2205

**Ellis, John**
*The Dealings of Daniel Kesserich* - Fritz
　Leiber　*s*　3417

**Evjenial**
*The Light in Exile* - Cheryl J. Franklin　*s*　2038

**Fairchild, Kimberly**
*The Fungus* - Harry Adam Knight　*h*　3192

**Falke, Egidius Maximillian**
*Out of the House of Life* - Chelsea Quinn
　Yarbro　*h*　6018

**Farrell, Gene**
*Kiss of Death* - Daniel Rhodes　*h*　4569

**Feinman, Jacob**
*Specters* - J.M. Dillard　*h*　1555

**Fielder, John**
*Dead in the Water* - Nancy Holder　*h*　2732

**Finley, Sarah**
*Descent* - Ron Dee　*h*　1465

**Fletcher, Evelyn**
*Solomon's Knife* - Victor Koman　*s*　3200

**Fletcher, Howard**
*Contagion* - John David Connor　*h*　1136

**Ford, Marcus**
*Omega* - Patrick Lynch　*h*　3577

**Frank, Victor**
*Mutation* - Robin Cook　*s*　1165

**Frankel, Cathy**
*Cross of Blood* - K.W. Jeter　*s*　2909

**French, Jessica**
*Little Boy Lost* - T.M. Wright　*h*　5992

**Friendly, Tod T.**
*Time's Arrow* - Martin Amis　*s*　96

**Gates, Lawrence**
*Sibs* - F. Paul Wilson　*h*　5898

**Ghere, Rhule**
*The Parafaith War* - L.E. Modesitt Jr.　*s*　3937

**Gibson, John "Gibby"**
*Black Ice* - Pat Graversen　*h*　2333

**Glasser, Stephen**
*Death's Door* - John Wooley　*h*　5969

**Gleason, Tommy**
*Spree* - Lucy Taylor　*h*　5415

**Goldman, David**
*A Reasonable Madness* - Fran Dorf　*h*　1580

**Gordon, Eathan**
*Mirage* - F. Paul Wilson　*h*　5892

**Gray, Simon**
*Archangel* - Michael Conner　*s*　1133

**Gray, Stewart**
*Flying in Place* - Susan Palwick　*h*　4240

**Graydon, Roland**
*Dead Voices* - Rick Hautala　*h*　2607

**Greville, Richard**
*Running Wild* - J.G. Ballard　*h*　320

**Gujerat, Mandvi "Manny"**
*Forests of the Night* - S. Andrew Swann　*s*　5363

**Gull**
*The Women of Whitechapel and Jack the Ripper* - Paul
　West　*h*　5761

**Haggard, Edward**
*Dr. Haggard's Disease* - Patrick McGrath　*h*　3813

**Hakoni, Kyosti Bitterleaf**
*Revolution's Shore* - Alis A. Rasmussen　*s*　4484

**Hansen, Randolf**
*Liquid Diet* - William Tedford　*h*　5419

**Harper, Toby**
*Life Support* - Tess Gerritsen　*h*　2206

**Harrington, Allison**
*Echoes of Honor* - David Weber　*s*　5669

**Harting, William Jameson "Jay"**
*Deadly Breed* - T.J. Kirby　*h*　3153

**Helms, Mary**
*Kids* - Trevor Hoyle　*h*　2787

**Howards, Tom**
*Dark Souls* - Barry Porter　*h*　4369

**Hrluska, Jenn**
*Daughter of Darkness* - Steven Spruill　*h*　5183

**Hunt, Gregory**
*Tech-Heaven* - Linda Nagata　*s*　4066

**Huston, Noah**
*Monday's Child* - Patricia Wallace　*h*　5623

**Inda, Sinykin**
*Mentor* - Kris Jensen　*s*　2898

**Jansen, Karen**
*Blade* - Mel Odom　*h*　4190

**Jeffries, S.C.**
*Voyage to the Red Planet* - Terry Bisson　*s*　508

**Jekyll, Henry**
*The Darker Passions: Dr. Jekyll and Mr. Hyde* -
　Amarantha Knight　*h*　3178
*Mary Reilly* - Valerie Martin　*h*　3654

**Jessan**
*The Price of the Stars* - Debra Doyle　*s*　1604

**Jessan, Nyls**
*Starpilot's Grave* - Debra Doyle　*s*　1606

**K**
*The Face of Another* - Kobo Abe　*h*　19

**Kane, Emily**
*Immortal* - Jason Nickles　*h*　4102

**Kasselman, Philip**
*Button Bright* - Michael Kurland　*h*　3251

**Keating, Michael**
*Night of Broken Souls* - Thomas F.
　Monteleone　*h*　3964

**Keenan, Daniel**
*Minds Apart* - Margaret Davis　*s*　1408

**Kent, Henry**
*Deathscape* - Michael Cecilione　*h*　945

**Ketcham, Roger**
*Pitfall* - Ronald Kelly　*h*　3054

**Kleiffer, Milton**
*Retro Lives* - Lee Grimes　*s*　2446

**Koda-Levin, Anais**
*Dark Water's Embrace* - Stephen Leigh　*s*　3426

**Koscuisko, Andrej**
*An Exchange of Hostages* - Susan R.
　Matthews　*s*　3692
*Prisoner of Conscience* - Susan R.
　Matthews　*s*　3693

**Kramer, Alan**
*Fatal Outcome* - Patricia Wallace　*h*　5622

**Kune**
*The Off Season* - Jack Cady　*f*　820

**Kurtz, Rupert**
*Headhunter* - Timothy Findley　*h*　1939

**Lacroix, Marc**
*Machine* - Rene Belletto　*h*　436

**Lambert, Natalie**
*Forever Knight: A Stirring of Dust* - Susan
　Sizemore　*h*　5078
*Forever Knight: Intimations of Mortality* - Susan M.
　Garrett　*h*　2149

**Lambert, Tom**
*Tomorrow and Tomorrow* - Charles
　Sheffield　*s*　4966

**LaPorte, Eva**
*Bloodletter* - Warren Newton Beath　*h*　426

**Larkin, Samuel**
*Lasher* - Anne Rice　*h*　4570

**Laski, Saul**
*Carrion Comfort* - Dan Simmons　*h*　5040

**Lassiter, Charles**
*Hopeship* - Simon Lang　*s*　3315

**Lawler, Valben**
*The Face of the Waters* - Robert Silverberg　*s*　5029

**Lawrence, Felix**
*Perfect Little Angels* - Andrew Neiderman　*h*　4090

**Leo, Sam**
*Kaleidoscope Eyes* - Graham Watkins　*h*　5631

**Lerner, Reed**
*The Basement* - Bari Wood　*h*　5961

**Leverett, Anthony**
*Lori* - Robert Bloch　*h*　536

**Lioren**
*The Genocidal Healer* - James White　*s*　5779

**Lockhart, Ximena**
*Death of an Adept* - Katherine Kurtz　*f*　3257

**Logan, Janet**
*Deathgift* - Ann Tonsor Zeddies　*s*　6061

**Lord, Suzannah**
*My Soul to Take* - Steven Spruill　*s*　5184

**Lowenstein, David**
*Beauty* - Brian D'Amato　*h*　1334

**Lucille**
*Strange Invasion* - Michael Kandel　*s*　3012

**Lyle, Nona**
*Horses of the Night* - Michael Cadnum　*h*　811

**Lynskey, Lucy**
*The Frighteners* - Michael Jahn　*h*　2856

**MacDonald, Murdo**
*Snowbeast!* - Peter Tremayne　*h*　5482

**Maclean, Ramsey**
*The Matrix* - Jonathan Aycliffe　*h*　280

**Mahafny**
*Finders-Seekers* - Gayle Greeno　*s*　2421

**Mallory, David**
*The Twelfth Child* - Raymond Van Over　*h*　5538

**Marik, Dao**
*Hopeship* - Simon Lang　*s*　3315
*The Trumpets of Tagan* - Simon Lang　*s*　3316

**Marks, Paul**
*The Man Upstairs* - T.L. Parkinson　*h*　4248

**Marling, Oliver Fonteyn**
*Dance of Death* - P.N. Elrod　*h*　1794

**Marlow, Charles**
*Headhunter* - Timothy Findley　*h*　1939

**Marsh, Harold**
*Black Death* - R. Karl Largent　*h*　3337

**Marshak, Arthur**
*Brothers* - Ben Bova　*s*　581

**Marshak, Jessie**
*Brothers* - Ben Bova   s   581

**Massenet, Charles**
*Them* - William W. Johnstone   h   2935

**Mayfair, Rowan**
*The Witching Hour* - Anne Rice   h   4580

**McCoy, Leonard**
*Doctor's Orders* - Diane Duane   s   1659
*Enemy Unseen* - V.E. Mitchell   s   3918
*First Frontier* - Diane Carey   s   902
*Prime Directive* - Judith Reeves-Stevens   s   4514
*Renegade* - Gene DeWeese   s   1511
*Sanctuary* - John Vornholt   s   5597
*Shadows on the Sun* - Michael Jan
   Friedman   s   2069
*Star Trek VI: The Undiscovered Country* - J.M.
   Dillard   s   1556
*Star Trek: The Classic Episodes 1* - James
   Blish   s   526
*Star Trek: The Classic Episodes 2* - James
   Blish   s   527
*Star Trek: The Classic Episodes 3* - James
   Blish   s   528
*Vulcan's Forge* - Susan Shwartz   s   5019

**Meadows, Catherine**
*Batman: Captured by the Engines* - Joe R.
   Lansdale   h   3320

**Medalont**
*Final Diagnosis* - James White   s   5777

**Mespil, Lunzie**
*The Death of Sleep* - Anne McCaffrey   s   3727
*Generation Warrior* - Anne McCaffrey   s   3735

**Michaels, William "Billy"**
*The M.D.: A Horror Story* - Thomas M.
   Disch   h   1561

**Mika**
*Tower of Doom* - Mark Anthony   h   155

**Mike**
*Wolf Flow* - K.W. Jeter   h   2918

**Miller, Desmond**
*Supernova* - Roger MacBride Allen   s   82

**Miloslavic, Dragos**
*St. Vitus Dances Eternity: A Sarajevo Ghost Story* -
   Stewart Von Allmen   h   5585

**Mohamonero**
*Eggheads* - Emily Devenport   s   1500

**Moran, John J.**
*The Lighthouse at the End of the World* - Stephen
   Marlowe   h   3631

**Mordenheim, Victor**
*Mordenheim* - Chet Williamson   h   5847

**Moses, Libby**
*Echoes of Issel* - Diann Thornley   s   5466

**Murchison**
*The Galactic Gourmet* - James White   s   5778

**Mussina, Isabella**
*Night of Broken Souls* - Thomas F.
   Monteleone   h   3964

**Nahvah**
*The Belly of the Wolf* - R.A. MacAvoy   f   3580

**Neumann, Kate**
*Children of the Night* - Dan Simmons   h   5050

**Ngoni, Beatrice**
*A Miracle of Rare Design* - Mike Resnick   s   4550

**Nicholson, Shawna**
*The Unknown Soldier* - Mickey Zucker
   Reichert   s   4525

**Nolan**
*The Silent Stars Go By* - James White   s   5781

**Norman**
*Chaingang* - Rex Miller   h   3899

**O'Keefe, Katie**
*Rulers of Darkness* - Steven Spruill   h   5185

**Opal, Sam**
*The Judas Glass* - Michael Cadnum   h   812

**Patou, Lucy**
*Omega* - Patrick Lynch   h   3577

**Patterson, Red**
*Skyscape* - Michael Cadnum   h   814

**Pearl, Michael**
*The Beyond* - Barry Harrington   h   2556

**Peekner**
*Dead in the West* - Joe R. Lansdale   h   3325

**Penn, Martin**
*Testament* - Valerie J. Freireich   s   2051

**Penninger, Greta**
*Distraction* - Bruce Sterling   s   5256

**Perlman, William**
*Afterage* - Yvonne Navarro   h   4072

**Phillips, Warren**
*Darkness* - John Saul   h   4840

**Plume, Jerry**
*Passive Intruder* - Michael Upchurch   h   5530

**Poole, Michael**
*Koko* - Peter Straub   h   5328

**Porsena, L. Robert**
*Red Orc's Rage* - Philip Jose Farmer   f   1873

**Praisegood, William R.**
*Blood and Roses* - Sharon Bainbridge   h   292

**Purdoe, Tim**
*The Great Wheel* - Ian R. MacLeod   s   3599

**Quiet**
*Bad Brains* - Kathe Koja   h   3193

**Quindell, Mason**
*Bring Me Children* - David Martin   h   3637

**Quong, Sue-Ling**
*The Singers of Time* - Frederik Pohl   s   4354

**Railly, Kathryn**
*12 Monkeys* - Elizabeth Hand   s   2532

**Raleigh, Bryan**
*Nightmare* - S.K. Epperson   h   1832

**Rhodes, Jeffrey**
*Harmful Intent* - Robin Cook   s   1164

**Rich**
*Invitation to the Game* - Monica Hughes   s   2807

**Roberts, Mark**
*Virus* - Graham Watkins   h   5632

**Roswell, Harry I.**
*Summerland* - L. Dean James   f   2865

**Royal, Solomon**
*Butcher* - Rex Miller   h   3898

**Ruquel**
*The Book of the Beast* - Tanith Lee   f   3405

**Samson, Leonard "Doc"**
*What Savage Beast* - Peter David   s   1390

**Sartorius**
*The Waterworks* - E.L. Doctorow   s   1564

**Schreber, D.P.**
*Dark City* - Frank Lauria   h   3351

**Scully, Dana**
*Antibodies* - Kevin J. Anderson   h   99
*Goblins* - Charles L. Grant   s   2309
*Ground Zero* - Kevin J. Anderson   h   106
*Ruins* - Kevin J. Anderson   h   112
*Whirlwind* - Charles L. Grant   f   2320

*The X-Files: Fight the Future* - Chris Carter   h   924

**Seguy, Eva**
*Mutant Star* - Karen Haber   s   2475

**Seward, John**
*Anno Dracula* - Kim Newman   h   4094

**Seward, Jonathan**
*Lord of the Vampires* - Jeanne Kalogridis   h   3005

**Sinclair, Adam**
*The Adept* - Katherine Kurtz   f   3254
*Dagger Magic* - Katherine Kurtz   f   3256
*Death of an Adept* - Katherine Kurtz   f   3257
*The Lodge of the Lynx* - Katherine Kurtz   f   3259
*The Templar Treasure* - Katherine Kurtz   f   3261

**Singleton, Eric**
*Cold White Fury* - Beth Amos   h   97

**Smith, Benjamin Franklin**
*The First Immortal* - James L. Halperin   s   2498

**Smith, Desi "Daisy Smeet"**
*Chaos Come Again* - Wilhelmina Baird   s   293

**Smith, Gary Franklin**
*The First Immortal* - James L. Halperin   s   2498

**Spencer, Simon**
*The Werewolf's Touch* - Cheri Scotch   h   4892

**Stallman, Connie**
*Evil Reincarnate* - Leigh Clark   h   1050

**Standish, Brian**
*Witch Hill* - Marion Zimmer Bradley   h   654

**Starbridge, Thanakar**
*Sugar Rain* - Paul Park   s   4243

**Swinton, Byron**
*Contagion* - John David Connor   h   1136

**Swire, Harvey**
*Twilight* - Peter James   h   2876

**Tachyon**
*Ace in the Hole* - George R.R. Martin   s   3641
*Jokertown Shuffle* - George R.R. Martin   s   3646

**Tate, Augustus "Gus"**
*The Demolished Man* - Alfred Bester   s   476

**Taylor, Shona**
*Medicine Show* - Jody Lynn Nye   s   4172
*Taylor's Ark* - Jody Lynn Nye   s   4176

**Terton, Ama "Ama-la"**
*Nothing Sacred* - Elizabeth Ann
   Scarborough   f   4867

**Thompson, Ewha**
*The Bushido Incident* - Betty Anne
   Crawford   s   1248

**Thorne, Emerson**
*The Hunted* - Kathryn Ptacek   h   4442

**Todd, Emma**
*The Man Who Turned into Himself* - David
   Ambrose   h   89

**Tolnismer, Alysess**
*The Host* - Peter R. Emshwiller   s   1819
*Short Blade* - Peter R. Emshwiller   s   1820

**Trap, Clyde**
*Requiem* - Clifford Mohr   h   3950

**Tremayne, Evan**
*Carnivores* - Penelope Banka Kreps   h   3232

**Uhua-Sorg, Kennet**
*The Ship Who Searched* - Anne McCaffrey   s   3749

**Ulkanov, Andre**
*The Multiplex Man* - James P. Hogan   s   2727

**Usher, Madeline**
*Return to the House of Usher* - Robert Poe   h   4345

**Usher, Roderick**
*Return to the House of Usher* - Robert Poe   h   4345

**Valdheim, M.R.**
*The Multiplex Man* - James P. Hogan   s   2727

**Van Helsing, Abraham**
*Lord of the Vampires* - Jeanne Kalogridis   h   3005

**Van Helsing, Stefan**
*Children of the Vampire* - Jeanne
　Kalogridis   h   3003

**Van Richten, Rudolph**
*I, Strahd* - P.N. Elrod   h   1797

**Vaughan, Elsie Crawford**
*The Lilith Factor* - Jean Paiva   h   4236

**Vertue, Leon**
*Mistworld* - Simon R. Green   s   2372

**Wahler, Jukes**
*Shade of Pale* - Greg Kihn   h   3104

**Wakefield, Nicole des Jardins**
*The Garden of Rama* - Arthur C. Clarke   s   1055

**Walker, Jason**
*The Unknown Soldier* - Mickey Zucker
　Reichert   s   4525

**Wallenberg, Carl**
*Life Support* - Tess Gerritsen   h   2206

**Wallich, Darren**
*Bloom* - Wil McCarthy   s   3761

**Walthers, Danielle "Dani"**
*Parliament of Blood* - Scott Ciencin   h   1031

**Walton, Alex**
*Virus* - Graham Watkins   h   5632

**Ward**
*Not Broken, Not Belonging* - Randy Fox   h   2030

**Warren**
*Act of Love* - Joe R. Lansdale   h   3319

**Watson, John**
*Seance for a Vampire* - Fred Saberhagen   h   4773

**Watson, John H.**
*Sherlock Holmes in Orbit* - Mike Resnick   s   4556

**Waxman, Will**
*Fallen Angels* - Larry Niven   s   4120

**Webb, Fiona**
*Website* - Ray Garton   h   2157

**Wendeen, Wendy**
*Drifter* - William C. Dietz   s   1543

**Wheeler, Matt**
*The Harvest* - Robert Charles Wilson   s   5909

**White**
*The Midnight Club* - Christopher Pike   h   4329

**Winstead, Samantha**
*Cries of the Children* - Clare McNally   h   3856

**Wren, Mason**
*Alien Resurrection* - A.C. Crispin   s   1258

**Xavier, Eileen**
*Godspeed* - Charles Sheffield   s   4957

**Yamaguchi, Motofusa**
*Half Asleep in Frog Pajamas* - Tom
　Robbins   s   4606

**Zobolotsky, Vladimir**
*Indiana Jones and the Genesis Deluge* - Rob
　MacGregor   f   3589

## DRIFTER

**Blackburn, Jimmy**
*Blackburn* - Bradley Denton   h   1489

**Corder, Rachel**
*Jackals* - Charles L. Grant   h   2313

**Dell**
*The Book of Webster's* - J.N. Williamson   h   5853

**Diaz, Lupe**
*The Orchid Eater* - Marc Laidlaw   h   3312

**Hogan, Stan**
*Symphony* - Charles L. Grant   h   2318

**Lavanic, Cruise**
*Night Cruise* - Billie Sue Mosiman   h   4041

**Moonlight, Charlie**
*Thunder Rise* - G. Wayne Miller   h   3895

**O'Hearn, Travis**
*Practical Demonkeeping* - Christopher
　Moore   h   3989

**Palmer, Clay**
*Prototype* - Brian Hodge   h   2704

**Pixie, Ephram**
*Wetbones* - John Shirley   h   5010

**Thorn, Robert**
*Shadow Dance* - Douglas Borton   h   577

**Unger, Alejandro "Alex"**
*Heavy Weather* - Bruce Sterling   s   5258

## DRIVER

**Nygerski, Cyrus "Moondog"**
*Room 13* - Henry Garfield   h   2139

**Scott**
*House of the Sun* - Nigel Findley   s   1936

## DRUG DEALER

**Bathory, David**
*Ancestral Hungers* - Scott Baker   h   303

**Campos, Juana "Juan"**
*Gods of the Well of Souls* - Jack L. Chalker   s   954

**Chung, Feng Hwa**
*Gold Dragon* - Robert Cain   s   831

**Diaz, Sal**
*The Orchid Eater* - Marc Laidlaw   h   3312

**Hakori, Sonny**
*TekWar* - William Shatner   s   4941

**Natter, Cody**
*Creekers* - Edward Lee   h   3391

**Nirobus**
*My Son, the Wizard* - Christopher Stasheff   f   5218

**Watkins, Classy Jack**
*Living Hell* - Ric Meyers   h   3882

**Windemere, Gideon**
*Necrom* - Mick Farren   s   1881

**Zodiac, Jack**
*Captain Jack Zodiac* - Michael Kandel   f   3009

## ECONOMIST

**Proctor, Ottoken**
*Krokodil Tears* - Jack Yeovil   f   6023

## EDITOR

**Albright, Harper**
*The Uncanny* - Andrew Klavan   h   3164

**Aylesworth, Jesse**
*An Exaltation of Larks* - Robert Reed   s   4506

**Bogen, Nancy**
*Bagatelle—Guinevere* - Nancy Bogen   f   558

**Cameron, Jenny**
*Shadow of the Beast* - Margaret L. Carter   h   926

**Camillia**
*Pluto, Animal Lover* - Laren Stover   h   5318

**Carter, Richard**
*The Summoning* - Bentley Little   h   3498

**Chancel, Davey**
*The Hellfire Club* - Peter Straub   h   5326

**Collings, Reed**
*Bleeder* - Gene Lazuta   h   3374

**Corvan, Kim**
*Mars Prime* - William C. Dietz   s   1548

**Dean, Scarlet**
*Cyberbooks* - Ben Bova   s   582

**Game Cat**
*Vurt* - Jeff Noon   s   4136

**Gerome, Pluto Hellbender**
*Pluto, Animal Lover* - Laren Stover   h   5318

**Gunn, Erik**
*Moondog* - Henry Garfield   h   2138

**Hollander, Tom**
*The Children of Hamelin* - Norman Spinrad   s   5170

**Larsen, Alexandra**
*The Gris-Gris Man* - Don Davis   h   1403

**Lowell, Greg**
*The Well* - Michael B. Sirota   h   5077

**Maxwell, Jillian**
*Facade* - Kristine Kathryn Rusch   h   4716

**McIlvane**
*The Waterworks* - E.L. Doctorow   s   1564

**Metcalf, Oliver**
*The Blackstone Chronicles* - John Saul   h   4838

**Mulloy, Cynthia "Lady Cyndara"**
*Knights of the Morningstar* - Melanie Rawn   s   4487

**Murasaki, Rose**
*Suckers* - Anne Billson   h   490

**Owen, Davey**
*Live Girls* - Ray Garton   h   2151

**Parker, Jim**
*University* - Bentley Little   h   3499

**Rick**
*God's Dice* - S. Andrew Swann   f   5364

**Sandford, Nancy**
*The Ragged World: A Novel of the Hefn on Earth* -
　Judith Moffett   s   3943

**Tom**
*Remake* - Connie Willis   s   5873

## EMPATH

**Arry**
*The Dubious Hills* - Pamela Dean   f   1444

**Famber, Leelson**
*Shadow's End* - Sheri S. Tepper   s   5435

**Farhallen, Annadale**
*Children of Enchantment* - Anne Kelleher
　Bush   f   787

**Fletcher, Diane**
*Passion Play* - Sean Stewart   s   5276

**Keller, Yates**
*The War Minstrels* - Karen Haber   s   2477
*Woman Without a Shadow* - Karen Haber   s   2478

**Khan, Rukmani**
*The Khan's Persuasion* - Cynthia Felice   s   1914

**Kr, Duncan**
*Glory's People* - Alfred Coppel   s   1183
*Glory's War* - Alfred Coppel   s   1184

**Noressa**
*Token of Dragonsblood* - Damaris Cole   f   1114

**Ranier**
*The Remarkables* - Robert Reed   s   4507

**Reed, Kayla**
*Sister Blood* - Karen Haber  *s*  2476
*The War Minstrels* - Karen Haber  *s*  2477
*Woman Without a Shadow* - Karen Haber  *s*  2478

**Spark, Charles**
*The Flies of Memory* - Ian Watson  *s*  5635

**Stryke, Modra**
*The Demons at Rainbow Bridge* - Jack L.
   Chalker  *s*  952

**Troi, Deanna**
*Chains of Command* - Bill McCay  *s*  3767
*Guises of the Mind* - Rebecca Neason  *s*  4081
*Imzadi* - Peter David  *s*  1383
*Triangle: Imzadi II* - Peter David  *s*  1388

## ENGINEER

**al-Kharif, Yasin**
*Bright Messengers* - Gentry Lee  *s*  3398

**Al Shei, Katmer**
*Fool's War* - Sarah Zettel  *s*  6079

**Augustus, Caleb**
*Jovah's Angel* - Sharon Shinn  *s*  5001

**Banning, Mitch**
*The Singularity Project* - F.M. Busby  *s*  784

**Barclay, Reginald**
*Requiem* - Michael Jan Friedman  *s*  2067

**Bell Dog**
*Through the Heart* - Richard Grant  *f*  2328

**Borg, Cy**
*Drifter's Run* - William C. Dietz  *s*  1544
*Drifter's War* - William C. Dietz  *s*  1545

**Bradley, Jason**
*The Ghost From the Grand Banks* - Arthur C.
   Clarke  *s*  1056

**Casey, Paddy**
*The Rising* - James Doohan  *s*  1579

**Cedar, Hugh Rock**
*Fossil* - Hal Clement  *s*  1083

**Davison, Wesley**
*Thrill* - Patricia Wallace  *h*  5624

**Doheny, Mike**
*Sunstroke* - David Kagan  *s*  2999

**Dorrin**
*The Magic Engineer* - L.E. Modesitt Jr.  *f*  3933

**Eberhardt, Johann**
*Bright Messengers* - Gentry Lee  *s*  3398

**Faith, Charlie**
*The Embedding* - Ian Watson  *s*  5634

**Forester, Clay**
*The Humanoids* - Jack Williamson  *s*  5865

**Fowke, William G.**
*A Journal of the Flood Year* - David Ely  *s*  1805

**Graham, Jason "Jase"**
*Inheritor* - C.J. Cherryh  *s*  997

**Grimm**
*Inquisitor* - Ian Watson  *s*  5637

**Gunar**
*The Order War* - L.E. Modesitt Jr.  *f*  3936

**Hackworth, John Percival**
*The Diamond Age* - Neal Stephenson  *s*  5253

**Halloran, Jack**
*Hell on High* - Holly Lisle  *f*  3483

**Hamilton, Jack**
*Eye in the Sky* - Philip K. Dick  *s*  1521

**Harmon, Dale**
*Moon Walker* - Rick Hautala  *h*  2610

**Hobart, Rollin**
*The Undesired Princess and the Enchanted Bunny* - L.
   Sprague de Camp  *f*  1419

**Hobson, Peter**
*The Terminal Experiment* - Robert J.
   Sawyer  *s*  4860

**Hutton, George**
*Earth* - David Brin  *s*  685

**Ironsmith, Frank**
*The Humanoids* - Jack Williamson  *s*  5865

**Ishimaru, Kazumasa**
*Through the Arc of the Rain Forest* - Karen Tei
   Yamashita  *f*  6008

**Jacobi, Henry**
*The Engines of God* - Jack McDevitt  *s*  3787

**Jaffey**
*Zeta Base* - Judith Alguire  *s*  74

**Jahns, Carter**
*Mars Underground* - William Hartmann  *s*  2584

**Justen**
*The Order War* - L.E. Modesitt Jr.  *f*  3936

**kai Ortega, Maeru "Kai"**
*Alpha Centauri* - William Barton  *s*  378

**Ko, Melody**
*Nightfeeder* - Judith Reeves-Stevens  *f*  4513
*Shifter* - Judith Reeves-Stevens  *f*  4515

**La Forge, Geordi**
*Balance of Power* - Dafydd ab Hugh  *s*  7
*Dark Mirror* - Diane Duane  *s*  1658
*Doomsday World* - Carmen Carter  *s*  923
*Relics* - Michael Jan Friedman  *s*  2066
*Requiem* - Michael Jan Friedman  *s*  2067
*Vendetta* - Peter David  *s*  1389

**Lanier, Garry**
*Eon* - Greg Bear  *s*  417

**Lassiter, Diane**
*Days of the Dead* - Ashley McConnell  *h*  3774

**Leving, Fredda**
*Caliban* - Roger MacBride Allen  *s*  77

**Magyar, Cherry**
*Slow River* - Nicola Griffith  *s*  2445

**McPherson, Dennis**
*The Gold Coast* - Kim Stanley Robinson  *s*  4632

**Ngu, Emerson**
*Pallas* - L. Neil Smith  *s*  5132

**Nylan**
*The Chaos Balance* - L.E. Modesitt Jr.  *f*  3925
*Fall of Angels* - L.E. Modesitt Jr.  *f*  3930

**O'Brien, Miles**
*Bloodletter* - K.W. Jeter  *s*  2908
*Vengeance* - Dafydd ab Hugh  *s*  10

**Powderdry, Lars**
*The Zap Gun* - Philip K. Dick  *s*  1523

**Quarrels, David**
*The Khan's Persuasion* - Cynthia Felice  *s*  1914

**Raeder, Peter**
*The Rising* - James Doohan  *s*  1579

**Russell, Paul**
*Lake of the Sun* - Wynne Whiteford  *s*  5787

**Sanderheim, Doug**
*Slow Funeral* - Rebecca Ore  *f*  4221

**Santorini, Dan**
*Death Dream* - Ben Bova  *s*  583

**Schwatzendale, Fay**
*Ports of Call* - Jack Vance  *s*  5549

**Scott, Montgomery**
*Crossover* - Michael Jan Friedman  *s*  2063
*Relics* - Michael Jan Friedman  *s*  2066

**Sealock, Brendan**
*Iris* - William Barton  *s*  381

**Severyn, Todd**
*Ill Wind* - Kevin J. Anderson  *s*  108

**Shan, Rafael Zhong "China Mountain"**
*China Mountain Zhang* - Maureen F.
   McHugh  *s*  3817

**Stargard, Conrad**
*Conrad's Quest for Rubber* - Leo
   Frankowski  *s*  2043
*The Flying Warlord* - Leo Frankowski  *s*  2044
*The High-Tech Knight* - Leo Frankowski  *s*  2045
*Lord Conrad's Lady* - Leo Frankowski  *s*  2046
*The Radiant Warrior* - Leo Frankowski  *s*  2047

**Steffan**
*Iron Dragons: Mountains and Madness* - Rose
   Estes  *f*  1839

**Stewart, Bill**
*Weapon* - Robert Mason  *s*  3666

**Thorpe, Thomas**
*Thunder Strike!* - Michael McCollum  *s*  3772

**Topchek, Lilo**
*The Zap Gun* - Philip K. Dick  *s*  1523

**Torres, B'Elanna**
*The Escape* - Dean Wesley Smith  *s*  5113
*The Final Fury* - Dafydd ab Hugh  *s*  9
*Her Klingon Soul* - Michael Jan Friedman  *s*  2064
*Pathways* - Jeri Taylor  *s*  5404

**Traveller, Josiah**
*Anti-Ice* - Stephen Baxter  *s*  398

**Underhill**
*The Humanoids* - Jack Williamson  *s*  5865

**Wakefield, Richard**
*Rama II* - Arthur C. Clarke  *s*  1058

**Winters, Kelly Ann**
*March or Die* - Andrew Keith  *s*  3035

**Ye Armonk, Louise**
*Ring* - Stephen Baxter  *s*  402

**Yeager, Max**
*The Gatekeepers* - Daniel Graham Jr.  *s*  2301

## ENTERTAINER

**Bishop, Nigel**
*The California Voodoo Game* - Larry Niven  *s*  4117

**Bloss, Bibi**
*Skin* - Kathe Koja  *h*  3196

**Chan, Dahlia**
*Cytheria* - Richard Calder  *s*  835

**Daggett, Tace**
*Night Hunter* - Michael Reaves  *h*  4496

**Destin, Elissa**
*Destiny's Carnival* - Warren Murphy  *h*  4057

**Gadded, Elizabeth**
*Prophets for the End of Time* - Marcos
   Donnelly  *f*  1577

**Garcia, Acacia "Panthesilea"**
*The California Voodoo Game* - Larry Niven  *s*  4117

**Impresario, Throng**
*Past Imperative* - Dave Duncan  *f*  1684

**Kateralbin, Crispin**
*The War in the Waste* - Felicity Savage  *f*  4851

**Kayrlis**
*Ancient Games* - Scott Ciencin  *f*  1028

**Khuzud, Kami**
*D'Shai* - Joel Rosenberg  *f*  4670

**Komus**
*Song of the Gargoyle* - Zilpha Keatley
Snyder  f  5153

**Michaelson, Hari**
*Heroes Die* - Matthew Woodring Stover  s  5319

**Miranda, Carmen**
*Carmen Miranda's Ghost Is Haunting Space Station
Three* - Don Sakers  s  4785

**O'Brien, Coley**
*Destiny's Carnival* - Warren Murphy  h  4057

**Performer**
*Puppet Master* - Barry T. Hawkins  h  2632

**Rackstraw, Jeremiah**
*Escardy Gap* - Peter Crowther  h  1282

**Rhys-Whitney, Harper**
*The Fear in Yesterday's Rings* - George C.
Chesbro  h  1007

**Rylus**
*When the Gods Are Silent* - Jane M.
Lindskold  f  3477

**Sathilda**
*Conan the Gladiator* - Leonard Carpenter  f  907

**Shellabarger, Vince**
*Dinosaur Summer* - Greg Bear  s  416

**Sinclair, Monique**
*Sacred Prey* - Vivian Schilling  h  4875

**Toei, Rei**
*Idoru* - William Gibson  s  2218

**Zooty**
*Day of the Dead* - Neil Gaiman  s  2102

## EQUESTRIAN

**Grenlaarin, Karah**
*The Rose Sea* - S.M. Stirling  f  5296

## EXPATRIATE

**Freds**
*Escape From Kathmandu* - Kim Stanley
Robinson  s  4630

**George**
*Escape From Kathmandu* - Kim Stanley
Robinson  s  4630

**Guglioli, Johnny**
*White Queen* - Gwyneth Jones  s  2955

## EXPERIMENTAL SUBJECT

**Barchar, Jason "Jase" Lee**
*Naked to the Stars/The Alien Way* - Gordon R.
Dickson  s  1537

**Barnes, Parker**
*Virtuosity* - Terry Bisson  s  507

**Billy the Kid**
*The Illegal Rebirth of Billy the Kid* - Rebecca
Ore  s  4220

**The Brown Oxford**
*The Collected Stories of Philip K. Dick, Volume One:
The Short Happy Life of the Brown Oxford* - Philip
K. Dick  s  1519

**Cozzano, William Anthony**
*Interface* - Stephen Bury  s  781

**De Leone, "Deus X"**
*Deus X* - Norman Spinrad  s  5171

**Develos, Debi**
*Blood* - Ron Dee  h  1463

**Donohue, Gabriela "Gaby"**
*Doc Sidhe* - Aaron Allston  f  85

**Fullin**
*Commitment Hour* - James Alan Gardner  s  2134

**Haflinger, Nickie**
*The Shockwave Rider* - John Brunner  s  736

**Jarrow, Richard**
*The Multiplex Man* - James P. Hogan  s  2727

**Jiang-Tibayan, Nikko**
*The Bohr Maker* - Linda Nagata  s  4064

**Jonson, Kenneth**
*Aggressor Six* - Wil McCarthy  s  3760

**Lieserl**
*Ring* - Stephen Baxter  s  402

**Matalon, Cynthia**
*The Hot-Wired Dodo* - Jack L. Chalker  s  956

**Quare, Joshua Ali**
*Kaleidoscope Century* - John Barnes  s  352

**Ranes, Josev T.**
*Aggressor Six* - Wil McCarthy  s  3760

**Reyes, Adrien**
*Someone to Watch over Me* - Tricia
Sullivan  s  5355

**Rogers, Buck**
*A Life in the Future* - Martin Caidin  s  827

**Royal, Paul**
*Nanoware Time/The Persistence of Vision* - Ian
Watson  s  5638

**Sil**
*Species* - Yvonne Navarro  s  4075

**Stavenger, Douglas**
*Moonrise* - Ben Bova  s  587

**Stewart, Hope**
*Dark of the Eye* - Douglas Clegg  h  1078

**Sutter, Frank**
*Innerverse* - John DeChancie  s  1458

**Tallant, Benno**
*Run for the Stars/Echoes of Thunder* - Harlan
Ellison  s  1788

**Toledo, Harry**
*Burn* - Bill Ransom  s  4476

**Toledo, Rico**
*Burn* - Bill Ransom  s  4476
*ViraVax* - Bill Ransom  s  4478

**Washington, Arlene "Lady El"**
*Lady El* - Jim Starlin  s  5213

## EXPLORER

**Alpha, Pamayers**
*The Weigher* - Eric Vinicoff  s  5574

**Alvin**
*Beyond the Fall of Night* - Arthur C. Clarke  s  1054

**Ansa**
*The Poisoned Lands* - John Maddox
Roberts  f  4619
*Queens of Land and Sea* - John Maddox
Roberts  f  4620

**Anthea**
*I Who Have Never Known Men* - Jacqueline
Harpman  s  2554

**Arak, Bashir**
*The Planet Beyond* - Steve Mudd  s  4043

**Bedlam, Wellen**
*Dragon Tome* - Richard A. Knaak  f  3169

**Blondell, Mark Anthony "Tony"**
*Tyrannosaurus Rex* - J.F. Rivkin  s  4597

**Breanna**
*Zombie Lover* - Piers Anthony  f  197

**Burton, Richard Francis**
*To Your Scattered Bodies Go* - Philip Jose
Farmer  s  1876

**Carson, Aloysius Byron**
*Uncharted Territory* - Connie Willis  s  5875

**Columbus, Christopher**
*Pastwatch: The Redemption of Christopher Columbus* -
Orson Scott Card  s  895

**Conti, Niccolo Dei**
*The Venetian's Wife: A Strangely Sensual Tale of a
Renaissance Explorer, a Computer, and a
Metamorphosis* - Nick Bantock  f  336

**Dain, Benn**
*Mazeway* - Jack Williamson  s  5866

**De Soto, Hernando**
*Tatham Mound* - Piers Anthony  f  191

**Denison, Arthur**
*Dinotopia* - James Gurney  f  2468
*The World Beneath* - James Gurney  f  2469

**Denness, Leonov Opener**
*Mirabile* - Janet Kagan  s  3001

**Endrada, Deirdre "Deedee"**
*Halfway Human* - Carolyn Ives Gilman  s  2237

**Enrique, Dom**
*Mansions of Darkness* - Chelsea Quinn
Yarbro  h  6016

**Ettalira**
*To Fear the Light* - Ben Bova  s  595

**Fawcett, Christine**
*Tyrannosaurus Rex* - J.F. Rivkin  s  4597

**Finriddy, Sarah "Fin"**
*Uncharted Territory* - Connie Willis  s  5875

**Gray Wolf, Josiah**
*Beyond Eden* - J.M. Morgan  s  3999
*Desert Eden* - J.M. Morgan  s  4000

**Gray Wolf, Willow**
*Future Eden* - J.M. Morgan  s  4001

**Greta**
*I Who Have Never Known Men* - Jacqueline
Harpman  s  2554

**Harms, Harry**
*Heaven's Reach* - David Brin  s  687

**Hawk, Carin**
*Ark Liberty* - Will Bradley  s  656

**Hawkins, Danny**
*A Thunder on Neptune* - Gordon Eklund  s  1768

**I**
*I Who Have Never Known Men* - Jacqueline
Harpman  s  2554

**Jamail, Dierdre**
*Delta Pavonis* - Eric Kotani  s  3221

**Kadiya**
*Golden Trillium* - Andre Norton  f  4153

**Kairn**
*The Steel Kings* - John Maddox Roberts  f  4621

**Katelo, Jonathan**
*Beyond Eden* - J.M. Morgan  s  3999

**Katelo, Seth**
*Beyond Eden* - J.M. Morgan  s  3999
*Future Eden* - J.M. Morgan  s  4001

**Kenner, Erin Elizabeth**
*Mother Lode* - Zach Hughes  s  2812

**Law, Guilford**
*Darwinia* - Robert Charles Wilson  s  5906

**Lennox, Xavier William**
*A Miracle of Rare Design* - Mike Resnick  s  4550

**Manan, Mattine "Mattie"**
*Mutagenesis* - Helen Collins  *s*  1116

**Mayland, Gia**
*The Expediter* - J. Brian Clarke  *s*  1062

**Profitt, Dennis**
*Star Precinct* - Kevin D. Randle  *s*  4470

**Reille y Sanchez, Estrellita**
*Contact and Commune* - L. Neil Smith  *s*  5129

**Saari, Juna "Eerin"**
*The Color of Distance* - Amy Thomson  *s*  5461

**St. Ives, Langdon**
*Lord Kelvin's Machine* - James P. Blaylock  *f*  520

**Sidra**
*Future Eden* - J.M. Morgan  *s*  4001

**Sobieski, Josip**
*Conrad's Quest for Rubber* - Leo
  Frankowski  *s*  2043

**Stafford, Alwyn Bryan**
*Mars Underground* - William Hartmann  *s*  2584

**Toch, Van**
*War With the Newts* - Karel Capek  *s*  874

**Weyland, Cadmann**
*Beowulf's Children* - Larry Niven  *s*  4116

**Zhang**
*Shangri-La: The Return to the World of Lost Horizon* -
  Eleanor Cooney  *f*  1169

## FANATIC

**Cayne, Candy**
*Cold Iron* - Melisa Michaels  *f*  3886

**Cornelian, Prime**
*Exile* - Al Sarrantonio  *s*  4829

**Matthews, Gabriel**
*Deathgrip* - Brian Hodge  *h*  2700

**Tscharka, Gerald**
*The Voices of Heaven* - Frederik Pohl  *s*  4356

**Unger, Juanita "Jane"**
*Heavy Weather* - Bruce Sterling  *s*  5258

## FARMER

**Allen**
*The Persistence of Memory* - Karen Ripley  *s*  4592

**al'Thor, Rand**
*The Eye of the World* - Robert Jordan  *f*  2986

**Amelia**
*Return to Isis* - Jean Stewart  *s*  5268

**Bender, Jack**
*Mutants Amok* - Mark Grant  *s*  2325

**Benta**
*Invitation to the Game* - Monica Hughes  *s*  2807

**Berg-Benson, Sephony**
*An Eye for Dark Places* - Norma Marder  *s*  3622

**Cephus**
*Flickering Shadows* - Kwadwo Agymah
  Kamau  *f*  3006

**Coll, Lorand**
*Competition* - Sharon Green  *f*  2355

**Coll, Lorand "Lor"**
*Challenges* - Sharon Green  *f*  2354
*Convergence* - Sharon Green  *f*  2356

**Corlaiys, Aitchley**
*Cathedral of Thorns* - Steven Frankos  *f*  2041

**Cosmo, Jason**
*Dirty Work* - Dan McGirt  *f*  3810
*Jason Cosmo* - Dan McGirt  *f*  3811

**Craven, Dudley**
*Blood Kin* - Ronald Kelly  *h*  3051

**de Marion, Raoul**
*Shaman* - Robert Shea  *f*  4946

**Dorthansdotter, Paksenarrion "Paks"**
*Sheepfarmer's Daughter* - Elizabeth Moon  *f*  3973

**Firinne**
*Faery in Shadow* - C.J. Cherryh  *f*  987

**Flitworth, Renata**
*Reaper Man* - Terry Pratchett  *f*  4399

**Gird**
*Surrender None: The Legacy of Gird* - Elizabeth
  Moon  *f*  3975

**Greeley, Dan**
*The Drylands* - Mary Rosenblum  *s*  4678

**Greene, Cathy**
*The Taking* - Donald Beman  *h*  438

**Harris, Dutch**
*Wake Up Screaming* - Vincent Courtney  *h*  1215

**Hirmin**
*The Wooden Sword* - Lynn Abbey  *f*  18

**Hulhe**
*When the Gods Are Silent* - Jane M.
  Lindskold  *f*  3477

**Lasker, Tom**
*Ancient Shores* - Jack McDevitt  *s*  3786

**MacLean, Henry**
*Other* - Gordon R. Dickson  *s*  1538

**Macurdy, Curtis**
*The Lion of Farside* - John Dalmas  *f*  1324

**McFarland, Henry Lee**
*Petrogypsies* - Rory Harper  *s*  2549

**McMurphy, Robie**
*The Reluctant Sorcerer* - Simon Hawke  *f*  2622

**Meara, Ray**
*Butcher* - Rex Miller  *h*  3898

**Morrow, Rachel**
*A Gift upon the Shore* - M.K. Wren  *s*  5982

**Mulliner, Jasper**
*The Barrens* - F. Paul Wilson  *h*  5884

**Nugent, Efram**
*Girl in Landscape* - Jonathan Lethem  *s*  3440

**Old Mose**
*Over the River & through the Woods* - Clifford D.
  Simak  *s*  5047

**Pink**
*Nanoware Time/The Persistence of Vision* - Ian
  Watson  *s*  5638

**Potter, Evelyn Sylvia**
*Cloven Hooves* - Megan Lindholm  *f*  3470

**Puckett, Max**
*Rama Revealed* - Arthur C. Clarke  *s*  1059

**Rahn**
*They Fly at Ciron* - Samuel R. Delany  *s*  1482

**Redthorn, Jeremy**
*The Face of Apollo* - Fred Saberhagen  *s*  4766

**Roo, Luger**
*The Case of the Police Officer's Cock Ring and the
  Piano Player Who Had No Fingers* - Edward
  Lee  *h*  3388

**Shepherd, Carolyn Crespin**
*Gibbon's Decline and Fall* - Sheri S.
  Tepper  *s*  5430

**Siladri**
*The Painted Alphabet* - Diana Darling  *f*  1356

**Sorensson, Eldon**
*Night Calls* - Katharine Eliska Kimbriel  *h*  3119

**Tanner, Tarleton "Sonny"**
*Promised Land* - Connie Willis  *s*  5872

**Tom**
*The Lizard War* - John Dalmas  *s*  1325

**Tradescant, John**
*Sexing the Cherry* - Jeanette Winterson  *f*  5927

**Troop, Jan**
*Trinity Grove* - David van Meter Smith  *h*  5112

**Valdemar "Val"**
*Wayfinder's Story: The Seventh Book of Lost Swords* -
  Fred Saberhagen  *f*  4777

**Vandervelde**
*In the Land of the Dead* - K.W. Jeter  *h*  2912

## FBI AGENT

**Alvarez, Edward**
*Doomsday Exam* - Nick Pollotta  *f*  4363

**Anderson, Richard**
*Bureau 13* - Nick Pollotta  *f*  4362

**Bayley, James**
*The Silicon Man* - Charles Platt  *s*  4343

**Bellamy, Frank**
*The Ebon Mask* - Richard Lee Byers  *h*  797

**Black, Frank**
*The Frenchman* - Elizabeth Hand  *h*  2534
*Gehenna* - Lewis Gannett  *h*  2114

**Booker, Sam**
*Midnight* - Dean R. Koontz  *h*  3212

**Cavanaugh, Robert**
*Oaths and Miracles* - Nancy Kress  *s*  3242

**Chase, Richard**
*The Devouring* - Douglas D. Hawk  *h*  2615

**Donaher, Michael**
*Bureau 13* - Nick Pollotta  *f*  4362
*Full Moonster* - Nick Pollotta  *f*  4364

**Dunn, Jim**
*The Ebon Mask* - Richard Lee Byers  *h*  797

**Edwardo "Ed"**
*Full Moonster* - Nick Pollotta  *f*  4364

**Fletcher, Lenora**
*The Hanged Man* - T.J. MacGregor  *h*  3594

**Horta, Raul**
*Doomsday Exam* - Nick Pollotta  *f*  4363

**Hubbard, Scott**
*The Eleventh Plague: A Novel of Medical Terror* -
  John S. Marr  *h*  3632

**Jamison, Diane**
*Infectress* - Tom Cool  *s*  1167

**Kavanaugh, Robert**
*Stinger* - Nancy Kress  *s*  3243

**Kersh, Jeremy**
*Naming the Flowers* - Kate Wilhelm  *s*  5809

**Kreident, Craig**
*Lethal Exposure* - Kevin J. Anderson  *s*  110
*Virtual Destruction* - Kevin J. Anderson  *s*  118

**Levitt, Ira**
*Thinning the Predators* - Daina Graziunas  *h*  2341

**McGruder, Jim**
*Bright Shadow* - Elizabeth Forrest  *h*  1971

**Mulder, Fox**
*Antibodies* - Kevin J. Anderson  *h*  99
*Goblins* - Charles L. Grant  *s*  2309
*Ground Zero* - Kevin J. Anderson  *h*  106
*Ruins* - Kevin J. Anderson  *h*  112
*Whirlwind* - Charles L. Grant  *f*  2320
*The X-Files: Fight the Future* - Chris Carter  *h*  924

**Sanders, Kenneth**
*Doomsday Exam* - Nick Pollotta  f  4363

**Scully, Dana**
*Antibodies* - Kevin J. Anderson  h  99
*Goblins* - Charles L. Grant  s  2309
*Ground Zero* - Kevin J. Anderson  h  106
*Ruins* - Kevin J. Anderson  h  112
*Whirlwind* - Charles L. Grant  h  2320
*The X-Files: Fight the Future* - Chris Carter  h  924

**Shedian, Taylor Caroline**
*Souls* - Katina Alexis  h  71

**Shelby, Kathe**
*Father's Little Helper* - Ronald Kelly  h  3052

**Starling, Clarice**
*The Silence of the Lambs* - Thomas Harris  h  2566

**Taylor, Jessica**
*Bureau 13* - Nick Pollotta  f  4362
*Full Moonster* - Nick Pollotta  f  4364

**Turpin, Richard**
*The World of Darkness: Watcher* - Charles L. Grant  h  2321

**Woczniak, Hal**
*The Forever King* - Molly Cochran  f  1092

## FEMINIST

**Amos, Renee**
*Star Sister* - Juanita Coulson  s  1211

**Goblin, Gwenny**
*The Color of Her Panties* - Piers Anthony  f  167

**Tesuawane, Sovawanea "Sophy" a**
*Gibbon's Decline and Fall* - Sheri S. Tepper  s  5430

## FEMME FATALE

**Aedrea**
*Saint Leibowitz and the Wild Horse Woman* - Walter M. Miller Jr.  s  3908

**de Noux, Leanna**
*Leanna: Possession of a Woman* - Marie Kiraly  h  3149

**Fancy, Jan "Jeanette"**
*Succumb* - Ron Dee  h  1468

**Nikki**
*Dark Winds* - Graham Watkins  h  5630

**Walker, Betsy**
*Last Rites* - David Darke  h  1354

## FIANCE(E)

**Addams, Fester**
*Addams Family Values* - Todd Strasser  f  5324

**an Treves, Sheyrena "Rena"**
*Elvenblood* - Andre Norton  f  4150

**Anyr**
*The Sleep of Stone* - Louise Cooper  f  1179

**Brightglade, Douglas**
*Aquamancer* - Don Callander  f  841
*Geomancer* - Don Callander  f  845

**Creslin**
*The Towers of the Sunset* - L.E. Modesitt Jr.  f  3941

**Elionbel**
*Palace of Kings* - Mike Jefferies  f  2887

**Fairburn, Pamela**
*The Ambivalent Magician* - Simon Hawke  f  2616

**Flynn, Maggie**
*Beyond the Gate* - Dave Wolverton  s  5949

**Garlick, Magrat**
*Lords and Ladies* - Terry Pratchett  f  4394

**Gwenhwyfar**
*The Kingmaking* - Helen Hollick  f  2745

**Hazel**
*Belladonna* - Michael Stewart  h  5271

**Hirmin**
*The Wooden Sword* - Lynn Abbey  f  18

**Keleios**
*Nightseer* - Laurell K. Hamilton  f  2521

**Lockhart, Ximena**
*Death of an Adept* - Katherine Kurtz  f  3257

**Lothor**
*Nightseer* - Laurell K. Hamilton  f  2521

**Manstar, Myrn**
*Aquamancer* - Don Callander  f  841
*Geomancer* - Don Callander  f  845

**Mati, Gwendolyn "Gwen"**
*Half Asleep in Frog Pajamas* - Tom Robbins  s  4606

**Matt**
*The Oathbound Wizard* - Christopher Stasheff  f  5219

**Melliandra "Melli"**
*The Baker's Boy* - J.V. Jones  f  2956

**Neville-Smythe, Brian**
*The Dragon and the Djinn* - Gordon R. Dickson  f  1528

**Peldyrin, Alix**
*Stranger at the Wedding* - Barbara Hambly  f  2509

**Quarrels, David**
*The Khan's Persuasion* - Cynthia Felice  s  1914

**Redbird**
*Shaman* - Robert Shea  f  4946

**Shelagh**
*Sweetheart, Sweetheart* - Bernard Taylor  h  5402

**Troi, Deanna**
*Triangle: Imzadi II* - Peter David  s  1388

**Vandermeer, Constance**
*A Wish and a Dream* - Ingrid Weaver  f  5658

**L'var y Smid, Vida**
*The Eyes of God* - Mark Kreighbaum  s  3231
*Palace* - Katharine Kerr  s  3072

**ViKay**
*Hour of the Octopus* - Joel Rosenberg  f  4673

**Worf**
*Triangle: Imzadi II* - Peter David  s  1388

## FILMMAKER

**Brad**
*I, Said the Fly* - Michael Shea  h  4944

**Haller, Buzzy**
*Horror Show* - Greg Kihn  h  3103

**Holdstrom, Roy**
*A Graveyard for Lunatics* - Ray Bradbury  h  620

**My Secret Agent Lover Man**
*Witch Baby* - Francesca Lia Block  f  552

**Seyirshi, Ginbiryol**
*Shadowkill* - Jo Clayton  s  1069
*Shadowplay* - Jo Clayton  s  1070
*Shadowspeer* - Jo Clayton  s  1071

**Thorpe, Leonard**
*Glimmering* - Elizabeth Hand  s  2535

**Tom**
*Remake* - Connie Willis  s  5873

**Worth, Andrew**
*Distress* - Greg Egan  s  1760

## FINANCIER

**Curtis, Richard**
*Dreamer* - Peter James  h  2871

**Ritz**
*Living with the Reptiles* - Roger L. DiSilvestro  s  1563

**Soo, Hannah**
*Take Back Plenty* - Colin Greenland  s  2419

## FIRE FIGHTER

**Nolan, Wulf**
*Borderland: A Novel of Terror* - S.K. Epperson  h  1828

## FISHERMAN

**Alemi**
*The Dolphins of Pern* - Anne McCaffrey  s  3729

**Carmody, Michael**
*Sailor Song* - Ken Kesey  s  3082

**Darling, William Somers "Whip"**
*Beast* - Peter Benchley  h  440

**Fleming, Ed**
*Raven Stole the Moon* - Garth Stein  h  5249

**Paco, Chico**
*Through the Arc of the Rain Forest* - Karen Tei Yamashita  f  6008

**Sargent, Gideon**
*The Innsmouth Heritage* - Brian Stableford  h  5194

## FOREMAN

**Church, Andy**
*Where the Chill Waits* - T. Chris Martindale  h  3658

**Qian**
*China Mountain Zhang* - Maureen F. McHugh  s  3817

## FORTUNE HUNTER

**Pennyman**
*The Last Coin* - James P. Blaylock  f  519

## FOSTER PARENT

**Attila the Hun**
*Attila's Treasure* - Stephan Grundy  f  2453

## FOUNDLING

**Acorna**
*Acorna* - Anne McCaffrey  s  3717

**Adam**
*Child of Shadows* - John Coyne  h  1236

**Alnosha "Nosh"**
*The Hands of Lyr* - Andre Norton  f  4154

**Artos**
*The Dragon's Boy* - Jane Yolen  f  6030

**Bryant, Bonnie**
*The Godsend* - Bernard Taylor  h  5401

**Caitlin**
*The Spellkey Trilogy* - Ann Downer  f  1592

**Douglas, Medoret**
*A Whisper of Time* - Paula E. Downing  s  1595

**Fath, Jaro**
*Night Lamp* - Jack Vance  s  5548

**Floris**
*Out of the Ordinary* - Annie Dalton  f  1330

**Kelly, Ista**
*Night Sky Mine* - Melissa Scott  s  4898

**Penthesilea**
*The Amazon Chronicles* - Jane E.M.
    Robinson  f  4627

**Tristen**
*Fortress in the Eye of Time* - C.J. Cherryh  f  991

**Witch Baby**
*Witch Baby* - Francesca Lia Block  f  552

## FRIEND

**Beasley, Marjorie "Mouse"**
*The Witch Returns* - Phyllis Reynolds
    Naylor  f  4079
*The Witch's Eye* - Phyllis Reynolds Naylor  f  4080

**Brenlek, Parke**
*Reunion on Neverend* - John E. Stith  s  5306

**Caroline**
*Jed the Dead* - Alan Dean Foster  s  2007

**Chen, Laura**
*Resurrection Man* - Sean Stewart  f  5277

**Mancy, Katherine "Kat"**
*Her Monster* - Jeff Collignon  h  1115

**Mordance of Barquist**
*The Queen of Ashes* - Deborah Turner
    Harris  f  2561

**Olaffson, Egil**
*Egil's Book* - C.J. Mills  s  3910

**Patrick**
*The Secret of the Indian* - Lynne Reid Banks  f  332

**Rosa**
*Correspondence* - Sue Thomas  s  5450

**Sander**
*Through the Heart* - Richard Grant  f  2328

**Tummelier, Peter**
*Tap, Tap* - David Martin  h  3640

**Vizuelos, Ramon**
*Meeting the Minotaur* - Carol Dawson  f  1409

## FUGITIVE

**Adams, Frankly**
*Virtual Death* - Shale Aaron  s  5

**Akamu**
*The Bones of Time* - Kathleen Ann Goonan  s  2273

**Amelia**
*Further Adventures* - Jon Stephen Fink  f  1940

**Aregeni, Callion**
*In the Rift* - Marion Zimmer Bradley  f  639

**Avery, Rupert "Roo"**
*Shadow of a Dark Queen* - Raymond E.
    Feist  f  1911

**Bailey, Penelope**
*Soothsayer* - Mike Resnick  s  4557

**Batik**
*Wolf in Shadow* - David Gemmell  s  2191

**Beeblebrox, Zaphod**
*The Illustrated Hitchhiker's Guide to the Galaxy* -
    Douglas Adams  s  29

**Belacqua, Lyra**
*The Subtle Knife* - Philip Pullman  f  4448

**Beneforte, Fiametta**
*The Spirit Ring* - Lois McMaster Bujold  f  763

**Bloocher, Jemmy "Tim Hann"**
*Destiny's Road* - Larry Niven  s  4119

**Brewster, Mike**
*Starswarm* - Jerry Pournelle  s  4379

**Bronwyn**
*Palaces and Prisons* - Ron Miller  f  3904
*Silk and Steel* - Ron Miller  f  3905

**Callen, Kevin**
*Come Before Christ and Murder Love* - Stewart
    Home  f  2754

**Cha'dune, Hezhi Yehd**
*The Blackgod* - J. Gregory Keyes  f  3095

**Chevette**
*Virtual Light* - William Gibson  s  2219

**Chiara**
*The Thirteenth Daughter of the Moon* - Steven
    Nightingale  f  4104

**Conyers, Pamela**
*The Enigma Variations* - John Maddox
    Roberts  s  4618        ·

**Crawford, Michael**
*The Stress of Her Regard* - Tim Powers  h  4385

**Daine, Truro**
*The Night Mayor* - Kim Newman  s  4099

**Danio, Kiera**
*Wheel of Dreams* - Salinda Tyson  f  5529

**Door**
*Neverwhere* - Neil Gaiman  f  2104

**Dorvin, Jan**
*The Sky Lords* - John Brosnan  s  720

**Dredd, Joseph "Judge"**
*Judge Dredd* - Neal Barrett Jr.  s  366

**Elayne**
*The Path of Daggers* - Robert Jordan  f  2989

**Endicott, Carl "Johnson"**
*Delta Search* - William Shatner  s  4930

**Iphigenia, Alusz**
*The Demon Princes: Volume One* - Jack
    Vance  s  5544

**ir Var, Zorn**
*Demon Moon* - Jack Williamson  s  5862

**Jake**
*Further Adventures* - Jon Stephen Fink  f  1940

**Jessa**
*Deathweave* - Cary Osborne  s  4226

**Johnny**
*Johnny Mnemonic* - Terry Bisson  s  505

**Kestrel**
*People of the Sea* - W. Michael Gear  s  2169

**King**
*River Rats* - Caroline Stevermer  s  5267

**Kochevikov, Pyetr**
*Rusalka* - C.J. Cherryh  f  1002

**Larkspur, Evan**
*The Unwound Way* - William Adams  s  35

**Larsdatter, Alea**
*A Wizard in Midgard* - Christopher Stasheff  s  5231

**Lissar, Lissla "Deerskin"**
*Deerskin* - Robin McKinley  f  3844

**Lucian**
*The Arkadians* - Lloyd Alexander  f  67

**Melmoth, Lydia**
*Virtual Death* - Shale Aaron  s  5

**Melmoth, Stamen**
*Virtual Death* - Shale Aaron  s  5

**Murdoch, John**
*Dark City* - Frank Lauria  h  3351

**Naso**
*The Last World* - Christoph Ransmayr  f  4475

**Neal, Porsche**
*Beneath the Gated Sky* - Robert Reed  s  4502

**Nolan, Carly**
*Cyberweb* - Lisa Mason  s  3662

**Novak, Cornell**
*Beneath the Gated Sky* - Robert Reed  s  4502

**Nyateneri**
*The Innkeeper's Song* - Peter S. Beagle  f  409

**Orgoru**
*A Wizard in Peace* - Christopher Stasheff  s  5233

**Oshima, Lynn**
*The Bones of Time* - Kathleen Ann Goonan  s  2273

**Parry, William "Will"**
*The Subtle Knife* - Philip Pullman  f  4448

**Randolph, Dan**
*Empire Builders* - Ben Bova  s  584

**Reed, Kayla**
*Woman Without a Shadow* - Karen Haber  s  2478

**Renar of Dagothrin**
*Lady of Mercy* - Michelle Sagara  f  4784

**Reynolds, Mason Algiers**
*The Hollow Earth: The Narrative of Mason Algiers
    Reynolds of Virginia* - Rudy Rucker  s  4705

**Riva**
*The Eyes of God* - Mark Kreighbaum  s  3231

**Russie, Moishe**
*Worldwar: Tilting the Balance* - Harry
    Turtledove  s  5517

**Ryder**
*Kamikaze L'Amour* - Richard Kadrey  s  2998

**Ryder, Gordon**
*Pirates of the Universe* - Terry Bisson  s  506

**Scorpio**
*Dragon's Blood* - Alex McDonough  s  3799
*Dragon's Claw* - Alex McDonough  s  3800
*Dragon's Eye* - Alex McDonough  s  3801
*Scorpio* - Alex McDonough  s  3802
*Scorpio Descending* - Alex McDonough  s  3803
*Scorpio Rising* - Alex McDonough  s  3804

**Shido, Jamisia "Jamie Capra"**
*This Alien Shore* - C.S. Friedman  s  2059

**Simon, Chuck**
*Haven* - David Peters  f  4304

**Sloan, Philip**
*Come Before Christ and Murder Love* - Stewart
    Home  f  2754

**Stephen "Scribble"**
*Vurt* - Jeff Noon  s  4136

**Tal, Haemas Sennay**
*Moonspeaker* - K.D. Wentworth  s  5754

**Tamar**
*The Alleluia Files* - Sharon Shinn  s  4999

**Telford, Jason**
*This Side of Judgment* - J.R. Dunn  s  1696

**Thompson, Emily**
*The Night Watch* - Sean Stewart  s  5274

**Turkel, Maximillian**
*Mutants Amok* - Mark Grant  s  2325

**Turner, Bud**
*Tombley's Walk* - Crosland Brown  h  723

**Vale, Oliver**
*Buddy Holly Is Alive and Well on Ganymede* - Bradley
  Denton  s  1490

**Villiers, Caroline "Cara Deaver" Tara**
*Night's Pawn* - Tom Dowd  s  1591

**vlith-Arkad, Brandon**
*A Prison Unsought* - Sherwood Smith  s  5139
*Ruler of Naught* - Sherwood Smith  s  5141

**von Darkmoor, Erik**
*Shadow of a Dark Queen* - Raymond E.
  Feist  f  1911

**Windrose, Antryg**
*Dog Wizard* - Barbara Hambly  f  2503

**Winters, Talia**
*Voices* - John Vornholt  s  5598

**Zapata, Xolotl**
*High Aztec* - Ernest Hogan  s  2722

**Zwakh, Ignatz**
*Dead Girls* - Richard Calder  s  837

## GAMBLER

**Blayke, Arcole**
*Exile's Children* - Angus Wells  f  5735

**Bobcat**
*The Blood Jaguar* - Michael H. Payne  f  4271

**Crane, Scott**
*Last Call* - Tim Powers  f  4384

**Daniel**
*The Door to Ambermere* - J. Calvin Pierce  f  4316

**Falkirk, Trey**
*Chariot* - Charles L. Grant  h  2304

**Karaquazian, Jack**
*Blood: A Southern Fantasy* - Michael
  Moorcock  f  3977
*Fabulous Harbors* - Michael Moorcock  f  3981
*The War Amongst the Angels* - Michael
  Moorcock  f  3986

**Knox, Edward**
*The 7th Guest* - Matthew J. Costello  h  1192

**Larice, Aldin**
*The Napoleon Wager* - William R.
  Forstchen  s  1980

**McNamara, Deuce**
*The Six Families* - Nancy Holder  s  2733

**Oakenhurst, Sam**
*Blood: A Southern Fantasy* - Michael
  Moorcock  f  3977

**Rado**
*Thorn and Needle* - Paul B. Thompson  f  5456

**Sanchi**
*Sphynxes Wild* - Esther Friesner  f  2083

**Schwatzendale, Fay**
*Ports of Call* - Jack Vance  s  5549

## GAME WARDEN

**Little Hawk, Jay**
*Crota* - Owl Goingback  h  2251

## GANG MEMBER

**Hart, Lola**
*Random Acts of Senseless Violence* - Jack
  Womack  f  5959

**Iz**
*Random Acts of Senseless Violence* - Jack
  Womack  f  5959

**Jude**
*Random Acts of Senseless Violence* - Jack
  Womack  f  5959

**Lynx**
*Bad Voltage* - Jonathan Littell  s  3491

**Mara**
*Bad Voltage* - Jonathan Littell  s  3491

**Pope, Francisco**
*Cybernetic Jungle* - S.N. Lewitt  s  3449

**Sulvia, Paulo "Jackal"**
*Cybernetic Jungle* - S.N. Lewitt  s  3449

## GARDENER

**Beauty**
*Rose Daughter* - Robin McKinley  f  3847

**Boone, Clayton**
*Father of Frankenstein* - Christopher Bram  h  659

**Faun, Forrest**
*Faun & Games* - Piers Anthony  f  169

**Tanner, Karin**
*Deadweight* - Robert Devereaux  h  1505

## GENETICALLY ALTERED BEING

**Adda**
*Flux* - Stephen Baxter  s  399

**Aenea**
*The Rise of Endymion* - Dan Simmons  s  5059

**Akili**
*Distress* - Greg Egan  s  1760

**Alias**
*Masquerades* - Kate Novak  f  4166

**Angelica, Pearl**
*Tower of the Gods* - Thomas A. Easton  s  1726

**Apolinario, Lot**
*Deception Well* - Linda Nagata  s  4065

**August**
*Becoming Human* - Valerie J. Freireich  s  2049

**Avens, Isobel**
*Signs of Life* - M. John Harrison  s  2580

**Barbtail, Dotson**
*Seeds of Destiny* - Thomas A. Easton  s  1724

**Bashir, Julian**
*Vengeance* - Dafydd ab Hugh  s  10

**Bell, Alice**
*Woodsman* - Thomas A. Easton  s  1727

**Binewski, Olympia**
*Geek Love* - Katherine Dunn  h  1697

**Bishop, Killeen**
*Furious Gulf* - Gregory Benford  s  447

**Bishop, Toby**
*Furious Gulf* - Gregory Benford  s  447

**Blacktop**
*Tower of the Gods* - Thomas A. Easton  s  1726

**Blaze**
*Mississippi Blues* - Kathleen Ann Goonan  s  2274

**Bloat**
*Dealer's Choice* - George R.R. Martin  s  3643
*Jokertown Shuffle* - George R.R. Martin  s  3646

**Blossom, Gypsy**
*Seeds of Destiny* - Thomas A. Easton  s  1724

**Boda**
*Pollen* - Jeff Noon  s  4135

**Brice, Marcer Joseph**
*Imposter* - Valerie J. Freireich  s  2050

**Bridger, Mead**
*Testament* - Valerie J. Freireich  s  2051

**Brik**
*The Middle of Nowhere* - David Gerrold  s  2209

**Cage, Peter**
*Wildlife* - James Patrick Kelly  s  3049

**Cage, Wynne**
*Wildlife* - James Patrick Kelly  s  3049

**Caldwell, John**
*Mojave Wells* - L. Dean James  s  2864

**Camden, Alice "Leisha"**
*Beggars in Spain* - Nancy Kress  s  3237

**Cameron, Dev**
*Warstrider: Netlink* - William H. Keith Jr.  s  3038

**Castanaveras, Denice**
*The Last Dancer* - Daniel Keys Moran  s  3994
*The Long Run* - Daniel Keys Moran  s  3995

**Clarris, Peter**
*Changeling* - Christopher Kubasik  f  3245

**C'mel**
*Norstrilia* - Cordwainer Smith  s  5105

**Cody**
*Black Milk* - Robert Reed  s  4504

**Covington, Diana**
*Beggars and Choosers* - Nancy Kress  s  3236

**Coyote**
*Pollen* - Jeff Noon  s  4135

**Crenson, Croyd "The Sleeper"**
*Black Trump* - George R.R. Martin  s  3642
*Marked Cards* - George R.R. Martin  s  3647
*Turn of the Cards* - Victor Milan  s  3891

**Cross, Tom**
*Greenhouse* - Thomas A. Easton  s  1723

**Darke, Makellen**
*Dancer of the Sixth* - Michelle Shirey
  Crean  s  1254

**DaSilva, Renli**
*The Shapes of Their Hearts* - Melissa Scott  s  4901

**Delilah "Lilah"**
*Jovah's Angel* - Sharon Shinn  s  5001

**Delta, Ralphayers**
*The Weigher* - Eric Vinicoff  s  5574

**Doresh, Barc**
*Stepwater* - L. Warren Douglas  s  1588

**Dorset, Byron**
*Specters of the Dawn* - S. Andrew Swann  s  5368

**Dribble**
*Clipjoint* - Wilhelmina Baird  s  294

**Dura**
*Flux* - Stephen Baxter  s  399

**Elisa**
*The Silent City* - Elisabeth Vonarburg  s  5592

**Endicott, James "Jimmy"**
*Delta Search* - William Shatner  s  4930

**Ethemark**
*City on Fire* - Walter Jon Williams  s  5835

**Fairfax, Aaron Lee**
*Rewind* - Terry England  s  1825

**Farkas, Victor**
*Hot Sky at Midnight* - Robert Silverberg  s  5032

**Francie**
*Naming the Flowers* - Kate Wilhelm  s  5809

**Galele, Tedla**
*Halfway Human* - Carolyn Ives Gilman  s  2237

**G'hana, 'jum**
*The Children Star* - Joan Slonczewski  s  5090

**Gillian**
*Ash Ock* - Christopher Hinz  *s*  2690
*The Paratwa* - Christopher Hinz  *s*  2691

**Girelf**
*Stepwater* - L. Warren Douglas  *s*  1588

**Gomez, Catseye**
*The Nine Lives of Catseye Gomez* - Simon
  Hawke  *f*  2620

**Grizzly**
*Vengeance Strike* - David Robbins  *s*  4604

**Gujerat, Mandvi "Manny"**
*Forests of the Night* - S. Andrew Swann  *s*  5363

**Halton, John**
*Looking for the Mahdi* - N. Lee Wood  *s*  5966

**Hangman**
*Rememory* - John Gregory Betancourt  *s*  481

**Harms, Harry**
*Heaven's Reach* - David Brin  *s*  687

**Hartmann, Gregg**
*Ace in the Hole* - George R.R. Martin  *s*  3641
*Marked Cards* - George R.R. Martin  *s*  3647

**Hazard, Arthur**
*Brain Child* - George Turner  *s*  5491

**Hork**
*Flux* - Stephen Baxter  *s*  399

**Hume, Edna "Aten"**
*GodHeads* - Emily Devenport  *s*  1501

**Hunter, Lucel**
*The Centurion's Empire* - Sean McMullen  *s*  3854

**Ingolfsson, Gwendolyn**
*Drakon* - S.M. Stirling  *s*  5294

**Isham, Evi**
*Emperors of the Twilight* - S. Andrew
  Swann  *s*  5362

**Jagun**
*Golden Trillium* - Andre Norton  *f*  4153

**Jared**
*The Alleluia Files* - Sharon Shinn  *s*  4999

**Jiang-Tibayan, Nikko**
*The Bohr Maker* - Linda Nagata  *s*  4064

**Jodahs**
*Imago* - Octavia E. Butler  *s*  791

**Joreth**
*OtherWhere* - Margaret Wander Bonanno  *s*  566

**Kaa**
*Infinity's Shore* - David Brin  *s*  688

**Khat**
*City of Bones* - Martha Wells  *f*  5748

**Kim, Jenae**
*Lethe* - Tricia Sullivan  *s*  5354

**Kren**
*The Lanterns of God* - Ron Sarti  *s*  4835

**Kullervo, Reede Kulleva**
*The Summer Queen* - Joan D. Vinge  *s*  5572

**Lennox, Xavier William**
*A Miracle of Rare Design* - Mike Resnick  *s*  4550

**Lewis**
*Prisoner of Dreams* - Karen Ripley  *s*  4593
*The Tenth Class* - Karen Ripley  *s*  4594

**Lilisaire**
*The Stars Are Also Fire* - Poul Anderson  *s*  134

**Lilith**
*The Shape-Changer's Wife* - Sharon Shinn  *f*  5002

**Lirion**
*Harvest the Fire* - Poul Anderson  *s*  128

**Lopez, Angelica "Angel" Lorenzo**
*Specters of the Dawn* - S. Andrew Swann  *s*  5368

**Lovelock**
*Lovelock* - Orson Scott Card  *s*  892

**Lucinda**
*The Alleluia Files* - Sharon Shinn  *s*  4999

**Lutz, Klaue**
*Lives of the Monster Dogs* - Kirsten Bakis  *s*  305

**Mahtra**
*Cinnabar Shadows* - Lynn Abbey  *f*  15

**Manx, Leo**
*Proteus Unbound* - Charles Sheffield  *s*  4963

**Marisovna, Cora**
*Climbing Olympus* - Kevin J. Anderson  *s*  102

**Martin, Helix**
*Accidental Creatures* - Anne Harris  *s*  2558

**Mason, Estelle "Lysistrata"**
*Cannon's Orb* - L. Warren Douglas  *s*  1586

**Maude**
*Conrad's Quest for Rubber* - Leo
  Frankowski  *s*  2043

**Meadows, Mark "Captain Trips"**
*Black Trump* - George R.R. Martin  *s*  3642
*Turn of the Cards* - Victor Milan  *s*  3891

**Milo**
*The Sky Lords* - John Brosnan  *s*  720

**Oar**
*Expendable* - James Alan Gardner  *s*  2135

**Oimu, Harriet**
*Celestis* - Paul Park  *s*  4241

**Pan, Miss Scarlet**
*Winterlong* - Elizabeth Hand  *s*  2539

**Phousita**
*The Bohr Maker* - Linda Nagata  *s*  4064

**Pukai, Pualeiokekai**
*Reefsong* - Carol Severance  *s*  4923

**Qox, J'briol**
*Primary Inversion* - Catherine Asaro  *s*  220

**Rache of Scole**
*Blueheart* - Alison Sinclair  *s*  5068

**Rajasthan, Nohar**
*Emperors of the Twilight* - S. Andrew
  Swann  *s*  5362
*Forests of the Night* - S. Andrew Swann  *s*  5363

**Ranji**
*The False Mirror* - Alan Dean Foster  *s*  2004

**Reive**
*AEstival Tide* - Elizabeth Hand  *s*  2533

**Reva**
*Mainline* - Deborah Christian  *s*  1026

**Rolfa**
*The Child Garden* - Geoff Ryman  *s*  4756

**Ryder**
*Black Milk* - Robert Reed  *s*  4504

**Saturna**
*Saturn's Child* - Nichelle Nichols  *s*  4101

**Sharifi, Jennifer**
*Beggars Ride* - Nancy Kress  *s*  3238

**Shaw, John**
*The Divide* - Robert Charles Wilson  *s*  5907

**Shongili, Sean**
*Power Lines* - Anne McCaffrey  *s*  3743

**Sil**
*Species* - Yvonne Navarro  *s*  4075

**Slash**
*Rememory* - John Gregory Betancourt  *s*  481

**Sokol**
*Legacy of the Ancients* - Ron Sarti  *s*  4836

**Soledad, Zeide**
*Cybernetic Jungle* - S.N. Lewitt  *s*  3449

**Stavenger, Douglas**
*Moonwar* - Ben Bova  *s*  588

**Stewart, Genevieve "Genny"**
*Jupiter's Daughter* - Tom Hyman  *s*  2820

**Stigg**
*My Father Immortal* - Michael D. Weaver  *s*  5659

**Styreme, Katharine**
*Celestis* - Paul Park  *s*  4241

**Suida, Frederick**
*Woodsman* - Thomas A. Easton  *s*  1727

**Taya**
*Star Child* - James P. Hogan  *s*  2730

**Tetsami, Kari**
*Partisan* - S. Andrew Swann  *s*  5365
*Profiteer* - S. Andrew Swann  *s*  5366
*Revolutionary* - S. Andrew Swann  *s*  5367

**Thomas, Stephen**
*Nautilus* - Vonda N. McIntyre  *s*  3823

**Tiban, Boris**
*Climbing Olympus* - Kevin J. Anderson  *s*  102

**Torx, BrainGeneral**
*Mutant Hell* - Mark Grant  *s*  2324
*Mutants Amok* - Mark Grant  *s*  2325

**Troy, Linda Ellen "Sparta"**
*The Diamond Moon* - Paul Preuss  *s*  4417
*Hide and Seek* - Paul Preuss  *s*  4418
*The Medusa Encounter* - Paul Preuss  *s*  4419
*The Shining Ones* - Paul Preuss  *s*  4421

**Tsering**
*Lethe* - Tricia Sullivan  *s*  5354

**Tsia**
*Cat Scratch Fever* - Tara K. Harper  *s*  2550

**Two Bears**
*Shadowboxer* - Nick Pollotta  *s*  4366

**Ullrich, Nils**
*Armed Memory* - Jim Young  *s*  6048

**Urt**
*Lords of the Sky* - Angus Wells  *f*  5738

**Valdoria, Sauscony**
*Primary Inversion* - Catherine Asaro  *s*  220

**Vaun**
*Hero* - Dave Duncan  *s*  1680

**Veate**
*The Albino Knife* - Steve Perry  *s*  4288

**Verity**
*Mississippi Blues* - Kathleen Ann Goonan  *s*  2274

**von Sacher, Ludwig**
*Lives of the Monster Dogs* - Kirsten Bakis  *s*  305

**Wali, Linnet**
*Imposter* - Valerie J. Freireich  *s*  2050

**Wandel, Timothy J.**
*Armed Memory* - Jim Young  *s*  6048

**Wanders, Wendy**
*Winterlong* - Elizabeth Hand  *s*  2539

**Wang-mu**
*Xenocide* - Orson Scott Card  *s*  899

**Wellin, Alleluia "Alleya"**
*Jovah's Angel* - Sharon Shinn  *s*  5001

**Wrasselly, Bleth**
*The Wells of Phyre* - L. Warren Douglas  *s*  1589

**Wrasselly, Slith**
*The Wells of Phyre* - L. Warren Douglas  *s*  1589

**Xtasca the Cherub**
*Mother of Plenty* - Colin Greenland  s  2417
*Seasons of Plenty* - Colin Greenland  s  2418

**Yaeylie, Frenna**
*Hand of Prophecy* - Severna Park  s  4244

## GENIUS

**Ahrens, Bleys**
*Other* - Gordon R. Dickson  s  1538

**Brewster, Marvin "Doc"**
*The Ambivalent Magician* - Simon Hawke  f  2616
*The Inadequate Adept* - Simon Hawke  f  2617
*The Reluctant Sorcerer* - Simon Hawke  f  2622

**Cocciolone, Carol Jeanne**
*Lovelock* - Orson Scott Card  s  892

**da Vinci, Leonardo**
*Pasquale's Angel* - Paul J. McAuley  f  3714

**Dead Man**
*Red Iron Nights* - Glen Cook  f  1153

**Dore, Michael**
*Lunar Justice* - Charles L. Harness  s  2545

**Duberville, Myron**
*Outer Space and All That Junk* - Mel
  Gilden  s  2227

**Eklunk, Hans-Bjorn "Mokey/Moke"**
*Psykosis* - Wilhelmina Baird  s  296

**Faust, Johannes "Jack"**
*Jack Faust* - Michael Swanwick  s  5372

**Hazelhof, Cornelia**
*Timeshare* - Joshua Dann  s  1344

**Kalakaua, Cen**
*The Bones of Time* - Kathleen Ann Goonan  s  2273

**Lowrey, Jason**
*Death Dream* - Ben Bova  s  583

**Miller, Quintus**
*Walkers* - Graham Masterton  h  3681

**Mulcahey, Gerald "Jerry"**
*Heavy Weather* - Bruce Sterling  s  5258

**Ned**
*Hope of Earth* - Piers Anthony  s  175

**Okun, Brackish**
*Silent Zone* - Stephen Molstad  s  3952

**Quilp**
*A Game of Universe* - Eric S. Nylund  f  4178

**Rogers, Clive**
*The Tooth Fairy* - Graham Joyce  f  2995

**Rogers, Newman "Warren G. Menso"**
*Circuit of Heaven* - Dennis Danvers  s  1348

**Savage, Clark "Doc" Jr.**
*The Frightened Fish* - Kenneth Robeson  f  4622
*The Jade Ogre* - Kenneth Robeson  f  4623
*White Eyes* - Kenneth Robeson  f  4625

**Seafort, Philip**
*Voices of Hope* - David Feintuch  s  1903

**Sharifi, Jennifer**
*Beggars Ride* - Nancy Kress  s  3238

**T.**
*The Smithsonian Institution* - Gore Vidal  f  5570

**Tweep, Jonathan B.**
*Through the Arc of the Rain Forest* - Karen Tei
  Yamashita  f  6008

## GENTLEMAN

**Aerich of House Lyorn**
*The Phoenix Guards* - Steven Brust  f  747

**Aranow, Jackson**
*Beggars Ride* - Nancy Kress  s  3238

**Calmady, Pollexfen**
*The Architecture of Desire* - Mary Gentle  f  2195

**Khaavren of House Tiassa**
*The Phoenix Guards* - Steven Brust  f  747

**Mardimil, Rion**
*Challenges* - Sharon Green  f  2354
*Competition* - Sharon Green  f  2355

**Watkins, Daniel J.**
*The Golden Nineties* - Lisa Mason  s  3663

**Wooster, Bertie**
*Scream for Jeeves: A Parody* - P.H. Cannon  h  867

## GENTLEWOMAN

**Althea**
*The Forge of Virtue* - Lynn Abbey  f  16

**Door**
*Neverwhere* - Neil Gaiman  f  2104

**Kendry, Alicen**
*Season of Storms* - Ellen Foxxe  f  2032

**Matalon, Cynthia**
*The Hot-Wired Dodo* - Jack L. Chalker  s  956

**Morlock, Endora**
*Madman Run* - David Robbins  s  4600

**Tazendra of House Dzur**
*The Phoenix Guards* - Steven Brust  f  747

**Vorder, Sera**
*The Gnome's Engine* - Teresa Edgerton  f  1742
*Goblin Moon* - Teresa Edgerton  f  1743

**Westbrook, Louisa**
*Flameweaver* - Margaret Ball  f  314

## GIRLFRIEND

**Anica**
*Senor Vivo and the Coca Lord* - Louis de
  Bernieres  f  1411

**Barber, Cissy**
*Land O'Goshen* - Charles McNair  s  3855

**Beaumont, Andrea**
*Mask of the Phantasm* - Geary Gravel  s  2331

**Becky**
*See You Later* - Christopher Pike  f  4332

**Carlisle, Bari**
*Count Geiger's Blues* - Michael Bishop  s  499

**Christensen, Maryanne "Maggie"**
*The Crimson Sky* - Joel Rosenberg  f  4669
*The Silver Stone* - Joel Rosenberg  f  4676

**Cind**
*Empire's End* - Allan Cole  s  1103

**Delores**
*Bride of the Slime Monster* - Craig Shaw
  Gardner  f  2125

**Donna**
*Pirates of the Universe* - Terry Bisson  s  506

**Donohue, Gabriela "Gaby"**
*Doc Sidhe* - Aaron Allston  f  85

**Fava**
*Serpent Catch* - Dave Wolverton  s  5956

**Frydys**
*The Deepest Sea* - Charles Barnitz  f  363

**Gwen**
*Rehearsal for a Renaissance* - Douglas W.
  Clark  f  1045

**Lane, Lois**
*The Death and Life of Superman* - Roger
  Stern  s  5262
*Lois & Clark* - C.J. Cherryh  s  999

**Lavalle, Linda**
*Why Do Birds* - Damon Knight  s  3190

**Loola**
*Night of the Living 'Gator!* - Richard A.
  Lupoff  s  3573
*Night of the Living Rat!* - Debra Doyle  s  1603

**Lucy**
*That's All, Folks!* - Greg Snow  f  5148

**Maler, Vicki**
*Psychosphere* - Brian Lumley  h  3563

**Marian**
*Sherwood* - Parke Godwin  f  2248

**Martine**
*Time and Light* - William Bornefeld  s  574

**McGiven, Mary**
*The Haunt* - John Fogarty  h  1966

**Millicent "Millie"**
*Jumper* - Steven Gould  s  2290

**Qian, San-xiang**
*China Mountain Zhang* - Maureen F.
  McHugh  s  3817

**Sanderson, Merry**
*Wolf and Iron* - Gordon R. Dickson  s  1539

**Six, Nicola**
*London Fields* - Martin Amis  s  95

**Snick, Panthea**
*Dayworld Breakup* - Philip Jose Farmer  s  1869

**Sommers, Serena**
*Forest of the Night* - S.P. Somtow  f  5156

**Taylor, Lura**
*Dumford Blood* - S.K. Epperson  h  1829

**Tinnie**
*Dread Brass Shadows* - Glen Cook  f  1149

## GLADIATOR

**E'non, Caelan**
*Realm of Light* - Deborah Chester  f  1008
*Reign of Shadows* - Deborah Chester  f  1009

**O'Connor, Corbo**
*The Fourth Guardian* - Ronald Anthony
  Cross  s  1273
*The Lost Guardian* - Ronald Anthony Cross  s  1274
*The White Guardian* - Ronald Anthony
  Cross  s  1275

## GOVERNESS

**Claire**
*The Night Watch* - Sean Stewart  f  5274

**Martinique, Speranza**
*Moon Dance* - S.P. Somtow  h  5158

**Sto-Helit, Susan**
*Hogfather* - Terry Pratchett  f  4391

## GOVERNMENT OFFICIAL

**Adler, Mark**
*Ursus* - David Dvorkin  s  1708

**Altman, Gibson**
*Pallas* - L. Neil Smith  s  5132

**Barchar, Jason "Jase" Lee**
*Naked to the Stars/The Alien Way* - Gordon R.
  Dickson  s  1537

**Battacharia, Rustum "Bat"**
*Cold as Ice* - Charles Sheffield  *s*  4950

**Bohlen, Ross**
*This Side of Judgment* - J.R. Dunn  *s*  1696

**Borden, Samantha**
*Dusk* - Ron Dee  *h*  1466

**Byrd, Tom**
*Living Real* - James C. Bassett  *s*  386

**Carri, Michael**
*Man o' War* - William Shatner  *s*  4932

**Cassiday, Robert**
*Otherworld* - Kenneth C. Flint  *h*  1959

**Cavan, Andrew**
*Mirror to the Sky* - Mark S. Geston  *s*  2213

**Chandler, Jeff**
*Deus-X: A Novel of Spiritual Terror* - Joseph A. Citro  *h*  1037

**Chang, Marte**
*Burn* - Bill Ransom  *s*  4476
*ViraVax* - Bill Ransom  *s*  4478

**Cochrane, William**
*Rage of Spirits* - Noel Hynd  *h*  2824

**Coeccias, Aedile**
*Fanuilh* - Daniel Hood  *f*  2757

**Cork, Joe**
*The Faery Convention* - Brett Davis  *f*  1399

**Cormack, Leonard**
*Faraday's Orphans* - N. Lee Wood  *s*  5965

**Dahl, Deha**
*The Last Hawk* - Catherine Asaro  *s*  219

**Dahl, Lars**
*Crystal Line* - Anne McCaffrey  *s*  3724

**Denturian, Maaron**
*Dark Sky Legion* - William Barton  *s*  379

**Drexel, David**
*Firelance* - David Mace  *s*  3586

**Dykes, Joe**
*Operation Damocles* - Oscar L. Fellows  *s*  1916

**Edwards, James "Jay"**
*Men in Black* - Steve Perry  *s*  4298

**Einstein, Albert**
*Einstein's Dreams* - Alan Lightman  *f*  3459

**Elspeth**
*Winds of Change* - Mercedes Lackey  *f*  3304
*Winds of Fate* - Mercedes Lackey  *f*  3305

**Esmelda "Esme"**
*Northlight* - Deborah Wheeler  *s*  5775

**Everett, Radmilla**
*Rewind* - Terry England  *s*  1825

**fab Maelgwyn, Tryffin**
*The Castle of the Silver Wheel* - Teresa Edgerton  *f*  1741

**Falconer, Fay**
*The Painter Knight* - Fiona Patton  *f*  4258

**Fisher, David**
*The Case of the Toxic Spell Dump* - Harry Turtledove  *f*  5497

**Forrest, Winn**
*Half-Light* - Denise Vitola  *s*  5575

**Foskins**
*The Rats* - James Herbert  *h*  2671

**Funcitti, Benito**
*The Man in the Moon Must Die* - Jeff Bredenberg  *s*  665

**Gabriel**
*Aristoi* - Walter Jon Williams  *s*  5834

**Gladstone, Meina**
*The Fall of Hyperion* - Dan Simmons  *s*  5052

**Gregory**
*The Dream Vessel* - Jeff Bredenberg  *s*  664

**Hanks, Deana**
*Invader* - C.J. Cherryh  *s*  998

**Hawkes, Benton**
*The Law of War* - William Shatner  *s*  4931

**Holton, Clare**
*Dream Maker* - W.A. Harbinson  *s*  2542

**Hork**
*Flux* - Stephen Baxter  *s*  399

**Illyan, Simon**
*Memory* - Lois McMaster Bujold  *s*  761

**Jarrod**
*Earthling* - Tony Daniel  *s*  1336

**Jivar, Michael**
*Iceman* - Cynthia Felice  *s*  1913

**Kalvin, Walter**
*Silent Thunder/Universe* - Dean Ing  *s*  2829

**Kay**
*Men in Black* - Steve Perry  *s*  4298

**Kendall, James William**
*Sunstroke* - David Kagan  *s*  2999

**Kintner, Edward**
*Paths to Otherwhere* - James P. Hogan  *s*  2728

**Krystel**
*Hellworld* - Simon R. Green  *s*  2371

**Laidcliff, Cullen**
*Looking for the Mahdi* - N. Lee Wood  *s*  5966

**Lang, Edward Winslow**
*Sheltered Lives* - Charles Oberndorf  *s*  4188

**Lewis, Claude**
*Way Station* - Clifford D. Simak  *s*  5048

**Linn, Holly**
*A Second Infinity* - Michael D. Weaver  *s*  5660

**Marouk, Kemal**
*The Joy Machine* - James Gunn  *s*  2458

**Matsuko, Estelle**
*On Basilisk Station* - David Weber  *s*  5679

**Mazdan, Jennifer "Jennie"**
*Unquenchable Fire* - Rachel Pollack  *f*  4361

**McCullough, Carson**
*The Seraphim Rising* - Elisabeth De Vos  *s*  1442

**Meagar**
*The Outlander: Captivity* - B.J. Salterberg  *s*  4792

**Melmoth, Stamen**
*Virtual Death* - Shale Aaron  *s*  5

**Miro, Roy**
*Dark Rivers of the Heart* - Dean R. Koontz  *h*  3204

**Mornay, Peter**
*Glory's War* - Alfred Coppel  *s*  1184

**Morrisey, Hilda Jeanne**
*The Siege of Eternity* - Frederik Pohl  *s*  4353

**Myklathun, Einar**
*Dragon's Domain* - Thorarinn Gunnarsson  *f*  2461

**na Juriam dro Sarn, Perolys**
*The Queen of Ashes* - Deborah Turner Harris  *f*  2561

**Nanchen, Kedar**
*Exile* - Michael P. Kube-McDowell  *s*  3248

**Nichols, Harford**
*Night of Broken Souls* - Thomas F. Monteleone  *h*  3964

**Nimziki, Albert Alexander**
*Silent Zone* - Stephen Molstad  *s*  3952

**Nobilio, Francis "Frank"**
*Illegal Alien* - Robert J. Sawyer  *s*  4858

**Nomikos, Conrad**
*This Immortal* - Roger Zelazny  *s*  6074

**Overed, Martin**
*To a Highland Nation* - Christopher Rowley  *s*  4698

**Pembun, Jawj Pero**
*Rule Golden and Double Meaning* - Damon Knight  *s*  3189

**Penetanguishene**
*The Queen's Squadron* - R.M. Meluch  *s*  3874

**Perry, Max**
*Summertide* - Charles Sheffield  *s*  4965

**Phoe, Sam**
*Key West 2720 A.D.* - William Eakins  *s*  1720

**Powell, Adrian**
*Indiana Jones and the Dance of the Giants* - Rob MacGregor  *f*  3588

**Primer**
*The Gaia Websters* - Kim Antieau  *s*  198

**Remson, Vincent**
*The Stalk* - Janet Morris  *s*  4016

**Renard, Eris**
*Green Lake* - S.K. Epperson  *h*  1830

**Renya, Jacinta**
*Iceman* - Cynthia Felice  *s*  1913

**Richter**
*Buddy Holly Is Alive and Well on Ganymede* - Bradley Denton  *s*  1490

**Russell, Dale**
*Green Lake* - S.K. Epperson  *h*  1830

**Saigo**
*Aristoi* - Walter Jon Williams  *s*  5834

**St. James, Nicholas**
*The Penultimate Truth* - Philip K. Dick  *s*  1522

**Selius, Overseer**
*Tangled Webs* - Steve Mudd  *s*  4044

**Sheehan, Matt**
*Manhattan Transfer* - John E. Stith  *s*  5303

**Sherwood, Iris "Butcher of Boston"**
*In the Cube* - David Alexander Smith  *s*  5109

**Shiloh, Luna**
*Flies From the Amber* - Wil McCarthy  *s*  3763

**Silk, Venture**
*Spindoc* - Steve Perry  *s*  4300

**Skif**
*Winds of Fate* - Mercedes Lackey  *f*  3305

**Smith**
*Murder at the Galactic Writers' Society* - Janet Asimov  *s*  251

**Soul, Derek**
*A Second Infinity* - Michael D. Weaver  *s*  5660

**Tar'krim, Stereth**
*Guilt-Edged Ivory* - Doris Egan  *s*  1756

**Tharpit, Jaxian**
*The Reaver Road* - Dave Duncan  *f*  1687

**Ticktockman**
*"Repent, Harlequin!" Said the Ticktockman* - Harlan Ellison  *s*  1782

**Truant, Cal**
*Naked to the Stars/The Alien Way* - Gordon R. Dickson  *s*  1537

**Two Feathers, Jimmy "the Injun"**
*Oracle* - Mike Resnick  *s*  4551

**Valarian, Nickolai**
*Red Devil* - David Saperstein  *h*  4816

Valdheim, M.R.
*The Multiplex Man* - James P. Hogan   *s*   2727

Water Spider
*The Night Watch* - Sean Stewart   *f*   5274

Wentworth, Ford
*The Trinity Vector* - Steve Perry   *s*   4302

Wolf, Behrooz "Bey"
*Proteus Unbound* - Charles Sheffield   *s*   4963

Yeager, Galen
*The Sounding Stillness* - Kenneth Von
   Gunden   *s*   5587

## GRANDPARENT

Bat, Charlie
*Missing Angel Juan* - Francesca Lia Block   *f*   550

Bink
*Zombie Lover* - Piers Anthony   *f*   197

Brown, Emma
*The Summer I Shrank My Grandmother* - Elvira
   Woodruff   *f*   5968

Deveraux, Rosalie
*Blood Roots* - Richie Tankersley Cusick   *h*   1300

Grandma Fifi
*Baby Be-Bop* - Francesca Lia Block   *f*   545

Harris, Dutch
*Wake Up Screaming* - Vincent Courtney   *h*   1215

Mandlestein, Gemma Rose
*Briar Rose* - Jane Yolen   *f*   6029

Maya
*The Fifth Sacred Thing* - Starhawk   *f*   5209

Mennym, Tulip
*The Mennyms* - Sylvia Waugh   *f*   5654
*Mennyms Alive* - Sylvia Waugh   *f*   5655

Partridge
*Slow Funeral* - Rebecca Ore   *f*   4221

Wandigaux, Rowena
*Never Land* - Douglas Clegg   *h*   1081

## GUARD

Clayton, Wilbur
*Tunnelvision* - R. Patrick Gates   *h*   2162

Cork, Stan
*Tower of Evil* - James Kisner   *h*   3161

Dad
*Pet Store* - M.T. Coffin   *h*   1097

Edgecomb, Paul
*The Green Mile* - Stephen King   *h*   3134

Elroy, Shannon
*Tower of Evil* - James Kisner   *h*   3161

Garwood, Tony
*Children of the End* - Mark A. Clements   *h*   1084

Ilya
*Firebird* - Mercedes Lackey   *f*   3281

Reandn
*Touched by Magic* - Doranna Durgin   *f*   1705

Shaws, Adams
*The Streeter* - Scott Ian Barry   *h*   373

Sullivan, Richard
*The Forgotten* - Stephen R. George   *h*   2200

Talbot
*When Demons Walk* - Patricia Briggs   *f*   683

Von Rabenaue, Walter
*Lord of the Dark Lake* - Ron Faust   *h*   1894

Wetmore, Percy
*The Green Mile* - Stephen King   *h*   3134

## GUARDIAN

Bandylegs, Ahira
*The Road Home* - Joel Rosenberg   *f*   4674

Bevol, Osraed
*The Meri* - Maya Kaathryn Bohnhoff   *f*   561

Brewster, Mike
*Starswarm* - Jerry Pournelle   *s*   4379

Brita
*Conan the Rogue* - John Maddox Roberts   *f*   4617

Cincinnati, Chime
*Last Refuge* - Elizabeth Ann Scarborough   *f*   4866

Cloud, Nelda
*Quasar* - Jamil Nasir   *s*   4071

Earth
*The Book of Earth* - Marjorie Bradley
   Kellogg   *f*   3044

Endymion, Raul
*Endymion* - Dan Simmons   *s*   5051
*The Rise of Endymion* - Dan Simmons   *s*   5059

Hayaka, Reyna
*Wild Magic* - Jo Clayton   *f*   1072

Helling, Suzanne "Alouzon"
*Dragon Death* - Gael Baudino   *f*   390
*Duel of Dragons* - Gael Baudino   *f*   391

Kadolan "Kade"
*Faery Lands Forlorn* - Dave Duncan   *f*   1677
*Perilous Seas* - Dave Duncan   *f*   1685

Lealor
*Dragon's Queen* - Carol L. Dennis   *f*   1488

Mother Night
*Godmother Night* - Rachel Pollack   *f*   4358

Myrddin
*In the Shadow of the Oak King* - Courtway
   Jones   *f*   2939

Pagemaster
*The Pagemaster* - David Kirschner   *f*   3156

Sess, Medusa "Glory"
*Psychoshop* - Alfred Bester   *s*   477

Terton, Ama "Ama-la"
*Nothing Sacred* - Elizabeth Ann
   Scarborough   *f*   4867

Vanian
*Guardian's Key* - Anne Logston   *f*   3511

## GUIDE

Aburto, Manuel "Manny"
*Tyrannosaurus Rex* - J.F. Rivkin   *s*   4597

al-Hakim, Sharif
*The Calling* - Kathryn Meyer Griffith   *h*   2439

Aurelico, Karvonen
*The Raven Ring* - Patricia C. Wrede   *f*   5978

Bento, Jake
*Atlantis Found* - R. Garcia y Robertson   *s*   2119
*The Virgin and the Dinosaur* - R. Garcia y
   Robertson   *s*   2122

Bix
*Dinotopia* - James Gurney   *f*   2468

Bridger, Gray
*Testament* - Valerie J. Freireich   *s*   2051

Centaur, Cathryn
*Faun & Games* - Piers Anthony   *f*   169

Chanly, Bel, Margasdotter
*The Outskirter's Secret* - Rosemary Kirstein   *s*   3157

D'Noch
*The Book of Water* - Marjorie Bradley
   Kellogg   *f*   3045

Elf, Jenny
*Demons Don't Dream* - Piers Anthony   *f*   168

Freese, Neil
*Snowmen* - Jerry Earl Brown   *s*   725

Gall, Dennis
*Snowmen* - Jerry Earl Brown   *s*   725

Gato, Coyote
*Coyote* - Peter Gadol   *f*   2100

Goosequill
*Milton in America* - Peter Ackroyd   *f*   25

Hali
*Witch and Wombat* - Carolyn Cushman   *f*   1299

Jagun
*Golden Trillium* - Andre Norton   *f*   4153

Johnson, Cloud Hunter
*When Wolves Cry* - Chris N. Africa   *h*   41

Joshua
*Groogleman* - Debra Doyle   *s*   1600

Katelo, Jonathon
*Desert Eden* - J.M. Morgan   *s*   4000

Kathinka
*The Flies of Memory* - Ian Watson   *s*   5635

Kenning, Valerie
*Antarctica* - Kim Stanley Robinson   *s*   4628

Korinaam the Shapeshifter
*The Mountains of Majipoor* - Robert
   Silverberg   *s*   5037

Majicou
*The Wild Road* - Gabriel King   *f*   3120

Marie
*Correspondence* - Sue Thomas   *s*   5450

Moore, Malcolm
*Time Scout* - Robert Asprin   *s*   263

Naguchi, Machiko
*Hunter's Planet* - David Bischoff   *s*   492

Raven of Lao-tzu
*Blood Lines* - William R. Burkett Jr.   *s*   774

Rivers, Reginald
*Rivers of Time* - L. Sprague de Camp   *s*   1417

Rollie
*Sing the Light* - Louise Marley   *s*   3629

Roth, Peter
*Monster* - John Tigges   *h*   5474

Salandra
*Indiana Jones and the Interior World* - Rob
   MacGregor   *f*   3590

Seeker After Patterns
*Beyond the Fall of Night* - Arthur C. Clarke   *s*   1054

Service
*The Remarkables* - Robert Reed   *s*   4507

Summer
*Pigs Don't Fly* - Mary Brown   *f*   727

Tyeewapi, Anevai
*Ground-Ties* - Jane S. Fancher   *s*   1861
*Uplink* - Jane S. Fancher   *s*   1865

Virgil
*Quest for Apollo* - Michael Lahey   *f*   3309

von Mannheim De Soto, Igor
*Cat-A-Lyst* - Alan Dean Foster   *s*   1997

## GUNFIGHTER

Diego
*Time: The Semi-Final Frontier* - Lionel
   Fenn   *s*   1921

**Gerlach, Midas**
*The Bars on Satan's Jailhouse* - Norman
    Partridge   *h*   4251

**Roland**
*The Drawing of the Three* - Stephen King   *h*   3131

**Roland of Gilead**
*The Waste Lands* - Stephen King   *h*   3143
*Wizard and Glass* - Stephen King   *h*   3144

**Shaddock, Tolman**
*Demon Dance* - T. Chris Martindale   *h*   3655

**Stackalee**
*The Bars on Satan's Jailhouse* - Norman
    Partridge   *h*   4251

## GYPSY

**Cigany**
*The Gypsy* - Steven Brust   *f*   744

**Janusz, Ekaterina "Kate" Marya**
*Maia's Veil* - P.K. McAllister   *s*   3707

**Janusz, Pov**
*Maia's Veil* - P.K. McAllister   *s*   3707
*Orion's Dagger* - P.K. McAllister   *s*   3708
*Siduri's Net* - P.K. McAllister   *s*   3709

**Petalo, Vadoma**
*Dead Time* - Richard Lee Byers   *h*   796

**Stefano, Yuri**
*Taltos* - Anne Rice   *h*   4577

**Zagala**
*Yesterday We Saw Mermaids* - Esther
    Friesner   *f*   2086

## HAIRDRESSER

**Vaughn, Rosalyn**
*The Book of the Damned* - D.A. Fowler   *h*   2022

## HANDICAPPED

**Anne**
*The Time Tree* - Enid Richemont   *f*   4585

**Beatrice**
*The Broken Sword* - Molly Cochran   *f*   1091

**Bonivard, Francois**
*Wildlife* - James Patrick Kelly   *s*   3049

**Braganca, Alphonso**
*God's Fires* - Patricia Anthony   *s*   159

**Brodski**
*The Nihilesthete* - Richard Kalich   *h*   3002

**Bustamante, Robby**
*The Hollow Man* - Dan Simmons   *s*   5054

**Carter, Sharon**
*Jacob's Hands* - Aldous Huxley   *f*   2817

**Cat**
*Mistworld* - Simon R. Green   *s*   2372

**Chakliux**
*Song of the River* - Sue Harrison   *f*   2583

**Coal, Hugo**
*The Grotesque* - Patrick McGrath   *h*   3814

**Creeping Sword**
*Spell of Apocalypse* - Mayer Alan Brenner   *f*   672

**Curran, Baal**
*Killobyte* - Piers Anthony   *f*   179

**D'Halldt, Lian**
*Legacies* - Alison Sinclair   *s*   5069

**dunMheric, Mikhyel Rhomandi**
*Ring of Intrigue* - Jane S. Fancher   *f*   1863

**Er'ril**
*Wit'ch Fire* - James Clemens   *f*   1082

**Fileli**
*The Broken Land* - Ian McDonald   *s*   3791

**Formosus, Musculus Herodes**
*Whose Song Is Sung* - Frank Schaefer   *f*   4872

**Gandharva**
*Bhagavati* - Kara Dalkey   *f*   1316

**Gardner, Peter**
*Captain Quad* - Sean Costello   *h*   1203

**Gilman**
*Pigs Don't Fly* - Mary Brown   *f*   727

**Hawson, Jordan**
*The Temper of Wisdom* - Lynn Abbey   *f*   17

**Heather**
*Lorien Lost* - Michael King   *f*   3124

**Holmes, Odetta**
*The Waste Lands* - Stephen King   *h*   3143

**Hunsacker, Patty**
*Blind Hunger* - David Darke   *h*   1352

**Igor**
*Goblins in the Castle* - Bruce Coville   *f*   1218

**Innowen**
*Shadowdance* - Robin Wayne Bailey   *f*   290

**Juvell, Tyler**
*Iron Shadows* - Steven Barnes   *f*   362

**Lannister, Tyrion**
*A Game of Thrones* - George R.R. Martin   *f*   3645

**Little Girl**
*The Mer-Child: A Legend for Children and Other
    Adults* - Robin Morgan   *f*   4008

**Lyim**
*The Seventh Sentinel* - Mary Kirchoff   *f*   3154

**Maddox, Cory**
*The March Hare Network* - Jack L. Chalker   *s*   957

**Majere, Raistlin**
*The Soulforge* - Margaret Weis   *f*   5728

**Maxon, Max**
*Bodyguard* - William C. Dietz   *s*   1542

**Perez, Theresa "Terry"**
*Shadow of the Well of Souls* - Jack L.
    Chalker   *s*   961

**Presteign, Olivia**
*The Stars My Destination* - Alfred Bester   *s*   478

**R-T "Artie"**
*R-T, Margaret, and the Rats of NIMH* - Jane Leslie
    Conly   *f*   1132

**Raim**
*Dark Heart* - Betsy James   *f*   2857

**Rebecca**
*Gate of Darkness, Circle of Light* - Tanya
    Huff   *f*   2797

**Ritz**
*Living with the Reptiles* - Roger L.
    DiSilvestro   *s*   1563

**Robert**
*Legacy of the Ancients* - Ron Sarti   *s*   4836

**Sarah**
*Brother to Dragons, Companion to Owls* - Jane M.
    Lindskold   *f*   3473

**Sarin, Robert**
*The Plague Tales* - Ann Benson   *s*   453

**Singer, Eleal**
*Past Imperative* - Dave Duncan   *f*   1684

**Smedley, Julian**
*Present Tense* - Dave Duncan   *f*   1686

**Stonewall, Annie Casteel**
*Gates of Paradise* - V.C. Andrews   *h*   145

**Sylvarresta, Iome**
*The Runelords: The Sum of All Men* - David
    Farland   *f*   1866

**Tesa "Good Eyes"**
*Silent Dances* - A.C. Crispin   *s*   1263

**Therru**
*Tehanu: The Last Book of Earthsea* - Ursula K. Le
    Guin   *f*   3383

**Toland, Walter**
*Killobyte* - Piers Anthony   *f*   179

**Tremulis, Victor Anthony "Tremble"**
*The Holy Terror* - Wayne Allen Sallee   *h*   4787

**Troys, Taylor Thaddeus "Taytay"**
*Meeting the Minotaur* - Carol Dawson   *f*   1409

**Uhua-Sorg, Kennet**
*The Ship Who Searched* - Anne McCaffrey   *s*   3749

**Voerster, Broni**
*Glory* - Alfred Coppel   *s*   1182

**Winter, Catty**
*Well Wished* - Franny Billingsley   *f*   489

**Winthrop, Montana "Tana"**
*The Earth Saver* - Catherine Wells   *s*   5745

**Wort**
*Tower of Doom* - Mark Anthony   *h*   155

**X(A/N)ᵗʰ "Nimby"**
*Yon Ill Wind* - Piers Anthony   *f*   196

**Ylon**
*Mirror of Destiny* - Andre Norton   *f*   4159

## HANDYMAN

**Barnett, Schuyler "Sky"**
*My Soul to Keep* - Judith Hawkes   *h*   2631

**Buford, Tommy**
*Let There Be Dark* - Allen Lee Harris   *h*   2557

**Clewe, Harry**
*The Blood of Angels* - Stephen Gregory   *h*   2428

**Kane, Bowie**
*Pitfall* - Ronald Kelly   *h*   3054

**Landry, Jack**
*Dark Debts* - Karen Hall   *h*   2494

**Orfindel "Hosea Lincoln"**
*The Fire Duke* - Joel Rosenberg   *f*   4671

**St. George, Joe**
*Dolores Claiborne* - Stephen King   *h*   3130

**Santillanes, Gil**
*Days of the Dead* - Ashley McConnell   *h*   3774

**Singer, John Wolfe**
*Uwharrie* - Eugene E. Pfaff Jr.   *h*   4309

**Skyler**
*Blood Roots* - Richie Tankersley Cusick   *h*   1300

**Sloan, Cotter**
*Makoto* - Kelley Wilde   *h*   5801

**Williams, Billy**
*The Sixth Dog* - Jane Rice   *h*   4582

## HEALER

**Adler, Keisha**
*Owlsight* - Mercedes Lackey   *f*   3292

**Amberdrake**
*The Black Gryphon* - Mercedes Lackey   *f*   3270
*The White Gryphon* - Mercedes Lackey   *f*   3303

**Ash, Hatty**
*Devil's Tower* - Mark Sumner   *f*   5357

**Campbell, Brianne**
*Journeyman Wizard* - Mary Frances
Zambreno  *f*  6057

**Darby, Beacontor "Beau"**
*Into the Fire* - Dennis L. McKiernan  *f*  3834
*Into the Forge* - Dennis L. McKiernan  *f*  3835

**Darian**
*Owlsight* - Mercedes Lackey  *f*  3292

**Davos**
*The Itinerant Exorcist* - Ashley McConnell  *f*  3776

**Dion**
*Shadow Leader* - Tara K. Harper  *f*  2552
*Wolfwalker* - Tara K. Harper  *f*  2553

**Eircelly, Talarrie**
*If Wishes Were Horses* - Anne McCaffrey  *f*  3737

**Ericson, Jacob**
*Jacob's Hands* - Aldous Huxley  *f*  2817

**Erin of Elliath**
*Chains of Darkness, Chains of Light* - Michelle
Sagara  *f*  4781
*Into the Dark Lands* - Michelle Sagara  *f*  4783
*Lady of Mercy* - Michelle Sagara  *f*  4784

**Fyana**
*The Poisoned Lands* - John Maddox
Roberts  *f*  4619

**Herb-Woman**
*Strange Deliverance* - Mary Brown  *s*  728

**Johnson, Lezzie**
*Groogleman* - Debra Doyle  *s*  1600

**Kelene**
*City of the Sorcerers* - Mary H. Herbert  *f*  2673
*Winged Magic* - Mary H. Herbert  *f*  2678

**Leyladin**
*The White Order* - L.E. Modesitt Jr.  *f*  3942

**Madrone**
*The Fifth Sacred Thing* - Starhawk  *f*  5209

**Mama Yaya**
*I, Tituba, Black Witch of Salem* - Maryse
Conde  *f*  1130

**Mami Gros-Jeanne**
*Brown Girl in the Ring* - Nalo Hopkinson  *f*  2771

**Monmart, Kevisson**
*House of Moons* - K.D. Wentworth  *s*  5752
*Moonspeaker* - K.D. Wentworth  *s*  5754

**Myrilandel "Myri"**
*The Dragon's Touchstone* - Irene Radford  *f*  4459

**Nolar**
*Flight of Vengeance* - Andre Norton  *f*  4152

**Oonan**
*The Dubious Hills* - Pamela Dean  *f*  1444

**Pinheiro, Berenice**
*God's Fires* - Patricia Anthony  *s*  159

**Rethia**
*Touched by Magic* - Doranna Durgin  *f*  1705

**Sarai**
*The Children Star* - Joan Slonczewski  *s*  5090

**Sari**
*Branch and Crown* - Gael Baudino  *f*  389

**Saun**
*Athyra* - Steven Brust  *f*  739

**Senungatuk, Clodagh**
*Power Lines* - Anne McCaffrey  *s*  3743

**Shiloh**
*The Halloween Man* - Douglas Clegg  *h*  1080

**Stone, Gloria**
*The Gaia Websters* - Kim Antieau  *s*  198

**Thenike**
*Ammonite* - Nicola Griffith  *s*  2443

**Thuryn, Rhysel**
*The Bastard Prince* - Katherine Kurtz  *f*  3255

**Tris**
*Steal the Dragon* - Patricia Briggs  *f*  682

**Twilla**
*Mirror of Destiny* - Andre Norton  *f*  4159

**Varden**
*Spires of Spirit* - Gael Baudino  *f*  395

# HEALTH CARE PROFESSIONAL

**Ayers, Jane**
*The Illegal Rebirth of Billy the Kid* - Rebecca
Ore  *s*  4220

**Barnes, Nick**
*Reaper* - Ben Mizrich  *h*  3923

**Berquist, Kate**
*Nightmare* - S.K. Epperson  *h*  1832

**Bev**
*My Cousin, My Gastroenterologist* - Mark
Leyner  *s*  3456

**Campbell, Trey**
*Bad Karma* - Andrew Harper  *h*  2548

**Chirwl**
*Medicine Show* - Jody Lynn Nye  *s*  4172

**Crawford, Jonathan**
*The Callahan Touch* - Spider Robinson  *f*  4637

**Dieudonne, Genevieve**
*Anno Dracula* - Kim Newman  *h*  4094

**Frede**
*Orion Among the Stars* - Ben Bova  *s*  589

**Frost, Melanie**
*The Seventh Heart* - Marina Fitch  *f*  1943

**Griffin, Beth**
*Nazareth Hill* - Ramsey Campbell  *h*  861

**Johanna**
*Strange Angels* - Kathe Koja  *h*  3197

**Martina, Jewel**
*Chimera* - Mary Rosenblum  *s*  4677

**Nacker the Teach**
*The Pharaoh Contract* - Ray Aldridge  *s*  63

**Stillwater, Paige**
*Mr. Murder* - Dean R. Koontz  *h*  3213

# HEIR

**Aidan**
*Flight of the Raven* - Jennifer Roberson  *f*  4608

**Alastair**
*The Heirs of Hammerfell* - Marion Zimmer
Bradley  *s*  638

**Anderson, Carter**
*The High House* - James Stoddard  *f*  5311

**Benjarth, Paul**
*The Cloud People* - Robert B. Kelly  *f*  3050

**Blessing, Arthur**
*The Forever King* - Molly Cochran  *f*  1092

**Cannon, Vassily "Bass" James**
*A Plague of Change* - L. Warren Douglas  *s*  1587

**Cheever, Shelby V**
*The Billion Dollar Boy* - Charles Sheffield  *s*  4948

**Chevenga, Fourth**
*Lion's Heart* - Karen Wehrstein  *f*  5683

**Coerlis, Jack-Jax Landsdowne**
*Mid-Flinx* - Alan Dean Foster  *s*  2010

**Conn**
*The Heirs of Hammerfell* - Marion Zimmer
Bradley  *s*  638

**Crowell**
*Iroshi* - Cary Osborne  *s*  4228

**Doresh, Barc**
*Stepwater* - L. Warren Douglas  *s*  1588

**Draus, Morry**
*I Wake From a Dream of a Drowned Star City* - S.P.
Somtow  *s*  5157

**D'Rosselin, Jens Metadi Jessan**
*The Long Hunt* - Debra Doyle  *s*  1602

**Elspeth**
*Winds of Change* - Mercedes Lackey  *f*  3304
*Winds of Fate* - Mercedes Lackey  *f*  3305

**Fundan, Dane**
*The Founder* - Christopher Rowley  *s*  4696

**Gavrilli, David**
*Interface Masque* - Shariann Lewitt  *s*  3453

**Girelf**
*Stepwater* - L. Warren Douglas  *s*  1588

**Hawke**
*Far Harbor* - Melisa C. Michaels  *s*  3888

**Hawken, Garrick**
*Allamanda* - Michael Williams  *f*  5817

**Kelligan, Sam Houston**
*Beachhead* - Jack Williamson  *s*  5859

**Kopal, Jefferson "Jeff"**
*The Cyborg From Earth* - Charles Sheffield  *s*  4952

**Kyl**
*The Dragon Crown* - Richard A. Knaak  *f*  3168

**Little Father**
*Lion Time in Timbuctoo* - Robert Silverberg  *s*  5036

**Lynn, Corbet**
*Winter Rose* - Patricia A. McKillip  *f*  3843

**Lyonz**
*Drum Warning* - Jo Clayton  *f*  1066

**mac Brian, Murcha**
*Brian Boru: Emperor of the Irish* - Morgan
Llywelyn  *f*  3501

**MacCallum, Dierdre**
*The Door through Washington Square* - Elaine
Bergstrom  *f*  464

**MacIntyre, Sean Horus**
*Heirs of Empire* - David Weber  *s*  5672

**Medwin, Earl**
*Jacob's Hands* - Aldous Huxley  *f*  2817

**Panthera**
*The Fulfillments of Fate and Desire* - Storm
Constantine  *s*  1142

**Pasmore, Tom**
*Mystery* - Peter Straub  *h*  5330

**Pelucir, Talis**
*The Book of Atrix Wolfe* - Patricia A.
McKillip  *f*  3838

**Pendragon, Arthur**
*The Saxon Shore* - Jack Whyte  *f*  5793

**Phostis**
*Krispos the Emperor* - Harry Turtledove  *f*  5508

**Qox, J'briol**
*Primary Inversion* - Catherine Asaro  *s*  220

**Radon**
*Firewalk* - Anne Logston  *f*  3509

**Raschad, Meesha**
*Mistwalker* - Denise Lopez Heald  *s*  2637

**Starfire, Dion**
*King's Sacrifice* - Margaret Weis  *s*  5717

*The Lost King* - Margaret Weis   s   5720

**Swift**
*Bewitchments of Love and Hate* - Storm
   Constantine   s   1140

**Thompson, Emily**
*The Night Watch* - Sean Stewart   f   5274

**von Schuss, Nicholas**
*Kit's Book* - C.J. Mills   s   3911

**Widdick, Harry**
*Retro Lives* - Lee Grimes   s   2446

**X, Aaron**
*Conglomeros* - Jesse Browner   f   729

**Yuan, Li**
*The Middle Kingdom* - David Wingrove   s   5919

## HEIR—DISPOSSESSED

**Aletto**
*One Land, One Duke* - Ru Emerson   f   1809
*The Two in Hiding* - Ru Emerson   f   1812

**Calliope**
*One for the Morning Glory* - John Barnes   f   355

**Dunladry, Duncan**
*Caledon of the Mists* - Deborah Turner
   Harris   f   2560

**Evander, Danais**
*The Wizard and the Floating City* - Christopher
   Rowley   f   4699

**Freelorn "Lorn"**
*The Door into Sunset* - Diane Duane   f   1660

**Garth One-eye**
*Arena* - William R. Forstchen   f   1977

**Giraud**
*Curse of the Black Heron* - Holly Lisle   f   3479

**ir Var, Zorn**
*Demon Moon* - Jack Williamson   s   5862

**Islay, Arran "Henry Martyn"**
*Henry Martyn* - L. Neil Smith   s   5131

**Julian of Stansvale**
*The Wind Crystal* - Diana L. Paxson   f   4269

**Kryn**
*The Hands of Lyr* - Andre Norton   f   4154

**Renar of Dagothrin**
*Lady of Mercy* - Michelle Sagara   f   4784

**Rodrigo**
*The Still* - David Feintuch   f   1902

**Sharbaraz**
*The Stolen Throne* - Harry Turtledove   f   5510

**Stronsi, Felitzia "Flitz"**
*Throy* - Jack Vance   s   5550

**Telmah, Lord Cima**
*The White Abacus* - Damien Broderick   s   708

**vlith-Arkad, Brandon**
*A Prison Unsought* - Sherwood Smith   s   5139
*Ruler of Naught* - Sherwood Smith   s   5141

## HEIR—LOST

**Brewster, Kip**
*Starswarm* - Jerry Pournelle   s   4379

**dav Leydon, Kian "Mouse"**
*Kingmaker's Sword* - Ann Marston   f   3635

**Floris**
*Out of the Ordinary* - Annie Dalton   f   1330

**Morkaarin, Bren**
*The Rose Sea* - S.M. Stirling   f   5296

**Ohmsford, Par**
*The Scions of Shannara* - Terry Brooks   f   716

**Thayer, Danny**
*Street Magic* - Michael Reaves   f   4497

**Tomjon**
*Wyrd Sisters* - Terry Pratchett   f   4405

## HEIRESS

**Alton, Marguerida "Margaret"**
*The Shadow Matrix* - Marion Zimmer
   Bradley   s   645

**Baxter, Anna Elizabeth**
*Sheltered Lives* - Charles Oberndorf   s   4188

**Bohentin, Caroline**
*Brain Rose* - Nancy Kress   s   3239

**Chios, Maia**
*Dragon Season* - Michael Cassutt   f   936

**Clermont, Selena**
*Kiss of Death* - Daniel Rhodes   h   4569

**Craig, Edith**
*Lucifer's Eye* - Hugh B. Cave   h   943

**Crockett, Selena**
*Archangel* - Michael Conner   s   1133

**Elayne**
*A Crown of Swords* - Robert Jordan   f   2984
*The Dragon Reborn* - Robert Jordan   f   2985
*The Fires of Heaven* - Robert Jordan   f   2987

**Elspeth**
*Winds of Fury* - Mercedes Lackey   f   3306

**Genoud, Rochelle**
*Oktober* - Stephen Gallagher   h   2112

**Hoffman, Vivien**
*Skull Session* - Daniel Hecht   h   2638

**Julien, Maria**
*Unholy Fire* - Whitley Strieber   h   5342

**Liwellan, Sarra Ambrai**
*The Ruins of Ambrai* - Melanie Rawn   f   4489

**Mariell, Christina**
*Haunted* - James Herbert   h   2669

**Metadi, Beka Rosselin**
*The Price of the Stars* - Debra Doyle   s   1604

**Milleflores, Delanna**
*Promised Land* - Connie Willis   s   5872

**Olyvria**
*Krispos the Emperor* - Harry Turtledove   f   5508

**Pallenberg, Rachel**
*Galilee* - Clive Barker   h   340

**Priscian**
*Beggar's Banquet* - Daniel Hood   f   2756

**Ransome, Lilyaka**
*A Passage of Stars* - Alis A. Rasmussen   s   4482

**Scillia**
*The One-Armed Queen* - Jane Yolen   f   6037

**Soerensen, Terese "Tess"**
*An Earthly Crown* - Kate Elliott   s   1771

**Stratford, Julie**
*The Mummy, or Ramses the Damned* - Anne
   Rice   h   4572

**Tyrell, Sarah**
*Blade Runner 2: The Edge of Human* - K.W.
   Jeter   s   2906

**van de Oest, Frances Lorien "Lore"**
*Slow River* - Nicola Griffith   s   2445

**van Huyten, Mariesa Gorley**
*Firestar* - Michael Flynn   s   1962
*Rogue Star* - Michael Flynn   s   1965

**Wade, Laura Gardner**
*A Reasonable Madness* - Fran Dorf   h   1580

**Welsh, Ariel**
*Changeling* - Stephen Leigh   s   3425
*Renegade* - Cordell Scotten   s   4903

**Windsor, Bethany**
*Cluster Command* - David Drake   s   1630

## HEIRESS—DISPOSSESSED

**Dunladry, Mhairi**
*Caledon of the Mists* - Deborah Turner
   Harris   f   2560

**Kandaki**
*The Land of Gold* - Gillian Bradshaw   f   658

**McCabe, Sarah/Melissa**
*The Catswold Portal* - Shirley Rousseau
   Murphy   f   4055

**Nona**
*Fractal Mode* - Piers Anthony   f   171

**Noressa**
*Token of Dragonsblood* - Damaris Cole   f   1114

**Tal, Haemas Sennay**
*House of Moons* - K.D. Wentworth   s   5752

**L'var y Smid, Vida**
*Palace* - Katharine Kerr   s   3072

**Vestrit, Althea**
*The Ship of Magic* - Robin Hobb   f   2696

## HEIRESS—LOST

**Farthing, Sophie**
*Harm's Way* - Colin Greenland   s   2416

**Kastazi, Marko**
*Hawk's Flight* - Carol Chase   f   980

**Saro**
*The Book of Atrix Wolfe* - Patricia A.
   McKillip   f   3838

## HERBALIST

**Fenton, Mariah**
*The Changeling Garden* - Winifred Elze   h   1806

**Katin**
*Season of Storms* - Ellen Foxxe   f   2032

**Mami Gros-Jeanne**
*Brown Girl in the Ring* - Nalo Hopkinson   f   2771

**Pinheiro, Berenice**
*God's Fires* - Patricia Anthony   s   159

## HERO

**Alias**
*Masquerades* - Kate Novak   f   4166

**al'Thor, Rand "Dragon Reborn"**
*The Shadow Rising* - Robert Jordan   f   2990

**Appenfell, Rudgar "Rudy"**
*A Breach in the Watershed* - Douglas Niles   f   4105
*Darkenheight* - Douglas Niles   f   4107
*War of the Three Waters* - Douglas Niles   f   4110

**Arthur "Artos"**
*A Prince Among Men* - Robert N. Charrette   f   977

**Atare, Sheen**
*Hidden Fires* - Katharine Eliska Kimbriel   s   3117

**Barku, Perkar Kar**
*The Blackgod* - J. Gregory Keyes   f   3095
*The Waterborn* - J. Gregory Keyes   f   3098

**Beowulf**
*The Tower of Beowulf* - Parke Godwin   f   2250

*Whose Song Is Sung* - Frank Schaefer   *f*   4872

**Bishop**
*Alien 3* - Alan Dean Foster   *s*   1993

**Blackthorn**
*Hunter of the Light* - Risa Aratyr   *f*   203

**Breo-Saight "Brie"**
*Fire Arrow* - Edith Pattou   *f*   4260

**Caine, Tycho**
*Evil Triumphant* - Michael A. Stackpole   *s*   5199

**Caramon**
*The Second Generation* - Margaret Weis   *f*   5724

**Charming**
*Slay and Rescue* - John Moore   *f*   3991

**Cohen, Ghenghiz "Cohen the Barbarian"**
*Interesting Times* - Terry Pratchett   *f*   4392

**Corleau**
*The Sorceress and the Cygnet* - Patricia A. McKillip   *f*   3842

**Cosmo, Jason**
*Dirty Work* - Dan McGirt   *f*   3810
*Jason Cosmo* - Dan McGirt   *f*   3811

**Crowley, Damon**
*Evil Triumphant* - Michael A. Stackpole   *s*   5199

**Darith**
*Blood of the Colyn Muir* - Paul Edwin Zimmer   *f*   6083

**dav Leydon, Kian "Mouse"**
*Kingmaker's Sword* - Ann Marston   *f*   3635

**de Oro, Irving**
*Horrors of the Dancing Gods* - Jack L. Chalker   *f*   955

**de Oro, Joe**
*Songs of the Dancing Gods* - Jack L. Chalker   *f*   962

**Derry, Jerry**
*Ye Gods!* - Tom Holt   *f*   2753

**Dryhope, Wat**
*A History Maker* - Alasdair Gray   *s*   2338

**Endymion, Raul**
*Endymion* - Dan Simmons   *s*   5051
*The Rise of Endymion* - Dan Simmons   *s*   5059

**Evans, Bill "Bill the Just"**
*The League of the Crimson Crescent* - James E. Reagen   *f*   4495

**Feree, Harper**
*The Friendship Song* - Nancy Springer   *f*   5179

**Firemayne, Rowan**
*Cup of Clay* - Carole Nelson Douglas   *f*   1583
*Seed upon the Wind* - Carole Nelson Douglas   *f*   1584

**Fleetfox**
*Barrow* - John Deakins   *f*   1443

**Gersen, Kirth**
*The Demon Princes: Volume One* - Jack Vance   *s*   5544
*The Demon Princes: Volume Two* - Jack Vance   *s*   5545

**Geryam**
*The Birth of the Blade* - Dennis McCarty   *f*   3766

**Gordon, Evelyn Cyril "Oscar/Scar"**
*Glory Road* - Robert A. Heinlein   *f*   2644

**Gordon, Roger Jr.**
*Revenge of the Fluffy Bunnies* - Craig Shaw Gardner   *f*   2132

**Great and Powerful Turtle**
*Dealer's Choice* - George R.R. Martin   *s*   3643

**Grover**
*Heroes, Inc.* - Kyle Crocco   *f*   1268
*Heroes Wanted* - Kyle Crocco   *f*   1267

**Hackleberry, Kelvin Knight**
*Chimaera's Copper* - Piers Anthony   *f*   166
*Mouvar's Magic* - Piers Anthony   *f*   182
*Orc's Opal* - Piers Anthony   *f*   183

**Harrington, Honor**
*Echoes of Honor* - David Weber   *s*   5669

**Hercules**
*Atlantis Found* - R. Garcia y Robertson   *s*   2119
*By the Sword* - Timothy Boggs   *f*   559
*The First Casualty* - David L. Seidman   *f*   4912

**Hood, Robin**
*The Fantastic Adventures of Robin Hood* - Martin H. Greenberg   *f*   2389
*The Oathbound Wizard* - Christopher Stasheff   *f*   5219
*The Outlaws of Sherwood* - Robin McKinley   *f*   3846
*Robin and the King* - Parke Godwin   *f*   2247
*The Sheriff of Nottingham* - Richard Kluger   *f*   3165

**Jack**
*A Man Betrayed* - J.V. Jones   *f*   2958
*Master and Fool* - J.V. Jones   *f*   2959

**Jayal**
*The Forging of the Shadows* - Oliver Johnson   *f*   2924
*Nations of the Night* - Oliver Johnson   *f*   2925

**Jetboy**
*Night of the Cooters* - Howard Waldrop   *s*   5614

**Kahless**
*Kahless* - Michael Jan Friedman   *s*   2065

**Kerrigan, Joshua "Josh"**
*Putting Up Roots* - Charles Sheffield   *s*   4964

**Kochevikov, Pyetr**
*Chernevog* - C.J. Cherryh   *f*   982
*Rusalka* - C.J. Cherryh   *f*   1002
*Yvgenie* - C.J. Cherryh   *f*   1005

**Lamaril**
*Golden Trillium* - Andre Norton   *f*   4153

**Lashana "Shana"**
*Elvenblood* - Andre Norton   *f*   4150

**Lee, Houlka**
*A Dozen Tough Jobs* - Howard Waldrop   *f*   5612

**Leger, Gary**
*The Dragon's Dagger* - R.A. Salvatore   *f*   4797
*Dragonslayer's Return* - R.A. Salvatore   *f*   4798
*The Woods out Back* - R.A. Salvatore   *f*   4809

**Long, Huey "Hal" Alphonse**
*The Trinity Vector* - Steve Perry   *s*   4302

**Mac Cool, Finn**
*Finn Mac Cool* - Morgan Llywelyn   *f*   3504

**mac Cumhall, Fionn "Demne"**
*Master of Earth and Water* - Diana L. Paxson   *f*   4266
*The Shield between the Worlds* - Diana L. Paxson   *f*   4267
*Sword of Fire and Shadow* - Diana L. Paxson   *f*   4268

**MacDuff**
*The Spawn of Loki* - Jason Henderson   *f*   2658

**Mace, Jarek**
*Morningstar* - David Gemmell   *f*   2190

**MacGregor, Sandy**
*A Name to Conjure With* - Donald Aamodt   *f*   3
*A Troubling Along the Border* - Donald Aamodt   *f*   4

**MacLoed, Alex**
*Fallen Angels* - Larry Niven   *s*   4120

**Maddox, Cory**
*The Cybernetic Walrus* - Jack L. Chalker   *s*   951
*The Hot-Wired Dodo* - Jack L. Chalker   *s*   956

**Malledd**
*Touched by the Gods* - Lawrence Watt-Evans   *f*   5651

**MaqqRee, Desmond "Doc Sidhe"**
*Doc Sidhe* - Aaron Allston   *f*   85

**Melvinge**
*Night of the Living 'Gator!* - Richard A. Lupoff   *s*   3573
*Night of the Living Rat!* - Debra Doyle   *s*   1603
*Night of the Living Shark!* - David Bischoff   *s*   493

**Mirakles**
*The Zork Chronicles* - George Alec Effinger   *s*   1754

**Nicholas "Santa Claus"**
*The Autobiography of Santa Claus: It's Better to Give* - Jeff Guinn   *f*   2456

**O'Day, Gallen**
*Beyond the Gate* - Dave Wolverton   *s*   5949
*The Golden Queen* - Dave Wolverton   *s*   5951

**Oghmal**
*Search for the Starblade* - Keith Taylor   *f*   5408

**Oonitsaupivia, Nijon**
*By the Sword* - Greg Costikyan   *f*   1207

**Oryolin, Alexander**
*Peter Nevsky and the True Story of the Russian Moon Landing* - John Calvin Batchelor   *s*   388

**Parker, Peter "Spider-Man"**
*Spider-Man: The Venom Factor* - Diane Duane   *s*   1667
*The Ultimate Spider-Man* - Stan Lee   *s*   3403

**Raistlin**
*The Second Generation* - Margaret Weis   *f*   5724

**Raven**
*Out of This World* - Lawrence Watt-Evans   *f*   5645

**Reeve, Todd**
*Crisis on Doona* - Anne McCaffrey   *s*   3723

**Rhodes, Jim "War Machine"**
*Iron Man: The Armor Trap* - Greg Cox   *s*   1227

**Richer the Quick**
*Men Like Rats* - Rob Chilson   *s*   1015

**Rifkin, Bernie "Power Man"**
*Captain Jack Zodiac* - Michael Kandel   *f*   3009

**Ripley**
*Alien Resurrection* - A.C. Crispin   *s*   1258

**Roan**
*Waking in Dreamland* - Jody Lynn Nye   *f*   4177

**Roarke, Jason**
*Flare Star* - Paula E. Downing   *s*   1594

**Shielder's Mark**
*Nobody's Son* - Sean Stewart   *f*   5275

**Sigvarthsson, Shef**
*The Hammer and the Cross* - Harry Harrison   *f*   2570

**Silverhand, Caeled**
*Silverlight* - Morgan Llywelyn   *f*   3507

**Silverstein, Ian**
*The Crimson Sky* - Joel Rosenberg   *f*   4669
*The Fire Duke* - Joel Rosenberg   *f*   4671
*The Silver Stone* - Joel Rosenberg   *f*   4676

**Skywalker, Luke**
*Ambush at Corellia* - Roger MacBride Allen   *s*   76
*Before the Storm* - Michael P. Kube-McDowell   *s*   3247
*Children of the Jedi* - Barbara Hambly   *s*   2500
*The Courtship of Princess Leia* - Dave Wolverton   *s*   5950
*The Crystal Star* - Vonda N. McIntyre   *s*   3820
*Dark Force Rising* - Timothy Zahn   *s*   6052
*Darksaber* - Kevin J. Anderson   *s*   103

*The Glove of Darth Vader* - Paul Davids  s  1392
*Heir to the Empire* - Timothy Zahn  s  6054
*Jedi Search* - Kevin J. Anderson  s  109
*The Last Command* - Timothy Zahn  s  6055
*The Lost City of the Jedi* - Paul Davids  s  1393
*The New Rebellion* - Kristine Kathryn
   Rusch  s  4719
*Shadows of the Empire* - Steve Perry  s  4299
*The Truce at Bakura* - Kathy Tyers  s  5527

**Snorrison, Bran**
*The Deepest Sea* - Charles Barnitz  f  363

**Spring-Heeled Jack**
*Spring-Heeled Jack* - Philip Pullman  f  4447

**Stark, Tony "Iron Man"**
*Iron Man: The Armor Trap* - Greg Cox  s  1227

**Stello, Rawnie**
*The Friendship Song* - Nancy Springer  f  5179

**Stoner, Keith**
*Star Brothers* - Ben Bova  s  594

**Strand, Paul**
*The Queen's Squadron* - R.M. Meluch  s  3874

**Thaxton, Xavier**
*Count Geiger's Blues* - Michael Bishop  s  499

**Thompson, Peter**
*My Teacher Flunked the Planet* - Bruce
   Coville  s  1222

**Tiger**
*Sword-Maker* - Jennifer Roberson  f  4614

**Tull**
*Serpent Catch* - Dave Wolverton  s  5956

**Tyner, Gil**
*The Hero King* - Rick Shelley  f  4970
*The Hero of Varay* - Rick Shelley  f  4971

**Vaun**
*Hero* - Dave Duncan  s  1680

**Warner, Seth**
*Through the Ice* - Piers Anthony  f  192

**Washi**
*Dark Legend* - Jamake Highwater  f  2686

**Wayne, Bruce "Batman"**
*Batman: Captured by the Engines* - Joe R.
   Lansdale  h  3320
*Batman: Knightfall* - Dennis O'Neil  s  4215
*Batman Returns* - Craig Shaw Gardner  s  2124
*Catwoman* - Lynn Abbey  s  14
*The Further Adventures of Batman 2: Featuring the
   Penguin* - Martin H. Greenberg  s  2391
*The Further Adventures of Batman 3: Featuring
   Catwoman* - Martin H. Greenberg  s  2392
*Mask of the Phantasm* - Geary Gravel  s  2331

**York, Dennison**
*Thoughts of God* - Michael Kanaly  s  3007

**Zhukovsky, Dmitry**
*Peter Nevsky and the True Story of the Russian Moon
   Landing* - John Calvin Batchelor  s  388

## HEROINE

**Birnbaum, Maureen**
*Maureen Birnbaum, Barbarian Swordsperson: The
   Complete Stories* - George Alec Effinger  f  1752

**Borden, Lizzie**
*Lizzie Borden* - Elizabeth Engstrom  h  1826

**Cilla**
*Heroes, Inc.* - Kyle Crocco  f  1268
*Heroes Wanted* - Kyle Crocco  f  1267

**Cley**
*Beyond the Fall of Night* - Arthur C. Clarke  s  1054

**D'Ame, Celia "Lee"**
*A Roil of Stars* - Don Wismer  s  5930

**Harker, Mina**
*The Dracula Tape* - Fred Saberhagen  h  4765

**Jenna**
*Sister Light, Sister Dark* - Jane Yolen  f  6039
*White Jenna* - Jane Yolen  f  6041

**Kaeler, Lanen**
*Song in the Silence* - Elizabeth Kerner  f  3065

**Kendoro, Judit**
*Acorna* - Anne McCaffrey  s  3717

**Kiakra, Minerva**
*Minerva Wakes* - Holly Lisle  f  3487

**Kyle, Selena "Catwoman"**
*Batman Returns* - Craig Shaw Gardner  s  2124
*Catwoman* - Lynn Abbey  s  14
*The Further Adventures of Batman 3: Featuring
   Catwoman* - Martin H. Greenberg  s  2392

**LaBrae, Jael**
*Dragon Rigger* - Jeffrey A. Carver  s  929

**Lessis of Valmes**
*Bazil Broketail* - Christopher Rowley  f  4692

**Madouc**
*Madouc* - Jack Vance  f  5547

**McCormick, Lianne**
*When the Bough Breaks* - Mercedes Lackey  f  3302

**McCray, Abbey**
*Leap Point* - Kay Kenyon  s  3063

**Melior, Laurel**
*Winter Rose* - Patricia A. McKillip  f  3843

**Melior, Rois**
*Winter Rose* - Patricia A. McKillip  f  3843

**Mitsuko, Fujiwara "Little Puddle" no**
*Little Sister* - Kara Dalkey  f  1320

**no Mitsuko, Fujiwara**
*The Heavenward Path* - Kara Dalkey  f  1319

**Nona**
*Fractal Mode* - Piers Anthony  f  171

**O'Dell, Judith**
*Imajica* - Clive Barker  h  343

**Ogg, Nanny**
*Lords and Ladies* - Terry Pratchett  f  4394

**Orphan**
*A Plague of Angels* - Sheri S. Tepper  s  5433

**Ripley**
*Alien 3* - Alan Dean Foster  s  1993

**Schechter, Kate**
*The Long Dark Tea-Time of the Soul* - Douglas
   Adams  s  30

**Star Shell**
*People of the Lakes* - Kathleen O'Neal Gear  f  2164

**Tamai**
*Changeweaver* - Margaret Ball  f  313

**Thalassa**
*The Forging of the Shadows* - Oliver
   Johnson  f  2924
*Nations of the Night* - Oliver Johnson  f  2925

**Troy, Linda Ellen "Sparta"**
*The Shining Ones* - Paul Preuss  s  4421

**Weatherwax, Granny**
*Lords and Ladies* - Terry Pratchett  f  4394
*Witches Abroad* - Terry Pratchett  f  4404
*Wyrd Sisters* - Terry Pratchett  f  4405

**Westriding, Margorie "Jory"**
*Sideshow* - Sheri S. Tepper  s  5436

## HIGHWAYMAN

**deBurrows, Oliver**
*The Sword of Bedwyr* - R.A. Salvatore  f  4808

## HIPPIE

**Farrell**
*The Folk of the Air* - Peter S. Beagle  f  407

**Hollander, Tom**
*The Children of Hamelin* - Norman Spinrad  s  5170

## HISTORIAN

**Alis**
*Remake* - Connie Willis  s  5873

**Allen-Shimmura, Elio**
*Dark Water's Embrace* - Stephen Leigh  s  3426

**Backmaker, Hodgins "Hodge"**
*Bring the Jubilee* - Ward Moore  s  3993

**Balfour, Alex**
*Till the End of Time* - Allen Appel  f  201

**Braeth, Rikard**
*Crown of the Serpent* - Allen L. Wold  s  5932
*Lair of the Cyclops* - Allen L. Wold  s  5933

**Cavewood, Matthew**
*Belladonna* - Michael Stewart  h  5271

**Chance, Lester**
*Blue Light* - Walter Mosley  s  4042

**Croaker**
*Dreams of Steel* - Glen Cook  f  1150

**Dawson, Joe**
*Scotland the Brave* - Jennifer Roberson  f  4611
*Shadow of Obsession* - Rebecca Neason  f  4082

**Dubchek, Jackson**
*Stranded!* - Warren Norwood  s  4164

**Duratan**
*Flight of Vengeance* - Andre Norton  f  4152

**Faron, Theodore**
*The Children of Men* - P.D. James  f  2870

**Henry, Ned**
*To Say Nothing of the Dog* - Connie Willis  s  5874

**Kindle, Verity**
*To Say Nothing of the Dog* - Connie Willis  s  5874

**Lalelelang**
*The Spoils of War* - Alan Dean Foster  s  2016

**Lindstrom, Flynn**
*Day of the Snake* - Matthew J. Costello  s  1196

**Lingri**
*The Others* - Margaret Wander Bonanno  s  565
*OtherWhere* - Margaret Wander Bonanno  s  566
*OtherWise* - Margaret Wander Bonanno  s  567

**Magnus, Mei-Ling**
*Standing Wave* - Howard V. Hendrix  s  2661

**Mays, Randolph**
*The Diamond Moon* - Paul Preuss  s  4417

**Neskat, Merinda**
*Nightsword* - Margaret Weis  f  5722
*Sentinels* - Margaret Weis  s  5725

**Raeburn, Francis**
*The Lodge of the Lynx* - Katherine Kurtz  f  3259

**Shedemei**
*Earthborn* - Orson Scott Card  s  884

**Shn'dar, Queekat**
*Sentinels* - Margaret Weis  s  5725

**Stone, Roger**
*Ancient Images* - Ramsey Campbell  h  852

**Taub, Judy**
*Dictator* - William F. Wu  s  5996

**Toledo, Indira**
*Mother of Demons* - Eric Flint  s  1956

**Tsang-jieh**
*Bronze Mirror* - Jeanne Larsen  *f*  3338

**Tylar**
*Legacy* - Steve White  *s*  5785

**Verlith, Zjhanne**
*Zjhanne's Book* - C.J. Mills  *s*  3912

**von Sacher, Ludwig**
*Lives of the Monster Dogs* - Kirsten Bakis  *s*  305

**Wallace, Indra**
*3001: The Final Odyssey* - Arthur C.
　Clarke  *s*  1053

**Watanabe, Kenji**
*The Garden of Rama* - Arthur C. Clarke  *s*  1055

**Zurzal**
*Brother to Shadows* - Andre Norton  *s*  4142

## HISTORICAL FIGURE

**Alexander the Great**
*Dark Prince* - David Gemmell  *f*  2187
*Lord of the Two Lands* - Judith Tarr  *f*  5395

**Antonius, Marcus**
*Throne of Isis* - Judith Tarr  *f*  5397

**Asimov, Issac**
*Back in the USSA* - Kim Newman  *s*  4095

**Attila the Hun**
*Attila's Treasure* - Stephan Grundy  *f*  2453

**Augustine**
*Blameless in Abaddon* - James Morrow  *f*  4029

**Bathori, Elizabeth**
*Daughter of the Night* - Elaine Bergstrom  *h*  463

**Bathory, Elizabeth**
*Blood Countess* - Andrei Codrescu  *h*  1094

**Baum, L. Frank**
*Was* - Geoff Ryman  *f*  4758

**Benson, E.F.**
*The Haunting of Lamb House* - Joan Aiken  *h*  45

**Bonaparte, Napoleon**
*The Napoleon Wager* - William R.
　Forstchen  *s*  1980

**Borden, Lizzie**
*Lizzie Borden* - Elizabeth Engstrom  *h*  1826

**Botticelli, Sandro**
*The Memory Cathedral* - Jack Dann  *s*  1341

**Brady, Julia**
*The Gallery of His Dreams* - Kristine Kathryn
　Rusch  *f*  4717

**Brady, Mathew B.**
*The Gallery of His Dreams* - Kristine Kathryn
　Rusch  *f*  4717

**Bruno, Giordano**
*Love & Sleep* - John Crowley  *f*  1277

**Burton, Richard Francis**
*To Your Scattered Bodies Go* - Philip Jose
　Farmer  *s*  1876

**Bush, George Herbert Walker**
*Reality Is What You Can Get Away With: An
　Illustrated Screenplay* - Robert Anton
　Wilson  *s*  5904

**Byron, George Gordon**
*Lord of the Dead* - Tom Holland  *h*  2741
*The Stress of Her Regard* - Tim Powers  *h*  4385

**Caesar, Julius**
*Caesar's Bicycle* - John Barnes  *s*  350

**Capone, Al**
*Consolidation* - Peter F. Hamilton  *s*  2523
*Timeshare: Second Time Around* - Joshua
　Dann  *s*  1345

**Capone, Alphonse**
*Back in the USSA* - Kim Newman  *s*  4095

**Charlemagne**
*His Majesty's Elephant* - Judith Tarr  *f*  5394

**Chekhov, Anton**
*Chekhov's Journey* - Ian Watson  *s*  5633

**Christian, Fletcher**
*Conflict* - Peter F. Hamilton  *s*  2522

**Churchill, Winston**
*Triumph* - Ben Bova  *s*  598

**Clemens, Sam**
*How Few Remain* - Harry Turtledove  *s*  5504

**Cleopatra**
*Throne of Isis* - Judith Tarr  *f*  5397

**Cody, William**
*Devil's Engine* - Mark Sumner  *f*  5356

**Coleridge, Samuel Taylor**
*Walford's Oak* - Jill M. Phillips  *f*  4310

**Columbus, Christopher**
*Pastwatch: The Redemption of Christopher Columbus* -
　Orson Scott Card  *s*  895

**Craven, Wes**
*Wes Craven's New Nightmare* - David
　Bergantino  *h*  460

**Crowley, Aleister**
*The Door through Washington Square* - Elaine
　Bergstrom  *f*  464
*The Woman between the Worlds* - F. Gwynplaine
　MacIntyre  *s*  3596

**Custer, George A.**
*How Few Remain* - Harry Turtledove  *s*  5504

**Custer, George Armstrong**
*Devil's Tower* - Mark Sumner  *f*  5357

**da Vinci, Leonardo**
*The Memory Cathedral* - Jack Dann  *s*  1341

**de Medici, Caterina**
*The Stars Dispose* - Michaela Roessner  *f*  4651

**De Soto, Hernando**
*Tatham Mound* - Piers Anthony  *f*  191

**Dean, James**
*Spyder* - Norman Partridge  *h*  4255

**Dickinson, Emily**
*The Steampunk Trilogy* - Paul Di Filippo  *s*  1518

**Douglass, Frederick**
*How Few Remain* - Harry Turtledove  *s*  5504

**Doyle, Arthur Conan**
*Believe: A Novel* - William Shatner  *f*  4929
*Nevermore* - William Hjortsberg  *h*  2692
*Photographing Fairies* - Steve Szilagyi  *f*  5379

**Einstein, Albert**
*Einstein's Dreams* - Alan Lightman  *f*  3459

**Eiriksdottir, Freydis**
*The Ice-Shirt* - William T. Vollmann  *f*  5580

**Eiriksson, Leif**
*The Ice-Shirt* - William T. Vollmann  *f*  5580

**Fermi, Enrico**
*Worldwar: In the Balance* - Harry
　Turtledove  *s*  5515

**Gable, Clark**
*Who P-P-Plugged Roger Rabbit?* - Gary K.
　Wolf  *f*  5934

**Geronimo**
*Apacheria* - Jake Page  *s*  4233

**Goebbels, Joseph "Joseph Gable"**
*The Resurrections* - Simon Louvish  *s*  3528

**Goering, Hermann**
*To Your Scattered Bodies Go* - Philip Jose
　Farmer  *s*  1876

**Gorbachev, Mikhail Sergeevich**
*Fellow Traveller* - William Barton  *s*  380

**Guevara, Ernesto "Che"**
*The Resurrections* - Simon Louvish  *s*  3528

**Harrison, Benjamin**
*The Smithsonian Institution* - Gore Vidal  *f*  5570

**Henry, Wiiliam**
*Queen's Gambit Declined* - Melinda M.
　Snodgrass  *f*  5147

**Hitler, Adolf**
*Dark Legacy* - Mark A. Kostrubula  *h*  3220
*The Resurrections* - Simon Louvish  *s*  3528
*Triumph* - Ben Bova  *s*  598

**Houdini, Harry**
*Believe: A Novel* - William Shatner  *f*  4929
*Nevermore* - William Hjortsberg  *h*  2692

**James, Henry**
*The Haunting of Lamb House* - Joan Aiken  *h*  45

**Jarry, Alfred**
*Night of the Cooters* - Howard Waldrop  *s*  5614

**Jefferson, Thomas**
*Arc d'X* - Steve Erickson  *f*  1835

**John**
*The Sheriff of Nottingham* - Richard Kluger  *f*  3165

**Karloff, Boris**
*Father of Frankenstein* - Christopher Bram  *h*  659

**Kennedy, John F.**
*Time Station Berlin* - David Evans  *s*  1852

**Lagenkamp, Heather**
*Wes Craven's New Nightmare* - David
　Bergantino  *h*  460

**Lee, Robert E.**
*The Guns of the South: A Novel of the Civil War* -
　Harry Turtledove  *s*  5502

**Lincoln, Abraham**
*Skeletons* - Al Sarrantonio  *h*  4834
*The Smithsonian Institution* - Gore Vidal  *f*  5570

**Louis XIV**
*The Moon and the Sun* - Vonda N.
　McIntyre  *f*  3822
*Queen's Gambit Declined* - Melinda M.
　Snodgrass  *f*  5147

**mac Cumhall, Fionn "Demne"**
*Master of Earth and Water* - Diana L.
　Paxson  *f*  4266
*The Shield between the Worlds* - Diana L.
　Paxson  *f*  4267
*Sword of Fire and Shadow* - Diana L.
　Paxson  *f*  4268

**mac Kennedy, Brian**
*Brian Boru: Emperor of the Irish* - Morgan
　Llywelyn  *f*  3501

**Machiavelli, Niccolo**
*The Memory Cathedral* - Jack Dann  *s*  1341

**Mack the Knife**
*Spring-Heeled Jack* - Philip Pullman  *f*  4447

**Marlowe, Christopher**
*Strange Devices of the Sun and Moon* - Lisa
　Goldstein  *f*  2262

**Mata Hari**
*The Mata Hari Adventure* - James Luceno  *f*  3544

**Mozart, Wolfgang Amadeus**
*I, Vampire* - Michael Romkey  *h*  4665

**Philip of Macedon**
*Lion of Macedon* - David Gemmell  *f*  2189
*Orion and the Conqueror* - Ben Bova  *s*  590

**Poe, Edgar Allan**
*The Bloody Red Baron* - Kim Newman  *h*  4097
*The Lighthouse at the End of the World* - Stephen Marlowe  *h*  3631
*Madeline: After the Fall of Usher* - Marie Kiraly  *h*  3150

**Polo, Marco**
*If at Faust You Don't Succeed* - Roger Zelazny  *f*  6070

**Presley, Elvis**
*Armageddon: The Musical* - Robert Rankin  *s*  4473
*Bone Music* - Alan Rodgers  *h*  4646
*Comeback Tour: The Sky Belongs to the Stars* - Jack Yeovil  *s*  6020
*Elvis Rising: Stories on the King* - Kay Sloan  *f*  5089
*The King Is Dead: Tales of Elvis Post Mortem* - Paul M. Sammon  *h*  4810

**Ramses the Great**
*The Mummy, or Ramses the Damned* - Anne Rice  *h*  4572

**Rasputin**
*I, Vampire* - Michael Romkey  *h*  4665

**Reagan, Ronald "Dutch"**
*Time on My Hands* - Peter Delacorte  *s*  1480

**Roosevelt, Franklin Delano**
*Triumph* - Ben Bova  *s*  598

**Roosevelt, Theodore**
*1901* - Robert Conroy  *s*  1139
*Bully!* - Mike Resnick  *s*  4539

**Runyon, Damon**
*Nevermore* - William Hjortsberg  *h*  2692

**Scott, Walter**
*Picking the Ballad's Bones* - Elizabeth Ann Scarborough  *f*  4869

**Shelley, Mary**
*Gothic Romance* - Emmanuel Carrere  *h*  912

**Shelley, Percy Bysshe**
*Lord of the Dead* - Tom Holland  *h*  2741
*Wall, Stone, Craft* - Walter Jon Williams  *h*  5842

**Sherman, William Tecumseh**
*Under the Shadow* - Jane Toombs  *h*  5481

**Siegel, Benjamin "Bugsy"**
*Last Call* - Tim Powers  *f*  4384

**Skorzeny, Otto**
*1945* Newt Gingrich  *s*  2239

**Stoker, Bram**
*Dracula Unbound* - Brian W. Aldiss  *h*  55

**Tesla, Nikola**
*The Prestige* - Christopher Priest  *s*  4432

**Thorbjornsdottir, Gudrid**
*The Ice-Shirt* - William T. Vollmann  *f*  5580

**Tituba**
*I, Tituba, Black Witch of Salem* - Maryse Conde  *f*  1130

**Wilde, Oscar**
*The Hunger and Ecstasy of Vampires* - Brian Stableford  *h*  5192

**William**
*Robin and the King* - Parke Godwin  *f*  2247

**Wilson, Brian**
*Glimpses* - Lewis Shiner  *h*  4997

## HOMOSEXUAL

**Ashkevron, Vanyel**
*Magic's Price* - Mercedes Lackey  *f*  3288

**Atuli, Cameron**
*Maximum Light* - Nancy Kress  *s*  3241

**Callaway, Chris**
*Out for Blood* - John Peyton Cooke  *h*  1166

**Compton, Andrew**
*Exquisite Corpse* - Poppy Z. Brite  *h*  695

**Cramer, Eddie**
*Vampires Anonymous* - Jeffrey N. McMahan  *h*  3853

**Enkidu**
*Mirage* - Perry Brass  *s*  662

**Gibb**
*Key West 2720 A.D.* - William Eakins  *s*  1720

**Greeland**
*Mirage* - Perry Brass  *s*  662

**Hagan**
*Attila's Treasure* - Stephan Grundy  *f*  2453

**Jarrat, Kevin**
*Death's Head* - Mel Keegan  *s*  3029

**Justin, Rangsey**
*Night Sky Mine* - Melissa Scott  *s*  4898

**Kelahnus**
*The Stone Prince* - Fiona Patton  *f*  4259

**Kidd, Christian**
*That's All, Folks!* - Greg Snow  *f*  5148

**Leonard, Wyatt**
*From the Teeth of Angels* - Jonathan Carroll  *h*  918

**McDonald, Dirk**
*Baby Be-Bop* - Francesca Lia Block  *f*  545
*Witch Baby* - Francesca Lia Block  *f*  552

**Merlin**
*Mordred's Curse* - Ian McDowell  *f*  3806

**Phoe, Sam**
*Key West 2720 A.D.* - William Eakins  *s*  1720

**Reichart, Carlos**
*Boys of Life* - Paul Russell  *h*  4737

**Shan, Rafael Zhong "China Mountain"**
*China Mountain Zhang* - Maureen F. McHugh  *s*  3817

**Stefan**
*Magic's Price* - Mercedes Lackey  *f*  3288

**Stone, Jerry**
*Death's Head* - Mel Keegan  *s*  3029

**Tarasov, Sein**
*Night Sky Mine* - Melissa Scott  *s*  4898

**van Liesvelt, Butch**
*Trouble and Her Friends* - Melissa Scott  *s*  4902

**Vanyel**
*Magic's Pawn* - Mercedes Lackey  *f*  3287

**Whale, James**
*Father of Frankenstein* - Christopher Bram  *h*  659

## HORSE TRAINER

**Cabot, Jaime**
*Changespell* - Doranna Durgin  *f*  1703
*Dun Lady's Jess* - Doranna Durgin  *f*  1704

**Cassidy**
*The Persistence of Memory* - Karen Ripley  *s*  4592

**Delaney, Cathy "Cassidy"**
*The Warden of Horses* - Karen Ripley  *s*  4595

**Ellis, Cindy**
*The Godmother's Web* - Elizabeth Ann Scarborough  *f*  4864

**Eve, Glennys**
*The Stalking Horse* - Constance Ash  *f*  222

**Fletcher, Ben**
*Darkscope* - Margaret Falk  *h*  1860

**Rialla**
*Steal the Dragon* - Patricia Briggs  *f*  682

**Slater, Matthew**
*The Tallow Image* - Jane Brindle  *h*  690

**Varianus, Galwin Gaius**
*Black Horses for the King* - Anne McCaffrey  *f*  3720

## HOTEL OWNER

**Rand, Phylis**
*Darkling* - Michael O'Rourke  *h*  4223

## HOTEL WORKER

**Farris, Duffy**
*The Jimjams* - Michael Green  *h*  2345

**Farris, Rose**
*The Jimjams* - Michael Green  *h*  2345

**Marden, Kim**
*Chiller* - Randall Boyll  *h*  610

**Pascal**
*A Face at the Window* - Dennis McFarland  *h*  3809

## HOUSEKEEPER

**Callahan, Myra**
*Borderland: A Novel of Terror* - S.K. Epperson  *h*  1828

**Cortez, Rafaela**
*Tropic of Orange* - Karen Tei Yamashita  *f*  6009

**Griffin**
*The Thief of Always* - Clive Barker  *h*  347

**Timpson, Jean**
*Sweetheart, Sweetheart* - Bernard Taylor  *h*  5402

**Zapata, Carmen**
*Panic* - Chris Curry  *h*  1295

## HOUSEWIFE

**Albin, Tritia**
*The Mailman* - Bentley Little  *h*  3494

**Ann**
*The Cormorant* - Stephen Gregory  *h*  2429

**Benson, Rachal**
*Shadow Twin* - Dale Hoover  *h*  2762

**Black, Catherine**
*The Frenchman* - Elizabeth Hand  *h*  2534

**Blervaque, Rose**
*Living Real* - James C. Bassett  *s*  386

**Boxletter, Marion**
*Duplicates* - Andrew Neiderman  *h*  4086

**Boyle, Heather**
*Website* - Ray Garton  *h*  2157

**Bradley, Angela**
*Metal Angel* - Nancy Springer  *f*  5181

**Brown, Oenone**
*Firefly* - Piers Anthony  *h*  170

**Burlingame, Jessie**
*Gerald's Game* - Stephen King  *h*  3133

**Caffre, Marie**
*Return to Camerein* - Rick Shelley  *s*  4974

**Carson, Casey**
*Darkside* - Dennis Etchison  *h*  1845

**Carter, Annie**
*The Changeling Garden* - Winifred Elze  *h*  1806

**Chancel, Nora**
*The Hellfire Club* - Peter Straub  *h*  5326

**Collins, Camisa**
*Flesh and Blood* - D.A. Fowler   h   2024

**Collins, Maggie**
*The Sweetheart Season* - Karen Joy Fowler   f   2029

**Daimler, Rachel**
*Lullaby* - Diane Guest   h   2455

**Dalton, Susan Benning**
*Watchers in the Woods* - William W.
   Johnstone   h   2936

**DeSalvo, Lara**
*Shades of Night* - Rick Hautala   h   2612

**Douglas, Jill**
*The Baby* - Stephanie Kegan   h   3033

**Edwards, Cynthia**
*The Immortals* - Andrew Neiderman   h   4087

**Elisabeth**
*What's Wrong with Valerie?* - D.A. Fowler   h   2026

**Fletcher, DeAnne**
*Lost Boys* - Orson Scott Card   f   891

**Forrest, Connie**
*Evil Intent* - Bernard Taylor   h   5400

**Gaetan, Mary**
*Lie to Me* - David Martin   h   3639

**Gordon, Sr.**
*Revenge of the Fluffy Bunnies* - Craig Shaw
   Gardner   f   2132

**Harker, Mina**
*Bram Stoker's Dracula* - Fred Saberhagen   h   4763

**Julia**
*The Hellbound Heart* - Clive Barker   h   342

**Kennedy, Colquitt**
*The House Next Door* - Anne Rivers
   Siddons   h   5021

**Lacroix, Marie**
*Machine* - Rene Belletto   h   436

**Lacuna**
*Question Quest* - Piers Anthony   f   186

**Lamont, Gail**
*Dead Voices* - Abigail McDaniels   h   3783

**Lowry, Mary**
*Fear* - L. Ron Hubbard   h   2789

**Lundens, Myra**
*The Basement* - Bari Wood   h   5961

**Lydyard, Cordelia**
*The Angel of Pain* - Brian Stableford   h   5189

**Manning, Zoe**
*Night Games* - Marilyn Harris   h   2562

**Marlowe, Kate**
*The Godsend* - Bernard Taylor   h   5401

**Marshall, Meg**
*Seeds of Evil* - Margaret Bingley   h   491

**Martin, Vicki**
*Goblins* - Vincent Courtney   h   1212

**McGarvey, Heather**
*Winter Moon* - Dean R. Koontz   h   3218

**Merrick, Melanie**
*Fear Itself* - Ric Meyers   h   3881
*Living Hell* - Ric Meyers   h   3882

**Moore, Rebecca**
*Cemetery of Angels* - Noel Hynd   h   2821

**Murphy, Annie**
*The Elementals* - Morgan Llywelyn   f   3503

**Nolan, Celia**
*Celia* - Ruby Jean Jensen   h   2900

**Pinchot, Arlen**
*The Basement* - Bari Wood   h   5961

**Raphael, Stella**
*Asylum* - Patrick McGrath   h   3812

**Roberts, Kristen**
*Neighbors* - Maureen S. Pusti   h   4450

**Robinson, Tracy Zempelios**
*Second Chance* - Chet Williamson   h   5850

**Russell, Katrinka**
*Violin* - Anne Rice   h   4579

**Schroeder, Lauren**
*Dark Channel* - Ray Garton   h   2150

**Speke, Clara**
*Ghostwright* - Michael Cadnum   h   810

**Stewart, Kate**
*Dark of the Eye* - Douglas Clegg   h   1078

**Sue**
*The Interior Life* - Katherine Blake   f   515

**Tanner, Sharon**
*Creature* - John Saul   h   4839

**Taylor, Miriam**
*The Devil's Advocate* - Andrew Neiderman   h   4085

**Walker, Janet**
*Playmates* - Abigail McDaniels   h   3784

**Whitcome, Pamela**
*Shadow Child* - Joseph A. Citro   h   1038

**White, Karen**
*Gypsies* - Robert Charles Wilson   s   5908

**Wilmore, Cally**
*Apocalypse* - Nancy Springer   f   5176

**Worthington, Kara Noble**
*Bloody Waters* - B.L. Winters   h   5926

## HUMAN

**Alvin**
*Beyond the Fall of Night* - Arthur C. Clarke   s   1054

**Cardiff, Melisan**
*Hooray for Hellywood* - Esther Friesner   f   2077

**Cley**
*Beyond the Fall of Night* - Arthur C. Clarke   s   1054

**Graciosa**
*Child of Faerie, Child of Earth* - Josepha
   Sherman   f   4985

**I**
*My Cousin, My Gastroenterologist* - Mark
   Leyner   s   3456

**Isham, Evi**
*Emperors of the Twilight* - S. Andrew
   Swann   s   5362

**Jason**
*Master of Many Treasures* - Mary Brown   f   726

**Lieserl**
*Ring* - Stephen Baxter   s   402

**Mayaram, Simon**
*Celestis* - Paul Park   s   4241

**Oren, Eichra**
*Converse and Conflict* - L. Neil Smith   s   5130

**Passman, Breyten**
*River of Dust* - Alexander Jablokov   s   2840

**Pomegranate**
*Bronze Mirror* - Jeanne Larsen   f   3338

**Rand**
*Path of Fire* - Charles Ingrid   s   2832

**Starbuck, Ron**
*Elsewhere* - Will Shetterly   f   4993

**Straat-ien, Nevan**
*The Spoils of War* - Alan Dean Foster   s   2016

**Suida, Frederick**
*Woodsman* - Thomas A. Easton   s   1727

**Theon**
*Seeking the Dream Brother* - Marcia J.
   Bennett   s   451

**Womack, Jeff**
*Brother Termite* - Patricia Anthony   s   156

## HUNTER

**Baalgor "Grayface"**
*Ancient Echoes* - Robert Holdstock   f   2735

**Bart**
*Initiation* - Marian Hughes   s   2806

**Brostek**
*Shadow-Maze* - Mark Smith   f   5133

**Coconino**
*The Earth Is All That Lasts* - Catherine
   Wells   s   5744

**Complain, Roy**
*Non-Stop* - Brian W. Aldiss   s   58

**Darian**
*Owlflight* - Mercedes Lackey   f   3291

**Davidsen, Gunnar**
*Bright Shadow* - Elizabeth Forrest   h   1971

**Eloise**
*Nicoji* - M. Shayne Bell   s   434

**Gaultry**
*Wind From a Foreign Sky* - Katya Reimann   f   4528

**Gilliam**
*Hunter's Death* - Michelle West   f   5758
*Hunter's Oath* - Michelle West   f   5759

**Hamr**
*Hunting the Ghost Dancer* - A.A. Attanasio   f   268

**Jake**
*Nicoji* - M. Shayne Bell   s   434

**Jondalar**
*The Plains of Passage* - Jean M. Auel   f   275

**Kori**
*The Animal Wife* - Elizabeth Marshall
   Thomas   f   5444

**Lewin, Bonnie**
*Conflict* - Peter F. Hamilton   s   2522

**Lily**
*The Dog King* - Christoph Ransmayr   f   4474

**Maliwal**
*The Sacred Stones* - William Sarabande   f   4818

**Masau**
*The Sacred Stones* - William Sarabande   f   4818

**McKay, Debra**
*Children of the Earth* - Catherine Wells   s   5743
*The Earth Is All That Lasts* - Catherine
   Wells   s   5744

**Mikhail**
*Initiation* - Marian Hughes   s   2806

**Milana, Chaka**
*Eternity Road* - Jack McDevitt   s   3788

**Mist**
*Shadow Dance* - Anne Logston   f   3513

**Nafai**
*The Ships of Earth* - Orson Scott Card   s   897

**Nemet "Greenface"**
*Ancient Echoes* - Robert Holdstock   f   2735

**Ohaern**
*The Shaman* - Christopher Stasheff   f   5223

**or-Reise, Garric**
*Lord of the Isles* - David Drake   f   1636

**Ramsey, Keith**
*Blood Lines* - William R. Burkett Jr.   s   774

**Robin**
*Passager* - Jane Yolen   f   6038

**Rockdream**
*The Goblin Plain War* - Carl Miller   f   3892

**Rolfson, Bjorn**
*Magelord: The Awakening* - Thomas K.
   Martin   f   3651

**Rucker, Judgement**
*The Cellar* - Richard Laymon   h   3365

**Runs in Light**
*People of the Wolf* - W. Michael Gear   f   2170

**Sam**
*Nicoji* - M. Shayne Bell   s   434

**Sherwood, John**
*Dancing Bears* - Fred Saberhagen   f   4764

**Songa**
*Conan the Savage* - Leonard Carpenter   f   909

**Stone, Enoch**
*A Hunger in the Soul* - Mike Resnick   s   4545

**Swift**
*The Animal Wife* - Elizabeth Marshall
   Thomas   f   5444

**Taelor, Chris**
*When Wolves Cry* - Chris N. Africa   h   41

**Tikki "Striper"**
*Striper Assassin* - Nyx Smith   f   5135

**Varo**
*Shadow-Maze* - Mark Smith   f   5133

**Washington, Billy**
*Beggars and Choosers* - Nancy Kress   s   3236

**Wolf**
*The Hunter Returns* - David Drake   f   1632

## IMMIGRANT

**Atare, Darame "Silver" Meath**
*Hidden Fires* - Katharine Eliska Kimbriel   s   3117

**Brigitta, Maeve**
*The Scathach and the Maeve's Daughter* - Mary
   Alexander Walker   f   5618

**Casruel, Aru**
*Mother of Storms* - Adrian Cole   f   1101

**Dagda**
*The Enchanted Isles* - Casey Flynn   f   1960
*Most Ancient Song* - Casey Flynn   f   1961

**Giyt, Evesham**
*O Pioneer!* - Frederik Pohl   s   4350

**Harrison, Theophilius "Ted"**
*Orbital Resonance* - John Barnes   s   356

**Heron, John**
*The Schizogenic Man* - Raymond Harris   s   2563

**Mondragon, Carlos**
*The Black Sun* - Jack Williamson   s   5860

**Nolan**
*The Silent Stars Go By* - James White   s   5781

**Nuada**
*The Enchanted Isles* - Casey Flynn   f   1960
*Most Ancient Song* - Casey Flynn   f   1961

**Sharissa**
*The Shrouded Realm* - Richard A. Knaak   f   3174

**Zeree, Dru**
*The Shrouded Realm* - Richard A. Knaak   f   3174

## IMMORTAL

**Abaddon**
*Wolf in Shadow* - David Gemmell   s   2191

**Alegretta**
*Outnumbering the Dead* - Frederik Pohl   s   4352

**an Jiar yn Aliria dur Hamley, Quinzaine**
*Fire Crossing* - Cheryl J. Franklin   s   2036

**Anij**
*Insurrection* - J.M. Dillard   s   1554

**Ashata/Maya**
*The Queen's Squadron* - R.M. Meluch   s   3874

**Aten**
*Orion Among the Stars* - Ben Bova   s   589

**Bardsey, Geoffrey**
*The Merlin Effect* - T.A. Barron   f   371

**Barlstilkin, Talbeck**
*Eternal Light* - Paul J. McAuley   s   3710

**Barr, Dallas**
*Buying Time* - Joe Haldeman   s   2487

**Bawn, Caitlin**
*Legends Reborn* - Kenneth C. Flint   f   1958

**Brazil, Nathan**
*Echoes of the Well of Souls* - Jack L.
   Chalker   s   953
*Gods of the Well of Souls* - Jack L. Chalker   s   954
*Shadow of the Well of Souls* - Jack L.
   Chalker   s   961

**Cantrell, Barry**
*Prey* - William W. Johnstone   h   2932

**Chang, Mavra**
*Echoes of the Well of Souls* - Jack L.
   Chalker   s   953
*Gods of the Well of Souls* - Jack L. Chalker   s   954
*Shadow of the Well of Souls* - Jack L.
   Chalker   s   961

**Cole, Cassandra**
*A Logical Magician* - Robert Weinberg   f   5697

**Darius**
*Shadow of Obsession* - Rebecca Neason   f   4082

**Denturian, Maaron**
*Dark Sky Legion* - William Barton   s   379

**Devlin, Annie**
*Scotland the Brave* - Jennifer Roberson   f   4611

**Elavel**
*White Queen* - Gwyneth Jones   s   2955

**Ersh**
*Beholder's Eye* - Julie E. Czerneda   s   1303

**Esen-Alit-Quar**
*Beholder's Eye* - Julie E. Czerneda   s   1303

**Gilgamesh**
*How Like a God* - Brenda W. Clough   f   1089

**Gi'Suei'Obodi'Sedon**
*The Last Dancer* - Daniel Keys Moran   s   3994

**Gi'Tbad'Eovad'Dvan, "William Devane"**
*The Last Dancer* - Daniel Keys Moran   s   3994

**Hanno**
*The Boat of a Million Years* - Poul Anderson   s   125

**Hera**
*Orion and the Conqueror* - Ben Bova   s   590

**James, Will**
*Warpath* - Tony Daniel   s   1337

**Joseph**
*In the Garden of Iden* - Kage Baker   s   298

**Khordas**
*The Element of Fire* - Jason Henderson   f   2657

**Kundry**
*The Grail of Hearts* - Susan Shwartz   f   5015

**Kusaka, Michael**
*The Dark Beyond the Stars* - Frank M.
   Robinson   s   4626

**lach Feragh, Culain**
*Ghost King* - David Gemmell   f   2188

**Lansing, Gilbert "Keith"**
*Starplex* - Robert J. Sawyer   s   4859

**Lomallin**
*The Shaman* - Christopher Stasheff   f   5223

**Luki**
*Fire Crossing* - Cheryl J. Franklin   s   2036

**MacLeod, Connor**
*The Element of Fire* - Jason Henderson   f   2657

**MacLeod, Duncan**
*The Element of Fire* - Jason Henderson   f   2657
*Scotland the Brave* - Jennifer Roberson   f   4611
*Shadow of Obsession* - Rebecca Neason   f   4082

**Marconi, Maria**
*Buying Time* - Joe Haldeman   s   2487

**Mauryl**
*Fortress of Owls* - C.J. Cherryh   f   993

**McIntosh, Alexander**
*Gryphon* - Crawford Kilian   s   3106

**Mendoza**
*In the Garden of Iden* - Kage Baker   s   298

**Mertz, Harry**
*A Covenant of Justice* - David Gerrold   s   2207

**Milo**
*The Sky Lords* - John Brosnan   s   720

**Moran, California**
*Gryphon* - Crawford Kilian   s   3106

**Morgiana**
*The Dagger and the Cross: A Novel of the Crusades* -
   Judith Tarr   f   5393

**Mosay**
*Outnumbering the Dead* - Frederik Pohl   s   4352

**Nomikos, Conrad**
*This Immortal* - Roger Zelazny   s   6074

**O'Mor, Rury**
*Legends Reborn* - Kenneth C. Flint   f   1958

**Orilson, Wend**
*The Crown of Dalemark* - Diana Wynne
   Jones   f   2945

**Orion**
*Orion Among the Stars* - Ben Bova   s   589
*Orion and the Conqueror* - Ben Bova   s   590
*Orion in the Dying Time* - Ben Bova   s   591

**Picket**
*Darwinia* - Robert Charles Wilson   s   5906

**Q**
*Q-Space* - Greg Cox   s   1228
*Q-Zone* - Greg Cox   s   1229

**Quetzal**
*A King Beneath the Mountain* - Robert N.
   Charrette   f   973

**Red Orc**
*More than Fire* - Philip Jose Farmer   s   1871

**Riatha**
*The Eye of the Hunter* - Dennis L.
   McKiernan   f   3833

**Rufus**
*The Boat of a Million Years* - Poul Anderson   s   125

**Sadi**
*Kaleidoscope Century* - John Barnes   s   352

**Saladin**
*The Forever King* - Molly Cochran   *f*   1092

**Sanglant**
*Prince of Dogs* - Kate Elliott   *f*   1775

**Sharra**
*Mall, Mayhem and Magic* - Holly Lisle   *f*   3485

**Shawdell**
*Green Rider* - Kristen Britain   *f*   692

**Shedemei**
*Earthborn* - Orson Scott Card   *s*   884

**Smith, Benjamin Franklin**
*The First Immortal* - James L. Halperin   *s*   2498

**Snorrison, Bran**
*The Deepest Sea* - Charles Barnitz   *f*   363

**Stefanos**
*Chains of Darkness, Chains of Light* - Michelle
   Sagara   *f*   4781
*Children of the Blood: Book Two of The Sundered* -
   Michelle Sagara   *f*   4782
*Into the Dark Lands* - Michelle Sagara   *f*   4783

**Sterling, Justin**
*Dark Heart* - Margaret Weis   *f*   5707
*Testament of the Dragon* - Margaret Weis   *f*   5729

**Stheno**
*Bhagavati* - Kara Dalkey   *f*   1316

**Summerson, Natil**
*Strands of Sunlight* - Gael Baudino   *f*   396

**Susan**
*The Spawn of Loki* - Jason Henderson   *f*   2658

**Taliesin**
*The Broken Sword* - Molly Cochran   *f*   1091

**Talon**
*The Last Wizard* - Simon Hawke   *f*   2619

**Vanderdecker, Cornelius**
*Flying Dutch* - Tom Holt   *f*   2750

**Verid**
*Daughter of Elysium* - Joan Slonczewski   *s*   5091

**Walmsley, Nigel**
*Sailing Bright Eternity* - Gregory Benford   *s*   449

**Wu, Oliver**
*Star Bridge* - James Gunn   *s*   2459

## IMPORTER/EXPORTER

**Fisher, Steve**
*Chase the Morning* - Michael Scott Rohan   *f*   4658
*Cloud Castles* - Michael Scott Rohan   *f*   4659
*The Gates of Noon* - Michael Scott Rohan   *f*   4661

## IMPOSTER

**Arbol**
*Split Heirs* - Lawrence Watt-Evans   *f*   5649

**Caine, Tycho**
*Evil Ascending* - Michael A. Stackpole   *s*   5198

**Carlotta**
*Castle of Deception* - Mercedes Lackey   *f*   3275

**Cerebus**
*When Dreams Collide* - Wm. Mark
   Simmons   *f*   5063

**Claus, Bob "Santa"**
*Santa's Twin* - Dean R. Koontz   *f*   3214

**Davenger/Daven, Harla**
*Dancer of the Sixth* - Michelle Shirey
   Crean   *s*   1254

**Dooley, Paul**
*The Tranquility Alternative* - Allen Steele   *s*   5248

**Faust, Johann**
*If at Faust You Don't Succeed* - Roger
   Zelazny   *f*   6070

**Grandier, Urbain**
*The Element of Fire* - Martha Wells   *f*   5750

**Hal Jam**
*The Bear Went over the Mountain* - William
   Kotzwinkle   *f*   3222

**Hastings, Kyle Stevens**
*Down the Bright Way* - Robert Reed   *s*   4505

**liMarchborg, Tradain**
*The White Tribunal* - Paula Volsky   *f*   5583

**Marceline**
*Fools* - Pat Cadigan   *s*   805

**Mike**
*The Moon Is a Harsh Mistress* - Robert A.
   Heinlein   *s*   2645

**Orgoru**
*A Wizard in Peace* - Christopher Stasheff   *s*   5233

**Quigley, Joe**
*Lady Slings the Booze* - Spider Robinson   *s*   4640

**Rahl, Drefan**
*Temple of the Winds* - Terry Goodkind   *f*   2270

**Sulula "Philiope"**
*Conan of the Red Brotherhood* - Leonard
   Carpenter   *f*   906

**Tibbon, Rachel**
*Kingdom of the Grail* - A.A. Attanasio   *f*   269

**Trioculus**
*The Glove of Darth Vader* - Paul Davids   *s*   1392
*The Lost City of the Jedi* - Paul Davids   *s*   1393
*Zorba the Hutt's Revenge* - Paul Davids   *s*   1394

**Tyrell, Sarah**
*Blade Runner: Replicant Night* - K.W. Jeter   *s*   2907

**Weston, Jamie**
*Summerland* - L. Dean James   *f*   2865

## INDIAN

**Aeslu "Moon's Stead" of Vmatta**
*Fire and Ice* - Edward Myers   *f*   4061
*The Mountain Made of Light* - Edward
   Myers   *f*   4062
*The Summit* - Edward Myers   *f*   4063

**Amgigh**
*My Sister the Moon* - Sue Harrison   *f*   2582

**Anasan**
*Sing for a Gentle Rain* - J. Alison James   *f*   2861

**Animiki-Waewidum, Gahzee**
*Svaha* - Charles de Lint   *s*   1437

**Aqamdax**
*Song of the River* - Sue Harrison   *f*   2583

**Atwood, Clancy "Kolo"**
*Demon Dance* - T. Chris Martindale   *h*   3655

**Aurelio**
*The War of Don Emmanuel's Nether Parts* - Louis de
   Bernieres   *f*   1412

**Bad Belly/Still Water**
*People of the Earth* - W. Michael Gear   *f*   2166

**Bear, Bagese**
*Dead Voices: Natural Agonies in the Real World* -
   Gerald Vizenor   *f*   5578

**Bear, Tom**
*The Charm* - Adam Niswander   *h*   4111

**Bigthorn, Henry**
*Clarke County, Space* - Allen Steele   *s*   5241

**Bitterhand, Calvin**
*The Trickster* - Muriel Gray   *h*   2340

**Bluecrane, Will**
*Earthsong* - Suzette Haden Elgin   *s*   1769

**Boles, Danny**
*Brittle Innings* - Michael Bishop   *h*   498

**Broken Echo**
*Spirit Crossings* - Claudia Peck   *f*   4275

**Broken-finger, Leonard**
*High Steel* - Jack C. Haldeman II   *s*   2486

**Carmody, Alice Levertov**
*Sailor Song* - Ken Kesey   *s*   3082

**Chagak**
*Mother Earth, Father Sky* - Sue Harrison   *f*   2581

**Chakotay**
*Pathways* - Jeri Taylor   *s*   5404
*Ragnarok* - Nathan Archer   *s*   206

**Chato del Klinne**
*Ghost Dance* - Kathryn Ptacek   *h*   4441

**Coconino**
*Children of the Earth* - Catherine Wells   *s*   5743
*The Earth Is All That Lasts* - Catherine
   Wells   *s*   5744
*The Earth Saver* - Catherine Wells   *s*   5745

**Crow**
*Crow and Weasel* - Barry Lopez   *f*   3523

**Digging Woman**
*Walking Wolf* - Nancy A. Collins   *h*   1126

**Eleazar**
*Whisper* - Raymond Van Over   *h*   5539

**Elk Charm**
*People of the Fire* - W. Michael Gear   *f*   2167

**Fall, Thomas**
*Warpath* - Tony Daniel   *s*   1337

**Geronimo**
*Apacheria* - Jake Page   *s*   4233

**Green Spider**
*People of the Lakes* - Kathleen O'Neal Gear   *f*   2164

**Gultec**
*Feathered Dragon* - Douglas Niles   *f*   4108

**Hawk-That-Settles**
*Krokodil Tears* - Jack Yeovil   *f*   6023

**Hunt, Sam**
*The Trickster* - Muriel Gray   *h*   2340

**Icefalcon**
*Icefalcon's Quest* - Barbara Hambly   *f*   2504

**Idera**
*Dark Legend* - Jamake Highwater   *f*   2686

**Juh**
*Apacheria* - Jake Page   *s*   4233

**Kane, Bowie**
*Pitfall* - Ronald Kelly   *h*   3054

**Katelo, Jonathan**
*Beyond Eden* - J.M. Morgan   *s*   3999

**Katelo, Jonathon**
*Desert Eden* - J.M. Morgan   *s*   4000

**Katelo, Seth**
*Beyond Eden* - J.M. Morgan   *s*   3999
*Future Eden* - J.M. Morgan   *s*   4001

**Kerac, John**
*Wake of the Werewolf* - Geoffrey Caine   *h*   834

**Kerebawa**
*Nightlife* - Brian Hodge   *h*   2702

**Kiin**
*My Sister the Moon* - Sue Harrison   *f*   2582

**K'os**
*Song of the River* - Sue Harrison   *f*   2583

**Kuwai**
*Dark Legend* - Jamake Highwater   f   2686

**Lichen**
*People of the River* - W. Michael Gear   f   2168

**Little Bear**
*The Key to the Indian* - Lynne Reid Banks   f   331
*The Secret of the Indian* - Lynne Reid Banks   f   332

**Little Spring**
*Apacheria* - Jake Page   s   4233

**Lowell, Jacob**
*Nadya: The Wolf Chronicles* - Pat Murphy   f   4052

**McIntosh, Calvin**
*Stoneskin's Revenge* - Tom Deitz   f   1476
*Sunshaker's War* - Tom Deitz   f   1477

**Medicine Plant**
*Dawn Land* - Joseph Bruchac   f   731

**Miriam**
*The Spirit Stalker* - Nina Romberg   h   4664

**Miss Bird**
*The Gilda Stories* - Jewelle Gomez   h   2267

**Montes, Samta**
*A Whisper of Time* - Paula E. Downing   s   1595

**Moonlight, Charlie**
*Thunder Rise* - G. Wayne Miller   h   3895

**Mortega, Dyani**
*Blood Siege* - G. Harry Stine   s   5278

**Nahadeh, Yute**
*Ember From the Sun* - Mark Canter   s   870

**Ninekiller, Amos**
*The Wild Blue and the Gray* - William Sanders   s   4814

**O'Connor, Thunderbird Devlin "Bird"**
*Above the Lower Sky* - Tom Deitz   f   1469

**Ooljee, Paul**
*Cyber Way* - Alan Dean Foster   s   2000

**Otter**
*People of the Lakes* - Kathleen O'Neal Gear   f   2164

**Renard, Eris**
*Green Lake* - S.K. Epperson   h   1830

**Sahacat**
*People of the Sky* - Clare Bell   s   431

**Salazar, Bettina**
*Ghost Dance* - Kathryn Ptacek   h   4441

**Sallas, Ike "the Bakatcha Bandit"**
*Sailor Song* - Ken Kesey   s   3082

**Samiq**
*My Sister the Moon* - Sue Harrison   f   2582

**Shuganan**
*Mother Earth, Father Sky* - Sue Harrison   f   2581

**Sky-fire-trail**
*Collidescope* - Grace Chetwin   s   1011

**Spotted Horse, David**
*Sacred Ground* - Mercedes Lackey   f   3294

**Spring Rain**
*Sing for a Gentle Rain* - J. Alison James   f   2861

**Star Shell**
*People of the Lakes* - Kathleen O'Neal Gear   f   2164

**Stone, Charlie**
*Wendigo Border* - Catherine Montrose   h   3967

**Stranger, John**
*High Steel* - Jack C. Haldeman II   s   2486
*Run for the Stars/Echoes of Thunder* - Harlan Ellison   s   1788

**Tale Teller**
*Tatham Mound* - Piers Anthony   f   191

**Talldeer, Frank**
*Sacred Ground* - Mercedes Lackey   f   3294

**Temiya, Kesbe**
*People of the Sky* - Clare Bell   s   431

**Tesuawane, Sovawanea "Sophy"** a
*Gibbon's Decline and Fall* - Sheri S. Tepper   s   5430

**Tharon**
*People of the River* - W. Michael Gear   f   2168

**Thaxton, Wendall**
*The Higher Space* - Jamil Nasir   s   4070

**Thunder, Anna**
*The Grass Dancer* - Susan Power   f   4380

**Thunder, Charlene**
*The Grass Dancer* - Susan Power   f   4380

**Tumkis "Lady Sun"**
*Madoc's Hundred* - Pat Winter   f   5925

**Uhatatse**
*People of the Mesa* - Ardath Mayhar   f   3704

**Uta**
*Raptor* - Paul Zindel   s   6084

**Utlunta**
*Stoneskin's Revenge* - Tom Deitz   f   1476

**Wakandagi, Ptesa "Tesa/Good Eyes"**
*Silent Songs* - A.C. Crispin   s   1264

**Wanachtee**
*The Silent Stars Go By* - James White   s   5781

**Wanbli**
*The Third Eagle: Lessons Along a Minor String* - R.A. MacAvoy   s   3583

**Washi**
*Dark Legend* - Jamake Highwater   f   2686

**Waterman, James "Jamie" Fox**
*Mars* - Ben Bova   s   586

**Weasel**
*Crow and Weasel* - Barry Lopez   f   3523

**Webb, Danny**
*The Serpent Slayers* - Adam Niswander   h   4113

**Webster, Grandma**
*The Godmother's Web* - Elizabeth Ann Scarborough   f   4864

**White Eagle, Zacxk**
*Shaman Woods* - Morgan Fields   h   1931

**Whitefeather, Matthew**
*The Last Vampire* - Kathryn Meyer Griffith   h   2440

**Winchester, Miriam**
*Shadow Walkers* - Nina Romberg   h   4663

**Wind Soldier, Harley**
*The Grass Dancer* - Susan Power   f   4380

## INDUSTRIALIST

**Brown, Frank**
*White Horse, Dark Dragon* - Robert C. Fleet   f   1947

**Camerata, Jo**
*Star Brothers* - Ben Bova   s   594

**Darby, Abraham III**
*The Iron Bridge* - David Morse   s   4036

**Evans, Philip**
*Mindstar Rising* - Peter F. Hamilton   s   2526

**Hutton, George**
*Earth* - David Brin   s   685

**Ingles, Benton**
*Outworld Cats* - Jack Lovejoy   s   3536

## INNKEEPER

**Anara**
*India's Story* - Kathlyn S. Starbuck   s   5208

**Bates, Norman**
*Psycho* - Robert Bloch   h   540

**Caramon**
*The Second Generation* - Margaret Weis   f   5724

**Karsh**
*The Innkeeper's Song* - Peter S. Beagle   f   409

**Luisa**
*Cambio Bay* - Kate Wilhelm   f   5806

**Parker, Caroline**
*Winter Wolves* - Earle Wescott   h   5756

**Solith, Gwin Nien**
*The Cursed* - Dave Duncan   f   1674

## INSPECTOR

**Quiles, Phil**
*Water Rites* - Guy N. Smith   h   5121

## INSURANCE AGENT

**Cochrane, Rick**
*Time and Chance* - Alan Brennert   f   676

**Croft, Samantha**
*Demon Within* - Dana Reed   h   4499

**Priestley, Oswald**
*Nazareth Hill* - Ramsey Campbell   h   861

## INSURANCE INVESTIGATOR

**Hake, Elliot**
*Out of Body* - Thomas Baum   h   397

**Kullervo, Vyra**
*Greenthieves* - Alan Dean Foster   s   2005

**Lincoln, Bojake "Buffalo"**
*Double Jeopardy* - Aaron Allston   s   86

**Manz, Broderick**
*Greenthieves* - Alan Dean Foster   s   2005

**Parker, James "Spark"**
*Double Jeopardy* - Aaron Allston   s   86

## INTERIOR DECORATOR

**Hollander, Mariele**
*Graythings* - Pat Graversen   h   2335

## INVALID

**Maddock, Yanaba**
*Powers That Be* - Anne McCaffrey   s   3745

**Unger, Alejandro "Alex"**
*Heavy Weather* - Bruce Sterling   s   5258

**Young, Pat**
*Obsessed* - Rick R. Reed   h   4500

## INVENTOR

**Bailey, David "Herbert" Clancy**
*The Modular Man* - Roger MacBride Allen   s   79

**Blervaque, Carver**
*Living Real* - James C. Bassett   s   386

**Boles, Barrington**
*Parallelities* - Alan Dean Foster   s   2012

**Brenner, Hugh**
*Paths to Otherwhere* - James P. Hogan   s   2728

**Burke, Martin**
*/ -* Greg Bear  *s*  413

**Chang, Marte**
*Burn* - Bill Ransom  *s*  4476
*ViraVax* - Bill Ransom  *s*  4478

**Claiborne, Kevin**
*Pacific Edge* - Kim Stanley Robinson  *s*  4634

**Cowperthwait, Cosmo**
*The Steampunk Trilogy* - Paul Di Filippo  *s*  1518

**da Vinci, Leonardo**
*The Memory Cathedral* - Jack Dann  *s*  1341

**D'Auber MacLeod, Carli**
*Proxies* - Laura J. Mixon  *s*  3922

**Demopoulos, Demetrios "Dr. Dimension"**
*Dr. Dimension* - John DeChancie  *s*  1456

**Dietz, Tre**
*Freeware* - Rudy Rucker  *s*  4703

**Edison, Thomas**
*Expiration Date* - Tim Powers  *f*  4383

**Habeggar**
*Slow Freight* - F.M. Busby  *s*  785

**Haggerwells, Barbara**
*Bring the Jubilee* - Ward Moore  *s*  3993

**Hawk**
*The Hunter Returns* - David Drake  *f*  1632

**Helmish**
*Top Dog* - Jerry Jay Carroll  *f*  915

**Kazenstein, Morris**
*Sewer, Gas & Electric* - Matt Ruff  *s*  4708

**Leclerc, Louis**
*Witch* - Donald E. McQuinn  *s*  3864

**Leonard**
*Jingo* - Terry Pratchett  *f*  4393

**Lewis, Carl**
*Cyberbooks* - Ben Bova  *s*  582

**Lowe, Saul**
*Door Number Three* - Patrick O'Leary  *s*  4210

**Lowrey, Jason**
*Death Dream* - Ben Bova  *s*  583

**Macafee, Simon**
*The Cyborg From Earth* - Charles Sheffield  *s*  4952

**Mallory, Quinn**
*Sliders: The Novel* - Brad Linaweaver  *s*  3467

**McDougal, Marta**
*Core* - Paul Preuss  *s*  4416

**Mobarak, Cyrus "Torquemada"**
*Cold as Ice* - Charles Sheffield  *s*  4950

**Newton, Isaac**
*Newton's Cannon* - J. Gregory Keyes  *f*  3097

**Portaris, Anne**
*Arrow From Earth* - F.M. Busby  *s*  782

**Rook, August**
*The Rim-World Legacy and Beyond* - Frank A. Javor  *s*  2882

**Samuels, Albert**
*The Clouds of Magellan* - David F. Nighbert  *s*  4103

**Sanders, Johnny**
*Armed Memory* - Jim Young  *s*  6048

**Sartorius**
*The Waterworks* - E.L. Doctorow  *s*  1564

**Tesla, Nikola**
*The Prestige* - Christopher Priest  *s*  4432

**Traveller, Josiah**
*Anti-Ice* - Stephen Baxter  *s*  398

# INVESTIGATOR

**Adkins, Merrill**
*A Chill in the Blood* - P.N. Elrod  *h*  1793

**Ambrose, Jonathan**
*Death of a Darklord* - Laurell K. Hamilton  *h*  2516

**Byron**
*The Queen of Darkness* - Miguel Conner  *s*  1134

**Christman, Barbara**
*Sole Survivor* - Dean R. Koontz  *h*  3215

**Cutter, Lance**
*Mr. Sandman* - Lyle Howard  *h*  2779

**Gamaliel, Cartee**
*Kindred* - John Gideon  *h*  2222

**Hutsenreiter, Skirlet**
*Night Lamp* - Jack Vance  *s*  5548

**McKenzie, Chia**
*Idoru* - William Gibson  *s*  2218

# JEWELER

**Baird, Jason**
*The Jade Ogre* - Kenneth Robeson  *f*  4623

# JOURNALIST

**Adashek, David**
*Meg* - Steve Alten  *h*  88

**Andreyeva, Maya Tayanichna**
*The Fortunate Fall* - Raphael Carter  *s*  927

**Bankole, Larkin "Asha Vere"**
*Parable of the Talents* - Octavia E. Butler  *s*  793

**Barbee, Will**
*Darker than You Think* - Jack Williamson  *h*  5861

**Barlowe, Philip**
*Act of Love* - Joe R. Lansdale  *h*  3319

**Barris, Michael Albert**
*The Immortals* - Tracy Hickman  *s*  2681

**Bathory-Kereshtur, Drake**
*Blood Countess* - Andrei Codrescu  *h*  1094

**Baylor, Katti**
*Rockabilly Hell* - William W. Johnstone  *h*  2933

**Behler, Simon William**
*The Last Voyage of Somebody the Sailor* - John Barth  *f*  374

**Belzoni, Peter**
*Dinosaur Summer* - Greg Bear  *s*  416

**Benedek, Walter**
*Live Girls* - Ray Garton  *h*  2151

**Benedict, Sally**
*Infinity's Child* - Harry Stein  *h*  5250

**Bennett, Laura**
*Echoes* - Jackie Hyman  *h*  2818

**Bolton, Maxwell "Max"**
*Shade and Shadow* - Francine G. Woodbury  *f*  5967

**Bratenahl, Robert**
*I, Robot: The Illustrated Screenplay* - Harlan Ellison  *s*  1785

**Breen, Matthew**
*Paradise: A Chronicle of a Distant World* - Mike Resnick  *s*  4552

**Brenda**
*Steel Beach* - John Varley  *s*  5566

**Cage, Wynne**
*Wildlife* - James Patrick Kelly  *s*  3049

**Cain, Martin**
*Empire's Horizon* - John Brizzolara  *s*  707

**Carlsen, Anita**
*Sorcerers of Sodom* - Roger Elwood  *h*  1804

**Carpenter, Joe**
*Sole Survivor* - Dean R. Koontz  *h*  3215

**Carver, Alison**
*Cup of Clay* - Carole Nelson Douglas  *f*  1583
*Seed upon the Wind* - Carole Nelson Douglas  *f*  1584

**Clayborne, Laura**
*Mine* - Robert R. McCammon  *h*  3756

**Clemens, Sam**
*How Few Remain* - Harry Turtledove  *s*  5504

**Coley, J.J.**
*Boneman* - Lisa Cantrell  *h*  871

**Colter, Daniel**
*Into the Deep* - Ken Grimwood  *s*  2450

**Constantine, Danny**
*Archangel* - Michael Conner  *s*  1133

**Converse, Maggie**
*The Burning Man* - Michael Hammond  *h*  2530

**Corvan, Rex**
*Mars Prime* - William C. Dietz  *s*  1548
*Matrix Man* - William C. Dietz  *s*  1549

**Costello, T.P.**
*Evolution's Shore* - Ian McDonald  *s*  3792

**Cotter, Wolf**
*Mastery* - Kelley Wilde  *h*  5802

**Crandall, Samantha "Sam"**
*The Modular Man* - Roger MacBride Allen  *s*  79

**Cross, Joanna**
*Superstition* - David Ambrose  *h*  90

**Davenport, Geoff**
*The Last Voice They Hear* - Ramsey Campbell  *h*  858

**Davis, Hannah**
*Marked Cards* - George R.R. Martin  *s*  3647

**Davis, Kelly Brynn**
*Shapes* - Steve Vance  *h*  5552

**DeLuca, Neil**
*The Gilgul* - Henry W. Hocherman  *h*  2697

**Dewey, Thomas E. "Ted"**
*The Lurker* - James V. Smith  *h*  5123

**Donovan, Lincoln "Link"**
*The Devil's Laughter* - William W. Johnstone  *h*  2930

**Douglass, Frederick**
*How Few Remain* - Harry Turtledove  *s*  5504

**Driscoll, Guy**
*The Moons of Summer* - S.K. Epperson  *h*  1831

**Duke, Nicholas**
*Majestic* - Whitley Strieber  *s*  5341

**Dunlap, Gordon**
*The Totem* - David Morrell  *h*  4012

**Durbin, Ashley**
*Hair of the Dog* - Brett Davis  *f*  1400

**Eberhart, George**
*Good News From Outer Space* - John Kessel  *s*  3084

**Elgin, Edith**
*Moonwar* - Ben Bova  *s*  588

**Elliot, Dan**
*Beneath Still Waters* - Matthew J. Costello  *h*  1193

**Falco, Ray**
*Vodoun* - David Madsen  *h*  3605

**Faronya, Kelmer**
*The Regiment's War* - John Dalmas  *s*  1326

**Fleming, Jack**
*Blood on the Water* - P.N. Elrod   *h*   1791
*Bloodlist* - P.N. Elrod   *h*   1792
*A Chill in the Blood* - P.N. Elrod   *h*   1793
*Fire in the Blood* - P.N. Elrod   *h*   1796

**Fouts, Marian**
*Murder in the Solid State* - Wil McCarthy   *s*   3764

**Freeman, Giles**
*Candle Night* - Phil Rickman   *h*   4586

**Friendly, Bud**
*Silent Moon* - William Relling Jr.   *h*   4531

**Frolatti, Victor**
*The Golden Mean* - Nick Bantock   *f*   334

**Gale, Brad**
*Thunder Rise* - G. Wayne Miller   *h*   3895

**Gallagher, Dori**
*Trickster* - Chris Curry   *h*   1297

**Garrith, Lance**
*The Specialist* - Wynne Whiteford   *s*   5788

**Gaylen, Linda**
*Brainstorm* - Steven M. Krauzer   *h*   3230

**Gibbs, Hank**
*Psycho House* - Robert Bloch   *h*   542

**Glenn, Molly**
*Till the End of Time* - Allen Appel   *f*   201

**Gorlay, Rankin**
*The Dark One* - Guy N. Smith   *h*   5118

**Grimes, Griff**
*Serial Killer Days* - David Prill   *h*   4436

**Guglioli, Johnny**
*White Queen* - Gwyneth Jones   *s*   2955

**Haig, Gudrun "Dauna"**
*The Singularity Project* - F.M. Busby   *s*   784

**Hammond, Lech**
*Mars—The Red Planet* - Mick Farren   *s*   1880

**Hayes, Terry**
*The Season of Passage* - Christopher Pike   *h*   4331

**Hemingway, Kate**
*Twilight* - Peter James   *h*   2876

**Hendricks, Cara**
*Shadow World* - A.C. Crispin   *s*   1262

**Hobbs, Alexandra**
*Red Angel* - Roxanne Longstreet   *h*   3518

**Hodges, Laren**
*The Lurker* - James V. Smith   *h*   5123

**Hph-wayuo "Alvin"**
*Heaven's Reach* - David Brin   *s*   687

**Inconnu, Jane "Jade" Avril**
*Sam Gunn, Unlimited* - Ben Bova   *s*   593

**Inman, Toby**
*Pictures at 11* - Norman Spinrad   *s*   5173

**Jacobs, Peter**
*The Cold One* - Christopher Pike   *h*   4327

**Jacobs-Wolde, Jessica**
*My Soul to Keep* - Tannarive Due   *h*   1670

**Jayson, Darby**
*The Homecoming* - Kimberly Rangel   *h*   4471

**Jeffers, Anne**
*Black Lightning* - John Saul   *h*   4837

**Johnson, Hildy**
*Steel Beach* - John Varley   *s*   5566

**Jones, Cory**
*City of Pain* - John Terra   *f*   5438

**Jones, Jeremiah "Jonesy"**
*Chaos Come Again* - Wilhelmina Baird   *s*   293

**Kar, Ann**
*Century 21* - Ewa Kuryluk   *s*   3263

**Kay, Laura**
*Catamount* - Michael Peak   *f*   4273

**Keegan, Caroline**
*Wyrm Wolf* - Edo van Belkom   *h*   5535

**Kennison, Rogers**
*Deadly Dreams* - Gerald A. Schiller   *h*   4874

**Kent, Clark "Superman"**
*The Death and Life of Superman* - Roger
   Stern   *s*   5262
*The Further Adventures of Superman* - Martin H.
   Greenberg   *s*   2393
*Lois & Clark* - C.J. Cherryh   *s*   999

**Kirby, Paul**
*The Chosen* - Edward Lee   *h*   3389

**Knight, Stormy**
*Prey* - William W. Johnstone   *h*   2932

**Kozinski, Judy**
*Oaths and Miracles* - Nancy Kress   *s*   3242

**Kroft, Brian**
*The Undine* - Michael O'Rourke   *h*   4224

**Kurimoto, Eva**
*Protektor* - Charles Platt   *s*   4342

**Lane, Lois**
*The Death and Life of Superman* - Roger
   Stern   *s*   5262
*Lois & Clark* - C.J. Cherryh   *s*   999

**Lang, Alice "Lancaster"**
*Einstein's Bridge* - John Cramer   *s*   1244

**Law, Lily**
*Darwinia* - Robert Charles Wilson   *s*   5906

**Leung, Kathy**
*Vespers* - Jeff Rovin   *h*   4688

**Lyell, Thomasina**
*The Pure Cold Light* - Gregory Frost   *s*   2087

**Lyon, John**
*Bring Me Children* - David Martin   *h*   3637

**Maas, Ellen**
*The Forbidden Zone* - Whitley Strieber   *h*   5340

**Machiavelli, Niccolo**
*Pasquale's Angel* - Paul J. McAuley   *f*   3714

**MacPherson, Maggie**
*Force of Arms* - G. Harry Stine   *s*   5279

**Maguire, Charlotte "Charlie"**
*Fatherland* - Robert Harris   *s*   2564

**Mallernee, Jay**
*My Soul to Take* - Steven Spruill   *s*   5184

**Marat, Mike**
*Thirst of the Vampire* - T. Lucien Wright   *h*   5988

**Markham, Robert**
*A Hunger in the Soul* - Mike Resnick   *s*   4545

**Marsh, Maxwell**
*Rage* - Elizabeth Ergas   *h*   1834

**Marshall, Deidi**
*Flesh and Blood* - D.A. Fowler   *h*   2024

**Mash, Madeleine**
*Coyote* - Peter Gadol   *f*   2100

**Masterson, Rick**
*Darkling* - Michael O'Rourke   *h*   4223

**Matthews, Susan**
*Dancing on Air* - Nancy Kress   *s*   3240

**Maxwell, James**
*The Mysterium* - Eric McCormack   *h*   3780

**McAslan, Gabriel "Gaby"**
*Evolution's Shore* - Ian McDonald   *s*   3792

**McKinnon, Savvy**
*Insanity, Illinois* - Mark Sumner   *s*   5358

**McPherson, Mark**
*Seed upon the Wind* - Carole Nelson
   Douglas   *f*   1584

**Mitchell, Kelly**
*Domination* - Michael Cecilione   *h*   946

**Moon, Donovan**
*Morningstar* - Peter Atkins   *h*   265

**Moravec, Alan**
*This Symbiotic Fascination* - Charlee Jacob   *h*   2843

**Morelli, Berry**
*Candle Night* - Phil Rickman   *h*   4586

**Morrison, Faye**
*Curfew* - Phil Rickman   *h*   4587

**Musik, Peter**
*The End-of-Everything Man* - Tom De
   Haven   *f*   1421

**Myshtigo, Cort**
*This Immortal* - Roger Zelazny   *s*   6074

**Nicholson, Graeme**
*Expansion* - Peter F. Hamilton   *s*   2525

**Nielson, Anne**
*Bad Dreams* - Kim Newman   *h*   4096

**Noble, Bentley**
*Shackled* - Ray Garton   *h*   2156

**Noir, Alfred "Alf"**
*Psychoshop* - Alfred Bester   *s*   477

**Nygerski, Cyrus "Moondog"**
*Moondog* - Henry Garfield   *h*   2138

**O'Connor, Dennis**
*The Hunger of the Beast* - John Driver   *h*   1656

**Paik, Anna**
*Cortez on Jupiter* - Ernest Hogan   *s*   2721

**Parker, Max**
*Parallelities* - Alan Dean Foster   *s*   2012

**Pascal, David**
*Carnosaur* - Harry Adam Knight   *s*   3191

**Pemberton, Martin**
*The Waterworks* - E.L. Doctorow   *s*   1564

**Perez, Theresa "Terry"**
*Echoes of the Well of Souls* - Jack L.
   Chalker   *s*   953
*Shadow of the Well of Souls* - Jack L.
   Chalker   *s*   961

**Perry, Brenda**
*The Wishing Well* - Charles de Lint   *f*   1441

**Perry, Jerrica**
*The Bighead* - Edward Lee   *h*   3387

**Phillips, Randa**
*Dark Debts* - Karen Hall   *h*   2494

**Pierce, Melinda**
*Goon* - Edward Lee   *h*   3392

**Piper, Rick**
*Panic* - Chris Curry   *h*   1295

**Poe, John Charles**
*The Black Cat* - Robert Poe   *h*   4344
*Return to the House of Usher* - Robert Poe   *h*   4345

**Pohaku, Annie**
*Mars Underground* - William Hartmann   *s*   2584

**Prescott, Elaine**
*Soul Snatchers* - Michael Cecilione   *h*   947

**Prosky, Ronald**
*The New Neighbor* - Ray Garton   *h*   2154

**Quadrun, Ben**
*Nightmare Logic* - Matthew Hall   *h*   2495

**Quinn**
*Silicon Embrace* - John Shirley　*s*　5009

**Raleigh, David**
*Nightmare* - S.K. Epperson　*h*　1832

**Ravanski, Magda**
*The Frighteners* - Michael Jahn　*h*　2856

**Rebecca "Becca"**
*Briar Rose* - Jane Yolen　*f*　6029

**Reed, Kate**
*Judgment of Tears: Anno Dracula 1959* - Kim
Newman　*h*　4098

**Reynolds, Kelly**
*Area 51* - Robert Doherty　*s*　1565

**Robbins, Maggie**
*The Dig* - Alan Dean Foster　*s*　2002

**Roberts, Roy**
*Grave Markings* - Michael A. Arnzen　*h*　212

**Roberts, Veronica "Ronnie"**
*Universal Soldier* - Robert Tine　*s*　5476

**Rosen, Gerry**
*The Jericho Iteration* - Allen Steele　*s*　5242

**Runyon, Damon**
*Nevermore* - William Hjortsberg　*h*　2692

**Sawyer, Meredith**
*The Long Midnight* - Daniel Ransom　*h*　4480

**Saxton, Drake**
*The Black Carousel* - Charles L. Grant　*h*　2303

**Shade, Kathleen**
*Portrait of the Psychopath as a Young Woman* -
Edward Lee　*h*　3395

**Sloan, Susan**
*Beneath Still Waters* - Matthew J. Costello　*h*　1193

**Smithback, Bill**
*Relic* - Douglas Preston　*h*　4414
*Reliquary* - Douglas Preston　*h*　4415

**Spencer, Arlene**
*Revenge of the Seventh Carrier* - Peter Albano　*s*　49

**Stevens, Jim**
*Reborn* - F. Paul Wilson　*h*　5895

**Stiller, Dennis**
*The Nexus* - Mike McQuay　*f*　3860

**Stone, Walker**
*Whipping Boy* - John Byrne　*h*　800

**Strasheim, John**
*Bloom* - Wil McCarthy　*s*　3761

**Suilin, Dick**
*Rolling Hot* - David Drake　*s*　1642

**Sulaiman, Kahlili "Kay Bee" bint Munadi**
*Looking for the Mahdi* - N. Lee Wood　*s*　5966

**Sumner, Shaelyn**
*Distant Dreams* - Jenny Lykins　*f*　3576

**Thaxton, Xavier**
*Count Geiger's Blues* - Michael Bishop　*s*　499

**Theremon 762**
*Nightfall* - Isaac Asimov　*s*　248

**Thomas, Fran**
*Winter Wolves* - Earle Wescott　*h*　5756

**Thorne, Holly**
*Cold Fire* - Dean R. Koontz　*h*　3203

**Tiernan, John**
*The Jericho Iteration* - Allen Steele　*s*　5242

**Trask, Victor**
*Savant* - Rex Miller　*h*　3901

**Tremaine, Bernard**
*Black Dogs* - Ian McEwan　*h*　3808

**Tremaine, Ian**
*Carlucci's Edge* - Richard Paul Russo　*s*　4747

**Urmila**
*The Calcutta Chromosome* - Amitav Ghosh　*h*　2214

**Vigeant, Alison**
*Angel Souls and Devil Hearts* - Christopher
Golden　*h*　2255
*Of Masques and Martyrs* - Christopher
Golden　*h*　2258

**Wallace, Ditsy**
*The Square Deal* - David Drake　*s*　1644

**Watkins, Beverly**
*Operation Damocles* - Oscar L. Fellows　*s*　1915

**Watterson, Sam**
*Silent Scream* - Dan Schmidt　*h*　4883

**Webster, Torie**
*The Eyes of Torie Webster* - Roy Sorrels　*h*　5164

**Wilkins, John**
*Silent Scream* - Dan Schmidt　*h*　4883

**Wilson, Braemer**
*White Queen* - Gwyneth Jones　*s*　2955

**Windsor, Marion**
*The Blood of the Lamb* - Thomas F.
Monteleone　*h*　3958

**Wing, Sue**
*The Summoning* - Bentley Little　*h*　3498

**Woodbury, Gillian**
*Silent Moon* - William Relling Jr.　*h*　4531

**Worth, Andrew**
*Distress* - Greg Egan　*s*　1760

**Wright, Paul**
*Nightlight* - Michael Cadnum　*h*　813

**Yokusuka, Jory**
*Berserker Fury* - Fred Saberhagen　*s*　4760

**Zarnicke, Marion**
*A World Lost* - James B. Johnson　*s*　2921

## JUDGE

**Acari, Stefan**
*The Beacon* - Valerie J. Freireich　*s*　2048

**Brody, Aloysius**
*Pallas* - L. Neil Smith　*s*　5132

**Candle, Martin**
*Blameless in Abaddon* - James Morrow　*f*　4029

**Fastet, Meer**
*Exile* - Michael P. Kube-McDowell　*s*　3248

**Gundhalinu, BZ**
*The Summer Queen* - Joan D. Vinge　*s*　5572

**James, Dede**
*The Between* - Tannarive Due　*h*　1669

**Mertz, Harry**
*A Covenant of Justice* - David Gerrold　*s*　2207

**Phillips, Triune Adjudicator**
*Tangled Webs* - Steve Mudd　*s*　4044

**Questioner II**
*Six Moon Dance* - Sheri S. Tepper　*s*　5437

**Rile, Martin**
*Lunar Justice* - Charles L. Harness　*s*　2545

**Skerow**
*Flesh and Gold* - Phyllis Gotlieb　*s*　2286

**Svensdotter, Esther "Star"**
*Red Planet Run* - Dana Stabenow　*s*　5187

**Tarkenton, Lewis**
*Echoes* - Jackie Hyman　*h*　2818

**Underbridge, Kin**
*Wrath of the Princes* - Holly Lisle　*f*　3490

## KIDNAPPER

**Boldface, Byron**
*Dragon Tempest* - Don Callander　*f*　844

**Carton, Sidney "Sid"**
*North Wind* - Gwyneth Jones　*s*　2953

**Crawford, Stony**
*The Halloween Man* - Douglas Clegg　*h*　1080

**de Clifford, Robert**
*The Dragon and the Gnarly King* - Gordon R.
Dickson　*f*　1529

**Falushe, Viole**
*The Demon Princes: Volume One* - Jack
Vance　*s*　5544

**Pong, Mustapha**
*McCade's Bounty* - William C. Dietz　*s*　1550

**Pook**
*Voices of Hope* - David Feintuch　*s*　1903

**Tucker, Randy Karl**
*Freeware* - Rudy Rucker　*s*　4703

## KNIGHT

**Amaury**
*King & Raven* - Cary James　*f*　2858

**Amfortas**
*The Grail of Hearts* - Susan Shwartz　*f*　5015

**Bedwyr**
*The Last Pendragon* - Robert Rice　*f*　4584

**Bright**
*Gawain and Lady Green* - Anne Eliot
Crompton　*f*　1269

**Byron**
*Henry's Gift: The Magic Eye* - David
Worsick　*f*　5972

**Connor**
*Merlin's Legacy: Dawn of Camelot* - Quinn Taylor
Evans　*f*　1857

**Darius**
*Kaz the Minotaur* - Richard A. Knaak　*f*　3172

**de Beq, Henri**
*Knights of the Blood* - Scott MacMillan　*f*　3602

**de Courcy, Guiscard**
*King Javan's Year* - Katherine Kurtz　*f*　3258

**de Verdeur, Michel "Raven"**
*King & Raven* - Cary James　*f*　2858

**Drummond, Cathan**
*The Bastard Prince* - Katherine Kurtz　*f*　3255

**Durendal**
*The Gilded Chain: A Tale of the King's Blades* - Dave
Duncan　*f*　1679

**Eckert, Jim/Gorbash**
*The Dragon and the Djinn* - Gordon R.
Dickson　*f*　1528
*The Dragon and the Gnarly King* - Gordon R.
Dickson　*f*　1529
*The Dragon at War* - Gordon R. Dickson　*f*　1530
*The Dragon in Lyonesse* - Gordon R.
Dickson　*f*　1531
*The Dragon Knight* - Gordon R. Dickson　*f*　1532
*The Dragon on the Border* - Gordon R.
Dickson　*f*　1533
*The Dragon, the Earl, and the Troll* - Gordon R.
Dickson　*f*　1534

**Ector**
*The Dragon's Boy* - Jane Yolen　*f*　6030

**Elric**
*The Spellkey Trilogy* - Ann Downer　*f*　1592

**Eveningstar, Dasmaria**
*Shadowborn* - William W. Connors   *h*   1137

**Falc of Risskor**
*Deathknight* - Andrew J. Offutt   *f*   4201

**Fitz-Gerald, Ralf**
*Sherwood* - Parke Godwin   *f*   2248

**Gawain**
*Gawain and Lady Green* - Anne Eliot
    Crompton   *f*   1269

**Gawaine**
*Blood and Honor* - Simon R. Green   *f*   2361

**Gilman**
*Pigs Don't Fly* - Mary Brown   *f*   727

**Gistere, Rurak**
*The Day of the Tempest* - Jean Rabe   *f*   4457

**Gwalchavad**
*Grail* - Stephen R. Lawhead   *f*   3355

**Hawson, Jordan**
*The Forge of Virtue* - Lynn Abbey   *f*   16
*The Temper of Wisdom* - Lynn Abbey   *f*   17

**Jaqueth, Falcon**
*The Falcon and the Serpent* - Cheryl A.
    Smith   *f*   5101

**Jayal**
*The Forging of the Shadows* - Oliver
    Johnson   *f*   2924
*Nations of the Night* - Oliver Johnson   *f*   2925

**Kaz**
*Kaz the Minotaur* - Richard A. Knaak   *f*   3172

**Lancelot**
*The Child Queen* - Nancy McKenzie   *f*   3827
*Chronicles of King Arthur* - Andrea
    Hopkins   *f*   2767
*Guinevere: The Legend in Autumn* - Persia
    Woolley   *f*   5970
*Queen of the Summer Stars* - Persia
    Woolley   *f*   5971

**Launcelot**
*The King* - Donald Barthelme   *f*   375

**mac Cuel, Ceilyn**
*The Work of the Sun* - Teresa Edgerton   *f*   1746

**Mathen**
*The Time of Madness* - Thomas K. Martin   *f*   3652

**Morrough**
*StarSpawn* - Kenneth Von Gunden   *s*   5588

**Neville-Smythe, Brian**
*The Dragon and the Djinn* - Gordon R.
    Dickson   *f*   1528
*The Dragon in Lyonesse* - Gordon R.
    Dickson   *f*   1531
*The Dragon, the Earl, and the Troll* - Gordon R.
    Dickson   *f*   1534

**Odosson, William "Will"**
*Knight's Wyrd* - Debra Doyle   *f*   1601

**Parsifal**
*Parsifal* - Peter Vansittart   *f*   5560

**Ra-Hir**
*The Children of Wrath* - Mickey Zucker
    Reichert   *f*   4518

**Ra-khir of Erythane**
*Beyond Ragnarok* - Mickey Zucker Reichert   *f*   4516

**Rainaut, Valence**
*Crusader's Torch* - Chelsea Quinn Yarbro   *h*   6015

**Shadowborn, Alexi**
*Shadowborn* - William W. Connors   *h*   1137

**Simon "Seoman/Snowlock"**
*To Green Angel Tower* - Tad Williams   *f*   5832

**Sparhawk**
*The Diamond Throne* - David Eddings   *f*   1731
*Domes of Fire* - David Eddings   *f*   1732
*The Hidden City* - David Eddings   *f*   1733
*The Ruby Knight* - David Eddings   *f*   1736
*The Sapphire Rose* - David Eddings   *f*   1737

**Stardust, Baijon "Tiggy"**
*Archangel Blues* - eluki bes shahar   *s*   471
*Darktraders* - eluki bes shahar   *s*   472

**Tancred, Tolwyn**
*Storm Knights* - Bill Slavicsek   *f*   5087

**Tawl**
*Master and Fool* - J.V. Jones   *f*   2959

**William**
*Here There Be Dragons* - Roger Zelazny   *f*   6069

**Woczniak, Hal**
*The Forever King* - Molly Cochran   *f*   1092

## LAIRD

**Montana, Kent**
*668: The Neighbor of the Beast* - Lionel
    Fenn   *h*   1917
*Kent Montana and the Really Ugly Thing From Mars* -
    Lionel Fenn   *s*   1918
*Kent Montana and the Reasonably Invisible Man* -
    Lionel Fenn   *s*   1919
*The Mark of the Moderately Vicious Vampire* - Lionel
    Fenn   *h*   1920

**Tuchman, Ward**
*Enemy of My Enemy* - Ben Ohlander   *s*   4204

## LANDLORD

**Connaghan, Connor**
*Child of Shadows* - John Coyne   *h*   1236

**Daez, Henry**
*Makoto* - Kelley Wilde   *h*   5801

**Stone, David**
*Sati* - Christopher Pike   *f*   4330

## LANDOWNER

**Caoimhghin**
*The Adventures of Threadwell the Tailor, or
    Alterations Made While You Wait* - P.D.
    Cacek   *h*   801

**Sylvie**
*Moonwise* - Greer Ilene Gilman   *f*   2238

**Thinking Man of Moha**
*Fish Soup* - Ursula K. Le Guin   *f*   3378

**Vehmund, Marsall**
*Heart-Beast* - Tanith Lee   *h*   3411

**Writing Woman of Maho**
*Fish Soup* - Ursula K. Le Guin   *f*   3378

## LANDSCAPER

**Lakeman, Max**
*Max Lakeman and the Beautiful Stranger* - Jon
    Cohen   *f*   1098

## LAWMAN

**Adwon, Jay**
*Dusk* - Ron Dee   *h*   1466

**Allen**
*The Persistence of Memory* - Karen Ripley   *s*   4592

**Bill**
*Dusk* - Ron Dee   *h*   1466

**Bird, Jake**
*Devil's Engine* - Mark Sumner   *f*   5356

**Booth, Felix**
*Pitfall* - Ronald Kelly   *h*   3054

**Cantrell, Boone**
*Spirit Catcher* - Elizabeth Hallam   *f*   2497

**deLacey, William**
*Lady of the Forest* - Jennifer Roberson   *f*   4609

**Erickson, Richard**
*Shadows Fall* - Simon R. Green   *f*   2373

**Fitz-Gerald, Ralf**
*Sherwood* - Parke Godwin   *f*   2248

**Kresh, Alvar**
*Caliban* - Roger MacBride Allen   *s*   77
*Inferno* - Roger MacBride Allen   *s*   78

**Laker, Tom**
*Among Madmen* - Jim Starlin   *s*   5212

**Mark, Philip**
*The Sheriff of Nottingham* - Richard Kluger   *f*   3165

**Narn, Roger K. "RK"**
*Mojo and the Pickle Jar* - Douglas Bell   *f*   433

**Pale Boy**
*Batman: Captured by the Engines* - Joe R.
    Lansdale   *h*   3320

**Presley, Elvis**
*Comeback Tour: The Sky Belongs to the Stars* - Jack
    Yeovil   *s*   6020

**Sinjaria, Nolan ra**
*Talion: Revenant* - Michael A. Stackpole   *f*   5206

**Smith, Alamo**
*Destination: Showdown* - Jake Davis   *s*   1405
*The Last Rangers* - Jake Davis   *s*   1406

**Watt, Al**
*Darkly the Thunder* - William W.
    Johnstone   *h*   2929

## LAWYER

**Adair, Hugh**
*Breeder* - Douglas Clegg   *h*   1076

**Adair, Rachel**
*Breeder* - Douglas Clegg   *h*   1076

**Allison, Harold**
*The Man Who Turned into Himself* - David
    Ambrose   *h*   89

**Ananda**
*The Thirteenth Daughter of the Moon* - Steven
    Nightingale   *f*   4104

**Ballard, Kurt**
*Shadow of the Beast* - Margaret L. Carter   *h*   926

**Banner, Clint**
*Quake* - Richard Laymon   *h*   3370

**Banning, Peter "Peter Pan"**
*Hook* - Terry Brooks   *f*   713

**Beaumont, Greg**
*Midnight's Lair* - Richard Laymon   *h*   3369

**Becker, Max**
*Second Contact* - Mike Resnick   *s*   4555

**Bellman, Craig**
*The House That Jack Built* - Graham
    Masterton   *h*   3675

**Birkett, Alison**
*Temporary Agency* - Rachel Pollack   *f*   4360

**Blaine, Maggie**
*The Dark* - Andrew Neiderman   *h*   4084

**Burke, Moira Janelle**
*Overshoot* - Mona Clee   *s*   1075

**Burlingame, Gerald**
*Gerald's Game* - Stephen King　*h*　3133

**Cray, Jennifer**
*One Land, One Duke* - Ru Emerson　*f*　1809
*The Two in Hiding* - Ru Emerson　*f*　1812

**Dad**
*Thor* - Wayne Smith　*h*　5146

**Dittimore, Jeffry**
*The Land of Nod* - Mark A. Clements　*h*　1085

**Duinngan, Will**
*Darkborn* - Matthew J. Costello　*h*　1195

**Everett, Radmilla**
*Rewind* - Terry England　*s*　1825

**Galen, Michelle**
*The Double* - Don Webb　*h*　5661

**Grange, Florida**
*Mucho Mojo* - Joe R. Lansdale　*h*　3330

**Harker, Jonathan**
*The Darker Passions: Dracula* - Amarantha
　Knight　*h*　3179
*Mina* - Marie Kiraly　*h*　3151

**Harshaw, Jubal**
*Stranger in a Strange Land* - Robert A.
　Heinlein　*s*　2649

**Hastings, Julie**
*Darkman* - Randall Boyll　*h*　611
*Darkman #2: The Price of Fear* - Randall
　Boyll　*h*　613

**Horton, Carol**
*Althea* - Abigail McDaniels　*h*　3782

**Jones, T. Bowser**
*Murder in the Solid State* - Wil McCarthy　*s*　3764

**Judge, Paul**
*Soul Catcher* - Colin Kersey　*h*　3081

**Kalimuni**
*The Broken Land* - Ian McDonald　*s*　3791

**Kwan, Martin**
*Cutthroat* - Michael Slade　*h*　5084

**Labonta, Anthony**
*Flesh and Gold* - Phyllis Gotlieb　*s*　2286

**Malone, Billy**
*The Devil's Churn* - Kristine Kathryn
　Rusch　*h*　4715

**Maury, Paul**
*Whiteout* - Sage Walker　*s*　5619

**Maxwell, Thomas F.**
*Relife* - Dan Barton　*h*　376

**Mikolajczak, Adam**
*Seaward* - Brad Leithauser　*h*　3433

**Milton, John**
*The Devil's Advocate* - Andrew Neiderman　*h*　4085

**Morrell, Charlie**
*Dead of Night* - Alex Abella　*h*　20
*The Killing of the Saints* - Alex Abella　*h*　21

**Nolan, Carly**
*Arachne* - Lisa Mason　*s*　3661

**Novak, Shea**
*Fatal Outcome* - Patricia Wallace　*h*　5622

**O'Neill, Marcus Quilligan**
*I Met a Man Who Wasn't There* - Mary R.
　Callaghan　*h*　840

**Parker, Melody**
*Tombley's Walk* - Crosland Brown　*h*　723

**Popescu, Liliana**
*The Lost* - Jonathan Aycliffe　*h*　279

**Radix, William**
*The Good Children* - Kate Wilhelm　*h*　5808

**Rice, Dale**
*Illegal Alien* - Robert J. Sawyer　*s*　4858

**Roche, Allison**
*Mefisto in Onyx* - Harlan Ellison　*h*　1786

**Ross, Malcolm**
*The Jewel of Seven Stars* - Bram Stoker　*h*　5312

**Segretti, Paolo**
*Mindplayers* - Pat Cadigan　*s*　806

**Semnarek, Robert**
*The Colors of Hell* - Michael Paine　*h*　4234

**Seward, Terry**
*Seaward* - Brad Leithauser　*h*　3433

**Shears, Melvin**
*The Mirror Maze* - James P. Hogan　*s*　2726

**Shepherd, Carolyn Crespin**
*Gibbon's Decline and Fall* - Sheri S.
　Tepper　*s*　5430

**Starborne, Angela**
*California Ghosting* - William Hill　*h*　2687

**Sterling, Alice**
*Sacrifice* - Richard Kinion　*h*　3146

**Stevenson, Tom**
*Return of the Wolfman* - Jeff Rovin　*h*　4687

**Stiller, Warreven "Raven"**
*Shadow Man* - Melissa Scott　*s*　4900

**Stirling, Richard**
*The Judas Glass* - Michael Cadnum　*h*　812

**Stryker, Elliot**
*The Eyes of Darkness* - Dean R. Koontz　*s*　3206

**Tanner, Frank**
*Deadweight* - Robert Devereaux　*h*　1505

**Taylor, Kevin**
*The Devil's Advocate* - Andrew Neiderman　*h*　4085

**Thomas, Quentin**
*Lunar Justice* - Charles L. Harness　*s*　2545

**Timoteo**
*Blood of the Goddess* - Kara Dalkey　*f*　1318

**Tyr**
*Crucible* - Troy Denning　*f*　1484

**Vandermark, David**
*Thinning the Predators* - Daina Graziunas　*h*　2341

**Vaughan, Celestine**
*Cold Kiss* - Roxanne Longstreet　*h*　3517

**Wilcox, Bradford C.**
*Thirst* - Pyotr Kurtinski　*h*　3253

**Wilkes, Ron**
*Bitter Blood* - Karen E. Taylor　*h*　5405

**Wilson, Bob**
*The Higher Space* - Jamil Nasir　*s*　4070

**Winters, Jennifer**
*Fury* - John Coyne　*h*　1237

**Witney, Tom**
*Sweet Heart* - Peter James　*h*　2875

**Wolfe, D.**
*Arachne* - Lisa Mason　*s*　3661

**Woody**
*My Stepfather Shrank!* - Barbara Dillon　*s*　1558

**Worthington, John**
*Bloody Waters* - B.L. Winters　*h*　5926

## LEADER

**ab Owen, Madoc "Weather Eyes"**
*Madoc's Hundred* - Pat Winter　*f*　5925

**Adair, Devon**
*Earth 2* - Melissa Crandall　*s*　1247

**Aiysha**
*Blood Feuds* - S.M. Stirling　*s*　5292

**Alain, Jahnel**
*Fallway* - Paula E. Downing　*s*　1593

**Aldived**
*The Heldan* - Deborah Talmadge-Bickmore　*f*　5383

**Alhammittson, Alhammitt "Mitt"**
*The Crown of Dalemark* - Diana Wynne
　Jones　*f*　2945

**Alldera**
*The Furies* - Suzy McKee Charnas　*s*　968

**al'Thor, Rand**
*The Path of Daggers* - Robert Jordan　*f*　2989

**al'Thor, Rand "Dragon Reborn"**
*A Crown of Swords* - Robert Jordan　*f*　2984
*The Dragon Reborn* - Robert Jordan　*f*　2985
*The Fires of Heaven* - Robert Jordan　*f*　2987
*Lord of Chaos* - Robert Jordan　*f*　2988
*The Shadow Rising* - Robert Jordan　*f*　2990

**Amalfi, Julia**
*Full Tide of Night* - J.R. Dunn　*s*　1695

**Amberdrake**
*The White Gryphon* - Mercedes Lackey　*f*　3303

**Ambras "Dog King"**
*The Dog King* - Christoph Ransmayr　*f*　4474

**Amnel, Kahlan**
*Temple of the Winds* - Terry Goodkind　*f*　2270

**Amnell, Kahlan**
*Blood of the Fold* - Terry Goodkind　*f*　2268
*Stone of Tears* - Terry Goodkind　*f*　2269
*Wizard's First Rule* - Terry Goodkind　*f*　2271

**Andrachis, Shil**
*Shadows on the Sun* - Michael Jan
　Friedman　*s*　2069

**Aoibhell, Brendan**
*The Deer's Cry: A Book of the Keltiad* - Patricia
　Kennealy-Morrison　*f*　3060

**Atvar**
*Worldwar: In the Balance* - Harry
　Turtledove　*s*　5515
*Worldwar: Tilting the Balance* - Harry
　Turtledove　*s*　5517

**Azak**
*Emperor and Clown* - Dave Duncan　*f*　1676

**Badrang the Tyrant**
*Martin the Warrior* - Brian Jacques　*f*　2851

**Bailey, Penelope**
*Prophet* - Mike Resnick　*s*　4553

**Bakhtiian, Ilyakoria "Ilya"**
*An Earthly Crown* - Kate Elliott　*s*　1771

**Bammer, Mortimer**
*Kill Crazy* - L.S. Riker　*s*　4590

**Bankole, Lauren Oya "Olamina"**
*Parable of the Talents* - Octavia E. Butler　*s*　793

**Barra the Pict**
*Iron Dawn* - Matthew Woodring Stover　*f*　5320
*Jericho Moon* - Matthew Woodring Stover　*f*　5321

**Bell, Howard**
*The Return of the Breakneck Boys* - Geary
　Gravel　*s*　2332

**ben Sierra Nueva, Amos "Simeon"**
*The City Who Fought* - Anne McCaffrey　*s*　3722

**Beowulf**
*Cry Wolf* - Kenneth Von Gunden　*s*　5586
*Under Fire* - Kenneth Von Gunden　*s*　5589

**Bird**
*The Fifth Sacred Thing* - Starhawk　*f*　5209

**Bonney, Jessamyn "Krokodil"**
*Krokodil Tears* - Jack Yeovil  *f*  6023

**Brave Man**
*People of the Earth* - W. Michael Gear  *f*  2166

**Britannicus, Caius**
*The Skystone* - Jack Whyte  *f*  5794

**Britannicus, Caius Merlyn**
*The Eagles' Brood* - Jack Whyte  *f*  5792
*The Saxon Shore* - Jack Whyte  *f*  5793

**Brownpony, Elia**
*Saint Leibowitz and the Wild Horse Woman* - Walter
  M. Miller Jr.  *s*  3908

**Cahanagh, Athyn "Blackmantle"**
*Blackmantle: A Triumph* - Patricia Kennealy-
  Morrison  *f*  3059

**Caribou**
*The Woman Who Loved Reindeer* - Meredith Ann
  Pierce  *f*  4320

**Catahn, Ren**
*The Crystal Rose* - Maya Kaathryn Bohnhoff  *f*  560

**Chakthi**
*Exile's Challenge* - Angus Wells  *f*  5734

**Chalkin**
*Dragonseye* - Anne McCaffrey  *s*  3730

**Chior**
*OtherWise* - Margaret Wander Bonanno  *s*  567

**Click**
*The Warden of Horses* - Karen Ripley  *s*  4595

**Coke, Matthew**
*The Sharp End* - David Drake  *s*  1643

**Connor, Islaen**
*Call to Arms* - P.M. Griffin  *s*  2435

**Cordell**
*Feathered Dragon* - Douglas Niles  *f*  4108

**Cutter**
*Captives of the Blue Mountain* - Wendy
  Pini  *f*  4336
*The Quest Begins* - Wendy Pini  *f*  4337

**deJanes, Ecktor**
*Adiamante* - L.E. Modesitt Jr.  *s*  3924

**DeVore, Howard**
*White Moon, Red Dragon* - David
  Wingrove  *s*  5921
*The White Mountain* - David Wingrove  *s*  5922

**Dios, Warden**
*The Gap into Ruin: This Day All Gods Die* - Stephen
  R. Donaldson  *s*  1575

**Donough**
*Pride of Lions* - Morgan Llywelyn  *f*  3506

**Doom**
*Between Floors* - Thomas F. Monteleone  *h*  3957

**Dread, Doctor**
*Revenge of the Fluffy Bunnies* - Craig Shaw
  Gardner  *f*  2132

**Duncan, George Thomas**
*Ecstasy Club* - Douglas Rushkoff  *s*  4732

**Edwardo "Ed"**
*Full Moonster* - Nick Pollotta  *f*  4364

**Egdril**
*No One Noticed the Cat* - Anne McCaffrey  *f*  3740

**El-ahrairah**
*Tales From Watership Down* - Richard Adams  *f*  32

**Elemak**
*The Ships of Earth* - Orson Scott Card  *s*  897

**Ember**
*Isle of Woman* - Piers Anthony  *f*  178

**Erkenbert**
*One King's Way* - Harry Harrison  *s*  2572

**Estmere**
*King's Son, Magic's Son* - Josepha Sherman  *f*  4986

**Etzilios**
*Hammer and Anvil* - Harry Turtledove  *f*  5503

**Eve, Glennys**
*The Stallion Queen* - Constance Ash  *f*  223

**Ewine, Zarel**
*Arena* - William R. Forstchen  *f*  1977

**Exeter, Edward**
*Future Indefinite* - Dave Duncan  *f*  1678

**Farblood, Corri**
*Soothslayer: A Magickal Fantasy* - D.J.
  Conway  *f*  1143

**Fieran**
*Dragon Moon* - Chris Claremont  *f*  1040

**Fitch, Xavier**
*Species* - Yvonne Navarro  *s*  4075

**Flagg, Randall**
*The Stand: The Complete and Uncut Edition* - Stephen
  King  *h*  3142

**Foxfire**
*Silver Shadows* - Elaine Cunningham  *f*  1292

**Fundan, Fair**
*To a Highland Nation* - Christopher
  Rowley  *s*  4698

**Galore, B.S.**
*Star Wreck II: The Attack of the Jargonites* - Leah
  Rewolinski  *s*  4563

**Gelasaar III**
*The Phoenix in Flight* - Sherwood Smith  *s*  5138

**Gird**
*Liar's Oath* - Elizabeth Moon  *f*  3969

**Gordon, Martin "Marty"**
*Anvil of Stars* - Greg Bear  *s*  414

**Greenway, Dorian**
*Irrational Fears* - William Browning
  Spencer  *h*  5167

**Gull**
*Final Sacrifice* - Clayton Emery  *f*  1814
*Shattered Chains* - Clayton Emery  *f*  1816

**Harlan, Richard**
*Brander's Book* - C.J. Mills  *s*  3909

**Hauser, Wolfgang "Karl Wolf"**
*Cohort of the Damned* - Andrew Keith  *s*  3034

**Hederick**
*Hederick, the Theocrat* - Ellen Dodge
  Severson  *f*  4925

**Hutchings, Ian McFarland**
*Fortress on the Sun* - Paul Cook  *s*  1157

**Islay, Arran "Henry Martyn"**
*Bretta Martyn* - L. Neil Smith  *s*  5128

**Ivanova, Susan**
*The Touch of Your Shadow, the Whisper of Your Name*
  - Neal Barrett Jr.  *s*  367

**Izmailova, Ekaterina**
*Griffin's Egg* - Michael Swanwick  *s*  5370

**Jalanopi**
*Purgatory: A Chronicle of a Distant World* - Mike
  Resnick  *s*  4554

**Jamas**
*No One Noticed the Cat* - Anne McCaffrey  *f*  3740

**Janeway, Kathryn**
*The Chance Factor* - Diana G. Gallagher  *s*  2109

**Jared**
*The Alleluia Files* - Sharon Shinn  *s*  4999

**Jarth, Christopher**
*Escape to the Wind* - Jennifer DiMarco  *s*  1559

**Jean-Claude**
*The Killing Dance* - Laurell K. Hamilton  *h*  2518

**Jerno**
*Wrath of the Princes* - Holly Lisle  *f*  3490

**Jordan, John James**
*Project Farcry* - Pauline Ashwell  *s*  230

**Josef**
*The Run to Chaos Keep* - Jack L. Chalker  *s*  960

**Juh**
*Apacheria* - Jake Page  *s*  4233

**Jute, Tabitha**
*Mother of Plenty* - Colin Greenland  *s*  2417
*Seasons of Plenty* - Colin Greenland  *s*  2418

**Jy**
*Down the Bright Way* - Robert Reed  *s*  4505

**Kami, Minamoto no**
*Glory's People* - Alfred Coppel  *s*  1183

**Kennedy, John F.**
*Time Station Berlin* - David Evans  *s*  1852

**Kesair**
*The Elementals* - Morgan Llywelyn  *f*  3503

**Kham**
*Never Trust an Elf* - Robert N. Charrette  *f*  976

**Kifo, Ndug "Brother Death"**
*Brother Death* - Steve Perry  *s*  4292

**Kurosov'e, Malyene Andreivne "Malye"**
*The Fall of Sirius* - Wil McCarthy  *s*  3762

**K'vin**
*Dragonseye* - Anne McCaffrey  *s*  3730

**Lashana "Shana"**
*Elvenblood* - Andre Norton  *f*  4150

**Lehman, Stefan**
*The Stone Within* - David Wingrove  *s*  5920

**Lenk, Able**
*Legacy* - Greg Bear  *s*  420

**Lessa**
*All the Weyrs of Pern* - Anne McCaffrey  *s*  3719

**Li Yuan**
*White Moon, Red Dragon* - David
  Wingrove  *s*  5921

**Little Spring**
*Apacheria* - Jake Page  *s*  4233

**Lloth**
*Siege of Darkness* - R.A. Salvatore  *f*  4804

**Lottick, Vaclav**
*Bloom* - Wil McCarthy  *s*  3761

**Mac Airt, Cormac**
*Finn Mac Cool* - Morgan Llywelyn  *f*  3504

**mac Kennedy, Brian**
*Brian Boru: Emperor of the Irish* - Morgan
  Llywelyn  *f*  3501

**MacIntyre, Colin**
*The Armageddon Inheritance* - David
  Weber  *s*  5668

**Malachy the Great**
*Brian Boru: Emperor of the Irish* - Morgan
  Llywelyn  *f*  3501

**Markhamwit**
*Design for Great-Day* - Alan Dean Foster  *s*  2001

**Marta**
*Hungry for Home: A Wolf Odyssey* - 'Asta
  Bowen  *f*  599

**Matar, Kitiara "Kit"**
*Steel and Stone* - Ellen Porath  *f*  4368

**Mayhew, Benjamin**
*Flag in Exile* - David Weber   s   5671
*The Honor of the Queen* - David Weber   s   5674

**Mayhew IX, Benjamin**
*Echoes of Honor* - David Weber   s   5669

**McCay, Debra**
*The Earth Saver* - Catherine Wells   s   5745

**McKenzie, Victoria**
*Metaphase* - Vonda N. McIntyre   s   3821
*Starfarers* - Vonda N. McIntyre   s   3824
*Transition* - Vonda N. McIntyre   s   3825

**Merlin**
*The Eagle and the Sword* - A.A. Attanasio   f   267
*The Faery Convention* - Brett Davis   f   1399

**Metzgar, Joachim**
*Mutant Legacy* - Karen Haber   s   2474

**Michaelson, Hal**
*Virtual Destruction* - Kevin J. Anderson   s   118

**Mikhail**
*Initiation* - Marian Hughes   s   2806

**Milton, John**
*Milton in America* - Peter Ackroyd   f   25

**Minarik**
*Shadowdance* - Robin Wayne Bailey   f   290

**Mission**
*Ghost of Chance* - William S. Burroughs   s   780

**Mithra**
*The Falcon Rises* - Michael C. Staudinger   f   5235

**Moonbrow, Aljan "Jan"**
*The Son of Summer Stars* - Meredith Ann
    Pierce   f   4319

**Moondark, Gan**
*Warrior* - Donald E. McQuinn   s   3863
*Witch* - Donald E. McQuinn   s   3864

**Morgannan, Warrick**
*The Ambivalent Magician* - Simon Hawke   f   2616
*The Inadequate Adept* - Simon Hawke   f   2617

**Murdan of Overhall**
*Dragon Companion* - Don Callander   f   842

**Nafai**
*Earthfall* - Orson Scott Card   s   885

**Nathalorial, Kaylana**
*Villains by Necessity* - Eve Forward   f   1985

**NicCuinn, Meghan**
*The Witches of Eileanan* - Kate Forsyth   f   1984

**Nicodareus**
*Darkenheight* - Douglas Niles   f   4107

**Nikolaus**
*Guilty Pleasures* - Laurell K. Hamilton   f   2517

**Nuada**
*The Enchanted Isles* - Casey Flynn   f   1960
*Most Ancient Song* - Casey Flynn   f   1961

**Nugent, Efram**
*Girl in Landscape* - Jonathan Lethem   s   3440

**O'Connor, John**
*The Flight of Michael McBride* - Midori
    Snyder   f   5151

**O'Neill, Jack**
*StarGate* - Dean Devlin   s   1509

**Ooslaxt**
*Christmas Slaughter* - Mark Grant   s   2323

**Parnell, Eugene M.**
*The Tranquility Alternative* - Allen Steele   s   5248

**Pendragon, Arthur**
*The Kingmaking* - Helen Hollick   f   2745
*Pendragon's Banner* - Helen Hollick   f   2746

**Pendragon, Uther**
*The Dragon and the Unicorn* - A.A.
    Attanasio   f   266

**Perin, Antonio "Tony"**
*Full Tide of Night* - J.R. Dunn   s   1695

**Philip of Macedon**
*Lion of Macedon* - David Gemmell   f   2189

**Piero**
*Outpost* - Scott Mackay   s   3597

**Podlowski, Eric**
*Flames of the Dragon* - Robin Wayne Bailey   f   287

**Polo, Marco**
*If at Faust You Don't Succeed* - Roger
    Zelazny   f   6070

**Polyta**
*Under the Healing Sign* - Nick O'Donohoe   f   4198

**Rahl, Darken**
*Wizard's First Rule* - Terry Goodkind   f   2271

**Raihna**
*Conan the Relentless* - Roland J. Green   f   2348

**Ras, Pawasar Pawasar**
*Earthgrip* - Harry Turtledove   s   5499

**Ratha**
*Ratha and Thistle-Chaser* - Clare Bell   f   432

**Ratio**
*The White Abacus* - Damien Broderick   s   708

**Redman, Stu**
*The Stand: The Complete and Uncut Edition* - Stephen
    King   h   3142

**Renagi**
*Tegne: Soul Warrior* - Richard La Plante   f   3268

**Rhisadel, Teressa**
*Wren's War* - Sherwood Smith   f   5144

**Ridenau, Roderic**
*Children of Enchantment* - Anne Kelleher
    Bush   f   787

**Rille, Cailet Ambrai**
*The Mageborn Traitor* - Melanie Rawn   f   4488

**Ritter, Alexis**
*The Venom Trees of Sunga* - L. Sprague de
    Camp   s   1420

**Roebeck, Nan**
*The Fourth Rome* - David Drake   s   1631

**Roele, Michael**
*The Iron Throne* - Simon Hawke   f   2618

**Rosemont, Alexander F.**
*Finger of God* - Michael Kasner   s   3013

**Ryba**
*Fall of Angels* - L.E. Modesitt Jr.   f   3930

**Sardoll, Dirac**
*Berserker Kill* - Fred Saberhagen   s   4761

**Sauventreen, Verna**
*Blood of the Fold* - Terry Goodkind   f   2268

**Sayyed**
*Winged Magic* - Mary H. Herbert   f   2678

**Sean Horus MacIntyre**
*The Armageddon Inheritance* - David
    Weber   s   5668

**Seetoo "Jolly"**
*Marooned on Eden* - Robert L. Forward   s   1986

**Service**
*The Remarkables* - Robert Reed   s   4507

**Sheridan, John**
*The Touch of Your Shadow, the Whisper of Your Name*
    - Neal Barrett Jr.   s   367

**Siglen**
*The Rowan* - Anne McCaffrey   s   3747

**Sisko, Benjamin**
*Bloodletter* - K.W. Jeter   s   2908
*Fallen Heroes* - Dafydd ab Hugh   s   8
*Warped* - K.W. Jeter   s   2917

**Skandranon**
*The White Gryphon* - Mercedes Lackey   f   3303

**Solo, Leia Organa**
*Ambush at Corellia* - Roger MacBride Allen   s   76
*Before the Storm* - Michael P. Kube-
    McDowell   s   3247
*Children of the Jedi* - Barbara Hambly   s   2500
*Darksaber* - Kevin J. Anderson   s   103
*The Last Command* - Timothy Zahn   s   6055
*The New Rebellion* - Kristine Kathryn
    Rusch   s   4719

**Stavenger, Douglas**
*Moonwar* - Ben Bova   s   588

**Talbott, Marshe "Queen"**
*Aggressor Six* - Wil McCarthy   s   3760

**Taller**
*Silent Dances* - A.C. Crispin   s   1263
*Silent Songs* - A.C. Crispin   s   1264

**Thanehand**
*Palace of Kings* - Mike Jefferies   f   2887

**Tharn, Bulion**
*The Cursed* - Dave Duncan   f   1674

**Tharon**
*People of the River* - W. Michael Gear   f   2168

**Tharpit, Jaxian**
*The Reaver Road* - Dave Duncan   f   1687

**Thibodeau, Skida "Skilly"**
*Prince of Sparta* - Jerry Pournelle   s   4378

**Thrawn**
*The Last Command* - Timothy Zahn   s   6055

**Tighe, Dan**
*The Trikon Deception* - Ben Bova   s   597

**Toikella**
*The Mountains of Majipoor* - Robert
    Silverberg   s   5037

**Torriner, Sheel**
*The Furies* - Suzy McKee Charnas   s   968

**Tragen, Aaron**
*Beowulf's Children* - Larry Niven   s   4116

**Tyger**
*Escape to the Wind* - Jennifer DiMarco   s   1559

**Ursht, Oman**
*Alastor* - Jack Vance   s   5543

**Urthstripe the Strong**
*Salamandastron* - Brian Jacques   f   2855

**Valdez, Maria**
*Under Fire* - Kenneth Von Gunden   s   5589

**Valeur, Whiss**
*Illusion* - Paula Volsky   f   5582

**Valorian**
*Valorian* - Mary H. Herbert   f   2677

**Van Chou, Ngen**
*The Web of Spider* - W. Michael Gear   s   2173

**Vanyi**
*Spear of Heaven* - Judith Tarr   f   5396

**Vayhawk**
*The Heldan* - Deborah Talmadge-Bickmore   f   5383

**Vega, Carlos**
*The Faces of Ceti* - Mary Caraker   s   877

**Veriam, Lizora "Lizra"**
*Gold Unicorn* - Tanith Lee   f   3410

**Volemak**
*The Memory of Earth* - Orson Scott Card   s   894

**Vordegh**
*Star Ascendant* - Louise Cooper   *f*   1180

**Vosnesensky, Mikhail Andreivitch**
*Mars* - Ben Bova   *s*   586

**Walter of Jacin**
*The Wild Hunt: Vengeance Moon* - Jocelin
  Foxe   *f*   2031

**Wargallow, Simon**
*The Gods in Anger* - Adrian Cole   *f*   1100

**Warhurst, Montgomery**
*Semper Mars* - Ian Douglas   *s*   1585

**Weisser, Erich "Erich Alois"**
*Children of the Dusk* - Janet Berliner   *f*   467

**Wellin, Alleluia "Alleya"**
*Jovah's Angel* - Sharon Shinn   *s*   5001

**Wheeler, Matt**
*The Harvest* - Robert Charles Wilson   *s*   5909

**Wide**
*Starstrike* - W. Michael Gear   *s*   2172

**Windruth**
*Dragon Rigger* - Jeffrey A. Carver   *s*   929

**Wok**
*The Pixilated Peeress* - L. Sprague de
  Camp   *f*   1416

**Ye Armonk, Louise**
*Ring* - Stephen Baxter   *s*   402

**Yuan, Li**
*The Stone Within* - David Wingrove   *s*   5920
*The White Mountain* - David Wingrove   *s*   5922

### LESBIAN

**Alston, Marian**
*Island in the Sea of Time* - S.M. Stirling   *s*   5295

**Antero, Rali Emilie**
*The Warrior Returns* - Allan Cole   *f*   1109

**Antiope**
*The Amazon Chronicles* - Jane E.M.
  Robinson   *f*   4627

**Ardyn**
*Escape to the Wind* - Jennifer DiMarco   *s*   1559

**Brown**
*Phaze Doubt* - Piers Anthony   *f*   184

**Carless, India "Trouble"**
*Trouble and Her Friends* - Melissa Scott   *s*   4902

**Cerise**
*Trouble and Her Friends* - Melissa Scott   *s*   4902

**Cidiera "Cid"**
*The Nature of Smoke* - Anne Harris   *s*   2559

**Cohen, Lauren "Laurie"**
*Godmother Night* - Rachel Pollack   *f*   4358

**Elayna**
*Heartstone and Silver* - Jacqui Singleton   *f*   5071

**Erica**
*Clicking Stones* - Nancy Tyler Glenn   *s*   2242

**Gilda**
*The Gilda Stories* - Jewelle Gomez   *h*   2267

**Ginny**
*Virago* - Karen Marie Christa Minns   *h*   3915

**Harmon, Anne Marie "Annie"**
*Waking the Moon* - Elizabeth Hand   *f*   2538

**Hart**
*In the Blood* - Lauren Wright Douglas   *s*   1590

**Hartell, Kathryn**
*Shadows After Dark* - Ouida Crozier   *f*   1286

**Jian, Reverdy**
*Dreaming Metal* - Melissa Scott   *s*   4895

**Dreamships** - Melissa Scott   *s*   4896

**Lang, Jacqueline "Jaqe"**
*Godmother Night* - Rachel Pollack   *f*   4358

**Lauri**
*Spires of Spirit* - Gael Baudino   *f*   395

**Magnolia**
*The Nature of Smoke* - Anne Harris   *s*   2559

**Manilla**
*Virago* - Karen Marie Christa Minns   *h*   3915

**Morgan**
*Clicking Stones* - Nancy Tyler Glenn   *s*   2242

**Mully, Katharine**
*Memory and Dream* - Charles de Lint   *f*   1433

**Pierson, Ellen**
*Temporary Agency* - Rachel Pollack   *f*   4360

**Ra Sadiin, Cydell**
*Heartstone and Silver* - Jacqui Singleton   *f*   5071

**Rhannet, Prima**
*Sword-Born* - Jennifer Roberson   *f*   4612

**Ryder, Christine**
*The Tranquility Alternative* - Allen Steele   *s*   5248

**Sandoval**
*In the Blood* - Lauren Wright Douglas   *s*   1590

**Spanner**
*Slow River* - Nicola Griffith   *s*   2445

**Tyger**
*Escape to the Wind* - Jennifer DiMarco   *s*   1559

**Videla, Pilar**
*Whiteout* - Sage Walker   *s*   5619

### LIBERAL

**Hamilton, Marsha**
*Eye in the Sky* - Philip K. Dick   *s*   1521

### LIBRARIAN

**Ackley, Robert**
*The Lodger* - Fred Chappell   *h*   966

**Bergsndot, Ravna**
*A Fire upon the Deep* - Vernor Vinge   *s*   5573

**Braun, Susan**
*Ladies Night* - Jack Ketchum   *h*   3091

**Brightlaw, Nic**
*The Cup of Morning Shadows* - Rosemary
  Edghill   *f*   1747

**Dowd, Katherine "Katy"**
*Flames of the Dragon* - Robin Wayne Bailey   *f*   287

**Dwyer**
*Painted Devil* - Michael Bedard   *f*   430

**Ghan**
*The Waterborn* - J. Gregory Keyes   *f*   3098

**Giles**
*The Harvest* - Richie Tankersley Cusick   *h*   1302

**Giles, Rupert**
*Return to Chaos* - Craig Shaw Gardner   *h*   2131

**Goodlooking/Bella**
*North Wind* - Gwyneth Jones   *s*   2953

**Hale, David**
*Uwharrie* - Eugene E. Pfaff Jr.   *h*   4309

**Hausmann, Elena**
*The Third Force* - Marc Laidlaw   *s*   3313

**Howgath, Lizzy**
*Kent Montana and the Reasonably Invisible Man* -
  Lionel Fenn   *s*   1919

**Huxley, Dorothy**
*Rune* - Christopher Fowler   *h*   2020

**Kite, Dorothy**
*The Devil's Cradle* - Kate Stewart   *h*   5269

**Lerille, Jack**
*Paddywhack* - John Stchur   *h*   5236

**Library**
*Genetic Soldier* - George Turner   *s*   5492

**Marian**
*The Fermata* - Nicholson Baker   *s*   302

**Marlowe, Ruth**
*The Cup of Morning Shadows* - Rosemary
  Edghill   *f*   1747
*The Sword of Maiden's Tears* - Rosemary
  Edghill   *f*   1748

**McCutcheon, Christopher**
*The Quiet Pools* - Michael P. Kube-
  McDowell   *s*   3249

**Morrison, Rebecca**
*The Blackstone Chronicles* - John Saul   *h*   4838

**Nokar**
*Bones of the Past* - Holly Lisle   *f*   3478

**Osmirik**
*Castle Spellbound* - John DeChancie   *s*   1454

**Pagemaster**
*The Pagemaster* - David Kirschner   *f*   3156

**Penn, Simon**
*Blood of the Covenant* - Brent Monahan   *h*   3954
*The Book of Common Dread* - Brent
  Monahan   *h*   3955

**Rowan**
*The Outskirter's Secret* - Rosemary Kirstein   *s*   3157

**Taja**
*Summer King, Winter Fool* - Lisa Goldstein   *f*   2263

**Vanderveen, Frederika**
*Blood of the Covenant* - Brent Monahan   *h*   3954
*The Book of Common Dread* - Brent
  Monahan   *h*   3955

**Whitehead, Tom**
*Dragon Companion* - Don Callander   *f*   842
*Dragon Tempest* - Don Callander   *f*   844

**Yont, Felicity "Lissy"**
*Homebody* - Orson Scott Card   *h*   890

### LINGUIST

**Aeslu "Moon's Stead" of Vmatta**
*The Mountain Made of Light* - Edward
  Myers   *f*   4062
*The Summit* - Edward Myers   *f*   4063

**An**
*Eggheads* - Emily Devenport   *s*   1500

**Cameron, Bren**
*Foreigner* - C.J. Cherryh   *s*   990
*Inheritor* - C.J. Cherryh   *s*   997
*Invader* - C.J. Cherryh   *s*   998

**Chornyak, Delina Meloran**
*Earthsong* - Suzette Haden Elgin   *s*   1769

**Ea**
*Black Wine* - Candas Jane Dorsey   *s*   1582

**Elemak**
*Earthfall* - Orson Scott Card   *s*   885

**Feldberg, David**
*Requiem* - Graham Joyce   *h*   2994

**Fisher, Johanna**
*St. Peter's Wolf* - Michael Cadnum   *h*   816

**Hanks, Deana**
*Invader* - C.J. Cherryh   *s*   998

**Ivanova, Sonya**
*Russian Spring* - Norman Spinrad   *s*   5174

**Izakar "Izzy"**
*The Family Tree* - Sheri S. Tepper   s   5429

**Jackson, Daniel**
*StarGate* - Dean Devlin   s   1509

**Janna**
*Mission Child* - Maureen F. McHugh   s   3819

**Jing, Jong**
*Stones of the Dalai Lama* - Ken Mitchell   f   3916

**Katelo, Jonathon**
*Desert Eden* - J.M. Morgan   s   4000

**Koolhan, Sara**
*Heaven's Reach* - David Brin   s   687

**Korinaam the Shapeshifter**
*The Mountains of Majipoor* - Robert
   Silverberg   s   5037

**Liang, Sindon**
*The Khan's Persuasion* - Cynthia Felice   s   1914

**Lixia, Li**
*A Woman of the Iron People* - Eleanor
   Arnason   s   211

**mac Cainnech, Aidan**
*Byzantium* - Stephen R. Lawhead   f   3353

**Macinnes, Matt**
*The Starry Child* - Lynn Hanna   f   2540

**Morden**
*The Shadow Within* - Jeanne Cavelos   s   944

**Obed**
*The Off Season* - Jack Cady   f   820

**Parent, Lucy**
*The Magnificent Wilf* - Gordon R. Dickson   s   1536

**Perez, Magdalena**
*Voices of Chaos* - A.C. Crispin   s   1266

**Pesca, Walter**
*Dreadnought* - Thorarinn Gunnarsson   s   2464

**Saber, Karen**
*Marks of Our Brothers* - Jane M. Lindskold   s   3475

**St. George, Blacktooth "Nimmy"**
*Saint Leibowitz and the Wild Horse Woman* - Walter
   M. Miller Jr.   s   3908

**Sanders, Nicholas**
*Ring of Swords* - Eleanor Arnason   s   210

**Sandoz, Emilio**
*Children of God* - Mary Doria Russell   s   4735
*The Sparrow* - Mary Doria Russell   s   4736

**Schweigman, Marianne**
*Being Alien* - Rebecca Ore   s   4217

**Soerensen, Terese "Tess"**
*An Earthly Crown* - Kate Elliott   s   1771

**Tallstaff, Lutha**
*Shadow's End* - Sheri S. Tepper   s   5435

**Taylor, Nugan**
*Genetic Soldier* - George Turner   s   5492

**Terza, Abby**
*Manhattan Transfer* - John E. Stith   s   5303

**Tesa "Good Eyes"**
*Silent Dances* - A.C. Crispin   s   1263

**Theodoulos**
*Cross and Crescent* - Susan Shwartz   f   5014

**Varianus, Galwin Gaius**
*Black Horses for the King* - Anne
   McCaffrey   f   3720

**Wheatley, Gillian**
*The Seventh Heart* - Marina Fitch   f   1943

**Windclan, Raincloud**
*Daughter of Elysium* - Joan Slonczewski   s   5091

**Wolde, David**
*My Soul to Keep* - Tannarive Due   h   1670

## LOVER

**Arden**
*The Lightless Kingdom* - Jonathan Wylie   f   6007

**Attercop, Karen**
*Webs* - Scott Baker   h   304

**Drew, Laura**
*The Unseen* - Joseph A. Citro   h   1039

**Efstathiou, Garcia**
*Descent* - Ron Dee   h   1465

**Endymion, Raul**
*The Rise of Endymion* - Dan Simmons   s   5059

**Harker, Mina**
*The Dracula Tape* - Fred Saberhagen   h   4765

**Stevenson, Walker**
*The Deathless* - Myles Murchison   h   4048

## MADAM

**Callahan, Sally**
*Callahan's Lady* - Spider Robinson   s   4638
*Lady Slings the Booze* - Spider Robinson   s   4640

**Malone, Jessie**
*The Golden Nineties* - Lisa Mason   s   3663

## MAGICIAN

**Aderyn**
*A Time of Exile* - Katharine Kerr   f   3077

**ae'Magi, Geoffrey**
*Masques* - Patricia Briggs   f   681

**Alexia**
*Dark Mirror, Dark Dreams* - Sharon Green   f   2357
*Silver Princess, Golden Knight* - Sharon
   Green   f   2359
*Wind Whispers, Shadow Shouts* - Sharon
   Green   f   2360

**Allalie, Fentrice**
*Walking the Labyrinth* - Lisa Goldstein   f   2266

**Ambrose, Tereza**
*Death of a Darklord* - Laurell K. Hamilton   h   2516

**Amnel, Kahlan**
*Temple of the Winds* - Terry Goodkind   f   2270

**Amnell, Kahlan**
*Blood of the Fold* - Terry Goodkind   f   2268
*Stone of Tears* - Terry Goodkind   f   2269
*Wizard's First Rule* - Terry Goodkind   f   2271

**Amrey, Murl "Kar Kalim"**
*Kar Kalim* - Deborah Christian   f   1025

**Ancar**
*Winds of Fury* - Mercedes Lackey   f   3306

**An'desha**
*Storm Breaking* - Mercedes Lackey   f   3296
*Storm Rising* - Mercedes Lackey   f   3297
*Storm Warning* - Mercedes Lackey   f   3298

**Andry**
*The Dragon Token* - Melanie Rawn   f   4485
*Stronghold* - Melanie Rawn   f   4492
*Sunrunner's Fire* - Melanie Rawn   f   4493

**Angier, Rupert**
*The Prestige* - Christopher Priest   s   4432

**ap Don, Gwydion**
*The Island of the Mighty* - Evangeline
   Walton   f   5626

**ap Kian, Donaugh**
*The Western King* - Ann Marston   f   3636

**ap Mathonwy, Math**
*The Island of the Mighty* - Evangeline
   Walton   f   5626

**ap Nia, Aidan**
*King's Son, Magic's Son* - Josepha Sherman   f   4986

**Apolon**
*Tiger Burning Bright* - Marion Zimmer
   Bradley   f   652

**Arianrhod**
*The Island of the Mighty* - Evangeline
   Walton   f   5626

**Aroha**
*Sable, Shadow and Ice* - Cheryl J. Franklin   f   2039

**Arthre, Roy "Ratha"**
*The Falcon Rises* - Michael C. Staudinger   f   5235

**Ashkevron, Savil**
*Magic's Price* - Mercedes Lackey   f   3288

**Ashkevron, Vanyel**
*Magic's Price* - Mercedes Lackey   f   3288

**Atrus**
*Myst: The Book of Atrus* - Rand Miller   f   3896
*Myst: The Book of D'ni* - Rand Miller   f   3897

**Aurian**
*Aurian* - Maggie Furey   f   2095
*Dhiammara* - Maggie Furey   f   2096
*Harp of Winds* - Maggie Furey   f   2097
*Sword of Flame* - Maggie Furey   f   2098

**Avran**
*Aurian* - Maggie Furey   f   2095
*Harp of Winds* - Maggie Furey   f   2097
*Sword of Flame* - Maggie Furey   f   2098

**Ayth, Argoth**
*Demon Moon* - Jack Williamson   s   5862

**Baenre, Liriel**
*Daughter of the Drow* - Elaine Cunningham   f   1287

**Beneforte, Fiametta**
*The Spirit Ring* - Lois McMaster Bujold   f   763

**Blackburn, Thorne**
*Ghostlight* - Marion Zimmer Bradley   f   634

**Boh, Walker**
*The Talismans of Shannara* - Terry Brooks   f   717

**Borden, Alfred**
*The Prestige* - Christopher Priest   s   4432

**Brailsford, Jane**
*A College of Magics* - Caroline Stevermer   f   5266

**Breivik, Allan**
*Make Way for Dragons!* - Thorarinn
   Gunnarsson   f   2465

**Brown**
*Phaze Doubt* - Piers Anthony   f   184

**Brown, Pellimore "Pel"**
*The Reign of the Brown Magician* - Lawrence Watt-
   Evans   f   5647

**Calindor**
*Redmagic* - Crawford Kilian   f   3107

**Cameron, Jason**
*The Fire Rose* - Mercedes Lackey   f   3280

**Casaubon**
*The Architecture of Desire* - Mary Gentle   f   2195
*Rats and Gargoyles* - Mary Gentle   f   2196

**Celine, Sigismundo**
*Nature's God* - Robert Anton Wilson   f   5903

**Collins, Jack**
*A Calculated Magic* - Robert Weinberg   f   5694

**Corwyn**
*Rehearsal for a Renaissance* - Douglas W.
   Clark   f   1045

**Courtak, Jarrod**
*The Unicorn Peace* - John Lee  *f*  3399
*The Unicorn Solution* - John Lee  *f*  3400
*The Unicorn War* - John Lee  *f*  3401

**Cray, Jennifer**
*One Land, One Duke* - Ru Emerson  *f*  1809
*The Two in Hiding* - Ru Emerson  *f*  1812

**Crowley, Aleister**
*The Door through Washington Square* - Elaine
  Bergstrom  *f*  464
*The Woman between the Worlds* - F. Gwynplaine
  MacIntyre  *s*  3596

**Danan, Elora**
*Shadow Dawn* - Chris Claremont  *f*  1042

**Dara**
*Guardian's Key* - Anne Logston  *f*  3511

**Daruya**
*Spear of Heaven* - Judith Tarr  *f*  5396

**D'Asperge, Timaeus**
*Another Day, Another Dungeon* - Greg
  Costikyan  *f*  1206
*One Quest, Hold the Dragons* - Greg
  Costikyan  *f*  1208

**de Draconis, Rejiia**
*The Loneliest Magician* - Irene Radford  *f*  4461

**Decutonius**
*Elfwood* - Rose Estes  *f*  1837
*Twisted Dragon* - Kevin Stein  *f*  5251

**Dee, John**
*Scorpio Rising* - Alex McDonough  *s*  3804

**Delacorte, Emil**
*Now You See It. . .* - Richard Matheson  *h*  3688

**Delacorte, Maximillian**
*Now You See It. . .* - Richard Matheson  *h*  3688

**Dhu, Zeldan**
*Elvendude* - Mark Shepherd  *f*  4980

**Didge**
*The End-of-Everything Man* - Tom De
  Haven  *f*  1421

**Dion**
*Mage Heart* - Jane Routley  *f*  4686

**d'Iste, Tiran**
*Dark Mirror, Dark Dreams* - Sharon Green  *f*  2357
*Silver Princess, Golden Knight* - Sharon
  Green  *f*  2359
*Wind Whispers, Shadow Shouts* - Sharon
  Green  *f*  2360

**Dobbs, Melvin**
*Resurrection Dreams* - Richard Laymon  *h*  3371

**Domenico**
*The Devil's Day* - James Blish  *h*  525

**Donaltsson, Marta**
*Kindred Rites* - Katharine Eliska Kimbriel  *f*  3118

**Dorrin**
*The Magic Engineer* - L.E. Modesitt Jr.  *f*  3933

**Drake, Tannim**
*Chrome Circle* - Mercedes Lackey  *f*  3277

**Eckert, Jim/Gorbash**
*The Dragon and the Djinn* - Gordon R.
  Dickson  *f*  1528
*The Dragon and the Gnarly King* - Gordon R.
  Dickson  *f*  1529
*The Dragon at War* - Gordon R. Dickson  *f*  1530
*The Dragon in Lyonesse* - Gordon R.
  Dickson  *f*  1531
*The Dragon Knight* - Gordon R. Dickson  *f*  1532
*The Dragon on the Border* - Gordon R.
  Dickson  *f*  1533
*The Dragon, the Earl, and the Troll* - Gordon R.
  Dickson  *f*  1534

**Eleuth**
*Songs of Earth and Power* - Greg Bear  *f*  424

**Eliseth**
*Dhiammara* - Maggie Furey  *f*  2096
*Sword of Flame* - Maggie Furey  *f*  2098

**Elof**
*The Forge in the Forest* - Michael Scott
  Rohan  *f*  4660

**Elspeth**
*Winds of Fury* - Mercedes Lackey  *f*  3306

**Ferenczy, Janos**
*Deadspeak* - Brian Lumley  *h*  3551

**Firesong**
*Storm Breaking* - Mercedes Lackey  *f*  3296
*Storm Warning* - Mercedes Lackey  *f*  3298

**Flowerstalk, Flarman**
*Pyromancer* - Don Callander  *f*  847

**Fortune, Celinde "Cissy"**
*Dreaming Metal* - Melissa Scott  *s*  4895

**Frost**
*Demon Blade* - Mark A. Garland  *f*  2141

**Fry, Theodore**
*The Fair Rules of Evil* - David C. Smith  *h*  5111

**Galvin**
*Red Magic* - Jean Rabe  *f*  4458

**Gehn**
*Myst: The Book of Atrus* - Rand Miller  *f*  3896

**Gray Mouser**
*Farewell to Lankhmar* - Fritz Leiber  *f*  3418
*Swords Against the Shadowland* - Robin Wayne
  Bailey  *f*  291

**Great Chaffalo**
*The Midnight Horse* - Sid Fleischman  *f*  1948

**Gregorian**
*Stations of the Tide* - Michael Swanwick  *s*  5373

**Greyson, Hunter "Grey"**
*Witchlight* - Marion Zimmer Bradley  *f*  655

**Gunar**
*The Order War* - L.E. Modesitt Jr.  *f*  3936

**Halanyn, SharMarali "Shar"**
*Chrome Circle* - Mercedes Lackey  *f*  3277

**Hawke, Michael**
*Night Magic* - Thomas Tryon  *h*  5485

**Hawken, Solomon**
*Arcady* - Michael Williams  *f*  5818

**Herewiss**
*The Door into Sunset* - Diane Duane  *f*  1660

**Houdini, Harry**
*Believe: A Novel* - William Shatner  *f*  4929
*Nevermore* - William Hjortsberg  *h*  2692

**Humfrey**
*Question Quest* - Piers Anthony  *f*  186

**Impossumble**
*An Impossumble Summer* - Brenda W.
  Clough  *f*  1090

**Incarnadine**
*Bride of the Castle* - John DeChancie  *s*  1452
*Castle Dreams* - John DeChancie  *s*  1453
*Castle War!* - John DeChancie  *s*  1455

**Irith**
*Taking Flight* - Lawrence Watt-Evans  *f*  5650

**Jaad**
*Ronin* - D.A. Heeley  *f*  2639

**Jack**
*The Loneliest Magician* - Irene Radford  *f*  4461

**Justen**
*The Order War* - L.E. Modesitt Jr.  *f*  3936

**Kayli**
*Firewalk* - Anne Logston  *f*  3509

**Keatley, Thompson**
*A Dry Spell* - Susan Moloney  *h*  3951

**Keeper, Tom**
*Ancient Games* - Scott Ciencin  *f*  1028
*Night of Glory* - Scott Ciencin  *f*  1030
*The Ways of Magic* - Scott Ciencin  *f*  1033

**Kevin**
*Castle of Deception* - Mercedes Lackey  *f*  3275

**Kew, Horris**
*The Tangle Box* - Terry Brooks  *f*  718

**Kheperu**
*Iron Dawn* - Matthew Woodring Stover  *f*  5320
*Jericho Moon* - Matthew Woodring Stover  *f*  5321

**Kim**
*Magician's Ward* - Patricia C. Wrede  *f*  5976

**Kirtha**
*Mind of the Magic* - Holly Lisle  *f*  3486

**Laela**
*Twisted Dragon* - Kevin Stein  *f*  5251

**Linda**
*Bride of the Castle* - John DeChancie  *s*  1452

**Luap**
*Liar's Oath* - Elizabeth Moon  *f*  3969

**Maguire, Aaron**
*The Wizard's Apprentice* - S.P. Somtow  *f*  5163

**Mairelon**
*Mairelon the Magician* - Patricia C. Wrede  *f*  5977

**Mano, Iuti**
*Demon Drums* - Carol Severance  *f*  4922
*Storm Caller* - Carol Severance  *f*  4924

**Maria**
*Aunt Maria* - Diana Wynne Jones  *f*  2943

**Marita**
*Sable, Shadow and Ice* - Cheryl J. Franklin  *f*  2039

**Master**
*Mythology Abroad* - Jody Lynn Nye  *f*  4174

**McLaud, Jaren**
*Sage of Sare* - Julie Dean Smith  *f*  5126

**Merlin**
*The Camelot Chronicles* - Mike Ashley  *f*  224
*Merlin and the Dragons* - Jane Yolen  *f*  6036
*The Merlin Chronicles* - Mike Ashley  *f*  227
*Merlin's Harp* - Anne Eliot Crompton  *f*  1270

**Merrill, Richard "Mairelon"**
*Magician's Ward* - Patricia C. Wrede  *f*  5976

**Miathan**
*Aurian* - Maggie Furey  *f*  2095
*Dhiammara* - Maggie Furey  *f*  2096
*Harp of Winds* - Maggie Furey  *f*  2097

**Mizzamir**
*Villains by Necessity* - Eve Forward  *f*  1985

**Moncrief, Marcel**
*Ports of Call* - Jack Vance  *s*  5549

**Moon, Jeremy**
*Wizard's Mole* - Brad Strickland  *f*  5337

**Mordeth**
*The Falcon Rises* - Michael C. Staudinger  *f*  5235

**Nallaneen, Faris**
*A College of Magics* - Caroline Stevermer  *f*  5266

**Nandan**
*The Adventures of King Midas* - Lynne Reid
  Banks  *f*  329

**Nashram, Mika**
*By the Sword* - Greg Costikyan  *f*  1207

**Navarre**
*The Magic Wars* - Jo Clayton   *f*   1068

**Nazaual**
*Redmagic* - Crawford Kilian   *f*   3107

**ni Bron, Deir**
*Redmagic* - Crawford Kilian   *f*   3107

**Niad**
*The Cursed* - Dave Duncan   *f*   1674

**Nightingale "Lyrebird"**
*The Eagle and the Nightingales* - Mercedes
   Lackey   *f*   3278

**Nimbulan "Lan"**
*The Dragon's Touchstone* - Irene Radford   *f*   4459

**Nokias**
*The Ship Who Won* - Anne McCaffrey   *s*   3750

**Nunn**
*Dragon Burning* - Craig Shaw Gardner   *f*   2126
*Dragon Sleeping* - Craig Shaw Gardner   *f*   2127
*Dragon Waking* - Craig Shaw Gardner   *f*   2128

**Obar**
*Dragon Waking* - Craig Shaw Gardner   *f*   2128

**Ohmsford, Par**
*The Scions of Shannara* - Terry Brooks   *f*   716

**Old Nathan**
*Old Nathan* - David Drake   *f*   1639

**O'Shay, Padrig**
*City of Pain* - John Terra   *f*   5438

**Osmirik**
*Castle Spellbound* - John DeChancie   *s*   1454

**Parody, Paskal**
*Kirins: The Secret of the Hanging Stones* - James D.
   Priest   *f*   4434

**Pec-Pec**
*The Dream Vessel* - Jeff Bredenberg   *s*   664

**Pilgrim, Julian**
*Ghostlight* - Marion Zimmer Bradley   *f*   634

**Platho, Aivlys**
*Clock Strikes Sword* - Ian Hammell   *f*   2529

**Platho, Endimin**
*Clock Strikes Sword* - Ian Hammell   *f*   2529

**Pol**
*Skybowl* - Melanie Rawn   *f*   4490

**Quinn, Roger**
*A Calculated Magic* - Robert Weinberg   *f*   5694

**Raeburn, Francis**
*Death of an Adept* - Katherine Kurtz   *f*   3257

**Rand**
*Four & Twenty Blackbirds* - Mercedes
   Lackey   *f*   3283

**Redwyn**
*The Lost History of Redwyn* - William Jay   *f*   2883

**Reed, Sharon**
*The Road to Hell, Volume I* - Robert
   Weinberg   *h*   5701
*The Road to Hell, Volume II* - Robert
   Weinberg   *h*   5702

**Rhiana**
*In the Rift* - Marion Zimmer Bradley   *f*   639

**Road Man**
*Soulsmith* - Tom Deitz   *f*   1475

**Rosie**
*Wild Blood* - Nancy A. Collins   *h*   1127

**Rufo**
*Glory Road* - Robert A. Heinlein   *f*   2644

**Sabriel**
*Sabriel* - Garth Nix   *f*   4129

**St. Brendan, Caitlin**
*Indiana Jones and the White Witch* - Martin
   Caidin   *f*   826

**Salmalin, Numair**
*The Realms of the Gods* - Tamora Pierce   *f*   4321
*Wolf-Speaker* - Tamora Pierce   *f*   4324

**Sarrasri, Diane**
*The Realms of the Gods* - Tamora Pierce   *f*   4321
*Wild Magic* - Tamora Pierce   *f*   4323
*Wolf-Speaker* - Tamora Pierce   *f*   4324

**Sauventreen, Verna**
*Blood of the Fold* - Terry Goodkind   *f*   2268

**Seymour**
*The White Mists of Power* - Kristine Kathryn
   Rusch   *f*   4730

**s'Falenn, Arithon**
*Curse of the Mistwraith* - Janny Wurts   *f*   6001
*Ships of Merior* - Janny Wurts   *f*   6004

**Shaa, Zalzyn**
*Catastrophe's Spell* - Mayer Alan Brenner   *f*   671

**Shamandar, Serrin**
*Streets of Blood* - Carl Sargent   *f*   4821

**s'Ilessid, Lysaer**
*Curse of the Mistwraith* - Janny Wurts   *f*   6001
*Ships of Merior* - Janny Wurts   *f*   6004

**Sioned**
*Stronghold* - Melanie Rawn   *f*   4492

**Skeeve**
*Sweet Myth-tery of Life* - Robert Asprin   *f*   262

**Smith, Kayla**
*Bedlam Boyz* - Ellen Guon   *f*   2467

**Smythe, Raoul "Rags"**
*Shade and Shadow* - Francine G. Woodbury   *f*   5967

**Solith, Gwin Nien**
*The Cursed* - Dave Duncan   *f*   1674

**Sorensson, Alfreda "Allie"**
*Kindred Rites* - Katharine Eliska Kimbriel   *f*   3118

**Southwell, Roger**
*The Printer's Devil* - Chico Kidd   *f*   3099

**Speckarin**
*Kirins: The Flight of the Ain* - James D.
   Priest   *f*   4433
*Kirins: The Secret of the Hanging Stones* - James D.
   Priest   *f*   4434
*Kirins: The Spell of No'an* - James D.
   Priest   *f*   4435

**Tannim**
*Born to Run* - Mercedes Lackey   *f*   3271

**Tarawe**
*Demon Drums* - Carol Severance   *f*   4922
*Storm Caller* - Carol Severance   *f*   4924

**Telgrin**
*The Floating Castle* - Craig Mills   *f*   3913

**Temple, Hamilton**
*The 7th Guest* - Matthew J. Costello   *h*   1192

**Thorne, Peter**
*Death Channels* - Robert E. Vardeman   *h*   5562

**Tianna**
*Iron Dragons: Mountains and Madness* - Rose
   Estes   *f*   1839

**Touchstone**
*Sabriel* - Garth Nix   *f*   4129

**Trent**
*Harpy Thyme* - Piers Anthony   *f*   174

**Tryon**
*Wren to the Rescue* - Sherwood Smith   *f*   5142

**Tyrr**
*Demon Blade* - Mark A. Garland   *f*   2141

**Urtho**
*The Black Gryphon* - Mercedes Lackey   *f*   3270

**Valorian**
*Valorian* - Mary H. Herbert   *f*   2677

**Vangerdahast**
*Cormyr: A Novel* - Ed Greenwood   *f*   2426

**Vanyel**
*Magic's Pawn* - Mercedes Lackey   *f*   3287

**Vanyi**
*Spear of Heaven* - Judith Tarr   *f*   5396

**Victor**
*Blood and Honor* - Simon R. Green   *f*   2361

**Vordegh**
*Star Ascendant* - Louise Cooper   *f*   1180

**Wanderson, Balthan**
*The Temper of Wisdom* - Lynn Abbey   *f*   17

**Ware, Theron**
*The Devil's Day* - James Blish   *h*   525

**White Crow, Valentine**
*The Architecture of Desire* - Mary Gentle   *f*   2195
*Rats and Gargoyles* - Mary Gentle   *f*   2196

**Wilum**
*Flight to Hollow Mountain* - Mark Sebanc   *f*   4908

**Winters, Elizabet**
*Bedlam Boyz* - Ellen Guon   *f*   2467

**Wolf**
*Masques* - Patricia Briggs   *f*   681

**Wolfe, Atrix**
*The Book of Atrix Wolfe* - Patricia A.
   McKillip   *f*   3838

**Worabex**
*Red Unicorn* - Tanith Lee   *f*   3414

**Wren**
*The True Knight* - Susan Dexter   *f*   1513
*Wren to the Rescue* - Sherwood Smith   *f*   5142
*Wren's War* - Sherwood Smith   *f*   5144

**Wurlitzer, Max**
*Night Magic* - Thomas Tryon   *h*   5485

**Wyvernspur, Finder "Nameless"**
*Song of the Saurials* - Kate Novak   *f*   4167

**X-ray, Foxtrot "Fox"**
*Chrome Circle* - Mercedes Lackey   *f*   3277

**Zambendorf, Karl**
*The Immortality Option* - James P. Hogan   *s*   2725

**Zodiac, Saskia**
*Seasons of Plenty* - Colin Greenland   *s*   2418

## MAIDEN

**Arden, Rose Red**
*Snow White and Rose Red* - Patricia C.
   Wrede   *f*   5981

**Arden, Snow White**
*Snow White and Rose Red* - Patricia C.
   Wrede   *f*   5981

**Flitworth, Renata**
*Reaper Man* - Terry Pratchett   *f*   4399

**Lissa**
*The Birth of the Blade* - Dennis McCarty   *f*   3766

**Marian**
*Sherwood* - Parke Godwin   *f*   2248

**Rinna**
*The Birth of the Blade* - Dennis McCarty   *f*   3766

**Suisan**
*Suisan* - Phyllis Carol Agins   *f*   42

## MAINTENANCE WORKER

**Bell, Howard**
*A Key for the Nonesuch* - Geary Gravel   *s*   2330

**Bird, Jake**
*Devil's Tower* - Mark Sumner   *f*   5357

**Cleg, Horace**
*Spider* - Patrick McGrath   *h*   3815

**Demerit, Geode**
*Firefly* - Piers Anthony   *h*   170

**Hawkins, Ron**
*Fire* - Alan Rodgers   *h*   4647

**Hunt, Sam**
*The Trickster* - Muriel Gray   *h*   2340

**LeGuerre, Tessa**
*The Passion* - Donna Boyd   *h*   603

**Linares, Segismundo**
*The Secret Weavers: Stories of the Fantastic by Latin
   American Women* - Marjorie Agosin   *f*   43

**McIssac, Dean**
*Summon the Keeper* - Tanya Huff   *f*   2800

**Morcey, Paul**
*The Things That Are Not There* - Robert
   Morgan   *h*   4007

**Perry, Harlan**
*The Death Crystal* - J. Edward Ames   *h*   91

**Quimby, Byron**
*Lot Lizards* - Ray Garton   *h*   2152

**Rickard, Robert**
*Room 13* - Henry Garfield   *h*   2139

**Ridge, Freeman**
*Dark Visions* - T. Lucien Wright   *h*   5987

**Torrance, Jack**
*The Shining* - Stephen King   *h*   3141

**Vlaicu, Elena**
*The Lost* - Jonathan Aycliffe   *h*   279

## MANUFACTURER

**McLaris, Duncan**
*Lifeline* - Kevin J. Anderson   *s*   111

## MARTIAL ARTS EXPERT

**Agenos, Mordion "the Servant"**
*Hexwood* - Diana Wynne Jones   *s*   2948

**al Jorddyn, Kerridwen**
*Kingmaker's Sword* - Ann Marston   *f*   3635

**ap Hywel, Dafydd**
*The Dragon on the Border* - Gordon R.
   Dickson   *f*   1533

**Aralorn**
*Masques* - Patricia Briggs   *f*   681

**Aranur**
*Shadow Leader* - Tara K. Harper   *f*   2552

**Attila**
*Hunter's Planet* - David Bischoff   *s*   492

**Aw, Ruiz**
*The Pharaoh Contract* - Ray Aldridge   *s*   63

**Baenre, Dantrag**
*Starless Night* - R.A. Salvatore   *f*   4807

**Bannering, Charlan "Arlin"**
*King of the Dead* - R.A. MacAvoy   *f*   3581

**Bannon**
*Fifth Quarter* - Tanya Huff   *f*   2795
*No Quarter* - Tanya Huff   *f*   2798

**Bariden**
*The Hidden Realms* - Sharon Green   *f*   2358

**Barrow, Simon**
*The First Duelist* - Rutledge Etheridge   *s*   1849

**Birnbaum, Maureen**
*Maureen Birnbaum, Barbarian Swordsperson: The
   Complete Stories* - George Alec Effinger   *f*   1752

**Blayke, Arcole**
*Exile's Children* - Angus Wells   *f*   5735

**Bork, Saval**
*Brother Death* - Steve Perry   *s*   4292

**Breo-Saight "Brie"**
*Fire Arrow* - Edith Pattou   *f*   4260

**Callista**
*Darksaber* - Kevin J. Anderson   *s*   103

**Campbell, Laicy "Iroshi"**
*The Glaive* - Cary Osborne   *s*   4227
*Iroshi* - Cary Osborne   *s*   4228

**Chase, Jason**
*Night's Pawn* - Tom Dowd   *s*   1591

**Christensen, Maryanne "Maggie"**
*The Crimson Sky* - Joel Rosenberg   *f*   4669
*The Silver Stone* - Joel Rosenberg   *f*   4676

**Cierto, Hoja**
*Black Steel* - Steve Perry   *s*   4291

**Cole, Cassandra**
*A Logical Magician* - Robert Weinberg   *f*   5697

**Corson**
*Mistress of Ambiguities* - J.F. Rivkin   *f*   4596

**Cromwell, Willard**
*Indiana Jones and the Sky Pirates* - Martin
   Caidin   *f*   825

**Crowell**
*Iroshi* - Cary Osborne   *s*   4228

**Curran, Joslire**
*An Exchange of Hostages* - Susan R.
   Matthews   *s*   3692

**Cypher, Richard "the Seeker"**
*Wizard's First Rule* - Terry Goodkind   *f*   2271

**Danica**
*Canticle* - R.A. Salvatore   *f*   4793

**Darcy, Jade**
*Jade Darcy and the Zen Pirates* - Stephen
   Goldin   *s*   2260

**deBurrows, Oliver**
*Luthien's Gamble* - R.A. Salvatore   *f*   4802

**Dion**
*Shadow Leader* - Tara K. Harper   *f*   2552
*Wolfwalker* - Tara K. Harper   *f*   2553

**Drake, Christopher**
*End Game* - Robert Cain   *s*   830

**Dunreith, Cassandra "Cass"**
*Dragon Moon* - Chris Claremont   *f*   1040

**Ellis, Cander**
*Shadow of the Crown* - Craig Mills   *f*   3914

**Ensi**
*The Glaive* - Cary Osborne   *s*   4227

**Eride "Thorn"**
*Thorn and Needle* - Paul B. Thompson   *f*   5456

**Fieran**
*Dragon Moon* - Chris Claremont   *f*   1040

**Greene, Harris**
*Doc Sidhe* - Aaron Allston   *f*   85

**Heredes**
*A Passage of Stars* - Alis A. Rasmussen   *s*   4482

**Hernandez, Corinne**
*The First Duelist* - Rutledge Etheridge   *s*   1849

**Javere "Javerri"**
*Ladylord* - Sasha Miller   *f*   3906

**Jewelbright, Taynad**
*Brother to Shadows* - Andre Norton   *s*   4142

**Jofre**
*Brother to Shadows* - Andre Norton   *s*   4142

**Juvell, Cat**
*Iron Shadows* - Steven Barnes   *f*   362

**Kang, Liu**
*Mortal Kombat* - Martin Delrio   *f*   1483

**Kethry**
*Oathblood* - Mercedes Lackey   *f*   3290

**Khadaji, Emile**
*The Albino Knife* - Steve Perry   *s*   4288

**Kifo, Ndug "Brother Death"**
*Brother Death* - Steve Perry   *s*   4292

**Kinoshita, Ito**
*The Widowmaker Reborn* - Mike Resnick   *s*   4560

**Knight, Aubrey**
*Firedance* - Steven Barnes   *s*   360
*Gorgon Child* - Steven Barnes   *s*   361

**Lasker, Burt**
*Fortress of Forbidden Destiny* - Ryder
   Syvertson   *s*   5378

**Lescevre, Thibault**
*Anvil of the Sun* - Anne Lesley Groell   *f*   2451
*Bridge of Valor* - Anne Lesley Groell   *f*   2452

**Lidjun, Dun**
*Hour of the Octopus* - Joel Rosenberg   *f*   4673

**MacLeod, Duncan**
*The Element of Fire* - Jason Henderson   *f*   2657
*Scotland the Brave* - Jennifer Roberson   *f*   4611
*Shadow of Obsession* - Rebecca Neason   *f*   4082

**Mishima, Ken**
*The Unwound Way* - William Adams   *s*   35

**Morane, Reynard**
*The Death of the Necromancer* - Martha
   Wells   *f*   5749

**Mushimo**
*Iroshi* - Cary Osborne   *s*   4228

**Nimesin, Kymil**
*Elfshadow* - Elaine Cunningham   *f*   1288

**Pine, Leonard**
*Mucho Mojo* - Joe R. Lansdale   *h*   3330
*Savage Season* - Joe R. Lansdale   *h*   3332

**Podlowski, Eric**
*Brothers of the Dragon* - Robin Wayne
   Bailey   *f*   286
*Flames of the Dragon* - Robin Wayne Bailey   *f*   287

**Podlowski, Robert**
*Brothers of the Dragon* - Robin Wayne
   Bailey   *f*   286
*Flames of the Dragon* - Robin Wayne Bailey   *f*   287

**Protagonist, Hiro**
*Snow Crash* - Neal Stephenson   *s*   5254

**Rachelle**
*The Anubis Murders* - Gary Gygax   *f*   2472
*Death in Delhi* - Gary Gygax   *f*   2473

**Radineaux, Jenifleur**
*Anvil of the Sun* - Anne Lesley Groell   *f*   2451
*Bridge of Valor* - Anne Lesley Groell   *f*   2452

**Radineaux, Viera**
*Anvil of the Sun* - Anne Lesley Groell   *f*   2451

**Raven**
*Snow Crash* - Neal Stephenson   *s*   5254

**Ripley, Robert Remington III**
*When Dreams Collide* - Wm. Mark
   Simmons   *f*   5063

**Rosen, Charlina "Charley"**
*Helm* - Steven Gould   s   2289

**Samson, Daniel "Dan"**
*Union Fires* - John Barnes   f   358
*Wartide* - John Barnes   f   359

**Segnbora**
*The Door into Sunset* - Diane Duane   f   1660

**Shadrack**
*Ronin* - D.A. Heeley   f   2639

**Shuyun**
*Gatherer of Clouds* - Sean Russell   f   4741
*The Initiate Brother* - Sean Russell   f   4742

**Silverstein, Ian**
*The Crimson Sky* - Joel Rosenberg   f   4669
*The Fire Duke* - Joel Rosenberg   f   4671
*The Silver Stone* - Joel Rosenberg   f   4676

**Simon, Chuck**
*Psi-Man* - David Peters   s   4305

**Siobahn**
*Luthien's Gamble* - R.A. Salvatore   f   4802

**Skywalker, Luke**
*Ambush at Corellia* - Roger MacBride Allen   s   76
*Before the Storm* - Michael P. Kube-
    McDowell   s   3247
*Children of the Jedi* - Barbara Hambly   s   2500
*The Courtship of Princess Leia* - Dave
    Wolverton   s   5950
*The Crystal Star* - Vonda N. McIntyre   s   3820
*Dark Force Rising* - Timothy Zahn   s   6052
*Darksaber* - Kevin J. Anderson   s   103
*The Glove of Darth Vader* - Paul Davids   s   1392
*Heir to the Empire* - Timothy Zahn   s   6054
*Jedi Search* - Kevin J. Anderson   s   109
*The Last Command* - Timothy Zahn   s   6055
*The Lost City of the Jedi* - Paul Davids   s   1393
*The New Rebellion* - Kristine Kathryn
    Rusch   s   4719
*Shadows of the Empire* - Steve Perry   s   4299
*The Truce at Bakura* - Kathy Tyers   s   5527

**Slaven, Eleret**
*The Raven Ring* - Patricia C. Wrede   f   5978

**Sleel**
*Black Steel* - Steve Perry   s   4291

**Stone, Jack**
*Dead Time* - Richard Lee Byers   h   796

**Swag**
*Kill Crazy* - L.S. Riker   s   4590

**Taltos, Vlad**
*Athyra* - Steven Brust   f   739
*Dragon* - Steven Brust   f   741
*Orca* - Steven Brust   f   745
*Phoenix* - Steven Brust   f   746

**Tarma**
*Oathblood* - Mercedes Lackey   f   3290

**Tegne**
*Tegne: Soul Warrior* - Richard La Plante   f   3268

**Terminationer**
*Samurai Cat Goes to the Movies* - Mark E.
    Rogers   s   4656

**Thorsen, Thorian "Torrie"**
*The Crimson Sky* - Joel Rosenberg   f   4669
*The Fire Duke* - Joel Rosenberg   f   4671
*The Silver Stone* - Joel Rosenberg   f   4676

**Topaz**
*Mistworld* - Simon R. Green   s   2372

**Vader, Darth**
*Shadows of the Empire* - Steve Perry   s   4299

**Vallaniri, Daner**
*The Raven Ring* - Patricia C. Wrede   f   5978

**Veate**
*The Albino Knife* - Steve Perry   s   4288

**Venabili, Dors**
*Forward the Foundation* - Isaac Asimov   s   236

**Vree**
*Fifth Quarter* - Tanya Huff   f   2795
*No Quarter* - Tanya Huff   f   2798

**Wu, Kildee**
*Black Steel* - Steve Perry   s   4291

## MASSEUSE

**Galloway, Katt**
*Walking Wounded* - Robert Devereaux   h   1507

## MATCHMAKER

**Sparrow**
*Justice* - David Drake   s   1635

## MECHANIC

**Bowers, Sidney**
*Mojave Wells* - L. Dean James   s   2864

**Cugnet, Vern**
*Stones of the Dalai Lama* - Ken Mitchell   f   3916

**Damen, Clyde**
*Cats Raise the Dead* - Shirley Rousseau
    Murphy   f   4054

**Frank**
*Spacer Dreams* - Larry Segriff   s   4911

**Hummingbird, Kinsey**
*Drawing Blood* - Poppy Z. Brite   h   694

**Kateralbin, Crispin**
*The War in the Waste* - Felicity Savage   f   4851

**Petway, Boomer**
*Skinny Legs and All* - Tom Robbins   f   4607

**Sam**
*The Unfinished* - Jay B. Laws   h   3362

**Semmlar, Wayne**
*Near Dead* - Stephen R. George   h   2202

**Solis, Rudy**
*Mother of Winter* - Barbara Hambly   f   2506

**Spenser, Vernon**
*Bright Shadow* - Elizabeth Forrest   h   1971

**Tick-Tick**
*Finder* - Emma Bull   f   769

**Whipple, Frank "Weasel"**
*Mongster* - Randall Boyll   h   616

## MENTALLY ILL PERSON

**Calder, Reginald**
*No Blood Spilled* - Les Daniels   h   1338

**Carol**
*Century 21* - Ewa Kuryluk   s   3263

**Chance, Lester**
*Blue Light* - Walter Mosley   s   4042

**Cochrane, Miles "David Gilman"**
*Alpha Centauri* - William Barton   s   378

**Creed, Victor "Sabertooth"**
*Codename Wolverine* - Christopher Golden   s   2256

**di Hoa, Barry**
*The Voices of Heaven* - Frederik Pohl   s   4356

**Goldblatt, Steve**
*Landscape of Demons and the Book of Sara* - Gabriel
    Devlin Kessler   h   3088

**Jack**
*Lunatics* - Bradley Denton   f   1491

**Liddy, Mary**
*The Uprising* - Brent Monahan   h   3956

**Masada, Kio**
*This Alien Shore* - C.S. Friedman   s   2059

**Nina**
*Planar Powers* - J. Robert King   f   3122

**Plumtree, Janis**
*Earthquake Weather* - Tim Powers   f   4382

**Sloan, Philip**
*Come Before Christ and Murder Love* - Stewart
    Home   f   2754

**Soul Catcher**
*She Is the Darkness* - Glen Cook   f   1154

**Ted**
*The Kronos Condition* - Emily Devenport   s   1502

**Tobias, Cameron**
*Making Love* - Melanie Tem   h   5422

**Tobias, Robin**
*Strange Angels* - Kathe Koja   h   3197

**Typhoid Mary**
*Twilight of the Empire* - Simon R. Green   s   2374

**Valentine, Kenneth "Sparky"**
*The Golden Globe* - John Varley   s   5565

**Wade, Tamara**
*Bad Blood* - D.A. Fowler   h   2021

## MERCENARY

**Alon**
*The Nomad Queen* - James Gordon White   f   5783

**Barek, A.E.**
*Created By* - Richard Christian Matheson   h   3691

**Barra the Pict**
*Iron Dawn* - Matthew Woodring Stover   f   5320
*Jericho Moon* - Matthew Woodring Stover   f   5321

**Belmonte, Rodrigo**
*The Lions of Al-Rassan* - Guy Gavriel Kay   f   3016

**Bruno**
*Harm's Way* - Colin Greenland   s   2416

**Byrnison, Iorek**
*The Golden Compass* - Philip Pullman   f   4446

**Calis**
*Shadow of a Dark Queen* - Raymond E.
    Feist   f   1911

**Calmady, Pollexfen**
*The Architecture of Desire* - Mary Gentle   f   2195

**Canby, Gordon**
*Canby's Legion* - Bill Baldwin   s   308

**Carson, Chev**
*Warp Angel* - Stuart Hopen   s   2766

**Clay, John Sebastian**
*A Landscape of Darkness* - John Blair   s   513

**Cooke, Daniel**
*Surface Action* - David Drake   s   1646

**dav Aidan, Kenzie "Catfoot"**
*Broken Blade* - Ann Marston   f   3634

**dav Medroch, Cullin**
*Kingmaker's Sword* - Ann Marston   f   3635

**Dawson, Jack**
*Hell-Storm* - James A. Moore   h   3990

**de Garsenc, Blaise**
*A Song for Arbonne* - Guy Gavriel Kay   f   3017

**d'Iste, Tiran**
*Dark Mirror, Dark Dreams* - Sharon Green   f   2357

**Silver Princess, Golden Knight** - Sharon
Green  *f*  2359

**Duran**
*Headhunters* - Mel Odom  *s*  4192

**Falkenberg, John Christian**
*Prince of Mercenaries* - Jerry Pournelle  *s*  4377

**Gordon, John**
*Surface Action* - David Drake  *s*  1646

**Grover**
*Heroes, Inc.* - Kyle Crocco  *f*  1268
*Heroes Wanted* - Kyle Crocco  *f*  1267

**Gustiano, Rinaldo**
*The Innamorati* - Midori Snyder  *f*  5152

**Horn, Alan**
*Star Bridge* - James Gunn  *s*  2459

**Hunter, Lucel**
*The Centurion's Empire* - Sean McMullen  *s*  3854

**Jes**
*Hope of Earth* - Piers Anthony  *s*  175

**Jill of Cerrmor**
*The Dragon Revenant* - Katharine Kerr  *f*  3069

**kar Therma, Staffa**
*Relic of Empire* - W. Michael Gear  *s*  2171

**Karolyi, Ignace**
*Traveling with the Dead* - Barbara Hambly  *h*  2511

**Kerowyn**
*By the Sword* - Mercedes Lackey  *f*  3273

**Kheperu**
*Iron Dawn* - Matthew Woodring Stover  *f*  5320
*Jericho Moon* - Matthew Woodring Stover  *f*  5321

**Korendir**
*The Master of Whitestorm* - Janny Wurts  *f*  6003

**Latro**
*Soldier of Arete* - Gene Wolfe  *f*  5944

**Leucas**
*Iron Dawn* - Matthew Woodring Stover  *f*  5320
*Jericho Moon* - Matthew Woodring Stover  *f*  5321

**Lyma, Skyla**
*Relic of Empire* - W. Michael Gear  *s*  2171

**Maelwaedd, Rhodry**
*Days of Air and Darkness* - Katharine Kerr  *f*  3067
*Days of Blood and Fire* - Katharine Kerr  *f*  3068
*The Dragon Revenant* - Katharine Kerr  *f*  3069
*A Time of Exile* - Katharine Kerr  *f*  3077

**Mark, Philip**
*The Sheriff of Nottingham* - Richard Kluger  *f*  3165

**Matar, Kitiara "Kit"**
*Steel and Stone* - Ellen Porath  *f*  4368

**Miri**
*Carpe Diem* - Steve Miller  *s*  3907

**Morrison, Athol**
*When Heaven Fell* - William Barton  *s*  383

**ni Errhyn, Bracht**
*Dark Magic* - Angus Wells  *f*  5733
*Forbidden Magic* - Angus Wells  *f*  5736
*Wild Magic* - Angus Wells  *f*  5741

**Nighthawk, Jefferson "Widowmaker"**
*The Widowmaker Reborn* - Mike Resnick  *s*  4560

**Owensford, Peter**
*Go Tell the Spartans* - Jerry Pournelle  *s*  4375
*Prince of Sparta* - Jerry Pournelle  *s*  4378

**Parmenion**
*Lion of Macedon* - David Gemmell  *f*  2189

**Ramok**
*Cat Scratch Fever* - Tara K. Harper  *s*  2550

**Ranson, June**
*Rolling Hot* - David Drake  *s*  1642

**Ranth**
*The Sands of Kalaven: A Novel of Shunlar* - Carol
Heller  *f*  2651

**Ravis**
*The Barbed Coil* - J.V. Jones  *f*  2957

**Reece**
*War* - Simon Hawke  *f*  2625

**Rhodry**
*A Time of Omens* - Katharine Kerr  *f*  3078

**Rico**
*Fade to Black* - Nyx Smith  *s*  5134

**Romlar, Artus**
*The Regiment's War* - John Dalmas  *s*  1326
*The White Regiment* - John Dalmas  *s*  1327

**Roshannon, Nikkael**
*Wheel of Dreams* - Salinda Tyson  *f*  5529

**Sadi**
*Kaleidoscope Century* - John Barnes  *s*  352

**Schonnegon, Teletha**
*Wizard of Bones* - Robert N. Charrette  *f*  979

**Shaman**
*The Quick* - Burt Cole  *s*  1113

**Shunlar**
*The Sands of Kalaven: A Novel of Shunlar* - Carol
Heller  *f*  2651

**Silverhorn, Aelfred**
*Into the Void* - Nigel Findley  *f*  1937

**Skater, Jack**
*Headhunters* - Mel Odom  *s*  4192

**Starhawk**
*The Dark Hand of Magic* - Barbara Hambly  *f*  2502

**Suilin, Dick**
*Rolling Hot* - David Drake  *s*  1642

**Sumara**
*The Nomad Queen* - James Gordon White  *f*  5783

**Sun Wolf**
*The Dark Hand of Magic* - Barbara Hambly  *f*  2502

**Tarlach**
*Flight of Vengeance* - Andre Norton  *f*  4152
*Storms of Victory* - Andre Norton  *f*  4162

**Theisiger, Carlo**
*Enemy of My Enemy* - Ben Ohlander  *s*  4204

**Whitlock, Megan**
*Shadow's Son* - Shirley Meier  *f*  3872

**Wolf**
*Konrad* - David Ferring  *f*  1927

**Xris**
*Knights of the Black Earth* - Margaret Weis  *s*  5718

**York, Dennison**
*Thoughts of God* - Michael Kanaly  *s*  3007

**Zakalwe, Cheradenine**
*Use of Weapons* - Iain M. Banks  *s*  328

## MIDWIFE

**Donaltsson, Marta**
*Kindred Rites* - Katharine Eliska Kimbriel  *f*  3118

**Sorensson, Alfreda "Allie"**
*Kindred Rites* - Katharine Eliska Kimbriel  *f*  3118

## MILITARY PERSONNEL

**a Cimabue, Damastes**
*The Demon King* - Chris Bunch  *f*  770
*The Seer King* - Chris Bunch  *f*  771

**Abivard**
*The Stolen Throne* - Harry Turtledove  *f*  5510

*The Thousand Cities* - Harry Turtledove  *f*  5512
*Videssos Besieged* - Harry Turtledove  *f*  5513

**Abrena, Mirielle**
*Legacy of Steel* - Mary H. Herbert  *f*  2675

**Agesilaus, "Agis"**
*Spartan Run* - David Robbins  *s*  4602

**Aidan**
*Way of the Clans* - Robert Thurston  *s*  5469

**al-Schouki, Esoch**
*Foragers* - Charles Oberndorf  *s*  4187

**Alain**
*King's Dragon* - Kate Elliott  *f*  1773

**Alaiya**
*The Return of the Breakneck Boys* - Geary
Gravel  *s*  2332

**Alex**
*Alien Dreams* - Larry Segriff  *s*  4910

**Alston, Marian**
*Island in the Sea of Time* - S.M. Stirling  *s*  5295

**Althor**
*Catch the Lightning* - Catherine Asaro  *s*  218

**Amilcar**
*Pendragon* - Stephen R. Lawhead  *f*  3357

**Andojar, Susan Smith**
*The Web of Spider* - W. Michael Gear  *s*  2173

**Angelus, Lucifer "Luke"**
*Chains of Light* - Quentin Thomas  *s*  5449

**Antero, Rali Emilie**
*The Warrior's Tale* - Allan Cole  *f*  1110

**Antilles, Wedge**
*Rogue Squadron* - Michael A. Stackpole  *s*  5205

**Antonius, Marcus**
*Throne of Isis* - Judith Tarr  *f*  5397

**Antonovich, Colonel**
*The Struggle* - Jerry Ahern  *s*  44

**APU-805 "Bird Dog"**
*Destination: Showdown* - Jake Davis  *s*  1405
*The Last Rangers* - Jake Davis  *s*  1406

**Armstrong, Alexander "the Great"**
*Martian Rainbow* - Robert L. Forward  *s*  1987

**Arthur**
*The Hawk's Gray Feather* - Patricia Kennealy-
Morrison  *f*  3061

**Arvin, Andro**
*Starfire Down* - Lee McKeone  *s*  3830

**Asado**
*The War of Don Emmanuel's Nether Parts* - Louis de
Bernieres  *f*  1412

**Ash, Mickey**
*The Daemon in the Machine* - Felicity
Savage  *f*  4848
*The War in the Waste* - Felicity Savage  *f*  4852

**Asher, Anat**
*Signs of Life* - Cherry Wilder  *s*  5804

**Atkins, Thomas "Soldier"**
*Genetic Soldier* - George Turner  *s*  5492

**Atle**
*Silent Songs* - A.C. Crispin  *s*  1264

**Atvar**
*Worldwar: Striking the Balance* - Harry
Turtledove  *s*  5516
*Worldwar: Upsetting the Balance* - Harry
Turtledove  *s*  5518

**Auganzar**
*Warlord of Heaven* - Adrian Cole  *f*  1102

**Augustine, Alexa**
*Dream of Glass* - Jean Mark Gawron  *s*  2163

**Bammer, Mortimer**
*Kill Crazy* - L.S. Riker   s   4590

**Bar-el, Shimon**
*Hero* - Joel Rosenberg   s   4672

**Baranyk, Valentin**
*Cold Allies* - Patricia Anthony   s   157

**Barnes, Randy**
*Sleipnir* - Linda Evans   f   1856

**Bashir, Julian**
*Armageddon Sky* - L.A. Graf   s   2296
*Time's Enemy* - L.A. Graf   s   2297

**Bavalius, Vitellan**
*The Centurion's Empire* - Sean McMullen   s   3854

**Begg, Albert**
*Fabulous Harbors* - Michael Moorcock   f   3981

**Belisarius**
*In the Heart of Darkness* - Eric Flint   s   1955
*An Oblique Approach* - David Drake   s   1638

**Belkassem, Ferhat Ben**
*Path of the Fury* - David Weber   s   5680

**Bezarian**
*Red Army* - Ralph Peters   s   4306

**Bickerstaff, Robert Luther**
*Terraplane* - Jack Womack   s   5960

**Bill**
*Planet of the Robot Slaves* - Harry Harrison   s   2573

**Birch, Wellington**
*Lurid Dreams* - Charles L. Harness   s   2546

**Black, Frank**
*Dead Heat* - Del Stone Jr.   h   5313

**Blackstone, Rex**
*Primary Inversion* - Catherine Asaro   s   220

**Blade, Sonya**
*Mortal Kombat* - Martin Delrio   f   1483

**Bloch, Jared**
*No Limits* - Nigel Findley   s   1938

**Blount, Mikal**
*The Clouds of Saturn* - Michael McCollum   s   3770

**Bonaparte, Napoleon**
*The Napoleon Wager* - William R.
   Forstchen   s   1980

**Braan**
*Genellan: Planetfall* - Scott G. Gier   s   2223

**Bradoukis, Matthew**
*Ground Zero* - Kevin J. Anderson   h   106

**Brainard**
*The Jungle* - David Drake   s   1634

**Brant, Arn**
*The Lanterns of God* - Ron Sarti   s   4835
*Legacy of the Ancients* - Ron Sarti   s   4836

**Brentwood, David**
*Battle Front* - Ian Slater   s   5086

**Brightlaw, Nic**
*The Cup of Morning Shadows* - Rosemary
   Edghill   f   1747

**Brim, Wilf**
*The Defenders* - Bill Baldwin   s   309
*The Defiance* - Bill Baldwin   s   310
*The Mercenaries* - Bill Baldwin   s   311
*The Siege* - Bill Baldwin   s   312

**Britannicus, Caius**
*The Skystone* - Jack Whyte   f   5794

**Broketail, Bazil**
*Battledragon* - Christopher Rowley   f   4691
*A Dragon at World's End* - Christopher
   Rowley   f   4693
*Dragons of Argonath* - Christopher Rowley   f   4694
*Dragons of War* - Christopher Rowley   f   4695

*A Sword for a Dragon* - Christopher
   Rowley   f   4697

**Brown, Zack**
*Darker Angels* - S.P. Somtow   h   5155

**Brutus, Marcus Junius**
*Child of the Eagle* - Esther Friesner   f   2073

**Buccari, Sharl**
*Genellan: Planetfall* - Scott G. Gier   s   2223

**Bueller**
*Aliens: Earth Hive* - Steve Perry   s   4289

**Burning**
*A Screaming Across the Sky* - Brian Daley   s   1315

**Burns, David**
*The War in the Waste* - Felicity Savage   f   4852

**Bushell, Thomas**
*The Two Georges* - Richard Dreyfuss   s   1655

**Caceras, Mimla**
*Traitors from Within* - R.A. Montgomery   s   3966

**Caesar, Julius**
*Caesar's Bicycle* - John Barnes   s   350

**Caillet, Bertrand**
*The Werewolf of Paris* - Guy Endore   h   1822

**Cain, Roth Tiberius**
*Cain* - James Byron Huggins   h   2802

**Calrissian, Lando**
*Before the Storm* - Michael P. Kube-
   McDowell   s   3247

**Cameron, Dev**
*Warstrider* - William H. Keith Jr.   s   3037

**Carlson, Curt**
*Blood Siege* - G. Harry Stine   s   5278
*Force of Arms* - G. Harry Stine   s   5279
*Guts and Glory* - G. Harry Stine   s   5280
*Judgment Day* - G. Harry Stine   s   5281
*Warrior Shield* - G. Harry Stine   s   5283

**Carmichael, Anson**
*The Alien Years* - Robert Silverberg   s   5027

**Carnes, Rebecca**
*Arc Riders* - David Drake   s   1626

**Carrigan**
*The Unknown Soldier* - Mickey Zucker
   Reichert   s   4525

**Castellan, Basil**
*Prince of Sunset* - Steve White   s   5786

**Cedric**
*One for the Morning Glory* - John Barnes   f   355

**Centuri, Ariann**
*Half-Light* - Denise Vitola   s   5575

**Chakotay**
*Pathways* - Jeri Taylor   s   5404
*Ragnarok* - Nathan Archer   s   206

**Chan**
*Dragon's Blood* - Alex McDonough   s   3799

**Chaney**
*Crown of Empire* - Chelsea Quinn Yarbro   s   6014

**Chapel, Christine**
*Crossroad* - Barbara Hambly   s   2501

**Charlie**
*Chains of Light* - Quentin Thomas   s   5449

**Chase**
*Deathweave* - Cary Osborne   s   4226

**Chekov, Pavel**
*The Ashes of Eden* - William Shatner   s   4927
*The Disinherited* - Peter David   s   1381
*Traitor Winds* - L.A. Graf   s   2298
*War Dragons* - L.A. Graf   s   2299
*Windows on a Lost World* - V.E. Mitchell   s   3920

**Chen, Kao**
*Beneath the Tree of Heaven* - David
   Wingrove   s   5917

**Chibisov**
*Red Army* - Ralph Peters   s   4306

**Christiansen, Mitch**
*Killjoy* - Elizabeth Forrest   h   1973

**Cind**
*Empire's End* - Allan Cole   s   1103

**Claire**
*The Night Watch* - Sean Stewart   f   5274

**Class, Julian**
*Forever Peace* - Joe Haldeman   s   2488

**Claypoole, Rachman**
*School of Fire* - David Sherman   s   4982

**Clendannan, Cherrid ris**
*Death's Gray Land* - Mike Shupp   s   5011

**Coke, Matthew**
*The Sharp End* - David Drake   s   1643

**Cole, Marcus**
*To Dream in the City of Sorrows* - Kathryn M.
   Drennan   s   1654

**Collins, Lysander**
*Prince of Sparta* - Jerry Pournelle   s   4378

**Connor, Islaen**
*Fire Planet* - P.M. Griffin   s   2436
*Jungle Assault* - P.M. Griffin   s   2437

**Coollege, Emma**
*Galactic MI* - Kevin D. Randle   s   4467

**Corry, William M.**
*Starsea Invaders: First Action* - G. Harry
   Stine   s   5282

**Cort**
*A Wizard in Chaos* - Christopher Stasheff   s   5230

**Court, Annalyn Reynolds**
*The Winds of Mars* - H.M. Hoover   s   2765

**Courvossier, Raoul**
*The Honor of the Queen* - David Weber   s   5674

**Craythorne**
*Mind Changer* - James White   s   5780

**Creaghan, Michael**
*Hellboy: The Lost Army* - Christopher
   Golden   h   2257

**Creighton, Abe "TC"**
*Afrikorps* - Bill Dolan   s   1566
*Cobra Curse* - Bill Dolan   s   1567
*Iron Horse* - Bill Dolan   s   1568
*White Rhino* - Bill Dolan   s   1569

**Crisco, Bungeeman**
*Star Wreck 6: Geek Space Nine* - Leah
   Rewolinski   s   4562

**Croaker**
*Bleak Seasons* - Glen Cook   f   1147
*Dreams of Steel* - Glen Cook   f   1150
*She Is the Darkness* - Glen Cook   f   1154

**Crusher, Wesley**
*Balance of Power* - Dafydd ab Hugh   s   7

**Custer, George A.**
*How Few Remain* - Harry Turtledove   s   5504

**Dacham, Klaus**
*Partisan* - S. Andrew Swann   s   5365

**Dai, David**
*Half the Day Is Night* - Maureen F.
   McHugh   s   3818

**Dallas, Korben**
*The Fifth Element* - Terry Bisson   s   504

**Damico, Mary**
*Dream Baby* - Bruce McAllister   s   3706

**Daniels, Kip**
*Godzilla 2000* - Marc Cerasini   *s*   949

**Danirov, Major**
*Suicide Attack* - John Sievert   *s*   5023

**Danner, Hannah**
*Ammonite* - Nicola Griffith   *s*   2443

**Dartmuth, Darcie**
*Dominion's Reach* - Diann Thornley   *s*   5465

**Data**
*The Devil's Heart* - Carmen Carter   *s*   922
*Doomsday World* - Carmen Carter   *s*   923
*Imzadi* - Peter David   *s*   1383
*Insurrection* - J.M. Dillard   *s*   1554
*Intellivore* - Diane Duane   *s*   1663
*The Last Stand* - Brad Ferguson   *s*   1923
*Metamorphosis* - Jean Lorrah   *s*   3524

**Datz, Harmis**
*Plague Demon* - Brian Craig   *f*   1239

**Daumier, Anatole**
*The Carnival of Destruction* - Brian
  Stableford   *h*   5190

**Davenger/Daven, Harla**
*Dancer of the Sixth* - Michelle Shirey
  Crean   *s*   1254

**Davies, Rachel**
*Jefferson's War: Death of a Regiment* - Kevin
  Randle   *s*   4466

**Dax, Jadzia**
*Call to Arms* - Diane Carey   *s*   901
*Time's Enemy* - L.A. Graf   *s*   2297

**de Barenton, Lucien**
*The Moon and the Sun* - Vonda N.
  McIntyre   *f*   3822

**de Laal, Leland**
*Helm* - Steven Gould   *s*   2289

**De Vore, Howard**
*The Broken Wheel* - David Wingrove   *s*   5918

**De Vries, Alicia "Tisiphone"**
*Path of the Fury* - David Weber   *s*   5680

**Deanc, Joseph**
*School of Fire* - David Sherman   *s*   4982

**DeChance, Megan**
*Hellworld* - Simon R. Green   *s*   2371

**Decius**
*The Light Bearer* - Donna Gillespie   *f*   2229

**Delacourte, Michaela "Mikey"**
*Spacer Dreams* - Larry Segriff   *s*   4911

**DeLorn, McLaren "Swordfish"**
*Psykosis* - Wilhelmina Baird   *s*   296

**Derigha, Yarrun**
*Expendable* - James Alan Gardner   *s*   2135

**Des Grieux, Samuel "Slick"**
*The Warrior* - David Drake   *s*   1651

**Desoll, Trystin**
*The Parafaith War* - L.E. Modesitt Jr.   *s*   3937

**DeWellesthar, Auglaise "Dancer"**
*Dancer of the Sixth* - Michelle Shirey
  Crean   *s*   1254

**Diamond, Tal**
*City of Diamond* - Jane Emerson   *s*   1807

**Dietrich, Martin**
*Darkness on the Ice* - Lois Tilton   *h*   5475

**DiFalco, Tiraena**
*Legacy* - Steve White   *s*   5785

**Distephano, Vincent**
*Alien Resurrection* - A.C. Crispin   *s*   1258

**Doorman, Lissea**
*The Voyage* - David Drake   *s*   1649

**Dorthansdotter, Paksenarrion "Paks"**
*Sheepfarmer's Daughter* - Elizabeth Moon   *f*   3973

**Douglas, Jardine Craig**
*A History Maker* - Alasdair Gray   *s*   2338

**Drake, Christopher**
*Cybernarc* - Robert Cain   *s*   829
*Gold Dragon* - Robert Cain   *s*   831

**Ducas, Leo**
*Cross and Crescent* - Susan Shwartz   *f*   5014
*Shards of Empire* - Susan Shwartz   *f*   5017

**Dulaine, Dirk**
*A Wizard in Chaos* - Christopher Stasheff   *s*   5230

**Dunbar, Sheik**
*Starstrike* - W. Michael Gear   *s*   2172

**Ehara**
*The Spellsong War* - L.E. Modesitt Jr.   *f*   3939

**Ehren**
*Barrenlands* - Doranna Durgin   *f*   1702

**E'non, Caelan**
*Shadow War* - Deborah Chester   *f*   1010

**Eslingen, Philip**
*Point of Hopes* - Melissa Scott   *f*   4899

**Essell, Lilly**
*Realtime Interrupt* - James P. Hogan   *s*   2729

**Esterhok, Quait**
*Eternity Road* - Jack McDevitt   *s*   3788

**Estes, Ken**
*Pandora* - Alan Rodgers   *h*   4650

**Etasalou**
*The Prisoner Within* - Donald E. McQuinn   *s*   3861

**Falkenberg, John Christian**
*Falkenberg's Legion* - Jerry Pournelle   *s*   4374

**Faulk, Carol**
*A Darker Geometry* - Mark O. Martin   *s*   3649

**Fergus**
*The Lost Prince* - Bridget Wood   *f*   5962

**Ferrier, Matt**
*Darkness on the Ice* - Lois Tilton   *h*   5475

**Fist, Sinklar**
*Relic of Empire* - W. Michael Gear   *s*   2171

**Flood, Reuben**
*Habu* - James B. Johnson   *s*   2920

**Folliot, Clive**
*The Final Battle* - Richard A. Lupoff   *f*   3572
*The Hidden City* - Charles de Lint   *f*   1429

**Fraser, Colin**
*March or Die* - Andrew Keith   *s*   3035

**Frede**
*Orion Among the Stars* - Ben Bova   *s*   589

**Freeman, Doug**
*Battle Front* - Ian Slater   *s*   5086

**Frey, Ezra**
*Emperors of the Twilight* - S. Andrew
  Swann   *s*   5362

**Freyer, Ulteena**
*The Parafaith War* - L.E. Modesitt Jr.   *s*   3937

**Frost**
*Deathstalker War* - Simon R. Green   *s*   2366

**Fujito, Hiroshi**
*Assault of the Super Carrier* - Peter Albano   *s*   47
*Super Carrier: The Ultimate Secret Weapon* - Peter
  Albano   *s*   50

**Gaffney, Arnold**
*Lieutenant* - Rick Shelley   *s*   4972

**Gailard**
*The Guardian* - Angus Wells   *f*   5737

**Galoran**
*Count Scar* - C. Dale Brittain   *f*   702

**Garibaldi, Michael**
*Voices* - John Vornholt   *s*   5598

**Garrison, Richard**
*Psychomech* - Brian Lumley   *h*   3562

**Garroway, Mark Alan**
*Semper Mars* - Ian Douglas   *s*   1585

**Gerin the Fox**
*Fox and Empire* - Harry Turtledove   *f*   5500
*Prince of the North* - Harry Turtledove   *f*   5509

**Geryam**
*The Birth of the Blade* - Dennis McCarty   *f*   3766

**Gift, Sebastian "Nifty"**
*Berserker Fury* - Fred Saberhagen   *s*   4760

**Giles**
*Beauty* - Sheri S. Tepper   *f*   5428

**Gloth**
*The Doom Brigade* - Margaret Weis   *f*   5708

**Glyndower, Evan**
*High Moon* - Diane Duane   *s*   1661
*Kill Station* - Diane Duane   *s*   1664
*Mindblast* - Diane Duane   *s*   1665

**Gomja, Herphan**
*Beyond the Moons* - David Cook   *f*   1144

**Gorbunova, Ludmila**
*Worldwar: Tilting the Balance* - Harry
  Turtledove   *s*   5517
*Worldwar: Upsetting the Balance* - Harry
  Turtledove   *s*   5518

**Grahame, John**
*The Templar Treasure* - Katherine Kurtz   *f*   3261

**Grant, John "Slick"**
*March or Die* - Andrew Keith   *s*   3035

**Gregg, Stephen**
*Igniting the Reaches* - David Drake   *s*   1633

**Grenlaarin, Karah**
*The Rose Sea* - S.M. Stirling   *f*   5296

**Greycloak, Janos**
*The Far Kingdoms* - Allan Cole   *f*   1104

**Gyhard**
*Fifth Quarter* - Tanya Huff   *f*   2795
*No Quarter* - Tanya Huff   *f*   2798

**Hadrak, Quisaz**
*Martian Deathtrap* - Nathan Archer   *s*   205

**Hagan, Kara**
*Warstrider: Netlink* - William H. Keith Jr.   *s*   3038

**Hammer, Alois**
*The Warrior* - David Drake   *s*   1651

**Hanavi, Ari**
*Hero* - Joel Rosenberg   *s*   4672

**Hanfor**
*The Spellsong War* - L.E. Modesitt Jr.   *f*   3939

**Harper, Timothy**
*Death's Gray Land* - Mike Shupp   *s*   5011
*The Last Reckoning* - Mike Shupp   *s*   5012

**Harrington, Honor**
*Echoes of Honor* - David Weber   *s*   5669
*Field of Dishonor* - David Weber   *s*   5670
*Flag in Exile* - David Weber   *s*   5671
*Honor Among Enemies* - David Weber   *s*   5673
*The Honor of the Queen* - David Weber   *s*   5674
*In Enemy Hands* - David Weber   *s*   5675
*On Basilisk Station* - David Weber   *s*   5679
*The Short Victorious War* - David Weber   *s*   5681

**Hasgard, David**
*Traitors from Within* - R.A. Montgomery   *s*   3966

**Hauser, Wolfgang "Karl Wolf"**
*Cohort of the Damned* - Andrew Keith    s    3034

**Hausmann, Louis**
*The Third Force* - Marc Laidlaw    s    3313

**Havoc, Mike**
*L.A. Strike* - David Robbins    s    4599

**Hawke, Christopher**
*No Blood Spilled* - Les Daniels    h    1338

**Hawken, Jos**
*Yamato: A Rage in Heaven* - Ken Kato    s    3014

**Hawkins, Ethan**
*Mutant Star* - Karen Haber    s    2475

**Heller, Prescott "Sean Toole"**
*Union Fires* - John Barnes    f    358

**Hightower, Belisarius**
*Pandora* - Alan Rodgers    h    4650

**Hiller, Steven**
*Independence Day* - Dean Devlin    s    1508

**Hilton, Jim**
*Deep Trek* - James Axler    s    278

**Himmels, Peter**
*The Sandman: Book of Dreams* - Neil
    Gaiman    f    2105

**Hiroshi, Kajiwara**
*Fire on the Border* - Kevin O'Donnell Jr.    s    4194

**Hitler, Adolf**
*Dark Legacy* - Mark A. Kostrubula    h    3220

**Holser, Vax**
*Midshipman's Hope* - David Feintuch    s    1901

**Horn, Corran**
*Rogue Squadron* - Michael A. Stackpole    s    5205

**Houston, Jackson**
*Wartide* - John Barnes    f    359

**Howell, Clarence**
*Hour of the Scorpion* - Matthew J. Costello    s    1199

**Humidyear VII, Fivetide**
*Excession* - Iain M. Banks    s    324

**Hunter, Gregory**
*Blood Alone* - Elaine Bergstrom    h    462

**Hunter, Scott**
*Hellworld* - Simon R. Green    s    2371

**Hunter, Travis**
*Search and Destroy* - Keith William
    Andrews    s    141
*Sink the Armada* - Keith William Andrews    s    142
*Treason in Time* - Keith William Andrews    s    143

**I**
*The Veils of Snows* - Mark Helprin    f    2654

**ibn Khairan, Ammar**
*The Lions of Al-Rassan* - Guy Gavriel Kay    f    3016

**Icefalcon**
*Icefalcon's Quest* - Barbara Hambly    f    2504

**Ivanova, Susan**
*Voices* - John Vornholt    s    5598

**Jamie**
*Alien Dreams* - Larry Segriff    s    4910

**Jamil/Alasil**
*The Watcher's Mask* - Laurie J. Marks    f    3627

**Janeway, Kathryn**
*Chrysalis* - David Niall Wilson    s    5880
*The Escape* - Dean Wesley Smith    s    5113
*The Final Fury* - Dafydd ab Hugh    s    9
*Her Klingon Soul* - Michael Jan Friedman    s    2064
*Mosaic* - Jeri Taylor    s    5403
*Ragnarok* - Nathan Archer    s    206

**Jarrat, Kevin**
*Death's Head* - Mel Keegan    s    3029

**Jarrow, Richard**
*The Multiplex Man* - James P. Hogan    s    2727

**Jarth, Christopher**
*Escape to the Wind* - Jennifer DiMarco    s    1559

**Jefferson, David Steven**
*The Galactic Silver Star* - Kevin D. Randle    s    4468
*Jefferson's War: Death of a Regiment* - Kevin
    Randle    s    4466

**Jenkins, Tom**
*Alien Dreams* - Larry Segriff    s    4910

**Jessan**
*The Price of the Stars* - Debra Doyle    s    1604

**Jessan, Nyls**
*Starpilot's Grave* - Debra Doyle    s    1606

**Jiltanith**
*Mutineers' Moon* - David Weber    s    5677

**Joanna**
*Way of the Clans* - Robert Thurston    s    5469

**Jonas, Paul**
*River of Blue Fire* - Tad Williams    f    5830

**Jones, Indiana "Indy"**
*The Mata Hari Adventure* - James Luceno    f    3544

**Jones, Virginia "Jinjur"**
*Marooned on Eden* - Robert L. Forward    s    1986
*Ocean under the Ice* - Robert L. Forward    s    1988
*Return to Rocheworld* - Robert L. Forward    s    1989
*Rocheworld* - Robert L. Forward    s    1990

**Jonson, Kenneth**
*Aggressor Six* - Wil McCarthy    s    3760

**Joyner, Griffin**
*The First Duelist* - Rutledge Etheridge    s    1849

**Julius Caesar, Gaius**
*Child of the Eagle* - Esther Friesner    f    2073

**Kadaffi, "Captain Cadaver"**
*Bill, the Galactic Hero: The Final Incoherent
    Adventure* - Harry Harrison    s    2568

**Kaid**
*Fire Margins* - Lisanne Norman    s    4137
*Razor's Edge* - Lisanne Norman    s    4139

**Kammaeman**
*Present Tense* - Dave Duncan    f    1686

**Kang**
*The Doom Brigade* - Margaret Weis    f    5708

**Karmikal, Jake**
*Jungle Assault* - P.M. Griffin    s    2437

**Kasuga**
*On the Verge* - Roland J. Green    s    2350

**Kateralbin, Crispin**
*The Daemon in the Machine* - Felicity
    Savage    f    4848
*The War in the Waste* - Felicity Savage    f    4852

**Kawalsky**
*Stargate SG-1* - Ashley McConnell    s    3777

**Keane, Andrew**
*Never Sound Retreat* - William R.
    Forstchen    s    1981
*Rally Cry!* - William R. Forstchen    s    1982
*Terrible Swift Sword* - William R.
    Forstchen    s    1983

**Keita, Arthur**
*Path of the Fury* - David Weber    s    5680

**Kelly, Bryan**
*Beyond the Void* - Sean Dalton    s    1331
*Destination: Mutiny* - Sean Dalton    s    1332
*The Salukan Gambit* - Sean Dalton    s    1333

**Kemra**
*Adiamante* - L.E. Modesitt Jr.    s    3924

**Keynes, Daniel "Butch"**
*The War in the Waste* - Felicity Savage    f    4851

**Khaavren of House Tiassa**
*Five Hundred Years After* - Steven Brust    f    742

**Kilgour, Alex**
*Vortex* - Allan Cole    s    1108

**Kim, Harry**
*Her Klingon Soul* - Michael Jan Friedman    s    2064

**Kincaid, Astrid**
*The Transmigration of Souls* - William
    Barton    s    382

**King, Greg**
*Sink the Armada* - Keith William Andrews    s    142
*Treason in Time* - Keith William Andrews    s    143

**Kinnison, Kimball**
*Galactic Patrol* - Edward E. Smith    s    5116
*Gray Lensman* - Edward E. Smith    s    5117

**Kira**
*Bloodletter* - K.W. Jeter    s    2908
*Devil in the Sky* - Greg Cox    s    1226

**Kire**
*They Fly at Ciron* - Samuel R. Delany    s    1482

**Kirk, James T.**
*Traitor Winds* - L.A. Graf    s    2298

**Kit**
*A Hero Born* - Michael A. Stackpole    f    5202

**Kluge, Wilhelm**
*At Sword's Point* - Scott MacMillan    f    3601
*Knights of the Blood* - Scott MacMillan    f    3602

**Knifedancer, Railu**
*The Illusionists* - Faren Miller    f    3894

**Konnor**
*The Outlander: Captivity* - B.J. Salterberg    s    4792

**Kontsandas, Esteban**
*Winning Colors* - Elizabeth Moon    s    3976

**Korie, Jonathan Thomas**
*Voyage of the Star Wolf* - David Gerrold    s    2212

**Kren**
*The Lanterns of God* - Ron Sarti    s    4835

**Krim**
*The Hidden War* - Michael Armstrong    s    209

**Krystal**
*The Death of Chaos* - L.E. Modesitt Jr.    f    3926

**Kun, Holger**
*A Knight Among Knaves* - Robert N.
    Charrette    f    974

**Kurasawa, Sho**
*The Painful Field* - Roland J. Green    s    2351
*The Sum of Things* - Roland J. Green    s    2353

**La Forge, Geordi**
*Balance of Power* - Dafydd ab Hugh    s    7
*Dark Mirror* - Diane Duane    s    1658
*Doomsday World* - Carmen Carter    s    923
*Relics* - Michael Jan Friedman    s    2066
*Requiem* - Michael Jan Friedman    s    2067
*Vendetta* - Peter David    s    1389

**Lachlan "Locke"**
*A Hero Born* - Michael A. Stackpole    f    5202

**Lady**
*Dreams of Steel* - Glen Cook    f    1150

**Laine**
*Barrenlands* - Doranna Durgin    f    1702

**Lannan**
*The Price of the Stars* - Debra Doyle    s    1604

**Lannat**
*The Prisoner Within* - Donald E. McQuinn    s    3861
*With Full Honors* - Donald E. McQuinn    s    3865

**Lara, Katherine**
*Berserker* - S.D. Perry   s   4285

**Larson, Al**
*By Chaos Cursed* - Mickey Zucker Reichert   f   4517
*Dragonrank Master* - Mickey Zucker
   Reichert   f   4519
*Shadow's Realm* - Mickey Zucker Reichert   f   4523

**Leary, Daniel**
*With the Lightnings* - David Drake   s   1652

**Lee, Darcy**
*Fire on the Border* - Kevin O'Donnell Jr.   s   4194

**Lee, Robert E.**
*The Guns of the South: A Novel of the Civil War* -
   Harry Turtledove   s   5502

**Leopold**
*Tiger Burning Bright* - Marion Zimmer
   Bradley   f   652

**Lieutenant**
*Final Blackout* - L. Ron Hubbard   s   2790

**Lindquist, Anna Catarina**
*McLendon's Syndrome* - Robert Frezza   s   2053

**Lipschitz, Isadore**
*Hero* - Joel Rosenberg   s   4672

**Liss, Benetan**
*Star Ascendant* - Louise Cooper   f   1180

**Livia**
*Nocturnas* - Shawn Ryan   h   4755

**Llannat**
*Starpilot's Grave* - Debra Doyle   s   1606

**Lochley, Elizabeth**
*Day of the Dead* - Neil Gaiman   s   2102

**Longchamp, Jimmy**
*Secrets of the Morning* - V.C. Andrews   h   146

**Lucas, James**
*The Wild Blue and the Gray* - William
   Sanders   s   4814

**Lucifer**
*Angels & Visitations: A Miscellany* - Neil
   Gaiman   f   2101

**Ma Li "Sister"**
*Shangri-La: The Return to the World of Lost Horizon* -
   Eleanor Cooney   f   1169

**Mac Kay, Kenneth "Ken"**
*McLendon's Syndrome* - Robert Frezza   s   2053

**MacBride, Johnny**
*Bats* - William W. Johnstone   h   2926

**MacIntyre, Colin**
*Mutineers' Moon* - David Weber   s   5677

**MacIntyre, Sean Horus**
*Heirs of Empire* - David Weber   s   5672

**MacMahan, Hector**
*Mutineers' Moon* - David Weber   s   5677

**MacNeil, Duncan**
*Down Among the Dead Men* - Simon R.
   Green   f   2367

**Maddock, Yanaba**
*Power Lines* - Anne McCaffrey   s   3743
*Power Play* - Anne McCaffrey   s   3744
*Powers That Be* - Anne McCaffrey   s   3745

**Maenial**
*The Silver Wolf* - Alice Borchardt   h   572

**Mahan, Patrick**
*1901* - Robert Conroy   s   1139

**Mahoney, Ian**
*The Return of the Emperor* - Allan Cole   s   1106
*Vortex* - Allan Cole   s   1108

**Maniakes**
*Hammer and Anvil* - Harry Turtledove   f   5503

**Videssos Besieged** - Harry Turtledove   f   5513

**Mapstone, Laren**
*Green Rider* - Kristen Britain   f   692

**Margulies, Mary**
*The Sharp End* - David Drake   s   1643

**Marik, Dao**
*Hopeship* - Simon Lang   s   3315
*The Trumpets of Tagan* - Simon Lang   s   3316

**Martel, James Mannheim**
*1945* - Newt Gingrich   s   2239

**Matsika, Amadeus**
*The Ear, the Eye, and the Arm* - Nancy
   Farmer   f   1867

**Matsuhara, Yoshi**
*Assault of the Super Carrier* - Peter Albano   s   47
*Ordeal of the Seventh Carrier* - Peter Albano   s   48
*Revenge of the Seventh Carrier* - Peter Albano   s   49

**Matthieson, Jonah**
*Man-Kzin Wars V* - Larry Niven   s   4125

**McAusland, James**
*Flameweaver* - Margaret Ball   f   314

**McCarthy, James Edward**
*A Rage for Revenge* - David Gerrold   s   2210
*A Season for Slaughter* - David Gerrold   s   2211

**McCulley, Kitty**
*The Healer's War* - Elizabeth Ann
   Scarborough   f   4865

**McCullough, Mike**
*Secret Realms* - Tom Cool   s   1168

**McGill, Henderson**
*Deep Trek* - James Axler   s   278

**McKay**
*Devil's Deal* - Richard Austin   s   277

**McKay, Kenneth "Ken"**
*The VMR Theory* - Robert Frezza   s   2055

**McKeon, Alister**
*On Basilisk Station* - David Weber   s   5679

**McShane, Terry**
*seaQuest DSV: Fire Below* - Matthew J.
   Costello   s   1201

**Means, Gordon**
*Cold Allies* - Patricia Anthony   s   157

**Merikur, Anson**
*Cluster Command* - David Drake   s   1630

**Meyers, Max**
*The Final Battle* - William C. Dietz   s   1546

**Minarik**
*Shadowdance* - Robin Wayne Bailey   f   290

**Mint**
*Exodus From the Long Sun* - Gene Wolfe   s   5941

**Mitford, Chuck**
*Freedom's Challenge* - Anne McCaffrey   s   3732
*Freedom's Choice* - Anne McCaffrey   s   3733
*Freedom's Landing* - Anne McCaffrey   s   3734

**Moden, Sten**
*The Sharp End* - David Drake   s   1643

**Mohatsa, Phila**
*Beyond the Void* - Sean Dalton   s   1331

**Montagu, Edmund**
*The Mummy!: A Tale of the Twenty-Second Century* -
   Jane Webb Loudon   h   3526

**Moon, Paul**
*Shadows of War* - Thomas S. Gressman   s   2432

**Morkaarin, Bren**
*The Rose Sea* - S.M. Stirling   f   5296

**Mortega, Dyani**
*Blood Siege* - G. Harry Stine   s   5278

**Mosby, Marianne**
*Legion of the Damned* - William C. Dietz   s   1547

**Moses, Libby**
*Echoes of Issel* - Diann Thornley   s   5466

**Muadhen, Seamus**
*Nature's God* - Robert Anton Wilson   f   5903

**Murgen**
*Bleak Seasons* - Glen Cook   f   1147
*She Is the Darkness* - Glen Cook   f   1154

**Naomia**
*Chains of Light* - Quentin Thomas   s   5449

**Nimrod**
*Solo* - Robert Mason   s   3665

**Nina**
*Planar Powers* - J. Robert King   f   3122

**Nolan, Lon**
*Lieutenant* - Rick Shelley   s   4972
*Officer Cadet* - Rick Shelley   s   4973

**Normandy, Claire**
*Shiva in Steel* - Fred Saberhagen   s   4775

**Norreen**
*Shattered Chains* - Clayton Emery   f   1816

**Norris**
*Bodyguard* - William C. Dietz   s   1542

**North**
*Vengeance* - David Drake   s   1648

**Norwood, Natalie**
*The Final Battle* - William C. Dietz   s   1546

**O'Bannion, Joss**
*High Moon* - Diane Duane   s   1661
*Kill Station* - Diane Duane   s   1664
*Mindblast* - Diane Duane   s   1665

**O'Brian, Launa**
*First Dawn* - Mike Moscoe   s   4038
*Lost Days* - Mike Moscoe   s   4039
*Second Fire* - Mike Moscoe   s   4040

**O'Brien, Miles**
*Bloodletter* - K.W. Jeter   s   2908
*Vengeance* - Dafydd ab Hugh   s   10

**Oit-Makidom, Maraakuks**
*Runes of Autumn* - Larry Elmore   f   1790

**Olon, Sammis Arloff**
*Timediver's Dawn* - L.E. Modesitt Jr.   s   3940

**O'Neill, Jack**
*Reconnaissance* - Bill McCay   s   3769
*StarGate* - Dean Devlin   s   1509
*Stargate SG-1* - Ashley McConnell   s   3777

**O'Reilly, Theo**
*Mask of the Night* - Mary Ryan   h   4753

**Orlis**
*Officer Cadet* - Rick Shelley   s   4973

**Osic, Angelo**
*On My Way to Paradise* - Dave Wolverton   s   5955

**Owensford, Peter**
*Go Tell the Spartans* - Jerry Pournelle   s   4375
*Prince of Sparta* - Jerry Pournelle   s   4378

**Paris, Tom**
*Chrysalis* - David Niall Wilson   s   5880
*Pathways* - Jeri Taylor   s   5404

**Parker, Evan**
*The Winds of Mars* - H.M. Hoover   s   2765

**Parkes, John**
*The Mountain Walks* - Roland J. Green   s   2349

**Pauley, Nigel**
*Limbo Search* - Parke Godwin   s   2245

**Pesca, Walter**
*Dreadnought* - Thorarinn Gunnarsson   s   2464

**Pettis**
*Moonbane* - Al Sarrantonio  *s*  4831

**Philippe**
*Canal Dreams* - Iain M. Banks  *s*  323

**Phillips, Mark**
*The Crystal Sorcerers* - William R. Forstchen  *f*  1979

**Phineas**
*Daughter of Prophecy* - Anne Kelleher Bush  *f*  788

**Phule, Willard**
*Phule's Company* - Robert Asprin  *s*  260
*Phule's Paradise* - Robert Asprin  *s*  261

**Picard, Jean-Luc**
*All Good Things...* - Michael Jan Friedman  *s*  2061
*Balance of Power* - Dafydd ab Hugh  *s*  7
*A Call to Darkness* - Michael Jan Friedman  *s*  2062
*Chains of Command* - Bill McCay  *s*  3767
*Crossover* - Michael Jan Friedman  *s*  2063
*Dark Mirror* - Diane Duane  *s*  1658
*Debtors' Planet* - William R. Thompson  *s*  5457
*The Devil's Heart* - Carmen Carter  *s*  922
*Dragon's Honor* - Kij Johnson  *s*  2922
*Federation* - Judith Reeves-Stevens  *s*  4511
*Guises of the Mind* - Rebecca Neason  *s*  4081
*Kahless* - Michael Jan Friedman  *s*  2065
*The Last Stand* - Brad Ferguson  *s*  1923
*Q-in-Law* - Peter David  *s*  1384
*Q-Squared* - Peter David  *s*  1385
*Q-Zone* - Greg Cox  *s*  1229
*Relics* - Michael Jan Friedman  *s*  2066
*Requiem* - Michael Jan Friedman  *s*  2067
*The Return* - William Shatner  *s*  4933
*Reunion* - Michael Jan Friedman  *s*  2068
*The Soldiers of Fear* - Dean Wesley Smith  *s*  5115
*Vendetta* - Peter David  *s*  1389

**Pike, Eli**
*The Rim-World Legacy and Beyond* - Frank A. Javor  *s*  2882

**Porter, Aloysius Graham**
*The Sand Dwellers* - Adam Niswander  *h*  4112

**Poseen-Ka**
*The Final Battle* - William C. Dietz  *s*  1546

**Price, Joshua**
*Galactic MI* - Kevin D. Randle  *s*  4467

**Prien, Rube**
*From Time to Time* - Jack Finney  *s*  1941

**Pyramors**
*Warlord of Heaven* - Adrian Cole  *f*  1102

**Rabin, David**
*Vulcan's Forge* - Susan Shwartz  *s*  5019

**Rady, Sonja**
*Prince of Sunset* - Steve White  *s*  5786

**Ragem, Paul**
*Beholder's Eye* - Julie E. Czerneda  *s*  1303

**Raines, Ingrid**
*The Children's Hour* - Jerry Pournelle  *s*  4372

**Ramos, Festina**
*Expendable* - James Alan Gardner  *s*  2135

**Ranes, Josev T.**
*Aggressor Six* - Wil McCarthy  *s*  3760

**Rankin, Howard S.**
*A Landscape of Darkness* - John Blair  *s*  513

**Razkili**
*Shadowdance* - Robin Wayne Bailey  *f*  290

**Reandn**
*Wolf Justice* - Doranna Durgin  *f*  1706

**Rebello, Joseph "Joe" Z.**
*In the Wrong Hands* - Edward Gibson  *s*  2215

**Relkin**
*Battledragon* - Christopher Rowley  *f*  4691

*Bazil Broketail* - Christopher Rowley  *f*  4692
*A Dragon at World's End* - Christopher Rowley  *f*  4693
*Dragons of Argonath* - Christopher Rowley  *f*  4694
*Dragons of War* - Christopher Rowley  *f*  4695
*A Sword for a Dragon* - Christopher Rowley  *f*  4697

**Renier, Mordan**
*Ganwold's Child* - Diann Thornley  *s*  5467

**Renner, Kevin**
*The Gripping Hand* - Larry Niven  *s*  4122

**Rhoodie, Andries**
*The Guns of the South: A Novel of the Civil War* - Harry Turtledove  *s*  5502

**Riker, William**
*A Call to Darkness* - Michael Jan Friedman  *s*  2062
*Imbalance* - V.E. Mitchell  *s*  3919
*Imzadi* - Peter David  *s*  1383
*Q-Zone* - Greg Cox  *s*  1229
*Ship of the Line* - Diane Carey  *s*  904
*The Soldiers of Fear* - Dean Wesley Smith  *s*  5115
*Triangle: Imzadi II* - Peter David  *s*  1388

**Riley, David**
*Operation Synbat* - Bob Mayer  *h*  3701

**Riley, Kevin**
*A Flag Full of Stars* - Brad Ferguson  *s*  1922

**Ripley**
*Alien 3* - Alan Dean Foster  *s*  1993

**Robbins, Cynthia**
*The Rising* - James Doohan  *s*  1579

**Roberts, Amelia**
*Priorities* - Lynda Lyons  *s*  3579

**Rockdream**
*The Warrior and the Witch* - Carl Miller  *f*  3893

**Roker**
*Hero* - Dave Duncan  *s*  1680

**Romlar, Artus**
*The Regiment's War* - John Dalmas  *s*  1326
*The White Regiment* - John Dalmas  *s*  1327

**Rosemont, Alexander F.**
*Finger of God* - Michael Kasner  *s*  3013

**Roshak, Ter**
*Way of the Clans* - Robert Thurston  *s*  5469

**Ross, Brent**
*Assault of the Super Carrier* - Peter Albano  *s*  47
*Revenge of the Seventh Carrier* - Peter Albano  *s*  49
*Super Carrier: The Ultimate Secret Weapon* - Peter Albano  *s*  50

**Rourke, John T.**
*The Struggle* - Jerry Ahern  *s*  44

**Rovin, Elli**
*Limbo Search* - Parke Godwin  *s*  2245

**Sagan, Derek**
*King's Sacrifice* - Margaret Weis  *s*  5717
*The Lost King* - Margaret Weis  *s*  5720

**Sampson, Matt**
*Traitors from Within* - R.A. Montgomery  *s*  3966

**Sandoval**
*In the Blood* - Lauren Wright Douglas  *s*  1590

**Sanglant**
*Prince of Dogs* - Kate Elliott  *f*  1775

**Sanmartin, Raul**
*A Small Colonial War* - Robert Frezza  *s*  2054

**Sarnac, Robert**
*Legacy* - Steve White  *s*  5785

**Savage, Clark "Doc" Jr.**
*Escape From Loki* - Philip Jose Farmer  *f*  1870
*Python Isle* - Kenneth Robeson  *f*  4624

**Savitsky**
*Lunching with the Antichrist* - Michael Moorcock  *f*  3984

**Sawyer, Daniel**
*Solo* - Robert Mason  *s*  3665

**Schonnegon, Teletha**
*Timespell* - Robert N. Charrette  *f*  978

**Scolari, Paula**
*Legion of the Damned* - William C. Dietz  *s*  1547

**Scott, Lisa**
*Cohort of the Damned* - Andrew Keith  *s*  3034

**Scott, Montgomery**
*Crossover* - Michael Jan Friedman  *s*  2063
*Relics* - Michael Jan Friedman  *s*  2066

**Seafort, Nicholas**
*Challenger's Hope* - David Feintuch  *s*  1899
*Fisherman's Hope* - David Feintuch  *s*  1900
*Midshipman's Hope* - David Feintuch  *s*  1901

**Senea**
*The Heldan* - Deborah Talmadge-Bickmore  *f*  5383

**Serege, Lujan Ansellic**
*Dominion's Reach* - Diann Thornley  *s*  5465
*Echoes of Issel* - Diann Thornley  *s*  5466

**Serege, Tristan "Tris"**
*Dominion's Reach* - Diann Thornley  *s*  5465

**Serrano**
*Once a Hero* - Elizabeth Moon  *s*  3970

**Serrano, Heris**
*Hunting Party* - Elizabeth Moon  *s*  3968
*Sporting Chance* - Elizabeth Moon  *s*  3974
*Winning Colors* - Elizabeth Moon  *s*  3976

**Shanto**
*The Initiate Brother* - Sean Russell  *f*  4742

**Sharp, Marcus**
*Beast* - Peter Benchley  *h*  440

**Shea, Nicole**
*Grounded!* - Chris Claremont  *s*  1041
*Sundowner* - Chris Claremont  *s*  1043

**Sheridan, John**
*Thirdspace* - Peter David  *s*  1387

**Sherman, William Tecumseh**
*Under the Shadow* - Jane Toombs  *h*  5481

**Shonto**
*Gatherer of Clouds* - Sean Russell  *f*  4741

**Shores, Candice**
*The Painful Field* - Roland J. Green  *s*  2351
*The Sum of Things* - Roland J. Green  *s*  2353

**Silence, John**
*Deathstalker Rebellion* - Simon R. Green  *s*  2365
*Twilight of the Empire* - Simon R. Green  *s*  2374

**Siluricus, Gaius Macellius Severus**
*The Forest House* - Marion Zimmer Bradley  *f*  633

**Silverblade "Blade"**
*The Silver Gryphon* - Mercedes Lackey  *f*  3295

**Sinclair, Jeffrey**
*To Dream in the City of Sorrows* - Kathryn M. Drennan  *s*  1654

**Sisko, Benjamin**
*Armageddon Sky* - L.A. Graf  *s*  2296
*Bloodletter* - K.W. Jeter  *s*  2908
*Devil in the Sky* - Greg Cox  *s*  1226
*Fallen Heroes* - Dafydd ab Hugh  *s*  8
*Time's Enemy* - L.A. Graf  *s*  2297
*Warped* - K.W. Jeter  *s*  2917

**Skandrakae, Tadrith "Tad"**
*The Silver Gryphon* - Mercedes Lackey  *f*  3295

**Skorzeny, Otto**
*1945* - Newt Gingrich  *s*  2239

**Slade, Ned**
*The Voyage* - David Drake   s   1649

**Smedley, Julian**
*Present Tense* - Dave Duncan   f   1686

**Smith, George**
*Some of Your Blood* - Theodore Sturgeon   h   5347

**Smith, Tom**
*Ai! Pedrito!: When Intelligence Goes Wrong* - L. Ron Hubbard   s   2788

**Smolte, Hampton**
*Elephantasm* - Tanith Lee   h   3408

**Smythe, Peter**
*Arthur War Lord* - Dafydd ab Hugh   f   6

**Snatch**
*The Knights of Cawdor* - Mike Jefferies   f   2886

**Sobel, Charles**
*Turn of the Cards* - Victor Milan   s   3891

**Sobieski, Josip**
*Conrad's Quest for Rubber* - Leo Frankowski   s   2043

**Sogan, Varn Tarl**
*Call to Arms* - P.M. Griffin   s   2435
*Fire Planet* - P.M. Griffin   s   2436

**Solo, Jacen**
*Trouble on Cloud City* - Kevin J. Anderson   s   117

**Solo, Jaina**
*Trouble on Cloud City* - Kevin J. Anderson   s   117

**Soloman**
*Cain* - James Byron Huggins   h   2802

**Spencer, Allison**
*The War Machine* - David Drake   s   1650

**Spencer, David**
*Return to Camerein* - Rick Shelley   s   4974

**Spots-Son of Chotrz-Shaa**
*Man-Kzin Wars V* - Larry Niven   s   4125

**Stanley, Samuel**
*The Two Georges* - Richard Dreyfuss   s   1655

**Stasov, Ilya Sergeiivich**
*A Deeper Sea* - Alexander Jablokov   s   2838

**Steiner-Davion, Victor**
*Prince of Havoc* - Michael A. Stackpole   s   5204

**Sten**
*Empire's End* - Allan Cole   s   1103
*The Return of the Emperor* - Allan Cole   s   1106
*Vortex* - Allan Cole   s   1108

**Stone, Jerry**
*Death's Head* - Mel Keegan   s   3029

**Stone, Wallace "Rocky"**
*Galactic MI* - Kevin D. Randle   s   4467

**Stoner, Charley**
*Limbo Search* - Parke Godwin   s   2245

**Storm, Jack**
*Alien Salute* - Charles Ingrid   s   2830
*Return Fire* - Charles Ingrid   s   2833

**Straat-ien, Nevan**
*The Spoils of War* - Alan Dean Foster   s   2016

**Strand, Paul**
*The Queen's Squadron* - R.M. Meluch   s   3874

**Sturgis, Dean**
*Suicide Attack* - John Sievert   s   5023

**Suiza, Esmay**
*Once a Hero* - Elizabeth Moon   s   3970

**Sulu**
*The Kobayashi Maru* - Julia Ecklar   s   1728

**Sulu, Hikaru**
*The Ashes of Eden* - William Shatner   s   4927
*Traitor Winds* - L.A. Graf   s   2298

**sus-Airaalin, Theio syn-Ricte**
*By Honor Betray'd* - Debra Doyle   s   1598

**Sweet**
*Call to Battle* - Doug Murray   h   4059

**Takagama, Brund**
*A Darker Geometry* - Mark O. Martin   s   3649

**Tarimenloku, Igsat**
*The White Regiment* - John Dalmas   s   1327

**Tast'annin, Margalis**
*AEstival Tide* - Elizabeth Hand   s   2533
*Icarus Descending* - Elizabeth Hand   s   2536

**Tate, Donnacee**
*Wanderer* - Donald E. McQuinn   s   3862
*Warrior* - Donald E. McQuinn   s   3863
*Witch* - Donald E. McQuinn   s   3864

**Telerhyde**
*The Stone Movers* - Patricia Mullen   f   4045

**Thor, Odin**
*Timediver's Dawn* - L.E. Modesitt Jr.   s   3940

**Thorsson, Thor**
*Article 23* - William R. Forstchen   s   1978

**Thrawn**
*The Last Command* - Timothy Zahn   s   6055

**Tighe, Justin**
*Mosaic* - Jeri Taylor   s   5403

**Tirelli, Elizabeth "Lizard"**
*A Season for Slaughter* - David Gerrold   s   2211

**Tissaurd, Nadia**
*The Mercenaries* - Bill Baldwin   s   311

**Tokoyuni, Mitsuo**
*Blood on the Sun* - Brian Herbert   h   2664

**Toledo, Rico**
*Burn* - Bill Ransom   s   4476
*ViraVax* - Bill Ransom   s   4478

**Tolliver, Edgar "Eddie"**
*Fisherman's Hope* - David Feintuch   s   1900

**Tolwyn, Geoffrey**
*Action Stations* - William R. Forstchen   s   1976

**Tornsaarin, Willek**
*The Rose Sea* - S.M. Stirling   f   5296

**Torraway, Roger**
*Man Plus* - Frederik Pohl   s   4348

**Torrence, Victoria**
*The Galactic Silver Star* - Kevin D. Randle   s   4468
*Jefferson's War: Death of a Regiment* - Kevin Randle   s   4466

**Torx, BrainGeneral**
*Mutant Hell* - Mark Grant   s   2324
*Mutants Amok* - Mark Grant   s   2325

**Trace, Donalt**
*Tactical Error* - Thorarinn Gunnarsson   s   2466

**Tremane**
*Storm Rising* - Mercedes Lackey   f   3297

**Trillby, Samatha**
*Time Station London* - David Evans   s   1853

**Trondheim, Heida**
*The False Mirror* - Alan Dean Foster   s   2004

**Truant, Cal**
*Naked to the Stars/The Alien Way* - Gordon R. Dickson   s   1537

**Tsikas**
*Videssos Besieged* - Harry Turtledove   f   5513

**Tsingar**
*Tears of Time* - Nancy Asire   f   256
*To Fall Like Stars* - Nancy Asire   f   257

**Turcotte, Mike**
*Area 51* - Robert Doherty   s   1565

**Turenne**
*Wartide* - John Barnes   f   359

**Turnbull, Jack**
*Maze of Worlds* - Brian Lumley   h   3559

**Turner, Winston**
*Action Stations* - William R. Forstchen   s   1976

**Tusk-Anini**
*Phule's Paradise* - Robert Asprin   s   261

**Tyler, John**
*The Harvest* - Robert Charles Wilson   s   5909

**Tyre, Philip**
*Challenger's Hope* - David Feintuch   s   1899

**Tyrranis**
*Valorian* - Mary H. Herbert   f   2677

**Tyson, Joseph**
*The Galactic Silver Star* - Kevin D. Randle   s   4468

**Tzikas**
*The Thousand Cities* - Harry Turtledove   f   5512

**Uhura**
*The Disinherited* - Peter David   s   1381

**Ursis, Nikolai Yanuarievich**
*The Siege* - Bill Baldwin   s   312

**Valentine**
*Priorities* - Lynda Lyons   s   3579

**Valentinian**
*An Oblique Approach* - David Drake   s   1638

**van Worden, Alphonse**
*The Manuscript Found in Sragossa* - Jan Potocki   h   4371

**Vanachek, Viveka "Viv" Jeng**
*Nothing Sacred* - Elizabeth Ann Scarborough   f   4867

**Vandiver**
*Extinct* - Charles Wilson   h   5877

**Var, Tomas**
*Exile's Challenge* - Angus Wells   f   5734

**Varrus, Gaius Publius**
*The Skystone* - Jack Whyte   f   5794

**Vereshchagin, Anton**
*Fire in a Faraway Place* - Robert Frezza   s   2052
*A Small Colonial War* - Robert Frezza   s   2054

**Vernon, Gary**
*Sleipnir* - Linda Evans   f   1856

**vlith-Arkad, Brandon**
*A Prison Unsought* - Sherwood Smith   s   5139
*Ruler of Naught* - Sherwood Smith   s   5141

**Volkova, Ekaterina Alexandrova**
*Glory's War* - Alfred Coppel   s   1184

**Voltaire, Carter**
*The Drylands* - Mary Rosenblum   s   4678

**von Darkmoor, Erik**
*Rage of a Demon King* - Raymond E. Feist   f   1908
*Rise of a Merchant Prince* - Raymond E. Feist   f   1909
*Shadow of a Dark Queen* - Raymond E. Feist   f   1911
*Shards of a Broken Crown* - Raymond E. Feist   f   1912

**von Hessel**
*Escape From Loki* - Philip Jose Farmer   f   1870

**von Richtofen, Manfred**
*The Bloody Red Baron* - Kim Newman   h   4097

**Vorkosigan, Miles**
*Borders of Infinity* - Lois McMaster Bujold   s   757
*Cetaganda* - Lois McMaster Bujold   s   758
*Komarr* - Lois McMaster Bujold   s   760
*Memory* - Lois McMaster Bujold   s   761
*Mirror Dance* - Lois McMaster Bujold   s   762

*The Vor Game* - Lois McMaster Bujold   s   764

**Vorpatril, Ivan**
*Memory* - Lois McMaster Bujold   s   761

**Vozmozho, Vozmuzhalnoy "Moozh"**
*The Call of Earth* - Orson Scott Card   s   882

**Vusca**
*The Book of the Beast* - Tanith Lee   f   3405

**Walders, Shana**
*Maximum Light* - Nancy Kress   s   3241

**Walking Bear, Jack**
*First Dawn* - Mike Moscoe   s   4038
*Lost Days* - Mike Moscoe   s   4039
*Second Fire* - Mike Moscoe   s   4040

**Wallace, Enoch**
*Way Station* - Clifford D. Simak   s   5048

**Walsh, Richard Earl**
*Dragon Season* - Michael Cassutt   f   936

**Wanderman, Aubrey**
*Honor Among Enemies* - David Weber   s   5673

**Wanker, David L.**
*The Kruton Interface* - John DeChancie   s   1459

**Ward, Alan**
*Midsummer* - Matthew J. Costello   h   1200

**Warhurst, Montgomery**
*Semper Mars* - Ian Douglas   s   1585

**Warson, Toll**
*The Voyage* - David Drake   s   1649

**Washington, George**
*Two Crowns for America* - Katherine Kurtz   f   3262

**Webber, Mitch**
*Icefire* - Judith Reeves-Stevens   s   4512

**Webster, Joshua**
*Deep Freeze* - Zach Hughes   s   2811

**Whitaker, Tomyris "Whit Hastings"**
*Return to Isis* - Jean Stewart   s   5268

**White Crow, Valentine**
*The Architecture of Desire* - Mary Gentle   f   2195
*Rats and Gargoyles* - Mary Gentle   f   2196

**Whitefeather, Steven "Brian Moore"**
*Time Station London* - David Evans   s   1853

**Wilks**
*Aliens: Earth Hive* - Steve Perry   s   4289
*Aliens: The Female War* - Steve Perry   s   4290

**Winkler, Gene "Wink"**
*Signs of Life* - Cherry Wilder   s   5804

**Winslow, Dirk**
*Time: The Semi-Final Frontier* - Lionel Fenn   s   1921

**Winston, Ariana**
*Shadows of War* - Thomas S. Gressman   s   2432

**Winters, Kelly Ann**
*March or Die* - Andrew Keith   s   3035

**Winthrop, Edwin**
*The Bloody Red Baron* - Kim Newman   h   4097

**Witzko, Damion**
*On the Verge* - Roland J. Green   s   2350

**Wolff, Hauptsturmfuhrer**
*Darkness on the Ice* - Lois Tilton   h   5475

**Worf**
*Armageddon Sky* - L.A. Graf   s   2296
*Call to Arms* - Diane Carey   s   901
*Doomsday World* - Carmen Carter   s   923
*Kahless* - Michael Jan Friedman   s   2065
*Reunion* - Michael Jan Friedman   s   2068
*Triangle: Imzadi II* - Peter David   s   1388

**Wu, Nyima**
*Nothing Sacred* - Elizabeth Ann Scarborough   f   4867

**Yeager, Pauli**
*Heritage of Flight* - Susan Shwartz   s   5016

**Yeager, Sam**
*Worldwar: In the Balance* - Harry Turtledove   s   5515
*Worldwar: Upsetting the Balance* - Harry Turtledove   s   5518

**Yellow Hare**
*Celestial Matters* - Richard Garfinkle   s   2140

**Yoshio, Ikawa**
*The Crystal Sorcerers* - William R. Forstchen   f   1979

**Zhang**
*Shangri-La: The Return to the World of Lost Horizon* - Eleanor Cooney   f   1169

**Zhiming, Lao**
*Crossroad* - Barbara Hambly   s   2501

**Zigramson, Thorolf**
*The Pixilated Peeress* - L. Sprague de Camp   f   1416

**Zorin, Lavrenti Borisovich**
*Branch Point* - Mona Clee   s   1074

# MINER

**Allard**
*Suisan* - Phyllis Carol Agins   f   42

**Bandicut, John**
*Neptune Crossing* - Jeffrey A. Carver   s   933

**Bloodyluck, Kithri**
*Jaydium* - Deborah Wheeler   s   5774

**Calum**
*Acorna's Quest* - Anne McCaffrey   s   3718

**Dillon**
*Alien 3* - Alan Dean Foster   s   1993

**Gioglie III, Declan "Gill"**
*Acorna* - Anne McCaffrey   s   3717

**Kennet, Spencer**
*Monsoon* - Peter L. Rice   s   4583

**Kostner, Harry**
*Unearthed* - Ashley McConnell   h   3778

**Ochs, Thur**
*The Spirit Ring* - Lois McMaster Bujold   f   763

**Raschad, Meesha**
*Mistwalker* - Denise Lopez Heald   s   2637

**Ree, Killashandra**
*Crystal Line* - Anne McCaffrey   s   3724

**Sheen**
*Raft* - Stephen Baxter   s   401

**Trask, Grace**
*The Billion Dollar Boy* - Charles Sheffield   s   4948

**Trask, Lana**
*The Billion Dollar Boy* - Charles Sheffield   s   4948

**Wade, Jonathan**
*What's Wrong with Tamara?* - D.A. Fowler   h   2025

# MINSTREL

**ab Meredydd, Rhys "Sun Eyes"**
*Madoc's Hundred* - Pat Winter   f   5925

**Alaric**
*In the Red Lord's Reach* - Phyllis Eisenstein   f   1765

**Angharad**
*Into the Green* - Charles de Lint   f   1430

**Annice**
*Sing the Four Quarters* - Tanya Huff   f   2799

**Banyon, Eric**
*Bedlam's Bard* - Mercedes Lackey   f   3269
*Knight of Ghosts and Shadows* - Mercedes Lackey   f   3285
*Summoned to Tourney* - Mercedes Lackey   f   3299

**Birdsong, Starling**
*Assassin's Quest* - Robin Hobb   f   2694

**Blackthorn**
*Hunter of the Light* - Risa Aratyr   f   203

**Brandarkson, Brandark**
*Oath of Swords* - David Weber   f   5678

**Bruchan**
*The Boy From the Burren* - Sheila Gilluly   f   2236

**Carbri**
*Search for the Starblade* - Keith Taylor   f   5408

**Cross, Prosper**
*The World Next Door* - Brad Ferguson   s   1924

**de Talair, Bertran**
*A Song for Arbonne* - Guy Gavriel Kay   f   3017

**Ecklundson, Dword**
*Captains Outrageous, or, For Doom the Bell Tolls* - Roy V. Young   f   6049

**Emereck**
*Shadows over Lyra* - Patricia C. Wrede   f   5980

**Ewin, Cors Cant**
*Arthur War Lord* - Dafydd ab Hugh   f   6

**Eydryth of Kar Garudwyn**
*Songsmith* - Andre Norton   f   4161

**Garfield, Jake**
*The World Next Door* - Brad Ferguson   s   1924

**Kestrel**
*The Robin and the Kestrel* - Mercedes Lackey   f   3293

**Lisseut of Vezet**
*A Song for Arbonne* - Guy Gavriel Kay   f   3017

**Lukas, Harkon**
*Death of a Darklord* - Laurell K. Hamilton   h   2516

**Magpie**
*A Cast of Corbies* - Mercedes Lackey   f   3274

**Mantrell, Matthew "Matt"**
*The Secular Wizard* - Christopher Stasheff   f   5222

**Natil**
*Maze of Moonlight* - Gael Baudino   f   393

**Odell, Owen**
*Morningstar* - David Gemmell   f   2190

**Orfeo**
*Storm Warriors* - Brian Craig   f   1240
*Zaragoz* - Brian Craig   f   1241

**Polijn**
*The Sure Death of a Mouse* - Dan Crawford   f   1250
*A Wild Dog and Lone* - Dan Crawford   f   1251

**Raven**
*A Cast of Corbies* - Mercedes Lackey   f   3274

**Robin**
*The Robin and the Kestrel* - Mercedes Lackey   f   3293

**Rosvenir, Collan**
*The Mageborn Traitor* - Melanie Rawn   f   4488

**Stasya**
*Sing the Four Quarters* - Tanya Huff   f   2799

**Stefan**
*Magic's Price* - Mercedes Lackey   f   3288

**Strann**
*The Avenger* - Louise Cooper   *f*   1174

**Taliesen**
*The Hawk's Gray Feather* - Patricia Kennealy-Morrison   *f*   3061
*The Hedge of Mist* - Patricia Kennealy-Morrison   *s*   3062
*The Oak Above the Kings: A Book of the Keltiad* - Patricia Kennealy   *s*   3058

**Talisen**
*Hero's Song* - Edith Pattou   *f*   4261

**Tegrid**
*The Silver Hand* - Stephen R. Lawhead   *f*   3358

**Thomas**
*Thomas the Rhymer* - Ellen Kushner   *f*   3265

**Trystan**
*Storm Warriors* - Brian Craig   *f*   1240

**Tualha**
*A Wizard Abroad* - Diane Duane   *f*   1668

## MODEL

**Curio**
*Majyk by Design* - Esther Friesner   *f*   2080

**Jagoda, Barbara**
*Chicago Loop* - Paul Theroux   *h*   5443

**Jaishree/Minaz**
*Beauty* - Brian D'Amato   *h*   1334

**Macaree, Anne**
*Obsessed* - Rick R. Reed   *h*   4500

**Marks, Barbie**
*I Was a Teenage Fairy* - Francesca Lia Block   *f*   549

**Patricia**
*The Man Upstairs* - T.L. Parkinson   *h*   4248

**Patton, Hallie**
*Private Demons* - Robert Masello   *h*   3660

**Shanna**
*Pelts* - F. Paul Wilson   *h*   5894

**Tyrell, Sarah**
*Blade Runner 2: The Edge of Human* - K.W. Jeter   *s*   2906

**Warner, Valerie**
*The Devil's Auction* - Robert Weinberg   *h*   5696

## MONSTER

**Baat**
*Hunting the Ghost Dancer* - A.A. Attanasio   *f*   268

**Caliban**
*Caliban's Hour* - Tad Williams   *f*   5826

**Conglomeros**
*Conglomeros* - Jesse Browner   *f*   729

**Doomsday**
*The Death and Life of Superman* - Roger Stern   *s*   5262

**Fades**
*The Eye of the World* - Robert Jordan   *f*   2986

**Frankenstein's Monster**
*The Final Battle* - Richard A. Lupoff   *f*   3572

**Frostwing**
*Frostwing* - Richard A. Knaak   *f*   3170

**Ghidorah**
*Godzilla 2000* - Marc Cerasini   *s*   949

**Godzilla**
*Godzilla 2000* - Marc Cerasini   *s*   949

**Graylord**
*Shadowlight* - Jackie Hyman   *f*   2819

**Grendel**
*The Tower of Beowulf* - Parke Godwin   *f*   2250

**Grundbur**
*Whose Song Is Sung* - Frank Schaefer   *f*   4872

**Kaeot**
*A Whisper of Wings* - Steven Ray Fulgham   *h*   2091

**Mama**
*India's Story* - Kathlyn S. Starbuck   *s*   5208

**Nicodareus**
*Darkenheight* - Douglas Niles   *f*   4107

**Poduano, Dominic**
*Shapes* - Steve Vance   *h*   5552

**Shadowman**
*Dark Souls* - Barry Porter   *h*   4369

**Shudde-M'ell**
*The Burrowers Beneath* - Brian Lumley   *h*   3548

**Sikes, Jesse**
*Sins of the Flesh* - Don Davis   *h*   1404

**Skogskra, Haakon**
*The Gnome's Engine* - Teresa Edgerton   *f*   1742

**Utlunta**
*Stoneskin's Revenge* - Tom Deitz   *f*   1476

**Verner, Janice**
*Find Your Own Truth* - Robert N. Charrette   *f*   972

**Vril, Dietrich**
*The Armageddon Box* - Robert Weinberg   *h*   5690

**Ward, Alan**
*Midsummer* - Matthew J. Costello   *h*   1200

## MORGUE ATTENDANT

**Radburn, Adam**
*The Undead* - Roxanne Longstreet   *h*   3519

**Washburn, Corky**
*Bring on the Night* - Don Davis   *h*   1402

## MOUNTAIN MAN

**Digby, Digger**
*The World Next Door* - Brad Ferguson   *s*   1924

**Kindle, Tom**
*The Harvest* - Robert Charles Wilson   *s*   5909

**Malone, Amos "Mad Amos"**
*Mad Amos* - Alan Dean Foster   *f*   2009

## MOUNTAINEER

**Appenfell, Rudgar "Rudy"**
*A Breach in the Watershed* - Douglas Niles   *f*   4105
*Darkenheight* - Douglas Niles   *f*   4107
*War of the Three Waters* - Douglas Niles   *f*   4110

**Glover, Tony**
*Snowbeast!* - Peter Tremayne   *h*   5482

## MURDERER

**Bates, Norman**
*Psycho* - Robert Bloch   *h*   540
*Psycho II* - Robert Bloch   *h*   541

**Bergeron, Carolyn**
*Nightmare Logic* - Matthew Hall   *h*   2495

**Black Heron**
*Curse of the Black Heron* - Holly Lisle   *f*   3479

**Blade**
*Shadow Hunt* - Anne Logston   *f*   3514

**Bothari**
*Barrayar* - Lois McMaster Bujold   *s*   756

**Brandsetter, Earl**
*Lethal Interface* - Mel Odom   *s*   4193

**Caiper, Watly**
*The Host* - Peter R. Emshwiller   *s*   1819

**Cassidy, Lylah**
*Looker* - Jorge Saralegui   *h*   4820

**Chandler, Joshua "the Whistler" Jeremiah**
*Oracle* - Mike Resnick   *s*   4551

**Chucky**
*Child's Play III* - Matthew J. Costello   *h*   1194

**Dagon**
*Dead Boys* - Richard Calder   *s*   836

**Dennis**
*Frisk* - Dennis Cooper   *h*   1170

**Ell, Pe**
*The Druid of Shannara* - Terry Brooks   *f*   710

**Felmet**
*Wyrd Sisters* - Terry Pratchett   *f*   4405

**Gaimes, Gary**
*House Haunted* - Al Sarrantonio   *h*   4830

**Garrett, Carl**
*The Dead Man's Kiss* - Robert Weinberg   *h*   5695

**Garza, Tony**
*In the Mood* - Charles L. Grant   *h*   2312

**Gavel, Kevin**
*Junkyard* - Barry Porter   *h*   4370

**Growler, Donald**
*Cul-De-Sac* - David Martin   *h*   3638

**Helman, Granger**
*Bloodshift* - Garfield Reeves-Stevens   *h*   4508

**Johnny**
*The Bad Thing* - Michael O'Rourke   *h*   4222

**Kane**
*Kane* - Douglas Borton   *h*   576

**King, Depard**
*Spindoc* - Steve Perry   *s*   4300

**LaFontaine, Horace "Gray Redstar"**
*Blue Light* - Walter Mosley   *s*   4042

**Laker, Maria**
*Among Madmen* - Jim Starlin   *s*   5212

**Lector, Hannibal "Cannibal"**
*The Silence of the Lambs* - Thomas Harris   *h*   2566

**Lewis, Jonathan Thomas**
*In Double Jeopardy* - Andrew Neiderman   *h*   4088

**Marrah, Rabh**
*The Light in Exile* - Cheryl J. Franklin   *s*   2038

**Mishwe, Dajaj**
*ViraVax* - Bill Ransom   *s*   4478

**Newman, Greg**
*Impulse* - Rick Hautala   *h*   2609

**Ostrow, Henry**
*Clarke County, Space* - Allen Steele   *s*   5241

**Page, Scott**
*This Side of Judgment* - J.R. Dunn   *s*   1696

**Phoenix, Simon**
*Demolition Man* - Richard Osborne   *s*   4229

**Primavera**
*Dead Girls* - Richard Calder   *s*   837

**Prince, Mick**
*Quoth the Crow* - David Bischoff   *h*   494

**Reich, Ben**
*The Demolished Man* - Alfred Bester   *s*   476

**Royal, Barton**
*Billy* - Whitley Strieber   *h*   5338

**Saladin**
*The Forever King* - Molly Cochran   *f*   1092

**Saunders, Clay**
*Wildest Dreams* - Norman Partridge   *h*   4256

**Sikes, Jesse**
*Sins of the Flesh* - Don Davis   *h*   1404

**Stark, George**
*The Dark Half* - Stephen King   *h*   3128

**Steve**
*Sacrifice* - Richard Kinion   *h*   3146

**Succubus**
*The Hacker* - Chet Day   *h*   1410

**Teatime, Jonathan**
*Hogfather* - Terry Pratchett   *f*   4391

**Thibodeau, Skida "Skilly"**
*Prince of Sparta* - Jerry Pournelle   *s*   4378

**Tomaso**
*Polar City Blues* - Katharine Kerr   *s*   3073

**Two Feathers, Jimmy "the Injun"**
*Oracle* - Mike Resnick   *s*   4551

**Vitarosa**
*Mind Snare* - Gayle Greeno   *s*   2422

**Walford, John**
*Walford's Oak* - Jill M. Phillips   *f*   4310

**Wolf, Billy "Slider"**
*Dreamer* - Peter James   *h*   2871

## MUSEUM CURATOR

**Barton, Howard**
*The Paper Grail* - James P. Blaylock   *f*   522

**Chapman, Tony**
*Desmond: A Novel of Love and the Modern Vampire* - Ulysses G. Dietz   *h*   1541

**Flannery, Kathleen**
*The Two Georges* - Richard Dreyfuss   *s*   1655

**Hunt, Katie**
*The Trickster* - Muriel Gray   *h*   2340

**Jordan, Miles**
*End of an Era* - Robert J. Sawyer   *s*   4853

**Kawakita, Gregory**
*Relic* - Douglas Preston   *h*   4414

**Larraby, Luke**
*The Boss in the Wall* - Avram Davidson   *h*   1396

**Roberts, Karin**
*Blood Sabbath* - Leigh Clark   *h*   1048

**Schenk, Madeline Leuoir**
*Warsprite* - Jefferson P. Swycaffer   *s*   5375

**Sheridan, Denise**
*Son of Darkness* - Josepha Sherman   *f*   4990

**Stone, Enoch**
*A Hunger in the Soul* - Mike Resnick   *s*   4545

**Thackeray, Brandon**
*End of an Era* - Robert J. Sawyer   *s*   4853

**Wisnewski, Leonard**
*Legion of the Dead* - Geoffrey Caine   *h*   833

**Ystilog, Erpad**
*Brotherhood of the Stars* - Kirby Greene   *s*   2414

## MUSICIAN

**Alton, Margaret**
*Exile's Song* - Marion Zimmer Bradley   *s*   632

**Alvarez, Dan**
*Bone Music* - Alan Rodgers   *h*   4646

**Amy**
*Stranded* - Camarin Grae   *s*   2295

**Ananda**
*The Thirteenth Daughter of the Moon* - Steven Nightingale   *f*   4104

**Angel Juan**
*Missing Angel Juan* - Francesca Lia Block   *f*   550

**Arlen, Drew**
*Beggars and Choosers* - Nancy Kress   *s*   3236

**Asgard, Paula**
*Carlucci's Edge* - Richard Paul Russo   *s*   4747

**Baby Baby**
*Rock 'n' Roll Babes From Outer Space* - Linda Javin   *s*   2880

**Banyon, Eric**
*Bedlam's Bard* - Mercedes Lackey   *f*   3269
*Knight of Ghosts and Shadows* - Mercedes Lackey   *f*   3285
*Summoned to Tourney* - Mercedes Lackey   *f*   3299

**Bat, Cherokee**
*Cherokee Bat and the Goat Guys* - Francesca Lia Block   *f*   546

**Batterberry, Lesli**
*Ghosts of Wind and Shadow* - Charles de Lint   *f*   1427

**Bauer, Robert**
*Requiem* - Clifford Mohr   *h*   3950

**Becker, Triana**
*Violin* - Anne Rice   *h*   4579

**Bellman, Alan**
*The Printer's Devil* - Chico Kidd   *f*   3099

**Bellman, Kim**
*The Printer's Devil* - Chico Kidd   *f*   3099

**Billy**
*Cowboy Feng's Space Bar and Grille* - Steven Brust   *s*   740

**Blaze**
*Mississippi Blues* - Kathleen Ann Goonan   *s*   2274

**Breivik, Allan**
*Make Way for Dragons!* - Thorarinn Gunnarsson   *f*   2465

**Briam**
*Changing Fate* - Elisabeth Waters   *f*   5629

**Brown, Rembrandt "Cryin' Man"**
*Sliders: The Novel* - Brad Linaweaver   *s*   3467

**Byron**
*The White Mists of Power* - Kristine Kathryn Rusch   *f*   4730

**Cairns, Moira**
*December* - Phil Rickman   *h*   4588

**Caladrius, Rook**
*Song for the Basilisk* - Patricia A. McKillip   *f*   3841

**Cameron, Tim**
*Shadow of the Beast* - Margaret L. Carter   *h*   926

**Carbri**
*Search for the Starblade* - Keith Taylor   *f*   5408

**Casey, Matt**
*Our Lady of the Harbour* - Charles de Lint   *f*   1434

**Celine, Sigismundo**
*Nature's God* - Robert Anton Wilson   *f*   5903

**Celyn, Imp y**
*Soul Music* - Terry Pratchett   *f*   4401

**Chang, Emily**
*Night Magic* - Thomas Tryon   *h*   5485

**Charly**
*The Making of a Monster* - Gail Petersen   *h*   4307

**Clewe, Elizabeth**
*The Blood of Angels* - Stephen Gregory   *h*   2428

**Clisser**
*Dragonseye* - Anne McCaffrey   *s*   3730

**Crecilius, Hallie**
*The Devil's Cradle* - Kate Stewart   *h*   5269

**Cruitaire, Christa**
*Gossamer Axe* - Gael Baudino   *f*   392

**Daffyd**
*The Soprano Sorceress* - L.E. Modesitt Jr.   *f*   3938

**"Damnbanna" Deil**
*Damnbanna* - Nancy Springer   *f*   5177

**Davis, Kate**
*The Making of a Monster* - Gail Petersen   *h*   4307

**de Saint-Germain, Francois**
*Blood Roses* - Chelsea Quinn Yarbro   *h*   6012

**Dirk**
*The Abraxas Marvel Circus* - Stephen Leigh   *f*   3423

**Douglas, Morric**
*Blackmantle: A Triumph* - Patricia Kennealy-Morrison   *f*   3059

**Drew**
*The Making of a Monster* - Gail Petersen   *h*   4307

**Dulcet, Giulia**
*Song for the Basilisk* - Patricia A. McKillip   *f*   3841

**Erik**
*Phantom* - Susan Kay   *h*   3020

**Fiolon**
*Lady of the Trillium* - Marion Zimmer Bradley   *f*   641

**Firemayne, Rowan**
*Cup of Clay* - Carole Nelson Douglas   *f*   1583
*Seed upon the Wind* - Carole Nelson Douglas   *f*   1584

**Foxxe, Johnny "Fox"**
*The Wood Wife* - Terri Windling   *f*   5916

**Frida**
*Kamikaze L'Amour* - Richard Kadrey   *s*   2998

**Fullin**
*Commitment Hour* - James Alan Gardner   *s*   2134

**Gandharva**
*Bhagavati* - Kara Dalkey   *f*   1316

**Gavin, Felix**
*The Little Country* - Charles de Lint   *f*   1432

**Gawaine**
*Fortress of Frost and Fire* - Mercedes Lackey   *f*   3282

**Geiger, Rolf**
*The Prodigy* - Noel Hynd   *h*   2823

**Ghost**
*Lost Souls* - Poppy Z. Brite   *h*   697

**Greystoke, David**
*Ocean under the Ice* - Robert L. Forward   *s*   1988

**Gurden, Tom**
*The Mask of Loki* - Roger Zelazny   *f*   6071

**Halliday, Arden**
*Gone South* - Robert R. McCammon   *h*   3755

**Harmon, Anne Marie "Annie"**
*Waking the Moon* - Elizabeth Hand   *f*   2538

**Hinckel, Hieronymus**
*Chorus Skating* - Alan Dean Foster   *f*   1998

**Holley, Charles Hardin**
*Back in the USSA* - Kim Newman   *s*   4095

**Hu "Hugh"**
*Shame of Man* - Piers Anthony   *s*   188

**Indigo**
*The Unicorn Sonata* - Peter S. Beagle   *f*   412

**Jamie**
*Cowboy Feng's Space Bar and Grille* - Steven Brust   s   740

**Joel**
*Finder's Bane* - Kate Novak   f   4165

**Jones, Fanning "Fan"**
*Dreaming Metal* - Melissa Scott   s   4895

**Jorandel "Jorie"**
*Cold Iron* - Melisa Michaels   f   3886

**Joreth**
*OtherWise* - Margaret Wander Bonanno   s   567

**Joy, Sandy "Sana"**
*Strands of Sunlight* - Gael Baudino   f   396

**Keith**
*Stainless* - Todd Grimson   h   2449

**Kelledy, Meran**
*Ghosts of Wind and Shadow* - Charles de Lint   f   1427

**Kentraine, Beth**
*Knight of Ghosts and Shadows* - Mercedes Lackey   f   3285
*Summoned to Tourney* - Mercedes Lackey   f   3299

**Kevin**
*Castle of Deception* - Mercedes Lackey   f   3275

**King**
*River Rats* - Caroline Stevermer   s   5267

**Kostanuik, April**
*Torment* - Stephen R. George   h   2204

**LaRoche, Serge**
*Serpent's Gift* - A.C. Crispin   s   1261

**Lazarich, Sabina**
*Someone to Watch over Me* - Tricia Sullivan   s   5355

**Little, Janey**
*The Little Country* - Charles de Lint   f   1432

**Lobey, Lo**
*The Einstein Intersection* - Samuel R. Delany   s   1481

**Longchamp, Dawn**
*Secrets of the Morning* - V.C. Andrews   h   146

**MacKai, Willie**
*Phantom Banjo* - Elizabeth Ann Scarborough   f   4868
*Picking the Ballad's Bones* - Elizabeth Ann Scarborough   f   4869
*Strum Again?* - Elizabeth Ann Scarborough   f   4870

**Manzara, Vincent**
*Fantasma* - Thomas F. Monteleone   h   3963

**Maria Elena**
*Humans* - Donald E. Westlake   f   5768

**Marlowe, Trip**
*Glimmering* - Elizabeth Hand   s   2535

**Martin, Julianne**
*Phantom Banjo* - Elizabeth Ann Scarborough   f   4868
*Strum Again?* - Elizabeth Ann Scarborough   f   4870

**Meriones**
*The Elementals* - Morgan Llywelyn   f   3503

**Meriweather, Buncan**
*Son of Spellsinger* - Alan Dean Foster   f   2015

**Meriweather, Jon-Tom**
*Chorus Skating* - Alan Dean Foster   f   1998

**Merlin, Walter Drake**
*Tomorrow and Tomorrow* - Charles Sheffield   s   4966

**Miller, Zeke**
*Night Music* - Sheila Bristow Garner   h   2147

**Moore, Melinda**
*Gossamer Axe* - Gael Baudino   f   392

**Murphy, James**
*Landslayer's Law* - Tom Deitz   f   1474

**Naitachal**
*Fortress of Frost and Fire* - Mercedes Lackey   f   3282

**Nesbitt, Justin**
*The Beyond* - Barry Harrington   h   2556

**Nightingale "Lyrebird"**
*The Eagle and the Nightingales* - Mercedes Lackey   f   3278

**Onado, Hisako**
*Canal Dreams* - Iain M. Banks   s   323

**Pennant, Rebecca**
*The Judas Glass* - Michael Cadnum   h   812

**Petiron**
*The Masterharper of Pern* - Anne McCaffrey   s   3739

**Presley, Elvis**
*Armageddon: The Musical* - Robert Rankin   s   4473
*Bone Music* - Alan Rodgers   h   4646
*Elvis Rising: Stories on the King* - Kay Sloan   s   5089
*Elvissey* - Jack Womack   s   5957
*The King Is Dead: Tales of Elvis Post Mortem* - Paul M. Sammon   h   4810

**Quinsonnas**
*Paris in the Twentieth Century* - Jules Verne   s   5568

**Rafe**
*Ecstasia* - Francesca Lia Block   f   547

**Redwing, T'fyrr**
*The Eagle and the Nightingales* - Mercedes Lackey   f   3278

**Reilly, Dave**
*December* - Phil Rickman   h   4588

**Ribson, Joe**
*Necrom* - Mick Farren   s   1881

**Rivera, Josephine "Joey"**
*The Unicorn Sonata* - Peter S. Beagle   f   412

**Robinson, Woody**
*Second Chance* - Chet Williamson   h   5850

**Roland**
*Gate of Darkness, Circle of Light* - Tanya Huff   f   2797

**Rune**
*The Lark and the Wren* - Mercedes Lackey   f   3286

**Ryder**
*Kamikaze L'Amour* - Richard Kadrey   s   2998

**St. John, Simon**
*December* - Phil Rickman   h   4588

**Sanchez, Monica**
*Gossamer Axe* - Gael Baudino   f   392

**Sandeen, Michael**
*Night Music* - Sheila Bristow Garner   h   2147

**Scallan, Amy**
*Our Lady of the Harbour* - Charles de Lint   f   1434

**Seregil**
*Luck in the Shadows* - Lynn Flewelling   f   1952

**s'Falenn, Arithon**
*Fugitive Prince* - Janny Wurts   f   6002

**Simba**
*Twisted* - Sue Hollister Barr   h   364

**Singer**
*Deathgift* - Ann Tonsor Zeddies   s   6061

**Steengo**
*The Stainless Steel Rat Sings the Blues* - Harry Harrison   s   2575

**Stefanovsky, Stephan**
*Violin* - Anne Rice   h   4579

**Styreme, Katharine**
*Celestis* - Paul Park   s   4241

**Summers, Nick**
*The Calling* - Kathryn Meyer Griffith   h   2439

**Thann, Danilo "Dan"**
*Elfsong* - Elaine Cunningham   f   1289
*Silver Shadows* - Elaine Cunningham   f   1292

**Tomkins, Icanus**
*Out of the Ordinary* - Annie Dalton   f   1330

**Valentine, Timmy**
*Vanitas: Escape From Vampire Junction* - S.P. Somtow   h   5162

**Voyaging Moon**
*The Remarkable Journey of Prince Jen* - Lloyd Alexander   f   69

**Wilson, Brian**
*Glimpses* - Lewis Shiner   h   4997

**Witch Baby**
*Cherokee Bat and the Goat Guys* - Francesca Lia Block   f   546
*Missing Angel Juan* - Francesca Lia Block   f   550
*Witch Baby* - Francesca Lia Block   f   552

**Woodrow, Melissa**
*Torment* - Stephen R. George   h   2204

**Wyvernspur, Finder "Nameless"**
*Song of the Saurials* - Kate Novak   f   4167

**Young, Beau**
*Big Rock Beat* - Greg Kihn   h   3102

**Zacharias, Michael**
*Lost Futures* - Lisa Tuttle   s   5520

# MUTANT

**Aedrea**
*Saint Leibowitz and the Wild Horse Woman* - Walter M. Miller Jr.   s   3908

**Akimura, Rick**
*Mutant Legacy* - Karen Haber   s   2474

**Calanthe**
*The Enchantments of Flesh and Spirit* - Storm Constantine   s   1141

**Chichelski, Chango**
*Accidental Creatures* - Anne Harris   s   2558

**Creed, Victor "Sabertooth"**
*Codename Wolverine* - Christopher Golden   s   2256

**Dahlgren, Sven**
*Heart of Red Iron* - Phyllis Gotlieb   s   2287

**Darkholme, Raven "Mystique"**
*Codename Wolverine* - Christopher Golden   s   2256

**Denethan**
*The Marked Man* - Charles Ingrid   s   2831

**Dodger**
*Choose Your Enemies Carefully* - Robert N. Charrette   s   971
*Find Your Own Truth* - Robert N. Charrette   f   972
*Never Deal with a Dragon* - Robert N. Charrette   s   975

**Gojiro**
*Gojiro* - Mark Jacobson   f   2847

**Gregory, Joe-Jim**
*Silent Thunder/Universe* - Dean Ing   s   2829

**Jon**
*The Tery* - F. Paul Wilson   s   5900

**Kid Death**
*The Einstein Intersection* - Samuel R.
Delany   s   1481

**Lobey, Lo**
*The Einstein Intersection* - Samuel R.
Delany   s   1481

**Logan "Wolverine"**
*Codename Wolverine* - Christopher Golden   s   2256

**Melisande**
*The Widowmaker* - Mike Resnick   s   4559

**Nebogipfel**
*The Time Ships* - Stephen Baxter   s   403

**Ooslaxt**
*Christmas Slaughter* - Mark Grant   s   2323

**Pellaz**
*The Enchantments of Flesh and Spirit*   Storm
Constantine   s   1141

**Portman, William T. "Orde"**
*Blue Light* - Walter Mosley   s   4042

**Remillard, Jon**
*Diamond Mask: A Novel* - Julian May   s   3697

**Ryton, Melanie**
*The Mutant Season* - Robert Silverberg   s   5039

**Ryton, Michael**
*The Mutant Season* - Robert Silverberg   s   5039

**Sanders, Kenneth**
*Doomsday Exam* - Nick Pollotta   f   4363

**Spider**
*The Einstein Intersection* - Samuel R.
Delany   s   1481

**VJ**
*Mutation* - Robin Cook   s   1165

**Weena**
*The Time Ships* - Stephen Baxter   s   403

## MYTHICAL CREATURE

**Aarundel**
*Once a Hero* - Michael A. Stackpole   f   5203

**Acila**
*Changing Fate* - Elisabeth Waters   f   5629

**Adana "the Snake Mother"**
*The Face in the Abyss* - A. Merritt   f   3878

**Aidan**
*Alamut* - Judith Tarr   f   5390

**Akhor**
*Song in the Silence* - Elizabeth Kerner   f   3065

**Alara**
*The Elvenbane* - Andre Norton   f   4149

**Albin**
*The Wild Wood* - Charles de Lint   f   1440

**Aleshire, Puck**
*The Iron Dragon's Daughter* - Michael
Swanwick   f   5371

**Algooth**
*The Gates of Vensunor* - Carol Heller   f   2650

**Alinor**
*Wheels of Fire* - Mercedes Lackey   f   3301

**Allard**
*Suisan* - Phyllis Carol Agins   f   42

**Allerum**
*Shadow's Realm* - Mickey Zucker Reichert   f   4523

**Amaranth**
*The Dragon's Touchstone* - Irene Radford   f   4459

**Ampelus**
*Thessalonica* - Harry Turtledove   f   5511

**an Treves, Sheyrena "Rena"**
*Elvenblood* - Andre Norton   f   4150

**Anlon**
*Morigu: The Dead* - Mark C. Perry   f   4284

**Apollo**
*Ye Gods!* - Tom Holt   f   2753

**Aralorn**
*Masques* - Patricia Briggs   f   681

**Aravan**
*The Eye of the Hunter* - Dennis L.
McKiernan   f   3833
*Voyage of the Fox Rider* - Dennis L.
McKiernan   f   3837

**Archangel**
*Headhunters* - Mel Odom   s   4192

**Arin**
*The Dragonstone* - Dennis L. McKiernan   t   3832

**Aryadyss**
*Donnerjack* - Roger Zelazny   s   6063

**Aurealis, Gannd**
*War* - Simon Hawke   f   2625

**Ayesha**
*Dragon's Domain* - Thorarinn Gunnarsson   f   2461

**Azak**
*Emperor and Clown* - Dave Duncan   f   1676

**Azdra'ik**
*The Goblin Mirror* - C.J. Cherryh   f   994

**Azriel**
*Servant of the Bones* - Anne Rice   h   4575

**Baba Yaga**
*Weirdos of the Universe, Unite!* - Pamela F.
Service   f   4921

**Baenre, Liriel**
*Daughter of the Drow* - Elaine Cunningham   f   1287

**Bandylegs, Ahira**
*The Road Home* - Joel Rosenberg   f   4674

**Bedlam, Wellen**
*Dragon Tome* - Richard A. Knaak   f   3169

**Belevairn**
*A Two-Edged Sword* - Thomas K. Martin   f   3653

**Bennett**
*A Knight Among Knaves* - Robert N.
Charrette   f   974

**Berengar**
*The Shadow Gate* - Margaret Ball   f   317

**Betwixt and Between**
*Brother to Dragons, Companion to Owls* - Jane M.
Lindskold   f   3473

**Bhelliom "Blue Rose"**
*The Hidden City* - David Eddings   f   1733

**Binah**
*Cross and Crescent* - Susan Shwartz   f   5014

**Birkwelch**
*Minerva Wakes* - Holly Lisle   f   3487

**Blathine**
*The Isles of the Blest* - Morgan Llywelyn   f   3505

**The Bleeding Man**
*Night* - Alan Rodgers   h   4649

**Bonita**
*Polymorph* - Scott Westerfeld   s   5767

**Bressanone, Rana**
*The Broken Goddess* - Hans Bemmann   f   439

**Broketail, Bazil**
*Battledragon* - Christopher Rowley   f   4691
*Bazil Broketail* - Christopher Rowley   f   4692
*A Dragon at World's End* - Christopher
Rowley   f   4693

*Dragons of Argonath* - Christopher Rowley   f   4694
*Dragons of War* - Christopher Rowley   f   4695
*A Sword for a Dragon* - Christopher
Rowley   f   4697

**Bruenor, Catti-Brie**
*Passage to Dawn* - R.A. Salvatore   f   4803
*Siege of Darkness* - R.A. Salvatore   f   4804
*Sojourn* - R.A. Salvatore   f   4806
*Starless Night* - R.A. Salvatore   f   4807

**Bryarmote**
*Pyromancer* - Don Callander   f   847

**Burrfoot, Tasslehoff**
*Wanderlust* - Mary Kirchoff   f   3155

**Calis**
*Shadow of a Dark Queen* - Raymond E.
Feist   f   1911

**Calyx**
*Cathedral of Thorns* - Steven Frankos   f   2041

**Carabosse**
*Beauty* - Sheri S. Tepper   f   5428

**Carlotta**
*Castle of Deception* - Mercedes Lackey   f   3275

**Catti-Brie**
*The Silent Blade* - R.A. Salvatore   f   4805

**Centaur, Cathryn**
*Faun & Games* - Piers Anthony   f   169

**Centaur, Che**
*Isle of View* - Piers Anthony   f   177

**Chentelle**
*Quest for the Fallen Star* - Piers Anthony   f   185

**Chyrie**
*Greendaughter* - Anne Logston   f   3510

**Clarris, Peter**
*Changeling* - Christopher Kubasik   f   3245

**Collins, Maggie**
*The Sweetheart Season* - Karen Joy Fowler   f   2029

**Concord, Tappuah "Tappy"**
*The Caterpillar's Question* - Piers Anthony   f   164

**Constable, Arbitrance**
*Dragon Rescue* - Don Callander   f   843

**Constable, Retruance**
*Dragon Companion* - Don Callander   f   842

**Cork, Joe**
*The Faery Convention* - Brett Davis   f   1399

**Craulnober, Elaith**
*Elfsong* - Elaine Cunningham   f   1289

**Cray, Robyn**
*The Two in Hiding* - Ru Emerson   f   1812

**Crystal**
*Troll-Quest* - Rose Estes   f   1841

**Cumber**
*Dragoncharm* - Graham Edwards   f   1749

**Cutter**
*Captives of the Blue Mountain* - Wendy
Pini   f   4336
*The Quest Begins* - Wendy Pini   f   4337

**Cymel**
*Drum Warning* - Jo Clayton   f   1066

**Dalamar**
*Tears of the Night Sky* - Linda P. Baker   f   299

**Darby, Beacontor "Beau"**
*Into the Fire* - Dennis L. McKiernan   f   3834
*Into the Forge* - Dennis L. McKiernan   f   3835

**Darkling, Katastrofa "Kathy"**
*Riverrun* - S.P. Somtow   f   5159

**Dead Man**
*Pretty Pewter Gods* - Glen Cook   f   1152

**Death**
*Donnerjack* - Roger Zelazny  s  6063
*Hogfather* - Terry Pratchett  f  4391
*Maskerade* - Terry Pratchett  f  4395
*The Sandman: Book of Dreams* - Neil
Gaiman  f  2105

**Death "Bill Door"**
*Reaper Man* - Terry Pratchett  f  4399

**Death of Rats**
*Soul Music* - Terry Pratchett  f  4401

**Debauchery Devil/Torchy Burns**
*Strum Again?* - Elizabeth Ann Scarborough  f  4870

**deBurrows, Oliver**
*Luthien's Gamble* - R.A. Salvatore  f  4802
*The Sword of Bedwyr* - R.A. Salvatore  f  4808

**Dh'arlo'me**
*Prince of Demons* - Mickey Zucker
Reichert  f  4522

**Dhu, Zeldan**
*Elvendude* - Mark Shepherd  f  4980

**Diliani**
*Kirins: The Flight of the Ain* - James D.
Priest  f  4433

**Dimblethum**
*Into the Land of the Unicorns* - Bruce
Coville  f  1219

**DiThorn, Bram**
*The Seventh Sentinel* - Mary Kirchoff  f  3154

**Djinn**
*The Djinn in the Nightingale's Eye* - A.S.
Byatt  f  794

**Donya**
*Shadow* - Anne Logston  f  3512
*Shadow Dance* - Anne Logston  f  3513

**Dorcas**
*Diggers* - Terry Pratchett  s  4386
*Truckers* - Terry Pratchett  s  4402

**Dorfl**
*Feet of Clay* - Terry Pratchett  f  4389

**Do'Urden, Drizzt**
*The Legacy* - R.A. Salvatore  f  4801
*Siege of Darkness* - R.A. Salvatore  f  4804
*The Silent Blade* - R.A. Salvatore  f  4805
*Sojourn* - R.A. Salvatore  f  4806
*Starless Night* - R.A. Salvatore  f  4807

**Dragon**
*Dragon Tome* - Richard A. Knaak  f  3169

**Drizzt Do'Urden**
*Passage to Dawn* - R.A. Salvatore  f  4803

**Drulethen "Dru"**
*The Qualinesti* - Paul B. Thompson  f  5455

**Drumheller, Thorn**
*Shadow Moon* - George Lucas  f  3540

**Dubhain**
*Faery in Shadow* - C.J. Cherryh  f  987

**Duran**
*Headhunters* - Mel Odom  s  4192

**Earth**
*The Book of Earth* - Marjorie Bradley
Kellogg  f  3044
*The Book of Water* - Marjorie Bradley
Kellogg  f  3045

**Eleighanaran "Leigh"**
*Shadows on the Hill* - Jackie Cassada  f  935

**Elessedil, Wren**
*The Talismans of Shannara* - Terry Brooks  f  717

**Eleuth**
*Songs of Earth and Power* - Greg Bear  f  424

**Elf, Jenny**
*Demons Don't Dream* - Piers Anthony  f  168
*Isle of View* - Piers Anthony  f  177

**Elsie**
*Galatea in 2-D* - Aaron Allston  f  87

**Erato**
*Zeus and Co.* - David Lee Jones  f  2942

**Essessili**
*The Dragon at War* - Gordon R. Dickson  f  1530

**Evander**
*Days of Air and Darkness* - Katharine Kerr  f  3067

**Fafleen**
*Dragon's Queen* - Carol L. Dennis  f  1488

**Fairy Godmother**
*Spell Bound* - Ru Emerson  f  1810

**Fallon**
*The Stone Movers* - Patricia Mullen  f  4045

**Fanuilh**
*Beggar's Banquet* - Daniel Hood  f  2756
*Fanuilh* - Daniel Hood  f  2757
*Scales of Justice* - Daniel Hood  f  2758
*Wizard's Heir* - Daniel Hood  f  2759

**Faun, Forrest**
*Faun & Games* - Piers Anthony  f  169

**Feinstein, Rose**
*The Magic Touch* - Jody Lynn Nye  f  4171

**Ferdulf**
*Fox and Empire* - Harry Turtledove  f  5500

**Fin, Adam**
*Something Rich and Strange* - Patricia A.
McKillip  f  3840

**Fir**
*Above the Lower Sky* - Tom Deitz  f  1469

**Fireforge, Flint**
*Kindred Spirits* - Mark Anthony  f  154
*Wanderlust* - Mary Kirchoff  f  3155

**Florida**
*Nevernever* - Will Shetterly  f  4995

**Fortune**
*Dragoncharm* - Graham Edwards  f  1749

**Fortune, Felicity**
*The Godmother* - Elizabeth Ann
Scarborough  f  4862
*The Godmother's Apprentice* - Elizabeth Ann
Scarborough  f  4863

**Foxfire**
*Silver Shadows* - Elaine Cunningham  f  1292

**Foxfire, Dalvenjah**
*Dragons on the Town* - Thorarinn
Gunnarsson  f  2463
*Make Way for Dragons!* - Thorarinn
Gunnarsson  f  2465

**Froister, Albert**
*The Magic Touch* - Jody Lynn Nye  f  4171

**Gali**
*Mall, Mayhem and Magic* - Holly Lisle  f  3485

**Galweigh, Kait**
*Diplomacy of Wolves* - Holly Lisle  f  3481

**Gargoyle, Gary**
*Geis of the Gargoyle* - Piers Anthony  f  172

**Garlthik**
*The Longing Ring* - Christopher Kubasik  f  3246

**Garroc**
*The Panther's Hoard* - Nancy Varian
Berberick  f  458
*Shadow of the Seventh Moon* - Nancy Varian
Berberick  f  459

**Garuda**
*The Iron Ring* - Lloyd Alexander  f  68

**Genevera "Gena"**
*Once a Hero* - Michael A. Stackpole  f  5203

**Ghysla**
*The Sleep of Stone* - Louise Cooper  f  1179

**Gil-Ravandry, Kelsenellenelvial**
*The Dragon's Dagger* - R.A. Salvatore  f  4797
*The Woods out Back* - R.A. Salvatore  f  4809

**Gloth**
*The Doom Brigade* - Margaret Weis  f  5708

**Goblin, Gwenny**
*The Color of Her Panties* - Piers Anthony  f  167

**Goranu**
*The Heavenward Path* - Kara Dalkey  f  1319
*Little Sister* - Kara Dalkey  f  1320

**Gorbo**
*The Marvellous Land of Snergs* - E.A. Wyke-
Smith  f  6006

**Graeboe**
*Harpy Thyme* - Piers Anthony  f  174

**Greenhands "Silveran"**
*The Qualinesti* - Paul B. Thompson  f  5455

**Grendel**
*The Tower of Beowulf* - Parke Godwin  f  2250

**Griffin**
*The Healing of Crossroads* - Nick
O'Donohoe  f  4195

**Grimi, Garni ben**
*Another Day, Another Dungeon* - Greg
Costikyan  f  1206

**Grimma**
*Diggers* - Terry Pratchett  s  4386

**Gryphon**
*Wolfhelm* - Richard A. Knaak  f  3175

**Gurder**
*Wings* - Terry Pratchett  s  4403

**Guthrum**
*The Clan of the Warlord* - Elizabeth H.
Boyer  f  604

**Halanyn, SharMarali "Shar"**
*Chrome Circle* - Mercedes Lackey  f  3277

**Half-Elvin, Tanthalas "Tanis"**
*Kindred Spirits* - Mark Anthony  f  154
*Steel and Stone* - Ellen Porath  f  4368
*Wanderlust* - Mary Kirchoff  f  3155

**Haran, Shaidar**
*Lord of Chaos* - Robert Jordan  f  2988

**Hardgreip**
*War of the Gods* - Poul Anderson  f  136

**Hardy, Dominic**
*Juniper, Gentian and Rosemary* - Pamela
Dean  f  1445

**Harpy-Goblin, Gloha**
*Harpy Thyme* - Piers Anthony  f  174

**Hasruel**
*Castle in the Air* - Diana Wynne Jones  f  2944

**Hathor**
*Horrible Humes* - Stephen Billias  f  487
*The Land of Gold* - Gillian Bradshaw  f  658
*Outcasts* - Clayton Emery  f  1815

**Hauberin**
*A Strange and Ancient Name* - Josepha
Sherman  f  4991

**Herky**
*Goblins in the Castle* - Bruce Coville  f  1218

**Highborn, Ilaron**
*Son of Darkness* - Josepha Sherman  f  4990

**Hisvet**
*Return to Lankhmar* - Fritz Leiber  *f*  3422

**Hobkin**
*Hobkin* - Peni R. Griffin  *f*  2438

**Holl**
*Higher Mythology* - Jody Lynn Nye  *f*  4170
*Mythology Abroad* - Jody Lynn Nye  *f*  4174

**Horace**
*Mouvar's Magic* - Piers Anthony  *f*  182

**Hunt, Nicholas "Pygmalion"**
*Evil Triumphant* - Michael A. Stackpole  *s*  5199

**Iff**
*Haroun and the Sea of Stories* - Salman
　Rushdie  *f*  4731

**Immugio**
*Final Sacrifice* - Clayton Emery  *f*  1814

**Indian**
*An Exaltation of Larks* - Robert Reed  *s*  4506

**Infinity**
*Unicorn Highway* - David Lee Jones  *f*  2941

**Irith**
*Taking Flight* - Lawrence Watt-Evans  *f*  5650

**Islief the Watcher**
*A Child of Elvish* - Nancy Varian Berberick  *f*  457

**Jael**
*Dagger's Edge* - Anne Logston  *f*  3508

**Jared**
*A Call to Arms* - Thomas K. Martin  *f*  3650

**Jasmine "Jas"**
*Finder's Bane* - Kate Novak  *f*  4165

**Jason**
*Master of Many Treasures* - Mary Brown  *f*  726

**Jeffrey**
*Clan of the Shape-Changers* - Robert Levy  *f*  3446

**Jewel**
*The Changeling* - Kristine Kathryn Rusch  *f*  4714

**Jinnarin**
*Voyage of the Fox Rider* - Dennis L.
　McKiernan  *f*  3837

**Jo**
*Clouds End* - Sean Stewart  *f*  5272

**Jorandel "Jorie"**
*Cold Iron* - Melisa Michaels  *f*  3886

**Juraviel, Belli'mar**
*The Demon Spirit* - R.A. Salvatore  *f*  4795

**Kakzim**
*Cinnabar Shadows* - Lynn Abbey  *f*  15

**Kalavek**
*Dragon's Domain* - Thorarinn Gunnarsson  *f*  2461

**Kang**
*The Doom Brigade* - Margaret Weis  *f*  5708

**Katrina**
*Our Lady of the Harbour* - Charles de Lint  *f*  1434

**Kaz**
*Kaz the Minotaur* - Richard A. Knaak  *f*  3172

**Kazul**
*Calling on Dragons* - Patricia C. Wrede  *f*  5974
*Dealing with Dragons* - Patricia C. Wrede  *f*  5975

**Keighvin**
*Born to Run* - Mercedes Lackey  *f*  3271

**Kelledy, Cerin**
*Ghosts of Wind and Shadow* - Charles de
　Lint  *f*  1427

**Kelledy, Meran**
*Ghosts of Wind and Shadow* - Charles de
　Lint  *f*  1427

**Kellin**
*A Tapestry of Lions* - Jennifer Roberson  *f*  4615

**Keman**
*Elvenblood* - Andre Norton  *f*  4150

**Khalid**
*Wishing Season* - Esther Friesner  *f*  2085

**Kham**
*Never Trust an Elf* - Robert N. Charrette  *f*  976

**Kharendaen**
*Dragonmage of Mystara* - Thorarinn
　Gunnarsson  *f*  2462

**Kicva**
*A Child of Elvish* - Nancy Varian Berberick  *f*  457

**Kith-Kanan**
*Firstborn* - Paul B. Thompson  *f*  5454
*The Kinslayer Wars* - Douglas Niles  *f*  4109
*The Qualinesti* - Paul B. Thompson  *f*  5455

**Korendil**
*Bedlam's Bard* - Mercedes Lackey  *f*  3269
*Knight of Ghosts and Shadows* - Mercedes
　Lackey  *f*  3285
*Summoned to Tourney* - Mercedes Lackey  *f*  3299

**Kyl**
*The Dragon Crown* - Richard A. Knaak  *f*  3168

**Laela**
*Twisted Dragon* - Kevin Stein  *f*  5251

**Lakshmi**
*My Son, the Wizard* - Christopher Stasheff  *f*  5218

**Laril**
*The Moonbane Mage* - Laurie J. Marks  *f*  3626

**Larson, Al**
*By Chaos Cursed* - Mickey Zucker Reichert  *f*  4517
*Dragonrank Master* - Mickey Zucker
　Reichert  *f*  4519
*Shadow's Realm* - Mickey Zucker Reichert  *f*  4523

**Lauri**
*Spires of Spirit* - Gael Baudino  *f*  395

**Leda**
*Nevernever* - Will Shetterly  *f*  4995

**Lee**
*Polymorph* - Scott Westerfeld  *s*  5767

**Leetah**
*Captives of the Blue Mountain* - Wendy
　Pini  *f*  4336
*The Quest Begins* - Wendy Pini  *f*  4337

**Lesseth**
*Kar Kalim* - Deborah Christian  *f*  1025

**Lightfoot**
*Into the Land of the Unicorns* - Bruce
　Coville  *f*  1219

**Liosh**
*Dragon* - Steven Brust  *f*  741

**Lithaniel, Ardagh**
*The Shattered Oath* - Josepha Sherman  *f*  4989

**Lohmatski, Gregori**
*Dancing Bears* - Fred Saberhagen  *f*  4764

**Loiosh**
*Phoenix* - Steven Brust  *f*  746

**Lomallin**
*The Shaman* - Christopher Stasheff  *f*  5223

**Loola**
*Night of the Living 'Gator!* - Richard A.
　Lupoff  *s*  3573
*Night of the Living Rat!* - Debra Doyle  *s*  1603

**Luccia**
*Vinas Solamnus* - J. Robert King  *f*  3123

**Lugh**
*Landslayer's Law* - Tom Deitz  *f*  1474

**Mab**
*I Was a Teenage Fairy* - Francesca Lia
　Block  *f*  549

**mac Ailill, Fionchadd**
*Sunshaker's War* - Tom Deitz  *f*  1477

**Maclyn of Elfhame Outremer**
*When the Bough Breaks* - Mercedes Lackey  *f*  3302

**Maelwaedd, Rhodry**
*Days of Air and Darkness* - Katharine Kerr  *f*  3067
*Days of Blood and Fire* - Katharine Kerr  *f*  3068
*The Dragon Revenant* - Katharine Kerr  *f*  3069
*A Time of Exile* - Katharine Kerr  *f*  3077

**Ma'eva**
*Storm Caller* - Carol Severance  *f*  4924

**Makepeace, Sebastian**
*The Last Wizard* - Simon Hawke  *f*  2619

**Malendor**
*Dark Divide* - Mark Acres  *f*  27

**Malystryx**
*The Day of the Tempest* - Jean Rabe  *f*  4457
*Spirit of the Wind* - Chris Pierson  *f*  4326

**Mama**
*India's Story* - Kathlyn S. Starbuck  *s*  5208

**Margawt "The Morigu"**
*Morigu: The Dead* - Mark C. Perry  *f*  4284

**Marge**
*Horrors of the Dancing Gods* - Jack L.
　Chalker  *f*  955

**Masklin**
*Truckers* - Terry Pratchett  *s*  4402
*Wings* - Terry Pratchett  *s*  4403

**Master**
*Mythology Abroad* - Jody Lynn Nye  *f*  4174

**McBride, Michael**
*The Flight of Michael McBride* - Midori
　Snyder  *f*  5151

**McCogg, Gus "Aengus Mac Og"**
*The Friendship Song* - Nancy Springer  *f*  5179

**McDaris, Samantha "Sammi"**
*Elvendude* - Mark Shepherd  *f*  4980

**McMickey, Mickey**
*Dragonslayer's Return* - R.A. Salvatore  *f*  4798

**Melanchthon "7332"**
*The Iron Dragon's Daughter* - Michael
　Swanwick  *f*  5371

**Melior, Rohannan**
*The Cup of Morning Shadows* - Rosemary
　Edghill  *f*  1747
*The Sword of Maiden's Tears* - Rosemary
　Edghill  *f*  1748

**Mennym, Appleby**
*The Mennyms* - Sylvia Waugh  *f*  5654
*Mennyms Under Siege* - Sylvia Waugh  *f*  5656

**Mennym, Pilbeam**
*Mennyms Under Siege* - Sylvia Waugh  *f*  5656

**Mennym, Soobie**
*Mennyms Alive* - Sylvia Waugh  *f*  5655

**Mennym, Tulip**
*The Mennyms* - Sylvia Waugh  *f*  5654
*Mennyms Alive* - Sylvia Waugh  *f*  5655

**Mennym, Vinetta**
*The Mennyms* - Sylvia Waugh  *f*  5654

**Mer-Child**
*The Mer-Child: A Legend for Children and Other
　Adults* - Robin Morgan  *f*  4008

**Merwoman, Mela**
*The Color of Her Panties* - Piers Anthony  *f*  167

**Mharyon**
*Dragon Moon* - Chris Claremont  *f*  1040

**Minerva**
*Ye Gods!* - Tom Holt  *f*  2753

**Mist**
*Shadow Dance* - Anne Logston  *f*  3513

**Mnrogar**
*The Dragon, the Earl, and the Troll* - Gordon R. Dickson  *f*  1534

**Mollockle, Thud**
*Hearts and Armor* - Ron Miller  *f*  3903
*Palaces and Prisons* - Ron Miller  *f*  3904
*Silk and Steel* - Ron Miller  *f*  3905

**Molok**
*Kaz the Minotaur* - Richard A. Knaak  *f*  3172

**Monkey**
*Dragon Cauldron* - Laurence Yep  *f*  6024
*Dragon War* - Laurence Yep  *f*  6025

**Moonbrow, Aljan "Jan"**
*The Son of Summer Stars* - Meredith Ann Pierce  *f*  4319

**Mooner**
*Elsewhere* - Will Shetterly  *f*  4993

**Moql'nkkn "Moql/Saaski"**
*The Moorchild* - Eloise Jarvis McGraw  *f*  3816

**Morgis, Duke**
*Wolfhelm* - Richard A. Knaak  *f*  3175

**Morpheus**
*The Sandman: Book of Dreams* - Neil Gaiman  *f*  2105

**Morrolan**
*Dragon* - Steven Brust  *f*  741

**Morwyne the Powershaper**
*Darkthunder's Way* - Tom Deitz  *f*  1470

**Mother Night**
*Godmother Night* - Rachel Pollack  *f*  4358

**Mumbo**
*The Adventures of King Midas* - Lynne Reid Banks  *f*  329

**Naitachal**
*Fortress of Frost and Fire* - Mercedes Lackey  *f*  3282

**Narlh**
*The Oathbound Wizard* - Christopher Stasheff  *f*  5219

**Nastrus**
*The Unicorn War* - John Lee  *f*  3401

**Natil**
*Maze of Moonlight* - Gael Baudino  *f*  393

**Nepe/Flach**
*Phaze Doubt* - Piers Anthony  *f*  184

**Nia**
*The Deer's Cry: A Book of the Keltiad* - Patricia Kennealy-Morrison  *f*  3060

**Nimesin, Kymil**
*Elfshadow* - Elaine Cunningham  *f*  1288

**Niviene**
*Merlin's Harp* - Anne Eliot Crompton  *f*  1270

**Norton**
*Steel Rose* - Kara Dalkey  *f*  1321

**Novari**
*The Warrior Returns* - Allan Cole  *f*  1109

**Nym**
*A Prince Among Men* - Robert N. Charrette  *f*  977

**O'Fallon, Michael Timothy**
*The Reluctant Sorcerer* - Simon Hawke  *f*  2622

**Ogress, Okra**
*The Color of Her Panties* - Piers Anthony  *f*  167

**Ohmsford, Par**
*The Talismans of Shannara* - Terry Brooks  *f*  717

**Ohmsford, Wren**
*The Elf Queen of Shannara* - Terry Brooks  *f*  711

**Old Man of the Mountain**
*A Calculated Magic* - Robert Weinberg  *f*  5694

**Old Ric**
*The Shadow Eater* - Adam Lee  *f*  3386

**Oxyle**
*Mirror of Destiny* - Andre Norton  *f*  4159

**Ozzie**
*The Other Sinbad* - Craig Shaw Gardner  *f*  2130

**Paithan**
*Elven Star* - Margaret Weis  *f*  5712

**Pan**
*Cloven Hooves* - Megan Lindholm  *f*  3470

**Pellia**
*The Unicorn Solution* - John Lee  *f*  3400

**Percinet**
*Child of Faerie, Child of Earth* - Josepha Sherman  *f*  4985

**Petrus**
*Spiritride* - Mark Shepherd  *f*  4981

**Phanes**
*Making Love* - Melanie Tem  *h*  5422

**Pie 'oh' Pah**
*Imajica* - Clive Barker  *h*  343

**Polyta**
*Under the Healing Sign* - Nick O'Donohoe  *f*  4198

**Rabble**
*When the Gods Are Silent* - Jane M. Lindskold  *f*  3477

**Raganda**
*The Gates of Noon* - Michael Scott Rohan  *f*  4661

**Ralph**
*Steel Rose* - Kara Dalkey  *f*  1321

**Rasputin**
*Shadows on the Hill* - Jackie Cassada  *f*  935

**Rathan, Linden**
*The Last Dragonlord* - Joanne Bertin  *f*  470

**Red Mare**
*A Ride on the Red Mare's Back* - Ursula K. Le Guin  *f*  3382

**Reddy, John**
*A King Beneath the Mountain* - Robert N. Charrette  *f*  973
*A Knight Among Knaves* - Robert N. Charrette  *f*  974

**Regis**
*The Legacy* - R.A. Salvatore  *f*  4801

**Reindeer**
*The Woman Who Loved Reindeer* - Meredith Ann Pierce  *f*  4320

**Riatha**
*The Eye of the Hunter* - Dennis L. McKiernan  *f*  3833

**Rictus**
*The Thief of Always* - Clive Barker  *h*  347

**Rikus**
*The Verdant Passage* - Troy Denning  *f*  1487

**Riversong**
*The Warrior and the Witch* - Carl Miller  *f*  3893

**Rizalli, Arvin "Harek"**
*User Unfriendly* - Vivian Vande Velde  *f*  5558

**Robin**
*Street Magic* - Michael Reaves  *f*  4497

**Roc, Roxanne**
*Roc and a Hard Place* - Piers Anthony  *f*  187

**Rool**
*Shadow Moon* - George Lucas  *f*  3540

**Ruskettle, Olive**
*Song of the Saurials* - Kate Novak  *f*  4167

**Ryan-Turriy, Adlayra**
*Dancer's Rise* - Jo Clayton  *f*  1064

**Sadira**
*The Verdant Passage* - Troy Denning  *f*  1487

**Santa Claus**
*Santa Steps Out: A Fairy Tale for Grownups* - Robert Devereaux  *h*  1506

**Scathach**
*The Scathach and the Maeve's Daughter* - Mary Alexander Walker  *f*  5618

**Scope**
*Dragoncharm* - Graham Edwards  *f*  1749

**Scott**
*House of the Sun* - Nigel Findley  *s*  1936

**Selendrile**
*Dragon's Bait* - Vivian Vande Velde  *f*  5556

**Seraphina**
*A Wish and a Dream* - Ingrid Weaver  *f*  5658

**Shadow**
*Dagger's Edge* - Anne Logston  *f*  3508
*Shadow* - Anne Logston  *f*  3512
*Shadow Dance* - Anne Logston  *f*  3513
*Shadow Hunt* - Anne Logston  *f*  3514
*Shadowlight* - Jackie Hyman  *f*  2819

**Shamandar, Serrin**
*Streets of Blood* - Carl Sargent  *f*  4821

**Shea, Ernie "Lucky Duck"**
*The Callahan Touch* - Spider Robinson  *f*  4637

**Sherwood, John**
*Dancing Bears* - Fred Saberhagen  *f*  4764

**Shimmer**
*Dragon Cauldron* - Laurence Yep  *f*  6024
*Dragon War* - Laurence Yep  *f*  6025

**Shulana**
*Dragonspawn* - Mark Acres  *f*  28

**Sianna**
*Lady of Avalon* - Marion Zimmer Bradley  *f*  640

**Sigfrid**
*The Dragons of the Rhine* - Diana L. Paxson  *f*  4264
*The Wolf and the Raven* - Diana L. Paxson  *f*  4270

**Sigfrith**
*Rhinegold* - Stephan Grundy  *f*  2454

**Sigyn**
*The Tower of Beowulf* - Parke Godwin  *f*  2250

**Silbakor**
*Dragon Death* - Gael Baudino  *f*  390
*Duel of Dragons* - Gael Baudino  *f*  391

**Silkweb Empress**
*Bronze Mirror* - Jeanne Larsen  *f*  3338

**Sinjin**
*Some Enchanted Evening* - Alice Alfonsi  *f*  73

**Siobahn**
*Luthien's Gamble* - R.A. Salvatore  *f*  4802

**Sithas**
*Firstborn* - Paul B. Thompson  *f*  5454
*The Kinslayer Wars* - Douglas Niles  *f*  4109

**Skandrakae, Tadrith "Tad"**
*The Silver Gryphon* - Mercedes Lackey  *f*  3295

**Skandranon**
*The Black Gryphon* - Mercedes Lackey  f  3270
*The White Gryphon* - Mercedes Lackey  f  3303

**Skywise**
*The Quest Begins* - Wendy Pini  f  4337

**Sorak**
*The Outcast* - Simon Hawke  f  2621
*The Seeker* - Simon Hawke  f  2624

**Speckarin**
*Kirins: The Flight of the Ain* - James D.
   Priest  f  4433
*Kirins: The Secret of the Hanging Stones* - James D.
   Priest  f  4434
*Kirins: The Spell of No'an* - James D.
   Priest  f  4435

**Steffan**
*Iron Dragons: Mountains and Madness* - Rose
   Estes  f  1839

**Stheno**
*Bhagavati* - Kara Dalkey  f  1316

**Summerson, Natil**
*Strands of Sunlight* - Gael Baudino  f  396

**Susan**
*Clan of the Shape-Changers* - Robert Levy  f  3446
*The Spawn of Loki* - Jason Henderson  f  2658

**Tamerlane, Rebecca "Michael Kerr"**
*Afterimage* - Kristine Kathryn Rusch  f  4709

**Tanis**
*Dragons of Summer Flame* - Margaret Weis  f  5711
*The Second Generation* - Margaret Weis  f  5724

**Tek**
*The Son of Summer Stars* - Meredith Ann
   Pierce  f  4319

**Telery of Limerick**
*Gnome Man's Land* - Esther Friesner  f  2075
*Harpy High* - Esther Friesner  f  2076

**Teyle**
*Conan the Formidable* - Steve Perry  f  4293

**Theodoulos**
*Cross and Crescent* - Susan Shwartz  f  5014

**Thistledown, Tipperton "Tip"**
*Into the Fire* - Dennis L. McKiernan  f  3834
*Into the Forge* - Dennis L. McKiernan  f  3835

**Thorvin**
*Fade to Black* - Nyx Smith  s  5134

**Tiamat**
*Jeremy Thatcher, Dragon Hatcher* - Bruce
   Coville  f  1221

**Tick-Tick**
*Finder* - Emma Bull  f  769

**Tikki "Striper"**
*Striper Assassin* - Nyx Smith  f  5135

**Tinkerbell**
*Hook* - Terry Brooks  f  713

**Toq**
*Warriorwards* - Dafydd ab Hugh  f  11

**Tor**
*Shadows on the Hill* - Jackie Cassada  f  935

**Touriq**
*The Unicorn Sonata* - Peter S. Beagle  f  412

**Troll**
*Angels & Visitations: A Miscellany* - Neil
   Gaiman  f  2101
*A Ride on the Red Mare's Back* - Ursula K. Le
   Guin  f  3382

**Tsang-jieh**
*Bronze Mirror* - Jeanne Larsen  f  3338

**Tuiereann, Aedham "Adam"**
*Elvendude* - Mark Shepherd  f  4980

**Ulahane**
*The Shaman* - Christopher Stasheff  f  5223

**Unicorn**
*Blue Moon Rising* - Simon R. Green  f  2362
*Last Mountain* - Robert C. Fleet  f  1946

**Vallus**
*The Radiant Dragon* - Elaine Cunningham  f  1291

**Vanderdecker**
*The Marvellous Land of Snergs* - E.A. Wyke-
   Smith  f  6006

**Vanessa**
*Maze of Moonlight* - Gael Baudino  f  393

**Varden**
*Spires of Spirit* - Gael Baudino  f  395

**Vicia-Heinox**
*The Faithful Traitor* - Robert Don Hughes  f  2809

**Voyvodan**
*Fortress of Frost and Fire* - Mercedes
   Lackey  f  3282

**Water**
*The Book of Water* - Marjorie Bradley
   Kellogg  f  3045

**Winnowill**
*Captives of the Blue Mountain* - Wendy
   Pini  f  4336

**Winters, Theodore "TK" Karlington**
*Strands of Sunlight* - Gael Baudino  f  396

**Wok**
*The Pixilated Peeress* - L. Sprague de
   Camp  f  1416

**Wurm**
*The Wizardry Consulted* - Rick Cook  f  1161

**Wynter**
*Red Magic* - Jean Rabe  f  4458

**X-ray, Foxtrot "Fox"**
*Chrome Circle* - Mercedes Lackey  f  3277

**Yocote**
*The Sage* - Christopher Stasheff  f  5221

**Zephyr**
*Fool on the Hill* - Matt Ruff  f  4707

**Zinixo**
*The Living God* - Dave Duncan  f  1682
*The Stricken Field* - Dave Duncan  f  1688
*Upland Outlaws* - Dave Duncan  f  1690

# NATURALIST

**Cottington, Angelica**
*Lady Cottington's Pressed Fairy Book* - Terry
   Jones  f  2981

**Cowperthwait, Cosmo**
*The Steampunk Trilogy* - Paul Di Filippo  s  1518

**Flattery, Tristam**
*Sea Without a Shore* - Sean Russell  f  4743
*World Without End* - Sean Russell  f  4744

# NEIGHBOR

**Boxer, Hugh**
*Sweet Heart* - Peter James  h  2875

**Forrest, Pete**
*Beyond the Veil of Stars* - Robert Reed  s  4503

# NOBLEMAN

**Abivard**
*The Stolen Throne* - Harry Turtledove  f  5510

**Alain**
*Prince of Dogs* - Kate Elliott  f  1775

**Andry**
*Sunrunner's Fire* - Melanie Rawn  f  4493

**Ankoku**
*Dragon's Winter* - Elizabeth A. Lynn  f  3578

**Arbuthnot, Farquhar**
*Strong Spirits* - Elisa DeCarlo  f  1451

**Artos**
*Black Horses for the King* - Anne
   McCaffrey  f  3720

**Aryton, Antony**
*Whispers in the Dark* - Jonathan Aycliffe  h  283

**Asan**
*Requiem for Anthi* - Jay D. Blakeney  s  517

**Atani, Karadur**
*Dragon's Winter* - Elizabeth A. Lynn  f  3578

**Atreus**
*Faces of Deception* - Troy Denning  f  1485

**Bassarab**
*One Foot in the Grave* - Wm. Mark
   Simmons  f  5062

**Bennett**
*A Knight Among Knaves* - Robert N.
   Charrette  f  974

**Berengar**
*The Shadow Gate* - Margaret Ball  f  317

**Briam**
*Changing Fate* - Elisabeth Waters  f  5629

**Bright**
*Gawain and Lady Green* - Anne Eliot
   Crompton  f  1269

**Brock, Dire-Lord**
*The Goda War* - Jay D. Blakeney  s  516

**Caidin**
*Tower of Doom* - Mark Anthony  h  155

**Caitin, Bedyr**
*Wrath of Ashar* - Angus Wells  f  5742

**Camron**
*The Barbed Coil* - J.V. Jones  f  2957

**Carruthers, Ronald "Ronnie"**
*Hunting Party* - Elizabeth Moon  s  3968

**Casaubon**
*The Architecture of Desire* - Mary Gentle  f  2195
*Rats and Gargoyles* - Mary Gentle  f  2196

**Charles**
*Daughter of the Night* - Elaine Bergstrom  h  463

**Chee, Diren**
*House of Moons* - K.D. Wentworth  s  5752

**Coal, Hugo**
*The Grotesque* - Patrick McGrath  h  3814

**Connelly, Misha**
*Phoenix Cafe* - Gwyneth Jones  s  2954

**Crowley**
*Lady Cottington's Pressed Fairy Book* - Terry
   Jones  f  2981

**Cullinane, Jason**
*The Road Home* - Joel Rosenberg  f  4674

**Dahven**
*One Land, One Duke* - Ru Emerson  f  1809

**Damfels, Sylvan Bon**
*Grass* - Sheri S. Tepper  s  5431

**Dan, Issachar**
*Wind From a Foreign Sky* - Katya Reimann  f  4528

**Dart**
*The Wooden Sword* - Lynn Abbey  f  18

**Dash**
*Shards of a Broken Crown* - Raymond E. Feist  *f*  1912

**D'Asperge, Timaeus**
*Another Day, Another Dungeon* - Greg Costikyan  *f*  1206
*One Quest, Hold the Dragons* - Greg Costikyan  *f*  1208

**dav Aidan, Kenzie "Catfoot"**
*Broken Blade* - Ann Marston  *f*  3634

**dav Medroch, Cullin**
*Kingmaker's Sword* - Ann Marston  *f*  3635

**de Barenton, Lucien**
*The Moon and the Sun* - Vonda N. McIntyre  *f*  3822

**de Carabas**
*Neverwhere* - Neil Gaiman  *f*  2104

**de Clifford, Robert**
*The Dragon and the Gnarly King* - Gordon R. Dickson  *f*  1529

**de Garsenc, Blaise**
*A Song for Arbonne* - Guy Gavriel Kay  *f*  3017

**de la von Zaguar, Lamar**
*The Mark of the Moderately Vicious Vampire* - Lionel Fenn  *h*  1920

**de Richlieu**
*The Devil Rides Out* - Dennis Wheatley  *h*  5773

**de Talair, Bertran**
*A Song for Arbonne* - Guy Gavriel Kay  *f*  3017

**d'Eath, Edward**
*Men at Arms* - Terry Pratchett  *f*  4396

**Deathstalker, Owen**
*Deathstalker Honor* - Simon R. Green  *s*  2364
*Deathstalker Rebellion* - Simon R. Green  *s*  2365
*Deathstalker War* - Simon R. Green  *s*  2366

**deLacey, William**
*Lady of the Forest* - Jennifer Roberson  *f*  4609

**delAurvre, Christopher**
*Maze of Moonlight* - Gael Baudino  *f*  393

**Denton, Eric**
*Black Body* - H.C. Turk  *h*  5488

**Dinaos**
*The Belly of the Wolf* - R.A. MacAvoy  *f*  3580

**DiThorn, Bram**
*The Seventh Sentinel* - Mary Kirchoff  *f*  3154

**do'Verrada, Alejandro**
*The Golden Key* - Melanie Rawn  *f*  4486

**Dracula**
*The Mammoth Book of Dracula* - Stephen Jones  *h*  2972

**Duone, Morgan**
*Emerald House Rising* - Peg Kerr  *f*  3080

**Duzon**
*Touched by the Gods* - Lawrence Watt-Evans  *f*  5651

**Eckert, Jim/Gorbash**
*The Dragon and the Djinn* - Gordon R. Dickson  *f*  1528
*The Dragon and the Gnarly King* - Gordon R. Dickson  *f*  1529
*The Dragon at War* - Gordon R. Dickson  *f*  1530
*The Dragon in Lyonesse* - Gordon R. Dickson  *f*  1531
*The Dragon Knight* - Gordon R. Dickson  *f*  1532
*The Dragon on the Border* - Gordon R. Dickson  *f*  1533
*The Dragon, the Earl, and the Troll* - Gordon R. Dickson  *f*  1534

**Ehara**
*The Spellsong War* - L.E. Modesitt Jr.  *f*  3939

**Erelvar**
*A Call to Arms* - Thomas K. Martin  *f*  3650
*A Two-Edged Sword* - Thomas K. Martin  *f*  3653

**Ewine, Zarel**
*Arena* - William R. Forstchen  *f*  1977

**Felmet**
*Wyrd Sisters* - Terry Pratchett  *f*  4405

**Fiolon**
*Lady of the Trillium* - Marion Zimmer Bradley  *f*  641

**Firdun**
*The Warding of Witch World* - Andre Norton  *f*  4163

**Flutirr**
*Flute Song Magic* - Andrea Shettle  *f*  4996

**Gallowglass, Geoffrey**
*M'Lady Witch* - Christopher Stasheff  *f*  5217
*Quicksilver's Knight* - Christopher Stasheff  *f*  5220

**Galoran**
*Count Scar* - C. Dale Brittain  *f*  702

**Garon**
*A Man Betrayed* - J.V. Jones  *f*  2958

**Geoffrey**
*Blood and Roses* - Sharon Bainbridge  *h*  292

**Gift**
*The Resistance* - Kristine Kathryn Rusch  *f*  4727

**Gilliam**
*Hunter's Death* - Michelle West  *f*  5758
*Hunter's Oath* - Michelle West  *f*  5759

**Godwinesson, Harold**
*Lord of Sunset* - Parke Godwin  *f*  2246

**Gordon, George**
*Wall, Stone, Craft* - Walter Jon Williams  *h*  5842

**Gordon, Winston**
*Mina* - Marie Kiraly  *h*  3151

**Graham, James**
*The Ebon Mask* - Richard Lee Byers  *h*  797

**Grijalva, Sario**
*The Golden Key* - Melanie Rawn  *f*  4486

**Gustiano, Rinaldo**
*The Innamorati* - Midori Snyder  *f*  5152

**Gwalchavad**
*Grail* - Stephen R. Lawhead  *f*  3355

**Halarek, Karne**
*Brander's Book* - C.J. Mills  *s*  3909
*Egil's Book* - C.J. Mills  *s*  3910
*Kit's Book* - C.J. Mills  *s*  3911
*Zjhanne's Book* - C.J. Mills  *s*  3912

**Harlan, Brander**
*Brander's Book* - C.J. Mills  *s*  3909

**Hong**
*Interesting Times* - Terry Pratchett  *f*  4392

**Jaeme**
*Elfwood* - Rose Estes  *f*  1837

**Jaxom**
*All the Weyrs of Pern* - Anne McCaffrey  *s*  3719

**Jayal**
*The Forging of the Shadows* - Oliver Johnson  *f*  2924
*Nations of the Night* - Oliver Johnson  *f*  2925

**Kent, Averil**
*Sea Without a Shore* - Sean Russell  *f*  4743

**Kermovan**
*The Forge in the Forest* - Michael Scott Rohan  *f*  4660

**Kronis**
*Sons of the Titans* - Patrick H. Adkins  *f*  36

**Lanart-Hastur, Mikhail**
*Exile's Song* - Marion Zimmer Bradley  *s*  632
*The Shadow Matrix* - Marion Zimmer Bradley  *s*  645

**Lanfranc, Guy**
*Kingdom of the Grail* - A.A. Attanasio  *f*  269

**Larath, Deveren**
*King's Man and Thief* - Christie Golden  *f*  2253

**Laszlo, Count Dracula**
*The Secret Life of Laszlo, Count Dracula* - Roderick Anscombe  *h*  152

**Lecouveurs, Alain**
*In Hot Blood* - Petru Popescu  *h*  4367

**Lidjun, Dun**
*Hour of the Octopus* - Joel Rosenberg  *f*  4673

**Llanfrechfa, Geraint**
*Streets of Blood* - Carl Sargent  *f*  4821

**Locklear**
*Krondor, the Betrayal* - Raymond E. Feist  *f*  1905

**Lohmatski, Gregori**
*Dancing Bears* - Fred Saberhagen  *f*  4764

**Lugard**
*The Hunger and Ecstasy of Vampires* - Brian Stableford  *h*  5192

**MacAuley, Alasdair**
*The Last Highlander* - Claire Cross  *f*  1271

**Maijstral, Drake**
*Rock of Ages* - Walter Jon Williams  *s*  5840

**Mandrol**
*The Janus Mask* - Richard A. Knaak  *f*  3171

**McCann, Rorin**
*Caledon of the Mists* - Deborah Turner Harris  *f*  2560

**Melior, Rohannan**
*The Cup of Morning Shadows* - Rosemary Edghill  *f*  1747

**NaBlaine, Ruairi**
*Bridge of Valor* - Anne Lesley Groell  *f*  2452

**Narrion**
*Summer King, Winter Fool* - Lisa Goldstein  *f*  2263

**Orc**
*Red Orc's Rage* - Philip Jose Farmer  *f*  1873

**Orien**
*On Fortune's Wheel* - Cynthia Voigt  *f*  5579

**Ottokar**
*The Duke of Sumava* - Sara J. Wrench  *f*  5983

**Ourousov, Prince**
*The Princess and the Dragon* - Roberto Pazzi  *f*  4272

**Paladyr**
*The Endless Knot* - Stephen R. Lawhead  *f*  3354

**Pel of House Yendi**
*Five Hundred Years After* - Steven Brust  *f*  742

**Penward, Darren**
*Carnosaur* - Harry Adam Knight  *s*  3191

**Pjerin**
*Sing the Four Quarters* - Tanya Huff  *f*  2799

**Prosper**
*The Shining Company* - Rosemary Sutcliff  *f*  5359

**Quordane, Holis**
*Shadow of the Crown* - Craig Mills  *f*  3914

**Ranulf**
*Changing Fate* - Elisabeth Waters  *f*  5629

**Rap**
*The Living God* - Dave Duncan  *f*  1682

*The Stricken Field* - Dave Duncan  f  1688

**Ravis**
*The Barbed Coil* - J.V. Jones  f  2957

**ReAth**
*Shaper's Legacy* - Sheila Finch  s  1933

**Robert "Robin Hood" of Locksley**
*Lady of the Forest* - Jennifer Roberson  f  4609

**Rosvenir, Collan**
*The Mageborn Traitor* - Melanie Rawn  f  4488

**Sadir**
*Canby's Legion* - Bill Baldwin  s  308

**Sahr, Leon**
*Fire Angels* - Jane Routley  f  4685

**Sakhalin, Anatoly**
*The Law of Becoming* - Kate Elliott  s  1774

**Santos, Ramon**
*Iceman* - Cynthia Felice  s  1913

**Sessine, Alandre VII**
*Feersum Endjinn* - Iain M. Banks  s  325

**Sethiyan, Hattim**
*The Usurper* - Angus Wells  f  5739

**Shinji, Matsumura**
*The Yngling in Yamato* - John Dalmas  s  1329

**Shonto**
*Gatherer of Clouds* - Sean Russell  f  4741

**Skogskra, Haakon**
*The Gnome's Engine* - Teresa Edgerton  f  1742

**sorMeklan, Driskolt "Dart"**
*Beneath the Web* - Lynn Abbey  f  12

**Stalker, Martin**
*A Tremor in the Bitter Earth* - Katya
    Reimann  f  4527

**Stark, Eddard**
*A Game of Thrones* - George R.R. Martin  f  3645

**Steadford, Sir Harry**
*The Meddlesome Ghost* - Sheila Rosalynd
    Allen  f  84

**Strelsau, Mathias**
*Silk and Steel* - Ron Miller  f  3905

**Tarrant, Gerald**
*Black Sun Rising* - C.S. Friedman  f  2056
*When True Night Falls* - C.S. Friedman  f  2060

**Thann, Danilo "Dan"**
*Elfshadow* - Elaine Cunningham  f  1288

**Tolivar**
*Sky Trillium* - Julian May  f  3700

**Tremane**
*Storm Rising* - Mercedes Lackey  f  3297

**Urghart, Ian**
*The Time of Madness* - Thomas K. Martin  f  3652

**Valdoria kva Skolia, Kelricson Garlin**
*The Last Hawk* - Catherine Asaro  s  219

**Valemar**
*Summer King, Winter Fool* - Lisa Goldstein  f  2263

**Valiarde, Nicholas "Donatien"**
*The Death of the Necromancer* - Martha
    Wells  f  5749

**Vallaniri, Daner**
*The Raven Ring* - Patricia C. Wrede  f  5978

**Villette, Louis**
*The Judas Cross* - Charles Sheffield  h  4960

**Viroslav, Alexander**
*The Kiss* - Kathryn Reines  h  4529

**Volmar**
*Castle of Deception* - Mercedes Lackey  f  3275

---

**von Amerningen, Lutz**
*Cloud Castles* - Michael Scott Rohan  f  4659

**von Darkmoor, Erik**
*Rise of a Merchant Prince* - Raymond E.
    Feist  f  1909

**von Glower, Friedrich**
*The Beast Within: A Gabriel Knight Mystery* - Jane
    Jensen  h  2895

**von Hessel**
*Escape From Loki* - Philip Jose Farmer  f  1870

**von Schuss, Nicholas**
*Kit's Book* - C.J. Mills  s  3911

**Vorkosigan, Aral**
*Barrayar* - Lois McMaster Bujold  s  756

**Vorkosigan, Miles**
*Borders of Infinity* - Lois McMaster Bujold  s  757
*Cetaganda* - Lois McMaster Bujold  s  758
*Komarr* - Lois McMaster Bujold  s  760
*Memory* - Lois McMaster Bujold  s  761
*Mirror Dance* - Lois McMaster Bujold  s  762
*The Vor Game* - Lois McMaster Bujold  s  764

**Vorpatril, Ivan**
*Cetaganda* - Lois McMaster Bujold  s  758
*Memory* - Lois McMaster Bujold  s  761

**Xar**
*The Seventh Gate* - Margaret Weis  f  5727

**Young, Pavel**
*Field of Dishonor* - David Weber  s  5670

**Youngman, Cai**
*The Dragon's Boy* - Jane Yolen  f  6030

**zu Blas und Fiersing, Dalain "Wisp"**
*An Exchange of Gifts* - Anne McCaffrey  f  3731

## NOBLEWOMAN

**Acila**
*Changing Fate* - Elisabeth Waters  f  5629

**Agramonte, Maran**
*The Demon King* - Chris Bunch  f  770
*The Seer King* - Chris Bunch  f  771

**Aiko**
*The Dragonstone* - Dennis L. McKiernan  f  3832

**al Jorddyn, Kerridwen**
*Kingmaker's Sword* - Ann Marston  f  3635

**al Keylan, Brynda**
*Broken Blade* - Ann Marston  f  3634

**Albain, Elandra**
*Reign of Shadows* - Deborah Chester  f  1009

**Alice**
*The Prince and the Pilgrim* - Mary Stewart  f  5270

**Altunin, Roberta**
*Rock of Ages* - Walter Jon Williams  s  5840

**Amalayna**
*Chains of Darkness, Chains of Light* - Michelle
    Sagara  f  4781

**Amalia, Lady**
*The Interior Life* - Katherine Blake  f  515

**Aradia**
*A Heroine of the World* - Tanith Lee  f  3412

**Arianna**
*The Resistance* - Kristine Kathryn Rusch  f  4727

**Arin**
*The Dragonstone* - Dennis L. McKiernan  f  3832

**Aryton, Antonia**
*Whispers in the Dark* - Jonathan Aycliffe  h  283

**Astiar, Meliara "Mel"**
*Court Duel* - Sherwood Smith  f  5137

---

**Avignon, Kitten "Our Lady of Roses"**
*Mage Heart* - Jane Routley  f  4686

**Bannering, Charlan "Arlin"**
*King of the Dead* - R.A. MacAvoy  f  3581

**Bathori, Elizabeth**
*Daughter of the Night* - Elaine Bergstrom  h  463

**Bathory, Elizabeth**
*Blood Countess* - Andrei Codrescu  h  1094

**Beauty**
*Beauty* - Sheri S. Tepper  f  5428

**Catelyn**
*A Game of Thrones* - George R.R. Martin  f  3645

**Ciara**
*Ciara's Song* - Andre Norton  f  4146

**da Brabant, Huegenet**
*Blood Roses* - Chelsea Quinn Yarbro  h  6012

**Damarr, Amala**
*The Mace of Souls* - Bruce Fergusson  f  1925

**dar Dero, Halleyne**
*Wrath of the Princes* - Holly Lisle  f  3490

**de Brus, Marjory**
*Quest for a Maid* - Frances Mary Hendry  f  2662

**de Gris, Daria**
*The Changeling Prince* - Vivian Vande
    Velde  f  5554

**de la Crois, Marie-Josephe**
*The Moon and the Sun* - Vonda N.
    McIntyre  f  3822

**de Marktos, Cecelia**
*Hunting Party* - Elizabeth Moon  s  3968
*Sporting Chance* - Elizabeth Moon  s  3974
*Winning Colors* - Elizabeth Moon  s  3976

**de Remy, Mireille**
*The Eight* - Katherine Neville  f  4092

**di'Marano, Diora**
*The Broken Crown* - Michelle West  f  5757

**du Pres, Josette**
*Angelique's Descent* - Lara Parker  h  4246

**Duone, Kestrienne**
*Emerald House Rising* - Peg Kerr  f  3080

**Eckert, Angie**
*The Dragon and the Gnarly King* - Gordon R.
    Dickson  f  1529

**Eleighanaran "Leigh"**
*Shadows on the Hill* - Jackie Cassada  f  935

**Erzsebet**
*The Secret Weavers: Stories of the Fantastic by Latin
    American Women* - Marjorie Agosin  f  43

**FitzWalter, Marion "Marion of Ravenskeep"**
*Lady of the Forest* - Jennifer Roberson  f  4609

**Francine**
*Lord Conrad's Lady* - Leo Frankowski  s  2046

**Gallowglass, Cordelia**
*M'Lady Witch* - Christopher Stasheff  f  5217

**Graciosa**
*Child of Faerie, Child of Earth* - Josepha
    Sherman  f  4985

**Halarek, Kathryn "Kit" Magdalena Alysha**
*Kit's Book* - C.J. Mills  s  3911

**Harlan, Kathryn "Kit"**
*Zjhanne's Book* - C.J. Mills  s  3912

**Harrington, Honor**
*Field of Dishonor* - David Weber  s  5670
*Flag in Exile* - David Weber  s  5671
*Honor Among Enemies* - David Weber  s  5673
*The Honor of the Queen* - David Weber  s  5674
*In Enemy Hands* - David Weber  s  5675
*On Basilisk Station* - David Weber  s  5679

*The Short Victorious War* - David Weber   *s*   5681

**Helen**
*Helen's Passage* - Diana M. Concannon   *f*   1129
*The Princess and the Dragon* - Roberto
   Pazzi   *f*   4272

**Hutsenreiter, Skirlet**
*Night Lamp* - Jack Vance   *s*   5548

**Indes, Richenza**
*The Wild Hunt: Vengeance Moon* - Jocelin
   Foxe   *f*   2031

**Jaeme**
*Twisted Dragon* - Kevin Stein   *f*   5251

**Javere "Javerri"**
*Ladylord* - Sasha Miller   *f*   3906

**Kalena**
*Wolf Justice* - Doranna Durgin   *f*   1706

**Katrina**
*War* - Simon Hawke   *f*   2625

**Kayli**
*Firewalk* - Anne Logston   *f*   3509

**Kessallia**
*The Prince of Ill Luck* - Susan Dexter   *f*   1512

**Kiarda**
*Spirit Fox* - Mickey Zucker Reichert   *f*   4524

**Lisa**
*Demon Knight* - Ken Hood   *f*   2760

**Liwellan, Sarra Ambrai**
*The Mageborn Traitor* - Melanie Rawn   *f*   4488

**Lohmatski, Natalya**
*Dancing Bears* - Fred Saberhagen   *f*   4764

**Lysia**
*Hammer and Anvil* - Harry Turtledove   *f*   5503

**Marian**
*The Outlaws of Sherwood* - Robin
   McKinley   *f*   3846

**Matilde**
*A Strange and Ancient Name* - Josepha
   Sherman   *f*   4991

**Melania**
*The Eagle and the Sword* - A.A. Attanasio   *f*   267

**Melliandra "Melli"**
*The Baker's Boy* - J.V. Jones   *f*   2956
*A Man Betrayed* - J.V. Jones   *f*   2958

**Morgiana**
*The Dagger and the Cross: A Novel of the Crusades* -
   Judith Tarr   *f*   5393

**Morianna, Maigrey**
*King's Sacrifice* - Margaret Weis   *s*   5717
*The Lost King* - Margaret Weis   *s*   5720

**Myat**
*An Enemy Reborn* - Michael A. Stackpole   *f*   5197

**Naismith, Cordelia**
*Barrayar* - Lois McMaster Bujold   *s*   756

**Nia**
*The Deer's Cry: A Book of the Keltiad* - Patricia
   Kennealy-Morrison   *f*   3060

**Nordbo, Tyra**
*Inconstant Star* - Poul Anderson   *s*   129

**Pentacoste**
*Better in the Dark* - Chelsea Quinn Yarbro   *h*   6011

**Penward, Jan**
*Carnosaur* - Harry Adam Knight   *s*   3191

**Percy, Anne**
*The Spiral Dance* - R. Garcia y Robertson   *f*   2121

**Raine of the Three Waters**
*A Breach in the Watershed* - Douglas Niles   *f*   4105
*Darkenheight* - Douglas Niles   *f*   4107

*War of the Three Waters* - Douglas Niles   *f*   4110

**Ramkin, Sybil**
*Guards! Guards!* - Terry Pratchett   *f*   4390

**Rangegonda**
*Better in the Dark* - Chelsea Quinn Yarbro   *h*   6011

**Renya, Jacinta**
*Iceman* - Cynthia Felice   *s*   1913

**Rhiana**
*In the Rift* - Marion Zimmer Bradley   *f*   639

**St. Du Lac, Lynn**
*The Lost History of Redwyn* - William Jay   *f*   2883

**Scatha**
*The Endless Knot* - Stephen R. Lawhead   *f*   3354

**Soerensen, Terese "Tess"**
*Jaran* - Kate Elliott   *s*   1772

**Soolis, Yveena**
*The Thirteenth Majestral* - Hayford Peirce   *s*   4277

**Steiner, Katrina**
*Prince of Havoc* - Michael A. Stackpole   *s*   5204

**Sto-Helit, Susan**
*Hogfather* - Terry Pratchett   *f*   4391

**Trovagh**
*Ciara's Song* - Andre Norton   *f*   4146

**Valaise, Ailena**
*Kingdom of the Grail* - A.A. Attanasio   *f*   269

**Vantara**
*The Fugitive Worlds* - Bob Shaw   *s*   4942

**ViKay**
*Hour of the Octopus* - Joel Rosenberg   *f*   4673

**Viroslav, Maria**
*The Kiss* - Kathryn Reines   *h*   4529

**vo Derrivalle, Eliste**
*Illusion* - Paula Volsky   *f*   5582

**Voerster, Eliana Ehrengraf**
*Glory* - Alfred Coppel   *s*   1182

**Volkova, Ekaterina Alexandrova**
*Glory's War* - Alfred Coppel   *s*   1184

**von Alte, Erde**
*The Book of Earth* - Marjorie Bradley
   Kellogg   *f*   3044

**Vorsoisson, Ekaterin "Kat"**
*Komarr* - Lois McMaster Bujold   *s*   760

**Yvette of Grintz**
*The Pixilated Peeress* - L. Sprague de
   Camp   *f*   1416

**Zaula**
*Requiem for Anthi* - Jay D. Blakeney   *s*   517

**Ziemann, Mia**
*Holy Fire* - Bruce Sterling   *s*   5259

**Zillabar**
*A Covenant of Justice* - David Gerrold   *s*   2207

## NURSE

**Armstrong, Vera**
*Werewolf* - Peter Rubie   *h*   4702

**Barrett, Kitty**
*Night Music* - Sheila Bristow Garner   *h*   2147

**Boardman, Gillian**
*Stranger in a Strange Land* - Robert A.
   Heinlein   *s*   2649

**Brigit**
*The World I Made for Her* - Thomas
   Moran   *h*   3996

**Chapel, Christine**
*Crossroad* - Barbara Hambly   *s*   2501

**Charlie**
*Chains of Light* - Quentin Thomas   *s*   5449

**Coughlin, Molly**
*Dry Skull Dreams* - Michael Green   *h*   2344

**Damico, Mary**
*Dream Baby* - Bruce McAllister   *s*   3706

**Everson, Kelly**
*Harmful Intent* - Robin Cook   *s*   1164

**Fellowes, Edith**
*The Ugly Little Boy* - Isaac Asimov   *s*   250

**Halloran, Myrna**
*Flying in Place* - Susan Palwick   *h*   4240

**Kelly, Dorothea**
*Systems* - W.T. Quick   *s*   4452

**Kuttner, Dayne**
*Sympathy for the Devil* - Holly Lisle   *f*   3488

**MacDougall, Clarissa**
*Gray Lensman* - Edward E. Smith   *s*   5117

**Matheson, Honor**
*Fatal Outcome* - Patricia Wallace   *h*   5622

**McCulley, Kitty**
*The Healer's War* - Elizabeth Ann
   Scarborough   *f*   4865

**Nuala**
*The World I Made for Her* - Thomas
   Moran   *h*   3996

**Prawdzik, Ed**
*Night Sounds* - Warner Lee   *h*   3415

**Sannazarro, Sally**
*Treasure Box* - Orson Scott Card   *h*   898

**Shikome, Lily**
*The Twelfth Child* - Raymond Van Over   *h*   5538

**Waller, Enid**
*Fiends* - John Farris   *h*   1884

## OCCULTIST

**Alice, Ti**
*Tempter* - Nancy A. Collins   *h*   1125

**Callow, John**
*Evil Intent* - Bernard Taylor   *h*   5400

**Mander, Otto**
*The Burning* - Graham Masterton   *h*   3672

**Mandrax**
*Master of Lies* - Graham Masterton   *h*   3676

**Miller, Quintus**
*Walkers* - Graham Masterton   *h*   3681

**Raeburn, Francis**
*The Lodge of the Lynx* - Katherine Kurtz   *f*   3259

**Talbot, David**
*The Tale of the Body Thief* - Anne Rice   *h*   4576

## OFFICE WORKER

**Bobby**
*Steam* - Jay B. Laws   *h*   3361

**Carpenter, Paul**
*Hot Sky at Midnight* - Robert Silverberg   *s*   5032

**Craig, Alice**
*Down River* - Stephen Gallagher   *h*   2110

**Frankl, Victor**
*The Suiting* - Kelley Wilde   *h*   5803

**Harrison, Sally**
*The Eyes of the Beast* - Steve Harris   *h*   2565

**Kennedy, Jill**
*Insatiable* - David Dvorkin   *h*   1707

**Mick**
*Steam* - Jay B. Laws   h   3361

**Roode, Tanya**
*Lethal Delivery* - J.G. Maxon   h   3695

**Sciascia, Francesca**
*Catacomb* - Andrew Laurance   h   3347

**Thompson, Patty**
*Seed of Evil* - Edmund Plante   h   4340

**Toplin**
*Toplin* - Michael McDowell   h   3807

## OIL INDUSTRY WORKER

**McFarland, Henry Lee**
*Petrogypsies* - Rory Harper   s   2549

**Miller, Doc**
*Petrogypsies* - Rory Harper   s   2549

## ORGANIZED CRIME FIGURE

**Bey, Friedlander**
*The Exile Kiss* - George Alec Effinger   s   1750

**Capone, Al**
*Timeshare: Second Time Around* - Joshua
   Dann   s   1345

**Catalano, Serena**
*Protektor* - Charles Platt   s   4342

**Gaetano, Rafaelo**
*Empire Builders* - Ben Bova   s   584

**Jabba the Hutt**
*Tales From Jabba's Palace* - Kevin J.
   Anderson   s   114

**Kyler, Vaughan**
*Blood on the Water* - P.N. Elrod   h   1791

**Paco, Frank**
*Bloodlist* - P.N. Elrod   h   1792

**Pruet, Maxine**
*Phule's Paradise* - Robert Asprin   s   261

**Raven**
*Snow Crash* - Neal Stephenson   s   5254

**Scanwell, Jane**
*Empire Builders* - Ben Bova   s   584

**Stoogeone, Anthony**
*Something Out There* - Ronald Kelly   h   3056

**Tatsuo, Tamenaga**
*The Art of Arrow Cutting* - Stephen
   Dedman   f   1462

**Xisor**
*Shadows of the Empire* - Steve Perry   s   4299

## ORPHAN

**a-Lagan, Meredydd**
*The Meri* - Maya Kaathryn Bohnhoff   f   561

**Acorna**
*Acorna's Quest* - Anne McCaffrey   s   3718

**Blessing, Arthur**
*The Forever King* - Molly Cochran   f   1092

**Brita**
*Conan the Rogue* - John Maddox Roberts   f   4617

**Buddy**
*Land O'Goshen* - Charles McNair   s   3855

**Cahanagh, Athyn "Blackmantle"**
*Blackmantle: A Triumph* - Patricia Kennealy-
   Morrison   f   3059

**Calliope**
*Ecstasia* - Francesca Lia Block   f   547

**Chance, David**
*Brain Child* - George Turner   s   5491

**Concord, Tappuah "Tappy"**
*The Caterpillar's Question* - Piers Anthony   f   164

**Destree**
*Storms of Victory* - Andre Norton   f   4162

**Dillon, Ronny**
*Soulsmith* - Tom Deitz   f   1475

**Dufrenoy, Michael**
*Paris in the Twentieth Century* - Jules
   Verne   s   5568

**Francie**
*In the Heart of the Valley of Love* - Cynthia
   Kadohata   s   2997

**Gael, Dorothy "Dotty"**
*Was* - Geoff Ryman   f   4758

**Gwynn, Angharad "the Rowan"**
*The Rowan* - Anne McCaffrey   s   3747

**Halfnight, Andrew**
*First Blast of the Trumpet Against the Monstrous
   Regiment of Women* - Eric McCormack   h   3779

**Harris, Nora**
*Grandma's Little Darling* - Stephen R.
   George   h   2201

**Harth, Beren "Brat" SanDyllin**
*Wheel of Dreams* - Salinda Tyson   f   5529

**Hasmara, Faan "Fa"**
*The Magic Wars* - Jo Clayton   f   1068
*Wildfire* - Jo Clayton   f   1073

**Hawkins, Rosalind "Rose"**
*The Fire Rose* - Mercedes Lackey   f   3280

**Henry of Veldran**
*Henry's Gift: The Magic Eye* - David
   Worsick   f   5972

**I**
*A City in Winter* - Mark Helprin   f   2653

**Jenkins, Tom**
*Spacer Dreams* - Larry Segriff   s   4911

**Jenna**
*Sister Light, Sister Dark* - Jane Yolen   f   6039
*White Jenna* - Jane Yolen   f   6041

**Keven**
*The Road West* - Gary Wright   f   5984

**Kim**
*Mairelon the Magician* - Patricia C. Wrede   f   5977

**Kiriel**
*The Broken Crown* - Michelle West   f   5757

**Kirk**
*Elfwood* - Rose Estes   f   1837

**Kristinsson, Garth**
*Hidden Fires* - Katharine Eliska Kimbriel   s   3117

**Lace, Invictus Ovidius "I.O."**
*A Dozen Tough Jobs* - Howard Waldrop   f   5612

**Laitha "Gian Avur"**
*Ghost King* - David Gemmell   f   2188

**Leda**
*Nevernever* - Will Shetterly   f   4995

**Merlin**
*Merlin* - Jane Yolen   f   6035

**Metcalf, Charlotte**
*Whispers in the Dark* - Jonathan Aycliffe   h   283

**Montoneros, Juan Ramirez**
*Catacomb* - Andrew Laurance   h   3347

**Ned**
*Hope of Earth* - Piers Anthony   s   175
*Spring-Heeled Jack* - Philip Pullman   f   4447

**Neihart, Fletcher Robert**
*Finity's End* - C.J. Cherryh   s   988

**Nevsky, Peter**
*Peter Nevsky and the True Story of the Russian Moon
   Landing* - John Calvin Batchelor   s   388

**Nimue**
*The Winter King* - Bernard Cornwell   f   1191

**Number Ten Ox**
*The Chronicles of Master Li and Number Ten Ox* -
   Barry Hughart   f   2803

**Nuria**
*Well Wished* - Franny Billingsley   f   489

**Nyara**
*Winds of Change* - Mercedes Lackey   f   3304

**O'Meara, Beverly**
*In the Cube* - David Alexander Smith   s   5109

**Pinch "Janol"**
*King Pinch* - David Cook   f   1146

**Piyolss, Faan Korispais**
*Wild Magic* - Jo Clayton   f   1072

**Rae**
*The War in the Waste* - Felicity Savage   f   4851

**Rafe**
*Ecstasia* - Francesca Lia Block   f   547

**Rybak, Nadya**
*Nadya: The Wolf Chronicles* - Pat Murphy   f   4052

**Salk, Job Napoleon**
*Brother to Dragons* - Charles Sheffield   s   4949

**Scillia**
*The One-Armed Queen* - Jane Yolen   f   6037

**Shana**
*The Elvenbane* - Andre Norton   f   4149

**Skylda "Skyla"**
*The Clan of the Warlord* - Elizabeth H.
   Boyer   f   604

**Smith, Valentine Michael**
*Stranger in a Strange Land* - Robert A.
   Heinlein   s   2649

**Steven**
*Hunter's Oath* - Michelle West   f   5759

**Summer**
*Pigs Don't Fly* - Mary Brown   f   727

**Thuro "Uther Pendragon"**
*Ghost King* - David Gemmell   f   2188

**Touch**
*The Midnight Horse* - Sid Fleischman   f   1948

**Tragen, Aaron**
*Beowulf's Children* - Larry Niven   s   4116

**Tywi**
*The Dark Shore* - Adam Lee   f   3385

**William**
*Goblins in the Castle* - Bruce Coville   f   1218

**Wren**
*Wren to the Rescue* - Sherwood Smith   f   5142
*Wren's Quest* - Sherwood Smith   f   5143
*Wren's War* - Sherwood Smith   f   5144

**Xylina**
*If I Pay Thee Not in Gold* - Piers Anthony   f   176

**Yatima**
*Diaspora* - Greg Egan   s   1759

## OUTCAST

**Arity "Ari"**
*Delta City* - Felicity Savage   f   4849

**Chang, Deanna**
*Scorpion Shards* - Neal Shusterman   s   5013

## Character Description Index — Outlaw / Paralegal / Paranormal Investigator / Parent

**Cole, Dillon**
*Scorpion Shards* - Neal Shusterman   s   5013

**Duin, Mael**
*The Voyage of Mael Duin's Curragh* - Patricia Aakhus   f   2

**Hidalgo, Lourdes**
*Scorpion Shards* - Neal Shusterman   s   5013

**Indigo**
*Aisling* - Louise Cooper   f   1172
*Avatar* - Louise Cooper   f   1173
*Infanta* - Louise Cooper   f   1176
*Revenant* - Louise Cooper   f   1178
*Troika* - Louise Cooper   f   1181

**Jofre**
*Brother to Shadows* - Andre Norton   s   4142

**Kerrigan, Joshua "Josh"**
*Putting Up Roots* - Charles Sheffield   s   4964

**McCall, Dante**
*Songs of Chaos* - S.N. Lewitt   s   3452

**Starling, Ugly**
*Far Harbor* - Melisa C. Michaels   s   3888

**Steck**
*Commitment Hour* - James Alan Gardner   s   2134

**Tomeas**
*Beyond the Door* - Gary L. Blackwood   s   510

**Zigmunn**
*Brotherhood of the Stars* - Kirby Greene   s   2414

## OUTLAW

**Boren, Troy**
*Blindfold* - Kevin J. Anderson   s   101

**Cripplemaker, General**
*Farewell Horizontal* - K.W. Jeter   s   2911

**Falushe, Viole**
*The Demon Princes: Volume One* - Jack Vance   s   5544

**Fowke, William G.**
*A Journal of the Flood Year* - David Ely   s   1805

**Hood, Robin**
*The Fantastic Adventures of Robin Hood* - Martin H. Greenberg   f   2389
*The Oathbound Wizard* - Christopher Stasheff   f   5219
*The Outlaws of Sherwood* - Robin McKinley   f   3846
*Robin and the King* - Parke Godwin   f   2247
*The Sheriff of Nottingham* - Richard Kluger   f   3165

**Jane "Quicksilver"**
*Quicksilver's Knight* - Christopher Stasheff   f   5220

**Kid Zero**
*Ghost Dancers* - Brian Craig   s   1238

**Kryn**
*The Hands of Lyr* - Andre Norton   f   4154

**Larque, Lens**
*The Demon Princes: Volume Two* - Jack Vance   s   5545

**Longdirk, Tobias**
*Demon Knight* - Ken Hood   f   2760

**mac Sliabhin, Caith**
*Faery in Shadow* - C.J. Cherryh   f   987

**Paladyr**
*The Endless Knot* - Stephen R. Lawhead   f   3354

**Robert "Robin Hood" of Locksley**
*Lady of the Forest* - Jennifer Roberson   f   4609

**Tar'krim, Stereth**
*Guilt-Edged Ivory* - Doris Egan   s   1756
*Two-Bit Heroes* - Doris Egan   s   1757

**Verner, Samuel**
*Choose Your Enemies Carefully* - Robert N. Charrette   s   971

## PARALEGAL

**Fortune, Alison Crandall**
*Devil's Gate* - Elizabeth Ergas   h   1833

## PARANORMAL INVESTIGATOR

**Ash, David**
*The Ghosts of Sleath* - James Herbert   h   2668
*Haunted* - James Herbert   h   2669

**Bannister, Frank**
*The Frighteners* - Michael Jahn   h   2856

**Barrett, Lionel**
*Hell House* - Richard Matheson   h   3685

**Collins, Amanda**
*Deadly Friend* - Keith Ferrario   h   1926

**Crow, Titus**
*The Burrowers Beneath* - Brian Lumley   h   3548
*Titus Crow, Volume One* - Brian Lumley   h   3566
*Titus Crow, Volume Three* - Brian Lumley   h   3567
*Titus Crow, Volume Two* - Brian Lumley   h   3568
*The Transition of Titus Crow* - Brian Lumley   h   3569

**Curtiss, David**
*Julian's House* - Judith Hawkes   h   2630

**Curtiss, Sally**
*Julian's House* - Judith Hawkes   h   2630

**Cutter, Sam**
*The Burning Man* - Michael Hammond   h   2530

**de Marigny, Henri Laurent**
*Titus Crow, Volume One* - Brian Lumley   h   3566
*Titus Crow, Volume Three* - Brian Lumley   h   3567
*Titus Crow, Volume Two* - Brian Lumley   h   3568
*The Transition of Titus Crow* - Brian Lumley   h   3569

**Forbes, Melanie**
*The Link* - Andrew Laurance   h   3348
*The Premonition* - Andrew Laurance   h   3349
*The Unborn* - Andrew Laurance   h   3350

**Hale, Ebeneezer**
*The Messenger* - Donald Tyson   h   5528

**Henning, J. Benjamin**
*Something's Alive on the Titanic* - Robert Serling   h   4915

**Jourdemayne, Truth**
*Ghostlight* - Marion Zimmer Bradley   f   634
*Gravelight* - Marion Zimmer Bradley   f   636
*Witchlight* - Marion Zimmer Bradley   f   655

**Leffing, Lucius**
*The Adventures of Lucius Leffing* - Joseph Payne Brennan   h   670

**MacLaren, Colin**
*Heartlight* - Marion Zimmer Bradley   f   637

**Monroe, Wade**
*The Possession* - Ronald Kelly   h   3055

**Rathel, Amanda**
*Black Body* - H.C. Turk   h   5488

**Stratford, Earl**
*The Committee* - Raymond Buckland   h   752

**Thorne, Peter**
*Death Channels* - Robert E. Vardeman   h   5562

**Trask, Julian**
*Absolute Power* - Ray Russell   h   4738

**Tregarde, Diana**
*Burning Water* - Mercedes Lackey   h   3272

## PARENT

**Addams, Morticia**
*Addams Family Values* - Todd Strasser   f   5324

**Ajani, Korinna "Kori" Kassemi**
*The March Hare Network* - Jack L. Chalker   s   957

**Allaird, Clarence Engels "Clancy"**
*Arrow From Earth* - F.M. Busby   s   782

**Anderson, Ted**
*Darkness* - John Saul   h   4840

**Ann "Annai"**
*Shame of Man* - Piers Anthony   s   188

**Anwara**
*The Moorchild* - Eloise Jarvis McGraw   f   3816

**Artemisia**
*Split Heirs* - Lawrence Watt-Evans   f   5649

**Aurian**
*Harp of Winds* - Maggie Furey   f   2097

**Barris, Michael Albert**
*The Immortals* - Tracy Hickman   s   2681

**Bauer, Libby**
*Requiem* - Clifford Mohr   h   3950

**Beauchamp, Elena**
*Mockingbird* - Sean Stewart   f   5273

**Beynac, Dagny**
*The Stars Are Also Fire* - Poul Anderson   s   134

**Binewski, Olympia**
*Geek Love* - Katherine Dunn   h   1697

**Blackburn, Thorne**
*Ghostlight* - Marion Zimmer Bradley   f   634

**Bowe, Austin**
*Tripoint* - C.J. Cherryh   s   1003

**Bradley, Richard**
*The Hollowing* - Robert Holdstock   f   2738

**Brand, Anne-Marie**
*Secret Passages* - Paul Preuss   s   4420

**Brook**
*Clouds End* - Sean Stewart   f   5272

**Buccari, Sharl**
*In the Shadow of the Moon* - Scott G. Gier   s   2224

**Butler, Mark**
*After Sundown* - Randall Boyll   h   609

**Calliope**
*Primavera* - Francesca Lia Block   f   551

**Caraval, Julio**
*Spirits of the Ordinary* - Kathleen Alcala   f   52

**Carpenter, Mary Anne**
*Guardian* - John Saul   h   4841

**Chandler, Karen**
*Solomon's Knife* - Victor Koman   s   3200

**Clayborne, Laura**
*Mine* - Robert R. McCammon   h   3756

**Cleg, Horace**
*Spider* - Patrick McGrath   h   3815

**Cohen, Lauren "Laurie"**
*Godmother Night* - Rachel Pollack   f   4358

**Cortez, Rosita "Rose" Carmelita**
*Timemaster* - Robert L. Forward   s   1992

**Crowell, Eve**
*Eden's Eyes* - Sean Costello   h   1205

**Crystal**
*Troll-Quest* - Rose Estes   f   1841

**Cuthberton-Jones**
*Angela and Diabola* - Lynne Reid Banks   f   330

**Dad**
*The Key to the Indian* - Lynne Reid Banks   f   331

*Songs of Enchantment* - Ben Okri  *f*  4208

**Danilov, Sonya**
*These Fallen Angels* - Wendy Haley  *h*  2492

**Deeds, A.J.**
*Meeting the Minotaur* - Carol Dawson  *f*  1409

**Dryhope, Kate "Kittock"**
*A History Maker* - Alasdair Gray  *s*  2338

**Edith of Shaftsbury**
*Lord of Sunset* - Parke Godwin  *f*  2246

**Eilan**
*The Forest House* - Marion Zimmer Bradley  *f*  633

**Ellington, Lucas**
*The Kill Riff* - David J. Schow  *h*  4887

**Ember**
*Isle of Woman* - Piers Anthony  *f*  178

**Farthing, Jacob**
*Harm's Way* - Colin Greenland  *s*  2416

**Felice**
*User Unfriendly* - Vivian Vande Velde  *f*  5558

**Figueroa, Poppy**
*Kalifornia* - Marc Laidlaw  *s*  3311

**Gilmour, Sarah**
*Nighteyes* - Garfield Reeves-Stevens  *s*  4510

**Girat, Phaed**
*Raising the Stones* - Sheri S. Tepper  *s*  5434

**Han, Liu**
*Worldwar: Striking the Balance* - Harry Turtledove  *s*  5516

**Harrington, Allison**
*Echoes of Honor* - David Weber  *s*  5669

**Hawkins, Marie**
*Tripoint* - C.J. Cherryh  *s*  1003

**Herb-Woman**
*Strange Deliverance* - Mary Brown  *s*  728

**Hightower, Alex**
*Possession* - Peter James  *h*  2873

**Holiday, Ben**
*The Tangle Box* - Terry Brooks  *f*  718
*Witches' Brew* - Terry Brooks  *f*  719

**Hu "Hugh"**
*Shame of Man* - Piers Anthony  *s*  188

**Hudder, Cyrus**
*Core* - Paul Preuss  *s*  4416

**Julian**
*The Children of Men* - P.D. James  *f*  2870

**Khadaji, Emile**
*The Albino Knife* - Steve Perry  *s*  4288

**Kiakra, Darryl**
*Minerva Wakes* - Holly Lisle  *f*  3487

**Kiakra, Minerva**
*Minerva Wakes* - Holly Lisle  *f*  3487

**Killeen**
*Sailing Bright Eternity* - Gregory Benford  *s*  449

**Kirk, George Samuel**
*Best Destiny* - Diane Carey  *s*  900

**Knight, Dean**
*The Monastery* - J.N. Williamson  *h*  5856

**Koussevitzky, Clifford "Cliff"**
*Captain Jack Zodiac* - Michael Kandel  *f*  3009

**Laine, Bonnie**
*Nightscape* - Stephen R. George  *h*  2203

**Lang, Jacqueline "Jaqe"**
*Godmother Night* - Rachel Pollack  *f*  4358

**Lawford, Arthur**
*The Return* - Walter de la Mare  *h*  1424

**Lawrence, Sally**
*The Offspring* - Kenneth McKenney  *h*  3826

**Lilith**
*Imago* - Octavia E. Butler  *s*  791

**Mackenson, Tom**
*Boy's Life* - Robert R. McCammon  *h*  3754

**Madeleine**
*Phantom* - Susan Kay  *h*  3020

**Martin, Paul**
*Shaman Woods* - Morgan Fields  *h*  1931

**Matthews, Susan**
*Dancing on Air* - Nancy Kress  *s*  3240

**McCray, Abbey**
*Leap Point* - Kay Kenyon  *s*  3063

**Medlocke, Stephen**
*Brethren* - Shawn Ryan  *h*  4754

**Mennym, Vinetta**
*The Mennyms* - Sylvia Waugh  *f*  5654

**Merelan**
*The Masterharper of Pern* - Anne McCaffrey  *s*  3739

**Michaels, William "Billy"**
*The M.D.: A Horror Story* - Thomas M. Disch  *h*  1561

**Miranda**
*Caliban's Hour* - Tad Williams  *f*  5826

**Moon, Miranda**
*The Trinity Vector* - Steve Perry  *s*  4302

**Mother**
*Don't Forget Your Spacesuit, Dear* - Jody Lynn Nye  *s*  4169

**Ness**
*Shadow's Daughter* - Shirley Meier  *f*  3871

**Night, Noel**
*The Monastery* - J.N. Williamson  *h*  5856

**Ogre**
*The Ogre Downstairs* - Diana Wynne Jones  *f*  2949

**Pardu**
*Heart Readers* - Kristine Kathryn Rusch  *f*  4718

**Quijance, Natasha**
*Red Planet Run* - Dana Stabenow  *s*  5187

**Rasa**
*The Call of Earth* - Orson Scott Card  *s*  882
*The Memory of Earth* - Orson Scott Card  *s*  894

**Raven, Jeff**
*Lyon's Pride* - Anne McCaffrey  *s*  3738

**Reilly, Rosemary**
*Son of Rosemary* - Ira Levin  *h*  3445

**Reynar III**
*Silver Princess, Golden Knight* - Sharon Green  *f*  2359

**Ringess, Mallory**
*The Wild* - David Zindell  *s*  6086

**Rissedotte, Faia**
*Mind of the Magic* - Holly Lisle  *f*  3486

**Rivakonneva "Riva"**
*Mathemagics* - Margaret Ball  *f*  316

**Rodriguez**
*Senora Rodriguez and Other Worlds* - Martha Cerda  *f*  950

**Savage, Lucy**
*Where Does Kissing End?* - Kate Pullinger  *h*  4445

**Scott, Michael**
*The Black School* - J.N. Williamson  *h*  5851

**Semele, Alice**
*Dominion* - Bentley Little  *h*  3492

**Serege, Lujan Ansellic**
*Echoes of Issel* - Diann Thornley  *s*  5466

**Sinclair, Katherine**
*Troll-Quest* - Rose Estes  *f*  1841
*Troll-Taken* - Rose Estes  *f*  1842

**Sparhawk**
*The Hidden City* - David Eddings  *f*  1733

**Stewart, Anne**
*Jupiter's Daughter* - Tom Hyman  *s*  2820

**Sudek, Tina Miner**
*The Amulet* - A.R. Morlan  *h*  4009

**Sue**
*The Interior Life* - Katherine Blake  *f*  515

**Talbot, Annie**
*Her Monster* - Jeff Collignon  *h*  1115

**Tallstaff, Iutha**
*Shadow's End* - Sheri S. Tepper  *s*  5435

**Teppish, Vladimir X. III**
*The Vampire's Beautiful Daughter* - S.P. Somtow  *h*  5161

**Tompkins, Ben**
*Blood of the Children* - Alan Rodgers  *h*  4645

**Torfinn, Karine**
*One Mind's Eye* - Kathy Tyers  *s*  5525

**Trayne, Robert**
*Whipping Boy* - John Byrne  *h*  800

**Ttan**
*Devil in the Sky* - Greg Cox  *s*  1226

**Tyler, Erica**
*Midsummer* - Matthew J. Costello  *h*  1200

**Valaise, Ailena**
*Kingdom of the Grail* - A.A. Attanasio  *f*  269

**Valentine, John Barrymore**
*The Golden Globe* - John Varley  *s*  5565

**Volemak**
*The Memory of Earth* - Orson Scott Card  *s*  894

**Wade, Tamara**
*Bad Blood* - D.A. Fowler  *h*  2021

**Walker, Janet**
*Playmates* - Abigail McDaniels  *h*  3784

**Walker, Mark**
*Playmates* - Abigail McDaniels  *h*  3784

**Walthers, Samantha "Sam"**
*Parliament of Blood* - Scott Ciencin  *h*  1031
*The Vampire Odyssey* - Scott Ciencin  *h*  1032
*The Wildlings* - Scott Ciencin  *h*  1034

**White, Diane**
*Hell-Storm* - James A. Moore  *h*  3990

**Widdick, Robert**
*Retro Lives* - Lee Grimes  *s*  2446

**Willson, Matthew**
*Dark Reunion* - Stephen R. George  *h*  2198

**Windclan, Raincloud**
*Daughter of Elysium* - Joan Slonczewski  *s*  5091

**Woody**
*My Stepfather Shrank!* - Barbara Dillon  *s*  1558

**Zimmerman, Debra**
*Panda Ray* - Michael Kandel  *s*  3011

**Zorba the Hutt**
*Zorba the Hutt's Revenge* - Paul Davids  *s*  1394

## PAROLE OFFICER

**Ortega, Felix**
*Out of Body* - Thomas Baum  *h*  397

## PASSENGER

**Cleo**
*Checkmate* - Eric T. Baker   *s*   297

**Cline, Tara**
*Redshift Rendezvous* - John E. Stith   *s*   5305

**Stripe**
*A Maze of Stars* - John Brunner   *s*   734

**Volar**
*A Maze of Stars* - John Brunner   *s*   734

## PATIENT

**Adda**
*Flux* - Stephen Baxter   *s*   399

**Andrews, Laura**
*Quarantine* - Greg Egan   *s*   1762

**Billie**
*Aliens: Earth Hive* - Steve Perry   *s*   4289

**Canary, Sarah**
*Sarah Canary* - Karen Joy Fowler   *f*   2028

**Cleg, Dennis "Spider"**
*Spider* - Patrick McGrath   *h*   3815

**Engel, Emily**
*Zod Wallop* - William Browning Spencer   *h*   5169

**Evans, Katy**
*The Homecoming* - Kimberly Rangel   *h*   4471

**Fraser, Mike**
*Dark Silence* - Rick Hautala   *h*   2606

**Griffith, Wally**
*Strange Invasion* - Michael Kandel   *s*   3012

**Hatcher, Agnes**
*Bad Karma* - Andrew Harper   *h*   2548

**Hewlitt**
*Final Diagnosis* - James White   *s*   5777

**Horsfall, Arne**
*Fiends* - John Farris   *h*   1884

**Johnson, Laura**
*Door Number Three* - Patrick O'Leary   *s*   4210

**Kevin**
*The Midnight Club* - Christopher Pike   *h*   4329

**Lassiter, Charles**
*Hopeship* - Simon Lang   *s*   3315

**Lockheart, Karen**
*Eden's Eyes* - Sean Costello   *h*   1205

**Owens, Tiffany "Tif"**
*Resurrection* - Katharine Kerr   *s*   3075

**Pawluk, Ilonka**
*The Midnight Club* - Christopher Pike   *h*   4329

**Serege, Lujan Ansellic**
*Dominion's Reach* - Diann Thornley   *s*   5465

**Story, Raymond**
*Zod Wallop* - William Browning Spencer   *h*   5169

**Voisard, B.J.**
*Sarah Canary* - Karen Joy Fowler   *f*   2028

## PATRIOT

**Vivo, Dionisio**
*Senor Vivo and the Coca Lord* - Louis de
   Bernieres   *f*   1411

## PAWNBROKER

**Steiner, Bill**
*Rose Madder* - Stephen King   *h*   3139

## PEDDLER

**Crocken**
*The Wizard's Shadow* - Susan Dexter   *f*   1514

**Gunn**
*Primavera* - Francesca Lia Block   *f*   551

## PHARMACIST

**Aiken, Robert**
*The Mysterium* - Eric McCormack   *h*   3780

**Kole, Polly**
*Flesh* - Gus Weill   *h*   5685

**Small, Elmo**
*The Devil's Cradle* - Kate Stewart   *h*   5269

## PHILANTHROPIST

**Cornish, Francis**
*The Cornish Trilogy* - Robertson Davies   *f*   1397

**Dore, Michael**
*Lunar Justice* - Charles L. Harness   *s*   2545

**Flitheimer, Samuel**
*Dr. Dimension* - John DeChancie   *s*   1456

**Maule, Matthew**
*A Matter of Taste* - Fred Saberhagen   *h*   4770

## PHILOSOPHER

**Caraval, Julio**
*Spirits of the Ordinary* - Kathleen Alcala   *f*   52

**Dogbrick**
*The Dark Shore* - Adam Lee   *f*   3385

**Johnson, Mark "Hobbes"**
*Mosaic* - Jeri Taylor   *s*   5403

**Malu**
*Children of the Mind* - Orson Scott Card   *s*   883

**Tradescant, John**
*Sexing the Cherry* - Jeanette Winterson   *f*   5927

## PHOTOGRAPHER

**Brady, Mathew B.**
*The Gallery of His Dreams* - Kristine Kathryn
   Rusch   *f*   4717

**Brand, Anne-Marie**
*Secret Passages* - Paul Preuss   *s*   4420

**Brenner, Robin**
*The Feeding* - Leigh Clark   *h*   1051

**Burke, Peter**
*Cold at Heart* - Brian Hopkins   *h*   2768

**Cadigan, Risha "Rusty"**
*Love Bite* - Sherry Gottlieb   *h*   2288

**Castle, Charles**
*Photographing Fairies* - Steve Szilagyi   *f*   5379

**Chase, Adam**
*Nocturnas* - Shawn Ryan   *h*   4755

**Cotto, Grant**
*Strange Angels* - Kathe Koja   *h*   3197

**Fender, Duncan**
*Suckers* - Anne Billson   *h*   490

**Freeman, Claire**
*Candle Night* - Phil Rickman   *h*   4586

**Gray, Doreen**
*Fire in the Blood* - P.N. Elrod   *h*   1796

**Hazel**
*Belladonna* - Michael Stewart   *h*   5271

**Hitchcock, Frank**
*The School* - T.M. Wright   *h*   5994

**Landon, Harry**
*I'll Be Watching You* - Samuel M. Key   *h*   3094

**Law, Guilford**
*Darwinia* - Robert Charles Wilson   *s*   5906

**Lewis, Dafydd**
*Naomi's Room* - Jonathan Aycliffe   *h*   281

**Lewis, Leonard**
*Nightlight* - Michael Cadnum   *h*   813

**Lucas, Annabel "Nan"**
*My Soul to Keep* - Judith Hawkes   *h*   2631

**Magistrale, Michelangelo "Mage"**
*The Art of Arrow Cutting* - Stephen
   Dedman   *f*   1462

**Marlow, Lee**
*Double Edge* - Dennis Etchison   *h*   1846

**McClure, Katy**
*The Dwelling* - Tom Elliott   *h*   1776

**McGann, Jim**
*From a Whisper to a Scream* - Samuel M.
   Key   *h*   3093

**Pike, Eli**
*The Rim-World Legacy and Beyond* - Frank A.
   Javor   *s*   2882

**Poe, Jared**
*The Lazarus Heart* - Poppy Z. Brite   *h*   696

**Popman, Walker**
*Passive Intruder* - Michael Upchurch   *h*   5530

**Preston, Natalie**
*Carrion Comfort* - Dan Simmons   *h*   5049

**Rabjohns, Will**
*Sacrament* - Clive Barker   *h*   345

**Ted**
*Thor* - Wayne Smith   *h*   5146

**Williams, Stanley**
*The Undine* - Michael O'Rourke   *h*   4224

**Zivic, Leland**
*From the Teeth of Angels* - Jonathan Carroll   *h*   918

## PHOTOJOURNALIST

**Carson, Lily**
*Someplace to Be Flying* - Charles de Lint   *f*   1435

**McKeane, Fletcher**
*In the Shadows of the Moonglade* - Riley St.
   James   *h*   5186

**Nash, Scott**
*Lagoon* - Alison Drake   *h*   1625

**Pike, Eli**
*The Ice Beast* - Frank A. Javor   *s*   2881

## PILOT

**Amaya, Anya**
*Glory's People* - Alfred Coppel   *s*   1183

**Antilles, Wedge**
*Rogue Squadron* - Michael A. Stackpole   *s*   5205

**Arbok**
*Prison Ship* - Martin Caidin   *s*   828

**Ashata/Maya**
*The Queen's Squadron* - R.M. Meluch   *s*   3874

**Bass, Rocket Man**
*Voyage to the Red Planet* - Terry Bisson   *s*   508

**Baxter, Carl**
*The Homecoming* - Barry B. Longyear   *s*   3521

**Beautiful Maria**
*Angel Station* - Walter Jon Williams   s   5833

**Bird, Morris**
*Heavy Time* - C.J. Cherryh   s   995

**Blackstone, Rex**
*Primary Inversion* - Catherine Asaro   s   220

**Blaze, Chastity**
*Saturn Rukh* - Robert L. Forward   s   1991

**Bloodyluck, Kithri**
*Jaydium* - Deborah Wheeler   s   5774

**Boggs, W.J.**
*Labyrinth of Night* - Allen Steele   s   5244

**Bottlenose**
*Starplex* - Robert J. Sawyer   s   4859

**Buccari, Sharl**
*In the Shadow of the Moon* - Scott G. Gier   s   2224

**Callista**
*Darksaber* - Kevin J. Anderson   s   103

**Cargo**
*Cyberstealth* - S.N. Lewitt   s   3450
*Dancing Vac* - S.N. Lewitt   s   3451

**Chin, Gun Roh**
*The Run to Chaos Keep* - Jack L. Chalker   s   960

**Collingwood, Max**
*Ancient Shores* - Jack McDevitt   s   3786

**Cormack, Leonard**
*Faraday's Orphans* - N. Lee Wood   s   5965

**Davis, Kyra**
*Harvest of Stars* - Poul Anderson   s   127

**Deering, Wilma**
*A Life in the Future* - Martin Caidin   s   827

**Dekker, Paul**
*Heavy Time* - C.J. Cherryh   s   995
*Hellburner* - C.J. Cherryh   s   996

**di Hoa, Barry**
*The Voices of Heaven* - Frederik Pohl   s   4356

**Dooley, Samantha "Sam"**
*No Limits* - Nigel Findley   s   1938

**Dulcimer**
*Transcendence* - Charles Sheffield   s   4967

**Falcon, Nikki**
*Falcon* - Emma Bull   s   768

**Faulkner, William**
*The Wild Blue and the Gray* - William
    Sanders   s   4814

**Finn, Clio**
*The Seeds of Time* - Kay Kenyon   s   3064

**Gorbunova, Ludmila**
*Worldwar: Tilting the Balance* - Harry
    Turtledove   s   5517
*Worldwar: Upsetting the Balance* - Harry
    Turtledove   s   5518

**Haines, Carolyn**
*Extinct* - Charles Wilson   h   5877

**Hawksmoor, Nicholas**
*Berserker Kill* - Fred Saberhagen   s   4761

**Hiller, Steven**
*Independence Day* - Dean Devlin   s   1508

**Hoke**
*'48* - James Herbert   h   2667

**Horn, Corran**
*Rogue Squadron* - Michael A. Stackpole   s   5205

**Hutchins, Priscilla "Hutch"**
*The Engines of God* - Jack McDevitt   s   3787

**Jasmine "Jas"**
*Finder's Bane* - Kate Novak   f   4165

**Jaynes, Jennifer**
*In the Shadows of the Moonglade* - Riley St.
    James   h   5186

**Jenkins, Tom**
*Alien Dreams* - Larry Segriff   s   4910

**Jetboy**
*Night of the Cooters* - Howard Waldrop   s   5614

**Jian, Reverdy**
*Dreaming Metal* - Melissa Scott   s   4895
*Dreamships* - Melissa Scott   s   4896

**Jiltanith**
*Mutineers' Moon* - David Weber   s   5677

**Kaa**
*Infinity's Shore* - David Brin   s   688

**Kady, Meg**
*Hellburner* - C.J. Cherryh   s   996

**Kan-Kon**
*Dragon Rigger* - Jeffrey A. Carver   s   929

**Keff**
*The Ship Errant* - Jody Lynn Nye   s   4175

**Kruger, Clayton Allen**
*Deadly Breed* - T.J. Kirby   h   3153

**Kustaa, Captain Fred**
*Under the Yoke* - S.M. Stirling   s   5301

**Kymri**
*Grounded!* - Chris Claremont   s   1041

**LaBrae, Jael**
*Dragon Rigger* - Jeffrey A. Carver   s   929

**Low, Boston**
*The Dig* - Alan Dean Foster   s   2002

**Lukas, Greg**
*Mind Light* - Margaret Davis   s   1407
*Minds Apart* - Margaret Davis   s   1408

**MacLoed, Alex**
*Fallen Angels* - Larry Niven   s   4120

**Malone, Patrick**
*Alien Tongue* - Stephen Leigh   s   3424

**Maraquine, Toller II**
*The Fugitive Worlds* - Bob Shaw   s   4942

**Marconi, Maria**
*Buying Time* - Joe Haldeman   s   2487

**Matthieson, Jonah**
*Man-Kzin Wars V* - Larry Niven   s   4125

**Mendez, Sofia**
*The Sparrow* - Mary Doria Russell   s   4736

**Michaelson, Kiley**
*Mind Light* - Margaret Davis   s   1407

**Morales, Daire**
*Lethe* - Tricia Sullivan   s   5354

**Morianna, Maigrey**
*King's Sacrifice* - Margaret Weis   s   5717
*The Lost King* - Margaret Weis   s   5720

**Newell, Charlie**
*Wildside* - Steven Gould   s   2291

**Nguyen, Marie**
*Wildside* - Steven Gould   s   2291

**Nielsen, Berkeley "Berk"**
*Faraday's Orphans* - N. Lee Wood   s   5965

**Ninekiller, Amos**
*The Wild Blue and the Gray* - William
    Sanders   s   4814

**Northfield, Anthony**
*War Birds* - R.M. Meluch   s   3875

**Nussem, Alis Mary**
*Reckoning Infinity* - John E. Stith   s   5304

**O'Tennis, Ned**
*The Last Legends of Earth* - A.A. Attanasio   s   270

**Owens, Tiffany "Tif"**
*Resurrection* - Katharine Kerr   s   3075

**Pallas**
*Raft* - Stephen Baxter   s   401

**Paris, Tom**
*Chrysalis* - David Niall Wilson   s   5880
*Pathways* - Jeri Taylor   s   5404

**Pollard, Ben**
*Heavy Time* - C.J. Cherryh   s   995
*Hellburner* - C.J. Cherryh   s   996

**Prentice, Clara**
*Wildside* - Steven Gould   s   2291

**Randolph, Jake**
*The Torching* - Marcy Heidish   h   2642

**Raqella**
*Sundowner* - Chris Claremont   s   1043

**Renner, Kevin**
*The Gripping Hand* - Larry Niven   s   4122

**Ringess, Danlo**
*The Broken God* - David Zindell   s   6085
*The Wild* - David Zindell   s   6086

**Rogers, Buck**
*A Life in the Future* - Martin Caidin   s   827

**Roy, Ubu**
*Angel Station* - Walter Jon Williams   s   5833

**Ryder, Christine**
*The Tranquility Alternative* - Allen Steele   s   5248

**St. John, Ian "Hunter"**
*Wing Commander: Freedom Flight* - Mercedes
    Lackey   s   3307

**Sakai, Catherine**
*To Dream in the City of Sorrows* - Kathryn M.
    Drennan   s   1654

**Sands, Larson Clarke**
*The Clouds of Saturn* - Michael McCollum   s   3770

**Sangre, Ryne**
*A Roil of Stars* - Don Wismer   s   5930

**Scoresby, Lee**
*The Golden Compass* - Philip Pullman   f   4446
*The Subtle Knife* - Philip Pullman   f   4448

**Sebasten-Janurias**
*Mighty Good Road* - Melissa Scott   s   4897

**Shannon, Rip**
*A Mind for Trade* - Andre Norton   s   4158

**Shea, Nicole**
*Grounded!* - Chris Claremont   s   1041
*Sundowner* - Chris Claremont   s   1043

**Siggerson, Olaf**
*Destination: Mutiny* - Sean Dalton   s   1332

**Silver, Harry**
*Shiva in Steel* - Fred Saberhagen   s   4775

**Spinner-of-Rope**
*Ring* - Stephen Baxter   s   402

**Stanton, Karl**
*Reckoning Infinity* - John E. Stith   s   5304

**Stern**
*'48* - James Herbert   h   2667

**Thibodeaux, Suzanne "Suzy Falcon" Marie**
*Eternal Light* - Paul J. McAuley   s   3710

**Toad of Toad Hall**
*The Willows in Winter* - William Horwood   f   2776

**Trioran, Eril**
*Jaydium* - Deborah Wheeler   s   5774

**Trudeau, Arielle**
*Return to Rocheworld* - Robert L. Forward   s   1989

**Vantara**
*The Fugitive Worlds* - Bob Shaw  *s*  4942

**Vaughan, James**
*Dr. Haggard's Disease* - Patrick McGrath  *h*  3813

**von Richthofen, Manfred**
*The Bloody Red Baron* - Kim Newman  *h*  4097

**Walthers, Audee**
*The Gateway Trip: Tales and Vignettes of the Heechee* - Frederik Pohl  *s*  4346

**Wysaigh, "Wy"**
*Faraday's Orphans* - N. Lee Wood  *s*  5965

**Yeager, Pauli**
*Heritage of Flight* - Susan Shwartz  *s*  5016

**Young, "Mighty" Joe**
*Lunar Descent* - Allen Steele  *s*  5245

## PIONEER

**Hunter**
*Twilight of the Empire* - Simon R. Green  *s*  2374

## PIRATE

**Blackstrap**
*Dinotopia Lost* - Alan Dean Foster  *f*  2003

**de Wolf, Mike**
*Typewriter in the Sky* - L. Ron Hubbard  *f*  2791

**Deadmon**
*Dragon's Plunder* - Brad Strickland  *f*  5336

**Engor**
*Engor's Sword Arm* - David C. Smith  *h*  5110

**Frank**
*Spacer Dreams* - Larry Segriff  *s*  4911

**Gabool**
*Mariel of Redwall* - Brian Jacques  *f*  2850

**Gregg, Stephen**
*Through the Breach* - David Drake  *s*  1647

**Helmuth**
*Galactic Patrol* - Edward E. Smith  *s*  5116

**Hook, James**
*Hook* - Terry Brooks  *f*  713

**Islay, Arran "Henry Martyn"**
*Henry Martyn* - L. Neil Smith  *s*  5131

**Ivard**
*Ruler of Naught* - Sherwood Smith  *s*  5141

**Khordas**
*The Element of Fire* - Jason Henderson  *f*  2657

**Kobir, Nikolai**
*Canby's Legion* - Bill Baldwin  *s*  308

**Louchard, Onidi "Dinah O'Neill"**
*Power Play* - Anne McCaffrey  *s*  3744

**Magon**
*The Warrior Returns* - Allan Cole  *f*  1109

**Marth, Jarem**
*Ash Ock* - Christopher Hinz  *s*  2690
*The Paratwa* - Christopher Hinz  *s*  2691

**McDonald**
*Cat's Gambit* - Leslie Gadallah  *s*  2099

**Merrick the Blackbird**
*Sister Blood* - Karen Haber  *s*  2476

**Mission**
*Ghost of Chance* - William S. Burroughs  *s*  780

**Pong, Mustapha**
*McCade's Bounty* - William C. Dietz  *s*  1550

**Rhannet, Prima**
*Sword-Born* - Jennifer Roberson  *f*  4612

**Ricimer, Piet**
*Through the Breach* - David Drake  *s*  1647

**Smiggens, Preister**
*Dinotopia Lost* - Alan Dean Foster  *f*  2003

**Succorso, Nick**
*Forbidden Knowledge* - Stephen R. Donaldson  *s*  1571
*The Gap into Madness: Chaos and Order* - Stephen R. Donaldson  *s*  1573

**Thermopyle, Angus**
*The Gap into Conflict: The Real Story* - Stephen R. Donaldson  *s*  1572

## PLANTATION OWNER

**Colleton, Anne**
*The Great War: American Front* - Harry Turtledove  *s*  5501

## POLICE OFFICER

**Abbot, Thomas**
*The Reckoning* - Ruby Jean Jensen  *h*  2904

**Adair, Kirsten**
*The Bohr Maker* - Linda Nagata  *s*  4064

**Aiah**
*City on Fire* - Walter Jon Williams  *s*  5835

**Audran, Marid**
*A Fire in the Sun* - George Alec Effinger  *s*  1751

**Austin, Steve**
*Slippin' into Darkness* - Norman Partridge  *h*  4254

**Barnes, Parker**
*Virtuosity* - Terry Bisson  *s*  507

**Benton, David**
*Return of the Living Dead* - John Russo  *h*  4746

**Bigthorn, Henry**
*Clarke County, Space* - Allen Steele  *s*  5241

**Bilbo, Charlie**
*Charlie's Bones* - L.L. Thrasher  *h*  5468

**Bilbo, Jonathan**
*Charlie's Bones* - L.L. Thrasher  *h*  5468

**Bileux, Peter**
*Nightshade* - Stanley R. Moore  *h*  3992

**Bish, Michael**
*The Moons of Summer* - S.K. Epperson  *h*  1831

**Blair, Reeve**
*The Mysterium* - Eric McCormack  *h*  3780

**Blakemore, Mark**
*Black Lightning* - John Saul  *h*  4837

**Blatchley, James**
*The World I Made for Her* - Thomas Moran  *h*  3996

**Blaze, Christopher**
*Vampire Beat* - Vincent Courtney  *h*  1214

**Blossom**
*Nightwatch* - Robin Wayne Bailey  *f*  289

**Blount, Alan**
*Shadow Dance* - Jessica Palmer  *h*  4238

**Bogner, C. Lane "Rusty"**
*Black Death* - R. Karl Largent  *h*  3337

**Bolt, Mike**
*Treasure Box* - Orson Scott Card  *h*  898

**Bork, Tazzimi "Taz"**
*Brother Death* - Steve Perry  *s*  4292

**Brackett, Richard**
*Mind Slayer* - Kevin D. Randle  *s*  4469

**Braco, Jag**
*Inquisitor* - Ian Watson  *s*  5637

**Brill, Janna**
*Dragon's Teeth* - Lee Killough  *s*  3109

**Bromton, Stu**
*Greely's Cove* - John Gideon  *h*  2221

**Brooks, Tim**
*Ghosts* - Noel Hynd  *h*  2822

**Bryce, Neal**
*The Death Crystal* - J. Edward Ames  *h*  91

**Burge**
*Nightwatch* - Robin Wayne Bailey  *f*  289

**Byrne, Marianne**
*Dying Breath* - Jon A. Harrald  *h*  2555

**Cage, Bill**
*Deathwalker* - R. Patrick Gates  *h*  2159

**Caldwell, Frank**
*Manhattan Heat* - Ken Eulo  *h*  1851

**Camel, Teddy**
*Cul-De-Sac* - David Martin  *h*  3638
*Lie to Me* - David Martin  *h*  3639

**Cardenas, Angel**
*Montezuma Strip* - Alan Dean Foster  *s*  2011

**Carlisle, Harry**
*The Armageddon Crazy* - Mick Farren  *s*  1877

**Carson, Dave**
*Funland* - Richard Laymon  *h*  3366

**Carter, Robert**
*The Summoning* - Bentley Little  *h*  3498

**Carver, Zachary**
*Soul Snatchers* - Michael Cecilione  *h*  947

**Celluci, Mike**
*Blood Price* - Tanya Huff  *h*  2793
*Blood Trail* - Tanya Huff  *h*  2794

**Chandler, Zinc**
*Cutthroat* - Michael Slade  *h*  5084

**Chilke, Eustace**
*Throy* - Jack Vance  *s*  5550

**Choy, Mary**
*/ -* Greg Bear  *s*  413
*Queen of Angels* - Greg Bear  *s*  423

**Chu**
*Stations of the Tide* - Michael Swanwick  *s*  5373

**Church, Louis Edward**
*Whisper* - Raymond Van Over  *h*  5539

**Clark, Elliot**
*Cold Whisper* - Rick Hautala  *h*  2605

**Clattuc, Glawen**
*Ecce and Old Earth* - Jack Vance  *s*  5546
*Throy* - Jack Vance  *s*  5550

**Clements, Yolanda Free**
*Alien Heat* - Lynn S. Hightower  *s*  2684

**Cofflin, Jared**
*Island in the Sea of Time* - S.M. Stirling  *s*  5295

**Coleridge, Stuart**
*The Orpheus Process* - Daniel H. Gower  *h*  2293

**Conway, H.W.**
*Vyrmin* - Gene Lazuta  *h*  3376

**Cook, Dan**
*Waltz with Evil* - P.D. Rozzi  *h*  4701

**Cramer, Eddie**
*Vampires Anonymous* - Jeffrey N. McMahan  *h*  3853

**Cummings, Stewart**
*Header* - Edward Lee  *h*  3393

**D'Agosta, Vincent**
*Reliquary* - Douglas Preston  *h*  4415

**Dario, Ramon**
*Senor Vivo and the Coca Lord* - Louis de
Bernieres  *f*  1411

**Darkling, Katastrofa "Kathy"**
*Riverrun* - S.P. Somtow  *f*  5159

**Dawson, DeWitt**
*Happy Policeman* - Patricia Anthony  *s*  160

**De Clerq, Robert**
*Cutthroat* - Michael Slade  *h*  5084

**Deckard, Rick**
*Blade Runner 2: The Edge of Human* - K.W.
Jeter  *s*  2906
*Blade Runner: Replicant Night* - K.W. Jeter  *s*  2907

**Delaney, Joan**
*Funland* - Richard Laymon  *h*  3366

**Dillon, Lan**
*Reunion on Neverend* - John E. Stith  *s*  5306

**Dios, Warden**
*The Gap into Ruin: This Day All Gods Die* - Stephen
R. Donaldson  *s*  1575

**Dragelman, Dan**
*Claw* - Ken Eulo  *h*  1850

**Dredd, Joseph "Judge"**
*Judge Dredd* - Neal Barrett Jr.  *s*  366

**Drew, Jonathan**
*Night Blood* - Eric Flanders  *h*  1945

**Eberle, Markus**
*At Sword's Point* - Scott MacMillan  *f*  3601

**Entragion, Collie**
*Desperation* - Stephen King  *h*  3129
*The Regulators* - Richard Bachman  *h*  284

**Erskine, Glenn**
*In a Dark Dream* - Charles L. Grant  *h*  2310

**Ethemark**
*City on Fire* - Walter Jon Williams  *s*  5835

**Fenn**
*The Fleet of Stars* - Poul Anderson  *s*  126

**Fisher, Isobel**
*The Bones of Haven* - Simon R. Green  *f*  2363
*The God Killer* - Simon R. Green  *f*  2368
*Guard Against Dishonor* - Simon R. Green  *f*  2369
*Hawk & Fisher* - Simon R. Green  *f*  2370
*Winner Takes All* - Simon R. Green  *f*  2375
*Wolf in the Fold* - Simon R. Green  *f*  2376

**Flynn, Charlie**
*Far Edge of Darkness* - Linda Evans  *s*  1855

**Fogarty, Bill**
*Mind Kill* - Richard La Plante  *h*  3267

**Ford, Morgan**
*Skull Session* - Daniel Hecht  *h*  2638

**Franks, Leo**
*Night Mask* - William W. Johnstone  *h*  2931

**Frazier, Nick**
*Down River* - Stephen Gallagher  *h*  2110

**Friedman, Jack**
*Homecoming* - Matthew J. Costello  *h*  1198

**Fuentes, Jose**
*Star Prey* - Ehren M. Ehly  *h*  1763

**Gates, Bill**
*Tunnelvision* - R. Patrick Gates  *h*  2162

**Gatlin, Ben**
*Father's Little Helper* - Ronald Kelly  *h*  3052

**Gavel, Kevin**
*Junkyard* - Barry Porter  *h*  4370

**Gilbert, Cyrus**
*Between the Devil and the Deep* - J.M.
Morgan  *h*  3998

**Gimlet, Carrot**
*Feet of Clay* - Terry Pratchett  *f*  4389
*Guards! Guards!* - Terry Pratchett  *f*  4390
*Men at Arms* - Terry Pratchett  *f*  4396

**Gray, Frank**
*The Lazarus Heart* - Poppy Z. Brite  *h*  696

**Gulliver, Connie**
*Dragon Tears* - Dean R. Koontz  *h*  3205

**Gundhalinu, BZ**
*The Summer Queen* - Joan D. Vinge  *s*  5572

**Gutierrez, Osvaldo**
*Shango* - James Roberto Curtis  *h*  1298

**Hamilton, Case**
*Death's Door* - John Wooley  *h*  5969

**Hamilton, Diana**
*Death's Door* - John Wooley  *h*  5969

**Hansen, Nils**
*Justice* - David Drake  *s*  1635
*Northworld* - David Drake  *s*  1637
*Vengeance* - David Drake  *s*  1648

**Hanson, Marvin**
*Act of Love* - Joe R. Lansdale  *h*  3319

**Harding, Skip**
*Crota* - Owl Goingback  *h*  2251

**Hardrim, Mel**
*The Argus Gambit* - David D. Ross  *s*  4681

**Hawk**
*The Bones of Haven* - Simon R. Green  *f*  2363
*The God Killer* - Simon R. Green  *f*  2368
*Guard Against Dishonor* - Simon R. Green  *f*  2369
*Hawk & Fisher* - Simon R. Green  *f*  2370
*Winner Takes All* - Simon R. Green  *f*  2375
*Wolf in the Fold* - Simon R. Green  *f*  2376

**Hawn, Loren**
*Days of Atonement* - Walter Jon Williams  *s*  5836

**Hayden, Mark**
*Bats* - William W. Johnstone  *h*  2926

**Hays, Micah**
*The Case of the Police Officer's Cock Ring and the
Piano Player Who Had No Fingers* - Edward
Lee  *h*  3388
*Splatterspunk: The Micah Hays Stories* - Edward
Lee  *h*  3397

**Helwig, Mitch**
*Blue Limbo* - Terrence M. Green  *s*  2377

**Hendricks, Clint**
*Stone Dead* - Ellen Jamison  *h*  2878

**Henry, Dora**
*The Family Tree* - Sheri S. Tepper  *s*  5429

**Hershey**
*Judge Dredd* - Neal Barrett Jr.  *s*  366

**Huxley, Lenina**
*Demolition Man* - Richard Osborne  *s*  4229

**Hyland, Morn**
*Forbidden Knowledge* - Stephen R.
Donaldson  *s*  1571
*The Gap into Conflict: The Real Story* - Stephen R.
Donaldson  *s*  1572
*The Gap into Madness: Chaos and Order* - Stephen R.
Donaldson  *s*  1573
*The Gap into Power: A Dark and Hungry God Arises*
- Stephen R. Donaldson  *s*  1574
*The Gap into Ruin: This Day All Gods Die* - Stephen
R. Donaldson  *s*  1575

**Ingalls, Ray**
*The Devil's Laughter* - William W.
Johnstone  *h*  2930

**Izeki, Hitedoro**
*Anvil* - Nicolas van Pallandt  *s*  5540

**Johnson, Greg**
*The Charm* - Adam Niswander  *h*  4111

**Karoulis, Sam**
*Blue Limbo* - Terrence M. Green  *s*  2377

**Kastlin, Vask**
*Mainline* - Deborah Christian  *s*  1026

**Kelly, Bob**
*The Forbidden Zone* - Whitley Strieber  *h*  5340

**Killany, Mark**
*Night Cruise* - Billie Sue Mosiman  *h*  4041

**Killdeer, Hunter**
*Living with the Reptiles* - Roger L.
DiSilvestro  *s*  1563

**Kimball, Joel**
*Night* - Alan Rodgers  *h*  4649

**Kimmler, Vic**
*Borderland: A Novel of Terror* - S.K.
Epperson  *h*  1828

**Kinion, Richard**
*The Case of the Police Officer's Cock Ring and the
Piano Player Who Had No Fingers* - Edward
Lee  *h*  3388

**Kirkpatrick, Stanley**
*The Spider #8: The Devil's Paymaster/Legions of the
Accursed Light* - Grant Stockbridge  *f*  5309

**Knudsen, Arne**
*Master of Lies* - Graham Masterton  *h*  3676

**Kostal, Miriam**
*River of Dust* - Alexander Jablokov  *s*  2840

**Lacey, Bobbie**
*Polar City Blues* - Katharine Kerr  *s*  3073

**Laidlaw, Alison**
*Cloud Castles* - Michael Scott Rohan  *f*  4659

**Langston, Fred**
*Blood* - Ron Dee  *h*  1463

**Laughing More, Anna**
*Wake of the Werewolf* - Geoffrey Caine  *h*  834

**Laverne, Vernon**
*The Death Prayer* - David Bowker  *h*  602

**Lawson, John**
*Moonfall* - Tamara Thorne  *h*  5464

**Llewellyn, George**
*Werewolf* - Peter Rubie  *h*  4702

**Locke, Ryan**
*Bloody Valentine* - Stephen R. George  *h*  2197

**Lockerman, John**
*Grave Markings* - Michael A. Arnzen  *h*  212

**Loman, Bill**
*Yours Truly, Jackie the Stripper* - Edo van
Belkom  *h*  5536

**Luckinbill, Tom**
*Yellow Moon* - David J. Searls  *h*  4907

**Lyon, Harry**
*Dragon Tears* - Dean R. Koontz  *h*  3205

**Mahan, Sherry**
*The Bad Thing* - Michael O'Rourke  *h*  4222

**Mallory, Thomas**
*The Wizard of Camelot* - Simon Hawke  *f*  2627

**Marceline**
*Fools* - Pat Cadigan  *s*  805

**March, Xavier**
*Fatherland* - Robert Harris  *s*  2564

**Maxwell, Mahlon Sumner "Mama"**
*Dragon's Teeth* - Lee Killough  *s*  3109

**Mays, Johnny**
*Down River* - Stephen Gallagher  *h*  2110

**McCardle, Box "Texas"**
*Metal Angel* - Nancy Springer  *f*  5181

**McClellan, Conan**
*Return of the Living Dead* - John Russo  *h*  4746

**McCormick, Sandra**
*Dark Heart* - Margaret Weis  *f*  5707

**McElroy, Jud**
*The Headsman* - James Neal Harvey  *h*  2599

**McGarvey, Jack**
*Winter Moon* - Dean R. Koontz  *h*  3218

**McKinnan**
*The Third Beast* - Peter Loughran  *h*  3527

**McLeod, Noel**
*The Adept* - Katherine Kurtz  *f*  3254
*Dagger Magic* - Katherine Kurtz  *f*  3256

**McRay, Kevin**
*Nine Levels Down* - William Dantz  *h*  1347

**Meagher, Richard**
*The Uprising* - Brent Monahan  *h*  3956

**Melrose, Frank**
*Dead Voices* - Rick Hautala  *h*  2607

**Minster, Joanne**
*The World of Darkness: Watcher* - Charles L.
  Grant  *h*  2321

**Mullins, Lawrence**
*Creekers* - Edward Lee  *h*  3391

**Munro, Dan**
*Reign* - Chet Williamson  *h*  5849

**Nanopoulos, Sheila**
*Glass Houses* - Laura J. Mixon  *s*  3921

**Nathan, Corliss**
*Genesis* - Charles L. Grant  *h*  2308

**Obo**
*Mind Slayer* - Kevin D. Randle  *s*  4469

**O'Brien, Ed**
*Leannu: Possession of a Woman* - Marie
  Kiraly  *h*  3149

**O'Brien, Richard**
*The Crawling Dark* - Pauline Dunn  *h*  1698

**O'Donnell, Erin**
*Deathwalker* - Patrick Whalen  *h*  5769

**O'Hara, Frank**
*A Room for the Dead* - Noel Hynd  *h*  2825

**Okata, Gail**
*Demon Fire* - Gary L. Holleman  *h*  2743

**Ooljee, Paul**
*Cyber Way* - Alan Dean Foster  *s*  2000

**Ortiveda, Phyllis**
*Ursus* - David Dvorkin  *s*  1708

**Outhwaite, Terence**
*Virgins and Martyrs* - Simon Maginn  *h*  3607

**Owldark, Fringe Dorwalk**
*Sideshow* - Sheri S. Tepper  *s*  5436

**Packard, Nick**
*Wet Work* - Philip Nutman  *h*  4168

**Pangborn, Alan**
*Needful Things* - Stephen King  *h*  3137

**Parsons**
*Twisted* - Sue Hollister Barr  *h*  364

**Payne**
*Running Wild* - J.G. Ballard  *h*  320

**Peters, George**
*Offspring* - Jack Ketchum  *h*  3092

**Plase, Janice**
*Kent Montana and the Reasonably Invisible Man* -
  Lionel Fenn  *s*  1919

**Plon**
*The Prisoner Within* - Donald E. McQuinn  *s*  3861

**Portlock, Ben**
*Dumford Blood* - S.K. Epperson  *h*  1829

**Powell, Lincoln**
*The Demolished Man* - Alfred Bester  *s*  476

**Prejean, Lani**
*Night Mask* - William W. Johnstone  *h*  2931

**Rafin**
*Runes of Autumn* - Larry Elmore  *f*  1790

**Ramsey, Quinn**
*Demon Fire* - Gary L. Holleman  *h*  2743

**Randall, Mick**
*Shadows* - Kimberly Rangel  *h*  4472

**Rathe, Nicolas "Nico"**
*Point of Hopes* - Melissa Scott  *f*  4899

**Rocky**
*God's Dice* - S. Andrew Swann  *f*  5364

**Rossi, Eric**
*Domination* - Michael Cecilione  *h*  946

**Rufin, Tal**
*Four & Twenty Blackbirds* - Mercedes
  Lackey  *f*  3283

**Rydell, Berry**
*Virtual Light* - William Gibson  *s*  2219

**Sanders, John A.**
*Dark Visions* - T. Lucien Wright  *h*  5987

**Sanders, Phillipe "Phil" Montoya**
*The Modular Man* - Roger MacBride Allen  *s*  79

**Savik, Bob**
*Hair of the Dog* - Brett Davis  *f*  1400

**Shepard, Natalie**
*Spider Legs* - Piers Anthony  *s*  189

**Silver, David**
*Alien Blues* - Lynn S. Hightower  *s*  2682
*Alien Eyes* - Lynn S. Hightower  *s*  2683
*Alien Heat* - Lynn S. Hightower  *s*  2684
*Alien Rites* - Lynn S. Hightower  *s*  2685

**Sinclair, Travis**
*Prank Night* - David Robbins  *h*  4601

**Singer, Helen**
*Symphony* - Adrian Savage  *h*  4847

**Slaughter, Nathan**
*The Totem* - David Morrell  *h*  4012

**Solo, Jay**
*The Nine Lives of Catseye Gomez* - Simon
  Hawke  *f*  2620

**Specter, Alan**
*Time Station Berlin* - David Evans  *s*  1852

**Stablits, Dothan**
*Hard Landing* - Algis Budrys  *s*  753

**Stack, Nathan**
*Demon Download* - Jack Yeovil  *f*  6021

**Stanley, Rodman**
*Night Beasts* - T.W. Stetson  *h*  5263

**Stark, Emmett**
*The Headsman* - James Neal Harvey  *h*  2599

**Starlen, Garett**
*Nightwatch* - Robin Wayne Bailey  *f*  289

**Stavrianos, Nick**
*Quarantine* - Greg Egan  *s*  1762

**Stepovich, Mike**
*The Gypsy* - Steven Brust  *f*  744

**Stone, Alexandra**
*Testament of the Dragon* - Margaret Weis  *f*  5729

**Stone, Neil**
*Deathscape* - Michael Cecilione  *h*  945

**Straker, Phil**
*Creekers* - Edward Lee  *h*  3391

**Stratton, Dan**
*Night Hunter* - Michael Reaves  *h*  4496

**String**
*Alien Blues* - Lynn S. Hightower  *s*  2682
*Alien Eyes* - Lynn S. Hightower  *s*  2683
*Alien Heat* - Lynn S. Hightower  *s*  2684
*Alien Rites* - Lynn S. Hightower  *s*  2685

**Sutton, Henry**
*Out of the Night* - Patrick Whalen  *h*  5771

**Sweeney, Jim**
*The Keeper* - Robert D. Lee  *h*  3402

**Thomas, Peter**
*Wolfsong* - Traci Briery  *h*  680

**Thomas, Shep**
*Nightscape* - Stephen R. George  *h*  2203

**Thomason, John "Jean Vitterand"**
*Time Station Paris* - David Evans  *s*  1854

**Tishner, Frank**
*Firefly* - Piers Anthony  *h*  170

**Tucker, Graham**
*The Homecoming* - Kimberly Rangel  *h*  4471

**Vess, Edgler Foreman**
*Intensity* - Dean R. Koontz  *h*  3210

**Vimes, Samuel**
*Feet of Clay* - Terry Pratchett  *f*  4389
*Guards! Guards!* - Terry Pratchett  *f*  4390
*Jingo* - Terry Pratchett  *f*  4393

**Vorbis**
*Small Gods* - Terry Pratchett  *f*  4400

**Walker, Max**
*Timecop* - S.D. Perry  *s*  4286

**Walker, Ross**
*Spook* - Steve Vance  *h*  5553

**Walsmear, Michael**
*Photographing Fairies* - Steve Szilagyi  *f*  5379

**Warden**
*The Tetherballs of Bougainville* - Mark
  Leyner  *f*  3457

**Warrick, Susan**
*OtherSyde* - J. Michael Straczynski  *h*  5323

**Waterman, Phil**
*Trickster* - Chris Curry  *h*  1297

**Wayland, Richard**
*Dying Breath* - Jon A. Harrald  *h*  2555

**Weldon, Jim**
*The Revelation* - Bentley Little  *h*  3496

**Willson, Matthew**
*Dark Reunion* - Stephen R. George  *h*  2198

**Woodruff, Bodeen**
*Happy Policeman* - Patricia Anthony  *s*  160

**Yail, Jiron**
*The Glaive* - Cary Osborne  *s*  4227

**Yates, Sam**
*Target* - Janet Morris  *s*  4017

**Younger, Jesse "Cole"**
*Rockabilly Hell* - William W. Johnstone  *h*  2933
*Rockabilly Limbo* - William W. Johnstone  *h*  2934

## POLITICAL FIGURE

**Abivard**
*Videssos Besieged* - Harry Turtledove  *f*  5513

**Agis**
*The Verdant Passage* - Troy Denning  *f*  1487

**Agyar**
*The Vampire Memoirs* - Mara McCuniff  *h*  3781

**a'Husain, Idryis Khan**
*Imposter* - Valerie J. Freireich  *s*  2050

**Aiah**
*City on Fire* - Walter Jon Williams  *s*  5835

**Anniyas, Avira**
*The Ruins of Ambrai* - Melanie Rawn  *f*  4489

**Armstrong, Alexander "the Great"**
*Martian Rainbow* - Robert L. Forward  *s*  1907

**Ascher, Emily**
*The Broken Wheel* - David Wingrove  *s*  5918

**Beeblebrox, Zaphod**
*The Illustrated Hitchhiker's Guide to the Galaxy* - Douglas Adams  *s*  29

**Beynac, Dagny**
*The Stars Are Also Fire* - Poul Anderson  *s*  134

**Bigelow, Walter T.**
*Journals of the Plague Years* - Norman Spinrad  *s*  5172

**Bonfim, Ana Maria**
*Cradle of Splendor* - Patricia Anthony  *s*  158

**Boorman**
*Ignition* - Kevin J. Anderson  *s*  107

**Bouriere, Tira**
*Crown of Empire* - Chelsea Quinn Yarbro  *s*  6014

**Bouriere, Wiley**
*Crown of Empire* - Chelsea Quinn Yarbro  *s*  6014

**Brady, Tedman**
*A Fearful Symmetry* - James Luceno  *s*  3542

**Brauna, Sanda**
*Becoming Human* - Valerie J. Freireich  *s*  2049

**Brookmeyer, Warren**
*Tek Power* - William Shatner  *s*  4937

**Brownbenttalon**
*O Pioneer!* - Frederik Pohl  *s*  4350

**Brutus, Marcus Junius**
*Child of the Eagle* - Esther Friesner  *f*  2073

**Bruwer-Sanmartin, Hanna**
*Fire in a Faraway Place* - Robert Frezza  *s*  2052

**Bush, George Herbert Walker**
*Reality Is What You Can Get Away With: An Illustrated Screenplay* - Robert Anton Wilson  *s*  5904

**Cannon, Ben**
*Cannon's Orb* - L. Warren Douglas  *s*  1586

**Capone, Alphonse**
*Back in the USSA* - Kim Newman  *s*  4095

**Carri, Michael**
*The Law of War* - William Shatner  *s*  4931

**Carson, Ilene**
*Tech-Heaven* - Linda Nagata  *s*  4066

**Cavanagh, Stewart**
*Conqueror's Pride* - Timothy Zahn  *s*  6051

**Cedric**
*One for the Morning Glory* - John Barnes  *f*  355

**Churchill, Winston**
*Triumph* - Ben Bova  *s*  598

**Claiborne, Kevin**
*Pacific Edge* - Kim Stanley Robinson  *s*  4634

**Constantine**
*City on Fire* - Walter Jon Williams  *s*  5835
*Metropolitan* - Walter Jon Williams  *s*  5839

**Cotto, Vir**
*Personal Agendas* - Al Sarrantonio  *s*  4833

**Cozzano, William Anthony**
*Interface* - Stephen Bury  *s*  781

**Crane, Peter**
*Hunting the Corrigan's Blood* - Holly Lisle  *s*  3484

**Crawford, Lee**
*Dark Genesis* - J. Gregory Keyes  *s*  3096

**Crocker, Thad**
*Yellow Moon* - David J. Searls  *h*  4907

**Croft, Michael "Mickey"**
*The Stalk* - Janet Morris  *s*  4016
*Trust Territory* - Janet Morris  *s*  4019

**Dad**
*Songs of Enchantment* - Ben Okri  *f*  4208

**Davis, Jefferson**
*Stars and Stripes Forever* - Harry Harrison  *s*  2577

**De Styx, Marquande**
*The Silent City* - Elisabeth Vonarburg  *s*  5592

**De Vore, Howard**
*The Broken Wheel* - David Wingrove  *s*  5918

**Decker, Andrew Jackson**
*Storm Knights* - Bill Slavicsek  *f*  5087

**DeMarian, Melesandra III**
*The Stone Prince* - Fiona Patton  *f*  4259

**Denning, John**
*The Beacon* - Valerie J. Freireich  *s*  2048

**Emory, Ariane**
*Cyteen* - C.J. Cherryh  *s*  984

**Erzul, Ti Sandra**
*Moving Mars* - Greg Bear  *s*  421

**Eusabian, Jerrode**
*The Phoenix in Flight* - Sherwood Smith  *s*  5138
*The Rifter's Covenant* - Sherwood Smith  *s*  5140

**Feich, Daimhin**
*The Crystal Rose* - Maya Kaathryn Bohnhoff  *f*  560

**Flanagan, Thomas**
*The Resurrectionist* - Thomas F. Monteleone  *h*  3965

**Frazier, Rhea**
*Shadows Fall* - Simon R. Green  *f*  2373

**Gaetano, Rafaelo**
*Empire Builders* - Ben Bova  *s*  584

**Gorbachev, Mikhail Sergeevich**
*Fellow Traveller* - William Barton  *s*  380

**Green, Paul**
*Fire* - Alan Rodgers  *h*  4647

**Harrison, Andrew**
*1945* - Newt Gingrich  *s*  2239

**Hartmann, Gregg**
*Ace in the Hole* - George R.R. Martin  *s*  3641
*Marked Cards* - George R.R. Martin  *s*  3647

**Haskell, Charles L. "Charlie"**
*Moonfall* - Jack McDevitt  *s*  3789

**Haven, Dextra**
*A Screaming Across the Sky* - Brian Daley  *s*  1315

**Hawkins, Nirgal**
*Blue Mars* - Kim Stanley Robinson  *s*  4629
*Green Mars* - Kim Stanley Robinson  *s*  4633

**Heiratikus**
*Wind From a Foreign Sky* - Katya Reimann  *f*  4528

**Highland, Bill**
*The Committee* - Raymond Buckland  *h*  752

**Hitler, Adolf**
*The Resurrections* - Simon Louvish  *s*  3528
*Triumph* - Ben Bova  *s*  598

**Holland, Martin**
*Carnival* - William W. Johnstone  *h*  2927

**Hrrestan**
*Treaty at Doona* - Anne McCaffrey  *s*  3752

**Huger, Willy**
*Root of All Evil* - David A. Farrow  *h*  1888

**Ivanova, Sonya**
*Russian Spring* - Norman Spinrad  *s*  5174

**Joubert, Mireille**
*Semper Mars* - Ian Douglas  *s*  1585

**Kalass, Et**
*In the Shadow of the Moon* - Scott G. Gier  *s*  2224

**Koto**
*Songs of Enchantment* - Ben Okri  *f*  4208

**Kresh, Alvar**
*Utopia* - Roger MacBride Allen  *s*  83

**Lancaster, Whitney**
*Breeder* - Ed Kelleher  *h*  3041

**Lang, Gabriel**
*Rage of Spirits* - Noel Hynd  *h*  2824

**Larissa**
*Queens of Land and Sea* - John Maddox Roberts  *f*  4620
*The Steel Kings* - John Maddox Roberts  *f*  4621

**Lattimore, Sam**
*The Resurrectionist* - Thomas F. Monteleone  *h*  3965

**Lee, Jeroen**
*Becoming Human* - Valerie J. Freireich  *s*  2049

**Lilisaire**
*The Stars Are Also Fire* - Poul Anderson  *s*  134

**Lincoln, Abraham**
*Stars and Stripes Forever* - Harry Harrison  *s*  2577

**Liwellan, Sarra Ambrai**
*The Mageborn Traitor* - Melanie Rawn  *f*  4488

**Lyppiatt, Xan**
*The Children of Men* - P.D. James  *f*  2870

**Macdonald, Dorothea**
*Diamond Mask: A Novel* - Julian May  *s*  3697

**MacFarlane, Nelly**
*Furnace* - Muriel Gray  *h*  2339

**Machiavelli, Niccolo**
*Pasquale's Angel* - Paul J. McAuley  *f*  3714

**Mackenzie, Lyle**
*Sister Blood* - Karen Haber  *s*  2476

**Majamdar, Casseia**
*Moving Mars* - Greg Bear  *s*  421

**Mayhew IX, Benjamin**
*Echoes of Honor* - David Weber  *s*  5669

**Mayor, Mayor**
*Escardy Gap* - Peter Crowther  *h*  1282

**McComb, Aaron**
*Timecop* - S.D. Perry  *s*  4286

**McIntyre, Scott**
*Footprints of Thunder* - James F. David  *s*  1379

**Mollari, Londo**
*Personal Agendas* - Al Sarrantonio  *s*  4833

**O'Connor, Katherine**
*The Last Wizard* - Simon Hawke  *f*  2619

**Parker, Evan**
*The Winds of Mars* - H.M. Hoover  *s*  2765

**Parker, Janis**
*The Winds of Mars* - H.M. Hoover  *s*  2765

**Parsons**
*The Totem* - David Morrell   *h*   4012

**Pashikov, Ilya**
*Russian Spring* - Norman Spinrad   *s*   5174

**Passman, Hektor**
*River of Dust* - Alexander Jablokov   *s*   2840

**Pickard, Joe**
*Echoes* - Jackie Hyman   *h*   2818

**Polmaire**
*Deepwater Dreams* - Sydney J. Van Scyoc   *s*   5541

**Prothore, Alfred**
*The Jekyll Legacy* - Robert Bloch   *h*   535

**Purcell, Harry**
*Worlds Enough and Time* - Joe Haldeman   *s*   2491

**Pyramors**
*Warlord of Heaven* - Adrian Cole   *f*   1102

**Reagan, Ronald**
*The Atrocity Exhibition* - J.G. Ballard   *s*   319

**Reem "First Cousin Brother"**
*Brother Termite* - Patricia Anthony   *s*   156

**Reeve, Todd**
*Treaty at Doona* - Anne McCaffrey   *s*   3752

**Renier, Mordan**
*Ganwold's Child* - Diann Thornley   *s*   5467

**Richmond, Eleanor Boxwood**
*Interface* - Stephen Bury   *s*   781

**Rollie, Steve**
*Dark Tide* - Elizabeth Forrest   *h*   1972

**Roosevelt, Franklin Delano**
*Triumph* - Ben Bova   *s*   598

**Roosevelt, Theodore**
*1901* - Robert Conroy   *s*   1139
*Bully!* - Mike Resnick   *s*   4539

**Scanwell, Jane**
*Empire Builders* - Ben Bova   *s*   584

**Seldon, Hari**
*Foundation's Fear* - Gregory Benford   *s*   446

**Shazad**
*Queens of Land and Sea* - John Maddox
   Roberts   *f*   4620

**Sheba**
*Traitors* - Kristine Kathryn Rusch   *f*   4729

**Shefferton, Jeffrey**
*The Argus Gambit* - David D. Ross   *s*   4681
*The Eighth Rank* - David D. Ross   *s*   4682

**Stane, Temelathe**
*Shadow Man* - Melissa Scott   *s*   4900

**Steinmetz, Saul**
*Aftermath* - Charles Sheffield   *s*   4947

**Tali**
*Brother Termite* - Patricia Anthony   *s*   156

**Travassa, Daisainia**
*Legacies* - Alison Sinclair   *s*   5069

**L'var y Smid, Vida**
*The Eyes of God* - Mark Kreighbaum   *s*   3231

**Verid**
*Daughter of Elysium* - Joan Slonczewski   *s*   5091

**Wakefield, Nicole des Jardins**
*Rama Revealed* - Arthur C. Clarke   *s*   1059

**Welch, Lewis**
*Dreambuilder* - Tom Deitz   *f*   1471

**Weston, Quinton**
*The Immortals* - Tracy Hickman   *s*   2681

**Whitmore, Thomas**
*Independence Day* - Dean Devlin   *s*   1508

**Womack, Jeff**
*Brother Termite* - Patricia Anthony   *s*   156

**Wycliff, Walter**
*The President's Astrologer* - Barbara
   Shafferman   *f*   4926

**Zellorian**
*Warlord of Heaven* - Adrian Cole   *f*   1102

# PORNOGRAPHER

**Shutterbug**
*Slippin' into Darkness* - Norman Partridge   *h*   4254

# POSTAL WORKER

**Bethune, Casey**
*The Black Carousel* - Charles L. Grant   *h*   2303

**Chevette**
*Virtual Light* - William Gibson   *s*   2219

**Jaffe, Randolph**
*The Great and Secret Show* - Clive Barker   *h*   341

**Simon**
*Wishbringer* - Craig Shaw Gardner   *f*   2133

**Smith, John**
*The Mailman* - Bentley Little   *h*   3494

# PREHISTORIC HUMAN

**Amgigh**
*My Sister the Moon* - Sue Harrison   *f*   2582

**Ayla**
*The Plains of Passage* - Jean M. Auel   *f*   275

**Bad Belly/Still Water**
*People of the Earth* - W. Michael Gear   *f*   2166

**Ban-ya**
*The Edge of the World* - William Sarabande   *f*   4817

**Brave Man**
*People of the Earth* - W. Michael Gear   *f*   2166

**Catchstraw**
*People of the Sea* - W. Michael Gear   *f*   2169

**Cha-kwena**
*The Edge of the World* - William Sarabande   *f*   4817
*Thunder in the Sky* - William Sarabande   *f*   4819

**Chagak**
*Mother Earth, Father Sky* - Sue Harrison   *f*   2581

**Doban**
*Shiva: An Adventure of the Ice Age* - J.H.
   Brennan   *f*   669

**Elk Charm**
*People of the Fire* - W. Michael Gear   *f*   2167

**Fava**
*Serpent Catch* - Dave Wolverton   *s*   5956

**Hawk**
*The Hunter Returns* - David Drake   *f*   1632

**Helen**
*No Enemy but Time* - Michael Bishop   *s*   502

**Heron**
*People of the Wolf* - W. Michael Gear   *f*   2170

**Hiram**
*Shiva Accused: An Adventure of the Ice Age* - J.H.
   Brennan   *f*   667
*Shiva: An Adventure of the Ice Age* - J.H.
   Brennan   *f*   669
*Shiva's Challenge: An Adventure of the Ice Age* - J.H.
   Brennan   *f*   668

**Jondalar**
*The Plains of Passage* - Jean M. Auel   *f*   275

**Kazzintuitruaabemss "Kazz"**
*To Your Scattered Bodies Go* - Philip Jose
   Farmer   *s*   1876

**Kestrel**
*People of the Sea* - W. Michael Gear   *f*   2169

**Kiin**
*My Sister the Moon* - Sue Harrison   *f*   2582

**Kori**
*The Animal Wife* - Elizabeth Marshall
   Thomas   *f*   5444

**Little Dancer**
*People of the Fire* - W. Michael Gear   *f*   2167

**Lolita**
*Cathouse* - Dean Ing   *s*   2828

**Mah-ree**
*The Edge of the World* - William Sarabande   *f*   4817

**Maliwal**
*The Sacred Stones* - William Sarabande   *f*   4818

**Masau**
*The Sacred Stones* - William Sarabande   *f*   4818

**Monkey, King**
*The Kronos Condition* - Emily Devenport   *s*   1502

**Ozette, Ember**
*Ember From the Sun* - Mark Canter   *s*   870

**Raven Hunter**
*People of the Wolf* - W. Michael Gear   *f*   2170

**Runs in Light**
*People of the Wolf* - W. Michael Gear   *f*   2170

**Samiq**
*My Sister the Moon* - Sue Harrison   *f*   2582

**Shiva**
*Shiva Accused: An Adventure of the Ice Age* - J.H.
   Brennan   *f*   667
*Shiva: An Adventure of the Ice Age* - J.H.
   Brennan   *f*   669
*Shiva's Challenge: An Adventure of the Ice Age* - J.H.
   Brennan   *f*   668

**Sunchaser**
*People of the Sea* - W. Michael Gear   *t*   2169

**Swift**
*The Animal Wife* - Elizabeth Marshall
   Thomas   *f*   5444

**Talker**
*Dawn Land* - Joseph Bruchac   *f*   731

**Thag**
*Shiva's Challenge: An Adventure of the Ice Age* - J.H.
   Brennan   *f*   668

**Timmie**
*The Ugly Little Boy* - Isaac Asimov   *s*   250

**Tull**
*Serpent Catch* - Dave Wolverton   *s*   5956

**White Ash**
*People of the Earth* - W. Michael Gear   *f*   2166

**Willow**
*The Hunter Returns* - David Drake   *f*   1632

**Wolf**
*The Hunter Returns* - David Drake   *f*   1632

**Young Hunter**
*Dawn Land* - Joseph Bruchac   *f*   731

**Ysuna**
*The Sacred Stones* - William Sarabande   *f*   4818

# PRINCIPAL

**Hanley, Matthew**
*The School* - Ed Kelleher   *h*   3042

**Stiles**
*Mysteries of the Word* - Stanley Wiater   *h*   5796

## PRINTER

**Wolsey, Faye**
*The Palm Dome* - Liz Fulton   *h*   2094

## PRISONER

**a Cimabue, Damastes**
*The Demon King* - Chris Bunch   *f*   770
*The Seer King* - Chris Bunch   *f*   771

**Armand, Pamela**
*The Living Evil* - Ruby Jean Jensen   *h*   2902

**Baram**
*The Outlanders* - David B. Coe   *f*   1096

**Bladestone, Hugh**
*Fortress on the Sun* - Paul Cook   *s*   1157

**Bowe-Hawkins, Thomas "Tom"**
*Tripoint* - C.J. Cherryh   *s*   1003

**Braldt**
*The Hunter on Arena* - Rose Estes   *s*   1838

**Case, Jamie**
*Wheels of Fire* - Mercedes Lackey   *f*   3301

**Chappy**
*The End of Alice* - A.M. Homes   *h*   2755

**Chinnery, Thomas**
*Bijapur* - Kara Dalkey   *f*   1317

**Coffey, John**
*The Green Mile* - Stephen King   *h*   3134

**DeWitt, Katherine "Kate" Ariella**
*Fortress on the Sun* - Paul Cook   *s*   1157

**Dillon**
*Alien 3* - Alan Dean Foster   *s*   1993

**Elionbel**
*Palace of Kings* - Mike Jefferies   *f*   2887

**Endymion, Raul**
*Endymion* - Dan Simmons   *s*   5051

**Faronya, Tain**
*The Kalif's War* - John Dalmas   *s*   1322

**Felicitas**
*Outpost* - Scott Mackay   *s*   3597

**Gabriel, Justin**
*Mind Kill* - Richard La Plante   *h*   3267

**Gaetan, Philip**
*Lie to Me* - David Martin   *h*   3639

**Gerick**
*Hard Crash* - Ryan Hughes   *s*   2810

**G'Kar**
*Personal Agendas* - Al Sarrantonio   *s*   4833

**Griffin, Alan**
*Cold Whisper* - Rick Hautala   *h*   2605

**Harlan, Richard**
*Brander's Book* - C.J. Mills   *s*   3909

**Hyland, Morn**
*The Gap into Madness: Chaos and Order* - Stephen R. Donaldson   *s*   1573

**Kerac, John**
*Wake of the Werewolf* - Geoffrey Caine   *h*   834

**Keri**
*The Hunter on Arena* - Rose Estes   *s*   1838

**Kinsey, Doc**
*The Night Seasons* - J.N. Williamson   *h*   5858

**Kitatimate, Alexander "Sander"**
*Cinderblock* - Janine Ellen Young   *s*   6047

**Lewin, Alma Marie**
*Days of Cain* - J.R. Dunn   *s*   1694

**Mendez, Marla**
*Prison Planet* - William C. Dietz   *s*   1551

**Motzin, Rebeka**
*Days of Cain* - J.R. Dunn   *s*   1694

**Osokin**
*Brute Orbits* - George Zebrowski   *s*   6059

**Piero**
*Outpost* - Scott Mackay   *s*   3597

**Randi**
*The Hunter on Arena* - Rose Estes   *s*   1838

**Renn, Jonathan**
*Prison Planet* - William C. Dietz   *s*   1551

**Seventeen**
*The Road to Hell, Volume I* - Robert Weinberg   *h*   5701

**Sharbaraz**
*The Stolen Throne* - Harry Turtledove   *f*   5510

**Simmanye, Ioska**
*Prisoner of Conscience* - Susan R. Matthews   *s*   3693

**Tasarov, Yevgeny**
*Brute Orbits* - George Zebrowski   *s*   6059

**Zofia**
*Hard Crash* - Ryan Hughes   *s*   2810

## PRIVATEER

**Metadi, Jos**
*The Gathering Flame* - Debra Doyle   *s*   1599

**Vendeley, Rolande**
*Season of Storms* - Ellen Foxxe   *f*   2032

## PROBATION OFFICER

**St. Charles, Lia**
*Voodoo Child* - Michael Reaves   *h*   4498

## PRODUCER

**Boggs, Buffalo Odersby**
*Visitors From Oz: The Wild Adventures of Dorothy, the Scarecrow and the Tin Woodman* - Martin Gardner   *f*   2136

**Curtis, Samantha "Sam"**
*Dreamer* - Peter James   *h*   2871

**Dyckman, Alicia "Lish"**
*The Swords of Zinjaban* - L. Sprague de Camp   *s*   1418

**Evans, Christina**
*The Eyes of Darkness* - Dean R. Koontz   *s*   3206

**Garbage, Roger**
*Skeletons* - Al Sarrantonio   *h*   4834

**Goff, Max**
*Curfew* - Phil Rickman   *h*   4587

**Gold, Samuel**
*Visitors From Oz: The Wild Adventures of Dorothy, the Scarecrow and the Tin Woodman* - Martin Gardner   *f*   2136

**Hamilton, Dennis**
*Reign* - Chet Williamson   *h*   5849

**Hudson, Cal**
*Symphony* - Adrian Savage   *h*   4847

**Hudson, Graham**
*Glimpses* - Lewis Shiner   *h*   4997

**Kravitz, Sol**
*Big Rock Beat* - Greg Kihn   *h*   3102

**LaBianca, Diana**
*The Hunger of the Beast* - John Driver   *h*   1656

**Martin**
*The Informers* - Brett Easton Ellis   *h*   1778

**Rippen, Jack**
*Celestial Dogs* - J.S. Russell   *h*   4734

**Storm, Richard**
*The Uncanny* - Andrew Klavan   *h*   3164

**White, Alan**
*Created By* - Richard Christian Matheson   *h*   3691

## PROFESSOR

**Ackerman, Larry**
*The Voice in the Basement* - T. Chris Martindale   *h*   3657

**Aigar**
*Lost in Translation* - Margaret Ball   *f*   315

**Aisling, Algernon**
*Voyage of the Basset* - James C. Christensen   *f*   1024

**Arthre, Roy "Ratha"**
*The Falcon Rises* - Michael C. Staudinger   *f*   5235

**Arturo, Maximillian**
*Sliders: The Novel* - Brad Linaweaver   *s*   3467

**Asher, James**
*Those Who Hunt the Night* - Barbara Hambly   *h*   2510
*Traveling with the Dead* - Barbara Hambly   *h*   2511

**Bagnell, Edward E.**
*The Boss in the Wall* - Avram Davidson   *h*   1396

**Baird, John**
*The Hemingway Hoax* - Joe Haldeman   *s*   2489

**Ballard, Cathy**
*The Voice in the Basement* - T. Chris Martindale   *h*   3657

**Barringer, Warren**
*Cursed Be the Child* - Mort Castle   *h*   937

**Beauduc, Clarence**
*Smoke and Mirrors* - Jane M. Lindskold   *s*   3476

**Belecamus, Dorian**
*Indiana Jones and the Peril at Delphi* - Rob MacGregor   *f*   3591

**Besser, Dudley J.**
*Coven* - Edward Lee   *h*   3390

**Blessing, William**
*Quoth the Crow* - David Bischoff   *h*   494

**Bramhall, Arthur**
*The Bear Went over the Mountain* - William Kotzwinkle   *f*   3222

**Brandon, Richard**
*God's Dice* - S. Andrew Swann   *f*   5364

**Briggs, Garner**
*Hence* - Brad Leithauser   *s*   3431

**Cable, John**
*Out of the Night* - Patrick Whalen   *h*   5771

**Camfrey, Maurizio**
*The Palm Dome* - Liz Fulton   *h*   2094

**Cassidy, Lylah**
*Looker* - Jorge Saralegui   *h*   4820

**Cept, Claire**
*Bring Me Children* - David Martin   *h*   3637

**Chiara**
*The Thirteenth Daughter of the Moon* - Steven Nightingale   *f*   4104

**Clisser**
*Dragonseye* - Anne McCaffrey   *s*   3730

**Collins, Elliot**
*Dark Winds* - Graham Watkins   *h*   5630

**Crane, George "Trip" III**
*The First Immortal* - James L. Halperin   *s*   2498

**Cross, Michael**
*Garden* - Matthew J. Costello  *h*  1197
*Wurm* - Matthew J. Costello  *h*  1202

**D'Auber MacLeod, Carli**
*Proxies* - Laura J. Mixon  *s*  3922

**Dobbs, Charles "Sugar" Franklin**
*The Healing of Crossroads* - Nick
    O'Donohoe  *f*  4195
*The Magic and the Healing* - Nick
    O'Donohoe  *f*  4196

**Doyle, Lionel**
*The Beast* - Marie Ardell White  *h*  5784

**Dunlet, Kate**
*Deep Quarry* - John E. Stith  *s*  5302

**Dunworthy, James**
*Doomsday Book* - Connie Willis  *s*  5868

**Emerson, Ian**
*University* - Bentley Little  *h*  3499

**Eschbach, Johan**
*The Ghost of the Revelator* - L.E. Modesitt
    Jr.  *s*  3931
*Of Tangible Ghosts* - L.E. Modesitt Jr.  *f*  3935

**Estrand, Philip**
*As She Climbed Across the Table* - Jonathan
    Lethem  *s*  3439

**Feit, Sherry**
*Walking Wounded* - Robert Devereaux  *h*  1507

**Ferro-Maine, Sylvia**
*The Ecolitan Enigma* - L.E. Modesitt Jr.  *s*  3927

**Forster, J.Q.R.**
*The Diamond Moon* - Paul Preuss  *s*  4417
*The Shining Ones* - Paul Preuss  *s*  4421

**Frankel, Sidney**
*Roadkill* - Richard Sanford  *h*  4815

**Galloway, Marcus**
*Walking Wounded* - Robert Devereaux  *h*  1507

**Gerard, Brian**
*Webs* - Scott Baker  *h*  304

**Ghormley, Richard**
*Wendigo Border* - Catherine Montrose  *h*  3967

**Gobi, Frank**
*Rim: A Novel of Virtual Reality* - Alexander
    Besher  *s*  475

**Grant, Alan**
*Jurassic Park* - Michael Crichton  *s*  1255

**Grossclout**
*Roc and a Hard Place* - Piers Anthony  *f*  187

**Habeggar**
*Slow Freight* - F.M. Busby  *s*  785

**Harding, Amelia "Blaze"**
*Forever Peace* - Joe Haldeman  *s*  2488

**Harlow, Robert "Bob"**
*Stones of the Dalai Lama* - Ken Mitchell  *f*  3916

**Hartke, Eugene Debs**
*Hocus Pocus or, What's the Hurry, Son?* - Kurt
    Vonnegut Jr.  *s*  5593

**Hasagawa, Padraic Hakim**
*Reality Is What You Can Get Away With: An
    Illustrated Screenplay* - Robert Anton
    Wilson  *s*  5904

**Hazzard, Calvin**
*Rough Beast* - Gary Goshgarian  *h*  2284

**Hillenbrand, Charles**
*Naomi's Room* - Jonathan Aycliffe  *h*  281

**Holbrook, Miller**
*One Wish* - C.J. Card  *f*  880

**James, Joshua**
*Darkborn* - Matthew J. Costello  *h*  1195

**Jennings, Patricia**
*The Taking* - Donald Beman  *h*  438

**Jones, Kellogg "Doc"**
*Laying the Music to Rest* - Dean Wesley
    Smith  *h*  5114

**Jordan, Richard**
*Otherworld* - Kenneth C. Flint  *h*  1959

**Kane, Michael**
*Kane of Old Mars* - Michael Moorcock  *s*  3983

**Kenley, Joshua Claybourne**
*A Time for Us* - Christine Holden  *f*  2731

**King, Schuyler "Skye"**
*MagicNet* - John DeChancie  *f*  1461

**Lansen, Mark**
*Golden Eyes* - John Gideon  *h*  2220

**Li, Harry**
*Eyes of the Empress* - Camille Bacon-Smith  *f*  285

**Lowry, Jack**
*Irrational Fears* - William Browning
    Spencer  *h*  5167

**Lowry, James**
*Fear* - L. Ron Hubbard  *h*  2789

**Macleod, Andrew**
*The Matrix* - Jonathan Aycliffe  *h*  280

**Marchenko, Ivan "Burian Klimus"**
*Frameshift* - Robert J. Sawyer  *s*  4856

**McClare, D.J.**
*Unwillingly to Earth* - Pauline Ashwell  *s*  231

**Meral, Katerin "Kitri Terry"**
*Fire Crossing* - Cheryl J. Franklin  *s*  2036

**Michaels, Kevin**
*October* - Al Sarrantonio  *h*  4832

**Milano, Gretta**
*Fallen* - Dee Graham  *h*  2302

**Morgan, Liam**
*Superstitious* - R.L. Stine  *h*  5290

**Morrow, Julian**
*The Secret History* - Donna Tartt  *h*  5398

**Murphy, Pilar**
*Puppet Master* - Barry T. Hawkins  *h*  2632

**Nigel**
*Specterworld* - Isidore Haiblum  *s*  2480

**Northfield, Anthony**
*War Birds* - R.M. Meluch  *s*  3875

**O'Sullivan, Mike**
*The Haunt* - John Fogarty  *h*  1966

**Pendeers, Kristine**
*Songs of Earth and Power* - Greg Bear  *f*  424

**Perkins, Blair**
*Bats* - William W. Johnstone  *h*  2926

**Perry, Eleanor**
*Fires of Eden* - Dan Simmons  *h*  5053

**Rivers, Neal**
*Keeper of the King* - Nigel Bennett  *h*  452

**Roberts, Tom**
*Neighbors* - Maureen S. Pusti  *h*  4450

**Rogers, Mara**
*Indiana Jones and the Unicorn's Legacy* - Rob
    MacGregor  *f*  3593

**Ross, John**
*A Knight of the Word* - Terry Brooks  *f*  714

**Sanderson, Loki**
*Destiny's Carnival* - Warren Murphy  *h*  4057

**Seguy, Eva**
*Mutant Star* - Karen Haber  *s*  2475

**Shrewsbury, Laban**
*The Trail of Cthulhu* - August Derleth  *h*  1497

**Singh, Alan**
*Brother to Dragons* - Charles Sheffield  *s*  4949

**Skena, Harry**
*Patton's Spaceship* - John Barnes  *s*  357

**Slakey, Justin**
*The Stainless Steel Rat Goes to Hell* - Harry
    Harrison  *s*  2574

**Slater, Peter**
*Secret Passages* - Paul Preuss  *s*  4420

**Smith, Vlad**
*The Boss in the Wall* - Avram Davidson  *h*  1396

**Smythe, Raoul "Rags"**
*Shade and Shadow* - Francine G. Woodbury  *f*  5967

**Standish, William**
*Mrs. God* - Peter Straub  *h*  5329

**Stephen**
*Lunatics* - Bradley Denton  *f*  1491

**Stern, Andrew**
*The Streeter* - Scott Ian Barry  *h*  373

**Summers, Erik**
*Wilderness* - Dennis Danvers  *h*  1349

**Tagge, Geoff**
*Mind Stealer* - Lee Duigon  *h*  1672

**Talley, Herbert**
*Beast* - Peter Benchley  *h*  440

**Thomas, Stephen**
*Nautilus* - Vonda N. McIntyre  *s*  3823

**Tyler, Maurice**
*Black Sun* - Robert Leininger  *s*  3429

**Wagner, Jeff**
*Twilight Time* - Rick Hautala  *h*  2613

**Walcott, Roland**
*Indiana Jones and the Unicorn's Legacy* - Rob
    MacGregor  *f*  3593

**Walther, Jeeris Belamy "Jeebee"**
*Wolf and Iron* - Gordon R. Dickson  *s*  1539

**Warner, Alex**
*The Armageddon Box* - Robert Weinberg  *h*  5690
*The Devil's Auction* - Robert Weinberg  *h*  5696

**Whaler, Nathaniel Firstborne**
*The Ecolitan Enigma* - L.E. Modesitt Jr.  *s*  3927

**Whitman, Lisl**
*Reprisal* - F. Paul Wilson  *h*  5896

**Williams, Tommy**
*Fear* - L. Ron Hubbard  *h*  2789

**Winfield, Angela**
*The Werewolf's Touch* - Cheri Scotch  *h*  4892

**Xanthus**
*The Fabulist* - John Vornholt  *f*  5595

## PROSPECTOR

**Baran, Theodore**
*The Ice Beast* - Frank A. Javor  *s*  2881

**Bird, Morris**
*Heavy Time* - C.J. Cherryh  *s*  995

**Caraval, Zacarias**
*Spirits of the Ordinary* - Kathleen Alcala  *f*  52

**Darch, Jack**
*The Specialist* - Wynne Whiteford  *s*  5788

**Dekker, Paul**
*Heavy Time* - C.J. Cherryh  *s*  995

**Pollard, Ben**
*Heavy Time* - C.J. Cherryh  *s*  995

## PROSTITUTE

**Calanthe**
*The Fulfillments of Fate and Desire* - Storm
 Constantine  *s*  1142

**Chapman, Annie**
*From Hell* - Alan Moore  *h*  3987

**Coachman, Dosh**
*Future Indefinite* - Dave Duncan  *f*  1678

**Delaney, Tania Jane**
*Born to Run* - Mercedes Lackey  *f*  3271

**Doshky "Dosh"**
*Crashcourse* - Wilhelmina Baird  *s*  295

**Gerard, Sybil**
*The Difference Engine* - William Gibson  *s*  2217

**Hafford, Jovvi**
*Challenges* - Sharon Green  *f*  2354
*Competition* - Sharon Green  *f*  2355

**Kathy**
*Dark Prince* - Keith Herber  *h*  2663

**Lawrence, Rod**
*Sheltered Lives* - Charles Oberndorf  *s*  4188

**Mary**
*Beautiful Strangers* - Melanie Tem  *h*  5420

**Maureen**
*Callahan's Lady* - Spider Robinson  *s*  4638

**Melina**
*Total Recall* - Piers Anthony  *s*  193

**Naomia**
*Chains of Light* - Quentin Thomas  *s*  5449

**Panthera**
*The Fulfillments of Fate and Desire* - Storm
 Constantine  *s*  1142

**Rima**
*The Last Rangers* - Jake Davis  *s*  1406

**Rumer**
*Waking Beauty* - Paul Witcover  *f*  5931

**SaDiablo, Daemon**
*Daughter of the Blood* - Anne Bishop  *f*  495

**Smoke, Smokey**
*Smoke and Mirrors* - Jane M. Lindskold  *s*  3476

**Stevens, Kathleen "Zero"**
*Near Death* - Nancy Kilpatrick  *h*  3113

**Stone, Cheryl**
*Dead Time* - Richard Lee Byers  *h*  796

**Sunshine, Mary**
*Vampire Junkies* - Norman Spinrad  *h*  5175

**Swann, Wanda**
*Pluto, Animal Lover* - Laren Stover  *h*  5318

**Thalassa**
*The Forging of the Shadows* - Oliver
 Johnson  *f*  2924

**Vanity**
*Dead Boys* - Richard Calder  *s*  836

**Vita**
*And Eternity* - Piers Anthony  *f*  162

**Wali, Linnet**
*Imposter* - Valerie J. Freireich  *s*  2050

**Wilkinson, Hilda**
*Spider* - Patrick McGrath  *h*  3815

## PSYCHIC

**Agis**
*The Verdant Passage* - Troy Denning  *f*  1487

**Ahlwen, Anders**
*The Snows of Jaspre* - Mary Caraker  *s*  878

**Akimura, Julian**
*Mutant Legacy* - Karen Haber  *s*  2474
*Mutant Star* - Karen Haber  *s*  2475

**Akimura, Rick**
*Mutant Legacy* - Karen Haber  *s*  2474

**Alfvaen, Tinling**
*Hellspark* - Janet Kagan  *s*  3000

**Alsnor, Lotta**
*The White Regiment* - John Dalmas  *s*  1327

**Alta**
*White Horse, Dark Dragon* - Robert C.
 Fleet  *f*  1947

**Althor**
*Catch the Lightning* - Catherine Asaro  *s*  218

**Althorpe, Cory**
*World Without End* - Molly Cochran  *f*  1093

**Alton, Lew**
*Exile's Song* - Marion Zimmer Bradley  *s*  632

**Alton, Margaret**
*Exile's Song* - Marion Zimmer Bradley  *s*  632

**Amber**
*Return Fire* - Charles Ingrid  *s*  2833

**Amby**
*Merlin's Bones* - Fred Saberhagen  *f*  4771

**Anniyas, Avira**
*The Ruins of Ambrai* - Melanie Rawn  *f*  4489

**Arbuthnot, Aubrey**
*The Devil You Say* - Elisa DeCarlo  *f*  1450
*Strong Spirits* - Elisa DeCarlo  *f*  1451

**Austin**
*Summon the Keeper* - Tanya Huff  *f*  2800

**Azaro**
*The Famished Road* - Ben Okri  *f*  4207
*Songs of Enchantment* - Ben Okri  *f*  4208

**Bailey, Penelope**
*Prophet* - Mike Resnick  *s*  4553
*Soothsayer* - Mike Resnick  *s*  4557

**Baines, Ti-Jeanne**
*Brown Girl in the Ring* - Nalo Hopkinson  *f*  2771

**Baker, Lenny**
*The Ascending* - T.M. Wright  *h*  5989

**Beatrice**
*The Broken Sword* - Molly Cochran  *f*  1091

**Beauchamp, Antoinette "Toni"**
*Mockingbird* - Sean Stewart  *f*  5273

**Beauchamp, Candace Jane "Candy"**
*Mockingbird* - Sean Stewart  *f*  5273

**Beauchamp, Elena**
*Mockingbird* - Sean Stewart  *f*  5273

**Beautiful Maria**
*Angel Station* - Walter Jon Williams  *s*  5833

**Bevol, Osraed**
*Taminy* - Maya Kaathryn Bohnhoff  *f*  563

**Biergarten, Ryerson**
*The Ascending* - T.M. Wright  *h*  5989
*Goodlow's Ghosts* - T.M. Wright  *h*  5991

**Billy**
*Aliens: The Female War* - Steve Perry  *s*  4290

**Blade, Thomas**
*The Marked Man* - Charles Ingrid  *s*  2831

**Bolte, Laura**
*The Thread That Binds the Bones* - Nina Kiriki
 Hoffman  *f*  2717

**Bond, Molly**
*Frameshift* - Robert J. Sawyer  *s*  4856

**Born, Eric**
*Reclamation* - Sarah Zettel  *s*  6081

**Bremen, Jeremy "Jerry"**
*The Hollow Man* - Dan Simmons  *s*  5054

**Brewster, Mackenzie**
*The Witch of Maple Park* - Stephanie S.
 Tolan  *f*  5478

**Briggs, Marilyn**
*Near Dead* - Stephen R. George  *h*  2202

**Bustamante, Robby**
*The Hollow Man* - Dan Simmons  *s*  5054

**Calanthe**
*The Enchantments of Flesh and Spirit* - Storm
 Constantine  *s*  1141

**Calliope**
*Ecstasia* - Francesca Lia Block  *f*  547
*Primavera* - Francesca Lia Block  *f*  551

**Cardenas, Angel**
*Montezuma Strip* - Alan Dean Foster  *s*  2011

**Carrie**
*Fire Margins* - Lisanne Norman  *s*  4137
*Fortune's Wheel* - Lisanne Norman  *s*  4138
*Razor's Edge* - Lisanne Norman  *s*  4139
*Turning Point* - Lisanne Norman  *s*  4140

**Cat "Bian"**
*Dreamfall* - Joan D. Vinge  *s*  5571

**C'boath, Joruus**
*Dark Force Rising* - Timothy Zahn  *s*  6052

**Chatwin, Jack**
*Ancient Echoes* - Robert Holdstock  *f*  2735

**Coddington, Quentin**
*Strange Stains and Mysterious Smells* - Terry
 Jones  *f*  2982

**Costa**
*Speaking Dreams* - Severna Park  *s*  4245

**Creedath**
*The Gates of Vensunor* - Carol Heller  *f*  2650

**Cuthberton-Jones, Angelica**
*Angela and Diabola* - Lynne Reid Banks  *f*  330

**Cuthberton-Jones, Diabola**
*Angela and Diabola* - Lynne Reid Banks  *f*  330

**Dakar**
*Ships of Merior* - Janny Wurts  *f*  6004

**Danio, Kiera**
*Wheel of Dreams* - Salinda Tyson  *f*  5529

**Darke, Makellen**
*Dancer of the Sixth* - Michelle Shirey
 Crean  *s*  1254

**d'Armand, Magnus Gallowglass "Gar Pike"**
*Warlock and Son* - Christopher Stasheff  *s*  5224
*A Wizard in Absentia* - Christopher Stasheff  *s*  5229
*A Wizard in Chaos* - Christopher Stasheff  *s*  5230
*A Wizard in Midgard* - Christopher Stasheff  *s*  5231
*A Wizard in Mind* - Christopher Stasheff  *s*  5232
*A Wizard in Peace* - Christopher Stasheff  *s*  5233
*A Wizard in War* - Christopher Stasheff  *s*  5234

**Dart, Kathy**
*Fury* - John Coyne  *h*  1237

**Dawn, Rhoda**
*Outworld Cats* - Jack Lovejoy  *s*  3536

**de Courcy, Guiscard**
*King Javan's Year* - Katherine Kurtz  *f*  3258

**DeChance, Megan**
*Hellworld* - Simon R. Green  *s*  2371

**Derae**
*Dark Prince* - David Gemmell  *f*  2187

**Desse, Gorynal**
*The Ruins of Ambrai* - Melanie Rawn  *f*  4489

**Destree**
*Storms of Victory* - Andre Norton  *f*  4162

**DeVries, Harlan**
*The Place* - T.M. Wright  *h*  5993

**Dhalvad**
*Seeking the Dream Brother* - Marcia J.
    Bennett  *s*  451

**Dions**
*Throne of Isis* - Judith Tarr  *f*  5397

**Dorothea "Diamond Mask"**
*Magnificat* - Julian May  *s*  3699

**Dulay**
*Inhuman Beings* - Jerry Jay Carroll  *s*  914

**Elen**
*City of Bones* - Martha Wells  *f*  5748

**Ella**
*Shade's Children* - Garth Nix  *s*  4130

**Emrys**
*The Lost Years of Merlin* - T.A. Barron  *f*  370
*Merlin and the Dragons* - Jane Yolen  *f*  6036

**E'non, Caelan**
*Realm of Light* - Deborah Chester  *f*  1008
*Reign of Shadows* - Deborah Chester  *f*  1009
*Shadow War* - Deborah Chester  *f*  1010

**Erskine, Harry**
*Burial* - Graham Masterton  *h*  3671

**Etchison, Theo**
*Forest of the Night* - S.P. Somtow  *f*  5156
*Riverrun* - S.P. Somtow  *f*  5159

**Eth**
*Dream-Weaver* - Louise Lawrence  *s*  3359

**Farhallen, Nydia**
*Daughter of Prophecy* - Anne Kelleher Bush  *f*  788

**Farseer, FitzChivalry "Fitz"**
*Assassin's Apprentice* - Robin Hobb  *f*  2693
*Assassin's Quest* - Robin Hobb  *f*  2694
*Royal Assassin* - Robin Hobb  *f*  2695

**Farseer, Verity**
*Royal Assassin* - Robin Hobb  *f*  2695

**Finister "Moraga"**
*Quicksilver's Knight* - Christopher Stasheff  *f*  5220

**Fischer, Benjamin Franklin**
*Hell House* - Richard Matheson  *h*  3685

**Fischer, Tim**
*Night* - Alan Rodgers  *h*  4649

**Foyle, Gulliver "Gully"**
*The Stars My Destination* - Alfred Bester  *s*  478

**Freund, Solomon**
*Child of the Light* - Janet Gluckman  *f*  2244

**Freund, Solomon "Sol"**
*Child of the Journey* - Janet Berliner  *f*  466
*Children of the Dusk* - Janet Berliner  *f*  467

**Frewin, Mary**
*The Red-Eared Ghosts* - Vivian Alcock  *f*  53

**Fuller, Maude**
*Slow Funeral* - Rebecca Ore  *f*  4221

**Furth, Dafyd**
*Exile's Challenge* - Angus Wells  *f*  5734
*Exile's Children* - Angus Wells  *f*  5735

**Fury**
*Jack the Bodiless* - Julian May  *s*  3698

**Gently, Dirk**
*The Long Dark Tea-Time of the Soul* - Douglas
    Adams  *s*  30

**Gilbert, India**
*India's Story* - Kathlyn S. Starbuck  *s*  5208

**Gold-eye**
*Shade's Children* - Garth Nix  *s*  4130

**Golding, Juniper**
*The Juniper Game* - Sherryl Jordan  *f*  2992

**Gotti, Guillemo**
*The Book of Earth* - Marjorie Bradley
    Kellogg  *f*  3044

**Grahame, John**
*The Templar Treasure* - Katherine Kurtz  *f*  3261

**Grandpa Rowe**
*The Cartoonist* - Sean Costello  *h*  1204

**Green Spider**
*People of the Lakes* - Kathleen O'Neal Gear  *f*  2164

**Guerner, Margaret "Peggy"**
*Alvin Journeyman* - Orson Scott Card  *f*  881

**Guester, Peggy**
*Prentice Alvin* - Orson Scott Card  *f*  896

**Gumby**
*The Lost Guardian* - Ronald Anthony Cross  *s*  1274

**Gwynn, Angharad "the Rowan"**
*The Rowan* - Anne McCaffrey  *s*  3747

**Gwynn-Raven, Angharad "the Rowan"**
*Damia* - Anne McCaffrey  *s*  3725

**Gwynn-Raven, Damia**
*Damia* - Anne McCaffrey  *s*  3725

**Haldane, Javan Jashan Urien**
*King Javan's Year* - Katherine Kurtz  *f*  3258

**Haldane, Rhys Michael Alister**
*The Bastard Prince* - Katherine Kurtz  *f*  3255

**Hansen, Claire Beth**
*Summon the Keeper* - Tanya Huff  *f*  2800

**Harootunian, Larque "Lark"**
*Larque on the Wing* - Nancy Springer  *f*  5180

**Huffington, Q-Jo**
*Half Asleep in Frog Pajamas* - Tom
    Robbins  *s*  4606

**Iban**
*Sing the Warmth* - Louise Marley  *s*  3630

**Inda, Sinykin**
*Mentor* - Kris Jensen  *s*  2898

**Iquar, Kryx**
*Catch the Lightning* - Catherine Asaro  *s*  218

**Jack the Bodiless**
*Magnificat* - Julian May  *s*  3699

**Jakri**
*Receive the Gift* - Louise Marley  *s*  3628

**Jane "Quicksilver"**
*Quicksilver's Knight* - Christopher Stasheff  *f*  5220

**Jarrett, Ma**
*Lucifer's Eye* - Hugh B. Cave  *h*  943

**Jemeret**
*Commencement* - Roby James  *s*  2877

**Jewel**
*Hunter's Death* - Michelle West  *f*  5758

**Jilseponie "Pony"**
*The Demon Spirit* - R.A. Salvatore  *f*  4795

**Jobber**
*Beldan's Fire* - Midori Snyder  *f*  5150

**Jones, Jeremiah "Jonesy"**
*Chaos Come Again* - Wilhelmina Baird  *s*  293

**Joy, Sandy "Sana"**
*Strands of Sunlight* - Gael Baudino  *f*  396

**Kastlin, Vask**
*Mainline* - Deborah Christian  *s*  1026

**Keelie**
*The Jigsaw Woman* - Kim Antieau  *f*  199

**Kemp, Lilah**
*Headhunter* - Timothy Findley  *h*  1939

**Kendrick, Amanda**
*When the Bough Breaks* - Mercedes Lackey  *f*  3302

**Kentraine, Beth**
*Knight of Ghosts and Shadows* - Mercedes
    Lackey  *f*  3285
*Summoned to Tourney* - Mercedes Lackey  *f*  3299

**Keogh, Harry**
*Deadspawn* - Brian Lumley  *h*  3550
*Deadspeak* - Brian Lumley  *h*  3551
*Necroscope: The Lost Years* - Brian
    Lumley  *h*  3560
*Resurgence* - Brian Lumley  *h*  3564
*The Source* - Brian Lumley  *h*  3565

**Keogh, Nathan**
*Bloodwars* - Brian Lumley  *h*  3547

**Ketral, Jarid Tal**
*Moonspeaker* - K.D. Wentworth  *s*  5754

**Kiklu, Nathan**
*Blood Brothers* - Brian Lumley  *h*  3546
*The Last Aerie* - Brian Lumley  *h*  3557

**Kiklu, Nestor**
*Blood Brothers* - Brian Lumley  *h*  3546
*The Last Aerie* - Brian Lumley  *h*  3557

**King, Greta**
*The Place* - T.M. Wright  *h*  5993

**Kinnison, Kimball**
*Galactic Patrol* - Edward E. Smith  *s*  5116
*Gray Lensman* - Edward E. Smith  *s*  5117

**Kirkland, Larry**
*Bloody Bones* - Laurell K. Hamilton  *h*  2512
*Circus of the Damned* - Laurell K.
    Hamilton  *h*  2515

**Kline, Felix**
*Sepulchre* - James Herbert  *h*  2672

**Kolkey, Alan**
*Walker between the Worlds* - Diane
    DesRochers  *f*  1499

**Korsakov, Jahn**
*One Mind's Eye* - Kathy Tyers  *s*  5525

**Kusac**
*Fire Margins* - Lisanne Norman  *s*  4137
*Fortune's Wheel* - Lisanne Norman  *s*  4138
*Razor's Edge* - Lisanne Norman  *s*  4139
*Turning Point* - Lisanne Norman  *s*  4140

**Kyle, Amy**
*The Nexus* - Mike McQuay  *f*  3860

**Lanart-Hastur, Mikhail**
*Exile's Song* - Marion Zimmer Bradley  *s*  632
*The Shadow Matrix* - Marion Zimmer
    Bradley  *s*  645

**Lannan**
*The Price of the Stars* - Debra Doyle  *s*  1604

**Lanta**
*Wanderer* - Donald E. McQuinn  *s*  3862

**LaSarde, Dawn**
*Walker between the Worlds* - Diane
    DesRochers  *f*  1499

**Laurel**
*The Hanged Man* - Francesca Lia Block  *f*  548

**Lavra**
*The Chymical Wedding* - Lindsay Clarke  *f*  1063

**Leith**
*The Prince of Ill Luck* - Susan Dexter  *f*  1512

**Lewis**
*Prisoner of Dreams* - Karen Ripley  *s*  4593
*The Tenth Class* - Karen Ripley  *s*  4594

**Library**
*Genetic Soldier* - George Turner  *s*  5492

**Lichen**
*People of the River* - W. Michael Gear   f   2168

**Lillorigga "Lilli"**
*The Red Wyvern* - Katharine Kerr   f   3074

**Lisane**
*Nameless Magery* - Delia Marshall Turner   f   5490

**Lisbei of Bethely**
*In the Mothers' Land* - Elisabeth Vonarburg   s   5590

**Llannat**
*Starpilot's Grave* - Debra Doyle   s   1606

**London, Claire**
*Heartlight* - Marion Zimmer Bradley   f   637

**Lovat, Peregrine**
*The Adept* - Katherine Kurtz   f   3254
*Dagger Magic* - Katherine Kurtz   f   3256
*The Lodge of the Lynx* - Katherine Kurtz   f   3259
*The Templar Treasure* - Katherine Kurtz   f   3261

**Lu**
*Sing the Light* - Louise Marley   s   3629

**Luet**
*The Ships of Earth* - Orson Scott Card   s   897

**Luz**
*The Secret Weavers: Stories of the Fantastic by Latin American Women* - Marjorie Agosin   f   43

**Lynx, Philip "Flinx"**
*Mid-Flinx* - Alan Dean Foster   s   2010

**Lyon, Afra**
*Damia* - Anne McCaffrey   s   3725

**Lyon, Isthian "Thian"**
*Damia's Children* - Anne McCaffrey   s   3726

**Lyon, Laria**
*Damia's Children* - Anne McCaffrey   s   3726

**Lyon, Rojer**
*Damia's Children* - Anne McCaffrey   s   3726
*Lyon's Pride* - Anne McCaffrey   s   3738

**Macaffrey, Lester Hill**
*Heathern* - Jack Womack   s   5958

**Macdonald, Dorothea**
*Diamond Mask: A Novel* - Julian May   s   3697

**Mandel, Greg**
*Mindstar Rising* - Peter F. Hamilton   s   2526
*A Quantum Murder* - Peter F. Hamilton   s   2527

**Masters, Gil**
*Fragments* - James F. David   h   1380

**Mazdan, Jennifer "Jennie"**
*Unquenchable Fire* - Rachel Pollack   f   4361

**McBride, Ronica**
*Commencement* - Roby James   s   2877

**McCabe, Darian**
*World Without End* - Molly Cochran   f   1093

**McConnell, Celeste**
*Assemblers of Infinity* - Kevin J. Anderson   s   100

**McLeod, Noel**
*The Adept* - Katherine Kurtz   f   3254
*Dagger Magic* - Katherine Kurtz   f   3256

**Medicine Plant**
*Dawn Land* - Joseph Bruchac   f   731

**Mendelssohn, Olivia**
*The Flies of Memory* - Ian Watson   s   5635

**Merlin, Emrys**
*The Seven Songs of Merlin* - T.A. Barron   f   372

**Metzgar, Joachim**
*Mutant Legacy* - Karen Haber   s   2474

**Miller, Alvin "Maker"**
*Alvin Journeyman* - Orson Scott Card   f   881
*Heartfire* - Orson Scott Card   f   889
*Prentice Alvin* - Orson Scott Card   f   896

**Miller, Calvin**
*Alvin Journeyman* - Orson Scott Card   f   881
*Heartfire* - Orson Scott Card   f   889

**Miller, Margaret "Peggy"**
*Heartfire* - Orson Scott Card   f   889

**Minnie "Miin"**
*Shame of Man* - Piers Anthony   s   188

**Miya**
*Dreamfall* - Joan D. Vinge   s   5571

**Monmart, Kevisson**
*House of Moons* - K.D. Wentworth   s   5752
*Moonspeaker* - K.D. Wentworth   s   5754

**Montoya, Nita**
*The Drylands* - Mary Rosenblum   s   4678

**Morales, Mira**
*The Hanged Man* - T.J. MacGregor   h   3594

**Morrison, Gertie**
*Threshold* - Bill Myers   s   4060

**Mreen**
*Receive the Gift* - Louise Marley   s   3628

**Muir, Oona**
*Fog Heart* - Thomas Tessier   h   5440

**Mulligan, Jack**
*Polar City Blues* - Katharine Kerr   s   3073

**Murgen**
*She Is the Darkness* - Glen Cook   f   1154

**Nahadeh, Nika**
*Ember From the Sun* - Mark Canter   s   870

**Nemony**
*Dream-Weaver* - Louise Lawrence   s   3359

**Niall**
*The Delta* - Colin Wilson   s   5878

**Novak, Simon**
*Graythings* - Pat Graversen   h   2335

**Nyushka**
*Death Channels* - Robert E. Vardeman   h   5562

**Onyx**
*Marks of Our Brothers* - Jane M. Lindskold   s   3475

**or-Reise, Garric**
*Queen of Demons* - David Drake   f   1640

**Orient, Finder**
*Finder* - Emma Bull   f   769

**Ousensky**
*The Boy Who Cried Werewolf* - Elvira   h   1800

**Ozette, Ember**
*Ember From the Sun* - Mark Canter   s   870

**Pairis, Rudy**
*Mefisto in Onyx* - Harlan Ellison   h   1786

**Parganas, Koot "Kootie" Hoomie**
*Expiration Date* - Tim Powers   f   4383

**Pellaz**
*The Enchantments of Flesh and Spirit* - Storm Constantine   s   1141

**Pidgely, Dylan**
*The Juniper Game* - Sherryl Jordan   f   2992

**Powell, Lincoln**
*The Demolished Man* - Alfred Bester   s   476

**Prilicla**
*The Galactic Gourmet* - James White   s   5778
*Mind Changer* - James White   s   5780

**Proteus**
*Exit to Reality* - Edith Forbes   s   1968

**Psycho, Jenny**
*Deathstalker War* - Simon R. Green   s   2366

**Pulivok, Akushtina "Tina" Santis**
*Catch the Lightning* - Catherine Asaro   s   218

**Radcliffe, Milton**
*Lorien Lost* - Michael King   f   3124

**Raeburn, Francis**
*Death of an Adept* - Katherine Kurtz   f   3257

**Ragman**
*The Host* - Peter R. Emshwiller   s   1819

**Raines, Michael**
*The Fugitive Stars* - Daniel Ransom   s   4479

**Ransome, Errec**
*By Honor Betray'd* - Debra Doyle   s   1598
*The Gathering Flame* - Debra Doyle   s   1599
*The Long Hunt* - Debra Doyle   s   1602

**Rap**
*Emperor and Clown* - Dave Duncan   f   1676
*Faery Lands Forlorn* - Dave Duncan   f   1677
*The Living God* - Dave Duncan   f   1682
*Magic Casement* - Dave Duncan   f   1683
*Perilous Seas* - Dave Duncan   f   1685
*The Stricken Field* - Dave Duncan   f   1688
*Upland Outlaws* - Dave Duncan   f   1690

**Ratkay, Dante**
*Resurrection Man* - Sean Stewart   f   5277

**Raven, Jeff**
*Lyon's Pride* - Anne McCaffrey   s   3738
*The Rowan* - Anne McCaffrey   s   3747

**Ravenwood, Janice**
*Wildest Dreams* - Norman Partridge   h   4256

**Remillard, Jon**
*Diamond Mask: A Novel* - Julian May   s   3697

**Remillard, Mark**
*Magnificat* - Julian May   s   3699

**Remillard, Rogatien**
*Diamond Mask: A Novel* - Julian May   s   3697
*Jack the Bodiless* - Julian May   s   3698

**Renfield, Tom**
*The Thread That Binds the Bones* - Nina Kiriki Hoffman   f   2717

**Rhia**
*The Lost Years of Merlin* - T.A. Barron   f   370

**Rhiannon "Rhia"**
*The Seven Songs of Merlin* - T.A. Barron   f   372

**Rogillard, Jack**
*Jack the Bodiless* - Julian May   s   3698

**Roshannon, Nikkael**
*Wheel of Dreams* - Salinda Tyson   f   5529

**Ross, John**
*Running with the Demon* - Terry Brooks   f   715

**Sally**
*The Kronos Condition* - Emily Devenport   s   1502

**Sarah**
*Brother to Dragons, Companion to Owls* - Jane M. Lindskold   f   3473

**Seale, Willow**
*The Silent Strength of Stones* - Nina Kiriki Hoffman   f   2716

**Senea**
*The Heldan* - Deborah Talmadge-Bickmore   f   5383

**sen'Laurea, Terricel "Terris"**
*Northlight* - Deborah Wheeler   s   5775

**Shackleford, Ray**
*Glimpses* - Lewis Shiner   h   4997

**Shadith**
*Fire in the Sky* - Jo Clayton   s   1067
*Shadowkill* - Jo Clayton   s   1069
*Shadowplay* - Jo Clayton   s   1070
*Shadowspeer* - Jo Clayton   s   1071

**Shar, Moabet**
*The Illusionists* - Faren Miller   f   3894

**Sharrea**
*Bone Danc: A Fantasy for Technophiles* - Emma Bull  s  766

**Shedwyn**
*Beldan's Fire* - Midori Snyder  f  5150

**Shunlar**
*The Gates of Vensunor* - Carol Heller  f  2650

**Siglen**
*The Rowan* - Anne McCaffrey  s  3747

**Silver, Mier**
*Mission: Tori* - Johanna Bolton  s  564

**Simon, Chuck**
*Psi-Man* - David Peters  s  4305

**Sinclair, Adam**
*The Adept* - Katherine Kurtz  f  3254
*Dagger Magic* - Katherine Kurtz  f  3256
*Death of an Adept* - Katherine Kurtz  f  3257
*The Lodge of the Lynx* - Katherine Kurtz  f  3259
*The Templar Treasure* - Katherine Kurtz  f  3261

**Singer**
*Deathgift* - Ann Tonsor Zeddies  s  6061

**Sira**
*Sing the Light* - Louise Marley  s  3629
*Sing the Warmth* - Louise Marley  s  3630

**Siri**
*Receive the Gift* - Louise Marley  s  3628

**Smith, Desi "Daisy Smeet"**
*Chaos Come Again* - Wilhelmina Baird  s  293

**Smith, Sam**
*World Without End* - Molly Cochran  f  1093

**Snout**
*Aliens Stole My Body* - Bruce Coville  s  1217

**Sorak**
*The Outcast* - Simon Hawke  f  2621
*The Seeker* - Simon Hawke  f  2624

**Sprits**
*Concrete Hotel* - C. Christopher Caldon  h  839

**Stewart, Genevieve "Genny"**
*Jupiter's Daughter* - Tom Hyman  s  2820

**Stone, Arla**
*Reclamation* - Sarah Zettel  s  6081

**Straker, Ellis**
*Yamato: A Rage in Heaven* - Ken Kato  s  3014

**Stroud, Abraham Hale**
*Curse of the Vampire* - Geoffrey Caine  h  832
*Legion of the Dead* - Geoffrey Caine  h  833
*Wake of the Werewolf* - Geoffrey Caine  h  834

**Sullivan, Pete**
*Expiration Date* - Tim Powers  f  4383

**sus-Airaalin, Theio syn-Ricte**
*By Honor Betray'd* - Debra Doyle  s  1598

**Taine, Sid**
*The Black Lodge* - Robert Weinberg  h  5692

**Tal, Haemas Sennay**
*House of Moons* - K.D. Wentworth  s  5752
*Moonspeaker* - K.D. Wentworth  s  5754

**Tamai**
*Flameweaver* - Margaret Ball  f  314

**Taminy-a-Cuinn**
*The Crystal Rose* - Maya Kaathryn Bohnhoff  f  560
*Taminy* - Maya Kaathryn Bohnhoff  f  563

**Tamis**
*Lion of Macedon* - David Gemmell  f  2189

**Tanaka, Joey**
*Mind Kill* - Richard La Plante  h  3267

**Tanith**
*The Nightwalker* - Thomas Tessier  h  5442

**Tanner, Florence**
*Hell House* - Richard Matheson  h  3685

**Tate, Augustus "Gus"**
*The Demolished Man* - Alfred Bester  s  476

**Ted**
*The Kronos Condition* - Emily Devenport  s  1502

**Thomas, Quentin**
*Lunar Justice* - Charles L. Harness  s  2545

**Thuryn, Rhysel**
*The Bastard Prince* - Katherine Kurtz  f  3255

**Tierney, Rose**
*The Parasite* - Ramsey Campbell  h  863

**Tomaso**
*Polar City Blues* - Katharine Kerr  s  3073

**Topaz**
*Mistworld* - Simon R. Green  s  2372

**Torfinn, Llyn**
*One Mind's Eye* - Kathy Tyers  s  5525

**Torrance, Danny**
*The Shining* - Stephen King  h  3141

**Tregarde, Diana**
*Children of the Night* - Mercedes Lackey  h  3276

**Trigg, Dino**
*Megalomania* - Ian Wallace  s  5621

**Troi, Deanna**
*Q-Space* - Greg Cox  s  1228

**Tula**
*In the Mothers' Land* - Elisabeth Vonarburg  s  5590

**Tye, Asher**
*A Roil of Stars* - Don Wismer  s  5930

**Typhoid Mary**
*Twilight of the Empire* - Simon R. Green  s  2374

**Ussemitus**
*Mother of Storms* - Adrian Cole  f  1101

**Vader, Darth**
*Shadows of the Empire* - Steve Perry  s  4299

**Valdez, Mark**
*Burning Water* - Mercedes Lackey  h  3272

**Valdoria kva Skolia, Kelricson Garlin**
*The Last Hawk* - Catherine Asaro  s  219

**van Hooven, Karen**
*Burial* - Graham Masterton  h  3671

**Varia**
*The Lion of Farside* - John Dalmas  f  1324

**Veronica**
*Guises of the Mind* - Rebecca Neason  s  4081

**Verrou, Nick**
*The Silent Strength of Stones* - Nina Kiriki Hoffman  f  2716

**von Alte, Erde**
*The Book of Earth* - Marjorie Bradley Kellogg  f  3044

**Wan, Lai**
*Some Things Never Die* - Robert Morgan  h  4005

**Westbrook, Louisa**
*Flameweaver* - Margaret Ball  f  314

**Wheele, Catherine**
*Sunglasses After Dark* - Nancy A. Collins  h  1124

**White, Carrie**
*Carrie* - Stephen King  h  3127

**White Ash**
*People of the Earth* - W. Michael Gear  f  2166

**Wilson, Karen**
*The Headsman* - James Neal Harvey  h  2599

**Yoshida, Dorthy**
*Eternal Light* - Paul J. McAuley  s  3710

**Zakri**
*Sing the Warmth* - Louise Marley  s  3630

**Zambendorf, Karl**
*The Immortality Option* - James P. Hogan  s  2725

**Zverkov, Alexey**
*Spellcaster* - J. Edward Ames  h  92

# PSYCHOLOGIST

**Akimura, Julian**
*Mutant Legacy* - Karen Haber  s  2474

**Belman, Lola**
*The Ganymede Club* - Charles Sheffield  s  4955

**Bond, Molly**
*Frameshift* - Robert J. Sawyer  s  4856

**Braithwaite**
*Final Diagnosis* - James White  s  5777

**Brandon, Richard**
*God's Dice* - S. Andrew Swann  f  5364

**Brennan, Ted**
*House Haunted* - Al Sarrantonio  h  4830

**Burke, Martin**
*/ -* Greg Bear  s  413
*Queen of Angels* - Greg Bear  s  423

**Byrd, Benjamin**
*St. Peter's Wolf* - Michael Cadnum  h  816

**Calvin, Susan**
*I, Robot: The Illustrated Screenplay* - Harlan Ellison  s  1785

**Chalmers, Reed**
*The Enchanter Reborn* - L. Sprague de Camp  f  1413

**Craslowe, Hadrian**
*Greely's Cove* - John Gideon  h  2221

**Craythorne**
*Mind Changer* - James White  s  5780

**Creighton, Jonathan**
*The Barrens* - F. Paul Wilson  h  5884

**Davison, Bill**
*Was* - Geoff Ryman  f  4758

**Decker, Henry**
*Sick* - Jay R. Bonansinga  h  571

**Deering, Wilma**
*A Life in the Future* - Martin Caidin  s  827

**Dobbs, Evelyn**
*Fool's War* - Sarah Zettel  s  6079

**Donnelly, John**
*Door Number Three* - Patrick O'Leary  s  4210

**Franklyn, Kit**
*Blood on the Bayou* - D.J. Donaldson  h  1570

**Gable, Robert**
*Serpent's Gift* - A.C. Crispin  s  1261
*Starbridge* - A.C. Crispin  s  1265
*Voices of Chaos* - A.C. Crispin  s  1266

**Haas, Alexandria Victoria**
*Mindplayers* - Pat Cadigan  s  806

**Halburton, Gustav**
*Dark Dreaming* - Pat Franklin  h  2040

**Hinson, Jody**
*The Halflife* - Sharon Webb  s  5664

**Kane, Anna**
*Nine Levels Down* - William Dantz  h  1347

**Lasalle, Stevie**
*The Death Crystal* - J. Edward Ames  h  91

**MacLaren, Colin**
*Heartlight* - Marion Zimmer Bradley  f  637

**Martin, Wes**
*Fragments* - James F. David   *h*   1380

**McClane**
*The Collected Stories of Philip K. Dick, Volume Two: We Can Remember It for You Wholesale* - Philip K. Dick   *s*   1520

**Metcalf, Lily**
*Resume with Monsters* - William Browning Spencer   *h*   5168

**Moore, Julie**
*The Cold One* - Christopher Pike   *h*   4327

**Morgan, Meredith**
*Dark Dreaming* - Pat Franklin   *h*   2040

**Murphy, Pilar**
*Puppet Master* - Barry T. Hawkins   *h*   2632

**O'Mara**
*The Genocidal Healer* - James White   *s*   5779
*Mind Changer* - James White   *s*   5780

**Outerbridge, Philip**
*Some of Your Blood* - Theodore Sturgeon   *h*   5347

**Puerta, Raul**
*The Between* - Tannarive Due   *h*   1669

**Rand, Adrienne**
*Prototype* - Brian Hodge   *h*   2704

**Reeling, Kate**
*Manhattan Heat* - Ken Eulo   *h*   1851

**Ryan, Holly**
*Sacrifice* - Richard Kinion   *h*   3146

**Schafer, Justin**
*Alien Influences* - Kristine Kathryn Rusch   *s*   4711

**Segretti, Paolo**
*Mindplayers* - Pat Cadigan   *s*   806

**Selden, Penelope**
*The Whims of Creation* - Simon Hawke   *s*   2626

**Shea, Harold**
*The Enchanter Reborn* - L. Sprague de Camp   *f*   1413

**Sheerin 501**
*Nightfall* - Isaac Asimov   *s*   248

**Sieyes**
*A Whisper of Time* - Paula E. Downing   *s*   1595

**Stern, Andrew**
*The Streeter* - Scott Ian Barry   *h*   373

**Todd, Redmond "Red" Eugene**
*Lovelock* - Orson Scott Card   *s*   892

**Torfinn, Karine**
*One Mind's Eye* - Kathy Tyers   *s*   5525

**Towne, Sam**
*Superstition* - David Ambrose   *h*   90

**Troi, Deanna**
*Chains of Command* - Bill McCay   *s*   3767
*Guises of the Mind* - Rebecca Neason   *s*   4081
*Imzadi* - Peter David   *s*   1383
*The Last Stand* - Brad Ferguson   *s*   1923
*Q-Space* - Greg Cox   *s*   1228
*The Soldiers of Fear* - Dean Wesley Smith   *s*   5115
*Triangle: Imzadi II* - Peter David   *s*   1388

**Turner, Marian**
*Night Glow* - Martin James   *h*   2867

**Veering, Albert**
*7 Steps to Midnight* - Richard Matheson   *h*   3682

**Weiss, Rachel**
*Shadow Dance* - Douglas Borton   *h*   577

**Westerman, Stacy**
*Lorelei* - Mark A. Clements   *h*   1086

**Wiggin, Andrew**
*Xenocide* - Orson Scott Card   *s*   899

**Williams, Albert**
*Some of Your Blood* - Theodore Sturgeon   *h*   5347

**Winters, Elizabet**
*Bedlam Boyz* - Ellen Guon   *f*   2467

## PUBLIC RELATIONS

**Baker, Denise**
*Soul Catcher* - Colin Kersey   *h*   3081

**Chapel, John**
*Red Bride* - Christopher Fowler   *h*   2019

**Collier, Rance**
*Slow Freight* - F.M. Busby   *s*   785

**Dobbs**
*Kill Crazy* - L.S. Riker   *s*   4590

**Farraday**
*Silicon Embrace* - John Shirley   *s*   5009

**Gordon, Roger Jr.**
*Bride of the Slime Monster* - Craig Shaw Gardner   *f*   2125

**Hanover, June**
*Burning Bright* - J.S. Russell   *h*   4733

**Kaiser, Valentine**
*A Matter of Taste* - Fred Saberhagen   *h*   4770

**McGlinn, Desiree**
*Mask of the Night* - Mary Ryan   *h*   4753

**Mitchell, Paige**
*Lethal Exposure* - Kevin J. Anderson   *s*   110

**Ogle, Cyrus "Cy"**
*Interface* - Stephen Bury   *s*   781

**Silk, Venture**
*The Forever Drug* - Steve Perry   *s*   4296

**Spano, Constance "Connie"**
*Independence Day* - Dean Devlin   *s*   1508

**Taylor**
*The Tenth Class* - Karen Ripley   *s*   4594

**Wishart, Adam**
*The Walking Shadow* - Brian Stableford   *s*   5195

## PUBLISHER

**Dixon, Travis**
*Night Brothers* - Sidney Williams   *h*   5824

**Finnegan, Jack**
*Glimmering* - Elizabeth Hand   *s*   2535

**Gibbs, Hank**
*Psycho House* - Robert Bloch   *h*   542

**Hamilton, Rick**
*The Man Who Turned into Himself* - David Ambrose   *h*   89

**James, Will**
*Warpath* - Tony Daniel   *s*   1337

**Seton, Winston**
*Naming the Flowers* - Kate Wilhelm   *s*   5809

**Sturdley, Harry**
*Crossover* - Bill McCay   *f*   3768

**Walton, Robert**
*Gothic Romance* - Emmanuel Carrere   *h*   912

**Wasserman, Janus Cornelius**
*The House of the Toad* - Richard L. Tierney   *h*   5470

## RACIST

**Bracher, Frederick**
*Mark of the Werewolf* - Jeffrey Sackett   *h*   4780

**McKendree**
*Devil's Deal* - Richard Austin   *s*   277

## RADIO

**Alexander, Sam**
*SETI* - Frederick Fichman   *s*   1930

**Hale, Dick**
*Night Mask* - William W. Johnstone   *h*   2931

## RADIO PERSONALITY

**Cooley, Dan**
*The Devil and Dan Cooley* - Holly Lisle   *f*   3480

**Csejthe, Christopher**
*One Foot in the Grave* - Wm. Mark Simmons   *f*   5062

**Goodall, Sasha**
*Fear Nothing* - Dean R. Koontz   *h*   3207

**Handler, Paul**
*Deathgrip* - Brian Hodge   *h*   2700

**LaCroix, Lucien**
*Forever Knight: A Stirring of Dust* - Susan Sizemore   *h*   5078

**Russie, Moishe**
*Worldwar: Striking the Balance* - Harry Turtledove   *s*   5516

**Scott, Aaron "Sunset"**
*Shock Radio* - Leigh Clark   *h*   1052

**Sigmond, Jerry**
*Dust* - Charles Pellegrino   *h*   4279

## RAKE

**Skelbrooke, Francis**
*The Gnome's Engine* - Teresa Edgerton   *f*   1742

## RANCHER

**Abernathy, Tom**
*Thunder Road* - Chris Curry   *h*   1296

**Alfonso**
*Under the Shadow* - Jane Toombs   *h*   5481

**Carmichael, Anson**
*The Alien Years* - Robert Silverberg   *s*   5027

**Ericson, Jacob**
*Jacob's Hands* - Aldous Huxley   *f*   2817

**Fundan, Fair**
*To a Highland Nation* - Christopher Rowley   *s*   4698

**Hawkes, Benton**
*Man o' War* - William Shatner   *s*   4932

**Kinner's Son, Kensher**
*The Blood of a Dragon* - Lawrence Watt-Evans   *f*   5640

**Reeve, Todd**
*Crisis on Doona* - Anne McCaffrey   *s*   3723

**Shade, John**
*Nightshade* - Jack Butler   *s*   789

**Spenotex, Arakaho Blundy**
*Stopping at Slowyear* - Frederik Pohl   *s*   4355

**Wiltin, Hof**
*To a Highland Nation* - Christopher Rowley   *s*   4698

## RANGER

**De Brouchee, Montolio**
*Sojourn* - R.A. Salvatore   *f*   4806

**Linders, Martin**
*The Quiet* - Patrick Billings   h   488

**Michaels, Steve**
*Carmilla: The Return* - Kyle Marffin   h   3623

**Norris, Robert**
*Vyrmin* - Gene Lazuta   h   3376

**Pirelli, Peter**
*Swamp* - Peter Tremayne   h   5483

**Ranger Dan**
*Camp Vamp* - Elvira   h   1801

**Tanner, John**
*The Quiet* - Patrick Billings   h   488

## REAL ESTATE AGENT

**Barnes, Collee**
*Black Death* - R. Karl Largent   h   3337

**Chessner, Barbara**
*Infernal Affairs* - Jane Heller   h   2652

**Demos, Maria**
*Souls* - Katina Alexis   h   71

**Dvorak, Teresa**
*Frostwing* - Richard A. Knaak   f   3170

**Harker, Jonathan**
*Bram Stoker's Dracula* - Fred Saberhagen   h   4763

**Lutz, Frances**
*Infernal Affairs* - Jane Heller   h   2652

**Masterson, Gordon**
*Killing Frost* - Dan I. Blake   h   514

**Maxwell, Maureen**
*Relife* - Dan Barton   h   376

**Niley, Frank**
*Blue Moon* - Laurell K. Hamilton   h   2513

**Poker, Susan**
*The Hacker and the Ants* - Rudy Rucker   s   4704

**Roberts, Katie**
*The Haunting* - Ruby Jean Jensen   h   2901

**S-, Delia**
*First Love: A Gothic Tale* - Joyce Carol
   Oates   h   4183

**Stebbins, Ivy**
*All the Bells on Earth* - James P. Blaylock   f   518

**Willson, Andrea**
*Dark Reunion* - Stephen R. George   h   2198

## REANIMATED DEAD

**Ash, Leanard**
*Shadows Fall* - Simon R. Green   f   2373

**Bogert, Norman**
*I, Robot: The Illustrated Screenplay* - Harlan
   Ellison   s   1785

**Capone, Al**
*Consolidation* - Peter F. Hamilton   s   2523

**Cheops**
*The Mummy!: A Tale of the Twenty-Second Century* -
   Jane Webb Loudon   h   3526

**Christian, Fletcher**
*Conflict* - Peter F. Hamilton   s   2522

**Clerval, Henry**
*Brittle Innings* - Michael Bishop   h   498

**Crea**
*The Darker Passions: Frankenstein* - Amarantha
   Knight   h   3180

**Daniels, Danny**
*Deadweight* - Robert Devereaux   h   1505

**Devreaux, Luc**
*Universal Soldier* - Robert Tine   s   5476

**Gorobec, Anton**
*I Am Frankenstein* - C. Dean Andersson   h   140

**Herrin, Ashley**
*Harrowgate* - Daniel H. Gower   h   2292

**Hitch**
*Dead Heat* - Del Stone Jr.   h   5313

**Jed**
*Jed the Dead* - Alan Dean Foster   s   2007

**Keelie**
*The Jigsaw Woman* - Kim Antieau   f   199

**LaFontaine, Horace "Gray Redstar"**
*Blue Light* - Walter Mosley   s   4042

**Lewin, Bonnie**
*Conflict* - Peter F. Hamilton   s   2522

**Merrick, Geoffrey Robert**
*Fear Itself* - Ric Meyers   h   3881
*Living Hell* - Ric Meyers   h   3882
*Worst Nightmare* - Ric Meyers   h   3883

**Nolan, Durk**
*Celia* - Ruby Jean Jensen   h   2900

**Nuwen, Pham**
*A Fire upon the Deep* - Vernor Vinge   s   5573

**Old Ric**
*The Shadow Eater* - Adam Lee   f   3386

**Outis, Charles "Mr. Charlie"**
*Solis* - A.A. Attanasio   s   272

**Poons, Windle**
*Reaper Man* - Terry Pratchett   f   4399

**Protarus, Iraj**
*Wolves of the Gods* - Allan Cole   f   1111

**Ramses the Great**
*The Mummy, or Ramses the Damned* - Anne
   Rice   h   4572

**Scott, Andrew**
*Universal Soldier* - Robert Tine   s   5476

**Smithers, Albert**
*Black as Blood* - Rob Chilson   f   1014

**Soo, Hannah**
*Take Back Plenty* - Colin Greenland   s   2419

**Tucker, William Alec III**
*A King of Infinite Space* - Allen Steele   s   5243

**Wolfe, Jacob**
*Deathstalker Honor* - Simon R. Green   s   2364

**Zachary**
*Guilty Pleasures* - Laurell K. Hamilton   f   2517

## REBEL

**Akma**
*Earthborn* - Orson Scott Card   s   884

**Ashton, Choe**
*Signs of Life* - M. John Harrison   s   2580

**Falsche, Viktor**
*The Janus Mask* - Richard A. Knaak   f   3171

**Gi'Suei'Obodi'Sedon**
*The Last Dancer* - Daniel Keys Moran   s   3994

**Harrowslough, Holly**
*Finder's Bane* - Kate Novak   f   4165

**Khalid, Ibn ben**
*The Widowmaker Reborn* - Mike Resnick   s   4560

**Kylie, Gabriel**
*Anvil* - Nicolas van Pallandt   s   5540

**Linn-Campbell, Neena**
*A Covenant of Justice* - David Gerrold   s   2207

**Maniakes**
*Hammer and Anvil* - Harry Turtledove   f   5503

**McCann, Rorin**
*Caledon of the Mists* - Deborah Turner
   Harris   f   2560

**Sobek, Yoo**
*Hostile Takeover* - Jack McKinney   s   3849

## RECEPTIONIST

**Cobb, Phoebe**
*Everville* - Clive Barker   h   338

**Gregory, Libby**
*Ghost Boy* - Jean Simon   h   5064

**King, Ellen**
*The Faery Convention* - Brett Davis   f   1399

**Pond, Susan**
*Passive Intruder* - Michael Upchurch   h   5530

## RECLUSE

**Anderson, Duskin**
*The High House* - James Stoddard   f   5311

**Barber, Clem**
*The Sand Dwellers* - Adam Niswander   h   4112

**Finnegan, Jack**
*Glimmering* - Elizabeth Hand   s   2535

**Gravel, Edmund**
*The Haunted Tea Cosy: A Dispirited and Distasteful
   Diversion for Christmas* - Edward Gorey   h   2276

**Haramis**
*Lady of the Trillium* - Marion Zimmer
   Bradley   f   641

**Inya**
*Kar Kalim* - Deborah Christian   f   1025

**Kubick, Ruby**
*Glass Houses* - Laura J. Mixon   s   3921

**Rushkin, Vincent Adjani**
*Memory and Dream* - Charles de Lint   f   1433

**Smith, Brandon**
*Virtual Girl* - Amy Thomson   s   5462

**Talbot, Edward "Eddie"**
*Her Monster* - Jeff Collignon   h   1115

**Wallace, Enoch**
*Way Station* - Clifford D. Simak   s   5048

**Wolf, Behrooz "Bey"**
*Proteus in the Underworld* - Charles
   Sheffield   s   4962

## REFUGEE

**Ayyah**
*Cat's Gambit* - Leslie Gadallah   s   2099

**ben Sierra Nueva, Amos "Simeon"**
*The City Who Fought* - Anne McCaffrey   s   3722

**Bishop, Toby**
*Furious Gulf* - Gregory Benford   s   447

**Casey, Jerry**
*Cold Allies* - Patricia Anthony   s   157

**du Boise, Llysette**
*The Ghost of the Revelator* - L.E. Modesitt
   Jr.   s   3931

**Fileli, Mathembe**
*The Broken Land* - Ian McDonald   s   3791

**Galele, Tedla**
*Halfway Human* - Carolyn Ives Gilman   s   2237

**Lisane**
*Nameless Magery* - Delia Marshall Turner   f   5490

**Mondragon, Tom**
*Endgame* - C.J. Cherryh   *s*   986

**ni Bron, Deir**
*Redmagic* - Crawford Kilian   *f*   3107

**Russie, Moishe**
*Worldwar: Striking the Balance* - Harry
   Turtledove   *s*   5516

**Rusty**
*A Time for Dragons* - Gary Gentile   *s*   2193

**Sam**
*Hope of Earth* - Piers Anthony   *s*   175

**Scott**
*A Time for Dragons* - Gary Gentile   *s*   2193

**Serege, Tristan "Tris"**
*Echoes of Issel* - Diann Thornley   *s*   5466

**Waesc, Dorias**
*Reclamation* - Sarah Zettel   *s*   6081

**Zwakh, Ignatz**
*Dead Boys* - Richard Calder   *s*   836

## REINCARNATED PERSON

**Fiona**
*Ronin* - D.A. Heeley   *f*   2639

**Jaad**
*Ronin* - D.A. Heeley   *f*   2639

**Nielson, Sasha**
*The Starry Child* - Lynn Hanna   *f*   2540

**Severn, Joseph**
*The Fall of Hyperion* - Dan Simmons   *s*   5052

**Shadrack**
*Ronin* - D.A. Heeley   *f*   2639

**Thaxton, Wendall**
*The Higher Space* - Jamil Nasir   *s*   4070

**Wiggin, Peter**
*Children of the Mind* - Orson Scott Card   *s*   883

## RELATIVE

**Casteel, Luke Jr.**
*Gates of Paradise* - V.C. Andrews   *h*   145

**Chambers, Christel**
*The Misconceiver* - Lucy Ferriss   *s*   1929

**Claus, Bob "Santa"**
*Santa's Twin* - Dean R. Koontz   *f*   3214

**Davis, Shannon**
*The Store* - Bentley Little   *h*   3497

**Jack the Bodiless**
*Magnificat* - Julian May   *s*   3699

**Lee, Amy**
*The Earth Giant* - Melvin Burgess   *s*   773

**Lee, Peter**
*The Earth Giant* - Melvin Burgess   *s*   773

**Madison, Jay**
*The Gryphon King* - Tom Deitz   *f*   1473

**Marat, Beverly**
*Thirst of the Vampire* - T. Lucien Wright   *h*   5988

**Michaels, Judge**
*The M.D.: A Horror Story* - Thomas M.
   Disch   *h*   1561

**Miller, Alvin "Maker"**
*Alvin Journeyman* - Orson Scott Card   *f*   881

**Miller, Calvin**
*Alvin Journeyman* - Orson Scott Card   *f*   881
*Heartfire* - Orson Scott Card   *f*   889

**Nahadeh, Nika**
*Ember From the Sun* - Mark Canter   *s*   870

**Ratkay, Jet**
*Resurrection Man* - Sean Stewart   *f*   5277

**Risinger, Werner**
*Oktober* - Stephen Gallagher   *h*   2112

**Rosen, Jenna**
*Raven Stole the Moon* - Garth Stein   *h*   5249

**Shiro, Miaowara**
*Samurai Cat Goes to Hell* - Mark E. Rogers   *f*   4655

**Stout, Thomas A.**
*Humpty Dumpty: An Oval* - Damon Knight   *s*   3186

**Susan**
*Fade* - Robert Cormier   *h*   1188

**Tolar, Rob**
*The Gryphon King* - Tom Deitz   *f*   1473

**Troys, Taylor Thaddeus "Taytay"**
*Meeting the Minotaur* - Carol Dawson   *f*   1409

## RELIGIOUS

**Aenea**
*Endymion* - Dan Simmons   *s*   5051
*The Rise of Endymion* - Dan Simmons   *s*   5059

**Ainvar**
*Druids* - Morgan Llywelyn   *f*   3502

**Akiba**
*Freeze Frames* - Katharine Kerr   *s*   3071

**Alanda, Marcus**
*Quest for the Fallen Star* - Piers Anthony   *f*   185

**Alexander**
*The Bighead* - Edward Lee   *h*   3387

**Alston, John "Skiddle"**
*The Great Wheel* - Ian R. MacLeod   *s*   3599

**al'Vere, Egwene**
*A Crown of Swords* - Robert Jordan   *f*   2984
*The Dragon Reborn* - Robert Jordan   *f*   2985
*The Path of Daggers* - Robert Jordan   *f*   2989

**Anaral**
*An Acceptable Time* - Madeleine L'Engle   *f*   3436

**Anthony**
*Catacomb* - Andrew Laurance   *h*   3347

**Arcangelo**
*Zaragoz* - Brian Craig   *f*   1241

**Ardis**
*Four & Twenty Blackbirds* - Mercedes
   Lackey   *f*   3283

**Arnez, Jorge "Mal Sangre"**
*Voodoo Child* - Michael Reaves   *h*   4498

**Augustine**
*Blameless in Abaddon* - James Morrow   *f*   4029

**Auk, Maytera**
*Exodus From the Long Sun* - Gene Wolfe   *s*   5941

**Auriane**
*The Light Bearer* - Donna Gillespie   *f*   2229

**Avelyn**
*The Demon Awakens* - R.A. Salvatore   *f*   4794

**Ayth, Argoth**
*Demon Moon* - Jack Williamson   *s*   5862

**Bach, Arthur**
*Night Prophets* - Paul F. Olson   *h*   4213

**Bain**
*The Thing That Darkness Hides* - Robert
   Morgan   *h*   4006

**Bankole, Lauren Oya "Olamina"**
*Parable of the Talents* - Octavia E. Butler   *s*   793

**Bardsey, Geoffrey**
*The Merlin Effect* - T.A. Barron   *f*   371

**Barron, Paul**
*Wurm* - Matthew J. Costello   *h*   1202

**Barthlomew, Lucy**
*Moonfall* - Tamara Thorne   *h*   5464

**Batik**
*Wolf in Shadow* - David Gemmell   *s*   2191

**Bayley, Frank**
*Unholy Fire* - Whitley Strieber   *h*   5342

**Beatrice**
*Bright Messengers* - Gentry Lee   *s*   3398

**Beelson, Raymond**
*Armageddon Summer* - Jane Yolen   *s*   6028

**Begg, Edwin**
*Lunching with the Antichrist* - Michael
   Moorcock   *f*   3984

**Belkin, Gregory**
*Servant of the Bones* - Anne Rice   *h*   4575

**Ben Yussef, Essaj**
*The Riddled Man* - Mark E. Rogers   *f*   4654

**Benedict**
*Sable, Shadow and Ice* - Cheryl J. Franklin   *f*   2039

**Benjamin, Papa**
*The Black Lodge* - Robert Weinberg   *h*   5692

**Boro**
*Brand New Cherry Flavor* - Todd Grimson   *h*   2448

**Braco, Jag**
*Inquisitor* - Ian Watson   *s*   5637

**Brendan**
*The Book of Brendan* - Ann Curry   *f*   1294

**Breyd**
*The Sword and the Lion* - Roberta Cray   *f*   1253

**Brownpony, Elia**
*Saint Leibowitz and the Wild Horse Woman* - Walter
   M. Miller Jr.   *s*   3908

**Bruno, Giordano**
*Love & Sleep* - John Crowley   *f*   1277

**Brutha**
*Small Gods* - Terry Pratchett   *f*   4400

**Bryce, Christopher**
*Storm Knights* - Bill Slavicsek   *f*   5087

**Bryce, Pat**
*The Priest: A Gothic Romance* - Thomas M.
   Disch   *h*   1562

**Cadderly**
*In Sylvan Shadows* - R.A. Salvatore   *f*   4800

**Cahill, Joseph**
*Midnight Mass* - F. Paul Wilson   *h*   5891

**Caillean**
*The Forest House* - Marion Zimmer Bradley   *f*   633
*Lady of Avalon* - Marion Zimmer Bradley   *f*   640

**Callahan**
*Aqua Sancta* - Edward Bryant   *h*   748

**Calyx**
*Sunder, Eclipse and Seed* - Elise Guttenberg   *f*   2471

**Carenza, Peter**
*The Blood of the Lamb* - Thomas F.
   Monteleone   *h*   3958

**Carpenter, Tom**
*Dark Fortune* - Richard Lee Byers   *h*   795

**Carrie**
*Virgin* - Mary Elizabeth Murphy   *h*   4050

**Cassia**
*The Cult of Loving Kindness* - Paul Park   *s*   4242

**Catalina, Mother**
*Yesterday We Saw Mermaids* - Esther
   Friesner   *f*   2086

**Catcher, Selene**
*Renaissance Moon* - Linda Nevins   *f*   4093

**Catherine**
*Phoenix Cafe* - Gwyneth Jones   *s*   2954

**Celeste**
*Private Demons* - Robert Masello   *h*   3660

**Centuri, Ariann**
*Half-Light* - Denise Vitola   *s*   5575

**Champion, Dragonbait**
*Masquerades* - Kate Novak   *f*   4166

**Chisolm, Casey**
*Symphony* - Charles L. Grant   *h*   2318

**Chomanche**
*A Miracle of Rare Design* - Mike Resnick   *s*   4550

**Church, Thomas**
*The Gaia Websters* - Kim Antieau   *s*   198

**Cincinnati, Chime**
*Last Refuge* - Elizabeth Ann Scarborough   *f*   4866

**Clement VII, Pope**
*Scorpio* - Alex McDonough   *s*   3802

**Cleopatra**
*Throne of Isis* - Judith Tarr   *f*   5397

**Columcille**
*The Throne of Tara* - John Desjarlais   *f*   1498

**Corey, Elizabeth "Betty"**
*The World on Blood* - Jonathan Nasaw   *h*   4069

**Corio, Giovanna**
*Renaissance Moon* - Linda Nevins   *f*   4093

**Cornelius, Vito**
*The Fifth Element* - Terry Bisson   *s*   504

**Crane, Scott**
*Earthquake Weather* - Tim Powers   *f*   4382

**Crookleg, Poilar**
*Kingdoms of the Wall* - Robert Silverberg   *s*   5033

**Crysania**
*Tears of the Night Sky* - Linda P. Baker   *f*   299

**Dakar**
*Ships of Merior* - Janny Wurts   *f*   6004

**Darby, Abraham III**
*The Iron Bridge* - David Morse   *s*   4036

**Darcourt, Simon**
*The Cornish Trilogy* - Robertson Davies   *f*   1397

**Darin of Culverne**
*Children of the Blood: Book Two of The Sundered* - Michelle Sagara   *f*   4782
*Lady of Mercy* - Michelle Sagara   *f*   4784

**Darius**
*Elephantasm* - Tanith Lee   *h*   3408

**Darrow, Iselia**
*Star Ascendant* - Louise Cooper   *f*   1180

**Dawson, Donny**
*Deathgrip* - Brian Hodge   *h*   2700

**de Uzeda, Pedro**
*The Manuscript Found in Sragossa* - Jan Potocki   *h*   4371

**Deaver, Herman**
*The Folk of the Fringe* - Orson Scott Card   *s*   886

**Dev**
*Sunder, Eclipse and Seed* - Elise Guttenberg   *f*   2471

**Deveaux, Jacques**
*City of Pain* - John Terra   *f*   5438

**Dexter, Quinn**
*Emergence* - Peter F. Hamilton   *s*   2524

**di Rienzi, Angelica**
*Waking the Moon* - Elizabeth Hand   *f*   2538

---

**Dions**
*Throne of Isis* - Judith Tarr   *f*   5397

**Dixon, Benjamin**
*Blood Lust* - Ron Dee   *h*   1464

**Dobbs, J.R. "BoB"**
*Reality Is What You Can Get Away With: An Illustrated Screenplay* - Robert Anton Wilson   *s*   5904

**Domenico**
*The Devil's Day* - James Blish   *h*   525

**Donaher, Michael**
*Bureau 13* - Nick Pollotta   *f*   4362
*Full Moonster* - Nick Pollotta   *f*   4364

**Doron**
*Rainbow Man* - M.J. Engh   *s*   1824

**Dreen**
*The Hands of Lyr* - Andre Norton   *f*   4154

**Duncan**
*Eternity* - Maggie Shayne   *f*   4943

**Duran, Marcus**
*Parable of the Talents* - Octavia E. Butler   *s*   793

**Duroc, Roger**
*Comeback Tour: The Sky Belongs to the Stars* - Jack Yeovil   *s*   6020

**Eiden, Paul**
*Owl Light* - Michael Paine   *h*   4235

**Eilan**
*The Forest House* - Marion Zimmer Bradley   *f*   633

**Elias**
*The Revelation* - Bentley Little   *h*   3496

**Ellington, Dan**
*The Blood of the Lamb* - Thomas F. Monteleone   *h*   3958

**Elmara**
*Elminster: The Making of a Mage* - Ed Greenwood   *f*   2427

**Erelvar**
*A Call to Arms* - Thomas K. Martin   *f*   3650
*A Two-Edged Sword* - Thomas K. Martin   *f*   3653

**Eride "Thorn"**
*Thorn and Needle* - Paul B. Thompson   *f*   5456

**Erkenbert**
*One King's Way* - Harry Harrison   *s*   2572

**Falconi, Giovanni**
*The Sister* - Elleston Trevor   *h*   5484

**Farrand, Louis**
*Garden* - Matthew J. Costello   *h*   1197

**Faust, Prometheus "Bruce Payne"**
*Symphony* - Adrian Savage   *h*   4847

**Felipe**
*The Great Wheel* - Ian R. MacLeod   *s*   3599

**Ferro, Dante**
*Blood of the Covenant* - Brent Monahan   *h*   3954

**Figueroa, Calafia "Kali"**
*Kalifornia* - Marc Laidlaw   *s*   3311

**Fitzpatrick, Al-Hajji Brian**
*The Missing Matter* - Thomas R. McDonough   *s*   3805

**Fitzpatrick, Dan**
*Virgin* - Mary Elizabeth Murphy   *h*   4050

**Flanagan, Jeffrey**
*Lords of Creation* - Tim Sullivan   *s*   5351

**Fletcher, Step**
*Lost Boys* - Orson Scott Card   *f*   891

**Forrest, Winn**
*Half-Light* - Denise Vitola   *s*   5575

---

**Galvin**
*Red Magic* - Jean Rabe   *f*   4458

**Ganganelli, Patrizio**
*Cardinal's Sin* - Raymond Buckland   *h*   751

**Garcia-Mesa, Rosa**
*Shango* - James Roberto Curtis   *h*   1298

**Garden, Beauty "Beau"**
*Humility Garden* - Felicity Savage   *f*   4850

**Garden, Humility "Humi"**
*Humility Garden* - Felicity Savage   *f*   4850

**Garner**
*Wetbones* - John Shirley   *h*   5010

**Gawen**
*Lady of Avalon* - Marion Zimmer Bradley   *f*   640

**Gerbert**
*Ars Magica* - Judith Tarr   *f*   5392

**Gervinus**
*The Shattered Oath* - Josepha Sherman   *f*   4989

**Gilray, Jimmy-Don**
*Good News From Outer Space* - John Kessel   *s*   3084

**Gotti, Guillemo**
*The Book of Earth* - Marjorie Bradley Kellogg   *f*   3044

**Grebb, Richard**
*Penance* - Rick R. Reed   *h*   4501

**Green, Jerome**
*Dead Voices* - Abigail McDaniels   *h*   3783

**Gregory**
*The Secret Life of Laszlo, Count Dracula* - Roderick Anscombe   *h*   152
*StarSpawn* - Kenneth Von Gunden   *s*   5588

**Greylocks, Lysander**
*Shadowborn* - William W. Connors   *h*   1137

**Gurden, Tom**
*The Mask of Loki* - Roger Zelazny   *f*   6071

**Hadrian**
*The Silver Wolf* - Alice Borchardt   *h*   572

**Handrar, Ser**
*Wizard of Bones* - Robert N. Charrette   *f*   979

**Hari**
*The Willing Spirit* - Piers Anthony   *f*   195

**Harpole, Nicholas**
*In the Garden of Iden* - Kage Baker   *s*   298

**Harrowslough, Holly**
*Finder's Bane* - Kate Novak   *f*   4165

**Haven, Dextra**
*A Screaming Across the Sky* - Brian Daley   *s*   1315

**Hawk-That-Settles**
*Krokodil Tears* - Jack Yeovil   *f*   6023

**Hay, Matthew**
*Witch Hill* - Marion Zimmer Bradley   *h*   654

**Hederick**
*Hederick, the Theocrat* - Ellen Dodge Severson   *f*   4925

**Heisenberg, Paul**
*The Walking Shadow* - Brian Stableford   *s*   5195

**Herewiss**
*The Door into Sunset* - Diane Duane   *f*   1660

**Hodierna**
*The Notorious Abbess* - Vera Chapman   *f*   965

**Hopewell, Norman**
*Darkman #3: The Gods of Hell* - Randall Boyll   *h*   614

**Hoyt, Father**
*Hyperion* - Dan Simmons   *s*   5055

**Hudson, Cal**
*Symphony* - Adrian Savage   *h*   4847

**Inhetep, Setne**
*The Anubis Murders* - Gary Gygax   *f*   2472
*Death in Delhi* - Gary Gygax   *f*   2473

**Ix**
*Earth Made of Glass* - John Barnes   *s*   351

**Jenkins, Obadiah**
*Branch and Crown* - Gael Baudino   *f*   389
*O Greenest Branch!* - Gael Baudino   *f*   394

**Jeremy, Clark**
*Blood Siege* - G. Harry Stine   *s*   5278

**Joachim**
*The Wood Nymph and the Cranky Saint* - C. Dale
   Brittain   *f*   706

**Joe**
*Wheels of Fire* - Mercedes Lackey   *f*   3301

**Joel**
*Finder's Bane* - Kate Novak   *f*   4165

**Joel-Andrew**
*The Off Season* - Jack Cady   *f*   820

**Johnson, Samuel**
*The Iron Bridge* - David Morse   *s*   4036

**Jolyon**
*The Arm of the Stone* - Victoria Strauss   *f*   5333

**Jones, Lucifer**
*Lucifer Jones* - Mike Resnick   *f*   4549

**Jones, Ritcher**
*Dawn's Uncertain Light* - Neal Barrett Jr.   *s*   365

**Jonnah's-kin, Maihu**
*Snow Brother* - S.M. Stirling   *f*   5299

**Jorem**
*The Boy From the Burren* - Sheila Gilluly   *f*   2236

**Kakzim**
*Cinnabar Shadows* - Lynn Abbey   *f*   15

**Kalimuni**
*The Broken Land* - Ian McDonald   *s*   3791

**Kang, Liu**
*Mortal Kombat* - Martin Delrio   *f*   1483

**Karal**
*Storm Rising* - Mercedes Lackey   *f*   3297

**Kathinka**
*The Flies of Memory* - Ian Watson   *s*   5635

**Keeper, Tom**
*Ancient Games* - Scott Ciencin   *f*   1028

**Kelly, Gideon**
*The Time of Feasting* - Mick Farren   *h*   1882

**Khargi**
*Disciples of Dread* - Hugh B. Cave   *h*   941

**KhriNyad-Son**
*The Gates of Twilight* - Paula Volsky   *f*   5581

**Kidd, Malachy**
*Eyes of Silver* - Michael A. Stackpole   *f*   5200

**Kinney, Michael**
*Dark Debts* - Karen Hall   *h*   2494

**Koja**
*Horselords* - David Cook   *f*   1145

**Koriba**
*Kirinyaga: A Fable of Utopia* - Mike
   Resnick   *s*   4548

**Korrey, Eula**
*Chariot* - Charles L. Grant   *h*   2304

**Krishna the Holy Mendoro**
*The Ninety Trillion Fausts* - Jack L. Chalker   *s*   958

**Kuan Yu-Chen**
*The Only Thing to Fear* - Robert Morgan   *h*   4003

**LaFitte, Shane**
*Voodoo Child* - Michael Reaves   *h*   4498

**Lanta**
*Wanderer* - Donald E. McQuinn   *s*   3862

**Lasker, Burt**
*Fortress of Forbidden Destiny* - Ryder
   Syvertson   *s*   5378

**Lewin, Linda**
*Journals of the Plague Years* - Norman
   Spinrad   *s*   5172

**Lightstorm, Allan "Al"**
*Unquenchable Fire* - Rachel Pollack   *f*   4361

**Lion, Maurice**
*Jackals* - Charles L. Grant   *h*   2313

**Lissa**
*King Pinch*   David Cook   *f*   1146

**Lockwood, Edmund**
*The Ghosts of Sleath* - James Herbert   *h*   2668

**Loeffler, Brian**
*Sorcerers of Sodom* - Roger Elwood   *h*   1804

**Losang**
*Fortress of Forbidden Destiny* - Ryder
   Syvertson   *s*   5378

**Luke**
*Thessalonica* - Harry Turtledove   *f*   5511

**mac Cainnech, Aidan**
*Byzantium* - Stephen R. Lawhead   *f*   3353

**mac Calprin, Patraic "Patricius Calpurnius"**
*The Deer's Cry: A Book of the Keltiad* - Patricia
   Kennealy-Morrison   *f*   3060

**MacDonald, Warren**
*Blood Lust* - Ron Dee   *h*   1464

**Magnalucius**
*Quest: In Search of the Dragontooth* - Michael
   Green   *f*   2346

**Mama Pitie**
*Portent* - James Herbert   *h*   2670

**Mara**
*Time Blender* - Michael Dorn   *s*   1581

**Marapper, Henry**
*Non-Stop* - Brian W. Aldiss   *s*   58

**Marble, Maytera**
*Lake of the Long Sun* - Gene Wolfe   *s*   5942

**Marius**
*Pandora* - Anne Rice   *h*   4573

**Markham, Clare**
*The Colors of Hell* - Michael Paine   *h*   4234

**Marley, Andrew**
*The Werewolf's Touch* - Cheri Scotch   *h*   4892

**Martin, Fred**
*Blood Feud* - Sam Siciliano   *h*   5020

**Matthias**
*The Changeling* - Kristine Kathryn Rusch   *f*   4714

**Maya**
*The Fifth Sacred Thing* - Starhawk   *f*   5209

**McFarley, Andrew**
*Purgatory: A Chronicle of a Distant World* - Mike
   Resnick   *s*   4554

**McGann, Agnes "Aggie"**
*Gibbon's Decline and Fall* - Sheri S.
   Tepper   *s*   5430

**McMurtrey, Evander Harold**
*The Race for God* - Brian Herbert   *s*   2666

**Medlocke, Stephen**
*Brethren* - Shawn Ryan   *h*   4754

**Melchior**
*Count Scar* - C. Dale Brittain   *f*   702

**Mercer, Jebidiah**
*Dead in the West* - Joe R. Lansdale   *h*   3325

**Merchant, Liliane**
*The Arm of the Stone* - Victoria Strauss   *f*   5333

**Meriamon**
*Lord of the Two Lands* - Judith Tarr   *f*   5395

**Merlin**
*Enemy of God* - Bernard Cornwell   *f*   1189
*Excalibur* - Bernard Cornwell   *f*   1190

**Michael**
*The Eyes of Torie Webster* - Roy Sorrels   *h*   5164

**Milam, Hank**
*Rockabilly Limbo* - William W. Johnstone   *h*   2934

**Milk, Billy**
*Only Begotten Daughter* - James Morrow   *f*   4034

**Miner, Bron "Selwyn Forester"**
*The Arm of the Stone* - Victoria Strauss   *f*   5333

**Mint, Maytera**
*Calde of the Long Sun* - Gene Wolfe   *s*   5937

**Mirabar**
*In Legend Born* - Laura Resnick   *f*   4533

**Montoneros, Juan Ramirez**
*Catacomb* - Andrew Laurance   *h*   3347

**Moon, Miranda**
*The Trinity Vector* - Steve Perry   *s*   4302

**Mornay, Peter**
*Glory's War* - Alfred Coppel   *s*   1184

**Mulkerrin**
*Of Saints and Shadows* - Christopher
   Golden   *h*   2259

**Nathalorial, Kaylana**
*Villains by Necessity* - Eve Forward   *f*   1985

**Nazaual**
*Redmagic* - Crawford Kilian   *f*   3107

**Nessarose**
*Wicked: The Life and Times of the Wicked Witch of
   the West* - Gregory Maguire   *f*   3609

**Newcombe, Dan**
*Richter 10* - Arthur C. Clarke   *s*   1060

**Nicodemus**
*Plague Demon* - Brian Craig   *f*   1239

**Nuwen, Pham**
*A Fire upon the Deep* - Vernor Vinge   *s*   5573

**Nyateneri**
*The Innkeeper's Song* - Peter S. Beagle   *f*   409

**Olamina, Lauren Oya**
*Parable of the Sower* - Octavia E. Butler   *s*   792

**Oldman, Wendel**
*Wyrm Wolf* - Edo van Belkom   *h*   5535

**O'Riordan**
*The Silent Stars Go By* - James White   *s*   5781

**O'Rourke, Mike**
*Children of the Night* - Dan Simmons   *h*   5050

**Osaro, George**
*Ghosts* - Noel Hynd   *h*   2822

**Padrik**
*The Robin and the Kestrel* - Mercedes
   Lackey   *f*   3293

**Paul**
*The Twelfth Child* - Raymond Van Over   *h*   5538

**Paulin**
*King Javan's Year* - Katherine Kurtz   *f*   3258

**Pavek of Urik**
*The Brazen Gambit* - Lynn Abbey   *f*   13
*Cinnabar Shadows* - Lynn Abbey   *f*   15

**Peach-Frog-At-Twilight**
*Jade Darcy and the Zen Pirates* - Stephen Goldin   s   2260

**Pec-Pec**
*The Dream Vessel* - Jeff Bredenberg   s   664

**Pessoa, Manoel**
*God's Fires* - Patricia Anthony   s   159

**Phniangsak, Sam**
*Paths to Otherwhere* - James P. Hogan   s   2728

**Pinkes, Clayton**
*Prophets for the End of Time* - Marcos Donnelly   f   1577

**Poke, Mica**
*Night Prayers* - P.D. Cacek   h   803

**Ponce, Armando**
*Dead of Night* - Alex Abella   h   20

**Portman, William T. "Orde"**
*Blue Light* - Walter Mosley   s   4042

**Presley, Elvis**
*Elvissey* - Jack Womack   s   5957

**Prince, Hugo**
*The Death Prayer* - David Bowker   h   602

**Prowier, Isaac**
*Soul Snatchers* - Michael Cecilione   h   947

**Pyrrhos**
*Krispos Rising* - Harry Turtledove   f   5507

**Quauhtli**
*The Chalchiuhite Dragon* - Kenneth Morris   f   4020

**Quetzal**
*Calde of the Long Sun* - Gene Wolfe   s   5937

**Quillan**
*The Face of the Waters* - Robert Silverberg   s   5029

**Rael**
*The Cult of Loving Kindness* - Paul Park   s   4242

**Rafferty, John**
*Unholy Fire* - Whitley Strieber   h   5342

**Rasnar, Patriarch**
*Rally Cry!* - William R. Forstchen   s   1982

**Rasputin**
*I, Vampire* - Michael Romkey   h   4665

**Regina**
*A Cast of Corbies* - Mercedes Lackey   f   3274

**Rhodonite "Rod"**
*The Children Star* - Joan Slonczewski   s   5090

**Ritter, Alexis**
*The Venom Trees of Sunga* - L. Sprague de Camp   s   1420

**Roche**
*Doomsday Book* - Connie Willis   s   5868

**Rose**
*Madeleine's Ghost* - Robert Girardi   h   2240

**Ryan, William**
*Nightworld* - F. Paul Wilson   h   5893

**Ryana**
*The Seeker* - Simon Hawke   f   2624

**Sabah, Hasan al**
*The Mask of Loki* - Roger Zelazny   f   6071

**St. Brendan, Caitlin**
*Indiana Jones and the White Witch* - Martin Caidin   f   826

**St. George, Blacktooth "Nimmy"**
*Saint Leibowitz and the Wild Horse Woman* - Walter M. Miller Jr.   s   3908

**Sal**
*The Face of Apollo* - Fred Saberhagen   s   4766

**Salvatore, Dominga**
*The Laughing Corpse* - Laurell K. Hamilton   f   2519

**Sandburg, Elaine "Nefret"**
*Thebes of the Hundred Gates* - Robert Silverberg   s   5043

**Sandoz, Emilio**
*Children of God* - Mary Doria Russell   s   4735
*The Sparrow* - Mary Doria Russell   s   4736

**Sawalha, Erim**
*The Riddled Man* - Mark E. Rogers   f   4654

**Sayyed**
*City of the Sorcerers* - Mary H. Herbert   f   2673

**Seaton, Thomas**
*Vampire Bytes* - Linda Grant   h   2322

**Selatre**
*Prince of the North* - Harry Turtledove   f   5509

**Sennen, David**
*The Black Death* - Basil Copper   h   1185

**Seth, Nguyen**
*Demon Download* - Jack Yeovil   f   6021

**Shore, Oliver**
*Avatar* - Donald Beman   h   437

**Shuyun**
*Gatherer of Clouds* - Sean Russell   f   4741
*The Initiate Brother* - Sean Russell   f   4742

**Sien**
*Shadow War* - Deborah Chester   f   1010

**Silk**
*Nightside the Long Sun* - Gene Wolfe   s   5943

**Silk, Patera**
*Calde of the Long Sun* - Gene Wolfe   s   5937
*Exodus From the Long Sun* - Gene Wolfe   s   5941
*Lake of the Long Sun* - Gene Wolfe   s   5942

**Simon**
*Corrupting Dr. Nice* - John Kessel   s   3083

**Smith, Joseph**
*The Ghost of the Revelator* - L.E. Modesitt Jr.   s   3931

**Sokolowska, Marya**
*Under the Yoke* - S.M. Stirling   s   5301

**Solamnus, Vinas**
*Vinas Solamnus* - J. Robert King   f   3123

**Soothslayer**
*Soothslayer: A Magickal Fantasy* - D.J. Conway   f   1143

**Suarra**
*The Face in the Abyss* - A. Merritt   f   3878

**Sullivan, William T.**
*Deus-X: A Novel of Spiritual Terror* - Joseph A. Citro   h   1037

**Sylah**
*Wanderer* - Donald E. McQuinn   s   3862
*Warrior* - Donald E. McQuinn   s   3863

**Taminy-a-Cuinn**
*The Crystal Rose* - Maya Kaathryn Bohnhoff   f   560
*Taminy* - Maya Kaathryn Bohnhoff   f   563

**Tarrant, Gerald**
*Crown of Shadows* - C.S. Friedman   s   2057

**Tenar**
*Tehanu: The Last Book of Earthsea* - Ursula K. Le Guin   f   3383

**Thayer, Philip**
*Afternoon of the Gosling* - Marlys Huffman   h   2801

**Thomas**
*Towing Jehovah* - James Morrow   f   4035

**Timoteo**
*Blood of the Goddess* - Kara Dalkey   f   1318

**Timothy "Timmy"**
*Live From Golgotha: A Novel* - Gore Vidal   s   5569

**Timura, Safar**
*Wolves of the Gods* - Allan Cole   f   1111

**Traiben**
*Kingdoms of the Wall* - Robert Silverberg   s   5033

**Trask, Lanyon**
*In the Mood* - Charles L. Grant   h   2312

**Trayne, Robert**
*Whipping Boy* - John Byrne   h   800

**Ulrich**
*Storm Warning* - Mercedes Lackey   f   3298

**Uluye**
*Avatar* - Louise Cooper   f   1173

**Uthred**
*Nations of the Night* - Oliver Johnson   f   2925

**Uthred of Ravenspur**
*The Forging of the Shadows* - Oliver Johnson   f   2924

**Vadeviya**
*Touched by the Gods* - Lawrence Watt-Evans   f   5651

**Vadim, Lux**
*Desert Fire* - David Alexander   s   65

**Valdez, Ramon**
*The Killing of the Saints* - Alex Abella   h   21

**Vanyel**
*Magic's Promise* - Mercedes Lackey   f   3289

**Vanyi**
*Arrows of the Sun* - Judith Tarr   f   5391

**Vaughan, Lucus**
*Spiritride* - Mark Shepherd   f   4981

**Ventan, Daniel**
*Mission of Magic* - Julie Dean Smith   f   5125

**Veronica**
*Cardmaster* - Clayton Emery   f   1813
*Guises of the Mind* - Rebecca Neason   s   4081

**Vitarosa**
*Mind Snare* - Gayle Greeno   s   2422

**Vorbis**
*Small Gods* - Terry Pratchett   f   4400

**Vost, Harlic**
*Thorn and Needle* - Paul B. Thompson   f   5456

**Vryce, Damien Kilcannon**
*Black Sun Rising* - C.S. Friedman   f   2056
*Crown of Shadows* - C.S. Friedman   s   2057
*When True Night Falls* - C.S. Friedman   f   2060

**Walsh, Dalton**
*The Reckoning* - Ruby Jean Jensen   h   2904

**Webster, Grandma**
*The Godmother's Web* - Elizabeth Ann Scarborough   f   4864

**Wendeen, Wendy**
*Drifter* - William C. Dietz   s   1543

**Weston, Quinton**
*The Immortals* - Tracy Hickman   s   2681

**Wheele, Catherine**
*Sunglasses After Dark* - Nancy A. Collins   h   1124

**Wilburfoss, Jon**
*Wulfsyarn: A Mosaic* - Phillip Mann   s   3617

**Wisdom**
*The Curse* - John Tigges   h   5472

**Wolpin, Zev**
*Midnight Mass* - F. Paul Wilson   h   5891

**Woodhouse, Andy**
*Son of Rosemary* - Ira Levin   h   3445

Wynett
*The Usurper* - Angus Wells  *f*  5739
*The Way Beneath* - Angus Wells  *f*  5740

Wyth
*Taminy* - Maya Kaathryn Bohnhoff  *f*  563

Xavier
*The Vampire Virus* - Michael Romkey  *h*  4668

Ysuna
*The Sacred Stones* - William Sarabande  *f*  4818

Zalman
*A Blessing on the Moon* - Joseph Skibell  *f*  5079

## RENEGADE

**den Karynth, Calandryll**
*Wild Magic* - Angus Wells  *t*  5741

**Elemak**
*Earthfall* - Orson Scott Card  *s*  885

## REPAIRMAN

**Shackleford, Ray**
*Glimpses* - Lewis Shiner  *h*  4997

**Slavanovot, Viktor**
*The Fall of Sirius* - Wil McCarthy  *s*  3762

**Walker, Greg**
*Sacrifice* - John Farris  *h*  1886

## RESEARCHER

**Butterworth, Alicia**
*Cosm* - Gregory Benford  *s*  444

**Campbell, Katie**
*Rapid Growth* - Mary K. Hanner  *h*  2541

**Cedar, Janice**
*Fossil* - Hal Clement  *s*  1083

**Coddington, Quentin**
*Strange Stains and Mysterious Smells* - Terry
    Jones  *f*  2982

**Correa, Marissa**
*Lightpaths* - Howard V. Hendrix  *s*  2660

**Cortland, Roger**
*Lightpaths* - Howard V. Hendrix  *s*  2660

**Davakinapwottapellazanzis**
*The Expediter* - J. Brian Clarke  *s*  1062

**Dearborn, Sondra**
*Proteus in the Underworld* - Charles
    Sheffield  *s*  4962

**Deepneau, Ed**
*Insomnia* - Stephen King  *h*  3135

**Didi "Deeds"**
*Circle of One* - Eric James Fullilove  *s*  2092

**Dworkin, Sam**
*Silent Zone* - Stephen Molstad  *s*  3952

**Foster, Neda**
*The Abductors: Conspiracy* - Jonathan
    Frakes  *s*  2034

**Foster, Sandra "Sandy"**
*Bellwether* - Connie Willis  *s*  5867

**Gatzalumendi, Isadora Katarina Manuela**
*Anvil* - Nicolas van Pallandt  *s*  5540

**Harrison, Bailey**
*The Vampire Virus* - Michael Romkey  *h*  4668

**Hartell, Kathryn**
*Shadows After Dark* - Ouida Crozier  *f*  1286

**Hogopian, Aaron**
*Playing God* - Sarah Zettel  *s*  6080

**Italiano, Dorothy**
*A Reasonable World* - Damon Knight  *s*  3188

**Kavanaugh, Louise**
*Nightshade* - Stanley R. Moore  *h*  3992

**Keller, Sally**
*Probe* - Edward M. Lerner  *s*  3437

**Kullervo, Reede Kulleva**
*The Summer Queen* - Joan D. Vinge  *s*  5572

**Laney, Colin**
*Idoru* - William Gibson  *s*  2218

**Magnus, Mei-Ling**
*Standing Wave* - Howard V. Hendrix  *s*  2661

**Marshak, Arthur**
*Brothers* - Ben Bova  *s*  581

**Martin, Hector**
*Accidental Creatures* - Anne Harris  *s*  2558

**Mayland, Gia**
*The Expediter* - J. Brian Clarke  *s*  1062

**McDarvid, Jack**
*The Green Progression* - L.E. Modesitt Jr.  *s*  3932

**McMichaels, Scott**
*Infectress* - Tom Cool  *s*  1167

**Meniskos, Jhana**
*Lightpaths* - Howard V. Hendrix  *s*  2660

**Messenger, Karen**
*Host* - Peter James  *h*  2872

**Mirabara, Keishi**
*The Fortunate Fall* - Raphael Carter  *s*  927

**Moffett, Pierce**
*Love & Sleep* - John Crowley  *f*  1277

**Morton, John**
*Night Glow* - Martin James  *h*  2867

**Myers, Didi "Deeds"**
*The Stranger* - Eric James Fullilove  *s*  2093

**Myers, Edward**
*The Summit* - Edward Myers  *f*  4063

**Nguyen, Phat "Zak"**
*Cosm* - Gregory Benford  *s*  444

**Okun, Brackish**
*Silent Zone* - Stephen Molstad  *s*  3952

**O'Reilly, Bennett "Ben"**
*Bellwether* - Connie Willis  *s*  5867

**Owen, Harriet Cleaver**
*A Reasonable World* - Damon Knight  *s*  3188

**Pendeers, Kristine**
*Songs of Earth and Power* - Greg Bear  *f*  424

**Phelan, Andrew**
*The Trail of Cthulhu* - August Derleth  *h*  1497

**Potter, Jack**
*Signal to Noise* - Eric S. Nylund  *s*  4179

**Prien, Rube**
*From Time to Time* - Jack Finney  *s*  1941

**Rae, Dorcas**
*Gaia's Toys* - Rebecca Ore  *s*  4218

**Renzie**
*Vanishing Point* - Michaela Roessner  *s*  4652

**Rojas, Duncan**
*Ivory: A Legend of Past and Future* - Mike
    Resnick  *s*  4547

**Sandoval, Mickey**
*Heads* - Greg Bear  *s*  419

**S'Nash**
*Fossil* - Hal Clement  *s*  1083

**Spae, Elizabeth**
*A King Beneath the Mountain* - Robert N.
    Charrette  *f*  973

**Stewart, Anne**
*Jupiter's Daughter* - Tom Hyman  *s*  2820

**Stilman, Shyh**
*Lightwing* - Tara K. Harper  *s*  2551

**Tardivel, Pierre**
*Frameshift* - Robert J. Sawyer  *s*  4856

**Ulkanov, Andre**
*The Multiplex Man* - James P. Hogan  *s*  2727

**Unger, Juanita "Jane"**
*Heavy Weather* - Bruce Sterling  *s*  5258

**Weintraub, Sarah**
*Threshold* - Bill Myers  *s*  4060

## RESISTANCE FIGHTER

**Garcia, Bud**
*Martian Deathtrap* - Nathan Archer  *s*  205

**Spock**
*Spectre* - William Shatner  *s*  4934

**Winters, Katie**
*Martian Deathtrap* - Nathan Archer  *s*  205

## RESTAURATEUR

**Aaron, Lily**
*After Silence* - Jonathan Carroll  *h*  916

**Abbott, Vera**
*The Chosen* - Edward Lee  *h*  3389

**Bryant, Sandra**
*The Crawling Dark* - Pauline Dunn  *h*  1698

**Denman, Lloyd**
*The Burning* - Graham Masterton  *h*  3672

**Dohen, Spike**
*Skinny Legs and All* - Tom Robbins  *f*  4607

**Lacey, Joey**
*Vampire Blood* - Kathryn Meyer Griffith  *h*  2441

**Maclaren, Neil**
*Raven* - Charles L. Grant  *h*  2314

**Selway, Cookson**
*A Face at the Window* - Dennis McFarland  *h*  3809

## REVOLUTIONARY

**Alice**
*Innerverse* - John DeChancie  *s*  1458

**Alta**
*Deception Well* - Linda Nagata  *s*  4065

**al'Thor, Rand "Dragon Reborn"**
*The Dragon Reborn* - Robert Jordan  *f*  2985
*The Fires of Heaven* - Robert Jordan  *f*  2987

**Apolinario, Lot**
*Deception Well* - Linda Nagata  *s*  4065

**Arabella "Infectress"**
*Infectress* - Tom Cool  *s*  1167

**Ascher, Emily**
*Beneath the Tree of Heaven* - David
    Wingrove  *s*  5917

**Ash of Ashland**
*Dancing Jack* - Laurie J. Marks  *f*  3624

**Astrahn**
*A City in Winter* - Mark Helprin  *f*  2653

**Babcock, Maria**
*Nature's God* - Robert Anton Wilson  *f*  5903

**Bender, Jack**
*Mutant Hell* - Mark Grant  *s*  2324
*Mutants Amok* - Mark Grant  *s*  2325

**Berg-Benson, Sephony**
*An Eye for Dark Places* - Norma Marder   s   3622

**Bird**
*The Fifth Sacred Thing* - Starhawk   f   5209

**Boysie**
*Flickering Shadows* - Kwadwo Agymah
   Kamau   f   3006

**Bronwyn**
*Thornhold* - Elaine Cunningham   f   1293

**Brooks, Jenny**
*Cathy IV* - Frances Lucas   s   3539

**Caliban**
*Inferno* - Roger MacBride Allen   s   78

**Carmichael, Justin**
*Two Crowns for America* - Katherine Kurtz   f   3262

**Cephus**
*Flickering Shadows* - Kwadwo Agymah
   Kamau   f   3006

**Constantine**
*City on Fire* - Walter Jon Williams   s   5835

**d'Ark, Hazel**
*Deathstalker Honor* - Simon R. Green   s   2364

**d'Armand, Magnus Gallowglass "Gar Pike"**
*A Wizard in Mind* - Christopher Stasheff   s   5232
*A Wizard in Peace* - Christopher Stasheff   s   5233

**Death Wind**
*Dragons Past* - Gary Gentile   s   2192

**Deathstalker, Owen**
*Deathstalker Rebellion* - Simon R. Green   s   2365
*Deathstalker War* - Simon R. Green   s   2366

**Dennehy, Nuala Maebh**
*The Rising of the Moon* - Flynn Connolly   s   1135

**Derveet**
*Flowerdust* - Gwyneth Jones   s   2952

**Desse, Gorynal**
*The Ruins of Ambrai* - Melanie Rawn   f   4489

**Devlin, Annie**
*Scotland the Brave* - Jennifer Roberson   f   4611

**DeVore, Howard**
*White Moon, Red Dragon* - David
   Wingrove   s   5921
*The White Mountain* - David Wingrove   s   5922

**Dexter, Fiona**
*Dark Genesis* - J. Gregory Keyes   s   3096

**Doc**
*Dragons Past* - Gary Gentile   s   2192

**Duncan, George Thomas**
*Ecstasy Club* - Douglas Rushkoff   s   4732

**Duncan, William St.-George**
*Dayworld Breakup* - Philip Jose Farmer   s   1869

**Ebert, Hans**
*Beneath the Tree of Heaven* - David
   Wingrove   s   5917

**Faron, Theodore**
*The Children of Men* - P.D. James   f   2870

**Fastet, Meer**
*Exile* - Michael P. Kube-McDowell   s   3248

**Fenn**
*The Fleet of Stars* - Poul Anderson   s   126

**Gallandro, Anja**
*Trouble on Cloud City* - Kevin J. Anderson   s   117

**Garden, Humility "Humi"**
*Delta City* - Felicity Savage   f   4849

**Garoit, Darrell**
*Infinity Hold* - Barry B. Longyear   s   3522

**Gird**
*Liar's Oath* - Elizabeth Moon   f   3969

**Greensleeves**
*Surrender None: The Legacy of Gird* - Elizabeth
   Moon   f   3975

**Greensleeves**
*Final Sacrifice* - Clayton Emery   f   1814
*Shattered Chains* - Clayton Emery   f   1816

**Gregory**
*The Dream Vessel* - Jeff Bredenberg   s   664

**Guevara, Ernesto "Che"**
*The Resurrections* - Simon Louvish   s   3528

**Gull**
*Final Sacrifice* - Clayton Emery   f   1814
*Shattered Chains* - Clayton Emery   f   1816

**Hall, Courtney**
*Out on Blue Six* - Ian McDonald   s   3794

**Han, Liu**
*Worldwar: Striking the Balance* - Harry
   Turtledove   s   5516

**Harlan, Brander**
*Brander's Book* - C.J. Mills   s   3909

**Harvey, Emily**
*Memorymakers* - Brian Herbert   s   2665

**Hathor**
*Horrible Humes* - Stephen Billias   f   487

**Hausmann, Elena**
*The Third Force* - Marc Laidlaw   s   3313

**Hawkins, Nirgal**
*Green Mars* - Kim Stanley Robinson   s   4633

**Holley, Charles Hardin**
*Back in the USSA* - Kim Newman   s   4095

**Igraine**
*The Rising of the Moon* - Flynn Connolly   s   1135

**Jobber**
*Beldan's Fire* - Midori Snyder   f   5150

**Journey, Ruby**
*Deathstalker Rebellion* - Simon R. Green   s   2365

**Julian**
*The Children of Men* - P.D. James   f   2870

**Junknowitz, Lucky**
*Free Radicals* - Jack McKinney   s   3848
*Hostile Takeover* - Jack McKinney   s   3849

**Kenmuir, Ian**
*The Stars Are Also Fire* - Poul Anderson   s   134

**Kishida, Katie**
*Tech-Heaven* - Linda Nagata   s   4066

**Knott, Wyoming "Wyoh"**
*The Moon Is a Harsh Mistress* - Robert A.
   Heinlein   s   2645

**LaNague, Peter**
*The LaNague Chronicles* - F. Paul Wilson   s   5889

**Lander**
*The Parched Sea* - Troy Denning   f   1486

**Lecotta, Angel**
*Time: The Semi-Final Frontier* - Lionel
   Fenn   s   1921

**Lindsay, Abelard**
*Schismatrix Plus* - Bruce Sterling   s   5260

**Lirion**
*Harvest the Fire* - Poul Anderson   s   128

**Lohmatski, Natalya**
*Dancing Bears* - Fred Saberhagen   f   4764

**Ma Li "Sister"**
*Shangri-La: The Return to the World of Lost Horizon* -
   Eleanor Cooney   f   1169

**Madrone**
*The Fifth Sacred Thing* - Starhawk   f   5209

**Margaret**
*A Million Open Doors* - John Barnes   s   353

**Marm, Everett C. "Harlequin"**
*"Repent, Harlequin!" Said the Ticktockman* - Harlan
   Ellison   s   1782

**Martin, Andrew**
*The Positronic Man* - Isaac Asimov   s   249

**Masul**
*The Star Scroll* - Melanie Rawn   f   4491

**Miraflores, Pedro**
*Ai! Pedrito!: When Intelligence Goes Wrong* - L. Ron
   Hubbard   s   2788

**Mitroff, Seryi**
*The Frightened Fish* - Kenneth Robeson   f   4622

**Mondragon, Tom**
*Endgame* - C.J. Cherryh   s   986

**Moorcock, Margaret Rose**
*The War Amongst the Angels* - Michael
   Moorcock   f   3986

**Munk**
*Solis* - A.A. Attanasio   s   272

**Nanchen, Kedar**
*Exile* - Michael P. Kube-McDowell   s   3248

**Naoh**
*Dreamfall* - Joan D. Vinge   s   5571

**Niall**
*The Delta* - Colin Wilson   s   5878

**Nili, Mei**
*Solis* - A.A. Attanasio   s   272

**Notorincus**
*A City in Winter* - Mark Helprin   f   2653

**Oimu, Harriet**
*Celestis* - Paul Park   s   4241

**O'Kelly, Manuel "Mannie"**
*The Moon Is a Harsh Mistress* - Robert A.
   Heinlein   s   2645

**Pepon, Buko**
*Paradise: A Chronicle of a Distant World* - Mike
   Resnick   s   4552

**Perin, Antonio "Tony"**
*Full Tide of Night* - J.R. Dunn   s   1695

**Pinvey**
*Hall of Whispers* - Mike Jefferies   f   2884

**Potter, Prat'han**
*Future Indefinite* - Dave Duncan   f   1678

**Psycho, Jenny**
*Deathstalker War* - Simon R. Green   s   2366

**Quath'jutt'kkal'thon "Quath"**
*Furious Gulf* - Gregory Benford   s   447
*Tides of Light* - Gregory Benford   s   450

**Ragman**
*The Host* - Peter R. Emshwiller   s   1819

**Reed, Kayla**
*Sister Blood* - Karen Haber   s   2476

**Remillard, Mark**
*Magnificat* - Julian May   s   3699

**Reno**
*Solip: System* - Walter Jon Williams   s   5841

**Riva**
*The Eyes of God* - Mark Kreighbaum   s   3231

**Robin**
*The Robin and the Kestrel* - Mercedes
   Lackey   f   3293

**Ronay, Kinna**
*The Fleet of Stars* - Poul Anderson   s   126

**Rozak, Jay**
*Islands of Tomorrow* - F.M. Busby   s   783

**Russell, Saxifrage "Sax"**
*Green Mars* - Kim Stanley Robinson   s   4633

**Saigo**
*Aristoi* - Walter Jon Williams   s   5834

**Saint-Germain**
*Two Crowns for America* - Katherine Kurtz   f   3262

**Scott**
*Dragons Past* - Gary Gentile   s   2192

**Shedwyn**
*Beldan's Fire* - Midori Snyder   f   5150

**Shira**
*Timelike Infinity* - Stephen Baxter   s   404

**Snick, Panthea**
*Dayworld Breakup* - Philip Jose Farmer   s   1869

**Sorya**
*Metropolitan* - Walter Jon Williams   s   5839

**Spinner, Probe**
*Arachne* - Lisa Mason   s   3661

**Stanton, Chris-John**
*Chicago Red* - R.M. Meluch   s   3873

**Steele, Vanessa**
*The Woman between the Worlds* - F. Gwynplaine
   MacIntyre   s   3596

**Steinfeld**
*Eclipse Corona* - John Shirley   s   5006

**Stone, Edwin L. "Ed"**
*Why Do Birds* - Damon Knight   s   3190

**Storm, Jack**
*Alien Salute* - Charles Ingrid   s   2830
*Return Fire* - Charles Ingrid   s   2833

**Sucre**
*Canal Dreams* - Iain M. Banks   s   323

**Tamar**
*The Alleluia Files* - Sharon Shinn   s   4999

**Tembo**
*Phoenix Fire* - Elizabeth Forrest   f   1974

**Toitovna, Maya**
*Green Mars* - Kim Stanley Robinson   s   4633

**Tolnismer, Alysess**
*Short Blade* - Peter R. Emshwiller   s   1820

**Torrence, Daniel "Hardeyes"**
*Eclipse Corona* - John Shirley   s   5006

**Turkel, Maximillian**
*Christmas Slaughter* - Mark Grant   s   2323
*Mutant Hell* - Mark Grant   s   2324
*Mutants Amok* - Mark Grant   s   2325

**Urban**
*Deception Well* - Linda Nagata   s   4065

**VaGayjur, Supaari**
*Children of God* - Mary Doria Russell   s   4735

**Valeur, Whiss**
*Illusion* - Paula Volsky   f   5582

**Van Chou, Ngen**
*The Web of Spider* - W. Michael Gear   s   2173

**Vanelli, MONDO**
*How to Mutate and Take Over the World* - R.U.
   Sirius   s   5074

**Vierran**
*Hexwood* - Diana Wynne Jones   s   2948

**Washington, George**
*Two Crowns for America* - Katherine Kurtz   f   3262

**West, Kilimanjaro**
*Out on Blue Six* - Ian McDonald   s   3794

**Withers, Virgil "Rip"**
*Clash by Night* - Chet Williamson   h   5844

**Zeenoson, Dref**
*Illusion* - Paula Volsky   f   5582

**Zhu Wong**
*The Golden Nineties* - Lisa Mason   s   3663

**Zorin, Lavrenti Borisovich**
*Branch Point* - Mona Clee   s   1074

**Zwakh, Ignatz**
*Dead Things* - Richard Calder   s   838

## ROBOT

**APU-805 "Bird Dog"**
*Destination: Showdown* - Jake Davis   s   1405
*The Last Rangers* - Jake Davis   s   1406

**Arthur**
*The Immortality Option* - James P. Hogan   s   2725

**Bailey, David "Herbert" Clancy**
*The Modular Man* - Roger MacBride Allen   s   79

**Bill**
*Hawaiian U.F.O. Aliens* - Mel Gilden   s   2226
*Tubular Android Superheroes* - Mel Gilden   s   2228

**C-3PO**
*The Glove of Darth Vader* - Paul Davids   s   1392

**Caliban**
*Inferno* - Roger MacBride Allen   s   78
*Utopia* - Roger MacBride Allen   s   83

**CBN-001 "Caliban"**
*Caliban* - Roger MacBride Allen   s   77

**Celia**
*Automated Alice* - Jeff Noon   f   4134

**Cge**
*Backblast* - Lee McKeone   s   3828
*The Clone Crisis* - Lee McKeone   s   3829

**Claude**
*Title Deleted for Security Reasons* - Ed
   Blome   s   553

**Delta**
*Warsprite* - Jefferson P. Swycaffer   s   5375

**Didi "Deeds"**
*Circle of One* - Eric James Fullilove   s   2092

**Doggie**
*Daughter of Elysium* - Joan Slonczewski   s   5091

**Eleanor of Aquitaine**
*Rama Revealed* - Arthur C. Clarke   s   1059

**Elvis**
*The Man in the Moon Must Die* - Jeff
   Bredenberg   s   665

**Fess**
*The Warlock Insane* - Christopher Stasheff   f   5225
*The Warlock Rock* - Christopher Stasheff   s   5226
*A Wizard in Absentia* - Christopher Stasheff   s   5229

**Flere-Imsaho**
*The Player of Games* - Iain M. Banks   s   326

**Gaunt**
*Checkmate* - Eric T. Baker   s   297

**Hunter**
*Dictator* - William F. Wu   s   5996
*Predator* - William F. Wu   s   5998
*Warrior* - William F. Wu   s   6000

**Jakobot "Jacko" 490,9000**
*Extreme Paranoia: Nobody Knows the Trouble I've
   Shot* - Ken Rolston   s   4662

**Jin the Plarnjarn**
*The Race for God* - Brian Herbert   s   2666

**Karli Dog**
*Vurt* - Jeff Noon   s   4136

**Kort**
*Star Child* - James P. Hogan   s   2730

**Kryten**
*Better than Life* - Grant Naylor   s   4076

**Mandrake**
*Nightshade* - Jack Butler   s   789

**Marble, Maytera**
*Lake of the Long Sun* - Gene Wolfe   s   5942

**Martin, Andrew**
*The Positronic Man* - Isaac Asimov   s   249

**Monique**
*Freeware* - Rudy Rucker   s   4703

**Moses**
*Greenthieves* - Alan Dean Foster   s   2005

**Mthembu, Lucas "Venator"**
*Harvest the Fire* - Poul Anderson   s   128

**Myers, Didi "Deeds"**
*The Stranger* - Eric James Fullilove   s   2093

**Myth, Urban**
*Cinderblock* - Janine Ellen Young   s   6047

**Nimrod**
*Solo* - Robert Mason   s   3665

**Norby**
*Norby and the Court Jester* - Janet Asimov   s   252
*Norby and the Oldest Dragon* - Janet
   Asimov   s   253
*Norby and Yobo's Great Adventure* - Janet
   Asimov   s   254
*Norby Down to Earth* - Janet Asimov   s   255

**Olivaw, R. Daneel "Eto Demerzel"**
*Forward the Foundation* - Isaac Asimov   s   236
*Foundation's Fear* - Gregory Benford   s   446

**Oliver**
*Stationfall* - Arthur Byron Cover   s   1216

**Paolo**
*Diaspora* - Greg Egan   s   1759

**Prospero**
*Inferno* - Roger MacBride Allen   s   78

**RAMROD Mark I "Rod"**
*Cybernarc* - Robert Cain   s   829
*End Game* - Robert Cain   s   830
*Gold Dragon* - Robert Cain   s   831

**Solo**
*Solo* - Robert Mason   s   3665
*Weapon* - Robert Mason   s   3666

**Spinner, Probe**
*Arachne* - Lisa Mason   s   3661

**Stone, Gloria**
*The Gaia Websters* - Kim Antieau   s   198

**Terminationer**
*Samurai Cat Goes to the Movies* - Mark E.
   Rogers   s   4656

**Trema, Lodovik**
*Foundation and Chaos* - Greg Bear   s   418

**TW-O: 114-84-1311825**
*Cathedral of Thorns* - Steven Frankos   f   2041

**Unnamed Character**
*A Prophecy of Monsters* - Clark Ashton
   Smith   h   5103

**Wu, Victor "Orf"**
*Earthling* - Tony Daniel   s   1336

**X41**
*Specterworld* - Isidore Haiblum   s   2480

## ROGUE

**Crowley**
*Lady Cottington's Pressed Fairy Book* - Terry
   Jones   f   2981

**Devlin, Johnny**
*Trader* - Charles de Lint   f   1438

**Elemak**
*The Ships of Earth* - Orson Scott Card   s   897

## ROYALTY

**Adric**
*The White Mists of Power* - Kristine Kathryn
   Rusch   f   4730

**Aeid**
*O Greenest Branch!* - Gael Baudino   f   394

**Ahten, Raj**
*The Runelords: The Sum of All Men* - David
   Farland   f   1866

**Aidan**
*Alamut* - Judith Tarr   f   5390
*The Dagger and the Cross: A Novel of the Crusades* -
   Judith Tarr   f   5393

**Akhor**
*Song in the Silence* - Elizabeth Kerner   f   3065

**al-Badr, Arwa Bint Muhammad**
*Guts and Glory* - G. Harry Stine   s   5280

**Alain**
*M'Lady Witch* - Christopher Stasheff   f   5217

**Alderan, Kermiak**
*Rediscovery: A Novel of Darkover* - Marion Zimmer
   Bradley   s   643

**Alexander**
*The Floating Castle* - Craig Mills   f   3913
*The Prince and the Pilgrim* - Mary Stewart   f   5270

**Alexia**
*Dark Mirror, Dark Dreams* - Sharon Green   f   2357
*Silver Princess, Golden Knight* - Sharon
   Green   f   2359
*Wind Whispers, Shadow Shouts* - Sharon
   Green   f   2360

**Allic**
*The Crystal Sorcerers* - William R.
   Forstchen   f   1979

**Altir "Tir"**
*Icefalcon's Quest* - Barbara Hambly   f   2504

**Alya, Princess**
*Strings* - Dave Duncan   s   1689

**Amatus**
*One for the Morning Glory* - John Barnes   f   355

**Ambrose**
*The Gilded Chain: A Tale of the King's Blades* - Dave
   Duncan   f   1679

**Amelia**
*Dragon's Plunder* - Brad Strickland   f   5336

**Ancar**
*Winds of Fury* - Mercedes Lackey   f   3306

**Anghara, Princess**
*Nemesis* - Louise Cooper   f   1177

**Anigel**
*Black Trillium* - Marion Zimmer Bradley   f   630

**Anlawdd**
*Arthur War Lord* - Dafydd ab Hugh   f   6

**Annice**
*Sing the Four Quarters* - Tanya Huff   f   2799

**ap Don, Gwydion**
*The Island of the Mighty* - Evangeline
   Walton   f   5626

**ap Hywel, Dafydd**
*The Dragon on the Border* - Gordon R.
   Dickson   f   1533

**ap Kian, Donaugh**
*The Western King* - Ann Marston   f   3636

**ap Kian, Tiernyn**
*The Western King* - Ann Marston   f   3636

**ap Mathonwy, Math**
*The Island of the Mighty* - Evangeline
   Walton   f   5626

**ap Medrault, Irion**
*The Last Pendragon* - Robert Rice   f   4584

**ap Nia, Aidan**
*King's Son, Magic's Son* - Josepha Sherman   f   4986

**Apuilana, Nialli**
*The New Springtime* - Robert Silverberg   s   5040

**Arbol**
*Split Heirs* - Lawrence Watt-Evans   f   5649

**Arianrhod**
*The Island of the Mighty* - Evangeline
   Walton   f   5626

**Artemisia**
*Split Heirs* - Lawrence Watt-Evans   f   5649

**Arthur**
*The Autobiography of Santa Claus: It's Better to Give*
   - Jeff Guinn   f   2456
*The Book of Brendan* - Ann Curry   f   1294
*The Camelot Chronicles* - Mike Ashley   f   224
*Enemy of God* - Bernard Cornwell   f   1189
*Excalibur* - Bernard Cornwell   f   1190
*Grail* - Stephen R. Lawhead   f   3355
*The Hawk's Gray Feather* - Patricia Kennealy-
   Morrison   f   3061
*In the Shadow of the Oak King* - Courtway
   Jones   f   2939
*The King* - Donald Barthelme   f   375
*Shadow of the King* - Helen Hollick   f   2747
*Witch of the North* - Courtway Jones   f   2940

**Asbrak**
*The Door to Ambermere* - J. Calvin Pierce   f   4316

**Aster "Star"**
*Glory Road* - Robert A. Heinlein   f   2644

**Avril**
*The Price of Blood and Honor* - Elizabeth
   Willey   f   5811

**Azdra'ik**
*The Goblin Mirror* - C.J. Cherryh   f   994

**Bahnakson, Bahzell**
*Oath of Swords* - David Weber   f   5678

**bar Valentin, Alessan**
*Tigana* - Guy Gavriel Kay   f   3018

**Bastable**
*Charmed* - Marilyn Singer   f   5070

**Belkis "Bell"**
*Here There Be Dragons* - Roger Zelazny   f   6069

**Beryt**
*Shaper's Legacy* - Sheila Finch   s   1933

**Berzel**
*Kedrigern and the Charming Couple* - John
   Morressy   f   4013

**Bink**
*Zombie Lover* - Piers Anthony   f   197

**Borric**
*Prince of the Blood* - Raymond E. Feist   f   1907

**Braganca, Alphonso**
*God's Fires* - Patricia Anthony   s   159

**Brant, Arn**
*The Lanterns of God* - Ron Sarti   s   4835
*Legacy of the Ancients* - Ron Sarti   s   4836

**Bronwyn**
*Hearts and Armor* - Ron Miller   f   3903
*Palaces and Prisons* - Ron Miller   f   3904
*Silk and Steel* - Ron Miller   f   3905

**Brunahild "Sigdrifa"**
*The Dragons of the Rhine* - Diana L.
   Paxson   f   4264
*The Wolf and the Raven* - Diana L. Paxson   f   4270

**Brunichild**
*Rhinegold* - Stephan Grundy   f   2454

**Bruno**
*King and Emperor* - Harry Harrison   f   2571

**Bryarmote**
*Pyromancer* - Don Callander   f   847

**Byriver, Jerno**
*Thunder of the Captains* - Holly Lisle   f   3489

**Caitin, Kedryn**
*The Usurper* - Angus Wells   f   5739
*The Way Beneath* - Angus Wells   f   5740
*Wrath of Ashar* - Angus Wells   f   5742

**Cale**
*Invasion America* - Christie Golden   s   2252
*On the Run* - Christie Golden   s   2254

**Calliope**
*One for the Morning Glory* - John Barnes   f   355

**Carrion, Kade**
*The Element of Fire* - Martha Wells   f   5750

**Casey**
*With Full Honors* - Donald E. McQuinn   s   3865

**Cefwyn**
*Fortress in the Eye of Time* - C.J. Cherryh   f   991
*Fortress of Eagles* - C.J. Cherryh   f   992
*Fortress of Owls* - C.J. Cherryh   f   993

**Cerdic**
*Shadow of the King* - Helen Hollick   f   2747

**Cha'dune, Hezhi Yehd**
*The Blackgod* - J. Gregory Keyes   f   3095
*The Waterborn* - J. Gregory Keyes   f   3098

**Chandra**
*The Fire's Stone* - Tanya Huff   f   2796

**Charming**
*Slay and Rescue* - John Moore   f   3991

**Cimorene**
*Calling on Dragons* - Patricia C. Wrede   f   5974
*Dealing with Dragons* - Patricia C. Wrede   f   5975
*Searching for Dragons* - Patricia C. Wrede   f   5979

**Collins, Lysander**
*Prince of Sparta* - Jerry Pournelle   s   4378

**Columcille**
*The Throne of Tara* - John Desjarlais   f   1498

**Conan III**
*Rouse a Sleeping Cat* - Dan Crawford   f   1249

**Cormac**
*Wolfking* - Bridget Wood   f   5963

**Cwan, Si**
*End Game* - Peter David   s   1382

**Cwenn**
*Suisan* - Phyllis Carol Agins   f   42

**Cyron**
*Star Child* - James P. Hogan   s   2730

**Danan, Elora**
*Shadow Dawn* - Chris Claremont   f   1042
*Shadow Moon* - George Lucas   f   3540

**Danu**
*The Enchanted Isles* - Casey Flynn   f   1960

**Dara**
*Krispos of Videssos* - Harry Turtledove   f   5506

**Daruya**
*Spear of Heaven* - Judith Tarr   f   5396

**Darville**
*The Perfect Princess* - Irene Radford   f   4462

**Darvish**
*The Fire's Stone* - Tanya Huff  f  2796

**Darynson, Davyn "Davi"**
*Book of Stones* - L. Dean James  f  2862

**d'Aurca, Adamus**
*Fair Peril* - Nancy Springer  f  5178

**de Draconis, Rejiia**
*The Loneliest Magician* - Irene Radford  f  4461

**de Laal, Leland**
*Helm* - Steven Gould  s  2289

**de Noram, Marilyn**
*Helm* - Steven Gould  s  2289

**de Saumur et Navarre y Cordova, Anastasia "Meanne"**
*An Exchange of Gifts* - Anne McCaffrey  f  3731

**de'Leonne, Valedan kai**
*The Broken Crown* - Michelle West  f  5757

**DeMarian, Demnor**
*The Stone Prince* - Fiona Patton  f  4259

**DeMarian, Kassandra**
*The Painter Knight* - Fiona Patton  f  4258

**DeMarian, Melesandra III**
*The Stone Prince* - Fiona Patton  f  4259

**den Karynth, Calandryll**
*Dark Magic* - Angus Wells  f  5733
*Forbidden Magic* - Angus Wells  f  5736
*Wild Magic* - Angus Wells  f  5741

**Desio**
*Servant of the Empire* - Raymond E. Feist  f  1910

**Diaspad**
*The Work of the Sun* - Teresa Edgerton  f  1746

**Dirona**
*Search for the Starblade* - Keith Taylor  f  5408

**Dolph**
*Isle of View* - Piers Anthony  f  177

**Dragon**
*Dragon Tome* - Richard A. Knaak  f  3169

**Du Lucent, Andrea**
*The War of the Sky Lords* - John Brosnan  s  721

**Dulay**
*Inhuman Beings* - Jerry Jay Carroll  s  914

**Dunladry, Duncan**
*Caledon of the Mists* - Deborah Turner Harris  f  2560

**Dunladry, Mhairi**
*Caledon of the Mists* - Deborah Turner Harris  f  2560
*The Queen of Ashes* - Deborah Turner Harris  f  2561

**dunMheric, Deymorin Rhomandi**
*Ring of Intrigue* - Jane S. Fancher  f  1863
*Ring of Lightning* - Jane S. Fancher  f  1864

**dunMheric, Mikhyel Rhomandi**
*Ring of Intrigue* - Jane S. Fancher  f  1863
*Ring of Lightning* - Jane S. Fancher  f  1864

**dunMheric, Nikaenor "Nikki" Rhomandi**
*Ring of Lightning* - Jane S. Fancher  f  1864

**Durmontov, Alexei**
*Magician's Ward* - Patricia C. Wrede  f  5976

**Edhadeya**
*Earthborn* - Orson Scott Card  s  884

**Edward**
*Lord of Sunset* - Parke Godwin  f  2246

**Edward, Albert Victor Christian**
*The Women of Whitechapel and Jack the Ripper* - Paul West  h  5761

**Eedrah**
*Myst: The Book of D'ni* - Rand Miller  f  3897

**Egdril**
*No One Noticed the Cat* - Anne McCaffrey  f  3740

**Ehlana**
*Domes of Fire* - David Eddings  f  1732
*The Sapphire Rose* - David Eddings  f  1737

**Eithne**
*The Shattered Oath* - Josepha Sherman  f  4989

**e'Kieron, Aliera**
*Five Hundred Years After* - Steven Brust  f  742

**Elaine**
*Wolf's Cub* - Mackay Wood  f  5964

**Elayne**
*A Crown of Swords* - Robert Jordan  f  2984
*The Dragon Reborn* - Robert Jordan  f  2985
*The Fires of Heaven* - Robert Jordan  f  2987
*The Path of Daggers* - Robert Jordan  f  2989

**Ellyn**
*The Guardian* - Angus Wells  f  5737

**Elminster**
*Elminster: The Making of a Mage* - Ed Greenwood  f  2427

**Elric of Melnibone**
*The Fortress of the Pearl* - Michael Moorcock  f  3982
*The Revenge of the Rose* - Michael Moorcock  f  3985
*Tales of the White Wolf* - Edward E. Kramer  f  3227

**Elryc**
*The Still* - David Feintuch  f  1902

**Emberella**
*Witches Abroad* - Terry Pratchett  f  4404

**Erland**
*Prince of the Blood* - Raymond E. Feist  f  1907

**Erwyn**
*Go Quest, Young Man* - K.B. Bogen  f  557

**Estmere**
*King's Son, Magic's Son* - Josepha Sherman  f  4986

**Evander, Danais**
*The Wizard and the Floating City* - Christopher Rowley  f  4699

**Everynne**
*The Golden Queen* - Dave Wolverton  s  5951

**fab Maelgwyn, Tryffin**
*The Castle of the Silver Wheel* - Teresa Edgerton  f  1741

**Falcon, Nikki**
*Falcon* - Emma Bull  s  768

**Farseer, Verity**
*Royal Assassin* - Robin Hobb  f  2695

**Feritayl, Irma**
*Bill, the Galactic Hero: On the Planet of Tasteless Pleasure* - Harry Harrison  s  2567

**Fernholz the Wise**
*The Fools' War* - Lee Kisling  f  3159

**Fire, Fen "Fire Queen"**
*The Fire Queen* - Jack Holland  f  2740

**Flowerbender**
*Marbleheart* - Don Callander  f  846

**Formidable**
*A Remembrance for Kedrigern* - John Morressy  f  4014

**Fox-Eyes, Thelvyn**
*Dragonmage of Mystara* - Thorarinn Gunnarsson  f  2462

**Freelorn "Lorn"**
*The Door into Sunset* - Diane Duane  f  1660

**Gail**
*Nobody's Son* - Sean Stewart  s  5275

**Garion**
*The Seeress of Kell* - David Eddings  f  1738
*Sorceress of Darshiva* - David Eddings  f  1739

**Gasam**
*The Poisoned Lands* - John Maddox Roberts  f  4619

**Gavilan, Kemal**
*Matrix Cubed* - Britton Bloom  s  554

**Gavin**
*Magelord: The Awakening* - Thomas K. Martin  f  3651
*The Time of Madness* - Thomas K. Martin  f  3652

**Gelasaar III**
*The Phoenix in Flight* - Sherwood Smith  s  5138

**Gerin the Fox**
*Fox and Empire* - Harry Turtledove  f  5500

**Gilgamesh**
*To the Land of the Living* - Robert Silverberg  f  5044

**Goro**
*Mortal Kombat* - Martin Delrio  f  1483

**Gorthyn**
*The Shining Company* - Rosemary Sutcliff  f  5359

**Grainne**
*The Lost Prince* - Bridget Wood  f  5962

**Griffiths, Jeremy**
*Nightsword* - Margaret Weis  f  5722

**Guenevere**
*The Camelot Chronicles* - Mike Ashley  f  224
*Witch of the North* - Courtway Jones  f  2940

**Guinevere**
*The Child Queen* - Nancy McKenzie  f  3827
*Guinevere: The Legend in Autumn* - Persia Woolley  f  5970
*The King* - Donald Barthelme  f  375
*Queen of the Summer Stars* - Persia Woolley  f  5971

**Gwenhwyfar**
*Pendragon's Banner* - Helen Hollick  f  2746
*Shadow of the King* - Helen Hollick  f  2747

**Gwydion**
*The Well-Favored Man: The Tale of the Sorcerer's Nephew* - Elizabeth Willey  f  5813

**Hael**
*The Steel Kings* - John Maddox Roberts  f  4621

**hai-Arkad, Brandon**
*The Rifter's Covenant* - Sherwood Smith  s  5140

**Haldane, Javan Jashan Urien**
*King Javan's Year* - Katherine Kurtz  f  3258

**Hanorissia, Juliassa**
*The Lantern of God* - John Dalmas  s  1323

**Haramis**
*Black Trillium* - Marion Zimmer Bradley  f  630
*Blood Trillium* - Julian May  f  3696
*Lady of the Trillium* - Marion Zimmer Bradley  f  641
*Sky Trillium* - Julian May  f  3700

**Harnak**
*Oath of Swords* - David Weber  f  5678

**Harpirias of Muldemar**
*The Mountains of Majipoor* - Robert Silverberg  s  5037

**Hauberin**
*A Strange and Ancient Name* - Josepha Sherman  f  4991

**Heliokleia**
*Horses of Heaven* - Gillian Bradshaw   f   657

**Hemlock**
*Sweet Myth-tery of Life* - Robert Asprin   f   262

**Herla**
*Storm Warriors* - Brian Craig   f   1240

**Herric**
*Wolf's Cub* - Mackay Wood   f   5964

**Ho, Gordon**
*House of the Sun* - Nigel Findley   s   1936

**Holbian**
*The Road to Underfall* - Mike Jefferies   f   2888

**Hr.Tyi.Bei.k.ai**
*Alien Tongue* - Stephen Leigh   s   3424

**I**
*A City in Winter* - Mark Helprin   f   2653

**Incarnadine**
*Bride of the Castle* - John DeChancie   s   1452
*Castle Dreams* - John DeChancie   s   1453
*Castle War!* - John DeChancie   s   1455

**Ingolfsson, Yolande**
*The Stone Dogs* - S.M. Stirling   s   5300

**Inosolan "Inos"**
*Emperor and Clown* - Dave Duncan   f   1676
*Faery Lands Forlorn* - Dave Duncan   f   1677
*Magic Casement* - Dave Duncan   f   1683
*Perilous Seas* - Dave Duncan   f   1685

**Iowyn**
*Tears of Time* - Nancy Asire   f   256

**Iris**
*Geis of the Gargoyle* - Piers Anthony   f   172

**Irrylath**
*The Pearl of the Soul of the World* - Meredith Ann Pierce   f   4318

**Irsei, Corum Jhaelen**
*Corum: The Coming of Chaos* - Michael Moorcock   f   3978

**Ivy**
*Man From Mundania* - Piers Anthony   f   180

**Jael**
*Dagger's Edge* - Anne Logston   f   3508

**Jamas**
*No One Noticed the Cat* - Anne McCaffrey   f   3740

**Jathondi**
*The Gates of Twilight* - Paula Volsky   f   5581

**Javas**
*To Save the Sun* - Ben Bova   s   596

**Jemson "Jem"**
*The One-Armed Queen* - Jane Yolen   f   6037

**Jen**
*The Remarkable Journey of Prince Jen* - Lloyd Alexander   f   69

**Jerno**
*Wrath of the Princes* - Holly Lisle   f   3490

**Jessa**
*Darkloom* - Cary Osborne   s   4225
*Deathweave* - Cary Osborne   s   4226

**Jewel**
*The Changeling* - Kristine Kathryn Rusch   f   4714

**John**
*The Sheriff of Nottingham* - Richard Kluger   f   3165

**Jones, Shadrach**
*The Collected Stories of Philip K. Dick, Volume One: The Short Happy Life of the Brown Oxford* - Philip K. Dick   s   1519

**Josua**
*To Green Angel Tower* - Tad Williams   f   5832

**Julia**
*Blue Moon Rising* - Simon R. Green   f   2362

**Julian of Stansvale**
*The Jewel of Fire* - Diana L. Paxson   f   4265
*The Wind Crystal* - Diana L. Paxson   f   4269

**Kadiya**
*Black Trillium* - Marion Zimmer Bradley   f   630
*Golden Trillium* - Andre Norton   f   4153

**Kadolan "Kade"**
*Faery Lands Forlorn* - Dave Duncan   f   1677
*Perilous Seas* - Dave Duncan   f   1685

**Kahn, Tae**
*The Children of Wrath* - Mickey Zucker Reichert   f   4518

**Kahsir**
*Tears of Time* - Nancy Asire   f   256

**kai de'Leonne, Valedan**
*The Uncrowned King* - Michelle West   f   5760

**Kaihan**
*Nameless Magery* - Delia Marshall Turner   f   5490

**Kandaki**
*The Land of Gold* - Gillian Bradshaw   f   658

**Karin**
*Voima* - C. Dale Brittain   f   704

**Kashir**
*To Fall Like Stars* - Nancy Asire   f   257

**Katin**
*Season of Storms* - Ellen Foxxe   f   2032

**Kazul**
*Calling on Dragons* - Patricia C. Wrede   f   5974

**Kendrick, Robyn**
*The Coral Kingdom* - Douglas Niles   f   4106

**Kestrel**
*The Robin and the Kestrel* - Mercedes Lackey   f   3293

**Khyriz**
*Voices of Chaos* - A.C. Crispin   s   1266

**Kilgour, Alex**
*Vortex* - Allan Cole   s   1108

**Kith-Kanan**
*Firstborn* - Paul B. Thompson   f   5454

**Korendil**
*Bedlam's Bard* - Mercedes Lackey   f   3269
*Knight of Ghosts and Shadows* - Mercedes Lackey   f   3285
*Summoned to Tourney* - Mercedes Lackey   f   3299

**Korsibar**
*Sorcerers of Majipoor* - Robert Silverberg   s   5041

**Kristin**
*The Sixth Book of Lost Swords: Mindsword's Story* - Fred Saberhagen   f   4776

**Kuwai**
*Dark Legend* - Jamake Highwater   f   2686

**Larissa**
*Queens of Land and Sea* - John Maddox Roberts   f   4620
*The Steel Kings* - John Maddox Roberts   f   4621

**LeFarge, Frederick**
*The Stone Dogs* - S.M. Stirling   s   5300

**LeFarge, Marya**
*The Stone Dogs* - S.M. Stirling   s   5300

**Leith**
*The Prince of Ill Luck* - Susan Dexter   f   1512

**Leon**
*The Stallion Queen* - Constance Ash   f   223

**Leopold**
*Tiger Burning Bright* - Marion Zimmer Bradley   f   652

**Lha**
*Python Isle* - Kenneth Robeson   f   4624

**Lionheart, Richard**
*The Empire of Fear* - Brian Stableford   h   5191

**Lissar, Lissla "Deerskin"**
*Deerskin* - Robin McKinley   f   3844

**Lithaniel, Ardagh**
*The Shattered Oath* - Josepha Sherman   f   4989

**Lizra**
*Black Unicorn* - Tanith Lee   f   3404

**Llyndreth**
*The Shadow Warrior* - Pat Zettner   f   6082

**Louis XIV**
*The Moon and the Sun* - Vonda N. McIntyre   f   3822

**Luap**
*Liar's Oath* - Elizabeth Moon   f   3969

**Lucas, Prince**
*Rats and Gargoyles* - Mary Gentle   f   2196

**Lugh**
*Landslayer's Law* - Tom Deitz   f   1474

**Lysander**
*Prince of Mercenaries* - Jerry Pournelle   s   4377

**Mac Airt, Cormac**
*Finn Mac Cool* - Morgan Llywelyn   f   3504

**Madia**
*Demon Blade* - Mark A. Garland   f   2141

**Magon**
*The Warrior Returns* - Allan Cole   f   1109

**Malachy the Great**
*Brian Boru: Emperor of the Irish* - Morgan Llywelyn   f   3501

**Mara**
*Mistress of the Empire* - Raymond E. Feist   f   1906
*Servant of the Empire* - Raymond E. Feist   f   1910

**Maryn**
*The Red Wyvern* - Katharine Kerr   f   3074

**Matsuko, Estelle**
*On Basilisk Station* - David Weber   s   5679

**McDaris, Samantha "Sammi"**
*Elvendude* - Mark Shepherd   f   4980

**Meiglan**
*The Dragon Token* - Melanie Rawn   f   4485
*Skybowl* - Melanie Rawn   f   4490

**Meldron**
*The Silver Hand* - Stephen R. Lawhead   f   3358

**Meriamon**
*Lord of the Two Lands* - Judith Tarr   f   5395

**Merlin**
*Prince of Chaos* - Roger Zelazny   f   6073

**Midas**
*The Adventures of King Midas* - Lynne Reid Banks   f   329

**Mikayla**
*Lady of the Trillium* - Marion Zimmer Bradley   f   641

**Miriamele**
*To Green Angel Tower* - Tad Williams   f   5832

**Mordred**
*Mordred's Curse* - Ian McDowell   f   3806

**Morgan le Fay**
*The Prince and the Pilgrim* - Mary Stewart   f   5270

**Morgan le Fey**
*Witch of the North* - Courtway Jones   f   2940

**Morgen**
*Reunion* - Michael Jan Friedman   s   2068

**Morgeu**
*The Dragon and the Unicorn* - A.A.
  Attanasio  *f*  266

**Morgian**
*Grail* - Stephen R. Lawhead  *f*  3355

**Murat**
*The Sixth Book of Lost Swords: Mindsword's Story* -
  Fred Saberhagen  *f*  4776

**Mynauzet**
*King of the Dead* - R.A. MacAvoy  *f*  3581

**Nallaneen, Faris**
*A College of Magics* - Caroline Stevermer  *f*  5266

**Nargol, Edward**
*The Legend of Nightfall* - Mickey Zucker
  Reichert  *f*  4521

**Naxania**
*The Unicorn Peace* - John Lee  *f*  3399

**Nicholas**
*The Changeling* - Kristine Kathryn Rusch  *f*  4714
*The King's Buccaneer* - Raymond E. Feist  *f*  1904
*To Save the Sun* - Ben Bova  *s*  596

**Nisa**
*Emperor of Everything* - Ray Aldridge  *s*  62
*The Pharaoh Contract* - Ray Aldridge  *s*  63

**Nishima**
*The Initiate Brother* - Sean Russell  *f*  4742

**Nlavi**
*By the Sword* - Greg Costikyan  *f*  1207

**Nopal**
*The Chalchiuhite Dragon* - Kenneth Morris  *f*  4020

**Ohanscai, Natalya**
*Eyes of Silver* - Michael A. Stackpole  *f*  5200

**Organa, Leia**
*The Courtship of Princess Leia* - Dave
  Wolverton  *s*  5950
*The Crystal Star* - Vonda N. McIntyre  *s*  3820
*Dark Force Rising* - Timothy Zahn  *s*  6052
*The Truce at Bakura* - Kathy Tyers  *s*  5527
*Zorba the Hutt's Revenge* - Paul Davids  *s*  1394

**Oswald**
*Drachenfels* - Jack Yeovil  *f*  6022

**Palamon**
*Across the Thlassa Mey* - Dennis McCarty  *f*  3765

**Pardu**
*Heart Readers* - Kristine Kathryn Rusch  *f*  4718

**Pelagia, Iolanthe "Io"**
*City of Diamond* - Jane Emerson  *s*  1807

**Pellior, Arioso**
*Song for the Basilisk* - Patricia A. McKillip  *f*  3841

**Pelucir, Talis**
*The Book of Atrix Wolfe* - Patricia A.
  McKillip  *f*  3838

**Penarvon, Arthur**
*The Oak Above the Kings: A Book of the Keltiad* -
  Patricia Kennealy  *s*  3058

**Pendragon, Arthur**
*The Kingmaking* - Helen Hollick  *f*  2745
*Merlin and the Dragons* - Jane Yolen  *f*  6036
*Pendragon's Banner* - Helen Hollick  *f*  2746

**Pendreic, Gweniver**
*The Oak Above the Kings: A Book of the Keltiad* -
  Patricia Kennealy  *s*  3058

**Pendreic, Morguenna**
*The Hedge of Mist* - Patricia Kennealy-
  Morrison  *s*  3062

**Percinet**
*Child of Faerie, Child of Earth* - Josepha
  Sherman  *f*  4985

**Pol**
*The Dragon Token* - Melanie Rawn  *f*  4485
*Skybowl* - Melanie Rawn  *f*  4490
*Sunrunner's Fire* - Melanie Rawn  *f*  4493

**Prestimion**
*Sorcerers of Majipoor* - Robert Silverberg  *s*  5041

**Princess**
*A Remembrance for Kedrigern* - John
  Morressy  *f*  4014

**Prospero**
*The Price of Blood and Honor* - Elizabeth
  Willey  *f*  5811
*A Sorcerer and a Gentleman* - Elizabeth
  Willey  *f*  5812
*The Well-Favored Man: The Tale of the Sorcerer's
  Nephew* - Elizabeth Willey  *f*  5813

**Protarus, Iraj**
*Wolves of the Gods* - Allan Cole  *f*  1111

**Queen**
*The Veils of Snows* - Mark Helprin  *f*  2654

**Quisling, Emann**
*Vinas Solamnus* - J. Robert King  *f*  3123

**Ramifon Blayl, Ram**
*Letters From Atlantis* - Robert Silverberg  *f*  5035

**Rance**
*Bride of the Castle* - John DeChancie  *s*  1452

**Rania**
*The Promise* - Monica Hughes  *s*  2808

**Rasha of the Thousand Doors**
*Yesterday We Saw Mermaids* - Esther
  Friesner  *f*  2086

**Rhisadel, Teressa**
*Wren's War* - Sherwood Smith  *f*  5144

**Ridenau, Roderic**
*Children of Enchantment* - Anne Kelleher
  Bush  *f*  787

**Robert**
*Legacy of the Ancients* - Ron Sarti  *s*  4836

**Rodrigo**
*The Still* - David Feintuch  *f*  1902

**Roele, Michael**
*The Iron Throne* - Simon Hawke  *f*  2618

**Rohan**
*The Star Scroll* - Melanie Rawn  *f*  4491
*Stronghold* - Melanie Rawn  *f*  4492

**Romanov, George Alexandrovich**
*The Princess and the Dragon* - Roberto
  Pazzi  *f*  4272

**Rose**
*Question Quest* - Piers Anthony  *f*  186

**Rosselin Metadi, Beka**
*By Honor Betray'd* - Debra Doyle  *s*  1598

**Rossemikka "Mikka"**
*The Perfect Princess* - Irene Radford  *f*  4462

**Rowforth**
*Chimaera's Copper* - Piers Anthony  *f*  166

**Rudolph "Rudy"**
*Being of Two Minds* - Pamela F. Service  *f*  4918

**Rupert**
*Blue Moon Rising* - Simon R. Green  *f*  2362

**Rustin**
*The Still* - David Feintuch  *f*  1902

**Sarai**
*The Spell of the Black Dagger* - Lawrence Watt-
  Evans  *f*  5648

**Scathach**
*Lavondyss: Journey to an Unknown Region* - Robert
  Holdstock  *f*  2739

**Scour**
*Starliner* - David Drake  *s*  1645

**Serena**
*The Wizard and the Floating City* - Christopher
  Rowley  *f*  4699

**s'Falenn, Arithon**
*Curse of the Mistwraith* - Janny Wurts  *f*  6001
*Ships of Merior* - Janny Wurts  *f*  6004

**Shahryar**
*The Last Arabian Night* - Craig Shaw
  Gardner  *f*  2129

**Shalindra**
*The Wolf of Winter* - Paula Volsky  *f*  5584

**Shaltar, Connor**
*Wren to the Rescue* - Sherwood Smith  *f*  5142
*Wren's Quest* - Sherwood Smith  *f*  5143
*Wren's War* - Sherwood Smith  *f*  5144

**Shazad**
*Queens of Land and Sea* - John Maddox
  Roberts  *f*  4620

**Sheela**
*The Nomad Queen* - James Gordon White  *f*  5783

**Shelyra "Raymonda"**
*Tiger Burning Bright* - Marion Zimmer
  Bradley  *f*  652

**Shimmer**
*Dragon Cauldron* - Laurence Yep  *f*  6024
*Dragon War* - Laurence Yep  *f*  6025

**Sianna**
*Lady of Avalon* - Marion Zimmer Bradley  *f*  640

**Sigvarthsson, Shef**
*King and Emperor* - Harry Harrison  *f*  2571
*One King's Way* - Harry Harrison  *s*  2572

**s'Ilessid, Lysaer**
*Curse of the Mistwraith* - Janny Wurts  *f*  6001
*Fugitive Prince* - Janny Wurts  *f*  6002
*Ships of Merior* - Janny Wurts  *f*  6004

**Silkweb Empress**
*Bronze Mirror* - Jeanne Larsen  *f*  3338

**Silver Hand, Llew**
*The Endless Knot* - Stephen R. Lawhead  *f*  3354
*The Silver Hand* - Stephen R. Lawhead  *f*  3358

**Silver Snow**
*Imperial Lady* - Andre Norton  *f*  4155

**Simon**
*The Gift* - Patrick O'Leary  *f*  4211

**Sioned**
*Skybowl* - Melanie Rawn  *f*  4490

**Sithas**
*Firstborn* - Paul B. Thompson  *f*  5454
*The Kinslayer Wars* - Douglas Niles  *f*  4109

**Sogan, Varn Tarl**
*Call to Arms* - P.M. Griffin  *s*  2435
*Jungle Assault* - P.M. Griffin  *s*  2437

**Solo, Leia Organa**
*Ambush at Corellia* - Roger MacBride Allen  *s*  76
*Before the Storm* - Michael P. Kube-
  McDowell  *s*  3247
*Children of the Jedi* - Barbara Hambly  *s*  2500
*Darksaber* - Kevin J. Anderson  *s*  103
*Heir to the Empire* - Timothy Zahn  *s*  6054
*The Last Command* - Timothy Zahn  *s*  6055
*The New Rebellion* - Kristine Kathryn
  Rusch  *s*  4719

**sorRodion, Rinchen "Wolf"**
*Beneath the Web* - Lynn Abbey  *f*  12

**Starfire, Dion**
*King's Sacrifice* - Margaret Weis  *s*  5717
*The Lost King* - Margaret Weis  *s*  5720

**Steiner-Davion, Victor**
*Prince of Havoc* - Michael A. Stackpole   s   5204

**Stephen**
*The Last Book of Swords: Shieldbreaker's Story* - Fred Saberhagen   f   4768

**Sumara**
*The Nomad Queen* - James Gordon White   f   5783

**Sylvarresta, Iome**
*The Runelords: The Sum of All Men* - David Farland   f   1866

**Tabini**
*Invader* - C.J. Cherryh   s   998

**Tamar**
*The Iron Ring* - Lloyd Alexander   f   68

**Tamas of Maggiar**
*The Goblin Mirror* - C.J. Cherryh   f   994

**Tel'anh, Alethia**
*Shadows over Lyra* - Patricia C. Wrede   f   5980

**Tenedos, Laish**
*The Demon King* - Chris Bunch   f   770
*The Seer King* - Chris Bunch   f   771

**Thaiter, Leot**
*The Wild Hunt: Vengeance Moon* - Jocelin Foxe   f   2031

**Theovere**
*The Eagle and the Nightingales* - Mercedes Lackey   f   3278

**Theseus**
*Whilom* - Robert Watson   f   5639

**Thismet**
*Sorcerers of Majipoor* - Robert Silverberg   s   5041

**Thorian**
*The Reaver Road* - Dave Duncan   f   1687

**Thuro "Uther Pendragon"**
*Ghost King* - David Gemmell   f   2188

**Tianna**
*Iron Dragons: Mountains and Madness* - Rose Estes   f   1839

**Toikella**
*The Mountains of Majipoor* - Robert Silverberg   s   5037

**Tolivar**
*Blood Trillium* - Julian May   f   3696

**Trelane, Athaya**
*Call of Madness* - Julie Dean Smith   f   5124
*Mission of Magic* - Julie Dean Smith   f   5125
*Sage of Sare* - Julie Dean Smith   f   5126
*The Wizard King* - Julie Dean Smith   f   5127

**Trelane, Durek**
*Mission of Magic* - Julie Dean Smith   f   5125
*Sage of Sare* - Julie Dean Smith   f   5126

**Trent**
*Castle Dreams* - John DeChancie   s   1453
*Castle Spellbound* - John DeChancie   s   1454

**Trerzian**
*Bewitchments of Love and Hate* - Storm Constantine   s   1140

**Trusslo, Alix Amanda**
*Dragon Rescue* - Don Callander   f   843

**Tupac, Acanna**
*Mansions of Darkness* - Chelsea Quinn Yarbro   h   6016

**Tyner, Gil**
*The Hero King* - Rick Shelley   f   4970
*The Hero of Varay* - Rick Shelley   f   4971

**Val Orden, Gaborn**
*The Runelords: The Sum of All Men* - David Farland   f   1866

**Valmar**
*Voima* - C. Dale Brittain   f   704

**Varis**
*The Wolf of Winter* - Paula Volsky   f   5584

**Venkatna**
*Justice* - David Drake   s   1635

**Veriam, Lizora "Lizra"**
*Gold Unicorn* - Tanith Lee   f   3410

**Victor**
*Blood and Honor* - Simon R. Green   f   2361

**Wenceslas, Rudyard "Waldo" Riding**
*The Wealdwife's Tale* - Paul Hazel   f   2636

**William**
*Robin and the King* - Parke Godwin   f   2247

**Willow**
*The Tangle Box* - Terry Brooks   f   718

**Wizenbeak**
*Lord of the Troll-Bats* - Alexis A. Gilliland   f   2234

**Wynett**
*The Usurper* - Angus Wells   f   5739
*The Way Beneath* - Angus Wells   f   5740

**Xena**
*The Empty Throne* - Ru Emerson   f   1808
*The Thief of Hermes* - Ru Emerson   f   1811

**Xizor**
*The Mandalorian Armor* - K.W. Jeter   s   2914

**Yambu**
*Wayfinder's Story: The Seventh Book of Lost Swords* - Fred Saberhagen   f   4777

**Yamun**
*Horselords* - David Cook   f   1145

**Ylon**
*Mirror of Destiny* - Andre Norton   f   4159

**Yuan, Li**
*The Middle Kingdom* - David Wingrove   s   5919

**Zeus**
*Sons of the Titans* - Patrick H. Adkins   f   36

**Zoltan**
*Wayfinder's Story: The Seventh Book of Lost Swords* - Fred Saberhagen   f   4777

# RULER

**Abaddon**
*Wolf in Shadow* - David Gemmell   s   2191

**Aetheric III**
*Conspiracy* - J. Robert King   f   3121

**Agamemnon**
*Helen's Passage* - Diana M. Concannon   f   1129

**Agricola, Caesar Germanicus**
*Cry Republic* - Kirk Mitchell   s   3917

**Albain, Elandra**
*Realm of Light* - Deborah Chester   f   1008
*Shadow War* - Deborah Chester   f   1010

**Anadon, Oren**
*Exile* - Michael P. Kube-McDowell   s   3248

**Andry**
*The Dragon Token* - Melanie Rawn   f   4485
*Stronghold* - Melanie Rawn   f   4492

**Anthimos**
*Krispos Rising* - Harry Turtledove   f   5507

**ap Kian, Keylan**
*The Western King* - Ann Marston   f   3636

**Archon of Lycanth**
*The Warrior's Tale* - Allan Cole   f   1110

**Arthur**
*The Autobiography of Santa Claus: It's Better to Give* - Jeff Guinn   f   2456
*The Child Queen* - Nancy McKenzie   f   3827
*Chronicles of King Arthur* - Andrea Hopkins   f   2767
*Guinevere: The Legend in Autumn* - Persia Woolley   f   5970
*King & Raven* - Cary James   f   2858
*Mordred's Curse* - Ian McDowell   f   3806
*Pendragon* - Stephen R. Lawhead   f   3357
*Queen of the Summer Stars* - Persia Woolley   f   5971

**Arthur "Artos"**
*A Prince Among Men* - Robert N. Charrette   f   977

**Atare, Darame "Silver" Meath**
*Hidden Fires* - Katharine Eliska Kimbriel   s   3117

**Atare, Sheen**
*Hidden Fires* - Katharine Eliska Kimbriel   s   3117

**Avril**
*A Sorcerer and a Gentleman* - Elizabeth Willey   f   5812

**Azoun**
*Crusade* - James Lowder   f   3537

**Azoun IV**
*Cormyr: A Novel* - Ed Greenwood   f   2425

**bad-Jam, Gilan "Gilan the Third"**
*The Swords of Zinjaban* - L. Sprague de Camp   s   1418

**Biilathkamoro, Chodrisei "Coso"**
*The Kalif's War* - John Dalmas   s   1322

**Bloat**
*Dealer's Choice* - George R.R. Martin   s   3643
*Jokertown Shuffle* - George R.R. Martin   s   3646

**Boncorro**
*The Secular Wizard* - Christopher Stasheff   f   5222

**Brandin of Ygrath**
*Tigana* - Guy Gavriel Kay   f   3018

**Brown, Pellimore "Pel"**
*The Reign of the Brown Magician* - Lawrence Watt-Evans   f   5647

**Bull-Roar, Harold**
*Byzantium* - Stephen R. Lawhead   f   3353

**Charlemagne**
*His Majesty's Elephant* - Judith Tarr   f   5394

**Chevenga**
*Shadow's Son* - Shirley Meier   f   3872

**Chevenga, Fourth**
*Lion's Heart* - Karen Wehrstein   f   5683
*Lion's Soul* - Karen Wehrstein   f   5684

**Cleon, I**
*Foundation's Fear* - Gregory Benford   s   446

**The Computer**
*Extreme Paranoia: Nobody Knows the Trouble I've Shot* - Ken Rolston   s   4662

**Conan III**
*A Wild Dog and Lone* - Dan Crawford   f   1251

**Cornelian, Prime**
*Exile* - Al Sarrantonio   s   4829

**Darius**
*Fractal Mode* - Piers Anthony   f   171
*Virtual Mode* - Piers Anthony   f   194

**Diogenes, Romanus**
*Shards of Empire* - Susan Shwartz   f   5017

**d'Iste, Tiran**
*Wind Whispers, Shadow Shouts* - Sharon Green   f   2360

**Dragit**
*On the Run* - Christie Golden   s   2254

**Drev**
*The Dark Shore* - Adam Lee   f   3385

**Dy-Dybo**
*Fossil Hunter* - Robert J. Sawyer   s   4855

**Edward III**
*Chicago Red* - R.M. Meluch   s   3873

**Elessedil, Wren**
*The Talismans of Shannara* - Terry Brooks   f   717

**Elric of Melnibone**
*Elric: Song of the Black Sword* - Michael
　Moorcock   f   3980

**Emshander IV**
*Upland Outlaws* - Dave Duncan   f   1690

**Emshander V**
*The Living God* - Dave Duncan   f   1682
*The Stricken Field* - Dave Duncan   f   1688

**Estarion**
*Arrows of the Sun* - Judith Tarr   f   5391

**Friend**
*Swan Song* - Robert R. McCammon   h   3757

**Gampo, Songstan**
*The Yngling and the Circle of Power* - John
　Dalmas   s   1328

**Garden, Humility "Humi"**
*Delta City* - Felicity Savage   f   4849

**Gawen**
*Lady of Avalon* - Marion Zimmer Bradley   f   640

**Gerin the Fox**
*Prince of the North* - Harry Turtledove   f   5509

**Gleese, Eacon**
*The Stone Movers* - Patricia Mullen   f   4045

**Greene, Andy "the Warden"**
*The Warden of Horses* - Karen Ripley   s   4595

**Gwenhwyvar**
*Pendragon* - Stephen R. Lawhead   f   3357

**Ha'ark**
*Never Sound Retreat* - William R.
　Forstchen   s   1981

**Hadding**
*War of the Gods* - Poul Anderson   f   136

**Halarek, Karne**
*Brander's Book* - C.J. Mills   s   3909
*Egil's Book* - C.J. Mills   s   3910
*Kit's Book* - C.J. Mills   s   3911
*Zjhanne's Book* - C.J. Mills   s   3912

**Haldane, Rhys Michael Alister**
*The Bastard Prince* - Katherine Kurtz   f   3255

**Hemlock**
*Sweet Myth-tery of Life* - Robert Asprin   f   262

**Henry, Wiiliam**
*Queen's Gambit Declined* - Melinda M.
　Snodgrass   f   5147

**Holiday, Ben**
*The Tangle Box* - Terry Brooks   f   718
*Witches' Brew* - Terry Brooks   f   719

**Ilisidi**
*Inheritor* - C.J. Cherryh   s   997

**Ineluki the Storm King**
*Stone of Farewell* - Tad Williams   f   5831

**Irtuk-Saa**
*The Triad Worlds* - F.M. Busby   s   786

**Jenna**
*The One-Armed Queen* - Jane Yolen   f   6037

**Jessa**
*Darkloom* - Cary Osborne   s   4225

**Julius Caesar, Gaius**
*Child of the Eagle* - Esther Friesner   f   2073

**Justinian**
*In the Heart of Darkness* - Eric Flint   s   1955

**Kerim**
*When Demons Walk* - Patricia Briggs   f   683

**Kostimon**
*Reign of Shadows* - Deborah Chester   f   1009

**Koyil**
*Fallway* - Paula E. Downing   s   1593

**Krispos**
*Krispos of Videssos* - Harry Turtledove   f   5506
*Krispos the Emperor* - Harry Turtledove   f   5508

**Lamruil**
*Evermeet: Island of Elves* - Elaine
　Cunningham   f   1290

**Langelleik, Holjpip**
*Crystal Witness* - Kathy Tyers   s   5524

**Lephi the White**
*The Chaos Balance* - L.E. Modesitt Jr.   f   3925

**Loran, Luroc I**
*Firehand* - Andre Norton   s   4151

**Louis XIV**
*Queen's Gambit Declined* - Melinda M.
　Snodgrass   f   5147

**MacIntyre, Colin**
*Heirs of Empire* - David Weber   s   5672

**Ma'elKoth**
*Heroes Die* - Matthew Woodring Stover   s   5319

**Maniakes**
*Videssos Besieged* - Harry Turtledove   f   5513

**Marrimian**
*Hall of Whispers* - Mike Jefferies   f   2884

**Marth, Jarem**
*Ash Ock* - Christopher Hinz   s   2690
*The Paratwa* - Christopher Hinz   s   2691

**Mauakes**
*Horses of Heaven* - Gillian Bradshaw   f   657

**McCullough, Dusty**
*Free Zone* - Charles Platt   s   4341

**Medoc**
*The Lost Prince* - Bridget Wood   f   5962

**Mendanbar**
*Searching for Dragons* - Patricia C. Wrede   f   5979

**Mercati, Adrian**
*City of Diamond* - Jane Emerson   s   1807

**Minder XXIII, John**
*Stepwater* - L. Warren Douglas   s   1588
*The Wells of Phyre* - L. Warren Douglas   s   1589

**Mon, Ismail**
*The Pleistocene Redemption* - Dan
　Gallagher   s   2107

**MoonQueen**
*The Queen of Darkness* - Miguel Conner   s   1134

**Morbius**
*Strange Tales From the Nile Empire* - Greg
　Farshtey   f   1889

**Mordeth**
*The Falcon Rises* - Michael C. Staudinger   f   5235

**Nakar**
*Tower of Fear* - Glen Cook   f   1155

**Naxania**
*The Unicorn Peace* - John Lee   f   3399

**Nyctasia**
*Mistress of Ambiguities* - J.F. Rivkin   f   4596

**Oliderval**
*The Unicorn Peace* - John Lee   f   3399

**O'Meara, Patrick**
*Masters of the Fist* - Edward P. Hughes   s   2805

**Onrad**
*The Defenders* - Bill Baldwin   s   309

**Orlovsky, Paulo**
*The Third Force* - Marc Laidlaw   s   3313

**Orwen, Feng**
*The White Abacus* - Damien Broderick   s   708

**Panshinea**
*Path of Fire* - Charles Ingrid   s   2832

**Pati**
*Delta City* - Felicity Savage   f   4849

**Pendragon, Arthor**
*The Wolf and the Crown* - A.A. Attanasio   f   273

**Pendragon, Arthur**
*Arthur* - Stephen R. Lawhead   f   3352
*Changer* - Jane M. Lindskold   f   3474

**Pendrelc, Arthur "Artos"**
*The Hedge of Mist* - Patricia Kennealy-
　Morrison   s   3062

**Pepon, Buko**
*Paradise: A Chronicle of a Distant World* - Mike
　Resnick   s   4552

**Philip of Macedon**
*Orion and the Conqueror* - Ben Bova   s   590

**Pitt, Janus**
*Nemesis* - Isaac Asimov   s   247

**Pol**
*The Dragon Token* - Melanie Rawn   f   4485

**Queen of Ice**
*Horrible Humes* - Stephen Billias   f   487

**Ra Sadiin, Cydell**
*Heartstone and Silver* - Jacqui Singleton   f   5071

**Rahl, Richard "the Seeker"**
*Temple of the Winds* - Terry Goodkind   f   2270

**Rap**
*The Cutting Edge* - Dave Duncan   f   1675
*Upland Outlaws* - Dave Duncan   f   1690

**Reatur**
*A World of Difference* - Harry Turtledove   s   5514

**Rex, Arthur**
*The Whispers* - Dan Parkinson   s   4247

**Reynar III**
*Silver Princess, Golden Knight* - Sharon
　Green   f   2359

**Reysson, Gaylon**
*Book of Stones* - L. Dean James   f   2862
*Kingslayer* - L. Dean James   f   2863

**Rhodry**
*A Time of Omens* - Katharine Kerr   f   3078

**Ridenau, Abelard**
*Daughter of Prophecy* - Anne Kelleher Bush   f   788

**Rohan**
*The Star Scroll* - Melanie Rawn   f   4491
*Stronghold* - Melanie Rawn   f   4492

**Rosselin, Perada "Rada"**
*The Gathering Flame* - Debra Doyle   s   1599

**Rosselin Metadi, Beka**
*Starpilot's Grave* - Debra Doyle   s   1606

**Rugad**
*The Resistance* - Kristine Kathryn Rusch   f   4727

**Sage of Sare**
*The Wizard King* - Julie Dean Smith   f   5127

**Sethiyan, Hattim**
*The Usurper* - Angus Wells   f   5739

**Shalaman**
*The White Gryphon* - Mercedes Lackey   f   3303

**Shar, Dalin**
*Exile* - Al Sarrantonio   s   4829

**Sharbaraz**
*The Thousand Cities* - Harry Turtledove  f  5512

**Siddonie**
*The Catswold Portal* - Shirley Rousseau
   Murphy  f  4055

**Silver Hand, Llew**
*The Endless Knot* - Stephen R. Lawhead  f  3354

**Sioned**
*Stronghold* - Melanie Rawn  f  4492

**Soerensen, Terese "Tess"**
*The Law of Becoming* - Kate Elliott  s  1774

**Stefanos**
*Chains of Darkness, Chains of Light* - Michelle
   Sagara  f  4781
*Children of the Blood: Book Two of The Sundered* -
   Michelle Sagara  f  4782
*Into the Dark Lands* - Michelle Sagara  f  4783

**Strelsau, Mathias**
*Silk and Steel* - Ron Miller  f  3905

**Suettay**
*The Witch Doctor* - Christopher Stasheff  f  5228

**Sultan of Alpha Centauri**
*A Gathering of Stars* - Donald Moffitt  s  3947

**Summer, Moon Dawntreader**
*The Summer Queen* - Joan D. Vinge  s  5572

**Taniane**
*The New Springtime* - Robert Silverberg  s  5040

**Teaqua**
*Look into the Sun* - James Patrick Kelly  s  3047

**Thiede**
*The Fulfillments of Fate and Desire* - Storm
   Constantine  s  1142

**Tirrell**
*Talion: Revenant* - Michael A. Stackpole  f  5206

**Todtmann, Jeremiah**
*King of the Grey* - Richard A. Knaak  f  3173

**Toshtai**
*D'Shai* - Joel Rosenberg  f  4670

**Trioculus**
*The Glove of Darth Vader* - Paul Davids  s  1392
*The Lost City of the Jedi* - Paul Davids  s  1393
*Zorba the Hutt's Revenge* - Paul Davids  s  1394

**Ublaz Mad Eyes**
*The Pearls of Lutra* - Brian Jacques  f  2854

**Ulga, Jubadi va**
*Terrible Swift Sword* - William R.
   Forstchen  s  1983

**Una**
*Storms of Victory* - Andre Norton  f  4162

**Varodias**
*The Unicorn War* - John Lee  f  3401

**Von Zarovich, Strahd**
*I, Strahd* - P.N. Elrod  h  1797

**Vorbarra, Gregor**
*The Vor Game* - Lois McMaster Bujold  s  764

**Vorkosigan, Aral**
*Barrayar* - Lois McMaster Bujold  s  756

**Wittelsbach, Ludwig**
*From Prussia with Love* - John DeChancie  f  1457

**Woodgate, Lisa**
*Bretta Martyn* - L. Neil Smith  s  5128

**Ygorla**
*The Avenger* - Louise Cooper  f  1174
*The Deceiver* - Louise Cooper  f  1175

**Yildiz**
*Conan of the Red Brotherhood* - Leonard
   Carpenter  f  906

**Zorah**
*Beldan's Fire* - Midori Snyder  f  5150

## RUNAWAY

**Adric**
*The White Mists of Power* - Kristine Kathryn
   Rusch  f  4730

**Aletto**
*The Two in Hiding* - Ru Emerson  f  1812

**Batterberry, Lesli**
*Ghosts of Wind and Shadow* - Charles de
   Lint  f  1427

**Biale**
*On Fortune's Wheel* - Cynthia Voigt  f  5579

**Chlorine**
*Yon Ill Wind* - Piers Anthony  f  196

**Delaney, Tania Jane**
*Born to Run* - Mercedes Lackey  f  3271

**Eleeri**
*The Key of the Keplian* - Andre Norton  f  4156

**Falfurrias, Ofelia Damareux**
*Remnant Population* - Elizabeth Moon  s  3972

**Farthing, Sophie**
*Harm's Way* - Colin Greenland  s  2416

**Fels, Jimmy**
*Penance* - Rick R. Reed  h  4501

**Gavrilli, David**
*Interface Masque* - Shariann Lewitt  s  3453

**Goldberg, Honeylou Emmyjane "Marshmallow"**
*The Red Tape War* - Jack L. Chalker  s  959

**Ingoldesdaughter, Berika**
*The Wooden Sword* - Lynn Abbey  f  18

**Larissa**
*Larissa* - Emily Devenport  s  1503

**Lila Anne**
*Summerland* - L. Dean James  f  2865

**Magnolia**
*The Nature of Smoke* - Anne Harris  s  2559

**Ogress, Okra**
*The Color of Her Panties* - Piers Anthony  f  167

**Popsy**
*Shadow Walkers* - Nina Romberg  h  4663

**Rice, David "Davy"**
*Jumper* - Steven Gould  s  2290

**Robyn**
*Stoneskin's Revenge* - Tom Deitz  f  1476

**Ryn "Robin"**
*The War of the Sky Lords* - John Brosnan  s  721

**Shade**
*Shade* - Emily Devenport  s  1504

**Smith, Kayla**
*Bedlam Boyz* - Ellen Guon  f  2467

**Starbuck, Ron**
*Elsewhere* - Will Shetterly  f  4993

**Stein, Susan "Starbright"**
*Summer of Love* - Lisa Mason  s  3664

**Tenere, Jared**
*Voices of Hope* - David Feintuch  s  1903

**Welch, Melissa "Kay Franklin"**
*Hobkin* - Peni R. Griffin  f  2438

**Welch, Sara "Liza Franklin"**
*Hobkin* - Peni R. Griffin  f  2438

**Willa**
*The Lone Sentinel* - Jo Dereske  s  1493

**Williams, Sadie**
*Shadow Walkers* - Nina Romberg  h  4663

**Yvette of Grintz**
*The Pixilated Peeress* - L. Sprague de
   Camp  f  1416

## SAILOR

**Ap Sennon, Olmy**
*Legacy* - Greg Bear  s  420

**Barbarossa, Galilee**
*Galilee* - Clive Barker  h  340

**Boysie**
*Flickering Shadows* - Kwadwo Agymah
   Kamau  f  3006

**Brooks, Connor**
*Ill Wind* - Kevin J. Anderson  s  108

**Chinnery, Thomas**
*Blood of the Goddess* - Kara Dalkey  f  1318

**Cook, Jeremy**
*Infernal Affairs* - Jane Heller  h  2652

**Enos, George**
*The Great War: American Front* - Harry
   Turtledove  s  5501

**Gavin, Felix**
*The Little Country* - Charles de Lint  f  1432

**Greene, Harry**
*First Blast of the Trumpet Against the Monstrous
   Regiment of Women* - Eric McCormack  h  3779

**Hanno**
*The Boat of a Million Years* - Poul Anderson  s  125

**Hart, Sally**
*Hunger* - William Dantz  h  1346

**Hart, Thomas J.**
*Hunger* - William Dantz  h  1346

**Jyp**
*Chase the Morning* - Michael Scott Rohan  f  4658

**"Lal" Lalkhamsin-Khamsolal**
*The Innkeeper's Song* - Peter S. Beagle  f  409

**Mad Mall**
*Chase the Morning* - Michael Scott Rohan  f  4658

**Marsh, Obediah**
*The Shadow over Innsmouth* - H.P.
   Lovecraft  h  3533

**McCabe, Darian**
*World Without End* - Molly Cochran  f  1093

**Palmer, Tall Man**
*White Shark* - Peter Benchley  h  441

**Parkinson, Rupert**
*The Ghost From the Grand Banks* - Arthur C.
   Clarke  s  1056

**Rope**
*Clouds End* - Sean Stewart  f  5272

**Rork, Paddy**
*Signs of Life* - Cherry Wilder  s  5804

**Rys**
*Dancing Jack* - Laurie J. Marks  f  3624

**Sallas, Ike "the Bakatcha Bandit"**
*Sailor Song* - Ken Kesey  s  3082

**Talbot**
*When Demons Walk* - Patricia Briggs  f  683

**Tomcat**
*River Rats* - Caroline Stevermer  s  5267

**Ulfilo**
*Conan and the Treasure of Python* - John Maddox
   Roberts  f  4616

**Wulfrede**
*Conan and the Treasure of Python* - John Maddox Roberts  *f*  4616

## SALESMAN

**Fong, Len**
*An Enemy Reborn* - Michael A. Stackpole  *f*  5197

**Hoover, Rod**
*Lethal Delivery* - J.G. Maxon  *h*  3695

**Papago Joe**
*Burial* - Graham Masterton  *h*  3671

**Salmoneus**
*The First Casualty* - David L. Seidman  *f*  4912

**Stebbins, Walt**
*All the Bells on Earth* - James P. Blaylock  *f*  518

**Tyler, Zane**
*Netherworld* - Richard Lee Byers  *h*  798

## SALOON HOSTESS

**Drew, Laura**
*The Unseen* - Joseph A. Citro  *h*  1039

**Rivaudais, Antoinette**
*Madeleine's Ghost* - Robert Girardi  *h*  2240

## SALOON KEEPER/OWNER

**Guinan**
*The Devil's Heart* - Carmen Carter  *s*  922
*Vendetta* - Peter David  *s*  1389

**Jacobson, Auston**
*Vampire Diary: The Embrace* - Robert Weinberg  *h*  5705

**Jones, Kellogg "Doc"**
*Laying the Music to Rest* - Dean Wesley Smith  *h*  5114

**Koto**
*The Famished Road* - Ben Okri  *f*  4207
*Songs of Enchantment* - Ben Okri  *f*  4208

**MacAuliffe, Judy**
*The Keeper* - Robert D. Lee  *h*  3402

**Marcus**
*Wagers of Sin* - Robert Asprin  *s*  264

**Mendoza, Carlos "Iceman"**
*Oracle* - Mike Resnick  *s*  4551
*Prophet* - Mike Resnick  *s*  4553
*Soothsayer* - Mike Resnick  *s*  4557

**Mirlu, Bonnie Jean "B.J."**
*Necroscope: The Lost Years* - Brian Lumley  *h*  3560
*Resurgence* - Brian Lumley  *h*  3564

**Newton, Roger**
*The Unseen* - Joseph A. Citro  *h*  1039

**Quark**
*Fallen Heroes* - Dafydd ab Hugh  *s*  8

**Stonebender, Jake**
*The Callahan Touch* - Spider Robinson  *f*  4637
*Callahan's Legacy* - Spider Robinson  *s*  4639

**Turner, Augusta "Gussie"**
*Phantom Banjo* - Elizabeth Ann Scarborough  *f*  4868
*Picking the Ballad's Bones* - Elizabeth Ann Scarborough  *f*  4869

**Wilder, Travis**
*Beyond the Pale* - Mark Anthony  *f*  153

## SCAVENGER

**Keebler, Micah "the Scavenger"**
*Trust Territory* - Janet Morris  *s*  4019

**Little, Loy**
*Men Like Rats* - Rob Chilson  *s*  1015

**Richer the Quick**
*Men Like Rats* - Rob Chilson  *s*  1015

## SCHOLAR

**Addams, Helen "Kyria"**
*Duel of Dragons* - Gael Baudino  *f*  391

**Afsan**
*Fossil Hunter* - Robert J. Sawyer  *s*  4855

**Ariane**
*Moonwise* - Greer Ilene Gilman  *f*  2238

**Arouetto**
*The Secular Wizard* - Christopher Stasheff  *f*  5222

**Brice, Marcer Joseph**
*Imposter* - Valerie J. Freireich  *s*  2050

**Cadderly**
*Canticle* - R.A. Salvatore  *f*  4793
*In Sylvan Shadows* - R.A. Salvatore  *f*  4800

**Cameron, Daren**
*Warstrider: Netlink* - William H. Keith Jr.  *s*  3038

**Carville, Rebecca**
*Lord of the Dead* - Tom Holland  *h*  2741

**Catcher, Selene**
*Renaissance Moon* - Linda Nevins  *f*  4093

**Dagref**
*Fox and Empire* - Harry Turtledove  *f*  5500

**Darcourt, Simon**
*The Cornish Trilogy* - Robertson Davies  *f*  1397

**den Karynth, Calandryll**
*Forbidden Magic* - Angus Wells  *f*  5736

**Dikobe, Pauline**
*Foragers* - Charles Oberndorf  *s*  4187

**Endang**
*Flowerdust* - Gwyneth Jones  *s*  2952

**Fall-Levchenko, Anna Leah**
*Branch Point* - Mona Clee  *s*  1074

**Faust, Johannes "Jack"**
*Jack Faust* - Michael Swanwick  *s*  5372

**Flynn, Evon**
*Nightsword* - Margaret Weis  *f*  5722

**Foth**
*The Tides of God* - Ted Reynolds  *s*  4567

**Geddarms, Volothamp "Volo"**
*The Mage in the Iron Mask* - Brian Thomsen  *f*  5458

**Haramis**
*Blood Trillium* - Julian May  *f*  3696

**Hawken, Solomon**
*Arcady* - Michael Williams  *f*  5818

**Hawkins, Rosalind "Rose"**
*The Fire Rose* - Mercedes Lackey  *f*  3280

**Herric**
*Wolf's Cub* - Mackay Wood  *f*  5964

**Hulhe**
*When the Gods Are Silent* - Jane M. Lindskold  *f*  3477

**Jackson, Daniel**
*StarGate* - Dean Devlin  *s*  1509

**Jenk, Gottfried**
*Goblin Moon* - Teresa Edgerton  *f*  1743

**Karageorge, Vanessa**
*Carve the Sky* - Alexander Jablokov  *s*  2836

**Karriaagzh**
*Human to Human* - Rebecca Ore  *s*  4219

**Lennuick, Peyto**
*Timespell* - Robert N. Charrette  *f*  978

**Locklear, Carroll**
*Cathouse* - Dean Ing  *s*  2828

**Medwind Song**
*Bones of the Past* - Holly Lisle  *f*  3478

**Milana, Chaka**
*Eternity Road* - Jack McDevitt  *s*  3788

**Mundy, Adele**
*With the Lightnings* - David Drake  *s*  1652

**Nolar**
*Flight of Vengeance* - Andre Norton  *f*  4152

**Patterson, Gil**
*Mother of Winter* - Barbara Hambly  *f*  2506

**Perholt, Gillian**
*The Djinn in the Nightingale's Eye* - A.S. Byatt  *f*  794

**Psellus, Micheal**
*Shards of Empire* - Susan Shwartz  *f*  5017

**Rhenford, Liam**
*Beggar's Banquet* - Daniel Hood  *f*  2756
*Fanuilh* - Daniel Hood  *f*  2757
*Scales of Justice* - Daniel Hood  *f*  2758
*Wizard's Heir* - Daniel Hood  *f*  2759

**Sanda**
*Initiation* - Marian Hughes  *s*  2806

**Saryon**
*Legacy of the Darksword* - Margaret Weis  *f*  5719

**Sheridan, Denise**
*Son of Darkness* - Josepha Sherman  *f*  4990

**Soerensen, Terese "Tess"**
*Jaran* - Kate Elliott  *s*  1772

**Solinari, Kelly**
*Crisis on Doona* - Anne McCaffrey  *s*  3723

**Song, Medwind**
*Mind of the Magic* - Holly Lisle  *f*  3486

**Southwell, Roger**
*The Printer's Devil* - Chico Kidd  *f*  3099

**Stone, Linneth**
*Mysterium* - Robert Charles Wilson  *s*  5911

**Theodora of Pyrene**
*Two-Bit Heroes* - Doris Egan  *s*  1757

**Theotohy, Maria Magdalena**
*The Cornish Trilogy* - Robertson Davies  *f*  1397

**Trevayne, Pagadon Alphen**
*The Fortress of Eternity* - Andrew Whitmore  *f*  5790

**Universal Historian**
*The Dechronization of Sam Magruder* - George Gaylord Simpson  *s*  5067

**Wolling, Jen**
*Earth* - David Brin  *s*  685

**Yalso**
*Dragon Tome* - Richard A. Knaak  *f*  3169

**Zigramson, Thorolf**
*The Pixilated Peeress* - L. Sprague de Camp  *f*  1416

**Zurvan**
*Servant of the Bones* - Anne Rice  *h*  4575

## SCIENTIST

**Adams, Rafe**
*Heritage of Flight* - Susan Shwartz   s   5016

**Adcock, Patrice "Pat"**
*The Other End of Time* - Frederik Pohl   s   4351
*The Siege of Eternity* - Frederik Pohl   s   4353

**Aias**
*Celestial Matters* - Richard Garfinkle   s   2140

**Al Qaseem, Zero**
*Signal to Noise* - Eric S. Nylund   s   4179

**Albee, David**
*Lords of Creation* - Tim Sullivan   s   5351

**Anastasi, Janet**
*Maverick* - Bruce Bethke   s   484

**Animiki-Waewidum, Gahzee**
*Svaha* - Charles de Lint   s   1437

**Ari**
*Cyteen* - C.J. Cherryh   s   984

**Armstrong, Augustus "Gus"**
*Martian Rainbow* - Robert L. Forward   s   1987

**Ash, Leon**
*The Invisible Company* - Scott Russell
   Sanders   s   4813

**Asher, Lydia**
*Traveling with the Dead* - Barbara Hambly   h   2511

**Augustus, Caleb**
*Jovah's Angel* - Sharon Shinn   s   5001

**Avichenko, Emily "Avi"**
*Only Child* - H.M. Hoover   s   2764

**Banner, Robert Bruce "Incredible Hulk"**
*What Savage Beast* - Peter David   s   1390

**Barbarossa, Edwin Amadeus**
*How Like a God* - Brenda W. Clough   f   1089

**Barton, Chris**
*7 Steps to Midnight* - Richard Matheson   h   3682

**Beaufort, Victor**
*The Jigsaw Woman* - Kim Antieau   f   199

**Beckett, Sam**
*Angels Unaware* - L. Elizabeth Storm   s   5315
*Knights of the Morningstar* - Melanie Rawn   s   4487

**Beenay 25**
*Nightfall* - Isaac Asimov   s   248

**Blanca**
*Diaspora* - Greg Egan   s   1759

**Bodeland, Joe**
*Dracula Unbound* - Brian W. Aldiss   h   55

**Bogert, Norman**
*I, Robot: The Illustrated Screenplay* - Harlan
   Ellison   s   1785

**Boles, Barrington**
*Parallelities* - Alan Dean Foster   s   2012

**Bomarigala**
*GodHeads* - Emily Devenport   s   1501

**Boone, Jack**
*Red Mars* - Kim Stanley Robinson   s   4635

**Boyle, Simon**
*The Illegal Rebirth of Billy the Kid* - Rebecca
   Ore   s   4220

**Bracken, Gary**
*Virus Clans* - Michael Kanaly   s   3008

**Brady-Phillips, Graysha**
*Shivering World* - Kathy Tyers   s   5526

**Brand, Matthew Tyler**
*The Hot-Wired Dodo* - Jack L. Chalker   s   956

**Brenner, Hugh**
*Paths to Otherwhere* - James P. Hogan   s   2728

**Brewster, Bobby Joe**
*Manhattan Transfer* - John E. Stith   s   5303

**Brewster, Marvin "Doc"**
*The Ambivalent Magician* - Simon Hawke   f   2616
*The Inadequate Adept* - Simon Hawke   f   2617
*The Reluctant Sorcerer* - Simon Hawke   f   2622

**Bridger, Nathan Hale**
*seaQuest DSV: Fire Below* - Matthew J.
   Costello   s   1201
*seaQuest DSV: The Novel* - Diane Duane   s   1666

**Brink, Ludger**
*The Dig* - Alan Dean Foster   s   2002

**Brown, Nelly**
*The Summer I Shrank My Grandmother* - Elvira
   Woodruff   f   5968

**Brumado, Joanna**
*Mars* - Ben Bova   s   586

**Bruno, Richard**
*Journals of the Plague Years* - Norman
   Spinrad   s   5172

**Brusen, Elaine**
*Merlin's Bones* - Fred Saberhagen   f   4771

**Burnham, Harold**
*Carnivores* - Penelope Banka Kreps   h   3232

**Burton, Paige**
*Between the Devil and the Deep* - J.M.
   Morgan   h   3998

**Butterworth, Alicia**
*Cosm* - Gregory Benford   s   444

**Byrne, Jack**
*The Eleventh Plague: A Novel of Medical Terror* -
   John S. Marr   h   3632

**Byron, Ada**
*The Difference Engine* - William Gibson   s   2217

**Cameron, Daren**
*Warstrider: Netlink* - William H. Keith Jr.   s   3038

**Cannon, April**
*Ancient Shores* - Jack McDevitt   s   3786

**Capthorne, Mya**
*Hidden Echoes* - Mike Jefferies   f   2885

**Carne, Stephanie**
*The Mirror Maze* - James P. Hogan   s   2726

**Carpenter, Harold**
*Icebound* - Dean R. Koontz   h   3209

**Carr, Sultana**
*Flare* - Roger Zelazny   s   6065

**Carson, Aloysius Byron**
*Uncharted Territory* - Connie Willis   s   5875

**Carson, Guy**
*Mount Dragon* - Douglas Preston   h   4413

**Chalmers, Frank**
*Red Mars* - Kim Stanley Robinson   s   4635

**Chao, Larry O'Shawnessy**
*The Ring of Charon* - Roger MacBride Allen   s   80
*The Shattered Sphere* - Roger MacBride Allen   s   81

**Chapman, Julie**
*Mr. Sandman* - Lyle Howard   h   2779

**Chase, Simon**
*White Shark* - Peter Benchley   h   441

**Chior**
*OtherWise* - Margaret Wander Bonanno   s   567

**Chornyak, Delina Meloran**
*Earthsong* - Suzette Haden Elgin   s   1769

**Chowdhury, Ralph**
*Sparrowhawk* - Thomas A. Easton   s   1725

**Cidiera "Cid"**
*The Nature of Smoke* - Anne Harris   s   2559

**Class, Julian**
*Forever Peace* - Joe Haldeman   s   2488

**Claudia**
*Agviq* - Michael Armstrong   s   208

**Clayborn, Robert**
*Phylum Monsters* - Hayford Peirce   s   4276

**Clayborne, Ann**
*Blue Mars* - Kim Stanley Robinson   s   4629

**Cocciolone, Carol Jeanne**
*Lovelock* - Orson Scott Card   s   892

**Cochrane, Miles "David Gilman"**
*Alpha Centauri* - William Barton   s   378

**Cochrane, Zefrem**
*Federation* - Judith Reeves-Stevens   s   4511

**Cohen, Julius**
*Mother of Demons* - Eric Flint   s   1956

**Colette, Sianna**
*The Shattered Sphere* - Roger MacBride Allen   s   81

**Collins, Jack**
*A Calculated Magic* - Robert Weinberg   f   5694

**Coombs, Alice**
*As She Climbed Across the Table* - Jonathan
   Lethem   s   3439

**Cooper, Marjorie**
*Father to the Man* - John Gribbin   s   2434

**Cope, Edward Drinker**
*Bone Wars* - Brett Davis   s   1398

**Copplestone, Edward**
*The Hunger and Ecstasy of Vampires* - Brian
   Stableford   h   5192

**Cordery, Noell**
*The Empire of Fear* - Brian Stableford   h   5191

**Cortland, Roger**
*Lightpaths* - Howard V. Hendrix   s   2660
*Standing Wave* - Howard V. Hendrix   s   2661

**Cory, Patrick**
*Donovan's Brain/Hauser's Memory* - Curt
   Siodmak   h   5072
*Gabriel's Body* - Curt Siodmak   h   5073

**Coulton, Roger**
*Einstein's Bridge* - John Cramer   s   1244

**Craig, Samantha**
*Reaper* - Ben Mizrich   h   3923

**Crane, George "Trip" III**
*The First Immortal* - James L. Halperin   s   2498

**Crane, Lewis**
*Richter 10* - Arthur C. Clarke   s   1060

**Cross, Anthony**
*Dark Matter* - Garfield Reeves-Stevens   h   4509

**Dad**
*Eva* - Peter Dickinson   s   1525

**Dana, Gregory**
*Voyager* - Stephen Baxter   s   406

**Danziger, E.E.**
*From Time to Time* - Jack Finney   s   1941

**Darrow, Troy**
*Carnivore* - Leigh Clark   h   1049

**de Montgarde, Adela**
*To Fear the Light* - Ben Bova   s   595
*To Save the Sun* - Ben Bova   s   596

**de Montpalau, Antoni**
*Natural History* - Juan Perucho   h   4303

**De Ramaira, David**
*Of the Fall* - Paul J. McAuley   s   3713

**Deepneau, Ed**
*Insomnia* - Stephen King   h   3135

**Delaney, Brian**
*The Turing Option* - Harry Harrison  s  2579

**DelGiudice, Jeff**
*Echoes of the Fourth Magic* - R.A.
  Salvatore  f  4799

**Delp, Albert**
*Lights Out in the Reptile House* - Jim
  Shepard  f  4976

**Delvano, Gwen**
*Dying of the Light* - George R.R. Martin  s  3644

**Demopoulos, Demetrios "Dr. Dimension"**
*Dr. Dimension* - John DeChancie  s  1456

**Denison, Arthur**
*Dinotopia* - James Gurney  f  2468
*The World Beneath* - James Gurney  f  2469

**Denness, Leonov Opener**
*Mirabile* - Janet Kagan  s  3001

**Derec**
*Changeling* - Stephen Leigh  s  3425
*Renegade* - Cordell Scotten  s  4903

**Devlin**
*The Coachman Rat* - David Henry Wilson  f  5879

**Dinsmuir, Harold "Dirty"**
*Insatiable* - David Dvorkin  h  1707

**Dominque, Nyota**
*Saturn's Child* - Nichelle Nichols  s  4101

**Dorman, Jeremy**
*Antibodies* - Kevin J. Anderson  h  99

**D'oud**
*The False Mirror* - Alan Dean Foster  s  2004

**Dowornobb**
*Genellan: Planetfall* - Scott G. Gier  s  2223

**Drake, Michael**
*A Hunger in the Soul* - Mike Resnick  s  4545

**Drake, Michaeline**
*Ancient Heavens* - Robert E. Vardeman  s  5561

**Drake, Richard**
*Ancient Heavens* - Robert E. Vardeman  s  5561

**Dravie, Lena**
*Stranger Suns* - George Zebrowski  s  6060

**Dumenco, Georg**
*Lethal Exposure* - Kevin J. Anderson  s  110

**Durancy, Abraham**
*Queen City Jazz* - Kathleen Ann Goonan  s  2275

**Easterman, Nesta Christiana**
*Vanishing Point* - Michaela Roessner  s  4652

**Einhorn, Carl**
*Rage of Spirits* - Noel Hynd  h  2824

**Ellen**
*The Red Queen* - Dirk Draulans  s  1653

**Emory, Ariane**
*Cyteen* - C.J. Cherryh  s  984

**Fairburn, Pamela**
*The Ambivalent Magician* - Simon Hawke  f  2616

**f'ath, Riitha**
*The Alien Dark* - Diana G. Gallagher  s  2108

**Feldman, Malachi**
*The Asylum* - John E. Ames  h  93

**Fermi, Enrico**
*Worldwar: In the Balance* - Harry
  Turtledove  s  5515

**Fiar, Jacobious**
*Jonas McFee, A.T.P.* - Sarah Sargent  s  4827

**Finriddy, Sarah "Fin"**
*Uncharted Territory* - Connie Willis  s  5875

**Fitch, Xavier**
*Species* - Yvonne Navarro  s  4075

**Fitzpatrick, Al-Hajji Brian**
*The Missing Matter* - Thomas R.
  McDonough  s  3805

**Fletcher, Richard Wesley**
*The Great and Secret Show* - Clive Barker  h  341

**Flood, Reuben**
*Habu* - James B. Johnson  s  2920

**Florey, Rick**
*Of the Fall* - Paul J. McAuley  s  3713

**Forester, Clay**
*The Humanoids* - Jack Williamson  s  5865

**Forsyte, Adrian**
*Shifter* - Judith Reeves-Stevens  f  4515

**Foster, Sandra "Sandy"**
*Bellwether* - Connie Willis  s  5867

**Frank, Victor**
*Mutation* - Robin Cook  s  1165

**Frankenstein, Gunthar Thunnar**
*I Am Frankenstein* - C. Dean Andersson  h  140

**Frankenstein, Victor**
*The Darker Passions: Frankenstein* - Amarantha
  Knight  h  3180
*The Memoirs of Elizabeth Frankenstein* - Theodore
  Roszak  h  4684
*The Secret Laboratory Journals of Dr. Victor
  Frankenstein* - Jeremy Kay  h  3019

**Franklin, Charles**
*Moving Mars* - Greg Bear  s  421

**Freede, Hannibal**
*Flare* - Roger Zelazny  s  6065

**Freeman, Alan**
*Extinct* - Charles Wilson  h  5877

**Freetz, Jhoe**
*Flies From the Amber* - Wil McCarthy  s  3763

**Friedkin**
*The Quick* - Burt Cole  s  1113

**Gadfium, Hortis**
*Feersum Endjinn* - Iain M. Banks  s  325

**G'Dath**
*A Flag Full of Stars* - Brad Ferguson  s  1922

**Gill, Spencer**
*The House of Doors* - Brian Lumley  h  3554
*Maze of Worlds* - Brian Lumley  h  3559

**Gillespie, William**
*Something's Alive on the Titanic* - Robert
  Serling  h  4915

**Gilman, Emily**
*Sparrowhawk* - Thomas A. Easton  s  1725

**Goble, Samuel**
*A Thunder on Neptune* - Gordon Eklund  s  1768

**Gordon, Julie**
*Mirage* - F. Paul Wilson  h  5892

**Gordon, Nathan**
*Mirage* - F. Paul Wilson  h  5892

**Gottbaum, Leo**
*The Silicon Man* - Charles Platt  s  4343

**Grant, Alan**
*Jurassic Park* - Michael Crichton  s  1255

**Gray, Simon**
*Archangel* - Michael Conner  s  1133

**Gray Wolf, Josiah**
*Beyond Eden* - J.M. Morgan  s  3999
*Desert Eden* - J.M. Morgan  s  4000

**Graydon, Nicholas**
*The Face in the Abyss* - A. Merritt  f  3878

**Green, Sandra**
*Saturn Rukh* - Robert L. Forward  s  1991

**Gregorian**
*Stations of the Tide* - Michael Swanwick  s  5373

**Gregory, Stephen Thomas**
*Starfarers* - Vonda N. McIntyre  s  3824

**Griffin, George**
*Einstein's Bridge* - John Cramer  s  1244

**Hake**
*Vanishing Point* - Michaela Roessner  s  4652

**Haley, Adam**
*Howl* - Christine Tanasiuk  h  5388

**Hamid-Jones, Abdul**
*Crescent in the Sky* - Donald Moffitt  s  3946
*A Gathering of Stars* - Donald Moffitt  s  3947

**Hanley, Roderick**
*Reborn* - F. Paul Wilson  h  5895

**Harding, Amelia "Blaze"**
*Forever Peace* - Joe Haldeman  s  2488

**Harding, Sarah**
*The Lost World* - Michael Crichton  s  1256

**Harrigan, Kevin G.**
*The Pleistocene Redemption* - Dan
  Gallagher  s  2107

**Harris, Samantha**
*Howl* - Christine Tanasiuk  h  5388

**Harrison, Bailey**
*The Vampire Virus* - Michael Romkey  h  4668

**Harrison, David**
*Twistor* - John Cramer  s  1245

**Hart**
*In the Blood* - Lauren Wright Douglas  s  1590

**Hastings, Amber**
*Thunder Strike!* - Michael McCollum  s  3772

**Hayes**
*Time and Light* - William Bornefeld  s  574

**Heber, Vanessa**
*Bug Park* - James P. Hogan  s  2723

**Helier, Conrad**
*Inherit the Earth* - Brian Stableford  s  5193

**Helmond, Orville**
*The Orpheus Process* - Daniel H. Gower  h  2293

**Henderson, Carl**
*The Homing* - John Saul  h  4842

**Henning, Johanna**
*Memento Mori* - Shariann Lewitt  s  3454

**Hillerman, Walter "Walt"**
*Lady El* - Jim Starlin  s  5213

**Hobson, Peter**
*The Terminal Experiment* - Robert J.
  Sawyer  s  4860

**Hoffman, Judith**
*Eon* - Greg Bear  s  417

**Holdsworth, Adrian**
*The Voice of Cepheus* - Ken Appleby  s  202

**Holland, R. Paul**
*Infinity's Child* - Harry Stein  h  5250

**Hooker, Nicodemus**
*Kent Montana and the Really Ugly Thing From Mars* -
  Lionel Fenn  s  1918

**Hoskins, Gerald**
*The Ugly Little Boy* - Isaac Asimov  s  250

**Hrecker, Marcus Aurelius**
*Seeds of Destiny* - Thomas A. Easton  s  1724

**Hudder, Cyrus**
*Core* - Paul Preuss  s  4416

**Hudder, Leiden "Leidy"**
*Core* - Paul Preuss  s  4416

**Hugo**
*Outer Space and All That Junk* - Mel
  Gilden  s  2227

**Hunt, Gregory**
*Tech-Heaven* - Linda Nagata  s  4066

**Hunt, Victor**
*Entoverse* - James P. Hogan  s  2724

**Hutchings, Ian McFarland**
*Fortress on the Sun* - Paul Cook  s  1157

**Hutton, Andrew**
*Earthling* - Tony Daniel  s  1336

**ih'iie-u Ulak!ha', Hwii**
*Dark Mirror* - Diane Duane  s  1658

**Ishikawa, Keiko**
*Imbalance* - V.E. Mitchell  s  3919

**Izmailova, Ekatarina**
*Griffin's Egg* - Michael Swanwick  s  5370

**Jackson, Daniel**
*Reconnaissance* - Bill McCay  s  3769

**Jacoby**
*Virus Clans* - Michael Kanaly  s  3008

**James, Henderson**
*Over the River & through the Woods* - Clifford D.
  Simak  s  5047

**Johnson, Mark "Hobbes"**
*Mosaic* - Jeri Taylor  s  5403

**Jordan, Miles**
*End of an Era* - Robert J. Sawyer  s  4853

**Joubert, Mireille**
*Semper Mars* - Ian Douglas  s  1585

**Joyce, Nancy**
*Vespers* - Jeff Rovin  h  4688

**Kalakaua, Cen**
*The Bones of Time* - Kathleen Ann Goonan  s  2273

**Kamehameha, Cesar**
*Blueheart* - Alison Sinclair  s  5068

**Kameron, Theodore R.G.**
*The Eleventh Plague: A Novel of Medical Terror* -
  John S. Marr  h  3632

**Kami, Minamoto no**
*Glory's People* - Alfred Coppel  s  1183

**Kastle**
*Devil's Engine* - Mark Sumner  f  5356

**Katayev, Nadezhda**
*Pacific Edge* - Kim Stanley Robinson  s  4634

**Kee-Toroca**
*Fossil Hunter* - Robert J. Sawyer  s  4855

**Kelly, Brian**
*The Forbidden Zone* - Whitley Strieber  h  5340

**Kendoro, Judit**
*Acorna* - Anne McCaffrey  s  3717

**Kenmore, Harold**
*Of Beginnings and Endings* - Robert Adams  s  33

**Kesserich, Daniel**
*The Dealings of Daniel Kesserich* - Fritz
  Leiber  s  3417

**Kintner, Edward**
*Paths to Otherwhere* - James P. Hogan  s  2728

**Kitchener, Edward**
*A Quantum Murder* - Peter F. Hamilton  s  2527

**Knight, Rachel**
*The Serpent Slayers* - Adam Niswander  h  4113

**Kolkey, Alan**
*Walker between the Worlds* - Diane
  DesRochers  f  1499

**Kominsky, Katerina "Kate"**
*The Secret Oceans* - Betty Ballantine  s  318

**Koolhan, Sara**
*Heaven's Reach* - David Brin  s  687

**Kornfeld-Taggert, Sieglinde**
*Delta Pavonis* - Eric Kotani  s  3221

**Kramer, Paul "Papa"**
*The Silent City* - Elisabeth Vonarburg  s  5592

**Kramer, Richard**
*Deadly Dreams* - Gerald A. Schiller  h  4874

**Kreider, Tomus**
*Flies From the Amber* - Wil McCarthy  s  3763

**Kurtzweill, Alvin**
*The X-Files: Fight the Future* - Chris Carter  h  924

**Kuvasc, Paval**
*Regenesis* - Julia Ecklar  s  1729

**Labyrinth, Doc**
*The Collected Stories of Philip K. Dick, Volume One:
  The Short Happy Life of the Brown Oxford* - Philip
  K. Dick  s  1519

**Lacan, Arnauld**
*The Hollowing* - Robert Holdstock  f  2738

**Lan, Song**
*Bright Angel* - John Blair  s  512

**Lang, Darya**
*Convergence* - Charles Sheffield  s  4951
*Divergence* - Charles Sheffield  s  4954
*Summertide* - Charles Sheffield  s  4965
*Transcendence* - Charles Sheffield  s  4967

**Larrin, Marty**
*Forever Peace* - Joe Haldeman  s  2488

**Larsson, Gunvald**
*Icebound* - Dean R. Koontz  h  3209

**Lee, Richard**
*Father to the Man* - John Gribbin  s  2434

**Lehman, Roger "Senmut-Ptah"**
*Thebes of the Hundred Gates* - Robert
  Silverberg  s  5043

**Lentrall, Davlo**
*Utopia* - Roger MacBride Allen  s  83

**Levine, Charles**
*Mount Dragon* - Douglas Preston  h  4413

**Levine, Richard**
*The Lost World* - Michael Crichton  s  1256

**Levitt, Irv**
*A World of Difference* - Harry Turtledove  s  5514

**Li, Stefan**
*Ark Liberty* - Will Bradley  s  656

**Libermann, E.F.**
*The Discovery of Dragons* - Graeme Base  f  385

**Lightnin' Lil**
*Mississippi Blues* - Kathleen Ann Goonan  s  2274

**Little Girl**
*The Mer-Child: A Legend for Children and Other
  Adults* - Robin Morgan  f  4008

**Locklear, Carroll**
*Cathouse* - Dean Ing  s  2828

**Lockwood, Spencer**
*Ill Wind* - Kevin J. Anderson  s  108

**Lovell, Willa**
*Judgment Day* - G. Harry Stine  s  5281

**Lustig, Alex**
*Earth* - David Brin  s  685

**Lydyard, David**
*The Angel of Pain* - Brian Stableford  h  5189
*The Carnival of Destruction* - Brian
  Stableford  h  5190

**Lynch, Raymond**
*Infinity's Child* - Harry Stein  h  5250

**Maggie**
*Cain* - James Byron Huggins  h  2802
*The Cat* - R.L. Stine  h  5285

**Magruder, Sam**
*The Dechronization of Sam Magruder* - George
  Gaylord Simpson  s  5067

**Malcolm, Ian**
*The Lost World* - Michael Crichton  s  1256

**Mallory, Edward**
*The Difference Engine* - William Gibson  s  2217

**Mallory, Quinn**
*Sliders: The Novel* - Brad Linaweaver  s  3467

**Manan, Mattine "Mattie"**
*Mutagenesis* - Helen Collins  s  1116

**Manderley, Alexander**
*Thunder Road* - Chris Curry  h  1296

**Margison, Tom**
*Kids* - Trevor Hoyle  h  2787

**Markos**
*The Eternal Enemy* - Michael Berlyn  s  469

**Marlowe, Jim**
*White Horse, Dark Dragon* - Robert C.
  Fleet  f  1947

**Marouk, Kemal**
*The Joy Machine* - James Gunn  s  2458

**Marquard, Pat**
*A World of Difference* - Harry Turtledove  s  5514

**Marsh, Othniel Charles**
*Bone Wars* - Brett Davis  s  1398

**Martin, Hector**
*Accidental Creatures* - Anne Harris  s  2558

**Maryk, Peter**
*The Blood Artists* - Chuck Hogan  h  2720

**Masmajean, Anna "Mama" Jason**
*Mirabile* - Janet Kagan  s  3001

**Massey, Caleb**
*Beamriders!* - Martin Caidin  s  824

**Maxey, Warren**
*Dangerous Nature* - T.J. Kirby  h  3152

**McAndrews, Arthur Morton**
*One Man's Universe* - Charles Sheffield  s  4961

**McClare, D.J.**
*Unwillingly to Earth* - Pauline Ashwell  s  231

**McDougal, Marta**
*Core* - Paul Preuss  s  4416

**McHenry, Mark**
*Worf's First Adventure* - Peter David  s  1391

**McKay, Debra**
*Children of the Earth* - Catherine Wells  s  5743
*The Earth Is All That Lasts* - Catherine
  Wells  s  5744

**McKenzie, Victoria**
*Metaphase* - Vonda N. McIntyre  s  3821
*Starfarers* - Vonda N. McIntyre  s  3824
*Transition* - Vonda N. McIntyre  s  3825

**Meacher, Henry**
*Moonseed* - Stephen Baxter  s  400

**Meadows, Mark "Captain Trips"**
*Black Trump* - George R.R. Martin  s  3642
*Turn of the Cards* - Victor Milan  s  3891

**Medea, Helene**
*Light Raid* - Connie Willis   s   5870

**Mendoza**
*In the Garden of Iden* - Kage Baker   s   298

**Meniskos, Jhana**
*Lightpaths* - Howard V. Hendrix   s   2660

**Meriweather, Gentian**
*Juniper, Gentian and Rosemary* - Pamela Dean   f   1445

**Merrit, Robin**
*Operation Synbat* - Bob Mayer   h   3701

**Messenger, Joe**
*Host* - Peter James   h   2872

**Minakis, Manolis**
*Secret Passages*   Paul Preuss   s   4420

**Mirskaya, Daria Nicolaeuna**
*Scorpio Descending* - Alex McDonough   s   3803

**Mishwe, Dajaj**
*ViraVax* - Bill Ransom   s   4478

**Mokoena, Mamphela**
*Starfarers* - Poul Anderson   s   133

**Monlux, Cassandra**
*Slow Freight* - F.M. Busby   s   785

**Mora, Chad**
*Predator* - William F. Wu   s   5998

**Morrison, Ryan**
*Journey to Terezor* - Frank Asch   s   221

**Mosala, Violet**
*Distress* - Greg Egan   s   1760

**Mulcahey, Gerald "Jerry"**
*Heavy Weather* - Bruce Sterling   s   5258

**Munsen, Luke**
*Fire* - Alan Rodgers   h   4647

**Myers, Jeremy**
*The Serpent Slayers* - Adam Niswander   h   4113

**Mzu, Alkad**
*Conflict* - Peter F. Hamilton   s   2522

**Nagashima, Galvanix**
*The Oxygen Barons* - Gregory Feeley   s   1897

**Narbando, Ignatio**
*Lord Kelvin's Machine* - James P. Blaylock   f   520

**Narrow Leg**
*The Ship Errant* - Jody Lynn Nye   s   4175

**Nathan, Jessica**
*Desert Eden* - J.M. Morgan   s   4000

**Neale, Charis**
*Dark Matter* - Garfield Reeves-Stevens   h   4509

**Newcombe, Dan**
*Richter 10* - Arthur C. Clarke   s   1060

**Nobilio, Francis "Frank"**
*Illegal Alien* - Robert J. Sawyer   s   4858

**Noreen**
*Time and Light* - William Bornefeld   s   574

**Nussbaumer, Lynn**
*Playing God* - Sarah Zettel   s   6080

**Nystrom, Wayne**
*Dictator* - William F. Wu   s   5996
*Predator* - William F. Wu   s   5998
*Warrior* - William F. Wu   s   6000

**O'Brian, James**
*Gabriel's Body* - Curt Siodmak   h   5073

**Obrion, Juan**
*Stranger Suns* - George Zebrowski   s   6060

**O'Donnell, Hugh**
*The Trikon Deception* - Ben Bova   s   597

**O'Hara, Liam**
*Time, Like an Ever-Rolling Stream* - Judith Moffett   s   3944

**O'Reilly, Bennett "Ben"**
*Bellwether* - Connie Willis   s   5867

**Osic, Angelo**
*On My Way to Paradise* - Dave Wolverton   s   5955

**Ozzie**
*Dreams of Gods and Men* - W.T. Quick   s   4451

**Pearse, Stephen**
*The Blood Artists* - Chuck Hogan   h   2720

**Peg**
*The Virgin and the Dinosaur* - R. Garcia y Robertson   s   2122

**Pendergast, George Irving**
*Children of the End* - Mark A. Clements   h   1084

**Perez, Anna**
*Ring of Swords* - Eleanor Arnason   s   210

**Perry, Jon**
*Cold as Ice* - Charles Sheffield   s   4950

**Poggs, Hugo**
*Portent* - James Herbert   h   2670

**Poole, Michael**
*Timelike Infinity* - Stephen Baxter   s   404

**Precieux, Pierre**
*The Dechronization of Sam Magruder* - George Gaylord Simpson   s   5067

**Prescott, George**
*Supernova* - Roger MacBride Allen   s   82

**Pruitt, Pam**
*Time, Like an Ever-Rolling Stream* - Judith Moffett   s   3944

**Pulaski, Toya**
*Converse and Conflict* - L. Neil Smith   s   5130

**Quinn, Jimmy**
*The Sparrow* - Mary Doria Russell   s   4736

**Rae, Dorcas**
*Gaia's Toys* - Rebecca Ore   s   4218

**Rant, Paul**
*I, Said the Fly* - Michael Shea   h   4944

**Rashid**
*Commitment Hour* - James Alan Gardner   s   2134

**Razin, Fyodor Alexeyevich**
*Landscape Painted with Tea* - Milorad Pavic   f   4263

**Reed, Jerry**
*Russian Spring* - Norman Spinrad   s   5174

**Rees**
*Raft* - Stephen Baxter   s   401

**Reichner, Helmut**
*Threshold* - Bill Myers   s   4060

**Relorn, Wryan**
*Timediver's Dawn* - L.E. Modesitt Jr.   s   3940

**Rey, Cory**
*Icefire* - Judith Reeves-Stevens   s   4512

**Rivers, James**
*Portent* - James Herbert   h   2670

**Robillard, Zac**
*Isaac Asimov's I-Bots* - Steve Perry   s   4297

**Rosenberg, Isaac**
*Titan* - Stephen Baxter   s   405

**Rowan**
*The Steerswoman* - Rosemary Kirstein   s   3158

**Ruskin, Willard**
*From a Changeling Star* - Jeffrey A. Carver   s   931

**Russell, Paul**
*Lake of the Sun* - Wynne Whiteford   s   5787

**Russell, Saxifrage "Sax"**
*Blue Mars* - Kim Stanley Robinson   s   4629
*Green Mars* - Kim Stanley Robinson   s   4633

**Ryan, Jayne**
*Beachhead* - Jack Williamson   s   5859

**Rydell, Tony**
*Dream Maker* - W.A. Harbinson   s   2542

**Saari, Juna "Eerin"**
*The Color of Distance* - Amy Thomson   s   5461

**Saint-Alaban, Justice**
*Winterlong* - Elizabeth Hand   s   2539

**St. Clair, Adrienne**
*Bloodshift* - Garfield Reeves-Stevens   h   4508

**St. Ives, Langdon**
*Lord Kelvin's Machine* - James P. Blaylock   f   520

**Salib, Tariq**
*The Missing Matter* - Thomas R. McDonough   s   3805

**Samules, Martha**
*Spider Legs* - Piers Anthony   s   189

**Sandford, Nancy**
*The Ragged World: A Novel of the Hefn on Earth* - Judith Moffett   s   3943

**Sanger, David**
*Murder in the Solid State* - Wil McCarthy   s   3764

**Sara**
*Brightness Reef* - David Brin   s   684

**Sarai**
*The Children Star* - Joan Slonczewski   s   5090

**Sattler, Ellie**
*Jurassic Park* - Michael Crichton   s   1255

**Sauvage, J.D.**
*Metaphase* - Vonda N. McIntyre   s   3821
*Nautilus* - Vonda N. McIntyre   s   3823
*Transition* - Vonda N. McIntyre   s   3825

**Sawyer, Kelly**
*Carnivore* - Leigh Clark   h   1049

**Schlessinger, David**
*The Secret Oceans* - Betty Ballantine   s   318

**Seaforth, Fawn**
*The Howling Stones* - Alan Dean Foster   s   2006

**Sealock, Brendan**
*Iris* - William Barton   s   381

**Seldon, Hari**
*Forward the Foundation* - Isaac Asimov   s   236
*Foundation and Chaos* - Greg Bear   s   418
*Foundation's Fear* - Gregory Benford   s   446

**Sena, Miranda**
*Rewind* - Terry England   s   1825

**Shank, Billy**
*Echoes of the Fourth Magic* - R.A. Salvatore   f   4799

**Sharma, Govinda**
*The Cold One* - Christopher Pike   h   4327

**Sheerin 501**
*Nightfall* - Isaac Asimov   s   248

**Shepard, M.**
*Evolution's Shore* - Ian McDonald   s   3792

**Sigvarthsson, Shef**
*King and Emperor* - Harry Harrison   f   2571

**Simna, Jack**
*Life Form* - Alan Dean Foster   s   2008

**Sinclair, Richard**
*Dust* - Charles Pellegrino   h   4279

**Skardon, John**
*Mixed Doubles* - Daniel Da Cruz   s   1305

**Slater, Peter**
*Secret Passages* - Paul Preuss   s   4420

**Snow, David**
*Cold at Heart* - Brian Hopkins   h   2768

**Sole, Chris**
*The Embedding* - Ian Watson   s   5634

**Soleta**
*End Game* - Peter David   s   1382

**Sonnenberg, Bryce**
*The Ganymede Club* - Charles Sheffield   s   4955

**Sorricaine, Viktor**
*The World at the End of Time* - Frederik
   Pohl   s   4357

**Speke, Vernon**
*Hunger* - William Dantz   h   1346

**Spock**
*The City on the Edge of Forever* - Harlan
   Ellison   s   1784
*Crossover* - Michael Jan Friedman   s   2063
*Crossroad* - Barbara Hambly   s   2501
*First Frontier* - Diane Carey   s   902
*First Strike* - Diane Carey   s   903
*The Joy Machine* - James Gunn   s   2458
*Prime Directive* - Judith Reeves-Stevens   s   4514
*Probe* - Margaret Wander Bonanno   s   569
*Renegade* - Gene DeWeese   s   1511
*The Return* - William Shatner   s   4933
*The Rift* - Peter David   s   1386
*Sanctuary* - John Vornholt   s   5597
*Sarek* - A.C. Crispin   s   1260
*Star Trek: The Classic Episodes 1* - James
   Blish   s   526
*Star Trek: The Classic Episodes 2* - James
   Blish   s   527
*Star Trek: The Classic Episodes 3* - James
   Blish   s   528
*Star Trek: The Lost Years* - J.M. Dillard   s   1557
*Vulcan's Glory* - D.C. Fontana   s   1967
*Windows on a Lost World* - V.E. Mitchell   s   3920

**Spring, Juliet**
*Host* - Peter James   h   2872

**Stafford, Alwyn Bryan**
*Mars Underground* - William Hartmann   s   2584

**Stark, Tony "Iron Man"**
*Iron Man: The Armor Trap* - Greg Cox   s   1227

**Stasov, Ilya Sergeiivich**
*A Deeper Sea* - Alexander Jablokov   s   2838

**Stavi, Kira**
*Remnant Population* - Elizabeth Moon   s   3972

**Stein, Rachel**
*Search and Destroy* - Keith William
   Andrews   s   141

**Stevenson, David**
*The Innsmouth Heritage* - Brian Stableford   h   5194

**Stilman, Shyh**
*Lightwing* - Tara K. Harper   s   2551

**Straachen, Dianus**
*Faces under Water* - Tanith Lee   h   3409

**Summers, Erik**
*Wilderness* - Dennis Danvers   h   1349

**Susan**
*Laying the Music to Rest* - Dean Wesley
   Smith   h   5114

**Tagak**
*Shaping the Dawn* - Sheila Finch   s   1934

**Takiuji, Sukihara**
*Limbo System* - Rick Cook   s   1158

**Talbott, Marshe "Queen"**
*Aggressor Six* - Wil McCarthy   s   3760

**Talmadge, Jessica**
*Supernova* - Roger MacBride Allen   s   82

**Tanaka, Joey**
*Mind Kill* - Richard La Plante   h   3267

**Tanaka, Terry**
*Meg* - Steve Alten   h   88

**Tangaloa, George**
*The Hand of Zei* - L. Sprague de Camp   s   1414

**Taramasco, Sam**
*Warsprite* - Jefferson P. Swycaffer   s   5375

**Tarosh, Valentine**
*Carnivore* - Leigh Clark   h   1049

**Taylor, Jonas**
*Meg* - Steve Alten   h   88

**Tellentyre, Edward**
*The Werewolves of London* - Brian
   Stableford   h   5196

**Teller, Edward**
*Operation Damocles* - Oscar L. Fellows   s   1915

**Tenzer, Paul**
*Kalimantan* - Lucius Shepard   h   4979

**Thackeray, Brandon**
*End of an Era* - Robert J. Sawyer   s   4853

**Thomas, Signy**
*Whiteout* - Sage Walker   s   5619

**Thyme, Jordan "Antiquity"**
*Zeta Base* - Judith Alguire   s   74

**T'Larien, Dirk**
*Dying of the Light* - George R.R. Martin   s   3644

**Toitovna, Maya**
*Green Mars* - Kim Stanley Robinson   s   4633
*Red Mars* - Kim Stanley Robinson   s   4635

**Tomeas**
*Beyond the Door* - Gary L. Blackwood   s   510

**Tomochelor, Pulickel**
*The Howling Stones* - Alan Dean Foster   s   2006

**Tovin, Rahel**
*Regenesis* - Julia Ecklar   s   1729

**Trace, Erika**
*Assemblers of Infinity* - Kevin J. Anderson   s   100

**Tripolk, Anna**
*Lifeline* - Kevin J. Anderson   s   111

**Trreggerthann, Umber**
*The Gift of the Gorboduc Vandal* - Paul O.
   Williams   s   5821

**Tsia**
*Cat Scratch Fever* - Tara K. Harper   s   2550

**Tucker, Rose**
*Sole Survivor* - Dean R. Koontz   h   3215

**Tyeewapi, Anevai**
*Ground-Ties* - Jane S. Fancher   s   1861
*Uplink* - Jane S. Fancher   s   1865

**Tyler, Maurice**
*Black Sun* - Robert Leininger   s   3429

**Vadim, Lux**
*Desert Fire* - David Alexander   s   65

**Vannice, Owen**
*Corrupting Dr. Nice* - John Kessel   s   3083

**Venabili, Dors**
*Forward the Foundation* - Isaac Asimov   s   236

**Vernon, Vivian**
*Dr. Dimension* - John DeChancie   s   1456

**Virili, Rima**
*The Black Sun* - Jack Williamson   s   5860

**Wakefield, Richard**
*The Garden of Rama* - Arthur C. Clarke   s   1055

**Walden, Jerome**
*The Infinity Plague* - Robert E. Vardeman   s   5564

**Walker, Mark**
*Playmates* - Abigail McDaniels   h   3784

**Ward, David**
*Operation Synbat* - Bob Mayer   h   3701

**Ward, Kim**
*The Stone Within* - David Wingrove   s   5920
*White Moon, Red Dragon* - David
   Wingrove   s   5921
*The White Mountain* - David Wingrove   s   5922

**Waterman, James "Jamie" Fox**
*Mars* - Ben Bova   s   586

**Wayville, Chris**
*Flying to Valhalla* - Charles Pellegrino   s   4280

**Wayville, Clarice**
*Flying to Valhalla* - Charles Pellegrino   s   4280

**Webster, Tania**
*Sister, Sister* - Andrew Neiderman   h   4091

**Weintraub, Sarah**
*Threshold* - Bill Myers   s   4060

**Westlake, Peyton**
*Darkman* - Randall Boyll   h   611
*Darkman #1: The Hangman* - Randall Boyll   h   612
*Darkman #2: The Price of Fear* - Randall
   Boyll   h   613
*Darkman #3: The Gods of Hell* - Randall
   Boyll   h   614
*Darkman #4: The Face of Death* - Randall
   Boyll   h   615

**Wilson, Barry**
*The Fungus* - Harry Adam Knight   h   3192

**Withrow, Dennis "Dennis Dithrovvu"**
*Mathemagics* - Margaret Ball   f   316

**Wojciechowski, Thaddaios "Wolf" Alexandru**
*In the Wrong Hands* - Edward Gibson   s   2215

**Wolf, Behrooz "Bey"**
*Proteus in the Underworld* - Charles
   Sheffield   s   4962
*Proteus Unbound* - Charles Sheffield   s   4963

**Wolling, Jen**
*Earth* - David Brin   s   685

**Wood, Max**
*The Frightened Fish* - Kenneth Robeson   f   4622

**Wren, Mason**
*Alien Resurrection* - A.C. Crispin   s   1258

**Wu, Victor "Orf"**
*Earthling* - Tony Daniel   s   1336

**Xavier, Adolph**
*Mr. Sandman* - Lyle Howard   h   2779

**Xu-Tzu, Phan**
*Celestial Matters* - Richard Garfinkle   s   2140

**York, Natalie**
*Voyager* - Stephen Baxter   s   406

**Zambelli, Ruggerio**
*From Prussia with Love* - John DeChancie   f   1457

**Zellorian**
*Warlord of Heaven* - Adrian Cole   f   1102

## SCOUT

**Cody, William**
*Devil's Engine* - Mark Sumner   f   5356

**Dakota**
*The Lanterns of God* - Ron Sarti   s   4835

**Darkwind**
*Winds of Change* - Mercedes Lackey   *f*   3304
*Winds of Fate* - Mercedes Lackey   *f*   3305
*Winds of Fury* - Mercedes Lackey   *f*   3306

**Dash**
*Shards of a Broken Crown* - Raymond E. Feist   *f*   1912

**Hunter, Scott**
*Hellworld* - Simon R. Green   *s*   2371

**Krystel**
*Hellworld* - Simon R. Green   *s*   2371

**Looks-at-Charts**
*Quozl* - Alan Dean Foster   *s*   2013

**Ravenloft, Kinson**
*First King of Shannara* - Terry Brooks   *f*   712

**Wakefield, Wallace "Wake"**
*The Unnatural* - David Prill   *h*   4437

## SEA CAPTAIN

**Aravan**
*Voyage of the Fox Rider* - Dennis L. McKiernan   *f*   3837

**Bedford, Richard**
*Firelance* - David Mace   *s*   3586

**Blackstrap**
*Dinotopia Lost* - Alan Dean Foster   *f*   2003

**Brazil, Nathan**
*Echoes of the Well of Souls* - Jack L. Chalker   *s*   953

**Bridger, Nathan Hale**
*seaQuest DSV: Fire Below* - Matthew J. Costello   *s*   1201
*seaQuest DSV: The Novel* - Diane Duane   *s*   1666

**Carmody, Michael**
*Sailor Song* - Ken Kesey   *s*   3082

**Carpenter, Paul**
*Hot Sky at Midnight* - Robert Silverberg   *s*   5032

**Corry, William M.**
*Starsea Invaders: First Action* - G. Harry Stine   *s*   5282

**de Novau, Isidre**
*Natural History* - Juan Perucho   *h*   4303

**Deadmon**
*Dragon's Plunder* - Brad Strickland   *f*   5336

**Dollar, John**
*John Dollar* - Marianne Wiggins   *h*   5799

**Enos, George**
*The Great War: American Front* - Harry Turtledove   *s*   5501

**Haven, Kyle**
*The Ship of Magic* - Robin Hobb   *f*   2696

**Hook, James**
*Hook* - Terry Brooks   *f*   713

**Kominsky, Katerina "Kate"**
*The Secret Oceans* - Betty Ballantine   *s*   318

**Maurynna**
*The Last Dragonlord* - Joanne Bertin   *f*   470

**Naill, Clarence "Rusty"**
*Back to the Time Trap* - Keith Laumer   *s*   3343

**Ro, Vallant**
*Convergence* - Sharon Green   *f*   2356

**Stark, Marilyn**
*seaQuest DSV: The Novel* - Diane Duane   *s*   1666

**Van Horne, Anthony**
*Towing Jehovah* - James Morrow   *f*   4035

**Vanderdecker**
*The Marvellous Land of Snergs* - E.A. Wyke-Smith   *f*   6006

**Vanderdecker, Cornelius**
*Flying Dutch* - Tom Holt   *f*   2750

## SECRETARY

**Andrada, Rosa**
*The House of the Toad* - Richard L. Tierney   *h*   5470

**Banks, Stanley**
*Quake* - Richard Laymon   *h*   3370

**Blaine, Dee Dee**
*Jumpers* - R. Patrick Gates   *h*   2161

**Burton, Denise**
*Deadly Dreams* - Gerald A. Schiller   *h*   4874

**Downing, Rae**
*Orphans* - Jean Simon   *h*   5065

**Farrell, Lizbeth**
*Homecoming* - Matthew J. Costello   *h*   1198

**Harpole, Nicholas**
*In the Garden of Iden* - Kage Baker   *s*   298

**Jervis, Katherine**
*Milton in America* - Peter Ackroyd   *f*   25

**Kharyat, Judy**
*Son of Rosemary* - Ira Levin   *h*   3445

**Koenig, Willy**
*Psychomech* - Brian Lumley   *h*   3562

**Lisa**
*The Shadow Gate* - Margaret Ball   *f*   317

**MacDonald, Ellen**
*Snowbeast!* - Peter Tremayne   *h*   5482

**Pendrake, Matthew**
*Mind Slayer* - Kevin D. Randle   *s*   4469

**Reuven**
*Legacy of the Darksword* - Margaret Weis   *f*   5719

**Stalker, Darmen**
*Fire Angels* - Jane Routley   *f*   4685

**Vehmund, Daniel**
*Heart-Beast* - Tanith Lee   *h*   3411

**Wilson, Karen**
*The Headsman* - James Neal Harvey   *h*   2599

**Wroke, Alice**
*The Demon Princes: Volume Two* - Jack Vance   *s*   5545

## SECRETARY—LEGAL

**Foster, Katherine**
*Twilight Time* - Rick Hautala   *h*   2613

**Larsen, Penny**
*Darkman #1: The Hangman* - Randall Boyll   *h*   612

**Spellman, Karen**
*The Homing* - John Saul   *h*   4842

## SECURITY OFFICER

**Dunjer, Tom**
*Specterworld* - Isidore Haiblum   *s*   2480

**Farthing, Jacob**
*Harm's Way* - Colin Greenland   *s*   2416

**Garibaldi, Michael**
*The Touch of Your Shadow, the Whisper of Your Name* - Neal Barrett Jr.   *s*   367
*Voices* - John Vornholt   *s*   5598

**Gi'Tbad'Eovad'Dvan, "William Devane"**
*The Last Dancer* - Daniel Keys Moran   *s*   3994

**Griffin, Alex**
*The California Voodoo Game* - Larry Niven   *s*   4117

**Harijadi, Anjeillo "Angel"**
*The Shapes of Their Hearts* - Melissa Scott   *s*   4901

**James-B-OND-1**
*Title Deleted for Security Reasons* - Ed Blome   *s*   553

**Joe**
*Wheels of Fire* - Mercedes Lackey   *f*   3301

**Kincannon, Aidan**
*Red, Red Robin* - Stephen Gallagher   *h*   2113

**Mendelssohn, Olivia**
*The Flies of Memory* - Ian Watson   *s*   5635

**Nash, August**
*Labyrinth of Night* - Allen Steele   *s*   5244

**Odo**
*Fallen Heroes* - Dafydd ab Hugh   *s*   8
*Warped* - K.W. Jeter   *s*   2917

**Quinn, Adam**
*Conqueror's Pride* - Timothy Zahn   *s*   6051

**Reddy, John**
*A Prince Among Men* - Robert N. Charrette   *f*   977

**Rourke, Kenneth Christian**
*Random Factor* - Joel Henry Sherman   *s*   4984

**Surrey, John**
*Timeshare* - Joshua Dann   *s*   1344

**Tuvok**
*The Escape* - Dean Wesley Smith   *s*   5113
*Ragnarok* - Nathan Archer   *s*   206

**Waverly, Tim**
*Outworld Cats* - Jack Lovejoy   *s*   3536

**Westin, Andy**
*Mall Purchase Night* - Rick Cook   *f*   1159

**Weyland, Cadmann**
*Beowulf's Children* - Larry Niven   *s*   4116

**Worf**
*Doomsday World* - Carmen Carter   *s*   923

## SERIAL KILLER

**Bateman, Patrick**
*American Psycho* - Brett Easton Ellis   *h*   1777

**Blackburn, Jimmy**
*Blackburn* - Bradley Denton   *h*   1489

**Breen, Arthur Quentin**
*The Safety of Unknown Cities* - Lucy Taylor   *h*   5414

**Bunkowski, Daniel "Chaingang"**
*Butcher* - Rex Miller   *h*   3898
*Chaingang* - Rex Miller   *h*   3899
*Savant* - Rex Miller   *h*   3901
*Slice* - Rex Miller   *h*   3902

**Byrne, Lysander "Jay"**
*Exquisite Corpse* - Poppy Z. Brite   *h*   695

**Compton, Andrew**
*Exquisite Corpse* - Poppy Z. Brite   *h*   695

**Cross, Anthony**
*Dark Matter* - Garfield Reeves-Stevens   *h*   4509

**Dart, Dick**
*The Hellfire Club* - Peter Straub   *h*   5326

**DeVries, Harlan**
*The Place* - T.M. Wright   *h*   5993

**Diver Dan**
*Bloodletter* - Warren Newton Beath   *h*   426

**Dyson, T.T.**
*Fiend* - C. Dean Andersson   *h*   138

**Haid, Francis Madsen "Painkiller"**
*The Holy Terror* - Wayne Allen Sallee  *h*  4787

**Jack the Ripper**
*A Night in the Lonesome October* - Roger Zelazny  *h*  6072

**Jarrow, Tod**
*Evil Reincarnate* - Leigh Clark  *h*  1050

**Jordan**
*The Lazarus Heart* - Poppy Z. Brite  *h*  696

**Kilpatrick, Mark Michael**
*Grave Markings* - Michael A. Arnzen  *h*  212

**Lavanic, Cruise**
*Night Cruise* - Billie Sue Mosiman  *h*  4041

**Ledbetter, Gary**
*A Room for the Dead* - Noel Hynd  *h*  2825

**Lorelei**
*Lorelei* - Mark A. Clements  *h*  1086

**Lugosh, James D.**
*Order of the Arrow* - Michael T. Hinkemeyer  *h*  2689

**Marsh, Gregory Bradford**
*Nightmare's Disciple* - Joseph S. Pulver Jr.  *h*  4449

**Nasty Andrew**
*Bleeder* - Gene Lazuta  *h*  3374

**Performer**
*Puppet Master* - Barry T. Hawkins  *h*  2632

**Semmlar, Wayne**
*Near Dead* - Stephen R. George  *h*  2202

**Spoda, Arthur**
*Iceman* - Rex Miller  *h*  3900

**Turch, Averell "The Needle"**
*Soulcatchers* - Jan Lara  *h*  3336

**Vassago**
*Hideaway* - Dean R. Koontz  *h*  3208

**Vess, Edgler Foreman**
*Intensity* - Dean R. Koontz  *h*  3210

**Watts, Arnie**
*Thoughts of God* - Michael Kanaly  *s*  3007

**Zyto, Michael**
*Machine* - Rene Belletto  *h*  436

## SERVANT

**Avran**
*Aurian* - Maggie Furey  *f*  2095

**Aziz**
*Crescent in the Sky* - Donald Moffitt  *s*  3946

**Bascombe, Jeryline A.**
*Tales From the Crypt: Demon Knight* - Randall Boyll  *h*  617

**Beeker**
*Phule's Company* - Robert Asprin  *s*  260

**Bouchard, Angelique**
*Angelique's Descent* - Lara Parker  *h*  4246

**Caillet, Josephine**
*The Werewolf of Paris* - Guy Endore  *h*  1822

**Dara**
*Guardian's Key* - Anne Logston  *f*  3511

**Duvet, Berthe**
*The Porcelain Dove* - Delia Sherman  *f*  4983

**Ember, Annie**
*Elephantasm* - Tanith Lee  *h*  3408

**Fledge**
*The Grotesque* - Patrick McGrath  *h*  3814

**Frike**
*Bring Me the Head of Prince Charming* - Roger Zelazny  *f*  6062

**Goosequill**
*Milton in America* - Peter Ackroyd  *f*  25

**Gregor**
*Dr. Haggard's Disease* - Patrick McGrath  *h*  3813

**Hornchurch, Anthony**
*The Devil You Say* - Elisa DeCarlo  *f*  1450
*Strong Spirits* - Elisa DeCarlo  *f*  1451

**Jaimah**
*The Apprentice* - Deborah Talmadge-Bickmore  *f*  5382

**Jasper**
*Murder in Cormyr* - Chet Williamson  *f*  5848

**Jeeves**
*Scream for Jeeves: A Parody* - P.H. Cannon  *h*  867

**Konrad**
*Konrad* - David Ferring  *f*  1927

**Lewis**
*Prisoner of Dreams* - Karen Ripley  *s*  4593

**Mafoo**
*The Remarkable Journey of Prince Jen* - Lloyd Alexander  *f*  69

**Magda**
*The Angry Angel* - Chelsea Quinn Yarbro  *h*  6010

**Michael**
*Dark Dance* - Tanith Lee  *h*  3406

**Miss Bird**
*The Gilda Stories* - Jewelle Gomez  *h*  2267

**Polijn**
*The Sure Death of a Mouse* - Dan Crawford  *f*  1250

**Pomegranate**
*Bronze Mirror* - Jeanne Larsen  *f*  3338

**Ranira "Renra"**
*Shadows over Lyra* - Patricia C. Wrede  *f*  5980

**Reilly, Mary**
*Mary Reilly* - Valerie Martin  *h*  3654

**Roman**
*Rock of Ages* - Walter Jon Williams  *s*  5840

**Ruto**
*Glory Road* - Robert A. Heinlein  *f*  2644

**Saluez**
*Shadow's End* - Sheri S. Tepper  *s*  5435

**Singh, Ram**
*The Spider #8: The Devil's Paymaster/Legions of the Accursed Light* - Grant Stockbridge  *f*  5309

**Sulula "Philiope"**
*Conan of the Red Brotherhood* - Leonard Carpenter  *f*  906

**Underbridge, Kin**
*Thunder of the Captains* - Holly Lisle  *f*  3489

**Valcourt, Guy-Luc**
*Adversary* - Daniel Rhodes  *h*  4568

**Vierran**
*Hexwood* - Diana Wynne Jones  *s*  2948

**Wang-mu**
*Xenocide* - Orson Scott Card  *s*  899

**Zaman**
*Viper* - Alan Riefe  *h*  4589

## SETTLER

**Adair, Devon**
*Earth 2* - Melissa Crandall  *s*  1247

**Anij**
*Insurrection* - J.M. Dillard  *s*  1554

**Barrera, Ramis**
*Lifeline* - Kevin J. Anderson  *s*  111

**Bjornsen, Kristin "Kris"**
*Freedom's Landing* - Anne McCaffrey  *s*  3734

**Bjornson, Kristen "Kris"**
*Freedom's Challenge* - Anne McCaffrey  *s*  3732

**Calhoun, Janey**
*Warpath* - Tony Daniel  *s*  1337

**Cohen, Julius**
*Mother of Demons* - Eric Flint  *s*  1956

**Dura**
*Flux* - Stephen Baxter  *s*  399

**Gart, Maya**
*The Faces of Ceti* - Mary Caraker  *s*  877

**Harris, James**
*Bright Angel* - John Blair  *s*  512

**Hrriss**
*Crisis on Doona* - Anne McCaffrey  *s*  3723

**Indergard, Cejo**
*The Dazzle of Day* - Molly Gloss  *s*  2243

**Maddock, Yanaba**
*Power Lines* - Anne McCaffrey  *s*  3743

**Magnus, Brock**
*The Faces of Ceti* - Mary Caraker  *s*  877

**Metcalf, Elizabeth**
*Nadya: The Wolf Chronicles* - Pat Murphy  *f*  4052

**Mitford, Chuck**
*Freedom's Challenge* - Anne McCaffrey  *s*  3732
*Freedom's Landing* - Anne McCaffrey  *s*  3734

**Negrete, Dolores**
*The Dazzle of Day* - Molly Gloss  *s*  2243

**O'Hara, Marianne**
*Worlds Enough and Time* - Joe Haldeman  *s*  2491

**Raven, Jeff**
*The Rowan* - Anne McCaffrey  *s*  3747

**Rourke, Buneka**
*Powers That Be* - Anne McCaffrey  *s*  3745

**Toledo, Indira**
*Mother of Demons* - Eric Flint  *s*  1956

**Tucker, Paris**
*Red Genesis* - S.C. Sykes  *s*  5377

**Vega, Carlos**
*The Faces of Ceti* - Mary Caraker  *s*  877

**Watanabe, Kenji**
*The Garden of Ruma* - Arthur C. Clarke  *s*  1055

**Zainal**
*Freedom's Challenge* - Anne McCaffrey  *s*  3732
*Freedom's Choice* - Anne McCaffrey  *s*  3733
*Freedom's Landing* - Anne McCaffrey  *s*  3734

## SHAMAN

**Alara**
*The Elvenbane* - Andre Norton  *f*  4149

**Anasan**
*Sing for a Gentle Rain* - J. Alison James  *f*  2861

**Asakeiri, Adline**
*The Watcher's Mask* - Laurie J. Marks  *f*  3627

**Ata'al**
*The Watcher's Mask* - Laurie J. Marks  *f*  3627

**Aurelio**
*The War of Don Emmanuel's Nether Parts* - Louis de Bernieres  *f*  1412

**Ayla**
*The Plains of Passage* - Jean M. Auel  *f*  275

**Bandit**
*Fade to Black* - Nyx Smith  *s*  5134

**Bear, Tom**
*The Charm* - Adam Niswander  *h*  4111

**Bitterhand, Calvin**
*The Trickster* - Muriel Gray   *h*   2340

**Broken-finger, Leonard**
*High Steel* - Jack C. Haldeman II   *s*   2486

**Carver, Alison**
*Seed upon the Wind* - Carole Nelson
    Douglas   *f*   1584

**Cha-kwena**
*The Edge of the World* - William Sarabande   *f*   4817
*Thunder in the Sky* - William Sarabande   *f*   4819

**Coyote**
*Cherokee Bat and the Goat Guys* - Francesca Lia
    Block   *f*   546

**Crone**
*Shiva Accused: An Adventure of the Ice Age* - J.H.
    Brennan   *f*   667

**de Marion, Auguste "White Bear"**
*Shaman* - Robert Shea   *f*   4946

**Dibiaja, Mpu**
*The Painted Alphabet* - Diana Darling   *f*   1356

**Dzaminid**
*Spirits of Cavern and Hearth* - M. Coleman
    Easton   *f*   1722

**Gallegher, P.J.**
*Valentine* - S.P. Somtow   *h*   5160

**Heron**
*People of the Wolf* - W. Michael Gear   *f*   2170

**Kies, Wolfgang**
*Wolf and Raven* - Michael A. Stackpole   *f*   5207

**Little Dancer**
*People of the Fire* - W. Michael Gear   *f*   2167

**Livingstone, David**
*Raven Stole the Moon* - Garth Stein   *h*   5249

**Lorat**
*Rinn's Star* - Paula E. Downing   *s*   1719

**McAusland, Louisa**
*Changeweaver* - Margaret Ball   *f*   313

**Ouija**
*Cyberweb* - Lisa Mason   *s*   3662

**Ravinga**
*The Mark of the Cat* - Andre Norton   *f*   4157

**Ria**
*Shaman* - Sandra Miesel   *f*   3889

**Sahacat**
*People of the Sky* - Clare Bell   *s*   431

**Sandwriter**
*The Promise* - Monica Hughes   *s*   2808

**Sibatia**
*Dry Skull Dreams* - Michael Green   *h*   2344

**Spring Rain**
*Sing for a Gentle Rain* - J. Alison James   *f*   2861

**Sunchaser**
*People of the Sea* - W. Michael Gear   *f*   2169

**Talker**
*Dawn Land* - Joseph Bruchac   *f*   731

**Talldeer, Jennifer**
*Sacred Ground* - Mercedes Lackey   *f*   3294

**Tamai**
*Changeweaver* - Margaret Ball   *f*   313

**Tanaka**
*Mind Stealer* - Lee Duigon   *h*   1672

**Ulahane**
*The Shaman* - Christopher Stasheff   *f*   5223

**Verner, Samuel**
*Find Your Own Truth* - Robert N. Charrette   *f*   972

**Webb, Danny**
*The Serpent Slayers* - Adam Niswander   *h*   4113

**White Eagle, Zacxk**
*Shaman Woods* - Morgan Fields   *h*   1931

**Winchester, Miriam**
*Shadow Walkers* - Nina Romberg   *h*   4663

**Wolf**
*Spiritride* - Mark Shepherd   *f*   4981

**Wyungare**
*Dealer's Choice* - George R.R. Martin   *s*   3643

**Yocote**
*The Sage* - Christopher Stasheff   *f*   5221

## SHEPHERD

**Ingoldesdaughter, Berika**
*Beneath the Web* - Lynn Abbey   *f*   12
*The Wooden Sword* - Lynn Abbey   *f*   18

**Rissedote, Faia**
*Fire in the Mist* - Holly Lisle   *f*   3482

**Roanhorse, Michael**
*Eye Killers* - A.A. Carr   *h*   911

## SIDEKICK

**Bill**
*Hawaiian U.F.O. Aliens* - Mel Gilden   *s*   2226
*Tubular Android Superheroes* - Mel Gilden   *s*   2228

**Brand**
*The Hammer and the Cross* - Harry
    Harrison   *f*   2570
*One King's Way* - Harry Harrison   *s*   2572

**Brennan, Joseph Payne**
*The Adventures of Lucius Leffing* - Joseph Payne
    Brennan   *h*   670

**Cge**
*Backblast* - Lee McKeone   *s*   3828
*The Clone Crisis* - Lee McKeone   *s*   3829

**Claude**
*Title Deleted for Security Reasons* - Ed
    Blome   *s*   553

**de Marigny, Henri Laurent**
*Titus Crow, Volume One* - Brian Lumley   *h*   3566
*Titus Crow, Volume Three* - Brian Lumley   *h*   3567
*Titus Crow, Volume Two* - Brian Lumley   *h*   3568
*The Transition of Titus Crow* - Brian
    Lumley   *h*   3569

**Dead Man**
*Red Iron Nights* - Glen Cook   *f*   1153

**Dulaine, Dirk**
*A Wizard in Chaos* - Christopher Stasheff   *s*   5230
*A Wizard in Peace* - Christopher Stasheff   *s*   5233
*A Wizard in War* - Christopher Stasheff   *s*   5234

**Gabrielle**
*The Empty Throne* - Ru Emerson   *f*   1808

**Hangman**
*Rememory* - John Gregory Betancourt   *s*   481

**Jakobot "Jacko" 490,9000**
*Extreme Paranoia: Nobody Knows the Trouble I've
    Shot* - Ken Rolston   *s*   4662

**Kalencka**
*Rally Cry!* - William R. Forstchen   *s*   1982

**Lochlainn, Sean O.**
*A Study in Sorcery* - Michael Kurland   *f*   3252

**Mona**
*Enemy of My Enemy* - Ben Ohlander   *s*   4204

**Murphy, Clarence "Cookie"**
*Judson's Eden* - Keith Laumer   *s*   3344

**Number Ten Ox**
*Eight Skilled Gentlemen* - Barry Hughart   *f*   2804

**Pulon**
*Ganwold's Child* - Diann Thornley   *s*   5467

**Salmoneus**
*The First Casualty* - David L. Seidman   *f*   4912

**Snuff**
*A Night in the Lonesome October* - Roger
    Zelazny   *h*   6072

**Wendell**
*Slay and Rescue* - John Moore   *f*   3991

**Ya-Mash, Yam**
*The Return of the Breakneck Boys* - Geary
    Gravel   *s*   2332

## SINGER

**Brill**
*The Soprano Sorceress* - L.E. Modesitt Jr.   *f*   3938

**Carter, Sharon**
*Jacob's Hands* - Aldous Huxley   *f*   2817

**Chentelle**
*Quest for the Fallen Star* - Piers Anthony   *f*   185

**Daae, Christine**
*Phantom* - Susan Kay   *h*   3020

**Delilah "Lilah"**
*Jovah's Angel* - Sharon Shinn   *s*   5001

**du Boise, Llysette**
*The Ghost of the Revelator* - L.E. Modesitt
    Jr.   *s*   3931

**Du Boise, Llysette**
*Of Tangible Ghosts* - L.E. Modesitt Jr.   *f*   3935

**Elizabeth**
*Ladies Night* - Jack Ketchum   *h*   3091

**Gabriel**
*Archangel* - Sharon Shinn   *s*   5000

**Heather**
*Lorien Lost* - Michael King   *f*   3124

**Ingham, Justine**
*Circuit of Heaven* - Dennis Danvers   *s*   1348

**Jakri**
*Receive the Gift* - Louise Marley   *s*   3628

**Kidd, Billy Lee**
*Deathsong* - Douglas Borton   *h*   575

**Lina**
*Interface Masque* - Shariann Lewitt   *s*   3453

**Lucinda**
*The Alleluia Files* - Sharon Shinn   *s*   4999

**Madonette**
*The Stainless Steel Rat Sings the Blues* - Harry
    Harrison   *s*   2575

**Marshall, Anna**
*The Soprano Sorceress* - L.E. Modesitt Jr.   *f*   3938
*The Spellsong War* - L.E. Modesitt Jr.   *f*   3939

**Merelan**
*The Masterharper of Pern* - Anne
    McCaffrey   *s*   3739

**Merlin, Anastasia "Ana"**
*Tomorrow and Tomorrow* - Charles
    Sheffield   *s*   4966

**Nitt, Agnes**
*Maskerade* - Terry Pratchett   *f*   4395

**Nugget, Jain**
*Kaduna Memories* - Jack McKinney   *s*   3850

**Parker, Daria**
*Silk* - Caitlin R. Kiernan   *h*   3101

## Socialite (continued)

**Primavera**
*Primavera* - Francesca Lia Block   *f*   551

**Rachel**
*Archangel* - Sharon Shinn   *s*   5000

**Rathenau, Miriam**
*Child of the Journey* - Janet Berliner   *f*   466
*Child of the Light* - Janet Gluckman   *f*   2244

**Rossiter, Adam**
*Tempter* - Nancy A. Collins   *h*   1125

**Singer, Eleal**
*Past Imperative* - Dave Duncan   *f*   1684

**Sira**
*Sing the Light* - Louise Marley   *s*   3629
*Sing the Warmth* - Louise Marley   *s*   3630

**Siri**
*Receive the Gift* - Louise Marley   *s*   3628

**Stannard, Gabriel**
*The Kill Riff* - David J. Schow   *h*   4887

**Taylor, Tamara**
*The Werewolf Chronicles* - Traci Briery   *h*   679
*Wolfsong* - Traci Briery   *h*   680

**Thissizz**
*The Merro Tree* - Katie Waitman   *s*   5609

**Zakri**
*Sing the Warmth* - Louise Marley   *s*   3630

## SINGLE PARENT

**Baines, Ti-Jeanne**
*Brown Girl in the Ring* - Nalo Hopkinson   *f*   2771

**Corey, Maggie**
*Freeze Frames* - Katharine Kerr   *s*   3071

**Cray, Robyn**
*The Two in Hiding* - Ru Emerson   *f*   1812

**Golding, Marsha**
*The Juniper Game* - Sherryl Jordan   *f*   2992

**Matthews, Lydia**
*Carnivores* - Penelope Banka Kreps   *h*   3232

**Mooney, Shawana**
*The Arbitrary Placement of Walls* - Martha Soukup   *f*   5165

**Rede, Pippa**
*In the Land of Winter* - Richard Grant   *f*   2326

**Sinclair, Felice**
*The Fagin* - Pat Graversen   *h*   2334

**Sloan, Susan**
*Beneath Still Waters* - Matthew J. Costello   *h*   1193

**Trey, Annie**
*Alien Rites* - Lynn S. Hightower   *s*   2685

## SLAVE

**Annalise**
*Black Wine* - Candas Jane Dorsey   *s*   1582

**Astrahn**
*A City in Winter* - Mark Helprin   *f*   2653

**Aw, Ruiz**
*Emperor of Everything* - Ray Aldridge   *s*   62

**Bjornsen, Kristin "Kris"**
*Freedom's Landing* - Anne McCaffrey   *s*   3734

**Bjornson, Kristen "Kris"**
*Freedom's Challenge* - Anne McCaffrey   *s*   3732
*Freedom's Choice* - Anne McCaffrey   *s*   3733

**Breith**
*Drum Calls* - Jo Clayton   *f*   1065

**Cadarn, Derfel**
*The Winter King* - Bernard Cornwell   *f*   1191

**Conn**
*The Shining Company* - Rosemary Sutcliff   *f*   5359

**Curran, Joslire**
*An Exchange of Hostages* - Susan R. Matthews   *s*   3692

**d'Anton, Charlotte Marie**
*The Virgin and the Dinosaur* - R. Garcia y Robertson   *s*   2122

**Dawson**
*Warp Angel* - Stuart Hopen   *s*   2766

**Decius**
*The Light Bearer* - Donna Gillespie   *f*   2229

**Endang**
*Flowerdust* - Gwyneth Jones   *s*   2952

**Essa**
*Black Wine* - Candas Jane Dorsey   *s*   1582

**Faro**
*If I Pay Thee Not in Gold* - Piers Anthony   *f*   176

**Flavius**
*Pandora* - Anne Rice   *h*   4573

**Garfield, Joanne**
*Parable of the Sower* - Octavia E. Butler   *s*   792

**Hemings, Sally**
*Arc d'X* - Steve Erickson   *f*   1835

**Indian, John**
*I, Tituba, Black Witch of Salem* - Maryse Conde   *f*   1130

**Long-Reach**
*Man-Kzin Wars IV* - Larry Niven   *s*   4124

**mac Calprin, Patraic "Patricius Calpurnius"**
*The Deer's Cry: A Book of the Keltiad* - Patricia Kennealy-Morrison   *f*   3060

**Marcus**
*Wagers of Sin* - Robert Asprin   *s*   264

**Martin the Warrior**
*Martin the Warrior* - Brian Jacques   *f*   2851

**Nisa**
*Emperor of Everything* - Ray Aldridge   *s*   62
*The Pharaoh Contract* - Ray Aldridge   *s*   63

**Notorincus**
*A City in Winter* - Mark Helprin   *f*   2653

**Otha**
*The Hollow Earth: The Narrative of Mason Algiers Reynolds of Virginia* - Rudy Rucker   *s*   4705

**Radience**
*Warriorwards* - Dafydd ab Hugh   *f*   11

**Rakam, Radosse**
*Four Ways to Forgiveness* - Ursula K. Le Guin   *s*   3380

**Reyes, Adrien**
*Someone to Watch over Me* - Tricia Sullivan   *s*   5355

**Ryson, Kerryl**
*The Thirteenth Majestral* - Hayford Peirce   *s*   4277

**Sadira**
*The Verdant Passage* - Troy Denning   *f*   1487

**Tiana**
*Songs of the Dancing Gods* - Jack L. Chalker   *f*   962

**Timkin**
*The Red King* - Victor Kelleher   *f*   3043

**Vashanna**
*Cat Scratch Fever* - Tara K. Harper   *s*   2550

**Willow Leaf**
*The Road to Underfall* - Mike Jefferies   *f*   2888

**Yaeylie, Frenna**
*Hand of Prophecy* - Severna Park   *s*   4244

**Yaroslavich, Yuri**
*Terrible Swift Sword* - William R. Forstchen   *s*   1983

## SMUGGLER

**Barabbas**
*Woman Without a Shadow* - Karen Haber   *s*   2478

**Dalamini, Ming**
*Crystal Witness* - Kathy Tyers   *s*   5524

**Hinton, Blackbird**
*Python Isle* - Kenneth Robeson   *f*   4624

**Iger**
*The War Minstrels* - Karen Haber   *s*   2477

**Lando, Pik**
*Drifter* - William C. Dietz   *s*   1543
*Drifter's Run* - William C. Dietz   *s*   1544
*Drifter's War* - William C. Dietz   *s*   1545

**Mogurn, Deuteronomous**
*Dragons in the Stars* - Jeffrey A. Carver   *s*   930

**Reed, Kayla**
*The War Minstrels* - Karen Haber   *s*   2477

**St. Cyr, Butterfly**
*Archangel Blues* - eluki bes shahar   *s*   471
*Darktraders* - eluki bes shahar   *s*   472
*Hellflower* - eluki bes shahar   *s*   473

**Tanner, Louis**
*Destroying Angel* - Richard Paul Russo   *s*   4749

**Valentine, Patrick**
*Prototype* - Brian Hodge   *h*   2704

**Vasquez, Juanita**
*Mojo and the Pickle Jar* - Douglas Bell   *f*   433

**X, Aaron**
*Conglomeros* - Jesse Browner   *f*   729

## SOCIAL WORKER

**Block, Hillary**
*Deathchain* - Ken Greenhall   *h*   2415

**Fairfax, Eugenia**
*Black Night* - S.J. Strayhorn   *h*   5334

**Foxworth, Elizabeth**
*Fragments* - James F. David   *h*   1380

**Haberman**
*The Nihilesthete* - Richard Kalich   *h*   3002

**James, Hilton**
*The Between* - Tannarive Due   *h*   1669

**Janos, Teodor**
*The Death of Sleep* - Anne McCaffrey   *s*   3727

**Jo**
*The Parasite War* - Tim Sullivan   *s*   5352

**Johnston, Jerry**
*Prodigal* - Melanie Tem   *h*   5423

**Samson, Rosalie "Rose"**
*The Godmother* - Elizabeth Ann Scarborough   *f*   4862

**Stevens, Carol**
*Reborn* - F. Paul Wilson   *h*   5895

**Vaughn, Melissa**
*Child of Shadows* - John Coyne   *h*   1236

**Winchell, Anne**
*Bone* - George C. Chesbro   *h*   1006

## SOCIALITE

**Cobri, Amy**
*Sundowner* - Chris Claremont   *s*   1043

**de Conde, Sarah Webster**
*Deep Freeze* - Zach Hughes   s   2811

**Evans, Constanza**
*The War of Don Emmanuel's Nether Parts* - Louis de Bernieres   f   1412

**Galinda "Glinda the Good"**
*Wicked: The Life and Times of the Wicked Witch of the West* - Gregory Maguire   f   3609

**Leyner, Mark**
*Et Tu, Babe* - Mark Leyner   s   3455

**Rogers, Troi**
*Treks Not Taken: What if Stephen King, Anne Rice, Bret Easton Ellis, and Other Literary Greats Had Written Episodes of Star Trek: The Next Generation?* - Steven R. Boyett   s   607

**Zant, Quasar**
*Quasar* - Jamil Nasir   s   4071

## SOCIOLOGIST

**Baker, Jonathan**
*Red Genesis* - S.C. Sykes   s   5377

**Dove, Amy**
*God's World* - Ian Watson   s   5636

**Lixia, Li**
*A Woman of the Iron People* - Eleanor Arnason   s   211

**Massif, Sheila**
*The Living One* - Lewis Gannett   h   2115

**Morris, Claudia**
*Children of the Thunder* - John Brunner   s   733

## SONGWRITER

**Bradley, Angela**
*Metal Angel* - Nancy Springer   f   5181

## SORCERER

**Al-Ra,ma, Khaddam**
*The Riddled Man* - Mark E. Rogers   f   4654

**Arunsun, Khelben**
*Thornhold* - Elaine Cunningham   f   1293

**Asandir**
*Curse of the Mistwraith* - Janny Wurts   f   6001

**Avril**
*The Price of Blood and Honor* - Elizabeth Willey   f   5811
*A Sorcerer and a Gentleman* - Elizabeth Willey   f   5812

**Azrael**
*Evil Reincarnate* - Leigh Clark   h   1050

**Balor**
*Fire Arrow* - Edith Pattou   f   4260

**Baralis**
*The Baker's Boy* - J.V. Jones   f   2956
*Master and Fool* - J.V. Jones   f   2959

**Bariden**
*The Hidden Realms* - Sharon Green   f   2358

**Belgarath**
*Belgarath the Sorcerer* - David Eddings   f   1730
*The Rivan Codex* - David Eddings   f   1735

**ben Shaqar, Sharif**
*The Devouring Void* - Mark E. Rogers   f   4653

**Bilitu**
*Engor's Sword Arm* - David C. Smith   h   5110

**Bonaduce, Aballister**
*Canticle* - R.A. Salvatore   f   4793

**Brandin of Ygrath**
*Tigana* - Guy Gavriel Kay   f   3018

**Brandis**
*Wind Whispers, Shadow Shouts* - Sharon Green   f   2360

**Caolin "Blood Lord"**
*The Jewel of Fire* - Diana L. Paxson   f   4265

**Constance**
*Down Among the Dead Men* - Simon R. Green   f   2367

**Creeping Sword**
*Spell of Apocalypse* - Mayer Alan Brenner   f   672

**Custer, George Armstrong**
*Devil's Tower* - Mark Sumner   f   5357

**Darynson, Davyn "Davi"**
*Book of Stones* - L. Dean James   f   2862

**Deite, Manuel "Childe"**
*Raven* - S.A. Swiniarski   h   5374

**Dewar**
*The Price of Blood and Honor* - Elizabeth Willey   f   5811
*A Sorcerer and a Gentleman* - Elizabeth Willey   f   5812

**Diaz, Ricardo**
*Dead of Night* - Alex Abella   h   20

**Drulethen "Dru"**
*The Qualinesti* - Paul B. Thompson   f   5455

**Dur**
*Drum Warning* - Jo Clayton   f   1066

**Elena**
*The Fourth Guardian* - Ronald Anthony Cross   s   1273
*The Lost Guardian* - Ronald Anthony Cross   s   1274

**Elminster**
*Elminster: The Making of a Mage* - Ed Greenwood   f   2427

**Erwyn**
*Go Quest, Young Man* - K.B. Bogen   f   557

**Evander**
*Days of Air and Darkness* - Katharine Kerr   f   3067

**Farblood, Corri**
*Soothslayer: A Magickal Fantasy* - D.J. Conway   f   1143

**Gervinus**
*The Shattered Oath* - Josepha Sherman   f   4989

**Grandier, Urbain**
*The Element of Fire* - Martha Wells   f   5750

**Great Karlini**
*Spell of Apocalypse* - Mayer Alan Brenner   f   672

**Gwydion**
*The Well-Favored Man: The Tale of the Sorcerer's Nephew* - Elizabeth Willey   f   5813

**Jack**
*The Baker's Boy* - J.V. Jones   f   2956
*A Man Betrayed* - J.V. Jones   f   2958
*Master and Fool* - J.V. Jones   f   2959

**Jazen**
*The Courts of Sorcery* - Ashley McConnell   f   3773
*The Fountains of Mirlacca* - Ashley McConnell   f   3775

**Jones, Umber**
*Rook* - Graham Masterton   h   3678

**Kaftus**
*The Sure Death of a Mouse* - Dan Crawford   f   1250

**Kateralbin, Crispin**
*The Daemon in the Machine* - Felicity Savage   f   4848
*The War in the Waste* - Felicity Savage   f   4852

**Klingsor**
*The Grail of Hearts* - Susan Shwartz   f   5015

**Lady**
*Dreams of Steel* - Glen Cook   f   1150

**liMarchborg, Tradain**
*The White Tribunal* - Paula Volsky   f   5583

**Litzenreich**
*Shadowbreed* - David Ferring   f   1928

**Lothor**
*Nightseer* - Laurell K. Hamilton   f   2521

**Lukasha**
*The Spirit Gate* - Maya Kaathryn Bohnhoff   f   562

**Macumba the Dark Man**
*Howl-O-Ween* - Gary L. Holleman   h   2744

**Malone, Amos "Mad Amos"**
*Mad Amos* - Alan Dean Foster   f   2009

**Maximillian**
*Catastrophe's Spell* - Mayer Alan Brenner   f   671
*Spell of Apocalypse* - Mayer Alan Brenner   f   672
*Spell of Fate* - Mayer Alan Brenner   f   673

**Merlin**
*Arthur* - Stephen R. Lawhead   f   3352

**Mikal**
*Broken Blade* - Ann Marston   f   3634

**Mocata**
*The Devil Rides Out* - Dennis Wheatley   h   5773

**Murphy, Grey**
*Man From Mundania* - Piers Anthony   f   180

**Mylne, Duncan**
*The Matrix* - Jonathan Aycliffe   h   280

**Nevyn**
*The Dragon Revenant* - Katharine Kerr   f   3069

**O'Connor, Corbo**
*The Fourth Guardian* - Ronald Anthony Cross   s   1273
*The Lost Guardian* - Ronald Anthony Cross   s   1274
*The White Guardian* - Ronald Anthony Cross   s   1275

**Orogastus**
*Sky Trillium* - Julian May   f   3700

**Orogastus/Portolanus**
*Blood Trillium* - Julian May   f   3696

**Orris**
*The Outlanders* - David B. Coe   f   1096

**Preposteror, Beelzebub**
*The Night of Wishes: Or, The Satanarchaeolidealcohellish Notion Potion* - Michael Ende   f   1821

**Prospero**
*The Price of Blood and Honor* - Elizabeth Willey   f   5811
*A Sorcerer and a Gentleman* - Elizabeth Willey   f   5812
*The Well-Favored Man: The Tale of the Sorcerer's Nephew* - Elizabeth Willey   f   5813

**Raphael**
*The White Guardian* - Ronald Anthony Cross   s   1275

**Ross, John**
*A Knight of the Word* - Terry Brooks   f   714

**Sawalha, Erim**
*The Riddled Man* - Mark E. Rogers   f   4654

**Sayyed**
*City of the Sorcerers* - Mary H. Herbert   f   2673
*Winged Magic* - Mary H. Herbert   f   2678

**Semjaza**
*Zaragoz* - Brian Craig   f   1241

**Shawdell**
*Green Rider* - Kristen Britain   *f*   692

**Sheldon, Rudolph "Rudy"**
*Brown Girl in the Ring* - Nalo Hopkinson   *f*   2771

**Shoth**
*An Enemy Reborn* - Michael A. Stackpole   *f*   5197

**Silverhair, Imandoff**
*Soothslayer: A Magickal Fantasy* - D.J.
   Conway   *f*   1143

**Simon**
*The Dragonbone Chair* - Tad Williams   *f*   5829
*Stone of Farewell* - Tad Williams   *f*   5831

**Soothslayer**
*Soothslayer: A Magickal Fantasy* - D.J.
   Conway   *f*   1143

**sr'Yat, Jazen**
*The Itinerant Exorcist* - Ashley McConnell   *f*   3776

**Suldris, James**
*This Dark Paradise* - Wendy Haley   *h*   2493

**Taltos, Vlad**
*Athyra* - Steven Brust   *f*   739
*Dragon* - Steven Brust   *f*   741
*Orca* - Steven Brust   *f*   745
*Phoenix* - Steven Brust   *f*   746

**Tarrant, Gerald**
*When True Night Falls* - C.S. Friedman   *f*   2060

**Tirand**
*The Deceiver* - Louise Cooper   *f*   1175

**Tornsaarin, Willek**
*The Rose Sea* - S.M. Stirling   *f*   5296

**Ufgood, Torquil**
*Shadow Dawn* - Chris Claremont   *f*   1042

**Varis**
*The Wolf of Winter* - Paula Volsky   *f*   5584

**Zal'honan, Firan**
*King of the Dead* - Gene DeWeese   *h*   1510

**Zeree, Dru**
*Children of the Drake* - Richard A. Knaak   *f*   3166
*The Shrouded Realm* - Richard A. Knaak   *f*   3174

**Zhadnoboth**
*A Name to Conjure With* - Donald Aamodt   *f*   3
*A Troubling Along the Border* - Donald Aamodt   *f*   4

## SORCERESS

**Addams, Helen "Kyria"**
*Dragon Death* - Gael Baudino   *f*   390
*Duel of Dragons* - Gael Baudino   *f*   391

**Aditi**
*Bijapur* - Kara Dalkey   *f*   1317
*Blood of the Goddess* - Kara Dalkey   *f*   1318

**Aeriel**
*The Pearl of the Soul of the World* - Meredith Ann
   Pierce   *f*   4318

**Antissa, Sybil**
*Owl Light* - Michael Paine   *h*   4235

**Arletta, Simone**
*Valentine* - S.P. Somtow   *h*   5160

**Averil**
*Plague Demon* - Brian Craig   *f*   1239

**Brill**
*The Soprano Sorceress* - L.E. Modesitt Jr.   *f*   3938

**Carrion, Kade**
*The Element of Fire* - Martha Wells   *f*   5750

**Chalaine**
*Dark Mirror, Dark Dreams* - Sharon Green   *f*   2357
*The Hidden Realms* - Sharon Green   *f*   2358

**Coral**
*The Goblin Plain War* - Carl Miller   *f*   3892
*The Warrior and the Witch* - Carl Miller   *f*   3893

**dar Dero, Halleyne**
*Wrath of the Princes* - Holly Lisle   *f*   3490

**de Gris, Daria**
*The Changeling Prince* - Vivian Vande
   Velde   *f*   5554

**Dirona**
*Search for the Starblade* - Keith Taylor   *f*   5408

**Drusilla**
*The Fourth Guardian* - Ronald Anthony
   Cross   *s*   1273

**Elena**
*Wit'ch Fire* - James Clemens   *f*   1082

**Elizebith of Morea**
*Dark Divide* - Mark Acres   *f*   27
*Outcasts* - Clayton Emery   *f*   1815
*The Stone of Time* - Rose Estes   *f*   1840

**Elyssa**
*Konrad* - David Ferring   *f*   1927

**Erek**
*Hall of Whispers* - Mike Jefferies   *f*   2884

**Felaya**
*Token of Dragonsblood* - Damaris Cole   *f*   1114

**Freemark, Nest**
*A Knight of the Word* - Terry Brooks   *f*   714
*Running with the Demon* - Terry Brooks   *f*   715

**Gabria**
*Dark Horse* - Mary H. Herbert   *f*   2674
*Lightning's Daughter* - Mary H. Herbert   *f*   2676
*Winged Magic* - Mary H. Herbert   *f*   2678

**Gantha**
*Afterimage* - Kristine Kathryn Rusch   *f*   4709

**Gemma**
*The Lightless Kingdom* - Jonathan Wylie   *f*   6007

**Green**
*Gawain and Lady Green* - Anne Eliot
   Crompton   *f*   1269

**Haramis**
*Black Trillium* - Marion Zimmer Bradley   *f*   630
*Blood Trillium* - Julian May   *f*   3696
*Lady of the Trillium* - Marion Zimmer
   Bradley   *f*   641
*Sky Trillium* - Julian May   *f*   3700

**Hasmara, Faan "Fa"**
*The Magic Wars* - Jo Clayton   *f*   1068
*Wildfire* - Jo Clayton   *f*   1073

**Ingoldesdaughter, Berika**
*Beneath the Web* - Lynn Abbey   *f*   12

**Inya**
*Kar Kalim* - Deborah Christian   *f*   1025

**Ithariel**
*The Master of Whitestorm* - Janny Wurts   *f*   6003

**Ivy**
*Man From Mundania* - Piers Anthony   *f*   180

**Jennedote, Yaji**
*Fire in the Mist* - Holly Lisle   *f*   3482

**Jill**
*Days of Air and Darkness* - Katharine Kerr   *f*   3067
*Days of Blood and Fire* - Katharine Kerr   *f*   3068
*A Time of Exile* - Katharine Kerr   *f*   3077
*A Time of Omens* - Katharine Kerr   *f*   3078

**Karuth**
*The Avenger* - Louise Cooper   *f*   1174
*The Deceiver* - Louise Cooper   *f*   1175

**Keleios**
*Nightseer* - Laurell K. Hamilton   *f*   2521

**Kelene**
*City of the Sorcerers* - Mary H. Herbert   *f*   2673
*Winged Magic* - Mary H. Herbert   *f*   2678

**Kethry**
*Oathblood* - Mercedes Lackey   *f*   3290

**Leather-Woman**
*Spires of Spirit* - Gael Baudino   *f*   395

**Liant**
*Prince of Dogs* - Kate Elliott   *f*   1775

**Lila Anne**
*Summerland* - L. Dean James   *f*   2865

**Lonat, Bosanka**
*The Golden Thread* - Suzy McKee Charnas   *f*   969

**Madeline**
*The Death of the Necromancer* - Martha
   Wells   *f*   5749

**Marsh, Valentine**
*The Golden Thread* - Suzy McKee Charnas   *f*   969

**Marshall, Anna**
*The Soprano Sorceress* - L.E. Modesitt Jr.   *f*   3938
*The Spellsong War* - L.E. Modesitt Jr.   *f*   3939

**Megan**
*Merlin's Legacy: Dawn of Camelot* - Quinn Taylor
   Evans   *f*   1857

**Mira**
*Dragons on the Town* - Thorarinn
   Gunnarsson   *f*   2463

**Morgan le Fay**
*Merlin's Bones* - Fred Saberhagen   *f*   4771
*The Prince and the Pilgrim* - Mary Stewart   *f*   5270

**Morgian**
*Grail* - Stephen R. Lawhead   *f*   3355

**Mystra**
*Elminster: The Making of a Mage* - Ed
   Greenwood   *f*   2427

**ni Pendaron, Teleri**
*The Work of the Sun* - Teresa Edgerton   *f*   1746

**NicCuinn, Meghan**
*The Witches of Eileanan* - Kate Forsyth   *f*   1984

**Nimue**
*The Merlin Effect* - T.A. Barron   *f*   371
*The Winter King* - Bernard Cornwell   *f*   1191

**Polgara**
*Polgara the Sorceress* - David Eddings   *f*   1734

**Ravanna**
*The Pearl of the Soul of the World* - Meredith Ann
   Pierce   *f*   4318

**Rissedote, Faia**
*Fire in the Mist* - Holly Lisle   *f*   3482

**Rissedotte, Faia**
*Mind of the Magic* - Holly Lisle   *f*   3486

**Ro, Nyx**
*The Cygnet and the Firebird* - Patricia A.
   McKillip   *f*   3839

**Rose**
*Question Quest* - Piers Anthony   *f*   186

**Ruha**
*The Parched Sea* - Troy Denning   *f*   1486

**Segnbora**
*The Door into Sunset* - Diane Duane   *f*   1660

**Sephrenia**
*The Diamond Throne* - David Eddings   *f*   1731
*The Ruby Knight* - David Eddings   *f*   1736

**Serroi**
*Dancer's Rise* - Jo Clayton   *f*   1064
*The Magic Wars* - Jo Clayton   *f*   1068

**Shamera "Sham"**
*When Demons Walk* - Patricia Briggs   *f*   683

Sharissa
*Children of the Drake* - Richard A. Knaak   *f*   3166
*The Shrouded Realm* - Richard A. Knaak   *f*   3174

Shiara
*The Wiz Biz* - Rick Cook   *f*   1160

Siddonie
*The Catswold Portal* - Shirley Rousseau
   Murphy   *f*   4055

Silme
*By Chaos Cursed* - Mickey Zucker Reichert   *f*   4517

Song, Medwind
*Fire in the Mist* - Holly Lisle   *f*   3482
*Mind of the Magic* - Holly Lisle   *f*   3486

Thayla
*Beyond the Pale* - Jack Koke   *f*   3198

Veriam, Tanaquil
*Gold Unicorn* - Tanith Lee   *f*   3410
*Red Unicorn* - Tanith Lee   *f*   3414

Vettazen
*The Fountains of Mirlacca* - Ashley
   McConnell   *f*   3775

Warner, Valerie
*The Armageddon Box* - Robert Weinberg   *h*   5690
*The Devil's Auction* - Robert Weinberg   *h*   5696

Whistler, Circe
*Wildest Dreams* - Norman Partridge   *h*   4256

Ygorla
*The Avenger* - Louise Cooper   *f*   1174
*The Deceiver* - Louise Cooper   *f*   1175

Zandramas
*The Seeress of Kell* - David Eddings   *f*   1738

## SPACE EXPLORER

Barclay, Reginald
*Requiem* - Michael Jan Friedman   *s*   2067

Boone, Jack
*Red Mars* - Kim Stanley Robinson   *s*   4635

Cameron, Dev
*Warstrider: Netlink* - William H. Keith Jr.   *s*   3038

Chekov, Pavel
*The Ashes of Eden* - William Shatner   *s*   4927
*The Disinherited* - Peter David   *s*   1381
*Traitor Winds* - L.A. Graf   *s*   2298
*War Dragons* - L.A. Graf   *s*   2299
*Windows on a Lost World* - V.E. Mitchell   *s*   3920

Christian, Paige
*The Starlight Crystal* - Christopher Pike   *s*   4333

Cochrane, Zefrem
*Federation* - Judith Reeves-Stevens   *s*   4511

Crusher, Beverly
*Chains of Command* - Bill McCay   *s*   3767
*Dragon's Honor* - Kij Johnson   *s*   2922
*Imbalance* - V.E. Mitchell   *s*   3919
*Intellivore* - Diane Duane   *s*   1663

Dan
*Douglas Adams's Starship Titanic* - Terry
   Jones   *s*   2979

Data
*Imzadi* - Peter David   *s*   1383
*Insurrection* - J.M. Dillard   *s*   1554
*Intellivore* - Diane Duane   *s*   1663
*The Last Stand* - Brad Ferguson   *s*   1923
*Metamorphosis* - Jean Lorrah   *s*   3524

Datum
*Treks Not Taken: What if Stephen King, Anne Rice,
   Bret Easton Ellis, and Other Literary Greats Had
   Written Episodes of Star Trek: The Next
   Generation?* - Steven R. Boyett   *s*   607

Derigha, Yarrun
*Expendable* - James Alan Gardner   *s*   2135

Erhsham, Ling
*The Transmigration of Souls* - William
   Barton   *s*   382

Hunter, Harold "Randy" Randolph
*Timemaster* - Robert L. Forward   *s*   1992

Ishikawa, Keiko
*Imbalance* - V.E. Mitchell   *s*   3919

Janeway, Kathryn
*Chrysalis* - David Niall Wilson   *s*   5880
*The Escape* - Dean Wesley Smith   *s*   5113
*The Final Fury* - Dafydd ab Hugh   *s*   9
*Her Klingon Soul* - Michael Jan Friedman   *s*   2064
*Mosaic* - Jeri Taylor   *s*   5403
*Ragnarok* - Nathan Archer   *s*   206

Kincaid, Astrid
*The Transmigration of Souls* - William
   Barton   *s*   382

Lucy
*Douglas Adams's Starship Titanic* - Terry
   Jones   *s*   2979

Macafee, Simon
*The Cyborg From Earth* - Charles Sheffield   *s*   4952

Nettie
*Douglas Adams's Starship Titanic* - Terry
   Jones   *s*   2979

Nira, Val
*The Longest Voyage/Slow Lightning* - Poul
   Anderson   *s*   130

Ramos, Festina
*Expendable* - James Alan Gardner   *s*   2135

Riker, William
*Imbalance* - V.E. Mitchell   *s*   3919
*Imzadi* - Peter David   *s*   1383
*The Soldiers of Fear* - Dean Wesley Smith   *s*   5115

Shaffer, Beowulf
*Crashlander* - Larry Niven   *s*   4118

Sparrow
*The Dark Beyond the Stars* - Frank M.
   Robinson   *s*   4626

Spinner-of-Rope
*Ring* - Stephen Baxter   *s*   402

Taylor, Shona
*Medicine Show* - Jody Lynn Nye   *s*   4172
*Taylor's Ark* - Jody Lynn Nye   *s*   4176

Tichy, Ijon
*Peace on Earth* - Stanislaw Lem   *s*   3435

Troi, Deanna
*The Last Stand* - Brad Ferguson   *s*   1923

Uhura
*The Disinherited* - Peter David   *s*   1381

Zahmekoses
*Encounter with Tiber* - Buzz Aldrin   *s*   64

Zeq, Ahmad
*The Transmigration of Souls* - William
   Barton   *s*   382

## SPACEMAN

Apollo
*Armageddon* - Richard Hatch   *s*   2602

Austin, Gregory
*Fallway* - Paula E. Downing   *s*   1593

Bandicut, John
*The Infinite Sea* - Jeffrey A. Carver   *s*   932
*Neptune Crossing* - Jeffrey A. Carver   *s*   933
*Strange Attractors* - Jeffrey A. Carver   *s*   934

Barlow, Frank
*The Ring of Charon* - Roger MacBride Allen   *s*   80

Barzac, Ree
*Brotherhood of the Stars* - Kirby Greene   *s*   2414

Bede, Strebban "Badger"
*Hunting the Corrigan's Blood* - Holly Lisle   *s*   3484

Bell, Justin Wood
*Article 23* - William R. Forstchen   *s*   1978

Bill
*Bill, the Galactic Hero: On the Planet of Tasteless
   Pleasure* - Harry Harrison   *s*   2567
*Bill, the Galactic Hero: The Final Incoherent
   Adventure* - Harry Harrison   *s*   2568

Bowe-Hawkins, Thomas "Tom"
*Tripoint* - C.J. Cherryh   *s*   1003

Caleb
*PartnerShip* - Anne McCaffrey   *s*   3741

Calvert, Joshua
*Emergence* - Peter F. Hamilton   *s*   2524
*Expansion* - Peter F. Hamilton   *s*   2525

Casey, Paddy
*The Rising* - James Doohan   *s*   1579

Chen, Robert
*Starseed* - Spider Robinson   *s*   4643

Clavius, Black
*Glory* - Alfred Coppel   *s*   1182

Colville, Randall "Ran"
*Starliner* - David Drake   *s*   1645

Cortland, Roger
*Standing Wave* - Howard V. Hendrix   *s*   2661

Crisco, Bungeeman
*Star Wreck 6: Geek Space Nine* - Leah
   Rewolinski   *s*   4562

Dannerman, Jim Daniel "Dan"
*The Other End of Time* - Frederik Pohl   *s*   4351

Danziger
*Earth 2* - Melissa Crandall   *s*   1247

Davis, Kyra
*Harvest of Stars* - Poul Anderson   *s*   127

DeWoe, Dekker
*Mining the Oort* - Frederik Pohl   *s*   4349

Enderton, Paddy
*Godspeed* - Charles Sheffield   *s*   4957

Everett, Matt
*Article 23* - William R. Forstchen   *s*   1978

Eye on Sky
*Anvil of Stars* - Greg Bear   *s*   414

Fath, Jaro
*Night Lamp* - Jack Vance   *s*   5548

Ferrol, Chayne
*Warhorse* - Timothy Zahn   *s*   6056

Forister
*PartnerShip* - Anne McCaffrey   *s*   3741

Foyle, Gulliver "Gully"
*The Stars My Destination* - Alfred Bester   *s*   478

Freetz, Jhoe
*Flies From the Amber* - Wil McCarthy   *s*   3763

Fundan, Dane
*The Founder* - Christopher Rowley   *s*   4696

Gatineau, Robert
*The Middle of Nowhere* - David Gerrold   *s*   2209

Gift, Sebastian "Nifty"
*Berserker Fury* - Fred Saberhagen   *s*   4760

Gioglie III, Declan "Gill"
*Acorna* - Anne McCaffrey   *s*   3717

**Gordon, Martin "Marty"**
*Anvil of Stars* - Greg Bear   s   414

**Graham, Jason "Jase"**
*Inheritor* - C.J. Cherryh   s   997

**Gregory, Joe-Jim**
*Silent Thunder/Universe* - Dean Ing   s   2829

**Greystoke, David**
*Ocean under the Ice* - Robert L. Forward   s   1988

**Hahn**
*Collidescope* - Grace Chetwin   s   1011

**Hakoni, Kyosti Bitterleaf**
*Revolution's Shore* - Alis A. Rasmussen   s   4484

**Hap, Channa**
*The City Who Fought* - Anne McCaffrey   s   3722

**Hara, Jay**
*Godspeed* - Charles Sheffield   s   4957

**Hathaway**
*The Martian Chronicles* - Ray Bradbury   s   621

**Hawkins, Ethan**
*Mutant Star* - Karen Haber   s   2475

**Hawthorn, Ariel**
*Anvil of Stars* - Greg Bear   s   414

**Heredes, Lilyaka Ash**
*Revolution's Shore* - Alis A. Rasmussen   s   4484

**Holly, Wanda**
*Starliner* - David Drake   s   1645

**Hoyland, Hugh**
*Silent Thunder/Universe* - Dean Ing   s   2829

**Hunter, Homer**
*Stationfall* - Arthur Byron Cover   s   1216

**Iger**
*The War Minstrels* - Karen Haber   s   2477

**Jo**
*Eggheads* - Emily Devenport   s   1500

**Joli-Chanteu, Alexander**
*The Ship Who Searched* - Anne McCaffrey   s   3749

**Jordan, John James**
*Project Farcry* - Pauline Ashwell   s   230

**Joshim**
*A Matter of Oaths* - Helen S. Wright   s   5985

**kai Ortega, Maeru "Kai"**
*Alpha Centauri* - William Barton   s   378

**Keff**
*The Ship Errant* - Jody Lynn Nye   s   4175

**Kilgour, Alex**
*Revenge of the Damned* - Allan Cole   s   1107

**Kirk, George Samuel**
*Best Destiny* - Diane Carey   s   900

**Klemay, Keff**
*The Ship Who Won* - Anne McCaffrey   s   3750

**Kraft, Jason**
*Redshift Rendezvous* - John E. Stith   s   5305

**Kreider, Tomus**
*Flies From the Amber* - Wil McCarthy   s   3763

**Krim**
*The Hidden War* - Michael Armstrong   s   209

**Lazarian, Ramou**
*A Company of Stars* - Christopher Stasheff   s   5215
*We Open on Venus* - Christopher Stasheff   s   5227

**Lennart**
*Jaydium* - Deborah Wheeler   s   5774

**Lister, David**
*Better than Life* - Grant Naylor   s   4076
*Red Dwarf: Infinity Welcomes Careful Drivers* - Grant
   Naylor   s   4077

**Lot**
*Vast* - Linda Nagata   s   4067

**Lujan, Derek**
*Children of the Earth* - Catherine Wells   s   5743

**Lukas, Greg**
*Mind Light* - Margaret Davis   s   1407
*Minds Apart* - Margaret Davis   s   1408

**Lyon, Rojer**
*Lyon's Pride* - Anne McCaffrey   s   3738

**MacDonald, Mercy**
*Stopping at Slowyear* - Frederik Pohl   s   4355

**Malone, Patrick**
*Alien Tongue* - Stephen Leigh   s   3424

**McAndrews, Arthur Morton**
*One Man's Universe* - Charles Sheffield   s   4961

**McCall, Dante**
*Songs of Chaos* - S.N. Lewitt   s   3452

**McCoy, Leonard**
*Vulcan's Forge* - Susan Shwartz   s   5019

**McDonald**
*Cat's Gambit* - Leslie Gadallah   s   2099

**Metaxos, Diego**
*Powers That Be* - Anne McCaffrey   s   3745

**Morales, Daire**
*Lethe* - Tricia Sullivan   s   5354

**Morgen**
*Mad Roy's Light* - Paula King   s   3125

**Morrison, Troy**
*Dream-Weaver* - Louise Lawrence   s   3359

**Muncie, Lance**
*The Trikon Deception* - Ben Bova   s   597

**Nevsky, Peter**
*Peter Nevsky and the True Story of the Russian Moon
   Landing* - John Calvin Batchelor   s   388

**Operative 41**
*The Salukan Gambit* - Sean Dalton   s   1333

**Oryolin, Alexander**
*Peter Nevsky and the True Story of the Russian Moon
   Landing* - John Calvin Batchelor   s   388

**Palaton**
*Path of Fire* - Charles Ingrid   s   2832

**Parnell, Eugene M.**
*The Tranquility Alternative* - Allen Steele   s   5248

**Pirelli, Vince**
*Warlords of Jupiter* - William H. Keith Jr.   s   3036

**Putakin, Yuri**
*Orion's Dagger* - P.K. McAllister   s   3708

**Quinn, Jimmy**
*The Sparrow* - Mary Doria Russell   s   4736

**Raeder, Peter**
*The Rising* - James Doohan   s   1579

**Rafe**
*A Matter of Oaths* - Helen S. Wright   s   5985

**Ragem, Paul**
*Beholder's Eye* - Julie E. Czerneda   s   1303

**Ramey**
*Rimrunners* - C.J. Cherryh   s   1001

**Ransome, Errec**
*The Gathering Flame* - Debra Doyle   s   1599

**Ransome, Lilyaka**
*A Passage of Stars* - Alis A. Rasmussen   s   4482

**Rarberticandornan, "Ar"**
*Dragons in the Stars* - Jeffrey A. Carver   s   930

**Rebello, Joseph "Joe" Z.**
*In the Wrong Hands* - Edward Gibson   s   2215

**Renna**
*Glory Season* - David Brin   s   686

**Ricimer, Piet**
*Igniting the Reaches* - David Drake   s   1633
*Through the Breach* - David Drake   s   1647

**Riddell, Lester**
*Lunar Descent* - Allen Steele   s   5245

**Rimmer, Arnold J.**
*Red Dwarf: Infinity Welcomes Careful Drivers* - Grant
   Naylor   s   4077

**Roarke, Jason**
*Flare Star* - Paula E. Downing   s   1594

**Rossman, Aaron**
*Golden Fleece* - Robert J. Sawyer   s   4857

**Ryder, Gunther "Gun"**
*Pirates of the Universe* - Terry Bisson   s   506

**Saint-Just, Emile**
*Blind Justice* - S.N. Lewitt   s   3448

**Sasaki, Jay**
*Starmind* - Spider Robinson   s   4642

**Shannon, Rip**
*A Mind for Trade* - Andre Norton   s   4158

**Sheridan, John**
*The Touch of Your Shadow, the Whisper of Your Name*
   - Neal Barrett Jr.   s   367

**South, Joe**
*The Stalk* - Janet Morris   s   4016
*Threshold* - Janet Morris   s   4018
*Trust Territory* - Janet Morris   s   4019

**Stanton, Karl**
*Reckoning Infinity* - John E. Stith   s   5304

**Starbuck**
*Armageddon* - Richard Hatch   s   2602

**Stranger, John**
*High Steel* - Jack C. Haldeman II   s   2486

**Succorso, Nick**
*Forbidden Knowledge* - Stephen R
   Donaldson   s   1571
*The Gap into Madness: Chaos and Order* - Stephen R.
   Donaldson   s   1573

**Takagama, Brund**
*A Darker Geometry* - Mark O. Martin   s   3649

**Thorson, Dane**
*Derelict for Trade* - Andre Norton   s   4148
*A Mind for Trade* - Andre Norton   s   4158

**Tyre, Philip**
*Challenger's Hope* - David Feintuch   s   1899

**Urban**
*Vast* - Linda Nagata   s   4067

**Vorlund, Krip**
*Dare to Go A-Hunting* - Andre Norton   s   4147

**Vosnesensky, Mikhail Andreivitch**
*Mars* - Ben Bova   s   586

**Young, "Mighty" Joe**
*Lunar Descent* - Allen Steele   s   5245

**Zhukovsky, Dmitry**
*Peter Nevsky and the True Story of the Russian Moon
   Landing* - John Calvin Batchelor   s   388

**Zigmunn**
*Brotherhood of the Stars* - Kirby Greene   s   2414

**Zolotin, Peter**
*Burster* - Michael Capobianco   s   876

## SPACESHIP CAPTAIN

**Aguilar, Ricardo**
*Starfarers* - Poul Anderson   s   133

**Allaird, Clarence Engels "Clancy"**
*Arrow From Earth* - F.M. Busby  s  782

**Andreos, Leonidas**
*Siduri's Net* - P.K. McAllister  s  3709

**Aoibhell, Brendan**
*The Deer's Cry: A Book of the Keltiad* - Patricia
   Kennealy-Morrison  f  3060

**Atle**
*Silent Songs* - A.C. Crispin  s  1264

**Bartlett, Jennan**
*Mad Roy's Light* - Paula King  s  3125

**Bateson, Morgan**
*Ship of the Line* - Diane Carey  s  904

**Bishop, Killeen**
*Furious Gulf* - Gregory Benford  s  447

**Bowe, Austin**
*Tripoint* - C.J. Cherryh  s  1003

**Brim, Wilf**
*The Defenders* - Bill Baldwin  s  309
*The Mercenaries* - Bill Baldwin  s  311

**Calhoun, Forrest**
*Rogue Star* - Michael Flynn  s  1965

**Calhoun, Mackenzie**
*End Game* - Peter David  s  1382

**Calvert, Joshua**
*Consolidation* - Peter F. Hamilton  s  2523

**Canby, Gordon**
*Canby's Legion* - Bill Baldwin  s  308

**Cantrell, Loren**
*Ground-Ties* - Jane S. Fancher  s  1861
*Harmonies of the 'Net* - Jane S. Fancher  s  1862

**Carrasco, Solomon**
*The Artifact* - W. Michael Gear  s  2165

**Cavanagh, Pheylan**
*Conqueror's Pride* - Timothy Zahn  s  6051

**Chanur, Hilfy**
*Chanur's Legacy* - C.J. Cherryh  s  981

**Chin, Gun Roh**
*The Ninety Trillion Fausts* - Jack L. Chalker  s  958

**Christian, Karl**
*The Starlight Crystal* - Christopher Pike  s  4333

**Crusher, Beverly**
*All Good Things. . .* - Michael Jan Friedman  s  2061

**Crusher, Jack**
*Q-Squared* - Peter David  s  1385

**Degahv, Rieka**
*Earth Herald* - Jan Clark  s  1046
*Prodigy* - Jan Clark  s  1047

**DeWellesthar, Auglaise "Dancer"**
*Dancer of the Sixth* - Michelle Shirey
   Crean  s  1254

**d'jehn, Tahl**
*The Alien Dark* - Diana G. Gallagher  s  2108

**Dominque, Nyota**
*Saturn's Child* - Nichelle Nichols  s  4101

**Doorman, Lissea**
*The Voyage* - David Drake  s  1649

**Drake, Cadence "Cady"**
*Hunting the Corrigan's Blood* - Holly Lisle  s  3484

**du Cheyne, Gaetan**
*Acts of Conscience* - William Barton  s  377

**elan Emok, Stuk**
*Half-Light* - Denise Vitola  s  5575

**Estriss**
*The Radiant Dragon* - Elaine Cunningham  f  1291

**Fairouz**
*The Missing Matter* - Thomas R.
   McDonough  s  3805

**Falstaff, Raymond**
*Border Dispute* - Daniel R. Kerns  s  3066

**Faulk, Carol**
*A Darker Geometry* - Mark O. Martin  s  3649

**Gen-93-Beta, John**
*Alien Earth* - Megan Lindholm  s  3469

**Gowdy, Samuel "Sam" Hall**
*The Triad Worlds* - F.M. Busby  s  786

**Greenberg, Bernard**
*Earthgrip* - Harry Turtledove  s  5499

**Griffiths, Jeremy**
*Nightsword* - Margaret Weis  f  5722
*Sentinels* - Margaret Weis  s  5725

**Grzzeearoghh "Grizz"**
*Treaty at Doona* - Anne McCaffrey  s  3752

**Hardesty**
*Voyage of the Star Wolf* - David Gerrold  s  2212

**Hawken, Jos**
*Yamato: A Rage in Heaven* - Ken Kato  s  3014

**Hayden, Conek**
*Backblast* - Lee McKeone  s  3828
*The Clone Crisis* - Lee McKeone  s  3829
*Starfire Down* - Lee McKeone  s  3830

**Icor, Gella**
*Starfire Down* - Lee McKeone  s  3830

**Indiw**
*Border Dispute* - Daniel R. Kerns  s  3066

**Janeway, Kathryn**
*Chrysalis* - David Niall Wilson  s  5880
*The Escape* - Dean Wesley Smith  s  5113
*The Final Fury* - Dafydd ab Hugh  s  9
*Her Klingon Soul* - Michael Jan Friedman  s  2064
*Mosaic* - Jeri Taylor  s  5403
*Ragnarok* - Nathan Archer  s  206

**Janusz, Pov**
*Maia's Veil* - P.K. McAllister  s  3707
*Orion's Dagger* - P.K. McAllister  s  3708
*Siduri's Net* - P.K. McAllister  s  3709

**Jellico, Miceal**
*Redline the Stars* - Andre Norton  s  4160

**Jenkins, Peter**
*Limbo System* - Rick Cook  s  1158

**Jo-lac**
*Prisoner of Dreams* - Karen Ripley  s  4593

**Jo-Lac**
*The Tenth Class* - Karen Ripley  s  4594

**Jones, Virginia "Jinjur"**
*Marooned on Eden* - Robert L. Forward  s  1986
*Ocean under the Ice* - Robert L. Forward  s  1988
*Return to Rocheworld* - Robert L. Forward  s  1989
*Rocheworld* - Robert L. Forward  s  1990

**Jones, Walter Tai-Ching**
*Homecoming* - David Alexander Smith  s  5108

**Judson, Marl**
*Judson's Eden* - Keith Laumer  s  3344

**Jute, Tabitha**
*Mother of Plenty* - Colin Greenland  s  2417
*Seasons of Plenty* - Colin Greenland  s  2418
*Take Back Plenty* - Colin Greenland  s  2419

**Kenmuir, Ian**
*The Stars Are Also Fire* - Poul Anderson  s  134

**Kenner, Erin Elizabeth**
*Mother Lode* - Zach Hughes  s  2812

**Killeen**
*Tides of Light* - Gregory Benford  s  450

**Kimberlin, Elwyn**
*The Tides of God* - Ted Reynolds  s  4567

**Kirk, James T.**
*The Ashes of Eden* - William Shatner  s  4927
*Assignment: Eternity* - Greg Cox  s  1225
*Avenger* - William Shatner  s  4928
*The City on the Edge of Forever* - Harlan
   Ellison  s  1784
*The Disinherited* - Peter David  s  1381
*Doctor's Orders* - Diane Duane  s  1659
*Enemy Unseen* - V.E. Mitchell  s  3918
*The Fearful Summons* - Denny Martin Flinn  s  1954
*Federation* - Judith Reeves-Stevens  s  4511
*First Frontier* - Diane Carey  s  902
*First Strike* - Diane Carey  s  903
*A Flag Full of Stars* - Brad Ferguson  s  1922
*The Joy Machine* - James Gunn  s  2458
*The Kobayashi Maru* - Julia Ecklar  s  1728
*Mind Meld* - John Vornholt  s  5596
*Prime Directive* - Judith Reeves-Stevens  s  4514
*Probe* - Margaret Wander Bonanno  s  569
*Renegade* - Gene DeWeese  s  1511
*The Return* - William Shatner  s  4933
*The Rift* - Peter David  s  1386
*Rules of Engagement* - Peter Morwood  s  4037
*Sanctuary* - John Vornholt  s  5597
*Spectre* - William Shatner  s  4934
*Star Trek VI: The Undiscovered Country* - J.M.
   Dillard  s  1556
*Star Trek: The Classic Episodes 1* - James
   Blish  s  526
*Star Trek: The Classic Episodes 2* - James
   Blish  s  527
*Star Trek: The Classic Episodes 3* - James
   Blish  s  528
*Star Trek: The Lost Years* - J.M. Dillard  s  1557
*Starfleet Academy* - Diane Carey  s  905
*Traitor Winds* - L.A. Graf  s  2298
*War Dragons* - L.A. Graf  s  2299
*Windows on a Lost World* - V.E. Mitchell  s  3920

**Kirov, Natasha Alyosha Katerina**
*Voyage to the Red Planet* - Terry Bisson  s  508

**K'Kai**
*Wing Commander: Freedom Flight* - Mercedes
   Lackey  s  3307

**Kobir, Nikolai**
*Canby's Legion* - Bill Baldwin  s  308

**Korie, Jonathan Thomas**
*The Middle of Nowhere* - David Gerrold  s  2209

**Kr, Duncan**
*Glory's People* - Alfred Coppel  s  1183
*Glory's War* - Alfred Coppel  s  1184

**Krake, Francis**
*The Singers of Time* - Frederik Pohl  s  4354

**Krecis**
*Saturn's Child* - Nichelle Nichols  s  4101

**Kusaka, Michael**
*The Dark Beyond the Stars* - Frank M.
   Robinson  s  4626

**Lando, Pik**
*Drifter* - William C. Dietz  s  1543
*Drifter's Run* - William C. Dietz  s  1544
*Drifter's War* - William C. Dietz  s  1545

**Lastwell, Franklin**
*Life Form* - Alan Dean Foster  s  2008

**Liddell, Rose**
*The Painful Field* - Roland J. Green  s  2351
*Squadron Alert* - Roland J. Green  s  2352
*The Sum of Things* - Roland J. Green  s  2353

**Linn-Campbell, Neena**
*A Covenant of Justice* - David Gerrold  s  2207

**MacIntyre, Colin**
*The Armageddon Inheritance* - David Weber   s   5668
*Heirs of Empire* - David Weber   s   5672
*Mutineers' Moon* - David Weber   s   5677

**MacKenzie, Ian S.**
*Outbanker* - Timothy A. Madden   s   3603

**Maldari**
*The Fearful Summons* - Denny Martin Flinn   s   1954

**Mallory, Signy**
*Downbelow Station* - C.J. Cherryh   s   985

**Marceau, Yves**
*Flare Star* - Paula E. Downing   s   1594

**Marteen, Triscoe**
*Prodigy* - Jan Clark   s   1047

**May, James**
*Desperate Measures* - Joe Clifford Faust   s   1891
*Precious Cargo* - Joe Clifford Faust   s   1893

**McAlois, Lois**
*Tower of the Gods* - Thomas A. Easton   s   1726
*Woodsman* - Thomas A. Easton   s   1727

**McCade, Sam**
*McCade's Bounty* - William C. Dietz   s   1550

**Metadi, Beka Rosselin**
*The Price of the Stars* - Debra Doyle   s   1604

**Metadi, Jos**
*The Gathering Flame* - Debra Doyle   s   1599

**Mogurn, Deuteronomous**
*Dragons in the Stars* - Jeffrey A. Carver   s   930

**Moore, Teldin**
*The Ultimate Helm* - Russ T. Howard   f   2785

**Morgan, Jason**
*A Thousand Words for Stranger* - Julie E. Czerneda   s   1304

**Morgan, Rod**
*Saturn Rukh* - Robert L. Forward   s   1991

**Morgen**
*Reunion* - Michael Jan Friedman   s   2068

**Nafai**
*Earthfall* - Orson Scott Card   s   885

**Ng, Margot O'Reilly**
*Ruler of Naught* - Sherwood Smith   s   5141

**Nicol, Jesse**
*Harvest the Fire* - Poul Anderson   s   128

**nu-Aten, Ha'riel**
*Smoke and Mirrors* - Jane M. Lindskold   s   3476

**O'Malley, Wolf**
*White Light* - William Barton   s   384

**Pak, So**
*The Bushido Incident* - Betty Anne Crawford   s   1248

**Picard, Jean-Luc**
*All Good Things. . .* - Michael Jan Friedman   s   2061
*Avenger* - William Shatner   s   4928
*Balance of Power* - Dafydd ab Hugh   s   7
*A Call to Darkness* - Michael Jan Friedman   s   2062
*Chains of Command* - Bill McCay   s   3767
*Crossover* - Michael Jan Friedman   s   2063
*Dark Mirror* - Diane Duane   s   1658
*Debtors' Planet* - William R. Thompson   s   5457
*The Devil's Heart* - Carmen Carter   s   922
*Dragon's Honor* - Kij Johnson   s   2922
*Federation* - Judith Reeves-Stevens   s   4511
*Guises of the Mind* - Rebecca Neason   s   4081
*Insurrection* - J.M. Dillard   s   1554
*Intellivore* - Diane Duane   s   1663
*Kahless* - Michael Jan Friedman   s   2065
*The Last Stand* - Brad Ferguson   s   1923
*Q-in-Law* - Peter David   s   1384
*Q-Space* - Greg Cox   s   1228

*Q-Squared* - Peter David   s   1385
*Q-Zone* - Greg Cox   s   1229
*Relics* - Michael Jan Friedman   s   2066
*Requiem* - Michael Jan Friedman   s   2067
*The Return* - William Shatner   s   4933
*Reunion* - Michael Jan Friedman   s   2068
*Ship of the Line* - Diane Carey   s   904
*The Soldiers of Fear* - Dean Wesley Smith   s   5115
*Spectre* - William Shatner   s   4934
*Vendetta* - Peter David   s   1389

**Pickhard, Jean-Alex**
*Treks Not Taken: What if Stephen King, Anne Rice, Bret Easton Ellis, and Other Literary Greats Had Written Episodes of Star Trek: The Next Generation?* - Steven R. Boyett   s   607

**Pike, Christopher**
*The Rift* - Peter David   s   1386

**Prowl Captain**
*A Darker Geometry* - Mark O. Martin   s   3649

**Qing-an, Virginia "Ginny" Vonzel**
*Alpha Centauri* - William Barton   s   378

**Quinn, Rachel**
*Moonfall* - Jack McDevitt   s   3789

**Rallya**
*A Matter of Oaths* - Helen S. Wright   s   5985

**Ransome, Lilyaka**
*The Price of Ransom* - Alis A. Rasmussen   s   4483

**Reese, Frances**
*Double Planet* - John Gribbin   s   2433

**Reille y Sanchez, Estrellita**
*Contact and Commune* - L. Neil Smith   s   5129

**Ricardo, Jean-Lucy**
*Star Wreck II: The Attack of the Jargonites* - Leah Rewolinski   s   4563
*Star Wreck III: Time Warped* - Leah Rewolinski   s   4564
*Star Wreck IV: Live Long and Profit* - Leah Rewolinski   s   4565
*Star Wreck 6: Geek Space Nine* - Leah Rewolinski   s   4562
*Star Wreck: The Generation Gap* - Leah Rewolinski   s   4566

**Rick**
*Bill, the Galactic Hero: On the Planet of Tasteless Pleasure* - Harry Harrison   s   2567

**Riker, Paul Whitfield**
*The Trumpets of Tagan* - Simon Lang   s   3316

**Roman, Haml**
*Warhorse* - Timothy Zahn   s   6056

**Rosselin Metadi, Beka**
*By Honor Betray'd* - Debra Doyle   s   1598
*Starpilot's Grave* - Debra Doyle   s   1606

**St. Cyr, Butterfly**
*Archangel Blues* - eluki bes shahar   s   471
*Darktraders* - eluki bes shahar   s   472
*Hellflower* - eluki bes shahar   s   473

**Sarrault, Elizabeth**
*Blind Justice* - S.N. Lewitt   s   3448

**Sassinak**
*Generation Warrior* - Anne McCaffrey   s   3735
*Sassinak* - Anne McCaffrey   s   3748

**Saxtorph, Eric**
*Inconstant Star* - Poul Anderson   s   129

**Selenkov, Yuri Ivanovich**
*Rinn's Star* - Paula E. Downing   s   1719

**Serrano, Heris**
*Hunting Party* - Elizabeth Moon   s   3968
*Sporting Chance* - Elizabeth Moon   s   3974
*Winning Colors* - Elizabeth Moon   s   3976

**Shaffer, Beowulf**
*Crashlander* - Larry Niven   s   4118

**Simeon-Hap, Joat**
*The Ship Avenged* - S.M. Stirling   s   5298

**Singh, Robert**
*The Hammer of God* - Arthur C. Clarke   s   1057

**Sisko, Benjamin**
*Armageddon Sky* - L.A. Graf   s   2296
*Call to Arms* - Diane Carey   s   901
*Time's Enemy* - L.A. Graf   s   2297
*Vengeance* - Dafydd ab Hugh   s   10

**Smirk, James T.**
*Star Wreck II: The Attack of the Jargonites* - Leah Rewolinski   s   4563
*Star Wreck III: Time Warped* - Leah Rewolinski   s   4564
*Star Wreck IV: Live Long and Profit* - Leah Rewolinski   s   4565
*Star Wreck 6: Geek Space Nine* - Leah Rewolinski   s   4562
*Star Wreck: The Generation Gap* - Leah Rewolinski   s   4566

**Solo, Han**
*Ambush at Corellia* - Roger MacBride Allen   s   76
*Children of the Jedi* - Barbara Hambly   s   2500
*The Courtship of Princess Leia* - Dave Wolverton   s   5950
*Heir to the Empire* - Timothy Zahn   s   6054
*Jedi Search* - Kevin J. Anderson   s   109
*The New Rebellion* - Kristine Kathryn Rusch   s   4719
*The Truce at Bakura* - Kathy Tyers   s   5527

**Spock**
*Vulcan's Forge* - Susan Shwartz   s   5019

**Steiger, Dianne**
*The Ring of Charon* - Roger MacBride Allen   s   80

**Sten**
*Revenge of the Damned* - Allan Cole   s   1107

**Straker, Ellis**
*Yamato: A Rage in Heaven* - Ken Kato   s   3014

**Sulu, Hikaru**
*The Ashes of Eden* - William Shatner   s   4927
*The Fearful Summons* - Denny Martin Flinn   s   1954
*Starfleet Academy* - Diane Carey   s   905
*War Dragons* - L.A. Graf   s   2299

**Susumu, Tocohl**
*Hellspark* - Janet Kagan   s   3000

**sutai-Khornezh, Kasak**
*Rules of Engagement* - Peter Morwood   s   4037

**Swann, Chia**
*Earthfall* - Jerry Earl Brown   s   724

**Taranga, Eugenia**
*Burster* - Michael Capobianco   s   876

**Tarrel, Janus**
*Dreadnought* - Thorarinn Gunnarsson   s   2464

**Thermopyle, Angus**
*The Gap into Madness: Chaos and Order* - Stephen R. Donaldson   s   1573
*The Gap into Power: A Dark and Hungry God Arises* - Stephen R. Donaldson   s   1574
*The Gap into Ruin: This Day All Gods Die* - Stephen R. Donaldson   s   1575

**Thornekan, Roald**
*Down the Stream of Stars* - Jeffrey A. Carver   s   928

**Trask, Grace**
*The Billion Dollar Boy* - Charles Sheffield   s   4948

**Trask, Lana**
*The Billion Dollar Boy* - Charles Sheffield   s   4948

**Tscharka, Gerald**
*The Voices of Heaven* - Frederik Pohl   s   4356

**Tug**
*Alien Earth* - Megan Lindholm   s   3469

**Van Pelt**
*The Eternal Enemy* - Michael Berlyn   s   469

**Velmeran**
*Battle of the Ring* - Thorarinn Gunnarsson   s   2460
*Tactical Error* - Thorarinn Gunnarsson   s   2466

**Vikktakkht**
*Chanur's Legacy* - C.J. Cherryh   s   981

**Wallace, Rollingham Boregard "Rusty"**
*A World Lost* - James B. Johnson   s   2921

**Wallich, Darren**
*Bloom* - Wil McCarthy   s   3761

**Wanker, David L.**
*The Kruton Interface* - John DeChancie   s   1459

**Webster, Daniel**
*Deep Freeze* - Zach Hughes   s   2811

**Wilburfoss, Jon**
*Wulfsyarn: A Mosaic* - Phillip Mann   s   3617

**Wilder**
*The Martian Chronicles* - Ray Bradbury   s   621

**Williams, Jonathan**
*The Martian Chronicles* - Ray Bradbury   s   622

**York, Nathaniel**
*The Martian Chronicles* - Ray Bradbury   s   622

**Zebara**
*The Death of Sleep* - Anne McCaffrey   s   3727

**Zennor**
*First Strike* - Diane Carey   s   903

## SPACEWOMAN

**Adcock, Patrice "Pat"**
*The Other End of Time* - Frederik Pohl   s   4351

**An**
*Eggheads* - Emily Devenport   s   1500

**Benacerraf, Paula**
*Titan* - Stephen Baxter   s   405

**Blaze, Chastity**
*Saturn Rukh* - Robert L. Forward   s   1991

**Bronson, Victoria "Tory"**
*The Sails of Tau Ceti* - Michael McCollum   s   3771

**Carialle**
*The Ship Who Won* - Anne McCaffrey   s   3750

**Claridge, Kit**
*The Sails of Tau Ceti* - Michael McCollum   s   3771

**Cofort, Rael**
*Derelict for Trade* - Andre Norton   s   4148
*Redline the Stars* - Andre Norton   s   4160

**Desmon, Lilah**
*The Cyborg From Earth* - Charles Sheffield   s   4952

**Dikobe, Pauline**
*Foragers* - Charles Oberndorf   s   4187

**Dobbs, Evelyn**
*Fool's War* - Sarah Zettel   s   6079

**Easter, Brandi**
*Standing Wave* - Howard V. Hendrix   s   2661

**Green, Sandra**
*Saturn Rukh* - Robert L. Forward   s   1991

**Guimaraes, Veronica**
*Songs of Chaos* - S.N. Lewitt   s   3452

**Harris, Jenny**
*Expansion* - Peter F. Hamilton   s   2525

**Hawkins, Marie**
*Tripoint* - C.J. Cherryh   s   1003

**Hutchins, Priscilla "Hutch"**
*The Engines of God* - Jack McDevitt   s   3787

**Ivanova, Susan**
*The Touch of Your Shadow, the Whisper of Your Name*
  - Neal Barrett Jr.   s   367

**Jansky, Thalia**
*White Light* - William Barton   s   384

**Janusz, Ekaterina "Kate" Marya**
*Maia's Veil* - P.K. McAllister   s   3707

**Kozel, Dina**
*Siduri's Net* - P.K. McAllister   s   3709

**Le Roux, Reiki Momoku**
*Marooned on Eden* - Robert L. Forward   s   1986

**LeBrae, Jael**
*Dragons in the Stars* - Jeffrey A. Carver   s   930

**Lightner, Sydnie "Charel Secour"**
*The Triad Worlds* - F.M. Busby   s   786

**Lindquist, Anna Catarina**
*The VMR Theory* - Robert Frezza   s   2055

**Lioe, Quin**
*Burning Bright* - Melissa Scott   s   4894

**Liss, Trojan nine zero eight**
*Rainbow Man* - M.J. Engh   s   1824

**Macintosh, Elizabeth**
*Rediscovery: A Novel of Darkover* - Marion Zimmer
  Bradley   s   643

**Murchison**
*The Galactic Gourmet* - James White   s   5778

**Nussem, Alis Mary**
*Reckoning Infinity* - John E. Stith   s   5304

**Ohasi, Juko**
*The Dazzle of Day* - Molly Gloss   s   2243

**Porlock, Leona**
*Rainbow Man* - M.J. Engh   s   1824

**Portaris, Anne**
*Arrow From Earth* - F.M. Busby   s   782

**Quinn, Rachel**
*Moonfall* - Jack McDevitt   s   3789

**Robbins, Cynthia**
*The Rising* - James Doohan   s   1579

**Rogers, Troi**
*Treks Not Taken: What if Stephen King, Anne Rice,*
  *Bret Easton Ellis, and Other Literary Greats Had*
  *Written Episodes of Star Trek: The Next*
  *Generation?* - Steven R. Boyett   s   607

**Selenko, Avi**
*Maia's Veil* - P.K. McAllister   s   3707

**Serrano**
*Once a Hero* - Elizabeth Moon   s   3970

**Sirkin**
*Sporting Chance* - Elizabeth Moon   s   3974

**Stone, Julie**
*The Infinite Sea* - Jeffrey A. Carver   s   932

**Suiza, Esmay**
*Once a Hero* - Elizabeth Moon   s   3970

**Svensdotter, Esther "Star"**
*Red Planet Run* - Dana Stabenow   s   5187

**Tamura, Eiko**
*Harvest of Stars* - Poul Anderson   s   127

**Taylor, Nugan**
*Genetic Soldier* - George Turner   s   5492

**Trask, Jovanna**
*Warlords of Jupiter* - William H. Keith Jr.   s   3036

**Voss, Natalie**
*Where the Ships Die* - William C. Dietz   s   1553

**Yeager, Elizabeth**
*Rimrunners* - C.J. Cherryh   s   1001

## SPINSTER

**Borden, Emma**
*Lizzie Borden* - Elizabeth Engstrom   h   1826

## SPIRIT

**Aguilana, Haros**
*King of the Grey* - Richard A. Knaak   f   3173

**Alliar**
*A Strange and Ancient Name* - Josepha
  Sherman   f   4991

**Anne**
*The Time Tree* - Enid Richemont   f   4585

**Arbuthnot, Farquhar**
*Strong Spirits* - Elisa DeCarlo   f   1451

**Balyet**
*Balyet* - Patricia Wrightson   f   5995

**Bat, Charlie**
*Missing Angel Juan* - Francesca Lia Block   f   550

**Bessledorf, Jonathon**
*Bernie and the Bessledorf Ghost* - Phyllis Reynolds
  Naylor   f   4078

**Bilbo, Charlie**
*Charlie's Bones* - L.L. Thrasher   h   5468

**Boofuls**
*Mirror* - Graham Masterton   h   3677

**Bouchette, Jean-Paul**
*The Suiting* - Kelley Wilde   h   5803

**Broken Echo**
*Spirit Crossings* - Claudia Peck   f   4275

**Caitria**
*The Deepest Sea* - Charles Barnitz   f   363

**Candace**
*The Seventh Heart* - Marina Fitch   f   1943

**Cantrell, Boone**
*Spirit Catcher* - Elizabeth Hallam   f   2497

**Carlton, Billy**
*Cemetery of Angels* - Noel Hynd   h   2821

**Carter, Ellie**
*The Wishing Well* - Charles de Lint   f   1441

**Chernevog, Kavi**
*Yvgenie* - C.J. Cherryh   f   1005

**Clarkston, Rachel**
*Waltz with Evil* - P.D. Rozzi   h   4701

**Crane, Scott**
*Earthquake Weather* - Tim Powers   f   4382

**Darffot, Tex "Bear"**
*Tex and Molly in the Afterlife* - Richard
  Grant   f   2327

**Death**
*Kindred Rites* - Katharine Eliska Kimbriel   f   3118

**Delaney, Sylvie**
*Homebody* - Orson Scott Card   h   890

**Ensi**
*The Glaive* - Cary Osborne   s   4227

**Ghost**
*The Time of the Ghost* - Diana Wynne
  Jones   f   2951

**Grace, Peter**
*The Parasite* - Ramsey Campbell   h   863

**Great Chaffalo**
*The Midnight Horse* - Sid Fleischman   *f*   1948

**Green, Antony**
*Aunt Maria* - Diana Wynne Jones   *f*   2943

**Harrison, Benjamin**
*The Smithsonian Institution* - Gore Vidal   *f*   5570

**Hightower, Fabian**
*Possession* - Peter James   *h*   2873

**Holmes, Shadrach**
*Double Trouble Squared* - Kathryn Lasky   *f*   3340

**Jade**
*Familiar Spirit* - Lisa Tuttle   *h*   5519

**Jim**
*Agyar* - Steven Brust   *f*   738

**Jolie**
*And Eternity* - Piers Anthony   *f*   162

**Kregler, Timothy**
*The Land of Nod* - Mark A. Clements   *h*   1085

**Lara**
*The Shadow Eater* - Adam Lee   *f*   3386

**Lincoln, Abraham**
*The Smithsonian Institution* - Gore Vidal   *f*   5570

**Lissette**
*Cursed Be the Child* - Mort Castle   *h*   937

**Louise, Zoe**
*Stonewords: A Ghost Story* - Pam Conrad   *f*   1138

**Malloy, D'Arcy**
*Second Child* - John Saul   *h*   4844

**Mama Yaya**
*I, Tituba, Black Witch of Salem* - Maryse Conde   *f*   1130

**Maybelle**
*The Witch House* - Norma Tadlock Johnson   *f*   2923

**Miranda, Carmen**
*Carmen Miranda's Ghost Is Haunting Space Station Three* - Don Sakers   *s*   4785

**Mogget**
*Sabriel* - Garth Nix   *f*   4129

**Molly**
*Tex and Molly in the Afterlife* - Richard Grant   *f*   2327

**Monet, Claude**
*Monet's Ghost* - Chelsea Quinn Yarbro   *f*   6017

**O'Neill, Marcus Quilligan**
*I Met a Man Who Wasn't There* - Mary R. Callaghan   *h*   840

**Orlene**
*And Eternity* - Piers Anthony   *f*   162

**Pascale**
*The Ghost Inside the Monitor* - Margaret J. Anderson   *f*   122

**Patience**
*A Witch Across Time* - Gilbert B. Cross   *f*   1272

**Peregrine**
*The Thread That Binds the Bones* - Nina Kiriki Hoffman   *f*   2717

**Picket**
*Darwinia* - Robert Charles Wilson   *s*   5906

**Queenie**
*The Influence* - Ramsey Campbell   *h*   857

**Ransome, Errec**
*The Long Hunt* - Debra Doyle   *s*   1602

**Raynor, Sara**
*Darkling* - Michael O'Rourke   *h*   4223

**Rohr, Gail**
*The Land of Nod* - Mark A. Clements   *h*   1085

**Rowan, Jack**
*Dead Lines* - John Skipp   *h*   5082

**Scathach**
*The Scathach and the Maeve's Daughter* - Mary Alexander Walker   *f*   5618

**Scott, Walter**
*Picking the Ballad's Bones* - Elizabeth Ann Scarborough   *f*   4869

**Scrooge, Ebenezer**
*Carol for Another Christmas* - Elizabeth Ann Scarborough   *f*   4861

**Seth, Nguyen**
*Demon Download* - Jack Yeovil   *f*   6021

**Skibelski, Chaim**
*A Blessing on the Moon* - Joseph Skibell   *f*   5079

**Smith, Joseph**
*The Ghost of the Revelator* - L.E. Modesitt Jr.   *s*   3931

**Stanovich, Martin Philip**
*Ghost Boy* - Jean Simon   *h*   5064

**Steadford, Sir Harry**
*The Meddlesome Ghost* - Sheila Rosalynd Allen   *f*   84

**Stefanovsky, Stephan**
*Violin* - Anne Rice   *h*   4579

**Tuggle**
*The Witch's Eye* - Phyllis Reynolds Naylor   *f*   4080

**Vivian**
*Black Snow Days* - Claudia O'Keefe   *s*   4205

**Walford, John**
*Walford's Oak* - Jill M. Phillips   *f*   4310

**Wyatt, Adam**
*Superstition* - David Ambrose   *h*   90

**Yang**
*Unicorn U.* - Esther Friesner   *f*   2084

## SPORTS FIGURE

**Angel**
*Damnbanna* - Nancy Springer   *f*   5177

**Asakeiri, Adline**
*The Watcher's Mask* - Laurie J. Marks   *f*   3627

**Boles, Danny**
*Brittle Innings* - Michael Bishop   *h*   498

**Briggs, Timothy**
*Hence* - Brad Leithauser   *s*   3431

**Clerval, Henry**
*Brittle Innings* - Michael Bishop   *h*   498

**David**
*Gameplay* - Kevin J. Anderson   *f*   105
*Game's End* - Kevin J. Anderson   *f*   104

**Doyle, Irini**
*The Sweetheart Season* - Karen Joy Fowler   *f*   2029

**Drake, Tannim**
*Chrome Circle* - Mercedes Lackey   *f*   3277

**El Gran Mojado**
*Tropic of Orange* - Karen Tei Yamashita   *f*   6009

**Freemark, Nest**
*A Knight of the Word* - Terry Brooks   *f*   714

**Goon**
*Goon* - Edward Lee   *h*   3392

**Greene, Harris**
*Doc Sidhe* - Aaron Allston   *f*   85

**Gurgeh, Jernau**
*The Player of Games* - Iain M. Banks   *s*   326

**Haas, Peter**
*Memento Mori* - Shariann Lewitt   *s*   3454

**Halloway, Bobby**
*Fear Nothing* - Dean R. Koontz   *h*   3207

**Hoey, Buck**
*Brittle Innings* - Michael Bishop   *h*   498

**Knight, Aubrey**
*Gorgon Child* - Steven Barnes   *s*   361

**Lily**
*Ecstasia* - Francesca Lia Block   *f*   547

**Major, Cyrus "Cy" Lance**
*Zeus and Co.* - David Lee Jones   *f*   2942

**Melanie**
*Gameplay* - Kevin J. Anderson   *f*   105
*Game's End* - Kevin J. Anderson   *f*   104

**Parmenion**
*Lion of Macedon* - David Gemmell   *f*   2189

**Sands, Max**
*The Barsoom Project* - Larry Niven   *s*   4115

**Seavers, Kim**
*Beamriders!* - Martin Caidin   *s*   824

**Shomer, Jillian**
*Achilles' Choice* - Larry Niven   *s*   4114

**Silk, Venture**
*Spindoc* - Steve Perry   *s*   4300

**Sonnenberg, Bryce**
*The Ganymede Club* - Charles Sheffield   *s*   4955

**Tanner, Mark**
*Creature* - John Saul   *h*   4839

## SPOUSE

**Adair, Hugh**
*Breeder* - Douglas Clegg   *h*   1076

**Addams, Morticia**
*Addams Family Values* - Todd Strasser   *f*   5324

**Banner, Elizabeth "Betty Tanner"**
*What Savage Beast* - Peter David   *s*   1390

**Barton, Alex**
*The Circus of the Earth and Air* - Brooke Stevens   *f*   5264

**Bednacort, Loria**
*Destiny's Road* - Larry Niven   *s*   4119

**Bellman, Effie**
*The House That Jack Built* - Graham Masterton   *h*   3675

**Bellman, Kim**
*The Printer's Devil* - Chico Kidd   *f*   3099

**Bird, Marianne**
*Tap, Tap* - David Martin   *h*   3640

**Bonney, Isabel "Iz"**
*Elvissey* - Jack Womack   *s*   5957

**Bonney, John**
*Elvissey* - Jack Womack   *s*   5957

**Brady, Julia**
*The Gallery of His Dreams* - Kristine Kathryn Rusch   *f*   4717

**Carpenter, Rebecca**
*Dark Fortune* - Richard Lee Byers   *h*   795

**Casaubon**
*The Architecture of Desire* - Mary Gentle   *f*   2195

**Cedar, Janice**
*Fossil* - Hal Clement   *s*   1083

**Claus, Anya**
*Santa Steps Out: A Fairy Tale for Grownups* - Robert Devereaux   *h*   1506

**Cooper, Ellen**
*Earthbound* - Richard Matheson   *h*   3684

**Cortez, Rosita "Rose" Carmelita**
*Timemaster* - Robert L. Forward  s  1992

**Curtis, Richard**
*Dreamer* - Peter James  h  2871

**Dalton, Tom**
*Watchers in the Woods* - William W.
Johnstone  h  2936

**Dartmuth, Darcie**
*Dominion's Reach* - Diann Thornley  s  5465

**Defoe, Piper**
*Storytellers* - Julie Anne Parks  h  4249

**Doreen**
*Flickering Shadows* - Kwadwo Agymah
Kamau  f  3006

**Duke, Cindy**
*The Wild* - Whitley Strieber  h  5343

**Eckert, Angie**
*The Dragon and the Gnarly King* - Gordon R.
Dickson  f  1529

**Edith of Shaftsbury**
*Lord of Sunset* - Parke Godwin  f  2246

**Eichord, Donna**
*Iceman* - Rex Miller  h  3900

**Elizabeth**
*The Secret Life of Laszlo, Count Dracula* - Roderick
Anscombe  h  152

**Elspeth**
*Thomas the Rhymer* - Ellen Kushner  f  3265

**Elvis**
*The Man in the Moon Must Die* - Jeff
Bredenberg  s  665

**Fiona**
*Ronin* - D.A. Heeley  f  2639

**Francine**
*Lord Conrad's Lady* - Leo Frankowski  s  2046

**Gail**
*Nobody's Son* - Sean Stewart  f  5275

**Glivven, Miranda**
*Cat's Paw* - L.A. Taylor  f  5409

**Gold, Michael "Mike"**
*Unquenchable Fire* - Rachel Pollack  f  4361

**Guenevere**
*The Camelot Chronicles* - Mike Ashley  f  224
*Witch of the North* - Courtway Jones  f  2940

**Gwenhwyfar**
*Pendragon's Banner* - Helen Hollick  f  2746

**Harootunian, Geoffrey "Hoot"**
*Larque on the Wing* - Nancy Springer  f  5180

**Harris, Druce**
*Howl* - Christine Tanasiuk  h  5388

**Heln**
*Chimaera's Copper* - Piers Anthony  f  166

**Hillenbrand, Laura**
*Naomi's Room* - Jonathan Aycliffe  h  281

**Indian, John**
*I, Tituba, Black Witch of Salem* - Maryse
Conde  f  1130

**Julia**
*The Hellbound Heart* - Clive Barker  h  342

**K, Ylla**
*The Martian Chronicles* - Ray Bradbury  s  622

**Knight, Aubrey**
*Firedance* - Steven Barnes  s  360

**Laker, Maria**
*Among Madmen* - Jim Starlin  s  5212

**Larking, Lorien**
*Lorien Lost* - Michael King  f  3124

**Lilith**
*The Shape-Changer's Wife* - Sharon Shinn  f  5002

**Lowell, Janet**
*The Well* - Michael B. Sirota  h  5077

**Luet**
*The Ships of Earth* - Orson Scott Card  s  897

**Mandel, Eleanor**
*A Quantum Murder* - Peter F. Hamilton  s  2527

**Marian**
*Robin and the King* - Parke Godwin  f  2247

**Marshak, Julia**
*Brothers* - Ben Bova  s  581

**Maxwell, Maureen**
*Relife* - Dan Barton  h  376

**Messenger, Karen**
*Host* - Peter James  h  28/2

**Milleflores, Delanna**
*Promised Land* - Connie Willis  s  5872

**Miller, Alvin "Maker"**
*Heartfire* - Orson Scott Card  f  889

**Miller, Margaret "Peggy"**
*Heartfire* - Orson Scott Card  f  889

**Moira**
*The Wizardry Quested* - Rick Cook  f  1163

**Morgan, Richard**
*Dark Dreaming* - Pat Franklin  h  2040

**Murra**
*Stopping at Slowyear* - Frederik Pohl  s  4355

**Nailer, Diane**
*Grimm Memorials* - R. Patrick Gates  h  2160

**Orchard, Julia**
*The Count of Eleven* - Ramsey Campbell  h  853

**Paixao, Rhea**
*Starmind* - Spider Robinson  s  4642

**Pauling, Judd**
*Lullaby* - Diane Guest  h  2455

**Peebles**
*My Stepfather Shrank!* - Barbara Dillon  s  1558

**Pendreic, Morguenna**
*The Hedge of Mist* - Patricia Kennealy-
Morrison  s  3062

**Porter, Rand**
*Starmind* - Spider Robinson  s  4642

**Potter, Evelyn Sylvia**
*Cloven Hooves* - Megan Lindholm  f  3470

**Princess**
*A Remembrance for Kedrigern* - John
Morressy  f  4014

**Promise**
*Firedance* - Steven Barnes  s  360

**Rabbit, Roger**
*Who P-P-Plugged Roger Rabbit?* - Gary K.
Wolf  f  5934

**Rachel**
*Archangel* - Sharon Shinn  s  5000

**Radon**
*Firewalk* - Anne Logston  f  3509

**Ransom, Lauren**
*Night Things* - Michael Talbot  h  5380

**Rasha of the Thousand Doors**
*Yesterday We Saw Mermaids* - Esther
Friesner  f  2086

**Rathenau, Miriam**
*Child of the Journey* - Janet Berliner  f  466
*Children of the Dusk* - Janet Berliner  f  467

**Rider, Emily**
*Other Nature* - Stephanie A. Smith  s  5145

**Rider, Sean**
*Other Nature* - Stephanie A. Smith  s  5145

**Rodriguez**
*Senora Rodriguez and Other Worlds* - Martha
Cerda  f  950

**Roshnani**
*The Stolen Throne* - Harry Turtledove  f  5510

**Sadb**
*The Shield between the Worlds* - Diana L.
Paxson  f  4267

**Scheherazade**
*The Last Arabian Night* - Craig Shaw
Gardner  f  2129

**Shahryar**
*The Last Arabian Night* - Craig Shaw
Gardner  f  2129

**Shielder's Mark**
*Nobody's Son* - Sean Stewart  f  5275

**Shongili, Sean**
*Power Lines* - Anne McCaffrey  s  3743

**Strayhorn, Leslie**
*Shock Lines* - Warren Newton Beath  h  427

**Tanner, Tarleton "Sonny"**
*Promised Land* - Connie Willis  s  5872

**Todd, Redmond "Red" Eugene**
*Lovelock* - Orson Scott Card  s  892

**Varia**
*The Lion of Farside* - John Dalmas  f  1324

**Verlith, Zjhanne**
*Zjhanne's Book* - C.J. Mills  s  3912

**Wade, Zach**
*A Reasonable Madness* - Fran Dorf  h  1580

**White Crow, Valentine**
*The Architecture of Desire* - Mary Gentle  f  2195

# SPY

**Alec of Kerry**
*Luck in the Shadows* - Lynn Flewelling  f  1952
*Stalking Darkness* - Lynn Flewelling  f  1953

**Arda**
*Murder at the Galactic Writers' Society* - Janet
Asimov  s  251

**Ashe, Timothy**
*The Seeds of Time* - Kay Kenyon  s  3064

**Ball**
*Blood Lines* - William R. Burkett Jr.  s  774

**Began, Ttar**
*Mission: Tori* - Johanna Bolton  s  564

**Bennet, Hal**
*The Hanged Man* - T.J. MacGregor  h  3594

**Bond, Hamish**
*Judgment of Tears: Anno Dracula 1959* - Kim
Newman  h  4098

**Bruckner, Bill**
*Nomad* - David Alexander  s  66

**Caludius, Alexsandra**
*7 Steps to Midnight* - Richard Matheson  h  3682

**Carelias, Caroline "Sarah"**
*Union Fires* - John Barnes  f  358

**Cargo**
*Cyberstealth* - S.N. Lewitt  s  3450
*Dancing Vac* - S.N. Lewitt  s  3451

**Carlson, Winnie**
*Putting Up Roots* - Charles Sheffield  s  4964

**Carvalho, Edson**
*Cradle of Splendor* - Patricia Anthony   *s*   158

**Cincinnatus**
*The Great War: American Front* - Harry
   Turtledove   *s*   5501

**Clark, Darcy**
*Deadspawn* - Brian Lumley   *h*   3550

**Colburn, Croft**
*The Forever Drug* - Steve Perry   *s*   4296

**Con, Val**
*Carpe Diem* - Steve Miller   *s*   3907

**Coollege, Emma**
*Galactic MI* - Kevin D. Randle   *s*   4467

**Corvino, Dominic**
*Wet Work* - Philip Nutman   *h*   4168

**Coughlan, Demeter**
*Man Plus* - Frederik Pohl   *s*   4348

**Covington, Diana**
*Beggars and Choosers* - Nancy Kress   *s*   3236

**Crane**
*Lake of the Long Sun* - Gene Wolfe   *s*   5942
*Nightside the Long Sun* - Gene Wolfe   *s*   5943

**Dalt, Steven**
*The LaNague Chronicles* - F. Paul Wilson   *s*   5889
*The Tery* - F. Paul Wilson   *s*   5900

**Dannerman, Jim Daniel "Dan"**
*The Other End of Time* - Frederik Pohl   *s*   4351
*The Siege of Eternity* - Frederik Pohl   *s*   4353

**Darkholme, Raven "Mystique"**
*Codename Wolverine* - Christopher Golden   *s*   2256

**Darkwind**
*Winds of Fate* - Mercedes Lackey   *f*   3305

**Dawson, Joe**
*Scotland the Brave* - Jennifer Roberson   *f*   4611
*Shadow of Obsession* - Rebecca Neason   *f*   4082

**Del Valle, Ryan**
*Wet Work* - Philip Nutman   *h*   4168

**Delacourte, Michaela "Mikey"**
*Spacer Dreams* - Larry Segriff   *s*   4911

**Du Boise, Llysette**
*Of Tangible Ghosts* - L.E. Modesitt Jr.   *f*   3935

**Ellis, Cander**
*Shadow of the Crown* - Craig Mills   *f*   3914

**Eschbach, Johan**
*The Ghost of the Revelator* - L.E. Modesitt
   Jr.   *s*   3931
*Of Tangible Ghosts* - L.E. Modesitt Jr.   *f*   3935

**Evans, Owain**
*The Winnowing* - Gherbod Fleming   *h*   1950

**Ferguson, Harold "Rondo"**
*Darkman #4: The Face of Death* - Randall
   Boyll   *h*   615

**Ferris, Robert**
*The Devouring* - Douglas D. Hawk   *h*   2615

**Gallatin, Michael**
*The Wolf's Hour* - Robert R. McCammon   *h*   3759

**Ghoster**
*Cyberstealth* - S.N. Lewitt   *s*   3450
*Dancing Vac* - S.N. Lewitt   *s*   3451

**Halloran, Lawrence "Fixer-of-Weapons"**
*Man-Kzin Wars IV* - Larry Niven   *s*   4124

**Harris, Laika**
*City of Iron* - Chet Williamson   *h*   5843
*Empire of Dust* - Chet Williamson   *h*   5846

**Heller, Prescott "Sean Toole"**
*Union Fires* - John Barnes   *f*   358

**Heslin, Camnor**
*Dancer's Rise* - Jo Clayton   *f*   1064

**Hubbard, Scott**
*The Eleventh Plague: A Novel of Medical Terror* -
   John S. Marr   *h*   3632

**Hughes, Mary**
*Charmed Life* - Bernard Taylor   *h*   5399

**Hunt, Michael**
*Name of the Beast* - Daniel Easterman   *h*   1721

**Jacob**
*Falcon* - Emma Bull   *s*   768

**Jamil/Alasil**
*The Watcher's Mask* - Laurie J. Marks   *f*   3627

**Jin the Plarnjarn**
*The Race for God* - Brian Herbert   *s*   2666

**Jonesy**
*Brain Child* - George Turner   *s*   5491

**Jordan, Matt**
*Watchers in the Woods* - William W.
   Johnstone   *h*   2936

**Kastrouni, Dimitrious**
*Demogorgon* - Brian Lumley   *h*   3552

**Kendry, Alicen**
*Season of Storms* - Ellen Foxxe   *f*   2032

**Keogh, Harry**
*Deadspawn* - Brian Lumley   *h*   3550
*Deadspeak* - Brian Lumley   *h*   3551
*Necroscope: The Lost Years* - Brian
   Lumley   *h*   3560
*Resurgence* - Brian Lumley   *h*   3564
*The Source* - Brian Lumley   *h*   3565

**Kesev, Chaim**
*Virgin* - Mary Elizabeth Murphy   *h*   4050

**King, Depard**
*Spindoc* - Steve Perry   *s*   4300

**Kline, Cynthia**
*The Armageddon Crazy* - Mick Farren   *s*   1877

**Kro, Gulthar**
*The Regiment's War* - John Dalmas   *s*   1326

**Kromman**
*The Gilded Chain: A Tale of the King's Blades* - Dave
   Duncan   *f*   1679

**Kurz**
*Fire in the Sky* - Jo Clayton   *s*   1067

**Lomax, Felix "Gravedancer"**
*Prophet* - Mike Resnick   *s*   4553

**Luciano, Tony**
*City of Iron* - Chet Williamson   *h*   5843
*Empire of Dust* - Chet Williamson   *h*   5846

**Mary**
*The Puppet Masters* - Robert A. Heinlein   *s*   2646

**Mata Hari**
*The Mata Hari Adventure* - James Luceno   *f*   3544

**Medallia**
*A Wizard in Mind* - Christopher Stasheff   *s*   5232

**Meh'Lindi**
*Inquisitor* - Ian Watson   *s*   5637

**Mendoza, Carlos "Iceman"**
*Oracle* - Mike Resnick   *s*   4551
*Prophet* - Mike Resnick   *s*   4553
*Soothsayer* - Mike Resnick   *s*   4557

**Merchant, Liliane**
*The Arm of the Stone* - Victoria Strauss   *f*   5333

**Mercury, Ryan**
*Beyond the Pale* - Jack Koke   *f*   3198

**Miraflores, Pedro**
*Ai! Pedrito!: When Intelligence Goes Wrong* - L. Ron
   Hubbard   *s*   2788

**Moonblade, Arilyn**
*Elfshadow* - Elaine Cunningham   *f*   1288
*Silver Shadows* - Elaine Cunningham   *f*   1292

**Morganstern, Jack**
*Dead Girls* - Richard Calder   *s*   837

**Morris "Mauricio di Mauro"**
*The Night of Wishes: Or, The
   Satanarchaeolidealcohellish Notion Potion* - Michael
   Ende   *f*   1821

**Multiple Entity "ME"**
*ME: A Novel of Self Discovery* - Thomas T.
   Thomas   *s*   5452

**Nash, August**
*Labyrinth of Night* - Allen Steele   *s*   5244

**Nivens, Sam**
*The Puppet Masters* - Robert A. Heinlein   *s*   2646

**Nysander**
*Luck in the Shadows* - Lynn Flewelling   *f*   1952

**Ochs, Thur**
*The Spirit Ring* - Lois McMaster Bujold   *f*   763

**Old Man**
*The Puppet Masters* - Robert A. Heinlein   *s*   2646

**Potter, Jack**
*Signal to Noise* - Eric S. Nylund   *s*   4179

**Pulaski, Toya**
*Converse and Conflict* - L. Neil Smith   *s*   5130

**Quail, Douglas**
*The Collected Stories of Philip K. Dick, Volume Two:
   We Can Remember It for You Wholesale* - Philip K.
   Dick   *s*   1520

**Quinn "Nomad"**
*Nomad* - David Alexander   *s*   66

**Ramsey**
*Nomad* - David Alexander   *s*   66

**Reed, James**
*Operation Damocles* - Oscar L. Fellows   *s*   1915

**Relanj, Zia**
*The Forever Drug* - Steve Perry   *s*   4296
*Spindoc* - Steve Perry   *s*   4300

**Reydak, Karl**
*A Fearful Symmetry* - James Luceno   *s*   3542

**Rialla**
*Steal the Dragon* - Patricia Briggs   *f*   682

**Ring, Ethan**
*Scissors Cut Paper Wrap Stone* - Ian
   McDonald   *s*   3795

**Rourke, John T.**
*The Struggle* - Jerry Ahern   *s*   44

**Santoul, Remy**
*Illegal Alien* - James Luceno   *s*   3543

**Scribble, Jacob**
*The Night of Wishes: Or, The
   Satanarchaeolidealcohellish Notion Potion* - Michael
   Ende   *f*   1821

**Seavers, Kim**
*Beamriders!* - Martin Caidin   *s*   824

**Seregil**
*Luck in the Shadows* - Lynn Flewelling   *f*   1952
*Stalking Darkness* - Lynn Flewelling   *f*   1953

**Seven, Gary**
*Assignment: Eternity* - Greg Cox   *s*   1225

**Shin, Praeis**
*Playing God* - Sarah Zettel   *s*   6080

**Silver, Mier**
*Mission: Tori* - Johanna Bolton   *s*   564

**Sims, Dolores**
*Cradle of Splendor* - Patricia Anthony   *s*   158

**Sma, Diziet**
*Use of Weapons* - Iain M. Banks   s   328

**Somoroff, Peter**
*Red Devil* - David Saperstein   h   4816

**Sperin, Bro**
*The Ship Avenged* - S.M. Stirling   s   5298

**Steengo**
*The Stainless Steel Rat Sings the Blues* - Harry
    Harrison   s   2575

**Stein, Joseph**
*City of Iron* - Chet Williamson   h   5843
*Empire of Dust* - Chet Williamson   h   5846

**Steiner, Clara**
*The Werewolf's Revenge* - Richard Jaccoma   h   2841

**Stone, Will**
*Majestic* - Whitley Strieber   s   5341

**Sutter, Frank**
*Innerverse* - John DeChancie   s   1458

**Tamara**
*On My Way to Paradise* - Dave Wolverton   s   5955

**Thann, Danilo "Dan"**
*Silver Shadows* - Elaine Cunningham   f   1292

**Thibaudeaux, Catherine "Cat"**
*Delta Search* - William Shatner   s   4930

**Tower, Josh**
*Systems* - W.T. Quick   s   4452

**Trask, Ben**
*Bloodwars* - Brian Lumley   h   3547
*The Last Aerie* - Brian Lumley   h   3557

**Trilling, Kate**
*The Invisible Company* - Scott Russell
    Sanders   s   4813

**Tristan**
*Masque* - F. Paul Wilson   s   5890

**Underhill, Jimmy**
*The Werewolf's Revenge* - Richard Jaccoma   h   2841

**Van Dorne, Chesna "Echo"**
*The Wolf's Hour* - Robert R. McCammon   h   3759

**Van Ryn, Rex**
*The Devil Rides Out* - Dennis Wheatley   h   5773

**Vear, Nick**
*The Ridge* - Lisa Cantrell   h   872

**Watt, Peter**
*Gehenna* - Lewis Gannett   h   2114

**Wei**
*Rule Golden and Double Meaning* - Damon
    Knight   s   3189

**Whitaker, Tomyris "Whit Hastings"**
*Return to Isis* - Jean Stewart   s   5268

**Winter, John**
*Deathwalker* - Patrick Whalen   h   5769

**Wright, Jimjoy Earle**
*The Ecolitan Operation* - L.E. Modesitt Jr.   s   3928
*The Ecologic Secession* - L.E. Modesitt Jr.   s   3929

**Wroke, Alice**
*The Demon Princes: Volume Two* - Jack
    Vance   s   5545

**Xu-Tzu, Phan**
*Celestial Matters* - Richard Garfinkle   s   2140

**Zakalwe, Cheradenine**
*Use of Weapons* - Iain M. Banks   s   328

## STATISTICIAN

**Marcsson, Azamat**
*Dreaming in Smoke* - Tricia Sullivan   s   5353

---

**Tremaine, Elspeth "Beth"**
*The Convocation* - John R. Holt   h   2748

## STEP-PARENT

**Branwen**
*The Lost Years of Merlin* - T.A. Barron   f   370

**Burrich**
*Assassin's Apprentice* - Robin Hobb   f   2693

**Cwenn**
*Suisan* - Phyllis Carol Agins   f   42

**Heber, Vanessa**
*Bug Park* - James P. Hogan   s   2723

**Peter**
*Bones* - Joyce Thompson   h   5453

**Robin**
*Passager* - Jane Yolen   f   6038

**Sherwood, Iris "Butcher of Boston"**
*In the Cube* - David Alexander Smith   s   5109

**Wilkinson, Hilda**
*Spider* - Patrick McGrath   h   3815

**Willson, Andrea**
*Dark Reunion* - Stephen R. George   h   2198

## STEWARD

**Lindgren, Anton**
*Carve the Sky* - Alexander Jablokov   s   2836

**McGulvey, Mr.**
*In between Dragons* - Michael Kandel   f   3010

## STOCK BROKER

**Duke, Bob**
*The Wild* - Whitley Strieber   h   5343

**Mati, Gwendolyn "Gwen"**
*Half Asleep in Frog Pajamas* - Tom
    Robbins   s   4606

**Rotciv, Victor**
*The Convocation* - John R. Holt   h   2748

## STORE OWNER

**Baxter, Spyder**
*Silk* - Caitlin R. Kiernan   h   3101

**Beacham, Kate**
*In the Rift* - Marion Zimmer Bradley   f   639

**Deeters, Nathan**
*Cross a Dark Bridge* - Deborah
    Churchman   h   1027

**Gypsy Pete**
*Frisk* - Dennis Cooper   h   1170

**Hodge, Benton**
*Sineater* - Elizabeth Massie   h   3668

**Jonah**
*Something Rich and Strange* - Patricia A.
    McKillip   f   3840

**Katts, Wesley**
*Anthony Shriek* - Jessica Amanda
    Salmonson   h   4790

**Kopp, Curly**
*Seaward* - Brad Leithauser   h   3433

**Markham, Dan**
*California Gothic* - Dennis Etchison   h   1843

**Markham, Evie**
*California Gothic* - Dennis Etchison   h   1843

---

**Moriarity, Pepper**
*The House That Jack Built* - Graham
    Masterton   h   3675

**Somersby, Nadine**
*Prank Night* - David Robbins   h   4601

**Soper, Helen**
*Head Injuries* - Conrad Williams   h   5816

## STORYTELLER

**Chakliux**
*Song of the River* - Sue Harrison   f   2583

**Dandilion**
*Tales From Watership Down* - Richard Adams   f   32

**Gabrielle**
*The Thief of Hermes* - Ru Emerson   f   1811

**Khalifa, Rashid**
*Haroun and the Sea of Stories* - Salman
    Rushdie   f   4731

**Magara**
*Shadow-Maze* - Mark Smith   f   5133

**McCaffrey, Anne**
*A Diversity of Dragons* - Anne McCaffrey   f   3728

**Mikhailovych, Lixand**
*Shadow's Daughter* - Shirley Meier   f   3871

**Murphy, Buffy**
*Fair Peril* - Nancy Springer   f   5178

**Nazir, Nassifeh "Opalears"**
*The Family Tree* - Sheri S. Tepper   s   5429

**Quijance, Natasha**
*Red Planet Run* - Dana Stabenow   s   5187

**Scheherazade**
*The Last Arabian Night* - Craig Shaw
    Gardner   f   2129

**Teller**
*The Gift* - Patrick O'Leary   f   4211

**Tighe, Epiphanius "Eppy"**
*A Diversity of Dragons* - Anne McCaffrey   f   3728

## STOWAWAY

**Allaird, Margaret "Marnie"**
*Arrow From Earth* - F.M. Busby   s   782

**Chase-Frisson L'Zalle, Trevarre**
*Shivering World* - Kathy Tyers   s   5526

**Colter, Daniel**
*Into the Deep* - Ken Grimwood   s   2450

**Mondragon, Carlos**
*The Black Sun* - Jack Williamson   s   5860

## STREETPERSON

**Allen, Zadok**
*The Shadow over Innsmouth* - H.P.
    Lovecraft   h   3533

**Bone**
*Bone* - George C. Chesbro   h   1006
*A Hidden Place* - Robert Charles Wilson   s   5910

**Elgin**
*Street* - Jack Cady   h   822

**Holt, Kenneth**
*Wyrm Wolf* - Edo van Belkom   h   5535

**Julian**
*Wilding* - Melanie Tem   h   5425

**Peru, Mattie**
*Breeder* - Douglas Clegg   h   1076

**Phousita**
*The Bohr Maker* - Linda Nagata   s   4064

**Pook**
*Voices of Hope* - David Feintuch  *s*  1903

**Silk**
*Street* - Jack Cady  *h*  822

**Symptomatic Nerve Gas**
*Street* - Jack Cady  *h*  822

## STRIPPER

**Strangelove, Jacqueline**
*Yours Truly, Jackie the Stripper* - Edo van
  Belkom  *h*  5536

## STUDENT

**a-Lagan, Meredydd**
*The Meri* - Maya Kaathryn Bohnhoff  *f*  561

**Adelrune**
*The Book of Knights* - Yves Meynard  *f*  3884

**Ahrens, Bleys**
*Young Bleys* - Gordon R. Dickson  *s*  1540

**Alderberry, Jane**
*The Iron Dragon's Daughter* - Michael
  Swanwick  *f*  5371

**Alexander, Ardeth**
*The Night Inside* - Nancy Baker  *h*  301

**Alnosha "Nosh"**
*The Hands of Lyr* - Andre Norton  *f*  4154

**Anderson, Marion**
*Flesh* - Gus Weill  *h*  5685

**Angelo, Jamie**
*Beauty* - Brian D'Amato  *h*  1334

**Anhand, Deteras "Detter"**
*Nameless Magery* - Delia Marshall Turner  *f*  5490

**Ariadne, Helene**
*Light Raid* - Connie Willis  *s*  5870

**Ashenden, Turner**
*Views from the Oldest House* - Richard
  Grant  *s*  2329

**Attercop, Karen**
*Webs* - Scott Baker  *h*  304

**Aubrey**
*The Shape-Changer's Wife* - Sharon Shinn  *f*  5002

**Aurian**
*Aurian* - Maggie Furey  *f*  2095

**Bankhead, Tallulah "Tulley"**
*Beyond the Door* - Gary L. Blackwood  *s*  510

**Barclay, Andy**
*Child's Play III* - Matthew J. Costello  *h*  1194

**Barrett, Jonathan**
*Red Death* - P.N. Elrod  *h*  1798

**Bittan, Rebecca**
*The Kiss* - Kathryn Reines  *h*  4529

**Blatchley, James**
*The World I Made for Her* - Thomas
  Moran  *h*  3996

**Blennerhassett, Daniel**
*Virgins and Martyrs* - Simon Maginn  *h*  3607

**Bradley, Alexander "Alex"**
*The Hollowing* - Robert Holdstock  *f*  2738

**Briar**
*Tris's Book* - Tamora Pierce  *f*  4322

**Brown, Tim**
*The Select* - F. Paul Wilson  *h*  5897

**Bruckner, Teresa**
*Angels Unaware* - L. Elizabeth Storm  *s*  5315

**Bryant, Martin**
*The Crawling Dark* - Pauline Dunn  *h*  1698

**Burkhardt, Jared Jr.**
*First Love: A Gothic Tale* - Joyce Carol
  Oates  *h*  4183

**C.**
*Galatea 2.2* - Richard M. Powers  *s*  4381

**Cadderly**
*Canticle* - R.A. Salvatore  *f*  4793

**Caeser, Justin**
*Flesh* - Gus Weill  *h*  5685

**Caldwell, Jay**
*Call to Battle* - Doug Murray  *h*  4059

**Campbell, Deirdre**
*Indiana Jones and the Dance of the Giants* - Rob
  MacGregor  *f*  3588
*Indiana Jones and the Seven Veils* - Rob
  MacGregor  *f*  3592

**Cannon, Ben**
*Cannon's Orb* - L. Warren Douglas  *s*  1586

**Cannon, Bobby**
*The School* - Ed Kelleher  *h*  3042

**Carter, Janet**
*Tam Lin* - Pamela Dean  *f*  1446

**Champion, Ned**
*The Wilds* - Richard Laymon  *h*  3373

**Chios, Maia**
*Dragon Season* - Michael Cassutt  *f*  936

**Christie**
*The Informers* - Brett Easton Ellis  *h*  1778

**Cleary, Quinn**
*The Select* - F. Paul Wilson  *h*  5897

**Colette, Sianna**
*The Shattered Sphere* - Roger MacBride Allen  *s*  81

**Collins, Jack**
*A Logical Magician* - Robert Weinberg  *f*  5697

**Collins, Karen Cecile "Casey"**
*Islands of Tomorrow* - F.M. Busby  *s*  783

**Conti, Ned**
*Madeleine's Ghost* - Robert Girardi  *h*  2240

**Correa, Marissa**
*Lightpaths* - Howard V. Hendrix  *s*  2660

**Coughlan, Demeter**
*Man Plus* - Frederik Pohl  *s*  4348

**Crowe, Janie**
*The Plague Tales* - Ann Benson  *s*  453

**Crusher, Wesley**
*Debtors' Planet* - William R. Thompson  *s*  5457

**Cymel**
*Drum Calls* - Jo Clayton  *f*  1065

**Daae, Christine**
*Phantom* - Susan Kay  *h*  3020

**Dain, Benn**
*Mazeway* - Jack Williamson  *s*  5866

**Daja**
*Tris's Book* - Tamora Pierce  *f*  4322

**Daley, Cameron**
*The Vanishing* - Marilyn Kaye  *s*  3021

**David**
*Gameplay* - Kevin J. Anderson  *f*  105
*Game's End* - Kevin J. Anderson  *f*  104

**Davis, Anne**
*Order of the Arrow* - Michael T.
  Hinkemeyer  *h*  2689

**de Kreshtur, Andrei**
*Blood Countess* - Andrei Codrescu  *h*  1094

**DeWoe, Dekker**
*Mining the Oort* - Frederik Pohl  *s*  4349

**Diaz, Rafael**
*The Terror* - Graham Masterton  *h*  3679

**Dion**
*Mage Heart* - Jane Routley  *f*  4686

**Dougal, Duncan**
*My Teacher Fried My Brains* - Bruce
  Coville  *s*  1223

**Doyle, Keith**
*Higher Mythology* - Jody Lynn Nye  *f*  4170
*Mythology Abroad* - Jody Lynn Nye  *f*  4174

**Drib**
*The Knights of Cawdor* - Mike Jefferies  *f*  2886

**Ehlers, Lou**
*Who Killed James Dean?* - Warren Newton
  Beath  *h*  428

**Ellerman, Amy**
*The Quiet* - Patrick Billings  *h*  488

**Endrada, Valerie "Val"**
*Halfway Human* - Carolyn Ives Gilman  *s*  2237

**Engle, Kivrin**
*Doomsday Book* - Connie Willis  *s*  5868

**Evans, Sean**
*A Diversity of Dragons* - Anne McCaffrey  *f*  3728

**Exeter, Edward**
*Past Imperative* - Dave Duncan  *f*  1684

**Farley, Heather**
*Serpent's Gift* - A.C. Crispin  *s*  1261

**Forbes, Vanessa**
*The School* - Ed Kelleher  *h*  3042

**Forester, David**
*Starfleet Academy* - Diane Carey  *s*  905

**Gangle, Kendar "Ratwacker"**
*Majyk by Accident* - Esther Friesner  *f*  2079

**Gardner, Sam**
*Captain Quad* - Sean Costello  *h*  1203

**Gates, John**
*Flicker* - Theodore Roszak  *h*  4683

**Gerchak, Julie**
*My Ishmael* - Daniel Quinn  *s*  4456

**Gilbert, India**
*India's Story* - Kathlyn S. Starbuck  *s*  5208

**Ginny**
*Virago* - Karen Marie Christa Minns  *h*  3915

**Gladheon, Karigan**
*Green Rider* - Kristen Britain  *f*  692

**Gorse**
*Wizard's Hall* - Jane Yolen  *f*  6043

**Green, Margo**
*Relic* - Douglas Preston  *h*  4414

**Grey, Liza**
*The Messenger* - Donald Tyson  *h*  5528

**Harper, Fay**
*Jinx High* - Mercedes Lackey  *h*  3284

**Harrison, Lee Anne**
*The Magic and the Healing* - Nick
  O'Donohoe  *f*  4196
*Under the Healing Sign* - Nick O'Donohoe  *f*  4198

**Harrison, Theophilius "Ted"**
*Orbital Resonance* - John Barnes  *s*  356

**Hart, Lola**
*Random Acts of Senseless Violence* - Jack
  Womack  *f*  5959

**Helit, Susan Sto**
*Soul Music* - Terry Pratchett  *f*  4401

**Helling, Suzanne "Alouzon"**
*Dragon Death* - Gael Baudino   *f*   390
*Duel of Dragons* - Gael Baudino   *f*   391

**Henry "Thornmallow"**
*Wizard's Hall* - Jane Yolen   *f*   6043

**Hoyland, Hugh**
*Silent Thunder/Universe* - Dean Ing   *s*   2829

**Hph-wayuo "Alvin"**
*Brightness Reef* - David Brin   *s*   684

**I**
*Ishmael* - Daniel Quinn   *s*   4455

**James, Mike**
*The Orchid Eater* - Marc Laidlaw   *h*   3312

**Janeway, Kathryn**
*The Chance Factor* - Diana G. Gallagher   *s*   2109

**Jankowitz, Sheldon**
*User Unfriendly* - Vivian Vande Velde   *f*   5558

**Jasper**
*Murder in Cormyr* - Chet Williamson   *f*   5848

**Jennedote, Yaji**
*Fire in the Mist* - Holly Lisle   *f*   3482

**Joanna**
*The Time Tree* - Enid Richemont   *f*   4585

**Johnson, Duffy**
*Wolf Moon* - John R. Holt   *h*   2749

**Johnson, Sibyl**
*Far Edge of Darkness* - Linda Evans   *s*   1855

**Kane, Laura**
*Deathscape* - Michael Cecilione   *h*   945

**Keane, Abel**
*The Trail of Cthulhu* - August Derleth   *h*   1497

**Ken**
*The Lost City of the Jedi* - Paul Davids   *s*   1393

**Kenner, Mark**
*Shadow World* - A.C. Crispin   *s*   1262

**Kestrel, Derek "Deke"**
*Jinx High* - Mercedes Lackey   *h*   3284

**Khalid**
*Wishing Season* - Esther Friesner   *f*   2085

**Kirk, Peter James**
*Sarek* - A.C. Crispin   *s*   1260

**Kittridge, Valerie**
*Witch-Light* - Nancy Holder   *h*   2734

**Koscuisko, Andrej**
*An Exchange of Hostages* - Susan R.
   Matthews   *s*   3692

**Krebs, Scott**
*But What of Earth?* - Piers Anthony   *s*   163

**Lane, Thomas**
*Tam Lin* - Pamela Dean   *f*   1446

**LaRoche, Serge**
*Serpent's Gift* - A.C. Crispin   *s*   1261

**Latcher, Dan**
*Stitch* - Mark Morris   *h*   4024

**Latimer, Sarah**
*Witch Hill* - Marion Zimmer Bradley   *h*   654

**Lazarian, Ramou**
*A Company of Stars* - Christopher Stasheff   *s*   5215
*We Open on Venus* - Christopher Stasheff   *s*   5227

**Lealbhallain**
*The Meri* - Maya Kaathryn Bohnhoff   *f*   561

**Lee, Lysistrata "Lizzie"**
*Unwillingly to Earth* - Pauline Ashwell   *s*   231

**Leong, Allan**
*The Robin Hood Ambush* - William F. Wu   *s*   5999

**Lescevre, Thibault**
*Bridge of Valor* - Anne Lesley Groell   *f*   2452

**Lewis, Jonathan**
*Looker* - Jorge Saralegui   *h*   4820

**Leydon, B.**
*Unwillingly to Earth* - Pauline Ashwell   *s*   231

**Io Lyrane, Lyrane**
*Demon Moon* - Jack Williamson   *s*   5862

**Lockwood, Grace**
*The Ghosts of Sleath* - James Herbert   *h*   2668

**Lombard, Nick**
*Trinity Grove* - David van Meter Smith   *h*   5112

**Longchamp, Dawn**
*Secrets of the Morning* - V.C. Andrews   *h*   146

**Lugosh, James D.**
*Order of the Arrow* - Michael T.
   Hinkemeyer   *h*   2689

**Luther**
*Fool on the Hill* - Matt Ruff   *f*   4707

**Magruder, Bernie**
*Bernie and the Bessledorf Ghost* - Phyllis Reynolds
   Naylor   *f*   4078

**Mandy**
*Weirdos of the Universe, Unite!* - Pamela F.
   Service   *f*   4921

**Manilla**
*Virago* - Karen Marie Christa Minns   *h*   3915

**Margaret**
*A Million Open Doors* - John Barnes   *s*   353

**Margison, Tom**
*Kids* - Trevor Hoyle   *h*   2787

**Marling, Oliver Fonteyn**
*Red Death* - P.N. Elrod   *h*   1798

**Marlowe, Jim**
*Red Planet* - Robert A. Heinlein   *s*   2647

**Marlowe, Ruth**
*The Cup of Morning Shadows* - Rosemary
   Edghill   *f*   1747
*The Sword of Maiden's Tears* - Rosemary
   Edghill   *f*   1748

**Mason, Estelle "Lysistrata"**
*Cannon's Orb* - L. Warren Douglas   *s*   1586

**Mathews, Sheilagh**
*The Voice of Cepheus* - Ken Appleby   *s*   202

**Maupin, Emily**
*Anthony Shriek* - Jessica Amanda
   Salmonson   *h*   4790

**McDowell, Josie**
*Belladonna* - Michael Stewart   *h*   5271

**McHenry, Mark**
*Worf's First Adventure* - Peter David   *s*   1391

**McLeod, Morgan**
*Starseed* - Spider Robinson   *s*   4643

**Melanie**
*Gameplay* - Kevin J. Anderson   *f*   105
*Game's End* - Kevin J. Anderson   *f*   104

**Merlino, Pepper**
*Seattle Ghost Story* - Nick DiMartino   *h*   1560

**Mikayla**
*Lady of the Trillium* - Marion Zimmer
   Bradley   *f*   641

**Montagu, Edric**
*The Mummy!: A Tale of the Twenty-Second Century* -
   Jane Webb Loudon   *h*   3526

**Moore, Julie**
*The Cold One* - Christopher Pike   *h*   4327

**Moreau, Alessandra "Ale"**
*Day of the Snake* - Matthew J. Costello   *s*   1196
*Hour of the Scorpion* - Matthew J. Costello   *s*   1199

**Morgan, Sara**
*Superstitious* - R.L. Stine   *h*   5290

**Morley, Lynn**
*The Witch Returns* - Phyllis Reynolds
   Naylor   *f*   4079
*The Witch's Eye* - Phyllis Reynolds Naylor   *f*   4080

**Mosca, Piero**
*Flare* - Roger Zelazny   *s*   6065

**Mouche**
*Six Moon Dance* - Sheri S. Tepper   *s*   5437

**Murdley, Jennifer**
*Jennifer Murdley's Toad* - Bruce Coville   *f*   1220

**Murray, Melpomene**
*Orbital Resonance* - John Barnes   *s*   356

**Nafai**
*The Memory of Earth* - Orson Scott Card   *s*   894
*The Ships of Earth* - Orson Scott Card   *s*   897

**Nicole, Maeve**
*The Scathach and the Maeve's Daughter* - Mary
   Alexander Walker   *f*   5618

**Noycannir, Mergau**
*An Exchange of Hostages* - Susan R.
   Matthews   *s*   3692

**Nuela**
*Deepwater Dreams* - Sydney J. Van Scyoc   *s*   5541

**O'Donnell, Annie**
*Stitch* - Mark Morris   *h*   4024

**O'Keefe, Polly**
*An Acceptable Time* - Madeleine L'Engle   *f*   3436

**Omri**
*The Secret of the Indian* - Lynne Reid Banks   *f*   332

**Owen**
*Weirdos of the Universe, Unite!* - Pamela F.
   Service   *f*   4921

**P, Quentin**
*Zombie* - Joyce Carol Oates   *h*   4185

**Pantera, Black Malachi**
*Views from the Oldest House* - Richard
   Grant   *s*   2329

**Parker, Jim**
*University* - Bentley Little   *h*   3499

**Pfahl, Susan**
*Agyar* - Steven Brust   *f*   738

**Pira, Cleo**
*Lives of the Monster Dogs* - Kirsten Bakis   *s*   305

**Potter, Curt**
*Night Prophets* - Paul F. Olson   *h*   4213

**Potter, Harry**
*Harry Potter and the Sorcerer's Stone* - J.K.
   Rowling   *f*   4700

**Powell, Kim**
*Looker* - Jorge Saralegui   *h*   4820

**Prescott, George**
*Supernova* - Roger MacBride Allen   *s*   82

**Pullen, Faith**
*University* - Bentley Little   *h*   3499

**Rachel**
*The Time Tree* - Enid Richemont   *f*   4585

**Radineaux, Jenifleur**
*Anvil of the Sun* - Anne Lesley Groell   *f*   2451

**Rand**
*Path of Fire* - Charles Ingrid   *s*   2832

**Ranieri, Tony**
*Beyond the Shroud* - Rick Hautala   *h*   2604

**Raoulin**
*The Book of the Beast* - Tanith Lee  *f*  3405

**Raven, Ian**
*Stitch* - Mark Morris  *h*  4024

**Reynolds, William**
*Lurid Dreams* - Charles L. Harness  *s*  2546

**Rizalli, Arvin "Harek"**
*User Unfriendly* - Vivian Vande Velde  *f*  5558

**Robbins, Jake**
*The Vanishing* - Marilyn Kaye  *s*  3021

**Ross, Elaine**
*In Double Jeopardy* - Andrew Neiderman  *h*  4088

**Rozhenko, Worf**
*Worf's First Adventure* - Peter David  *s*  1391

**St. Claire, Nicole**
*Wolf Moon* - John R. Holt  *h*  2749

**St. John, Wade**
*Coven* - Edward Lee  *h*  3390

**Salazar, Kirk**
*The Venom Trees of Sunga* - L. Sprague de
Camp  *s*  1420

**Sanders, Alison**
*The Priest: A Gothic Romance* - Thomas M.
Disch  *h*  1562

**Schell, Alix**
*Lurid Dreams* - Charles L. Harness  *s*  2546

**Schwartz, Randomly Distributed "Randy"**
*Orbital Resonance* - John Barnes  *s*  356

**sen'Laurea, Terricel "Terris"**
*Northlight* - Deborah Wheeler  *s*  5775

**Shaffer, Walter Scott Jr.**
*Beyond the Door* - Gary L. Blackwood  *s*  510

**Shelton, Brett C.**
*Child's Play III* - Matthew J. Costello  *h*  1194

**Sheppard, Lee**
*The Messenger* - Donald Tyson  *h*  5528

**Simmons, Susan**
*My Teacher Fried My Brains* - Bruce
Coville  *s*  1223

**Sloane, Ed**
*Dawn Song* - Michael Marano  *h*  3620

**Soledad, Zeide**
*Cybernetic Jungle* - S.N. Lewitt  *s*  3449

**Soleta**
*Worf's First Adventure* - Peter David  *s*  1391

**Spider**
*Fine Prey* - Scott Westerfeld  *s*  5766

**Sturgis, Wally**
*The Shattered Sphere* - Roger MacBride Allen  *s*  81

**Susan**
*The Divide* - Robert Charles Wilson  *s*  5907

**Susi**
*Way Up High* - Roger Zelazny  *f*  6076

**Sutton, Frank**
*Red Planet* - Robert A. Heinlein  *s*  2647

**Sweetsong, Stanley**
*Shoebag Returns* - Mary James  *f*  2869

**Talmadge, Jessica**
*Supernova* - Roger MacBride Allen  *s*  82

**Theodora of Pyrene**
*The Gate of Ivory* - Doris Egan  *s*  1755

**Thompson, Peter**
*My Teacher Flunked the Planet* - Bruce
Coville  *s*  1222
*My Teacher Glows in the Dark* - Bruce
Coville  *s*  1224

**Tobin, Sara Ann**
*Angel Light* - Andrew M. Greeley  *f*  2342

**Tooley, Nick**
*Tam Lin* - Pamela Dean  *f*  1446

**Torres, Rogelio**
*Meridian 144* - Meg Files  *s*  1932

**Trevisan, David**
*The Fair Rules of Evil* - David C. Smith  *h*  5111

**Tris**
*Tris's Book* - Tamora Pierce  *f*  4322

**Tugelbend, Victor**
*Moving Pictures* - Terry Pratchett  *f*  4398

**Turch, Averell "The Needle"**
*Soulcatchers* - Jan Lara  *h*  3336

**Ulrich, Will**
*The Robin Hood Ambush* - William F. Wu  *s*  5999

**Voss, Dorn**
*Where the Ships Die* - William C. Dietz  *s*  1553

**Wae, Kiondili**
*Lightwing* - Tara K. Harper  *s*  2551

**Wagner**
*Jack Faust* - Michael Swanwick  *s*  5372

**Walsh, Charity**
*The Bighead* - Edward Lee  *h*  3387

**Walthers, Danielle "Dani"**
*The Vampire Odyssey* - Scott Ciencin  *h*  1032
*The Wildlings* - Scott Ciencin  *h*  1034

**Washburn, Bob**
*The Robin Hood Ambush* - William F. Wu  *s*  5999

**Wells, Jeff**
*Norby and the Court Jester* - Janet Asimov  *s*  252
*Norby and the Oldest Dragon* - Janet
Asimov  *s*  253
*Norby and Yobo's Great Adventure* - Janet
Asimov  *s*  254
*Norby Down to Earth* - Janet Asimov  *s*  255

**Winter, James**
*Sing for a Gentle Rain* - J. Alison James  *f*  2861

**Wren**
*Wren's Quest* - Sherwood Smith  *f*  5143

**!Xabbu**
*City of Golden Shadow* - Tad Williams  *s*  5828

**Zach**
*Ecstasy Club* - Douglas Rushkoff  *s*  4732

**Zeeman, Richard**
*Blue Moon* - Laurell K. Hamilton  *h*  2513

**Zoe**
*The Silver Kiss* - Annette Curtis Klause  *f*  3163

## STUDENT—COLLEGE

**Allie**
*Lost in Translation* - Margaret Ball  *f*  315

**Aylesworth, Jesse**
*An Exaltation of Larks* - Robert Reed  *s*  4506

**Bainbridge**
*Ferman's Devils* - Joe Clifford Faust  *s*  1892

**Bird, Marianne**
*Tap, Tap* - David Martin  *h*  3640

**Calderon, Miguel**
*Shango* - James Roberto Curtis  *h*  1298

**Caldwell, John**
*Mojave Wells* - L. Dean James  *s*  2864

**Callare, Jesse**
*Mother of Storms* - John Barnes  *s*  354

**Clark, Joe**
*Fiend* - C. Dean Andersson  *h*  138

**Collier, Marcy**
*Mythology 101* - Jody Lynn Nye  *f*  4173

**Copley, Isabelle "Izzy"**
*Memory and Dream* - Charles de Lint  *f*  1433

**Crusher, Wesley**
*Balance of Power* - Dafydd ab Hugh  *s*  7

**Daniels, Aikin**
*Dreamseeker's Road* - Tom Deitz  *f*  1472

**Desmond, Timothy Alfred**
*Unicorn U.* - Esther Friesner  *f*  2084

**Devery, Nell**
*When Darkness Falls* - Sidney Williams  *h*  5825

**Domerc**
*Lost in Translation* - Margaret Ball  *f*  315

**Doyle, Keith**
*Mythology 101* - Jody Lynn Nye  *f*  4173

**Faulkner, Sully**
*An Exaltation of Larks* - Robert Reed  *s*  4506

**Fortunato, Amelia**
*Dark Visions* - T. Lucien Wright  *h*  5987

**Freemark, Nest**
*A Knight of the Word* - Terry Brooks  *f*  714

**Harris, Tina**
*The Abductors: Conspiracy* - Jonathan
Frakes  *s*  2034

**Jacoby, Darcy**
*Wendigo Border* - Catherine Montrose  *h*  3967

**Kaminski, Tiffany Jeanine "T.J."**
*Steel Rose* - Kara Dalkey  *f*  1321

**Kaplan, T'ing Hau**
*Unicorn U.* - Esther Friesner  *f*  2084

**Lahikainen, Sarah**
*Cold Whisper* - Rick Hautala  *h*  2605

**Madison, Jay**
*The Gryphon King* - Tom Deitz  *f*  1473

**McLean, Alec**
*Dreamseeker's Road* - Tom Deitz  *f*  1472

**Murphy, Grey**
*Man From Mundania* - Piers Anthony  *f*  180

**Papen, Richard**
*The Secret History* - Donna Tartt  *h*  5398

**Rob**
*Agviq* - Michael Armstrong  *s*  208

**Roberts, Sheila**
*Into the Deep* - Ken Grimwood  *s*  2450

**Sullivan, David**
*Darkthunder's Way* - Tom Deitz  *f*  1470
*Dreamseeker's Road* - Tom Deitz  *f*  1472
*Landslayer's Law* - Tom Deitz  *f*  1474
*Sunshaker's War* - Tom Deitz  *f*  1477

**Swenson, Colter**
*Footprints of Thunder* - James F. David  *s*  1379

**Tolar, Rob**
*The Gryphon King* - Tom Deitz  *f*  1473

**Wilkinson, Steve "The Dreamer"**
*A Call to Arms* - Thomas K. Martin  *f*  3650
*A Two-Edged Sword* - Thomas K. Martin  *f*  3653

**Winter, Henry**
*The Secret History* - Donna Tartt  *h*  5398

**Zalewski, Petra**
*Footprints of Thunder* - James F. David  *s*  1379

## STUDENT—EXCHANGE

**Lonat, Bosanka**
*The Golden Thread* - Suzy McKee Charnas  *f*  969

## STUDENT—GRADUATE

**Chance, Angela**
*Time Station Berlin* - David Evans   s   1852

**Davies, Stewart**
*Target Earth* - Steve Perry   s   4301

**Kaye, Peter**
*Chiller* - Randall Boyll   h   610

**Losmara, Rafe**
*Reprisal* - F. Paul Wilson   h   5896

**Marqueete, Donald**
*Quoth the Crow* - David Bischoff   h   494

**Nguyen, Phat "Zak"**
*Cosm* - Gregory Benford   s   444

**Shepherd, Chyna**
*Intensity* - Dean R. Koontz   h   3210

**Tabor, Lucian "Luke"**
*Islands of Tomorrow* - F.M. Busby   s   783

**Timmers, Lacy**
*Soulcatchers* - Jan Lara   h   3336

**Verruckt, Steven**
*Vampires Anonymous* - Jeffrey N.
   McMahan   h   3853

**Zolotin, Peter**
*Burster* - Michael Capobianco   s   876

## STUDENT—HIGH SCHOOL

**Alexander, Sam**
*SETI* - Frederick Fichman   s   1930

**Angel**
*Damnbanna* - Nancy Springer   f   5177

**Bryge, Larry**
*Spirit Crossings* - Claudia Peck   f   4275

**Carter, David**
*Invasion America* - Christie Golden   s   2252
*On the Run* - Christie Golden   s   2254

**"Damnbanna" Deil**
*Damnbanna* - Nancy Springer   f   5177

**Desmond, Timothy Alfred**
*Harpy High* - Esther Friesner   f   2076

**Dillon, Ronny**
*Soulsmith* - Tom Deitz   f   1475

**Freemark, Nest**
*Running with the Demon* - Terry Brooks   f   715

**Harper, Marty**
*The Cat* - R.L. Stine   h   5285

**Marsh, Valentine**
*The Golden Thread* - Suzy McKee Charnas   f   969

**Martino, Chris**
*OtherSyde* - J. Michael Straczynski   h   5323

**Oakland, Brian**
*Stunts* - Charles L. Grant   h   2317

**Obst, Roger**
*OtherSyde* - J. Michael Straczynski   h   5323

**Roeder, Karel**
*Lights Out in the Reptile House* - Jim
   Shepard   f   4976

**Sherman**
*In between Dragons* - Michael Kandel   f   3010

**Welch, Lewis**
*Soulsmith* - Tom Deitz   f   1475

## STUDENT—JUNIOR HIGH SCHOOL

**De Witt, Ryan**
*Red Wizard* - Nancy Springer   f   5182

## STUDENT—MIDDLE SCHOOL

**Jeff**
*On Meeting Witches at Wells* - Judith
   Gorog   f   2283

## STUNTMAN

**Takumo, Charles "Charlie" Willis**
*The Art of Arrow Cutting* - Stephen
   Dedman   f   1462

## SUPERNATURAL BEING

**Bahhum Bug**
*The Haunted Tea Cosy: A Dispirited and Distasteful
   Diversion for Christmas* - Edward Gorey   h   2276

**Changer**
*Changer* - Jane M. Lindskold   f   3474

**Chet**
*Thirsty* - M.T. Anderson   h   120

**Dog Brother**
*Tooth and Claw* - Graham Masterton   h   3680

**Harkender, Jacob**
*The Carnival of Destruction* - Brian
   Stableford   h   5190

**Hellboy**
*Hellboy: The Lost Army* - Christopher
   Golden   h   2257

**James, Raglan**
*The Tale of the Body Thief* - Anne Rice   h   4576

**McGee, Rosa**
*Sacrament* - Clive Barker   h   345

**Pangloss**
*In the Blood* - Nancy A. Collins   h   1121

**Steep, Jacob**
*Sacrament* - Clive Barker   h   345

**Takumo, Charles "Charlie" Willis**
*The Art of Arrow Cutting* - Stephen
   Dedman   f   1462

**Tooth Fairy**
*The Tooth Fairy* - Graham Joyce   f   2995

**Tristen**
*Fortress of Eagles* - C.J. Cherryh   f   992
*Fortress of Owls* - C.J. Cherryh   f   993

**Zo'e'minira "Zoe"**
*The Duke of Sumava* - Sara J. Wrench   f   5983

## SURVEYOR

**Sakai, Catherine**
*To Dream in the City of Sorrows* - Kathryn M.
   Drennan   s   1654

## SURVIVOR

**Gelasias, Crystal**
*Red Shadows* - Yvonne Navarro   s   4074

**Laski, Saul**
*Carrion Comfort* - Dan Simmons   h   5049

**Lily**
*Red Shadows* - Yvonne Navarro   s   4074

## TAILOR

**Mulvihill, Travest**
*The Ways of Magic* - Scott Ciencin   f   1033

**Rae**
*The War in the Waste* - Felicity Savage   f   4851

**Threadwell**
*The Adventures of Threadwell the Tailor, or
   Alterations Made While You Wait* - P.D.
   Cacek   h   801

## TAXI DRIVER

**Boda**
*Pollen* - Jeff Noon   s   4135

**Coyote**
*Pollen* - Jeff Noon   s   4135

**Dallas, Korben**
*The Fifth Element* - Terry Bisson   s   504

**Davenport, Ben**
*The Last Voice They Hear* - Ramsey
   Campbell   h   858

**Denton, Pete**
*The Last Voice They Hear* - Ramsey
   Campbell   h   858

**Spencer, Jake**
*Bloodlines* - J.N. Williamson   h   5852

**Warner, Hank "Joey Bennett"**
*Someplace to Be Flying* - Charles de Lint   f   1435

## TAXIDERMIST

**Reed, Matt**
*The Reckoning* - Ruby Jean Jensen   h   2904

## TEACHER

**Al-Ra,ma, Khaddam**
*The Riddled Man* - Mark E. Rogers   f   4654

**Albin, Doug**
*The Mailman* - Bentley Little   h   3494

**Almond, Donna**
*Dead in the Water* - Nancy Holder   h   2732

**Anara**
*India's Story* - Kathlyn S. Starbuck   s   5208

**Anaxagoras**
*The Wizard's Apprentice* - S.P. Somtow   f   5163

**Anthony**
*Catacomb* - Andrew Laurance   h   3347

**Archer, Ann**
*Otherworld* - Kenneth C. Flint   h   1959

**Baker, Bob**
*After Life* - Andrew Neiderman   h   4083

**Bevol, Osraed**
*The Meri* - Maya Kaathryn Bohnhoff   f   561
*Taminy* - Maya Kaathryn Bohnhoff   f   563

**Bird, Roscoe**
*Tap, Tap* - David Martin   h   3640

**Bjornsen, Paula**
*Night Sounds* - Warner Lee   h   3415

**Bloch, Jared**
*No Limits* - Nigel Findley   s   1938

**Bodbmall**
*Master of Earth and Water* - Diana L.
   Paxson   f   4266

**Bolton, Jennifer**
*Cold White Fury* - Beth Amos   h   97

**Bonnie**
*Expiry Date* - Carol Anne Davis   *h*   1401

**Bowen, Tess**
*The Uprising* - Abigail McDaniels   *h*   3785

**Buchanan, Victoria**
*The Vampire Papers* - Michael Romkey   *h*   4666

**Callare, Jesse**
*Mother of Storms* - John Barnes   *s*   354

**Carter, Travis**
*Demon's Fright* - Penelope Banka Kreps   *h*   3233

**Chapin, Francis**
*Blood of Innocents* - John Arbucci   *h*   204

**Chen, Robert**
*Starseed* - Spider Robinson   *s*   4643

**Cierto, Hoja**
*Black Steel* - Steve Perry   *s*   4291

**Coffey, Malcolm "Cup"**
*Goat Dance* - Douglas Clegg   *h*   1079

**Connely, Mary**
*Blood Feud* - Sam Siciliano   *h*   5020

**Craven, Tammy**
*Blood Kin* - Ronald Kelly   *h*   3051

**Crindle**
*Mysteries of the Word* - Stanley Wiater   *h*   5796

**Cruitaire, Christa**
*Gossamer Axe* - Gael Baudino   *f*   392

**Defoe, Piper**
*Storytellers* - Julie Anne Parks   *h*   4249

**Denisovitch, Pavel**
*The Nanotech Chronicles* - Michael Flynn   *s*   1964

**Dennehy, Nuala Maebh**
*The Rising of the Moon* - Flynn Connolly   *s*   1135

**Drake, Christopher**
*End Game* - Robert Cain   *s*   830

**Dulcet, Giulia**
*Song for the Basilisk* - Patricia A. McKillip   *f*   3841

**Dunbar, Maggie**
*Dark Tide* - Elizabeth Forrest   *h*   1972

**Edhadeya**
*Earthborn* - Orson Scott Card   *s*   884

**Evans, Jonna**
*Monster* - John Tigges   *h*   5474

**Fast, Barry**
*Firestar* - Michael Flynn   *s*   1962

**Feinstein, Rose**
*The Magic Touch* - Jody Lynn Nye   *f*   4171

**Feraru, Michael**
*The Lost* - Jonathan Aycliffe   *h*   279

**Frame, Max**
*Dead End* - Guy N. Smith   *h*   5119

**Freleng, Rachel**
*Cries of the Children* - Clare McNally   *h*   3856

**Galbraith, Jenn**
*Good Night, Sweet Angel* - Clare McNally   *h*   3857

**Ghan**
*The Waterborn* - J. Gregory Keyes   *f*   3098

**Graham, Dexter**
*Mysterium* - Robert Charles Wilson   *s*   5911

**Graves, Elliott**
*Dark Lullaby* - Jessica Palmer   *h*   4237

**Grout**
*The Knights of Cawdor* - Mike Jefferies   *f*   2886

**Halver**
*The Dubious Hills* - Pamela Dean   *f*   1444

**Harker, Mina**
*Mina* - Marie Kiraly   *h*   3151


**Harper, Jim**
*Oktober* - Stephen Gallagher   *h*   2112

**Harris**
*The Rats* - James Herbert   *h*   2671

**Hawthorne, Sara**
*Moonfall* - Tamara Thorne   *h*   5464

**Heredes**
*A Passage of Stars* - Alis A. Rasmussen   *s*   4482

**Hickory, Magister**
*Wizard's Hall* - Jane Yolen   *f*   6043

**Holman, Guy**
*Charmed Life* - Bernard Taylor   *h*   5399

**Ironhart, Jim**
*Cold Fire* - Dean R. Koontz   *h*   3203

**Jackson, Andrew**
*Spirit Crossings* - Claudia Peck   *f*   4275

**John, Mortel**
*Commencement* - Roby James   *s*   2877

**Johnson, Harriette**
*Inagehi* - Jack Cady   *h*   817

**Johnson, Hildy**
*Steel Beach* - John Varley   *s*   5566

**Kallisti, Magdalen**
*Specters* - J.M. Dillard   *h*   1555

**Karpou, Betty Lou**
*My Teacher Fried My Brains* - Bruce Coville   *s*   1223

**Kelys**
*In the Mothers' Land* - Elisabeth Vonarburg   *s*   5590

**Kendal, Evan**
*Stunts* - Charles L. Grant   *h*   2317

**La Cotta, Paul**
*Dawn Song* - Michael Marano   *h*   3620

**Lambert, Constance**
*The Stone Circle* - Gary Goshgarian   *h*   2285

**Lasalle, Stevie**
*The Death Crystal* - J. Edward Ames   *h*   91

**Leigh, Makoto Shirata**
*Makoto* - Kelley Wilde   *h*   5801

**Leones, Giraut**
*A Million Open Doors* - John Barnes   *s*   353

**Lewes, Charlotte**
*John Dollar* - Marianne Wiggins   *h*   5799

**Linnie**
*The Wall at the Edge of the World* - Jim Aikin   *s*   46

**Logan, Diana**
*Eye Killers* - A.A. Carr   *h*   911

**Logan, Jennifer**
*Earthgrip* - Harry Turtledove   *s*   5499

**Lu**
*Sing the Light* - Louise Marley   *s*   3629

**Macaffrey, Lester Hill**
*Heathern* - Jack Womack   *s*   5958

**Makepeace, Sebastian**
*The Last Wizard* - Simon Hawke   *f*   2619

**Manning, Kitty**
*Meridian 144* - Meg Files   *s*   1932

**Martin, Paul**
*Shaman Woods* - Morgan Fields   *h*   1931

**Matthews, Charles**
*I Met a Man Who Wasn't There* - Mary R. Callaghan   *h*   840

**McCarthy, Mary Margaret**
*Substitute Teacher* - Jordan Storm   *h*   5314


**McCormick, Lianne**
*When the Bough Breaks* - Mercedes Lackey   *f*   3302

**McCormick, Marilou**
*Room 13* - Henry Garfield   *h*   2139

**McCready**
*Damnbanna* - Nancy Springer   *f*   5177

**McPherson, Jim**
*The Gold Coast* - Kim Stanley Robinson   *s*   4632

**Milburn, Annie**
*Charmed Life* - Bernard Taylor   *h*   5399

**Mint, Maytera**
*Calde of the Long Sun* - Gene Wolfe   *s*   5937

**Morgasdotte, Roba**
*Bones of the Past* - Holly Lisle   *f*   3478

**Nailer, Steve**
*Grimm Memorials* - R. Patrick Gates   *h*   2160

**Neary, Mark**
*Billy* - Whitley Strieber   *h*   5338

**Nielson**
*When Darkness Falls* - Sidney Williams   *h*   5825

**Nolan, Eric**
*Shadow Child* - Joseph A. Citro   *h*   1038

**O'Donnell, Charley**
*Fog Heart* - Thomas Tessier   *h*   5440

**Overstreet, Lee**
*After Life* - Andrew Neiderman   *h*   4083

**Oykib**
*Earthfall* - Orson Scott Card   *s*   885

**Paarman, Martin**
*Succumb* - Ron Dee   *h*   1468

**Palmer, Jane**
*Panda Ray* - Michael Kandel   *s*   3011

**Podlowski, Eric**
*Brothers of the Dragon* - Robin Wayne Bailey   *f*   286

**Potts, Edward "Potty"**
*The Red-Eared Ghosts* - Vivian Alcock   *f*   53

**Powell, Richard**
*The Bell Witch: An American Haunting* - Brent Monahan   *h*   3953

**Powers, Richard**
*Galatea 2.2* - Richard M. Powers   *s*   4381

**Powl**
*Lens of the World* - R.A. MacAvoy   *f*   3582

**Rakam, Radosse**
*Four Ways to Forgiveness* - Ursula K. Le Guin   *s*   3380

**Rasa**
*The Call of Earth* - Orson Scott Card   *s*   882
*The Memory of Earth* - Orson Scott Card   *s*   894

**Reeves, Gail**
*The Immaculate* - Mark Morris   *h*   4023

**Reichmann, Wolfgang "Wolfie"**
*Being of Two Minds* - Pamela F. Service   *f*   4918

**Rhymer, Catherine**
*Reluctant Voyagers* - Elisabeth Vonarburg   *s*   5591

**Richards, Neil**
*Sister, Sister* - Andrew Neiderman   *h*   4091

**Rille, Cailet Ambrai**
*The Mageborn Traitor* - Melanie Rawn   *f*   4488

**Robinson, Sarah**
*Beyond the Shroud* - Rick Hautala   *h*   2604

**Rook, Jim**
*Rook* - Graham Masterton   *h*   3678
*The Terror* - Graham Masterton   *h*   3679
*Tooth and Claw* - Graham Masterton   *h*   3680

**Ross, Angie**
*Impulse* - Rick Hautala  *h*  2609

**Scott, Michael**
*The Black School* - J.N. Williamson  *h*  5851

**Sensar**
*Minds Apart* - Margaret Davis  *s*  1408

**Sharpless, Carril**
*The Ragged World: A Novel of the Hefn on Earth* -
Judith Moffett  *s*  3943

**Shelagh**
*Sweetheart, Sweetheart* - Bernard Taylor  *h*  5402

**Simms, Nanci**
*Deep Trek* - James Axler  *s*  278

**Strayhorn, Philip**
*Shock Lines* - Warren Newton Beath  *h*  427

**Succor-of-Yellowways-Sands**
*Nanoware Time/The Persistence of Vision* - Ian
Watson  *s*  5638

**Sulaweyo, Irene**
*River of Blue Fire* - Tad Williams  *f*  5830

**Sulaweyo, Renie**
*City of Golden Shadow* - Tad Williams  *s*  5828

**Sutton, Michael**
*Secrets of the Morning* - V.C. Andrews  *h*  146

**Tamar**
*The Iron Ring* - Lloyd Alexander  *f*  68

**Tekkitho, Chin**
*Homegoing* - Frederik Pohl  *s*  4347

**Thakur**
*Ratha and Thistle-Chaser* - Clare Bell  *f*  432

**Timpson, Freda**
*The Red-Eared Ghosts* - Vivian Alcock  *f*  53

**Tobias, Charlotte**
*Making Love* - Melanie Tem  *h*  5422

**Travis, Susanne**
*The One Safe Place* - Ramsey Campbell  *h*  862

**Von Karlsfeld, Hilda**
*Mordenheim* - Chet Williamson  *h*  5847

**Wallace, Brandy**
*Dreambuilder* - Tom Deitz  *f*  1471

**Warwick, David**
*Sweetheart, Sweetheart* - Bernard Taylor  *h*  5402

**Webster, Tom**
*Requiem* - Graham Joyce  *h*  2994

**Weir, Jacob**
*The Black School* - J.N. Williamson  *h*  5851

**Wells, Nancy**
*Dark Twilight* - Joseph A. Citro  *h*  1036

**Wheeler, Kelly**
*Captain Quad* - Sean Costello  *h*  1203

**Withrow, Dennis "Dennis Dithrovvu"**
*Mathemagics* - Margaret Ball  *f*  316

**Wu, Kildee**
*Black Steel* - Steve Perry  *s*  4291

**Wyatt, Ren**
*Storytellers* - Julie Anne Parks  *h*  4249

**Zach**
*Ecstasy Club* - Douglas Rushkoff  *s*  4732

**Zeeman, Richard**
*Blue Moon* - Laurell K. Hamilton  *h*  2513
*The Killing Dance* - Laurell K. Hamilton  *h*  2518
*The Lunatic Cafe* - Laurell K. Hamilton  *h*  2520

## TECHNICIAN

**Carlson, Winnie**
*Putting Up Roots* - Charles Sheffield  *s*  4964

**Castor, Charlie**
*Operation Damocles* - Oscar L. Fellows  *s*  1916

**Craig, James Christopher**
*Psychamok* - Brian Lumley  *h*  3561

**Fortune, Celinde "Cissy"**
*Dreaming Metal* - Melissa Scott  *s*  4895

**Heber, Kevin**
*Bug Park* - James P. Hogan  *s*  2723

**Karmade, Theodore "Ted"**
*Quasar* - Jamil Nasir  *s*  4071

**Lee, Wei**
*Red Dust* - Paul J. McAuley  *s*  3715

**Mirabara, Keishi**
*The Fortunate Fall* - Raphael Carter  *s*  927

**Ornis, Frederik Ry**
*Legacy* - Greg Bear  *s*  420

**Peter**
*Ecstasy Club* - Douglas Rushkoff  *s*  4732

**Sharkey, Alex**
*Fairyland* - Paul J. McAuley  *s*  3711

**Sullivan, Pete**
*Expiration Date* - Tim Powers  *f*  4383

**Taki**
*Bug Park* - James P. Hogan  *s*  2723

**Tamura, Eiko**
*Harvest of Stars* - Poul Anderson  *s*  127

**Trapp, Phillip**
*Blood Work* - Fay Zachary  *h*  6050

## TEENAGER

**Aaron, Lincoln**
*After Silence* - Jonathan Carroll  *h*  916

**Adams, Nicola Chelsea "Niki"**
*From a Whisper to a Scream* - Samuel M.
Key  *h*  3093

**Adler, Keisha**
*Owlsight* - Mercedes Lackey  *f*  3292

**Aguilar, Carlos**
*Days of the Dead* - Ashley McConnell  *h*  3774

**Aisling, Miranda**
*Voyage of the Basset* - James C.
Christensen  *f*  1024

**Alexander**
*The Prince and the Pilgrim* - Mary Stewart  *f*  5270

**Alice**
*The Prince and the Pilgrim* - Mary Stewart  *f*  5270

**Allaird, Margaret "Marnie"**
*Arrow From Earth* - F.M. Busby  *s*  782

**Alys**
*Dragon's Bait* - Vivian Vande Velde  *f*  5556

**Amy**
*The Kingdom of Kevin Malone* - Suzy McKee
Charnas  *f*  970

**Anatole**
*Silicon Embrace* - John Shirley  *s*  5009

**Anderson, Aaron**
*Oasis* - Brian Hodge  *h*  2703

**Anderson, Chris**
*Oasis* - Brian Hodge  *h*  2703

**Anderson, Kelly**
*Darkness* - John Saul  *h*  4840

**Andrea**
*The Third Beast* - Peter Loughran  *h*  3527

**Angel Juan**
*Missing Angel Juan* - Francesca Lia Block  *f*  550

**Antero, Amalric**
*The Far Kingdoms* - Allan Cole  *f*  1104

**Anthony**
*The First Horror* - R.L. Stine  *h*  5288

**Aradia**
*A Heroine of the World* - Tanith Lee  *f*  3412

**Arry**
*The Dubious Hills* - Pamela Dean  *f*  1444

**Arthor**
*The Eagle and the Sword* - A.A. Attanasio  *f*  267

**Aryl**
*Under Alien Stars* - Pamela F. Service  *s*  4919

**Asgar, Klia**
*Foundation and Chaos* - Greg Bear  *s*  418

**Astiar, Meliara "Mel"**
*Court Duel* - Sherwood Smith  *f*  5137

**Atbin**
*The Promise* - Monica Hughes  *s*  2808

**Baldwin, Sean**
*Yon Ill Wind* - Piers Anthony  *f*  196

**Balter, Harry**
*Parable of the Sower* - Octavia E. Butler  *s*  792

**Barrow, Simon**
*The First Duelist* - Rutledge Etheridge  *s*  1849

**Basker, Tem**
*The Starlight Crystal* - Christopher Pike  *s*  4333

**Bat, Cherokee**
*Cherokee Bat and the Goat Guys* - Francesca Lia
Block  *f*  546

**Battacharia, Rustum "Bat"**
*The Ganymede Club* - Charles Sheffield  *s*  4955

**Beckett, Kerry**
*Irrational Fears* - William Browning
Spencer  *h*  5167

**Becky**
*See You Later* - Christopher Pike  *f*  4332

**Bell, Justin Wood**
*Article 23* - William R. Forstchen  *s*  1978

**Bellard, Fern**
*Something Stirs* - Charles L. Grant  *h*  2316

**Belle, Amy**
*Witch* - Christopher Pike  *f*  4334

**Belzoni, Peter**
*Dinosaur Summer* - Greg Bear  *s*  416

**Benedict, Whitney**
*The Boy Who Cried Werewolf* - Elvira  *h*  1800

**Bering**
*The Dog King* - Christoph Ransmayr  *f*  4474

**Bidding, Philippa**
*Rebel From Alphorion* - Robyn Tallis  *s*  5381

**Bird, Catherine White**
*Tooth and Claw* - Graham Masterton  *h*  3680

**Bishop, Bryan**
*Away Is a Strange Place to Be* - H.M.
Hoover  *s*  2763

**Black, Charlie**
*When Darkness Falls* - Sidney Williams  *h*  5825

**Blade**
*Dark Lord of Derkholm* - Diana Wynne
Jones  *f*  2946
*Madman Run* - David Robbins  *s*  4600

**Blair, Tony**
*Boys of Life* - Paul Russell  *h*  4737

**Blake, Nick**
*Dragon Burning* - Craig Shaw Gardner  *f*  2126
*Dragon Sleeping* - Craig Shaw Gardner  *f*  2127
*Dragon Waking* - Craig Shaw Gardner  *f*  2128

**Bouriere, Tira**
*Crown of Empire* - Chelsea Quinn Yarbro  *s*  6014

**Bouriere, Wiley**
*Crown of Empire* - Chelsea Quinn Yarbro  *s*  6014

**Brazil, Bubbles**
*Negrophobia: An Urban Parable* - Darius
    James  *f*  2859

**Breanna**
*Zombie Lover* - Piers Anthony  *f*  197

**Bremmers, Lana**
*The Devil's End* - D.A. Fowler  *h*  2023

**Brett/Natalie**
*Holy Fire* - Bruce Sterling  *s*  5259

**Brewster, Kip**
*Starswarm* - Jerry Pournelle  *s*  4379

**Brewster, Mackenzie**
*The Witch of Maple Park* - Stephanie S.
    Tolan  *f*  5478

**Brightblade, Douglas**
*Pyromancer* - Don Callander  *f*  847

**Brill, Lucy**
*Prodigal* - Melanie Tem  *h*  5423

**Brill, Rae**
*Prodigal* - Melanie Tem  *h*  5423

**Bronson, Raymond**
*I Know What You Did Last Summer* - Lois
    Duncan  *h*  1692

**Brostek**
*Shadow-Maze* - Mark Smith  *f*  5133

**Brown, Max**
*Thrill* - Patricia Wallace  *h*  5624

**Bryge, Larry**
*Spirit Crossings* - Claudia Peck  *f*  4275

**Buckland, Ulysses**
*The Whims of Creation* - Simon Hawke  *s*  2626

**Buddy**
*Land O'Goshen* - Charles McNair  *s*  3855

**Burroughs, Mahree**
*Starbridge* - A.C. Crispin  *s*  1265

**Byrns, Scott**
*Something Stirs* - Charles L. Grant  *h*  2316

**Caceras, Mimla**
*Traitors from Within* - R.A. Montgomery  *s*  3966

**Callahan, Jessica**
*Sweet Revenge* - Jean Simon  *h*  5066

**Callahan, Juanita "Nita"**
*A Wizard Abroad* - Diane Duane  *f*  1668

**Campbell, Brianne**
*Journeyman Wizard* - Mary Frances
    Zambreno  *f*  6057

**Carpenter, Alison**
*Guardian* - John Saul  *h*  4841

**Carpenter, Corey**
*Dark Time* - Maxine O'Callaghan  *h*  4189

**Carruthers, Ronald "Ronnie"**
*Hunting Party* - Elizabeth Moon  *s*  3968

**Carson, Erin**
*Darkside* - Dennis Etchison  *h*  1845

**Cart**
*The Time of the Ghost* - Diana Wynne
    Jones  *f*  2951

**Carter, David**
*The Eyes of the Beast* - Steve Harris  *h*  2565

**Casad, Sasha**
*Bodyguard* - William C. Dietz  *s*  1542

**Casey, Jerry**
*Cold Allies* - Patricia Anthony  *s*  157

**Caspar**
*The Ogre Downstairs* - Diana Wynne Jones  *f*  2949

**Cassia**
*The Cult of Loving Kindness* - Paul Park  *s*  4242

**Cavish, Beka**
*Stalking Darkness* - Lynn Flewelling  *f*  1953

**Cayne, Candy**
*Cold Iron* - Melisa Michaels  *f*  3886

**Cedric**
*Strings* - Dave Duncan  *s*  1689

**Chakallakak, Chakallakak "Chaka" ngha**
*The Long Hunt* - Debra Doyle  *s*  1602

**Challer, Bo**
*A Whisper of Wings* - Steven Ray Fulgham  *h*  2091

**Chang, Deanna**
*Scorpion Shards* - Neal Shusterman  *s*  5013

**Chase, Danny**
*The Magic Bicycle* - William Hill  *f*  2688

**Chase-Frisson L'Zalle, Trevarre**
*Shivering World* - Kathy Tyers  *s*  5526

**Cheever, Shelby V**
*The Billion Dollar Boy* - Charles Sheffield  *s*  4948

**Chloe**
*Camp Vamp* - Elvira  *h*  1801

**Chris**
*Thirsty* - M.T. Anderson  *h*  120

**Christian, Paige**
*The Starlight Crystal* - Christopher Pike  *s*  4333

**Clark, Steve**
*Disturbing Behavior* - John Whitman  *h*  5789

**Clemmy**
*The Fools' War* - Lee Kisling  *f*  3159

**Cofield, Aaron**
*Ray Bradbury Presents: Dinosaur Planet* - Stephen
    Leigh  *s*  3427
*Ray Bradbury Presents: Dinosaur World* - Stephen
    Leigh  *s*  3428

**Cole, Dillon**
*Scorpion Shards* - Neal Shusterman  *s*  5013

**Colene**
*Chaos Mode* - Piers Anthony  *f*  165
*Fractal Mode* - Piers Anthony  *f*  171
*Virtual Mode* - Piers Anthony  *f*  194

**Collins, Chad**
*Quozl* - Alan Dean Foster  *s*  2013

**Corrigan, Casey**
*The Witch of Maple Park* - Stephanie S.
    Tolan  *f*  5478

**Costello, Joey**
*Something Stirs* - Charles L. Grant  *h*  2316

**Cottington, Angelica**
*Lady Cottington's Pressed Fairy Book* - Terry
    Jones  *f*  2981

**Crandall, Raymond E. Jr.**
*The Magic Touch* - Jody Lynn Nye  *f*  4171

**Cuchlainn**
*The Raid* - Randy Lee Eickhoff  *f*  1764

**Culley, Mance**
*The Living Dark* - Stephen Gresham  *h*  2431

**Curran, Baal**
*Killobyte* - Piers Anthony  *f*  179

**Cutler, Philip**
*Dawn* - V.C. Andrews  *h*  144

**Dafoe, Mary Lou "Merrilu"**
*Dragon Sleeping* - Craig Shaw Gardner  *f*  2127

**Dafoe, Rafe**
*Blood and Chocolate* - Annette Curtis
    Klause  *h*  3162

**Dagref**
*Fox and Empire* - Harry Turtledove  *f*  5500

**Daley, Cameron**
*The Vanishing* - Marilyn Kaye  *s*  3021

**Daneam, Penelope**
*Dominion* - Bentley Little  *h*  3492

**Daniels, Kip**
*Godzilla 2000* - Marc Cerasini  *s*  949

**Danilov, Justin**
*These Fallen Angels* - Wendy Haley  *h*  2492

**Danya**
*Vampire Diary: The Embrace* - Robert
    Weinberg  *h*  5705

**Darian**
*Owlsight* - Mercedes Lackey  *f*  3292

**David**
*Medallion of the Black Hound* - Shirley Rousseau
    Murphy  *f*  4056

**Davidson, Troy**
*Liquid Diet* - William Tedford  *h*  5419

**Davis, Shannon**
*The Store* - Bentley Little  *h*  3497

**Deal, Brian**
*The Square Deal* - David Drake  *s*  1644

**Deborah**
*Wilding* - Melanie Tem  *h*  5425

**Debra**
*The Sister* - Elleston Trevor  *h*  5484

**deCotmer, Ailith**
*A Time for Us* - Christine Holden  *f*  2731

**Delacroix, Ivy**
*Tunnelvision* - R. Patrick Gates  *h*  2162

**Delane, Ariel**
*Intensity* - Dean R. Koontz  *h*  3210

**Delgado, Susan**
*Wizard and Glass* - Stephen King  *h*  3144

**Delgato, Amy**
*Dark Time* - Maxine O'Callaghan  *h*  4189

**Demarest, Patti**
*Demon's Fright* - Penelope Banka Kreps  *h*  3233

**DeMarian, Demnor**
*The Stone Prince* - Fiona Patton  *f*  4259

**Denison, Will**
*Dinotopia* - James Gurney  *f*  2468

**Dentata, Regina**
*Shock Lines* - Warren Newton Beath  *h*  427

**Desmond, Emily**
*King of Morning, Queen of Day* - Ian
    McDonald  *f*  3793

**Desmond, Timothy Alfred**
*Gnome Man's Land* - Esther Friesner  *f*  2075

**Doheny, Shannon**
*Elvira: Transylvania 90210* - Elvira  *h*  1802

**Donatello, Kevin**
*The Uprising* - Abigail McDaniels  *h*  3785

**Doot**
*Wolf Flow* - K.W. Jeter  *h*  2918

**Douay, Deldragon Drakedon "Drake"**
*Lords of the Sword* - Hugh Cook  *f*  1156

**D'Rosselin, Jens Metadi Jessan**
*The Long Hunt* - Debra Doyle  *s*  1602

**Duberville, Myron**
*Outer Space and All That Junk* - Mel
   Gilden   s   2227
**Dug**
*Demons Don't Dream* - Piers Anthony   f   168
**DuMar, Theresa "T.J." Jr.**
*T.J.'s Ghost* - Shirley Climo   h   1087
**Dunbar, Lane**
*The Stake* - Richard Laymon   h   3372
**Dwayne**
*The Cat* - R.L. Stine   h   5285
**Eagen, Wesley**
*Hell-O-Ween* - David Robbins   h   4598
**Elena**
*Wit'ch Fire* - James Clemens   f   1082
**Ella**
*I Feel Like the Morning Star* - Gregory
   Maguire   s   3608
*Shade's Children* - Garth Nix   s   4130
**Elliott, Kate**
*Vision Quest* - Pamela F. Service   f   4920
**Elliott, Noah**
*Bloodstream* - Tess Gerritsen   h   2205
**Ember, Annie**
*Elephantasm* - Tanith Lee   h   3408
**Emerson, Dirk**
*Demon's Fright* - Penelope Banka Kreps   h   3233
**Emily**
*The House on Hound Hill* - Maggie Prince   f   4438
**Endicott, James "Jimmy"**
*Delta Search* - William Shatner   s   4930
**Erik**
*The Lone Sentinel* - Jo Dereske   s   1493
**Esterbrook, Diana**
*The Higher Space* - Jamil Nasir   s   4070
**Etchison, Theo**
*Riverrun* - S.P. Somtow   f   5159
**Eva**
*Eva* - Peter Dickinson   s   1525
*Into the Forest* - Jean Hegland   s   2640
**Everett, Matt**
*Article 23* - William R. Forstchen   s   1978
**Fels, Jimmy**
*Penance* - Rick R. Reed   h   4501
**Fleming, Cory**
*Hell-O-Ween* - David Robbins   h   4598
**Florence, Julia**
*Witch* - Christopher Pike   f   4334
**Fong, Jimmy**
*Vision Quest* - Pamela F. Service   f   4920
**Francie**
*In the Heart of the Valley of Love* - Cynthia
   Kadohata   s   2997
**Francy, Lizzie**
*Beggars Ride* - Nancy Kress   s   3238
**Frankel, Melissa**
*Roadkill* - Richard Sanford   h   4815
**Frankie**
*Collidescope* - Grace Chetwin   s   1011
**Frasier, Cally**
*The First Horror* - R.L. Stine   h   5288
**Frasier, Cody**
*The First Horror* - R.L. Stine   h   5288
**Freeman, Justine**
*Perfect Little Angels* - Andrew Neiderman   h   4090

**Freemark, Nest**
*Running with the Demon* - Terry Brooks   f   715
**French, Melissa**
*Liquid Diet* - William Tedford   h   5419
**Fuller, Stan**
*The Summoned* - Steven Ray Fulgham   h   2090
**Gale, C.J.**
*Little Boy Lost* - T.M. Wright   h   5992
**Gale, Dorothy**
*Visitors From Oz: The Wild Adventures of Dorothy,
   the Scarecrow and the Tin Woodman* - Martin
   Gardner   f   2136
**Gandillon, Vivian**
*Blood and Chocolate* - Annette Curtis
   Klause   h   3162
**Garcia-Chase, Isabel**
*The Wall Around Eden* - Joan Slonczewski   s   5092
**Garfield, Joanne**
*Parable of the Sower* - Octavia E. Butler   s   792
**Gart, Maya**
*The Faces of Ceti* - Mary Caraker   s   877
**Gelly**
*Flight to Hollow Mountain* - Mark Sebanc   f   4908
**Geronimo**
*Madman Run* - David Robbins   s   4600
**Gilmour, Wendy**
*Nighteyes* - Garfield Reeves-Stevens   s   4510
**Gina**
*All's Faire* - Pamela F. Service   f   4917
**Golding, Juniper**
*The Juniper Game* - Sherryl Jordan   f   2992
**Gordon, Kate**
*The Merlin Effect* - T.A. Barron   f   371
**Grant, Kip**
*Spook Night* - David Robbins   h   4603
**Grant, Shery**
*Spook Night* - David Robbins   h   4603
**Grimson, Jim**
*Red Orc's Rage* - Philip Jose Farmer   f   1873
**Guenther, Spiro**
*The Devil's End* - D.A. Fowler   h   2023
**Gurney, Molly**
*Out of the Ordinary* - Annie Dalton   f   1330
**Hague, Scott**
*Witch* - Christopher Pike   f   4334
**Hara, Jay**
*Godspeed* - Charles Sheffield   s   4957
**Harper, Fay**
*Jinx High* - Mercedes Lackey   h   3284
**Harper, Marty**
*The Cat* - R.L. Stine   h   5285
**Harper, Willie**
*Dark Fortune* - Richard Lee Byers   h   795
**Hart, Adragon**
*Sweet Blood* - Pat Graversen   h   2337
**Hart, Beth**
*Precious Blood* - Pat Graversen   h   2336
**Hart, Lola**
*Random Acts of Senseless Violence* - Jack
   Womack   f   5959
**Hasgard, David**
*Traitors from Within* - R.A. Montgomery   s   3966
**Hawk-Hobby**
*Merlin* - Jane Yolen   f   6035
**Hayes, Drew**
*Living with Aliens* - John DeChancie   s   1460

**Heber, Kevin**
*Bug Park* - James P. Hogan   s   2723
**Hector**
*The Lake at the End of the World* - Caroline
   MacDonald   s   3584
**Helmond, Alexandra "Ally"**
*The Orpheus Process* - Daniel H. Gower   h   2293
**Henchard, Daniel**
*Groogleman* - Debra Doyle   s   1600
**Hendricks, Cara**
*Shadow World* - A.C. Crispin   s   1262
**Hendricks, Connie**
*Being of Two Minds* - Pamela F. Service   f   4918
**Hidalgo, Lourdes**
*Scorpion Shards* - Neal Shusterman   s   5013
**Higginson, Alice**
*Painted Devil* - Michael Bedard   f   430
**Hildegund**
*Attila's Treasure* - Stephan Grundy   f   2453
**Hilton, Matt**
*Journey to Terezor* - Frank Asch   s   221
**Holland, Linda**
*Carnival* - William W. Johnstone   h   2927
**Holloway, Melissa**
*Second Child* - John Saul   h   4844
**Holmes, Sherlock**
*Muddle Earth* - John Brunner   s   735
**Holscomb, Ray**
*Junkyard* - Barry Porter   h   4370
**Horton, Lisa**
*Althea* - Abigail McDaniels   h   3782
**Howe, Geena**
*Monet's Ghost* - Chelsea Quinn Yarbro   f   6017
**Hph-wayuo "Alvin"**
*Infinity's Shore* - David Brin   s   688
**Indigo**
*The Unicorn Sonata* - Peter S. Beagle   f   412
**Islay, Robretta "Bretta Martyn"**
*Bretta Martyn* - L. Neil Smith   s   5128
**Iz**
*Random Acts of Senseless Violence* - Jack
   Womack   f   5959
**Jack**
*After the Blue* - Russel Like   s   3465
**Jacoby, Daniel**
*The Wall Around Eden* - Joan Slonczewski   s   5092
**James**
*The Dying Sun* - Gary L. Blackwood   s   511
**James, Julie**
*I Know What You Did Last Summer* - Lois
   Duncan   h   1692
**Janozek, Magda**
*Flare Star* - Paula E. Downing   s   1594
**Jed**
*Armageddon Summer* - Jane Yolen   s   6028
**Jeffrey**
*Clan of the Shape-Changers* - Robert Levy   f   3446
**Jilseponie "Pony"**
*The Demon Awakens* - R.A. Salvatore   f   4794
**Jo**
*Balyet* - Patricia Wrightson   f   5995
**Johnson, Lezzie**
*Groogleman* - Debra Doyle   s   1600
**Jonah**
*The House on Hound Hill* - Maggie Prince   f   4438

**Jones, Indiana "Indy"**
*The Mata Hari Adventure* - James Luceno *f* 3544

**Jones, T.J.**
*Rook* - Graham Masterton *h* 3678

**Jordan, Andy**
*65mm* - Dale Hoover *h* 2761

**Jordan, Richard "Rivername"**
*Project Farcry* - Pauline Ashwell *s* 230

**J'role**
*The Longing Ring* - Christopher Kubasik *f* 3246

**Jude**
*Random Acts of Senseless Violence* - Jack
   Womack *f* 5959

**Julia**
*Blue Moon* - Hila Feil *f* 1898

**Kaantille, Katrina**
*The Loneliest Magician* - Irene Radford *f* 4461

**Kahn, Tae**
*Beyond Ragnarok* - Mickey Zucker Reichert *f* 4516

**Kal**
*Flight to Hollow Mountain* - Mark Sebanc *f* 4908

**Kaplan, T'ing Hau**
*Gnome Man's Land* - Esther Friesner *f* 2075

**Kara**
*Flight of the Dragon Kyn* - Susan Fletcher *f* 1951

**Kat**
*Dark Heart* - Betsy James *f* 2857

**Kate**
*The Ancient One* - T.A. Barron *f* 368

**Kawaguchi, Mike**
*The Summoned* - Steven Ray Fulgham *h* 2090

**Kayrlis**
*Ancient Games* - Scott Ciencin *f* 1028

**Kee**
*The Book of Webster's* - J.N. Williamson *h* 5853

**Keeper, Tom**
*The Ways of Magic* - Scott Ciencin *f* 1033

**Keeton, Tallis**
*Lavondyss: Journey to an Unknown Region* - Robert
   Holdstock *f* 2739

**Kelly, Ista**
*Night Sky Mine* - Melissa Scott *s* 4898

**Kem**
*Through the Heart* - Richard Grant *f* 2328

**Ken**
*The Lost City of the Jedi* - Paul Davids *s* 1393

**Kestrel, Derek "Deke"**
*Jinx High* - Mercedes Lackey *h* 3284

**Kevin**
*All's Faire* - Pamela F. Service *f* 4917
*The Midnight Club* - Christopher Pike *h* 4329

**Killany, Molly**
*Night Cruise* - Billie Sue Mosiman *h* 4041

**Kim**
*Demons Don't Dream* - Piers Anthony *f* 168

**Kincaid, Hannah**
*A Witch Across Time* - Gilbert B. Cross *f* 1272

**Kirk, James T. "Jimmy"**
*Best Destiny* - Diane Carey *s* 900

**Klein, Alice**
*Higher Education* - Charles Sheffield *s* 4958

**Knox, Emily**
*Blood Lust* - Ron Dee *h* 1464

**Komodo**
*Gojiro* - Mark Jacobson *f* 2847

**Kruickshank, Jenny**
*The Whims of Creation* - Simon Hawke *s* 2626

**Laker, Naomi "Mig" Margaret**
*Aunt Maria* - Diana Wynne Jones *f* 2943

**Lamai, Leie**
*Glory Season* - David Brin *s* 686

**Lamai, Maia**
*Glory Season* - David Brin *s* 686

**Larissa**
*Larissa* - Emily Devenport *s* 1503

**LeBrae, Jael**
*Dragons in the Stars* - Jeffrey A. Carver *s* 930

**Lee, Afriqua**
*Jaguar* - Bill Ransom *s* 4477

**Lee, Lysistrata "Lizzie"**
*Unwillingly to Earth* - Pauline Ashwell *s* 231

**Lewis, Laura**
*The Third Beast* - Peter Loughran *h* 3527

**Leyner, Mark**
*The Tetherballs of Bougainville* - Mark
   Leyner *f* 3457

**Li, Beth**
*The Werewolf's Revenge* - Richard Jaccoma *h* 2841

**Lindsey, Alison**
*Midnight Is a Lonely Place* - Barbara
   Erskine *h* 1836

**Littlefield, Eric**
*Monkey Station* - Ardath Mayhar *s* 3703

**Longchamp, Dawn**
*Dawn* - V.C. Andrews *h* 144

**Luban, Rick**
*Higher Education* - Charles Sheffield *s* 4958

**Luz**
*The Secret Weavers: Stories of the Fantastic by Latin
   American Women* - Marjorie Agosin *f* 43

**Lyon, Isthian "Thian"**
*Damia's Children* - Anne McCaffrey *s* 3726

**Lyon, Laria**
*Damia's Children* - Anne McCaffrey *s* 3726

**Lyon, Rojer**
*Damia's Children* - Anne McCaffrey *s* 3726

**MacFarlane, Griffin**
*Furnace* - Muriel Gray *h* 2339

**MacIver, Teri**
*Second Child* - John Saul *h* 4844

**Madlen**
*The Sister* - Elleston Trevor *h* 5484

**Magnus, Brock**
*The Faces of Ceti* - Mary Caraker *s* 877

**Maguire, Aaron**
*The Wizard's Apprentice* - S.P. Somtow *f* 5163

**Malcolm**
*The Ogre Downstairs* - Diana Wynne Jones *f* 2949

**Malone, Kevin**
*The Kingdom of Kevin Malone* - Suzy McKee
   Charnas *f* 970

**Mancy, Katherine "Kat"**
*Her Monster* - Jeff Collignon *h* 1115

**Mandy**
*Weirdos of the Universe, Unite!* - Pamela F.
   Service *f* 4921

**Marbon, Diccon**
*Sunderlies Seeking* - Gayle Greeno *f* 2424

**Marbon, Jenneth**
*Sunderlies Seeking* - Gayle Greeno *f* 2424

**Marina**
*Armageddon Summer* - Jane Yolen *s* 6028

**Mark**
*The Transall Saga* - Gary Paulsen *s* 4262

**Marks, Barbie**
*I Was a Teenage Fairy* - Francesca Lia
   Block *f* 549

**Marlene**
*Nemesis* - Isaac Asimov *s* 247

**Marsh, Pella**
*Girl in Landscape* - Jonathan Lethem *s* 3440

**Mart**
*I Feel Like the Morning Star* - Gregory
   Maguire *s* 3608

**Martin, Justin**
*Thunder Road* - Chris Curry *h* 1296

**Martino, Chris**
*OtherSyde* - J. Michael Straczynski *h* 5323

**Mary**
*A Tie to the Past* - David Wiseman *f* 5928

**Mason, Jennifer**
*Ray Bradbury Presents: Dinosaur Planet* - Stephen
   Leigh *s* 3427
*Ray Bradbury Presents: Dinosaur World* - Stephen
   Leigh *s* 3428

**Masters, Amber**
*Haunted* - Tamara Thorne *h* 5463

**Mattison, Petie**
*Wake Up Screaming* - Vincent Courtney *h* 1215

**Max**
*Strange Attractors* - William Sleator *s* 5088

**Maxwell, Alicia**
*Facade* - Kristine Kathryn Rusch *h* 4716

**McDonald, Dirk**
*Baby Be-Bop* - Francesca Lia Block *f* 545
*Witch Baby* - Francesca Lia Block *f* 552

**McFarland, Sonny**
*Father's Little Helper* - Ronald Kelly *h* 3052

**McFee, Jonas**
*Jonas McFee, A.T.P.* - Sarah Sargent *s* 4827

**McKenzie, Chia**
*Idoru* - William Gibson *s* 2218

**McNamara, Alice**
*Along Came a Spider* - Athena Alexis *h* 70

**Menaker, Mikhail "the Mick" Geoffrey**
*Count Geiger's Blues* - Michael Bishop *s* 499

**Mennym, Appleby**
*The Mennyms* - Sylvia Waugh *f* 5654
*Mennyms Under Siege* - Sylvia Waugh *f* 5656

**Meriweather, Buncan**
*Son of Spellsinger* - Alan Dean Foster *f* 2015

**Meriweather, Gentian**
*Juniper, Gentian and Rosemary* - Pamela
   Dean *f* 1445

**Metaxos, Diego**
*Powers That Be* - Anne McCaffrey *s* 3745

**Milena "Alfred Russell Wallace"**
*Fairyland* Paul J. McAuley *s* 3711

**Miles, Janna**
*Speak to the Rain* - Helen K. Passey *h* 4257

**Mitsuko, Fujiwara "Little Puddle" no**
*Little Sister* - Kara Dalkey *f* 1320

**Mordock, Kyle**
*Midnight's Lair* - Richard Laymon *h* 3369

**Mornette, Will**
*Rebel From Alphorion* - Robyn Tallis *s* 5381

**Morning, Debbie Sue**
*Serial Killer Days* - David Prill   *h*   4436

**Morris**
*Under Siege* - Elisabeth Mace   *f*   3587

**Morrison, Troy**
*Dream-Weaver* - Louise Lawrence   *s*   3359

**Mouche**
*Six Moon Dance* - Sheri S. Tepper   *s*   5437

**Murdley, Jennifer**
*Jennifer Murdley's Toad* - Bruce Coville   *f*   1220

**Murphy, Emily**
*Fair Peril* - Nancy Springer   *f*   5178

**Nafai**
*The Call of Earth* - Orson Scott Card   *s*   882

**Neihart, Fletcher Robert**
*Finity's End* - C.J. Cherryh   *s*   988

**Nell**
*Into the Forest* - Jean Hegland   *s*   2640

**Nelson, MaryAnn "Spook"**
*Spook* - Steve Vance   *h*   5553

**Nelson, Zack**
*Sweet Revenge* - Jean Simon   *h*   5066

**Newell, Charlie**
*Wildside* - Steven Gould   *s*   2291

**Newkirk, Bobby**
*Double Date* - R.L. Stine   *h*   5287

**Newman, Sandy**
*The Mountain King* - Rick Hautala   *h*   2611

**Nguyen, Marie**
*Wildside* - Steven Gould   *s*   2291

**Niad**
*The Cursed* - Dave Duncan   *f*   1674

**Nicholas**
*The King's Buccaneer* - Raymond E. Feist   *f*   1904

**Nickerson, Josh**
*Kindred* - John Gideon   *h*   2222

**no Mitsuko, Fujiwara**
*The Heavenward Path* - Kara Dalkey   *f*   1319

**Noir, Julie**
*The Black Cat* - Robert Poe   *h*   4344

**Nolan, Ronan**
*A Wizard Abroad* - Diane Duane   *f*   1668

**Norak, Zach**
*Raptor* - Paul Zindel   *s*   6084

**Nothing**
*Lost Souls* - Poppy Z. Brite   *h*   697

**Oakland, Brian**
*Stunts* - Charles L. Grant   *h*   2317

**Oakton, Cody**
*Only Child* - H.M. Hoover   *s*   2764

**Obst, Roger**
*OtherSyde* - J. Michael Straczynski   *h*   5323

**O'Connor, Tim**
*Entity* - Nina Mandelik   *h*   3615

**O'Hara, Emerald**
*Quake* - Richard Laymon   *h*   3370

**Olamina, Lauren Oya**
*Parable of the Sower* - Octavia E. Butler   *s*   792

**Orc**
*Red Orc's Rage* - Philip Jose Farmer   *f*   1873

**Osborn, Winston D.**
*T.J.'s Ghost* - Shirley Climo   *h*   1087

**O'Shea, Devin**
*Moon of the Werewolf* - Ronald Kelly   *h*   3053

**O'Shea, Rosie**
*Moon of the Werewolf* - Ronald Kelly   *h*   3053

**Owen**
*Weirdos of the Universe, Unite!* - Pamela F. Service   *f*   4921

**Pablo "Sam Krueger"**
*Proxies* - Laura J. Mixon   *s*   3922

**Parganas, Koot "Kootie" Hoomie**
*Expiration Date* - Tim Powers   *f*   4383

**Parmenter, Casey**
*Tourists* - Lisa Goldstein   *f*   2264

**Patterson, Lizzie**
*Where the Towers Pierce the Sky* - Marie D. Goodwin   *f*   2272

**Pawluk, Ilonka**
*The Midnight Club* - Christopher Pike   *h*   4329

**Pink**
*Nanoware Time/The Persistence of Vision* - Ian Watson   *s*   5638

**Pop**
*Baby Be-Bop* - Francesca Lia Block   *f*   545

**Prentice, Clara**
*Wildside* - Steven Gould   *s*   2291

**Prettiance "Pretty"**
*Strange Deliverance* - Mary Brown   *s*   728

**Priestley, Amy**
*Nazareth Hill* - Ramsey Campbell   *h*   861

**Rael**
*The Cult of Loving Kindness* - Paul Park   *s*   4242

**Raitt, Johnny**
*The Vampire's Beautiful Daughter* - S.P. Somtow   *h*   5161

**Ramirez, Rafael**
*Blood Sport* - Lisa Smedman   *f*   5096

**Redfern, Diana**
*The Lake at the End of the World* - Caroline MacDonald   *s*   3584

**Rees**
*Raft* - Stephen Baxter   *s*   401

**Reyes, Eddie**
*Jaguar* - Bill Ransom   *s*   4477

**Rice, David "Davy"**
*Jumper* - Steven Gould   *s*   2290

**Riley, Ray**
*The Last Vampire* - Christopher Pike   *h*   4328

**Rivera, Josephine "Joey"**
*The Unicorn Sonata* - Peter S. Beagle   *f*   412

**Robbins, Jake**
*The Vanishing* - Marilyn Kaye   *s*   3021

**Robert**
*The Dying Sun* - Gary L. Blackwood   *s*   511

**Roberts, Heather**
*Blood Sabbath* - Leigh Clark   *h*   1048

**Rogers, Clive**
*The Tooth Fairy* - Graham Joyce   *f*   2995

**Ronay, Matthias "Matt"**
*Growing Up Weightless* - John M. Ford   *s*   1970

**Rosenberg, Willow**
*Return to Chaos* - Craig Shaw Gardner   *h*   2131

**Ross, Brandy**
*Impulse* - Rick Hautala   *h*   2609

**Rourke, Buneka**
*Powers That Be* - Anne McCaffrey   *s*   3745

**Rusty**
*A Time for Dragons* - Gary Gentile   *s*   2193

**Ryan, Lacey**
*Shackled* - Ray Garton   *h*   2156

**Ryder, Howie**
*Dawn's Uncertain Light* - Neal Barrett Jr.   *s*   365

**Sabriel**
*Sabriel* - Garth Nix   *f*   4129

**Sam**
*No Kidding* - Bruce Brooks   *s*   709

**Sampson, Matt**
*Traitors from Within* - R.A. Montgomery   *s*   3966

**Sander**
*Through the Heart* - Richard Grant   *f*   2328

**Santiago, Martina**
*The Vanishing* - Marilyn Kaye   *s*   3021

**Saxon, Bonnie**
*The Stake* - Richard Laymon   *h*   3372

**Scott**
*A Time for Dragons* - Gary Gentile   *s*   2193

**Seale, Evan**
*The Silent Strength of Stones* - Nina Kiriki Hoffman   *f*   2716

**Seale, Willow**
*The Silent Strength of Stones* - Nina Kiriki Hoffman   *f*   2716

**Semele, Dion**
*Dominion* - Bentley Little   *h*   3492

**Serege, Tristan "Tris"**
*Dominion's Reach* - Diann Thornley   *s*   5465
*Echoes of Issel* - Diann Thornley   *s*   5466
*Ganwold's Child* - Diann Thornley   *s*   5467

**Shade**
*Shade* - Emily Devenport   *s*   1504

**Shiva**
*Shiva Accused: An Adventure of the Ice Age* - J.H. Brennan   *f*   667
*Shiva: An Adventure of the Ice Age* - J.H. Brennan   *f*   669
*Shiva's Challenge: An Adventure of the Ice Age* - J.H. Brennan   *f*   668

**Sikes, Jason**
*Under Alien Stars* - Pamela F. Service   *s*   4919

**Silver, Jake**
*Them* - William W. Johnstone   *h*   2935

**Slaven, Eleret**
*The Raven Ring* - Patricia C. Wrede   *f*   5978

**Snell, Nancy**
*The Devil's End* - D.A. Fowler   *h*   2023

**Snell, Susan**
*Carrie* - Stephen King   *h*   3127

**Solo, Jacen**
*Trouble on Cloud City* - Kevin J. Anderson   *s*   117

**Solo, Jaina**
*Trouble on Cloud City* - Kevin J. Anderson   *s*   117

**Southall, Sam**
*The Tooth Fairy* - Graham Joyce   *f*   2995

**Spellman, Julie**
*The Homing* - John Saul   *h*   4842

**Spiro, Jason**
*Deadrush* - Yvonne Navarro   *h*   4073

**Spoor, Torrance**
*The Living One* - Lewis Gannett   *h*   2115

**Stanislaus, Glynn Webster**
*Mind Snare* - Gayle Greeno   *s*   2422

**Starbuck, Ron**
*Nevernever* - Will Shetterly   *f*   4995

**Stavenger, Douglas**
*Moonrise* - Ben Bova   *s*   587

**Stein, Susan "Starbright"**
*Summer of Love* - Lisa Mason   *s*   3664

**Stephen**
*The Last Book of Swords: Shieldbreaker's Story* - Fred
  Saberhagen  *f*  4768

**Strick, Gavin**
*Disturbing Behavior* - John Whitman  *h*  5789

**Suarez, Corazon "Cory"**
*White Light* - William Barton  *s*  384

**Summers, Buffy**
*Buffy the Vampire Slayer* - Richie Tankersley
  Cusick  *h*  1301
*The Harvest* - Richie Tankersley Cusick  *h*  1302
*Return to Chaos* - Craig Shaw Gardner  *h*  2131

**Sundquist, Michael**
*The Presence* - John Saul  *h*  4843

**Susan**
*Clan of the Shape-Changers* - Robert Levy  *f*  3446

**Swinton, Robby**
*Contagion* - John David Connor  *h*  1136

**Sylvan, Eve**
*Strange Attractors* - William Sleator  *s*  5088

**T.**
*The Smithsonian Institution* - Gore Vidal  *f*  5570

**Tabor, Abby**
*Away Is a Strange Place to Be* - H.M.
  Hoover  *s*  2763

**Taki**
*Bug Park* - James P. Hogan  *s*  2723

**Tamerlane "Tam"**
*Strange Deliverance* - Mary Brown  *s*  728

**Tanaquil**
*Black Unicorn* - Tanith Lee  *f*  3404

**Tanner, Mark**
*Creature* - John Saul  *h*  4839

**Teague, Aiden**
*Blood and Chocolate* - Annette Curtis
  Klause  *h*  3162

**Teppish, Rebecca**
*The Vampire's Beautiful Daughter* - S.P.
  Somtow  *h*  5161

**Thompkins, Maryellen**
*Jaguar* - Bill Ransom  *s*  4477

**Tim**
*The Gift* - Patrick O'Leary  *f*  4211

**T'lion**
*The Dolphins of Pern* - Anne McCaffrey  *s*  3729

**Toledo, Harry**
*Burn* - Bill Ransom  *s*  4476

**Tolivar**
*Sky Trillium* - Julian May  *f*  3700

**Tomcat**
*River Rats* - Caroline Stevermer  *s*  5267

**Trayne, Paul**
*Whipping Boy* - John Byrne  *h*  800

**Trickster**
*Secret Realms* - Tom Cool  *s*  1168

**Triplett, Michael**
*Entity* - Nina Mandelik  *h*  3615

**Truely, Yours "Y.T."**
*Snow Crash* - Neal Stephenson  *s*  5254

**Turner, Lucas "Yip"**
*Virtually Perfect* - Dan Gutman  *s*  2470

**Tyler, Gail**
*Raven* - S.A. Swiniarski  *h*  5374

**Tyler, Griffin**
*I Was a Teenage Fairy* - Francesca Lia
  Block  *f*  549

**Tymmon**
*Song of the Gargoyle* - Zilpha Keatley
  Snyder  *f*  5153

**Uta**
*Raptor* - Paul Zindel  *s*  6084

**Valdez, Vido**
*Higher Education* - Charles Sheffield  *s*  4958

**Varo**
*Shadow-Maze* - Mark Smith  *f*  5133

**Veriam, Tanaquil**
*Gold Unicorn* - Tanith Lee  *f*  3410

**Verrou, Nick**
*The Silent Strength of Stones* - Nina Kiriki
  Hoffman  *f*  2716

**Vestrit, Althea**
*The Ship of Magic* - Robin Hobb  *f*  2696

**Voerster, Broni**
*Glory* - Alfred Coppel  *s*  1182

**Voss, Dorn**
*Where the Ships Die* - William C. Dietz  *s*  1553

**Wade, Bree**
*Double Date* - R.L. Stine  *h*  5287

**Wade, Samantha**
*Double Date* - R.L. Stine  *h*  5287

**Wagner, Jennifer**
*The Season of Passage* - Christopher Pike  *h*  4331

**Walders, Shana**
*Maximum Light* - Nancy Kress  *s*  3241

**Walker, Sharissa**
*Sacrifice* - John Farris  *h*  1886

**Walthers, Danielle "Dani"**
*The Vampire Odyssey* - Scott Ciencin  *h*  1032
*The Wildlings* - Scott Ciencin  *h*  1034

**Weatherby, Ann**
*Hell-O-Ween* - David Robbins  *h*  4598

**Weiland**
*The Changeling Prince* - Vivian Vande
  Velde  *f*  5554

**Wells, Jeff**
*Norby and the Court Jester* - Janet Asimov  *s*  252
*Norby and the Oldest Dragon* - Janet
  Asimov  *s*  253
*Norby and Yobo's Great Adventure* - Janet
  Asimov  *s*  254
*Norby Down to Earth* - Janet Asimov  *s*  255

**Wheeler, Belinda "Bobbie"**
*Witch Spell* - Guy N. Smith  *h*  5122

**White, Carrie**
*Carrie* - Stephen King  *h*  3127

**Wilkerson, Joey**
*Guardian* - John Saul  *h*  4841

**Williams, Bryce**
*WiZrD* - Steve Zell  *h*  6078

**Williams, Megan**
*WiZrD* - Steve Zell  *h*  6078

**Willson, Peter**
*Dark Reunion* - Stephen R. George  *h*  2198

**Witch Baby**
*Missing Angel Juan* - Francesca Lia Block  *f*  550
*Witch Baby* - Francesca Lia Block  *f*  552

**Withers, Jonella "Johnnie"**
*The Living Dark* - Stephen Gresham  *h*  2431

**Wolenczak, Lucas**
*seaQuest DSV: Fire Below* - Matthew J.
  Costello  *s*  1201

**Woolcott, Jeremy**
*Along Came a Spider* - Athena Alexis  *h*  70

**Wright, Tracy**
*The Uprising* - Abigail McDaniels  *h*  3785

**Wyndon, Elbryan**
*The Demon Awakens* - R.A. Salvatore  *f*  4794

**X, Brandon "Brand"**
*Killjoy* - Elizabeth Forrest  *h*  1973

**Young, Miranda Jane**
*Breeder* - Ed Kelleher  *h*  3041

**Young Hunter**
*Dawn Land* - Joseph Bruchac  *f*  731

**Zoe**
*The Silver Kiss* - Annette Curtis Klause  *f*  3163

## TELEPATH

**Abe**
*The Clouds of Magellan* - David F.
  Nighbert  *s*  4103

**Acorna**
*Acorna's Quest* - Anne McCaffrey  *s*  3718

**Alderan, Kermiak**
*Rediscovery: A Novel of Darkover* - Marion Zimmer
  Bradley  *s*  643

**Alexander, Lyta**
*Thirdspace* - Peter David  *s*  1387

**Alton, Marguerida "Margaret"**
*The Shadow Matrix* - Marion Zimmer
  Bradley  *s*  645

**Aramina**
*The Renegades of Pern* - Anne McCaffrey  *s*  3746

**Asgar, Klia**
*Foundation and Chaos* - Greg Bear  *s*  418

**Bandit**
*Fire Planet* - P.M. Griffin  *s*  2436

**Big Sword**
*Project Farcry* - Pauline Ashwell  *s*  230

**Castanaveras, Denice**
*The Last Dancer* - Daniel Keys Moran  *s*  3994
*The Long Run* - Daniel Keys Moran  *s*  3995

**Cloud**
*Cloud's Rider* - C.J. Cherryh  *s*  983
*Rider at the Gate* - C.J. Cherryh  *s*  1000

**Connor, Islaen**
*Call to Arms* - P.M. Griffin  *s*  2435

**Dara**
*Feather Stroke* - Sydney J. Van Scyoc  *f*  5542

**Dellon, Melusine "Sinah"**
*Gravelight* - Marion Zimmer Bradley  *f*  636

**Demir**
*City of the Sorcerers* - Mary H. Herbert  *f*  2673

**Dexter, Fiona**
*Dark Genesis* - J. Gregory Keyes  *s*  3096

**Dickory, Tracy**
*Time and the Clock Mice, Etcetera* - Peter
  Dickinson  *f*  1527

**Dillon, Ronny**
*Dreambuilder* - Tom Deitz  *f*  1471
*Wordwright* - Tom Deitz  *f*  1478

**Droagn, Endark**
*Lair of the Cyclops* - Allen L. Wold  *s*  5933

**Dwiri**
*OtherWhere* - Margaret Wander Bonanno  *s*  566

**Endicott, Rob**
*The Gifted* - Jack Caravela  *h*  879

**Estriss**
*Into the Void* - Nigel Findley  *f*  1937

**Eve, Glennys**
*The Stallion Queen* - Constance Ash   *f*   223

**Ezekiel "Zeke"**
*The Seraphim Rising* - Elisabeth De Vos   *s*   1442

**Farley, Heather**
*Serpent's Gift* - A.C. Crispin   *s*   1261

**Fisher, Danny**
*Cloud's Rider* - C.J. Cherryh   *s*   983
*Rider at the Gate* - C.J. Cherryh   *s*   1000

**Goss, Brionne**
*Cloud's Rider* - C.J. Cherryh   *s*   983

**Grimya**
*Aisling* - Louise Cooper   *f*   1172
*Avatar* - Louise Cooper   *f*   1173
*Infanta* - Louise Cooper   *f*   1176
*Revenant* - Louise Cooper   *f*   1178
*Troika* - Louise Cooper   *f*   1181

**Gubwa, Charon**
*Psychosphere* - Brian Lumley   *h*   3563

**Halloran, Lawrence "Fixer-of-Weapons"**
*Man-Kzin Wars IV* - Larry Niven   *s*   4124

**Hanna**
*The Master of Chaos* - Terry A. Adams   *s*   34

**Hastur, Leonie**
*Rediscovery: A Novel of Darkover* - Marion Zimmer
　Bradley   *s*   643

**Hendricks, Connie**
*Being of Two Minds* - Pamela F. Service   *f*   4918

**Hilliard, Terrence**
*The Shadow Within* - Jeanne Cavelos   *s*   944

**Horace**
*Mouvar's Magic* - Piers Anthony   *f*   182

**Hume, Edna "Aten"**
*GodHeads* - Emily Devenport   *s*   1501

**Hunnul**
*Valorian* - Mary H. Herbert   *f*   2677

**Ishmael**
*Ishmael* - Daniel Quinn   *s*   4455
*My Ishmael* - Daniel Quinn   *s*   4456

**Ivanova, Susan**
*Voices* - John Vornholt   *s*   5598

**Jarnhann, Nils**
*The Yngling and the Circle of Power* - John
　Dalmas   *s*   1328
*The Yngling in Yamato* - John Dalmas   *s*   1329

**Jenny Sixa**
*Circle of One* - Eric James Fullilove   *s*   2092

**Jones, Sibyl**
*Pollen* - Jeff Noon   *s*   4135

**Jordan, Richard "Rivername"**
*Project Farcry* - Pauline Ashwell   *s*   230

**Kalliana**
*Blindfold* - Kevin J. Anderson   *s*   101

**Kes**
*Chrysalis* - David Niall Wilson   *s*   5880

**Khar'pern**
*Exiles' Return* - Gayle Greeno   *s*   2420
*Finders-Seekers* - Gayle Greeno   *s*   2421
*Mind-Speakers' Call* - Gayle Greeno   *s*   2423

**KLse**
*GodHeads* - Emily Devenport   *s*   1501

**Krishna the Holy Mendoro**
*The Ninety Trillion Fausts* - Jack L. Chalker   *s*   958

**Kyllikki**
*Dreamspy* - Jacqueline Lichtenberg   *s*   3458

**Lanart-Hastur, Mikhail**
*Exile's Song* - Marion Zimmer Bradley   *s*   632

**The Shadow Matrix** - Marion Zimmer
　Bradley   *s*   645

**Lewis, Rob**
*How Like a God* - Brenda W. Clough   *f*   1089

**Liosh**
*Dragon* - Steven Brust   *f*   741

**Macintosh, Elizabeth**
*Rediscovery: A Novel of Darkover* - Marion Zimmer
　Bradley   *s*   643

**Marbon, Doyce**
*Exiles' Return* - Gayle Greeno   *s*   2420
*Finders-Seekers* - Gayle Greeno   *s*   2421
*Mind-Speakers' Call* - Gayle Greeno   *s*   2423

**McBan, Rod**
*Norstrilia* - Cordwainer Smith   *s*   5105

**McCray, Jimmy**
*The Demons at Rainbow Bridge* - Jack L.
　Chalker   *s*   952
*The Ninety Trillion Fausts* - Jack L. Chalker   *s*   958
*The Run to Chaos Keep* - Jack L. Chalker   *s*   960

**McCrea, Rinn**
*Rinn's Star* - Paula E. Downing   *s*   1719

**Murrinder, Ainne**
*The Wall at the Edge of the World* - Jim
　Aikin   *s*   46

**Naufts, Tom**
*The Gifted* - Jack Caravela   *h*   879

**Nigheyes**
*Royal Assassin* - Robin Hobb   *f*   2695

**Nighteyes**
*Assassin's Quest* - Robin Hobb   *f*   2694

**Noelle**
*Starborne* - Robert Silverberg   *s*   5042

**Owen, Rhyssa**
*Pegasus in Flight* - Anne McCaffrey   *s*   3742

**Oykib**
*Earthfall* - Orson Scott Card   *s*   885

**Pelleas**
*In the Shadow of the Oak King* - Courtway
　Jones   *f*   2939

**Pellia**
*The Unicorn Solution* - John Lee   *f*   3400

**Pendrake, Matthew**
*Mind Slayer* - Kevin D. Randle   *s*   4469

**Rand, Aino**
*Marks of Our Brothers* - Jane M. Lindskold   *s*   3475

**Ree, Danlo**
*The Wall at the Edge of the World* - Jim
　Aikin   *s*   46

**Ripley, Ellen**
*Aliens: The Female War* - Steve Perry   *s*   4290

**Robinton**
*The Masterharper of Pern* - Anne
　McCaffrey   *s*   3739

**Rudolph "Rudy"**
*Being of Two Minds* - Pamela F. Service   *f*   4918

**Sarrasri, Diane**
*The Realms of the Gods* - Tamora Pierce   *f*   4321
*Wild Magic* - Tamora Pierce   *f*   4323
*Wolf-Speaker* - Tamora Pierce   *f*   4324

**Saturna**
*Saturn's Child* - Nichelle Nichols   *s*   4101

**Seqiro**
*Chaos Mode* - Piers Anthony   *f*   165
*Virtual Mode* - Piers Anthony   *f*   194

**Silberhutte, Hank**
*Titus Crow, Volume Three* - Brian Lumley   *h*   3567
*Titus Crow, Volume Two* - Brian Lumley   *h*   3568

**Sixa, Jenny**
*The Stranger* - Eric James Fullilove   *s*   2093

**Smoke, Smokey**
*Smoke and Mirrors* - Jane M. Lindskold   *s*   3476

**Sogan, Varn Tarl**
*Jungle Assault* - P.M. Griffin   *s*   2437

**Starbuck, July**
*Double Trouble Squared* - Kathryn Lasky   *f*   3340
*Shadows in the Water* - Kathryn Lasky   *s*   3341

**Starbuck, Liberty**
*Double Trouble Squared* - Kathryn Lasky   *f*   3340
*Shadows in the Water* - Kathryn Lasky   *s*   3341

**Stewart, Guil**
*Rider at the Gate* - C.J. Cherryh   *s*   1000

**Stone, Richard**
*Psychamok* - Brian Lumley   *h*   3561

**Streak**
*Shadows in the Water* - Kathryn Lasky   *s*   3341

**Summer**
*Master of Many Treasures* - Mary Brown   *f*   726

**Taylor, Jessica**
*Bureau 13* - Nick Pollotta   *f*   4362
*Full Moonster* - Nick Pollotta   *f*   4364

**Teska**
*Mind Meld* - John Vornholt   *s*   5596

**Tharion**
*Blindfold* - Kevin J. Anderson   *s*   101

**Tharna**
*The Key of the Keplian* - Andre Norton   *f*   4156

**Thorpe, Proserpine**
*The Reign of the Brown Magician* - Lawrence Watt-
　Evans   *f*   5647

**Troi, Lwaxana**
*Q-in-Law* - Peter David   *s*   1384

**Troit, Deanna "Dee"**
*Star Wreck IV: Live Long and Profit* - Leah
　Rewolinski   *s*   4565

**Vacit, Kevin**
*Dark Genesis* - J. Gregory Keyes   *s*   3096

**Valdez, Maria**
*Under Fire* - Kenneth Von Gunden   *s*   5589

**Wae, Kiondili**
*Lightwing* - Tara K. Harper   *s*   2551

**Waterfall, Kylene**
*Death's Gray Land* - Mike Shupp   *s*   5011
*The Last Reckoning* - Mike Shupp   *s*   5012

**Weisser, Erich**
*Child of the Light* - Janet Gluckman   *f*   2244

**Weisser, Erich "Erich Alois"**
*Child of the Journey* - Janet Berliner   *f*   466
*Children of the Dusk* - Janet Berliner   *f*   467

**Welch, Lewis**
*Dreambuilder* - Tom Deitz   *f*   1471

**Welch, Lewis Owen**
*Wordwright* - Tom Deitz   *f*   1478

**Whitehorse, Janara**
*Enemy Unseen* - V.E. Mitchell   *s*   3918

**Winters, Talia**
*Voices* - John Vornholt   *s*   5598

**Wycherley, Jenret**
*Exiles' Return* - Gayle Greeno   *s*   2420
*Mind-Speakers' Call* - Gayle Greeno   *s*   2423

## TELEVISION

**Allen, Sandy**
*Ancient Images* - Ramsey Campbell   *h*   852

## Character Description Index

**Claypoole, Chester "Chet" W.**
*Live From Golgotha: A Novel* - Gore Vidal  s  5569

**Franker, Edward "Eddie"**
*Pictures at 11* - Norman Spinrad  s  5173

### TELEVISION PERSONALITY

**Asimov, Issac**
*Back in the USSA* - Kim Newman  s  4095

**Collier, Samantha**
*Shock Radio* - Leigh Clark  h  1052

**Collins, Rikka**
*Satellite Night News* - Jack Hopkins  s  2770

**Feirn**
*Hero* - Dave Duncan  s  1680

**Figueroa, Calafia "Kali"**
*Kalifornia* - Marc Laidlaw  s  3311

**Figueroa, Poppy**
*Kalifornia* - Marc Laidlaw  s  3311

**Figueroa, Sandy**
*Kalifornia* - Marc Laidlaw  s  3311

**Inman, Toby**
*Pictures at 11* - Norman Spinrad  s  5173

**Jeremy, Clark**
*Blood Siege* - G. Harry Stine  s  5278

**Lyon, John**
*Bring Me Children* - David Martin  h  3637

**Martens, Billy**
*The Wizard of Camelot* - Simon Hawke  f  2627

**Mays, Randolph**
*The Diamond Moon* - Paul Preuss  s  4417

**Mendoza, Carl**
*Pictures at 11* - Norman Spinrad  s  5173

**Snyder, Harry**
*Satellite Night News* - Jack Hopkins  s  2770

**Wanda-Jean**
*The Feelies* - Mick Farren  s  1878

**Waterhouse, Mary Ann "Synthi Venture"**
*Mother of Storms* - John Barnes  s  354

### TERRORIST

**Aarons, Keith "Pan"**
*Second Chance* - Chet Williamson  h  5850

**al-Qurtubi**
*Name of the Beast* - Daniel Easterman  h  1721

**Dread, Doctor**
*Revenge of the Fluffy Bunnies* - Craig Shaw
   Gardner  f  2132

**Jeremiah**
*The Quiet Pools* - Michael P. Kube-
   McDowell  s  3249

**O'Connor, Padraic**
*Shade of Pale* - Greg Kihn  h  3104

**Philipe**
*The Ignored* - Bentley Little  h  3493

**Terrell, Mary "Merry Terror"**
*Mine* - Robert R. McCammon  h  3756

**Wade**
*Antarctica* - Kim Stanley Robinson  s  4628

### THIEF

**Aaron**
*The Fire's Stone* - Tanya Huff  f  2796

**Aladdin**
*A Bad Day for Ali Baba* - Craig Shaw
   Gardner  f  2123

**Alderberry, Jane**
*The Iron Dragon's Daughter* - Michael
   Swanwick  f  5371

**Allika**
*King's Man and Thief* - Christie Golden  f  2253

**Asrubal**
*Night Lamp* - Jack Vance  s  5548

**Aurelico, Karvonen**
*The Raven Ring* - Patricia C. Wrede  f  5978

**Bagsby**
*Dragonspawn* - Mark Acres  f  28

**Blaine, Cassandra "Cass"**
*Clipjoint* - Wilhelmina Baird  s  294
*Crashcourse* - Wilhelmina Baird  s  295

**Brayker, Silas**
*Tales From the Crypt: Demon Knight* - Randall
   Boyll  h  617

**Brekke, Robbie**
*Brain Rose* - Nancy Kress  s  3239

**Breks, Falca**
*The Mace of Souls* - Bruce Fergusson  f  1925

**Brenn**
*A Sorcerer's Apprentice* - Michael Williams  f  5820

**Castanaveras, Trent**
*The Long Run* - Daniel Keys Moran  s  3995

**Cat**
*Mistworld* - Simon R. Green  s  2372

**Chichelski, Chango**
*Accidental Creatures* - Anne Harris  s  2558

**Christmas**
*The Widowmaker* - Mike Resnick  s  4559

**Crane, Mary**
*Psycho* - Robert Bloch  h  540

**Cumberland, Jack**
*Mongster* - Randall Boyll  h  616

**Dogbrick**
*The Dark Shore* - Adam Lee  f  3385

**Donya**
*Shadow* - Anne Logston  f  3512
*Shadow Dance* - Anne Logston  f  3513

**Etcher**
*Arc d'X* - Steve Erickson  f  1835

**Fafhrd**
*Farewell to Lankhmar* - Fritz Leiber  f  3418
*Ill Met in Lankhmar* - Fritz Leiber  f  3419
*Lean Times in Lankhmar* - Fritz Leiber  f  3420
*Return to Lankhmar* - Fritz Leiber  f  3422
*Swords Against the Shadowland* - Robin Wayne
   Bailey  f  291

**Faust, Johann**
*If at Faust You Don't Succeed* - Roger
   Zelazny  f  6070

**Felice**
*User Unfriendly* - Vivian Vande Velde  f  5558

**Garlthik**
*The Longing Ring* - Christopher Kubasik  f  3246

**Gray Mouser**
*Farewell to Lankhmar* - Fritz Leiber  f  3418
*Swords Against the Shadowland* - Robin Wayne
   Bailey  f  291

**Grey Mouser**
*Ill Met in Lankhmar* - Fritz Leiber  f  3419
*Lean Times in Lankhmar* - Fritz Leiber  f  3420
*Return to Lankhmar* - Fritz Leiber  f  3422

**Habbazu**
*Between the Rivers* - Harry Turtledove  f  5496

**Hammen**
*Arena* - William R. Forstchen  f  1977

**Helarion**
*The Thief of Hermes* - Ru Emerson  f  1811

**Hinckel, Hieronymus**
*Chorus Skating* - Alan Dean Foster  f  1998

**Josarian**
*In Legend Born* - Laura Resnick  f  4533

**J'role**
*The Longing Ring* - Christopher Kubasik  f  3246

**Kemp, Jerod**
*Shadow of the Crown* - Craig Mills  f  3914

**Kiera**
*Orca* - Steven Brust  f  745

**Kwip**
*Castle Spellbound* - John DeChancie  s  1454

**Larath, Deveren**
*King's Man and Thief* - Christie Golden  f  2253

**Larque, Lens**
*The Demon Princes: Volume Two* - Jack
   Vance  s  5545

**Lucas, Prince**
*Rats and Gargoyles* - Mary Gentle  f  2196

**Lucy**
*But What of Earth?* - Piers Anthony  s  163

**Macero**
*Songs of the Dancing Gods* - Jack L. Chalker  f  962

**Madeline**
*The Death of the Necromancer* - Martha
   Wells  f  5749

**Maijstral, Drake**
*Rock of Ages* - Walter Jon Williams  s  5840

**Malkin**
*The Wizardry Consulted* - Rick Cook  f  1161

**Marrika**
*King's Man and Thief* - Christie Golden  f  2253

**Medakan, Taziar**
*By Chaos Cursed* - Mickey Zucker Reichert  f  4517
*Shadow's Realm* - Mickey Zucker Reichert  f  4523

**Mosquito**
*Cytheria* - Richard Calder  s  835

**Mouse**
*Soothsayer* - Mike Resnick  s  4557

**Mwili-Ferret**
*The 97th Step* - Steve Perry  s  4287

**Nightfall**
*The Legend of Nightfall* - Mickey Zucker
   Reichert  f  4521

**Orien**
*On Fortune's Wheel* - Cynthia Voigt  f  5579

**Petie**
*The Red King* - Victor Kelleher  f  3043

**Pinch "Janol"**
*King Pinch* - David Cook  f  1146

**Pope, Justin**
*Mixed Doubles* - Daniel Da Cruz  s  1305

**Sataru, Hidaka**
*The Yngling in Yamato* - John Dalmas  s  1329

**Seregil**
*Stalking Darkness* - Lynn Flewelling  f  1953

**Shadow**
*Dagger's Edge* - Anne Logston  f  3508
*Shadow* - Anne Logston  f  3512
*Shadow Dance* - Anne Logston  f  3513
*Shadow Hunt* - Anne Logston  f  3514

**Shadowspawn**
*The Shadow of Sorcery* - Andrew J. Offutt   f   4202

**Shamera "Sham"**
*When Demons Walk* - Patricia Briggs   f   683

**Sharrow**
*Against a Dark Background* - Iain M. Banks   s   322

**Shile**
*The Changeling Prince* - Vivian Vande
   Velde   f   5554

**Slash**
*Rememory* - John Gregory Betancourt   s   481

**Tabaea**
*The Spell of the Black Dagger* - Lawrence Watt-
   Evans   f   5648

**Tainharsdartter, Kevral**
*Beyond Ragnarok* - Mickey Zucker Reichert   f   4516

**Talen**
*The Ruby Knight* - David Eddings   f   1736

**Trace, Charlie**
*Demogorgon* - Brian Lumley   h   3552

**Valiarde, Nicholas "Donatien"**
*The Death of the Necromancer* - Martha
   Wells   f   5749

## TIME TRAVELER

**Aburto, Manuel "Manny"**
*Tyrannosaurus Rex* - J.F. Rivkin   s   4597

**Antiope**
*Amazon: A Novel* - Barbara G. Walker   f   5616

**Ashe, Timothy**
*The Seeds of Time* - Kay Kenyon   s   3064

**Backmaker, Hodgins "Hodge"**
*Bring the Jubilee* - Ward Moore   s   3993

**Bartlett, Tony "Antonius Caelerus"**
*Far Edge of Darkness* - Linda Evans   s   1855

**Basehart, Diana**
*Time Station London* - David Evans   s   1853

**Bavalius, Vitellan**
*The Centurion's Empire* - Sean McMullen   s   3854

**Beauty**
*Beauty* - Sheri S. Tepper   f   5428

**Beckett, Sam**
*Angels Unaware* - L. Elizabeth Storm   s   5315
*Knights of the Morningstar* - Melanie Rawn   s   4487

**Bentley, Abigail Porterhouse**
*Friends in Time* - Grace Chetwin   f   1012

**Bento, Jake**
*Atlantis Found* - R. Garcia y Robertson   s   2119
*The Virgin and the Dinosaur* - R. Garcia y
   Robertson   s   2122

**Birch, Wellington**
*Lurid Dreams* - Charles L. Harness   s   2546

**Blondell, Mark Anthony "Tony"**
*Tyrannosaurus Rex* - J.F. Rivkin   s   4597

**Bonhomme, Jacques**
*The Centurion's Empire* - Sean McMullen   s   3854

**Bonney, Isabel "Iz"**
*Elvissey* - Jack Womack   s   5957

**Bonney, John**
*Elvissey* - Jack Womack   s   5957

**Borgel**
*Borgel* - Daniel Manus Pinkwater   f   4338

**Callahan, Mike**
*Callahan's Legacy* - Spider Robinson   s   4639

**Carelias, Caroline "Sarah"**
*Union Fires* - John Barnes   f   358

**Carnelian, Jherek**
*The Dancers at the End of Time* - Michael
   Moorcock   s   3979

**Carnes, Rebecca**
*Arc Riders* - David Drake   s   1626

**Carrigan**
*The Unknown Soldier* - Mickey Zucker
   Reichert   s   4525

**Carson, Kenneth "Kit"**
*Time Scout* - Robert Asprin   s   263

**Chance, Angela**
*Time Station Berlin* - David Evans   s   1852

**Chang, Steve**
*Warrior* - William F. Wu   s   6000

**Chiron Cat's Eye in Draco**
*Summer of Love* - Lisa Mason   s   3664

**Coconino**
*Children of the Earth* - Catherine Wells   s   5743
*The Earth Saver* - Catherine Wells   s   5745

**Cofield, Aaron**
*Ray Bradbury Presents: Dinosaur Planet* - Stephen
   Leigh   s   3427
*Ray Bradbury Presents: Dinosaur World* - Stephen
   Leigh   s   3428

**Cole, James**
*12 Monkeys* - Elizabeth Hand   s   2532

**Collier, Ben**
*A Bridge of Years* - Robert Charles Wilson   s   5905

**Collins, Karen Cecile "Casey"**
*Islands of Tomorrow* - F.M. Busby   s   783

**Dad**
*The Key to the Indian* - Lynne Reid Banks   f   331

**d'Anton, Charlotte Marie**
*The Virgin and the Dinosaur* - R. Garcia y
   Robertson   s   2122

**Davis, Edward**
*Thebes of the Hundred Gates* - Robert
   Silverberg   s   5043

**Devane, Elizabeth**
*The Trinity Paradox* - Kevin J. Anderson   s   116

**Diego**
*Time: The Semi-Final Frontier* - Lionel
   Fenn   s   1921

**DiFalco, Tiraena**
*Legacy* - Steve White   s   5785

**Diko**
*Pastwatch: The Redemption of Christopher Columbus* -
   Orson Scott Card   s   895

**Dobbs, Karl**
*The Lincoln Hunters* - Wilson Tucker   s   5487

**Donnelly, John**
*Door Number Three* - Patrick O'Leary   s   4210

**Dubchek, Jackson**
*Stranded!* - Warren Norwood   s   4164

**Durvash**
*Man-Kzin Wars V* - Larry Niven   s   4125

**Eakins, Daniel Jamieson**
*The Man Who Folded Himself* - David
   Gerrold   s   2208

**Eakins, Diane Jane**
*The Man Who Folded Himself* - David
   Gerrold   s   2208

**Engle, Kivrin**
*Doomsday Book* - Connie Willis   s   5868

**Faison, Genevieva**
*Corrupting Dr. Nice* - John Kessel   s   3083

**Fall-Levchenko, Anna Leah**
*Branch Point* - Mona Clee   s   1074

**Faracon, George**
*Time Station Paris* - David Evans   s   1854

**Fawcett, Christine**
*Tyrannosaurus Rex* - J.F. Rivkin   s   4597

**Fergus**
*The Lost Prince* - Bridget Wood   f   5962

**Finn, Clio**
*The Seeds of Time* - Kay Kenyon   s   3064

**Flynn, Charlie**
*Far Edge of Darkness* - Linda Evans   s   1855

**Foster, Bass**
*Of Beginnings and Endings* - Robert Adams   s   33

**Foster, Maggie**
*The Iron Bridge* - David Morse   s   4036

**Gaspar, James**
*Days of Cain* - J.R. Dunn   s   1694

**Gibbs, Rinpoche**
*Muddle Earth* - John Brunner   s   735

**Gibson, Emma**
*Friends in Time* - Grace Chetwin   f   1012

**Gina**
*All's Faire* - Pamela F. Service   f   4917

**Grady, Joanna**
*Wolfking* - Bridget Wood   f   5963

**Grainger, Tim**
*Arc Riders* - David Drake   s   1626
*The Fourth Rome* - David Drake   s   1631

**Haggerwells, Barbara**
*Bring the Jubilee* - Ward Moore   s   3993

**Harper, Timothy**
*Death's Gray Land* - Mike Shupp   s   5011
*The Last Reckoning* - Mike Shupp   s   5012

**Hatshepsut**
*Dragon's Claw* - Alex McDonough   s   3800

**Henry, Ned**
*To Say Nothing of the Dog* - Connie Willis   s   5874

**Heron, John**
*The Schizogenic Man* - Raymond Harris   s   2563

**Indian**
*An Exaltation of Larks* - Robert Reed   s   4506

**Izakar "Izzy"**
*The Family Tree* - Sheri S. Tepper   s   5429

**ja N'Wook, Chrysamen "Chrys"**
*Caesar's Bicycle* - John Barnes   s   350

**Jackson, Skeeter**
*Wagers of Sin* - Robert Asprin   s   264

**Johnson, Laura**
*Door Number Three* - Patrick O'Leary   s   4210

**Johnson, Sibyl**
*Far Edge of Darkness* - Linda Evans   s   1855

**Kampa, Joshua**
*No Enemy but Time* - Michael Bishop   s   502

**Kate**
*The Ancient One* - T.A. Barron   f   368

**Kenmore, Harold**
*Of Beginnings and Endings* - Robert Adams   s   33

**Kevin**
*All's Faire* - Pamela F. Service   f   4917

**Kharitonov, Jeffrey**
*Branch Point* - Mona Clee   s   1074

**Kindle, Verity**
*To Say Nothing of the Dog* - Connie Willis   s   5874

**Kirk, James T.**
*The City on the Edge of Forever* - Harlan
   Ellison   s   1784

**Korsyzczy, Nela Zy-Czorsky**
*Sideshow* - Sheri S. Tepper   s   5436

**Krieger, Stefan**
*Lightning* - Dean R. Koontz   h   3211

**Leclerc, Louis**
*Witch* - Donald E. McQuinn   s   3864

**Lecotta, Angel**
*Time: The Semi-Final Frontier* - Lionel
    Fenn   s   1921

**Lehman, Roger "Senmut-Ptah"**
*Thebes of the Hundred Gates* - Robert
    Silverberg   s   5043

**Lewin, Alma Marie**
*Days of Cain* - J.R. Dunn   s   1694

**Liddell, Alice Pleasance**
*Automated Alice* - Jeff Noon   f   4134

**Limmer, Edwin**
*The Whispers* - Dan Parkinson   s   4247

**Lowe, Saul**
*Door Number Three* - Patrick O'Leary   s   4210

**Lujan, Derek**
*Children of the Earth* - Catherine Wells   s   5743

**Lund, Jack "Mr. Was"**
*Mr. Was* - Pete Hautman   s   2614

**Lungo Muso**
*Outpost* - Scott Mackay   s   3597

**Macairty, Adam Maser**
*Psychoshop* - Alfred Bester   s   477

**MacCallum, Bridget**
*The Door through Washington Square* - Elaine
    Bergstrom   f   464

**Magruder, Sam**
*The Dechronization of Sam Magruder* - George
    Gaylord Simpson   s   5067

**Magus, Stheneleos XLIV**
*Web of Futures* - Jefferson P. Swycaffer   f   5376

**Mason, Jennifer**
*Ray Bradbury Presents: Dinosaur Planet* - Stephen
    Leigh   s   3427
*Ray Bradbury Presents: Dinosaur World* - Stephen
    Leigh   s   3428

**Matamoros, Hunahpu**
*Pastwatch: The Redemption of Christopher Columbus* -
    Orson Scott Card   s   895

**Melvin**
*Borgel* - Daniel Manus Pinkwater   f   4338

**Moore, Malcolm**
*Time Scout* - Robert Asprin   s   263

**Moreau, Alessandra "Ale"**
*Day of the Snake* - Matthew J. Costello   s   1196
*Hour of the Scorpion* - Matthew J. Costello   s   1199

**Morley, Simon "Si"**
*From Time to Time* - Jack Finney   s   1941

**Murdoch, Ross**
*Firehand* - Andre Norton   s   4151

**Naill, Clarence "Rusty"**
*Back to the Time Trap* - Keith Laumer   s   3343

**Nazir, Nassifeh "Opalears"**
*The Family Tree* - Sheri S. Tepper   s   5429

**Nebogipfel**
*The Time Ships* - Stephen Baxter   s   403

**Noir, Alfred "Alf"**
*Psychoshop* - Alfred Bester   s   477

**Nystrom, Wayne**
*Dictator* - William F. Wu   s   5996
*Predator* - William F. Wu   s   5998
*Warrior* - William F. Wu   s   6000

**O'Brian, Launa**
*First Dawn* - Mike Moscoe   s   4038
*Lost Days* - Mike Moscoe   s   4039
*Second Fire* - Mike Moscoe   s   4040

**O'Connor, Flynn**
*Wolfking* - Bridget Wood   f   5963

**Olam, Thomas "Tom" Edward**
*From Prussia with Love* - John DeChancie   f   1457

**Omri**
*The Key to the Indian* - Lynne Reid Banks   f   331

**O'Shaughnessy, Maddock**
*Web of Futures* - Jefferson P. Swycaffer   f   5376

**Parz, Jasoft**
*Timelike Infinity* - Stephen Baxter   s   404

**Peg**
*The Virgin and the Dinosaur* - R. Garcia y
    Robertson   s   2122

**Philips, Jethro**
*Mercy's Mill* - Betty Levin   f   3444

**Pinky**
*Mr. Was* - Pete Hautman   s   2614

**Prince, Gabriel**
*Time on My Hands* - Peter Delacorte   s   1480

**Quinn "Nomad"**
*Desert Fire* - David Alexander   s   65

**Reynolds, William**
*Lurid Dreams* - Charles L. Harness   s   2546

**Rhoodie, Andries**
*The Guns of the South: A Novel of the Civil War* -
    Harry Turtledove   s   5502

**Riordan, Eveleen**
*Firehand* - Andre Norton   s   4151

**Rivers, Reginald**
*Rivers of Time* - L. Sprague de Camp   s   1417

**Roebeck, Nan**
*Arc Riders* - David Drake   s   1626
*The Fourth Rome* - David Drake   s   1631

**Rose**
*The Revenge of the Rose* - Michael
    Moorcock   f   3985

**Roy**
*Letters From Atlantis* - Robert Silverberg   f   5035

**Rozak, Jay**
*Islands of Tomorrow* - F.M. Busby   s   783

**Samson, Daniel "Dan"**
*Union Fires* - John Barnes   f   358
*Wartide* - John Barnes   f   359

**Sandburg, Elaine "Nefret"**
*Thebes of the Hundred Gates* - Robert
    Silverberg   s   5043

**Sarnac, Robert**
*Legacy* - Steve White   s   5785

**Sauromanta**
*Atlantis Found* - R. Garcia y Robertson   s   2119

**Sess, Medusa "Glory"**
*Psychoshop* - Alfred Bester   s   477

**Seven, Gary**
*Assignment: Eternity* - Greg Cox   s   1225

**Shira**
*Timelike Infinity* - Stephen Baxter   s   404

**Silver, Michelle "Micki" Ann**
*The Silver Tree* - Ruth L. Williams   f   5822

**Simon**
*Corrupting Dr. Nice* - John Kessel   s   3083

**Singer, Mayelbridwen "Maewen"**
*The Crown of Dalemark* - Diana Wynne
    Jones   f   2945

**Skena, Harry**
*Patton's Spaceship* - John Barnes   s   357

**Skoro, Andrea "Andie"**
*Mr. Was* - Pete Hautman   s   2614

**Smythe, Peter**
*Arthur War Lord* - Dafydd ab Hugh   f   6

**South, Joe**
*The Stalk* - Janet Morris   s   4016
*Threshold* - Janet Morris   s   4018
*Trust Territory* - Janet Morris   s   4019

**Specter, Alan**
*Time Station Berlin* - David Evans   s   1852

**Stargard, Conrad**
*Conrad's Quest for Rubber* - Leo
    Frankowski   s   2043
*The Flying Warlord* - Leo Frankowski   s   2044
*The High-Tech Knight* - Leo Frankowski   s   2045
*Lord Conrad's Lady* - Leo Frankowski   s   2046
*The Radiant Warrior* - Leo Frankowski   s   2047

**Steward, Ben**
*The Lincoln Hunters* - Wilson Tucker   s   5487

**Strang, Mark**
*Caesar's Bicycle* - John Barnes   s   350

**Surrey, John**
*Timeshare* - Joshua Dann   s   1344
*Timeshare: Second Time Around* - Joshua
    Dann   s   1345

**Susan**
*Laying the Music to Rest* - Dean Wesley
    Smith   h   5114

**Tabor, Lucian "Luke"**
*Islands of Tomorrow* - F.M. Busby   s   783

**Tate, Donnacee**
*Wanderer* - Donald E. McQuinn   s   3862
*Warrior* - Donald E. McQuinn   s   3863
*Witch* - Donald E. McQuinn   s   3864

**Teeg, Harper**
*The Seeds of Time* - Kay Kenyon   s   3064

**Thomason, John "Jean Vitterand"**
*Time Station Paris* - David Evans   s   1854

**Tiber, Jim**
*Day of the Snake* - Matthew J. Costello   s   1196
*Hour of the Scorpion* - Matthew J. Costello   s   1199

**Tylar**
*Legacy* - Steve White   s   5785

**Tyson, Roger**
*Back to the Time Trap* - Keith Laumer   s   3343

**van Wyyck, Margo**
*Time Scout* - Robert Asprin   s   263

**Vannice, Owen**
*Corrupting Dr. Nice* - John Kessel   s   3083

**Walker, Max**
*Timecop* - S.D. Perry   s   4286

**Walking Bear, Jack**
*First Dawn* - Mike Moscoe   s   4038
*Lost Days* - Mike Moscoe   s   4039
*Second Fire* - Mike Moscoe   s   4040

**Waterfall, Kylene**
*Death's Gray Land* - Mike Shupp   s   5011
*The Last Reckoning* - Mike Shupp   s   5012

**Weigand, Pauli**
*The Fourth Rome* - David Drake   s   1631

**Whitefeather, Steven "Brian Moore"**
*Time Station London* - David Evans   s   1853

**Winter, Tom**
*A Bridge of Years* - Robert Charles Wilson   s   5905

**Writer**
*The Time Ships* - Stephen Baxter   s   403

**Zhu Wong**
*The Golden Nineties* - Lisa Mason   s   3663

**Zimmerman, Christopher**
*Panda Ray* - Michael Kandel   s   3011

## TINKER

**Click**
*The Warden of Horses* - Karen Ripley   s   4595

## TOUR GUIDE

**Blume, Sandy**
*The Midnight Tour* - Richard Laymon   h   3368

**Lake, Dana**
*The Midnight Tour* - Richard Laymon   h   3368

**Raines, Darcy**
*Midnight's Lair* - Richard Laymon   h   3369

**Reith, Fergus**
*The Swords of Zinjaban* - L. Sprague de Camp   s   1418

**Tucker, Lynn**
*The Midnight Tour* - Richard Laymon   h   3368

## TOURIST

**Anangaranga-Jones, Nixy**
*Muddle Earth* - John Brunner   s   735

**Beauduc, Clarence**
*Smoke and Mirrors* - Jane M. Lindskold   s   3476

**Cotta**
*The Last World* - Christoph Ransmayr   f   4475

**Hager, Ross Ed**
*Jed the Dead* - Alan Dean Foster   s   2007

**Hobbs, Maggie**
*A Love through Time* - Terri Brisbin   f   691

**LaFayette, Morgan**
*The Last Highlander* - Claire Cross   f   1271

**MacKendimen, Alex**
*A Love through Time* - Terri Brisbin   f   691

**Onoda, Norio**
*Meridian 144* - Meg Files   s   1932

**Penn, Martin**
*Testament* - Valerie J. Freireich   s   2051

## TOY

**Elita**
*Stone Dead* - Ellen Jamison   h   2878

## TRADER

**Abba-Bashti**
*The Amazon Chronicles* - Jane E.M. Robinson   f   4627

**Chinnery, Thomas**
*Bhagavati* - Kara Dalkey   f   1316

**Cofort, Rael**
*Derelict for Trade* - Andre Norton   s   4148

**Donato, Rinio**
*Vaporetto 13* - Robert Girardi   h   2241

**Greenberg, Bernard**
*Earthgrip* - Harry Turtledove   s   5499

**Heiclaro, Corean**
*Emperor of Everything* - Ray Aldridge   s   62

**Hodge, Birk "Birkaj"**
*The Inquisitor* - Cheryl J. Franklin   s   2037

**Jayge**
*The Renegades of Pern* - Anne McCaffrey   s   3746

**Jellico, Miceal**
*Redline the Stars* - Andre Norton   s   4160

**Jones, Altair**
*Endgame* - C.J. Cherryh   s   986

**Ki**
*Luck of the Wheels* - Megan Lindholm   f   3471

**Liedral**
*The Magic Engineer* - L.E. Modesitt Jr.   f   3933

**Logan, Jennifer**
*Earthgrip* - Harry Turtledove   s   5499

**Otter**
*People of the Lakes* - Kathleen O'Neal Gear   f   2164

**Roy, Ubu**
*Angel Station* - Walter Jon Williams   s   5833

**Sharur**
*Between the Rivers* - Harry Turtledove   f   5496

**Sparrow**
*Bone Danc: A Fantasy for Technophiles* - Emma Bull   s   766

**Squires, Jack**
*Vaporetto 13* - Robert Girardi   h   2241

**Susumo, Tocohl**
*Hellspark* - Janet Kagan   s   3000

**Tarz, Auriel**
*World Spirits* - Aline Boucher-Kaplan   s   580

**Thorne, Newman "Nemo"**
*Circuit of Heaven* - Dennis Danvers   s   1348

**Thorson, Dane**
*Derelict for Trade* - Andre Norton   s   4148

## TRAITOR

**Baralis**
*The Baker's Boy* - J.V. Jones   f   2956
*Master and Fool* - J.V. Jones   f   2959

**Kozel, Dina**
*Siduri's Net* - P.K. McAllister   s   3709

**Marrika**
*King's Man and Thief* - Christie Golden   f   2253

**Siebold, Howard**
*Afterage* - Yvonne Navarro   h   4072

**Smith, Zachariah**
*Leap Point* - Kay Kenyon   s   3063

**Teeg, Harper**
*The Seeds of Time* - Kay Kenyon   s   3064

**Trinidad**
*Beneath the Gated Sky* - Robert Reed   s   4502

**Tris**
*Steal the Dragon* - Patricia Briggs   f   682

**Tsikas**
*Videssos Besieged* - Harry Turtledove   f   5513

**Tzikas**
*The Thousand Cities* - Harry Turtledove   f   5512

**Volmar**
*Castle of Deception* - Mercedes Lackey   f   3275

## TRAPPER

**Jameson, Gary**
*Pelts* - F. Paul Wilson   h   5894

## TRAVEL AGENT

**Brent**
*The Unfinished* - Jay B. Laws   h   3362

**Hawthorn, Lucas**
*The Whispers* - Dan Parkinson   s   4247

**Hayes, Donna**
*The Cellar* - Richard Laymon   h   3365

**Raphaella "Rae"**
*Angel Light* - Andrew M. Greeley   f   2342

**Savage, Mina**
*Where Does Kissing End?* - Kate Pullinger   h   4445

**Shaeler, Anita**
*The Forsaken* - Steven Ray Fulgham   h   2089

**White, Alice**
*Wilderness* - Dennis Danvers   h   1349

## TRAVELER

**Aesop**
*The Fabulist* - John Vornholt   f   5595

**Anglith of Arkraz, Omar "Trader of Tales"**
*The Hunters' Haunt* - Dave Duncan   f   1681
*The Reaver Road* - Dave Duncan   f   1687

**Aster "Star"**
*Glory Road* - Robert A. Heinlein   f   2644

**Balter, Harry**
*Parable of the Sower* - Octavia E. Butler   s   792

**Bawn, Caitlin**
*Legends Reborn* - Kenneth C. Flint   f   1958

**Beatrice**
*Bright Messengers* - Gentry Lee   s   3398

**Bennington, Jay Jay**
*Glenraven* - Marion Zimmer Bradley   f   635

**Berenice, Teal Blane**
*Blueheart* - Alison Sinclair   s   5068

**Brooks, Jenny**
*Cathy IV* - Frances Lucas   s   3539

**Campbell, Hamish**
*Demon Knight* - Ken Hood   f   2760

**Carrington, Charles Francis**
*Changeweaver* - Margaret Ball   f   313

**Cermit, Abasio**
*A Plague of Angels* - Sheri S. Tepper   f   5433

**Chris**
*The Tattooed Map* - Barbara Hodgson   f   2706

**Cortiss, Sophie**
*Glenraven* - Marion Zimmer Bradley   f   635

**Dan**
*Douglas Adams's Starship Titanic* - Terry Jones   s   2979

**Daviot**
*Lords of the Sky* - Angus Wells   f   5738

**Dent, Arthur**
*The Illustrated Hitchhiker's Guide to the Galaxy* - Douglas Adams   s   29
*Mostly Harmless* - Douglas Adams   s   31

**Doyle, Keith**
*Mythology Abroad* - Jody Lynn Nye   f   4174

**Dumery of Shiphaven**
*The Blood of a Dragon* - Lawrence Watt-Evans   f   5640

**Ehomba, Etjole**
*Carnivores of Light and Darkness* - Alan Dean Foster   f   1996

**Elizabeth**
*Mutagenesis* - Helen Collins   s   1116

**Exeter, Edward**
*Future Indefinite* - Dave Duncan   f   1670
*Present Tense* - Dave Duncan   f   1686

**Forrest, Pete**
*Beyond the Veil of Stars* - Robert Reed  s  4503

**Gale, Dorothy**
*Visitors From Oz: The Wild Adventures of Dorothy, the Scarecrow and the Tin Woodman* - Martin Gardner  f  2136

**Geddarms, Volothamp "Volo"**
*The Mage in the Iron Mask* - Brian Thomsen  f  5458

**Gordon, Evelyn Cyril "Oscar/Scar"**
*Glory Road* - Robert A. Heinlein  f  2644

**Gunnar**
*Byzantium* - Stephen R. Lawhead  f  3353

**ibn-Rushd, Damon**
*Destiny's Road* - Larry Niven  s  4119

**Jack**
*The End-of-Everything Man* - Tom De Haven  f  1421
*The Last Human* - Tom De Haven  f  1422
*Walker of Worlds* - Tom De Haven  f  1423

**Janna**
*Mission Child* - Maureen F. McHugh  s  3819

**Jimi**
*Lunching with the Antichrist* - Michael Moorcock  f  3984

**Keven**
*The Road West* - Gary Wright  f  5984

**Klaverel-va-Hynkkel**
*The Mark of the Cat* - Andre Norton  f  4157

**Kristinsson, Garth**
*Hidden Fires* - Katharine Eliska Kimbriel  s  3117

**Lafall, Teksan**
*Delan the Mislaid* - Laurie J. Marks  f  3625

**Lamai, Maia**
*Glory Season* - David Brin  s  686

**Lee, Wei**
*Red Dust* - Paul J. McAuley  s  3715

**Logan, Matthew**
*The Jewel of Equilibrant* - Steven Frankos  f  2042

**Lucy**
*Douglas Adams's Starship Titanic* - Terry Jones  s  2979

**Lydia**
*The Tattooed Map* - Barbara Hodgson  f  2706

**Mairelon**
*Mairelon the Magician* - Patricia C. Wrede  f  5977

**Miller, Jack**
*The Ultimate Bike Path* - Michael B. Sirota  s  5076

**Mooney, Shawana**
*The Arbitrary Placement of Walls* - Martha Soukup  f  5165

**Moreno, Alexandra "Alix"**
*When Heaven Fell* - William Barton  s  383

**Neal, Porsche**
*Beyond the Veil of Stars* - Robert Reed  s  4503

**Nettie**
*Douglas Adams's Starship Titanic* - Terry Jones  s  2979

**Nopal**
*The Chalchiuhite Dragon* - Kenneth Morris  f  4020

**Novak, Cornell**
*Beyond the Veil of Stars* - Robert Reed  s  4503

**Olmstead, Robert**
*The Shadow over Innsmouth* - H.P. Lovecraft  h  3533

**Orun**
*Hidden Echoes* - Mike Jefferies  f  2885

**Paolo**
*Diaspora* - Greg Egan  s  1759

**Petrillo, Val**
*The Safety of Unknown Cities* - Lucy Taylor  h  5414

**Quantrill, Snohomish "Sno"**
*The Godmother's Apprentice* - Elizabeth Ann Scarborough  f  4863

**Rado**
*Thorn and Needle* - Paul B. Thompson  f  5456

**Ranulfson, Murdo**
*The Iron Lance* - Stephen R. Lawhead  f  3356

**Rebecca "Becca"**
*Briar Rose* - Jane Yolen  f  6029

**Ree, Danlo**
*The Wall at the Edge of the World* - Jim Aikin  s  46

**Road Man**
*Soulsmith* - Tom Deitz  f  1475

**Salazar, Kirk**
*The Venom Trees of Sunga* - L. Sprague de Camp  s  1420

**Sari**
*Branch and Crown* - Gael Baudino  f  389
*O Greenest Branch!* - Gael Baudino  f  394

**Scoresby, Lee**
*The Subtle Knife* - Philip Pullman  f  4448

**Self, Melinda**
*Amnesia Moon* - Jonathan Lethem  f  3438

**Shannow, Jon**
*Wolf in Shadow* - David Gemmell  s  2191

**Shirley**
*Correspondence* - Sue Thomas  s  5450

**Summer**
*Master of Many Treasures* - Mary Brown  f  726

**Susri "Fawn"**
*Child of an Ancient City* - Tad Williams  f  5827

**Thistleknot, Kronn-alin**
*Spirit of the Wind* - Chris Pierson  f  4326

**Thorian**
*The Reaver Road* - Dave Duncan  f  1687

**Tobin, G. Patrick "Toby"**
*Angel Light* - Andrew M. Greeley  f  2342

**Trusla**
*The Warding of Witch World* - Andre Norton  f  4163

**Valdemar "Val"**
*Wayfinder's Story: The Seventh Book of Lost Swords* - Fred Saberhagen  f  4777

**Westriding, Margorie "Jory"**
*Sideshow* - Sheri S. Tepper  s  5436

**Whit, Beatrice**
*The Beacon* - Valerie J. Freireich  s  2048

**!Xabbu**
*City of Golden Shadow* - Tad Williams  s  5828

**Ying, Soong Mei**
*The Discovery of Dragons* - Graeme Base  f  385

**Zoltan**
*Wayfinder's Story: The Seventh Book of Lost Swords* - Fred Saberhagen  f  4777

## TROUBLESHOOTER

**d'Armand, Magnus Gallowglass "Gar Pike"**
*A Wizard in Chaos* - Christopher Stasheff  s  5230
*A Wizard in Midgard* - Christopher Stasheff  s  5231

**Dearborn, Sondra**
*Proteus in the Underworld* - Charles Sheffield  s  4962

**Dinsman, Angela**
*Reefsong* - Carol Severance  s  4923

**Homer-R-ICK-3**
*Extreme Paranoia: Nobody Knows the Trouble I've Shot* - Ken Rolston  s  4662

**McCray, Tom**
*Protektor* - Charles Platt  s  4342

**Sheehan, Matt**
*Manhattan Transfer* - John E. Stith  s  5303

**Sparrow**
*Bone Danc: A Fantasy for Technophiles* - Emma Bull  s  766

## TRUCK DRIVER

**Ashton, Choe**
*Signs of Life* - M. John Harrison  s  2580

**Ben**
*Night of the Living Dead* - John Russo  h  4745

**Cohen, Sophie**
*The Black Mariah* - Jay R. Bonansinga  h  570

**Crispian, Grace**
*Rune* - Christopher Fowler  h  2020

**Hardin, Charlie**
*Roadkill* - Richard Sanford  h  4815

**Hynde, Lucas**
*The Black Mariah* - Jay R. Bonansinga  h  570

**Ketter, Bill**
*Lot Lizards* - Ray Garton  h  2152

**Mel**
*Celia* - Ruby Jean Jensen  h  2900

**Rose, Mick "China"**
*Signs of Life* - M. John Harrison  s  2580

**Spiller, Josh**
*Furnace* - Muriel Gray  h  2339

**Winters, Michael**
*Sati* - Christopher Pike  f  4330

## TWIN

**Akimura, Julian**
*Mutant Star* - Karen Haber  s  2475

**Alastair**
*The Heirs of Hammerfell* - Marion Zimmer Bradley  s  638

**Ankoku**
*Dragon's Winter* - Elizabeth A. Lynn  f  3578

**Atani, Karadur**
*Dragon's Winter* - Elizabeth A. Lynn  f  3578

**Conn**
*The Heirs of Hammerfell* - Marion Zimmer Bradley  s  638

**Daniel**
*Dark Father* - Tom Piccirilli  h  4312

**de Conde, Sarah Webster**
*Deep Freeze* - Zach Hughes  s  2811

**Dennessy, Beth**
*The Darkness Within* - Shawn MacDonald  h  3585

**Dennessy, Carol**
*The Darkness Within* - Shawn MacDonald  h  3585

**Dion**
*Shadow Leader* - Tara K. Harper  f  2552

**Grason, Missy**
*Cross a Dark Bridge* - Deborah
    Churchman   *h*   1027

**Harrah, Talia Crawford**
*The Lilith Factor* - Jean Paiva   *h*   4236

**Harvey, Emily**
*Memorymakers* - Brian Herbert   *s*   2665

**Harvey, Thomas**
*Memorymakers* - Brian Herbert   *s*   2665

**Keogh, Nathan**
*Bloodwars* - Brian Lumley   *h*   3547

**Kiklu, Nathan**
*Blood Brothers* - Brian Lumley   *h*   3546
*The Last Aerie* - Brian Lumley   *h*   3557

**Kiklu, Nestor**
*Blood Brothers* - Brian Lumley   *h*   3546
*Bloodwars* - Brian Lumley   *h*   3547
*The Last Aerie* - Brian Lumley   *h*   3557

**Korsyzczy, Nela Zy-Czorsky**
*Sideshow* - Sheri S. Tepper   *s*   5436

**Lamai, Leie**
*Glory Season* - David Brin   *s*   686

**Marshall, Olivia**
*Seeds of Evil* - Margaret Bingley   *h*   491

**Marshall, Orlando**
*Seeds of Evil* - Margaret Bingley   *h*   491

**Oshita, Joy**
*Iron Shadows* - Steven Barnes   *f*   362

**Rhom**
*Shadow Leader* - Tara K. Harper   *f*   2552

**Samuel**
*Dark Father* - Tom Piccirilli   *h*   4312

**Santiago, Martina**
*The Vanishing* - Marilyn Kaye   *s*   3021

**Starbuck, July**
*Double Trouble Squared* - Kathryn Lasky   *f*   3340
*Shadows in the Water* - Kathryn Lasky   *s*   3341

**Starbuck, Liberty**
*Double Trouble Squared* - Kathryn Lasky   *f*   3340
*Shadows in the Water* - Kathryn Lasky   *s*   3341

**Vaughan, Elsie Crawford**
*The Lilith Factor* - Jean Paiva   *h*   4236

**Wade, Arlo**
*Bad Blood* - D.A. Fowler   *h*   2021

**Wade, Austin**
*Bad Blood* - D.A. Fowler   *h*   2021

**Wade, Bree**
*Double Date* - R.L. Stine   *h*   5287

**Wade, Samantha**
*Double Date* - R.L. Stine   *h*   5287

## UNDERTAKER

**Archway, Andy**
*The Unnatural* - David Prill   *h*   4437

**Diest, Vernon**
*The Moons of Summer* - S.K. Epperson   *h*   1831

**Grimm, Eleanor**
*Grimm Memorials* - R. Patrick Gates   *h*   2160

**Mitsumishi, Ecclesiastes**
*The Abraxas Marvel Circus* - Stephen Leigh   *f*   3423

**O'Shea, Patrick**
*Moon of the Werewolf* - Ronald Kelly   *h*   3053

**Rodgers, Franklin**
*Moon Walker* - Rick Hautala   *h*   2610

**Simpson, Beth Ann**
*Buried Screams* - C. Dean Andersson   *h*   137

**Sunnyside, P.T.**
*The Unnatural* - David Prill   *h*   4437

## UNEMPLOYED

**Allen, Harrison**
*Dark Twilight* - Joseph A. Citro   *h*   1036

**Ballard, Mitch**
*The Voice in the Basement* - T. Chris
    Martindale   *h*   3657

**Douglas, Doug**
*Slippin' into Darkness* - Norman Partridge   *h*   4254

**Nimitz, Brent**
*Dark Journey* - A.R. Morlan   *h*   4010

## VACATIONER

**Baldwin, Sean**
*Yon Ill Wind* - Piers Anthony   *f*   196

**Deanna**
*A Well-Timed Enchantment* - Vivian Vande
    Velde   *f*   5559

**Heffer, John Wilson**
*The Feelies* - Mick Farren   *s*   1878

## VAGRANT

**Flanders, Ted "Dead Ted"**
*Tower of Evil* - James Kisner   *h*   3161

**Frost, Joni**
*Stone Angels* - Mike Jefferies   *h*   2889

**Laurie**
*Dark Father* - Tom Piccirilli   *h*   4312

**Parsons, Ronna**
*Twisted* - Sue Hollister Barr   *h*   364

**Shustak, Evan "American Dream"**
*The Holy Terror* - Wayne Allen Sallee   *h*   4787

## VAMPIRE

**Adler, Stephen**
*Less than Human* - Gary L. Raisor   *h*   4464

**Agenor, Roland**
*The Golden* - Lucius Shepard   *h*   4978

**Aguilana, Haros**
*King of the Grey* - Richard A. Knaak   *f*   3173

**Agyar, Janos "Jack"**
*Agyar* - Steven Brust   *f*   738

**Akasha**
*The Queen of the Damned* - Anne Rice   *h*   4574

**Aleron**
*Sex and the Single Vampire* - Nancy
    Kilpatrick   *h*   3114

**Allogiamento, Maria Theresa**
*The Vampire Journals* - Traci Briery   *h*   678

**Alucard, Sevil**
*Elvira: Transylvania 90210* - Elvira   *h*   1802

**Angel**
*Dark Prince* - Keith Herber   *h*   2663

**Antonio**
*To Dream of Dreamers Lost* - David Niall
    Wilson   *h*   5882

**Anya**
*Live Girls* - Ray Garton   *h*   2151

**Anyelet**
*Afterage* - Yvonne Navarro   *h*   4072

**ap Ieuan, Owain**
*The Devil's Advocate* - Gherbod Fleming   *h*   1949

**Aragon, Julian**
*Thirst* - Michael Cecilione   *h*   948

**Armand**
*The Vampire Armand* - Anne Rice   *h*   4578

**Asher**
*Burnt Offerings* - Laurell K. Hamilton   *h*   2514

**Astare, T.**
*Morningstar* - Peter Atkins   *h*   265

**Austra, Catherine**
*Daughter of the Night* - Elaine Bergstrom   *h*   463

**Austra, Laurence**
*Blood Alone* - Elaine Bergstrom   *h*   462

**Bach, Arthur**
*Night Prophets* - Paul F. Olson   *h*   4213

**Banaker, Oliver**
*Curse of the Vampire* - Geoffrey Caine   *h*   832

**Barrett, Jonathan**
*Dance of Death* - P.N. Elrod   *h*   1794
*Death Masque* - P.N. Elrod   *h*   1795

**Bassarab**
*One Foot in the Grave* - Wm. Mark
    Simmons   *f*   5062

**Bathory, Elizabeth**
*Lord of the Vampires* - Jeanne Kalogridis   *h*   3005

**Beckwith, Desmond**
*Desmond: A Novel of Love and the Modern Vampire* -
    Ulysses G. Dietz   *h*   1541

**Beheim, Michel**
*The Golden* - Lucius Shepard   *h*   4978

**Ben Sapir, Elijah**
*Bloodsucking Fiends: A Love Story* - Christopher
    Moore   *h*   3988

**Beth**
*Out for Blood* - John Peyton Cooke   *h*   1166

**Bianka**
*As One Dead* - Don Bassingthwaite   *h*   387

**Blacke, Austin**
*Mastery* - Kelley Wilde   *h*   5802

**Blade**
*Blade* - Mel Odom   *h*   4190

**Blake, Alexander**
*Netherworld* - Richard Lee Byers   *h*   798

**Blaze, Christopher**
*Harvest of Blood* - Vincent Courtney   *h*   1213
*Vampire Beat* - Vincent Courtney   *h*   1214

**Bloodworth, Emma**
*The Last Vampire* - Kathryn Meyer Griffith   *h*   2440

**Blue, Sonja**
*A Dozen Black Roses* - Nancy A. Collins   *h*   1119
*In the Blood* - Nancy A. Collins   *h*   1121
*Midnight Blue: The Sonja Blue Collection* - Nancy A.
    Collins   *h*   1122
*Sunglasses After Dark* - Nancy A. Collins   *h*   1124

**Bowman, Michael**
*Cold Kiss* - Roxanne Longstreet   *h*   3517

**Braille**
*Night Thirst* - Patrick Whalen   *h*   5770

**Brent, David**
*The Vampire's Apprentice* - Richard Lee
    Byers   *h*   799

**Brissot, Phillipe**
*Thirst of the Vampire* - T. Lucien Wright   *h*   5988

**Burlow, Kurt**
*Salem's Lot* - Stephen King   *h*   3140

**Cadigan, Risha "Rusty"**
*Love Bite* - Sherry Gottlieb   *h*   2288

**Callaway, Chris**
*Out for Blood* - John Peyton Cooke   *h*   1166

**Carfax, Kurt**
*The Time of Feasting* - Mick Farren   *h*   1882

**Carmilla**
*The Darker Passions: Carmilla* - Amarantha
   Knight   *h*   3177

**Carnitch, Richard**
*Nightlife* - Jack Ellis   *h*   1779

**Cassandra**
*Sweet Myth-tery of Life* - Robert Asprin   *f*   262

**Cavanaugh, Carter**
*The Vampire's Apprentice* - Richard Lee
   Byers   *h*   799

**Chapman, Merrick**
*Rulers of Darkness* - Steven Spruill   *h*   5185

**Chapman, Zane**
*Daughter of Darkness* - Steven Spruill   *h*   5183
*Rulers of Darkness* - Steven Spruill   *h*   5185

**Charles**
*Daughter of the Night* - Elaine Bergstrom   *h*   463

**Cheryl**
*Sex and the Single Vampire* - Nancy
   Kilpatrick   *h*   3114

**Chris**
*Thirsty* - M.T. Anderson   *h*   120

**Christopher**
*The Silver Kiss* - Annette Curtis Klause   *f*   3163

**Claudius**
*Vampire Diary: The Embrace* - Robert
   Weinberg   *h*   5705

**Clemens, Atta Olivia**
*A Candle for D'Artagnan* - Chelsea Quinn
   Yarbro   *h*   6013
*Crusader's Torch* - Chelsea Quinn Yarbro   *h*   6015

**Cody, Will**
*Angel Souls and Devil Hearts* - Christopher
   Golden   *h*   2255
*Of Masques and Martyrs* - Christopher
   Golden   *h*   2258

**Collins, Barnabas**
*Angelique's Descent* - Lara Parker   *h*   4246

**Conforti, Alexandra**
*The Golden* - Lucius Shepard   *h*   4978

**Constantine, Miquel Kaliq**
*Ragged Angels* - Della Van Hise   *h*   5537

**Cortinez, Don Lazaro Ruiz**
*The Vampire Virus* - Michael Romkey   *h*   4668

**Crouper, Martin**
*Immortal* - Jason Nickles   *h*   4102

**Csejthe, Christopher**
*One Foot in the Grave* - Wm. Mark
   Simmons   *f*   5062

**da Clovina, Antonio**
*The Vampire Journals* - Traci Briery   *h*   678

**Danilov, Alexander**
*These Fallen Angels* - Wendy Haley   *h*   2492
*This Dark Paradise* - Wendy Haley   *h*   2493

**Darsen**
*Virago* - Karen Marie Christa Minns   *h*   3915

**Darte, Novak**
*Tooth: A Tale of Love and Death in Paradox* - Novak
   Kruger   *h*   3244

**Davidson, Troy**
*Liquid Diet* - William Tedford   *h*   5419

**Davis, Kate**
*The Making of a Monster* - Gail Petersen   *h*   4307

**Day, Rachaela**
*Darkness, I* - Tanith Lee   *h*   3407

**de Beq, Henri**
*Knights of the Blood* - Scott MacMillan   *f*   3602

**de Dip, Onofre**
*Natural History* - Juan Perucho   *h*   4303

**de la von Zaguar, Lamar**
*The Mark of the Moderately Vicious Vampire* - Lionel
   Fenn   *h*   1920

**de Lioncourt, Lestat**
*Memnoch the Devil* - Anne Rice   *h*   4571
*The Queen of the Damned* - Anne Rice   *h*   4574
*The Tale of the Body Thief* - Anne Rice   *h*   4576

**de Montalia, Madelaine**
*Out of the House of Life* - Chelsea Quinn
   Yarbro   *h*   6018

**De Romanus, Marius**
*The Vampire Armand* - Anne Rice   *h*   4578

**de Saint-Germain, Francois**
*Blood Roses* - Chelsea Quinn Yarbro   *h*   6012

**De Vilbiss, Vincent**
*The Book of Common Dread* - Brent
   Monahan   *h*   3955

**de Villanueva, Don Sebastian**
*No Blood Spilled* - Les Daniels   *h*   1338

**Deland, Roger**
*Desmond: A Novel of Love and the Modern Vampire* -
   Ulysses G. Dietz   *h*   1541

**Delaney, Tawne**
*This Symbiotic Fascination* - Charlee Jacob   *h*   2843

**Desmodus, Eli**
*Desmodus* - Melanie Tem   *h*   5421

**Desmodus, Joel**
*Desmodus* - Melanie Tem   *h*   5421

**Desmodus, Rory**
*Desmodus* - Melanie Tem   *h*   5421

**Develos, Debi**
*Blood* - Ron Dee   *h*   1463

**DeWinter**
*As One Dead* - Don Bassingthwaite   *h*   387

**di Medusa, Nicoletta Vittorini**
*The Vampire Princess* - Michael Romkey   *h*   4667

**Diego y Rey, Eduardo**
*Bloodshift* - Garfield Reeves-Stevens   *h*   4508

**Dieudonne, Genevieve**
*Anno Dracula* - Kim Newman   *h*   4094
*Drachenfels* - Jack Yeovil   *f*   6022
*Judgment of Tears: Anno Dracula 1959* - Kim
   Newman   *h*   4098

**Dracul, Vlad**
*Vampire Junkies* - Norman Spinrad   *h*   5175

**Dracula**
*The Angry Angel* - Chelsea Quinn Yarbro   *h*   6010
*Anno Dracula* - Kim Newman   *h*   4094
*Blood of the Impaler* - Jeffrey Sackett   *h*   4779
*Bram Stoker's Dracula* - Fred Saberhagen   *h*   4763
*Dracul: An Eternal Love Story* - Nancy
   Kilpatrick   *h*   3110
*The Dracula Tape* - Fred Saberhagen   *h*   4765
*Dracula Unbound* - Brian W. Aldiss   *h*   55
*The Holmes-Dracula File* - Fred
   Saberhagen   *h*   4767
*The Mammoth Book of Dracula* - Stephen
   Jones   *h*   2972
*Seance for a Vampire* - Fred Saberhagen   *h*   4773

**Dracula, Radu**
*A Sharpness on the Neck* - Fred
   Saberhagen   *h*   4774

**Dracula, Vlad**
*A Sharpness on the Neck* - Fred
   Saberhagen   *h*   4774

**Drake, Franz**
*Kiss of the Vampire* - Lee Weathersby   *h*   5657

**Drake, Simon Tepes**
*Kiss of the Vampire* - Lee Weathersby   *h*   5657

**Drummond, John**
*At Sword's Point* - Scott MacMillan   *f*   3601

**Dun, Richard**
*Keeper of the King* - Nigel Bennett   *h*   452

**Elizabeth**
*Virgintooth* - Mark Ivanhoe   *h*   2834

**Erickson, Dirk**
*The Informers* - Brett Easton Ellis   *h*   1778

**Erzsebet**
*The Secret Weavers: Stories of the Fantastic by Latin
   American Women* - Marjorie Agosin   *f*   43

**Esher**
*A Dozen Black Roses* - Nancy A. Collins   *h*   1119

**Evans, Owain**
*The Winnowing* - Gherbod Fleming   *h*   1950

**Falke**
*Eye Killers* - A.A. Carr   *h*   911

**Ferenczy, Janos**
*Deadspeak* - Brian Lumley   *h*   3551

**Fitzroy, Henry**
*Blood Debt* - Tanya Huff   *h*   2792
*Blood Price* - Tanya Huff   *h*   2793
*Blood Trail* - Tanya Huff   *h*   2794

**Fleming, Jack**
*Blood on the Water* - P.N. Elrod   *h*   1791
*Bloodlist* - P.N. Elrod   *h*   1792
*A Chill in the Blood* - P.N. Elrod   *h*   1793
*Fire in the Blood* - P.N. Elrod   *h*   1796

**Florescu, Ilana**
*Domination* - Michael Cecilione   *h*   946

**French, Melissa**
*Liquid Diet* - William Tedford   *h*   5419

**Frost, Deacon**
*Blade* - Mel Odom   *h*   4190

**Garret, Allison**
*Night Prayers* - P.D. Cacek   *h*   803

**Geoffrey**
*Blood and Roses* - Sharon Bainbridge   *h*   292

**Gersten, Clovis**
*Golden Eyes* - John Gideon   *h*   2220

**Gilda**
*The Gilda Stories* - Jewelle Gomez   *h*   2267

**Giovanni, Madeleine**
*The Road to Hell, Volume II* - Robert
   Weinberg   *h*   5702
*The Unbeholden* - Robert Weinberg   *h*   5703
*Unholy Allies* - Robert Weinberg   *h*   5704

**Gloria**
*The Vampire Journals* - Traci Briery   *h*   678

**Greer, Mitchell**
*Blood Ties* - Karen E. Taylor   *h*   5407

**Gregory**
*Night Thirst* - Patrick Whalen   *h*   5770

**Griffin, Deirdre**
*Bitter Blood* - Karen E. Taylor   *h*   5405
*Blood Secrets* - Karen E. Taylor   *h*   5406
*Blood Ties* - Karen E. Taylor   *h*   5407

**Guitierrez, Rafael**
*Diary of a Vampire* - Gary Bowen   *h*   600

**Haal, Daetrin Ungashak To-Alym**
*The Madness Season* - C.S. Friedman   *s*   2058

**Hall, Cassandra**
*Thirst* - Michael Cecilione    *h*   948

**Hardwick, David Lyle**
*Near Death* - Nancy Kilpatrick    *h*   3113

**Hart, Adragon**
*Precious Blood* - Pat Graversen    *h*   2336
*Sweet Blood* - Pat Graversen    *h*   2337

**Hart, Beth**
*Precious Blood* - Pat Graversen    *h*   2336

**Hart, Elsbeth**
*Sweet Blood* - Pat Graversen    *h*   2337

**Hodge, J. Benison**
*The Devil's Advocate* - Gherbod Fleming    *h*   1949

**Hunsacker, Matt**
*Blind Hunger* - David Darke    *h*   1352

**Jackson, Kendall**
*The Devil's Advocate* - Gherbod Fleming    *h*   1949

**Jean-Claude**
*Bloody Bones* - Laurell K. Hamilton    *h*   2512
*Burnt Offerings* - Laurell K. Hamilton    *h*   2514
*Circus of the Damned* - Laurell K.
    Hamilton    *h*   2515
*The Killing Dance* - Laurell K. Hamilton    *h*   2518
*The Laughing Corpse* - Laurell K. Hamilton    *f*   2519

**Jody**
*Bloodsucking Fiends: A Love Story* - Christopher
    Moore    *h*   3988

**Jonathan**
*Virgintooth* - Mark Ivanhoe    *h*   2834

**Jones, Nora**
*Dance of Death* - P.N. Elrod    *h*   1794
*Red Death* - P.N. Elrod    *h*   1798

**Jorhsa**
*Some Things Never Die* - Robert Morgan    *h*   4005

**Justine**
*Stainless* - Todd Grimson    *h*   2449

**Kaiser, Valentine**
*A Matter of Taste* - Fred Saberhagen    *h*   4770

**Kane, Nathan**
*Bring on the Night* - Don Davis    *h*   1402

**Karros, Dimitri Alexander**
*Ragged Angels* - Della Van Hise    *h*   5537

**Keelan, Delphine**
*Sweet Blood* - Pat Graversen    *h*   2337

**Kennedy, Simon**
*Vampire$* - John Steakley    *h*   5237

**Kiklu, Nestor**
*Bloodwars* - Brian Lumley    *h*   3547

**Kirilovich, Vasily "Temsik"**
*Out for Blood* - John Peyton Cooke    *h*   1166

**Kluge, Wilhelm**
*At Sword's Point* - Scott MacMillan    *f*   3601
*Knights of the Blood* - Scott MacMillan    *f*   3602

**Knight, Nicholas**
*Forever Knight: A Stirring of Dust* - Susan
    Sizemore    *h*   5078
*Forever Knight: Intimations of Mortality* - Susan M.
    Garrett    *h*   2149

**Kodesh, Kli**
*To Speak in Lifeless Tongues* - David Niall
    Wilson    *h*   5883
*The Winnowing* - Gherbod Fleming    *h*   1950

**Kraeken**
*Shrines and Desecrations* - Brian Hodge    *h*   2705

**LaCroix, Lucien**
*Forever Knight: A Stirring of Dust* - Susan
    Sizemore    *h*   5078

**LeBrel, Andre**
*Children of the Night* - Mercedes Lackey    *h*   3276

**Lecouveurs, Alain**
*In Hot Blood* - Petru Popescu    *h*   4367

**Lethe**
*Shifters* - Edward Lee    *h*   3396

**Lindquist, Anna Catarina**
*McLendon's Syndrome* - Robert Frezza    *s*   2053
*The VMR Theory* - Robert Frezza    *s*   2055

**Lot**
*As One Dead* - Don Bassingthwaite    *h*   387

**Lothos**
*Buffy the Vampire Slayer* - Richie Tankersley
    Cusick    *h*   1301

**Luci**
*Night Prayers* P.D. Cacek    *h*   803

**Lyall, Andrew**
*Vampires Anonymous* - Jeffrey N.
    McMahan    *h*   3853

**Lydia "Pandora"**
*Pandora* - Anne Rice    *h*   4573

**Lykan, Radu**
*Necroscope: The Lost Years* - Brian
    Lumley    *h*   3560
*Resurgence* - Brian Lumley    *h*   3564

**Madison, Marshall**
*Bloodlines* - J.N. Williamson    *h*   5852

**Magda**
*The Darker Passions: Dracula* - Amarantha
    Knight    *h*   3179

**Malach**
*Personal Darkness* - Tanith Lee    *h*   3413

**Malendor**
*Dark Divide* - Mark Acres    *f*   27

**Mariana**
*Blood Relations* - Doug Murray    *h*   4058

**Martin, Larry**
*Blood Ties* - Karen E. Taylor    *h*   5407

**Master**
*Virgintooth* - Mark Ivanhoe    *h*   2834

**Matheson, Harry**
*Blood Brothers* - T. Lucien Wright    *h*   5986

**Maule, Matthew**
*A Matter of Taste* - Fred Saberhagen    *h*   4770

**McCunniff, Mara**
*The Vampire Memoirs* - Mara McCuniff    *h*   3781

**McKay, Kenneth "Ken"**
*The VMR Theory* - Robert Frezza    *s*   2055

**Michelson, Terry**
*Vampire Blood* - Kathryn Meyer Griffith    *h*   2441

**Millarca**
*Carmilla: The Return* - Kyle Marffin    *h*   3623

**Mirlu, Bonnie Jean "B.J."**
*Necroscope: The Lost Years* - Brian
    Lumley    *h*   3560
*Resurgence* - Brian Lumley    *h*   3564

**Montrovant**
*To Dream of Dreamers Lost* - David Niall
    Wilson    *h*   5882
*To Speak in Lifeless Tongues* - David Niall
    Wilson    *h*   5883

**Mulkerrin, Liam**
*Angel Souls and Devil Hearts* - Christopher
    Golden    *h*   2255

**Murasaki, Rose**
*Suckers* - Anne Billson    *h*   490

**Navarra**
*Night Brothers* - Sidney Williams    *h*   5824

**Nest, Henrich Joseph**
*The Harvest* - Richie Tankersley Cusick    *h*   1302

**Nicholas**
*The Winnowing* - Gherbod Fleming    *h*   1950

**Nightshade**
*Sex and the Single Vampire* - Nancy
    Kilpatrick    *h*   3114

**Nightwing**
*Vampire Breath* - R.L. Stine    *h*   5291

**Nikolaus**
*Guilty Pleasures* - Laurell K. Hamilton    *f*   2517

**Octavian, Peter**
*Of Masques and Martyrs* - Christopher
    Golden    *h*   2258
*Of Saints and Shadows* - Christopher
    Golden    *h*   2259

**Parker, David**
*I, Vampire* - Michael Romkey    *h*   4665
*The Vampire Papers* - Michael Romkey    *h*   4666
*The Vampire Princess* - Michael Romkey    *h*   4667

**Perne, Alisa**
*The Last Vampire* - Christopher Pike    *h*   4328

**Pierce**
*Human Resources* - Floyd Kemske    *h*   3057

**Quetzal**
*Calde of the Long Sun* - Gene Wolfe    *s*   5937

**Quinn**
*Precious Blood* - Pat Graversen    *h*   2336

**Radburn, Adam**
*The Undead* - Roxanne Longstreet    *h*   3519

**Rakz, Yosekaat**
*Vampire Beat* - Vincent Courtney    *h*   1214

**Reed, Kate**
*Judgment of Tears: Anno Dracula 1959* - Kim
    Newman    *h*   4098

**Renquist, Victor**
*The Time of Feasting* - Mick Farren    *h*   1882

**Rice, Caddie**
*Blood of Mugwump* - Doug Rice    *h*   4581

**Rice, Doug**
*Blood of Mugwump* - Doug Rice    *h*   4581

**Rivers, Neal**
*Keeper of the King* - Nigel Bennett    *h*   452

**Romero, Val**
*Night Blood* - Eric Flanders    *h*   1945

**Rozokov, Dimitri**
*The Night Inside* - Nancy Baker    *h*   301

**Ruth**
*Personal Darkness* - Tanith Lee    *h*   3413

**Sabra**
*Keeper of the King* - Nigel Bennett    *h*   452

**SaDiablo, Saetan**
*Daughter of the Blood* - Anne Bishop    *f*   495

**Sadler, Ben**
*Sins of the Blood* - Kristine Kathryn Rusch    *h*   4728

**St. Clair, Adrienne**
*Bloodshift* - Garfield Reeves-Stevens    *h*   4508

**Saint-Germain**
*Better in the Dark* - Chelsea Quinn Yarbro    *h*   6011
*Mansions of Darkness* - Chelsea Quinn
    Yarbro    *h*   6016
*Out of the House of Life* - Chelsea Quinn
    Yarbro    *h*   6018
*Writ in Blood* - Chelsea Quinn Yarbro    *h*   6019

**Santos**
*To Speak in Lifeless Tongues* - David Niall
    Wilson    *h*   5883

Santos, Nick
*The World on Blood* - Jonathan Nasaw   *h*   4069

Sartak
*Netherworld* - Richard Lee Byers   *h*   798

Shade, John
*Nightshade* - Jack Butler   *s*   789

Shade, Scarlett
*Shade* - David Darke   *h*   1355

Shaithis
*Deadspawn* - Brian Lumley   *h*   3550

Shelly, Byron
*The Last Vampire* - Kathryn Meyer Griffith   *h*   2440

Simon
*The Silver Kiss* - Annette Curtis Klause   *f*   3163

Simon, Althene
*Darkness, I* - Tanith Lee   *h*   3407

Sinjon
*A Dozen Black Roses* - Nancy A. Collins   *h*   1119

Skinner
*Bad Dreams* - Kim Newman   *h*   4096

Smith, Desidra
*Blood on the Sun* - Brian Herbert   *h*   2664

Stiles, Alex
*Nightblood* - T. Chris Martindale   *h*   3656

Stirling, Richard
*The Judas Glass* - Michael Cadnum   *h*   812

Striescu, Aldo
*Shadows* - Jonathan Nasaw   *h*   4068

Sullivan
*Dark Prince* - Keith Herber   *h*   2663

Tabor, Martin
*Some Things Come Back* - Robert Morgan   *h*   4004

Talamasca
*The Vampire Armand* - Anne Rice   *h*   4578

Tarrant, Gerald
*Crown of Shadows* - C.S. Friedman   *s*   2057

Tatyana
*I, Strahd* - P.N. Elrod   *h*   1797

Tch'muchgar
*Thirsty* - M.T. Anderson   *h*   120

Tepes, Vlad
*The Darker Passions: Dracula* - Amarantha
   Knight   *h*   3179
*The Empire of Fear* - Brian Stableford   *h*   5191
*I Am Dracula* - C. Dean Andersson   *h*   139

Teppish, Rebecca
*The Vampire's Beautiful Daughter* - S.P.
   Somtow   *h*   5161

Teppish, Vladimir X. III
*The Vampire's Beautiful Daughter* - S.P.
   Somtow   *h*   5161

Tessler
*Blood Relations* - Doug Murray   *h*   4058

Thorne, Becker
*The Vampire Papers* - Michael Romkey   *h*   4666

Tomley, Marissa
*The Wildlings* - Scott Ciencin   *h*   1034

Torgov, Grandma Mugwump
*Blood of Mugwump* - Doug Rice   *h*   4581

Tsepesh, Arkady
*Children of the Vampire* - Jeanne
   Kalogridis   *h*   3003

Tsepesh, Vlad
*Children of the Vampire* - Jeanne
   Kalogridis   *h*   3003
*Covenant with the Vampire* - Jeanne
   Kalogridis   *h*   3004

Tyler, Devin
*Parliament of Blood* - Scott Ciencin   *h*   1031

Val
*Blood Relations* - Doug Murray   *h*   4058

Vampire
*Aqua Sancta* - Edward Bryant   *h*   748

Vampyr
*Child of an Ancient City* - Tad Williams   *f*   5827

Van Diemen, William
*Thirst* - Pyotr Kurtinski   *h*   3253

Vanderveen, Frederika
*Blood of the Covenant* - Brent Monahan   *h*   3954

Varney, Alicia
*Blood War* - Robert Weinberg   *h*   5693
*The Unbeholden* - Robert Weinberg   *h*   5703
*Unholy Allies* - Robert Weinberg   *h*   5704

Vaughan, Celestine
*Cold Kiss* - Roxanne Longstreet   *h*   3517

Venneman, Richard
*Insatiable* - David Dvorkin   *h*   1707

Vertok, Kyril
*Shadows After Dark* - Ouida Crozier   *f*   1286

Vigor
*Tooth: A Tale of Love and Death in Paradox* - Novak
   Kruger   *h*   3244

Viroslav, Alexander
*The Kiss* - Kathryn Reines   *h*   4529

Viroslav, Maria
*The Kiss* - Kathryn Reines   *h*   4529

von Cragga, Ivo
*The Ruby Tear* - Rebecca Brand   *h*   660

Von Zarovich, Strahd
*I, Strahd* - P.N. Elrod   *h*   1797

Vril, Dietrich
*The Armageddon Box* - Robert Weinberg   *h*   5690

Walthers, Danielle "Dani"
*Parliament of Blood* - Scott Ciencin   *h*   1031
*The Vampire Odyssey* - Scott Ciencin   *h*   1032
*The Wildlings* - Scott Ciencin   *h*   1034

Whistler, Jamey
*Shadows* - Jonathan Nasaw   *h*   4068
*The World on Blood* - Jonathan Nasaw   *h*   4069

Wilson, Christopher T.
*Blood on the Sun* - Brian Herbert   *h*   2664

Wolff, Hauptsturmfuhrer
*Darkness on the Ice* - Lois Tilton   *h*   5475

Wratha, the Unrisen
*Blood Brothers* - Brian Lumley   *h*   3546

Yoshino, Bill
*The Vampire Odyssey* - Scott Ciencin   *h*   1032

Ysidro, Don Simon
*Those Who Hunt the Night* - Barbara
   Hambly   *h*   2510

Zillabar
*A Covenant of Justice* - David Gerrold   *s*   2207

Zillah
*Lost Souls* - Poppy Z. Brite   *h*   697

Zuchmul
*Dreamspy* - Jacqueline Lichtenberg   *s*   3458

## VAMPIRE HUNTER

Blake, Anita
*Bloody Bones* - Laurell K. Hamilton   *h*   2512
*Blue Moon* - Laurell K. Hamilton   *h*   2513
*Burnt Offerings* - Laurell K. Hamilton   *h*   2514
*Circus of the Damned* - Laurell K.
   Hamilton   *h*   2515

*Guilty Pleasures* - Laurell K. Hamilton   *f*   2517
*The Killing Dance* - Laurell K. Hamilton   *h*   2518
*The Laughing Corpse* - Laurell K. Hamilton   *f*   2519
*The Lunatic Cafe* - Laurell K. Hamilton   *h*   2520

Crow, Jack
*Vampire$* - John Steakley   *h*   5237

Dixon, Benjamin
*Blood Lust* - Ron Dee   *h*   1464

Eliason, Scott
*Sins of the Blood* - Kristine Kathryn Rusch   *h*   4728

Felix, William Charles "Gunman"
*Vampire$* - John Steakley   *h*   5237

Kirkland, Larry
*Bloody Bones* - Laurell K. Hamilton   *h*   2512
*Circus of the Damned* - Laurell K.
   Hamilton   *h*   2515

Merrick
*Buffy the Vampire Slayer* - Richie Tankersley
   Cusick   *h*   1301

Noirceuil
*To Dream of Dreamers Lost* - David Niall
   Wilson   *h*   5882

Summers, Buffy
*Buffy the Vampire Slayer* - Richie Tankersley
   Cusick   *h*   1301
*The Harvest* - Richie Tankersley Cusick   *h*   1302
*Return to Chaos* - Craig Shaw Gardner   *h*   2131

Timms, Camilla
*Sins of the Blood* - Kristine Kathryn Rusch   *h*   4728

## VETERAN

Ives, Bobby
*The Nightwalker* - Thomas Tessier   *h*   5442

Justinian
*Subterranean Gallery* - Richard Paul Russo   *s*   4750

Kiff, Jim
*Darkborn* - Matthew J. Costello   *h*   1195

Kindred, Lewis
*Kindred* - John Gideon   *h*   2222

Lambert, Dan
*Gone South* - Robert R. McCammon   *h*   3755

Lucier, Kevin
*Jumpers* - R. Patrick Gates   *h*   2161

Poole, Michael
*Koko* - Peter Straub   *h*   5328

Stiles, Chris
*Nightblood* - T. Chris Martindale   *h*   3656

Underhill, Tim
*Koko* - Peter Straub   *h*   5328
*The Throat* - Peter Straub   *h*   5332

Ward, Alex
*The Parasite War* - Tim Sullivan   *s*   5352

Winters, Theodore "TK" Karlington
*Strands of Sunlight* - Gael Baudino   *f*   396

Wolf
*Spiritride* - Mark Shepherd   *f*   4981

## VETERINARIAN

Brooks, Anne
*The Devil's Laughter* - William W.
   Johnstone   *h*   2930

Cully, Lawrence
*The Black Cat* - Robert Poe   *h*   4344

Dobbs, Charles "Sugar" Franklin
*The Magic and the Healing* - Nick
   O'Donohoe   *f*   4196

**Harrison, Lee Anne**
*The Magic and the Healing* - Nick
  O'Donohoe  *f*  4196
*Under the Healing Sign* - Nick O'Donohoe  *f*  4198

**Henshaw, William**
*Hard Landing* - Algis Budrys  *s*  753

**Mallau, Olney**
*Hand of Prophecy* - Severna Park  *s*  4244

**Nicole, Maeve**
*The Scathach and the Maeve's Daughter* - Mary
  Alexander Walker  *f*  5618

**Perkins, Blair**
*Bats* - William W. Johnstone  *h*  2926

**Stewart, Meg**
*Claw* - Ken Eulo  *h*  1850

**Vaughan, BJ**
*The Healing of Crossroads* - Nick
  O'Donohoe  *f*  4195
*The Magic and the Healing* - Nick
  O'Donohoe  *f*  4196
*Under the Healing Sign* - Nick O'Donohoe  *f*  4198

## VIGILANTE

**Kies, Wolfgang**
*Wolf and Raven* - Michael A. Stackpole  *f*  5207

**Raven, Richard**
*Wolf and Raven* - Michael A. Stackpole  *f*  5207

**Repairman Jack**
*Nightworld* - F. Paul Wilson  *h*  5893

## VILLAIN

**BKR**
*Aliens Stole My Body* - Bruce Coville  *s*  1217

**Chee, Diren**
*House of Moons* - K.D. Wentworth  *s*  5752

**Hasloch, Toller**
*Heartlight* - Marion Zimmer Bradley  *f*  637

**Hong**
*Interesting Times* - Terry Pratchett  *f*  4392

**Ice**
*Chaos Come Again* - Wilhelmina Baird  *s*  293

**Ingles, Benton**
*Outworld Cats* - Jack Lovejoy  *s*  3536

## VINTNER

**Clermont, Donald**
*Kiss of Death* - Daniel Rhodes  *h*  4569

**Cochran, Sid**
*Earthquake Weather* - Tim Powers  *f*  4382

## VOLUNTEER

**Wilkinson, Steve "The Dreamer"**
*A Two-Edged Sword* - Thomas K. Martin  *f*  3653

## WAITER/WAITRESS

**Ajani, Korinna "Kori" Kassemi**
*The March Hare Network* - Jack L. Chalker  *s*  957

**Beauchamp, Candace Jane "Candy"**
*Mockingbird* - Sean Stewart  *f*  5273

**Blyushkina, Marta Aleksandrova**
*Toplin* - Michael McDowell  *h*  3807

**Caldwell, Jessica**
*King of Morning, Queen of Day* - Ian
  McDonald  *f*  3793

**Charles, Ellen Cherry**
*Skinny Legs and All* - Tom Robbins  *f*  4607

**Chavez, Rafael**
*Black Night* - S.J. Strayhorn  *h*  5334

**Cobal, Flysse**
*Exile's Children* - Angus Wells  *f*  5735

**D'Ame, Celia "Lee"**
*A Roil of Stars* - Don Wismer  *s*  5930

**Deal, Sissy**
*Resume with Monsters* - William Browning
  Spencer  *h*  5168

**Dennessy, Anne**
*The Darkness Within* - Shawn MacDonald  *h*  3585

**E'lan, Misele**
*The Itinerant Exorcist* - Ashley McConnell  *f*  3776

**Gable, Helen**
*Symphony* - Charles L. Grant  *h*  2318

**Greene, Maggie**
*Entity* - Nina Mandelik  *h*  3615

**Jane**
*Animals* - John Skipp  *h*  5080

**Juarel, Chita**
*Kent Montana and the Really Ugly Thing From Mars* -
  Lionel Fenn  *s*  1918

**Keene, Valerie**
*Dark Rivers of the Heart* - Dean R. Koontz  *h*  3204

**Lacerda, Zefty**
*Trader* - Charles de Lint  *f*  1438

**Lange, Lizbet**
*Charlie's Bones* - L.L. Thrasher  *h*  5468

**MacCallum, Brenda**
*Shadows* - John Saul  *h*  4845

**Masterson, Jenny**
*Practical Demonkeeping* - Christopher
  Moore  *h*  3989

**Nakota**
*The Cipher* - Kathe Koja  *h*  3194

**Payne, Deliverance "Del"**
*Ticktock* - Dean R. Koontz  *h*  3217

**Podlowski, Robert**
*Brothers of the Dragon* - Robin Wayne
  Bailey  *f*  286

**Pulivok, Akushtina "Tina" Santis**
*Catch the Lightning* - Catherine Asaro  *s*  218

**Sanders, Julia**
*Raven* - Charles L. Grant  *h*  2314

**Smith, Shanifa**
*Dead End* - Guy N. Smith  *h*  5119

**Steinberg, Leah**
*Shock Radio* - Leigh Clark  *h*  1052

**Wickes, Margaret**
*The Quagmire* - James Kisner  *h*  3160

## WANDERER

**Aderyn**
*A Time of Exile* - Katharine Kerr  *f*  3077

**Angharad**
*Into the Green* - Charles de Lint  *f*  1430

**Beppu, Chan-ti**
*The Last Legends of Earth* - A.A. Attanasio  *s*  270

**Bishop, Toby**
*Sailing Bright Eternity* - Gregory Benford  *s*  449

**Brompton, Arnold**
*Virtual Girl* - Amy Thomson  *s*  5462

**Byron**
*The White Mists of Power* - Kristine Kathryn
  Rusch  *f*  4730

**Calanthe**
*Bewitchments of Love and Hate* - Storm
  Constantine  *s*  1140
*The Fulfillments of Fate and Desire* - Storm
  Constantine  *s*  1142

**Campbell, Laicy "Iroshi"**
*Iroshi* - Cary Osborne  *s*  4228

**Canary, Sarah**
*Sarah Canary* - Karen Joy Fowler  *f*  2028

**Canches, Alejandro**
*The Plague Tales* - Ann Benson  *s*  453

**Chin, Ah Kin**
*Sarah Canary* - Karen Joy Fowler  *f*  2028

**Clavius, Black**
*Glory* - Alfred Coppel  *s*  1182

**Cross, Prosper**
*The World Next Door* - Brad Ferguson  *s*  1924

**Dara**
*Ancestral Hungers* - Scott Baker  *h*  303

**Delan**
*Delan the Mislaid* - Laurie J. Marks  *f*  3625

**Duin, Mael**
*The Voyage of Mael Duin's Curragh* - Patricia
  Aakhus  *f*  2

**Essa**
*Black Wine* - Candas Jane Dorsey  *s*  1582

**Fall, Thomas**
*Warpath* - Tony Daniel  *s*  1337

**Garfield, Jake**
*The World Next Door* - Brad Ferguson  *s*  1924

**Hamr**
*Hunting the Ghost Dancer* - A.A. Attanasio  *f*  268

**Hastings, Kyle Stevens**
*Down the Bright Way* - Robert Reed  *s*  4505

**Joel-Andrew**
*The Off Season* - Jack Cady  *f*  820

**Jy**
*Down the Bright Way* - Robert Reed  *s*  4505

**Kelys**
*In the Mothers' Land* - Elisabeth Vonarburg  *s*  5590

**Killeen**
*Sailing Bright Eternity* - Gregory Benford  *s*  449

**Knobil**
*West of January* - Dave Duncan  *s*  1691

**Kundry**
*The Grail of Hearts* - Susan Shwartz  *f*  5015

**Kwan, Roxane**
*Mazeway* - Jack Williamson  *s*  5866

**Langtry, Cimarron**
*The Earth Remembers* - Susan Torian Olan  *s*  4209

**Lynx, Philip "Flinx"**
*Mid-Flinx* - Alan Dean Foster  *s*  2010

**McIntosh, Calvin**
*Stoneskin's Revenge* - Tom Deitz  *f*  1476
*Sunshaker's War* - Tom Deitz  *f*  1477

**Moliak**
*Down the Bright Way* - Robert Reed  *s*  4505

**O'Rourke**
*Earthfall* - Jerry Earl Brown  *s*  724

**Quejaches, Xia**
*The Stone Garden* - Mary Rosenblum  *s*  4679

**Rahn**
*They Fly at Ciron* - Samuel R. Delany  *s*  1482

**Raishan, Marguerite "Marghe" Angelica**
*Ammonite* - Nicola Griffith  s  2443

**Rance**
*Bride of the Castle* - John DeChancie  s  1452

**Rowan**
*The Steerswoman* - Rosemary Kirstein  s  3158

**Sanderson, Paul**
*Wolf and Iron* - Gordon R. Dickson  s  1539

**Thenike**
*Ammonite* - Nicola Griffith  s  2443

**T'Larien, Dirk**
*Dying of the Light* - George R.R. Martin  s  3644

**Veriam, Tanaquil**
*Red Unicorn* - Tanith Lee  f  3414

**Wu, Oliver**
*Star Bridge* - James Gunn  s  2459


## WARD

**Hammond, Fiona**
*The Black Death* - Basil Copper  h  1185


## WARLOCK

**Alaric**
*In the Red Lord's Reach* - Phyllis
  Eisenstein  f  1765

**Cardiff, Noel**
*Hooray for Hellywood* - Esther Friesner  f  2077

**Gallowglass, Geoffrey**
*M'Lady Witch* - Christopher Stasheff  f  5217
*Quicksilver's Knight* - Christopher Stasheff  f  5220

**Gallowglass, Rod**
*Warlock and Son* - Christopher Stasheff  s  5224
*The Warlock Insane* - Christopher Stasheff  f  5225
*The Warlock Rock* - Christopher Stasheff  s  5226

**Jones, Lloyd Merlin**
*MagicNet* - John DeChancie  f  1461

**Wheeler, Alec**
*Witch Spell* - Guy N. Smith  h  5122


## WARRIOR

**Aarundel**
*Once a Hero* - Michael A. Stackpole  f  5203

**Abivard**
*The Stolen Throne* - Harry Turtledove  f  5510

**Achilles**
*Yellowstone Run* - David Robbins  s  4605

**Aiko**
*The Dragonstone* - Dennis L. McKiernan  f  3832

**Ala-eh-din Beyh**
*Tower of Fear* - Glen Cook  f  1155

**Alexander**
*Helen's Passage* - Diana M. Concannon  f  1129

**Alexander the Great**
*Lord of the Two Lands* - Judith Tarr  f  5395

**Alhammittson, Alhammitt "Mitt"**
*The Crown of Dalemark* - Diana Wynne
  Jones  f  2945

**Amrey, Murl "Kar Kalim"**
*Kar Kalim* - Deborah Christian  f  1025

**Ansa**
*The Poisoned Lands* - John Maddox
  Roberts  f  4619
*Queens of Land and Sea* - John Maddox
  Roberts  f  4620

**Antiope**
*Amazon: A Novel* - Barbara G. Walker  f  5616
*The Amazon Chronicles* - Jane E.M.
  Robinson  f  4627

**Anya**
*Orion in the Dying Time* - Ben Bova  s  591

**ap Hywel, Dafydd**
*The Dragon in Lyonesse* - Gordon R.
  Dickson  f  1531

**ap Kian, Tiernyn**
*The Western King* - Ann Marston  f  3636

**Apollo**
*Armageddon* - Richard Hatch  s  2602

**Arianna**
*The Resistance* - Kristine Kathryn Rusch  f  4727

**Arthur**
*The Child Queen* - Nancy McKenzie  f  3827
*Chronicles of King Arthur* - Andrea
  Hopkins  f  2767
*Mordred's Curse* - Ian McDowell  f  3806
*The Winter King* - Bernard Cornwell  f  1191

**Artos**
*Black Horses for the King* - Anne
  McCaffrey  f  3720

**Attila the Hun**
*The Autobiography of Santa Claus: It's Better to Give*
  - Jeff Guinn  f  2456

**Aurealis, Gannd**
*War* - Simon Hawke  f  2625

**Auriane**
*The Light Bearer* - Donna Gillespie  f  2229

**Aviendha**
*The Fires of Heaven* - Robert Jordan  f  2987

**Bahnakson, Bahzell**
*Oath of Swords* - David Weber  f  5678
*The War God's Own* - David Weber  f  5682

**Baram**
*The Outlanders* - David B. Coe  f  1096

**Barku, Perkar Kar**
*The Blackgod* - J. Gregory Keyes  f  3095

**Barra the Pict**
*Iron Dawn* - Matthew Woodring Stover  f  5320
*Jericho Moon* - Matthew Woodring Stover  f  5321

**Bedwyr, Luthien "Crimson Shadow"**
*The Dragon King* - R.A. Salvatore  f  4796
*Luthien's Gamble* - R.A. Salvatore  f  4802
*The Sword of Bedwyr* - R.A. Salvatore  f  4808

**Beroth of Firoze**
*Clock Strikes Sword* - Ian Hammell  f  2529

**Beryl**
*The Oxygen Barons* - Gregory Feeley  s  1897

**bin Sind, Simna**
*Carnivores of Light and Darkness* - Alan Dean
  Foster  f  1996

**Bjorn of Bromme**
*The Discovery of Dragons* - Graeme Base  f  385

**Blackburn, Trebor**
*Captains Outrageous, or, For Doom the Bell Tolls* -
  Roy V. Young  f  6049

**Blade**
*L.A. Strike* - David Robbins  s  4599
*Madman Run* - David Robbins  s  4600
*Spartan Run* - David Robbins  s  4602
*Vengeance Strike* - David Robbins  s  4604
*Yellowstone Run* - David Robbins  s  4605

**Blade, Sonya**
*Mortal Kombat* - Martin Delrio  f  1483

**Blake, Nick**
*Dragon Burning* - Craig Shaw Gardner  f  2126

**Dragon Sleeping** - Craig Shaw Gardner  f  2127
*Dragon Waking* - Craig Shaw Gardner  f  2128

**Bodbmall**
*Master of Earth and Water* - Diana L.
  Paxson  f  4266

**Boh, Walker**
*The Talismans of Shannara* - Terry Brooks  f  717

**Braldt**
*The Hunter on Arena* - Rose Estes  s  1838

**Brand**
*The Hammer and the Cross* - Harry
  Harrison  f  2570
*One King's Way* - Harry Harrison  s  2572

**Brandarkson, Brandark**
*Oath of Swords* - David Weber  f  5678

**Breyd**
*The Sword and the Lion* - Roberta Cray  f  1253

**Brock, Dire-Lord**
*The Goda War* - Jay D. Blakeney  s  516

**Broketail, Bazil**
*Bazil Broketail* - Christopher Rowley  f  4692

**Bronwyn**
*Hearts and Armor* - Ron Miller  f  3903

**Bruenor, Catti-Brie**
*Starless Night* - R.A. Salvatore  f  4807

**Brunahild "Sigdrifa"**
*The Dragons of the Rhine* - Diana L.
  Paxson  f  4264
*The Wolf and the Raven* - Diana L. Paxson  f  4270

**Brunichild**
*Rhinegold* - Stephan Grundy  f  2454

**Cadarn, Derfel**
*Enemy of God* - Bernard Cornwell  f  1189
*Excalibur* - Bernard Cornwell  f  1190
*The Winter King* - Bernard Cornwell  f  1191

**Caitin, Bedyr**
*Wrath of Ashar* - Angus Wells  f  5742

**Caitin, Kedryn**
*The Usurper* - Angus Wells  f  5739
*The Way Beneath* - Angus Wells  f  5740
*Wrath of Ashar* - Angus Wells  f  5742

**Caldaq**
*A Call to Arms* - Alan Dean Foster  s  1995

**Calistinsson, Colbey**
*Prince of Demons* - Mickey Zucker
  Reichert  f  4522
*The Western Wizard* - Mickey Zucker
  Reichert  f  4526

**Camron**
*The Barbed Coil* - J.V. Jones  f  2957

**Cavish, Beka**
*Stalking Darkness* - Lynn Flewelling  f  1953

**Cerdic**
*Shadow of the King* - Helen Hollick  f  2747

**Chakthi**
*Exile's Challenge* - Angus Wells  f  5734

**Champion, Dragonbait**
*Song of the Saurials* - Kate Novak  f  4167

**Chanly, Bel, Margasdotter**
*The Outskirter's Secret* - Rosemary Kirstein  s  3157

**Christensen, Maryanne "Maggie"**
*The Crimson Sky* - Joel Rosenberg  f  4669

**Cleedis**
*King Pinch* - David Cook  f  1146

**Conan**
*Conan and the Treasure of Python* - John Maddox
  Roberts  f  4616
*The Conan Chronicles* - Robert Jordan  f  2983

*Conan of the Red Brotherhood* - Leonard
    Carpenter  *f*  906
*Conan, Scourge of the Bloody Coast* - Leonard
    Carpenter  *f*  910
*Conan the Formidable* - Steve Perry  *f*  4293
*Conan the Gladiator* - Leonard Carpenter  *f*  907
*Conan the Guardian* - Roland J. Green  *f*  2347
*Conan the Indomitable* - Steve Perry  *f*  4294
*Conan the Outcast* - Leonard Carpenter  *f*  908
*Conan the Relentless* - Roland J. Green  *f*  2348
*Conan the Rogue* - John Maddox Roberts  *f*  4617
*Conan the Savage* - Leonard Carpenter  *f*  909
*Hour of the Dragon* - Robert E. Howard  *f*  2783

**Connla**
*The Isles of the Blest* - Morgan Llywelyn  *f*  3505

**Cordell**
*Feathered Dragon* - Douglas Niles  *f*  4108

**Crowley, Damon**
*Evil Triumphant* - Michael A. Stackpole  *s*  5199

**Cuchlainn**
*The Raid* - Randy Lee Eickhoff  *f*  1764

**Culaehra**
*The Sage* - Christopher Stasheff  *f*  5221

**Cullinane, Jason**
*The Road Home* - Joel Rosenberg  *f*  4674

**Dan, Issachar**
*Wind From a Foreign Sky* - Katya Reimann  *f*  4528

**Danica**
*Canticle* - R.A. Salvatore  *f*  4793

**Darcy, Jade**
*Jade Darcy and the Zen Pirates* - Stephen
    Goldin  *s*  2260

**d'Armand, Magnus Gallowglass "Gar Pike"**
*Warlock and Son* - Christopher Stasheff  *s*  5224
*A Wizard in War* - Christopher Stasheff  *s*  5234

**D'Artagnan, Charles**
*A Candle for D'Artagnan* - Chelsea Quinn
    Yarbro  *h*  6013

**Darthoridan**
*Evermeet: Island of Elves* - Elaine
    Cunningham  *f*  1290

**de Oro, Irving**
*Horrors of the Dancing Gods* - Jack L.
    Chalker  *f*  955

**Deal, John "J.C."**
*The Square Deal* - David Drake  *s*  1644

**Deering, Wilma**
*Hammer of Mars* - M.S. Murdock  *s*  4049

**Del**
*Sword-Born* - Jennifer Roberson  *f*  4612

**Delilah "Del"**
*Sword-Breaker* - Jennifer Roberson  *f*  4613

**DenUyl, Luis Raoul**
*The Lizard War* - John Dalmas  *s*  1325

**Donough**
*Pride of Lions* - Morgan Llywelyn  *f*  3506

**Dryhope, Wat**
*A History Maker* - Alasdair Gray  *s*  2338

**Dunstan, Sara**
*Legacy of Steel* - Mary H. Herbert  *f*  2675

**Duzon**
*Touched by the Gods* - Lawrence Watt-
    Evans  *f*  5651

**Dyfed**
*Shadow of the Seventh Moon* - Nancy Varian
    Berberick  *f*  459

**Ecklundson, Dword**
*Captains Outrageous, or, For Doom the Bell Tolls* -
    Roy V. Young  *f*  6049

**Egil**
*The Dragonstone* - Dennis L. McKiernan  *f*  3832

**Eh'rik**
*Snow Brother* - S.M. Stirling  *f*  5299

**Elric of Melnibone**
*Elric: Song of the Black Sword* - Michael
    Moorcock  *f*  3980
*The Fortress of the Pearl* - Michael
    Moorcock  *f*  3982
*The Revenge of the Rose* - Michael
    Moorcock  *f*  3985
*Tales of the White Wolf* - Edward E.
    Kramer  *f*  3227

**Erin of Elliath**
*Chains of Darkness, Chains of Light* - Michelle
    Sagara  *f*  4781
*Into the Dark Lands* - Michelle Sagara  *f*  4783
*Lady of Mercy* - Michelle Sagara  *f*  4784

**Er'ril**
*Wit'ch Fire* - James Clemens  *f*  1082

**Fafhrd**
*Farewell to Lankhmar* - Fritz Leiber  *f*  3418
*Ill Met in Lankhmar* - Fritz Leiber  *f*  3419
*Lean Times in Lankhmar* - Fritz Leiber  *f*  3420
*Return to Lankhmar* - Fritz Leiber  *f*  3422
*Swords Against the Shadowland* - Robin Wayne
    Bailey  *f*  291

**Falmah-Al, Kezi**
*The Goda War* - Jay D. Blakeney  *s*  516

**Ferahgo the Assassin**
*Salamandastron* - Brian Jacques  *f*  2855

**Fire, Fen "Fire Queen"**
*The Fire Queen* - Jack Holland  *f*  2740

**Formidable**
*A Remembrance for Kedrigern* - John
    Morressy  *f*  4014

**Foster, Bass**
*Of Beginnings and Endings* - Robert Adams  *s*  33

**Fyodor of Rashemen**
*Daughter of the Drow* - Elaine Cunningham  *f*  1287

**Gabria**
*Dark Horse* - Mary H. Herbert  *f*  2674
*Lightning's Daughter* - Mary H. Herbert  *f*  2676
*Winged Magic* - Mary H. Herbert  *f*  2678

**Gabrielle**
*The Thief of Hermes* - Ru Emerson  *f*  1811

**Garon**
*A Man Betrayed* - J.V. Jones  *f*  2958

**Garroc**
*The Panther's Hoard* - Nancy Varian
    Berberick  *f*  458
*Shadow of the Seventh Moon* - Nancy Varian
    Berberick  *f*  459

**Garth One-eye**
*Arena* - William R. Forstchen  *f*  1977

**Gasam**
*The Poisoned Lands* - John Maddox
    Roberts  *f*  4619

**Genevera "Gena"**
*Once a Hero* - Michael A. Stackpole  *f*  5203

**Geronimo**
*Madman Run* - David Robbins  *s*  4600

**Gilbert, Renard**
*No Limits* - Nigel Findley  *s*  1938

**Gilgamesh**
*To the Land of the Living* - Robert
    Silverberg  *f*  5044

**Gillian**
*Ash Ock* - Christopher Hinz  *s*  2690
*The Paratwa* - Christopher Hinz  *s*  2691

**Glass Warrior**
*The Glass Warrior* - Robert E. Vardeman  *f*  5563

**Godwinesson, Harold**
*Lord of Sunset* - Parke Godwin  *f*  2246

**Goro**
*Mortal Kombat* - Martin Delrio  *f*  1483

**Grimm**
*Inquisitor* - Ian Watson  *s*  5637

**Grizzly**
*Vengeance Strike* - David Robbins  *s*  4604

**Guiwenneth**
*Gate of Ivory, Gate of Horn* - Robert
    Holdstock  *f*  2737

**Gultec**
*Feathered Dragon* - Douglas Niles  *f*  4108

**Gunnar**
*Byzantium* - Stephen R. Lawhead  *f*  3353

**Hadding**
*War of the Gods* - Poul Anderson  *f*  136

**Hael**
*The Steel Kings* - John Maddox Roberts  *f*  4621

**Hagan**
*Attila's Treasure* - Stephan Grundy  *f*  2453

**Haji, Hool**
*Kane of Old Mars* - Michael Moorcock  *s*  3983

**Half-Elvin, Tanthalas "Tanis"**
*Kindred Spirits* - Mark Anthony  *f*  154
*Steel and Stone* - Ellen Porath  *f*  4368
*Wanderlust* - Mary Kirchoff  *f*  3155

**Han Rosie**
*Mariel of Redwall* - Brian Jacques  *f*  2850

**Hanavi, Ari**
*Hero* - Joel Rosenberg  *s*  4672

**Hanse**
*The Shadow of Sorcery* - Andrew J. Offutt  *f*  4202

**Harnak**
*Oath of Swords* - David Weber  *f*  5678

**Hasloch, Toller**
*Heartlight* - Marion Zimmer Bradley  *f*  637

**Helwin, Owen**
*The Bridge of Dawn* - Neil Hancock  *f*  2531

**Hercules**
*By the Sword* - Timothy Boggs  *f*  559

**Hickock**
*Yellowstone Run* - David Robbins  *s*  4605

**Hirsch, Magen**
*Warp Angel* - Stuart Hopen  *s*  2766

**Holbian**
*The Road to Underfall* - Mike Jefferies  *f*  2888

**Idera**
*Dark Legend* - Jamake Highwater  *f*  2686

**Iowyn**
*Tears of Time* - Nancy Asire  *f*  256

**Isaf**
*The Fortress of Eternity* - Andrew
    Whitmore  *f*  5790

**Ivar**
*The Hammer and the Cross* - Harry
    Harrison  *f*  2570

**ja N'Wook, Chrysamen "Chrys"**
*Caesar's Bicycle* - John Barnes  *s*  350

**Jaeme**
*Twisted Dragon* - Kevin Stein  *f*  5251

**Jarnhann, Nils**
*The Yngling and the Circle of Power* - John
    Dalmas  *s*  1328
*The Yngling in Yamato* - John Dalmas  *s*  1329

**Jenna**
*The One-Armed Queen* - Jane Yolen   f   6037

**Jiana**
*Warriorwards* - Dafydd ab Hugh   f   11

**Jones, Cory**
*City of Pain* - John Terra   f   5438

**Juraviel, Belli'mar**
*The Demon Spirit* - R.A. Salvatore   f   4795

**Kadumi**
*The Parched Sea* - Troy Denning   f   1486

**Kahless**
*Kahless* - Michael Jan Friedman   s   2065

**Kahn, Tae**
*Beyond Ragnarok* - Mickey Zucker Reichert   f   4516

**Kahsir**
*Tears of Time* - Nancy Asire   f   256

**Kairn**
*The Steel Kings* - John Maddox Roberts   f   4621

**Kallmirsson, Rache**
*The Last of the Renshai* - Mickey Zucker
   Reichert   f   4520

**Kardith**
*Northlight* - Deborah Wheeler   s   5775

**Kashir**
*To Fall Like Stars* - Nancy Asire   f   257

**Kastring**
*Shadowbreed* - David Ferring   f   1928

**Kelahnus**
*The Stone Prince* - Fiona Patton   f   4259

**Kelemvor**
*Crucible* - Troy Denning   f   1484

**Kern**
*Conspiracy* - J. Robert King   f   3121

**Khast, Rafiq**
*Eyes of Silver* - Michael A. Stackpole   f   5200

**Kidd, Malachy**
*Eyes of Silver* - Michael A. Stackpole   f   5200

**Kikun**
*Shadowkill* - Jo Clayton   s   1069
*Shadowplay* - Jo Clayton   s   1070
*Shadowspeer* - Jo Clayton   s   1071

**Kireyevsky, Vasily "Vasha"**
*The Law of Becoming* - Kate Elliott   s   1774

**Kirha**
*Wing Commander: Freedom Flight* - Mercedes
   Lackey   s   3307

**Kith-Kanan**
*The Kinslayer Wars* - Douglas Niles   f   4109
*The Qualinesti* - Paul B. Thompson   f   5455

**Konrad**
*Shadowbreed* - David Ferring   f   1928

**Kruickshank, Jenny**
*The Whims of Creation* - Simon Hawke   s   2626

**Kurosawa, Oishi**
*The Napoleon Wager* - William R.
   Forstchen   s   1980

**lach Feragh, Culain**
*Ghost King* - David Gemmell   f   2188

**Lamaril**
*Golden Trillium* - Andre Norton   f   4153

**Latticus, Gaarius "Gaar"**
*The Vampire Memoirs* - Mara McCuniff   h   3781

**Leiria**
*Wolves of the Gods* - Allan Cole   f   1111

**Leucas**
*Iron Dawn* - Matthew Woodring Stover   f   5320
*Jericho Moon* - Matthew Woodring Stover   f   5321

**Loran, Luroc I**
*Firehand* - Andre Norton   s   4151

**Lorhaiden**
*To Fall Like Stars* - Nancy Asire   f   257

**mac Brian, Murcha**
*Brian Boru: Emperor of the Irish* - Morgan
   Llywelyn   f   3501

**Mac Cool, Finn**
*Finn Mac Cool* - Morgan Llywelyn   f   3504

**Mac Morna, Goll**
*Finn Mac Cool* - Morgan Llywelyn   f   3504

**mac Morna, Goll**
*The Shield between the Worlds* - Diana L.
   Paxson   f   4267

**Macurdy, Curtis**
*The Lion of Farside* - John Dalmas   f   1324

**Mad Mall**
*Chase the Morning* - Michael Scott Rohan   f   4658

**Maddock**
*Spirit Fox* - Mickey Zucker Reichert   f   4524

**Majere, Caramon**
*The Soulforge* - Margaret Weis   f   5728

**Mana**
*Lion's Heart* - Karen Wehrstein   f   5683

**Mandaka, Bukoba**
*Ivory: A Legend of Past and Future* - Mike
   Resnick   s   4547

**Mano, Iuti**
*Demon Drums* - Carol Severance   f   4922
*Storm Caller* - Carol Severance   f   4924

**Margawt "The Morigu"**
*Morigu: The Dead* - Mark C. Perry   f   4284

**Mariel**
*The Bellmaker* - Brian Jacques   f   2848
*Mariel of Redwall* - Brian Jacques   f   2850

**Marliir, Dauneth**
*Cormyr: A Novel* - Ed Greenwood   f   2425

**Matthias**
*Mattimeo* - Brian Jacques   f   2852

**Mek Kermak's-kin, Shkai'ra**
*Saber & Shadow* - S.M. Stirling   f   5297
*Snow Brother* - S.M. Stirling   f   5299

**Melody**
*The Lion of Farside* - John Dalmas   f   1324

**Miaowara Tomokato**
*Samurai Cat Goes to the Movies* - Mark E.
   Rogers   s   4656
*The Sword of Samurai Cat* - Mark E.
   Rogers   s   4657

**Minstrel Boy**
*The Last Stand of the DNA Cowboys* - Mick
   Farren   s   1879

**Mitrian**
*The Last of the Renshai* - Mickey Zucker
   Reichert   f   4520

**Moonblade, Arilyn**
*Elfshadow* - Elaine Cunningham   f   1288
*Silver Shadows* - Elaine Cunningham   f   1292

**Moondark, Gan**
*Warrior* - Donald E. McQuinn   s   3863
*Witch* - Donald E. McQuinn   s   3864

**Moore, Teldin**
*Beyond the Moons* - David Cook   f   1144
*Into the Void* - Nigel Findley   f   1937
*The Radiant Dragon* - Elaine Cunningham   f   1291

**Morgis, Duke**
*Wolfhelm* - Richard A. Knaak   f   3175

**Mwili-Ferret**
*The 97th Step* - Steve Perry   s   4287

**Naguchi, Machiko**
*Hunter's Planet* - David Bischoff   s   492

**Nazhuret**
*The Belly of the Wolf* - R.A. MacAvoy   f   3580
*King of the Dead* - R.A. MacAvoy   f   3581
*Lens of the World* - R.A. MacAvoy   f   3582

**Nick**
*The Paratwa* - Christopher Hinz   s   2691

**Nimbulan "Lan"**
*The Dragon's Touchstone* - Irene Radford   f   4459

**No-man's Son, Roric**
*Voima* - C. Dale Brittain   f   704

**Nukurren**
*Mother of Demons* - Eric Flint   s   1956

**Oblivion, Billy**
*The Last Stand of the DNA Cowboys* - Mick
   Farren   s   1879

**O'Day, Gallen**
*Beyond the Gate* - Dave Wolverton   s   5949
*The Golden Queen* - Dave Wolverton   s   5951

**Oghmal**
*Search for the Starblade* - Keith Taylor   f   5408

**Ohaern**
*The Sage* - Christopher Stasheff   f   5221
*The Shaman* - Christopher Stasheff   f   5223

**O'Meara, Patrick**
*Masters of the Fist* - Edward P. Hughes   s   2805

**or-Reise, Garric**
*Lord of the Isles* - David Drake   f   1636
*Queen of Demons* - David Drake   f   1640

**Orion**
*Orion Among the Stars* - Ben Bova   s   589
*Orion and the Conqueror* - Ben Bova   s   590
*Orion in the Dying Time* - Ben Bova   s   591

**O'Shay, Padrig**
*City of Pain* - John Terra   f   5438

**Parmenion**
*Dark Prince* - David Gemmell   f   2187

**Patterson, Gil**
*Mother of Winter* - Barbara Hambly   f   2506

**Pendragon, Uther**
*The Dragon and the Unicorn* - A.A.
   Attanasio   f   266
*The Eagles' Brood* - Jack Whyte   f   5792

**Penthesilea**
*The Amazon Chronicles* - Jane E.M.
   Robinson   f   4627

**Petrus**
*Spiritride* - Mark Shepherd   f   4981

**Phillips, Mark**
*The Crystal Sorcerers* - William R.
   Forstchen   f   1979

**Pirelli, Vince**
*Warlords of Jupiter* - William H. Keith Jr.   s   3036

**Potter, Prat'han**
*Future Indefinite* - Dave Duncan   f   1678

**Quinn "Nomad"**
*Desert Fire* - David Alexander   s   65
*Nomad* - David Alexander   s   66

**Rabble**
*When the Gods Are Silent* - Jane M.
   Lindskold   f   3477

**Raihna**
*Conan the Relentless* - Roland J. Green   f   2348

**Ranji**
*The False Mirror* - Alan Dean Foster   s   2004

**Rap**
*Emperor and Clown* - Dave Duncan    f   1676

**Raven Hunter**
*People of the Wolf* - W. Michael Gear    f   2170

**Renagi**
*Tegne: Soul Warrior* - Richard La Plante    f   3268

**Renzie**
*Vanishing Point* - Michaela Roessner    s   4652

**Rikki-Tikki-Tavi**
*Spartan Run* - David Robbins    s   4602

**Rikus**
*The Verdant Passage* - Troy Denning    f   1487

**Ripley, Ellen**
*Aliens: The Female War* - Steve Perry    s   4290

**Rivakonneva "Riva"**
*Mathemagics* - Margaret Ball    f   316

**Rockdream**
*The Goblin Plain War* - Carl Miller    f   3892

**Roclawzi, Neal "Dun Wolf"**
*Once a Hero* - Michael A. Stackpole    f   5203

**Rogers, Buck**
*Hammer of Mars* - M.S. Murdock    s   4049

**Roland**
*Charlemagne's Champion* - Gail Van Asten    f   5534

**Rose**
*The Revenge of the Rose* - Michael
     Moorcock    f   3985

**Sakhalin, Anatoly**
*The Law of Becoming* - Kate Elliott    s   1774

**Sal**
*The Face of Apollo* - Fred Saberhagen    s   4766

**Sam**
*Hope of Earth* - Piers Anthony    s   175

**Sandtiger "Tiger"**
*Sword-Breaker* - Jennifer Roberson    f   4613

**Santagithi**
*The Western Wizard* - Mickey Zucker
     Reichert    f   4526

**Sauromanta**
*Atlantis Found* - R. Garcia y Robertson    s   2119

**Serroi**
*Dancer's Rise* - Jo Clayton    f   1064
*The Magic Wars* - Jo Clayton    f   1068

**Shannow, Jon**
*Wolf in Shadow* - David Gemmell    s   2191

**Shantow**
*The Wolves of Autumn* - Scott Ciencin    f   1035

**Sharrow**
*Against a Dark Background* - Iain M. Banks    s   322

**Shile**
*The Conjurer Princess* - Vivian Vande
     Velde    f   5555

**Shinji, Matsumura**
*The Yngling in Yamato* - John Dalmas    s   1329

**Shiro, Miaowara**
*Samurai Cat Goes to Hell* - Mark E. Rogers    f   4655

**Shkai'ra**
*The Cage* - S.M. Stirling    f   5293
*Shadow's Son* - Shirley Meier    f   3872

**Shunlar**
*The Gates of Vensunor* - Carol Heller    f   2650

**Sigfrid**
*The Dragons of the Rhine* - Diana L.
     Paxson    f   4264
*The Wolf and the Raven* - Diana L. Paxson    f   4270

**Sigfrith**
*Rhinegold* - Stephan Grundy    f   2454

**Sigvarthsson, Shef**
*One King's Way* - Harry Harrison    s   2572

**Silver Hand, Llew**
*The Silver Hand* - Stephen R. Lawhead    f   3358

**Silver Snow**
*Imperial Lady* - Andre Norton    f   4155

**Silverhand, Caeled**
*Silverlight* - Morgan Llywelyn    f   3507

**Simms, Nanci**
*Deep Trek* - James Axler    s   278

**Simon, Chuck**
*Haven* - David Peters    f   4304

**Sims, Christopher**
*A Talent for War* - Jack McDevitt    s   3790

**Singh, Ram**
*The Spider #8: The Devil's Paymaster/Legions of the*
     *Accursed Light* - Grant Stockbridge    f   5309

**Sixclaw, Swartt**
*Outcast of Redwall* - Brian Jacques    f   2853

**Slate**
*The Enigma Variations* - John Maddox
     Roberts    s   4618

**Slovotsky, Walter**
*The Road Home* - Joel Rosenberg    f   4674
*The Road to Ehvenor* - Joel Rosenberg    f   4675

**Snaugenhutt**
*Son of Spellsinger* - Alan Dean Foster    f   2015

**Solamnus, Vinas**
*Vinas Solamnus* - J. Robert King    f   3123

**Solo, Han**
*Ambush at Corellia* - Roger MacBride Allen    s   76
*Children of the Jedi* - Barbara Hambly    s   2500
*The Courtship of Princess Leia* - Dave
     Wolverton    s   5950
*Heir to the Empire* - Timothy Zahn    s   6054
*Jedi Search* - Kevin J. Anderson    s   109
*The New Rebellion* - Kristine Kathryn
     Rusch    s   4719
*The Truce at Bakura* - Kathy Tyers    s   5527

**Songa**
*Conan the Savage* - Leonard Carpenter    f   909

**Stalker, Martin**
*A Tremor in the Bitter Earth* - Katya
     Reimann    f   4527

**Starbuck**
*Armageddon* - Richard Hatch    s   2602

**Strang, Mark**
*Caesar's Bicycle* - John Barnes    s   350

**Sunflash**
*Outcast of Redwall* - Brian Jacques    f   2853

**Tainharsdarter, Kevral**
*The Children of Wrath* - Mickey Zucker
     Reichert    f   4518

**Tainharsdartter, Kevral**
*Prince of Demons* - Mickey Zucker
     Reichert    f   4522

**Talienson, Caltus "Cal"**
*Dark Divide* - Mark Acres    f   27
*Horrible Humes* - Stephen Billias    f   487
*The Stone of Time* - Rose Estes    f   1840

**Tanis**
*The Second Generation* - Margaret Weis    f   5724

**Tansen**
*In Legend Born* - Laura Resnick    f   4533

**Tarawe**
*Demon Drums* - Carol Severance    f   4922

**Tarlach**
*Flight of Vengeance* - Andre Norton    f   4152

**Tarma**
*Oathblood* - Mercedes Lackey    f   3290

**Teenager, Orlando**
*City of Golden Shadow* - Tad Williams    s   5828

**Tek**
*The Son of Summer Stars* - Meredith Ann
     Pierce    f   4319

**Tepes, Vlad**
*The Empire of Fear* - Brian Stableford    h   5191

**Thanehand**
*Palace of Kings* - Mike Jefferies    f   2887
*The Road to Underfall* - Mike Jefferies    f   2888

**Thromar**
*The Jewel of Equilibrant* - Steven Frankos    f   2042

**Tiger**
*Sword-Born* - Jennifer Roberson    f   4612

**Tind**
*A Landscape of Darkness* - John Blair    s   513

**Titch**
*The True Knight* - Susan Dexter    f   1513

**Tomokato, Miaowara**
*Samurai Cat Goes to Hell* - Mark E. Rogers    f   4655

**Tor**
*Shadows on the Hill* - Jackie Cassada    f   935

**Toren**
*The Schemes of Dragons* - Dave Smeds    f   5097

**Trask, Jovanna**
*Warlords of Jupiter* - William H. Keith Jr.    s   3036

**Tregarth, Keris**
*The Warding of Witch World* - Andre
     Norton    f   4163

**Trreggerthann, Umber**
*The Gift of the Gorboduc Vandal* - Paul O.
     Williams    s   5821

**Turkel, Maximillian**
*Mutant Hell* - Mark Grant    s   2324

**Tye, Asher**
*A Roil of Stars* - Don Wismer    s   5930

**Ulfilo**
*Conan and the Treasure of Python* - John Maddox
     Roberts    f   4616

**Vandien**
*Luck of the Wheels* - Megan Lindholm    f   3471

**Vayhawk**
*The Heldan* - Deborah Talmadge-Bickmore    f   5383

**Vercingetorix**
*Druids* - Morgan Llywelyn    f   3502

**Vervaine, Meguet**
*The Cygnet and the Firebird* - Patricia A.
     McKillip    f   3839

**Vryce, Damien Kilcannon**
*Black Sun Rising* - C.S. Friedman    f   2056
*Crown of Shadows* - C.S. Friedman    s   2057
*When True Night Falls* - C.S. Friedman    f   2060

**Wanbli**
*The Third Eagle: Lessons Along a Minor String* - R.A.
     MacAvoy    s   3583

**Whitlock, Megan**
*The Cage* - S.M. Stirling    f   5293
*Saber & Shadow* - S.M. Stirling    f   5297
*Shadow's Son* - Shirley Meier    f   3872

**Wiggin, Andrew**
*Xenocide* - Orson Scott Card    s   899

**Wiltin, Hof**
*To a Highland Nation* - Christopher
     Rowley    s   4698

**Storms of Victory** - Andre Norton    f   4162

**Wolf**
*Masques* - Patricia Briggs  *f*  681

**Wood, Leo "Lobo"**
*L.A. Strike* - David Robbins  *s*  4599

**Wulfgar**
*The Silent Blade* - R.A. Salvatore  *f*  4805

**Wulfrede**
*Conan and the Treasure of Python* - John Maddox
Roberts  *f*  4616

**Wyndon, Elbryan**
*The Demon Awakens* - R.A. Salvatore  *f*  4794
*The Demon Spirit* - R.A. Salvatore  *f*  4795

**Xena**
*The Empty Throne* - Ru Emerson  *f*  1808
*The Thief of Hermes* - Ru Emerson  *f*  1811

**Yor**
*Captains Outrageous, or, For Doom the Bell Tolls* -
Roy V. Young  *f*  6049

**Yoshio, Ikawa**
*The Crystal Sorcerers* - William R.
Forstchen  *f*  1979

## WEALTHY

**Bernard, Cynthia**
*The Gatekeepers* - Daniel Graham Jr.  *s*  2301

**Cobham, James**
*Freedom & Necessity* - Steven Brust  *f*  743

**Cobham, Richard**
*Freedom & Necessity* - Steven Brust  *f*  743

**Collins, George**
*The Thing That Darkness Hides* - Robert
Morgan  *h*  4006

**Deeds, A.J.**
*Meeting the Minotaur* - Carol Dawson  *f*  1409

**Evans, Harrington-Smith**
*Bereavement* - Richard Lortz  *h*  3525

**Garrison, David**
*Psychosphere* - Brian Lumley  *h*  3563

**Hagar, Jonathan**
*The Beast* - Marie Ardell White  *h*  5784

**Kane, Chandler**
*Order of the Arrow* - Michael T.
Hinkemeyer  *h*  2689

**Khoronos, Erim**
*Incubi* - Edward Lee  *h*  3394

**Khumeni, George**
*Demogorgon* - Brian Lumley  *h*  3552

**Krisos, Alexander**
*Lord of the Dark Lake* - Ron Faust  *h*  1894

**Medwin, Earl**
*Jacob's Hands* - Aldous Huxley  *f*  2817

**Melford, Trudy**
*Proteus in the Underworld* - Charles
Sheffield  *s*  4962

**Schrapnell**
*To Say Nothing of the Dog* - Connie Willis  *s*  5874

**Scott, Jim**
*Jackals* - Charles L. Grant  *h*  2313

**Shannon, Royston**
*Water Rites* - Guy N. Smith  *h*  5121

**Southerland, John**
*A Matter of Taste* - Fred Saberhagen  *h*  4770

**Tummelier, Peter**
*Tap, Tap* - David Martin  *h*  3640

**Voight, Susan**
*Freedom & Necessity* - Steven Brust  *f*  743

**Zant, Quasar**
*Quasar* - Jamil Nasir  *s*  4071

## WEREWOLF

**Antonov, Denis**
*The Passion* - Donna Boyd  *h*  603

**Bell, April**
*Darker than You Think* - Jack Williamson  *h*  5861

**Berzel**
*Kedrigern and the Charming Couple* - John
Morressy  *f*  4013

**Blanchard, Miles**
*The World of Darkness: Watcher* - Charles L.
Grant  *h*  2321

**Cade, Skinner**
*Wild Blood* - Nancy A. Collins  *h*  1127

**Caillet, Bertrand**
*The Werewolf of Paris* - Guy Endore  *h*  1822

**Caldwell, Jay**
*Call to Battle* - Doug Murray  *h*  4059

**Cameron, Jason**
*The Fire Rose* - Mercedes Lackey  *f*  3280

**Devoncroix, Alexander**
*The Passion* - Donna Boyd  *h*  603

**Duke, Bob**
*The Wild* - Whitley Strieber  *h*  5343

**Gallatin, Michael**
*The Wolf's Hour* - Robert R. McCammon  *h*  3759

**Gandillon, Vivian**
*Blood and Chocolate* - Annette Curtis
Klause  *h*  3162

**Garou, Lupe**
*One Foot in the Grave* - Wm. Mark
Simmons  *f*  5062

**Haal, Daetrin Ungashak To-Alym**
*The Madness Season* - C.S. Friedman  *s*  2058

**Halver**
*The Dubious Hills* - Pamela Dean  *f*  1444

**Ives, Bobby**
*The Nightwalker* - Thomas Tessier  *h*  5442

**Jez**
*Wild Blood* - Nancy A. Collins  *h*  1127

**Jock o' the Syde**
*The Spiral Dance* - R. Garcia y Robertson  *f*  2121

**Kaldy, Janos**
*Mark of the Werewolf* - Jeffrey Sackett  *h*  4780

**Kinkaid, Johnny**
*Moon Dance* - S.P. Somtow  *h*  5158

**Koshka, Ulysses**
*Under the Shadow* - Jane Toombs  *h*  5481

**Leith**
*Tapestry of Dark Souls* - Elaine Bergstrom  *h*  465

**Lycaon**
*The Last World* - Christoph Ransmayr  *f*  4475

**mac Cuel, Ceilyn**
*The Work of the Sun* - Teresa Edgerton  *f*  1746

**Marley, Andrew**
*The Werewolf's Touch* - Cheri Scotch  *h*  4892

**Melvinge**
*Night of the Living 'Gator!* - Richard A.
Lupoff  *s*  3573
*Night of the Living Rat!* - Debra Doyle  *s*  1603
*Night of the Living Shark!* - David Bischoff  *s*  493

**Merrick, Ty**
*Opalite Moon* - Denise Vitola  *f*  5577

**Moreau, Paul**
*Hair of the Dog* - Brett Davis  *f*  1400

**Nora**
*Animals* - John Skipp  *h*  5080

**Nygerski, Cyrus "Moondog"**
*Room 13* - Henry Garfield  *h*  2139

**Oldman, Wendel**
*Wyrm Wolf* - Edo van Belkom  *h*  5535

**O'Shea, Devin**
*Moon of the Werewolf* - Ronald Kelly  *h*  3053

**O'Shea, Patrick**
*Moon of the Werewolf* - Ronald Kelly  *h*  3053

**O'Shea, Rosie**
*Moon of the Werewolf* - Ronald Kelly  *h*  3053

**Penz**
*Conan the Formidable* - Steve Perry  *f*  4293

**Regeane**
*The Silver Wolf* - Alice Borchardt  *h*  572

**Roo, Luger**
*The Case of the Police Officer's Cock Ring and the
Piano Player Who Had No Fingers* - Edward
Lee  *h*  3388

**Rybak, Nadya**
*Nadya: The Wolf Chronicles* - Pat Murphy  *f*  4052

**St. Claire, Nicole**
*Wolf Moon* - John R. Holt  *h*  2749

**Skillet, William "Billy"**
*Walking Wolf* - Nancy A. Collins  *h*  1126

**Talbot, Larry**
*A Night in the Lonesome October* - Roger
Zelazny  *h*  6072
*Return of the Wolfman* - Jeff Rovin  *h*  4687

**Ted**
*Thor* - Wayne Smith  *h*  5146

**Turner, Loraine "Phyllis"**
*The Werewolf Chronicles* - Traci Briery  *h*  679
*Wolfsong* - Traci Briery  *h*  680

**Turpin, Richard**
*The World of Darkness: Watcher* - Charles L.
Grant  *h*  2321

**Unnamed Character**
*A Prophecy of Monsters* - Clark Ashton
Smith  *h*  5103

**Vehmund, Daniel**
*Heart-Beast* - Tanith Lee  *h*  3411

**Warhelski, Maxim**
*All Things under the Moon* - Robert
Morgan  *h*  4002

**White, Alice**
*Wilderness* - Dennis Danvers  *h*  1349

**White, Gabriel**
*Hell-Storm* - James A. Moore  *h*  3990

**Zeeman, Richard**
*Blue Moon* - Laurell K. Hamilton  *h*  2513
*The Killing Dance* - Laurell K. Hamilton  *h*  2518
*The Lunatic Cafe* - Laurell K. Hamilton  *h*  2520

## WIDOW(ER)

**Aditi**
*Blood of the Goddess* - Kara Dalkey  *f*  1318

**Alderson, Charlotte**
*The Colors of Hell* - Michael Paine  *h*  4234

**Baxter, Anna Elizabeth**
*Sheltered Lives* - Charles Oberndorf  *s*  4188

**Bremen, Jeremy "Jerry"**
*The Hollow Man* - Dan Simmons  *s*  5054

**Brewer, Tom**
*Dreamthorp* - Chet Williamson   *h*   5845

**Deems, Ann**
*Reign* - Chet Williamson   *h*   5849

**deJanes, Ecktor**
*Adiamante* - L.E. Modesitt Jr.   *s*   3924

**di'Marano, Diora**
*The Broken Crown* - Michelle West   *f*   5757

**Gormlaith**
*Pride of Lions* - Morgan Llywelyn   *f*   3506

**Grainger, Laura**
*Darker Angels* - S.P. Somtow   *h*   5155

**Hamilton, Ruth**
*Dead in the Water* - Nancy Holder   *h*   2732

**Heron, Madeleine**
*Green Lake* - S.K. Epperson   *h*   1830

**Hunsacker, Patty**
*Blind Hunger* - David Darke   *h*   1352

**Kimmler, Vic**
*Borderland: A Novel of Terror* - S.K.
  Epperson   *h*   1828

**Kishida, Katie**
*Tech-Heaven* - Linda Nagata   *s*   4066

**Kung, Evelyn**
*The Lincoln Hunters* - Wilson Tucker   *s*   5487

**Lark, Don**
*Homebody* - Orson Scott Card   *h*   890

**Lewes, Charlotte**
*John Dollar* - Marianne Wiggins   *h*   5799

**Lewis, Mary**
*Nightlight* - Michael Cadnum   *h*   813

**Merwoman, Mela**
*The Color of Her Panties* - Piers Anthony   *f*   167

**Miles, Dora**
*The Baby* - Stephanie Kegan   *h*   3033

**Mordance of Barquist**
*The Queen of Ashes* - Deborah Turner
  Harris   *f*   2561

**Nielson, Rainey**
*The Starry Child* - Lynn Hanna   *f*   2540

**O'Hallahan, Emma Delaney**
*What's Wrong with America* - Scott
  Bradfield   *h*   627

**Ruha**
*The Parched Sea* - Troy Denning   *f*   1486

**Starbridge, Charity**
*Sugar Rain* - Paul Park   *s*   4243

**Stumpf, Cordie**
*Fires of Eden* - Dan Simmons   *h*   5053

**Telek, Kassia**
*The Spirit Gate* - Maya Kaathryn Bohnhoff   *f*   562

**Tenar**
*Tehanu: The Last Book of Earthsea* - Ursula K. Le
  Guin   *f*   3383

**Tyrell, Sarah**
*A Question of Time* - Fred Saberhagen   *h*   4772

**Ward, Donna**
*Heathen* - Shaun Hutson   *h*   2816

## WITCH

**al'Vere, Egwene**
*A Crown of Swords* - Robert Jordan   *f*   2984
*The Dragon Reborn* - Robert Jordan   *f*   2985
*The Path of Daggers* - Robert Jordan   *f*   2989

**Antonia**
*Daughter of Magic* - C. Dale Brittain   *f*   703

**Ariodne**
*The Wolves of Autumn* - Scott Ciencin   *f*   1035

**Aurelia**
*The Pit and the Pendulum* - Amarantha
  Knight   *h*   3183

**Avris**
*Songsmith* - Andre Norton   *f*   4161

**Baba Yaga**
*Harpy High* - Esther Friesner   *f*   2076

**Bedlam, Gwen**
*Wolfhelm* - Richard A. Knaak   *f*   3175

**Belou, Sylvia**
*When Shadows Fall* - Brian Scott Smith   *h*   5100

**Black, Angela**
*Fetish* - Edward Bryant   *h*   749

**Brevelan**
*The Glass Dragon* - Irene Radford   *f*   4460

**Caitlin**
*The Spellkey Trilogy* - Ann Downer   *f*   1592

**Carewe, Eliza "Bettina"**
*Absolute Power* - Ray Russell   *h*   4738

**Ceridwen**
*Dragonslayer's Return* - R.A. Salvatore   *f*   4798

**Civet**
*Dragon Cauldron* - Laurence Yep   *f*   6024

**Coxe, Rachel**
*Witches* - Kathryn Meyer Griffith   *h*   2442

**Curry, Rowan Mayfair**
*Lasher* - Anne Rice   *h*   4570

**Daniels, Molly**
*Witchcraft* - Bill Michaels   *h*   3885

**Datu, Dayu**
*The Painted Alphabet* - Diana Darling   *f*   1356

**Demidas, Tanya**
*Cardinal's Sin* - Raymond Buckland   *h*   751

**Denton, Alba**
*Black Body* - H.C. Turk   *h*   5488

**Dorella**
*Dorella* - Mark A. Garland   *f*   2142

**Drake, Selma**
*The Quagmire* - James Kisner   *h*   3160

**Eithne**
*The Shattered Oath* - Josepha Sherman   *f*   4989

**Ela**
*The Goblin Mirror* - C.J. Cherryh   *f*   994

**Elayna**
*Heartstone and Silver* - Jacqui Singleton   *f*   5071

**Ellel, Quince**
*A Plague of Angels* - Sheri S. Tepper   *f*   5433

**Elphaba**
*Wicked: The Life and Times of the Wicked Witch of
  the West* - Gregory Maguire   *f*   3609

**Elspet**
*Coven* - Steven William Rimmer   *h*   4591

**Esk**
*Equal Rites* - Terry Pratchett   *f*   4387

**Eva**
*Witchcraft* - Bill Michaels   *h*   3885

**Fat Woman**
*Nice Guys Finish Last* - Gary Jonas   *h*   2938

**Florence, Julia**
*Witch* - Christopher Pike   *f*   4334

**Fuller, Maude**
*Slow Funeral* - Rebecca Ore   *f*   4221

**Galinda "Glinda the Good"**
*Wicked: The Life and Times of the Wicked Witch of
  the West* - Gregory Maguire   *f*   3609

**Gallowglass, Cordelia**
*M'Lady Witch* - Christopher Stasheff   *f*   5217

**Gallowglass, Gwen**
*The Warlock Rock* - Christopher Stasheff   *s*   5226

**Garlick, Magrat**
*Lords and Ladies* - Terry Pratchett   *f*   4394
*Witches Abroad* - Terry Pratchett   *f*   4404

**Givens, Amanda**
*Witches* - Kathryn Meyer Griffith   *h*   2442

**Glendil**
*The Moon's Wife: A Hystery* - A.A.
  Attanasio   *f*   271

**Gowdie, Maggie**
*The Rebirth of Wonder* - Lawrence Watt-
  Evans   *f*   5646

**Granny Weatherwax**
*Maskerade* - Terry Pratchett   *f*   4395

**Grimm, Eleanor**
*Grimm Memorials* - R. Patrick Gates   *h*   2160

**Gullone, Greta**
*The Witch Returns* - Phyllis Reynolds
  Naylor   *f*   4079

**Hali**
*Witch and Wombat* - Carolyn Cushman   *f*   1299

**Hardgreip**
*War of the Gods* - Poul Anderson   *f*   136

**Inge**
*Quest for a Maid* - Frances Mary Hendry   *f*   2662

**Kadar**
*The Fagin* - Pat Graversen   *h*   2334

**Lara**
*The Shadow Eater* - Adam Lee   *f*   3386

**Latimer, Sarah**
*Witch Hill* - Marion Zimmer Bradley   *h*   654

**Layla**
*Spyder* - Norman Partridge   *h*   4255

**Lessis of Valmes**
*Bazil Broketail* - Christopher Rowley   *f*   4692

**Luz, Gabriel**
*Witch-Light* - Nancy Holder   *h*   2734

**Lydi**
*Shadow of the Seventh Moon* - Nancy Varian
  Berberick   *f*   459

**Margery**
*Strange Devices of the Sun and Moon* - Lisa
  Goldstein   *f*   2262

**Margrett**
*Coven* - Steven William Rimmer   *h*   4591

**Mayfair, Rowan**
*The Witching Hour* - Anne Rice   *h*   4580

**Medea**
*Fiend* - C. Dean Andersson   *h*   138

**Moira**
*The Wiz Biz* - Rick Cook   *f*   1160
*The Wizardry Cursed* - Rick Cook   *f*   1162
*The Wizardry Quested* - Rick Cook   *f*   1163

**Morwen**
*Calling on Dragons* - Patricia C. Wrede   *f*   5974

**Musser, Joanie**
*Apocalypse* - Nancy Springer   *f*   5176

**Naismith, Gladys**
*A Sudden Wild Magic* - Diana Wynne Jones   *f*   2950

**Nessarose**
*Wicked: The Life and Times of the Wicked Witch of the West* - Gregory Maguire   f  3609

**Niahrin**
*Aisling* - Louise Cooper   f  1172

**Norman, Eliza**
*Neighbors* - Maureen S. Pusti   h  4450

**Norman, Rebecca**
*The Tallow Image* - Jane Brindle   h  690

**Oakes**
*On Meeting Witches at Wells* - Judith Gorog   f  2283

**Ogg, Nanny**
*Lords and Ladies* - Terry Pratchett   f  4394

**Olon, Sammis Arloff**
*Timediver's Dawn* - L.E. Modesitt Jr.   s  3940

**Owens, Gillian**
*Practical Magic* - Alice Hoffman   f  ?713

**Owens, Sally**
*Practical Magic* - Alice Hoffman   f  2713

**Partridge**
*Slow Funeral* - Rebecca Ore   f  4221

**Prokash, Magda**
*Blood Sabbath* - Leigh Clark   h  1048

**Relorn, Wryan**
*Timediver's Dawn* - L.E. Modesitt Jr.   s  3940

**Rhea of Coos**
*Wizard and Glass* - Stephen King   h  3144

**Rhiannon**
*Overshoot* - Mona Clee   s  1075

**Rowan**
*His Majesty's Elephant* - Judith Tarr   f  5394

**St. James, Raven**
*Eternity* - Maggie Shayne   f  4943

**Seraphina**
*The Memoirs of Elizabeth Frankenstein* - Theodore Roszak   h  4684

**Skylda "Skyla"**
*The Clan of the Warlord* - Elizabeth H. Boyer   f  604

**Smith, Evangeline**
*The Torching* - Marcy Heidish   h  2642

**Telek, Kassia**
*The Spirit Gate* - Maya Kaathryn Bohnhoff   f  562

**Teneria of Fishertown**
*The Blood of a Dragon* - Lawrence Watt-Evans   f  5640

**Theodora**
*Daughter of Magic* - C. Dale Brittain   f  703
*The Witch and the Cathedral* - C. Dale Brittain   f  705

**Thunder, Anna**
*The Grass Dancer* - Susan Power   f  4380

**Tituba**
*I, Tituba, Black Witch of Salem* - Maryse Conde   f  1130

**Tregarde, Diana**
*Jinx High* - Mercedes Lackey   h  3284

**Tuggle**
*The Witch's Eye* - Phyllis Reynolds Naylor   f  4080

**Tzigane**
*I Am Dracula* - C. Dean Andersson   h  139

**Weatherwax, Granny**
*Lords and Ladies* - Terry Pratchett   f  4394
*Witches Abroad* - Terry Pratchett   f  4404
*Wyrd Sisters* - Terry Pratchett   f  4405

**Weiss, Selene**
*Shadows* - Jonathan Nasaw   h  4068

**Wheeler, Yvonne**
*Witch Spell* - Guy N. Smith   h  5122

**Wickes, Margaret**
*The Quagmire* - James Kisner   h  3160

**Witch Baby**
*Cherokee Bat and the Goat Guys* - Francesca Lia Block   f  546

**Zady**
*Mouvar's Magic* - Piers Anthony   f  182
*Orc's Opal* - Piers Anthony   f  183

**Zagala**
*Yesterday We Saw Mermaids* - Esther Friesner   f  2086

**Zumwalt, William Irving "Wiz"**
*The Wiz Biz* - Rick Cook   f  1160

# WIZARD

**Ahten, Raj**
*The Runelords: The Sum of All Men* - David Farland   f  1866

**Aigar**
*Lost in Translation* - Margaret Ball   f  315

**Ala-eh-din Beyh**
*Tower of Fear* - Glen Cook   f  1155

**Alamar**
*Voyage of the Fox Rider* - Dennis L. McKiernan   f  3837

**Alayna**
*Children of Amarid* - David B. Coe   f  1095

**Alfred**
*Fire Sea* - Margaret Weis   f  5714
*Into the Labyrinth* - Margaret Weis   f  5716
*Serpent Mage* - Margaret Weis   f  5726
*The Seventh Gate* - Margaret Weis   f  5727

**Alyna**
*Runes of Autumn* - Larry Elmore   f  1790

**Ambrosius, Merlin**
*The Wizard of Camelot* - Simon Hawke   f  2627

**Ambrosius, Merlinus**
*The Wolf and the Crown* - A.A. Attanasio   f  273

**Ambrosius, Merlinus "Myrddin/Lailoken"**
*The Dragon and the Unicorn* - A.A. Attanasio   f  266

**an Jiar yn Aliria dur Hamley, Quinzaine**
*Fire Crossing* - Cheryl J. Franklin   s  2036

**Anaxagoras**
*The Wizard's Apprentice* - S.P. Somtow   f  5163

**Anderson, Richard**
*Bureau 13* - Nick Pollotta   f  4362

**Anhand, Deteras "Detter"**
*Nameless Magery* - Delia Marshall Turner   f  5490

**Antero, Rali Emilie**
*The Warrior Returns* - Allan Cole   f  1109

**Antimodes**
*The Soulforge* - Margaret Weis   f  5728

**Ape**
*The Gates of Noon* - Michael Scott Rohan   f  4661

**Archon of Lycanth**
*The Warrior's Tale* - Allan Cole   f  1110

**A'stoc**
*Quest for the Fallen Star* - Piers Anthony   f  185

**Aubrey**
*The Shape-Changer's Wife* - Sharon Shinn   f  5002

**Avelyn**
*The Demon Awakens* - R.A. Salvatore   f  4794

**Bal-Simba**
*The Wizardry Cursed* - Rick Cook   f  1162
*The Wizardry Quested* - Rick Cook   f  1163

**Baloran**
*Shadow Hunt* - Anne Logston   f  3514

**Barnard, Jacques**
*2XS* - Nigel Findley   f  1935

**Bedlam, Cabe**
*The Crystal Dragon* - Richard A. Knaak   f  3167

**Belevairn**
*A Two-Edged Sword* - Thomas K. Martin   f  3653

**Benelaius**
*Murder in Cormyr* - Chet Williamson   f  5848

**Beogoat**
*Heroes Wanted* - Kyle Crocco   f  1267

**Bird, Jake**
*Devil's Engine* - Mark Sumner   f  5356

**Black-Robe, Harvas**
*Krispos of Videssos* - Harry Turtledove   f  5506

**Blade**
*Dark Lord of Derkholm* - Diana Wynne Jones   f  2946

**Blas, Gaultry**
*A Tremor in the Bitter Earth* - Katya Reimann   f  4527

**Boncorro**
*The Secular Wizard* - Christopher Stasheff   f  5222

**Breith**
*Drum Calls* - Jo Clayton   f  1065

**Bremen**
*First King of Shannara* - Terry Brooks   f  712

**Bremener, Saul**
*The Witch Doctor* - Christopher Stasheff   f  5228

**Briar**
*Tris's Book* - Tamora Pierce   f  4322

**Brightglade, Douglas**
*Aquamancer* - Don Callander   f  841
*Geomancer* - Don Callander   f  845

**Buckland, Ulysses**
*The Whims of Creation* - Simon Hawke   s  2626

**Byron**
*Cardmaster* - Clayton Emery   f  1813

**Callahan, Juanita "Nita"**
*A Wizard Abroad* - Diane Duane   f  1668

**Callen, Kevin**
*Come Before Christ and Murder Love* - Stewart Home   f  2754

**Carpenter, Aaron**
*The Hero King* - Rick Shelley   f  4970

**Carpinski, Wyrdrune**
*The Samurai Wizard* - Simon Hawke   f  2623
*The Wizard of Santa Fe* - Simon Hawke   f  2628
*The Wizard of Sunset Strip* - Simon Hawke   f  2629

**Cerryl**
*The White Order* - L.E. Modesitt Jr.   f  3942

**Chandra**
*The Fire's Stone* - Tanya Huff   f  2796

**Chernevog, Kavi**
*Chernevog* - C.J. Cherryh   f  982

**Clootie**
*Split Heirs* - Lawrence Watt-Evans   f  5649

**Coll, Lorand**
*Competition* - Sharon Green   f  2355

**Coll, Lorand "Lor"**
*Challenges* - Sharon Green   f  2354
*Convergence* - Sharon Green   f  2356

**Cormallon, Ran**
*The Gate of Ivory* - Doris Egan   s   1755
*Guilt-Edged Ivory* - Doris Egan   s   1756
*Two-Bit Heroes* - Doris Egan   s   1757

**Creslin**
*The Towers of the Sunset* - L.E. Modesitt
   Jr.   f   3941

**Crotalus**
*Conan, Scourge of the Bloody Coast* - Leonard
   Carpenter   f   910
*The Falcon and the Serpent* - Cheryl A.
   Smith   f   5101

**Cullinane, Andrea**
*The Road to Ehvenor* - Joel Rosenberg   f   4675

**Cymel**
*Drum Calls* - Jo Clayton   f   1065

**Cypher, Richard "the Seeker"**
*Stone of Tears* - Terry Goodkind   f   2269

**Daimbert**
*A Bad Spell in Yurt* - C. Dale Brittain   f   701
*Daughter of Magic* - C. Dale Brittain   f   703
*The Witch and the Cathedral* - C. Dale
   Brittain   f   705
*The Wood Nymph and the Cranky Saint* - C. Dale
   Brittain   f   706

**Dairine**
*High Wizardry* - Diane Duane   f   1662

**Daja**
*Tris's Book* - Tamora Pierce   f   4322

**Dalamar**
*Dragons of Summer Flame* - Margaret Weis   f   5711

**Darcalus**
*King of the Dead* - Gene DeWeese   h   1510

**Dark Lord**
*Outcasts* - Clayton Emery   f   1815

**d'Armand, Magnus Gallowglass "Gar Pike"**
*Warlock and Son* - Christopher Stasheff   s   5224
*A Wizard in Absentia* - Christopher Stasheff   s   5229
*A Wizard in Chaos* - Christopher Stasheff   s   5230
*A Wizard in Midgard* - Christopher Stasheff   s   5231
*A Wizard in Mind* - Christopher Stasheff   s   5232
*A Wizard in Peace* - Christopher Stasheff   s   5233
*A Wizard in War* - Christopher Stasheff   s   5234

**Delroy, Lylene**
*The Conjurer Princess* - Vivian Vande
   Velde   f   5555

**Demandred**
*Lord of Chaos* - Robert Jordan   f   2988

**Derk**
*Dark Lord of Derkholm* - Diana Wynne
   Jones   f   2946

**Desmond, Timothy Alfred**
*Harpy High* - Esther Friesner   f   2076
*Unicorn U.* - Esther Friesner   f   2084

**Dismarum**
*Wit'ch Fire* - James Clemens   f   1082

**DiThorn, Guerrand**
*The Seventh Sentinel* - Mary Kirchoff   f   3154

**Domerc**
*Lost in Translation* - Margaret Ball   f   315

**Domon, Tamrissa**
*Convergence* - Sharon Green   f   2356

**Drev**
*The Dark Shore* - Adam Lee   f   3385

**Drumheller, Thorn**
*Shadow Dawn* - Chris Claremont   f   1042
*Shadow Moon* - George Lucas   f   3540

**Duone, Kestrienne**
*Emerald House Rising* - Peg Kerr   f   3080

**Duone, Morgan**
*Emerald House Rising* - Peg Kerr   f   3080

**Durmontov, Alexei**
*Magician's Ward* - Patricia C. Wrede   f   5976

**Elaine**
*Wolf's Cub* - Mackay Wood   f   5964

**Elaira**
*Fugitive Prince* - Janny Wurts   f   6002

**Eldrich**
*Beneath the Vaulted Hills* - Sean Russell   f   4739
*The Compass of the Soul* - Sean Russell   f   4740

**Ellyn**
*The Guardian* - Angus Wells   f   5737

**Elric of Melnibone**
*Elric: Song of the Black Sword* - Michael
   Moorcock   f   3980
*The Fortress of the Pearl* - Michael
   Moorcock   f   3982
*The Revenge of the Rose* - Michael
   Moorcock   f   3985
*Tales of the White Wolf* - Edward E.
   Kramer   f   3227

**Eschar, William**
*A Plague of Sorcerers* - Mary Frances
   Zambreno   f   6058

**Eveshka**
*Yvgenie* - C.J. Cherryh   f   1005

**Falconer, Jamie**
*Dragon's Plunder* - Brad Strickland   f   5336

**Fallon**
*The Stone Movers* - Patricia Mullen   f   4045

**Falsche, Viktor**
*The Janus Mask* - Richard A. Knaak   f   3171

**Faltar**
*The White Order* - L.E. Modesitt Jr.   f   3942

**Farren**
*Touched by Magic* - Doranna Durgin   f   1705

**Fence**
*The Whim of the Dragon* - Pamela Dean   f   1447

**Fielding, Anna**
*The Compass of the Soul* - Sean Russell   f   4740

**Fiendlord, Zoltan**
*Majyk by Accident* - Esther Friesner   f   2079
*Majyk by Design* - Esther Friesner   f   2080

**Flowerstalk, Flarman**
*Pyromancer* - Don Callander   f   847

**Gadjung**
*The Wizard and the Floating City* - Christopher
   Rowley   f   4699

**Gamelan**
*The Warrior's Tale* - Allan Cole   f   1110

**Gangle, Kendar "Ratwacker"**
*Majyk by Accident* - Esther Friesner   f   2079
*Majyk by Design* - Esther Friesner   f   2080
*Majyk by Hook or Crook* - Esther Friesner   f   2081

**Garion**
*The Seeress of Kell* - David Eddings   f   1738
*Sorceress of Darshiva* - David Eddings   f   1739

**Gaultry**
*Wind From a Foreign Sky* - Katya Reimann   f   4528

**Gemcutter, Jena**
*Emerald House Rising* - Peg Kerr   f   3080

**Gestaurien, Mauryl**
*Fortress in the Eye of Time* - C.J. Cherryh   f   991

**Glyrenden**
*The Shape-Changer's Wife* - Sharon Shinn   f   5002

**G'Meni**
*The Janus Mask* - Richard A. Knaak   f   3171

**Graves, Jermyn**
*Journeyman Wizard* - Mary Frances
   Zambreno   f   6057

**Greensleeves**
*Final Sacrifice* - Clayton Emery   f   1814
*Shattered Chains* - Clayton Emery   f   1816

**Grey Mouser**
*Ill Met in Lankhmar* - Fritz Leiber   f   3419
*Lean Times in Lankhmar* - Fritz Leiber   f   3420
*Return to Lankhmar* - Fritz Leiber   f   3422

**Greycloak, Janos**
*The Far Kingdoms* - Allan Cole   f   1104

**Gwenlliant**
*The Castle of the Silver Wheel* - Teresa
   Edgerton   f   1741
*The Grail and the Ring* - Teresa Edgerton   f   1744

**Hattord, Jovvi**
*Challenges* - Sharon Green   f   2354
*Competition* - Sharon Green   f   2355

**Handrar, Ser**
*Wizard of Bones* - Robert N. Charrette   f   979

**Haplo**
*Elven Star* - Margaret Weis   f   5712
*Fire Sea* - Margaret Weis   f   5714
*The Hand of Chaos* - Margaret Weis   f   5715
*Into the Labyrinth* - Margaret Weis   f   5716
*Serpent Mage* - Margaret Weis   f   5726
*The Seventh Gate* - Margaret Weis   f   5727

**Harkta**
*The Conjurer Princess* - Vivian Vande
   Velde   f   5555

**Heiratikus**
*Wind From a Foreign Sky* - Katya Reimann   f   4528

**Hickory, Magister**
*Wizard's Hall* - Jane Yolen   f   6043

**Holyhands, Dion**
*Fire Angels* - Jane Routley   f   4685

**Hooded One**
*Lord of the Isles* - David Drake   f   1636

**Horta, Raul**
*Doomsday Exam* - Nick Pollotta   f   4363

**Immugio**
*Final Sacrifice* - Clayton Emery   f   1814

**Inglorion, Ingold**
*Icefalcon's Quest* - Barbara Hambly   f   2504
*Mother of Winter* - Barbara Hambly   f   2506

**Inhetep, Setne**
*The Anubis Murders* - Gary Gygax   f   2472
*Death in Delhi* - Gary Gygax   f   2473

**Innisfree, Merle "Myrddin"**
*The Rebirth of Wonder* - Lawrence Watt-
   Evans   f   5646

**Irsei, Corum Jhaelen**
*Corum: The Coming of Chaos* - Michael
   Moorcock   f   3978

**Jaldis the Blind**
*The Rainbow Abyss* - Barbara Hambly   f   2507

**Jankowitz, Sheldon**
*User Unfriendly* - Vivian Vande Velde   f   5558

**Jaryd**
*Children of Amarid* - David B. Coe   f   1095

**Jaylor**
*The Glass Dragon* - Irene Radford   f   4460

**Kaihan**
*Nameless Magery* - Delia Marshall Turner   f   5490

**Katsuleris, Aubrey**
*The Broken Sword* - Molly Cochran   f   1091

**Kedrigern**
*Kedrigern and the Charming Couple* - John
Morressy  f  4013
*A Remembrance for Kedrigern* - John
Morressy  f  4014

**Keman**
*Elvenblood* - Andre Norton  f  4150

**Ko, Shang**
*Bride of the Rat God* - Barbara Hambly  f  2499

**Kromman**
*The Gilded Chain: A Tale of the King's Blades* - Dave
Duncan  f  1679

**Lawre, Jocchario**
*The Mage in the Iron Mask* - Brian
Thomsen  f  5458

**Leyladin**
*The White Order* - L.E. Modesitt Jr.  f  3942

**Lindavar**
*Murder in Cormyr* - Chet Williamson  f  5848

**Longshadow**
*Bleak Seasons* - Glen Cook  f  1147

**Loremaster, Barach**
*Wizard's Mole* - Brad Strickland  f  5337

**Lyim**
*The Seventh Sentinel* - Mary Kirchoff  f  3154

**MacGregor, Sandy**
*A Name to Conjure With* - Donald Aamodt  f  3
*A Troubling Along the Border* - Donald Aamodt  f  4

**Magaera**
*The Towers of the Sunset* - L.E. Modesitt
Jr.  f  3941

**Magistrale, Michelangelo "Mage"**
*The Art of Arrow Cutting* - Stephen
Dedman  f  1462

**Majere, Palin**
*The Day of the Tempest* - Jean Rabe  f  4457

**Majere, Raistlin**
*Dragons of Summer Flame* - Margaret Weis  f  5711
*The Soulforge* - Margaret Weis  f  5728

**Maligor**
*Red Magic* - Jean Rabe  f  4458

**Mandrol**
*The Janus Mask* - Richard A. Knaak  f  3171

**Manstar, Myrn**
*Geomancer* - Don Callander  f  845

**Mantrell, Matthew "Matt"**
*My Son, the Wizard* - Christopher Stasheff  f  5218
*The Secular Wizard* - Christopher Stasheff  f  5222

**Mardimil, Rion**
*Challenges* - Sharon Green  f  2354
*Competition* - Sharon Green  f  2355

**Matt**
*The Oathbound Wizard* - Christopher
Stasheff  f  5219

**Matthiall**
*Glenraven* - Marion Zimmer Bradley  f  635

**Mauryl**
*Fortress of Owls* - C.J. Cherryh  f  993

**McCamfrey, Tessa**
*The Barbed Coil* - J.V. Jones  f  2957

**Medoc**
*The Lost Prince* - Bridget Wood  f  5962

**Melchior**
*Count Scar* - C. Dale Brittain  f  702

**Merlin**
*The Eagle and the Sword* - A.A. Attanasio  f  267
*Enemy of God* - Bernard Cornwell  f  1189
*Excalibur* - Bernard Cornwell  f  1190

*The Faery Convention* - Brett Davis  f  1399
*Mordred's Curse* - Ian McDowell  f  3806

**Mikhalevviko "Mikh"**
*Mathemagics* - Margaret Ball  f  316

**Mistislaus**
*The Clan of the Warlord* - Elizabeth H.
Boyer  f  604

**Misurov, Sasha**
*Chernevog* - C.J. Cherryh  f  982
*Rusalka* - C.J. Cherryh  f  1002

**Monkey**
*Dragon Cauldron* - Laurence Yep  f  6024
*Dragon War* - Laurence Yep  f  6025

**Moonfeather**
*Shadowboxer* - Nick Pollotta  s  4366

**Morgannan, Warrick**
*The Ambivalent Magician* - Simon Hawke  f  2616
*The Inadequate Adept* - Simon Hawke  f  2617

**Mornan**
*The Sleep of Stone* - Louise Cooper  f  1179

**Mosiah**
*Legacy of the Darksword* - Margaret Weis  f  5719

**Nakar**
*Tower of Fear* - Glen Cook  f  1155

**Narantir**
*D'Shai* - Joel Rosenberg  f  4670

**Nestor**
*The Guardian* - Angus Wells  f  5737

**Ningauble of the Seven Eyes**
*Ill Met in Lankhmar* - Fritz Leiber  f  3419

**Nirobus**
*My Son, the Wizard* - Christopher Stasheff  f  5218

**Nolan, Ronan**
*A Wizard Abroad* - Diane Duane  f  1668

**Nysander**
*Luck in the Shadows* - Lynn Flewelling  f  1952

**Parthet "Uncle Parker"**
*The Hero King* - Rick Shelley  f  4970
*The Hero of Varay* - Rick Shelley  f  4971

**Peldyrin, Kyra**
*Stranger at the Wedding* - Barbara Hambly  f  2509

**Pendaron, Telerini**
*The Moon in Hiding* - Teresa Edgerton  f  1745

**Persyvaunce**
*Red Wizard* - Nancy Springer  f  5182

**Poons, Windle**
*Reaper Man* - Terry Pratchett  f  4399

**Psamathos**
*Roverandom* - J.R.R. Tolkien  f  5479

**Rahl, Darken**
*Wizard's First Rule* - Terry Goodkind  f  2271

**Rahl, Richard "the Seeker"**
*Blood of the Fold* - Terry Goodkind  f  2268
*Temple of the Winds* - Terry Goodkind  f  2270

**Raistlin**
*The Second Generation* - Margaret Weis  f  5724

**Randall**
*School of Wizardry* - Debra Doyle  f  1605

**Reysson, Gaylon**
*Book of Stones* - L. Dean James  f  2862
*Kingslayer* - L. Dean James  f  2863

**Rhion the Brown**
*The Magicians of Night* - Barbara Hambly  f  2505
*The Rainbow Abyss* - Barbara Hambly  f  2507

**Rhiow**
*The Book of Night with Moon* - Diane
Duane  f  1657

**Rincewind**
*Eric* - Terry Pratchett  f  4388
*Interesting Times* - Terry Pratchett  f  4392

**Ro, Vallant**
*Convergence* - Sharon Green  f  2356

**Rogan the Inept**
*The Door to Ambermere* - J. Calvin Pierce  f  4316

**Rolfson, Bjorn**
*Magelord: The Awakening* - Thomas K.
Martin  f  3651

**Rwyan**
*Lords of the Sky* - Angus Wells  f  5738

**Saash**
*The Book of Night with Moon* - Diane
Duane  f  1657

**SaDiablo, Daemon**
*Daughter of the Blood* - Anne Bishop  f  495

**SaDiablo, Saetan**
*Daughter of the Blood* - Anne Bishop  f  495

**Sage of Sare**
*The Wizard King* - Julie Dean Smith  f  5127

**Sataru, Hidaka**
*The Yngling in Yamato* - John Dalmas  s  1329

**Seagryn**
*The Faithful Traitor* - Robert Don Hughes  f  2809

**s'Falenn, Arithon**
*Fugitive Prince* - Janny Wurts  f  6002

**Shadimar**
*The Last of the Renshai* - Mickey Zucker
Reichert  f  4520
*The Western Wizard* - Mickey Zucker
Reichert  f  4526

**Shulana**
*Dragonspawn* - Mark Acres  f  28

**Sien**
*Shadow War* - Deborah Chester  f  1010

**s'Ilessid, Lysaer**
*Fugitive Prince* - Janny Wurts  f  6002

**Silvas**
*The Wizard at Home* - Rick Shelley  f  4975

**Sinistrad**
*Dragon Wing* - Margaret Weis  f  5709

**Sinjaria, Nolan ra**
*Talion: Revenant* - Michael A. Stackpole  f  5206

**Slade, Billy**
*The Samurai Wizard* - Simon Hawke  f  2623
*The Wizard of Santa Fe* - Simon Hawke  f  2628

**Smythe**
*The Jewel of Equilibrant* - Steven Frankos  f  2042

**Solis, Rudy**
*Mother of Winter* - Barbara Hambly  f  2506

**Soul Catcher**
*She Is the Darkness* - Glen Cook  f  1154

**Suliman**
*Castle in the Air* - Diana Wynne Jones  f  2944

**Sun Wolf**
*The Dark Hand of Magic* - Barbara Hambly  f  2502

**Taja**
*Summer King, Winter Fool* - Lisa Goldstein  f  2263

**Taliesin**
*The Broken Sword* - Molly Cochran  f  1091

**Talon**
*The Last Wizard* - Simon Hawke  f  2619

**Tanafres, Yan**
*Timespell* - Robert N. Charrette  f  978
*Wizard of Bones* - Robert N. Charrette  f  979

**Tatsuo, Tamenaga**
*The Art of Arrow Cutting* - Stephen Dedman   *f*   1462

**Tenedos, Laish**
*The Demon King* - Chris Bunch   *f*   770
*The Seer King* - Chris Bunch   *f*   771

**Tenoctris**
*Lord of the Isles* - David Drake   *f*   1636
*Queen of Demons* - David Drake   *f*   1640

**Terek**
*Fall of Angels* - L.E. Modesitt Jr.   *f*   3930

**Terrance**
*A Forest Lord* - Michael Williams   *f*   5819
*A Sorcerer's Apprentice* - Michael Williams   *f*   5820

**Thews, Questor**
*Witches' Brew* - Terry Brooks   *f*   719

**Thurid**
*The Dragon's Carbuncle* - Elizabeth H. Boyer   *f*   605

**Thursley, Eric**
*Eric* - Terry Pratchett   *f*   4388

**Tibbeth of Hale**
*Stranger at the Wedding* - Barbara Hambly   *f*   2509

**Timura, Safar**
*Wolves of the Gods* - Allan Cole   *f*   1111

**Trelane, Athaya**
*Call of Madness* - Julie Dean Smith   *f*   5124
*Mission of Magic* - Julie Dean Smith   *f*   5125
*Sage of Sare* - Julie Dean Smith   *f*   5126
*The Wizard King* - Julie Dean Smith   *f*   5127

**Tris**
*Tris's Book* - Tamora Pierce   *f*   4322

**Tugelbend, Victor**
*Moving Pictures* - Terry Pratchett   *f*   4398

**Urghart, Ian**
*The Time of Madness* - Thomas K. Martin   *f*   3652

**Urruah**
*The Book of Night with Moon* - Diane Duane   *f*   1657

**Uthred of Ravenspur**
*The Forging of the Shadows* - Oliver Johnson   *f*   2924

**Val Orden, Gaborn**
*The Runelords: The Sum of All Men* - David Farland   *f*   1866

**Valdaimon**
*Dragonspawn* - Mark Acres   *f*   28

**Valerian**
*Magelord: The Awakening* - Thomas K. Martin   *f*   3651

**Vallus**
*The Radiant Dragon* - Elaine Cunningham   *f*   1291

**Varien**
*Barrenlands* - Doranna Durgin   *f*   1702

**Vilkata**
*The Last Book of Swords: Shieldbreaker's Story* - Fred Saberhagen   *f*   4768

**Vyledaar, Alessa**
*Dragonmage of Mystara* - Thorarinn Gunnarsson   *f*   2462

**Windrose, Antryg**
*Dog Wizard* - Barbara Hambly   *f*   2503

**Wizard**
*The Adventures of Threadwell the Tailor, or Alterations Made While You Wait* - P.D. Cacek   *h*   801

**Wizenbeak**
*Lord of the Troll-Bats* - Alexis A. Gilliland   *f*   2234

*The Shadow Shaia* - Alexis A. Gilliland   *f*   2235

**Worgan**
*Wolf's Cub* - Mackay Wood   *f*   5964

**Xar**
*The Seventh Gate* - Margaret Weis   *f*   5727

**Zellorian**
*Mother of Storms* - Adrian Cole   *f*   1101

**Zinixo**
*The Living God* - Dave Duncan   *f*   1682
*The Stricken Field* - Dave Duncan   *f*   1688
*Upland Outlaws* - Dave Duncan   *f*   1690

**Zorander, Zeddicus "Zedd" Zu'l**
*Stone of Tears* - Terry Goodkind   *f*   2269

**Zumwalt, William Irving "Wiz"**
*The Wiz Biz* - Rick Cook   *f*   1160
*The Wizardry Consulted* - Rick Cook   *f*   1161
*The Wizardry Cursed* - Rick Cook   *f*   1162
*The Wizardry Quested* - Rick Cook   *f*   1163

# WOODSMAN

**Alec of Kerry**
*Luck in the Shadows* - Lynn Flewelling   *f*   1952

**Cypher, Richard "the Seeker"**
*Wizard's First Rule* - Terry Goodkind   *f*   2271

**Scarecrow Jack**
*Down Among the Dead Men* - Simon R. Green   *f*   2367

# WORKER

**Acton, Joe**
*Moondog* - Henry Garfield   *h*   2138

**Boyle, Martin**
*Website* - Ray Garton   *h*   2157

**Braun, Caleb**
*Goblin Moon* - Teresa Edgerton   *f*   1743

**Case, David**
*Boundaries* - T.M. Wright   *h*   5990

**Chin, Ah Kin**
*Sarah Canary* - Karen Joy Fowler   *f*   2028

**Cincinnatus**
*The Great War: American Front* - Harry Turtledove   *s*   5501

**Collins, Hap**
*Mucho Mojo* - Joe R. Lansdale   *h*   3330
*Savage Season* - Joe R. Lansdale   *h*   3332

**Douglas, Doug**
*Slippin' into Darkness* - Norman Partridge   *h*   4254

**Ehomba, Etjole**
*Carnivores of Light and Darkness* - Alan Dean Foster   *f*   1996

**Endicott, Rob**
*The Gifted* - Jack Caravela   *h*   879

**Fairfax, Lena**
*Black Night* - S.J. Strayhorn   *h*   5334

**Flynn, Evon**
*Nightsword* - Margaret Weis   *f*   5722

**Foster, Sunny Mae**
*Ghost Dance* - Kathryn Ptacek   *h*   4441

**Gold, Michael "Mike"**
*Unquenchable Fire* - Rachel Pollack   *f*   4361

**Harris, Alex**
*Ghost Light* - Rick Hautala   *h*   2608

**Hawkins, Ethorne**
*Dogland* - Will Shetterly   *f*   4992

**Hirazawa, Suki**
*Angel Kiss* - Kelley Wilde   *h*   5800

**Howard**
*Toplin* - Michael McDowell   *h*   3807

**Jarrett, Syd**
*Animals* - John Skipp   *h*   5080

**Lambert, Dan**
*Gone South* - Robert R. McCammon   *h*   3755

**Lindholm, Erik Robert**
*Buried Screams* - C. Dean Andersson   *h*   137

**Mackenson, Tom**
*Boy's Life* - Robert R. McCammon   *h*   3754

**Madonette**
*The Stainless Steel Rat Sings the Blues* - Harry Harrison   *s*   2575

**Martin, Neil**
*The Quorum* - Kim Newman   *h*   4100

**Nakimura, Grace**
*Gabriel Knight: Sins of the Fathers* - Jane Jensen   *h*   2896

**Newman, Mark**
*The Mountain King* - Rick Hautala   *h*   2611

**Purdue, Frederick**
*The Eyes of the Beast* - Steve Harris   *h*   2565

**Ransom, Cliff**
*Dark Twilight* - Joseph A. Citro   *h*   1036

**Rap**
*Faery Lands Forlorn* - Dave Duncan   *f*   1677
*Magic Casement* - Dave Duncan   *f*   1683
*Perilous Seas* - Dave Duncan   *f*   1685

**Resner, Jacob**
*A Question of Time* - Fred Saberhagen   *h*   4772

**Rowena**
*The Persistence of Memory* - Karen Ripley   *s*   4592

**Ryerson, Will**
*Reprisal* - F. Paul Wilson   *h*   5896

**Saad, Khalil**
*The Nightmare People* - Lawrence Watt-Evans   *h*   5643

**Savage, Lucy**
*Where Does Kissing End?* - Kate Pullinger   *h*   4445

**Sawyer, Phil**
*The Mountain King* - Rick Hautala   *h*   2611

**Sheldon, Peter**
*Lucifer's Eye* - Hugh B. Cave   *h*   943

**Sheridan, Alan**
*Twisted Images* - Don D'Ammassa   *h*   1335

**Sinbad the Porter**
*The Other Sinbad* - Craig Shaw Gardner   *f*   2130

**Slonimsky, Waldo**
*The Burning* - Graham Masterton   *h*   3672

**Strasheim, John**
*Bloom* - Wil McCarthy   *s*   3761

**Sudek, Anna**
*The Amulet* - A.R. Morlan   *h*   4009

**Sudek, Tina Miner**
*The Amulet* - A.R. Morlan   *h*   4009

**Taylor, Gary**
*The Bridge: A Horror Story* - John Skipp   *h*   5081

**Weil, Gunther**
*Griffin's Egg* - Michael Swanwick   *s*   5370

**Whitcomb, Johnny**
*Inagehi* - Jack Cady   *h*   817

**Whitefeather, Matthew**
*The Last Vampire* - Kathryn Meyer Griffith   *h*   2440

**Womack, Ewa**
*Chicago Loop* - Paul Theroux   *h*   5443

# WRITER

**Adams, Joseph**
*The Penultimate Truth* - Philip K. Dick   s   1522

**Aesop**
*The Fabulist* - John Vornholt   f   5595

**Albright, Steven**
*Bloodletter* - Warren Newton Beath   h   426

**Alburton, Denso**
*Hidden Echoes* - Mike Jefferies   f   2885

**Alderini, Delbert**
*Quest for Apollo* - Michael Lahey   f   3309

**Angier, Rupert**
*The Prestige* - Christopher Priest   s   4432

**Anglith of Arkraz, Omar "Trader of Tales"**
*The Hunters' Haunt* - Dave Duncan   f   1681
*The Reaver Road* - Dave Duncan   f   1687

**Ann**
*Gothic Romance* - Emmanuel Carrere   h   912

**Aragon, Julian**
*Thirst* - Michael Cecilione   h   948

**Archangel**
*Tropic of Orange* - Karen Tei Yamashita   f   6009

**Aretino, Pietro**
*A Farce to Be Reckoned With* - Roger
   Zelazny   f   6064

**Atrus**
*Myst: The Book of D'ni* - Rand Miller   f   3897

**Bandy, Emily**
*Bad Brains* - Kathe Koja   h   3193

**Banning, Mitch**
*The Singularity Project* - F.M. Busby   s   784

**Bannock, John**
*In the Mood* - Charles L. Grant   h   2312

**Barbarossa, Maddox**
*Galilee* - Clive Barker   h   340

**Barnevelt, Dirk**
*The Hand of Zei* - L. Sprague de Camp   s   1414

**Baum, L. Frank**
*Was* - Geoff Ryman   f   4758

**Baylor, Katti**
*Rockabilly Limbo* - William W. Johnstone   h   2934

**Beaumont, Thad**
*The Dark Half* - Stephen King   h   3128

**Bell, Howard**
*A Key for the Nonesuch* - Geary Gravel   s   2330

**Bellman, Alan**
*The Printer's Devil* - Chico Kidd   f   3099

**Bennington, Jay Jay**
*Glenraven* - Marion Zimmer Bradley   f   635

**Benson, E.F.**
*The Haunting of Lamb House* - Joan Aiken   h   45

**Bishopric, Susan**
*The Night Mayor* - Kim Newman   s   4099

**Black, Marguerita "Maggie"**
*The Wood Wife* - Terri Windling   f   5916

**Blake, Jason**
*Moonbane* - Al Sarrantonio   s   4831

**Blaylock, Morgan**
*The Devouring* - Douglas D. Hawk   h   2615

**Blessing, William**
*Quoth the Crow* - David Bischoff   h   494

**Borden, Alfred**
*The Prestige* - Christopher Priest   s   4432

**Boscage, A.D.**
*The Priest: A Gothic Romance* - Thomas M.
   Disch   h   1562

**Bramhall, Arthur**
*The Bear Went over the Mountain* - William
   Kotzwinkle   f   3222

**Braun, Tom**
*Ladies Night* - Jack Ketchum   h   3091

**Britannicus, Caius Merlyn**
*The Eagles' Brood* - Jack Whyte   f   5792
*The Saxon Shore* - Jack Whyte   f   5793

**Bugmeier, Neil**
*Horror Show* - Greg Kihn   h   3103

**Byron, George Gordon**
*Lord of the Dead* - Tom Holland   h   2741
*The Stress of Her Regard* - Tim Powers   h   4385

**Carlson-Wade, Bruno David**
*Bereavement* - Richard Lortz   h   3525

**Carrington, Charles Francis**
*Changeweaver* - Margaret Ball   f   313

**Carson, Roberta**
*Rogue Star* - Michael Flynn   s   1965

**Chasen, Liz**
*Demon Night* - J. Michael Straczynski   h   5322

**Chekhov, Anton**
*Chekhov's Journey* - Ian Watson   s   5633

**Clare, Peter**
*The Vanishment* - Jonathan Aycliffe   h   282

**Clavel**
*North Wind* - Gwyneth Jones   s   2953

**Clayburn, Karl Thomas**
*Buried Screams* - C. Dean Andersson   h   137

**Cobham, James**
*Freedom & Necessity* - Steven Brust   f   743

**Cobham, Richard**
*Freedom & Necessity* - Steven Brust   f   743

**Coleridge, Samuel Taylor**
*Walford's Oak* - Jill M. Phillips   f   4310

**Colloway, Stephen**
*Shackled* - Ray Garton   h   2156

**Connel, Eileen**
*October* - Al Sarrantonio   h   4832

**Conner, Daphne "Dee"**
*Cat's Eye* - William W. Johnstone   h   2928

**Cooper, Arlene**
*The Children of Hamelin* - Norman Spinrad   s   5170

**Cooper, David**
*Earthbound* - Richard Matheson   h   3684

**Corbett, Blake**
*Shapes* - Steve Vance   h   5552

**Coventry, Martina**
*City of Truth* - James Morrow   s   4030

**Crazy**
*Death Is a Lonely Business* - Ray Bradbury   h   619

**Crowe, Derek**
*The 37th Mandala* - Marc Laidlaw   h   3310

**Davis, Bill**
*The Store* - Bentley Little   h   3497

**Defoe, Braxton**
*Storytellers* - Julie Anne Parks   h   4249

**Delacroix, Conway**
*Fetish* - Edward Bryant   h   749

**Dero, Halleyne dar**
*Thunder of the Captains* - Holly Lisle   f   3489

**Devereaux, Cleveland Carroll**
*Who Killed James Dean?* - Warren Newton
   Beath   h   428

**Diane**
*Amazon: A Novel* - Barbara G. Walker   f   5616

**Dickinson, Emily**
*The Steampunk Trilogy* - Paul Di Filippo   s   1518

**Diehrenn**
*Encounter with Tiber* - Buzz Aldrin   s   64

**Donner, Bruce**
*Stage Fright* - Clare McNally   h   3858

**Donner, Greg**
*Dreamer* - Daniel Quinn   h   4454

**Doughterty, Brian**
*Icebound* - Dean R. Koontz   h   3209

**Doyle, Arthur Conan**
*Believe: A Novel* - William Shatner   f   4929
*Nevermore* - William Hjortsberg   h   2692
*Photographing Fairies* - Steve Szilagyi   f   5379

**Dufrenoy, Michael**
*Paris in the Twentieth Century* - Jules
   Verne   s   5568

**Dunbar, Larry**
*The Stake* - Richard Laymon   h   3372

**Dunreith, Cassandra "Cass"**
*Dragon Moon* - Chris Claremont   f   1040

**Duvet, Berthe**
*The Porcelain Dove* - Delia Sherman   f   4983

**Eliot, Ann**
*The Innsmouth Heritage* - Brian Stableford   h   5194

**Esher, David**
*Unearthed* - Ashley McConnell   h   3778

**Etchison, Phil**
*Forest of the Night* - S.P. Somtow   f   5156

**Eupolis of Pallene**
*Goatsong* - Tom Holt   f   2751
*The Walled Orchard* - Tom Holt   f   2752

**Faulkner, William**
*The Wild Blue and the Gray* - William
   Sanders   s   4814

**Fettle, Richard**
*Queen of Angels* - Greg Bear   s   423

**Fitzroy, Henry**
*Blood Debt* - Tanya Huff   h   2792
*Blood Price* - Tanya Huff   h   2793
*Blood Trail* - Tanya Huff   h   2794

**Fleming, Paul**
*Demon Shadows* - Michael B. Sirota   h   5075

**Flood, C. Thomas**
*Bloodsucking Fiends: A Love Story* - Christopher
   Moore   h   3988

**Forrest, Jack**
*Evil Intent* - Bernard Taylor   h   5400

**Fortizak "Zak"**
*Murder at the Galactic Writers' Society* - Janet
   Asimov   s   251

**Fowler, Cassie**
*Towing Jehovah* - James Morrow   f   4035

**Frisson**
*The Witch Doctor* - Christopher Stasheff   f   5228

**Fronto**
*The Arkadians* - Lloyd Alexander   f   67

**Gainsborough, Harry**
*Zod Wallop* - William Browning Spencer   h   5169

**Galliez, Aymar**
*The Werewolf of Paris* - Guy Endore   h   1822

**Gardner, Joe**
*The Children's Hour* - Douglas Clegg   *h*   1077

**Grey, Agnes**
*Pillow Friend* - Lisa Tuttle   *h*   5522

**Grey, Alice**
*The Torching* - Marcy Heidish   *h*   2642

**Grey, Marjorie**
*Pillow Friend* - Lisa Tuttle   *h*   5522

**Griffin, Nic**
*The Ruby Tear* - Rebecca Brand   *h*   660

**Guerreri, Karen Rohmer**
*Preternatural* - Margaret Wander Bonanno   *s*   568

**Gwent, Donson**
*Wordwright* - Tom Deitz   *f*   1478

**Hackett, Horace**
*Typewriter in the Sky* - L. Ron Hubbard   *f*   2791

**Haines, Amelia "Amy"**
*Psycho House* - Robert Bloch   *h*   542

**Hardison, Matt**
*Let There Be Dark* - Allen Lee Harris   *h*   2557

**Hardwick, David Lyle**
*Near Death* - Nancy Kilpatrick   *h*   3113

**Hardy, Gorman**
*Beast House* - Richard Laymon   *h*   3364

**Harshaw, Jubal**
*Stranger in a Strange Land* - Robert A.
   Heinlein   *s*   2649

**Hart, Elsbeth**
*Sweet Blood* - Pat Graversen   *h*   2337

**Hitchcock, Allison**
*The School* - T.M. Wright   *h*   5994

**Hope, Mary**
*A Gift upon the Shore* - M.K. Wren   *s*   5982

**I**
*The Broken Goddess* - Hans Bemmann   *f*   439
*Dance Dance Dance* - Haruki Murakami   *s*   4046
*Flying Saucers over Hennepin* - Peter
   Gelman   *f*   2186
*Hard-Boiled Wonderland and the End of the World* -
   Haruki Murakami   *s*   4047
*I Who Have Never Known Men* - Jacqueline
   Harpman   *s*   2554
*Ishmael* - Daniel Quinn   *s*   4455
*Time and the Clock Mice, Etcetera* - Peter
   Dickinson   *f*   1527
*The Veils of Snows* - Mark Helprin   *f*   2654
*The Wall* - Marlen Haushofer   *s*   2603

**I "Laundry"**
*Dead Voices: Natural Agonies in the Real World* -
   Gerald Vizenor   *f*   5578

**James, Cullen**
*A Child Across the Sky* - Jonathan Carroll   *h*   917

**James, Henry**
*The Haunting of Lamb House* - Joan Aiken   *h*   45

**Jarry, Alfred**
*Night of the Cooters* - Howard Waldrop   *s*   5614

**Jeremy**
*Black Dogs* - Ian McEwan   *h*   3808

**Johnson, Joe**
*The Undesired Princess and the Enchanted Bunny* - L.
   Sprague de Camp   *f*   1419

**Jones, Bob**
*The Ignored* - Bentley Little   *h*   3493

**Jones, David**
*Deus Ex Machina* - J.V. Brummels   *s*   732

**Kar, Ann**
*Century 21* - Ewa Kuryluk   *s*   3263

**Kenan, Philip**
*Resume with Monsters* - William Browning
   Spencer   *h*   5168

**Kennedy, Kate**
*Midnight Is a Lonely Place* - Barbara
   Erskine   *h*   1836

**Knight, Gabriel**
*The Beast Within: A Gabriel Knight Mystery* - Jane
   Jensen   *h*   2895
*Gabriel Knight: Sins of the Fathers* - Jane
   Jensen   *h*   2896

**Kosarek, Deborah**
*Children of the End* - Mark A. Clements   *h*   1084

**Kramer, George**
*The Dealings of Daniel Kesserich* - Fritz
   Leiber   *s*   3417

**Kreutzer, Friedrich**
*Mordenheim* - Chet Williamson   *h*   5847

**Lacey, Jenny**
*Vampire Blood* - Kathryn Meyer Griffith   *h*   2441

**Laker, Naomi "Mig" Margaret**
*Aunt Maria* - Diana Wynne Jones   *f*   2943

**Landers, Diana**
*The Beast* - Marie Ardell White   *h*   5784

**Lane, Hester**
*The Jekyll Legacy* - Robert Bloch   *h*   535

**Lang, Alice "Lancaster"**
*Einstein's Bridge* - John Cramer   *s*   1244

**Latcher, Dan**
*Stitch* - Mark Morris   *h*   4024

**Levin, Peter**
*Children of the Thunder* - John Brunner   *s*   733

**Leyner, Mark**
*Et Tu, Babe* - Mark Leyner   *s*   3455
*The Tetherballs of Bougainville* - Mark
   Leyner   *f*   3457

**Lingri**
*The Others* - Margaret Wander Bonanno   *s*   565
*OtherWhere* - Margaret Wander Bonanno   *s*   566
*OtherWise* - Margaret Wander Bonanno   *s*   567

**Locke, Laura**
*The Possession* - Ronald Kelly   *h*   3055

**Locke, Richard**
*Shifters* - Edward Lee   *h*   3396

**MacDonald, Sean**
*Avatar* - Donald Beman   *h*   437
*The Taking* - Donald Beman   *h*   438

**Magnalucius**
*Quest: In Search of the Dragontooth* - Michael
   Green   *f*   2346

**Mara, Vincent**
*Thirst* - Pyotr Kurtinski   *h*   3253

**Marinville, Johnny**
*Desperation* - Stephen King   *h*   3129
*The Regulators* - Richard Bachman   *h*   284

**Marlow, Jenny**
*Double Edge* - Dennis Etchison   *h*   1846

**Marlowe, Christopher**
*Strange Devices of the Sun and Moon* - Lisa
   Goldstein   *f*   2262

**Marqueete, Donald**
*Quoth the Crow* - David Bischoff   *h*   494

**Martin, Gina**
*Entoverse* - James P. Hogan   *s*   2724

**Martin, Hailey**
*Leanna: Possession of a Woman* - Marie
   Kiraly   *h*   3149

**Masters, David**
*Haunted* - Tamara Thorne   *h*   5463

**Matheson, Harry**
*Blood Brothers* - T. Lucien Wright   *h*   5986

**Matheson, Jerry**
*Blood Brothers* - T. Lucien Wright   *h*   5986

**Mauney, Kevin**
*Above the Lower Sky* - Tom Deitz   *f*   1469

**McCaffrey, Anne**
*A Diversity of Dragons* - Anne McCaffrey   *f*   3728

**McCullough, Caitlin**
*Control Freak* - Christa Faust   *h*   1890

**McDowell, Allison**
*Sweet William* - Jessica Palmer   *h*   4239

**McGilray, Aidan**
*Stage Fright* - Clare McNally   *h*   3858

**McPherson, Jim**
*The Gold Coast* - Kim Stanley Robinson   *s*   4632

**Mears, Ben**
*Salem's Lot* - Stephen King   *h*   3140

**Milton, John**
*Milton in America* - Peter Ackroyd   *f*   25

**Monahan, Tim**
*The Halflife* - Sharon Webb   *s*   5664

**Moreaux, Paul**
*Fade* - Robert Cormier   *h*   1188

**Morris, Anne**
*Winter Tides* - James P. Blaylock   *h*   524

**Mully, Katharine**
*Memory and Dream* - Charles de Lint   *f*   1433

**Munn, Alex**
*The Shift* - George Foy   *s*   2033

**Murray, Melpomene**
*Orbital Resonance* - John Barnes   *s*   356

**Myers, Edward**
*The Summit* - Edward Myers   *f*   4063

**Nailer, Steve**
*Grimm Memorials* - R. Patrick Gates   *h*   2160

**Narrator**
*The House on the Borderland* - William Hope
   Hodgson   *h*   2711

**Naso**
*The Last World* - Christoph Ransmayr   *f*   4475

**Nell**
*Into the Forest* - Jean Hegland   *s*   2640

**Nesbit, Edward**
*The Chymical Wedding* - Lindsay Clarke   *f*   1063

**Newns, Margaret**
*Skyscape* - Michael Cadnum   *h*   814

**Nicol, Jesse**
*Harvest the Fire* - Poul Anderson   *s*   128

**Nielson, Cameron**
*Bad Dreams* - Kim Newman   *h*   4096

**Noonan, Mike**
*Bag of Bones* - Stephen King   *h*   3126

**Nordbo, Tyra**
*Inconstant Star* - Poul Anderson   *s*   129

**O'Brien, Anne**
*I Met a Man Who Wasn't There* - Mary R.
   Callaghan   *h*   840

**Olson, Zenobia**
*Flying Saucers over Hennepin* - Peter
   Gelman   *f*   2186

**Orfeo**
*Zaragoz* - Brian Craig   *f*   1241

**Overstreet, Jessie**
*After Life* - Andrew Neiderman   *h*   4083

**Paixao, Rhea**
*Starmind* - Spider Robinson   *s*   4642

**Phan, Tommy**
*Ticktock* - Dean R. Koontz   *h*   3217

**Platt, Maxwell**
*Portrait of the Psychopath as a Young Woman* -
   Edward Lee   *h*   3395

**Podlowski, Robert**
*Flames of the Dragon* - Robin Wayne Bailey   *f*   287

**Poe, Edgar Allan**
*The Bloody Red Baron* - Kim Newman   *h*   4097
*The Lighthouse at the End of the World* - Stephen
   Marlowe   *h*   3631
*Madeline: After the Fall of Usher* - Marie
   Kiraly   *h*   3150

**Powers, Richard**
*Galatea 2.2* - Richard M. Powers   *s*   4381

**Powys, Joe M.**
*Curfew* - Phil Rickman   *h*   4587

**Prefect, Ford**
*The Illustrated Hitchhiker's Guide to the Galaxy* -
   Douglas Adams   *s*   29
*Mostly Harmless* - Douglas Adams   *s*   31

**Prentice, Tom**
*Wetbones* - John Shirley   *h*   5010

**Prince, Gabriel**
*Time on My Hands* - Peter Delacorte   *s*   1480

**Prince, Mick**
*Quoth the Crow* - David Bischoff   *h*   494

**Raine of the Three Waters**
*Darkenheight* - Douglas Niles   *f*   4107
*War of the Three Waters* - Douglas Niles   *f*   4110

**Ramsey, Keith**
*Blood Lines* - William R. Burkett Jr.   *s*   774

**Randolph, Jake**
*The Torching* - Marcy Heidish   *h*   2642

**Ransom, Lucas**
*Exquisite Corpse* - Poppy Z. Brite   *h*   695

**Raven of Lao-tzu**
*Blood Lines* - William R. Burkett Jr.   *s*   774

**Ravenwood, Janice**
*Wildest Dreams* - Norman Partridge   *h*   4256

**Reynman, John**
*The Double* - Don Webb   *h*   5661

**Rimbaud, Ole**
*Serial Killer Days* - David Prill   *h*   4436

**Ripley, Robert Remington III**
*When Dreams Collide* - Wm. Mark
   Simmons   *f*   5063

**Robinson, David**
*Beyond the Shroud* - Rick Hautala   *h*   2604

**Rothman, Felice**
*Bagatelle—Guinevere* - Nancy Bogen   *f*   558

**Rowan, Jack**
*Dead Lines* - John Skipp   *h*   5082

**Rutledge, Andrew**
*Root of All Evil* - David A. Farrow   *h*   1888

**St. Jacques, Adela Rogers**
*Night of the Living 'Gator!* - Richard A.
   Lupoff   *s*   3573

**Santangelo, Kaye**
*The Shift* - George Foy   *s*   2033

**Santos, Nick**
*The World on Blood* - Jonathan Nasaw   *h*   4069

**Scoresby, Lyman**
*The Lodger* - Fred Chappell   *h*   966

**Scott, Valerie**
*What's Wrong with Valerie?* - D.A. Fowler   *h*   2026

**Selway, Ellen**
*A Face at the Window* - Dennis McFarland   *h*   3809

**Severanko, Nick**
*Bleeder* - Gene Lazuta   *h*   3374

**Shade, Scarlett**
*Shade* - David Darke   *h*   1355

**Shane, Laura**
*Lightning* - Dean R. Koontz   *h*   3211

**Shea, Bill**
*Deadly Vengeance* - Stephen R. George   *h*   2199

**Shelley, Mary**
*Gothic Romance* - Emmanuel Carrere   *h*   912

**Shelley, Percy Bysshe**
*Lord of the Dead* - Tom Holland   *h*   2741
*Wall, Stone, Craft* - Walter Jon Williams   *h*   5842

**Shields, Ben**
*Prank Night* - David Robbins   *h*   4601

**Sierek, Detlef**
*Drachenfels* - Jack Yeovil   *f*   6022

**Silenus, Martin**
*The Rise of Endymion* - Dan Simmons   *s*   5059

**Smith, Stephen**
*Where Does Kissing End?* - Kate Pullinger   *h*   4445

**Snow, Chris**
*Fear Nothing* - Dean R. Koontz   *h*   3207

**Speke, Hamilton**
*Ghostwright* - Michael Cadnum   *h*   810

**Spenotex, Arakaho Blundy**
*Stopping at Slowyear* - Frederik Pohl   *s*   4355

**Stenvall, Richard**
*The Night Seasons* - J.N. Williamson   *h*   5858

**Sterling, Ben**
*Midnight Sun* - Ramsey Campbell   *h*   860

**Stevens, Jim**
*Reborn* - F. Paul Wilson   *h*   5895

**Stillwater, Marty**
*Mr. Murder* - Dean R. Koontz   *h*   3213

**Stoker, Bram**
*Dracula Unbound* - Brian W. Aldiss   *h*   55
*Slave of My Thirst* - Tom Holland   *h*   2742

**Stone, Jack**
*The Immaculate* - Mark Morris   *h*   4023

**Storey, Graham**
*Pillow Friend* - Lisa Tuttle   *h*   5522

**Strine, Arnold**
*The Fermata* - Nicholson Baker   *s*   302

**Talbot, Edward "Eddie"**
*Her Monster* - Jeff Collignon   *h*   1115

**Taliesen**
*The Hawk's Gray Feather* - Patricia Kennealy-
   Morrison   *f*   3061
*The Hedge of Mist* - Patricia Kennealy-
   Morrison   *s*   3062
*The Oak Above the Kings: A Book of the Keltiad* -
   Patricia Kennealy   *s*   3058

**Taylor, Lucian**
*The Hill of Dreams* - Arthur Machen   *h*   3595

**Tichy, Ijon**
*Peace on Earth* - Stanislaw Lem   *s*   3435

**Timmerson, Ray**
*Immortal* - Jason Nickles   *h*   4102

**Timothy "Timmy"**
*Live From Golgotha: A Novel* - Gore Vidal   *s*   5569

**Torrance, Jack**
*The Shining* - Stephen King   *h*   3141

**Tregarde, Diana**
*Burning Water* - Mercedes Lackey   *h*   3272
*Jinx High* - Mercedes Lackey   *h*   3284

**Tremaine, June**
*Black Dogs* - Ian McEwan   *h*   3808

**Trout, Kilgore**
*Timequake* - Kurt Vonnegut Jr.   *s*   5594

**Underbridge, Kin**
*Thunder of the Captains* - Holly Lisle   *f*   3489

**Underhill, Tim**
*Koko* - Peter Straub   *h*   5328
*The Throat* - Peter Straub   *h*   5332

**Virgil**
*Quest for Apollo* - Michael Lahey   *f*   3309

**Voight, Susan**
*Freedom & Necessity* - Steven Brust   *f*   743

**Vonnegut, Kurt "Junior"**
*Timequake* - Kurt Vonnegut Jr.   *s*   5594

**Wade, Kara**
*Sibs* - F. Paul Wilson   *h*   5898

**Walker, David**
*Steam* - Jay B. Laws   *h*   3361

**Walker, Hillary "Hilly"**
*The Forgotten* - Stephen R. George   *h*   2200

**Wallace, Wendy**
*The Hunted* - Kathryn Ptacek   *h*   4442

**Warren, Carol**
*In the Deep Woods* - Nicholas Conde   *h*   1131

**Watson, John H.**
*Sherlock Holmes in Orbit* - Mike Resnick   *s*   4556

**Webster, Duncan**
*Cardinal's Sin* - Raymond Buckland   *h*   751
*The Committee* - Raymond Buckland   *h*   752

**Wheldrake**
*The Revenge of the Rose* - Michael
   Moorcock   *f*   3985

**White, Alan**
*Created By* - Richard Christian Matheson   *h*   3691

**Whitman, Walt**
*Darker Angels* - S.P. Somtow   *h*   5155

**Wilde, Oscar**
*The Hunger and Ecstasy of Vampires* - Brian
   Stableford   *h*   5192

**Williams, Martin**
*Mirror* - Graham Masterton   *h*   3677

**Wilson, Barry**
*The Fungus* - Harry Adam Knight   *h*   3192

**Wollstonecraft, Mary**
*Wall, Stone, Craft* - Walter Jon Williams   *h*   5842

**Writer**
*The Time Ships* - Stephen Baxter   *s*   403

**Writing Woman of Maho**
*Fish Soup* - Ursula K. Le Guin   *f*   3378

**Wulf**
*Wulfsyarn: A Mosaic* - Phillip Mann   *s*   3617

**Young, Samson**
*London Fields* - Martin Amis   *s*   95

## YOUNG MAN

**Andrew**
*The Last Coin* - James P. Blaylock   *f*   519

**Azod**
*The Forsaken* - Steven Ray Fulgham   *h*   2089

**Baedecker, Scott**
*Phases of Gravity* - Dan Simmons   s   5057

**Bryan**
*The Night in Fog* - David B. Silva   h   5026

**Cade, Skinner**
*Wild Blood* - Nancy A. Collins   h   1127

**Casteel, Luke Jr.**
*Web of Dreams* - V.C. Andrews   h   147

**Cope, Seamus**
*Head Injuries* - Conrad Williams   h   5816

**Dallaugher, Danny**
*When Shadows Fall* - Brian Scott Smith   h   5100

**Deeping, Gabriel**
*Gabriel's Body* - Curt Siodmak   h   5073

**Donner, Mark**
*Disciples of Dread* - Hugh B. Cave   h   941

**Drackman, Bryan "Ticktock"**
*Dragon Tears* - Dean R. Koontz   h   3205

**Dylan**
*Gehenna* - Lewis Gannett   h   2114

**Gray, Zachary**
*An Acceptable Time* - Madeleine L'Engle   f   3436

**Grieg, Christian**
*Boundaries* - T.M. Wright   h   5990

**Hawthorne, Royce**
*Chaingang* - Rex Miller   h   3899

**Hightower, Fabian**
*Possession* - Peter James   h   2873

**Jonathan**
*Tapestry of Dark Souls* - Elaine Bergstrom   h   465

**Julian**
*Orphans* - Jean Simon   h   5065

**Justin**
*The Living Evil* - Ruby Jean Jensen   h   2902

**Lawrence, Mark**
*The Offspring* - Kenneth McKenney   h   3826

**Leonidas**
*The Pit and the Pendulum* - Amarantha
  Knight   h   3183

**Lydyard, David**
*The Werewolves of London* - Brian
  Stableford   h   5196

**Majeed**
*The Safety of Unknown Cities* - Lucy
  Taylor   h   5414

**Matthews, Eric**
*Demon Night* - J. Michael Straczynski   h   5322

**Michaels, Judge**
*The M.D.: A Horror Story* - Thomas M.
  Disch   h   1561

**Radcliffe, Phillip**
*A Sharpness on the Neck* - Fred
  Saberhagen   h   4774

**Rice, Doug**
*Blood of Mugwump* - Doug Rice   h   4581

**Rick**
*The Night in Fog* - David B. Silva   h   5026

**Rork, Paddy**
*Signs of Life* - Cherry Wilder   s   5804

**Saralyn, Paul**
*The Link* - Andrew Laurance   h   3348

**Sikes, Stephen**
*Sins of the Flesh* - Don Davis   h   1404

**Smith, Eugene**
*Nice Guys Finish Last* - Gary Jonas   h   2938

**Stranger**
*Black Sun* - Douglas E. Winter   h   5923

**Thorsen, Thorian "Torrie"**
*The Crimson Sky* - Joel Rosenberg   f   4669
*The Fire Duke* - Joel Rosenberg   f   4671
*The Silver Stone* - Joel Rosenberg   f   4676

**Tsepesh, Arkady**
*Covenant with the Vampire* - Jeanne
  Kalogridis   h   3004

**Van Buren, Peter**
*Silent Witness* - Robert Arthur Smith   h   5136

**Washington, Sandy**
*Homegoing* - Frederik Pohl   s   4347

**Wilkinson, Esau**
*The Hunger of the Beast* - John Driver   h   1656

**Wilson, Collingsworth**
*I Know What You Did Last Summer* - Lois
  Duncan   h   1692

# YOUNG WOMAN

**Adderstone, Susannah**
*The Vanishment* - Jonathan Aycliffe   h   282

**Anghara, Princess**
*Nemesis* - Louise Cooper   f   1177

**Barbara**
*Night of the Living Dead* - John Russo   h   4745

**Barrett, Elizabeth**
*Death Masque* - P.N. Elrod   h   1795

**Barrington, Cathy**
*The Tallow Image* - Jane Brindle   h   690

**Bell, Celina**
*The Unborn* - Andrew Laurance   h   3350

**Blaise, Anna**
*A Hidden Place* - Robert Charles Wilson   s   5910

**Caitlin**
*The Druid's Gift* - Margaret J. Anderson   f   121
*Expiry Date* - Carol Anne Davis   h   1401

**Castillo, Lourdes Maria**
*The Halloween Man* - Douglas Clegg   h   1080

**Chen Li**
*Twisted Images* - Don D'Ammassa   h   1335

**Cissie**
*'48* - James Herbert   h   2667

**Conner, Katie**
*Dead Lines* - John Skipp   h   5082

**Craig, Julie**
*Heathen* - Shaun Hutson   h   2816

**Crawford, Oilvia**
*Blood Roots* - Richie Tankersley Cusick   h   1300

**Crogan, Janice**
*Beast House* - Richard Laymon   h   3364

**Cross, Jo**
*Garden* - Matthew J. Costello   h   1197

**Dalton, Jennifer "Darla"**
*Darkman #4: The Face of Death* - Randall
  Boyll   h   615

**Deacon, Jane**
*The Hill of Dreams* - Arthur Machen   h   3595

**Delaney, Sylvie**
*Homebody* - Orson Scott Card   h   890

**Donaldson, Pamela**
*Madeline: After the Fall of Usher* - Marie
  Kiraly   h   3150

**Duffy, Karen**
*Boundaries* - T.M. Wright   h   5990

**Dun Lady's Jess**
*Dun Lady's Jess* - Doranna Durgin   f   1704

**Effie**
*The Gilda Stories* - Jewelle Gomez   h   2267

**Elvira**
*The Boy Who Cried Werewolf* - Elvira   h   1800
*Camp Vamp* - Elvira   h   1801
*Elvira: Transylvania 90210* - Elvira   h   1802

**Emma**
*Westlin Wind* - Charles de Lint   f   1439

**Fairclough, Jude**
*The Night in Fog* - David B. Silva   h   5026

**Falco, Josie**
*Orphans* - Jean Simon   h   5065

**Foyan, Esmeralda**
*Westlin Wind* - Charles de Lint   f   1439

**Frankenstein, Elizabeth**
*The Darker Passions: Frankenstein* - Amarantha
  Knight   h   3180
*The Memoirs of Elizabeth Frankenstein* - Theodore
  Roszak   h   4684

**Gloria**
*The Wilds* - Richard Laymon   h   3373

**Gordon, Karen**
*The Gilgul* - Henry W. Hocherman   h   2697

**Hart, Carolyn**
*A Room for the Dead* - Noel Hynd   h   2825

**Henderson, Lisa**
*Bone Music* - Alan Rodgers   h   4646

**Herbert, Grisel**
*The Return* - Walter de la Mare   h   1424

**Holmes, Lori**
*Lori* - Robert Bloch   h   536

**Huru**
*The Adventures of Huru on the Road to Baghdad* -
  Guneli Gun   f   2457

**Jess**
*Changespell* - Doranna Durgin   f   1703

**Juarel, Chita**
*668: The Neighbor of the Beast* - Lionel
  Fenn   h   1917

**Julia**
*Spree* - Lucy Taylor   h   5415

**Karen**
*Black Sun* - Douglas E. Winter   h   5923

**Karis**
*Tooth: A Tale of Love and Death in Paradox* - Novak
  Kruger   h   3244

**Karpov, Sapphire**
*Putting Up Roots* - Charles Sheffield   s   4964

**Katiasi**
*I Am Frankenstein* - C. Dean Andersson   h   140

**Kelene**
*The Angry Angel* - Chelsea Quinn Yarbro   h   6010

**Kyla**
*Engor's Sword Arm* - David C. Smith   h   5110

**Laitha "Gian Avur"**
*Ghost King* - David Gemmell   f   2188

**Laster, Vickie**
*Descent* - Ron Dee   h   1465

**Laura**
*The Darker Passions: Carmilla* - Amarantha
  Knight   h   3177

**Lawford, Sheila**
*The Return* - Walter de la Mare   h   1424

**Lawrence, Ursula**
*The Darker Passions: Dr. Jekyll and Mr. Hyde* - Amarantha Knight   *h*   3178

**Leta**
*The Stone Giant* - James P. Blaylock   *f*   523

**Lie**
*The Bars on Satan's Jailhouse* - Norman Partridge   *h*   4251

**Lockland, Tessa**
*Midnight* - Dean R. Koontz   *h*   3212

**Lopez, Maria Elena**
*Witch-Light* - Nancy Holder   *h*   2734

**Lott, Roxanne**
*The Mark of the Moderately Vicious Vampire* - Lionel Fenn   *h*   1920

**Lowe, Cherie**
*Who Killed James Dean?* - Warren Newton Beath   *h*   428

**MacDavid, Kate**
*Night Beasts* - T.W. Stetson   *h*   5263

**MacLaren, Sherideen**
*For You, the Living* - Wayne Allen Sallee   *h*   4786

**Mara**
*Cry Republic* - Kirk Mitchell   *s*   3917

**Marianne**
*Marianne, the Matchbox and the Malachite Mouse* - Sheri S. Tepper   *f*   5432

**Marshall, Jenny**
*The Judas Cross* - Charles Sheffield   *h*   4960

**Mary**
*The House on the Borderland* - William Hope Hodgson   *h*   2711

**Milton, Annie**
*Cul-De-Sac* - David Martin   *h*   3638

**Mirri**
*The Iron Ring* - Lloyd Alexander   *f*   68

**Morris, Zenoa**
*The Living Evil* - Ruby Jean Jensen   *h*   2902

**Murray, Mina**
*Dracul: An Eternal Love Story* - Nancy Kilpatrick   *h*   3110

**Ngamuku, Larae**
*Horrors of the Dancing Gods* - Jack L. Chalker   *f*   955

**Partrick, Nicole**
*Adversary* - Daniel Rhodes   *h*   4568

**Portland, Elaine**
*Blood and Roses* - Sharon Bainbridge   *h*   292

**Pritchard, Jen**
*The New Neighbor* - Ray Garton   *h*   2154

**Rachaela**
*Personal Darkness* - Tanith Lee   *h*   3413

**Renada**
*The Stars Must Wait* - Keith Laumer   *s*   3346

**Renzler, Lenore**
*The 37th Mandala* - Marc Laidlaw   *h*   3310

**Reynolds, Jessie**
*Forget Me Not* - Gene Lazuta   *h*   3375

**Rice, Caddie**
*Blood of Mugwump* - Doug Rice   *h*   4581

**Rios, Judy**
*California Gothic* - Dennis Etchison   *h*   1843

**Rivi**
*Shaping the Dawn* - Sheila Finch   *s*   1934

**Rose, Janie**
*Rage* - Elizabeth Ergas   *h*   1834

**Sarah**
*Familiar Spirit* - Lisa Tuttle   *h*   5519

**Selima**
*Lion Time in Timbuctoo* - Robert Silverberg   *s*   5036

**Smith, Kamryn**
*Killjoy* - Elizabeth Forrest   *h*   1973

**Snow, Julie**
*Cold at Heart* - Brian Hopkins   *h*   2768

**Soamosa**
*The Ship Avenged* - S.M. Stirling   *s*   5298

**Sondra**
*Tapestry of Dark Souls* - Elaine Bergstrom   *h*   465

**Sophie**
*Spell Bound* - Ru Emerson   *f*   1810

**Sorensson, Alfreda "Allie"**
*Night Calls* - Katharine Eliska Kimbriel   *h*   3119

**Stark, Laura**
*Dreamthorp* - Chet Williamson   *h*   5845

**Stephenson, Jenny**
*Mask of the Night* - Mary Ryan   *h*   4753

**Susie**
*The Wilds* - Richard Laymon   *h*   3373

**Toland, Cindy**
*Ghost Light* - Rick Hautala   *h*   2608

**Trelawney, Margaret**
*The Jewel of Seven Stars* - Bram Stoker   *h*   5312

**Tsepesh, Mary Wyndham**
*Covenant with the Vampire* - Jeanne Kalogridis   *h*   3004

**Van Voreen, Leigh**
*Web of Dreams* - V.C. Andrews   *h*   147

**Vendramin, Caterina**
*Vaporetto 13* - Robert Girardi   *h*   2241

**Walker, Laura**
*In Hot Blood* - Petru Popescu   *h*   4367

**Weena**
*The Time Ships* - Stephen Baxter   *s*   403

**Westenra, Lucy**
*Dracul: An Eternal Love Story* - Nancy Kilpatrick   *h*   3110

**Whalley, Vida**
*A Dry Spell* - Susan Moloney   *h*   3951

**Wheelwright, Laura**
*Heart-Beast* - Tanith Lee   *h*   3411

**Xylina**
*If I Pay Thee Not in Gold* - Piers Anthony   *f*   176

## ZEALOT

**Duran, Marcus**
*Parable of the Talents* - Octavia E. Butler   *s*   793

**Jolyon**
*The Arm of the Stone* - Victoria Strauss   *f*   5333

## ZOO KEEPER

**Roueche, Philip**
*Claw* - Ken Eulo   *h*   1850

# Author Index

This index alphabetically lists authors of books featured or mentioned in entries in the main section. For each author, the titles of books written and entry numbers are shown. A bold entry number indicates a featured main entry under the title and author in question; lightface numbers refer to main entries that mention the title in question under the rubric "Other books you might like."

## A

**Aakhus, Patricia**
*The Voyage of Mael Duin's Curragh* **2**, 3846

**Aamodt, Donald**
*A Name to Conjure With* **3**, 671, 1072, 2862, 4481, 5820
*A Troubling Along the Border* **4**, 673, 1072

**Aardema, Verna**
*Why Mosquitoes Buzz in People's Ears* 3382

**Aaron, Shale**
*Virtual Death* **5**, 506

**ab Hugh, Dafydd**
*Arthur War Lord* **6**, 5785
*Balance of Power* 7, 905
*Endgame* 3467
*Fallen Heroes* **8**, 2917
*Far Beyond the Wave* 5785
*The Final Fury* **9**, 903, 1663, 2297, 5115, 5404
*Knee Deep in the Dead* 3467
*Vengeance* **10**
*Warriorwards* **11**

**Abbey, Lynn**
*Beneath the Web* **12**, 5752
*The Black Flame* 2651, 3477, 4871, 5741
*The Brazen Gambit* **13**, 2624
*Catwoman* **14**, 2124, 2391, 2392, 4215
*Cinnabar Shadows* **15**, 1290
*Daughter of the Bright Moon* 2095, 2987, 4265, 5733
*The Forge of Virtue* **16**
*Simbul's Gift* 2425
*The Temper of Wisdom* **17**
*Unicorn and Dragon* 459, 3097, 6041
*The Wooden Sword* **18**, 1030, 2097, 3098, 4159, 4699, 5983

**Abbott, Edwin A.**
*Flatland* 4070

**Abe, Kobo**
*Beyond the Curve* 3250
*The Face of Another* **19**, 1334, 3020, 5073

**Abella, Alex**
*Dead of Night* **20**
*The Killing of the Saints* **21**, 1298, 1403, 1851, 2150, 2896, 3605, 4498

**Abner, Ken**
*Terminal Frights, Volume One* **22**

**Abrahams, Roger D.**
*Afro-American Folk Tales* 2771, 4207

**Achilli, Justin**
*Dark Tyrants* **23**, 5798, 5882, 5883

**Acker, Kathy**
*Empire of the Senseless* 3457, 4581
*Pussy, King of the Pirates* 780

**Ackerman, Forrest J.**
*Ackermanthology!* **24**
*I, Vampire: Interviews with the Undead* **5284**
*New Eves: Science Fiction about the Extraordinary Women of Today and Tomorrow* **2035**

**Ackroyd, Peter**
*First Light* 815
*Hawksmoor* 1094, 3984
*Milton in America* **25**
*The Trial of Elizabeth Cree* **26**

**Acres, Mark**
*Dark Divide* **27**, 487, 1533, 1840
*Dragonspawn* **28**, 3578

**Adair, Gilbert**
*Alice through the Needle's Eye: The Further Adventures of Lewis Carroll's "Alice"* 4134, 5713

**Adams, Douglas**
*Dirk Gently's Holistic Detective Agency* 1453, 1919, 2228, 2480, 4247, 4389, 4390
*The Hitchhiker's Guide to the Galaxy* 483, 553, 735, 959, 1216, 1453, 1455, 1456, 1459, 1504, 1918, 1921, 1999, 2055, 2075, 2123, 2130, 2132, 2133, 2172, 2208, 2226, 2332, 2567, 2568, 2622, 2750, 2880, 2979, 3465, 4076, 4077, 4388, 4392, 4562, 4563, 4564, 4565, 4566, 4656, 4662, 4785, 5076, 6008

*The Illustrated Hitchhiker's Guide to the Galaxy* **29**
*Life, the Universe, and Everything* 1918, 4077
*The Long Dark Tea-Time of the Soul* **30**, 1919, 2228, 4391, 4399
*Mostly Harmless* **31**
*The Original Hitchhiker's Radio Scripts* 1784
*The Restaurant at the End of the Universe* 493, 959, 1459, 1603, 1918, 2055, 2123, 2130, 2979, 4076, 4077, 5076
*So Long, and Thanks for All the Fish* 1918, 3573, 4077

**Adams, Richard**
*Girl in a Swing* 2019, 2713
*Maia* 3412, 4850
*The Plague Dogs* 3152, 3701
*Shardik* 4273, 4692
*Tales From Watership Down* **32**, 408, 2849, 2854
*Watership Down* 432, 599, 1132, 2850, 2852, 3115, 4271, 4273, 5755

**Adams, Robert**
*Alternatives* 3466
*Castaways in Time* 5295
*The Coming of the Horseclans* 2397
*Of Beginnings and Endings* **33**
*The Seven Magical Jewels of Ireland* 4619, 5500
*Stairway to Forever* 4519

**Adams, Terry A.**
*The Master of Chaos* **34**
*Sentience: A Novel of First Contact* 133

**Adams, William**
*The Unwound Way* **35**, 3750, 5198, 5201

**Addison, Joseph**
*Tesseract* 4339

**Adkins, Patrick H.**
*Sons of the Titans* **36**, 458, 1979, 2404, 2658

**Adler, C.S.**
*Ghost Brother* 1898

**Adrian, Jack**
*The Ash-Tree Press Annual Macabre 1997* **37**

*The Ash-Tree Press Annual Macabre 1998* **38**
*Strange Tales From the Strand* **39**, 4026

**Aesop**
*Aesop's Fables* **40**, 2447

**Afanas'ev, Aleksandr**
*Russian Fairy Tales* 3281

**Africa, Chris N.**
*When Wolves Cry* **41**, 2768, 5388

**Agins, Phyllis Carol**
*Suisan* **42**

**Agosin, Marjorie**
*The Secret Weavers: Stories of the Fantastic by Latin American Women* **43**, 51, 1411, 1412, 1818, 2035, 4169, 5814, 5815

**Ahern, Jerry**
*The Battle Begins* 5086
*Final Rain* 277
*The Quest* 278
*The Struggle* **44**, 1924
*To End All War* 2324, 2325
*Werewolves* 2841

**Aickman, Robert**
*Cold Hand in Mine* 3879, 3880, 5329
*The Fontana Book of Ghost Stories Series* 1309
*Pages From a Young Girl's Journal* 5419
*Painted Devils* 5329
*Unsettled Dust* 5763, 5764, 5765
*The Wine-Dark Sea* 851, 864, 865, 866, 3462, 3463, 3779, 5329

**Aiken, Joan**
*Black Hearts in Battersea* 5976, 5977
*A Fit of Shivers* 1526
*The Haunting of Lamb House* **45**, 666, 5762
*The Last Slice of Rainbow and Other Stories* 3610
*Nightbirds on Nantucket* 5977
*The Shadow Guests* 4257
*A Touch of Chill* 1526

**Aikin, Jim**
*Walk the Moon's Road* 2414, 2450
*The Wall at the Edge of the World* **46**, 4478

**Akers, Alan Burt**
*Arena of Antares* 1977
*Transit to Scorpio* 3983

**Albano, Peter**
*Assault of the Super Carrier* **47**
*Ordeal of the Seventh Carrier* **48**
*Revenge of the Seventh Carrier* **49**
*Super Carrier: The Ultimate Secret Weapon* **50**

**Alcala, Kathleen**
*Mrs. Vargas and the Dead Naturalist* **51**
*Spirits of the Ordinary* **52**

**Alcock, Vivian**
*The Haunting of Cassie Palmer* 4257
*The Red-Eared Ghosts* **53**

**Aldiss, Brian W.**
*Bow Down to Nul* 5027
*Common Clay: 20 Odd Stories* **54**
*Cryptozoic* 175, 188
*Dracula Unbound* **55**, 1134, 3003, 4094, 4098, 4772
*Frankenstein Unbound* 140, 498, 912, 1305, 3019, 3180, 3631, 4385, 4684
*Greybeard* 2870
*Helliconia Spring* 4242, 5040, 5940
*Helliconia Summer* 884, 4242, 5040, 5940
*The Helliconia Trilogy* 4243
*Helliconia Winter* 418, 4242, 5040, 5940
*Hothouse* 2847, 5659
*An Island Called Moreau* 2107, 5940
*Last Orders* **56**, 5940
*Man in His Time: The Best Science Fiction Stories of Brian W. Aldiss* **57**, 123, 624, 5940
*Non-Stop* **58**, 4626, 5937, 5943
*A Romance of the Equator: The Best Fantasy Stories of Brian W. Aldiss* **59**, 244, 415, 2736, 3876
*The Saliva Tree and Other Strange Growths* 5747
*Somewhere East of Life* **60**, 352, 4071
*Spaceship* 2829
*Starship* 297, 2243, 2626
*A Tupelov Too Far and Other Stories* **61**
*Vanguard From Alpha* 5766
*The Year Before Tomorrow* 5517
*The Year Before Yesterday* 2564, 5518

**Aldridge, Ray**
*Emperor of Everything* **62**
*The Pharaoh Contract* **63**, 1604

**Aldrin, Buzz**
*Encounter with Tiber* **64**

**Alexander, David**
*Death Race* 1405
*Desert Fire* **65**
*Fane* 2688
*Nomad* 47, 50, **66**, 830, 1405

**Alexander, Lloyd**
*The Arkadians* **67**, 2869
*The Beggar Queen* 5142
*The Book of Three* 1601, 2944, 2986, 5359
*The Drackenberg Adventure* 5928
*The High King* 658, 6042
*The Iron Ring* **68**, 5479
*The Kestrel* 5142
*Prydain Chronicles* 4056

**Alexis, Athena**
*Along Came a Spider* **70**, 146, 1300, 5808, 5926

**Alexis, Katina**
*Souls* **71**, 2023

**Alfonsi, Alice**
*Dark Seductions* **72**
*Some Enchanted Evening* **73**, 880, 5658

**Alguire, Judith**
*Zeta Base* **74**, 662, 3539

**Allen, Mary Elizabeth**
*All Hallow's Eve. Tales of Love and the Supernatural* **75**

**Allen, Roger MacBride**
*Allies and Aliens* 2254
*Ambush at Corellia* **76**, 103, 114, 115, 3247, 3820, 4719, 5205, 5950
*Caliban* **77**, 446, 1336, 2005, 2906
*Farside Cannon* 1916
*Inferno* **78**, 418, 4297
*The Modular Man* **79**, 665, 5462
*Orphan of Creation* 175, 188, 502, 733, 1525, 2434, 2725, 3703, 4039, 4547, 4552
*The Ring of Charon* **80**, 100, 378, 379, 382, 401, 402, 421, 447, 449, 478, 597, 685, 784, 932, 933, 934, 1055, 1183, 1244, 1247, 1407, 1509, 1537, 1565, 1573, 1575, 1897, 1989, 1990, 1993, 1999, 2000, 2002, 2060, 2226, 2417, 2524, 2602, 2649, 2812, 2921, 3398, 3429, 3710, 3734, 3760, 3762, 3763, 3787, 3805, 3823, 3825, 4000, 4018, 4122, 4126, 4179, 4241, 4281, 4302, 4351, 4354, 4416, 4505, 4760, 4761, 4762, 4769, 4947, 5188, 5244, 5260, 5303, 5304, 5573, 5677, 5865, 5866, 6065, 6079, 6085, 6086
*Rogue Powers* 2211
*The Shattered Sphere* **81**, 382, 383, 934, 1183, 3760, 3762, 3823, 4760
*Supernova* **82**, 354, 4652
*The Torch of Honor* 589, 1326, 4378
*Utopia* **83**, 198, 1695
*The War Machine* **1650**

**Allen, Sheila Rosalynd**
*The Meddlesome Ghost* **84**

**Allmen, Stewart Von**
*Conspicuous Consumption* 5535

**Allston, Aaron**
*Doc Sidhe* **85**, 1472, 1474, 3490
*Double Jeopardy* **86**
*Galatea in 2-D* **87**, 1433, 1438, 1461, 2082, 2735, 2791, 3173, 3490, 4486
*Thunder of the Captains* **3489**
*Wrath of the Princes* **3490**

**Almquist, Gregg**
*Beast Rising* 1036

**Alsobrook, Rosalyn**
*Time Storm* 2731, 3576

**Alten, Steve**
*Meg* **88**, 5877

**Altieri, Daniel**
*Shangri-La: The Return to the World of Lost Horizon* **1169**

**Ambrose, David**
*The Man Who Turned into Himself* **89**, 858, 2613, 4086, 5661
*Superstition* **90**

**Ames, J. Edward**
*The Death Crystal* **91**
*Spellcaster* **92**

**Ames, John E.**
*The Asylum* **93**, 1939, 5897

**Ames, Mel D.**
*Tales of Titillation and Terror* **94**, 5335

**Amis, Kingsley**
*The Green Man* 982, 1002
*Spectrum* 4721
*Spectrum 2* 242
*Spectrum 3* 243

**Amis, Martin**
*London Fields* **95**
*Night Train* 5661
*Time's Arrow* **96**, 466, 467, 1341, 1663, 2244, 2446, 2542, 6029

**Amos, Beth**
*Cold White Fury* **97**

**Andersen, Hans Christian**
*The Complete Fairy Tales and Stories* 2447

**Anderson, Chester**
*The Butterfly Kid* **87**, 735, 2014, 2228, 2913, 3173, 3664, 4388, 4392, 4565, 4641, 4862, 4863, 4864, 5170

**Anderson, Dana**
*Cafe Purgatorium* **98**, 4314

**Anderson, Dennis Lee**
*Arthur, King* 973, 977, 1344, 1853

**Anderson, Edward**
*Thieves Like Us* 3330

**Anderson, Jani**
*Bringing Down the Moon* **22**

**Anderson, Kevin J.**
*Afterimage* **4709**
*Afterimage Aftershock* **4710**
*Ai! Pedrito!: When Intelligence Goes Wrong* **2788**
*Antibodies* **99**, 924
*Assemblers of Infinity* **100**, 587, 588, 1770, 2275, 3710, 4955
*Blindfold* **101**, 2477, 2478, 2788, 4829, 5548
*Climbing Olympus* **102**, 2788
*Darksaber* **103**, 4299
*Gamearth* 390, 391, 4709
*Gameplay* **105**, 3309, 4709, 5432
*Game's End* **104**, 1662, 4709
*Ground Zero* **106**, 924, 2320, 2788, 4874, 5843
*Ignition* **107**
*Ill Wind* **108**, 506, 4218
*Jedi Search* **76**, **109**, 2500, 3247, 3820, 4719, 5205, 5950
*Lethal Exposure* **110**
*Lifeline* **111**
*Ruins* **112**, 924, 2308, 2788, 3679, 5846
*Shifting the Boundaries: The Selected Works of Kevin J. Anderson* **113**, 578, 4313, 5881
*Tales From Jabba's Palace* **114**

*Tales From the Bounty Hunters* 2914
*Tales From the Mos Eisley Cantina* **115**
*The Trinity Paradox* **116**, 895, 1852, 1854, 2239, 5516, 5518
*Trouble on Cloud City* **117**
*Virtual Destruction* **118**, 957, 1858, 3242
*War of the Worlds: Global Dispatches* **119**, 205, 607, 2398, 6077
*The X-Files: Ruins* 2114, 2534

**Anderson, M.T.**
*Thirsty* **120**

**Anderson, Margaret J.**
*The Druid's Gift* **121**, 561, 563, 1498, 2121, 2883
*The Ghost Inside the Monitor* **122**, 2283, 3444, 4971, 5558
*In the Circle of Time* 2688
*To Nowhere and Back* 2992

**Anderson, Paul Dale**
*Claw Hammer* 2599

**Anderson, Poul**
*Alight in the Void* 349
*All One Universe* **123**
*The Armies of Elfland* **124**
*The Boat of a Million Years* **125**, 175, 178, 188, 298, 590, 591, 734, 789, 884, 1053, 1876, 2459, 2626, 2829, 3854, 5039, 5496, 5942, 6074
*The Book of Poul Anderson* 4956
*The Broken Sword* 2246, 2783, 3934, 3980, 4163, 4284, 4518, 4989
*A Circus of Hells* 3907, 3928
*The Corridors of Time* 4164, 5999
*The Dancer From Atlantis* 5295
*The Day of Their Return* 4151
*The Devil's Game* 714
*Earthman, Go Home!* 1652, 2437, 3928
*Earthman's Burden* 1536, 5875
*The Enemy Stars* 3777
*Ensign Flandry* 1900, 3735, 3861, 3928, 3970, 5403, 5514, 5922
*Fire Time* 2810
*Flandry of Terra* 1633, 4037
*The Fleet of Stars* **126**
*Gallicenae* 3260
*The Game of Empire* 2459, 2476, 3907, 3928, 5319, 5503, 5510
*Guardians of Time* 1225, 1631, 1855, 2119, 3083, 4040
*Harvest of Stars* **127**, 593, 2526, 2907
*Harvest the Fire* **128**
*The High Crusade* 1325, 4365, 5131, 5588, 5900
*Hoka!* 197, 259, 1414, 4785, 5875
*Hrolf Kraki's Saga* 363, 2571, 3910, 4526
*Inconstant Star* **129**, 2828, 3649, 4124, 4125, 4372
*The King of Ys: Roma Mater* 1191, 2747
*Kingship with the Stars* 592
*A Knight of Ghosts and Shadows* 1041, 3907, 3928
*The Longest Voyage/Slow Lightning* **130**
*Man-Kzin Wars III* **4123**
*The Merman's Children* 5511
*A Midsummer Tempest* 314, 2570, 2945, 3079, 3097, 3700, 3822
*Mirkheim* 2459

*The Night Face* 1913
*The Night Fantastic* 1717, 2413, 4543
*Operation Chaos* 162, 2574, 4055, 4360
*Orion Shall Rise* 3788, 4602
*People of the Wind* 2223, 2224, 3723
*The Peregrine* 1719
*The Psychotechnic League* 584
*The Queen of Air and Darkness* 1182
*Question and Answer* 1248
*The Rebel Worlds* 3907, 3928
*Satan's World* 3125
*The Shield of Time* 6, **131**, 895, 1196, 1199, 1854, 1983, 5011, 5487, 5906, 5999
*The Snows of Ganymede* 5561
*Space Folk* **132**
*Starfarers* **133**
*The Stars Are Also Fire* **134**, 445, 3715, 3795
*A Stone in Heaven* 248, 5917
*Tau Zero* 445, 5305
*There Will Be Time* 2012, 5999
*Three Hearts and Three Lions* 169, 635, 962, 1534, 1678, 3505, 4153, 4159, 4595, 4743, 5231, 5647
*The Time Patrol* 65, **135**, 263, 264, 357, 1074, 1196, 1417, 1626, 1694, 1852, 1941, 1980, 1983, 2122, 2532, 3427, 3428, 4525, 5315, 5487, 5921, 5922
*Time Patrolman* 904, 1344, 1345, 1631, 1853, 2067, 4164, 5113, 5996, 5998, 6000
*Trader to the Stars* 1647, 4148, 4160, 5499, 5549
*Twilight World* 4600
*War of the Gods* **136**
*War of the Wing-Men* 3769
*The Winter of the World* 4619, 4620, 4621
*The Year of the Ransom* 4164

**Andersson, C. Dean**
*Buried Screams* **137**, 2302
*Fiend* **138**
*I Am Dracula* **139**, 678, 3004, 3005, 3179, 6011
*I Am Frankenstein* **140**

**Andrews, Allen**
*Pig Plantagenet* 2849, 2853, 2854

**Andrews, Keith William**
*Freedom's Rangers* 359, 5011
*The Freedom's Rangers Series* 3038
*Search and Destroy* 116, **141**, 1199, 5012
*Sink the Armada* 65, **142**, 5559
*Treason in Time* **143**, 1199

**Andrews, V.C.**
*All That Glitters* 2492
*Dawn* **144**
*The Dollanganger Saga* 1300
*Flowers in the Attic* 70, 5808, 5926
*Gates of Paradise* **145**
*Secrets of the Morning* **146**, 5484
*Web of Dreams* **147**

**Aniolowski, Scott David**
*Return to Lovecraft Country* **148**, 4427

**Anonymous**
*The Book of Irish Weirdness* **149**
*A Century of Ghost Stories* 1310
*The Darkest Thirst: A Vampire Anthology* **150**
*Fifty Years of Ghost Stories* 1310

*Ghost Tales of the Villa Deodati* 5389
*The Kiss of Death: An Anthology of Vampire Stories* **151**

**Anscombe, Roderick**
*The Secret Life of Laszlo, Count Dracula* **152**, 3003, 3005, 6010

**Anstey, F.**
*The Brass Bottle* 73

**Anthony, Mark**
*Beyond the Pale* **153**, 1484
*Crypt of the Shadowking* 1290, 3538
*Kindred Spirits* **154**, 3155, 4925
*Tower of Doom* **155**, 1510, 2516

**Anthony, Patricia**
*Brother Termite* **156**, 2087, 2254, 2417, 4353
*Cold Allies* **157**, 5515, 5517
*Cradle of Splendor* **158**
*Flanders* 5501
*God's Fires* **159**, 3599
*Happy Policeman* **160**, 2286, 5576

**Anthony, Piers**
*Alien Plot* **161**
*And Eternity* **162**, 4047
*Battle Circle* 1328
*Bearing an Hourglass* 96
*Being a Green Mother* 4153, 4159, 4783
*Bio of a Space Tyrant* 2212
*But What of Earth?* **163**, 1689, 3249
*Castle Roogna* 30, 677
*The Caterpillar's Question* **164**, 558, 951, 1478, 2644
*Centaur Aisle* 677
*Chaos Mode* **165**
*Chimaera's Copper* **166**
*Chthon* 3693
*Cluster* 958, 1995
*The Color of Her Panties* **167**
*Demons Don't Dream* **168**, 2015, 4171, 4393
*Dragon's Gold* 5222
*Faith of Tarot* 4926
*Faun & Games* **169**
*Firefly* **170**, 5771
*For Love of Evil* 652, 4781, 4782
*Fractal Mode* **171**
*Geis of the Gargoyle* **172**
*Hard Sell* **173**
*Harpy Thyme* **174**
*Hasan* 73, 618, 880
*Hope of Earth* **175**
*If I Pay Thee Not in Gold* **176**, 882, 4159, 4784
*Isle of View* **177**
*Isle of Woman* **178**, 5496
*Killobyte* **179**, 507, 583, 1461, 2082, 2791, 4283, 5753
*Kirlian Quest* 1871
*Macroscope* 4354
*Man From Mundania* **180**, 671, 1206, 1809, 1812, 2132, 2133, 4316
*Mercycle* **181**, 2450, 5726
*Mouvar's Magic* **182**
*On a Pale Horse* 1416, 4358
*Orc's Opal* **183**
*Orn* 2575, 4595
*Out of Phaze* 5225, 5226
*Phaze Doubt* **184**
*Prostho Plus* 5779
*Quest for the Fallen Star* **185**
*Question Quest* **186**
*Refugee* 5132, 5889
*The Ring* 4178
*Rings of Ice* 82, 354, 400
*Robot Adept* 5225, 5226

*Roc and a Hard Place* **187**
*Shame of Man* **188**
*Sos the Rope* 4619, 4621
*The Source of Magic* 30, 677
*A Spell for Chameleon* 30, 671, 677, 1267, 2123, 2130, 5219, 5224, 6049
*Spider Legs* **189**
*Split Infinity* 676, 1421, 1812
*Steppe* 590
*Tales From the Great Turtle* **190**, 2686
*Tarot* 637, 2406, 2574, 4359, 4384
*Tatham Mound* **191**
*Thousandstar* 953
*Through the Ice* **192**, 4799
*Total Recall* **193**, 805, 1304, 1878, 4635
*Unicorn Point* 5225, 5226
*Var the Stick* 1324
*Virtual Mode* **194**, 1471, 2943, 4156
*Vision of Tarot* 960
*Wielding a Red Sword* 355, 3696
*The Willing Spirit* **195**, 1316, 1317, 1318
*Yon Ill Wind* **196**
*Zombie Lover* **197**, 1014

**Antieau, Kim**
*The Gaia Websters* **198**, 1481, 3922
*The Jigsaw Woman* **199**, 4070, 4850
*Trudging to Eden* 113, **200**

**Anvil, Christopher**
*Pandora's Planet* 2880, 4124

**Appel, Allen**
*Till the End of Time* **201**, 4047
*Time After Time* 5114

**Appleby, Ken**
*The Voice of Cepheus* **202**

**Aratyr, Risa**
*Hunter of the Light* **203**

**Arbucci, John**
*Blood of Innocents* **204**, 879, 2704, 3637, 4480, 4840, 4843, 4845, 5622
*The Innocent* 3230

**Archer, Nathan**
*Cold War* 4285
*Martian Deathtrap* **205**
*Ragnarok* **206**, 1923

**Archer, Peter**
*Rath and Storm* **207**

**Ardai, Charles**
*Future Crime: An Anthology of the Shape of Crime to Come* **3619**

**Armstrong, Michael**
*Agviq* **208**, 870, 1632, 3862, 4000, 5444, 5743
*The Hidden War* **209**

**Arnason, Eleanor**
*Daughter of the Bear King* 271, 1065, 1491, 1678, 1684, 1686, 1703, 1704, 1747, 2504, 2506, 3386, 3939, 4448, 4669, 4798, 4868, 5178, 5364, 5591, 5719
*Ring of Swords* **210**, 219, 351, 377, 684, 686, 758, 988, 990, 997, 1043, 1116, 1264, 1407, 1408, 1586, 1593, 1824, 1849, 2016, 2051, 2052, 2338, 3000, 3380, 3475, 3752, 3760, 3762, 3972, 4067, 4128, 4140, 4187, 4241, 4244, 4356, 4736, 4900, 4902, 5090, 5091, 5466, 5467, 5492, 5674, 5681

*The Sword Smith* 16, 409, 667, 669, 987, 1042, 1292, 1592, 1790, 2263, 2362, 3098, 3385, 3401, 3540, 3652, 3728, 3925, 3930, 5579
*To the Resurrection Station* 874, 2196
*A Woman of the Iron People* **211**, 250, 558, 566, 686, 792, 793, 877, 968, 1583, 1584, 2037, 2637, 2683, 3046, 3157, 3424, 3972, 4038, 4325, 4855, 4923, 5091, 5450, 5461, 5574, 5590, 5616, 5872

**Arnold, Mark Alan**
*Borderland* 5913

**Arnzen, Michael A.**
*Grave Markings* **212**, 2159
*Needles and Sins* 113, **213**, 776, 2698, 3667, 4230, 4313, 5316, 5881

**Aronica, Lou**
*Full Spectrum* 501, 755, 887, 1363, 1365, 1621, 2634, 2679, 5045
*Full Spectrum 2* **214**, 238, 239, 500, 1363, 1365, 1616, 1621, 2634, 2679
*Full Spectrum 3* **215**, 1363, 1620, 2679, 4031, 4032
*Full Spectrum 3-4* 2634, 2635
*Full Spectrum 4* **216**, 1364, 1617, 1622, 2679

**Arthur, Ruth**
*The Autumn People* 1898

**Arthurs, Bruce D.**
*Copper Star* **217**
*Olympus* 2404

**Asaro, Catherine**
*Catch the Lightning* **218**
*The Last Hawk* **219**
*Primary Inversion* **220**, 2877, 4736

**Asch, Frank**
*Journey to Terezor* **221**, 1493, 2227, 2763, 2868, 5381

**Ash, Constance**
*The Horsegirl* 2397, 2676, 4156
*The Stalking Horse* **222**, 1743, 2397, 3627, 4493, 5296, 5547
*The Stallion Queen* **223**, 2673, 2678

**Ashley, Mike**
*The Best of British SF* 4439
*The Camelot Chronicles* **224**, 2745, 2767, 4610
*The Mammoth Book of Fairy Tales* **225**
*The Mammoth Book of Short Horror Novels* **226**, 2974
*The Merlin Chronicles* **227**, 369, 370, 372, 1270
*The Pendragon Chronicles* 266, 267, 640, 1531, 2745, 2746, 2767, 3062
*The Random House Book of Fantasy Stories* **228**, 1613, 5030, 5721, 5730
*The Random House Book of Science Fiction Stories* **229**, 2594

**Ashwell, Pauline**
*Project Farcry* **230**, 4858
*Unwillingly to Earth* **231**, 762, 2551, 2832, 3724, 3974, 4030, 4160, 5403

**Asimov, Isaac**
*100 Great Fantasy Short Short Stories* 1710, 1714, 5687
*The Asimov Chronicles: Fifty Years of Isaac Asimov* **232**
*Atlantis* 5035
*The Best of Isaac Asimov* 4956
*The Bicentennial Man* 5171
*The Book of Dragons* 801
*The Caves of Steel* 77, 160, 253, 254, 255, 476, 830, 1336, 2005, 2093, 2527, 2684, 2685, 3000, 3315, 3425, 3918, 4121, 4389, 4470, 4747, 4903, 5836
*The Complete Robot* 78, 3425, 4903
*The Complete Stories - Volume 1* **233**, 4706, 5551
*The Complete Stories - Volume 2* **234**
*The Currents of Space* 4043, 4940
*David Starr, Space Ranger* 2765
*Dragon Tales* 2479, 4408, 5239
*The End of Eternity* 2012, 2489, 3979, 4164
*Faeries* **235**, 2388
*Fantastic Voyage II: Destination Brain* 5892
*Forward the Foundation* **236**, 418
*Foundation* 894, 984, 2645, 4044, 4375, 4682, 5116, 5917, 5920, 5921, 5922
*Foundation and Earth* 882, 885
*Foundation and Empire* 392, 984, 1538, 2051, 2171, 3873, 4044, 4305, 4375, 4553, 5141
*The Foundation Trilogy* 446, 1540, 3072, 5865
*Foundation's Edge* 984
*The Gods Themselves* 4, 2724, 4019
*Gold: The Final Science Fiction Collection* **237**, 2490
*The Hugo Winners 1-5* 2401, 2405, 5871
*I, Robot* 253, 254, 255, 4297
*I, Robot: The Illustrated Screenplay* **1785**
*Isaac Asimov Presents the Best Horror and Supernatural Tales of the 19th Century* 39
*Isaac Asimov Presents the Great SF Stories* 422, 2585
*Isaac Asimov Presents the Great SF Stories: 1-25* 24, 2401, 2594, 2595, 2596, 2597, 2598, 5871
*Isaac Asimov Presents the Great SF Stories: 15 (1953)* 5948
*Isaac Asimov Presents the Great SF Stories: 20 (1958)* **238**
*Isaac Asimov Presents the Great SF Stories: 21 (1959)* 214, **239**
*Isaac Asimov Presents the Great SF Stories: 22 (1959)* **240**
*Isaac Asimov Presents the Great SF Stories: 23 (1961)* **241**
*Isaac Asimov Presents the Great SF Stories: 24 (1962)* **242**
*Isaac Asimov Presents the Great SF Stories: 25 (1963)* **243**
*Isaac Asimov Presents the Great SF Stories Series* 1612, 1614
*Isaac Asimov's Magical Worlds of Fantasy #10: Ghosts* 1610
*Lucky Starr and the Big Sun of Mercury* 2764
*Lucky Starr and the Pirates of the Asteroids* 1382, 4910, 4958
*Lucky Starr and the Rings of Saturn* 4952
*Magic: The Final Fantasy Collection* **244**

*The Mammoth Book of Fantastic Science Fiction* **245**
*The Mammoth Book of Modern Science Fiction: Short Novels of the 1980s* **246**
*The Mammoth Book of Vintage Science Fiction* 5954
*The Martian Way* 586, 5377
*Microcosmic Tales* 4828, 5946
*Mythical Beasties* 4988
*The Naked Sun* 77, 253, 254, 255, 830, 2011, 3425, 4903, 5836
*Nemesis* **247**, 4417, 4421, 4962
*The New Hugo Winners* 888, 2401, 2405
*Nightfall* **248**, 4762
*Norby and the Court Jester* **252**
*Norby and the Oldest Dragon* **253**
*Norby and Yobo's Great Adventure* **254**
*Norby Down to Earth* **255**
*Opus 200* 5938
*Opus 300* 5938
*Our Angry Earth* 3932
*The Positronic Man* **249**
*The Rest of the Robots* 253, 254, 255
*Robot Dreams* 253, 254, 255, 3666, 4197
*Robots and Empire* 83, 446, 484, 984, 2730, 3425, 4903, 5865
*The Robots of Dawn* 78, 484, 708, 2725, 3425, 4903, 5051, 5059, 5375, 5836
*Second Foundation* 984, 4044, 4304, 4375
*Sherlock Holmes through Time and Space* 4556
*The Stars Like Dust* 5546
*Tales of the Black Widowers* 585, 3619
*The Ugly Little Boy* **250**
*The Ugly Little Boy/The Widget, the Wadget, and Boff* 130
*Young Extraterrestrials* 5238

**Asimov, Janet**
*Murder at the Galactic Writers' Society* **251**
*Norby and the Court Jester* **252**
*Norby and the Oldest Dragon* **253**
*Norby and Yobo's Great Adventure* **254**
*The Norby Chronicles* 1217
*Norby Down to Earth* **255**, 5381
*Norby, the Mixed-up Robot* 1223, 4338
*Norby Through Time and Space* 3803

**Asire, Nancy**
*Tears of Time* **256**
*To Fall Like Stars* **257**
*Wizard Spawn* **1004**

**Askew, Alice**
*Aylmer Vance: Ghost-Seer* **258**

**Askew, Claude**
*Aylmer Vance: Ghost-Seer* **258**

**Asprin, Robert**
*Another Fine Myth* 167, 168, 169, 172, 177, 184, 186, 196, 1045, 1160, 1208, 1416, 1998, 2075, 2076, 2081, 2145, 2362, 2616, 2946, 4120, 4388, 4392, 4393, 4395, 4396, 4401, 5219, 5224
*The Bug Wars* 513, 1627, 2211, 2224, 3035, 3037, 4373
*Catwoman* **14**
*The Cold Cash War* 4932, 5457
*Little Myth Marker* 1603
*M.Y.T.H. Inc. in Action* **259**

*M.Y.T.H. Inc. Link* 4390
*Myth-ing Persons* 187, 671, 4391, 4399
*Myth-Nomers and Im-Pervections* 180
*Phule's Company* **260**, 1267, 2575, 3811
*Phule's Paradise* 7, **261**, 4148, 4350
*Stealer's Sky* 2783
*Sweet Myth-tery of Life* 197, **262**
*Thieves' World* 630, 986, 1148, 1150, 1152, 1153, 1207, 2363, 2368, 2369, 2375, 2376, 3300, 3836, 4202, 4335, 5214, 5216
*Time Scout* **263**, 1855, 5785
*Wagers of Sin* **264**, 350, 1855

**Asquith, Cynthia**
*The Ghost Book* 38, 1310
*This Mortal Coil* 601, 3360, 5772

**Asten, Gail Van**
*Charlemagne's Champion* 2662

**Atherton, Gertrude**
*The Bell in the Fog and Other Stories* 485, 1673, 2919, 4968

**Atherton, Nancy**
*Aunt Dimity and the Duke* 1451

**Atkins, Peter**
*Big Thunder* 3326
*Morningstar* **265**, 1031, 1945, 4496, 4728, 6050

**Attanasio, A.A.**
*Arthur* 3386
*The Dark Shore* **3385**
*The Dragon and the Unicorn* **266**, 1657, 2126, 2735, 4178, 5793
*The Eagle and the Sword* **267**
*Hunting the Ghost Dancer* **268**
*Kingdom of the Grail* **269**, 2231, 3385, 3386
*The Last Legends of Earth* **270**
*The Moon's Wife: A Hystery* **271**, 1435, 1438, 1491, 2538, 3385, 3386, 4093, 5180
*The Shadow Eater* **3386**
*Solis* **272**
*The Wolf and the Crown* **273**
*Wyvern* 3386

**Attebery, Brian**
*The Norton Book of Science Fiction: North American Science Fiction, 1960-1990* **3381**

**Atwood, Margaret**
*Good Bones and Simple Murders* **274**, 794, 1578, 1942, 2144, 2146, 3384, 5557, 5617
*The Handmaid's Tale* 968, 1135, 1653, 1817, 1877, 1929, 3241, 3622, 4325, 5268, 5276, 5430, 5911

**Auel, Jean M.**
*Clan of the Cave Bear* 178, 268, 667, 668, 669, 731, 870, 881, 889, 1539, 1632, 1838, 2166, 2167, 2168, 2169, 2170, 2581, 2582, 2583, 4320, 4817, 4818, 4819, 5444
*The Mammoth Hunters* 667, 669, 1207, 2170, 4817, 4818, 4819
*The Plains of Passage* **275**, 669, 5444
*The Valley of Horses* 667, 669, 2571, 4040, 4817, 4818, 4819, 5444

**Auerbach, Nina**
*Forbidden Journeys: Fairy Tales and Fantasies by Victorian Women Writers* 37, **276**, 648, 2035, 5814, 5815, 6089

**August, Michael**
*New Year's Evil* 5288

**Auster, Paul**
*The New York Trilogy* 3201, 3780, 5661

**Austin, A.J.**
*To Fear the Light* 595
*To Save the Sun* 596

**Austin, Richard**
*Devil's Deal* 44, **277**

**Avi**
*Devil's Race* 5286, 5289
*Something Upstairs: A Tale of Ghosts* 1898

**Awlinson, Richard**
*Shadowdale* 1287, 2427, 4106, 4800, 4803, 4804, 4805
*Waterdeep* 1293, 5723

**Axler, James**
*Death Lands: Time Nomads* 2324, 2325
*Deep Trek* **278**
*Red Equinox* 44, 277

**Aycliffe, Jonathan**
*The Lost* **279**
*The Matrix* **280**
*Naomi's Room* **281**, 521, 1836, 2292, 2642, 2874, 3433, 3607, 3675, 5064, 5271, 5463, 5991, 5992
*The Vanishment* **282**, 608, 666
*Whispers in the Dark* 45, **283**, 3164

**Ayrton, Michael**
*The Maze Maker* 1129, 2404


**B**


**Bach, Richard**
*Jonathan Livingston Seagull* 4455, 4456

**Bachman, Richard**
*The Regulators* **284**, 839, 2318
*The Running Man* 1052

**Bacon-Smith, Camille**
*Eyes of the Empress* **285**

**Bailey, Robin Wayne**
*Brothers of the Dragon* 85, **286**, 2126, 2127, 2424
*Enchanter* 1754, 1839, 3913
*Flames of the Dragon* **287**
*The Lake of Fire* 1429, 3572
*The Lost City of Zork* **288**, 1839
*Nightwatch* 17, **289**, 844, 4390, 5087
*Shadowdance* **290**
*Swords Against the Shadowland* **291**, 3418

**Bainbridge, Sharon**
*Blood and Roses* **292**

**Baird, Wilhelmina**
*Chaos Come Again* **293**, 4353, 5890
*Clipjoint* **294**, 3484, 3711, 5576, 6048
*Crashcourse* 251, **295**, 5173, 5259, 5619

*Psykosis* 296

**Baker, Eric T.**
*Checkmate* 297

**Baker, Kage**
*In the Garden of Iden* 298, 3854, 4036

**Baker, Linda P.**
*Tears of the Night Sky* 299

**Baker, Mike**
*Young Blood* 300

**Baker, Nancy**
*The Night Inside* 301, 3253, 4068

**Baker, Nicholson**
*The Fermata* 302, 3459, 3493

**Baker, Scott**
*Ancestral Hungers* 303, 2255, 2259, 2512, 5183, 5421, 5693
*Dhampire* 1499, 2754
*Drink the Fire From the Flames* 290, 1009, 1010, 1109, 1928, 4360, 4612, 5321, 5931
*Firedance* 4943
*Webs* 304, 811, 3815, 4716

**Baker, Sharon**
*Burning Tears of Sassurum* 3871
*Quarreling, They Met the Dragon* 3157

**Bakis, Kirsten**
*Lives of the Monster Dogs* 305

**Bakker, Robert T.**
*Raptor Red* 306, 416, 1256, 1379, 2386, 5067, 6084

**Baldick, Chris**
*The Oxford Book of Gothic Tales* 307, 848, 1314, 3574, 4027, 4180, 5418, 5439, 5936
*The Vampyre and Other Tales of the Macabre* 4026

**Baldwin, Bill**
*Canby's Legion* 308, 1552, 4829, 4973
*The Defenders* 309, 4525, 4974, 5668
*The Defiance* 310, 1652
*Galactic Convoy* 1976
*The Helmsman* 3034
*The Mercenaries* 311, 2350
*The Siege* 312, 1546, 4982

**Baldwin, David**
*Dark Heart* 5707

**Baldwin, John**
*The Eleventh Plague: A Novel of Medical Terror* 3632

**Balfour, Bruce**
*Star Crusader* 4495, 5204

**Ball, Margaret**
*Acorna* 3717
*Acorna's Quest* 3718
*Changeweaver* 313, 1042, 1104, 3098, 4146
*Flameweaver* 314, 563, 633, 2424, 3303, 3304, 3878, 5757
*Lost in Translation* 315
*Mathemagics* 316, 2074, 3717, 4981
*PartnerShip* 3741
*The Shadow Gate* 317, 634, 1477, 2357, 2359, 3077, 3717, 4869, 4971, 4991, 5223

**Ballantine, Betty**
*The Secret Oceans* 318, 1024, 2469, 2982, 3729

**Ballard, J.G.**
*The Atrocity Exhibition* 319, 443, 3460, 3619
*The Best Short Stories of J.G. Ballard* 61, 624, 5345, 5348
*Billennium and Other Stories* 56, 57
*Concrete Island* 323, 2580
*Crash* 780, 2580
*The Crystal World* 3192, 3612, 3792, 4135
*The Drought* 2535
*The Drowned World* 56, 57, 354, 2998, 3612, 5906
*Hello America* 837, 4474
*Love and Napalm: Export U.S.A.* 555
*Memories of the Space Ages* 5369
*Running Wild* 320, 2787, 5799
*Terminal Beach* 56, 57, 59
*The Unlimited Dream Company* 3612
*Vermilion Sands* 56, 57, 59, 3876
*War Fever* 321, 3648, 3796, 4636

**Banks, Iain M.**
*Against a Dark Background* 322, 5543
*The Bridge* 319, 2028, 3473, 3791, 5927
*Canal Dreams* 323
*Consider Phlebas* 2365, 2366, 5116, 5365, 5637
*Excession* 324, 2523, 2525
*Feersum Endjinn* 325, 838, 5828
*The Player of Games* 219, 326, 1067, 1633, 1938, 2364, 2374, 3106, 4044, 4114, 4115, 4277, 5069, 5140, 5722
*The State of the Art* 327, 3106
*Use of Weapons* 328, 2522, 5117, 5138

**Banks, Lynne Reid**
*The Adventures of King Midas* 329
*Angela and Diabola* 330
*The Farthest-Away Mountain* 3545
*The Indian in the Cupboard* 430, 773, 1132, 1218, 2719, 3587, 5654, 5655, 5656
*The Key to the Indian* 331
*The Secret of the Indian* 332

**Bantock, Nick**
*The Forgetting Room* 52, 333
*The Golden Mean* 334
*Griffin & Sabine* 2706, 3124, 5450
*Sabine's Notebook* 335, 5450
*The Venetian's Wife: A Strangely Sensual Tale of a Renaissance Explorer, a Computer, and a Metamorphosis* 336

**Barber, Richard**
*The Arthurian Legends* 5560

**Barbet, Pierre**
*Baphomet's Meteor* 3261
*The Napoleons of Eridanus* 3800

**Barker, Clive**
*The Age of Desire* 4786
*The Books of Blood Series* 855
*Books of Blood Series* 2153, 3138, 3362, 3674
*Cabal* 337, 3336, 3759, 4745, 4746, 5007
*The Damnation Game* 2672, 3808, 3902, 4085
*Everville* 338, 4575, 5190, 5414
*Forms of Heaven* 339, 1022, 1112
*Galilee* 340, 3126
*The Great and Secret Show* 341, 2214, 3143, 3144, 5190, 5414

*The Hellbound Heart* 342, 2222, 3351, 3364, 3368, 4499, 5010
*Imajica* 343, 495, 1117, 3143, 5931
*Incarnations* 344, 1022
*Sacrament* 345, 3620, 4579
*Sex, Death and Starshine* 428, 5849
*Tapping the Vein: Book One* 3334
*Tapping the Vein: Books One and Two* 346
*The Thief of Always* 347, 2995, 3779
*"Twilight at the Towers"* 4702
*Weaveworld* 1423, 1957, 3131, 3143, 3677

**Barker, M.A.R.**
*Flamesong* 1317, 1318, 1904, 1906, 1909, 1910, 2887, 2888, 4020, 5391
*Man of Gold* 15, 104, 770, 771, 1008, 1109, 1111, 1316, 1317, 1318, 1904, 1906, 1908, 1909, 1910, 1912, 2041, 2330, 2473, 2887, 2888, 3581, 3925, 4020, 5391, 5731

**Barlow, Robert H.**
*The Hoard of the Wizard Beast and One Other* 348, 3516

**Barnes, John**
*Apostrophes and Apocalypses* 349
*Caesar's Bicycle* 350
*Earth Made of Glass* 351, 1316
*Encounter with Tiber* 64
*Kaleidoscope Century* 352, 413, 957, 1762, 4218
*The Man Who Pulled Down the Sky* 4620, 5032
*A Million Open Doors* 64, 353, 1970, 4175, 4679
*Mother of Storms* 64, 108, 354, 5258
*One for the Morning Glory* 169, 355, 1082, 5178
*Orbital Resonance* 64, 356, 782, 1970, 4349, 4643
*Patton's Spaceship* 357, 384, 1054, 4641
*Sin of Origin* 3617, 4550
*Union Fires* 358
*Wartide* 359

**Barnes, Steven**
*Achilles' Choice* 4114
*The Barsoom Project* 4115
*Beowulf's Children* 4116
*The California Voodoo Game* 4117
*Firedance* 360
*Gorgon Child* 361, 720, 4117
*Iron Shadows* 362
*Streetlethal* 4117, 4227, 4366, 4747, 6075

**Barnes-Svarney, Patricia**
*Quarantine* 2109

**Barnett, Jill**
*Imagine* 3280

**Barnett, Lisa A.**
*Point of Hopes* 4899

**Barnitz, Charles**
*The Deepest Sea* 136, 363, 4518

**Barr, Sue Hollister**
*Twisted* 364

**Barrett, Neal Jr.**
*Dawn's Uncertain Light* 163, 188, 277, 365, 886, 4602
*Judge Dredd* 366, 4075
*The Karma Corps* 1326
*Slightly Off Center* 3327, 3328, 3329

*Through Darkest America* 163, 277, 886, 1996, 2603, 4604, 4621, 5092, 5982
*The Touch of Your Shadow, the Whisper of Your Name* 367, 944, 1654, 2102, 4833

**Barrett, William F.**
*The Lady and the Lotus* 3260

**Barrie, J.M.**
*Peter Pan* 713

**Barron, T.A.**
*The Ancient One* 368
*The Fires of Merlin* 369
*The Lost Years of Merlin* 370
*The Merlin Effect* 371, 6035, 6038
*The Seven Songs of Merlin* 372

**Barry, Scott Ian**
*The Streeter* 373, 488

**Barth, John**
*Chimera* 2129, 4731
*The Last Voyage of Somebody the Sailor* 374, 2123, 2129, 2130, 6087

**Barthelme, Donald**
*City Life* 2641
*The King* 375, 973, 977, 1092, 5427

**Barton, Dan**
*Relife* 376

**Barton, William**
*Acts of Conscience* 377
*Alpha Centauri* 378
*Dark Sky Legion* 379, 1337, 5449, 5745, 5951
*Fellow Traveller* 380, 388, 2433
*Iris* 381, 5052
*The Transmigration of Souls* 382
*When Heaven Fell* 383, 2254
*White Light* 384

**Base, Graeme**
*The Discovery of Dragons* 385, 1024, 2980, 2982, 5479

**Basile, Giambattista**
*Pentameron or Entertainment for the Little Ones* 849

**Bassett, James C.**
*Living Real* 386, 1348, 6063

**Bassingthwaite, Don**
*As One Dead* 387, 1119, 1949, 2512, 2664, 5703
*Breathe Deeply* 5535
*Such Pain* 2321, 5535

**Bassler, Thomas J.**
*Half Past Human* 4662

**Batchelor, John Calvin**
*The Birth of the People's Republic of Antarctica* 4628
*Peter Nevsky and the True Story of the Russian Moon Landing* 388

**Battin, B.W.**
*Night Sounds* 3415

**Baudino, Gael**
*Branch and Crown* 389
*Dragon Death* 390, 2505
*Dragonsword* 286, 1161, 1749, 3067, 3659, 3872, 3982, 4695, 4697
*Duel of Dragons* 391, 843, 2462, 2465, 2797, 3578, 4173, 4691, 4693, 4694, 4695, 4707

*Gossamer Axe*  **392**, 1181, 1409, 1430, 1434, 1436, 1499, 1583, 1958, 2950, 3264, 3284, 3285, 3286, 3293, 3299, 3301, 3423, 3886, 3887, 4596, 4655, 4870, 4993, 5177, 5179, 5293, 5915
*Maze of Moonlight*  **393**, 3017, 5983
*O Greenest Branch!*  **394**, 3297
*Spires of Spirit*  **395**, 3356
*Strands of Starlight*  750, 2121, 2799, 3078, 3274, 4337
*Strands of Sunlight*  **396**, 2800, 4171, 4221, 4862, 4863, 4864, 5912

**Bauer, Marion Dane**
*Am I Blue?*  545

**Baum, L. Frank**
*Dorothy and the Wizard in Oz*  3609
*The Emerald City of Oz*  197
*The Land of Oz*  3609, 6006
*The Life and Adventures of Santa Claus*  2456
*The Master Key: An Electrical Fairy Tale*  1218
*The Patchwork Girl of Oz*  5654, 5655, 5656
*The Wonderful Wizard of Oz*  2136, 3144, 4758

**Baum, Thomas**
*Out of Body*  **397**, 3134, 3267, 5415

**Baxter, Stephen**
*Anti-Ice*  **398**, 4628
*Flux*  **399**, 932
*Moonseed*  **400**
*Raft*  81, **401**, 447, 449, 596, 1003, 1247, 1262, 1593, 1645, 1986, 2215, 2829, 3050, 3750, 3763, 3805, 4000, 4122, 4950, 4957, 5000, 5233, 5540, 5937, 5943
*Ring*  384, **402**, 4333, 6086
*The Time Ships*  **403**, 1759, 2906, 4040
*Timelike Infinity*  **404**, 4353, 4961
*Titan*  **405**, 3199, 3789, 4947
*Voyager*  **406**

**Bayer, Sandy**
*The Crystal Curtain*  3852

**Bayley, Barrington J.**
*The Fall of Chronopolis*  2489

**Beagle, Peter S.**
*A Fine and Private Place*  271, 2687, 3201, 3433, 4023, 4383, 5530
*The Folk of the Air*  **407**, 727, 987, 1747, 1748, 1841, 3170
*Giant Bones*  **408**
*The Innkeeper's Song*  **409**
*The Last Unicorn*  1219, 1343, 1946, 3399, 3401, 3540, 4319
*Lila the Werewolf*  1349, 3162, 5425
*Peter S. Beagle's Immortal Unicorn*  **410**, 466, 467, 2398
*The Rhinoceros Who Quoted Nietzsche and Other Odd Acquaintances*  **411**, 3240
*The Unicorn Sonata*  **412**, 3414, 3938

**Bear, Greg**
*/*  378, **413**
*Anvil of Stars*  **414**, 3726
*Bear's Fantasies*  **415**
*Beyond Heaven's River*  2996
*Blood Music*  100, 836, 1133, 1348, 1760, 1770, 2058, 2163, 2275, 2443, 2681, 3008, 3049, 3245, 3792, 4476, 4478, 4748, 4756, 5172, 5255
*Corona*  527

*Dinosaur Summer*  **416**, 6084
*Eon*  127, 326, 381, 382, 399, 403, **417**, 444, 447, 784, 785, 786, 928, 930, 931, 953, 954, 985, 1337, 1557, 1565, 1876, 1897, 1992, 2002, 2417, 2882, 3014, 3064, 3117, 3771, 3786, 4103, 4333, 4351, 4353, 4420, 4505, 4705, 4951, 5052, 5304
*Eternity*  326, 381, 590, 783, 1855, 1871, 2140, 2525, 4705, 5052
*The Forge of God*  82, 402, 405, 685, 753, 1057, 1258, 1651, 2646, 2955, 4281, 4416, 4775, 5677
*Foundation and Chaos*  **418**
*Great Sky River*  5834
*Heads*  79, 272, **419**, 588, 665
*The Infinity Concerto*  635, 1470, 3939, 4658, 4661
*Legacy*  **420**, 5571
*Moving Mars*  102, **421**, 1585, 2584, 2765, 4629, 4633, 5187
*New Legends*  **422**, 2596, 2597, 2598, 2634, 2635, 2679, 4169
*Queen of Angels*  126, 127, 294, **423**, 476, 583, 761, 1968, 2727, 2882, 3604, 3921, 4121, 5451
*Slant*  4179
*Songs of Earth and Power*  185, 203, **424**, 1321, 1472, 2737, 3059, 3269, 3886, 4659, 4981, 5221, 5223, 5817, 5818
*Tangents*  **425**, 4998, 5255, 5837
*The Wind From a Burning Woman*  3048, 3086, 3234, 5257, 5369

**Beard, Henry N.**
*Bored of the Rings*  2567, 2568, 4562, 4563, 4564, 4565, 4566, 4656, 4657

**Beason, Doug**
*Assemblers of Infinity*  **100**
*Ignition*  **107**
*Ill Wind*  **108**
*Lethal Exposure*  **110**
*Lifeline*  **111**
*The Trinity Paradox*  **116**
*Virtual Destruction*  **118**

**Beath, Warren Newton**
*Bloodletter*  **426**, 4327, 4496
*Shock Lines*  **427**, 2734, 4710, 5631
*Who Killed James Dean?*  **428**, 3102

**Beaumont, Charles**
*Charles Beaumont: Selected Stories*  531, 579
*Collected Stories*  532
*The Howling Man*  **429**
*Omnibus of Speed*  4308
*Selected Stories*  529, 530, 533, 537, 623, 3683, 3686, 3687, 3689, 4132, 4916, 5901

**Bebris, Carrie A.**
*Shadowborn*  **1137**

**Bedard, Michael**
*A Darker Magic*  4079
*Painted Devil*  330, **430**, 5654, 5655, 5656

**Bell, Clare**
*Clan Ground*  846, 1895, 4143
*People of the Sky*  **431**, 878, 3469, 4147, 5016, 5743, 5744
*Ratha and Thistle-Chaser*  **432**, 4143
*Ratha's Creature*  4143, 4144, 4145, 4157

**Bell, Douglas**
*Mojo and the Pickle Jar*  **433**, 891, 1584, 4458, 5456

**Bell, M. Shayne**
*Nicoji*  **434**
*Washed by a Wave of Wind*  **435**

**Bellairs, John**
*The Eyes of the Killer Robot*  253, 254, 255
*The Face in the Frost*  520, 2075, 4395, 4396, 4400, 5626
*The House with a Clock in Its Walls*  1294
*The Trolley to Yesterday*  2688

**Bellamy, Edward**
*Looking Back 2000-1887*  5568

**Belletto, Rene**
*Machine*  397, **436**, 1786, 4875

**Beman, Donald**
*Avatar*  **437**
*The Taking*  **438**

**Bemmann, Hans**
*The Broken Goddess*  **439**
*The Stone and the Flute*  273

**Benary-Isbert, Margot**
*The Wicked Enchantment*  2196

**Benchley, Peter**
*Beast*  88, **440**, 1346, 3232, 3998, 4415, 5877
*Jaws*  88, 1346, 3998, 5877
*White Shark*  189, **441**, 1850, 3220

**Bendixen, Alfred**
*Haunted Dusk*  5439
*Haunted Women: The Best Supernatural Tales by American Women Writers*  3570, 4180

**Benford, Gregory**
*Across the Sea of Suns*  1058, 2216, 2646
*Alternate Americas*  **442**, 4536, 4537, 4538, 5498
*Alternate Empires*  2044, 2045, 2047, 4537, 4538, 5301, 5498, 5505
*Alternate Heroes*  4536, 4537, 4538, 4540, 5498, 5505
*Alternate Wars*  **443**, 1074, 1196, 1980, 3867, 4537, 4538, 4814, 5498, 5502, 5515
*Beyond the Fall of Night*  **1054**
*Big Sky River*  1015
*Cosm*  **444**, 793, 5830
*A Darker Geometry*  3649
*Far Futures*  402, **445**, 4066
*Foundation's Fear*  418, **446**
*Furious Gulf*  384, 399, **447**, 684, 3763, 3823, 4353
*Great Sky River*  272, 417, 423, 806, 808, 985, 2036, 2690, 2691, 3522, 3604, 4065, 4418, 4419, 5108, 5431, 5449, 5541, 5878
*Heart of the Comet*  381, 928, 931, 1057, 1058, 2216, 2433, 3772, 3824, 4417
*Hitler Victorious: Eleven Stories of the German Victory in World War II*  2564, 5300, 5301
*If the Stars Are Gods*  1991, 3617
*In Alien Flesh*  349, 425
*In the Ocean of Night*  1058, 2216
*Jupiter Project*  3922, 4952, 4964, 5561
*Matter's End*  **448**, 823
*Sailing Bright Eternity*  **449**
*Shiva Descending*  1057, 3772
*The Stars in Shroud*  351, 1248

*Tides of Light*  34, 417, 423, **450**, 985, 1015, 1689, 2460, 2690, 2691, 3117, 3604, 4418, 4419, 4696, 5108, 5129, 5431, 5787, 6056
*Timescape*  782, 1245, 3786, 4420, 5774, 6060
*What Might Have Been*  5633

**Bengtsson, Frans G.**
*The Long Ships*  136, 269, 363, 633, 640, 1104, 1105, 1498, 2189, 2248, 2250, 2453, 2454, 2572, 3353, 3502, 4270, 4872, 5014

**Bennett, Janice**
*Forever in Time*  1271, 3576

**Bennett, Marcia J.**
*Seeking the Dream Brother*  **451**, 4147

**Bennett, Nigel**
*Keeper of the King*  **452**, 1579

**Benson, A.C.**
*Basil Netherby*  456
*Ghosts in the House*  456

**Benson, Ann**
*The Plague Tales*  **453**

**Benson, D.R.**
*The Unknown*  5700

**Benson, Donald**
*And Having Writ*  5501

**Benson, E.F.**
*The Collected Ghost Stories of E.F. Benson*  45, **454**, 779, 1243, 2846, 3633, 4141, 5610, 5611
*The Terror by Night*  **455**, 875

**Benson, Robert Hugh**
*The Light Invisible*  454, **456**

**Bently, Thomas**
*Celestial Chess*  4092

**Berberick, Nancy Varian**
*A Child of Elvish*  **457**, 1290
*The Jewels of Elvish*  4434
*The Panther's Hoard*  **458**, 5223
*Shadow of the Seventh Moon*  **459**, 5580
*Stormblade*  3155, 5454, 5455, 5711
*Tears of the Night Sky*  **299**

**Bergantino, David**
*Wes Craven's New Nightmare*  **460**

**Berger, Thomas**
*Arthur Rex*  3474

**Berger, William**
*Little Big Man*  1126

**Berglund, Edward P.**
*Disciples of Cthulhu*  148, **461**, 2399, 2978, 3535, 4422, 4423, 4425, 4426, 4427, 4428, 4429, 4430, 4431, 5325, 5698, 5884

**Bergstrom, Elaine**
*Baronness of Blood*  2516
*Blood Alone*  **462**
*Daughter of the Night*  **463**, 1286
*The Door through Washington Square*  **464**
*Leanna: Possession of a Woman*  3149
*Madeline: After the Fall of Usher*  3150
*Mina*  3151
*Shattered Glass*  279, 4234, 4529, 4755, 5475, 5690
*Tapestry of Dark Souls*  155, **465**, 2516, 2663, 584/

**Berkman, Edwina**
*Demon Within* **4499**

**Berliner, Janet**
*Child of the Journey* **466**
*Children of the Dusk* **467**
*David Copperfield's Beyond Imagination* **1186**
*David Copperfield's Tales of the Impossible* **1187**
*Desire Burn: Women's Stories From the Dark Side of Passion* **468**, 2891
*Peter S. Beagle's Immortal Unicorn* **410**

**Berlyn, Michael**
*The Eternal Enemy* **469**, 785, 1586, 1587, 1594, 2812, 4030, 5930

**Bernard, Diane**
*Eternally Yours* 691

**Bertin, Joanne**
*The Last Dragonlord* **470**

**bes shahar, eluki**
*Archangel Blues* **471**
*Darktraders* **472**
*Hellflower* **473**

**Besher, Alexander**
*Mir* **474**, 5353
*Rim: A Novel of Virtual Reality* **475**, 483, 3662, 4283

**Bester, Alfred**
*The Computer Connection* 927, 1861, 3994
*The Demolished Man* **476**, 1696, 1968, 2093, 2330, 2474, 2475, 2527, 3073, 4121, 4469, 4557, 5054, 5276, 5373, 5754, 5835
*Golem* [100] 1723, 5109
*The Light Fantastic* 321, 3187
*Psychoshop* 444, **477**
*Star Light, Star Bright* 54, 233, 234, 243, 321, 624, 850, 1874, 2569, 3187, 3308, 3342, 4706, 5028, 5344, 5349, 5551, 5641, 5869
*The Stars My Destination* **478**, 1514, 1664, 2171, 2209, 2290, 2545, 2645, 3452, 4280, 4304, 4511, 4557, 5232, 5260, 5598
*Virtual Unrealities: The Short Fiction of Alfred Bester* **479**, 1963, 3219, 3971, 5346, 5613

**Betancourt, John Gregory**
*The Best of Weird Tales* **480**, 3028
*The Best of Weird Tales: 1923* **3023**
*Devil in the Sky* **1226**
*The Hag's Contract* 2625
*Rememory* **481**
*The Ultimate Alien* **4406**
*The Ultimate Dragon* **4408**
*The Ultimate Witch* **4411**
*The Ultimate Zombie* **4412**
*The Vengeance of Hera* 4912
*Weird Tales: Seven Decades of Terror* **482**, 3023
*The Wrath of Poseidon* 4912

**Bethke, Bruce**
*Headcrash* 118, 386, 474, **483**, 505, 2916, 3662, 4893, 5259
*Maverick* **484**

**Bianco, Margery Williams**
*A Street of Little Shops* 3610

**Bierce, Ambrose**
*Can Such Things Be?* 963, 964, 4275
*Ghost and Horror Stories* 1243
*The Moonlit Road and Other Ghost and Horror Stories* **485**

*Poems of Ambrose Bierce* **486**

**Biggle, Lloyd**
*All the Colors of Darkness* 2996
*The Light That Never Was* 4350
*Monument* 884, 3344, 5550
*This Darkening Universe* 1659
*The Whirligig of Time* 3343
*The World Menders* 5230, 5231

**Biggs, Cheryl**
*Yesterday's Passion* 3039

**Billias, Stephen**
*The Holo Men* 2470
*Horrible Humes* 27, **487**, 1840, 4433, 4675
*The Quest for the 36* 5612

**Billings, Patrick**
*The Quiet* **488**

**Billingsley, Franny**
*Well Wished* **489**

**Billson, Anne**
*Suckers* **490**, 1802, 3988, 4445, 5406

**Bingley, Margaret**
*Seeds of Evil* **491**, 2021, 4091, 5065, 5118, 5269, 5484

**Birkin, Charles**
*My Name Is Death* 533

**Birnbaum, Alfred**
*Hard-Boiled Wonderland and the End of the World* **4047**

**Bischoff, David**
*Abduction: The UFO Conspiracy* 2034
*Bill, the Galactic Hero: On the Planet of Tasteless Pleasure* **2567**
*Christmas Slaughter* **2323**
*Dr. Dimension* **1456**
*Hunter's Planet* **492**, 4075
*The Judas Cross* **4960**
*Mutant Hell* **2324**
*Mutants Amok* **2325**
*Night of the Living Shark!* **493**, 1456, 1603, 3573, 5934
*Quoth the Crow* **494**, 696, 4186, 5844
*seaQuest DSV: The Ancient* 318, 1201
*The Vampires of Nightworld* 1134

**Bishop, Anne**
*Daughter of the Blood* **495**

**Bishop, Michael**
*Ancient of Days* 1525, 2434
*Apartheid, Superstrings, and Mordecai Thubana* **496**
*At the City Limits of Fate* **497**, 3981
*Blooded on Arachne* 3086, 3116, 3234, 5369
*Brittle Innings* 199, **498**, 2029, 3977
*Close Encounters with the Deity* 6067
*Count Geiger's Blues* **499**, 2393, 3642, 3647, 3768, 3891, 3977, 5148, 5262, 5567
*Eyes of Fire* 353
*A Little Knowledge* 1877
*Nebula Awards 23* 4031, 4032, 4033
*Nebula Awards 23-25* 1342, 4824
*Nebula Awards 24* 246, **500**, 887, 4031, 4032, 4033, 4822, 4823, 5871
*Nebula Awards 25* 215, **501**, 1363, 1616, 1620, 1622, 4031, 4032, 4033, 4558, 4822, 4823, 5871
*No Enemy but Time* 175, 188, **502**, 1525, 2434, 4039

*One Winter in Eden* 3086, 5369
*The Secret Ascension* 789, 1519, 1520, 1521, 1522, 1523, 4546
*Transfigurations* 3617, 4550
*Unicorn Mountain* 1343
*Who Made Stevie Crye?* 2873

**Bisson, Terry**
*Bears Discover Fire* **503**
*The Fifth Element* **504**
*Fire on the Mountain* 496, 1133, 2577, 3867, 3993, 5502, 5633
*Johnny Mnemonic* 118, **505**, 2033
*Pirates of the Universe* **506**
*Virtuosity* **507**, 4075
*Voyage to the Red Planet* **508**, 1418, 3082, 4095, 5215, 5227, 5859

**Black, Campbell**
*Letters From the Dead* 4701, 5519
*Raiders of the Lost Ark* 825, 826, 922, 1581, 2257, 3588, 3589, 3590, 3591, 3592, 3593, 3916, 4549

**Blackburn, John**
*Children of the Night* 4733
*For Fear of Little Men* 1038, 2541, 2672, 3091

**Blackwood, Algernon**
*Best Ghost Stories of Algernon Blackwood* 454, 1243, 2710, 3658
*The Complete John Silence Stories* 258, **509**
*The Doll and One Other* 2025, 2899, 2902, 3782
*The Human Chord* 3595
*John Silence* 670
*Julius LeVallon: An Episode* 4586
*The Listener and Other Stories* 2712
*Pan's Garden: A Volume of Nature Stories* 456
*Shocks* 455

**Blackwood, Gary L.**
*Beyond the Door* **510**, 970, 2948
*The Dying Sun* **511**, 709, 3584, 3608

**Blair, John**
*Bright Angel* **512**
*A Landscape of Darkness* **513**

**Blake, Adrian**
*Unholy Communion* 5342

**Blake, Dan I.**
*Killing Frost* **514**

**Blake, Katherine**
*The Interior Life* **515**, 2622, 4658, 4659, 4661

**Blake, Sterling**
*Chiller* 2498, 4066

**Blakeney, Jay D.**
*The Goda War* **516**, 3888
*Requiem for Anthi* **517**, 3888, 4482

**Blankman, Lynn**
*Ghost Beyond the Garden* 5286, 5289

**Blatty, William Peter**
*Demons Five, Exorcists Nothing* 2448
*The Exorcist* 661, 937, 1048, 1804, 2494, 2697, 4239, 5342, 5896
*Legion* 5342, 5896
*The Ninth Configuration* 5898

**Blaylock, James P.**
*All the Bells on Earth* **518**, 715, 3497, 3957
*The Digging Leviathan* 1520
*The Elfin Ship* 2132, 2133, 2750

*Homunculus* 25, 714, 1014, 1564, 2329, 2546, 3097, 3124, 4385, 4740
*Land of Dreams* 545, 546, 549, 550, 551, 552, 820, 2329, 3423, 3793, 4448
*The Last Coin* **519**, 1172, 2232, 2304, 2329
*Lord Kelvin's Machine* **520**, 3596, 4432
*Night Relics* **521**, 608, 1560, 2687, 4383
*The Paper Grail* 389, **522**, 819, 919, 1091, 1397, 1519, 2028, 2231, 2627, 2717, 3262, 4104, 4382, 4384, 4992, 5614, 5615, 5903
*The Stone Giant* **523**, 1208, 2132, 2133, 3811
*Winter Tides* **524**

**Blayre, Christopher**
*The Strange Papers of Dr. Blayre* 3360

**Bleiler, Everett F.**
*The Collected Ghost Stories of Mrs. J.H. Riddell* 4968
*A Treasury of Victorian Ghost Stories* 1234, 1235, 2300

**Blish, James**
*The Best of James Blish* 233, 234
*Black Easter* 2658, 4647, 6071
*A Case of Conscience* 707, 2523, 3599, 4567, 4736, 5635
*Cities in Flight* 9, 232, 402, 445, 1055, 1627, 3722, 5303
*Common Time* 5305
*The Day After Judgment* 4647
*The Devil's Day* **525**, 3416
*Earthman, Come Home* 734, 5499
*Jack of Eagles* 4305, 4918
*A Life for the Stars* 356, 734, 1003, 2626, 3770, 5499, 5937, 5943
*Midsummer Century* 884
*The Seedling Stars* 399, 5788
*Spock Must Die* 1922
*Star Trek 3* 1658
*Star Trek: The Classic Episodes 1* **526**
*Star Trek: The Classic Episodes 2* **527**
*Star Trek: The Classic Episodes 3* **528**
*There Shall Be No Darkness* 4764
*They Shall Have Stars* 401
*A Torrent of Faces* 1057
*The Triumph of Time* 404, 508, 2208, 2501, 3710

**Bloch, Robert**
*American Gothic* 1830, 2612
*The Best of Robert Bloch* 5104
*Catnip* 3145
*The Complete Stories of Robert Bloch, Volume 1: Final Reckonings* **531**
*The Complete Stories of Robert Bloch, Volume 2: Bitter Ends* **529**
*The Complete Stories of Robert Bloch, Volume 3: Last Rites* **530**
*The Early Fears* **532**, 1494, 1495, 1496, 3529, 3532, 3534, 5627
*The Eighth Stage of Fandom: Selections From 25 Years of Fan Writing* 4546
*Fear and Trembling* **533**
*Fiddler's Fee* 3950
*Flowers From the Moon and Other Lunacies* **534**
*The Jekyll Legacy* **535**
*The Kidnapper* 5338

*Lori* **536**, 5468
*Midnight Pleasures* **537**
*Monsters in Our Midst* **538**, 1018, 2280
*The Mysteries of the Worm* **539**, 925, 3266
*Night of the Ripper* 535, 2931, 5761
*Psycho* **540**, 576, 1131, 1777, 2428, 2566, 2638, 3088, 3208, 3336, 3716, 3815, 4185, 4222
*Psycho II* 426, **541**, 620, 1052, 1846, 3103
*Psycho House* **542**, 4664
*Psycho-Paths* **543**, 1018, 1019, 2280, 2282, 2600, 3324
*Robert Bloch's Psychos* **544**
*The Scarf* 2548, 3815, 4084
*Screams* 3690
*The Selected Stories of Robert Bloch* 625, 3683, 4131
*The Shooting Star* 1763
*The Star Stalker* 619, 620, 1763, 4131
*Strange Eons* 1497, 2743, 2748, 3548, 3566, 3567, 3568, 3569, 4007, 4112, 4449, 5053, 5470
*There Is a Serpent in Eden* 1834
*The Will to Kill* 5443

**Block, Francesca Lia**
*Baby Be-Bop* **545**
*Cherokee Bat and the Goat Guys* **546**
*Ecstasia* **547**
*The Hanged Man* **548**
*I Was a Teenage Fairy* **549**
*Missing Angel Juan* **550**
*Primavera* **551**, 5959
*Weetzie Bat* 4104
*Witch Baby* **552**, 636

**Block, Lawrence**
*Ariel* 320, 2801, 4237, 5623

**Blome, Ed**
*Title Deleted for Security Reasons* 483, **553**, 3313, 3435, 4076, 4298, 5074

**Bloom, Britton**
*Matrix Cubed* **554**, 3036

**Blum, Robert S.**
*The Girl From the Emerald Island* 5490

**Blumlein, Michael**
*The Brains of Rats* 319, **555**, 674, 675, 821, 913, 3456, 4053, 4253, 4977, 5005, 5058, 5899

**Blunt, Giles**
*Cold Eye* 437, **556**, 694, 1204, 1975, 2030, 2292, 3193, 3196, 3197, 3640, 3691, 4790

**Bogart, Bonnie**
*The Ewoks Join the Fight* 1392, 1393, 1394

**Bogen, K.B.**
*Go Quest, Young Man* 196, **557**, 6049

**Bogen, Nancy**
*Bagatelle—Guinevere* **558**

**Boggs, Timothy**
*By the Sword* **559**, 1808, 4912
*The Eye of the Ram* 4912
*Serpent's Shadow* 1808, 4912

**Bohnhoff, Maya Kaathryn**
*The Crystal Rose* **560**
*The Meri* 394, 396, **561**, 633, 640, 1135, 1356, 1478, 3628, 4207, 4863, 5266, 5456

*The Spirit Gate* **562**, 1143, 1943
*Taminy* 396, **563**, 1135, 4159

**Boileau, Pierre**
*Choice Cuts* 1205

**Bolton, Johanna**
*The Alien Within* 3125
*Mission: Tori* **564**, 1913, 2414, 2811, 3771, 5550

**Bonanno, Margaret Wander**
*Dwellers in the Crucible* 527, 900, 1260, 1388, 1511, 1954, 2063, 2064, 3316, 3767, 4081, 4138, 5019, 6051
*The Others* 453, **565**, 643, 653, 766, 788, 1956, 2909, 3581, 3719, 3817, 3994, 4008, 4062, 4101, 4756, 5174, 5430
*OtherWhere* **566**
*OtherWise* **567**, 5037
*Preternatural* **568**, 4333
*Probe* **569**
*Saturn's Child* **4101**
*Strangers From the Sky* 526, 528, 902, 1225, 1386, 2065, 2298, 4511, 5375

**Bonansinga, Jay R.**
*The Black Mariah* **570**, 2313
*Sick* **571**, 3178

**Bone, J.F.**
*Confederation Matador* 2575, 5230

**Borchardt, Alice**
*The Silver Wolf* **572**, 4573

**Borden, William**
*Superstoe* 499, 2186, 2393, 3222, 3439, 3455, 4606

**Borges, Jorge Luis**
*The Book of Fantasy* 1576, 2592
*Collected Fictions* **573**, 818
*Ficciones* 3460, 3461, 3464
*Labyrinths* 950, 3462, 3463

**Bornefeld, William**
*Time and Light* **574**

**Borton, Douglas**
*Deathsong* **575**
*Kane* **576**, 2314, 3052, 3899
*Shadow Dance* **577**

**Boston, Bruce**
*Dark Tales and Light* **578**

**Boston, L.M.**
*Children of Green Knowe* 2949
*An Enemy at Green Knowe* 4080
*The Stones of Green Knowe* 1138
*The Treasure of Green Knowe* 4585

**Bouchard, Robert A.**
*Count Scar* **702**

**Boucher, Anthony**
*The Best From Fantasy and Science Fiction: 7* 240
*The Best From Fantasy and Science Fiction: 8* 241
*The Compleat Werewolf and Other Tales of Fantasy and Science Fiction* **579**
*Far and Away* 59

**Boucher-Kaplan, Aline**
*World Spirits* **580**, 5575

**Boulle, Pierre**
*Planet of the Apes* 1982, 5514

**Bova, Ben**
*As on a Darkling Plain* 885, 897, 1248
*Brothers* **581**

*Colony* 3199, 4962, 5241
*Cyberbooks* 481, **582**
*Death Dream* 107, 475, 507, **583**, 956, 957, 2011, 2275, 2791, 4283, 4342, 4860, 5753
*Empire Builders* **584**
*Exiled From Earth* 6059
*Future Crime* **585**, 3619
*The Kinsman Saga* 2143, 2726, 5870
*Mars* 102, 406, 421, **586**, 1585, 2584, 2840, 4348, 4349, 4629, 4633
*Millennium* 2645
*Moonrise* **587**, 4952
*Moonwar* **588**
*The Multiple Man* 5890
*Orion* 1324, 1871, 5544
*Orion Among the Stars* **589**, 3937
*Orion and the Conqueror* **590**, 2140, 2572
*Orion in the Dying Time* **591**
*Peacekeepers* 2143, 2726, 4632, 4634, 5193
*The Privateers* 2245
*Sam Gunn Forever* **592**
*Sam Gunn, Unlimited* 236, **593**
*Star Brothers* **594**
*The Starcrossed* 1918, 2996, 3573
*Test of Fire* 111, 400
*To Fear the Light* **595**
*To Save the Sun* **596**
*The Trikon Deception* **597**, 2727, 5377
*Triumph* **598**, 895, 1854, 2239, 3528, 5516, 5517, 5518, 5996
*Voyagers II: The Alien Within* 824
*Voyagers III: Star Brothers* 824
*The Winds of Altair* 2764

**Bowen, 'Asta**
*Hungry for Home: A Wolf Odyssey* **599**, 4271

**Bowen, Elizabeth**
*The Cat Jumps and Other Stories* 3360
*The Demon Lover and Other Stories* 601

**Bowen, Gary**
*Diary of a Vampire* **600**, 948, 1541, 4069

**Bowen, Marjorie**
*Kecksies and Other Twilight Tales* 3360, 5772
*Twilight and Other Supernatural Romances* **601**

**Bowes, Richard**
*Minions of the Moon* 2995

**Bowker, David**
*The Death Prayer* **602**

**Bowker, Richard**
*Dover Beach* 160, 1751, 4121, 4941, 5302, 5644, 5887
*Forbidden Sanctuary* 2870
*Marlborough Street* 4469, 4604

**Bowles, Paul**
*The Sheltering Sky* 5414

**Boyd, Donna**
*The Passion* 572, **603**

**Boyd, John**
*The Andromeda Gun* 1398

**Boyer, Elizabeth H.**
*The Clan of the Warlord* **604**, 844, 4491
*The Curse of Slagfid* 2760
*The Dragon's Carbuncle* **605**

*The Elves and the Otterskin* 1685, 2424
*The Lord of Chaos* 993

**Boyer, Robert H.**
*Visions & Imaginings: Classic Fantasy Fiction* **606**, 1576, 1613, 2592, 5003, 5030, 5721, 5730

**Boyett, Steven R.**
*The Answer Tree* 917, 3541
*Ariel: A Book of the Change* 177, 184
*Treks Not Taken: What if Stephen King, Anne Rice, Bret Easton Ellis, and Other Literary Greats Had Written Episodes of Star Trek: The Next Generation?* 119, **607**, 2398, 6077

**Boyle, Josephine**
*Holy Terror* **608**, 3607

**Boyll, Randall**
*After Sundown* **609**, 1828, 3033, 3092, 4223, 4369, 5685
*Chiller* **610**, 1078, 1080, 1971
*Darkman* 19, **611**, 1334, 3881, 3882, 3883, 5073
*Darkman #1: The Hangman* **612**
*Darkman #2: The Price of Fear* **613**
*Darkman #3: The Gods of Hell* **614**
*Darkman #4: The Face of Death* 112, **615**
*Mongster* **616**, 4240
*Shocker* 4088
*Tales From the Crypt: Demon Knight* **617**

**Brackett, Leigh**
*The Book of Skaith* 3746
*Eric John Stark, Outlaw of Mars* 3746
*The Ginger Star* 2575, 5647
*The Long Tomorrow* 1328, 3788, 4074
*The Nemesis From Terra/Battle for the Stars* 2829
*People of the Talisman* 3696
*The Starmen of the Lyrdis* 5645, 5864
*The Sword of Rhiannon* 2414, 4151, 5752

**Bradbury, Ray**
*Ahmed and the Oblivion Machines* **618**
*The Autumn People* 3334
*Dandelion Wine* 3136, 3754, 4131, 5060
*Death Is a Lonely Business* **619**
*Driving Blind* 2641
*Fahrenheit 451* 5568
*A Graveyard for Lunatics* **620**, 3688, 4131
*The Halloween Tree* 5796
*The Illustrated Man* 4131
*The Martian Chronicles* 435, **621**, **622**, 2416, 4548
*A Memory of Murder* 2281
*The October Country* **623**, 819, 2319, 4832, 4916, 5901
*Quicker than the Eye* **624**, 5348
*Ray Bradbury on Stage: A Chrestomathy of His Plays* 1022
*Something Wicked This Way Comes* 347, 518, 1081, 1282, 2303, 2316, 2557, 2565, 2817, 3137, 3477, 4010, 4057, 4131, 4486, 5060, 5264
*The Stories of Ray Bradbury* 429, 532, 893, 3683, 3686, 3687, 4131, 4132, 5929

''The Homecoming''  3053
''The Wonderful Ice Cream Suit''  5803
Tomorrow Midnight  3334
The Toynbee Convector  625, 4131, 4636

**Braddock, Hanovi**
Ashes of the Sun  2827

**Bradfield, Scott**
Animal Planet  3222
Dream of the Wolf  626, 816, 1349, 5343
Greetings From Earth  818
What's Wrong with America  627, 1396, 5167, 5168

**Bradley, Marion Zimmer**
The Best of Marion Zimmer Bradley  3845
The Best of Marion Zimmer Bradley's Fantasy Magazine  628, 6005, 6046
The Best of Marion Zimmer Bradley's Fantasy Magazine, Volume II  629
Black Trillium  630, 3696, 3700, 4153
The Bloody Sun  3747
The Catch Trap  5264
City of Sorcery  3746, 4269
Darkover Landfall  4147
Domains of Darkover  631, 4269
The Door through Space  2414
Exile's Song  632
The Fall of Atlantis  4146
The Firebrand  1253, 2036, 3356, 3725, 4553, 5017, 5434, 6053
The Forbidden Tower  218, 219, 1862, 2354, 2357, 3697, 5752
The Forest House  266, 267, 633, 692, 1270, 3260, 5792, 5793, 5794
Free Amazons of Darkover  408, 3290, 3300, 5293
Ghostlight  634
Glenraven  635
Gravelight  636
Hawkmistress!  313, 314, 4515, 5542
Heartlight  637
The Heirs of Hammerfell  638, 3255, 4081, 4269
The Heritage of Hastur  1933, 1934, 3288, 4334, 5754
The House Between the Worlds  515, 962, 5218
Hunters of the Red Moon  3800
In the Rift  639
The Keeper's Price  2991
Lady of Avalon  640, 1775, 4573
Lady of the Trillium  641, 3700
Leroni of Darkover  642
Lythande  745
Lythandeer People  1765
The Mists of Avalon  224, 227, 1092, 1190, 1191, 1269, 1270, 1409, 1498, 1531, 1582, 1741, 1857, 1960, 1961, 2039, 2188, 2231, 2232, 2572, 2740, 2745, 2746, 2767, 2858, 2883, 2939, 2940, 3017, 3062, 3077, 3352, 3355, 3357, 3636, 3827, 4265, 4609, 4610, 4877, 5015, 5270, 5359, 5397, 5757, 5792, 5793, 5970, 5971, 6071
Rediscovery: A Novel of Darkover  643, 3629, 3630, 5862
Renunciates of Darkover  644
The Shadow Matrix  645
Sharra's Exile  922, 986, 3746

The Shattered Chain  62, 1141, 1755, 2050, 2550, 3634, 5071, 5978
Star of Danger  2764
Stormqueen!  256, 3746, 3940
Sword and Sorceress I-XII  765, 4759
Sword and Sorceress VIII  646
Sword and Sorceress IX  647
Sword and Sorceress XI  648
Sword and Sorceress XII  649
Sword and Sorceress XIII  650
Sword and Sorceress XIV  651
The Sword and Sorceress Series  316, 1808, 1811, 2072, 2074, 3076, 3290, 3670, 3906, 4610, 5018
Thendara House  1004, 1177, 1755, 3746, 5434
Tiger Burning Bright  652
Towers of Darkover  653
Two to Conquer  894
Web of Darkness  5035, 6041
Web of Light  5035
Witch Hill  654
Witchlight  655, 1462
The World Wreckers  2372, 3426, 3726, 4140

**Bradley, Will**
Ark Liberty  656, 664, 1569, 3999

**Bradshaw, Gillian**
Hawk of May  224, 1190, 2745, 2747, 2760, 2939, 2940, 3058, 3062, 3827, 5970, 5971
Horses of Heaven  657
In Winter's Shadow  2939, 5971
Kingdom of Summer  2939, 2940, 5971
The Land of Gold  67, 658, 1867, 1868, 4321, 4544, 5391

**Brady, Joan**
God on a Harley  1577, 4926

**Bram, Christopher**
Father of Frankenstein  659, 1094

**Brand, Rebecca**
The Ruby Tear  660

**Brandewyne, Rebecca**
Passion Moon Rising  84

**Brandner, Gary**
Cat People  4472
Doomstalker  661, 2703
The Howling  723, 3376

**Branscome, Anna**
The Essential World of Darkness  5797
The Quintessential World of Darkness  5798

**Brass, Perry**
Mirage  74, 662

**Braunbeck, Gary A.**
Isaac Asimov's I-Bots  4297
Things Left Behind  663, 1789, 2701, 3495, 4231

**Brautigan, Richard**
The Hawkline Monster  499, 2847, 3439, 3456, 4233, 5151, 5817
In Watermelon Sugar  1787, 2554, 2603, 2640, 4720, 5145
Revenge of the Lawn: Stories 1962-1970  3222
Trout Fishing in America  3455

**Bredenberg, Jeff**
The Dream Vessel  664
The Man in the Moon Must Die  665, 2788

**Brenchley, Chaz**
The Keys to D'Esperance  666

**Brennan, C.M.**
The Genesis Web  3036

**Brennan, J.H.**
Shiva Accused: An Adventure of the Ice Age  667
Shiva: An Adventure of the Ice Age  669, 1632
Shiva's Challenge: An Adventure of the Ice Age  668, 2857

**Brennan, Joseph Payne**
The Adventures of Lucius Leffing  670
Nightmare Need  4752
Nine Horrors and a Dream  534, 2844, 5211
Stories of Darkness and Dread  2319, 4463

**Brenner, Mayer Alan**
Catastrophe's Spell  3, 4, 605, 671, 1206
Spell of Apocalypse  672, 1030
Spell of Fate  673

**Brennert, Alan**
Her Pilgrim Soul  674
Kindred Spirits  2412, 2589, 5024
Ma Qui and Other Phantoms  675, 2078, 3250
Time and Chance  201, 676

**Brentano, Clemens Maria**
Fairy Tales From Brentano  2447

**Bretnor, Reginald**
The Collected Feghoot  677
The Schimmelhorn File  677, 2227
Schimmelhorn's Gold  677

**Brett, Brian**
The Fungus Garden  2544

**Brett, Jan**
The First Dog  3377

**Bretton, Barbara**
Somewhere in Time  3576

**Briarton, Grendel**
The Collected Feghoot  677, 4637, 4639

**Briery, Traci**
The Vampire Journals  292, 678, 1794, 1795, 1798, 3113, 3151, 3623, 4246
The Vampire Memoirs  3781
The Werewolf Chronicles  679, 926, 4472
Wolfsong  680, 4472

**Briggs, Patricia**
Masques  681, 717, 718, 845
Steal the Dragon  682
When Demons Walk  683

**Brightfield, Richard**
Valley of the Kings: Egypt, May 1908  3544

**Brin, David**
Brightness Reef  159, 296, 684, 786, 932, 988, 998, 1259, 1589, 2010, 3007, 3359, 3732, 3733, 3972, 4128, 4241, 4351, 5059, 5429, 5437, 5571, 5777, 5778, 5780, 6081

Earth  79, 82, 100, 108, 205, 295, 354, 382, 400, 405, 413, 414, 510, 596, 656, 656, 685, 753, 792, 806, 808, 1056, 1057, 1075, 1167, 1258, 1336, 1382, 1549, 1581, 1594, 1651, 1805, 1897, 1989, 1990, 2328, 2491, 2579, 2645, 2997, 2999, 3311, 3437, 3449, 3503, 3604, 3661, 3744, 3745, 3789, 3805, 3921, 3932, 3944, 3952, 4000, 4126, 4218, 4281, 4357, 4416, 4421, 4503, 4629, 4633, 4634, 4635, 4652, 4677, 4682, 4704, 4708, 4769, 4895, 4947, 4949, 4950, 4961, 5132, 5173, 5174, 5209, 5241, 5242, 5303, 5351, 5433, 5540, 5566, 5573, 5677, 5744, 5745, 5834, 5839, 5873, 5956, 5966, 6065
Glory Season  210, 686, 1104, 1116, 1588, 1824, 2134, 3241, 3380, 3426, 3440, 3453, 4900, 4957, 5091, 5187, 5368, 5804
Heaven's Reach  687, 1501, 1759
Infinity's Shore  688, 5669
Otherness  349, 592, 689, 823
The Postman  365, 435, 728, 788, 792, 793, 886, 1405, 1569, 1924, 2603, 2640, 2805, 3082, 3346, 3864, 4074, 4209, 4599, 4678, 4836, 5086, 5242, 5267, 5982
The Practice Effect  2574, 4595, 5830
The River of Time  124, 132, 161, 244, 411, 415, 425, 772, 804, 1431, 1515, 1608, 2576, 5240, 5945
Startide Rising  80, 126, 130, 132, 181, 309, 311, 322, 324, 404, 450, 874, 892, 958, 1056, 1067, 1083, 1255, 1262, 1264, 1503, 1504, 1535, 1545, 1557, 1587, 1634, 1725, 1729, 1995, 2037, 2172, 2224, 2332, 2371, 2419, 2434, 2450, 2649, 2838, 3721, 3729, 3730, 3823, 3830, 3994, 4019, 4122, 4123, 4124, 4217, 4219, 4418, 4419, 4483, 4505, 4557, 4919, 4923, 4951, 4967, 4984, 5108, 5282, 5354, 5431, 5436, 5587, 5589, 5779, 5949, 6051, 6056
Sundiver  401, 567, 1157, 2223, 4416, 6065
The Uplift War  132, 250, 326, 450, 451, 469, 874, 876, 981, 990, 1261, 1503, 1634, 1725, 1729, 2016, 2434, 2551, 2898, 3000, 3703, 3735, 3976, 4160, 4217, 4241, 4418, 4419, 4547, 4552, 5108, 5431, 5526, 5586, 5779, 5866

**Brindle, Jane**
The Tallow Image  690, 3146, 5334

**Brinkley, William**
The Last Ship  3586

**Brisbin, Terri**
A Love through Time  691

**Britain, Kristen**
Green Rider  692

**Brite, Poppy Z.**
Are You Loathsome Tonight?  693, 1401, 5005
Drawing Blood  212, 437, 547, 694, 1845, 2494, 2901, 3101, 3197, 3364, 3368, 3675, 5414, 5463
Exquisite Corpse  695, 1890, 3183

*The Lazarus Heart*   494, **696**, 4186, 5844

*Lost Souls*   490, 548, 600, **697**, 799, 803, 946, 1031, 1032, 1034, 1121, 1122, 1127, 1301, 1707, 1778, 1882, 1945, 2151, 2336, 2337, 2449, 3151, 3312, 3407, 3413, 3623, 4307, 4464, 4978, 5160, 5162, 5175, 5183, 5347, 5406, 5419, 5852

*Love in Vein*   **698**, 748, 2508, 3030, 3181, 3182, 3618, 4690, 5385, 5386, 5387

*Love in Vein II*   **699**, 3177, 3618, 4689, 4690, 5386, 5387

*Swamp Foetus*   **700**, 1123, 2698, 2860, 3090, 3100, 3318, 3393, 3667, 3669, 3673, 4886, 5008, 5411, 5412, 5413, 5416

**Brittain, C. Dale**
*A Bad Spell in Yurt*   187, 557, **701**, 2079, 2081, 5163
*Count Scar*   **702**
*Daughter of Magic*   **703**
*Mage Quest*   5219
*Voima*   **704**
*The Witch and the Cathedral*   **705**
*The Wood Nymph and the Cranky Saint*   **706**, 1014, 2080

**Brittain, William**
*Who Knew There'd Be Ghosts?*   5286, 5289

**Brizzolara, John**
*Empire's Horizon*   **707**, 1210

**Brock, Darryl**
*If I Never Get Back*   2029

**Broderick, Damien**
*Strange Attractors: Original Australian Speculative Fiction*   2593, 4713
*Striped Holes*   2013
*The White Abacus*   **708**, 1442, 4060

**Brooke, William J.**
*Teller of Tales*   1257, 1578, 1942, 2144, 2146, 2845, 5557
*A Telling of the Tales: Five Stories*   5557

**Brookes, Owen**
*Deadly Communion*   3128, 3203, 4471
*Inheritance*   1580

**Brooks, Bruce**
*No Kidding*   511, **709**

**Brooks, Cecil**
*The Unwound Way*   35

**Brooks, Stanwood**
*The Seventh Child*   2317

**Brooks, Terry**
*The Druid of Shannara*   **710**
*The Elf Queen of Shannara*   **711**
*First King of Shannara*   **712**
*Hook*   **713**, 5143
*A Knight of the Word*   **714**, 3620
*Magic Kingdom for Sale—Sold!*   4397
*Running with the Demon*   **715**, 1117
*The Scions of Shannara*   **716**
*The Sword of Shannara*   2884, 3634, 4284, 5757
*The Talismans of Shannara*   681, **717**, 5716
*The Tangle Box*   **718**
*Witches' Brew*   **719**

**Brosnan, John**
*Carnosaur*   3191
*The Fungus*   3192

*The Sky Lords*   **720**, 3050
*The War of the Sky Lords*   **721**

**Brown, Charles Brockden**
*Three Gothic Novels*   **722**

**Brown, Crosland**
*Tombley's Walk*   514, 679, 680, **723**, 816, 1127, 2138, 3376, 4002, 5080, 5552

**Brown, Dale**
*Day of the Cheetah*   2143, 3450, 3875
*The Silver Tower*   2143, 2726

**Brown, Fredric**
*The Best of Fredric Brown*   529, 530
*Martians, Go Home*   4546
*The Mind Thing*   914, 2542
*What Mad Universe*   1521, 4546, 5169

**Brown, Jerry Earl**
*Earthfall*   163, **724**, 1924
*Snowmen*   **725**, 5281, 5378

**Brown, Mary**
*Master of Many Treasures*   **726**, 2462
*Pigs Don't Fly*   **727**
*Strange Deliverance*   **728**
*The Unlikely Ones*   32, 67, 2774, 2775, 2776, 2848, 2849, 2850, 2851, 2853, 2854, 2855, 3625, 5382

**Brown, Rosel George**
*Sibyl Sue Blue*   2685

**Browne, Robert**
*The New Atoms' Bombshell*   2029

**Browner, Jesse**
*Conglomeros*   558, **729**, 1444, 2186, 3263, 3855, 4046

**Brownwood, Mark**
*Destiny's Carnival*   **4057**

**Brownworth, Victoria**
*Night Bites: Vampire Stories by Women*   **730**, 1713, 2891

**Broxon, Mildred Downey**
*Too Long a Sacrifice*   3254, 3259, 5428

**Bruchac, Joseph**
*Dawn Land*   **731**

**Brugalette, Philip**
*The Nine Gates*   1293

**Brummels, J.V.**
*Deus Ex Machina*   **732**

**Brunner, John**
*Age of Miracles*   2954, 4506, 4966, 5027, 5909
*The Astronauts Must Not Land*   2252
*Bedlam Planet*   1595
*Born Under Mars*   353
*Catch a Falling Star*   882, 885
*Children of the Thunder*   **733**, 874, 1165, 1637, 1648, 2474, 2475, 3742, 4343, 4504, 4827, 4950, 5258, 5907, 6008
*The Dramaturges of Yan*   5561
*The Dreaming Earth*   2807
*The Infinitive of Go*   2012
*The Jagged Orbit*   3243
*A Maze of Stars*   595, **734**, 1182, 4175, 5042, 5549
*Muddle Earth*   **735**
*A Planet of Your Own*   1574, 3344
*Polymath*   2393, 5781
*The Productions of Time*   3979, 4197
*The Rites of Ohe*   2414

*The Sheep Look Up*   5081, 5867
*The Shockwave Rider*   **736**, 1760, 1915, 1965, 3786, 3818, 4821, 5256
*The Skynappers*   2996
*The Squares of the City*   160
*Stand on Zanzibar*   1785, 4296, 4678, 5173, 5193
*The Tides of Time*   178, 188, 4592, 4595
*Times Without Number*   1852, 1854, 2563, 6000
*Timescoop*   1345
*Total Eclipse*   1248, 3221
*The Traveler in Black*   195
*The Web of Everywhere*   3777
*The Whole Man*   5048
*The World Swappers*   379, 5048

**Brush, Karen**
*Demon Pig*   **737**, 846, 1821, 2848, 2850, 2851, 2853, 2855, 5974, 6025
*The Pig, the Prince and the Unicorn*   1821, 2850, 2855

**Brust, Steven**
*Agyar*   660, **738**, 1286, 1355, 1425, 1433, 3954, 3955
*Athyra*   **739**
*Brokedown Palace*   3018
*Cowboy Feng's Space Bar and Grille*   173, 392, **740**, 1454, 2299, 3285, 3299, 4637, 4638, 4639
*Dragon*   **741**
*Five Hundred Years After*   **742**
*Freedom & Necessity*   **743**
*The Gypsy*   **744**, 1249
*Jhereg*   15, 104, 289, 702, 1239, 1240, 1241, 1292, 1529, 1813, 2031, 2042, 2069, 2330, 2362, 2363, 2367, 2451, 2452, 2463, 2620, 2639, 2756, 2757, 2759, 2795, 2798, 3069, 3246, 3273, 3419, 3420, 3422, 3512, 3514, 3894, 4142, 4165, 4166, 4390, 4405, 4488, 4521, 4612, 4613, 4670, 4671, 4673, 4674, 4676, 4794, 4849, 4975, 4994, 5337, 5558, 5813, 5819, 5848, 5978, 5980, 6022, 6073
*Orca*   **745**, 1030
*Phoenix*   **746**, 1072, 1737
*The Phoenix Guards*   **747**, 1702, 1706, 1730, 1734, 1816, 5017, 5458, 5840
*The Sun, the Moon, and the Stars*   42, 375, 1005, 1446, 1479, 2236, 3281, 5981, 6001, 6088, 6090
*Teckla*   5197
*To Reign in Hell*   4670

**Bryant, Dorothy**
*The Kin of Ata Are Waiting for You*   6028

**Bryant, Edward**
*Aqua Sancta*   **748**, 2705, 3388
*Darker Passions*   213
*Fetish*   **749**, 1834, 2938, 4570
*Neon Twilight*   1753, 3237, 3945, 6068
*Particle Theory*   1753

**Bryant, Peter**
*Red Alert*   5023, 5174

**Buchan, John**
*The Far Islands and Tales of Fantasy*   5762
*Witchwood*   **750**

**Buckland, Raymond**
*Cardinal's Sin*   **751**
*The Committee*   397, **752**, 2824

**Budrys, Algis**
*Hard Landing*   **753**, 4196
*L. Ron Hubbard Presents Writers of the Future, Volume II*   4713
*L. Ron Hubbard Presents Writers of the Future, Volume VII*   **754**
*L. Ron Hubbard Presents Writers of the Future, Volume VIII*   **755**
*L. Ron Hubbard Presents Writers of the Future, Volumes I-VIII*   1766, 1767, 5952, 5953
*Michaelmas*   592, 5766
*Rogue Moon*   665, 3435, 3554, 3559, 4954, 4965
*Some Will Not Die*   277, 1903, 2805, 3346, 4209, 4605

**Bujold, Lois McMaster**
*Adventures of Miles Vorkosian*   1540
*Barrayar*   **756**, 1633, 1680, 1756, 1913, 3909, 3911, 3912, 4972, 5041, 5674, 5717
*Borders of Infinity*   173, 260, **757**, 1326, 1332, 1630, 1650, 4288, 4375, 4484, 4984, 5128, 5466
*Brothers in Arms*   311, 1103, 1538, 1544, 1628, 1661, 2435, 3748, 4191, 4225, 4484, 4963, 5131, 5234, 5550, 5718
*Cetaganda*   **758**, 5548
*Dreamweaver's Dilemma*   **759**, 1969, 3430, 5782, 5838
*Ethan of Athos*   4148
*Falling Free*   356, 1589, 2558, 2763, 2766, 3824, 4418, 4419, 4504, 4643, 4963, 5491, 5541, 5809
*Komarr*   **760**, 3861
*Memory*   **761**, 5465, 5544
*Mirror Dance*   **762**, 1003, 1602, 5362, 5672
*Shards of Honor*   1184, 1254, 1331, 1333, 1503, 1542, 1604, 1756, 1913, 2052, 2209, 2350, 2445, 2683, 2766, 2921, 3909, 3912, 3968, 3970, 3976, 4228, 4291, 5669, 5670, 5671, 5673, 5675, 5679
*The Spirit Ring*   726, 727, **763**, 841, 1249, 1450, 1451, 1841, 1953, 2079, 2141, 2195, 2269, 2271, 2499, 2503, 2519, 2653, 2862, 2956, 3080, 3168, 3170, 3256, 3293, 3306, 3508, 3509, 3511, 3844, 3941, 4129, 4323, 4462, 4686, 4718, 4768, 4983, 5144, 5163, 5217, 5222, 5251, 5394, 5555, 5584, 5648, 5716, 5749, 5750, 5813, 5978, 5980
*The Vor Game*   309, 745, **764**, 1543, 1550, 1900, 2212, 4982, 5283, 5298, 5545, 5722
*The Warrior's Apprentice*   231, 260, 310, 986, 988, 1003, 1047, 1261, 1544, 1571, 1599, 1630, 1650, 1652, 1901, 3748, 3974, 4375, 4378, 4974, 5139, 5280, 5283, 5681, 6061
*Women at War*   **765**

**Bulfinch, Thomas**
*Bulfinch's Mythology*   5533

**Bull, Emma**
*Bone Danc: A Fantasy for Technophiles*   **766**

*Bone Dance: A Fantasy for Technophiles* 46, 62, 198, 218, 473, 728, 743, 744, 971, 974, 975, 976, 986, 1425, 1499, 1819, 1849, 1861, 1903, 1936, 3170, 3940, 4117, 4949, 5134, 5179, 5433, 5839
*Double Feature* **767**, 1969, 2947, 5782, 5973
*Falcon* 517, 580, 756, **768**, 985, 1102, 1557, 3450, 3451, 3458, 3748, 3875, 3928, 3929, 4226, 4287
*Finder* 424, 743, **769**, 1148, 1152, 2373, 3294, 3487, 4995, 5409, 5555, 5694, 5818, 5914
*Freedom & Necessity* **743**
*Liavek: Festival Week* **4994**
*The Princess and the Lord of Night* 743
*War for the Oaks* 235, 271, 317, 392, 393, 424, 546, 550, 714, 743, 935, 987, 1040, 1159, 1181, 1321, 1434, 1436, 1471, 1475, 1476, 1478, 1491, 1742, 1747, 1837, 1841, 1947, 1958, 2076, 2077, 2083, 2465, 2521, 2717, 2771, 2942, 3077, 3264, 3274, 3277, 3284, 3285, 3286, 3299, 3302, 3488, 3886, 3887, 3938, 4120, 4149, 4173, 4174, 4317, 4394, 4434, 4658, 4659, 4661, 4675, 4798, 4821, 4868, 4870, 4981, 4989, 4990, 4993, 4995, 4996, 5062, 5096, 5179, 5181, 5642, 5646, 5913, 5914, 5915

**Bulmer, Kenneth**
*The Chariots of Ra* 3777
*The Earth Gods Are Coming* 2810
*No Man's World* 3861

**Bunch, Chris**
*The Demon King* **770**
*Empire's End* **1103**
*The Far Kingdoms* **1104**
*Kingdoms of the Night* **1105**
*The Return of the Emperor* **1106**
*Revenge of the Damned* **1107**
*The Seer King* **771**, 1111, 1154, 4258
*Vortex* **1108**
*The Warrior's Tale* **1110**

**Bunch, David R.**
*Bunch!* **772**
*Moderan* 506

**Bunyan, John**
*The Pilgrim's Progress* 1803

**Burgess, Anthony**
*A Clockwork Orange* 862, 3716
*The Eve of Saint Venus* 2073

**Burgess, Melvin**
*The Earth Giant* 53, **773**

**Burke, John**
*The Devil's Footsteps* 1833, 3272, 4591
*Dracula, Prince of Darkness* 4687
*The Hammer Horror Omnibus* 1022, 4687
*Ladygrove* 438
*The Second Hammer Horror Film Omnibus* 1022

**Burke, Martin R.**
*The Chance Factor* **2109**

**Burkett, William R. Jr.**
*Blood Lines* **774**
*Sleeping Planet* 914

**Burks, Arthur J.**
*Black Medicine* 942, 3515, 4904, 4905, 5149, 5627

**Burleson, Donald**
*Beyond the Lamplight* **775**
*Flute Song* 1296, 4650
*Four Shadowings* **776**
*Lemon Drops and Other Horrors* **777**, 3321, 4891

**Burnell, Mark**
*Freak* 3965
*Glittering Savages* 5183, 5185

**Burns, Cliff**
*The Reality Machine* **778**, 3851, 4231, 5663

**Burrage, A.M.**
*Intruders: New Weird Tales* 2846
*The Occult Files of Francis Chard: Some Ghost Stories* 258, 509
*Some Ghost Stories* 1350, 3633
*Someone in the House: Strange Stories Old and New* 5610
*Someone in the Room: Strange Tales Old and New* **779**, 5611
*Warning Whispers* 454, 455

**Burroughs, Edgar Rice**
*At the Earth's Core* 2257, 3590
*The Eternal Lover* 3877
*The Gods of Mars* 2416
*Pellucidar* 3590, 4705
*Pirates of Venus* 1414
*A Princess of Mars* 1414, 3983
*Synthetic Men of Mars* 1414

**Burroughs, William S.**
*Ghost of Chance* 25, **780**
*Interzone* 778, 4532, 5662, 5663
*Junky* 548
*Naked Lunch* 319, 2859, 3455, 3456
*Nova Express* 3457, 4581

**Burton, Richard F.**
*The Book of the Thousand Nights and a Night: A Plain and Literal Translation of the Arabian Nights Entertainments* 374, 6087

**Bury, Stephen**
*Interface* 352, 413, **781**, 2723, 5009, 5253, 5259, 5355

**Busby, F.M.**
*The Alien Debt* 2437, 4373
*All These Earths* 5781
*Arrow From Earth* **782**, 1602, 2766
*The Breeds of Man* 2870, 3236
*Cage a Man* 2811
*The Demu Trilogy* 1901, 3708, 3738, 5672
*Islands of Tomorrow* **783**
*Rebel's Quest* 2459
*Rebel's Seed* 877
*Rissa Kerguelen* 762, 1003, 1108, 1254, 1571, 1574, 2445, 2459, 3699, 3725, 4484, 5128, 5466, 5821, 5872
*The Singularity Project* **784**
*Slow Freight* **785**, 1594, 1899, 4300, 5042
*Star Rebel* 1900, 5403
*The Triad Worlds* **786**
*Young Rissa* 1071, 3603

**Bush, Anne Kelleher**
*Children of Enchantment* **787**, 1513, 2625
*Daughter of Prophecy* **788**, 5748

**Butler, Jack**
*Nightshade* **789**, 2440, 3244, 3458, 3547, 4072

**Butler, Octavia E.**
*Adulthood Rites* 469, 685, 1255, 1408, 1723, 1726, 1727, 1768, 1871, 2058, 2213, 2287, 2539, 3001, 3047, 3188, 3792, 3999, 4217, 4219, 4242, 5016, 5373, 6074
*Bloodchild and Other Stories* **790**, 3384
*Clay's Ark* 3236
*Dawn* 100, 156, 278, 296, 327, 377, 379, 383, 404, 469, 566, 594, 656, 664, 685, 686, 838, 1054, 1055, 1056, 1116, 1157, 1255, 1362, 1569, 1586, 1587, 1593, 1634, 1723, 1727, 1771, 1924, 1932, 1964, 2008, 2037, 2056, 2058, 2108, 2211, 2213, 2215, 2287, 2419, 2539, 2578, 2603, 2649, 2898, 2953, 2955, 2997, 3000, 3001, 3047, 3063, 3064, 3188, 3238, 3424, 3469, 3476, 3792, 3944, 4000, 4016, 4019, 4042, 4075, 4101, 4122, 4123, 4126, 4217, 4219, 4241, 4290, 4325, 4347, 4479, 4626, 4635, 4756, 4761, 4762, 4853, 4933, 4950, 5016, 5090, 5091, 5092, 5108, 5130, 5157, 5303, 5354, 5363, 5368, 5373, 5431, 5435, 5436, 5461, 5492, 5499, 5515, 5526, 5590, 5591, 5677, 5956, 6048, 6080
*Imago* 469, 685, **791**, 876, 1179, 1255, 1304, 1559, 1723, 1726, 1727, 2058, 2213, 2287, 2539, 3001, 3047, 3188, 3446, 3792, 4001, 4217, 4219, 4242, 4900, 5016, 5373, 5461
*Kindred* 1130, 1835, 2614, 3243, 3874, 5180
*Mind of My Mind* 632, 645, 876, 1502, 2795, 2798, 5430, 5590
*Parable of the Sower* 788, **792**, 1769, 2637, 2771, 3380, 3862, 3864, 4836, 4856, 5965, 6009
*Parable of the Talents* **793**, 1075
*Patternmaster* 4952, 5041, 5510, 5754
*Survivor* 210, 1595, 1914, 2223, 2224, 2542, 3157, 3871, 4116
*Wild Seed* 394, 876, 881, 889, 2771
*Xenogenesis Series* 899
*The Xenogenesis Trilogy* 5609

**Butner, Richard**
*Intersections: The Sycamore Hill Anthology* **3085**

**Buzzati, Dino**
*Catastrophe* 3443, 3461, 3464

**Byatt, A.S.**
*The Djinn in the Nightingale's Eye* **794**, 1358, 6040
*Possession: A Romance* 334, 336, 1276, 1277

**Byers, Richard Lee**
*Dark Fortune* **795**
*Dead Time* **796**
*The Ebon Mask* **797**, 5701, 5702
*Netherworld* **798**, 2321, 2515, 2663, 2664, 4058, 5535
*On a Darkling Plain* 2513, 2515, 2604, 5585
*The Vampire's Apprentice* **799**, 1166, 2337, 2834, 5537

**Byfield, Barbara Ninde**
*Andrew and the Alchemist* 6030

**Byrne, Beverly**
*A Matter of Time* 3039

**Byrne, Eugene**
*Back in the USSA* **4095**

**Byrne, John**
*Fear Book* 2022, 5784
*Whipping Boy* 795, **800**, 1507, 2700, 3668, 4073, 4787

**Byson, Brian**
*Have to Go: Planet R-101* 319


# C

**Cabell, James Branch**
*Jurgen* 3980
*The Silver Stallion* 1699

**Cacek, P.D.**
*The Adventures of Threadwell the Tailor, or Alterations Made While You Wait* **801**
*Leavings* **802**, 2937
*Night Prayers* **803**, 3623

**Cadigan, Pat**
*Dirty Work* **804**
*Fools* 60, 505, **805**, 1449, 1696, 2092, 2163, 2527, 2727, 2839, 2907, 3829, 4071, 4192, 4590, 4747, 4860, 5171, 5184, 5213
*Mindplayers* 60, 79, 419, 505, **806**, 927, 1449, 1519, 1750, 1820, 1873, 1878, 1881, 1935, 1964, 1968, 2545, 2839, 3049, 3075, 3604, 3661, 3711, 3921, 4071, 4099, 4136, 4342, 4704, 5170, 5254, 5376, 5491, 5638, 5828
*Patterns* **807**, 1520, 1615, 1827, 2261, 2715, 3442, 4053, 4118, 4216, 4977, 4998, 5058, 5255, 5257, 5521, 5614, 5837
*The Power and the Passion* 265
*Synners* 294, 295, 386, 419, 483, 548, 766, 781, **808**, 835, 1418, 1449, 1549, 1760, 1878, 1936, 2218, 2219, 2488, 2535, 2721, 2723, 2955, 2998, 3046, 3082, 3311, 3559, 3604, 3661, 3764, 3818, 3850, 3921, 3922, 4099, 4135, 4366, 4677, 4748, 4821, 5134, 5171, 5184, 5213, 5253, 5254, 5256, 5259, 5491, 5619, 5873, 5959
*Tea From an Empty Cup* **809**

**Cadnum, Michael**
*Ghostwright* **810**, 858, 3213, 3691
*Horses of the Night* **811**
*The Judas Glass* **812**, 3396, 4445
*Nightlight* **813**, 2638, 4830, 5402
*St. Peter's Wolf* **816**, 1349, 1822, 4892, 5080, 5146, 5343, 5425, 5481
*Skyscape* 212, **814**, 3812, 4084
*Sleepwalker* **815**

**Cady, Jack**
*Inagehi* **817**, 4221
*The Night We Buried Road Dog* **818**, 819
*The Off Season* 389, 518, 636, **820**, 2029, 2104, 2240, 2687, 2817, 3124, 3809, 4104, 4382, 4383, 4992, 5145, 5440, 5530, 5570

*The Sons of Noah and Other
  Stories* 200, **821**, 5165
*Street* **822**
*The Well* 666, 890, 1776, 3141,
  3953

**Cahill, James**
*Lamps on the Brow* **823**

**Caidin, Martin**
*Beamriders!* **824**
*Cyborg* 5476
*Indiana Jones and the Sky
  Pirates* **825**, 5309
*Indiana Jones and the White
  Witch* **826**
*A Life in the Future* **827**, 1053
*The Messiah Stone* 1092, 4771
*Prison Ship* **828**, 3693, 4017, 4365

**Cain, Robert**
*Cybernarc* **829**, 1406, 3665, 4590,
  4935, 4936, 4938, 4939
*End Game* **830**
*Gold Dragon* **831**, 4590, 4939

**Caine, Geoffrey**
*Curse of the Dead* 5562
*Curse of the Vampire* **832**
*Legion of the Dead* **833**, 5562
*Wake of the Werewolf* **834**, 3376,
  5562

**Caine, Peter**
*Virus* 1164

**Calder, Richard**
*Cytheria* **835**
*Dead Boys* **836**
*Dead Girls* 780, **837**
*Dead Things* **838**

**Calder-Marshall, Arthur**
*The Scarlet Boy* 5519

**Caldon, C. Christopher**
*Concrete Hotel* **839**

**Caldwell, Taylor**
*Your Sins and Mine* 6028

**Callaghan, Mary R.**
*I Met a Man Who Wasn't There* **840**,
  5468

**Callander, Don**
*Aquamancer* **841**, 1469
*Dragon Companion* 726, **842**, 2126,
  2462, 4691
*Dragon Rescue* **843**
*Dragon Tempest* **844**
*Geomancer* **845**
*Marbleheart* **846**
*Pyromancer* **847**, 1035, 3775, 4045,
  4154, 5002

**Callenbach, Ernest**
*Ecotopia: A Novel about Ecology,
  People and Politics in 1999* 4631
*Ecotopia Emerging* 4631

**Calvino, Italo**
*The Castle of Crossed Destinies* 2406,
  4263, 4359
*Cosmicomics* 677, 3443
*Fantastic Tales: Visionary and
  Everyday* **848**
*Invisible Cities* 3443
*Italian Folktales* **849**, 2680
*Numbers in the Dark and Other
  Stories* **850**, 3571
*T Zero* 677
*The Watcher and Other Stories* 3443

**Cameron, Eleanor**
*Beyond Silence* 4917

*The Court of the Stone
  Children* 2614, 2951, 3444, 5559
*The Wonderful Flight to the Mushroom
  Planet* 252, 1217

**Campbell, John W.**
*Who Goes There?* 1197, 3188
*Who Goes There? and Other
  Stories* 5767

**Campbell, Marilyn**
*Just in Time* 3039

**Campbell, Ramsey**
*Alone with the Horrors* **851**, 3462
*Ancient Images* **852**, 917, 1473,
  2241, 2448, 3025, 3103, 4683,
  4734
*Best New Horror* **2961**
*Best New Horror 2* **2962**
*Best New Horror 4* **2963**
*The Claw* 3408, 5085
*Cold Print* 539, 1494, 3532
*The Count of Eleven* **853**, 1489,
  4436
*Dark Companions* 2017, 2866, 5329
*Deathport* **854**, 2311, 5331
*Demons by Daylight* **855**, 3447,
  3461, 3463, 3464
*The Doll Who Ate His Mother* 541,
  1131
*The Face That Must Die* 540, 2110,
  2755, 3088, 3716, 3807, 3902,
  4088, 4185, 4248, 5318, 5327
*Far Away and Never* **856**, 2781,
  2782, 5110, 5471
*Ghosts and Grisly Things* 2018
*The Gruesome Book* 4274, 4282
*The Height of the Scream* 5329
*The Hungry Moon* 3496, 3951,
  3965, 4024, 4531, 4587, 4733,
  4907
*Incarnate* 90, 284, 813, 898, 1380,
  2197, 2530, 2789, 3267, 4841,
  5522, 5816
*The Influence* 280, 282, 666, **857**,
  937, 2201, 2455, 3774, 4023,
  4239
*The Inhabitant of the Lake and Less
  Welcome Tenants* 1495, 1496,
  3266
*The Last Voice They Hear* **858**
*The Long Lost* **859**, 3104, 3668,
  5400
*Medusa* 5420
*Meeting the Author* 966
*Midnight Sun* **860**, 2711, 3310,
  5189, 5350
*The Nameless* 937, 3885, 4254
*Nazareth Hill* **861**
*New Tales of the Cthulhu
  Mythos* 2978, 3531, 4425, 4426,
  4431, 5493, 5494, 5698
*New Terrors* 2307, 5924
*Obsession* 1195, 2339, 2415, 2652,
  4085, 5400
*The One Safe Place* **862**, 4011
*The Parasite* 839, **863**, 4310
*Scared Stiff* 700, 938, 2153, 2180,
  5007, 5360, 5416
*Strange Things and Stranger
  Places* **864**, 3530, 5600
*Superhorror* 2307, 3961
*To Wake the Dead* 524, 1048, 1195,
  1215, 2201, 3040, 3233, 3552,
  3958, 4239, 4340
*Two Obscure Tales* **865**
*Uncanny Banquet* 1306, 2590, 2993,
  4644
*Waking Nightmares* **866**

**Canning, John**
*50 Great Ghost Stories* 2543, 2643

**Cannon, P.H.**
*Pulptime* 1859, 4345, 4751, 5426
*Scream for Jeeves: A Parody* **867**,
  1451, 2826
*Tales of Lovecraftian Horror and
  Humor* **868**
*The Thing in the Bathtub and Other
  Lovecraftian Tales* **869**

**Canter, Mark**
*Ember From the Sun* **870**

**Cantrell, Lisa**
*Boneman* 20, **871**, 2699, 3093, 4498
*The Manse* 4832
*The Ridge* **872**
*Torments* 342, **873**

**Capek, Karel**
*War With the Newts* **874**

**Capes, Bernard**
*The Black Reaper* 455, **875**, 5610

**Capobianco, Michael**
*Alpha Centauri* **378**
*Burster* 378, 380, **876**, 1594, 4626
*Fellow Traveller* **380**
*Iris* **381**
*White Light* **384**

**Capote, Truman**
*In Cold Blood* 1489

**Caraker, Mary**
*The Faces of Ceti* **877**
*Seven Worlds* 4147
*The Snows of Jaspre* **878**, 4147

**Caravela, Jack**
*The Gifted* **879**, 3230, 4480

**Card, C.J.**
*One Wish* **880**, 5658

**Card, Orson Scott**
*The Abyss* 318, 440, 1062, 1201,
  1202, 4915, 5282
*Alvin Journeyman* **881**, 3257, 5504
*The Call of Earth* **882**
*Children of the Mind* **883**
*Dragons of Darkness* 2014, 2413,
  2479, 3728, 4408, 5556, 5710,
  6032
*Dragons of Light* 801, 2014, 2413,
  2479, 3574, 3728, 4408, 5710,
  6032
*Earthborn* **884**
*Earthfall* **885**
*Ender's Game* 250, 414, 469, 478,
  566, 785, 903, 1054, 1168, 1254,
  1381, 1627, 1641, 1680, 1896,
  1987, 2807, 3037, 3398, 3692,
  3726, 3760, 3790, 3937, 4117,
  4290, 4373, 4505, 4762, 4884,
  5955, 6051
*Eye for Eye/The Tunesmith* 3189
*The Folk of the Fringe* 435, **886**,
  1457, 3931, 4152, 4620, 5383
*Future on Fire* **887**
*Future on Ice* **888**
*Heartfire* **889**
*Homebody* **890**, 2241
*Lost Boys* **891**, 1130, 1502, 3007,
  3375, 4170, 4758, 4899
*Lovelock* **892**, 968, 1729
*Maps in a Mirror* 124, 161, 244,
  415, 435, **893**, 1874, 2736, 5028
*The Memory of Earth* **894**, 5000,
  5001, 5033, 5041, 5233, 5546,
  5862

*Pastwatch: The Redemption of
  Christopher Columbus* 298, **895**,
  3083, 4036
*Prentice Alvin* **896**, 2086, 3842,
  5820
*Red Prophet* 394, 2086, 2570, 3580,
  4233, 5580, 5925
*Seventh Son* 162, 191, 389, 394,
  435, 442, 1583, 1746, 2086, 2191,
  2236, 3118, 4433, 4435, 4814,
  4946, 5034, 5333, 5356, 5357,
  5920
*The Ships of Earth* **897**
*Songmaster* 729, 1571, 1583, 3286,
  3453, 4729
*Speaker for the Dead* 230, 1054,
  1183, 2297, 3047, 3713, 3790,
  3823, 4547, 5434
*Treasure Box* **898**, 5522
*The Worthing Saga* 1053, 2422,
  2498, 3854, 4548, 5609
*Wyrms* 1574, 1930, 3717, 5128,
  5157, 5436, 6082
*Xenocide* **899**, 930, 1549, 2343,
  4896

**Cardarelle, Andria**
*To Sleep with Evil* 1137

**Carey, Diane**
*Battlestations!* 7
*Best Destiny* **900**
*Call to Arms* **901**
*First Frontier* **902**, 1225
*First Strike* 9, **903**, 1663, 2297,
  5115
*Ghost Ship* 923, 1384, 2068
*The Search* 2917
*Ship of the Line* **904**
*Starfleet Academy* **905**

**Carl, Lillian Stewart**
*Wings of Power* 3303

**Carlow, Joyce**
*Timeswept* 691, 1271, 2731

**Carnell, John**
*New Writings in SF 1* 4721

**Carney, William**
*Witchcraft* **3885**

**Caron, Mona**
*Harvest Tales and Midnight Revels:
  Stories for the Waning of the
  Year* **3705**

**Carpenter, Leonard**
*Conan of the Red Brotherhood* **906**
*Conan, Scourge of the Bloody
  Coast* **910**
*Conan the Gladiator* **907**, 2983
*Conan the Great* 4293, 4617
*Conan the Outcast* **908**
*Conan the Savage* **909**
*Conan the Warlord* 2347, 2348

**Carr, A.A.**
*Eye Killers* **911**, 3967, 4668

**Carr, Caleb**
*The Alienist* 26

**Carr, John Dickson**
*The Devil in Velvet* 464, 5061

**Carr, John F.**
*CoDominium: Revolt on War
  World* 4373
*Life Among the Asteroids* 4376

**Carr, Terry**
*The Best From Universe* 1618, 5045,
  5046

*The Best Science Fiction Novellas of the Year 1-2* 5045, 5046
*The Best Science Fiction of the Year 1-16* 5045, 5046
*On Our Way to the Future* 1609
*The Science Fiction Hall of Fame, Volume 4* 245, 246, 1618
*Terry Carr's Best Science Fiction and Fantasy of the Year #16* 501
*Universe 1* 4721

**Carrere, Emmanuel**
*Gothic Romance* 498, 659, **912**, 1836, 2642, 4684, 5192, 5271, 5842
*Two by Carrere* **913**

**Carroll, Jerry Jay**
*Inhuman Beings* **914**
*Top Dog* **915**

**Carroll, Jim**
*The Basketball Diaries* 5959

**Carroll, Jonathan**
*After Silence* 345, **916**
*Bones of the Moon* 655, 1089, 1278, 2101, 2105, 2995, 4210
*A Child Across the Sky* 460, 620, 898, **917**, 1085, 1278, 2995, 3541, 4683, 4734
*From the Teeth of Angels* 5, 898, **918**, 2995, 4210, 4579
*The Land of Laughs* 2557, 3441, 4546, 4582, 5167, 5169, 5311, 5358
*Outside the Dog Museum* **919**, 1089
*The Panic Hand* **920**, 1789, 2842, 5166
*Sleeping in Flame* 739, 1278, 4943
*The Voice of Our Shadow* 858

**Carroll, Lewis**
*Alice's Adventures in Wonderland* 4134, 5713
*Through the Looking Glass and What Alice Found There* 3156, 4134, 5713

**Carson, Dave**
*H.P. Lovecraft's Book of Horror* **2968**

**Carter, Angela**
*The Bloody Chamber* 1140, 1142, 3195, 4182
*Burning Your Boats: The Collected Short Stories* 920, **921**, 4181
*The Infernal Desire Machines of Dr. Hoffman* 1818
*The Magic Toyshop* 144, 4183
*Nights at the Circus* 1697, 2091
*The Old Wives' Fairy Tale Book* 3574, 5814

**Carter, Carmen**
*The Children of Hamlin* 1384, 2064
*The Devil's Heart* **922**, 2065, 3920
*Doomsday World* **923**, 2066, 3524
*Dreams of the Raven* 5880

**Carter, Chris**
*The X-Files: Fight the Future* **924**, 5843, 5846

**Carter, Lin**
*The City Outside the World* 2414
*Discoveries in Fantasy* 606, 1576
*Dragons, Elves and Heroes* 2378, 2388, 4906
*The Fishers From Outside* 3555
*Golden Cities, Far* 606
*Great Short Novels of Adult Fantasy 1* 606, 5102
*Great Short Novels of Adult Fantasy 2* 606

*Invisible Death* 1940, 4623, 5307, 5309
*New Worlds for Old* 606
*The Spawn of Cthulhu* 461, 2399, 3535, 4422, 4423, 4425, 4428, 4430, 4431, 5698
*The Volcano Ogre* 4622, 5308
*Weird Tales* 4724, 4726
*The Xothic Legend Cycle* 3556, 3859, 4444
*The Xothic Legend Cycle: The Complete Mythos Fiction of Lin Carter* **925**
*The Year's Best Fantasy Stories Series* 1371, 1374, 1377
*The Young Magicians* 5239

**Carter, Margaret L.**
*Demon Lovers and Strange Seductions* 72, 1357, 1367, 3026, 4465, 5093
*Shadow of the Beast* **926**

**Carter, Raphael**
*The Fortunate Fall* 386, 809, **927**, 1458, 2092, 2394, 3072, 3711, 5248, 5355, 5619, 5966, 6063, 6079

**Carter, Tonya R.**
*Firstborn* **5454**
*The Qualinesti* **5455**

**Cartmill, Cleve**
*Hell Hath Fury* 4006
*Prelude to Armageddon* 2889, 3676

**Carver, Jeffrey A.**
*Down the Stream of Stars* **928**, 3710, 3725, 3726, 3821, 5208, 5215, 5573, 6085
*Dragon Rigger* **929**, 2060, 2163
*Dragons in the Stars* 220, **930**, 1083, 1337, 2059, 2163, 2832, 3722, 4896, 5575
*From a Changeling Star* 785, **931**, 1458, 1964, 3075, 3764, 4114, 4756, 5201, 5245, 5638, 5680, 5905
*The Infinite Sea* **932**
*Neptune Crossing* **933**, 1183, 3762, 6086
*The Rapture Effect* 806, 808, 1537, 1549, 1805, 2579, 3398, 3661, 4188, 4219, 4483, 4857, 5566, 5592
*Strange Attractors* **934**

**Case, David**
*The Cell* 5442
*The Third Grave* 616, 815

**Caspian, Jonatha Adriane**
*The Nightmare Dream* 5438

**Cassada, Jackie**
*Shadows on the Hill* **935**, 5701, 5702

**Cassedy, Sylvia**
*Behind the Attic Wall* 2438

**Casserly, Gordon**
*Tiger Girl* 3145

**Cassutt, Michael**
*Dragon Season* **936**, 2142, 2463, 2722, 5714
*Sacred Visions* **2343**

**Castle, Mort**
*Cursed Be the Child* **937**

**Castro, Adam-Troy**
*Lost in Booth Nine* 213, **938**, 5412

**Causey, Michael**
*Uwharrie* **4309**

**Cave, Hugh B.**
*Bitter/Sweet* **939**
*Death Stalks the Night* **940**, 3571, 5628
*Disciples of Dread* 20, 21, 871, **941**, 2699, 2744, 3594, 3605, 5692
*The Door Below* 534, **942**
*The Evil* 1125
*Legion of the Dead* 4498, 5155
*The Lower Deep* 1298, 5692
*Lucifer's Eye* **943**
*Murgunstrumm and Others* 537, 1088, 1700, 2780, 2844, 3515, 3516, 5149, 5628
*Shades of Evil* 1403

**Cavelos, Jeanne**
*The Shadow Within* **944**, 1387, 1654, 3096, 4833

**Cecilione, Michael**
*Deathscape* **945**
*Domination* 803, **946**, 1890, 2151, 2288, 5800
*The Parliament of Blood* 5405, 5407
*Soul Snatchers* **947**
*Thirst* **948**, 2151

**Cerasini, Marc**
*Godzilla 2000* **949**

**Cercone, Karen Rose**
*Armageddon Sky* **2296**

**Cerda, Martha**
*Senora Rodriguez and Other Worlds* 52, **950**, 6009

**Cerf, Bennett**
*Famous Ghost Stories* 1309

**Chadbourn, Mark**
*The Eternal* 3215

**Chalker, Jack L.**
*And the Devil Will Drag You Under* 3483, 3488, 3848
*The Birth of Flux and Anchor* 5647
*The Cybernetic Walrus* 110, **951**, 2470, 4898
*Dance Band on the Titanic* 5114
*The Demons at Rainbow Bridge* **952**, 1046, 1719
*Demons of the Dancing Gods* 169, 652
*Downtiming the Night Side* 895, 1852, 2012, 2208
*Echoes of the Well of Souls* **953**
*The Four Lords of the Diamond Series* 5544, 5545
*Gods of the Well of Souls* **954**
*Horrors of the Dancing Gods* 185, **955**
*The Hot-Wired Dodo* **956**
*The Identity Matrix* 4470
*The Labyrinth of Dreams* 5830
*The March Hare Network* **957**, 5353
*The Messiah Choice* 637
*Midnight at the Well of Souls* 1876, 5130
*The Ninety Trillion Fausts* **958**
*Pirates of the Thunder* 4594
*The Red Tape War* 553, **959**, 1459, 1752, 3435
*The River of Dancing Gods* 194, 630, 635, 1267, 1419, 1809, 1812, 2235, 5224, 5500, 5645
*The Run to Chaos Keep* **960**, 1871
*Shadow of the Well of Souls* **961**
*Songs of the Dancing Gods* 197, **962**, 5218
*Vengeance of the Dancing Gods* 4055, 5197

*War of Shadows* 66
*Warriors of the Storm* 3861
*When the Changewinds Blow* 165, 171, 2235, 4269

**Chambers, Robert W.**
*The King in Yellow* 485, **963**, 1252, 2225
*Out of the Dark: Origins* **964**

**Chandler, A. Bertram**
*The Alternate Martians* 3983
*The Big Black Mark* 1899, 1900
*Frontier of the Dark* 1248
*Gateway to Never* 3125
*Kelly Country* 2563
*The Road to the Rim* 5403
*Space Mercenaries* 3747
*The Wild Ones* 2575, 5549

**Chant, Joy**
*The Grey Mane of Morning* 1025, 3068, 3404, 4156
*Red Moon and Black Mountain* 1447, 1809, 3069, 3383, 3436, 4163, 5984

**Chapman, Vera**
*The Green Knight* 273, 1269
*King Arthur's Daughter* 1857
*The King's Damosel* 4877
*The Notorious Abbess* **965**

**Chappell, Fred**
*Dagon* 3533, 3548, 3566, 5167
*I Am One of You Forever* 817
*The Lodger* 868, 869, **966**, 1424, 2826, 5168
*More Shapes than One* 818, 821, 868, 869, 939, **967**, 2842, 3327, 3575, 4184, 5166, 5417

**Charles, Robert**
*Flowers of Evil* 1625, 5081, 5858
*The Scream of the Dove* 5086

**Charnas, Suzy McKee**
*The Bronze King* 550
*Dorothea Dreams* 4943
*The Furies* **968**, 4627
*The Golden Thread* 605, **969**, 2272, 2623, 4387, 5977, 5995
*The Kingdom of Kevin Malone* 549, **970**, 2879, 6017
*Merlin's King* 5070
*Motherlines* 208, 1590, 2242, 3863, 4792, 5268
*The Ruby Tear* 660
*The Vampire Tapestry* 738, 1124, 1286, 1426, 2267, 3458, 3915, 4574, 4665
*Walk to the End of the World* 208, 1590, 2242, 3863, 4792, 5268, 5477, 5590

**Charnee, David**
*Sensei* 4742

**Charrette, Robert N.**
*Choose Your Enemies Carefully* 566, **971**, 1591, 1935, 3245, 4304, 5135, 5731
*Find Your Own Truth* **972**, 1591, 1935, 3245, 4304, 5135, 5731
*Just Compensation* 5207
*A King Beneath the Mountain* **973**
*A Knight Among Knaves* **974**
*Never Deal with a Dragon* 726, **975**, 1591, 1935, 2077, 2463, 3245, 3641, 4191, 4304, 4363, 4513, 4821, 4909, 5135, 5731
*Never Trust an Elf* 172, **976**, 1591, 1977, 3245, 5135, 5731

*A Prince Among Men* **977**, 2619, 4771, 5203
*Timespell* **978**
*Wizard of Bones* **979**
*Wolf Pack* 5469
*Wolves on the Border* 1938

**Chase, Carol**
*Hawk's Flight* 313, **980**, 1029, 3766, 3904

**Chase, Robert**
*The Game of Fox and Lion* 2212

**Chaucer, Geoffrey**
*The Canterbury Tales* 1045

**Chayefsky, Paddy**
*Altered States* 364, 571, 2702, 2918, 3101, 4979, 5520

**Chelsea, Jane**
*Winter Harvest* 3377

**Cherryh, C.J.**
*Angel with the Sword* 12, 176, 289, 631, 894, 2236, 2361, 3580, 3643, 3646, 4043, 5033, 5038, 5596, 5760, 5862
*Brothers of the Earth* 6051
*Chanur's Homecoming* 1997, 2099, 3307, 4137, 5141
*Chanur's Legacy* **981**, 1988, 4855, 4967, 5363
*Chanur's Venture* 2099, 4350, 5985
*Chernevog* **982**, 3281, 4699, 5741
*Cloud's Rider* **983**, 2289
*Cuckoo's Egg* 1595, 2194, 2416, 5548
*Cyteen* 326, 566, 567, 928, 931, **984**, 1538, 1554, 1574, 1606, 1865, 2050, 2051, 2065, 2171, 2248, 2389, 2466, 3000, 3236, 3248, 3735, 3994, 4559, 4560, 4898, 4933, 4955, 5354, 5434, 5525, 5572, 5637, 5732, 5917, 5920, 5921, 5922
*A Dirge for Stabis* 256, 314, 2570
*Downbelow Station* 10, 923, **985**, 1226, 1861, 1865, 2296, 2351, 2464, 2466, 3014, 4016, 5833, 5922
*The Dreamstone* 393, 4265
*Endgame* **986**, 1388
*Exile's Gate* 922, 1631, 2359, 2436, 3777
*The Faded Sun: Kesrith* 513, 517, 631, 1067, 1381, 1771, 2038, 2194, 2224, 3316, 3839, 4550, 5019, 5469
*The Faded Sun: Kutath* 1923, 2194
*The Faded Sun: Shon'Jir* 1774, 2194
*Faery in Shadow* **987**, 3636, 4674
*Festival Moon* 647, 3643, 3646, 5038
*Finity's End* **988**, 1978, 4910
*The Fires of Azeroth* 1581, 2436, 4152, 4520, 5741, 5951
*Flood Tide* **989**
*Foreigner* 684, 688, 786, 932, **990**, 1259, 1303, 1500, 1589, 1825, 1956, 2922, 3000, 3732, 3750, 3760, 3972, 4138, 4241, 4356, 4711, 4735, 4736, 4932, 5461, 5757
*Fortress in the Eye of Time* **991**, 1065, 3506, 4259, 4714, 5200
*Fortress of Eagles* **992**
*Fortress of Owls* **993**

*Forty Thousand in Gehenna* 35, 565, 756, 785, 894, 1184, 1323, 1537, 1956, 1986, 2049, 2135, 2421, 3713, 3719, 3723, 3727, 3911, 4038, 4244, 5351, 5404, 5457, 6081
*Gate of Ivrel* 644, 1025, 1173, 1178, 1660, 3477, 3634, 3635, 3920, 3940, 3969, 4109, 4163, 5683, 5951, 6001
*The Goblin Mirror* 955, **994**, 4727, 5251
*Heavy Time* 761, **995**, 1862, 3994
*Hellburner* 584, 905, **996**, 2298, 2832, 3315, 4927
*Hestia* 5880
*Hunter of Worlds* 3800
*Inheritor* **997**
*Invader* **998**, 4128, 4241, 5760
*The Kif Strike Back* 2099, 5833, 5985
*Lois & Clark* **999**
*Merchanter's Luck* 1891, 1893, 2476, 3830, 4593, 5833
*The Paladin* 11, 1815, 2095, 2188, 3934, 3973, 4167, 5220
*Port Eternity* 1386
*The Pride of Chanur* 1041, 1043, 1333, 1384, 1543, 1645, 1647, 1895, 2016, 2099, 2108, 2733, 3125, 3307, 3536, 3735, 4122, 4139, 4143, 4157, 4347, 4657, 5141, 5833, 5917, 5922, 5985
*Reap the Whirlwind* 3982
*Rider at the Gate* **1000**, 1703, 2289, 2420
*Rimrunners* 768, 901, **1001**, 1265, 1719, 2064, 2435, 3748, 4148, 4194, 5188, 5246, 5833
*Rusalka* 18, 194, 393, **1002**, 1176, 1592, 3098, 3281, 3776, 4013, 4776, 4781, 5733, 5983
*Serpent's Reach* 1069, 1116, 1389, 2058, 3752, 3909, 3910, 3911, 3919, 4081, 4140, 4698, 4894, 5574, 5788, 5949
*Sunfall* 2533
*The Tree of Swords and Jewels* 17, 459, 2097, 2098, 3841, 4146, 5832
*Tripoint* **1003**, 1899, 3974, 5298
*Voyager in Night* 133, 512, 2207, 2811
*Wave Without a Shore* 951, 4592
*Well of Shiuan* 257, 1174, 4153, 5733, 5951
*Wizard Spawn* 11, 256, **1004**, 2674, 5739, 5742
*Yvgenie* **1005**, 3281

**Chesbro, George C.**
*Bone* 822, **1006**, 1779, 3202, 3319, 4787
*The Fear in Yesterday's Rings* **1007**, 1570, 2138, 5552

**Chester, Deborah**
*Beyond the Void* **1331**
*Destination: Mutiny* **1332**
*Realm of Light* **1008**
*Reign of Shadows* 702, 770, **1009**, 3123, 5964
*The Salukan Gambit* **1333**
*Shadow War* **1010**

**Chesterton, G.K.**
*The Man Who Was Thursday* 1564

**Chetwin, Grace**
*Collidescope* 221, **1011**, 5088
*The Crystal Stair* 3043

*Friends in Time* **1012**
*Gom on Windy Mountain* 329, 3043, 5142, 6030
*Out of the Dark World* 1319, 1320
*The Riddle and the Rune* 3043, 6030

**Chetwynd-Hayes, R.**
*Gaslight Tales of Terror* 1233
*Tales From the Shadows* 939
*The Vampire Stories of R. Chetwynd-Hayes* **1013**, 3549

**Chiba, Milan**
*Noonblaze* 1916

**Child, Lincoln**
*Mount Dragon* 99, **4413**
*Relic* **4414**
*Reliquary* **4415**

**Chilson, Rob**
*Black as Blood* **1014**, 1396
*Men Like Rats* **1015**, 2193, 2954, 5878
*The Shores of Kansas* 4039

**Chizmar, Richard**
*Monsters and Other Stories* **1016**

**Chizmar, Richard T.**
*The Best of Cemetery Dance* 22, **1017**
*Blood Brothers* 2157
*Chillers* **1018**, 4314
*Cold Blood* 538, 544, **1019**, 2278, 2280, 2600, 3598
*Cold Chills* 3324
*The Earth Strikes Back* **1020**
*Midnight Promises* 663, **1021**, 1789, 2155, 2701, 2714, 5026
*Screamplays* **1022**

**Cholfin, Bryan**
*The Best of Crank!* **1023**

**Chown, Marcus**
*Double Planet* **2433**

**Christensen, James C.**
*Voyage of the Basset* 68, 385, **1024**, 2654, 2719

**Christian, Deborah**
*Kar Kalim* **1025**
*Mainline* 357, **1026**, 1694, 3186, 5531

**Christopher, John**
*Beyond the Burning Lands* 658
*The City of Gold and Lead* 221
*The Death of Grass* 4279
*Empty World* 1133
*Fireball* 2647
*The Little People* 2107
*The Long Winter* 511, 3429
*New Found Land* 1655
*No Blade of Grass* 4262
*Pendulum* 1141
*The Pool of Fire* 221
*The Possessors* 609, 2302, 3141, 4369, 5643
*The Prince in Waiting* 4919, 5508
*The Sword of the Spirits* 3255
*The Tripods Trilogy* 5870
*When the Tripods Came* 5027
*The White Mountains* 221, 1781, 4919
*Wild Jack* 511

**Chupp, Sam**
*Sins of the Fathers* 797, 2604, 5585

**Churchman, Deborah**
*Cross a Dark Bridge* **1027**, 4344, 5808

**Ciencin, Scott**
*Ancient Games* **1028**
*Godzilla Invades America* 949
*Godzilla: King of the Monsters* 949
*The Lotus and the Rose* **1029**
*Night of Glory* **1030**
*The Night Parade* 1289, 1290, 3538, 4800
*Parliament of Blood* **1031**, 4666, 5852
*The Vampire Odyssey* **1032**, 2336, 2748, 4190, 4576, 4667, 5693, 5705, 5852
*The Ways of Magic* **1033**, 1082
*The Wildlings* **1034**, 5852
*Windchaser* 2003, 2469
*The Wolves of Autumn* 846, **1035**

**Citro, Joseph A.**
*Dark Twilight* **1036**, 2285, 3778
*Deus-X: A Novel of Spiritual Terror* **1037**, 1296
*Shadow Child* **1038**
*The Unseen* **1039**, 2200, 2936, 3056, 3160, 5112

**Claremont, Chris**
*Dragon Moon* **1040**, 4487
*First Flight* 2256, 3307
*Grounded!* **1041**, 3029
*Shadow Dawn* **1042**
*Shadow Moon* **3540**
*Sundowner* **1043**

**Clark, Douglas W.**
*Alchemy Unlimited* 174, 4397
*Rehearsal for a Renaissance* **1045**, 3409
*Whirlwind Alchemy* 706, 845, 2079

**Clark, Jan**
*Earth Herald* **1046**
*Prodigy* **1047**, 5669

**Clark, Leigh**
*Blood Sabbath* 1032, **1048**, 1215, 1354, 3233, 5100
*Carnivore* **1049**
*Evil Reincarnate* 690, **1050**, 4710, 4753
*The Feeding* 1038, **1051**, 1295, 2203, 3369
*Shock Radio* **1052**

**Clark, Simon**
*The Derelict of Death* 2709

**Clarke, Arthur C.**
*2001: A Space Odyssey* 381, 512, 4857, 4954, 4965
*2010: Odyssey Two* 381, 512, 4954, 4965
*2061: Odyssey Three* 381, 512, 4950, 4954, 4965
*3001: The Final Odyssey* **1053**
*Beyond the Fall of Night* **1054**
*Childhood's End* 156, 202, 402, 594, 3238, 3521, 3792, 4016, 4506, 4642, 5636, 5660, 5860, 5909
*The City and the Stars* 445, 4065
*Cradle* 3398
*The Deep Range* 318, 2838
*Dolphin Island* 318, 3341, 3729, 4948
*Earthlight* 1916
*A Fall of Moondust* 2881, 2882, 5597
*The Garden of Rama* **1055**, 2419, 2807, 3398, 5244
*The Ghost From the Grand Banks* **1056**
*The Hammer of God* 83, **1057**
*Imperial Earth* 3924

*Islands in the Sky* 2647, 3199
*A Meeting with Medusa/Green
    Mars* 3189
*More than One Universe* 2547
*The Nine Billion Names of God* 4956
*Rama II* 247, **1058**, 2165, 2216,
    3398, 4421
*Rama Revealed* **1059**, 3398
*Rendezvous with Rama* 380, 381,
    417, 2067, 2165, 2216, 2433,
    3398, 4280, 4417, 4967
*Richter 10* **1060**, 1962, 4420
*The Sands of Mars* 421, 586, 2881,
    5187, 5377, 5561
*The Songs of Distant Earth* 351,
    1182, 2006, 3924, 4548, 5804
*Tales From Planet Earth* 234, 443,
    **1061**
*Tales From the White Hart* 115,
    2299, 4637, 4639

**Clarke, J. Brian**
*The Expediter* **1062**, 4219

**Clarke, Lindsay**
*The Chymical Wedding* 84, **1063**,
    1397, 1746

**Clarke, Pauline**
*The Return of the Twelves* 331, 332,
    430, 1132, 3587, 5654, 5655,
    5656

**Clavell, James**
*Shogun* 4673, 4742

**Clayton, Jo**
*Dancer's Rise* 641, **1064**, 5127
*Diadem from the Stars* 1439, 3973
*Drinker of Souls* 982, 1002
*Drum Calls* **1065**
*Drum Warning* 1033, **1066**
*Fire in the Sky* **1067**
*The Magic Wars* **1068**
*Shadowkill* **1069**
*Shadowplay* **1070**
*Shadowspeer* **1071**
*Wild Magic* 4, 604, 673, **1072**,
    1114, 3486, 3766
*Wildfire* 673, **1073**, 3766, 4674

**Clee, Mona**
*Branch Point* 357, **1074**, 2614,
    3467, 4039, 5067, 5315
*Overshoot* 793, **1075**, 3761

**Clegg, Douglas**
*Bad Karma* 2548
*Breeder* **1076**, 1465
*The Children's Hour* **1077**
*Dark of the Eye* 571, **1078**, 1843,
    1971, 4012, 5850
*Eye of the Needle* 97
*Goat Dance* 137, 859, 860, **1079**,
    1931, 2285, 2557, 2749, 2929,
    3129, 3137, 3615, 3778, 4754,
    4907, 5077, 5112, 5398, 5472,
    5769, 5771, 5961
*The Halloween Man* **1080**, 5026
*Never Land* **1081**, 3310

**Clemens, James**
*Wit'ch Fire* **1082**

**Clement, Hal**
*Cycle of Fire* 377, 434
*Fossil* 251, **1083**, 1729, 3734
*Mission of Gravity* 401, 1956, 1986,
    1988, 5597
*Needle* 621, 2542, 4017
*Still River* 133

**Clements, Mark A.**
*Children of the End* **1084**, 2779,
    3204

*The Land of Nod* 898, **1085**
*Lorelei* **1086**, 4224

**Clifton, Mark**
*When They Come From Space* 5766

**Climo, Shirley**
*T.J.'s Ghost* **1087**

**Cline, Leonard**
*The Dark Chamber* 2702
*The Lady of the Frozen Death and
    Other Weird Tales* **1088**

**Clough, Brenda W.**
*How Like a God* 362, **1089**
*An Impossumble Summer* **1090**

**Clowes, Carolyn**
*The Pandora Principle* 7, 905, **1389**,
    4514

**Clute, John**
*Interzone: The 1st Anthology* 4439
*Interzone: The 2nd Anthology* 4439
*Interzone: The 3rd Anthology* 4439
*Interzone: The 4th Anthology* 4439

**Cochran, Molly**
*The Broken Sword* **1091**
*The Forever King* 973, 977, **1092**,
    4771
*World Without End* **1093**

**Codrescu, Andrei**
*Blood Countess* 279, **1094**, 4529

**Coe, David B.**
*Children of Amarid* **1095**
*The Outlanders* **1096**

**Coffin, M.T.**
*Blood Red Eightball* 5291
*Pet Store* **1097**

**Cohen, Barney**
*Blood on the Moon* 584, 588, 4121,
    4470
*The Taking of Satcon Station* 1665,
    4469, 5032

**Cohen, Jon**
*Max Lakeman and the Beautiful
    Stranger* 433, **1098**

**Cohen, Stephen Paul**
*Night Launch* 2143

**Colchie, Thomas**
*A Hammock Beneath the
    Mangoes* **1099**

**Cole, Adrian**
*The Gods in Anger* **1100**
*Mother of Storms* 563, **1101**, 3268,
    5456, 5575, 5582
*A Place Among the Fallen* 1155,
    1927, 2885
*Warlord of Heaven* **1102**

**Cole, Allan**
*Empire's End* **1103**, 1598
*The Far Kingdoms* **1104**, 1251,
    1912, 3353, 4744
*Kingdoms of the Night* **1105**
*The Return of the Emperor* **1106**,
    1332
*Revenge of the Damned* **1107**, 1551,
    4288
*Sten* 63, 309, 312, 771, 1254, 1331,
    1333, 1535, 1550, 1573, 1575,
    1604, 2364, 2366, 4375, 4939,
    5138, 6014, 6052, 6054
*Vortex* **1108**
*The Warrior Returns* **1109**
*The Warrior's Tale* **1110**
*Wolves of the Gods* **1111**

**Cole, Alonzo Dean**
*The Witch's Tale* **1112**

**Cole, Burt**
*The Quick* 66, **1113**

**Cole, Damaris**
*Token of Dragonsblood* **1114**, 1937,
    3404

**Coleman, Wim**
*Terminal Games* 4283

**Collignon, Jeff**
*Her Monster* 729, **1115**, 5826

**Collins, Helen**
*Mutagenesis* 134, 210, **1116**, 1247,
    1586, 1769, 2681, 2820, 3236,
    3426, 4119, 4476, 5090, 5231,
    5430, 5492

**Collins, Nancy A.**
*Angels on Fire* **1117**
*Dark Love* **1118**, 1367, 2176, 2177,
    2178, 2179, 2182, 2185, 2893
*A Dozen Black Roses* 387, **1119**,
    1949, 1950, 2258, 2512, 2514,
    2518, 2664, 5703
*Forbidden Acts* **1120**, 3024
*In the Blood* **1121**, 1286
*Midnight Blue: The Sonja Blue
    Collection* **1122**
*Nameless Sins* **1123**, 3100, 3327,
    3328, 3329, 3673, 5339
*Sunglasses After Dark* 490, 600, 697,
    799, 948, 1124, 1707, 1882, 2151,
    2336, 2449, 2510, 3405, 3407,
    3564, 4464, 4513, 5419
*Tempter* 697, **1125**, 1465, 1888,
    2147, 2494, 2896, 3950, 4307,
    4464, 5160
*The Tortuga Hill Gang's Last
    Ride* 4251
*Walking Wolf* **1126**, 3119, 4052,
    4251, 4256
*Wild Blood* 679, 680, 926, **1127**,
    1800, 2520, 3564, 4472

**Collins, Paul**
*Metaworlds* 4439

**Colombo, John Robert**
*Other Canadas* 2593

**Colson, S. Darnbrook**
*People of the Night* 94, **1128**, 2137,
    2655, 2656, 2769, 2860, 3667,
    4789, 5335, 5416
*Snakes* 1467

**Compton, D.G.**
*Chronocules* 160
*Farewell, Earth's Bliss* 421, 586,
    5377

**Concannon, Diana M.**
*Helen's Passage* **1129**

**Conde, Maryse**
*I, Tituba, Black Witch of Salem* **1130**,
    1835

**Conde, Nicholas**
*In the Deep Woods* **1131**, 4664,
    5123
*The Religion* 20, 21, 1076, 1298,
    1403, 1851, 2150, 2744, 3605

**Condon, Richard**
*The Manchurian Candidate* 5664

**Coney, Michael Greatrex**
*King of the Scepter'd Isle* 5428

**Conford, Ellen**
*Genie with the Light Blue Hair* 5182

**Congdon, Don**
*Tales of Love and Horror* 75, 1357,
    3026, 4465

**Conklin, Groff**
*12 Great Classics of Science
    Fiction* 240, 1614
*17 X Infinity* 242
*Another Part of the Galaxy* 241,
    1614
*The Best of Science Fiction* 24, 214,
    238, 239, 1621, 3648, 4127, 4725,
    5004, 5238, 5948
*Giants Unleashed* 241, 1614
*Great Science Fiction about
    Doctors* 5604, 5886
*Great Stories of Space Travel* 243
*Invaders of Earth* 4406
*Science Fiction Adventures in
    Dimension* 241
*Science Fiction Oddities* 240
*The Science Fiction Omnibus* 240,
    1061
*Science Fiction Terror Tales* 5691
*A Treasury of Science Fiction* 1061

**Conly, Jane Leslie**
*R-T, Margaret, and the Rats of
    NIMH* **1132**

**Conner, Michael**
*Archangel* **1133**, 3244, 3977, 4748,
    5172

**Conner, Miguel**
*The Queen of Darkness* **1134**

**Conners, Aaron**
*The Pandora Directive: A Tex Murphy
    Novel* 4495

**Connolly, Flynn**
*The Rising of the Moon* **1135**, 3622,
    5276

**Connor, John David**
*Contagion* **1136**, 3577, 4786

**Connors, William W.**
*Shadowborn* **1137**

**Conrad, Joseph**
*Heart of Darkness* 4979

**Conrad, Pam**
*Stonewords: A Ghost Story* 122,
    1012, **1138**, 1272, 2283, 4078

**Conroy, Robert**
*1901* **1139**, 5501

**Constantine, Storm**
*Bewitchments of Love and Hate* **1140**,
    2295
*Burying the Shadow* 738
*The Enchantments of Flesh and
    Spirit* **1141**, 2295, 3405, 3742
*The Fulfillments of Fate and
    Desire* **1142**
*Wraeththu* 551, 4849, 4851, 5931

**Contreras, Ernie**
*The Pagemaster* 3156

**Conway, D.J.**
*The Dream Warrior* 2639
*Soothslayer: A Magickal
    Fantasy* **1143**

**Cook, David**
*Beyond the Moons* 1114, **1144**,
    1291, 1937, 2618, 2785, 2985,
    4909
*Horselords* 657, **1145**, 3537, 4108,
    4807
*King Pinch* **1146**, 4808

Author Index

## Cook, Glen
*Bitter Gold Hearts* 2629
*The Black Company* 15, 28, 164, 290, 739, 745, 771, 991, 992, 1009, 1010, 1102, 1110, 1156, 1173, 1178, 1239, 1240, 1682, 1688, 1690, 1733, 1816, 1908, 1927, 1928, 1979, 2031, 2190, 2191, 2367, 2884, 2984, 2985, 2988, 2990, 3171, 3227, 3246, 3273, 3540, 3653, 3833, 3834, 3837, 3930, 4201, 4526, 4674, 4693, 4694, 4730, 4777, 4945, 5017, 5203, 5206, 5509, 5599, 5682, 5683, 5737, 6002, 6003
*Bleak Seasons* **1147**, 5197
*Deadly Quicksilver Lies* **1148**, 5061, 5459
*The Dragon Never Sleeps* 35, 81, 209, 309, 310, 311, 322, 328, 471, 472, 473, 478, 734, 883, 1103, 1183, 1184, 1573, 1575, 1598, 1633, 1645, 1664, 1995, 2364, 2365, 2374, 2417, 2418, 2419, 2464, 2466, 2523, 2812, 3448, 3710, 3722, 3749, 3821, 3823, 3825, 4288, 4354, 4375, 4483, 4505, 4553, 4626, 4760, 4859, 4896, 4951, 4984, 5116, 5138, 5139, 5140, 5260, 5365, 5543, 5573, 5637, 5668, 5679, 5680, 5718, 5834, 5835, 6079, 6081, 6085
*Dread Brass Shadows* **1149**, 2125, 2228, 4673
*Dreams of Steel* **1150**
*The Fire in His Hands* 3016, 3154
*The Heirs of Babylon* 3586
*A Matter of Time* 442, 4477
*Old Tin Sorrows* **1151**, 2228
*Pretty Pewter Gods* **1152**, 5848
*Red Iron Nights* **1153**, 1250, 4709
*A Shadow of All Night Falling* 1176, 1640, 2989, 3175, 4258
*Shadows Linger* 2990, 3833
*She Is the Darkness* **1154**
*Sweet Silver Blues* 1665, 1935, 2226, 2228, 2363, 2369, 2370, 2375, 2376, 2620, 2628, 2756, 2757, 2759, 3441, 3512, 3514, 4166, 4362, 4673, 5232, 6022
*The Swordbearer* 978, 979, 1636, 1790, 1902, 2356, 2886, 3122, 3385, 3652, 3982, 4165, 4294, 4457, 4766, 4777, 4975, 5458
*Tower of Fear* 605, 1111, **1155**, 1528, 1866, 3893, 3894, 3925, 3942, 4015, 4493, 4533
*The White Rose* 2990, 3833

## Cook, Hugh
*Lords of the Sword* **1156**
*The Women and the Warlords* 3339

## Cook, Paul
*Fortress on the Sun* **1157**

## Cook, Rick
*Limbo System* 828, **1158**, 1325, 4017, 5564, 5932
*Mall Purchase Night* **1159**, 3198, 3485
*The Wiz Biz* **1160**, 1703
*The Wizardry Compiled* 1858
*The Wizardry Consulted* **1161**
*The Wizardry Cursed* **1162**, 1461
*The Wizardry Quested* **1163**
*Wizard's Bane* 1419, 2264, 2622, 5063

## Cook, Robin
*Coma* 93, 1561, 1832, 1939, 2206, 2867, 3996, 4874, 5897
*Godplayer* 581, 1832
*Harmful Intent* **1164**, 3200
*Mutation* **1165**
*Outbreak* 2720

## Cooke, Catherine
*Mask of the Wizard* 2471, 4523, 4806

## Cooke, John Peyton
*Out for Blood* 600, 799, **1166**, 1541, 1707, 1920, 2116, 2337, 3853, 5537

## Cool, Tom
*Infectress* 378, **1167**, 1348, 3761, 4703, 6047
*Secret Realms* **1168**

## Coon, Susan
*Rahne* 2811

## Cooney, Caroline B.
*The Terrorist* 5285

## Cooney, Eleanor
*Shangri-La: The Return to the World of Lost Horizon* **1169**

## Cooper, Dennis
*Frisk* 695, **1170**, 2162, 2448, 3312, 4185, 4734, 4737
*Wrong* **1171**

## Cooper, Edmund
*All Fool's Day* 6028
*The Cloud Walker* 4152, 4602, 4619, 5383
*A Far Sunset* 5496
*The Last Continent* 4628
*The Overman Culture* 5890
*Prisoner of Fire* 583
*Seahorse in the Sky* 160, 2828, 3800, 5303
*The Seed of Light* 297
*Transit* 2996

## Cooper, Louise
*Aisling* **1172**
*Avatar* **1173**
*The Avenger* 1068, **1174**
*The Book of Paradox* 4926
*The Deceiver* 1072, **1175**, 2521
*Infanta* **1176**
*Nemesis* 1069, **1177**, 1739, 2862, 3227, 3973
*The Pretender* 604, 1072
*Revenant* **1178**
*The Sleep of Stone* **1179**, 2636, 3159, 3410, 3545, 4615, 4985, 5177, 5336, 5394, 5556, 5827, 6017, 6042
*Star Ascendant* **1180**
*Troika* **1181**

## Cooper, Richard
*The Road to Corlay* 1852

## Cooper, Susan
*The Dark Is Rising* 371, 1033, 1330, 1447, 1668, 3078
*Greenwitch* 371
*The Grey King* 371, 1330
*Over Sea, under Stone* 977, 1601, 2232, 3436, 3720, 4322, 4771, 6036
*Silver on the Tree* 172, 196

## Cooper, Susan Rogers
*Other People's Houses* 1829

## Coppel, Alfred
*Glory* **1182**, 5298, 5549

*Glory's People* **1183**
*Glory's War* **1184**, 2476, 3970, 5403

## Copper, Basil
*The Black Death* 690, **1185**, 3571
*The Great White Space* 1497, 2711, 5350, 5482
*The House of the Wolf* 5158

## Copper, Edmund
*The Amber Print* 852
*From Evil's Pillow* 852

## Copper, Merian C.
*King Kong* 5474

## Copperfield, David
*David Copperfield's Beyond Imagination* 1186
*David Copperfield's Tales of the Impossible* 410, **1187**

## Corelli, Marie
*The Sorrows of Satan* 4571

## Corman, Avery
*Oh God!* 1577

## Cormier, Robert
*The Chocolate War* 5789
*Fade* 709, **1188**, 3493, 5013

## Cornwell, Bernard
*Enemy of God* **1189**
*Excalibur* **1190**
*The Winter King* 267, **1191**, 2747, 3355

## Correy, Lee
*The Abode of Life* 526

## Cosgrove, Rachel R.
*The Hidden Valley of Oz* 3609

## Costello, Matthew J.
*The 7th Guest* **1192**, 3913, 4495
*Beneath Still Waters* **1193**, 1972, 2094, 2333, 2822, 2929, 3783, 4715, 5114
*Child's Play III* **1194**, 2878, 2899, 2902, 3217, 3782, 3784
*Darkborn* **1195**, 3233, 4085, 5398
*Day of the Snake* 783, **1196**, 5890
*Garden* **1197**, 4279
*Homecoming* **1198**, 3375, 3518
*Hour of the Scorpion* **1199**
*Masque* 5890
*Midsummer* **1200**, 5890
*Mirage* 5892
*seaQuest DSV: Fire Below* **1201**
*The Seventh Guest* 3364, 3368
*Wurm* 88, 440, 441, **1202**, 5890

## Costello, Sean
*Captain Quad* 397, 611, **1203**, 2876, 3996, 4240, 4788, 5415
*The Cartoonist* 138, **1204**, 2904, 5398
*Eden's Eyes* **1205**

## Costikyan, Greg
*Another Day, Another Dungeon* **1206**
*By the Sword* **1207**
*One Quest, Hold the Dragons* **1208**

## Coulson, Juanita
*Legacy of Earth* **1209**
*The Past of Forever* **1210**
*Star Sister* **1211**
*Tomorrow's Heritage* 2048, 4301

## Coulson, Robert
*Charles Fort Never Mentioned Wombats* 4546

## The Council of Four
*The Science Fictional Sherlock Holmes* 4556

## Courtney, Vincent
*Goblins* 1038, **1212**
*Harvest of Blood* **1213**, 2699
*Vampire Beat* **1214**, 1791, 1793, 2149, 2792, 3108, 3517, 3560, 5078, 5374
*Wake Up Screaming* **1215**, 2606

## Cover, Arthur Byron
*Planetfall* 288, 1754, 4495
*Stationfall* 288, **1216**, 1754

## Coville, Bruce
*Aliens Stole My Body* **1217**
*Armageddon Summer* 6028
*The Dark Abyss* 1429, 3572
*Goblins in the Castle* **1218**
*Into the Land of the Unicorns* **1219**
*Jennifer Murdley's Toad* **1220**, 3378
*Jeremy Thatcher, Dragon Hatcher* **1221**, 1558, 3378, 5822
*My Teacher Flunked the Planet* **1222**, 1391, 4921
*My Teacher Fried My Brains* **1223**
*My Teacher Glows in the Dark* **1224**
*My Teacher Is an Alien* 773, 5286, 5289
*The Unicorn Treasury* 410, 412, 1343, 1946, 4319, 6033

## Cowles, Frederick
*Fear Walks the Night* 779, 875, 3633

## Cowper, Richard
*Clone* 2870, 5890
*A Dream of Kinship* 3696
*The Road to Corlay* 2945, 4151, 5508

## Cox, Glen E.
*Going Mobile* 2938

## Cox, Greg
*Assignment: Eternity* **1225**
*Devil in the Sky* 10, **1226**, 2296, 2917, 2922
*Dragon's Honor* **2922**
*Iron Man: The Armor Trap* **1227**, 1390
*Q-Space* **1228**
*Q-Zone* **1229**
*Tomorrow Bites* **1230**, 2410
*Tomorrow Sucks* **1231**, 1611

## Cox, Michael
*The Oxford Book of English Ghost Stories* 1309, 2300, 2483, 3432
*The Oxford Book of Twentieth Century Ghost Stories* **1232**, 2483
*Twelve Tales of the Supernatural* **1233**
*Twelve Victorian Ghost Stories* **1234**
*Victorian Ghost Stories: An Oxford Anthology* **1235**, 2300, 3432

## Coyle, Harold
*Team Yankee* 1642, 4306

## Coyne, John
*Child of Shadows* 1080, **1236**, 2334, 4340
*Fury* **1237**, 2873, 5186
*Hobgoblin* 2322

## Crace, Jim
*The Gift of Stones* 4320

## Cragg, Dan
*School of Fire* **4982**

## Craig, Brian
*Ghost Dancers* **1238**, 1935

*Plague Demon* **1239**, 1979
*Storm Warriors* **1240**, 4109
*Zaragoz* **1241**, 4653, 5087

**Craig, Patricia**
*Twelve Irish Ghost Stories* **1242**, 2481

**Cram, Ralph Adams**
*Black Spirits and White* 485, 963, 964, **1243**

**Cramer, John**
*Einstein's Bridge* 110, 444, **1244**, 4179
*Twistor* 824, **1245**, 2807, 5088

**Cramer, Kathryn**
*The Architecture of Fear* 2396, 5902
*The Ascent of Wonder: The Evolution of Hard SF* **2585**
*Christmas Ghosts* 1307, 1311, 1313, 4541
*Spirits of Christmas* 1307, 1311, 2588, 2894, 4541, 4861
*Walls of Fear* **1246**, 2396, 5902

**Cramer, Kathyrn**
*Christmas Ghosts* 2276

**Crandall, Melissa**
*Earth 2* **1247**
*Search and Rescue* 4487

**Crawford, Betty Anne**
*The Bushido Incident* **1248**, 4955

**Crawford, Dan**
*Rouse a Sleeping Cat* **1249**
*The Sure Death of a Mouse* **1250**
*A Wild Dog and Lone* **1251**

**Crawford, F. Marion**
*For the Blood Is the Life and Other Stories* **1252**
*Wandering Ghosts* 2633

**Cray, Roberta**
*The Sword and the Lion* **1253**, 3268

**Crean, Michelle Shirey**
*Dancer of the Sixth* 220, 312, **1254**, 1598, 3968, 5670

**Creighton, Lee**
*Two Queens of Lochrie* 4481

**Cresswell, Helen**
*A Game of Catch* 2438
*Moondial* 1011

**Crichton, Michael**
*The Andromeda Strain* 99, 1136, 1164, 1698, 2048, 2685, 2720, 2999, 3337, 3361, 3577, 3632, 3703, 3923, 4012, 4413, 4786, 4928
*Jurassic Park* 581, 591, 902, 949, 1049, **1255**, 1379, 1417, 1729, 2107, 2291, 2820, 3191, 3232, 4075, 4117, 4279, 4597, 4853, 5351, 6084
*The Lost World* 949, 1049, **1256**, 1379, 4415
*Sphere* 440, 1202, 4915
*The Terminal Man* 581, 1164, 1347, 2206, 2638, 2872, 3200, 4232
*Westworld* 4117

**Crider, Bill**
*Shotgun Saturday Night* 1829

**Crimmins, Cathy**
*Revenge of the Christmas Box* **1257**, 3214

**Crispin, A.C.**
*Alien Resurrection* **1258**
*Ancestor's World* **1259**, 1500

*The Eyes of the Beholders* 1389, 2066, 2068, 3524
*The Paradise Snare* 117
*Sarek* 1226, **1260**
*Serpent's Gift* 230, 1083, **1261**
*Shadow World* **1262**, 1391
*Silent Dances* **1263**, 1391, 1594, 1865, 1956, 2550, 3752, 3767, 4128
*Silent Songs* **1264**, 2001, 5037
*Songsmith* **4161**
*Starbridge* 231, 517, **1265**, 1333, 1391, 1978, 2551, 3066, 4160, 4349, 5048, 5780
*Time for Yesterday* 527, 902, 922, 3316
*V* 504, 1508, 2910, 2948, 3952, 5282, 5575
*Voices of Chaos* **1266**
*Yesterday's Son* 527, 528, 922, 1383, 3316

**Crocco, Kyle**
*Heroes, Inc.* 167, 559, 1208, **1268**, 2080, 2803, 2950, 3810, 3991, 4458, 5649, 6066
*Heroes Wanted* 262, **1267**, 3810, 5649

**Crompton, Anne Eliot**
*Gawain and Lady Green* **1269**, 3355, 3884
*Merlin's Harp* **1270**, 1857

**Crosland, Margaret**
*The Gothic Tales of the Marquis de Sade* 5389

**Cross, Claire**
*The Last Highlander* **1271**

**Cross, Gilbert B.**
*A Witch Across Time* 122, 1012, **1272**, 3444

**Cross, John Keir**
*The Angry Planet* 2647

**Cross, Ronald Anthony**
*The Fourth Guardian* **1273**, 3262
*The Lost Guardian* 1093, **1274**
*Prisoners of Paradise* 58, 1691
*The White Guardian* **1275**

**Crowe, Catherine**
*Night-Side of Nature* 2158

**Crowley, John**
*Aegypt* 25, 333, 518, 1457, 2262, 2329, 3714, 4740, 5591
*Antiquities* 819, **1276**, 1431, 2106, 2265, 2537, 4757, 5165
*Beasts* 305, 721, 3243, 3797, 4604
*Little, Big* 271, 334, 335, 336, 439, 547, 551, 820, 919, 1063, 1397, 1423, 1445, 2101, 2104, 2105, 2238, 2329, 2533, 2706, 2817, 3791, 3793, 3984, 4104, 4360, 4382, 4383, 4448, 4475, 5274, 5927
*Love & Sleep* 655, **1277**, 4992, 5273
*Novelty* **1278**, 5633, 5945

**Crowther, Peter**
*Blue Motel* **1279**
*Dante's Disciples* **1280**
*Destination Unknown* **1281**
*Escardy Gap* **1282**
*Heaven Sent: 18 Glorious Tales of the Angels* **1283**, 1339, 2342, 3112, 6031
*Narrow Houses* **1284**, 2175, 2777, 3112, 3962, 5667
*Tombs* **3228**

*Touch Wood* **1285**

**Crozier, Ouida**
*Shadows After Dark* **1286**, 5071

**Cuddon, J.A.**
*The Penguin Book of Ghost Stories* 1309

**Cummings, Ray**
*Brigands of the Moon* 5864
*Wandl the Invader* 5864

**Cunningham, Elaine**
*Daughter of the Drow* **1287**
*Elfshadow* **1288**, 1486, 1487, 3538, 4800, 4803, 4804, 4805, 4807
*Elfsong* **1289**
*Evermeet: Island of Elves* **1290**, 5022
*The Radiant Dragon* **1291**, 2785
*Silver Shadows* **1292**
*Thornhold* **1293**

**Cunningham, Jere**
*The Abyss* 1884

**Curry, Ann**
*The Book of Brendan* 369, 370, 372, **1294**, 4447, 6035, 6038

**Curry, Chris**
*Haunted* **5463**
*Moonfall* **5464**
*Panic* 1038, **1295**
*Thunder Road* **1296**
*Trickster* 427, **1297**, 3680

**Curry, Jane Louise**
*Over the Sea's Edge* 4917

**Curtis, James Roberto**
*Shango* **1298**

**Cushman, Carolyn**
*Witch and Wombat* 315, 703, 915, **1299**, 2946

**Cusick, Richie Tankersley**
*Blood Roots* **1300**, 3406
*Buffy the Vampire Slayer* 1032, 1034, **1301**, 1801, 1802, 2131, 5161, 5324
*The Harvest* **1302**, 2131
*The Mall* 1692
*Vampire* 120, 4328

**Cussler, Clive**
*Raise the Titanic!* 5114

**Cymri, Chris**
*Dragons Can Only Rust* 299

**Czerneda, Julie E.**
*Beholder's Eye* **1303**, 1501
*A Thousand Words for Stranger* **1304**, 2059, 3597

## D

**Da Cruz, Daniel**
*The Ayes of Texas* 48, 49
*Mixed Doubles* 33, **1305**, 1473, 1919, 2044, 2045, 2047
*Texas on the Rocks* 47, 48, 49, 50, 66
*Texas Triumphant* 47, 48, 49, 50

**Dahl, Roald**
*Charlie and the Chocolate Factory* 4338
*Roald Dahl's Book of Ghost Stories* **1306**
*The Witches* 2949, 4079, 4080

**Dalby, Richard**
*The Best of Ghosts and Scholars* 2866
*Chillers for Christmas* **1307**, 2894
*Dracula's Brood* 1013, **1308**, 1360, 1370, 2387, 2484, 2972, 2975
*Edwardian Ghost Stories by Eminent Women Writers* 37
*Ghosts and Scholars* 283
*Ghosts for Christmas* 4541, 4861
*The Mammoth Book of Ghost Stories* 1232, 1233, 1306, **1309**, 1709
*The Mammoth Book of Ghost Stories 2* 1232, 1709
*The Mammoth Book of Victorian and Edwardian Ghost Stories* 38, 1234, **1310**, 2483
*Mistletoe Mayhem* **1311**, 2276, 2894
*Modern Ghost Stories by Eminent Women Writers* **1312**, 1715, 2483, 5814, 5815
*Shivers for Christmas* **1313**
*Tales of Witchcraft* 1711
*Thrillers for Christmas* 4541
*Twelve Gothic Tales* **1314**
*Vampire Stories* 4879, 4881, 5688
*Victorian Ghost Stories by Eminent Women Writers* 1235, 5814
*The Virago Book of Ghost Stories* 4443
*The Virago Book of Ghost Stories: The Twentieth Century* 4443, 5523
*The Virago Book of Victorian Ghost Stories* 1234

**Daley, Brian**
*The Doomfarers of Coramonde* 162, 1008, 1065, 1066, 1147, 1154, 1419, 1754, 1809, 1812, 1814, 3650, 3653, 4316, 4523, 4794
*Fall of the White Ship Avatar* 260, 261, 1103, 1106, 1144, 1572
*The Han Solo Adventures* 76, 103, 109, 115, 2500, 2914, 3247, 5527, 5950, 6055
*Han Solo and the Lost Legacy* 6052, 6054
*Han Solo at Star's End* 6052, 6054
*Han Solo's Revenge* 6052, 6054
*Jinx on a Terran Inheritance* 260, 261, 1106, 1144, 1331, 1333, 1542, 1572, 1604, 1606, 4291, 5668
*Requiem for a Ruler of Worlds* 260, 261, 309, 312, 473, 1106, 1108, 1144, 1572, 1937, 3735, 5668, 6014
*A Screaming Across the Sky* **1315**
*Starfollowers of Coramonde* 1754
*A Tapestry of Magics* 259, 747, 4670
*Tron* 5171, 5753

**Dalkey, Kara**
*Bhagavati* **1316**
*Bijapur* **1317**
*Blood of the Goddess* **1318**
*The Curse of Sagamore* 1514, 4387
*Euryale* 3309
*Goa* 195, 770, 771, 1111, 1154, 2995
*The Heavenward Path* **1319**
*Little Sister* 68, **1320**, 1462, 1868, 2614, 4129
*The Nightingale* 42, 375, 1358, 1446, 1479, 6088, 6090
*Steel Rose* **1321**, 3886, 3887, 5273
*The Sword of Sagamore* 1514

**Dalmas, John**
*The Bavarian Gate* 1981

*Fanglith* 3801, 5588
*Homecoming* 885, 2004
*The Kalif's War* **1322**, 1628, 4972, 4984
*The Lantern of God* **1323**, 1876, 3907, 5588, 5900
*The Lion of Farside* **1324**
*The Lizard War* 1158, **1325**, 1976, 2193, 2353, 5588, 5900, 5932
*The Regiment* 308, 589, 1546, 4378
*The Regiment's War* **1326**
*The Walkaway Clause* 1182
*The White Regiment* **1327**, 1552, 4373, 5930
*The Yngling* 47, 50, 4600, 4602, 4619, 4621
*The Yngling and the Circle of Power* **1328**
*The Yngling in Yamato* **1329**

**Dalton, Annie**
*Out of the Ordinary* 1220, **1330**

**Dalton, Sean**
*Beyond the Void* 929, **1331**, 2683
*Destination: Mutiny* **1332**
*The Salukan Gambit* **1333**
*Showdown* 1398

**D'Amato, Brian**
*Beauty* 437, **1334**, 3196

**D'Ammassa, Don**
*Twisted Images* **1335**

**Daniel, Les**
*Don Sebastian Series* 4767

**Daniel, Tony**
*Earthling* **1336**, 1481
*Warpath* **1337**, 5745

**Daniell, Tina**
*The Companions* 4368
*Dark Heart* 154, 3155, 4368

**Daniels, Les**
*The Black Castle* 463, 1797, 4303, 6012, 6013, 6015, 6016, 6018
*The Chronicles of Don Sebastian* 5191
*Citizen Vampire* 1794, 1795
*No Blood Spilled* **1338**, 2742, 4097, 4770, 6011
*The Silver Skull* 4573, 4668, 6016
*Yellow Fog* 2511, 2742, 6019

**Daniels, Patricia**
*Sinbad the Sailor* 374, 2130, 4731, 6087

**Dann, Jack**
*Aliens!* 4406
*Angels!* 1028, 1283, **1339**, 2342, 3480, 6031
*Dinosaurs!* 2386, 2468, 4543
*Dinosaurs II* 2386
*Dragons!* 801, 2479, 4408, 5710
*Hackers* 2394
*High Steel* **2486**
*Little People!* **1340**, 2388, 4906, 4988
*Magicats!* 1369, 3377, 4144, 4145, 4273, 5252
*Magicats II* 4144, 5252
*The Man Who Melted* 1788
*The Memory Cathedral* **1341**, 3409, 4651, 5152
*Nebula Awards 32* **1342**, 1619, 4824, 5489
*Run for the Stars/Echoes of Thunder* **1788**
*Sorcerers!* 3076
*Unicorns!* 410, 412, 2397, 2941, 6033

*Unicorns II* 410, 412, 1219, **1343**, 2941, 6033
*Wandering Stars: An Anthology of Jewish Fantasy and Science Fiction* 1788

**Dann, Jeanne Van Buren**
*In the Field of Fire* 3706

**Dann, Joshua**
*Timeshare* **1344**, 4247, 5565
*Timeshare: Second Time Around* **1345**, 4247

**Dantz, William**
*Hunger* 88, 373, 441, **1346**, 3232, 3998, 5877
*Nine Levels Down* **1347**

**Danvers, Dennis**
*Circuit of Heaven* **1348**
*Wilderness* 679, 680, 816, 926, **1349**, 4472, 5146, 5343, 5425

**Danziger, Paula**
*This Place Has No Atmosphere* 4919

**Dare, M.P.**
*Unholy Relics* 455, 875, **1350**, 4141, 5611

**Dark, Larry**
*The Literary Ghost* 1232, 1306, **1351**

**Darke, David**
*Blind Hunger* **1352**, 4083
*Horrorshow* 428, 460, **1353**, 2761, 3102, 3103, 3326
*Last Rites* **1354**
*Shade* **1355**, 5537

**Darling, Diana**
*The Painted Alphabet* **1356**

**Darnay, Arsen**
*A Hostage for Hinterland* 4678
*The Purgatory Zone* 1981, 2574

**Datlow, Ellen**
*Alien Sex* 72, 75, **1357**, 1607, 2174, 2178, 2179, 2180, 2181, 3026, 4406, 5093, 5094
*Black Swan, White Raven* **1358**, 3847
*Black Thorn, White Rose* **1359**, 5973, 6045, 6046
*Blood Is Not Enough* 698, 1231, **1360**, 1611, 1718, 2071, 2387, 2409, 2508, 2975, 3031, 3112, 3758, 4407, 4876, 4879, 4880, 4881, 5284, 5688, 5935
*Little Deaths* 1118, 1120, **1361**, 1367, 2174, 2176, 2177, 2178, 2179, 2182, 2185, 3181, 5385
*Off Limits: Tales of Alien Sex* **1362**, 1607
*Omni Best Science Fiction One* **1363**
*Omni Best Science Fiction Three* 216, **1364**, 1622
*Omni Visions One* **1365**
*Ruby Slippers, Golden Tears* **1366**, 5912
*Sirens and Other Daemon Lovers* **1367**
*Snow White, Blood Red* **1368**, 3844, 4791, 6044, 6045, 6046
*Twists of the Tale* **1369**
*A Whisper of Blood* 698, 1231, 1286, **1370**, 1718, 2071, 2387, 3031, 4407, 5688
*The Year's Best Fantasy and Horror: Eighth Annual Collection* 2964
*The Year's Best Fantasy and Horror: Eleventh Annual Collection* **1371**

*The Year's Best Fantasy and Horror: Fifth Annual Collection* **1372**
*The Year's Best Fantasy and Horror: Fourth Annual Collection* 215, 646, **1373**, 2962, 4025, 4031, 4032, 5601
*The Year's Best Fantasy and Horror: Ninth Annual Collection* **1374**, 2969
*The Year's Best Fantasy and Horror Series* 228, 2970, 2971, 5003, 5602, 5603, 5606, 5912, 6032, 6044
*The Year's Best Fantasy and Horror: Seventh Annual Collection* **1375**, 5608
*The Year's Best Fantasy and Horror: Sixth Annual Collection* **1376**, 2963, 5607
*The Year's Best Fantasy and Horror: Tenth Annual Collection* **1377**
*The Year's Best Fantasy and Horror: Third Annual Collection* 59, 647, **1378**, 1428, 2961, 4723, 5605
*The Year's Best Fantasy: First Annual Collection* 4131, 4723, 6044

**Davenport, Basil**
*Deals with the Devil: An Anthology* 1280, 4542

**David, James F.**
*Footprints of Thunder* 1049, 1256, **1379**
*Fragments* 90, **1380**

**David, Peter**
*Body and Soul* 2909, 2910, 3520
*The Disinherited* **1381**
*Doomsday World* **923**
*End Game* **1382**
*Howling Mad* 2125, 3280, 4387
*Imzadi* **1383**, 1658
*In the Beginning* 2102
*Q-in-Law* 1228, 1229, **1384**
*Q-Squared* 1226, 1228, 1229, **1385**, 2501
*The Rift* **1386**
*A Rock and a Hard Place* 2066, 2068, 3524
*The Siege* 2908
*Thirdspace* **1387**
*Triangle: Imzadi II* **1388**
*Vendetta* **1389**
*What Savage Beast* 1227, **1390**
*Worf's First Adventure* **1391**, 2109, 4910

**Davids, Hollace**
*The Glove of Darth Vader* **1392**
*The Lost City of the Jedi* **1393**
*Zorba the Hutt's Revenge* **1394**

**Davids, Paul**
*The Glove of Darth Vader* 1391, **1392**, 6055
*The Lost City of the Jedi* 1391, **1393**
*Zorba the Hutt's Revenge* **1394**

**Davidson, Avram**
*The Adventurers of Dr. Eszterhazy* 4851
*Adventures in Unhistory* 818
*The Avram Davidson Treasury* **1395**, 2641
*The Best From Fantasy and Science Fiction: 12* 242
*The Best From Fantasy and Science Fiction: 12-14* 4712
*The Best From Fantasy and Science Fiction: 13* 243
*The Boss in the Wall* **1396**

*Marco Polo and the Sleeping Beauty* 523

**Davies, Robertson**
*The Cornish Trilogy* **1397**
*The Depford Trilogy* 2817
*High Spirits* 2813, 2814
*What's Bred in the Bone* 518, 1277

**Davis, Brett**
*Bone Wars* **1398**, 6084
*The Faery Convention* 315, **1399**, 4389, 5459
*Hair of the Dog* **1400**

**Davis, Carol**
*Quantum Leap: Obsessions: A Novel* 5315

**Davis, Carol Anne**
*Expiry Date* **1401**

**Davis, Don**
*Bring on the Night* **1402**, 1779, 2288, 3498, 3519, 4102
*The Gris-Gris Man* 1298, **1403**, 1888, 2744, 2896, 3678, 4498
*Sins of the Flesh* **1404**, 1443

**Davis, Grania**
*The Boss in the Wall* **1396**

**Davis, Jake**
*Destination: Showdown* **1405**
*The Last Rangers* **1406**, 1567, 4590

**Davis, Jay**
*Bring on the Night* **1402**
*Sins of the Flesh* **1404**

**Davis, Margaret**
*Mind Light* **1407**, 1899, 4160
*Minds Apart* **1408**, 4175

**Davis, Robert**
*Padre Porko: The Gentlemanly Pig* 2786

**Dawson, Carol**
*Meeting the Minotaur* **1409**

**Dawson, Coningsby**
*The Road to Avalon* 5270

**Day, Chet**
*The Hacker* **1410**, 2322

**de Bernieres, Louis**
*Senor Vivo and the Coca Lord* **1411**, 3006, 4208
*The War of Don Emmanuel's Nether Parts* **1412**, 1657, 3006, 4208

**de Camp, Catherine Crook**
*The Pixilated Peeress* **1416**
*The Swords of Zinjaban* **1418**

**de Camp, L. Sprague**
*The Carnelian Cube* 5645, 5647
*The Complete Compleat Enchanter* 1812, 2014, 2080, 2616, 3015, 3650, 4392, 4395, 4399, 4404, 4971, 5694
*The Dragon of the Ishtar Gate* 2140, 5496
*The Enchanter Reborn* **1413**, 3015, 5219
*The Fantastic Swordsmen* 2657, 4082, 4611, 4759, 5599
*The Golden Wind* 195, 1316, 1317
*The Hand of Zei* 631, **1414**, 1772, 4152
*The Honorable Barbarian* 523, **1415**, 2463, 2465, 3471
*The Incomplete Enchanter* 1532, 4517
*The Land of Unreason* 652, 1809, 3015, 4161, 4162, 4371

*Lest Darkness Fall* 350, 895, 1045, 1341, 1631, 1638, 2043, 2044, 2045, 2046, 2047, 2570, 2571, 3663, 3917, 4036, 4040, 5295, 5505, 6000
*The Pixilated Peeress* 639, **1416**, 5222
*The Prisoner of Zhamanak* 1914, 5319
*Rivers of Time* 263, 264, **1417**, 1855
*Rogue Queen* 1211
*Solomon's Stone* 3989
*Swords and Sorcery* 4759, 5599
*The Swords of Zinjaban* **1418**, 1757, 5227
*Tales From Gavagan's Bar* 2299, 4637, 4639
*The Unbeheaded King* 4163
*The Undesired Princess and the Enchanted Bunny* **1419**, 2751, 5639
*The Venom Trees of Sunga* **1420**, 4545
*The Virgin of Zesh* 1914
*Warlocks and Warriors* 3420, 5599

**de Cles, Jon**
*Blood of the Colyn Muir* **6083**

**De Haven, Tom**
*The End-of-Everything Man* **1421**
*Freak's Amour* 1940
*The Last Human* **1422**
*Walker of Worlds* **1423**, 1426

**de la Mare, Walter**
*The Collected Tales of Walter de la Mare* 5763, 5764, 5765
*The Return* **1424**
*The Riddle and Other Stories* 3360

**de Larrabeiti, Michael**
*The Borribles* 1841, 3271, 3301, 4497
*The Borribles Go for Broke* 3271, 4497

**de Lint, Charles**
*Cafe Purgatorium* **98**
*The Dreaming Place* 1475, 3545, 5336, 5827, 6017
*Dreams Underfoot* 395, 818, **1425**, 3702, 5912
*Drink Down the Moon* 166, 183, 1423, **1426**
*From a Whisper to a Scream* **3093**
*Ghosts of Wind and Shadow* **1427**, 2078, 4497
*Greenmantle* 203, 1040, 2797, 3470
*The Harp of the Grey Rose* 3269
*Hedgework and Guessery* **1428**, 5810
*The Hidden City* **1429**, 3572
*I'll Be Watching You* **3094**
*Into the Green* **1430**
*The Ivory and the Horn* 395, **1431**, 2106
*Jack of Kinrowan* 935
*Jack, the Giant-Killer* 42, 375, 1005, 1446, 1479, 2797, 3285, 6088, 6090
*The Little Country* 87, 164, 424, 522, 1101, 1356, **1432**, 1452, 1471, 1478, 1584, 1835, 1873, 2627, 2644, 2735, 2737, 2738, 2791, 3275, 3354, 4384, 4671, 4717, 4970, 5159, 5626
*Memory and Dream* 439, 1399, **1433**, 1445, 1472, 2082, 2266, 2538, 2735, 2737, 2738, 3118, 3283, 3838, 3887, 3896, 3897, 4195, 4358, 4486, 5180, 5916

*Moonheart: A Romance* 203, 1040, 1159, 1321, 1472, 1474, 1947, 1958, 3299, 4382, 4989, 4990, 4995, 5818, 5913
*Mulengro: A Romany Tale* 738, 744, 1249, 2771, 5061
*Our Lady of the Harbour* **1434**, 4171, 4864
*Someplace to Be Flying* **1435**, 2104
*Spiritwalk* 1159, **1436**, 1958, 2736, 3299, 3470, 4757, 5913
*Svaha* 431, 974, **1437**, 1477, 1499, 1936, 3583, 4192, 4991, 5134, 6008
*Trader* **1438**, 3773, 5273
*The Valley of Thunder* 3572
*Westlin Wind* **1439**, 1925
*The Wild Wood* **1440**, 2088, 2980, 3840, 5916
*The Wishing Well* **1441**
*Wolf Moon* 1349, 3625, 4397
*Yarrow* 1241, 3294

**De Vos, Elisabeth**
*The Seraphim Rising* **1442**

**Deakins, John**
*Barrow* 166, 183, 1206, **1443**, 3842, 4284, 5153

**Dean, Lisa**
*Trickster* **1297**

**Dean, Pamela**
*The Dubious Hills* 728, **1444**, 1705, 2865, 3280, 3731, 3816, 3843, 4324, 4899, 5409, 5577, 5848
*The Hidden Land* 4, 1488, 3400, 5235
*Juniper, Gentian and Rosemary* **1445**
*The Secret Country* 4, 286, 410, 412, 1343, 1440, 1488, 1744, 1816, 2359, 2879, 3400, 3487, 4045, 4319, 4797, 4798, 4809, 5182, 5235, 5311, 5364, 6033
*Tam Lin* 42, 375, 391, 637, 935, 1005, 1409, 1434, **1446**, 2538, 4008, 4870, 5178, 5428
*The Whim of the Dragon* 4, **1447**, 1488, 5182, 5235, 5311

**Deane, Hamilton**
*Dracula: The Ultimate Illustrated Edition of the World-Famous Vampire Play* 339, 344, 1112, **1448**, 3110

**DeBrandt, Don H.**
*The Quicksilver Screen* **1449**

**DeCandido, Keith R.A.**
*The Ultimate Alien* **4406**
*The Ultimate Dragon* **4408**

**DeCarlo, Elisa**
*The Devil You Say* **1450**
*Strong Spirits* **1451**

**Decarnin, Camilla**
*Worlds Apart* 2117, 2295, 2444, 5154

**DeChancie, John**
*Bride of the Castle* **1452**
*Castle Dreams* **1453**
*Castle Fantastic* 2380
*Castle for Rent* 4362
*Castle Kidnapped* 5939
*Castle Perilous* 166, 182, 183, 1529, 1584, 1979, 2617, 2622, 2623, 2627, 2628, 2644, 2804, 4316, 4387, 4405, 4435, 4970, 5208, 5337, 5646
*Castle Spellbound* **1454**
*Castle War!* **1455**

*Dr. Dimension* **1456**
*From Prussia with Love* **1457**
*Innerverse* **1458**
*The Kruton Interface* **1459**
*Living with Aliens* **1460**, 3952
*MagicNet* **1461**
*Paradox Alley* 31, 86, 493, 959, 1055, 1490, 2226, 2770, 2804, 3821, 3825, 4505, 4662, 5076, 5933
*Red Limit Freeway* 31, 86, 493, 959, 1490, 1545, 2226, 2770, 2804, 3424, 3741, 3825, 4505, 4662, 5076, 5933
*Starrigger* 31, 86, 493, 959, 1144, 1337, 1490, 1645, 2002, 2226, 2332, 2770, 2804, 2836, 3424, 3722, 3741, 3825, 4076, 4077, 4302, 4505, 4662, 4859, 5076, 5227, 5933

**Dedman, Stephen**
*The Art of Arrow Cutting* **1462**

**Dee, Ron**
*Blind Hunger* **1352**
*Blood* **1463**, 5120
*Blood Lust* **1464**, 1945, 2152, 3372, 5237
*Descent* **1465**
*Dusk* 723, 1127, **1466**, 1945, 2152, 3051, 3372, 3498, 4102, 4464, 5237, 5770
*Horrorshow* **1353**
*Last Rites* **1354**
*Sex and Blood* **1467**, 2655, 2778, 3111, 3114, 3388, 3393, 3397
*Shade* **1355**
*Succumb* 138, 1086, **1468**, 4224

**Defalco, Tom**
*The Past* 2256

**DeFelitta, Frank**
*Audrey Rose* 4237, 4442

**DeFord, Miriam Allen**
*Space, Time and Crime* 3619

**Deighton, Len**
*SS-GB* 598, 2667, 3528

**Deitz, Tom**
*Above the Lower Sky* **1469**, 1943
*Darkthunder's Way* **1470**
*Dreambuilder* **1471**
*Dreamseeker's Road* 1321, **1472**, 2737, 2957
*The Gryphon King* **1473**, 3423
*Landslayer's Law* **1474**
*Soulsmith* 522, 563, **1475**, 1512, 1639, 2057, 2060, 2552, 2716, 2717, 2942, 3256, 3624, 4060, 4221, 5277, 5529
*Stoneskin's Revenge* 487, **1476**
*Sunshaker's War* 1432, **1477**, 3077, 3294
*Windmaster's Bane* 391, 935, 974, 1162, 1947, 3285, 3354, 3357, 3799, 3802, 3804, 4798
*Wordwright* **1478**

**Del Rey, Lester**
*The Eleventh Commandment* 1135, 3242
*Once upon a Time: A Treasury of Modern Fairy Tales* 225, 606, 1359, 1366, 1368, **1479**, 1576, 2378, 6044, 6045, 6046, 6087, 6088, 6090
*Police Your Planet* 4931
*Pstalemate* 2290, 3011
*Step to the Stars* 3199

*The Year After Tomorrow: An Anthology of Science Fiction Stories* 6027

**Delacorte, Peter**
*Time on My Hands* **1480**, 5874

**Delaney, Laurence**
*The Triton Ultimatum* 4512

**Delany, Samuel R.**
*Babel-17* 5254, 5634
*The Ballad of Beta-2* 5042
*The Bridge of Lost Desire* 1720, 4046, 4047, 4263
*Dhalgren* 43, 805, 1720, 2771, 3456, 4051
*Driftglass: 10 Tales of Speculative Fiction* 1608, 5945
*The Einstein Intersection* **1481**, 1879, 6074
*Neveryona* 2457
*Nova* 5943
*Quark 1* 4721
*The Splendor and Misery of Bodies, of Cities* 1720, 5634
*Stars in My Pocket Like Grains of Sand* 1720, 5634
*Tales of Neveryon* 729, 746, 2328, 3872, 5684, 5937, 5945
*They Fly at Ciron* 567, 793, **1482**, 2243, 2338, 3380, 3692, 3855, 5132, 5492, 5942
*Triton* 1720, 4051

**Delrio, Martin**
*Mortal Kombat* **1483**

**DeMarinis, Rick**
*Cinder* 618
*Scimitar* 1916

**Denning, Troy**
*The Amber Enchantress* 1293, 2621, 2624
*The Cerulean Storm* 2621
*The Crimson Legion* 13, 2621, 2624
*Crucible* **1484**
*Dragonwall* 3537, 4108
*Faces of Deception* **1485**
*The Obsidian Oracle* 2621
*The Parched Sea* 1287, 1288, 1289, **1486**, 2427, 3121, 3537, 3538, 4106, 4800, 4803, 4804, 4805, 4807, 5682
*The Veiled Dragon* 4326, 5708
*The Verdant Passage* 13, **1487**, 2618, 2621, 2624

**Dennis, Carol L.**
*Dragon's Knight* 470, 3578
*Dragon's Queen* **1488**

**Dennis, Ian**
*Bagdad* 618

**Dent, Lester**
*Python Isle* **4624**

**Denton, Bradley**
*Blackburn* **1489**, 3088
*Buddy Holly Is Alive and Well on Ganymede* **1490**, 2418, 3083, 3190, 4997, 5089, 5768, 6020
*Lunatics* **1491**, 4093
*One Day Closer to Death* **1492**

**Denton, Terry**
*Felix and Alexander* 3377

**Dereske, Jo**
*The Lone Sentinel* 221, 878, **1493**, 2227, 5381

**Derleth, August**
*The Cthulhu Mythos* **1494**, 3566,
  3567, 3568
*Harrigan's File*  4904, 4905
*In Lovecraft's Shadow*  **1495**
*The Lurker at the Threshold*  4007
*The Mask of Cthulhu*  **1496**, 3531,
  3532
*Not Long for This World*  534
*The Other Side of the Moon*  5691
*Someone in the Dark*  1088, 3515,
  4141
*Strange Ports of Call*  5691
*Tales of the Cthulhu Mythos*  539,
  3535, 4425, 4431
*The Trail of Cthulhu*  **1497**, 5470
*The Watchers out of Time*  3535

**Desjarlais, John**
*The Throne of Tara*  561, **1498**,
  3265, 3358, 4584, 5101, 5392

**DesRochers, Diane**
*Walker between the Worlds*  **1499**

**Devenport, Emily**
*Eggheads*  774, **1500**, 2877, 5571
*GodHeads*  **1501**, 1759
*The Kronos Condition*  1442, **1502**
*Larissa*  **1503**
*Shade*  294, **1504**, 1805, 3921,
  4142, 4930, 5462

**Deveraux, Jude**
*A Knight in Shining Armor*  1704,
  4517

**Devereaux, Robert**
*Deadweight*  **1505**
*Santa Steps Out: A Fairy Tale for
  Grownups*  **1506**
*Walking Wounded*  **1507**

**Devlin, Dean**
*Independence Day*  504, **1508**, 2034,
  3952, 4301
*StarGate*  1483, **1509**, 4286

**DeWeese, Gene**
*Chain of Attack*  526, 903, 1663,
  1923
*The Final Nexus*  5115
*King of the Dead*  1137, **1510**
*Lord of the Necropolis*  1137
*Now You See It/Him/Them. . .*  4546,
  5697
*The Peacekeepers*  923, 1384, 2067,
  2068, 2922, 3524
*Renegade*  **1511**

**Dexter, Catherine**
*Mazemaker*  5559

**Dexter, Susan**
*The Mountains of Channadran*  844
*The Prince of Ill Luck*  **1512**, 5151
*The Sword of Calandra*  993, 3121
*The True Knight*  **1513**
*The Wizard's Shadow*  172, 672, 718,
  **1514**, 2858, 3099, 3277, 3773,
  3838, 3914, 4809, 5583, 6042

**Di Filippo, Paul**
*Fractal Paisleys*  1023, 1492, **1515**,
  1758
*Lost Pages*  **1516**
*Ribofunk*  578, **1517**
*The Steampunk Trilogy*  403, **1518**,
  3931

**Diamond, Graham**
*Captain Sinbad*  618

**Dick, Philip K.**
*The Best of Philip K. Dick*  321, 4216

*Blade Runner*  77, 79, 249, 366, 708,
  837, 1725, 2011, 2377, 2536,
  2539, 2906, 2907, 3484, 4193,
  4220, 4229, 4286, 4300, 4748,
  4749, 4939, 5375, 5462, 5966
*The Collected Short Stories of Philip K.
  Dick*  5346
*The Collected Stories of Philip K.
  Dick*  54, 1753, 5344, 5349
*The Collected Stories of Philip K. Dick,
  Volume One: The Short Happy Life
  of the Brown Oxford*  **1519**
*The Collected Stories of Philip K. Dick,
  Volume Two: We Can Remember It
  for You Wholesale*  **1520**
*The Divine Invasion*  3012
*Do Androids Dream of Electric
  Sheep?*  193, 836, 2684, 2685,
  3012, 3204, 3434, 3579, 4071,
  4117, 4325, 4342, 4555, 5476
*Dr. Bloodmoney*  1133, 5906
*Eye in the Sky*  951, 956, 957, **1521**,
  3012
*Flow My Tears, the Policeman
  Said*  193, 3612
*The Game-Players of Titan*  4114,
  4115
*The Man in the High Castle*  201,
  443, 598, 1518, 1658, 1982, 2239,
  2564, 2667, 3528, 4272, 4474,
  4536, 4546, 5300, 5515, 5516,
  5918, 5919
*The Man Who Japed*  1782, 5642
*Martian Time-Slip*  586, 622, 3012,
  3612, 4555
*A Maze of Death*  160, 805, 1453
*Our Friends From Frolix 8*  2254
*The Penultimate Truth*  **1522**, 4205
*A Scanner Darkly*  193, 294, 805,
  830, 1411, 1696, 3612, 4935,
  4936, 4937, 4940, 5173, 5254,
  5593, 5867
*Solar Lottery*  5048
*The Three Stigmata of Palmer
  Eldritch*  568, 829, 1411, 2093,
  2722, 2907, 3012, 3780, 4454,
  4979, 5520, 5661
*Time Out of Joint*  193
*The Transmigration of Timothy
  Archer*  3612
*Ubik*  96, 1762, 1835, 2789, 2913,
  3012, 3351, 3456, 3459, 4454,
  5156, 5487
*The Unteleported Man*  708, 784,
  1458, 1509, 1565, 2882, 2907,
  2913, 4505, 4682, 5156, 5159,
  5306, 6060
*Valis*  2754, 3012, 3186, 3612
*We Can Build You*  4297
*The Zap Gun*  **1523**

**Dickens, Charles**
*A Christmas Carol*  2276
*The Complete Ghost Stories of Charles
  Dickens*  1597
*The D. Case: The Truth about the
  Mystery of Edwin Drood*  **1524**

**Dickey, James**
*Deliverance*  2279

**Dickinson, Peter**
*The Blue Hawk*  658, 3404, 4156
*Eva*  **1525**, 2808, 2868, 3703
*The Gift*  2992, 3340
*Healer*  4334, 5478
*Heartsease*  6038
*The Lion Tamer's Daughter*  **1526**
*Merlin Dreams*  6030

*Time and the Clock Mice,
  Etcetera*  **1527**

**Dicks, Terrance**
*The Claws of Axos*  5261
*Doctor Who: The Mind of Evil*  5261

**Dickson, Gordon R.**
*Alien Art*  2721
*The Alien Way*  933, 990, 997, 998,
  2108, 2864, 5574, 5575
*The Chantry Guild*  353, 418
*Dorsai!*  308, 310, 513, 589, 996,
  1041, 1315, 1646, 1651, 2049,
  2435, 3034, 3035, 3037, 3698,
  3865, 4142, 4226, 4227, 4288,
  4292, 4374, 4378, 4466, 4560,
  4583, 5294, 5378, 5469, 6075
*The Dorsai Companion*  4346
*The Dragon and the Djinn*  **1528**,
  5218
*The Dragon and the George*  6, 85,
  131, 286, 842, 843, 915, 1160,
  1161, 1163, 1196, 1207, 1324,
  1685, 1704, 1747, 1873, 1985,
  2042, 2127, 2362, 2616, 2617,
  3728, 3934, 3938, 4014, 4055,
  4316, 4399, 4401, 4404, 4457,
  4669, 4671, 4697, 4809, 5228,
  5235, 5337, 5694, 5719, 6049,
  6069
*The Dragon and the Gnarly
  King*  **1529**
*The Dragon at War*  842, **1530**,
  2234, 3169, 4691, 4695, 4697,
  4924
*The Dragon in Lyonesse*  **1531**
*The Dragon Knight*  131, 393, 841,
  1045, **1532**, 1985, 4971
*The Dragon on the Border*  **1533**,
  4697
*The Dragon, the Earl, and the
  Troll*  **1534**, 2360, 4671
*The Earth Lords*  1443
*The Far Call*  380, 388, 586, 597,
  1248
*The Final Encyclopedia*  2054, 4377,
  5917, 5920, 5921, 5922
*The Forever Man*  132, 1389, 6051
*The Harriers*  **1535**
*Home From the Shore*  1469, 4923,
  5541
*Jamie the Red*  4201
*The Lifeship*  5781
*Lost Dorsai*  132, 2054, 2349, 3790,
  4377, 4468
*The Magnificent Wilf*  **1536**
*Masters of Everon*  2421, 2550,
  3307, 3769, 4280
*Naked to the Stars/The Alien
  Way*  130, **1537**, 1593, 5467
*Necromancer*  127
*None but Man*  595
*Other*  **1538**, 5545
*The Pritcher Mass*  421, 5032
*Secret Under the Caribbean*  3341
*Soldier, Ask Not*  206, 513, 901,
  2054, 2349, 3035, 3790, 4194,
  4374, 4377, 4466, 5469
*The Space Swimmers; Science Fiction
  by Gordon Dickson*  2450
*Space Winners*  2647, 3341, 3729
*The Spirit of Dorsai*  4377
*The Tactics of Mistake*  1322, 1326,
  1327, 1641, 2054, 2349, 2351,
  2353, 3790, 3875, 4468, 4672
*Time Storm*  131, 403, 1581, 1941,
  1983, 2808, 3920, 3940, 4641,
  5012, 5087, 5487, 5999

*Way of the Pilgrim*  132, 1493, 1774,
  2192, 2254, 3767, 3817, 5027,
  5918, 5919
*Wolf and Iron*  208, 1328, **1539**,
  1838, 1932, 2603, 3470, 3863,
  4678
*Wolfling*  1595, 1995, 2004
*Young Bleys*  **1540**

**Dietz, Ulysses G.**
*Desmond: A Novel of Love and the
  Modern Vampire*  **1541**

**Dietz, William C.**
*Bodyguard*  **1542**, 4225
*Cluster Command*  **1630**
*Drifter*  473, **1543**
*Drifter's Run*  **1544**
*Drifter's War*  **1545**
*The Final Battle*  **1546**, 2432, 4972
*Freehold*  2350
*Legion of the Damned*  **1547**, 3034,
  4982, 5670, 5718
*Mars Prime*  **1548**, 2584, 4629, 4633
*Matrix Man*  295, **1549**, 2087, 5173
*McCade's Bounty*  **1550**
*Prison Planet*  1107, **1551**, 3693,
  6059
*Steelheart*  **1552**
*War World*  5930
*Where the Ships Die*  **1553**

**Dillard, Anne**
*Specters*  1926, 5064

**Dillard, J.M.**
*Emissary*  1247, 1654, 2061, 2908,
  4295, 5598
*Insurrection*  **1554**
*The Lost Years*  1511, 1922, 2069,
  4927, 5019
*Recovery*  1954
*Specters*  **1555**, 2024, 2556, 3585,
  4442, 4501, 5314
*Star Trek V: The Final Frontier*  1728,
  1967, 2062, 2666
*Star Trek VI: The Undiscovered
  Country*  **1556**, 3307
*Star Trek: Generations*  2061, 2063
*Star Trek: The Lost Years*  **1557**,
  1728, 1967, 2062

**Dillon, Barbara**
*My Stepfather Shrank!*  **1558**

**DiMarco, Jennifer**
*Escape to the Wind*  **1559**, 4882,
  5209

**DiMartino, Nick**
*Seattle Ghost Story*  **1560**

**Dimenstein, Catherine Wells**
*Children of the Earth*  **5743**
*The Earth Is All That Lasts*  **5744**
*The Earth Saver*  **5745**

**Disch, Thomas M.**
*The Brave Little Toaster: A Bedtime
  Story for Small Appliances*  252
*The Brave Little Toaster Goes to
  Mars*  252
*The Businessman: A Tale of
  Terror*  627, 1396, 1672, 3057,
  3660, 3957, 4436
*The Genocides*  1015, 2252, 2646,
  2811, 5027
*Getting into Death*  337
*The M.D.: A Horror Story*  627, **1561**,
  2700, 3494, 4437, 5167
*Mankind under the Leash*  1015, 5878
*The New Improved Sun: An Anthology
  of Utopian Science Fiction*  4959

*The Priest: A Gothic Romance* 627, **1562**
*The Ruins of Earth: An Anthology of the Immediate Future* 4959

**DiSilvestro, Roger L.**
*Living with the Reptiles* 65, 141, 142, 143, 522, 1417, **1563**, 3427, 3428, 4564, 5559
*Ursula's Gift* 5939

**Dixon, Larry**
*The Black Gryphon* **3270**
*Born to Run* **3271**
*Chrome Circle* **3277**
*Owlflight* **3291**
*Owlsight* **3292**
*The Silver Gryphon* **3295**
*The White Gryphon* **3303**

**Doctorow, E.L.**
*The Waterworks* 26, 453, **1564**

**Dodge, Jim**
*Stone Junction* 4607

**Doherty, Robert**
*Area 51* **1565**, 3952

**Dolan, Bill**
*Afrikorps* 1405, **1566**, 4678
*Cobra Curse* **1567**, 3013
*Iron Horse* 1405, **1568**
*White Rhino* **1569**, 4544

**Donaldson, D.J.**
*Blood on the Bayou* 1007, **1570**, 1888, 2138

**Donaldson, Stephen R.**
*Chronicles of Thomas Covenant* 896
*Forbidden Knowledge* **1571**
*The Gap into Conflict: The Real Story* **1572**, 3692
*The Gap into Madness: Chaos and Order* **1573**
*The Gap into Power: A Dark and Hungry God Arises* **1574**
*The Gap into Ruin: This Day All Gods Die* **1575**
*The Gap into Vision: Forbidden Knowledge* 930
*The Illearth War* 1911, 2887, 5235, 5741, 6058
*Lord Foul's Bane* 17, 182, 713, 1035, 2888, 2987, 3581, 4014, 4520, 4776, 4797, 4809, 5235, 5364, 5651, 5682, 5733, 5832, 5921, 5922, 6058
*The Mirror of Her Dreams* 515, 2505, 2507, 3659
*The Power That Preserves* 5235, 6058
*Strange Dreams* **1576**
*The Wounded Land* 5832

**Donnelly, J.W.**
*Babylon Gardens* 578

**Donnelly, Joe**
*The Shee* 3104

**Donnelly, Marcos**
*Prophets for the End of Time* **1577**

**Donoghue, Emma**
*Kissing the Witch: Old Tales in New Skins* 794, 1358, **1578**, 2845

**Doohan, James**
*The Rising* **1579**

**Dorf, Fran**
*A Reasonable Madness* **1580**

**Dorfman, Ariel**
*Mascara* 19, 1334, 5073

**Dorn, Michael**
*Time Blender* **1581**

**Dorsey, Candas Jane**
*Black Wine* **1582**, 4244

**Douglas, Carole Nelson**
*Cup of Clay* 286, 563, **1583**, 2042, 2127, 2358, 2617
*Keepers of Edanvant* 1731, 1736
*Probe* 1304
*Seed upon the Wind* **1584**
*Six of Swords* 2502, 4614

**Douglas, Ian**
*Semper Mars* **1585**

**Douglas, John**
*The Late Show* 3326

**Douglas, L. Warren**
*Bright Islands in a Dark Sea* 1647, 2010
*Cannon's Orb* 296, 420, 684, 688, 933, 998, 1303, **1586**, 2008, 2637, 2681, 3440, 3730, 3739, 3752, 4119, 4476, 4479, 4711, 4859, 5068, 5467
*A Plague of Change* 988, **1587**, 1599, 2008, 2637, 2953, 3475, 4642, 5363, 5461, 5466
*Stepwater* 708, 758, 1266, 1500, 1553, 1582, **1588**, 1807, 2059, 2135, 4101, 5437, 5465, 5543
*The Wells of Phyre* **1589**, 5780

**Douglas, Lauren Wright**
*In the Blood* 74, 662, **1590**, 1720, 2242, 3579, 3915

**Douglis, Marjie**
*Matrix Witch* 5542

**Dowd, Tom**
*Night's Pawn* **1591**, 5096, 5135

**Downer, Ann**
*The Spellkey Trilogy* **1592**

**Downing, Paula E.**
*Fallway* 1586, **1593**, 2223, 2224, 2476, 2683, 3707, 3708, 3709, 3723, 3752, 3760, 5467
*Flare Star* 996, **1594**, 1899, 3707, 3708, 3709, 4148, 5403, 6065
*Maia's Veil* **3707**
*Rinn's Star* 632, 645, 897, 1046, 1772, 3708, 3709, 4140
*Siduri's Net* **3709**
*A Whisper of Time* 351, **1595**, 3707, 3708, 3709, 4175, 5429, 5548

**Doyle, Arthur Conan**
*The Best Horror Stories of Arthur Conan Doyle* **1596**, 3694
*The Best Supernatural Tales of Arthur Conan Doyle* 2680, 3147, 4021
*The Horror of the Heights and Other Tales of Suspense* **1597**, 5746
*The Lost World* 306, 416, 1256, 1379, 1417, 2468, 4597, 5067

**Doyle, Debra**
*By Honor Betray'd* **1598**
*The Gathering Flame* **1599**
*Groogleman* **1600**
*Knight's Wyrd* **1601**
*The Long Hunt* **1602**
*Night of the Living Rat!* 493, **1603**, 3573
*The Price of the Stars* 310, 645, 929, 1043, 1047, 1503, 1553, **1604**, 1901, 2053, 2374, 3722, 3749, 4957, 5138, 5139, 5140, 5141, 5672, 5673, 5674, 5675, 5680, 5681, 6086

*School of Wizardry* 847, **1605**, 4700, 5640, 6043, 6057, 6058
*Starpilot's Grave* **1606**, 4148, 5674

**Dozois, Gardner**
*Angels!* **1339**
''Down Among the Dead Men'' 5690
*Dying for It: More Erotic Tales of Unearthly Love* **1607**, 2177, 2178, 2179
*Future Earths: Under African Skies* **4544**
*Geodesic Dreams: The Best Short Fiction of Gardner Dozois* 61, 804, **1608**
*The Good Old Stuff* **1609**
*Isaac Asimov's Aliens* 4406
*Isaac Asimov's Ghosts* **1610**
*Isaac Asimov's Vampires* **1611**
*Little People!* **1340**
*Modern Classic Short Novels of Science Fiction* **1612**, 3381, 5954
*Modern Classics of Fantasy* 225, 228, **1613**, 5030, 5721
*Modern Classics of Science Fiction* 229, 246, 422, **1614**, 2585, 2594, 2595, 3381
*Ripper!* 1763, 5761
*Slow Dancing through Time* **1615**
*Strangers* 791
*Unicorns II* **1343**
*The Year's Best Science Fiction: Eighth Annual Collection* 215, 1363, **1616**, 4031, 4558
*The Year's Best Science Fiction: Eleventh Annual Collection* **1617**, 5046
*The Year's Best Science Fiction: Fifteenth Annual Collection* **1618**, 5954
*The Year's Best Science Fiction: Fourteenth Annual Collection* **1619**
*The Year's Best Science Fiction: Ninth Annual Collection* **1620**, 4032
*The Year's Best Science Fiction Series* 246, 888, 1339, 1342, 2593, 2594, 2595, 2596, 2597, 2598, 4439, 4824, 5489
*The Year's Best Science Fiction: Seventh Annual Collection* 214, 238, 500, 501, 887, **1621**, 4725, 5948
*The Year's Best Science Fiction: Tenth Annual Collection* 216, 1364, 1365, **1622**
*The Year's Best Science Fiction: Thirteenth Annual Collection* **1623**
*The Year's Best Science Fiction: Twelfth Annual Collection* **1624**, 2679, 3751

**Drake, Alison**
*Lagoon* **1625**, 1806, 5081

**Drake, David**
*Arc Riders* **1626**, 1853, 2119
*At Any Price* 308
*Battlestation* **1627**, 3037
*Birds of Prey* 1855, 1955
*Bridgehead* 1955
*The Butcher's Bill* 4972
*Caught in the Crossfire* **1628**
*A Century of Horror: 1970-1979: The Greatest Stories of the Decade* **1629**
*Cluster Command* **1630**, 4374, 6014
*Counter Attack* 1896
*Counting the Cost* 2054, 3937, 4982
*Cross the Stars* 2004
*Dagger* 1955, 4202

*The Dragon Lord* 1189, 1190, 2747, 3474, 3806
*Enemy of My Enemy* **4204**
*The Fleet* 1896, 4373
*The Fleet 1-6* 6005
*The Forlorn Hope* 1327, 4672, 4973
*Fortress* 3586, 5300
*The Fourth Rome* **1631**, 4040
*From the Heart of Darkness* 674, 675, 2780, 2784, 3753
*Hammer's Slammers* 1315, 1326, 2052, 2054, 2323, 2805, 4194, 4226, 4306, 4374, 4377, 4583, 5676
*The Hammer's Slammers Series* 4829
*Heads to the Storm* 3147, 3148
*An Honorable Defense* 1650, 6014
*The Hunter Returns* **1632**
*Igniting the Reaches* 308, **1633**, 5294
*In the Heart of Darkness* **1955**
*The Jungle* 1547, 1567, **1634**, 2371, 2437, 4507, 4974, 5280
*Justice* **1635**, 4204
*Lord of the Isles* **1636**, 1866, 3834
*The Military Dimension* 1552
*More than Honor* 5676
*Northworld* 1315, **1637**, 1661, 1862, 1955, 2350, 4204, 5294
*An Oblique Approach* 770, **1638**, 1956
*Old Nathan* **1639**, 2191, 2367, 3118, 5356, 5357
*Queen of Demons* **1640**
*Ranks of Bronze* 206, 1955, 1980, 1983, 2188
*Redliners* **1641**, 1976
*Rolling Hot* **1642**, 4306, 4377, 4672
*The Sea Hag* 1415
*The Sharp End* **1643**
*The Square Deal* 86, **1644**
*Starliner* 10, 782, **1645**, 2053, 3315, 3968, 3974, 4967, 5676, 5679
*Surface Action* **1646**, 4911
*Target* **4017**
*Through the Breach* 308, **1647**, 1955
*The Undesired Princess and the Enchanted Bunny* 1419
*Vengeance* **1648**, 4204
*Vettius and His Friends* 856, 1110, 2781, 2782, 3356, 5110, 5471, 5505
*The Voyage* **1649**
*The War Machine* **1650**, 6014
*The Warrior* 312, 1547, **1651**
*With the Lightnings* **1652**

**Drake, H.B.**
*The Shadowy Thing* 1424

**Draulans, Dirk**
*The Red Queen* **1653**

**Dreadstone, Carl**
*The Bride of Frankenstein* 4687
*The Wolfman* 1800

**Drennan, Kathryn M.**
*To Dream in the City of Sorrows* 944, 1387, **1654**, 2102, 3096, 4833

**Drew, Wayland**
*Willow* 1042, 1483, 3540

**Dreyfuss, Richard**
*The Two Georges* **1655**, 5504

**Driscoll, Richard**
*Mind Slayer* **4469**
*Star Precinct* **4470**

**Driver, John**
*The Hunger of the Beast* **1656**, 2200, 3133, 3391, 3402, 4222

**Du Maurier, Daphne**
*"Don't Look Now"* 3348, 3349, 3350, 3433
*Rebecca* 2612, 2875

**Duane, Diane**
*The Book of Night with Moon* **1657**, 3120
*Dark Mirror* 1385, **1658**, 2788, 4934
*Deep Wizardry* 4323
*Doctor's Orders* 526, 569, 900, 1381, 1556, **1659**, 1922, 4514
*The Door into Fire* 978, 1109, 1444, 1902, 1985, 2796, 2799, 2987, 3068, 3078, 3175, 3296, 3297, 3298, 3304, 3305, 3306, 3401, 4322, 4608, 4975, 5684
*The Door into Shadow* 1444, 2796, 3078, 3304
*The Door into Sunset* **1660**, 1985, 2560, 3078, 3304
*High Moon* **1661**, 3029
*High Wizardry* 605, 969, **1662**, 2623, 2628, 4323, 5558, 5646
*Intellivore* **1663**
*Kill Station* **1664**
*Mindblast* **1665**
*My Enemy, My Ally* **1728**, 2062, 2063, 2064, 2296, 3918
*The Romulan Way* 1226, 2063, 2069, 5019
*seaQuest DSV: The Novel* 1201, **1666**, 5282
*So You Want to Be a Wizard?* 168, 641, 847, 1267, 1605, 2949, 4323, 4338, 4404, 5002, 5070, 5977
*Spectres* 3130, 3898
*Spider-Man: The Venom Factor* 1227, 1390, **1667**, 3403
*Spock's World* 1260, 1384, 1861, 2062, 4137, 5019
*A Wizard Abroad* **1668**, 4260
*The Wounded Sky* 528, 1228, 1386, 2501, 4511
*X-Men: Empire's End* 2256

**Due, Tannarive**
*The Between* **1669**, 2161
*My Soul to Keep* **1670**, 3164

**Duffy, Steve**
*The Night Comes On* **1671**, 3314, 5776

**Dugan, Bill**
*Geronimo* 4233

**Duigon, Lee**
*Mind Stealer* **1672**

**Dumas, Alexandre**
*The Three Musketeers* 747, 5017
*Twenty Years After* 742

**Dunbar, Olivia Howard**
*The Shell of Sense* **1673**, 2633, 2919

**Duncan, Dave**
*The Coming of Wisdom* 993
*The Cursed* **1674**, 5735
*The Cutting Edge* 712, 717, 719, 1105, **1675**, 1732, 1733, 2271, 3486, 3624, 4986, 5391
*The Destiny of the Sword* 5709, 5712
*Emperor and Clown* **1676**, 5221
*Faery Lands Forlorn* **1677**
*Future Indefinite* **1678**
*The Gilded Chain: A Tale of the King's Blades* **1679**

*Hero* 958, 1547, **1680**, 2215, 2466, 2536, 3829, 4229, 5201, 5476, 5718, 5949
*The Hunters' Haunt* **1681**
*The Living God* **1682**
*Magic Casement* 992, 1146, **1683**, 1732, 2076, 2984, 3834, 3837, 5735
*Past Imperative* **1684**
*Perilous Seas* **1685**
*Present Tense* **1686**
*The Reaver Road* **1687**, 5595
*The Reluctant Swordsman* 4809, 5651
*The Stricken Field* **1688**
*Strings* **1689**, 4696
*Upland Outlaws* **1690**, 3926
*West of January* **1691**

**Duncan, Lois**
*I Know What You Did Last Summer* **1692**
*I Walk at Night* 5285
*Night Terrors: Stories of Shadow and Substance* **1693**
*Summer of Fear* 1801

**Dunn, J.R.**
*Days of Cain* 467, **1694**, 3064, 5874
*Full Tide of Night* 1348, **1695**
*This Side of Judgment* **1696**, 2907, 3743

**Dunn, Katherine**
*Geek Love* 789, 1027, **1697**, 3206, 4057, 5264, 5899

**Dunn, Pauline**
*The Crawling Dark* 1136, **1698**, 2934

**Dunsany**
*At the Edge of the World* 5102
*The Complete Pegana* **1699**
*A Dreamer's Tales* 3530, 3859, 5103
*Ghosts of the Heaviside Layer and Other Fantasies* 348
*The Hashish Man and Other Stories by Lord Dunsany* **1700**
*The King of Elfland's Daughter* 3980
*The Travel Tales of Mr. Joseph Jorkens* 3147, 3148, 4021

**Dupree, Tom**
*Full Spectrum 5* **2679**

**Durant, Alan**
*Vampire and Werewolf Stories* **1701**

**Durgin, Doranna**
*Barrenlands* **1702**
*Changespell* **1703**, 4669, 5554
*Dun Lady's Jess* **1704**, 2673, 2678, 2869
*Touched by Magic* **1705**
*Wolf Justice* **1706**

**Durrenmatt, Friedrich**
*It Happened in Broad Daylight* 1131

**Dvorkin, David**
*The Captain's Honor* 2068
*Insatiable* **1707**, 3517
*Timetrap* 2501
*Ursus* 41, 373, 488, **1708**, 4831, 5388

**Dziemianowicz, Stefan**
*100 Creepy Little Creature Stories* **5686**
*100 Ghastly Little Ghost Stories* **1709**, 4828
*100 Tiny Tales of Terror* **5687**
*100 Twisted Little Tales of Torment* **1710**

*100 Vicious Little Vampire Stories* **5688**
*100 Wicked Little Witch Stories* **1711**
*100 Wild Little Weird Tales* **5689**
*Between Time and Terror* **5691**
*Famous Fantastic Mysteries* **1712**
*Girls' Night Out* **1713**
*Horrors: 365 Scary Stories* **1714**
*Mistresses of the Dark* **1715**
*Nursery Crimes* **1716**
*Rivals of Dracula* **5699**
*Rivals of Weird Tales* **5700**
*Sea Cursed: Thirty Terrifying Tales of the Deep* **3798**
*A Taste for Blood* **2407**
*To Sleep, Perchance to Dream. . .Nightmare* **1717**
*Virtuous Vampires* **1718**
*Weird Tales: 32 Unearthed Terrors* 480, 482, 2485, 3023, 3028
*Weird Vampire Tales* **5706**


# E

**E. Downing, Paula**
*Rinn's Star* **1719**

**Eager, Edward**
*Half Magic* 2944, 5822
*Knight's Castle* 332, 1218, 3587
*Seven-Day Magic* 1294

**Eakins, William**
*Key West 2720 A.D.* **1720**

**Easterman, Daniel**
*Name of the Beast* **1721**, 2312, 5196

**Easton, Edward**
*The Miscast Gentleman* 3097

**Easton, M. Coleman**
*Spirits of Cavern and Hearth* 1145, 1470, **1722**, 3626, 5097, 5831

**Easton, Thomas A.**
*Greenhouse* **1723**, 2536, 3932, 5429
*Seeds of Destiny* **1724**
*Silicon Karma* 5353
*Sparrowhawk* 892, **1725**, 2215, 2536, 3503, 3932, 4218, 5157, 5260, 5363, 5368, 6048
*Tower of the Gods* **1726**
*Woodsman* **1727**

**Eberhard, Wolfram**
*Folktales of China* 6026

**Eccarius, J.G.**
*The Last Days of Christ the Vampire* 3244

**Ecklar, Julia**
*Armageddon Sky* **2296**
*The Kobayashi Maru* 905, 1381, **1728**, 1967, 2069, 4514, 5404
*Regenesis* 1589, **1729**, 2006, 2011, 2291, 4548
*Time's Enemy* **2297**
*Traitor Winds* **2298**

**Eco, Umberto**
*Foucault's Pendulum* 334, 335, 1063, 1093, 1273, 1274, 1277, 1397, 2214, 3262, 3682, 4683, 5903
*The Name of the Rose* 3256

**Eddings, David**
*Belgarath the Sorcerer* 712, 1096, **1730**, 4852

*The Belgariad Series* 4284
*The Diamond Throne* **1731**, 4045, 6007
*Domes of Fire* **1732**
*Guardians of the West* 1177, 3926
*The Hidden City* **1733**, 1905
*Magician's Gambit* 1904, 2531, 2990
*Pawn of Prophecy* 287, 704, 717, 994, 1029, 1105, 1675, 1682, 1688, 1690, 1904, 1909, 1911, 2096, 2190, 2268, 2269, 2270, 2271, 2531, 2618, 2676, 2959, 2984, 2985, 2988, 2990, 3489, 3765, 3766, 3833, 3834, 3837, 3892, 3985, 4490, 4908, 5150, 5203, 5650, 5651, 5727, 5736, 6073
*Polgara the Sorceress* **1734**
*Queen of Sorcery* 1904, 2531, 2990
*The Rivan Codex* **1735**
*The Ruby Knight* **1736**
*The Sapphire Rose* 4, 1072, **1737**
*The Seeress of Kell* **1738**, 5832
*Sorceress of Darshiva* **1739**, 1842, 5125, 5820

**Eddings, Leigh**
*Belgarath the Sorcerer* **1730**
*Polgara the Sorceress* **1734**
*The Rivan Codex* **1735**

**Edelman, Scott**
*The Gift* 1166, 1541, 2116, 3853
*Suicide Art* 693, 700, 1021, **1740**, 3318, 5411, 5413

**Edgerton, Teresa**
*The Castle of the Silver Wheel* **1741**, 5002
*The Gnome's Engine* **1742**
*Goblin Moon* **1743**, 2032, 2354, 2355, 2356, 4851
*The Grail and the Ring* 681, **1744**, 1842
*The Moon in Hiding* **1745**, 3510
*The Work of the Sun* **1746**, 2809

**Edghill, Rosemary**
*The Book of Moons* 637
*The Cup of Morning Shadows* **1747**
*The Sword of Maiden's Tears* **1748**, 2141

**Edmonds, I.G.**
*Trickster Tales* 4987

**Edmondson, G.C.**
*The Man Who Corrupted Earth* 1962

**Edwards, Claudia J.**
*Eldrie the Healer* 5547
*Taming the Forest King* 2651

**Edwards, Graham**
*Dragoncharm* 1705, **1749**, 1984, 2650, 3045, 3065, 3728, 4461, 4739, 4848

**Effinger, George Alec**
*The Exile Kiss* **1750**
*A Fire in the Sun* **1751**, 3946, 3947, 4941, 5644
*Look Away* 3075
*Maureen Birnbaum, Barbarian Swordsperson: The Complete Stories* 262, 316, 648, 649, 650, 651, **1752**, 1808, 1811, 2072, 2074, 2144, 4610, 5617
*The Old Funny Stuff* **1753**
*The Red Tape War* 959

*When Gravity Fails* 360, 481, 505, 746, 805, 806, 808, 1153, 1504, 1572, 1680, 1762, 1820, 1889, 1964, 2913, 3946, 3947, 4193, 4291, 4544, 4749, 4941, 5210, 5363, 5644, 5887, 5966
*The Zork Chronicles* 288, **1754**, 1839, 3479

**Egan, Doris**
*The Gate of Ivory* 1486, **1755**, 2264, 3158
*Guilt-Edged Ivory* **1756**
*Two-Bit Heroes* **1757**

**Egan, Greg**
*Axiomatic* **1758**
*Diaspora* **1759**, 2661
*Distress* **1760**, 5256
*Permutation City* **1761**, 2729, 3831
*Quarantine* **1762**, 2273, 4420, 4502

**Egan, Robert**
*Little Shop of Horrors* 5324

**Egbert, H.M.**
*Mrs. Aladdin* 73, 880, 5658

**Ehly, Ehren M.**
*Star Prey* **1763**, 1846, 4716, 5562

**Ehrlich, Amy**
*The Ewoks and the Lost Children* 1392, 1393, 1394

**Ehrlich, Max**
*The Reincarnation of Peter Proud* 1050, 1237, 2901, 4442

**Eickhoff, Randy Lee**
*The Raid* **1764**

**Eisenstein, Phyllis**
*Born to Exile* 18, 176, 1096, 1430, 1583, 1584, 2095, 2290, 2361, 3086, 3580, 4161, 4520, 5153, 5369, 5984
*The Crystal Palace* 16, 1042, 3765
*In the Hands of Glory* 2436, 2437, 4468
*In the Red Lord's Reach* 12, 257, 845, 1430, 1530, **1765**, 2290, 3278, 3293, 3410, 3414, 4294, 4808, 5199
*Shadow of Earth* 6, 142, 442, 1196, 1199, 1530, 1581, 1658, 3920, 4517, 4934, 4971, 5011, 5150, 5364
*Sorcerer's Son* 1104, 5143, 5153
*Spec-Lit: Speculative Fiction, Number 1* **1766**
*Spec-Lit: Speculative Fiction, Number 2* **1767**

**Eklund, Gordon**
*Space Pirates* 1647
*A Thunder on Neptune* **1768**, 1991, 4963

**Elder, Joseph**
*Eros in Orbit* 1362, 1607

**Elgin, Suzette Haden**
*And Then There'll Be Fireworks* 186, 515, 2084, 2950, 4361, 5235, 5616
*Communipath Worlds* 642, 653, 1263
*Earthsong* **1769**, 3622, 3628, 3629, 3630, 4999
*The Grand Jubilee* 186, 515, 2084, 2950, 3696, 3697, 3699, 4361, 4405, 5235, 5337, 5616
*The Judas Rose* 1135, 3622, 4325, 5634

*Native Tongue* 642, 968, 1135, 1582, 1929, 2295, 2445, 3622, 4325, 4486, 4736, 5209, 5268, 5276, 5430, 5634, 5867, 5956
*Star Anchored, Star Angered* 4330
*Twelve Fair Kingdoms* 167, 174, 184, 186, 187, 515, 560, 563, 1045, 1695, 2015, 2084, 2950, 3118, 3278, 3719, 3747, 4221, 4361, 4866, 5219, 5235, 5574, 5616

**Eliot, Marc**
*How Dear the Dawn* 462

**Eliot, T.S.**
*Old Possum's Book of Practical Cats* 4273

**Elizabeth, Suzanne**
*Destined to Love* 2497
*Destiny in Disguise* 2497

**Elliot, Jeffrey M.**
*Kindred Spirits* 2116, 2117, 2295, 2444, 5154

**Elliott, Elton**
*Nanodreams* **1770**, 2394, 4064

**Elliott, Jannean**
*Shadow World* **1262**

**Elliott, Kate**
*An Earthly Crown* **1771**, 4138, 4486, 5227
*The Golden Key* 4486
*Jaran* **1772**, 1809, 5544
*King's Dragon* 992, **1773**
*The Law of Becoming* **1774**
*Prince of Dogs* **1775**

**Elliott, Tom**
*The Dwelling* 342, 364, 861, 873, 890, 1192, **1776**, 2040, 2875, 2901, 3055, 3685, 3953, 4663, 4778, 4830, 5424

**Ellis, Brett Easton**
*American Psycho* 695, 1170, 1401, **1777**, 2755, 3807, 4185, 5326, 5443
*The Informers* 812, **1778**, 3396

**Ellis, Jack**
*Nightlife* **1779**
*Seeing Eye* **1780**, 1975

**Ellis, Peter Berresford**
*Snowbeast!* **5482**
*Swamp* **5483**

**Ellis, Terry**
*Invasion of Willow Wood Springs* **1781**

**Ellison, Harlan**
*Again, Dangerous Visions* 1023, 4713, 4721
*Angry Candy* 625, 1492, **1783**, 3421, 5058
*The City on the Edge of Forever* 1225, **1784**, 1853
*Dangerous Visions* 214, 215, 238, 239, 501, 1023, 1614, 1616, 1620, 4031, 4713, 4721, 5004, 5948
*Deathbird Stories* 3421, 4977
*The Essential Ellison: A 35-Year Retrospective* 893, 3421, 4889
*The Fantasies of Harlan Ellison* 3222
*I Have No Mouth and I Must Scream* 4232
*I, Robot: The Illustrated Screenplay* 29, **1785**

*Medea: Harlan's World* 3641, 3643, 3646, 3647, 4725, 5038, 5214, 5216
*Mefisto in Onyx* 397, 436, **1786**, 4875
*Mind Fields: The Art of Jacek Yerka* **1787**
*Partners in Wonder: Harlan Ellison in Collaboration with...* 1615
''Repent, Harlequin!'' Said the Ticktockman* **1782**
*Run for the Stars/Echoes of Thunder* **1788**
*Slippage* 663, 778, **1789**, 2701, 4886, 5663
*Strange Wine* 3421

**Elmore, Larry**
*Runes of Autumn* **1790**

**Elmore, Robert**
*Runes of Autumn* **1790**

**Elrod, P.N.**
*Blood on the Water* **1791**
*Bloodlist* 285, **1792**, 2149, 2517, 2792, 3108, 5078, 5374
*A Chill in the Blood* **1793**
*Dance of Death* **1794**
*Death Masque* **1795**
*Fire in the Blood* **1796**
*I, Strahd* 155, 465, 1510, **1797**, 2516, 2663, 5847, 6011
*Keeper of the King* 452
*Red Death* 292, **1798**, 4774
*The Time of the Vampires* **1799**
*The Vampire Chronicles* 4464
*The Vampire Files Series* 1121, 1213, 1214, 2793

**Elvira**
*The Boy Who Cried Werewolf* **1800**
*Camp Vamp* **1801**
*Elvira: Transylvania 90210* **1802**
*Transylvania 90210* 1302, 2131, 5161

**Elwood, Roger**
*Angelwalk: A Modern Fable* **1803**, 2802, 5101
*Horror Hunters* 5653
*Six Science Fiction Plays* 1784, 1785, 5904
*Sorcerers of Sodom* **1804**, 1959, 2930

**Ely, David**
*A Journal of the Flood Year* **1805**
*Seconds* 89, 376, 4086

**Elze, Winifred**
*The Changeling Garden* **1806**

**Emerson, Jane**
*City of Diamond* **1807**, 3927, 5725

**Emerson, Ru**
*The Calling of the Three* 1421, 3282
*The Craft of Light* 3282
*The Empty Throne* 559, **1808**
*Fortress of Frost and Fire* 3282
*Masques* 559
*One Land, One Duke* **1809**, 3282
*The Princess of Flames* 2651, 2799, 4871
*Spell Bound* **1810**, 3846, 5534
*The Thief of Hermes* **1811**, 4912
*To the Haunted Mountains* 2471, 6007
*The Two in Hiding* 1584, **1812**, 3282, 4784
*Voices of Chaos* **1266**

**Emery, Clayton**
*Cardmaster* **1813**

*Final Sacrifice* **1814**
*Outcasts* 27, 487, **1815**, 1840
*Shattered Chains* **1816**, 1977, 2529, 2827
*Tales of Robin Hood* 2248, 2389
*Whispering Woods* 207, 1977

**Emmerich, Roland**
*Independence Day* **1508**
*StarGate* **1509**

**Emshwiller, Carol**
*Carmen Dog* **1817**, 4034, 5616
*The Start of the End of It All* **1818**, 5641

**Emshwiller, Peter R.**
*The Host* 805, 1438, **1819**, 2727, 3449, 3817, 4030, 4709, 4710, 4949, 5355, 5642
*Short Blade* 805, **1820**, 4709

**Ende, Michael**
*The Neverending Story* 87, 713, 1294, 1299, 1432, 3010, 3156, 3468, 3884, 4917, 5972
*The Night of Wishes: Or, The Satanarchaeolidealcohellish Notion Potion* 489, 1527, **1821**
*The Night of Wishes: or The Satanarchaeolidealcohellish Notion Potion* 2085, 2776, 5163

**Endore, Guy**
*The Werewolf of Paris* 572, 603, **1822**, 5481

**Enfantino, Peter**
*Quick Chills* 300, 1378, **1823**, 2960, 2961, 4199, 4200, 4846, 5602, 5603, 5605
*Quick Chills II* **4025**

**Engel, Alan**
*Variant* 1164

**Engh, M.J.**
*Rainbow Man* 686, **1824**, 2134, 2237, 3426, 3440, 4900

**England, Terry**
*Rewind* **1825**

**Engstrom, Elizabeth**
*Black Ambrosia* 3519, 4576, 5347, 5419
*Imagination Fully Dilated* **1044**, 4186
*Lizzie Borden* **1826**
*Nightmare Flower* 802, **1827**, 5521

**Ennis, Catherine**
*To the Lightning* 4882

**Enright, D.J.**
*The Oxford Book of the Supernatural* 2543, 2643

**Epperson, S.K.**
*Borderland: A Novel of Terror* **1828**, 4582
*Dumford Blood* **1829**, 2599, 5332
*Green Lake* **1830**
*The Moons of Summer* **1831**, 4344, 5334
*Nightmare* **1832**, 5464

**Erdoes, Richard**
*American Indian Myths and Legends* 40, 190, 849, 5578, 5751

**Ergas, Elizabeth**
*Devil's Gate* 947, **1833**, 3389, 5100
*Rage* **1834**

**Erickson, Steve**
*Arc d'X* **1835**, 5209

**Erskine, Barbara**
*Midnight Is a Lonely Place* 1050,
  **1836**, 2903, 4753, 5463

**Eshbach, Lloyd Arthur**
*The Land Beyond the Gate* 1957

**Estes, Rose**
*Elfwood* **1837**, 5251
*The Hunter* 4294, 5097
*The Hunter on Arena* **1838**
*Iron Dragons: Mountains and
  Madness* **1839**
*Skryling's Blade* 27, 487, 1815
*The Stone of Time* **1840**, 3169
*Troll-Quest* **1841**
*Troll-Taken* 636, 703, 1744, **1842**,
  2326, 3487, 3816, 4170, 5409

**Estey, Dale**
*A Lost Tale* 184, 639, 2943, 3257

**Estleman, Loren D.**
*Deals with the Devil* **4542**

**Etchison, Dennis**
*The Blood Kiss* 555, 5339, 5600
*California Gothic* **1843**, 3640
*The Complete Masters of
  Darkness* 1629, **1844**, 2590, 5031
*Cutting Edge* 2965, 3959, 3960,
  4278, 4812, 4888, 5855
*The Dark Country* 429, 623, 864,
  865, 866, 2319, 3687, 4530, 4886,
  4889
*Darkside* 916, **1845**, 3312, 3785,
  5064, 5332, 5990
*Double Edge* **1846**
*Metahorror* 1740, **1847**, 4278, 5795
*Red Dreams* 3322, 4889, 5007
*Shadow Man* 284, **1848**, 2448, 3103

**Etheridge, Rutledge**
*The First Duelist* **1849**

**Eulo, Ken**
*The Brownstone* 3033, 3141, 5519
*Claw* **1850**, 2779, 3701, 4414,
  4415, 4688
*Manhattan Heat* **1851**, 4847

**Evans, David**
*Time Station Berlin* **1852**
*Time Station London* 1344, **1853**
*Time Station Paris* **1854**

**Evans, Linda**
*Far Edge of Darkness* 264, 350,
  1638, **1855**
*Sleipnir* 263, 458, **1856**, 2572,
  4516, 4522
*Time Scout* 263
*Wagers of Sin* 264

**Evans, Quinn Taylor**
*Merlin's Legacy: Dawn of
  Camelot* **1857**

**Everett, H.D.**
*The Death Mask and Other
  Ghosts* 1673

**Ewers, Hanz Heine**
*Alraune* 5690


**F**


**Fabi, Mark**
*Wyrm* **1858**

**Faig, Kenneth W. Jr.**
*Tales of the Lovecraft
  Collectors* **1859**

**Fairman, Paul W.**
*The Runaway Robot* 252

**Falk, Margaret**
*Darkscope* **1860**, 2198

**Fancher, Jane S.**
*Ground-Ties* **1861**, 2051, 2351,
  2733, 3994, 4927
*Harmonies of the 'Net* 1774, **1862**,
  2048, 2298, 5660
*Ring of Intrigue* **1863**
*Ring of Lightning* **1864**
*Uplink* **1865**

**Farland, David**
*The Runelords: The Sum of All
  Men* 1082, **1866**

**Farmer, Nancy**
*The Ear, the Eye, and the Arm* 1600,
  **1867**, 3045, 3283, 4262, 5145
*A Girl Named Disaster* **1868**, 1996

**Farmer, Philip Jose**
*A Barnstormer in Oz* 2136, 3609
*Dare* 3543
*Dayworld* 4720, 5546
*Dayworld Breakup* **1869**
*Dayworld Rebel* 5193
*Doc Savage: His Apocalyptic
  Life* 1940, 3643, 4624, 4625
*Escape From Loki* 85, 725, **1870**,
  4622, 4623, 4624, 4625, 5307,
  5308, 5309
*The Fabulous Riverboat* 961
*Flesh* 3543, 5490
*The Green Odyssey* 2414, 4545
*The Image of the Beast* 3543
*The Lovers* 2050
*The Mad Goblin* 4624, 4625
*The Maker of Universes* 164, 953,
  1324, 3848, 5033, 5830
*More than Fire* **1871**
*Night of Light* 3617
*Quest to Riverworld* **1872**
*Red Orc's Rage* 87, 164, 179, 507,
  970, 1100, 1461, **1873**, 2082,
  2791, 3831, 4458, 4921, 5063,
  5558
*Riders of the Purple Wage* **1874**,
  3736
*Strange Relations* 1362, 4139
*Tales of Riverworld* **1875**, 4929
*Tarzan Alive* 3643
*Time's Last Gift* 175, 5998
*To Your Scattered Bodies Go* 270,
  1422, 1581, **1876**, 2332, 5044,
  5714, 5726, 6071
*Tongues of the Moon* 111
*Traitor to the Living* 188
*Two Hawks From Earth* 4814
*The Unreasoning Mask* 4942
*Venus on the Half Shell* 4546
*The Wind Whales of Ishmael* 3800
*A Woman a Day* 3543

**Farren, Mick**
*The Armageddon Crazy* **1877**, 6028
*The Feelies* 805, **1878**, 3311, 4339,
  5353
*The Last Stand of the DNA
  Cowboys* **1879**
*Mars—The Red Planet* **1880**
*Necrom* **1881**, 3071
*The Texts of Festival* 3664, 5170
*The Time of Feasting* **1882**, 2258,
  4190, 4667

**Farris, John**
*All Heads Turn When the Hunt Goes
  By* 21, 654, 1076, 1888, 2494,
  4009, 4738

*The Axman Cometh* 1777, 1826,
  **1883**, 2202, 2689, 2871, 3638,
  3695, 5845
*Catacombs* 2672, 3551, 3565, 4816
*Fiends* 1204, **1884**, 2091, 2936,
  5553
*The Fury* 97, 204, 872, 879, 941,
  1580, 2530, 2704, 3211, 3215,
  3230, 3251, 3594, 4843, 4883
*I Scream. You Scream. We All Scream
  for Ice Cream* 3494
*Night Visions 8* **1885**
*Sacrifice* 1670, **1886**, 2113, 4668
*Scare Tactics* **1887**, 2305, 3673,
  3753
*Son of the Endless Night* 5896
*When Michael Calls* 536
*Wildwood* 1039, 2091, 2936, 3056,
  3681, 4224, 5380

**Farrow, David A.**
*Root of All Evil* **1888**

**Farshtey, Greg**
*Strange Tales From the Nile
  Empire* **1889**, 2472, 3015, 4909,
  5210, 5438

**Faulkner, William**
*Absalom, Absalom* 340

**Faust, Christa**
*Control Freak* **1890**

**Faust, Joe Clifford**
*Desperate Measures* **1891**, 3828
*The Essence of Evil* 3828
*Ferman's Devils* **1892**
*Precious Cargo* **1893**, 3828

**Faust, Ron**
*Lord of the Dark Lake* **1894**, 3492

**Fawcett, Bill**
*Battlestation* 1627
*Blessings and Curses* 5214
*Cats in Space and Other Places* **1895**,
  3536, 4054, 4144, 4145, 5252
*The Crafters* 5216
*Honor of the Regiment* **1896**
*Lords of Dragonclaw* 4608
*The Siege of Arista* 1627, 5216

**Feeley, Gregory**
*The Oxygen Barons* 596, 1594,
  **1897**, 2433, 3449, 4678, 4682,
  4950, 5526

**Feil, Hila**
*Blue Moon* 1475, **1898**

**Feintuch, David**
*Challenger's Hope* **1899**, 4973
*Fisherman's Hope* **1900**, 4972
*Midshipman's Hope* 1047, **1901**,
  1978, 3970, 5403, 5673, 5675
*The Still* **1902**
*Voices of Hope* **1903**, 4930

**Feist, Raymond E.**
*A Darkness at Sethanon* 2724, 4852
*Daughter of the Empire* 3303, 3339,
  3581, 3906, 3985, 4741, 6001,
  6003, 6004
*Faerie Tale* 338, 343, 1432, 2160,
  3144, 3779, 5207, 5879
*The King's Buccaneer* **1904**
*Krondor, the Betrayal* 1706, **1905**,
  4727
*Magician* 1685, 1730, 1733, 1738,
  2271, 2425, 2724, 2984, 2985,
  3095, 3172, 5034
*Magician: Apprentice* 4493
*Mistress of the Empire* **1906**
*Prince of the Blood* 1775, **1907**

*Rage of a Demon King* **1908**, 4685
*Rise of a Merchant Prince* **1909**
*Servant of the Empire* **1910**, 4741
*Shadow of a Dark Queen* **1911**,
  3295, 4848
*Shards of a Broken Crown* **1912**
*Silverthorn* 2724

**Felice, Cynthia**
*Double Nocturne* 353, 897, 1757
*Downtime* 1041, **1865**, 2067, 2069,
  4927
*Eclipses* 5572
*Godsfire* 165
*Iceman* **1913**, 3912
*The Khan's Persuasion* 1771, 1772,
  **1914**, 2069
*Light Raid* **5870**
*Promised Land* **5872**
*The Sunbound* 1719, 3718

**Fellows, Oscar L.**
*Operation Damocles* **1915**, **1916**

**Fenn, Lionel**
*668: The Neighbor of the Beast* **1917**,
  4398, 6072
*Kent Montana and the Really Ugly
  Thing From Mars* **1918**, 4398,
  5934
*Kent Montana and the Reasonably
  Invisible Man* **1919**
*The Mark of the Moderately Vicious
  Vampire* 1802, **1920**, 3057
*Once upon a Time in the East* 1398
*The Seven Spears of the
  W'dch'ck* 1603
*Time: The Semi-Final Frontier* **1921**

**Ferguson, Brad**
*A Flag Full of Stars* 905, 1260,
  1511, **1922**, 2296
*The Last Stand* 206, 901, 903, **1923**,
  2922
*The World Next Door* 160, 1133,
  **1924**, 2574, 5906

**Fergusson, Bruce**
*The Mace of Souls* 1439, **1925**

**Ferman, Edward L.**
*The Best From Fantasy and Science
  Fiction: 15-20* 4712
*The Best From Fantasy & Science
  Fiction: A 40th Anniversary
  Anthology* 888, 4712
*The Best From Fantasy & Science
  Fiction: A 45th Anniversary
  Anthology* **4712**
*The Best From Fantasy and Science
  Fiction: A Special 25th Anniversary
  Anthology* 4712
*The Best Horror From Fantasy &
  Science Fiction* 5700

**Ferrario, Keith**
*Deadly Friend* **1926**, 2821, 3785,
  5064

**Ferring, David**
*Konrad* 1241, **1927**
*Shadowbreed* **1928**, 5819

**Ferriss, Lucy**
*The Misconceiver* **1929**

**Fichman, Frederick**
*SETI* **1930**

**Fields, Morgan**
*Shaman Woods* **1931**, 2198, 2734,
  3655, 3895, 4111, 4113, 4309,
  5077, 5961

**Files, Meg**
*Meridian 144* **1932**

**Finch, Sheila**
*Infinity's Web* 2012
*Shaper's Legacy* **1933**
*Shaping the Dawn* **1934**

**Findley, Nigel**
*2XS* 972, 974, 976, 1238, 1591,
 **1935**, 3245, 4821, 5134, 5135,
 5731, 6020
*The Broken Sphere* 2785
*House of the Sun* **1936**, 3198
*Into the Void* 1114, 1144, 1291,
 **1937**, 2785
*No Limits* **1938**, 5828
*Shadowplay* 1591, 5135

**Findley, Timothy**
*Headhunter* **1939**, 4086, 5897

**Fine, Stephen**
*Molly Dear: The Autobiography of an
 Android* 2544

**Fink, Jon Stephen**
*Further Adventures* **1940**, 4622,
 4623, 5307, 5308, 5309

**Finney, Charles G.**
*The Circus of Dr. Lao* 1282, 2303,
 2565, 3137, 4010, 4057, 5264

**Finney, Jack**
*The Body Snatchers* 137, 662, 1037,
 1200, 1723, 1727, 2302, 2344,
 2345, 3212, 3218, 4090, 4944,
 5643
*From Time to Time* 464, 1480, **1941**,
 5594
*Marion's Wall* 3149
*Three by Finney* 3690
*Time After Time* 4036
*Time and Again* 464, 1480, 3690,
 4036, 4332, 5873

**Finney, Walter Braden**
*From Time to Time* **1941**

**Finnis, A.**
*13 Again* 2395
*Bone Meal: Seven More Tales of
 Terror* 1693, 2772
*The Cat-Dogs* 1693, 2772

**Fisher, David**
*Legally Correct Fairy Tales* 1257,
 1578, **1942**, 2845

**Fitch, Marina**
*The Seventh Heart* **1943**, 2540

**Fitzgerald, M.J.**
*The Princess and the Dragon* **4272**

**Flanders, Eric**
*The Forever Children* **1944**, 3637,
 4845, 5250, 5314, 5789
*Night Blood* 570, **1945**, 2313

**Fleet, Robert C.**
*Last Mountain* **1946**
*White Horse, Dark Dragon* **1947**

**Fleischman, Sid**
*The Midnight Horse* **1948**, 4447

**Fleisher, Beth**
*Dragon Moon* **1040**

**Fleming, Gherbod**
*The Devil's Advocate* **1949**, 5701,
 5702, 5882, 5883
*The Winnowing* **1950**, 5882

**Fleming, Ian**
*Chitty Chitty Bang Bang* 4338
*You Only Live Twice* 4560

**Fletcher, Susan**
*Dragon's Milk* 329, 5975, 6030

*Flight of the Dragon Kyn* 1249, **1951**

**Flewelling, Lynn**
*Luck in the Shadows* 683, 692, 1773,
 **1952**, 1984, 2253, 2268, 2270,
 2452, 2650, 2694, 2695, 2696,
 2756, 2925, 2957, 2959, 3481,
 3645, 3651, 3832, 3835, 4686,
 4739, 4796, 5320, 5333, 5581,
 5734, 5735, 5749, 5758
*Stalking Darkness* **1953**, 2096, 2253,
 2270, 2694, 3080, 3835, 5320,
 5758

**Flinn, Denny Martin**
*The Fearful Summons* **1954**

**Flint, Eric**
*In the Heart of Darkness* **1955**
*Mother of Demons* **1956**
*An Oblique Approach* **1638**

**Flint, Kenneth C.**
*Challenge of the Clans* 3059, 3060,
 3501, 3504, 3506, 4266, 4267,
 4268, 5962, 5963
*Cromm* 1498, **1957**, 4174
*The Dark Druid* 5962, 5963
*The Enchanted Isles* **1960**
*Isle of Destiny* 2, 3061
*Legends Reborn* **1958**
*Most Ancient Song* **1961**
*Otherworld* **1959**
*Riders of the Sidhe* 203, 3358
*Storm Shield* 5962, 5963
*A Storm upon Ulster* 1764, 5408

**Flood, Eloise**
*Chains of Command* **3767**

**Flynn, Casey**
*The Enchanted Isles* **1960**, 2677,
 3166, 3174, 3358, 3969
*Most Ancient Song* 203, 1240, **1961**,
 3166, 3174, 3358, 3969

**Flynn, Michael**
*The Country of the Blind* 2217
*Fallen Angels* **4120**
*Firestar* 405, 1244, **1962**, 2660,
 4295, 5248, 5860
*The Forest of Time and Other
 Stories* **1963**
*In the Country of the Blind* 116, 442,
 443, 483, 596, 598, 781, 895,
 1093, 1199, 1274, 1655, 1987,
 2087, 2480, 2488, 2564, 2839,
 3662, 3764, 3854, 3931, 4120,
 4288, 4292, 4682, 4937, 5248,
 5694, 5903
*The Nanotech Chronicles* 100, 772,
 804, 1517, 1770, **1964**, 2569,
 2576, 3001, 3087, 3796, 4118,
 4127, 4216, 4706, 4953, 5257,
 5259, 5369, 5638
*Rogue Star* **1965**, 3789

**Fogarty, John**
*The Haunt* **1966**

**Foglio, Phil**
*Illegal Aliens* **4365**

**Fontana, D.C.**
*Vulcan's Glory* 1386, 1728, **1967**

**Forbes, Caroline**
*The Needle on Full* 4882

**Forbes, Edith**
*Exit to Reality* **1968**

**Ford, John M.**
*Casting Fortune* 409, 767, 1473,
 3154, 4994

*The Dragon Waiting* 314, 652, 738,
 1638, 2507, 2570, 2945, 4272,
 4793, 5014, 5017, 5503, 5511,
 5513
*The Final Reflection* 528, 1922, 4037
*From the End of the Twentieth
 Century* **1969**
*Fugue State/The Death of Dr.
 Island* 130
*Growing Up Weightless* 588, 782,
 927, **1970**, 3359, 4911
*How Much for Just the Planet?* 7,
 526, 607, 1382, 1459, 1536, 1659,
 1918, 1921, 1922, 2567, 2568,
 2880, 4562, 4563, 4564, 4565,
 4566, 4656, 4785, 4870, 5875
*The Princes of Air* 927

**Ford, Patrick K.**
*The Mabinogi and Other Medieval
 Welsh Tales* 5626

**Forrest, Elizabeth**
*Bright Shadow* **1971**
*Dark Tide* 441, 955, **1972**, 2557,
 2749, 3783, 4715, 5121
*Killjoy* **1973**, 5892
*Phoenix Fire* 973, 1159, 1514,
 1748, **1974**, 2142, 2309, 2320,
 2499, 2658, 3167, 3277, 3485,
 3838, 5497, 5697
*Retribution* 437, **1975**, 3267

**Forrest, Felix C.**
*Carola* 5105, 5106
*Ria* 5105, 5106

**Forrest, Katherine V.**
*Dreams and Swords* 1286, 4882

**Forstchen, William R.**
*1945* **2239**
*Action Stations* **1976**, 5204
*Arena* 207, 1483, 1814, 1816,
 **1977**, 2827
*Article 23* **1978**
*The Crystal Sorcerers* **1979**
*The Crystal Warriors* 2042, 2463
*A Darkness upon the Ice* 66
*Ice Prophet* 897, 2870, 4373
*Into the Sea of Stars* 1182, 5042,
 5549
*The Napoleon Wager* **1980**
*Never Sound Retreat* **1981**
*Rally Cry!* 1199, **1982**, 3034, 4799,
 5011
*Terrible Swift Sword* **1983**, 2239

**Forsyth, Kate**
*The Witches of Eileanan* **1984**

**Fortier, Ron**
*Monkey Station* **3703**

**Fortune, Dion**
*The Secrets of Dr. Taverner* 509,
 5696

**Forward, Eve**
*Villains by Necessity* 683, **1985**,
 2451, 2639, 4676, 5678

**Forward, Martha Dodson**
*Marooned on Eden* **1986**
*Ocean under the Ice* **1988**

**Forward, Robert L.**
*Dragon's Egg* 80, 81, 401, 1244,
 1245, 1537, 3398, 3805, 4123,
 4280, 4554, 6065
*The Flight of the Dragonfly* 1245
*Indistinguishable From Magic* 237
*Marooned on Eden* 1083, **1986**,
 3721

*Martian Rainbow* 596, 1548, **1987**,
 4635, 5859
*Ocean under the Ice* **1988**
*Return to Rocheworld* **1989**, 3738,
 3823
*Rocheworld* 64, 1184, 1770, 1964,
 **1990**, 4126, 4357, 4942
*Saturn Rukh* **1991**
*Starquake* 401, 404, 1245
*Timemaster* 236, 404, 593, **1992**

**Foster, Alan Dean**
*Alien* 492, 4289, 4290, 4331
*Alien 3* 492, **1993**, 4289, 4290
*Alien Nation* 504, 1062, 1247, 2682,
 2683, 2684, 2909, 2910, 3520,
 4938, 4939, 5107, 5109
*Aliens* 9, 492, 4075, 4289, 4290
*Betcha Can't Read Just One* **1994**
*Cachalot* 2450, 4923
*A Call to Arms* **1995**, 2810
*Carnivores of Light and
 Darkness* **1996**
*Cat-A-Lyst* 1895, **1997**, 2036, 2620,
 3536, 4143, 4157, 4288, 5589,
 6060
*Chorus Skating* 197, **1998**, 3269,
 4524
*Codgerspace* **1999**
*Cyber Way* 35, 118, 158, 164, 190,
 433, 522, 753, 784, 891, 936, 995,
 1159, 1725, 1788, 1858, 1974,
 **2000**, 2084, 2309, 2320, 2343,
 2486, 2499, 2658, 2682, 2836,
 2861, 3109, 3485, 3704, 4121,
 4302, 4364, 4864, 4940, 5109,
 5199, 5278, 5497, 5744, 5751,
 5836, 6023
*Dark Star* 2979, 4298, 4626, 5280
*Design for Great-Day* **2001**, 4859,
 5565
*The Dig* **2002**, 3897
*Dinotopia Lost* **2003**
*The False Mirror* **2004**, 4378
*Glory Lane* 356, 493, 958, 1222,
 1267, 1453, 1455, 1752, 1871,
 2332, 2629, 2797, 3800, 3811,
 4350, 4562, 4662, 5639
*Greenthieves* **2005**
*The Hour of the Gate* 2946
*The Howling Stones* **2006**, 3769,
 4067
*The I Inside* 583, 4469
*Into the Out Of* 4207
*Jed the Dead* **2007**
*The Last Starfighter* 949, 1509
*Life Form* **2008**
*Mad Amos* **2009**, 5356, 5357, 5504
*The Man Who Used the Universe* 584
*Metrognome* 4173
*Mid-Flinx* **2010**, 5571
*Midworld* 3344
*Montezuma Strip* **2011**, 2033, 2377
*Orphan Star* 1948
*Outland* 829, 831, 2369, 4935,
 4938, 4940
*Parallelities* **2012**
*Quozl* 173, 1419, 1454, 1455, 1930,
 **2013**, 2053, 3063, 3910, 4077,
 4298, 4365, 5379, 5429, 6062
*Sentenced to Prism* 5319
*Smart Dragons, Foolish Elves* **2014**,
 2077, 2413, 4723
*Son of Spellsinger* 169, 187, **2015**
*Spellsinger* 167, 168, 184, 186, 194,
 196, 635, 1416, 1426, 2081, 2946,
 3939, 4163, 4401, 4519, 5224
*Spellsinger at the Gate* 172

*Splinter of the Mind's Eye* 76, 2477, 6052, 6054, 6055
*The Spoils of War* **2016**
*Star Trek Log One* 527
*Star Trek Log Ten* 526
*Starman* 5375
*The Tar-Aiym Krang* 322, 741, 1553, 3359, 3717, 4711, 4829, 4930
*The Thing* 1200
*To the Vanishing Point* 31, 165, 171, 936, 951, 962, 1435, 1454, 1455, 1456, 2327, 2644, 3173, 3343, 3439, 3485, 3805, 3810, 4178, 4364, 4384, 4394, 4473, 4970, 5156, 5159, 5199, 5208, 5497, 5647, 5817, 6062
*Voyage of the Basset* **1024**
*Voyage to the City of the Dead* 4545
*With Friends Like These. . .* 3308, 4127, 4706

**Foster, M.A.**
*Preserver* 4592, 4595
*The Warriors of Dawn* 1326, 1757, 4594

**Fowler, Christopher**
*The Bureau of Lost Souls* **2017**
*City Jitters* 4133
*Flesh Wounds* 3673
*Personal Demons* **2018**
*Red Bride* 1086, **2019**, 2428, 4224
*Roofworld* 2089
*Rune* **2020**, 2339, 3957, 4733, 5400
*Sharper Knives* 94, 775, 3674

**Fowler, D.A.**
*Bad Blood* **2021**, 5118, 5484
*The Book of the Damned* **2022**, 5784
*The Devil's End* 71, **2023**, 2816, 3233, 4598
*Flesh and Blood* **2024**
*What's Wrong with Tamara?* **2025**
*What's Wrong with Valerie?* **2026**

**Fowler, Karen Joy**
*Artificial Things* 2261, 5807
*Black Glass: Short Fictions* **2027**
*Sarah Canary* **2028**, 2265, 3473, 4758, 5151
*The Sweetheart Season* **2029**, 4992

**Fowles, John**
*The Collector* 1656, 2113, 2428, 3002, 3094, 3133, 3402, 4185
*The Magus* 2160, 5485

**Fox, Randy**
*Not Broken, Not Belonging* 1044, **2030**, 2137

**Foxe, Jocelin**
*The Wild Hunt: Vengeance Moon* **2031**

**Foxxe, Ellen**
*Season of Storms* **2032**

**Foy, George**
*The Shift* **2033**

**Frakes, Jonathan**
*The Abductors: Conspiracy* 1579, **2034**

**Frakes, Randall**
*The Terminator* 65, 142, 143, 1199, 1941, 2546, 4333, 5012
*Terminator 2: Judgment Day* 1074, 2532, 4333, 4525

**France, Anatole**
*Revolt of the Angels* 4571

**Frank, Janrae**
*New Eves: Science Fiction about the Extraordinary Women of Today and Tomorrow* 24, 765, **2035**, 4825, 4826

**Frank, Pat**
*Alas, Babylon* 728, 3608

**Franklin, Cheryl J.**
*Fire Crossing* 471, 472, 510, 929, 1101, 1756, **2036**, 2524, 2724, 3725, 4485, 5951
*Fire Get* 930, 2524, 2724, 3933, 5124, 5125, 5449, 6073
*Fire Lord* 2524, 2724
*The Inquisitor* **2037**
*The Light in Exile* 632, 645, **2038**, 2372, 2724, 4594, 5752
*Sable, Shadow and Ice* **2039**

**Franklin, Debra**
*The Admirer* 5287

**Franklin, Pat**
*Dark Dreaming* **2040**, 3657

**Frankos, Steven**
*Cathedral of Thorns* **2041**
*The Jewel of Equilibrant* **2042**

**Frankowski, Leo**
*Conrad's Quest for Rubber* **2043**
*The Cross-Time Engineer* 1328, 1341, 1677, 1982, 4151, 4523, 4799, 5036, 5694
*The Flying Warlord* 33, **2044**, 4814
*The High-Tech Knight* 33, 1982, **2045**
*Lord Conrad's Lady* **2046**
*The Radiant Warrior* 33, 1982, **2047**

**Frayling, Christopher**
*The Vampire* 1308

**Frayn, Michael**
*Sweet Dreams* 519

**Freireich, Valerie J.**
*The Beacon* 1046, **2048**, 4301, 5027
*Becoming Human* 1807, **2049**, 2274, 2559, 3038, 3241, 3927, 4064, 4065
*Imposter* **2050**, 3426
*Testament* 1807, **2051**, 2558

**French, Joseph Lewis**
*The Short Story Omnibus* 1310

**Frezza, Robert**
*Fire in a Faraway Place* **2052**
*McLendon's Syndrome* **2053**, 3484
*A Small Colonial War* **2054**, 5786
*The VMR Theory* **2055**

**Friedberg, Gertrude**
*The Revolving Boy* 4827

**Friedman, C.S.**
*Black Sun Rising* 604, 2037, **2056**, 3438, 3473, 3646, 4485, 4490, 4652, 5277, 5333, 5572, 5629
*Crown of Shadows* **2057**, 5941
*In Conquest Born* 4049, 5821
*The Madness Season* 1586, 1587, 1593, 1602, **2058**, 2665, 2954, 3469, 3476, 4124, 4984, 5451, 5572
*This Alien Shore* **2059**, 2237, 3761, 4901, 5540
*When True Night Falls* 560, **2060**, 5371

**Friedman, M.J.**
*Exile* 999
*Heat Wave* 999

**Friedman, Michael Jan**
*All Good Things. . .* 1228, 1229, 1388, **2061**
*A Call to Darkness* **2062**
*Crossover* **2063**, 5019, 5596
*Deadly Games* 999
*The Disinherited* **1381**
*Doomsday World* **923**
*Double, Double* 1658, 1967, 4514, 4934
*Fortune's Light* 1383, 3524
*Her Klingon Soul* **2064**
*Kahless* 10, 904, **2065**, 4559, 4933
*Legacy* 1954
*Relics* **2066**, 4934
*Requiem* **2067**
*Reunion* **2068**, 3919, 4081, 4928
*Shadows on the Sun* **2069**, 3315, 4139

**Friesner, Esther**
*Alien Pregnant by Elvis* **2070**, 2384, 4169, 4540
*Blood Muse: Timeless Tales of Vampires in the Arts* **2071**, 5448
*Chicks in Chainmail* 316, 649, 650, 651, 765, 1808, 1811, **2072**, 2144, 3290, 5018
*Child of the Eagle* 350, **2073**, 5511
*Demon Blues* 1014, 5649
*Did You Say Chicks?!* **2074**
*Druid's Blood* 4556
*Elf Defense* 1426, 3269, 4393, 5649
*Gnome Man's Land* **2075**, 4317, 4394
*Happy High* 2800
*Harpy High* **2076**, 4317
*Hooray for Hellywood* **2077**, 3989, 4363, 5649
*It's Been Fun* **2078**
*Majyk by Accident* 197, **2079**, 5163, 5649
*Majyk by Design* **2080**
*Majyk by Hook or Crook* **2081**
*New York by Knight* 3474, 4926, 5096, 5311, 5642
*The Psalms of Herod* 1653
*The Sherwood Game* **2082**, 2470
*Sphynxes Wild* 1098, **2083**, 5939
*Split Heirs* 5649
*Unicorn U.* **2084**, 4317, 5649
*Warchild* 8, 2917
*The Water King's Laughter* 1765, 5153
*Wishing Season* 73, 489, 557, 880, **2085**, 2129, 4863, 5163, 5218, 5658, 6017
*Yesterday We Saw Mermaids* **2086**

**Frost, Brian J.**
*Book of the Werewolf* 1230, 2410, 2892, 2976, 4410, 5384

**Frost, Gregory**
*Lyrec* 846
*The Pure Cold Light* **2087**, 2728

**Frost, Mark**
*The List of 7* 2692, 3631, 4773

**Froud, Brian**
*The Goblin Companion* **2980**
*Good Faeries, Bad Faeries* **2088**
*Something Rich and Strange* **3840**
*Strange Stains and Mysterious Smells* **2982**

**Fruttero, Carlo**
*The D. Case: The Truth about the Mystery of Edwin Drood* 1524

**Fry, Rosalie**
*The Secret of Roan Inish* 773, 3731, 3816, 5554

**Fulgham, Steven Ray**
*The Forsaken* **2089**, 4499
*The Summoned* **2090**, 3394, 4598
*A Whisper of Wings* **2091**

**Fuller, Julie Forward**
*Return to Rocheworld* **1989**

**Fullilove, Eric James**
*Circle of One* **2092**, 4192, 5576, 5596
*The Stranger* **2093**

**Fulton, Liz**
*The Palm Dome* **2094**, 2822

**Furey, Maggie**
*Aurian* 741, 1066, 1095, **2095**, 3107
*Dhiammara* **2096**
*Harp of Winds* **2097**, 4795
*Sword of Flame* **2098**

**Furlong, Monica**
*Wise Child* 1746

**Furness, Ray**
*The Dedalus Book of German Decadence* 3089

## G

**Gabaldon, Diana**
*Dragonfly in Amber* 691, 2731, 3261
*Outlander* 2121, 2540

**Gadallah, Leslie**
*Cat's Gambit* 451, **2099**

**Gadol, Peter**
*Coyote* **2100**, 3523, 5361, 5578

**Gaiman, Neil**
*Angels & Visitations: A Miscellany* **2101**, 3460, 5165
*Day of the Dead* **2102**
*Good Omens: The Nice and Accurate Prophecies of Agnes Nutter, Witch* 262, 453, 672, 1268, 1283, 1339, 1577, 2084, 2100, **2103**, 2327, 2342, 2658, 2750, 2753, 2803, 2880, 2950, 3009, 3071, 3311, 3480, 3483, 3488, 3810, 3811, 3908, 3986, 4028, 4029, 4035, 4060, 4391, 4399, 4400, 4401, 4404, 4607, 4655, 5456, 5532, 5569, 5768, 5958, 6031, 6049, 6062, 6064, 6070
*Neverwhere* **2104**
*Now We Are Sick* 486, 4274
*The Sandman: Book of Dreams* **2105**, 4186
*Smoke and Mirrors* 578, **2106**

**Galen, Mitchell**
*Tales From the Darkside, Volume 1* 2402, 2403, 5473

**Gallagher, Dan**
*The Pleistocene Redemption* **2107**

**Gallagher, Diana G.**
*The Alien Dark* 35, 64, 100, 210, 419, 643, 933, 981, 990, 998, 1587, 1875, **2108**, 2764, 2864, 3001, 3469, 3721, 3738, 3770, 3771, 4124, 4372, 4626, 4761, 4762, 4853, 4855, 4867, 5244, 5280, 5376, 5526, 5574, 5809, 5933
*Arcade* 2470
*The Chance Factor* **2109**

**Gallagher, Stephen**
*Down River* **2110**, 2279, 2608, 2900, 3695, 3899, 3900, 3901, 4088
*Night Visions 8* **1885**
*Nightmare, with Angel* **2111**, 2755
*Oktober* **2112**
*Red, Red Robin* **2113**
*Valley of Lights* 1792, 2288, 2302, 2610, 2793, 3129, 4004, 4005, 4327, 5010

**Gallery, Daniel V.**
*The Brink* 4512

**Galouye, Daniel F.**
*Dark Universe* 656, 664, 3608
*Lords of the Psychon* 2954

**Gannett, Lewis**
*Gehenna* **2114**, 2308, 2534, 5843, 5846
*The Living One* 1027, 1562, 1800, **2115**, 4445, 5705

**Garber, Eric**
*Embracing the Dark* 1740, **2116**
*Swords of the Rainbow* **2117**, 2444

**Garcia, Robert T.**
*Chilled to the Bone* **2118**, 3224, 3228

**Garcia Marquez, Gabriel**
*One Hundred Years of Solitude* 52, 950, 1411, 1412, 4263, 4475

**Garcia y Robertson, R.**
*Atlantis Found* **2119**
*The Moon Maid and Other Fantastic Adventures* **2120**
*The Spiral Dance* **2121**, 3261
*The Virgin and the Dinosaur* 403, **2122**

**Gardner, Craig Shaw**
*The 7th Guest* **1192**
*A Bad Day for Ali Baba* **2123**, 4393
*Batman* 14, 366, 611, 612, 613, 614, 615, 2391, 2392
*The Batman Murders* 14, 2331, 2391, 2392, 4215
*Batman Returns* 14, **2124**, 2391, 2392
*Bride of the Slime Monster* 1149, **2125**, 4398, 5934
*Dragon Burning* **2126**
*Dragon Sleeping* 1180, **2127**, 4676
*Dragon Waking* **2128**
*An Excess of Enchantments* 671
*The Last Arabian Night* **2129**
*A Malady of Magicks* 4400
*A Multitude of Monsters* 2083
*The Other Sinbad* 374, 2081, 2085, **2130**, 4396, 4401, 4549, 6070, 6087
*Return to Chaos* **2131**
*Revenge of the Fluffy Bunnies* 1268, 1603, 2084, **2132**, 3768, 4398, 5934
*Slaves of the Volcano God* 1413, 1418, 4398, 5934

*Wishbringer* 288, 1206, 1839, **2133**

**Gardner, James Alan**
*Commitment Hour* **2134**, 2237
*Expendable* 1303, **2135**

**Gardner, John**
*Grendel* 2250, 4872

**Gardner, Martin**
*Visitors From Oz: The Wild Adventures of Dorothy, the Scarecrow and the Tin Woodman* **2136**

**Gardner, S. Anthony**
*A Few Bricks Shy* **2137**

**Garfield, Henry**
*Moondog* **2138**, 2768
*Room 13* **2139**

**Garfinkle, Richard**
*Celestial Matters* **2140**, 5321, 5512, 5513

**Garland, Mark A.**
*Demon Blade* **2141**
*Dorella* **2142**

**Garn, Jake**
*Night Launch* **2143**

**Garner, Alan**
*Elidor* 165, 171, 1330
*The Owl Service* 1011
*Red Shift* 1011, 2992
*The Weirdstone of Brisingamen* 1005, 1294, 2283, 2943, 3436, 3737, 5977, 6006

**Garner, James Finn**
*Once upon a More Enlightened Time* 1578, 1942, 2845, 5557, 5617
*Once upon a More Enlightened Time: More Politically Correct Bedtime Stories* **2144**
*Politically Correct Bedtime Stories* 274, 1257, 1578, 1942, **2145**, 2845, 5557, 6089
*Politically Correct Holiday Stories* 1257, 1578, 1942, 2845, 3214, 4861, 5557
*Politically Correct Holiday Stories: For an Enlightened Yuletide Season* **2146**

**Garner, Sheila Bristow**
*Night Music* **2147**, 3950

**Garnett, David**
*New Worlds* **2148**, 2635

**Garrett, Michael**
*Deadly After Dark* **2174**
*Fear the Fever* **2176**
*Hot Blood X* **2177**
*Hot Blood: Crimes of Passion* **2178**
*Hot Blood: Kiss and Kill* **2179**
*Hotter Blood: More Tales of Erotic Horror* **2180**
*Hottest Blood: The Ultimate in Erotic Horror* **2181**
*Seeds of Fear* **2182**
*Stranger by Night* **2185**

**Garrett, Randall**
*The Gandalara Cycle I* 4143
*Lord Darcy Investigates* 2472, 3254
*Murder and Magic* 3254, 4673, 4793
*Takeoff!* 119, 607, 1752, 2398, 4134, 5713, 6077
*Takeoff, Too* 119, 607, 1752, 2398, 6077

*Too Many Magicians* 17, 971, 975, 1148, 1152, 1153, 1518, 1534, 1655, 2217, 2363, 2368, 2369, 2370, 2473, 2628, 2804, 3109, 3254, 3259, 3261, 3276, 4047, 4673, 5506, 5507, 5967, 5976, 6058

**Garrett, Susan M.**
*Forever Knight: Intimations of Mortality* **2149**

**Garton, Ray**
*Cafe Purgatorium* **98**
*Crucifax* 697, 1048, 2147, 3312
*Crucifax Autumn* 1301, 1845, 2935, 3679, 5323
*Dark Channel* **2150**, 3310, 4024, 5562
*Live Girls* 490, 803, 946, 948, 1890, **2151**, 3988, 5175, 5406
*Lot Lizards* 570, **2152**, 2313
*Methods of Madness* 192, 700, 938, 1171, **2153**, 2656, 3318, 5360, 5411
*The New Neighbor* **2154**
*Pieces of Hate* 1021, **2155**, 5536
*Shackled* **2156**
*Website* **2157**

**Gary, Romain**
*The Gasp* 1577, 4926

**Gascoigne, Marc**
*Streets of Blood* **4821**

**Gaskell, Elizabeth Cleghorn**
*Cranford* 1743, 3383
*A Dark Night's Work and Other Stories* **2158**
*Mrs. Gaskell's Tales of Mystery and Horror* 4968

**Gates, R. Patrick**
*Deathwalker* **2159**, 3210
*Grimm Memorials* **2160**
*Jumpers* **2161**
*Tunnelvision* **2162**, 3585

**Gath, G.G.**
*Driven to Kill* 5287

**Gawron, Jean Mark**
*Dream of Glass* 157, 1761, **2163**, 2486, 2729, 2839, 2955, 3049, 3186, 3438, 3795, 4130, 4136, 4177, 4677, 4703, 4894, 4902, 5171, 5450, 5462

**Gear, Kathleen O'Neal**
*People of the Earth* **2166**
*People of the Fire* **2167**
*People of the Lakes* **2164**
*People of the River* **2168**
*People of the Sea* **2169**
*People of the Wolf* **2170**
*Song of the Wolf* 870

**Gear, W. Michael**
*The Artifact* 1880, **2165**, 2352, 2460, 2830, 2831, 2833
*People of the Earth* 2164, **2166**, 3704
*People of the Fire* 275, 2164, **2167**, 2581, 5751
*People of the Lakes* **2164**
*People of the River* 731, 2164, **2168**
*People of the Sea* 2164, **2169**
*People of the Wolf* 178, 208, 268, 275, 1632, 2164, **2170**, 2583, 4320, 4817, 4818, 4819, 5444
*Relic of Empire* 1067, **2171**, 4225, 5786
*Starstrike* 1504, **2172**, 2432

*The Warriors of Spider* 2460, 2830, 2831, 2833
*The Way of Spider* 2460, 2830, 2831, 2833
*The Web of Spider* **2173**, 2460, 2830, 2831, 2833, 3929

**Gee, Maurice**
*The Halfmen of O* 5070

**Gelb, Jeff**
*Deadly After Dark* 1361, **2174**
*Fear Itself* 1279, 1285, **2175**, 2777, 3024, 5666
*Fear the Fever* **2176**
*Hot Blood* 1367, 1401
*Hot Blood X* **2177**
*Hot Blood: Crimes of Passion* **2178**
*Hot Blood: Kiss and Kill* **2179**
*Hot Blood: Stranger by Night* 5536
*Hot Blood: Tales of Provocative Horror* 72, 75, 302, 1118, 1120, 1357, 1361, 1607, 3026, 4465, 5056, 5093, 5094
*Hotter Blood: More Tales of Erotic Horror* 72, 75, 1120, 1357, 1361, **2180**, 4465, 5056, 5093, 5094
*Hottest Blood: The Ultimate in Erotic Horror* 72, 75, 1120, 1361, **2181**, 2893, 5056, 5094, 5385
*Seeds of Fear* 1361, **2182**
*Shock Rock* 2183, 4810
*Shock Rock II* **2184**, 4810
*Stranger by Night* 1361, **2185**

**Gellis, Roberta**
*Shimmering Splendor* 1129

**Gelman, Peter**
*Flying Saucers over Hennepin* **2186**

**Gemmell, David**
*Dark Prince* **2187**, 5395
*Ghost King* **2188**
*Lion of Macedon* 1129, **2189**, 5395, 5595, 5738
*Morningstar* 287, **2190**, 2247, 4808, 5200, 5202, 5221
*Wolf in Shadow* **2191**, 4835

**Gems, Jonathan**
*Mars Attacks!* 205, 504, 1508

**Gentile, Gary**
*Dragons Past* **2192**, 3428
*A Time for Dragons* **2193**

**Gentle, Mary**
*Ancient Light* 517, 707, 1210, 1323, 1599, 1774, 1933, 1934, **2194**, 2897, 2999, 3047, 3484, 3888, 3933, 4976, 5372, 5726, 5727, 5748
*The Architecture of Desire* 1250, **2195**, 2509, 4983
*Golden Witchbreed* 517, 565, 567, 580, 621, 707, 758, 990, 997, 1062, 1101, 1210, 1323, 1757, 1771, 1861, 1914, 1933, 1934, 2057, 2069, 2420, 2423, 2443, 2897, 2898, 3047, 3157, 3158, 3424, 3484, 3763, 3787, 3830, 3888, 3911, 3919, 4137, 4139, 4188, 4242, 4976, 5543, 5572
*Rats and Gargoyles* 672, 673, 994, 1035, 1068, 1073, 1251, 2056, **2196**, 2521, 2538, 3095, 3274, 3486, 3627, 3766, 4522, 4653, 4654, 4850, 4983, 5203, 5221, 5223, 5371, 5726

**Gentry, Georgina**
*Timeless Warrior* 2497

**George, J. Frederick**
*Interface* **781**

**George, Peter**
*Dr. Strangelove* 5174

**George, Stephen R.**
*Bloody Valentine* **2197**
*Dark Reunion* 1295, **2198**
*Deadly Vengeance* **2199**
*The Forgotten* 1656, **2200**, 4499
*Grandma's Little Darling* **2201**
*Near Dead* **2202**, 3899
*Nightscape* **2203**, 2555, 2748
*Torment* **2204**, 2823, 4239

**Gerritsen, Tess**
*Bloodstream* **2205**
*Life Support* **2206**, 3577

**Gerrold, David**
*Chess with a Dragon* 1493, 3345, 3521, 4217
*A Covenant of Justice* **2207**
*A Day for Damnation* 2954, 5352
*Deathbeast* 5998
*Encounter at Farpoint* 1229, 1247, 2061, 2066
*Flying Sorcerers* 4785
*The Man Who Folded Himself* 135, 2012, **2208**
*A Matter for Men* 383, 1900, 2646, 5352
*The Middle of Nowhere* **2209**
*Moonstar Odyssey* 5561
*A Rage for Revenge* **2210**, 5352, 5878
*A Season for Slaughter* **2211**
*Voyage of the Star Wolf* 1899, **2212**, 4775, 5725
*When HARLIE Was One: Release 2.0* 249, 3437, 5452

**Geston, Mark S.**
*Mirror to the Sky* **2213**, 4679
*The Siege of Wonder* 1343

**Ghidalia, Vic**
*The Devil's Generation* 1716
*Little Monsters* 1716

**Ghosh, Amitav**
*The Calcutta Chromosome* 1316, **2214**

**Gibbon, Floyd**
*The Red Napoleon* 4621

**Gibbons, Stella**
*Cold Comfort Farm* 1027

**Gibson, Edward**
*In the Wrong Hands* 781, **2215**, 3199, 4896, 4950
*Reach* 202, 388, 450, 1058, 2143, **2216**, 5057

**Gibson, Walter B.**
*Norgil, More Tales of Prestidigetection* 1187
*Norgil the Magician* 1187

**Gibson, William**
*Burning Chrome* 927, 4366, 4747, 4998, 5007, 5255, 5257, 5837
*Count Zero* 2911, 2916, 3491, 3890, 4099, 4451, 4452, 5841, 5960
*The Difference Engine* 398, 443, 520, 1139, 1457, 1518, **2217**, 3931, 5450, 5501
*Idoru* 835, **2218**
*Mona Lisa Overdrive* 2911, 3491, 3890, 4099, 4451, 4452, 5841, 5960

*Neuromancer* 5, 474, 481, 505, 736, 789, 972, 1238, 1750, 1751, 1862, 1865, 1936, 2011, 2911, 3204, 3431, 3491, 3559, 3604, 3661, 3818, 3850, 3890, 3921, 3995, 4099, 4117, 4135, 4451, 4452, 4821, 5254, 5255, 5635, 5841, 5960, 6020
*Virtual Light* 1903, **2219**, 5959

**Gideon, John**
*Golden Eyes* **2220**
*Greely's Cove* **2221**, 3389, 3415
*Kindred* **2222**

**Gier, Scott G.**
*Genellan: Planetfall* **2223**
*In the Shadow of the Moon* **2224**, 5465

**Gilbert, R.A.**
*Victorian Ghost Stories: An Oxford Anthology* **1235**

**Gilbert, Stephen**
*Ratman's Notebooks* 3807, 5327

**Gilchrist, R. Murray**
*The Stone Dragon and Other Tragic Romances* 964, **2225**

**Gilden, Mel**
*Hawaiian U.F.O. Aliens* 1456, 1935, 1997, 2007, **2226**, 2480
*Outer Space and All That Junk* 173, **2227**, 4338
*Surfing Samurai Robots* 31, 1935, 2007, 2013, 3441, 4341, 4473, 4640, 5934
*Tubular Android Superheroes* 1892, 1935, 2005, 2007, **2228**

**Gillespie, Donna**
*The Light Bearer* **2229**, 2453, 2454, 4264

**Gilliam, Richard**
*Ancient Enchantresses* **3670**
*Confederacy of the Dead* **2230**, 4880, 5098, 5099, 5155
*Excalibur* 4759
*Grails: Quests of the Dawn* 190, **2231**, 2346, 3670, 4987, 6005
*Grails: Visitations of the Night* **2232**, 2346
*More Phobias* **5666**
*Phantoms of the Night* **2233**, 2381, 5665
*Phobias: Stories of Your Deepest Fears* **5667**
*Somewhere South of Midnight* 5098, 5099
*Tales From the Great Turtle* **190**

**Gilliland, Alexis A.**
*Lord of the Troll-Bats* 706, 841, **2234**
*The Revolution From Rosinante* 584, 4962
*The Shadow Shaia* **2235**, 3905
*Wizenbeak* 2132, 2133

**Gilluly, Sheila**
*The Boy From the Burren* 457, **2236**, 3871, 3905, 4167, 4717, 4801, 4806
*Greenbriar Queen* 1288, 1660, 1683, 2819
*Ritnym's Daughter* 3412

**Gilman, Carolyn Ives**
*Halfway Human* 1266, 2134, **2237**

**Gilman, Charlotte Perkins**
*Herland* 4627
*"The Yellow Wallpaper"* 1673

*The Yellow Wallpaper and Other Writings of Charlotte Perkins Gilman* 2158

**Gilman, Greer Ilene**
*Moonwise* 43, 335, 1276, 1471, 2105, **2238**, 2739, 3470, 3793, 4475

**Gilman, Robert Cham**
*The Rebel of Rhada* 1182

**Gilmour, H.B.**
*The Eyes of Laura Mars* 1780, 1975, 4471

**Gingrich, Newt**
*1945* 1854, **2239**, 5516, 5517

**Girardi, Robert**
*Madeleine's Ghost* **2240**, 3149
*Vaporetto 13* **2241**, 3409

**Gladney, Heather**
*Teot's War* 744, 1150, 1486, 1487, 3018, 3157, 3270, 3288, 3296, 3298, 3862, 3864, 3872, 3911, 4521, 4613, 4976, 5684

**Glasgow, Ellen**
*The Shadowy Third and Other Stories* 601, 1673

**Glenn, Nancy Tyler**
*Clicking Stones* 74, 662, 1590, **2242**, 2295, 3579, 3915, 4882

**Gloss, Molly**
*The Dazzle of Day* 297, **2243**, 4735

**Gluckman, Janet**
*Child of the Light* 466, **2244**, 5079, 6029

**Glut, Donald F.**
*The Empire Strikes Back* 2171, 4299, 5279, 6052, 6054, 6075

**Godwin, Malcolm**
*The Holy Grail* 2231, 2232

**Godwin, Parke**
*Beloved Exile* 1092, 3352
*Firelord* 273, 2188, 3017
*Invitation to Camelot* 5270
*The Last Rainbow* 459, 1191, 5925
*Limbo Search* **2245**
*Lord of Sunset* **2246**
*A Memory of Lions* 363
*Robin and the King* 2190, **2247**
*Sherwood* 269, 2190, **2248**, 2389, 2570, 3165, 3502, 4584, 4609, 4985
*The Snake Oil Wars* 433, 2100, 2103, **2249**, 2753, 2859, 3810, 3986, 4028, 4029, 4034, 4035, 4473, 5351, 5532, 5569, 5616, 5636, 5768, 6062, 6064, 6070
*The Tower of Beowulf* **2250**, 2453, 4872
*Waiting for the Galactic Bus* 5, 31, 156, 159, 433, 1803, 2084, 2100, 2103, 2342, 2343, 2666, 2750, 2753, 2859, 2942, 3007, 3083, 3311, 3908, 4028, 4029, 4030, 4034, 4035, 4473, 5101, 5181, 5277, 5351, 5532, 5569, 5616, 5636, 5768, 5958, 6060, 6064

**Godwin, Tom**
*Space Prison* 6059

**Goingback, Owl**
*Crota* **2251**, 3129, 5249

**Goldblatt, Andrew**
*The Bully Pulpit* 4455, 4456

**Golden, Christie**
*Dance of the Dead* 155, 465, 1014, 3613, 5847
*The Enemy Within* 155, 2516
*Invasion America* **2252**
*King's Man and Thief* **2253**
*On the Run* **2254**

**Golden, Christopher**
*Angel Souls and Devil Hearts* **2255**, 5407
*Armageddon* **2602**
*Codename Wolverine* **2256**
*Hellboy: The Lost Army* **2257**
*Of Masques and Martyrs* **2258**
*Of Saints and Shadows* 303, **2259**, 2512, 2518, 2602, 3409, 5421

**Goldin, Stephen**
*The Alien Condition* 4406
*And Not Make Dreams Your Master* 583
*Crystals of Air and Water* 6087
*The Eternity Brigade* 589, **2211**, 5204
*Jade Darcy and the Affair of Honor* 63, 360, 631, 756, 1106, 1262, 1331, 1503, 1542, 1547, 1571, 1572, 1604, 1606, 1661, 1680, 2209, 2812, 3603, 3665, 3724, 3968, 4228, 4229, 4288, 4291, 4296, 4484, 4637, 4640, 4984, 5362, 5476, 5670, 5680, 5779
*Jade Darcy and the Zen Pirates* 293, 360, 981, 1420, 1454, 1572, **2260**, 2766, 3665, 4291, 4720, 5234, 5679, 6060
*Shrine of the Desert Mage* 374, 1528, 1687, 2130, 6087
*The Storyteller and the Jahn* 6087

**Golding, William**
*The Inheritors* 502, 4039
*Lord of the Flies* 862, 3021, 3606, 4663, 5486, 5799

**Goldman, Randy**
*Werewolf Wars* 2768, 5388

**Goldman, William**
*Magic* 2025, 2632, 3217
*The Princess Bride* 69, 713, 1432, 2653, 3010, 5178, 5232

**Goldstein, Lisa**
*Daily Voices* **2261**, 3945
*The Dream Years* 43, 323, 333, 334, 335, 336, 676, 919, 2028, 2104, 3663, 4272, 4732, 5614, 5635
*A Mask for the General* 744, 3791, 4051, 4360, 4750, 5272, 5274, 6009
*The Red Magician* 314, 466, 467, 4272, 5079, 5983
*Strange Devices of the Sun and Moon* 1679, **2262**, 3822
*Summer King, Winter Fool* 1814, 1866, **2263**, 3838, 3841, 3925, 4528, 5728, 5811
*Tourists* **2264**, 2706, 2952, 3423, 5939
*Travelers in Magic* 819, 1431, 2106, **2265**, 2537, 3279, 3984, 5165
*Walking the Labyrinth* 636, 637, **2266**, 3283, 3847, 4093, 5916

**Gomez, Jewelle**
*The Gilda Stories* 1286, 2116, **2267**, 3031, 3853, 4315, 5421, 5802
*Swords of the Rainbow* **2117**

**Goodkind, Terry**
*Blood of the Fold* 1775, **2268**, 4524
*Stone of Tears* 1674, 1734, 2126,
2128, **2269**, 2958, 3936, 4107,
4337, 4527, 4739, 4795, 6004
*Temple of the Winds* 2096, **2270**
*Wizard's First Rule* 287, 692, 704,
712, 979, 1009, 1105, 1147, 1172,
1292, 1513, 1733, 1744, 1814,
1905, 1952, 1953, 2141, **2271**,
2506, 2657, 2693, 2694, 2695,
2696, 2924, 2925, 2956, 2957,
2959, 2984, 2989, 3044, 3095,
3296, 3507, 3651, 3832, 3835,
3838, 3926, 4110, 4528, 4685,
4768, 4794, 4796, 4908, 4986,
5034, 5202, 5203, 5275, 5320,
5554, 5651, 5734, 5748, 5972,
5978

**Goodstone, Tony**
*The Pulps* 1712

**Goodwin, Marie D.**
*Where the Towers Pierce the
Sky* **2272**

**Goonan, Kathleen Ann**
*The Bones of Time* **2273**
*Mississippi Blues* **2274**, 3931
*Queen City Jazz* 774, **2275**, 3236,
3788, 4858

**Gorden, Greg**
*Prophecy* 2529
*Strange Tales From the Nile
Empire* **1889**

**Gordon, John**
*The Burning Baby and Other
Ghosts* 5762, 5763, 5764, 5765
*The Edge of the World* 1319, 1320

**Gordon, Karen Elizabeth**
*Paris out of Hand* 333, 336

**Gordon, Stuart**
*Fire in the Abyss* 5927
*Smile on the Void* 1063, 1499, 2535,
2754, 4732, 4946, 5903

**Gorey, Edward**
*Amphigorey Also* 1044, 3334
*The Haunted Tea Cosy: A Dispirited
and Distasteful Diversion for
Christmas* **2276**

**Gorman, Ed**
*Cages* 1016, 1021, **2277**, 2714,
3216, 4250, 5885
*Dark Crimes II: Modern Masters of
Noir* 538, 544
*Dark Crimes: Great Noir Fiction From
the '50's to the '90's* 2600, 3324
*Dracula: Prince of Darkness* **2387**
*The Fugitive Stars* **4479**
*The Long Midnight* **4480**
*Moonchasers and Other Stories* 2155
*Night Screams* **2278**
*Out There in the Darkness* **2279**
*Predators* 544, **2280**
*Prisoners and Other Stories* 777,
**2281**, 3321, 3327, 3328, 3329,
3367, 4253, 5339
*Shadow Games* 1830
*Stalkers* 538, 544, 1019, **2282**,
2600, 3228

**Gormley, Beatrice**
*Mail-Order Wings* 1558, 2949

**Gorog, Judith**
*On Meeting Witches at Wells* **2283**
*Winning Scheherazade* 329, 618

**Goshgarian, Gary**
*Rough Beast* 2205, **2284**, 4843
*The Stone Circle* **2285**

**Gotlieb, Phyllis**
*Flesh and Gold* **2286**
*Heart of Red Iron* **2287**

**Gottlieb, Sherry**
*Love Bite* **2288**

**Goudge, Elizabeth**
*The Little White Horse* 1219
*The Middle Window* 4943

**Goulart, Ron**
*After Things Fell Apart* 735, 2882
*Big Bang* 1216
*Brainz, Inc.* 1999, 4363
*Brinkman* 2573
*The Chameleon Corps* 2921, 3345
*Cowboy Heaven* 5997
*Hail Hibbler* 4363
*Hellquad* 1216, 2573, 4341
*The Prisoner of Blackwood Castle* 30,
5997
*Shaggy Planet* 4341
*Skyrocket Steele* 1216, 4341
*Skyrocket Steele Conquers the Universe
and Other Media Tales* 1428,
3945, 6068
*Starpirate's Brain* 30, 3345, 5997
*A Talent for the Invisible* 3345, 4362
*Upside Downside* 30
*When the Waker Sleeps* 735, 5243
*The Wicked Cyborg* 2573, 4940,
5997

**Gould, Sabine Baring**
*A Book of Ghosts* 3633

**Gould, Steven**
*Helm* 2246, **2289**
*Jumper* 302, 970, **2290**, 2474,
2717, 3011, 4070
*Wildside* 298, 1981, **2291**, 4502,
4948

**Gower, Daniel H.**
*Harrowgate* **2292**, 2335, 5784
*The Orpheus Process* 610, 1078,
1971, 2157, **2293**, 2872, 3204,
3207, 4232, 5632

**Goyen, William**
*Arcadio* 1697

**Grabinski, Stefan**
*The Dark Domain* 573, 2225, **2294**,
3447, 5317

**Grae, Camarin**
*Stranded* 74, 662, **2295**, 3539, 4245

**Graf, L.A.**
*Armageddon Sky* **2296**
*Caretaker* 1729, 2061
*Crossroad* 10
*Extreme Prejudice* 1729
*Firestorm* 2064
*Ice Trap* 3767
*Time's Enemy* 9, 903, 904, **2297**,
5115
*Traitor Winds* 905, 1729, **2298**,
4927
*War Dragons* **2299**

**Grafton, John**
*Great Ghost Stories* **2300**

**Graham, Daniel Jr.**
*The Gatekeepers* **2301**

**Graham, Dee**
*Fallen* **2302**, 4710

**Grahame, Kenneth**
*The Wind in the Willows* 32, 737,
1821, 2774, 2775, 2776, 2848,
2849, 2850, 2851, 2852, 2853,
2854, 2855, 3115

**Grant, Charles L.**
*668: The Neighbor of the Beast* **1917**
*The Best of Shadows* 1017, 1629,
3959, 3961, 3962, 4873
*The Black Carousel* **2303**
*Blood River Down* 2014
*Chariot* **2304**
*The Chronicles of Greystone
Bay* 5888
*The Dark Cry of the Moon* 2768,
5861
*Dialing the Wind* **2305**
*The Dodd Mead Gallery of
Horror* 5924
*Doom City* 4212
*Fears* 1284, 2175, 2777, 5666,
5667
*Final Shadows* **2306**, 3962, 4206,
5795
*For Fear of the Night* 918, 1468,
4832
*Gallery of Horror* **2307**
*Genesis* **2308**, 2638, 5843, 5846
*Goblins* 106, 112, 924, **2309**, 5358
*Gothic Ghosts* **5665**
*Greystone Bay* 4212
*The Greystone Bay Series* 2118
*The Hour of the Oxrun Dead* 832,
1185, 2339, 2930, 3041, 3212,
4838, 5111
*In a Dark Dream* 284, **2310**, 5522
*In the Fog* **2311**
*In the Mood* **2312**
*Jackals* **2313**
*Kent Montana and the Really Ugly
Thing From Mars* **1918**
*Kent Montana and the Reasonably
Invisible Man* **1919**
*The Last Call of Mourning* 4832
*The Long Night of the Grave* 616,
2439, 3526, 4572, 5695
*The Mark of the Moderately Vicious
Vampire* **1920**
*The Nestling* 834, 2430, 2929, 3140,
3655, 3679, 4441, 5077, 5483,
5769
*Night Songs* 4715
*Night Visions 2* 1885
*Nightmare Seasons* 3132
*The Pet* 811, 2197, 2431, 2915,
2935, 3127, 4022, 4841, 5323,
5825
*Raven* **2314**
*The SeaHarp Hotel* **2315**, 4212
*The Shadows Series* 3960
*The Soft Whisper of the Dead* 1013,
1402, 2220, 3498
*Something Stirs* **2316**, 3137
*Stunts* **2317**, 4009, 4601, 4603
*Symphony* **2318**
*Tales From the Nightside* 623, **2319**,
4463, 4891
*Time. The Semi-Final Frontier* **1921**
*Whirlwind* 106, 112, 924, **2320**,
5358
*The World of Darkness:
Watcher* **2321**
*The X-Files: Goblins* 2114, 2534

**Grant, Glenn**
*Northern Stars: The Anthology of
Canadian Science Fiction* 2593

**Grant, Kathryn**
*The Willow Garden* 69, 3338, 3339,
4155

**Grant, Linda**
*Vampire Bytes* 2322

**Grant, Mark**
*Christmas Slaughter* 2323
*Mutant Hell* 2324
*Mutants Amok* 1406, **2325**, 3891,
4599

**Grant, Richard**
*In the Land of Winter* **2326**
*Rumors of Spring* 1278, 3794
*Tex and Molly in the Afterlife* **2327**,
4732, 5079
*Through the Heart* 1482, **2328**,
2533, 3855, 5433
*Views from the Oldest House* 1278,
**2329**

**Grant, Rob**
*Better than Life* **4076**
*Red Dwarf: Infinity Welcomes Careful
Drivers* **4077**

**Gravel, Geary**
*The Dreamwright* 3479
*A Key for the Nonesuch* 104, 929,
1026, 1331, 1332, 1584, 1838,
1881, 1979, 2042, **2330**, 2463,
2644, 4652, 4671, 4970, 5159,
5306, 5774, 5775
*Mask of the Phantasm* **2331**
*The Return of the Breakneck
Boys* **2332**, 5159

**Graversen, Pat**
*Black Ice* **2333**
*Dollies* 1194, 2025, 2878, 2899,
2902, 3217, 3782, 3784, 5823
*The Fagin* 2203, **2334**, 2748, 2930
*Graythings* **2335**
*Precious Blood* **2336**, 3413
*Sweet Blood* **2337**, 4666, 5705,
5852

**Graves, Robert**
*Greek Myths* 5533
*Hercules, My Shipmate* 2404
*Watch the Northwind Rise* 5490

**Gray, Alasdair**
*A History Maker* **2338**

**Gray, Muriel**
*Furnace* **2339**
*The Trickster* 911, 2251, **2340**,
3680, 3967, 4710

**Graziunas, Daina**
*Among Madmen* **5212**
*Lady El* **5213**
*Thinning the Predators* **2341**

**Greeley, Andrew M.**
*Angel Fire* 1803, 5101
*Angel Light* 1339, **2342**
*The Final Planet* 4081
*God Game* 583
*The Magic Cup* 2231, 2232
*Sacred Visions* **2343**

**Green, Kate**
*Contrarywise* 4519

**Green, Michael**
*Dry Skull Dreams* **2344**
*The Jimjams* 1894, **2345**, 4907,
5053
*Quest: In Search of the
Dragontooth* 1024, **2346**, 3044

**Green, Roger Lancelyn**
*The Tale of Troy* 1129

**Green, Roland J.**
*Conan at the Demon's Gate*   907, 910, **2983**
*Conan the Guardian*   908, 909, **2347**, 4616
*Conan the Relentless*   906, **2348**
*Conan the Valiant*   4293
*Division of the Spoils*   4973
*The Great King's War*   5495, 5513
*The Mountain Walks*   **2349**, 4982
*On the Verge*   **2350**
*The Painful Field*   1552, **2351**
*Squadron Alert*   **2352**, 4672
*Starcruiser Shenandoah*   2173
*The Sum of Things*   **2353**
*These Green Foreign Hills*   4974
*Warriors for the Working Day*   3861
*The Wayward Knights*   5723
*Women at War*   **765**

**Green, Sharon**
*Challenges*   **2354**
*Competition*   **2355**
*Convergence*   1943, **2356**
*The Crystals of Mida*   1071
*Dark Mirror, Dark Dreams*   **2357**
*Hellhound Magic*   1731, 1736
*The Hidden Realms*   **2358**, 5133
*Lady Blade, Lord Fighter*   1004
*Silver Princess, Golden Knight*   641, **2359**, 5217, 5220
*Wind Whispers, Shadow Shouts*   **2360**

**Green, Simon R.**
*Blood and Honor*   **2361**, 3636, 4699, 5678
*Blue Moon Rising*   12, 1207, 1702, 1703, 2357, 2360, **2362**, 2987, 3635, 4685, 6001
*The Bones of Haven*   1249, 1484, **2363**
*Deathstalker Honor*   **2364**
*Deathstalker Rebellion*   **2365**
*Deathstalker War*   **2366**
*Down Among the Dead Men*   **2367**
*The God Killer*   **2368**, 2472, 2620, 3303
*Guard Against Dishonor*   769, **2369**, 4935
*Hawk & Fisher*   290, 745, 1148, 1152, 1153, 1250, 1251, 1705, 1706, 2041, **2370**, 2473, 2756, 2757, 2758, 2759, 3122, 3276, 3283, 4015, 4166, 4612, 4640, 4673, 4899, 4975, 5848
*Hellworld*   1643, **2371**
*Mistworld*   **2372**, 2414
*Shadows Fall*   **2373**
*Twilight of the Empire*   **2374**
*Winner Takes All*   1838, **2375**
*Wolf in the Fold*   **2376**

**Green, Terrence M.**
*Blue Limbo*   **2377**

**Greenberg, Martin H.**
*100 Creepy Little Creature Stories*   **5686**
*100 Ghastly Little Ghost Stories*   **1709**
*100 Hair-Raising Little Horror Stories*   **4828**
*100 Tiny Tales of Terror*   **5687**
*100 Twisted Little Tales of Torment*   **1710**
*100 Vicious Little Vampire Stories*   **5688**
*100 Wicked Little Witch Stories*   **1711**
*100 Wild Little Weird Tales*   **5689**

*After the King: Stories in Honor of J.R.R. Tolkien*   422, 606, 1576, **2378**, 2380, 3227, 5214, 5216, 6044, 6077
*Aladdin: Master of the Lamp*   **4534**
*Alien Pregnant by Elvis*   **2070**
*Alternate Americas*   **442**
*Alternate Wars*   **443**
*Amazing Science Fiction Stories: The War Years 1936-1945*   3948, 3949
*Amazing Science Fiction Stories: The Wild Years 1946-1955*   3948, 3949
*Amazing Science Fiction Stories: The Wonder Years 1926-1935*   3948, 3949
*Ancient Enchantresses*   **3670**
*Back From the Dead*   **2379**
*Battle Magic*   **2380**
*Between Time and Terror*   **5691**
*Black Cats and Broken Mirrors*   **2381**
*Blood Lines: Vampire Stories From New England*   **4876**
*Blood Muse: Timeless Tales of Vampires in the Arts*   **2071**
*Bootcamp 3000*   **4373**
*The Bradbury Chronicles: Stories in Honor of Ray Bradbury*   **4131**
*By Any Other Fame*   **4540**
*Camelot Fantastic*   **4877**
*Catfantastic II*   **4143**
*Catfantastic III*   **4144**
*Catfantastic IV*   **4145**
*Celebrity Vampires*   1799, 2071, **2382**, 5688
*Christmas Bestiary*   **2412**
*Christmas Ghosts*   **4541**
*Christmas on Ganymede and Other Stories*   2412, 2456, 2587, 2588, 2589, 4720, 5024
*Civil War Ghosts*   **2383**
*Classic Tales of Horror and the Supernatural*   **4440**
*Confederacy of the Dead*   **2230**
*The Conspiracy Files*   **2384**
*Cults of Horror*   2601
*Dark Love*   **1118**
*Deals with the Devil*   **4542**
*Desire Burn: Women's Stories From the Dark Side of Passion*   **468**
*Devil Worshippers*   **2385**, 4411, 4542
*Dinosaur Fantastic*   **4543**
*Dinosaurs*   **2386**
*Dracula: Prince of Darkness*   748, 1013, 1799, **2387**, 2705, 2972, 3226, 5688, 5699
*Dragon Fantastic*   **2413**
*Elf Fantastic*   **2388**
*Enchanted Forests*   **3070**
*Faeries*   **235**
*Famous Fantastic Mysteries*   **1712**
*The Fantastic Adventures of Robin Hood*   2248, **2389**, 4534
*Fields of Blood: Vampire Stories of the Heartland*   **4879**
*Forbidden Acts*   **1120**
*Foundation's Friends*   **232**
*Frankenstein: The Monster Wakes*   **2390**, 2973, 3019, 3180
*The Further Adventures of Batman*   14, 2124, 2331, 3403
*The Further Adventures of Batman 2: Featuring the Penguin*   14, 2124, **2391**
*The Further Adventures of Batman 3: Featuring Catwoman*   **2392**, 4215
*The Further Adventures of Superman*   999, **2393**, 3403, 3768, 5262

*The Further Adventures of the Joker*   14, 2124
*Future Net*   **2394**
*Girls' Night Out*   **1713**
*Grails: Quests of the Dawn*   **2231**
*Grails: Visitations of the Night*   **2232**
*Great American Ghost Stories*   **3869**
*Great Writers and Kids Write Spooky Stories*   **2395**, 3705, 4274, 4282
*Haunted Houses: The Greatest Stories*   **2396**
*Heaven Sent: 18 Glorious Tales of the Angels*   **1283**
*The Horror Hall of Fame*   **5031**
*Horrors: 365 Scary Stories*   **1714**
*Horse Fantastic*   2380, **2397**, 4543
*Isaac Asimov Presents the Great SF Stories: 20 (1958)*   **238**
*Isaac Asimov Presents the Great SF Stories: 21 (1959)*   **239**
*Isaac Asimov Presents the Great SF Stories: 22 (1959)*   **240**
*Isaac Asimov Presents the Great SF Stories: 23 (1961)*   **241**
*Isaac Asimov Presents the Great SF Stories: 24 (1962)*   **242**
*Isaac Asimov Presents the Great SF Stories: 25 (1963)*   **243**
*It Came From the Drive-In*   **4252**
*Lord of the Fantastic: Stories in Honor of Roger Zelazny*   2380, **2398**
*Love in Vein II*   **699**
*Lovecraft's Legacy*   **5698**
*The Mammoth Book of Fantastic Science Fiction*   **245**
*The Mammoth Book of Modern Science Fiction: Short Novels of the 1980s*   **246**
*Miskatonic University*   **2399**
*Mob Magic*   **5459**
*More Phobias*   **5666**
*Mummy Stories*   **2400**
*Murasaki*   **5038**
*The New Hugo Winners, Volume III*   **5871**
*The New Hugo Winners, Volume IV*   **2401**
*New Legends*   **422**
*New Stories From the Twilight Zone*   **2402**, 4913, 4914
*Night Screams*   **2278**
*Nightmares on Elm Street: Freddy Krueger's Seven Sweetest Dreams*   460, **2403**
*Nursery Crimes*   **1716**
*Olympus*   **2404**
*Orphans of the Night*   **4988**
*Phantoms of the Night*   **2233**
*Phobias: Stories of Your Deepest Fears*   **5667**
*Predators*   **2280**
*Psycho-Paths*   **543**
*Red Jack*   **5761**
*The Reel Stuff*   **5460**
*Rivals of Dracula*   **5699**
*Rivals of Weird Tales*   **5700**
*Sea Cursed: Thirty Terrifying Tales of the Deep*   **3798**
*Sherlock Holmes in Orbit*   **4556**
*Sisters in Fantasy 2*   **5018**
*Sisters of the Night*   **2508**
*Smart Dragons, Foolish Elves*   **2014**
*Southern Blood: Vampire Stories From the American South*   **4880**
*Stalkers*   **2282**
*Streets of Blood: Vampire Stories From New York City*   **4881**
*The Super Hugos*   **2405**
*Supernatural Sleuths*   **5653**

*Tales of Riverworld*   **1875**
*Tarot Fantastic*   **2406**
*A Taste for Blood*   1370, 1611, **2407**, 2975, 4407, 5265, 5935
*The Time of the Vampires*   **1799**
*To Sleep, Perchance to Dream. . .Nightmare*   **1717**
*The Twilight Zone: The Original Stories*   4913, 4914
*Urban Horrors*   **4133**
*Vampire Detectives*   1718, **2408**, 3108, 5459
*Vampires: The Greatest Stories*   150, 151, **2409**, 2484, 5265
*Vamps*   730, 1360, 1370, 1713, 2508, 2975, 3030, 3031
*Virtuous Vampires*   **1718**
*Warrior Princesses*   **4871**
*Warriors of Blood and Dream*   **6075**
*Weird Tales From Shakespeare*   **3079**
*Weird Vampire Tales*   **5706**
*Werewolves*   1230, **2410**, 3032, 4988
*White House Horrors*   **2411**

**Greenberg, Rosalind M.**
*Christmas Bestiary*   **2412**, 2587, 2588, 2589, 5024
*Dragon Fantastic*   **2413**, 2479, 4408, 4543, 5710
*Horse Fantastic*   **2397**

**Greenberger, Robert**
*The Disinherited*   **1381**

**Greene, Kirby**
*Brotherhood of the Stars*   **2414**

**Greenfield, Irving A.**
*Julius Caesar Is Alive and Well*   2073

**Greenhall, Ken**
*Deathchain*   853, **2415**

**Greenland, Colin**
*Harm's Way*   **2416**
*Mother of Plenty*   **2417**
*Seasons of Plenty*   **2418**, 2837
*Take Back Plenty*   929, 1059, **2419**, 3190, 3448, 4019, 4421, 4896, 5227

**Greeno, Gayle**
*Exiles' Return*   **2420**, 3096, 4137
*Finders-Seekers*   1000, **2421**, 2550, 3298, 3776
*Mind Snare*   **2422**
*Mind-Speakers' Call*   983, **2423**
*Sunderlies Seeking*   **2424**

**Greenwood, Ed**
*All Shadows Fled*   299, 1293
*Cormyr: A Novel*   **2425**, **2426**
*Elminster: The Making of a Mage*   **2427**
*Spellfire*   1485, 3537, 4106

**Gregory, Stephen**
*The Blood of Angels*   **2428**
*The Cormorant*   **2429**, 4249
*The Woodwitch*   1185, 3373

**Gresham, Stephen**
*Blood Wings*   **2430**, 5483
*The Living Dark*   **2431**, 4841, 5825

**Gressman, Thomas S.**
*Shadows of War*   **2432**

**Gribbin, John**
*Double Planet*   **2433**
*Father to the Man*   1165, 1525, **2434**

**Griffin, P.M.**
*Call to Arms*   **2435**
*Fire Planet*   **2436**
*Firehand*   **4151**

*Flight of Vengeance* **4152**
*Jungle Assault* 1326, **2437**
*Redline the Stars* **4160**
*Star Commandos* 1665
*Storms of Victory* **4162**

**Griffin, Peni R.**
*Hobkin* 970, 1441, **2438**, 3444, 3816
*Otto From Otherwhere* 192, 605

**Griffith, Helen V.**
*Journal of a Teenage Genius* 2949

**Griffith, Kathryn Meyer**
*The Calling* **2439**, 5312
*The Last Vampire* 1463, **2440**, 4072
*Vampire Blood* **2441**, 5657, 5986
*Witches* 690, **2442**, 4577, 5122

**Griffith, Nicola**
*Ammonite* 210, 792, 1116, 1482, 1586, 1649, 1769, 2051, **2443**, 2806, 3440, 4172, 4176, 4187, 5090, 5172, 5430, 5435, 5461, 5804
*Bending the Landscape: Fantasy* **2444**
*Slow River* 1304, 1582, 2273, 2274, **2445**, 2558, 2559, 3453, 4064, 4218, 4898

**Grimes, Lee**
*Retro Lives* **2446**

**Grimm, Jacob Ludwig**
*The Complete Fairy Tales of the Brothers Grimm* 225, **2447**, 3844

**Grimm, Wilhelm Carl**
*The Complete Fairy Tales of the Brothers Grimm* **2447**

**Grimson, Todd**
*Brand New Cherry Flavor* **2448**, 3103, 4256, 5085
*Stainless* **2449**, 4069

**Grimwood, Ken**
*Into the Deep* **2450**
*Replay* 96, 201, 376, 676, 796, 1089, 2208, 2446, 3459, 4966, 5594, 5905

**Groell, Anne Lesley**
*Anvil of the Sun* **2451**
*Bridge of Valor* **2452**

**Grubb, Davis**
*The Night of the Hunter* 1489, 3208, 4183
*You Never Believe Me and Other Stories* 3328, 3329, 3333, 3335

**Grubb, Jeff**
*Azure Bonds* 4166
*Cormyr: A Novel* **2425**, **2426**
*Finder's Bane* **4165**
*Lord Teode* 2426
*Masquerades* **4166**
*Song of the Saurials* **4167**

**Grundy, Stephan**
*Attila's Treasure* **2453**
*Rhinegold* 2229, 2250, **2454**, 2572, 2686, 4264, 4270, 4872

**Guest, Diane**
*Lullaby* 2198, **2455**, 4701

**Guest, Judith**
*Ordinary People* 4240

**Guin, Chris**
*Mall, Mayhem and Magic* **3485**

**Guinn, Jeff**
*The Autobiography of Santa Claus: It's Better to Give* **2456**

**Gun, Guneli**
*The Adventures of Huru on the Road to Baghdad* **2457**

**Guneli, Gun**
*On the Road to Baghdad* 6082

**Gunn, James**
*The Immortals* 581
*The Joy Machine* **2458**, 4711, 4893
*Nebula Award Stories 10* 245
*Star Bridge* **2459**, 3874

**Gunnarsson, Thorarinn**
*Battle of the Ring* 2352, **2460**, 6056
*The Dragonlord of Mystara* 470
*Dragonmage of Mystara* **2462**, 4326
*Dragon's Domain* 726, 1749, **2461**, 4460
*Dragons on the Town* **2463**, 3169, 4615
*Dreadnought* **2464**
*Make Way for Dragons!* 1221, 1268, 2076, 2077, **2465**, 5337
*Song of the Dwarves* 4518
*Tactical Error* **2466**

**Guon, Ellen**
*Bedlam Boyz* **2467**, 3277, 3302, 4862, 4980, 4995
*Bedlam's Bard* **3269**
*Knight of Ghosts and Shadows* **3285**
*Summoned to Tourney* **3299**
*Wing Commander: Freedom Flight* **3307**

**Gurney, James**
*Dinotopia* 29, 306, 318, 385, 416, 1024, 1256, 2003, 2122, 2346, 2386, **2468**, 2654, 2980, 2981, 2982, 3156, 3382, 3427, 3428, 4456, 4543, 4597, 4854, 4855, 5479, 5972, 6032, 6069, 6076
*The World Beneath* 385, 1024, 2003, **2469**, 2980, 2982, 5479

**Guthridge, George**
*Child of the Journey* **466**
*Child of the Light* **2244**
*Children of the Dusk* **467**

**Gutman, Dan**
*Virtually Perfect* **2470**

**Guttenberg, Elise**
*Sunder, Eclipse and Seed* **2471**, 6039

**Gygax, Gary**
*The Anubis Murders* 1250, **2472**
*Death in Delhi* **2473**

# H

**Haber, Karen**
*Mutant Legacy* **2474**
*The Mutant Season* **5039**, 6053
*Mutant Star* **2475**, 3726, 4551
*Sister Blood* **2476**
*Thieves' Carnival/The Jewel of Bas* 2829
*Universe 2* **5045**
*Universe 3* **5046**
*The War Minstrels* 101, **2477**
*Woman Without a Shadow* 101, **2478**

**Hackett, John**
*The Third World War, August 1985* **4306**

**Hagar, Jean**
*Nightwalker* 1829

**Haggard, H. Rider**
*She* 3877, 4235, 4572

**Hague, Michael**
*The Book of Dragons* 385, 801, **2479**, 6036

**Hahn, Mary Downing**
*The Doll in the Garden* 2688

**Haiblum, Isidore**
*Out of Sync* 592
*Specterworld* **2480**

**Haining, Peter**
*The Black Magic Omnibus* 2385
*Black Tales* 5418
*A Circle of Witches* 4411, 6034
*The Evil People* 2385
*The Ghost Companion* 3432
*The Ghouls* 5460, 5947
*Gothic Tales of Terror* 307, 1314, 2718, 5389
*Gothic Tales of Terror, Volume II* 4180
*Great Irish Stories of the Supernatural* 149, **2481**
*Great Irish Tales of Horror* 149, 1242, **2482**
*Great Irish Tales of Terror and the Supernatural* 1242
*Great Irish Tales of the Unimaginable* 149
*Great Tales of Terror From Europe and America* 848, 2586, 4026, 5418, 5439
*The Hollywood Nightmare* 4252, 5460, 5947
*The Lucifer Society* 38, 3616, 4311
*The Mammoth Book of Twentieth Century Ghost Stories* **2483**
*Peter Cushing's Tales of a Monster Hunter* 5653
*The Shilling Shockers* 307, 1314
*Stories of the Walking Dead* 2379, 2977, 4412, 5083
*Supernatural Sleuths* 5653
*The Vampire Hunters' Casebook* **2484**
*Weird Tales* 480, 482, **2485**, 5689
*Wild Night Company* 4203
*The Witchcraft Reader* 1711

**Haldeman, Jack C. II**
*High Steel* 128, 157, 1337, **2486**, 4635, 4677, 4679, 5745
*Perry's Planet* 528
*Run for the Stars/Echoes of Thunder* **1788**
*Vector Analysis* 1788

**Haldeman, Joe**
*All My Sins Remembered* 1849, 4467
*Buying Time* 125, **2487**, 2920, 3239, 3874, 4681, 4813
*Forever Peace* **2488**, 3922
*The Forever War* 206, 352, 398, 513, 589, 901, 904, 1053, 1103, 1627, 1641, 2211, 2245, 2351, 2353, 2464, 2546, 2790, 3937, 4038, 4194, 4204, 4374, 4466, 4477, 4775, 4966, 5115, 5294, 5955
*The Hemingway Hoax* 1473, 1875, **2489**, 2546
*None So Blind* 2120, **2490**
*Planet of Judgment* 528
*There Is No Darkness* 2486
*Vietnam and Other Alien Worlds* 759, 1969, 2947, 5782
*World Without End* 528
*Worlds: A Novel of the Near Future* 127, 3242

*Worlds Apart* 5909
*Worlds Enough and Time* **2491**, 4116, 4350

**Haldeman, Linda**
*The Lastborn of Elvinwood* 177, 2945

**Hale, Edward E.**
*The Man Without a Country* 5377

**Hale, F.J.**
*Ogre Castle* 4397

**Hales, E.E.Y.**
*Chariot of Fire* 960

**Haley, Wendy**
*These Fallen Angels* **2492**, 4246
*This Dark Paradise* **2493**, 3413, 4666

**Hall, Karen**
*Dark Debts* 1888, **2494**

**Hall, Matthew**
*Nightmare Logic* **2495**

**Hall, Melissa Mia**
*Wild Women* **2496**

**Hallahan, William**
*The Search for Joseph Tully* 1237

**Hallam, Elizabeth**
*Spirit Catcher* **2497**

**Halperin, James L.**
*The First Immortal* **2498**

**Ham, Bob**
*Rolling Vengeance* 2324, 2325
*Tennessee Terror* 44

**Hambly, Barbara**
*The Armies of Daylight* 256, 257, 1175, 1703, 1746, 2987, 3273, 4613, 5832
*Beauty and the Beast* 559, 1808, 3020, 3882, 3883, 5474
*Bride of the Rat God* **2499**, 3099, 3485, 3838
*Children of the Jedi* 76, 103, 114, 117, **2500**, 2914, 4299
*Crossroad* **2501**
*The Dark Hand of Magic* 289, 1534, 2098, **2502**, 3107, 3634, 4614, 4699, 5741
*Dog Wizard* 12, 1985, 2357, **2503**, 2616, 3839, 5497, 5715, 5716
*Dragonsbane* 28, 470, 727, 971, 975, 994, 1207, 1685, 1732, 2757, 2809, 3044, 4013, 4014, 4513, 4517, 4674, 5087, 5509
*Ghost Walker* 900, 1663
*Icefalcon's Quest* 1679, **2504**, 4524, 4727
*Immortal Blood* 1792, 1793
*Ishmael* 528, 569, 1225, 1383, 1385, 1511, 1556, 1658, 1922, 2067, 2297, 4040, 5113, 5597
*The Ladies of Mandrigyn* 289, 644, 702, 1029, 1147, 1150, 2095, 2360, 3016, 3635, 3839, 4488, 4596, 4614, 4674, 4714, 4784, 5206, 5220, 5678, 5735
*The Magicians of Night* **2505**
*Mother of Winter* 1813, **2506**
*The Rainbow Abyss* 704, 739, 747, **2507**
*The Silent Tower* 105, 317, 393, 424, 439, 683, 718, 1161, 1162, 1163, 1419, 1662, 1842, 1985, 2629, 3471, 3840, 3930, 4446, 4669, 4671, 4676, 4793, 5719
*The Silicon Mage* 317, 1160, 1985, 2097, 3121

*The Silver Tower* 915
*Sisters of the Night* 730, 1713, **2508**
*Stranger at the Wedding* **2509**, 2958, 3776, 5127
*Those Who Hunt the Night* 131, 135, 265, 832, 1013, 1121, 1791, **2510**, 2514, 2517, 3252, 4508, 6050
*The Time of the Dark* 153, 391, 562, 635, 718, 1008, 1009, 1066, 1155, 1173, 1174, 1175, 1178, 1181, 1239, 1421, 1422, 1477, 1640, 1660, 1678, 1732, 1746, 1747, 1809, 1812, 1863, 1866, 1907, 1911, 1983, 2235, 2361, 2367, 2560, 2561, 2623, 2628, 2796, 2885, 2886, 2985, 3157, 3246, 3270, 3296, 3297, 3304, 3305, 3306, 3386, 3482, 3650, 3652, 3653, 3938, 3939, 3942, 4517, 4520, 4523, 4526, 4798, 5150, 5251, 5736, 5737, 5738, 6073
*Traveling with the Dead* **2511**
*The Walls of Air* 1175, 1746
*The Witches of Wenshar* 289, 389, 394, 3839, 5733, 5760

**Hamilton, Edith**
*Mythology* 5533

**Hamilton, Edmond**
*Doomstar* 1916
*The Haunted Stars* 133
*The Sun Smashers* 5863

**Hamilton, Laurell K.**
*Bloody Bones* **2512**
*Blue Moon* **2513**
*Burnt Offerings* **2514**
*Circus of the Damned* 2255, **2515**
*Death of a Darklord* 1137, 1510, **2516**
*Guilty Pleasures* 262, 285, 803, 1152, 1399, 2053, 2055, 2092, 2149, 2309, 2320, **2517**, 3441, 3484, 5062, 5078, 5324, 5405, 5407, 5577
*The Killing Dance* **2518**
*The Laughing Corpse* **2519**, 5707
*The Lunatic Cafe* 1400, **2520**, 5577
*Nightseer* 172, 673, 681, 763, 841, 994, 1253, 1674, 1687, 1744, 1837, 2039, 2268, 2269, 2358, 2503, 2509, **2521**, 2862, 2956, 3074, 3080, 3105, 3167, 3168, 3277, 3306, 3486, 3509, 3511, 3514, 3775, 3839, 3936, 4129, 4323, 4459, 4489, 4527, 4686, 4768, 4804, 5127, 5144, 5266, 5584, 5750, 5812, 5967, 5978, 5980
*Nightshade* 1383

**Hamilton, Peter F.**
*Conflict* **2522**
*Consolidation* **2523**
*Emergence* 687, **2524**
*Expansion* **2525**
*Mindstar Rising* 110, 1168, **2526**
*A Quantum Murder* **2527**

**Hamilton, Virginia**
*Her Stories* **2528**
*House of Dies Drear* 331
*Justice and Her Brothers* 362

**Hammell, Ian**
*Clock Strikes Sword* **2529**

**Hammond, Michael**
*The Burning Man* **2530**, 5622

**Hancock, Neil**
*Across the Far Mountain* 3077

*The Bridge of Dawn* **2531**

**Hand, Elizabeth**
*12 Monkeys* 1258, **2532**
*AEstival Tide* 836, **2533**, 4381
*The Frenchman* 2114, 2308, **2534**
*Glimmering* **2535**, 6028
*Icarus Descending* 400, **2536**, 5105
*Last Summer at Mars Hill* **2537**
*Waking the Moon* 715, 1180, 1445, **2538**, 3099, 3257, 4093, 4358
*Winterlong* **2539**
*The X-Files: Fight the Future* **924**

**Hanlon, John**
*Death's Loving Arms and Other Terror Tales* 4494
*The House of Living Death and Other Terror Tales* 4494

**Hanna, Lynn**
*The Starry Child* **2540**

**Hanner, Mary K.**
*Rapid Growth* **2541**

**Hansen, Karl**
*War Games* 2432

**Hansen, Ron**
*Mariette in Ecstasy* 4050
*Nebraska* 626

**Harbinson, W.A.**
*Dream Maker* 156, **2542**

**Hardin, Terri**
*American Gothic* 5439
*Supernatural Tales From around the World* **2543**, 2643

**Hardy, Lyndon**
*Master of the Five Magics* 1683, 1813

**Hardy, Robin**
*The Wicker Man* 852

**Harington, Donald**
*The Cockroaches of Stay More* **2544**, 5612

**Harness, Charles L.**
*Lunar Justice* **2545**
*Lurid Dreams* 1196, **2546**
*An Ornament to His Profession* **2547**

**Harper, Andrew**
*Bad Karma* **2548**, 4084

**Harper, Rory**
*Petrogypsies* 1891, 1893, **2549**

**Harper, Tara K.**
*Cat Scratch Fever* **2550**
*Cataract* 3500
*Lightwing* 231, 996, **2551**, 2832, 3718
*Shadow Leader* **2552**, 4324
*Wolfwalker* 1176, **2553**

**Harpman, Jacqueline**
*I Who Have Never Known Men* **2554**

**Harrald, Jon A.**
*Dying Breath* **2555**

**Harrington, Alan**
*Life in the Crystal Palace* 1782

**Harrington, Barry**
*The Beyond* **2556**

**Harris, Allen Lee**
*Deliver Us From Evil* 3160
*Let There Be Dark* **2557**, 2749, 4715

**Harris, Anne**
*Accidental Creatures* **2558**, 4339
*The Nature of Smoke* **2559**

**Harris, David**
*Bill, the Galactic Hero: The Final Incoherent Adventure* **2568**

**Harris, Deborah Turner**
*The Adept* **3254**
*Caledon of the Mists* **2560**, 4045
*Dagger Magic* **3256**
*Death of an Adept* **3257**
*The Lodge of the Lynx* **3259**
*The Queen of Ashes* **2561**
*The Templar Treasure* **3261**

**Harris, Geraldine**
*Prince of the Godborn* 5142, 6037

**Harris, Marilyn**
*Night Games* **2562**
*The Portent* 1625

**Harris, Raymond**
*The Broken Worlds* 4162, 4594, 5550
*The Schizogenic Man* 350, 590, **2563**
*Shadows of the White Sun* 351, 353, 882, 1914, 5377, 5546, 5548

**Harris, Robert**
*Fatherland* 598, 2239, **2564**, 2667, 3528, 3601, 4474, 5517, 5518

**Harris, Steve**
*The Eyes of the Beast* **2565**
*Straker's Island* 4249

**Harris, Thomas**
*Red Dragon* 2110, 2159, 2341, 2534, 2825, 3319, 3518, 3899, 3900, 3902, 5084, 5085, 5326, 5328
*The Silence of the Lambs* 695, 1170, 1555, 2428, **2566**, 2931, 3210, 3395, 3402, 3756, 3855, 4084, 4222, 4501, 4509, 5318, 5326, 5328, 5338, 5453

**Harrison, Harry**
*The Adventures of the Stainless Steel Rat* 3849, 4467
*Bill, the Galactic Hero* 260, 261, 1382, 1536, 1919, 3828, 4563, 4564, 4566, 4657
*Bill, the Galactic Hero: On the Planet of Tasteless Pleasure* 1420, **2567**
*Bill, the Galactic Hero: On the Planet of Zombie Vampires* 2486
*Bill, the Galactic Hero: The Final Incoherent Adventure* **2568**
*Bill, the Galactic Hero: The Planet of the Robot Slaves* 173, 553
*Captive Universe* 58
*The Daleth Effect* 1666
*Deathworld* 1107, 1551, 1641, 2210, 3522, 4884
*Deathworld 3* 1025
*The Deathworld Trilogy* 420, 785, 1247, 1540, 1634, 1643, 2010, 2056, 2371, 3744, 4957
*Galactic Dreams* 2490, 2547, **2569**
*The Hammer and the Cross* 363, 889, 1191, 1856, 2229, 2246, 2250, 2453, 2454, **2570**, 3501, 3636, 4264, 4270, 4518, 4872
*Invasion: Earth* 914
*King and Emperor* **2571**, 5500
*Make Room, Make Room* 1878
*One King's Way* **2572**
*Planet of the Damned* 564, 2414, 5231, 5319
*Planet of the Robot Slaves* **2573**
*Planet Story* 29, 1787
*A Rebel in Time* 2046, 3343
*Return to Eden* 591, 885

*S.F.: Author's Choice* 240
*Science Fiction Novellas* 6027
*A Science Fiction Reader* 6027
*The Stainless Steel Rat* 5232
*The Stainless Steel Rat Goes to Hell* **2574**, 4655
*The Stainless Steel Rat Saves the World* 3343, 3801
*The Stainless Steel Rat Sings the Blues* **2575**
*Stainless Steel Visions* **2576**
*Star Smashers and Galaxy Rangers* 3543
*Stars and Stripes Forever* **2577**, 5495
*The Technicolor Time Machine* 508, 1344, 1418, 3082, 5043, 5565
*There Won't Be War* **2578**, 4959
*Tunnel through the Deeps* 1655
*The Turing Option* **2579**
*West of Eden* 165, 591, 4853
*Winter in Eden* 591

**Harrison, M. John**
*The Pastel City* 3791, 3797
*Signs of Life* **2580**, 3241
*A Storm of Wings* 5547

**Harrison, Shirley**
*The Diary of Jack the Ripper: The Discovery, the Investigation, the Debate* 3987

**Harrison, Sue**
*Mother Earth, Father Sky* 191, 561, 668, 870, 2166, 2167, 2168, 2169, **2581**, 2857, 3503, 3704, 4320, 4817, 4818, 4819, 5925
*My Sister the Moon* 2169, **2582**
*Song of the River* **2583**

**Hart, James V.**
*Bram Stoker's Dracula* **4763**

**Hartley, L.P.**
*The Travelling Grave, and Other Stories* 779
*The Travelling Grave and Other Stories* 4141, 5610, 5611

**Hartman, Darlene**
*Hopeship* 3315
*The Trumpets of Tagan* 3316

**Hartmann, William**
*Mars Underground* 1585, **2584**

**Hartwell, David G.**
*The Ascent of Wonder: The Evolution of Hard SF* 229, 422, 448, 1617, 1623, 1624, **2585**
*Bodies of the Dead* **2586**, 5439
*Christmas Forever* 2456, **2587**
*Christmas Magic* 2146, **2588**
*Christmas Stars* 2412, **2589**, 5024
*The Color of Evil* 1373
*The Dark Descent* 226, 1629, 1844, **2590**, 3027, 4440, 5031, 5924
*Foundations of Fear* 226, **2591**, 4440
*Masterpieces of Fantasy and Wonder* **2592**, 6046
*Northern Stars: The Anthology of Canadian Science Fiction* 1767, **2593**, 4439
*The Science Fiction Century* **2594**
*Visions of Wonder: The Science Fiction Research Association Anthology* 229, **2595**
*The World Treasury of Science Fiction* 850, 887, 1612, 3381, 4725, 5004, 5489
*Year's Best SF* 1619, **2596**
*Year's Best SF 2* 1619, **2597**

*Year's Best SF 3* **2598**
*The Year's Best SF 13* 1623

**Hartzell, Susan**
*The Crawling Dark* **1698**

**Harvey, Frank**
*Air Force!* 5247

**Harvey, James Neal**
*The Headsman* 1831, **2599**, 3210

**Harvey, William Fryer**
*The Beast with Five Fingers and Other
Stories* 4141
*Midnight Tales* 454, 455, 5610

**Hasford, Gustav**
*Phantom Blooper* 4477
*The Short Timers* 4865

**Hatch, George**
*Guignoir and Other Furies* 22, 2280,
**2600**, 2966, 4200, 5447
*Sinistre: An Anthology of Rituals* 22,
1281, **2601**, 3112
*Souls in Pawn* 1281

**Hatch, Richard**
*Armageddon* **2602**

**Hatch, Robert**
*Dark Tyrants* 23

**Hatvary, George Egon**
*The Murder of Edgar Allan Poe* 3150

**Hauff, Wilhelm**
*The Fairy Tales of Wilhelm
Hauff* 2447

**Haushofer, Marlen**
*The Wall* 1787, 2554, **2603**, 2640

**Hautala, Rick**
*Beyond the Shroud* 797, 839, 2161,
**2604**, 4256, 5249, 5585
*Cold Whisper* **2605**, 2631, 3040,
3640
*Dark Silence* **2606**, 5472
*Dead Voices* **2607**
*Ghost Light* 1505, **2608**, 3139,
3205, 3365, 3857, 3858
*Impulse* **2609**
*Moon Walker* **2610**, 2928
*The Mountain King* **2611**
*Night Visions 9* **5441**
*Shades of Night* **2612**
*Twilight Time* **2613**

**Hautman, Pete**
*Mr. Was* **2614**, 5594

**Hawk, Douglas D.**
*The Devouring* **2615**

**Hawke, Simon**
*The Ambivalent Magician* **2616**
*The Argonaut Affair* 33
*Batman: To Stalk a Specter* 14, 2124,
2331, 2391, 2392, 4215
*The Inadequate Adept* **2617**
*The Iron Throne* **2618**, 3489
*The Ivanhoe Gambit* 1162, 3799,
3802, 3803, 3804, 3849
*The Kyber Connection* 33, 4164
*The Last Wizard* **2619**
*The Nine Lives of Catseye
Gomez* **2620**
*The Nomad* 1977
*The Outcast* 13, **2621**, 5723
*Predator 2* 492
*The Reluctant Sorcerer* 847, **2622**
*The Samurai Wizard* **2623**
*The Seeker* 13, 299, 394, 1485,
**2624**
*War* **2625**

*The Whims of Creation* 107, 2243,
**2626**, 5941
*The Wizard of 4th Street* 227, 433,
973, 1091, 1160, 1273, 4391,
4771, 5646, 5697
*The Wizard of Camelot* 973, 977,
**2627**, 4771, 5203
*The Wizard of Santa Fe* **2628**
*The Wizard of Sunset Strip* **2629**,
2797, 4362

**Hawkes, Judith**
*Julian's House* 281, 282, 861, 890,
2040, 2240, **2630**, 2669, 2856,
3055, 3201, 5334, 5402, 5528,
5991
*My Soul to Keep* **2631**

**Hawkins, Barry T.**
*Puppet Master* 2159, **2632**

**Hawkins, Ward**
*Red Flame Burning* 165, 2574

**Hawthorne, Hildegarde**
*Faded Garden: The Collected Ghost
Stories of Hildegarde
Hawthorne* 2919

**Hawthorne, Julian**
*The Rose of Death and Other
Mysterious Delusions* **2633**

**Hawthorne, Nathaniel**
*The Celestial Railroad and Other
Stories* 722
*The House of the Seven Gables* 340
*The Scarlet Letter* 1130

**Hayden, Laura**
*A Margin in Time* 3039

**Hayden, Patrick Nielsen**
*Starlight 1* **2634**
*Starlight 2* **2635**

**Haydock, Tim**
*The Mammoth Book of Classic
Chillers* 226

**Hazel, Paul**
*The Wealdwife's Tale* **2636**, 2739

**Heald, Denise Lopez**
*Mistwalker* **2637**

**Healy, Raymond J.**
*Adventures in Time and Space* 24,
214, 238, 239, 422, 501, 1616,
1620, 1621, 2405, 3308, 3381,
4127, 5004, 5238

**Heard, Gerald**
*The Doppelgangers* 2788

**Heard, H.F.**
*A Taste for Honey* 4842

**Hearn, Lafcadio**
*Kwaidan* 5801
*Some Chinese Ghosts* 3250

**Hearn, Michael Patrick**
*The Victorian Fairy Tale Book* 276,
2447, 3574, 6088, 6090

**Heath, Peter**
*Assassins From Tomorrow* 3979

**Hecht, Daniel**
*Skull Session* **2638**

**Heeley, D.A.**
*Lilith* 1143
*Ronin* **2639**

**Hegland, Jean**
*Into the Forest* 2554, **2640**

**Heide, Florence P.**
*The Shrinking of Treehorn* 5968

**Heidel, R. Andrew**
*Beyond the Wall of Sleep* **2641**

**Heidish, Marcy**
*The Torch* 1050
*The Torching* 71, 966, 1836, 2023,
**2642**, 2874, 4753, 5186, 5271,
5290

**Hein, Ruth D.**
*Ghostly Tales of Iowa* **2643**, 5211

**Heinlein, Robert A.**
*Beyond This Horizon* 4296
*Citizen of the Galaxy* 62, 1903,
1948, 3767, 4043, 4453, 4952
*The Door into Summer* 1345, 1895,
3663, 4143, 4157, 4247, 4332,
4559
*Double Star* 1987, 2361, 2375,
2422, 2459, 2788, 4937, 5215,
5227, 5248, 5609
*Expanded Universe* 5938
*Farmer in the Sky* 380, 1768, 2549,
4964
*Farnham's Freehold* 116, 435, 3873,
4018, 4599, 5659
*Friday* 1071, 1571
*Glory Road* 135, 1229, 1414, 1429,
1452, 1453, 1684, 1754, 1983,
2357, **2644**, 3098, 3572, 3848,
3849, 4014, 4674
*The Green Hills of Earth* 4956, 5247,
5345
*Have Spacesuit—Will Travel* 1217,
1460, 2491, 2763, 4930
*I Will Fear No Evil* 2498, 4066
*Job: A Comedy of Justice* 956, 2103,
2753, 2942, 3908, 3986, 4028,
5532, 5636, 6070
*The Man Who Sold the Moon* 593
*Methuselah's Children* 127, 1554,
2491, 4955
*The Moon Is a Harsh Mistress* 77,
79, 126, 134, 419, 478, 587, 588,
894, 1548, 1915, 1965, 1993,
2196, 2459, **2645**, 2733, 3437,
3466, 3603, 3994, 4895, 4931,
4932, 5132, 5213, 5234, 5241,
5245, 5365, 5366, 5367, 5370,
5452, 5566, 5889
*The Number of the Beast* 135, 302,
951, 5159
*Orphans of the Sky* 58, 297, 4626,
5042, 5942, 5943
*The Past through Tomorrow* 479,
2829, 4118, 4123, 4127, 4346,
5106, 5349, 5551
*Podkayne of Mars* 1265, 1970, 2416,
2418, 2763
*The Puppet Masters* 156, 383, 564,
1197, 2034, 2211, 2344, 2345,
**2646**, 3063, 3188, 3218, 3476,
4510, 4944, 5027, 5341, 5352
*Red Planet* 421, 586, 1585, 1768,
2584, **2647**, 2765, 5859
*Requiem* **2648**, 5480
*Revolt in 2100* 1869
*The Rolling Stones* 1970, 2808, 4919
*Silent Thunder/Universe* 2829
*Sixth Column* 1869, 1877, 2323,
3873
*Space Cadet* 1900, 4911, 4948,
4958
*The Star Beast* 3500
*Starman Jones* 905, 1899, 1978,
5246

*Starship Troopers* 206, 310, 589,
1327, 1382, 1508, 1635, 1641,
1651, 2004, 2210, 2211, 2351,
2353, 2436, 2464, 2790, 4204,
4377, 4378, 4466, 4583, 4672,
4910, 4911, 5023, 5246, 5278,
5279, 5280, 5283, 5469
*Stranger in a Strange Land* 362,
1587, 1862, 2103, 2343, **2649**,
2722, 3924, 3943, 3944, 4139,
4242, 4330, 4347, 5373, 5436,
5449, 5532
*Time Enough for Love* 125, 1962,
2446, 2487, 2498, 2920, 3663,
4813
*Time for the Stars* 3249, 4918
*To Sail Beyond the Sunset* 2489
*Tunnel in the Sky* 2290, 2807, 3011,
4262, 5295
*The Unpleasant Profession of Jonathan
Hoag* 3252, 3351
*Waldo and Magic, Inc.* 162, 5694

**Helfers, John**
*Black Cats and Broken Mirrors* **2381**

**Heller, Carol**
*The Gates of Vensunor* 1984, **2650**,
3481, 4459
*The Sands of Kalaven: A Novel of
Shunlar* **2651**

**Heller, Jane**
*Infernal Affairs* **2652**

**Helprin, Mark**
*A City in Winter* **2653**
*The Veils of Snows* **2654**
*Winter's Tale* 896, 1276, 5272,
5570

**Hemingway, Hilary**
*Time Blender* **1581**

**Hemmingson, Michael**
*Nice Little Stories Jam-Packed with
Depraved Sex and Violence* **2655**,
2778, 3176, 3392, 3393, 3397,
5316, 5536
*Snuff Flique* **2656**

**Henderson, C.J.**
*All Things under the Moon* **4002**
*The Only Thing to Fear* **4003**
*Some Things Come Back* **4004**
*Some Things Never Die* **4005**
*The Thing That Darkness Hides* **4006**
*The Things That Are Not There* **4007**

**Henderson, Jason**
*The Element of Fire* **2657**
*Highlander: The Element of Fire* 559,
1808, 4082, 4611, 5707, 5729
*The Spawn of Loki* 458, **2658**, 4516,
4522

**Henderson, Zenna**
*Ingathering: The Complete People
Stories of Zenna Henderson* 759,
1460, 1502, 1969, **2659**, 2716,
3430, 3981, 4502, 5838
*The People: No Different Flesh* 2717

**Hendrix, Howard V.**
*Lightpaths* **2660**, 4295
*Standing Wave* **2661**

**Hendry, Frances Mary**
*Quest for a Maid* 269, 658, 2636,
**2662**, 4008

**Henry, Will**
*Genesis Five* 2107

**Herber, Keith**
*Dark Prince* **2663**

*Prince of the City* 798, 2664, 4058

**Herbert, Brian**
*Blood on the Sun* 387, 1119, 1949,
   1950, **2664**, 4058
*Memorymakers* **2665**
*The Race for God* **2666**, 4507, 5033

**Herbert, Frank**
*The Ascension Factor* 4478
*Chapterhouse: Dune* 4551
*Children of Dune* 707, 5561
*Destination: Void* 126
*The Dosadi Experiment* 959, 2545
*Dune* 35, 231, 324, 434, 554, 566,
   567, 580, 622, 707, 756, 1102,
   1103, 1108, 1254, 1566, 1598,
   1637, 1648, 1654, 1807, 1861,
   2194, 2365, 2366, 2459, 2523,
   2524, 3014, 3231, 3316, 3599,
   3710, 3735, 3909, 3910, 3911,
   3927, 3937, 3946, 3947, 4287,
   4483, 4557, 4698, 4729, 5019,
   5051, 5059, 5117, 5138, 5140,
   5141, 5278, 5292, 5434, 5526,
   5575, 5637, 5671, 5672, 5673,
   5675, 5717, 5720, 5722, 5739,
   5740, 5742, 5744, 5835, 5917,
   5920, 5921, 5922, 5941, 5985,
   6008, 6052
*Dune Messiah* 707, 1538, 5941
*The God-Emperor of Dune* 4553
*Hellstrom's Hive* 4662, 4842, 4944,
   5755
*Heretics of Dune* 2464, 2722, 3507,
   4551
*The Jesus Incident* 4476, 4478
*The Lazarus Effect* 4476, 4478
*Nebula Winners 15* 500, 501, 4031,
   4032
*Whipping Star* 1992, 2343, 2666,
   4019, 4357, 5042
*The White Plague* 1133, 1167, 1724,
   2681, 2870, 3008, 3242, 3641,
   3642, 4476, 4478, 4748, 4756,
   4856, 5054, 5172, 5212, 5258

**Herbert, James**
*'48* **2667**, 2720
*The Dark* 943, 3370
*Domain* 3192, 3992
*Fluke* 4582
*The Fog* 800, 943, 2787, 2867,
   3370
*The Ghosts of Sleath* **2668**
*Haunted* 283, 2094, **2669**
*Lair* 3192, 3992
*The Magic Cottage* 2160, 2562,
   4249
*Moon* 1580, 3128, 3203, 4471
*Portent* **2670**, 2824
*The Rats* **2671**, 3192, 3992, 4370
*Sepulchre* **2672**, 3594, 4508
*The Spear* 4960
*Survivor* 3215

**Herbert, Mary H.**
*City of the Sorcerers* **2673**, 5529
*Dark Horse* 223, 2397, 2552, **2674**,
   4323, 4493
*Legacy of Steel* **2675**
*Lightning's Daughter* 223, 1293,
   2397, **2676**
*Valorian* 1029, **2677**
*Winged Magic* **2678**

**Herley, Richard**
*The Stone Arrow* 275, 1632, 2167,
   2168, 2169, 2581, 4818, 4819,
   5444

**Heron, E.**
*Flaxman Low, Psychic Detective* 509

**Herriot, James**
*Blossom Comes Home* 3377

**Hersey, John**
*White Lotus* 3817, 5301, 5918, 5919

**Hershey, Jennifer**
*Full Spectrum 5* 1619, 1623, 1624,
   2596, 2597, 2598, 2634, 2635,
   **2679**

**Herzog, Arthur III**
*Earthsound* 1060

**Hesse, Hermann**
*The Fairy Tales of Hermann*
   *Hesse* **2680**

**Hichens, Robert**
*Tongues of Conscience* 1252

**Hickman, Tracy**
*Dragon Wing* 5709
*Dragons of Summer Flame* 5711
*Elven Star* 5712
*Fire Sea* 5714
*The Hand of Chaos* 5715
*The Immortals* **2681**, 5722, 5725
*Into the Labyrinth* 5716
*Legacy of the Darksword* 5719
*Nightsword* 5722
*Relics and Omens* 5723
*The Second Generation* 5724
*Sentinels* 5725
*Serpent Mage* 5726
*The Seventh Gate* 5727
*Treasures of Fantasy* 5730

**Higgs, Eric**
*Doppelganger* 3178, 3320

**Highsmith, Patricia**
*Strangers on a Train* 2415

**Hightower, Lynn S.**
*Alien Blues* 2421, **2682**, 4117, 4389,
   4935, 4936, 4938, 4939, 5596
*Alien Eyes* **2683**
*Alien Heat* 2093, 2286, **2684**
*Alien Rites* **2685**, 4928

**Highwater, Jamake**
*Dark Legend* **2686**, 4264

**Hildick, E.W.**
*The Active-Enzyme Lemon-Freshened*
   *Junior High School Witch* 2949,
   5478

**Hilgartner, Beth**
*Colors in the Dreamweaver's*
   *Loom* 5070

**Hill, David**
*The Way of the Werewolf* 2410,
   2976, 5384

**Hill, Douglas**
*Exiles of Colsec* 3966

**Hill, Susan**
*The Woman in Black* 5519

**Hill, William**
*California Ghosting* **2687**
*The Magic Bicycle* **2688**

**Hilton, James**
*Lost Horizon* 1105, 1169, 4020,
   4061, 4062, 4063, 4866, 4867,
   5396

**Hinkemeyer, Michael T.**
*Order of the Arrow* 1894, **2689**
*Soulcatchers* 3336

**Hinsenbrock, Vicky L.**
*Ghostly Tales of Iowa* **2643**

**Hinz, Christopher**
*Ash Ock* **2690**, 4049
*Liege-Killer* 3072, 4049, 4287, 5366
*The Paratwa* **2691**

**Hitchcock, Alfred**
*Alfred Hitchcock Presents: Stories for*
   *Late at Night* 543, 2282
*Alfred Hitchcock Presents: Stories My*
   *Mother Never Told Me* 543
*Alfred Hitchcock Presents: Stories Not*
   *for the Nervous* 543, 1019

**Hite, Shere**
*The Divine Comedy of Ariadne and*
   *Jupiter: The Amazing and*
   *Spectacular Adventures of Ariadne*
   *and Jupiter in Heaven and on*
   *Earth* 5397

**Hjortsberg, William**
*Falling Angel* 21, 619, 1125, 1792,
   2110, 4006, 4085, 4100
*Nevermore* 26, 1564, **2692**, 3150,
   3596, 3631, 4344, 4345, 4773

**Hoban, Russell**
*Riddley Walker* 325

**Hobb, Robin**
*Assassin's Apprentice* 682, 1008,
   1082, 1513, 1636, 1773, 1863,
   1952, 1953, 2268, 2270, 2426,
   2451, 2452, 2504, 2653, **2693**,
   2795, 2798, 2956, 2958, 2959,
   2989, 3074, 3123, 3278, 3385,
   3481, 3645, 3651, 3775, 3832,
   3896, 4165, 4796, 4808, 5202,
   5275, 5583, 5737, 5759
*Assassin's Quest* **2694**
*Royal Assassin* 466, **2695**, 4802
*The Ship of Magic* **2696**

**Hocherman, Henry W.**
*The Gilgul* **2697**

**Hodge, Brian**
*The Convulsion Factory* 663, 1789,
   **2698**, 3667, 4313, 5600
*The Darker Saints* 20, 1298, **2699**,
   4498
*Deathgrip* 795, 800, **2700**
*Falling Idols* 1016, **2701**, 5026
*Nightlife* **2702**, 3101
*Oasis* 858, **2703**, 5472
*Prototype* **2704**, 3207
*Shrines and Desecrations* 748, 1467,
   **2705**, 3111, 3114, 3549

**Hodgell, P.C.**
*Dark of the Moon* 4, 673, 936, 1068,
   1072, 1073, 3175, 3421, 4653
*God Stalk* 4, 672, 673, 682, 936,
   1068, 1072, 1073, 1251, 1253,
   1856, 2196, 2521, 2538, 3095,
   3421, 3486, 3766, 3773, 3894,
   4521, 4522, 4653, 4654, 4849,
   4850, 5203, 5371, 5509, 5741

**Hodgson, Barbara**
*The Tattooed Map* 333, 336, **2706**

**Hodgson, Sheila**
*The Fellow Travellers and Other Ghost*
   *Stories* 1671, **2707**, 5776

**Hodgson, William Hope**
*Beyond the Dawning: The Poems of*
   *William Hope Hodgson* 486
*Carnacki the Ghost Finder* 258, 509,
   670
*Deep Waters* 3798
*Demons of the Sea* **2708**, 3798

*Down Among the Weeds: The Sargasso*
   *Sea Stories of William Hope*
   *Hodgson* **2709**
*The Ghost Pirates* 2732
*The Haunted Pampero* **2710**
*The House on the Borderland* **2711**
*The Night Land* 4371
*Out of the Storm* 5746
*Terrors of the Sea* **2712**

**Hoffman, Alice**
*Practical Magic* 1445, **2713**

**Hoffman, Barry**
*Firefly...Burning Bright* 1016, 2155,
   2656, **2714**
*Hungry Eyes* 3395

**Hoffman, Curtis H.**
*Project: Millennium* 2753

**Hoffman, Nina Kiriki**
*Child of an Ancient City* 5827
*Common Threads* 200
*Legacy of Fire* 2078, **2715**, 4878
*The Silent Strength of Stones* 636,
   **2716**
*The Thread That Binds the*
   *Bones* 1444, 1478, 1502, 1512,
   2659, **2717**, 2942, 3628, 3630,
   3935, 4221

**Hoffmann, E.T.A.**
*The Best Tales of Hoffmann* 5389
*The Golden Pot and Other*
   *Tales* **2718**
*Nutcracker* 2654, **2719**
*The Tales of Hoffmann* 5418

**Hogan, Chuck**
*The Blood Artists* **2720**, 3632

**Hogan, Ernest**
*Cortez on Jupiter* 766, 1449, **2721**,
   2847, 3046, 3082, 3452, 4642,
   4643, 4679, 5565
*High Aztec* 829, 2369, **2722**, 4935,
   4936, 5254

**Hogan, James P.**
*Bug Park* 386, 1168, **2723**, 3922,
   5755
*Code of the Lifemaker* 83, 446
*Endgame Enigma* 597, 2301
*Entoverse* 472, 1981, **2724**
*The Genesis Machine* 1245
*The Immortality Option* **2725**, 5051,
   5059
*The Mirror Maze* **2726**
*The Multiplex Man* 1762, 2163,
   **2727**, 3049, 4130, 4136, 4677,
   5680
*Paths to Otherwhere* 357, 1026,
   **2728**, 3186, 5531
*The Proteus Operation* 1245, 5516,
   5996
*Realtime Interrupt* 956, 1761, 2033,
   **2729**, 3831
*Star Child* **2730**
*Thrice upon a Time* 110, 1345
*The Two Faces of Tomorrow* 3454
*Voyage From Yesteryear* 3344, 3924,
   5788, 5804

**Hogg, James**
*Private Memoirs and Confessions of a*
   *Justified Sinner* 722
*Selected Stories and Sketches* 2905

**Hoh, Diane**
*The Accident* 1692
*Book of Horrors* 5285

**Hoklin, Lonn**
*Kindred* 2222

**Holden, Christine**
*A Time for Us*  **2731**

**Holder, Nancy**
*Cannibal Dwight's Special
    Purpose*  4255, 5685
*Dead in the Water*  **2732**, 4715
*Making Love*  5422
*The Six Families*  **2733**
*Witch-Light*  **2734**

**Holdstock, Robert**
*Ancient Echoes*  1491, **2735**, 4093
*The Bone Forest*  395, 415, 1431,
    2106, **2736**, 3845, 4757, 4809
*Gate of Ivory, Gate of Horn*  **2737**
*The Hollowing*  **2738**
*Lavondyss: Journey to an Unknown
    Region*  1423, 2238, 2636, **2739**,
    4797, 4809, 4992, 5806
*Mythago Wood*  153, 271, 439, 820,
    919, 935, 1435, 1438, 1440, 2101,
    2105, 2238, 2636, 3291, 3292,
    3470, 3793, 3843, 3878, 4159,
    4382, 4475, 4797, 4809, 5806,
    5817, 5818, 5927

**Holland, Jack**
*The Fire Queen*  633, **2740**, 5783

**Holland, Tom**
*Lord of the Dead*  **2741**
*Slave of My Thirst*  **2742**

**Holleman, Gary L.**
*Demon Fire*  **2743**, 3885, 5100, 5463
*Howl-O-Ween*  **2744**

**Hollick, Helen**
*The Kingmaking*  1190, **2745**, 4877
*Pendragon's Banner*  **2746**, 3474
*Shadow of the King*  **2747**, 3355

**Hollister, Bernard**
*You and Science Fiction: A Humanistic
    Aproach to Tomorrow*  6027

**Holm, John**
*The Hammer and the Cross*  **2570**
*King and Emperor*  **2571**
*One King's Way*  **2572**

**Holmen, Rachel E.**
*Sword and Sorceress XIV*  651

**Holt, John R.**
*The Convocation*  **2748**
*Wilderness*  926
*Wolf Moon*  514, **2749**

**Holt, Tom**
*Expecting Someone Taller*  36, 355,
    4056, 4393, 4400
*Flying Dutch*  1752, **2750**
*Goatsong*  67, 2189, **2751**, 5595,
    5639
*The Walled Orchard*  2189, **2752**,
    5595
*Who's Afraid of Beowulf?*  1273
*Ye Gods!*  **2753**

**Home, Stewart**
*Come Before Christ and Murder
    Love*  **2754**, 4732

**Homes, A.M.**
*The End of Alice*  **2755**, 4183
*The Safety of Objects*  3195, 4181

**Hone, Joseph**
*Irish Ghost Stories*  1242, 2481,
    2482, 4203

**Hood, Daniel**
*Beggar's Banquet*  **2756**
*Fanuilh*  **2757**, 5848
*Scales of Justice*  **2758**, 5749
*Wizard's Heir*  **2759**

**Hood, Ken**
*Demon Knight*  **2760**, 4852

**Hoover, Dale**
*65mm*  460, 1085, 1353, **2761**,
    3103, 3326
*Shadow Twin*  **2762**

**Hoover, H.M.**
*Away Is a Strange Place to Be*  **2763**
*The Bell Tree*  878
*Children of Morrow*  878, 4827
*Only Child*  230, **2764**
*Orvis*  253, 254, 255
*This Time of Darkness*  3584
*Treasures of Morrow*  878
*The Winds of Mars*  **2765**

**Hopen, Stuart**
*Warp Angel*  **2766**, 5051, 5767

**Hopkins, Andrea**
*Chronicles of King Arthur*  227, 266,
    267, 1270, 2745, 2746, **2767**,
    3062, 4987

**Hopkins, Brian**
*Cold at Heart*  41, **2768**, 5388
*Something Haunts Us All*  94, 802,
    **2769**, 2937, 3495, 3667, 4231,
    4313, 5316, 5335, 5445, 5620,
    5881

**Hopkins, Jack**
*Satellite Night News*  **2770**

**Hopkinson, Nalo**
*Brown Girl in the Ring*  **2771**

**Horlak, E.E.**
*Still Life*  2819

**Horowitz, Anthony**
*Death Walks Tonight*  **2772**
*The Puffin Book of Horror
    Stories*  1701, 2395

**Horseman, Elaine**
*Hubble's Bubble*  5968

**Horsting, Jessica**
*Midnight Graffiti*  1017, 1281, **2773**,
    5025

**Horvitz, Leslie**
*The Dying*  1625

**Horwood, William**
*Duncton Wood*  32, 432
*Toad Triumphant*  **2774**
*The Willows and Beyond*  **2775**
*The Willows in Winter*  **2776**, 2848

**Hoskins, Robert**
*To Control the Stars*  3777

**Houarner, Gerard Daniel**
*Going Postal*  2384, **2777**
*Inside the Works*  4314
*Painfreak*  2656, **2778**, 3318, 3495,
    5413, 5445, 5620

**Household, Geoffrey**
*The Sending*  1580

**Hovorka, Robert**
*Derelict*  4285

**Howard, Hayden**
*The Eskimo Invasion*  5766

**Howard, Joseph**
*Damien*  3445

**Howard, Lyle**
*Mr. Sandman*  **2779**, 4874

**Howard, Robert E.**
*Beyond the Borders*  **2780**, 3981
*Bran Mak Morn*  906
*The Coming of Conan*  5599

*Conan the Barbarian*  906, 907, 909,
    910, 2347, 2348, 2782, 2983,
    3501, 5110, 5599
*Conan the Conqueror*  909, 1838,
    1856, 2347, 2348, 3172, 4621
*Cthulhu: The Mythos and Kindred
    Horrors*  3531
*Eons of the Night*  **2781**
*Ghor, Kin-Slayer: The Saga of
    Genseric's Fifth-Born Son*  **2782**
*Hour of the Dragon*  291, 906, 907,
    **2783**, 2983, 3420, 4294, 4616
*King Conan*  906, 907, 909, 4617
*The Last Ride*  3335
*The People of the Black Circle*  4616
*Red Nails*  4616
*Skull-Face*  616, 942, 5695
*Skulls in the Stars*  3418
*Solomon Kane*  856
*The Sword of Conan*  4617
*Trails in Darkness*  **2784**

**Howard, Russ T.**
*The Ultimate Helm*  **2785**

**Howard, Stella**
*Prophecy of Darkness*  1811, 4912

**Howatch, Susan**
*Glittering Images*  5392

**Howe, Deborah**
*Bunnicula: A Rabbit Tale of
    Mystery*  1090

**Howe, James**
*How the Ewoks Saved the Trees: An
    Old Ewok Legend*  1392, 1393,
    1394
*Return to Howliday Inn*  **2786**

**Hoyle, Fred**
*A for Andromeda*  5766
*The Inferno*  82, 354
*October the First Is Too Late*  5295,
    5906

**Hoyle, Trevor**
*Kids*  **2787**
*The Last Gasp*  4512, 4628

**Hubbard, L. Ron**
*Ai! Pedrito!: When Intelligence Goes
    Wrong*  **2788**
*The Case of the Friendly
    Corpse*  3989
*Death's Deputy*  3415
*The Doomed Planet*  828
*Fear*  **2789**, 3417
*Final Blackout*  1113, **2790**
*Typewriter in the Sky*  **2791**
*Typewriter in the Sky/Fear*  5072,
    5791

**Huff, Tanya**
*Blood Debt*  **2792**, 3108
*Blood Pact*  301
*Blood Price*  1355, 1400, 1791,
    1793, 1796, 2149, 2376, 2441,
    2513, 2517, 2519, **2793**, 3053,
    3276, 3284, 3602, 4847, 5062,
    5078, 5374, 5406, 5577
*Blood Trail*  2514, 2517, 2518,
    2519, 2520, **2794**
*Child of the Grove*  739
*Fifth Quarter*  **2795**, 4524
*The Fire's Stone*  **2796**, 3288, 3305,
    3512, 3514, 3914, 4521
*Gate of Darkness, Circle of
    Light*  681, 1098, 1426, 1781,
    2619, **2797**, 3285, 3299, 4173,
    4995, 5379, 5646
*No Quarter*  **2798**
*Scholar of Decay*  1137, 1510

*Sing the Four Quarters*  **2799**, 3278,
    3298
*Summon the Keeper*  1657, **2800**

**Huffman, Marlys**
*Afternoon of the Gosling*  **2801**

**Huggins, James Byron**
*Cain*  **2802**, 3632

**Hugh, Zachary**
*Mother Lode*  **2812**

**Hughart, Barry**
*Bridge of Birds*  69, 409, 559, 746,
    1268, 1677, **3338**, 3991, 4155,
    4400, 4673, 4742, 6022, 6026,
    6066
*The Chronicles of Master Li and
    Number Ten Ox*  **2803**
*Eight Skilled Gentlemen*  69, **2804**,
    3338, 4742
*The Story of the Stone*  3338, 4742

**Hughes, Edward P.**
*Masters of the Fist*  1642, 2790,
    **2805**, 3346

**Hughes, Marian**
*Initiation*  2289, **2806**, 4119

**Hughes, Monica**
*Invitation to the Game*  **2807**
*The Promise*  641, **2808**, 3446, 4154
*Sandwriter*  1356

**Hughes, Robert Don**
*The Faithful Traitor*  **2809**
*The Forging of the Dragon*  2234
*Prophet of Lamath*  701, 1532, 3578

**Hughes, Ryan**
*The Darkness Before the Dawn*  13,
    2624
*Hard Crash*  **2810**

**Hughes, Zach**
*Deep Freeze*  **2811**
*Mother Lode*  **2812**

**Hurry, Graeme**
*Northern Chills*  2815

**Hutchinson, Bobby**
*Now and Then*  691

**Hutchison, Don**
*Northern Frights*  **2813**
*Northern Frights 2*  **2814**
*Northern Frights 3*  **2815**

**Hutson, Shaun**
*Heathen*  **2816**, 5120

**Huxley, Aldous**
*Brave New World*  574, 1782, 2558,
    3794, 5157, 5469, 5491, 5568
*Jacob's Hands*  **2817**

**Huysmans, J.K.**
*A Rebours*  3595

**Hyde, Christopher**
*Jericho Falls*  1136, 3337

**Hyman, Jackie**
*Echoes*  2154, **2818**, 3494
*Shadowlight*  1837, **2819**, 3383,
    5820

**Hyman, Tom**
*Jupiter's Daughter*  **2820**

**Hynd, Noel**
*Cemetery of Angels*  **2821**, 5468
*Ghosts*  840, **2822**, 3126
*The Prodigy*  **2823**
*Rage of Spirits*  **2824**
*A Room for the Dead*  **2825**

**Hynes, James**
*Publish and Perish* **2826**

## I

**Ice, Kathy**
*Distant Planes* **2827**

**Ing, Dean**
*Anasazi* 2861, 3704
*Cathouse* 129, **2828**, 3649, 3723, 4124, 4125, 4372, 4640
*The Ransom of Black Stealth One* 2143
*Silent Thunder/Universe* **2829**
*Systemic Shock* 3966, 4343, 4602

**Ingalls, Rachel**
*The End of Tragedy* 920, 2842, 3195, 4182, 5166

**Ingrid, Charles**
*Alien Salute* **2830**, 5261, 5564
*The Marked Man* 720, **2831**
*Path of Fire* **2832**
*Return Fire* **2833**, 3425, 4903, 5261

**Ingulphus**
*Tedious Brief Tales of Granta and Gramarye* 1350

**Ionesco, Eugene**
*Rhinoceros* 1817

**Ireson, Barbara**
*Tales out of Time* 4917

**Irving, Washington**
*The Legend of Sleepy Hollow and Other Stories* 722

**Irwin, Robert**
*The Arabian Nightmare* 2706

**Isherwood, Christopher**
*Jacob's Hands* **2817**

**Ivanhoe, Mark**
*Virgintooth* 600, 799, 2337, **2834**, 5537

## J

**Jablokov, Alexander**
*The Breath of Suspension* **2835**, 3600, 4680
*Carve the Sky* **2836**, 4103, 5107
*Deepdrive* **2837**
*A Deeper Sea* **2838**, 5107, 5587
*Nimbus* **2839**
*River of Dust* **2840**

**Jac, Cherlyn**
*Shadows in Time* 1271, 2731, 3576

**Jaccoma, Richard**
*The Werewolf's Revenge* **2841**, 4002
*The Werewolf's Tale* 2520, 2794, 4002, 4005, 4702, 5085

**Jackson, Basil**
*State of Emergency* 4512

**Jackson, Shirley**
*The Haunting of Hill House* 281, 282, 873, 1192, 2040, 2630, 2669, 3684, 3685, 4580, 4663, 5021, 5329, 5402, 5424, 5528, 5991, 5994
*Just an Ordinary Day* **2842**

*The Lottery, or the Adventures of James Harris* 623, 626, 5901
*The Magic of Shirley Jackson* 3575, 4181, 4182
*One Ordinary Day, with Peanuts* 5166
*The Sundial* 2314
*We Have Always Lived in the Castle* 2026, 3815, 4312

**Jacob, Charlee**
*This Symbiotic Fascination* **2843**

**Jacobi, Carl**
*Revelations in Black* 534, 942, 1088, 4904, 4905, 5627, 5628
*Smoke of the Snake* 939, 940, 942, **2844**, 3515, 5149, 5211

**Jacobs, A.J.**
*Fractured Fairy Tales* **2845**, 6040

**Jacobs, Joseph**
*English Fairy Tales* 2636

**Jacobs, W.W.**
*The Monkey's Paw and Other Tales of Mystery and the Macabre* **2846**

**Jacobson, Karie**
*Simulations* 2394

**Jacobson, Mark**
*Gojiro* 499, 729, **2847**, 4046

**Jacques, Brian**
*The Bellmaker* **2848**
*The Long Patrol* **2849**
*Mariel of Redwall* 32, **2850**
*Martin the Warrior* 32, **2851**
*Mattimeo* 737, **2852**, 3115
*Mossflower* 737
*Outcast of Redwall* **2853**
*The Pearls of Lutra* **2854**
*Redwall* 68, 599, 737, 1527, 1998, 2774, 2775, 2776, 4271
*Salamandastron* **2855**

**Jaffery, Sheldon**
*The Weirds* 940, 4494

**Jahn, Michael**
*The Frighteners* **2856**, 5468

**Jakes, John**
*Black in Time* 2577
*Brak the Barbarian* 3418, 4294
*The Mark of the Demons* 4848
*Six Gun Planet* 1398
*Time Gate* 3801

**James, Betsy**
*Dark Heart* 731, **2857**

**James, Cary**
*King & Raven* 273, **2858**, 3884, 5270

**James, Darius**
*Negrophobia: An Urban Parable* **2859**, 3455

**James, Del**
*The Language of Fear* **2860**

**James, Henry**
*The Ghostly Tales of Henry James* 2633
*Stories of the Supernatural* 45, 5772
*The Turn of the Screw* 3813
*The Two Magics: The Turn of the Screw, Covering End* 4275

**James, J. Alison**
*Sing for a Gentle Rain* 191, 331, 368, 1583, 2166, 2167, 2168, 2170, 2857, **2861**, 2865, 3436, 3545, 3704, 4380, 4918, 5035, 5751

**James, L. Dean**
*Book of Stones* **2862**
*Kingslayer* **2863**, 4326
*Mojave Wells* **2864**
*Summerland* 153, 1180, **2865**, 3843, 3936, 4105, 4107, 4908

**James, M.R.**
*The Best Ghost Stories of M.R. James* 4275
*"Casting the Runes"* 2020, 5111
*Casting the Runes and Other Ghost Stories* 283, 1243
*The Collected Ghost Stories of M.R. James* 2905, 3633
*A Warning to the Curious* **2866**

**James, Martin**
*Night Glow* 2112, **2867**

**James, Mary**
*Shoebag* 67, **2868**, 5656
*Shoebag Returns* **2869**

**James, P.D.**
*The Children of Men* **2870**

**James, Peter**
*Dreamer* **2871**
*Host* **2872**
*Possession* **2873**, 4310
*Prophecy* **2874**
*Sweet Heart* **2875**
*Twilight* **2876**

**James, Roby**
*Commencement* **2877**

**James, Valerie**
*Bewitching Beloved* 4943

**Jamison, Ellen**
*Stone Dead* **2878**, 3217, 3784

**Jansson, Tove**
*Finn Family Moomintroll* 6006

**Jarrow, Gail**
*Beyond the Magic Sphere* 489, **2879**

**Javin, Linda**
*Rock 'n' Roll Babes From Outer Space* **2880**

**Javor, Frank A.**
*The Ice Beast* **2881**
*The Rim-World Legacy and Beyond* **2882**

**Jay, William**
*The Lost History of Redwyn* **2883**

**Jefferies, Mike**
*Hall of Whispers* **2884**
*Hidden Echoes* 2760, **2885**
*The Knights of Cawdor* **2886**
*Palace of Kings* **2887**
*The Road to Underfall* 1156, **2888**
*Stone Angels* **2889**, 4852

**Jelloun, Tahar Ben**
*The Sand Child* 4263

**Jenkins, Vivan Knight**
*The Outlaw Heart* 2497

**Jenkins, William Fitzgerald**
*First Contacts: The Essential Murray Leinster* 3430

**Jennings, Phillip C.**
*The Bug Life Chronicles* **2890**
*Tower to the Sky* 5621

**Jens, Tina L.**
*Dangerous Dames* **2891**
*Strange Creatures* **2892**
*Tales of Forbidden Passion* **2893**
*Winter Tales* **2894**

**Jensen, Jane**
*The Beast Within: A Gabriel Knight Mystery* **2895**
*Gabriel Knight: Sins of the Fathers* 452, **2896**

**Jensen, Kris**
*FreeMaster* **2897**, 3907
*Mentor* 643, 990, **2898**, 4485

**Jensen, Ruby Jean**
*Baby Dolly* 364, 690, 2025, 2878, **2899**, 3217, 3782, 3784
*Celia* 1505, 2333, 2608, 2609, 2612, **2900**, 3130, 3139, 3205, 3365, 3857, 3858
*Chain Letter* 853, 2415
*The Haunting* **2901**, 2933, 3146, 3368
*The Living Evil* 2878, **2902**, 3784
*Night Thunder* **2903**
*The Reckoning* **2904**, 4501
*Victoria* 3782

**Jeppson, Janet O.**
*The Last Immortal* 251
*The Second Experiment* 251

**Jerome, Jerome K.**
*Three Men in a Boat* 5874

**Jessop, Augustus**
*The Phantom Coach and Other Ghost Stories of an Antiquary* **2905**

**Jeter, K.W.**
*Blade Runner 2: The Edge of Human* **2906**
*Blade Runner: Replicant Night* **2907**
*Bloodletter* 8, **2908**
*Cross of Blood* **2909**
*Dark Horizon* 2683, **2910**, 3243, 3520
*Dark Seeker* 3101, 4979, 5899
*Death's Arms* 474
*Farewell Horizontal* **2911**, 5899
*The Glass Hammer* 1519, 1520
*In the Land of the Dead* **2912**, 5899
*Infernal Devices* 520, 1186, 3596, 4432
*Madlands* 976, 1567, **2913**, 2997, 3009, 3245, 5109, 5145, 5156, 5254
*The Mandalorian Armor* 117, **2914**
*Morlock Night* 403, 1091
*The Night Man* 862, 2431, **2915**, 2935, 3127, 3679, 4022, 5323, 5825
*Noir* **2916**
*Soul Eater* 304, 2201, 5879
*Warped* **2917**
*Wolf Flow* 871, **2918**

**Jewett, Sarah Orne**
*Lady Ferry and Other Uncanny People* **2919**

**Johnson, Annabel**
*Prisoner of Psi* 5013

**Johnson, James B.**
*Daystar and Shadow* 4600
*Habu* **2920**
*A World Lost* **2921**

**Johnson, Kij**
*Dragon's Honor* 1225, 1226, 1228, 1229, 1382, **2922**

**Johnson, Norma Tadlock**
*The Witch House* **2923**

**Johnson, Oliver**
*The Forging of the Shadows* **2924**, 4685
*Nations of the Night* **2925**

**Johnston, Joe**
*The Adventures of Peebo: A Tale of Magic and Suspense* 1392, 1393, 1394

**Johnston, William L.**
*Asylum* 4838

**Johnstone, William W.**
*Bats* 2615, **2926**, 4688, 4815, 5263
*Carnival* **2927**, 3366, 4010, 5624
*Cat's Eye* **2928**, 3371
*Darkly the Thunder* 2316, **2929**
*The Devil's Laughter* **2930**
*Night Mask* 2825, **2931**
*Prey* 2824, **2932**
*Rockabilly Hell* **2933**, 5119
*Rockabilly Limbo* **2934**
*Them* **2935**, 3559, 3856
*Toy Cemetery* 5823
*Trapped in the Ashes* 44
*Watchers in the Woods* **2936**, 3092, 5685

**Jonas, Gary**
*By Death Abused* 2137
*Curse of the Magazine Killers* **2937**
*Nice Guys Finish Last* 2137, **2938**

**Jones, Courtway**
*In the Shadow of the Oak King* 224, 227, 266, 267, 2745, 2858, **2939**, 4266, 4270, 4458, 5792, 5793, 5794, 5970
*Witch of the North* **2940**, 5270

**Jones, D.F.**
*Colossus* 126, 4232, 4381, 4857, 5632
*Denver Is Missing* 354

**Jones, David Lee**
*Unicorn Highway* **2941**
*Zeus and Co.* 2404, 2716, **2942**

**Jones, Diana Wynne**
*Archer's Goon* 5979
*Aunt Maria* 545, 546, 549, 552, **2943**
*Cart and Cwidder* 1444, 1668, 3871, 4322, 4446, 4448, 5579, 5977, 5980, 6037
*Castle in the Air* 187, 355, 847, **2944**, 5218, 6043
*The Crown of Dalemark* **2945**, 4163, 5510, 5512
*Dark Lord of Derkholm* **2946**
*Drowned Ammet* 1444
*Eight Days of Luke* 171
*Everard's Ride* **2947**, 3279, 3981, 5782, 5973
*Fire and Hemlock* 194, 5428
*Hexwood* 196, 635, **2948**
*The Homeward Bounders* 165, 4338
*Howl's Moving Castle* 174, 1220, 1668, 1677, 2075, 5975, 5979
*The Lives of Christopher Chant* 1601, 1605, 4334, 4920, 5976
*The Ogre Downstairs* 1220, 2075, 2076, **2949**, 5478, 5968
*The Power of Three* 2015
*The Spellcoats* 1444, 5496
*A Sudden Wild Magic* **2950**
*A Tale of Time City* 121, 2272, 5822
*The Time of the Ghost* 53, **2951**
*Warlock at the Wheel and Other Stories* 3611, 3845, 5239
*Witch Week* 330, 5490
*Witch's Business* 4079, 4080

**Jones, Gwyneth**
*Flowerdust* **2952**
*North Wind* **2953**

*Phoenix Cafe* **2954**
*Seven Tales and a Table* 497
*White Queen* 157, 2486, 2837, **2955**, 3711, 4130, 4136, 4503, 4554, 4703, 5450

**Jones, J.V.**
*The Baker's Boy* 683, 1513, 1773, 1902, 1952, 1953, 2268, 2270, 2426, 2452, 2619, 2694, 2695, 2696, 2798, 2924, 2925, **2956**, 3074, 3489, 3509, 3645, 3775, 3832, 3835, 4150, 4461, 5320, 5529, 5583, 5734, 5737, 5758, 5964
*The Barbed Coil* **2957**
*A Man Betrayed* **2958**, 4796, 5529
*Master and Fool* **2959**, 4802

**Jones, Marti**
*Star Dust* 3576

**Jones, Neil**
*Deathwing* 6023

**Jones, Richard Glyn**
*Cybersex* 1362
*The Penguin Book of Modern Fantasy by Women* 5815

**Jones, Stephen**
*The Best Horror From Fantasy Tales* **2960**
*Best New Horror* 1372, 1378, **2961**, 5602, 5603, 5605, 5606
*Best New Horror 2* **2962**, 4025, 5601
*Best New Horror 4* 1376, **2963**, 5607
*Best New Horror 5* 5608
*Best New Horror 6* **2964**
*Fantasy Tales #2* **2965**
*Fantasy Tales #4* **2966**
*Fantasy Tales #6* **2967**
*Gaslight and Ghosts* 217
*H.P. Lovecraft's Book of Horror* 848, **2968**
*The Mammoth Book of Best New Horror* 1374, **2969**
*The Mammoth Book of Best New Horror 8* 1377, **2970**
*The Mammoth Book of Best New Horror 9* 1371, **2971**
*The Mammoth Book of Dracula* **2972**, 3226, 5699
*The Mammoth Book of Frankenstein* 140, 2892, **2973**, 3019, 3180, 5691, 5886
*The Mammoth Book of Terror* 226, **2974**
*The Mammoth Book of Vampires* 150, 151, 1013, 1611, 1799, 2382, 2408, 2409, 2484, **2975**, 3031, 4876, 4879, 4880, 4881, 5265, 5284, 5688, 5935
*The Mammoth Book of Werewolves* 1230, 2410, **2976**, 3032, 5384
*The Mammoth Book of Zombies* **2977**, 4412
*Shadows over Innsmouth* **2978**, 3533, 4424, 4426, 4430, 5493, 5494

**Jones, Terry**
*Douglas Adams's Starship Titanic* **2979**
*The Goblin Companion* 385, 2088, **2980**
*Lady Cottington's Pressed Fairy Book* 29, 2088, **2981**, 3214
*Strange Stains and Mysterious Smells* 2088, **2982**

**Jordan, Brenda**
*The Brentwood Witches* 2713

**Jordan, Robert**
*The Conan Chronicles* **2983**
*Conan the Invincible* 906, 908, 909, 4293, 4617
*Conan the Magnificent* 2347, 2348, 4616
*Conan the Victorious* 908, 909, 2347, 2348
*A Crown of Swords* 1775, **2984**
*The Dragon Reborn* 2097, **2985**, 3107, 5760
*The Eye of the World* 164, 287, 457, 487, 712, 717, 979, 994, 1010, 1096, 1422, 1592, 1675, 1682, 1685, 1688, 1690, 1730, 1732, 1733, 1734, 1790, 1837, 1864, 1909, 1911, 2042, 2126, 2128, 2190, 2268, 2269, 2270, 2271, 2677, **2986**, 3044, 3068, 3172, 3305, 3306, 3626, 3765, 3832, 3837, 3892, 3926, 3930, 3985, 4105, 4107, 4154, 4489, 4515, 4526, 4741, 5034, 5203, 5221, 5251, 5320, 5650, 5651, 5711, 5715, 5727, 5734, 5736, 5757, 5829, 5831, 6073
*The Fires of Heaven* 257, 2098, **2987**
*The Great Hunt* 4524, 5831
*Lord of Chaos* 1702, 1905, 2425, **2988**, 5678
*The Path of Daggers* **2989**
*The Shadow Rising* **2990**
*The World of Robert Jordan's The Wheel of Time* 1735, **2991**

**Jordan, Sherryl**
*The Juniper Game* **2992**, 3340

**Joshi, S.T.**
*Great Weird Tales* **2993**

**Joyce, Graham**
*Requiem* **2994**, 4575
*The Tooth Fairy* 1506, **2995**

**Jurasik, Peter**
*Diplomatic Act* **2996**

**Juster, Norton**
*Alberic the Wise and Other Journeys* 329
*The Phantom Tollbooth* 1217, 2868, 4731

## K

**Kadohata, Cynthia**
*In the Heart of the Valley of Love* 1835, **2997**

**Kadrey, Richard**
*Kamikaze L'Amour* 52, **2998**, 6009
*Metrophage* 361, 808, 4205, 4940, 5254, 5960

**Kafka, Franz**
*Stories, 1904-1924* 573, 3460, 5317

**Kagan, David**
*Sunstroke* 2301, **2999**, 4416

**Kagan, Janet**
*Hellspark* 230, 785, 877, 952, 990, 998, 1504, 1537, 1643, 2058, 2764, **3000**, 3475, 3744, 3752, 3928, 4140, 4554, 5090

*Mirabile* 100, 413, 1420, 1517, 1589, 1593, 1723, 1724, 1726, 1727, 1729, 1769, 1964, 1988, 1997, 2008, 2037, 2659, 2800, **3001**, 3646, 3721, 3730, 3738, 4176, 4195, 4196, 4198, 4479, 4633, 4953, 5038, 5363, 5369, 5499, 5809
*Uhura's Song* 527, 569, 1381, 1556, 2421, 3918

**Kahn, James**
*Indiana Jones and the Temple of Doom* 713, 825, 826, 3588, 3589, 3590, 3591, 3592, 3593, 3916, 4549
*Return of the Jedi* 114, 2171, 6052, 6054

**Kahn, Joan**
*The Edge of the Chair* 543, 2282
*Hanging by a Thread* 543, 1019, 2282

**Kalich, Richard**
*The Nihilesthete* **3002**

**Kalogridis, Jeanne**
*Children of the Vampire* 279, **3003**
*Covenant with the Vampire* **3004**, 6010
*Lord of the Vampires* 2742, **3005**

**Kamau, Kwadwo Agymah**
*Flickering Shadows* 1462, **3006**

**Kanaly, Michael**
*Thoughts of God* 2661, **3007**
*Virus Clans* **3008**

**Kandel, Michael**
*Captain Jack Zodiac* 499, 830, **3009**, 3642, 3647, 3891, 4590, 4606, 5148, 5567
*In between Dragons* 1662, **3010**, 3156, 4008, 5478
*Panda Ray* 444, 1502, 2837, **3011**
*Strange Invasion* 1452, 1454, 1522, 1999, **3012**, 3106, 3434, 4365, 5009

**Kane, Kathleen**
*This Time for Keeps* 2731, 3039, 5658

**Kangilaski, Joan**
*The Seeking Sword* 3601

**Kao, Karl S.Y.**
*Classical Chinese Tales of the Supernatural and the Fantastic* 6026

**Kaplan, Aline Boucher**
*Khyren* 4481

**Kapp, Colin**
*The Ion War* 1326
*The Survival Game* 1248, 1641, 2016, 4964, 5781
*The Wizard of Anharitte* 882, 1757, 5230, 5231

**Karr, Phyllis Ann**
*Frostflower and Thorn* 4614, 6041
*Frostflower and Windbourne* 5293
*The Idylls of the Queen* 1189, 1190, 1269, 1857, 2747, 3355, 3806

**Kasner, Michael**
*Finger of God* **3013**

**Kast, Pierre**
*The Vampires of Alfama* 4574, 4578, 6011, 6012, 6013, 6015, 6016, 6018

**Kato, Ken**
*Yamato: A Rage in Heaven* 566,
1145, **3014**

**Katz, Welwyn Wilton**
*The Third Magic* 121

**Kaufman, Douglas**
*The Dark Realm* 5438
*Dragons over England* 1889, **3015**,
4909, 5210, 5438

**Kay, Guy Gavriel**
*The Darkest Road* 3068, 5759
*The Lions of Al-Rassan* 770, 1111,
1154, **3016**, 3356, 3942, 4259,
4533, 4743, 5218, 6002
*A Song for Arbonne* 965, **3017**,
4651, 4686, 5222, 5397
*The Summer Tree* 28, 391, 1010,
1288, 1474, 1476, 1660, 1686,
1739, 1947, 2471, 2506, 2986,
2988, 3058, 3059, 3062, 3068,
3069, 3357, 3401, 3650, 3653,
3765, 4457, 4493, 4659, 4661,
4730, 5719
*Tigana* 771, 1147, 1292, 1660,
1960, 2424, 2504, **3018**, 3105,
3171, 3175, 3872, 3925, 3975,
4167, 5206, 5812
*The Wandering Fire* 3068

**Kay, Jeremy**
*The Secret Laboratory Journals of Dr.
Victor Frankenstein* **3019**

**Kay, Susan**
*Phantom* 1115, 2200, **3020**

**Kaye, M.M.**
*The Ordinary Princess* 5975

**Kaye, Marilyn**
*Amy, Number Seven* 1217
*The Vanishing* **3021**

**Kaye, Marvin**
*13 Plays of Ghosts and the
Supernatural* 1448
*Angels of Darkness* 468, **3022**
*The Best of Weird Tales: 1923* **3023**
*A Cold Blue Light* 2245
*Devils and Demons* 1280, 4542
*Don't Open This Book!* **3024**
*Fantastique* 2428, **3025**, 4588
*Ghosts* 2233, 5665
*Haunted America* 2383, 2586, 3866,
3868, 3869, 3870
*Lovers and Other Monsters* 1118,
**3026**
*Masterpieces of Terror and the
Unknown* 2993, **3027**
*The Masters of Solitude* 1101, 2245
*Thirteen Plays of Ghosts and the
Supernatural* 339, 344, 1022,
1112
*Weird Tales: The Magazine That Never
Dies* 480, 482, 3023, **3028**
*Wintermind* 2245
*Witches and Warlocks: Tales of Black
Magic Old and New* 1711

**Kazantzakis, Nikos**
*Alexander the Great* 2187, 5395

**Keaney, Brian**
*No Need for Heroes* 5995

**Keegan, Mel**
*Death's Head* **3029**

**Keesey, Pam**
*Dark Angels: Lesbian Vampire
Stories* 730, 2117, 2508, 5387

*Darker Angels: Lesbian Vampire
Stories* 699, 1713, 2444, **3030**,
3177, 3618, 4689, 5386
*Daughters of Darkness: Lesbian
Vampire Stories* 730, 1286, 1713,
2117, 2444, 2508, **3031**, 3177,
3181, 3182, 4689, 5154, 5385,
5387
*Women Who Run with Werewolves:
Tales of Blood, Lust and
Metamorphosis* 2496, **3032**, 3112

**Kegan, Stephanie**
*The Baby* 1076, 2875, **3033**, 3774,
4450, 5269

**Kehret, Peg**
*Horror at the Haunted House* 5288

**Keith, Andrew**
*Cohort of the Damned* 1546, **3034**
*Honor and Fidelity* 3037
*March or Die* 1547, **3035**

**Keith, William H. Jr.**
*Bolo Brigade* 4973, 5204
*Diplomatic Act* **2996**
*March or Die* **3035**
*Mercenary's Star* 1976
*Operation Excalibur* 2350
*Renegade's Honor* 4583
*Warlords of Jupiter* **3036**
*Warstrider* **3037**, 4974
*Warstrider: Netlink* 1184, **3038**

**Kelleher, Anne**
*A Once and Future Love* **3039**

**Kelleher, Ed**
*Animus* **3040**
*Breeder* **3041**
*The School* 1354, 2023, 2139, **3042**,
3499, 5122, 5314

**Kelleher, Victor**
*The Red King* 2986, **3043**, 3105

**Keller, Donald G.**
*The Horns of Elfland* **3264**

**Kelley, Leo P.**
*The Counterfeits* 2882

**Kellogg, Marjorie Bradley**
*The Book of Earth* 2126, 2128,
2795, 2799, **3044**, 3298, 3507,
4150, 4461
*The Book of Water* **3045**
*Harmony* 46, 209, 656, 721, 792,
1449, 1482, 1559, 2328, **3046**,
3082, 3452, 4000, 4325, 4642,
5370, 5592, 5873, 5965
*Reign of Fire* 3157
*The Wave and the Flame* 3157

**Kelly, Erin**
*City of Darkness* 3229
*City of Darkness: Unseen* 23, 3224,
5797
*The Splendour Falls* 23, 3225, 3229,
5797, 5798

**Kelly, James Patrick**
*Heroines* 3945
*Look into the Sun* 919, 1062, 2721,
3046, **3047**, 3084, 4276, 4643
*Think Like a Dinosaur and Other
Stories* **3048**
*Wildlife* 352, 1696, **3049**

**Kelly, Robert B.**
*The Cloud People* **3050**

**Kelly, Ronald**
*Blood Kin* **3051**, 4102
*Father's Little Helper* 916, 2755,
**3052**

*Moon of the Werewolf* 514, **3053**,
3162
*Pitfall* 373, **3054**
*The Possession* **3055**
*Something Out There* 2794, **3056**,
5425

**Kemp, Gene**
*Ghosts, Ghouls and Other
Nightmares* 2772

**Kemske, Floyd**
*Human Remains* 4667
*Human Resources* **3057**, 3957

**Kendall, Carol**
*The Gammage Cup* 6006

**Kendall, Gordon**
*White Wing* 3454, 5292

**Kenneally, Patricia**
*The Oak Above the Kings: A Book of
the Keltiad* **3058**
*The Throne of Scone* 3060

**Kennealy-Morrison, Patricia**
*Blackmantle: A Triumph* **3059**
*The Copper Crown* 392, 1476, 1660,
1961, 3060, 3068, 3078, 3305,
3354, 3357, 3358, 3502, 3697,
4492, 4608, 4989, 5684
*The Deer's Cry: A Book of the
Keltiad* **3060**
*The Hawk's Gray Feather* 1092,
3060, **3061**, 4584
*The Hedge of Mist* **3062**
*The Silver Branch* 392, 1960
*The Throne of Scone* 392

**Kennedy, Leigh**
*The Journal of Nicholas the
American* 709

**Kennedy, Richard**
*Amy's Eyes* 332

**Kenyon, Kay**
*Leap Point* **3063**, 4042, 6080
*The Seeds of Time* 298, 1694, **3064**,
5429

**Kerner, Elizabeth**
*Song in the Silence* **3065**

**Kerns, Daniel R.**
*Border Dispute* **3066**

**Kerr, Katharine**
*The Bristling Wood* 3061, 3295,
5715
*Daggerspell* 704, 742, 1288, 1660,
2031, 3018, 3060, 3273, 3291,
3292, 3839, 3926, 3975, 4462,
4980, 5715, 5727, 5734
*Darkspell* 5715
*Days of Air and Darkness* **3067**
*Days of Blood and Fire* **3068**, 3936
*The Dragon Revenant* **3069**, 3904,
4718, 5819
*Enchanted Forests* 2381, **3070**
*Freeze Frames* **3071**
*Palace* 687, 760, 1501, 1695, 2730,
**3072**, 3231, 3453, 4244, 4342,
6079, 6080
*Polar City Blues* 476, 761, 805, 891,
1664, 1696, 1725, 1819, 2000,
2092, 2372, 2377, 2475, 2545,
2682, 2684, 2685, 2722, 2757,
2913, **3073**, 3109, 3256, 3830,
4295, 4300, 4305, 4469, 4551,
4747, 4748, 4749, 4858, 4939,
4940, 5109, 5276, 5451, 5836
*The Red Wyvern* **3074**
*Resurrection* 60, 442, 1441, **3075**,
5410, 5531

*The Shimmering Door* **3076**
*A Time of Exile* **3077**
*A Time of Omens* **3078**
*Weird Tales From Shakespeare* **3079**,
5826

**Kerr, Peg**
*Emerald House Rising* 1010, 2253,
2758, 3074, **3080**, 3509, 3651,
4459, 4739, 5137, 5490, 5555,
5749

**Kerr, Philip**
*The Second Angel* 2720, 3923

**Kerruish, Jessie**
*The Undying Monster* 3826

**Kersey, Colin**
*Soul Catcher* 911, 2340, 2670,
**3081**, 3680

**Kesey, Ken**
*Sailor Song* **3082**, 5145

**Kessel, John**
*Corrupting Dr. Nice* **3083**, 4247,
5874
*Freedom Beach* 3048, 3049
*Good News From Outer Space* 156,
327, 1877, 2100, 2249, **3084**,
3542, 4034, 4555, 4567, 4630,
4632, 5958
*Intersections: The Sycamore Hill
Anthology* 1766, 1767, 2635,
**3085**
*Meeting in Infinity* 2835, 3048,
**3086**, 3234, 3442, 3712, 4680,
5240, 5257
*The Pure Product* **3087**

**Kessler, Gabriel Devlin**
*Landscape of Demons and the Book of
Sara* **3088**

**Kessler, Joan C.**
*Demons of the Night: Tales of the
Fantastic, Madness, and the
Supernatural From Nineteenth
Century France* **3089**

**Kessler, Risa**
*Once upon a Time: A Treasury of
Modern Fairy Tales* **1479**

**Ketchum, Jack**
*The Exit at Toledo Blade
Boulevard* **3090**, 5005
*Ladies Night* **3091**
*Off Season* 2611, 3387, 3391
*Offspring* 1051, 1828, 2611, **3092**,
3369, 3387, 3391, 5474, 5685

**Key, Alexander**
*The Forgotten Door* 510, 2948

**Key, Samuel M.**
*From a Whisper to a Scream* 1848,
2825, **3093**, 3375, 3518, 3857
*I'll Be Watching You* 2113, **3094**

**Key, Ted**
*The Cat From Outer Space* 3500

**Keyes, Daniel**
*Flowers for Algernon* 1460, 3200,
5907

**Keyes, J. Gregory**
*The Blackgod* 992, **3095**, 3773,
4110, 4527, 4795
*Dark Genesis* 1387, **3096**
*Deadly Relations* 2102
*Newton's Cannon* **3097**
*The Waterborn* 1042, 1095, 1943,
2924, 2925, **3098**, 3773, 4110,
5583, 5757, 5817

**Kidd, Chico**
*The Printer's Devil* **3099**

**Kidd, Kathryn H.**
*Lovelock* **892**

**Kidd, Virginia**
*Millennial Women* 4825, 4826

**Kiernan, Caitlin R.**
*Candles for Elizabeth* **3100**
*Silk* 1890, **3101**

**Kihn, Greg**
*Big Rock Beat* **3102**
*Horror Show* 2448, **3103**
*Shade of Pale* 840, **3104**

**Kilian, Crawford**
*The Empire of Time* 178, 188, 895,
2563, 4151
*Greenmagic* **3105**, 4154
*Gryphon* **3106**
*Icequake* 4628
*Redmagic* **3107**
*Rogue Emperor* 264, 350, 590,
1855, 1955, 6000

**Killough, Lee**
*Blood Hunt* 1213, 1214, 1792,
2793, 3560, 3602, 4004, 4005,
5374
*Blood Links* 1791, 1792, 1793,
1796, 4508
*Blood Walk* 2792, **3108**
*Deadly Silents* 476, 2286, 3073
*The Doppelganger Gambit* 2682
*Dragon's Teeth* 2000, 2682, 2683,
**3109**, 4121, 4940, 5576
*The Leopard's Daughter* 1996
*Liberty's World* 1757, 2223, 4175,
4545, 5230
*Spider Play* 1153, 1665, 2369,
2370, 2375, 2682, 4339
*A Voice out of Ramah* 1182

**Kilpatrick, Nancy**
*As One Dead* 387
*The Darker Passions: Carmilla* **3177**
*The Darker Passions: Dr. Jekyll and
Mr. Hyde* **3178**
*The Darker Passions: Dracula* **3179**
*The Darker Passions:
Frankenstein* **3180**
*The Darker Passions Reader* **3176**
*Demon Sex* **3181**
*Dracul: An Eternal Love Story* **3110**
*Endorphins* **3111**
*In the Shadow of the Gargoyle* **3112**
*Near Death* **3113**, 3253, 3517, 4246
*The Pit and the Pendulum* **3183**
*Sex and the Single Vampire* 748,
1467, 2705, **3114**, 3388, 3549,
5175

**Kilworth, Garry**
*Angel* 602, 1117, 2534, 2802, 3620
*Archangel* 2802
*The Foxes of Firstdark* 32, 40, 306,
599, 737, **3115**, 3378, 3523, 4008,
4271
*Highlander* 3854
*Hogfoot Right and Bird-Hands* 497,
772, **3116**, 3250, 3702
*In Solitary* 3800
*The Night of Kadar* 877, 1595, 4592,
4595
*Split Second* 175, 188, 5998

**Kimbriel, Katharine Eliska**
*Hidden Fires* **3117**
*Kindred Rites* 2326, **3118**
*Night Calls* **3119**

**King, Bernard**
*Demon Shield* 2889
*Starkadder* 4518

**King, Gabriel**
*The Wild Road* 846, **3120**

**King, J. Robert**
*Carnival of Fear* 155, 465, 2516,
5847
*Conspiracy* **3121**
*Planar Powers* **3122**
*The Summerhill Hounds* 1485
*Vinas Solamnus* **3123**

**King, Michael**
*Lorien Lost* **3124**, 4486, 5570

**King, Paula**
*Mad Roy's Light* 1593, 1594, 1595,
**3125**, 3709, 5930
*Orion's Dagger* **3708**

**King, Stephen**
*Apt Pupil* 2755
*Bag of Bones* 1560, **3126**, 5026
*Carrie* 1203, 1926, 2915, **3127**,
3284, 3785, 4334, 4832, 5486,
5553
*Christine* 2316, 2915, 3320, 4022,
5323, 5486
*The Crate* 4414
*Cujo* 1708, 2199, 2429, 5146,
5236, 5539, 5894
*The Dark Half* 426, 810, 1846,
**3128**, 3206, 3213, 3374, 3691,
5169, 5422, 5823, 5849
*The Dark Tower Series* 343
*The Dark Tower: The
Gunslinger* 341, 576, 2009, 2191,
5151, 5504
*The Dead Zone* 795, 800, 945, 1669,
1780, 1975, 2318, 3193, 3203,
3678, 3965, 4363, 4649, 5399,
5987
*Desperation* **3129**
*Different Seasons* 2305, 5056, 5060
*Dolores Claiborne* **3130**
*The Drawing of the Three* **3131**
*The Eyes of the Dragon* 347
*Firestarter* 93, 97, 610, 879, 1971,
2112, 2284, 2530, 2704, 3211,
3215, 3230, 3251, 3594, 3860,
4480, 4841, 5850
*Four Past Midnight* **3132**, 3216,
5056
*Gerald's Game* **3133**
*The Green Mile* **3134**, 4838
*The Gunslinger* 5034
*Insomnia* 1669, 2161, **3135**, 3493,
5399
*It* 616, 918, 1077, 1195, 2316,
3206, 3754, 4370, 5464, 5522
*Misery* 810, 3002
*The Mist* 5263
*My Pretty Pony* **3136**
*Needful Things* 859, 2154, 2652,
**3137**, 3497, 4085, 4100
*Night Shift* 3753
*Nightmares and Dreamscapes* **3138**
*Pet Sematary* 937, 2030, 2293,
2607, 3206, 3658, 4327, 5539
*The Regulators* 284
*Rose Madder* 2609, 2612, **3139**,
3210, 3365, 3858, 5414
*Salem's Lot* 832, 1402, 1466, 1920,
2152, 2220, 2441, 3051, **3140**,
3205, 3496, 3498, 4102, 5322,
5770, 5891

*The Shining* 282, 521, 609, 890,
1966, 2314, 2631, 2732, **3141**,
3149, 3675, 3953, 4223, 4249,
5380, 5463, 5528, 5625, 5993,
5994
*Silver Bullet* 4515
*Skeleton Crew* 777, 3321, 3753
*The Stand* 338, 341, 525, 2934,
3370, 3757, 4413, 5190
*The Stand: The Complete and Uncut
Edition* 343, **3142**, 4384, 4647
*The Talisman* 341, 347, 3551, 3565,
3779, 4009
''The Children of the Corn'' 320
*The Tommyknockers* 137, 1037,
1200, 3206
''Trucks'' 3320
*The Waste Lands* **3143**
*Wizard and Glass* **3144**

**King, T. Jackson**
*Ancestor's World* **1259**
*Retread Shop* 493, 1259, 1261,
1262, 1456, 3469, 3974, 4160,
5779

**Kingsbury, Donald**
*The Moon Goddess and the Son* 127,
584, 588

**Kingsley, Amanda**
*Hellcat* **3145**

**Kinion, Richard**
*Sacrifice* **3146**, 3387

**Kinsella, W.P.**
*The Iowa Baseball Confederacy* 2029

**Kipling, Rudyard**
*Famous Tales of India* 195, 1316,
1317
*The Jungle Book* 3610
*Just So Stories* 3610, 3611
*Kim* 314
*Kipling's Fantasy* 2680, **3147**, 4021,
5310
*Kipling's Science Fiction* **3148**
*Puck of Pook's Hill* 459, 5310

**Kiraly, Marie**
*Leanna: Possession of a Woman* **3149**
*Madeline: After the Fall of
Usher* **3150**, 4344, 4345
*Mina* 3004, **3151**, 3179, 3180,
3623, 4684, 6010

**Kirby, T.J.**
*Dangerous Nature* 2541, **3152**,
3701, 3901
*Deadly Breed* 373, 488, 1346, 1850,
2779, **3153**, 3701

**Kirchoff, Mary**
*The Black Wing* 470, 4925, 5708
*Flint the King* 5454, 5455
*Kendermore* 2675, 5711, 5724
*The Seventh Sentinel* **3154**
*Wanderlust* 154, **3155**, 4368

**Kirkland, James I.**
*First Frontier* **902**

**Kirkwood, Kathleen**
*A Slip in Time* 691, 1271

**Kirschner, David**
*The Pagemaster* 318, 2981, **3156**,
3214, 5713, 5972

**Kirstein, Rosemary**
*The Outskirter's Secret* 420, 567,
656, 664, 760, 1643, 1805, 1956,
2271, 2421, 2443, 2999, **3157**,
3231, 3399, 3478, 3721, 3732,
3733, 3734, 3739, 3750, 3819,
3912, 4038, 4957, 5001, 5037,
5090, 5456
*The Steerswoman* 394, 580, 692,
1756, 1815, 2038, 2260, 2443,
2796, 2799, 2812, 3043, 3050,
**3158**, 3231, 3399, 3471, 3627,
3628, 3629, 3630, 3719, 3721,
3724, 3748, 3862, 3872, 4119,
4147, 4596, 4999, 5091, 5097,
5233, 5296, 5748, 5984

**Kisling, Lee**
*The Fools' War* **3159**

**Kisner, James**
*Night Visions 9* **5441**
*The Quagmire* **3160**
*Tower of Evil* **3161**, 5989

**Kjelgaard, Jim**
*The Hunter Returns* **1632**

**Klass, Judy**
*The Cry of the Onlies* 1554

**Klause, Annette Curtis**
*Blood and Chocolate* 514, **3162**
*The Silver Kiss* **3163**

**Klavan, Andrew**
*The Uncanny* **3164**

**Klaw, Richard**
*Weird Business* **3334**

**Klein, T.E.D.**
*The Ceremonies* 137, 860, 1079,
2929, 3496, 3615, 4003, 4568,
4754, 5112, 5340, 5893
*Dark Gods* 851, 864, 866

**Kline, Otis Adelbert**
*The Outlaws of Mars* 3983

**Kline, Robert**
*Campfire Story* 4598

**Kluger, Richard**
*The Sheriff of Nottingham* 2247,
**3165**, 4609

**Knaak, Richard A.**
*Children of the Drake* **3166**
*The Crystal Dragon* **3167**
*The Dragon Crown* **3168**
*Dragon Tome* 2234, **3169**
*Firedrake* 5563, 5708, 5790
*Frostwing* 2760, **3170**
*The Ice Dragon* 470
*The Janus Mask* **3171**
*Kaz the Minotaur* 154, 1485, **3172**,
5022, 5724
*King of the Grey* 1040, 1435, 1842,
2127, 2791, **3173**
*The Legend of Huma* 1485, 3155,
5454, 5455, 5711, 5724
*The Shrouded Realm* 3067, **3174**
*Wolfhelm* 1096, **3175**, 4991

**Kneale, Nigel**
*Quatermass and the Pit* 833
*The Quatermass Experiment* 99,
1022, 4331
*The Year of the Sex Olympics and
Other TV Plays* 1022

**Knight, Amarantha**
*The Darker Passions: Carmilla* **3177**
*The Darker Passions: Dr. Jekyll and
Mr. Hyde* **3178**
*The Darker Passions: Dracula* **3179**

*The Darker Passions:*
  *Frankenstein* 199, 1409, **3180**
*The Darker Passions Reader* **3176**
*Demon Sex* 2177, **3181**
*Love Bites* 698, 699, 3030, **3182**,
  3618, 4689, 5386, 5387
*The Pit and the Pendulum* **3183**
*Seductive Spectres* 2177, **3184**,
  3618, 5386
*Sex Macabre* 3618, 5386

**Knight, Damon**
*Beyond Tomorrow* 1609
*The Clarion Awards* 1618
*CV* 594, 1666, 2732, 3008, 4923
*The Dark Side* 5691
*First Contact* 4406
*God's Nose* 1428, 2078, **3185**
*Humpty Dumpty: An Oval* **3186**
*Late Knight Edition* 4535
*Mind Switch* 436, 1786, 4875
*Nebula Award Stories 1965* 500, 501,
  4031, 4032
*Now Begins Tomorrow* 1609
*The Observers* 594, 1666
*One Hundred Years of Science*
  *Fiction* 1618
*One Side Laughing: Stories Unlike*
  *Other Stories* 61, 503, 2547,
  **3187**, 3796, 5805
*Orbit 1* 4721
*Perchance to Dream* 1717
*A Reasonable World* 1666, 2955,
  **3188**, 3944, 5677
*Rule Golden and Double*
  *Meaning* **3189**
*Tomorrow and Tomorrow* 5641
*Why Do Birds* 2418, **3190**

**Knight, Harry Adam**
*Carnosaur* 1256, 1379, **3191**
*The Fungus* 2671, **3192**, 3992

**Knight, Stephen**
*Jack the Ripper: The Final*
  *Solution* 3987

**Knoepflmacher, U.C.**
*Forbidden Journeys: Fairy Tales and*
  *Fantasies by Victorian Women*
  *Writers* 276

**Koja, Kathe**
*Bad Brains* 93, 814, 945, 1939,
  2030, **3193**, 4790, 5969
*The Cipher* 2762, **3194**
*Extremities* **3195**, 4181
*Skin* 212, 437, 548, 2030, **3196**
*Strange Angels* 212, 814, 2030,
  2548, **3197**, 3812, 4084

**Koke, Jack**
*Beyond the Pale* **3198**
*Dead Air* 5096

**Koman, Victor**
*The Jehovah Contract* 1856, 2525,
  2865, 3860, 4029, 4035, 5302,
  5768, 5887
*Kings of the High Frontier* **3199**
*Solomon's Knife* **3200**

**Komarnicki, Todd**
*Famine* **3201**, 3525

**Koontz, Dean R.**
*The Bad Place* 602, 2341, 2704,
  **3202**, 4189, 4509
*Beastchild* 1595
*Cold Fire* 655, 3134, **3203**, 3415,
  3678
*Dark Rivers of the Heart* 1973, 2157,
  2322, **3204**
*Darkfall* 661, 1125

*Demon Seed* 2157, 2872
*Dragon Tears* 284, 571, 2341, **3205**,
  4883
*The Eyes of Darkness* **3206**, 5664
*Fear Nothing* **3207**
*The Haunted Earth* 5497
*Hideaway* 376, 916, 945, 1078,
  1669, 2161, 2202, 2293, 3052,
  **3208**, 4327, 4837, 5969, 5987
*The House of Thunder* 376, 1832,
  4874
*Icebound* **3209**
*Intensity* **3210**
*Lightning* 97, 2608, **3211**, 3251,
  3979, 4363, 4843, 5399
*Midnight* 99, 800, 2112, 3152,
  **3212**, 3632, 4509, 4845
*Mr. Murder* 858, **3213**
*Oddkins* 40, 347, 3523
*Phantoms* 1698, 2934, 3337, 4413,
  5358
*Santa's Twin* 1506, **3214**
*The Servants of Twilight* 1080, 1236,
  2203, 2555, 4840, 5250, 5895
*Shadowfires* 1084, 1505, 2608,
  2802, 2900, 3130, 3139, 3152,
  3365, 5895
*Sole Survivor* 1971, **3215**
*Strange Highways* 2277, 2714, **3216**,
  5885
*Strangers* 1380, 4189
*Ticktock* **3217**
*Twilight Eyes* 1282, 2160, 2927,
  3366
*The Vision* 1780, 1975, 2871, 3135,
  3594, 4471, 5987, 5993
*Warlock* 4621
*Watchers* 41, 373, 488, 1084, 1346,
  1349, 1539, 1708, 1780, 1850,
  2284, 2429, 2611, 2779, 3152,
  3153, 3701, 4756, 5388, 5474,
  5586, 5589
*Whispers* 2609, 4088
*Winter Moon* **3218**

**Kornbluth, C.M.**
*His Share of Glory: The Complete Short*
  *Science Fiction of C.M.*
  *Kornbluth* **3219**, 5348
*''The Little Black Bag''* 1561

**Kornwise, Robert**
*Through the Ice* **192**

**Kosinski, Jerzy**
*Being There* 3222
*The Painted Bird* 4303

**Kostrubula, Mark A.**
*Dark Legacy* 2932, **3220**

**Kotani, Eric**
*Act of God* 584, 930
*Between the Stars* 82, 421
*Delta Pavonis* **3221**
*The Island Worlds* 82
*Supernova* **82**

**Kotzwinkle, William**
*The Bear Went over the*
  *Mountain* 915, **3222**
*E.T.: The Extra-Terrestrial* 2227
*The Fan Man* 3011, 3455
*Fata Morgana* 1151
*The Hot Jazz Trio* **3223**
*Superman III* 5262

**Kramer, Edward E.**
*Confederacy of the Dead* **2230**
*The Crow: Shattered Lives and Broken*
  *Dreams* **4186**
*Dante's Disciples* **1280**, 1281

*Dark Destiny* 23, **3224**, 3229, 5797,
  5798, 5882
*Dark Destiny II: Proprietors of*
  *Fate* 23, **3225**, 5797, 5798
*Dark Destiny III: Children of*
  *Dracula* 23, **3226**, 5797, 5798
*Dark Love* **1118**
*Forbidden Acts* **1120**
*Free Space* **3466**
*Grails: Quests of the Dawn* **2231**
*Grails: Visitations of the Night* **2232**
*More Phobias* **5666**
*Phobias: Stories of Your Deepest*
  *Fears* **5667**
*The Sandman: Book of Dreams* **2105**
*Tales of the White Wolf* **3227**, 3980,
  4759
*Tombs* 1187, 1281, 1283, **3228**

**Kramer-Rolls, Dana**
*Home Is the Hunter* 902, 5404

**Krause, Staley**
*Strange City* 23, **3225**, **3229**, 3613,
  5797
*Truth Until Paradox* 3227, 5701,
  5702

**Krauzer, Steven M.**
*Brainstorm* 752, **3230**, 4480

**Kreighbaum, Mark**
*The Eyes of God* 760, **3231**
*Palace* **3072**

**Kreps, Penelope Banka**
*Carnivores* 1049, 2779, **3232**
*Demon's Fright* 1215, **3233**

**Kress, Nancy**
*The Aliens of Earth* 503, 624, 772,
  790, 804, 1515, 2027, 2835, 3048,
  **3234**, 3379, 3384, 3600, 3736,
  3971, 4216, 4680, 5240, 5410
*Beaker's Dozen* **3235**
*Beggars and Choosers* 2274, 2580,
  **3236**, 3792, 4064
*Beggars in Spain* 305, 1965, 2522,
  2820, 3008, 3075, **3237**, 4064,
  4210, 4355, 4850, 4955
*The Beggars in Spain Trilogy* 2558,
  4065
*Beggars Ride* **3238**
*Brain Rose* 60, 352, 568, 583, 2275,
  2446, 3075, **3239**, 4071, 5193,
  5531, 5767
*Dancing on Air* 411, **3240**
*The Golden Grove* 5002
*Maximum Light* **3241**
*Oaths and Miracles* **3242**
*Stinger* **3243**

**Kressing, Harry**
*The Cook* 3497, 3814

**Kropp, Lloyd**
*The Drift* 2708

**Kruger, Novak**
*Tooth: A Tale of Love and Death in*
  *Paradox* **3244**

**Kubasik, Christopher**
*Changeling* 976, 1591, 1889, **3245**,
  4821, 5135, 5731
*The Longing Ring* **3246**

**Kube-McDowell, Michael P.**
*Alternities* 2208, 2489, 5088, 5908
*Before the Storm* 114, 117, **3247**,
  4719
*Empery* 3821, 3825, 5933
*Emprise* 1184, 2301, 2836, 3448,
  3719, 3825, 4062, 5788, 5933

*Enigma* 953, 1992, 2836, 3398,
  3821, 3824, 4062, 4483, 4505,
  5933, 6085
*Exile* **3248**
*Odyssey* 78
*The Quiet Pools* 127, **3249**, 4682,
  5909

**Kurahashi, Yumiko**
*The Woman with the Flying Head and*
  *Other Stories* **3250**

**Kurland, Lynn**
*Stardust of Yesterday* 2540

**Kurland, Michael**
*Bottom Right* 4843
*Button Bright* 97, 2704, 3230, **3251**
*A Study in Sorcery* 1151, 1153,
  2370, 2627, 2628, **3252**
*Ten Little Wizards* 2804, 3109, 3259
*Transmission Error* 2882
*The Unicorn Girl* 2913, 5170
*The Whenabouts of Burr* 5495

**Kurtinski, Pyotr**
*Thirst* **3253**

**Kurtz, Katherine**
*The Adept* 639, 751, 2375, 2560,
  2992, **3254**
*The Bastard Prince* **3255**, 4488,
  4781, 5041, 5222, 5512
*Camber of Culdi* 2883, 5393, 5506,
  5510, 5752
*Camber the Heretic* 2883
*Chronicle of Deryni* 5542
*Dagger Magic* **3256**, 3408
*Death of an Adept* **3257**, 5773
*The Deryni Archives* 1735, 2991,
  4793
*Deryni Checkmate* 256, 1175, 2360,
  3399, 4163
*Deryni Rising* 17, 256, 393, 630,
  1110, 1174, 1175, 1702, 1742,
  1863, 2188, 2560, 2561, 2988,
  3016, 3058, 3123, 3154, 3171,
  3284, 3288, 3304, 3305, 3399,
  3436, 3482, 3540, 3635, 3652,
  3697, 3699, 4258, 4259, 4485,
  4492, 4533, 4714, 4730, 4783,
  5581, 5737, 5754, 5811, 6002,
  6003
*The Harrowing of Gwynedd* 638,
  750, 1745, 4782, 4783, 5126,
  5508, 5868
*High Deryni* 256, 1175, 2098, 2987,
  3399, 4265, 5832
*King Javan's Year* 2424, **3258**,
  4784, 5126, 5500, 5503
*Lammas Night* 1275, 2244, 2505,
  2507
*The Lodge of the Lynx* 6, 637, **3259**
*On Crusade* **3260**
*The Quest for Saint Camber* 638,
  3696, 4162
*Saint Camber* 2883, 3580, 3776,
  4081, 5015
*The Templar Treasure* **3261**
*Two Crowns for America* 889, **3262**

**Kuryluk, Ewa**
*Century 21* **3263**

**Kushner, Ellen**
*Basilisk* 646, 647
*The Horns of Elfland* **3264**
*Outlaws of Sherwood Forest* 3846
*Swordspoint* 290, 409, 1140, 1142,
  1679, 1902, 2032, 2263, 2355,
  2759, 3288, 3405, 3419, 3422,
  3841, 4612, 4743, 5458, 5579,
  5811, 5813, 5976

*Thomas the Rhymer* 166, 183, 1434, 2636, **3265**, 3269, 3505, 4161

**Kuttner, Henry**
*The Best of Henry Kuttner* 529, 530, 624, 3219, 3971, 5047, 5348
*The Book of Iod* 1495, **3266**
*The Dark World* 3877
*Elak of Atlantis* 1699
*Mutant* 2474, 2475, 3725, 3726, 3742, 4600, 5039, 6053
*Robots Have No Tails* 1456, 1999, 2979, 4662
*The Startling Worlds of Henry Kuttner* 3416

# L

**La Plante, Richard**
*Mind Kill* **3267**
*Tegne: Soul Warrior* **3268**

**La Spina, Greye**
*Invaders From the Dark* 3877

**Lackey, Mercedes**
*Arrow's Fall* 2674, 5783
*Arrow's Flight* 5682, 5783
*Arrows of the Queen* 176, 692, 1029, 1095, 1952, 2236, 2796, 3482, 4150, 5124, 5125, 5202, 5684, 5783, 6073
*Bardic Voices* 1427, 1430, 1583, 3404, 3545, 4149, 5179
*Bedlam's Bard* **3269**
*The Black Gryphon* **3270**
*Born to Run* 1436, 2467, **3271**, 4862, 4980, 5912
*Burning Water* 1153, 1450, 1451, 1665, 2320, 2370, 2375, 2856, 3073, 3254, **3272**, 4315, 4709, 5276, 5630, 5696
*By the Sword* 176, 2795, 2798, 3121, **3273**, 5127, 5783
*A Cast of Corbies* **3274**, 4986, 4989, 4991
*Castle of Deception* 1839, **3275**, 3490, 4495, 4991
*Children of the Night* 891, 1151, 1450, 2370, 2517, 3073, 3254, 3259, **3276**, 4362, 4709
*Chrome Circle* 1321, **3277**, 3887, 4980
*The Eagle and the Nightingales* 682, 705, **3278**, 4146, 4808
*The Elvenbane* **4149**
*Elvenblood* **4150**
*Fiddler Fair* **3279**
*The Fire Rose* 1462, **3280**, 3663, 4764
*Firebird* **3281**
*Fortress of Frost and Fire* 1839, **3282**, 3490, 3913
*Four & Twenty Blackbirds* **3283**
*Freedom Flight* 1976
*If I Pay Thee Not in Gold* **176**
*Jinx High* 1450, **3284**, 4709, 5266
*Knight of Ghosts and Shadows* 180, 185, 392, 396, 1432, 2467, **3285**, 4868, 4980, 4991, 4993, 5618, 5646, 5915
*The Lark and the Wren* 560, 1143, 2799, **3286**, 3446, 4150, 5275
*Magic's Pawn* 1660, **3287**, 3383, 4793, 4801, 5542
*Magic's Price* **3288**, 4167
*Magic's Promise* 742, **3289**
*Oathblood* **3290**

*The Oathbound* 2553, 3906, 4596, 4613
*Owlflight* **3291**
*Owlsight* **3292**
*Prison of Souls* 1839, 3490, 4980, 4981
*Rediscovery: A Novel of Darkover* **643**
*The Robin and the Kestrel* 705, 845, 2195, 2653, **3293**, 3410, 3933
*Sacred Ground* **3294**
*The Ship Who Searched* **3749**
*The Silver Gryphon* **3295**
*Storm Breaking* **3296**
*Storm Rising* **3297**
*Storm Warning* **3298**
*Summoned to Tourney* 1436, 2467, **3299**, 4862, 4980
*Sword of Ice and Other Tales of Valdemar* 1735, 2991, **3300**
*Tiger Burning Bright* **652**
*Wheels of Fire* 639, 2467, **3301**, 4862, 4980, 4981
*When the Bough Breaks* 396, **3302**, 3478, 3482, 3487, 3776, 5296
*The White Gryphon* **3303**
*Winds of Change* **3304**
*Winds of Fate* **3305**, 4433, 4718
*Winds of Fury* **3306**, 4491
*Wing Commander: Freedom Flight* 643, 1043, **3307**, 5681

**Lafferty, R.A.**
*The Devil Is Dead* 523
*Lafferty in Orbit* 321, 1492, **3308**
*The Reefs of Earth* 3011

**Lagerkvist, Pars**
*The Dwarf* 556

**Lahey, Michael**
*Quest for Apollo* 960, 1129, **3309**, 3700, 5511

**Laidlaw, Marc**
*The 37th Mandala* 655, 2222, 2312, **3310**, 4449
*Kalifornia* 2820, **3311**, 5209
*Neon Lotus* 118, 313, 358, 433, 522, 560, 562, 725, 763, 936, 980, 1145, 1169, 1172, 1328, 1514, 1543, 1680, 1737, 1881, 1943, 1974, 1997, 2000, 2141, 2231, 2232, 2343, 2499, 2619, 2717, 2771, 2836, 2952, 3167, 3478, 3507, 3591, 3916, 3935, 3966, 3985, 4020, 4060, 4061, 4062, 4630, 4744, 4777, 4866, 4867, 4970, 5198, 5199, 5253, 5376, 5378, 5532, 5584, 5714, 5744, 6071, 6073
*The Orchid Eater* **3312**
*The Third Force* **3313**

**Laing, Alexander**
*The Haunted Omnibus* 1, 1310, 2968

**Lake, Simon**
*Daughter of Darkness* 5288

**Lamb, Hugh**
*Forgotten Tales of Terror* 1233, 1306, 2993
*Return From the Grave* 2379, 2973
*Victorian Nightmares* 1234

**L'Amour, Louis**
*Haunted Mesa* 2009, 2291, 4062, 5151

**Lampman, Evelyn Sibley**
*The Shy Stegosaurus of Cricket Creek* 2468, 6076

*The Shy Stegosaurus of Indian Springs* 2468

**Lamsley, Terry**
*Conference with the Dead* 1671
*Under the Crust* **3314**, 5776

**Landis, Marie**
*Blood on the Sun* **2664**
*Memorymakers* **2665**

**Lane, Andy**
*All-Consuming Fire* 4556

**Lane, Joel**
*The Earth Wire and Other Stories* 4878, 5816

**Lang, Andrew**
*The Arabian Nights Entertainments* 374, 1687, 2123, 2130, 4534, 4731, 6087
*The Blue Fairy Book* 225, 235, 1479, 2447, 5310, 6087, 6088, 6090
*The Green Fairy Book* 2447, 5310, 6090
*The Red Fairy Book* 235, 1479, 2447, 5310, 6088, 6090

**Lang, Simon**
*Hopeship* **3315**
*The Trumpets of Tagan* 1649, **3316**

**Langford, David**
*Irrational Numbers* 775, 2018, **3317**, 3533, 3556, 4444, 5446
*The Leaky Establishment* 1918, 3573

**Langguth, A.J.**
*Jesus Christs* 2753, 4330, 5015, 5569

**Lanier, Sterling E.**
*Hiero's Journey* 664, 1481, 1996, 2640, 3788, 4001, 4153, 4162, 4209, 4621, 4836, 5267
*Menace Under Marwood* 586
*The Peculiar Exploits of Brigadier Ffellowes* 4638

**Lanigan, Catherine**
*Jewel of the Nile* 3589, 3591, 4549
*Romancing the Stone* 3592, 4549

**Lannes, Roberta**
*The Mirror of the Night* 3100, **3318**, 5413

**Lansdale, Joe R.**
*Act of Love* 1831, 3209, 3210, **3319**
*Batman: Captured by the Engines* 14, 2124, 2391, **3320**
*Bestsellers Guaranteed* **3321**
*By Bizarre Hands* 555, 776, 777, 1123, 1128, 2281, 2784, **3322**, 3367, 3553, 3558, 4250, 4253, 4885, 5600, 5885
*Captured by the Engines* 2331, 2392, 4215
*Cold in July* 1831, 2162, 3052, **3323**
*Dark at Heart* 544, 1018, 2278, 2279, 2600, **3324**, 3598
*Dead in the West* 617, 1126, 1804, **3325**, 4255
*The Drive-In: A Double Omnibus* **3326**
*Electric Gumbo: A Lansdale Reader* **3327**
*A Fist Full of Stories (and Articles)* **3328**
*The Good, the Bad, and the Indifferent* **3329**, 4011
*The Magic Wagon* 4251, 4946, 5615
*Mucho Mojo* 1830, **3330**
*The New Frontier* 217, 3331, 3870

*Night Visions 8* **1885**
*The Nightrunners* 862, 945, 2341, 2556, 2871, 3208, 3527, 3638, 4254, 4471, 4837, 5969, 5987
*On the Far Side of the Cadillac Desert with Dead Folks* 4251
*Razored Saddles* 217, **3331**, 3870
*Savage Season* 1843, **3332**, 3755, 5850
*The Steel Valentine* 2279
*Stories by Mama Lansdale's Youngest Boy* 2078, **3333**, 6068
*Tarzan: The Lost Adventure* 2257
*Weird Business* 1044, **3334**
*Writer of the Purple Rage* **3335**, 4250

**Lansdale, Karen**
*Dark at Heart* **3324**

**Lara, Jan**
*Soulcatchers* 2689, **3336**

**Lardo, Vincent**
*China House* 3852

**Largent, R. Karl**
*Black Death* **3337**, 3577

**Larsen, Jeanne**
*Bronze Mirror* 374, 2803, **3338**, 5827, 6026
*Silk Road* 69, 313, 1145, 2804, **3339**, 4155, 4742, 5918

**Larson, Glen A.**
*Battlestar Galactica* 2602
*The Cylon Death Machine* 2602
*The Living Legend* 2602
*The Long Patrol* 2602

**Lasky, Kathryn**
*Double Trouble Squared* 1218, **3340**, 3468, 4918
*Shadows in the Water* 318, **3341**, 3729

**Laubenthal, Sanders Anne**
*Excalibur* 4877

**Laumer, Keith**
*Alien Minds* **3342**, 3796, 5641
*Back to the Time Trap* **3343**
*Bolo: The Annals of the Dinochrome Brigade* 1896, 1938, 2464, 4374, 5278, 5279, 5281
*The Complete Bolo* 1642, 1896, 4194
*End as a Hero* 2252
*The Glory Game* 4378
*The Great Time Machine Hoax* 5645
*Judson's Eden* 2810, **3344**
*Nine by Laumer* 592
*The Other Sky/The House in November* 2829
*Retief and the Warlords* 2001
*Retief at Large* 1536, 3919, 4560, 4932, 5875
*Retief: Diplomat at Arms* 1659
*Retief's Ransom* 30
*The Return of Retief* 30, 2013
*Reward for Retief* 30, 173, 2013, **3345**, 4037
*Rogue Bolo* 1628, 1651, 1896, 2725, 4769, 5278, 5279, 5280, 5283
*Star Colony* 734, 2491, 4373
*The Stars Must Wait* 163, 1642, 2805, **3346**, 3586
*The Time Bender* 3848
*Worlds of the Imperium* 1655, 5517
*Zone Yellow* 5130

**Laurance, Alice**
*Cassandra Rising* 4825, 4826

**Laurance, Andrew**
*Blood of Nostradamus: The
   Unborn* 3561
*Catacomb* 2312, **3347**, 3958
*The Link* **3348**
*The Premonition* **3349**
*The Unborn* **3350**

**Lauria, Frank**
*Dark City* **3351**

**Lawhead, Stephen R.**
*Arthur* 1498, 3061, **3352**, 4877,
   5560
*Byzantium* **3353**, 5014, 5017, 5513
*The Endless Knot* **3354**
*Grail* **3355**
*In the Hall of the Dragon King* 4654,
   5124
*The Iron Lance* **3356**
*Merlin* 227
*Pendragon* **3357**
*The Silver Hand* **3358**

**Lawrence, J.A.**
*Mudd's Angels* 526, 527, 528
*Star Trek: The Classic Episodes
   1* **526**
*Star Trek: The Classic Episodes
   3* **528**

**Lawrence, Louise**
*Dream-Weaver* **3359**

**Lawrence, Margery**
*Nights of the Round Table* **3360**
*Number Seven, Queer Street* 601

**Laws, Jay B.**
*Steam* 2116, **3361**
*The Unfinished* 345, **3362**

**Laws, Stephen**
*Daemonic* 1894, 5119
*Macabre* 602, 4733, 5119
*Voyages into Darkness* **3363**

**Laymon, Richard**
*Beast House* **3364**
*The Cellar* **3365**, 5120
*Funland* 2565, 2927, **3366**, 4010,
   5119, 5624
*A Good, Secret Place* 3090, **3367**,
   3553, 3558, 3674
*The Midnight Tour* **3368**
*Midnight's Lair* 1051, 1347, 1894,
   2611, 3209, **3369**, 5474, 5685
*The Mop Up* 4786
*Out Are the Lights* 3674
*Quake* 3209, **3370**
*Resurrection Dreams* 2610, **3371**
*The Stake* 810, 2220, 2441, **3372**,
   3498
*The Wilds* **3373**
*The Woods Are Dark* 3092, 3387

**Lazuta, Gene**
*Bleeder* **3374**, 5823
*Forget Me Not* **3375**
*Vyrmin* **3376**

**Le Fanu, J. Sheridan**
*Best Ghost Stories* 2866
*In a Glass Darkly* 258, 509

**Le Guin, Ursula K.**
*Always Coming Home* 211, 686,
   2037, 3627, 3771, 4361, 4631,
   5092, 5383, 5580, 5743, 5745
*The Beginning Place* 3731, 4971
*Buffalo Gals and Other Animal
   Presences* 274, 2120, 5807
*Catwings* **3377**, 3740, 6076
*City of Illusions* 4153, 4592, 4595
*The Compass Rose* 790, 5807

*The Dispossessed* 1923, 4420, 4932,
   5366, 5367, 5377, 5889
*The Eye of the Heron* 877, 2575
*The Farthest Shore* 1175, 2461,
   2865, 4149, 4265, 5142, 5832,
   6024, 6025
*Fish Soup* 2144, **3378**, 6089
*A Fisherman of the Inland Sea* 274,
   1653, 3235, **3379**, 5410
*Four Ways to Forgiveness* **3380**
*The Lathe of Heaven* 157, 512, 788,
   1521, 1523, 2486, 2754, 3186,
   3438, 3896, 4177, 4353, 4361,
   4553, 4678, 5515, 5591, 5660
*The Left Hand of Darkness* 211,
   1141, 1362, 1771, 2194, 2237,
   2295, 2423, 2443, 2881, 3047,
   3426, 3819, 3910, 3919, 4245,
   4325, 4900, 5477, 5580, 5592
*Nebula Award Stories 11* 245
*The Norton Book of Science Fiction:
   North American Science Fiction,
   1960-1990* 229, 246, 422, 888,
   1612, 1617, 1619, 1622, 1623,
   1624, 2585, 2593, 2594, 2595,
   **3381**
*Planet of Exile* 595, 2870
*A Ride on the Red Mare's Back* **3382**
*Tehanu: The Last Book of
   Earthsea* 314, 1175, 1177, **3383**,
   3731, 4149, 4152, 4211, 6025
*The Tombs of Atuan* 1175, 2461,
   3098, 4149, 4150, 5142, 5741,
   6024, 6025
*Unlocking the Air and Other
   Stories* **3384**
*The Wind's Twelve Quarters* 2120,
   5807
*A Wizard of Earthsea* 18, 371, 561,
   978, 1161, 1175, 1221, 1528,
   1529, 1530, 1531, 1533, 1605,
   1636, 1742, 1743, 1816, 1984,
   2128, 2354, 2356, 2461, 2650,
   3065, 3169, 3477, 3482, 3582,
   3884, 4149, 4321, 4324, 4334,
   4461, 4462, 4691, 4693, 4694,
   4924, 5034, 5142, 5272, 5728,
   5974, 5984, 6024, 6025, 6032,
   6036, 6037, 6069
*The Word for World Is Forest* 580,
   622, 1263, 3730, 4044, 4273,
   4539, 5069, 5880

**Lee, Adam**
*The Dark Shore* **3385**
*The Shadow Eater* **3386**

**Lee, Edward**
*The Bighead* 3373, **3387**
*The Case of the Police Officer's Cock
   Ring and the Piano Player Who Had
   No Fingers* **3388**
*The Chosen* 2743, **3389**, 5100
*Coven* 3042, 3183, **3390**
*Creekers* **3391**
*Edward Lee's Quest for Sex, Truth and
   Reality* 1467, 2778, 3367, 3553,
   3558, 5411, 5412, 5416, 5854
*Goon* **3392**
*Header* 2655, **3393**
*Incubi* 2090, **3394**, 5120, 5856
*Inside the Works* **4314**
*Portrait of the Psychopath as a Young
   Woman* **3395**
*Shifters* **3396**
*Splatterspunk: The Micah Hays
   Stories* **3397**, 5536

**Lee, Gentry**
*Bright Messengers* **3398**

*The Garden of Rama* **1055**
*Rama II* **1058**
*Rama Revealed* **1059**

**Lee, John**
*The Unicorn Dilemma* 2941
*The Unicorn Peace* **3399**
*The Unicorn Quest* 1100, 1946,
   2941, 4319
*The Unicorn Solution* 2941, **3400**,
   3892
*The Unicorn War* **3401**

**Lee, Robert D.**
*The Keeper* 3373, 3387, 3391,
   **3402**, 4222

**Lee, Sharon**
*Carpe Diem* **3907**

**Lee, Stan**
*The Ultimate Silver Surfer* 1390
*The Ultimate Spider-Man* 1227,
   1390, 1667, **3403**, 5567

**Lee, Tanith**
*Black Unicorn* 330, 549, 701, 1090,
   1219, 1343, 1440, 1946, 2941,
   3400, **3404**, 3545, 3720, 4319,
   4321, 4985, 5336, 5394, 5827,
   5979, 6017, 6033
*The Book of the Beast* **3405**, 4851
*The Book of the Damned* 43, 1140
*Dark Dance* 2115, 2220, 2492,
   2493, **3406**
*Darkness, I* 303, 3253, **3407**, 4068,
   4575, 4578
*Death's Master* 495, 4849, 5931
*Don't Bite the Sun* 5890
*Dreams of Dark and Light* 5369
*The Electric Forest* 957
*Elephantasm* **3408**
*Faces under Water* **3409**
*Gold Unicorn* **3410**, 5144
*Heart-Beast* 572, 603, 2895, **3411**
*A Heroine of the World* **3412**, 5390,
   5393
*Kill the Dead* 3624
*Night's Master* 1140
*Personal Darkness* **3413**
*Quest for the White Witch* 2760
*Red as Blood: Or Tales from the Sisters
   Grimmer* 1142, 1359, 1366, 1810,
   5428
*Red Unicorn* **3414**
*Sabella: Or, The Blood Stone* 1124,
   1134, 2207
*The Silver Metal Lover* 5181
*The Storm Lord* 5683
*Tamastara, or, the Indian
   Nights* 1316, 1317, 1318, 1699
*Volkhavaar* 5682

**Lee, Vernon**
*The Snake Lady and Other
   Stories* 4969, 5772
*Supernatural Tales: Excursions into
   Fantasy* 4968

**Lee, Warner**
*Night Sounds* **3415**

**Leiber, Fritz**
*Bazaar of the Bizarre* 291
*The Best of Fritz Leiber* 3683
*The Big Time* 350, 358, 359, 590,
   598, 1626, 1635, 1694, 2119,
   2564, 2790, 3064, 4164
*The Change War* 1275, 4164
*Conjure Wife* 280, 438, 2713, 2826,
   3390, 3499, 4738, 5290
*Conjure Wife/Our Lady of
   Darkness* **3416**, 3690, 5072, 5791

*The Dealings of Daniel
   Kesserich* **3417**
*The Demons of the Upper Air* 4752
*Farewell to Lankhmar* **3418**
*Four Ghosts in Hamlet* 5849
*Gather, Darkness!* 652
*Heroes and Horrors* 2781
*Ill Met in Lankhmar* 290, 291, 495,
   683, 1109, 1147, 1292, 1636,
   1813, 2253, 2451, 2452, 2759,
   **3419**, 3980, 4165, 4166, 4849,
   4945, 5206, 5458, 5471
*Ill Met in Lankhmar/The Fair in Emain
   Macha* 3189
*The Knight and Knave of
   Swords* 1532, 3172, 3175, 3982,
   3985, 4015
*Lean Times in Lankhmar* 291, 1484,
   2253, **3420**
*The Leiber Chronicles* 674, 675, 893,
   3219, **3421**, 5106, 5599
*Night's Black Agents* 5047
*Our Lady of Darkness* 2335, 3128,
   3161, 3194, 4248
*Return to Lankhmar* **3422**
*Ship of Shadows* 58, 4626, 5942,
   5943
*The Silver Eggheads* 419
*The Sinful Ones* 914, 951, 956,
   3493, 5643
*A Specter Is Haunting Texas* 5626
*Swords Against Death* 2362, 5102
*Swords Against Wizardry* 3836
*Swords and Deviltry* 259, 1239,
   1241, 1979, 2101, 2363, 2368,
   3246, 3512, 4316, 4975, 4994,
   5840
*The Swords of Lankhmar* 1706, 2783
*Two Sought Adventure: Exploits of
   Fafhrd and the Gray Mouser* 2190
*The Wanderer* 354, 3106, 4510,
   5303, 5341
*You Are All Alone* 3351

**Leiber, Justin**
*The Sword and the Eye* 2367
*The Sword and the Tower* 993

**Leigh, Stephen**
*The Abraxas Marvel Circus* 522,
   3097, 3286, **3423**
*Alien Tongue* 981, 1989, 2683,
   2898, **3424**
*Changeling* 2830, 2831, 2833, **3425**
*Dark Water's Embrace* **3426**
*Dinosaur Samurai* 1417
*Ray Bradbury Presents: Dinosaur
   Planet* 416, 2122, **3427**, 4854
*Ray Bradbury Presents: Dinosaur
   World* 306, 1379, 2468, **3428**,
   4597, 4853, 4854, 4855

**Leininger, Robert**
*Black Sun* 74, **3429**

**Leinster, Murray**
*Creatures of the Abyss* 189
*First Contacts: The Essential Murray
   Leinster* 2547, **3430**
*Land of the Giants* 4403
*The Med Series* 4172, 4176, 5777,
   5778, 5779, 5780
*Unknown Danger* 4386

**Leithauser, Brad**
*Hence* **3431**
*The Norton Book of Ghost
   Stories* 2483, **3432**
*Seaward* **3433**, 3809, 5440, 5530

**Lem, Stanislaw**
*The Cyberiad* 850, 3431

*Eden* **3434**
*Memoirs of a Space Traveler* 3431
*Mortal Engines* 850, 3431
*Peace on Earth* 3313, **3435**, 5074
*Return From the Stars* 3431
*Solaris* 3617, 4884

**L'Engle, Madeleine**
*An Acceptable Time* 371, 1033,
   **3436**, 4438
*The Moon by Night* 1898
*A Swiftly Tilting Planet* 1343
*A Wrinkle in Time* 510, 2948, 5013
*The Young Unicorns* 3276

**Lerner, Alan J.**
*Brigadoon: A Musical Play in Two
   Acts* 1958

**Lerner, Edward M.**
*Probe* 2215, **3437**, 6060

**Leroux, Gaston**
*The Phantom of the Opera* 19, 611,
   1115, 3020, 4395

**Lessing, Doris**
*The Fifth Child* 95, 330, 1141
*The Memoirs of a Survivor* 1141

**Lethem, Jonathan**
*Amnesia Moon* 2535, **3438**, 4135,
   4177
*As She Climbed Across the
   Table* **3439**
*Girl in Landscape* **3440**
*Gun, with Occasional Music* 1152,
   **3441**, 5362
*The Wall of the Sky, the Wall of the
   Eye* 411, 1023, 3087, **3442**, 3712

**Levi, Primo**
*The Mirror Maker* **3443**

**Levie, Rex Dean**
*Insect Warriors* 5755

**Levin, Betty**
*Mercy's Mill* 970, **3444**
*The Sword of Culann* 1294

**Levin, Ira**
*The Boys From Brazil* 3672, 3964,
   5136, 5732, 5895
*Rosemary's Baby* 863, 1076, 1212,
   1465, 3033, 3552, 3958, 4340,
   4577, 5269, 5401, 5538, 5895
*Sliver* 1777, 3094, 3208, 4248
*Son of Rosemary* **3445**
*The Stepford Wives* 1817, 1944,
   3041, 4083, 4087, 4090, 5021,
   5789

**Levinson, Bruce Scott**
*The Green Progression* 3932

**Levy, Robert**
*Clan of the Shape-Changers* **3446**

**Lewin, Leonard C.**
*Report from Iron Mountain* 1522

**Lewis, C.S.**
*The Chronicles of Narnia* 1447, 1803
*The Horse and His Boy* 3404, 4156
*The Last Battle* 5364
*The Lion, the Witch, and the
   Wardrobe* 368, 4330, 5182
*The Magician's Nephew* 1704
*Out of the Silent Planet* 2342, 2416,
   4654
*Perelandra: A Novel* 1803
*Pilgrim's Regress* 1803
*Prince Caspian* 368
*The Screwtape Letters* 4868
*That Hideous Strength* 4455, 4456
*The Voyage of the Dawn Treader* 368

**Lewis, D.F.**
*The Best of D.F. Lewis* **3447**, 3614,
   4230

**Lewis, Sinclair**
*If This Goes On* 5086

**Lewitt, S.N.**
*Angel at Apogee* 3454, 4594
*Blind Justice* **3448**, 3453, 3454
*Cybernetic Jungle* **3449**, 4339
*Cyberstealth* 1535, **3450**, 3453,
   3454, 3875, 4618
*Dancing Vac* **3451**, 3453, 3454,
   3875, 4618
*Songs of Chaos* **3452**

**Lewitt, Shariann**
*Interface Masque* 2274, **3453**
*Memento Mori* 5, **3454**

**Leyner, Mark**
*Et Tu, Babe* **3455**
*My Cousin, My
   Gastroenterologist* 158, 319, 2186,
   2847, 2859, **3456**, 3855, 4046,
   4606, 5593, 5867
*The Tetherballs of Bougainville* **3457**

**Lichtenberg, Jacqueline**
*Border Dispute* 3066
*Dreamspy* **3458**
*Dushau* 418, 954, 1772, 3066, 4350
*First Channel* 1304, 2665, 2806,
   4735
*House of Zeor* 220, 1134, 1408,
   2665, 4318
*Molt Brother* 2037, 2665, 3066,
   5109, 5467, 5572
*Unto Zeor Forever* 2665, 4318
*Zelerod's Doom* 4784

**Lieberman, Herbert**
*City of the Dead* 1410

**Lightman, Alan**
*Einstein's Dreams* 302, 1758, **3459**

**Lightner, A.M.**
*The Day of the Drones* 3243

**Ligotti, Thomas**
*The Agonizing Resurrection of Victor
   Frankenstein and Other Gothic
   Tales* **3460**, 5876
*Grimscribe: His Lives and
   Works* 864, 866, 3447, **3461**
*The Nightmare Factory* 573, **3462**,
   3532
*Noctuary* 3447, **3463**, 3530, 5876
*Songs of a Dead Dreamer* 851, 864,
   865, 866, 921, 2294, 2866, 3447,
   **3464**, 3530, 5317
*Vastarien* 966, 2022

**Like, Russel**
*After the Blue* **3465**

**Linaker, Michael R.**
*Scorpion* 3054

**Linaweaver, Brad**
*Free Space* **3466**
*Moon of Ice* 443, 1915, 2239, 4474,
   5517, 5518, 5889
*Sliders: The Novel* **3467**

**Lindbergh, Anne**
*Travel Far, Pay No Fare* 3156, **3468**

**Lindgren, Astrid**
*Mio My Son* 1330

**Lindholm, Megan**
*Alien Earth* 399, 404, 1046, 1726,
   **3469**, 4019, 4957, 5429, 5435,
   5492, 5743
*Alien Nation* 1247

*Assassin's Apprentice* **2693**
*Assassin's Quest* **2694**
*Cloven Hooves* 639, 744, 1440,
   1471, 2693, 3173, **3470**, 4985,
   5177, 5180, 5916
*The Gypsy* 744
*Harpy's Flight* 4924
*The Limbreth Gate* 2693
*Luck of the Wheels* 2465, 2507,
   3289, **3471**, 3871, 4013
*The Reindeer People* 1765
*Royal Assassin* **2695**
*The Ship of Magic* **2696**
*The Windsingers* 4924
*Wizard of the Pigeons* 738, 744,
   1425, 1431, 2104, 2105, 2537,
   2693, 2694, 2695, 2696, 2817,
   4383, 5274, 5697, 5913

**Lindley, Charles**
*The Ghost Book of Charles Lindley,
   Viscount Halifax* 2543, **3472**

**Lindsay, Jeffrey P.**
*Time Blender* 1581

**Lindskold, Jane M.**
*Brother to Dragons, Companion to
   Owls* 558, **3473**, 5133
*Changer* **3474**
*Donnerjack* 6063
*Marks of Our Brothers* 786, **3475**,
   6063
*The Pipes of Orpheus* 2404
*Smoke and Mirrors* **3476**
*When the Gods Are Silent* **3477**

**Linebarger, Paul Myron Anthony**
*Atomsk* 5174
*Norstrilia* **5105**
*The Rediscovery of Man* **5106**

**Linzner, Gordon**
*The Oni* 1335, 5800
*The Troupe* 822, 1851, 4787, 4847,
   5405, 5407

**Lippincott, David**
*Tremor Violet* 1060

**Lisle, Holly**
*Bones of the Past* 3302, **3478**
*Curse of the Black Heron* **3479**
*The Devil and Dan Cooley* **3480**
*Diplomacy of Wolves* **3481**
*Fire in the Mist* 1413, 3302, **3482**,
   5296
*Glenraven* 635
*Hell on High* **3483**
*Hunting the Corrigan's Blood* **3484**
*In the Rift* 639
*Mall, Mayhem and Magic* 639, 3099,
   **3485**
*Mind of the Magic* 719, **3486**
*Minerva Wakes* 316, 703, 1033,
   1299, 1744, 2141, 2326, 2737,
   2738, 3099, **3487**, 3843, 4129,
   4797, 5409, 5555, 5697
*The Rose Sea* 5296
*Sympathy for the Devil* 639, **3488**
*Thunder of the Captains* **3489**
*When the Bough Breaks* 3302
*Wrath of the Princes* **3490**

**Littell, Jonathan**
*Bad Voltage* 547, 836, 837, 838,
   972, 2219, **3491**, 4451, 4452,
   5959

**Little, Bentley**
*Dominion* 438, **3492**
*The Ignored* **3493**
*The Mailman* **3494**

*Murmerous Haunts* **3495**, 4231,
   5445, 5620
*The Revelation* 1079, 1884, 2318,
   2928, 2929, **3496**, 3615, 3668,
   3951, 5176, 5322
*The Store* **3497**
*The Summoning* 1335, 2220, **3498**,
   4003, 5800
*University* **3499**

**Little, Denise**
*Alien Pets* 2892, **3500**
*Mistresses of the Dark* **1715**

**Lively, Penelope**
*The Ghost of Thomas Kempe* 122,
   1272, 2438, 2923, 2951, 4078,
   4438
*Uninvited Ghosts and Other
   Stories* 1526, 3611

**Llewellyn, Edward**
*Fugitive in Transit* 5550
*Prelude to Chaos* 2870

**Llewelyn, Morgan**
*The Isles of the Blest* 1423

**Llywelyn, Morgan**
*Bard: The Odyssey of the Irish* 203,
   657, 1961, 2229, 2572, 3354,
   3358, 5408
*Brian Boru: Emperor of the
   Irish* **3501**, 4260
*Druids* 266, 633, 640, 1476, 2229,
   2454, 2740, **3502**, 3588, 3592,
   4264, 4270, 4989, 5792, 5793,
   5794
*The Elementals* 1482, 2716, **3503**,
   5433
*Finn Mac Cool* **3504**, 4266, 4267,
   4268
*Grania: She-King of the Irish
   Seas* 3059, 5962
*The Horse Goddess* 561, 657, 1961,
   5408, 5626
*The Isles of the Blest* 1810, 1960,
   2662, **3505**, 4519, 5534
*Lion of Ireland* 2572, 5408
*Pride of Lions* 2746, **3506**
*Red Branch* 1764, 1960, 5359
*Silverlight* 2619, **3507**

**Lobdell, Scott**
*Generation X* 2256

**LoBrutto, Pat**
*Razored Saddles* 3331

**Locke, Joseph**
*Vampire Heart* 120, 1302, 2131,
   4328, 5161

**Lofts, Norah**
*The Devil's Own* 4048, 4591
*The Lute Player* 3017

**Logston, Anne**
*Dagger's Edge* **3508**
*Firewalk* 3080, **3509**, 3652
*Greendaughter* **3510**
*Guardian's Key* **3511**
*Shadow* 15, 2368, 2376, 2452,
   2473, **3512**, 4596, 5648
*Shadow Dance* **3513**
*Shadow Hunt* 2473, **3514**, 3914

**London, Jack**
*Before Adam* 268
*Curious Fragments* 5746
*Selected Science Fiction and Fantasy
   Stories* 2680, 3147, 3148, 5310

**Long, Frank Belknap**
*Escape From Tomorrow* **3515**, 5149

*The Eye Above the Mantel and Other
  Stories* **3516**
*The Horror From the Hills* 4414,
  4415
*The Hounds of Tindalos* 942, 1495,
  1496, 2844, 3529, 3534, 4904,
  4905, 5627, 5628
*In Mayan Splendor* 4752
*Return to Tomorrow* 939
*The Rim of the Unknown* 5104

**Longstreet, Roxanne**
*Cold Kiss* 2149, **3517**, 5078
*Red Angel* 2159, 2825, 2931, **3518**
*The Undead* 301, 1779, **3519**, 5185,
  5347, 6050

**Longyear, Barry B.**
*The Change* 2909, **3520**
*Circus World* 5215
*City of Baraboo* 5215, 5264
*Elephant Song* 5215
*Enemy Mine* 434, 4125
*Enemy Mine/Another Orphan* 3189
*The God Box* 519, 4404, 4707
*The Homecoming* **3521**, 5129
*Infinity Hold* 1107, 1113, 1551,
  **3522**, 3693, 6059
*Naked Came the Robot* 1216, 2573,
  4297

**Lopez, Barry**
*Crow and Weasel* 40, 190, 1356,
  1527, 1867, 2100, **3523**, 4008,
  4380, 5578

**Lorrah, Jean**
*The IDIC Epidemic* 526, 1554, 2685,
  4928
*Metamorphosis* 2066, **3524**
*The Night of the Twin Moons* 528
*Survivors* 2068
*The Vulcan Academy Murders* 527,
  1260, 3315, 4928, 5596

**Lortz, Richard**
*Bereavement* **3525**

**Loudon, Jane Webb**
*The Mummy!: A Tale of the Twenty-
  Second Century* **3526**, 5312

**Loughran, Peter**
*The Third Beast* **3527**

**Louvish, Simon**
*The Resurrections* **3528**

**Lovecraft, H.P.**
*The Annotated H.P. Lovecraft* **3529**
*At the Mountains of Madness* 2711,
  5482
*At the Mountains of Madness and Other
  Novels* 5189
*The Best of H.P. Lovecraft:
  Bloodcurdling Tales of Horror and
  the Macabre* 1700, 5104
*The Case of Charles Dexter
  Ward* 1125, 1424, 3675, 3953
*Collected Poems* 486
*The Colour out of Space and
  Others* 728
*Dagon and Other Macabre
  Tales* 5104
*The Dream Cycle of H.P. Lovecraft:
  Dreams of Terror and Death* **3530**
*The Dream Quest of Unknown
  Kadath* 3595, 3859, 5102
*The Dunwich Horror and
  Others* 2710, 2712, 3462
*The Horror in the Museum and Other
  Revisions* **3531**
*The Lurker at the Threshold* 342,
  5470

*Road to Madness: The Transition of
  H.P. Lovecraft* **3532**
*The Shadow over Innsmouth* **3533**
*Tales of H.P. Lovecraft* **3534**
*Tales of the Cthulhu Mythos* 148,
  4429
*Tales of the Cthulhu Mythos: Golden
  Anniversary Anthology* 461, 2978,
  4422, 4423, 4424, 4428, 4430,
  4431, 5325, 5698
*The Thing on the Doorstep* 436
*The Watchers out of Time* 539, 3266,
  **3535**
*The Watchers out of Time and
  Others* 925

**Lovegrove, James**
*Escardy Gap* **1282**

**Lovejoy, Jack**
*The Hunters* 2211, 2811, 3800
*Outworld Cats* **3536**

**Lovejoy, William H.**
*White Night* 4512

**Lowder, James**
*Crusade* **3537**, 4108
*Knight of the Black Rose* 4326
*Prince of Lies* 1287, 5723
*The Ring of Winter* 1146, 1289,
  **3538**, 4800, 4803, 4804, 4805,
  4807

**Lowndes, Marie Belloc**
*The Lodger* 5761

**Lucas, Frances**
*Cathy IV* 1559, **3539**, 4245

**Lucas, George**
*Shadow Moon* 1042, **3540**
*Star Wars* 2171, 2365, 5023, 5116,
  5141, 5720, 6052, 6054
*The Star Wars Trilogy* 76, 114,
  2500, 5205, 5527, 5950, 6055

**Lucas, Tim**
*Throat Sprockets* 3103, **3541**, 4734

**Luceno, James**
*A Fearful Symmetry* **3542**
*Illegal Alien* 1420, **3543**
*The Mata Hari Adventure* **3544**

**Lucentini, Franco**
*The D. Case: The Truth about the
  Mystery of Edwin Drood* **1524**

**Luenn, Janet**
*The Root Cellar* 4917

**Luenn, Nancy**
*Goldclimbers* **3545**, 4615, 5143,
  5640

**Luke, Melinda**
*The Baby Ewok's Picnic
  Surprise* 1392, 1393, 1394
*Wicket Finds a Way: An Ewok
  Adventure* 1392, 1393, 1394

**Lumley, Brian**
*Blood Brothers* **3546**
*Bloodwars* **3547**
*The Burrowers Beneath* 1497, **3548**,
  4007, 4112, 4449, 5340, 5470
*The Caller of the Black* 3266
*The Compleate Crow* 4315
*A Coven of Vampires* 3111, **3549**
*Dagon's Bell and Other
  Discords* 1494, 1495, 1496
*Deadspawn* **3550**
*Deadspeak* **3551**
*Demogorgon* 3220, **3552**
*Fruiting Bodies and Other
  Fungi* 2780, 2784, 3367, **3553**

*The House of Cthulhu and Other Tales
  of the Primal Land* 3702
*The House of Doors* 1894, **3554**
*Iced on Aran and Other Dream
  Quests* 856, **3555**, 3613, 5471
*In His Own Write: Brian Lumley,
  Necroscribe* **3556**, 4444
*The Last Aerie* **3557**
*The Last Rite* **3558**
*Maze of Worlds* **3559**
*Necroscope* 1214, 2530, 3347,
  4496, 5020, 5120, 5212, 5773
*The Necroscope Series* 3349
*Necroscope: The Lost Years* **3560**,
  5704
*Psychamok* 752, **3561**
*Psychomech* 751, 752, **3562**
*Psychosphere* 752, **3563**
*Resurgence* **3564**
*The Second Wish and Other
  Exhalations* 3673
*The Source* **3565**
*Titus Crow, Volume One* **3566**
*Titus Crow, Volume Three* **3567**
*Titus Crow, Volume Two* **3568**
*The Transition of Titus Crow* **3569**,
  4112
*Vamphyri!* 463

**Lundie, Catherine A.**
*Restless Spirits* 37, **3570**, 5439

**Lupoff, Richard**
*Circumpolar!* 5830

**Lupoff, Richard A.**
*Before...12:01...and After* 925,
  **3571**
*The Black Tower* 1429
*Buck Rogers in the 25th Century* 554
*The Final Battle* 1429, **3572**
*Lovecraft's Book* 1859, 4751
*Night of the Living 'Gator!* 1603,
  **3573**
*That Man on Beta II* 554
*What If? Stories That Should Have Won
  the Hugo* 2405

**Lurie, Alison**
*The Oxford Book of Modern Fairy
  Tales* 225, 228, 1613, 2592,
  **3574**, 5003, 5030, 5721, 5730,
  5814
*Women and Ghosts* 2826, 2842,
  **3575**, 4184, 5166

**Luserke, Uwe**
*Desire Burn: Women's Stories From the
  Dark Side of Passion* 468

**Lykins, Jenny**
*Distant Dreams* **3576**

**Lymington, John**
*Night of the Big Heat* 914

**Lynch, Patrick**
*Carriers* 99, 2720, 3337, 4413
*Omega* 2206, **3577**, 3632

**Lyndell, Catherine**
*Stolen Dreams* 313

**Lynn, Elizabeth A.**
*The Dancers of Arun* 644, 653
*Dragon's Winter* **3578**
*The Northern Girl* 644
*The Sardonyx Net* 3692
*Tales From a Vanished
  Country* 1428, 3945, 5810
*Watchtower* 3268, 5750, 6075

**Lyons, Lynda**
*Priorities* 74, 662, 2295, **3579**,
  4245

**Lyris, Sonia Orin**
*And Peace Shall Sleep* 207, 2827

**Lytton, Edward Bulwer**
*The Haunters and the Haunted; or, the
  House and the Brain* 1597

**M**

**Mac Rauch, Earl**
*Buckaroo Banzai* 5009

**MacApp, C.C.**
*Prisoners of the Sky* 2246

**MacAvoy, R.A.**
*The Belly of the Wolf* 2195, **3580**
*The Book of Kells* 2, 317, 363, 1386,
  1957, 2359, 2570, 3261, 3502
*Damiano* 3714, 4869
*Damiano's Lute* 4869, 5222
*The Grey Horse* 1000, 1703, 1704,
  3840
*King of the Dead* **3581**, 5582
*Lens of the World* 2986, **3582**, 5391,
  5582, 5584, 6039
*Tea with the Black Dragon* 285, 634,
  636, 714, 1450, 1451, 1477, 1528,
  1531, 1841, 2847, 4055, 4517,
  5176, 5556, 5618
*The Third Eagle: Lessons Along a
  Minor String* 353, 431, 1070,
  1414, 1691, 1891, 1893, **3583**,
  4262, 4453, 5131, 5743, 5744,
  5925
*Twisting the Rope* 285, 4868, 4870

**MacDonald, Caroline**
*The Lake at the End of the
  World* **3584**

**MacDonald, George**
*The Complete Fairy Tales of George
  MacDonald* 2447
*The Fantasy Stories of George
  MacDonald* 4021

**MacDonald, James D.**
*By Honor Betray'd* **1598**
*The Gathering Flame* **1599**
*Groogleman* **1600**
*Knight's Wyrd* **1601**
*The Long Hunt* **1602**
*Night of the Living Rat!* **1603**
*The Price of the Stars* **1604**
*School of Wizardry* **1605**
*Starpilot's Grave* **1606**

**MacDonald, John D.**
*The Executioners* 1198, 2111, 2843,
  3518, 3756
*The Girl, the Gold Watch, and
  Everything* 302
*Wine of the Dreamers* 4361

**MacDonald, Shawn**
*The Darkness Within* **3585**, 5926

**Mace, David**
*Firelance* 1924, **3586**

**Mace, Elisabeth**
*Under Siege* 332, **3587**

**MacEoin, Denis**
*The Lost* 279
*The Matrix* 280
*Name of the Beast* 1721
*Naomi's Room* 281
*The Vanishment* 282
*Whispers in the Dark* 283

**MacGregor, Rob**
*Indiana Jones and the Dance of the Giants* 825, 826, **3588**, 5307
*Indiana Jones and the Genesis Deluge* 825, 826, **3589**, 4622
*Indiana Jones and the Interior World* 825, 826, **3590**
*Indiana Jones and the Last Crusade* 825, 826, 2231, 4549
*Indiana Jones and the Peril at Delphi* 825, 826, **3591**, 4549, 4623, 5308
*Indiana Jones and the Seven Veils* 825, 826, **3592**, 4549
*Indiana Jones and the Unicorn's Legacy* 825, 826, **3593**

**MacGregor, T.J.**
*The Hanged Man* **3594**

**Machen, Arthur**
*The Great God Pan* 4235
*The Green Round* 4586
*The Hill of Dreams* **3595**, 4586
*Tales of Horror and the Supernatural* 2710
*The Terror* 456
*"The White People"* 1081
*The Three Impostors* 2712

**MacIntyre, F. Gwynplaine**
*The Woman between the Worlds* **3596**

**Mackay, Scott**
*Outpost* **3597**

**Maclay, John**
*Voices From the Night* 2278, **3598**, 4278, 4722

**MacLean, Alistair**
*Ice Station Zebra* 3209

**Maclean, Charles**
*The Watcher* 1237

**MacLeod, Ian R.**
*The Great Wheel* **3599**
*Voyages by Starlight* **3600**

**MacMillan, Scott**
*At Sword's Point* 3260, **3601**
*Knights of the Blood* 3260, **3602**

**Madden, Timothy A.**
*Outbanker* 379, 3448, **3603**, 5930

**Maddox, Tom**
*Halo* **3604**, 5462

**Madsen, David**
*Vodoun* **3605**

**Maeder, Tom**
*Revenge of the Christmas Box* **1257**

**Maeve, Henry**
*The Witch King* 4056

**Maggin, Elliot S.**
*Superman: Last Son of Krypton* 999, 2393, 5262
*Superman: Miracle Monday* 999, 2393, 5262

**Maginn, Simon**
*Sheep* **3606**
*Virgins and Martyrs* 2548, 2994, 3149, **3607**

**Maguire, Gregory**
*I Feel Like the Morning Star* 3584, **3608**
*Wicked: The Life and Times of the Wicked Witch of the West* 2136, **3609**

**Mahy, Margaret**
*The Changeover* 330, 1179, 3163, 4079, 4080
*The Girl with the Green Ear: Stories about Magic in Nature* **3610**
*The Haunting* 4257
*The Pirates' Mixed-Up Voyage* 3156
*A Tall Story and Other Tales* **3611**
*The Tricksters* 53, 1668, 2951

**Mailer, Norman**
*The Executioner's Song* 1489

**Maine, Charles Eric**
*Alph* 1653, 2870

**Mainhardt, Ricia**
*Robert Bloch: Appreciations of the Master* **3689**
*Superheroes* **5567**

**Malacypse the Younger**
*Principia Discordia* 5904

**Malden, R.H.**
*Nine Ghosts* 1350, 5611

**Mallory, Thomas**
*Le Morte d'Arthur* 5359

**Maloney, Jack**
*Freedom Express* 2324, 2325

**Malterre, Elona**
*The Celts* 3502

**Malzberg, Barry**
*Beyond Apollo* **3612**, 5057
*Classic Tales of Horror and the Supernatural* **4440**
*The Falling Astronauts* 5057

**Manachino, Albert J.**
*Noctet: Tales of Madonna-Moloch* **3613**
*The Odd Lot: The Selected Works of Albert J. Manachino* **3614**, 4463, 5335, 5881

**Mancour, T.L.**
*Spartacus* 3767

**Mandelik, Nina**
*Entity* 1077, **3615**

**Manguel, Alberto**
*Black Water 2: More Tales of the Fantastic* 1099, **3616**, 5936
*Black Water: The Book of Fantastic Literature* 1099, 5936
*The Oxford Book of Canadian Ghost Stories* 2813, 2814, 2815

**Manley, Seon**
*Christmas Ghosts: An Anthology* 1311, 1313, 2276, 2894, 4541
*Ghostly Gentlewomen* 3570
*Ladies of Horror* 3570
*Women of the Weird* 1715, 3022

**Mann, Phillip**
*Wulfsyarn: A Mosaic* **3617**

**Mann, William J.**
*Grave Passions* **3618**, 5386

**Mano, D. Keith**
*The Bridge* 5081

**Manson, Cynthia**
*Future Crime: An Anthology of the Shape of Crime to Come* **3619**

**Marano, Michael**
*Dawn Song* 1117, **3620**

**Marasco, Robert**
*Burnt Offerings* 2455, 3033, 3141, 3774

**March, Melisand**
*The Site* 3161, 3364, **3621**, 4499, 5164, 5961, 5989

**March, William**
*The Bad Seed* 320, 3606, 4844

**Marcus, Greil**
*Dead Elvis* 4810

**Marder, Norma**
*An Eye for Dark Places* 968, **3622**

**Marfinn, Kyle**
*Carmilla: The Return* **3623**

**Margroff, Robert E.**
*The Caterpillar's Question* **164**
*Chimaera's Copper* **166**
*Mouvar's Magic* **182**

**Margulies, Leo**
*My Best Science Fiction Story* 1844, 2405
*Weird Tales* 2485, 5689
*Worlds of Weird* 2485, 5689

**Marks, Laurie J.**
*Dancing Jack* **3624**, 4146
*Delan the Mislaid* **3625**
*The Moonbane Mage* 1035, 1815, 2819, 3626
*The Watcher's Mask* **3627**, 5296

**Marley, Louise**
*Receive the Gift* **3628**
*Sing the Light* 2877, **3629**, 3730, 3739, 4999, 5001
*Sing the Warmth* **3630**

**Marlowe, Stephen**
*The Lighthouse at the End of the World* 1516, 3150, **3631**

**Marr, John S.**
*The Eleventh Plague: A Novel of Medical Terror* **3632**

**Marsh, Geoffrey**
*Fangs and the Hooded Demon* 1415

**Marsh, Richard**
*The Haunted Chair and Other Stories* 875, **3633**

**Marshak, Sondra**
*Star Trek: The New Voyages* 527
*Star Trek: The New Voyages II* 527

**Marshall, Deborah A.**
*Serpent's Gift* **1261**

**Marshall, Edison**
*Conqueror* 2187, 5395

**Marston, Ann**
*Broken Blade* 993, **3634**
*Kingmaker's Sword* **3635**
*The Western King* **3636**

**Marter, Ian**
*Dr. Who and the Ribos Operation* 4338

**Martin, David**
*Bring Me Children* 822, **3637**, 4501, 4845, 5250, 5314
*Cul-De-Sac* **3638**
*Lie to Me* 1829, **3639**, 5453
*Tap, Tap* **3640**

**Martin, George R.R.**
*Ace in the Hole* 989, **3641**
*The Armageddon Rag* 575, 3664, 3756, 4887, 4997, 5170, 5615
*Black Trump* **3642**
*Dealer's Choice* **3643**
*Down and Dirty* 989
*Dying of the Light* **3644**, 5544, 5545

*Fevre Dream* 1124, 2009, 2191, 3602, 3977, 5151
*A Game of Thrones* 1154, 1640, 1912, 2989, **3645**, 4258, 4259, 4533, 5034, 6002
*The John W. Campbell Awards, Volume 5* 754, 755, 5952, 5953
*Jokertown Shuffle* 986, **3646**
*Marked Cards* **3647**
*New Voices I-IV* 754, 755, 5952, 5953
*Night Visions 3* 1885, 3363
*Portraits of His Children* 625, 1753, **3648**, 5641
*Songs the Dead Men Sing* 1783, 4889, 5058
*"The Skin Trade"* 2794
*Wild Cards* 499, 1535, 2256, 3009, 4363, 5038, 5148, 5214, 5216, 5642, 6048
*The Wild Cards Series* 1674, 3891, 4130, 5567

**Martin, Jack**
*Halloween* 1555, 5026
*Halloween III: Season of the Witch* 2317, 4009, 4601, 4603
*Scanners* 752, 879, 3561, 3563
*Videodrome* 1353, 3326

**Martin, Les**
*Field of Death* 3544
*Trek of Doom* 3544

**Martin, Marcia**
*The Weigher* **5574**

**Martin, Mark O.**
*A Darker Geometry* **3649**

**Martin, Thomas K.**
*A Call to Arms* **3650**
*Magelord: The Awakening* **3651**
*A Matter of Honor* 562, 1143, 5197
*The Time of Madness* **3652**
*A Two-Edged Sword* **3653**

**Martin, Valerie**
*The Consolation of Nature, and Other Stories* 3195
*Mary Reilly* 535, **3654**, 5826

**Martindale, T. Chris**
*Demon Dance* 2251, 3325, **3655**, 3967
*Nightblood* **3656**, 4213
*The Voice in the Basement* 2292, 3364, **3657**, 5784
*Where the Chill Waits* 41, 834, 2936, **3658**, 3895, 5769

**Martine-Barnes, Adrienne**
*The Crystal Sword* 4266, 4267, 4268
*The Fire Sword* 4266, 4267, 4268, 4608, 4920, 4991
*Master of Earth and Water* **4266**
*The Rainbow Sword* 407, 1815, 2083, **3659**, 4266, 4267, 4268, 6083
*The Shield between the Worlds* **4267**
*Sword of Fire and Shadow* **4268**

**Martinson, Harry**
*Aniara* 58

**Masefield, John**
*The Box of Delights, or, When the Wolves Were Running* 1294
*The Midnight Folk* 4079, 4080

**Masello, Robert**
*Private Demons* 2652, **3660**, 4006, 4085, 4100

**Mason, Anne**
*The Stolen Law* 4158, 4911, 5609

**Mason, Arthur**
*The Wee Men of Ballywooden* 2438

**Mason, David**
*The Sorcerer's Skull* 1996

**Mason, Lisa**
*Arachne* 77, **3661**, 3764, 3921,
4893, 5462
*Cyberweb* 483, **3662**
*The Golden Nineties* 264, 2120,
3597, **3663**, 4036
*Summer of Love* 1345, 1480, 3071,
**3664**, 5873

**Mason, Mary**
*Jade Darcy and the Zen Pirates* **2260**

**Mason, Robert**
*Solo* **3665**
*Weapon* 1113, **3666**

**Massie, Elizabeth**
*Shadow Dreams* 94, 663, 693, 802,
1789, 2698, 2701, 3495, **3667**
*Sineater* 859, 2318, 3104, **3668**
*Southern Discomfort: Selected Works of
Elizabeth Massie* 113, 1123, **3669**,
4463, 5316, 5881

**Massie-Ferch, Kathleen M.**
*Ancient Enchantresses* 649, 650, 651,
3070, 3076, **3670**, 4610
*Warrior Enchantresses* 3076

**Masterton, Graham**
*Burial* 602, 2670, 2743, 3081,
3325, **3671**, 5053
*The Burning* **3672**, 4847
*Flights of Fear* 2018, **3673**
*Fortnight of Fear* 3549, **3674**
*The House That Jack Built* **3675**,
3953
*Hurry, Monster* 5796
*The Manitou* 41, 860, 3081, 3325,
3658, 5350
*Master of Lies* 3620, **3676**, 5085
*Mirror* **3677**
*Revenge of the Manitou* 3325, 3658
*Rook* 397, 1403, **3678**, 5415
*The Terror* **3679**
*Tooth and Claw* **3680**
*Walkers* 3033, **3681**

**Matheson, Richard**
*7 Past Midnight* 4875
*7 Seconds to Midnight* 89
*7 Steps to Midnight* **3682**
*Bid Time Return* 4753
*Collected Stories* 429, 529, 530,
532, 533, 537, 623, 2277, 3138,
3333, **3683**, 3689, 5901
*The Dance of the Dead* 5923
*Earthbound* 524, 1468, 1560, 2019,
3178, **3684**
*Hell House* 90, 281, 861, 1192,
1776, 2630, 2669, 3607, 3657,
**3685**, 4830, 5329, 5424, 5528,
5991
*I Am Legend* 2440, 3361, 3458,
**3686**, 3758, 4072, 4831, 5050,
5212, 5770, 5891, 5923
*The Incredible Shrinking Man* **3687**
*Now You See It...* **3688**, 5485
*Richard Matheson: Collected
Stories* 531, 4132
*Robert Bloch: Appreciations of the
Master* **3689**
*Somewhere in Time/What Dreams May
Come* **3690**
*A Stir of Echoes* 2613, 2874, 3135,
3965
*The Twilight Zone Scripts* 4916

**Matheson, Richard Christian**
*Created By* 138, 426, 1846, 3213,
**3691**, 5422
*Scars and Other Distinguishing
Marks* 4530, 4885, 5005

**Matschatt, Cecile**
*Fiction Stories* 6027

**Matthews, Caitlin**
*Tarot Tales* **4359**

**Matthews, Rodney**
*Yendor* 6076

**Matthews, Susan R.**
*An Exchange of Hostages* **3692**
*Hour of Judgment* 2286
*Prisoner of Conscience* **3693**

**Maturin, Charles**
*Melmoth the Wanderer* 4371

**Mauck, Joe**
*Claw* **1850**

**Maupassant, Guy de**
*The Dark Side: Tales of Terror and the
Supernatural* 1596, **3694**

**Maxim, John R.**
*Abel/Baker/Charley* 1826, 2197,
2613, 3128, 3374, 3691, 5422
*Platforms* 2668, 2687, 4256
*Time Out of Mind* 464

**Maxon, J.G.**
*Lethal Delivery* **3695**

**Maxwell, Ann**
*Fire Dancer* 1772

**May, Julian**
*Black Trillium* **630**
*Blood Trillium* 641, **3696**, 4153
*Diamond Mask: A Novel* **3697**
*Jack the Bodiless* 645, **3698**
*Magnificat* 2526, **3699**
*The Many-Colored Land* 15, 987,
1324, 1421, 2119, 2122, 3058,
3059, 3060, 3062, 3427, 5754,
5998
*Sky Trillium* **3700**

**Mayer, Bob**
*Operation Synbat* 1850, 2779, **3701**,
3901, 4414

**Mayhar, Ardath**
*Mean Little Old Lady at Work* 113,
578, **3702**, 5881
*Monkey Station* **3703**
*People of the Mesa* 2166, **3704**

**Mayhew, Michael**
*Harvest Tales and Midnight Revels:
Stories for the Waning of the
Year* **3705**

**Mayne, William**
*Earthfasts* 1138
*A Game of Dark* 4917
*Supernatural Stories* 1693, 1701,
4282

**Mayr, Dallas**
*Ladies Night* **3091**

**McAllister, Bruce**
*Dream Baby* 3206, **3706**, 4865
*There Won't Be War* **2578**

**McAllister, P.K.**
*Maia's Veil* **3707**
*Orion's Dagger* **3708**
*Siduri's Net* 3476, **3709**

**McAuley, Paul J.**
*Child of the River* 3440, 3819
*Eternal Light* **3710**

*Fairyland* 835, 2218, **3711**
*Four Hundred Billion Stars* 952,
2365, 5108
*In Dreams* 2184, 4810
*The Invisible Country* **3712**
*Of the Fall* **3713**, 3946, 4547
*Pasquale's Angel* 1341, 1457, 2043,
**3714**, 3841, 4651, 5152
*Red Dust* 2840, **3715**, 5865

**McBain, Ed**
*Lizzie* 1826

**McCabe, Patrick**
*The Butcher Boy* 862, 3638, **3716**

**McCaffrey, Anne**
*Acorna* **3717**
*Acorna's Quest* **3718**
*Alchemy and Academe* 671, 4397
*All the Weyrs of Pern* 3050, **3719**
*Black Horses for the King* 2654,
**3720**, 5794, 6035, 6038
*The Chronicles of Pern: First
Fall* 2371, **3721**, 4999, 5001
*The City Who Fought* 83, **3722**, 5298
*The Coelura* 3840
*Crisis on Doona* 3066, **3723**, 4137,
4138, 4170, 4176, 4300, 4350
*Crystal Line* **3724**
*Crystal Singer* 1071, 2477, 2478,
3286, 3888, 3938, 4870, 4996,
5774
*Damia* 101, 2478, **3725**, 4553,
6053
*Damia's Children* **3726**, 5672
*The Death of Sleep* 1070, **3727**,
4170, 4176
*Decision at Doona* 1263, 1595,
1956, 2421
*Dinosaur Planet* 1986, 3221
*A Diversity of Dragons* **3728**
*The Dolphins of Pern* 2450, **3729**
*Dragon Song* 4996
*Dragondrums* 1066, 1221
*Dragonflight* 222, 894, 1000, 1114,
2036, 2421, 2423, 3044, 3045,
3065, 3157, 3940, 4149, 4485,
4490, 4492, 4493, 4692, 4695,
4697, 5034, 5708, 5862
*Dragonquest* 4149, 4692, 4697
*Dragonriders of Pern* 842, 843,
4691, 4693, 4694
*The Dragonriders of Pern
Series* 2553, 3289, 5829
*Dragonsdawn* 638, 983, 1247, 2371,
3001
*Dragonseye* **3730**
*Dragonsinger* 1221, 4161
*Dragonsong* 1221, 2015
*Drangonsinger* 1765
*An Exchange of Gifts* **3731**
*Freedom's Challenge* **3732**
*Freedom's Choice* **3733**
*Freedom's Landing* 383, 420, 1500,
1501, 2034, 2223, **3734**, 3952,
4116
*Generation Warrior* 1070, **3735**
*Get Off the Unicorn* 3845
*The Girl Who Heard Dragons* 3065,
**3736**
*If Wishes Were Horses* **3737**
*Killashandra* 1772
*Lyon's Pride* **3738**
*The Masterharper of Pern* **3739**
*Moreta, Dragonlady of Pern* 692
*Moreta's Story* 3044
*Nerilka's Story* 638
*No One Noticed the Cat* **3740**, 4054
*PartnerShip* 313, 315, **3741**

*Pegasus in Flight* 101, 2474, 2475,
**3742**
*Power Lines* **3743**
*Power Play* **3744**
*Powers That Be* 293, 632, 1988,
2010, 2476, 3359, 3503, **3745**,
4356, 5433, 5435, 5437, 5745
*The Renegades of Pern* 638, **3746**
*Restoree* 1913
*The Rowan* 101, 218, 643, 645, 653,
2416, 2474, 2475, 2478, 2551,
3060, 3096, 3628, 3629, 3630,
3699, **3747**, 4101, 4139, 6053
*Sassinak* 62, 757, 764, 1041, 1070,
2436, 3307, **3748**, 4482, 4910
*The Ship Who Sang* 734, 1389,
1627, 2135, 2419, 2890, 3038,
3888, 4175, 5298, 5375, 5680
*The Ship Who Searched* 643, **3749**
*The Ship Who Won* **3750**, 4175
*Space Opera* 3264, **3751**
*To Ride Pegasus* 101, 642, 788,
2420, 5208
*Treaty at Doona* 1259, 1264, 1546,
1586, 2001, **3752**
*The White Dragon* 222, 4149, 4692,
4697, 5640

**McCammon, Robert R.**
*Blue World* 700, 967, 1887, 2281,
2319, 3138, 3216, 3321, 3328,
3329, 3335, **3753**, 4648, 5339,
5600, 5899
*Boy's Life* **3754**
*Gone South* 3373, **3755**
*Mine* 1843, 2111, 2548, 2555,
3130, 3332, 3695, **3756**, 4887
*Mystery Walk* 1886, 4073, 5484,
5485
*The Night Boat* 3220, 3964
*Stinger* 576, 617, 1037, 2314, 3129
*Swan Song* 338, 341, 343, 525,
3142, 3143, **3757**, 4647, 5190
*They Thirst* 1402, 1463, 1464, 1466,
1882, 2152, 2258, 3140, 3142,
3550, 3551, 3564, 3565, 4072,
4102, 4190, 5158, 5237, 5770,
5891
*Under the Fang* 854, 1373, 2118,
2315, 2387, **3758**, 5448, 5888
*Usher's Passing* 70, 340, 1888,
2115, 2494, 2557, 2749, 4344,
4601, 4603, 4778
*The Wolf's Hour* 462, 2841, 2895,
**3759**, 4702, 4780

**McCarthy, Wil**
*Aggressor Six* 1315, **3760**, 4775
*Bloom* 1695, **3761**, 5068
*The Fall of Sirius* 1315, **3762**, 4775
*Flies From the Amber* 1157, **3763**
*Murder in the Solid State* 2723,
2916, **3764**

**McCarty, Dennis**
*Across the Thlassa Mey* **3765**
*The Birth of the Blade* 844, **3766**

**McCauley, Kirby**
*Dark Forces* 1629, 1847, 2307,
2965, 5924
*Frights* 2965
*Night Chills* 1844, 2965, 2974

**McCay, Bill**
*Chains of Command* **3767**, 5457
*Crossover* **3768**
*Reconnaissance* **3769**

**McCloy, Helen**
*Through a Glass Darkly* 2562

**McCollum, Michael**
*Antares Dawn*  353, 882
*Antares Passage*  1182, 2016
*The Clouds of Saturn*  1986, **3770**
*A Greater Infinity*  953, 3343
*Life Probe*  5788
*The Sails of Tau Ceti*  **3771**
*Thunder Strike!*  **3772**

**McConchie, Lyn**
*Ciara's Song*  **4146**
*The Key of the Keplian*  **4156**

**McConnell, Ashley**
*The Courts of Sorcery*  **3773**
*Days of the Dead*  1886, 2734, 2903,
   **3774**, 4601, 4603, 5631
*The Fountains of Mirlacca*  3280,
   **3775**
*Highlander: Scimitar*  2657, 4082,
   4611, 5707, 5729
*The Itinerant Exorcist*  **3776**
*Prelude*  4487
*Quantum Leap: The Novel*  3467,
   4487
*Stargate SG-1*  **3777**
*Too Close for Comfort*  4487
*Unearthed*  **3778**
*The Wall*  4487

**McCormack, Eric**
*First Blast of the Trumpet Against the
   Monstrous Regiment of
   Women*  **3779**
*Inspecting the Vaults*  626, 1171
*The Mysterium*  **3780**
*The Paradise Motel*  1468, 5661

**McCrumb, Sharyn**
*Bimbos of the Death Sun*  251, 316,
   568, 2567, 4120, 4546, 4785
*If Ever I Return, Pretty Peggy-
   O*  1829
*Zombies of the Gene Pool*  4120

**McCullough, Colleen**
*A Creed for the Third
   Millennium*  2093, 4678

**McCuniff, Mara**
*The Vampire Memoirs*  139, 2267,
   3113, 3151, **3781**, 4763, 4774,
   6016

**McCuniff, Maura**
*The Vampire Memoirs*  6012

**McDaniels, Abigail**
*Althea*  **3782**
*Dead Voices*  2903, 2933, **3783**
*Playmates*  2878, 2902, **3784**
*The Uprising*  1926, 2821, 2933,
   **3785**, 5064

**McDevitt, Jack**
*Ancient Shores*  870, **3786**, 5867
*The Engines of God*  378, 684, 1258,
   1259, 1500, 1565, 3763, **3787**,
   4281, 4859, 5372
*Eternity Road*  **3788**
*The Hercules Text*  202
*Moonfall*  **3789**
*A Talent for War*  443, 516, **3790**

**McDonald, Ian**
*The Broken Land*  2952, **3791**, 4241
*Desolation Road*  328, 547, 551, 622,
   820, 1880, 2101, 2533, 5069
*Empire Dreams*  1278
*Evolution's Shore*  1825, 3476, **3792**,
   4858, 5068
*King of Morning, Queen of
   Day*  1471, 1960, 2238, 3354,
   3357, 3470, **3793**, 3854

*Out on Blue Six*  1278, **3794**, 4750,
   5918, 5919
*Scissors Cut Paper Wrap Stone*  **3795**,
   4296
*Speaking in Tongues*  2576, **3796**
*Terminal Cafe*  305, 325, 835, 836,
   837, 838, 1348, 1760, 2218, 2377,
   2522, 3238, **3797**, 3818, 4192,
   4381, 4703, 5105, 5253, 5256,
   5828, 6009

**McDonald, T. Liam**
*Sea Cursed: Thirty Terrifying Tales of
   the Deep*  2709, 2732, **3798**

**McDonough, Alex**
*Dragon's Blood*  **3799**
*Dragon's Claw*  **3800**
*Dragon's Eye*  **3801**
*Scorpio*  403, 1476, **3802**, 4302
*Scorpio Descending*  **3803**
*Scorpio Rising*  **3804**

**McDonough, Thomas R.**
*The Missing Matter*  110, 2480, **3805**,
   4019

**McDowell, Ian**
*Merlin's Gift*  3474
*Mordred's Curse*  1189, 1269, **3806**

**McDowell, Michael**
*The Amulet*  1205
*Blackwater*  70, 145, 147, 340, 4838,
   5808, 5926
*The Blackwater Series*  1300
*Cold Moon over Babylon*  1860
*Toplin*  **3807**, 5327

**McElroy, Joseph**
*Plus*  3996, 4581

**McEwan, Ian**
*Black Dogs*  **3808**
*The Cement Garden*  1027, 2111,
   5808
*In between the Sheets*  626, 920

**McFadden, Kevin**
*The Cold One*  4327
*The Last Vampire*  4328
*The Midnight Club*  4329
*Sati*  4330
*The Season of Passage*  4331
*See You Later*  4332
*The Starlight Crystal*  4333
*Witch*  4334

**McFarland, Dennis**
*A Face at the Window*  2241, **3809**,
   5440

**McGann, Michael**
*The Ghost Warriors*  2324, 2325

**McGarry, Jim**
*Irish Tales of Terror*  149, 1242,
   2481, 2482, 4203

**McGinley, Phyllis**
*The Plain Princess*  329

**McGirt, Dan**
*Dirty Work*  **3810**, 6066
*Jason Cosmo*  982, 1002, 1268, **3811**

**McGrath, Patrick**
*Asylum*  **3812**, 4084
*Blood and Water and Other
   Tales*  921, 3984, 4027, 4181
*Dr. Haggard's Disease*  3779, **3813**
*The Grotesque*  627, 2115, 3002,
   3688, **3814**, 4788
*The New Gothic*  4027
*Spider*  811, 2548, **3815**, 4185

**McGraw, Charles G.**
*Demon Blade*  2141

*Dorella*  2142

**McGraw, Eloise Jarvis**
*Merry-Go-Round in Oz*  3609
*The Moorchild*  1143, 1319, 1320,
   **3816**

**McHugh, Maureen F.**
*China Mountain Zhang*  927, 1968,
   2952, 3029, **3817**, 5253
*Half the Day Is Night*  1760, **3818**,
   5256
*Mission Child*  **3819**

**McIntyre, Vonda N.**
*Aurora: Beyond Equality*  4825, 4826
*The Crystal Star*  103, 109, 2500,
   **3820**, 4299, 5527, 5950
*Dreamsnake*  642, 1722, 2120, 2806,
   4176, 4836
*Enterprise*  526, 900
*The Entropy Effect*  526, 1386
*The Exile Waiting*  2477, 3718, 4043
*The Girl Who Was Plugged In*  5525
*Metaphase*  81, 322, 324, 384, 404,
   1059, 1333, 1726, 1989, 1992,
   2522, 3469, 3743, 3745, 3749,
   **3821**, 4356, 4961, 4967, 5304
*The Moon and the Sun*  **3822**, 5152
*Nautilus*  **3823**
*Screwtop/The Girl Who Was Plugged
   In*  130
*The Search for Spock*  527, 1556
*Star Trek II: The Wrath of Khan*  526,
   1556
*Star Trek III: The Search for
   Spock*  1954
*Star Trek IV: The Voyage Home*  569,
   1556, 4273
*Starfarers*  107, 656, 732, 1559,
   1649, 1689, 1897, 2301, 2838,
   **3824**, 4696, 5188
*Superluminal*  181, 2838, 4349, 5985
*Transition*  81, 656, 1055, 1556,
   1645, 1897, 1992, 2048, 2491,
   2836, 3805, **3825**, 4505

**McKay, William**
*The Secret Peace*  3544

**McKee, Lynn Armistead**
*Woman of the Mists*  731, 2166, 2857

**McKenney, Kenneth**
*The Offspring*  **3826**

**McKenzie, Nancy**
*The Child Queen*  **3827**

**McKeone, Dixie**
*The Spider's Test*  2625

**McKeone, Dixie Lee**
*Greatheart*  2625
*The Sentinel*  3479

**McKeone, Lee**
*Backblast*  **3828**
*The Clone Crisis*  **3829**
*Starfire Down*  **3830**

**McKiernan, Dennis L.**
*Caverns of Socrates*  **3831**
*The Dark Tide*  710, /11, 716, 2884,
   2886
*Dragondoom*  28, 3578
*The Dragonstone*  844, **3832**
*The Eye of the Hunter*  **3833**, 5203
*Into the Fire*  **3834**
*Into the Forge*  **3835**
*Shadows of Doom*  710, 716
*Tales of Mithgar*  **3836**
*Voyage of the Fox Rider*  2271, **3837**

**McKillip, Patricia A.**
*The Book of Atrix Wolfe*  203, 1472,
   2354, 2538, 2653, 2654, 3070,
   3099, **3838**, 4105, 4211, 4908,
   5275, 6004, 6042
*The Changeling Sea*  1177, 1179,
   5293, 5629
*The Cygnet and the Firebird*  **3839**
*Fool's Run*  807, 1265, 2690, 5524
*The Forgotten Beasts of Eld*  727,
   4334
*Harpist in the Wind*  257, 2098,
   4265, 4727
*The House on Parchment Street*  122,
   1272, 2283, 2923, 4078, 4438
*Moon-Flash*  2647, 3404
*The Riddle-Master of Hed*  18, 185,
   409, 702, 978, 991, 1174, 1592,
   1660, 1682, 1688, 1690, 1814,
   1863, 1908, 2041, 2096, 2097,
   2263, 2361, 2471, 2504, 2506,
   2819, 2884, 2885, 2988, 3069,
   3122, 3154, 3171, 3401, 3414,
   3482, 3540, 3653, 3837, 3897,
   3939, 4446, 4448, 4457, 4528,
   4714, 4730, 5272, 5733, 5964,
   5983, 6002, 6003
*Something Rich and Strange*  1440,
   2088, 2981, 2982, **3840**, 5916
*Song for the Basilisk*  **3841**
*The Sorceress and the Cygnet*  1035,
   1734, **3842**
*Winter Rose*  153, 2957, **3843**, 3847,
   4358

**McKinley, Robin**
*Beauty*  3065, 5981
*The Blue Sword*  763, 2674, 2676,
   2796, 2819, 3871, 3973, 3975,
   4156, 4727, 5977
*Deerskin*  1358, **3844**, 5912
*The Hero and the Crown*  763, 2676,
   3412, 3941, 6037
*Imaginary Lands*  1340, 5239
*A Knot in the Grain and Other
   Stories*  **3845**
*The Outlaws of Sherwood*  2, 2247,
   2248, 2389, 3165, **3846**, 4519,
   4609
*Rose Daughter*  **3847**

**McKinney, Jack**
*Before the Invid Storm*  2432
*End of the Circle*  5204
*Free Radicals*  **3848**
*Hostile Takeover*  **3849**
*Kaduna Memories*  3771, **3850**

**McLaren, Teri**
*The Cursed Land*  2827

**McLaughlin, Dean**
*The Man Who Wanted Stars*  380,
   4511

**McLaughlin, Mark**
*Feeding the Glamour Hogs*  **3851**

**McMahan, Jeffrey N.**
*Somewhere in the Night*  2116, **3852**
*Vampires Anonymous*  1166, 2116,
   **3853**, 4069

**McMullen, Sean**
*The Centurion's Empire*  **3854**

**McNail, Stanley**
*Something Breathing*  4752

**McNair, Charles**
*Land O'Goshen*  **3855**

**McNally, Clare**
*Cries of the Children*  **3856**
*Good Night, Sweet Angel*  2609, **3857**

*Stage Fright* **3858**

**McNaughton, Brian**
*The Throne of Bones* **3859**

**McQuay, Mike**
*Escape From New York* 6059
*Hot Time in Old Town* 2916
*Jitterbug* 1060
*Lifekeeper* 1060
*Memories* 1305, 5195
*The Nexus* 1498, 1803, **3860**, 5101
*Richter 10* **1060**
*Suspicion* 78

**McQuinn, Donald E.**
*The Prisoner Within* **3861**
*Wanderer* **3862**
*Warrior* 208, 656, 720, 721, 1539, 3248, **3863**, 3873, 3999, 4000, 4001, 5574, 5743, 5965
*Witch* **3864**
*With Full Honors* **3865**, 5669, 5786

**McSherry, Frank Jr.**
*Civil War Ghosts* 5155

**McSherry, Frank D. Jr.**
*Civil War Ghosts* 2230, **2383**, 5098
*Eastern Ghosts* **3866**
*The Fantastic Civil War* 442, 443, **3867**, 4814, 5502
*Ghosts of the Heartland* **3868**
*Great American Ghost Stories* 2586, **3869**
*Hollywood Ghosts* 4252
*More Dixie Ghosts* 5098
*New England Ghosts* 4876
*Nightmares in Dixie* 2230, 5098, 5099, 5155
*Spooky Sea Stories* **5652**
*A Treasury of Great American Horror Stories* 2586, 3331
*Western Ghosts* 217, 3331, **3870**

**Meacham, Beth**
*Terry's Universe* 5045, 5046

**Meier, Shirley**
*The Cage* 1176, 4596, **5293**
*Saber & Shadow* **5297**
*Shadow's Daughter* 787, **3871**, 5297, 5299, 5684
*Shadow's Son* 787, **3872**, 5297, 5299

**Meluch, R.M.**
*Chicago Red* 208, 3863, **3873**
*The Queen's Squadron* 3722, 3749, **3874**, 5786
*War Birds* 1628, 2173, **3875**
*Wind Child* 3747, 4594

**Melville, Pauline**
*Shape-Shifter: Stories by Pauline Melville* 51, 2736, **3876**

**Meredith, Ann**
*Love Across Time* 1271

**Meredith, Richard**
*At the Narrow Passage* 1995, 2004
*Run, Come See Jerusalem* 5868
*Vestiges of Time* 2012

**Merle, Robert**
*The Day of the Dolphin* 2838

**Merril, Judith**
*5th Annual of the Year's Best S-F* 240
*6th Annual of the Year's Best S-F* 241
*7th Annual of the Year's Best S-F* 241
*8th Annual of the Year's Best S-F* 242
*9th Annual of the Year's Best S-F* 243
*The Best of Judith Merril* 448
*SF: 59, The Year's Greatest Science Fiction and Fantasy* 240
*Tesseracts* 4713

**Merritt, A.**
*Burn, Witch, Burn!* 1194, 2025
*Burn, Witch, Burn!/Creep, Shadow, Creep!* **3877**
*Dwellers in the Mirage* 4867, 5626
*The Face in the Abyss* **3878**, 5626
*The Moon Pool* 2257
*The Ship of Ishtar* 5496, 5626

**Merwin, Samuel**
*The House of Many Worlds* 264, 357, 1855

**Metcalfe, John**
*The Feasting Dead* 2111, 5423
*Nightmare Jack and Other Stories* **3879**, **3880**

**Metzger, Thom**
*Big Gurl* 2843, 3392

**Meyer, Nicholas**
*The Canary Trainer* 4773
*The Seven-Percent Solution* 4773

**Meyers, Ric**
*Fear Itself* 494, 612, 613, 614, 615, 696, **3881**, 5844
*Living Hell* 612, 613, 614, 615, **3882**
*Worst Nightmare* 612, 613, 615, **3883**

**Meyers, Roy**
*Dolphin Boy* 318

**Meynard, Yves**
*The Book of Knights* 369, **3884**

**Michael, David J.**
*Death Tour* 1625

**Michaels, Bill**
*Witchcraft* **3885**

**Michaels, Melisa**
*Cold Iron* 3264, **3886**, 5061
*Sister to the Rain* **3887**, 5061

**Michaels, Melisa C.**
*Far Harbor* 517, 3458, 3603, **3888**, 3929, 4482, 5524
*First Battle* 209, 1043, 1543, 2437
*Floater Factor* 4962
*Last War* 1043, 2435
*Pirate Prince* 1550, 5241
*Skirmish* 311, 356, 746, 1043, 1332, 1543, 1550, 1664, 2260, 2419, 2466, 4484, 4594, 4897, 5674

**Michelinie, David**
*Spider-Man: Carnage in New York* 1390

**Middleton, Richard**
*The Ghost Ship and Other Stories* 2712

**Miesel, Sandra**
*Shaman* **3889**, 5124, 5125, 5176

**Miklowitz, Gloria D.**
*Desperate Pursuit* 5287

**Milan, Victor**
*CLD* 1552
*The Cybernetic Samurai* 77, 79, 475, 806, 808, 1168, 2526, 2579, 3604, 3795, 4193, 4704, 5213, 5452
*The Cybernetic Shogun* **3890**
*Devil's Deal* **277**
*Turn of the Cards* 3642, 3647, **3891**, 5567
*War in Tethyr* 2675, 5022

**Miles, Bernard**
*Robin Hood: His Life and Legend* 2248, 2389, 4609

**Millard, Joseph**
*The Gods Hate Kansas* 1581

**Miller, Carl**
*The Goblin Plain War* **3892**
*The Warrior and the Witch* **3893**

**Miller, David C.**
*Contagion* **1136**

**Miller, Faren**
*The Illusionists* **3894**

**Miller, G. Wayne**
*Thunder Rise* 427, 577, 817, 911, 1297, 1886, 2251, 2340, 2903, 3081, 3680, 3778, **3895**, 4111, 4113, 4238, 4309, 4441, 5769, 6078

**Miller, John**
*First Power Play* 554, 827, 3036

**Miller, Rand**
*Myst: The Book of Atrus* **3896**
*Myst: The Book of D'ni* **3897**

**Miller, Rex**
*Butcher* **3898**
*Chaingang* **3899**
*Iceman* 3395, **3900**
*Savant* **3901**
*Slice* **3902**
*Slob* 1198, 2566, 2843, 3319, 3392, 5123

**Miller, Robyn**
*Myst: The Book of Atrus* **3896**

**Miller, Ron**
*Hearts and Armor* 3501, **3903**, 4871
*Palaces and Prisons* 980, **3904**
*Silk and Steel* 980, 2651, **3905**, 4490

**Miller, Sasha**
*Ladylord* **3906**

**Miller, Steve**
*Agent of Change* 1849, 4142, 4291, 4354, 4467, 4484, 4984, 5717
*Carpe Diem* 35, **3907**, 4142, 4291, 4354, 4467
*Conflict of Honors* 4142, 4291, 4354, 4467

**Miller, Walter M. Jr.**
*A Canticle for Leibowitz* 574, 724, 788, 4028, 4081, 4209, 4567, 4605, 4836, 5212, 5911
*Saint Leibowitz and the Wild Horse Woman* **3908**, 4835
*The Science Fiction Stories of Walter M. Miller, Jr.* 479, 4118, 5106, 5613

**Millhauser, Stephen**
*The Barnum Museum* 920
*In the Penny Arcade* 921

**Mills, C.J.**
*Brander's Book* 762, **3909**
*Egil's Book* **3910**
*Kit's Book* 1913, **3911**
*Winter World* 762, 1862, 5279
*Zjhanne's Book* **3912**

**Mills, Craig**
*The Floating Castle* **3913**, 4495
*Shadow of the Crown* **3914**

**Mills, Robert P.**
*The Best From Fantasy and Science Fiction: 9-11* 4712

**Milton, John**
*Paradise Lost* 4571

**Minns, Karen Marie Christa**
*Virago* 2242, 3579, **3915**

**Minsky, Marvin**
*The Turing Option* **2579**

**Mitchell, Betsy**
*Full Spectrum 3* **215**
*Full Spectrum 4* **216**

**Mitchell, Elizabeth**
*Alien Stars* 1627

**Mitchell, Ken**
*Stones of the Dalai Lama* **3916**

**Mitchell, Kirk**
*Cry Republic* 1955, **3917**
*Never the Twain* 5504
*Procurator* 590, 1955, 2140, 5036, 5503, 5511, 5512

**Mitchell, V.E.**
*Enemy Unseen* 569, 2552, **3918**
*Imbalance* **3919**
*Windows on a Lost World* **3920**

**Mitchison, Naomi**
*Memoirs of a Spacewoman* 2419

**Mittman, Stephanie**
*Bridge to Yesterday* 2497

**Mixon, Laura J.**
*Glass Houses* 231, 251, 294, 784, 2723, **3921**, 4077, 4708, 5362
*Proxies* **3922**

**Mizrich, Ben**
*Reaper* **3923**

**Modesitt, L.E. Jr.**
*Adiamante* **3924**
*The Chaos Balance* **3925**
*The Death of Chaos* **3926**
*The Ecolitan Enigma* **3927**
*The Ecolitan Operation* 3451, **3928**
*The Ecologic Envoy* 3451
*The Ecologic Secession* **3929**, 5717
*Fall of Angels* **3930**
*The Ghost of the Revelator* **3931**
*The Green Progression* **3932**
*The Hammer of Darkness* 5930
*The Magic Engineer* **3933**
*The Magic of Recluce* 712, 1096, 1905, **3934**
*Of Tangible Ghosts* 682, **3935**
*The Order War* 1180, **3936**, 6004
*The Parafaith War* **3937**
*The Soprano Sorceress* **3938**
*The Spellsong War* **3939**
*Timediver's Dawn* **3940**
*The Towers of the Sunset* 1674, 1741, 2677, **3941**, 3969, 4150, 5735
*The White Order* **3942**

**Moesta, Rebecca**
*Trouble on Cloud City* **117**

**Moffett, Judith**
*Pennterra* 211, 2897, 3249, 4552, 5092
*The Ragged World: A Novel of the Hefn on Earth* **3943**
*Time, Like an Ever-Rolling Stream* **3944**
*Two That Came True* 1428, 3185, 3237, **3945**, 4355, 6068

**Moffitt, Donald**
*Crescent in the Sky* **3946**
*A Gathering of Stars* **3947**

**Mohan, Kim**
*Amazing Stories: The Anthology* 1023, 2148, **3948**, 4439, 5489
*More Amazing Stories* 3949

**Mohr, Clifford**
*Requiem* 2204, 2823, **3950**, 4239, 4646

**Moloney, Susan**
*A Dry Spell* 3951

**Molstad, Stephen**
*Independence Day* **1508**
*Silent Zone* 3952

**Monaco, Richard**
*The Grail War* 273
*Parsifal* 3356

**Monahan, Brent**
*The Bell Witch: An American Haunting* 3953
*Blood of the Covenant* 3954, 5290
*The Book of Common Dread* 660, 2259, 2994, 3113, **3955**, 4050
*The Uprising* 2285, 2903, **3956**, 4586, 4754

**Monette, Paul**
*Predator* 492, 1483

**Monteleone, Elizabeth**
*Borderlands 4* **3962**

**Monteleone, Thomas F.**
*Between Floors* 2157, **3957**
*The Blood of the Lamb* 751, 1507, 1721, 2150, 2318, 2700, **3958**, 4050, 4073
*Borderlands* **3959**, 4724, 4726
*Borderlands 1* 1847
*Borderlands 2* **3960**, 4278
*Borderlands 3* 3598, **3961**, 4206, 5795
*Borderlands 4* **3962**, 4722
*The Borderlands Series* 2306, 5855
*Fantasma* **3963**
*Lyrica* 4236, 4569
*The Magnificent Gallery* 1282, 2303, 2565, 4010
*Night of Broken Souls* **3964**
*Night Things* 3054
*The Resurrectionist* 1507, 2304, 2824, **3965**, 4073

**Montgomery, R.A.**
*Traitors from Within* **3966**

**Montrose, Catherine**
*Wendigo Border* 3119, **3967**, 5249

**Moon, Elizabeth**
*The Deed of Paksenarrion* 4693, 4694, 5529
*Divided Allegiance* 962, 1156, 1702, 1737, 1738, 3069, 3892, 3903, 5739, 5740, 5742
*Generation Warrior* **3735**
*Hunting Party* 1542, **3968**, 5671, 5966
*Liar's Oath* 2677, 3282, 3941, **3969**, 4150, 4488, 4489, 4986
*Lunar Activity* 6005
*Oath of Gold* 962, 1101, 1156, 1737, 1738, 3069, 3077, 3892, 3903, 4490, 5714, 5739, 5740, 5742
*Once a Hero* 1046, 2432, **3970**, 5669
*Phases* 2027, 3279, **3971**
*Remnant Population* 622, 988, 997, 1695, 1825, 2135, 3732, **3972**, 4119, 4187, 4856, 5437, 5872

*Sassinak* **3748**
*Sheepfarmer's Daughter* 11, 18, 631, 936, 962, 994, 1110, 1143, 1156, 1253, 1674, 1675, 1732, 1737, 1738, 1815, 2031, 2195, 2457, 2639, 2985, 3069, 3273, 3295, 3296, 3297, 3508, 3513, 3624, 3627, 3892, 3903, 3904, 3934, 3941, **3973**, 4924, 5202, 5296, 5333, 5509, 5650, 5678, 5739, 5740, 5742, 5790, 5962, 5963
*Sporting Chance* 2766, **3974**
*Surrender None: The Legacy of Gird* 673, 936, 1156, 3105, 3510, 3539, 3846, 3904, 3934, **3975**, 4167, 4802, 4806, 5507, 5712, 5790, 5819, 6082
*Winning Colors* **3976**

**Moorcock, Michael**
*An Alien Heat* 326, 3106
*The Bane of the Black Sword* 5648
*Behold the Man* 1305, 5195, 5569
*Blood: A Southern Fantasy* 2304, **3977**
*The Chronicles of Corum* 1240
*Corum: The Coming of Chaos* 3418, **3978**
*The Dancers at the End of Time* **3979**, 4247
*Elric of Melnibone* 1102, 1173, 1174, 1178, 1181, 1241, 1637, 1648, 1754, 1881, 1927, 1928, 2529, 2885, 3227, 3419, 3420, 4109, 5408, 5683
*Elric: Song of the Black Sword* **3980**
*Fabulous Harbors* **3981**
*The Final Programme* 1879
*The Fireclown* 1879
*The Fortress of the Pearl* 1422, 1470, **3982**, 4515, 4777
*Gloriana, or the Unfulfilled Queen* 2262, 5547
*The Ice Schooner* 511
*Kane of Old Mars* **3983**
*Lunching with the Antichrist* **3984**
*New Worlds 5* 2148
*New Worlds Quarterly Number 1- 4* 2148
*The Revenge of the Rose* **3985**, 4777, 5650, 5736, 5740
*The Runestaff* 1635
*Sailor on the Seas of Fate* 5648
*Stormbringer* 2781
*The Swords Trilogy* 1147, 1961, 3358
*The War Amongst the Angels* **3986**, 4178
*The Warlord of the Air* 1655

**Moore, Alan**
*From Hell* **3987**

**Moore, C.L.**
*The Best of C.L. Moore* 790, 3219, 5047
*Jirel of Joiry* 644, 649, 650, 651, 2072, 2074, 2360, 2651, 3290, 3418, 3634, 3906, 4161, 4162, 4520, 4610, 4871, 5220, 5383
*Judgment Night* 5645
*Northwest Smith* 1069

**Moore, Christopher**
*Bloodsucking Fiends: A Love Story* 1800, 1802, 2449, **3988**, 4069, 5062
*Practical Demonkeeping* 617, 867, 868, 869, 1917, 2519, 3483, 3488, **3989**, 4317, 4395, 4396, 5168, 5324

**Moore, James A.**
*Hell-Storm* **3990**, 4059
*The House of Secrets* 798, 5703

**Moore, John**
*Slay and Rescue* 262, 557, 559, 1208, 1512, 2079, 2080, 2803, 3810, **3991**, 4945, 5219, 5649, 6049, 6066

**Moore, Roger E.**
*The Maelstrom's Eye* 1291, 2785

**Moore, Stanley R.**
*Nightshade* **3992**

**Moore, Ward**
*Bring the Jubilee* 442, 443, 2043, 2563, 2577, 3867, **3993**, 4814, 5502
*Joyleg* 5232

**Moran, Daniel Keys**
*The Armageddon Blues* 1880, 5621
*Emerald Eyes* 733, 1933, 1934, 4504, 5039, 5621, 5907
*The Last Dancer* **3994**
*The Long Run* 361, 733, 768, **3995**, 4451, 5039, 5621

**Moran, Thomas**
*The World I Made for Her* **3996**

**Morey, Joe**
*Glimring Night and Other Tales of Fantasy* **3997**

**Morgan, Chris**
*Dark Fantasies* 2306, 3961, 4206, 4644, 5795

**Morgan, J.M.**
*Between the Devil and the Deep* 88, 189, 441, 1346, 3232, **3998**, 5877
*Beyond Eden* 278, **3999**
*Desert Eden* 656, 1482, 1566, 1568, 1932, 2328, 2999, 3429, 3862, **4000**, 5433, 5592, 5743
*Future Eden* 1569, **4001**

**Morgan, Jill**
*Great Writers and Kids Write Spooky Stories* **2395**

**Morgan, Robert**
*All Things under the Moon* **4002**, 5085
*The Only Thing to Fear* **4003**, 5989
*Some Things Come Back* **4004**
*Some Things Never Die* 1335, 2288, **4005**
*The Thing That Darkness Hides* 3294, **4006**
*The Things That Are Not There* 751, 2749, **4007**, 5773

**Morgan, Robin**
*The Mer-Child: A Legend for Children and Other Adults* 1356, 3378, 3816, **4008**, 4171, 4447, 6089

**Morlan, A.R.**
*The Amulet* 1834, **4009**
*Dark Journey* 2565, **4010**

**Moroz, Anne**
*No Safe Place* 3748, 4285

**Morr, Kenyon**
*Kingdom of Sorrow* 5357
*See No Weevil* 5357

**Morrell, David**
*Testament* 3658, 5844
*Testament: The Unpublished Prologues* **4011**
*The Totem* **4012**

**Morressy, John**
*Kedrigern and the Charming Couple* 3811, **4013**, 4316
*Kedrigern in Wanderland* 5337
*The Mansions of Space* 3617
*The Questing of Kedrigern* 1677, 2622
*A Remembrance for Kedrigern* **4014**

**Morris, Chris**
*City at the Edge of Time* **4015**
*The Stalk* **4016**
*Threshold* **4018**
*Trust Territory* **4019**

**Morris, Janet**
*Arc Riders* **1626**
*Beyond Sanctuary* 289
*Beyond the Veil* 4202
*Beyond Wizardwall* 4202
*City at the Edge of Time* 2502, **4015**, 4202, 4614
*Cruiser Dreams* 5524
*Dream Dancer* 209, 5524
*Earth Dreams* 5524
*The Fourth Rome* **1631**
*Heroes in Hell* 1280, 1626, 1631, 4388, 4605, 4655, 4869
*The High Couch of Silistra* 1071
*The Stalk* **4016**
*Target* **4017**, 5129, 5787, 5932
*Tempus* 4202
*Tempus Bound* 4201
*Threshold* 1626, **4018**
*Trust Territory* **4019**

**Morris, Kenneth**
*The Chalchiuhite Dragon* 3107, **4020**
*The Dragon Path: Collected Tales of Kenneth Morris* 2680, **4021**
*The Secret Mountain and Other Tales* 3147, 5310

**Morris, Mark**
*Close to the Bone* 775, 2018
*The Horror Club* **4022**
*The Immaculate* 3525, 3809, **4023**, 5530
*Stitch* 1354, **4024**
*Toady* 5398
*Voyages into Darkness* 3363

**Morris, William**
*Golden Wings and Other Stories* 1699

**Morris, Winifred**
*With Magical Horses to Ride* 5559

**Morrish, Robert**
*Quick Chills II* 300, 1017, 2773, 2962, **4025**, 4199, 5025, 5095, 5601
*The Quick Chills Series* 1372, 3997, 5606

**Morrison, Greg**
*The Crystal Sorcerers* 1979

**Morrison, Robert**
*The Vampyre and Other Tales of the Macabre* 4026

**Morrow, Bradford**
*The New Gothic* 307, 1351, **4027**, 4180

**Morrow, James**
*Bible Stories for Adults* 497, 1758, 3908, 3986, **4028**
*Blameless in Abaddon* 3986, **4029**
*City of Truth* 1727, 2338, **4030**
*The Continent of Lies* 583
*Nebula Awards 26* 1620, **4031**, 4822, 4823, 5871

*Nebula Awards 26-28*   1342, 2401, 4824

*Nebula Awards 27*   216, 1365, 1622, **4032**, 4822, 4823

*Nebula Awards 28*   1617, **4033**, 4822, 4823

*Only Begotten Daughter*   433, 1165, 1506, 1817, 1877, 2196, 2249, 3084, 3311, 3480, 3542, 3627, 3860, **4034**, 4567, 5195, 5277, 5616, 5911, 5958

*This Is the Way the World Ends*   95

*Towing Jehovah*   1577, 2327, 3986, **4035**

**Morrow, W.C.**
*The Ape, the Idiot, and Other People*   485, 963, 1243, 1597

**Morse, David**
*The Iron Bridge*   298, **4036**

**Mortimore, Jim**
*Clark's Law*   367, 1387, 1654, 3096, 4833, 5598

**Morwood, Peter**
*High Moon*   **1661**
*The Horse Lord*   223, 1731, 1736, 2397, 2673, 2678
*Kill Station*   **1664**
*Mindblast*   **1665**
*Rules of Engagement*   569, 1954, **4037**, 4514
*seaQuest DSV: The Novel*   **1666**

**Moscoe, Mike**
*First Dawn*   **4038**, 5496
*Lost Days*   **4039**
*Second Fire*   2043, **4040**

**Mosiman, Billie Sue**
*Death in Dixie*   5098, 5099
*Night Cruise*   570, 2313, **4041**, 5853

**Moskowitz, Sam**
*Ghostly by Gaslight*   39
*Great Untold Stories of Fantasy and Horror*   38, 39
*Hauntings and Horrors*   1712
*Horrors Unknown*   1712
*Masters of Horror*   1712
*Science Fiction by Gaslight*   39, 1712, 5746
*The Time Curve*   3459

**Mosley, Walter**
*Blue Light*   **4042**

**Mrozek, Slawomir**
*The Elephant*   2641

**Mudd, Steve**
*The Planet Beyond*   **4043**
*Tangled Webs*   **4044**

**Mula, Tom**
*Jacob Marley's Christmas Carol*   4861

**Mullen, Patricia**
*The Stone Movers*   **4045**, 4107, 4110, 4795

**Mulock, Diana**
*The Adventures of a Brownie as Told to My Child*   2438

**Munby, A.N.L.**
*The Alabaster Hand and Other Ghost Stories*   456, 1350, 2905, 5611

**Mundy, Talbot**
*Queen Cleopatra*   2073
*Tros of Samothrace*   2073

**Munn, H. Warner**
*The Werewolf of Ponkert*   4002, 4702, 5146, 5425, 5481

**Murakami, Haruki**
*Dance Dance Dance*   **4046**
*Hard-Boiled Wonderland and the End of the World*   2186, 3263, **4047**

**Murchison, Myles**
*The Deathless*   **4048**

**Murdock, M.S.**
*Armageddon Off Vesta*   554, 3036
*Hammer of Mars*   554, 3036, **4049**
*Prime Squared*   554, 827, 3036
*Rebellion 2456*   554, 827, 3036
*Web of the Romulans*   528

**Murphy, Mary Elizabeth**
*Virgin*   2994, 3607, **4050**

**Murphy, Pat**
*The City, Not Long After*   43, 46, 323, 334, 335, 496, 547, 551, 721, 766, 792, 820, 919, 2028, 2219, 2706, 2998, 3046, 3084, 3449, 4030, **4051**, 4104, 4325, 4360, 4474, 4631, 4750, 5209, 5268, 5592, 5909, 5911, 6009
*The Falling Woman*   351, 744, 1272, 4332, 5477, 5806
*Nadya: The Wolf Chronicles*   572, 680, 2029, 3119, **4052**, 4764
*Points of Departure*   790, 819, 1431, 1818, 1827, 2106, 2265, 2537, 2715, 3235, 3279, 3379, 3384, 3736, **4053**, 4878, 5058, 5165, 5410, 5521, 5615, 5641, 5805
*Rachel in Love*   1525

**Murphy, Shirley Rousseau**
*Cats Raise the Dead*   **4054**
*The Catswold Portal*   1657, 2358, 3120, **4055**, 5143
*Medallion of the Black Hound*   192, 2505, 2879, **4056**, 5070, 5182
*Nightpool*   4485, 4490, 4493
*The Ring of Fire*   4608

**Murphy, Warren**
*The Broken Sword*   **1091**
*Destiny's Carnival*   **4057**, 5264
*The Forever King*   **1092**
*World Without End*   **1093**

**Murray, Doug**
*Blood Relations*   2664, **4058**
*Call to Battle*   3990, **4059**, 5701, 5702

**Murray, Earl**
*The Quiet*   **488**

**Murray, Will**
*The Frightened Fish*   **4622**
*The Jade Ogre*   **4623**
*Python Isle*   **4624**
*White Eyes*   **4625**

**Murrill, Ray W.**
*War Dogs of the Golden Horde*   205

**Mustard, Helen M.**
*Parzival: A Romance of the Middle Ages*   5015

**Myers, Bill**
*Threshold*   **4060**

**Myers, Edward**
*Fire and Ice*   1169, 4020, **4061**, 5033
*The Mountain Made of Light*   1105, 3592, 3878, 4020, **4062**, 4207, 5033, 5037, 5396
*The Summit*   **4063**

**Myers, Gary**
*The House of the Worm*   925, 3555, 3859, 5102, 5103, 5471

**Myers, John Myers**
*Silverlock*   1856, 5178

**Myers, Walter Dean**
*Brainstorm*   1878

## N

**Nabokov, Vladimir**
*Pale Fire*   4263

**Nader, George**
*Chrome*   3029

**Nagata, Linda**
*The Bohr Maker*   2274, 2559, 3241, 3453, **4064**
*Deception Well*   2274, 2558, **4065**
*Tech-Heaven*   158, 581, 2498, **4066**
*Vast*   **4067**

**Naha, Ed**
*Robocop*   829, 830, 831, 1406, 3665, 4229, 5476
*Robocop 2*   366, 829, 830, 831, 5476

**Nance, Kathleen**
*Wishes Come True*   73, 880

**Nasaw, Jonathan**
*Shadows*   **4068**
*The World on Blood*   345, 600, 812, 1541, 2449, **4069**, 4445

**Nasir, Jamil**
*The Higher Space*   199, 2273, **4070**
*Quasar*   **4071**

**Navarro, Yvonne**
*Afterage*   301, **4072**
*Deadrush*   1507, **4073**
*Final Impact*   400
*Music of the Spears*   4285
*Red Shadows*   **4074**
*Species*   **4075**, 4224

**Naylor, Doug**
*Better than Life*   **4076**
*Red Dwarf: Infinity Welcomes Careful Drivers*   **4077**

**Naylor, Grant**
*Better than Life*   **4076**
*Red Dwarf: Infinity Welcomes Careful Drivers*   3313, **4077**

**Naylor, Phyllis Reynolds**
*Bernie and the Bessledorf Ghost*   2923, 2951, **4078**, 4438
*The Witch Returns*   **4079**
*The Witch's Eye*   **4080**, 4275

**Neason, Rebecca**
*Guises of the Mind*   2922, **4081**, 5880
*Shadow of Obsession*   **4082**

**Necker, Claire**
*Supernatural Cats*   1369, 3145, 5252

**Neiderman, Andrew**
*After Life*   **4083**
*The Dark*   **4084**
*Dawn*   144
*The Devil's Advocate*   **4085**
*Duplicates*   **4086**
*Gates of Paradise*   145
*The Immortals*   3139, **4087**
*In Double Jeopardy*   **4088**
*The Need*   **4089**
*Perfect Little Angels*   2205, **4090**, 4839, 4840, 5789
*Secrets of the Morning*   146

*Sister, Sister*   70, **4091**
*Web of Dreams*   147

**Neill, John Rea**
*The Wonder City of Oz*   3609

**Nesbit, E.**
*Five Children and It*   5968
*The House of Arden*   4585
*In the Dark*   4968, 5763, 5764, 5765
*The Magic World*   3587
*Story of the Amulet*   332

**Neville, Katherine**
*The Eight*   **4092**, 4983

**Neville, Kris**
*Bettyann*   1595

**Nevins, Linda**
*Renaissance Moon*   637, 2540, **4093**

**Newman, Kim**
*Anno Dracula*   292, 303, 659, 1139, 1518, 2511, 2692, 2741, 2742, 3005, 3564, 3596, 3631, **4094**, 4773, 5192, 5693, 5704, 6019
*Back in the USSA*   25, 1516, **4095**
*Bad Dreams*   265, 284, 660, 3267, 3808, **4096**, 5020, 5988, 6050
*The Bloody Red Baron*   1686, 2742, **4097**, 4755, 6019
*Comeback Tour: The Sky Belongs to the Stars*   6020
*Demon Download*   6021
*Drachenfels*   6022
*Famous Monsters*   2018
*Jago*   2312, 3310, 4024, 4587
*Judgment of Tears: Anno Dracula 1959*   **4098**
*Krokodil Tears*   6023
*The Night Mayor*   1615, 2470, 2839, 3559, **4099**, 4135, 5614
*The Original Dr. Shade and Other Stories*   5339
*The Quorum*   2652, 4085, **4100**
*Sago*   5189

**Newman, Sharan**
*The Chessboard Queen*   1857, 5970, 5971
*Guinevere*   224, 2939, 3827, 5970, 5971
*Guinevere Evermore*   5970, 5971

**Nichols, Nichelle**
*Saturn's Child*   568, **4101**

**Nickle, David**
*The Claus Effect*   1506

**Nickles, Jason**
*Immortal*   3051, **4102**

**Nighbert, David F.**
*The Clouds of Magellan*   2836, **4103**

**Nightingale, Steven**
*The Thirteenth Daughter of the Moon*   **4104**

**Niles, Douglas**
*A Breach in the Watershed*   1484, 2924, 2925, 3095, **4105**, 4794, 4908
*The Coral Kingdom*   **4106**
*Darkenheight*   **4107**, 4795
*Darkwalker on Moonshae*   2618, 4803
*Deathwalker on Moonshea*   4805
*The Dragons*   5708
*Emperor of Ansalon*   4925
*Feathered Dragon*   2675, **4108**
*Ironhelm*   3121
*The Kinslayer Wars*   **4109**, 5454, 5455
*Pawns Prevail*   299

*War of the Three Waters* **4110**

**Niles, Steve**
*Saturday Mourning Fly in My Eye* 346

**Niswander, Adam**
*The Charm* 911, 1886, 2340, 3081, 3671, 3680, 3967, **4111**, 4238, 4309, 5053, 5249, 6078
*The Sand Dwellers* **4112**, 4449
*The Serpent Slayers* **4113**

**Niven, Larry**
*Achilles' Choice* 360, 362, 1108, 3454, 4114, **4188**, 5174
*The Barsoom Project* **4115**
*Beowulf's Children* **4116**
*The California Voodoo Game* 1980, **4117**
*Crashlander* **4118**
*Destiny's Road* 2289, 3739, 3819, **4119**, 4999
*Dream Park* 360, 971, 975
*Fallen Angels* 553, 597, 677, 735, 1543, 1805, 1921, 1962, 2301, 2567, 2568, 3313, 3429, 3932, **4120**, 4546, 4639, 4641, 5209, 5499, 5697
*Flatlander* 4066, **4121**
*The Flight of the Horse* 131, 135, 1255, 1752, 3191, 4195, 4198, 5351, 5497, 5956
*Footfall* 108, 205, 414, 1057, 1258, 1508, 2646, 3429, 3944, 4281, 4301, 4760, 4775, 4858, 4919, 5516, 5517, 5677, 5866
*A Gift from Earth* 877
*The Gripping Hand* 990, 997, 1586, 1606, 1989, 3726, **4122**, 5778
*Inferno* 960, 2574
*The Integral Trees* 132, 401, 1897, 1986, 1991, 2289, 3050, 3770, 4957, 5233, 5526
*The Legacy of Heorot* 2210, 2211, 2491, 4884, 5016, 5431
*The Long Arm of Gil Hamilton* 585, 2527
*Lucifer's Hammer* 82, 108, 248, 354, 1057, 2296, 3429, 3772, 4000, 4947, 5242, 5295
*The Magic Goes Away* 1299, 1532, 2461, 4460, 4743, 5974
*Man-Kzin Wars* 828, 1158, 1535, 1627, 3649, 4372, 4373, 5917
*Man-Kzin Wars II* 828, 1158, 4372
*Man-Kzin Wars II-VII* 3649
*Man-Kzin Wars III* **4123**, 4372
*Man-Kzin Wars IV* 4103, **4124**, 4372
*Man-Kzin Wars V* **4125**
*The Mote in God's Eye* 132, 248, 296, 418, 1001, 1158, 1184, 1557, 1630, 1646, 1650, 1929, 2008, 2062, 2352, 3475, 3821, 4019, 4187, 4356, 5292, 5575, 5679
*N-Space* 123, 161, 237, 244, 349, 585, 2490, 2576, 2648, 3187, **4126**, 4953, 5345, 5480, 5551, 5938
*Neutron Star* 447, 4357, 4706, 4961, 5305
*Oath of Fealty* 585, 2349
*The Patchwork Girl* 585, 4470
*Playgrounds of the Mind* 237, 2648, 3648, **4127**, 5480, 5938
*Protector* 132, 596, 688, 1001, 1055, 1259, 1261, 1264, 1726, 1987, 1990, 2108, 2649, 2828, 2836, 2864, 3469, 3994, 4103, 4351, 5059, 5244

*Ringworld* 132, 417, 961, 1001, 1876, 1980, 2332, 2828, 4103, 5069, 5304, 5597
*Ringworld Engineers* 417, 2828, 3994
*The Ringworld Throne* **4128**
*The Smoke Ring* 1897, 1991, 2289, 3770, 5000
*Tales of Known Space* 129, 233, 234, 479, 1608, 1874, 2828, 3308, 3771, 4346, 4372, 4706, 4953, 4961, 5106, 5349, 5369, 5574
*A World out of Time* 445, 1053, 3924

**Nix, Garth**
*Sabriel* 68, 1868, 2654, **4129**
*Shade's Children* 2837, **4130**

**Nixon, Joan Lowery**
*Don't Scream* 5285
*The Stalker* 1801

**Noel, Atanielle Annyn**
*The Duchess of Kneedeep* 5550
*Murder on Usher's Planet* 4470
*Speaker to Heaven* 2286

**Nolan, Ted**
*Hell on High* **3483**

**Nolan, William F.**
*Blood Sky* 4255
*The Bradbury Chronicles: Stories in Honor of Ray Bradbury* 2398, 3689, **4131**, 6077
*Helltracks* 1489
*Logan's Run* 574, 4835
*Night Shapes: Excursions into Terror* 3216, 3686, 3687, **4132**, 5901
*Things Beyond Midnight* 532, 2281, 3683, 5854, 5857, 5885
*Urban Horrors* **4133**, 4212
*William F. Nolan's Logan: A Trilogy* 1449

**Noon, Jeff**
*Automated Alice* **4134**
*Pollen* **4135**
*Vurt* **4136**, 4703, 4732

**Norman, Howard**
*Northern Tales: Traditional Stories of Eskimo and Indian Peoples* 40, 190, 5578

**Norman, John**
*Magicians of Gor* 4294

**Norman, Lisanne**
*Fire Margins* 3718, **4137**
*Fortune's Wheel* **4138**
*Razor's Edge* **4139**
*Turning Point* 983, **4140**, 5404, 5525

**North, Eric**
*The Ant Men* 5755

**Northcote, Amyas**
*In Ghostly Company* **4141**

**Norton, Andre**
*The Beast Master* 431, 1070, 1437, 1951, 2552, 3583, 5545, 5759
*Black Trillium* 630
*The Book of Andre Norton* 823
*Breed to Come* 4054
*Brother to Shadows* 1598, 1602, **4142**, 4228, 5138
*Catfantastic* 1369, 1895, 2413, 3377, 3500, 3740, 4273, 4543, 5252
*Catfantastic II* 2413, **4143**, 4543, 5252

*Catfantastic III* **4144**
*Catfantastic IV* **4145**
*Catseye* 983, 1657, 2420, 4138
*Ciara's Song* **4146**
*The Crossroads of Time* 1626, 2119, 3993, 5996
*The Crystal Gryphon* 658, 5002
*Dare to Go A-Hunting* **4147**
*Dark Piper* 4801
*Daybreak, 2250 A.D.* 3788
*The Defiant Agents* 1011
*Derelict for Trade* **4148**
*Dragon Magic* 187, 4996
*Dread Companion* 169, 3259
*The Elvenbane* 457, 711, 1114, 1951, 1984, 2650, 2985, 3481, 3508, **4149**, 4174, 4615, 4675, 5556, 6024
*Elvenblood* 2650, 2678, 3045, 3065, 3292, 3295, 3728, 3936, **4150**, 4321, 4461, 4527, 4794
*Firehand* **4151**
*Flight in Yiktor* 3625
*Flight of Vengeance* **4152**
*Forerunner* 4592
*Galactic Derelict* 5113
*The Gate of the Cat* 638
*Gates to Tomorrow: An Introduction to Science Fiction* 5238
*Golden Trillium* 641, 3700, **4153**
*The Hands of Lyr* 1706, **4154**
*Here Abide Monsters* 196, 3800, 4595
*Horn Crown* 4269
*Ice Crown* 632, 3747
*Imperial Lady* 69, 1104, 3338, 3339, **4155**, 5014, 5015
*The Jekyll Legacy* **535**
*Judgment on Janus* 2372
*The Key of the Keplian* **4156**
*The Last Planet* 3727
*Lavender-Green Magic* 2992, 3436
*Lord of Thunder* 1437
*The Mark of the Cat* 3740, **4157**
*Merlin's Mirror* 459, 5534
*A Mind for Trade* **4158**
*Mirror of Destiny* **4159**, 5200
*Moon of Three Rings* 4055
*No Night Without Stars* 4619
*Octagon Magic* 2943
*On Wings of Magic* 3906
*Operation Time Search* 1011
*Ordeal in Otherwhere* 1265, 5752
*Quest Crosstime* 1011
*Red Hart Magic* 464
*Redline the Stars* **4160**
*Sargasso of Space* 3125, 5549
*The Sioux Space Man* 431, 3583
*Songsmith* 1430, **4161**
*Sorceress of the Witch World* 638, 3696
*Space Pioneers* 5247
*Star Born* 3769
*Star Gate* 3801, 5306, 6060
*Star Guard* 1628
*The Stars Are Ours* 2764, 4964
*Storms of Victory* **4162**
*Tiger Burning Bright* **652**
*The Time Traders* 5499
*Voodoo Planet* 1719
*Voorloper* 2437
*The Warding of Witch World* **4163**
*'Ware Hawk* 638
*Warlock of the Witch World* 4782
*Witch World* 219, 562, 2819, 3650, 4783
*The X Factor* 2764, 2810
*The Year of the Unicorn* 355

**Norton, Mary**
*The Borrowers* 1132, 1558, 4386, 4402, 4403, 6006
*The Borrowers Afield* 4386, 4402
*The Borrowers Afloat* 4386, 4402
*The Borrowers Aloft* 4402, 4403

**Norwood, Warren**
*Stranded!* 141, 1563, **4164**
*Trapped!* 141, 1563
*Vanished* 141, 143, 1563, 3428, 5012

**Nourse, Alan E.**
*The Fourth Horseman* 1625, 5081

**Novak, Kate**
*Azure Bonds* 4106, 4108
*Finder's Bane* **4165**
*Masquerades* **4166**
*Song of the Saurials* 2426, **4167**, 4806
*The Wyvern's Spur* 2426

**Nowlan, Philip Francis**
*Armageddon 2419 A.D.* 554, 827, 3036, 4049

**Nutman, Philip**
*Wet Work* **4168**, 4745, 4746, 5313

**Nye, Jody Lynn**
*Crisis on Doona* 3723
*The Death of Sleep* 3727
*Don't Forget Your Spacesuit, Dear* **4169**, 5617
*Higher Mythology* 1842, **4170**
*The Magic Touch* **4171**, 4864
*Medicine Show* **4172**, 4195, 4196, 4198, 5778
*Mythology 101* 235, 1471, 2438, 3910, **4173**, 4435
*Mythology Abroad* 1668, **4174**, 4863, 5379
*The Ship Errant* **4175**
*The Ship Who Won* 3750
*Taylor's Ark* 2443, 3752, 3968, 4176, 4195, 4196, 4198, 5777, 5778, 5780
*Treaty at Doona* 3752
*Waking in Dreamland* 2688, **4177**

**Nye, Robert**
*Merlin* 3806

**Nylund, Eric S.**
*Dry Water* 1089, 5817
*A Game of Universe* **4178**
*Signal to Noise* **4179**, 5353

# O

**Oates, Joyce Carol**
*American Gothic Tales* 1314, **4180**, 5439
*Bellefleur* 145, 147, 340, 1300, 2115
*The Collector of Hearts: New Tales of the Grotesque* 3195, **4181**
*Demon and Other Tales* **4182**
*First Love: A Gothic Tale* **4183**
*Haunted: Tales of the Grotesque* 921, 2842, **4184**, 5166, 5417
*Mysteries of Winterhurn* 5330
*Night-Side: Eighteen Tales* 626, 2641
*Zombie* 2755, 3002, **4185**, 5326

**O'Barr, James**
*The Crow: Shattered Lives and Broken Dreams* 494, 696, 1044, **4186**, 5844

Author Index

**Oberndorf, Charles**
*Foragers* **4187**
*Sheltered Lives* 574, **4188**, 4478, 5592

**Oboler, Arch**
*The Oboler Omnibus* 339, 344, 1022, 1112

**O'Brien, Fitz-James**
*The Supernatural Tales of Fitz-James O'Brien* 2633

**O'Brien, Flann**
*The Third Policeman* 982, 1002

**O'Brien, Robert C.**
*Mrs. Frisby and the Rats of NIMH* 1090, 1132, 1527, 2853
*Z for Zachariah* 3584, 3608

**O'Callaghan, Maxine**
*Dark Time* 1296, 3218, 3856, **4189**, 4650

**Odom, Mel**
*Blade* **4190**
*F.R.E.E.Lancers* **4191**
*Headhunters* **4192**
*Lethal Interface* **4193**, 4300, 4893, 4901, 4902, 5576
*Preying for Keeps* 3198
*Stranded!* **4164**

**O'Donnell, Elliott**
*Ghosts: Stories of the Supernatural* 2543
*Haunted and Hunted* 2905
*Strange Disappearances* 2543

**O'Donnell, Kevin Jr.**
*Fire on the Border* 1103, **4194**

**O'Donohoe, Nick**
*The Healing of Crossroads* **4195**
*The Magic and the Healing* **4196**
*Too, Too Solid Flesh* **4197**
*Under the Healing Sign* **4198**

**Oestreicher, Joy**
*Air Fish* 300, **4199**, 5095, 5447
*Alpha Gallery* 3997, **4200**, 5095

**Offutt, Andrew J.**
*Ardor on Aros* 3543
*The Castle Keeps* 4600
*Deathknight* **4201**
*King Dragon* 4592, 4595
*My Lord Barbarian* 5197, 5645
*The Shadow of Sorcery* **4202**
*The Sign of the Moonbow* 5962, 5963
*Sword of the Gael* 1960, 2572, 3358, 3501, 3504, 3506, 4266, 4267, 4268, 5962, 5963
*The Tower of Death* 5963
*The Undying Wizard* 5962, 5963
*When Death Birds Fly* 1960, 5963

**O'Griofa, Martin**
*Irish Tales of the Supernatural* **4203**

**O'Hearn, Marian**
*Soldiers of the Black Goat* 2442

**Ohlander, Ben**
*Enemy of My Enemy* **4204**

**O'Keefe, Claudia**
*Black Snow Days* **4205**
*Ghosttide* 2233, 3598, 3961, **4206**, 4644, 5331, 5795

**O'Keefe, Daniel**
*The Book of Famous Irish Ghost Stories* 4203

**Okri, Ben**
*The Famished Road* 1411, 1412, 1433, 1438, 1867, 1868, 2735, 2771, 3006, 3007, 3173, **4207**, 4358, 4544, 5273, 5578
*Songs of Enchantment* 1867, 1868, 3006, **4208**

**Olan, Susan Torian**
*The Earth Remembers* **4209**

**Olander, Joseph D.**
*School and Society Through Science Fiction* 6027

**O'Leary, Patrick**
*Door Number Three* 568, 3597, **4210**, 4333
*The Gift* **4211**

**Oleck, Jack**
*Tales From the Crypt* 2403, 5473

**Olesker, Jack**
*Confessional* 5342

**Oliphant, Margaret**
*Stories of the Seen and Unseen* 4969

**Oliver, Chad**
*Another Kind* 59, 3876
*The Edge of Forever* 59
*The Mists of Time* 5998
*Unearthly Neighbors* 595, 3342, 3769
*The Wolf Is My Brother* 4052

**Olson, Paul F.**
*Dead End: City Limits* **4212**
*Night Prophets* 3656, **4213**
*Post Mortem: New Tales of Ghostly Horror* 1610, 2233, 3869, 4206, **4214**, 4644, 5331, 5665

**Oltion, Jerry**
*Isaac Asimov's Robot City/Robots and Aliens Book 4: Alliance* 484

**O'Malley, Kathleen**
*Silent Dances* **1263**
*Silent Songs* **1264**

**O'Neil, Dennis**
*Batman: Knightfall* 1667, 2331, **4215**

**O'Neill, Joseph**
*The Land under England* 5747

**Onions, Oliver**
*The Collected Ghost Stories of Oliver Onions* 1252, 2846

**Onopa, Robert**
*The Pleasure Tube* 4976

**Opie, Iona**
*The Classic Fairy Tales* 4890

**Ore, Rebecca**
*Alien Bootlegger and Other Stories* 772, 1515, 1758, 2027, 3234, 3384, **4216**, 4680
*Becoming Alien* 231, 753, 757, 764, 828, 1209, 1408, 1460, 1493, 1537, 1587, 1594, 1930, 1995, 2048, 2224, 2549, 2551, 2898, 3424, 3452, 3521, 4116, 4347, 4349, 4550, 4894, 5048, 5449, 6061
*Being Alien* 757, 764, 828, 1062, 1209, 1261, 1262, 1493, 2016, 2549, 3521, 3723, 3752, 4140, **4217**, 4347
*Gaia's Toys* **4218**
*Human to Human* 764, **4219**

**Orgill, Douglas**
*The Sixth Winter* 3429

**Ormondroyd, Edward**
*David and the Phoenix* 1220, 1221, 6076
*Time at the Top* 4585

**O'Rourke, Michael**
*The Bad Thing* **4222**
*Darkling* **4223**
*The Undine* 3104, 3492, **4224**

**Orr, A.**
*The World in Amber* 4055

**Orwell, George**
*1984* 574, 781, 1782, 2215, 3808, 4188, 4976, 5568, 5592
*Animal Farm* 1817, 4976

**Osborne, Cary**
*Darkloom* **4225**
*Deathweave* **4226**
*The Glaive* **4227**
*Iroshi* 1462, **4228**

**Osborne, Richard**
*Demolition Man* 366, **4229**, 4286, 4559

**O'Shea, Pat**
*The Hounds of the Morrigan* 1220, 1294, 1330, 6042

**Osier, Jeffrey**
*Driftglider and Other Stories* 775, 776, 2769, 2937, **4230**
*Horizon Lines* 3495, **4231**, 4313, 5445, 5620

**O'Sullivan, Vincent**
*Master of the Fallen Years* 963, 2633

**Ouellette, Pierre**
*The Deus Machine* 3207, 3923, **4232**, 4283, 4860, 5632, 5753

**Over, Raymond Van**
*The Twelfth Child* 4340

**P**

**Page, Gerald**
*Horrorstory III* **5601**

**Page, Jake**
*Apacheria* **4233**

**Page, Thomas**
*The Spirit* 5075

**Pagel, Stephen**
*Bending the Landscape: Fantasy* **2444**

**Paine, Michael**
*Cities of the Dead* 2439, 3526, 4050, 5312, 5695
*The Colors of Hell* 3607, **4234**
*Owl Light* **4235**, 5630, 5824

**Paiva, Jean**
*Lilith* 5824
*The Lilith Factor* 491, **4236**, 4312, 4844

**The Illegal Rebirth of Billy the Kid** 951, 957, 995, 2049, **4220**, 4559, 4560
*Slow Funeral* **4221**, 5333

**Palmer, David R.**
*Emergence* 876, 1261, 1262, 1539, 1550, 1600, 1930, 2260, 2554, 2603, 2640, 2808, 2997, 3429, 3940, 3966, 4262, 4507, 4599, 4605, 4835, 5212, 5232, 5242, 5267, 6075
*Threshold* 3698

**Palmer, Jessica**
*Dark Lullaby* **4237**
*Shadow Dance* 3967, **4238**
*Sweet William* **4239**

**Palwick, Susan**
*Flying in Place* 396, 397, 970, 1130, 2326, 2445, 2614, 2876, 2951, 3007, 3302, 3473, 3844, 4183, **4240**, 4758, 4862, 5415, 5430, 5912

**Pamely, C.D.**
*Tales of Mystery and Terror* 964, 2225

**Pangborn, Edgar**
*The Company of Glory* 365, 886
*Davy* 365, 886, 3788, 4074, 5593
*The Judgment of Eve* 365, 886
*A Mirror for Observers* 565, 567, 4188

**Panshin, Alexei**
*Masque World* 1216, 2013, 3345, 3583, 5131
*Rite of Passage* 297, 1539, 2109, 2626, 4507
*Star Well* 1536, 2013, 3345, 3583, 5131
*The Thurb Revolution* 3345, 3583, 5131

**Paragon, John**
*The Boy Who Cried Werewolf* **1800**
*Camp Vamp* **1801**
*Elvira: Transylvania 90210* **1802**

**Park, Paul**
*Celestis* **4241**
*The Cult of Loving Kindness* 3539, **4242**
*Soldiers of Paradise* 56, 57, 5940
*Sugar Rain* 56, 57, **4243**, 5940

**Park, Ruth**
*Playing Beatie Bow* 1138, 4585

**Park, Severna**
*Hand of Prophecy* 1266, **4244**
*Speaking Dreams* 1559, **4245**

**Parker, Chauncey G. III**
*The Visitor* 4370

**Parker, Lara**
*Angelique's Descent* **4246**

**Parkinson, Dan**
*The Gates of Thorbardin* 2675, 5711
*The Gully Dwarves* 5022
*Viper's Spawn* 3979
*The Whispers* **4247**

**Parkinson, T.L.**
*The Man Upstairs* 89, 913, 1468, 3094, **4248**

**Parks, Julie Anne**
*Storytellers* **4249**

**Parry, Michel**
*Beware of the Cat* 1369, 3145, 5252
*Devil's Kisses* 75, 2178, 2179, 2181, 2893, 5093, 5094
*Great Black Magic Stories* 2385
*Reign of Terror* 1233, 1234
*The Rivals of Dracula: A Century of Vampire Fiction* 2972, 5699

*Rivals of Frankenstein*   140, 2390, 2973, 3019, 4409

**Partridge, Norman**
*Bad Intentions*   1016, 1021, 2277, **4250**, 5885
*The Bars on Satan's Jailhouse*   **4251**
*Guignoir*   2967
*It Came From the Drive-In*   **4252**, 5954
*Mr. Fox and Other Feral Tales*   2277, **4253**, 4463
*Slippin' into Darkness*   **4254**
*Spyder*   428, 2938, 3102, **4255**
*Wildest Dreams*   **4256**

**Pasechnik, Steve**
*The Best of the Rest*   3997

**Passey, Helen K.**
*Speak to the Rain*   1087, **4257**

**Paton Walsh, Jill**
*A Chance Child*   2614

**Patterson, Teresa**
*The World of Robert Jordan's The Wheel of Time*   **2991**

**Patton, Fiona**
*The Painter Knight*   **4258**
*The Stone Prince*   3509, **4259**, 4533

**Pattou, Edith**
*Fire Arrow*   **4260**
*Hero's Song*   **4261**, 4497

**Pattrick, William**
*Mysterious Sea Stories*   2708, 2709, 2732, 3798, 5652

**Paul, Barbara**
*The Three Minute Universe*   9, 903, 1663, 1923
*Under the Canopy*   5230

**Paulsen, Gary**
*The Transall Saga*   **4262**

**Pausacker, Jenny**
*Fast Forward*   1558

**Pavic, Milorad**
*Landscape Painted with Tea*   1524, 2186, 4046, 4047, **4263**

**Paxson, Diana L.**
*Brisingamen*   2083, 3276, 5176
*The Dragons of the Rhine*   **4264**, 4676
*The Jewel of Fire*   **4265**
*Master of Earth and Water*   1764, 3504, 3506, **4266**
*The Shield between the Worlds*   3059, 3504, **4267**
*Sword of Fire and Shadow*   **4268**
*The White Raven*   965, 1191, 3017, 3018, 3636, 5015, 5390, 5393
*The Wind Crystal*   3905, **4269**
*The Wolf and the Raven*   136, 363, 1856, 2229, 2246, 2250, 2453, 2454, 2571, 2572, 2686, **4270**, 4669

**Payne, John**
*The Book of the Thousand Nights and the One Night*   6087

**Payne, Michael H.**
*The Blood Jaguar*   **4271**

**Pazzi, Roberto**
*The Princess and the Dragon*   1005, **4272**, 5147

**Peabody, Richard**
*Mondo Elvis*   4540, 5089, 5957

**Peacock, Thomas Love**
*Nightmare Abbey*   3526

**Peak, Michael**
*Cat House*   1895, 3120, 3377, 4143, 4157
*Catamount*   4143, **4273**

**Peake, Mervyn**
*Gormenghast*   325
*Gormenghast Trilogy*   5829
*Sometime, Never*   98
*Titus Alone*   5311

**Pearce, Philippa**
*Dread and Delight: A Century of Children's Ghost Stories*   **4274**, 4282
*Tom's Midnight Garden*   1138, 2283, 4332, 4585

**Pearlman, Gilbert**
*Young Frankenstein*   5324

**Pearson, Kit**
*Handful of Time*   122

**Peattie, Elia**
*The Shape of Fear and Other Ghostly Tales*   2919

**Peck, Claudia**
*Spirit Crossings*   1471, **4275**

**Peck, Richard**
*The Ghost Belonged to Me*   2923, 4078
*Voices After Midnight*   121, 2272

**Pedler, Kit**
*Mutant 59, The Plastic Eater*   108

**Peel, John**
*Timewyrm: Genesys*   3799, 3803

**Peirce, Hayford**
*Napoleon Disentimed*   3343
*Phylum Monsters*   1165, 2107, **4276**
*The Thirteenth Majestral*   **4277**

**Pelan, John**
*The Case of the Police Officer's Cock Ring and the Piano Player Who Had No Fingers*   3388
*Darkside: Horror for the Next Millennium*   1281, 2176, 2893, 3184, **4278**, 5924
*Goon*   3392
*Shifters*   3396
*Splatterspunk: The Micah Hays Stories*   3397

**Pellegrino, Charles**
*Dust*   3008, **4279**
*Flying to Valhalla*   133, 2252, **4280**
*The Killing Star*   1244, 1258, **4281**

**Pepper, Dennis**
*The Young Oxford Book of Ghost Stories*   1693, 1701, 2772, **4282**

**Peretti, Frank E.**
*This Present Darkness*   750

**Perez-Reverte, Arturo**
*The Club Dumas*   333

**Perrault, Charles**
*Complete Fairy Tales*   849

**Perriman, Cole**
*Terminal Games*   507, **4283**, 4860, 5753

**Perrin, Don**
*The Doom Brigade*   **5708**
*Knights of the Black Earth*   **5718**
*Theros Ironfeld*   2425

**Perrin, Pat**
*Terminal Games*   **4283**

**Perry, Mark C.**
*Morigu: The Dead*   458, 704, 1068, 1180, 1443, 2128, 2674, 3044, 3510, 3842, **4284**, 5223

**Perry, S.D.**
*Berserker*   **4285**
*Timecop*   1853, 2119, 2532, **4286**, 5315

**Perry, Stephanie**
*Aliens: The Female War*   **4290**

**Perry, Steve**
*The 97th Step*   580, 1604, 4142, 4228, **4287**, 4305, 4467, 6075
*The Albino Knife*   **4288**
*Aliens: Earth Hive*   492, 1993, **4289**
*Aliens: Nightmare Asylum*   492
*Aliens: The Female War*   492, **4290**
*Black Steel*   **4291**
*Brother Death*   4225, **4292**
*Conan the Fearless*   2983
*Conan the Formidable*   906, 908, 909, 910, **4293**, 4617
*Conan the Free Lance*   2347, 2348, 4616
*Conan the Indomitable*   **4294**
*The Digital Effect*   2916, **4295**
*The Forever Drug*   **4296**
*Isaac Asimov's I-Bots*   **4297**
*The Man Who Never Missed*   63, 756, 761, 1184, 1332, 1333, 1503, 1535, 1542, 1661, 1849, 1869, 2364, 3539, 3873, 3975, 4120, 4225, 4226, 4227, 4228, 4304, 4467, 4521, 4583, 4637, 5229, 5365, 5366, 5889
*The Man Who Never Missed Series*   1540
*Matadora*   1331
*Men in Black*   3063, **4298**
*Prey*   492
*Shadows of the Empire*   **4299**, 4719, 5205
*Spindoc*   **4300**
*Stellar Ranger*   5151
*Target Earth*   **4301**
*The Trinity Vector*   **4302**, 4895

**Perucho, Juan**
*Natural History*   **4303**

**Peters, David**
*Haven*   **4304**
*Psi-Man*   **4305**

**Peters, Ralph**
*Red Army*   1642, **4306**, 5300

**Petersen, Gail**
*The Making of a Monster*   1122, 2449, **4307**, 5162

**Peterson, John**
*The Littles*   1558, 4386, 4402, 4403

**Peyton, Richard**
*Journey into Fear and Other Great Stories of Horror on the Railways*   **4308**

**Pfaff, Eugene E. Jr.**
*Uwharrie*   2251, 2340, 3081, 3325, 3671, 4111, 4113, 4238, **4309**, 6078

**Pfeffer, Susan Beth**
*Rewind to Yesterday*   1662

**Pfefferle, Seth**
*Stickman*   5075

**Phelps, Ethel Johnston**
*Tatterhood and Other Tales*   276, 794, 849, 1578, 2144, 2146, 2528, 2719, 4008, 4987, 5617, 6088, 6089

**Philbrick, Rodman**
*Hunger*   **1346**
*Nine Levels Down*   **1347**

**Phillifent, John T.**
*The Man From U.N.C.L.E.: The Mad Scientist Affair*   1853, 4296

**Phillips, Jill M.**
*Walford's Oak*   4275, **4310**

**Phillips, Robert**
*The Omnibus of Twentieth Century Ghost Stories*   **4311**
*Triumph of the Night*   1, 1232, 1306, 1351, 3616, 4214, 5417

**Piccirilli, Tom**
*Dark Father*   2021, 2334, 4091, **4312**, 4728, 4883, 5657, 5986, 5992
*The Dog Syndrome and Other Sick Puppies*   **4313**, 5445, 5620
*Inside the Works*   22, **4314**
*Pentacle*   3119, 3613, **4315**

**Pierce, Constance**
*Elvis Rising: Stories on the King*   5089

**Pierce, David**
*Forever Yours*   4329

**Pierce, J. Calvin**
*The Door to Ambermere*   **4316**
*The Wizard of Ambermere*   **4317**

**Pierce, Meredith Ann**
*The Dark-Angel*   1444
*The Pearl of the Soul of the World*   164, 847, 3159, 3842, 4129, 4154, **4318**, 5974
*The Son of Summer Stars*   **4319**
*The Woman Who Loved Reindeer*   668, 2166, 2167, 2168, 2169, 2170, 2581, 2582, 2583, **4320**

**Pierce, Tamora**
*Alanna: The First Adventure*   3737, 5629
*In the Hand of the Goddess*   4871
*The Realms of the Gods*   1319, 4260, **4321**
*Tris's Book*   **4322**
*Wild Magic*   68, **4323**
*Wolf-Speaker*   **4324**

**Piercy, Marge**
*He, She and It*   1824, **4325**, 5450, 5590
*Woman on the Edge of Time*   515, 968, 1130, 1835, 3622, 5180, 5905, 5908

**Pierson, Chris**
*Spirit of the Wind*   2425, **4326**

**Pike, Christopher**
*Chain Letter*   1692
*The Cold One*   **4327**, 4837
*The Creature in the Teacher*   1097, 5291
*Die Softly*   5285
*The Eternal Enemy*   568, 3597, 4210, 5013, 5372
*The Last Vampire*   120, 1302, **4328**, 5161
*The Lost Mind*   362
*The Midnight Club*   **4329**

*Remember Me*  1089
*Sati*  2056, **4330**
*The Season of Passage*  199, 1134, **4331**, 5860
*See You Later*  1272, 1475, **4332**
*The Starlight Crystal*  199, 568, 3597, **4333**, 4966, 5860
*The Tachyon Web*  2291
*Weekend*  1801
*Whisper of Death*  655
*Witch*  **4334**, 5478

**Pinckney, Josephine**
*Great Mischief*  2713

**Pine, Nicholas**
*The In Crowd*  4329
*The New Kid*  5287
*Night School*  1302, 4328, 5161

**Pines, T.**
*13 Tales of Horror*  2395
*Thirteen*  1693, 2395

**Pini, Richard**
*Against the Wind*  4336, 4337
*The Blood of Ten Chiefs*  408, 3300, 4336, 4337, 6005
*Captives of the Blue Mountain*  **4336**
*Dark Hours*  **4335**, 4336, 4337
*The Quest Begins*  **4337**
*Winds of Change*  4336, 4337
*Wolfsong*  4336, 4337

**Pini, Wendy**
*Captives of the Blue Mountain*  **4336**
*Elfquest: Journey to Sorrow's End*  4335
*The Quest Begins*  **4337**

**Pinkwater, Daniel Manus**
*The Afterlife Diet*  2327
*Borgel*  1222, 1224, 1603, 2133, 3573, **4338**, 4564
*Lizard Music*  1218, 1223
*The Snarkout Boys and the Avocado of Death*  1224
*Young Adults*  545, 546, 550, 552

**Piper, H. Beam**
*The Cosmic Computer*  897
*Fuzzies and Other People*  451
*Fuzzy Sapiens*  5457
*Little Fuzzy*  230, 434, 451, 1263, 1595, 2296, 2764, 3475, 3523, 3910, 4273, 4433, 4434, 4435, 4554
*Lord Kalvan of Otherwhen*  141, 142, 143, 1275, 1563, 1626, 1678, 2043, 2046, 4038, 4164, 4835, 5011
*The Other Human Race*  451, 1263, 3316
*Space Viking*  129, 1633, 2374, 5140, 5821
*Uller Uprising*  4378

**Piziks, Steven**
*In the Company of the Mind*  **4339**

**Plante, Edmund**
*Alone in the House*  5288
*Seed of Evil*  3040, **4340**, 5118, 5401

**Platt, Charles**
*Free Zone*  2013, **4341**
*Protektor*  **4342**
*The Silicon Man*  **4343**

**Playboy Editors**
*The Playboy Book of Science Fiction and Fantasy*  5489

**Poe, Edgar Allan**
*Complete Stories and Poems*  722
*The Fall of the House of Usher*  3813

*Ligeia*  3813
*The Narrative of A. Gordon Pym*  4371
*The Science Fiction of Edgar Allan Poe*  3148

**Poe, Robert**
*The Black Cat*  **4344**, 4778
*Return to the House of Usher*  3150, **4345**, 4778

**Pogue, Bill**
*The Trikon Deception*  597

**Pohl, Frederik**
*The Age of the Pussyfoot*  5243
*The Best Science Fiction for 1972*  245
*Beyond the Blue Event Horizon*  2006, 4511
*The Coming of the Quantum Cats*  582, 2012, 5908
*Drunkard's Walk*  2487, 2920, 4813
*The Eighth Galaxy Reader*  243
*Gateway*  247, 447, 449, 1509, 2006, 4067, 4103, 4961
*The Gateway Trip: Tales and Vignettes of the Heechee*  2836, 4103, **4346**, 5244, 5933
*Gladiator-at-Law*  1805, 1838, 2328, 2545, 2770, 3795, 4473, 4662, 5593
*Homegoing*  3943, **4347**
*Jem*  248, 1768
*Man Plus*  586, 1768, 2840, 3715, 4205, **4348**, 4963, 5377
*Midas World*  1892
*Mining the Oort*  83, 421, 2765, **4349**, 4379, 4911, 4948, 4958, 4962
*Narabedla, Ltd.*  1209, 1995, 4197, 4276, 5645
*Nebula Winners 14*  245
*O Pioneer!*  **4350**
*The Other End of Time*  159, 477, 688, 2002, 2417, **4351**, 4502, 4859
*Outnumbering the Dead*  2422, **4352**, 4955
*The Reefs of Space*  62, 2064
*The Science Fiction Roll of Honor*  245
*The Seventh Galaxy Reader*  242
*The Siege of Eternity*  **4353**
*The Singers of Time*  2273, 3597, **4354**, 4420, 4735, 5860
*The Space Merchants*  593, 1892, 3794
*Stopping at Slowyear*  2806, 3075, 3185, 3237, 4172, 4176, **4355**, 4949, 4957, 5809, 6068
*The Voices of Heaven*  1696, 1759, 2661, 4116, **4356**, 4964
*The World at the End of Time*  734, **4357**, 4506
*The Years of the City*  1819, 1820, 5642

**Polikarpus, Viido**
*Down Town*  1842, 4170

**Pollack, Rachel**
*Godmother Night*  715, 3118, 4211, **4358**, 5555
*Tarot Tales*  2406, **4359**
*Temporary Agency*  389, 3071, 3935, **4360**, 5274, 5529
*Unquenchable Fire*  3438, 3935, 4177, **4361**, 4631, 5145, 5529, 5591

**Pollotta, Nick**
*Bureau 13*  285, 390, 706, 1399, 1974, 2309, 2320, 2519, 2800, 4191, 4298, 4304, **4362**, 4394, 5497
*Doomsday Exam*  1159, 1974, 2309, 2320, 2363, **4363**
*Full Moonster*  1400, 2513, 3257, **4364**, 4394, 5497, 5577
*Illegal Aliens*  483, 1454, 1892, 1921, 2007, 2228, 2880, 4120, 4298, **4365**
*Satellite Night News*  **2770**
*Shadowboxer*  **4366**

**Pope, Elizabeth Marie**
*The Perilous Gard*  17, 317, 393, 3017, 3816, 3840, 4870, 5983
*The Sherwood Ring*  122, 1272, 4078

**Popescu, Petru**
*In Hot Blood*  **4367**

**Popkes, Steven**
*Caliban Landing*  130, 5107
*The Longest Voyage/Slow Lightning*  130
*Slow Lightning*  5107

**Porath, Ellen**
*Kindred Spirits*  154
*Steel and Stone*  **4368**, 4925

**Porter, Barry**
*Dark Souls*  **4369**
*Junkyard*  373, **4370**, 4815

**Posey, Ernest**
*Hormone Pirates of Xenobia and Dream Studs of Kama Loka*  2117

**Potocki, Jan**
*The Manuscript Found in Sragossa*  **4371**

**Pournelle, Jerry**
*Beowulf's Children*  **4116**
*Birth of Fire*  421, 2765, 4964
*The Children's Hour*  1331, 3649, 4124, 4125, **4372**
*CoDominium: Revolt on War World*  **4373**, 5292
*Exiles to Glory*  4952
*Falkenberg's Legion*  1322, 1326, 1327, 1546, 2171, 2351, 2353, 2435, 3035, **4374**, 4466, 4583, 4672, 5300, 5465, 5469
*Fallen Angels*  **4120**
*Go Tell the Spartans*  1641, **4375**, 5292
*The Gripping Hand*  **4122**
*Higher Education*  **4958**
*Janissaries*  359, 1547, 1635, 1642, 2349, 4201, 5512, 5513
*King David's Spaceship*  353, 1182, 4545
*Life Among the Asteroids*  **4376**
*Man-Kzin Wars III*  **4123**
*The Mercenary*  308, 1646, 2054
*Prince of Mercenaries*  129, 308, 1113, 1630, 1642, 1650, 1900, 2054, 2349, 3666, **4377**, 5377
*Prince of Sparta*  **4378**
*A Spaceship for the King*  1652
*Starswarm*  **4379**
*War World I: The Burning Eye*  2004, 5292
*War World II: Death's Head Rebellion*  5292
*War World III: Sauron Dominion*  5292
*West of Honor*  4948, 4958

**Power, Susan**
*The Grass Dancer*  636, **4380**

**Powers, Richard M.**
*Galatea 2.2*  **4381**

**Powers, Tim**
*The Anubis Gates*  520, 969, 1457, 1520, 1564, 1615, 2077, 2329, 2546, 3124, 3421, 3596, 3799, 3802, 3803, 3804, 4432, 4446, 4658, 4659
*Dinner at Deviant's Palace*  1519
*The Drawing of the Dark*  955, 1189, 2262, 3257, 3714, 3806, 3822
*Earthquake Weather*  **4382**
*Expiration Date*  2687, **4383**, 5570
*Last Call*  87, 518, 715, 1091, 1277, 2304, 2406, 3262, 4095, 4359, **4384**
*On Stranger Tides*  4661, 5842
*The Stress of Her Regard*  912, 1276, 2265, 2741, **4385**, 4546, 5052, 5614, 5615, 5842, 6018, 6022

**Poyer, David C.**
*The Shiloh Project*  5502

**Pratchett, Terry**
*The Colour of Magic*  174, 197, 2075, 2616, 5034, 5840
*Diggers*  1222, 1223, 1224, **4386**
*Equal Rites*  2573, 4013, **4387**
*Eric*  4171, **4388**
*Feet of Clay*  **4389**
*Good Omens: The Nice and Accurate Prophecies of Agnes Nutter, Witch*  **2103**
*Guards! Guards!*  1207, 3991, **4390**, 5649
*Hogfather*  **4391**
*Interesting Times*  **4392**
*Jingo*  **4393**
*The Light Fantastic*  355
*Lords and Ladies*  1160, **4394**
*Maskerade*  **4395**
*Men at Arms*  **4396**
*Mort*  1385, 4014, **4397**
*Moving Pictures*  3573, **4398**, 5875
*Reaper Man*  196, 1603, 2327, **4399**
*Small Gods*  **4400**, 5232
*Soul Music*  **4401**
*Sourcery*  180, 2125
*Strata*  3050
*Truckers*  1222, 1223, 1224, 1558, **4402**
*Wings*  1222, 1223, 1224, **4403**, 4434
*Witches Abroad*  187, 2145, **4404**
*Wyrd Sisters*  980, 1045, 1529, 2750, 2942, 3079, **4405**, 5337

**Pratt, Fletcher**
*The Blue Star*  5222, 5228, 5506, 5507, 5976
*Invaders From Rigel*  2172
*The Well of the Unicorn*  3980

**Preiss, Byron**
*The Ultimate Alien*  **4406**
*The Ultimate Dracula*  150, 151, 2387, **4407**, 5448
*The Ultimate Dragon*  801, 2479, **4408**
*The Ultimate Frankenstein*  2390, **4409**
*The Ultimate Werewolf*  1230, 2410, 2976, 3032, **4410**, 5384
*The Ultimate Witch*  2938, **4411**, 6034
*The Ultimate Zombie*  2892, **4412**, 4745, 4746

**Preston, Douglas**
*Mount Dragon* **4413**
*Relic* 3207, **4414**, 4688
*Reliquary* **4415**

**Preston, Richard**
*Cobra Event* 3577

**Preuss, Paul**
*Arthur C. Clarke's Venus Prime, Vol. 2:*
*Maelstrom* 1880
*Breaking Strain* 1646, 5930
*Core* **4416**
*The Diamond Moon* 1661, **4417**
*Hide and Seek* **4418**
*The Medusa Encounter* **4419**
*Secret Passages* **4420**
*The Shining Ones* **4421**
*Starfire* 5188, 5246

**Preussler, Otfried**
*The Satanic Mill* 1605, 3163

**Price, E. Hoffman**
*The Devil Wives of Li Fong* 4741
*Far Lands, Other Days* 940, 942,
1088, 1700, 2780, 4741, 5628
*The Jade Enchantress* 4741
*Strange Gateways* 3515

**Price, Robert M.**
*The Arkham Cycle* 2399
*The Azathoth Cycle* 461, **4422**
*The Cthulhu Cycle* **4423**
*The Dunwich Cycle* 2399
*The Dunwich Cycle: Where the Old*
*Gods Wait* **4424**
*The Hastur Cycle* 461, 2978, **4425**
*The Innsmouth Cycle: The Taint of the*
*Deep Ones in 13 Tales* **4426**
*The Lovecraft Circle* 5494
*The Necronomicon* **4427**
*The New Lovecraft Circle* 148, 461,
3571, **4428**
*The Nyarlathotep Cycle* **4429**
*The Shub Niggurath Cycle* 461, 2978,
**4430**
*Tales of the Lovecraft Mythos* 461,
2978, **4431**, 5325, 5494
*Tales of the Providence Pales* 1859

**Price, Susan**
*The Ghost Drum: A Cat's Tale* 3377,
5142
*Horror Stories* 1693, 1701, 2772,
4282

**Pridgen, William**
*Night of the Dragon's Blood* 4529

**Priest, Christopher**
*The Glamour* 982, 1002, 1098, 4776
*An Infinite Summer* 5747
*The Inverted World* 5305
*The Perfect Lover* 2580
*The Prestige* 1186, 2266, 3439,
**4432**

**Priest, James D.**
*Kirins: The Flight of the Ain* 2142,
**4433**
*Kirins: The Secret of the Hanging*
*Stones* **4434**
*Kirins: The Spell of No'an* 235, 565,
1299, 2142, 3077, 3513, 3910,
3943, 3944, 4061, 4062, 4403,
**4435**, 4709, 5379

**Prill, David**
*Serial Killer Days* 3497, **4436**
*The Unnatural* 1396, 3057, **4437**,
5167

**Prince, Maggie**
*The House on Hound Hill* **4438**

**Pringle, David**
*The Best of Interzone* 1023, 2148,
**4439**, 5489
*Route 666* 972, 6020, 6021

**Pronzini, Bill**
*The Arbor House Necropolis* 2973,
2977, 5083
*The Arbor House Treasury of Horror*
*and the Supernatural* 2590, 2591,
2974, 2993, 3027, 4311
*Classic Tales of Horror and the*
*Supernatural* **4440**
*Double* 1524
*Mummy!* 2400
*Werewolf!* 1230, 2410, 2976, 4410,
5384

**Ptacek, Kathryn**
*Ghost Dance* 427, 749, 911, 1297,
2251, 2340, 3081, 3655, 3671,
3680, 3895, 3967, 4111, 4113,
4309, **4441**, 5769, 6078
*The Hunted* 3898, 3964, **4442**, 5314
*In Silence Sealed* 912, 1086, 2741,
4569, 5192, 5842
*Shadoweyes* 2734
*Women of Darkness* 468, 1312,
2496, 2891, 3022, 5523
*Women of Darkness II* 468, 2496,
2891, 3022, **4443**, 5523
*Women of the West* 217

**Pugmire, W.H.**
*Tales of Sesqua Valley* 3556, **4444**,
4878

**Pullinger, Kate**
*Where Does Kissing End?* 2843,
**4445**

**Pullman, Philip**
*The Golden Compass* 1028, 3386,
4211, 4446, 6037
*Spring-Heeled Jack* **4447**
*The Subtle Knife* **4448**

**Pulver, Joseph S. Jr.**
*Nightmare's Disciple* 4112, **4449**

**Pulver, Mary Monica**
*Murder at the War* 1040

**Purtill, Richard**
*The Stolen Goddess* 5496

**Pusti, Maureen S.**
*Neighbors* **4450**

**Pyle, Howard**
*The Merry Adventures of Robin*
*Hood* 2247, 2248, 2389, 3165,
4609
*The Story of King Arthur and His*
*Knights* 224, 2767, 5970
*The Story of the Champions of the*
*Round Table* 224, 5970

**Pynchon, Thomas**
*Gravity's Rainbow* 2329, 4606,
4681, 5903

# Q

**Quick, W.T.**
*Chains of Light* **5449**
*Dreams of Flesh and Sand* 361,
3890, 5449
*Dreams of Gods and Men* 361, 3491,
3890, **4451**, 5449
*Systems* 361, 3995, **4452**, 4555,
5449

*Yesterday's Pawn* **4453**, 5449

**Quinn, Daniel**
*Dreamer* 89, 813, 1669, 2161,
2613, 2789, 3267, **4454**, 5520,
5816
*Ishmael* 2578, **4455**
*My Ishmael* **4456**

**Quinn, Seabury**
*The Devil's Bride* 5696
*The Phantom Fighter* 258, 670,
2856, 4315, 5562

**Quittner, Joshua**
*Flame War* 2322

# R

**Rabe, Jean**
*The Day of the Tempest* **4457**
*Red Magic* 1289, 3538, **4458**, 4800,
4807, 5723

**Rackham, John**
*The Anything Tree* 3727
*The Treasure of Tau Ceti* 3221

**Radford, Irene**
*The Dragon's Touchstone* 3292, **4459**
*The Glass Dragon* 1705, 1749, **4460**
*The Loneliest Magician* 3045, **4461**
*The Perfect Princess* **4462**

**Radin, Paul**
*African Folktales* 2771, 4207
*African Folktales and Sculpture* 2528
*The Trickster* 5578, 5751

**Rainey, Stephen Mark**
*The Best of Deathrealm* 2773, 5025
*Fugue Devil and Other Weird*
*Horrors* 113, 775, 776, 2769,
3317, 3669, 4230, 4231, **4463**,
5446, 5881

**Raisor, Gary L.**
*Less than Human* 1945, **4464**
*Obsessions* 1279, 1284, 1285, 2384,
2601, 2777, 3024, **4465**, 5666,
5667

**Ramanujan, A.K.**
*Folktales From India* 849

**Rand, Ayn**
*Atlas Shrugged* 3200, 4867, 4976

**Randall, Marta**
*Islands* 4352

**Randle, Kevin**
*Jefferson's War: Death of a*
*Regiment* **4466**
*Remember the Little Bighorn* 1852,
5504

**Randle, Kevin D.**
*Galactic MI* **4467**
*The Galactic Silver Star* 2436, **4468**,
5469
*Mind Slayer* 1696, **4469**
*Remember Gettysburg* 358, 3867,
3993, 5502
*Remember the Alamo!* 2046, 2563,
6000
*Star Precinct* **4470**

**Randle, Robert**
*Seeds of War* 3034

**Rangel, Kimberly**
*The Homecoming* **4471**
*Shadows* **4472**

**Rankin, Robert**
*Armageddon: The Musical* 31, 156,
1490, 2070, 3190, 3664, **4473**,
5089, 5768, 5957, 5958, 6020

**Ransmayr, Christoph**
*The Dog King* **4474**
*The Last World* 2238, 3793, **4475**

**Ransom, Bill**
*Burn* **4476**
*Jaguar* **4477**, 4517
*ViraVax* 453, 774, 1724, 2443,
2681, **4478**, 5258

**Ransom, Daniel**
*The Fugitive Stars* **4479**
*The Long Midnight* **4480**
*The Serpent's Kiss* 5084

**Raskin, Ellen**
*The Mysterious Disappearance of*
*Leon* 4263

**Rasmussen, Alis A.**
*An Earthly Crown* **1771**
*King's Dragon* **1773**
*The Labyrinth Gate* 85, 166, 183,
1532, 2125, 2505, 3582, 4438,
**4481**, 4799, 5712, 5726
*The Law of Becoming* **1774**
*A Passage of Stars* 220, 356, 473,
688, 756, 762, 774, 876, 928, 930,
981, 995, 996, 1003, 1108, 1262,
1332, 1337, 1407, 1478, 1503,
1544, 1545, 1553, 1571, 1574,
1599, 1604, 1606, 1645, 1661,
1756, 1774, 1824, 1970, 1986,
2260, 2419, 2551, 2649, 2785,
2812, 3014, 3072, 3117, 3248,
3452, 3707, 3719, 3724, 3735,
3821, 3830, 3976, 4101, 4123,
4126, 4160, 4302, 4467, **4482**,
4557, 4643, 4682, 4897, 4951,
4957, 4967, 4984, 5229, 5541,
5671, 5679, 5717, 5720, 5777,
5821, 5917, 5920, 5921, 5922,
6079, 6082, 6086
*The Price of Ransom* 311, 356, 876,
1108, 1144, 1407, 1544, 1545,
1588, 1649, 1771, 1937, 1992,
2260, 2649, 2785, 2953, 3117,
3452, 3741, 3821, 3823, 3830,
4123, 4467, **4483**, 4505, 4557,
4897, 4900, 5229, 5367, 5466,
5670, 5672, 5720
*Revolution's Shore* 309, 356, 684,
876, 1103, 1108, 1407, 1543,
1544, 1545, 1598, 1606, 1664,
1680, 1771, 1849, 1992, 2053,
2260, 2466, 2649, 2785, 3117,
3452, 3821, 3830, 3873, 3910,
3912, 4123, 4375, 4467, **4484**,
4557, 4895, 4897, 5139, 5229,
5234, 5571, 5674, 5720

**Raven, Simon**
*Doctors Wear Scarlet* 4236

**Rawn, Melanie**
*Dragon Prince* 683, 692, 1143,
1486, 1487, 1773, 1864, 1907,
1908, 1912, 2060, 2552, 3078,
3168, 3645, 3893, 4161, 4258,
4613, 5391, 5582, 5727, 5812,
5964
*The Dragon Token* **4485**
*The Golden Key* 1773, 3506, **4486**,
4611, 5017
*Knights of the Morningstar* 1040,
2657, **4487**
*The Mageborn Traitor* **4488**
*The Ruins of Ambrai* 1143, **4489**

*Skybowl* **4490**
*The Star Scroll* 604, 1155, 3306, **4491**, 5547, 5582, 5712
*Stronghold* 28, 182, 3067, 3581, 3839, **4492**
*Sunrunner's Fire* 3905, **4493**, 5582

**Ray, Fred Olen**
*Weird Menace* **4494**

**Reagen, James E.**
*The League of the Crimson Crescent* 3913, **4495**

**Reamy, Tom**
*Blind Voices* 896, 1186, 1282, 2303, 4776, 5176

**Reaves, Michael**
*Night Hunter* 1793, 2322, 2792, 3108, **4496**
*The Shattered World* 171
*Street Magic* 3271, 3301, 4261, **4497**, 4675, 4993
*Voodoo Child* 1403, 2896, **4498**

**Reed, Dana**
*Demon Within* **4499**

**Reed, Morton**
*Requiem* 3950

**Reed, Rick R.**
*Obsessed* 695, 2156, 3585, **4500**
*Penance* 822, 1779, 3395, **4501**

**Reed, Robert**
*Beneath the Gated Sky* **4502**
*Beyond the Veil of Stars* 1762, **4503**, 5775
*Black Milk* 1165, 1933, 1934, **4504**, 4756, 5664, 5907
*Down the Bright Way* 31, 250, 358, 359, 449, 1574, 2213, 3467, 3805, 3874, **4505**, 5054, 5531, 5774
*An Exaltation of Larks* **4506**
*The Hormone Jungle* 2690, 2691
*The Remarkables* 4063, **4507**, 5033

**Rees, Simon**
*The Devil's Looking-Glass* 3677

**Reeves-Stevens, Garfield**
*The Ashes of Eden* **4927**
*Avenger* **4928**
*Bloodshift* **4508**
*Dark Matter* **4509**, 5453
*Federation* **4511**
*Gray Matter* 5084
*Icefire* **4512**
*Memory Prime* 1663, 4511, 4927
*Nighteyes* 157, 1930, 2542, **4510**, 5341
*Nightfeeder* **4513**
*Prime Directive* **4514**
*The Return* **4933**
*Shifter* **4515**
*Spectre* **4934**

**Reeves-Stevens, Judith**
*The Ashes of Eden* **4927**
*Avenger* **4928**
*The Day of Descent* 504, 1508, 2909, 2910, 3520
*Federation* 902, 904, 2065, **4511**, 4927, 4934
*Icefire* **4512**
*Nightfeeder* **4513**
*Prime Directive* 1554, 2298, 4037, **4514**, 4927, 4928, 4933, 5141
*The Return* **4933**
*Shifter* 2809, **4515**
*Spectre* **4934**

**Reichert, Mickey Zucker**
*Beyond Ragnarok* **4516**, 4899

*By Chaos Cursed* 390, **4517**
*The Children of Wrath* **4518**
*Dragonrank Master* 2, **4519**, 5790, 5944
*Godslayer* 2, 390, 391, 1683, 1979, 2369, 2375, 5741
*The Last of the Renshai* 3270, **4520**
*The Legend of Nightfall* 739, **4521**
*Prince of Demons* **4522**
*Shadow's Realm* **4523**, 4801, 4806
*Spirit Fox* **4524**
*The Unknown Soldier* **4525**, 5184
*The Western Wizard* **4526**, 5150

**Reidah, Alvah**
*Fault Lines* 1060

**Reiffel, Leonard**
*The Contaminant* 2787

**Reimann, Katya**
*A Tremor in the Bitter Earth* **4527**
*Wind From a Foreign Sky* 2031, 2958, 4459, **4528**

**Rein-Hagen, Mark**
*Vampire Diary: The Embrace* 5705

**Reines, Kathryn**
*The Kiss* 4246, **4529**

**Relling, William Jr.**
*Brujo* 2734, 5075
*The Infinite Man* 530, 537, 3328, 3329, 3333, **4530**, 4648, 5339
*The Infinite Man and Other Stories* 429, 5854
*New Moon* 833, 2288, 2793, 3900, 4004, 4005
*Silent Moon* **4531**

**Remick, Jack**
*Terminal Weird* 778, 2137, 3851, **4532**, 4789, 5662, 5663

**Renard, Maurice**
*The Hands of Orlac* 1205

**Renault, Mary**
*Fire From Heaven* 2187
*The Persian Boy* 5395

**Resnick, Laura**
*In Legend Born* **4533**

**Resnick, Mike**
*Aladdin: Master of the Lamp* **4534**
*An Alien Land* **4535**
*Alternate Kennedys* 442, 2411, **4536**, 5498
*Alternate Presidents* 442, 1139, 2411, **4537**, 5495, 5498
*Alternate Warriors* **4538**, 5498
*The Best Rootin' Tootin' Shootin' Gunslinger in the Whole Damned Galaxy* 5215
*Bully!* **4539**, 5501
*Bwana & Bully!* 4207, 5504
*By Any Other Fame* 2070, **4540**, 5089
*Christmas Ghosts* 1311, 1313, 2276, 2587, 2894, **4541**, 4861
*The Dark Lady: A Romance of the Far Future* 4781, 5548
*Deals with the Devil* 3071, 3483, 3488, **4542**
*Dinosaur Fantastic* 2386, **4543**
*Future Earths: Under African Skies* 1567, 1867, 1868, 2771, 4207, **4544**
*A Hunger in the Soul* **4545**
*Inside the Funhouse* 735, **4546**
*Ivory: A Legend of Past and Future* 496, 3790, **4547**, 5545
*Kirinyaga: A Fable of Utopia* **4548**

*Lucifer Jones* **4549**
*A Miracle of Rare Design* 1876, **4550**, 5549
*Oracle* **4551**
*Paradise: A Chronicle of a Distant World* 496, 1996, 3713, 3790, **4552**
*Prophet* 2475, 3064, **4553**
*Purgatory: A Chronicle of a Distant World* **4554**
*Pursuit on Ganymede* 3983
*The Red Tape War* 959
*Santiago* 5319
*Second Contact* 595, 2921, **4555**
*Sherlock Holmes in Orbit* **4556**
*Sideshow* 5215
*Soothsayer* 1238, 1544, **4557**, 4717, 5184, 5376
*Stalking the Unicorn: A Fable of Tonight* 1343, 5459, 5642
*The Three-Legged Hootch Dancer* 4638, 5215
*Whatdunits* 2005, 3619, **4558**
*The Widowmaker* **4559**
*The Widowmaker Reborn* **4560**
*The Wild Alien Tamer* 5215
*Will the Last Person to Leave the Planet Please Shut Off the Sun?* **4561**
*Witch Fantastic* 6034

**Rewolinski, Leah**
*Star Wreck II: The Attack of the Jargonites* 607, 1459, **4563**
*Star Wreck III: Time Warped* 1459, **4564**
*Star Wreck IV: Live Long and Profit* **4565**
*Star Wreck 6: Geek Space Nine* **4562**
*Star Wreck: The Generation Gap* 607, 1459, 2567, 2568, **4566**, 4656

**Reynolds, Mack**
*Amazon Planet* 176
*The Best Ye Breed* **4539**
*Blackman's Burden* 4539, 4561
*Border, Breed Nor Birth* **4539**
*Chaos in Lagrangia* 5188
*Lagrange Five* 5188
*The Other Time* 5036, 6000
*Perchance to Dream* 583
*Planetary Agent X* 5230
*The Rival Rigellians* 5231
*Space Search* 195
*Trojan Orbit* 584, 588

**Reynolds, Ted**
*The Tides of God* 2165, 2216, 2343, 2666, 2722, **4567**, 5195

**Rhodes, Daniel**
*Adversary* 2874, **4568**, 5271
*Kiss of Death* 3989, **4569**
*Next, After Lucifer* 283, 2889, 3164

**Rhodes, Jewell Martin**
*Voodoo Dreams* 3605

**Rice, Anne**
*Interview with the Vampire* 799, 812, 1121, 1124, 1140, 1166, 1286, 1541, 2267, 2337, 2510, 2834, 3151, 3405, 3519, 3602, 3853, 4318, 4367, 4665, 5347, 5537, 5705
*Lasher* **4570**, 5122
*Memnoch the Devil* 3908, 4028, 4029, **4571**, 5190
*The Mummy, or Ramses the Damned* 616, 2439, **4572**, 5312, 5695
*Pandora* **4573**

*The Queen of the Damned* 452, 575, 1882, 2258, 3407, 4096, 4098, 4318, **4574**
*Servant of the Bones* **4575**, 5312, 6016
*The Tale of the Body Thief* 2149, **4576**
*Taltos* **4577**
*The Vampire Armand* **4578**
*The Vampire Chronicles* 4464, 5191
*The Vampire Lestat* 152, 301, 463, 490, 600, 660, 678, 697, 1122, 1125, 1355, 1778, 1795, 1798, 2259, 2741, 3113, 3413, 3781, 3954, 3955, 4094, 4097, 4307, 4318, 4508, 4774, 4978, 5160, 5162, 5406, 5822, 6012, 6018
*Violin* 2823, **4579**
*The Witching Hour* 654, 690, 749, 2442, **4580**, 5122, 5421, 5488

**Rice, Doug**
*Blood of Mugwump* 3244, **4581**

**Rice, Jane**
*The Sixth Dog* **4582**
*"The Refugee"* 4702

**Rice, Jeff**
*The Night Stalker* 106, 112, 2114
*The Night Strangler* 106, 2114

**Rice, Peter L.**
*Monsoon* **4583**

**Rice, Robert**
*The Last Pendragon* 269, **4584**

**Richemont, Enid**
*The Time Tree* 1012, **4585**

**Richey, James**
*Quest for the Fallen Star* 185

**Rickman, Phil**
*Candle Night* **4586**, 5121
*Curfew* **4587**
*December* **4588**
*The Man in the Moss* 5400

**Riddell, J.H.**
*The Collected Ghost Stories of Mrs. J.H. Riddell* 2158, 2707, 4969

**Riefe, Alan**
*Viper* **4589**

**Riggs, Alan**
*Quest for the Fallen Star* 185

**Riker, L.S.**
*Kill Crazy* 830, **4590**, 4938

**Rimel, Duane**
*To Yith and Beyond* 3516

**Rimmer, Steven William**
*Coven* **4591**

**Ripley, Karen**
*The Alchemist of Time* 956
*The Persistence of Memory* 1876, 2673, 2678, 4156, **4592**
*Prisoner of Dreams* 1046, **4593**, 4955
*The Tenth Class* 762, **4594**
*The Warden of Horses* 4163, **4595**

**Rivkin, J.F.**
*The Dreamstone* 27, 487, 1840
*Mistress of Ambiguities* **4596**
*Runesword: The Dreamstone* 1815
*Silverglass* 2376
*Tyrannosaurus Rex* 1417, 2468, **4597**

**Robbins, David**
*The Fox Run* 278
*Hell-O-Ween* **4598**

*L.A. Strike* **4599**, 5023
*Madman Run* **4600**
*Prank Night* **4601**
*Spartan Run* **4602**
*Spook Night* 3146, **4603**
*Vengeance Strike* **4604**
*Yellowstone Run* 1406, 2324, 2325, **4605**, 5023

**Robbins, Todd**
*"Spurs"* 1697

**Robbins, Tom**
*Another Roadside Attraction* 1421, 2186, 5593
*Half Asleep in Frog Pajamas* **4606**
*Jitterbug Perfume* 3456
*Skinny Legs and All* **4607**, 5867

**Roberson, Jennifer**
*Flight of the Raven* **4608**
*The Golden Key* **4486**
*Lady of the Forest* 2247, 3165, **4609**, 5397
*Legacy of the Sword* 1179
*Return to Avalon: A Celebration of Marion Zimmer Bradley* 640, 2398, **4610**
*Scotland the Brave* 4082, **4611**, 4990, 5707, 5729
*Shapechangers* 1179, 2361, 4055, 4486, 4492, 5629, 5650, 5767
*The Song of Homana* 1179
*Sword-Born* **4612**
*Sword-Breaker* **4613**
*Sword-Dancer* 1004, 2502, 4521, 5293
*Sword-Maker* 3471, **4614**
*Sword-Singer* 1439, 1486, 1487
*A Tapestry of Lions* **4615**

**Roberts, John Maddox**
*Conan and the Manhunters* 907, 910
*Conan and the Treasure of Python* 2983, **4616**
*Conan the Bold* 908, 4293
*Conan the Champion* 908
*Conan the Rogue* **4617**
*Delta Pavonis* 3221
*The Enigma Variations* **4618**
*King of the Wood* 442, 1139, 1436, 1655, 2086, 5781
*The Poisoned Lands* **4619**
*Queens of Land and Sea* **4620**
*The Steel Kings* 1025, **4621**, 5500

**Roberts, Keith**
*Anita* 2713
*Kiteworld* 56, 57
*The Passing of the Dragons* 56, 57
*Pavane* 3917, 5301, 5633

**Roberts, Moss**
*Chinese Fairy Tales and Fantasies* 849

**Robeson, Kenneth**
*Doc Savage Omnibus #1* 85, 1870, 4624
*Doc Savage Omnibus #9* 1870
*Doc Savage Omnibus #10* 1870
*Doc Savage Omnibus #11* 1870
*Doc Savage Omnibus #12* 1870, 4624
*Doc Savage Omnibus #13* 1870, 4624
*The Frightened Fish* 1940, **4622**, 5307
*The Jade Ogre* **4623**, 5308, 5309
*Python Isle* 1870, **4624**
*White Eyes* 85, **4625**

**Robinson, Frank M.**
*The Dark Beyond the Stars* 1059, 1645, 1875, 1992, 2829, 3787, 3874, **4626**, 5000, 5198, 5201, 5937, 5943
*The Power* 46

**Robinson, Jane E.M.**
*The Amazon Chronicles* **4627**, 5071

**Robinson, Jeanne**
*Starmind* **4642**
*Starseed* **4643**

**Robinson, Kim Stanley**
*Antarctica* **4628**
*Blue Mars* 406, 1876, **4629**
*Escape From Kathmandu* 725, 2070, 4062, **4630**, 4866, 4867, 5378
*Future Primitive: The New Ecotopias* **4631**, 4959
*The Gold Coast* 95, 736, 3817, 3818, **4632**
*Green Mars* 134, 406, 1724, 2526, 2765, 2840, 3380, 3715, 4348, **4633**, 5187
*Icehenge* 1248, 4962
*The Memory of Whiteness* 1305
*Pacific Edge* **4634**
*The Planet on the Table* 5807, 6067
*Red Mars* 102, 406, 421, 586, 784, 1585, 2584, 3715, 3927, 4095, 4348, 4548, **4635**, 4932, 5187
*Remaking History* 321, 1199, **4636**, 5028
*A Sensitive Dependence on Initial Conditions* 1428
*A Short, Sharp Shock/The Dragon Masters* 3189
*The Wild Shore* 4619

**Robinson, Lynda S.**
*Murder at the Place of Anubis* 5321

**Robinson, Spider**
*Antinomy* 503, 4636
*Callahan and Company* 115, 263, 2659, 4636
*The Callahan Touch* **4637**
*Callahan's Crosstime Saloon* 582, 677, 740, 1858, 2055, 2125, 2299
*Callahan's Lady* 740, **4638**
*Callahan's Legacy* 2007, 2055, 2299, **4639**
*Callahan's Secret* 740, 2622
*Kill the Editor* 3237, 4355
*Lady Slings the Booze* **4640**
*Lifehouse* 357, **4641**
*Melancholy Elephants* 503
*Stardance* 1548, 2721, 2955, 3238, 3452, 4679, 5609, 5635
*Starmind* **4642**
*Starseed* **4643**
*Time Travelers Strictly Cash* 740
*True Minds* 1428, 5810

**Roche, Thomas S.**
*Brothers of the Night* **4689**
*In the Shadow of the Gargoyle* 3112
*Sons of Darkness: Tales of Men, Blood and Immortality* **4690**

**Roddenberry, Gene**
*Star Trek - The Motion Picture: A Novel* 1556

**Roden, Barbara**
*Midnight Never Comes* **4644**

**Roden, Christopher**
*Midnight Never Comes* **4644**

**Rodgers, Alan**
*Blood of the Children* **4645**
*Bone Music* **4646**

*Fire* 343, **4647**, 5190
*New Life for the Dead* **4648**
*Night* 338, 3445, 4050, 4575, **4649**
*Pandora* **4650**

**Roessner, Michaela**
*The Stars Dispose* 1679, 3822, **4651**, 5152
*Vanishing Point* 1026, 2266, 2273, 2535, 2728, 3021, 3438, 3710, 4177, 4502, 4553, **4652**, 5208, 5274, 5818, 5906
*Walkabout Woman* 3291, 3889

**Rogers, Joel Townsley**
*The Red Right Hand* 3756

**Rogers, Mark E.**
*The Adventures of Samurai Cat* 915, 1895, 4054, 4144, 4562, 5252
*The Devouring Void* **4653**
*The Expected One* 3016, 3154
*The Riddled Man* **4654**
*Samurai Cat Goes to Hell* **4655**
*Samurai Cat Goes to the Movies* **4656**
*Samurai Cat in the Real World* 4549
*The Sword of Samurai Cat* 4549, **4657**

**Rohan, Michael Scott**
*The Anvil of Ice* 1008, 1010, 1028, 1082, 1109, 1730, 1814, 1912, 2271, 2504, 2984, 3123, 3942, 4446, 4457, 5964
*Chase the Morning* 1475, 1947, 3849, **4658**
*Cloud Castles* **4659**
*The Forge in the Forest* 457, 1173, 1178, 1690, 2884, 2886, 3893, **4660**, 5206, 5738, 5831
*The Gates of Noon* **4661**

**Rohmer, Sax**
*The Brood of the Witch Queen* 5696
*The Dream Detective* 509

**Rolston, Ken**
*Extreme Paranoia: Nobody Knows the Trouble I've Shot* 553, 735, 959, 1452, 1805, 2323, 2480, 2567, 2568, 2770, 2979, 3313, 3829, 4076, 4298, 4562, **4662**, 4909, 5074

**Rolt, L.T.C.**
*Sleep No More* 1350, 2905, 5611

**Romberg, Nina**
*Shadow Walkers* 2901, 3146, 3964, 4442, **4663**, 5334, 5528
*The Spirit Stalker* 542, **4664**

**Romero, George**
*Dawn of the Dead* 4168, 4745, 4746, 4831, 4834, 5313

**Romkey, Michael**
*I, Vampire* 139, 292, 463, 678, 2267, 3781, 4097, **4665**, 4763, 5191, 6019
*The Vampire Papers* 152, 2492, 2493, 3253, 4068, **4666**, 5405, 5407
*The Vampire Princess* **4667**
*The Vampire Virus* **4668**

**Roscoe, Theodore**
*Z Is for Zombie* 3605

**Rose, Karen**
*Time's Enemy* 2297
*Traitor Winds* 2298

**Rosenberg, Joel**
*The Crimson Sky* **4669**

*D'Shai* 747, 2507, 3078, 3872, **4670**
*The Fire Duke* 741, 1529, 2639, 4522, **4671**
*Guardians of the Flame: The Warriors* 105
*Hero* 2004, 2052, 2351, 2353, 4373, **4672**
*Hour of the Octopus* 1250, 2756, 2803, **4673**
*Not for Glory* 589, 1322, 1327, 2435
*The Road Home* **4674**
*The Road to Ehvenor* 1837, 4149, **4675**, 4993, 5915
*The Silver Stone* **4676**
*The Sleeping Dragon* 104, 391, 1162, 1163, 3831, 4492, 5063, 5558

**Rosenblum, Mary**
*Chimera* 1761, 2729, **4677**
*The Drylands* **4678**, 5032
*The Stone Garden* 506, 2559, 3453, 3454, **4679**, 5565, 5609, 5777
*Synthesis & Other Virtual Realities* 2027, 2120, 3087, 3600, 3971, **4680**

**Roshwald, Mordecai**
*Level 7* 1522, 3608, 4205

**Rosny, J.H.**
*Quest for Fire* 275, 2166, 2170

**Ross, Adrian**
*The Hole of the Pit* 2711

**Ross, David D.**
*The Argus Gambit* 3449, **4681**
*The Eighth Rank* 2727, **4682**

**Ross, James**
*They Don't Dance Much* 3330

**Roszak, Theodore**
*Flicker* 428, 1353, 2214, 2448, 3541, 3682, **4683**, 4734
*The Memoirs of Elizabeth Frankenstein* 659, 3019, **4684**

**Rouch, James**
*Body Count* 2324, 2325
*Civilian Slaughter* 44

**Routley, Jane**
*Fire Angels* **4685**
*Mage Heart* **4686**

**Rovin, Jeff**
*Mortal Kombat* 1483
*Return of the Wolfman* 1800, **4687**
*Vespers* **4688**

**Rowe, Michael**
*Brothers of the Night* 699, 3618, **4689**, 5386
*Sons of Darkness: Tales of Men, Blood and Immortality* 3618, **4690**, 5386, 5387

**Rowlands, David G.**
*The Executor and Other Ghost Stories* 1671, 2707, 3314

**Rowley, Christopher**
*Battledragon* **4691**
*Bazil Broketail* 182, 842, 843, 1749, **4692**
*A Dragon at World's End* **4693**
*Dragons of Argonath* **4694**
*Dragons of War* **4695**
*The Founder* **4696**
*A Sword for a Dragon* **4697**
*To a Highland Nation* **4698**

*The Wizard and the Floating
    City* **4699**

**Rowling, J.K.**
*Harry Potter and the Sorcerer's
    Stone* **4700**

**Royle, Nicholas**
*Counterparts* 5816
*Darklands* 3363

**Rozzi, P.D.**
*Waltz with Evil* **4701**

**Rubie, Peter**
*Werewolf* 2895, **4702**

**Rubinstein, Gillian**
*Space Demons* 168

**Rucker, Rudy**
*Freeware* **4703**
*The Hacker and the Ants* **4704**
*The Hollow Earth: The Narrative of
    Mason Algiers Reynolds of
    Virginia* 2469, **4705**
*Live Robots* 272, 809, 927, 2645,
    3435
*Master of Space and Time* 4341
*Software* 79, 806, 808, 1873, 2579,
    3921, 4341, 5091, 5213, 5573
*Transreal!* **4706**
*Wetware* 79, 249, 419, 1820, 1964,
    2837, 3795, 3890, 4276, 4341,
    4381, 5245, 5451, 5452, 5573
*White Light, or What Is Cantor's
    Continuum Problem* 519

**Rudwin, Maximilian**
*Devil Stories* 1280

**Ruff, Matt**
*Fool on the Hill* 1206, 2465, **4707**,
    5153
*Sewer, Gas & Electric* 4042, **4708**

**Rumbelow, Donald**
*The Complete Jack the Ripper* 3987

**Rusch, Kristine Kathryn**
*Afterimage* **4709**
*Afterimage Aftershock* **4710**
*Alien Influences* **4711**
*The Best From Fantasy & Science
    Fiction: A 45th Anniversary
    Anthology* 629, 3948, 3949, **4712**
*The Best of Pulphouse: The Hardback
    Magazine* 216, 628, 629, 755,
    1023, 1363, 1364, 1365, 1373,
    1618, 2148, 2593, 2967, 3948,
    3949, **4713**, 5954, 6045
*The Changeling* 3123, 4259, **4714**
*The Devil's Churn* **4715**
*The Escape* 5113
*Facade* **4716**
*The Gallery of His Dreams* 1441,
    **4717**, 4758, 5379
*Heart Readers* **4718**, 5113
*The New Rebellion* **4719**
*Pulphouse, Issue 6: Fantasy* 1373,
    **4723**, 5945, 6044
*Pulphouse, Issue 7: Horror* **4724**
*Pulphouse, Issue 8: Science
    Fiction* 887, **4725**
*Pulphouse, Issue 9: Dark
    Fantasy* 1373, 4131, **4726**
*Pulphouse, Issue 10: Special
    Issue* 1257, 2146, 2412, 2456,
    2587, 2588, 2589, 3214, **4720**,
    4861, 5024
*Pulphouse, Issue 11: Speculative
    Fiction* 4558, **4721**
*Pulphouse, Issue 12: The Last
    Issue* **4722**
*The Resistance* **4727**

*Sins of the Blood* **4728**, 5062
*The Soldiers of Fear* **5115**
*Traitors* 1513, 1864, **4729**, 5113
*The White Mists of Power* 1065,
    1679, 3510, **4730**, 5113

**Rushdie, Salman**
*Haroun and the Sea of Stories* 374,
    1681, 2123, 2130, **4731**, 5827,
    6087
*The Satanic Verses* 2249

**Rushkoff, Douglas**
*Ecstasy Club* 2754, **4732**

**Russ, Joanna**
*And Chaos Died* 101, 3860
*The Female Man* 1211, 1590, 1653,
    1720, 2242, 4792, 5477
*Picnic on Paradise* 5597
*Souls/Houston, Houston, Do You
    Read?* 2829
*The Two of Them* 3579
*We Who Are About To. . .* 1590,
    2242, 3579, 4792

**Russell, Eric Frank**
*Design for Great-Day* **2001**
*Dreadful Sanctuary* 2001
*The Great Explosion* 1182
*Men, Martians, and Machines* 4297
*Sinister Barrier* 2001, 3188, 3351,
    4944, 5010
*The Space Willies* 1419
*Wasp* 1652, 2001

**Russell, J.S.**
*Burning Bright* **4733**
*Celestial Dogs* **4734**

**Russell, Mary Doria**
*Children of God* **4735**
*The Sparrow* 159, 1442, 3599,
    4067, 4711, **4736**, 5372

**Russell, Paul**
*Boys of Life* 1170, 2448, **4737**

**Russell, Ray**
*Absolute Power* 2816, **4738**
*Incubus* 170, 2090, 2154, 3361,
    3394

**Russell, Sean**
*Beneath the Vaulted Hills* **4739**
*The Compass of the Soul* **4740**
*Gatherer of Clouds* 1253, **4741**
*The Initiate Brother* 563, 1101,
    3268, **4742**, 5277
*Sea Without a Shore* **4743**
*World Without End* **4744**

**Russo, John**
*Inhuman* 5313
*Night of the Living Dead* 3091, **4745**,
    4834
*Return of the Living Dead* **4746**

**Russo, Richard Paul**
*Carlucci's Edge* 2033, 3231, **4747**
*Carlucci's Heart* **4748**, 4936
*Destroying Angel* 1548, 1825, 2033,
    2092, 2218, 2219, 2527, 4192,
    4300, 4366, **4749**, 5363
*Inner Eclipse* 2897
*Subterranean Gallery* 4051, **4750**,
    5910

**Rutherford, Brett**
*Night Gaunts: An Entertainment Based
    on the Life and Work of H.P.
    Lovecraft* **4751**
*Whippoorwill Road* **4752**

**Ryan, Alan**
*The Bones Wizard* 2319

*Cast a Cold Eye* 840
*Dead White* 1193, 2927, 5756
*Halloween Horrors* 3705
*Haunting Women* 37, 1312, 1715,
    2496, 3570, 4443, 5523
*The Kill* 2310, 4310
*Night Visions 1* 1885
*Perpetual Light* 1283, 1339, 6031
*Vampires: Two Centuries of Great
    Vampire Stories* 1231, 1308,
    1360, 1370, 1718, 1799, 2071,
    2382, 2407, 2408, 2409, 2975,
    3031, 4407, 4879, 4881, 5265,
    5688, 5706, 5935

**Ryan, Kevin**
*Requiem* **2067**

**Ryan, Mary**
*Mask of the Night* **4753**

**Ryan, Shawn**
*Brethren* **4754**, 5186
*Nocturnas* 279, 4529, **4755**

**Ryman, Geoff**
*The Child Garden* 2913, 2997, **4756**,
    5145, 5491
*Unconquered Countries: Four
    Novellas* **4757**
*The Unconquered Country* 2952,
    3791, 4630, 4866, 4867, 5396
*Was* 2136, 3609, **4758**, 5912


**S**

**Saberhagen, Fred**
*After the Fact* 5487
*An Armory of Swords* 2657, **4759**
*Berserker* 128, 516, 2165
*Berserker Fury* **4760**
*Berserker Kill* **4761**
*Berserker Lies* **4762**
*Berserker Man* 516
*The Berserker Throne* 516
*The Berserker Wars* 516
*Berserker's Planet* 516, 2460
*Bram Stoker's Dracula* 139, 3110,
    3179, **4763**
*Brother Assassin* 5294
*A Century of Progress* 5906
*Dancing Bears* 3281, 4052, **4764**
*Dominion* 3253
*The Dracula Tape* 55, **4765**, 4779,
    5050, 6010
*Earth Descended* 516
*Empire of the East* 2041
*The Face of Apollo* **4766**
*The Fifth Book of Lost Swords:
    Coinspinner's Story* 2863
*The First Book of Swords* 3507, 3978
*The Fourth Book of Lost Swords:
    Farslayer's Story* 2863
*The Frankenstein Papers* 140
*The Holmes-Dracula File* 1524, **4767**
*The Last Book of Swords:
    Shieldbreaker's Story* 1172, **4768**
*Machines That Kill* **4769**
*A Matter of Taste* 2492, 2493, 3003,
    **4770**
*Merlin's Bones* **4771**
*Octagon* 118, 1858
*An Old Friend of the Family* 2517,
    4097, 4098
*A Question of Time* **4772**
*Seance for a Vampire* 3560, **4773**,
    6019

*The Second Book of Lost Swords:
    Sightbinder's Story* 2863
*The Second Book of Swords* 1748
*A Sharpness on the Neck* 452, 660,
    1794, 4667, **4774**
*Shiva in Steel* **4775**
*The Sixth Book of Lost Swords:
    Mindsword's Story* 1748, 2863,
    **4776**
*A Spadeful of Spacetime* 3459
*The Third Book of Lost Swords:
    Stonecutter's Story* 2783, 2863
*The Ultimate Enemy* 516
*Wayfinder's Story: The Seventh Book of
    Lost Swords* **4777**
*Woundhealer's Story: The First Book of
    Lost Swords* 1150

**Sachs, Leslie Raymond**
*The Virginia Ghost Murders* **4778**

**Sackett, Jeffrey**
*Blood of the Impaler* 4765, **4779**
*Mark of the Werewolf* 2895, **4780**

**Sade, Marquis de**
*Eugenie de Franval and Other
    Stories* 3183

**Sadler, Barry**
*Casca: Panzer Soldier* 359
*Casca: The Eternal Mercenary* 358,
    359

**Sagan, Carl**
*Contact* 202, 380, 4280

**Sagara, Michelle**
*The Broken Crown* 5757
*Chains of Darkness, Chains of
    Light* 2096, **4781**, 5127
*Children of the Blood: Book Two of
    The Sundered* **4782**
*Into the Dark Lands* 604, 1146,
    3074, 3270, 4153, 4462, **4783**,
    4924
*Lady of Mercy* 1985, **4784**

**Saha, Arthur W.**
*The 1990 Annual World's Best Science
    Fiction* **5948**
*The Year's Best Fantasy Stories* 1374
*The Year's Best Fantasy Stories
    Series* 1371, 1377

**St. Clair, Margaret**
*The Dolphins of Altair* 2450

**Saint-Exupery, Antoine de**
*The Little Prince* 1356, 3010, 3378,
    4008, 4455, 4456

**St. James, Renwick**
*Voyage of the Basset* 1024

**St. James, Riley**
*In the Shadows of the
    Moonglade* 5186

**St. Jude**
*How to Mutate and Take Over the
    World* **5074**

**Sakers, Don**
*Carmen Miranda's Ghost Is Haunting
    Space Station Three* 3751, 4169,
    4637, **4785**

**Saki**
*The Complete Short Stories of
    Saki* 2846

**Sallee, Wayne Allen**
*Drinking Buddies* 4255
*For You, the Living* **4786**, 5923
*The Holy Terror* 822, 1779, **4787**
*Pain-Grin* 1128, 2137, 4230, **4788**

*With Wounds Still Wet* 2698, 4231, 4532, **4789**, 5662, 5663

**Salmonson, Jessica Amanda**
*Amazons!* 316, 628, 629, 648, 649, 650, 651, 765, 1808, 1811, 2072, 2074, 3290, 3670, 4627, 5071
*Anthony Shriek* 212, 694, 2030, 3124, 3193, 3196, 3197, **4790**
*Heroic Visions* 628, 629
*John Collier and Fredric Brown Went Quarrelling through My Head* 802, 1827, 2715, 3702, 4891, 5521
*The Mysterious Doom and Other Ghostly Tales of the Pacific Northwest* 2543, 2643, 3472, 3705, **4791**, 5211
*A Silver Thread of Madness* 4878
*Tales by Moonlight* 1823, 4846, 5447
*Tales by Moonlight II* 1823, 4200, 4846
*Tomoe Gozen* 3268, 3412, 3906, 4742
*What Did Miss Darrington See?: An Anthology of Feminist Supernatural Fiction* 37, 1312, 1715, 2035, 2496, 3570, 4443, 5523, 5814

**Salsitz, Rhondi**
*Retribution* **1975**

**Salterberg, B.J.**
*The Outlander: Captivity* 1211, **4792**

**Salvatore, R.A.**
*Canticle* 1290, 4108, **4793**
*The Crystal Shard* 3537, 4458
*The Demon Awakens* 1095, **4794**, 4848
*The Demon Spirit* **4795**
*The Dragon King* **4796**
*The Dragon's Dagger* **4797**
*Dragonslayer's Return* 1905, **4798**
*Echoes of the Fourth Magic* 1781, **4799**
*Exile* 2675
*Homeland* 3537, 4108
*In Sylvan Shadows* **4800**
*The Legacy* 1146, 1287, 2427, 2618, 3489, **4801**
*Luthien's Gamble* **4802**
*Passage to Dawn* 4326, **4803**
*Siege of Darkness* 1287, 2427, 2625, **4804**
*The Silent Blade* **4805**
*Sojourn* 299, 604, 1484, **4806**
*Starless Night* 1287, 2427, **4807**, 5022
*The Sword of Bedwyr* **4808**, 5200
*The Woods out Back* 439, 2127, 2739, **4809**

**Sammon, Paul M.**
*The King Is Dead: Tales of Elvis Post Mortem* 2070, 2184, 4540, **4810**
*Splatterpunks II: Over the Edge* **4811**
*Splatterpunks: Extreme Horror* **4812**

**Samson, Joan**
*The Auctioneer* 3497

**Sanders, Scott Russell**
*The Invisible Company* **4813**

**Sanders, William**
*Journey to Fusang* 4545, 5781
*The Wild Blue and the Gray* 1983, 2416, 3867, 3993, **4814**, 5501, 5502

**Sanford, Richard**
*Roadkill* 1049, 4279, **4815**

**Saperstein, David**
*Red Devil* **4816**

**Sapir, Richard**
*The Destroyer #1: Created, the Destroyer* 359, 1547, 4229, 5476

**Sarabande, William**
*Beyond the Sea of Ice* 191, 275, 668, 2166, 2167, 2168, 2169, 2170, 2581, 5444
*The Edge of the World* 881, **4817**
*The Sacred Stones* 2582, 2583, **4818**
*Thunder in the Sky* 731, **4819**

**Saralegui, Jorge**
*Looker* **4820**

**Sarban**
*The Doll Maker and Other Tales of the Uncanny* 749, 1194, 2025
*Ringstones, and Other Curious Tales* 3606, 3879, 3880
*The Sound of His Horn* 2667, 5301

**Sargent, Carl**
*Streets of Blood* 1591, **4821**, 5135

**Sargent, Pamela**
*Afterlives: An Anthology of Stories about Life After Death* 1283, 1872, 1875, 4929, 6031
*The Alien Upstairs* 5910
*Cloned Lives* 5732
*The Golden Space* 4352
*Nebula Awards 29* 1623, 1624, 3751, **4822**
*Nebula Awards 29-31* 1342, 5489
*Nebula Awards 30* 2596, 4439, **4823**
*Nebula Awards 31* 2597, 2598, **4824**
*The Shore of Women* 968, 4792
*Venus of Dreams* 127, 3824, 5377
*Venus of Shadows* 5572
*Women of Wonder: Science Fiction Stories by Women about Women* 628, 1609
*Women of Wonder, the Classic Years: Science Fiction by Women From the 1940s to the 1970s* 765, **4825**
*Women of Wonder, the Contemporary Years: Science Fiction by Women From the 1970s to the 1990s* 765, **4826**

**Sargent, Sarah**
*Jonas McFee, A.T.P.* 2868, **4827**, 5088
*Weird Henry Berg* 2868

**Sarrantonio, Al**
*100 Hair-Raising Little Horror Stories* 1709, 1710, 1714, **4828**, 5686, 5687
*Exile* **4829**
*House Haunted* 90, 342, 861, 1192, 1380, 2040, 2875, 3055, 3161, 3657, 3684, 3685, 4663, 4701, **4830**, 5631
*Moonbane* **4831**
*October* 2221, 3676, **4832**
*Personal Agendas* 1387, 3096, **4833**
*Skeletons* 3956, 4646, **4834**

**Sarti, Ron**
*The Lanterns of God* **4835**
*Legacy of the Ancients* **4836**

**Saul, John**
*Black Lightning* 2755, 3638, 4088, 4327, **4837**
*The Blackstone Chronicles* **4838**
*Creature* 1944, 2205, 2284, 3041, 3153, 4059, 4083, 4087, **4839**, 5789

*Darkness* 1944, 2156, 3164, 3637, **4840**, 5250, 5314
*Guardian* 3162, **4841**
*The Homing* 2284, 3207, **4842**
*The Presence* **4843**
*Second Child* 2822, 3126, **4844**
*Shadows* **4845**
*Suffer the Children* 1236, 1848, 2801, 4450, 4645, 5623

**Saunders, Elizabeth A.**
*When the Black Lotus Blooms* 1823, 2967, 3997, **4846**, 5447

**Saunders, Jake**
*The Texas-Israeli War: 1999* 4836

**Savage, Adrian**
*Symphony* 3389, 3885, 4588, 4646, 4754, **4847**

**Savage, Felicity**
*The Daemon in the Machine* **4848**
*Delta City* **4849**
*Humility Garden* **4850**
*The War in the Waste* **4851**, **4852**

**Sawyer, Robert J.**
*End of an Era* **4853**, 5067
*Far-Seer* 398, 416, 1988, 2122, 2386, 2468, 3427, 3738, 4743, 4744, **4854**
*Fossil Hunter* 1988, 3427, 4744, **4855**
*Frameshift* 444, **4856**
*Golden Fleece* 734, 1549, **4857**, 5042
*Illegal Alien* **4858**
*Starplex* 293, 384, 1157, 1759, 2002, 2135, 2417, 2661, 4351, **4859**, 4951, 5367
*The Terminal Experiment* 507, 2488, 3764, **4860**

**Saxon, Peter**
*The Curse of Rathlaw* 5843, 5846

**Scarborough, Elizabeth Ann**
*Bronwyn's Bane* 1045, 1683, 4699, 5220
*Carol for Another Christmas* 1409, **4861**
*The Christening Quest* 16, 3634
*The Drastic Dragon of Draco, Texas* 1207, 2145
*Final Recipe* 4061, 5199
*The Godmother* 395, 2800, **4862**
*The Godmother's Apprentice* 4171, **4863**
*The Godmother's Web* **4864**
*The Goldcamp Vampire; or The Sanguinary Sourdough* 2009, 4389, 5151
*The Harem of Aman Akbar* 1528, 2050, 2922
*The Healer's War* 1069, 1130, 1631, 3035, 3706, 3743, 3744, 4466, 4477, **4865**, 5383
*Last Refuge* 458, 563, 653, 1064, 1110, 1169, 1253, 1974, 2327, 2499, 2503, 3167, 3844, 3878, 3916, 3935, 4063, 4207, 4208, 4364, 4444, **4866**, 5716, 5750
*Nothing Sacred* 313, 314, 560, 562, 725, 891, 1169, 1328, 1412, 1881, 1932, 2552, 2578, 2716, 3503, 3744, 3745, 3878, 4020, 4061, 4062, 4063, **4867**, 5198, 5378, 5396, 5532, 5757
*Phantom Banjo* 393, 395, 424, 604, 634, 1289, 3274, 3886, 3938, **4868**

*Picking the Ballad's Bones* 1998, **4869**
*Power Lines* 3743
*Power Play* 3744
*Powers That Be* 3745
*Song of Sorcery* 393, 3731
*Space Opera* 3751
*Strum Again?* **4870**
*Warrior Princesses* **4871**

**Schaefer, Frank**
*Whose Song Is Sung* **4872**

**Schaub, Mary**
*Flight of Vengeance* 4152

**Schechter, Harold**
*Dying Breath* 2555
*Nevermore* 4778

**Scheckley, Robert**
*The Tenth Victim* 4115

**Schelling, Christopher**
*The Magic of Christmas* 5024

**Schevill, James**
*Lovecraft's Follies: A Play* 4751

**Schiff, Stuart David**
*The Best of Whispers* 22, 1017, 1629, 2307, 3962, **4873**
*Mad Scientists* 5886
*Whispers: An Anthology of Fantasy and Horror* 2960, 3961
*The Whispers Series* 1823, 2773, 2966, 4724, 4726, 4846, 5025

**Schiller, Gerald A.**
*Deadly Dreams* **4874**

**Schilling, Vivian**
*Sacred Prey* 2896, **4875**

**Schimel, Lawrence**
*Blood Lines: Vampire Stories From New England* 150, 151, **4876**
*Camelot Fantastic* **4877**
*The Drag Queen of Elfland* **4878**
*Fields of Blood: Vampire Stories of the Heartland* **4879**
*The Fortune Teller* 2381
*Southern Blood: Vampire Stories From the American South* **4880**, 5098, 5099
*Streets of Blood: Vampire Stories From New York City* **4881**
*Tarot Fantastic* 2406
*Things Invisible to See: Gay and Lesbian Tales of Magic Realism* **4882**

**Schmidt, Dan**
*Silent Scream* **4883**

**Schmidt, Dennis**
*Kensho* 1329, 4226, 4227, 4228
*Labyrinth* **4884**
*Satori* 3344
*Way-Farer* 4116, 6075

**Schmidt, Stanley**
*Unknown Worlds: Tales From Beyond* 5700

**Schmitz, James H.**
*The Best of James H. Schmitz* 759, 1969, 2947, 3430, 5782, 5838
*The Demon Breed* 595, 892, 899, 958, 1634, 1680, 2055, 2371, 2838, 2877, 3168, 3972, 4172, 4698, 4897, 5037, 5109, 5282, 5527, 5589, 5872
*The Telzey Toy* 632
*The Universe Against Her* 1000, 2420, 2421, 2423, 2684, 3359, 3918, 4139, 4560

*The Witches of Karres* 652, 703, 1384, 1536, 4392, 4405, 5234

**Schochet, Victoria**
*The Berkley Showcase: New Writings in Science Fiction and Fantasy, Volumes 1-4* 5952, 5953

**Schofield, Sandy**
*The Big Game* 8, 2908, 2917

**Schow, David J.**
*Black Leather Required* 1128, 3090, **4885**
*Crypt Orchids* **4886**, 5005
*The Kill Riff* 426, 1052, 1777, 3527, 3807, **4887**, 4997, 5443
*Lost Angels* 1128, 1171, 2656, 2860, **4888**, 5008
*Seeing Red* 700, 776, 1783, 3322, **4889**, 5007, 5008, 5360, 5413
*The Shaft* 871, 2918, 3161, 5692
*Silver Scream* 2183, 2761, 4252, 4811, 4812

**Schulz, Bruno**
*Sanatorium under the Sign of the Hourglass* 573, 2294, 5317
*The Street of Crocodiles* 950, 2294, 3460, 3461, 3464, 5876

**Schwartz, Howard**
*Lilith's Cave: Jewish Tales of the Supernatural* 4791, **4890**

**Schwartz, Susan**
*Byzantium's Crown* 2561, 3255, 3339, 5503, 5508, 5510
*Imperial Lady* **4155**

**Schweitzer, Darrell**
*Tom O'Bedlam's Night Out and Other Strange Excursions* 3859
*Transients and Other Disquieting Tales* 3614, **4891**, 5929

**Scithes, George H.**
*Another Round at the Spaceport Bar* 2125

**Scognamiglio, John**
*Dark Seductions* **72**

**Scortia, Thomas N.**
*Strange Bedfellows: Sex and Science Fiction* 1362, 1607

**Scotch, Cheri**
*The Werewolf's Kiss* 3411, 5481
*The Werewolf's Touch* 4246, **4892**

**Scott, Dixon**
*A Fresh Wind in the Willows* 2774, 2775, 2776

**Scott, Elkeanor**
*Randall's Round* 1673

**Scott, Gavin**
*Revolution* 3544

**Scott, Jefferson**
*Terminal Logic* **4893**, 4901

**Scott, Jody**
*I, Vampire* 1122

**Scott, Melissa**
*The Armor of Light* 1063, 2262, 2263, 3714, 4651, 5147
*Burning Bright* **4894**
*A Choice of Destinies* 350, 590, 1855, 2140, 5506, 5507, 5510, 5512
*Dreaming Metal* 2660, **4895**
*Dreamships* 79, 930, 2832, 3749, **4896**, 5229
*The Empress of Earth* 4593

*Five-Twelfths of Heaven* 882, 897, 4594, 4942, 5298, 5546
*The Kindly Ones* 353, 1757
*Mighty Good Road* 1041, 1056, 1332, 2476, 3727, 4289, **4897**
*Night Sky Mine* **4898**, 4930
*Point of Hopes* 1705, 2758, 3257, 3283, 4651, **4899**, 5152, 5758, 5976
*Shadow Man* 1588, 2059, 2134, 3426, 3440, **4900**, 5037, 5461
*The Shapes of Their Hearts* **4901**
*Silence in Solitude* 4593
*Trouble and Her Friends* 951, 956, 1761, 2445, 3072, 4179, **4902**, 5619

**Scotten, Cordell**
*Renegade* **4903**

**Searight, Richard F.**
*The Brain in the Jar and Others* **4904**
*The Sealed Casket and Other Stories* **4905**

**Searles, Baird**
*Halflings, Hobbits, Warrows & Weefolk: A Collection of Tales of Heroes Short in Stature* 1340, 1994, 2378, 2388, **4906**, 5239

**Searls, David J.**
*Yellow Moon* **4907**

**Sebanc, Mark**
*Flight to Hollow Mountain* 1042, **4908**

**Sechi, Stephen Michael**
*Tales of Talislanta* **4909**

**See, Carolyn**
*Making History* 2997

**Seeman, Elizabeth**
*The Talking Dog and the Barking Man* 2786

**Segriff, Larry**
*Alien Dreams* **4910**
*Battle Magic* 2380
*Future Net* 2394
*Spacer Dreams* 2478, 4158, 4379, **4911**, 4948, 4958

**Seidman, David L.**
*The First Casualty* **4912**

**Selby, Curt**
*Blood County* 2912

**Seltzer, David**
*The Omen* 2312, 3445, 3958, 5401, 5538

**Semeiks, Jonna Gormley**
*Dying Breath* **2555**

**Serling, Carol**
*Journeys to the Twilight Zone* 1281, **4913**, 4916
*Return to the Twilight Zone* 1281, **4914**, 4916

**Serling, Robert**
*Something's Alive on the Titanic* 1202, **4915**

**Serling, Rod**
*Devils and Demons* 2385
*The Gallery Reader* 4914
*More Stories From The Twilight Zone* 3132
*New Stories From The Twilight Zone* 3132
*The Night Gallery Reader* 2402, 2403, 4913, 5473
*Rod Serling's Triple W* 1711

*The Season to Be Wary* 4875
*Stories From the Twilight Zone* 2402, 3132, 4913, 4914, 5473
*The Twilight Zone: Complete Stories* 4916

**Service, Pamela F.**
*All's Faire* 53, 1040, 4487, **4917**
*Being of Two Minds* 3340, **4918**
*Under Alien Stars* 1262, 1504, 2808, **4919**
*Vision Quest* 3934, **4920**, 5928, 5995
*Weirdos of the Universe, Unite!* 167, **4921**
*When the Night Wind Howls* 773
*Winter of Magic's Return* 641, 2272, 3261

**Severance, Carol**
*Demon Drums* 4784, **4922**
*Reefsong* 63, 181, 1997, 4421, **4923**, 4964, 5029, 5541, 5744
*Storm Caller* **4924**

**Severson, Ellen Dodge**
*Hederick, the Theocrat* **4925**

**Seymour, L. Edward**
*The Bighead* 3387

**Shafferman, Barbara**
*The President's Astrologer* **4926**

**Shakespeare, William**
*The Merchant of Venice* 1045
*The Tempest* 5826

**Sharp, Margery**
*The Rescuers* 737, 1821, 2848, 2851, 2852, 3115

**Shatner, William**
*The Ashes of Eden* **4927**
*Avenger* **4928**
*Believe: A Novel* 1872, 1875, **4929**
*Delta Search* **4930**
*The Law of War* **4931**
*Man o' War* **4932**
*The Return* 2065, **4933**
*Spectre* **4934**
*Tek Money* **4935**
*Tek Net* **4936**
*Tek Power* **4937**
*Tek Vengeance* **4938**
*TekLab* 829, **4939**
*TekLords* 831, 4590, **4940**
*TekWar* 829, 1406, **4941**, 5302

**Shaw, Bob**
*The Fugitive Worlds* **4942**
*Orbitsville* 247
*The Two-Timers* 2489
*The Wooden Spaceships* 3344

**Shayne, Maggie**
*Eternity* **4943**

**Shea, Michael**
*The Colour out of Time* 1497, 3548, 3566, 3567, 3568, 4112, 4449, 5884
*Fat Face* 4007, 5426, 5446
*I, Said the Fly* **4944**
*The Mines of Behemoth* 3422, **4945**
*Nifft the Lean* 856, 1142, 1239, 1927, 1928, 2451, 3122, 3419, 5471, 5547

**Shea, Robert**
*The Illuminatus! Trilogy* 1093, 1273, 1274, 4302, 4662, 4708, 5009, 5074, 5170
*Shaman* 191, **4946**

**Sheckley, Robert**
*Alien Harvest* 4285
*Bring Me the Head of Prince Charming* **6062**
*A Call to Arms* 1387
*The Collected Robert Sheckley* 234, 5805
*Dimension of Miracles* 6062, 6070
*Dramocles: An Intergalactic Soap Opera* 6062
*A Farce to Be Reckoned With* **6064**
*If at Faust You Don't Succeed* **6070**
*Is THAT What People Do? The Selected Short Stories of Robert Sheckley* 1753
*Journey Beyond Tomorrow* 506, 6064
*Mindswap* 6064
*Minotaur Maze* 5810
*On the Planet of Bottled Brains* 6070
*Options* 6062, 6070
*The Status Civilization* 3522

**Sheffield, Charles**
*Aftermath* 3761, **4947**
*The Billion Dollar Boy* 4158, 4379, **4948**
*Brother to Dragons* **4949**, 5132
*Cold as Ice* 1254, 2476, **4950**, 5540, 5859
*Convergence* **4951**
*The Cyborg From Earth* 4379, **4952**
*Dancing with Myself* 123, 237, 244, **4953**
*Divergence* **4954**
*The Ganymede Club* **4955**
*Georgia on My Mind and Other Places* 1963, **4956**
*Godspeed* 420, **4957**
*Higher Education* 1962, 4379, **4958**
*How to Save the World* 888, 1962, **4959**
*The Judas Cross* **4960**
*The McAndrew Chronicles* 1990, 1992, 5247, 6065
*The Nimrod Hunt* 3665, 4289, 4557
*One Man's Universe* 236, 2979, **4961**
*Proteus Combined* 4550
*Proteus in the Underworld* **4962**
*Proteus Unbound* **4963**
*Putting Up Roots* 4379, **4964**
*The Selkie* 1179
*Sight of Proteus* 4470
*Summertide* **4965**
*Tomorrow and Tomorrow* 477, **4966**
*Trader's World* 4175
*Transcendence* 322, 1501, 2661, **4967**

**Sheldon, Alice**
*Her Smoke Rose Up Forever* 5477

**Shelley, Mary**
*Collected Tales and Stories* **4968**
*Frankenstein* 140, 199, 498, 1561, 2293, 3019, 3180, 3526, 4684, 5422, 5847
*The Mortal Immortal* 411, **4969**
*Tales and Stories of Mary Wollstonecraft Shelley* 2158

**Shelley, Rick**
*The Hero King* 286, **4970**
*The Hero of Varay* 4265, **4971**
*Lieutenant* **4972**
*Officer Cadet* **4973**
*Return to Camerein* **4974**
*Until Relieved* 5718
*The Wizard at Home* **4975**

**Shepard, Jim**
*Lights Out in the Reptile House* 164, 4949, **4976**

**Shepard, Leslie**
*The Dracula Book of Great Vampire Stories* 1308, 1360, 1370, 2407, 4407, 5265, 5706

**Shepard, Lucius**
*The Ends of the Earth* 2835, 3048, 3086, 3234, 3442, 4561, **4977**, 5056
*The Golden* 325, 572, 603, 812, 2511, 3601, 4094, 4098, **4978**
*The Jaguar Hunter* 674, 675, 821, 3086, 3706, 4053, 4630
*Kalimantan* 1356, 1435, 3101, 3173, 3478, 3916, 4020, 4061, 4062, 4207, **4979**, 5520
*Life During Wartime* 323, 3449, 3666, 3706, 5955, 6061
*Nantucket Slayrides* 98, 3363, 4314

**Shepherd, Mark**
*Elvendude* **4980**
*Escape From Roksamur* 3479, 3490
*Spiritride* **4981**
*Wheels of Fire* **3301**

**Sherman, David**
*School of Fire* **4982**

**Sherman, Delia**
*The Essential Bordertown* **5914**
*The Horns of Elfland* **3264**
*The Porcelain Dove* 1358, 2509, 2758, 3843, 3847, 4899, **4983**, 5275, 5914

**Sherman, Joel Henry**
*Random Factor* 3448, **4984**

**Sherman, Josepha**
*A Cast of Corbies* **3274**
*Castle of Deception* **3275**
*The Chaos Gate* 1839, 3479, 3489, 3490
*Child of Faerie, Child of Earth* 1741, 3275, **4985**, 5217
*The Horse of Flame* 657, 3275
*King's Son, Magic's Son* **4986**
*Once upon a Galaxy* **4987**
*Orphans of the Night* 3070, **4988**
*The Shattered Oath* **4989**
*The Shining Falcon* 3274, 3275, 5390, 5393
*Son of Darkness* **4990**
*A Strange and Ancient Name* 3274, 3275, **4991**

**Shetterly, Will**
*Cats Have No Lord* 259, 4921, 5063, 5159
*Dogland* 1445, **4992**
*Double Feature* 767
*Elsewhere* 235, 396, 545, 546, 549, 550, 552, 767, 769, 970, 976, 1101, 1159, 1427, 1436, 1474, 1837, 1841, 1958, 2142, 2373, 2467, 3245, 3271, 3299, 3301, 3302, 3468, 3513, 3871, 3884, 4149, 4174, 4261, 4497, 4615, 4675, 4985, 4990, **4993**, 5143, 5179, 5181, 5267, 5371, 5556, 5822, 5913, 5914, 5915, 5977
*Liavek* 408, 630, 646, 647, 767, 986, 989, 1683, 1889, 1969, 1994, 2376, 3300, 3643, 3646, 3836, 4166, 4335, 4405, 4723, 5038, 5210, 5214, 5216, 5599, 5913, 5915, 5945

*Liavek: Festival Week* 767, 989, 4723, **4994**, 5216, 5945
*The Liavek Series* 769, 5581
*Liavek: Spells of Binding* 646, 989, 5216, 5913, 5915
*Liavek: The Players of Luck* 989, 1994, 5216, 5973
*Liavek: Wizard's Row* 767, 989, 1427, 3076, 4390, 5210, 5216, 5913, 5915, 5945
*Nevernever* 767, 769, 1148, 1152, 1400, 2373, 3198, **4995**, 5914
*The Tangled Lands* 104, 105, 179, 180, 475, 1161, 1163, 1452, 1461, 1662, 1684, 2082, 2330, 2644, 2791, 3587, 3831, 5063, 5156, 5159, 5558, 5719

**Shettle, Andrea**
*Flute Song Magic* 1583, 3286, 4167, 4801, 4806, **4996**, 5179, 6043

**Shiel, M.P.**
*Xelucha and Others* 964

**Shiner, Lewis**
*Deserted Cities of the Heart* 2998, 3706, 5057
*Glimpses* 1835, 3664, 4553, 4579, **4997**, 5089, 5850, 5873
*Nine Hard Questions about the Nature of the Universe* **4998**
*Slam* 323
*When the Music's Over* 4959

**Shinn, Sharon**
*The Alleluia Files* **4999**
*Archangel* 1442, 3739, 3819, **5000**
*Jovah's Angel* **5001**
*The Shape-Changer's Wife* 3280, **5002**

**Shippey, Tom**
*The Oxford Book of Fantasy Stories* 228, 848, 1613, 2592, 3070, 3574, **5003**, 5030, 5721, 5730
*The Oxford Book of Science Fiction Stories* 229, 246, 422, 1612, 2585, 2594, 2595, 3381, 3574, **5004**

**Shiras, Wilmar H.**
*Children of the Atom* 3340

**Shirley, John**
*Black Butterflies: A Flock on the Dark Side* 1492, 3090, 4886, **5005**
*Cellars* 20
*Dracula in Love* 55
*Eclipse* 1750, 4343
*Eclipse Corona* 1750, **5006**
*Eclipse Penumbra* 1750
*Heatseeker* 555, 807, 4977, **5007**, 5255, 5899
*In Darkness Waiting* 2344, 2345, 4907
*New Noir* 1128, 2656, 2860, 4250, **5008**
*Silicon Embrace* **5009**
*Wetbones* 2156, 2313, 2843, 3396, 4041, **5010**, 5853

**Shuler, Linda Lay**
*She Who Remembers* 3889

**Shupp, Mike**
*Death's Gray Land* **5011**
*The Last Reckoning* **5012**

**Shusterman, Neal**
*Scorpion Shards* 4070, **5013**

**Shute, Nevil**
*On the Beach* 3966

**Shwartz, Susan**
*Arabesques II* 374, 2130, 4534, 6087
*Arabesques: More Tales of the Arabian Nights* 374, 1681, 1687, 2123, 2129, 2130, 4534, 5981, 6087
*Blood Feuds* **5292**
*Cross and Crescent* **5014**
*The Grail of Hearts* 965, 2571, 2883, **5015**
*Hecate's Cauldron* 6034
*Heritage of Flight* 3748, 4696, **5016**
*Shards of Empire* 965, **5017**, 5511, 5513
*Silk Roads and Shadows* 5292, 5506
*Sisters in Fantasy* 2380, 3670, 5815
*Sisters in Fantasy 2* **5018**
*Vulcan's Forge* **5019**

**Siciliano, Sam**
*The Angel of the Opera* 4773
*Blood Feud* **5020**

**Siddons, Anne Rivers**
*The House Next Door* 890, 3621, **5021**

**Siegel, Barbara**
*Tanis, the Shadow Years* 154, 3155, 5454, 5455

**Siegel, Scott**
*Tales From Tethedril* **5022**

**Sievert, John**
*Suicide Attack* 1567, **5023**, 5469

**Silbersack, John**
*The Magic of Christmas* 2412, 2587, 2588, 2589, **5024**
*Roger's Rangers* 554, 827, 3036

**Silke, James**
*Plague of Knives* 6083

**Silva, David B.**
*Best of The Horror Show* 1823, 2773, 2960, 2966, 3959, 3960, 3997, 4200, 4724, 4726, 4846, 4873
*Dead End: City Limits* **4212**
*The Definitive Best of the Horror Show* 1017, 2773, **5025**
*Disappeared* 97
*The Night in Fog* 1016, 2701, **5026**
*Post Mortem: New Tales of Ghostly Horror* **4214**

**Silverberg, Robert**
*The Alien Years* **5027**
*Alpha 1* 4721
*At Winter's End* 724, 884
*Beyond Control* 6027
*Beyond the Safe Zone* 4535
*The Book of Skulls* 2487, 2920, 3239, 4234, 4813
*Born with the Dead* 3797
*Car Sinister* 1644
*The Collected Stories of Robert Silverberg, Volume 1: Secret Sharers* **5028**
*Conquerers From the Darkness* 2252
*The Crystal Ship* 4825
*Downward to the Earth* 707, 5052, 5055
*Dying Inside* 2290, 3203, 3742, 3860
*Earth Is the Strangest Place* 6027
*The Face of the Waters* 4176, 4507, **5029**, 5726
*The Fantasy Hall of Fame* 228, 1613, 2592, 3574, 5003, **5030**, 5730
*The Gate of Worlds* 135, 783, 5868

*Gilgamesh the King* 178, 363, 3581, 5496, 5831
*Hawksbill Station* 2575, 3597
*The Horror Hall of Fame* 2590, **5031**
*Hot Sky at Midnight* **5032**
*Kingdoms of the Wall* 4063, 5000, **5033**, 5862
*Legends: Short Novels by the Masters of Modern Fantasy* **5034**
*Letters From Atlantis* 6, 331, 658, 1012, 1490, 1537, 1873, 2752, 2861, 3545, 4918, **5035**, 5336, 5827, 6017
*Lion Time in Timbuctoo* 1996, 4544, **5036**
*Lord Valentine's Castle* 882, 961, 2361, 3385, 3386, 3477, 3580, 4670, 4994, 5581, 5931
*The Masks of Time* 5195
*The Mountains of Majipoor* **5037**
*Murasaki* 689, 1517, **5038**
*The Mutant Season* 2474, 2477, 2478, **5039**
*The New Springtime* 724, **5040**
*Nightfall* 248
*Nightwings* 4152
*The Positronic Man* 249
*Recalled to Life* 379, 419, 1337
*The Science Fiction Hall of Fame, Volume 1* 24, 214, 215, 238, 239, 241, 500, 501, 1612, 1614, 1616, 1620, 1874, 2405, 2585, 3187, 3308, 3381, 4031, 4376, 5004, 5031, 5948, 6027
*The Science Fictional Dinosaur* 4543
*Son of Man* 3434
*Sorcerers of Majipoor* **5041**
*Starborne* 4333, **5042**, 5860
*Thebes of the Hundred Gates* 658, 3185, 3237, 3428, 4355, **5043**
*To Live Again* 3239
*To the Land of the Living* 1089, 1872, 1875, 3842, **5044**, 5831
*Tom O'Bedlam* 5193, 5909
*Tower of Glass* 2539, 4220, 5157, 5491
*The Ugly Little Boy* 250
*Universe 1* 1363, 1364, 1365
*Universe 1-3* 2634, 2635
*Universe 2* 216, 1363, 1364, 1365, 1620, 1622, **5045**
*Universe 3* 1617, 1623, 1624, 2596, **5046**
*Up the Line* 264, 1638, 5503, 5513
*Valentine Pontifex* 954, 5512

**Silverstein, Janna**
*Full Spectrum 5* **2679**

**Simak, Clifford D.**
*All Flesh Is Grass* 435
*Cemetery World* 885
*A Choice of Gods* 5909
*City* 252, 874, 3240, 5040, 5586, 5589
*The Cosmic Engineers* 5863
*Destiny Doll* 923
*The Fellowship of the Talisman* 185, 355, 630, 884, 955, 1998, 2945, 3822, 5228
*The Goblin Reservation* 3010, 3175, 4389, 4390
*A Heritage of Stars* 484, 882, 3788, 4619, 4620
*Mastodonia* 2192, 3428, 3920, 4233, 5998
*Our Children's Children* 2870

Author Index

*Out of Their Minds* 87, 1399, 1413, 1872, 2791, 3015, 3173, 3768, 4364, 4869, 4921, 5087, 5148, 5697, 5934

*Over the River & through the Woods* 411, 3712, **5047**, 5344, 5346, 5348

*Project Pope* 5171

*Ring Around the Sun* 5774, 6060

*Shakespeare's Planet* 209, 3079, 5826

*Skirmish: The Great Short Fiction of Clifford D. Simak* 624, 4535

*Special Deliverance* 635, 5113

*They Walked Like Men* 1157, 2048

*Time Is the Simplest Thing* 1581, 4016

*The Visitors* 3940

*Way Station* 125, 263, **5048**

*The Werewolf Principle* 1869

*Why Call Them Back From Heaven?* 2498, 4066, 5243

**Simmons, Dan**

*Carrion Comfort* 55, 462, 1094, 1670, 1778, 1959, 2493, 3206, 3396, 3547, 4096, 4580, 4666, 4978, 5010, 5020, **5049**, 5399, 5405, 5475, 5690, 5704, 5899

*Children of the Night* 279, 1463, 4755, **5050**, 5172, 5852

*Endymion* 1442, 2059, 2525, 3718, 4060, 5001, **5051**, 6081

*The Fall of Hyperion* 80, 96, 116, 272, 404, 414, 417, 423, 449, 883, 899, 952, 1054, 1184, 1634, 1820, 2036, 2480, 2725, 3014, 3437, 4099, 4507, 4762, 4769, 4857, 4954, 4965, 5029, **5052**, 5905

*Fires of Eden* 2743, **5053**

*The Hollow Man* 362, 1089, 1438, 2163, 2727, 3007, 3049, **5054**, 5680

*Hyperion* 80, 96, 116, 220, 270, 293, 328, 404, 414, 417, 423, 447, 449, 472, 478, 566, 708, 783, 899, 930, 952, 1054, 1106, 1184, 1634, 1681, 1819, 1820, 1993, 2036, 2056, 2057, 2060, 2480, 2666, 2727, 2729, 2766, 2882, 3014, 3117, 3398, 3437, 3644, 4099, 4136, 4281, 4507, 4641, 4708, 4736, 4762, 4769, 4857, 4867, 4896, 4901, 4951, 4954, 4965, 5012, 5029, **5055**, 5372, 5436, 5449, 5594, 5668, 5774, 5899, 5905

*The Hyperion Cantos* 3143

*Lost Summer* 4011

*Lovedeath* 938, 1362, **5056**

*Phases of Gravity* 388, 431, 3612, 4632, **5057**, 5247, 5540

*Prayers to Broken Stones* 821, 4253, **5058**

*The Rise of Endymion* 687, 2525, **5059**

*Song of Kali* 1338, 1670, 1886, 3408, 5851

*Summer of Night* 3754, 4907, **5060**

**Simmons, Trana Mae**

*Spell Bound* **5061**

**Simmons, Wm. Mark**

*In the Net of Dreams* 1461, 3831

*One Foot in the Grave* **5062**

*When Dreams Collide* 87, 179, 3173, **5063**

**Simon, Jean**

*Ghost Boy* 1926, 2821, 3785, **5064**

*Orphans* 3406, **5065**

*Sweet Revenge* **5066**

**Simons, Les**

*Gila* 3054

**Simos, Miriam**

*The Fifth Sacred Thing* **5209**

**Simpson, George Gaylord**

*The Dechronization of Sam Magruder* **5067**, 5315

**Simpson, Pamela**

*Partners in Time* 5390, 5393

**Sinclair, Alison**

*Blueheart* **5068**

*Legacies* **5069**

**Sinclair, May**

*The Intercessor and Other Stories* 601

**Singer, A.L.**

*Safari Sleuth* 3544

**Singer, Isaac Bashevis**

*Collected Stories* 4890

**Singer, Marilyn**

*Charmed* 1837, **5070**, 5559, 5822

**Singer, Richard**

*Air Fish* **4199**

**Singleton, Jacqui**

*Heartstone and Silver* 4627, **5071**

**Siodmak, Curt**

*Donovan's Brain/Hauser's Memory* 3562, 3563, **5072**, 5791

*Gabriel's Body* 436, 1786, 3561, 3562, 3563, **5073**

**Sirius, R.U.**

*How to Mutate and Take Over the World* 3457, **5074**

**Sirota, Michael B.**

*Demon Shadows* 1828, 4223, **5075**

*The Ultimate Bike Path* **5076**

*The Well* 3160, **5077**, 5121

**Sizemore, Susan**

*Forever Knight: A Stirring of Dust* **5078**

**Skal, David J.**

*Antibodies* 555, 3196

**Skarda, Patricia L.**

*The Evil Image: Two Centuries of Gothic Short Fiction and Poetry* 307, 848, 1314, **5439**

**Skibell, Joseph**

*A Blessing on the Moon* **5079**

**Skimin, Bob**

*Gray Victory* 896, 5147

**Skipp, John**

*Animals* **5080**

*Book of the Dead* 2118, 2379, 2977, 3758, 4168, 4412, 4745, 4746, 4786, 4811, 4812, 5313, 5888

*The Bridge: A Horror Story* 1020, 1806, 2541, 2670, 3091, 4279, **5081**

*The Cleanup* 1052, 3527

*Dead Lines* 2153, 3362, 4310, 4885, 5008, **5082**, 5360

*Fright Night* 1032, 1034

*The Light at the End* 490, 697, 946, 948, 1006, 1122, 1301, 1707, 1779, 2151, 3963, 4190, 5175

*The Scream* 2147, 2222, 3445, 3950, 4588, 4887, 4997, 5340, 5893

*Still Dead: Book of the Dead 2* 2977, 4168, 4412, 4745, 4746, 4786, 4811, **5083**, 5313, 5888

**Sky, Kathleen**

*Vulcan!* 528, 3919, 3920

*Witchdame* 2945, 3700

**Skye, Christina**

*Bride of the Mist* 2540

**Slade, Michael**

*Cutthroat* 2931, **5084**

*Evil Eye* **5085**

*Ghoul* 2638, 3899

*Headhunter* 2599

**Sladek, John**

*Mechasm* 1918, 1919, 3573

*Roderick* 3465

**Slater, Ian**

*Battle Front* **5086**

**Slavicsek, Bill**

*Storm Knights* 2056, 3015, **5087**, 5210, 5438

**Sleator, William**

*Interstellar Pig* 168, 2807

*Strange Attractors* 121, **5088**

**Sloan, Kay**

*Elvis Rising: Stories on the King* 2070, 4540, **5089**

**Sloane, Ben**

*Outland Strip* 831

*Ultimate Weapon* 831, 3665

**Sloane, William**

*The Edge of Running Water* 3417

*To Walk the Night* 3417, 4235

**Slonczewski, Joan**

*The Children Star* 760, 3000, 3231, 5068, **5090**, 5437, 6080

*Daughter of Elysium* 210, 236, 249, 447, 665, 686, 892, 1083, 1336, 1724, 1769, 1872, 2008, 2049, 2820, 3231, 4241, 4698, 4893, **5091**, 5368, 5587, 5745

*A Door into Ocean* 134, 181, 210, 211, 566, 580, 643, 686, 792, 899, 968, 1056, 1116, 1543, 1559, 1586, 1723, 1769, 1824, 2051, 2295, 2443, 2578, 3001, 3064, 3248, 3440, 3729, 3745, 4187, 4325, 4421, 4554, 4627, 4629, 4633, 4634, 4698, 4902, 4922, 4923, 5029, 5068, 5130, 5172, 5209, 5233, 5268, 5435, 5436, 5450, 5526, 5587, 5590, 5638, 5726, 5949, 5956, 6080

*Still Forms on Foxfield* 211, 2243, 2578, 2751, 3344

*The Wall Around Eden* 160, 211, 327, 365, 720, **5092**, 5878

**Slung, Michele**

*I Shudder at Your Touch* 75, 1118, 1120, 1357, 1361, 1367, 1607, 2176, 2178, 2179, 2181, 2182, 2185, 2893, 3024, 3026, 4465, 5056, **5093**

*Shudder Again* 1118, 1120, 1361, 2176, 2178, 2179, 2182, 2185, 5056, **5094**

**Smart, Brian**

*Best of the Midwest's Science Fiction, Fantasy and Horror, Volume I* 4199

*Best of the Midwest's Science Fiction, Fantasy and Horror, Volume II* 4199, **5095**

*The Best of the Midwest's Science Fiction, Fantasy and Horror, Volume II* 5447

**Smedman, Lisa**

*Blood Sport* **5096**

*The Lucifer Deck* 5207

**Smeds, Dave**

*The Schemes of Dragons* 1470, 4922, **5097**

*The Sorcery Within* 2502, 2553, 4922, 5563

**Smith, A.C.H.**

*The Dark Crystal: A Novel* 3404, 5572

*Labyrinth: A Novel* 718

**Smith, Beecher**

*Monsters From Memphis* **5098**

*More Monsters From Memphis* **5099**

**Smith, Brian Scott**

*When Shadows Fall* 3885, **5100**

**Smith, Carmichael**

*Atomsk* 5105, 5106

**Smith, Cheryl A.**

*The Falcon and the Serpent* **5101**

**Smith, Clark Ashton**

*The Book of Hyperborea* 3582, **5102**

*The Dweller in the Gulf* 348

*Mother of Toads* 348

*Other Dimensions* 1700, 5628

*Out of Space and Time* 1496, 3529, 3534

*A Prophecy of Monsters* **5103**

*A Rendezvous in Averoigne* 1494, 2225, 5627

*Tales of Zothique* 291, 1699, 1700, 3420, 3859, **5104**

*The Vaults of Yoh-Vombis* 348

*The Zothique* 4021

**Smith, Cordwainer**

*The Best of Cordwainer Smith* 233, 242, 321, 804, 892, 930, 1061, 1608, 1723, 1727, 1874, 1895, 2649, 2832, 3001, 3187, 3308, 3796, 4123, 4126, 4127, 4216, 4346, 4376, 4706, 4769, 5363, 5368, 5369, 5551, 5586, 5589, 5638, 5834

*Norstrilia* 77, 250, 1680, 1723, 1725, 2049, 2536, 2645, 2649, 3240, 3797, 4054, 4698, 4931, **5105**, 5117, 5157, 5213, 5452, 5566, 5586, 5589, 5809, 5834, 5835

*Quest of the Three Worlds* 897

*The Rediscovery of Man* 54, 445, 479, 689, 759, 850, 1588, 1787, 1969, 2569, 2576, 2947, 3240, 3430, 3441, 4071, 4118, 4136, **5106**, 5344, 5345, 5346, 5349, 5613, 5782, 5838, 5869

**Smith, David Alexander**

*Future Boston* **5107**

*Homecoming* 210, 469, 734, 1059, 1407, 1537, 1869, 1989, 2108, 2419, 2691, 2898, 3437, 3603, 3943, 4124, 4626, 4643, 4896, **5108**, 5452, 5573, 5574

*In the Cube* 156, 476, 478, 2087, 2092, 3520, 4748, **5109**, 5363, 5587

*Marathon* 64, 473, 2579, 3698, 3741, 3760, 5248

*Rendezvous* 34, 64, 202, 450, 1058, 1407, 1537, 1557, 2216, 2898, 2921, 3398, 3437, 4217, 4219, 5452, 5573, 5787

**Smith, David C.**
*Engor's Sword Arm* 2782, **5110**, 5471
*The Fair Rules of Evil* 2020, 2607, 4820, **5111**

**Smith, David van Meter**
*Trinity Grove* 1806, 3042, 3956, 4586, **5112**

**Smith, Dean Wesley**
*The Abductors: Conspiracy* **2034**
*The Escape* 2297, **5113**, 5880
*Laying the Music to Rest* 84, 1193, 1202, 1860, 1972, 2034, 2732, 4772, 4915, **5114**
*The Soldiers of Fear* 9, 901, 903, 2297, **5115**

**Smith, Deborah**
*Legends* 5639

**Smith, Dodie**
*The Hundred and One Dalmatians* 2786

**Smith, E.E. "Doc"**
*Triplanetary* 270

**Smith, Edward E.**
*Galactic Patrol* 270, **5116**
*The Galaxy Primes* 5864
*Gray Lensman* 270, **5117**
*The Lensman Series* 309
*The Skylark of Space* 270, 5141
*Skylark of Valeron* 270, 5863
*Triplanetary* 4103

**Smith, Ernest Bramah**
*Kai Lung Unrolls His Mat* 6026
*Kai Lung's Golden Hours* 6026

**Smith, George H.**
*Kar Kaballa* 261, 4814

**Smith, George O.**
*Nomad* 5864
*Pattern for Conquest* 5863

**Smith, Guy N.**
*The Black Fedora* 602
*The Dark One* **5118**
*Dead End* 2156, **5119**
*Dead Meat* **5120**
*Entombed* 3347
*The Killer Crabs Series* 2671
*Water Rites* **5121**
*Witch Spell* 690, **5122**

**Smith, James V.**
*The Lurker* **5123**

**Smith, Julia**
*Shadow-Maze* **5133**

**Smith, Julie Dean**
*Call of Madness* 1674, 2561, 3293, **5124**, 5783
*Mission of Magic* 4458, **5125**
*Sage of Sare* 1064, **5126**
*The Wizard King* **5127**, 5752

**Smith, Kim**
*Mysterious Cat Stories* **5252**

**Smith, L.J.**
*Dark Reunion* 120, 1302, 4328, **5161**
*Heart of Valor* 5070
*The Night of the Solstice* 5070
*Secret Vampire* 120

**Smith, L. Neil**
*Bretta Martyn* **5128**

*Brightsuit MacBear* 4350, 4435
*Contact and Commune* 129, 165, 211, 3603, 4017, **5129**, 5174, 5514, 5564, 5932
*Converse and Conflict* **5130**
*The Crystal Empire* 178, 5781, 5906
*The Gallatin Divergence* 141, 142, 4536, 5012
*Henry Martyn* 4277, **5131**
*The Lando Calrissian Adventures* 76, 103, 115, 2500, 3247, 3820, 4299, 5527
*Lando Calrissian and the Flamewind of Oseon* 6052, 6054, 6055
*Lando Calrissian and the Mindharp of Sharu* 6052, 6054, 6055
*Lando Calrissian and the Starcave of Thon Boka* 6052, 6054, 6055
*The Nagasaki Vector* 142, 143, 593, 783, 1196, 1199, 1563
*Pallas* 435, **5132**
*The Probability Broach* 1655, 1915, 2921, 3109, 3466, 5889
*Taflak Lysandra* 4435
*Their Majesties' Bucketeers* 981, 1988, 2108, 4855
*Tom Paine Maru* 593, 5403, 5549
*The Venus Belt* 83, 593, 2450

**Smith, Mark**
*Shadow-Maze* **5133**

**Smith, Martin Cruz**
*The Indians Won* 4814
*Nightwing* 2615, 2926, 4688, 4815, 5263

**Smith, Michael Marshall**
*Spares* 1973, 5892

**Smith, Nyx**
*Fade to Black* **5134**, 5207
*Striper Assassin* 1591, **5135**
*Who Hunts the Hunter* 3198

**Smith, Robert Arthur**
*Silent Witness* 3898, **5136**

**Smith, Sherwood**
*Court Duel* **5137**
*Derelict for Trade* **4148**
*A Mind for Trade* **4158**
*The Phoenix in Flight* 310, 1047, 1901, 2366, 4148, 4158, **5138**, 5671, 5673, 5675, 5681
*A Prison Unsought* 4158, **5139**
*The Rifter's Covenant* **5140**
*Ruler of Naught* **5141**
*Wren to the Rescue* 67, 599, 1605, 2869, 2944, 3159, 4700, **5142**, 5579, 5974, 6025, 6043, 6058
*Wren's Quest* 1319, 1320, 1600, **5143**
*Wren's War* 4321, **5144**

**Smith, Stephanie A.**
*Other Nature* **5145**

**Smith, Susan Mackay**
*Wolf's Cub* **5964**

**Smith, Thorne**
*The Night Life of the Gods* 1491, 5570
*Topper: An Improbable Adventure* 2327, 3470, 3989, 4275

**Smith, Wayne**
*Thor* **5146**

**Snodgrass, Melinda M.**
*Ace in the Hole* **3641**
*Dealer's Choice* **3643**

*Double Solitaire* 3642, 3647, 3891, 5567
*Queen's Gambit Declined* 652, 955, 2945, 3822, 5125, **5147**, 5510
*The Tears of the Singers* 526

**Snow, Greg**
*That's All, Folks!* 499, 4434, **5148**

**Snow, Jack**
*The Magical Mimics in Oz* 3609
*Spectral Snow: The Dark Fantasies of Jack Snow* **5149**

**Snyder, Midori**
*Beldan's Fire* 4489, **5150**
*The Flight of Michael McBride* 1512, 2009, 3118, 3280, **5151**, 5356, 5357
*Hatchling* 2003, 2469
*The Innamorati* **5152**
*New Moon* 3067, 3298

**Snyder, Zilpha Keatley**
*Song of the Gargoyle* **5153**

**Sohl, Jerry**
*Costigan's Needle* 5088, 5114
*Night Slaves* 5358

**Soles, Caro**
*Meltdown!* 2117, 2444, **5154**

**Somtow, S.P.**
*Aquila and the Iron Horse* 3917
*Aquila and the Sphinx* 3917
*Aquila in the New World* 3917
*Darker Angels* **5155**
*Forest of the Night* **5156**
*I Wake From a Dream of a Drowned Star* 4850, **5157**
*Moon Dance* 514, 603, 834, 1126, 1127, 1822, 2794, 2895, 3053, 3411, 4002, 4052, 4251, 4946, 5146, 5151, **5158**, 5421, 5481
*Riverrun* 1529, 1684, 2644, 4970, **5159**
*Valentine* 1301, **5160**
*Vampire Junction* 490, 697, 946, 1124, 3623, 3781, 4307, 4573, 4574, 5419
*The Vampire's Beautiful Daughter* 120, 2131, 3162, **5161**
*Vanitas: Escape From Vampire Junction* 1122, 3954, **5162**
*The Wizard's Apprentice* 489, 557, 2079, 2085, 4863, **5163**, 6017

**Sorrels, Roy**
*The Eyes of Torie Webster* 2606, **5164**, 5472, 5961

**Soukup, Martha**
*The Arbitrary Placement of Walls* **5165**

**Spark, Muriel**
*Open to the Public* 2842, **5166**

**Spector, Caroline**
*Worlds Without End* 5096

**Spector, Craig**
*Animals* **5080**
*The Bridge: A Horror Story* **5081**
*Dead Lines* **5082**
*Still Dead: Book of the Dead 2* **5083**

**Spector, Robert Donald**
*Seven Masterpieces of Gothic Horror* 4026

**Speer, Flora M.**
*Castle of Dreams* 6071

**Spence, Lewis**
*The Myths of the North American Indians* 5751

**Spence, Walter**
*The Devil and Dan Cooley* **3480**

**Spencer, William Browning**
*Irrational Fears* **5167**
*Resume with Monsters* 867, 868, 869, 1562, 3057, 3957, 4437, **5168**
*The Return of Count Electric and Other Stories* 2826
*Zod Wallop* 1085, **5169**

**Spielberg, Steven**
*Close Encounters of the Third Kind* 1490, 2048

**Spinrad, Norman**
*Bug Jack Barron* 125, 2487, 2920, 3239, 4813
*The Children of Hamelin* **5170**
*Deus X* 134, **5171**
*The Iron Dream* 2323, 2564, 3528, 5117
*Journals of the Plague Years* **5172**
*Little Heroes* 736, 789, 1751, 2911, 3491, 5181
*Pictures at 11* **5173**
*Riding the Torch* 4325
*Russian Spring* 388, 2727, **5174**
*Songs From the Stars* 5635, 5909
*Vampire Junkies* 3111, 3114, 3988, **5175**
*The Void Captain's Tale* 583, 734, 1899, 5042, 5544, 5550
*A World Between* 353

**Springer, Nancy**
*Apocalypse* **5176**
*Damnbanna* 497, 1441, 3264, **5177**
*Fair Peril* **5178**
*The Friendship Song* 489, 970, 1441, 2879, 3444, 3468, 4129, 4862, **5179**, 5267
*A Horse to Love* 4156
*Larque on the Wing* 1433, 1438, 2735, **5180**
*Metal Angel* 1028, 2342, 3480, **5181**
*Red Wizard* 183, 2879, 3043, 4799, 5163, **5182**, 5559
*The Sable Moon* 185
*Wings of Flame* 4985

**Spruill, Steven**
*Daughter of Darkness* **5183**
*My Soul to Take* **5184**
*Rulers of Darkness* **5185**

**Stabenow, Dana**
*Red Planet Run* 3294, **5187**
*Second Star* 1987, **5188**, 5859

**Stableford, Brian**
*The Angel of Pain* **5189**
*Balance of Power* 351, 2223
*The Carnival of Destruction* 1686, **5190**
*The Castaways of Tanagar* 564, 885, 1329
*The City of the Sun* 564
*Critical Threshold* 1248, 1719
*The Dedalus Book of Decadence: Moral Ruins* 3089
*The Empire of Fear* 463, 1463, 1797, 2741, 2834, 3143, 3546, 3550, 3601, 3602, 3954, 3955, 4094, 4096, 4097, 4098, 4508, 4576, 4578, 4668, 4770, 4781, 4784, 4978, 5050, 5185, **5191**, 5693, 5704, 5802, 6012, 6018
*Fables and Fantasies* 2225, 3859, 5103
*The Gates of Eden* 1248, 2491

*Ghost Dancers*  **1238**
*The Hunger and Ecstasy of*
   *Vampires*  2255, **5192**
*Inherit the Earth*  **5193**
*The Innsmouth Heritage*  3317, 3533,
   **5194**, 5426, 5446, 5884
*Journey to the Center*  953
*The Last Days of the Edge of the*
   *World*  172
*Optiman*  66
*The Paradise Game*  3344
*Plague Demon*  **1239**
*The Second Dedalus Book of*
   *Decadence: The Black Feast*  3089
*Sexual Chemistry: Sardonic Tales of the*
   *Genetic Revolution*  3116
*Slumming in Voodooland*  5923
*Storm Warriors*  **1240**
*The Walking Shadow*  **5195**, 5909
*The Werewolves of London*  1117,
   1277, 1721, 4740, 4766, **5196**,
   5828
*Wildeblood's Empire*  1182, 5231
*Young Blood*  303, 812, 4445, 4978,
   5183
*Zaragoz*  **1241**

**Stackpole, Michael A.**
*Battletech: Warrior: Coupe*  3425
*An Enemy Reborn*  **5197**
*Evil Ascending*  1819, **5198**
*Evil Triumphant*  **5199**
*Eyes of Silver*  **5200**
*A Gathering Evil*  1819, 1820, 1881,
   4364, 4909, **5201**
*A Hero Born*  **5202**
*Once a Hero*  973, 977, 1091, 4796,
   4808, **5203**
*Prince of Havoc*  **5204**
*Rogue Squadron*  2914, 3247, 4719,
   **5205**
*Talion: Revenant*  **5206**
*Warrior: Coup*  4903
*Wolf and Raven*  **5207**

**Stacy, Ryder**
*Doomsday Warrior*  5023

**Stadler, John**
*Eco-Fiction*  4631, 4959

**Stallman, Robert**
*The Orphan*  1188

**Stang, Ivan**
*Three-Fisted Tales of "Bob"*  5904

**Stanley, George Edward**
*Pet Store*  **1097**

**Stanton, Mary**
*The Heavenly Horse From the*
   *Outermost West*  223, 2397, 2673,
   2676, 2678, 3291
*Piper at the Gate*  223, 2397

**Stapledon, Olaf**
*Last and First Men*  445
*Star Maker*  445

**Starbuck, Kathlyn S.**
*India's Story*  **5208**

**Starhawk**
*The Fifth Sacred Thing*  1499, 1835,
   4631, **5209**

**Stark, Ed**
*Dragons over England*  **3015**
*Mysterious Cairo*  1889, 2472, 2473,
   3015, **5210**
*Strange Tales From the Nile*
   *Empire*  **1889**

**Stark, Kirt**
*13 Haunting Ghost Tales*  **5211**

**Starlin, Jim**
*Among Madmen*  **5212**
*Lady El*  272, **5213**
*Thinning the Predators*  2341

**Stasheff, Christopher**
*Blessings and Curses*  **5214**
*A Company of Stars*  1771, **5215**
*The Crafters*  **5216**
*The Enchanter Reborn*  **1413**
*Her Majesty's Wizard*  194, 1160,
   1324, 1413, 2560, 2616, 4391,
   4392
*King Kobold*  703
*King Kobold Revived*  27, 652, 1533,
   2226, 4922
*M'Lady Witch*  196, **5217**
*My Son, the Wizard*  639, **5218**
*The Oathbound Wizard*  **5219**
*Quicksilver's Knight*  **5220**
*The Sage*  **5221**
*The Secular Wizard*  955, **5222**
*The Shaman*  **5223**
*Warlock and Son*  197, **5224**
*The Warlock Heretical*  706
*The Warlock in Spite of Himself*  167,
   168, 172, 177, 180, 184, 186, 705,
   845, 1268, 1413, 1531, 1534,
   1755, 2041, 2079, 2235, 3296,
   3297, 3991, 4316, 4399, 4404,
   4433, 4435, 4766, 5235, 5694
*The Warlock Insane*  1755, 2809,
   3471, 4013, **5225**
*The Warlock Is Missing*  3010
*The Warlock Rock*  706, 1416, 1998,
   2015, **5226**
*The Warlock Unlocked*  169, 259, 701
*The Warlock Wandering*  1755
*We Open on Venus*  1771, 2575,
   **5227**
*The Witch Doctor*  635, 4671, **5228**,
   5500
*A Wizard in Absentia*  **5229**
*A Wizard in Chaos*  **5230**
*A Wizard in Midgard*  **5231**
*A Wizard in Mind*  **5232**
*A Wizard in Peace*  **5233**
*A Wizard in War*  **5234**

**Stashower, Daniel**
*The Adventure of the Ectoplasmic*
   *Man*  2692, 3688, 4345, 4929

**Staudinger, Michael C.**
*The Falcon Rises*  701, **5235**

**Stchur, John**
*Paddywhack*  2199, **5236**, 5539

**Steakley, John**
*Armor*  2245, 4204
*Vampire$*  3564, 3853, 4728, **5237**

**Stearns, Michael**
*A Starfarer's Dozen*  **5238**
*A Wizard's Dozen*  1994, 4988, **5239**,
   5973, 6040

**Steele, Allen**
*All-American Alien Boy*  1758, 3712,
   **5240**
*Clarke County, Space*  127, 134, 356,
   1055, 1788, 1965, 1970, 2100,
   2486, 2660, 3448, 3604, 3770,
   4295, 4483, 4937, 4955, 4962,
   5032, 5089, 5130, 5188, **5241**,
   5451, 5545, 5566, 5598, 5836,
   5840, 5957, 6020
*The Jericho Iteration*  761, 3242,
   **5242**
*A King of Infinite Space*  2498, **5243**
*Labyrinth of Night*  102, 421, 586,
   1565, 2864, 3787, **5244**

*Lunar Descent*  587, 588, 596, 597,
   1970, 2645, 4349, 4931, 4949,
   5234, **5245**, 5370, 5566, 5859
*Orbital Decay*  107, 181, 405, 584,
   597, 757, 764, 996, 1548, 1594,
   2301, 2433, 2486, 2549, 3789,
   4682, 4976, 5188, **5246**, 5258,
   6065
*Rude Astronauts*  4953, 4956, **5247**
*The Tranquility Alternative*  64, 587,
   2002, **5248**

**Steele, Danielle**
*Ghost*  4579

**Steffen, Elizabeth**
*Portrait of the Psychopath as a Young*
   *Woman*  3395

**Stein, Garth**
*Raven Stole the Moon*  4249, **5249**

**Stein, Harry**
*Infinity's Child*  1670, 2206, 3164,
   **5250**

**Stein, Kevin**
*Brothers Majere*  5711
*Twisted Dragon*  **5251**

**Stephens, John Richard**
*The Enchanted Cat*  3740, 4054,
   4144, 4145
*Mysterious Cat Stories*  4144, **5252**

**Stephenson, Andrew**
*Nightwatch*  111

**Stephenson, Neal**
*The Diamond Age*  107, 158, 809,
   1458, 1929, 2377, 2728, 3711,
   4708, **5253**, 5259, 5430, 5966
*Interface*  781
*Snow Crash*  31, 108, 118, 295, 471,
   472, 474, 475, 483, 505, 553, 781,
   792, 805, 809, 927, 1227, 1449,
   1518, 1761, 1805, 1862, 2087,
   2092, 2163, 2219, 2394, 2488,
   2579, 2729, 2770, 2839, 2997,
   3009, 3082, 3311, 3435, 3449,
   3455, 3662, 3921, 4076, 4191,
   4193, 4218, 4292, 4478, 4590,
   4677, 4704, 4749, 4893, 4894,
   4902, 5009, 5074, 5171, **5254**,
   5281, 5370, 5438, 5566, 5569,
   5573, 5619, 5834, 5957, 6047,
   6063, 6079

**Sterling, Bruce**
*Crystal Express*  423, 425, 804, 807,
   3086, 3234, 4053, 4998, 5007,
   **5255**, 5837, 6067
*The Difference Engine*  **2217**
*Distraction*  **5256**
*Globalhead*  **5257**
*Heavy Weather*  354, 2998, 3789,
   4218, **5258**
*Holy Fire*  **5259**
*Involution Ocean*  791, 3874
*Islands in the Net*  474, 736, 984,
   1750, 3431, 3491, 3794, 3850,
   3890, 3995, 4343, 4452, 4632,
   4634, 4681, 4682, 5006, 5254,
   5593, 5841, 5955, 5960
*Mirrorshades: The Cyberpunk*
   *Anthology*  804, 1516, 2394, 4713,
   4812
*Schismatrix*  328, 2890, 3850, 5833,
   5841
*Schismatrix Plus*  1965, 2660, **5260**

**Stern, David**
*Nightmare World*  **5261**

**Stern, Philip Van Doren**
*The Midnight Reader*  1, 2968

**Stern, Roger**
*The Death and Life of Superman*  999,
   1667, 2393, 3768, **5262**

**Sternau, Cynthia**
*The Secret Prophecies of*
   *Nostradamus*  2381

**Stetson, T.W.**
*Night Beasts*  2615, 2926, 3701,
   4815, **5263**

**Steussy, Marti**
*Dreams of Dawn*  2764, 3536, 3727,
   3800, 4143
*Forest of the Night*  1895, 3536,
   4143

**Stevens, Brooke**
*The Circus of the Earth and*
   *Air*  1186, 2266, 4432, **5264**,
   5409

**Stevens, John Richard**
*Vampires, Wine & Roses*  **5265**

**Stevenson, Robert Louis**
*The Strange Case of Dr. Jekyll and Mr.*
   *Hyde*  19, 535, 1424, 2702, 2818,
   3178, 3654, 4089

**Stevermer, Caroline**
*A College of Magics*  315, 557, 979,
   1065, 1790, 2032, 2263, 2269,
   2354, 2355, 2356, 2956, 3080,
   3278, 3303, 3509, 3511, 3942,
   4459, 4528, 4686, 4700, 4740,
   5137, **5266**, 5458, 5490, 5728,
   5811, 5967, 5976, 5978, 6057
*River Rats*  1430, 1600, 2274, 3624,
   **5267**

**Stewart, Fred Mustard**
*The Mephisto Waltz*  2204, 2823

**Stewart, George R.**
*Earth Abides*  3584, 4074, 4631

**Stewart, Jean**
*Return to Isis*  46, 5209, **5268**

**Stewart, Kate**
*The Devil's Cradle*  2748, **5269**

**Stewart, Mary**
*The Crystal Cave*  227, 991, 1189,
   1270, 2745, 2746, 3506, 3806,
   3827
*The Prince and the Pilgrim*  **5270**
*The Wicked Day*  2940, 4584

**Stewart, Michael**
*Belladonna*  966, 1050, 1836, 2642,
   2874, 4753, 5186, **5271**, 5290
*Monkey Shines*  2429, 5894

**Stewart, Ramona**
*The Possession of Joel Delaney*  1237,
   2204, 4837, 5066

**Stewart, Sean**
*Clouds End*  **5272**
*Mockingbird*  **5273**
*The Night Watch*  **5274**
*Nobody's Son*  3070, **5275**, 6066
*Passion Play*  **5276**
*Resurrection Man*  1339, 2342, 3257,
   3480, **5277**

**Stiegler, Marc**
*The Gentle Seduction*  54, 123, 448,
   689, 804, 850, 1515, 1517, 1770,
   1963, 1964, 3087, 3442, 4127,
   4216, 4376, 4706, 4953, 5028,
   5240, 5257, 5369, 5638, 5869

**Stine, G. Harry**
*The Bastard Rebellion* 1566, 1567, 1569, 4539, 4544
*Blood Siege* 1651, 2000, **5278**
*Force of Arms* 48, 3013, **5279**
*Guts and Glory* 1568, 3013, **5280**
*Judgment Day* **5281**
*The Lost Battalion* 831, 1651, 3013, 3037
*Operation Iron Fist* 49
*Operation Steel Band* 3013
*Sierra Madre* 830, 831, 1406, 1651, 4769
*Starsea Invaders: First Action* 1201, **5282**
*Warbots* 47, 48, 49, 50, 829, 1566, 1568, 1569, 1896, 1938, 2488
*Warrior Shield* **5283**

**Stine, Jean Marie**
*365 Science Fiction Short Stories* 24
*I, Vampire: Interviews with the Undead* 2382, 2408, **5284**, 5448
*New Eves: Science Fiction about the Extraordinary Women of Today and Tomorrow* **2035**

**Stine, Jovial Bob**
*Spaceballs: The Book* 4565, 4656

**Stine, R.L.**
*All-Night Party* 1801
*The Cat* **5285**
*The Curse of Camp Cold Lake* **5286**
*Double Date* **5287**
*The First Horror* **5288**
*Monster Blood II* 1097
*My Best Friend Is Invisible* **5289**
*Say Cheese and Die* 1097
*Superstitious* 1354, 2139, 3499, **5290**
*The Thrill Club* 4329
*Vampire Breath* **5291**
*The Wrong Number* 1692

**Stirling, S.M.**
*Betrayals* 367, 944, 4833, 5676
*Blood Feuds* **5292**, 5917
*The Cage* 986, **5293**, 5684
*The Children's Hour* 4372
*The City Who Fought* 3722
*Drakon* **5294**
*Go Tell the Spartans* 4375
*Island in the Sea of Time* 1981, **5295**
*Marching through Georgia* 442, 1322, 1579, 1641, 3867, 4372, 5502, 5676
*More than Honor* **5676**
*Prince of Sparta* **4378**
*The Rising* **1579**
*The Rose Sea* 5133, **5296**, 5383, 5678
*Saber & Shadow* 787, **5297**
*Shadow's Son* **3872**
*The Ship Avenged* 4148, **5298**
*Snow Brother* 787, 3871, 3872, **5299**, 5676
*The Stone Dogs* 1326, 1579, 4372, **5300**
*Under the Yoke* 1579, **5301**

**Stith, John E.**
*Deep Quarry* 2005, 2226, 4555, **5302**, 5644
*Manhattan Transfer* 934, 3734, **5303**
*Memory Blank* 1304
*Reckoning Infinity* **5304**
*Redshift Rendezvous* 80, 81, 118, 181, 402, 1548, 1579, 1990, 2000, 3603, 4193, 4241, 4357, 4470, 4640, 4952, 4961, 5298, **5305**

*Reunion on Neverend* 4502, **5306**, 5545, 5775

**Stockbridge, Grant**
*The Spider #1: The Spider and the Pain Master/Secret City of Crime* 1940, 4623
*The Spider #3: Death's Crimson Juggernaut/The Red Death Rain* 4622, **5307**
*The Spider #4: Death Reign of the Vampire King/The Pain Emperor* **5308**
*The Spider #8: The Devil's Paymaster/ Legions of the Accursed Light* **5309**
*The Spider: Master of Men* 3883

**Stockton, Frank**
*The Lady or the Tiger and Other Stories* **5310**

**Stoddard, James**
*The High House* **5311**

**Stoker, Bram**
*Dracula* 139, 152, 279, 292, 1112, 1402, 1448, 2742, 3004, 3110, 3163, 3179, 4094, 4763, 4770, 4779
*Dracula's Guest* 4969
*The Jewel of Seven Stars* **5312**

**Stone, Del Jr.**
*Dead Heat* **5313**

**Stone, Tom B.**
*The Fright Before Christmas* 1097, 5291

**Storm, Jordan**
*Substitute Teacher* **5314**

**Storm, L. Elizabeth**
*Angels Unaware* **5315**

**Storm, Sue**
*Star Bones Weep the Blood of Angels* 693, 802, 2769, 3100, 3318, 3667, **5316**

**Stotler, William R.**
*The Final Diary Entry of Kees Huijgens* **5317**, 5446

**Stout, Amy**
*Full Spectrum 3* **215**
*Full Spectrum 4* **216**

**Stout, Rex**
*Under the Andes* 3878, 4062

**Stover, Laren**
*Pluto, Animal Lover* 2429, **5318**

**Stover, Matthew Woodring**
*Heroes Die* **5319**
*Iron Dawn* 1640, 4612, **5320**
*Jericho Moon* **5321**

**Stowe, Harriet Beecher**
*Old Town Fireside Stories* 2919

**Straczynski, J. Michael**
*Demon Night* **5322**
*Other Syde* 3679
*OtherSyde* 192, 2935, 4022, **5323**
*Tales From the New Twilight Zone* 2402, 2403, 4913, 4914, 5473

**Strasser, Todd**
*Addams Family Values* **5324**

**Stratman, Thomas M.K.**
*Cthulhu's Heirs* 148, 461, 2399, 2978, 4422, 4423, 4424, 4425, 4426, 4428, 4430, **5325**

**Straub, Peter**
*Floating Dragon* 943, 1136, 2541, 3091, 3337, 3370, 4012, 5845
*Ghost Story* 524, 840, 1080, 1195, 1215, 1560, 2019, 2822, 2904, 3126, 3140, 3205, 3496, 4254, 4569, 5322, 5398
*Ghosts* 2233
*The Hellfire Club* 3088, **5326**
*Houses Without Doors* 3138, **5327**
*If You Could See Me Now* 1860, 1883, 2495, 5415
*Koko* 91, 2222, 3319, 3323, 3332, 3682, 3755, 3898, 3901, 4865, 5085, **5328**
*Mrs. God* 280, 2241, **5329**
*Mystery* **5330**
*Peter Straub's Ghosts* 1610, 2396, **5331**
*Shadowland* 2334, 2748, 5485
*The Throat* 1830, 3780, **5332**

**Strauss, Victoria**
*The Arm of the Stone* **5333**, 5554

**Strayhorn, S.J.**
*Black Night* 1830, **5334**, 5464

**Streeter, Newton E.**
*Noise and Other Night Terrors* 2937, **5335**

**Strete, Craig**
*The Bleeding Man and Other Stories* 1437
*Death in the Spirit House* 1437, 1470
*Dreams That Burn in the Night* 1437

**Strickland, Brad**
*Ark Liberty* **656**
*Crisis on Vulcan* 2109
*Dragon's Plunder* 2085, **5336**
*Nul's Quest* 3, 4, 3309
*Shadowshow* 460, 1353, 2761, 3102, 3541
*The Star Ghost* 2109
*Wizard's Mole* 1161, 1530, 2042, 2505, 2617, 3159, 4458, 4986, **5337**

**Strieber, Whitley**
*Billy* 1848, 3375, 3395, 3639, 4041, 4501, **5338**, 5992
*Communion: A True Story* 2034
*Evenings with Demons* **5339**
*The Forbidden Zone* 1037, 2345, 3310, **5340**
*The Hunger* 1882, 2019, 2510, 3253, 4068, 4089, 4367, 4508, 4574, 4665, 5824
*Majestic* 1296, 4510, 4650, **5341**
*Unholy Fire* 2889, **5342**
*The Wild* 679, 680, 729, 5080, **5343**
*The Wolfen* 373, 679, 1007, 1570, 1822, 2138, 3053, 3376, 4052, 4764, 5388, 5442

**Strugatsky, Arkadi**
*Hard to Be a God* 5230

**Strugatsky, Boris**
*Roadside Picnic* 3434
*The Snail on the Slope* 3434

**Stuart, W.J.**
*Forbidden Planet* 2864, 3079, 5244

**Sturgeon, Theodore**
*Alien Cargo* 5910
*Aliens 4* 1874, 4216
*Case and the Dreamer* 806
*Caviar* 233, 234
*The Complete Egoist* 448
*The Dreaming Jewels* 2303, 2458, 4642

*E Pluribus Unicorn* 674, 850, 1874, 3308, 5106, 5551
*Godbody* 5910
*The Golden Helix* 3342
*The Joy Machine* **2458**
*Killdozer!* **5344**
*Microcosmic God* 2458, **5345**
*More than Human* 653, 1380, 2290, 3011, 3238, 3697, 4643, 4918, 5065, 5910
*The Perfect Host* 349, **5346**
*Slow Sculpture* 5910
*Some of Your Blood* 3519, 3541, 4500, 4576, **5347**, 5423
*Sturgeon Is Alive and Well* 1608, 4561
*Thunder and Roses* 2547, 3219, **5348**
*A Touch of Sturgeon* 625, 4131
*The Ultimate Egoist* 54, 479, 2458, 2490, 2569, 2659, **5349**, 5594, 5613, 5869
*Venus Plus X* 1362, 1720
*Voyage to the Bottom of the Sea* 318, 1201, 1666, 5282
*A Way Home* 1061, 3308

**Sturgis, Susanna J.**
*Magic Realism by Women: Dreams in a Minor Key* 51, 2035, 4169, 5018, 5814, 5815

**Sturluson, Snorri**
*Egil's Saga* 136

**Sucharitkul, Somtow**
*The Fallen Country* 5163
*Forest of the Night* **5156**
*I Wake From a Dream of a Drowned Star City* **5157**
*Light on the Sound* 2890
*Mallworld* 493, 1603, 5163
*Moon Dance* **5158**
*Riverrun* **5159**
*The Throne of Madness* 2890
*The Utopia Hunters* 2890
*Valentine* **5160**
*The Vampire's Beautiful Daughter* **5161**
*Vanitas: Escape From Vampire Junction* **5162**
*The Wizard's Apprentice* **5163**

**Sue, Eugene**
*The Wandering Jew* 4371

**Suggs, Welch**
*Medallion of the Black Hound* **4056**

**Sullivan, C.W.**
*Welsh Celtic Myth in Modern Fantasy* 5560

**Sullivan, Jack**
*Lost Souls* 2300

**Sullivan, Tim**
*Cold Shocks* 2814, 2815, 3228, **5350**
*Lords of Creation* 1261, 3191, **5351**
*The Parasite War* 383, **5352**, 5878

**Sullivan, Tricia**
*Dreaming in Smoke* **5353**
*Lethe* 1000, 2051, 2274, 2558, 4064, 4065, **5354**, 5525, 5804
*Someone to Watch over Me* **5355**

**Sumner, Mark**
*Devil's Engine* **5356**
*Devil's Tower* 889, 3118, **5357**, 5504
*Insanity, Illinois* **5358**
*The Prodigal Sorcerer* 207

**Suskind, Patrick**
*The Pigeon* 913

**Sutcliff, Rosemary**
*The Light Beyond the Forest* 2232
*The Mark of the Horse Lord* 5928
*The Shining Company* 4584, **5359**
*Sun Horse, Moon Horse* 3876, 5618
*Sword at Sunset* 2188, 3501, 5015

**Sutherland, James**
*Stormtrack* 354

**Sutphen, Richard**
*Sexpunks & Savage Sagas* 1401,
3176, 3397, **5360**, 5416

**Sutton, David**
*The Best Horror From Fantasy
Tales* **2960**
*Fantasy Tales #2* **2965**
*Fantasy Tales #4* **2966**
*Fantasy Tales #6* **2967**

**Svendsen, Hanne Marie**
*The Gold Ball* 2264, 2662, **5361**

**Swain, E.G.**
*The Stoneground Ghost Tales* 1350

**Swann, S. Andrew**
*Emperors of the Twilight* **5362**, 6048
*Forests of the Night* 1588, 1589,
2906, 2909, 3066, 4476, 4479,
5105, **5363**, 6048
*God's Dice* **5364**
*Partisan* **5365**
*Profiteer* 1067, **5366**
*Revolutionary* **5367**
*Specters of the Dawn* 296, 2580,
**5368**
*Specters of the Twilight* 1825

**Swann, Thomas Burnett**
*Day of the Minotaur* 4159
*The Gods Abide* 36
*Lady of the Bees* 169
*The Tournament of Thorns* 5002
*Wolfwinter* 5511

**Swanwick, Michael**
*Gravity's Angels* 503, 772, 2835,
3086, 3234, 3442, 3600, 3648,
3796, 4680, 5028, 5257, **5369**,
5805
*Griffin's Egg* **5370**
*In the Drift* 1399, 5956
*The Iron Dragon's Daughter* 2738,
3933, 4136, 4850, **5371**
*Jack Faust* 714, 4179, **5372**
*Stations of the Tide* 472, 2728, 3186,
3604, 4030, 4176, 4652, 4950,
**5373**, 5436, 5717
*Vacuum Flowers* 60, 63, 79, 505,
805, 838, 927, 1543, 1723, 1819,
1964, 2163, 2536, 3075, 3921,
4071, 4342, 5198, 5201, 5241,
5451, 5638, 5809, 5839

**Swiniarski, S.A.**
*Raven* **5374**

**Swiniarski, Steven**
*Emperors of the Twilight* **5362**
*Forests of the Night* **5363**
*God's Dice* **5364**
*Partisan* **5365**
*Profiteer* **5366**
*Raven* **5374**
*Revolutionary* **5367**
*Specters of the Dawn* **5368**

**Swycaffer, Jefferson P.**
*Warsprite* **5375**
*Web of Futures* **5376**

**Sykes, S.C.**
*Red Genesis* 102, 421, 1585, 2584,
2765, 2840, 4348, 4629, 4633,
4635, **5377**

**Syvertson, Ryder**
*Fortress of Forbidden Destiny* 725,
**5378**

**Szilagyi, Steve**
*Photographing Fairies* 2980, 2981,
2982, 3263, 4929, **5379**

**T**

**Talbot, Michael**
*The Delicate Dependency* 4578, 4665
*Night Things* **5380**

**Tallis, Robyn**
*Children of the Storm* 6057
*Rebel From Alphorion* **5381**
*Visions from the Sea* 4158

**Talmadge-Bickmore, Deborah**
*The Apprentice* 1064, 2521, 3511,
3914, 5266, **5382**, 5820
*The Heldan* 5133, **5383**

**Tan, Cecilia**
*The Beast Within: Erotic Tales of
Werewolves* 3181, 3184, **5384**
*Blood Kiss: Vampire Erotica* 698,
3030, 3181, 3184, 4690, **5385**
*Cherished Blood* 699, 3177, **5386**
*Erotic Vampire Tales* 699, 3182
*Erotica Vampirica* 3177, 3184,
4689, **5387**
*Vampire Erotica* 699, 3177, 4689

**Tanasiuk, Christine**
*Howl* 41, 2768, **5388**

**Tannehill, Jayne**
*V: The Oregon Invasion* 2910, 4290

**Tarchetti, I.U.**
*Fantastic Tales* 2718, **5389**

**Tarr, Judith**
*Alamut* 1742, 3016, 3839, **5390**
*Arrows of the Sun* 5292, **5391**
*Ars Magica* 978, 1743, 2246, 2662,
3258, 5222, **5392**, 5503
*Blood Feuds* 5292
*The Dagger and the Cross: A Novel of
the Crusades* 965, 3261, 5014,
5015, **5393**, 5506
*The Eagle's Daughter* 965, 5500,
5513
*The Hall of the Mountain King* 4730
*His Majesty's Elephant* **5394**, 5511
*The Isle of Glass* 185, 1288
*Lord of the Two Lands* 2140, 2187,
2561, **5395**, 5510, 5738
*Spear of Heaven* 1105, 3295, 3353,
4063, **5396**
*Throne of Isis* **5397**
*A Wind in Cairo* 2457

**Tartt, Donna**
*The Secret History* **5398**, 5464

**Taylor, Bernard**
*Charmed Life* **5399**
*Evil Intent* 2339, **5400**
*The Godsend* 1212, 1236, 2801,
3606, **5401**, 5623
*Mother's Boys* 916
*Sweetheart, Sweetheart* 608, 3684,
4223, **5402**

**Taylor, Jeri**
*Mosaic* 1388, **5403**
*Pathways* **5404**
*Unification* 1260, 2061, 2063, 2066,
5596

**Taylor, Karen E.**
*Bitter Blood* 1086, 1670, 2288,
2492, 2493, 3517, 4666, **5405**
*Blood Secrets* 803, 948, 2149, 2151,
2288, 3517, 4667, 5078, **5406**,
5704, 5705
*Blood Ties* 5374, **5407**

**Taylor, Keith**
*Bard* 1240, 1960, 1961, 3358
*The Cauldron of Plenty* 1957
*Search for the Starblade* 1961, 4015,
**5408**
*The Sorcerer's Sacred Isle* 1961

**Taylor, L.A.**
*The Blossom of Erda* 585, 5019
*Cat's Paw* 1657, 3080, 3120, 3740,
4054, 4145, **5409**, 5967
*Women's Work* 790, 3384, **5410**

**Taylor, Lucy**
*Close to the Bone* 693, 938, 2655,
2860, 3100, 3176, 3367, 3393,
3669, 4885, **5411**
*The Flesh Artist* 1401, 1890, 2155,
2655, 2778, 3393, **5412**, 5536
*Painted in Blood* 2656, 3090, 3318,
**5413**
*The Safety of Unknown Cities* 3183,
**5414**
*Spree* 3373, **5415**
*Unnatural Acts* 213, 1467, 3669
*Unnatural Acts and Other
Stories* 693, 2655, 2778, 3392,
3397, **5416**

**Taylor, Peter**
*The Oracle at Stoneleigh Court* 3575,
4184, **5417**

**Taylor, Ronald**
*Six German Romantic Tales* 2718,
**5418**

**Tedford, William**
*Liquid Diet* 1301, 2336, **5419**, 5705

**Telep, Peter**
*Squire* 2858
*Squire's Blood* 2858

**Tella, Alfred**
*Sundered Soul* 1925
*The Willing Spirit* **195**

**Tem, Melanie**
*Beautiful Strangers* **5420**
*Desmodus* 3396, 4581, **5421**
*Making Love* 2733, **5422**, 5522
*Prodigal* 1845, 3525, 4023, 5064,
**5423**
*Revenant* 3525, 4023, **5424**
*Wilding* 926, 1822, 3492, 4841,
**5425**
*Witch-Light* **2734**

**Tem, Steve Rasnic**
*Beautiful Strangers* **5420**
*Celestial Inventory* 200, 5876
*Decoded Mirrors: Three Tales after
Lovecraft* 3317, 5194, **5426**,
5446, 5884
*Excavation* 1036, 1077, 2094, 2668,
3778, 3783, 3951
*Fairytales* **5427**

**Tenn, William**
*The Human Angle* 1874
*Of All Possible Worlds* 1874

*Of Men and Monsters* 1015, 3342,
5303
*The Seven Sexes* 233, 234, 243,
3342, 4706
*The Square Root of Man* 3500

**Tepper, Sheri S.**
*After Long Silence* 1261, 2287,
3713, 3729, 3743, 3745, 3750
*Beauty* 42, 783, 1479, 4008, **5428**,
6088, 6090
*The Family Tree* 1943, 2243, 3241,
**5429**
*The Gate to Women's Country* 720,
721, 1211, 1929, 2052, 3046,
4325, 4631, 5092, 5209, 5268,
5590, 5982
*Gibbon's Decline and Fall* 1075,
1167, 1336, 3241, **5430**
*Grass* 34, 129, 159, 296, 686, 708,
785, 883, 899, 1072, 1116, 1458,
1643, 1807, 1824, 1987, 2056,
2207, 2226, 2287, 2806, 2882,
3231, 3248, 3249, 3398, 3713,
3717, 3763, 3908, 3910, 3927,
3929, 3972, 4062, 4067, 4116,
4122, 4241, 4242, 4507, 4552,
4711, 4735, 4736, 4867, 5016,
5128, 5306, 5373, **5431**, 5759,
5775, 5949
*Jinian Footseer* 2674
*King's Blood Four* 742, 1416, 1816,
1866, 2507, 2885, 2886, 3399,
3802, 3804, 4766
*Marianne, the Magus, and the
Manticore* 315
*Marianne, the Matchbox and the
Malachite Mouse* 105, **5432**
*Necromancer Nine* 1030, 3399
*A Plague of Angels* 198, 558, 1399,
1433, 1481, 1482, 2134, 2338,
2735, 2738, 4130, 5371, **5433**,
5748, 5942, 6047
*Raising the Stones* 35, 293, 377,
435, 566, 686, 1769, 1989, 2006,
2037, 3448, 3628, 3738, 4038,
4242, 4503, 4635, 5174, **5434**,
5543, 5575
*Shadow's End* 2057, **5435**
*Sideshow* 379, 686, 784, 2422,
2578, 5011, **5436**, 5592, 5941
*Six Moon Dance* 687, 774, 793,
1266, **5437**
*Song of Mavin Manyshaped* 5629
*Wizard's Eleven* 3399

**Terra, John**
*City of Pain* **5438**

**Terry, Elizabeth**
*American Gothic* 2586, 3570, **5439**

**Tessier, Thomas**
*The Dreams of Dr. Ladybank* 814,
1939, 5898
*Fog Heart* 839, 3126, **5440**
*Night Visions 9* **5441**
*The Nightwalker* 1349, 2222, 4780,
**5442**, 5861
*Phantom* 857, 1560

**Tevis, Walter**
*The Man Who Fell to Earth* 305, 621
*Mockingbird* 1968, 3465

**Theroux, Paul**
*The Black House* 5402
*Chicago Loop* **5443**

**Thigpen, Corbett H.**
*Three Faces of Eve* 5364

**Thomas, Elizabeth Marshall**
*The Animal Wife*   2582, 4818, 4819, **5444**
*Reindeer Moon*   502, 667, 668, 1632, 2166, 2167, 2168, 2169, 2581, 2582, 2583, 2857, 4320

**Thomas, Jane Resh**
*The Princess in the Pigpen*   329, 605, 969

**Thomas, Jeffrey**
*Black Walls, Red Glass*   **5445**, 5620
*The Bones of the Old Ones*   3556, 4444
*The Bones of the Old Ones and Other Lovecraftian Tales*   **5446**
*Terata: Anomalies of Literature*   **5447**
*A Vampire Bestiary*   **5448**

**Thomas, Quentin**
*Chains of Light*   **5449**

**Thomas, Sue**
*Correspondence*   **5450**, 5462

**Thomas, Thomas T.**
*Crygender*   4640, **5451**
*Flare*   **6065**
*Man Plus*   **4348**
*The Mask of Loki*   **6071**
*ME: A Novel of Self Discovery*   79, 249, 829, 1761, 2579, 2725, 3665, 4348, 4381, 5213, 5259, **5452**

**Thompson, Gene**
*Lupe*   3606

**Thompson, Harlan**
*Silent Running*   2660, 5303

**Thompson, Hunter S.**
*Fear and Loathing in Las Vegas*   3455, 3456

**Thompson, Jim**
*After Dark, My Sweet*   **5338**
*Pop. 1280*   1829
*South of Heaven*   3330

**Thompson, Joyce**
*Bones*   **5453**

**Thompson, Paul B.**
*The Dragonesti*   **5708**
*Firstborn*   4109, **5454**
*The Qualinesti*   4109, **5455**
*Red Sands*   374
*Riverwind the Plainsman*   5724
*Thorn and Needle*   **5456**

**Thompson, Ruth Plumly**
*The Royal Book of Oz*   3609

**Thompson, William R.**
*Debtors' Planet*   7, **5457**

**Thomsen, Brian**
*Halflings, Hobbits, Warrows & Weefolk: A Collection of Tales of Heroes Short in Stature*   **4906**
*The Mage in the Iron Mask*   **5458**
*Mob Magic*   **5459**
*The Reel Stuff*   **5460**
*Tales of Ravenloft*   155, 3224

**Thomson, Amy**
*The Color of Distance*   377, 1991, 2006, 2237, 2953, 3733, 4735, **5461**, 5804
*Virtual Girl*   77, 198, 835, 837, 892, 1582, 1903, 2051, 2093, 2163, 2445, 2729, 2730, 2839, 3049, 3797, 4677, 4704, 5450, **5462**, 5660

**Thorne, Tamara**
*Haunted*   2743, 3368, 3675, 3951, 5334, **5463**
*Moonfall*   1354, 5100, **5464**

**Thornley, Diann**
*Dominion's Reach*   **5465**
*Echoes of Issel*   **5466**
*Ganwold's Child*   2224, 5367, **5467**, 5544

**Thrasher, L.L.**
*Charlie's Bones*   **5468**

**Thurber, James**
*The 13 Clocks*   1527
*The Secret Life of Walter Mitty*   3010

**Thurston, Robert**
*Robot Jox*   1938
*Way of the Clans*   4583, **5469**

**Tichenor, H.M.**
*Irish Fairy Tales*   2481, 2482, 4203

**Tidyman, Ernest**
*Absolute Zero*   5243

**Tierney, Richard L.**
*The House of the Toad*   1497, 5121, **5470**
*Scroll of Thoth*   925, 2782, 3422, 5110, 5321, **5471**

**Tigges, John**
*The Curse*   5186, **5472**
*Kevin Browne's Nightales*   2402, **5473**
*Monster*   2611, **5474**
*Venom*   1672, 4589

**Tilton, Lois**
*Accusations*   367, 944, 4833, 5598
*Betrayal*   8, 2917
*Darkness on the Ice*   3601, 4755, **5475**
*Vampire Winter*   2440

**Tine, Robert**
*Chain Reaction*   504, 1508
*Universal Soldier*   366, 1547, 2532, 4229, 4286, **5476**

**Tiptree, James Jr.**
*Brightness Falls From the Air*   34, 3644
*Crown of Stars*   3644
*Her Smoke Rose Up Forever*   790, 1818, 2835, 3048, 3086, 3234, 3235, 3379, 3442, 3600, 3712, 3736, 4680, 5369, 5410, **5477**, 5641
*Up the Walls of the World*   512, 2297, 3644, 4280

**Titus, Eve**
*Basil of Baker Street*   2786

**Tobias, Michael**
*Believe: A Novel*   **4929**
*Voice of the Planet*   2578, 4455, 4456, 4929

**Tolan, Stephanie S.**
*The Witch of Maple Park*   **5478**

**Tolkien, J.R.R.**
*The Book of Lost Tales 1*   408
*The Father Christmas Letters*   2456
*The Fellowship of the Ring*   18, 487, 710, 711, 716, 717, 915, 991, 992, 1592, 1675, 1738, 1952, 1953, 2235, 2271, 2378, 2531, 2887, 2888, 2924, 2959, 2985, 3765, 3833, 3834, 3835, 3893, 4107, 4109, 4110, 4520, 4906, 4908, 5554, 5714, 6024

*The Hobbit*   16, 368, 711, 713, 1207, 1601, 2271, 2378, 3050, 3513, 3728, 3765, 3835, 4808, 4906, 5640, 5726, 6006, 6024, 6069
*The Lord of the Rings Trilogy*   1739, 3144, 4284, 4660, 5829
*The Return of the King*   257, 487, 710, 711, 716, 922, 1738, 2098, 2378, 2531, 2887, 2888, 3833, 4906, 5714, 5741, 5832
*Roverandom*   **5479**
*Sauron Defeated*   **5480**
*The Silmarillion*   1730, 1735, 2991, 3067, 3836
*Sir Gawain and the Green Knight, Pearl, and Sir Orfeo*   1269
*The Tolkien Reader*   4021
*The Two Towers*   256, 487, 710, 711, 716, 1738, 2378, 2531, 2887, 2888, 2987, 3833, 4906, 5714
*Unfinished Tales of Numenor and Middle-Earth*   1735, 2991, 3836

**Tolstoy, Leo**
*War and Peace*   2987

**Tolstoy, Nikolai**
*The Coming of the King*   3352, 5534

**Toole, John Kennedy**
*A Confederacy of Dunces*   5168

**Toombs, Jane**
*Under the Shadow*   3411, 4892, **5481**

**Topor, Roland**
*Joko's Anniversary*   3223
*The Tenant*   282, 913, 2294, 2789, 3094, 3149, 3194, 4234, 4248, 4499, 5082

**Tramontana, C.J.**
*Storm Knights*   **5087**

**Travers, Pamela L.**
*Mary Poppins*   2949

**Treece, Henry**
*The Golden Strangers*   5295

**Tremayne, Peter**
*The Ants*   3054
*Bloodmist*   3265, 3505
*Bloodright*   4765, 4779
*Dracula, My Love*   3110, 4367, 4765, 4779
*Dracula Unborn*   55, 3003, 3005, 4770, 5050, 6010
*Irish Masters of Fantasy*   149, 1242, 2481, 2482, 4203
*My Lady of Hi-Brasil*   3061
*The Revenge of Dracula*   4765, 4779
*Snowbeast!*   **5482**
*Swamp*   2430, **5483**

**Trent, Dan**
*Althea*   3782
*Dead Voices*   3783
*Playmates*   3784
*The Uprising*   3785

**Trent, Lynda**
*Althea*   3782
*Dead Voices*   3783
*Playmates*   3784
*The Uprising*   3785

**Trevor, Elleston**
*The Sister*   **5484**

**Trocchi, Alexander**
*Cain's Book*   548

**Trowbridge, Dave**
*The Phoenix in Flight*   **5138**
*A Prison Unsought*   **5139**
*The Rifter's Covenant*   **5140**

*Ruler of Naught*   **5141**

**Trumbo, Dalton**
*Johnny Got His Gun*   3996

**Tryon, Thomas**
*Harvest Home*   438, 860, 1185, 1833
*Night Magic*   3688, **5485**
*The Night of the Moonbow*   **5486**
*The Other*   491, 1081, 1212, 2021, 2024, 2631, 2632, 2818, 3088, 3606, 3640, 4091, 4237, 4240, 4312, 4844, 5065, 5401, 5484, 5625

**Tubb, E.C.**
*Toyman*   2330, 2921
*The Winds of Gath*   2332, 6081

**Tuchman, Barbara W.**
*A Distant Mirror*   393

**Tucker, Wilson**
*The Lincoln Hunters*   1480, 1980, 3993, **5487**
*The Time Masters*   116
*The Year of the Quiet Sun*   1133, 5048

**Turk, H.C.**
*Black Body*   3183, **5488**

**Turner, Alice K.**
*The Playboy Book of Science Fiction*   **5489**

**Turner, Delia Marshall**
*Nameless Magery*   **5490**

**Turner, George**
*Brain Child*   **5491**
*Genetic Soldier*   128, 1168, 2209, 2338, 2526, 2906, 4128, 4525, **5492**

**Turner, Jim**
*Cthulhu 2000*   148, 461, 4423, 4426, 4428, 4429, **5493**
*The Eternal Lovecraft: The Persistence of HPL in Popular Culture*   **5494**

**Turtledove, Harry**
*Agent of Byzantium*   264, 2140, 5036
*Alternate Generals*   **5495**
*Between the Rivers*   2577, **5496**
*Blood Feuds*   **5292**
*The Case of the Toxic Spell Dump*   672, 955, 1159, 1163, 1399, 2080, 3485, 4171, 4394, **5497**
*Departures*   **5498**
*A Different Flesh*   175, 188, 1655
*Earthgrip*   1420, 2055, 3001, 3648, 4120, 4160, **5499**
*An Emperor for the Legion*   1676
*Fox and Empire*   **5500**
*The Great War: American Front*   **5501**
*The Guns of the South: A Novel of the Civil War*   358, 598, 881, 1074, 1139, 1457, 1480, 1518, 1941, 2501, 2577, 3977, 3981, 3993, 4233, 4538, 5292, 5356, 5357, 5487, **5502**
*Hammer and Anvil*   **5503**
*How Few Remain*   1516, 5495, **5504**
*Kaleidoscope*   **5505**
*Krispos of Videssos*   3258, 4488, **5506**
*Krispos Rising*   3771, 4782, **5507**
*Krispos the Emperor*   3255, **5508**
*The Legion of Videssos*   1025, 1676
*The Misplaced Legion*   1324, 1638, 1676, 2752, 3353, 4782
*Prince of the North*   **5509**
*The Pugnacious Peacemaker*   5036

*The Pugnacious Peacemaker/The Wheels of If* 2829
*The Stolen Throne* 3913, 5041, **5510**
*Thessalonica* 5218, **5511**
*The Thousand Cities* **5512**
*The Two Georges* **1655**
*Videssos Besieged* **5513**
*Werenight* 5792, 5794
*A World of Difference* **5514**
*Worldwar: In the Balance* 1854, 1900, 3063, **5515**, 5996
*Worldwar: Striking the Balance* **5516**
*Worldwar: Tilting the Balance* 2239, **5517**
*Worldwar: Upsetting the Balance* **5518**

**Tuttle, Lisa**
*Familiar Spirit* **5519**
*Lost Futures* 796, **5520**
*Memories of the Body* 1827, 3116, 4182, **5521**
*A Nest of Nightmares* 1827, 2715
*Pillow Friend* 898, **5522**, 5816
*Skin of the Soul* 468, 2496, 2891, 3022, 4443, **5523**

**Twain, Mark**
*The Adventures of Huckleberry Finn* 5267
*A Connecticut Yankee in King Arthur's Court* 1419, 1532, 2044, 2045, 2047, 2616, 4971, 6035, 6038
*Satires and Burlesques* 2129

**Tyers, Kathy**
*Crystal Witness* 4044, **5524**
*Firebird* 1772
*One Mind's Eye* **5525**
*Shivering World* 231, 1805, 3021, 3745, 4652, 4856, **5526**
*The Truce at Bakura* 109, 4299, **5527**, 6055

**Tyson, Donald**
*The Messenger* **5528**

**Tyson, Salinda**
*Wheel of Dreams* 2958, **5529**


## U

**Undset, Sigrid**
*The Bridal Wreath* 136

**Upchurch, Michael**
*Passive Intruder* 2240, 3809, 5440, **5530**

**Updike, John**
*Toward the End of Time* **5531**
*The Witches of Eastwick* 749, 2442, 4570, 4577, 5021, 5488

**Urban, Scott H.**
*The Conspiracy Files* 2384

**Ustinov, Peter**
*The Old Man and Mr. Smith* **5532**, 5569, 5768

**Uttley, Alison**
*A Traveler in Time* 2992, 3261


## V

**Vachss, Andrew**
*Born Bad* 2714
*A Flash of White* 1021

**Vallejo, Doris**
*The Boy Who Saved the Stars* 6076
*Ladies: Retold Tales of Goddesses and Heroines* **5533**

**Van Allsburg, Chris**
*Two Bad Ants* 3382

**Van Asten, Gail**
*Charlemagne's Champion* 3846, 4519, **5534**

**van Belkom, Edo**
*Wyrm Wolf* 2321, 3990, 4059, **5535**
*Yours Truly, Jackie the Stripper* 3397, **5536**

**Van Gores, Alida**
*Mermaid's Song* 1155

**Van Hise, Della**
*Killing Time* 900, 922, 1385, 1386, 1511, 2297, 4280, 4933, 5113
*Ragged Angels* **5537**

**Van Hise, James**
*Midnight Graffiti* 2773

**Van Lustbader, Eric**
*Dai-San* 1329
*The Sunset Warrior* 3659, 3982

**Van Name, Mark L.**
*Intersections: The Sycamore Hill Anthology* 3085

**Van Over, Raymond**
*The Twelfth Child* **5538**
*Whisper* 2199, **5539**

**van Pallandt, Nicolas**
*Anvil* 1481, **5540**

**Van Scyoc, Sydney J.**
*Assignment: Nor'Dyren* 2414
*Bluesong* 1025, 4152
*Cloudcry* 2372
*Darkchild* 1595, 4996, 5548
*Deepwater Dreams* 63, 2450, 3341, 3729, 4421, 4923, 5029, **5541**, 5781
*Feather Stroke* 1757, 3287, 4162, 4515, **5542**

**Van Vogt, A.E.**
*The Battle of Forever* 2172
*Destination Universe* 823
*Null-A Three* 2217, 5621
*The Pawns of Null-A* 5621
*The Players of Null-A* 2217
*The Silkie* 1469, 5541
*Slan* 565, 567, 642, 733, 2290, 2420, 2545, 2665, 3994, 3995, 4081, 4305, 4918, 5039
*The Voyage of the Space Beagle* 1649, 5048, 5860
*The Weapon Makers* 446, 784, 1103, 1108, 1869, 4114, 5543, 5865
*The Weapon Shops of Isher* 1523, 1869, 2730, 3874, 4114, 5260, 5865
*The World of Null-A* 379, 2217, 3698, 3829, 4682, 5621

**Vance, Jack**
*Alastor* 418, 758, 883, 2135, 5465, **5543**, 5725
*The Anome* 1408, 3698, 5055
*Araminta Station* 4277
*The Asutra* 5055, 5130
*Big Planet* 897, 1691, 4545
*The Book of Dreams* 4277
*The Brave Free Men* 884, 2207
*City of the Chasch* 631
*Cugel's Saga* 4277, 4945

*The Demon Princes: Volume One* **5544**, 5722
*The Demon Princes: Volume Two* **5545**
*The Dirdir* 1025
*The Dragon Masters* 1015, 2058, 2193, 4277, 6056
*The Dying Earth* 3157, 3158
*The Dying Earth Series* 4397
*Ecce and Old Earth* **5546**
*Emphyrio* 176, 2192, 3696, 5457
*The Eyes of the Overworld* 3158
*The Five Gold Bands* 1871
*Galactic Effectuator* 4277
*The Green Pearl* 3700, 5512, 5582
*The Languages of Pao* 5634
*Lyonesse* 185, 630, 955, 2945, 3077, 5041, 5582
*Madouc* 632, 1743, 2662, 5128, **5547**, 5582, 5639
*Marune: Alastor 933* 4952
*Night Lamp* **5548**
*Planet of Adventure* 953
*Ports of Call* **5549**
*Rhialto the Marvellous* 4945
*Servants of the Wankh* 1329
*Showboat World* 1691, 2422, 2575, 4197, 5055
*Space Opera* 4197, 5215
*Space Pirate* 1647
*Suldrun's Garden* 222, 3822
*Throy* **5550**
*To Live Forever* 2487, 2920, 4813
*Trullion: Alastor 2262* 2414, 4121, 4634
*When the Five Moons Rise* **5551**

**Vance, Steve**
*Shapes* **5552**
*Spook* 1115, 1334, 3020, **5553**

**Vande Velde, Vivian**
*The Changeling Prince* **5554**
*The Conjurer Princess* **5555**
*Dragon's Bait* 1951, 5394, **5556**
*Tales From the Brothers Grimm and the Sisters Weird* 1366, **5557**
*User Unfriendly* 87, 179, 475, 507, 1218, 1461, 1600, 1873, 2082, 3468, 3487, 3831, 4433, 4671, 4921, 5063, **5558**
*A Well-Timed Enchantment* 1012, **5559**, 5822

**Vandermeer, Jeff**
*The Book of Lost Places* 3851

**Vansittart, Peter**
*Parsifal* 5153, **5560**

**Vardeman, Robert E.**
*Ancient Heavens* **5561**
*Dark Legacy* 207, 2827
*Death Channels* **5562**
*The Glass Warrior* **5563**
*The Infinity Plague* 3309, **5564**
*The Klingon Gambit* 527, 1511
*Mutiny on the Enterprise* 528
*Phantoms on the Wind* 1155, 1745

**Varian, Nancy**
*Berberick, Stormblade* 5724

**Various Authors**
*The Night Visions Series* 98, 4314

**Varley, John**
*The Barbie Murders and Other Stories* 3256, 4302, 4376, 5106, 5638

*Blue Champagne* 54, 61, 124, 161, 234, 479, 503, 624, 689, 772, 804, 850, 1515, 1608, 1874, 2569, 2576, 3187, 3235, 3308, 3571, 3648, 4070, 4118, 4123, 4126, 4127, 4216, 4302, 4376, 4561, 4636, 4643, 4706, 4956, 4961, 5028, 5106, 5245, 5247, 5257, 5344, 5346, 5349, 5369, 5551, 5638, 5807, 5869
*Demon* 508, 1418, 5234, 5840
*The Golden Globe* **5565**
*Millennium* 116, 141, 142, 143, 263, 824, 1563, 2546, 3064, 3467, 4942, 5011, 5282, 5487
*Nanoware Time/The Persistence of Vision* **5638**
*The Ophiuchi Hotline* 325, 1046, 1825, 2001, 2049, 2050, 2172, 3038, 3943, 4016, 4560, 4933, 4962, 5354, 5525, 5866
*The Persistence of Vision* 161, 233, 234, 448, 479, 503, 665, 804, 1061, 1517, 1608, 1874, 1963, 2295, 2490, 2576, 2649, 2659, 2721, 3087, 3185, 3187, 3308, 3604, 3736, 4118, 4123, 4126, 4127, 4346, 4376, 4561, 4636, 4643, 4706, 4953, 4961, 5106, 5245, 5257, 5345, 5348, 5369, 5551, 5613, 5638, 5805, 5807
*Press Enter/Hawksbill Station* 130
*Steel Beach* 5, 77, 79, 126, 128, 134, 236, 249, 587, 1336, 1664, 1695, 1970, 2087, 2218, 2458, 2579, 2645, 2660, 2730, 3263, 3454, 3662, 3761, 3944, 4283, 4342, 4348, 4761, 4860, 4895, 4901, 5242, 5248, 5254, 5370, **5566**, 5573, 5865, 6079
*Superheroes* 1227, 1390, 1667, 3403, **5567**
*Tango Charlie and Foxtrot Charlie/The Star Pit* 130
*Titan* 685, 954, 961, 1634, 2295, 2371, 3972, 4103, 4280, 4417, 4421, 4595, 4705, 4942, 5304, 5647, 5880
*Wizard* 1055, 3050, 5000, 5033

**Varma, Devendra P.**
*Voices From the Vault: Authentic Vampire Tales* 2407, 5706

**Vaughan, Ralph**
*Sherlock Holmes in the Adventure of the Ancient Gods* 867, 1859, 4751

**Vercors**
*You Shall Know Them* 2434

**Verne, Jules**
*From the Earth to the Moon* 398
*Journey to the Center of the Earth* 2468, 2469, 3590, 4705
*Mysterious Island* 5376
*Paris in the Twentieth Century* **5568**
*Twenty Thousand Leagues under the Sea* 398, 440, 1666
*Yesterday and Tomorrow* 3148

**Vidal, Gore**
*Live From Golgotha: A Novel* **5569**
*Messiah* 4330
*The Smithsonian Institution* **5570**
*Visit to a Small Planet* 1226, 1228, 1385

**Vidal, Harriette**
*Animus* 3040
*Breeder* 3041
*The School* 3042

**Vinge, Joan D.**
*Catspaw* 481, 2690, 2691, 3644, 4287, 5039
*Dreamfall* 2877, **5571**, 5872
*Mad Max Beyond Thunderdome* 1644
*The Outcasts of Heaven Belt* 1381
*Psion* 2474, 2475, 3725, 3726, 3742, 4898, 4930, 4964, 5039, 6053
*Return to Oz* 2136, 3609
*The Snow Queen* 176, 991, 1176, 3644, 5041, 5757, 5839, 5880
*The Summer Queen* 351, 721, 741, 758, 762, 953, 954, 961, 1388, 1469, 1593, 1606, 3729, 3745, 3750, 3927, 4729, 5548, **5572**, 5745
*World's End* 2050, 5760

**Vinge, Vernor**
*A Fire upon the Deep* 46, 79, 81, 236, 309, 322, 324, 382, 402, 414, 471, 478, 684, 687, 688, 708, 792, 883, 892, 933, 934, 983, 990, 1003, 1059, 1083, 1183, 1184, 1264, 1303, 1333, 1337, 1458, 1573, 1575, 1586, 1587, 1663, 1664, 1727, 1820, 1989, 1992, 1993, 1999, 2010, 2087, 2374, 2523, 2524, 2525, 2551, 2832, 3469, 3617, 3722, 3724, 3733, 3743, 3749, 3762, 3787, 3821, 3823, 4122, 4138, 4292, 4356, 4503, 4554, 4760, 4761, 4855, 4895, 4898, 4966, 4967, 5051, 5059, 5116, 5138, 5140, 5254, 5260, 5354, 5363, 5462, 5566, **5573**, 5668, 5679, 5834, 5949, 6079, 6085, 6086
*Marooned in Realtime* 401, 928, 931, 1055, 1986, 2328, 2603, 3021, 3256, 3734, 4000, 4018, 4019, 4506, 4652, 5043, 5067, 5660, 5909
*The Peace War* 2603, 2881, 4018, 4867, 5043
*Tatja Grimm's World* 1595, 4729, 5544
*Threats. . .and Other Promises* 425

**Vinicoff, Eric**
*The Weigher* 792, 1254, 2443, 2637, 3743, **5574**

**Vitola, Denise**
*Half-Light* 2053, 2864, 2948, 5282, **5575**
*Manjinn Moon* **5576**
*Opalite Moon* 1400, 2513, **5577**
*Quantum Moon* 1400

**Vizenor, Gerald**
*Dead Voices: Natural Agonies in the Real World* 190, 2686, 4207, 4208, 4380, **5578**, 5751

**Voigt, Cynthia**
*Jackaroo* 4447
*On Fortune's Wheel* 980, **5579**

**Vollmann, William T.**
*The Ice-Shirt* **5580**
*Whores for Gloria* 3362
*You Bright and Risen Angels* 780, 3457

**Volsky, Paula**
*The Gates of Twilight* 5333, **5581**

*Illusion* 705, 991, 1249, 1251, 1675, 1676, 1863, 1902, 1952, 2032, 2039, 2060, 2195, 2509, 2561, 2653, 2693, 2884, 2956, 3274, 3293, 3410, 3508, 3581, 3624, 3841, 3933, 4045, 4488, 4490, 4491, 4686, 4714, 4718, 4739, 4740, 4802, 4851, 4983, 5126, 5137, 5150, 5228, 5266, **5582**, 5648, 5750, 5758, 5813
*The Sorcerer's Curse* 4852
*The Sorcerer's Lady* 1030
*The White Tribunal* **5583**
*The Wolf of Winter* **5584**

**Von Allmen, Stewart**
*Conspicuous Consumption* 2321, 3990, 4059
*St. Vitus Dances Eternity: A Sarajevo Ghost Story* **5585**

**Von Gunden, Kenneth**
*Cry Wolf* **5586**
*The Sounding Stillness* **5587**
*StarSpawn* 1325, **5588**, 5900
*Under Fire* **5589**

**Von Harbou, Thea**
*Metropolis* 484

**Vonarburg, Elisabeth**
*In the Mothers' Land* **5590**
*Reluctant Voyagers* **5591**
*The Silent City* 4478, **5592**

**Vonnegut, Kurt Jr.**
*Between Time and Timbuktu* 1784, 1785, 5904
*Cat's Cradle* 1412, 2100, 2103, 2722, 2859, 3311, 3313, 3439, 4028, 4029, 4035, 4607
*Happy Birthday, Wanda June* 1784, 1785, 5904
*Hocus Pocus or, What's the Hurry, Son?* 2770, **5593**
*Player Piano* 506, 1523
*The Sirens of Titan* 96, 3343, 3459, 5531, 5905
*Slaughterhouse Five* 96, 1694, 2244, 2542, 3456, 4606, 5079, 6029
*Timequake* **5594**
*Welcome to the Monkey House* 124, 161, 321, 624, 850, 1515, 4636, 5551

**Vornholt, John**
*Antimatter* 8, 2917
*Blood Oath* 367, 944, 4833
*The Fabulist* 1681, 3504, **5595**
*Masks* 2068
*Mind Meld* **5596**
*River Quest* 2003, 2469
*Sanctuary* **5597**
*Voices* 367, 944, 1387, 2102, 3096, 4833, **5598**

**W**

**Wagner, Karl Edward**
*The Book of Kane* 856, 2781, 2782, 5110, 5471
*Darkness Weaves* 907, 910, 3172, 3420, 3422
*Death Angel's Shadow* 3172, 4617
*Echoes of Valor I* 2347, 2348, 4616
*Echoes of Valor I-III* 4759
*Echoes of Valor III* 4617, **5599**
*Exorcisms and Ecstasies* 3549, **5600**
*Horrorstory III* **5601**

*Horrorstory IV* **5602**
*Horrorstory V* **5603**
*In a Lonely Place* 2780, 2784
*Intensive Scare* **5604**, 5886
''The Fourth Seal'' 93, 1561
*Why Not You and I* 4886
*The Year's Best Horror Stories XVIII* 1378, 2961, **5605**
*The Year's Best Horror Stories XIX* 1373, 2962, 4025
*The Year's Best Horror Stories XX* **5606**
*The Year's Best Horror Stories XXI* 1376, 2963, **5607**
*The Year's Best Horror Stories XXII* 1375
*The Year's Best Horror Stories XXIII* **5608**
*The Year's Best Horror Stories Series* 1371, 1372, 1374, 1377, 2964, 2969, 2970, 2971

**Waitman, Katie**
*The Merro Tree* 2422, 3453, 3931, **5609**

**Wakefield, H. Russell**
*The Clock Strikes Twelve* 779, 875, **5610**
*Imagine a Man in a Box* 4141, **5611**
*They Return at Evening* 779, 2846, 3879, 3880

**Waldrop, Howard**
*A Dozen Tough Jobs* 36, 1810, 2549, 2751, **5612**, 5944
*Going Home Again* **5613**
*Night of the Cooters* 520, 1615, 3619, 4095, **5614**, 6022
*Strange Monsters of the Recent Past* 25, 5047, **5615**, 5641, 5805, 6020
*Them Bones* 3619, 5911

**Walker, Barbara G.**
*Amazon: A Novel* **5616**
*Feminist Fairy Tales* 794, **5617**

**Walker, Mary Alexander**
*The Scathach and the Maeve's Daughter* 2121, 3071, 3470, 3876, 4196, 5177, **5618**

**Walker, Sage**
*Whiteout* 386, 405, 809, 1075, 1167, 1168, 1244, 2243, 2291, 2394, 2488, 2723, 5355, **5619**

**Walker, William A. Jr.**
*Dystopia* **5620**

**Wallace, Ian**
*Megalomania* **5621**

**Wallace, Patricia**
*Fatal Outcome* 4480, **5622**
*Monday's Child* 2801, **5623**, 5625
*Thrill* **5624**

**Walpole, Hugh**
*All Souls' Night* 1252

**Walters, R.R.**
*Wind Chimes* 4240, **5625**

**Walton, Evangeline**
*The Children of Llyr* 1668, 1764
*The Island of the Mighty* 1961, **5626**
*The Prince of Annwn* 987, 3058

**Wandrei, Donald**
*Don't Dream* 534, 1494, 3529, 3534, **5627**
*The Eye and the Finger* 1496, 5628
*The Painted Mirror* 1335
*Strange Harvest* 4904, 4905

*The Web of Easter Island* 3569

**Wandrei, Howard**
*Time Burial* 1700, 3571, 5104, 5149, **5628**

**Ward, C.E.**
*Vengeful Ghosts* 1671, 2707, 5211

**Warner, Gertrude**
*The Boxcar Children* 3731

**Waters, Elisabeth**
*The Best of Marion Zimmer Bradley's Fantasy Magazine, Volume II* 629
*Changing Fate* **5629**

**Waters, T.A.**
*The Probability Pad* 2076, 2228, 2913, 5170

**Watkins, Graham**
*Dark Winds* **5630**
*Kaleidoscope Eyes* **5631**
*Virus* 3923, **5632**

**Watson, Ian**
*Chekhov's Journey* 508, 1418, **5633**
*The Embedding* **5634**
*The Flies of Memory* 2953, 2955, **5635**
*God's World* 2343, 2666, **5636**, 5717
*Inquisitor* 1108, 5087, **5637**, 6021
*The Martian Inca* 5561
*Nanoware Time/The Persistence of Vision* **5638**
*Oracle* 3854
*Queenmagic, Kingmagic* 4092, 4115, 4707
*The Very Slow Time Machine* 5747

**Watson, Robert**
*Whilom* 67, 2751, 2752, 5595, **5639**

**Watt-Evans, Lawrence**
*The Blood of a Dragon* 842, 1156, 1749, 2461, 3545, 4460, 4695, **5640**, 6069
*Crosstime Traffic* 206, 3648, **5641**
*Denner's Wreck* 3700, 5230, 6061
*The Lure of the Basilisk* 1469, 1682, 1688
*Martian Deathtrap* 205
*Newer York* 1819, **5642**
*The Nightmare People* 2302, 2344, 2345, 3091, **5643**
*Nightside City* **5644**
*Out of This World* 153, 206, **5645**
*Ragnarok* 206
*The Rebirth of Wonder* 1299, 1478, 2883, 2942, 4434, **5646**
*The Reign of the Brown Magician* 5207, **5647**
*Seven Altars of Dusarra* 4848
*The Spell of the Black Dagger* **5648**
*Split Heirs* 2073, 2079, **5649**
*Taking Flight* 3446, **5650**
*Touched by the Gods* 5273, **5651**
*With a Single Spell* 671

**Waugh, Charles G.**
*13 Short Horror Novels* 226, 2974
*Back From the Dead* 2379
*Civil War Ghosts* 2383
*Devil Worshippers* 2385
*East Coast Ghosts* 4214
*Eastern Ghosts* 3866
*Faeries* 235
*Ghosts of the Heartland* 3868
*Great American Ghost Stories* 3869
*House Shudders* 1246, 5902
*The Mammoth Book of Fantastic Science Fiction* 245

*The Mammoth Book of Modern Science Fiction: Short Novels of the 1980s* **246**
*Spooky Sea Stories* 2708, 2709, 4308, **5652**
*Supernatural Sleuths* 5459, **5653**
*Western Ghosts* 3870
*Yankee Witches* 1711

**Waugh, Evelyn**
*The Loved One* 4437

**Waugh, Sylvia**
*The Mennyms* 53, 430, 773, 2719, 2869, **5654**
*Mennyms Alive* **5655**
*Mennyms Under Siege* **5656**

**Way, John H.**
*Contagion* **1136**

**Weathersby, Lee**
*Kiss of the Vampire* 1352, 1795, 1798, 3557, 5020, **5657**, 5986, 5988

**Weaver, Ingrid**
*A Wish and a Dream* **5658**

**Weaver, Michael D.**
*My Father Immortal* 419, 499, 656, 720, 724, 968, 1405, 1568, 1569, 2446, 2536, 2847, 3786, 3891, 3999, 4352, 5491, 5492, 5589, 5592, **5659**, 5809
*A Second Infinity* 198, **5660**, 6047
*Wolf-Dreams* 2552, 2553

**Webb, Don**
*The Double* **5661**
*A Spell for the Fulfillment of Desire* 778, 2137, 4532, 4789, **5662**
*Stealing My Rules* 778, 3851, **5663**

**Webb, Sharon**
*The Halflife* 193, **5664**

**Webb, Wendy**
*Gothic Ghosts* 4644, **5665**
*More Phobias* 1279, 1284, 1285, 2175, **5666**
*Phobias: Stories of Your Deepest Fears* 1279, 1284, 1285, 2175, 2384, 2777, 3024, **5667**

**Weber, David**
*The Armageddon Inheritance* 3968, **5668**, 5785
*Crusade* 5785
*Echoes of Honor* **5669**
*Field of Dishonor* **5670**
*Flag in Exile* 1046, 1315, 2476, **5671**
*Heirs of Empire* **5672**
*Honor Among Enemies* 645, **5673**
*The Honor of the Queen* 312, 3976, **5674**
*In Enemy Hands* **5675**, 5786
*Insurrection* 5785
*More than Honor* **5676**
*Mutineers' Moon* 35, 378, 379, 382, 405, 753, 786, 933, 1553, 1565, 1599, 1645, 3732, 3733, 3750, 3762, 3944, 4042, 4301, 4421, 4479, 5282, **5677**, 5785, 5863
*Oath of Swords* **5678**
*On Basilisk Station* 310, 1043, 1047, 1254, 1546, 1598, 1901, 1978, 2366, 3865, 3970, 3974, 3976, 5117, 5138, 5139, 5140, 5362, **5679**, 5718

*Path of the Fury* 220, 293, 296, 471, 903, 929, 932, 934, 1602, 1824, 2209, 2832, 2942, 3037, 3049, 3710, 3762, 3865, 4348, 5138, 5355, **5680**, 6079
*The Short Victorious War* **5681**
*The War God's Own* **5682**

**Wehrstein, Karen**
*Lion's Heart* 164, 787, 2236, 3871, 3872, 3975, 5209, 5297, 5299, **5683**
*Lion's Soul* 787, 3871, 3872, 5071, 5209, 5297, 5299, **5684**
*Shadow's Son* 3872

**Weighell, Ron**
*The White Road* 2707, 3314, 5776

**Weill, Gus**
*Flesh* 627, 1027, 2115, 4437, **5685**

**Wein, Len**
*Mayhem in Manhattan* 1667, 3403
*Stalker From the Stars* 1390

**Weinbaum, Stanley G.**
*The Black Flame* 4620

**Weinberg, Robert**
*100 Creepy Little Creature Stories* 2892, 4828, **5686**
*100 Ghastly Little Ghost Stories* **1709**
*100 Tiny Tales of Terror* **5687**
*100 Twisted Little Tales of Torment* **1710**
*100 Vicious Little Vampire Stories* 150, 151, 2071, 4879, 4881, 5284, 5448, **5688**
*100 Wicked Little Witch Stories* **1711**, 2938
*100 Wild Little Weird Tales* 480, 482, 3023, 3028, **5689**
*The Armageddon Box* 462, 832, 2841, 3220, 3672, 3964, 4649, 4755, 4960, 5136, 5475, **5690**, 5773, 5895
*Between Time and Terror* **5691**
*The Black Lodge* 871, 1298, 1403, 2699, 2744, 2856, 2896, 3093, 3885, 4847, **5692**
*Blood War* 303, 387, 798, 1949, 1950, 2255, 2258, 2259, 2514, 2515, 2663, 3613, 4004, 4058, 4190, **5693**, 5883
*A Calculated Magic* **5694**
*The Dead Man's Kiss* 833, 1721, 2932, 4733, **5695**
*The Devil's Auction* 2304, 4315, 4960, **5696**, 5773
*The Eighth Green Man and Other Strange Folk* 480, 2485, 3023, 3028
*Famous Fantastic Mysteries* **1712**
*Far Below and Other Horrors* 480, 2485, 3028
*Girls' Night Out* 730, **1713**
*Great Writers and Kids Write Spooky Stories* 2395
*Horrors: 365 Scary Stories* **1714**
*A Logical Magician* 3487, **5697**, 5967
*Lovecraft's Legacy* 2315, 5493, 5494, 5698, 5884
*Miskatonic University* 148, **2399**, 4422, 4424, 4427
*Mistresses of the Dark* **1715**
*The Mists From Beyond* 1872
*Nursery Crimes* **1716**
*Rivals of Dracula* 1799, 2972, 3226, **5699**
*Rivals of Weird Tales* **5700**

*The Road to Hell, Volume I* **5701**
*The Road to Hell, Volume II* **5702**
*A Taste for Blood* **2407**
*To Sleep, Perchance to Dream. . .Nightmare* **1717**
*The Unbeholden* 387, 1119, 2512, 4058, **5703**, 5882, 5883
*The Unbidden* 1949
*Uncanny Tales* 940
*Unholy Allies* 387, 452, 798, 1949, 2514, 2515, 4058, **5704**, 5883
*Vampire Diary: The Embrace* 387, 2663, 2664, 3019, 5162, **5705**
*Virtuous Vampires* **1718**
*Weird Menace 1: The Corpse Factory* 4494
*Weird Menace 2: Satan's Roadhouse* 4494
*Weird Tales: Seven Decades of Terror* 482
*Weird Vampire Tales* 1231, **5706**
*World of Darkness: The Unbeholden* 2518

**Weiner, Ellis**
*National Lampoon's Doon* 2567, 2568, 4562, 4563, 4564, 4565, 4566, 4656, 4657

**Weinreich, Beatrice Silverman**
*Yiddish Folk Tales* 6090

**Weinstein, Howard**
*The Covenant of the Crown* 526, 2922, 4081
*Deep Domain* 2296, 5597
*Exiles* 2066
*Perchance to Dream* 1383
*Power Hungry* 1383, 2068

**Weis, Margaret**
*Dark Heart* **5707**
*The Doom Brigade* **5708**
*A Dragon-Lover's Treasury of the Fantastic* 2479, 4408, **5710**
*Dragon Wing* 457, 719, 1937, 2529, 3050, 4105, **5709**, 6004
*DragonLance Chronicles* 1287
*Dragons of Autumn Twilight* 154, 2271, 3155, 4106, 5454, 5455
*Dragons of Summer Flame* 2462, **5711**
*Elven Star* 3050, 4491, **5712**
*Fantastic Alice* 4134, **5713**
*Fire Sea* 27, 510, 681, 717, 1100, 1488, 1533, 2519, 3050, 3174, 4174, 4458, **5714**, 5740
*The Hand of Chaos* 2503, **5715**
*Into the Labyrinth* 681, 717, 4105, 4807, **5716**
*King's Sacrifice* **5717**
*Knights of Black Earth* 3927
*Knights of the Black Earth* **5718**
*Legacy of the Darksword* **5719**
*The Lost King* 1745, **5720**
*A Magic-Lover's Treasury of the Fantastic* **5721**
*Nightsword* **5722**
*Relics and Omens* **5723**
*The Second Generation* **5724**
*Sentinels* 1807, **5725**
*Serpent Mage* 1422, **5726**
*The Seventh Gate* **5727**
*The Soulforge* **5728**
*The Star of the Guardians Series* 4829
*Testament of the Dragon* **5729**
*Time of the Twins* 5454, 5455
*Treasures of Fantasy* **5730**
*War of the Twins* 5454, 5455

**Weiskopf, T.K.F.**
*Tomorrow Bites* **1230**
*Tomorrow Sucks* **1231**

**Weisman, Jordan K.**
*Into the Shadows* 976, 1591, 1889, 3245, 4821, 5135, **5731**

**Weiss, Bobbie J.G.**
*Lifeline* 2109

**Weldon, Fay**
*The Cloning of Joanna May* 95, **5732**
*Letters to Alice on First Reading Jane Austen* 950, 1397
*Lives and Loves of a She-Devil* 1818, 5477, 5927
*The Shrapnel Academy* 2028, 3473

**Wellman, Manly Wade**
*After Dark* 1396, 1639, 3272
*Cahena* 2528
*The Hanging Stones* 1639
*John the Balladeer* 1639, 1765, 3472, 4791
*The Lost and Lurking* 1639
*The Old Gods Waken* 715, 3272
*The School of Darkness* 2139, 2856, 3390
*Sherlock Holmes's War of the Worlds* 119, 1524
*The Valley So Low* 967, 3328, 3329, 3333
*Who Fears the Devil?* 817, 1639
*Worse Things Waiting* 537, 939, 942, 2844, 3515, 5155

**Wells, Angus**
*Dark Magic* 2987, 5296, **5733**
*Exile's Challenge* **5734**
*Exile's Children* **5735**
*Forbidden Magic* 702, **5736**
*The Guardian* **5737**
*Lords of the Sky* 726, 2462, **5738**
*The Usurper* **5739**
*The Way Beneath* **5740**
*Wild Magic* 1068, **5741**
*Wrath of Ashar* 1005, 3246, **5742**

**Wells, Catherine**
*Children of the Earth* 5492, **5743**
*The Earth Is All That Lasts* 191, 656, 1932, 3424, 3469, 3503, 3704, 3729, 3745, 3862, 3864, 4000, 4001, 5429, 5433, 5435, 5492, **5744**, 5965
*The Earth Saver* **5745**

**Wells, H.G.**
*28 Science Fiction Stories* 1597
*The Complete Short Stories of H.G. Wells* 3148
*The Food of the Gods* 874, 4842
*The Invisible Man* 611, 1188, 3493
*The Island of Doctor Moreau* 305, 874, 2580
*The Shape of Things to Come* 2790
*Thirty Strange Stories* **5746**, **5747**
*The Time Machine* 403, 1074, 1344, 3526, 5067, 5192, 5659, 5999
*The War of the Worlds* 119, 205, 2034, 2048, 2192, 5878
*When the Sleeper Wakes* 735, 5243, 5568

**Wells, Martha**
*City of Bones* **5748**
*The Death of the Necromancer* 2758, **5749**

*The Element of Fire*  718, 719, 841, 979, 1009, 1064, 1143, 1253, 1636, 1660, 1773, 1790, 1864, 2032, 2039, 2060, 2195, 2269, 2358, 2503, 2506, 2509, 2529, 2693, 2694, 2695, 2696, 2956, 2958, 2959, 2989, 3168, 3293, 3306, 3481, 3508, 3511, 3645, 3775, 3839, 3844, 3914, 3930, 3936, 3978, 4516, 4527, 4718, 4768, 4804, 4983, 5144, 5217, 5251, 5266, 5391, 5394, 5584, 5716, 5728, **5750**, 5811, 5812, 5813, 5978, 5980

**Welsch, Roger**
*Touching the Fire*  178, 190, 731, 2686, 4380, 4817, **5751**

**Wentworth, K.D.**
*House of Moons*  645, 3060, **5752**
*The Imperium Game*  **5753**
*Moonspeaker*  218, 219, **5754**

**Werber, Bernard**
*Empire of the Ants*  **5755**

**Wescott, Earle**
*Winter Wolves*  **5756**, 5894

**West, Michelle**
*The Broken Crown*  5200, **5757**
*Hunter's Death*  **5758**
*Hunter's Oath*  1095, 2695, 3291, 3292, **5759**
*The Uncrowned King*  **5760**

**West, Owen**
*The Funhouse*  5624

**West, Paul**
*Lord Byron's Doctor*  5842
*The Women of Whitechapel and Jack the Ripper*  26, 3987, **5761**

**Westall, Robert**
*Antique Dust*  283, 1671, 2866, 3314, 5776
*The Call and Other Stories*  1526, **5762**
*The Cats of Seroster*  2944
*Demons and Shadows: The Ghostly Best Stories of Robert Westall*  **5763**
*Ghost Stories*  1693, 1701, 2772, 4274, 4282
*In Camera and Other Stories*  1526, **5764**
*Shades of Darkness: More of the Ghostly Best Stories of Robert Westall*  **5765**
*Wind Eye*  1294

**Westerfeld, Scott**
*Fine Prey*  **5766**
*Polymorph*  **5767**

**Westlake, Donald E.**
*Humans*  729, 2753, 5532, **5768**, 6062

**Whalen, Patrick**
*Deathwalker*  427, 2251, 2340, 3081, 3325, 3671, 3895, 4111, 4113, 4238, 4309, 5249, **5769**, 6078
*Night Thirst*  3051, 4102, **5770**
*Out of the Night*  947, 2285, 3956, **5771**

**Wham, Tom**
*The Stone of Time*  **1840**

**Wharton, Edith**
*The Ghost-Feeler*  **5772**

**Wheatley, Dennis**
*A Century of Horror Stories*  1, 2968

*The Devil Rides Out*  751, 3408, 5111, 5692, 5696, **5773**
*The Irish Witch*  1185
*The Satanist*  4531
*Strange Conflict*  92, 637, 941
*They Used Dark Forces*  2932, 3220, 3672, 3759, 4960
*To the Devil, a Daughter*  4531, 4568

**Wheeler, David**
*No, but I Saw the Movie*  5460, 5947

**Wheeler, Deborah**
*Jaydium*  **5774**
*Northlight*  1026, **5775**

**Whitbourn, John**
*Binscombe Tales*  2707, 3314, **5776**
*Popes and Phantoms*  1276

**White, E.B.**
*Charlotte's Web*  1090, 2786

**White, Edward Lucas**
*Lukundoo and Other Stories*  1252, 3447, 3879, 3880

**White, James**
*The Dream Millennium*  897, 4066, 5042, 5243, 5860
*Escape Orbit*  3522
*Final Diagnosis*  **5777**
*The Galactic Gourmet*  **5778**
*The Genocidal Healer*  4176, **5779**
*Hospital Station*  4172, 4196
*Mind Changer*  1266, **5780**
*Sector General*  4195
*The Silent Stars Go By*  2491, 4116, **5781**
*The White Papers*  759, 1969, 3430, **5782**, 5838

**White, James Gordon**
*The Beast*  **5784**
*The Nomad Queen*  **5783**

**White, John Manchip**
*Whistling Past the Churchyard*  2543, 2643, 3472, 3705

**White, Marie Ardell**
*The Beast*  **5784**

**White, Steve**
*Legacy*  **5785**
*Prince of Sunset*  **5786**

**White, T.H.**
*The Once and Future King*  96, 266, 1092, 2188, 2572, 2745, 2767, 3352
*The Sword in the Stone*  370, 372, 3720, 6035, 6038

**White, Ted**
*Phoenix Prime*  5647
*The Sorceress of Qar*  1772

**Whiteford, Wynne**
*Lake of the Sun*  621, 5514, **5787**
*The Specialist*  4633, 4635, **5788**

**Whitehead, Henry S.**
*West India Lights*  3879, 3880

**Whiteside, Shaun**
*The Wall*  2603

**Whitman, John**
*Disturbing Behavior*  2205, **5789**

**Whitmore, Andrew**
*The Fortress of Eternity*  3934, 4167, **5790**

**Whittemore, Edward**
*Jerusalem Poker*  1093, 1274, 1275, 4359, 4384

**Whitten, Les**
*Moon of the Wolf*  1007, 1404, 1570, 2138, 5442
*Moon of the Wolf/Progeny of the Adder*  5072, **5791**
*Progeny of the Adder*  1402, 2288, 2510, 2792, 3108, 4004, 4005, 4496, 4508

**Whyte, Jack**
*The Eagles' Brood*  **5792**
*The Saxon Shore*  **5793**
*The Skystone*  266, 267, 640, 2746, **5794**

**Wiater, Stanley**
*After the Darkness*  2278, 3598, 3961, 4278, 4722, **5795**
*Mysteries of the Word*  3556, 4444, 5446, **5796**

**Wieck, Stewart**
*The Beast Within*  23, 3225, 3229, 5693, **5797**
*The Essential World of Darkness*  5701, 5702, **5797**
*The Quintessential World of Darkness*  **5798**
*St. Vitus Dances Eternity: A Sarajevo Ghost Story*  **5585**
*Strange City*  **3229**
*Toreador*  1950
*When Will You Rage*  23, 3224, 3229, 5797
*World of Darkness: Death and Damnation*  3224
*World of Darkness: Truth Until Paradox*  23, 3224, 5797

**Wiggins, Marianne**
*John Dollar*  **5799**

**Wilde, Kelley**
*Angel Kiss*  1335, 3492, **5800**
*Makoto*  4003, **5801**
*Mastery*  2255, **5802**
*The Suiting*  839, **5803**

**Wilde, Oscar**
*The Picture of Dorian Gray*  19, 87, 556, 2818, 3595

**Wilder, Cherry**
*Dealers in Light and Darkness*  497, 3240
*Signs of Life*  **5804**

**Wilhelm, Kate**
*And the Angels Sing*  415, 3379, 3736, 3751, **5805**
*Cambio Bay*  11, **5806**
*Children of the Wind: Five Novellas*  2261, **5807**
*The Clewiston Test*  5184
*The Clone*  5352
*Crazy Time*  582, 4276
*Death Qualified: A Mystery of Chaos*  891, 2559, 5054
*The Good Children*  **5808**
*Juniper Time*  5634
*Listen, Listen*  2261
*Margaret and I*  1932, 3263
*The Mile-Long Spaceship*  665
*Naming the Flowers*  1441, 2864, **5809**
*State of Grace*  497, 2078, 3185, 5177, **5810**
*Where Late the Sweet Birds Sang*  1932, 5732

**Wilkins, Cary**
*A Treasury of Fantasy: Heroic Adventures in Imaginary Lands*  5003

**Wilkins-Freeman, Mary E.**
*Collected Ghost Stories*  5772
*The Wind in the Rosebush and Other Stories of the Supernatural*  1673

**Willard, Nancy**
*Pish, Posh, Said Hieronymus Bosch*  3382
*Uncle Terrible: More Adventures of Anatole*  329

**Willey, Elizabeth**
*The Price of Blood and Honor*  **5811**
*A Sorcerer and a Gentleman*  2355, 5503, **5812**
*The Well-Favored Man: The Tale of the Sorcerer's Nephew*  718, 719, 1064, 2503, 2509, 4986, **5813**

**Williams, A. Susan**
*The Lifted Veil: The Book of Fantastic Literature by Women*  37, 629, 1715, 2035, 3574, 4826, 5018, **5814**
*The Penguin Book of Modern Fantasy by Women*  3670, 5018, **5815**

**Williams, Charles**
*Dead Calm*  3756
*The Greater Trumps*  2406, 4359
*The Hot Spot*  3330
*War in Heaven*  2231

**Williams, Conrad**
*Head Injuries*  **5816**

**Williams, Linda V.**
*Vampire Bytes*  **2322**

**Williams, Michael**
*Allamanda*  **5817**
*Arcady*  1474, **5818**
*Before the Mask*  4925
*A Forest Lord*  1146, 2627, **5819**
*Galen Beknighted*  5724
*The Oath and the Measure*  4368
*A Sorcerer's Apprentice*  1532, 4261, **5820**
*Weasel's Luck*  5711, 5724

**Williams, Paul O.**
*An Ambush of Shadows*  4604, 4621
*The Breaking of Northwall*  46, 208, 278, 394, 656, 720, 721, 787, 881, 889, 1075, 3501, 3862, 3863, 3864, 3873, 3908, 4001, 4488, 5500, 5590, 5743, 5745, 5920, 5965
*The Ends of the Circle*  394, 1324
*The Gift of the Gorboduc Vandal*  2038, 2173, **5821**
*The Song of the Axe*  3788, 4600, 4619
*The Sword of Forebearance*  1329, 4602

**Williams, Ruth L.**
*The Silver Tree*  **5822**

**Williams, Sheila**
*Hugo and Nebula Award Winners From Asimov's Science Fiction*  888
*Isaac Asimov's Ghosts*  **1610**
*Isaac Asimov's Vampires*  **1611**

**Williams, Sidney**
*Gnelfs*  1038, **5823**
*Night Brothers*  **5824**
*When Darkness Falls*  **5825**

**Williams, Tad**
*Caliban's Hour*  3079, 3409, **5826**
*Child of an Ancient City*  2085, 3410, 3414, 5336, **5827**
*City of Golden Shadow*  **5828**

*The Dragonbone Chair* 1146, 1909, 1911, 2095, 3581, 3893, 4489, 4513, 4526, 4660, 4776, 5034, 5715, 5727, 5736, 5750, 5790, **5829**, 6003
*River of Blue Fire* **5830**
*Stone of Farewell* 4167, 5750, **5831**
*Tailchaser's Song* 32, 432, 599, 737, 1657, 2421, 2423, 2774, 2775, 2848, 2849, 2850, 2851, 2852, 2853, 2854, 2855, 3115, 3120, 3377, 3740, 4054, 4143, 4144, 4145, 4157, 4271, 4273
*To Green Angel Tower* 3107, 5741, **5832**

**Williams, Walter Jon**
*Ambassador of Progress* 353, 5231
*Angel Station* 768, 984, 985, 1001, 1891, 1893, 2099, 3248, 3830, 3929, 4453, 4593, 5573, **5833**
*Aristoi* 2213, 3256, 4729, **5834**
*City on Fire* **5835**
*The Crown Jewels* 261
*Days of Atonement* 116, 1665, 2682, 3029, 3663, 4193, **5836**
*Elegy for Angels and Dogs/The Graveyard Heart* 3189
*Facets* **5837**
*Frankensteins and Foreign Devils* **5838**
*Hardwired* 66, 481, 766, 971, 972, 975, 1543, 1644, 1750, 1820, 2033, 3242, 3890, 3921, 4191, 4343, 4618, 4747, 5006, 6047
*Metropolitan* 218, 324, 2364, 2522, 4931, **5839**
*Rock of Ages* 3465, **5840**
*Solip: System* **5841**
*Voice of the Whirlwind* 79, 107, 110, 597, 805, 957, 974, 995, 996, 1936, 2275, 2536, 2579, 3741, 3795, 3850, 4193, 4366, 4618, 4747, 5134, 5245, 5680
*Wall, Stone, Craft* **5842**

**Williamson, Chet**
*Ash Wednesday* 2310, 2668, 2904, 4834, 5424, 5440, 5991
*City of Iron* 2308, **5843**
*Clash by Night* 494, 696, 4186, **5844**
*The Crow: City of Angels* 494, 696
*Dreamthorp* 427, 1297, 1931, 2689, 3336, 3655, 3895, 4664, 5077, **5845**, 5961
*Empire of Dust* 2308, **5846**
*Hell: A Cyberpunk Thriller* 4495
*The House of Fear* 200, 666, 5427, 5530, 5929
*Lowland Rider* 1347, 1851, 4787
*Mordenheim* 155, 1510, 2516, 3613, **5847**
*Murder in Cormyr* 2426, **5848**
*Reign* 660, 3025, 3858, 4716, **5849**
*Second Chance* 1843, **5850**
*Soulstorm* 281, 861, 1192, 1380, 2630, 3684, 3685, 4830, 5380

**Williamson, J.N.**
*Author's Choice Monthly Number 24: The Naked Flesh of Feeling* 3558
*The Best of Masques* 1847, 3959, 4724, 4726
*The Black School* 5464, **5851**
*Bloodlines* 5421, **5852**
*The Book of Webster's* **5853**
*The Fifth Season* **5854**
*Masques* 4278
*Masques III* 4200

*Masques IV* **5855**
*The Masques Series* 3960
*The Monastery* 3389, 5100, **5856**
*The Naked Flesh of Feeling* 3553, **5857**
*The Night Seasons* 3134, **5858**
*The Tulpa* 2605

**Williamson, Jack**
*Beachhead* 586, 4160, 4348, **5859**
*The Best of Jack Williamson* 4956
*The Black Sun* **5860**
*Darker than You Think* 603, 1822, 2789, 3053, 3877, 4582, 4604, 4764, 5756, **5861**
*Demon Moon* 3629, **5862**
*The Fortress of Utopia* **5863**
*The Girl from Mars & The Prince of Space* **5864**
*The Humanoid Touch* 1896
*The Humanoids* 126, 128, 134, 198, 232, 249, 446, 1782, 2458, 3715, 3794, 4903, **5865**
*The Legion of Space* 3035, 4468, 5048
*Mazeway* 2048, 2807, 3448, 4349, 4357, 4894, 5834, **5866**
*The Silicon Dagger* 5086
*The Singers of Time* **4354**
*Star Bridge* 2458, **2459**

**Willis, Connie**
*Bellwether* 4042, **5867**
*Doomsday Book* 453, 783, 1941, 2883, 3801, **5868**
*Fire Watch* 1854, 5807
*Impossible Things* 123, 274, 689, 790, 1758, 1963, 2027, 2120, 2537, 3235, 3384, 3971, 4535, 5240, 5410, **5869**
*Light Raid* 969, 1662, **5870**
*Lincoln's Dreams* 3993, 5806
*The New Hugo Winners, Volume III* 2401, **5871**
*Promised Land* **5872**
*Remake* 3083, **5873**
*To Say Nothing of the Dog* 1852, **5874**
*Uncharted Territory* 1536, **5875**

**Wiloch, Thomas**
*Mr. Templeton's Toyshop: Prose Poems and Short Fiction* 3851, **5876**

**Wilson, Charles**
*Extinct* 88, 189, **5877**

**Wilson, Colin**
*The Delta* **5878**
*The Mind Parasites* 3567, 3568, 5470
*The Space Vampires* 4331, 5049

**Wilson, David Henry**
*The Coachman Rat* 737, 1810, 5427, **5879**

**Wilson, David Niall**
*Chrysalis* **5880**
*The Fall of the House of Escher and Other Illusions* 94, 663, 802, 1789, 2769, 2937, 3495, 4231, 4313, 5316, 5335, 5445, 5620, **5881**
*To Dream of Dreamers Lost* 1950, **5882**
*To Speak in Lifeless Tongues* **5883**

**Wilson, F. Paul**
*The Barrens* 3556, 4444, 5194, 5446, **5884**
*The Barrens and Others* **5885**
*Black Wind* 4003

*Diagnosis: Terminal* **5886**
*Dydeetown World* 1751, 4941, 5302, 5644, **5887**
*Freak Show* 854, 2311, 3758, 4057, **5888**
*Implant* 1347, 4874
*The Keep* 3759, 4529
*The LaNague Chronicles* 328, 593, 1915, 3466, 5132, 5365, 5366, 5367, **5889**
*Masque* **5890**
*Midnight Mass* 1197, 2440, 3758, 4072, **5891**
*Mirage* 1973, **5892**
*Nightworld* 1721, 3445, 5340, **5893**
*Pelts* 5318, **5894**
*Reborn* **5895**
*Reprisal* **5896**
*The Select* 93, 1939, 2206, **5897**
*Sibs* 436, 1786, 2115, 2613, 5892, **5898**
*Soft and Others* 777, 1887, 2277, 3321, 3328, 3329, 4648, 5339, 5600, **5899**
*The Tery* 1323, 1325, 2193, 3158, 5132, 5225, 5226, 5588, **5900**
*The Tomb* 3882, 3883
*The Touch* 1410, 1507, 1561, 2700, 3134, 4073

**Wilson, Gahan**
*The Cleft and Other Odd Tales* **5901**
*Eddy Deco's Last Caper* 868, 869, 5168, 5796, 6072
*Everybody's Favorite Duck* 6072
*Gahan Wilson's The Ultimate Haunted House* 2396, 5665, **5902**
*Still Weird* 3334

**Wilson, Richard**
*And Then the Town Took Off* 5303
*The Girls from Planet 5* 5997

**Wilson, Robert Anton**
*The Earth Will Shake* 1273, 1275, 3262
*Masks of the Illuminati* 1063
*Nature's God* **5903**
*Reality Is What You Can Get Away With: An Illustrated Screenplay* 29, 1784, 1785, 2859, 3457, 5074, **5904**
*The Schrodinger's Cat Trilogy* 1093, 1274
*The Widow's Son* 2627

**Wilson, Robert Charles**
*A Bridge of Years* 65, 135, 510, 1074, 1852, 2532, 4286, 4525, 4641, 5043, 5868, **5905**
*Darwinia* **5906**
*The Divide* **5907**
*Gypsies* 1521, 3707, 5647, **5908**
*The Harvest* 4506, **5909**
*A Hidden Place* **5910**
*Memory Wire* 295, 4632
*Mysterium* 895, 956, 2239, 5295, **5911**
*Second Fire* 2615, 2926, 4688, 4815, 5263

**Wilson, Robin Scott**
*Clarion* 3085
*Clarion I-III* 1766, 1767, 5953
*Clarion II* 3085
*Clarion III* 3085
*Those Who Can: A Science Fiction Reader* 1766, 1767, 3085

**Wilson, Steve**
*The Lost Traveller* 1238

**Windling, Terri**
*The Armless Maiden and Other Tales for Childhood's Survivors* 1358, 1366, **5912**
*Black Swan, White Raven* 1358
*Black Thorn, White Rose* 1359
*Borderland* 235, 630, 646, 647, 767, 769, 971, 975, 986, 989, 1288, 1368, 1427, 1436, 1994, 2467, 3271, 3299, 3300, 3302, 4335, 4675, 4993, 4994, 4995, 5216, **5913**
*Bordertown* 235, 546, 552, 769, 971, 975, 989, 1427, 1436, 2373, 2467, 3271, 3299, 4675, 4993, 4994, 4995, 5216
*Elsewhere* 647, 1340, 1368, 1425, 6005
*Elsewhere II* 1340, 1368, 1425, 4335
*Elsewhere III* 1340, 1425
*The Essential Bordertown* **5914**
*Faery* 235, 1340, 1368, 2388, 4335
*Life on the Border* 235, 646, 648, 711, 767, 769, 976, 1159, 1179, 1359, 1368, 1373, 1427, 1434, 1436, 1837, 1958, 1960, 1994, 2373, 2378, 2461, 2467, 3245, 3271, 3299, 3301, 3302, 3643, 3646, 4174, 4335, 4497, 4675, 4866, 4971, 4985, 4993, 4995, 5038, 5156, 5214, 5216, 5428, 5818, **5915**, 5945, 6044, 6045
*Ruby Slippers, Golden Tears* 1366
*Sirens and Other Daemon Lovers* 1367
*Snow White, Blood Red* 1368
*The Wood Wife* 636, 1358, 2266, 2326, 4358, **5916**
*The Year's Best Fantasy and Horror: Eleventh Annual Collection* 1371
*The Year's Best Fantasy and Horror: Fifth Annual Collection* 1372
*The Year's Best Fantasy and Horror: Fourth Annual Collection* 1373
*The Year's Best Fantasy and Horror: Ninth Annual Collection* 1374
*The Year's Best Fantasy and Horror: Seventh Annual Collection* 1375
*The Year's Best Fantasy and Horror: Sixth Annual Collection* 1376
*The Year's Best Fantasy and Horror: Tenth Annual Collection* 1377
*The Year's Best Fantasy and Horror: Third Annual Collection* 1378

**Wingate, Anne**
*The Eye of Anna* 1829

**Wingert, Jennifer**
*Spirit Fox* 4524

**Wingrove, David**
*Beneath the Tree of Heaven* 3699, 5725, **5917**
*The Broken Wheel* 3896, **5918**
*The Middle Kingdom* 201, 657, 1145, 1538, 1573, 1575, 3817, 3896, 3897, 4682, 5253, **5919**
*Myst: The Book of Atrus* 3896
*Myst: The Book of D'ni* 3897
*The Stone Within* **5920**
*White Moon, Red Dragon* **5921**
*The White Mountain* **5922**

**Winter, Douglas E.**
*Black Sun* **5923**
*Night Visions 5* 1885
*Prime Evil* 2965, 4888
*Revelations* **5924**

**Winter, Pat**
*Madoc* 3166
*Madoc's Hundred* 2570, 3166, **5925**

**Winter, Steve**
*Wanderlust* 3155

**Winters, B.L.**
*Bloody Waters* **5926**

**Winterson, Jeanette**
*Sexing the Cherry* **5927**

**Winthrop, Elizabeth**
*Castle in the Attic* 331

**Wise, Herbert**
*Great Tales of Terror and the Supernatural* 1, 38, 848, 2590, 2591, 2968, 2993, 3027, 4311, 4440, 5031

**Wiseman, David**
*A Tie to the Past* **5928**

**Wisman, Ken**
*Weird Family Tales* 3614, **5929**

**Wismer, Don**
*A Roil of Stars* **5930**

**Witcover, Paul**
*Waking Beauty* **5931**

**Wittig, Monique**
*Les Guerilleres* 780, 5590

**Wold, Allen L.**
*Crown of the Serpent* 5129, 5564, **5932**
*Lair of the Cyclops* **5933**
*V: The Pursuit of Diana* 4290

**Wolf, Gary K.**
*Who Censored Roger Rabbit?* 1152, 1399, 1506, 1524, 2132, 3441, 3768, 5148
*Who P-P-Plugged Roger Rabbit?* 2620, 3441, 3768, 5148, **5934**

**Wolf, Jack C.**
*Ghosts, Castles and Victims* 4026
*Tales of the Occult* 4026

**Wolf, Leonard**
*Blood Thirst: 100 Years of Vampire Fiction* 2409, 5265, **5935**
*Doubles, Dummies and Dolls: 21 Terror Tales of Replication* **5936**

**Wolf, Milton T.**
*Visions of Wonder: The Science Fiction Research Association Anthology* **2595**

**Wolfe, Gene**
*The Book of the New Sun* 4243
*Calde of the Long Sun* **5937**
*Castle of Days* 237, 244, 2576, **5938**
*Castleview* 2622, 2623, 4173, 4362, 5903, **5939**
*The Citadel of the Autarch* 4242
*Claw of the Conciliator* 4242
*The Devil in a Forest* 5579
*Endangered Species* 61, 321, 621, 625, 823, 3379, **5940**, 6067
*Exodus From the Long Sun* **5941**
*The Fifth Head of Cerberus* 927, 5732
*Free Live Free* 4263
*Gene Wolfe's Book of Days* 2412, 2589, 4720, 5024
*The Island of Doctor Death and Other Stories and Other Stories* 6067
*Lake of the Long Sun* **5942**
*Nightside the Long Sun* 567, 892, 2057, 2243, 2626, **5943**

*Peace* 4211
*The Shadow of the Torturer* 248, 904, 1150, 1429, 1482, 1983, 2533, 2550, 3572, 3692, 3874, 4201, 4242, 5000, 5434, 5720
*Soldier of Arete* 2, 11, 2187, 2189, 2751, 2752, 4201, 5790, **5944**
*Soldier of the Mist* 11, 2187, 2189, 3170, 4272, 5321, 5595, 5738
*Storeys From the Old Hotel* 415, 1431, 1608, 2736, 4561, 4757, 5913, **5945**
*The Sword of the Lictor* 4242
*There Are Doors* 1521, 5806, 5908, 5960

**Wolfe, Ron**
*Death's Door* **5969**

**Wolfe, Sebastian**
*The Little Book of Horrors* 1709, 1710, 1714, 4828, 5686, 5687, **5946**
*Reel Terror* 4252, 5460, **5947**

**Wollheim, Donald A.**
*The 1990 Annual World's Best Science Fiction* 214, 215, 238, 239, 500, 501, 887, 1616, 1620, 1621, 4031, 4558, 4725, **5948**
*The Avon Ghost Reader* 4214
*The Pocket Book of Science Fiction* 5004

**Wolverton, Dave**
*Beyond the Gate* 4829, **5949**
*The Courtship of Princess Leia* 109, 2500, 3820, 4299, **5950**
*The Golden Queen* **5951**
*L. Ron Hubbard Presents Writers of the Future, Volume VIII* 755
*L. Ron Hubbard Presents Writers of the Future, Volume IX* **5952**
*L. Ron Hubbard Presents Writers of the Future, Volume XII* **5953**
*L. Ron Hubbard Presents Writers of the Future, Volume XIV* **5954**
*On My Way to Paradise* 475, 3037, 3450, 3451, 4191, 4193, 4618, 4884, 5006, 5278, 5279, 5280, 5281, 5283, 5841, **5955**, 6061
*Path of the Hero* 4854
*Serpent Catch* 250, 268, 1255, 3191, 4854, 4949, 5351, **5956**

**Womack, Jack**
*Ambient* 4095
*Elvissey* 5089, **5957**
*Heathern* 4030, 4856, 5642, **5958**
*Random Acts of Senseless Violence* 3312, **5959**
*Terraplane* **5960**

**Wood, Bari**
*The Basement* **5961**
*The Killing Gift* 1580
*The Tribe* 2697

**Wood, Bridget**
*The Lost Prince* **5962**
*Wolfking* 633, 2740, 3501, 3504, 3506, 4266, **5963**

**Wood, Mackay**
*Wolf's Cub* **5964**

**Wood, N. Lee**
*Faraday's Orphans* 3599, **5965**
*Looking for the Mahdi* **5966**

**Woodbury, Francine G.**
*Shade and Shadow* **5967**

**Woodruff, Elvira**
*The Summer I Shrank My Grandmother* **5968**

**Woods, Richard**
*A Diversity of Dragons* 3728

**Wooley, John**
*Death's Door* **5969**

**Woolley, Persia**
*Child of the Northern Spring* 2939, 3827
*Guinevere: The Legend in Autumn* 224, 269, 1737, 2939, 2940, **5970**
*Queen of the Summer Stars* 1741, 2939, 2940, **5971**

**Woolrich, Cornell**
*It Had to Be Murder* 4500

**Worsick, David**
*Henry's Gift: The Magic Eye* 2981, 3896, 3897, **5972**, 6036

**Wrede, Patricia C.**
*Book of Enchantments* **5973**, 6040
*Calling on Dragons* 1512, 4460, 5144, **5974**
*Caught in Crystal* 176, 642, 4323, 5509, 5733
*Daughter of Witches* 289, 4323
*Dealing with Dragons* 174, 329, 1220, 1221, 1488, 1534, 1951, 2014, 2362, 2413, 2944, 3941, 4390, 4447, 5217, 5556, 5640, **5975**, 6032, 6069
*Magician's Ward* 5137, **5976**
*Mairelon the Magician* 489, 763, 1742, 2355, 3776, 4899, 5002, 5490, **5977**
*The Raven Ring* 682, 1172, 1953, 2039, 2141, 2268, 2269, 2957, 3278, 3486, 4768, 5749, **5978**, 6057
*Searching for Dragons* 329, 843, 1488, 1533, 1951, 2015, 2461, 2463, 3070, 3513, 4324, **5979**, 6024, 6025
*The Seven Towers* 1477, 1685, 2359, 2362, 3171
*Shadow Magic* 12, 16, 176, 393, 3296, 3298, 3304, 3305, 3306, 3512, 3514
*Shadows over Lyra* **5980**
*Snow White and Rose Red* 42, 375, 1005, 1446, 1479, 1810, 2121, 2262, 2636, 5428, 5639, **5981**, 6062, 6088, 6090
*Sorcery and Cecelia* 314, 727, 743, 1742, 1921, 5137, 5266
*Talking to Dragons* 168, 703, 1220, 1488, 1668, 2014, 2946, 3070, 3728, 4322

**Wren, M.K.**
*A Gift upon the Shore* 2603, **5982**
*House of the Wolf* 3865
*Sword of the Lamb* 741, 3018, 5684

**Wrench, Sara J.**
*The Duke of Sumava* **5983**

**Wright, Gary**
*The Road West* **5984**

**Wright, Helen S.**
*A Matter of Oaths* 2436, 4468, **5985**, 6052

**Wright, S. Fowler**
*The Throne of Saturn* 5746

**Wright, Stephen**
*Going Native* 570

*M31: A Family Romance* 1831

**Wright, Susan**
*Violations* 206

**Wright, T. Lucien**
*Blood Brothers* 810, 1352, 1355, 2024, 3546, 3557, 4091, 4728, 4883, 5537, 5657, **5986**
*Dark Visions* 3135, **5987**
*Thirst of the Vampire* 452, 660, 1794, 1795, 1798, 3113, 4774, 5020, **5988**

**Wright, T.M.**
*The Ascending* 2335, 3620, 4003, **5989**
*Boundaries* 2556, **5990**
*Goodlow's Ghosts* 4256, 5468, **5991**
*The Island* 947, 2241, 2822, 3783
*Little Boy Lost* 521, 2292, 3657, 5784, 5969, **5992**
*A Manhattan Ghost Story* 3201
*The Place* 1198, 3639, **5993**
*The School* 2139, 3657, **5994**
*Sleepeasy* 2335

**Wrightson, Patricia**
*Balyet* 4310, 4920, **5995**
*The Dark Bright Water* 2170, 4946
*The Ice Is Coming* 2170, 4946
*Journey Behind the Wind* 2170, 4946

**Wu, William F.**
*Dictator* 5516, **5996**
*An Enemy Reborn* **5197**
*Hong on the Range* 1879, **5997**
*Predator* 78, 83, **5998**
*The Robin Hood Ambush* 2248, 2389, **5999**
*Warrior* 1855, **6000**

**Wurts, Janny**
*Curse of the Mistwraith* 1640, 1674, 1864, 1908, 4462, 4516, 4522, 4528, **6001**
*Cycle of Fire Trilogy* 5563
*Daughter of the Empire* 3338
*Fugitive Prince* 1775, **6002**
*Keeper of the Keys* 1906
*The Master of Whitestorm* 1904, 1906, **6003**
*Mistress of the Empire* **1906**
*Servant of the Empire* **1910**
*Shadowfane* 1906, 4685
*Ships of Merior* **6004**
*Stormwarden* 1906, 1907, 2356, 3270, 3385, 5728
*That Way Lies Camelot* 3279, **6005**

**Wyke-Smith, E.A.**
*The Marvellous Land of Snergs* **6006**

**Wylie, Jonathan**
*Dreams of Stone* 1731, 1736
*Dreams Street* 1722
*The First Named* 5133
*The Lightless Kingdom* 1731, 1736, 5715, **6007**

**Wylie, Philip**
*The Disappearance* 3021, 4652
*When Worlds Collide* 732, 4416

**Wyndham, John**
*Chocky* 2787
*The Crysalids* 3251
*The Day of the Triffids* 1806, 2344, 5858
*The Midwich Cuckoos* 491, 733, 2787, 3251, 3856, 4504, 4645, 5065
*Out of the Deeps* 189, 4923, 5541
*Re-Birth* 728, 4074, 4678

*Tales of Gooseflesh and
   Laughter* 5747
*The Trouble with Lichen* 4352

## Y

**Yamashita, Karen Tei**
*Through the Arc of the Rain
   Forest* **6008**
*Tropic of Orange* 52, 950, **6009**

**Yarbro, Chelsea Quinn**
*The Angry Angel* 4578, **6010**
*Ariosto* 1341, 3255, 3258, 4651,
   5218, 5228
*A Baroque Fable* 1207, 2144, 2145,
   2362, 4399
*Beastnights* 723, 2222, 5332
*Better in the Dark* 2246, **6011**
*Blood Games* 264, 4573
*Blood Roses* **6012**
*A Candle for D'Artagnan* 742, 3822,
   4513, 4784, **6013**
*Crown of Empire* **6014**
*Crusader's Torch* 3602, **6015**
*False Dawn* 4621
*Firecode* 3251
*A Flame in Byzantium* 5503
*The Godforsaken* 4892, 5861
*Hotel Transylvania* 1142, 1795,
   3110, 3163
*Hyacinths* 1535
*Mansions of Darkness* 4668, **6016**
*Monet's Ghost* **6017**
*The Olivia Trilogy* 678, 3151, 3781
*Out of the House of Life* 55, 4303,
   **6018**
*The Palace* 463, 1797, 3017, 4770,
   4782
*The Path of the Eclipse* 195, 1317,
   1318
*The Saint-Germain Chronicles* 2705,
   4767, 5191, 5802
*Signs and Portents* 2715
*Tempting Fate* 2511, 3759
*Time of the Fourth Horseman* 1133,
   1164, 1590, 3242, 5868
*Writ in Blood* 5501, **6019**

**Yeats, W.B.**
*A Treasury of Irish Myth, Legend and
   Folklore* **6090**

**Yeovil, Jack**
*Comeback Tour: The Sky Belongs to the
   Stars* 4821, 5089, 5957, **6020**
*Demon Download* 1238, 2323, **6021**
*Drachenfels* 1443, 1927, 1928, **6022**
*Krokodil Tears* 1238, **6023**

**Yep, Laurence**
*Dragon Cauldron* 2463, **6024**
*Dragon of the Lost Sea* 843, 1218,
   2461, 2865, 4324, 4460, 4462,
   5974
*Dragon War* 2850, **6025**
*The Rainbow People* 3610
*Tongues of Jade* 69, 1221, 4742,
   **6026**

**Yermakov, Nicholas**
*Clique* 4220
*Fall into Darkness* 1025

**Yolen, Jane**
*2041: Twelve Short Stories about the
   Future by Top Science Fiction
   Writers* 4558, 5238, **6027**
*Armageddon Summer* **6028**

*Briar Rose* 466, 467, 636, 728,
   1358, 1409, 1694, 1787, 2244,
   2265, 4404, 4758, 5079, 5143,
   5912, 5916, **6029**
*Camelot* 3720
*Child of Faerie* 3737
*The Devil's Arithmetic* 2244, 2272,
   5079
*Dove Isabeau* 5534
*Dragon's Blood* 4322, 5979
*The Dragon's Boy* 3382, **6030**
*The Faery Flag* 5995
*Favorite Folktales From around the
   World* 849, 2528, 4987
*The Girl Who Cried Flowers and Other
   Tales* 3610
*Here There Be Angels* **6031**
*Here There Be Dragons* 2346, 2479,
   4408, 5710, **6032**
*Here There Be Unicorns* 410, 412,
   1219, 1946, 2346, 3414, 3737,
   4319, **6033**
*Here There Be Witches* **6034**
*The Hobby* 370
*Merlin* **6035**
*Merlin and the Dragons* **6036**
*Merlin's Booke* 369, 372
*The One-Armed Queen* **6037**
*Passager* 369, 370, 372, 3720, **6038**
*The Robot and Rebecca and the Missing
   Owser* 253, 254, 255
*Shape Shifters: Fantasy and Science
   Fiction Tales about Humans Who
   Can Change Their Shapes* 3446,
   5239
*Sister Light, Sister Dark* 2471, 3582,
   3843, **6039**
*Sky Dogs* 3382
*Storyteller* 2947, 5782, 5973
*Tales of Wonder* 3845
*Tam Lin* 3523
*Twelve Impossible Things Before
   Breakfast* 794, **6040**
*Vampires* 4988
*White Jenna* 3582, **6041**
*The Wild Hunt* 1472, 3847, **6042**
*Wizard's Hall* 329, 701, 847, 1601,
   1605, 2944, 3159, 3545, 4260,
   4261, 4323, 4700, 5979, **6043**,
   6057, 6058
*Xanadu* 628, 1368, **6044**
*Xanadu 2* **6045**
*Xanadu 3* **6046**
*The Xanadu Series* 1359, 1366,
   2634, 2635
*Zoo 2000: Twelve Stories of Science
   Fiction and Fantasy Beasts* 3611

**Young, Janine Ellen**
*Cinderblock* 1167, 1348, **6047**, 6063

**Young, Jim**
*Armed Memory* 413, 3711, 4708,
   **6048**
*The Face of the Deep* 1861, 3919

**Young, Richard**
*African-American Folktales for Young
   Readers: Including Favorite Stories
   From African and African-American
   Storytellers* 2528

**Young, Roy V.**
*Captains Outrageous, or, For Doom the
   Bell Tolls* **6049**

**Youssef, Michael**
*Earth King* 3860

**Yulsman, Jerry**
*Elleander Morning* 5501, 5516,
   5517, 5518

## Z

**Zachary, Fay**
*Blood Work* **6050**

**Zachary, Hugh**
*Deep Freeze* 2811

**Zahn, Timothy**
*The Backlash Mission* 66
*The Blackcollar* 2211, 2212, 4602,
   4604, 5027
*Cobra* 589, 1322, 1326, 1900,
   2016, 2212, 2435, 4378, 4984
*A Coming of Age* 632
*Conqueror's Pride* **6051**
*Dark Force Rising* 5917, **6052**
*Deadman Switch* 4594, 5298
*Distant Friends and Others* **6053**
*Heir to the Empire* 76, 103, 109,
   114, 2500, 2914, 3247, 3820,
   4719, 5205, **6054**
*The Last Command* **6055**
*Specter of the Past* 117
*Spinneret* 564, 953, 2491, 3221
*Triplet* 165
*Warhorse* **6056**

**Zahorski, Kenneth J.**
*Visions & Imaginings: Classic Fantasy
   Fiction* 606

**Zambreno, Mary Frances**
*Journeyman Wizard* 641, 5002,
   5976, **6057**
*A Plague of Sorcerers* 701, 1218,
   4260, 4261, 4323, 5640, 5979,
   6043, **6058**
*A Plague of Wizards* 4700

**Zaring, Jane**
*The Return of the Dragon* 5975

**Zebrowski, George**
*Brute Orbits* 3693, **6059**
*The Killing Star* **4281**
*Nebula Awards 21* 501, 4031, 4032,
   4033
*Nebula Awards 21-22* 1342, 4824
*Nebula Awards 22* 215, 246, 500,
   501, 4031, 4032, 4033, 4822,
   4823
*Stranger Suns* 382, 472, 753, 782,
   786, 1026, 1509, 2036, 2728,
   3786, 4019, 4281, 4503, 4652,
   4859, 5054, 5306, 5449, 5774,
   5775, **6060**

**Zeddies, Ann Tonsor**
*Deathgift* **6061**

**Zelazny, Roger**
*The Black Throne* 4764, 5044
*Bridge of Ashes* 191, 1873, 2166,
   2861, 3704, 4380, 5035
*Bring Me the Head of Prince
   Charming* 1208, 1821, 2081,
   3810, 3991, 4396, 4401, 4404,
   **6062**
*Changeling* 4994
*Creatures of Light and Darkness* 36,
   1637, 1648, 1979, 2658, 5449
*Damnation Alley* 86, 1238, 1644,
   2323, 4600, 4602, 4604
*Donnerjack* 3477, **6063**
*Doorways in the Sand* 477, 995
*The Dream Master* 1521, 4210
*A Farce to Be Reckoned With* 2574,
   **6064**
*Flare* 399, 3789, 4416, 4947, 5258,
   **6065**
*Forever After* 5275, **6066**

*Frost and Fire* 425, 5837, **6067**
*Gone to Earth* 3648, **6068**
*The Guns of Avalon* 3978
*Here There Be Dragons* 6032, 6036,
   **6069**
*If at Faust You Don't Succeed* 3480,
   3483, 3991, 4388, 4404, 4655,
   **6070**
*Isle of the Dead* 3698
*Jack of Shadows* 1755, 3073
*Lord of Light* 195, 477, 591, 771,
   1028, 1316, 1317, 1318, 1635,
   2065, 2196, 3122, 3477, 4654,
   4766, 5532, 5637, 5660, 5835,
   5839
*The Mask of Loki* 2658, **6071**
*A Night in the Lonesome
   October* 5796, **6072**
*Nine Princes in Amber* 162, 164,
   477, 746, 747, 1102, 1162, 1180,
   1181, 1635, 1637, 1648, 1678,
   1684, 1686, 1732, 1813, 1864,
   1871, 2361, 2628, 2639, 3386,
   3635, 3636, 3645, 3799, 3802,
   3803, 3804, 3848, 3849, 3978,
   3980, 3985, 4165, 4488, 4517,
   4522, 4523, 4670, 4994, 5017,
   5041, 5364, 5683, 5716, 5727,
   5812, 5813, 6001
*Prince of Chaos* **6073**
*Psychoshop* **477**
*Roadmarks* 590
*Sign of the Unicorn* 3978, 5508
*This Immortal* 125, 789, 2487, 2920,
   3465, 4813, 4990, 5212, 5707,
   5729, 5866, **6074**
*Today We Choose Faces* 969
*Warriors of Blood and Dream* 4227,
   **6075**
*Way Up High* 2468, 3382, 5972,
   **6076**
*Wheel of Fortune* 1187, 2406
*The Williamson Effect* 2398, **6077**
*Wizard World* 1722

**Zell, Steve**
*WiZrD* 2903, **6078**

**Zettel, Sarah**
*Fool's War* 1303, 3231, **6079**
*Playing God* 760, **6080**
*Reclamation* 4244, 5069, **6081**

**Zettner, Pat**
*The Shadow Warrior* 3510, 5709,
   5712, **6082**

**Zimmer, Paul Edwin**
*Blood of the Colyn Muir* 1177, 1815,
   3061, 3659, **6083**

**Zindel, Paul**
*Raptor* **6084**

**Zindell, David**
*The Broken God* **6085**
*Neverness* 768
*The Wild* **6086**

**Zipes, Jack**
*Arabian Nights: The Marvels and
   Wonders of the Thousand and One
   Nights* 374, 1681, 1687, 2123,
   2129, 2130, 4534, **6087**
*Beauties, Beasts and
   Enchantments* 276, 849, 1359,
   1479, 2680, 3574, **6088**
*The Brothers Grimm: From Enchanted
   Forests to the Modern World* 849,
   5560
*Don't Bet on the Prince* 43, 276,
   648, 1366, 2528, 5617

*The Outspoken Princess and the Gentle
  Knight*   274, 794, 1366, 2144,
  2145, 2146, 5617, 6040, **6089**

*Spells of Enchantment*   276, 849,
  1368, 1479, 1576, 2680, 3844,
  4890, 4987, 5912, **6090**

**Zoline, Pamela**
*The Heat Death of the Universe*   2261

# Title Index

This index alphabetically lists all titles featured or mentioned in entries in the main section. Each title is followed by the name of the main author and the entry number(s) where the title can be found. A bold entry number indicates that the title in question is a featured main entry; lightface numbers refer to entries for other books that mention the title in question under the rubric "Other books you might like."

**/**
Bear, Greg   378, **413**

## A

*2XS*
Findley, Nigel   972, 974, 976, 1238, 1591, **1935**, 3245, 4821, 5134, 5135, 5731, 6020

*5th Annual of the Year's Best S-F*
Merril, Judith   240

*6th Annual of the Year's Best S-F*
Merril, Judith   241

*7 Past Midnight*
Matheson, Richard   4875

*7 Seconds to Midnight*
Matheson, Richard   89

*7 Steps to Midnight*
Matheson, Richard   **3682**

*7th Annual of the Year's Best S-F*
Merril, Judith   241

*The 7th Guest*
Costello, Matthew J.   **1192**, 3913, 4495

*8th Annual of the Year's Best S-F*
Merril, Judith   242

*9th Annual of the Year's Best S-F*
Merril, Judith   243

*12 Great Classics of Science Fiction*
Conklin, Groff   240, 1614

*12 Monkeys*
Hand, Elizabeth   1258, **2532**

*13 Again*
Finnis, A.   2395

*The 13 Clocks*
Thurber, James   1527

*13 Haunting Ghost Tales*
Stark, Kirt   **5211**

*13 Plays of Ghosts and the Supernatural*
Kaye, Marvin   1448

*13 Short Horror Novels*
Waugh, Charles G.   226, 2974

*13 Tales of Horror*
Pines, T.   2395

*17 X Infinity*
Conklin, Groff   242

*28 Science Fiction Stories*
Wells, H.G.   1597

*The 37th Mandala*
Laidlaw, Marc   655, 2222, 2312, **3310**, 4449

*'48*
Herbert, James   **2667**, 2720

*50 Great Ghost Stories*
Canning, John   2543, 2643

*65mm*
Hoover, Dale   460, 1085, 1353, **2761**, 3103, 3326

*The 97th Step*
Perry, Steve   580, 1604, 4142, 4228, **4287**, 4305, 4467, 6075

*100 Creepy Little Creature Stories*
Weinberg, Robert   2892, 4828, **5686**

*100 Ghastly Little Ghost Stories*
Dziemianowicz, Stefan   **1709**, 4828

*100 Great Fantasy Short Short Stories*
Asimov, Isaac   1710, 1714, 5687

*100 Hair-Raising Little Horror Stories*
Sarrantonio, Al   1709, 1710, 1714, **4828**, 5686, 5687

*100 Tiny Tales of Terror*
Weinberg, Robert   **5687**

*100 Twisted Little Tales of Torment*
Dziemianowicz, Stefan   **1710**

*100 Vicious Little Vampire Stories*
Weinberg, Robert   150, 151, 2071, 4879, 4881, 5284, 5448, **5688**

*100 Wicked Little Witch Stories*
Dziemianowicz, Stefan   **1711**

*100 Wicked Little Witch Stories*
Weinberg, Robert   2938

*100 Wild Little Weird Tales*
Weinberg, Robert   480, 482, 3023, 3028, **5689**

*365 Science Fiction Short Stories*
Stine, Jean Marie   24

*668: The Neighbor of the Beast*
Fenn, Lionel   **1917**, 4398, 6072

*1901*
Conroy, Robert   **1139**, 5501

*1945*
Gingrich, Newt   1854, **2239**, 5516, 5517

*1984*
Orwell, George   574, 781, 1782, 2215, 3808, 4188, 4976, 5568, 5592

*The 1990 Annual World's Best Science Fiction*
Wollheim, Donald A.   214, 215, 238, 239, 500, 501, 887, 1616, 1620, 1621, 4031, 4558, 4725, **5948**

*2001: A Space Odyssey*
Clarke, Arthur C.   381, 512, 4857, 4954, 4965

*2010: Odyssey Two*
Clarke, Arthur C.   381, 512, 4954, 4965

*2041: Twelve Short Stories about the Future by Top Science Fiction Writers*
Yolen, Jane   4558, 5238, **6027**

*2061: Odyssey Three*
Clarke, Arthur C.   381, 512, 4950, 4954, 4965

*3001: The Final Odyssey*
Clarke, Arthur C.   **1053**

*A for Andromeda*
Hoyle, Fred   5766

*Abduction: The UFO Conspiracy*
Bischoff, David   2034

*The Abductors: Conspiracy*
Frakes, Jonathan   1579, **2034**

*Abel/Baker/Charley*
Maxim, John R.   1826, 2197, 2613, 3128, 3374, 3691, 5422

*The Abode of Life*
Correy, Lee   526

*Above the Lower Sky*
Deitz, Tom   **1469**, 1943

*The Abraxas Marvel Circus*
Leigh, Stephen   522, 3097, 3286, **3423**

*Absalom, Absalom*
Faulkner, William   340

*Absolute Power*
Russell, Ray   2816, **4738**

*Absolute Zero*
Tidyman, Ernest   5243

*The Abyss*
Card, Orson Scott   318, 440, 1062, 1201, 1202, 4915, 5282

*The Abyss*
Cunningham, Jere   1884

*An Acceptable Time*
L'Engle, Madeleine   371, 1033, **3436**, 4438

*The Accident*
Hoh, Diane   1692

*Accidental Creatures*
Harris, Anne   **2558**, 4339

*Accusations*
Tilton, Lois   367, 944, 4833, 5598

*Ace in the Hole*
Martin, George R.R.   989, **3641**

*Achilles' Choice*
Niven, Larry   360, 362, 1108, 3454, **4114**, 4188, 5174

*Ackermanthology!*
Ackerman, Forrest J.   **24**

*Acorna*
McCaffrey, Anne **3717**

*Acorna's Quest*
McCaffrey, Anne **3718**

*Across the Far Mountain*
Hancock, Neil 3077

*Across the Sea of Suns*
Benford, Gregory 1058, 2216, 2646

*Across the Thlassa Mey*
McCarty, Dennis **3765**

*Act of God*
Kotani, Eric 584, 930

*Act of Love*
Lansdale, Joe R. 1831, 3209, 3210,
**3319**

*Action Stations*
Forstchen, William R. **1976**, 5204

*The Active-Enzyme Lemon-Freshened
Junior High School Witch*
Hildick, E.W. 2949, 5478

*Acts of Conscience*
Barton, William **377**

*Addams Family Values*
Strasser, Todd **5324**

*The Adept*
Kurtz, Katherine 639, 751, 2375,
2560, 2992, **3254**

*Adiamante*
Modesitt, L.E. Jr. **3924**

*The Admirer*
Franklin, Debra 5287

*Adulthood Rites*
Butler, Octavia E. 469, 685, 1255,
1408, 1723, 1726, 1727, 1768,
1871, 2058, 2213, 2287, 2539,
3001, 3047, 3188, 3792, 3999,
4217, 4219, 4242, 5016, 5373,
6074

*The Adventure of the Ectoplasmic
Man*
Stashower, Daniel 2692, 3688, 4345,
4929

*The Adventurers of Dr. Eszterhazy*
Davidson, Avram 4851

*Adventures in Time and Space*
Healy, Raymond J. 24, 214, 238,
239, 422, 501, 1616, 1620, 1621,
2405, 3308, 3381, 4127, 5004,
5238

*Adventures in Unhistory*
Davidson, Avram 818

*The Adventures of a Brownie as Told
to My Child*
Mulock, Diana 2438

*The Adventures of Huckleberry Finn*
Twain, Mark 5267

*The Adventures of Huru on the Road
to Baghdad*
Gun, Guneli **2457**

*The Adventures of King Midas*
Banks, Lynne Reid **329**

*The Adventures of Lucius Leffing*
Brennan, Joseph Payne **670**

*Adventures of Miles Vorkosian*
Bujold, Lois McMaster 1540

*The Adventures of Peebo: A Tale of
Magic and Suspense*
Johnston, Joe 1392, 1393, 1394

*The Adventures of Samurai Cat*
Rogers, Mark E. 915, 1895, 4054,
4144, 4562, 5252

*The Adventures of the Stainless Steel
Rat*
Harrison, Harry 3849, 4467

*The Adventures of Threadwell the
Tailor, or Alterations Made While
You Wait*
Cacek, P.D. **801**

*Adversary*
Rhodes, Daniel 2874, **4568**, 5271

*Aegypt*
Crowley, John 25, 333, 518, 1457,
2262, 2329, 3714, 4740, 5591

*Aesop's Fables*
Aesop **40**, 2447

*AEstival Tide*
Hand, Elizabeth 836, **2533**, 4381

*African-American Folktales for Young
Readers: Including Favorite Stories
From African and African-
American Storytellers*
Young, Richard 2528

*African Folktales*
Radin, Paul 2771, 4207

*African Folktales and Sculpture*
Radin, Paul 2528

*Afrikorps*
Dolan, Bill 1405, **1566**, 4678

*Afro-American Folk Tales*
Abrahams, Roger D. 2771, 4207

*After Dark*
Wellman, Manly Wade 1396, 1639,
3272

*After Dark, My Sweet*
Thompson, Jim 5338

*After Life*
Neiderman, Andrew **4083**

*After Long Silence*
Tepper, Sheri S. 1261, 2287, 3713,
3729, 3743, 3745, 3750

*After Silence*
Carroll, Jonathan 345, **916**

*After Sundown*
Boyll, Randall **609**, 1828, 3033,
3092, 4223, 4369, 5685

*After the Blue*
Like, Russel **3465**

*After the Darkness*
Wiater, Stanley 2278, 3598, 3961,
4278, 4722, **5795**

*After the Fact*
Saberhagen, Fred 5487

*After the King: Stories in Honor of
J.R.R. Tolkien*
Greenberg, Martin H. 422, 606,
1576, **2378**, 2380, 3227, 5214,
5216, 6044, 6077

*After Things Fell Apart*
Goulart, Ron 735, 2882

*Afterage*
Navarro, Yvonne 301, **4072**

*Afterimage*
Rusch, Kristine Kathryn **4709**

*Afterimage Aftershock*
Rusch, Kristine Kathryn **4710**

*The Afterlife Diet*
Pinkwater, Daniel Manus 2327

*Afterlives: An Anthology of Stories
about Life After Death*
Sargent, Pamela 1283, 1872, 1875,
4929, 6031

*Aftermath*
Sheffield, Charles 3761, **4947**

*Afternoon of the Gosling*
Huffman, Marlys **2801**

*Again, Dangerous Visions*
Ellison, Harlan 1023, 4713, 4721

*Against a Dark Background*
Banks, Iain M. **322**, 5543

*Against the Wind*
Pini, Richard 4336, 4337

*The Age of Desire*
Barker, Clive 4786

*Age of Miracles*
Brunner, John 2954, 4506, 4966,
5027, 5909

*The Age of the Pussyfoot*
Pohl, Frederik 5243

*Agent of Byzantium*
Turtledove, Harry 264, 2140, 5036

*Agent of Change*
Miller, Steve 1849, 4142, 4291,
4354, 4467, 4484, 4984, 5717

*Aggressor Six*
McCarthy, Wil 1315, **3760**, 4775

*The Agonizing Resurrection of Victor
Frankenstein and Other Gothic
Tales*
Ligotti, Thomas **3460**, 5876

*Agviq*
Armstrong, Michael **208**, 870, 1632,
3862, 4000, 5444, 5743

*Agyar*
Brust, Steven 660, **738**, 1286, 1355,
1425, 1433, 3954, 3955

*Ahmed and the Oblivion Machines*
Bradbury, Ray **618**

*Ai! Pedrito!: When Intelligence Goes
Wrong*
Hubbard, L. Ron **2788**

*Air Fish*
Oestreicher, Joy 300, **4199**, 5095,
5447

*Air Force!*
Harvey, Frank 5247

*Aisling*
Cooper, Louise **1172**

*The Alabaster Hand and Other Ghost
Stories*
Munby, A.N.L. 456, 1350, 2905,
5611

*Aladdin: Master of the Lamp*
Resnick, Mike **4534**

*Alamut*
Tarr, Judith 1742, 3016, 3839, **5390**

*Alanna: The First Adventure*
Pierce, Tamora 3737, 5629

*Alas, Babylon*
Frank, Pat 728, 3608

*Alastor*
Vance, Jack 418, 758, 883, 2135,
5465, **5543**, 5725

*Alberic the Wise and Other Journeys*
Juster, Norton 329

*The Albino Knife*
Perry, Steve **4288**

*The Alchemist of Time*
Ripley, Karen 956

*Alchemy and Academe*
McCaffrey, Anne 671, 4397

*Alchemy Unlimited*
Clark, Douglas W. 174, 4397

*Alexander the Great*
Kazantzakis, Nikos 2187, 5395

*Alfred Hitchcock Presents: Stories for
Late at Night*
Hitchcock, Alfred 543, 2282

*Alfred Hitchcock Presents: Stories
My Mother Never Told Me*
Hitchcock, Alfred 543

*Alfred Hitchcock Presents: Stories
Not for the Nervous*
Hitchcock, Alfred 543, 1019

*Alice through the Needle's Eye: The
Further Adventures of Lewis
Carroll's "Alice"*
Adair, Gilbert 4134, 5713

*Alice's Adventures in Wonderland*
Carroll, Lewis 4134, 5713

*Alien*
Foster, Alan Dean 492, 4289, 4290,
4331

*Alien 3*
Foster, Alan Dean 492, **1993**, 4289,
4290

*Alien Art*
Dickson, Gordon R. 2721

*Alien Blues*
Hightower, Lynn S. 2421, **2682**,
4117, 4389, 4935, 4936, 4938,
4939, 5596

*Alien Bootlegger and Other Stories*
Ore, Rebecca 772, 1515, 1758,
2027, 3234, 3384, **4216**, 4680

*Alien Cargo*
Sturgeon, Theodore 5910

*The Alien Condition*
Goldin, Stephen 4406

**The Alien Dark**
Gallagher, Diana G.   35, 64, 100, 210, 419, 643, 933, 981, 990, 998, 1587, 1875, **2108**, 2764, 2864, 3001, 3469, 3721, 3738, 3770, 3771, 4124, 4372, 4626, 4761, 4762, 4853, 4855, 4867, 5244, 5280, 5376, 5526, 5574, 5809, 5933

**The Alien Debt**
Busby, F.M.   2437, 4373

**Alien Dreams**
Segriff, Larry   **4910**

**Alien Earth**
Lindholm, Megan   399, 404, 1046, 1726, 4019, 4957, 5429, 5435, 5492, 5743

**Alien Eyes**
Hightower, Lynn S.   **2683**

**Alien Harvest**
Sheckley, Robert   4285

**Alien Heat**
Hightower, Lynn S.   2093, 2286, **2684**

**An Alien Heat**
Moorcock, Michael   326, 3106

**Alien Influences**
Rusch, Kristine Kathryn   **4711**

**An Alien Land**
Resnick, Mike   **4535**

**Alien Minds**
Laumer, Keith   **3342**, 3796, 5641

**Alien Nation**
Foster, Alan Dean   504, 1062, 1247, 2682, 2683, 2684, 2909, 2910, 3520, 4938, 4939, 5107, 5109

**Alien Nation**
Lindholm, Megan   1247

**Alien Pets**
Little, Denise   2892, **3500**

**Alien Plot**
Anthony, Piers   **161**

**Alien Pregnant by Elvis**
Friesner, Esther   **2070**, 2384, 4169, 4540

**Alien Resurrection**
Crispin, A.C.   **1258**

**Alien Rites**
Hightower, Lynn S.   **2685**, 4928

**Alien Salute**
Ingrid, Charles   **2830**, 5261, 5564

**Alien Sex**
Datlow, Ellen   72, 75, **1357**, 1607, 2174, 2178, 2179, 2180, 2181, 3026, 4406, 5093, 5094

**Alien Stars**
Mitchell, Elizabeth   1627

**Alien Tongue**
Leigh, Stephen   981, 1989, 2683, 2898, **3424**

**The Alien Upstairs**
Sargent, Pamela   5910

**The Alien Way**
Dickson, Gordon R.   933, 990, 997, 998, 2108, 2864, 5574, 5575

**The Alien Within**
Bolton, Johanna   3125

**The Alien Years**
Silverberg, Robert   **5027**

**The Alienist**
Carr, Caleb   26

**Aliens!**
Dann, Jack   4406

**Aliens**
Foster, Alan Dean   9, 492, 4075, 4289, 4290

**Aliens 4**
Sturgeon, Theodore   1874, 4216

**Aliens: Earth Hive**
Perry, Steve   492, 1993, **4289**

**Aliens: Nightmare Asylum**
Perry, Steve   492

**The Aliens of Earth**
Kress, Nancy   503, 624, 772, 790, 804, 1515, 2027, 2835, 3048, **3234**, 3379, 3384, 3600, 3736, 3971, 4216, 4680, 5240, 5410

**Aliens Stole My Body**
Coville, Bruce   **1217**

**Aliens: The Female War**
Perry, Steve   492, **4290**

**Alight in the Void**
Anderson, Poul   349

**All-American Alien Boy**
Steele, Allen   1758, 3712, **5240**

**All-Consuming Fire**
Lane, Andy   4556

**All Flesh Is Grass**
Simak, Clifford D.   435

**All Fool's Day**
Cooper, Edmund   6028

**All Good Things. . .**
Friedman, Michael Jan   1228, 1229, 1388, **2061**

**All Hallow's Eve: Tales of Love and the Supernatural**
Allen, Mary Elizabeth   **75**

**All Heads Turn When the Hunt Goes By**
Farris, John   21, 654, 1076, 1888, 2494, 4009, 4738

**All My Sins Remembered**
Haldeman, Joe   1849, 4467

**All-Night Party**
Stine, R.L.   1801

**All One Universe**
Anderson, Poul   **123**

**All Shadows Fled**
Greenwood, Ed   299, 1293

**All Souls' Night**
Walpole, Hugh   1252

**All That Glitters**
Andrews, V.C.   2492

**All the Bells on Earth**
Blaylock, James P.   **518**, 715, 3497, 3957

**All the Colors of Darkness**
Biggle, Lloyd   2996

**All the Weyrs of Pern**
McCaffrey, Anne   3050, **3719**

**All These Earths**
Busby, F.M.   5781

**All Things under the Moon**
Morgan, Robert   **4002**, 5085

**Allamanda**
Williams, Michael   **5817**

**The Alleluia Files**
Shinn, Sharon   **4999**

**Allies and Aliens**
Allen, Roger MacBride   2254

**All's Faire**
Service, Pamela F.   53, 1040, 4487, **4917**

**Alone in the House**
Plante, Edmund   5288

**Alone with the Horrors**
Campbell, Ramsey   **851**, 3462

**Along Came a Spider**
Alexis, Athena   **70**, 146, 1300, 5808, 5926

**Alph**
Maine, Charles Eric   1653, 2870

**Alpha 1**
Silverberg, Robert   4721

**Alpha Centauri**
Barton, William   **378**

**Alpha Gallery**
Oestreicher, Joy   3997, **4200**, 5095

**Alraune**
Ewers, Hanz Heine   5690

**Altered States**
Chayefsky, Paddy   364, 571, 2702, 2918, 3101, 4979, 5520

**Alternate Americas**
Benford, Gregory   **442**, 4536, 4537, 4538, 5498

**Alternate Empires**
Benford, Gregory   2044, 2045, 2047, 4537, 4538, 5301, 5498, 5505

**Alternate Generals**
Turtledove, Harry   **5495**

**Alternate Heroes**
Benford, Gregory   4536, 4537, 4538, 4540, 5498, 5505

**Alternate Kennedys**
Resnick, Mike   442, 2411, **4536**, 5498

**The Alternate Martians**
Chandler, A. Bertram   3983

**Alternate Presidents**
Resnick, Mike   442, 1139, 2411, **4537**, 5495, 5498

**Alternate Warriors**
Resnick, Mike   **4538**, 5498

**Alternate Wars**
Benford, Gregory   **443**, 1074, 1196, 1980, 3867, 4537, 4538, 4814, 5498, 5502, 5515

**Alternatives**
Adams, Robert   3466

**Alternities**
Kube-McDowell, Michael P.   2208, 2489, 5088, 5908

**Althea**
McDaniels, Abigail   **3782**

**Alvin Journeyman**
Card, Orson Scott   **881**, 3257, 5504

**Always Coming Home**
Le Guin, Ursula K.   211, 686, 2037, 3627, 3771, 4361, 4631, 5092, 5383, 5580, 5743, 5745

**Am I Blue?**
Bauer, Marion Dane   545

**Amazing Science Fiction Stories: The War Years 1936-1945**
Greenberg, Martin H.   3948, 3949

**Amazing Science Fiction Stories: The Wild Years 1946-1955**
Greenberg, Martin H.   3948, 3949

**Amazing Science Fiction Stories: The Wonder Years 1926-1935**
Greenberg, Martin H.   3948, 3949

**Amazing Stories: The Anthology**
Mohan, Kim   1023, 2148, **3948**, 4439, 5489

**Amazon: A Novel**
Walker, Barbara G.   **5616**

**The Amazon Chronicles**
Robinson, Jane E.M.   **4627**, 5071

**Amazon Planet**
Reynolds, Mack   176

**Amazons!**
Salmonson, Jessica Amanda   316, 628, 629, 648, 649, 650, 651, 765, 1808, 1811, 2072, 2074, 3290, 3670, 4627, 5071

**Ambassador of Progress**
Williams, Walter Jon   353, 5231

**The Amber Enchantress**
Denning, Troy   1293, 2621, 2624

**The Amber Print**
Copper, Edmund   852

**Ambient**
Womack, Jack   4095

**The Ambivalent Magician**
Hawke, Simon   **2616**

**Ambush at Corellia**
Allen, Roger MacBride   **76**, 103, 114, 115, 3247, 3820, 4719, 5205, 5950

**An Ambush of Shadows**
Williams, Paul O.   4604, 4621

**American Gothic**
Bloch, Robert   1830, 2612

**American Gothic**
Terry, Elizabeth   2586, 3570, **5439**

**American Gothic Tales**
Oates, Joyce Carol   1314, **4180**, 5439

**American Indian Myths and Legends**
Erdoes, Richard   40, 190, 849, 5578, 5751

**American Psycho**
Ellis, Brett Easton   695, 1170, 1401, **1777**, 2755, 3807, 4185, 5326, 5443

**Ammonite**
Griffith, Nicola   210, 792, 1116, 1482, 1586, 1649, 1769, 2051, **2443**, 2806, 3440, 4172, 4176, 4187, 5090, 5172, 5430, 5435, 5461, 5804

**Amnesia Moon**
Lethem, Jonathan   2535, **3438**, 4135, 4177

**Among Madmen**
Starlin, Jim   **5212**

**Amphigorey Also**
Gorey, Edward   1044, 3334

**The Amulet**
McDowell, Michael   1205

**The Amulet**
Morlan, A.R.   1834, **4009**

**Amy, Number Seven**
Kaye, Marilyn   1217

**Amy's Eyes**
Kennedy, Richard   332

**Anasazi**
Ing, Dean   2861, 3704

**Ancestor's World**
Crispin, A.C.   **1259**, 1500

**Ancestral Hungers**
Baker, Scott   **303**, 2255, 2259, 2512, 5183, 5421, 5693

**Ancient Echoes**
Holdstock, Robert   1491, **2735**, 4093

**Ancient Enchantresses**
Massie-Ferch, Kathleen M.   649, 650, 651, 3070, 3076, **3670**, 4610

**Ancient Games**
Ciencin, Scott   **1028**

**Ancient Heavens**
Vardeman, Robert E.   **5561**

**Ancient Images**
Campbell, Ramsey   **852**, 917, 1473, 2241, 2448, 3025, 3103, 4683, 4734

**Ancient Light**
Gentle, Mary   517, 707, 1210, 1323, 1599, 1774, 1933, 1934, **2194**, 2897, 2999, 3047, 3484, 3888, 3933, 4976, 5372, 5726, 5727, 5748

**Ancient of Days**
Bishop, Michael   1525, 2434

**The Ancient One**
Barron, T.A.   **368**

**Ancient Shores**
McDevitt, Jack   870, **3786**, 5867

**And Chaos Died**
Russ, Joanna   101, 3860

**And Eternity**
Anthony, Piers   **162**, 4047

**And Having Writ**
Benson, Donald   5501

**And Not Make Dreams Your Master**
Goldin, Stephen   583

**And Peace Shall Sleep**
Lyris, Sonia Orin   207, 2827

**And the Angels Sing**
Wilhelm, Kate   415, 3379, 3736, 3751, **5805**

**And the Devil Will Drag You Under**
Chalker, Jack L.   3483, 3488, 3848

**And Then the Town Took Off**
Wilson, Richard   5303

**And Then There'll Be Fireworks**
Elgin, Suzette Haden   186, 515, 2084, 2950, 4361, 5235, 5616

**Andrew and the Alchemist**
Byfield, Barbara Ninde   6030

**The Andromeda Gun**
Boyd, John   1398

**The Andromeda Strain**
Crichton, Michael   99, 1136, 1164, 1698, 2048, 2685, 2720, 2999, 3337, 3361, 3577, 3632, 3703, 3923, 4012, 4413, 4786, 4928

**Angel**
Kilworth, Garry   602, 1117, 2534, 2802, 3620

**Angel at Apogee**
Lewitt, S.N.   3454, 4594

**Angel Fire**
Greeley, Andrew M.   1803, 5101

**Angel Kiss**
Wilde, Kelley   1335, 3492, **5800**

**Angel Light**
Greeley, Andrew M.   1339, **2342**

**The Angel of Pain**
Stableford, Brian   **5189**

**The Angel of the Opera**
Siciliano, Sam   4773

**Angel Souls and Devil Hearts**
Golden, Christopher   **2255**, 5407

**Angel Station**
Williams, Walter Jon   768, 984, 985, 1001, 1891, 1893, 2099, 3248, 3830, 3929, 4453, 4593, 5573, **5833**

**Angel with the Sword**
Cherryh, C.J.   12, 176, 289, 631, 894, 2236, 2361, 3580, 3643, 3646, 4043, 5033, 5038, 5596, 5760, 5862

**Angela and Diabola**
Banks, Lynne Reid   **330**

**Angelique's Descent**
Parker, Lara   **4246**

**Angels!**
Dann, Jack   1028, 1283, **1339**, 2342, 3480, 6031

**Angels & Visitations: A Miscellany**
Gaiman, Neil   **2101**, 3460, 5165

**Angels of Darkness**
Kaye, Marvin   468, **3022**

**Angels on Fire**
Collins, Nancy A.   **1117**

**Angels Unaware**
Storm, L. Elizabeth   **5315**

**Angelwalk: A Modern Fable**
Elwood, Roger   **1803**, 2802, 5101

**The Angry Angel**
Yarbro, Chelsea Quinn   4578, **6010**

**Angry Candy**
Ellison, Harlan   625, 1492, **1783**, 3421, 5058

**The Angry Planet**
Cross, John Keir   2647

**Aniara**
Martinson, Harry   58

**Animal Farm**
Orwell, George   1817, 4976

**Animal Planet**
Bradfield, Scott   3222

**The Animal Wife**
Thomas, Elizabeth Marshall   2582, 4818, 4819, **5444**

**Animals**
Skipp, John   **5080**

**Animus**
Kelleher, Ed   **3040**

**Anita**
Roberts, Keith   2713

**Anno Dracula**
Newman, Kim   292, 303, 659, 1139, 1518, 2511, 2692, 2741, 2742, 3005, 3564, 3596, 3631, **4094**, 4773, 5192, 5693, 5704, 6019

**The Annotated H.P. Lovecraft**
Lovecraft, H.P.   **3529**

**The Anome**
Vance, Jack   1408, 3698, 5055

**Another Day, Another Dungeon**
Costikyan, Greg   **1206**

**Another Fine Myth**
Asprin, Robert   167, 168, 169, 172, 177, 184, 186, 196, 1045, 1160, 1208, 1416, 1998, 2075, 2076, 2081, 2145, 2362, 2616, 2946, 4120, 4388, 4392, 4393, 4395, 4396, 4401, 5219, 5224

**Another Kind**
Oliver, Chad   59, 3876

**Another Part of the Galaxy**
Conklin, Groff   241, 1614

**Another Roadside Attraction**
Robbins, Tom   1421, 2186, 5593

**Another Round at the Spaceport Bar**
Scithes, George H.   2125

**The Answer Tree**
Boyett, Steven R.   917, 3541

**The Ant Men**
North, Eric   5755

**Antarctica**
Robinson, Kim Stanley   **4628**

**Antares Dawn**
McCollum, Michael   353, 882

**Antares Passage**
McCollum, Michael   1182, 2016

**Anthony Shriek**
Salmonson, Jessica Amanda   212, 694, 2030, 3124, 3193, 3196, 3197, **4790**

**Anti-Ice**
Baxter, Stephen   398, 4628

**Antibodies**
Anderson, Kevin J.   **99**, 924

**Antibodies**
Skal, David J.   555, 3196

**Antimatter**
Vornholt, John   8, 2917

**Antinomy**
Robinson, Spider   503, 4636

**Antique Dust**
Westall, Robert   283, 1671, 2866, 3314, 5776

**Antiquities**
Crowley, John   819, **1276**, 1431, 2106, 2265, 2537, 4757, 5165

**The Ants**
Tremayne, Peter   3054

**The Anubis Gates**
Powers, Tim   520, 969, 1457, 1520, 1564, 1615, 2077, 2329, 2546, 3124, 3421, 3596, 3799, 3802, 3803, 3804, 4432, 4446, 4658, 4659

**The Anubis Murders**
Gygax, Gary   1250, **2472**

**Anvil**
van Pallandt, Nicolas   1481, **5540**

**The Anvil of Ice**
Rohan, Michael Scott   1008, 1010, 1028, 1082, 1109, 1730, 1814, 1912, 2271, 2504, 2984, 3123, 3942, 4446, 4457, 5964

**Anvil of Stars**
Bear, Greg   **414**, 3726

**Anvil of the Sun**
Groell, Anne Lesley   **2451**

**The Anything Tree**
Rackham, John   3727

**Apacheria**
Page, Jake   **4233**

**Apartheid, Superstrings, and Mordecai Thubana**
Bishop, Michael   **496**

**The Ape, the Idiot, and Other People**
Morrow, W.C.   485, 963, 1243, 1597

**Apocalypse**
Springer, Nancy   **5176**

**Apostrophes and Apocalypses**
Barnes, John   349

**The Apprentice**
Talmadge-Bickmore, Deborah   1064, 2521, 3511, 3914, 5266, **5382**, 5820

**Apt Pupil**
King, Stephen  2755

**Aqua Sancta**
Bryant, Edward  **748**, 2705, 3388

**Aquamancer**
Callander, Don  **841**, 1469

**Aquila and the Iron Horse**
Somtow, S.P.  3917

**Aquila and the Sphinx**
Somtow, S.P.  3917

**Aquila in the New World**
Somtow, S.P.  3917

**Arabesques II**
Shwartz, Susan  374, 2130, 4534,
6087

**Arabesques: More Tales of the
Arabian Nights**
Shwartz, Susan  374, 1681, 1687,
2123, 2129, 2130, 4534, 5981,
6087

**The Arabian Nightmare**
Irwin, Robert  2706

**The Arabian Nights Entertainments**
Lang, Andrew  374, 1687, 2123,
2130, 4534, 4731, 6087

**Arabian Nights: The Marvels and
Wonders of the Thousand and One
Nights**
Zipes, Jack  374, 1681, 1687, 2123,
2129, 2130, 4534, **6087**

**Arachne**
Mason, Lisa  77, **3661**, 3764, 3921,
4893, 5462

**Araminta Station**
Vance, Jack  4277

**The Arbitrary Placement of Walls**
Soukup, Martha  **5165**

**The Arbor House Necropolis**
Pronzini, Bill  2973, 2977, 5083

**The Arbor House Treasury of Horror
and the Supernatural**
Pronzini, Bill  2590, 2591, 2974,
2993, 3027, 4311

**Arc d'X**
Erickson, Steve  **1835**, 5209

**Arc Riders**
Drake, David  **1626**, 1853, 2119

**Arcade**
Gallagher, Diana G.  2470

**Arcadio**
Goyen, William  1697

**Arcady**
Williams, Michael  1474, **5818**

**Archangel**
Conner, Michael  **1133**, 3244, 3977,
4748, 5172

**Archangel**
Kilworth, Garry  2802

**Archangel**
Shinn, Sharon  1442, 3739, 3819,
**5000**

**Archangel Blues**
bes shahar, eluki  **471**

**Archer's Goon**
Jones, Diana Wynne  5979

**The Architecture of Desire**
Gentle, Mary  1250, **2195**, 2509,
4983

**The Architecture of Fear**
Cramer, Kathryn  2396, 5902

**Ardor on Aros**
Offutt, Andrew J.  3543

**Are You Loathsome Tonight?**
Brite, Poppy Z.  **693**, 1401, 5005

**Area 51**
Doherty, Robert  **1565**, 3952

**Arena**
Forstchen, William R.  207, 1483,
1814, 1816, **1977**, 2827

**Arena of Antares**
Akers, Alan Burt  1977

**The Argonaut Affair**
Hawke, Simon  33

**The Argus Gambit**
Ross, David D.  3449, **4681**

**Ariel**
Block, Lawrence  320, 2801, 4237,
5623

**Ariel: A Book of the Change**
Boyett, Steven R.  177, 184

**Ariosto**
Yarbro, Chelsea Quinn  1341, 3255,
3258, 4651, 5218, 5228

**Aristoi**
Williams, Walter Jon  2213, 3256,
4729, **5834**

**Ark Liberty**
Bradley, Will  **656**, 664, 1569, 3999

**The Arkadians**
Alexander, Lloyd  **67**, 2869

**The Arkham Cycle**
Price, Robert M.  2399

**The Arm of the Stone**
Strauss, Victoria  **5333**, 5554

**Armageddon**
Hatch, Richard  **2602**

**Armageddon 2419 A.D.**
Nowlan, Philip Francis  554, 827,
3036, 4049

**The Armageddon Blues**
Moran, Daniel Keys  1880, 5621

**The Armageddon Box**
Weinberg, Robert  462, 832, 2841,
3220, 3672, 3964, 4649, 4755,
4960, 5136, 5475, **5690**, 5773,
5895

**The Armageddon Crazy**
Farren, Mick  **1877**, 6028

**The Armageddon Inheritance**
Weber, David  3968, **5668**, 5785

**Armageddon Off Vesta**
Murdock, M.S.  554, 3036

**The Armageddon Rag**
Martin, George R.R.  575, 3664,
3756, 4887, 4997, 5170, 5615

**Armageddon Sky**
Graf, L.A.  **2296**

**Armageddon Summer**
Yolen, Jane  **6028**

**Armageddon: The Musical**
Rankin, Robert  31, 156, 1490, 2070,
3190, 3664, **4473**, 5089, 5768,
5957, 5958, 6020

**Armed Memory**
Young, Jim  413, 3711, 4708, **6048**

**The Armies of Daylight**
Hambly, Barbara  256, 257, 1175,
1703, 1746, 2987, 3273, 4613,
5832

**The Armies of Elfland**
Anderson, Poul  **124**

**The Armless Maiden and Other Tales
for Childhood's Survivors**
Windling, Terri  1358, 1366, **5912**

**Armor**
Steakley, John  2245, 4204

**The Armor of Light**
Scott, Melissa  1063, 2262, 2263,
3714, 4651, 5147

**An Armory of Swords**
Saberhagen, Fred  2657, **4759**

**Arrow From Earth**
Busby, F.M.  **782**, 1602, 2766

**Arrow's Fall**
Lackey, Mercedes  2674, 5783

**Arrow's Flight**
Lackey, Mercedes  5682, 5783

**Arrows of the Queen**
Lackey, Mercedes  176, 692, 1029,
1095, 1952, 2236, 2796, 3482,
4150, 5124, 5125, 5202, 5684,
5783, 6073

**Arrows of the Sun**
Tarr, Judith  5292, **5391**

**Ars Magica**
Tarr, Judith  978, 1743, 2246, 2662,
3258, 5222, **5392**, 5503

**The Art of Arrow Cutting**
Dedman, Stephen  **1462**

**Arthur**
Attanasio, A.A.  3386

**Arthur**
Lawhead, Stephen R.  1498, 3061,
**3352**, 4877, 5560

**Arthur C. Clarke's Venus Prime, Vol.
2: Maelstrom**
Preuss, Paul  1880

**Arthur, King**
Anderson, Dennis Lee  973, 977,
1344, 1853

**Arthur Rex**
Berger, Thomas  3474

**Arthur War Lord**
ab Hugh, Dafydd  **6**, 5785

**The Arthurian Legends**
Barber, Richard  5560

**Article 23**
Forstchen, William R.  **1978**

**The Artifact**
Gear, W. Michael  1880, **2165**, 2352,
2460, 2830, 2831, 2833

**Artificial Things**
Fowler, Karen Joy  2261, 5807

**As on a Darkling Plain**
Bova, Ben  885, 897, 1248

**As One Dead**
Bassingthwaite, Don  **387**, 1119,
1949, 2512, 2664, 5703

**As She Climbed Across the Table**
Lethem, Jonathan  **3439**

**The Ascending**
Wright, T.M.  2335, 3620, 4003,
**5989**

**The Ascension Factor**
Herbert, Frank  4478

**The Ascent of Wonder: The Evolution
of Hard SF**
Hartwell, David G.  229, 422, 448,
1617, 1623, 1624, **2585**

**Ash Ock**
Hinz, Christopher  **2690**, 4049

**The Ash-Tree Press Annual Macabre
1997**
Adrian, Jack  37

**The Ash-Tree Press Annual Macabre
1998**
Adrian, Jack  38

**Ash Wednesday**
Williamson, Chet  2310, 2668, 2904,
4834, 5424, 5440, 5991

**The Ashes of Eden**
Shatner, William  **4927**

**Ashes of the Sun**
Braddock, Hanovi  2827

**The Asimov Chronicles: Fifty Years of
Isaac Asimov**
Asimov, Isaac  232

**Assassin's Apprentice**
Hobb, Robin  682, 1008, 1082,
1513, 1636, 1773, 1863, 1952,
1953, 2268, 2270, 2426, 2451,
2452, 2504, 2653, **2693**, 2795,
2798, 2956, 2958, 2959, 2989,
3074, 3123, 3278, 3385, 3481,
3645, 3651, 3775, 3832, 3896,
4165, 4796, 4808, 5202, 5275,
5583, 5737, 5759

**Assassins From Tomorrow**
Heath, Peter  3979

**Assassin's Quest**
Hobb, Robin  **2694**

**Assault of the Super Carrier**
Albano, Peter  **47**

**Assemblers of Infinity**
Anderson, Kevin J.  **100**, 587, 588,
1770, 2275, 3710, 4955

**Assignment: Eternity**
Cox, Greg  **1225**

**Assignment: Nor'Dyren**
Van Scyoc, Sydney J.  2414

**The Astronauts Must Not Land**
Brunner, John  2252

*The Asutra*
Vance, Jack　5055, 5130

*The Asylum*
Ames, John E.　**93**, 1939, 5897

*Asylum*
Johnston, William L.　4838

*Asylum*
McGrath, Patrick　**3812**, 4084

*At Any Price*
Drake, David　308

*At Sword's Point*
MacMillan, Scott　3260, **3601**

*At the City Limits of Fate*
Bishop, Michael　**497**, 3981

*At the Earth's Core*
Burroughs, Edgar Rice　2257, 3590

*At the Edge of the World*
Dunsany　5102

*At the Mountains of Madness*
Lovecraft, H.P.　2711, 5482

*At the Mountains of Madness and
　Other Novels*
Lovecraft, H.P.　5189

*At the Narrow Passage*
Meredith, Richard　1995, 2004

*At Winter's End*
Silverberg, Robert　724, 884

*Athyra*
Brust, Steven　**739**

*Atlantis*
Asimov, Isaac　5035

*Atlantis Found*
Garcia y Robertson, R.　**2119**

*Atlas Shrugged*
Rand, Ayn　3200, 4867, 4976

*Atomsk*
Linebarger, Paul Myron
　Anthony　5174

*Atomsk*
Smith, Carmichael　5105, 5106

*The Atrocity Exhibition*
Ballard, J.G.　**319**, 443, 3460, 3619

*Attila's Treasure*
Grundy, Stephan　**2453**

*The Auctioneer*
Samson, Joan　3497

*Audrey Rose*
DeFelitta, Frank　4237, 4442

*Aunt Dimity and the Duke*
Atherton, Nancy　1451

*Aunt Maria*
Jones, Diana Wynne　545, 546, 549,
　552, **2943**

*Aurian*
Furey, Maggie　741, 1066, 1095,
　**2095**, 3107

*Aurora: Beyond Equality*
McIntyre, Vonda N.　4825, 4826

*Author's Choice Monthly Number
　24: The Naked Flesh of Feeling*
Williamson, J.N.　3558

*The Autobiography of Santa Claus:
　It's Better to Give*
Guinn, Jeff　**2456**

*Automated Alice*
Noon, Jeff　**4134**

*The Autumn People*
Arthur, Ruth　1898

*The Autumn People*
Bradbury, Ray　3334

*Avatar*
Beman, Donald　**437**

*Avatar*
Cooper, Louise　**1173**

*The Avenger*
Cooper, Louise　1068, **1174**

*Avenger*
Shatner, William　**4928**

*The Avon Ghost Reader*
Wollheim, Donald A.　4214

*The Avram Davidson Treasury*
Davidson, Avram　**1395**, 2641

*Away Is a Strange Place to Be*
Hoover, H.M.　**2763**

*Axiomatic*
Egan, Greg　**1758**

*The Axman Cometh*
Farris, John　1777, 1826, **1883**,
　2202, 2689, 2871, 3638, 3695,
　5845

*The Ayes of Texas*
Da Cruz, Daniel　48, 49

*Aylmer Vance: Ghost-Seer*
Askew, Alice　**258**

*The Azathoth Cycle*
Price, Robert M.　461, **4422**

*Azure Bonds*
Grubb, Jeff　4166

*Azure Bonds*
Novak, Kate　4106, 4108


**B**

*Babel-17*
Delany, Samuel R.　5254, 5634

*The Baby*
Kegan, Stephanie　1076, 2875, **3033**,
　3774, 4450, 5269

*Baby Be-Bop*
Block, Francesca Lia　**545**

*Baby Dolly*
Jensen, Ruby Jean　364, 690, 2025,
　2878, **2899**, 3217, 3782, 3784

*The Baby Ewok's Picnic Surprise*
Luke, Melinda　1392, 1393, 1394

*Babylon Gardens*
Donnelly, J.W.　578

*Back From the Dead*
Greenberg, Martin H.　**2379**

*Back in the USSA*
Newman, Kim　25, 1516, **4095**

*Back to the Time Trap*
Laumer, Keith　**3343**

*Backblast*
McKeone, Lee　**3828**

*The Backlash Mission*
Zahn, Timothy　66

*Bad Blood*
Fowler, D.A.　**2021**, 5118, 5484

*Bad Brains*
Koja, Kathe　93, 814, 945, 1939,
　2030, **3193**, 4790, 5969

*A Bad Day for Ali Baba*
Gardner, Craig Shaw　**2123**, 4393

*Bad Dreams*
Newman, Kim　265, 284, 660, 3267,
　3808, **4096**, 5020, 5988, 6050

*Bad Intentions*
Partridge, Norman　1016, 1021,
　2277, **4250**, 5885

*Bad Karma*
Harper, Andrew　**2548**, 4084

*The Bad Place*
Koontz, Dean R.　602, 2341, 2704,
　**3202**, 4189, 4509

*The Bad Seed*
March, William　320, 3606, 4844

*A Bad Spell in Yurt*
Brittain, C. Dale　187, 557, **701**,
　2079, 2081, 5163

*The Bad Thing*
O'Rourke, Michael　**4222**

*Bad Voltage*
Littell, Jonathan　547, 836, 837, 838,
　972, 2219, **3491**, 4451, 4452,
　5959

*Bag of Bones*
King, Stephen　1560, **3126**, 5026

*Bagatelle—Guinevere*
Bogen, Nancy　**558**

*Bagdad*
Dennis, Ian　618

*The Baker's Boy*
Jones, J.V.　683, 1513, 1773, 1902,
　1952, 1953, 2268, 2270, 2426,
　2452, 2619, 2694, 2695, 2696,
　2798, 2924, 2925, **2956**, 3074,
　3489, 3509, 3645, 3775, 3832,
　3835, 4150, 4461, 5320, 5529,
　5583, 5734, 5737, 5758, 5964

*Balance of Power*
ab Hugh, Dafydd　**7**, 905

*Balance of Power*
Stableford, Brian　351, 2223

*The Ballad of Beta-2*
Delany, Samuel R.　5042

*Balyet*
Wrightson, Patricia　4310, 4920,
　**5995**

*The Bane of the Black Sword*
Moorcock, Michael　5648

*Baphomet's Meteor*
Barbet, Pierre　3261

*The Barbed Coil*
Jones, J.V.　**2957**

*The Barbie Murders and Other
　Stories*
Varley, John　3256, 4302, 4376,
　5106, 5638

*Bard*
Taylor, Keith　1240, 1960, 1961,
　3358

*Bard: The Odyssey of the Irish*
Llywelyn, Morgan　203, 657, 1961,
　2229, 2572, 3354, 3358, 5408

*Bardic Voices*
Lackey, Mercedes　1427, 1430, 1583,
　3404, 3545, 4149, 5179

*A Barnstormer in Oz*
Farmer, Philip Jose　2136, 3609

*The Barnum Museum*
Millhauser, Stephen　920

*Baronness of Blood*
Bergstrom, Elaine　2516

*A Baroque Fable*
Yarbro, Chelsea Quinn　1207, 2144,
　2145, 2362, 4399

*Barrayar*
Bujold, Lois McMaster　**756**, 1633,
　1680, 1756, 1913, 3909, 3911,
　3912, 4972, 5041, 5674, 5717

*Barrenlands*
Durgin, Doranna　**1702**

*The Barrens*
Wilson, F. Paul　3556, 4444, 5194,
　5446, **5884**

*The Barrens and Others*
Wilson, F. Paul　**5885**

*Barrow*
Deakins, John　166, 183, 1206, **1443**,
　3842, 4284, 5153

*The Bars on Satan's Jailhouse*
Partridge, Norman　**4251**

*The Barsoom Project*
Niven, Larry　**4115**

*The Basement*
Wood, Bari　**5961**

*Basil Netherby*
Benson, A.C.　456

*Basil of Baker Street*
Titus, Eve　2786

*Basilisk*
Kushner, Ellen　646, 647

*The Basketball Diaries*
Carroll, Jim　5959

*The Bastard Prince*
Kurtz, Katherine　**3255**, 4488, 4781,
　5041, 5222, 5512

*The Bastard Rebellion*
Stine, G. Harry　1566, 1567, 1569,
　4539, 4544

*Batman*
Gardner, Craig Shaw　14, 366, 611,
　612, 613, 614, 615, 2391, 2392

**Batman: Captured by the Engines**
Lansdale, Joe R.   14, 2124, 2391, **3320**

**Batman: Knightfall**
O'Neil, Dennis   1667, 2331, **4215**

**The Batman Murders**
Gardner, Craig Shaw   14, 2331, 2391, 2392, 4215

**Batman Returns**
Gardner, Craig Shaw   14, **2124**, 2391, 2392

**Batman: To Stalk a Specter**
Hawke, Simon   14, 2124, 2331, 2391, 2392, 4215

**Bats**
Johnstone, William W.   2615, **2926**, 4688, 4815, 5263

**The Battle Begins**
Ahern, Jerry   5086

**Battle Circle**
Anthony, Piers   1328

**Battle Front**
Slater, Ian   **5086**

**Battle Magic**
Greenberg, Martin H.   **2380**

**The Battle of Forever**
Van Vogt, A.E.   2172

**Battle of the Ring**
Gunnarsson, Thorarinn   2352, **2460**, 6056

**Battledragon**
Rowley, Christopher   **4691**

**Battlestar Galactica**
Larson, Glen A.   2602

**Battlestation**
Drake, David   **1627**, 3037

**Battlestations!**
Carey, Diane   7

**Battletech: Warrior: Coupe**
Stackpole, Michael A.   3425

**The Bavarian Gate**
Dalmas, John   1981

**Bazaar of the Bizarre**
Leiber, Fritz   291

**Bazil Broketail**
Rowley, Christopher   182, 842, 843, 1749, **4692**

**Beachhead**
Williamson, Jack   586, 4160, 4348, **5859**

**The Beacon**
Freireich, Valerie J.   1046, **2048**, 4301, 5027

**Beaker's Dozen**
Kress, Nancy   **3235**

**Beamriders!**
Caidin, Martin   **824**

**The Bear Went over the Mountain**
Kotzwinkle, William   915, **3222**

**Bearing an Hourglass**
Anthony, Piers   96

**Bears Discover Fire**
Bisson, Terry   **503**

**Bear's Fantasies**
Bear, Greg   **415**

**Beast**
Benchley, Peter   88, **440**, 1346, 3232, 3998, 4415, 5877

**The Beast**
White, Marie Ardell   **5784**

**Beast House**
Laymon, Richard   **3364**

**The Beast Master**
Norton, Andre   431, 1070, 1437, 1951, 2552, 3583, 5545, 5759

**Beast Rising**
Almquist, Gregg   1036

**The Beast with Five Fingers and Other Stories**
Harvey, William Fryer   4141

**The Beast Within**
Wieck, Stewart   23, 3225, 3229, 5693, 5797

**The Beast Within: A Gabriel Knight Mystery**
Jensen, Jane   **2895**

**The Beast Within: Erotic Tales of Werewolves**
Tan, Cecilia   3181, 3184, **5384**

**Beastchild**
Koontz, Dean R.   1595

**Beastnights**
Yarbro, Chelsea Quinn   723, 2222, 5332

**Beasts**
Crowley, John   305, 721, 3243, 3797, 4604

**Beauties, Beasts and Enchantments**
Zipes, Jack   276, 849, 1359, 1479, 2680, 3574, **6088**

**Beautiful Strangers**
Tem, Melanie   **5420**

**Beauty**
D'Amato, Brian   437, **1334**, 3196

**Beauty**
McKinley, Robin   3065, 5981

**Beauty**
Tepper, Sheri S.   42, 783, 1479, 4008, **5428**, 6088, 6090

**Beauty and the Beast**
Hambly, Barbara   559, 1808, 3020, 3882, 3883, 5474

**Becoming Alien**
Ore, Rebecca   231, 753, 757, 764, 828, 1209, 1408, 1460, 1493, 1537, 1587, 1594, 1930, 1995, 2048, 2224, 2549, 2551, 2898, 3424, 3452, 3521, 4116, 4347, 4349, 4550, 4894, 5048, 5449, 6061

**Becoming Human**
Freireich, Valerie J.   1807, **2049**, 2274, 2559, 3038, 3241, 3927, 4064, 4065

**Bedlam Boyz**
Guon, Ellen   **2467**, 3277, 3302, 4862, 4980, 4995

**Bedlam Planet**
Brunner, John   1595

**Bedlam's Bard**
Lackey, Mercedes   **3269**

**Before Adam**
London, Jack   268

**Before the Invid Storm**
McKinney, Jack   2432

**Before the Mask**
Williams, Michael   4925

**Before the Storm**
Kube-McDowell, Michael P.   114, 117, **3247**, 4719

**Before. . .12:01. . .and After**
Lupoff, Richard A.   925, **3571**

**The Beggar Queen**
Alexander, Lloyd   5142

**Beggars and Choosers**
Kress, Nancy   2274, 2580, **3236**, 3792, 4064

**Beggar's Banquet**
Hood, Daniel   **2756**

**Beggars in Spain**
Kress, Nancy   305, 1965, 2522, 2820, 3008, 3075, **3237**, 4064, 4210, 4355, 4850, 4955

**The Beggars in Spain Trilogy**
Kress, Nancy   2558, 4065

**Beggars Ride**
Kress, Nancy   **3238**

**The Beginning Place**
Le Guin, Ursula K.   3731, 4971

**Behind the Attic Wall**
Cassedy, Sylvia   2438

**Behold the Man**
Moorcock, Michael   1305, 5195, 5569

**Beholder's Eye**
Czerneda, Julie E.   **1303**, 1501

**Being a Green Mother**
Anthony, Piers   4153, 4159, 4783

**Being Alien**
Ore, Rebecca   757, 764, 828, 1062, 1209, 1261, 1262, 1493, 2016, 2549, 3521, 3723, 3752, 4140, **4217**, 4347

**Being of Two Minds**
Service, Pamela F.   3340, **4918**

**Being There**
Kosinski, Jerzy   3222

**Beldan's Fire**
Snyder, Midori   4489, **5150**

**Belgarath the Sorcerer**
Eddings, David   712, 1096, **1730**, 4852

**The Belgariad Series**
Eddings, David   4284

**Believe: A Novel**
Shatner, William   1872, 1875, **4929**

**The Bell in the Fog and Other Stories**
Atherton, Gertrude   485, 1673, 2919, 4968

**The Bell Tree**
Hoover, H.M.   878

**The Bell Witch: An American Haunting**
Monahan, Brent   **3953**

**Belladonna**
Stewart, Michael   966, 1050, 1836, 2642, 2874, 4753, 5186, **5271**, 5290

**Bellefleur**
Oates, Joyce Carol   145, 147, 340, 1300, 2115

**The Bellmaker**
Jacques, Brian   **2848**

**Bellwether**
Willis, Connie   4042, **5867**

**The Belly of the Wolf**
MacAvoy, R.A.   2195, **3580**

**Beloved Exile**
Godwin, Parke   1092, 3352

**Bending the Landscape: Fantasy**
Griffith, Nicola   **2444**

**Beneath Still Waters**
Costello, Matthew J.   **1193**, 1972, 2094, 2333, 2822, 2929, 3783, 4715, 5114

**Beneath the Gated Sky**
Reed, Robert   **4502**

**Beneath the Tree of Heaven**
Wingrove, David   3699, 5725, **5917**

**Beneath the Vaulted Hills**
Russell, Sean   **4739**

**Beneath the Web**
Abbey, Lynn   **12**, 5752

**Beowulf's Children**
Niven, Larry   **4116**

**Berberick, Stormblade**
Varian, Nancy   5724

**Bereavement**
Lortz, Richard   **3525**

**The Berkley Showcase: New Writings in Science Fiction and Fantasy, Volumes 1-4**
Schochet, Victoria   5952, 5953

**Bernie and the Bessledorf Ghost**
Naylor, Phyllis Reynolds   2923, 2951, **4078**, 4438

**Berserker**
Perry, S.D.   **4285**

**Berserker**
Saberhagen, Fred   128, 516, 2165

**Berserker Fury**
Saberhagen, Fred   **4760**

**Berserker Kill**
Saberhagen, Fred   **4761**

**Berserker Lies**
Saberhagen, Fred   **4762**

**Berserker Man**
Saberhagen, Fred   516

*The Berserker Throne*
Saberhagen, Fred   516

*The Berserker Wars*
Saberhagen, Fred   516

*Berserker's Planet*
Saberhagen, Fred   516, 2460

*Best Destiny*
Carey, Diane   **900**

*The Best From Fantasy and Science Fiction: 7*
Boucher, Anthony   240

*The Best From Fantasy and Science Fiction: 8*
Boucher, Anthony   241

*The Best From Fantasy and Science Fiction: 9-11*
Mills, Robert P.   4712

*The Best From Fantasy and Science Fiction: 12*
Davidson, Avram   242

*The Best From Fantasy and Science Fiction: 12-14*
Davidson, Avram   4712

*The Best From Fantasy and Science Fiction: 13*
Davidson, Avram   243

*The Best From Fantasy and Science Fiction: 15-20*
Ferman, Edward L.   4712

*The Best From Fantasy & Science Fiction: A 40th Anniversary Anthology*
Ferman, Edward L.   888, 4712

*The Best From Fantasy & Science Fiction: A 45th Anniversary Anthology*
Rusch, Kristine Kathryn   629, 3948, 3949, **4712**

*The Best From Fantasy and Science Fiction: A Special 25th Anniversary Anthology*
Ferman, Edward L.   4712

*The Best From Universe*
Carr, Terry   1618, 5045, 5046

*Best Ghost Stories*
Le Fanu, J. Sheridan   2866

*Best Ghost Stories of Algernon Blackwood*
Blackwood, Algernon   454, 1243, 2710, 3658

*The Best Ghost Stories of M.R. James*
James, M.R.   4275

*The Best Horror From Fantasy & Science Fiction*
Ferman, Edward L.   5700

*The Best Horror From Fantasy Tales*
Jones, Stephen   **2960**

*The Best Horror Stories of Arthur Conan Doyle*
Doyle, Arthur Conan   **1596**, 3694

*Best New Horror*
Jones, Stephen   1372, 1378, **2961**, 5602, 5603, 5605, 5606

*Best New Horror 2*
Jones, Stephen   **2962**, 4025, 5601

*Best New Horror 4*
Jones, Stephen   1376, **2963**, 5607

*Best New Horror 5*
Jones, Stephen   5608

*Best New Horror 6*
Jones, Stephen   2964

*The Best of British SF*
Ashley, Mike   4439

*The Best of C.L. Moore*
Moore, C.L.   790, 3219, 5047

*The Best of Cemetery Dance*
Chizmar, Richard T.   22, **1017**

*The Best of Cordwainer Smith*
Smith, Cordwainer   233, 242, 321, 804, 892, 930, 1061, 1608, 1723, 1727, 1874, 1895, 2649, 2832, 3001, 3187, 3308, 3796, 4123, 4126, 4127, 4216, 4346, 4376, 4706, 4769, 5363, 5368, 5369, 5551, 5586, 5589, 5638, 5834

*The Best of Crank!*
Cholfin, Bryan   **1023**

*The Best of D.F. Lewis*
Lewis, D.F.   **3447**, 3614, 4230

*The Best of Deathrealm*
Rainey, Stephen Mark   2773, 5025

*The Best of Fredric Brown*
Brown, Fredric   529, 530

*The Best of Fritz Leiber*
Leiber, Fritz   3683

*The Best of Ghosts and Scholars*
Dalby, Richard   2866

*The Best of H.P. Lovecraft: Bloodcurdling Tales of Horror and the Macabre*
Lovecraft, H.P.   1700, 5104

*The Best of Henry Kuttner*
Kuttner, Henry   529, 530, 624, 3219, 3971, 5047, 5348

*The Best of Interzone*
Pringle, David   1023, 2148, **4439**, 5489

*The Best of Isaac Asimov*
Asimov, Isaac   4956

*The Best of Jack Williamson*
Williamson, Jack   4956

*The Best of James Blish*
Blish, James   233, 234

*The Best of James H. Schmitz*
Schmitz, James H.   759, 1969, 2947, 3430, 5782, 5838

*The Best of Judith Merril*
Merril, Judith   448

*The Best of Marion Zimmer Bradley*
Bradley, Marion Zimmer   3845

*The Best of Marion Zimmer Bradley's Fantasy Magazine*
Bradley, Marion Zimmer   628, 6005, 6046

*The Best of Marion Zimmer Bradley's Fantasy Magazine, Volume II*
Bradley, Marion Zimmer   629

*The Best of Masques*
Williamson, J.N.   1847, 3959, 4724, 4726

*The Best of Philip K. Dick*
Dick, Philip K.   321, 4216

*The Best of Pulphouse: The Hardback Magazine*
Rusch, Kristine Kathryn   216, 628, 629, 755, 1023, 1363, 1364, 1365, 1373, 1618, 2148, 2593, 2967, 3948, 3949, **4713**, 5954, 6045

*The Best of Robert Bloch*
Bloch, Robert   5104

*The Best of Science Fiction*
Conklin, Groff   24, 214, 238, 239, 1621, 3648, 4127, 4725, 5004, 5238, 5948

*The Best of Shadows*
Grant, Charles L.   1017, 1629, 3959, 3961, 3962, 4873

*Best of The Horror Show*
Silva, David B.   1823, 2773, 2960, 2966, 3959, 3960, 3997, 4200, 4724, 4726, 4846, 4873

*Best of the Midwest's Science Fiction, Fantasy and Horror, Volume I*
Smart, Brian   4199

*Best of the Midwest's Science Fiction, Fantasy and Horror, Volume II*
Smart, Brian   4199, **5095**

*The Best of the Midwest's Science Fiction, Fantasy and Horror, Volume II*
Smart, Brian   5447

*The Best of the Rest*
Pasechnik, Steve   3997

*The Best of Weird Tales*
Betancourt, John Gregory   480, 3028

*The Best of Weird Tales: 1923*
Kaye, Marvin   **3023**

*The Best of Whispers*
Schiff, Stuart David   22, 1017, 1629, 2307, 3962, **4873**

*The Best Rootin' Tootin' Shootin' Gunslinger in the Whole Damned Galaxy*
Resnick, Mike   5215

*The Best Science Fiction for 1972*
Pohl, Frederik   245

*The Best Science Fiction Novellas of the Year 1-2*
Carr, Terry   5045, 5046

*The Best Science Fiction of the Year 1-16*
Carr, Terry   5045, 5046

*The Best Short Stories of J.G. Ballard*
Ballard, J.G.   61, 624, 5345, 5348

*The Best Supernatural Tales of Arthur Conan Doyle*
Doyle, Arthur Conan   2680, 3147, 4021

*The Best Tales of Hoffmann*
Hoffmann, E.T.A.   5389

*The Best Ye Breed*
Reynolds, Mack   4539

*Bestsellers Guaranteed*
Lansdale, Joe R.   **3321**

*Betcha Can't Read Just One*
Foster, Alan Dean   **1994**

*Betrayal*
Tilton, Lois   8, 2917

*Betrayals*
Stirling, S.M.   367, 944, 4833, 5676

*Better in the Dark*
Yarbro, Chelsea Quinn   2246, **6011**

*Better than Life*
Naylor, Grant   **4076**

*Bettyann*
Neville, Kris   1595

*The Between*
Due, Tannarive   **1669**, 2161

*Between Floors*
Monteleone, Thomas F.   2157, **3957**

*Between the Devil and the Deep*
Morgan, J.M.   88, 189, 441, 1346, 3232, **3998**, 5877

*Between the Rivers*
Turtledove, Harry   2577, **5496**

*Between the Stars*
Kotani, Eric   82, 421

*Between Time and Terror*
Weinberg, Robert   **5691**

*Between Time and Timbuktu*
Vonnegut, Kurt Jr.   1784, 1785, 5904

*Beware of the Cat*
Parry, Michel   1369, 3145, 5252

*Bewitching Beloved*
James, Valerie   4943

*Bewitchments of Love and Hate*
Constantine, Storm   **1140**, 2295

*The Beyond*
Harrington, Barry   **2556**

*Beyond Apollo*
Malzberg, Barry   **3612**, 5057

*Beyond Control*
Silverberg, Robert   6027

*Beyond Eden*
Morgan, J.M.   278, **3999**

*Beyond Heaven's River*
Bear, Greg   2996

*Beyond Ragnarok*
Reichert, Mickey Zucker   **4516**, 4899

*Beyond Sanctuary*
Morris, Janet   289

*Beyond Silence*
Cameron, Eleanor   4917

*Beyond the Blue Event Horizon*
Pohl, Frederik   2006, 4511

*Beyond the Borders*
Howard, Robert E.   **2780**, 3981

**Beyond the Burning Lands**
Christopher, John   658

**Beyond the Curve**
Abe, Kobo   3250

**Beyond the Dawning: The Poems of William Hope Hodgson**
Hodgson, William Hope   486

**Beyond the Door**
Blackwood, Gary L.   **510**, 970, 2948

**Beyond the Fall of Night**
Clarke, Arthur C.   **1054**

**Beyond the Gate**
Wolverton, Dave   4829, **5949**

**Beyond the Lamplight**
Burleson, Donald   **775**

**Beyond the Magic Sphere**
Jarrow, Gail   489, **2879**

**Beyond the Moons**
Cook, David   1114, **1144**, 1291, 1937, 2618, 2785, 2985, 4909

**Beyond the Pale**
Anthony, Mark   **153**, 1484

**Beyond the Pale**
Koke, Jack   **3198**

**Beyond the Safe Zone**
Silverberg, Robert   4535

**Beyond the Sea of Ice**
Sarabande, William   191, 275, 668, 2166, 2167, 2168, 2169, 2170, 2581, 5444

**Beyond the Shroud**
Hautala, Rick   797, 839, 2161, **2604**, 4256, 5249, 5585

**Beyond the Veil**
Morris, Janet   4202

**Beyond the Veil of Stars**
Reed, Robert   1762, **4503**, 5775

**Beyond the Void**
Dalton, Sean   929, **1331**, 2683

**Beyond the Wall of Sleep**
Heidel, R. Andrew   **2641**

**Beyond This Horizon**
Heinlein, Robert A.   4296

**Beyond Tomorrow**
Knight, Damon   1609

**Beyond Wizardwall**
Morris, Janet   4202

**Bhagavati**
Dalkey, Kara   **1316**

**Bible Stories for Adults**
Morrow, James   497, 1758, 3908, 3986, **4028**

**The Bicentennial Man**
Asimov, Isaac   5171

**Bid Time Return**
Matheson, Richard   4753

**Big Bang**
Goulart, Ron   1216

**The Big Black Mark**
Chandler, A. Bertram   1899, 1900

**The Big Game**
Schofield, Sandy   8, 2908, 2917

**Big Gurl**
Metzger, Thom   2843, 3392

**Big Planet**
Vance, Jack   897, 1691, 4545

**Big Rock Beat**
Kihn, Greg   **3102**

**Big Sky River**
Benford, Gregory   1015

**Big Thunder**
Atkins, Peter   3326

**The Big Time**
Leiber, Fritz   350, 358, 359, 590, 598, 1626, 1635, 1694, 2119, 2564, 2790, 3064, 4164

**The Bighead**
Lee, Edward   3373, **3387**

**Bijapur**
Dalkey, Kara   **1317**

**Bill, the Galactic Hero**
Harrison, Harry   260, 261, 1382, 1536, 1919, 3828, 4563, 4564, 4566, 4657

**Bill, the Galactic Hero: On the Planet of Tasteless Pleasure**
Harrison, Harry   1420, **2567**

**Bill, the Galactic Hero: On the Planet of Zombie Vampires**
Harrison, Harry   2486

**Bill, the Galactic Hero: The Final Incoherent Adventure**
Harrison, Harry   **2568**

**Bill, the Galactic Hero: The Planet of the Robot Slaves**
Harrison, Harry   173, 553

**Billennium and Other Stories**
Ballard, J.G.   56, 57

**The Billion Dollar Boy**
Sheffield, Charles   4158, 4379, **4948**

**Billy**
Strieber, Whitley   1848, 3375, 3395, 3639, 4041, 4501, **5338**, 5992

**Bimbos of the Death Sun**
McCrumb, Sharyn   251, 316, 568, 2567, 4120, 4546, 4785

**Binscombe Tales**
Whitbourn, John   2707, 3314, **5776**

**Bio of a Space Tyrant**
Anthony, Piers   2212

**Birds of Prey**
Drake, David   1855, 1955

**Birth of Fire**
Pournelle, Jerry   421, 2765, 4964

**The Birth of Flux and Anchor**
Chalker, Jack L.   5647

**The Birth of the Blade**
McCarty, Dennis   844, **3766**

**The Birth of the People's Republic of Antarctica**
Batchelor, John Calvin   4628

**Bitter Blood**
Taylor, Karen E.   1086, 1670, 2288, 2492, 2493, 3517, 4666, **5405**

**Bitter Gold Hearts**
Cook, Glen   2629

**Bitter/Sweet**
Cave, Hugh B.   **939**

**Black Ambrosia**
Engstrom, Elizabeth   3519, 4576, 5347, 5419

**Black as Blood**
Chilson, Rob   **1014**, 1396

**Black Body**
Turk, H.C.   3183, **5488**

**Black Butterflies: A Flock on the Dark Side**
Shirley, John   1492, 3090, 4886, **5005**

**The Black Carousel**
Grant, Charles L.   **2303**

**The Black Castle**
Daniels, Les   463, 1797, 4303, 6012, 6013, 6015, 6016, 6018

**The Black Cat**
Poe, Robert   **4344**, 4778

**Black Cats and Broken Mirrors**
Greenberg, Martin H.   **2381**

**The Black Company**
Cook, Glen   15, 28, 164, 290, 739, 745, 771, 991, 992, 1009, 1010, 1102, 1110, 1156, 1173, 1178, 1239, 1240, 1682, 1688, 1690, 1733, 1816, 1908, 1927, 1928, 1979, 2031, 2190, 2191, 2367, 2884, 2984, 2985, 2988, 2990, 3171, 3227, 3246, 3273, 3540, 3653, 3833, 3834, 3837, 3930, 4201, 4526, 4674, 4693, 4694, 4730, 4777, 4945, 5017, 5203, 5206, 5509, 5599, 5682, 5683, 5737, 6002, 6003

**The Black Death**
Copper, Basil   690, **1185**, 3571

**Black Death**
Largent, R. Karl   **3337**, 3577

**Black Dogs**
McEwan, Ian   **3808**

**Black Easter**
Blish, James   2658, 4647, 6071

**The Black Fedora**
Smith, Guy N.   602

**The Black Flame**
Abbey, Lynn   2651, 3477, 4871, 5741

**The Black Flame**
Weinbaum, Stanley G.   4620

**Black Glass: Short Fictions**
Fowler, Karen Joy   **2027**

**The Black Gryphon**
Lackey, Mercedes   **3270**

**Black Hearts in Battersea**
Aiken, Joan   5976, 5977

**Black Horses for the King**
McCaffrey, Anne   2654, **3720**, 5794, 6035, 6038

**The Black House**
Theroux, Paul   5402

**Black Ice**
Graversen, Pat   **2333**

**Black in Time**
Jakes, John   2577

**Black Leather Required**
Schow, David J.   1128, 3090, **4885**

**Black Lightning**
Saul, John   2755, 3638, 4088, 4327, **4837**

**The Black Lodge**
Weinberg, Robert   871, 1298, 1403, 2699, 2744, 2856, 2896, 3093, 3885, 4847, **5692**

**The Black Magic Omnibus**
Haining, Peter   2385

**The Black Mariah**
Bonansinga, Jay R.   **570**, 2313

**Black Medicine**
Burks, Arthur J.   942, 3515, 4904, 4905, 5149, 5627

**Black Milk**
Reed, Robert   1165, 1933, 1934, **4504**, 4756, 5664, 5907

**Black Night**
Strayhorn, S.J.   1830, **5334**, 5464

**The Black Reaper**
Capes, Bernard   455, **875**, 5610

**The Black School**
Williamson, J.N.   5464, **5851**

**Black Snow Days**
O'Keefe, Claudia   **4205**

**Black Spirits and White**
Cram, Ralph Adams   485, 963, 964, **1243**

**Black Steel**
Perry, Steve   **4291**

**Black Sun**
Leininger, Robert   74, **3429**

**The Black Sun**
Williamson, Jack   **5860**

**Black Sun**
Winter, Douglas E.   **5923**

**Black Sun Rising**
Friedman, C.S.   604, 2037, **2056**, 3438, 3473, 3646, 4485, 4490, 4652, 5277, 5333, 5572, 5629

**Black Swan, White Raven**
Datlow, Ellen   **1358**, 3847

**Black Tales**
Haining, Peter   5418

**Black Thorn, White Rose**
Datlow, Ellen   **1359**, 5973, 6045, 6046

**The Black Throne**
Zelazny, Roger   4764, 5044

**The Black Tower**
Lupoff, Richard A.   1429

*Black Trillium*
Bradley, Marion Zimmer  **630**, 3696, 3700, 4153

*Black Trump*
Martin, George R.R.  **3642**

*Black Unicorn*
Lee, Tanith  330, 549, 701, 1090, 1219, 1343, 1440, 1946, 2941, 3400, **3404**, 3545, 3720, 4319, 4321, 4985, 5336, 5394, 5827, 5979, 6017, 6033

*Black Walls, Red Glass*
Thomas, Jeffrey  **5445**, 5620

*Black Water 2: More Tales of the Fantastic*
Manguel, Alberto  1099, **3616**, 5936

*Black Water: The Book of Fantastic Literature*
Manguel, Alberto  1099, 5936

*Black Wind*
Wilson, F. Paul  4003

*Black Wine*
Dorsey, Candas Jane  **1582**, 4244

*The Black Wing*
Kirchoff, Mary  470, 4925, 5708

*Blackburn*
Denton, Bradley  **1489**, 3088

*The Blackcollar*
Zahn, Timothy  2211, 2212, 4602, 4604, 5027

*The Blackgod*
Keyes, J. Gregory  992, **3095**, 3773, 4110, 4527, 4795

*Blackman's Burden*
Reynolds, Mack  4539, 4561

*Blackmantle: A Triumph*
Kennealy-Morrison, Patricia  **3059**

*The Blackstone Chronicles*
Saul, John  **4838**

*Blackwater*
McDowell, Michael  70, 145, 147, 340, 4838, 5808, 5926

*The Blackwater Series*
McDowell, Michael  1300

*Blade*
Odom, Mel  **4190**

*Blade Runner*
Dick, Philip K.  77, 79, 249, 366, 708, 837, 1725, 2011, 2377, 2536, 2539, 2906, 2907, 3484, 4193, 4220, 4229, 4286, 4300, 4748, 4749, 4939, 5375, 5462, 5966

*Blade Runner 2: The Edge of Human*
Jeter, K.W.  **2906**

*Blade Runner: Replicant Night*
Jeter, K.W.  **2907**

*Blameless in Abaddon*
Morrow, James  3986, **4029**

*Bleak Seasons*
Cook, Glen  **1147**, 5197

*Bleeder*
Lazuta, Gene  **3374**, 5823

*The Bleeding Man and Other Stories*
Strete, Craig  1437

*A Blessing on the Moon*
Skibell, Joseph  **5079**

*Blessings and Curses*
Stasheff, Christopher  **5214**

*Blind Hunger*
Darke, David  **1352**, 4083

*Blind Justice*
Lewitt, S.N.  **3448**, 3453, 3454

*Blind Voices*
Reamy, Tom  896, 1186, 1282, 2303, 4776, 5176

*Blindfold*
Anderson, Kevin J.  **101**, 2477, 2478, 2788, 4829, 5548

*Blood*
Dee, Ron  **1463**, 5120

*Blood: A Southern Fantasy*
Moorcock, Michael  2304, **3977**

*Blood Alone*
Bergstrom, Elaine  **462**

*Blood and Chocolate*
Klause, Annette Curtis  514, **3162**

*Blood and Honor*
Green, Simon R.  **2361**, 3636, 4699, 5678

*Blood and Roses*
Bainbridge, Sharon  **292**

*Blood and Water and Other Tales*
McGrath, Patrick  921, 3984, 4027, 4181

*The Blood Artists*
Hogan, Chuck  **2720**, 3632

*Blood Brothers*
Chizmar, Richard T.  2157

*Blood Brothers*
Lumley, Brian  **3546**

*Blood Brothers*
Wright, T. Lucien  810, 1352, 1355, 2024, 3546, 3557, 4091, 4728, 4883, 5537, 5657, **5986**

*Blood Countess*
Codrescu, Andrei  279, **1094**, 4529

*Blood County*
Selby, Curt  2912

*Blood Debt*
Huff, Tanya  **2792**, 3108

*Blood Feud*
Siciliano, Sam  **5020**

*Blood Feuds*
Stirling, S.M.  **5292**, 5917

*Blood Games*
Yarbro, Chelsea Quinn  264, 4573

*Blood Hunt*
Killough, Lee  1213, 1214, 1792, 2793, 3560, 3602, 4004, 4005, 5374

*Blood Is Not Enough*
Datlow, Ellen  698, 1231, **1360**, 1611, 1718, 2071, 2387, 2409, 2508, 2975, 3031, 3112, 3758, 4407, 4876, 4879, 4880, 4881, 5284, 5688, 5935

*The Blood Jaguar*
Payne, Michael H.  **4271**

*Blood Kin*
Kelly, Ronald  **3051**, 4102

*The Blood Kiss*
Etchison, Dennis  555, 5339, 5600

*Blood Kiss: Vampire Erotica*
Tan, Cecilia  698, 3030, 3181, 3184, 4690, **5385**

*Blood Lines*
Burkett, William R. Jr.  **774**

*Blood Lines: Vampire Stories From New England*
Schimel, Lawrence  150, 151, **4876**

*Blood Links*
Killough, Lee  1791, 1792, 1793, 1796, 4508

*Blood Lust*
Dee, Ron  **1464**, 1945, 2152, 3372, 5237

*Blood Muse: Timeless Tales of Vampires in the Arts*
Friesner, Esther  **2071**, 5448

*Blood Music*
Bear, Greg  100, 836, 1133, 1348, 1760, 1770, 2058, 2163, 2275, 2443, 2681, 3008, 3049, 3245, 3792, 4476, 4478, 4748, 4756, 5172, 5255

*Blood Oath*
Vornholt, John  367, 944, 4833

*The Blood of a Dragon*
Watt-Evans, Lawrence  842, 1156, 1749, 2461, 3545, 4460, 4695, **5640**, 6069

*The Blood of Angels*
Gregory, Stephen  **2428**

*Blood of Innocents*
Arbucci, John  **204**, 879, 2704, 3637, 4480, 4840, 4843, 4845, 5622

*Blood of Mugwump*
Rice, Doug  3244, **4581**

*Blood of Nostradamus: The Unborn*
Laurance, Andrew  3561

*The Blood of Ten Chiefs*
Pini, Richard  408, 3300, 4336, 4337, 6005

*Blood of the Children*
Rodgers, Alan  **4645**

*Blood of the Colyn Muir*
Zimmer, Paul Edwin  1177, 1815, 3061, 3659, **6083**

*Blood of the Covenant*
Monahan, Brent  **3954**, 5290

*Blood of the Fold*
Goodkind, Terry  1775, **2268**, 4524

*Blood of the Goddess*
Dalkey, Kara  **1318**

*Blood of the Impaler*
Sackett, Jeffrey  4765, **4779**

*The Blood of the Lamb*
Monteleone, Thomas F.  751, 1507, 1721, 2150, 2318, 2700, **3958**, 4050, 4073

*Blood on the Bayou*
Donaldson, D.J.  1007, **1570**, 1888, 2138

*Blood on the Moon*
Cohen, Barney  584, 588, 4121, 4470

*Blood on the Sun*
Herbert, Brian  387, 1119, 1949, 1950, **2664**, 4058

*Blood on the Water*
Elrod, P.N.  **1791**

*Blood Pact*
Huff, Tanya  301

*Blood Price*
Huff, Tanya  1355, 1400, 1791, 1793, 1796, 2149, 2376, 2441, 2513, 2517, 2519, **2793**, 3053, 3276, 3284, 3602, 4847, 5062, 5078, 5374, 5406, 5577

*Blood Red Eightball*
Coffin, M.T.  5291

*Blood Relations*
Murray, Doug  2664, **4058**

*Blood River Down*
Grant, Charles L.  2014

*Blood Roots*
Cusick, Richie Tankersley  **1300**, 3406

*Blood Roses*
Yarbro, Chelsea Quinn  **6012**

*Blood Sabbath*
Clark, Leigh  1032, **1048**, 1215, 1354, 3233, 5100

*Blood Secrets*
Taylor, Karen E.  803, 948, 2149, 2151, 2288, 3517, 4667, 5078, **5406**, 5704, 5705

*Blood Siege*
Stine, G. Harry  1651, 2000, **5278**

*Blood Sky*
Nolan, William F.  4255

*Blood Sport*
Smedman, Lisa  **5096**

*Blood Thirst: 100 Years of Vampire Fiction*
Wolf, Leonard  2409, 5265, **5935**

*Blood Ties*
Taylor, Karen E.  5374, **5407**

*Blood Trail*
Huff, Tanya  2514, 2517, 2518, 2519, 2520, **2794**

*Blood Trillium*
May, Julian  641, **3696**, 4153

*Blood Walk*
Killough, Lee  2792, **3108**

**Blood War**
Weinberg, Robert   303, 387, 798, 1949, 1950, 2255, 2258, 2259, 2514, 2515, 2663, 3613, 4004, 4058, 4190, **5693**, 5883

**Blood Wings**
Gresham, Stephen   **2430**, 5483

**Blood Work**
Zachary, Fay   **6050**

**Bloodchild and Other Stories**
Butler, Octavia E.   **790**, 3384

**Blooded on Arachne**
Bishop, Michael   3086, 3116, 3234, 5369

**Bloodletter**
Beath, Warren Newton   **426**, 4327, 4496

**Bloodletter**
Jeter, K.W.   8, **2908**

**Bloodlines**
Williamson, J.N.   5421, **5852**

**Bloodlist**
Elrod, P.N.   285, **1792**, 2149, 2517, 2792, 3108, 5078, 5374

**Bloodmist**
Tremayne, Peter   3265, 3505

**Bloodright**
Tremayne, Peter   4765, 4779

**Bloodshift**
Reeves-Stevens, Garfield   **4508**

**Bloodstream**
Gerritsen, Tess   **2205**

**Bloodsucking Fiends: A Love Story**
Moore, Christopher   1800, 1802, 2449, **3988**, 4069, 5062

**Bloodwars**
Lumley, Brian   **3547**

**Bloody Bones**
Hamilton, Laurell K.   **2512**

**The Bloody Chamber**
Carter, Angela   1140, 1142, 3195, 4182

**The Bloody Red Baron**
Newman, Kim   1686, 2742, **4097**, 4755, 6019

**The Bloody Sun**
Bradley, Marion Zimmer   3747

**Bloody Valentine**
George, Stephen R.   **2197**

**Bloody Waters**
Winters, B.L.   **5926**

**Bloom**
McCarthy, Wil   1695, **3761**, 5068

**Blossom Comes Home**
Herriot, James   3377

**The Blossom of Erda**
Taylor, L.A.   585, 5019

**Blue Champagne**
Varley, John   54, 61, 124, 161, 234, 479, 503, 624, 689, 772, 804, 850, 1515, 1608, 1874, 2569, 2576, 3187, 3235, 3308, 3571, 3648, 4070, 4118, 4123, 4126, 4127, 4216, 4302, 4376, 4561, 4636, 4643, 4706, 4956, 4961, 5028, 5106, 5245, 5247, 5257, 5344, 5346, 5349, 5369, 5551, 5638, 5807, 5869

**The Blue Fairy Book**
Lang, Andrew   225, 235, 1479, 2447, 5310, 6087, 6088, 6090

**The Blue Hawk**
Dickinson, Peter   658, 3404, 4156

**Blue Light**
Mosley, Walter   **4042**

**Blue Limbo**
Green, Terrence M.   **2377**

**Blue Mars**
Robinson, Kim Stanley   406, 1876, **4629**

**Blue Moon**
Feil, Hila   1475, **1898**

**Blue Moon**
Hamilton, Laurell K.   **2513**

**Blue Moon Rising**
Green, Simon R.   12, 1207, 1702, 1703, 2357, 2360, **2362**, 2987, 3635, 4685, 6001

**Blue Motel**
Crowther, Peter   **1279**

**The Blue Star**
Pratt, Fletcher   5222, 5228, 5506, 5507, 5976

**The Blue Sword**
McKinley, Robin   763, 2674, 2676, 2796, 2819, 3871, 3973, 3975, 4156, 4727, 5977

**Blue World**
McCammon, Robert R.   700, 967, 1887, 2281, 2319, 3138, 3216, 3321, 3328, 3329, 3335, **3753**, 4648, 5339, 5600, 5899

**Blueheart**
Sinclair, Alison   **5068**

**Bluesong**
Van Scyoc, Sydney J.   1025, 4152

**The Boat of a Million Years**
Anderson, Poul   **125**, 175, 178, 188, 298, 590, 591, 734, 789, 884, 1053, 1876, 2459, 2626, 2829, 3854, 5039, 5496, 5942, 6074

**Bodies of the Dead**
Hartwell, David G.   **2586**, 5439

**Body and Soul**
David, Peter   2909, 2910, 3520

**Body Count**
Rouch, James   2324, 2325

**The Body Snatchers**
Finney, Jack   137, 662, 1037, 1200, 1723, 1727, 2302, 2344, 2345, 3212, 3218, 4090, 4944, 5643

**Bodyguard**
Dietz, William C.   **1542**, 4225

**The Bohr Maker**
Nagata, Linda   2274, 2559, 3241, 3453, **4064**

**Bolo Brigade**
Keith, William H. Jr.   4973, 5204

**Bolo: The Annals of the Dinochrome Brigade**
Laumer, Keith   1896, 1938, 2464, 4374, 5278, 5279, 5281

**Bone**
Chesbro, George C.   822, **1006**, 1779, 3202, 3319, 4787

**Bone Danc: A Fantasy for Technophiles**
Bull, Emma   **766**

**Bone Dance: A Fantasy for Technophiles**
Bull, Emma   46, 62, 198, 218, 473, 728, 743, 744, 971, 974, 975, 976, 986, 1425, 1499, 1819, 1849, 1861, 1903, 1936, 3170, 3940, 4117, 4949, 5134, 5179, 5433, 5839

**The Bone Forest**
Holdstock, Robert   395, 415, 1431, 2106, **2736**, 3845, 4757, 4809

**Bone Meal: Seven More Tales of Terror**
Finnis, A.   1693, 2772

**Bone Music**
Rodgers, Alan   **4646**

**Bone Wars**
Davis, Brett   **1398**, 6084

**Boneman**
Cantrell, Lisa   20, **871**, 2699, 3093, 4498

**Bones**
Thompson, Joyce   **5453**

**The Bones of Haven**
Green, Simon R.   1249, 1484, **2363**

**Bones of the Moon**
Carroll, Jonathan   655, 1089, 1278, 2101, 2105, 2995, 4210

**The Bones of the Old Ones**
Thomas, Jeffrey   3556, 4444

**The Bones of the Old Ones and Other Lovecraftian Tales**
Thomas, Jeffrey   **5446**

**Bones of the Past**
Lisle, Holly   3302, **3478**

**The Bones of Time**
Goonan, Kathleen Ann   **2273**

**The Bones Wizard**
Ryan, Alan   2319

**The Book of Andre Norton**
Norton, Andre   823

**The Book of Atrix Wolfe**
McKillip, Patricia A.   203, 1472, 2354, 2538, 2653, 2654, 3070, 3099, **3838**, 4105, 4211, 4908, 5275, 6004, 6042

**The Book of Brendan**
Curry, Ann   369, 370, 372, **1294**, 4447, 6035, 6038

**The Book of Common Dread**
Monahan, Brent   660, 2259, 2994, 3113, **3955**, 4050

**The Book of Dragons**
Asimov, Isaac   801

**The Book of Dragons**
Hague, Michael   385, 801, **2479**, 6036

**The Book of Dreams**
Vance, Jack   4277

**The Book of Earth**
Kellogg, Marjorie Bradley   2126, 2128, 2795, 2799, **3044**, 3298, 3507, 4150, 4461

**Book of Enchantments**
Wrede, Patricia C.   **5973**, 6040

**The Book of Famous Irish Ghost Stories**
O'Keefe, Daniel   4203

**The Book of Fantasy**
Borges, Jorge Luis   1576, 2592

**A Book of Ghosts**
Gould, Sabine Baring   3633

**Book of Horrors**
Hoh, Diane   5285

**The Book of Hyperborea**
Smith, Clark Ashton   3582, **5102**

**The Book of Iod**
Kuttner, Henry   1495, **3266**

**The Book of Irish Weirdness**
Anonymous   **149**

**The Book of Kane**
Wagner, Karl Edward   856, 2781, 2782, 5110, 5471

**The Book of Kells**
MacAvoy, R.A.   2, 317, 363, 1386, 1957, 2359, 2570, 3261, 3502

**The Book of Knights**
Meynard, Yves   369, **3884**

**The Book of Lost Places**
Vandermeer, Jeff   3851

**The Book of Lost Tales 1**
Tolkien, J.R.R.   408

**The Book of Moons**
Edghill, Rosemary   637

**The Book of Night with Moon**
Duane, Diane   **1657**, 3120

**The Book of Paradox**
Cooper, Louise   4926

**The Book of Poul Anderson**
Anderson, Poul   4956

**The Book of Skaith**
Brackett, Leigh   3746

**The Book of Skulls**
Silverberg, Robert   2487, 2920, 3239, 4234, 4813

**Book of Stones**
James, L. Dean   2862

**The Book of the Beast**
Lee, Tanith   **3405**, 4851

**The Book of the Damned**
Fowler, D.A.   **2022**, 5784

*The Book of the Damned*
Lee, Tanith  43, 1140

*Book of the Dead*
Skipp, John  2118, 2379, 2977,
  3758, 4168, 4412, 4745, 4746,
  4786, 4811, 4812, 5313, 5888

*The Book of the New Sun*
Wolfe, Gene  4243

*The Book of the Thousand Nights
  and a Night: A Plain and Literal
  Translation of the Arabian Nights
  Entertainments*
Burton, Richard F.  374, 6087

*The Book of the Thousand Nights
  and the One Night*
Payne, John  6087

*Book of the Werewolf*
Frost, Brian J.  1230, 2410, 2892,
  2976, 4410, 5384

*The Book of Three*
Alexander, Lloyd  1601, 2944, 2986,
  5359

*The Book of Water*
Kellogg, Marjorie Bradley  3045

*The Book of Webster's*
Williamson, J.N.  5853

*The Books of Blood Series*
Barker, Clive  855

*Books of Blood Series*
Barker, Clive  2153, 3138, 3362,
  3674

*Bootcamp 3000*
Greenberg, Martin H.  4373

*Border, Breed Nor Birth*
Reynolds, Mack  4539

*Border Dispute*
Kerns, Daniel R.  3066

*Borderland*
Windling, Terri  235, 630, 646, 647,
  767, 769, 971, 975, 986, 989,
  1288, 1368, 1427, 1436, 1994,
  2467, 3271, 3299, 3300, 3302,
  4335, 4675, 4993, 4994, 4995,
  5216, **5913**

*Borderland: A Novel of Terror*
Epperson, S.K.  **1828**, 4582

*Borderlands*
Monteleone, Thomas F.  **3959**, 4724,
  4726

*Borderlands 1*
Monteleone, Thomas F.  1847

*Borderlands 2*
Monteleone, Thomas F.  **3960**, 4278

*Borderlands 3*
Monteleone, Thomas F.  3598, **3961**,
  4206, 5795

*Borderlands 4*
Monteleone, Thomas F.  **3962**, 4722

*The Borderlands Series*
Monteleone, Thomas F.  2306, 5855

*Borders of Infinity*
Bujold, Lois McMaster  173, 260,
  **757**, 1326, 1332, 1630, 1650,
  4288, 4375, 4484, 4984, 5128,
  5466

*Bordertown*
Windling, Terri  235, 546, 552, 769,
  971, 975, 989, 1427, 1436, 2373,
  2467, 3271, 3299, 4675, 4993,
  4994, 4995, 5216

*Bored of the Rings*
Beard, Henry N.  2567, 2568, 4562,
  4563, 4564, 4565, 4566, 4656,
  4657

*Borgel*
Pinkwater, Daniel Manus  1222, 1224,
  1603, 2133, 3573, **4338**, 4564

*Born Bad*
Vachss, Andrew  2714

*Born to Exile*
Eisenstein, Phyllis  18, 176, 1096,
  1430, 1583, 1584, 2095, 2290,
  2361, 3086, 3580, 4161, 4520,
  5153, 5369, 5984

*Born to Run*
Lackey, Mercedes  1436, 2467, **3271**,
  4862, 4980, 5912

*Born Under Mars*
Brunner, John  353

*Born with the Dead*
Silverberg, Robert  3797

*The Borribles*
de Larrabeiti, Michael  1841, 3271,
  3301, 4497

*The Borribles Go for Broke*
de Larrabeiti, Michael  3271, 4497

*The Borrowers*
Norton, Mary  1132, 1558, 4386,
  4402, 4403, 6006

*The Borrowers Afield*
Norton, Mary  4386, 4402

*The Borrowers Afloat*
Norton, Mary  4386, 4402

*The Borrowers Aloft*
Norton, Mary  4402, 4403

*The Boss in the Wall*
Davidson, Avram  **1396**

*Bottom Right*
Kurland, Michael  4843

*Boundaries*
Wright, T.M.  2556, **5990**

*Bow Down to Nul*
Aldiss, Brian W.  5027

*The Box of Delights, or, When the
  Wolves Were Running*
Masefield, John  1294

*The Boxcar Children*
Warner, Gertrude  3731

*The Boy From the Burren*
Gilluly, Sheila  457, **2236**, 3871,
  3905, 4167, 4717, 4801, 4806

*The Boy Who Cried Werewolf*
Elvira  **1800**

*The Boy Who Saved the Stars*
Vallejo, Doris  6076

*The Boys From Brazil*
Levin, Ira  3672, 3964, 5136, 5732,
  5895

*Boy's Life*
McCammon, Robert R.  **3754**

*Boys of Life*
Russell, Paul  1170, 2448, **4737**

*The Bradbury Chronicles: Stories in
  Honor of Ray Bradbury*
Nolan, William F.  2398, 3689, **4131**,
  6077

*Brain Child*
Turner, George  **5491**

*The Brain in the Jar and Others*
Searight, Richard F.  **4904**

*Brain Rose*
Kress, Nancy  60, 352, 568, 583,
  2275, 2446, 3075, **3239**, 4071,
  5193, 5531, 5767

*The Brains of Rats*
Blumlein, Michael  319, **555**, 674,
  675, 821, 913, 3456, 4053, 4253,
  4977, 5005, 5058, 5899

*Brainstorm*
Krauzer, Steven M.  752, **3230**, 4480

*Brainstorm*
Myers, Walter Dean  1878

*Brainz, Inc.*
Goulart, Ron  1999, 4363

*Brak the Barbarian*
Jakes, John  3418, 4294

*Bram Stoker's Dracula*
Saberhagen, Fred  139, 3110, 3179,
  **4763**

*Bran Mak Morn*
Howard, Robert E.  906

*Branch and Crown*
Baudino, Gael  **389**

*Branch Point*
Clee, Mona  357, **1074**, 2614, 3467,
  4039, 5067, 5315

*Brand New Cherry Flavor*
Grimson, Todd  **2448**, 3103, 4256,
  5085

*Brander's Book*
Mills, C.J.  762, **3909**

*The Brass Bottle*
Anstey, F.  73

*The Brave Free Men*
Vance, Jack  884, 2207

*The Brave Little Toaster: A Bedtime
  Story for Small Appliances*
Disch, Thomas M.  252

*The Brave Little Toaster Goes to
  Mars*
Disch, Thomas M.  252

*Brave New World*
Huxley, Aldous  574, 1782, 2558,
  3794, 5157, 5469, 5491, 5568

*The Brazen Gambit*
Abbey, Lynn  **13**, 2624

*A Breach in the Watershed*
Niles, Douglas  1484, 2924, 2925,
  3095, **4105**, 4794, 4908

*The Breaking of Northwall*
Williams, Paul O.  46, 208, 278, 394,
  656, 720, 721, 787, 881, 889,
  1075, 3501, 3862, 3863, 3864,
  3873, 3908, 4001, 4488, 5500,
  5590, 5743, 5745, 5920, 5965

*Breaking Strain*
Preuss, Paul  1646, 5930

*The Breath of Suspension*
Jablokov, Alexander  **2835**, 3600,
  4680

*Breathe Deeply*
Bassingthwaite, Don  5535

*Breed to Come*
Norton, Andre  4054

*Breeder*
Clegg, Douglas  **1076**, 1465

*Breeder*
Kelleher, Ed  **3041**

*The Breeds of Man*
Busby, F.M.  2870, 3236

*The Brentwood Witches*
Jordan, Brenda  2713

*Brethren*
Ryan, Shawn  **4754**, 5186

*Bretta Martyn*
Smith, L. Neil  **5128**

*Brian Boru: Emperor of the Irish*
Llywelyn, Morgan  **3501**, 4260

*Briar Rose*
Yolen, Jane  466, 467, 636, 728,
  1358, 1409, 1694, 1787, 2244,
  2265, 4404, 4758, 5079, 5143,
  5912, 5916, **6029**

*The Bridal Wreath*
Undset, Sigrid  136

*The Bride of Frankenstein*
Dreadstone, Carl  4687

*Bride of the Castle*
DeChancie, John  **1452**

*Bride of the Mist*
Skye, Christina  2540

*Bride of the Rat God*
Hambly, Barbara  **2499**, 3099, 3485,
  3838

*Bride of the Slime Monster*
Gardner, Craig Shaw  1149, **2125**,
  4398, 5934

*The Bridge*
Banks, Iain M.  319, 2028, 3473,
  3791, 5927

*The Bridge*
Mano, D. Keith  5081

*The Bridge: A Horror Story*
Skipp, John  1020, 1806, 2541,
  2670, 3091, 4279, **5081**

*Bridge of Ashes*
Zelazny, Roger  191, 1873, 2166,
  2861, 3704, 4380, 5035

**Bridge of Birds**
Hughart, Barry   69, 409, 559, 746, 1268, 1677, 3338, 3991, 4155, 4400, 4673, 4742, 6022, 6026, 6066

**The Bridge of Dawn**
Hancock, Neil   **2531**

**The Bridge of Lost Desire**
Delany, Samuel R.   1720, 4046, 4047, 4263

**Bridge of Valor**
Groell, Anne Lesley   **2452**

**A Bridge of Years**
Wilson, Robert Charles   65, 135, 510, 1074, 1852, 2532, 4286, 4525, 4641, 5043, 5868, **5905**

**Bridge to Yesterday**
Mittman, Stephanie   2497

**Bridgehead**
Drake, David   1955

**Brigadoon: A Musical Play in Two Acts**
Lerner, Alan J.   1958

**Brigands of the Moon**
Cummings, Ray   5864

**Bright Angel**
Blair, John   **512**

**Bright Islands in a Dark Sea**
Douglas, L. Warren   1647, 2010

**Bright Messengers**
Lee, Gentry   **3398**

**Bright Shadow**
Forrest, Elizabeth   **1971**

**Brightness Falls From the Air**
Tiptree, James Jr.   34, 3644

**Brightness Reef**
Brin, David   159, 296, **684**, 786, 932, 988, 998, 1259, 1589, 2010, 3007, 3359, 3732, 3733, 3972, 4128, 4241, 4351, 5059, 5429, 5437, 5571, 5777, 5778, 5780, 6081

**Brightsuit MacBear**
Smith, L. Neil   4350, 4435

**Bring Me Children**
Martin, David   822, **3637**, 4501, 4845, 5250, 5314

**Bring Me the Head of Prince Charming**
Zelazny, Roger   1208, 1821, 2081, 3810, 3991, 4396, 4401, 4404, **6062**

**Bring on the Night**
Davis, Don   **1402**, 1779, 2288, 3498, 3519, 4102

**Bring the Jubilee**
Moore, Ward   442, 443, 2043, 2563, 2577, 3867, **3993**, 4814, 5502

**Bringing Down the Moon**
Anderson, Jani   22

**The Brink**
Gallery, Daniel V.   4512

**Brinkman**
Goulart, Ron   2573

**Brisingamen**
Paxson, Diana L.   2083, 3276, 5176

**The Bristling Wood**
Kerr, Katharine   3061, 3295, 5715

**Brittle Innings**
Bishop, Michael   199, **498**, 2029, 3977

**Brokedown Palace**
Brust, Steven   3018

**Broken Blade**
Marston, Ann   993, **3634**

**The Broken Crown**
West, Michelle   5200, **5757**

**The Broken God**
Zindell, David   **6085**

**The Broken Goddess**
Bemmann, Hans   **439**

**The Broken Land**
McDonald, Ian   2952, **3791**, 4241

**The Broken Sphere**
Findley, Nigel   2785

**The Broken Sword**
Anderson, Poul   2246, 2783, 3934, 3980, 4163, 4284, 4518, 4989

**The Broken Sword**
Cochran, Molly   **1091**

**The Broken Wheel**
Wingrove, David   3896, **5918**

**The Broken Worlds**
Harris, Raymond   4162, 4594, 5550

**Bronwyn's Bane**
Scarborough, Elizabeth Ann   1045, 1683, 4699, 5220

**The Bronze King**
Charnas, Suzy McKee   550

**Bronze Mirror**
Larsen, Jeanne   374, 2803, **3338**, 5827, 6026

**The Brood of the Witch Queen**
Rohmer, Sax   5696

**Brother Assassin**
Saberhagen, Fred   5294

**Brother Death**
Perry, Steve   4225, **4292**

**Brother Termite**
Anthony, Patricia   **156**, 2087, 2254, 2417, 4353

**Brother to Dragons**
Sheffield, Charles   **4949**, 5132

**Brother to Dragons, Companion to Owls**
Lindskold, Jane M.   558, **3473**, 5133

**Brother to Shadows**
Norton, Andre   1598, 1602, **4142**, 4228, 5138

**Brotherhood of the Stars**
Greene, Kirby   **2414**

**Brothers**
Bova, Ben   **581**

**The Brothers Grimm: From Enchanted Forests to the Modern World**
Zipes, Jack   849, 5560

**Brothers in Arms**
Bujold, Lois McMaster   311, 1103, 1538, 1544, 1628, 1661, 2435, 3748, 4191, 4225, 4484, 4963, 5131, 5234, 5550, 5718

**Brothers Majere**
Stein, Kevin   5711

**Brothers of the Dragon**
Bailey, Robin Wayne   85, **286**, 2126, 2127, 2424

**Brothers of the Earth**
Cherryh, C.J.   6051

**Brothers of the Night**
Rowe, Michael   699, 3618, **4689**, 5386

**Brown Girl in the Ring**
Hopkinson, Nalo   **2771**

**The Brownstone**
Eulo, Ken   3033, 3141, 5519

**Brujo**
Relling, William Jr.   2734, 5075

**Brute Orbits**
Zebrowski, George   3693, **6059**

**Buck Rogers in the 25th Century**
Lupoff, Richard A.   554

**Buckaroo Banzai**
Mac Rauch, Earl   5009

**Buddy Holly Is Alive and Well on Ganymede**
Denton, Bradley   **1490**, 2418, 3083, 3190, 4997, 5089, 5768, 6020

**Buffalo Gals and Other Animal Presences**
Le Guin, Ursula K.   274, 2120, 5807

**Buffy the Vampire Slayer**
Cusick, Richie Tankersley   1032, 1034, **1301**, 1801, 1802, 2131, 5161, 5324

**Bug Jack Barron**
Spinrad, Norman   125, 2487, 2920, 3239, 4813

**The Bug Life Chronicles**
Jennings, Phillip C.   **2890**

**Bug Park**
Hogan, James P.   386, 1168, **2723**, 3922, 5755

**The Bug Wars**
Asprin, Robert   513, 1627, 2211, 2224, 3035, 3037, 4373

**Bulfinch's Mythology**
Bulfinch, Thomas   5533

**Bully!**
Resnick, Mike   **4539**, 5501

**The Bully Pulpit**
Goldblatt, Andrew   4455, 4456

**Bunch!**
Bunch, David R.   772

**Bunnicula: A Rabbit Tale of Mystery**
Howe, Deborah   1090

**Bureau 13**
Pollotta, Nick   285, 390, 706, 1399, 1974, 2309, 2320, 2519, 2800, 4191, 4298, 4304, **4362**, 4394, 5497

**The Bureau of Lost Souls**
Fowler, Christopher   **2017**

**Burial**
Masterton, Graham   602, 2670, 2743, 3081, 3325, **3671**, 5053

**Buried Screams**
Andersson, C. Dean   **137**, 2302

**Burn**
Ransom, Bill   **4476**

**Burn, Witch, Burn!**
Merritt, A.   1194, 2025

**Burn, Witch, Burn!/Creep, Shadow, Creep!**
Merritt, A.   **3877**

**The Burning**
Masterton, Graham   **3672**, 4847

**The Burning Baby and Other Ghosts**
Gordon, John   5762, 5763, 5764, 5765

**Burning Bright**
Russell, J.S.   **4733**

**Burning Bright**
Scott, Melissa   **4894**

**Burning Chrome**
Gibson, William   927, 4366, 4747, 4998, 5007, 5255, 5257, 5837

**The Burning Man**
Hammond, Michael   **2530**, 5622

**Burning Tears of Sassurum**
Baker, Sharon   3871

**Burning Water**
Lackey, Mercedes   1153, 1450, 1451, 1665, 2320, 2370, 2375, 2856, 3073, 3254, **3272**, 4315, 4709, 5276, 5630, 5696

**Burning Your Boats: The Collected Short Stories**
Carter, Angela   920, **921**, 4181

**Burnt Offerings**
Hamilton, Laurell K.   **2514**

**Burnt Offerings**
Marasco, Robert   2455, 3033, 3141, 3774

**The Burrowers Beneath**
Lumley, Brian   1497, **3548**, 4007, 4112, 4449, 5340, 5470

**Burster**
Capobianco, Michael   378, 380, **876**, 1594, 4626

**Burying the Shadow**
Constantine, Storm   738

**The Bushido Incident**
Crawford, Betty Anne   **1248**, 4955

**The Businessman: A Tale of Terror**
Disch, Thomas M.   627, 1396, 1672, 3057, 3660, 3957, 4436

**But What of Earth?**
Anthony, Piers   **163**, 1689, 3249

**Butcher**
Miller, Rex  **3898**

**The Butcher Boy**
McCabe, Patrick   862, 3638, **3716**

**The Butcher's Bill**
Drake, David   4972

**The Butterfly Kid**
Anderson, Chester   87, 735, 2014,
2228, 2913, 3173, 3664, 4388,
4392, 4565, 4641, 4862, 4863,
4864, 5170

**Button Bright**
Kurland, Michael   97, 2704, 3230,
**3251**

**Buying Time**
Haldeman, Joe   125, **2487**, 2920,
3239, 3874, 4681, 4813

**Bwana & Bully!**
Resnick, Mike   4207, 5504

**By Any Other Fame**
Resnick, Mike   2070, **4540**, 5089

**By Bizarre Hands**
Lansdale, Joe R.   555, 776, 777,
1123, 1128, 2281, 2784, **3322**,
3367, 3553, 3558, 4250, 4253,
4885, 5600, 5885

**By Chaos Cursed**
Reichert, Mickey Zucker   390, **4517**

**By Death Abused**
Jonas, Gary   2137

**By Honor Betray'd**
Doyle, Debra   **1598**

**By the Sword**
Boggs, Timothy   **559**, 1808, 4912

**By the Sword**
Costikyan, Greg   **1207**

**By the Sword**
Lackey, Mercedes   176, 2795, 2798,
3121, **3273**, 5127, 5783

**Byzantium**
Lawhead, Stephen R.   **3353**, 5014,
5017, 5513

**Byzantium's Crown**
Schwartz, Susan   2561, 3255, 3339,
5503, 5508, 5510

# C

**Cabal**
Barker, Clive   **337**, 3336, 3759,
4745, 4746, 5007

**Cachalot**
Foster, Alan Dean   2450, 4923

**Caesar's Bicycle**
Barnes, John   **350**

**Cafe Purgatorium**
Anderson, Dana   **98**, 4314

**The Cage**
Meier, Shirley   1176, 4596

**The Cage**
Stirling, S.M.   986, **5293**, 5684

**Cage a Man**
Busby, F.M.   2811

**Cages**
Gorman, Ed   1016, 1021, **2277**,
2714, 3216, 4250, 5885

**Cahena**
Wellman, Manly Wade   2528

**Cain**
Huggins, James Byron   **2802**, 3632

**Cain's Book**
Trocchi, Alexander   548

**A Calculated Magic**
Weinberg, Robert   **5694**

**The Calcutta Chromosome**
Ghosh, Amitav   1316, **2214**

**Calde of the Long Sun**
Wolfe, Gene   **5937**

**Caledon of the Mists**
Harris, Deborah Turner   **2560**, 4045

**Caliban**
Allen, Roger MacBride   **77**, 446,
1336, 2005, 2906

**Caliban Landing**
Popkes, Steven   130, 5107

**Caliban's Hour**
Williams, Tad   3079, 3409, **5826**

**California Ghosting**
Hill, William   **2687**

**California Gothic**
Etchison, Dennis   **1843**, 3640

**The California Voodoo Game**
Niven, Larry   1980, **4117**

**The Call and Other Stories**
Westall, Robert   1526, **5762**

**The Call of Earth**
Card, Orson Scott   **882**

**Call of Madness**
Smith, Julie Dean   1674, 2561, 3293,
**5124**, 5783

**Call to Arms**
Carey, Diane   **901**

**A Call to Arms**
Foster, Alan Dean   **1995**, 2810

**Call to Arms**
Griffin, P.M.   **2435**

**A Call to Arms**
Martin, Thomas K.   **3650**

**A Call to Arms**
Sheckley, Robert   1387

**Call to Battle**
Murray, Doug   3990, **4059**, 5701,
5702

**A Call to Darkness**
Friedman, Michael Jan   **2062**

**Callahan and Company**
Robinson, Spider   115, 263, 2659,
4636

**The Callahan Touch**
Robinson, Spider   **4637**

**Callahan's Crosstime Saloon**
Robinson, Spider   582, 677, 740,
1858, 2055, 2125, 2299

**Callahan's Lady**
Robinson, Spider   740, **4638**

**Callahan's Legacy**
Robinson, Spider   2007, 2055, 2299,
**4639**

**Callahan's Secret**
Robinson, Spider   740, 2622

**The Caller of the Black**
Lumley, Brian   3266

**The Calling**
Griffith, Kathryn Meyer   **2439**, 5312

**The Calling of the Three**
Emerson, Ru   1421, 3282

**Calling on Dragons**
Wrede, Patricia C.   1512, 4460,
5144, **5974**

**Camber of Culdi**
Kurtz, Katherine   2883, 5393, 5506,
5510, 5752

**Camber the Heretic**
Kurtz, Katherine   2883

**Cambio Bay**
Wilhelm, Kate   11, **5806**

**Camelot**
Yolen, Jane   3720

**The Camelot Chronicles**
Ashley, Mike   **224**, 2745, 2767,
4610

**Camelot Fantastic**
Schimel, Lawrence   **4877**

**Camp Vamp**
Elvira   **1801**

**Campfire Story**
Kline, Robert   4598

**Can Such Things Be?**
Bierce, Ambrose   963, 964, 4275

**Canal Dreams**
Banks, Iain M.   **323**

**The Canary Trainer**
Meyer, Nicholas   4773

**Canby's Legion**
Baldwin, Bill   **308**, 1552, 4829, 4973

**A Candle for D'Artagnan**
Yarbro, Chelsea Quinn   742, 3822,
4513, 4784, **6013**

**Candle Night**
Rickman, Phil   **4586**, 5121

**Candles for Elizabeth**
Kiernan, Caitlin R.   **3100**

**Cannibal Dwight's Special Purpose**
Holder, Nancy   4255, 5685

**Cannon's Orb**
Douglas, L. Warren   296, 420, 684,
688, 933, 998, 1303, **1586**, 2008,
2637, 2681, 3440, 3730, 3739,
3752, 4119, 4476, 4479, 4711,
4859, 5068, 5467

**The Canterbury Tales**
Chaucer, Geoffrey   1045

**Canticle**
Salvatore, R.A.   1290, 4108, **4793**

**A Canticle for Leibowitz**
Miller, Walter M. Jr.   574, 724, 788,
4028, 4081, 4209, 4567, 4605,
4836, 5212, 5911

**Captain Jack Zodiac**
Kandel, Michael   499, 830, **3009**,
3642, 3647, 3891, 4590, 4606,
5148, 5567

**Captain Quad**
Costello, Sean   397, 611, **1203**,
2876, 3996, 4240, 4788, 5415

**Captain Sinbad**
Diamond, Graham   618

**The Captain's Honor**
Dvorkin, David   2068

**Captains Outrageous, or, For Doom
the Bell Tolls**
Young, Roy V.   **6049**

**Captive Universe**
Harrison, Harry   58

**Captives of the Blue Mountain**
Pini, Wendy   **4336**

**Captured by the Engines**
Lansdale, Joe R.   2331, 2392, 4215

**Car Sinister**
Silverberg, Robert   1644

**Cardinal's Sin**
Buckland, Raymond   **751**

**Cardmaster**
Emery, Clayton   **1813**

**Caretaker**
Graf, L.A.   1729, 2061

**Carlucci's Edge**
Russo, Richard Paul   2033, 3231,
**4747**

**Carlucci's Heart**
Russo, Richard Paul   **4748**, 4936

**Carmen Dog**
Emshwiller, Carol   **1817**, 4034, 5616

**Carmen Miranda's Ghost Is Haunting
Space Station Three**
Sakers, Don   3751, 4169, 4637,
**4785**

**Carmilla: The Return**
Marfinn, Kyle   **3623**

**Carnacki the Ghost Finder**
Hodgson, William Hope   258, 509,
670

**The Carnelian Cube**
de Camp, L. Sprague   5645, 5647

**Carnival**
Johnstone, William W.   **2927**, 3366,
4010, 5624

**The Carnival of Destruction**
Stableford, Brian   1686, **5190**

**Carnival of Fear**
King, J. Robert   155, 465, 2516,
5847

**Carnivore**
Clark, Leigh   **1049**

*Carnivores*
Kreps, Penelope Banka   1049, 2779, **3232**

*Carnivores of Light and Darkness*
Foster, Alan Dean   **1996**

*Carnosaur*
Knight, Harry Adam   1256, 1379, **3191**

*Carol for Another Christmas*
Scarborough, Elizabeth Ann   1409, **4861**

*Carola*
Forrest, Felix C.   5105, 5106

*Carpe Diem*
Miller, Steve   35, **3907**, 4142, 4291, 4354, 4467

*Carrie*
King, Stephen   1203, 1926, 2915, **3127**, 3284, 3785, 4334, 4832, 5486, 5553

*Carriers*
Lynch, Patrick   99, 2720, 3337, 4413

*Carrion Comfort*
Simmons, Dan   55, 462, 1094, 1670, 1778, 1959, 2493, 3206, 3396, 3547, 4096, 4580, 4666, 4978, 5010, 5020, **5049**, 5399, 5405, 5475, 5690, 5704, 5899

*Cart and Cwidder*
Jones, Diana Wynne   1444, 1668, 3871, 4322, 4446, 4448, 5579, 5977, 5980, 6037

*The Cartoonist*
Costello, Sean   138, **1204**, 2904, 5398

*Carve the Sky*
Jablokov, Alexander   **2836**, 4103, 5107

*Casca: Panzer Soldier*
Sadler, Barry   359

*Casca: The Eternal Mercenary*
Sadler, Barry   358, 359

*Case and the Dreamer*
Sturgeon, Theodore   806

*The Case of Charles Dexter Ward*
Lovecraft, H.P.   1125, 1424, 3675, 3953

*A Case of Conscience*
Blish, James   707, 2523, 3599, 4567, 4736, 5635

*The Case of the Friendly Corpse*
Hubbard, L. Ron   3989

*The Case of the Police Officer's Cock Ring and the Piano Player Who Had No Fingers*
Lee, Edward   **3388**

*The Case of the Toxic Spell Dump*
Turtledove, Harry   672, 955, 1159, 1163, 1399, 2080, 3485, 4171, 4394, **5497**

*Cassandra Rising*
Laurance, Alice   4825, 4826

*Cast a Cold Eye*
Ryan, Alan   840

*A Cast of Corbies*
Lackey, Mercedes   **3274**, 4986, 4989, 4991

*Castaways in Time*
Adams, Robert   5295

*The Castaways of Tanagar*
Stableford, Brian   564, 885, 1329

*Casting Fortune*
Ford, John M.   409, 767, 1473, 3154, 4994

*"Casting the Runes"*
James, M.R.   2020, 5111

*Casting the Runes and Other Ghost Stories*
James, M.R.   283, 1243

*Castle Dreams*
DeChancie, John   **1453**

*Castle Fantastic*
DeChancie, John   2380

*Castle for Rent*
DeChancie, John   4362

*Castle in the Air*
Jones, Diana Wynne   187, 355, 847, **2944**, 5218, 6043

*Castle in the Attic*
Winthrop, Elizabeth   331

*The Castle Keeps*
Offutt, Andrew J.   4600

*Castle Kidnapped*
DeChancie, John   5939

*The Castle of Crossed Destinies*
Calvino, Italo   2406, 4263, 4359

*Castle of Days*
Wolfe, Gene   237, 244, 2576, **5938**

*Castle of Deception*
Lackey, Mercedes   1839, **3275**, 3490, 4495, 4991

*Castle of Dreams*
Speer, Flora M.   6071

*The Castle of the Silver Wheel*
Edgerton, Teresa   **1741**, 5002

*Castle Perilous*
DeChancie, John   166, 182, 183, 1529, 1584, 1979, 2617, 2622, 2623, 2627, 2628, 2644, 2804, 4316, 4387, 4405, 4435, 4970, 5208, 5337, 5646

*Castle Roogna*
Anthony, Piers   30, 677

*Castle Spellbound*
DeChancie, John   **1454**

*Castle War!*
DeChancie, John   **1455**

*Castleview*
Wolfe, Gene   2622, 2623, 4173, 4362, 5903, **5939**

*The Cat*
Stine, R.L.   **5285**

*Cat-A-Lyst*
Foster, Alan Dean   1895, **1997**, 2036, 2620, 3536, 4143, 4157, 4288, 5589, 6060

*The Cat-Dogs*
Finnis, A.   1693, 2772

*The Cat From Outer Space*
Key, Ted   3500

*Cat House*
Peak, Michael   1895, 3120, 3377, 4143, 4157

*The Cat Jumps and Other Stories*
Bowen, Elizabeth   3360

*Cat People*
Brandner, Gary   4472

*Cat Scratch Fever*
Harper, Tara K.   **2550**

*Catacomb*
Laurance, Andrew   2312, **3347**, 3958

*Catacombs*
Farris, John   2672, 3551, 3565, 4816

*Catamount*
Peak, Michael   4143, **4273**

*Cataract*
Harper, Tara K.   3500

*Catastrophe*
Buzzati, Dino   3443, 3461, 3464

*Catastrophe's Spell*
Brenner, Mayer Alan   3, 4, 605, **671**, 1206

*Catch a Falling Star*
Brunner, John   882, 885

*Catch the Lightning*
Asaro, Catherine   **218**

*The Catch Trap*
Bradley, Marion Zimmer   5264

*The Caterpillar's Question*
Anthony, Piers   **164**, 550, 951, 1478, 2644

*Catfantastic*
Norton, Andre   1369, 1895, 2413, 3377, 3500, 3740, 4273, 4543, 5252

*Catfantastic II*
Norton, Andre   2413, **4143**, 4543, 5252

*Catfantastic III*
Norton, Andre   **4144**

*Catfantastic IV*
Norton, Andre   **4145**

*Cathedral of Thorns*
Frankos, Steven   **2041**

*Cathouse*
Ing, Dean   129, **2828**, 3649, 3723, 4124, 4125, 4372, 4640

*Cathy IV*
Lucas, Frances   1559, **3539**, 4245

*Catnip*
Bloch, Robert   3145

*Cat's Cradle*
Vonnegut, Kurt Jr.   1412, 2100, 2103, 2722, 2859, 3311, 3313, 3439, 4028, 4029, 4035, 4607

*Cat's Eye*
Johnstone, William W.   **2928**, 3371

*Cat's Gambit*
Gadallah, Leslie   451, **2099**

*Cats Have No Lord*
Shetterly, Will   259, 4921, 5063, 5159

*Cats in Space and Other Places*
Fawcett, Bill   **1895**, 3536, 4054, 4144, 4145, 5252

*The Cats of Seroster*
Westall, Robert   2944

*Cat's Paw*
Taylor, L.A.   1657, 3080, 3120, 3740, 4054, 4145, **5409**, 5967

*Cats Raise the Dead*
Murphy, Shirley Rousseau   **4054**

*Catseye*
Norton, Andre   983, 1657, 2420, 4138

*Catspaw*
Vinge, Joan D.   481, 2690, 2691, 3644, 4287, 5039

*The Catswold Portal*
Murphy, Shirley Rousseau   1657, 2358, 3120, **4055**, 5143

*Catwings*
Le Guin, Ursula K.   **3377**, 3740, 6076

*Catwoman*
Abbey, Lynn   **14**, 2124, 2391, 2392, 4215

*Caught in Crystal*
Wrede, Patricia C.   176, 642, 4323, 5509, 5733

*Caught in the Crossfire*
Drake, David   **1628**

*The Cauldron of Plenty*
Taylor, Keith   1957

*Caverns of Socrates*
McKiernan, Dennis L.   **3831**

*The Caves of Steel*
Asimov, Isaac   77, 160, 253, 254, 255, 476, 830, 1336, 2005, 2093, 2527, 2684, 2685, 3000, 3315, 3425, 3918, 4121, 4389, 4470, 4747, 4903, 5836

*Caviar*
Sturgeon, Theodore   233, 234

*Celebrity Vampires*
Greenberg, Martin H.   1799, 2071, **2382**, 5688

*Celestial Chess*
Bently, Thomas   4092

*Celestial Dogs*
Russell, J.S.   **4734**

*Celestial Inventory*
Tem, Steve Rasnic   200, 5876

*Celestial Matters*
Garfinkle, Richard   **2140**, 5321, 5512, 5513

*The Celestial Railroad and Other Stories*
Hawthorne, Nathaniel   722

*Celestis*
Park, Paul   **4241**

*Celia*
Jensen, Ruby Jean  1505, 2333, 2608, 2609, 2612, **2900**, 3130, 3139, 3205, 3365, 3857, 3858

*The Cell*
Case, David  5442

*The Cellar*
Laymon, Richard  **3365**, 5120

*Cellars*
Shirley, John  20

*The Celts*
Malterre, Elona  3502

*The Cement Garden*
McEwan, Ian  1027, 2111, 5808

*Cemetery of Angels*
Hynd, Noel  **2821**, 5468

*Cemetery World*
Simak, Clifford D.  885

*Centaur Aisle*
Anthony, Piers  677

*The Centurion's Empire*
McMullen, Sean  **3854**

*Century 21*
Kuryluk, Ewa  **3263**

*A Century of Ghost Stories*
Anonymous  1310

*A Century of Horror: 1970-1979: The Greatest Stories of the Decade*
Drake, David  **1629**

*A Century of Horror Stories*
Wheatley, Dennis  1, 2968

*A Century of Progress*
Saberhagen, Fred  5906

*The Ceremonies*
Klein, T.E.D.  137, 860, 1079, 2929, 3496, 3615, 4003, 4568, 4754, 5112, 5340, 5893

*The Cerulean Storm*
Denning, Troy  2621

*Cetaganda*
Bujold, Lois McMaster  **758**, 5548

*Chain Letter*
Jensen, Ruby Jean  853, 2415

*Chain Letter*
Pike, Christopher  1692

*Chain of Attack*
DeWeese, Gene  526, 903, 1663, 1923

*Chain Reaction*
Tine, Robert  504, 1508

*Chaingang*
Miller, Rex  **3899**

*Chains of Command*
McCay, Bill  **3767**, 5457

*Chains of Darkness, Chains of Light*
Sagara, Michelle  2096, **4781**, 5127

*Chains of Light*
Thomas, Quentin  **5449**

*The Chalchiuhite Dragon*
Morris, Kenneth  3107, **4020**

*Challenge of the Clans*
Flint, Kenneth C.  3059, 3060, 3501, 3504, 3506, 4266, 4267, 4268, 5962, 5963

*Challenger's Hope*
Feintuch, David  **1899**, 4973

*Challenges*
Green, Sharon  **2354**

*The Chameleon Corps*
Goulart, Ron  2921, 3345

*A Chance Child*
Paton Walsh, Jill  2614

*The Chance Factor*
Gallagher, Diana G.  **2109**

*The Change*
Longyear, Barry B.  2909, **3520**

*The Change War*
Leiber, Fritz  1275, 4164

*Changeling*
Kubasik, Christopher  976, 1591, 1889, **3245**, 4821, 5135, 5731

*Changeling*
Leigh, Stephen  2830, 2831, 2833, **3425**

*The Changeling*
Rusch, Kristine Kathryn  3123, 4259, **4714**

*Changeling*
Zelazny, Roger  4994

*The Changeling Garden*
Elze, Winifred  **1806**

*The Changeling Prince*
Vande Velde, Vivian  **5554**

*The Changeling Sea*
McKillip, Patricia A.  1177, 1179, 5293, 5629

*The Changeover*
Mahy, Margaret  330, 1179, 3163, 4079, 4080

*Changer*
Lindskold, Jane M.  **3474**

*Changespell*
Durgin, Doranna  **1703**, 4669, 5554

*Changeweaver*
Ball, Margaret  **313**, 1042, 1104, 3098, 4146

*Changing Fate*
Waters, Elisabeth  **5629**

*The Chantry Guild*
Dickson, Gordon R.  353, 418

*Chanur's Homecoming*
Cherryh, C.J.  1997, 2099, 3307, 4137, 5141

*Chanur's Legacy*
Cherryh, C.J.  **981**, 1988, 4855, 4967, 5363

*Chanur's Venture*
Cherryh, C.J.  2099, 4350, 5985

*The Chaos Balance*
Modesitt, L.E. Jr.  **3925**

*Chaos Come Again*
Baird, Wilhelmina  **293**, 4353, 5890

*The Chaos Gate*
Sherman, Josepha  1839, 3479, 3489, 3490

*Chaos in Lagrangia*
Reynolds, Mack  5188

*Chaos Mode*
Anthony, Piers  **165**

*Chapterhouse: Dune*
Herbert, Frank  4551

*Chariot*
Grant, Charles L.  **2304**

*Chariot of Fire*
Hales, E.E.Y.  960

*The Chariots of Ra*
Bulmer, Kenneth  3777

*Charlemagne's Champion*
Asten, Gail Van  2662

*Charlemagne's Champion*
Van Asten, Gail  3846, 4519, **5534**

*Charles Beaumont: Selected Stories*
Beaumont, Charles  531, 579

*Charles Fort Never Mentioned Wombats*
Coulson, Robert  4546

*Charlie and the Chocolate Factory*
Dahl, Roald  4338

*Charlie's Bones*
Thrasher, L.L.  **5468**

*Charlotte's Web*
White, E.B.  1090, 2786

*The Charm*
Niswander, Adam  911, 1886, 2340, 3081, 3671, 3680, 3967, **4111**, 4238, 4309, 5053, 5249, 6078

*Charmed*
Singer, Marilyn  1837, **5070**, 5559, 5822

*Charmed Life*
Taylor, Bernard  **5399**

*Chase the Morning*
Rohan, Michael Scott  1475, 1947, 3849, **4658**

*Checkmate*
Baker, Eric T.  **297**

*Chekhov's Journey*
Watson, Ian  508, 1418, **5633**

*Cherished Blood*
Tan, Cecilia  699, 3177, **5386**

*Chernevog*
Cherryh, C.J.  **982**, 3281, 4699, 5741

*Cherokee Bat and the Goat Guys*
Block, Francesca Lia  **546**

*Chess with a Dragon*
Gerrold, David  1493, 3345, 3521, 4217

*The Chessboard Queen*
Newman, Sharan  1857, 5970, 5971

*Chicago Loop*
Theroux, Paul  **5443**

*Chicago Red*
Meluch, R.M.  208, 3863, **3873**

*Chicks in Chainmail*
Friesner, Esther  316, 649, 650, 651, 765, 1808, 1811, **2072**, 2144, 3290, 5018

*A Child Across the Sky*
Carroll, Jonathan  460, 620, 898, **917**, 1085, 1278, 2995, 3541, 4683, 4734

*The Child Garden*
Ryman, Geoff  2913, 2997, **4756**, 5145, 5491

*Child of an Ancient City*
Williams, Tad  2085, 3410, 3414, 5336, **5827**

*A Child of Elvish*
Berberick, Nancy Varian  **457**, 1290

*Child of Faerie*
Yolen, Jane  3737

*Child of Faerie, Child of Earth*
Sherman, Josepha  1741, 3275, **4985**, 5217

*Child of Shadows*
Coyne, John  1080, **1236**, 2334, 4340

*Child of the Eagle*
Friesner, Esther  350, **2073**, 5511

*Child of the Grove*
Huff, Tanya  739

*Child of the Journey*
Berliner, Janet  **466**

*Child of the Light*
Gluckman, Janet  466, **2244**, 5079, 6029

*Child of the Northern Spring*
Woolley, Persia  2939, 3827

*Child of the River*
McAuley, Paul J.  3440, 3819

*The Child Queen*
McKenzie, Nancy  **3827**

*Childhood's End*
Clarke, Arthur C.  156, 202, 402, 594, 3238, 3521, 3792, 4016, 4506, 4642, 5636, 5660, 5860, 5909

*Children of Amarid*
Coe, David B.  **1095**

*Children of Dune*
Herbert, Frank  707, 5561

*Children of Enchantment*
Bush, Anne Kelleher  **787**, 1513, 2625

*Children of God*
Russell, Mary Doria  **4735**

*Children of Green Knowe*
Boston, L.M.  2949

*The Children of Hamelin*
Spinrad, Norman  **5170**

*The Children of Hamlin*
Carter, Carmen  1384, 2064

*The Children of Llyr*
Walton, Evangeline  1668, 1764

*The Children of Men*
James, P.D.  **2870**

**Children of Morrow**
Hoover, H.M.   878, 4827

**Children of the Atom**
Shiras, Wilmar H.   3340

**Children of the Blood: Book Two of The Sundered**
Sagara, Michelle   **4782**

**Children of the Drake**
Knaak, Richard A.   **3166**

**Children of the Dusk**
Berliner, Janet   **467**

**Children of the Earth**
Wells, Catherine   5492, **5743**

**Children of the End**
Clements, Mark A.   **1084**, 2779, 3204

**Children of the Jedi**
Hambly, Barbara   76, 103, 114, 117, **2500**, 2914, 4299

**Children of the Mind**
Card, Orson Scott   **883**

**Children of the Night**
Blackburn, John   4733

**Children of the Night**
Lackey, Mercedes   891, 1151, 1450, 2370, 2517, 3073, 3254, 3259, **3276**, 4362, 4709

**Children of the Night**
Simmons, Dan   279, 1463, 4755, **5050**, 5172, 5852

**Children of the Storm**
Tallis, Robyn   6057

**Children of the Thunder**
Brunner, John   **733**, 874, 1165, 1637, 1648, 2474, 2475, 3742, 4343, 4504, 4827, 4950, 5258, 5907, 6008

**Children of the Vampire**
Kalogridis, Jeanne   279, **3003**

**Children of the Wind: Five Novellas**
Wilhelm, Kate   2261, **5807**

**The Children of Wrath**
Reichert, Mickey Zucker   **4518**

**The Children Star**
Slonczewski, Joan   760, 3000, 3231, 5068, **5090**, 5437, 6080

**The Children's Hour**
Clegg, Douglas   **1077**

**The Children's Hour**
Pournelle, Jerry   1331, 3649, 4124, 4125, **4372**

**Child's Play III**
Costello, Matthew J.   **1194**, 2878, 2899, 2902, 3217, 3782, 3784

**A Chill in the Blood**
Elrod, P.N.   **1793**

**Chilled to the Bone**
Garcia, Robert T.   **2118**, 3224, 3228

**Chiller**
Blake, Sterling   2498, 4066

**Chiller**
Boyll, Randall   **610**, 1078, 1080, 1971

**Chillers**
Chizmar, Richard T.   **1018**, 4314

**Chillers for Christmas**
Dalby, Richard   **1307**, 2894

**Chimaera's Copper**
Anthony, Piers   **166**

**Chimera**
Barth, John   2129, 4731

**Chimera**
Rosenblum, Mary   1761, 2729, **4677**

**China House**
Lardo, Vincent   3852

**China Mountain Zhang**
McHugh, Maureen F.   927, 1968, 2952, 3029, **3817**, 5253

**Chinese Fairy Tales and Fantasies**
Roberts, Moss   849

**Chitty Chitty Bang Bang**
Fleming, Ian   4338

**Chocky**
Wyndham, John   2787

**The Chocolate War**
Cormier, Robert   5789

**Choice Cuts**
Boileau, Pierre   1205

**A Choice of Destinies**
Scott, Melissa   350, 590, 1855, 2140, 5506, 5507, 5510, 5512

**A Choice of Gods**
Simak, Clifford D.   5909

**Choose Your Enemies Carefully**
Charrette, Robert N.   566, **971**, 1591, 1935, 3245, 4304, 5135, 5731

**Chorus Skating**
Foster, Alan Dean   197, **1998**, 3269, 4524

**The Chosen**
Lee, Edward   2743, **3389**, 5100

**The Christening Quest**
Scarborough, Elizabeth Ann   16, 3634

**Christine**
King, Stephen   2316, 2915, 3320, 4022, 5323, 5486

**Christmas Bestiary**
Greenberg, Rosalind M.   **2412**, 2587, 2588, 2589, 5024

**A Christmas Carol**
Dickens, Charles   2276

**Christmas Forever**
Hartwell, David G.   2456, **2587**

**Christmas Ghosts**
Cramer, Kathryn   1307, 1311, 1313, 4541

**Christmas Ghosts**
Cramer, Kathryn   2276

**Christmas Ghosts**
Resnick, Mike   1311, 1313, 2276, 2587, 2894, **4541**, 4861

**Christmas Ghosts: An Anthology**
Manley, Seon   1311, 1313, 2276, 2894, 4541

**Christmas Magic**
Hartwell, David G.   2146, **2588**

**Christmas on Ganymede and Other Stories**
Greenberg, Martin H.   2412, 2456, 2587, 2588, 2589, 4720, 5024

**Christmas Slaughter**
Grant, Mark   **2323**

**Christmas Stars**
Hartwell, David G.   2412, **2589**, 5024

**Chrome**
Nader, George   3029

**Chrome Circle**
Lackey, Mercedes   1321, **3277**, 3887, 4980

**Chronicle of Deryni**
Kurtz, Katherine   5542

**The Chronicles of Corum**
Moorcock, Michael   1240

**The Chronicles of Don Sebastian**
Daniels, Les   5191

**The Chronicles of Greystone Bay**
Grant, Charles L.   5888

**Chronicles of King Arthur**
Hopkins, Andrea   227, 266, 267, 1270, 2745, 2746, **2767**, 3062, 4987

**The Chronicles of Master Li and Number Ten Ox**
Hughart, Barry   **2803**

**The Chronicles of Narnia**
Lewis, C.S.   1447, 1803

**The Chronicles of Pern: First Fall**
McCaffrey, Anne   2371, **3721**, 4999, 5001

**Chronicles of Thomas Covenant**
Donaldson, Stephen R.   896

**Chronocules**
Compton, D.G.   160

**Chrysalis**
Wilson, David Niall   **5880**

**Chthon**
Anthony, Piers   3693

**The Chymical Wedding**
Clarke, Lindsay   84, **1063**, 1397, 1746

**Ciara's Song**
Norton, Andre   **4146**

**Cinder**
DeMarinis, Rick   618

**Cinderblock**
Young, Janine Ellen   1167, 1348, **6047**, 6063

**Cinnabar Shadows**
Abbey, Lynn   **15**, 1290

**The Cipher**
Koja, Kathe   2762, **3194**

**Circle of One**
Fullilove, Eric James   **2092**, 4192, 5576, 5596

**A Circle of Witches**
Haining, Peter   4411, 6034

**Circuit of Heaven**
Danvers, Dennis   **1348**

**Circumpolar!**
Lupoff, Richard   5830

**The Circus of Dr. Lao**
Finney, Charles G.   1282, 2303, 2565, 3137, 4010, 4057, 5264

**A Circus of Hells**
Anderson, Poul   3907, 3928

**Circus of the Damned**
Hamilton, Laurell K.   2255, **2515**

**The Circus of the Earth and Air**
Stevens, Brooke   1186, 2266, 4432, **5264**, 5409

**Circus World**
Longyear, Barry B.   5215

**The Citadel of the Autarch**
Wolfe, Gene   4242

**Cities in Flight**
Blish, James   9, 232, 402, 445, 1055, 1627, 3722, 5303

**Cities of the Dead**
Paine, Michael   2439, 3526, 4050, 5312, 5695

**Citizen of the Galaxy**
Heinlein, Robert A.   62, 1903, 1948, 3767, 4043, 4453, 4952

**Citizen Vampire**
Daniels, Les   1794, 1795

**City**
Simak, Clifford D.   252, 874, 3240, 5040, 5586, 5589

**The City and the Stars**
Clarke, Arthur C.   445, 4065

**City at the Edge of Time**
Morris, Janet   2502, **4015**, 4202, 4614

**A City in Winter**
Helprin, Mark   **2653**

**City Jitters**
Fowler, Christopher   4133

**City Life**
Barthelme, Donald   2641

**The City, Not Long After**
Murphy, Pat   43, 46, 323, 334, 335, 496, 547, 551, 721, 766, 792, 820, 919, 2028, 2219, 2706, 2998, 3046, 3084, 3449, 4030, **4051**, 4104, 4325, 4360, 4474, 4631, 4750, 5209, 5268, 5592, 5909, 5911, 6009

**City of Baraboo**
Longyear, Barry B.   5215, 5264

**City of Bones**
Wells, Martha   **5748**

**City of Darkness**
Kelly, Erin   3229

**City of Darkness: Unseen**
Kelly, Erin   23, 3224, 5797

**City of Diamond**
Emerson, Jane   **1807**, 3927, 5725

**The City of Gold and Lead**
Christopher, John   221

**City of Golden Shadow**
Williams, Tad  **5828**

**City of Illusions**
Le Guin, Ursula K.  4153, 4592, 4595

**City of Iron**
Williamson, Chet  2308, **5843**

**City of Pain**
Terra, John  **5438**

**City of Sorcery**
Bradley, Marion Zimmer  3746, 4269

**City of the Chasch**
Vance, Jack  631

**City of the Dead**
Lieberman, Herbert  1410

**City of the Sorcerers**
Herbert, Mary H.  **2673**, 5529

**The City of the Sun**
Stableford, Brian  564

**City of Truth**
Morrow, James  1727, 2338, **4030**

**City on Fire**
Williams, Walter Jon  **5835**

**The City on the Edge of Forever**
Ellison, Harlan  1225, **1784**, 1853

**The City Outside the World**
Carter, Lin  2414

**The City Who Fought**
McCaffrey, Anne  83, **3722**, 5298

**Civil War Ghosts**
Greenberg, Martin H.  **2383**

**Civil War Ghosts**
McSherry, Frank Jr.  5155

**Civil War Ghosts**
McSherry, Frank D. Jr.  2230, 5098

**Civilian Slaughter**
Rouch, James  44

**Clan Ground**
Bell, Clare  846, 1895, 4143

**Clan of the Cave Bear**
Auel, Jean M.  178, 268, 667, 668, 669, 731, 870, 881, 889, 1539, 1632, 1838, 2166, 2167, 2168, 2169, 2170, 2581, 2582, 2583, 4320, 4817, 4818, 4819, 5444

**Clan of the Shape-Changers**
Levy, Robert  **3446**

**The Clan of the Warlord**
Boyer, Elizabeth H.  **604**, 844, 4491

**Clarion**
Wilson, Robin Scott  3085

**Clarion I-III**
Wilson, Robin Scott  1766, 1767, 5953

**Clarion II**
Wilson, Robin Scott  3085

**Clarion III**
Wilson, Robin Scott  3085

**The Clarion Awards**
Knight, Damon  1618

**Clarke County, Space**
Steele, Allen  127, 134, 356, 1055, 1788, 1965, 1970, 2100, 2486, 2660, 3448, 3604, 3770, 4295, 4483, 4937, 4955, 4962, 5032, 5089, 5130, 5188, **5241**, 5451, 5545, 5566, 5598, 5836, 5840, 5957, 6020

**Clark's Law**
Mortimore, Jim  367, 1387, 1654, 3096, 4833, 5598

**Clash by Night**
Williamson, Chet  494, 696, 4186, **5844**

**The Classic Fairy Tales**
Opie, Iona  4890

**Classic Tales of Horror and the Supernatural**
Pronzini, Bill  **4440**

**Classical Chinese Tales of the Supernatural and the Fantastic**
Kao, Karl S.Y.  6026

**The Claus Effect**
Nickle, David  1506

**The Claw**
Campbell, Ramsey  3408, 5085

**Claw**
Eulo, Ken  **1850**, 2779, 3701, 4414, 4415, 4688

**Claw Hammer**
Anderson, Paul Dale  2599

**Claw of the Conciliator**
Wolfe, Gene  4242

**The Claws of Axos**
Dicks, Terrance  5261

**Clay's Ark**
Butler, Octavia E.  3236

**CLD**
Milan, Victor  1552

**The Cleanup**
Skipp, John  1052, 3527

**The Cleft and Other Odd Tales**
Wilson, Gahan  **5901**

**The Clewiston Test**
Wilhelm, Kate  5184

**Clicking Stones**
Glenn, Nancy Tyler  74, 662, 1590, **2242**, 2295, 3579, 3915, 4882

**Climbing Olympus**
Anderson, Kevin J.  **102**, 2788

**Clipjoint**
Baird, Wilhelmina  **294**, 3484, 3711, 5576, 6048

**Clique**
Yermakov, Nicholas  4220

**Clock Strikes Sword**
Hammell, Ian  2529

**The Clock Strikes Twelve**
Wakefield, H. Russell  779, 875, **5610**

**A Clockwork Orange**
Burgess, Anthony  862, 3716

**Clone**
Cowper, Richard  2870, 5890

**The Clone**
Wilhelm, Kate  5352

**The Clone Crisis**
McKeone, Lee  **3829**

**Cloned Lives**
Sargent, Pamela  5732

**The Cloning of Joanna May**
Weldon, Fay  95, **5732**

**Close Encounters of the Third Kind**
Spielberg, Steven  1490, 2048

**Close Encounters with the Deity**
Bishop, Michael  6067

**Close to the Bone**
Morris, Mark  775, 2018

**Close to the Bone**
Taylor, Lucy  693, 938, 2655, 2860, 3100, 3176, 3367, 3393, 3669, 4885, **5411**

**Cloud Castles**
Rohan, Michael Scott  **4659**

**The Cloud People**
Kelly, Robert B.  **3050**

**The Cloud Walker**
Cooper, Edmund  4152, 4602, 4619, 5383

**Cloudcry**
Van Scyoc, Sydney J.  2372

**Clouds End**
Stewart, Sean  **5272**

**The Clouds of Magellan**
Nighbert, David F.  2836, **4103**

**The Clouds of Saturn**
McCollum, Michael  1986, **3770**

**Cloud's Rider**
Cherryh, C.J.  **983**, 2289

**Cloven Hooves**
Lindholm, Megan  639, 744, 1440, 1471, 2693, 3173, **3470**, 4985, 5177, 5180, 5916

**The Club Dumas**
Perez-Reverte, Arturo  333

**Cluster**
Anthony, Piers  958, 1995

**Cluster Command**
Drake, David  **1630**, 4374, 6014

**The Coachman Rat**
Wilson, David Henry  737, 1810, 5427, **5879**

**Cobra**
Zahn, Timothy  589, 1322, 1326, 1900, 2016, 2212, 2435, 4378, 4984

**Cobra Curse**
Dolan, Bill  **1567**, 3013

**Cobra Event**
Preston, Richard  3577

**The Cockroaches of Stay More**
Harington, Donald  **2544**, 5612

**Code of the Lifemaker**
Hogan, James P.  83, 446

**Codename Wolverine**
Golden, Christopher  **2256**

**Codgerspace**
Foster, Alan Dean  **1999**

**CoDominium: Revolt on War World**
Pournelle, Jerry  **4373**, 5292

**The Coelura**
McCaffrey, Anne  3840

**Cohort of the Damned**
Keith, Andrew  1546, **3034**

**Cold Allies**
Anthony, Patricia  **157**, 5515, 5517

**Cold as Ice**
Sheffield, Charles  1254, 2476, **4950**, 5540, 5859

**Cold at Heart**
Hopkins, Brian  41, **2768**, 5388

**Cold Blood**
Chizmar, Richard T.  538, 544, **1019**, 2278, 2280, 2600, 3598

**A Cold Blue Light**
Kaye, Marvin  2245

**The Cold Cash War**
Asprin, Robert  4932, 5457

**Cold Chills**
Chizmar, Richard T.  3324

**Cold Comfort Farm**
Gibbons, Stella  1027

**Cold Eye**
Blunt, Giles  437, **556**, 694, 1204, 1975, 2030, 2292, 3193, 3196, 3197, 3640, 3691, 4790

**Cold Fire**
Koontz, Dean R.  655, 3134, **3203**, 3415, 3678

**Cold Hand in Mine**
Aickman, Robert  3879, 3880, 5329

**Cold in July**
Lansdale, Joe R.  1831, 2162, 3052, **3323**

**Cold Iron**
Michaels, Melisa  3264, **3886**, 5061

**Cold Kiss**
Longstreet, Roxanne  2149, **3517**, 5078

**Cold Moon over Babylon**
McDowell, Michael  1860

**The Cold One**
Pike, Christopher  **4327**, 4837

**Cold Print**
Campbell, Ramsey  539, 1494, 3532

**Cold Shocks**
Sullivan, Tim  2814, 2815, 3228, **5350**

**Cold War**
Archer, Nathan  4285

**Cold Whisper**
Hautala, Rick  **2605**, 2631, 3040, 3640

**Cold White Fury**
Amos, Beth  **97**

**The Collected Feghoot**
Briarton, Grendel  **677**, 4637, 4639

**Collected Fictions**
Borges, Jorge Luis  **573**, 818

**Collected Ghost Stories**
Wilkins-Freeman, Mary E.  5772

**The Collected Ghost Stories of E.F. Benson**
Benson, E.F.  45, **454**, 779, 1243, 2846, 3633, 4141, 5610, 5611

**The Collected Ghost Stories of M.R. James**
James, M.R.  2905, 3633

**The Collected Ghost Stories of Mrs. J.H. Riddell**
Bleiler, Everett F.  4968

**The Collected Ghost Stories of Mrs. J.H. Riddell**
Riddell, J.H.  2158, 2707, 4969

**The Collected Ghost Stories of Oliver Onions**
Onions, Oliver  1252, 2846

**Collected Poems**
Lovecraft, H.P.  486

**The Collected Robert Sheckley**
Sheckley, Robert  234, 5805

**The Collected Short Stories of Philip K. Dick**
Dick, Philip K.  5346

**Collected Stories**
Beaumont, Charles  532

**Collected Stories**
Matheson, Richard  429, 529, 530, 532, 533, 537, 623, 2277, 3138, 3333, **3683**, 3689, 5901

**Collected Stories**
Singer, Isaac Bashevis  4890

**The Collected Stories of Philip K. Dick**
Dick, Philip K.  54, 1753, 5344, 5349

**The Collected Stories of Philip K. Dick, Volume One: The Short Happy Life of the Brown Oxford**
Dick, Philip K.  **1519**

**The Collected Stories of Philip K. Dick, Volume Two: We Can Remember It for You Wholesale**
Dick, Philip K.  **1520**

**The Collected Stories of Robert Silverberg, Volume 1: Secret Sharers**
Silverberg, Robert  **5028**

**Collected Tales and Stories**
Shelley, Mary  **4968**

**The Collected Tales of Walter de la Mare**
de la Mare, Walter  5763, 5764, 5765

**The Collector**
Fowles, John  1656, 2113, 2428, 3002, 3094, 3133, 3402, 4185

**The Collector of Hearts: New Tales of the Grotesque**
Oates, Joyce Carol  3195, **4181**

**A College of Magics**
Stevermer, Caroline  315, 557, 979, 1065, 1790, 2032, 2263, 2269, 2354, 2355, 2356, 2956, 3080, 3278, 3303, 3509, 3511, 3942, 4459, 4528, 4686, 4700, 4740, 5137, **5266**, 5458, 5490, 5728, 5811, 5967, 5976, 5978, 6057

**Collidescope**
Chetwin, Grace  221, **1011**, 5088

**Colony**
Bova, Ben  3199, 4962, 5241

**The Color of Distance**
Thomson, Amy  377, 1991, 2006, 2237, 2953, 3733, 4735, **5461**, 5804

**The Color of Evil**
Hartwell, David G.  1373

**The Color of Her Panties**
Anthony, Piers  **167**

**Colors in the Dreamweaver's Loom**
Hilgartner, Beth  5070

**The Colors of Hell**
Paine, Michael  3607, **4234**

**Colossus**
Jones, D.F.  126, 4232, 4381, 4857, 5632

**The Colour of Magic**
Pratchett, Terry  174, 197, 2075, 2616, 5034, 5840

**The Colour out of Space and Others**
Lovecraft, H.P.  728

**The Colour out of Time**
Shea, Michael  1497, 3548, 3566, 3567, 3568, 4112, 4449, 5884

**Coma**
Cook, Robin  93, 1561, 1832, 1939, 2206, 2867, 3996, 4874, 5897

**Come Before Christ and Murder Love**
Home, Stewart  **2754**, 4732

**Comeback Tour: The Sky Belongs to the Stars**
Yeovil, Jack  4821, 5089, 5957, **6020**

**A Coming of Age**
Zahn, Timothy  632

**The Coming of Conan**
Howard, Robert E.  5599

**The Coming of the Horseclans**
Adams, Robert  2397

**The Coming of the King**
Tolstoy, Nikolai  3352, 5534

**The Coming of the Quantum Cats**
Pohl, Frederik  582, 2012, 5908

**The Coming of Wisdom**
Duncan, Dave  993

**Commencement**
James, Roby  **2877**

**Commitment Hour**
Gardner, James Alan  **2134**, 2237

**The Committee**
Buckland, Raymond  397, **752**, 2824

**Common Clay: 20 Odd Stories**
Aldiss, Brian W.  **54**

**Common Threads**
Hoffman, Nina Kiriki  200

**Common Time**
Blish, James  5305

**Communion: A True Story**
Strieber, Whitley  2034

**Communipath Worlds**
Elgin, Suzette Haden  642, 653, 1263

**The Companions**
Daniell, Tina  4368

**The Company of Glory**
Pangborn, Edgar  365, 886

**A Company of Stars**
Stasheff, Christopher  1771, **5215**

**The Compass of the Soul**
Russell, Sean  **4740**

**The Compass Rose**
Le Guin, Ursula K.  790, 5807

**Competition**
Green, Sharon  **2355**

**The Compleat Werewolf and Other Tales of Fantasy and Science Fiction**
Boucher, Anthony  **579**

**The Compleate Crow**
Lumley, Brian  4315

**The Complete Bolo**
Laumer, Keith  1642, 1896, 4194

**The Complete Compleat Enchanter**
de Camp, L. Sprague  1812, 2014, 2080, 2616, 3015, 3650, 4392, 4395, 4399, 4404, 4971, 5694

**The Complete Egoist**
Sturgeon, Theodore  448

**Complete Fairy Tales**
Perrault, Charles  849

**The Complete Fairy Tales and Stories**
Andersen, Hans Christian  2447

**The Complete Fairy Tales of George MacDonald**
MacDonald, George  2447

**The Complete Fairy Tales of the Brothers Grimm**
Grimm, Jacob Ludwig  225, **2447**, 3844

**The Complete Ghost Stories of Charles Dickens**
Dickens, Charles  1597

**The Complete Jack the Ripper**
Rumbelow, Donald  3987

**The Complete John Silence Stories**
Blackwood, Algernon  258, **509**

**The Complete Masters of Darkness**
Etchison, Dennis  1629, **1844**, 2590, 5031

**The Complete Pegana**
Dunsany  **1699**

**The Complete Robot**
Asimov, Isaac  78, 3425, 4903

**The Complete Short Stories of H.G. Wells**
Wells, H.G.  3148

**The Complete Short Stories of Saki**
Saki  2846

**Complete Stories and Poems**
Poe, Edgar Allan  722

**The Complete Stories of Robert Bloch, Volume 1: Final Reckonings**
Bloch, Robert  **531**

**The Complete Stories of Robert Bloch, Volume 2: Bitter Ends**
Bloch, Robert  **529**

**The Complete Stories of Robert Bloch, Volume 3: Last Rites**
Bloch, Robert  **530**

**The Complete Stories - Volume 1**
Asimov, Isaac  **233**, 4706, 5551

**The Complete Stories - Volume 2**
Asimov, Isaac  **234**

**The Computer Connection**
Bester, Alfred  927, 1861, 3994

**Conan and the Manhunters**
Roberts, John Maddox  907, 910

**Conan and the Treasure of Python**
Roberts, John Maddox  2983, **4616**

**Conan at the Demon's Gate**
Green, Roland J.  907, 910, 2983

**The Conan Chronicles**
Jordan, Robert  **2983**

**Conan of the Red Brotherhood**
Carpenter, Leonard  **906**

**Conan, Scourge of the Bloody Coast**
Carpenter, Leonard  **910**

**Conan the Barbarian**
Howard, Robert E.  906, 907, 909, 910, 2347, 2348, 2782, 2983, 3501, 5110, 5599

**Conan the Bold**
Roberts, John Maddox  908, 4293

**Conan the Champion**
Roberts, John Maddox  908

**Conan the Conqueror**
Howard, Robert E.  909, 1838, 1856, 2347, 2348, 3172, 4621

**Conan the Fearless**
Perry, Steve  2983

**Conan the Formidable**
Perry, Steve  906, 908, 909, 910, **4293**, 4617

**Conan the Free Lance**
Perry, Steve  2347, 2348, 4616

**Conan the Gladiator**
Carpenter, Leonard  **907**, 2983

**Conan the Great**
Carpenter, Leonard  4293, 4617

**Conan the Guardian**
Green, Roland J.  908, 909, **2347**, 4616

**Conan the Indomitable**
Perry, Steve  **4294**

**Conan the Invincible**
Jordan, Robert   906, 908, 909, 4293, 4617

**Conan the Magnificent**
Jordan, Robert   2347, 2348, 4616

**Conan the Outcast**
Carpenter, Leonard   **908**

**Conan the Relentless**
Green, Roland J.   906, **2348**

**Conan the Rogue**
Roberts, John Maddox   **4617**

**Conan the Savage**
Carpenter, Leonard   **909**

**Conan the Valiant**
Green, Roland J.   4293

**Conan the Victorious**
Jordan, Robert   908, 909, 2347, 2348

**Conan the Warlord**
Carpenter, Leonard   2347, 2348

**Concrete Hotel**
Caldon, C. Christopher   **839**

**Concrete Island**
Ballard, J.G.   323, 2580

**A Confederacy of Dunces**
Toole, John Kennedy   5168

**Confederacy of the Dead**
Gilliam, Richard   **2230**, 4880, 5098, 5099, 5155

**Confederation Matador**
Bone, J.F.   2575, 5230

**Conference with the Dead**
Lamsley, Terry   1671

**Confessional**
Olesker, Jack   5342

**Conflict**
Hamilton, Peter F.   **2522**

**Conflict of Honors**
Miller, Steve   4142, 4291, 4354, 4467

**Conglomeros**
Browner, Jesse   558, **729**, 1444, 2186, 3263, 3855, 4046

**Conjure Wife**
Leiber, Fritz   280, 438, 2713, 2826, 3390, 3499, 4738, 5290

**Conjure Wife/Our Lady of Darkness**
Leiber, Fritz   **3416**, 3690, 5072, 5791

**The Conjurer Princess**
Vande Velde, Vivian   **5555**

**A Connecticut Yankee in King Arthur's Court**
Twain, Mark   1419, 1532, 2044, 2045, 2047, 2616, 4971, 6035, 6038

**Conquerers From the Darkness**
Silverberg, Robert   2252

**Conqueror**
Marshall, Edison   2187, 5395

**Conqueror's Pride**
Zahn, Timothy   **6051**

**Conrad's Quest for Rubber**
Frankowski, Leo   **2043**

**Consider Phlebas**
Banks, Iain M.   2365, 2366, 5116, 5365, 5637

**The Consolation of Nature, and Other Stories**
Martin, Valerie   3195

**Consolidation**
Hamilton, Peter F.   **2523**

**Conspicuous Consumption**
Allmen, Stewart Von   5535

**Conspicuous Consumption**
Von Allmen, Stewart   2321, 3990, 4059

**Conspiracy**
King, J. Robert   **3121**

**The Conspiracy Files**
Greenberg, Martin H.   **2384**

**Contact**
Sagan, Carl   202, 380, 4280

**Contact and Commune**
Smith, L. Neil   129, 165, 211, 3603, 4017, **5129**, 5174, 5514, 5564, 5932

**Contagion**
Connor, John David   **1136**, 3577, 4786

**The Contaminant**
Reiffel, Leonard   2787

**The Continent of Lies**
Morrow, James   583

**Contrarywise**
Green, Kate   4519

**Control Freak**
Faust, Christa   **1890**

**Convergence**
Green, Sharon   1943, **2356**

**Convergence**
Sheffield, Charles   **4951**

**Converse and Conflict**
Smith, L. Neil   **5130**

**The Convocation**
Holt, John R.   **2748**

**The Convulsion Factory**
Hodge, Brian   663, 1789, **2698**, 3667, 4313, 5600

**The Cook**
Kressing, Harry   3497, 3814

**The Copper Crown**
Kennealy-Morrison, Patricia   392, 1476, 1660, 1961, 3060, 3068, 3078, 3305, 3354, 3357, 3358, 3502, 3697, 4492, 4608, 4989, 5684

**Copper Star**
Arthurs, Bruce D.   **217**

**The Coral Kingdom**
Niles, Douglas   **4106**

**Core**
Preuss, Paul   **4416**

**The Cormorant**
Gregory, Stephen   **2429**, 4249

**Cormyr: A Novel**
Greenwood, Ed   **2425**, **2426**

**The Cornish Trilogy**
Davies, Robertson   **1397**

**Corona**
Bear, Greg   527

**Correspondence**
Thomas, Sue   **5450**, 5462

**The Corridors of Time**
Anderson, Poul   4164, 5999

**Corrupting Dr. Nice**
Kessel, John   **3083**, 4247, 5874

**Cortez on Jupiter**
Hogan, Ernest   766, 1449, **2721**, 2847, 3046, 3082, 3452, 4642, 4643, 4679, 5565

**Corum: The Coming of Chaos**
Moorcock, Michael   3418, **3978**

**Cosm**
Benford, Gregory   **444**, 793, 5830

**The Cosmic Computer**
Piper, H. Beam   897

**The Cosmic Engineers**
Simak, Clifford D.   5863

**Cosmicomics**
Calvino, Italo   677, 3443

**Costigan's Needle**
Sohl, Jerry   5088, 5114

**Count Geiger's Blues**
Bishop, Michael   **499**, 2393, 3642, 3647, 3768, 3891, 3977, 5148, 5262, 5567

**The Count of Eleven**
Campbell, Ramsey   **853**, 1489, 4436

**Count Scar**
Brittain, C. Dale   **702**

**Count Zero**
Gibson, William   2911, 2916, 3491, 3890, 4099, 4451, 4452, 5841, 5960

**Counter Attack**
Drake, David   1896

**The Counterfeits**
Kelley, Leo P.   2882

**Counterparts**
Royle, Nicholas   5816

**Counting the Cost**
Drake, David   2054, 3937, 4982

**The Country of the Blind**
Flynn, Michael   2217

**Court Duel**
Smith, Sherwood   **5137**

**The Court of the Stone Children**
Cameron, Eleanor   2614, 2951, 3444, 5559

**The Courts of Sorcery**
McConnell, Ashley   **3773**

**The Courtship of Princess Leia**
Wolverton, Dave   109, 2500, 3820, 4299, **5950**

**Coven**
Lee, Edward   3042, 3183, **3390**

**Coven**
Rimmer, Steven William   **4591**

**A Coven of Vampires**
Lumley, Brian   3111, **3549**

**A Covenant of Justice**
Gerrold, David   **2207**

**The Covenant of the Crown**
Weinstein, Howard   526, 2922, 4081

**Covenant with the Vampire**
Kalogridis, Jeanne   **3004**, 6010

**Cowboy Feng's Space Bar and Grille**
Brust, Steven   173, 392, **740**, 1454, 2299, 3285, 3299, 4637, 4638, 4639

**Cowboy Heaven**
Goulart, Ron   5997

**Coyote**
Gadol, Peter   **2100**, 3523, 5361, 5578

**Cradle**
Clarke, Arthur C.   3398

**Cradle of Splendor**
Anthony, Patricia   **158**

**The Craft of Light**
Emerson, Ru   3282

**The Crafters**
Stasheff, Christopher   **5216**

**Cranford**
Gaskell, Elizabeth Cleghorn   1743, 3383

**Crash**
Ballard, J.G.   780, 2580

**Crashcourse**
Baird, Wilhelmina   251, **295**, 5173, 5259, 5619

**Crashlander**
Niven, Larry   **4118**

**The Crate**
King, Stephen   4414

**The Crawling Dark**
Dunn, Pauline   1136, **1698**, 2934

**Crazy Time**
Wilhelm, Kate   582, 4276

**Created By**
Matheson, Richard Christian   138, 426, 1846, 3213, **3691**, 5422

**Creature**
Saul, John   1944, 2205, 2284, 3041, 3153, 4059, 4083, 4087, **4839**, 5789

**The Creature in the Teacher**
Pike, Christopher   1097, 5291

**Creatures of Light and Darkness**
Zelazny, Roger   36, 1637, 1648, 1979, 2658, 5449

**Creatures of the Abyss**
Leinster, Murray   189

**A Creed for the Third Millennium**
McCullough, Colleen   2093, 4678

**Creekers**
Lee, Edward   **3391**

**Crescent in the Sky**
Moffitt, Donald **3946**

**Cries of the Children**
McNally, Clare **3856**

**The Crimson Legion**
Denning, Troy 13, 2621, 2624

**The Crimson Sky**
Rosenberg, Joel **4669**

**Crisis on Doona**
McCaffrey, Anne 3066, **3723**, 4137, 4138, 4170, 4176, 4300, 4350

**Crisis on Vulcan**
Strickland, Brad 2109

**Critical Threshold**
Stableford, Brian 1248, 1719

**Cromm**
Flint, Kenneth C. 1498, **1957**, 4174

**Cross a Dark Bridge**
Churchman, Deborah **1027**, 4344, 5808

**Cross and Crescent**
Shwartz, Susan **5014**

**Cross of Blood**
Jeter, K.W. **2909**

**Cross the Stars**
Drake, David 2004

**The Cross-Time Engineer**
Frankowski, Leo 1328, 1341, 1677, 1982, 4151, 4523, 4799, 5036, 5694

**Crossover**
Friedman, Michael Jan **2063**, 5019, 5596

**Crossover**
McCay, Bill **3768**

**Crossroad**
Graf, L.A. 10

**Crossroad**
Hambly, Barbara **2501**

**The Crossroads of Time**
Norton, Andre 1626, 2119, 3993, 5996

**Crosstime Traffic**
Watt-Evans, Lawrence 206, 3648, **5641**

**Crota**
Goingback, Owl **2251**, 3129, 5249

**Crow and Weasel**
Lopez, Barry 40, 190, 1356, 1527, 1867, 2100, **3523**, 4008, 4380, 5578

**The Crow: City of Angels**
Williamson, Chet 494, 696

**The Crow: Shattered Lives and Broken Dreams**
O'Barr, James 494, 696, 1044, **4186**, 5844

**The Crown Jewels**
Williams, Walter Jon 261

**The Crown of Dalemark**
Jones, Diana Wynne **2945**, 4163, 5510, 5512

**Crown of Empire**
Yarbro, Chelsea Quinn **6014**

**Crown of Shadows**
Friedman, C.S. **2057**, 5941

**Crown of Stars**
Tiptree, James Jr. 3644

**A Crown of Swords**
Jordan, Robert 1775, **2984**

**Crown of the Serpent**
Wold, Allen L. 5129, 5564, **5932**

**Crucible**
Denning, Troy **1484**

**Crucifax**
Garton, Ray 697, 1048, 2147, 3312

**Crucifax Autumn**
Garton, Ray 1301, 1845, 2935, 3679, 5323

**Cruiser Dreams**
Morris, Janet 5524

**Crusade**
Lowder, James **3537**, 4108

**Crusade**
Weber, David 5785

**Crusader's Torch**
Yarbro, Chelsea Quinn 3602, **6015**

**The Cry of the Onlies**
Klass, Judy 1554

**Cry Republic**
Mitchell, Kirk 1955, **3917**

**Cry Wolf**
Von Gunden, Kenneth **5586**

**Crygender**
Thomas, Thomas T. 4640, **5451**

**Crypt of the Shadowking**
Anthony, Mark 1290, 3538

**Crypt Orchids**
Schow, David J. **4886**, 5005

**Cryptozoic**
Aldiss, Brian W. 175, 188

**The Crysalids**
Wyndham, John 3251

**The Crystal Cave**
Stewart, Mary 227, 991, 1189, 1270, 2745, 2746, 3506, 3806, 3827

**The Crystal Curtain**
Bayer, Sandy 3852

**The Crystal Dragon**
Knaak, Richard A. **3167**

**The Crystal Empire**
Smith, L. Neil 178, 5781, 5906

**Crystal Express**
Sterling, Bruce 423, 425, 804, 807, 3086, 3234, 4053, 4998, 5007, **5255**, 5837, 6067

**The Crystal Gryphon**
Norton, Andre 658, 5002

**Crystal Line**
McCaffrey, Anne **3724**

**The Crystal Palace**
Eisenstein, Phyllis 16, 1042, 3765

**The Crystal Rose**
Bohnhoff, Maya Kaathryn 560

**The Crystal Shard**
Salvatore, R.A. 3537, 4458

**The Crystal Ship**
Silverberg, Robert 4825

**Crystal Singer**
McCaffrey, Anne 1071, 2477, 2478, 3286, 3888, 3938, 4870, 4996, 5774

**The Crystal Sorcerers**
Forstchen, William R. **1979**

**The Crystal Stair**
Chetwin, Grace 3043

**The Crystal Star**
McIntyre, Vonda N. 103, 109, 2500, **3820**, 4299, 5527, 5950

**The Crystal Sword**
Martine-Barnes, Adrienne 4266, 4267, 4268

**The Crystal Warriors**
Forstchen, William R. 2042, 2463

**Crystal Witness**
Tyers, Kathy 4044, **5524**

**The Crystal World**
Ballard, J.G. 3192, 3612, 3792, 4135

**Crystals of Air and Water**
Goldin, Stephen 6087

**The Crystals of Mida**
Green, Sharon 1071

**Cthulhu 2000**
Turner, Jim 148, 461, 4423, 4426, 4428, 4429, **5493**

**The Cthulhu Cycle**
Price, Robert M. **4423**

**The Cthulhu Mythos**
Derleth, August **1494**, 3566, 3567, 3568

**Cthulhu: The Mythos and Kindred Horrors**
Howard, Robert E. 3531

**Cthulhu's Heirs**
Stratman, Thomas M.K. 148, 461, 2399, 2978, 4422, 4423, 4424, 4425, 4426, 4428, 4430, **5325**

**Cuckoo's Egg**
Cherryh, C.J. 1595, 2194, 2416, 5548

**Cugel's Saga**
Vance, Jack 4277, 4945

**Cujo**
King, Stephen 1708, 2199, 2429, 5146, 5236, 5539, 5894

**Cul-De-Sac**
Martin, David **3638**

**The Cult of Loving Kindness**
Park, Paul 3539, **4242**

**Cults of Horror**
Greenberg, Martin H. 2601

**Cup of Clay**
Douglas, Carole Nelson 286, 563, **1583**, 2042, 2127, 2358, 2617

**The Cup of Morning Shadows**
Edghill, Rosemary **1747**

**Curfew**
Rickman, Phil **4587**

**Curious Fragments**
London, Jack 5746

**The Currents of Space**
Asimov, Isaac 4043, 4940

**The Curse**
Tigges, John 5186, **5472**

**The Curse of Camp Cold Lake**
Stine, R.L. **5286**

**The Curse of Rathlaw**
Saxon, Peter 5843, 5846

**The Curse of Sagamore**
Dalkey, Kara 1514, 4387

**The Curse of Slagfid**
Boyer, Elizabeth H. 2760

**Curse of the Black Heron**
Lisle, Holly **3479**

**Curse of the Dead**
Caine, Geoffrey 5562

**Curse of the Magazine Killers**
Jonas, Gary **2937**

**Curse of the Mistwraith**
Wurts, Janny 1640, 1674, 1864, 1908, 4462, 4516, 4522, 4528, **6001**

**Curse of the Vampire**
Caine, Geoffrey **832**

**The Cursed**
Duncan, Dave **1674**, 5735

**Cursed Be the Child**
Castle, Mort **937**

**The Cursed Land**
McLaren, Teri 2827

**Cutthroat**
Slade, Michael 2931, **5084**

**The Cutting Edge**
Duncan, Dave 712, 717, 719, 1105, **1675**, 1732, 1733, 2271, 3486, 3624, 4986, 5391

**Cutting Edge**
Etchison, Dennis 2965, 3959, 3960, 4278, 4812, 4888, 5855

**CV**
Knight, Damon 594, 1666, 2732, 3008, 4923

**Cyber Way**
Foster, Alan Dean 35, 118, 158, 164, 190, 433, 522, 753, 784, 891, 936, 995, 1159, 1725, 1788, 1858, 1974, **2000**, 2084, 2309, 2320, 2343, 2486, 2499, 2658, 2682, 2836, 2861, 3109, 3485, 3704, 4121, 4302, 4364, 4864, 4940, 5109, 5199, 5278, 5497, 5744, 5751, 5836, 6023

**Cyberbooks**
Bova, Ben 481, **582**

**The Cyberiad**
Lem, Stanislaw 850, 3431

**Cybernarc**
Cain, Robert **829**, 1406, 3665, 4590, 4935, 4936, 4938, 4939

**Cybernetic Jungle**
Lewitt, S.N. **3449**, 4339

**The Cybernetic Samurai**
Milan, Victor 77, 79, 475, 806, 808, 1168, 2526, 2579, 3604, 3795, 4193, 4704, 5213, 5452

**The Cybernetic Shogun**
Milan, Victor **3890**

**The Cybernetic Walrus**
Chalker, Jack L. 110, **951**, 2470, 4898

**Cybersex**
Jones, Richard Glyn 1362

**Cyberstealth**
Lewitt, S.N. 1535, **3450**, 3453, 3454, 3875, 4618

**Cyberweb**
Mason, Lisa 483, **3662**

**Cyborg**
Caidin, Martin 5476

**The Cyborg From Earth**
Sheffield, Charles 4379, **4952**

**Cycle of Fire**
Clement, Hal 377, 434

**Cycle of Fire Trilogy**
Wurts, Janny 5563

**The Cygnet and the Firebird**
McKillip, Patricia A. **3839**

**The Cylon Death Machine**
Larson, Glen A. 2602

**Cyteen**
Cherryh, C.J. 326, 566, 567, 928, 931, **984**, 1538, 1554, 1574, 1606, 1865, 2050, 2051, 2065, 2171, 2248, 2389, 2466, 3000, 3236, 3248, 3735, 3994, 4559, 4560, 4898, 4933, 4955, 5354, 5434, 5525, 5572, 5637, 5732, 5917, 5920, 5921, 5922

**Cytheria**
Calder, Richard **835**


**D**


**The D. Case: The Truth about the Mystery of Edwin Drood**
Dickens, Charles **1524**

**The Daemon in the Machine**
Savage, Felicity **4848**

**Daemonic**
Laws, Stephen 1894, 5119

**Dagger**
Drake, David 1955, 4202

**The Dagger and the Cross: A Novel of the Crusades**
Tarr, Judith 965, 3261, 5014, 5015, **5393**, 5506

**Dagger Magic**
Kurtz, Katherine **3256**, 3408

**Dagger's Edge**
Logston, Anne **3508**

**Daggerspell**
Kerr, Katharine 704, 742, 1288, 1660, 2031, 3018, 3060, 3273, 3291, 3292, 3839, 3926, 3975, 4462, 4980, 5715, 5727, 5734

**Dagon**
Chappell, Fred 3533, 3548, 3566, 5167

**Dagon and Other Macabre Tales**
Lovecraft, H.P. 5104

**Dagon's Bell and Other Discords**
Lumley, Brian 1494, 1495, 1496

**Dai-San**
Van Lustbader, Eric 1329

**Daily Voices**
Goldstein, Lisa **2261**, 3945

**The Daleth Effect**
Harrison, Harry 1666

**Damia**
McCaffrey, Anne 101, 2478, **3725**, 4553, 6053

**Damiano**
MacAvoy, R.A. 3714, 4869

**Damiano's Lute**
MacAvoy, R.A. 4869, 5222

**Damia's Children**
McCaffrey, Anne **3726**, 5672

**Damien**
Howard, Joseph 3445

**Damnation Alley**
Zelazny, Roger 86, 1238, 1644, 2323, 4600, 4602, 4604

**The Damnation Game**
Barker, Clive 2672, 3808, 3902, 4085

**Damnbanna**
Springer, Nancy 497, 1441, 3264, **5177**

**Dance Band on the Titanic**
Chalker, Jack L. 5114

**Dance Dance Dance**
Murakami, Haruki **4046**

**Dance of Death**
Elrod, P.N. **1794**

**Dance of the Dead**
Golden, Christie 155, 465, 1014, 3613, 5847

**The Dance of the Dead**
Matheson, Richard 5923

**The Dancer From Atlantis**
Anderson, Poul 5295

**Dancer of the Sixth**
Crean, Michelle Shirey 220, 312, **1254**, 1598, 3968, 5670

**The Dancers at the End of Time**
Moorcock, Michael **3979**, 4247

**The Dancers of Arun**
Lynn, Elizabeth A. 644, 653

**Dancer's Rise**
Clayton, Jo 641, **1064**, 5127

**Dancing Bears**
Saberhagen, Fred 3281, 4052, **4764**

**Dancing Jack**
Marks, Laurie J. **3624**, 4146

**Dancing on Air**
Kress, Nancy 411, **3240**

**Dancing Vac**
Lewitt, S.N. **3451**, 3453, 3454, 3875, 4618

**Dancing with Myself**
Sheffield, Charles 123, 237, 244, **4953**

**Dandelion Wine**
Bradbury, Ray 3136, 3754, 4131, 5060

**Dangerous Dames**
Jens, Tina L. **2891**

**Dangerous Nature**
Kirby, T.J. 2541, **3152**, 3701, 3901

**Dangerous Visions**
Ellison, Harlan 214, 215, 238, 239, 501, 1023, 1614, 1616, 1620, 4031, 4713, 4721, 5004, 5948

**Dante's Disciples**
Crowther, Peter **1280**

**Dante's Disciples**
Kramer, Edward E. 1281

**Dare**
Farmer, Philip Jose 3543

**Dare to Go A-Hunting**
Norton, Andre **4147**

**The Dark**
Herbert, James 943, 3370

**The Dark**
Neiderman, Andrew **4084**

**The Dark Abyss**
Coville, Bruce 1429, 3572

**The Dark-Angel**
Pierce, Meredith Ann 1444

**Dark Angels: Lesbian Vampire Stories**
Keesey, Pam 730, 2117, 2508, 5387

**Dark at Heart**
Lansdale, Joe R. 544, 1018, 2278, 2279, 2600, **3324**, 3598

**The Dark Beyond the Stars**
Robinson, Frank M. 1059, 1645, 1875, 1992, 2829, 3787, 3874, **4626**, 5000, 5198, 5201, 5937, 5943

**The Dark Bright Water**
Wrightson, Patricia 2170, 4946

**The Dark Chamber**
Cline, Leonard 2702

**Dark Channel**
Garton, Ray **2150**, 3310, 4024, 5562

**Dark City**
Lauria, Frank **3351**

**Dark Companions**
Campbell, Ramsey 2017, 2866, 5329

**The Dark Country**
Etchison, Dennis 429, 623, 864, 865, 866, 2319, 3687, 4530, 4886, 4889

**Dark Crimes II: Modern Masters of Noir**
Gorman, Ed 538, 544

**Dark Crimes: Great Noir Fiction From the '50's to the '90's**
Gorman, Ed 2600, 3324

**The Dark Cry of the Moon**
Grant, Charles L. 2768, 5861

**The Dark Crystal: A Novel**
Smith, A.C.H. 3404, 5572

**Dark Dance**
Lee, Tanith 2115, 2220, 2492, 2493, **3406**

**Dark Debts**
Hall, Karen 1888, **2494**

**The Dark Descent**
Hartwell, David G. 226, 1629, 1844, **2590**, 3027, 4440, 5031, 5924

**Dark Destiny**
Kramer, Edward E. 23, **3224**, 3229, 5797, 5798, 5882

**Dark Destiny II: Proprietors of Fate**
Kramer, Edward E. 23, **3225**, 5797, 5798

**Dark Destiny III: Children of Dracula**
Kramer, Edward E. 23, **3226**, 5797, 5798

**Dark Divide**
Acres, Mark **27**, 487, 1533, 1840

**The Dark Domain**
Grabinski, Stefan 573, 2225, **2294**, 3447, 5317

**Dark Dreaming**
Franklin, Pat **2040**, 3657

**The Dark Druid**
Flint, Kenneth C. 5962, 5963

**Dark Fantasies**
Morgan, Chris 2306, 3961, 4206, 4644, 5795

**Dark Father**
Piccirilli, Tom 2021, 2334, 4091, **4312**, 4728, 4883, 5657, 5986, 5992

**Dark Force Rising**
Zahn, Timothy 5917, **6052**

**Dark Forces**
McCauley, Kirby 1629, 1847, 2307, 2965, 5924

**Dark Fortune**
Byers, Richard Lee **795**

**Dark Genesis**
Keyes, J. Gregory 1387, **3096**

**Dark Gods**
Klein, T.E.D. 851, 864, 866

**The Dark Half**
King, Stephen 426, 810, 1846, **3128**, 3206, 3213, 3374, 3691, 5169, 5422, 5823, 5849

**The Dark Hand of Magic**
Hambly, Barbara   289, 1534, 2098, **2502**, 3107, 3634, 4614, 4699, 5741

**Dark Heart**
Daniell, Tina   154, 3155, 4368

**Dark Heart**
James, Betsy   731, **2857**

**Dark Heart**
Weis, Margaret   **5707**

**Dark Horizon**
Jeter, K.W.   2683, **2910**, 3243, 3520

**Dark Horse**
Herbert, Mary H.   223, 2397, 2552, **2674**, 4323, 4493

**Dark Hours**
Pini, Richard   **4335**, 4336, 4337

**The Dark Is Rising**
Cooper, Susan   371, 1033, 1330, 1447, 1668, 3078

**Dark Journey**
Morlan, A.R.   2565, **4010**

**The Dark Lady: A Romance of the Far Future**
Resnick, Mike   4781, 5548

**Dark Legacy**
Kostrubula, Mark A.   2932, **3220**

**Dark Legacy**
Vardeman, Robert E.   207, 2827

**Dark Legend**
Highwater, Jamake   **2686**, 4264

**Dark Lord of Derkholm**
Jones, Diana Wynne   **2946**

**Dark Love**
Collins, Nancy A.   **1118**, 1367, 2176, 2177, 2178, 2179, 2182, 2185, 2093

**Dark Lullaby**
Palmer, Jessica   **4237**

**Dark Magic**
Wells, Angus   2987, 5296, **5733**

**Dark Matter**
Reeves-Stevens, Garfield   **4509**, 5453

**Dark Mirror**
Duane, Diane   1385, **1658**, 2788, 4934

**Dark Mirror, Dark Dreams**
Green, Sharon   **2357**

**A Dark Night's Work and Other Stories**
Gaskell, Elizabeth Cleghorn   **2158**

**Dark of the Eye**
Clegg, Douglas   571, **1078**, 1843, 1971, 4012, 5850

**Dark of the Moon**
Hodgell, P.C.   4, 673, 936, 1068, 1072, 1073, 3175, 3421, 4653

**The Dark One**
Smith, Guy N.   **5118**

**Dark Piper**
Norton, Andre   4801

**Dark Prince**
Gemmell, David   **2187**, 5395

**Dark Prince**
Herber, Keith   **2663**

**The Dark Realm**
Kaufman, Douglas   5438

**Dark Reunion**
George, Stephen R.   1295, **2198**

**Dark Reunion**
Smith, L.J.   120, 1302, 4328, 5161

**Dark Rivers of the Heart**
Koontz, Dean R.   1973, 2157, 2322, **3204**

**Dark Seductions**
Alfonsi, Alice   **72**

**Dark Seeker**
Jeter, K.W.   3101, 4979, 5899

**The Dark Shore**
Lee, Adam   **3385**

**The Dark Side**
Knight, Damon   5691

**The Dark Side: Tales of Terror and the Supernatural**
Maupassant, Guy de   1596, **3694**

**Dark Silence**
Hautala, Rick   **2606**, 5472

**Dark Sky Legion**
Barton, William   **379**, 1337, 5449, 5745, 5951

**Dark Souls**
Porter, Barry   **4369**

**Dark Star**
Foster, Alan Dean   2979, 4298, 4626, 5280

**Dark Tales and Light**
Boston, Bruce   **578**

**Dark Tide**
Forrest, Elizabeth   441, 955, **1972**, 2557, 2749, 3783, 4715, 5121

**The Dark Tide**
McKiernan, Dennis L.   710, 711, 716, 2884, 2886

**Dark Time**
O'Callaghan, Maxine   1296, 3218, 3856, **4189**, 4650

**The Dark Tower Series**
King, Stephen   343

**The Dark Tower: The Gunslinger**
King, Stephen   341, 576, 2009, 2191, 5151, 5504

**Dark Twilight**
Citro, Joseph A.   **1036**, 2285, 3778

**Dark Tyrants**
Achilli, Justin   **23**, 5798, 5882, 5883

**Dark Universe**
Galouye, Daniel F.   656, 664, 3608

**Dark Visions**
Wright, T. Lucien   3135, **5987**

**Dark Water's Embrace**
Leigh, Stephen   **3426**

**Dark Winds**
Watkins, Graham   **5630**

**The Dark World**
Kuttner, Henry   3877

**Darkborn**
Costello, Matthew J.   **1195**, 3233, 4085, 5398

**Darkchild**
Van Scyoc, Sydney J.   1595, 4996, 5548

**Darkenheight**
Niles, Douglas   **4107**, 4795

**Darker Angels**
Somtow, S.P.   **5155**

**Darker Angels: Lesbian Vampire Stories**
Keesey, Pam   699, 1713, 2444, **3030**, 3177, 3618, 4689, 5386

**A Darker Geometry**
Martin, Mark O.   **3649**

**A Darker Magic**
Bedard, Michael   4079

**Darker Passions**
Bryant, Edward   213

**The Darker Passions: Carmilla**
Knight, Amarantha   **3177**

**The Darker Passions: Dr. Jekyll and Mr. Hyde**
Knight, Amarantha   **3178**

**The Darker Passions: Dracula**
Knight, Amarantha   **3179**

**The Darker Passions: Frankenstein**
Knight, Amarantha   199, 1409, **3180**

**The Darker Passions Reader**
Knight, Amarantha   **3176**

**The Darker Saints**
Hodge, Brian   20, 1298, **2699**, 4498

**Darker than You Think**
Williamson, Jack   603, 1822, 2789, 3053, 3877, 4582, 4604, 4764, 5756, **5861**

**The Darkest Road**
Kay, Guy Gavriel   3068, 5759

**The Darkest Thirst: A Vampire Anthology**
Anonymous   **150**

**Darkfall**
Koontz, Dean R.   661, 1125

**Darklands**
Royle, Nicholas   3363

**Darkling**
O'Rourke, Michael   **4223**

**Darkloom**
Osborne, Cary   **4225**

**Darkly the Thunder**
Johnstone, William W.   2316, **2929**

**Darkman**
Boyll, Randall   19, **611**, 1334, 3881, 3882, 3883, 5073

**Darkman #1: The Hangman**
Boyll, Randall   **612**

**Darkman #2: The Price of Fear**
Boyll, Randall   **613**

**Darkman #3: The Gods of Hell**
Boyll, Randall   **614**

**Darkman #4: The Face of Death**
Boyll, Randall   112, **615**

**Darkness**
Saul, John   1944, 2156, 3164, 3637, **4840**, 5250, 5314

**Darkness, I**
Lee, Tanith   303, 3253, **3407**, 4068, 4575, 4578

**A Darkness at Sethanon**
Feist, Raymond E.   2724, 4852

**The Darkness Before the Dawn**
Hughes, Ryan   13, 2624

**Darkness on the Ice**
Tilton, Lois   3601, 4755, **5475**

**A Darkness upon the Ice**
Forstchen, William R.   66

**Darkness Weaves**
Wagner, Karl Edward   907, 910, 3172, 3420, 3422

**The Darkness Within**
MacDonald, Shawn   **3585**, 5926

**Darkover Landfall**
Bradley, Marion Zimmer   4147

**Darksaber**
Anderson, Kevin J.   **103**, 4299

**Darkscope**
Falk, Margaret   **1860**, 2198

**Darkside**
Etchison, Dennis   916, **1845**, 3312, 3785, 5064, 5332, 5990

**Darkside: Horror for the Next Millennium**
Pelan, John   1281, 2176, 2893, 3184, **4278**, 5924

**Darkspell**
Kerr, Katharine   5715

**Darkthunder's Way**
Deitz, Tom   **1470**

**Darktraders**
bes shahar, eluki   **472**

**Darkwalker on Moonshae**
Niles, Douglas   2618, 4803

**Darwinia**
Wilson, Robert Charles   **5906**

**Daughter of Darkness**
Lake, Simon   5288

**Daughter of Darkness**
Spruill, Steven   **5183**

**Daughter of Elysium**
Slonczewski, Joan   210, 236, 249, 447, 665, 686, 892, 1083, 1336, 1724, 1769, 1872, 2008, 2049, 2820, 3231, 4241, 4698, 4893, **5091**, 5368, 5587, 5745

**Daughter of Magic**
Brittain, C. Dale   **703**

**Daughter of Prophecy**
Bush, Anne Kelleher   **788**, 5748

**Daughter of the Bear King**
Arnason, Eleanor  271, 1065, 1491,
   1678, 1684, 1686, 1703, 1704,
   1747, 2504, 2506, 3386, 3939,
   4448, 4669, 4798, 4868, 5178,
   5364, 5591, 5719

**Daughter of the Blood**
Bishop, Anne  **495**

**Daughter of the Bright Moon**
Abbey, Lynn  2095, 2987, 4265,
   5733

**Daughter of the Drow**
Cunningham, Elaine  **1287**

**Daughter of the Empire**
Feist, Raymond E.  3303, 3339,
   3581, 3906, 3905, 4741, 6001,
   6003, 6004

**Daughter of the Empire**
Wurts, Janny  3338

**Daughter of the Night**
Bergstrom, Elaine  **463**, 1286

**Daughter of Witches**
Wrede, Patricia C.  289, 4323

**Daughters of Darkness: Lesbian
   Vampire Stories**
Keesey, Pam  730, 1286, 1713,
   2117, 2444, 2508, **3031**, 3177,
   3181, 3182, 4689, 5154, 5385,
   5387

**David and the Phoenix**
Ormondroyd, Edward  1220, 1221,
   6076

**David Copperfield's Beyond
   Imagination**
Copperfield, David  **1186**

**David Copperfield's Tales of the
   Impossible**
Copperfield, David  410, **1187**

**David Starr, Space Ranger**
Asimov, Isaac  2765

**Davy**
Pangborn, Edgar  365, 886, 3788,
   4074, 5593

**Dawn**
Andrews, V.C.  **144**

**Dawn**
Butler, Octavia E.  100, 156, 278,
   296, 327, 377, 379, 383, 404, 469,
   566, 594, 656, 664, 685, 686, 838,
   1054, 1055, 1056, 1116, 1157,
   1255, 1362, 1569, 1586, 1587,
   1593, 1634, 1723, 1727, 1771,
   1924, 1932, 1964, 2008, 2037,
   2056, 2058, 2108, 2211, 2213,
   2215, 2287, 2419, 2539, 2578,
   2603, 2649, 2898, 2953, 2955,
   2997, 3000, 3001, 3047, 3063,
   3064, 3188, 3238, 3424, 3469,
   3476, 3792, 3944, 4000, 4016,
   4019, 4042, 4075, 4101, 4122,
   4123, 4126, 4217, 4219, 4241,
   4290, 4325, 4347, 4479, 4626,
   4635, 4756, 4761, 4762, 4853,
   4933, 4950, 5016, 5090, 5091,
   5092, 5108, 5130, 5157, 5303,
   5354, 5355, 5368, 5373, 5431,
   5435, 5436, 5461, 5492, 5499,
   5515, 5526, 5590, 5591, 5677,
   5956, 6048, 6080

**Dawn Land**
Bruchac, Joseph  **731**

**Dawn of the Dead**
Romero, George  4168, 4745, 4746,
   4831, 4834, 5313

**Dawn Song**
Marano, Michael  1117, **3620**

**Dawn's Uncertain Light**
Barrett, Neal Jr.  163, 188, 277, **365**,
   886, 4602

**The Day After Judgment**
Blish, James  4647

**A Day for Damnation**
Gerrold, David  2954, 5352

**The Day of Descent**
Reeves-Stevens, Judith  504, 1508,
   2909, 2910, 3520

**Day of the Cheetah**
Brown, Dale  2143, 3450, 3875

**Day of the Dead**
Gaiman, Neil  **2102**

**The Day of the Dolphin**
Merle, Robert  2838

**The Day of the Drones**
Lightner, A.M.  3243

**Day of the Minotaur**
Swann, Thomas Burnett  4159

**Day of the Snake**
Costello, Matthew J.  783, **1196**,
   5890

**The Day of the Tempest**
Rabe, Jean  **4457**

**The Day of the Triffids**
Wyndham, John  1806, 2344, 5858

**The Day of Their Return**
Anderson, Poul  4151

**Daybreak, 2250 A.D.**
Norton, Andre  3788

**Days of Air and Darkness**
Kerr, Katharine  **3067**

**Days of Atonement**
Williams, Walter Jon  116, 1665,
   2682, 3029, 3663, 4193, **5836**

**Days of Blood and Fire**
Kerr, Katharine  **3068**, 3936

**Days of Cain**
Dunn, J.R.  467, **1694**, 3064, 5874

**Days of the Dead**
McConnell, Ashley  1886, 2734,
   2903, **3774**, 4601, 4603, 5631

**Daystar and Shadow**
Johnson, James B.  4600

**Dayworld**
Farmer, Philip Jose  4720, 5546

**Dayworld Breakup**
Farmer, Philip Jose  **1869**

**Dayworld Rebel**
Farmer, Philip Jose  5193

**The Dazzle of Day**
Gloss, Molly  297, **2243**, 4735

**Dead Air**
Koke, Jack  5096

**Dead Boys**
Calder, Richard  **836**

**Dead Calm**
Williams, Charles  3756

**Dead Elvis**
Marcus, Greil  4810

**Dead End**
Smith, Guy N.  2156, **5119**

**Dead End: City Limits**
Olson, Paul F.  **4212**

**Dead Girls**
Calder, Richard  780, **837**

**Dead Heat**
Stone, Del Jr.  **5313**

**Dead in the Water**
Holder, Nancy  **2732**, 4715

**Dead in the West**
Lansdale, Joe R.  617, 1126, 1804,
   **3325**, 4255

**Dead Lines**
Skipp, John  2153, 3362, 4310,
   4885, 5008, **5082**, 5360

**The Dead Man's Kiss**
Weinberg, Robert  833, 1721, 2932,
   4733, **5695**

**Dead Meat**
Smith, Guy N.  **5120**

**Dead of Night**
Abella, Alex  **20**

**Dead Things**
Calder, Richard  **838**

**Dead Time**
Byers, Richard Lee  **796**

**Dead Voices**
Hautala, Rick  **2607**

**Dead Voices**
McDaniels, Abigail  2903, 2933,
   **3783**

**Dead Voices: Natural Agonies in the
   Real World**
Vizenor, Gerald  190, 2686, 4207,
   4208, 4380, **5578**, 5751

**Dead White**
Ryan, Alan  1193, 2927, 5756

**The Dead Zone**
King, Stephen  795, 800, 945, 1669,
   1780, 1975, 2318, 3193, 3203,
   3678, 3965, 4363, 4649, 5399,
   5987

**Deadly After Dark**
Gelb, Jeff  1361, **2174**

**Deadly Breed**
Kirby, T.J.  373, 488, 1346, 1850,
   2779, **3153**, 3701

**Deadly Communion**
Brookes, Owen  3128, 3203, 4471

**Deadly Dreams**
Schiller, Gerald A.  **4874**

**Deadly Friend**
Ferrario, Keith  **1926**, 2821, 3785,
   5064

**Deadly Games**
Friedman, Michael Jan  999

**Deadly Quicksilver Lies**
Cook, Glen  **1148**, 5061, 5459

**Deadly Relations**
Keyes, J. Gregory  2102

**Deadly Silents**
Killough, Lee  476, 2286, 3073

**Deadly Vengeance**
George, Stephen R.  **2199**

**Deadman Switch**
Zahn, Timothy  4594, 5298

**Deadrush**
Navarro, Yvonne  1507, **4073**

**Deadspawn**
Lumley, Brian  **3550**

**Deadspeak**
Lumley, Brian  **3551**

**Deadweight**
Devereaux, Robert  **1505**

**Dealer's Choice**
Martin, George R.R.  **3643**

**Dealers in Light and Darkness**
Wilder, Cherry  497, 3240

**Dealing with Dragons**
Wrede, Patricia C.  174, 329, 1220,
   1221, 1488, 1534, 1951, 2014,
   2362, 2413, 2944, 3941, 4390,
   4447, 5217, 5556, 5640, **5975**,
   6032, 6069

**The Dealings of Daniel Kesserich**
Leiber, Fritz  **3417**

**Deals with the Devil**
Resnick, Mike  3071, 3483, 3488,
   **4542**

**Deals with the Devil: An Anthology**
Davenport, Basil  1280, 4542

**The Death and Life of Superman**
Stern, Roger  999, 1667, 2393, 3768,
   **5262**

**Death Angel's Shadow**
Wagner, Karl Edward  3172, 4617

**Death Channels**
Vardeman, Robert E.  **5562**

**The Death Crystal**
Ames, J. Edward  **91**

**Death Dream**
Bova, Ben  107, 475, 507, **583**, 956,
   957, 2011, 2275, 2791, 4283,
   4342, 4860, 5753

**Death in Delhi**
Gygax, Gary  **2473**

**Death in Dixie**
Mosiman, Billie Sue  5098, 5099

**Death in the Spirit House**
Strete, Craig  1437, 1470

**Death Is a Lonely Business**
Bradbury, Ray  619

**Death Lands: Time Nomads**
Axler, James  2324, 2325

**The Death Mask and Other Ghosts**
Everett, H.D.  1673

**Death Masque**
Elrod, P.N. **1795**

**Death of a Darklord**
Hamilton, Laurell K. 1137, 1510,
**2516**

**Death of an Adept**
Kurtz, Katherine **3257**, 5773

**The Death of Chaos**
Modesitt, L.E. Jr. **3926**

**The Death of Grass**
Christopher, John 4279

**The Death of Sleep**
McCaffrey, Anne 1070, **3727**, 4170,
4176

**The Death of the Necromancer**
Wells, Martha 2758, **5749**

**The Death Prayer**
Bowker, David **602**

**Death Qualified: A Mystery of Chaos**
Wilhelm, Kate 891, 2559, 5054

**Death Race**
Alexander, David 1405

**Death Stalks the Night**
Cave, Hugh B. **940**, 3571, 5628

**Death Tour**
Michael, David J. 1625

**Death Walks Tonight**
Horowitz, Anthony **2772**

**Deathbeast**
Gerrold, David 5998

**Deathbird Stories**
Ellison, Harlan 3421, 4977

**Deathchain**
Greenhall, Ken 853, **2415**

**Deathgift**
Zeddies, Ann Tonsor **6061**

**Deathgrip**
Hodge, Brian 795, 800, **2700**

**Deathknight**
Offutt, Andrew J. **4201**

**The Deathless**
Murchison, Myles **4048**

**Deathport**
Campbell, Ramsey **854**, 2311, 5331

**Death's Arms**
Jeter, K.W. 474

**Death's Deputy**
Hubbard, L. Ron 3415

**Death's Door**
Wooley, John **5969**

**Death's Gray Land**
Shupp, Mike **5011**

**Death's Head**
Keegan, Mel **3029**

**Death's Loving Arms and Other Terror Tales**
Hanlon, John 4494

**Death's Master**
Lee, Tanith 495, 4849, 5931

**Deathscape**
Cecilione, Michael **945**

**Deathsong**
Borton, Douglas 575

**Deathstalker Honor**
Green, Simon R. **2364**

**Deathstalker Rebellion**
Green, Simon R. **2365**

**Deathstalker War**
Green, Simon R. **2366**

**Deathwalker**
Gates, R. Patrick **2159**, 3210

**Deathwalker**
Whalen, Patrick 427, 2251, 2340,
3081, 3325, 3671, 3895, 4111,
4113, 4238, 4309, 5249, **5769**,
6078

**Deathwalker on Moonshea**
Niles, Douglas 4805

**Deathweave**
Osborne, Cary **4226**

**Deathwing**
Jones, Neil **6023**

**Deathworld**
Harrison, Harry 1107, 1551, 1641,
2210, 3522, 4884

**Deathworld 3**
Harrison, Harry 1025

**The Deathworld Trilogy**
Harrison, Harry 420, 785, 1247,
1540, 1634, 1643, 2010, 2056,
2371, 3744, 4957

**Debtors' Planet**
Thompson, William R. 7, **5457**

**The Deceiver**
Cooper, Louise 1072, **1175**, 2521

**December**
Rickman, Phil **4588**

**Deception Well**
Nagata, Linda 2274, 2558, **4065**

**The Dechronization of Sam Magruder**
Simpson, George Gaylord **5067**,
5315

**Decision at Doona**
McCaffrey, Anne 1263, 1595, 1956,
2421

**Decoded Mirrors: Three Tales after Lovecraft**
Tem, Steve Rasnic 3317, 5194,
**5426**, 5446, 5884

**The Dedalus Book of Decadence: Moral Ruins**
Stableford, Brian 3089

**The Dedalus Book of German Decadence**
Furness, Ray 3089

**The Deed of Paksenarrion**
Moon, Elizabeth 4693, 4694, 5529

**Deep Domain**
Weinstein, Howard 2296, 5597

**Deep Freeze**
Hughes, Zach **2811**

**Deep Quarry**
Stith, John E. 2005, 2226, 4555,
**5302**, 5644

**The Deep Range**
Clarke, Arthur C. 318, 2838

**Deep Trek**
Axler, James **278**

**Deep Waters**
Hodgson, William Hope 3798

**Deep Wizardry**
Duane, Diane 4323

**Deepdrive**
Jablokov, Alexander **2837**

**A Deeper Sea**
Jablokov, Alexander **2838**, 5107,
5587

**The Deepest Sea**
Barnitz, Charles 136, **363**, 4518

**Deepwater Dreams**
Van Scyoc, Sydney J. 63, 2450,
3341, 3729, 4421, 4923, 5029,
**5541**, 5781

**The Deer's Cry: A Book of the Keltiad**
Kennealy-Morrison, Patricia **3060**

**Deerskin**
McKinley, Robin 1358, **3844**, 5912

**The Defenders**
Baldwin, Bill **309**, 4525, 4974, 5668

**The Defiance**
Baldwin, Bill **310**, 1652

**The Defiant Agents**
Norton, Andre 1011

**The Definitive Best of the Horror Show**
Silva, David B. 1017, 2773, **5025**

**Delan the Mislaid**
Marks, Laurie J. **3625**

**The Delicate Dependency**
Talbot, Michael 4578, 4665

**Deliver Us From Evil**
Harris, Allen Lee 3160

**Deliverance**
Dickey, James 2279

**The Delta**
Wilson, Colin **5878**

**Delta City**
Savage, Felicity 495, **4849**

**Delta Pavonis**
Kotani, Eric **3221**

**Delta Search**
Shatner, William **4930**

**Demogorgon**
Lumley, Brian 3220, **3552**

**The Demolished Man**
Bester, Alfred **476**, 1696, 1968,
2093, 2330, 2474, 2475, 2527,
3073, 4121, 4469, 4557, 5054,
5276, 5373, 5754, 5835

**Demolition Man**
Osborne, Richard 366, **4229**, 4286,
4559

**Demon**
Varley, John 508, 1418, 5234, 5840

**Demon and Other Tales**
Oates, Joyce Carol **4182**

**The Demon Awakens**
Salvatore, R.A. 1095, **4794**, 4848

**Demon Blade**
Garland, Mark A. **2141**

**Demon Blues**
Friesner, Esther 1014, 5649

**The Demon Breed**
Schmitz, James H. 595, 892, 899,
958, 1634, 1680, 2055, 2371,
2838, 2877, 3168, 3972, 4172,
4698, 4897, 5037, 5109, 5282,
5527, 5589, 5872

**Demon Dance**
Martindale, T. Chris 2251, 3325,
**3655**, 3967

**Demon Download**
Yeovil, Jack 1238, 2323, **6021**

**Demon Drums**
Severance, Carol 4784, **4922**

**Demon Fire**
Holleman, Gary L. **2743**, 3885,
5100, 5463

**The Demon King**
Bunch, Chris **770**

**Demon Knight**
Hood, Ken **2760**, 4852

**The Demon Lover and Other Stories**
Bowen, Elizabeth 601

**Demon Lovers and Strange Seductions**
Carter, Margaret L. 72, 1357, 1367,
3026, 4465, 5093

**Demon Moon**
Williamson, Jack 3629, **5862**

**Demon Night**
Straczynski, J. Michael **5322**

**Demon Pig**
Brush, Karen **737**, 846, 1821, 2848,
2850, 2851, 2853, 2855, 5974,
6025

**The Demon Princes: Volume One**
Vance, Jack **5544**, 5722

**The Demon Princes: Volume Two**
Vance, Jack **5545**

**Demon Seed**
Koontz, Dean R. 2157, 2872

**Demon Sex**
Knight, Amarantha 2177, **3181**

**Demon Shadows**
Sirota, Michael B. 1828, 4223, **5075**

**Demon Shield**
King, Bernard 2889

**The Demon Spirit**
Salvatore, R.A. **4795**

**Demon Within**
Reed, Dana **4499**

**Demons and Shadows: The Ghostly Best Stories of Robert Westall**
Westall, Robert **5763**

Title Index

**The Demons at Rainbow Bridge**
Chalker, Jack L.  **952**, 1046, 1719

**Demons by Daylight**
Campbell, Ramsey  **855**, 3447, 3461, 3463, 3464

**Demons Don't Dream**
Anthony, Piers  **168**, 2015, 4171, 4393

**Demons Five, Exorcists Nothing**
Blatty, William Peter  2448

**Demon's Fright**
Kreps, Penelope Banka  1215, **3233**

**Demons of the Dancing Gods**
Chalker, Jack L.  169, 652

**Demons of the Night: Tales of the Fantastic, Madness, and the Supernatural From Nineteenth Century France**
Kessler, Joan C.  **3089**

**Demons of the Sea**
Hodgson, William Hope  **2708**, 3798

**The Demons of the Upper Air**
Leiber, Fritz  4752

**The Demu Trilogy**
Busby, F.M.  1901, 3708, 3738, 5672

**Denner's Wreck**
Watt-Evans, Lawrence  3700, 5230, 6061

**Denver Is Missing**
Jones, D.F.  354

**Departures**
Turtledove, Harry  **5498**

**The Depford Trilogy**
Davies, Robertson  2817

**Derelict**
Hovorka, Robert  4285

**Derelict for Trade**
Norton, Andre  **4148**

**The Derelict of Death**
Clark, Simon  2709

**The Deryni Archives**
Kurtz, Katherine  1735, 2991, 4793

**Deryni Checkmate**
Kurtz, Katherine  256, 1175, 2360, 3399, 4163

**Deryni Rising**
Kurtz, Katherine  17, 256, 393, 630, 1110, 1174, 1175, 1702, 1742, 1863, 2188, 2560, 2561, 2988, 3016, 3058, 3123, 3154, 3171, 3284, 3288, 3304, 3305, 3399, 3436, 3482, 3540, 3635, 3652, 3697, 3699, 4258, 4259, 4485, 4492, 4533, 4714, 4730, 4783, 5581, 5737, 5754, 5811, 6002, 6003

**Descent**
Dee, Ron  **1465**

**Desert Eden**
Morgan, J.M.  656, 1482, 1566, 1568, 1932, 2328, 2999, 3429, 3862, **4000**, 5433, 5592, 5743

**Desert Fire**
Alexander, David  65

**Deserted Cities of the Heart**
Shiner, Lewis  2998, 3706, 5057

**Design for Great-Day**
Foster, Alan Dean  **2001**, 4859, 5565

**Desire Burn: Women's Stories From the Dark Side of Passion**
Berliner, Janet  **468**, 2891

**Desmodus**
Tem, Melanie  3396, 4581, **5421**

**Desmond: A Novel of Love and the Modern Vampire**
Dietz, Ulysses G.  **1541**

**Desolation Road**
McDonald, Ian  328, 547, 551, 622, 820, 1880, 2101, 2533, 5069

**Desperate Measures**
Faust, Joe Clifford  **1891**, 3828

**Desperate Pursuit**
Miklowitz, Gloria D.  5287

**Desperation**
King, Stephen  **3129**

**Destination: Mutiny**
Dalton, Sean  **1332**

**Destination: Showdown**
Davis, Jake  **1405**

**Destination Universe**
Van Vogt, A.E.  823

**Destination Unknown**
Crowther, Peter  **1281**

**Destination: Void**
Herbert, Frank  126

**Destined to Love**
Elizabeth, Suzanne  2497

**Destiny Doll**
Simak, Clifford D.  923

**Destiny in Disguise**
Elizabeth, Suzanne  2497

**The Destiny of the Sword**
Duncan, Dave  5709, 5712

**Destiny's Carnival**
Murphy, Warren  **4057**, 5264

**Destiny's Road**
Niven, Larry  2289, 3739, 3819, **4119**, 4999

**The Destroyer #1: Created, the Destroyer**
Sapir, Richard  359, 1547, 4229, 5476

**Destroying Angel**
Russo, Richard Paul  1548, 1825, 2033, 2092, 2218, 2219, 2527, 4192, 4300, 4366, **4749**, 5363

**Deus Ex Machina**
Brummels, J.V.  **732**

**The Deus Machine**
Ouellette, Pierre  3207, 3923, **4232**, 4283, 4860, 5632, 5753

**Deus X**
Spinrad, Norman  134, **5171**

**Deus-X: A Novel of Spiritual Terror**
Citro, Joseph A.  **1037**, 1296

**The Devil and Dan Cooley**
Lisle, Holly  **3480**

**The Devil in a Forest**
Wolfe, Gene  5579

**Devil in the Sky**
Cox, Greg  10, **1226**, 2296, 2917, 2922

**The Devil in Velvet**
Carr, John Dickson  464, 5061

**The Devil Is Dead**
Lafferty, R.A.  523

**The Devil Rides Out**
Wheatley, Dennis  751, 3408, 5111, 5692, 5696, **5773**

**Devil Stories**
Rudwin, Maximilian  1280

**The Devil Wives of Li Fong**
Price, E. Hoffman  4741

**Devil Worshippers**
Greenberg, Martin H.  **2385**, 4411, 4542

**The Devil You Say**
DeCarlo, Elisa  **1450**

**The Devil's Advocate**
Fleming, Gherbod  **1949**, 5701, 5702, 5882, 5883

**The Devil's Advocate**
Neiderman, Andrew  **4085**

**Devils and Demons**
Kaye, Marvin  1280, 4542

**Devils and Demons**
Serling, Rod  2385

**The Devil's Arithmetic**
Yolen, Jane  2244, 2272, 5079

**The Devil's Auction**
Weinberg, Robert  2304, 4315, 4960, **5696**, 5773

**The Devil's Bride**
Quinn, Seabury  5696

**The Devil's Churn**
Rusch, Kristine Kathryn  **4715**

**The Devil's Cradle**
Stewart, Kate  2748, **5269**

**The Devil's Day**
Blish, James  **525**, 3416

**Devil's Deal**
Austin, Richard  44, **277**

**The Devil's End**
Fowler, D.A.  71, **2023**, 2816, 3233, 4598

**Devil's Engine**
Sumner, Mark  **5356**

**The Devil's Footsteps**
Burke, John  1833, 3272, 4591

**The Devil's Game**
Anderson, Poul  714

**Devil's Gate**
Ergas, Elizabeth  947, **1833**, 3389, 5100

**The Devil's Generation**
Ghidalia, Vic  1716

**The Devil's Heart**
Carter, Carmen  **922**, 2065, 3920

**Devil's Kisses**
Parry, Michel  75, 2178, 2179, 2181, 2893, 5093, 5094

**The Devil's Laughter**
Johnstone, William W.  **2930**

**The Devil's Looking-Glass**
Rees, Simon  3677

**The Devil's Own**
Lofts, Norah  4048, 4591

**Devil's Race**
Avi  5286, 5289

**Devil's Tower**
Sumner, Mark  889, 3118, **5357**, 5504

**The Devouring**
Hawk, Douglas D.  **2615**

**The Devouring Void**
Rogers, Mark E.  **4653**

**Dhalgren**
Delany, Samuel R.  43, 805, 1720, 2771, 3456, 4051

**Dhampire**
Baker, Scott  1499, 2754

**Dhiammara**
Furey, Maggie  **2096**

**Diadem from the Stars**
Clayton, Jo  1439, 3973

**Diagnosis: Terminal**
Wilson, F. Paul  **5886**

**Dialing the Wind**
Grant, Charles L.  **2305**

**The Diamond Age**
Stephenson, Neal  107, 158, 809, 1458, 1929, 2377, 2728, 3711, 4708, **5253**, 5259, 5430, 5966

**Diamond Mask: A Novel**
May, Julian  **3697**

**The Diamond Moon**
Preuss, Paul  1661, **4417**

**The Diamond Throne**
Eddings, David  **1731**, 4045, 6007

**Diary of a Vampire**
Bowen, Gary  **600**, 948, 1541, 4069

**The Diary of Jack the Ripper: The Discovery, the Investigation, the Debate**
Harrison, Shirley  3987

**Diaspora**
Egan, Greg  **1759**, 2661

**Dictator**
Wu, William F.  5516, **5996**

**Did You Say Chicks?!**
Friesner, Esther  **2074**

**Die Softly**
Pike, Christopher  5285

**The Difference Engine**
Gibson, William   398, 443, 520, 1139, 1457, 1518, **2217**, 3931, 5450, 5501

**A Different Flesh**
Turtledove, Harry   175, 188, 1655

**Different Seasons**
King, Stephen   2305, 5056, 5060

**The Dig**
Foster, Alan Dean   **2002**, 3897

**Diggers**
Pratchett, Terry   1222, 1223, 1224, **4386**

**The Digging Leviathan**
Blaylock, James P.   1520

**The Digital Effect**
Perry, Steve   2916, **4295**

**Dimension of Miracles**
Sheckley, Robert   6062, 6070

**Dinner at Deviant's Palace**
Powers, Tim   1519

**Dinosaur Fantastic**
Resnick, Mike   2386, **4543**

**Dinosaur Planet**
McCaffrey, Anne   1986, 3221

**Dinosaur Samurai**
Leigh, Stephen   1417

**Dinosaur Summer**
Bear, Greg   **416**, 6084

**Dinosaurs!**
Dann, Jack   2386, 2468, 4543

**Dinosaurs**
Greenberg, Martin H.   **2386**

**Dinosaurs II**
Dann, Jack   2386

**Dinotopia**
Gurney, James   29, 306, 318, 385, 416, 1024, 1256, 2003, 2122, 2346, 2386, **2468**, 2654, 2980, 2981, 2982, 3156, 3382, 3427, 3428, 4456, 4543, 4597, 4854, 4855, 5479, 5972, 6032, 6069, 6076

**Dinotopia Lost**
Foster, Alan Dean   **2003**

**Diplomacy of Wolves**
Lisle, Holly   **3481**

**Diplomatic Act**
Jurasik, Peter   **2996**

**The Dirdir**
Vance, Jack   1025

**A Dirge for Stabis**
Cherryh, C.J.   256, 314, 2570

**Dirk Gently's Holistic Detective Agency**
Adams, Douglas   1453, 1919, 2228, 2480, 4247, 4389, 4390

**Dirty Work**
Cadigan, Pat   **804**

**Dirty Work**
McGirt, Dan   **3810**, 6066

**The Disappearance**
Wylie, Philip   3021, 4652

**Disappeared**
Silva, David B.   97

**Disciples of Cthulhu**
Berglund, Edward P.   148, **461**, 2399, 2978, 3535, 4422, 4423, 4425, 4426, 4427, 4428, 4429, 4430, 4431, 5325, 5698, 5884

**Disciples of Dread**
Cave, Hugh B.   20, 21, 871, **941**, 2699, 2744, 3594, 3605, 5692

**Discoveries in Fantasy**
Carter, Lin   606, 1576

**The Discovery of Dragons**
Base, Graeme   **385**, 1024, 2980, 2982, 5479

**The Disinherited**
David, Peter   **1381**

**The Dispossessed**
Le Guin, Ursula K.   1923, 4420, 4932, 5366, 5367, 5377, 5889

**Distant Dreams**
Lykins, Jenny   **3576**

**Distant Friends and Others**
Zahn, Timothy   **6053**

**A Distant Mirror**
Tuchman, Barbara W.   393

**Distant Planes**
Ice, Kathy   **2827**

**Distraction**
Sterling, Bruce   **5256**

**Distress**
Egan, Greg   **1760**, 5256

**Disturbing Behavior**
Whitman, John   2205, **5789**

**Divergence**
Sheffield, Charles   **4954**

**A Diversity of Dragons**
McCaffrey, Anne   **3728**

**The Divide**
Wilson, Robert Charles   **5907**

**Divided Allegiance**
Moon, Elizabeth   962, 1156, 1702, 1737, 1738, 3069, 3892, 3903, 5739, 5740, 5742

**The Divine Comedy of Ariadne and Jupiter: The Amazing and Spectacular Adventures of Ariadne and Jupiter in Heaven and on Earth**
Hite, Shere   5397

**The Divine Invasion**
Dick, Philip K.   3012

**Division of the Spoils**
Green, Roland J.   4973

**The Djinn in the Nightingale's Eye**
Byatt, A.S.   **794**, 1358, 6040

**Do Androids Dream of Electric Sheep?**
Dick, Philip K.   193, 836, 2684, 2685, 3012, 3204, 3434, 3579, 4071, 4117, 4325, 4342, 4555, 5476

**Doc Savage: His Apocalyptic Life**
Farmer, Philip Jose   1940, 3643, 4624, 4625

**Doc Savage Omnibus #1**
Robeson, Kenneth   85, 1870, 4624

**Doc Savage Omnibus #9**
Robeson, Kenneth   1870

**Doc Savage Omnibus #10**
Robeson, Kenneth   1870

**Doc Savage Omnibus #11**
Robeson, Kenneth   1870

**Doc Savage Omnibus #12**
Robeson, Kenneth   1870, 4624

**Doc Savage Omnibus #13**
Robeson, Kenneth   1870, 4624

**Doc Sidhe**
Allston, Aaron   **85**, 1472, 1474, 3490

**Dr. Bloodmoney**
Dick, Philip K.   1133, 5906

**Dr. Dimension**
DeChancie, John   **1456**

**Dr. Haggard's Disease**
McGrath, Patrick   3779, **3813**

**Dr. Strangelove**
George, Peter   5174

**Dr. Who and the Ribos Operation**
Marter, Ian   4338

**Doctor Who: The Mind of Evil**
Dicks, Terrance   5261

**Doctor's Orders**
Duane, Diane   526, 569, 900, 1381, 1556, **1659**, 1922, 4514

**Doctors Wear Scarlet**
Raven, Simon   4236

**The Dodd Mead Gallery of Horror**
Grant, Charles L.   5924

**The Dog King**
Ransmayr, Christoph   **4474**

**The Dog Syndrome and Other Sick Puppies**
Piccirilli, Tom   **4313**, 5445, 5620

**Dog Wizard**
Hambly, Barbara   12, 1985, 2357, **2503**, 2616, 3839, 5497, 5715, 5716

**Dogland**
Shetterly, Will   1445, **4992**

**The Doll and One Other**
Blackwood, Algernon   2025, 2899, 2902, 3782

**The Doll in the Garden**
Hahn, Mary Downing   2688

**The Doll Maker and Other Tales of the Uncanny**
Sarban   749, 1194, 2025

**The Doll Who Ate His Mother**
Campbell, Ramsey   541, 1131

**The Dollanganger Saga**
Andrews, V.C.   1300

**Dollies**
Graversen, Pat   1194, 2025, 2878, 2899, 2902, 3217, 3782, 3784, 5823

**Dolores Claiborne**
King, Stephen   **3130**

**Dolphin Boy**
Meyers, Roy   318

**Dolphin Island**
Clarke, Arthur C.   318, 3341, 3729, 4948

**The Dolphins of Altair**
St. Clair, Margaret   2450

**The Dolphins of Pern**
McCaffrey, Anne   2450, **3729**

**Domain**
Herbert, James   3192, 3992

**Domains of Darkover**
Bradley, Marion Zimmer   **631**, 4269

**Domes of Fire**
Eddings, David   **1732**

**Domination**
Cecilione, Michael   803, **946**, 1890, 2151, 2288, 5800

**Dominion**
Little, Bentley   438, **3492**

**Dominion**
Saberhagen, Fred   3253

**Dominion's Reach**
Thornley, Diann   **5465**

**Don Sebastian Series**
Daniel, Les   4767

**Donnerjack**
Zelazny, Roger   3477, **6063**

**Donovan's Brain/Hauser's Memory**
Siodmak, Curt   3562, 3563, **5072**, 5791

**Don't Bet on the Prince**
Zipes, Jack   43, 276, 648, 1366, 2528, 5617

**Don't Bite the Sun**
Lee, Tanith   5890

**Don't Dream**
Wandrei, Donald   534, 1494, 3529, 3534, **5627**

**Don't Forget Your Spacesuit, Dear**
Nye, Jody Lynn   **4169**, 5617

**"Don't Look Now"**
Du Maurier, Daphne   3348, 3349, 3350, 3433

**Don't Open This Book!**
Kaye, Marvin   **3024**

**Don't Scream**
Nixon, Joan Lowery   5285

**The Doom Brigade**
Weis, Margaret   **5708**

**Doom City**
Grant, Charles L.   4212

**The Doomed Planet**
Hubbard, L. Ron   828

**The Doomfarers of Coramonde**
Daley, Brian 162, 1008, 1065, 1066, 1147, 1154, 1419, 1754, 1809, 1812, 1814, 3650, 3653, 4316, 4523, 4794

**Doomsday Book**
Willis, Connie 453, 783, 1941, 2883, 3801, **5868**

**Doomsday Exam**
Pollotta, Nick 1159, 1974, 2309, 2320, 2363, **4363**

**Doomsday Warrior**
Stacy, Ryder 5023

**Doomsday World**
Carter, Carmen **923**, 2066, 3524

**Doomstalker**
Brandner, Gary **661**, 2703

**Doomstar**
Hamilton, Edmond 1916

**The Door Below**
Cave, Hugh B. 534, **942**

**The Door into Fire**
Duane, Diane 978, 1109, 1444, 1902, 1985, 2796, 2799, 2987, 3068, 3078, 3175, 3296, 3297, 3298, 3304, 3305, 3306, 3401, 4322, 4608, 4975, 5684

**A Door into Ocean**
Slonczewski, Joan 134, 181, 210, 211, 566, 580, 643, 686, 792, 899, 968, 1056, 1116, 1543, 1559, 1586, 1723, 1769, 1824, 2051, 2295, 2443, 2578, 3001, 3064, 3248, 3440, 3729, 3745, 4187, 4325, 4421, 4554, 4627, 4629, 4633, 4634, 4698, 4902, 4922, 4923, 5029, 5068, 5130, 5172, 5209, 5233, 5268, 5435, 5436, 5450, 5526, 5587, 5590, 5638, 5726, 5949, 5956, 6080

**The Door into Shadow**
Duane, Diane 1444, 2796, 3078, 3304

**The Door into Summer**
Heinlein, Robert A. 1345, 1895, 3663, 4143, 4157, 4247, 4332, 4559

**The Door into Sunset**
Duane, Diane **1660**, 1985, 2560, 3078, 3304

**Door Number Three**
O'Leary, Patrick 568, 3597, **4210**, 4333

**The Door through Space**
Bradley, Marion Zimmer 2414

**The Door through Washington Square**
Bergstrom, Elaine **464**

**The Door to Ambermere**
Pierce, J. Calvin **4316**

**Doorways in the Sand**
Zelazny, Roger 477, 995

**Doppelganger**
Higgs, Eric 3178, 3320

**The Doppelganger Gambit**
Killough, Lee 2682

**The Doppelgangers**
Heard, Gerald 2788

**Dorella**
Garland, Mark A. **2142**

**Dorothea Dreams**
Charnas, Suzy McKee 4943

**Dorothy and the Wizard in Oz**
Baum, L. Frank 3609

**Dorsai!**
Dickson, Gordon R. 308, 310, 513, 589, 996, 1041, 1315, 1646, 1651, 2049, 2435, 3034, 3035, 3037, 3698, 3865, 4142, 4226, 4227, 4288, 4292, 4374, 4378, 4466, 4560, 4583, 5294, 5378, 5469, 6075

**The Dorsai Companion**
Dickson, Gordon R. 4346

**The Dosadi Experiment**
Herbert, Frank 959, 2545

**Double**
Pronzini, Bill 1524

**The Double**
Webb, Don **5661**

**Double Date**
Stine, R.L. **5287**

**Double, Double**
Friedman, Michael Jan 1658, 1967, 4514, 4934

**Double Edge**
Etchison, Dennis **1846**

**Double Feature**
Bull, Emma **767**, 1969, 2947, 5782, 5973

**Double Jeopardy**
Allston, Aaron **86**

**Double Nocturne**
Felice, Cynthia 353, 897, 1757

**Double Planet**
Gribbin, John **2433**

**Double Solitaire**
Snodgrass, Melinda M. 3642, 3647, 3891, 5567

**Double Star**
Heinlein, Robert A. 1987, 2361, 2375, 2422, 2459, 2788, 4937, 5215, 5227, 5248, 5609

**Double Trouble Squared**
Lasky, Kathryn 1218, **3340**, 3468, 4918

**Doubles, Dummies and Dolls: 21 Terror Tales of Replication**
Wolf, Leonard **5936**

**Douglas Adams's Starship Titanic**
Jones, Terry **2979**

**Dove Isabeau**
Yolen, Jane **5534**

**Dover Beach**
Bowker, Richard 160, 1751, 4121, 4941, 5302, 5644, 5887

**"Down Among the Dead Men"**
Dozois, Gardner **5690**

**Down Among the Dead Men**
Green, Simon R. **2367**

**Down Among the Weeds: The Sargasso Sea Stories of William Hope Hodgson**
Hodgson, William Hope **2709**

**Down and Dirty**
Martin, George R.R. 989

**Down River**
Gallagher, Stephen **2110**, 2279, 2608, 2900, 3695, 3899, 3900, 3901, 4088

**Down the Bright Way**
Reed, Robert 31, 250, 358, 359, 449, 1574, 2213, 3467, 3805, 3874, **4505**, 5054, 5531, 5774

**Down the Stream of Stars**
Carver, Jeffrey A. **928**, 3710, 3725, 3726, 3821, 5208, 5215, 5573, 6085

**Down Town**
Polikarpus, Viido 1842, 4170

**Downbelow Station**
Cherryh, C.J. 10, 923, **985**, 1226, 1861, 1865, 2296, 2351, 2464, 2466, 3014, 4016, 5833, 5922

**Downtime**
Felice, Cynthia 1041, 1865, 2067, 2069, 4927

**Downtiming the Night Side**
Chalker, Jack L. 895, 1852, 2012, 2208

**Downward to the Earth**
Silverberg, Robert 707, 5052, 5055

**A Dozen Black Roses**
Collins, Nancy A. 387, **1119**, 1949, 1950, 2258, 2512, 2514, 2518, 2664, 5703

**A Dozen Tough Jobs**
Waldrop, Howard 36, 1810, 2549, 2751, **5612**, 5944

**Drachenfels**
Yeovil, Jack 1443, 1927, 1928, **6022**

**The Drackenberg Adventure**
Alexander, Lloyd 5928

**Dracul: An Eternal Love Story**
Kilpatrick, Nancy **3110**

**Dracula**
Stoker, Bram 139, 152, 279, 292, 1112, 1402, 1448, 2742, 3004, 3110, 3163, 3179, 4094, 4763, 4770, 4779

**The Dracula Book of Great Vampire Stories**
Shepard, Leslie 1308, 1360, 1370, 2407, 4407, 5265, 5706

**Dracula in Love**
Shirley, John 55

**Dracula, My Love**
Tremayne, Peter 3110, 4367, 4765, 4779

**Dracula, Prince of Darkness**
Burke, John 4687

**Dracula: Prince of Darkness**
Greenberg, Martin H. 748, 1013, 1799, **2387**, 2705, 2972, 3226, 5688, 5699

**The Dracula Tape**
Saberhagen, Fred 55, **4765**, 4779, 5050, 6010

**Dracula: The Ultimate Illustrated Edition of the World-Famous Vampire Play**
Deane, Hamilton 339, 344, 1112, **1448**, 3110

**Dracula Unborn**
Tremayne, Peter 55, 3003, 3005, 4770, 5050, 6010

**Dracula Unbound**
Aldiss, Brian W. **55**, 1134, 3003, 4094, 4098, 4772

**Dracula's Brood**
Dalby, Richard 1013, **1308**, 1360, 1370, 2387, 2484, 2972, 2975

**Dracula's Guest**
Stoker, Bram 4969

**The Drag Queen of Elfland**
Schimel, Lawrence **4878**

**Dragon**
Brust, Steven **741**

**The Dragon and the Djinn**
Dickson, Gordon R. **1528**, 5218

**The Dragon and the George**
Dickson, Gordon R. 6, 85, 131, 286, 842, 843, 915, 1160, 1161, 1163, 1196, 1207, 1324, 1685, 1704, 1747, 1873, 1985, 2042, 2127, 2362, 2616, 2617, 3728, 3934, 3938, 4014, 4055, 4316, 4399, 4401, 4404, 4457, 4669, 4671, 4697, 4809, 5228, 5235, 5337, 5694, 5719, 6049, 6069

**The Dragon and the Gnarly King**
Dickson, Gordon R. **1529**

**The Dragon and the Unicorn**
Attanasio, A.A. **266**, 1657, 2126, 2735, 4178, 5793

**The Dragon at War**
Dickson, Gordon R. 842, **1530**, 2234, 3169, 4691, 4695, 4697, 4924

**A Dragon at World's End**
Rowley, Christopher **4693**

**Dragon Burning**
Gardner, Craig Shaw **2126**

**Dragon Cauldron**
Yep, Laurence 2463, **6024**

**Dragon Companion**
Callander, Don 726, **842**, 2126, 2462, 4691

**The Dragon Crown**
Knaak, Richard A. **3168**

**Dragon Death**
Baudino, Gael **390**, 2505

**Dragon Fantastic**
Greenberg, Rosalind M. **2413**, 2479, 4408, 4543, 5710

**The Dragon in Lyonesse**
Dickson, Gordon R.   **1531**

**The Dragon King**
Salvatore, R.A.   **4796**

**The Dragon Knight**
Dickson, Gordon R.   131, 393, 841, 1045, **1532**, 1985, 4971

**The Dragon Lord**
Drake, David   1189, 1190, 2747, 3474, 3806

**A Dragon-Lover's Treasury of the Fantastic**
Weis, Margaret   2479, 4408, **5710**

**Dragon Magic**
Norton, Andre   187, 4996

**The Dragon Masters**
Vance, Jack   1015, 2058, 2193, 4277, 6056

**Dragon Moon**
Claremont, Chris   **1040**, 4487

**The Dragon Never Sleeps**
Cook, Glen   35, 81, 209, 309, 310, 311, 322, 328, 471, 472, 473, 478, 734, 883, 1103, 1183, 1184, 1573, 1575, 1598, 1633, 1645, 1664, 1995, 2364, 2365, 2374, 2417, 2418, 2419, 2464, 2466, 2523, 2812, 3448, 3710, 3722, 3749, 3821, 3823, 3825, 4288, 4354, 4375, 4483, 4505, 4553, 4626, 4760, 4859, 4896, 4951, 4984, 5116, 5138, 5139, 5140, 5260, 5365, 5543, 5573, 5637, 5668, 5679, 5680, 5718, 5834, 5835, 6079, 6081, 6085

**The Dragon of the Ishtar Gate**
de Camp, L. Sprague   2140, 5496

**Dragon of the Lost Sea**
Yep, Laurence   843, 1218, 2461, 2865, 4324, 4460, 4462, 5974

**The Dragon on the Border**
Dickson, Gordon R.   **1533**, 4697

**The Dragon Path: Collected Tales of Kenneth Morris**
Morris, Kenneth   2680, **4021**

**Dragon Prince**
Rawn, Melanie   683, 692, 1143, 1486, 1487, 1773, 1864, 1907, 1908, 1912, 2060, 2552, 3078, 3168, 3645, 3893, 4161, 4258, 4613, 5391, 5582, 5727, 5812, 5964

**The Dragon Reborn**
Jordan, Robert   2097, **2985**, 3107, 5760

**Dragon Rescue**
Callander, Don   **843**

**The Dragon Revenant**
Kerr, Katharine   **3069**, 3904, 4718, 5819

**Dragon Rigger**
Carver, Jeffrey A.   **929**, 2060, 2163

**Dragon Season**
Cassutt, Michael   **936**, 2142, 2463, 2722, 5714

**Dragon Sleeping**
Gardner, Craig Shaw   1180, **2127**, 4676

**Dragon Song**
McCaffrey, Anne   4996

**Dragon Tales**
Asimov, Isaac   2479, 4408, 5239

**Dragon Tears**
Koontz, Dean R.   284, 571, 2341, **3205**, 4883

**Dragon Tempest**
Callander, Don   **844**

**The Dragon, the Earl, and the Troll**
Dickson, Gordon R.   **1534**, 2360, 4671

**The Dragon Token**
Rawn, Melanie   **4485**

**Dragon Tome**
Knaak, Richard A.   2234, **3169**

**The Dragon Waiting**
Ford, John M.   314, 652, 738, 1638, 2507, 2570, 2945, 4272, 4793, 5014, 5017, 5503, 5511, 5513

**Dragon Waking**
Gardner, Craig Shaw   **2128**

**Dragon War**
Yep, Laurence   2850, **6025**

**Dragon Wing**
Weis, Margaret   457, 719, 1937, 2529, 3050, 4105, **5709**, 6004

**The Dragonbone Chair**
Williams, Tad   1146, 1909, 1911, 2095, 3581, 3893, 4489, 4513, 4526, 4660, 4776, 5034, 5715, 5727, 5736, 5750, 5790, **5829**, 6003

**Dragoncharm**
Edwards, Graham   1705, **1749**, 1984, 2650, 3045, 3065, 3728, 4461, 4739, 4848

**Dragondoom**
McKiernan, Dennis L.   28, 3578

**Dragondrums**
McCaffrey, Anne   1066, 1221

**The Dragonesti**
Thompson, Paul B.   5708

**Dragonflight**
McCaffrey, Anne   222, 894, 1000, 1114, 2036, 2421, 2423, 3044, 3045, 3065, 3157, 3940, 4149, 4485, 4490, 4492, 4493, 4692, 4695, 4697, 5034, 5708, 5862

**Dragonfly in Amber**
Gabaldon, Diana   691, 2731, 3261

**DragonLance Chronicles**
Weis, Margaret   1287

**The Dragonlord of Mystara**
Gunnarsson, Thorarinn   470

**Dragonmage of Mystara**
Gunnarsson, Thorarinn   **2462**, 4326

**Dragonquest**
McCaffrey, Anne   4149, 4692, 4697

**Dragonrank Master**
Reichert, Mickey Zucker   2, **4519**, 5790, 5944

**Dragonriders of Pern**
McCaffrey, Anne   842, 843, 4691, 4693, 4694

**The Dragonriders of Pern Series**
McCaffrey, Anne   2553, 3289, 5829

**Dragons!**
Dann, Jack   801, 2479, 4408, 5710

**The Dragons**
Niles, Douglas   5708

**Dragon's Bait**
Vande Velde, Vivian   1951, 5394, **5556**

**Dragon's Blood**
McDonough, Alex   **3799**

**Dragon's Blood**
Yolen, Jane   4322, 5979

**The Dragon's Boy**
Yolen, Jane   3382, **6030**

**Dragons Can Only Rust**
Cymri, Chris   299

**The Dragon's Carbuncle**
Boyer, Elizabeth H.   **605**

**Dragon's Claw**
McDonough, Alex   **3800**

**The Dragon's Dagger**
Salvatore, R.A.   **4797**

**Dragon's Domain**
Gunnarsson, Thorarinn   726, 1749, **2461**, 4460

**Dragon's Egg**
Forward, Robert L.   80, 81, 401, 1244, 1245, 1537, 3398, 3805, 4123, 4280, 4554, 6065

**Dragons, Elves and Heroes**
Carter, Lin   2378, 2388, 4906

**Dragon's Eye**
McDonough, Alex   **3801**

**Dragon's Gold**
Anthony, Piers   5222

**Dragon's Honor**
Johnson, Kij   1225, 1226, 1228, 1229, 1382, **2922**

**Dragons in the Stars**
Carver, Jeffrey A.   220, **930**, 1083, 1337, 2059, 2163, 2832, 3722, 4896, 5575

**Dragon's Knight**
Dennis, Carol L.   470, 3578

**Dragon's Milk**
Fletcher, Susan   329, 5975, 6030

**Dragons of Argonath**
Rowley, Christopher   **4694**

**Dragons of Autumn Twilight**
Weis, Margaret   154, 2271, 3155, 4106, 5454, 5455

**Dragons of Darkness**
Card, Orson Scott   2014, 2413, 2479, 3728, 4408, 5556, 5710, 6032

**Dragons of Light**
Card, Orson Scott   801, 2014, 2413, 2479, 3574, 3728, 4408, 5710, 6032

**Dragons of Summer Flame**
Weis, Margaret   2462, **5711**

**The Dragons of the Rhine**
Paxson, Diana L.   **4264**, 4676

**Dragons of War**
Rowley, Christopher   **4695**

**Dragons on the Town**
Gunnarsson, Thorarinn   **2463**, 3169, 4615

**Dragons over England**
Kaufman, Douglas   1889, **3015**, 4909, 5210, 5438

**Dragons Past**
Gentile, Gary   **2192**, 3428

**Dragon's Plunder**
Strickland, Brad   2085, **5336**

**Dragon's Queen**
Dennis, Carol L.   **1488**

**Dragon's Teeth**
Killough, Lee   2000, 2682, 2683, **3109**, 4121, 4940, 5576

**The Dragon's Touchstone**
Radford, Irene   3292, **4459**

**Dragon's Winter**
Lynn, Elizabeth A.   **3578**

**Dragonsbane**
Hambly, Barbara   28, 470, 727, 971, 975, 994, 1207, 1685, 1732, 2757, 2809, 3044, 4013, 4014, 4513, 4517, 4674, 5087, 5509

**Dragonsdawn**
McCaffrey, Anne   638, 983, 1247, 2371, 3001

**Dragonseye**
McCaffrey, Anne   **3730**

**Dragonsinger**
McCaffrey, Anne   1221, 4161

**Dragonslayer's Return**
Salvatore, R.A.   1905, **4798**

**Dragonsong**
McCaffrey, Anne   1221, 2015

**Dragonspawn**
Acres, Mark   **28**, 3578

**The Dragonstone**
McKiernan, Dennis L.   844, **3832**

**Dragonsword**
Baudino, Gael   286, 1161, 1749, 3067, 3659, 3872, 3982, 4695, 4697

**Dragonwall**
Denning, Troy   3537, 4108

**Drakon**
Stirling, S.M.   **5294**

**The Dramaturges of Yan**
Brunner, John   5561

**Dramocles: An Intergalactic Soap Opera**
Sheckley, Robert   6062

**Drangonsinger**
McCaffrey, Anne  1765

**The Drastic Dragon of Draco, Texas**
Scarborough, Elizabeth Ann  1207, 2145

**Drawing Blood**
Brite, Poppy Z.  212, 437, 547, **694**, 1845, 2494, 2901, 3101, 3197, 3364, 3368, 3675, 5414, 5463

**The Drawing of the Dark**
Powers, Tim  955, 1189, 2262, 3257, 3714, 3806, 3822

**The Drawing of the Three**
King, Stephen  **3131**

**Dread and Delight: A Century of Children's Ghost Stories**
Pearce, Philippa  **4274**, 4282

**Dread Brass Shadows**
Cook, Glen  **1149**, 2125, 2228, 4673

**Dread Companion**
Norton, Andre  169, 3259

**Dreadful Sanctuary**
Russell, Eric Frank  2001

**Dreadnought**
Gunnarsson, Thorarinn  2464

**Dream Baby**
McAllister, Bruce  3206, **3706**, 4865

**The Dream Cycle of H.P. Lovecraft: Dreams of Terror and Death**
Lovecraft, H.P.  **3530**

**Dream Dancer**
Morris, Janet  209, 5524

**The Dream Detective**
Rohmer, Sax  509

**Dream Maker**
Harbinson, W.A.  156, **2542**

**The Dream Master**
Zelazny, Roger  1521, 4210

**The Dream Millennium**
White, James  897, 4066, 5042, 5243, 5860

**Dream of Glass**
Gawron, Jean Mark  157, 1761, **2163**, 2486, 2729, 2839, 2955, 3049, 3186, 3438, 3795, 4130, 4136, 4177, 4677, 4703, 4894, 4902, 5171, 5450, 5462

**A Dream of Kinship**
Cowper, Richard  3696

**Dream of the Wolf**
Bradfield, Scott  **626**, 816, 1349, 5343

**Dream Park**
Niven, Larry  360, 971, 975

**The Dream Quest of Unknown Kadath**
Lovecraft, H.P.  3595, 3859, 5102

**The Dream Vessel**
Bredenberg, Jeff  **664**

**The Dream Warrior**
Conway, D.J.  2639

**Dream-Weaver**
Lawrence, Louise  **3359**

**The Dream Years**
Goldstein, Lisa  43, 323, 333, 334, 335, 336, 676, 919, 2028, 2104, 3663, 4272, 4732, 5614, 5635

**Dreambuilder**
Deitz, Tom  **1471**

**Dreamer**
James, Peter  **2871**

**Dreamer**
Quinn, Daniel  89, 813, 1669, 2161, 2613, 2789, 3267, **4454**, 5520, 5816

**A Dreamer's Tales**
Dunsany  3530, 3859, 5103

**Dreamfall**
Vinge, Joan D.  2877, **5571**, 5872

**The Dreaming Earth**
Brunner, John  2807

**Dreaming in Smoke**
Sullivan, Tricia  **5353**

**The Dreaming Jewels**
Sturgeon, Theodore  2303, 2458, 4642

**Dreaming Metal**
Scott, Melissa  2660, **4895**

**The Dreaming Place**
de Lint, Charles  1475, 3545, 5336, 5827, 6017

**Dreams and Swords**
Forrest, Katherine V.  1286, 4882

**Dreams of Dark and Light**
Lee, Tanith  5369

**Dreams of Dawn**
Steussy, Marti  2764, 3536, 3727, 3800, 4143

**The Dreams of Dr. Ladybank**
Tessier, Thomas  814, 1939, 5898

**Dreams of Flesh and Sand**
Quick, W.T.  361, 3890, 5449

**Dreams of Gods and Men**
Quick, W.T.  361, 3491, 3890, **4451**, 5449

**Dreams of Steel**
Cook, Glen  **1150**

**Dreams of Stone**
Wylie, Jonathan  1731, 1736

**Dreams of the Raven**
Carter, Carmen  5880

**Dreams Street**
Wylie, Jonathan  1722

**Dreams That Burn in the Night**
Strete, Craig  1437

**Dreams Underfoot**
de Lint, Charles  395, 818, **1425**, 3702, 5912

**Dreamseeker's Road**
Deitz, Tom  1321, **1472**, 2737, 2957

**Dreamships**
Scott, Melissa  79, 930, 2832, 3749, **4896**, 5229

**Dreamsnake**
McIntyre, Vonda N.  642, 1722, 2120, 2806, 4176, 4836

**Dreamspy**
Lichtenberg, Jacqueline  **3458**

**The Dreamstone**
Cherryh, C.J.  393, 4265

**The Dreamstone**
Rivkin, J.F.  27, 487, 1840

**Dreamthorp**
Williamson, Chet  427, 1297, 1931, 2689, 3336, 3655, 3895, 4664, 5077, **5845**, 5961

**Dreamweaver's Dilemma**
Bujold, Lois McMaster  **759**, 1969, 3430, 5782, 5838

**The Dreamwright**
Gravel, Geary  3479

**The Drift**
Kropp, Lloyd  2708

**Drifter**
Dietz, William C.  473, **1543**

**Drifter's Run**
Dietz, William C.  **1544**

**Drifter's War**
Dietz, William C.  **1545**

**Driftglass: 10 Tales of Speculative Fiction**
Delany, Samuel R.  1608, 5945

**Driftglider and Other Stories**
Osier, Jeffrey  775, 776, 2769, 2937, **4230**

**Drink Down the Moon**
de Lint, Charles  166, 183, 1423, **1426**

**Drink the Fire From the Flames**
Baker, Scott  290, 1009, 1010, 1109, 1928, 4360, 4612, 5321, 5931

**Drinker of Souls**
Clayton, Jo  982, 1002

**Drinking Buddies**
Sallee, Wayne Allen  4255

**The Drive-In: A Double Omnibus**
Lansdale, Joe R.  **3326**

**Driven to Kill**
Gath, G.G.  5287

**Driving Blind**
Bradbury, Ray  2641

**The Drought**
Ballard, J.G.  2535

**Drowned Ammet**
Jones, Diana Wynne  1444

**The Drowned World**
Ballard, J.G.  56, 57, 354, 2998, 3612, 5906

**The Druid of Shannara**
Brooks, Terry  **710**

**Druids**
Llywelyn, Morgan  266, 633, 640, 1476, 2229, 2454, 2740, **3502**, 3588, 3592, 4264, 4270, 4989, 5792, 5793, 5794

**Druid's Blood**
Friesner, Esther  4556

**The Druid's Gift**
Anderson, Margaret J.  **121**, 561, 563, 1498, 2121, 2883

**Drum Calls**
Clayton, Jo  **1065**

**Drum Warning**
Clayton, Jo  1033, **1066**

**Drunkard's Walk**
Pohl, Frederik  2487, 2920, 4813

**Dry Skull Dreams**
Green, Michael  **2344**

**A Dry Spell**
Moloney, Susan  **3951**

**Dry Water**
Nylund, Eric S.  1089, 5817

**The Drylands**
Rosenblum, Mary  **4678**, 5032

**D'Shai**
Rosenberg, Joel  747, 2507, 3078, 3872, **4670**

**The Dubious Hills**
Dean, Pamela  728, **1444**, 1705, 2865, 3280, 3731, 3816, 3843, 4324, 4899, 5409, 5577, 5848

**The Duchess of Kneedeep**
Noel, Atanielle Annyn  5550

**Duel of Dragons**
Baudino, Gael  **391**, 843, 2462, 2465, 2797, 3578, 4173, 4691, 4693, 4694, 4695, 4707

**The Duke of Sumava**
Wrench, Sara J.  **5983**

**Dumford Blood**
Epperson, S.K.  **1829**, 2599, 5332

**Dun Lady's Jess**
Durgin, Doranna  **1704**, 2673, 2678, 2869

**Duncton Wood**
Horwood, William  32, 432

**Dune**
Herbert, Frank  35, 231, 324, 434, 554, 566, 567, 580, 622, 707, 756, 1102, 1103, 1108, 1254, 1566, 1598, 1637, 1648, 1654, 1807, 1861, 2194, 2365, 2366, 2459, 2523, 2524, 3014, 3231, 3316, 3599, 3710, 3735, 3909, 3910, 3911, 3927, 3937, 3946, 3947, 4287, 4483, 4557, 4698, 4729, 5019, 5051, 5059, 5117, 5138, 5140, 5141, 5278, 5292, 5434, 5526, 5575, 5637, 5671, 5672, 5673, 5675, 5717, 5720, 5722, 5739, 5740, 5742, 5744, 5835, 5917, 5920, 5921, 5922, 5941, 5985, 6008, 6052

**Dune Messiah**
Herbert, Frank  707, 1538, 5941

**The Dunwich Cycle**
Price, Robert M.  2399

**The Dunwich Cycle: Where the Old Gods Wait**
Price, Robert M.  **4424**

**The Dunwich Horror and Others**
Lovecraft, H.P.  2710, 2712, 3462

**Duplicates**
Neiderman, Andrew  **4086**

**Dushau**
Lichtenberg, Jacqueline  418, 954, 1772, 3066, 4350

**Dusk**
Dee, Ron  723, 1127, **1466**, 1945, 2152, 3051, 3372, 3498, 4102, 4464, 5237, 5770

**Dust**
Pellegrino, Charles  3008, **4279**

**The Dwarf**
Lagerkvist, Pars  556

**The Dweller in the Gulf**
Smith, Clark Ashton  348

**Dwellers in the Crucible**
Bonanno, Margaret Wander  527, 900, 1260, 1388, 1511, 1954, 2063, 2064, 3316, 3767, 4081, 4138, 5019, 6051

**Dwellers in the Mirage**
Merritt, A.  4867, 5626

**The Dwelling**
Elliott, Tom  342, 364, 861, 873, 890, 1192, **1776**, 2040, 2875, 2901, 3055, 3685, 3953, 4663, 4778, 4830, 5424

**Dydeetown World**
Wilson, F. Paul  1751, 4941, 5302, 5644, **5887**

**The Dying**
Horvitz, Leslie  1625

**Dying Breath**
Harrald, Jon A.  **2555**

**The Dying Earth**
Vance, Jack  3157, 3158

**The Dying Earth Series**
Vance, Jack  4397

**Dying for It: More Erotic Tales of Unearthly Love**
Dozois, Gardner  **1607**, 2177, 2178, 2179

**Dying Inside**
Silverberg, Robert  2290, 3203, 3742, 3860

**Dying of the Light**
Martin, George R.R.  **3644**, 5544, 5545

**The Dying Sun**
Blackwood, Gary L.  **511**, 709, 3584, 3608

**Dystopia**
Walker, William A. Jr.  **5620**


**E**


**E Pluribus Unicorn**
Sturgeon, Theodore  674, 850, 1874, 3308, 5106, 5551

**E.T.: The Extra-Terrestrial**
Kotzwinkle, William  2227

**The Eagle and the Nightingales**
Lackey, Mercedes  682, 705, **3278**, 4146, 4808

**The Eagle and the Sword**
Attanasio, A.A.  267

**The Eagles' Brood**
Whyte, Jack  5792

**The Eagle's Daughter**
Tarr, Judith  965, 5500, 5513

**The Ear, the Eye, and the Arm**
Farmer, Nancy  1600, **1867**, 3045, 3283, 4262, 5145

**The Early Fears**
Bloch, Robert  **532**, 1494, 1495, 1496, 3529, 3532, 3534, 5627

**Earth**
Brin, David  79, 82, 100, 108, 205, 295, 354, 382, 400, 405, 413, 414, 510, 596, 656, 664, **685**, 753, 792, 806, 808, 1056, 1057, 1075, 1167, 1258, 1336, 1382, 1549, 1581, 1594, 1651, 1805, 1897, 1989, 1990, 2328, 2491, 2579, 2645, 2997, 2999, 3311, 3437, 3449, 3503, 3604, 3661, 3744, 3745, 3789, 3805, 3921, 3932, 3944, 3952, 4000, 4126, 4218, 4281, 4357, 4416, 4421, 4503, 4629, 4633, 4634, 4635, 4652, 4677, 4682, 4704, 4708, 4769, 4895, 4947, 4949, 4950, 4961, 5132, 5173, 5174, 5209, 5241, 5242, 5303, 5351, 5433, 5540, 5566, 5573, 5677, 5744, 5745, 5834, 5839, 5873, 5956, 5966, 6065

**Earth 2**
Crandall, Melissa  **1247**

**Earth Abides**
Stewart, George R.  3584, 4074, 4631

**Earth Descended**
Saberhagen, Fred  516

**Earth Dreams**
Morris, Janet  5524

**The Earth Giant**
Burgess, Melvin  53, **773**

**The Earth Gods Are Coming**
Bulmer, Kenneth  2810

**Earth Herald**
Clark, Jan  **1046**

**The Earth Is All That Lasts**
Wells, Catherine  191, 656, 1932, 3424, 3469, 3503, 3704, 3729, 3745, 3862, 3864, 4000, 4001, 5429, 5433, 5435, 5492, **5744**, 5965

**Earth Is the Strangest Place**
Silverberg, Robert  6027

**Earth King**
Youssef, Michael  3860

**The Earth Lords**
Dickson, Gordon R.  1443

**Earth Made of Glass**
Barnes, John  **351**, 1316

**The Earth Remembers**
Olan, Susan Torian  **4209**

**The Earth Saver**
Wells, Catherine  5745

**The Earth Strikes Back**
Chizmar, Richard T.  **1020**

**The Earth Will Shake**
Wilson, Robert Anton  1273, 1275, 3262

**The Earth Wire and Other Stories**
Lane, Joel  4878, 5816

**Earthborn**
Card, Orson Scott  884

**Earthbound**
Matheson, Richard  524, 1468, 1560, 2019, 3178, **3684**

**Earthfall**
Brown, Jerry Earl  163, **724**, 1924

**Earthfall**
Card, Orson Scott  885

**Earthfasts**
Mayne, William  1138

**Earthgrip**
Turtledove, Harry  1420, 2055, 3001, 3648, 4120, 4160, **5499**

**Earthlight**
Clarke, Arthur C.  1916

**Earthling**
Daniel, Tony  **1336**, 1481

**An Earthly Crown**
Elliott, Kate  **1771**, 4138, 4486, 5227

**Earthman, Come Home**
Blish, James  734, 5499

**Earthman, Go Home!**
Anderson, Poul  1652, 2437, 3928

**Earthman's Burden**
Anderson, Poul  1536, 5875

**Earthquake Weather**
Powers, Tim  **4382**

**Earthsong**
Elgin, Suzette Haden  **1769**, 3622, 3628, 3629, 3630, 4999

**Earthsound**
Herzog, Arthur III  1060

**East Coast Ghosts**
Waugh, Charles G.  4214

**Eastern Ghosts**
McSherry, Frank D. Jr.  **3866**

**The Ebon Mask**
Byers, Richard Lee  797, 5701, 5702

**Ecce and Old Earth**
Vance, Jack  **5546**

**Echoes**
Hyman, Jackie  2154, **2818**, 3494

**Echoes of Honor**
Weber, David  **5669**

**Echoes of Issel**
Thornley, Diann  **5466**

**Echoes of the Fourth Magic**
Salvatore, R.A.  1781, **4799**

**Echoes of the Well of Souls**
Chalker, Jack L.  953

**Echoes of Valor I**
Wagner, Karl Edward  2347, 2348, 4616

**Echoes of Valor I-III**
Wagner, Karl Edward  4759

**Echoes of Valor III**
Wagner, Karl Edward  4617, **5599**

**Eclipse**
Shirley, John  1750, 4343

**Eclipse Corona**
Shirley, John  1750, **5006**

**Eclipse Penumbra**
Shirley, John  1750

**Eclipses**
Felice, Cynthia  5572

**Eco-Fiction**
Stadler, John  4631, 4959

**The Ecolitan Enigma**
Modesitt, L.E. Jr.  **3927**

**The Ecolitan Operation**
Modesitt, L.E. Jr.  3451, **3928**

**The Ecologic Envoy**
Modesitt, L.E. Jr.  3451

**The Ecologic Secession**
Modesitt, L.E. Jr.  **3929**, 5717

**Ecotopia: A Novel about Ecology, People and Politics in 1999**
Callenbach, Ernest  4631

**Ecotopia Emerging**
Callenbach, Ernest  4631

**Ecstasia**
Block, Francesca Lia  **547**

**Ecstasy Club**
Rushkoff, Douglas  2754, **4732**

**Eddy Deco's Last Caper**
Wilson, Gahan  868, 869, 5168, 5796, 6072

**Eden**
Lem, Stanislaw  **3434**

**Eden's Eyes**
Costello, Sean  **1205**

**The Edge of Forever**
Oliver, Chad  59

**The Edge of Running Water**
Sloane, William  3417

**The Edge of the Chair**
Kahn, Joan  543, 2282

**The Edge of the World**
Gordon, John  1319, 1320

**The Edge of the World**
Sarabande, William  881, **4817**

**Edward Lee's Quest for Sex, Truth and Reality**
Lee, Edward  1467, 2778, 3367, 3553, 3558, 5411, 5412, 5416, 5854

**Edwardian Ghost Stories by Eminent Women Writers**
Dalby, Richard  37

**Eggheads**
Devenport, Emily  774, **1500**, 2877, 5571

Title Index

**Egil's Book**
Mills, C.J.   **3910**

**Egil's Saga**
Sturluson, Snorri   136

**The Eight**
Neville, Katherine   **4092**, 4983

**Eight Days of Luke**
Jones, Diana Wynne   171

**Eight Skilled Gentlemen**
Hughart, Barry   69, **2804**, 3338, 4742

**The Eighth Galaxy Reader**
Pohl, Frederik   243

**The Eighth Green Man and Other Strange Folk**
Weinberg, Robert   480, 2485, 3023, 3028

**The Eighth Rank**
Ross, David D.   2727, **4682**

**The Eighth Stage of Fandom: Selections From 25 Years of Fan Writing**
Bloch, Robert   4546

**The Einstein Intersection**
Delany, Samuel R.   **1481**, 1879, 6074

**Einstein's Bridge**
Cramer, John   110, 444, **1244**, 4179

**Einstein's Dreams**
Lightman, Alan   302, 1758, **3459**

**Elak of Atlantis**
Kuttner, Henry   1699

**Eldrie the Healer**
Edwards, Claudia J.   5547

**The Electric Forest**
Lee, Tanith   957

**Electric Gumbo: A Lansdale Reader**
Lansdale, Joe R.   **3327**

**Elegy for Angels and Dogs/The Graveyard Heart**
Williams, Walter Jon   3189

**The Element of Fire**
Henderson, Jason   **2657**

**The Element of Fire**
Wells, Martha   718, 719, 841, 979, 1009, 1064, 1143, 1253, 1636, 1660, 1773, 1790, 1864, 2032, 2039, 2060, 2195, 2269, 2358, 2503, 2506, 2509, 2529, 2693, 2694, 2695, 2696, 2956, 2958, 2959, 2989, 3168, 3293, 3306, 3481, 3508, 3511, 3645, 3775, 3839, 3844, 3914, 3930, 3936, 3978, 4516, 4527, 4718, 4768, 4804, 4983, 5144, 5217, 5251, 5266, 5391, 5394, 5584, 5716, 5728, **5750**, 5811, 5812, 5813, 5978, 5980

**The Elementals**
Llywelyn, Morgan   1482, 2716, **3503**, 5433

**The Elephant**
Mrozek, Slawomir   2641

**Elephant Song**
Longyear, Barry B.   5215

**Elephantasm**
Lee, Tanith   **3408**

**The Eleventh Commandment**
Del Rey, Lester   1135, 3242

**The Eleventh Plague: A Novel of Medical Terror**
Marr, John S.   **3632**

**Elf Defense**
Friesner, Esther   1426, 3269, 4393, 5649

**Elf Fantastic**
Greenberg, Martin H.   **2388**

**The Elf Queen of Shannara**
Brooks, Terry   **711**

**The Elfin Ship**
Blaylock, James P.   2132, 2133, 2750

**Elfquest: Journey to Sorrow's End**
Pini, Wendy   4335

**Elfshadow**
Cunningham, Elaine   **1288**, 1486, 1487, 3538, 4800, 4803, 4804, 4805, 4807

**Elfsong**
Cunningham, Elaine   **1289**

**Elfwood**
Estes, Rose   **1837**, 5251

**Elidor**
Garner, Alan   165, 171, 1330

**Elleander Morning**
Yulsman, Jerry   5501, 5516, 5517, 5518

**Elminster: The Making of a Mage**
Greenwood, Ed   **2427**

**Elric of Melnibone**
Moorcock, Michael   1102, 1173, 1174, 1178, 1181, 1241, 1637, 1648, 1754, 1881, 1927, 1928, 2529, 2885, 3227, 3419, 3420, 4109, 5408, 5683

**Elric: Song of the Black Sword**
Moorcock, Michael   **3980**

**Elsewhere**
Shetterly, Will   235, 396, 545, 546, 549, 550, 552, 767, 769, 970, 976, 1101, 1159, 1427, 1436, 1474, 1837, 1841, 1958, 2142, 2373, 2467, 3245, 3271, 3299, 3301, 3302, 3468, 3513, 3871, 3884, 4149, 4174, 4261, 4497, 4615, 4675, 4985, 4990, **4993**, 5143, 5179, 5181, 5267, 5371, 5556, 5822, 5913, 5914, 5915, 5977

**Elsewhere**
Windling, Terri   647, 1340, 1368, 1425, 6005

**Elsewhere II**
Windling, Terri   1340, 1368, 1425, 4335

**Elsewhere III**
Windling, Terri   1340, 1425

**Elven Star**
Weis, Margaret   3050, 4491, **5712**

**The Elvenbane**
Norton, Andre   457, 711, 1114, 1951, 1984, 2650, 2985, 3481, 3508, **4149**, 4174, 4615, 4675, 5556, 6024

**Elvenblood**
Norton, Andre   2650, 2678, 3045, 3065, 3292, 3295, 3728, 3936, **4150**, 4321, 4461, 4527, 4794

**Elvendude**
Shepherd, Mark   **4980**

**The Elves and the Otterskin**
Boyer, Elizabeth H.   1685, 2424

**Elvira: Transylvania 90210**
Elvira   **1802**

**Elvis Rising: Stories on the King**
Sloan, Kay   2070, 4540, **5089**

**Elvissey**
Womack, Jack   5089, **5957**

**The Embedding**
Watson, Ian   **5634**

**Ember From the Sun**
Canter, Mark   **870**

**Embracing the Dark**
Garber, Eric   1740, **2116**

**The Emerald City of Oz**
Baum, L. Frank   197

**Emerald Eyes**
Moran, Daniel Keys   733, 1933, 1934, 4504, 5039, 5621, 5907

**Emerald House Rising**
Kerr, Peg   1010, 2253, 2758, 3074, **3080**, 3509, 3651, 4459, 4739, 5137, 5490, 5555, 5749

**Emergence**
Hamilton, Peter F.   687, **2524**

**Emergence**
Palmer, David R.   876, 1261, 1262, 1539, 1550, 1600, 1930, 2260, 2554, 2603, 2640, 2808, 2997, 3429, 3940, 3966, 4262, 4507, 4599, 4605, 4835, 5212, 5232, 5242, 5267, 6075

**Emissary**
Dillard, J.M.   1247, 1654, 2061, 2908, 4295, 5598

**Emperor and Clown**
Duncan, Dave   **1676**, 5221

**An Emperor for the Legion**
Turtledove, Harry   1676

**Emperor of Ansalon**
Niles, Douglas   4925

**Emperor of Everything**
Aldridge, Ray   **62**

**Emperors of the Twilight**
Swann, S. Andrew   **5362**, 6048

**Empery**
Kube-McDowell, Michael P.   3821, 3825, 5933

**Emphyrio**
Vance, Jack   176, 2192, 3696, 5457

**Empire Builders**
Bova, Ben   **584**

**Empire Dreams**
McDonald, Ian   1278

**Empire of Dust**
Williamson, Chet   2308, **5846**

**The Empire of Fear**
Stableford, Brian   463, 1463, 1797, 2741, 2834, 3143, 3546, 3550, 3601, 3602, 3954, 3955, 4094, 4096, 4097, 4098, 4508, 4576, 4578, 4668, 4770, 4781, 4784, 4978, 5050, 5185, **5191**, 5693, 5704, 5802, 6012, 6018

**Empire of the Ants**
Werber, Bernard   **5755**

**Empire of the East**
Saberhagen, Fred   2041

**Empire of the Senseless**
Acker, Kathy   3457, 4581

**The Empire of Time**
Kilian, Crawford   178, 188, 895, 2563, 4151

**The Empire Strikes Back**
Glut, Donald F.   2171, 4299, 5279, 6052, 6054, 6075

**Empire's End**
Cole, Allan   **1103**, 1598

**Empire's Horizon**
Brizzolara, John   **707**, 1210

**The Empress of Earth**
Scott, Melissa   4593

**Emprise**
Kube-McDowell, Michael P.   1184, 2301, 2836, 3448, 3719, 3825, 4062, 5788, 5933

**The Empty Throne**
Emerson, Ru   559, **1808**

**Empty World**
Christopher, John   1133

**The Enchanted Cat**
Stephens, John Richard   3740, 4054, 4144, 4145

**Enchanted Forests**
Kerr, Katharine   2381, **3070**

**The Enchanted Isles**
Flynn, Casey   **1960**, 2677, 3166, 3174, 3358, 3969

**Enchanter**
Bailey, Robin Wayne   1754, 1839, 3913

**The Enchanter Reborn**
de Camp, L. Sprague   **1413**, 3015, 5219

**The Enchantments of Flesh and Spirit**
Constantine, Storm   **1141**, 2295, 3405, 3742

**Encounter at Farpoint**
Gerrold, David   1229, 1247, 2061, 2066

**Encounter with Tiber**
Aldrin, Buzz   **64**

**End as a Hero**
Laumer, Keith   2252

**End Game**
Cain, Robert   **830**

**End Game**
David, Peter  **1382**

**The End of Alice**
Homes, A.M.  **2755**, 4183

**End of an Era**
Sawyer, Robert J.  **4853**, 5067

**The End of Eternity**
Asimov, Isaac  2012, 2489, 3979, 4164

**The End-of-Everything Man**
De Haven, Tom  **1421**

**End of the Circle**
McKinney, Jack  5204

**The End of Tragedy**
Ingalls, Rachel  920, 2842, 3195, 4182, 5166

**Endangered Species**
Wolfe, Gene  61, 321, 621, 625, 823, 3379, **5940**, 6067

**Ender's Game**
Card, Orson Scott  250, 414, 469, 478, 566, 785, 903, 1054, 1168, 1254, 1381, 1627, 1641, 1680, 1896, 1987, 2807, 3037, 3398, 3692, 3726, 3760, 3790, 3937, 4117, 4290, 4373, 4505, 4762, 4884, 5955, 6051

**Endgame**
ab Hugh, Dafydd  3467

**Endgame**
Cherryh, C.J.  **986**, 1388

**Endgame Enigma**
Hogan, James P.  597, 2301

**The Endless Knot**
Lawhead, Stephen R.  **3354**

**Endorphins**
Kilpatrick, Nancy  **3111**

**The Ends of the Circle**
Williams, Paul O.  394, 1324

**The Ends of the Earth**
Shepard, Lucius  2835, 3048, 3086, 3234, 3442, 4561, **4977**, 5056

**Endymion**
Simmons, Dan  1442, 2059, 2525, 3718, 4060, 5001, **5051**, 6081

**An Enemy at Green Knowe**
Boston, L.M.  4080

**Enemy Mine**
Longyear, Barry B.  434, 4125

**Enemy Mine/Another Orphan**
Longyear, Barry B.  3189

**Enemy of God**
Cornwell, Bernard  **1189**

**Enemy of My Enemy**
Ohlander, Ben  **4204**

**An Enemy Reborn**
Stackpole, Michael A.  **5197**

**The Enemy Stars**
Anderson, Poul  3777

**Enemy Unseen**
Mitchell, V.E.  569, 2552, **3918**

**The Enemy Within**
Golden, Christie  155, 2516

**The Engines of God**
McDevitt, Jack  378, 684, 1258, 1259, 1500, 1565, 3763, **3787**, 4281, 4859, 5372

**English Fairy Tales**
Jacobs, Joseph  2636

**Engor's Sword Arm**
Smith, David C.  2782, **5110**, 5471

**Enigma**
Kube-McDowell, Michael P.  953, 1992, 2836, 3398, 3821, 3824, 4062, 4483, 4505, 5933, 6085

**The Enigma Variations**
Roberts, John Maddox  **4618**

**Ensign Flandry**
Anderson, Poul  1900, 3735, 3861, 3928, 3970, 5403, 5514, 5922

**Enterprise**
McIntyre, Vonda N.  526, 900

**Entity**
Mandelik, Nina  1077, **3615**

**Entombed**
Smith, Guy N.  3347

**Entoverse**
Hogan, James P.  472, 1981, **2724**

**The Entropy Effect**
McIntyre, Vonda N.  526, 1386

**Eon**
Bear, Greg  127, 326, 381, 382, 399, 403, **417**, 444, 447, 784, 785, 786, 928, 930, 931, 953, 954, 985, 1337, 1557, 1565, 1876, 1897, 1992, 2002, 2417, 2882, 3014, 3064, 3117, 3771, 3786, 4103, 4333, 4351, 4353, 4420, 4505, 4705, 4951, 5052, 5304

**Eons of the Night**
Howard, Robert E.  **2781**

**Equal Rites**
Pratchett, Terry  2573, 4013, **4387**

**Eric**
Pratchett, Terry  4171, **4388**

**Eric John Stark, Outlaw of Mars**
Brackett, Leigh  3746

**Eros in Orbit**
Elder, Joseph  1362, 1607

**Erotic Vampire Tales**
Tan, Cecilia  699, 3182

**Erotica Vampirica**
Tan, Cecilia  3177, 3184, 4689, **5387**

**The Escape**
Smith, Dean Wesley  2297, **5113**, 5880

**Escape From Kathmandu**
Robinson, Kim Stanley  725, 2070, 4062, **4630**, 4866, 4867, 5378

**Escape From Loki**
Farmer, Philip Jose  85, 725, **1870**, 4622, 4623, 4624, 4625, 5307, 5308, 5309

**Escape From New York**
McQuay, Mike  6059

**Escape From Roksamur**
Shepherd, Mark  3479, 3490

**Escape From Tomorrow**
Long, Frank Belknap  **3515**, 5149

**Escape Orbit**
White, James  3522

**Escape to the Wind**
DiMarco, Jennifer  **1559**, 4882, 5209

**Escardy Gap**
Crowther, Peter  **1282**

**The Eskimo Invasion**
Howard, Hayden  5766

**The Essence of Evil**
Faust, Joe Clifford  3828

**The Essential Bordertown**
Windling, Terri  **5914**

**The Essential Ellison: A 35-Year Retrospective**
Ellison, Harlan  893, 3421, 4889

**The Essential World of Darkness**
Wieck, Stewart  5701, 5702, **5797**

**Et Tu, Babe**
Leyner, Mark  **3455**

**The Eternal**
Chadbourn, Mark  3215

**The Eternal Enemy**
Berlyn, Michael  **469**, 785, 1586, 1587, 1594, 2812, 4030, 5930

**The Eternal Enemy**
Pike, Christopher  568, 3597, 4210, 5013, 5372

**Eternal Light**
McAuley, Paul J.  **3710**

**The Eternal Lovecraft: The Persistence of HPL in Popular Culture**
Turner, Jim  **5494**

**The Eternal Lover**
Burroughs, Edgar Rice  3877

**Eternally Yours**
Bernard, Diane  691

**Eternity**
Bear, Greg  326, 381, 590, 783, 1855, 1871, 2140, 2525, 4705, 5052

**Eternity**
Shayne, Maggie  **4943**

**The Eternity Brigade**
Goldin, Stephen  589, 2211, 5204

**Eternity Road**
McDevitt, Jack  **3788**

**Ethan of Athos**
Bujold, Lois McMaster  4148

**Eugenie de Franval and Other Stories**
Sade, Marquis de  3183

**Euryale**
Dalkey, Kara  3309

**Eva**
Dickinson, Peter  **1525**, 2808, 2868, 3703

**The Eve of Saint Venus**
Burgess, Anthony  2073

**Evenings with Demons**
Strieber, Whitley  **5339**

**Everard's Ride**
Jones, Diana Wynne  **2947**, 3279, 3981, 5782, 5973

**Evermeet: Island of Elves**
Cunningham, Elaine  **1290**, 5022

**Everville**
Barker, Clive  338, 4575, 5190, 5414

**Everybody's Favorite Duck**
Wilson, Gahan  6072

**The Evil**
Cave, Hugh B.  1125

**Evil Ascending**
Stackpole, Michael A.  1819, **5198**

**Evil Eye**
Slade, Michael  5085

**The Evil Image: Two Centuries of Gothic Short Fiction and Poetry**
Skarda, Patricia L.  307, 848, 1314, 5439

**Evil Intent**
Taylor, Bernard  2339, **5400**

**The Evil People**
Haining, Peter  2385

**Evil Reincarnate**
Clark, Leigh  690, **1050**, 4710, 4753

**Evil Triumphant**
Stackpole, Michael A.  **5199**

**Evolution's Shore**
McDonald, Ian  1825, 3476, **3792**, 4858, 5068

**The Ewoks and the Lost Children**
Ehrlich, Amy  1392, 1393, 1394

**The Ewoks Join the Fight**
Bogart, Bonnie  1392, 1393, 1394

**An Exaltation of Larks**
Reed, Robert  **4506**

**Excalibur**
Cornwell, Bernard  **1190**

**Excalibur**
Gilliam, Richard  4759

**Excalibur**
Laubenthal, Sanders Anne  4877

**Excavation**
Tem, Steve Rasnic  1036, 1077, 2094, 2668, 3778, 3783, 3951

**An Excess of Enchantments**
Gardner, Craig Shaw  671

**Excession**
Banks, Iain M.  324, 2523, 2525

**An Exchange of Gifts**
McCaffrey, Anne  **3731**

**An Exchange of Hostages**
Matthews, Susan R.  **3692**

**The Executioners**
MacDonald, John D.  1198, 2111, 2843, 3518, 3756

**The Executioner's Song**
Mailer, Norman  1489

*The Executor and Other Ghost Stories*
Rowlands, David G.   1671, 2707, 3314

*Exile*
Friedman, M.J.   999

*Exile*
Kube-McDowell, Michael P.   **3248**

*Exile*
Salvatore, R.A.   2675

*Exile*
Sarrantonio, Al   **4829**

*The Exile Kiss*
Effinger, George Alec   **1750**

*The Exile Waiting*
McIntyre, Vonda N.   2477, 3718, 4043

*Exiled From Earth*
Bova, Ben   6059

*Exiles*
Weinstein, Howard   2066

*Exile's Challenge*
Wells, Angus   **5734**

*Exile's Children*
Wells, Angus   **5735**

*Exile's Gate*
Cherryh, C.J.   922, 1631, 2359, 2436, 3777

*Exiles of Colsec*
Hill, Douglas   3966

*Exiles' Return*
Greeno, Gayle   **2420**, 3096, 4137

*Exile's Song*
Bradley, Marion Zimmer   **632**

*Exiles to Glory*
Pournelle, Jerry   4952

*The Exit at Toledo Blade Boulevard*
Ketchum, Jack   **3090**, 5005

*Exit to Reality*
Forbes, Edith   **1968**

*Exodus From the Long Sun*
Wolfe, Gene   **5941**

*Exorcisms and Ecstasies*
Wagner, Karl Edward   3549, **5600**

*The Exorcist*
Blatty, William Peter   661, 937, 1048, 1804, 2494, 2697, 4239, 5342, 5896

*Expanded Universe*
Heinlein, Robert A.   5938

*Expansion*
Hamilton, Peter F.   **2525**

*The Expected One*
Rogers, Mark E.   3016, 3154

*Expecting Someone Taller*
Holt, Tom   36, 355, 4056, 4393, 4400

*The Expediter*
Clarke, J. Brian   **1062**, 4219

*Expendable*
Gardner, James Alan   1303, **2135**

*Expiration Date*
Powers, Tim   2687, **4383**, 5570

*Expiry Date*
Davis, Carol Anne   **1401**

*Exquisite Corpse*
Brite, Poppy Z.   **695**, 1890, 3183

*Extinct*
Wilson, Charles   88, 189, **5877**

*Extreme Paranoia: Nobody Knows the Trouble I've Shot*
Rolston, Ken   553, 735, 959, 1452, 1805, 2323, 2480, 2567, 2568, 2770, 2979, 3313, 3829, 4076, 4298, 4562, **4662**, 4909, 5074

*Extreme Prejudice*
Graf, L.A.   1729

*Extremities*
Koja, Kathe   **3195**, 4181

*The Eye Above the Mantel and Other Stories*
Long, Frank Belknap   **3516**

*The Eye and the Finger*
Wandrei, Donald   1496, 5628

*An Eye for Dark Places*
Marder, Norma   968, **3622**

*Eye for Eye/The Tunesmith*
Card, Orson Scott   3189

*Eye in the Sky*
Dick, Philip K.   951, 956, 957, **1521**, 3012

*Eye Killers*
Carr, A.A.   **911**, 3967, 4668

*The Eye of Anna*
Wingate, Anne   1829

*The Eye of the Heron*
Le Guin, Ursula K.   877, 2575

*The Eye of the Hunter*
McKiernan, Dennis L.   **3833**, 5203

*Eye of the Needle*
Clegg, Douglas   97

*The Eye of the Ram*
Boggs, Timothy   4912

*The Eye of the World*
Jordan, Robert   164, 287, 457, 487, 712, 717, 979, 994, 1010, 1096, 1422, 1592, 1675, 1682, 1685, 1688, 1690, 1730, 1732, 1733, 1734, 1790, 1837, 1864, 1909, 1911, 2042, 2126, 2128, 2190, 2268, 2269, 2270, 2271, 2677, **2986**, 3044, 3068, 3172, 3305, 3306, 3626, 3765, 3832, 3837, 3892, 3926, 3930, 3985, 4105, 4107, 4154, 4489, 4515, 4526, 4741, 5034, 5203, 5221, 5251, 5320, 5650, 5651, 5711, 5715, 5727, 5734, 5736, 5757, 5829, 5831, 6073

*The Eyes of Darkness*
Koontz, Dean R.   **3206**, 5664

*Eyes of Fire*
Bishop, Michael   353

*The Eyes of God*
Kreighbaum, Mark   760, **3231**

*The Eyes of Laura Mars*
Gilmour, H.B.   1780, 1975, 4471

*Eyes of Silver*
Stackpole, Michael A.   **5200**

*The Eyes of the Beast*
Harris, Steve   2565

*The Eyes of the Beholders*
Crispin, A.C.   1389, 2066, 2068, 3524

*The Eyes of the Dragon*
King, Stephen   347

*Eyes of the Empress*
Bacon-Smith, Camille   285

*The Eyes of the Killer Robot*
Bellairs, John   253, 254, 255

*The Eyes of the Overworld*
Vance, Jack   3158

*The Eyes of Torie Webster*
Sorrels, Roy   2606, **5164**, 5472, 5961


**F**


*F.R.E.E.Lancers*
Odom, Mel   **4191**

*Fables and Fantasies*
Stableford, Brian   2225, 3859, 5103

*The Fabulist*
Vornholt, John   1681, 3504, **5595**

*Fabulous Harbors*
Moorcock, Michael   **3981**

*The Fabulous Riverboat*
Farmer, Philip Jose   961

*Facade*
Rusch, Kristine Kathryn   **4716**

*A Face at the Window*
McFarland, Dennis   2241, **3809**, 5440

*The Face in the Abyss*
Merritt, A.   **3878**, 5626

*The Face in the Frost*
Bellairs, John   520, 2075, 4395, 4396, 4400, 5626

*The Face of Another*
Abe, Kobo   **19**, 1334, 3020, 5073

*The Face of Apollo*
Saberhagen, Fred   **4766**

*The Face of the Deep*
Young, Jim   1861, 3919

*The Face of the Waters*
Silverberg, Robert   4176, 4507, **5029**, 5726

*The Face That Must Die*
Campbell, Ramsey   540, 2110, 2755, 3088, 3716, 3807, 3902, 4088, 4185, 4248, 5318, 5327

*The Faces of Ceti*
Caraker, Mary   **877**

*Faces of Deception*
Denning, Troy   **1485**

*Faces under Water*
Lee, Tanith   **3409**

*Facets*
Williams, Walter Jon   5837

*Fade*
Cormier, Robert   709, **1188**, 3493, 5013

*Fade to Black*
Smith, Nyx   **5134**, 5207

*Faded Garden: The Collected Ghost Stories of Hildegarde Hawthorne*
Hawthorne, Hildegarde   2919

*The Faded Sun: Kesrith*
Cherryh, C.J.   513, 517, 631, 1067, 1381, 1771, 2038, 2194, 2224, 3316, 3839, 4550, 5019, 5469

*The Faded Sun: Kutath*
Cherryh, C.J.   1923, 2194

*The Faded Sun: Shon'Jir*
Cherryh, C.J.   1774, 2194

*Faerie Tale*
Feist, Raymond E.   338, 343, 1432, 2160, 3144, 3779, 5207, 5879

*Faeries*
Asimov, Isaac   **235**, 2388

*Faery*
Windling, Terri   235, 1340, 1368, 2388, 4335

*The Faery Convention*
Davis, Brett   315, **1399**, 4389, 5459

*The Faery Flag*
Yolen, Jane   5995

*Faery in Shadow*
Cherryh, C.J.   **987**, 3636, 4674

*Faery Lands Forlorn*
Duncan, Dave   **1677**

*The Fagin*
Graversen, Pat   2203, **2334**, 2748, 2930

*Fahrenheit 451*
Bradbury, Ray   5568

*Fair Peril*
Springer, Nancy   **5178**

*The Fair Rules of Evil*
Smith, David C.   2020, 2607, 4820, **5111**

*Fairy Tales From Brentano*
Brentano, Clemens Maria   2447

*The Fairy Tales of Hermann Hesse*
Hesse, Hermann   **2680**

*The Fairy Tales of Wilhelm Hauff*
Hauff, Wilhelm   2447

*Fairyland*
McAuley, Paul J.   835, 2218, **3711**

*Fairytales*
Tem, Steve Rasnic   **5427**

*Faith of Tarot*
Anthony, Piers   4926

*The Faithful Traitor*
Hughes, Robert Don   **2809**

**Falcon**
Bull, Emma   517, 580, 756, **768**, 985, 1102, 1557, 3450, 3451, 3458, 3748, 3875, 3928, 3929, 4226, 4287

**The Falcon and the Serpent**
Smith, Cheryl A.   **5101**

**The Falcon Rises**
Staudinger, Michael C.   701, **5235**

**Falkenberg's Legion**
Pournelle, Jerry   1322, 1326, 1327, 1546, 2171, 2351, 2353, 2435, 3035, **4374**, 4466, 4583, 4672, 5300, 5465, 5469

**Fall into Darkness**
Yermakov, Nicholas   1025

**Fall of Angels**
Modesitt, L.E. Jr.   **3930**

**The Fall of Atlantis**
Bradley, Marion Zimmer   4146

**The Fall of Chronopolis**
Bayley, Barrington J.   2489

**The Fall of Hyperion**
Simmons, Dan   80, 96, 116, 272, 404, 414, 417, 423, 449, 883, 899, 952, 1054, 1184, 1634, 1820, 2036, 2480, 2725, 3014, 3437, 4099, 4507, 4762, 4769, 4857, 4954, 4965, 5029, **5052**, 5905

**A Fall of Moondust**
Clarke, Arthur C.   2881, 2882, 5597

**The Fall of Sirius**
McCarthy, Wil   1315, **3762**, 4775

**The Fall of the House of Escher and Other Illusions**
Wilson, David Niall   94, 663, 802, 1789, 2769, 2937, 3495, 4231, 4313, 5316, 5335, 5445, 5620, **5881**

**The Fall of the House of Usher**
Poe, Edgar Allan   3813

**Fall of the White Ship Avatar**
Daley, Brian   260, 261, 1103, 1106, 1144, 1572

**Fallen**
Graham, Dee   **2302**, 4710

**Fallen Angels**
Niven, Larry   553, 597, 677, 735, 1543, 1805, 1921, 1962, 2301, 2567, 2568, 3313, 3429, 3932, **4120**, 4546, 4639, 4641, 5209, 5499, 5697

**The Fallen Country**
Sucharitkul, Somtow   5163

**Fallen Heroes**
ab Hugh, Dafydd   **8**, 2917

**Falling Angel**
Hjortsberg, William   21, 619, 1125, 1792, 2110, 4006, 4085, 4100

**The Falling Astronauts**
Malzberg, Barry   5057

**Falling Free**
Bujold, Lois McMaster   356, 1589, 2558, 2763, 2766, 3824, 4418, 4419, 4504, 4643, 4963, 5491, 5541, 5809

**Falling Idols**
Hodge, Brian   1016, **2701**, 5026

**The Falling Woman**
Murphy, Pat   351, 744, 1272, 4332, 5477, 5806

**Fallway**
Downing, Paula E.   1586, **1593**, 2223, 2224, 2476, 2683, 3707, 3708, 3709, 3723, 3752, 3760, 5467

**False Dawn**
Yarbro, Chelsea Quinn   4621

**The False Mirror**
Foster, Alan Dean   **2004**, 4378

**Familiar Spirit**
Tuttle, Lisa   **5519**

**The Family Tree**
Tepper, Sheri S.   1943, 2243, 3241, **5429**

**Famine**
Komarnicki, Todd   **3201**, 3525

**The Famished Road**
Okri, Ben   1411, 1412, 1433, 1438, 1867, 1868, 2735, 2771, 3006, 3007, 3173, **4207**, 4358, 4544, 5273, 5578

**Famous Fantastic Mysteries**
Dziemianowicz, Stefan   **1712**

**Famous Ghost Stories**
Cerf, Bennett   1309

**Famous Monsters**
Newman, Kim   2018

**Famous Tales of India**
Kipling, Rudyard   195, 1316, 1317

**The Fan Man**
Kotzwinkle, William   3011, 3455

**Fane**
Alexander, David   2688

**Fanglith**
Dalmas, John   3801, 5588

**Fangs and the Hooded Demon**
Marsh, Geoffrey   1415

**The Fantasies of Harlan Ellison**
Ellison, Harlan   3222

**Fantasma**
Monteleone, Thomas F.   **3963**

**The Fantastic Adventures of Robin Hood**
Greenberg, Martin H.   2248, **2389**, 4534

**Fantastic Alice**
Weis, Margaret   4134, **5713**

**The Fantastic Civil War**
McSherry, Frank D. Jr.   442, 443, **3867**, 4814, 5502

**The Fantastic Swordsmen**
de Camp, L. Sprague   2657, 4082, 4611, 4759, 5599

**Fantastic Tales**
Tarchetti, I.U.   2718, **5389**

**Fantastic Tales: Visionary and Everyday**
Calvino, Italo   **848**

**Fantastic Voyage II: Destination Brain**
Asimov, Isaac   5892

**Fantastique**
Kaye, Marvin   2428, **3025**, 4588

**The Fantasy Hall of Fame**
Silverberg, Robert   228, 1613, 2592, 3574, 5003, **5030**, 5730

**The Fantasy Stories of George MacDonald**
MacDonald, George   4021

**Fantasy Tales #2**
Jones, Stephen   **2965**

**Fantasy Tales #4**
Jones, Stephen   **2966**

**Fantasy Tales #6**
Jones, Stephen   **2967**

**Fanuilh**
Hood, Daniel   **2757**, 5848

**Far and Away**
Boucher, Anthony   59

**Far Away and Never**
Campbell, Ramsey   **856**, 2781, 2782, 5110, 5471

**Far Below and Other Horrors**
Weinberg, Robert   480, 2485, 3028

**Far Beyond the Wave**
ab Hugh, Dafydd   5785

**The Far Call**
Dickson, Gordon R.   380, 388, 586, 597, 1248

**Far Edge of Darkness**
Evans, Linda   264, 350, 1638, **1855**

**Far Futures**
Benford, Gregory   402, **445**, 4066

**Far Harbor**
Michaels, Melisa C.   517, 3458, 3603, **3888**, 3929, 4482, 5524

**The Far Islands and Other Tales of Fantasy**
Buchan, John   5762

**The Far Kingdoms**
Cole, Allan   **1104**, 1251, 1912, 3353, 4744

**Far Lands, Other Days**
Price, E. Hoffman   940, 942, 1088, 1700, 2780, 4741, 5628

**Far-Seer**
Sawyer, Robert J.   398, 416, 1988, 2122, 2386, 2468, 3427, 3738, 4743, 4744, **4854**

**A Far Sunset**
Cooper, Edmund   5496

**Faraday's Orphans**
Wood, N. Lee   3599, **5965**

**A Farce to Be Reckoned With**
Zelazny, Roger   2574, **6064**

**Farewell, Earth's Bliss**
Compton, D.G.   421, 586, 5377

**Farewell Horizontal**
Jeter, K.W.   **2911**, 5899

**Farewell to Lankhmar**
Leiber, Fritz   **3418**

**Farmer in the Sky**
Heinlein, Robert A.   380, 1768, 2549, 4964

**Farnham's Freehold**
Heinlein, Robert A.   116, 435, 3873, 4018, 4599, 5659

**Farside Cannon**
Allen, Roger MacBride   1916

**The Farthest-Away Mountain**
Banks, Lynne Reid   3545

**The Farthest Shore**
Le Guin, Ursula K.   1175, 2461, 2865, 4149, 4265, 5142, 5832, 6024, 6025

**Fast Forward**
Pausacker, Jenny   1558

**Fat Face**
Shea, Michael   4007, 5426, 5446

**Fata Morgana**
Kotzwinkle, William   1151

**Fatal Outcome**
Wallace, Patricia   4480, **5622**

**The Father Christmas Letters**
Tolkien, J.R.R.   2456

**Father of Frankenstein**
Bram, Christopher   **659**, 1094

**Father to the Man**
Gribbin, John   1165, 1525, **2434**

**Fatherland**
Harris, Robert   598, 2239, **2564**, 2667, 3528, 3601, 4474, 5517, 5518

**Father's Little Helper**
Kelly, Ronald   916, 2755, **3052**

**Fault Lines**
Reidah, Alvah   1060

**Faun & Games**
Anthony, Piers   **169**

**Favorite Folktales From around the World**
Yolen, Jane   849, 2528, 4987

**Fear**
Hubbard, L. Ron   **2789**, 3417

**Fear and Loathing in Las Vegas**
Thompson, Hunter S.   3455, 3456

**Fear and Trembling**
Bloch, Robert   533

**Fear Book**
Byrne, John   2022, 5784

**The Fear in Yesterday's Rings**
Chesbro, George C.   **1007**, 1570, 2138, 5552

**Fear Itself**
Gelb, Jeff   1279, 1285, **2175**, 2777, 3024, 5666

**Fear Itself**
Meyers, Ric   494, 612, 613, 614, 615, 696, **3881**, 5844

**Fear Nothing**
Koontz, Dean R.   **3207**

**Fear the Fever**
Gelb, Jeff   **2176**

**Fear Walks the Night**
Cowles, Frederick   779, 875, 3633

**The Fearful Summons**
Flinn, Denny Martin   **1954**

**A Fearful Symmetry**
Luceno, James   **3542**

**Fears**
Grant, Charles L.   1284, 2175, 2777, 5666, 5667

**The Feasting Dead**
Metcalfe, John   2111, 5423

**Feather Stroke**
Van Scyoc, Sydney J.   1757, 3287, 4162, 4515, **5542**

**Feathered Dragon**
Niles, Douglas   2675, **4108**

**Federation**
Reeves-Stevens, Judith   902, 904, 2065, **4511**, 4927, 4934

**The Feeding**
Clark, Leigh   1038, **1051**, 1295, 2203, 3369

**Feeding the Glamour Hogs**
McLaughlin, Mark   **3851**

**The Feelies**
Farren, Mick   805, **1878**, 3311, 4339, 5353

**Feersum Endjinn**
Banks, Iain M.   **325**, 838, 5828

**Feet of Clay**
Pratchett, Terry   **4389**

**Felix and Alexander**
Denton, Terry   3377

**Fellow Traveller**
Barton, William   380, 388, 2433

**The Fellow Travellers and Other Ghost Stories**
Hodgson, Sheila   1671, **2707**, 5776

**The Fellowship of the Ring**
Tolkien, J.R.R.   18, 487, 710, 711, 716, 717, 915, 991, 992, 1592, 1675, 1738, 1952, 1953, 2235, 2271, 2378, 2531, 2887, 2888, 2924, 2959, 2985, 3765, 3833, 3834, 3835, 3893, 4107, 4109, 4110, 4520, 4906, 4908, 5554, 5714, 6024

**The Fellowship of the Talisman**
Simak, Clifford D.   185, 355, 630, 884, 955, 1998, 2945, 3822, 5228

**The Female Man**
Russ, Joanna   1211, 1590, 1653, 1720, 2242, 4792, 5477

**Feminist Fairy Tales**
Walker, Barbara G.   794, **5617**

**Ferman's Devils**
Faust, Joe Clifford   **1892**

**The Fermata**
Baker, Nicholson   **302**, 3459, 3493

**Festival Moon**
Cherryh, C.J.   647, 3643, 3646, 5038

**Fetish**
Bryant, Edward   **749**, 1834, 2938, 4570

**Fevre Dream**
Martin, George R.R.   1124, 2009, 2191, 3602, 3977, 5151

**A Few Bricks Shy**
Gardner, S. Anthony   **2137**

**Ficciones**
Borges, Jorge Luis   3460, 3461, 3464

**Fiction Stories**
Matschatt, Cecile   6027

**Fiddler Fair**
Lackey, Mercedes   **3279**

**Fiddler's Fee**
Bloch, Robert   3950

**Field of Death**
Martin, Les   3544

**Field of Dishonor**
Weber, David   **5670**

**Fields of Blood: Vampire Stories of the Heartland**
Schimel, Lawrence   **4879**

**Fiend**
Andersson, C. Dean   **138**

**Fiends**
Farris, John   1204, **1884**, 2091, 2936, 5553

**The Fifth Book of Lost Swords: Coinspinner's Story**
Saberhagen, Fred   2863

**The Fifth Child**
Lessing, Doris   95, 330, 1141

**The Fifth Element**
Bisson, Terry   **504**

**The Fifth Head of Cerberus**
Wolfe, Gene   927, 5732

**Fifth Quarter**
Huff, Tanya   **2795**, 4524

**The Fifth Sacred Thing**
Starhawk   1499, 1835, 4631, **5209**

**The Fifth Season**
Williamson, J.N.   **5854**

**Fifty Years of Ghost Stories**
Anonymous   1310

**The Final Battle**
Dietz, William C.   **1546**, 2432, 4972

**The Final Battle**
Lupoff, Richard A.   1429, **3572**

**Final Blackout**
Hubbard, L. Ron   1113, **2790**

**Final Diagnosis**
White, James   **5777**

**The Final Diary Entry of Kees Hujgens**
Stotler, William R.   **5317**, 5446

**The Final Encyclopedia**
Dickson, Gordon R.   2054, 4377, 5917, 5920, 5921, 5922

**The Final Fury**
ab Hugh, Dafydd   **9**, 903, 1663, 2297, 5115, 5404

**Final Impact**
Navarro, Yvonne   400

**The Final Nexus**
DeWeese, Gene   5115

**The Final Planet**
Greeley, Andrew M.   4081

**The Final Programme**
Moorcock, Michael   1879

**Final Rain**
Ahern, Jerry   277

**The Final Reflection**
Ford, John M.   528, 1922, 4037

**Final Refuge**
Scarborough, Elizabeth Ann   4061, 5199

**Final Sacrifice**
Emery, Clayton   **1814**

**Final Shadows**
Grant, Charles L.   **2306**, 3962, 4206, 5795

**Find Your Own Truth**
Charrette, Robert N.   **972**, 1591, 1935, 3245, 4304, 5135, 5731

**Finder**
Bull, Emma   424, 743, **769**, 1148, 1152, 2373, 3294, 3487, 4995, 5409, 5555, 5694, 5818, 5914

**Finder's Bane**
Novak, Kate   **4165**

**Finders-Seekers**
Greeno, Gayle   1000, **2421**, 2550, 3298, 3776

**A Fine and Private Place**
Beagle, Peter S.   271, 2687, 3201, 3433, 4023, 4383, 5530

**Fine Prey**
Westerfeld, Scott   **5766**

**Finger of God**
Kasner, Michael   **3013**

**Finity's End**
Cherryh, C.J.   **988**, 1978, 4910

**Finn Family Moomintroll**
Jansson, Tove   6006

**Finn Mac Cool**
Llywelyn, Morgan   **3504**, 4266, 4267, 4268

**Fire**
Rodgers, Alan   343, **4647**, 5190

**Fire and Hemlock**
Jones, Diana Wynne   194, 5428

**Fire and Ice**
Myers, Edward   1169, 4020, **4061**, 5033

**Fire Angels**
Routley, Jane   **4685**

**Fire Arrow**
Pattou, Edith   **4260**

**Fire Crossing**
Franklin, Cheryl J.   471, 472, 510, 929, 1101, 1756, **2036**, 2524, 2724, 3725, 4485, 5951

**Fire Dancer**
Maxwell, Ann   1772

**The Fire Duke**
Rosenberg, Joel   741, 1529, 2639, 4522, **4671**

**Fire From Heaven**
Renault, Mary   2187

**Fire Get**
Franklin, Cheryl J.   930, 2524, 2724, 3933, 5124, 5125, 5449, 6073

**Fire in a Faraway Place**
Frezza, Robert   **2052**

**The Fire in His Hands**
Cook, Glen   3016, 3154

**Fire in the Abyss**
Gordon, Stuart   5927

**Fire in the Blood**
Elrod, P.N.   **1796**

**Fire in the Mist**
Lisle, Holly   1413, 3302, **3482**, 5296

**Fire in the Sky**
Clayton, Jo   **1067**

**A Fire in the Sun**
Effinger, George Alec   **1751**, 3946, 3947, 4941, 5644

**Fire Lord**
Franklin, Cheryl J.   2524, 2724

**Fire Margins**
Norman, Lisanne   3718, **4137**

**Fire on the Border**
O'Donnell, Kevin Jr.   1103, **4194**

**Fire on the Mountain**
Bisson, Terry   496, 1133, 2577, 3867, 3993, 5502, 5633

**Fire Planet**
Griffin, P.M.   **2436**

**The Fire Queen**
Holland, Jack   633, **2740**, 5783

**The Fire Rose**
Lackey, Mercedes   1462, **3280**, 3663, 4764

**Fire Sea**
Weis, Margaret   27, 510, 681, 717, 1100, 1488, 1533, 2519, 3050, 3174, 4174, 4458, **5714**, 5740

**The Fire Sword**
Martine-Barnes, Adrienne   4266, 4267, 4268, 4608, 4920, 4991

**Fire Time**
Anderson, Poul   2810

*A Fire upon the Deep*
Vinge, Vernor   46, 79, 81, 236, 309,
    322, 324, 382, 402, 414, 471, 478,
    684, 687, 688, 708, 792, 883, 892,
    933, 934, 983, 990, 1003, 1059,
    1083, 1183, 1184, 1264, 1303,
    1333, 1337, 1458, 1573, 1575,
    1586, 1587, 1663, 1664, 1727,
    1820, 1989, 1992, 1993, 1999,
    2010, 2087, 2374, 2523, 2524,
    2525, 2551, 2832, 3469, 3617,
    3722, 3724, 3733, 3743, 3749,
    3762, 3787, 3821, 3823, 4122,
    4138, 4292, 4356, 4503, 4554,
    4760, 4761, 4855, 4895, 4898,
    4966, 4967, 5051, 5059, 5116,
    5138, 5140, 5254, 5260, 5354,
    5363, 5462, 5566, **5573**, 5668,
    5679, 5834, 5949, 6079, 6085,
    6086

*Fire Watch*
Willis, Connie   1854, 5807

*Fireball*
Christopher, John   2647

*Firebird*
Lackey, Mercedes   **3281**

*Firebird*
Tyers, Kathy   1772

*The Firebrand*
Bradley, Marion Zimmer   1253, 2036,
    3356, 3725, 4553, 5017, 5434,
    6053

*The Fireclown*
Moorcock, Michael   1879

*Firecode*
Yarbro, Chelsea Quinn   3251

*Firedance*
Baker, Scott   4943

*Firedance*
Barnes, Steven   **360**

*Firedrake*
Knaak, Richard A.   5563, 5708, 5790

*Firefly*
Anthony, Piers   **170**, 5771

*Firefly. . .Burning Bright*
Hoffman, Barry   1016, 2155, 2656,
    **2714**

*Firehand*
Norton, Andre   **4151**

*Firelance*
Mace, David   1924, **3586**

*Firelord*
Godwin, Parke   273, 2188, 3017

*The Fires of Azeroth*
Cherryh, C.J.   1581, 2436, 4152,
    4520, 5741, 5951

*Fires of Eden*
Simmons, Dan   2743, **5053**

*The Fires of Heaven*
Jordan, Robert   257, 2098, **2987**

*The Fires of Merlin*
Barron, T.A.   **369**

*The Fire's Stone*
Huff, Tanya   **2796**, 3288, 3305,
    3512, 3514, 3914, 4521

*Firestar*
Flynn, Michael   405, 1244, **1962**,
    2660, 4295, 5248, 5860

*Firestarter*
King, Stephen   93, 97, 610, 879,
    1971, 2112, 2284, 2530, 2704,
    3211, 3215, 3230, 3251, 3594,
    3860, 4480, 4841, 5850

*Firestorm*
Graf, L.A.   2064

*Firewalk*
Logston, Anne   3080, **3509**, 3652

*First Battle*
Michaels, Melisa C.   209, 1043,
    1543, 2437

*First Blast of the Trumpet Against the
    Monstrous Regiment of Women*
McCormack, Eric   **3779**

*The First Book of Swords*
Saberhagen, Fred   3507, 3978

*The First Casualty*
Seidman, David L.   **4912**

*First Channel*
Lichtenberg, Jacqueline   1304, 2665,
    2806, 4735

*First Contact*
Knight, Damon   4406

*First Contacts: The Essential Murray
    Leinster*
Leinster, Murray   2547, **3430**

*First Dawn*
Moscoe, Mike   **4038**, 5496

*The First Dog*
Brett, Jan   3377

*The First Duelist*
Etheridge, Rutledge   **1849**

*First Flight*
Claremont, Chris   2256, 3307

*First Frontier*
Carey, Diane   **902**, 1225

*The First Horror*
Stine, R.L.   **5288**

*The First Immortal*
Halperin, James L.   **2498**

*First King of Shannara*
Brooks, Terry   **712**

*First Light*
Ackroyd, Peter   815

*First Love: A Gothic Tale*
Oates, Joyce Carol   **4183**

*The First Named*
Wylie, Jonathan   5133

*First Power Play*
Miller, John   554, 827, 3036

*First Strike*
Carey, Diane   9, **903**, 1663, 2297,
    5115

*Firstborn*
Thompson, Paul B.   4109, **5454**

*Fish Soup*
Le Guin, Ursula K.   2144, **3378**,
    6089

*A Fisherman of the Inland Sea*
Le Guin, Ursula K.   274, 1653, 3235,
    **3379**, 5410

*Fisherman's Hope*
Feintuch, David   **1900**, 4972

*The Fishers From Outside*
Carter, Lin   3555

*A Fist Full of Stories (and Articles)*
Lansdale, Joe R.   **3328**

*A Fit of Shivers*
Aiken, Joan   1526

*Five Children and It*
Nesbit, E.   5968

*The Five Gold Bands*
Vance, Jack   1871

*Five Hundred Years After*
Brust, Steven   **742**

*Five-Twelfths of Heaven*
Scott, Melissa   882, 897, 4594, 4942,
    5298, 5546

*A Flag Full of Stars*
Ferguson, Brad   905, 1260, 1511,
    **1922**, 2296

*Flag in Exile*
Weber, David   1046, 1315, 2476,
    **5671**

*A Flame in Byzantium*
Yarbro, Chelsea Quinn   5503

*Flame War*
Quittner, Joshua   2322

*Flames of the Dragon*
Bailey, Robin Wayne   **287**

*Flamesong*
Barker, M.A.R.   1317, 1318, 1904,
    1906, 1909, 1910, 2887, 2888,
    4020, 5391

*Flameweaver*
Ball, Margaret   **314**, 563, 633, 2424,
    3303, 3304, 3878, 5757

*Flanders*
Anthony, Patricia   5501

*Flandry of Terra*
Anderson, Poul   1633, 4037

*Flare*
Zelazny, Roger   399, 3789, 4416,
    4947, 5258, **6065**

*Flare Star*
Downing, Paula E.   996, **1594**, 1899,
    3707, 3708, 3709, 4148, 5403,
    6065

*A Flash of White*
Vachss, Andrew   1021

*Flatland*
Abbott, Edwin A.   4070

*Flatlander*
Niven, Larry   4066, **4121**

*Flaxman Low, Psychic Detective*
Heron, E.   509

*The Fleet*
Drake, David   1896, 4373

*The Fleet 1-6*
Drake, David   6005

*The Fleet of Stars*
Anderson, Poul   **126**

*Flesh*
Farmer, Philip Jose   3543, 5490

*Flesh*
Weill, Gus   627, 1027, 2115, 4437,
    **5685**

*Flesh and Blood*
Fowler, D.A.   **2024**

*Flesh and Gold*
Gotlieb, Phyllis   **2286**

*The Flesh Artist*
Taylor, Lucy   1401, 1890, 2155,
    2655, 2778, 3393, **5412**, 5536

*Flesh Wounds*
Fowler, Christopher   3673

*Flicker*
Roszak, Theodore   428, 1353, 2214,
    2448, 3541, 3682, **4683**, 4734

*Flickering Shadows*
Kamau, Kwadwo Agymah   1462,
    **3006**

*Flies From the Amber*
McCarthy, Wil   1157, **3763**

*The Flies of Memory*
Watson, Ian   2953, 2955, **5635**

*Flight in Yiktor*
Norton, Andre   3625

*The Flight of Michael McBride*
Snyder, Midori   1512, 2009, 3118,
    3280, **5151**, 5356, 5357

*Flight of the Dragon Kyn*
Fletcher, Susan   1249, **1951**

*The Flight of the Dragonfly*
Forward, Robert L.   1245

*The Flight of the Horse*
Niven, Larry   131, 135, 1255, 1752,
    3191, 4195, 4198, 5351, 5497,
    5956

*Flight of the Raven*
Roberson, Jennifer   **4608**

*Flight of Vengeance*
Norton, Andre   **4152**

*Flight to Hollow Mountain*
Sebanc, Mark   1042, **4908**

*Flights of Fear*
Masterton, Graham   2018, **3673**

*Flint the King*
Kirchoff, Mary   5454, 5455

*Floater Factor*
Michaels, Melisa C.   4962

*The Floating Castle*
Mills, Craig   **3913**, 4495

*Floating Dragon*
Straub, Peter   943, 1136, 2541,
    3091, 3337, 3370, 4012, 5845

*Flood Tide*
Cherryh, C.J.   **989**

*Flow My Tears, the Policeman Said*
Dick, Philip K.   193, 3612

*Flowerdust*
Jones, Gwyneth   **2952**

Title Index

**Flowers for Algernon**
Keyes, Daniel   1460, 3200, 5907

**Flowers From the Moon and Other Lunacies**
Bloch, Robert   **534**

**Flowers in the Attic**
Andrews, V.C.   70, 5808, 5926

**Flowers of Evil**
Charles, Robert   1625, 5081, 5858

**Fluke**
Herbert, James   4582

**Flute Song**
Burleson, Donald   1296, 4650

**Flute Song Magic**
Shettle, Andrea   1583, 3286, 4167, 4801, 4806, **4996**, 5179, 6043

**Flux**
Baxter, Stephen   **399**, 932

**Flying Dutch**
Holt, Tom   1752, **2750**

**Flying in Place**
Palwick, Susan   396, 397, 970, 1130, 2326, 2445, 2614, 2876, 2951, 3007, 3302, 3473, 3844, 4183, **4240**, 4758, 4862, 5415, 5430, 5912

**Flying Saucers over Hennepin**
Gelman, Peter   **2186**

**Flying Sorcerers**
Gerrold, David   4785

**Flying to Valhalla**
Pellegrino, Charles   133, 2252, **4280**

**The Flying Warlord**
Frankowski, Leo   33, **2044**, 4814

**The Fog**
Herbert, James   800, 943, 2787, 2867, 3370

**Fog Heart**
Tessier, Thomas   839, 3126, **5440**

**The Folk of the Air**
Beagle, Peter S.   **407**, 727, 987, 1747, 1748, 1841, 3170

**The Folk of the Fringe**
Card, Orson Scott   435, **886**, 1457, 3931, 4152, 4620, 5383

**Folktales From India**
Ramanujan, A.K.   849

**Folktales of China**
Eberhard, Wolfram   6026

**The Fontana Book of Ghost Stories Series**
Aickman, Robert   1309

**The Food of the Gods**
Wells, H.G.   874, 4842

**Fool on the Hill**
Ruff, Matt   1206, 2465, **4707**, 5153

**Fools**
Cadigan, Pat   60, 505, **805**, 1449, 1696, 2092, 2163, 2527, 2727, 2839, 2907, 3829, 4071, 4192, 4590, 4747, 4860, 5171, 5184, 5213

**Fool's Run**
McKillip, Patricia A.   807, 1265, 2690, 5524

**The Fools' War**
Kisling, Lee   **3159**

**Fool's War**
Zettel, Sarah   1303, 3231, **6079**

**Footfall**
Niven, Larry   108, 205, 414, 1057, 1258, 1508, 2646, 3429, 3944, 4281, 4301, 4760, 4775, 4858, 4919, 5516, 5517, 5677, 5866

**Footprints of Thunder**
David, James F.   1049, 1256, **1379**

**For Fear of Little Men**
Blackburn, John   1038, 2541, 2672, 3091

**For Fear of the Night**
Grant, Charles L.   918, 1468, 4832

**For Love of Evil**
Anthony, Piers   652, 4781, 4782

**For the Blood Is the Life and Other Stories**
Crawford, F. Marion   **1252**

**For You, the Living**
Sallee, Wayne Allen   4786, 5923

**Foragers**
Oberndorf, Charles   **4187**

**Forbidden Acts**
Collins, Nancy A.   **1120**, 3024

**Forbidden Journeys: Fairy Tales and Fantasies by Victorian Women Writers**
Auerbach, Nina   37, **276**, 648, 2035, 5814, 5815, 6089

**Forbidden Knowledge**
Donaldson, Stephen R.   **1571**

**Forbidden Magic**
Wells, Angus   702, **5736**

**Forbidden Planet**
Stuart, W.J.   2864, 3079, 5244

**Forbidden Sanctuary**
Bowker, Richard   2870

**The Forbidden Tower**
Bradley, Marion Zimmer   218, 219, 1862, 2354, 2357, 3697, 5752

**The Forbidden Zone**
Strieber, Whitley   1037, 2345, 3310, **5340**

**Force of Arms**
Stine, G. Harry   48, 3013, **5279**

**Foreigner**
Cherryh, C.J.   684, 688, 786, 932, **990**, 1259, 1303, 1500, 1589, 1825, 1956, 2922, 3000, 3732, 3750, 3760, 3972, 4138, 4241, 4356, 4711, 4735, 4736, 4932, 5461, 5757

**Forerunner**
Norton, Andre   4592

**The Forest House**
Bradley, Marion Zimmer   266, 267, **633**, 692, 1270, 3260, 5792, 5793, 5794

**A Forest Lord**
Williams, Michael   1146, 2627, **5819**

**Forest of the Night**
Somtow, S.P.   **5156**

**Forest of the Night**
Steussy, Marti   1895, 3536, 4143

**The Forest of Time and Other Stories**
Flynn, Michael   **1963**

**Forests of the Night**
Swann, S. Andrew   1588, 1589, 2906, 2909, 3066, 4476, 4479, 5105, **5363**, 6048

**Forever After**
Zelazny, Roger   5275, **6066**

**The Forever Children**
Flanders, Eric   **1944**, 3637, 4845, 5250, 5314, 5789

**The Forever Drug**
Perry, Steve   **4296**

**Forever in Time**
Bennett, Janice   1271, 3576

**The Forever King**
Cochran, Molly   973, 977, **1092**, 4771

**Forever Knight: A Stirring of Dust**
Sizemore, Susan   **5078**

**Forever Knight: Intimations of Mortality**
Garrett, Susan M.   **2149**

**The Forever Man**
Dickson, Gordon R.   132, 1389, 6051

**Forever Peace**
Haldeman, Joe   **2488**, 3922

**The Forever War**
Haldeman, Joe   206, 352, 398, 513, 589, 901, 904, 1053, 1103, 1627, 1641, 2211, 2245, 2351, 2353, 2464, 2546, 2790, 3937, 4038, 4194, 4204, 4374, 4466, 4477, 4775, 4966, 5115, 5294, 5955

**Forever Yours**
Pierce, David   4329

**The Forge in the Forest**
Rohan, Michael Scott   457, 1173, 1178, 1690, 2884, 2886, 3893, **4660**, 5206, 5738, 5831

**The Forge of God**
Bear, Greg   82, 402, 405, 685, 753, 1057, 1258, 1651, 2646, 2955, 4281, 4416, 4775, 5677

**The Forge of Virtue**
Abbey, Lynn   **16**

**Forget Me Not**
Lazuta, Gene   **3375**

**The Forgetting Room**
Bantock, Nick   52, **333**

**The Forging of the Dragon**
Hughes, Robert Don   2234

**The Forging of the Shadows**
Johnson, Oliver   **2924**, 4685

**The Forgotten**
George, Stephen R.   1656, **2200**, 4499

**The Forgotten Beasts of Eld**
McKillip, Patricia A.   727, 4334

**The Forgotten Door**
Key, Alexander   510, 2948

**Forgotten Tales of Terror**
Lamb, Hugh   1233, 1306, 2993

**The Forlorn Hope**
Drake, David   1327, 4672, 4973

**Forms of Heaven**
Barker, Clive   **339**, 1022, 1112

**The Forsaken**
Fulgham, Steven Ray   **2089**, 4499

**Fortnight of Fear**
Masterton, Graham   3549, **3674**

**Fortress**
Drake, David   3586, 5300

**Fortress in the Eye of Time**
Cherryh, C.J.   **991**, 1065, 3506, 4259, 4714, 5200

**Fortress of Eagles**
Cherryh, C.J.   **992**

**The Fortress of Eternity**
Whitmore, Andrew   3934, 4167, **5790**

**Fortress of Forbidden Destiny**
Syvertson, Ryder   725, **5378**

**Fortress of Frost and Fire**
Lackey, Mercedes   1839, **3282**, 3490, 3913

**Fortress of Owls**
Cherryh, C.J.   **993**

**The Fortress of the Pearl**
Moorcock, Michael   1422, 1470, **3982**, 4515, 4777

**The Fortress of Utopia**
Williamson, Jack   **5863**

**Fortress on the Sun**
Cook, Paul   **1157**

**The Fortunate Fall**
Carter, Raphael   386, 809, **927**, 1458, 2092, 2394, 3072, 3711, 5248, 5355, 5619, 5966, 6063, 6079

**The Fortune Teller**
Schimel, Lawrence   2381

**Fortune's Light**
Friedman, Michael Jan   1383, 3524

**Fortune's Wheel**
Norman, Lisanne   4138

**Forty Thousand in Gehenna**
Cherryh, C.J.   35, 565, 756, 785, 894, 1184, 1323, 1537, 1956, 1986, 2049, 2135, 2421, 3713, 3719, 3723, 3727, 3911, 4038, 4244, 5351, 5404, 5457, 6081

**Forward the Foundation**
Asimov, Isaac   **236**, 418

**Fossil**
Clement, Hal   251, **1083**, 1729, 3734

**Fossil Hunter**
Sawyer, Robert J.   1988, 3427, 4744, **4855**

**Foucault's Pendulum**
Eco, Umberto  334, 335, 1063, 1093, 1273, 1274, 1277, 1397, 2214, 3262, 3682, 4683, 5903

**Foundation**
Asimov, Isaac  894, 984, 2645, 4044, 4375, 4682, 5116, 5917, 5920, 5921, 5922

**Foundation and Chaos**
Bear, Greg  **418**

**Foundation and Earth**
Asimov, Isaac  882, 885

**Foundation and Empire**
Asimov, Isaac  392, 984, 1538, 2051, 2171, 3873, 4044, 4305, 4375, 4553, 5141

**The Foundation Trilogy**
Asimov, Isaac  446, 1540, 3072, 5865

**Foundation's Edge**
Asimov, Isaac  984

**Foundation's Fear**
Benford, Gregory  418, **446**

**Foundation's Friends**
Greenberg, Martin H.  232

**Foundations of Fear**
Hartwell, David G.  226, **2591**, 4440

**The Founder**
Rowley, Christopher  **4696**

**The Fountains of Mirlacca**
McConnell, Ashley  3280, **3775**

**Four & Twenty Blackbirds**
Lackey, Mercedes  **3283**

**Four Ghosts in Hamlet**
Leiber, Fritz  5849

**Four Hundred Billion Stars**
McAuley, Paul J.  952, 2365, 5108

**The Four Lords of the Diamond Series**
Chalker, Jack L.  5544, 5545

**Four Past Midnight**
King, Stephen  **3132**, 3216, 5056

**Four Shadowings**
Burleson, Donald  **776**

**Four Ways to Forgiveness**
Le Guin, Ursula K.  **3380**

**The Fourth Book of Lost Swords: Farslayer's Story**
Saberhagen, Fred  2863

**The Fourth Guardian**
Cross, Ronald Anthony  **1273**, 3262

**The Fourth Horseman**
Nourse, Alan E.  1625, 5081

**The Fourth Rome**
Drake, David  **1631**, 4040

**Fox and Empire**
Turtledove, Harry  **5500**

**The Fox Run**
Robbins, David  278

**The Foxes of Firstdark**
Kilworth, Garry  32, 40, 306, 599, 737, **3115**, 3378, 3523, 4008, 4271

**Fractal Mode**
Anthony, Piers  **171**

**Fractal Paisleys**
Di Filippo, Paul  1023, 1492, **1515**, 1758

**Fractured Fairy Tales**
Jacobs, A.J.  **2845**, 6040

**Fragments**
David, James F.  90, **1380**

**Frameshift**
Sawyer, Robert J.  444, **4856**

**Frankenstein**
Shelley, Mary  140, 199, 498, 1561, 2293, 3019, 3180, 3526, 4684, 5422, 5847

**The Frankenstein Papers**
Saberhagen, Fred  140

**Frankenstein: The Monster Wakes**
Greenberg, Martin H.  **2390**, 2973, 3019, 3180

**Frankenstein Unbound**
Aldiss, Brian W.  140, 498, 912, 1305, 3019, 3180, 3631, 4385, 4684

**Frankensteins and Foreign Devils**
Williams, Walter Jon  **5838**

**Freak**
Burnell, Mark  3965

**Freak Show**
Wilson, F. Paul  854, 2311, 3758, 4057, **5888**

**Freak's Amour**
De Haven, Tom  1940

**Free Amazons of Darkover**
Bradley, Marion Zimmer  400, 3290, 3300, 5293

**Free Live Free**
Wolfe, Gene  4263

**Free Radicals**
McKinney, Jack  **3848**

**Free Space**
Linaweaver, Brad  **3466**

**Free Zone**
Platt, Charles  2013, **4341**

**Freedom & Necessity**
Brust, Steven  **743**

**Freedom Beach**
Kessel, John  3048, 3049

**Freedom Express**
Maloney, Jack  2324, 2325

**Freedom Flight**
Lackey, Mercedes  1976

**Freedom's Challenge**
McCaffrey, Anne  **3732**

**Freedom's Choice**
McCaffrey, Anne  **3733**

**Freedom's Landing**
McCaffrey, Anne  383, 420, 1500, 1501, 2034, 2223, **3734**, 3952, 4116

**Freedom's Rangers**
Andrews, Keith William  359, 5011

**The Freedom's Rangers Series**
Andrews, Keith William  3038

**Freehold**
Dietz, William C.  2350

**FreeMaster**
Jensen, Kris  **2897**, 3907

**Freeware**
Rucker, Rudy  **4703**

**Freeze Frames**
Kerr, Katharine  **3071**

**The Frenchman**
Hand, Elizabeth  2114, 2308, **2534**

**A Fresh Wind in the Willows**
Scott, Dixon  2774, 2775, 2776

**Friday**
Heinlein, Robert A.  1071, 1571

**Friends in Time**
Chetwin, Grace  **1012**

**The Friendship Song**
Springer, Nancy  489, 970, 1441, 2879, 3444, 3468, 4129, 4862, **5179**, 5267

**The Fright Before Christmas**
Stone, Tom B.  1097, 5291

**Fright Night**
Skipp, John  1032, 1034

**The Frightened Fish**
Robeson, Kenneth  1940, **4622**, 5307

**The Frighteners**
Jahn, Michael  **2856**, 5468

**Frights**
McCauley, Kirby  2965

**Frisk**
Cooper, Dennis  695, **1170**, 2162, 2448, 3312, 4185, 4734, 4737

**From a Changeling Star**
Carver, Jeffrey A.  785, **931**, 1458, 1964, 3075, 3764, 4114, 4756, 5201, 5245, 5638, 5680, 5905

**From a Whisper to a Scream**
Key, Samuel M.  1848, 2825, **3093**, 3375, 3518, 3857

**From Evil's Pillow**
Copper, Edmund  852

**From Hell**
Moore, Alan  **3987**

**From Prussia with Love**
DeChancie, John  **1457**

**From the Earth to the Moon**
Verne, Jules  398

**From the End of the Twentieth Century**
Ford, John M.  **1969**

**From the Heart of Darkness**
Drake, David  674, 675, 2780, 2784, 3753

**From the Teeth of Angels**
Carroll, Jonathan  5, 898, **918**, 2995, 4210, 4579

**From Time to Time**
Finney, Jack  464, 1480, **1941**, 5594

**Frontier of the Dark**
Chandler, A. Bertram  1248

**Frost and Fire**
Zelazny, Roger  425, 5837, **6067**

**Frostflower and Thorn**
Karr, Phyllis Ann  4614, 6041

**Frostflower and Windbourne**
Karr, Phyllis Ann  5293

**Frostwing**
Knaak, Richard A.  2760, **3170**

**Fruiting Bodies and Other Fungi**
Lumley, Brian  2780, 2784, 3367, **3553**

**Fugitive in Transit**
Llewellyn, Edward  5550

**Fugitive Prince**
Wurts, Janny  1775, **6002**

**The Fugitive Stars**
Ransom, Daniel  **4479**

**The Fugitive Worlds**
Shaw, Bob  **4942**

**Fugue Devil and Other Weird Horrors**
Rainey, Stephen Mark  113, 775, 776, 2769, 3317, 3669, 4230, 4231, **4463**, 5446, 5881

**Fugue State/The Death of Dr. Island**
Ford, John M.  130

**The Fulfillments of Fate and Desire**
Constantine, Storm  **1142**

**Full Moonster**
Pollotta, Nick  1400, 2513, 3257, **4364**, 4394, 5497, 5577

**Full Spectrum**
Aronica, Lou  501, 755, 887, 1363, 1365, 1621, 2634, 2679, 5045

**Full Spectrum 2**
Aronica, Lou  **214**, 238, 239, 500, 1363, 1365, 1616, 1621, 2634, 2679

**Full Spectrum 3**
Aronica, Lou  **215**, 1363, 1620, 2679, 4031, 4032

**Full Spectrum 3-4**
Aronica, Lou  2634, 2635

**Full Spectrum 4**
Aronica, Lou  **216**, 1364, 1617, 1622, 2679

**Full Spectrum 5**
Hershey, Jennifer  1619, 1623, 1624, 2596, 2597, 2598, 2634, 2635, **2679**

**Full Tide of Night**
Dunn, J.R.  1348, **1695**

**The Fungus**
Knight, Harry Adam  2671, **3192**, 3992

**The Fungus Garden**
Brett, Brian  2544

**The Funhouse**
West, Owen  5624

**Funland**
Laymon, Richard   2565, 2927, **3366**,
   4010, 5119, 5624

**The Furies**
Charnas, Suzy McKee   **968**, 4627

**Furious Gulf**
Benford, Gregory   384, 399, **447**,
   684, 3763, 3823, 4353

**Furnace**
Gray, Muriel   **2339**

**Further Adventures**
Fink, Jon Stephen   **1940**, 4622, 4623,
   5307, 5308, 5309

**The Further Adventures of Batman**
Greenberg, Martin H.   14, 2124,
   2331, 3403

**The Further Adventures of Batman 2:
   Featuring the Penguin**
Greenberg, Martin H.   14, 2124, **2391**

**The Further Adventures of Batman 3:
   Featuring Catwoman**
Greenberg, Martin H.   **2392**, 4215

**The Further Adventures of Superman**
Greenberg, Martin H.   999, **2393**,
   3403, 3768, 5262

**The Further Adventures of the Joker**
Greenberg, Martin H.   14, 2124

**Fury**
Coyne, John   **1237**, 2873, 5186

**The Fury**
Farris, John   97, 204, 872, 879, 941,
   1580, 2530, 2704, 3211, 3215,
   3230, 3251, 3594, 4843, 4883

**Future Boston**
Smith, David Alexander   **5107**

**Future Crime**
Bova, Ben   **585**, 3619

**Future Crime: An Anthology of the
   Shape of Crime to Come**
Manson, Cynthia   **3619**

**Future Earths: Under African Skies**
Resnick, Mike   1567, 1867, 1868,
   2771, 4207, **4544**

**Future Eden**
Morgan, J.M.   1569, **4001**

**Future Indefinite**
Duncan, Dave   **1678**

**Future Net**
Greenberg, Martin H.   **2394**

**Future on Fire**
Card, Orson Scott   **887**

**Future on Ice**
Card, Orson Scott   **888**

**Future Primitive: The New Ecotopias**
Robinson, Kim Stanley   **4631**, 4959

**Fuzzies and Other People**
Piper, H. Beam   451

**Fuzzy Sapiens**
Piper, H. Beam   5457

# G

**Gabriel Knight: Sins of the Fathers**
Jensen, Jane   452, **2896**

**Gabriel's Body**
Siodmak, Curt   436, 1786, 3561,
   3562, 3563, **5073**

**Gahan Wilson's The Ultimate
   Haunted House**
Wilson, Gahan   2396, 5665, **5902**

**The Gaia Websters**
Antieau, Kim   **198**, 1481, 3922

**Gaia's Toys**
Ore, Rebecca   **4218**

**Galactic Convoy**
Baldwin, Bill   1976

**Galactic Derelict**
Norton, Andre   5113

**Galactic Dreams**
Harrison, Harry   2490, 2547, **2569**

**Galactic Effectuator**
Vance, Jack   4277

**The Galactic Gourmet**
White, James   **5778**

**Galactic MI**
Randle, Kevin D.   **4467**

**Galactic Patrol**
Smith, Edward E.   270, **5116**

**The Galactic Silver Star**
Randle, Kevin D.   2436, **4468**, 5469

**Galatea 2.2**
Powers, Richard M.   **4381**

**Galatea in 2-D**
Allston, Aaron   **87**, 1433, 1438,
   1461, 2082, 2735, 2791, 3173,
   3490, 4486

**The Galaxy Primes**
Smith, Edward E.   5864

**Galen Beknighted**
Williams, Michael   5724

**Galilee**
Barker, Clive   **340**, 3126

**The Gallatin Divergence**
Smith, L. Neil   141, 142, 4536, 5012

**The Gallery of His Dreams**
Rusch, Kristine Kathryn   1441, **4717**,
   4758, 5379

**Gallery of Horror**
Grant, Charles L.   **2307**

**The Gallery Reader**
Serling, Rod   4914

**Gallicenae**
Anderson, Poul   3260

**A Game of Catch**
Cresswell, Helen   2438

**A Game of Dark**
Mayne, William   4917

**The Game of Empire**
Anderson, Poul   2459, 2476, 3907,
   3928, 5319, 5503, 5510

**The Game of Fox and Lion**
Chase, Robert   2212

**A Game of Thrones**
Martin, George R.R.   1154, 1640,
   1912, 2989, **3645**, 4258, 4259,
   4533, 5034, 6002

**A Game of Universe**
Nylund, Eric S.   **4178**

**The Game-Players of Titan**
Dick, Philip K.   4114, 4115

**Gamearth**
Anderson, Kevin J.   390, 391, 4709

**Gameplay**
Anderson, Kevin J.   **105**, 3309, 4709,
   5432

**Game's End**
Anderson, Kevin J.   **104**, 1662, 4709

**The Gammage Cup**
Kendall, Carol   6006

**The Gandalara Cycle I**
Garrett, Randall   4143

**Ganwold's Child**
Thornley, Diann   2224, 5367, **5467**,
   5544

**The Ganymede Club**
Sheffield, Charles   **4955**

**The Gap into Conflict: The Real
   Story**
Donaldson, Stephen R.   **1572**, 3692

**The Gap into Madness: Chaos and
   Order**
Donaldson, Stephen R.   **1573**

**The Gap into Power: A Dark and
   Hungry God Arises**
Donaldson, Stephen R.   **1574**

**The Gap into Ruin: This Day All
   Gods Die**
Donaldson, Stephen R.   **1575**

**The Gap into Vision: Forbidden
   Knowledge**
Donaldson, Stephen R.   930

**Garden**
Costello, Matthew J.   **1197**, 4279

**The Garden of Rama**
Clarke, Arthur C.   **1055**, 2419, 2807,
   3398, 5244

**Gaslight and Ghosts**
Jones, Stephen   217

**Gaslight Tales of Terror**
Chetwynd-Hayes, R.   1233

**The Gasp**
Gary, Romain   1577, 4926

**Gate of Darkness, Circle of Light**
Huff, Tanya   681, 1098, 1426, 1781,
   2619, **2797**, 3285, 3299, 4173,
   4995, 5379, 5646

**The Gate of Ivory**
Egan, Doris   1486, **1755**, 2264, 3158

**Gate of Ivory, Gate of Horn**
Holdstock, Robert   **2737**

**Gate of Ivrel**
Cherryh, C.J.   644, 1025, 1173,
   1178, 1660, 3477, 3634, 3635,
   3920, 3940, 3969, 4109, 4163,
   5683, 5951, 6001

**The Gate of the Cat**
Norton, Andre   638

**The Gate of Worlds**
Silverberg, Robert   135, 783, 5868

**The Gate to Women's Country**
Tepper, Sheri S.   720, 721, 1211,
   1929, 2052, 3046, 4325, 4631,
   5092, 5209, 5268, 5590, 5982

**The Gatekeepers**
Graham, Daniel Jr.   **2301**

**The Gates of Eden**
Stableford, Brian   1248, 2491

**The Gates of Noon**
Rohan, Michael Scott   **4661**

**Gates of Paradise**
Andrews, V.C.   **145**

**The Gates of Thorbardin**
Parkinson, Dan   2675, 5711

**The Gates of Twilight**
Volsky, Paula   5333, **5581**

**The Gates of Vensunor**
Heller, Carol   1984, **2650**, 3481,
   4459

**Gates to Tomorrow: An Introduction
   to Science Fiction**
Norton, Andre   5238

**Gateway**
Pohl, Frederik   247, 447, 449, 1509,
   2006, 4067, 4103, 4961

**Gateway to Never**
Chandler, A. Bertram   3125

**The Gateway Trip: Tales and
   Vignettes of the Heechee**
Pohl, Frederik   2836, 4103, **4346**,
   5244, 5933

**Gather, Darkness!**
Leiber, Fritz   652

**Gatherer of Clouds**
Russell, Sean   1253, **4741**

**A Gathering Evil**
Stackpole, Michael A.   1819, 1820,
   1881, 4364, 4909, **5201**

**The Gathering Flame**
Doyle, Debra   **1599**

**A Gathering of Stars**
Moffitt, Donald   **3947**

**Gawain and Lady Green**
Crompton, Anne Eliot   **1269**, 3355,
   3884

**Geek Love**
Dunn, Katherine   789, 1027, **1697**,
   3206, 4057, 5264, 5899

**Gehenna**
Gannett, Lewis   **2114**, 2308, 2534,
   5843, 5846

**Geis of the Gargoyle**
Anthony, Piers   **172**

*Gene Wolfe's Book of Days*
Wolfe, Gene   2412, 2589, 4720, 5024

*Genellan: Planetfall*
Gier, Scott G.   **2223**

*Generation Warrior*
McCaffrey, Anne   1070, **3735**

*Generation X*
Lobdell, Scott   2256

*Genesis*
Grant, Charles L.   **2308**, 2638, 5843, 5846

*Genesis Five*
Henry, Will   2107

*The Genesis Machine*
Hogan, James P.   1245

*The Genesis Web*
Brennan, C.M.   3036

*Genetic Soldier*
Turner, George   128, 1168, 2209, 2338, 2526, 2906, 4128, 4525, **5492**

*Genie with the Light Blue Hair*
Conford, Ellen   5182

*The Genocidal Healer*
White, James   4176, **5779**

*The Genocides*
Disch, Thomas M.   1015, 2252, 2646, 2811, 5027

*The Gentle Seduction*
Stiegler, Marc   54, 123, 448, 689, 804, 850, 1515, 1517, 1770, 1963, 1964, 3087, 3442, 4127, 4216, 4376, 4706, 4953, 5028, 5240, 5257, 5369, 5638, 5869

*Geodesic Dreams: The Best Short Fiction of Gardner Dozois*
Dozois, Gardner   61, 804, **1608**

*Geomancer*
Callander, Don   **845**

*Georgia on My Mind and Other Places*
Sheffield, Charles   1963, **4956**

*Gerald's Game*
King, Stephen   **3133**

*Geronimo*
Dugan, Bill   4233

*Get Off the Unicorn*
McCaffrey, Anne   3845

*Getting into Death*
Disch, Thomas M.   337

*Ghor, Kin-Slayer: The Saga of Genseric's Fifth-Born Son*
Howard, Robert E.   **2782**

*Ghost*
Steele, Danielle   4579

*Ghost and Horror Stories*
Bierce, Ambrose   1243

*The Ghost Belonged to Me*
Peck, Richard   2923, 4078

*Ghost Beyond the Garden*
Blankman, Lynn   5286, 5289

*The Ghost Book*
Asquith, Cynthia   38, 1310

*The Ghost Book of Charles Lindley, Viscount Halifax*
Lindley, Charles   2543, **3472**

*Ghost Boy*
Simon, Jean   1926, 2821, 3785, **5064**

*Ghost Brother*
Adler, C.S.   1898

*The Ghost Companion*
Haining, Peter   3432

*Ghost Dance*
Ptacek, Kathryn   427, 749, 911, 1297, 2251, 2340, 3081, 3655, 3671, 3680, 3895, 3967, 4111, 4113, 4309, **4441**, 5769, 6078

*Ghost Dancers*
Craig, Brian   **1238**, 1935

*The Ghost Drum: A Cat's Tale*
Price, Susan   3377, 5142

*The Ghost-Feeler*
Wharton, Edith   **5772**

*The Ghost From the Grand Banks*
Clarke, Arthur C.   **1056**

*The Ghost Inside the Monitor*
Anderson, Margaret J.   **122**, 2283, 3444, 4921, 5558

*Ghost King*
Gemmell, David   **2188**

*Ghost Light*
Hautala, Rick   1505, **2608**, 3139, 3205, 3365, 3857, 3858

*Ghost of Chance*
Burroughs, William S.   25, **780**

*The Ghost of the Revelator*
Modesitt, L.E. Jr.   **3931**

*The Ghost of Thomas Kempe*
Lively, Penelope   122, 1272, 2438, 2923, 2951, 4078, 4438

*The Ghost Pirates*
Hodgson, William Hope   2732

*Ghost Ship*
Carey, Diane   923, 1384, 2068

*The Ghost Ship and Other Stories*
Middleton, Richard   2712

*Ghost Stories*
Westall, Robert   1693, 1701, 2772, 4274, 4282

*Ghost Story*
Straub, Peter   524, 840, 1080, 1195, 1215, 1560, 2019, 2822, 2904, 3126, 3140, 3205, 3496, 4254, 4569, 5322, 5398

*Ghost Tales of the Villa Deodati*
Anonymous   5389

*Ghost Walker*
Hambly, Barbara   900, 1663

*The Ghost Warriors*
McGann, Michael   2324, 2325

*Ghostlight*
Bradley, Marion Zimmer   **634**

*Ghostly by Gaslight*
Moskowitz, Sam   39

*Ghostly Gentlewomen*
Manley, Seon   3570

*The Ghostly Tales of Henry James*
James, Henry   2633

*Ghostly Tales of Iowa*
Hein, Ruth D.   **2643**, 5211

*Ghosts*
Hynd, Noel   840, **2822**, 3126

*Ghosts*
Kaye, Marvin   2233, 5665

*Ghosts*
Straub, Peter   2233

*Ghosts and Grisly Things*
Campbell, Ramsey   2018

*Ghosts and Scholars*
Dalby, Richard   283

*Ghosts, Castles and Victims*
Wolf, Jack C.   4026

*Ghosts for Christmas*
Dalby, Richard   4541, 4861

*Ghosts, Ghouls and Other Nightmares*
Kemp, Gene   2772

*Ghosts in the House*
Benson, A.C.   456

*The Ghosts of Sleath*
Herbert, James   **2668**

*Ghosts of the Heartland*
McSherry, Frank D. Jr.   **3868**

*Ghosts of the Heaviside Layer and Other Fantasies*
Dunsany   348

*Ghosts of Wind and Shadow*
de Lint, Charles   **1427**, 2078, 4497

*Ghosts: Stories of the Supernatural*
O'Donnell, Elliott   2543

*Ghosttide*
O'Keefe, Claudia   2233, 3598, 3961, **4206**, 4644, 5331, 5795

*Ghostwright*
Cadnum, Michael   **810**, 858, 3213, 3691

*Ghoul*
Slade, Michael   2638, 3899

*The Ghouls*
Haining, Peter   5460, 5947

*Giant Bones*
Beagle, Peter S.   **408**

*Giants Unleashed*
Conklin, Groff   241, 1614

*Gibbon's Decline and Fall*
Tepper, Sheri S.   1075, 1167, 1336, 3241, **5430**

*The Gift*
Dickinson, Peter   2992, 3340

*The Gift*
Edelman, Scott   1166, 1541, 2116, 3853

*The Gift*
O'Leary, Patrick   **4211**

*A Gift from Earth*
Niven, Larry   877

*The Gift of Stones*
Crace, Jim   4320

*The Gift of the Gorboduc Vandal*
Williams, Paul O.   2038, 2173, **5821**

*A Gift upon the Shore*
Wren, M.K.   2603, **5982**

*The Gifted*
Caravela, Jack   **879**, 3230, 4480

*Gila*
Simons, Les   3054

*The Gilda Stories*
Gomez, Jewelle   1286, 2116, **2267**, 3031, 3853, 4315, 5421, 5802

*The Gilded Chain: A Tale of the King's Blades*
Duncan, Dave   **1679**

*Gilgamesh the King*
Silverberg, Robert   178, 363, 3581, 5496, 5831

*The Gilgul*
Hocherman, Henry W.   **2697**

*The Ginger Star*
Brackett, Leigh   2575, 5647

*The Girl from Mars & The Prince of Space*
Williamson, Jack   **5864**

*The Girl From the Emerald Island*
Blum, Robert S.   5490

*Girl in a Swing*
Adams, Richard   2019, 2713

*Girl in Landscape*
Lethem, Jonathan   **3440**

*A Girl Named Disaster*
Farmer, Nancy   **1868**, 1996

*The Girl, the Gold Watch, and Everything*
MacDonald, John D.   302

*The Girl Who Cried Flowers and Other Tales*
Yolen, Jane   3610

*The Girl Who Heard Dragons*
McCaffrey, Anne   3065, **3736**

*The Girl Who Was Plugged In*
McIntyre, Vonda N.   5525

*The Girl with the Green Ear: Stories about Magic in Nature*
Mahy, Margaret   3610

*The Girls from Planet 5*
Wilson, Richard   5997

*Girls' Night Out*
Dziemianowicz, Stefan   **1713**

*Girls' Night Out*
Weinberg, Robert   730

*Gladiator-at-Law*
Pohl, Frederik   1805, 1838, 2328, 2545, 2770, 3795, 4473, 4662, 5593

**The Glaive**
Osborne, Cary   **4227**

**The Glamour**
Priest, Christopher   982, 1002, 1098, 4776

**The Glass Dragon**
Radford, Irene   1705, 1749, **4460**

**The Glass Hammer**
Jeter, K.W.   1519, 1520

**Glass Houses**
Mixon, Laura J.   231, 251, 294, 784, 2723, **3921**, 4077, 4708, 5362

**The Glass Warrior**
Vardeman, Robert E.   **5563**

**Glenraven**
Bradley, Marion Zimmer   **635**

**Glimmering**
Hand, Elizabeth   **2535**, 6028

**Glimpses**
Shiner, Lewis   1835, 3664, 4553, 4579, **4997**, 5089, 5850, 5873

**Glimring Night and Other Tales of Fantasy**
Morey, Joe   **3997**

**Glittering Images**
Howatch, Susan   5392

**Glittering Savages**
Burnell, Mark   5183, 5185

**Globalhead**
Sterling, Bruce   **5257**

**Gloriana, or the Unfulfilled Queen**
Moorcock, Michael   2262, 5547

**Glory**
Coppel, Alfred   **1182**, 5298, 5549

**The Glory Game**
Laumer, Keith   4378

**Glory Lane**
Foster, Alan Dean   356, 493, 958, 1222, 1267, 1453, 1455, 1752, 1871, 2332, 2629, 2797, 3800, 3811, 4350, 4562, 4662, 5639

**Glory Road**
Heinlein, Robert A.   135, 1229, 1414, 1429, 1452, 1453, 1684, 1754, 1983, 2357, **2644**, 3098, 3572, 3848, 3849, 4014, 4674

**Glory Season**
Brin, David   210, **686**, 1104, 1116, 1588, 1824, 2134, 3241, 3380, 3426, 3440, 3453, 4900, 4957, 5091, 5187, 5368, 5804

**Glory's People**
Coppel, Alfred   **1183**

**Glory's War**
Coppel, Alfred   **1184**, 2476, 3970, 5403

**The Glove of Darth Vader**
Davids, Paul   1391, **1392**, 6055

**Gnelfs**
Williams, Sidney   1038, **5823**

**Gnome Man's Land**
Friesner, Esther   **2075**, 4317, 4394

**The Gnome's Engine**
Edgerton, Teresa   **1742**

**Go Quest, Young Man**
Bogen, K.B.   196, **557**, 6049

**Go Tell the Spartans**
Pournelle, Jerry   1641, **4375**, 5292

**Goa**
Dalkey, Kara   195, 770, 771, 1111, 1154, 2995

**Goat Dance**
Clegg, Douglas   137, 859, 860, **1079**, 1931, 2285, 2557, 2749, 2929, 3129, 3137, 3615, 3778, 4754, 4907, 5077, 5112, 5398, 5472, 5769, 5771, 5961

**Goatsong**
Holt, Tom   67, 2189, **2751**, 5595, 5639

**The Goblin Companion**
Jones, Terry   385, 2088, **2980**

**The Goblin Mirror**
Cherryh, C.J.   955, **994**, 4727, 5251

**Goblin Moon**
Edgerton, Teresa   **1743**, 2032, 2354, 2355, 2356, 4851

**The Goblin Plain War**
Miller, Carl   **3892**

**The Goblin Reservation**
Simak, Clifford D.   3010, 3175, 4389, 4390

**Goblins**
Courtney, Vincent   1038, **1212**

**Goblins**
Grant, Charles L.   106, 112, 924, **2309**, 5358

**Goblins in the Castle**
Coville, Bruce   **1218**

**The God Box**
Longyear, Barry B.   519, 4404, 4707

**The God-Emperor of Dune**
Herbert, Frank   4553

**God Game**
Greeley, Andrew M.   583

**The God Killer**
Green, Simon R.   **2368**, 2472, 2620, 3303

**God on a Harley**
Brady, Joan   1577, 4926

**God Stalk**
Hodgell, P.C.   4, 672, 673, 682, 936, 1068, 1072, 1073, 1251, 1253, 1856, 2196, 2521, 2538, 3095, 3421, 3486, 3766, 3773, 3894, 4521, 4522, 4653, 4654, 4849, 4850, 5203, 5371, 5509, 5741

**The Goda War**
Blakeney, Jay D.   **516**, 3888

**Godbody**
Sturgeon, Theodore   5910

**The Godforsaken**
Yarbro, Chelsea Quinn   4892, 5861

**GodHeads**
Devenport, Emily   **1501**, 1759

**The Godmother**
Scarborough, Elizabeth Ann   395, 2800, **4862**

**Godmother Night**
Pollack, Rachel   715, 3118, 4211, **4358**, 5555

**The Godmother's Apprentice**
Scarborough, Elizabeth Ann   4171, **4863**

**The Godmother's Web**
Scarborough, Elizabeth Ann   **4864**

**Godplayer**
Cook, Robin   581, 1832

**The Gods Abide**
Swann, Thomas Burnett   36

**God's Dice**
Swann, S. Andrew   **5364**

**God's Fires**
Anthony, Patricia   **159**, 3599

**The Gods Hate Kansas**
Millard, Joseph   1581

**The Gods in Anger**
Cole, Adrian   **1100**

**God's Nose**
Knight, Damon   1428, 2078, **3185**

**The Gods of Mars**
Burroughs, Edgar Rice   2416

**Gods of the Well of Souls**
Chalker, Jack L.   **954**

**The Gods Themselves**
Asimov, Isaac   4, 2724, 4019

**God's World**
Watson, Ian   2343, 2666, **5636**, 5717

**The Godsend**
Taylor, Bernard   1212, 1236, 2801, 3606, **5401**, 5623

**Godsfire**
Felice, Cynthia   165

**Godslayer**
Reichert, Mickey Zucker   2, 390, 391, 1683, 1979, 2369, 2375, 5741

**Godspeed**
Sheffield, Charles   420, **4957**

**Godzilla 2000**
Cerasini, Marc   **949**

**Godzilla Invades America**
Ciencin, Scott   949

**Godzilla: King of the Monsters**
Ciencin, Scott   949

**Going Home Again**
Waldrop, Howard   **5613**

**Going Mobile**
Cox, Glen E.   2938

**Going Native**
Wright, Stephen   570

**Going Postal**
Houarner, Gerard Daniel   2384, **2777**

**Gojiro**
Jacobson, Mark   499, 729, **2847**, 4046

**The Gold Ball**
Svendsen, Hanne Marie   2264, 2662, **5361**

**The Gold Coast**
Robinson, Kim Stanley   95, 736, 3817, 3818, **4632**

**Gold Dragon**
Cain, Robert   **831**, 4590, 4939

**Gold: The Final Science Fiction Collection**
Asimov, Isaac   **237**, 2490

**Gold Unicorn**
Lee, Tanith   **3410**, 5144

**The Goldcamp Vampire; or The Sanguinary Sourdough**
Scarborough, Elizabeth Ann   2009, 4389, 5151

**Goldclimbers**
Luenn, Nancy   **3545**, 4615, 5143, 5640

**The Golden**
Shepard, Lucius   325, 572, 603, 812, 2511, 3601, 4094, 4098, **4978**

**Golden Cities, Far**
Carter, Lin   606

**The Golden Compass**
Pullman, Philip   1028, 3386, 4211, **4446**, 6037

**Golden Eyes**
Gideon, John   **2220**

**Golden Fleece**
Sawyer, Robert J.   734, 1549, **4857**, 5042

**The Golden Globe**
Varley, John   **5565**

**The Golden Grove**
Kress, Nancy   5002

**The Golden Helix**
Sturgeon, Theodore   3342

**The Golden Key**
Rawn, Melanie   1773, 3506, **4486**, 4611, 5017

**The Golden Mean**
Bantock, Nick   **334**

**The Golden Nineties**
Mason, Lisa   264, 2120, 3597, **3663**, 4036

**The Golden Pot and Other Tales**
Hoffmann, E.T.A.   **2718**

**The Golden Queen**
Wolverton, Dave   **5951**

**The Golden Space**
Sargent, Pamela   4352

**The Golden Strangers**
Treece, Henry   5295

**The Golden Thread**
Charnas, Suzy McKee   605, **969**, 2272, 2623, 4387, 5977, 5995

**Golden Trillium**
Norton, Andre   641, 3700, **4153**

**The Golden Wind**
de Camp, L. Sprague   195, 1316, 1317

**Golden Wings and Other Stories**
Morris, William 1699

**Golden Witchbreed**
Gentle, Mary 517, 565, 567, 580, 621, 707, 758, 990, 997, 1062, 1101, 1210, 1323, 1757, 1771, 1861, 1914, 1933, 1934, 2057, 2069, 2420, 2423, 2443, 2897, 2898, 3047, 3157, 3158, 3424, 3484, 3763, 3787, 3830, 3888, 3911, 3919, 4137, 4139, 4188, 4242, 4976, 5543, 5572

**Golem** [100]
Bester, Alfred 1723, 5109

**Gom on Windy Mountain**
Chetwin, Grace 329, 3043, 5142, 6030

**Gone South**
McCammon, Robert R. 3373, **3755**

**Gone to Earth**
Zelazny, Roger 3648, **6068**

**Good Bones and Simple Murders**
Atwood, Margaret **274**, 794, 1578, 1942, 2144, 2146, 3384, 5557, 5617

**The Good Children**
Wilhelm, Kate **5808**

**Good Faeries, Bad Faeries**
Froud, Brian **2088**

**Good News From Outer Space**
Kessel, John 156, 327, 1877, 2100, 2249, **3084**, 3542, 4034, 4555, 4567, 4630, 4632, 5958

**Good Night, Sweet Angel**
McNally, Clare 2609, **3857**

**The Good Old Stuff**
Dozois, Gardner **1609**

**Good Omens: The Nice and Accurate Prophecies of Agnes Nutter, Witch**
Gaiman, Neil 262, 453, 672, 1268, 1283, 1339, 1577, 2084, 2100, **2103**, 2327, 2342, 2658, 2750, 2753, 2803, 2880, 2950, 3009, 3071, 3311, 3480, 3483, 3488, 3810, 3811, 3908, 3986, 4028, 4029, 4035, 4060, 4391, 4399, 4400, 4401, 4404, 4607, 4655, 5456, 5532, 5569, 5768, 5958, 6031, 6049, 6062, 6064, 6070

**A Good, Secret Place**
Laymon, Richard 3090, **3367**, 3553, 3558, 3674

**The Good, the Bad, and the Indifferent**
Lansdale, Joe R. **3329**, 4011

**Goodlow's Ghosts**
Wright, T.M. 4256, 5468, **5991**

**Goon**
Lee, Edward **3392**

**Gorgon Child**
Barnes, Steven **361**, 720, 4117

**Gormenghast**
Peake, Mervyn 325

**Gormenghast Trilogy**
Peake, Mervyn 5829

**Gossamer Axe**
Baudino, Gael **392**, 1181, 1409, 1430, 1434, 1436, 1499, 1583, 1958, 2950, 3264, 3284, 3285, 3286, 3293, 3299, 3301, 3423, 3886, 3887, 4596, 4655, 4870, 4993, 5177, 5179, 5293, 5915

**Gothic Ghosts**
Webb, Wendy 4644, **5665**

**Gothic Romance**
Carrere, Emmanuel 498, 659, **912**, 1836, 2642, 4684, 5192, 5271, 5842

**Gothic Tales of Terror**
Haining, Peter 307, 1314, 2718, 5389

**Gothic Tales of Terror, Volume II**
Haining, Peter 4180

**The Gothic Tales of the Marquis de Sade**
Crosland, Margaret 5389

**Grail**
Lawhead, Stephen R. **3355**

**The Grail and the Ring**
Edgerton, Teresa 681, **1744**, 1842

**The Grail of Hearts**
Shwartz, Susan 965, 2571, 2883, **5015**

**The Grail War**
Monaco, Richard 273

**Grails: Quests of the Dawn**
Gilliam, Richard 190, **2231**, 2346, 3670, 4987, 6005

**Grails: Visitations of the Night**
Gilliam, Richard **2232**, 2346

**The Grand Jubilee**
Elgin, Suzette Haden 186, 515, 2084, 2950, 3696, 3697, 3699, 4361, 4405, 5235, 5337, 5616

**Grandma's Little Darling**
George, Stephen R. **2201**

**Grania: She-King of the Irish Seas**
Llywelyn, Morgan 3059, 5962

**Grass**
Tepper, Sheri S. 34, 129, 159, 296, 686, 708, 785, 883, 899, 1072, 1116, 1458, 1643, 1807, 1824, 1987, 2056, 2207, 2226, 2287, 2806, 2882, 3231, 3248, 3249, 3398, 3713, 3717, 3763, 3908, 3910, 3927, 3929, 3972, 4062, 4067, 4116, 4122, 4241, 4242, 4507, 4552, 4711, 4735, 4736, 4867, 5016, 5128, 5306, 5373, **5431**, 5759, 5775, 5949

**The Grass Dancer**
Power, Susan 636, **4380**

**Grave Markings**
Arnzen, Michael A. **212**, 2159

**Grave Passions**
Mann, William J. **3618**, 5386

**Gravelight**
Bradley, Marion Zimmer **636**

**A Graveyard for Lunatics**
Bradbury, Ray **620**, 3688, 4131

**Gravity's Angels**
Swanwick, Michael 503, 772, 2835, 3086, 3234, 3442, 3600, 3648, 3796, 4680, 5028, 5257, **5369**, 5805

**Gravity's Rainbow**
Pynchon, Thomas 2329, 4606, 4681, 5903

**Gray Lensman**
Smith, Edward E. 270, **5117**

**Gray Matter**
Reeves-Stevens, Garfield 5084

**Gray Victory**
Skimin, Bob 896, 5147

**Graythings**
Graversen, Pat **2335**

**Great American Ghost Stories**
McSherry, Frank D. Jr. 2586, **3869**

**The Great and Secret Show**
Barker, Clive **341**, 2214, 3143, 3144, 5190, 5414

**Great Black Magic Stories**
Parry, Michel 2385

**The Great Explosion**
Russell, Eric Frank 1182

**Great Ghost Stories**
Grafton, John **2300**

**The Great God Pan**
Machen, Arthur 4235

**The Great Hunt**
Jordan, Robert 4524, 5831

**Great Irish Stories of the Supernatural**
Haining, Peter 149, **2481**

**Great Irish Tales of Horror**
Haining, Peter 149, 1242, **2482**

**Great Irish Tales of Terror and the Supernatural**
Haining, Peter 1242

**Great Irish Tales of the Unimaginable**
Haining, Peter 149

**The Great King's War**
Green, Roland J. 5495, 5513

**Great Mischief**
Pinckney, Josephine 2713

**Great Science Fiction about Doctors**
Conklin, Groff 5604, 5886

**Great Short Novels of Adult Fantasy 1**
Carter, Lin 606, 5102

**Great Short Novels of Adult Fantasy 2**
Carter, Lin 606

**Great Sky River**
Bear, Greg 5834

**Great Sky River**
Benford, Gregory 272, 417, 423, 806, 808, 985, 2036, 2690, 2691, 3522, 3604, 4065, 4418, 4419, 5108, 5431, 5449, 5541, 5878

**Great Stories of Space Travel**
Conklin, Groff 243

**Great Tales of Terror and the Supernatural**
Wise, Herbert 1, 38, 848, 2590, 2591, 2968, 2993, 3027, 4311, 4440, 5031

**Great Tales of Terror From Europe and America**
Haining, Peter 848, 2586, 4026, 5418, 5439

**The Great Time Machine Hoax**
Laumer, Keith 5645

**Great Untold Stories of Fantasy and Horror**
Moskowitz, Sam 38, 39

**The Great War: American Front**
Turtledove, Harry **5501**

**Great Weird Tales**
Joshi, S.T. **2993**

**The Great Wheel**
MacLeod, Ian R. **3599**

**The Great White Space**
Copper, Basil 1497, 2711, 5350, 5482

**Great Writers and Kids Write Spooky Stories**
Greenberg, Martin H. **2395**, 3705, 4274, 4282

**A Greater Infinity**
McCollum, Michael 953, 3343

**The Greater Trumps**
Williams, Charles 2406, 4359

**Greatheart**
McKeone, Dixie Lee 2625

**Greek Myths**
Graves, Robert 5533

**Greely's Cove**
Gideon, John **2221**, 3389, 3415

**The Green Fairy Book**
Lang, Andrew 2447, 5310, 6090

**The Green Hills of Earth**
Heinlein, Robert A. 4956, 5247, 5345

**The Green Knight**
Chapman, Vera 273, 1269

**Green Lake**
Epperson, S.K. **1830**

**The Green Man**
Amis, Kingsley 982, 1002

**Green Mars**
Robinson, Kim Stanley 134, 406, 1724, 2526, 2765, 2840, 3380, 3715, 4348, **4633**, 5187

**The Green Mile**
King, Stephen **3134**, 4838

**The Green Odyssey**
Farmer, Philip Jose 2414, 4545

**The Green Pearl**
Vance, Jack 3700, 5512, 5582

**The Green Progression**
Modesitt, L.E. Jr. **3932**

**Green Rider**
Britain, Kristen **692**

*The Green Round*
Machen, Arthur  4586

*Greenbriar Queen*
Gilluly, Sheila  1288, 1660, 1683, 2819

*Greendaughter*
Logston, Anne  **3510**

*Greenhouse*
Easton, Thomas A.  **1723**, 2536, 3932, 5429

*Greenmagic*
Kilian, Crawford  **3105**, 4154

*Greenmantle*
de Lint, Charles  203, 1040, 2797, 3470

*Greenthieves*
Foster, Alan Dean  **2005**

*Greenwitch*
Cooper, Susan  371

*Greetings From Earth*
Bradfield, Scott  818

*Grendel*
Gardner, John  2250, 4872

*The Grey Horse*
MacAvoy, R.A.  1000, 1703, 1704, 3840

*The Grey King*
Cooper, Susan  371, 1330

*The Grey Mane of Morning*
Chant, Joy  1025, 3068, 3404, 4156

*Greybeard*
Aldiss, Brian W.  2870

*Greystone Bay*
Grant, Charles L.  4212

*The Greystone Bay Series*
Grant, Charles L.  2118

*Griffin & Sabine*
Bantock, Nick  2706, 3124, 5450

*Griffin's Egg*
Swanwick, Michael  **5370**

*Grimm Memorials*
Gates, R. Patrick  **2160**

*Grimscribe: His Lives and Works*
Ligotti, Thomas  864, 866, 3447, **3461**

*The Gripping Hand*
Niven, Larry  990, 997, 1586, 1606, 1989, 3726, **4122**, 5778

*The Gris-Gris Man*
Davis, Don  1298, **1403**, 1888, 2744, 2896, 3678, 4498

*Groogleman*
Doyle, Debra  **1600**

*The Grotesque*
McGrath, Patrick  627, 2115, 3002, 3688, **3814**, 4788

*Ground-Ties*
Fancher, Jane S.  **1861**, 2051, 2351, 2733, 3994, 4927

*Ground Zero*
Anderson, Kevin J.  **106**, 924, 2320, 2788, 4874, 5843

*Grounded!*
Claremont, Chris  **1041**, 3029

*Growing Up Weightless*
Ford, John M.  588, 782, 927, **1970**, 3359, 4911

*The Gruesome Book*
Campbell, Ramsey  4274, 4282

*Gryphon*
Kilian, Crawford  **3106**

*The Gryphon King*
Deitz, Tom  **1473**, 3423

*Guard Against Dishonor*
Green, Simon R.  769, **2369**, 4935

*Guardian*
Saul, John  3162, **4841**

*The Guardian*
Wells, Angus  **5737**

*Guardian's Key*
Logston, Anne  **3511**

*Guardians of the Flame: The Warriors*
Rosenberg, Joel  105

*Guardians of the West*
Eddings, David  1177, 3926

*Guardians of Time*
Anderson, Poul  1225, 1631, 1855, 2119, 3083, 4040

*Guards! Guards!*
Pratchett, Terry  1207, 3991, **4390**, 5649

*Les Guerilleres*
Wittig, Monique  780, 5590

*Guignoir*
Partridge, Norman  2967

*Guignoir and Other Furies*
Hatch, George  22, 2280, **2600**, 2966, 4200, 5447

*Guilt-Edged Ivory*
Egan, Doris  **1756**

*Guilty Pleasures*
Hamilton, Laurell K.  262, 285, 803, 1152, 1399, 2053, 2055, 2092, 2149, 2309, 2320, **2517**, 3441, 3484, 5062, 5078, 5324, 5405, 5407, 5577

*Guinevere*
Newman, Sharan  224, 2939, 3827, 5970, 5971

*Guinevere Evermore*
Newman, Sharan  5970, 5971

*Guinevere: The Legend in Autumn*
Woolley, Persia  224, 269, 1737, 2939, 2940, **5970**

*Guises of the Mind*
Neason, Rebecca  2922, **4081**, 5880

*The Gully Dwarves*
Parkinson, Dan  5022

*Gun, with Occasional Music*
Lethem, Jonathan  1152, **3441**, 5362

*The Guns of Avalon*
Zelazny, Roger  3978

*The Guns of the South: A Novel of the Civil War*
Turtledove, Harry  358, 598, 881, 1074, 1139, 1457, 1480, 1518, 1941, 2501, 2577, 3977, 3981, 3993, 4233, 4538, 5292, 5356, 5357, 5487, **5502**

*The Gunslinger*
King, Stephen  5034

*Guts and Glory*
Stine, G. Harry  1568, 3013, **5280**

*Gypsies*
Wilson, Robert Charles  1521, 3707, 5647, **5908**

*The Gypsy*
Brust, Steven  **744**, 1249

# H

*H.P. Lovecraft's Book of Horror*
Jones, Stephen  848, **2968**

*Habu*
Johnson, James B.  **2920**

*The Hacker*
Day, Chet  **1410**, 2322

*The Hacker and the Ants*
Rucker, Rudy  **4704**

*Hackers*
Dann, Jack  2394

*The Hag's Contract*
Betancourt, John Gregory  2625

*Hail Hibbler*
Goulart, Ron  4363

*Hair of the Dog*
Davis, Brett  **1400**

*Half Asleep in Frog Pajamas*
Robbins, Tom  **4606**

*Half-Light*
Vitola, Denise  2053, 2864, 2948, 5282, **5575**

*Half Magic*
Eager, Edward  2944, 5822

*Half Past Human*
Bassler, Thomas J.  4662

*Half the Day Is Night*
McHugh, Maureen F.  1760, **3818**, 5256

*The Halflife*
Webb, Sharon  193, **5664**

*Halflings, Hobbits, Warrows & Weefolk: A Collection of Tales of Heroes Short in Stature*
Searles, Baird  1340, 1994, 2378, 2388, **4906**, 5239

*The Halfmen of O*
Gee, Maurice  5070

*Halfway Human*
Gilman, Carolyn Ives  1266, 2134, **2237**

*The Hall of the Mountain King*
Tarr, Judith  4730

*Hall of Whispers*
Jefferies, Mike  **2884**

*Halloween*
Martin, Jack  1555, 5026

*Halloween III: Season of the Witch*
Martin, Jack  2317, 4009, 4601, 4603

*Halloween Horrors*
Ryan, Alan  3705

*The Halloween Man*
Clegg, Douglas  **1080**, 5026

*The Halloween Tree*
Bradbury, Ray  5796

*Halo*
Maddox, Tom  **3604**, 5462

*Hammer and Anvil*
Turtledove, Harry  **5503**

*The Hammer and the Cross*
Harrison, Harry  363, 889, 1191, 1856, 2229, 2246, 2250, 2453, 2454, **2570**, 3501, 3636, 4264, 4270, 4518, 4872

*The Hammer Horror Omnibus*
Burke, John  1022, 4687

*The Hammer of Darkness*
Modesitt, L.E. Jr.  5930

*The Hammer of God*
Clarke, Arthur C.  83, **1057**

*Hammer of Mars*
Murdock, M.S.  554, 3036, **4049**

*Hammer's Slammers*
Drake, David  1315, 1326, 2052, 2054, 2323, 2805, 4194, 4226, 4306, 4374, 4377, 4583, 5676

*The Hammer's Slammers Series*
Drake, David  4829

*A Hammock Beneath the Mangoes*
Colchie, Thomas  **1099**

*The Han Solo Adventures*
Daley, Brian  76, 103, 109, 115, 2500, 2914, 3247, 5527, 5950, 6055

*Han Solo and the Lost Legacy*
Daley, Brian  6052, 6054

*Han Solo at Star's End*
Daley, Brian  6052, 6054

*Han Solo's Revenge*
Daley, Brian  6052, 6054

*The Hand of Chaos*
Weis, Margaret  2503, **5715**

*Hand of Prophecy*
Park, Severna  1266, **4244**

*The Hand of Zei*
de Camp, L. Sprague  631, **1414**, 1772, 4152

*Handful of Time*
Pearson, Kit  122

*The Handmaid's Tale*
Atwood, Margaret  968, 1135, 1653, 1817, 1877, 1929, 3241, 3622, 4325, 5268, 5276, 5430, 5911

*The Hands of Lyr*
Norton, Andre  1706, **4154**

**The Hands of Orlac**
Renard, Maurice  1205

**The Hanged Man**
Block, Francesca Lia  **548**

**The Hanged Man**
MacGregor, T.J.  **3594**

**Hanging by a Thread**
Kahn, Joan  543, 1019, 2282

**The Hanging Stones**
Wellman, Manly Wade  1639

**Happy Birthday, Wanda June**
Vonnegut, Kurt Jr.  1784, 1785, 5904

**Happy High**
Friesner, Esther  2800

**Happy Policeman**
Anthony, Patricia  **160**, 2286, 5576

**Hard-Boiled Wonderland and the End of the World**
Murakami, Haruki  2186, 3263, **4047**

**Hard Crash**
Hughes, Ryan  **2810**

**Hard Landing**
Budrys, Algis  **753**, 4196

**Hard Sell**
Anthony, Piers  **173**

**Hard to Be a God**
Strugatsky, Arkadi  5230

**Hardwired**
Williams, Walter Jon  66, 481, 766, 971, 972, 975, 1543, 1644, 1750, 1820, 2033, 3242, 3890, 3921, 4191, 4343, 4618, 4747, 5006, 6047

**The Harem of Aman Akbar**
Scarborough, Elizabeth Ann  1528, 2050, 2922

**Harmful Intent**
Cook, Robin  **1164**, 3200

**Harmonies of the 'Net**
Fancher, Jane S.  1774, **1862**, 2048, 2298, 5660

**Harmony**
Kellogg, Marjorie Bradley  46, 209, 656, 721, 792, 1449, 1482, 1559, 2328, **3046**, 3082, 3452, 4000, 4325, 4642, 5370, 5592, 5873, 5965

**Harm's Way**
Greenland, Colin  **2416**

**Haroun and the Sea of Stories**
Rushdie, Salman  374, 1681, 2123, 2130, **4731**, 5827, 6087

**The Harp of the Grey Rose**
de Lint, Charles  3269

**Harp of Winds**
Furey, Maggie  **2097**, 4795

**Harpist in the Wind**
McKillip, Patricia A.  257, 2098, 4265, 4727

**Harpy High**
Friesner, Esther  **2076**, 4317

**Harpy Thyme**
Anthony, Piers  **174**

**Harpy's Flight**
Lindholm, Megan  4924

**The Harriers**
Dickson, Gordon R.  **1535**

**Harrigan's File**
Derleth, August  4904, 4905

**Harrowgate**
Gower, Daniel H.  **2292**, 2335, 5784

**The Harrowing of Gwynedd**
Kurtz, Katherine  638, 750, 1745, 4782, 4783, 5126, 5508, 5868

**Harry Potter and the Sorcerer's Stone**
Rowling, J.K.  **4700**

**The Harvest**
Cusick, Richie Tankersley  **1302**, 2131

**The Harvest**
Wilson, Robert Charles  4506, **5909**

**Harvest Home**
Tryon, Thomas  438, 860, 1185, 1833

**Harvest of Blood**
Courtney, Vincent  **1213**, 2699

**Harvest of Stars**
Anderson, Poul  **127**, 593, 2526, 2907

**Harvest Tales and Midnight Revels: Stories for the Waning of the Year**
Mayhew, Michael  **3705**

**Harvest the Fire**
Anderson, Poul  **128**

**Hasan**
Anthony, Piers  73, 618, 880

**The Hashish Man and Other Stories by Lord Dunsany**
Dunsany  **1700**

**The Hastur Cycle**
Price, Robert M.  461, 2978, **4425**

**Hatchling**
Snyder, Midori  2003, 2469

**The Haunt**
Fogarty, John  **1966**

**Haunted**
Herbert, James  283, 2094, **2669**

**Haunted**
Thorne, Tamara  2743, 3368, 3675, 3951, 5334, **5463**

**Haunted America**
Kaye, Marvin  2383, 2586, 3866, 3868, 3869, 3870

**Haunted and Hunted**
O'Donnell, Elliott  2905

**The Haunted Chair and Other Stories**
Marsh, Richard  875, **3633**

**Haunted Dusk**
Bendixen, Alfred  5439

**The Haunted Earth**
Koontz, Dean R.  5497

**Haunted Houses: The Greatest Stories**
Greenberg, Martin H.  **2396**

**Haunted Mesa**
L'Amour, Louis  2009, 2291, 4062, 5151

**The Haunted Omnibus**
Laing, Alexander  1, 1310, 2968

**The Haunted Pampero**
Hodgson, William Hope  **2710**

**The Haunted Stars**
Hamilton, Edmond  133

**Haunted: Tales of the Grotesque**
Oates, Joyce Carol  921, 2842, **4184**, 5166, 5417

**The Haunted Tea Cosy: A Dispirited and Distasteful Diversion for Christmas**
Gorey, Edward  **2276**

**Haunted Women: The Best Supernatural Tales by American Women Writers**
Bendixen, Alfred  3570, 4180

**The Haunters and the Haunted; or, the House and the Brain**
Lytton, Edward Bulwer  1597

**The Haunting**
Jensen, Ruby Jean  **2901**, 2933, 3146, 3368

**The Haunting**
Mahy, Margaret  4257

**The Haunting of Cassie Palmer**
Alcock, Vivian  4257

**The Haunting of Hill House**
Jackson, Shirley  281, 282, 873, 1192, 2040, 2630, 2669, 3684, 3685, 4580, 4663, 5021, 5329, 5402, 5424, 5528, 5991, 5994

**The Haunting of Lamb House**
Aiken, Joan  45, 666, 5762

**Haunting Women**
Ryan, Alan  37, 1312, 1715, 2496, 3570, 4443, 5523

**Hauntings and Horrors**
Moskowitz, Sam  1712

**Have Spacesuit—Will Travel**
Heinlein, Robert A.  1217, 1460, 2491, 2763, 4930

**Have to Go: Planet R-101**
Byson, Brian  319

**Haven**
Peters, David  **4304**

**Hawaiian U.F.O. Aliens**
Gilden, Mel  1456, 1935, 1997, 2007, **2226**, 2480

**Hawk & Fisher**
Green, Simon R.  290, 745, 1148, 1152, 1153, 1250, 1251, 1705, 1706, 2041, **2370**, 2473, 2756, 2757, 2758, 2759, 3122, 3276, 3283, 4015, 4166, 4612, 4640, 4673, 4899, 4975, 5848

**Hawk of May**
Bradshaw, Gillian  224, 1190, 2745, 2747, 2760, 2939, 2940, 3058, 3062, 3827, 5970, 5971

**The Hawkline Monster**
Brautigan, Richard  499, 2847, 3439, 3456, 4233, 5151, 5817

**Hawkmistress!**
Bradley, Marion Zimmer  313, 314, 4515, 5542

**Hawk's Flight**
Chase, Carol  313, **980**, 1029, 3766, 3904

**The Hawk's Gray Feather**
Kennealy-Morrison, Patricia  1092, 3060, **3061**, 4584

**Hawksbill Station**
Silverberg, Robert  2575, 3597

**Hawksmoor**
Ackroyd, Peter  1094, 3984

**He, She and It**
Piercy, Marge  1824, **4325**, 5450, 5590

**Head Injuries**
Williams, Conrad  **5816**

**Headcrash**
Bethke, Bruce  118, 386, 474, **483**, 505, 2916, 3662, 4893, 5259

**Header**
Lee, Edward  2655, **3393**

**Headhunter**
Findley, Timothy  **1939**, 4086, 5897

**Headhunter**
Slade, Michael  2599

**Headhunters**
Odom, Mel  **4192**

**Heads**
Bear, Greg  79, 272, **419**, 588, 665

**Heads to the Storm**
Drake, David  3147, 3148

**The Headsman**
Harvey, James Neal  1831, **2599**, 3210

**Healer**
Dickinson, Peter  4334, 5478

**The Healer's War**
Scarborough, Elizabeth Ann  1069, 1130, 1631, 3035, 3706, 3743, 3744, 4466, 4477, **4865**, 5383

**The Healing of Crossroads**
O'Donohoe, Nick  **4195**

**Heart-Beast**
Lee, Tanith  572, 603, 2895, **3411**

**Heart of Darkness**
Conrad, Joseph  4979

**Heart of Red Iron**
Gotlieb, Phyllis  **2287**

**Heart of the Comet**
Benford, Gregory  381, 928, 931, 1057, 1058, 2216, 2433, 3772, 3824, 4417

**Heart of Valor**
Smith, L.J.  5070

**Heart Readers**
Rusch, Kristine Kathryn  **4718**, 5113

**Heartfire**
Card, Orson Scott  **889**

**Heartlight**
Bradley, Marion Zimmer **637**

**Hearts and Armor**
Miller, Ron 3501, **3903**, 4871

**Heartsease**
Dickinson, Peter 6038

**Heartstone and Silver**
Singleton, Jacqui 4627, **5071**

**The Heat Death of the Universe**
Zoline, Pamela 2261

**Heat Wave**
Friedman, M.J. 999

**Heathen**
Hutson, Shaun **2816**, 5120

**Heathern**
Womack, Jack 4030, 4856, 5642, **5958**

**Heatseeker**
Shirley, John 555, 807, 4977, **5007**, 5255, 5899

**Heaven Sent: 18 Glorious Tales of the Angels**
Crowther, Peter **1283**, 1339, 2342, 3112, 6031

**The Heavenly Horse From the Outermost West**
Stanton, Mary 223, 2397, 2673, 2676, 2678, 3291

**Heaven's Reach**
Brin, David **687**, 1501, 1759

**The Heavenward Path**
Dalkey, Kara **1319**

**Heavy Time**
Cherryh, C.J. 761, **995**, 1862, 3994

**Heavy Weather**
Sterling, Bruce 354, 2998, 3789, 4218, **5258**

**Hecate's Cauldron**
Shwartz, Susan 6034

**Hederick, the Theocrat**
Severson, Ellen Dodge **4925**

**The Hedge of Mist**
Kennealy-Morrison, Patricia **3062**

**Hedgework and Guessery**
de Lint, Charles **1428**, 5810

**The Height of the Scream**
Campbell, Ramsey 5329

**Heir to the Empire**
Zahn, Timothy 76, 103, 109, 114, 2500, 2914, 3247, 3820, 4719, 5205, **6054**

**The Heirs of Babylon**
Cook, Glen 3586

**Heirs of Empire**
Weber, David **5672**

**The Heirs of Hammerfell**
Bradley, Marion Zimmer **638**, 3255, 4081, 4269

**The Heldan**
Talmadge-Bickmore, Deborah 5133, **5383**

**Helen's Passage**
Concannon, Diana M. **1129**

**Hell: A Cyberpunk Thriller**
Williamson, Chet 4495

**Hell Hath Fury**
Cartmill, Cleve 4006

**Hell House**
Matheson, Richard 90, 281, 861, 1192, 1776, 2630, 2669, 3607, 3657, **3685**, 4830, 5329, 5424, 5528, 5991

**Hell-O-Ween**
Robbins, David **4598**

**Hell on High**
Lisle, Holly **3483**

**Hell-Storm**
Moore, James A. **3990**, 4059

**The Hellbound Heart**
Barker, Clive **342**, 2222, 3351, 3364, 3368, 4499, 5010

**Hellboy: The Lost Army**
Golden, Christopher **2257**

**Hellburner**
Cherryh, C.J. 584, 905, **996**, 2298, 2832, 3315, 4927

**Hellcat**
Kingsley, Amanda **3145**

**The Hellfire Club**
Straub, Peter 3088, **5326**

**Hellflower**
bes shahar, eluki **473**

**Hellhound Magic**
Green, Sharon 1731, 1736

**Helliconia Spring**
Aldiss, Brian W. 4242, 5040, 5940

**Helliconia Summer**
Aldiss, Brian W. 884, 4242, 5040, 5940

**The Helliconia Trilogy**
Aldiss, Brian W. 4243

**Helliconia Winter**
Aldiss, Brian W. 418, 4242, 5040, 5940

**Hello America**
Ballard, J.G. 837, 4474

**Hellquad**
Goulart, Ron 1216, 2573, 4341

**Hellspark**
Kagan, Janet 230, 785, 877, 952, 990, 998, 1504, 1537, 1643, 2058, 2764, **3000**, 3475, 3744, 3752, 3928, 4140, 4554, 5090

**Hellstrom's Hive**
Herbert, Frank 4662, 4842, 4944, 5755

**Helltracks**
Nolan, William F. 1489

**Hellworld**
Green, Simon R. 1643, **2371**

**Helm**
Gould, Steven 2246, **2289**

**The Helmsman**
Baldwin, Bill 3034

**The Hemingway Hoax**
Haldeman, Joe 1473, 1875, **2489**, 2546

**Hence**
Leithauser, Brad **3431**

**Henry Martyn**
Smith, L. Neil 4277, **5131**

**Henry's Gift: The Magic Eye**
Worsick, David 2981, 3896, 3897, **5972**, 6036

**Her Klingon Soul**
Friedman, Michael Jan **2064**

**Her Majesty's Wizard**
Stasheff, Christopher 194, 1160, 1324, 1413, 2560, 2616, 4391, 4392

**Her Monster**
Collignon, Jeff 729, **1115**, 5826

**Her Pilgrim Soul**
Brennert, Alan **674**

**Her Smoke Rose Up Forever**
Tiptree, James Jr. 790, 1818, 2835, 3048, 3086, 3234, 3235, 3379, 3442, 3600, 3712, 3736, 4680, 5369, 5410, **5477**, 5641

**Her Stories**
Hamilton, Virginia **2528**

**Hercules, My Shipmate**
Graves, Robert 2404

**The Hercules Text**
McDevitt, Jack 202

**Here Abide Monsters**
Norton, Andre 196, 3800, 4595

**Here There Be Angels**
Yolen, Jane **6031**

**Here There Be Dragons**
Yolen, Jane 2346, 2479, 4408, 5710, **6032**

**Here There Be Dragons**
Zelazny, Roger 6032, 6036, **6069**

**Here There Be Unicorns**
Yolen, Jane 410, 412, 1219, 1946, 2346, 3414, 3737, 4319, **6033**

**Here There Be Witches**
Yolen, Jane **6034**

**Heretics of Dune**
Herbert, Frank 2464, 2722, 3507, 4551

**Heritage of Flight**
Shwartz, Susan 3748, 4696, **5016**

**The Heritage of Hastur**
Bradley, Marion Zimmer 1933, 1934, 3288, 4334, 5754

**A Heritage of Stars**
Simak, Clifford D. 484, 882, 3788, 4619, 4620

**Herland**
Gilman, Charlotte Perkins 4627

**Hero**
Duncan, Dave 958, 1547, **1680**, 2215, 2466, 2536, 3829, 4229, 5201, 5476, 5718, 5949

**Hero**
Rosenberg, Joel 2004, 2052, 2351, 2353, 4373, **4672**

**The Hero and the Crown**
McKinley, Robin 763, 2676, 3412, 3941, 6037

**A Hero Born**
Stackpole, Michael A. **5202**

**The Hero King**
Shelley, Rick 286, **4970**

**The Hero of Varay**
Shelley, Rick 4265, **4971**

**Heroes and Horrors**
Leiber, Fritz 2781

**Heroes Die**
Stover, Matthew Woodring **5319**

**Heroes in Hell**
Morris, Janet 1280, 1626, 1631, 4388, 4605, 4655, 4869

**Heroes, Inc.**
Crocco, Kyle 167, 559, 1208, **1268**, 2080, 2803, 2950, 3810, 3991, 4458, 5649, 6066

**Heroes Wanted**
Crocco, Kyle 262, **1267**, 3810, 5649

**Heroic Visions**
Salmonson, Jessica Amanda 628, 629

**A Heroine of the World**
Lee, Tanith **3412**, 5390, 5393

**Heroines**
Kelly, James Patrick 3945

**Hero's Song**
Pattou, Edith **4261**, 4497

**Hestia**
Cherryh, C.J. 5880

**Hexwood**
Jones, Diana Wynne 196, 635, **2948**

**The Hidden City**
de Lint, Charles **1429**, 3572

**The Hidden City**
Eddings, David **1733**, 1905

**Hidden Echoes**
Jefferies, Mike 2760, **2885**

**Hidden Fires**
Kimbriel, Katharine Eliska **3117**

**The Hidden Land**
Dean, Pamela 4, 1488, 3400, 5235

**A Hidden Place**
Wilson, Robert Charles **5910**

**The Hidden Realms**
Green, Sharon **2358**, 5133

**The Hidden Valley of Oz**
Cosgrove, Rachel R. 3609

**The Hidden War**
Armstrong, Michael **209**

**Hide and Seek**
Preuss, Paul **4418**

**Hideaway**
Koontz, Dean R. 376, 916, 945, 1078, 1669, 2161, 2202, 2293, 3052, **3208**, 4327, 4837, 5969, 5987

**Hiero's Journey**
Lanier, Sterling E.   664, 1481, 1996, 2640, 3788, 4001, 4153, 4162, 4209, 4621, 4836, 5267

**High Aztec**
Hogan, Ernest   829, 2369, **2722**, 4935, 4936, 5254

**The High Couch of Silistra**
Morris, Janet   1071

**The High Crusade**
Anderson, Poul   1325, 4365, 5131, 5588, 5900

**High Deryni**
Kurtz, Katherine   256, 1175, 2098, 2987, 3399, 4265, 5832

**The High House**
Stoddard, James   **5311**

**The High King**
Alexander, Lloyd   658, 6042

**High Moon**
Duane, Diane   **1661**, 3029

**High Spirits**
Davies, Robertson   2813, 2814

**High Steel**
Haldeman, Jack C. II   128, 157, 1337, **2486**, 4635, 4677, 4679, 5745

**The High-Tech Knight**
Frankowski, Leo   33, 1982, **2045**

**High Wizardry**
Duane, Diane   605, 969, **1662**, 2623, 2628, 4323, 5558, 5646

**Higher Education**
Sheffield, Charles   1962, 4379, **4958**

**Higher Mythology**
Nye, Jody Lynn   1842, **4170**

**The Higher Space**
Nasir, Jamil   199, 2273, **4070**

**Highlander**
Kilworth, Garry   3854

**Highlander: Scimitar**
McConnell, Ashley   2657, 4082, 4611, 5707, 5729

**Highlander: The Element of Fire**
Henderson, Jason   559, 1808, 4082, 4611, 5707, 5729

**The Hill of Dreams**
Machen, Arthur   **3595**, 4586

**His Majesty's Elephant**
Tarr, Judith   **5394**, 5511

**His Share of Glory: The Complete Short Science Fiction of C.M. Kornbluth**
Kornbluth, C.M.   **3219**, 5348

**A History Maker**
Gray, Alasdair   **2338**

**The Hitchhiker's Guide to the Galaxy**
Adams, Douglas   483, 553, 735, 959, 1216, 1453, 1455, 1456, 1459, 1504, 1918, 1921, 1999, 2055, 2075, 2123, 2130, 2132, 2133, 2172, 2208, 2226, 2332, 2567, 2568, 2622, 2750, 2880, 2979, 3465, 4076, 4077, 4388, 4392, 4562, 4563, 4564, 4565, 4566, 4656, 4662, 4785, 5076, 6008

**Hitler Victorious: Eleven Stories of the German Victory in World War II**
Benford, Gregory   2564, 5300, 5301

**The Hoard of the Wizard Beast and One Other**
Barlow, Robert H.   348, 3516

**The Hobbit**
Tolkien, J.R.R.   16, 368, 711, 713, 1207, 1601, 2271, 2378, 3050, 3513, 3728, 3765, 3835, 4808, 4906, 5640, 5726, 6006, 6024, 6069

**The Hobby**
Yolen, Jane   370

**Hobgoblin**
Coyne, John   2322

**Hobkin**
Griffin, Peni R.   970, 1441, **2438**, 3444, 3816

**Hocus Pocus or, What's the Hurry, Son?**
Vonnegut, Kurt Jr.   2770, **5593**

**Hogfather**
Pratchett, Terry   **4391**

**Hogfoot Right and Bird-Hands**
Kilworth, Garry   497, 772, **3116**, 3250, 3702

**Hoka!**
Anderson, Poul   197, 259, 1414, 4785, 5875

**The Hole of the Pit**
Ross, Adrian   2711

**The Hollow Earth: The Narrative of Mason Algiers Reynolds of Virginia**
Rucker, Rudy   2469, **4705**

**The Hollow Man**
Simmons, Dan   362, 1089, 1438, 2163, 2727, 3007, 3049, **5054**, 5680

**The Hollowing**
Holdstock, Robert   **2738**

**Hollywood Ghosts**
McSherry, Frank D. Jr.   4252

**The Hollywood Nightmare**
Haining, Peter   4252, 5460, 5947

**The Holmes-Dracula File**
Saberhagen, Fred   1524, **4767**

**The Holo Men**
Billias, Stephen   2470

**Holy Fire**
Sterling, Bruce   **5259**

**The Holy Grail**
Godwin, Malcolm   2231, 2232

**Holy Terror**
Boyle, Josephine   **608**, 3607

**The Holy Terror**
Sallee, Wayne Allen   822, 1779, **4787**

**Home From the Shore**
Dickson, Gordon R.   1469, 4923, 5541

**Home Is the Hunter**
Kramer-Rolls, Dana   902, 5404

**Homebody**
Card, Orson Scott   **890**, 2241

**Homecoming**
Costello, Matthew J.   **1198**, 3375, 3518

**Homecoming**
Dalmas, John   885, 2004

**The Homecoming**
Longyear, Barry B.   **3521**, 5129

**The Homecoming**
Rangel, Kimberly   **4471**

**Homecoming**
Smith, David Alexander   210, 469, 734, 1059, 1407, 1537, 1869, 1989, 2108, 2419, 2691, 2898, 3437, 3603, 3943, 4124, 4626, 4643, 4896, **5108**, 5452, 5573, 5574

**Homegoing**
Pohl, Frederik   3943, **4347**

**Homeland**
Salvatore, R.A.   3537, 4108

**The Homeward Bounders**
Jones, Diana Wynne   165, 4338

**The Homing**
Saul, John   2284, 3207, **4842**

**Homunculus**
Blaylock, James P.   25, 714, 1014, 1564, 2329, 2546, 3097, 3124, 4385, 4740

**Hong on the Range**
Wu, William F.   1879, **5997**

**Honor Among Enemies**
Weber, David   645, **5673**

**Honor and Fidelity**
Keith, Andrew   3037

**The Honor of the Queen**
Weber, David   312, 3976, **5674**

**Honor of the Regiment**
Fawcett, Bill   **1896**

**The Honorable Barbarian**
de Camp, L. Sprague   523, **1415**, 2463, 2465, 3471

**An Honorable Defense**
Drake, David   1650, 6014

**Hook**
Brooks, Terry   **713**, 5143

**Hooray for Hellywood**
Friesner, Esther   **2077**, 3989, 4363, 5649

**Hope of Earth**
Anthony, Piers   175

**Hopeship**
Lang, Simon   **3315**

**Horizon Lines**
Osier, Jeffrey   3495, **4231**, 4313, 5445, 5620

**The Hormone Jungle**
Reed, Robert   2690, 2691

**Hormone Pirates of Xenobia and Dream Studs of Kama Loka**
Posey, Ernest   2117

**Horn Crown**
Norton, Andre   4269

**The Horns of Elfland**
Kushner, Ellen   **3264**

**Horrible Humes**
Billias, Stephen   27, **407**, 1840, 4433, 4675

**Horror at the Haunted House**
Kehret, Peg   5288

**The Horror Club**
Morris, Mark   **4022**

**The Horror From the Hills**
Long, Frank Belknap   4414, 4415

**The Horror Hall of Fame**
Silverberg, Robert   2590, **5031**

**Horror Hunters**
Elwood, Roger   5653

**The Horror in the Museum and Other Revisions**
Lovecraft, H.P.   **3531**

**The Horror of the Heights and Other Tales of Suspense**
Doyle, Arthur Conan   **1597**, 5746

**Horror Show**
Kihn, Greg   2448, **3103**

**Horror Stories**
Price, Susan   1693, 1701, 2772, 4282

**Horrors: 365 Scary Stories**
Dziemianowicz, Stefan   **1714**

**Horrors of the Dancing Gods**
Chalker, Jack L.   185, **955**

**Horrors Unknown**
Moskowitz, Sam   1712

**Horrorshow**
Darke, David   428, 460, **1353**, 2761, 3102, 3103, 3326

**Horrorstory III**
Wagner, Karl Edward   **5601**

**Horrorstory IV**
Wagner, Karl Edward   **5602**

**Horrorstory V**
Wagner, Karl Edward   **5603**

**The Horse and His Boy**
Lewis, C.S.   3404, 4156

**Horse Fantastic**
Greenberg, Martin H.   2380, **2397**, 4543

**The Horse Goddess**
Llywelyn, Morgan   561, 657, 1961, 5408, 5626

**The Horse Lord**
Morwood, Peter  223, 1731, 1736, 2397, 2673, 2678

**The Horse of Flame**
Sherman, Josepha  657, 3275

**A Horse to Love**
Springer, Nancy  4156

**The Horsegirl**
Ash, Constance  2397, 2676, 4156

**Horselords**
Cook, David  657, **1145**, 3537, 4108, 4807

**Horses of Heaven**
Bradshaw, Gillian  **657**

**Horses of the Night**
Cadnum, Michael  **811**

**Hospital Station**
White, James  4172, 4196

**The Host**
Emshwiller, Peter R.  805, 1438, **1819**, 2727, 3449, 3817, 4030, 4709, 4710, 4949, 5355, 5642

**Host**
James, Peter  **2872**

**A Hostage for Hinterland**
Darnay, Arsen  4678

**Hostile Takeover**
McKinney, Jack  **3849**

**Hot Blood**
Gelb, Jeff  1367, 1401

**Hot Blood X**
Gelb, Jeff  **2177**

**Hot Blood: Crimes of Passion**
Gelb, Jeff  **2178**

**Hot Blood: Kiss and Kill**
Gelb, Jeff  **2179**

**Hot Blood: Stranger by Night**
Gelb, Jeff  5536

**Hot Blood: Tales of Provocative Horror**
Gelb, Jeff  72, 75, 302, 1118, 1120, 1357, 1361, 1607, 3026, 4465, 5056, 5093, 5094

**The Hot Jazz Trio**
Kotzwinkle, William  **3223**

**Hot Sky at Midnight**
Silverberg, Robert  **5032**

**The Hot Spot**
Williams, Charles  3330

**Hot Time in Old Town**
McQuay, Mike  2916

**The Hot-Wired Dodo**
Chalker, Jack L.  **956**

**Hotel Transylvania**
Yarbro, Chelsea Quinn  1142, 1795, 3110, 3163

**Hothouse**
Aldiss, Brian W.  2847, 5659

**Hotter Blood: More Tales of Erotic Horror**
Gelb, Jeff  72, 75, 1120, 1357, 1361, **2180**, 4465, 5056, 5093, 5094

**Hottest Blood: The Ultimate in Erotic Horror**
Gelb, Jeff  72, 75, 1120, 1361, **2181**, 2893, 5056, 5094, 5385

**The Hounds of the Morrigan**
O'Shea, Pat  1220, 1294, 1330, 6042

**The Hounds of Tindalos**
Long, Frank Belknap  942, 1495, 1496, 2844, 3529, 3534, 4904, 4905, 5627, 5628

**Hour of Judgment**
Matthews, Susan R.  2286

**Hour of the Dragon**
Howard, Robert E.  291, 906, 907, **2783**, 2983, 3420, 4294, 4616

**The Hour of the Gate**
Foster, Alan Dean  2946

**Hour of the Octopus**
Rosenberg, Joel  1250, 2756, 2803, **4673**

**The Hour of the Oxrun Dead**
Grant, Charles L.  832, 1185, 2339, 2930, 3041, 3212, 4838, 5111

**Hour of the Scorpion**
Costello, Matthew J.  **1199**

**The House Between the Worlds**
Bradley, Marion Zimmer  515, 962, 5218

**House Haunted**
Sarrantonio, Al  90, 342, 861, 1192, 1380, 2040, 2875, 3055, 3161, 3657, 3684, 3685, 4663, 4701, **4830**, 5631

**The House Next Door**
Siddons, Anne Rivers  890, 3621, **5021**

**The House of Arden**
Nesbit, E.  4585

**The House of Cthulhu and Other Tales of the Primal Land**
Lumley, Brian  3702

**House of Dies Drear**
Hamilton, Virginia  331

**The House of Doors**
Lumley, Brian  1894, **3554**

**The House of Fear**
Williamson, Chet  200, 666, 5427, 5530, 5929

**The House of Living Death and Other Terror Tales**
Hanlon, John  4494

**The House of Many Worlds**
Merwin, Samuel  264, 357, 1855

**House of Moons**
Wentworth, K.D.  645, 3060, **5752**

**The House of Secrets**
Moore, James A.  798, 5703

**The House of the Seven Gables**
Hawthorne, Nathaniel  340

**House of the Sun**
Findley, Nigel  **1936**, 3198

**The House of the Toad**
Tierney, Richard L.  1497, 5121, **5470**

**The House of the Wolf**
Copper, Basil  5158

**House of the Wolf**
Wren, M.K.  3865

**The House of the Worm**
Myers, Gary  925, 3555, 3859, 5102, 5103, 5471

**The House of Thunder**
Koontz, Dean R.  376, 1832, 4874

**House of Zeor**
Lichtenberg, Jacqueline  220, 1134, 1408, 2665, 4318

**The House on Hound Hill**
Prince, Maggie  **4438**

**The House on Parchment Street**
McKillip, Patricia A.  122, 1272, 2283, 2923, 4078, 4438

**The House on the Borderland**
Hodgson, William Hope  **2711**

**House Shudders**
Waugh, Charles G.  1246, 5902

**The House That Jack Built**
Masterton, Graham  **3675**, 3953

**The House with a Clock in Its Walls**
Bellairs, John  1294

**Houses Without Doors**
Straub, Peter  3138, **5327**

**How Dear the Dawn**
Eliot, Marc  462

**How Few Remain**
Turtledove, Harry  1516, 5495, **5504**

**How Like a God**
Clough, Brenda W.  362, **1089**

**How Much for Just the Planet?**
Ford, John M.  7, 526, 607, 1382, 1459, 1536, 1659, 1918, 1921, 1922, 2567, 2568, 2880, 4562, 4563, 4564, 4565, 4566, 4656, 4785, 4870, 5875

**How the Ewoks Saved the Trees: An Old Ewok Legend**
Howe, James  1392, 1393, 1394

**How to Mutate and Take Over the World**
Sirius, R.U.  3457, **5074**

**How to Save the World**
Sheffield, Charles  888, 1962, **4959**

**Howl**
Tanasiuk, Christine  41, 2768, **5388**

**Howl-O-Ween**
Holleman, Gary L.  **2744**

**The Howling**
Brandner, Gary  723, 3376

**Howling Mad**
David, Peter  2125, 3280, 4387

**The Howling Man**
Beaumont, Charles  **429**

**The Howling Stones**
Foster, Alan Dean  **2006**, 3769, 4067

**Howl's Moving Castle**
Jones, Diana Wynne  174, 1220, 1668, 1677, 2075, 5975, 5979

**Hrolf Kraki's Saga**
Anderson, Poul  363, 2571, 3910, 4526

**Hubble's Bubble**
Horseman, Elaine  5968

**Hugo and Nebula Award Winners From Asimov's Science Fiction**
Williams, Sheila  888

**The Hugo Winners 1-5**
Asimov, Isaac  2401, 2405, 5871

**The Human Angle**
Tenn, William  1874

**The Human Chord**
Blackwood, Algernon  3595

**Human Remains**
Kemske, Floyd  4667

**Human Resources**
Kemske, Floyd  **3057**, 3957

**Human to Human**
Ore, Rebecca  764, **4219**

**The Humanoid Touch**
Williamson, Jack  1896

**The Humanoids**
Williamson, Jack  126, 128, 134, 198, 232, 249, 446, 1782, 2458, 3715, 3794, 4903, **5865**

**Humans**
Westlake, Donald E.  729, 2753, 5532, **5768**, 6062

**Humility Garden**
Savage, Felicity  **4850**

**Humpty Dumpty: An Oval**
Knight, Damon  **3186**

**The Hundred and One Dalmatians**
Smith, Dodie  2786

**Hunger**
Dantz, William  88, 373, 441, **1346**, 3232, 3998, 5877

**The Hunger**
Strieber, Whitley  1882, 2019, 2510, 3253, 4068, 4089, 4367, 4508, 4574, 4665, 5824

**The Hunger and Ecstasy of Vampires**
Stableford, Brian  2255, **5192**

**A Hunger in the Soul**
Resnick, Mike  **4545**

**The Hunger of the Beast**
Driver, John  **1656**, 2200, 3133, 3391, 3402, 4222

**Hungry Eyes**
Hoffman, Barry  3395

**Hungry for Home: A Wolf Odyssey**
Bowen, 'Asta  **599**, 4271

**The Hungry Moon**
Campbell, Ramsey  3496, 3951, 3965, 4024, 4531, 4587, 4733, 4907

**The Hunted**
Ptacek, Kathryn  3898, 3964, **4442**, 5314

**The Hunter**
Estes, Rose  4294, 5097

**Hunter of the Light**
Aratyr, Risa  **203**

**Hunter of Worlds**
Cherryh, C.J.  3800

**The Hunter on Arena**
Estes, Rose  **1838**

**The Hunter Returns**
Drake, David  **1632**

**The Hunters**
Lovejoy, Jack  2211, 2811, 3800

**Hunter's Death**
West, Michelle  **5758**

**The Hunters' Haunt**
Duncan, Dave  **1681**

**Hunter's Oath**
West, Michelle  1095, 2695, 3291, 3292, **5759**

**Hunters of the Red Moon**
Bradley, Marion Zimmer  3800

**Hunter's Planet**
Bischoff, David  **492**, 4075

**Hunting Party**
Moon, Elizabeth  1542, **3968**, 5671, 5966

**Hunting the Corrigan's Blood**
Lisle, Holly  **3484**

**Hunting the Ghost Dancer**
Attanasio, A.A.  **268**

**Hurry, Monster**
Masterton, Graham  5796

**Hyacinths**
Yarbro, Chelsea Quinn  1535

**Hyperion**
Simmons, Dan  80, 96, 116, 220, 270, 293, 328, 404, 414, 417, 423, 447, 449, 472, 478, 566, 708, 783, 899, 930, 952, 1054, 1106, 1184, 1634, 1681, 1819, 1820, 1993, 2036, 2056, 2057, 2060, 2480, 2666, 2727, 2729, 2766, 2882, 3014, 3117, 3398, 3437, 3644, 4099, 4136, 4281, 4507, 4641, 4708, 4736, 4762, 4769, 4857, 4867, 4896, 4901, 4951, 4954, 4965, 5012, 5029, **5055**, 5372, 5436, 5449, 5594, 5668, 5774, 5899, 5905

**The Hyperion Cantos**
Simmons, Dan  3143

**I**

**I Am Dracula**
Andersson, C. Dean  **139**, 678, 3004, 3005, 3179, 6011

**I Am Frankenstein**
Andersson, C. Dean  **140**

**I Am Legend**
Matheson, Richard  2440, 3361, 3458, **3686**, 3758, 4072, 4831, 5050, 5212, 5770, 5891, 5923

**I Am One of You Forever**
Chappell, Fred  817

**I Feel Like the Morning Star**
Maguire, Gregory  3584, **3608**

**I Have No Mouth and I Must Scream**
Ellison, Harlan  4232

**The I Inside**
Foster, Alan Dean  583, 4469

**I Know What You Did Last Summer**
Duncan, Lois  **1692**

**I Met a Man Who Wasn't There**
Callaghan, Mary R.  **840**, 5468

**I, Robot**
Asimov, Isaac  253, 254, 255, 4297

**I, Robot: The Illustrated Screenplay**
Ellison, Harlan  29, **1785**

**I, Said the Fly**
Shea, Michael  **4944**

**I Scream. You Scream. We All Scream for Ice Cream**
Farris, John  3494

**I Shudder at Your Touch**
Slung, Michele  75, 1118, 1120, 1357, 1361, 1367, 1607, 2176, 2178, 2179, 2181, 2182, 2185, 2893, 3024, 3026, 4465, 5056, **5093**

**I, Strahd**
Elrod, P.N.  155, 465, 1510, **1797**, 2516, 2663, 5847, 6011

**I, Tituba, Black Witch of Salem**
Conde, Maryse  **1130**, 1835

**I, Vampire**
Romkey, Michael  139, 292, 463, 678, 2267, 3781, 4097, **4665**, 4763, 5191, 6019

**I, Vampire**
Scott, Jody  1122

**I, Vampire: Interviews with the Undead**
Stine, Jean Marie  2382, 2408, **5284**, 5448

**I Wake From a Dream of a Drowned Star City**
Somtow, S.P.  4850, **5157**

**I Walk at Night**
Duncan, Lois  5285

**I Was a Teenage Fairy**
Block, Francesca Lia  **549**

**I Who Have Never Known Men**
Harpman, Jacqueline  **2554**

**I Will Fear No Evil**
Heinlein, Robert A.  2498, 4066

**Icarus Descending**
Hand, Elizabeth  400, **2536**, 5105

**The Ice Beast**
Javor, Frank A.  **2881**

**Ice Crown**
Norton, Andre  632, 3747

**The Ice Dragon**
Knaak, Richard A.  470

**The Ice Is Coming**
Wrightson, Patricia  2170, 4946

**Ice Prophet**
Forstchen, William R.  897, 2870, 4373

**The Ice Schooner**
Moorcock, Michael  511

**The Ice-Shirt**
Vollmann, William T.  **5580**

**Ice Station Zebra**
MacLean, Alistair  3209

**Ice Trap**
Graf, L.A.  3767

**Icebound**
Koontz, Dean R.  **3209**

**Iced on Aran and Other Dream Quests**
Lumley, Brian  856, **3555**, 3613, 5471

**Icefalcon's Quest**
Hambly, Barbara  1679, **2504**, 4524, 4727

**Icefire**
Reeves-Stevens, Judith  **4512**

**Icehenge**
Robinson, Kim Stanley  1248, 4962

**Iceman**
Felice, Cynthia  **1913**, 3912

**Iceman**
Miller, Rex  3395, **3900**

**Icequake**
Kilian, Crawford  4628

**The Identity Matrix**
Chalker, Jack L.  4470

**The IDIC Epidemic**
Lorrah, Jean  526, 1554, 2685, 4928

**Idoru**
Gibson, William  835, **2218**

**The Idylls of the Queen**
Karr, Phyllis Ann  1189, 1190, 1269, 1857, 2747, 3355, 3806

**If at Faust You Don't Succeed**
Zelazny, Roger  3480, 3483, 3991, 4388, 4404, 4655, **6070**

**If Ever I Return, Pretty Peggy-O**
McCrumb, Sharyn  1829

**If I Never Get Back**
Brock, Darryl  2029

**If I Pay Thee Not in Gold**
Anthony, Piers  **176**, 882, 4159, 4784

**If the Stars Are Gods**
Benford, Gregory  1991, 3617

**If This Goes On**
Lewis, Sinclair  5086

**If Wishes Were Horses**
McCaffrey, Anne  **3737**

**If You Could See Me Now**
Straub, Peter  1860, 1883, 2495, 5415

**Igniting the Reaches**
Drake, David  308, **1633**, 5294

**Ignition**
Anderson, Kevin J.  **107**

**The Ignored**
Little, Bentley  **3493**

**I'll Be Watching You**
Key, Samuel M.  2113, **3094**

**Ill Met in Lankhmar**
Leiber, Fritz  290, 291, 495, 683, 1109, 1147, 1292, 1636, 1813, 2253, 2451, 2452, 2759, **3419**, 3980, 4165, 4166, 4849, 4945, 5206, 5458, 5471

**Ill Met in Lankhmar/The Fair in Emain Macha**
Leiber, Fritz  3189

**Ill Wind**
Anderson, Kevin J.  **108**, 506, 4218

**The Illearth War**
Donaldson, Stephen R.  1911, 2887, 5235, 5741, 6058

**Illegal Alien**
Luceno, James  1420, **3543**

**Illegal Alien**
Sawyer, Robert J.  **4858**

**Illegal Aliens**
Pollotta, Nick  483, 1454, 1892, 1921, 2007, 2228, 2880, 4120, 4298, **4365**

**The Illegal Rebirth of Billy the Kid**
Ore, Rebecca  951, 957, 995, 2049, **4220**, 4559, 4560

**The Illuminatus! Trilogy**
Shea, Robert  1093, 1273, 1274, 4302, 4662, 4708, 5009, 5074, 5170

**Illusion**
Volsky, Paula  705, 991, 1249, 1251, 1675, 1676, 1863, 1902, 1952, 2032, 2039, 2060, 2195, 2509, 2561, 2653, 2693, 2884, 2956, 3274, 3293, 3410, 3508, 3581, 3624, 3841, 3933, 4045, 4488, 4490, 4491, 4686, 4714, 4718, 4739, 4740, 4802, 4851, 4983, 5126, 5137, 5150, 5228, 5266, **5582**, 5648, 5750, 5758, 5813

**The Illusionists**
Miller, Faren  **3894**

**The Illustrated Hitchhiker's Guide to the Galaxy**
Adams, Douglas  **29**

**The Illustrated Man**
Bradbury, Ray  4131

**The Image of the Beast**
Farmer, Philip Jose  3543

**Imaginary Lands**
McKinley, Robin  1340, 5239

**Imagination Fully Dilated**
Engstrom, Elizabeth  **1044**, 4186

**Imagine**
Barnett, Jill  3280

**Imagine a Man in a Box**
Wakefield, H. Russell  4141, **5611**

**Imago**
Butler, Octavia E.   469, 685, **791**, 876, 1179, 1255, 1304, 1559, 1723, 1726, 1727, 2058, 2213, 2287, 2539, 3001, 3047, 3188, 3446, 3792, 4001, 4217, 4219, 4242, 4900, 5016, 5373, 5461

**Imajica**
Barker, Clive   **343**, 495, 1117, 3143, 5931

**Imbalance**
Mitchell, V.E.   **3919**

**The Immaculate**
Morris, Mark   3525, 3809, **4023**, 5530

**Immortal**
Nickles, Jason   3051, **4102**

**Immortal Blood**
Hambly, Barbara   1792, 1793

**The Immortality Option**
Hogan, James P.   **2725**, 5051, 5059

**The Immortals**
Gunn, James   581

**The Immortals**
Hickman, Tracy   **2681**, 5722, 5725

**The Immortals**
Neiderman, Andrew   3139, **4087**

**Imperial Earth**
Clarke, Arthur C.   3924

**Imperial Lady**
Norton, Andre   69, 1104, 3338, 3339, **4155**, 5014, 5015

**The Imperium Game**
Wentworth, K.D.   **5753**

**Implant**
Wilson, F. Paul   1347, 4874

**Impossible Things**
Willis, Connie   123, 274, 689, 790, 1758, 1963, 2027, 2120, 2537, 3235, 3384, 3971, 4535, 5240, 5410, **5869**

**An Impossumble Summer**
Clough, Brenda W.   **1090**

**Imposter**
Freireich, Valerie J.   **2050**, 3426

**Impulse**
Hautala, Rick   **2609**

**Imzadi**
David, Peter   **1383**, 1658

**In a Dark Dream**
Grant, Charles L.   284, **2310**, 5522

**In a Glass Darkly**
Le Fanu, J. Sheridan   258, 509

**In a Lonely Place**
Wagner, Karl Edward   2780, 2784

**In Alien Flesh**
Benford, Gregory   349, 425

**In between Dragons**
Kandel, Michael   1662, **3010**, 3156, 4008, 5478

**In between the Sheets**
McEwan, Ian   626, 920

**In Camera and Other Stories**
Westall, Robert   1526, **5764**

**In Cold Blood**
Capote, Truman   1489

**In Conquest Born**
Friedman, C.S.   4049, 5821

**The In Crowd**
Pine, Nicholas   4329

**In Darkness Waiting**
Shirley, John   2344, 2345, 4907

**In Double Jeopardy**
Neiderman, Andrew   **4088**

**In Dreams**
McAuley, Paul J.   2184, 4810

**In Enemy Hands**
Weber, David   **5675**, 5786

**In Ghostly Company**
Northcote, Amyas   **4141**

**In His Own Write: Brian Lumley, Necroscribe**
Lumley, Brian   **3556**, 4444

**In Hot Blood**
Popescu, Petru   **4367**

**In Legend Born**
Resnick, Laura   **4533**

**In Lovecraft's Shadow**
Derleth, August   **1495**

**In Mayan Splendor**
Long, Frank Belknap   4752

**In Silence Sealed**
Ptacek, Kathryn   912, 1086, 2741, 4569, 5192, 5842

**In Solitary**
Kilworth, Garry   3800

**In Sylvan Shadows**
Salvatore, R.A.   **4800**

**In the Beginning**
David, Peter   2102

**In the Blood**
Collins, Nancy A.   **1121**, 1286

**In the Blood**
Douglas, Lauren Wright   74, 662, **1590**, 1720, 2242, 3579, 3915

**In the Circle of Time**
Anderson, Margaret J.   2688

**In the Company of the Mind**
Piziks, Steven   **4339**

**In the Country of the Blind**
Flynn, Michael   116, 442, 443, 483, 596, 598, 781, 895, 1093, 1199, 1274, 1615, 1987, 2087, 2480, 2488, 2564, 2839, 3662, 3764, 3854, 3931, 4120, 4288, 4292, 4682, 4937, 5248, 5694, 5903

**In the Cube**
Smith, David Alexander   156, 476, 478, 2087, 2092, 3520, 4748, **5109**, 5363, 5587

**In the Dark**
Nesbit, E.   4968, 5763, 5764, 5765

**In the Deep Woods**
Conde, Nicholas   **1131**, 4664, 5123

**In the Drift**
Swanwick, Michael   1399, 5956

**In the Field of Fire**
Dann, Jeanne Van Buren   3706

**In the Fog**
Grant, Charles L.   **2311**

**In the Garden of Iden**
Baker, Kage   **298**, 3854, 4036

**In the Hall of the Dragon King**
Lawhead, Stephen R.   4654, 5124

**In the Hand of the Goddess**
Pierce, Tamora   4871

**In the Hands of Glory**
Eisenstein, Phyllis   2436, 2437, 4468

**In the Heart of Darkness**
Flint, Eric   **1955**

**In the Heart of the Valley of Love**
Kadohata, Cynthia   1835, **2997**

**In the Land of the Dead**
Jeter, K.W.   **2912**, 5899

**In the Land of Winter**
Grant, Richard   **2326**

**In the Mood**
Grant, Charles L.   **2312**

**In the Mothers' Land**
Vonarburg, Elisabeth   **5590**

**In the Net of Dreams**
Simmons, Wm. Mark   1461, 3831

**In the Ocean of Night**
Benford, Gregory   1058, 2216

**In the Penny Arcade**
Millhauser, Stephen   921

**In the Red Lord's Reach**
Eisenstein, Phyllis   12, 257, 845, 1430, 1530, **1765**, 2290, 3278, 3293, 3410, 3414, 4294, 4808, 5599

**In the Rift**
Bradley, Marion Zimmer   **639**

**In the Shadow of the Gargoyle**
Kilpatrick, Nancy   **3112**

**In the Shadow of the Moon**
Gier, Scott G.   **2224**, 5465

**In the Shadow of the Oak King**
Jones, Courtway   224, 227, 266, 267, 2745, 2858, **2939**, 4266, 4270, 4458, 5792, 5793, 5794, 5970

**In the Shadows of the Moonglade**
St. James, Riley   **5186**

**In the Wrong Hands**
Gibson, Edward   781, **2215**, 3199, 4896, 4950

**In Watermelon Sugar**
Brautigan, Richard   1787, 2554, 2603, 2640, 4720, 5145

**In Winter's Shadow**
Bradshaw, Gillian   2939, 5971

**The Inadequate Adept**
Hawke, Simon   **2617**

**Inagehi**
Cady, Jack   **817**, 4221

**Incarnate**
Campbell, Ramsey   90, 284, 813, 898, 1380, 2197, 2530, 2789, 3267, 4841, 5522, 5816

**Incarnations**
Barker, Clive   **344**, 1022

**The Incomplete Enchanter**
de Camp, L. Sprague   1532, 4517

**Inconstant Star**
Anderson, Poul   **129**, 2828, 3649, 4124, 4125, 4372

**The Incredible Shrinking Man**
Matheson, Richard   **3687**

**Incubi**
Lee, Edward   2090, **3394**, 5120, 5856

**Incubus**
Russell, Ray   170, 2090, 2154, 3361, 3394

**Independence Day**
Devlin, Dean   504, **1508**, 2034, 3952, 4301

**The Indian in the Cupboard**
Banks, Lynne Reid   430, 773, 1132, 1218, 2719, 3587, 5654, 5655, 5656

**Indiana Jones and the Dance of the Giants**
MacGregor, Rob   825, 826, **3588**, 5307

**Indiana Jones and the Genesis Deluge**
MacGregor, Rob   825, 826, **3589**, 4622

**Indiana Jones and the Interior World**
MacGregor, Rob   825, 826, **3590**

**Indiana Jones and the Last Crusade**
MacGregor, Rob   825, 826, 2231, 4549

**Indiana Jones and the Peril at Delphi**
MacGregor, Rob   825, 826, **3591**, 4549, 4623, 5308

**Indiana Jones and the Seven Veils**
MacGregor, Rob   825, 826, **3592**, 4549

**Indiana Jones and the Sky Pirates**
Caidin, Martin   **825**, 5309

**Indiana Jones and the Temple of Doom**
Kahn, James   713, 825, 826, 3588, 3589, 3590, 3591, 3592, 3593, 3916, 4549

**Indiana Jones and the Unicorn's Legacy**
MacGregor, Rob   825, 826, **3593**

**Indiana Jones and the White Witch**
Caidin, Martin   **826**

**The Indians Won**
Smith, Martin Cruz   4814

**India's Story**
Starbuck, Kathlyn S.   **5208**

**Indistinguishable From Magic**
Forward, Robert L.   237

*Infanta*
Cooper, Louise   **1176**

*Infectress*
Cool, Tom   378, **1167**, 1348, 3761,
   4703, 6047

*Infernal Affairs*
Heller, Jane   **2652**

*The Infernal Desire Machines of Dr.
   Hoffman*
Carter, Angela   1818

*Infernal Devices*
Jeter, K.W.   520, 1186, 3596, 4432

*Inferno*
Allen, Roger MacBride   **78**, 418,
   4297

*The Inferno*
Hoyle, Fred   82, 354

*Inferno*
Niven, Larry   960, 2574

*The Infinite Man*
Relling, William Jr.   530, 537, 3328,
   3329, 3333, **4530**, 4648, 5339

*The Infinite Man and Other Stories*
Relling, William Jr.   429, 5854

*The Infinite Sea*
Carver, Jeffrey A.   **932**

*An Infinite Summer*
Priest, Christopher   5747

*The Infinitive of Go*
Brunner, John   2012

*The Infinity Concerto*
Bear, Greg   635, 1470, 3939, 4658,
   4661

*Infinity Hold*
Longyear, Barry B.   1107, 1113,
   1551, **3522**, 3693, 6059

*The Infinity Plague*
Vardeman, Robert E.   3309, **5564**

*Infinity's Child*
Stein, Harry   1670, 2206, 3164,
   **5250**

*Infinity's Shore*
Brin, David   **688**, 5669

*Infinity's Web*
Finch, Sheila   2012

*The Influence*
Campbell, Ramsey   280, 282, 666,
   **857**, 937, 2201, 2455, 3774, 4023,
   4239

*The Informers*
Ellis, Brett Easton   812, **1778**, 3396

*Ingathering: The Complete People
   Stories of Zenna Henderson*
Henderson, Zenna   759, 1460, 1502,
   1969, **2659**, 2716, 3430, 3981,
   4502, 5838

*The Inhabitant of the Lake and Less
   Welcome Tenants*
Campbell, Ramsey   1495, 1496, 3266

*Inherit the Earth*
Stableford, Brian   **5193**

*Inheritance*
Brookes, Owen   1580

*Inheritor*
Cherryh, C.J.   **997**

*The Inheritors*
Golding, William   502, 4039

*Inhuman*
Russo, John   5313

*Inhuman Beings*
Carroll, Jerry Jay   **914**

*The Initiate Brother*
Russell, Sean   563, 1101, 3268,
   **4742**, 5277

*Initiation*
Hughes, Marian   2289, **2806**, 4119

*The Innamorati*
Snyder, Midori   **5152**

*Inner Eclipse*
Russo, Richard Paul   2897

*Innerverse*
DeChancie, John   **1458**

*The Innkeeper's Song*
Beagle, Peter S.   **409**

*The Innocent*
Arbucci, John   3230

*The Innsmouth Cycle: The Taint of
   the Deep Ones in 13 Tales*
Price, Robert M.   **4426**

*The Innsmouth Heritage*
Stableford, Brian   3317, 3533, **5194**,
   5426, 5446, 5884

*The Inquisitor*
Franklin, Cheryl J.   **2037**

*Inquisitor*
Watson, Ian   1108, 5087, **5637**, 6021

*Insanity, Illinois*
Sumner, Mark   **5358**

*Insatiable*
Dvorkin, David   **1707**, 3517

*Insect Warriors*
Levie, Rex Dean   5755

*Inside the Funhouse*
Resnick, Mike   735, **4546**

*Inside the Works*
Piccirilli, Tom   22, **4314**

*Insomnia*
King, Stephen   1669, 2161, **3135**,
   3493, 5399

*Inspecting the Vaults*
McCormack, Eric   626, 1171

*Insurrection*
Dillard, J.M.   **1554**

*Insurrection*
Weber, David   5785

*The Integral Trees*
Niven, Larry   132, 401, 1897, 1986,
   1991, 2289, 3050, 3770, 4957,
   5233, 5526

*Intellivore*
Duane, Diane   **1663**

*Intensity*
Koontz, Dean R.   **3210**

*Intensive Scare*
Wagner, Karl Edward   **5604**, 5886

*The Intercessor and Other Stories*
Sinclair, May   601

*Interesting Times*
Pratchett, Terry   **4392**

*Interface*
Bury, Stephen   352, 413, **781**, 2723,
   5009, 5253, 5259, 5355

*Interface Masque*
Lewitt, Shariann   2274, **3453**

*The Interior Life*
Blake, Katherine   **515**, 2622, 4658,
   4659, 4661

*Intersections: The Sycamore Hill
   Anthology*
Kessel, John   1766, 1767, 2635,
   **3085**

*Interstellar Pig*
Sleator, William   168, 2807

*Interview with the Vampire*
Rice, Anne   799, 812, 1121, 1124,
   1140, 1166, 1286, 1541, 2267,
   2337, 2510, 2834, 3151, 3405,
   3519, 3602, 3853, 4318, 4367,
   4665, 5347, 5537, 5705

*Interzone*
Burroughs, William S.   778, 4532,
   5662, 5663

*Interzone: The 1st Anthology*
Clute, John   4439

*Interzone: The 2nd Anthology*
Clute, John   4439

*Interzone: The 3rd Anthology*
Clute, John   4439

*Interzone: The 4th Anthology*
Clute, John   4439

*Into the Dark Lands*
Sagara, Michelle   604, 1146, 3074,
   3270, 4153, 4462, **4783**, 4924

*Into the Deep*
Grimwood, Ken   **2450**

*Into the Fire*
McKiernan, Dennis L.   **3834**

*Into the Forest*
Hegland, Jean   2554, **2640**

*Into the Forge*
McKiernan, Dennis L.   **3835**

*Into the Green*
de Lint, Charles   **1430**

*Into the Labyrinth*
Weis, Margaret   681, 717, 4105,
   4807, **5716**

*Into the Land of the Unicorns*
Coville, Bruce   **1219**

*Into the Out Of*
Foster, Alan Dean   4207

*Into the Sea of Stars*
Forstchen, William R.   1182, 5042,
   5549

*Into the Shadows*
Weisman, Jordan K.   976, 1591,
   1889, 3245, 4821, 5135, **5731**

*Into the Void*
Findley, Nigel   1114, 1144, 1291,
   **1937**, 2785

*Intruders: New Weird Tales*
Burrage, A.M.   2846

*Invader*
Cherryh, C.J.   **998**, 4128, 4241, 5760

*Invaders From Rigel*
Pratt, Fletcher   2172

*Invaders From the Dark*
La Spina, Greye   3877

*Invaders of Earth*
Conklin, Groff   4406

*Invasion America*
Golden, Christie   **2252**

*Invasion: Earth*
Harrison, Harry   914

*Invasion of Willow Wood Springs*
Ellis, Terry   **1781**

*The Inverted World*
Priest, Christopher   5305

*Invisible Cities*
Calvino, Italo   3443

*The Invisible Company*
Sanders, Scott Russell   **4813**

*The Invisible Country*
McAuley, Paul J.   **3712**

*Invisible Death*
Carter, Lin   1940, 4623, 5307, 5309

*The Invisible Man*
Wells, H.G.   611, 1188, 3493

*Invitation to Camelot*
Godwin, Parke   5270

*Invitation to the Game*
Hughes, Monica   **2807**

*Involution Ocean*
Sterling, Bruce   791, 3874

*The Ion War*
Kapp, Colin   1326

*The Iowa Baseball Confederacy*
Kinsella, W.P.   2029

*Iris*
Barton, William   **381**, 5052

*Irish Fairy Tales*
Tichenor, H.M.   2481, 2482, 4203

*Irish Ghost Stories*
Hone, Joseph   1242, 2481, 2482,
   4203

*Irish Masters of Fantasy*
Tremayne, Peter   149, 1242, 2481,
   2482, 4203

*Irish Tales of Terror*
McGarry, Jim   149, 1242, 2481,
   2482, 4203

*Irish Tales of the Supernatural*
O'Griofa, Martin   **4203**

*The Irish Witch*
Wheatley, Dennis   1185

*The Iron Bridge*
Morse, David   298, **4036**

**Iron Dawn**
Stover, Matthew Woodring   1640,
   4612, **5320**

**The Iron Dragon's Daughter**
Swanwick, Michael   2738, 3933,
   4136, 4850, **5371**

**Iron Dragons: Mountains and
   Madness**
Estes, Rose   **1839**

**The Iron Dream**
Spinrad, Norman   2323, 2564, 3528,
   5117

**Iron Horse**
Dolan, Bill   1405, **1568**

**The Iron Lance**
Lawhead, Stephen R.   **3356**

**Iron Man: The Armor Trap**
Cox, Greg   **1227**, 1390

**The Iron Ring**
Alexander, Lloyd   **68**, 5479

**Iron Shadows**
Barnes, Steven   **362**

**The Iron Throne**
Hawke, Simon   **2618**, 3489

**Ironhelm**
Niles, Douglas   3121

**Iroshi**
Osborne, Cary   1462, **4228**

**Irrational Fears**
Spencer, William Browning   **5167**

**Irrational Numbers**
Langford, David   775, 2018, **3317**,
   3533, 3556, 4444, 5446

**Is THAT What People Do? The
   Selected Short Stories of Robert
   Sheckley**
Sheckley, Robert   1753

**Isaac Asimov Presents the Best
   Horror and Supernatural Tales of
   the 19th Century**
Asimov, Isaac   39

**Isaac Asimov Presents the Great SF
   Stories**
Asimov, Isaac   422, 2585

**Isaac Asimov Presents the Great SF
   Stories: 1-25**
Asimov, Isaac   24, 2401, 2594,
   2595, 2596, 2597, 2598, 5871

**Isaac Asimov Presents the Great SF
   Stories: 15 (1953)**
Asimov, Isaac   5948

**Isaac Asimov Presents the Great SF
   Stories: 20 (1958)**
Asimov, Isaac   **238**

**Isaac Asimov Presents the Great SF
   Stories: 21 (1959)**
Asimov, Isaac   214, **239**

**Isaac Asimov Presents the Great SF
   Stories: 22 (1959)**
Asimov, Isaac   **240**

**Isaac Asimov Presents the Great SF
   Stories: 23 (1961)**
Asimov, Isaac   **241**

**Isaac Asimov Presents the Great SF
   Stories: 24 (1962)**
Asimov, Isaac   **242**

**Isaac Asimov Presents the Great SF
   Stories: 25 (1963)**
Asimov, Isaac   **243**

**Isaac Asimov Presents the Great SF
   Stories Series**
Asimov, Isaac   1612, 1614

**Isaac Asimov's Aliens**
Dozois, Gardner   4406

**Isaac Asimov's Ghosts**
Dozois, Gardner   **1610**

**Isaac Asimov's I-Bots**
Perry, Steve   **4297**

**Isaac Asimov's Magical Worlds of
   Fantasy #10: Ghosts**
Asimov, Isaac   1610

**Isaac Asimov's Robot City/Robots
   and Aliens Book 4: Alliance**
Oltion, Jerry   484

**Isaac Asimov's Vampires**
Dozois, Gardner   **1611**

**Ishmael**
Hambly, Barbara   528, 569, 1225,
   1383, 1385, 1511, 1556, 1658,
   1922, 2067, 2297, 4040, 5113,
   5597

**Ishmael**
Quinn, Daniel   2578, **4455**

**The Island**
Wright, T.M.   947, 2241, 2822, 3783

**An Island Called Moreau**
Aldiss, Brian W.   2107, 5940

**Island in the Sea of Time**
Stirling, S.M.   1981, **5295**

**The Island of Doctor Death and
   Other Stories and Other Stories**
Wolfe, Gene   6067

**The Island of Doctor Moreau**
Wells, H.G.   305, 874, 2580

**The Island of the Mighty**
Walton, Evangeline   1961, **5626**

**The Island Worlds**
Kotani, Eric   82

**Islands**
Randall, Marta   4352

**Islands in the Net**
Sterling, Bruce   474, 736, 984, 1750,
   3431, 3491, 3794, 3850, 3890,
   3995, 4343, 4452, 4632, 4634,
   4681, 4682, 5006, 5254, 5593,
   5841, 5955, 5960

**Islands in the Sky**
Clarke, Arthur C.   2647, 3199

**Islands of Tomorrow**
Busby, F.M.   **783**

**Isle of Destiny**
Flint, Kenneth C.   2, 3061

**The Isle of Glass**
Tarr, Judith   185, 1288

**Isle of the Dead**
Zelazny, Roger   3698

**Isle of View**
Anthony, Piers   **177**

**Isle of Woman**
Anthony, Piers   **178**, 5496

**The Isles of the Blest**
Llewelyn, Morgan   1423

**The Isles of the Blest**
Llywelyn, Morgan   1810, 1960,
   2662, **3505**, 4519, 5534

**It**
King, Stephen   616, 918, 1077,
   1195, 2316, 3206, 3754, 4370,
   5464, 5522

**It Came From the Drive-In**
Partridge, Norman   **4252**, 5954

**It Had to Be Murder**
Woolrich, Cornell   4500

**It Happened in Broad Daylight**
Durrenmatt, Friedrich   1131

**Italian Folktales**
Calvino, Italo   849, 2680

**The Itinerant Exorcist**
McConnell, Ashley   **3776**

**It's Been Fun**
Friesner, Esther   **2078**

**The Ivanhoe Gambit**
Hawke, Simon   1162, 3799, 3802,
   3803, 3804, 3849

**Ivory: A Legend of Past and Future**
Resnick, Mike   496, 3790, **4547**,
   5545

**The Ivory and the Horn**
de Lint, Charles   395, **1431**, 2106


**J**

**Jack Faust**
Swanwick, Michael   714, 4179, **5372**

**Jack of Eagles**
Blish, James   4305, 4918

**Jack of Kinrowan**
de Lint, Charles   935

**Jack of Shadows**
Zelazny, Roger   1755, 3073

**Jack the Bodiless**
May, Julian   645, **3698**

**Jack, the Giant-Killer**
de Lint, Charles   42, 375, 1005,
   1446, 1479, 2797, 3285, 6088,
   6090

**Jack the Ripper: The Final Solution**
Knight, Stephen   3987

**Jackals**
Grant, Charles L.   **2313**

**Jackaroo**
Voigt, Cynthia   4447

**Jacob Marley's Christmas Carol**
Mula, Tom   4861

**Jacob's Hands**
Huxley, Aldous   2817

**Jade Darcy and the Affair of Honor**
Goldin, Stephen   63, 360, 631, 756,
   1106, 1262, 1331, 1503, 1542,
   1547, 1571, 1572, 1604, 1606,
   1661, 1680, 2209, 2812, 3603,
   3665, 3724, 3968, 4228, 4229,
   4288, 4291, 4296, 4484, 4637,
   4640, 4984, 5362, 5476, 5670,
   5680, 5779

**Jade Darcy and the Zen Pirates**
Goldin, Stephen   293, 360, 981,
   1420, 1454, 1572, **2260**, 2766,
   3665, 4291, 4720, 5234, 5679,
   6060

**The Jade Enchantress**
Price, E. Hoffman   4741

**The Jade Ogre**
Robeson, Kenneth   **4623**, 5308, 5309

**The Jagged Orbit**
Brunner, John   3243

**Jago**
Newman, Kim   2312, 3310, 4024,
   4587

**Jaguar**
Ransom, Bill   **4477**, 4517

**The Jaguar Hunter**
Shepard, Lucius   674, 675, 821,
   3086, 3706, 4053, 4630

**Jamie the Red**
Dickson, Gordon R.   4201

**Janissaries**
Pournelle, Jerry   359, 1547, 1635,
   1642, 2349, 4201, 5512, 5513

**The Janus Mask**
Knaak, Richard A.   **3171**

**Jaran**
Elliott, Kate   **1772**, 1809, 5544

**Jason Cosmo**
McGirt, Dan   982, 1002, 1268, **3811**

**Jaws**
Benchley, Peter   88, 1346, 3998,
   5877

**Jaydium**
Wheeler, Deborah   **5774**

**Jed the Dead**
Foster, Alan Dean   **2007**

**Jedi Search**
Anderson, Kevin J.   76, **109**, 2500,
   3247, 3820, 4719, 5205, 5950

**Jefferson's War: Death of a Regiment**
Randle, Kevin   **4466**

**The Jehovah Contract**
Koman, Victor   1856, 2525, 2865,
   3860, 4029, 4035, 5302, 5768,
   5887

**The Jekyll Legacy**
Bloch, Robert   **535**

**Jem**
Pohl, Frederik   248, 1768

**Jennifer Murdley's Toad**
Coville, Bruce   **1220**, 3378

**Jeremy Thatcher, Dragon Hatcher**
Coville, Bruce   **1221**, 1558, 3378,
   5822

**Jericho Falls**
Hyde, Christopher   1136, 3337

**The Jericho Iteration**
Steele, Allen   761, 3242, **5242**

**Jericho Moon**
Stover, Matthew Woodring   **5321**

**Jerusalem Poker**
Whittemore, Edward   1093, 1274, 1275, 4359, 4384

**Jesus Christs**
Langguth, A.J.   2753, 4330, 5015, 5569

**The Jesus Incident**
Herbert, Frank   4476, 4478

**The Jewel of Equilibrant**
Frankos, Steven   **2042**

**The Jewel of Fire**
Paxson, Diana L.   **4265**

**The Jewel of Seven Stars**
Stoker, Bram   **5312**

**Jewel of the Nile**
Lanigan, Catherine   3589, 3591, 4549

**The Jewels of Elvish**
Berberick, Nancy Varian   4434

**Jhereg**
Brust, Steven   15, 104, 289, 702, 1239, 1240, 1241, 1292, 1529, 1813, 2031, 2042, 2069, 2330, 2362, 2363, 2367, 2451, 2452, 2463, 2620, 2639, 2756, 2757, 2759, 2795, 2798, 3069, 3246, 3273, 3419, 3420, 3422, 3512, 3514, 3894, 4142, 4165, 4166, 4390, 4405, 4488, 4521, 4612, 4613, 4670, 4671, 4673, 4674, 4676, 4794, 4849, 4975, 4994, 5337, 5558, 5813, 5819, 5848, 5978, 5980, 6022, 6073

**The Jigsaw Woman**
Antieau, Kim   **199**, 4070, 4850

**The Jimjams**
Green, Michael   1894, **2345**, 4907, 5053

**Jingo**
Pratchett, Terry   **4393**

**Jinian Footseer**
Tepper, Sheri S.   2674

**Jinx High**
Lackey, Mercedes   1450, **3284**, 4709, 5266

**Jinx on a Terran Inheritance**
Daley, Brian   260, 261, 1106, 1144, 1331, 1333, 1542, 1572, 1604, 1606, 4291, 5668

**Jirel of Joiry**
Moore, C.L.   644, 649, 650, 651, 2072, 2074, 2360, 2651, 3290, 3418, 3634, 3906, 4161, 4162, 4520, 4610, 4871, 5220, 5383

**Jitterbug**
McQuay, Mike   1060

**Jitterbug Perfume**
Robbins, Tom   3456

**Job: A Comedy of Justice**
Heinlein, Robert A.   956, 2103, 2753, 2942, 3908, 3986, 4028, 5532, 5636, 6070

**John Collier and Fredric Brown Went Quarrelling through My Head**
Salmonson, Jessica Amanda   802, 1827, 2715, 3702, 4891, 5521

**John Dollar**
Wiggins, Marianne   **5799**

**John Silence**
Blackwood, Algernon   670

**John the Balladeer**
Wellman, Manly Wade   1639, 1765, 3472, 4791

**The John W. Campbell Awards, Volume 5**
Martin, George R.R.   754, 755, 5952, 5953

**Johnny Got His Gun**
Trumbo, Dalton   3996

**Johnny Mnemonic**
Bisson, Terry   118, **505**, 2033

**Jokertown Shuffle**
Martin, George R.R.   986, **3646**

**Joko's Anniversary**
Topor, Roland   3223

**Jonas McFee, A.T.P.**
Sargent, Sarah   2868, **4827**, 5088

**Jonathan Livingston Seagull**
Bach, Richard   4455, 4456

**Journal of a Teenage Genius**
Griffith, Helen V.   2949

**The Journal of Nicholas the American**
Kennedy, Leigh   709

**A Journal of the Flood Year**
Ely, David   **1805**

**Journals of the Plague Years**
Spinrad, Norman   **5172**

**Journey Behind the Wind**
Wrightson, Patricia   2170, 4946

**Journey Beyond Tomorrow**
Sheckley, Robert   506, 6064

**Journey into Fear and Other Great Stories of Horror on the Railways**
Peyton, Richard   **4308**

**Journey to Fusang**
Sanders, William   4545, 5781

**Journey to Terezor**
Asch, Frank   **221**, 1493, 2227, 2763, 2868, 5381

**Journey to the Center**
Stableford, Brian   953

**Journey to the Center of the Earth**
Verne, Jules   2468, 2469, 3590, 4705

**Journeyman Wizard**
Zambreno, Mary Frances   641, 5002, 5976, **6057**

**Journeys to the Twilight Zone**
Serling, Carol   1281, **4913**, 4916

**Jovah's Angel**
Shinn, Sharon   **5001**

**The Joy Machine**
Gunn, James   **2458**, 4711, 4893

**Joyleg**
Moore, Ward   5232

**The Judas Cross**
Sheffield, Charles   **4960**

**The Judas Glass**
Cadnum, Michael   **812**, 3396, 4445

**The Judas Rose**
Elgin, Suzette Haden   1135, 3622, 4325, 5634

**Judge Dredd**
Barrett, Neal Jr.   **366**, 4075

**Judgment Day**
Stine, G. Harry   **5281**

**Judgment Night**
Moore, C.L.   5645

**The Judgment of Eve**
Pangborn, Edgar   365, 886

**Judgment of Tears: Anno Dracula 1959**
Newman, Kim   **4098**

**Judgment on Janus**
Norton, Andre   2372

**Judson's Eden**
Laumer, Keith   2810, **3344**

**Julian's House**
Hawkes, Judith   281, 282, 861, 890, 2040, 2240, **2630**, 2669, 2856, 3055, 3201, 5334, 5402, 5528, 5991

**Julius Caesar Is Alive and Well**
Greenfield, Irving A.   2073

**Julius LeVallon: An Episode**
Blackwood, Algernon   4586

**Jumper**
Gould, Steven   302, 970, **2290**, 2474, 2717, 3011, 4070

**Jumpers**
Gates, R. Patrick   **2161**

**The Jungle**
Drake, David   1547, 1567, **1634**, 2371, 2437, 4507, 4974, 5280

**Jungle Assault**
Griffin, P.M.   1326, **2437**

**The Jungle Book**
Kipling, Rudyard   3610

**The Juniper Game**
Jordan, Sherryl   **2992**, 3340

**Juniper, Gentian and Rosemary**
Dean, Pamela   **1445**

**Juniper Time**
Wilhelm, Kate   5634

**Junky**
Burroughs, William S.   548

**Junkyard**
Porter, Barry   373, **4370**, 4815

**Jupiter Project**
Benford, Gregory   3922, 4952, 4964, 5561

**Jupiter's Daughter**
Hyman, Tom   **2820**

**Jurassic Park**
Crichton, Michael   581, 591, 902, 949, 1049, **1255**, 1379, 1417, 1729, 2107, 2291, 2820, 3191, 3232, 4075, 4117, 4279, 4597, 4853, 5351, 6084

**Jurgen**
Cabell, James Branch   3980

**Just an Ordinary Day**
Jackson, Shirley   **2842**

**Just Compensation**
Charrette, Robert N.   5207

**Just in Time**
Campbell, Marilyn   3039

**Just So Stories**
Kipling, Rudyard   3610, 3611

**Justice**
Drake, David   **1635**, 4204

**Justice and Her Brothers**
Hamilton, Virginia   362

### K

**Kaduna Memories**
McKinney, Jack   3771, **3850**

**Kahless**
Friedman, Michael Jan   10, 904, **2065**, 4559, 4933

**Kai Lung Unrolls His Mat**
Smith, Ernest Bramah   6026

**Kai Lung's Golden Hours**
Smith, Ernest Bramah   6026

**Kaleidoscope**
Turtledove, Harry   **5505**

**Kaleidoscope Century**
Barnes, John   **352**, 413, 957, 1762, 4218

**Kaleidoscope Eyes**
Watkins, Graham   **5631**

**Kalifornia**
Laidlaw, Marc   2820, **3311**, 5209

**The Kalif's War**
Dalmas, John   **1322**, 1628, 4972, 4984

**Kalimantan**
Shepard, Lucius   1356, 1435, 3101, 3173, 3478, 3916, 4020, 4061, 4062, 4207, **4979**, 5520

**Kamikaze L'Amour**
Kadrey, Richard   52, **2998**, 6009

**Kane**
Borton, Douglas   **576**, 2314, 3052, 3899

**Kane of Old Mars**
Moorcock, Michael   **3983**

**Kar Kaballa**
Smith, George H.   261, 4814

**Kar Kalim**
Christian, Deborah   **1025**

*The Karma Corps*
Barrett, Neal Jr. 1326

*Kaz the Minotaur*
Knaak, Richard A. 154, 1485, **3172**, 5022, 5724

*Kecksies and Other Twilight Tales*
Bowen, Marjorie 3360, 5772

*Kedrigern and the Charming Couple*
Morressy, John 3811, **4013**, 4316

*Kedrigern in Wanderland*
Morressy, John 5337

*The Keep*
Wilson, F. Paul 3759, 4529

*The Keeper*
Lee, Robert D. 3373, 3387, 3391, **3402**, 4222

*Keeper of the Keys*
Wurts, Janny 1906

*Keeper of the King*
Bennett, Nigel **452**, 1579

*Keepers of Edanvant*
Douglas, Carole Nelson 1731, 1736

*The Keeper's Price*
Bradley, Marion Zimmer 2991

*Kelly Country*
Chandler, A. Bertram 2563

*Kendermore*
Kirchoff, Mary 2675, 5711, 5724

*Kensho*
Schmidt, Dennis 1329, 4226, 4227, 4228

*Kent Montana and the Really Ugly Thing From Mars*
Fenn, Lionel **1918**, 4398, 5934

*Kent Montana and the Reasonably Invisible Man*
Fenn, Lionel **1919**

*The Kestrel*
Alexander, Lloyd 5142

*Kevin Browne's Nightales*
Tigges, John 2402, **5473**

*A Key for the Nonesuch*
Gravel, Geary 104, 929, 1026, 1331, 1332, 1584, 1838, 1881, 1979, 2042, **2330**, 2463, 2644, 4652, 4671, 4970, 5159, 5306, 5774, 5775

*The Key of the Keplian*
Norton, Andre **4156**

*The Key to the Indian*
Banks, Lynne Reid **331**

*Key West 2720 A.D.*
Eakins, William **1720**

*The Keys to D'Esperance*
Brenchley, Chaz **666**

*The Khan's Persuasion*
Felice, Cynthia 1771, 1772, **1914**, 2069

*Khyren*
Kaplan, Aline Boucher 4481

*The Kidnapper*
Bloch, Robert 5338

*Kids*
Hoyle, Trevor **2787**

*The Kif Strike Back*
Cherryh, C.J. 2099, 5833, 5985

*The Kill*
Ryan, Alan 2310, 4310

*Kill Crazy*
Riker, L.S. 830, **4590**, 4938

*The Kill Riff*
Schow, David J. 426, 1052, 1777, 3527, 3807, **4887**, 4997, 5443

*Kill Station*
Duane, Diane **1664**

*Kill the Dead*
Lee, Tanith 3624

*Kill the Editor*
Robinson, Spider 3237, 4355

*Killashandra*
McCaffrey, Anne 1772

*Killdozer!*
Sturgeon, Theodore **5344**

*The Killer Crabs Series*
Smith, Guy N. 2671

*The Killing Dance*
Hamilton, Laurell K. **2518**

*Killing Frost*
Blake, Dan I. **514**

*The Killing Gift*
Wood, Bari 1580

*The Killing of the Saints*
Abella, Alex **21**, 1298, 1403, 1851, 2150, 2896, 3605, 4498

*The Killing Star*
Pellegrino, Charles 1244, 1258, **4281**

*Killing Time*
Van Hise, Della 900, 922, 1385, 1386, 1511, 2297, 4280, 4933, 5113

*Killjoy*
Forrest, Elizabeth **1973**, 5892

*Killobyte*
Anthony, Piers **179**, 507, 583, 1461, 2082, 2791, 4283, 5753

*Kim*
Kipling, Rudyard 314

*The Kin of Ata Are Waiting for You*
Bryant, Dorothy 6028

*The Kindly Ones*
Scott, Melissa 353, 1757

*Kindred*
Butler, Octavia E. 1130, 1835, 2614, 3243, 3874, 5180

*Kindred*
Gideon, John **2222**

*Kindred Rites*
Kimbriel, Katharine Eliska 2326, **3118**

*Kindred Spirits*
Anthony, Mark **154**, 3155, 4925

*Kindred Spirits*
Brennert, Alan 2412, 2589, 5024

*Kindred Spirits*
Elliot, Jeffrey M. 2116, 2117, 2295, 2444, 5154

*The King*
Barthelme, Donald **375**, 973, 977, 1092, 5427

*King and Emperor*
Harrison, Harry **2571**, 5500

*King & Raven*
James, Cary 273, **2858**, 3884, 5270

*King Arthur's Daughter*
Chapman, Vera 1857

*A King Beneath the Mountain*
Charrette, Robert N. **973**

*King Conan*
Howard, Robert E. 906, 907, 909, 4617

*King David's Spaceship*
Pournelle, Jerry 353, 1182, 4545

*King Dragon*
Offutt, Andrew J. 4592, 4595

*The King in Yellow*
Chambers, Robert W. 485, **963**, 1252, 2225

*The King Is Dead: Tales of Elvis Post Mortem*
Sammon, Paul M. 2070, 2184, 4540, **4810**

*King Javan's Year*
Kurtz, Katherine 2424, **3258**, 4784, 5126, 5500, 5503

*King Kobold*
Stasheff, Christopher 703

*King Kobold Revived*
Stasheff, Christopher 27, 652, 1533, 2226, 4922

*King Kong*
Copper, Merian C. 5474

*The King of Elfland's Daughter*
Dunsany 3980

*A King of Infinite Space*
Steele, Allen 2498, **5243**

*King of Morning, Queen of Day*
McDonald, Ian 1471, 1960, 2238, 3354, 3357, 3470, **3793**, 3854

*King of the Dead*
DeWeese, Gene 1137, **1510**

*King of the Dead*
MacAvoy, R.A. **3581**, 5582

*King of the Grey*
Knaak, Richard A. 1040, 1435, 1842, 2127, 2791, **3173**

*King of the Scepter'd Isle*
Coney, Michael Greatrex 5428

*King of the Wood*
Roberts, John Maddox 442, 1139, 1436, 1655, 2086, 5781

*The King of Ys: Roma Mater*
Anderson, Poul 1191, 2747

*King Pinch*
Cook, David **1146**, 4808

*The Kingdom of Kevin Malone*
Charnas, Suzy McKee 549, **970**, 2879, 6017

*Kingdom of Sorrow*
Morr, Kenyon 5357

*Kingdom of Summer*
Bradshaw, Gillian 2939, 2940, 5971

*Kingdom of the Grail*
Attanasio, A.A. **269**, 2231, 3385, 3386

*Kingdoms of the Night*
Cole, Allan **1105**

*Kingdoms of the Wall*
Silverberg, Robert 4063, 5000, **5033**, 5862

*Kingmaker's Sword*
Marston, Ann **3635**

*The Kingmaking*
Hollick, Helen 1190, **2745**, 4877

*King's Blood Four*
Tepper, Sheri S. 742, 1416, 1816, 1866, 2507, 2885, 2886, 3399, 3802, 3804, 4766

*The King's Buccaneer*
Feist, Raymond E. **1904**

*The King's Damosel*
Chapman, Vera 4877

*King's Dragon*
Elliott, Kate 992, **1773**

*King's Man and Thief*
Golden, Christie **2253**

*Kings of the High Frontier*
Koman, Victor **3199**

*King's Sacrifice*
Weis, Margaret **5717**

*King's Son, Magic's Son*
Sherman, Josepha **4986**

*Kingship with the Stars*
Anderson, Poul 592

*Kingslayer*
James, L. Dean **2863**, 4326

*The Kinslayer Wars*
Niles, Douglas **4109**, 5454, 5455

*The Kinsman Saga*
Bova, Ben 2143, 2726, 5870

*Kipling's Fantasy*
Kipling, Rudyard 2680, **3147**, 4021, 5310

*Kipling's Science Fiction*
Kipling, Rudyard **3148**

*Kirins: The Flight of the Ain*
Priest, James D. 2142, **4433**

*Kirins: The Secret of the Hanging Stones*
Priest, James D. **4434**

*Kirins: The Spell of No'an*
Priest, James D. 235, 565, 1299, 2142, 3077, 3513, 3910, 3943, 3944, 4061, 4062, 4403, **4435**, 4709, 5379

*Kirinyaga: A Fable of Utopia*
Resnick, Mike **4548**

**Kirlian Quest**
Anthony, Piers   1871

**The Kiss**
Reines, Kathryn   4246, **4529**

**Kiss of Death**
Rhodes, Daniel   3989, **4569**

**The Kiss of Death: An Anthology of Vampire Stories**
Anonymous   **151**

**Kiss of the Vampire**
Weathersby, Lee   1352, 1795, 1798, 3557, 5020, **5657**, 5986, 5988

**Kissing the Witch: Old Tales in New Skins**
Donoghue, Emma   794, 1358, **1578**, 2845

**Kiteworld**
Roberts, Keith   56, 57

**Kit's Book**
Mills, C.J.   1913, **3911**

**The Klingon Gambit**
Vardeman, Robert E.   527, 1511

**Knee Deep in the Dead**
ab Hugh, Dafydd   3467

**A Knight Among Knaves**
Charrette, Robert N.   **974**

**The Knight and Knave of Swords**
Leiber, Fritz   1532, 3172, 3175, 3982, 3985, 4015

**A Knight in Shining Armor**
Deveraux, Jude   1704, 4517

**A Knight of Ghosts and Shadows**
Anderson, Poul   1041, 3907, 3928

**Knight of Ghosts and Shadows**
Lackey, Mercedes   180, 185, 392, 396, 1432, 2467, **3285**, 4868, 4980, 4991, 4993, 5618, 5646, 5915

**Knight of the Black Rose**
Lowder, James   4326

**A Knight of the Word**
Brooks, Terry   **714**, 3620

**Knight's Castle**
Eager, Edward   332, 1218, 3587

**Knights of Black Earth**
Weis, Margaret   3927

**The Knights of Cawdor**
Jefferies, Mike   **2886**

**Knights of the Black Earth**
Weis, Margaret   **5718**

**Knights of the Blood**
MacMillan, Scott   3260, **3602**

**Knights of the Morningstar**
Rawn, Melanie   1040, 2657, **4487**

**Knight's Wyrd**
Doyle, Debra   **1601**

**A Knot in the Grain and Other Stories**
McKinley, Robin   **3845**

**The Kobayashi Maru**
Ecklar, Julia   905, 1381, **1728**, 1967, 2069, 4514, 5404

**Koko**
Straub, Peter   91, 2222, 3319, 3323, 3332, 3682, 3755, 3898, 3901, 4865, 5085, **5328**

**Komarr**
Bujold, Lois McMaster   **760**, 3861

**Konrad**
Ferring, David   1241, **1927**

**Krispos of Videssos**
Turtledove, Harry   3258, 4488, **5506**

**Krispos Rising**
Turtledove, Harry   3771, 4782, **5507**

**Krispos the Emperor**
Turtledove, Harry   3255, **5508**

**Krokodil Tears**
Yeovil, Jack   1238, **6023**

**Krondor, the Betrayal**
Feist, Raymond E.   1706, **1905**, 4727

**The Kronos Condition**
Devenport, Emily   1442, **1502**

**The Kruton Interface**
DeChancie, John   **1459**

**Kwaidan**
Hearn, Lafcadio   5801

**The Kyber Connection**
Hawke, Simon   33, 4164

## L

**L.A. Strike**
Robbins, David   **4599**, 5023

**L. Ron Hubbard Presents Writers of the Future, Volume II**
Budrys, Algis   4713

**L. Ron Hubbard Presents Writers of the Future, Volume VII**
Budrys, Algis   **754**

**L. Ron Hubbard Presents Writers of the Future, Volume VIII**
Budrys, Algis   **755**

**L. Ron Hubbard Presents Writers of the Future, Volume IX**
Wolverton, Dave   **5952**

**L. Ron Hubbard Presents Writers of the Future, Volume XII**
Wolverton, Dave   **5953**

**L. Ron Hubbard Presents Writers of the Future, Volume XIV**
Wolverton, Dave   **5954**

**L. Ron Hubbard Presents Writers of the Future, Volumes I-VIII**
Budrys, Algis   1766, 1767, 5952, 5953

**Labyrinth**
Schmidt, Dennis   **4884**

**Labyrinth: A Novel**
Smith, A.C.H.   718

**The Labyrinth Gate**
Rasmussen, Alis A.   85, 166, 183, 1532, 2125, 2505, 3582, 4438, **4481**, 4799, 5712, 5726

**The Labyrinth of Dreams**
Chalker, Jack L.   5830

**Labyrinth of Night**
Steele, Allen   102, 421, 586, 1565, 2864, 3787, **5244**

**Labyrinths**
Borges, Jorge Luis   950, 3462, 3463

**Ladies Night**
Ketchum, Jack   3091

**Ladies of Horror**
Manley, Seon   3570

**The Ladies of Mandrigyn**
Hambly, Barbara   289, 644, 702, 1029, 1147, 1150, 2095, 2360, 3016, 3635, 3839, 4488, 4596, 4614, 4674, 4714, 4784, 5206, 5220, 5678, 5735

**Ladies: Retold Tales of Goddesses and Heroines**
Vallejo, Doris   **5533**

**The Lady and the Lotus**
Barrett, William F.   3260

**Lady Blade, Lord Fighter**
Green, Sharon   1004

**Lady Cottington's Pressed Fairy Book**
Jones, Terry   29, 2088, **2981**, 3214

**Lady El**
Starlin, Jim   272, **5213**

**Lady Ferry and Other Uncanny People**
Jewett, Sarah Orne   **2919**

**Lady of Avalon**
Bradley, Marion Zimmer   **640**, 1775, 4573

**Lady of Mercy**
Sagara, Michelle   1985, **4784**

**Lady of the Bees**
Swann, Thomas Burnett   169

**Lady of the Forest**
Roberson, Jennifer   2247, 3165, **4609**, 5397

**The Lady of the Frozen Death and Other Weird Tales**
Cline, Leonard   **1088**

**Lady of the Trillium**
Bradley, Marion Zimmer   **641**, 3700

**The Lady or the Tiger and Other Stories**
Stockton, Frank   **5310**

**Lady Slings the Booze**
Robinson, Spider   **4640**

**Ladygrove**
Burke, John   438

**Ladylord**
Miller, Sasha   **3906**

**Lafferty in Orbit**
Lafferty, R.A.   321, 1492, **3308**

**Lagoon**
Drake, Alison   **1625**, 1806, 5081

**Lagrange Five**
Reynolds, Mack   5188

**Lair**
Herbert, James   3192, 3992

**Lair of the Cyclops**
Wold, Allen L.   **5933**

**The Lake at the End of the World**
MacDonald, Caroline   3584

**The Lake of Fire**
Bailey, Robin Wayne   1429, 3572

**Lake of the Long Sun**
Wolfe, Gene   **5942**

**Lake of the Sun**
Whiteford, Wynne   621, 5514, **5787**

**Lammas Night**
Kurtz, Katherine   1275, 2244, 2505, 2507

**Lamps on the Brow**
Cahill, James   **823**

**The LaNague Chronicles**
Wilson, F. Paul   328, 593, 1915, 3466, 5132, 5365, 5366, 5367, **5889**

**The Land Beyond the Gate**
Eshbach, Lloyd Arthur   1957

**Land of Dreams**
Blaylock, James P.   545, 546, 549, 550, 551, 552, 820, 2329, 3423, 3793, 4448

**The Land of Gold**
Bradshaw, Gillian   67, **658**, 1867, 1868, 4321, 4544, 5391

**The Land of Laughs**
Carroll, Jonathan   2557, 3441, 4546, 4582, 5167, 5169, 5311, 5358

**The Land of Nod**
Clements, Mark A.   898, **1085**

**The Land of Oz**
Baum, L. Frank   3609, 6006

**Land of the Giants**
Leinster, Murray   4403

**The Land of Unreason**
de Camp, L. Sprague   652, 1809, 3015, 4161, 4162, 4371

**Land O'Goshen**
McNair, Charles   **3855**

**The Land under England**
O'Neill, Joseph   5747

**The Lando Calrissian Adventures**
Smith, L. Neil   76, 103, 115, 2500, 3247, 3820, 4299, 5527

**Lando Calrissian and the Flamewind of Oseon**
Smith, L. Neil   6052, 6054, 6055

**Lando Calrissian and the Mindharp of Sharu**
Smith, L. Neil   6052, 6054, 6055

**Lando Calrissian and the Starcave of Thon Boka**
Smith, L. Neil   6052, 6054, 6055

**A Landscape of Darkness**
Blair, John   **513**

**Landscape of Demons and the Book of Sara**
Kessler, Gabriel Devlin   **3088**

**Landscape Painted with Tea**
Pavic, Milorad  1524, 2186, 4046, 4047, **4263**

**Landslayer's Law**
Deitz, Tom  **1474**

**The Language of Fear**
James, Del  **2860**

**The Languages of Pao**
Vance, Jack  5634

**The Lantern of God**
Dalmas, John  **1323**, 1876, 3907, 5588, 5900

**The Lanterns of God**
Sarti, Ron  **4835**

**Larissa**
Devenport, Emily  **1503**

**The Lark and the Wren**
Lackey, Mercedes  560, 1143, 2799, **3286**, 3446, 4150, 5275

**Larque on the Wing**
Springer, Nancy  1433, 1438, 2735, **5180**

**Lasher**
Rice, Anne  **4570**, 5122

**The Last Aerie**
Lumley, Brian  **3557**

**Last and First Men**
Stapledon, Olaf  445

**The Last Arabian Night**
Gardner, Craig Shaw  **2129**

**The Last Battle**
Lewis, C.S.  5364

**The Last Book of Swords: Shieldbreaker's Story**
Saberhagen, Fred  1172, **4768**

**Last Call**
Powers, Tim  87, 518, 715, 1091, 1277, 2304, 2406, 3262, 4095, 4359, **4384**

**The Last Call of Mourning**
Grant, Charles L.  4832

**The Last Coin**
Blaylock, James P.  **519**, 1172, 2232, 2304, 2329

**The Last Command**
Zahn, Timothy  **6055**

**The Last Continent**
Cooper, Edmund  4628

**The Last Dancer**
Moran, Daniel Keys  **3994**

**The Last Days of Christ the Vampire**
Eccarius, J.G.  3244

**The Last Days of the Edge of the World**
Stableford, Brian  172

**The Last Dragonlord**
Bertin, Joanne  **470**

**The Last Gasp**
Hoyle, Trevor  4512, 4628

**The Last Hawk**
Asaro, Catherine  **219**

**The Last Highlander**
Cross, Claire  **1271**

**The Last Human**
De Haven, Tom  **1422**

**The Last Immortal**
Jeppson, Janet O.  251

**The Last Legends of Earth**
Attanasio, A.A.  **270**

**Last Mountain**
Fleet, Robert C.  **1946**

**The Last of the Renshai**
Reichert, Mickey Zucker  3270, **4520**

**Last Orders**
Aldiss, Brian W.  **56**, 5940

**The Last Pendragon**
Rice, Robert  269, **4584**

**The Last Planet**
Norton, Andre  3727

**The Last Rainbow**
Godwin, Parke  459, 1191, 5925

**The Last Rangers**
Davis, Jake  **1406**, 1567, 4590

**The Last Reckoning**
Shupp, Mike  **5012**

**Last Refuge**
Scarborough, Elizabeth Ann  458, 563, 653, 1064, 1110, 1169, 1253, 1974, 2327, 2499, 2503, 3167, 3844, 3878, 3916, 3935, 4063, 4207, 4208, 4364, 4744, **4866**, 5716, 5750

**The Last Ride**
Howard, Robert E.  3335

**The Last Rite**
Lumley, Brian  **3558**

**Last Rites**
Darke, David  **1354**

**The Last Ship**
Brinkley, William  3586

**The Last Slice of Rainbow and Other Stories**
Aiken, Joan  3610

**The Last Stand**
Ferguson, Brad  206, 901, 903, **1923**, 2922

**The Last Stand of the DNA Cowboys**
Farren, Mick  **1879**

**The Last Starfighter**
Foster, Alan Dean  949, 1509

**Last Summer at Mars Hill**
Hand, Elizabeth  **2537**

**The Last Unicorn**
Beagle, Peter S.  1219, 1343, 1946, 3399, 3401, 3540, 4319

**The Last Vampire**
Griffith, Kathryn Meyer  1463, **2440**, 4072

**The Last Vampire**
Pike, Christopher  120, 1302, **4328**, 5161

**The Last Voice They Hear**
Campbell, Ramsey  **858**

**The Last Voyage of Somebody the Sailor**
Barth, John  **374**, 2123, 2129, 2130, 6087

**Last War**
Michaels, Melisa C.  1043, 2435

**The Last Wizard**
Hawke, Simon  **2619**

**The Last World**
Ransmayr, Christoph  2238, 3793, **4475**

**The Lastborn of Elvinwood**
Haldeman, Linda  177, 2945

**Late Knight Edition**
Knight, Damon  4535

**The Late Show**
Douglas, John  3326

**The Lathe of Heaven**
Le Guin, Ursula K.  157, 512, 788, 1521, 1523, 2486, 2754, 3186, 3438, 3896, 4177, 4353, 4361, 4553, 4678, 5515, 5591, 5660

**The Laughing Corpse**
Hamilton, Laurell K.  **2519**, 5707

**Lavender-Green Magic**
Norton, Andre  2992, 3436

**Lavondyss: Journey to an Unknown Region**
Holdstock, Robert  1423, 2238, 2636, **2739**, 4797, 4809, 4992, 5806

**The Law of Becoming**
Elliott, Kate  **1774**

**The Law of War**
Shatner, William  **4931**

**Laying the Music to Rest**
Smith, Dean Wesley  84, 1193, 1202, 1860, 1972, 2034, 2732, 4772, 4915, **5114**

**The Lazarus Effect**
Herbert, Frank  4476, 4478

**The Lazarus Heart**
Brite, Poppy Z.  494, **696**, 4186, 5844

**Le Morte d'Arthur**
Mallory, Thomas  5359

**The League of the Crimson Crescent**
Reagen, James E.  3913, **4495**

**The Leaky Establishment**
Langford, David  1918, 3573

**Lean Times in Lankhmar**
Leiber, Fritz  291, 1484, 2253, **3420**

**Leanna: Possession of a Woman**
Kiraly, Marie  **3149**

**Leap Point**
Kenyon, Kay  **3063**, 4042, 6080

**Leavings**
Cacek, P.D.  **802**, 2937

**The Left Hand of Darkness**
Le Guin, Ursula K.  211, 1141, 1362, 1771, 2194, 2237, 2295, 2423, 2443, 2881, 3047, 3426, 3819, 3910, 3919, 4245, 4325, 4900, 5477, 5580, 5592

**Legacies**
Sinclair, Alison  **5069**

**Legacy**
Bear, Greg  **420**, 5571

**Legacy**
Friedman, Michael Jan  1954

**The Legacy**
Salvatore, R.A.  1146, 1287, 2427, 2618, 3489, **4801**

**Legacy**
White, Steve  **5785**

**Legacy of Earth**
Coulson, Juanita  **1209**

**Legacy of Fire**
Hoffman, Nina Kiriki  2078, **2715**, 4878

**The Legacy of Heorot**
Niven, Larry  2210, 2211, 2491, 4884, 5016, 5431

**Legacy of Steel**
Herbert, Mary H.  **2675**

**Legacy of the Ancients**
Sarti, Ron  **4836**

**Legacy of the Darksword**
Weis, Margaret  **5719**

**Legacy of the Sword**
Roberson, Jennifer  1179

**Legally Correct Fairy Tales**
Fisher, David  1257, 1578, **1942**, 2845

**The Legend of Huma**
Knaak, Richard A.  1485, 3155, 5454, 5455, 5711, 5724

**The Legend of Nightfall**
Reichert, Mickey Zucker  739, **4521**

**The Legend of Sleepy Hollow and Other Stories**
Irving, Washington  722

**Legends**
Smith, Deborah  5639

**Legends Reborn**
Flint, Kenneth C.  **1958**

**Legends: Short Novels by the Masters of Modern Fantasy**
Silverberg, Robert  **5034**

**Legion**
Blatty, William Peter  5342, 5896

**The Legion of Space**
Williamson, Jack  3035, 4468, 5048

**Legion of the Damned**
Dietz, William C.  **1547**, 3034, 4982, 5670, 5718

**Legion of the Dead**
Caine, Geoffrey  **833**, 5562

**Legion of the Dead**
Cave, Hugh B.  4498, 5155

**The Legion of Videssos**
Turtledove, Harry  1025, 1676

**The Leiber Chronicles**
Leiber, Fritz  674, 675, 893, 3219, **3421**, 5106, 5599

**Lemon Drops and Other Horrors**
Burleson, Donald **777**, 3321, 4891

**Lens of the World**
MacAvoy, R.A. 2986, **3582**, 5391, 5582, 5584, 6039

**The Lensman Series**
Smith, Edward E. 309

**The Leopard's Daughter**
Killough, Lee 1996

**Leroni of Darkover**
Bradley, Marion Zimmer **642**

**Less than Human**
Raisor, Gary L. 1945, **4464**

**Lest Darkness Fall**
de Camp, L. Sprague 350, 895, 1045, 1341, 1631, 1638, 2043, 2044, 2045, 2046, 2047, 2570, 2571, 3663, 3917, 4036, 4040, 5295, 5505, 6000

**Let There Be Dark**
Harris, Allen Lee **2557**, 2749, 4715

**Lethal Delivery**
Maxon, J.G. **3695**

**Lethal Exposure**
Anderson, Kevin J. **110**

**Lethal Interface**
Odom, Mel **4193**, 4300, 4893, 4901, 4902, 5576

**Lethe**
Sullivan, Tricia 1000, 2051, 2274, 2558, 4064, 4065, **5354**, 5525, 5804

**Letters From Atlantis**
Silverberg, Robert 6, 331, 658, 1012, 1490, 1537, 1873, 2752, 2861, 3545, 4918, **5035**, 5336, 5827, 6017

**Letters From the Dead**
Black, Campbell 4701, 5519

**Letters to Alice on First Reading Jane Austen**
Weldon, Fay 950, 1397

**Level 7**
Roshwald, Mordecai 1522, 3608, 4205

**Liar's Oath**
Moon, Elizabeth 2677, 3282, 3941, **3969**, 4150, 4488, 4489, 4986

**Liavek**
Shetterly, Will 408, 630, 646, 647, 767, 986, 989, 1683, 1889, 1969, 1994, 2376, 3300, 3643, 3646, 3836, 4166, 4335, 4405, 4723, 5038, 5210, 5214, 5216, 5599, 5913, 5915, 5945

**Liavek: Festival Week**
Shetterly, Will 767, 989, 4723, **4994**, 5216, 5945

**The Liavek Series**
Shetterly, Will 769, 5581

**Liavek: Spells of Binding**
Shetterly, Will 646, 989, 5216, 5913, 5915

**Liavek: The Players of Luck**
Shetterly, Will 989, 1994, 5216, 5973

**Liavek: Wizard's Row**
Shetterly, Will 767, 989, 1427, 3076, 4390, 5210, 5216, 5913, 5915, 5945

**Liberty's World**
Killough, Lee 1757, 2223, 4175, 4545, 5230

**Lie to Me**
Martin, David 1829, **3639**, 5453

**Liege-Killer**
Hinz, Christopher 3072, 4049, 4287, 5366

**Lieutenant**
Shelley, Rick **4972**

**Life Among the Asteroids**
Pournelle, Jerry **4376**

**The Life and Adventures of Santa Claus**
Baum, L. Frank 2456

**Life During Wartime**
Shepard, Lucius 323, 3449, 3666, 3706, 5955, 6061

**A Life for the Stars**
Blish, James 356, 734, 1003, 2626, 3770, 5499, 5937, 5943

**Life Form**
Foster, Alan Dean **2008**

**Life in the Crystal Palace**
Harrington, Alan 1782

**A Life in the Future**
Caidin, Martin **827**, 1053

**Life on the Border**
Windling, Terri 235, 646, 648, 711, 767, 769, 976, 1159, 1179, 1359, 1368, 1373, 1427, 1434, 1436, 1837, 1958, 1960, 1994, 2373, 2378, 2461, 2467, 3245, 3271, 3277, 3299, 3301, 3302, 3643, 3646, 4174, 4335, 4497, 4675, 4866, 4971, 4985, 4993, 4995, 5038, 5156, 5214, 5216, 5428, 5818, **5915**, 5945, 6044, 6045

**Life Probe**
McCollum, Michael 5788

**Life Support**
Gerritsen, Tess **2206**, 3577

**Life, the Universe, and Everything**
Adams, Douglas 1918, 4077

**Lifehouse**
Robinson, Spider 357, **4641**

**Lifekeeper**
McQuay, Mike 1060

**Lifeline**
Anderson, Kevin J. **111**

**Lifeline**
Weiss, Bobbie J.G. 2109

**The Lifeship**
Dickson, Gordon R. 5781

**The Lifted Veil: The Book of Fantastic Literature by Women**
Williams, A. Susan 37, 629, 1715, 2035, 3574, 4826, 5018, **5814**

**Ligeia**
Poe, Edgar Allan 3813

**The Light at the End**
Skipp, John 490, 697, 946, 948, 1006, 1122, 1301, 1707, 1779, 2151, 3963, 4190, 5175

**The Light Bearer**
Gillespie, Donna **2229**, 2453, 2454, 4264

**The Light Beyond the Forest**
Sutcliff, Rosemary 2232

**The Light Fantastic**
Bester, Alfred 321, 3187

**The Light Fantastic**
Pratchett, Terry 355

**The Light in Exile**
Franklin, Cheryl J. 632, 645, **2038**, 2372, 2724, 4594, 5752

**The Light Invisible**
Benson, Robert Hugh 454, **456**

**Light on the Sound**
Sucharitkul, Somtow 2890

**Light Raid**
Willis, Connie 969, 1662, **5870**

**The Light That Never Was**
Biggle, Lloyd 4350

**The Lighthouse at the End of the World**
Marlowe, Stephen 1516, 3150, **3631**

**The Lightless Kingdom**
Wylie, Jonathan 1731, 1736, 5715, **6007**

**Lightning**
Koontz, Dean R. 97, 2608, **3211**, 3251, 3979, 4363, 4843, 5399

**Lightning's Daughter**
Herbert, Mary H. 223, 1293, 2397, **2676**

**Lightpaths**
Hendrix, Howard V. **2660**, 4295

**Lights Out in the Reptile House**
Shepard, Jim 164, 4949, **4976**

**Lightwing**
Harper, Tara K. 231, 996, **2551**, 2832, 3718

**Lila the Werewolf**
Beagle, Peter S. 1349, 3162, 5425

**Lilith**
Heeley, D.A. 1143

**Lilith**
Paiva, Jean 5824

**The Lilith Factor**
Paiva, Jean 491, **4236**, 4312, 4844

**Lilith's Cave: Jewish Tales of the Supernatural**
Schwartz, Howard 4791, **4890**

**Limbo Search**
Godwin, Parke **2245**

**Limbo System**
Cook, Rick 828, **1158**, 1325, 4017, 5564, 5932

**The Limbreth Gate**
Lindholm, Megan 2693

**The Lincoln Hunters**
Tucker, Wilson 1480, 1980, 3993, **5487**

**Lincoln's Dreams**
Willis, Connie 3993, 5806

**The Link**
Laurance, Andrew **3348**

**The Lion of Farside**
Dalmas, John **1324**

**Lion of Ireland**
Llywelyn, Morgan 2572, 5408

**Lion of Macedon**
Gemmell, David 1129, **2189**, 5395, 5595, 5738

**The Lion Tamer's Daughter**
Dickinson, Peter **1526**

**The Lion, the Witch, and the Wardrobe**
Lewis, C.S. 368, 4330, 5182

**Lion Time in Timbuctoo**
Silverberg, Robert 1996, 4544, **5036**

**Lion's Heart**
Wehrstein, Karen 164, 787, 2236, 3871, 3872, 3975, 5209, 5297, 5299, **5683**

**The Lions of Al-Rassan**
Kay, Guy Gavriel 770, 1111, 1154, **3016**, 3356, 3942, 4259, 4533, 4743, 5218, 6002

**Lion's Soul**
Wehrstein, Karen 787, 3871, 3872, 5071, 5209, 5297, 5299, **5684**

**Liquid Diet**
Tedford, William 1301, 2336, **5419**, 5705

**The List of 7**
Frost, Mark 2692, 3631, 4773

**Listen, Listen**
Wilhelm, Kate 2261

**The Listener and Other Stories**
Blackwood, Algernon 2712

**The Literary Ghost**
Dark, Larry 1232, 1306, **1351**

**Little, Big**
Crowley, John 271, 334, 335, 336, 439, 547, 551, 820, 919, 1063, 1397, 1423, 1445, 2101, 2104, 2105, 2238, 2329, 2533, 2706, 2817, 3791, 3793, 3984, 4104, 4360, 4382, 4383, 4448, 4475, 5274, 5927

**Little Big Man**
Berger, William 1126

**The Little Book of Horrors**
Wolfe, Sebastian 1709, 1710, 1714, 4828, 5686, 5687, **5946**

**Little Boy Lost**
Wright, T.M. 521, 2292, 3657, 5784, 5969, **5992**

**The Little Country**
de Lint, Charles   87, 164, 424, 522,
1101, 1356, **1432**, 1452, 1471,
1478, 1584, 1835, 1873, 2627,
2644, 2735, 2737, 2738, 2791,
3275, 3354, 4384, 4671, 4717,
4970, 5159, 5626

**Little Deaths**
Datlow, Ellen   1118, 1120, **1361**,
1367, 2174, 2176, 2177, 2178,
2179, 2182, 2185, 3181, 5385

**Little Fuzzy**
Piper, H. Beam   230, 434, 451, 1263,
1595, 2296, 2764, 3475, 3523,
3910, 4273, 4433, 4434, 4435,
4554

**Little Heroes**
Spinrad, Norman   736, 789, 1751,
2911, 3491, 5181

**A Little Knowledge**
Bishop, Michael   1877

**Little Monsters**
Ghidalia, Vic   1716

**Little Myth Marker**
Asprin, Robert   1603

**The Little People**
Christopher, John   2107

**Little People!**
Dann, Jack   **1340**, 2388, 4906, 4988

**The Little Prince**
Saint-Exupery, Antoine de   1356,
3010, 3378, 4008, 4455, 4456

**Little Shop of Horrors**
Egan, Robert   5324

**Little Sister**
Dalkey, Kara   68, **1320**, 1462, 1868,
2614, 4129

**The Little White Horse**
Goudge, Elizabeth   1219

**The Littles**
Peterson, John   1558, 4386, 4402,
4403

**Live From Golgotha: A Novel**
Vidal, Gore   **5569**

**Live Girls**
Garton, Ray   490, 803, 946, 948,
1890, **2151**, 3988, 5175, 5406

**Live Robots**
Rucker, Rudy   272, 809, 927, 2645,
3435

**Lives and Loves of a She-Devil**
Weldon, Fay   1818, 5477, 5927

**The Lives of Christopher Chant**
Jones, Diana Wynne   1601, 1605,
4334, 4920, 5976

**Lives of the Monster Dogs**
Bakis, Kirsten   305

**The Living Dark**
Gresham, Stephen   **2431**, 4841, 5825

**The Living Evil**
Jensen, Ruby Jean   2878, **2902**, 3784

**The Living God**
Duncan, Dave   **1682**

**Living Hell**
Meyers, Ric   612, 613, 614, 615,
**3882**

**The Living Legend**
Larson, Glen A.   2602

**The Living One**
Gannett, Lewis   1027, 1562, 1800,
**2115**, 4445, 5705

**Living Real**
Bassett, James C.   **386**, 1348, 6063

**Living with Aliens**
DeChancie, John   **1460**, 3952

**Living with the Reptiles**
DiSilvestro, Roger L.   65, 141, 142,
143, 522, 1417, **1563**, 3427, 3428,
4564, 5559

**Lizard Music**
Pinkwater, Daniel Manus   1218, 1223

**The Lizard War**
Dalmas, John   1158, **1325**, 1976,
2193, 2353, 5588, 5900, 5932

**Lizzie**
McBain, Ed   1826

**Lizzie Borden**
Engstrom, Elizabeth   **1826**

**The Lodge of the Lynx**
Kurtz, Katherine   6, 637, **3259**

**The Lodger**
Chappell, Fred   868, 869, **966**, 1424,
2826, 5168

**The Lodger**
Lowndes, Marie Belloc   5761

**Logan's Run**
Nolan, William F.   574, 4835

**A Logical Magician**
Weinberg, Robert   3487, **5697**, 5967

**Lois & Clark**
Cherryh, C.J.   **999**

**London Fields**
Amis, Martin   **95**

**The Lone Sentinel**
Dereske, Jo   221, 878, **1493**, 2227,
5381

**The Loneliest Magician**
Radford, Irene   3045, **4461**

**The Long Arm of Gil Hamilton**
Niven, Larry   585, 2527

**The Long Dark Tea-Time of the Soul**
Adams, Douglas   30, 1919, 2228,
4391, 4399

**The Long Hunt**
Doyle, Debra   **1602**

**The Long Lost**
Campbell, Ramsey   **859**, 3104, 3668,
5400

**The Long Midnight**
Ransom, Daniel   **4480**

**The Long Night of the Grave**
Grant, Charles L.   616, 2439, 3526,
4572, 5695

**The Long Patrol**
Jacques, Brian   **2849**

**The Long Patrol**
Larson, Glen A.   2602

**The Long Run**
Moran, Daniel Keys   361, 733, 768,
**3995**, 4451, 5039, 5621

**The Long Ships**
Bengtsson, Frans G.   136, 269, 363,
633, 640, 1104, 1105, 1498, 2189,
2248, 2250, 2453, 2454, 2572,
3353, 3502, 4270, 4872, 5014

**The Long Tomorrow**
Brackett, Leigh   1328, 3788, 4074

**The Long Winter**
Christopher, John   511, 3429

**The Longest Voyage/Slow Lightning**
Anderson, Poul   **130**

**The Longing Ring**
Kubasik, Christopher   **3246**

**Look Away**
Effinger, George Alec   3075

**Look into the Sun**
Kelly, James Patrick   919, 1062,
2721, 3046, **3047**, 3084, 4276,
4643

**Looker**
Saralegui, Jorge   **4820**

**Looking Back 2000-1887**
Bellamy, Edward   5568

**Looking for the Mahdi**
Wood, N. Lee   **5966**

**Lord Byron's Doctor**
West, Paul   5842

**Lord Conrad's Lady**
Frankowski, Leo   **2046**

**Lord Darcy Investigates**
Garrett, Randall   2472, 3254

**Lord Foul's Bane**
Donaldson, Stephen R.   17, 182, 713,
1035, 2888, 2987, 3581, 4014,
4520, 4776, 4797, 4809, 5235,
5364, 5651, 5682, 5733, 5832,
5921, 5922, 6058

**Lord Kalvan of Otherwhen**
Piper, H. Beam   141, 142, 143, 1275,
1563, 1626, 1678, 2043, 2046,
4038, 4164, 4835, 5011

**Lord Kelvin's Machine**
Blaylock, James P.   **520**, 3596, 4432

**The Lord of Chaos**
Boyer, Elizabeth H.   993

**Lord of Chaos**
Jordan, Robert   1702, 1905, 2425,
**2988**, 5678

**Lord of Light**
Zelazny, Roger   195, 477, 591, 771,
1028, 1316, 1317, 1318, 1635,
2065, 2196, 3122, 3477, 4654,
4766, 5532, 5637, 5660, 5835,
5839

**Lord of Sunset**
Godwin, Parke   **2246**

**Lord of the Dark Lake**
Faust, Ron   **1894**, 3492

**Lord of the Dead**
Holland, Tom   **2741**

**Lord of the Fantastic: Stories in
Honor of Roger Zelazny**
Greenberg, Martin H.   2380, **2398**

**Lord of the Flies**
Golding, William   862, 3021, 3606,
4663, 5486, 5799

**Lord of the Isles**
Drake, David   **1636**, 1866, 3834

**Lord of the Necropolis**
DeWeese, Gene   1137

**The Lord of the Rings Trilogy**
Tolkien, J.R.R.   1739, 3144, 4284,
4660, 5829

**Lord of the Troll-Bats**
Gilliland, Alexis A.   706, 841, **2234**

**Lord of the Two Lands**
Tarr, Judith   2140, 2187, 2561,
**5395**, 5510, 5738

**Lord of the Vampires**
Kalogridis, Jeanne   2742, **3005**

**Lord of Thunder**
Norton, Andre   1437

**Lord Teode**
Grubb, Jeff   2426

**Lord Valentine's Castle**
Silverberg, Robert   882, 961, 2361,
3385, 3386, 3477, 3580, 4670,
4994, 5581, 5931

**Lords and Ladies**
Pratchett, Terry   1160, **4394**

**Lords of Creation**
Sullivan, Tim   1261, 3191, **5351**

**Lords of Dragonclaw**
Fawcett, Bill   4608

**Lords of the Psychon**
Galouye, Daniel F.   2954

**Lords of the Sky**
Wells, Angus   726, 2462, **5738**

**Lords of the Sword**
Cook, Hugh   **1156**

**Lorelei**
Clements, Mark A.   **1086**, 4224

**Lori**
Bloch, Robert   **536**, 5468

**Lorien Lost**
King, Michael   **3124**, 4486, 5570

**The Lost**
Aycliffe, Jonathan   **279**

**The Lost and Lurking**
Wellman, Manly Wade   1639

**Lost Angels**
Schow, David J.   1128, 1171, 2656,
2860, **4888**, 5008

**The Lost Battalion**
Stine, G. Harry   831, 1651, 3013,
3037

**Lost Boys**
Card, Orson Scott   **891**, 1130, 1502,
3007, 3375, 4170, 4758, 4899

**The Lost City of the Jedi**
Davids, Paul   1391, **1393**

**The Lost City of Zork**
Bailey, Robin Wayne   **288**, 1839

**Lost Days**
Moscoe, Mike   **4039**

**Lost Dorsai**
Dickson, Gordon R.   132, 2054, 2349, 3790, 4377, 4468

**Lost Futures**
Tuttle, Lisa   796, **5520**

**The Lost Guardian**
Cross, Ronald Anthony   1093, **1274**

**The Lost History of Redwyn**
Jay, William   **2883**

**Lost Horizon**
Hilton, James   1105, 1169, 4020, 4061, 4062, 4063, 4866, 4867, 5396

**Lost in Booth Nine**
Castro, Adam-Troy   213, **938**, 5412

**Lost in Translation**
Ball, Margaret   **315**

**The Lost King**
Weis, Margaret   1745, **5720**

**The Lost Mind**
Pike, Christopher   362

**Lost Pages**
Di Filippo, Paul   **1516**

**The Lost Prince**
Wood, Bridget   **5962**

**Lost Souls**
Brite, Poppy Z.   490, 548, 600, **697**, 799, 803, 946, 1031, 1032, 1034, 1121, 1122, 1127, 1301, 1707, 1778, 1882, 1945, 2151, 2336, 2337, 2449, 3151, 3312, 3407, 3413, 3623, 4307, 4464, 4978, 5160, 5162, 5175, 5183, 5347, 5406, 5419, 5852

**Lost Souls**
Sullivan, Jack   2300

**Lost Summer**
Simmons, Dan   4011

**A Lost Tale**
Estey, Dale   184, 639, 2943, 3257

**The Lost Traveller**
Wilson, Steve   1238

**The Lost World**
Crichton, Michael   949, 1049, **1256**, 1379, 4415

**The Lost World**
Doyle, Arthur Conan   306, 416, 1256, 1379, 1417, 2468, 4597, 5067

**The Lost Years**
Dillard, J.M.   1511, 1922, 2069, 4927, 5019

**The Lost Years of Merlin**
Barron, T.A.   370

**Lot Lizards**
Garton, Ray   570, **2152**, 2313

**The Lottery, or the Adventures of James Harris**
Jackson, Shirley   623, 626, 5901

**The Lotus and the Rose**
Ciencin, Scott   **1029**

**Love Across Time**
Meredith, Ann   1271

**Love and Napalm: Export U.S.A.**
Ballard, J.G.   555

**Love & Sleep**
Crowley, John   655, **1277**, 4992, 5273

**Love Bite**
Gottlieb, Sherry   **2288**

**Love Bites**
Knight, Amarantha   698, 699, 3030, **3182**, 3618, 4689, 5386, 5387

**Love in Vein**
Brite, Poppy Z.   **698**, 748, 2508, 3030, 3181, 3182, 3618, 4690, 5385, 5386, 5387

**Love in Vein II**
Brite, Poppy Z.   **699**, 3177, 3618, 4689, 4690, 5386, 5387

**A Love through Time**
Brisbin, Terri   **691**

**The Lovecraft Circle**
Price, Robert M.   5494

**Lovecraft's Book**
Lupoff, Richard A.   1859, 4751

**Lovecraft's Follies: A Play**
Schevill, James   4751

**Lovecraft's Legacy**
Weinberg, Robert   2315, 5493, 5494, **5698**, 5884

**The Loved One**
Waugh, Evelyn   4437

**Lovedeath**
Simmons, Dan   938, 1362, **5056**

**Lovelock**
Card, Orson Scott   **892**, 968, 1729

**The Lovers**
Farmer, Philip Jose   2050

**Lovers and Other Monsters**
Kaye, Marvin   1118, **3026**

**The Lower Deep**
Cave, Hugh B.   1298, 5692

**Lowland Rider**
Williamson, Chet   1347, 1851, 4787

**The Lucifer Deck**
Smedman, Lisa   5207

**Lucifer Jones**
Resnick, Mike   **4549**

**The Lucifer Society**
Haining, Peter   38, 3616, 4311

**Lucifer's Eye**
Cave, Hugh B.   **943**

**Lucifer's Hammer**
Niven, Larry   82, 108, 248, 354, 1057, 2296, 3429, 3772, 4000, 4947, 5242, 5295

**Luck in the Shadows**
Flewelling, Lynn   683, 692, 1773, **1952**, 1984, 2253, 2268, 2270, 2452, 2650, 2694, 2695, 2696, 2756, 2925, 2957, 2959, 3481, 3645, 3651, 3832, 3835, 4686, 4739, 4796, 5320, 5333, 5581, 5734, 5735, 5749, 5758

**Luck of the Wheels**
Lindholm, Megan   2465, 2507, 3289, **3471**, 3871, 4013

**Lucky Starr and the Big Sun of Mercury**
Asimov, Isaac   2764

**Lucky Starr and the Pirates of the Asteroids**
Asimov, Isaac   1382, 4910, 4958

**Lucky Starr and the Rings of Saturn**
Asimov, Isaac   4952

**Lukundoo and Other Stories**
White, Edward Lucas   1252, 3447, 3879, 3880

**Lullaby**
Guest, Diane   2198, **2455**, 4701

**Lunar Activity**
Moon, Elizabeth   6005

**Lunar Descent**
Steele, Allen   587, 588, 596, 597, 1970, 2645, 4349, 4931, 4949, 5234, **5245**, 5370, 5566, 5859

**Lunar Justice**
Harness, Charles L.   **2545**

**The Lunatic Cafe**
Hamilton, Laurell K.   1400, **2520**, 5577

**Lunatics**
Denton, Bradley   **1491**, 4093

**Lunching with the Antichrist**
Moorcock, Michael   **3984**

**Lupe**
Thompson, Gene   3606

**The Lure of the Basilisk**
Watt-Evans, Lawrence   1469, 1682, 1688

**Lurid Dreams**
Harness, Charles L.   1196, **2546**

**The Lurker**
Smith, James V.   **5123**

**The Lurker at the Threshold**
Derleth, August   4007

**The Lurker at the Threshold**
Lovecraft, H.P.   342, 5470

**The Lute Player**
Lofts, Norah   3017

**Luthien's Gamble**
Salvatore, R.A.   **4802**

**Lyonesse**
Vance, Jack   185, 630, 955, 2945, 3077, 5041, 5582

**Lyon's Pride**
McCaffrey, Anne   **3738**

**Lyrec**
Frost, Gregory   846

**Lyrica**
Monteleone, Thomas F.   4236, 4569

**Lythande**
Bradley, Marion Zimmer   745

**Lythandedeer People**
Bradley, Marion Zimmer   1765

## M

**The M.D.: A Horror Story**
Disch, Thomas M.   627, **1561**, 2700, 3494, 4437, 5167

**M.Y.T.H. Inc. in Action**
Asprin, Robert   **259**

**M.Y.T.H. Inc. Link**
Asprin, Robert   4390

**M31: A Family Romance**
Wright, Stephen   1831

**Ma Qui and Other Phantoms**
Brennert, Alan   **675**, 2078, 3250

**The Mabinogi and Other Medieval Welsh Tales**
Ford, Patrick K.   5626

**Macabre**
Laws, Stephen   602, 4733, 5119

**The Mace of Souls**
Fergusson, Bruce   1439, **1925**

**Machine**
Belletto, Rene   397, **436**, 1786, 4875

**Machines That Kill**
Saberhagen, Fred   **4769**

**Macroscope**
Anthony, Piers   4354

**Mad Amos**
Foster, Alan Dean   **2009**, 5356, 5357, 5504

**The Mad Goblin**
Farmer, Philip Jose   4624, 4625

**Mad Max Beyond Thunderdome**
Vinge, Joan D.   1644

**Mad Roy's Light**
King, Paula   1593, 1594, 1595, **3125**, 3709, 5930

**Mad Scientists**
Schiff, Stuart David   5886

**Madeleine's Ghost**
Girardi, Robert   **2240**, 3149

**Madeline: After the Fall of Usher**
Kiraly, Marie   **3150**, 4344, 4345

**Madlands**
Jeter, K.W.   976, 1567, **2913**, 2997, 3009, 3245, 5109, 5145, 5156, 5254

**Madman Run**
Robbins, David   4600

**The Madness Season**
Friedman, C.S.   1586, 1587, 1593, 1602, **2058**, 2665, 2954, 3469, 3476, 4124, 4984, 5451, 5572

**Madoc**
Winter, Pat   3166

Title Index

**Madoc's Hundred**
Winter, Pat　2570, 3166, **5925**

**Madouc**
Vance, Jack　632, 1743, 2662, 5128, **5547**, 5582, 5639

**The Maelstrom's Eye**
Moore, Roger E.　1291, 2785

**Mage Heart**
Routley, Jane　**4686**

**The Mage in the Iron Mask**
Thomsen, Brian　**5458**

**Mage Quest**
Brittain, C. Dale　**5219**

**The Mageborn Traitor**
Rawn, Melanie　**4488**

**Magelord: The Awakening**
Martin, Thomas K.　**3651**

**Magic**
Goldman, William　2025, 2632, 3217

**The Magic and the Healing**
O'Donohoe, Nick　**4196**

**The Magic Bicycle**
Hill, William　**2688**

**Magic Casement**
Duncan, Dave　992, 1146, **1683**, 1732, 2076, 2984, 3834, 3837, 5735

**The Magic Cottage**
Herbert, James　2160, 2562, 4249

**The Magic Cup**
Greeley, Andrew M.　2231, 2232

**The Magic Engineer**
Modesitt, L.E. Jr.　**3933**

**The Magic Goes Away**
Niven, Larry　1299, 1532, 2461, 4460, 4743, 5974

**Magic Kingdom for Sale—Sold!**
Brooks, Terry　**4397**

**A Magic-Lover's Treasury of the Fantastic**
Weis, Margaret　**5721**

**The Magic of Christmas**
Silbersack, John　2412, 2587, 2588, 2589, **5024**

**The Magic of Recluce**
Modesitt, L.E. Jr.　712, 1096, 1905, **3934**

**The Magic of Shirley Jackson**
Jackson, Shirley　3575, 4181, 4182

**Magic Realism by Women: Dreams in a Minor Key**
Sturgis, Susanna J.　51, 2035, 4169, 5018, 5814, 5815

**Magic: The Final Fantasy Collection**
Asimov, Isaac　**244**

**The Magic Touch**
Nye, Jody Lynn　**4171**, 4864

**The Magic Toyshop**
Carter, Angela　144, 4183

**The Magic Wagon**
Lansdale, Joe R.　4251, 4946, 5615

**The Magic Wars**
Clayton, Jo　**1068**

**The Magic World**
Nesbit, E.　3587

**The Magical Mimics in Oz**
Snow, Jack　3609

**Magicats!**
Dann, Jack　1369, 3377, 4144, 4145, 4273, 5252

**Magicats II**
Dann, Jack　4144, 5252

**Magician**
Feist, Raymond E.　1685, 1730, 1733, 1738, 2271, 2425, 2724, 2984, 2985, 3095, 3172, 5034

**Magician: Apprentice**
Feist, Raymond E.　4493

**Magician's Gambit**
Eddings, David　1904, 2531, 2990

**The Magician's Nephew**
Lewis, C.S.　1704

**Magicians of Gor**
Norman, John　4294

**The Magicians of Night**
Hambly, Barbara　**2505**

**Magician's Ward**
Wrede, Patricia C.　5137, **5976**

**MagicNet**
DeChancie, John　**1461**

**Magic's Pawn**
Lackey, Mercedes　1660, **3287**, 3383, 4793, 4801, 5542

**Magic's Price**
Lackey, Mercedes　**3288**, 4167

**Magic's Promise**
Lackey, Mercedes　742, **3289**

**Magnificat**
May, Julian　2526, **3699**

**The Magnificent Gallery**
Monteleone, Thomas F.　1282, 2303, 2565, 4010

**The Magnificent Wilf**
Dickson, Gordon R.　**1536**

**The Magus**
Fowles, John　2160, 5485

**Maia**
Adams, Richard　3412, 4850

**Maia's Veil**
McAllister, P.K.　**3707**

**Mail-Order Wings**
Gormley, Beatrice　1558, 2949

**The Mailman**
Little, Bentley　**3494**

**Mainline**
Christian, Deborah　357, **1026**, 1694, 3186, 5531

**Mairelon the Magician**
Wrede, Patricia C.　489, 763, 1742, 2355, 3776, 4899, 5002, 5490, **5977**

**Majestic**
Strieber, Whitley　1296, 4510, 4650, **5341**

**Majyk by Accident**
Friesner, Esther　197, **2079**, 5163, 5649

**Majyk by Design**
Friesner, Esther　**2080**

**Majyk by Hook or Crook**
Friesner, Esther　**2081**

**Make Room, Make Room**
Harrison, Harry　1878

**Make Way for Dragons!**
Gunnarsson, Thorarinn　1221, 1268, 2076, 2077, **2465**, 5337

**The Maker of Universes**
Farmer, Philip Jose　164, 953, 1324, 3848, 5033, 5830

**Making History**
See, Carolyn　2997

**Making Love**
Tem, Melanie　2733, **5422**, 5522

**The Making of a Monster**
Petersen, Gail　1122, 2449, **4307**, 5162

**Makoto**
Wilde, Kelley　4003, **5801**

**A Malady of Magicks**
Gardner, Craig Shaw　4400

**The Mall**
Cusick, Richie Tankersley　1692

**Mall, Mayhem and Magic**
Lisle, Holly　639, 3099, **3485**

**Mall Purchase Night**
Cook, Rick　**1159**, 3198, 3485

**Mallworld**
Sucharitkul, Somtow　493, 1603, 5163

**The Mammoth Book of Best New Horror**
Jones, Stephen　1374, **2969**

**The Mammoth Book of Best New Horror 8**
Jones, Stephen　1377, **2970**

**The Mammoth Book of Best New Horror 9**
Jones, Stephen　1371, **2971**

**The Mammoth Book of Classic Chillers**
Haydock, Tim　226

**The Mammoth Book of Dracula**
Jones, Stephen　**2972**, 3226, 5699

**The Mammoth Book of Fairy Tales**
Ashley, Mike　225

**The Mammoth Book of Fantastic Science Fiction**
Asimov, Isaac　245

**The Mammoth Book of Frankenstein**
Jones, Stephen　140, 2892, **2973**, 3019, 3180, 5691, 5886

**The Mammoth Book of Ghost Stories**
Dalby, Richard　1232, 1233, 1306, **1309**, 1709

**The Mammoth Book of Ghost Stories 2**
Dalby, Richard　1232, 1709

**The Mammoth Book of Modern Science Fiction: Short Novels of the 1980s**
Asimov, Isaac　246

**The Mammoth Book of Short Horror Novels**
Ashley, Mike　**226**, 2974

**The Mammoth Book of Terror**
Jones, Stephen　226, **2974**

**The Mammoth Book of Twentieth Century Ghost Stories**
Haining, Peter　**2483**

**The Mammoth Book of Vampires**
Jones, Stephen　150, 151, 1013, 1611, 1799, 2382, 2408, 2409, 2484, **2975**, 3031, 4876, 4879, 4880, 4881, 5265, 5284, 5688, 5935

**The Mammoth Book of Victorian and Edwardian Ghost Stories**
Dalby, Richard　38, 1234, **1310**, 2483

**The Mammoth Book of Vintage Science Fiction**
Asimov, Isaac　5954

**The Mammoth Book of Werewolves**
Jones, Stephen　1230, 2410, **2976**, 3032, 5384

**The Mammoth Book of Zombies**
Jones, Stephen　**2977**, 4412

**The Mammoth Hunters**
Auel, Jean M.　667, 669, 1207, 2170, 4817, 4818, 4819

**A Man Betrayed**
Jones, J.V.　**2958**, 4796, 5529

**Man From Mundania**
Anthony, Piers　**180**, 671, 1206, 1809, 1812, 2132, 2133, 4316

**The Man From U.N.C.L.E.: The Mad Scientist Affair**
Phillifent, John T.　1853, 4296

**Man in His Time: The Best Science Fiction Stories of Brian W. Aldiss**
Aldiss, Brian W.　57, 123, 624, 5940

**The Man in the High Castle**
Dick, Philip K.　201, 443, 598, 1518, 1658, 1982, 2239, 2564, 2667, 3528, 4272, 4474, 4536, 4546, 5300, 5515, 5516, 5918, 5919

**The Man in the Moon Must Die**
Bredenberg, Jeff　**665**, 2788

**The Man in the Moss**
Rickman, Phil　5400

**Man-Kzin Wars**
Niven, Larry　828, 1158, 1535, 1627, 3649, 4372, 4373, 5917

**Man-Kzin Wars II**
Niven, Larry　828, 1158, 4372

**Man-Kzin Wars II-VII**
Niven, Larry　3649

**Man-Kzin Wars III**
Niven, Larry　**4123**, 4372

**Man-Kzin Wars IV**
Niven, Larry   4103, **4124**, 4372

**Man-Kzin Wars V**
Niven, Larry   **4125**

**Man o' War**
Shatner, William   **4932**

**Man of Gold**
Barker, M.A.R.   15, 104, 770, 771,
1008, 1109, 1111, 1316, 1317,
1318, 1904, 1906, 1908, 1909,
1910, 1912, 2041, 2330, 2473,
2887, 2888, 3581, 3925, 4020,
5391, 5731

**Man Plus**
Pohl, Frederik   586, 1768, 2840,
3715, 4205, **4348**, 4963, 5377

**The Man Upstairs**
Parkinson, T.L.   89, 913, 1468, 3094,
**4248**

**The Man Who Corrupted Earth**
Edmondson, G.C.   1962

**The Man Who Fell to Earth**
Tevis, Walter   305, 621

**The Man Who Folded Himself**
Gerrold, David   135, 2012, **2208**

**The Man Who Japed**
Dick, Philip K.   1782, 5642

**The Man Who Melted**
Dann, Jack   1788

**The Man Who Never Missed**
Perry, Steve   63, 756, 761, 1184,
1332, 1333, 1503, 1535, 1542,
1661, 1849, 1869, 2364, 3539,
3873, 3975, 4120, 4225, 4226,
4227, 4228, 4304, 4467, 4521,
4583, 4637, 5229, 5365, 5366,
5889

**The Man Who Never Missed Series**
Perry, Steve   1540

**The Man Who Pulled Down the Sky**
Barnes, John   4620, 5032

**The Man Who Sold the Moon**
Heinlein, Robert A.   593

**The Man Who Turned into Himself**
Ambrose, David   **89**, 858, 2613,
4086, 5661

**The Man Who Used the Universe**
Foster, Alan Dean   584

**The Man Who Wanted Stars**
McLaughlin, Dean   380, 4511

**The Man Who Was Thursday**
Chesterton, G.K.   1564

**The Man Without a Country**
Hale, Edward E.   5377

**The Manchurian Candidate**
Condon, Richard   5664

**The Mandalorian Armor**
Jeter, K.W.   117, **2914**

**A Manhattan Ghost Story**
Wright, T.M.   3201

**Manhattan Heat**
Eulo, Ken   **1851**, 4847

**Manhattan Transfer**
Stith, John E.   934, 3734, **5303**

**The Manitou**
Masterton, Graham   41, 860, 3081,
3325, 3658, 5350

**Manjinn Moon**
Vitola, Denise   **5576**

**Mankind under the Leash**
Disch, Thomas M.   1015, 5878

**The Manse**
Cantrell, Lisa   4832

**Mansions of Darkness**
Yarbro, Chelsea Quinn   4668, **6016**

**The Mansions of Space**
Morressy, John   3617

**The Manuscript Found in Saragossa**
Potocki, Jan   **4371**

**The Many-Colored Land**
May, Julian   15, 987, 1324, 1421,
2119, 2122, 3058, 3059, 3060,
3062, 3427, 5754, 5998

**Maps in a Mirror**
Card, Orson Scott   124, 161, 244,
415, 435, **893**, 1874, 2736, 5028

**Marathon**
Smith, David Alexander   64, 473,
2579, 3698, 3741, 3760, 5248

**Marbleheart**
Callander, Don   **846**

**The March Hare Network**
Chalker, Jack L.   **957**, 5353

**March or Die**
Keith, Andrew   1547, **3035**

**Marching through Georgia**
Stirling, S.M.   442, 1322, 1579,
1641, 3867, 4372, 5502, 5676

**Marco Polo and the Sleeping Beauty**
Davidson, Avram   523

**Margaret and I**
Wilhelm, Kate   1932, 3263

**A Margin in Time**
Hayden, Laura   3039

**Marianne, the Magus, and the
Manticore**
Tepper, Sheri S.   315

**Marianne, the Matchbox and the
Malachite Mouse**
Tepper, Sheri S.   105, **5432**

**Mariel of Redwall**
Jacques, Brian   32, **2850**

**Mariette in Ecstasy**
Hansen, Ron   4050

**Marion's Wall**
Finney, Jack   3149

**The Mark of the Cat**
Norton, Andre   3740, **4157**

**The Mark of the Demons**
Jakes, John   4848

**The Mark of the Horse Lord**
Sutcliff, Rosemary   5928

**The Mark of the Moderately Vicious
Vampire**
Fenn, Lionel   1802, **1920**, 3057

**Mark of the Werewolf**
Sackett, Jeffrey   2895, **4780**

**Marked Cards**
Martin, George R.R.   **3647**

**The Marked Man**
Ingrid, Charles   720, **2831**

**Marks of Our Brothers**
Lindskold, Jane M.   786, **3475**, 6063

**Marlborough Street**
Bowker, Richard   4469, 4604

**Marooned in Realtime**
Vinge, Vernor   401, 928, 931, 1055,
1986, 2328, 2603, 3021, 3256,
3734, 4000, 4018, 4019, 4506,
4652, 5043, 5067, 5660, 5909

**Marooned on Eden**
Forward, Robert L.   1083, **1986**,
3721

**Mars**
Bova, Ben   102, 406, 421, **586**,
1585, 2584, 2840, 4348, 4349,
4629, 4633

**Mars Attacks!**
Gems, Jonathan   205, 504, 1508

**Mars Prime**
Dietz, William C.   **1548**, 2584, 4629,
4633

**Mars—The Red Planet**
Farren, Mick   **1880**

**Mars Underground**
Hartmann, William   1585, **2584**

**The Martian Chronicles**
Bradbury, Ray   435, **621**, **622**, 2416,
4548

**Martian Deathtrap**
Archer, Nathan   **205**

**The Martian Inca**
Watson, Ian   5561

**Martian Rainbow**
Forward, Robert L.   596, 1548, **1987**,
4635, 5859

**Martian Time-Slip**
Dick, Philip K.   586, 622, 3012,
3612, 4555

**The Martian Way**
Asimov, Isaac   586, 5377

**Martians, Go Home**
Brown, Fredric   4546

**Martin the Warrior**
Jacques, Brian   32, **2851**

**Marune: Alastor 933**
Vance, Jack   4952

**The Marvellous Land of Snergs**
Wyke-Smith, E.A.   **6006**

**Mary Poppins**
Travers, Pamela L.   2949

**Mary Reilly**
Martin, Valerie   535, **3654**, 5826

**Mascara**
Dorfman, Ariel   19, 1334, 5073

**A Mask for the General**
Goldstein, Lisa   744, 3791, 4051,
4360, 4750, 5272, 5274, 6009

**The Mask of Cthulhu**
Derleth, August   **1496**, 3531, 3532

**The Mask of Loki**
Zelazny, Roger   2658, **6071**

**Mask of the Night**
Ryan, Mary   **4753**

**Mask of the Phantasm**
Gravel, Geary   **2331**

**Mask of the Wizard**
Cooke, Catherine   2471, 4523, 4806

**Maskerade**
Pratchett, Terry   **4395**

**Masks**
Vornholt, John   2068

**Masks of the Illuminati**
Wilson, Robert Anton   1063

**The Masks of Time**
Silverberg, Robert   5195

**Masque**
Wilson, F. Paul   **5890**

**Masque World**
Panshin, Alexei   1216, 2013, 3345,
3583, 5131

**Masquerades**
Novak, Kate   **4166**

**Masques**
Briggs, Patricia   **681**, 717, 718, 845

**Masques**
Emerson, Ru   559

**Masques**
Williamson, J.N.   4278

**Masques III**
Williamson, J.N.   4200

**Masques IV**
Williamson, J.N.   **5855**

**The Masques Series**
Williamson, J.N.   3960

**Master and Fool**
Jones, J.V.   **2959**, 4802

**The Master Key: An Electrical Fairy
Tale**
Baum, L. Frank   1218

**The Master of Chaos**
Adams, Terry A.   **34**

**Master of Earth and Water**
Paxson, Diana L.   1764, 3504, 3506,
**4266**

**Master of Lies**
Masterton, Graham   3620, **3676**,
5085

**Master of Many Treasures**
Brown, Mary   726, 2462

**Master of Space and Time**
Rucker, Rudy   4341

**Master of the Fallen Years**
O'Sullivan, Vincent   963, 2633

**Master of the Five Magics**
Hardy, Lyndon   1683, 1813

*The Master of Whitestorm*
Wurts, Janny   1904, 1906, **6003**

*The Masterharper of Pern*
McCaffrey, Anne   **3739**

*Masterpieces of Fantasy and Wonder*
Hartwell, David G.   **2592**, 6046

*Masterpieces of Terror and the Unknown*
Kaye, Marvin   2993, **3027**

*Masters of Everon*
Dickson, Gordon R.   2421, 2550, 3307, 3769, 4280

*Masters of Horror*
Moskowitz, Sam   1712

*The Masters of Solitude*
Kaye, Marvin   1101, 2245

*Masters of the Fist*
Hughes, Edward P.   1642, 2790, **2805**, 3346

*Mastery*
Wilde, Kelley   2255, **5802**

*Mastodonia*
Simak, Clifford D.   2192, 3428, 3920, 4233, 5998

*The Mata Hari Adventure*
Luceno, James   **3544**

*Matadora*
Perry, Steve   1331

*Mathemagics*
Ball, Margaret   **316**, 2074, 3717, 4981

*The Matrix*
Aycliffe, Jonathan   **280**

*Matrix Cubed*
Bloom, Britton   **554**, 3036

*Matrix Man*
Dietz, William C.   295, **1549**, 2087, 5173

*Matrix Witch*
Douglis, Marjie   5542

*A Matter for Men*
Gerrold, David   383, 1900, 2646, 5352

*A Matter of Honor*
Martin, Thomas K.   562, 1143, 5197

*A Matter of Oaths*
Wright, Helen S.   2436, 4468, **5985**, 6052

*A Matter of Taste*
Saberhagen, Fred   2492, 2493, 3003, **4770**

*A Matter of Time*
Byrne, Beverly   3039

*A Matter of Time*
Cook, Glen   442, 4477

*Matter's End*
Benford, Gregory   **448**, 823

*Mattimeo*
Jacques, Brian   737, **2852**, 3115

*Maureen Birnbaum, Barbarian Swordsperson: The Complete Stories*
Effinger, George Alec   262, 316, 648, 649, 650, 651, **1752**, 1808, 1811, 2072, 2074, 2144, 4610, 5617

*Maverick*
Bethke, Bruce   **484**

*Max Lakeman and the Beautiful Stranger*
Cohen, Jon   433, **1098**

*Maximum Light*
Kress, Nancy   **3241**

*Mayhem in Manhattan*
Wein, Len   1667, 3403

*The Maze Maker*
Ayrton, Michael   1129, 2404

*A Maze of Death*
Dick, Philip K.   160, 805, 1453

*Maze of Moonlight*
Baudino, Gael   393, 3017, 5983

*A Maze of Stars*
Brunner, John   595, **734**, 1182, 4175, 5042, 5549

*Maze of Worlds*
Lumley, Brian   **3559**

*Mazemaker*
Dexter, Catherine   5559

*Mazeway*
Williamson, Jack   2048, 2807, 3448, 4349, 4357, 4894, 5834, **5866**

*The McAndrew Chronicles*
Sheffield, Charles   1990, 1992, 5247, 6065

*McCade's Bounty*
Dietz, William C.   **1550**

*McLendon's Syndrome*
Frezza, Robert   **2053**, 3484

*ME: A Novel of Self Discovery*
Thomas, Thomas T.   79, 249, 829, 1761, 2579, 2725, 3665, 4348, 4381, 5213, 5259, **5452**

*Mean Little Old Lady at Work*
Mayhar, Ardath   113, 578, **3702**, 5881

*Mechasm*
Sladek, John   1918, 1919, 3573

*The Med Series*
Leinster, Murray   4172, 4176, 5777, 5778, 5779, 5780

*Medallion of the Black Hound*
Murphy, Shirley Rousseau   192, 2505, 2879, **4056**, 5070, 5182

*The Meddlesome Ghost*
Allen, Sheila Rosalynd   **84**

*Medea: Harlan's World*
Ellison, Harlan   3641, 3643, 3646, 3647, 4725, 5038, 5214, 5216

*Medicine Show*
Nye, Jody Lynn   **4172**, 4195, 4196, 4198, 5778

*Medusa*
Campbell, Ramsey   5420

*The Medusa Encounter*
Preuss, Paul   **4419**

*Meeting in Infinity*
Kessel, John   2835, 3048, **3086**, 3234, 3442, 3712, 4680, 5240, 5257

*Meeting the Author*
Campbell, Ramsey   966

*Meeting the Minotaur*
Dawson, Carol   **1409**

*A Meeting with Medusa/Green Mars*
Clarke, Arthur C.   3189

*Mefisto in Onyx*
Ellison, Harlan   397, 436, **1786**, 4875

*Meg*
Alten, Steve   **88**, 5877

*Megalomania*
Wallace, Ian   **5621**

*Melancholy Elephants*
Robinson, Spider   503

*Melmoth the Wanderer*
Maturin, Charles   4371

*Meltdown!*
Soles, Caro   2117, 2444, **5154**

*Memento Mori*
Lewitt, Shariann   5, **3454**

*Memnoch the Devil*
Rice, Anne   3908, 4028, 4029, **4571**, 5190

*Memoirs of a Space Traveler*
Lem, Stanislaw   3431

*Memoirs of a Spacewoman*
Mitchison, Naomi   2419

*The Memoirs of a Survivor*
Lessing, Doris   1141

*The Memoirs of Elizabeth Frankenstein*
Roszak, Theodore   659, 3019, **4684**

*Memories*
McQuay, Mike   1305, 5195

*Memories of the Body*
Tuttle, Lisa   1827, 3116, 4182, **5521**

*Memories of the Space Ages*
Ballard, J.G.   5369

*Memory*
Bujold, Lois McMaster   **761**, 5465, 5544

*Memory and Dream*
de Lint, Charles   439, 1399, **1433**, 1445, 1472, 2082, 2266, 2538, 2735, 2737, 2738, 3118, 3283, 3838, 3887, 3896, 3897, 4195, 4358, 4486, 5180, 5916

*Memory Blank*
Stith, John E.   1304

*The Memory Cathedral*
Dann, Jack   **1341**, 3409, 4651, 5152

*The Memory of Earth*
Card, Orson Scott   **894**, 5000, 5001, 5033, 5041, 5233, 5546, 5862

*A Memory of Lions*
Godwin, Parke   363

*A Memory of Murder*
Bradbury, Ray   2281

*The Memory of Whiteness*
Robinson, Kim Stanley   1305

*Memory Prime*
Reeves-Stevens, Garfield   1663, 4511, 4927

*Memory Wire*
Wilson, Robert Charles   295, 4632

*Memorymakers*
Herbert, Brian   **2665**

*Men at Arms*
Pratchett, Terry   **4396**

*Men in Black*
Perry, Steve   3063, **4298**

*Men Like Rats*
Chilson, Rob   **1015**, 2193, 2954, 5878

*Men, Martians, and Machines*
Russell, Eric Frank   4297

*Menace Under Marwood*
Lanier, Sterling E.   586

*The Mennyms*
Waugh, Sylvia   53, 430, 773, 2719, 2869, **5654**

*Mennyms Alive*
Waugh, Sylvia   5655

*Mennyms Under Siege*
Waugh, Sylvia   5656

*Mentor*
Jensen, Kris   643, 990, **2898**, 4485

*The Mephisto Waltz*
Stewart, Fred Mustard   2204, 2823

*The Mer-Child: A Legend for Children and Other Adults*
Morgan, Robin   1356, 3378, 3816, **4008**, 4171, 4447, 6089

*The Mercenaries*
Baldwin, Bill   **311**, 2350

*The Mercenary*
Pournelle, Jerry   308, 1646, 2054

*Mercenary's Star*
Keith, William H. Jr.   1976

*The Merchant of Venice*
Shakespeare, William   1045

*Merchanter's Luck*
Cherryh, C.J.   1891, 1893, 2476, 3830, 4593, 5833

*Mercycle*
Anthony, Piers   **181**, 2450, 5726

*Mercy's Mill*
Levin, Betty   970, **3444**

*The Meri*
Bohnhoff, Maya Kaathryn   394, 396, **561**, 633, 640, 1135, 1356, 1478, 3628, 4207, 4863, 5266, 5456

*Meridian 144*
Files, Meg   **1932**

*Merlin*
Lawhead, Stephen R.   227

*Merlin*
Nye, Robert   3806

**Merlin**
Yolen, Jane **6035**

**Merlin and the Dragons**
Yolen, Jane **6036**

**The Merlin Chronicles**
Ashley, Mike **227**, 369, 370, 372, 1270

**Merlin Dreams**
Dickinson, Peter 6030

**The Merlin Effect**
Barron, T.A. **371**, 6035, 6038

**Merlin's Bones**
Saberhagen, Fred **4771**

**Merlin's Booke**
Yolen, Jane 369, 372

**Merlin's Gift**
McDowell, Ian 3474

**Merlin's Harp**
Crompton, Anne Eliot **1270**, 1857

**Merlin's King**
Charnas, Suzy McKee 5070

**Merlin's Legacy: Dawn of Camelot**
Evans, Quinn Taylor **1857**

**Merlin's Mirror**
Norton, Andre 459, 5534

**Mermaid's Song**
Van Gores, Alida 1155

**The Merman's Children**
Anderson, Poul 5511

**The Merro Tree**
Waitman, Katie 2422, 3453, 3931, **5609**

**The Merry Adventures of Robin Hood**
Pyle, Howard 2247, 2248, 2389, 3165, 4609

**Merry-Go-Round in Oz**
McGraw, Eloise Jarvis 3609

**The Messenger**
Tyson, Donald **5528**

**Messiah**
Vidal, Gore 4330

**The Messiah Choice**
Chalker, Jack L. 637

**The Messiah Stone**
Caidin, Martin 1092, 4771

**Metahorror**
Etchison, Dennis 1740, **1847**, 4278, 5795

**Metal Angel**
Springer, Nancy 1028, 2342, 3480, **5181**

**Metamorphosis**
Lorrah, Jean 2066, **3524**

**Metaphase**
McIntyre, Vonda N. 81, 322, 324, 384, 404, 1059, 1333, 1726, 1989, 1992, 2522, 3469, 3743, 3745, 3749, **3821**, 4356, 4961, 4967, 5304

**Metaworlds**
Collins, Paul 4439

**Methods of Madness**
Garton, Ray 192, 700, 938, 1171, **2153**, 2656, 3318, 5360, 5411

**Methuselah's Children**
Heinlein, Robert A. 127, 1554, 2491, 4955

**Metrognome**
Foster, Alan Dean 4173

**Metrophage**
Kadrey, Richard 361, 808, 4205, 4940, 5254, 5960

**Metropolis**
Von Harbou, Thea 484

**Metropolitan**
Williams, Walter Jon 218, 324, 2364, 2522, 4931, **5839**

**Michaelmas**
Budrys, Algis 592, 5766

**Microcosmic God**
Sturgeon, Theodore 2458, **5345**

**Microcosmic Tales**
Asimov, Isaac 4828, 5946

**Mid-Flinx**
Foster, Alan Dean **2010**, 5571

**Midas World**
Pohl, Frederik 1892

**The Middle Kingdom**
Wingrove, David 201, 657, 1145, 1538, 1573, 1575, 3817, 3896, 3897, 4682, 5253, **5919**

**The Middle of Nowhere**
Gerrold, David **2209**

**The Middle Window**
Goudge, Elizabeth 4943

**Midnight**
Koontz, Dean R. 99, 800, 2112, 3152, **3212**, 3632, 4509, 4845

**Midnight at the Well of Souls**
Chalker, Jack L. 1876, 5130

**Midnight Blue: The Sonja Blue Collection**
Collins, Nancy A. **1122**

**The Midnight Club**
Pike, Christopher **4329**

**The Midnight Folk**
Masefield, John 4079, 4080

**Midnight Graffiti**
Horsting, Jessica 1017, 1281, **2773**, 5025

**The Midnight Horse**
Fleischman, Sid **1948**, 4447

**Midnight Is a Lonely Place**
Erskine, Barbara 1050, **1836**, 2903, 4753, 5463

**Midnight Mass**
Wilson, F. Paul 1197, 2440, 3758, 4072, **5891**

**Midnight Never Comes**
Roden, Barbara **4644**

**Midnight Pleasures**
Bloch, Robert 537

**Midnight Promises**
Chizmar, Richard T. 663, **1021**, 1789, 2155, 2701, 2714, 5026

**The Midnight Reader**
Stern, Philip Van Doren 1, 2968

**Midnight Sun**
Campbell, Ramsey **860**, 2711, 3310, 5189, 5350

**Midnight Tales**
Harvey, William Fryer 454, 455, 5610

**The Midnight Tour**
Laymon, Richard **3368**

**Midnight's Lair**
Laymon, Richard 1051, 1347, 1894, 2611, 3209, **3369**, 5474, 5685

**Midshipman's Hope**
Feintuch, David 1047, **1901**, 1978, 3970, 5403, 5673, 5675

**Midsummer**
Costello, Matthew J. **1200**, 5890

**Midsummer Century**
Blish, James 884

**A Midsummer Tempest**
Anderson, Poul 314, 2570, 2945, 3079, 3097, 3700, 3822

**The Midwich Cuckoos**
Wyndham, John 491, 733, 2787, 3251, 3856, 4504, 4645, 5065

**Midworld**
Foster, Alan Dean 3344

**Mighty Good Road**
Scott, Melissa 1041, 1056, 1332, 2476, 3727, 4289, **4897**

**The Mile-Long Spaceship**
Wilhelm, Kate 665

**The Military Dimension**
Drake, David 1552

**Millennial Women**
Kidd, Virginia 4825, 4826

**Millennium**
Bova, Ben 2645

**Millennium**
Varley, John 116, 141, 142, 143, 263, 824, 1563, 2546, 3064, 3467, 4942, 5011, 5282, 5487

**A Million Open Doors**
Barnes, John 64, **353**, 1970, 4175, 4679

**Milton in America**
Ackroyd, Peter **25**

**Mina**
Kiraly, Marie 3004, **3151**, 3179, 3180, 3623, 4684, 6010

**Mind Changer**
White, James 1266, **5780**

**Mind Fields: The Art of Jacek Yerka**
Ellison, Harlan **1787**

**A Mind for Trade**
Norton, Andre **4158**

**Mind Kill**
La Plante, Richard **3267**

**Mind Light**
Davis, Margaret **1407**, 1899, 4160

**Mind Meld**
Vornholt, John **5596**

**Mind of My Mind**
Butler, Octavia E. 632, 645, 876, 1502, 2795, 2798, 5430, 5590

**Mind of the Magic**
Lisle, Holly 719, **3486**

**The Mind Parasites**
Wilson, Colin 3567, 3568, 5470

**Mind Slayer**
Randle, Kevin D. 1696, **4469**

**Mind Snare**
Greeno, Gayle **2422**

**Mind-Speakers' Call**
Greeno, Gayle 983, **2423**

**Mind Stealer**
Duigon, Lee **1672**

**Mind Switch**
Knight, Damon 436, 1786, 4875

**The Mind Thing**
Brown, Fredric 914, 2542

**Mindblast**
Duane, Diane **1665**

**Mindplayers**
Cadigan, Pat 60, 79, 419, 505, **806**, 927, 1449, 1519, 1750, 1820, 1873, 1878, 1881, 1935, 1964, 1968, 2545, 2839, 3049, 3075, 3604, 3661, 3711, 3921, 4071, 4099, 4136, 4342, 4704, 5170, 5254, 5376, 5491, 5638, 5828

**Minds Apart**
Davis, Margaret **1408**, 4175

**Mindstar Rising**
Hamilton, Peter F. 110, 1168, **2526**

**Mindswap**
Sheckley, Robert 6064

**Mine**
McCammon, Robert R. 1843, 2111, 2548, 2555, 3130, 3332, 3695, **3756**, 4887

**Minerva Wakes**
Lisle, Holly 316, 703, 1033, 1299, 1744, 2141, 2326, 2737, 2738, 3099, **3487**, 3843, 4129, 4797, 5409, 5555, 5697

**The Mines of Behemoth**
Shea, Michael 3422, **4945**

**Mining the Oort**
Pohl, Frederik 83, 421, 2765, **4349**, 4379, 4911, 4948, 4958, 4962

**Minions of the Moon**
Bowes, Richard 2995

**Minotaur Maze**
Sheckley, Robert 5810

**Mio My Son**
Lindgren, Astrid 1330

**Mir**
Besher, Alexander **474**, 5353

**Mirabile**
Kagan, Janet  100, 413, 1420, 1517,
  1589, 1593, 1723, 1724, 1726,
  1727, 1729, 1769, 1964, 1988,
  1997, 2008, 2037, 2659, 2800,
  **3001**, 3646, 3721, 3730, 3738,
  4176, 4195, 4196, 4198, 4479,
  4633, 4953, 5038, 5363, 5369,
  5499, 5809

**A Miracle of Rare Design**
Resnick, Mike  1876, **4550**, 5549

**Mirage**
Brass, Perry  74, **662**

**Mirage**
Wilson, F. Paul  1973, **5892**

**Mirkheim**
Anderson, Poul  2459

**Mirror**
Masterton, Graham  **3677**

**Mirror Dance**
Bujold, Lois McMaster  **762**, 1003,
  1602, 5362, 5672

**A Mirror for Observers**
Pangborn, Edgar  565, 567, 4188

**The Mirror Maker**
Levi, Primo  **3443**

**The Mirror Maze**
Hogan, James P.  **2726**

**Mirror of Destiny**
Norton, Andre  **4159**, 5200

**The Mirror of Her Dreams**
Donaldson, Stephen R.  515, 2505,
  2507, 3659

**The Mirror of the Night**
Lannes, Roberta  3100, **3318**, 5413

**Mirror to the Sky**
Geston, Mark S.  **2213**, 4679

**Mirrorshades: The Cyberpunk
  Anthology**
Sterling, Bruce  804, 1516, 2394,
  4713, 4812

**The Miscast Gentleman**
Easton, Edward  3097

**The Misconceiver**
Ferriss, Lucy  **1929**

**Misery**
King, Stephen  810, 3002

**Miskatonic University**
Greenberg, Martin H.  **2399**

**Miskatonic University**
Weinberg, Robert  148, 4422, 4424,
  4427

**The Misplaced Legion**
Turtledove, Harry  1324, 1638, 1676,
  2752, 3353, 4782

**Missing Angel Juan**
Block, Francesca Lia  **550**

**The Missing Matter**
McDonough, Thomas R.  110, 2480,
  **3805**, 4019

**Mission Child**
McHugh, Maureen F.  **3819**

**Mission of Gravity**
Clement, Hal  401, 1956, 1986,
  1988, 5597

**Mission of Magic**
Smith, Julie Dean  4458, **5125**

**Mission: Tori**
Bolton, Johanna  **564**, 1913, 2414,
  2811, 3771, 5550

**Mississippi Blues**
Goonan, Kathleen Ann  **2274**, 3931

**The Mist**
King, Stephen  5263

**Mistletoe Mayhem**
Dalby, Richard  **1311**, 2276, 2894

**Mistress of Ambiguities**
Rivkin, J.F.  **4596**

**Mistress of the Empire**
Feist, Raymond E.  **1906**

**Mistresses of the Dark**
Dziemianowicz, Stefan  **1715**

**The Mists From Beyond**
Weinberg, Robert  1872

**The Mists of Avalon**
Bradley, Marion Zimmer  224, 227,
  1092, 1190, 1191, 1269, 1270,
  1409, 1498, 1531, 1582, 1741,
  1857, 1960, 1961, 2039, 2188,
  2231, 2232, 2572, 2740, 2745,
  2746, 2767, 2858, 2883, 2939,
  2940, 3017, 3062, 3077, 3352,
  3355, 3357, 3636, 3827, 4265,
  4609, 4610, 4877, 5015, 5270,
  5359, 5397, 5757, 5792, 5793,
  5970, 5971, 6071

**The Mists of Time**
Oliver, Chad  5998

**Mistwalker**
Heald, Denise Lopez  **2637**

**Mistworld**
Green, Simon R.  **2372**, 2414

**Mixed Doubles**
Da Cruz, Daniel  33, **1305**, 1473,
  1919, 2044, 2045, 2047

**M'Lady Witch**
Stasheff, Christopher  196, **5217**

**Mob Magic**
Thomsen, Brian  **5459**

**Mockingbird**
Stewart, Sean  **5273**

**Mockingbird**
Tevis, Walter  1968, 3465

**Moderan**
Bunch, David R.  506

**Modern Classic Short Novels of
  Science Fiction**
Dozois, Gardner  **1612**, 3381, 5954

**Modern Classics of Fantasy**
Dozois, Gardner  225, 228, **1613**,
  5030, 5721

**Modern Classics of Science Fiction**
Dozois, Gardner  229, 246, 422,
  **1614**, 2585, 2594, 2595, 3381

**Modern Ghost Stories by Eminent
  Women Writers**
Dalby, Richard  **1312**, 1715, 2483,
  5814, 5815

**The Modular Man**
Allen, Roger MacBride  **79**, 665,
  5462

**Mojave Wells**
James, L. Dean  **2864**

**Mojo and the Pickle Jar**
Bell, Douglas  **433**, 891, 1584, 4458,
  5456

**Molly Dear: The Autobiography of an
  Android**
Fine, Stephen  2544

**Molt Brother**
Lichtenberg, Jacqueline  2037, 2665,
  3066, 5109, 5467, 5572

**Mona Lisa Overdrive**
Gibson, William  2911, 3491, 3890,
  4099, 4451, 4452, 5841, 5960

**The Monastery**
Williamson, J.N.  3389, 5100, **5856**

**Monday's Child**
Wallace, Patricia  2801, **5623**, 5625

**Mondo Elvis**
Peabody, Richard  4540, 5089, 5957

**Monet's Ghost**
Yarbro, Chelsea Quinn  **6017**

**Mongster**
Boyll, Randall  **616**, 4240

**Monkey Shines**
Stewart, Michael  2429, 5894

**Monkey Station**
Mayhar, Ardath  **3703**

**The Monkey's Paw and Other Tales
  of Mystery and the Macabre**
Jacobs, W.W.  **2846**

**Monsoon**
Rice, Peter L.  **4583**

**Monster**
Tigges, John  2611, **5474**

**Monster Blood II**
Stine, R.L.  1097

**Monsters and Other Stories**
Chizmar, Richard  **1016**

**Monsters From Memphis**
Smith, Beecher  **5098**

**Monsters in Our Midst**
Bloch, Robert  **538**, 1018, 2280

**Montezuma Strip**
Foster, Alan Dean  **2011**, 2033, 2377

**Monument**
Biggle, Lloyd  884, 3344, 5550

**Moon**
Herbert, James  1580, 3128, 3203,
  4471

**The Moon and the Sun**
McIntyre, Vonda N.  **3822**, 5152

**The Moon by Night**
L'Engle, Madeleine  1898

**Moon Dance**
Somtow, S.P.  514, 603, 834, 1126,
  1127, 1822, 2794, 2895, 3053,
  3411, 4002, 4052, 4251, 4946,
  5146, 5151, **5158**, 5421, 5481

**Moon-Flash**
McKillip, Patricia A.  2647, 3404

**The Moon Goddess and the Son**
Kingsbury, Donald  127, 584, 588

**The Moon in Hiding**
Edgerton, Teresa  **1745**, 3510

**The Moon Is a Harsh Mistress**
Heinlein, Robert A.  77, 79, 126,
  134, 419, 478, 587, 588, 894,
  1548, 1915, 1965, 1993, 2196,
  2459, **2645**, 2733, 3437, 3466,
  3603, 3994, 4895, 4931, 4932,
  5132, 5213, 5234, 5241, 5245,
  5365, 5366, 5367, 5370, 5452,
  5566, 5889

**The Moon Maid and Other Fantastic
  Adventures**
Garcia y Robertson, R.  **2120**

**Moon of Ice**
Linaweaver, Brad  443, 1915, 2239,
  4474, 5517, 5518, 5889

**Moon of the Werewolf**
Kelly, Ronald  514, **3053**, 3162

**Moon of the Wolf**
Whitten, Les  1007, 1404, 1570,
  2138, 5442

**Moon of the Wolf/Progeny of the
  Adder**
Whitten, Les  5072, **5791**

**Moon of Three Rings**
Norton, Andre  4055

**The Moon Pool**
Merritt, A.  2257

**Moon Walker**
Hautala, Rick  **2610**, 2928

**Moonbane**
Sarrantonio, Al  **4831**

**The Moonbane Mage**
Marks, Laurie J.  1035, 1815, 2819,
  **3626**

**Moonchasers and Other Stories**
Gorman, Ed  2155

**Moondial**
Cresswell, Helen  1011

**Moondog**
Garfield, Henry  **2138**, 2768

**Moonfall**
McDevitt, Jack  **3789**

**Moonfall**
Thorne, Tamara  1354, 5100, **5464**

**Moonheart: A Romance**
de Lint, Charles  203, 1040, 1159,
  1321, 1472, 1474, 1947, 1958,
  3299, 4382, 4989, 4990, 4995,
  5818, 5913

**The Moonlit Road and Other Ghost
  and Horror Stories**
Bierce, Ambrose  **485**

*Moonrise*
Bova, Ben **587**, 4952

*The Moons of Summer*
Epperson, S.K. **1831**, 4344, 5334

*The Moon's Wife: A Hystery*
Attanasio, A.A. **271**, 1435, 1438, 1491, 2538, 3385, 3386, 4093, 5180

*Moonseed*
Baxter, Stephen **400**

*Moonspeaker*
Wentworth, K.D. 218, 219, **5754**

*Moonstar Odyssey*
Gerrold, David 5561

*Moonwar*
Bova, Ben **588**

*Moonwise*
Gilman, Greer Ilene 43, 335, 1276, 1471, 2105, **2238**, 2739, 3470, 3793, 4475

*The Moorchild*
McGraw, Eloise Jarvis 1143, 1319, 1320, **3816**

*The Mop Up*
Laymon, Richard 4786

*Mordenheim*
Williamson, Chet 155, 1510, 2516, 3613, **5847**

*Mordred's Curse*
McDowell, Ian 1189, 1269, **3806**

*More Amazing Stories*
Mohan, Kim **3949**

*More Dixie Ghosts*
McSherry, Frank D. Jr. 5098

*More Monsters From Memphis*
Smith, Beecher **5099**

*More Phobias*
Webb, Wendy 1279, 1284, 1285, 2175, **5666**

*More Shapes than One*
Chappell, Fred 818, 821, 868, 869, 939, **967**, 2842, 3327, 3575, 4184, 5166, 5417

*More Stories From The Twilight Zone*
Serling, Rod 3132

*More than Fire*
Farmer, Philip Jose **1871**

*More than Honor*
Weber, David **5676**

*More than Human*
Sturgeon, Theodore 653, 1380, 2290, 3011, 3238, 3697, 4643, 4918, 5065, 5910

*More than One Universe*
Clarke, Arthur C. 2547

*Moreta, Dragonlady of Pern*
McCaffrey, Anne 692

*Moreta's Story*
McCaffrey, Anne 3044

*Morigu: The Dead*
Perry, Mark C. 458, 704, 1068, 1180, 1443, 2128, 2674, 3044, 3510, 3842, **4284**, 5223

*Morlock Night*
Jeter, K.W. 403, 1091

*Morningstar*
Atkins, Peter **265**, 1031, 1945, 4496, 4728, 6050

*Morningstar*
Gemmell, David 287, **2190**, 2247, 4808, 5200, 5202, 5221

*Mort*
Pratchett, Terry 1385, 4014, **4397**

*Mortal Engines*
Lem, Stanislaw 850, 3431

*The Mortal Immortal*
Shelley, Mary 411, **4969**

*Mortal Kombat*
Delrio, Martin **1483**

*Mortal Kombat*
Rovin, Jeff 1483

*Mosaic*
Taylor, Jeri 1388, **5403**

*Mossflower*
Jacques, Brian 737

*Most Ancient Song*
Flynn, Casey 203, 1240, **1961**, 3166, 3174, 3358, 3969

*Mostly Harmless*
Adams, Douglas **31**

*The Mote in God's Eye*
Niven, Larry 132, 248, 296, 418, 1001, 1158, 1184, 1557, 1630, 1646, 1650, 1929, 2008, 2062, 2352, 3475, 3821, 4019, 4187, 4356, 5292, 5575, 5679

*Mother Earth, Father Sky*
Harrison, Sue 191, 561, 668, 870, 2166, 2167, 2168, 2169, **2581**, 2857, 3503, 3704, 4320, 4817, 4818, 4819, 5925

*Mother Lode*
Hughes, Zach **2812**

*Mother of Demons*
Flint, Eric **1956**

*Mother of Plenty*
Greenland, Colin **2417**

*Mother of Storms*
Barnes, John 64, 108, **354**, 5258

*Mother of Storms*
Cole, Adrian 563, **1101**, 3268, 5456, 5575, 5582

*Mother of Toads*
Smith, Clark Ashton 348

*Mother of Winter*
Hambly, Barbara 1813, **2506**

*Motherlines*
Charnas, Suzy McKee 208, 1590, 2242, 3863, 4792, 5268

*Mother's Boys*
Taylor, Bernard 916

*Mount Dragon*
Child, Lincoln 99

*Mount Dragon*
Preston, Douglas **4413**

*The Mountain King*
Hautala, Rick **2611**

*The Mountain Made of Light*
Myers, Edward 1105, 3592, 3878, 4020, **4062**, 4207, 5033, 5037, 5396

*The Mountain Walks*
Green, Roland J. **2349**, 4982

*The Mountains of Channadran*
Dexter, Susan 844

*The Mountains of Majipoor*
Silverberg, Robert **5037**

*Mouvar's Magic*
Anthony, Piers **182**

*Moving Mars*
Bear, Greg 102, **421**, 1585, 2584, 2765, 4629, 4633, 5187

*Moving Pictures*
Pratchett, Terry 3573, **4398**, 5875

*Mr. Fox and Other Feral Tales*
Partridge, Norman 2277, **4253**, 4463

*Mr. Murder*
Koontz, Dean R. 858, **3213**

*Mr. Sandman*
Howard, Lyle **2779**, 4874

*Mr. Templeton's Toyshop: Prose Poems and Short Fiction*
Wiloch, Thomas 3851, **5876**

*Mr. Was*
Hautman, Pete **2614**, 5594

*Mrs. Aladdin*
Egbert, H.M. 73, 880, 5658

*Mrs. Frisby and the Rats of NIMH*
O'Brien, Robert C. 1090, 1132, 1527, 2853

*Mrs. Gaskell's Tales of Mystery and Horror*
Gaskell, Elizabeth Cleghorn 4968

*Mrs. God*
Straub, Peter 280, 2241, **5329**

*Mrs. Vargas and the Dead Naturalist*
Alcala, Kathleen **51**

*Mucho Mojo*
Lansdale, Joe R. 1830, **3330**

*Muddle Earth*
Brunner, John **735**

*Mudd's Angels*
Lawrence, J.A. 526, 527, 528

*Mulengro: A Romany Tale*
de Lint, Charles 738, 744, 1249, 2771, 5061

*The Multiple Man*
Bova, Ben 5890

*The Multiplex Man*
Hogan, James P. 1762, 2163, **2727**, 3049, 4130, 4136, 4677, 5680

*A Multitude of Monsters*
Gardner, Craig Shaw 2083

*Mummy!*
Pronzini, Bill 2400

*The Mummy!: A Tale of the Twenty-Second Century*
Loudon, Jane Webb **3526**, 5312

*The Mummy, or Ramses the Damned*
Rice, Anne 616, 2439, **4572**, 5312, 5695

*Mummy Stories*
Greenberg, Martin H. **2400**

*Murasaki*
Silverberg, Robert 689, 1517, **5038**

*Murder and Magic*
Garrett, Randall 3254, 4673, 4793

*Murder at the Galactic Writers' Society*
Asimov, Janet **251**

*Murder at the Place of Anubis*
Robinson, Lynda S. 5321

*Murder at the War*
Pulver, Mary Monica 1040

*Murder in Cormyr*
Williamson, Chet 2426, **5848**

*Murder in the Solid State*
McCarthy, Wil 2723, 2916, **3764**

*The Murder of Edgar Allan Poe*
Hatvary, George Egon 3150

*Murder on Usher's Planet*
Noel, Atanielle Annyn 4470

*Murgunstrumm and Others*
Cave, Hugh B. 537, 1088, 1700, 2780, 2844, 3515, 3516, 5149, 5628

*Murmerous Haunts*
Little, Bentley **3495**, 4231, 5445, 5620

*Music of the Spears*
Navarro, Yvonne 4285

*Mutagenesis*
Collins, Helen 134, 210, **1116**, 1247, 1586, 1769, 2681, 2820, 3236, 3426, 4119, 4476, 5090, 5231, 5430, 5492

*Mutant*
Kuttner, Henry 2474, 2475, 3725, 3726, 3742, 4600, 5039, 6053

*Mutant 59, The Plastic Eater*
Pedler, Kit 108

*Mutant Hell*
Grant, Mark **2324**

*Mutant Legacy*
Haber, Karen **2474**

*The Mutant Season*
Haber, Karen 6053

*The Mutant Season*
Silverberg, Robert 2474, 2477, 2478, **5039**

*Mutant Star*
Haber, Karen **2475**, 3726, 4551

*Mutants Amok*
Grant, Mark 1406, **2325**, 3891, 4599

*Mutation*
Cook, Robin **1165**

**Mutineers' Moon**
Weber, David   35, 378, 379, 382, 405, 753, 786, 933, 1553, 1565, 1599, 1645, 3732, 3733, 3750, 3762, 3944, 4042, 4301, 4421, 4479, 5282, **5677**, 5785, 5863

**Mutiny on the Enterprise**
Vardeman, Robert E.   528

**My Best Friend Is Invisible**
Stine, R.L.   5289

**My Best Science Fiction Story**
Margulies, Leo   1844, 2405

**My Cousin, My Gastroenterologist**
Leyner, Mark   158, 319, 2186, 2847, 2859, **3456**, 3855, 4046, 4606, 5593, 5867

**My Enemy, My Ally**
Duane, Diane   1728, 2062, 2063, 2064, 2296, 3918

**My Father Immortal**
Weaver, Michael D.   419, 499, 656, 720, 724, 968, 1405, 1568, 1569, 2446, 2536, 2847, 3786, 3891, 3999, 4352, 5491, 5492, 5589, 5592, **5659**, 5809

**My Ishmael**
Quinn, Daniel   **4456**

**My Lady of Hi-Brasil**
Tremayne, Peter   3061

**My Lord Barbarian**
Offutt, Andrew J.   5197, 5645

**My Name Is Death**
Birkin, Charles   533

**My Pretty Pony**
King, Stephen   **3136**

**My Sister the Moon**
Harrison, Sue   2169, **2582**

**My Son, the Wizard**
Stasheff, Christopher   639, **5218**

**My Soul to Keep**
Due, Tannarive   **1670**, 3164

**My Soul to Keep**
Hawkes, Judith   **2631**

**My Soul to Take**
Spruill, Steven   **5184**

**My Stepfather Shrank!**
Dillon, Barbara   **1558**

**My Teacher Flunked the Planet**
Coville, Bruce   **1222**, 1391, 4921

**My Teacher Fried My Brains**
Coville, Bruce   **1223**

**My Teacher Glows in the Dark**
Coville, Bruce   **1224**

**My Teacher Is an Alien**
Coville, Bruce   773, 5286, 5289

**Myst: The Book of Atrus**
Miller, Rand   **3896**

**Myst: The Book of D'ni**
Miller, Rand   **3897**

**Mysteries of the Word**
Wiater, Stanley   3556, 4444, 5446, **5796**

**The Mysteries of the Worm**
Bloch, Robert   **539**, 925, 3266

**Mysteries of Winterhurn**
Oates, Joyce Carol   5330

**Mysterious Cairo**
Stark, Ed   1889, 2472, 2473, 3015, **5210**

**Mysterious Cat Stories**
Stephens, John Richard   4144, **5252**

**The Mysterious Disappearance of Leon**
Raskin, Ellen   4263

**The Mysterious Doom and Other Ghostly Tales of the Pacific Northwest**
Salmonson, Jessica Amanda   2543, 2643, 3472, 3705, **4791**, 5211

**Mysterious Island**
Verne, Jules   5376

**Mysterious Sea Stories**
Pattrick, William   2708, 2709, 2732, 3798, 5652

**The Mysterium**
McCormack, Eric   **3780**

**Mysterium**
Wilson, Robert Charles   895, 956, 2239, 5295, **5911**

**Mystery**
Straub, Peter   **5330**

**Mystery Walk**
McCammon, Robert R.   1886, 4073, 5484, 5485

**Myth-ing Persons**
Asprin, Robert   187, 671, 4391, 4399

**Myth-Nomers and Im-Pervections**
Asprin, Robert   180

**Mythago Wood**
Holdstock, Robert   153, 271, 439, 820, 919, 935, 1435, 1438, 1440, 2101, 2105, 2238, 2636, 3291, 3292, 3470, 3793, 3843, 3878, 4159, 4382, 4475, 4797, 4809, 5806, 5817, 5818, 5927

**Mythical Beasties**
Asimov, Isaac   4988

**Mythology**
Hamilton, Edith   5533

**Mythology 101**
Nye, Jody Lynn   235, 1471, 2438, 3910, **4173**, 4435

**Mythology Abroad**
Nye, Jody Lynn   1668, **4174**, 4863, 5379

**The Myths of the North American Indians**
Spence, Lewis   5751

**N**

**N-Space**
Niven, Larry   123, 161, 237, 244, 349, 585, 2490, 2576, 2648, 3187, **4126**, 4953, 5345, 5480, 5551, 5938

**Nadya: The Wolf Chronicles**
Murphy, Pat   572, 680, 2029, 3119, **4052**, 4764

**The Nagasaki Vector**
Smith, L. Neil   142, 143, 593, 783, 1196, 1199, 1563

**Naked Came the Robot**
Longyear, Barry B.   1216, 2573, 4297

**The Naked Flesh of Feeling**
Williamson, J.N.   3553, **5857**

**Naked Lunch**
Burroughs, William S.   319, 2859, 3455, 3456

**The Naked Sun**
Asimov, Isaac   77, 253, 254, 255, 830, 2011, 3425, 4903, 5836

**Naked to the Stars/The Alien Way**
Dickson, Gordon R.   130, **1537**, 1593, 5467

**Name of the Beast**
Easterman, Daniel   **1721**, 2312, 5196

**The Name of the Rose**
Eco, Umberto   3256

**A Name to Conjure With**
Aamodt, Donald   **3**, 671, 1072, 2862, 4481, 5820

**The Nameless**
Campbell, Ramsey   937, 3885, 4254

**Nameless Magery**
Turner, Delia Marshall   **5490**

**Nameless Sins**
Collins, Nancy A.   **1123**, 3100, 3327, 3328, 3329, 3673, 5339

**Naming the Flowers**
Wilhelm, Kate   1441, 2864, **5809**

**Nanodreams**
Elliott, Elton   **1770**, 2394, 4064

**The Nanotech Chronicles**
Flynn, Michael   100, 772, 804, 1517, 1770, **1964**, 2569, 2576, 3001, 3087, 3796, 4118, 4127, 4216, 4706, 4953, 5257, 5259, 5369, 5638

**Nanoware Time/The Persistence of Vision**
Watson, Ian   **5638**

**Nantucket Slayrides**
Shepard, Lucius   98, 3363, 4314

**Naomi's Room**
Aycliffe, Jonathan   **281**, 521, 1836, 2292, 2642, 2874, 3433, 3607, 3675, 5064, 5271, 5463, 5991, 5992

**Napoleon Disentimed**
Peirce, Hayford   3343

**The Napoleon Wager**
Forstchen, William R.   **1980**

**The Napoleons of Eridanus**
Barbet, Pierre   3800

**Narabedla, Ltd.**
Pohl, Frederik   1209, 1995, 4197, 4276, 5645

**The Narrative of A. Gordon Pym**
Poe, Edgar Allan   4371

**Narrow Houses**
Crowther, Peter   **1284**, 2175, 2777, 3112, 3962, 5667

**National Lampoon's Doon**
Weiner, Ellis   2567, 2568, 4562, 4563, 4564, 4565, 4566, 4656, 4657

**Nations of the Night**
Johnson, Oliver   **2925**

**Native Tongue**
Elgin, Suzette Haden   642, 968, 1135, 1582, 1929, 2295, 2445, 3622, 4325, 4486, 4736, 5209, 5268, 5276, 5430, 5634, 5867, 5956

**Natural History**
Perucho, Juan   **4303**

**The Nature of Smoke**
Harris, Anne   **2559**

**Nature's God**
Wilson, Robert Anton   **5903**

**Nautilus**
McIntyre, Vonda N.   **3823**

**Nazareth Hill**
Campbell, Ramsey   **861**

**Near Dead**
George, Stephen R.   **2202**, 3899

**Near Death**
Kilpatrick, Nancy   **3113**, 3253, 3517, 4246

**Nebraska**
Hansen, Ron   626

**Nebula Award Stories 10**
Gunn, James   245

**Nebula Award Stories 11**
Le Guin, Ursula K.   245

**Nebula Award Stories 1965**
Knight, Damon   500, 501, 4031, 4032

**Nebula Awards 21**
Zebrowski, George   501, 4031, 4032, 4033

**Nebula Awards 21-22**
Zebrowski, George   1342, 4824

**Nebula Awards 22**
Zebrowski, George   215, 246, 500, 501, 4031, 4032, 4033, 4822, 4823

**Nebula Awards 23**
Bishop, Michael   4031, 4032, 4033

**Nebula Awards 23-25**
Bishop, Michael   1342, 4824

**Nebula Awards 24**
Bishop, Michael   246, **500**, 887, 4031, 4032, 4033, 4822, 4823, 5871

**Nebula Awards 25**
Bishop, Michael   215, **501**, 1363, 1616, 1620, 1622, 4031, 4032, 4033, 4558, 4822, 4823, 5871

**Nebula Awards 26**
Morrow, James   1620, **4031**, 4822, 4823, 5871

**Nebula Awards 26-28**
Morrow, James   1342, 2401, 4824

**Nebula Awards 27**
Morrow, James   216, 1365, 1622, **4032**, 4822, 4823

**Nebula Awards 28**
Morrow, James   1617, **4033**, 4822, 4823

**Nebula Awards 29**
Sargent, Pamela   1623, 1624, 3751, **4822**

**Nebula Awards 29-31**
Sargent, Pamela   1342, 5489

**Nebula Awards 30**
Sargent, Pamela   2596, 4439, **4823**

**Nebula Awards 31**
Sargent, Pamela   2597, 2598, **4824**

**Nebula Awards 32**
Dann, Jack   **1342**, 1619, 4824, 5489

**Nebula Winners 14**
Pohl, Frederik   245

**Nebula Winners 15**
Herbert, Frank   500, 501, 4031, 4032

**Necrom**
Farren, Mick   **1881**, 3071

**Necromancer**
Dickson, Gordon R.   127

**Necromancer Nine**
Tepper, Sheri S.   1030, 3399

**The Necronomicon**
Price, Robert M.   **4427**

**Necroscope**
Lumley, Brian   1214, 2530, 3347, 4496, 5020, 5120, 5212, 5773

**The Necroscope Series**
Lumley, Brian   3349

**Necroscope: The Lost Years**
Lumley, Brian   **3560**, 5704

**The Need**
Neiderman, Andrew   **4089**

**Needful Things**
King, Stephen   859, 2154, 2652, **3137**, 3497, 4085, 4100

**Needle**
Clement, Hal   621, 2542, 4017

**The Needle on Full**
Forbes, Caroline   4882

**Needles and Sins**
Arnzen, Michael A.   113, **213**, 776, 2698, 3667, 4230, 4313, 5316, 5881

**Negrophobia: An Urban Parable**
James, Darius   **2859**, 3455

**Neighbors**
Pusti, Maureen S.   **4450**

**Nemesis**
Asimov, Isaac   **247**, 4417, 4421, 4962

**Nemesis**
Cooper, Louise   1069, **1177**, 1739, 2862, 3227, 3973

**The Nemesis From Terra/Battle for the Stars**
Brackett, Leigh   2829

**Neon Lotus**
Laidlaw, Marc   118, 313, 358, 433, 522, 560, 562, 725, 763, 936, 980, 1145, 1169, 1172, 1328, 1514, 1543, 1680, 1737, 1881, 1943, 1974, 1997, 2000, 2141, 2231, 2232, 2343, 2499, 2619, 2717, 2771, 2836, 2952, 3167, 3478, 3507, 3591, 3916, 3935, 3966, 3985, 4020, 4060, 4061, 4062, 4630, 4744, 4777, 4866, 4867, 4970, 5198, 5199, 5253, 5376, 5378, 5532, 5584, 5714, 5744, 6071, 6073

**Neon Twilight**
Bryant, Edward   1753, 3237, 3945, 6068

**Neptune Crossing**
Carver, Jeffrey A.   **933**, 1183, 3762, 6086

**Nerilka's Story**
McCaffrey, Anne   638

**A Nest of Nightmares**
Tuttle, Lisa   1827, 2715

**The Nestling**
Grant, Charles L.   834, 2430, 2929, 3140, 3655, 3679, 4441, 5077, 5483, 5769

**Netherworld**
Byers, Richard Lee   **798**, 2321, 2515, 2663, 2664, 4058, 5535

**Neuromancer**
Gibson, William   5, 474, 481, 505, 736, 789, 972, 1238, 1750, 1751, 1862, 1865, 1936, 2011, 2911, 3204, 3431, 3491, 3559, 3604, 3661, 3818, 3850, 3890, 3921, 3995, 4099, 4117, 4135, 4451, 4452, 4821, 5254, 5255, 5635, 5841, 5960, 6020

**Neutron Star**
Niven, Larry   447, 4357, 4706, 4961, 5305

**Never Deal with a Dragon**
Charrette, Robert N.   726, **975**, 1591, 1935, 2077, 2463, 3245, 3641, 4191, 4304, 4363, 4513, 4821, 4909, 5135, 5731

**Never Land**
Clegg, Douglas   **1081**, 3310

**Never Sound Retreat**
Forstchen, William R.   **1981**

**Never the Twain**
Mitchell, Kirk   5504

**Never Trust an Elf**
Charrette, Robert N.   172, **976**, 1591, 1977, 3245, 5135, 5731

**The Neverending Story**
Ende, Michael   87, 713, 1294, 1299, 1432, 3010, 3156, 3468, 3884, 4917, 5972

**Nevermore**
Hjortsberg, William   26, 1564, **2692**, 3150, 3596, 3631, 4344, 4345, 4773

**Nevermore**
Schechter, Harold   4778

**Neverness**
Zindell, David   768

**Nevernever**
Shetterly, Will   767, 769, 1148, 1152, 1400, 2373, 3198, **4995**, 5914

**Neverwhere**
Gaiman, Neil   **2104**

**Neveryona**
Delany, Samuel R.   2457

**The New Atoms' Bombshell**
Browne, Robert   2029

**New England Ghosts**
McSherry, Frank D. Jr.   4876

**New Eves: Science Fiction about the Extraordinary Women of Today and Tomorrow**
Frank, Janrae   24, 765, **2035**, 4825, 4826

**New Found Land**
Christopher, John   1655

**The New Frontier**
Lansdale, Joe R.   217, 3331, 3870

**The New Gothic**
Morrow, Bradford   307, 1351, **4027**, 4180

**The New Hugo Winners**
Asimov, Isaac   888, 2401, 2405

**The New Hugo Winners, Volume III**
Willis, Connie   2401, **5871**

**The New Hugo Winners, Volume IV**
Greenberg, Martin H.   **2401**

**The New Improved Sun: An Anthology of Utopian Science Fiction**
Disch, Thomas M.   4959

**The New Kid**
Pine, Nicholas   5287

**New Legends**
Bear, Greg   **422**, 2596, 2597, 2598, 2634, 2635, 2679, 4169

**New Life for the Dead**
Rodgers, Alan   **4648**

**The New Lovecraft Circle**
Price, Robert M.   148, 461, 3571, **4428**

**New Moon**
Relling, William Jr.   833, 2288, 2793, 3900, 4004, 4005

**New Moon**
Snyder, Midori   3067, 3298

**The New Neighbor**
Garton, Ray   **2154**

**New Noir**
Shirley, John   1128, 2656, 2860, 4250, **5008**

**The New Rebellion**
Rusch, Kristine Kathryn   **4719**

**The New Springtime**
Silverberg, Robert   724, **5040**

**New Stories From the Twilight Zone**
Greenberg, Martin H.   **2402**, 4913, 4914

**New Stories From The Twilight Zone**
Serling, Rod   3132

**New Tales of the Cthulhu Mythos**
Campbell, Ramsey   2978, 3531, 4425, 4426, 4431, 5493, 5494, 5698

**New Terrors**
Campbell, Ramsey   2307, 5924

**New Voices I-IV**
Martin, George R.R.   754, 755, 5952, 5953

**New Worlds**
Garnett, David   **2148**, 2635

**New Worlds 5**
Moorcock, Michael   2148

**New Worlds for Old**
Carter, Lin   606

**New Worlds Quarterly Number 1-4**
Moorcock, Michael   2148

**New Writings in SF 1**
Carnell, John   4721

**New Year's Evil**
August, Michael   5288

**New York by Knight**
Friesner, Esther   3474, 4926, 5096, 5311, 5642

**The New York Trilogy**
Auster, Paul   3201, 3780, 5661

**Newer York**
Watt-Evans, Lawrence   1819, **5642**

**Newton's Cannon**
Keyes, J. Gregory   **3097**

**Next, After Lucifer**
Rhodes, Daniel   283, 2889, 3164

**The Nexus**
McQuay, Mike   1498, 1803, **3860**, 5101

**Nice Guys Finish Last**
Jonas, Gary   2137, **2938**

**Nice Little Stories Jam-Packed with Depraved Sex and Violence**
Hemmingson, Michael   **2655**, 2778, 3176, 3392, 3393, 3397, 5316, 5536

**Nicoji**
Bell, M. Shayne   **434**

**Nifft the Lean**
Shea, Michael   856, 1142, 1239, 1927, 1928, 2451, 3122, 3419, 5471, 5547

*Night*
Rodgers, Alan   338, 3445, 4050, 4575, **4649**

*Night Beasts*
Stetson, T.W.   2615, 2926, 3701, 4815, **5263**

*Night Bites: Vampire Stories by Women*
Brownworth, Victoria   **730**, 1713, 2891

*Night Blood*
Flanders, Eric   570, **1945**, 2313

*The Night Boat*
McCammon, Robert R.   3220, 3964

*Night Brothers*
Williams, Sidney   **5824**

*Night Calls*
Kimbriel, Katharine Eliska   **3119**

*Night Chills*
McCauley, Kirby   1844, 2965, 2974

*The Night Comes On*
Duffy, Steve   **1671**, 3314, 5776

*Night Cruise*
Mosiman, Billie Sue   570, 2313, **4041**, 5853

*The Night Face*
Anderson, Poul   1913

*The Night Fantastic*
Anderson, Poul   1717, 2413, 4543

*The Night Gallery Reader*
Serling, Rod   2402, 2403, 4913, 5473

*Night Games*
Harris, Marilyn   **2562**

*Night Gaunts: An Entertainment Based on the Life and Work of H.P. Lovecraft*
Rutherford, Brett   **4751**

*Night Glow*
James, Martin   2112, **2867**

*Night Hunter*
Reaves, Michael   1793, 2322, 2792, 3108, **4496**

*The Night in Fog*
Silva, David B.   1016, 2701, **5026**

*A Night in the Lonesome October*
Zelazny, Roger   5796, **6072**

*The Night Inside*
Baker, Nancy   **301**, 3253, 4068

*Night Lamp*
Vance, Jack   **5548**

*The Night Land*
Hodgson, William Hope   4371

*Night Launch*
Garn, Jake   **2143**

*The Night Life of the Gods*
Smith, Thorne   1491, 5570

*Night Magic*
Tryon, Thomas   3688, **5485**

*The Night Man*
Jeter, K.W.   862, 2431, **2915**, 2935, 3127, 3679, 4022, 5323, 5825

*Night Mask*
Johnstone, William W.   2825, **2931**

*The Night Mayor*
Newman, Kim   1615, 2470, 2839, 3559, **4099**, 4135, 5614

*Night Music*
Garner, Sheila Bristow   **2147**, 3950

*Night of Broken Souls*
Monteleone, Thomas F.   **3964**

*Night of Glory*
Ciencin, Scott   **1030**

*The Night of Kadar*
Kilworth, Garry   877, 1595, 4592, 4595

*Night of Light*
Farmer, Philip Jose   3617

*Night of the Big Heat*
Lymington, John   914

*Night of the Cooters*
Waldrop, Howard   520, 1615, 3619, 4095, **5614**, 6022

*Night of the Dragon's Blood*
Pridgen, William   4529

*The Night of the Hunter*
Grubb, Davis   1489, 3208, 4183

*Night of the Living Dead*
Russo, John   3091, **4745**, 4834

*Night of the Living 'Gator!*
Lupoff, Richard A.   1603, **3573**

*Night of the Living Rat!*
Doyle, Debra   493, **1603**, 3573

*Night of the Living Shark!*
Bischoff, David   **493**, 1456, 1603, 3573, 5934

*The Night of the Moonbow*
Tryon, Thomas   **5486**

*Night of the Ripper*
Bloch, Robert   535, 2931, 5761

*The Night of the Solstice*
Smith, L.J.   5070

*The Night of the Twin Moons*
Lorrah, Jean   528

*The Night of Wishes: Or, The Satanarchaeolidealcohellish Notion Potion*
Ende, Michael   489, 1527, **1821**

*The Night of Wishes: or The Satanarchaeolidealcohellish Notion Potion*
Ende, Michael   2085, 2776, 5163

*The Night Parade*
Ciencin, Scott   1289, 1290, 3538, 4800

*Night Prayers*
Cacek, P.D.   **803**, 3623

*Night Prophets*
Olson, Paul F.   3656, **4213**

*Night Relics*
Blaylock, James P.   **521**, 608, 1560, 2687, 4383

*Night School*
Pine, Nicholas   1302, 4328, 5161

*Night Screams*
Gorman, Ed   **2278**

*The Night Seasons*
Williamson, J.N.   3134, **5858**

*Night Shapes: Excursions into Terror*
Nolan, William F.   3216, 3686, 3687, **4132**, 5901

*Night Shift*
King, Stephen   3753

*Night-Side: Eighteen Tales*
Oates, Joyce Carol   626, 2641

*Night-Side of Nature*
Crowe, Catherine   2158

*Night Sky Mine*
Scott, Melissa   **4898**, 4930

*Night Slaves*
Sohl, Jerry   5358

*Night Songs*
Grant, Charles L.   4715

*Night Sounds*
Lee, Warner   **3415**

*The Night Stalker*
Rice, Jeff   106, 112, 2114

*The Night Strangler*
Rice, Jeff   106, 2114

*Night Terrors: Stories of Shadow and Substance*
Duncan, Lois   **1693**

*Night Things*
Monteleone, Thomas F.   3054

*Night Things*
Talbot, Michael   **5380**

*Night Thirst*
Whalen, Patrick   3051, 4102, **5770**

*Night Thunder*
Jensen, Ruby Jean   **2903**

*Night Train*
Amis, Martin   5661

*Night Visions 1*
Ryan, Alan   1885

*Night Visions 2*
Grant, Charles L.   1885

*Night Visions 3*
Martin, George R.R.   1885, 3363

*Night Visions 5*
Winter, Douglas E.   1885

*Night Visions 8*
Farris, John   1885

*Night Visions 9*
Tessier, Thomas   **5441**

*The Night Visions Series*
Various Authors   98, 4314

*The Night Watch*
Stewart, Sean   **5274**

*The Night We Buried Road Dog*
Cady, Jack   **818**, **819**

*Nightbirds on Nantucket*
Aiken, Joan   5977

*Nightblood*
Martindale, T. Chris   **3656**, 4213

*Nighteyes*
Reeves-Stevens, Garfield   157, 1930, 2542, **4510**, 5341

*Nightfall*
Asimov, Isaac   **248**, 4762

*Nightfeeder*
Reeves-Stevens, Judith   **4513**

*The Nightingale*
Dalkey, Kara   42, 375, 1358, 1446, 1479, 6088, 6090

*Nightlife*
Ellis, Jack   **1779**

*Nightlife*
Hodge, Brian   **2702**, 3101

*Nightlight*
Cadnum, Michael   **813**, 2638, 4830, 5402

*Nightmare*
Epperson, S.K.   **1832**, 5464

*Nightmare Abbey*
Peacock, Thomas Love   3526

*The Nightmare Dream*
Caspian, Jonatha Adriane   5438

*The Nightmare Factory*
Ligotti, Thomas   573, **3462**, 3532

*Nightmare Flower*
Engstrom, Elizabeth   802, **1827**, 5521

*Nightmare Jack and Other Stories*
Metcalfe, John   **3879**, **3880**

*Nightmare Logic*
Hall, Matthew   **2495**

*Nightmare Need*
Brennan, Joseph Payne   4752

*The Nightmare People*
Watt-Evans, Lawrence   2302, 2344, 2345, 3091, **5643**

*Nightmare Seasons*
Grant, Charles L.   3132

*Nightmare, with Angel*
Gallagher, Stephen   **2111**, 2755

*Nightmare World*
Stern, David   **5261**

*Nightmares and Dreamscapes*
King, Stephen   **3138**

*Nightmare's Disciple*
Pulver, Joseph S. Jr.   4112, **4449**

*Nightmares in Dixie*
McSherry, Frank D. Jr.   2230, 5098, 5099, 5155

*Nightmares on Elm Street: Freddy Krueger's Seven Sweetest Dreams*
Greenberg, Martin H.   460, **2403**

*Nightpool*
Murphy, Shirley Rousseau   4485, 4490, 4493

*The Nightrunners*
Lansdale, Joe R.   862, 945, 2341, 2556, 2871, 3208, 3527, 3638, 4254, 4471, 4837, 5969, 5987

*Nights at the Circus*
Carter, Angela   1697, 2091

**Night's Black Agents**
Leiber, Fritz  5047

**Night's Master**
Lee, Tanith  1140

**Nights of the Round Table**
Lawrence, Margery  3360

**Night's Pawn**
Dowd, Tom  **1591**, 5096, 5135

**Nightscape**
George, Stephen R.  **2203**, 2555, 2748

**Nightseer**
Hamilton, Laurell K.  172, 673, 681, 763, 841, 994, 1253, 1674, 1687, 1744, 1837, 2039, 2268, 2269, 2358, 2503, 2509, **2521**, 2862, 2956, 3074, 3080, 3105, 3167, 3168, 3277, 3306, 3486, 3509, 3511, 3514, 3775, 3839, 3936, 4129, 4323, 4459, 4489, 4527, 4686, 4768, 4804, 5127, 5144, 5266, 5584, 5750, 5812, 5967, 5978, 5980

**Nightshade**
Butler, Jack  **789**, 2440, 3244, 3458, 3547, 4072

**Nightshade**
Hamilton, Laurell K.  1383

**Nightshade**
Moore, Stanley R.  **3992**

**Nightside City**
Watt-Evans, Lawrence  **5644**

**Nightside the Long Sun**
Wolfe, Gene  567, 892, 2057, 2243, 2626, **5943**

**Nightsword**
Weis, Margaret  **5722**

**Nightwalker**
Hagar, Jean  1829

**The Nightwalker**
Tessier, Thomas  1349, 2222, 4780, **5442**, 5861

**Nightwatch**
Bailey, Robin Wayne  17, **289**, 844, 4390, 5087

**Nightwatch**
Stephenson, Andrew  111

**Nightwing**
Smith, Martin Cruz  2615, 2926, 4688, 4815, 5263

**Nightwings**
Silverberg, Robert  4152

**Nightworld**
Wilson, F. Paul  1721, 3445, 5340, **5893**

**The Nihilesthete**
Kalich, Richard  **3002**

**Nimbus**
Jablokov, Alexander  **2839**

**The Nimrod Hunt**
Sheffield, Charles  3665, 4289, 4557

**The Nine Billion Names of God**
Clarke, Arthur C.  4956

**Nine by Laumer**
Laumer, Keith  592

**The Nine Gates**
Brugalette, Philip  1293

**Nine Ghosts**
Malden, R.H.  1350, 5611

**Nine Hard Questions about the Nature of the Universe**
Shiner, Lewis  **4998**

**Nine Horrors and a Dream**
Brennan, Joseph Payne  534, 2844, 5211

**Nine Levels Down**
Dantz, William  **1347**

**The Nine Lives of Catseye Gomez**
Hawke, Simon  **2620**

**Nine Princes in Amber**
Zelazny, Roger  162, 164, 477, 746, 747, 1102, 1162, 1180, 1181, 1635, 1637, 1648, 1678, 1684, 1686, 1732, 1813, 1864, 1871, 2361, 2628, 2639, 3386, 3635, 3636, 3645, 3799, 3802, 3803, 3804, 3848, 3849, 3978, 3980, 3985, 4165, 4488, 4517, 4522, 4523, 4670, 4994, 5017, 5041, 5364, 5683, 5716, 5727, 5812, 5813, 6001

**The Ninety Trillion Fausts**
Chalker, Jack L.  **958**

**The Ninth Configuration**
Blatty, William Peter  5898

**No Blade of Grass**
Christopher, John  4262

**No Blood Spilled**
Daniels, Les  **1338**, 2742, 4097, 4770, 6011

**No, but I Saw the Movie**
Wheeler, David  5460, 5947

**No Enemy but Time**
Bishop, Michael  175, 188, **502**, 1525, 2434, 4039

**No Kidding**
Brooks, Bruce  511, **709**

**No Limits**
Findley, Nigel  **1938**, 5828

**No Man's World**
Bulmer, Kenneth  3861

**No Need for Heroes**
Keaney, Brian  5995

**No Night Without Stars**
Norton, Andre  4619

**No One Noticed the Cat**
McCaffrey, Anne  **3740**, 4054

**No Quarter**
Huff, Tanya  **2798**

**No Safe Place**
Moroz, Anne  3748, 4285

**Nobody's Son**
Stewart, Sean  3070, **5275**, 6066

**Noctet: Tales of Madonna-Moloch**
Manachino, Albert J.  **3613**

**Noctuary**
Ligotti, Thomas  3447, **3463**, 3530, 5876

**Nocturnas**
Ryan, Shawn  279, 4529, **4755**

**Noir**
Jeter, K.W.  **2916**

**Noise and Other Night Terrors**
Streeter, Newton E.  2937, **5335**

**Nomad**
Alexander, David  47, 50, **66**, 830, 1405

**The Nomad**
Hawke, Simon  1977

**Nomad**
Smith, George O.  5864

**The Nomad Queen**
White, James Gordon  **5783**

**Non-Stop**
Aldiss, Brian W.  **58**, 4626, 5937, 5943

**None but Man**
Dickson, Gordon R.  595

**None So Blind**
Haldeman, Joe  2120, **2490**

**Noonblaze**
Chiba, Milan  1916

**Norby and the Court Jester**
Asimov, Janet  **252**

**Norby and the Oldest Dragon**
Asimov, Janet  **253**

**Norby and Yobo's Great Adventure**
Asimov, Janet  **254**

**The Norby Chronicles**
Asimov, Janet  1217

**Norby Down to Earth**
Asimov, Janet  **255**, 5381

**Norby, the Mixed-up Robot**
Asimov, Janet  1223, 4338

**Norby Through Time and Space**
Asimov, Janet  3803

**Norgil, More Tales of Prestidigetection**
Gibson, Walter B.  1187

**Norgil the Magician**
Gibson, Walter B.  1187

**Norstrilia**
Smith, Cordwainer  77, 250, 1680, 1723, 1725, 2049, 2536, 2645, 2649, 3240, 3797, 4054, 4698, 4931, **5105**, 5117, 5157, 5213, 5452, 5566, 5586, 5589, 5809, 5834, 5835

**North Wind**
Jones, Gwyneth  **2953**

**Northern Chills**
Hurry, Graeme  2815

**Northern Frights**
Hutchison, Don  **2813**

**Northern Frights 2**
Hutchison, Don  **2814**

**Northern Frights 3**
Hutchison, Don  **2815**

**The Northern Girl**
Lynn, Elizabeth A.  644

**Northern Stars: The Anthology of Canadian Science Fiction**
Hartwell, David G.  1767, **2593**, 4439

**Northern Tales: Traditional Stories of Eskimo and Indian Peoples**
Norman, Howard  40, 190, 5578

**Northlight**
Wheeler, Deborah  1026, **5775**

**Northwest Smith**
Moore, C.L.  1069

**Northworld**
Drake, David  1315, **1637**, 1661, 1862, 1955, 2350, 4204, 5294

**The Norton Book of Ghost Stories**
Leithauser, Brad  2483, **3432**

**The Norton Book of Science Fiction: North American Science Fiction, 1960-1990**
Le Guin, Ursula K.  229, 246, 422, 888, 1612, 1617, 1619, 1622, 1623, 1624, 2585, 2593, 2594, 2595, **3381**

**Not Broken, Not Belonging**
Fox, Randy  1044, **2030**, 2137

**Not for Glory**
Rosenberg, Joel  589, 1322, 1327, 2435

**Not Long for This World**
Derleth, August  534

**Nothing Sacred**
Scarborough, Elizabeth Ann  313, 314, 560, 562, 725, 891, 1169, 1328, 1412, 1881, 1932, 2552, 2578, 2716, 3503, 3744, 3745, 3878, 4020, 4061, 4062, 4063, **4867**, 5198, 5378, 5396, 5532, 5757

**The Notorious Abbess**
Chapman, Vera  **965**

**Nova**
Delany, Samuel R.  5943

**Nova Express**
Burroughs, William S.  3457, 4581

**Novelty**
Crowley, John  **1278**, 5633, 5945

**Now and Then**
Hutchinson, Bobby  691

**Now Begins Tomorrow**
Knight, Damon  1609

**Now We Are Sick**
Gaiman, Neil  486, 4274

**Now You See It...**
Matheson, Richard  **3688**, 5485

**Now You See It/Him/Them...**
DeWeese, Gene  4546, 5697

**Null-A Three**
Van Vogt, A.E.  2217, 5621

**Nul's Quest**
Strickland, Brad  3, 4, 3309

**The Number of the Beast**
Heinlein, Robert A.   135, 302, 951, 5159

**Number Seven, Queer Street**
Lawrence, Margery   601

**Numbers in the Dark and Other Stories**
Calvino, Italo   **850**, 3571

**Nursery Crimes**
Dziemianowicz, Stefan   **1716**

**Nutcracker**
Hoffmann, E.T.A.   2654, **2719**

**The Nyarlathotep Cycle**
Price, Robert M.   **4429**


# O

**O Greenest Branch!**
Baudino, Gael   **394**, 3297

**O Pioneer!**
Pohl, Frederik   **4350**

**The Oak Above the Kings: A Book of the Keltiad**
Kennealy, Patricia   **3058**

**Oasis**
Hodge, Brian   858, **2703**, 5472

**The Oath and the Measure**
Williams, Michael   4368

**Oath of Fealty**
Niven, Larry   585, 2349

**Oath of Gold**
Moon, Elizabeth   962, 1101, 1156, 1737, 1738, 3069, 3077, 3892, 3903, 4490, 5714, 5739, 5740, 5742

**Oath of Swords**
Weber, David   **5678**

**Oathblood**
Lackey, Mercedes   **3290**

**The Oathbound**
Lackey, Mercedes   2553, 3906, 4596, 4613

**The Oathbound Wizard**
Stasheff, Christopher   **5219**

**Oaths and Miracles**
Kress, Nancy   **3242**

**An Oblique Approach**
Drake, David   770, **1638**, 1956

**The Oboler Omnibus**
Oboler, Arch   339, 344, 1022, 1112

**The Observers**
Knight, Damon   594, 1666

**Obsessed**
Reed, Rick R.   695, 2156, 3585, **4500**

**Obsession**
Campbell, Ramsey   1195, 2339, 2415, 2652, 4085, 5400

**Obsessions**
Raisor, Gary L.   1279, 1284, 1285, 2384, 2601, 2777, 3024, **4465**, 5666, 5667

**The Obsidian Oracle**
Denning, Troy   2621

**The Occult Files of Francis Chard: Some Ghost Stories**
Burrage, A.M.   258, 509

**Ocean under the Ice**
Forward, Robert L.   **1988**

**Octagon**
Saberhagen, Fred   118, 1858

**Octagon Magic**
Norton, Andre   2943

**October**
Sarrantonio, Al   2221, 3676, **4832**

**The October Country**
Bradbury, Ray   **623**, 819, 2319, 4832, 4916, 5901

**October the First Is Too Late**
Hoyle, Fred   5295, 5906

**The Odd Lot: The Selected Works of Albert J. Manachino**
Manachino, Albert J.   **3614**, 4463, 5335, 5881

**Oddkins**
Koontz, Dean R.   40, 347, 3523

**Odyssey**
Kube-McDowell, Michael P.   78

**Of All Possible Worlds**
Tenn, William   1874

**Of Beginnings and Endings**
Adams, Robert   **33**

**Of Masques and Martyrs**
Golden, Christopher   **2258**

**Of Men and Monsters**
Tenn, William   1015, 3342, 5303

**Of Saints and Shadows**
Golden, Christopher   303, **2259**, 2512, 2518, 2602, 3409, 5421

**Of Tangible Ghosts**
Modesitt, L.E. Jr.   682, **3935**

**Of the Fall**
McAuley, Paul J.   **3713**, 3946, 4547

**Off Limits: Tales of Alien Sex**
Datlow, Ellen   **1362**, 1607

**The Off Season**
Cady, Jack   389, 518, 636, **820**, 2029, 2104, 2240, 2687, 2817, 3124, 3809, 4104, 4382, 4383, 4992, 5145, 5440, 5530, 5570

**Off Season**
Ketchum, Jack   2611, 3387, 3391

**Officer Cadet**
Shelley, Rick   **4973**

**Offspring**
Ketchum, Jack   1051, 1828, 2611, **3092**, 3369, 3387, 3391, 5474, 5685

**The Offspring**
McKenney, Kenneth   3826

**Ogre Castle**
Hale, F.J.   4397

**The Ogre Downstairs**
Jones, Diana Wynne   1220, 2075, 2076, **2949**, 5478, 5968

**Oh God!**
Corman, Avery   1577

**Oktober**
Gallagher, Stephen   **2112**

**An Old Friend of the Family**
Saberhagen, Fred   2517, 4097, 4098

**The Old Funny Stuff**
Effinger, George Alec   **1753**

**The Old Gods Waken**
Wellman, Manly Wade   715, 3272

**The Old Man and Mr. Smith**
Ustinov, Peter   **5532**, 5569, 5768

**Old Nathan**
Drake, David   **1639**, 2191, 2367, 3118, 5356, 5357

**Old Possum's Book of Practical Cats**
Eliot, T.S.   4273

**Old Tin Sorrows**
Cook, Glen   **1151**, 2228

**Old Town Fireside Stories**
Stowe, Harriet Beecher   2919

**The Old Wives' Fairy Tale Book**
Carter, Angela   3574, 5814

**The Olivia Trilogy**
Yarbro, Chelsea Quinn   678, 3151, 3781

**Olympus**
Greenberg, Martin H.   **2404**

**Omega**
Lynch, Patrick   2206, **3577**, 3632

**The Omen**
Seltzer, David   2312, 3445, 3958, 5401, 5538

**Omni Best Science Fiction One**
Datlow, Ellen   **1363**

**Omni Best Science Fiction Three**
Datlow, Ellen   216, **1364**, 1622

**Omni Visions One**
Datlow, Ellen   **1365**

**Omnibus of Speed**
Beaumont, Charles   4308

**The Omnibus of Twentieth Century Ghost Stories**
Phillips, Robert   **4311**

**On a Darkling Plain**
Byers, Richard Lee   2513, 2515, 2604, 5585

**On a Pale Horse**
Anthony, Piers   1416, 4358

**On Basilisk Station**
Weber, David   310, 1043, 1047, 1254, 1546, 1598, 1901, 1978, 2366, 3865, 3970, 3974, 3976, 5117, 5138, 5139, 5140, 5362, **5679**, 5718

**On Crusade**
Kurtz, Katherine   3260

**On Fortune's Wheel**
Voigt, Cynthia   980, **5579**

**On Meeting Witches at Wells**
Gorog, Judith   **2283**

**On My Way to Paradise**
Wolverton, Dave   475, 3037, 3450, 3451, 4191, 4193, 4618, 4884, 5006, 5278, 5279, 5280, 5281, 5283, 5841, **5955**, 6061

**On Our Way to the Future**
Carr, Terry   1609

**On Stranger Tides**
Powers, Tim   4661, 5842

**On the Beach**
Shute, Nevil   3966

**On the Far Side of the Cadillac Desert with Dead Folks**
Lansdale, Joe R.   4251

**On the Planet of Bottled Brains**
Sheckley, Robert   6070

**On the Road to Baghdad**
Guneli, Gun   6082

**On the Run**
Golden, Christie   **2254**

**On the Verge**
Green, Roland J.   **2350**

**On Wings of Magic**
Norton, Andre   3906

**Once a Hero**
Moon, Elizabeth   1046, 2432, **3970**, 5669

**Once a Hero**
Stackpole, Michael A.   973, 977, 1091, 4796, 4808, **5203**

**The Once and Future King**
White, T.H.   96, 266, 1092, 2188, 2572, 2745, 2767, 3352

**A Once and Future Love**
Kelleher, Anne   **3039**

**Once upon a Galaxy**
Sherman, Josepha   **4987**

**Once upon a More Enlightened Time**
Garner, James Finn   1578, 1942, 2845, 5557, 5617

**Once upon a More Enlightened Time: More Politically Correct Bedtime Stories**
Garner, James Finn   **2144**

**Once upon a Time: A Treasury of Modern Fairy Tales**
Del Rey, Lester   225, 606, 1359, 1366, 1368, **1479**, 1576, 2378, 6044, 6045, 6046, 6087, 6088, 6090

**Once upon a Time in the East**
Fenn, Lionel   1398

**The One-Armed Queen**
Yolen, Jane   **6037**

**One Day Closer to Death**
Denton, Bradley   **1492**

**One Foot in the Grave**
Simmons, Wm. Mark   5062

**One for the Morning Glory**
Barnes, John   169, **355**, 1082, 5178

**One Hundred Years of Science Fiction**
Knight, Damon   1618

**One Hundred Years of Solitude**
Garcia Marquez, Gabriel   52, 950,
   1411, 1412, 4263, 4475

**One King's Way**
Harrison, Harry   **2572**

**One Land, One Duke**
Emerson, Ru   **1809**, 3282

**One Man's Universe**
Sheffield, Charles   236, 2979, **4961**

**One Mind's Eye**
Tyers, Kathy   **5525**

**One Ordinary Day, with Peanuts**
Jackson, Shirley   5166

**One Quest, Hold the Dragons**
Costikyan, Greg   **1208**

**The One Safe Place**
Campbell, Ramsey   **862**, 4011

**One Side Laughing: Stories Unlike
   Other Stories**
Knight, Damon   61, 503, 2547, **3187**,
   3796, 5805

**One Winter in Eden**
Bishop, Michael   3086, 5369

**One Wish**
Card, C.J.   **880**, 5658

**The Oni**
Linzner, Gordon   1335, 5800

**Only Begotten Daughter**
Morrow, James   433, 1165, 1506,
   1817, 1877, 2196, 2249, 3084,
   3311, 3480, 3542, 3627, 3860,
   **4034**, 4567, 5195, 5277, 5616,
   5911, 5958

**Only Child**
Hoover, H.M.   230, **2764**

**The Only Thing to Fear**
Morgan, Robert   **4003**, 5989

**Opalite Moon**
Vitola, Denise   1400, 2513, **5577**

**Open to the Public**
Spark, Muriel   2842, **5166**

**Operation Chaos**
Anderson, Poul   162, 2574, 4055,
   4360

**Operation Damocles**
Fellows, Oscar L.   **1915**, **1916**

**Operation Excalibur**
Keith, William H. Jr.   2350

**Operation Iron Fist**
Stine, G. Harry   49

**Operation Steel Band**
Stine, G. Harry   3013

**Operation Synbat**
Mayer, Bob   1850, 2779, **3701**,
   3901, 4414

**Operation Time Search**
Norton, Andre   1011

**The Ophiuchi Hotline**
Varley, John   325, 1046, 1825, 2001,
   2049, 2050, 2172, 3038, 3943,
   4016, 4560, 4933, 4962, 5354,
   5525, 5866

**Optiman**
Stableford, Brian   66

**Options**
Sheckley, Robert   6062, 6070

**Opus 200**
Asimov, Isaac   5938

**Opus 300**
Asimov, Isaac   5938

**Oracle**
Resnick, Mike   **4551**

**Oracle**
Watson, Ian   3854

**The Oracle at Stoneleigh Court**
Taylor, Peter   3575, 4184, **5417**

**Orbit 1**
Knight, Damon   4721

**Orbital Decay**
Steele, Allen   107, 181, 405, 584,
   597, 757, 764, 996, 1548, 1594,
   2301, 2433, 2486, 2549, 3789,
   4682, 4976, 5188, **5246**, 5258,
   6065

**Orbital Resonance**
Barnes, John   64, **356**, 782, 1970,
   4349, 4643

**Orbitsville**
Shaw, Bob   247

**Orca**
Brust, Steven   **745**, 1030

**The Orchid Eater**
Laidlaw, Marc   **3312**

**Orc's Opal**
Anthony, Piers   **183**

**Ordeal in Otherwhere**
Norton, Andre   1265, 5752

**Ordeal of the Seventh Carrier**
Albano, Peter   **48**

**Order of the Arrow**
Hinkemeyer, Michael T.   1894, **2689**

**The Order War**
Modesitt, L.E. Jr.   1180, **3936**, 6004

**Ordinary People**
Guest, Judith   4240

**The Ordinary Princess**
Kaye, M.M.   5975

**The Original Dr. Shade and Other
   Stories**
Newman, Kim   5339

**The Original Hitchhiker's Radio
   Scripts**
Adams, Douglas   1784

**Orion**
Bova, Ben   1324, 1871, 5544

**Orion Among the Stars**
Bova, Ben   **589**, 3937

**Orion and the Conqueror**
Bova, Ben   **590**, 2140, 2572

**Orion in the Dying Time**
Bova, Ben   **591**

**Orion Shall Rise**
Anderson, Poul   3788, 4602

**Orion's Dagger**
McAllister, P.K.   **3708**

**Orn**
Anthony, Piers   2575, 4595

**An Ornament to His Profession**
Harness, Charles L.   **2547**

**The Orphan**
Stallman, Robert   1188

**Orphan of Creation**
Allen, Roger MacBride   175, 188,
   502, 733, 1525, 2434, 2725, 3703,
   4039, 4547, 4552

**Orphan Star**
Foster, Alan Dean   1948

**Orphans**
Simon, Jean   3406, **5065**

**Orphans of the Night**
Sherman, Josepha   3070, **4988**

**Orphans of the Sky**
Heinlein, Robert A.   58, 297, 4626,
   5042, 5942, 5943

**The Orpheus Process**
Gower, Daniel H.   610, 1078, 1971,
   2157, **2293**, 2872, 3204, 3207,
   4232, 5632

**Orvis**
Hoover, H.M.   253, 254, 255

**Other**
Dickson, Gordon R.   **1538**, 5545

**The Other**
Tryon, Thomas   491, 1081, 1212,
   2021, 2024, 2631, 2632, 2818,
   3088, 3606, 3640, 4091, 4237,
   4240, 4312, 4844, 5065, 5401,
   5484, 5625

**Other Canadas**
Colombo, John Robert   2593

**Other Dimensions**
Smith, Clark Ashton   1700, 5628

**The Other End of Time**
Pohl, Frederik   159, 477, 688, 2002,
   2417, **4351**, 4502, 4859

**The Other Human Race**
Piper, H. Beam   451, 1263, 3316

**Other Nature**
Smith, Stephanie A.   **5145**

**Other People's Houses**
Cooper, Susan Rogers   1829

**The Other Side of the Moon**
Derleth, August   5691

**The Other Sinbad**
Gardner, Craig Shaw   374, 2081,
   2085, **2130**, 4396, 4401, 4549,
   6070, 6087

**The Other Sky/The House in
   November**
Laumer, Keith   2829

**Other Syde**
Straczynski, J. Michael   3679

**The Other Time**
Reynolds, Mack   5036, 6000

**Otherness**
Brin, David   349, 592, **689**, 823

**The Others**
Bonanno, Margaret Wander   453, **565**,
   643, 653, 766, 788, 1956, 2909,
   3581, 3719, 3817, 3994, 4008,
   4062, 4101, 4756, 5174, 5430

**OtherSyde**
Straczynski, J. Michael   192, 2935,
   4022, **5323**

**OtherWhere**
Bonanno, Margaret Wander   **566**

**OtherWise**
Bonanno, Margaret Wander   **567**,
   5037

**Otherworld**
Flint, Kenneth C.   **1959**

**Otto From Otherwhere**
Griffin, Peni R.   192, 605

**Our Angry Earth**
Asimov, Isaac   3932

**Our Children's Children**
Simak, Clifford D.   2870

**Our Friends From Frolix 8**
Dick, Philip K.   2254

**Our Lady of Darkness**
Leiber, Fritz   2335, 3128, 3161,
   3194, 4248

**Our Lady of the Harbour**
de Lint, Charles   **1434**, 4171, 4864

**Out Are the Lights**
Laymon, Richard   3674

**Out for Blood**
Cooke, John Peyton   600, 799, **1166**,
   1541, 1707, 1920, 2116, 2337,
   3853, 5537

**Out of Body**
Baum, Thomas   **397**, 3134, 3267,
   5415

**Out of Phaze**
Anthony, Piers   5225, 5226

**Out of Space and Time**
Smith, Clark Ashton   1496, 3529,
   3534

**Out of Sync**
Haiblum, Isidore   592

**Out of the Dark: Origins**
Chambers, Robert W.   **964**

**Out of the Dark World**
Chetwin, Grace   1319, 1320

**Out of the Deeps**
Wyndham, John   189, 4923, 5541

**Out of the House of Life**
Yarbro, Chelsea Quinn   55, 4303,
   **6018**

**Out of the Night**
Whalen, Patrick   947, 2285, 3956,
   **5771**

**Out of the Ordinary**
Dalton, Annie   1220, **1330**

**Out of the Silent Planet**
Lewis, C.S.   2342, 2416, 4654

**Out of the Storm**
Hodgson, William Hope   5746

*Out of Their Minds*
Simak, Clifford D.   87, 1399, 1413,
   1872, 2791, 3015, 3173, 3768,
   4364, 4869, 4921, 5087, 5148,
   5697, 5934

*Out of This World*
Watt-Evans, Lawrence   153, 206,
   **5645**

*Out on Blue Six*
McDonald, Ian   1278, **3794**, 4750,
   5918, 5919

*Out There in the Darkness*
Gorman, Ed   **2279**

*Outbanker*
Madden, Timothy A.   379, 3448,
   **3603**, 5930

*Outbreak*
Cook, Robin   2720

*The Outcast*
Hawke, Simon   13, **2621**, 5723

*Outcast of Redwall*
Jacques, Brian   **2853**

*Outcasts*
Emery, Clayton   27, 487, **1815**, 1840

*The Outcasts of Heaven Belt*
Vinge, Joan D.   1381

*Outer Space and All That Junk*
Gilden, Mel   173, **2227**, 4338

*Outland*
Foster, Alan Dean   829, 831, 2369,
   4935, 4938, 4940

*Outland Strip*
Sloane, Ben   831

*Outlander*
Gabaldon, Diana   2121, 2540

*The Outlander: Captivity*
Salterberg, B.J.   1211, **4792**

*The Outlanders*
Coe, David B.   **1096**

*The Outlaw Heart*
Jenkins, Vivan Knight   2497

*The Outlaws of Mars*
Kline, Otis Adelbert   3983

*The Outlaws of Sherwood*
McKinley, Robin   2, 2247, 2248,
   2389, 3165, **3846**, 4519, 4609

*Outlaws of Sherwood Forest*
Kushner, Ellen   3846

*Outnumbering the Dead*
Pohl, Frederik   2422, **4352**, 4955

*Outpost*
Mackay, Scott   **3597**

*Outside the Dog Museum*
Carroll, Jonathan   **919**, 1089

*The Outskirter's Secret*
Kirstein, Rosemary   420, 567, 656,
   664, 760, 1643, 1805, 1956, 2271,
   2421, 2443, 2999, **3157**, 3231,
   3399, 3478, 3721, 3732, 3733,
   3734, 3739, 3750, 3819, 3912,
   4038, 4957, 5001, 5037, 5090,
   5456

*The Outspoken Princess and the
   Gentle Knight*
Zipes, Jack   274, 794, 1366, 2144,
   2145, 2146, 5617, 6040, **6089**

*Outworld Cats*
Lovejoy, Jack   **3536**

*Over Sea, under Stone*
Cooper, Susan   977, 1601, 2232,
   3436, 3720, 4322, 4771, 6036

*Over the River & through the Woods*
Simak, Clifford D.   411, 3712, **5047**,
   5344, 5346, 5348

*Over the Sea's Edge*
Curry, Jane Louise   4917

*The Overman Culture*
Cooper, Edmund   5890

*Overshoot*
Clee, Mona   793, **1075**, 3761

*Owl Light*
Paine, Michael   **4235**, 5630, 5824

*The Owl Service*
Garner, Alan   1011

*Owlflight*
Lackey, Mercedes   **3291**

*Owlsight*
Lackey, Mercedes   **3292**

*The Oxford Book of Canadian Ghost
   Stories*
Manguel, Alberto   2813, 2814, 2815

*The Oxford Book of English Ghost
   Stories*
Cox, Michael   1309, 2300, 2483,
   3432

*The Oxford Book of Fantasy Stories*
Shippey, Tom   228, 848, 1613, 2592,
   3070, 3574, **5003**, 5030, 5721,
   5730

*The Oxford Book of Gothic Tales*
Baldick, Chris   **307**, 848, 1314,
   3574, 4027, 4180, 5418, 5439,
   5936

*The Oxford Book of Modern Fairy
   Tales*
Lurie, Alison   225, 228, 1613, 2592,
   **3574**, 5003, 5030, 5721, 5730,
   5814

*The Oxford Book of Science Fiction
   Stories*
Shippey, Tom   229, 246, 422, 1612,
   2585, 2594, 2595, 3381, 3574,
   **5004**

*The Oxford Book of the Supernatural*
Enright, D.J.   2543, 2643

*The Oxford Book of Twentieth
   Century Ghost Stories*
Cox, Michael   **1232**, 2483

*The Oxygen Barons*
Feeley, Gregory   596, 1594, **1897**,
   2433, 3449, 4678, 4682, 4950,
   5526

**P**

*Pacific Edge*
Robinson, Kim Stanley   **4634**

*Paddywhack*
Stchur, John   2199, **5236**, 5539

*Padre Porko: The Gentlemanly Pig*
Davis, Robert   2786

*The Pagemaster*
Kirschner, David   318, 2981, **3156**,
   3214, 5713, 5972

*Pages From a Young Girl's Journal*
Aickman, Robert   5419

*Pain-Grin*
Sallee, Wayne Allen   1128, 2137,
   4230, **4788**

*Painfreak*
Houarner, Gerard Daniel   2656, **2778**,
   3318, 3495, 5413, 5445, 5620

*The Painful Field*
Green, Roland J.   1552, **2351**

*The Painted Alphabet*
Darling, Diana   **1356**

*The Painted Bird*
Kosinski, Jerzy   4303

*Painted Devil*
Bedard, Michael   330, **430**, 5654,
   5655, 5656

*Painted Devils*
Aickman, Robert   5329

*Painted in Blood*
Taylor, Lucy   2656, 3090, 3318,
   **5413**

*The Painted Mirror*
Wandrei, Donald   1335

*The Painter Knight*
Patton, Fiona   **4258**

*Palace*
Kerr, Katharine   687, 760, 1501,
   1695, 2730, **3072**, 3231, 3453,
   4244, 4342, 6079, 6080

*The Palace*
Yarbro, Chelsea Quinn   463, 1797,
   3017, 4770, 4782

*Palace of Kings*
Jefferies, Mike   **2887**

*Palaces and Prisons*
Miller, Ron   980, **3904**

*The Paladin*
Cherryh, C.J.   11, 1815, 2095, 2188,
   3934, 3973, 4167, 5220

*Pale Fire*
Nabokov, Vladimir   4263

*Pallas*
Smith, L. Neil   435, **5132**

*The Palm Dome*
Fulton, Liz   **2094**, 2822

*Panda Ray*
Kandel, Michael   444, 1502, 2837,
   **3011**

*Pandora*
Rice, Anne   **4573**

*Pandora*
Rodgers, Alan   **4650**

*The Pandora Directive: A Tex
   Murphy Novel*
Conners, Aaron   **4495**

*The Pandora Principle*
Clowes, Carolyn   7, 905, 1389, 4514

*Pandora's Planet*
Anvil, Christopher   2880, 4124

*Panic*
Curry, Chris   1038, **1295**

*The Panic Hand*
Carroll, Jonathan   **920**, 1789, 2842,
   5166

*Pan's Garden: A Volume of Nature
   Stories*
Blackwood, Algernon   456

*The Panther's Hoard*
Berberick, Nancy Varian   **458**, 5223

*The Paper Grail*
Blaylock, James P.   389, **522**, 819,
   919, 1091, 1397, 1519, 2028,
   2231, 2627, 2717, 3262, 4104,
   4382, 4384, 4992, 5614, 5615,
   5903

*Parable of the Sower*
Butler, Octavia E.   788, **792**, 1769,
   2637, 2771, 3380, 3862, 3864,
   4836, 4856, 5965, 6009

*Parable of the Talents*
Butler, Octavia E.   **793**, 1075

*Paradise: A Chronicle of a Distant
   World*
Resnick, Mike   496, 1996, 3713,
   3790, **4552**

*The Paradise Game*
Stableford, Brian   3344

*Paradise Lost*
Milton, John   4571

*The Paradise Motel*
McCormack, Eric   1468, 5661

*The Paradise Snare*
Crispin, A.C.   117

*Paradox Alley*
DeChancie, John   31, 86, 493, 959,
   1055, 1490, 2226, 2770, 2804,
   3821, 3825, 4505, 4662, 5076,
   5933

*The Parafaith War*
Modesitt, L.E. Jr.   **3937**

*Parallelities*
Foster, Alan Dean   **2012**

*The Parasite*
Campbell, Ramsey   839, **863**, 4310

*The Parasite War*
Sullivan, Tim   383, **5352**, 5878

*The Paratwa*
Hinz, Christopher   **2691**

*The Parched Sea*
Denning, Troy   1287, 1288, 1289,
   **1486**, 2427, 3121, 3537, 3538,
   4106, 4800, 4803, 4804, 4805,
   4807, 5682

**Paris in the Twentieth Century**
Verne, Jules  **5568**

**Paris out of Hand**
Gordon, Karen Elizabeth  333, 336

**The Parliament of Blood**
Cecilione, Michael  5405, 5407

**Parliament of Blood**
Ciencin, Scott  **1031**, 4666, 5852

**Parsifal**
Monaco, Richard  3356

**Parsifal**
Vansittart, Peter  5153, **5560**

**Particle Theory**
Bryant, Edward  1753

**Partisan**
Swann, S. Andrew  **5365**

**Partners in Time**
Simpson, Pamela  5390, 5393

**Partners in Wonder: Harlan Ellison in
  Collaboration with. . .**
Ellison, Harlan  1615

**PartnerShip**
McCaffrey, Anne  313, 315, **3741**

**Parzival: A Romance of the Middle
  Ages**
Mustard, Helen M.  5015

**Pasquale's Angel**
McAuley, Paul J.  1341, 1457, 2043,
  **3714**, 3841, 4651, 5152

**A Passage of Stars**
Rasmussen, Alis A.  220, 356, 473,
  688, 756, 762, 774, 876, 928, 930,
  981, 995, 996, 1003, 1108, 1262,
  1332, 1337, 1407, 1478, 1503,
  1544, 1545, 1553, 1571, 1574,
  1599, 1604, 1606, 1645, 1661,
  1756, 1774, 1824, 1970, 1986,
  2260, 2419, 2551, 2649, 2785,
  2812, 3014, 3072, 3117, 3248,
  3452, 3707, 3719, 3724, 3735,
  3821, 3830, 3976, 4101, 4123,
  4126, 4160, 4302, 4467, **4482**,
  4557, 4643, 4682, 4897, 4951,
  4957, 4967, 4984, 5229, 5541,
  5671, 5679, 5717, 5720, 5777,
  5821, 5917, 5920, 5921, 5922,
  6079, 6082, 6086

**Passage to Dawn**
Salvatore, R.A.  4326, **4803**

**Passager**
Yolen, Jane  369, 370, 372, 3720,
  **6038**

**The Passing of the Dragons**
Roberts, Keith  56, 57

**The Passion**
Boyd, Donna  572, **603**

**Passion Moon Rising**
Brandewyne, Rebecca  84

**Passion Play**
Stewart, Sean  **5276**

**Passive Intruder**
Upchurch, Michael  2240, 3809,
  5440, **5530**

**The Past**
Defalco, Tom  2256

**Past Imperative**
Duncan, Dave  **1684**

**The Past of Forever**
Coulson, Juanita  **1210**

**The Past through Tomorrow**
Heinlein, Robert A.  479, 2829, 4118,
  4123, 4127, 4346, 5106, 5349,
  5551

**The Pastel City**
Harrison, M. John  3791, 3797

**Pastwatch: The Redemption of
  Christopher Columbus**
Card, Orson Scott  298, **895**, 3083,
  4036

**The Patchwork Girl**
Niven, Larry  585, 4470

**The Patchwork Girl of Oz**
Baum, L. Frank  5654, 5655, 5656

**The Path of Daggers**
Jordan, Robert  **2989**

**Path of Fire**
Ingrid, Charles  **2832**

**The Path of the Eclipse**
Yarbro, Chelsea Quinn  195, 1317,
  1318

**Path of the Fury**
Weber, David  220, 293, 296, 471,
  903, 929, 932, 934, 1602, 1824,
  2209, 2832, 2942, 3037, 3049,
  3710, 3762, 3865, 4348, 5138,
  5355, **5680**, 6079

**Path of the Hero**
Wolverton, Dave  4854

**Paths to Otherwhere**
Hogan, James P.  357, 1026, **2728**,
  3186, 5531

**Pathways**
Taylor, Jeri  **5404**

**Pattern for Conquest**
Smith, George O.  5863

**Patternmaster**
Butler, Octavia E.  4952, 5041, 5510,
  5754

**Patterns**
Cadigan, Pat  **807**, 1520, 1615, 1827,
  2261, 2715, 3442, 4053, 4118,
  4216, 4977, 4998, 5058, 5255,
  5257, 5521, 5614, 5837

**Patton's Spaceship**
Barnes, John  **357**, 384, 1854, 4641

**Pavane**
Roberts, Keith  3917, 5301, 5633

**Pawn of Prophecy**
Eddings, David  287, 704, 717, 994,
  1029, 1105, 1675, 1682, 1688,
  1690, 1904, 1909, 1911, 2096,
  2190, 2268, 2269, 2270, 2271,
  2531, 2618, 2676, 2959, 2984,
  2985, 2988, 2990, 3489, 3765,
  3766, 3833, 3834, 3837, 3892,
  3985, 4490, 4908, 5150, 5203,
  5650, 5651, 5727, 5736, 6073

**The Pawns of Null-A**
Van Vogt, A.E.  5621

**Pawns Prevail**
Niles, Douglas  299

**Peace**
Wolfe, Gene  4211

**Peace on Earth**
Lem, Stanislaw  3313, **3435**, 5074

**The Peace War**
Vinge, Vernor  2603, 2881, 4018,
  4867, 5043

**Peacekeepers**
Bova, Ben  2143, 2726, 4632, 4634,
  5193

**The Peacekeepers**
DeWeese, Gene  923, 1384, 2067,
  2068, 2922, 3524

**The Pearl of the Soul of the World**
Pierce, Meredith Ann  164, 847,
  3159, 3842, 4129, 4154, **4318**,
  5974

**The Pearls of Lutra**
Jacques, Brian  **2854**

**The Peculiar Exploits of Brigadier
  Ffellowes**
Lanier, Sterling E.  4638

**Pegasus in Flight**
McCaffrey, Anne  101, 2474, 2475,
  **3742**

**Pellucidar**
Burroughs, Edgar Rice  3590, 4705

**Pelts**
Wilson, F. Paul  5318, **5894**

**Penance**
Reed, Rick R.  822, 1779, 3395,
  **4501**

**Pendragon**
Lawhead, Stephen R.  **3357**

**The Pendragon Chronicles**
Ashley, Mike  266, 267, 640, 1531,
  2745, 2746, 2767, 3062

**Pendragon's Banner**
Hollick, Helen  **2746**, 3474

**Pendulum**
Christopher, John  1141

**The Penguin Book of Ghost Stories**
Cuddon, J.A.  1309

**The Penguin Book of Modern Fantasy
  by Women**
Williams, A. Susan  3670, 5018,
  **5815**

**Pennterra**
Moffett, Judith  211, 2897, 3249,
  4552, 5092

**Pentacle**
Piccirilli, Tom  3119, 3613, **4315**

**Pentameron or Entertainment for the
  Little Ones**
Basile, Giambattista  849

**The Penultimate Truth**
Dick, Philip K.  **1522**, 4205

**The People: No Different Flesh**
Henderson, Zenna  2717

**The People of the Black Circle**
Howard, Robert E.  4616

**People of the Earth**
Gear, W. Michael  2164, **2166**, 3704

**People of the Fire**
Gear, W. Michael  275, 2164, **2167**,
  2581, 5751

**People of the Lakes**
Gear, Kathleen O'Neal  2164

**People of the Mesa**
Mayhar, Ardath  2166, **3704**

**People of the Night**
Colson, S. Darnbrook  94, **1128**,
  2137, 2655, 2656, 2769, 2860,
  3667, 4789, 5335, 5416

**People of the River**
Gear, W. Michael  731, 2164, **2168**

**People of the Sea**
Gear, W. Michael  2164, **2169**

**People of the Sky**
Bell, Clare  **431**, 878, 3469, 4147,
  5016, 5743, 5744

**People of the Talisman**
Brackett, Leigh  3696

**People of the Wind**
Anderson, Poul  2223, 2224, 3723

**People of the Wolf**
Gear, W. Michael  178, 208, 268,
  275, 1632, 2164, **2170**, 2583,
  4320, 4817, 4818, 4819, 5444

**Perchance to Dream**
Knight, Damon  1717

**Perchance to Dream**
Reynolds, Mack  583

**Perchance to Dream**
Weinstein, Howard  1383

**The Peregrine**
Anderson, Poul  1719

**Perelanda: A Novel**
Lewis, C.S.  1803

**The Perfect Host**
Sturgeon, Theodore  349, **5346**

**Perfect Little Angels**
Neiderman, Andrew  2205, **4090**,
  4839, 4840, 5789

**The Perfect Lover**
Priest, Christopher  2580

**The Perfect Princess**
Radford, Irene  **4462**

**The Perilous Gard**
Pope, Elizabeth Marie  17, 317, 393,
  3017, 3816, 3840, 4870, 5983

**Perilous Seas**
Duncan, Dave  **1685**

**Permutation City**
Egan, Greg  **1761**, 2729, 3831

**Perpetual Light**
Ryan, Alan  1283, 1339, 6031

**Perry's Planet**
Haldeman, Jack C. II  528

**The Persian Boy**
Renault, Mary  5395

**The Persistence of Memory**
Ripley, Karen  1876, 2673, 2678, 4156, **4592**

**The Persistence of Vision**
Varley, John  161, 233, 234, 448, 479, 503, 665, 804, 1061, 1517, 1608, 1874, 1963, 2295, 2490, 2576, 2649, 2659, 2721, 3087, 3185, 3187, 3308, 3604, 3736, 4118, 4123, 4126, 4127, 4346, 4376, 4561, 4636, 4643, 4706, 4953, 4961, 5106, 5245, 5257, 5345, 5348, 5369, 5551, 5613, 5638, 5805, 5807

**Personal Agendas**
Sarrantonio, Al  1387, 3096, **4833**

**Personal Darkness**
Lee, Tanith  **3413**

**Personal Demons**
Fowler, Christopher  **2018**

**The Pet**
Grant, Charles L.  811, 2197, 2431, 2915, 2935, 3127, 4022, 4841, 5323, 5825

**Pet Sematary**
King, Stephen  937, 2030, 2293, 2607, 3206, 3658, 4327, 5539

**Pet Store**
Coffin, M.T.  **1097**

**Peter Cushing's Tales of a Monster Hunter**
Haining, Peter  5653

**Peter Nevsky and the True Story of the Russian Moon Landing**
Batchelor, John Calvin  **388**

**Peter Pan**
Barrie, J.M.  713

**Peter S. Beagle's Immortal Unicorn**
Beagle, Peter S.  **410**, 466, 467, 2398

**Peter Straub's Ghosts**
Straub, Peter  1610, 2396, **5331**

**Petrogypsies**
Harper, Rory  1891, 1893, **2549**

**Phantom**
Kay, Susan  1115, 2200, **3020**

**Phantom**
Tessier, Thomas  857, 1560

**Phantom Banjo**
Scarborough, Elizabeth Ann  393, 395, 424, 604, 634, 1289, 3274, 3886, 3938, **4868**

**Phantom Blooper**
Hasford, Gustav  4477

**The Phantom Coach and Other Ghost Stories of an Antiquary**
Jessop, Augustus  **2905**

**The Phantom Fighter**
Quinn, Seabury  258, 670, 2856, 4315, 5562

**The Phantom of the Opera**
Leroux, Gaston  19, 611, 1115, 3020, 4395

**The Phantom Tollbooth**
Juster, Norton  1217, 2868, 4731

**Phantoms**
Koontz, Dean R.  1698, 2934, 3337, 4413, 5358

**Phantoms of the Night**
Gilliam, Richard  **2233**, 2381, 5665

**Phantoms on the Wind**
Vardeman, Robert E.  1155, 1745

**The Pharaoh Contract**
Aldridge, Ray  **63**, 1604

**Phases**
Moon, Elizabeth  2027, 3279, **3971**

**Phases of Gravity**
Simmons, Dan  388, 431, 3612, 4632, **5057**, 5247, 5540

**Phaze Doubt**
Anthony, Piers  **184**

**Phobias: Stories of Your Deepest Fears**
Webb, Wendy  1279, 1284, 1285, 2175, 2384, 2777, 3024, **5667**

**Phoenix**
Brust, Steven  **746**, 1072, 1737

**Phoenix Cafe**
Jones, Gwyneth  **2954**

**Phoenix Fire**
Forrest, Elizabeth  973, 1159, 1514, 1748, **1974**, 2142, 2309, 2320, 2499, 2658, 3167, 3277, 3485, 3838, 5497, 5697

**The Phoenix Guards**
Brust, Steven  **747**, 1702, 1706, 1730, 1734, 1816, 5017, 5458, 5840

**The Phoenix in Flight**
Smith, Sherwood  310, 1047, 1901, 2366, 4148, 4158, **5138**, 5671, 5673, 5675, 5681

**Phoenix Prime**
White, Ted  5647

**Photographing Fairies**
Szilagyi, Steve  2980, 2981, 2982, 3263, 4929, **5379**

**Phule's Company**
Asprin, Robert  **260**, 1267, 2575, 3811

**Phule's Paradise**
Asprin, Robert  7, **261**, 4148, 4350

**Phylum Monsters**
Peirce, Hayford  1165, 2107, **4276**

**Picking the Ballad's Bones**
Scarborough, Elizabeth Ann  1998, **4869**

**Picnic on Paradise**
Russ, Joanna  5597

**The Picture of Dorian Gray**
Wilde, Oscar  19, 87, 556, 2818, 3595

**Pictures at 11**
Spinrad, Norman  **5173**

**Pieces of Hate**
Garton, Ray  1021, **2155**, 5536

**Pig Plantagenet**
Andrews, Allen  2849, 2853, 2854

**The Pig, the Prince and the Unicorn**
Brush, Karen  1821, 2850, 2855

**The Pigeon**
Suskind, Patrick  913

**Pigs Don't Fly**
Brown, Mary  **727**

**The Pilgrim's Progress**
Bunyan, John  1803

**Pilgrim's Regress**
Lewis, C.S.  1803

**Pillow Friend**
Tuttle, Lisa  898, **5522**, 5816

**Piper at the Gate**
Stanton, Mary  223, 2397

**The Pipes of Orpheus**
Lindskold, Jane M.  2404

**Pirate Prince**
Michaels, Melisa C.  1550, 5241

**The Pirates' Mixed-Up Voyage**
Mahy, Margaret  3156

**Pirates of the Thunder**
Chalker, Jack L.  4594

**Pirates of the Universe**
Bisson, Terry  **506**

**Pirates of Venus**
Burroughs, Edgar Rice  1414

**Pish, Posh, Said Hieronymus Bosch**
Willard, Nancy  3382

**The Pit and the Pendulum**
Knight, Amarantha  **3183**

**Pitfall**
Kelly, Ronald  373, **3054**

**The Pixilated Peeress**
de Camp, L. Sprague  639, **1416**, 5222

**The Place**
Wright, T.M.  1198, 3639, **5993**

**A Place Among the Fallen**
Cole, Adrian  1155, 1927, 2885

**Plague Demon**
Craig, Brian  **1239**, 1979

**The Plague Dogs**
Adams, Richard  3152, 3701

**A Plague of Angels**
Tepper, Sheri S.  198, 558, 1399, 1433, 1481, 1482, 2134, 2338, 2735, 2738, 4130, 5371, **5433**, 5748, 5942, 6047

**A Plague of Change**
Douglas, L. Warren · 988, **1587**, 1599, 2008, 2637, 2953, 3475, 4642, 5363, 5461, 5466

**Plague of Knives**
Silke, James  6083

**A Plague of Sorcerers**
Zambreno, Mary Frances  701, 1218, 4260, 4261, 4323, 5640, 5979, 6043, **6058**

**A Plague of Wizards**
Zambreno, Mary Frances  4700

**The Plague Tales**
Benson, Ann  **453**

**The Plain Princess**
McGinley, Phyllis  329

**The Plains of Passage**
Auel, Jean M.  **275**, 669, 5444

**Planar Powers**
King, J. Robert  **3122**

**The Planet Beyond**
Mudd, Steve  **4043**

**Planet of Adventure**
Vance, Jack  953

**Planet of Exile**
Le Guin, Ursula K.  595, 2870

**Planet of Judgment**
Haldeman, Joe  528

**Planet of the Apes**
Boulle, Pierre  1982, 5514

**Planet of the Damned**
Harrison, Harry  564, 2414, 5231, 5319

**Planet of the Robot Slaves**
Harrison, Harry  **2573**

**A Planet of Your Own**
Brunner, John  1574, 3344

**The Planet on the Table**
Robinson, Kim Stanley  5807, 6067

**Planet Story**
Harrison, Harry  29, 1787

**Planetary Agent X**
Reynolds, Mack  5230

**Planetfall**
Cover, Arthur Byron  288, 1754, 4495

**Platforms**
Maxim, John R.  2668, 2687, 4256

**The Playboy Book of Science Fiction**
Turner, Alice K.  **5489**

**The Playboy Book of Science Fiction and Fantasy**
Playboy Editors  5489

**The Player of Games**
Banks, Iain M.  219, **326**, 1067, 1633, 1938, 2364, 2374, 3106, 4044, 4114, 4115, 4277, 5069, 5140, 5722

**Player Piano**
Vonnegut, Kurt Jr.  506, 1523

**The Players of Null-A**
Van Vogt, A.E.  2217

**Playgrounds of the Mind**
Niven, Larry  237, 2648, 3648, **4127**, 5480, 5938

**Playing Beatie Bow**
Park, Ruth  1138, 4585

**Playing God**
Zettel, Sarah  760, **6080**

**Playmates**
McDaniels, Abigail  2878, 2902, **3784**

**The Pleasure Tube**
Onopa, Robert  4976

**The Pleistocene Redemption**
Gallagher, Dan  **2107**

**Plus**
McElroy, Joseph  3996, 4581

**Pluto, Animal Lover**
Stover, Laren  2429, **5318**

**The Pocket Book of Science Fiction**
Wollheim, Donald A.  5004

**Podkayne of Mars**
Heinlein, Robert A.  1265, 1970, 2416, 2418, 2763

**Poems of Ambrose Bierce**
Bierce, Ambrose  **486**

**Point of Hopes**
Scott, Melissa  1705, 2758, 3257, 3283, 4651, **4899**, 5152, 5758, 5976

**Points of Departure**
Murphy, Pat  790, 819, 1431, 1818, 1827, 2106, 2265, 2537, 2715, 3235, 3279, 3379, 3384, 3736, **4053**, 4878, 5058, 5165, 5410, 5521, 5615, 5641, 5805

**The Poisoned Lands**
Roberts, John Maddox  **4619**

**Polar City Blues**
Kerr, Katharine  476, 761, 805, 891, 1664, 1696, 1725, 1819, 2000, 2092, 2372, 2377, 2475, 2545, 2682, 2684, 2685, 2722, 2757, 2913, **3073**, 3109, 3256, 3830, 4295, 4300, 4305, 4469, 4551, 4747, 4748, 4749, 4858, 4939, 4940, 5109, 5276, 5451, 5836

**Polgara the Sorceress**
Eddings, David  **1734**

**Police Your Planet**
Del Rey, Lester  4931

**Politically Correct Bedtime Stories**
Garner, James Finn  274, 1257, 1578, 1942, **2145**, 2845, 5557, 6089

**Politically Correct Holiday Stories**
Garner, James Finn  1257, 1578, 1942, 2845, 3214, 4861, 5557

**Politically Correct Holiday Stories: For an Enlightened Yuletide Season**
Garner, James Finn  **2146**

**Pollen**
Noon, Jeff  **4135**

**Polymath**
Brunner, John  2393, 5781

**Polymorph**
Westerfeld, Scott  **5767**

**The Pool of Fire**
Christopher, John  221

**Pop. 1280**
Thompson, Jim  1829

**Popes and Phantoms**
Whitbourn, John  1276

**The Porcelain Dove**
Sherman, Delia  1358, 2509, 2758, 3843, 3847, 4899, **4983**, 5275, 5914

**Port Eternity**
Cherryh, C.J.  1386

**The Portent**
Harris, Marilyn  1625

**Portent**
Herbert, James  **2670**, 2824

**Portrait of the Psychopath as a Young Woman**
Lee, Edward  3395

**Portraits of His Children**
Martin, George R.R.  625, 1753, **3648**, 5641

**Ports of Call**
Vance, Jack  **5549**

**The Positronic Man**
Asimov, Isaac  **249**

**Possession**
James, Peter  **2873**, 4310

**The Possession**
Kelly, Ronald  **3055**

**Possession: A Romance**
Byatt, A.S.  334, 336, 1276, 1277

**The Possession of Joel Delaney**
Stewart, Ramona  1237, 2204, 4837, 5066

**The Possessors**
Christopher, John  609, 2302, 3141, 4369, 5643

**Post Mortem: New Tales of Ghostly Horror**
Olson, Paul F.  1610, 2233, 3869, 4206, **4214**, 4644, 5331, 5665

**The Postman**
Brin, David  365, 435, 728, 788, 792, 793, 886, 1405, 1569, 1924, 2603, 2640, 2805, 3082, 3346, 3864, 4074, 4209, 4599, 4678, 4836, 5086, 5212, 5267, 5982

**The Power**
Robinson, Frank M.  46

**The Power and the Passion**
Cadigan, Pat  265

**Power Hungry**
Weinstein, Howard  1383, 2068

**Power Lines**
McCaffrey, Anne  3743

**The Power of Three**
Jones, Diana Wynne  2015

**Power Play**
McCaffrey, Anne  3744

**The Power That Preserves**
Donaldson, Stephen R.  5235, 6058

**Powers That Be**
McCaffrey, Anne  293, 632, 1988, 2010, 2476, 3359, 3503, **3745**, 4356, 5433, 5435, 5437, 5745

**Practical Demonkeeping**
Moore, Christopher  617, 867, 868, 869, 1917, 2519, 3483, 3488, **3989**, 4317, 4395, 4396, 5168, 5324

**Practical Magic**
Hoffman, Alice  1445, **2713**

**The Practice Effect**
Brin, David  2574, 4595, 5830

**Prank Night**
Robbins, David  **4601**

**Prayers to Broken Stones**
Simmons, Dan  821, 4253, **5058**

**Precious Blood**
Graversen, Pat  **2336**, 3413

**Precious Cargo**
Faust, Joe Clifford  **1893**, 3828

**Predator**
Monette, Paul  492, 1483

**Predator**
Wu, William F.  78, 83, **5998**

**Predator 2**
Hawke, Simon  492

**Predators**
Gorman, Ed  544, **2280**

**Prelude**
McConnell, Ashley  4487

**Prelude to Armageddon**
Cartmill, Cleve  2889, 3676

**Prelude to Chaos**
Llewellyn, Edward  2870

**The Premonition**
Laurance, Andrew  **3349**

**Prentice Alvin**
Card, Orson Scott  **896**, 2086, 3842, 5820

**The Presence**
Saul, John  **4843**

**Present Tense**
Duncan, Dave  **1686**

**Preserver**
Foster, M.A.  4592, 4595

**The President's Astrologer**
Shafferman, Barbara  **4926**

**Press Enter/Hawksbill Station**
Varley, John  130

**The Prestige**
Priest, Christopher  1186, 2266, 3439, **4432**

**The Pretender**
Cooper, Louise  604, 1072

**Preternatural**
Bonanno, Margaret Wander  **568**, 4333

**Pretty Pewter Gods**
Cook, Glen  **1152**, 5848

**Prey**
Johnstone, William W.  2824, **2932**

**Prey**
Perry, Steve  492

**Preying for Keeps**
Odom, Mel  3198

**The Price of Blood and Honor**
Willey, Elizabeth  **5811**

**The Price of Ransom**
Rasmussen, Alis A.  311, 356, 876, 1108, 1144, 1407, 1544, 1545, 1588, 1649, 1771, 1937, 1992, 2260, 2649, 2785, 2953, 3117, 3452, 3741, 3821, 3823, 3830, 4123, 4467, **4483**, 4505, 4557, 4897, 4900, 5229, 5367, 5466, 5670, 5672, 5720

**The Price of the Stars**
Doyle, Debra  310, 645, 929, 1043, 1047, 1503, 1553, **1604**, 1901, 2053, 2374, 3722, 3749, 4957, 5138, 5139, 5140, 5141, 5672, 5673, 5674, 5675, 5680, 5681, 6086

**The Pride of Chanur**
Cherryh, C.J.  1041, 1043, 1333, 1384, 1543, 1645, 1647, 1895, 2016, 2099, 2108, 2733, 3125, 3307, 3536, 3735, 4122, 4139, 4143, 4157, 4347, 4657, 5141, 5833, 5917, 5922, 5985

**Pride of Lions**
Llywelyn, Morgan  2746, **3506**

**The Priest: A Gothic Romance**
Disch, Thomas M.  627, **1562**

**Primary Inversion**
Asaro, Catherine  **220**, 2877, 4736

**Primavera**
Block, Francesca Lia  **551**, 5959

**Prime Directive**
Reeves-Stevens, Judith  1554, 2298, 4037, **4514**, 4927, 4928, 4933, 5141

**Prime Evil**
Winter, Douglas E.  2965, 4888

**Prime Squared**
Murdock, M.S.  554, 827, 3036

**A Prince Among Men**
Charrette, Robert N.  **977**, 2619, 4771, 5203

**The Prince and the Pilgrim**
Stewart, Mary  **5270**

**Prince Caspian**
Lewis, C.S.  368

**The Prince in Waiting**
Christopher, John  4919, 5508

**The Prince of Annwn**
Walton, Evangeline  987, 3058

**Prince of Chaos**
Zelazny, Roger  **6073**

**Prince of Demons**
Reichert, Mickey Zucker  **4522**

**Prince of Dogs**
Elliott, Kate  **1775**

**Prince of Havoc**
Stackpole, Michael A.  **5204**

**The Prince of Ill Luck**
Dexter, Susan  **1512**, 5151

**Prince of Lies**
Lowder, James  1287, 5723

**Prince of Mercenaries**
Pournelle, Jerry   129, 308, 1113, 1630, 1642, 1650, 1900, 2054, 2349, 3666, **4377**, 5377

**Prince of Sparta**
Pournelle, Jerry   **4378**

**Prince of Sunset**
White, Steve   **5786**

**Prince of the Blood**
Feist, Raymond E.   1775, **1907**

**Prince of the City**
Herber, Keith   798, 2664, 4058

**Prince of the Godborn**
Harris, Geraldine   5142, 6037

**Prince of the North**
Turtledove, Harry   **5509**

**The Princes of Air**
Ford, John M.   927

**The Princess and the Dragon**
Pazzi, Roberto   1005, **4272**, 5147

**The Princess and the Lord of Night**
Bull, Emma   743

**The Princess Bride**
Goldman, William   69, 713, 1432, 2653, 3010, 5178, 5232

**The Princess in the Pigpen**
Thomas, Jane Resh   329, 605, 969

**The Princess of Flames**
Emerson, Ru   2651, 2799, 4871

**A Princess of Mars**
Burroughs, Edgar Rice   1414, 3983

**Principia Discordia**
Malacypse the Younger   5904

**The Printer's Devil**
Kidd, Chico   **3099**

**Priorities**
Lyons, Lynda   74, 662, 2295, **3579**, 4245

**Prison of Souls**
Lackey, Mercedes   1839, 3490, 4980, 4981

**Prison Planet**
Dietz, William C.   1107, **1551**, 3693, 6059

**Prison Ship**
Caidin, Martin   **828**, 3693, 4017, 4365

**A Prison Unsought**
Smith, Sherwood   4158, **5139**

**The Prisoner of Blackwood Castle**
Goulart, Ron   30, 5997

**Prisoner of Conscience**
Matthews, Susan R.   **3693**

**Prisoner of Dreams**
Ripley, Karen   1046, **4593**, 4955

**Prisoner of Fire**
Cooper, Edmund   583

**Prisoner of Psi**
Johnson, Annabel   5013

**The Prisoner of Zhamanak**
de Camp, L. Sprague   1914, 5319

**The Prisoner Within**
McQuinn, Donald E.   **3861**

**Prisoners and Other Stories**
Gorman, Ed   777, **2281**, 3321, 3327, 3328, 3329, 3367, 4253, 5339

**Prisoners of Paradise**
Cross, Ronald Anthony   58, 1691

**Prisoners of the Sky**
MacApp, C.C.   2246

**The Pritcher Mass**
Dickson, Gordon R.   421, 5032

**Private Demons**
Masello, Robert   2652, **3660**, 4006, 4085, 4100

**Private Memoirs and Confessions of a Justified Sinner**
Hogg, James   722

**The Privateers**
Bova, Ben   2245

**The Probability Broach**
Smith, L. Neil   1655, 1915, 2921, 3109, 3466, 5889

**The Probability Pad**
Waters, T.A.   2076, 2228, 2913, 5170

**Probe**
Bonanno, Margaret Wander   **569**

**Probe**
Douglas, Carole Nelson   1304

**Probe**
Lerner, Edward M.   2215, **3437**, 6060

**Procurator**
Mitchell, Kirk   590, 1955, 2140, 5036, 5503, 5511, 5512

**Prodigal**
Tem, Melanie   1845, 3525, 4023, 5064, **5423**

**The Prodigal Sorcerer**
Sumner, Mark   207

**Prodigy**
Clark, Jan   **1047**, 5669

**The Prodigy**
Hynd, Noel   **2823**

**The Productions of Time**
Brunner, John   3979, 4197

**Profiteer**
Swann, S. Andrew   1067, **5366**

**Progeny of the Adder**
Whitten, Les   1402, 2288, 2510, 2792, 3108, 4004, 4005, 4496, 4508

**Project Farcry**
Ashwell, Pauline   **230**, 4858

**Project: Millennium**
Hoffman, Curtis H.   2753

**Project Pope**
Simak, Clifford D.   5171

**The Promise**
Hughes, Monica   641, **2808**, 3446, 4154

**Promised Land**
Willis, Connie   **5872**

**Prophecy**
Gorden, Greg   2529

**Prophecy**
James, Peter   **2874**

**Prophecy of Darkness**
Howard, Stella   1811, 4912

**A Prophecy of Monsters**
Smith, Clark Ashton   **5103**

**Prophet**
Resnick, Mike   2475, 3064, **4553**

**Prophet of Lamath**
Hughes, Robert Don   701, 1532, 3578

**Prophets for the End of Time**
Donnelly, Marcos   **1577**

**Prostho Plus**
Anthony, Piers   5779

**Protector**
Niven, Larry   132, 596, 688, 1001, 1055, 1259, 1261, 1264, 1726, 1987, 1990, 2108, 2649, 2828, 2836, 2864, 3469, 3994, 4103, 4351, 5059, 5244

**Protektor**
Platt, Charles   **4342**

**Proteus Combined**
Sheffield, Charles   4550

**Proteus in the Underworld**
Sheffield, Charles   **4962**

**The Proteus Operation**
Hogan, James P.   1245, 5516, 5996

**Proteus Unbound**
Sheffield, Charles   **4963**

**Prototype**
Hodge, Brian   **2704**, 3207

**Proxies**
Mixon, Laura J.   **3922**

**Prydain Chronicles**
Alexander, Lloyd   4056

**The Psalms of Herod**
Friesner, Esther   1653

**Psi-Man**
Peters, David   **4305**

**Psion**
Vinge, Joan D.   2474, 2475, 3725, 3726, 3742, 4898, 4930, 4964, 5039, 6053

**Pstalemate**
Del Rey, Lester   2290, 3011

**Psychamok**
Lumley, Brian   752, **3561**

**Psycho**
Bloch, Robert   **540**, 576, 1131, 1777, 2428, 2566, 2638, 3088, 3208, 3336, 3716, 3815, 4185, 4222

**Psycho II**
Bloch, Robert   426, **541**, 620, 1052, 1846, 3103

**Psycho House**
Bloch, Robert   **542**, 4664

**Psycho-Paths**
Bloch, Robert   **543**, 1018, 1019, 2280, 2282, 2600, 3324

**Psychomech**
Lumley, Brian   751, 752, **3562**

**Psychoshop**
Bester, Alfred   444, **477**

**Psychosphere**
Lumley, Brian   752, **3563**

**The Psychotechnic League**
Anderson, Poul   584

**Psykosis**
Baird, Wilhelmina   **296**

**Publish and Perish**
Hynes, James   **2826**

**Puck of Pook's Hill**
Kipling, Rudyard   459, 5310

**The Puffin Book of Horror Stories**
Horowitz, Anthony   1701, 2395

**The Pugnacious Peacemaker**
Turtledove, Harry   5036

**The Pugnacious Peacemaker/The Wheels of If**
Turtledove, Harry   2829

**Pulphouse, Issue 6: Fantasy**
Rusch, Kristine Kathryn   1373, **4723**, 5945, 6044

**Pulphouse, Issue 7: Horror**
Rusch, Kristine Kathryn   4724

**Pulphouse, Issue 8: Science Fiction**
Rusch, Kristine Kathryn   887, **4725**

**Pulphouse, Issue 9: Dark Fantasy**
Rusch, Kristine Kathryn   1373, 4131, **4726**

**Pulphouse, Issue 10: Special Issue**
Rusch, Kristine Kathryn   1257, 2146, 2412, 2456, 2587, 2588, 2589, 3214, **4720**, 4861, 5024

**Pulphouse, Issue 11: Speculative Fiction**
Rusch, Kristine Kathryn   4558, **4721**

**Pulphouse, Issue 12: The Last Issue**
Rusch, Kristine Kathryn   4722

**The Pulps**
Goodstone, Tony   1712

**Pulptime**
Cannon, P.H.   1859, 4345, 4751, 5426

**Puppet Master**
Hawkins, Barry T.   2159, **2632**

**The Puppet Masters**
Heinlein, Robert A.   156, 383, 564, 1197, 2034, 2211, 2344, 2345, **2646**, 3063, 3188, 3218, 3476, 4510, 4944, 5027, 5341, 5352

**The Pure Cold Light**
Frost, Gregory   2087, 2728

**The Pure Product**
Kessel, John   3087

**Purgatory: A Chronicle of a Distant World**
Resnick, Mike   4554

**The Purgatory Zone**
Darnay, Arsen   1981, 2574

**Pursuit on Ganymede**
Resnick, Mike   3983

**Pussy, King of the Pirates**
Acker, Kathy   780

**Putting Up Roots**
Sheffield, Charles   4379, **4964**

**Pyromancer**
Callander, Don   **847**, 1035, 3775, 4045, 4154, 5002

**Python Isle**
Robeson, Kenneth   1870, **4624**

## Q

**Q-in-Law**
David, Peter   1228, 1229, **1384**

**Q-Space**
Cox, Greg   **1228**

**Q-Squared**
David, Peter   1226, 1228, 1229, **1385**, 2501

**Q-Zone**
Cox, Greg   **1229**

**The Quagmire**
Kisner, James   **3160**

**Quake**
Laymon, Richard   3209, **3370**

**The Qualinesti**
Thompson, Paul B.   4109, **5455**

**Quantum Leap: Obsessions: A Novel**
Davis, Carol   5315

**Quantum Leap: The Novel**
McConnell, Ashley   3467, 4487

**Quantum Moon**
Vitola, Denise   1400

**A Quantum Murder**
Hamilton, Peter F.   **2527**

**Quarantine**
Barnes-Svarney, Patricia   2109

**Quarantine**
Egan, Greg   **1762**, 2273, 4420, 4502

**Quark 1**
Delany, Samuel R.   4721

**Quarrelling, They Met the Dragon**
Baker, Sharon   3157

**Quasar**
Nasir, Jamil   **4071**

**Quatermass and the Pit**
Kneale, Nigel   833

**The Quatermass Experiment**
Kneale, Nigel   99, 1022, 4331

**Queen City Jazz**
Goonan, Kathleen Ann   774, **2275**, 3236, 3788, 4858

**Queen Cleopatra**
Mundy, Talbot   2073

**The Queen of Air and Darkness**
Anderson, Poul   1182

**Queen of Angels**
Bear, Greg   126, 127, 294, **423**, 476, 583, 761, 1968, 2727, 2882, 3604, 3921, 4121, 5451

**The Queen of Ashes**
Harris, Deborah Turner   2561

**The Queen of Darkness**
Conner, Miguel   **1134**

**Queen of Demons**
Drake, David   **1640**

**Queen of Sorcery**
Eddings, David   1904, 2531, 2990

**The Queen of the Damned**
Rice, Anne   452, 575, 1882, 2258, 3407, 4096, 4098, 4318, **4574**

**Queen of the Summer Stars**
Woolley, Persia   1741, 2939, 2940, **5971**

**Queenmagic, Kingmagic**
Watson, Ian   4092, 4115, 4707

**Queen's Gambit Declined**
Snodgrass, Melinda M.   652, 955, 2945, 3822, 5125, **5147**, 5510

**Queens of Land and Sea**
Roberts, John Maddox   **4620**

**The Queen's Squadron**
Meluch, R.M.   3722, 3749, **3874**, 5786

**The Quest**
Ahern, Jerry   278

**The Quest Begins**
Pini, Wendy   **4337**

**Quest Crosstime**
Norton, Andre   1011

**Quest for a Maid**
Hendry, Frances Mary   269, 658, 2636, **2662**, 4008

**Quest for Apollo**
Lahey, Michael   960, 1129, **3309**, 3700, 5511

**Quest for Fire**
Rosny, J.H.   275, 2166, 2170

**The Quest for Saint Camber**
Kurtz, Katherine   638, 3696, 4162

**The Quest for the 36**
Billias, Stephen   5612

**Quest for the Fallen Star**
Anthony, Piers   **185**

**Quest for the White Witch**
Lee, Tanith   2760

**Quest: In Search of the Dragontooth**
Green, Michael   1024, **2346**, 3044

**Quest of the Three Worlds**
Smith, Cordwainer   897

**Quest to Riverworld**
Farmer, Philip Jose   **1872**

**The Questing of Kedrigern**
Morressy, John   1677, 2622

**Question and Answer**
Anderson, Poul   1248

**A Question of Time**
Saberhagen, Fred   **4772**

**Question Quest**
Anthony, Piers   **186**

**The Quick**
Cole, Burt   66, **1113**

**Quick Chills**
Enfantino, Peter   300, 1378, **1823**, 2960, 2961, 4199, 4200, 4846, 5602, 5603, 5605

**Quick Chills II**
Morrish, Robert   300, 1017, 2773, 2962, **4025**, 4199, 5025, 5095, 5601

**The Quick Chills Series**
Morrish, Robert   1372, 3997, 5606

**Quicker than the Eye**
Bradbury, Ray   **624**, 5348

**The Quicksilver Screen**
DeBrandt, Don H.   **1449**

**Quicksilver's Knight**
Stasheff, Christopher   **5220**

**The Quiet**
Billings, Patrick   **488**

**The Quiet Pools**
Kube-McDowell, Michael P.   127, **3249**, 4682, 5909

**The Quintessential World of Darkness**
Wieck, Stewart   **5798**

**The Quorum**
Newman, Kim   2652, 4085, **4100**

**Quoth the Crow**
Bischoff, David   **494**, 696, 4186, 5844

**Quozl**
Foster, Alan Dean   173, 1419, 1454, 1455, 1930, **2013**, 2053, 3063, 3910, 4077, 4298, 4365, 5379, 5429, 6062

## R

**R-T, Margaret, and the Rats of NIMH**
Conly, Jane Leslie   **1132**

**The Race for God**
Herbert, Brian   **2666**, 4507, 5033

**Rachel in Love**
Murphy, Pat   1525

**The Radiant Dragon**
Cunningham, Elaine   **1291**, 2785

**The Radiant Warrior**
Frankowski, Leo   33, 1982, **2047**

**Raft**
Baxter, Stephen   81, **401**, 447, 449, 596, 1003, 1247, 1262, 1593, 1645, 1986, 2215, 2829, 3050, 3750, 3763, 3805, 4000, 4122, 4950, 4957, 5000, 5233, 5540, 5937, 5943

**Rage**
Ergas, Elizabeth   **1834**

**A Rage for Revenge**
Gerrold, David   **2210**, 5352, 5878

**Rage of a Demon King**
Feist, Raymond E.   **1908**, 4685

**Rage of Spirits**
Hynd, Noel   **2824**

**Ragged Angels**
Van Hise, Della   **5537**

**The Ragged World: A Novel of the Hefn on Earth**
Moffett, Judith   **3943**

**Ragnarok**
Archer, Nathan   **206**, 1923

**Rahne**
Coon, Susan   2811

**The Raid**
Eickhoff, Randy Lee   **1764**

**Raiders of the Lost Ark**
Black, Campbell   825, 826, 922, 1581, 2257, 3588, 3589, 3590, 3591, 3592, 3593, 3916, 4549

**The Rainbow Abyss**
Hambly, Barbara   704, 739, 747, **2507**

**Rainbow Man**
Engh, M.J.   686, **1824**, 2134, 2237, 3426, 3440, 4900

**The Rainbow People**
Yep, Laurence   3610

**The Rainbow Sword**
Martine-Barnes, Adrienne   407, 1815, 2083, **3659**, 4266, 4267, 4268, 6083

**Raise the Titanic!**
Cussler, Clive   5114

**Raising the Stones**
Tepper, Sheri S.   35, 293, 377, 435, 566, 686, 1769, 1989, 2006, 2037, 3448, 3628, 3738, 4038, 4242, 4503, 4635, 5174, **5434**, 5543, 5575

**Rally Cry!**
Forstchen, William R.   1199, **1982**, 3034, 4799, 5011

**Rama II**
Clarke, Arthur C.   247, **1058**, 2165, 2216, 3398, 4421

**Rama Revealed**
Clarke, Arthur C.   **1059**, 3398

**Randall's Round**
Scott, Elkeanor   1673

**Random Acts of Senseless Violence**
Womack, Jack   3312, **5959**

**Random Factor**
Sherman, Joel Henry   3448, **4984**

**The Random House Book of Fantasy Stories**
Ashley, Mike   **228**, 1613, 5030, 5721, 5730

**The Random House Book of Science Fiction Stories**
Ashley, Mike   **229**, 2594

**Ranks of Bronze**
Drake, David   206, 1955, 1980, 1983, 2188

**The Ransom of Black Stealth One**
Ing, Dean   2143

**Rapid Growth**
Hanner, Mary K.　**2541**

**Raptor**
Zindel, Paul　**6084**

**Raptor Red**
Bakker, Robert T.　**306**, 416, 1256, 1379, 2386, 5067, 6084

**The Rapture Effect**
Carver, Jeffrey A.　806, 808, 1537, 1549, 1805, 2579, 3398, 3661, 4188, 4219, 4483, 4857, 5566, 5592

**Rath and Storm**
Archer, Peter　**207**

**Ratha and Thistle-Chaser**
Bell, Clare　**432**, 4143

**Ratha's Creature**
Bell, Clare　4143, 4144, 4145, 4157

**Ratman's Notebooks**
Gilbert, Stephen　3807, 5327

**The Rats**
Herbert, James　**2671**, 3192, 3992, 4370

**Rats and Gargoyles**
Gentle, Mary　672, 673, 994, 1035, 1068, 1073, 1251, 2056, **2196**, 2521, 2538, 3095, 3274, 3486, 3627, 3766, 4522, 4653, 4654, 4850, 4983, 5203, 5221, 5223, 5371, 5726

**Raven**
Grant, Charles L.　**2314**

**Raven**
Swiniarski, S.A.　**5374**

**The Raven Ring**
Wrede, Patricia C.　682, 1172, 1953, 2039, 2141, 2268, 2269, 2957, 3278, 3486, 4768, 5749, **5978**, 6057

**Raven Stole the Moon**
Stein, Garth　4249, **5249**

**Ray Bradbury on Stage: A Chrestomathy of His Plays**
Bradbury, Ray　1022

**Ray Bradbury Presents: Dinosaur Planet**
Leigh, Stephen　416, 2122, **3427**, 4854

**Ray Bradbury Presents: Dinosaur World**
Leigh, Stephen　306, 1379, 2468, **3428**, 4597, 4853, 4854, 4855

**Razored Saddles**
Lansdale, Joe R.　217, **3331**, 3870

**Razor's Edge**
Norman, Lisanne　**4139**

**Re-Birth**
Wyndham, John　728, 4074, 4678

**Reach**
Gibson, Edward　202, 388, 450, 1058, 2143, **2216**, 5057

**Reality Is What You Can Get Away With: An Illustrated Screenplay**
Wilson, Robert Anton　29, 1784, 1785, 2859, 3457, 5074, **5904**

**The Reality Machine**
Burns, Cliff　778, 3851, 4231, 5663

**Realm of Light**
Chester, Deborah　**1008**

**The Realms of the Gods**
Pierce, Tamora　1319, 4260, **4321**

**Realtime Interrupt**
Hogan, James P.　956, 1761, 2033, **2729**, 3831

**Reap the Whirlwind**
Cherryh, C.J.　3982

**Reaper**
Mizrich, Ben　**3923**

**Reaper Man**
Pratchett, Terry　196, 1603, 2327, **4399**

**A Reasonable Madness**
Dorf, Fran　**1580**

**A Reasonable World**
Knight, Damon　1666, 2955, **3188**, 3944, 5677

**The Reaver Road**
Duncan, Dave　**1687**, 5595

**Rebecca**
Du Maurier, Daphne　2612, 2875

**Rebel From Alphorion**
Tallis, Robyn　**5381**

**A Rebel in Time**
Harrison, Harry　2046, 3343

**The Rebel of Rhada**
Gilman, Robert Cham　1182

**The Rebel Worlds**
Anderson, Poul　3907, 3928

**Rebellion 2456**
Murdock, M.S.　554, 827, 3036

**Rebel's Quest**
Busby, F.M.　2459

**Rebel's Seed**
Busby, F.M.　877

**The Rebirth of Wonder**
Watt-Evans, Lawrence　1299, 1478, 2883, 2942, 4434, **5646**

**Reborn**
Wilson, F. Paul　**5895**

**A Rebours**
Huysmans, J.K.　3595

**Recalled to Life**
Silverberg, Robert　379, 419, 1337

**Receive the Gift**
Marley, Louise　**3628**

**The Reckoning**
Jensen, Ruby Jean　**2904**, 4501

**Reckoning Infinity**
Stith, John E.　**5304**

**Reclamation**
Zettel, Sarah　4244, 5069, **6081**

**Reconnaissance**
McCay, Bill　**3769**

**Recovery**
Dillard, J.M.　1954

**Red Alert**
Bryant, Peter　5023, 5174

**Red Angel**
Longstreet, Roxanne　2159, 2825, 2931, **3518**

**Red Army**
Peters, Ralph　1642, **4306**, 5300

**Red as Blood: Or Tales from the Sisters Grimmer**
Lee, Tanith　1142, 1359, 1366, 1810, 5428

**Red Branch**
Llywelyn, Morgan　1764, 1960, 5359

**Red Bride**
Fowler, Christopher　1086, **2019**, 2428, 4224

**Red Death**
Elrod, P.N.　292, **1798**, 4774

**Red Devil**
Saperstein, David　**4816**

**Red Dragon**
Harris, Thomas　2110, 2159, 2341, 2534, 2825, 3319, 3518, 3899, 3900, 3902, 5084, 5085, 5326, 5328

**Red Dreams**
Etchison, Dennis　3322, 4889, 5007

**Red Dust**
McAuley, Paul J.　2840, **3715**, 5865

**Red Dwarf: Infinity Welcomes Careful Drivers**
Naylor, Grant　3313, **4077**

**The Red-Eared Ghosts**
Alcock, Vivian　**53**

**Red Equinox**
Axler, James　44, 277

**The Red Fairy Book**
Lang, Andrew　235, 1479, 2447, 5310, 6088, 6090

**Red Flame Burning**
Hawkins, Ward　165, 2574

**Red Genesis**
Sykes, S.C.　102, 421, 1585, 2584, 2765, 2840, 4348, 4629, 4633, 4635, **5377**

**Red Hart Magic**
Norton, Andre　464

**Red Iron Nights**
Cook, Glen　**1153**, 1250, 4709

**Red Jack**
Greenberg, Martin H.　5761

**The Red King**
Kelleher, Victor　2986, **3043**, 3105

**Red Limit Freeway**
DeChancie, John　31, 86, 493, 959, 1490, 1545, 2226, 2770, 2804, 3424, 3741, 3825, 4505, 4662, 5076, 5933

**Red Magic**
Rabe, Jean　1289, 3538, **4458**, 4800, 4807, 5723

**The Red Magician**
Goldstein, Lisa　314, 466, 467, 4272, 5079, 5983

**Red Mars**
Robinson, Kim Stanley　102, 406, 421, 586, 784, 1585, 2584, 3715, 3927, 4095, 4348, 4548, **4635**, 4932, 5187

**Red Moon and Black Mountain**
Chant, Joy　1447, 1809, 3069, 3383, 3436, 4163, 5984

**Red Nails**
Howard, Robert E.　4616

**The Red Napoleon**
Gibbon, Floyd　4621

**Red Orc's Rage**
Farmer, Philip Jose　87, 164, 179, 507, 970, 1100, 1461, **1873**, 2082, 2791, 3831, 4458, 4921, 5063, 5558

**Red Planet**
Heinlein, Robert A.　421, 586, 1585, 1768, 2584, **2647**, 2765, 5859

**Red Planet Run**
Stabenow, Dana　3294, **5187**

**Red Prophet**
Card, Orson Scott　394, 2086, 2570, 3580, 4233, 5580, 5925

**The Red Queen**
Draulans, Dirk　**1653**

**Red, Red Robin**
Gallagher, Stephen　**2113**

**The Red Right Hand**
Rogers, Joel Townsley　3756

**Red Sands**
Thompson, Paul B.　374

**Red Shadows**
Navarro, Yvonne　**4074**

**Red Shift**
Garner, Alan　1011, 2992

**The Red Tape War**
Chalker, Jack L.　553, **959**, 1459, 1752, 3435

**Red Unicorn**
Lee, Tanith　**3414**

**Red Wizard**
Springer, Nancy　183, 2879, 3043, 4799, 5163, **5182**, 5559

**The Red Wyvern**
Kerr, Katharine　3074

**Rediscovery: A Novel of Darkover**
Bradley, Marion Zimmer　**643**, 3629, 3630, 5862

**The Rediscovery of Man**
Smith, Cordwainer　54, 445, 479, 689, 759, 850, 1588, 1787, 1969, 2569, 2576, 2947, 3240, 3430, 3441, 4071, 4118, 4136, **5106**, 5344, 5345, 5346, 5349, 5613, 5782, 5838, 5869

**Redline the Stars**
Norton, Andre　**4160**

**Redliners**
Drake, David　**1641**, 1976

**Redmagic**
Kilian, Crawford　**3107**

**Redshift Rendezvous**
Stith, John E.   80, 81, 118, 181, 402, 1548, 1579, 1990, 2000, 3603, 4193, 4241, 4357, 4470, 4640, 4952, 4961, 5298, **5305**

**Redwall**
Jacques, Brian   68, 599, 737, 1527, 1998, 2774, 2775, 2776, 4271

**The Reefs of Earth**
Lafferty, R.A.   3011

**The Reefs of Space**
Pohl, Frederik   62, 2064

**Reefsong**
Severance, Carol   63, 181, 1997, 4421, **4923**, 4964, 5029, 5541, 5744

**The Reel Stuff**
Thomsen, Brian   **5460**

**Reel Terror**
Wolfe, Sebastian   4252, 5460, **5947**

**Refugee**
Anthony, Piers   5132, 5889

**Regenesis**
Ecklar, Julia   1589, **1729**, 2006, 2011, 2291, 4548

**The Regiment**
Dalmas, John   308, 589, 1546, 4378

**The Regiment's War**
Dalmas, John   **1326**

**The Regulators**
Bachman, Richard   **284**, 839, 2318

**Rehearsal for a Renaissance**
Clark, Douglas W.   **1045**, 3409

**Reign**
Williamson, Chet   660, 3025, 3858, 4716, **5849**

**Reign of Fire**
Kellogg, Marjorie Bradley   3157

**Reign of Shadows**
Chester, Deborah   702, 770, **1009**, 3123, 5964

**Reign of Terror**
Parry, Michel   1233, 1234

**The Reign of the Brown Magician**
Watt-Evans, Lawrence   5207, **5647**

**The Reincarnation of Peter Proud**
Ehrlich, Max   1050, 1237, 2901, 4442

**Reindeer Moon**
Thomas, Elizabeth Marshall   502, 667, 668, 1632, 2166, 2167, 2168, 2169, 2581, 2582, 2583, 2857, 4320

**The Reindeer People**
Lindholm, Megan   1765

**Relic**
Preston, Douglas   3207, **4414**, 4688

**Relic of Empire**
Gear, W. Michael   1067, **2171**, 4225, 5786

**Relics**
Friedman, Michael Jan   **2066**, 4934

**Relics and Omens**
Weis, Margaret   **5723**

**Relife**
Barton, Dan   **376**

**The Religion**
Conde, Nicholas   20, 21, 1076, 1298, 1403, 1851, 2150, 2744, 3605

**Reliquary**
Preston, Douglas   **4415**

**The Reluctant Sorcerer**
Hawke, Simon   847, **2622**

**The Reluctant Swordsman**
Duncan, Dave   4809, 5651

**Reluctant Voyagers**
Vonarburg, Elisabeth   **5591**

**Remake**
Willis, Connie   3083, **5873**

**Remaking History**
Robinson, Kim Stanley   321, 1199, **4636**, 5028

**The Remarkable Journey of Prince Jen**
Alexander, Lloyd   **69**

**The Remarkables**
Reed, Robert   4063, **4507**, 5033

**Remember Gettysburg**
Randle, Kevin D.   358, 3867, 3993, 5502

**Remember Me**
Pike, Christopher   1089

**Remember the Alamo!**
Randle, Kevin D.   2046, 2563, 6000

**Remember the Little Bighorn**
Randle, Kevin   1852, 5504

**A Remembrance for Kedrigern**
Morressy, John   **4014**

**Rememory**
Betancourt, John Gregory   **481**

**Remnant Population**
Moon, Elizabeth   622, 988, 997, 1695, 1825, 2135, 3732, **3972**, 4119, 4187, 4856, 5437, 5872

**Renaissance Moon**
Nevins, Linda   637, 2540, **4093**

**Rendezvous**
Smith, David Alexander   34, 64, 202, 450, 1058, 1407, 1537, 1557, 2216, 2898, 2921, 3398, 3437, 4217, 4219, 5452, 5573, 5787

**A Rendezvous in Averoigne**
Smith, Clark Ashton   1494, 2225, 5627

**Rendezvous with Rama**
Clarke, Arthur C.   380, 381, 417, 2067, 2165, 2216, 2433, 3398, 4280, 4417, 4967

**Renegade**
DeWeese, Gene   **1511**

**Renegade**
Scotten, Cordell   **4903**

**Renegade's Honor**
Keith, William H. Jr.   4583

**The Renegades of Pern**
McCaffrey, Anne   638, **3746**

**Renunciates of Darkover**
Bradley, Marion Zimmer   **644**

**"Repent, Harlequin!" Said the Ticktockman**
Ellison, Harlan   **1782**

**Replay**
Grimwood, Ken   96, 201, 376, 676, 796, 1089, 2208, 2446, 3459, 4966, 5594, 5905

**Report from Iron Mountain**
Lewin, Leonard C.   1522

**Reprisal**
Wilson, F. Paul   **5896**

**Requiem**
Friedman, Michael Jan   **2067**

**Requiem**
Heinlein, Robert A.   **2648**, 5480

**Requiem**
Joyce, Graham   **2994**, 4575

**Requiem**
Mohr, Clifford   2204, 2823, **3950**, 4239, 4646

**Requiem for a Ruler of Worlds**
Daley, Brian   260, 261, 309, 312, 473, 1106, 1108, 1144, 1572, 1937, 3735, 5668, 6014

**Requiem for Anthi**
Blakeney, Jay D.   **517**, 3888, 4482

**The Rescuers**
Sharp, Margery   737, 1821, 2848, 2851, 2852, 3115

**The Resistance**
Rusch, Kristine Kathryn   **4727**

**The Rest of the Robots**
Asimov, Isaac   253, 254, 255

**The Restaurant at the End of the Universe**
Adams, Douglas   493, 959, 1459, 1603, 1918, 2055, 2123, 2130, 2979, 4076, 4077, 5076

**Restless Spirits**
Lundie, Catherine A.   37, **3570**, 5439

**Restoree**
McCaffrey, Anne   1913

**Resume with Monsters**
Spencer, William Browning   867, 868, 869, 1562, 3057, 3957, 4437, **5168**

**Resurgence**
Lumley, Brian   **3564**

**Resurrection**
Kerr, Katharine   60, 442, 1441, **3075**, 5410, 5531

**Resurrection Dreams**
Laymon, Richard   2610, **3371**

**Resurrection Man**
Stewart, Sean   1339, 2342, 3257, 3480, **5277**

**The Resurrectionist**
Monteleone, Thomas F.   1507, 2304, 2824, **3965**, 4073

**The Resurrections**
Louvish, Simon   **3528**

**Retief and the Warlords**
Laumer, Keith   2001

**Retief at Large**
Laumer, Keith   1536, 3919, 4560, 4932, 5875

**Retief: Diplomat at Arms**
Laumer, Keith   1659

**Retief's Ransom**
Laumer, Keith   30

**Retread Shop**
King, T. Jackson   493, 1259, 1261, 1262, 1456, 3469, 3974, 4160, 5779

**Retribution**
Forrest, Elizabeth   437, **1975**, 3267

**Retro Lives**
Grimes, Lee   **2446**

**The Return**
de la Mare, Walter   **1424**

**The Return**
Shatner, William   2065, **4933**

**Return Fire**
Ingrid, Charles   **2833**, 3425, 4903, 5261

**Return From the Grave**
Lamb, Hugh   2379, 2973

**Return From the Stars**
Lem, Stanislaw   3431

**The Return of Count Electric and Other Stories**
Spencer, William Browning   2826

**The Return of Retief**
Laumer, Keith   30, 2013

**The Return of the Breakneck Boys**
Gravel, Geary   **2332**, 5159

**The Return of the Dragon**
Zaring, Jane   5975

**The Return of the Emperor**
Cole, Allan   **1106**, 1332

**Return of the Jedi**
Kahn, James   114, 2171, 6052, 6054

**The Return of the King**
Tolkien, J.R.R.   257, 487, 710, 711, 716, 922, 1738, 2098, 2378, 2531, 2887, 2888, 3833, 4906, 5714, 5741, 5832

**Return of the Living Dead**
Russo, John   **4746**

**The Return of the Twelves**
Clarke, Pauline   331, 332, 430, 1132, 3587, 5654, 5655, 5656

**Return of the Wolfman**
Rovin, Jeff   1800, **4687**

**Return to Avalon: A Celebration of Marion Zimmer Bradley**
Roberson, Jennifer   640, 2398, **4610**

**Return to Camerein**
Shelley, Rick   **4974**

**Return to Chaos**
Gardner, Craig Shaw   **2131**

**Return to Eden**
Harrison, Harry 591, 885

**Return to Howliday Inn**
Howe, James **2786**

**Return to Isis**
Stewart, Jean 46, 5209, **5268**

**Return to Lankhmar**
Leiber, Fritz **3422**

**Return to Lovecraft Country**
Aniolowski, Scott David **148**, 4427

**Return to Oz**
Vinge, Joan D. 2136, 3609

**Return to Rocheworld**
Forward, Robert L. **1989**, 3738, 3823

**Return to the House of Usher**
Poe, Robert 3150, **4345**, 4778

**Return to the Twilight Zone**
Serling, Carol 1281, **4914**, 4916

**Return to Tomorrow**
Long, Frank Belknap 939

**Reunion**
Friedman, Michael Jan **2068**, 3919, 4081, 4928

**Reunion on Neverend**
Stith, John E. 4502, **5306**, 5545, 5775

**The Revelation**
Little, Bentley 1079, 1884, 2318, 2928, 2929, **3496**, 3615, 3668, 3951, 5176, 5322

**Revelations**
Winter, Douglas E. **5924**

**Revelations in Black**
Jacobi, Carl 534, 942, 1088, 4904, 4905, 5627, 5628

**Revenant**
Cooper, Louise **1178**

**Revenant**
Tem, Melanie 3525, 4023, **5424**

**The Revenge of Dracula**
Tremayne, Peter 4765, 4779

**Revenge of the Christmas Box**
Crimmins, Cathy **1257**, 3214

**Revenge of the Damned**
Cole, Allan **1107**, 1551, 4288

**Revenge of the Fluffy Bunnies**
Gardner, Craig Shaw 1268, 1603, 2084, **2132**, 3768, 4398, 5934

**Revenge of the Lawn: Stories 1962-1970**
Brautigan, Richard 3222

**Revenge of the Manitou**
Masterton, Graham 3325, 3658

**The Revenge of the Rose**
Moorcock, Michael **3985**, 4777, 5650, 5736, 5740

**Revenge of the Seventh Carrier**
Albano, Peter **49**

**Revolt in 2100**
Heinlein, Robert A. 1869

**Revolt of the Angels**
France, Anatole 4571

**Revolution**
Scott, Gavin 3544

**The Revolution From Rosinante**
Gilliland, Alexis A. 584, 4962

**Revolutionary**
Swann, S. Andrew **5367**

**Revolution's Shore**
Rasmussen, Alis A. 309, 356, 684, 876, 1103, 1108, 1407, 1543, 1544, 1545, 1598, 1606, 1664, 1680, 1771, 1849, 1992, 2053, 2260, 2466, 2649, 2785, 3117, 3452, 3821, 3830, 3873, 3910, 3912, 4123, 4375, 4467, **4484**, 4557, 4895, 4897, 5139, 5229, 5234, 5571, 5674, 5720

**The Revolving Boy**
Friedberg, Gertrude 4827

**Reward for Retief**
Laumer, Keith 30, 173, 2013, **3345**, 4037

**Rewind**
England, Terry **1825**

**Rewind to Yesterday**
Pfeffer, Susan Beth 1662

**Rhialto the Marvellous**
Vance, Jack 4945

**Rhinegold**
Grundy, Stephan 2229, 2250, **2454**, 2572, 2686, 4264, 4270, 4872

**Rhinoceros**
Ionesco, Eugene 1817

**The Rhinoceros Who Quoted Nietzsche and Other Odd Acquaintances**
Beagle, Peter S. **411**, 3240

**Ria**
Forrest, Felix C. 5105, 5106

**Ribofunk**
Di Filippo, Paul 578, **1517**

**Richard Matheson: Collected Stories**
Matheson, Richard 531, 4132

**Richter 10**
Clarke, Arthur C. **1060**, 1962, 4420

**The Riddle and Other Stories**
de la Mare, Walter 3360

**The Riddle and the Rune**
Chetwin, Grace 3043, 6030

**The Riddle-Master of Hed**
McKillip, Patricia A. 18, 185, 409, 702, 978, 991, 1174, 1592, 1660, 1682, 1688, 1690, 1814, 1863, 1908, 2041, 2096, 2097, 2263, 2361, 2471, 2504, 2506, 2819, 2884, 2885, 2988, 3069, 3122, 3154, 3171, 3401, 3414, 3482, 3540, 3653, 3837, 3897, 3939, 4446, 4448, 4457, 4528, 4714, 4730, 5272, 5733, 5964, 5983, 6002, 6003

**The Riddled Man**
Rogers, Mark E. **4654**

**Riddley Walker**
Hoban, Russell 325

**A Ride on the Red Mare's Back**
Le Guin, Ursula K. **3382**

**Rider at the Gate**
Cherryh, C.J. **1000**, 1703, 2289, 2420

**Riders of the Purple Wage**
Farmer, Philip Jose **1874**, 3736

**Riders of the Sidhe**
Flint, Kenneth C. ·203, 3358

**The Ridge**
Cantrell, Lisa **872**

**Riding the Torch**
Spinrad, Norman 4325

**The Rift**
David, Peter **1386**

**The Rifter's Covenant**
Smith, Sherwood **5140**

**Rim: A Novel of Virtual Reality**
Besher, Alexander **475**, 483, 3662, 4283

**The Rim of the Unknown**
Long, Frank Belknap 5104

**The Rim-World Legacy and Beyond**
Javor, Frank A. **2882**

**Rimrunners**
Cherryh, C.J. 768, 901, **1001**, 1265, 1719, 2064, 2435, 3748, 4148, 4194, 5188, 5246, 5833

**The Ring**
Anthony, Piers 4178

**Ring**
Baxter, Stephen 384, **402**, 4333, 6086

**Ring Around the Sun**
Simak, Clifford D. 5774, 6060

**The Ring of Charon**
Allen, Roger MacBride **80**, 100, 378, 379, 382, 401, 402, 421, 447, 449, 478, 597, 685, 784, 932, 933, 934, 1055, 1183, 1244, 1247, 1407, 1509, 1537, 1565, 1573, 1575, 1897, 1989, 1990, 1993, 1999, 2000, 2002, 2060, 2226, 2417, 2524, 2602, 2649, 2812, 2921, 3398, 3429, 3710, 3734, 3760, 3762, 3763, 3787, 3805, 3823, 3825, 4000, 4018, 4122, 4126, 4179, 4241, 4281, 4302, 4351, 4354, 4416, 4505, 4760, 4761, 4762, 4769, 4947, 5188, 5244, 5260, 5303, 5304, 5573, 5677, 5865, 5866, 6065, 6079, 6085, 6086

**The Ring of Fire**
Murphy, Shirley Rousseau 4608

**Ring of Intrigue**
Fancher, Jane S. **1863**

**Ring of Lightning**
Fancher, Jane S. **1864**

**Ring of Swords**
Arnason, Eleanor **210**, 219, 351, 377, 684, 686, 758, 988, 990, 997, 1043, 1116, 1264, 1407, 1408, 1586, 1593, 1824, 1849, 2016, 2051, 2052, 2338, 3000, 3380, 3475, 3752, 3760, 3762, 3972, 4067, 4128, 4140, 4187, 4241, 4244, 4356, 4736, 4900, 4902, 5090, 5091, 5466, 5467, 5492, 5674, 5681

**The Ring of Winter**
Lowder, James 1146, 1289, **3538**, 4800, 4803, 4804, 4805, 4807

**Rings of Ice**
Anthony, Piers 82, 354, 400

**Ringstones, and Other Curious Tales**
Sarban 3606, 3879, 3880

**Ringworld**
Niven, Larry 132, 417, 961, 1001, 1876, 1980, 2332, 2828, 4103, 5069, 5304, 5597

**Ringworld Engineers**
Niven, Larry 417, 2828, 3994

**The Ringworld Throne**
Niven, Larry **4128**

**Rinn's Star**
Downing, Paula E. 632, 645, 897, 1046, 1772, 3708, 3709, 4140

**Rinn's Star**
E. Downing, Paula **1719**

**Ripper!**
Dozois, Gardner 1763, 5761

**Rise of a Merchant Prince**
Feist, Raymond E. **1909**

**The Rise of Endymion**
Simmons, Dan 687, 2525, **5059**

**The Rising**
Doohan, James **1579**

**The Rising of the Moon**
Connolly, Flynn **1135**, 3622, 5276

**Rissa Kerguelen**
Busby, F.M. 762, 1003, 1108, 1254, 1571, 1574, 2445, 2459, 3699, 3725, 4484, 5128, 5466, 5821, 5872

**Rite of Passage**
Panshin, Alexei 297, 1539, 2109, 2626, 4507

**The Rites of Ohe**
Brunner, John 2414

**Ritnym's Daughter**
Gilluly, Sheila 3412

**The Rival Rigellians**
Reynolds, Mack 5231

**Rivals of Dracula**
Weinberg, Robert 1799, 2972, 3226, **5699**

**The Rivals of Dracula: A Century of Vampire Fiction**
Parry, Michel 2972, 5699

**Rivals of Frankenstein**
Parry, Michel 140, 2390, 2973, 3019, 4409

**Rivals of Weird Tales**
Weinberg, Robert  **5700**

**The Rivan Codex**
Eddings, David  **1735**

**River of Blue Fire**
Williams, Tad  **5830**

**The River of Dancing Gods**
Chalker, Jack L.  194, 630, 635,
  1267, 1419, 1809, 1812, 2235,
  5224, 5500, 5645

**River of Dust**
Jablokov, Alexander  **2840**

**The River of Time**
Brin, David  124, 132, 161, 244,
  411, 415, 425, 772, 804, 1431,
  1515, 1608, 2576, 5240, 5945

**River Quest**
Vornholt, John  2003, 2469

**River Rats**
Stevermer, Caroline  1430, 1600,
  2274, 3624, **5267**

**Riverrun**
Somtow, S.P.  1529, 1684, 2644,
  4970, **5159**

**Rivers of Time**
de Camp, L. Sprague  263, 264,
  **1417**, 1855

**Riverwind the Plainsman**
Thompson, Paul B.  5724

**The Road Home**
Rosenberg, Joel  **4674**

**The Road to Avalon**
Dawson, Coningsby  5270

**The Road to Corlay**
Cooper, Richard  1852

**The Road to Corlay**
Cowper, Richard  2945, 4151, 5508

**The Road to Ehvenor**
Rosenberg, Joel  1837, 4149, **4675**,
  4993, 5915

**The Road to Hell, Volume I**
Weinberg, Robert  **5701**

**The Road to Hell, Volume II**
Weinberg, Robert  **5702**

**Road to Madness: The Transition of
  H.P. Lovecraft**
Lovecraft, H.P.  **3532**

**The Road to the Rim**
Chandler, A. Bertram  5403

**The Road to Underfall**
Jefferies, Mike  1156, **2888**

**The Road West**
Wright, Gary  **5984**

**Roadkill**
Sanford, Richard  1049, 4279, **4815**

**Roadmarks**
Zelazny, Roger  590

**Roadside Picnic**
Strugatsky, Boris  3434

**Roald Dahl's Book of Ghost Stories**
Dahl, Roald  **1306**

**Robert Bloch: Appreciations of the
  Master**
Matheson, Richard  **3689**

**Robert Bloch's Psychos**
Bloch, Robert  **544**

**The Robin and the Kestrel**
Lackey, Mercedes  705, 845, 2195,
  2653, **3293**, 3410, 3933

**Robin and the King**
Godwin, Parke  2190, **2247**

**The Robin Hood Ambush**
Wu, William F.  2248, 2389, **5999**

**Robin Hood: His Life and Legend**
Miles, Bernard  2248, 2389, 4609

**Robocop**
Naha, Ed  829, 830, 831, 1406,
  3665, 4229, 5476

**Robocop 2**
Naha, Ed  366, 829, 830, 831, 5476

**Robot Adept**
Anthony, Piers  5225, 5226

**The Robot and Rebecca and the
  Missing Owser**
Yolen, Jane  253, 254, 255

**Robot Dreams**
Asimov, Isaac  253, 254, 255, 3666,
  4197

**Robot Jox**
Thurston, Robert  1938

**Robots and Empire**
Asimov, Isaac  83, 446, 484, 984,
  2730, 3425, 4903, 5865

**Robots Have No Tails**
Kuttner, Henry  1456, 1999, 2979,
  4662

**The Robots of Dawn**
Asimov, Isaac  78, 484, 708, 2725,
  3425, 4903, 5051, 5059, 5375,
  5836

**Roc and a Hard Place**
Anthony, Piers  **187**

**Rocheworld**
Forward, Robert L.  64, 1184, 1770,
  1964, **1990**, 4126, 4357, 4942

**A Rock and a Hard Place**
David, Peter  2066, 2068, 3524

**Rock 'n' Roll Babes From Outer
  Space**
Javin, Linda  **2880**

**Rock of Ages**
Williams, Walter Jon  3465, **5840**

**Rockabilly Hell**
Johnstone, William W.  **2933**, 5119

**Rockabilly Limbo**
Johnstone, William W.  **2934**

**Rod Serling's Triple W**
Serling, Rod  1711

**Roderick**
Sladek, John  3465

**Roger's Rangers**
Silbersack, John  554, 827, 3036

**Rogue Bolo**
Laumer, Keith  1628, 1651, 1896,
  2725, 4769, 5278, 5279, 5280,
  5283

**Rogue Emperor**
Kilian, Crawford  264, 350, 590,
  1855, 1955, 6000

**Rogue Moon**
Budrys, Algis  665, 3435, 3554,
  3559, 4954, 4965

**Rogue Powers**
Allen, Roger MacBride  2211

**Rogue Queen**
de Camp, L. Sprague  1211

**Rogue Squadron**
Stackpole, Michael A.  2914, 3247,
  4719, **5205**

**Rogue Star**
Flynn, Michael  **1965**, 3789

**A Roil of Stars**
Wismer, Don  **5930**

**Rolling Hot**
Drake, David  **1642**, 4306, 4377,
  4672

**The Rolling Stones**
Heinlein, Robert A.  1970, 2808,
  4919

**Rolling Vengeance**
Ham, Bob  2324, 2325

**A Romance of the Equator: The Best
  Fantasy Stories of Brian W. Aldiss**
Aldiss, Brian W.  59, 244, 415, 2736,
  3876

**Romancing the Stone**
Lanigan, Catherine  3592, 4549

**The Romulan Way**
Duane, Diane  1226, 2063, 2069,
  5019

**Ronin**
Heeley, D.A.  **2639**

**Roofworld**
Fowler, Christopher  2089

**Rook**
Masterton, Graham  397, 1403, **3678**,
  5415

**Room 13**
Garfield, Henry  **2139**

**A Room for the Dead**
Hynd, Noel  **2825**

**The Root Cellar**
Luenn, Janet  4917

**Root of All Evil**
Farrow, David A.  **1888**

**Rose Daughter**
McKinley, Robin  **3847**

**Rose Madder**
King, Stephen  2609, 2612, **3139**,
  3210, 3365, 3858, 5414

**The Rose of Death and Other
  Mysterious Delusions**
Hawthorne, Julian  **2633**

**The Rose Sea**
Stirling, S.M.  5133, **5296**, 5383,
  5678

**Rosemary's Baby**
Levin, Ira  863, 1076, 1212, 1465,
  3033, 3552, 3958, 4340, 4577,
  5269, 5401, 5538, 5895

**Rough Beast**
Goshgarian, Gary  2205, **2284**, 4843

**Rouse a Sleeping Cat**
Crawford, Dan  **1249**

**Route 666**
Pringle, David  972, 6020, 6021

**Roverandom**
Tolkien, J.R.R.  **5479**

**The Rowan**
McCaffrey, Anne  101, 218, 643,
  645, 653, 2416, 2474, 2475, 2478,
  2551, 3060, 3096, 3628, 3629,
  3630, 3699, **3747**, 4101, 4139,
  6053

**Royal Assassin**
Hobb, Robin  466, **2695**, 4802

**The Royal Book of Oz**
Thompson, Ruth Plumly  3609

**The Ruby Knight**
Eddings, David  **1736**

**Ruby Slippers, Golden Tears**
Datlow, Ellen  **1366**, 5912

**The Ruby Tear**
Brand, Rebecca  **660**

**Rude Astronauts**
Steele, Allen  4953, 4956, **5247**

**Ruins**
Anderson, Kevin J.  **112**, 924, 2308,
  2788, 3679, 5846

**The Ruins of Ambrai**
Rawn, Melanie  1143, **4489**

**The Ruins of Earth: An Anthology of
  the Immediate Future**
Disch, Thomas M.  4959

**Rule Golden and Double Meaning**
Knight, Damon  **3189**

**Ruler of Naught**
Smith, Sherwood  **5141**

**Rulers of Darkness**
Spruill, Steven  **5185**

**Rules of Engagement**
Morwood, Peter  569, 1954, **4037**,
  4514

**Rumors of Spring**
Grant, Richard  1278, 3794

**Run, Come See Jerusalem**
Meredith, Richard  5868

**Run for the Stars/Echoes of Thunder**
Ellison, Harlan  **1788**

**The Run to Chaos Keep**
Chalker, Jack L.  **960**, 1871

**The Runaway Robot**
Fairman, Paul W.  252

**Rune**
Fowler, Christopher  **2020**, 2339,
  3957, 4733, 5400

**The Runelords: The Sum of All Men**
Farland, David   1082, **1866**

**Runes of Autumn**
Elmore, Larry   **1790**

**The Runestaff**
Moorcock, Michael   1635

**Runesword: The Dreamstone**
Rivkin, J.F.   1815

**The Running Man**
Bachman, Richard   1052

**Running Wild**
Ballard, J.G.   320, 2787, 5799

**Running with the Demon**
Brooks, Terry   **715**, 1117

**Rusalka**
Cherryh, C.J.   18, 194, 393, **1002**, 1176, 1592, 3098, 3281, 3776, 4013, 4776, 4781, 5733, 5983

**Russian Fairy Tales**
Afanas'ev, Aleksandr   3281

**Russian Spring**
Spinrad, Norman   388, 2727, **5174**

## S

**S.F.: Author's Choice**
Harrison, Harry   240

**Sabella: Or, The Blood Stone**
Lee, Tanith   1124, 1134, 2207

**Saber & Shadow**
Stirling, S.M.   787, **5297**

**Sabine's Notebook**
Bantock, Nick   **335**, 5450

**The Sable Moon**
Springer, Nancy   185

**Sable, Shadow and Ice**
Franklin, Cheryl J.   **2039**

**Sabriel**
Nix, Garth   68, 1868, 2654, **4129**

**Sacrament**
Barker, Clive   **345**, 3620, 4579

**Sacred Ground**
Lackey, Mercedes   **3294**

**Sacred Prey**
Schilling, Vivian   2896, **4875**

**The Sacred Stones**
Sarabande, William   2582, 2583, **4818**

**Sacred Visions**
Greeley, Andrew M.   **2343**

**Sacrifice**
Farris, John   1670, **1886**, 2113, 4668

**Sacrifice**
Kinion, Richard   **3146**, 3387

**Safari Sleuth**
Singer, A.L.   3544

**The Safety of Objects**
Homes, A.M.   3195, 4181

**The Safety of Unknown Cities**
Taylor, Lucy   3183, **5414**

**The Sage**
Stasheff, Christopher   **5221**

**Sage of Sare**
Smith, Julie Dean   1064, **5126**

**Sago**
Newman, Kim   5189

**Sailing Bright Eternity**
Benford, Gregory   **449**

**Sailor on the Seas of Fate**
Moorcock, Michael   5648

**Sailor Song**
Kesey, Ken   3082, 5145

**The Sails of Tau Ceti**
McCollum, Michael   **3771**

**Saint Camber**
Kurtz, Katherine   2883, 3580, 3776, 4081, 5015

**The Saint-Germain Chronicles**
Yarbro, Chelsea Quinn   2705, 4767, 5191, 5802

**Saint Leibowitz and the Wild Horse Woman**
Miller, Walter M. Jr.   **3908**, 4835

**St. Peter's Wolf**
Cadnum, Michael   **816**, 1349, 1822, 4892, 5080, 5146, 5343, 5425, 5481

**St. Vitus Dances Eternity: A Sarajevo Ghost Story**
Von Allmen, Stewart   **5585**

**Salamandastron**
Jacques, Brian   **2855**

**Salem's Lot**
King, Stephen   832, 1402, 1466, 1920, 2152, 2220, 2441, 3051, **3140**, 3205, 3496, 3498, 4102, 5322, 5770, 5891

**The Saliva Tree and Other Strange Growths**
Aldiss, Brian W.   5747

**The Salukan Gambit**
Dalton, Sean   **1333**

**Sam Gunn Forever**
Bova, Ben   592

**Sam Gunn, Unlimited**
Bova, Ben   236, **593**

**Samurai Cat Goes to Hell**
Rogers, Mark E.   **4655**

**Samurai Cat Goes to the Movies**
Rogers, Mark E.   **4656**

**Samurai Cat in the Real World**
Rogers, Mark E.   4549

**The Samurai Wizard**
Hawke, Simon   **2623**

**Sanatorium under the Sign of the Hourglass**
Schulz, Bruno   573, 2294, 5317

**Sanctuary**
Vornholt, John   **5597**

**The Sand Child**
Jelloun, Tahar Ben   4263

**The Sand Dwellers**
Niswander, Adam   **4112**, 4449

**The Sandman: Book of Dreams**
Gaiman, Neil   **2105**, 4186

**The Sands of Kalaven: A Novel of Shunlar**
Heller, Carol   **2651**

**The Sands of Mars**
Clarke, Arthur C.   421, 586, 2881, 5187, 5377, 5561

**Sandwriter**
Hughes, Monica   1356

**Santa Steps Out: A Fairy Tale for Grownups**
Devereaux, Robert   **1506**

**Santa's Twin**
Koontz, Dean R.   1506, **3214**

**Santiago**
Resnick, Mike   5319

**The Sapphire Rose**
Eddings, David   4, 1072, **1737**

**Sarah Canary**
Fowler, Karen Joy   **2028**, 2265, 3473, 4758, 5151

**The Sardonyx Net**
Lynn, Elizabeth A.   3692

**Sarek**
Crispin, A.C.   1226, **1260**

**Sargasso of Space**
Norton, Andre   3125, 5549

**Sassinak**
McCaffrey, Anne   62, 757, 764, 1041, 1070, 2436, 3307, **3748**, 4482, 4910

**The Satanic Mill**
Preussler, Otfried   1605, 3163

**The Satanic Verses**
Rushdie, Salman   2249

**The Satanist**
Wheatley, Dennis   4531

**Satan's World**
Anderson, Poul   3125

**Satellite Night News**
Hopkins, Jack   **2770**

**Sati**
Pike, Christopher   2056, **4330**

**Satires and Burlesques**
Twain, Mark   2129

**Satori**
Schmidt, Dennis   3344

**Saturday Mourning Fly in My Eye**
Niles, Steve   346

**Saturn Rukh**
Forward, Robert L.   **1991**

**Saturn's Child**
Nichols, Nichelle   568, **4101**

**Sauron Defeated**
Tolkien, J.R.R.   **5480**

**Savage Season**
Lansdale, Joe R.   1843, **3332**, 3755, 5850

**Savant**
Miller, Rex   **3901**

**The Saxon Shore**
Whyte, Jack   **5793**

**Say Cheese and Die**
Stine, R.L.   1097

**Scales of Justice**
Hood, Daniel   **2758**, 5749

**A Scanner Darkly**
Dick, Philip K.   193, 294, 805, 830, 1411, 1696, 3612, 4935, 4936, 4937, 4940, 5173, 5254, 5593, 5867

**Scanners**
Martin, Jack   752, 879, 3561, 3563

**Scare Tactics**
Farris, John   **1887**, 2305, 3673, 3753

**Scared Stiff**
Campbell, Ramsey   700, 938, 2153, 2180, 5007, 5360, 5416

**The Scarf**
Bloch, Robert   2548, 3815, 4084

**The Scarlet Boy**
Calder-Marshall, Arthur   5519

**The Scarlet Letter**
Hawthorne, Nathaniel   1130

**Scars and Other Distinguishing Marks**
Matheson, Richard Christian   4530, 4885, 5005

**The Scathach and the Maeve's Daughter**
Walker, Mary Alexander   2121, 3071, 3470, 3876, 4196, 5177, **5618**

**The Schemes of Dragons**
Smeds, Dave   1470, 4922, **5097**

**The Schimmelhorn File**
Bretnor, Reginald   677, 2227

**Schimmelhorn's Gold**
Bretnor, Reginald   677

**Schismatrix**
Sterling, Bruce   328, 2890, 3850, 5833, 5841

**Schismatrix Plus**
Sterling, Bruce   1965, 2660, **5260**

**The Schizogenic Man**
Harris, Raymond   350, 590, **2563**

**Scholar of Decay**
Huff, Tanya   1137, 1510

**The School**
Kelleher, Ed   1354, 2023, 2139, **3042**, 3499, 5122, 5314

**The School**
Wright, T.M.   2139, 3657, **5994**

**School and Society Through Science Fiction**
Olander, Joseph D.   6027

**The School of Darkness**
Wellman, Manly Wade   2139, 2856, 3390

**School of Fire**
Sherman, David   **4982**

**School of Wizardry**
Doyle, Debra   847, **1605**, 4700, 5640, 6043, 6057, 6058

*The Schrodinger's Cat Trilogy*
Wilson, Robert Anton 1093, 1274

*Science Fiction Adventures in Dimension*
Conklin, Groff 241

*Science Fiction by Gaslight*
Moskowitz, Sam 39, 1712, 5746

*The Science Fiction Century*
Hartwell, David G. 2594

*The Science Fiction Hall of Fame, Volume 1*
Silverberg, Robert 24, 214, 215, 238, 239, 241, 500, 501, 1612, 1614, 1616, 1620, 1874, 2405, 2585, 3187, 3308, 3381, 4031, 4376, 5004, 5031, 5948, 6027

*The Science Fiction Hall of Fame, Volume 4*
Carr, Terry 245, 246, 1618

*Science Fiction Novellas*
Harrison, Harry 6027

*Science Fiction Oddities*
Conklin, Groff 240

*The Science Fiction of Edgar Allan Poe*
Poe, Edgar Allan 3148

*The Science Fiction Omnibus*
Conklin, Groff 240, 1061

*A Science Fiction Reader*
Harrison, Harry 6027

*The Science Fiction Roll of Honor*
Pohl, Frederik 245

*The Science Fiction Stories of Walter M. Miller, Jr.*
Miller, Walter M. Jr. 479, 4118, 5106, 5613

*Science Fiction Terror Tales*
Conklin, Groff 5691

*The Science Fictional Dinosaur*
Silverberg, Robert 4543

*The Science Fictional Sherlock Holmes*
The Council of Four 4556

*Scimitar*
DeMarinis, Rick 1916

*The Scions of Shannara*
Brooks, Terry **716**

*Scissors Cut Paper Wrap Stone*
McDonald, Ian **3795**, 4296

*Scorpio*
McDonough, Alex 403, 1476, **3802**, 4302

*Scorpio Descending*
McDonough, Alex **3803**

*Scorpio Rising*
McDonough, Alex **3804**

*Scorpion*
Linaker, Michael R. 3054

*Scorpion Shards*
Shusterman, Neal 4070, **5013**

*Scotland the Brave*
Roberson, Jennifer 4082, **4611**, 4990, 5707, 5729

*The Scream*
Skipp, John 2147, 2222, 3445, 3950, 4588, 4887, 4997, 5340, 5893

*Scream for Jeeves: A Parody*
Cannon, P.H. **867**, 1451, 2826

*The Scream of the Dove*
Charles, Robert 5086

*A Screaming Across the Sky*
Daley, Brian **1315**

*Screamplays*
Chizmar, Richard T. **1022**

*Screams*
Bloch, Robert 3690

*The Screwtape Letters*
Lewis, C.S. 4868

*Screwtop/The Girl Who Was Plugged In*
McIntyre, Vonda N. 130

*Scroll of Thoth*
Tierney, Richard L. 925, 2782, 3422, 5110, 5321, **5471**

*Sea Cursed: Thirty Terrifying Tales of the Deep*
McDonald, T. Liam 2709, 2732, **3798**

*The Sea Hag*
Drake, David 1415

*Sea Without a Shore*
Russell, Sean **4743**

*The SeaHarp Hotel*
Grant, Charles L. **2315**, 4212

*Seahorse in the Sky*
Cooper, Edmund 160, 2828, 3800, 5303

*The Sealed Casket and Other Stories*
Searight, Richard F. **4905**

*Seance for a Vampire*
Saberhagen, Fred 3560, **4773**, 6019

*seaQuest DSV: Fire Below*
Costello, Matthew J. **1201**

*seaQuest DSV: The Ancient*
Bischoff, David 318, 1201

*seaQuest DSV: The Novel*
Duane, Diane 1201, **1666**, 5282

*The Search*
Carey, Diane 2917

*Search and Destroy*
Andrews, Keith William 116, **141**, 1199, 5012

*Search and Rescue*
Crandall, Melissa 4487

*The Search for Joseph Tully*
Hallahan, William 1237

*The Search for Spock*
McIntyre, Vonda N. 527, 1556

*Search for the Starblade*
Taylor, Keith 1961, 4015, **5408**

*Searching for Dragons*
Wrede, Patricia C. 329, 843, 1488, 1533, 1951, 2015, 2461, 2463, 3070, 3513, 4324, **5979**, 6024, 6025

*A Season for Slaughter*
Gerrold, David **2211**

*The Season of Passage*
Pike, Christopher 199, 1134, **4331**, 5860

*Season of Storms*
Foxxe, Ellen **2032**

*The Season to Be Wary*
Serling, Rod 4875

*Seasons of Plenty*
Greenland, Colin **2418**, 2837

*Seattle Ghost Story*
DiMartino, Nick **1560**

*Seaward*
Leithauser, Brad **3433**, 3809, 5440, 5530

*The Second Angel*
Kerr, Philip 2720, 3923

*The Second Book of Lost Swords: Sightbinder's Story*
Saberhagen, Fred 2863

*The Second Book of Swords*
Saberhagen, Fred 1748

*Second Chance*
Williamson, Chet 1843, **5850**

*Second Child*
Saul, John 2822, 3126, **4844**

*Second Contact*
Resnick, Mike 595, 2921, **4555**

*The Second Dedalus Book of Decadence: The Black Feast*
Stableford, Brian 3089

*The Second Experiment*
Jeppson, Janet O. 251

*Second Fire*
Moscoe, Mike 2043, **4040**

*Second Fire*
Wilson, Robert Charles 2615, 2926, 4688, 4815, 5263

*Second Foundation*
Asimov, Isaac 984, 4044, 4304, 4375

*The Second Generation*
Weis, Margaret **5724**

*The Second Hammer Horror Film Omnibus*
Burke, John 1022

*A Second Infinity*
Weaver, Michael D. 198, **5660**, 6047

*Second Star*
Stabenow, Dana 1987, **5188**, 5859

*The Second Wish and Other Exhalations*
Lumley, Brian 3673

*Seconds*
Ely, David 89, 376, 4086

*The Secret Ascension*
Bishop, Michael 789, 1519, 1520, 1521, 1522, 1523, 4546

*The Secret Country*
Dean, Pamela 4, 286, 410, 412, 1343, 1440, 1488, 1744, 1816, 2359, 2879, 3400, 3487, 4045, 4319, 4797, 4798, 4809, 5182, 5235, 5311, 5364, 6033

*The Secret History*
Tartt, Donna 5398, 5464

*The Secret Laboratory Journals of Dr. Victor Frankenstein*
Kay, Jeremy **3019**

*The Secret Life of Laszlo, Count Dracula*
Anscombe, Roderick 152, 3003, 3005, 6010

*The Secret Life of Walter Mitty*
Thurber, James 3010

*The Secret Mountain and Other Tales*
Morris, Kenneth 3147, 5310

*The Secret Oceans*
Ballantine, Betty **318**, 1024, 2469, 2982, 3729

*The Secret of Roan Inish*
Fry, Rosalie 773, 3731, 3816, 5554

*The Secret of the Indian*
Banks, Lynne Reid **332**

*Secret Passages*
Preuss, Paul **4420**

*The Secret Peace*
McKay, William 3544

*The Secret Prophecies of Nostradamus*
Sternau, Cynthia 2381

*Secret Realms*
Cool, Tom **1168**

*Secret Under the Caribbean*
Dickson, Gordon R. 3341

*Secret Vampire*
Smith, L.J. 120

*The Secret Weavers: Stories of the Fantastic by Latin American Women*
Agosin, Marjorie 43, 51, 1411, 1412, 1818, 2035, 4169, 5814, 5815

*The Secrets of Dr. Taverner*
Fortune, Dion 509, 5696

*Secrets of the Morning*
Andrews, V.C. 146, 5484

*Sector General*
White, James 4195

*The Secular Wizard*
Stasheff, Christopher 955, **5222**

*Seductive Spectres*
Knight, Amarantha 2177, **3184**, 3618, 5386

*See No Weevil*
Morr, Kenyon 5357

*See You Later*
Pike, Christopher 1272, 1475, **4332**

*Seed of Evil*
Plante, Edmund 3040, **4340**, 5118, 5401

**The Seed of Light**
Cooper, Edmund  297

**Seed upon the Wind**
Douglas, Carole Nelson  **1584**

**The Seedling Stars**
Blish, James  399, 5788

**Seeds of Destiny**
Easton, Thomas A.  **1724**

**Seeds of Evil**
Bingley, Margaret  **491**, 2021, 4091,
5065, 5118, 5269, 5484

**Seeds of Fear**
Gelb, Jeff  1361, **2182**

**The Seeds of Time**
Kenyon, Kay  298, 1694, **3064**, 5429

**Seeds of War**
Randle, Robert  3034

**Seeing Eye**
Ellis, Jack  **1780**, 1975

**Seeing Red**
Schow, David J.  700, 776, 1783,
3322, **4889**, 5007, 5008, 5360,
5413

**The Seeker**
Hawke, Simon  13, 299, 394, 1485,
**2624**

**The Seeking Sword**
Kangilaski, Joan  3601

**Seeking the Dream Brother**
Bennett, Marcia J.  **451**, 4147

**The Seer King**
Bunch, Chris  **771**, 1111, 1154, 4258

**The Seeress of Kell**
Eddings, David  **1738**, 5832

**The Select**
Wilson, F. Paul  93, 1939, 2206,
**5897**

**Selected Science Fiction and Fantasy
Stories**
London, Jack  2680, 3147, 3148,
5310

**Selected Stories**
Beaumont, Charles  529, 530, 533,
537, 623, 3683, 3686, 3687, 3689,
4132, 4916, 5901

**Selected Stories and Sketches**
Hogg, James  2905

**The Selected Stories of Robert Bloch**
Bloch, Robert  625, 3683, 4131

**The Selkie**
Sheffield, Charles  1179

**Semper Mars**
Douglas, Ian  **1585**

**The Sending**
Household, Geoffrey  1580

**Senor Vivo and the Coca Lord**
de Bernieres, Louis  **1411**, 3006,
4208

**Senora Rodriguez and Other Worlds**
Cerda, Martha  52, **950**, 6009

**Sensei**
Charnee, David  4742

**A Sensitive Dependence on Initial
Conditions**
Robinson, Kim Stanley  1428

**Sentenced to Prism**
Foster, Alan Dean  5319

**Sentience: A Novel of First Contact**
Adams, Terry A.  133

**The Sentinel**
McKeone, Dixie Lee  3479

**Sentinels**
Weis, Margaret  1807, **5725**

**Sepulchre**
Herbert, James  **2672**, 3594, 4508

**The Seraphim Rising**
De Vos, Elisabeth  **1442**

**Serial Killer Days**
Prill, David  3497, **4436**

**Serpent Catch**
Wolverton, Dave  250, 268, 1255,
3191, 4854, 4949, 5351, **5956**

**Serpent Mage**
Weis, Margaret  1422, **5726**

**The Serpent Slayers**
Niswander, Adam  **4113**

**Serpent's Gift**
Crispin, A.C.  230, 1083, **1261**

**The Serpent's Kiss**
Ransom, Daniel  5084

**Serpent's Reach**
Cherryh, C.J.  1069, 1116, 1389,
2058, 3752, 3909, 3910, 3911,
3919, 4081, 4140, 4698, 4894,
5574, 5788, 5949

**Serpent's Shadow**
Boggs, Timothy  1808, 4912

**Servant of the Bones**
Rice, Anne  **4575**, 5312, 6016

**Servant of the Empire**
Feist, Raymond E.  **1910**, 4741

**Servants of the Wankh**
Vance, Jack  1329

**The Servants of Twilight**
Koontz, Dean R.  1080, 1236, 2203,
2555, 4840, 5250, 5895

**SETI**
Fichman, Frederick  **1930**

**Seven Altars of Dusarra**
Watt-Evans, Lawrence  4848

**Seven-Day Magic**
Eager, Edward  1294

**The Seven Magical Jewels of Ireland**
Adams, Robert  4619, 5500

**Seven Masterpieces of Gothic Horror**
Spector, Robert Donald  4026

**The Seven-Percent Solution**
Meyer, Nicholas  4773

**The Seven Sexes**
Tenn, William  233, 234, 243, 3342,
4706

**The Seven Songs of Merlin**
Barron, T.A.  **372**

**The Seven Spears of the W'dch'ck**
Fenn, Lionel  1603

**Seven Tales and a Table**
Jones, Gwyneth  497

**The Seven Towers**
Wrede, Patricia C.  1477, 1685,
2359, 2362, 3171

**Seven Worlds**
Caraker, Mary  4147

**The Seventh Child**
Brooks, Stanwood  2317

**The Seventh Galaxy Reader**
Pohl, Frederik  242

**The Seventh Gate**
Weis, Margaret  **5727**

**The Seventh Guest**
Costello, Matthew J.  3364, 3368

**The Seventh Heart**
Fitch, Marina  **1943**, 2540

**The Seventh Sentinel**
Kirchoff, Mary  **3154**

**Seventh Son**
Card, Orson Scott  162, 191, 389,
394, 435, 442, 1583, 1746, 2086,
2191, 2236, 3118, 4433, 4435,
4814, 4946, 5034, 5333, 5356,
5357, 5920

**Sewer, Gas & Electric**
Ruff, Matt  4042, **4708**

**Sex and Blood**
Dee, Ron  **1467**, 2655, 2778, 3111,
3114, 3388, 3393, 3397

**Sex and the Single Vampire**
Kilpatrick, Nancy  748, 1467, 2705,
**3114**, 3388, 3549, 5175

**Sex, Death and Starshine**
Barker, Clive  428, 5849

**Sex Macabre**
Knight, Amarantha  3618, 5386

**Sexing the Cherry**
Winterson, Jeanette  **5927**

**Sexpunks & Savage Sagas**
Sutphen, Richard  1401, 3176, 3397,
**5360**, 5416

**Sexual Chemistry: Sardonic Tales of
the Genetic Revolution**
Stableford, Brian  3116

**SF: 59, The Year's Greatest Science
Fiction and Fantasy**
Merril, Judith  240

**Shackled**
Garton, Ray  **2156**

**Shade**
Darke, David  **1355**, 5537

**Shade**
Devenport, Emily  294, **1504**, 1805,
3921, 4142, 4930, 5462

**Shade and Shadow**
Woodbury, Francine G.  **5967**

**Shade of Pale**
Kihn, Greg  840, **3104**

**Shade's Children**
Nix, Garth  2837, **4130**

**Shades of Darkness: More of the
Ghostly Best Stories of Robert
Westall**
Westall, Robert  **5765**

**Shades of Evil**
Cave, Hugh B.  1403

**Shades of Night**
Hautala, Rick  **2612**

**Shadow**
Logston, Anne  15, 2368, 2376,
2452, 2473, **3512**, 4596, 5648

**Shadow Child**
Citro, Joseph A.  **1038**

**Shadow Dance**
Borton, Douglas  577

**Shadow Dance**
Logston, Anne  3513

**Shadow Dance**
Palmer, Jessica  3967, **4238**

**Shadow Dawn**
Claremont, Chris  **1042**

**Shadow Dreams**
Massie, Elizabeth  94, 663, 693, 802,
1789, 2698, 2701, 3495, **3667**

**The Shadow Eater**
Lee, Adam  3386

**Shadow Games**
Gorman, Ed  1830

**The Shadow Gate**
Ball, Margaret  317, 634, 1477,
2357, 2359, 3077, 3717, 4869,
4971, 4991, 5223

**The Shadow Guests**
Aiken, Joan  4257

**Shadow Hunt**
Logston, Anne  2473, **3514**, 3914

**Shadow Leader**
Harper, Tara K.  **2552**, 4324

**Shadow Magic**
Wrede, Patricia C.  12, 16, 176, 393,
3296, 3298, 3304, 3305, 3306,
3512, 3514

**Shadow Man**
Etchison, Dennis  284, **1848**, 2448,
3103

**Shadow Man**
Scott, Melissa  1588, 2059, 2134,
3426, 3440, **4900**, 5037, 5461

**The Shadow Matrix**
Bradley, Marion Zimmer  **645**

**Shadow-Maze**
Smith, Mark  **5133**

**Shadow Moon**
Lucas, George  1042, **3540**

**Shadow of a Dark Queen**
Feist, Raymond E.  **1911**, 3295, 4848

**A Shadow of All Night Falling**
Cook, Glen  1176, 1640, 2989,
3175, 4258

**Shadow of Earth**
Eisenstein, Phyllis   6, 142, 442,
   1196, 1199, 1530, 1581, 1658,
   3920, 4517, 4934, 4971, 5011,
   5150, 5364

**Shadow of Obsession**
Neason, Rebecca   **4082**

**The Shadow of Sorcery**
Offutt, Andrew J.   **4202**

**Shadow of the Beast**
Carter, Margaret L.   **926**

**Shadow of the Crown**
Mills, Craig   **3914**

**Shadow of the King**
Hollick, Helen   **2747**, 3355

**Shadow of the Seventh Moon**
Berberick, Nancy Varian   **459**, 5580

**The Shadow of the Torturer**
Wolfe, Gene   248, 904, 1150, 1429,
   1482, 1983, 2533, 2550, 3572,
   3692, 3874, 4201, 4242, 5000,
   5434, 5720

**Shadow of the Well of Souls**
Chalker, Jack L.   **961**

**The Shadow over Innsmouth**
Lovecraft, H.P.   **3533**

**The Shadow Rising**
Jordan, Robert   **2990**

**The Shadow Shaia**
Gilliland, Alexis A.   **2235**, 3905

**Shadow Twin**
Hoover, Dale   **2762**

**Shadow Walkers**
Romberg, Nina   2901, 3146, 3964,
   4442, **4663**, 5334, 5528

**Shadow War**
Chester, Deborah   **1010**

**The Shadow Warrior**
Zettner, Pat   3510, 5709, 5712, **6082**

**The Shadow Within**
Cavelos, Jeanne   **944**, 1387, 1654,
   3096, 4833

**Shadow World**
Crispin, A.C.   **1262**, 1391

**Shadowborn**
Connors, William W.   **1137**

**Shadowboxer**
Pollotta, Nick   **4366**

**Shadowbreed**
Ferring, David   **1928**, 5819

**Shadowdale**
Awlinson, Richard   1287, 2427,
   4106, 4800, 4803, 4804, 4805

**Shadowdance**
Bailey, Robin Wayne   **290**

**Shadoweyes**
Ptacek, Kathryn   2734

**Shadowfane**
Wurts, Janny   1906, 4685

**Shadowfires**
Koontz, Dean R.   1084, 1505, 2608,
   2802, 2900, 3130, 3139, 3152,
   3365, 5895

**Shadowkill**
Clayton, Jo   **1069**

**Shadowland**
Straub, Peter   2334, 2748, 5485

**Shadowlight**
Hyman, Jackie   1837, **2819**, 3383,
   5820

**Shadowplay**
Clayton, Jo   **1070**

**Shadowplay**
Findley, Nigel   1591, 5135

**Shadows**
Nasaw, Jonathan   **4068**

**Shadows**
Rangel, Kimberly   **4472**

**Shadows**
Saul, John   **4845**

**Shadows After Dark**
Crozier, Ouida   **1286**, 5071

**Shadow's Daughter**
Meier, Shirley   787, **3871**, 5297,
   5299, 5684

**Shadow's End**
Tepper, Sheri S.   2057, **5435**

**Shadows Fall**
Green, Simon R.   **2373**

**Shadows in the Water**
Lasky, Kathryn   318, **3341**, 3729

**Shadows in Time**
Jac, Cherlyn   1271, 2731, 3576

**Shadows Linger**
Cook, Glen   2990, 3833

**Shadows of Doom**
McKiernan, Dennis L.   710, 716

**Shadows of the Empire**
Perry, Steve   **4299**, 4719, 5205

**Shadows of the White Sun**
Harris, Raymond   351, 353, 882,
   1914, 5377, 5546, 5548

**Shadows of War**
Gressman, Thomas S.   **2432**

**Shadows on the Hill**
Cassada, Jackie   **935**, 5701, 5702

**Shadows on the Sun**
Friedman, Michael Jan   **2069**, 3315,
   4139

**Shadows over Innsmouth**
Jones, Stephen   **2978**, 3533, 4424,
   4426, 4430, 5493, 5494

**Shadows over Lyra**
Wrede, Patricia C.   **5980**

**Shadow's Realm**
Reichert, Mickey Zucker   **4523**, 4801,
   4806

**The Shadows Series**
Grant, Charles L.   3960

**Shadow's Son**
Meier, Shirley   787, **3872**, 5297,
   5299

**Shadowshow**
Strickland, Brad   460, 1353, 2761,
   3102, 3541

**Shadowspeer**
Clayton, Jo   **1071**

**The Shadowy Thing**
Drake, H.B.   1424

**The Shadowy Third and Other
   Stories**
Glasgow, Ellen   601, 1673

**The Shaft**
Schow, David J.   871, 2918, 3161,
   5692

**Shaggy Planet**
Goulart, Ron   4341

**Shakespeare's Planet**
Simak, Clifford D.   209, 3079, 5826

**Shaman**
Miesel, Sandra   **3889**, 5124, 5125,
   5176

**Shaman**
Shea, Robert   191, **4946**

**The Shaman**
Stasheff, Christopher   **5223**

**Shaman Woods**
Fields, Morgan   **1931**, 2198, 2734,
   3655, 3895, 4111, 4113, 4309,
   5077, 5961

**Shame of Man**
Anthony, Piers   **188**

**Shango**
Curtis, James Roberto   **1298**

**Shangri-La: The Return to the World
   of Lost Horizon**
Cooney, Eleanor   **1169**

**The Shape-Changer's Wife**
Shinn, Sharon   3280, **5002**

**The Shape of Fear and Other Ghostly
   Tales**
Peattie, Elia   2919

**The Shape of Things to Come**
Wells, H.G.   **2790**

**Shape-Shifter: Stories by Pauline
   Melville**
Melville, Pauline   51, 2736, **3876**

**Shape Shifters: Fantasy and Science
   Fiction Tales about Humans Who
   Can Change Their Shapes**
Yolen, Jane   3446, 5239

**Shapechangers**
Roberson, Jennifer   1179, 2361,
   4055, 4486, 4492, 5629, 5650,
   5767

**Shaper's Legacy**
Finch, Sheila   **1933**

**Shapes**
Vance, Steve   **5552**

**The Shapes of Their Hearts**
Scott, Melissa   **4901**

**Shaping the Dawn**
Finch, Sheila   **1934**

**Shardik**
Adams, Richard   4273, 4692

**Shards of a Broken Crown**
Feist, Raymond E.   **1912**

**Shards of Empire**
Shwartz, Susan   965, **5017**, 5511,
   5513

**Shards of Honor**
Bujold, Lois McMaster   1184, 1254,
   1331, 1333, 1503, 1542, 1604,
   1756, 1913, 2052, 2209, 2350,
   2445, 2683, 2766, 2921, 3909,
   3912, 3968, 3970, 3976, 4228,
   4291, 5669, 5670, 5671, 5673,
   5675, 5679

**The Sharp End**
Drake, David   **1643**

**Sharper Knives**
Fowler, Christopher   94, 775, 3674

**A Sharpness on the Neck**
Saberhagen, Fred   452, 660, 1794,
   4667, **4774**

**Sharra's Exile**
Bradley, Marion Zimmer   922, 986,
   3746

**The Shattered Chain**
Bradley, Marion Zimmer   62, 1141,
   1755, 2050, 2550, 3634, 5071,
   5978

**Shattered Chains**
Emery, Clayton   **1816**, 1977, 2529,
   2827

**Shattered Glass**
Bergstrom, Elaine   279, 4234, 4529,
   4755, 5475, 5690

**The Shattered Oath**
Sherman, Josepha   **4989**

**The Shattered Sphere**
Allen, Roger MacBride   **81**, 382, 383,
   934, 1183, 3760, 3762, 3823,
   4760

**The Shattered World**
Reaves, Michael   171

**She**
Haggard, H. Rider   3877, 4235, 4572

**She Is the Darkness**
Cook, Glen   **1154**

**She Who Remembers**
Shuler, Linda Lay   3889

**The Shee**
Donnelly, Joe   3104

**Sheep**
Maginn, Simon   **3606**

**The Sheep Look Up**
Brunner, John   5081, 5867

**Sheepfarmer's Daughter**
Moon, Elizabeth   11, 18, 631, 936,
   962, 994, 1110, 1143, 1156, 1253,
   1674, 1675, 1732, 1737, 1738,
   1815, 2031, 2195, 2457, 2639,
   2985, 3069, 3273, 3295, 3296,
   3297, 3508, 3513, 3624, 3627,
   3892, 3903, 3904, 3934, 3941,
   **3973**, 4924, 5202, 5296, 5333,
   5509, 5650, 5678, 5739, 5740,
   5742, 5790, 5962, 5963

**The Shell of Sense**
Dunbar, Olivia Howard   **1673**, 2633,
   2919

**Sheltered Lives**
Oberndorf, Charles   574, **4188**, 4478, 5592

**The Sheltering Sky**
Bowles, Paul   5414

**The Sheriff of Nottingham**
Kluger, Richard   2247, **3165**, 4609

**Sherlock Holmes in Orbit**
Resnick, Mike   **4556**

**Sherlock Holmes in the Adventure of the Ancient Gods**
Vaughan, Ralph   867, 1859, 4751

**Sherlock Holmes through Time and Space**
Asimov, Isaac   4556

**Sherlock Holmes's War of the Worlds**
Wellman, Manly Wade   119, 1524

**Sherwood**
Godwin, Parke   269, 2190, **2248**, 2389, 2570, 3165, 3502, 4584, 4609, 4985

**The Sherwood Game**
Friesner, Esther   **2082**, 2470

**The Sherwood Ring**
Pope, Elizabeth Marie   122, 1272, 4078

**The Shield between the Worlds**
Paxson, Diana L.   3059, 3504, **4267**

**The Shield of Time**
Anderson, Poul   6, **131**, 895, 1196, 1199, 1854, 1983, 5011, 5487, 5906, 5999

**The Shift**
Foy, George   **2033**

**Shifter**
Reeves-Stevens, Judith   2809, **4515**

**Shifters**
Lee, Edward   **3396**

**Shifting the Boundaries: The Selected Works of Kevin J. Anderson**
Anderson, Kevin J.   **113**, 578, 4313, 5881

**The Shilling Shockers**
Haining, Peter   307, 1314

**The Shiloh Project**
Poyer, David C.   5502

**The Shimmering Door**
Kerr, Katharine   **3076**

**Shimmering Splendor**
Gellis, Roberta   1129

**The Shining**
King, Stephen   282, 521, 609, 890, 1966, 2314, 2631, 2732, **3141**, 3149, 3675, 3953, 4223, 4249, 5380, 5463, 5528, 5625, 5993, 5994

**The Shining Company**
Sutcliff, Rosemary   4584, **5359**

**The Shining Falcon**
Sherman, Josepha   3274, 3275, 5390, 5393

**The Shining Ones**
Preuss, Paul   **4421**

**The Ship Avenged**
Stirling, S.M.   4148, **5298**

**The Ship Errant**
Nye, Jody Lynn   **4175**

**The Ship of Ishtar**
Merritt, A.   5496, 5626

**The Ship of Magic**
Hobb, Robin   **2696**

**Ship of Shadows**
Leiber, Fritz   58, 4626, 5942, 5943

**Ship of the Line**
Carey, Diane   **904**

**The Ship Who Sang**
McCaffrey, Anne   734, 1389, 1627, 2135, 2419, 2890, 3038, 3888, 4175, 5298, 5375, 5680

**The Ship Who Searched**
McCaffrey, Anne   643, **3749**

**The Ship Who Won**
McCaffrey, Anne   **3750**, 4175

**The Ships of Earth**
Card, Orson Scott   **897**

**Ships of Merior**
Wurts, Janny   **6004**

**Shiva Accused: An Adventure of the Ice Age**
Brennan, J.H.   **667**

**Shiva: An Adventure of the Ice Age**
Brennan, J.H.   **669**, 1632

**Shiva Descending**
Benford, Gregory   1057, 3772

**Shiva in Steel**
Saberhagen, Fred   **4775**

**Shiva's Challenge: An Adventure of the Ice Age**
Brennan, J.H.   **668**, 2857

**Shivering World**
Tyers, Kathy   231, 1805, 3021, 3745, 4652, 4856, **5526**

**Shivers for Christmas**
Dalby, Richard   **1313**

**Shock Lines**
Beath, Warren Newton   **427**, 2734, 4710, 5631

**Shock Radio**
Clark, Leigh   **1052**

**Shock Rock**
Gelb, Jeff   **2183**, 4810

**Shock Rock II**
Gelb, Jeff   **2184**, 4810

**Shocker**
Boyll, Randall   4088

**Shocks**
Blackwood, Algernon   455

**The Shockwave Rider**
Brunner, John   **736**, 1760, 1915, 1965, 3786, 3818, 4821, 5256

**Shoebag**
James, Mary   67, **2868**, 5656

**Shoebag Returns**
James, Mary   **2869**

**Shogun**
Clavell, James   4673, 4742

**The Shooting Star**
Bloch, Robert   1763

**The Shore of Women**
Sargent, Pamela   968, 4792

**The Shores of Kansas**
Chilson, Rob   4039

**Short Blade**
Emshwiller, Peter R.   805, **1820**, 4709

**A Short, Sharp Shock/The Dragon Masters**
Robinson, Kim Stanley   3189

**The Short Story Omnibus**
French, Joseph Lewis   1310

**The Short Timers**
Hasford, Gustav   4865

**The Short Victorious War**
Weber, David   **5681**

**Shotgun Saturday Night**
Crider, Bill   1829

**Showboat World**
Vance, Jack   1691, 2422, 2575, 4197, 5055

**Showdown**
Dalton, Sean   1398

**The Shrapnel Academy**
Weldon, Fay   2028, 3473

**Shrine of the Desert Mage**
Goldin, Stephen   374, 1528, 1687, 2130, 6087

**Shrines and Desecrations**
Hodge, Brian   748, 1467, **2705**, 3111, 3114, 3549

**The Shrinking of Treehorn**
Heide, Florence P.   5968

**The Shrouded Realm**
Knaak, Richard A.   3067, **3174**

**The Shub Niggurath Cycle**
Price, Robert M.   461, 2978, **4430**

**Shudder Again**
Slung, Michele   1118, 1120, 1361, 2176, 2178, 2179, 2182, 2185, 5056, **5094**

**The Shy Stegosaurus of Cricket Creek**
Lampman, Evelyn Sibley   2468, 6076

**The Shy Stegosaurus of Indian Springs**
Lampman, Evelyn Sibley   2468

**Sibs**
Wilson, F. Paul   436, 1786, 2115, 2613, 5892, **5898**

**Sibyl Sue Blue**
Brown, Rosel George   2685

**Sick**
Bonansinga, Jay R.   **571**, 3178

**Sideshow**
Resnick, Mike   5215

**Sideshow**
Tepper, Sheri S.   379, 686, 784, 2422, 2578, 5011, **5436**, 5592, 5941

**Siduri's Net**
McAllister, P.K.   3476, **3709**

**The Siege**
Baldwin, Bill   **312**, 1546, 4982

**The Siege**
David, Peter   2908

**The Siege of Arista**
Fawcett, Bill   1627, 5216

**Siege of Darkness**
Salvatore, R.A.   1287, 2427, 2625, **4804**

**The Siege of Eternity**
Pohl, Frederik   **4353**

**The Siege of Wonder**
Geston, Mark S.   1343

**Sierra Madre**
Stine, G. Harry   830, 831, 1406, 1651, 4769

**Sight of Proteus**
Sheffield, Charles   4470

**The Sign of the Moonbow**
Offutt, Andrew J.   5962, 5963

**Sign of the Unicorn**
Zelazny, Roger   3978, 5508

**Signal to Noise**
Nylund, Eric S.   **4179**, 5353

**Signs and Portents**
Yarbro, Chelsea Quinn   2715

**Signs of Life**
Harrison, M. John   **2580**, 3241

**Signs of Life**
Wilder, Cherry   **5804**

**Silence in Solitude**
Scott, Melissa   4593

**The Silence of the Lambs**
Harris, Thomas   695, 1170, 1555, 2428, **2566**, 2931, 3210, 3395, 3402, 3756, 3855, 4084, 4222, 4501, 4509, 5318, 5326, 5328, 5338, 5453

**The Silent Blade**
Salvatore, R.A.   **4805**

**The Silent City**
Vonarburg, Elisabeth   4478, **5592**

**Silent Dances**
Crispin, A.C.   **1263**, 1391, 1594, 1865, 1956, 2550, 3752, 3767, 4128

**Silent Moon**
Relling, William Jr.   **4531**

**Silent Running**
Thompson, Harlan   2660, 5303

**Silent Scream**
Schmidt, Dan   **4883**

**Silent Songs**
Crispin, A.C.   **1264**, 2001, 5037

**The Silent Stars Go By**
White, James   2491, 4116, **5781**

**The Silent Strength of Stones**
Hoffman, Nina Kiriki   636, **2716**

**Silent Thunder/Universe**
Ing, Dean   **2829**

**The Silent Tower**
Hambly, Barbara   105, 317, 393,
   424, 439, 683, 718, 1161, 1162,
   1163, 1419, 1662, 1842, 1985,
   2629, 3471, 3840, 3930, 4446,
   4669, 4671, 4676, 4793, 5719

**Silent Witness**
Smith, Robert Arthur   3898, **5136**

**Silent Zone**
Molstad, Stephen   **3952**

**The Silicon Dagger**
Williamson, Jack   5086

**Silicon Embrace**
Shirley, John   **5009**

**Silicon Karma**
Easton, Thomas A.   5353

**The Silicon Mage**
Hambly, Barbara   317, 1160, 1985,
   2097, 3121

**The Silicon Man**
Platt, Charles   **4343**

**Silk**
Kiernan, Caitlin R.   1890, **3101**

**Silk and Steel**
Miller, Ron   980, 2651, **3905**, 4490

**Silk Road**
Larsen, Jeanne   69, 313, 1145, 2804,
   **3339**, 4155, 4742, 5918

**Silk Roads and Shadows**
Shwartz, Susan   5292, 5506

**The Silkie**
Van Vogt, A.E.   1469, 5541

**The Silmarillion**
Tolkien, J.R.R.   1730, 1735, 2991,
   3067, 3836

**The Silver Branch**
Kennealy-Morrison, Patricia   392,
   1960

**Silver Bullet**
King, Stephen   4515

**The Silver Eggheads**
Leiber, Fritz   419

**The Silver Gryphon**
Lackey, Mercedes   **3295**

**The Silver Hand**
Lawhead, Stephen R.   **3358**

**The Silver Kiss**
Klause, Annette Curtis   **3163**

**The Silver Metal Lover**
Lee, Tanith   5181

**Silver on the Tree**
Cooper, Susan   172, 196

**Silver Princess, Golden Knight**
Green, Sharon   641, **2359**, 5217,
   5220

**Silver Scream**
Schow, David J.   2183, 2761, 4252,
   4811, 4812

**Silver Shadows**
Cunningham, Elaine   **1292**

**The Silver Skull**
Daniels, Les   4573, 4668, 6016

**The Silver Stallion**
Cabell, James Branch   1699

**The Silver Stone**
Rosenberg, Joel   **4676**

**A Silver Thread of Madness**
Salmonson, Jessica Amanda   4878

**The Silver Tower**
Brown, Dale   2143, 2726

**The Silver Tower**
Hambly, Barbara   915

**The Silver Tree**
Williams, Ruth L.   **5822**

**The Silver Wolf**
Borchardt, Alice   572, 4573

**Silverglass**
Rivkin, J.F.   2376

**Silverlight**
Llywelyn, Morgan   2619, **3507**

**Silverlock**
Myers, John Myers   1856, 5178

**Silverthorn**
Feist, Raymond E.   2724

**Simbul's Gift**
Abbey, Lynn   2425

**Simulations**
Jacobson, Karie   2394

**Sin of Origin**
Barnes, John   3617, 4550

**Sinbad the Sailor**
Daniels, Patricia   374, 2130, 4731,
   6087

**Sineater**
Massie, Elizabeth   859, 2318, 3104,
   **3668**

**The Sinful Ones**
Leiber, Fritz   914, 951, 956, 3493,
   5643

**Sing for a Gentle Rain**
James, J. Alison   191, 331, 368,
   1583, 2166, 2167, 2168, 2170,
   2857, **2861**, 2865, 3436, 3545,
   3704, 4380, 4918, 5035, 5751

**Sing the Four Quarters**
Huff, Tanya   **2799**, 3278, 3298

**Sing the Light**
Marley, Louise   2877, **3629**, 3730,
   3739, 4999, 5001

**Sing the Warmth**
Marley, Louise   **3630**

**The Singers of Time**
Pohl, Frederik   2273, 3597, **4354**,
   4420, 4735, 5860

**The Singularity Project**
Busby, F.M.   **784**

**Sinister Barrier**
Russell, Eric Frank   2001, 3188,
   3351, 4944, 5010

**Sinistre: An Anthology of Rituals**
Hatch, George   22, 1281, **2601**, 3112

**Sink the Armada**
Andrews, Keith William   65, **142**,
   5559

**Sins of the Blood**
Rusch, Kristine Kathryn   **4728**, 5062

**Sins of the Fathers**
Chupp, Sam   797, 2604, 5585

**Sins of the Flesh**
Davis, Don   **1404**, 1443

**The Sioux Space Man**
Norton, Andre   431, 3583

**Sir Gawain and the Green Knight,
   Pearl, and Sir Orfeo**
Tolkien, J.R.R.   1269

**Sirens and Other Daemon Lovers**
Datlow, Ellen   **1367**

**The Sirens of Titan**
Vonnegut, Kurt Jr.   96, 3343, 3459,
   5531, 5905

**The Sister**
Trevor, Elleston   **5484**

**Sister Blood**
Haber, Karen   **2476**

**Sister Light, Sister Dark**
Yolen, Jane   2471, 3582, 3843, **6039**

**Sister, Sister**
Neiderman, Andrew   70, **4091**

**Sister to the Rain**
Michaels, Melisa   **3887**, 5061

**Sisters in Fantasy**
Shwartz, Susan   2380, 3670, 5815

**Sisters in Fantasy 2**
Shwartz, Susan   **5018**

**Sisters of the Night**
Hambly, Barbara   730, 1713, **2508**

**The Site**
March, Melisand   3161, 3364, **3621**,
   4499, 5164, 5961, 5989

**The Six Families**
Holder, Nancy   **2733**

**Six German Romantic Tales**
Taylor, Ronald   2718, **5418**

**Six Gun Planet**
Jakes, John   1398

**Six Moon Dance**
Tepper, Sheri S.   687, 774, 793,
   1266, **5437**

**Six of Swords**
Douglas, Carole Nelson   2502, 4614

**Six Science Fiction Plays**
Elwood, Roger   1784, 1785, 5904

**The Sixth Book of Lost Swords:
   Mindsword's Story**
Saberhagen, Fred   1748, 2863, **4776**

**Sixth Column**
Heinlein, Robert A.   1869, 1877,
   2323, 3873

**The Sixth Dog**
Rice, Jane   **4582**

**The Sixth Winter**
Orgill, Douglas   3429

**Skeleton Crew**
King, Stephen   777, 3321, 3753

**Skeletons**
Sarrantonio, Al   3956, 4646, **4834**

**Skin**
Koja, Kathe   212, 437, 548, 2030,
   **3196**

**Skin of the Soul**
Tuttle, Lisa   468, 2496, 2891, 3022,
   4443, **5523**

**Skinny Legs and All**
Robbins, Tom   **4607**, 5867

**Skirmish**
Michaels, Melisa C.   311, 356, 746,
   1043, 1332, 1543, 1550, 1664,
   2260, 2419, 2466, 4484, 4594,
   4897, 5674

**Skirmish: The Great Short Fiction of
   Clifford D. Simak**
Simak, Clifford D.   624, 4535

**Skryling's Blade**
Estes, Rose   27, 487, 1815

**Skull-Face**
Howard, Robert E.   616, 942, 5695

**Skull Session**
Hecht, Daniel   **2638**

**Skulls in the Stars**
Howard, Robert E.   3418

**Sky Dogs**
Yolen, Jane   3382

**The Sky Lords**
Brosnan, John   **720**, 3050

**Sky Trillium**
May, Julian   **3700**

**Skybowl**
Rawn, Melanie   **4490**

**The Skylark of Space**
Smith, Edward E.   270, 5141

**Skylark of Valeron**
Smith, Edward E.   270, 5863

**The Skynappers**
Brunner, John   2996

**Skyrocket Steele**
Goulart, Ron   1216, 4341

**Skyrocket Steele Conquers the
   Universe and Other Media Tales**
Goulart, Ron   1428, 3945, 6068

**Skyscape**
Cadnum, Michael   212, **814**, 3812,
   4084

**The Skystone**
Whyte, Jack   266, 267, 640, 2746,
   **5794**

**Slam**
Shiner, Lewis   323

**Slan**
Van Vogt, A.E.   565, 567, 642, 733,
   2290, 2420, 2545, 2665, 3994,
   3995, 4081, 4305, 4918, 5039

**Slant**
Bear, Greg   4179

**Slaughterhouse Five**
Vonnegut, Kurt Jr.   96, 1694, 2244,
   2542, 3456, 4606, 5079, 6029

**Slave of My Thirst**
Holland, Tom   **2742**

**Slaves of the Volcano God**
Gardner, Craig Shaw   1413, 1418, 4398, 5934

**Slay and Rescue**
Moore, John   262, 557, 559, 1208, 1512, 2079, 2080, 2803, 3810, **3991**, 4945, 5219, 5649, 6049, 6066

**Sleep No More**
Rolt, L.T.C.   1350, 2905, 5611

**The Sleep of Stone**
Cooper, Louise   **1179**, 2636, 3159, 3410, 3545, 4615, 4985, 5177, 5336, 5394, 5556, 5827, 6017, 6042

**Sleepeasy**
Wright, T.M.   2335

**The Sleeping Dragon**
Rosenberg, Joel   104, 391, 1162, 1163, 3831, 4492, 5063, 5558

**Sleeping in Flame**
Carroll, Jonathan   739, 1278, 4943

**Sleeping Planet**
Burkett, William R. Jr.   914

**Sleepwalker**
Cadnum, Michael   **815**

**Sleipnir**
Evans, Linda   263, 458, **1856**, 2572, 4516, 4522

**Slice**
Miller, Rex   **3902**

**Sliders: The Novel**
Linaweaver, Brad   **3467**

**Slightly Off Center**
Barrett, Neal Jr.   3327, 3328, 3329

**A Slip in Time**
Kirkwood, Kathleen   691, 1271

**Slippage**
Ellison, Harlan   663, 778, **1789**, 2701, 4886, 5663

**Slippin' into Darkness**
Partridge, Norman   **4254**

**Sliver**
Levin, Ira   1777, 3094, 3208, 4248

**Slob**
Miller, Rex   1198, 2566, 2843, 3319, 3392, 5123

**Slow Dancing through Time**
Dozois, Gardner   **1615**

**Slow Freight**
Busby, F.M.   **785**, 1594, 1899, 4300, 5042

**Slow Funeral**
Ore, Rebecca   **4221**, 5333

**Slow Lightning**
Popkes, Steven   5107

**Slow River**
Griffith, Nicola   1304, 1582, 2273, 2274, **2445**, 2558, 2559, 3453, 4064, 4218, 4898

**Slow Sculpture**
Sturgeon, Theodore   5910

**Slumming in Voodooland**
Stableford, Brian   5923

**A Small Colonial War**
Frezza, Robert   **2054**, 5786

**Small Gods**
Pratchett, Terry   **4400**, 5232

**Smart Dragons, Foolish Elves**
Foster, Alan Dean   **2014**, 2077, 2413, 4723

**Smile on the Void**
Gordon, Stuart   1063, 1499, 2535, 2754, 4732, 4946, 5903

**The Smithsonian Institution**
Vidal, Gore   **5570**

**Smoke and Mirrors**
Gaiman, Neil   578, **2106**

**Smoke and Mirrors**
Lindskold, Jane M.   **3476**

**Smoke of the Snake**
Jacobi, Carl   939, 940, 942, **2844**, 3515, 5149, 5211

**The Smoke Ring**
Niven, Larry   1897, 1991, 2289, 3770, 5000

**The Snail on the Slope**
Strugatsky, Boris   3434

**The Snake Lady and Other Stories**
Lee, Vernon   4969, 5772

**The Snake Oil Wars**
Godwin, Parke   433, 2100, 2103, **2249**, 2753, 2859, 3810, 3986, 4028, 4029, 4034, 4035, 4473, 5351, 5532, 5569, 5616, 5636, 5768, 6062, 6064, 6070

**Snakes**
Colson, S. Darnbrook   1467

**The Snarkout Boys and the Avocado of Death**
Pinkwater, Daniel Manus   1224

**Snow Brother**
Stirling, S.M.   787, 3871, 3872, **5299**, 5676

**Snow Crash**
Stephenson, Neal   31, 108, 118, 295, 471, 472, 474, 475, 483, 505, 553, 781, 792, 805, 809, 927, 1227, 1449, 1518, 1761, 1805, 1862, 2087, 2092, 2163, 2219, 2394, 2488, 2579, 2729, 2770, 2839, 2997, 3009, 3082, 3311, 3435, 3449, 3455, 3662, 3921, 4076, 4191, 4193, 4218, 4292, 4478, 4590, 4677, 4704, 4749, 4893, 4894, 4902, 5009, 5074, 5171, **5254**, 5281, 5370, 5438, 5566, 5569, 5573, 5619, 5834, 5957, 6047, 6063, 6079

**The Snow Queen**
Vinge, Joan D.   176, 991, 1176, 3644, 5041, 5757, 5839, 5880

**Snow White and Rose Red**
Wrede, Patricia C.   42, 375, 1005, 1446, 1479, 1810, 2121, 2262, 2636, 5428, 5639, **5981**, 6062, 6088, 6090

**Snow White, Blood Red**
Datlow, Ellen   **1368**, 3844, 4791, 6044, 6045, 6046

**Snowbeast!**
Tremayne, Peter   **5482**

**Snowmen**
Brown, Jerry Earl   725, 5281, 5378

**The Snows of Ganymede**
Anderson, Poul   5561

**The Snows of Jaspre**
Caraker, Mary   **878**, 4147

**Snuff Flique**
Hemmingson, Michael   **2656**

**So Long, and Thanks for All the Fish**
Adams, Douglas   1918, 3573, 4077

**So You Want to Be a Wizard?**
Duane, Diane   168, 641, 847, 1267, 1605, 2949, 4323, 4338, 4404, 5002, 5070, 5977

**Soft and Others**
Wilson, F. Paul   777, 1887, 2277, 3321, 3328, 3329, 4648, 5339, 5600, **5899**

**The Soft Whisper of the Dead**
Grant, Charles L.   1013, 1402, 2220, 3498

**Software**
Rucker, Rudy   79, 806, 808, 1873, 2579, 3921, 4341, 5091, 5213, 5573

**Sojourn**
Salvatore, R.A.   299, 604, 1484, **4806**

**Solar Lottery**
Dick, Philip K.   5048

**Solaris**
Lem, Stanislaw   3617, 4884

**Soldier, Ask Not**
Dickson, Gordon R.   206, 513, 901, 2054, 2349, 3035, 3790, 4194, 4374, 4377, 4466, 5469

**Soldier of Arete**
Wolfe, Gene   2, 11, 2187, 2189, 2751, 2752, 4201, 5790, **5944**

**Soldier of the Mist**
Wolfe, Gene   11, 2187, 2189, 3170, 4272, 5321, 5595, 5738

**The Soldiers of Fear**
Smith, Dean Wesley   9, 901, 903, 2297, **5115**

**Soldiers of Paradise**
Park, Paul   56, 57, 5940

**Soldiers of the Black Goat**
O'Hearn, Marian   2442

**Sole Survivor**
Koontz, Dean R.   1971, **3215**

**Solip: System**
Williams, Walter Jon   **5841**

**Solis**
Attanasio, A.A.   **272**

**Solo**
Mason, Robert   **3665**

**Solomon Kane**
Howard, Robert E.   856

**Solomon's Knife**
Koman, Victor   **3200**

**Solomon's Stone**
de Camp, L. Sprague   3989

**Some Chinese Ghosts**
Hearn, Lafcadio   3250

**Some Enchanted Evening**
Alfonsi, Alice   **73**, 880, 5658

**Some Ghost Stories**
Burrage, A.M.   1350, 3633

**Some of Your Blood**
Sturgeon, Theodore   3519, 3541, 4500, 4576, **5347**, 5423

**Some Things Come Back**
Morgan, Robert   **4004**

**Some Things Never Die**
Morgan, Robert   1335, 2288, **4005**

**Some Will Not Die**
Budrys, Algis   277, 1903, 2805, 3346, 4209, 4605

**Someone in the Dark**
Derleth, August   1088, 3515, 4141

**Someone in the House: Strange Stories Old and New**
Burrage, A.M.   5610

**Someone in the Room: Strange Tales Old and New**
Burrage, A.M.   **779**, 5611

**Someone to Watch over Me**
Sullivan, Tricia   **5355**

**Someplace to Be Flying**
de Lint, Charles   **1435**, 2104

**Something Breathing**
McNail, Stanley   4752

**Something Haunts Us All**
Hopkins, Brian   94, 802, **2769**, 2937, 3495, 3667, 4231, 4313, 5316, 5335, 5445, 5620, 5881

**Something Out There**
Kelly, Ronald   2794, **3056**, 5425

**Something Rich and Strange**
McKillip, Patricia A.   1440, 2088, 2981, 2982, **3840**, 5916

**Something Stirs**
Grant, Charles L.   **2316**, 3137

**Something Upstairs: A Tale of Ghosts**
Avi   1898

**Something Wicked This Way Comes**
Bradbury, Ray   347, 518, 1081, 1282, 2303, 2316, 2557, 2565, 2817, 3137, 3477, 4010, 4057, 4131, 4486, 5060, 5264

**Something's Alive on the Titanic**
Serling, Robert   1202, **4915**

**Sometime, Never**
Peake, Mervyn   98

**Somewhere East of Life**
Aldiss, Brian W.  **60**, 352, 4071

**Somewhere in the Night**
McMahan, Jeffrey N.  2116, **3852**

**Somewhere in Time**
Bretton, Barbara  3576

**Somewhere in Time/What Dreams May Come**
Matheson, Richard  **3690**

**Somewhere South of Midnight**
Gilliam, Richard  5098, 5099

**Son of Darkness**
Sherman, Josepha  **4990**

**Son of Man**
Silverberg, Robert  3434

**Son of Rosemary**
Levin, Ira  **3445**

**Son of Spellsinger**
Foster, Alan Dean  169, 187, **2015**

**The Son of Summer Stars**
Pierce, Meredith Ann  **4319**

**Son of the Endless Night**
Farris, John  5896

**A Song for Arbonne**
Kay, Guy Gavriel  965, **3017**, 4651, 4686, 5222, 5397

**Song for the Basilisk**
McKillip, Patricia A.  **3841**

**Song in the Silence**
Kerner, Elizabeth  **3065**

**The Song of Homana**
Roberson, Jennifer  1179

**Song of Kali**
Simmons, Dan  1338, 1670, 1886, 3408, 5851

**Song of Mavin Manyshaped**
Tepper, Sheri S.  5629

**Song of Sorcery**
Scarborough, Elizabeth Ann  393, 3731

**The Song of the Axe**
Williams, Paul O.  3788, 4600, 4619

**Song of the Dwarves**
Gunnarsson, Thorarinn  4518

**Song of the Gargoyle**
Snyder, Zilpha Keatley  **5153**

**Song of the River**
Harrison, Sue  **2583**

**Song of the Saurials**
Novak, Kate  2426, **4167**, 4806

**Song of the Wolf**
Gear, Kathleen O'Neal  870

**Songmaster**
Card, Orson Scott  729, 1571, 1583, 3286, 3453, 4729

**Songs From the Stars**
Spinrad, Norman  5635, 5909

**Songs of a Dead Dreamer**
Ligotti, Thomas  851, 864, 865, 866, 921, 2294, 2866, 3447, **3464**, 3530, 5317

**Songs of Chaos**
Lewitt, S.N.  **3452**

**The Songs of Distant Earth**
Clarke, Arthur C.  351, 1182, 2006, 3924, 4548, 5804

**Songs of Earth and Power**
Bear, Greg  185, 203, **424**, 1321, 1472, 2737, 3059, 3269, 3886, 4659, 4981, 5221, 5223, 5817, 5818

**Songs of Enchantment**
Okri, Ben  1867, 1868, 3006, **4208**

**Songs of the Dancing Gods**
Chalker, Jack L.  197, **962**, 5218

**Songs the Dead Men Sing**
Martin, George R.R.  1783, 4889, 5058

**Songsmith**
Norton, Andre  1430, **4161**

**Sons of Darkness: Tales of Men, Blood and Immortality**
Rowe, Michael  3618, **4690**, 5386, 5387

**The Sons of Noah and Other Stories**
Cady, Jack  200, **821**, 5165

**Sons of the Titans**
Adkins, Patrick H.  **36**, 458, 1979, 2404, 2658

**Soothsayer**
Resnick, Mike  1238, 1544, **4557**, 4717, 5184, 5376

**Soothslayer: A Magickal Fantasy**
Conway, D.J.  **1143**

**The Soprano Sorceress**
Modesitt, L.E. Jr.  **3938**

**A Sorcerer and a Gentleman**
Willey, Elizabeth  2355, 5503, **5812**

**Sorcerers!**
Dann, Jack  3076

**A Sorcerer's Apprentice**
Williams, Michael  1532, 4261, **5820**

**The Sorcerer's Curse**
Volsky, Paula  4852

**The Sorcerer's Lady**
Volsky, Paula  1030

**Sorcerers of Majipoor**
Silverberg, Robert  **5041**

**Sorcerers of Sodom**
Elwood, Roger  **1804**, 1959, 2930

**The Sorcerer's Sacred Isle**
Taylor, Keith  1961

**The Sorcerer's Skull**
Mason, David  1996

**Sorcerer's Son**
Eisenstein, Phyllis  1104, 5143, 5153

**The Sorceress and the Cygnet**
McKillip, Patricia A.  1035, 1734, **3842**

**Sorceress of Darshiva**
Eddings, David  **1739**, 1842, 5125, 5820

**The Sorceress of Qar**
White, Ted  1772

**Sorceress of the Witch World**
Norton, Andre  638, 3696

**Sorcery and Cecelia**
Wrede, Patricia C.  314, 727, 743, 1742, 1921, 5137, 5266

**The Sorcery Within**
Smeds, Dave  2502, 2553, 4922, 5563

**The Sorrows of Satan**
Corelli, Marie  4571

**Sos the Rope**
Anthony, Piers  4619, 4621

**Soul Catcher**
Kersey, Colin  911, 2340, 2670, **3081**, 3680

**Soul Eater**
Jeter, K.W.  304, 2201, 5879

**Soul Music**
Pratchett, Terry  **4401**

**Soul Snatchers**
Cecilione, Michael  **947**

**Soulcatchers**
Lara, Jan  2689, **3336**

**The Soulforge**
Weis, Margaret  **5728**

**Souls**
Alexis, Katina  **71**, 2023

**Souls/Houston, Houston, Do You Read?**
Russ, Joanna  2829

**Souls in Pawn**
Hatch, George  1281

**Soulsmith**
Deitz, Tom  522, 563, **1475**, 1512, 1639, 2057, 2060, 2552, 2716, 2717, 2942, 3256, 3624, 4060, 4221, 5277, 5529

**Soulstorm**
Williamson, Chet  281, 861, 1192, 1380, 2630, 3684, 3685, 4830, 5380

**The Sound of His Horn**
Sarban  2667, 5301

**The Sounding Stillness**
Von Gunden, Kenneth  **5587**

**The Source**
Lumley, Brian  **3565**

**The Source of Magic**
Anthony, Piers  30, 677

**Sourcery**
Pratchett, Terry  180, 2125

**South of Heaven**
Thompson, Jim  3330

**Southern Blood: Vampire Stories From the American South**
Schimel, Lawrence  **4880**, 5098, 5099

**Southern Discomfort: Selected Works of Elizabeth Massie**
Massie, Elizabeth  113, 1123, **3669**, 4463, 5316, 5881

**Space Cadet**
Heinlein, Robert A.  1900, 4911, 4948, 4958

**Space Demons**
Rubinstein, Gillian  168

**Space Folk**
Anderson, Poul  **132**

**Space Mercenaries**
Chandler, A. Bertram  3747

**The Space Merchants**
Pohl, Frederik  593, 1892, 3794

**Space Opera**
McCaffrey, Anne  3264, **3751**

**Space Opera**
Vance, Jack  4197, 5215

**Space Pioneers**
Norton, Andre  5247

**Space Pirate**
Vance, Jack  1647

**Space Pirates**
Eklund, Gordon  1647

**Space Prison**
Godwin, Tom  6059

**Space Search**
Reynolds, Mack  195

**The Space Swimmers; Science Fiction by Gordon Dickson**
Dickson, Gordon R.  2450

**Space, Time and Crime**
DeFord, Miriam Allen  3619

**The Space Vampires**
Wilson, Colin  4331, 5049

**Space Viking**
Piper, H. Beam  129, 1633, 2374, 5140, 5821

**The Space Willies**
Russell, Eric Frank  1419

**Space Winners**
Dickson, Gordon R.  2647, 3341, 3729

**Spaceballs: The Book**
Stine, Jovial Bob  4565, 4656

**Spacer Dreams**
Segriff, Larry  2478, 4158, 4379, **4911**, 4948, 4958

**Spaceship**
Aldiss, Brian W.  2829

**A Spaceship for the King**
Pournelle, Jerry  1652

**A Spadeful of Spacetime**
Saberhagen, Fred  3459

**Spares**
Smith, Michael Marshall  1973, 5892

**The Sparrow**
Russell, Mary Doria  159, 1442, 3599, 4067, 4711, **4736**, 5372

**Sparrowhawk**
Easton, Thomas A.  892, **1725**, 2215, 2536, 3503, 3932, 4218, 5157, 5260, 5363, 5368, 6048

**Spartacus**
Mancour, T.L.  3767

**Spartan Run**
Robbins, David  **4602**

**The Spawn of Cthulhu**
Carter, Lin 461, 2399, 3535, 4422, 4423, 4425, 4428, 4430, 4431, 5698

**The Spawn of Loki**
Henderson, Jason 458, **2658**, 4516, 4522

**Speak to the Rain**
Passey, Helen K. 1087, **4257**

**Speaker for the Dead**
Card, Orson Scott 230, 1054, 1183, 2297, 3047, 3713, 3790, 3823, 4547, 5434

**Speaker to Heaven**
Noel, Atanielle Annyn 2286

**Speaking Dreams**
Park, Severna 1559, **4245**

**Speaking in Tongues**
McDonald, Ian 2576, **3796**

**The Spear**
Herbert, James 4960

**Spear of Heaven**
Tarr, Judith 1105, 3295, 3353, 4063, **5396**

**Spec-Lit: Speculative Fiction, Number 1**
Eisenstein, Phyllis **1766**

**Spec-Lit: Speculative Fiction, Number 2**
Eisenstein, Phyllis **1767**

**Special Deliverance**
Simak, Clifford D. 635, 5113

**The Specialist**
Whiteford, Wynne 4633, 4635, **5788**

**Species**
Navarro, Yvonne 4075, 4224

**A Specter Is Haunting Texas**
Leiber, Fritz 5626

**Specter of the Past**
Zahn, Timothy 117

**Specters**
Dillard, Anne 1926, 5064

**Specters**
Dillard, J.M. **1555**, 2024, 2556, 3585, 4442, 4501, 5314

**Specters of the Dawn**
Swann, S. Andrew 296, 2580, **5368**

**Specters of the Twilight**
Swann, S. Andrew 1825

**Specterworld**
Haiblum, Isidore **2480**

**Spectral Snow: The Dark Fantasies of Jack Snow**
Snow, Jack **5149**

**Spectre**
Shatner, William **4934**

**Spectres**
Duane, Diane 3130, 3898

**Spectrum**
Amis, Kingsley 4721

**Spectrum 2**
Amis, Kingsley 242

**Spectrum 3**
Amis, Kingsley 243

**Spell Bound**
Emerson, Ru **1810**, 3846, 5534

**Spell Bound**
Simmons, Trana Mae **5061**

**A Spell for Chameleon**
Anthony, Piers 30, 671, 677, 1267, 2123, 2130, 5219, 5224, 6049

**A Spell for the Fulfillment of Desire**
Webb, Don 778, 2137, 4532, 4789, **5662**

**Spell of Apocalypse**
Brenner, Mayer Alan **672**, 1030

**Spell of Fate**
Brenner, Mayer Alan **673**

**The Spell of the Black Dagger**
Watt-Evans, Lawrence **5648**

**Spellcaster**
Ames, J. Edward **92**

**The Spellcoats**
Jones, Diana Wynne 1444, 5496

**Spellfire**
Greenwood, Ed 1485, 3537, 4106

**The Spellkey Trilogy**
Downer, Ann **1592**

**Spells of Enchantment**
Zipes, Jack 276, 849, 1368, 1479, 1576, 2680, 3844, 4890, 4987, 5912, **6090**

**Spellsinger**
Foster, Alan Dean 167, 168, 184, 186, 194, 196, 635, 1416, 1426, 2081, 2946, 3939, 4163, 4401, 4519, 5224

**Spellsinger at the Gate**
Foster, Alan Dean 172

**The Spellsong War**
Modesitt, L.E. Jr. **3939**

**Sphere**
Crichton, Michael 440, 1202, 4915

**Sphynxes Wild**
Friesner, Esther 1098, **2083**, 5939

**Spider**
McGrath, Patrick 811, 2548, **3815**, 4185

**The Spider #1: The Spider and the Pain Master/Secret City of Crime**
Stockbridge, Grant 1940, 4623

**The Spider #3: Death's Crimson Juggernaut/The Red Death Rain**
Stockbridge, Grant 4622, **5307**

**The Spider #4: Death Reign of the Vampire King/The Pain Emperor**
Stockbridge, Grant **5308**

**The Spider #8: The Devil's Paymaster/Legions of the Accursed Light**
Stockbridge, Grant **5309**

**Spider Legs**
Anthony, Piers **189**

**Spider-Man: Carnage in New York**
Michelinie, David 1390

**Spider-Man: The Venom Factor**
Duane, Diane 1227, 1390, **1667**, 3403

**The Spider: Master of Men**
Stockbridge, Grant 3883

**Spider Play**
Killough, Lee 1153, 1665, 2369, 2370, 2375, 2682, 4339

**The Spider's Test**
McKeone, Dixie 2625

**Spindoc**
Perry, Steve **4300**

**Spinneret**
Zahn, Timothy 564, 953, 2491, 3221

**The Spiral Dance**
Garcia y Robertson, R. **2121**, 3261

**Spires of Spirit**
Baudino, Gael **395**, 3356

**The Spirit**
Page, Thomas 5075

**Spirit Catcher**
Hallam, Elizabeth **2497**

**Spirit Crossings**
Peck, Claudia 1471, **4275**

**Spirit Fox**
Reichert, Mickey Zucker **4524**

**The Spirit Gate**
Bohnhoff, Maya Kaathryn **562**, 1143, 1943

**The Spirit of Dorsai**
Dickson, Gordon R. **4377**

**Spirit of the Wind**
Pierson, Chris 2425, **4326**

**The Spirit Ring**
Bujold, Lois McMaster 726, 727, **763**, 841, 1249, 1450, 1451, 1841, 1953, 2079, 2141, 2195, 2269, 2271, 2499, 2503, 2519, 2653, 2862, 2956, 3080, 3168, 3170, 3256, 3293, 3306, 3508, 3509, 3511, 3844, 3941, 4129, 4323, 4462, 4686, 4718, 4768, 4983, 5144, 5163, 5217, 5222, 5251, 5394, 5555, 5584, 5648, 5716, 5749, 5750, 5813, 5978, 5980

**The Spirit Stalker**
Romberg, Nina 542, **4664**

**Spiritride**
Shepherd, Mark **4981**

**Spirits of Cavern and Hearth**
Easton, M. Coleman 1145, 1470, **1722**, 3626, 5097, 5831

**Spirits of Christmas**
Cramer, Kathryn 1307, 1311, 2588, 2894, 4541, 4861

**Spirits of the Ordinary**
Alcala, Kathleen **52**

**Spiritwalk**
de Lint, Charles 1159, **1436**, 1958, 2736, 3299, 3470, 4757, 5913

**Splatterpunks II: Over the Edge**
Sammon, Paul M. **4811**

**Splatterpunks: Extreme Horror**
Sammon, Paul M. **4812**

**Splatterspunk: The Micah Hays Stories**
Lee, Edward **3397**, 5536

**The Splendor and Misery of Bodies, of Cities**
Delany, Samuel R. 1720, 5634

**The Splendour Falls**
Kelly, Erin 23, 3225, 3229, 5797, 5798

**Splinter of the Mind's Eye**
Foster, Alan Dean 76, 2477, 6052, 6054, 6055

**Split Heirs**
Watt-Evans, Lawrence 2073, 2079, **5649**

**Split Infinity**
Anthony, Piers 676, 1421, 1812

**Split Second**
Kilworth, Garry 175, 188, 5998

**Spock Must Die**
Blish, James 1922

**Spock's World**
Duane, Diane 1260, 1384, 1861, 2062, 4137, 5019

**The Spoils of War**
Foster, Alan Dean **2016**

**Spook**
Vance, Steve 1115, 1334, 3020, **5553**

**Spook Night**
Robbins, David 3146, **4603**

**Spooky Sea Stories**
Waugh, Charles G. 2708, 2709, 4308, **5652**

**Sporting Chance**
Moon, Elizabeth 2766, **3974**

**Spree**
Taylor, Lucy 3373, **5415**

**Spring-Heeled Jack**
Pullman, Philip **4447**

**"Spurs"**
Robbins, Todd 1697

**Spyder**
Partridge, Norman 428, 2938, 3102, **4255**

**Squadron Alert**
Green, Roland J. **2352**, 4672

**The Square Deal**
Drake, David 86, **1644**

**The Square Root of Man**
Tenn, William 3500

**The Squares of the City**
Brunner, John 160

**Squire**
Telep, Peter 2858

**Squire's Blood**
Telep, Peter 2858

**SS-GB**
Deighton, Len 598, 2667, 3528

**Stage Fright**
McNally, Clare   **3858**

**Stainless**
Grimson, Todd   **2449**, 4069

**The Stainless Steel Rat**
Harrison, Harry   **5232**

**The Stainless Steel Rat Goes to Hell**
Harrison, Harry   **2574**, 4655

**The Stainless Steel Rat Saves the World**
Harrison, Harry   3343, 3801

**The Stainless Steel Rat Sings the Blues**
Harrison, Harry   **2575**

**Stainless Steel Visions**
Harrison, Harry   **2576**

**Stairway to Forever**
Adams, Robert   4519

**The Stake**
Laymon, Richard   810, 2220, 2441, **3372**, 3498

**The Stalk**
Morris, Janet   **4016**

**The Stalker**
Nixon, Joan Lowery   1801

**Stalker From the Stars**
Wein, Len   1390

**Stalkers**
Gorman, Ed   538, 544, 1019, **2282**, 2600, 3228

**Stalking Darkness**
Flewelling, Lynn   **1953**, 2096, 2253, 2270, 2694, 3080, 3835, 5320, 5758

**The Stalking Horse**
Ash, Constance   **222**, 1743, 2397, 3627, 4493, 5296, 5547

**Stalking the Unicorn: A Fable of Tonight**
Resnick, Mike   1343, 5459, 5642

**The Stallion Queen**
Ash, Constance   **223**, 2673, 2678

**The Stand**
King, Stephen   338, 341, 525, 2934, 3370, 3757, 4413, 5190

**Stand on Zanzibar**
Brunner, John   1785, 4296, 4678, 5173, 5193

**The Stand: The Complete and Uncut Edition**
King, Stephen   343, **3142**, 4384, 4647

**Standing Wave**
Hendrix, Howard V.   **2661**

**Star Anchored, Star Angered**
Elgin, Suzette Haden   4330

**Star Ascendant**
Cooper, Louise   **1180**

**The Star Beast**
Heinlein, Robert A.   3500

**Star Bones Weep the Blood of Angels**
Storm, Sue   693, 802, 2769, 3100, 3318, 3667, **5316**

**Star Born**
Norton, Andre   3769

**Star Bridge**
Gunn, James   **2459**, 3874

**Star Bridge**
Williamson, Jack   2458

**Star Brothers**
Bova, Ben   **594**

**Star Child**
Hogan, James P.   **2730**

**Star Colony**
Laumer, Keith   734, 2491, 4373

**Star Commandos**
Griffin, P.M.   1665

**Star Crusader**
Balfour, Bruce   4495, 5204

**Star Dust**
Jones, Marti   3576

**Star Gate**
Norton, Andre   3801, 5306, 6060

**The Star Ghost**
Strickland, Brad   2109

**Star Guard**
Norton, Andre   1628

**Star Light, Star Bright**
Bester, Alfred   54, 233, 234, 243, 321, 624, 850, 1874, 2569, 3187, 3308, 3342, 4706, 5028, 5344, 5349, 5551, 5641, 5869

**Star Maker**
Stapledon, Olaf   445

**Star of Danger**
Bradley, Marion Zimmer   2764

**The Star of the Guardians Series**
Weis, Margaret   4829

**Star Precinct**
Randle, Kevin D.   **4470**

**Star Prey**
Ehly, Ehren M.   **1763**, 1846, 4716, 5562

**Star Rebel**
Busby, F.M.   1900, 5403

**The Star Scroll**
Rawn, Melanie   604, 1155, 3306, **4491**, 5547, 5582, 5712

**Star Sister**
Coulson, Juanita   **1211**

**Star Smashers and Galaxy Rangers**
Harrison, Harry   3543

**The Star Stalker**
Bloch, Robert   619, 620, 1763, 4131

**Star Trek II: The Wrath of Khan**
McIntyre, Vonda N.   526, 1556

**Star Trek 3**
Blish, James   1658

**Star Trek III: The Search for Spock**
McIntyre, Vonda N.   1954

**Star Trek IV: The Voyage Home**
McIntyre, Vonda N.   569, 1556, 4273

**Star Trek V: The Final Frontier**
Dillard, J.M.   1728, 1967, 2062, 2666

**Star Trek VI: The Undiscovered Country**
Dillard, J.M.   **1556**, 3307

**Star Trek: Generations**
Dillard, J.M.   2061, 2063

**Star Trek Log One**
Foster, Alan Dean   527

**Star Trek Log Ten**
Foster, Alan Dean   526

**Star Trek: The Classic Episodes 1**
Blish, James   **526**

**Star Trek: The Classic Episodes 2**
Blish, James   **527**

**Star Trek: The Classic Episodes 3**
Blish, James   **528**

**Star Trek: The Lost Years**
Dillard, J.M.   **1557**, 1728, 1967, 2062

**Star Trek - The Motion Picture: A Novel**
Roddenberry, Gene   1556

**Star Trek: The New Voyages**
Marshak, Sondra   527

**Star Trek: The New Voyages II**
Marshak, Sondra   527

**Star Wars**
Lucas, George   2171, 2365, 5023, 5116, 5141, 5720, 6052, 6054

**The Star Wars Trilogy**
Lucas, George   76, 114, 2500, 5205, 5527, 5950, 6055

**Star Well**
Panshin, Alexei   1536, 2013, 3345, 3583, 5131

**Star Wreck II: The Attack of the Jargonites**
Rewolinski, Leah   607, 1459, **4563**

**Star Wreck III: Time Warped**
Rewolinski, Leah   1459, **4564**

**Star Wreck IV: Live Long and Profit**
Rewolinski, Leah   **4565**

**Star Wreck 6: Geek Space Nine**
Rewolinski, Leah   **4562**

**Star Wreck: The Generation Gap**
Rewolinski, Leah   607, 1459, 2567, 2568, **4566**, 4656

**Starborne**
Silverberg, Robert   4333, **5042**, 5860

**Starbridge**
Crispin, A.C.   231, 517, **1265**, 1333, 1391, 1978, 2551, 3066, 4160, 4349, 5048, 5780

**The Starcrossed**
Bova, Ben   1918, 2996, 3573

**Starcruiser Shenandoah**
Green, Roland J.   2173

**Stardance**
Robinson, Spider   1548, 2721, 2955, 3238, 3452, 4679, 5609, 5635

**Stardust of Yesterday**
Kurland, Lynn   2540

**Starfarers**
Anderson, Poul   **133**

**Starfarers**
McIntyre, Vonda N.   107, 656, 732, 1559, 1649, 1689, 1897, 2301, 2838, **3824**, 4696, 5188

**A Starfarer's Dozen**
Stearns, Michael   **5238**

**Starfire**
Preuss, Paul   5188, 5246

**Starfire Down**
McKeone, Lee   **3830**

**Starfleet Academy**
Carey, Diane   **905**

**Starfollowers of Coramonde**
Daley, Brian   1754

**StarGate**
Devlin, Dean   1483, **1509**, 4286

**Stargate SG-1**
McConnell, Ashley   **3777**

**Starkadder**
King, Bernard   4518

**Starless Night**
Salvatore, R.A.   1287, 2427, **4807**, 5022

**Starlight 1**
Hayden, Patrick Nielsen   **2634**

**Starlight 2**
Hayden, Patrick Nielsen   **2635**

**The Starlight Crystal**
Pike, Christopher   199, 568, 3597, **4333**, 4966, 5860

**Starliner**
Drake, David   10, 782, **1645**, 2053, 3315, 3968, 3974, 4967, 5676, 5679

**Starman**
Foster, Alan Dean   5375

**Starman Jones**
Heinlein, Robert A.   905, 1899, 1978, 5246

**The Starmen of the Lyrdis**
Brackett, Leigh   5645, 5864

**Starmind**
Robinson, Spider   **4642**

**Starpilot's Grave**
Doyle, Debra   **1606**, 4148, 5674

**Starpirate's Brain**
Goulart, Ron   30, 3345, 5997

**Starplex**
Sawyer, Robert J.   293, 384, 1157, 1759, 2002, 2135, 2417, 2661, 4351, **4859**, 4951, 5367

**Starquake**
Forward, Robert L.   401, 404, 1245

**Starrigger**
DeChancie, John   31, 86, 493, 959, 1144, 1337, 1490, 1645, 2002, 2226, 2332, 2770, 2804, 2836, 3424, 3722, 3741, 3825, 4076, 4077, 4302, 4505, 4662, 4859, 5076, 5227, 5933

**The Starry Child**
Hanna, Lynn   **2540**

**Stars and Stripes Forever**
Harrison, Harry   2577, 5495

**The Stars Are Also Fire**
Anderson, Poul   **134**, 445, 3715, 3795

**The Stars Are Ours**
Norton, Andre   2764, 4964

**The Stars Dispose**
Roessner, Michaela   1679, 3822, **4651**, 5152

**Stars in My Pocket Like Grains of Sand**
Delany, Samuel R.   1720, 5634

**The Stars in Shroud**
Benford, Gregory   351, 1248

**The Stars Like Dust**
Asimov, Isaac   5546

**The Stars Must Wait**
Laumer, Keith   163, 1642, 2805, **3346**, 3586

**The Stars My Destination**
Bester, Alfred   **478**, 1514, 1664, 2171, 2209, 2290, 2545, 2645, 3452, 4280, 4304, 4511, 4557, 5232, 5260, 5598

**Starsea Invaders: First Action**
Stine, G. Harry   1201, **5282**

**Starseed**
Robinson, Spider   **4643**

**Starship**
Aldiss, Brian W.   297, 2243, 2626

**Starship Troopers**
Heinlein, Robert A.   206, 310, 589, 1327, 1382, 1508, 1635, 1641, 1651, 2004, 2210, 2211, 2351, 2353, 2436, 2464, 2790, 4204, 4377, 4378, 4466, 4583, 4672, 4910, 4911, 5023, 5246, 5278, 5279, 5280, 5283, 5469

**StarSpawn**
Von Gunden, Kenneth   1325, **5588**, 5900

**Starstrike**
Gear, W. Michael   1504, **2172**, 2432

**Starswarm**
Pournelle, Jerry   **4379**

**The Start of the End of It All**
Emshwiller, Carol   **1818**, 5641

**Startide Rising**
Brin, David   80, 126, 130, 132, 181, 309, 311, 322, 324, 404, 450, 874, 892, 958, 1056, 1067, 1083, 1255, 1262, 1264, 1503, 1504, 1535, 1545, 1557, 1587, 1634, 1725, 1729, 1995, 2037, 2172, 2224, 2332, 2371, 2419, 2434, 2450, 2649, 2838, 3721, 3729, 3730, 3823, 3830, 3994, 4019, 4122, 4123, 4124, 4217, 4219, 4418, 4419, 4483, 4505, 4557, 4919, 4923, 4951, 4967, 4984, 5108, 5282, 5354, 5431, 5436, 5587, 5589, 5779, 5949, 6051, 6056

**The Startling Worlds of Henry Kuttner**
Kuttner, Henry   3416

**State of Emergency**
Jackson, Basil   4512

**State of Grace**
Wilhelm, Kate   497, 2078, 3185, 5177, **5810**

**The State of the Art**
Banks, Iain M.   **327**, 3106

**Stationfall**
Cover, Arthur Byron   288, **1216**, 1754

**Stations of the Tide**
Swanwick, Michael   472, 2728, 3186, 3604, 4030, 4176, 4652, 4950, **5373**, 5436, 5717

**The Status Civilization**
Sheckley, Robert   3522

**Steal the Dragon**
Briggs, Patricia   **682**

**Stealer's Sky**
Asprin, Robert   2783

**Stealing My Rules**
Webb, Don   778, 3851, **5663**

**Steam**
Laws, Jay B.   2116, **3361**

**The Steampunk Trilogy**
Di Filippo, Paul   403, **1518**, 3931

**Steel and Stone**
Porath, Ellen   **4368**, 4925

**Steel Beach**
Varley, John   5, 77, 79, 126, 128, 134, 236, 249, 587, 1336, 1664, 1695, 1970, 2087, 2218, 2458, 2579, 2645, 2660, 2730, 3263, 3454, 3662, 3761, 3944, 4283, 4342, 4348, 4761, 4860, 4895, 4901, 5242, 5248, 5254, 5370, **5566**, 5573, 5865, 6079

**The Steel Kings**
Roberts, John Maddox   1025, **4621**, 5500

**Steel Rose**
Dalkey, Kara   **1321**, 3886, 3887, 5273

**The Steel Valentine**
Lansdale, Joe R.   2279

**Steelheart**
Dietz, William C.   **1552**

**The Steerswoman**
Kirstein, Rosemary   394, 580, 692, 1756, 1815, 2038, 2260, 2443, 2796, 2799, 2812, 3043, 3050, **3158**, 3231, 3399, 3471, 3627, 3628, 3629, 3630, 3719, 3721, 3724, 3748, 3862, 3872, 4119, 4147, 4596, 4999, 5091, 5097, 5233, 5296, 5748, 5984

**Stellar Ranger**
Perry, Steve   5151

**Sten**
Cole, Allan   63, 309, 312, 771, 1254, 1331, 1333, 1535, 1550, 1573, 1575, 1604, 2364, 2366, 4375, 4939, 5138, 6014, 6052, 6054

**Step to the Stars**
Del Rey, Lester   3199

**The Stepford Wives**
Levin, Ira   1817, 1944, 3041, 4083, 4087, 4090, 5021, 5789

**Steppe**
Anthony, Piers   590

**Stepwater**
Douglas, L. Warren   708, 758, 1266, 1500, 1553, 1582, **1588**, 1807, 2059, 2135, 4101, 5437, 5465, 5543

**Stickman**
Pfefferle, Seth   5075

**The Still**
Feintuch, David   **1902**

**Still Dead: Book of the Dead 2**
Skipp, John   2977, 4168, 4412, 4745, 4746, 4786, 4811, **5083**, 5313, 5888

**Still Forms on Foxfield**
Slonczewski, Joan   211, 2243, 2578, 2751, 3344

**Still Life**
Horlak, E.E.   2819

**Still River**
Clement, Hal   133

**Still Weird**
Wilson, Gahan   3334

**Stinger**
Kress, Nancy   **3243**

**Stinger**
McCammon, Robert R.   576, 617, 1037, 2314, 3129

**A Stir of Echoes**
Matheson, Richard   2613, 2874, 3135, 3965

**Stitch**
Morris, Mark   1354, **4024**

**Stolen Dreams**
Lyndell, Catherine   313

**The Stolen Goddess**
Purtill, Richard   5496

**The Stolen Law**
Mason, Anne   4158, 4911, 5609

**The Stolen Throne**
Turtledove, Harry   3913, 5041, **5510**

**The Stone and the Flute**
Bemmann, Hans   273

**Stone Angels**
Jefferies, Mike   **2889**, 4852

**The Stone Arrow**
Herley, Richard   275, 1632, 2167, 2168, 2169, 2581, 4818, 4819, 5444

**The Stone Circle**
Goshgarian, Gary   **2285**

**Stone Dead**
Jamison, Ellen   **2878**, 3217, 3784

**The Stone Dogs**
Stirling, S.M.   1326, 1579, 4372, **5300**

**The Stone Dragon and Other Tragic Romances**
Gilchrist, R. Murray   964, **2225**

**The Stone Garden**
Rosenblum, Mary   506, 2559, 3453, 3454, **4679**, 5565, 5609, 5777

**The Stone Giant**
Blaylock, James P.   **523**, 1208, 2132, 2133, 3811

**A Stone in Heaven**
Anderson, Poul   248, 5917

**Stone Junction**
Dodge, Jim   4607

**The Stone Movers**
Mullen, Patricia   **4045**, 4107, 4110, 4795

**Stone of Farewell**
Williams, Tad   4167, 5750, **5831**

**Stone of Tears**
Goodkind, Terry   1674, 1734, 2126, 2128, **2269**, 2958, 3936, 4107, 4337, 4527, 4739, 4795, 6004

**The Stone of Time**
Estes, Rose   **1840**, 3169

**The Stone Prince**
Patton, Fiona   3509, **4259**, 4533

**The Stone Within**
Wingrove, David   **5920**

**The Stoneground Ghost Tales**
Swain, E.G.   1350

**The Stones of Green Knowe**
Boston, L.M.   1138

**Stones of the Dalai Lama**
Mitchell, Ken   **3916**

**Stoneskin's Revenge**
Deitz, Tom   487, **1476**

**Stonewords: A Ghost Story**
Conrad, Pam   122, 1012, **1138**, 1272, 2283, 4078

**Stopping at Slowyear**
Pohl, Frederik   2806, 3075, 3185, 3237, 4172, 4176, **4355**, 4949, 4957, 5809, 6068

**The Store**
Little, Bentley   3497

**Storeys From the Old Hotel**
Wolfe, Gene   415, 1431, 1608, 2736, 4561, 4757, 5913, **5945**

**Stories, 1904-1924**
Kafka, Franz   573, 3460, 5317

**Stories by Mama Lansdale's Youngest Boy**
Lansdale, Joe R.   2078, **3333**, 6068

**Stories From the Twilight Zone**
Serling, Rod   2402, 3132, 4913, 4914, 5473

**Stories of Darkness and Dread**
Brennan, Joseph Payne   2319, 4463

**The Stories of Ray Bradbury**
Bradbury, Ray   429, 532, 893, 3683, 3686, 3687, 4131, 4132, 5929

**Stories of the Seen and Unseen**
Oliphant, Margaret   4969

**Stories of the Supernatural**
James, Henry   45, 5772

**Stories of the Walking Dead**
Haining, Peter   2379, 2977, 4412, 5083

**Storm Breaking**
Lackey, Mercedes   **3296**

**Storm Caller**
Severance, Carol   **4924**

**Storm Knights**
Slavicsek, Bill   2056, 3015, **5087**, 5210, 5438

**The Storm Lord**
Lee, Tanith   5683

**A Storm of Wings**
Harrison, M. John   5547

**Storm Rising**
Lackey, Mercedes   **3297**

**Storm Shield**
Flint, Kenneth C.   5962, 5963

**A Storm upon Ulster**
Flint, Kenneth C.   1764, 5408

**Storm Warning**
Lackey, Mercedes   **3298**

**Storm Warriors**
Craig, Brian   **1240**, 4109

**Stormblade**
Berberick, Nancy Varian   3155, 5454, 5455, 5711

**Stormbringer**
Moorcock, Michael   2781

**Stormqueen!**
Bradley, Marion Zimmer   256, 3746, 3940

**Storms of Victory**
Norton, Andre   **4162**

**Stormtrack**
Sutherland, James   354

**Stormwarden**
Wurts, Janny   1906, 1907, 2356, 3270, 3385, 5728

**The Story of King Arthur and His Knights**
Pyle, Howard   224, 2767, 5970

**Story of the Amulet**
Nesbit, E.   332

**The Story of the Champions of the Round Table**
Pyle, Howard   224, 5970

**The Story of the Stone**
Hughart, Barry   3338, 4742

**Storyteller**
Yolen, Jane   2947, 5782, 5973

**The Storyteller and the Jahn**
Goldin, Stephen   6087

**Storytellers**
Parks, Julie Anne   **4249**

**Straker's Island**
Harris, Steve   4249

**Stranded**
Grae, Camaren   74, 662, **2295**, 3539, 4245

**Stranded!**
Norwood, Warren   141, 1563, **4164**

**Strands of Starlight**
Baudino, Gael   750, 2121, 2799, 3078, 3274, 4337

**Strands of Sunlight**
Baudino, Gael   396, 2800, 4171, 4221, 4862, 4863, 4864, 5912

**A Strange and Ancient Name**
Sherman, Josepha   3274, 3275, **4991**

**Strange Angels**
Koja, Kathe   212, 814, 2030, 2548, **3197**, 3812, 4084

**Strange Attractors**
Carver, Jeffrey A.   **934**

**Strange Attractors**
Sleator, William   121, **5088**

**Strange Attractors: Original Australian Speculative Fiction**
Broderick, Damien   2593, 4713

**Strange Bedfellows: Sex and Science Fiction**
Scortia, Thomas N.   1362, 1607

**The Strange Case of Dr. Jekyll and Mr. Hyde**
Stevenson, Robert Louis   19, 535, 1424, 2702, 2818, 3178, 3654, 4089

**Strange City**
Krause, Staley   23, 3225, **3229**, 3613, 5797

**Strange Conflict**
Wheatley, Dennis   92, 637, 941

**Strange Creatures**
Jens, Tina L.   **2892**

**Strange Deliverance**
Brown, Mary   **728**

**Strange Devices of the Sun and Moon**
Goldstein, Lisa   1679, **2262**, 3822

**Strange Disappearances**
O'Donnell, Elliott   2543

**Strange Dreams**
Donaldson, Stephen R.   **1576**

**Strange Eons**
Bloch, Robert   1497, 2743, 2748, 3548, 3566, 3567, 3568, 3569, 4007, 4112, 4449, 5053, 5470

**Strange Gateways**
Price, E. Hoffman   3515

**Strange Harvest**
Wandrei, Donald   4904, 4905

**Strange Highways**
Koontz, Dean R.   2277, 2714, **3216**, 5885

**Strange Invasion**
Kandel, Michael   1452, 1454, 1522, 1999, **3012**, 3106, 3434, 4365, 5009

**Strange Monsters of the Recent Past**
Waldrop, Howard   25, 5047, **5615**, 5641, 5805, 6020

**The Strange Papers of Dr. Blayre**
Blayre, Christopher   3360

**Strange Ports of Call**
Derleth, August   5691

**Strange Relations**
Farmer, Philip Jose   1362, 4139

**Strange Stains and Mysterious Smells**
Jones, Terry   2088, **2982**

**Strange Tales From the Nile Empire**
Farshtey, Greg   **1889**, 2472, 3015, 4909, 5210, 5438

**Strange Tales From the Strand**
Adrian, Jack   **39**, 4026

**Strange Things and Stranger Places**
Campbell, Ramsey   **864**, 3530, 5600

**Strange Wine**
Ellison, Harlan   3421

**The Stranger**
Fullilove, Eric James   **2093**

**Stranger at the Wedding**
Hambly, Barbara   **2509**, 2958, 3776, 5127

**Stranger by Night**
Gelb, Jeff   1361, **2185**

**Stranger in a Strange Land**
Heinlein, Robert A.   362, 1587, 1862, 2103, 2343, **2649**, 2722, 3924, 3943, 3944, 4139, 4242, 4330, 4347, 5373, 5436, 5449, 5532

**Stranger Suns**
Zebrowski, George   382, 472, 753, 782, 786, 1026, 1509, 2036, 2728, 3786, 4019, 4281, 4503, 4652, 4859, 5054, 5306, 5449, 5774, 5775, **6060**

**Strangers**
Dozois, Gardner   791

**Strangers**
Koontz, Dean R.   1380, 4189

**Strangers From the Sky**
Bonanno, Margaret Wander   526, 528, 902, 1225, 1386, 2065, 2298, 4511, 5375

**Strangers on a Train**
Highsmith, Patricia   2415

**Strata**
Pratchett, Terry   3050

**Street**
Cady, Jack   **822**

**Street Magic**
Reaves, Michael   3271, 3301, 4261, **4497**, 4675, 4993

**The Street of Crocodiles**
Schulz, Bruno   950, 2294, 3460, 3461, 3464, 5876

**A Street of Little Shops**
Bianco, Margery Williams   3610

**The Streeter**
Barry, Scott Ian   **373**, 488

**Streetlethal**
Barnes, Steven   4117, 4227, 4366, 4747, 6075

**Streets of Blood**
Sargent, Carl   1591, **4821**, 5135

**Streets of Blood: Vampire Stories From New York City**
Schimel, Lawrence   **4881**

**The Stress of Her Regard**
Powers, Tim   912, 1276, 2265, 2741, **4385**, 4546, 5052, 5614, 5615, 5842, 6018, 6022

**The Stricken Field**
Duncan, Dave   **1688**

**Strings**
Duncan, Dave   **1689**, 4696

**Striped Holes**
Broderick, Damien   2013

**Striper Assassin**
Smith, Nyx   1591, **5135**

**Strong Spirits**
DeCarlo, Elisa   **1451**

**Stronghold**
Rawn, Melanie   28, 182, 3067, 3581, 3839, **4492**

**The Struggle**
Ahern, Jerry   **44**, 1924

**Strum Again?**
Scarborough, Elizabeth Ann   **4870**

**A Study in Sorcery**
Kurland, Michael   1151, 1153, 2370, 2627, 2628, **3252**

**Stunts**
Grant, Charles L.   **2317**, 4009, 4601, 4603

**Sturgeon Is Alive and Well**
Sturgeon, Theodore   1608, 4561

**Substitute Teacher**
Storm, Jordan   **5314**

**Subterranean Gallery**
Russo, Richard Paul   4051, **4750**, 5910

**The Subtle Knife**
Pullman, Philip   **4448**

**Succumb**
Dee, Ron   138, 1086, **1468**, 4224

**Such Pain**
Bassingthwaite, Don   2321, 5535

**Suckers**
Billson, Anne   **490**, 1802, 3988, 4445, 5406

**A Sudden Wild Magic**
Jones, Diana Wynne   **2950**

**Suffer the Children**
Saul, John   1236, 1848, 2801, 4450, 4645, 5623

**Sugar Rain**
Park, Paul   56, 57, **4243**, 5940

**Suicide Art**
Edelman, Scott   693, 700, 1021, **1740**, 3318, 5411, 5413

**Suicide Attack**
Sievert, John   1567, **5023**, 5469

**Suisan**
Agins, Phyllis Carol   **42**

**The Suiting**
Wilde, Kelley   839, **5803**

**Suldrun's Garden**
Vance, Jack   222, 3822

**The Sum of Things**
Green, Roland J.   **2353**

**The Summer I Shrank My Grandmother**
Woodruff, Elvira   **5968**

**Summer King, Winter Fool**
Goldstein, Lisa   1814, 1866, **2263**, 3838, 3841, 3925, 4528, 5728, 5811

**Summer of Fear**
Duncan, Lois   1801

**Summer of Love**
Mason, Lisa   1345, 1480, 3071, **3664**, 5873

**Summer of Night**
Simmons, Dan   3754, 4907, **5060**

**The Summer Queen**
Vinge, Joan D.   351, 721, 741, 758, 762, 953, 954, 961, 1388, 1469, 1593, 1606, 3729, 3745, 3750, 3927, 4729, 5548, **5572**, 5745

**The Summer Tree**
Kay, Guy Gavriel   28, 391, 1010, 1288, 1474, 1476, 1660, 1686, 1739, 1947, 2471, 2506, 2986, 2988, 3058, 3059, 3062, 3068, 3069, 3357, 3401, 3650, 3653, 3765, 4457, 4493, 4659, 4661, 4730, 5719

**The Summerhill Hounds**
King, J. Robert   1485

**Summerland**
James, L. Dean   153, 1180, **2865**, 3843, 3936, 4105, 4107, 4908

**Summertide**
Sheffield, Charles   **4965**

**The Summit**
Myers, Edward   **4063**

**Summon the Keeper**
Huff, Tanya   1657, **2800**

**The Summoned**
Fulgham, Steven Ray   **2090**, 3394, 4598

**Summoned to Tourney**
Lackey, Mercedes   1436, 2467, **3299**, 4862, 4980

**The Summoning**
Little, Bentley   1335, 2220, **3498**, 4003, 5800

**Sun Horse, Moon Horse**
Sutcliff, Rosemary   3876, 5618

**The Sun Smashers**
Hamilton, Edmond   5863

**The Sun, the Moon, and the Stars**
Brust, Steven   42, 375, 1005, 1446, 1479, 2236, 3281, 5981, 6001, 6088, 6090

**The Sunbound**
Felice, Cynthia   1719, 3718

**Sunder, Eclipse and Seed**
Guttenberg, Elise   **2471**, 6039

**Sundered Soul**
Tella, Alfred   1925

**Sunderlies Seeking**
Greeno, Gayle   **2424**

**The Sundial**
Jackson, Shirley   2314

**Sundiver**
Brin, David   401, 567, 1157, 2223, 4416, 6065

**Sundowner**
Claremont, Chris   **1043**

**Sunfall**
Cherryh, C.J.   2533

**Sunglasses After Dark**
Collins, Nancy A.   490, 600, 697, 799, 948, **1124**, 1707, 1882, 2151, 2336, 2449, 2510, 3405, 3407, 3564, 4464, 4513, 5419

**Sunrunner's Fire**
Rawn, Melanie   3905, **4493**, 5582

**The Sunset Warrior**
Van Lustbader, Eric   3659, 3982

**Sunshaker's War**
Deitz, Tom   1432, **1477**, 3077, 3294

**Sunstroke**
Kagan, David   2301, **2999**, 4416

**Super Carrier: The Ultimate Secret Weapon**
Albano, Peter   **50**

**The Super Hugos**
Greenberg, Martin H.   **2405**

**Superheroes**
Varley, John   1227, 1390, 1667, 3403, **5567**

**Superhorror**
Campbell, Ramsey   2307, 3961

**Superluminal**
McIntyre, Vonda N.   181, 2838, 4349, 5985

**Superman III**
Kotzwinkle, William   5262

**Superman: Last Son of Krypton**
Maggin, Elliot S.   999, 2393, 5262

**Superman: Miracle Monday**
Maggin, Elliot S.   999, 2393, 5262

**Supernatural Cats**
Necker, Claire   1369, 3145, 5252

**Supernatural Sleuths**
Haining, Peter   5653

**Supernatural Sleuths**
Waugh, Charles G.   5459, **5653**

**Supernatural Stories**
Mayne, William   1693, 1701, 4282

**Supernatural Tales: Excursions into Fantasy**
Lee, Vernon   4968

**Supernatural Tales From around the World**
Hardin, Terri   **2543**, 2643

**The Supernatural Tales of Fitz-James O'Brien**
O'Brien, Fitz-James   2633

**Supernova**
Allen, Roger MacBride   **82**, 354, 4652

**Superstition**
Ambrose, David   **90**

**Superstitious**
Stine, R.L.   1354, 2139, 3499, **5290**

**Superstoe**
Borden, William   499, 2186, 2393, 3222, 3439, 3455, 4606

**The Sure Death of a Mouse**
Crawford, Dan   **1250**

**Surface Action**
Drake, David   **1646**, 4911

**Surfing Samurai Robots**
Gilden, Mel   31, 1935, 2007, 2013, 3441, 4341, 4473, 4640, 5934

**Surrender None: The Legacy of Gird**
Moon, Elizabeth   673, 936, 1156, 3105, 3510, 3539, 3846, 3904, 3934, **3975**, 4167, 4802, 4806, 5507, 5712, 5790, 5819, 6082

**The Survival Game**
Kapp, Colin   1248, 1641, 2016, 4964, 5781

**Survivor**
Butler, Octavia E.   210, 1595, 1914, 2223, 2224, 2542, 3157, 3871, 4116

**Survivor**
Herbert, James   3215

**Survivors**
Lorrah, Jean   2068

**Suspicion**
McQuay, Mike   78

**Svaha**
de Lint, Charles   431, 974, **1437**, 1477, 1499, 1936, 3583, 4192, 4991, 5134, 6008

**Swamp**
Tremayne, Peter   2430, **5483**

**Swamp Foetus**
Brite, Poppy Z.   **700**, 1123, 2698, 2860, 3090, 3100, 3318, 3393, 3667, 3669, 3673, 4886, 5008, 5411, 5412, 5413, 5416

**Swan Song**
McCammon, Robert R.   338, 341, 343, 525, 3142, 3143, **3757**, 4647, 5190

**Sweet Blood**
Graversen, Pat   **2337**, 4666, 5705, 5852

**Sweet Dreams**
Frayn, Michael   519

**Sweet Heart**
James, Peter   **2875**

**Sweet Myth-tery of Life**
Asprin, Robert   197, **262**

**Sweet Revenge**
Simon, Jean   **5066**

**Sweet Silver Blues**
Cook, Glen   1665, 1935, 2226, 2228, 2363, 2369, 2370, 2375, 2376, 2620, 2628, 2756, 2757, 2759, 3441, 3512, 3514, 4166, 4362, 4673, 5232, 6022

**Sweet William**
Palmer, Jessica   **4239**

**The Sweetheart Season**
Fowler, Karen Joy   **2029**, 4992

**Sweetheart, Sweetheart**
Taylor, Bernard   608, 3684, 4223, **5402**

**A Swiftly Tilting Planet**
L'Engle, Madeleine   1343

**Sword and Sorceress I-XII**
Bradley, Marion Zimmer   765, 4759

**Sword and Sorceress VIII**
Bradley, Marion Zimmer   **646**

**Sword and Sorceress IX**
Bradley, Marion Zimmer   **647**

**Sword and Sorceress XI**
Bradley, Marion Zimmer   **648**

**Sword and Sorceress XII**
Bradley, Marion Zimmer   **649**

**Sword and Sorceress XIII**
Bradley, Marion Zimmer   **650**

**Sword and Sorceress XIV**
Bradley, Marion Zimmer   **651**

**The Sword and Sorceress Series**
Bradley, Marion Zimmer   316, 1808, 1811, 2072, 2074, 3076, 3290, 3670, 3906, 4610, 5018

**The Sword and the Eye**
Leiber, Justin   2367

**The Sword and the Lion**
Cray, Roberta   **1253**, 3268

**The Sword and the Tower**
Leiber, Justin   993

**Sword at Sunset**
Sutcliff, Rosemary   2188, 3501, 5015

**Sword-Born**
Roberson, Jennifer   **4612**

**Sword-Breaker**
Roberson, Jennifer   **4613**

**Sword-Dancer**
Roberson, Jennifer   1004, 2502, 4521, 5293

*A Sword for a Dragon*
Rowley, Christopher  **4697**

*The Sword in the Stone*
White, T.H.  370, 372, 3720, 6035,
6038

*Sword-Maker*
Roberson, Jennifer  3471, **4614**

*The Sword of Bedwyr*
Salvatore, R.A.  **4808**, 5200

*The Sword of Calandra*
Dexter, Susan  993, 3121

*The Sword of Conan*
Howard, Robert E.  4617

*The Sword of Culann*
Levin, Betty  1294

*Sword of Fire and Shadow*
Paxson, Diana L.  **4268**

*Sword of Flame*
Furey, Maggie  **2098**

*The Sword of Forebearance*
Williams, Paul O.  1329, 4602

*Sword of Ice and Other Tales of
Valdemar*
Lackey, Mercedes  1735, 2991, **3300**

*The Sword of Maiden's Tears*
Edghill, Rosemary  **1748**, 2141

*The Sword of Rhiannon*
Brackett, Leigh  2414, 4151, 5752

*The Sword of Sagamore*
Dalkey, Kara  1514

*The Sword of Samurai Cat*
Rogers, Mark E.  4549, **4657**

*The Sword of Shannara*
Brooks, Terry  2884, 3634, 4284,
5757

*Sword of the Gael*
Offutt, Andrew J.  1960, 2572, 3358,
3501, 3504, 3506, 4266, 4267,
4268, 5962, 5963

*Sword of the Lamb*
Wren, M.K.  741, 3018, 5684

*The Sword of the Lictor*
Wolfe, Gene  4242

*The Sword of the Spirits*
Christopher, John  3255

*Sword-Singer*
Roberson, Jennifer  1439, 1486, 1487

*The Sword Smith*
Arnason, Eleanor  16, 409, 667, 669,
987, 1042, 1292, 1592, 1790,
2263, 2362, 3098, 3385, 3401,
3540, 3652, 3728, 3925, 3930,
5579

*The Swordbearer*
Cook, Glen  978, 979, 1636, 1790,
1902, 2356, 2886, 3122, 3385,
3652, 3982, 4165, 4294, 4457,
4766, 4777, 4975, 5458

*Swords Against Death*
Leiber, Fritz  2362, 5102

*Swords Against the Shadowland*
Bailey, Robin Wayne  **291**, 3418

*Swords Against Wizardry*
Leiber, Fritz  3836

*Swords and Deviltry*
Leiber, Fritz  259, 1239, 1241, 1979,
2101, 2363, 2368, 3246, 3512,
4316, 4975, 4994, 5840

*Swords and Sorcery*
de Camp, L. Sprague  4759, 5599

*The Swords of Lankhmar*
Leiber, Fritz  1706, 2783

*Swords of the Rainbow*
Garber, Eric  **2117**, 2444

*The Swords of Zinjaban*
de Camp, L. Sprague  **1418**, 1757,
5227

*The Swords Trilogy*
Moorcock, Michael  1147, 1961,
3358

*Swordspoint*
Kushner, Ellen  290, 409, 1140,
1142, 1679, 1902, 2032, 2263,
2355, 2759, 3288, 3405, 3419,
3422, 3841, 4612, 4743, 5458,
5579, 5811, 5813, 5976

*Sympathy for the Devil*
Lisle, Holly  639, **3488**

*Symphony*
Grant, Charles L.  **2318**

*Symphony*
Savage, Adrian  3389, 3885, 4588,
4646, 4754, **4847**

*Synners*
Cadigan, Pat  294, 295, 386, 419,
483, 548, 766, 781, **808**, 835,
1418, 1449, 1549, 1760, 1878,
1936, 2218, 2219, 2488, 2535,
2721, 2723, 2955, 2998, 3046,
3082, 3311, 3559, 3604, 3661,
3764, 3818, 3850, 3921, 3922,
4099, 4135, 4366, 4677, 4748,
4821, 5134, 5171, 5184, 5213,
5253, 5254, 5256, 5259, 5491,
5619, 5873, 5959

*Synthesis & Other Virtual Realities*
Rosenblum, Mary  2027, 2120, 3087,
3600, 3971, **4680**

*Synthetic Men of Mars*
Burroughs, Edgar Rice  1414

*Systemic Shock*
Ing, Dean  3966, 4343, 4602

*Systems*
Quick, W.T.  361, 3995, **4452**, 4555,
5449


**T**

*T.J.'s Ghost*
Climo, Shirley  **1087**

*T Zero*
Calvino, Italo  677

*The Tachyon Web*
Pike, Christopher  2291

*Tactical Error*
Gunnarsson, Thorarinn  **2466**

*The Tactics of Mistake*
Dickson, Gordon R.  1322, 1326,
1327, 1641, 2054, 2349, 2351,
2353, 3790, 3875, 4468, 4672

*Taflak Lysandra*
Smith, L. Neil  4435

*Tailchaser's Song*
Williams, Tad  32, 432, 599, 737,
1657, 2421, 2423, 2774, 2775,
2848, 2849, 2850, 2851, 2852,
2853, 2854, 2855, 3115, 3120,
3377, 3740, 4054, 4143, 4144,
4145, 4157, 4271, 4273

*Take Back Plenty*
Greenland, Colin  929, 1059, **2419**,
3190, 3448, 4019, 4421, 4896,
5227

*Takeoff!*
Garrett, Randall  119, 607, 1752,
2398, 4134, 5713, 6077

*Takeoff, Too*
Garrett, Randall  119, 607, 1752,
2398, 6077

*The Taking*
Beman, Donald  **438**

*Taking Flight*
Watt-Evans, Lawrence  3446, **5650**

*The Taking of Satcon Station*
Cohen, Barney  1665, 4469, 5032

*The Tale of the Body Thief*
Rice, Anne  2149, **4576**

*A Tale of Time City*
Jones, Diana Wynne  121, 2272,
5822

*The Tale of Troy*
Green, Roger Lancelyn  1129

*A Talent for the Invisible*
Goulart, Ron  3345, 4362

*A Talent for War*
McDevitt, Jack  443, 516, **3790**

*Tales and Stories of Mary
Wollstonecraft Shelley*
Shelley, Mary  2158

*Tales by Moonlight*
Salmonson, Jessica Amanda  1823,
4846, 5447

*Tales by Moonlight II*
Salmonson, Jessica Amanda  1823,
4200, 4846

*Tales From a Vanished Country*
Lynn, Elizabeth A.  1428, 3945, 5810

*Tales From Gavagan's Bar*
de Camp, L. Sprague  2299, 4637,
4639

*Tales From Jabba's Palace*
Anderson, Kevin J.  **114**

*Tales From Planet Earth*
Clarke, Arthur C.  234, 443, **1061**

*Tales From Tethedril*
Siegel, Scott  **5022**

*Tales From the Bounty Hunters*
Anderson, Kevin J.  2914

*Tales From the Brothers Grimm and
the Sisters Weird*
Vande Velde, Vivian  1366, **5557**

*Tales From the Crypt*
Oleck, Jack  2403, 5473

*Tales From the Crypt: Demon Knight*
Boyll, Randall  **617**

*Tales From the Darkside, Volume 1*
Galen, Mitchell  2402, 2403, 5473

*Tales From the Great Turtle*
Anthony, Piers  **190**, 2686

*Tales From the Mos Eisley Cantina*
Anderson, Kevin J.  **115**

*Tales From the New Twilight Zone*
Straczynski, J. Michael  2402, 2403,
4913, 4914, **5473**

*Tales From the Nightside*
Grant, Charles L.  623, **2319**, 4463,
4891

*Tales From the Shadows*
Chetwynd-Hayes, R.  939

*Tales From the White Hart*
Clarke, Arthur C.  115, 2299, 4637,
4639

*Tales From Watership Down*
Adams, Richard  32, 408, 2849, 2854

*Tales of Forbidden Passion*
Jens, Tina L.  **2893**

*Tales of Gooseflesh and Laughter*
Wyndham, John  5747

*Tales of H.P. Lovecraft*
Lovecraft, H.P.  **3534**

*The Tales of Hoffmann*
Hoffmann, E.T.A  5418

*Tales of Horror and the Supernatural*
Machen, Arthur  2710

*Tales of Known Space*
Niven, Larry  129, 233, 234, 479,
1608, 1874, 2828, 3308, 3771,
4346, 4372, 4706, 4953, 4961,
5106, 5349, 5369, 5574

*Tales of Love and Horror*
Congdon, Don  75, 1357, 3026, 4465

*Tales of Lovecraftian Horror and
Humor*
Cannon, P.H.  **868**

*Tales of Mithgar*
McKiernan, Dennis L.  **3836**

*Tales of Mystery and Terror*
Pamely, C.D.  964, 2225

*Tales of Neveryon*
Delany, Samuel R.  729, 746, 2328,
3872, 5684, 5937, 5945

*Tales of Ravenloft*
Thomsen, Brian  155, 3224

*Tales of Riverworld*
Farmer, Philip Jose  **1875**, 4929

*Tales of Robin Hood*
Emery, Clayton  2248, 2389

*Tales of Sesqua Valley*
Pugmire, W.H.  3556, **4444**, 4878

**Tales of Talislanta**
Sechi, Stephen Michael  **4909**

**Tales of the Black Widowers**
Asimov, Isaac  585, 3619

**Tales of the Cthulhu Mythos**
Derleth, August  539, 3535, 4425, 4431

**Tales of the Cthulhu Mythos**
Lovecraft, H.P.  148, 4429

**Tales of the Cthulhu Mythos: Golden Anniversary Anthology**
Lovecraft, H.P.  461, 2978, 4422, 4423, 4424, 4428, 4430, 4431, 5325, 5698

**Tales of the Lovecraft Collectors**
Faig, Kenneth W. Jr.  **1859**

**Tales of the Lovecraft Mythos**
Price, Robert M.  461, 2978, **4431**, 5325, 5494

**Tales of the Occult**
Wolf, Jack C.  4026

**Tales of the Providence Pales**
Price, Robert M.  1859

**Tales of the White Wolf**
Kramer, Edward E.  **3227**, 3980, 4759

**Tales of Titillation and Terror**
Ames, Mel D.  **94**, 5335

**Tales of Witchcraft**
Dalby, Richard  1711

**Tales of Wonder**
Yolen, Jane  3845

**Tales of Zothique**
Smith, Clark Ashton  291, 1699, 1700, 3420, 3859, **5104**

**Tales out of Time**
Ireson, Barbara  4917

**Talion: Revenant**
Stackpole, Michael A.  **5206**

**The Talisman**
King, Stephen  341, 347, 3551, 3565, 3779, 4009

**The Talismans of Shannara**
Brooks, Terry  681, **717**, 5716

**The Talking Dog and the Barking Man**
Seeman, Elizabeth  2786

**Talking to Dragons**
Wrede, Patricia C.  168, 703, 1220, 1488, 1668, 2014, 2946, 3070, 3728, 4322

**A Tall Story and Other Tales**
Mahy, Margaret  **3611**

**The Tallow Image**
Brindle, Jane  **690**, 3146, 5334

**Taltos**
Rice, Anne  **4577**

**Tam Lin**
Dean, Pamela  42, 375, 391, 637, 935, 1005, 1409, 1434, **1446**, 2538, 4008, 4870, 5178, 5428

**Tam Lin**
Yolen, Jane  3523

**Tamastara, or, the Indian Nights**
Lee, Tanith  1316, 1317, 1318, 1699

**Taming the Forest King**
Edwards, Claudia J.  2651

**Taminy**
Bohnhoff, Maya Kaathryn  396, **563**, 1135, 4159

**Tangents**
Bear, Greg  **425**, 4998, 5255, 5837

**The Tangle Box**
Brooks, Terry  **718**

**The Tangled Lands**
Shetterly, Will  104, 105, 179, 180, 475, 1161, 1163, 1452, 1461, 1662, 1684, 2082, 2330, 2644, 2791, 3587, 3831, 5063, 5156, 5159, 5558, 5719

**Tangled Webs**
Mudd, Steve  **4044**

**Tango Charlie and Foxtrot Charlie/ The Star Pit**
Varley, John  130

**Tanis, the Shadow Years**
Siegel, Barbara  154, 3155, 5454, 5455

**Tap, Tap**
Martin, David  **3640**

**Tapestry of Dark Souls**
Bergstrom, Elaine  155, **465**, 2516, 2663, 5847

**A Tapestry of Lions**
Roberson, Jennifer  **4615**

**A Tapestry of Magics**
Daley, Brian  259, 747, 4670

**Tapping the Vein: Book One**
Barker, Clive  3334

**Tapping the Vein: Books One and Two**
Barker, Clive  **346**

**The Tar-Aiym Krang**
Foster, Alan Dean  322, 741, 1553, 3359, 3717, 4711, 4829, 4930

**Target**
Morris, Janet  **4017**, 5129, 5787, 5932

**Target Earth**
Perry, Steve  **4301**

**Tarot**
Anthony, Piers  637, 2406, 2574, 4359, 4384

**Tarot Fantastic**
Greenberg, Martin H.  **2406**

**Tarot Tales**
Pollack, Rachel  2406, **4359**

**Tarzan Alive**
Farmer, Philip Jose  3643

**Tarzan: The Lost Adventure**
Lansdale, Joe R.  2257

**A Taste for Blood**
Greenberg, Martin H.  1370, 1611, **2407**, 2975, 4407, 5265, 5935

**A Taste for Honey**
Heard, H.F.  4842

**Tatham Mound**
Anthony, Piers  **191**

**Tatja Grimm's World**
Vinge, Vernor  1595, 4729, 5544

**Tatterhood and Other Tales**
Phelps, Ethel Johnston  276, 794, 849, 1578, 2144, 2146, 2528, 2719, 4008, 4987, 5617, 6088, 6089

**The Tattooed Map**
Hodgson, Barbara  333, 336, **2706**

**Tau Zero**
Anderson, Poul  445, 5305

**Taylor's Ark**
Nye, Jody Lynn  2443, 3752, 3968, **4176**, 4195, 4196, 4198, 5777, 5778, 5780

**Tea From an Empty Cup**
Cadigan, Pat  **809**

**Tea with the Black Dragon**
MacAvoy, R.A.  285, 634, 636, 714, 1450, 1451, 1477, 1528, 1531, 1841, 2847, 4055, 4517, 5176, 5556, 5618

**Team Yankee**
Coyle, Harold  1642, 4306

**Tears of the Night Sky**
Baker, Linda P.  **299**

**The Tears of the Singers**
Snodgrass, Melinda M.  526

**Tears of Time**
Asire, Nancy  **256**

**Tech-Heaven**
Nagata, Linda  158, 581, 2498, **4066**

**The Technicolor Time Machine**
Harrison, Harry  508, 1344, 1418, 3082, 5043, 5565

**Teckla**
Brust, Steven  5197

**Tedious Brief Tales of Granta and Gramarye**
Ingulphus  1350

**Tegne: Soul Warrior**
La Plante, Richard  **3268**

**Tehanu: The Last Book of Earthsea**
Le Guin, Ursula K.  314, 1175, 1177, **3383**, 3731, 4149, 4152, 4211, 6025

**Tek Money**
Shatner, William  **4935**

**Tek Net**
Shatner, William  **4936**

**Tek Power**
Shatner, William  **4937**

**Tek Vengeance**
Shatner, William  **4938**

**TekLab**
Shatner, William  829, **4939**

**TekLords**
Shatner, William  831, 4590, **4940**

**TekWar**
Shatner, William  829, 1406, **4941**, 5302

**Teller of Tales**
Brooke, William J.  1257, 1578, 1942, 2144, 2146, 2845, 5557

**A Telling of the Tales: Five Stories**
Brooke, William J.  5557

**The Telzey Toy**
Schmitz, James H.  632

**The Temper of Wisdom**
Abbey, Lynn  **17**

**The Tempest**
Shakespeare, William  5826

**The Templar Treasure**
Kurtz, Katherine  **3261**

**Temple of the Winds**
Goodkind, Terry  2096, **2270**

**Temporary Agency**
Pollack, Rachel  389, 3071, 3935, **4360**, 5274, 5529

**Tempter**
Collins, Nancy A.  697, **1125**, 1465, 1888, 2147, 2494, 2896, 3950, 4307, 4464, 5160

**Tempting Fate**
Yarbro, Chelsea Quinn  2511, 3759

**Tempus**
Morris, Janet  4202

**Tempus Bound**
Morris, Janet  4201

**Ten Little Wizards**
Kurland, Michael  2804, 3109, 3259

**The Tenant**
Topor, Roland  282, 913, 2294, 2789, 3094, 3149, 3194, 4234, 4248, 4499, 5082

**Tennessee Terror**
Ham, Bob  44

**The Tenth Class**
Ripley, Karen  762, **4594**

**The Tenth Victim**
Scheckley, Robert  4115

**Teot's War**
Gladney, Heather  744, 1150, 1486, 1487, 3018, 3157, 3270, 3288, 3296, 3298, 3862, 3864, 3872, 3911, 4521, 4613, 4976, 5684

**Terata: Anomalies of Literature**
Thomas, Jeffrey  **5447**

**Terminal Beach**
Ballard, J.G.  56, 57, 59

**Terminal Cafe**
McDonald, Ian  305, 325, 835, 836, 837, 838, 1348, 1760, 2218, 2377, 2522, 3238, **3797**, 3818, 4192, 4381, 4703, 5105, 5253, 5256, 5828, 6009

**The Terminal Experiment**
Sawyer, Robert J.  507, 2488, 3764, **4860**

**Terminal Frights, Volume One**
Abner, Ken  **22**

**Terminal Games**
Perriman, Cole  507, **4283**, 4860, 5753

**Terminal Logic**
Scott, Jefferson **4893**, 4901

**The Terminal Man**
Crichton, Michael 581, 1164, 1347, 2206, 2638, 2872, 3200, 4232

**Terminal Weird**
Remick, Jack 778, 2137, 3851, **4532**, 4789, 5662, 5663

**The Terminator**
Frakes, Randall 65, 142, 143, 1199, 1941, 2546, 4333, 5012

**Terminator 2: Judgment Day**
Frakes, Randall 1074, 2532, 4333, 4525

**Terraplane**
Womack, Jack **5960**

**Terrible Swift Sword**
Forstchen, William R. **1983**, 2239

**The Terror**
Machen, Arthur 456

**The Terror**
Masterton, Graham **3679**

**The Terror by Night**
Benson, E.F. **455**, 875

**The Terrorist**
Cooney, Caroline B. 5285

**Terrors of the Sea**
Hodgson, William Hope **2712**

**Terry Carr's Best Science Fiction and Fantasy of the Year #16**
Carr, Terry 501

**Terry's Universe**
Meacham, Beth 5045, 5046

**The Tery**
Wilson, F. Paul 1323, 1325, 2193, 3158, 5132, 5225, 5226, 5588, **5900**

**Tesseract**
Addison, Joseph 4339

**Tesseracts**
Merril, Judith 4713

**Test of Fire**
Bova, Ben 111, 400

**Testament**
Freireich, Valerie J. 1807, **2051**, 2558

**Testament**
Morrell, David 3658, 5844

**Testament of the Dragon**
Weis, Margaret **5729**

**Testament: The Unpublished Prologues**
Morrell, David **4011**

**The Tetherballs of Bougainville**
Leyner, Mark **3457**

**Tex and Molly in the Afterlife**
Grant, Richard **2327**, 4732, 5079

**The Texas-Israeli War: 1999**
Saunders, Jake 4836

**Texas on the Rocks**
Da Cruz, Daniel 47, 48, 49, 50, 66

**Texas Triumphant**
Da Cruz, Daniel 47, 48, 49, 50

**The Texts of Festival**
Farren, Mick 3664, 5170

**That Hideous Strength**
Lewis, C.S. 4455, 4456

**That Man on Beta II**
Lupoff, Richard A. 554

**That Way Lies Camelot**
Wurts, Janny 3279, **6005**

**That's All, Folks!**
Snow, Greg 499, 4434, **5148**

**"The Children of the Corn"**
King, Stephen 320

**"The Fourth Seal"**
Wagner, Karl Edward 93, 1561

**"The Homecoming"**
Bradbury, Ray 3053

**"The Little Black Bag"**
Kornbluth, C.M. 1561

**"The Refugee"**
Rice, Jane 4702

**"The Skin Trade"**
Martin, George R.R. 2794

**"The White People"**
Machen, Arthur 1081

**"The Wonderful Ice Cream Suit"**
Bradbury, Ray 5803

**"The Yellow Wallpaper"**
Gilman, Charlotte Perkins 1673

**Thebes of the Hundred Gates**
Silverberg, Robert 658, 3185, 3237, 3428, 4355, **5043**

**Their Majesties' Bucketeers**
Smith, L. Neil 981, 1988, 2108, 4855

**Them**
Johnstone, William W. **2935**, 3559, 3856

**Them Bones**
Waldrop, Howard 3619, 5911

**Thendara House**
Bradley, Marion Zimmer 1004, 1177, 1755, 3746, 5434

**There Are Doors**
Wolfe, Gene 1521, 5806, 5908, 5960

**There Is a Serpent in Eden**
Bloch, Robert 1834

**There Is No Darkness**
Haldeman, Joe 2486

**There Shall Be No Darkness**
Blish, James 4764

**There Will Be Time**
Anderson, Poul 2012, 5999

**There Won't Be War**
Harrison, Harry **2578**, 4959

**Theros Ironfeld**
Perrin, Don 2425

**These Fallen Angels**
Haley, Wendy **2492**, 4246

**These Green Foreign Hills**
Green, Roland J. 4974

**Thessalonica**
Turtledove, Harry 5218, **5511**

**They Don't Dance Much**
Ross, James 3330

**They Fly at Ciron**
Delany, Samuel R. 567, 793, **1482**, 2243, 2338, 3380, 3692, 3855, 5132, 5492, 5942

**They Return at Evening**
Wakefield, H. Russell 779, 2846, 3879, 3880

**They Shall Have Stars**
Blish, James 401

**They Thirst**
McCammon, Robert R. 1402, 1463, 1464, 1466, 1882, 2152, 2258, 3140, 3142, 3550, 3551, 3564, 3565, 4072, 4102, 4190, 5158, 5237, 5770, 5891

**They Used Dark Forces**
Wheatley, Dennis 2932, 3220, 3672, 3759, 4960

**They Walked Like Men**
Simak, Clifford D. 1157, 2048

**The Thief of Always**
Barker, Clive 347, 2995, 3779

**The Thief of Hermes**
Emerson, Ru **1811**, 4912

**Thieves' Carnival/The Jewel of Bas**
Haber, Karen 2829

**Thieves Like Us**
Anderson, Edward 3330

**Thieves' World**
Asprin, Robert 630, 986, 1148, 1150, 1152, 1153, 1207, 2363, 2368, 2369, 2375, 2376, 3300, 3836, 4202, 4335, 5214, 5216

**The Thing**
Foster, Alan Dean 1200

**The Thing in the Bathtub and Other Lovecraftian Tales**
Cannon, P.H. 869

**The Thing on the Doorstep**
Lovecraft, H.P. 436

**The Thing That Darkness Hides**
Morgan, Robert 3294, **4006**

**Things Beyond Midnight**
Nolan, William F. 532, 2281, 3683, 5854, 5857, 5885

**Things Invisible to See: Gay and Lesbian Tales of Magic Realism**
Schimel, Lawrence 4882

**Things Left Behind**
Braunbeck, Gary A. **663**, 1789, 2701, 3495, 4231

**The Things That Are Not There**
Morgan, Robert 751, 2749, **4007**, 5773

**Think Like a Dinosaur and Other Stories**
Kelly, James Patrick **3048**

**Thinning the Predators**
Graziunas, Daina **2341**

**The Third Beast**
Loughran, Peter **3527**

**The Third Book of Lost Swords: Stonecutter's Story**
Saberhagen, Fred 2783, 2863

**The Third Eagle: Lessons Along a Minor String**
MacAvoy, R.A. 353, 431, 1070, 1414, 1691, 1891, 1893, **3583**, 4262, 4453, 5131, 5743, 5744, 5925

**The Third Force**
Laidlaw, Marc **3313**

**The Third Grave**
Case, David 616, 815

**The Third Magic**
Katz, Welwyn Wilton 121

**The Third Policeman**
O'Brien, Flann 982, 1002

**The Third World War, August 1985**
Hackett, John 4306

**Thirdspace**
David, Peter **1387**

**Thirst**
Cecilione, Michael **948**, 2151

**Thirst**
Kurtinski, Pyotr **3253**

**Thirst of the Vampire**
Wright, T. Lucien 452, 660, 1794, 1795, 1798, 3113, 4774, 5020, **5988**

**Thirsty**
Anderson, M.T. **120**

**Thirteen**
Pines, T. 1693, 2395

**Thirteen Plays of Ghosts and the Supernatural**
Kaye, Marvin 339, 344, 1022, 1112

**The Thirteenth Daughter of the Moon**
Nightingale, Steven **4104**

**The Thirteenth Majestral**
Peirce, Hayford **4277**

**Thirty Strange Stories**
Wells, H.G. **5746**, **5747**

**This Alien Shore**
Friedman, C.S. **2059**, 2237, 3761, 4901, 5540

**This Dark Paradise**
Haley, Wendy **2493**, 3413, 4666

**This Darkening Universe**
Biggle, Lloyd 1659

**This Immortal**
Zelazny, Roger 125, 789, 2487, 2920, 3465, 4813, 4990, 5212, 5707, 5729, 5866, **6074**

**This Is the Way the World Ends**
Morrow, James 95

**This Mortal Coil**
Asquith, Cynthia 601, 3360, 5772

**This Place Has No Atmosphere**
Danziger, Paula  4919

**This Present Darkness**
Peretti, Frank E.   750

**This Side of Judgment**
Dunn, J.R.   **1696**, 2907, 3743

**This Symbiotic Fascination**
Jacob, Charlee  **2843**

**This Time for Keeps**
Kane, Kathleen   2731, 3039, 5658

**This Time of Darkness**
Hoover, H.M.   3584

**Thomas the Rhymer**
Kushner, Ellen   166, 183, 1434,
2636, **3265**, 3269, 3505, 4161

**Thor**
Smith, Wayne   **5146**

**Thorn and Needle**
Thompson, Paul B.   **5456**

**Thornhold**
Cunningham, Elaine   **1293**

**Those Who Can: A Science Fiction
Reader**
Wilson, Robin Scott   1766, 1767,
3085

**Those Who Hunt the Night**
Hambly, Barbara   131, 135, 265,
832, 1013, 1121, 1791, **2510**,
2514, 2517, 3252, 4508, 6050

**Thoughts of God**
Kanaly, Michael   2661, **3007**

**The Thousand Cities**
Turtledove, Harry   **5512**

**A Thousand Words for Stranger**
Czerneda, Julie E.   **1304**, 2059, 3597

**Thousandstar**
Anthony, Piers   953

**The Thread That Binds the Bones**
Hoffman, Nina Kiriki   1444, 1478,
1502, 1512, 2659, **2717**, 2942,
3628, 3630, 3935, 4221

**Threats. . .and Other Promises**
Vinge, Vernor   425

**Three by Finney**
Finney, Jack   3690

**Three Faces of Eve**
Thigpen, Corbett H.   5364

**Three-Fisted Tales of "Bob"**
Stang, Ivan   5904

**Three Gothic Novels**
Brown, Charles Brockden   **722**

**Three Hearts and Three Lions**
Anderson, Poul   169, 635, 962, 1534,
1678, 3505, 4153, 4159, 4595,
4743, 5231, 5647

**The Three Impostors**
Machen, Arthur   2712

**The Three-Legged Hootch Dancer**
Resnick, Mike   4638, 5215

**Three Men in a Boat**
Jerome, Jerome K.   5874

**The Three Minute Universe**
Paul, Barbara   9, 903, 1663, 1923

**The Three Musketeers**
Dumas, Alexandre   747, 5017

**The Three Stigmata of Palmer
Eldritch**
Dick, Philip K.   568, 829, 1411,
2093, 2722, 2907, 3012, 3780,
4454, 4979, 5520, 5661

**Threshold**
Morris, Janet   1626, **4018**

**Threshold**
Myers, Bill   **4060**

**Threshold**
Palmer, David R.   3698

**Thrice upon a Time**
Hogan, James P.   110, 1345

**Thrill**
Wallace, Patricia   **5624**

**The Thrill Club**
Stine, R.L.   4329

**Thrillers for Christmas**
Dalby, Richard   4541

**The Throat**
Straub, Peter   1830, 3780, **5332**

**Throat Sprockets**
Lucas, Tim   3103, **3541**, 4734

**The Throne of Bones**
McNaughton, Brian   **3859**

**Throne of Isis**
Tarr, Judith   **5397**

**The Throne of Madness**
Sucharitkul, Somtow   2890

**The Throne of Saturn**
Wright, S. Fowler   5746

**The Throne of Scone**
Kennealy, Patricia   3060

**The Throne of Scone**
Kennealy-Morrison, Patricia   392

**The Throne of Tara**
Desjarlais, John   561, **1498**, 3265,
3358, 4584, 5101, 5392

**Through a Glass Darkly**
McCloy, Helen   2562

**Through Darkest America**
Barrett, Neal Jr.   163, 277, 886,
1996, 2603, 4604, 4621, 5092,
5982

**Through the Arc of the Rain Forest**
Yamashita, Karen Tei   **6008**

**Through the Breach**
Drake, David   308, **1647**, 1955

**Through the Heart**
Grant, Richard   1482, **2328**, 2533,
3855, 5433

**Through the Ice**
Anthony, Piers   192, 4799

**Through the Looking Glass and What
Alice Found There**
Carroll, Lewis   3156, 4134, 5713

**Throy**
Vance, Jack   **5550**

**Thunder and Roses**
Sturgeon, Theodore   2547, 3219,
**5348**

**Thunder in the Sky**
Sarabande, William   731, **4819**

**Thunder of the Captains**
Lisle, Holly   **3489**

**A Thunder on Neptune**
Eklund, Gordon   **1768**, 1991, 4963

**Thunder Rise**
Miller, G. Wayne   427, 577, 817,
911, 1297, 1886, 2251, 2340,
2903, 3081, 3680, 3778, **3895**,
4111, 4113, 4238, 4309, 4441,
5769, 6078

**Thunder Road**
Curry, Chris   **1296**

**Thunder Strike!**
McCollum, Michael   **3772**

**The Thurb Revolution**
Panshin, Alexei   3345, 3583, 5131

**Ticktock**
Koontz, Dean R.   **3217**

**The Tides of God**
Reynolds, Ted   2165, 2216, 2343,
2666, 2722, **4567**, 5195

**Tides of Light**
Benford, Gregory   34, 417, 423, **450**,
985, 1015, 1689, 2460, 2690,
2691, 3117, 3604, 4418, 4419,
4696, 5108, 5129, 5431, 5787,
6056

**The Tides of Time**
Brunner, John   178, 188, 4592, 4595

**A Tie to the Past**
Wiseman, David   **5928**

**Tigana**
Kay, Guy Gavriel   771, 1147, 1292,
1660, 1960, 2424, 2504, **3018**,
3105, 3171, 3175, 3872, 3925,
3975, 4167, 5206, 5812

**Tiger Burning Bright**
Bradley, Marion Zimmer   **652**

**Tiger Girl**
Casserly, Gordon   3145

**Till the End of Time**
Appel, Allen   **201**, 4047

**Time After Time**
Appel, Allen   5114

**Time After Time**
Finney, Jack   4036

**Time and Again**
Finney, Jack   464, 1480, 3690, 4036,
4332, 5873

**Time and Chance**
Brennert, Alan   201, **676**

**Time and Light**
Bornefeld, William   **574**

**Time and the Clock Mice, Etcetera**
Dickinson, Peter   **1527**

**Time at the Top**
Ormondroyd, Edward   4585

**The Time Bender**
Laumer, Keith   3848

**Time Blender**
Dorn, Michael   **1581**

**Time Burial**
Wandrei, Howard   1700, 3571, 5104,
5149, **5628**

**The Time Curve**
Moskowitz, Sam   3459

**Time Enough for Love**
Heinlein, Robert A.   125, 1962, 2446,
2487, 2498, 2920, 3663, 4813

**A Time for Dragons**
Gentile, Gary   **2193**

**Time for the Stars**
Heinlein, Robert A.   3249, 4918

**A Time for Us**
Holden, Christine   **2731**

**Time for Yesterday**
Crispin, A.C.   527, 902, 922, 3316

**Time Gate**
Jakes, John   3801

**Time Is the Simplest Thing**
Simak, Clifford D.   1581, 4016

**Time, Like an Ever-Rolling Stream**
Moffett, Judith   **3944**

**The Time Machine**
Wells, H.G.   403, 1074, 1344, 3526,
5067, 5192, 5659, 5999

**The Time Masters**
Tucker, Wilson   116

**A Time of Exile**
Kerr, Katharine   **3077**

**The Time of Feasting**
Farren, Mick   **1882**, 2258, 4190,
4667

**The Time of Madness**
Martin, Thomas K.   **3652**

**A Time of Omens**
Kerr, Katharine   **3078**

**The Time of the Dark**
Hambly, Barbara   153, 391, 562,
635, 718, 1008, 1009, 1066, 1155,
1173, 1174, 1175, 1178, 1181,
1239, 1421, 1422, 1477, 1640,
1660, 1678, 1732, 1746, 1747,
1809, 1812, 1863, 1866, 1907,
1911, 1983, 2235, 2361, 2367,
2560, 2561, 2623, 2628, 2796,
2885, 2886, 2985, 3157, 3246,
3270, 3296, 3297, 3304, 3305,
3306, 3386, 3482, 3650, 3652,
3653, 3938, 3939, 3942, 4517,
4520, 4523, 4526, 4798, 5150,
5251, 5736, 5737, 5738, 6073

**Time of the Fourth Horseman**
Yarbro, Chelsea Quinn   1133, 1164,
1590, 3242, 5868

**The Time of the Ghost**
Jones, Diana Wynne   53, **2951**

**Time of the Twins**
Weis, Margaret   5454, 5455

**The Time of the Vampires**
Elrod, P.N.   **1799**

**Time on My Hands**
Delacorte, Peter **1480**, 5874

**Time Out of Joint**
Dick, Philip K.   193

**Time Out of Mind**
Maxim, John R.   464

**The Time Patrol**
Anderson, Poul   65, **135**, 263, 264,
   357, 1074, 1196, 1417, 1626,
   1694, 1852, 1941, 1980, 1983,
   2122, 2532, 3427, 3428, 4525,
   5315, 5487, 5921, 5922

**Time Patrolman**
Anderson, Poul   904, 1344, 1345,
   1631, 1853, 2067, 4164, 5113,
   5996, 5998, 6000

**Time Scout**
Asprin, Robert   263, 1855, 5785

**The Time Ships**
Baxter, Stephen   **403**, 1759, 2906,
   4040

**Time Station Berlin**
Evans, David   **1852**

**Time Station London**
Evans, David   1344, **1853**

**Time Station Paris**
Evans, David   **1854**

**Time Storm**
Alsobrook, Rosalyn   2731, 3576

**Time Storm**
Dickson, Gordon R.   131, 403, 1581,
   1941, 1983, 2808, 3920, 3940,
   4641, 5012, 5087, 5487, 5999

**Time: The Semi-Final Frontier**
Fenn, Lionel   **1921**

**The Time Traders**
Norton, Andre   5499

**Time Travelers Strictly Cash**
Robinson, Spider   740

**The Time Tree**
Richemont, Enid   1012, **4585**

**Timecop**
Perry, S.D.   1853, 2119, 2532, **4286**,
   5315

**Timediver's Dawn**
Modesitt, L.E. Jr.   **3940**

**Timeless Warrior**
Gentry, Georgina   2497

**Timelike Infinity**
Baxter, Stephen   **404**, 4353, 4961

**Timemaster**
Forward, Robert L.   236, 404, 593,
   **1992**

**Timequake**
Vonnegut, Kurt Jr.   **5594**

**Time's Arrow**
Amis, Martin   **96**, 466, 467, 1341,
   1663, 2244, 2446, 2542, 6029

**Time's Enemy**
Graf, L.A.   9, 903, 904, **2297**, 5115

**Time's Last Gift**
Farmer, Philip Jose   175, 5998

**Times Without Number**
Brunner, John   1852, 1854, 2563,
   6000

**Timescape**
Benford, Gregory   782, 1245, 3786,
   4420, 5774, 6060

**Timescoop**
Brunner, John   1345

**Timeshare**
Dann, Joshua   **1344**, 4247, 5565

**Timeshare: Second Time Around**
Dann, Joshua   **1345**, 4247

**Timespell**
Charrette, Robert N.   **978**

**Timeswept**
Carlow, Joyce   691, 1271, 2731

**Timetrap**
Dvorkin, David   2501

**Timewyrm: Genesys**
Peel, John   3799, 3803

**Titan**
Baxter, Stephen   **405**, 3199, 3789,
   4947

**Titan**
Varley, John   685, 954, 961, 1634,
   2295, 2371, 3972, 4103, 4280,
   4417, 4421, 4595, 4705, 4942,
   5304, 5647, 5880

**Title Deleted for Security Reasons**
Blome, Ed   483, **553**, 3313, 3435,
   4076, 4298, 5074

**Titus Alone**
Peake, Mervyn   5311

**Titus Crow, Volume One**
Lumley, Brian   3566

**Titus Crow, Volume Three**
Lumley, Brian   3567

**Titus Crow, Volume Two**
Lumley, Brian   3568

**To a Highland Nation**
Rowley, Christopher   **4698**

**To Control the Stars**
Hoskins, Robert   3777

**To Dream in the City of Sorrows**
Drennan, Kathryn M.   944, 1387,
   **1654**, 2102, 3096, 4833

**To Dream of Dreamers Lost**
Wilson, David Niall   1950, **5882**

**To End All War**
Ahern, Jerry   2324, 2325

**To Fall Like Stars**
Asire, Nancy   **257**

**To Fear the Light**
Bova, Ben   595

**To Green Angel Tower**
Williams, Tad   3107, 5741, **5832**

**To Live Again**
Silverberg, Robert   3239

**To Live Forever**
Vance, Jack   2487, 2920, 4813

**To Nowhere and Back**
Anderson, Margaret J.   2992

**To Reign in Hell**
Brust, Steven   4670

**To Ride Pegasus**
McCaffrey, Anne   101, 642, 788,
   2420, 5208

**To Sail Beyond the Sunset**
Heinlein, Robert A.   2489

**To Save the Sun**
Bova, Ben   **596**

**To Say Nothing of the Dog**
Willis, Connie   1852, **5874**

**To Sleep, Perchance to
   Dream. . .Nightmare**
Dziemianowicz, Stefan   **1717**

**To Sleep with Evil**
Cardarelle, Andria   1137

**To Speak in Lifeless Tongues**
Wilson, David Niall   **5883**

**To the Devil, a Daughter**
Wheatley, Dennis   4531, 4568

**To the Haunted Mountains**
Emerson, Ru   2471, 6007

**To the Land of the Living**
Silverberg, Robert   1089, 1872, 1875,
   3842, **5044**, 5831

**To the Lightning**
Ennis, Catherine   4882

**To the Resurrection Station**
Arnason, Eleanor   874, 2196

**To the Vanishing Point**
Foster, Alan Dean   31, 165, 171,
   936, 951, 962, 1435, 1454, 1455,
   1456, 2327, 2644, 3173, 3343,
   3439, 3485, 3805, 3810, 4178,
   4364, 4384, 4394, 4473, 4970,
   5156, 5159, 5199, 5208, 5497,
   5647, 5817, 6062

**To Wake the Dead**
Campbell, Ramsey   524, 1048, 1195,
   1215, 2201, 3040, 3233, 3552,
   3958, 4239, 4340

**To Walk the Night**
Sloane, William   3417, 4235

**To Yith and Beyond**
Rimel, Duane   3516

**To Your Scattered Bodies Go**
Farmer, Philip Jose   270, 1422, 1581,
   **1876**, 2332, 5044, 5714, 5726,
   6071

**Toad Triumphant**
Horwood, William   **2774**

**Toady**
Morris, Mark   5398

**Today We Choose Faces**
Zelazny, Roger   969

**Token of Dragonsblood**
Cole, Damaris   **1114**, 1937, 3404

**The Tolkien Reader**
Tolkien, J.R.R.   4021

**Tom O'Bedlam**
Silverberg, Robert   5193, 5909

**Tom O'Bedlam's Night Out and
   Other Strange Excursions**
Schweitzer, Darrell   3859

**Tom Paine Maru**
Smith, L. Neil   593, 5403, 5549

**The Tomb**
Wilson, F. Paul   3882, 3883

**Tombley's Walk**
Brown, Crosland   514, 679, 680,
   **723**, 816, 1127, 2138, 3376, 4002,
   5080, 5552

**Tombs**
Kramer, Edward E.   1187, 1281,
   1283, **3228**

**The Tombs of Atuan**
Le Guin, Ursula K.   1175, 2461,
   3098, 4149, 4150, 5142, 5741,
   6024, 6025

**The Tommyknockers**
King, Stephen   137, 1037, 1200,
   3206

**Tomoe Gozen**
Salmonson, Jessica Amanda   3268,
   3412, 3906, 4742

**Tomorrow and Tomorrow**
Knight, Damon   5641

**Tomorrow and Tomorrow**
Sheffield, Charles   477, **4966**

**Tomorrow Bites**
Cox, Greg   **1230**, 2410

**Tomorrow Midnight**
Bradbury, Ray   3334

**Tomorrow Sucks**
Cox, Greg   **1231**, 1611

**Tomorrow's Heritage**
Coulson, Juanita   2048, 4301

**Tom's Midnight Garden**
Pearce, Philippa   1138, 2283, 4332,
   4585

**Tongues of Conscience**
Hichens, Robert   1252

**Tongues of Jade**
Yep, Laurence   69, 1221, 4742, **6026**

**Tongues of the Moon**
Farmer, Philip Jose   111

**Too Close for Comfort**
McConnell, Ashley   4487

**Too Long a Sacrifice**
Broxon, Mildred Downey   3254,
   3259, 5428

**Too Many Magicians**
Garrett, Randall   17, 971, 975, 1148,
   1152, 1153, 1518, 1534, 1655,
   2217, 2363, 2368, 2369, 2370,
   2473, 2628, 2804, 3109, 3254,
   3259, 3261, 3276, 4047, 4673,
   5506, 5507, 5967, 5976, 6058

**Too, Too Solid Flesh**
O'Donohoe, Nick   **4197**

**Tooth: A Tale of Love and Death in
   Paradox**
Kruger, Novak   **3244**

**Tooth and Claw**
Masterton, Graham   **3680**

*The Tooth Fairy*
Joyce, Graham  1506, **2995**

*Top Dog*
Carroll, Jerry Jay  **915**

*Toplin*
McDowell, Michael  **3807**, 5327

*Topper: An Improbable Adventure*
Smith, Thorne  2327, 3470, 3989, 4275

*The Torch*
Heidish, Marcy  1050

*The Torch of Honor*
Allen, Roger MacBride  589, 1326, 4378

*The Torching*
Heidish, Marcy  71, 966, 1836, 2023, **2642**, 2874, 4753, 5186, 5271, 5290

*Toreador*
Wieck, Stewart  1950

*Torment*
George, Stephen R.  **2204**, 2823, 4239

*Torments*
Cantrell, Lisa  342, **873**

*A Torrent of Faces*
Blish, James  1057

*The Tortuga Hill Gang's Last Ride*
Collins, Nancy A.  4251

*Total Eclipse*
Brunner, John  1248, 3221

*Total Recall*
Anthony, Piers  **193**, 805, 1304, 1878, 4635

*The Totem*
Morrell, David  **4012**

*The Touch*
Wilson, F. Paul  1410, 1507, 1561, 2700, 3134, 4073

*A Touch of Chill*
Aiken, Joan  1526

*A Touch of Sturgeon*
Sturgeon, Theodore  625, 4131

*The Touch of Your Shadow, the Whisper of Your Name*
Barrett, Neal Jr.  **367**, 944, 1654, 2102, 4833

*Touch Wood*
Crowther, Peter  **1285**

*Touched by Magic*
Durgin, Doranna  **1705**

*Touched by the Gods*
Watt-Evans, Lawrence  5273, **5651**

*Touching the Fire*
Welsch, Roger  178, 190, 731, 2686, 4380, 4817, **5751**

*Tourists*
Goldstein, Lisa  **2264**, 2706, 2952, 3423, 5939

*The Tournament of Thorns*
Swann, Thomas Burnett  5002

*Toward the End of Time*
Updike, John  **5531**

*The Tower of Beowulf*
Godwin, Parke  **2250**, 2453, 4872

*The Tower of Death*
Offutt, Andrew J.  5963

*Tower of Doom*
Anthony, Mark  **155**, 1510, 2516

*Tower of Evil*
Kisner, James  **3161**, 5989

*Tower of Fear*
Cook, Glen  605, 1111, **1155**, 1528, 1866, 3893, 3894, 3925, 3942, 4015, 4493, 4533

*Tower of Glass*
Silverberg, Robert  2539, 4220, 5157, 5491

*Tower of the Gods*
Easton, Thomas A.  **1726**

*Tower to the Sky*
Jennings, Phillip C.  5621

*Towers of Darkover*
Bradley, Marion Zimmer  **653**

*The Towers of the Sunset*
Modesitt, L.E. Jr.  1674, 1741, 2677, **3941**, 3969, 4150, 5735

*Towing Jehovah*
Morrow, James  1577, 2327, 3986, **4035**

*Toy Cemetery*
Johnstone, William W.  5823

*Toyman*
Tubb, E.C.  2330, 2921

*The Toynbee Convector*
Bradbury, Ray  **625**, 4131, 4636

*Trader*
de Lint, Charles  **1438**, 3773, 5273

*Trader to the Stars*
Anderson, Poul  1647, 4148, 4160, 5499, 5549

*Trader's World*
Sheffield, Charles  4175

*The Trail of Cthulhu*
Derleth, August  **1497**, 5470

*Trails in Darkness*
Howard, Robert E.  **2784**

*Traitor to the Living*
Farmer, Philip Jose  188

*Traitor Winds*
Graf, L.A.  905, 1729, **2298**, 4927

*Traitors*
Rusch, Kristine Kathryn  1513, 1864, **4729**, 5113

*Traitors from Within*
Montgomery, R.A.  **3966**

*The Tranquility Alternative*
Steele, Allen  64, 587, 2002, **5248**

*The Transall Saga*
Paulsen, Gary  **4262**

*Transcendence*
Sheffield, Charles  322, 1501, 2661, **4967**

*Transfigurations*
Bishop, Michael  3617, 4550

*Transients and Other Disquieting Tales*
Schweitzer, Darrell  3614, **4891**, 5929

*Transit*
Cooper, Edmund  2996

*Transit to Scorpio*
Akers, Alan Burt  3983

*Transition*
McIntyre, Vonda N.  81, 656, 1055, 1556, 1645, 1897, 1992, 2048, 2491, 2836, 3805, **3825**, 4505

*The Transition of Titus Crow*
Lumley, Brian  **3569**, 4112

*The Transmigration of Souls*
Barton, William  **382**

*The Transmigration of Timothy Archer*
Dick, Philip K.  3612

*Transmission Error*
Kurland, Michael  2882

*Transreal!*
Rucker, Rudy  **4706**

*Transylvania 90210*
Elvira  1302, 2131, 5161

*Trapped!*
Norwood, Warren  141, 1563

*Trapped in the Ashes*
Johnstone, William W.  44

*Travel Far, Pay No Fare*
Lindbergh, Anne  3156, **3468**

*The Travel Tales of Mr. Joseph Jorkens*
Dunsany  3147, 3148, 4021

*The Traveler in Black*
Brunner, John  195

*A Traveler in Time*
Uttley, Alison  2992, 3261

*Travelers in Magic*
Goldstein, Lisa  819, 1431, 2106, **2265**, 2537, 3279, 3984, 5165

*Traveling with the Dead*
Hambly, Barbara  **2511**

*The Travelling Grave, and Other Stories*
Hartley, L.P.  779

*The Travelling Grave and Other Stories*
Hartley, L.P.  4141, 5610, 5611

*Treason in Time*
Andrews, Keith William  **143**, 1199

*Treasure Box*
Card, Orson Scott  **898**, 5522

*The Treasure of Green Knowe*
Boston, L.M.  4585

*The Treasure of Tau Ceti*
Rackham, John  3221

*Treasures of Fantasy*
Weis, Margaret  **5730**

*Treasures of Morrow*
Hoover, H.M.  878

*A Treasury of Fantasy: Heroic Adventures in Imaginary Lands*
Wilkins, Cary  5003

*A Treasury of Great American Horror Stories*
McSherry, Frank D. Jr.  2586, 3331

*A Treasury of Irish Myth, Legend and Folklore*
Yeats, W.B.  6090

*A Treasury of Science Fiction*
Conklin, Groff  1061

*A Treasury of Victorian Ghost Stories*
Bleiler, Everett F.  1234, 1235, 2300

*Treaty at Doona*
McCaffrey, Anne  1259, 1264, 1546, 1586, 2001, **3752**

*The Tree of Swords and Jewels*
Cherryh, C.J.  17, 459, 2097, 2098, 3841, 4146, 5832

*Trek of Doom*
Martin, Les  3544

*Treks Not Taken: What if Stephen King, Anne Rice, Bret Easton Ellis, and Other Literary Greats Had Written Episodes of Star Trek: The Next Generation?*
Boyett, Steven R.  119, **607**, 2398, 6077

*A Tremor in the Bitter Earth*
Reimann, Katya  **4527**

*Tremor Violet*
Lippincott, David  1060

*The Triad Worlds*
Busby, F.M.  **786**

*The Trial of Elizabeth Cree*
Ackroyd, Peter  **26**

*Triangle: Imzadi II*
David, Peter  **1388**

*The Tribe*
Wood, Bari  2697

*Trickster*
Curry, Chris  427, **1297**, 3680

*The Trickster*
Gray, Muriel  911, 2251, **2340**, 3680, 3967, 4710

*The Trickster*
Radin, Paul  5578, 5751

*Trickster Tales*
Edmonds, I.G.  4987

*The Tricksters*
Mahy, Margaret  53, 1668, 2951

*The Trikon Deception*
Bova, Ben  **597**, 2727, 5377

*Trinity Grove*
Smith, David van Meter  1806, 3042, 3956, 4586, **5112**

*The Trinity Paradox*
Anderson, Kevin J.  **116**, 895, 1852, 1854, 2239, 5516, 5518

*The Trinity Vector*
Perry, Steve  **4302**, 4895

*Triplanetary*
Smith, E.E. ''Doc''  270

*Triplanetary*
Smith, Edward E.   4103

*Triplet*
Zahn, Timothy   165

*The Tripods Trilogy*
Christopher, John   5870

*Tripoint*
Cherryh, C.J.   **1003**, 1899, 3974, 5298

*Tris's Book*
Pierce, Tamora   **4322**

*Triton*
Delany, Samuel R.   1720, 4051

*The Triton Ultimatum*
Delaney, Laurence   4512

*Triumph*
Bova, Ben   **598**, 895, 1854, 2239, 3528, 5516, 5517, 5518, 5996

*Triumph of the Night*
Phillips, Robert   1, 1232, 1306, 1351, 3616, 4214, 5417

*The Triumph of Time*
Blish, James   404, 508, 2208, 2501, 3710

*Troika*
Cooper, Louise   **1181**

*Trojan Orbit*
Reynolds, Mack   584, 588

*Troll-Quest*
Estes, Rose   **1841**

*Troll-Taken*
Estes, Rose   636, 703, 1744, **1842**, 2326, 3487, 3816, 4170, 5409

*The Trolley to Yesterday*
Bellairs, John   2688

*Tron*
Daley, Brian   5171, 5753

*Tropic of Orange*
Yamashita, Karen Tei   52, 950, **6009**

*Tros of Samothrace*
Mundy, Talbot   2073

*Trouble and Her Friends*
Scott, Melissa   951, 956, 1761, 2445, 3072, 4179, **4902**, 5619

*Trouble on Cloud City*
Anderson, Kevin J.   **117**

*The Trouble with Lichen*
Wyndham, John   4352

*A Troubling Along the Border*
Aamodt, Donald   **4**, 673, 1072

*The Troupe*
Linzner, Gordon   822, 1851, 4787, 4847, 5405, 5407

*Trout Fishing in America*
Brautigan, Richard   3455

*The Truce at Bakura*
Tyers, Kathy   109, 4299, **5527**, 6055

*Truckers*
Pratchett, Terry   1222, 1223, 1224, 1558, **4402**

*"Trucks"*
King, Stephen   3320

*Trudging to Eden*
Antieau, Kim   113, **200**

*The True Knight*
Dexter, Susan   **1513**

*True Minds*
Robinson, Spider   1428, 5810

*Trullion: Alastor 2262*
Vance, Jack   2414, 4121, 4634

*The Trumpets of Tagan*
Lang, Simon   1649, **3316**

*Trust Territory*
Morris, Janet   **4019**

*Truth Until Paradox*
Krause, Staley   3227, 5701, 5702

*Tubular Android Superheroes*
Gilden, Mel   1892, 1935, 2005, 2007, **2228**

*The Tulpa*
Williamson, J.N.   2605

*Tunnel in the Sky*
Heinlein, Robert A.   2290, 2807, 3011, 4262, 5295

*Tunnel through the Deeps*
Harrison, Harry   1655

*Tunnelvision*
Gates, R. Patrick   **2162**, 3585

*A Tupelov Too Far and Other Stories*
Aldiss, Brian W.   **61**

*The Turing Option*
Harrison, Harry   **2579**

*Turn of the Cards*
Milan, Victor   3642, 3647, **3891**, 5567

*The Turn of the Screw*
James, Henry   3813

*Turning Point*
Norman, Lisanne   983, **4140**, 5404, 5525

*The Twelfth Child*
Over, Raymond Van   4340

*The Twelfth Child*
Van Over, Raymond   5538

*Twelve Fair Kingdoms*
Elgin, Suzette Haden   167, 174, 184, 186, 187, 515, 560, 563, 1045, 1695, 2015, 2084, 2950, 3118, 3278, 3719, 3747, 4221, 4361, 4866, 5219, 5235, 5574, 5616

*Twelve Gothic Tales*
Dalby, Richard   **1314**

*Twelve Impossible Things Before Breakfast*
Yolen, Jane   794, **6040**

*Twelve Irish Ghost Stories*
Craig, Patricia   **1242**, 2481

*Twelve Tales of the Supernatural*
Cox, Michael   **1233**

*Twelve Victorian Ghost Stories*
Cox, Michael   **1234**

*Twenty Thousand Leagues under the Sea*
Verne, Jules   398, 440, 1666

*Twenty Years After*
Dumas, Alexandre   742

*Twilight*
James, Peter   **2876**

*Twilight and Other Supernatural Romances*
Bowen, Marjorie   **601**

*"Twilight at the Towers"*
Barker, Clive   4702

*Twilight Eyes*
Koontz, Dean R.   1282, 2160, 2927, 3366

*Twilight of the Empire*
Green, Simon R.   **2374**

*Twilight Time*
Hautala, Rick   **2613**

*Twilight World*
Anderson, Poul   4600

*The Twilight Zone: Complete Stories*
Serling, Rod   **4916**

*The Twilight Zone Scripts*
Matheson, Richard   4916

*The Twilight Zone: The Original Stories*
Greenberg, Martin H.   4913, 4914

*Twisted*
Barr, Sue Hollister   **364**

*Twisted Dragon*
Stein, Kevin   **5251**

*Twisted Images*
D'Ammassa, Don   **1335**

*Twisting the Rope*
MacAvoy, R.A.   285, 4868, 4870

*Twistor*
Cramer, John   824, **1245**, 2807, 5088

*Twists of the Tale*
Datlow, Ellen   **1369**

*Two Bad Ants*
Van Allsburg, Chris   3382

*Two-Bit Heroes*
Egan, Doris   **1757**

*Two by Carrere*
Carrere, Emmanuel   **913**

*Two Crowns for America*
Kurtz, Katherine   889, **3262**

*A Two-Edged Sword*
Martin, Thomas K.   **3653**

*The Two Faces of Tomorrow*
Hogan, James P.   3454

*The Two Georges*
Dreyfuss, Richard   **1655**, 5504

*Two Hawks From Earth*
Farmer, Philip Jose   4814

*The Two in Hiding*
Emerson, Ru   1584, **1812**, 3282, 4784

*The Two Magics: The Turn of the Screw, Covering End*
James, Henry   4275

*Two Obscure Tales*
Campbell, Ramsey   **865**

*The Two of Them*
Russ, Joanna   3579

*Two Queens of Lochrie*
Creighton, Lee   4481

*Two Sought Adventure: Exploits of Fafhrd and the Gray Mouser*
Leiber, Fritz   2190

*Two That Came True*
Moffett, Judith   1428, 3185, 3237, **3945**, 4355, 6068

*The Two-Timers*
Shaw, Bob   2489

*Two to Conquer*
Bradley, Marion Zimmer   894

*The Two Towers*
Tolkien, J.R.R.   256, 487, 710, 711, 716, 1738, 2378, 2531, 2887, 2888, 2987, 3833, 4906, 5714

*Typewriter in the Sky*
Hubbard, L. Ron   **2791**

*Typewriter in the Sky/Fear*
Hubbard, L. Ron   5072, 5791

*Tyrannosaurus Rex*
Rivkin, J.F.   1417, 2468, **4597**

**U**

*Ubik*
Dick, Philip K.   96, 1762, 1835, 2789, 2913, 3012, 3351, 3456, 3459, 4454, 5156, 5487

*The Ugly Little Boy*
Asimov, Isaac   **250**

*The Ugly Little Boy/The Widget, the Wadget, and Boff*
Asimov, Isaac   130

*Uhura's Song*
Kagan, Janet   527, 569, 1381, 1556, 2421, 3918

*Uller Uprising*
Piper, H. Beam   4378

*The Ultimate Alien*
Preiss, Byron   **4406**

*The Ultimate Bike Path*
Sirota, Michael B.   **5076**

*The Ultimate Dracula*
Preiss, Byron   150, 151, 2387, **4407**, 5448

*The Ultimate Dragon*
Preiss, Byron   801, 2479, **4408**

*The Ultimate Egoist*
Sturgeon, Theodore   54, 479, 2458, 2490, 2569, 2659, **5349**, 5594, 5613, 5869

*The Ultimate Enemy*
Saberhagen, Fred   516

*The Ultimate Frankenstein*
Preiss, Byron   2390, **4409**

*The Ultimate Helm*
Howard, Russ T.   2785

*The Ultimate Silver Surfer*
Lee, Stan   1390

**The Ultimate Spider-Man**
Lee, Stan  1227, 1390, 1667, **3403**, 5567

**Ultimate Weapon**
Sloane, Ben  831, 3665

**The Ultimate Werewolf**
Preiss, Byron  1230, 2410, 2976, 3032, **4410**, 5384

**The Ultimate Witch**
Preiss, Byron  2938, **4411**, 6034

**The Ultimate Zombie**
Preiss, Byron  2892, **4412**, 4745, 4746

**The Unbeheaded King**
de Camp, L. Sprague  4163

**The Unbeholden**
Weinberg, Robert  387, 1119, 2512, 4058, **5703**, 5882, 5883

**The Unbidden**
Weinberg, Robert  1949

**The Unborn**
Laurance, Andrew  3350

**The Uncanny**
Klavan, Andrew  **3164**

**Uncanny Banquet**
Campbell, Ramsey  1306, 2590, 2993, 4644

**Uncanny Tales**
Weinberg, Robert  940

**Uncharted Territory**
Willis, Connie  1536, **5875**

**Uncle Terrible: More Adventures of Anatole**
Willard, Nancy  329

**Unconquered Countries: Four Novellas**
Ryman, Geoff  **4757**

**The Unconquered Country**
Ryman, Geoff  2952, 3791, 4630, 4866, 4867, 5396

**The Uncrowned King**
West, Michelle  **5760**

**The Undead**
Longstreet, Roxanne  301, 1779, **3519**, 5185, 5347, 6050

**Under Alien Stars**
Service, Pamela F.  1262, 1504, 2808, **4919**

**Under Fire**
Von Gunden, Kenneth  **5589**

**Under Siege**
Mace, Elisabeth  332, **3587**

**Under the Andes**
Stout, Rex  3878, 4062

**Under the Canopy**
Paul, Barbara  5230

**Under the Crust**
Lamsley, Terry  **3314**, 5776

**Under the Fang**
McCammon, Robert R.  854, 1373, 2118, 2315, 2387, **3758**, 5448, 5888

**Under the Healing Sign**
O'Donohoe, Nick  **4198**

**Under the Shadow**
Toombs, Jane  3411, 4892, **5481**

**Under the Yoke**
Stirling, S.M.  1579, **5301**

**The Undesired Princess and the Enchanted Bunny**
de Camp, L. Sprague  **1419**, 2751, 5639

**The Undine**
O'Rourke, Michael  3104, 3492, **4224**

**The Undying Monster**
Kerruish, Jessie  3826

**The Undying Wizard**
Offutt, Andrew J.  5962, 5963

**Unearthed**
McConnell, Ashley  **3778**

**Unearthly Neighbors**
Oliver, Chad  595, 3342, 3769

**The Unfinished**
Laws, Jay B.  345, **3362**

**Unfinished Tales of Numenor and Middle-Earth**
Tolkien, J.R.R.  1735, 2991, 3836

**Unholy Allies**
Weinberg, Robert  387, 452, 798, 1949, 2514, 2515, 4058, **5704**, 5883

**Unholy Communion**
Blake, Adrian  5342

**Unholy Fire**
Strieber, Whitley  2889, **5342**

**Unholy Relics**
Dare, M.P.  455, 875, **1350**, 4141, 5611

**Unicorn and Dragon**
Abbey, Lynn  459, 3097, 6041

**The Unicorn Dilemma**
Lee, John  2941

**The Unicorn Girl**
Kurland, Michael  2913, 5170

**Unicorn Highway**
Jones, David Lee  **2941**

**Unicorn Mountain**
Bishop, Michael  1343

**The Unicorn Peace**
Lee, John  **3399**

**Unicorn Point**
Anthony, Piers  5225, 5226

**The Unicorn Quest**
Lee, John  1100, 1946, 2941, 4319

**The Unicorn Solution**
Lee, John  2941, **3400**, 3892

**The Unicorn Sonata**
Beagle, Peter S.  **412**, 3414, 3938

**The Unicorn Treasury**
Coville, Bruce  410, 412, 1343, 1946, 4319, 6033

**Unicorn U.**
Friesner, Esther  **2084**, 4317, 5649

**The Unicorn War**
Lee, John  **3401**

**Unicorns!**
Dann, Jack  410, 412, 2397, 2941, 6033

**Unicorns II**
Dann, Jack  410, 412, 1219, **1343**, 2941, 6033

**Unification**
Taylor, Jeri  1260, 2061, 2063, 2066, 5596

**Uninvited Ghosts and Other Stories**
Lively, Penelope  1526, 3611

**Union Fires**
Barnes, John  358

**Universal Soldier**
Tine, Robert  366, 1547, 2532, 4229, 4286, **5476**

**Universe 1**
Carr, Terry  4721

**Universe 1**
Silverberg, Robert  1363, 1364, 1365

**Universe 1-3**
Silverberg, Robert  2634, 2635

**Universe 2**
Silverberg, Robert  216, 1363, 1364, 1365, 1620, 1622, **5045**

**Universe 3**
Silverberg, Robert  1617, 1623, 1624, 2596, **5046**

**The Universe Against Her**
Schmitz, James H.  1000, 2420, 2421, 2423, 2684, 3359, 3918, 4139, 4560

**University**
Little, Bentley  **3499**

**The Unknown**
Benson, D.R.  5700

**Unknown Danger**
Leinster, Murray  4386

**The Unknown Soldier**
Reichert, Mickey Zucker  **4525**, 5184

**Unknown Worlds: Tales From Beyond**
Schmidt, Stanley  5700

**The Unlikely Ones**
Brown, Mary  32, 67, **2774**, 2775, 2776, 2848, 2849, 2850, 2851, 2853, 2854, 2855, 3625, 5382

**The Unlimited Dream Company**
Ballard, J.G.  3612

**Unlocking the Air and Other Stories**
Le Guin, Ursula K.  **3384**

**The Unnatural**
Prill, David  1396, 3057, **4437**, 5167

**Unnatural Acts**
Taylor, Lucy  213, 1467, 3669

**Unnatural Acts and Other Stories**
Taylor, Lucy  693, 2655, 2778, 3392, 3397, **5416**

**The Unpleasant Profession of Jonathan Hoag**
Heinlein, Robert A.  3252, 3351

**Unquenchable Fire**
Pollack, Rachel  3438, 3935, 4177, **4361**, 4631, 5145, 5529, 5591

**The Unreasoning Mask**
Farmer, Philip Jose  4942

**The Unseen**
Citro, Joseph A.  **1039**, 2200, 2936, 3056, 3160, 5112

**Unsettled Dust**
Aickman, Robert  5763, 5764, 5765

**The Unteleported Man**
Dick, Philip K.  708, 784, 1458, 1509, 1565, 2882, 2907, 2913, 4505, 4682, 5156, 5159, 5306, 6060

**Until Relieved**
Shelley, Rick  5718

**Unto Zeor Forever**
Lichtenberg, Jacqueline  2665, 4318

**Unwillingly to Earth**
Ashwell, Pauline  **231**, 762, 2551, 2832, 3724, 3974, 4030, 4160, 5403

**The Unwound Way**
Adams, William  **35**, 3750, 5198, 5201

**Up the Line**
Silverberg, Robert  264, 1638, 5503, 5513

**Up the Walls of the World**
Tiptree, James Jr.  512, 2297, 3644, 4280

**Upland Outlaws**
Duncan, Dave  **1690**, 3926

**The Uplift War**
Brin, David  132, 250, 326, 450, 451, 469, 874, 876, 981, 990, 1261, 1503, 1634, 1725, 1729, 2016, 2434, 2551, 2898, 3000, 3703, 3735, 3976, 4160, 4217, 4241, 4418, 4419, 4547, 4552, 5108, 5431, 5526, 5586, 5779, 5866

**Uplink**
Fancher, Jane S.  **1865**

**The Uprising**
McDaniels, Abigail  1926, 2821, 2933, **3785**, 5064

**The Uprising**
Monahan, Brent  2285, 2903, **3956**, 4586, 4754

**Upside Downside**
Goulart, Ron  30

**Urban Horrors**
Nolan, William F.  **4133**, 4212

**Ursula's Gift**
DiSilvestro, Roger L.  5939

**Ursus**
Dvorkin, David  41, 373, 488, **1708**, 4831, 5388

**Use of Weapons**
Banks, Iain M.  **328**, 2522, 5117, 5138

**User Unfriendly**
Vande Velde, Vivian   87, 179, 475, 507, 1218, 1461, 1600, 1873, 2082, 3468, 3487, 3831, 4433, 4671, 4921, 5063, **5558**

**Usher's Passing**
McCammon, Robert R.   70, 340, 1888, 2115, 2494, 2557, 2749, 4344, 4601, 4603, 4778

**The Usurper**
Wells, Angus   **5739**

**Utopia**
Allen, Roger MacBride   **83**, 198, 1695

**The Utopia Hunters**
Sucharitkul, Somtow   2890

**Uwharrie**
Pfaff, Eugene E. Jr.   2251, 2340, 3081, 3325, 3671, 4111, 4113, 4238, **4309**, 6078


# V

**V**
Crispin, A.C.   504, 1508, 2910, 2948, 3952, 5282, 5575

**V: The Oregon Invasion**
Tannehill, Jayne   2910, 4290

**V: The Pursuit of Diana**
Wold, Allen L.   4290

**Vacuum Flowers**
Swanwick, Michael   60, 63, 79, 505, 805, 838, 927, 1543, 1723, 1819, 1964, 2163, 2536, 3075, 3921, 4071, 4342, 5198, 5201, 5241, 5451, 5638, 5809, 5839

**Valentine**
Somtow, S.P.   1301, **5160**

**Valentine Pontifex**
Silverberg, Robert   954, 5512

**Valis**
Dick, Philip K.   2754, 3012, 3186, 3612

**The Valley of Horses**
Auel, Jean M.   667, 669, 2571, 4040, 4817, 4818, 4819, 5444

**Valley of Lights**
Gallagher, Stephen   1792, 2288, 2302, 2610, 2793, 3129, 4004, 4005, 4327, 5010

**Valley of the Kings: Egypt, May 1908**
Brightfield, Richard   3544

**The Valley of Thunder**
de Lint, Charles   3572

**The Valley So Low**
Wellman, Manly Wade   967, 3328, 3329, 3333

**Valorian**
Herbert, Mary H.   1029, **2677**

**Vamphyri!**
Lumley, Brian   463

**Vampire**
Cusick, Richie Tankersley   120, 4328

**The Vampire**
Frayling, Christopher   1308

**Vampire$**
Steakley, John   3564, 3853, 4728, **5237**

**Vampire and Werewolf Stories**
Durant, Alan   **1701**

**The Vampire Armand**
Rice, Anne   **4578**

**Vampire Beat**
Courtney, Vincent   **1214**, 1791, 1793, 2149, 2792, 3108, 3517, 3560, 5078, 5374

**A Vampire Bestiary**
Thomas, Jeffrey   **5448**

**Vampire Blood**
Griffith, Kathryn Meyer   **2441**, 5657, 5986

**Vampire Breath**
Stine, R.L.   **5291**

**Vampire Bytes**
Grant, Linda   **2322**

**The Vampire Chronicles**
Elrod, P.N.   4464

**The Vampire Chronicles**
Rice, Anne   4464, 5191

**Vampire Detectives**
Greenberg, Martin H.   1718, **2408**, 3108, 5459

**Vampire Diary: The Embrace**
Weinberg, Robert   387, 2663, 2664, 3019, 5162, **5705**

**Vampire Erotica**
Tan, Cecilia   699, 3177, 4689

**Vampire Heart**
Locke, Joseph   120, 1302, 2131, 4328, 5161

**The Vampire Hunters' Casebook**
Haining, Peter   **2484**

**The Vampire Journals**
Briery, Traci   292, **678**, 1794, 1795, 1798, 3113, 3151, 3623, 4246

**Vampire Junction**
Somtow, S.P.   490, 697, 946, 1124, 3623, 3781, 4307, 4573, 4574, 5419

**Vampire Junkies**
Spinrad, Norman   3111, 3114, 3988, **5175**

**The Vampire Lestat**
Rice, Anne   152, 301, 463, 490, 600, 660, 678, 697, 1122, 1125, 1355, 1778, 1795, 1798, 2259, 2741, 3113, 3413, 3781, 3954, 3955, 4094, 4097, 4307, 4318, 4508, 4774, 4978, 5160, 5162, 5406, 5802, 6012, 6018

**The Vampire Memoirs**
McCuniff, Mara   139, 2267, 3113, 3151, **3781**, 4763, 4774, 6016

**The Vampire Memoirs**
McCuniff, Maura   6012

**The Vampire Odyssey**
Ciencin, Scott   **1032**, 2336, 2748, 4190, 4576, 4667, 5693, 5705, 5852

**The Vampire Papers**
Romkey, Michael   152, 2492, 2493, 3253, 4068, **4666**, 5405, 5407

**The Vampire Princess**
Romkey, Michael   **4667**

**Vampire Stories**
Dalby, Richard   4879, 4881, 5688

**The Vampire Stories of R. Chetwynd-Hayes**
Chetwynd-Hayes, R.   **1013**, 3549

**The Vampire Tapestry**
Charnas, Suzy McKee   738, 1124, 1286, 1426, 2267, 3458, 3915, 4574, 4665

**The Vampire Virus**
Romkey, Michael   **4668**

**Vampire Winter**
Tilton, Lois   2440

**Vampires**
Yolen, Jane   4988

**Vampires Anonymous**
McMahan, Jeffrey N.   1166, 2116, **3853**, 4069

**The Vampire's Apprentice**
Byers, Richard Lee   **799**, 1166, 2337, 2834, 5537

**The Vampire's Beautiful Daughter**
Somtow, S.P.   120, 2131, 3162, **5161**

**The Vampires of Alfama**
Kast, Pierre   4574, 4578, 6011, 6012, 6013, 6015, 6016, 6018

**The Vampires of Nightworld**
Bischoff, David   1134

**Vampires: The Greatest Stories**
Greenberg, Martin H.   150, 151, **2409**, 2484, 5265

**Vampires: Two Centuries of Great Vampire Stories**
Ryan, Alan   1231, 1308, 1360, 1370, 1718, 1799, 2071, 2382, 2407, 2408, 2409, 2975, 3031, 4407, 4879, 4881, 5265, 5688, 5706, 5935

**Vampires, Wine & Roses**
Stevens, John Richard   **5265**

**Vamps**
Greenberg, Martin H.   730, 1360, 1370, 1713, 2508, 2975, 3030, 3031

**The Vampyre and Other Tales of the Macabre**
Morrison, Robert   **4026**

**Vanguard From Alpha**
Aldiss, Brian W.   5766

**Vanished**
Norwood, Warren   141, 143, 1563, 3428, 5012

**The Vanishing**
Kaye, Marilyn   **3021**

**Vanishing Point**
Roessner, Michaela   1026, 2266, 2273, 2535, 2728, 3021, 3438, 3710, 4177, 4502, 4553, **4652**, 5208, 5274, 5818, 5906

**The Vanishment**
Aycliffe, Jonathan   **282**, 608, 666

**Vanitas: Escape From Vampire Junction**
Somtow, S.P.   1122, 3954, **5162**

**Vaporetto 13**
Girardi, Robert   **2241**, 3409

**Var the Stick**
Anthony, Piers   1324

**Variant**
Engel, Alan   1164

**Vast**
Nagata, Linda   **4067**

**Vastarien**
Ligotti, Thomas   966, 2022

**The Vaults of Yoh-Vombis**
Smith, Clark Ashton   348

**Vector Analysis**
Haldeman, Jack C. II   1788

**The Veiled Dragon**
Denning, Troy   4326, 5708

**The Veils of Snows**
Helprin, Mark   **2654**

**Vendetta**
David, Peter   **1389**

**The Venetian's Wife: A Strangely Sensual Tale of a Renaissance Explorer, a Computer, and a Metamorphosis**
Bantock, Nick   **336**

**Vengeance**
ab Hugh, Dafydd   **10**

**Vengeance**
Drake, David   **1648**, 4204

**The Vengeance of Hera**
Betancourt, John Gregory   4912

**Vengeance of the Dancing Gods**
Chalker, Jack L.   4055, 5197

**Vengeance Strike**
Robbins, David   **4604**

**Vengeful Ghosts**
Ward, C.E.   1671, 2707, 5211

**Venom**
Tigges, John   1672, 4589

**The Venom Trees of Sunga**
de Camp, L. Sprague   **1420**, 4545

**The Venus Belt**
Smith, L. Neil   83, 593, 2450

**Venus of Dreams**
Sargent, Pamela   127, 3824, 5377

**Venus of Shadows**
Sargent, Pamela   5572

**Venus on the Half Shell**
Farmer, Philip Jose   4546

**Venus Plus X**
Sturgeon, Theodore   1362, 1720

*The Verdant Passage*
Denning, Troy   13, **1487**, 2618, 2621, 2624

*Vermilion Sands*
Ballard, J.G.   56, 57, 59, 3876

*The Very Slow Time Machine*
Watson, Ian   5747

*Vespers*
Rovin, Jeff   **4688**

*Vestiges of Time*
Meredith, Richard   2012

*Vettius and His Friends*
Drake, David   856, 1110, 2781, 2782, 3356, 5110, 5471, 5505

*Victoria*
Jensen, Ruby Jean   3782

*The Victorian Fairy Tale Book*
Hearn, Michael Patrick   276, 2447, 3574, 6088, 6090

*Victorian Ghost Stories: An Oxford Anthology*
Cox, Michael   **1235**, 2300, 3432

*Victorian Ghost Stories by Eminent Women Writers*
Dalby, Richard   1235, 5814

*Victorian Nightmares*
Lamb, Hugh   1234

*Videodrome*
Martin, Jack   1353, 3326

*Videssos Besieged*
Turtledove, Harry   **5513**

*Vietnam and Other Alien Worlds*
Haldeman, Joe   759, 1969, 2947, 5782

*Views from the Oldest House*
Grant, Richard   1278, **2329**

*Villains by Necessity*
Forward, Eve   683, **1985**, 2451, 2639, 4676, 5678

*Vinas Solamnus*
King, J. Robert   **3123**

*Violations*
Wright, Susan   206

*Violin*
Rice, Anne   2823, **4579**

*Viper*
Riefe, Alan   **4589**

*Viper's Spawn*
Parkinson, Dan   3979

*Virago*
Minns, Karen Marie Christa   2242, 3579, **3915**

*The Virago Book of Ghost Stories*
Dalby, Richard   4443

*The Virago Book of Ghost Stories: The Twentieth Century*
Dalby, Richard   4443, 5523

*The Virago Book of Victorian Ghost Stories*
Dalby, Richard   1234

*ViraVax*
Ransom, Bill   453, 774, 1724, 2443, 2681, **4478**, 5258

*Virgin*
Murphy, Mary Elizabeth   2994, 3607, **4050**

*The Virgin and the Dinosaur*
Garcia y Robertson, R.   403, **2122**

*The Virgin of Zesh*
de Camp, L. Sprague   1914

*The Virginia Ghost Murders*
Sachs, Leslie Raymond   **4778**

*Virgins and Martyrs*
Maginn, Simon   2548, 2994, 3149, **3607**

*Virgintooth*
Ivanhoe, Mark   600, 799, 2337, **2834**, 5537

*Virtual Death*
Aaron, Shale   **5**, 506

*Virtual Destruction*
Anderson, Kevin J.   **118**, 957, 1858, 3242

*Virtual Girl*
Thomson, Amy   77, 198, 835, 837, 892, 1582, 1903, 2051, 2093, 2163, 2445, 2729, 2730, 2839, 3049, 3797, 4677, 4704, 5450, **5462**, 5660

*Virtual Light*
Gibson, William   1903, **2219**, 5959

*Virtual Mode*
Anthony, Piers   **194**, 1471, 2943, 4156

*Virtual Unrealities: The Short Fiction of Alfred Bester*
Bester, Alfred   **479**, 1963, 3219, 3971, 5346, 5613

*Virtually Perfect*
Gutman, Dan   **2470**

*Virtuosity*
Bisson, Terry   **507**, 4075

*Virtuous Vampires*
Dziemianowicz, Stefan   **1718**

*Virus*
Caine, Peter   1164

*Virus*
Watkins, Graham   3923, **5632**

*Virus Clans*
Kanaly, Michael   **3008**

*The Vision*
Koontz, Dean R.   1780, 1975, 2871, 3135, 3594, 4471, 5987, 5993

*Vision of Tarot*
Anthony, Piers   960

*Vision Quest*
Service, Pamela F.   3934, **4920**, 5928, 5995

*Visions & Imaginings: Classic Fantasy Fiction*
Boyer, Robert H.   **606**, 1576, 1613, 2592, 5003, 5030, 5721, 5730

*Visions from the Sea*
Tallis, Robyn   4158

*Visions of Wonder: The Science Fiction Research Association Anthology*
Hartwell, David G.   229, **2595**

*Visit to a Small Planet*
Vidal, Gore   1226, 1228, 1385

*The Visitor*
Parker, Chauncey G. III   4370

*The Visitors*
Simak, Clifford D.   3940

*Visitors From Oz: The Wild Adventures of Dorothy, the Scarecrow and the Tin Woodman*
Gardner, Martin   **2136**

*The VMR Theory*
Frezza, Robert   **2055**

*Vodoun*
Madsen, David   3605

*The Voice in the Basement*
Martindale, T. Chris   2292, 3364, **3657**, 5784

*The Voice of Cepheus*
Appleby, Ken   **202**

*The Voice of Our Shadow*
Carroll, Jonathan   858

*Voice of the Planet*
Tobias, Michael   2578, 4455, 4456, 4929

*Voice of the Whirlwind*
Williams, Walter Jon   79, 107, 110, 597, 805, 957, 974, 995, 996, 1936, 2275, 2536, 2579, 3741, 3795, 3850, 4193, 4366, 4618, 4747, 5134, 5245, 5680

*A Voice out of Ramah*
Killough, Lee   1182

*Voices*
Vornholt, John   367, 944, 1387, 2102, 3096, 4833, **5598**

*Voices After Midnight*
Peck, Richard   121, 2272

*Voices From the Night*
Maclay, John   2278, **3598**, 4278, 4722

*Voices From the Vault: Authentic Vampire Tales*
Varma, Devendra P.   2407, 5706

*Voices of Chaos*
Crispin, A.C.   **1266**

*The Voices of Heaven*
Pohl, Frederik   1696, 1759, 2661, 4116, **4356**, 4964

*Voices of Hope*
Feintuch, David   **1903**, 4930

*The Void Captain's Tale*
Spinrad, Norman   583, 734, 1899, 5042, 5544, 5550

*Voima*
Brittain, C. Dale   **704**

*The Volcano Ogre*
Carter, Lin   4622, 5308

*Volkhavaar*
Lee, Tanith   5682

*Voodoo Child*
Reaves, Michael   1403, 2896, **4498**

*Voodoo Dreams*
Rhodes, Jewell Martin   3605

*Voodoo Planet*
Norton, Andre   1719

*Voorloper*
Norton, Andre   2437

*The Vor Game*
Bujold, Lois McMaster   309, 745, **764**, 1543, 1550, 1900, 2212, 4982, 5283, 5298, 5545, 5722

*Vortex*
Cole, Allan   **1108**

*The Voyage*
Drake, David   **1649**

*Voyage From Yesteryear*
Hogan, James P.   3344, 3924, 5788, 5804

*The Voyage of Mael Duin's Curragh*
Aakhus, Patricia   **2**, 3846

*Voyage of the Basset*
Christensen, James C.   68, 385, **1024**, 2654, 2719

*The Voyage of the Dawn Treader*
Lewis, C.S.   368

*Voyage of the Fox Rider*
McKiernan, Dennis L.   2271, **3837**

*The Voyage of the Space Beagle*
Van Vogt, A.E.   1649, 5048, 5860

*Voyage of the Star Wolf*
Gerrold, David   1899, **2212**, 4775, 5725

*Voyage to the Bottom of the Sea*
Sturgeon, Theodore   318, 1201, 1666, 5282

*Voyage to the City of the Dead*
Foster, Alan Dean   4545

*Voyage to the Red Planet*
Bisson, Terry   **508**, 1418, 3082, 4095, 5215, 5227, 5859

*Voyager*
Baxter, Stephen   **406**

*Voyager in Night*
Cherryh, C.J.   133, 512, 2207, 2811

*Voyagers II: The Alien Within*
Bova, Ben   824

*Voyagers III: Star Brothers*
Bova, Ben   824

*Voyages by Starlight*
MacLeod, Ian R.   **3600**

*Voyages into Darkness*
Laws, Stephen   **3363**

*Vulcan!*
Sky, Kathleen   528, 3919, 3920

*The Vulcan Academy Murders*
Lorrah, Jean   527, 1260, 3315, 4928, 5596

*Vulcan's Forge*
Shwartz, Susan   **5019**

*Vulcan's Glory*
Fontana, D.C.   1386, 1728, **1967**

**Vurt**
Noon, Jeff  **4136**, 4703, 4732

**Vyrmin**
Lazuta, Gene  **3376**

## W

**Wagers of Sin**
Asprin, Robert  **264**, 350, 1855

**Waiting for the Galactic Bus**
Godwin, Parke  5, 31, 156, 159, 433, 1803, 2084, 2100, 2103, 2342, 2343, 2666, 2750, 2753, 2859, 2942, 3007, 3083, 3311, 3908, 4028, 4029, 4030, 4034, 4035, 4473, 5101, 5181, 5277, 5351, 5532, 5569, 5616, 5636, 5768, 5958, 6060, 6064

**Wake of the Werewolf**
Caine, Geoffrey  **834**, 3376, 5562

**Wake Up Screaming**
Courtney, Vincent  **1215**, 2606

**Waking Beauty**
Witcover, Paul  **5931**

**Waking in Dreamland**
Nye, Jody Lynn  2688, **4177**

**Waking Nightmares**
Campbell, Ramsey  **866**

**Waking the Moon**
Hand, Elizabeth  715, 1180, 1445, **2538**, 3099, 3257, 4093, 4358

**Waldo and Magic, Inc.**
Heinlein, Robert A.  162, 5694

**Walford's Oak**
Phillips, Jill M.  4275, **4310**

**Walk the Moon's Road**
Aikin, Jim  2414, 2450

**Walk to the End of the World**
Charnas, Suzy McKee  208, 1590, 2242, 3863, 4792, 5268, 5477, 5590

**Walkabout Woman**
Roessner, Michaela  3291, 3889

**The Walkaway Clause**
Dalmas, John  1182

**Walker between the Worlds**
DesRochers, Diane  **1499**

**Walker of Worlds**
De Haven, Tom  **1423**, 1426

**Walkers**
Masterton, Graham  3033, **3681**

**The Walking Shadow**
Stableford, Brian  **5195**, 5909

**Walking the Labyrinth**
Goldstein, Lisa  636, 637, **2266**, 3283, 3847, 4093, 5916

**Walking Wolf**
Collins, Nancy A.  **1126**, 3119, 4052, 4251, 4256

**Walking Wounded**
Devereaux, Robert  **1507**

**The Wall**
Haushofer, Marlen  1787, 2554, **2603**, 2640

**The Wall**
McConnell, Ashley  4487

**The Wall Around Eden**
Slonczewski, Joan  160, 211, 327, 365, 720, **5092**, 5878

**The Wall at the Edge of the World**
Aikin, Jim  **46**, 4478

**The Wall of the Sky, the Wall of the Eye**
Lethem, Jonathan  411, 1023, 3087, **3442**, 3712

**Wall, Stone, Craft**
Williams, Walter Jon  **5842**

**The Walled Orchard**
Holt, Tom  2189, **2752**, 5595

**The Walls of Air**
Hambly, Barbara  1175, 1746

**Walls of Fear**
Cramer, Kathryn  **1246**, 2396, 5902

**Waltz with Evil**
Rozzi, P.D.  **4701**

**The Wanderer**
Leiber, Fritz  354, 3106, 4510, 5303, 5341

**Wanderer**
McQuinn, Donald E.  **3862**

**The Wandering Fire**
Kay, Guy Gavriel  3068

**Wandering Ghosts**
Crawford, F. Marion  2633

**The Wandering Jew**
Sue, Eugene  4371

**Wandering Stars: An Anthology of Jewish Fantasy and Science Fiction**
Dann, Jack  1788

**Wanderlust**
Kirchoff, Mary  154, **3155**, 4368

**Wandl the Invader**
Cummings, Ray  5864

**War**
Hawke, Simon  **2625**

**The War Amongst the Angels**
Moorcock, Michael  **3986**, 4178

**War and Peace**
Tolstoy, Leo  2987

**War Birds**
Meluch, R.M.  1628, 2173, **3875**

**War Dogs of the Golden Horde**
Murrill, Ray W.  205

**War Dragons**
Graf, L.A.  **2299**

**War Fever**
Ballard, J.G.  **321**, 3648, 3796, 4636

**War for the Oaks**
Bull, Emma  235, 271, 317, 392, 393, 424, 546, 550, 634, 714, 743, 935, 987, 1040, 1159, 1181, 1321, 1434, 1436, 1471, 1475, 1476, 1478, 1491, 1742, 1747, 1837, 1841, 1947, 1958, 2076, 2077, 2083, 2465, 2521, 2717, 2771, 2942, 3077, 3264, 3274, 3277, 3284, 3285, 3286, 3299, 3302, 3488, 3886, 3887, 3938, 4120, 4149, 4173, 4174, 4317, 4394, 4434, 4658, 4659, 4661, 4675, 4798, 4821, 4868, 4870, 4981, 4989, 4990, 4993, 4995, 4996, 5062, 5096, 5179, 5181, 5642, 5646, 5913, 5914, 5915

**War Games**
Hansen, Karl  2432

**The War God's Own**
Weber, David  **5682**

**War in Heaven**
Williams, Charles  2231

**War in Tethyr**
Milan, Victor  2675, 5022

**The War in the Waste**
Savage, Felicity  **4851**, 4852

**The War Machine**
Drake, David  **1650**, 6014

**The War Minstrels**
Haber, Karen  101, **2477**

**The War of Don Emmanuel's Nether Parts**
de Bernieres, Louis  **1412**, 1657, 3006, 4208

**War of Shadows**
Chalker, Jack L.  66

**War of the Gods**
Anderson, Poul  **136**

**The War of the Sky Lords**
Brosnan, John  **721**

**War of the Three Waters**
Niles, Douglas  **4110**

**War of the Twins**
Weis, Margaret  5454, 5455

**War of the Wing-Men**
Anderson, Poul  3769

**The War of the Worlds**
Wells, H.G.  119, 205, 2034, 2048, 2192, 5878

**War of the Worlds: Global Dispatches**
Anderson, Kevin J.  **119**, 205, 607, 2398, 6077

**War With the Newts**
Capek, Karel  **874**

**War World**
Dietz, William C.  5930

**War World I: The Burning Eye**
Pournelle, Jerry  2004, 5292

**War World II: Death's Head Rebellion**
Pournelle, Jerry  5292

**War World III: Sauron Dominion**
Pournelle, Jerry  5292

**Warbots**
Stine, G. Harry  47, 48, 49, 50, 829, 1566, 1568, 1569, 1896, 1938, 2488

**Warchild**
Friesner, Esther  8, 2917

**The Warden of Horses**
Ripley, Karen  4163, **4595**

**The Warding of Witch World**
Norton, Andre  **4163**

**'Ware Hawk**
Norton, Andre  638

**Warhorse**
Zahn, Timothy  **6056**

**Warlock**
Koontz, Dean R.  4621

**Warlock and Son**
Stasheff, Christopher  197, **5224**

**Warlock at the Wheel and Other Stories**
Jones, Diana Wynne  3611, 3845, 5239

**The Warlock Heretical**
Stasheff, Christopher  706

**The Warlock in Spite of Himself**
Stasheff, Christopher  167, 168, 172, 177, 180, 184, 186, 705, 845, 1268, 1413, 1531, 1534, 1755, 2041, 2079, 2235, 3296, 3297, 3991, 4316, 4399, 4404, 4433, 4435, 4766, 5235, 5694

**The Warlock Insane**
Stasheff, Christopher  1755, 2809, 3471, 4013, **5225**

**The Warlock Is Missing**
Stasheff, Christopher  3010

**Warlock of the Witch World**
Norton, Andre  4782

**The Warlock Rock**
Stasheff, Christopher  706, 1416, 1998, 2015, **5226**

**The Warlock Unlocked**
Stasheff, Christopher  169, 259, 701

**The Warlock Wandering**
Stasheff, Christopher  1755

**Warlocks and Warriors**
de Camp, L. Sprague  3420, 5599

**Warlord of Heaven**
Cole, Adrian  **1102**

**The Warlord of the Air**
Moorcock, Michael  1655

**Warlords of Jupiter**
Keith, William H. Jr.  **3036**

**A Warning to the Curious**
James, M.R.  **2866**

**Warning Whispers**
Burrage, A.M.  454, 455

**Warp Angel**
Hopen, Stuart  **2766**, 5051, 5767

**Warpath**
Daniel, Tony  **1337**, 5745

**Warped**
Jeter, K.W.  **2917**

**The Warrior**
Drake, David   312, 1547, **1651**

**Warrior**
McQuinn, Donald E.   208, 656, 720, 721, 1539, 3248, **3863**, 3873, 3999, 4000, 4001, 5574, 5743, 5965

**Warrior**
Wu, William F.   1855, **6000**

**The Warrior and the Witch**
Miller, Carl   **3893**

**Warrior: Coup**
Stackpole, Michael A.   4903

**Warrior Enchantresses**
Massie-Ferch, Kathleen M.   3076

**Warrior Princesses**
Scarborough, Elizabeth Ann   **4871**

**The Warrior Returns**
Cole, Allan   **1109**

**Warrior Shield**
Stine, G. Harry   **5283**

**The Warrior's Apprentice**
Bujold, Lois McMaster   231, 260, 310, 986, 988, 1003, 1047, 1261, 1544, 1571, 1599, 1630, 1650, 1652, 1901, 3748, 3974, 4375, 4378, 4974, 5139, 5280, 5283, 5681, 6061

**Warriors for the Working Day**
Green, Roland J.   3861

**Warriors of Blood and Dream**
Zelazny, Roger   4227, **6075**

**The Warriors of Dawn**
Foster, M.A.   1326, 1757, 4594

**The Warriors of Spider**
Gear, W. Michael   2460, 2830, 2831, 2833

**Warriors of the Storm**
Chalker, Jack L.   3861

**The Warrior's Tale**
Cole, Allan   **1110**

**Warriorwards**
ab Hugh, Dafydd   **11**

**Warsprite**
Swycaffer, Jefferson P.   **5375**

**Warstrider**
Keith, William H. Jr.   **3037**, 4974

**Warstrider: Netlink**
Keith, William H. Jr.   1184, **3038**

**Wartide**
Barnes, John   **359**

**Was**
Ryman, Geoff   2136, 3609, **4758**, 5912

**Washed by a Wave of Wind**
Bell, M. Shayne   **435**

**Wasp**
Russell, Eric Frank   1652, 2001

**The Waste Lands**
King, Stephen   **3143**

**Watch the Northwind Rise**
Graves, Robert   5490

**The Watcher**
Maclean, Charles   1237

**The Watcher and Other Stories**
Calvino, Italo   3443

**Watchers**
Koontz, Dean R.   41, 373, 488, 1084, 1346, 1349, 1539, 1708, 1780, 1850, 2284, 2429, 2611, 2779, 3152, 3153, 3701, 4756, 5388, 5474, 5586, 5589

**Watchers in the Woods**
Johnstone, William W.   **2936**, 3092, 5685

**The Watcher's Mask**
Marks, Laurie J.   **3627**, 5296

**The Watchers out of Time**
Lovecraft, H.P.   539, 3266, **3535**

**The Watchers out of Time and Others**
Lovecraft, H.P.   925

**Watchtower**
Lynn, Elizabeth A.   3268, 5750, 6075

**The Water King's Laughter**
Friesner, Esther   1765, 5153

**Water Rites**
Smith, Guy N.   **5121**

**The Waterborn**
Keyes, J. Gregory   1042, 1095, 1943, 2924, 2925, **3098**, 3773, 4110, 5583, 5757, 5817

**Waterdeep**
Awlinson, Richard   1293, 5723

**Watership Down**
Adams, Richard   432, 599, 1132, 2850, 2852, 3115, 4271, 4273, 5755

**The Waterworks**
Doctorow, E.L.   26, 453, **1564**

**The Wave and the Flame**
Kellogg, Marjorie Bradley   3157

**Wave Without a Shore**
Cherryh, C.J.   951, 4592

**The Way Beneath**
Wells, Angus   **5740**

**Way-Farer**
Schmidt, Dennis   4116, 6075

**A Way Home**
Sturgeon, Theodore   1061, 3308

**The Way of Spider**
Gear, W. Michael   2460, 2830, 2831, 2833

**Way of the Clans**
Thurston, Robert   4583, **5469**

**Way of the Pilgrim**
Dickson, Gordon R.   132, 1493, 1774, 2192, 2254, 3767, 3817, 5027, 5918, 5919

**The Way of the Werewolf**
Hill, David   2410, 2976, 5384

**Way Station**
Simak, Clifford D.   125, 263, **5048**

**Way Up High**
Zelazny, Roger   2468, 3382, 5972, **6076**

**Wayfinder's Story: The Seventh Book of Lost Swords**
Saberhagen, Fred   **4777**

**The Ways of Magic**
Ciencin, Scott   **1033**, 1082

**The Wayward Knights**
Green, Roland J.   5723

**We Can Build You**
Dick, Philip K.   4297

**We Have Always Lived in the Castle**
Jackson, Shirley   2026, 3815, 4312

**We Open on Venus**
Stasheff, Christopher   1771, 2575, **5227**

**We Who Are About To...**
Russ, Joanna   1590, 2242, 3579, 4792

**The Wealdwife's Tale**
Hazel, Paul   **2636**, 2739

**Weapon**
Mason, Robert   1113, **3666**

**The Weapon Makers**
Van Vogt, A.E.   446, 784, 1103, 1108, 1869, 4114, 5543, 5865

**The Weapon Shops of Isher**
Van Vogt, A.E.   1523, 1869, 2730, 3874, 4114, 5260, 5865

**Weasel's Luck**
Williams, Michael   5711, 5724

**Weaveworld**
Barker, Clive   1423, 1957, 3131, 3143, 3677

**Web of Darkness**
Bradley, Marion Zimmer   5035, 6041

**Web of Dreams**
Andrews, V.C.   **147**

**The Web of Easter Island**
Wandrei, Donald   3569

**The Web of Everywhere**
Brunner, John   3777

**Web of Futures**
Swycaffer, Jefferson P.   5376

**Web of Light**
Bradley, Marion Zimmer   5035

**The Web of Spider**
Gear, W. Michael   **2173**, 2460, 2830, 2831, 2833, 3929

**Web of the Romulans**
Murdock, M.S.   528

**Webs**
Baker, Scott   **304**, 811, 3815, 4716

**Website**
Garton, Ray   **2157**

**The Wee Men of Ballywooden**
Mason, Arthur   2438

**Weekend**
Pike, Christopher   1801

**Weetzie Bat**
Block, Francesca Lia   4104

**The Weigher**
Vinicoff, Eric   792, 1254, 2443, 2637, 3743, **5574**

**Weird Business**
Lansdale, Joe R.   1044, **3334**

**Weird Family Tales**
Wisman, Ken   3614, **5929**

**Weird Henry Berg**
Sargent, Sarah   2868

**Weird Menace**
Ray, Fred Olen   **4494**

**Weird Menace 1: The Corpse Factory**
Weinberg, Robert   4494

**Weird Menace 2: Satan's Roadhouse**
Weinberg, Robert   4494

**Weird Tales**
Carter, Lin   4724, 4726

**Weird Tales**
Haining, Peter   480, 482, **2485**, 5689

**Weird Tales**
Margulies, Leo   2485, 5689

**Weird Tales: 32 Unearthed Terrors**
Dziemianowicz, Stefan   480, 482, 2485, 3023, 3028

**Weird Tales From Shakespeare**
Kerr, Katharine   **3079**, 5826

**Weird Tales: Seven Decades of Terror**
Betancourt, John Gregory   **482**, 3023

**Weird Tales: The Magazine That Never Dies**
Kaye, Marvin   480, 482, 3023, **3028**

**Weird Vampire Tales**
Weinberg, Robert   1231, **5706**

**Weirdos of the Universe, Unite!**
Service, Pamela F.   167, **4921**

**The Weirds**
Jaffery, Sheldon   940, 4494

**The Weirdstone of Brisingamen**
Garner, Alan   1005, 1294, 2283, 2943, 3436, 3737, 5977, 6006

**Welcome to the Monkey House**
Vonnegut, Kurt Jr.   124, 161, 321, 624, 850, 1515, 4636, 5551

**The Well**
Cady, Jack   666, 890, 1776, 3141, 3953

**The Well**
Sirota, Michael B.   3160, **5077**, 5121

**The Well-Favored Man: The Tale of the Sorcerer's Nephew**
Willey, Elizabeth   718, 719, 1064, 2503, 2509, 4986, **5813**

**Well of Shiuan**
Cherryh, C.J.   257, 1174, 4153, 5733, 5951

**The Well of the Unicorn**
Pratt, Fletcher   3980

**A Well-Timed Enchantment**
Vande Velde, Vivian   1012, **5559**, 5822

**Well Wished**
Billingsley, Franny   **489**

*The Wells of Phyre*
Douglas, L. Warren  **1589**, 5780

*Welsh Celtic Myth in Modern Fantasy*
Sullivan, C.W.  5560

*Wendigo Border*
Montrose, Catherine  3119, **3967**, 5249

*Werenight*
Turtledove, Harry  5792, 5794

*Werewolf!*
Pronzini, Bill  1230, 2410, 2976, 4410, 5384

*Werewolf*
Rubie, Peter  2895, **4702**

*The Werewolf Chronicles*
Bricry, Traci  **679**, 926, 4472

*The Werewolf of Paris*
Endore, Guy  572, 603, **1822**, 5481

*The Werewolf of Ponkert*
Munn, H. Warner  4002, 4702, 5146, 5425, 5481

*The Werewolf Principle*
Simak, Clifford D.  1869

*Werewolf Wars*
Goldman, Randy  2768, 5388

*The Werewolf's Kiss*
Scotch, Cheri  3411, 5481

*The Werewolf's Revenge*
Jaccoma, Richard  **2841**, 4002

*The Werewolf's Tale*
Jaccoma, Richard  2520, 2794, 4002, 4005, 4702, 5085

*The Werewolf's Touch*
Scotch, Cheri  4246, **4892**

*Werewolves*
Ahern, Jerry  2841

*Werewolves*
Greenberg, Martin H.  1230, **2410**, 3032, 4988

*The Werewolves of London*
Stableford, Brian  1117, 1277, 1721, 4740, 4766, **5196**, 5828

*Wes Craven's New Nightmare*
Bergantino, David  **460**

*West India Lights*
Whitehead, Henry S.  3879, 3880

*West of Eden*
Harrison, Harry  165, 591, 4853

*West of Honor*
Pournelle, Jerry  4948, 4958

*West of January*
Duncan, Dave  **1691**

*Western Ghosts*
McSherry, Frank D. Jr.  217, 3331, **3870**

*The Western King*
Marston, Ann  **3636**

*The Western Wizard*
Reichert, Mickey Zucker  **4526**, 5150

*Westlin Wind*
de Lint, Charles  **1439**, 1925

*Westmark*
Alexander, Lloyd  5142, 5579

*Westworld*
Crichton, Michael  4117

*Wet Work*
Nutman, Philip  **4168**, 4745, 4746, 5313

*Wetbones*
Shirley, John  2156, 2313, 2843, 3396, 4041, **5010**, 5853

*Wetware*
Rucker, Rudy  79, 249, 419, 1820, 1964, 2837, 3795, 3890, 4276, 4341, 4381, 5245, 5451, 5452, 5573

*What Did Miss Darrington See?: An Anthology of Feminist Supernatural Fiction*
Salmonson, Jessica Amanda  37, 1312, 1715, 2035, 2496, 3570, 4443, 5523, 5814

*What If? Stories That Should Have Won the Hugo*
Lupoff, Richard A.  2405

*What Mad Universe*
Brown, Fredric  1521, 4546, 5169

*What Might Have Been*
Benford, Gregory  5633

*What Savage Beast*
David, Peter  1227, **1390**

*Whatdunits*
Resnick, Mike  2005, 3619, **4558**

*What's Bred in the Bone*
Davies, Robertson  518, 1277

*What's Wrong with America*
Bradfield, Scott  **627**, 1396, 5167, 5168

*What's Wrong with Tamara?*
Fowler, D.A.  **2025**

*What's Wrong with Valerie?*
Fowler, D.A.  **2026**

*Wheel of Dreams*
Tyson, Salinda  2958, **5529**

*Wheel of Fortune*
Zelazny, Roger  1187, 2406

*Wheels of Fire*
Lackey, Mercedes  639, 2467, **3301**, 4862, 4980, 4981

*When Darkness Falls*
Williams, Sidney  **5825**

*When Death Birds Fly*
Offutt, Andrew J.  1960, 5963

*When Demons Walk*
Briggs, Patricia  **683**

*When Dreams Collide*
Simmons, Wm. Mark  87, 179, 3173, **5063**

*When Gravity Fails*
Effinger, George Alec  360, 481, 505, 746, 805, 806, 808, 1153, 1504, 1572, 1680, 1762, 1820, 1889, 1964, 2913, 3946, 3947, 4193, 4291, 4544, 4749, 4941, 5210, 5363, 5644, 5887, 5966

*When HARLIE Was One: Release 2.0*
Gerrold, David  249, 3437, 5452

*When Heaven Fell*
Barton, William  **383**, 2254

*When Michael Calls*
Farris, John  536

*When Shadows Fall*
Smith, Brian Scott  3885, **5100**

*When the Black Lotus Blooms*
Saunders, Elizabeth A.  1823, 2967, 3997, **4846**, 5447

*When the Bough Breaks*
Lackey, Mercedes  396, **3302**, 3478, 3482, 3487, 3776, 5296

*When the Changewinds Blow*
Chalker, Jack L.  165, 171, 2235, 4269

*When the Five Moons Rise*
Vance, Jack  **5551**

*When the Gods Are Silent*
Lindskold, Jane M.  **3477**

*When the Music's Over*
Shiner, Lewis  4959

*When the Night Wind Howls*
Service, Pamela F.  773

*When the Sleeper Wakes*
Wells, H.G.  735, 5243, 5568

*When the Tripods Came*
Christopher, John  5027

*When the Waker Sleeps*
Goulart, Ron  735, 5243

*When They Come From Space*
Clifton, Mark  5766

*When True Night Falls*
Friedman, C.S.  560, **2060**, 5371

*When Will You Rage*
Wieck, Stewart  23, 3224, 3229, 5797

*When Wolves Cry*
Africa, Chris N.  **41**, 2768, 5388

*When Worlds Collide*
Wylie, Philip  732, 4416

*The Whenabouts of Burr*
Kurland, Michael  5495

*Where Does Kissing End?*
Pullinger, Kate  2843, **4445**

*Where Late the Sweet Birds Sang*
Wilhelm, Kate  1932, 5732

*Where the Chill Waits*
Martindale, T. Chris  41, 834, 2936, **3658**, 3895, 5769

*Where the Ships Die*
Dietz, William C.  **1553**

*Where the Towers Pierce the Sky*
Goodwin, Marie D.  **2272**

*Whilom*
Watson, Robert  67, 2751, 2752, 5595, **5639**

*The Whim of the Dragon*
Dean, Pamela  4, **1447**, 1488, 5182, 5235, 5311

*The Whims of Creation*
Hawke, Simon  107, 2243, **2626**, 5941

*Whipping Boy*
Byrne, John  795, **800**, 1507, 2700, 3668, 4073, 4787

*Whipping Star*
Herbert, Frank  1992, 2343, 2666, 4019, 4357, 5042

*Whippoorwill Road*
Rutherford, Brett  **4752**

*The Whirligig of Time*
Biggle, Lloyd  3343

*Whirlwind*
Grant, Charles L.  106, 112, 924, **2320**, 5358

*Whirlwind Alchemy*
Clark, Douglas W.  706, 845, 2079

*Whisper*
Van Over, Raymond  2199, **5539**

*A Whisper of Blood*
Datlow, Ellen  698, 1231, 1286, **1370**, 1718, 2071, 2387, 3031, 4407, 5688

*Whisper of Death*
Pike, Christopher  655

*A Whisper of Time*
Downing, Paula E.  351, **1595**, 3707, 3708, 3709, 4175, 5429, 5548

*A Whisper of Wings*
Fulgham, Steven Ray  **2091**

*Whispering Woods*
Emery, Clayton  207, 1977

*Whispers*
Koontz, Dean R.  2609, 4088

*The Whispers*
Parkinson, Dan  **4247**

*Whispers: An Anthology of Fantasy and Horror*
Schiff, Stuart David  2960, 3961

*Whispers in the Dark*
Aycliffe, Jonathan  45, **283**, 3164

*The Whispers Series*
Schiff, Stuart David  1823, 2773, 2966, 4724, 4726, 4846, 5025

*Whistling Past the Churchyard*
White, John Manchip  2543, 2643, 3472, 3705

*The White Abacus*
Broderick, Damien  **708**, 1442, 4060

*The White Dragon*
McCaffrey, Anne  222, 4149, 4692, 4697, 5640

*White Eyes*
Robeson, Kenneth  85, **4625**

*The White Gryphon*
Lackey, Mercedes  **3303**

*The White Guardian*
Cross, Ronald Anthony  **1275**

*White Horse, Dark Dragon*
Fleet, Robert C.  **1947**

*White House Horrors*
Greenberg, Martin H.  **2411**

**White Jenna**
Yolen, Jane   3582, **6041**

**White Light**
Barton, William   **384**

**White Light, or What Is Cantor's Continuum Problem**
Rucker, Rudy   519

**White Lotus**
Hersey, John   3817, 5301, 5918, 5919

**The White Mists of Power**
Rusch, Kristine Kathryn   1065, 1679, 3510, **4730**, 5113

**White Moon, Red Dragon**
Wingrove, David   **5921**

**The White Mountain**
Wingrove, David   **5922**

**The White Mountains**
Christopher, John   221, 1781, 4919

**White Night**
Lovejoy, William H.   4512

**The White Order**
Modesitt, L.E. Jr.   **3942**

**The White Papers**
White, James   759, 1969, 3430, **5782**, 5838

**The White Plague**
Herbert, Frank   1133, 1167, 1724, 2681, 2870, 3008, 3242, 3641, 3642, 4476, 4478, 4748, 4756, 4856, 5054, 5172, 5212, 5258

**White Queen**
Jones, Gwyneth   157, 2486, 2837, **2955**, 3711, 4130, 4136, 4503, 4554, 4703, 5450

**The White Raven**
Paxson, Diana L.   965, 1191, 3017, 3018, 3636, 5015, 5390, 5393

**The White Regiment**
Dalmas, John   **1327**, 1552, 4373, 5930

**White Rhino**
Dolan, Bill   **1569**, 4544

**The White Road**
Weighell, Ron   2707, 3314, 5776

**The White Rose**
Cook, Glen   2990, 3833

**White Shark**
Benchley, Peter   189, **441**, 1850, 3220

**The White Tribunal**
Volsky, Paula   **5583**

**White Wing**
Kendall, Gordon   3454, 5292

**Whiteout**
Walker, Sage   386, 405, 809, 1075, 1167, 1168, 1244, 2243, 2291, 2394, 2488, 2723, 5355, **5619**

**Who Censored Roger Rabbit?**
Wolf, Gary K.   1152, 1399, 1506, 1524, 2132, 3441, 3768, 5148

**Who Fears the Devil?**
Wellman, Manly Wade   817, 1639

**Who Goes There?**
Campbell, John W.   1197, 3188

**Who Goes There? and Other Stories**
Campbell, John W.   5767

**Who Hunts the Hunter**
Smith, Nyx   3198

**Who Killed James Dean?**
Beath, Warren Newton   **428**, 3102

**Who Knew There'd Be Ghosts?**
Brittain, William   5286, 5289

**Who Made Stevie Crye?**
Bishop, Michael   2873

**Who P-P-Plugged Roger Rabbit?**
Wolf, Gary K.   2620, 3441, 3768, 5148, **5934**

**The Whole Man**
Brunner, John   5048

**Whores for Gloria**
Vollmann, William T.   3362

**Who's Afraid of Beowulf?**
Holt, Tom   1273

**Whose Song Is Sung**
Schaefer, Frank   **4872**

**Why Call Them Back From Heaven?**
Simak, Clifford D.   2498, 4066, 5243

**Why Do Birds**
Knight, Damon   2418, **3190**

**Why Mosquitoes Buzz in People's Ears**
Aardema, Verna   3382

**Why Not You and I**
Wagner, Karl Edward   4886

**The Wicked Cyborg**
Goulart, Ron   2573, 4940, 5997

**The Wicked Day**
Stewart, Mary   2940, 4584

**The Wicked Enchantment**
Benary-Isbert, Margot   2196

**Wicked: The Life and Times of the Wicked Witch of the West**
Maguire, Gregory   2136, **3609**

**The Wicker Man**
Hardy, Robin   852

**Wicket Finds a Way: An Ewok Adventure**
Luke, Melinda   1392, 1393, 1394

**The Widowmaker**
Resnick, Mike   **4559**

**The Widowmaker Reborn**
Resnick, Mike   **4560**

**The Widow's Son**
Wilson, Robert Anton   2627

**Wielding a Red Sword**
Anthony, Piers   355, 3696

**The Wild**
Strieber, Whitley   679, 680, 729, 5080, **5343**

**The Wild**
Zindell, David   **6086**

**The Wild Alien Tamer**
Resnick, Mike   5215

**Wild Blood**
Collins, Nancy A.   679, 680, 926, **1127**, 1800, 2520, 3564, 4472

**The Wild Blue and the Gray**
Sanders, William   1983, 2416, 3867, 3993, **4814**, 5501, 5502

**Wild Cards**
Martin, George R.R.   499, 1535, 2256, 3009, 4363, 5038, 5148, 5214, 5216, 5642, 6048

**The Wild Cards Series**
Martin, George R.R.   1674, 3891, 4130, 5567

**A Wild Dog and Lone**
Crawford, Dan   **1251**

**The Wild Hunt**
Yolen, Jane   1472, 3847, **6042**

**The Wild Hunt: Vengeance Moon**
Foxe, Jocelin   **2031**

**Wild Jack**
Christopher, John   511

**Wild Magic**
Clayton, Jo   4, 604, 673, **1072**, 1114, 3486, 3766

**Wild Magic**
Pierce, Tamora   68, **4323**

**Wild Magic**
Wells, Angus   1068, **5741**

**Wild Night Company**
Haining, Peter   4203

**The Wild Ones**
Chandler, A. Bertram   2575, 5549

**The Wild Road**
King, Gabriel   846, **3120**

**Wild Seed**
Butler, Octavia E.   394, 876, 881, 889, 2771

**The Wild Shore**
Robinson, Kim Stanley   4619

**Wild Women**
Hall, Melissa Mia   **2496**

**The Wild Wood**
de Lint, Charles   **1440**, 2088, 2980, 3840, 5916

**Wildeblood's Empire**
Stableford, Brian   1182, 5231

**Wilderness**
Danvers, Dennis   679, 680, 816, 926, **1349**, 4472, 5146, 5343, 5425

**Wilderness**
Holt, John R.   926

**Wildest Dreams**
Partridge, Norman   **4256**

**Wildfire**
Clayton, Jo   673, **1073**, 3766, 4674

**Wilding**
Tem, Melanie   926, 1822, 3492, 4841, **5425**

**Wildlife**
Kelly, James Patrick   352, 1696, **3049**

**The Wildlings**
Ciencin, Scott   **1034**, 5852

**The Wilds**
Laymon, Richard   3373

**Wildside**
Gould, Steven   298, 1981, **2291**, 4502, 4948

**Wildwood**
Farris, John   1039, 2091, 2936, 3056, 3681, 4224, 5380

**Will the Last Person to Leave the Planet Please Shut Off the Sun?**
Resnick, Mike   **4561**

**The Will to Kill**
Bloch, Robert   5443

**William F. Nolan's Logan: A Trilogy**
Nolan, William F.   1449

**The Williamson Effect**
Zelazny, Roger   2398, **6077**

**The Willing Spirit**
Anthony, Piers   **195**, 1316, 1317, 1318

**Willow**
Drew, Wayland   1042, 1483, 3540

**The Willow Garden**
Grant, Kathryn   69, 3338, 3339, 4155

**The Willows and Beyond**
Horwood, William   **2775**

**The Willows in Winter**
Horwood, William   **2776**, 2848

**Wind Child**
Meluch, R.M.   3747, 4594

**Wind Chimes**
Walters, R.R.   4240, **5625**

**The Wind Crystal**
Paxson, Diana L.   3905, **4269**

**Wind Eye**
Westall, Robert   1294

**The Wind From a Burning Woman**
Bear, Greg   3048, 3086, 3234, 5257, 5369

**Wind From a Foreign Sky**
Reimann, Katya   2031, 2958, 4459, **4528**

**A Wind in Cairo**
Tarr, Judith   2457

**The Wind in the Rosebush and Other Stories of the Supernatural**
Wilkins-Freeman, Mary E.   1673

**The Wind in the Willows**
Grahame, Kenneth   32, 737, 1821, 2774, 2775, 2776, 2848, 2849, 2850, 2851, 2852, 2853, 2854, 2855, 3115

**The Wind Whales of Ishmael**
Farmer, Philip Jose   3800

**Wind Whispers, Shadow Shouts**
Green, Sharon   2360

**Windchaser**
Ciencin, Scott   2003, 2469

**Windmaster's Bane**
Deitz, Tom   391, 935, 974, 1162, 1947, 3285, 3354, 3357, 3799, 3802, 3804, 4798

**Windows on a Lost World**
Mitchell, V.E.   **3920**

**The Winds of Altair**
Bova, Ben   2764

**Winds of Change**
Lackey, Mercedes   **3304**

**Winds of Change**
Pini, Richard   4336, 4337

**Winds of Fate**
Lackey, Mercedes   **3305**, 4433, 4718

**Winds of Fury**
Lackey, Mercedes   **3306**, 4491

**The Winds of Gath**
Tubb, E.C.   2332, 6081

**The Winds of Mars**
Hoover, H.M.   **2765**

**The Wind's Twelve Quarters**
Le Guin, Ursula K.   2120, 5807

**The Windsingers**
Lindholm, Megan   4924

**The Wine-Dark Sea**
Aickman, Robert   851, 864, 865, 866, 3462, 3463, 3779, 5329

**Wine of the Dreamers**
MacDonald, John D.   4361

**Wing Commander: Freedom Flight**
Lackey, Mercedes   643, 1043, **3307**, 5681

**Winged Magic**
Herbert, Mary H.   **2678**

**Wings**
Pratchett, Terry   1222, 1223, 1224, **4403**, 4434

**Wings of Flame**
Springer, Nancy   4985

**Wings of Power**
Carl, Lillian Stewart   3303

**Winner Takes All**
Green, Simon R.   1838, **2375**

**Winning Colors**
Moon, Elizabeth   **3976**

**Winning Scheherazade**
Gorog, Judith   329, 618

**The Winnowing**
Fleming, Gherbod   **1950**, 5882

**Winter Harvest**
Chelsea, Jane   3377

**Winter in Eden**
Harrison, Harry   591

**The Winter King**
Cornwell, Bernard   267, **1191**, 2747, 3355

**Winter Moon**
Koontz, Dean R.   **3218**

**Winter of Magic's Return**
Service, Pamela F.   641, 2272, 3261

**The Winter of the World**
Anderson, Poul   4619, 4620, 4621

**Winter Rose**
McKillip, Patricia A.   153, 2957, **3843**, 3847, 4358

**Winter Tales**
Jens, Tina L.   **2894**

**Winter Tides**
Blaylock, James P.   **524**

**Winter Wolves**
Wescott, Earle   **5756**, 5894

**Winter World**
Mills, C.J.   762, 1862, 5279

**Winterlong**
Hand, Elizabeth   **2539**

**Wintermind**
Kaye, Marvin   2245

**Winter's Tale**
Helprin, Mark   896, 1276, 5272, 5570

**Wise Child**
Furlong, Monica   1746

**A Wish and a Dream**
Weaver, Ingrid   **5658**

**Wishbringer**
Gardner, Craig Shaw   288, 1206, 1839, **2133**

**Wishes Come True**
Nance, Kathleen   73, 880

**Wishing Season**
Friesner, Esther   73, 489, 557, 880, **2085**, 2129, 4863, 5163, 5218, 5658, 6017

**The Wishing Well**
de Lint, Charles   **1441**

**Witch**
McQuinn, Donald E.   **3864**

**Witch**
Pike, Christopher   **4334**, 5478

**A Witch Across Time**
Cross, Gilbert B.   122, 1012, **1272**, 3444

**The Witch and the Cathedral**
Brittain, C. Dale   **705**

**Witch and Wombat**
Cushman, Carolyn   315, 703, 915, **1299**, 2946

**Witch Baby**
Block, Francesca Lia   **552**, 636

**The Witch Doctor**
Stasheff, Christopher   635, 4671, **5228**, 5500

**Witch Fantastic**
Resnick, Mike   6034

**Wit'ch Fire**
Clemens, James   **1082**

**Witch Hill**
Bradley, Marion Zimmer   **654**

**The Witch House**
Johnson, Norma Tadlock   **2923**

**The Witch King**
Maeve, Henry   4056

**Witch-Light**
Holder, Nancy   **2734**

**The Witch of Maple Park**
Tolan, Stephanie S.   **5478**

**Witch of the North**
Jones, Courtway   2940, 5270

**The Witch Returns**
Naylor, Phyllis Reynolds   **4079**

**Witch Spell**
Smith, Guy N.   690, **5122**

**Witch Week**
Jones, Diana Wynne   330, 5490

**Witch World**
Norton, Andre   219, 562, 2819, 3650, 4783

**Witchcraft**
Michaels, Bill   **3885**

**The Witchcraft Reader**
Haining, Peter   1711

**Witchdame**
Sky, Kathleen   2945, 3700

**The Witches**
Dahl, Roald   2949, 4079, 4080

**Witches**
Griffith, Kathryn Meyer   690, **2442**, 4577, 5122

**Witches Abroad**
Pratchett, Terry   187, 2145, **4404**

**Witches and Warlocks: Tales of Black Magic Old and New**
Kaye, Marvin   1711

**Witches' Brew**
Brooks, Terry   **719**

**The Witches of Eastwick**
Updike, John   749, 2442, 4570, 4577, 5021, 5488

**The Witches of Eileanan**
Forsyth, Kate   **1984**

**The Witches of Karres**
Schmitz, James H.   652, 703, 1384, 1536, 4392, 4405, 5234

**The Witches of Wenshar**
Hambly, Barbara   289, 389, 394, 3839, 5733, 5760

**The Witching Hour**
Rice, Anne   654, 690, 749, 2442, **4580**, 5122, 5421, 5488

**Witchlight**
Bradley, Marion Zimmer   **655**, 1462

**Witch's Business**
Jones, Diana Wynne   4079, 4080

**The Witch's Eye**
Naylor, Phyllis Reynolds   **4080**, 4275

**The Witch's Tale**
Cole, Alonzo Dean   **1112**

**Witchwood**
Buchan, John   750

**With a Single Spell**
Watt-Evans, Lawrence   671

**With Friends Like These...**
Foster, Alan Dean   3308, 4127, 4706

**With Full Honors**
McQuinn, Donald E.   **3865**, 5669, 5786

**With Magical Horses to Ride**
Morris, Winifred   5559

**With the Lightnings**
Drake, David   **1652**

**With Wounds Still Wet**
Sallee, Wayne Allen   2698, 4231, 4532, **4789**, 5662, 5663

**The Wiz Biz**
Cook, Rick   **1160**, 1703

**Wizard**
Varley, John   1055, 3050, 5000, 5033

**A Wizard Abroad**
Duane, Diane   **1668**, 4260

**Wizard and Glass**
King, Stephen   **3144**

**The Wizard and the Floating City**
Rowley, Christopher   **4699**

**The Wizard at Home**
Shelley, Rick   **4975**

**A Wizard in Absentia**
Stasheff, Christopher   **5229**

**A Wizard in Chaos**
Stasheff, Christopher   **5230**

**A Wizard in Midgard**
Stasheff, Christopher   **5231**

**A Wizard in Mind**
Stasheff, Christopher   **5232**

**A Wizard in Peace**
Stasheff, Christopher   **5233**

**A Wizard in War**
Stasheff, Christopher   **5234**

**The Wizard King**
Smith, Julie Dean   **5127**, 5752

**The Wizard of 4th Street**
Hawke, Simon   227, 433, 973, 1091, 1160, 1273, 4391, 4771, 5646, 5697

**The Wizard of Ambermere**
Pierce, J. Calvin   **4317**

**The Wizard of Anharitte**
Kapp, Colin   882, 1757, 5230, 5231

**Wizard of Bones**
Charrette, Robert N.   **979**

**The Wizard of Camelot**
Hawke, Simon   973, 977, **2627**, 4771, 5203

**A Wizard of Earthsea**
Le Guin, Ursula K.   18, 371, 561, 978, 1161, 1175, 1221, 1528, 1529, 1530, 1531, 1533, 1605, 1636, 1742, 1743, 1816, 1984, 2128, 2354, 2356, 2461, 2650, 3065, 3169, 3477, 3482, 3582, 3884, 4149, 4321, 4324, 4334, 4461, 4462, 4691, 4693, 4694, 4924, 5034, 5142, 5272, 5728, 5974, 5984, 6024, 6025, 6032, 6036, 6037, 6069

**The Wizard of Santa Fe**
Hawke, Simon   **2628**

**The Wizard of Sunset Strip**
Hawke, Simon   **2629**, 2797, 4362

**Wizard of the Pigeons**
Lindholm, Megan   738, 744, 1425,
1431, 2104, 2105, 2537, 2693,
2694, 2695, 2696, 2817, 4383,
5274, 5697, 5913

**Wizard Spawn**
Cherryh, C.J.   11, 256, **1004**, 2674,
5739, 5742

**Wizard World**
Zelazny, Roger   1722

**The Wizardry Compiled**
Cook, Rick   1858

**The Wizardry Consulted**
Cook, Rick   **1161**

**The Wizardry Cursed**
Cook, Rick   **1162**, 1461

**The Wizardry Quested**
Cook, Rick   **1163**

**The Wizard's Apprentice**
Somtow, S.P.   489, 557, 2079, 2085,
4863, **5163**, 6017

**Wizard's Bane**
Cook, Rick   1419, 2264, 2622, 5063

**A Wizard's Dozen**
Stearns, Michael   1994, 4988, **5239**,
5973, 6040

**Wizard's Eleven**
Tepper, Sheri S.   3399

**Wizard's First Rule**
Goodkind, Terry   287, 692, 704, 712,
979, 1009, 1105, 1147, 1172,
1292, 1513, 1733, 1744, 1814,
1905, 1952, 1953, 2141, **2271**,
2506, 2657, 2693, 2694, 2695,
2696, 2924, 2925, 2956, 2957,
2959, 2984, 2989, 3044, 3095,
3296, 3507, 3651, 3832, 3835,
3838, 3926, 4110, 4528, 4685,
4768, 4794, 4796, 4908, 4986,
5034, 5202, 5203, 5275, 5320,
5554, 5651, 5734, 5748, 5972,
5978

**Wizard's Hall**
Yolen, Jane   329, 701, 847, 1601,
1605, 2944, 3159, 3545, 4260,
4261, 4323, 4700, 5979, **6043**,
6057, 6058

**Wizard's Heir**
Hood, Daniel   **2759**

**Wizard's Mole**
Strickland, Brad   1161, 1530, 2042,
2505, 2617, 3159, 4458, 4986,
**5337**

**The Wizard's Shadow**
Dexter, Susan   172, 672, 718, **1514**,
2858, 3099, 3277, 3773, 3838,
3914, 4809, 5583, 6042

**Wizenbeak**
Gilliland, Alexis A.   2132, 2133

**WiZrD**
Zell, Steve   2903, **6078**

**Wolf and Iron**
Dickson, Gordon R.   208, 1328,
**1539**, 1838, 1932, 2603, 3470,
3863, 4678

**Wolf and Raven**
Stackpole, Michael A.   **5207**

**The Wolf and the Crown**
Attanasio, A.A.   **273**

**The Wolf and the Raven**
Paxson, Diana L.   136, 363, 1856,
2229, 2246, 2250, 2453, 2454,
2571, 2572, 2686, **4270**, 4669

**Wolf-Dreams**
Weaver, Michael D.   2552, 2553

**Wolf Flow**
Jeter, K.W.   871, **2918**

**Wolf in Shadow**
Gemmell, David   **2191**, 4835

**Wolf In the Fold**
Green, Simon R.   **2376**

**The Wolf Is My Brother**
Oliver, Chad   4052

**Wolf Justice**
Durgin, Doranna   **1706**

**Wolf Moon**
de Lint, Charles   1349, 3625, 4397

**Wolf Moon**
Holt, John R.   514, **2749**

**The Wolf of Winter**
Volsky, Paula   5584

**Wolf Pack**
Charrette, Robert N.   5469

**Wolf-Speaker**
Pierce, Tamora   **4324**

**The Wolfen**
Strieber, Whitley   373, 679, 1007,
1570, 1822, 2138, 3053, 3376,
4052, 4764, 5388, 5442

**Wolfhelm**
Knaak, Richard A.   1096, **3175**, 4991

**Wolfking**
Wood, Bridget   633, 2740, 3501,
3504, 3506, 4266, **5963**

**Wolfling**
Dickson, Gordon R.   1595, 1995,
2004

**The Wolfman**
Dreadstone, Carl   1800

**Wolf's Cub**
Wood, Mackay   **5964**

**The Wolf's Hour**
McCammon, Robert R.   462, 2841,
2895, **3759**, 4702, 4780

**Wolfsong**
Briery, Traci   **680**, 4472

**Wolfsong**
Pini, Richard   4336, 4337

**Wolfwalker**
Harper, Tara K.   1176, **2553**

**Wolfwinter**
Swann, Thomas Burnett   5511

**The Wolves of Autumn**
Ciencin, Scott   846, **1035**

**Wolves of the Gods**
Cole, Allan   **1111**

**Wolves on the Border**
Charrette, Robert N.   1938

**A Woman a Day**
Farmer, Philip Jose   3543

**The Woman between the Worlds**
MacIntyre, F. Gwynplaine   **3596**

**The Woman in Black**
Hill, Susan   5519

**A Woman of the Iron People**
Arnason, Eleanor   211, 250, 558,
566, 686, 792, 793, 877, 968,
1583, 1584, 2037, 2637, 2683,
3046, 3157, 3424, 3972, 4038,
4325, 4855, 4923, 5091, 5450,
5461, 5574, 5590, 5616, 5872

**Woman of the Mists**
McKee, Lynn Armistead   731, 2166,
2857

**Woman on the Edge of Time**
Piercy, Marge   515, 968, 1130, 1835,
3622, 5180, 5905, 5908

**The Woman Who Loved Reindeer**
Pierce, Meredith Ann   668, 2166,
2167, 2168, 2169, 2170, 2581,
2582, 2583, **4320**

**The Woman with the Flying Head
and Other Stories**
Kurahashi, Yumiko   **3250**

**Woman Without a Shadow**
Haber, Karen   101, **2478**

**Women and Ghosts**
Lurie, Alison   2826, 2842, **3575**,
4184, 5166

**The Women and the Warlords**
Cook, Hugh   3339

**Women at War**
Bujold, Lois McMaster   **765**

**Women of Darkness**
Ptacek, Kathryn   468, 1312, 2496,
2891, 3022, 5523

**Women of Darkness II**
Ptacek, Kathryn   468, 2496, 2891,
3022, **4443**, 5523

**Women of the Weird**
Manley, Seon   1715, 3022

**Women of the West**
Ptacek, Kathryn   217

**The Women of Whitechapel and Jack
the Ripper**
West, Paul   26, 3987, **5761**

**Women of Wonder: Science Fiction
Stories by Women about Women**
Sargent, Pamela   628, 1609

**Women of Wonder, the Classic
Years: Science Fiction by Women
From the 1940s to the 1970s**
Sargent, Pamela   765, **4825**

**Women of Wonder, the
Contemporary Years: Science
Fiction by Women From the 1970s
to the 1990s**
Sargent, Pamela   765, **4826**

**Women Who Run with Werewolves:
Tales of Blood, Lust and
Metamorphosis**
Keesey, Pam   2496, **3032**, 3112

**Women's Work**
Taylor, L.A.   790, 3384, **5410**

**The Wonder City of Oz**
Neill, John Rea   3609

**The Wonderful Flight to the
Mushroom Planet**
Cameron, Eleanor   252, 1217

**The Wonderful Wizard of Oz**
Baum, L. Frank   2136, 3144, 4758

**The Wood Nymph and the Cranky
Saint**
Brittain, C. Dale   **706**, 1014, 2080

**The Wood Wife**
Windling, Terri   636, 1358, 2266,
2326, 4358, **5916**

**The Wooden Spaceships**
Shaw, Bob   3344

**The Wooden Sword**
Abbey, Lynn   **18**, 1030, 2097, 3098,
4159, 4699, 5983

**The Woods Are Dark**
Laymon, Richard   3092, 3387

**The Woods out Back**
Salvatore, R.A.   439, 2127, 2739,
**4809**

**Woodsman**
Easton, Thomas A.   **1727**

**The Woodwitch**
Gregory, Stephen   1185, 3373

**The Word for World Is Forest**
Le Guin, Ursula K.   580, 622, 1263,
3730, 4044, 4273, 4539, 5069,
5880

**Wordwright**
Deitz, Tom   **1478**

**Worf's First Adventure**
David, Peter   **1391**, 2109, 4910

**The Work of the Sun**
Edgerton, Teresa   **1746**, 2809

**The World at the End of Time**
Pohl, Frederik   734, **4357**, 4506

**The World Beneath**
Gurney, James   385, 1024, 2003,
**2469**, 2980, 2982, 5479

**A World Between**
Spinrad, Norman   353

**The World I Made for Her**
Moran, Thomas   3996

**The World in Amber**
Orr, A.   4055

**A World Lost**
Johnson, James B.   **2921**

**The World Menders**
Biggle, Lloyd   5230, 5231

**The World Next Door**
Ferguson, Brad   160, 1133, **1924**,
2574, 5906

**World of Darkness: Death and Damnation**
Wieck, Stewart  3224

**World of Darkness: The Unbeholden**
Weinberg, Robert  2518

**World of Darkness: Truth Until Paradox**
Wieck, Stewart  23, 3224, 5797

**The World of Darkness: Watcher**
Grant, Charles L.  **2321**

**A World of Difference**
Turtledove, Harry  **5514**

**The World of Null-A**
Van Vogt, A.E.  379, 2217, 3698, 3829, 4682, 5621

**The World of Robert Jordan's The Wheel of Time**
Jordan, Robert  1735, **2991**

**The World on Blood**
Nasaw, Jonathan  345, 600, 812, 1541, 2449, **4069**, 4445

**A World out of Time**
Niven, Larry  445, 1053, 3924

**World Spirits**
Boucher-Kaplan, Aline  **580**, 5575

**The World Swappers**
Brunner, John  379, 5048

**The World Treasury of Science Fiction**
Hartwell, David G.  850, 887, 1612, 3381, 4725, 5004, 5489

**World Without End**
Cochran, Molly  **1093**

**World Without End**
Haldeman, Joe  528

**World Without End**
Russell, Sean  **4744**

**The World Wreckers**
Bradley, Marion Zimmer  2372, 3426, 3726, 4140

**Worlds: A Novel of the Near Future**
Haldeman, Joe  127, 3242

**Worlds Apart**
Decarnin, Camilla  2117, 2295, 2444, 5154

**Worlds Apart**
Haldeman, Joe  5909

**World's End**
Vinge, Joan D.  2050, 5760

**Worlds Enough and Time**
Haldeman, Joe  **2491**, 4116, 4350

**Worlds of the Imperium**
Laumer, Keith  1655, 5517

**Worlds of Weird**
Margulies, Leo  2485, 5689

**Worlds Without End**
Spector, Caroline  5096

**Worldwar: In the Balance**
Turtledove, Harry  1854, 1900, 3063, **5515**, 5996

**Worldwar: Striking the Balance**
Turtledove, Harry  **5516**

**Worldwar: Tilting the Balance**
Turtledove, Harry  2239, **5517**

**Worldwar: Upsetting the Balance**
Turtledove, Harry  **5518**

**Worse Things Waiting**
Wellman, Manly Wade  537, 939, 942, 2844, 3515, 5155

**Worst Nightmare**
Meyers, Ric  612, 613, 615, **3883**

**The Worthing Saga**
Card, Orson Scott  1053, 2422, 2498, 3854, 4548, 5609

**The Wounded Land**
Donaldson, Stephen R.  5832

**The Wounded Sky**
Duane, Diane  528, 1228, 1386, 2501, 4511

**Woundhealer's Story: The First Book of Lost Swords**
Saberhagen, Fred  1150

**Wraeththu**
Constantine, Storm  551, 4849, 4851, 5931

**Wrath of Ashar**
Wells, Angus  1005, 3246, **5742**

**The Wrath of Poseidon**
Betancourt, John Gregory  4912

**Wrath of the Princes**
Lisle, Holly  **3490**

**Wren to the Rescue**
Smith, Sherwood  67, 599, 1605, 2869, 2944, 3159, 4700, **5142**, 5579, 5974, 6025, 6043, 6058

**Wren's Quest**
Smith, Sherwood  1319, 1320, 1600, **5143**

**Wren's War**
Smith, Sherwood  4321, **5144**

**A Wrinkle in Time**
L'Engle, Madeleine  510, 2948, 5013

**Writ in Blood**
Yarbro, Chelsea Quinn  5501, **6019**

**Writer of the Purple Rage**
Lansdale, Joe R.  **3335**, 4250

**Wrong**
Cooper, Dennis  **1171**

**The Wrong Number**
Stine, R.L.  1692

**Wulfsyarn: A Mosaic**
Mann, Phillip  **3617**

**Wurm**
Costello, Matthew J.  88, 440, 441, **1202**, 5890

**Wyrd Sisters**
Pratchett, Terry  980, 1045, 1529, 2750, 2942, 3079, **4405**, 5337

**Wyrm**
Fabi, Mark  **1858**

**Wyrm Wolf**
van Belkom, Edo  2321, 3990, 4059, **5535**

**Wyrms**
Card, Orson Scott  1574, 1930, 3717, 5128, 5157, 5436, 6082

**Wyvern**
Attanasio, A.A.  3386

**The Wyvern's Spur**
Novak, Kate  2426


**X**

**The X Factor**
Norton, Andre  2764, 2810

**The X-Files: Fight the Future**
Carter, Chris  **924**, 5843, 5846

**The X-Files: Goblins**
Grant, Charles L.  2114, 2534

**The X-Files: Ruins**
Anderson, Kevin J.  2114, 2534

**X-Men: Empire's End**
Duane, Diane  2256

**Xanadu**
Yolen, Jane  628, 1368, **6044**

**Xanadu 2**
Yolen, Jane  **6045**

**Xanadu 3**
Yolen, Jane  **6046**

**The Xanadu Series**
Yolen, Jane  1359, 1366, 2634, 2635

**Xelucha and Others**
Shiel, M.P.  964

**Xenocide**
Card, Orson Scott  **899**, 930, 1549, 2343, 4896

**Xenogenesis Series**
Butler, Octavia E.  899

**The Xenogenesis Trilogy**
Butler, Octavia E.  5609

**The Xothic Legend Cycle**
Carter, Lin  3556, 3859, 4444

**The Xothic Legend Cycle: The Complete Mythos Fiction of Lin Carter**
Carter, Lin  **925**


**Y**

**Yamato: A Rage in Heaven**
Kato, Ken  566, 1145, **3014**

**Yankee Witches**
Waugh, Charles G.  1711

**Yarrow**
de Lint, Charles  1241, 3294

**Ye Gods!**
Holt, Tom  **2753**

**The Year After Tomorrow: An Anthology of Science Fiction Stories**
Del Rey, Lester  6027

**The Year Before Tomorrow**
Aldiss, Brian W.  5517

**The Year Before Yesterday**
Aldiss, Brian W.  2564, 5518

**The Year of the Quiet Sun**
Tucker, Wilson  1133, 5048

**The Year of the Ransom**
Anderson, Poul  4164

**The Year of the Sex Olympics and Other TV Plays**
Kneale, Nigel  1022

**The Year of the Unicorn**
Norton, Andre  355

**The Year's Best Fantasy and Horror: Eighth Annual Collection**
Datlow, Ellen  2964

**The Year's Best Fantasy and Horror: Eleventh Annual Collection**
Datlow, Ellen  **1371**

**The Year's Best Fantasy and Horror: Fifth Annual Collection**
Datlow, Ellen  **1372**

**The Year's Best Fantasy and Horror: Fourth Annual Collection**
Datlow, Ellen  215, 646, **1373**, 2962, 4025, 4031, 4032, 5601

**The Year's Best Fantasy and Horror: Ninth Annual Collection**
Datlow, Ellen  **1374**, 2969

**The Year's Best Fantasy and Horror Series**
Datlow, Ellen  228, 2970, 2971, 5003, 5602, 5603, 5606, 5912, 6032, 6044

**The Year's Best Fantasy and Horror: Seventh Annual Collection**
Datlow, Ellen  **1375**, 5608

**The Year's Best Fantasy and Horror: Sixth Annual Collection**
Datlow, Ellen  **1376**, 2963, 5607

**The Year's Best Fantasy and Horror: Tenth Annual Collection**
Datlow, Ellen  **1377**

**The Year's Best Fantasy and Horror: Third Annual Collection**
Datlow, Ellen  59, 647, **1378**, 1428, 2961, 4723, 5605

**The Year's Best Fantasy: First Annual Collection**
Datlow, Ellen  4131, 4723, 6044

**The Year's Best Fantasy Stories**
Saha, Arthur W.  1374

**The Year's Best Fantasy Stories Series**
Carter, Lin  1371, 1374, 1377

**The Year's Best Fantasy Stories Series**
Saha, Arthur W.  1371, 1377

**The Year's Best Horror Stories XVIII**
Wagner, Karl Edward  1378, 2961, **5605**

**The Year's Best Horror Stories XIX**
Wagner, Karl Edward  1373, 2962, 4025

**The Year's Best Horror Stories XX**
Wagner, Karl Edward  **5606**

Title Index

**The Year's Best Horror Stories XXI**
Wagner, Karl Edward　1376, 2963, **5607**

**The Year's Best Horror Stories XXII**
Wagner, Karl Edward　1375

**The Year's Best Horror Stories XXIII**
Wagner, Karl Edward　**5608**

**The Year's Best Horror Stories Series**
Wagner, Karl Edward　1371, 1372, 1374, 1377, 2964, 2969, 2970, 2971

**The Year's Best Science Fiction: Eighth Annual Collection**
Dozois, Gardner　215, 1363, **1616**, 4031, 4558

**The Year's Best Science Fiction: Eleventh Annual Collection**
Dozois, Gardner　**1617**, 5046

**The Year's Best Science Fiction: Fifteenth Annual Collection**
Dozois, Gardner　**1618**, 5954

**The Year's Best Science Fiction: Fourteenth Annual Collection**
Dozois, Gardner　**1619**

**The Year's Best Science Fiction: Ninth Annual Collection**
Dozois, Gardner　**1620**, 4032

**The Year's Best Science Fiction Series**
Dozois, Gardner　246, 888, 1339, 1342, 2593, 2594, 2595, 2596, 2597, 2598, 4439, 4824, 5489

**The Year's Best Science Fiction: Seventh Annual Collection**
Dozois, Gardner　214, 238, 500, 501, 887, **1621**, 4725, 5948

**The Year's Best Science Fiction: Tenth Annual Collection**
Dozois, Gardner　216, 1364, 1365, **1622**

**The Year's Best Science Fiction: Thirteenth Annual Collection**
Dozois, Gardner　**1623**

**The Year's Best Science Fiction: Twelfth Annual Collection**
Dozois, Gardner　**1624**, 2679, 3751

**Year's Best SF**
Hartwell, David G.　1619, **2596**

**Year's Best SF 2**
Hartwell, David G.　1619, **2597**

**Year's Best SF 3**
Hartwell, David G.　**2598**

**The Year's Best SF 13**
Hartwell, David G.　1623

**The Years of the City**
Pohl, Frederik　1819, 1820, 5642

**Yellow Fog**
Daniels, Les　2511, 2742, 6019

**Yellow Moon**
Searls, David J.　**4907**

**The Yellow Wallpaper and Other Writings of Charlotte Perkins Gilman**
Gilman, Charlotte Perkins　2158

**Yellowstone Run**
Robbins, David　1406, 2324, 2325, **4605**, 5023

**Yendor**
Matthews, Rodney　6076

**Yesterday and Tomorrow**
Verne, Jules　3148

**Yesterday We Saw Mermaids**
Friesner, Esther　**2086**

**Yesterday's Passion**
Biggs, Cheryl　3039

**Yesterday's Pawn**
Quick, W.T.　**4453**, 5449

**Yesterday's Son**
Crispin, A.C.　527, 528, 922, 1383, 3316

**Yiddish Folk Tales**
Weinreich, Beatrice Silverman　6090

**The Yngling**
Dalmas, John　47, 50, 4600, 4602, 4619, 4621

**The Yngling and the Circle of Power**
Dalmas, John　**1328**

**The Yngling in Yamato**
Dalmas, John　**1329**

**Yon Ill Wind**
Anthony, Piers　196

**You and Science Fiction: A Humanistic Aproach to Tomorrow**
Hollister, Bernard　6027

**You Are All Alone**
Leiber, Fritz　3351

**You Bright and Risen Angels**
Vollmann, William T.　780, 3457

**You Never Believe Me and Other Stories**
Grubb, Davis　3328, 3329, 3333, 3335

**You Only Live Twice**
Fleming, Ian　4560

**You Shall Know Them**
Vercors　2434

**Young Adults**
Pinkwater, Daniel Manus　545, 546, 550, 552

**Young Bleys**
Dickson, Gordon R.　**1540**

**Young Blood**
Baker, Mike　**300**

**Young Blood**
Stableford, Brian　303, 812, 4445, 4978, 5183

**Young Extraterrestrials**
Asimov, Isaac　5238

**Young Frankenstein**
Pearlman, Gilbert　5324

**The Young Magicians**
Carter, Lin　5239

**The Young Oxford Book of Ghost Stories**
Pepper, Dennis　1693, 1701, 2772, **4282**

**Young Rissa**
Busby, F.M.　1071, 3603

**The Young Unicorns**
L'Engle, Madeleine　3276

**Your Sins and Mine**
Caldwell, Taylor　6028

**Yours Truly, Jackie the Stripper**
van Belkom, Edo　3397, **5536**

**Yvgenie**
Cherryh, C.J.　**1005**, 3281

## Z

**Z for Zachariah**
O'Brien, Robert C.　3584, 3608

**Z Is for Zombie**
Roscoe, Theodore　3605

**The Zap Gun**
Dick, Philip K.　**1523**

**Zaragoz**
Craig, Brian　**1241**, 4653, 5087

**Zelerod's Doom**
Lichtenberg, Jacqueline　4784

**Zeta Base**
Alguire, Judith　**74**, 662, 3539

**Zeus and Co.**
Jones, David Lee　2404, 2716, **2942**

**Zjhanne's Book**
Mills, C.J.　3912

**Zod Wallop**
Spencer, William Browning　1085, **5169**

**Zombie**
Oates, Joyce Carol　2755, 3002, **4185**, 5326

**Zombie Lover**
Anthony, Piers　**197**, 1014

**Zombies of the Gene Pool**
McCrumb, Sharyn　4120

**Zone Yellow**
Laumer, Keith　5130

**Zoo 2000: Twelve Stories of Science Fiction and Fantasy Beasts**
Yolen, Jane　3611

**Zorba the Hutt's Revenge**
Davids, Paul　**1394**

**The Zork Chronicles**
Effinger, George Alec　288, **1754**, 1839, 3479

**The Zothique**
Smith, Clark Ashton　4021